PrincetonReview.com

THE COMPLETE
BOOK OF COLLEGES

Random House, Inc., New York
2014 Edition

The Princeton Review, Inc.
111 Speen St., Suite 550
Framingham, MA 01701
Email: editorialsupport@review.com

© 2013 by TPR Education IP Holdings, LLC

ISBN: 978-0-307-94628-7
ISSN: 1088-8594

SVP, Publisher: Robert Franek
Editor: Kristen O'Toole
Production: Best Content Solutions, LLC
Production Editor: Melissa Duclos-Yourdon

Printed in the United States of America.

9 8 7 6 5 4 3 2 1

2014 Edition

The Princeton Review is not affiliated with Princeton University.

ACKNOWLEDGMENTS

Each year we assemble an awe-inspiringly talented group of colleagues who work together to produce our guidebooks; this year is no exception. Everyone involved in this effort—authors, editors, data collectors, production specialists, and designers—gives so much more than is required to make *The Complete Book of Colleges* an exceptional student resource guide.

My sincere thanks go to the many who contributed to this tremendous project. Very special thanks go to Kristen O'Toole for her editorial commitment and vision. A warm and special thank you goes to our Student Survey expert, Stephen Koch, who continues to work in partnership with school administrators and students alike. My continued thanks go to our data collection pro, David Soto, for his successful efforts in collecting and accurately representing the statistical data that appear with each college profile and to Melissa Duclos-Yourdon for her dedication to reading through the massive amounts of data. The enormousness of this project and its deadline constraints could not have been realized without the calm presence of our production partner, Scott Harris. Scott's many years of dedication and focus continue to delight and remind me of what a pleasure it is to work together on this project each year. Special thanks also go to Jeanne Krier, our Random House publicist, for the dedicated work she continues to do on this book and the overall series since its inception. Jeanne continues to be my trusted colleague, media advisor, and friend. I would also like to make special mention of Tom Russell and Nicole Benhabib, our Random House publishing team, for their continuous investment and faith in our ideas. Last, I thank my TPR Partner Team, Deborah Ellinger, Scott Kirkpatrick, Michael Bleyhl, and Paul Kanarek for their confidence in me and my content team and for their commitment to providing students the resources they need to find the right fit school for them. Again, to all who contributed so much to this publication, thank you for your efforts; they do not go unnoticed.

Robert Franek
SVP—Publisher

CONTENTS

CONTENTS

FOREWORD

Welcome. You have found the best place to begin, fine-tune, and execute the search for your perfect college. With the understanding that choosing a school wisely is a top priority for each prospective student, we have provided a significant breadth of information in this text to help you navigate the exciting, amazing, and sometimes confusing process of choosing the right college.

The design of this guidebook will allow you to narrow your search of colleges from 1,567 to a few dozen. Here you'll find all the individual college statistics you'll need to make informed choices about the competitiveness, size, location, and academic offerings of the schools available to you. In addition, you can find even more information about individual schools at The Princeton Review's website, PrincetonReview.com. The site includes college search features, college profiles, college discussion boards, a college majors search engine, and much more.

By using this book, you can search for, choose, and apply to colleges with the confidence of a pro—or at the very least a well-informed undergraduate hopeful! We supply the information and guidance, and you ultimately make your own decision.

The college selection, application, and interview processes can be overwhelming at times. They can also be rewarding experiences. For most, choosing a college is the first major life decision. I know it was mine. Remember that your college decision is yours alone, so arm yourself with the best available information. Badger teachers, friends, high school and college admissions counselors, brothers, sisters, and parents; ask them how they chose their colleges and why. The more you know when beginning the process, the more in control of the situation you'll feel.

Whatever it is that you choose as your path in life, your college selection will forever be your first step in that direction. The friends you make, the professors you meet, and the classes you take are all springboards to the next phase of your life.

I wish you much luck and success at whichever college you decide to attend. My sincere hope is that this publication and other Princeton Review tools will be helpful in the process.

Robert Franek
SVP, Publisher

INTRODUCTION

Before you dive into *The Complete Book of Colleges*, we want to give you some tips for your college search—especially on how to get the most out of this book and what to do once you've made your choices and are ready to apply. Since the most important thing for you to do now is to start your search, we want to start right off by revealing the secret to getting admitted to the college of your choice.

It's almost never the focus of talk about college admissions in the media, and parents and students discuss the subject all the time without even realizing that it's the crucial element to getting admitted. We're talking about matchmaking: That is, finding colleges that have the educational and social environments you're looking for, where you are well-suited academically and have something the college is looking for in return. You have a lot more control over where you end up going to college than you might think.

Matchmaking is a two-step process. You should begin with a thorough self-examination or personal inventory. Your personal inventory is best structured in the form of a chart, so that when you begin to consider your options, you can check off those colleges that satisfy the various needs or wants you've identified. In this way, your best college choices will gradually begin to identify themselves.

Divide your inventory into two sections. One section should be biographical, including your high school course selection, GPA, SAT or ACT scores, class rank, and personal information like extracurricular activities—especially those you plan to continue in college. This will help you to assess how you stack up against each college's admissions standards and student body. The second section is a listing of the characteristics you need or want in the college you'll choose to attend. This list should include anything and everything you consider important, such as location, size of the student body, availability of scholarships, dormitory options, clubs and activities, even school colors if you want. This part of your inventory should grow continuously as you become more and more aware of what is important to you in your choice of colleges.

Armed with your personal inventory, you can begin to take advantage of the numerous resources available to help you narrow your choices of where to apply. There are five sources for information and advice that have become standard for most college-bound students:

1. College admissions brochures, websites, videos, and catalogs

If you are a junior or senior in high school, you probably know more about the kinds of information these materials should include than the people who are responsible for designing and writing them. No college that spends half a million dollars on glossy literature is going to be objective about its content. In the best of this material, you can probably get a decent idea of the academic offerings and the basic admissions requirements. In all of it, you will never see anything but the most appealing architecture and the best-looking students on campus, nor will you hear about the recent tuition increases that were greater than the rate of inflation. Look these materials over, but don't make any decisions based solely on what you read or see.

2. Your friends

No one knows colleges and universities better than the students who currently attend them. Seek out any and all of your friends, sons and daughters of family friends, and recent graduates of your high school who attend colleges that you are considering. Talk to them when they come home. Arrange to stay with them when you visit their colleges. Pick their brains for everything they know. It doesn't get any more direct and honest than this.

3. Books and college guides

There are two types of books that can be helpful to you in your search: those that discuss specific aspects of going to college and college guides. A great narrative guide that stresses students' own opinions of colleges is our own *The Best 378 Colleges*. In addition, look at other guides for good second opinions. As for comprehensive guides—those that emphasize data over narrative content—you're holding the most up-to-date and useful one in your hands.

4. Computers

There's a lot of help out there. Using our site, PrincetonReview.com, is the best way to find the right school for you and prepare for college.

5. Your counselor

Since it's *critically* important, we'll say it again: Once you've developed some ideas about your personal inventory and college options, schedule a meeting with your guidance counselor. The more research you've done before you get together, the more help you're likely to get. Good advice comes out of thoughtful discussion, not from the expectation that your counselor will do your work. When it comes time to file applications, look over the materials and requirements together, and allow plenty of time to put forth your best.

USING COLLEGE INFORMATION IN *THE COMPLETE BOOK OF COLLEGES* AND ELSEWHERE

Throughout the course of your college search, you'll confront an amazing array of statistics and other data related to every college you consider. In order for all of this information to be helpful, you need to have some sense of how to interpret it. We've included a detailed key to the college entries in this book a few pages deeper into this introduction. Almost all the statistics we've compiled are self-explanatory, but there are a few that will be more useful with some elaboration.

Let's start with student/teacher ratio. Don't use it to assess average class size; they are not interchangeable terms. At almost every college, the average class size is larger than its student/teacher ratio. At many big universities, it is considerably larger. What is useful about the ratio is that it can give you an idea of how accessible your professors will be outside of the classroom. Once you are in college, you'll grow to realize just how important this is.

In the same way, the percentage of faculty who hold PhDs is useful information. When you're paying thousands of dollars in tuition each year, there's something comforting about knowing that your professors have a considerably broader and deeper grasp of what you're studying than you do. In contrast, teaching assistants (TAs) may often be just one or two steps ahead of you.

Another interesting group of statistics deals with the percentage of students who go on to graduate or professional school. Never allow yourself to be swayed by such statistics, unless you've taken the time to ponder their meaning and visited the college in question. High percentages almost always mean one of two things: that the college is an intellectual enclave that inspires students onward to further their education, or that it is a pre-professional bastion of aggressive careerists. There isn't anything inherently wrong with either scenario, but neither has universal appeal to prospective students. Colleges that are exceptions to this rule are rare and precious. The most misleading figures provided to prospective students are those for medical school acceptance rates. Virtually every college in the country can boast of high acceptance rates to medical school for its graduates; pre-med programs are designed to weed out those who will not be strong candidates before they even get to apply! If you're thinking about medical school, ask colleges how many of their students apply to medical school each year. Also, try to get a sense of the attrition rate within the pre-med program.

One final piece of advice about statistics relates to the college's acceptance rate. Simply knowing the percentage of applicants who are admitted each year is helpful, but it is even more helpful if you know how many applied, as well. When you compare these figures to the freshman profile, you have the most accurate picture of just how tough it is to get in. An 80 percent acceptance rate doesn't mean there's an open door if you don't match up well to the academic achievements of the college's typical freshman. Beyond this, keep an eye out for colleges that have relatively self-selecting applicant pools. In these cases, high acceptance rates may be misleading. When evaluating highly selective public colleges as an out-of-state applicant, remember that you will likely face a more selective evaluation than state residents.

A Few Final Thoughts

Once you've narrowed down your options and decided where to apply, find the applications on PrincetonReview.com and get to work filling them out. The admissions process is stressful enough without putting extra pressure on yourself by waiting until the last minute. The first thing you should do when you receive the necessary forms is go over them with your guidance counselor. Immediately remove the recommendation forms (if they are required) and give them to the teachers and counselor(s) who will be completing them for you. They'll have a better opportunity to write a thorough and supportive recommendation if you give them enough time to complete them. This is also the time to make your request for official transcripts. Again, it takes time to do these things. Plan ahead.

As for completing the applications, organize yourself and all the materials. Keep everything in folders and accessible in case you need to speak with an admissions officer over the telephone. When essays and information on your extracurricular activities are required, do some outlining and rough draft-writing before you commit yourself to the actual forms or online tools.

Paying for college requires some of your attention too. Though we don't have nearly enough space to go into such a complicated and stressful subject now, it's very important that you get to work on your financial circumstances right away. Keep in mind that while college is costly, few people pay the "sticker price." Regardless, you have to have your finances in order before you can get the most financial aid possible. We've developed a financial center on PrincetonReview.com to help demystify the sometimes bewildering task of financing your education. You can also find the most exhaustive strategies for financing your education in our book *Paying for College Without Going Broke*.

Last but not least, **don't take it easy during your senior year!** Colleges routinely request mid-year grades, and they expect you to continue taking challenging academic courses and keep your grades up throughout your high school career. Doing so takes you one step closer to getting good news. On behalf of The Princeton Review, have a good time, and good luck. See you on campus!

Nota Bene

The data reported in this book, unless otherwise noted, was collected from the profiled colleges from the fall of 2012 through the spring of 2013. In some cases, we were unable to publish the most recent data because schools did not report the necessary statistics to us in time, despite our repeated outreach efforts. Because enrollment and financial statistics as well as application and financial aid deadlines fluctuate from one year to another, we recommend that you check to make sure you have the most current information before applying. Best of luck!

HOW *THE COMPLETE BOOK OF COLLEGES* IS ORGANIZED

There are two types of profiles in this book. Not every school listed will have both. All of the 1,567 colleges and universities included in this book have their own informational profiles, and each entry follows the same basic format. Many of the institutions also have special two-page portraits located at the back of the book. These are written by the colleges and universities that wanted to present detailed descriptions of their campuses and programs.

Unless noted in the descriptions below, the Admissions Services Division of The Princeton Review collected all of the data presented in the informational profiles. As is customary with college guides, all data reflect figures for the academic year prior to publication, unless otherwise indicated. Since college offerings and demographics vary significantly from one institution to another and some colleges report data more thoroughly than others, few entries will include all of the individual data points described below.

The Heading

This section includes school name, address, telephone number, fax number, e-mail address, Internet site, financial aid telephone number, and college code numbers for both the College Board (CEEB) and the American College Testing Program (ACT) when applicable. All Internet site addresses were accurate and functioning at the time of publication. Check PrincetonReview.com for the most up-to-date links to colleges.

The Icons

The icons are a feature we hope will make using *The Complete Book of Colleges* easier. Icons appear under the school name for schools that are profiled in *The Best 378 Colleges*.

The Blurb

Describes the college or university. Includes all available data that relate to the date of founding of the school, religious affiliation, whether the school is public or private, and campus size.

Ratings

This section includes the school's Fire Safety Rating, its Admissions Selectivity Rating, and its Green Rating.

Admissions Selectivity Rating

The number listed for each college is The Princeton Review's exclusive rating of admissions competitiveness. It is a very general assessment determined by several factors, among which are the school's acceptance rate, and the class rank and average test scores of entering first-year students. By incorporating all these factors, the rating adjusts for "self-selecting" applicant pools. *Note:* The Selectivity Rating for visual and performing arts schools are approximations only. Estimated Selectivity Ratings are included to give you a general idea of where they fit in the selectivity scale, but auditions and portfolios carry the greatest weight in admissions decisions.

Schools that received an Admissions Selectivity rating of 60* did not supply sufficient data for proper calculation of this rating. By default, these schools are given this rating, although their rating may have been significantly higher had they supplied sufficient data.

Fire Safety

We asked all the schools from which we collect data annually to answer several questions about their efforts to ensure fire safety for campus residents. Each school's responses to nine of those questions were considered when calculating its Fire Safety Rating. The questions were developed in consultation with the Center for Campus Fire Safety (www.campusfire.org), and they cover: 1) The percentage of student housing sleeping rooms protected by an automatic fire sprinkler system with a fire sprinkler head located in the individual sleeping rooms; 2) The percentage of student housing sleeping rooms equipped with a smoke detector connected to a supervised fire alarm system; 3) The number of malicious fire alarms that occur in student housing per year; 4) The number of unwanted fire alarms that occur in student housing per year; 5) The banning of certain hazardous items and activities in residence halls, like candles, smoking, halogen lamps, etc.; 6) The percentage of student housing building fire alarm systems that, if activated, result in a signal being transmitted to a monitored location on campus or the fire department.

Schools that did not report answers to any of the above questions receive a Fire Safety Rating of 60*. The schools have an opportunity to update their fire safety data every year and will have their fire safety ratings re-calculated and published annually.

Each individual rating places a college on a continuum for purposes of comparing all colleges within this academic year only. Though similar, these ratings are not intended to be compared directly to those that appeared on PrincetonReview.com in any prior academic year or within any Princeton Review print publication, except for *The Best 378 Colleges, 2013 Edition*. Our ratings computations are refined and change annually.

Green Rating

We asked all the schools we collect data from annually to answer a number of questions that evaluate the comprehensive measure of their performance as an environmentally aware and responsible institution. The questions were developed in consultation with ecoAmerica, a research and partnership-based environmental nonprofit that convened an expert committee to design this comprehensive rating system, and cover: 1) whether students have a campus quality of life that is both healthy and sustainable; 2) how well a school is preparing students not only for employment in the clean energy economy of the 21st century, but also for citizenship in a world now defined by environmental challenges; and 3) how environmentally responsible a school's policies are.

Colleges that did not supply answers to a sufficient number of the green campus questions for us to fairly compare them to other colleges receive a Green Rating of 60*. The schools have an opportunity to update their green data every year and will have their green ratings re-calculated and published annually.

Each individual rating places a college on a continuum for purposes of comparing all colleges within this academic year only. Though similar, these ratings are not intended to be compared directly to those that appeared on PrincetonReview.com in any prior academic year or within any Princeton Review print publication, except for the those editions published in the same year, as our ratings computations are refined and change annually.

Students & Faculty

Enrollment
The total number of full-time undergraduates.

Student Body
The percentage of male, female, out-of-state, and international students, and the number of foreign countries represented.

Ethnic Representation
By percentage according to ethnic group. Figures may not add up to 100 percent, as student reporting of ethnicity is voluntary by law.

Retention and Graduation
The percentage of freshmen who return for sophomore year. The percentage of last year's seniors who entered as freshmen and graduated in four years. The percentage of graduates who pursue further study within one year. The percentage of graduates who pursue further study at law school. The percentage of graduates who pursue further study at business school. The percentage of graduates who pursue further study at medical school.

Faculty
The ratio of undergraduates to full-time faculty. The number of full-time instructional faculty. The percentage of faculty who hold PhDs. The percentage of faculty members who teach undergraduates.

Academics

Degrees
The types of degrees awarded to students.

Academic Requirements
Areas in which all or most students are required to complete some course work prior to graduation. Can include general education (nonspecific), arts/fine arts, computer literacy, philosophy, foreign languages, history, humanities, mathematics, English (including composition), sciences (biological or physical), social sciences, and other requirements as specified by each school.

Classes
Number of students in an average regular class and an average lab/discussion section.

Majors with Highest Enrollment
The most popular majors.

Special Study Options
May include accelerated programs, cross registration, cooperative (work-study) program, distance learning, double majors, dual enrollment, English as a Second Language, student exchange programs (domestic), external degree programs, honors programs, independent study, internships, liberal arts/career combinations, student-designed majors, study abroad, teacher certification programs, weekend college, and other options as specified by each school.

Facilities

Housing
Types of school-owned or affiliated housing available. May include coed dorms, women's dorms, men's dorms, apartments for married students, apartments for single students, special housing for disabled students, special housing for international students, fraternity/sorority housing, cooperative housing, and other options as specified by the school. The availability of assistance in finding off-campus housing. Any housing requirements that may exist, such as required on-campus residence for freshmen.

Special Academic Facilities/Equipment
Other facilities and equipment of note (e.g., nuclear reactor, on-campus elementary school for student teachers, scanning electron microscopes, and so forth).

Campus Life

Activities
Standard activities available. May include campus ministries, choral groups, concert band, dance, drama/theater, international student organization, jazz band, literary magazine, Model UN, musical ensembles, musical theater, opera, pep band, radio station, student film society, student government, student newspaper, symphony orchestra, television station, and yearbook.

Organizations

Total number of registered organizations, honor societies, religious organizations, fraternities, sororities.

Athletics

Intercollegiate athletics available, listed by sex.

Admissions

Freshman Academic Profile

Average high school GPA. Class rank distribution. The percentage from public high schools. Average SAT (Math, Critical Reading, and Writing sections) and/or ACT composite scores. Median range of SAT (Math, Critical Reading, and Writing sections) and/or ACT composite scores. Test of English as a Foreign Language (TOEFL) requirements for international students.

Basis for Candidate Selection

The criteria considered by the admissions committee in evaluating candidates. May include secondary school record, class rank, recommendations, standardized test scores, essay, interview, extracurricular activities, talent/ability, character/personal qualities, alumni-/-ae relations, geographic residence, state residency, religious affiliation/commitment, minority status, volunteer work, work experience.

Freshman Admission Requirements

High school diploma/GED requirements. The number of academic units required or recommended in total and by academic subject. (Individual subject totals may not equal the complete sum of academic units required; in most cases, the difference is made up with electives. Check with the admissions office for any additional requirements.)

Freshman Admissions Statistics

The number of students who applied, the percentage of applicants who were accepted, and the percentage of those accepted who ultimately enrolled.

Transfer Admissions Requirements

Application requirements (may include high school transcript, college transcript, essay, interview, standardized tests, statement of good standing from prior school). Minimum high school GPA required. Minimum college GPA required. Lowest course grade transferable.

General Admissions Information

Application fee. Application deadlines. Admission notification date. "Rolling" indicates that decisions are sent to candidates as they are made, rather than held for a common notification date. Registration policy for terms other than the fall term. Common Application participation. Credit policies for College Entrance Examination Board Advanced Placement tests. Deferred admission policy.

Costs and Financial Aid

Tuition, room & board, fees, and books.

Required Forms and Deadlines

Forms that applicants for financial aid must file and their respective deadlines. May include FAFSA, institution's own financial aid form, CSS/Financial Aid PROFILE, business/farm supplement, state aid form, noncustodial (divorced/separated) parent statement, and other forms specified by the school. Deadlines for filing financial aid forms.

Notification of Awards

The date that notification of financial aid awards occurs. "Rolling" indicates that notification is ongoing—the sooner you complete all of your required financial aid paperwork, the sooner you'll hear about your package.

Types of Aid

Need-based scholarships and grants may include Federal Pell, SEOG, state scholarships/grants, private scholarships, college/university gift aid from institutional funds, United Negro College Fund, Federal Nursing Scholarship, and other resources as specified by the school. Loans may include Direct Subsidized Stafford Loans, Direct Unsubsidized Stafford Loans, Direct PLUS Loans, Federal Perkins Loans, Federal Nursing Loans, state loans, college/university loans from institutional funds, and other resources as specified by the school.

Student Employment

Availability of Federal Work-Study, a federal program that is need-based and part of most financial aid packages. Availability of part-time jobs direct from the college that are not based on need. The college's own assessment of part-time employment opportunities off campus.

Financial Aid Statistics

The percentage of freshmen who received some form of need-based financial aid. The percentage of undergraduates who received some form of need-based financial aid. The number of freshmen and undergrads who received an athletic scholarship or grant. The average amount of freshman scholarships and grants. The average amount of freshman loans. The average income from an on-campus job.

The Best 378 Colleges Icon

 Indicates whether the school can be found in our book, *The Best 378 Colleges*. In that book, each school has a detailed profile that includes the results of our surveys regarding student opinion, about many aspects of their schools and their educations.

COLLEGE DIRECTORY

ABILENE CHRISTIAN UNIVERSITY

ACU Box 29000, Abilene, TX 79699
Phone: 325-674-2650 • **Financial Aid Phone:** 325-674-2300
E-mail: info@admissions.acu.edu • **CEEB Code:** 6001
Fax: 325-674-2130 • **Website:** www.acu.edu • **ACT Code:** 4050

This private school, affiliated with the Church of Christ Church, was founded in 1906. It has a 208-acre campus.

RATINGS
Admissions Selectivity Rating: 89   **Fire Safety Rating:** 72   **Green Rating:** 75

STUDENTS AND FACULTY
Enrollment: 3,570. **Student Body:** 56% female, 44% male, 16% out-of-state, 5% international (43 countries represented). Asian 1%, African American 7%, Caucasian 74%, Hispanic 10%, Native American 0%.
Retention and Graduation: 75% freshmen return for sophomore year. 43% freshmen graduate within 4 years. 27% grads go on to further study within 1 year. 1% grads pursue law degrees. 1% grads pursue business degrees. 3% grads pursue medical degrees. **Faculty:** Student/faculty ratio 14:1. 243 full-time faculty, 82% hold PhDs, 9% are members of minority groups, 34% are women. 1% of classes are taught by teaching assistants.

ACADEMICS
Degrees: associate, bachelor's, master's, post-bachelor's certificate, post-master's certificate. **Classes:** Most classes have 20–29 students. Most lab/discussion sessions have 10–19 students. **Majors with Highest Enrollment:** accounting and finance; business administration and management; psychology. **Special Study Options:** cross-registration, distance learning, double major, dual enrollment, English as a Second Language (ESL), honors program, independent study, internships, student-designed major, study abroad, teacher certification program. **Honors Programs:** The Honors College offers highly motivated students extra stimulation and recognition in their course work, opportunities to work with selected faculty members and the chance to do independent projects in their major field. Ten percent of the ACU students participate. To graduate with University Honors will require 30 hours of Honors Courses. **Disability Services:** Special programs offered to physically disabled students include note-taking services, reader services, tape recorders. **Career Services:** Alumni network, alumni services, career/job search classes, career assessment, internships Career Services highlights include Body and Soul Pre-med program. College of Business Administration Leadership Deveopment.

FACILITIES
Housing: special housing for disabled students, men's dorms, special housing for international students, women's dorms. 95% of campus accessible to physically disabled. **Special Academic Facilities/Equipment:** Museum of university's history, biblical restoration studies center, voice institute, demonstration farm and ranch, observatory. **Computers:** 100% of classrooms, 100% of dorms, 100% of libraries, 100% of dining areas, 100% of student union, 87% of common outdoor areas have wireless network access. Students can register for classes online. Administrative functions (other than registration) can be performed online.

CAMPUS LIFE
Environment: City. **Activities:** Choral groups, concert band, drama/theater, jazz band, literary magazine, marching band, music ensembles, musical theater, opera, radio station, student government, student newspaper, symphony orchestra, television station, yearbook, Campus Ministries, International St:udent Organization 108 registered organizations, 14 honor societies, 16 religious organizations. 4 fraternities, 7 sororities. **Athletics (Intercollegiate):** *Men:* baseball, basketball, cross-country, football, tennis, track/field (outdoor), track/field (indoor). *Women:* basketball, cross-country, soccer, softball, tennis, track/field (outdoor), track/field (indoor), volleyball. **On-Campus Highlights:** Learning Commons in Brown Library, Jacob's Dream Sculpture, World Famous Bean in McGlothlin Campus Cntr., Hunter Welcome Center, Williams Performing Arts Building, Abilene Christian University remains proud to be one of the first to catch the vision of the learning commons nationwide. The Learning Commons combines group work space with computers and Starbucks coffee inside the Library. **Environmental Initiatives:** Student initiatives Recycle Mania—Campus Sustainability Day Blue Bag Paper Recycling—Use of recycled paper products—stocked by ACU Central Stores', Shredding for Offices. Facilities—light fixture retrofit, HVAC—energy saving initiatives, use of effluent water for irrigation.

ADMISSIONS
Freshman Academic Profile: Average high school GPA 3.6. 23% in top 10% of high school class, 58% in top 25% of high school class, 88% in top 50% of high school class. 59% from public high schools. SAT Math middle 50% range 490-600. SAT Critical Reading middle 50% range 480-600. SAT Writing middle 50% range 470-580. ACT middle 50% range 22-27. Minimum web-based TOEFL 70. Minimum paper TOEFL 525. **Basis for Candidate Selection:** *Very important factors considered include:* Class rank, application essay, rigor of secondary school record, standardized test scores. *Important factors considered include:* academic GPA, character/personal qualities, talent/ability. *Other factors considered include:* recommendation(s), alumni/ae relation, extracurricular activities, first generation, level of applicant's interest, volunteer work, work experience. **Freshman Admission Requirements:** High school diploma is required and GED is accepted. **Freshman Admission Statistics:** 8,440 applied, 45% admitted, 25% enrolled. **Transfer Admission Requirements:** High school transcript, college transcript(s), interview, minimum college GPA of 2.0 required. Lowest grade transferable 2. **General Admission Information:** Application Fee $50. Regular application deadline 2/15. Regular notification 2/15. Nonfall registration accepted. Credit offered for CEEB Advanced Placement tests.

COSTS AND FINANCIAL AID
Annual tuition $26,770. Room and board $8,650. Average book expense $1,100. **Required Forms and Deadlines:** FAFSA, institution's own financial aid form. **Notification of Awards:** Applicants will be notified of awards on a rolling basis beginning 4/1. **Types of Aid:** *Need-based scholarships/grants:* Federal Pell, SEOG, state scholarships/grants, private scholarships, the school's own gift aid, United Negro College Fund. *Loans:* Subsidized Stafford, Unsubsidized Stafford, PLUS, Federal Perkins, state loans, college/university loans from institutional funds. **Student Employment:** Federal Work-Study Program available. Institutional employment available. Highest amount earned per year from on-campus jobs $1,500. Off-campus job opportunities are good. **Financial Aid Statistics:** 100% freshmen, 99% undergrads receive need-based scholarship or grant aid. 91% freshmen, 89% undergrads receive non-need-based scholarship or grant aid. 82% freshmen, 80% undergrads receive need-based self-help aid. 5% freshmen, 6% undergrads receive athletic scholarships. 100% freshmen, 93% undergrads receive any aid. 69% undergrads borrow to pay for school. Average cumulative indebtedness $39,508. **Criteria for awarding institutional aid:** *Non-need-based:* academics, art, athletics, leadership, minority status, music/drama, religious affiliation, state/district residency.

ACADEMY OF ART UNIVERSITY

79 New Montgomery St, San Francisco, CA 94105
Phone: 415-274-2222 • **Financial Aid Phone:** 800-544-2787
E-mail: info@academyart.edu
Fax: 415-618-6287 • **Website:** www.academyart.edu • **ACT Code:** 155

This proprietary school was founded in 1929. It has a 20-acre campus.

RATINGS
Admissions Selectivity Rating: 61   **Fire Safety Rating:** 85   **Green Rating:** 60*

STUDENTS AND FACULTY
Enrollment: 11,710. **Student Body:** 56% female, 44% male, 41% out-of-state, 20% international (118 countries represented). Asian 8%, African American 6%, Caucasian 27%, Hispanic 9%, Native American 1%.
Retention and Graduation: 71% freshmen return for sophomore year. 6% grads go on to further study within 1 year. 3% grads pursue arts and sciences degrees. **Faculty:** Student/faculty ratio 19:1. 264 full-time faculty, 18% hold PhDs, 14% are members of minority groups, 41% are women. 0% of classes are taught by teaching assistants.

ACADEMICS
Degrees: associate, bachelor's, certificate, master's. **Classes:** Most classes have 10–19 students. **Majors with Highest Enrollment:** animation, interactive technology, video graphics and special effects; cinematography and film/video production; fashion/apparel design. **Special Study Options:** Accelerated program, cooperative education program, distance learning, English as a Second Language (ESL), independent study, internships, weekend college, Portfolio Development, Personal Enrichment program. **Disability Services:** Special programs offered to physically disabled students include note-taking services, reader services, tape recorders, tutors. **Career Services:** Alumni network.

FACILITIES
Housing: Coed dorms, men's dorms, women's dorms, apartments for married students, apartments for single students. 80% of campus accessible to physically disabled. **Special Academic Facilities/Equipment:** 3 Art galleries (public) for display of student work. **Computers:** Students can register for classes online. Administrative functions (other than registration) can be performed online.

CAMPUS LIFE
Environment: Metropolis. **Activities:** dance, drama/theater, musical theater, student newspaper, student-run film society, International Student Organization

27 registered organizations. **Athletics (Intercollegiate):** *Men:* baseball, basketball, cross-country, golf, soccer, tennis, track/field (outdoor). *Women:* basketball, cross-country, golf, soccer, softball, tennis, track/field (outdoor), volleyball.

ADMISSIONS

Freshman Admission Requirements: High school diploma is required and GED is accepted. **Freshman Admission Statistics:** 3,055 applied, 100% admitted, 41% enrolled. **Transfer Admission Requirements:** High school transcript, college transcript(s), minimum college GPA of 2.0 required. Lowest grade transferable C. **General Admission Information:** Application Fee $100. Nonfall registration accepted. Admission may be deferred for a maximum of 24 months.

COSTS AND FINANCIAL AID

Annual tuition $23,550. Room and board $13,400. Required fees $290. Average book expense $1,710. **Required Forms and Deadlines:** FAFSA, institution's own financial aid form. **Types of Aid:** *Need-based scholarships/grants:* Federal Pell, SEOG, state scholarships/grants. *Loans:* Direct Subsidized Stafford, Direct Unsubsidized Stafford, Direct PLUS, Subsidized Stafford, Unsubsidized Stafford, PLUS. **Student Employment:** Federal Work-Study Program available. Off-campus job opportunities are good. **Financial Aid Statistics:** 67% freshmen, 68% undergrads receive need-based scholarship or grant aid. 22% freshmen, 16% undergrads receive non-need-based scholarship or grant aid. 100% freshmen, 98% undergrads receive need-based self-help aid. 3% freshmen, 3% undergrads receive athletic scholarships. 61% freshmen, 66% undergrads receive any aid. 61% undergrads borrow to pay for school. Average cumulative indebtedness $46,726. **Criteria for awarding institutional aid:** *Non-need-based:* academics, art, athletics.

ACADIA UNIVERSITY

Admissions Office, Wolfville, NS B4P 2R6
Phone: 1-902-585-1446 • **Financial Aid Phone:** 902-585-1016
E-mail: pam.dimock@acadiau.ca
Fax: 902-585-1092 • **Website:** www.acadiau.ca

This public school was founded in 1838. It has a 200-acre campus.

RATINGS
Admissions Selectivity Rating: 63   **Fire Safety Rating:** 60*   **Green Rating:** 60*

STUDENTS AND FACULTY
Enrollment: 2,928. **Student Body:** 55% female, 45% male, 42% out-of-state. **Retention and Graduation:** 83% freshmen return for sophomore year. **Faculty:** Student/faculty ratio 10:1. 243 full-time faculty, 36% are women. 0% of classes are taught by teaching assistants.

ACADEMICS
Degrees: bachelor's, certificate, diploma, master's. **Special Study Options:** cooperative education program, distance learning, double major, English as a Second Language (ESL), exchange student program (domestic), honors program, independent study, internships, study abroad. **Career Services:** career/job search classes, career assessment, internships.

FACILITIES
Housing: Coed dorms, special housing for disabled students, men's dorms, women's dorms, apartments for single students. **Computers:** Students can register for classes online. Administrative functions (other than registration) can be performed online.

CAMPUS LIFE
Environment: Rural. **Activities:** Choral groups, concert band, dance, drama/theater, jazz band, literary magazine, music ensembles, musical theater, opera, pep band, radio station, student government, student newspaper, symphony orchestra, yearbook, Campus Ministries, International Student Organization 60 registered organizations, 3 religious organizations. **Athletics (Intercollegiate):** *Men:* basketball, cheerleading, cross-country, football, ice hockey, rugby, soccer, track/field (outdoor), volleyball. *Women:* basketball, cheerleading, cross-country, ice hockey, rugby, soccer, track/field (outdoor), volleyball. **On-Campus Highlights:** KC Irving Environmental Science Centre, The Sheldon L. Fountain Learning Commons

ADMISSIONS
Basis for Candidate Selection: *Very important factors considered include:* academic GPA, rigor of secondary school record. *Important factors considered include:* recommendation(s), talent/ability. *Other factors considered include:* Class rank, standardized test scores, character/personal qualities, extracurricular activities, geographical residence, volunteer work, work experience. **Freshman Admission Requirements:** High school diploma is required and GED is not

accepted. *Academic units required:* 1 English, 1 mathematics. *Academic units recommended:* 1 English, 1 mathematics. **Freshman Admission Statistics:** 1,600 applied, 49% admitted, 68% enrolled. **Transfer Admission Requirements:** college transcript(s). **General Admission Information:** Application Fee $25. Notification on a rolling basis, beginning on or about 11/1. Nonfall registration accepted. Admission may be deferred for a maximum of 1. Credit and/or placement offered for CEEB Advanced Placement tests.

COSTS AND FINANCIAL AID
Annual in-state tuition $8,062. Annual out-of-state tuition $8,062. Room and board $8,284. Required fees $180. Average book expense $1,200. **Notification of Awards:** Applicants will be notified of awards on or about 4/15. **Types of Aid:** *Loans:* Direct Subsidized Stafford, Direct Unsubsidized Stafford, Direct PLUS. **Student Employment:** Off-campus job opportunities are excellent. **Criteria for awarding institutional aid:** *Non-need-based:* academics, leadership, music/drama, state/district residency.

ADAMS STATE COLLEGE

208 Edgemont Blvd, Alamosa, CO 81102
Phone: 719-587-7712 • **Financial Aid Phone:** 719-587-7306
E-mail: ascadmit@adams.edu • **CEEB Code:** 4001
Fax: 719-587-7522 • **Website:** • **ACT Code:** 496

This public school was founded in 1921. It has a 90-acre campus.

RATINGS
Admissions Selectivity Rating: 75   **Fire Safety Rating:** 66   **Green Rating:** 72

STUDENTS AND FACULTY
Enrollment: 2,422. **Student Body:** 55% female, 45% male, 19% out-of-state, 0% international (10 countries represented). Asian 1%, African American 6%, Caucasian 51%, Hispanic 32%, Native American 1%.
Retention and Graduation: 55% freshmen return for sophomore year. 7% freshmen graduate within 4 years. 24% freshmen graduate within 6 years. **Faculty:** Student/faculty ratio 17:1. 111 full-time faculty, 70% hold PhDs, 19% are members of minority groups, 47% are women. 0% of classes are taught by teaching assistants.

ACADEMICS
Degrees: associate, bachelor's, master's. **Classes:** Most classes have fewer than 10 students. Most lab/discussion sessions have 10–19 students. **Majors with Highest Enrollment:** business administration and management; kinesiology and exercise science; teacher education, multiple levels. **Special Study Options:** Accelerated program, distance learning, double major, independent study, internships, study abroad, teacher certification program, weekend college, High School dual enrollment. **Disability Services:** Special programs offered to physically disabled students include note-taking services, reader services, tutors. **Career Services:** Alumni network, career/job search classes, career assessment, internships Career Services highlights include On-Campus Interviews Career Fair Career Counseling Services.

FACILITIES
Housing: Coed dorms, men's dorms, women's dorms, apartments for married students, apartments for single students, Learning Community. 95% of campus accessible to physically disabled. **Special Academic Facilities/Equipment:** Luther Bean Museum, Hatfield Gallery, Gallery 114, Leon Memorial Music Hall, Zacheis Planetarium, Ryan Geology Museum **Computers:** 10% of classrooms, 100% of dorms, 100% of libraries, 100% of dining areas, 99% of student union, have wireless network access. Students can register for classes online. Administrative functions (other than registration) can be performed online.

CAMPUS LIFE
Environment: Village. **Activities:** Choral groups, concert band, dance, drama/theater, jazz band, literary magazine, marching band, music ensembles, musical theater, pep band, radio station, student government, student newspaper, Campus Ministries, Model UN 23 registered organizations, 2 religious organizations. **Athletics (Intercollegiate):** *Men:* basketball, cross-country, football, golf, soccer, track/field (outdoor), track/field (indoor), wrestling. *Women:* basketball, cross-country, golf, soccer, softball, swimming, track/field (outdoor), track/field (indoor), volleyball. **On-Campus Highlights:** Leon Memorial Concert Hall, Zacheis Planetarium, Nielson Library, Plachy Hall, Rex Activity Center, Student Union Building (SUB). **Environmental Initiatives:** Establishment of EARTH (Environmental Action for Resources, Transportation, & Health) group on campus Partnering with the City of Alamosa and Habitat for Humanity to increase recycling opportunities on our campus. 3. Water Project Phase 1—convert supply to non-potable water Phase 2—update inefficient system with one with a weather station. Note that phase 2 has not been implemented yet, and may not for a few years.

ADMISSIONS

Freshman Academic Profile: Average high school GPA 3.0. 9% in top 10% of high school class, 24% in top 25% of high school class, 54% in top 50% of high school class. % from public high schools. SAT Math middle 50% range 450-550. SAT Critical Reading middle 50% range 430-550. SAT Writing middle 50% range 410-520. ACT middle 50% range 17-22. Minimum web-based TOEFL 79. Minimum paper TOEFL 550. **Basis for Candidate Selection:** *Very important factors considered include:* rigor of secondary school record, standardized test scores. *Important factors considered include:* academic GPA. *Other factors considered include:* Class rank, recommendation(s), character/ personal qualities, extracurricular activities, geographical residence, interview, state residency. **Freshman Admission Requirements:** High school diploma is required and GED is accepted. **Freshman Admission Statistics:** 2,534 applied, 64% admitted, 37% enrolled. **Transfer Admission Requirements:** college transcript(s), minimum college GPA of 2.0 required. Lowest grade transferable D. **General Admission Information:** Application Fee $30. Non-fall registration accepted. Admission may be deferred for a maximum of 2 years. Credit offered for CEEB Advanced Placement tests.

COSTS AND FINANCIAL AID

Required Forms and Deadlines: FAFSA. **Notification of Awards:** Applicants will be notified of awards on a rolling basis beginning 3/1. **Types of Aid:** *Need-based scholarships/grants:* Federal Pell, SEOG, state scholarships/ grants, private scholarships, the school's own gift aid. *Loans:* Subsidized Stafford, Unsubsidized Stafford, PLUS, Federal Perkins, Alternative Loans. **Student Employment:** Federal Work-Study Program available. Institutional employment available. Highest amount earned per year from on-campus jobs $1,854. Off-campus job opportunities are good. **Financial Aid Statistics:** 83% freshmen, 83% undergrads receive need-based scholarship or grant aid. 70% freshmen receive need-based self-help aid. 95% freshmen, 94% undergrads receive any aid. 77% undergrads borrow to pay for school. Average cumulative indebtedness $23,860. **Criteria for awarding institutional aid:** *Non-need-based:* academics, alumni affiliation, art, athletics, leadership, minority status, music/drama, state/district residency.

ADELPHI UNIVERSITY

Levermore Hall 114, Garden City, NY 11530
Phone: 516-877-3050 • **Financial Aid Phone:** 516-877-3080
E-mail: admissions@adelphi.edu • **CEEB Code:** 2003
Fax: 516-877-3039 • **Website:** www.adelphi.edu • **ACT Code:** 2664

This private school was founded in 1896. It has a 75-acre campus.

RATINGS

Admissions Selectivity Rating: 81   **Fire Safety Rating:** 99   **Green Rating:** 93

STUDENTS AND FACULTY

Enrollment: 5,053. **Student Body:** 70% female, 30% male, 8% out-of-state, 3% international (48 countries represented). Asian 7%, African American 11%, Caucasian 54%, Hispanic 13%, Native American 0%.
Retention and Graduation: 82% freshmen return for sophomore year. 54% freshmen graduate within 4 years. 66% freshmen graduate within 6 years. 41% grads go on to further study within 1 year. 2% grads pursue law degrees. 13% grads pursue business degrees. 6% grads pursue medical degrees. **Faculty:** Student/faculty ratio 12:1. 322 full-time faculty, 87% hold PhDs, 19% are members of minority groups, 52% are women. 0% of classes are taught by teaching assistants.

ACADEMICS

Degrees: associate, bachelor's, master's, post-bachelor's certificate, post-master's certificate. **Classes:** Most classes have 10–19 students. Most lab/discussion sessions have 10–19 students. **Majors with Highest Enrollment:** business/ commerce; education; nursing, other. **Special Study Options:** Accelerated program, cross-registration, distance learning, double major, dual enrollment, English as a Second Language (ESL), honors program, independent study, internships, liberal arts/career combination, student-designed major, study abroad, teacher certification program, weekend college, Joint Degrees; Learning Disabilities Program; Distance Learning Program is being restructured.
Honors Programs: The Honors College seeks to prepare highly talented and motivated students to face the 21st century by providing them with the intellectual perspectives and critical skills necessary to exercise responsible leadership. It involves an intense curricular and extracurricular program that asks students to view themselves and their work with integrity, passion, and seriousness.
Combined Degree Programs: BA/JD, BA/MA, BA/DDS, BA/MEng, Optometry, Dentistry, Physical therapy, Law, Environment Stud, Osteopathic. **Disabil-**

ity Services: Special programs offered to physically disabled students include note-taking services, reader services, tape recorders, tutors. **Career Services:** Alumni network, alumni services, career/job search classes, career assessment, internships, regional alumni.

FACILITIES

Housing: Coed dorms, special housing for disabled students, theme housing. Honors students live in the same residence hall; EXCEL mentoring program. 95% of campus accessible to physically disabled. **Special Academic Facilities/Equipment:** Art gallery, sculpture and ceramics studios, bronze-casting foundry, theatre, language labs. **Computers:** 90% of dorms, 99% of libraries, 99% of dining areas, 90% of student union, 75% of common outdoor areas have wireless network access. Students can register for classes online. Administrative functions (other than registration) can be performed online.

CAMPUS LIFE

Environment: Metropolis. **Activities:** Choral groups, concert band, dance, drama/theater, jazz band, literary magazine, music ensembles, musical theater, opera, radio station, student government, student newspaper, student-run film society, symphony orchestra, yearbook, Campus Ministries, International Student Organization, Model UN 80 registered organizations, 21 honor societies, 5 religious organizations. 3 fraternities, 7 sororities. **Athletics (Intercollegiate):** *Men:* baseball, basketball, cross-country, golf, lacrosse, soccer, swimming, tennis, track/field (outdoor), track/field (indoor). *Women:* basketball, bowling, cross-country, field hockey, lacrosse, soccer, softball, swimming, tennis, track/ field (outdoor), track/field (indoor), volleyball. **On-Campus Highlights:** Ruth S. Harley University Center, UnderGround Cafe, Swirbul Library, New Fine Arts Building, New Recreational Center. **Environmental Initiatives:** LEED silver rating for the CSPA project 100% green electrical Use of Geo-thermal heating and cooling systems in the newly constructed and proposed residence halls

ADMISSIONS

Freshman Academic Profile: Average high school GPA 3.5. 23% in top 10% of high school class, 55% in top 25% of high school class, 85% in top 50% of high school class. 74% from public high schools. SAT Math middle 50% range 510-620. SAT Critical Reading middle 50% range 500-600. SAT Writing middle 50% range 510-620. ACT middle 50% range 22-28. Minimum paper TOEFL 550. **Basis for Candidate Selection:** *Very important factors considered include:* rigor of secondary school record. *Important factors considered include:* Class rank, application essay, academic GPA, standardized test scores, character/ personal qualities, extracurricular activities, talent/ability, volunteer work. *Other factors considered include:* alumni/ae relation, first generation, interview, level of applicant's interest, work experience. **Freshman Admission Requirements:** High school diploma is required and GED is accepted. **Freshman Admission Statistics:** 9,184 applied, 66% admitted, 16% enrolled. **Transfer Admission Requirements:** college transcript(s), essay or personal statement, minimum college GPA of 2.3 required. **General Admission Information:** Application Fee $35. Notification on a rolling basis, beginning on or about 10/1. Nonfall registration accepted. Credit and/or placement offered for CEEB Advanced Placement tests.

COSTS AND FINANCIAL AID

Annual tuition $27,870. Room and board $11,900. Required fees $1,450. Average book expense $1,400. **Required Forms and Deadlines:** FAFSA, state aid form. **Notification of Awards:** Applicants will be notified of awards on a rolling basis beginning 2/15. **Types of Aid:** *Need-based scholarships/grants:* Federal Pell, SEOG, state scholarships/grants, private scholarships, the school's own gift aid, United Negro College Fund. *Loans:* Subsidized Stafford, Unsubsidized Stafford, PLUS, Federal Perkins, Federal Nursing, New York HELP Program (private alternative). **Student Employment:** Federal Work-Study Program available. Institutional employment available. Highest amount earned per year from on-campus jobs $20,594. Off-campus job opportunities are good. **Financial Aid Statistics:** 66% freshmen, 60% undergrads receive need-based scholarship or grant aid. 91% freshmen, 91% undergrads receive non-need-based scholarship or grant aid. 88% freshmen, 90% undergrads receive need-based self-help aid. 3% freshmen, 2% undergrads receive athletic scholarships. 98% freshmen, 91% undergrads receive any aid. 72% undergrads borrow to pay for school. Average cumulative indebtedness $35,429. **Criteria for awarding institutional aid:** *Non-need-based:* academics, alumni affiliation, art, athletics, leadership, minority status, music/drama, religious affiliation.

ADRIAN COLLEGE

110 South Madison Street, Adrian, MI 49221
Phone: 517-265-5161 • **Financial Aid Phone:** 517-265-5161
E-mail: admissions@adrian.edu • **CEEB Code:** 1001
Fax: 517-264-3331 • **Website:** www.adrian.edu • **ACT Code:** 1954

This private school, affiliated with the Methodist Church, was founded in 1859. It has a 100-acre campus.

RATINGS
Admissions Selectivity Rating: 73   **Fire Safety Rating:** 63   **Green Rating:** 61

STUDENTS AND FACULTY
Enrollment: 1,308. **Student Body:** 47% female, 53% male, 24% out-of-state, 4% international (6 countries represented). Asian 1%, African American 4%, Caucasian 77%, Hispanic 2%, Native American 0%.
Retention and Graduation: 73% freshmen return for sophomore year. 40% freshmen graduate within 4 years. 50% freshmen graduate within 6 years. 25% grads go on to further study within 1 year. 51% grads pursue arts and sciences degrees. 9% grads pursue law degrees. 9% grads pursue business degrees. 22% grads pursue medical degrees. **Faculty:** Student/faculty ratio 12:1. 78 full-time faculty, 82% hold PhDs, 9% are members of minority groups, 41% are women. 0% of classes are taught by teaching assistants.

ACADEMICS
Degrees: associate, bachelor's, transfer associate. **Classes:** Most classes have 10–19 students. Most lab/discussion sessions have 10–19 students. **Majors with Highest Enrollment:** business/commerce; English language and literature; kinesiology and exercise science. **Special Study Options:** double major, dual enrollment, honors program, independent study, internships, student-designed major, study abroad, teacher certification program. **Combined Degree Programs:** BA/MEng. **Disability Services:** Special programs offered to physically disabled students include note-taking services, reader services, tape recorders, tutors. **Career Services:** Alumni network, alumni services, career assessment, internships, regional alumni. Career Services highlights include Internships.

FACILITIES
Housing: Coed dorms, men's dorms, women's dorms, fraternity/sorority housing, apartments for single students, special-interest houses. 50% of campus accessible to physically disabled. **Special Academic Facilities/Equipment:** Art gallery, studio theatre, arboretum, education resource center, language lab, observatory, planetarium, solar greenhouse, nuclear magnetic resonance spectrometer, differential scanning calorimeter. **Computers:** 100% of classrooms, 100% of dorms, 100% of libraries, 100% of dining areas, 100% of student union, 100% of common outdoor areas have wireless network access. Students can register for classes online. Administrative functions (other than registration) can be performed online.

CAMPUS LIFE
Environment: Town. **Activities:** Choral groups, concert band, dance, drama/theater, jazz band, literary magazine, marching band, music ensembles, musical theater, pep band, radio station, student government, student newspaper, symphony orchestra, yearbook, Campus Ministries, International Student Organization 68 registered organizations, 13 honor societies, 8 religious organizations. 4 fraternities, 3 sororities. **Athletics (Intercollegiate): Men:** baseball, basketball, cross-country, football, golf, ice hockey, lacrosse, soccer, tennis, track/field (outdoor). **Women:** basketball, bowling, cross-country, golf, ice hockey, lacrosse, soccer, softball, tennis, track/field (outdoor), volleyball. **On-Campus Highlights:** Caine Student Center, Shipman Library, Merillat Sport and Fitness Center.

ADMISSIONS
Freshman Academic Profile: Average high school GPA 3.3. 17% in top 10% of high school class, 46% in top 25% of high school class, 81% in top 50% of high school class. % from public high schools. SAT Math middle 50% range 410-535. SAT Critical Reading middle 50% range 430-515. ACT middle 50% range 20-25. Minimum paper TOEFL 500. **Basis for Candidate Selection:** *Very important factors considered include:* Class rank, rigor of secondary school record. *Important factors considered include:* academic GPA, standardized test scores, talent/ability. *Other factors considered include:* alumni/ae relation, character/personal qualities, extracurricular activities, interview, level of applicant's interest, volunteer work, work experience. **Freshman Admission Requirements:** High school diploma is required and GED is accepted. **Freshman Admission Statistics:** 3,709 applied, 64% admitted, 21% enrolled. **Transfer Admission Requirements:** High school transcript, college transcript(s), minimum college GPA of 2.7 required. Lowest grade transferable C. **General Admission Information:** Notification on a rolling basis, beginning on or about 9/1. Nonfall registration not accepted. Admission may be deferred for a maximum of 1 year. Credit and/or placement offered for CEEB Advanced Placement tests.

COSTS AND FINANCIAL AID
Annual tuition $23,090. Room and board $7,600. Required fees $300. Average book expense $400. **Required Forms and Deadlines:** FAFSA. **Notification of Awards:** Applicants will be notified of awards on a rolling basis beginning 3/15. **Types of Aid:** *Need-based scholarships/grants:* Federal Pell, SEOG, state scholarships/grants, private scholarships, the school's own gift aid. *Loans:* Subsidized Stafford, Unsubsidized Stafford, PLUS, Federal Perkins. **Student Employment:** Federal Work-Study Program available. Institutional employment available. Highest amount earned per year from on-campus jobs $1,700. Off-campus job opportunities are good. **Financial Aid Statistics:** 87% freshmen, 86% undergrads receive need-based scholarship or grant aid. 88% freshmen, 86% undergrads receive non-need-based scholarship or grant aid. 89% freshmen, 88% undergrads receive need-based self-help aid. 98% freshmen, 92% undergrads receive any aid. 81% undergrads borrow to pay for school. Average cumulative indebtedness $20,000. **Criteria for awarding institutional aid:** *Non-need-based:* academics, alumni affiliation, art, leadership, music/drama, religious affiliation.

AGNES SCOTT COLLEGE

141 E. College Ave., Decatur, GA 30030-3797
Phone: 404-471-6285 • **Financial Aid Phone:** 404-471-6395
E-mail: admission@agnesscott.edu • **CEEB Code:** 5002
Fax: 404-471-6414 • **Website:** www.agnesscott.edu • **ACT Code:** 780

This private school, affiliated with the Presbyterian Church, was founded in 1889. It has a 100-acre campus.

RATINGS
Admissions Selectivity Rating: 87   **Fire Safety Rating:** 96   **Green Rating:** 90

STUDENTS AND FACULTY
Enrollment: 831. **Student Body:** 100% female, 0% male, 37% out-of-state, 9% international (29 countries represented). Asian 3%, African American 35%, Caucasian 35%, Hispanic 8%, Native American 0%.
Retention and Graduation: 82% freshmen return for sophomore year. 57% freshmen graduate within 4 years. 64% freshmen graduate within 6 years. 25% grads go on to further study within 1 year. 15% grads pursue arts and sciences degrees. 4% grads pursue law degrees. 2% grads pursue business degrees. 2% grads pursue medical degrees. **Faculty:** Student/faculty ratio 11:1. 72 full-time faculty, 97% hold PhDs, 21% are members of minority groups, 63% are women. 0% of classes are taught by teaching assistants.

ACADEMICS
Degrees: bachelor's, master's, post-bachelor's certificate. **Classes:** Most classes have 10–19 students. Most lab/discussion sessions have 10–19 students. **Majors with Highest Enrollment:** English language and literature; history; psychology. **Special Study Options:** Accelerated program, cross-registration, double major, dual enrollment, exchange student program (domestic), external degree program, independent study, internships, student-designed major, study abroad, teacher certification program, Woodruff Scholars program for women beyond traditional college age; exchange program with Mills College, Atlanta Semester. **Combined Degree Programs:** BA/MA, BA/MA Arch. w/Wash. U., BA/BS Eng. BA/BSN w/Emory. **Disability Services:** Special programs offered to physically disabled students include note-taking services, reader services, tape recorders, tutors. **Career Services:** Alumni network, alumni services, career/job search classes, career assessment, internships, regional alumni. Career Services highlights include Internships.

FACILITIES
Housing: women's dorms, apartments for single students, theme housing. 90% of campus accessible to physically disabled. **Special Academic Facilities/Equipment:** Art galleries, state-of the art science building opened in January 2003, collaborative learning centers, language lab, electron microscope, observatory, 30-inch Beck telescope, planetarium, interactive learning center, multimedia presentation classrooms, instructional technology center, multimedia production facility. **Computers:** 50% of classrooms, 100% of libraries, 100% of student union, 10% of common outdoor areas have wireless network access. Students can register for classes online. Administrative functions (other than registration) can be performed online.

CAMPUS LIFE
Environment: Metropolis. **Activities:** Choral groups, dance, drama/theater, literary magazine, marching band, music ensembles, musical theater, pep band,

student government, student newspaper, symphony orchestra, television station, yearbook, Campus Ministries, International Student Organization, Model UN 80 registered organizations, 12 honor societies, 12 religious organizations. **Athletics (Intercollegiate):** *Women:* basketball, lacrosse, soccer, softball, tennis, volleyball. **On-Campus Highlights:** New $36.5 million Science Center, Alston Campus Center, Newly renovated Bradley Observatory, McCain Library, Several residence halls are on the National Regist. **Environmental Initiatives:** Converted to campus-wide single stream recycling and composting. Agnes Scott is committed to Zero Waste, and has already achived a 62% waste diversion rate. Implementing a climate action plan with major efficiency and renewable energy commitments. Continued guidance and leadership from an inclusive sustainability steering committee with active Board and alumnae representatives as well as students, faculty, staff, and all management.

ADMISSIONS

Freshman Academic Profile: Average high school GPA 3.6. 39% in top 10% of high school class, 69% in top 25% of high school class, 92% in top 50% of high school class. 71% from public high schools. SAT Math middle 50% range 510-620. SAT Critical Reading middle 50% range 520-670. SAT Writing middle 50% range 520-630. ACT middle 50% range 22-29. **Basis for Candidate Selection:** *Very important factors considered include:* Class rank, application essay, academic GPA, recommendation(s), rigor of secondary school record, standardized test scores, character/personal qualities, talent/ability. *Important factors considered include:* extracurricular activities, volunteer work, work experience. *Other factors considered include:* alumni/ae relation, first generation, geographical residence, interview, level of applicant's interest, racial/ethnic status, state residency. **Freshman Admission Requirements:** High school diploma is required and GED is accepted. **Freshman Admission Statistics:** 1,554 applied, 62% admitted, 24% enrolled. **Transfer Admission Requirements:** High school transcript, college transcript(s), essay or personal statement, statement of good standing from prior institution(s). Minimum college GPA of 3.0 required. Lowest grade transferable C. **General Admission Information:** Application Fee $35. Nonfall registration accepted. Admission may be deferred for a maximum of 1 year. Credit and/or placement offered for CEEB Advanced Placement tests.

COSTS AND FINANCIAL AID

Annual tuition $33,246. Room and board $10,230. Required fees $215. Average book expense $1,000. **Required Forms and Deadlines:** FAFSA. **Notification of Awards:** Applicants will be notified of awards on a rolling basis beginning 3/1. **Types of Aid:** *Need-based scholarships/grants:* Federal Pell, SEOG, state scholarships/grants, private scholarships, the school's own gift aid. *Loans:* Subsidized Stafford, Unsubsidized Stafford, PLUS. **Student Employment:** Federal Work-Study Program available. Institutional employment available. Off-campus job opportunities are excellent. **Financial Aid Statistics:** 100% freshmen, 100% undergrads receive need-based scholarship or grant aid. 17% freshmen, 25% undergrads receive non-need-based scholarship or grant aid. 91% freshmen, 91% undergrads receive need-based self-help aid. % freshmen, % undergrads receive athletic scholarships. 100% freshmen, 99% undergrads receive any aid. 77% undergrads borrow to pay for school. Average cumulative indebtedness $27,462. **Criteria for awarding institutional aid:** *Non-need-based:* academics, leadership, minority status, music/drama, religious affiliation, state/district residency.

ALABAMA A&M UNIVERSITY

P.O. Box 908, Normal, AL 35762
Phone: 256-851-5245
E-mail: juan.alexander@aamu.edu • **CEEB Code:** 1003
Fax: 256-851-5249 • **ACT Code:** 2

This public school was founded in 1875. It has a 880-acre campus.

RATINGS

Admissions Selectivity Rating: 78   Fire Safety Rating: 60*   Green Rating: 60*

STUDENTS AND FACULTY

Enrollment: 4,489. **Student Body:** 52% female, 48% male, 31% out-of-state, 1% international (42 countries represented). Asian 0%, African American 70%, Caucasian 2%, Hispanic 0%, Native American 0%.
Retention and Graduation: 77% grads go on to further study within 1 year. 40% grads pursue arts and sciences degrees. 2% grads pursue law degrees. 45% grads pursue business degrees. 11% grads pursue medical degrees. **Faculty:** Student/faculty ratio 14:1. 314 full-time faculty, 45% hold PhDs, 55% are members of minority groups, 39% are women. 1% of classes are taught by teaching assistants.

ACADEMICS

Degrees: bachelor's, master's, post-master's certificate. **Classes:** Most classes have fewer than 10 students. Most lab/discussion sessions have 20–29 students. **Majors with Highest Enrollment:** biology/biological sciences; elementary education and teaching; mechanical engineering related technologies/technicians, other. **Special Study Options:** Accelerated program, cooperative education program, distance learning, double major, dual enrollment, exchange student program (domestic), honors program, independent study, internships, study abroad, teacher certification program, weekend college. **Disability Services:** Special programs offered to physically disabled students include note-taking services, reader services, tape recorders, tutors. **Career Services:** career/job search classes, career assessment, internships, regional alumni.

FACILITIES

Housing: men's dorms, women's dorms, apartments for single students. 65% of campus accessible to physically disabled. **Special Academic Facilities/Equipment:** State Black Archives **Computers:** Students can register for classes online.

CAMPUS LIFE

Environment: City. **Activities:** Choral groups, concert band, dance, drama/theater, jazz band, literary magazine, marching band, music ensembles, pep band, radio station, student government, student newspaper, symphony orchestra, television station, yearbook, Campus Ministries, International Student Organization 76 registered organizations, 14 honor societies, 3 religious organizations. 4 fraternities, 4 sororities. **Athletics (Intercollegiate):** *Men:* baseball, basketball, cross-country, football, golf, soccer, track/field (outdoor). *Women:* basketball, cross-country, soccer, softball, track/field (outdoor), volleyball. **On-Campus Highlights:** Engineering Building, Cafeteria, Gym, Business School, Dawson Building.

ADMISSIONS

Freshman Academic Profile: 90% from public high schools. SAT Math middle 50% range 380-470. SAT Critical Reading middle 50% range 400-470. SAT Writing middle 50% range 380-460. ACT middle 50% range 16-19. Minimum paper TOEFL 550. **Basis for Candidate Selection:** *Very important factors considered include:* standardized test scores, alumni/ae relation, geographical residence, state residency. *Important factors considered include:* racial/ethnic status. *Other factors considered include:* Class rank, recommendation(s). **Freshman Admission Requirements:** High school diploma is required and GED is accepted. *Academic units required:* 4 English, 4 mathematics, 4 science, (2 science labs), 4 social studies, 4 history. *Academic units recommended:* 4 English, 4 mathematics, 4 science, (2 science labs), 4 social studies, 4 history. **Freshman Admission Statistics:** 5,697 applied, 47% admitted, 39% enrolled. **Transfer Admission Requirements:** High school transcript, college transcript(s), standardized test scores, statement of good standing from prior institution(s). Minimum college GPA of 2.5 required. Lowest grade transferable C. **General Admission Information:** Application Fee $10. Regular application deadline 7/1. Notification on a rolling basis, beginning on or about 4/15. Nonfall registration accepted. Admission may be deferred for a maximum of 12 months. Neither credit nor placement offered for CEEB Advanced Placement tests.

COSTS AND FINANCIAL AID

Annual in-state tuition $3,948. Annual out-of-state tuition $7,896. Room and board $5,350. Required fees $744. **Required Forms and Deadlines:** FAFSA, institution's own financial aid form. **Types of Aid:** *Need-based scholarships/grants:* Federal Pell, SEOG, state scholarships/grants, private scholarships, the school's own gift aid, United Negro College Fund. *Loans:* Direct Subsidized Stafford, Direct Unsubsidized Stafford, Direct PLUS, Federal Perkins, state loans, college/university loans from institutional funds. **Student Employment:** Highest amount earned per year from on-campus jobs $5,400.

ALABAMA STATE UNIVERSITY

915 South Jackson Street, Montgomery, AL 36104
Phone: 334-229-4291
E-mail: dlamar@asunet.alasu.edu
Fax: 334-229-4984 • **Website:** www.alasu.edu • **ACT Code:** 8

This public school was founded in 1867.

RATINGS

Admissions Selectivity Rating: 63   Fire Safety Rating: 60*   Green Rating: 60*

STUDENTS AND FACULTY

Enrollment: 5,125. **Student Body:** 59% female, 41% male, 35% out-of-state, 0% international (countries represented). Asian 0%, African American 95%, Caucasian 4%, Hispanic 0%, Native American 0%.

Retention and Graduation: 68% freshmen return for sophomore year. 50% grads go on to further study within 1 year. **Faculty:** Student/faculty ratio 19:1. 229 full-time faculty, 59% hold PhDs, 67% are members of minority groups, 54% are women. 0% of classes are taught by teaching assistants.

ACADEMICS

Degrees: bachelor's, master's. **Majors with Highest Enrollment:** computer and information science; criminal justice/safety studies; elementary education and teaching. **Special Study Options:** cooperative education program, cross-registration, double major, honors program, internships, teacher certification program. **Disability Services:** Special programs offered to physically disabled students include note-taking services, tape recorders. **Career Services:** career/job search classes, internships.

FACILITIES

Housing: men's dorms, women's dorms, apartments for single students, Honor dorms. 90% of campus accessible to physically disabled. **Special Academic Facilities/Equipment:** Levi Watkins Learning Center Special Collections. **Computers:** Students can register for classes online. Administrative functions (other than registration) can be performed online.

CAMPUS LIFE

Environment: Activities: Choral groups, concert band, dance, drama/theater, jazz band, marching band, music ensembles, musical theater, pep band, radio station, student government, student newspaper, symphony orchestra, yearbook 64 registered organizations, 17 honor societies, 5 fraternities, 4 sororities. **Athletics (Intercollegiate):** *Men:* baseball, basketball, cheerleading, cross-country, football, golf, tennis, track/field (outdoor), track/field (indoor). *Women:* basketball, cheerleading, cross-country, golf, softball, tennis, track/field (outdoor), track/field (indoor), volleyball.

ADMISSIONS

Freshman Academic Profile: Average high school GPA 2.7. SAT Math middle 50% range 340-444. SAT Critical Reading middle 50% range 350-457. ACT middle 50% range 14-18. Minimum paper TOEFL 500. **Basis for Candidate Selection:** *Very important factors considered include:* rigor of secondary school record. *Important factors considered include:* Class rank, standardized test scores. *Other factors considered include:* recommendation(s). **Freshman Admission Requirements:** High school diploma is required and GED is accepted. **Transfer Admission Requirements:** college transcript(s), minimum college GPA of 2.0 required. Lowest grade transferable C. **General Admission Information:** Regular application deadline 7/30. Notification on a rolling basis, beginning on or about 8/30. Nonfall registration accepted. Admission may be deferred for a maximum of semester. Credit and/or placement offered for CEEB Advanced Placement tests.

COSTS AND FINANCIAL AID

Annual in-state tuition $2,904. Annual out-of-state tuition $5,808. Room and board $3,700. Average book expense $800. **Required Forms and Deadlines:** FAFSA, state aid form. **Notification of Awards:** Applicants will be notified of awards on a rolling basis beginning 5/15. **Types of Aid:** *Need-based scholarships/grants:* Federal Pell, SEOG, state scholarships/grants, private scholarships, the school's own gift aid. *Loans:* Subsidized Stafford, Unsubsidized Stafford, PLUS, Federal Perkins. **Student Employment:** Federal Work-Study Program available. Institutional employment available. Highest amount earned per year from on-campus jobs $2,400. Off-campus job opportunities are good. **Financial Aid Statistics:** 82% freshmen, 79% undergrads receive need-based scholarship or grant aid. 21% freshmen, 24% undergrads receive non-need-based scholarship or grant aid. 80% freshmen, 88% undergrads receive need-based self-help aid. 3% freshmen, 5% undergrads receive athletic scholarships. 72% undergrads borrow to pay for school. Average cumulative indebtedness $34,430. **Criteria for awarding institutional aid:** *Non-need-based:* academics, athletics.

ALASKA BIBLE COLLEGE

P.O. Box 289, Glennallen, AK 99588
Phone: 907-822-3201
E-mail: info@akbible.edu
Fax: 907-822-5027 • **Website:** www.akbible.edu

This private school, affiliated with the Christian (Nondenominational) Church, was founded in 1966. It has a 90-acre campus.

RATINGS

Admissions Selectivity Rating: 61   **Fire Safety Rating:** 60*   **Green Rating:** 60*

STUDENTS AND FACULTY

Retention and Graduation: 67% freshmen return for sophomore year. **Faculty:** Student/faculty ratio 7:1. 4 full-time faculty, 25% hold PhDs.

ACADEMICS

Degrees: associate, bachelor's, certificate, terminal associate, transfer associate. **Special Study Options:** cooperative education program, double major, independent study, internships.

FACILITIES

Housing: men's dorms, women's dorms, apartments for married students, apartments for single students.

CAMPUS LIFE

Environment: Rural. **On-Campus Highlights:** Annette Ball Memorial Library, Food Cache, Murdock Campus Center, Vince Joy Hall, Firebreak.

ADMISSIONS

Freshman Academic Profile: Minimum paper TOEFL 500. **Basis for Candidate Selection:** *Very important factors considered include:* application essay, recommendation(s), rigor of secondary school record, standardized test scores, character/personal qualities, interview, religious affiliation/commitment. *Important factors considered include:* volunteer work, work experience. *Other factors considered include:* extracurricular activities, racial/ethnic status, talent/ability. **Freshman Admission Requirements:** High school diploma is required and GED is accepted. **Freshman Admission Statistics:** 11 applied, 100% admitted, 100% enrolled. **Transfer Admission Requirements:** High school transcript, college transcript(s), essay or personal statement, interview, standardized test scores, statement of good standing from prior institution(s). Minimum college GPA of 2.0 required. Lowest grade transferable C. **General Admission Information:** Application Fee $35. Regular application deadline 7/1. Nonfall registration accepted. Admission may be deferred for a maximum of 1 year.

COSTS AND FINANCIAL AID

Annual tuition $5,720. Room and board $4,570. Average book expense $400.

ALASKA PACIFIC UNIVERSITY

4101 University Drive, Anchorage, AK 99508-4625
Phone: 907-564-8248 • **Financial Aid Phone:** 907-564-8341
E-mail: admissions@alaskapacific.edu • **CEEB Code:** 4201
Fax: 907-564-8317 • **Website:** www.alaskapacific.edu • **ACT Code:** 62

This private school was founded in 1957. It has a 170-acre campus.

RATINGS

Admissions Selectivity Rating: 88   **Fire Safety Rating:** 86   **Green Rating:** 79

STUDENTS AND FACULTY

Enrollment: 455. **Student Body:** 65% female, 35% male, 32% out-of-state, 0% international (3 countries represented). Asian 2%, African American 3%, Caucasian 58%, Hispanic 3%, Native American 15%.
Retention and Graduation: 67% freshmen return for sophomore year. 20% freshmen graduate within 4 years. 27% freshmen graduate within 6 years. **Faculty:** Student/faculty ratio 10:1. 50 full-time faculty, 64% hold PhDs, 4% are members of minority groups, 58% are women. 0% of classes are taught by teaching assistants.

ACADEMICS

Degrees: associate, bachelor's, certificate, master's, post-bachelor's certificate, terminal associate. **Classes:** Most classes have fewer than 10 students. Most lab/discussion sessions have fewer than 10 students. **Majors with Highest Enrollment:** business administration and management; elementary education and teaching; parks, recreation and leisure facilities management. **Special Study Options:** distance learning, double major, exchange student program (domestic), independent study, internships, student-designed major, study abroad, teacher certification program, Degree Completion program for adult students and a distance education program for Rural Alaskan Native Adults. **Disability Services:** Special programs offered to physically disabled students include note-taking services, tape recorders, tutors. **Career Services:** career/job search classes, career assessment, internships.

FACILITIES

Housing: Coed dorms, cooperative housing, several theme houses - example "Nordic Skiers House" for ski team members. 75% of campus accessible to physically disabled. **Special Academic Facilities/Equipment:** Alaskana collection GIS lab gym with pool Student Center with weight room and indoor climbing wall Outdoor recreation center with classes and rental equipment Lake for canoeing and kayaking trails for running, skiing, hiking, biking, etc., connected to city's trail system **Computers:** 100% of classrooms, 100% of dorms, 100% of libraries, 100% of dining areas, 100% of student union, 100% of common outdoor areas have wireless network access. Students can register for classes online. Administrative functions (other than registration) can be performed online.

CAMPUS LIFE

Environment: City. **Activities:** drama/theater, literary magazine, music ensembles, student government, student newspaper, yearbook 15 registered organizations, 1 religious organizations. **On-Campus Highlights:** Student Center, Climbing wall and weight room, Pool, lounges in Grant Hall and in Carr Gottst **Environmental Initiatives:** Kellogg Farm dedicated to organic and sustainable enterprises. APU does not use paper plates, plastic silverware, etc. Also paperless initiative. Committed to building a LEEDs level student center.

ADMISSIONS

Freshman Academic Profile: Average high school GPA 3.3. 17% in top 10% of high school class, 31% in top 25% of high school class, 72% in top 50% of high school class. 95% from public high schools. SAT Math middle 50% range 470-560. SAT Critical Reading middle 50% range 490-600. SAT Writing middle 50% range 460-610. ACT middle 50% range 21-27. Minimum web-based TOEFL 79. Minimum paper TOEFL 550. **Basis for Candidate Selection:** *Very important factors considered include:* application essay, academic GPA, rigor of secondary school record. *Important factors considered include:* recommendation(s), standardized test scores, alumni/ae relation, level of applicant's interest. *Other factors considered include:* extracurricular activities, talent/ability, volunteer work, work experience. **Freshman Admission Requirements:** High school diploma is required and GED is accepted. **Freshman Admission Statistics:** 245 applied, 48% admitted, 43% enrolled. **Transfer Admission Requirements:** college transcript(s), essay or personal statement, statement of good standing from prior institution(s). Minimum college GPA of 2.0 required. Lowest grade transferable C. **General Admission Information:** Application Fee $25. Regular application deadline 8/15. Notification on a rolling basis, beginning on or about 1/15. Nonfall registration accepted. Admission may be deferred for a maximum of 12 months. Credit offered for CEEB Advanced Placement tests.

COSTS AND FINANCIAL AID

Annual tuition $26,250. Room and board $9,300. Required fees $110. Average book expense $1,000. **Required Forms and Deadlines:** FAFSA. **Notification of Awards:** Applicants will be notified of awards on a rolling basis beginning 2/1. **Types of Aid:** *Need-based scholarships/grants:* Federal Pell, SEOG, state scholarships/grants, private scholarships, the school's own gift aid. *Loans:* Subsidized Stafford, Unsubsidized Stafford, PLUS, state loans, college/university loans from institutional funds. **Student Employment:** Federal Work-Study Program available. Institutional employment available. Off-campus job opportunities are good. **Financial Aid Statistics:** 47% freshmen, 55% undergrads receive need-based scholarship or grant aid. 100% freshmen, 48% undergrads receive non-need-based scholarship or grant aid. 68% freshmen, 42% undergrads receive need-based self-help aid. 88% freshmen, 92% undergrads receive any aid. 93% undergrads borrow to pay for school. Average cumulative indebtedness $44,398. **Criteria for awarding institutional aid:** *Non-need-based:* academics, alumni affiliation, leadership, religious affiliation, state/district residency.

ALBANY COLLEGE OF PHARMACY

106 New Scotland Avenue, Albany, NY 12208
Phone: 518-694-7221 • **Financial Aid Phone:** 518-694-7256
E-mail: admissions@acp.edu • **CEEB Code:** 2013
Fax: 518-694-7322 • **Website:** www.acp.edu • **ACT Code:** 2672

This private school was founded in 1881. It has a 21-acre campus.

RATINGS
Admissions Selectivity Rating: 89   **Fire Safety Rating:** 63   **Green Rating:** 60*

STUDENTS AND FACULTY
Enrollment: 1,015. **Student Body:** 58% female, 42% male, 10% out-of-state, 8% international (6 countries represented). Asian 13%, African American 2%, Caucasian 73%, Hispanic 1%, Native American 0%.
Retention and Graduation: 79% freshmen return for sophomore year.
Faculty: Student/faculty ratio 16:1. 82 full-time faculty, 74% hold PhDs, 12% are members of minority groups, 49% are women. 0% of classes are taught by teaching assistants.

ACADEMICS
Degrees: bachelor's, certificate, first professional. **Classes:** Most classes have 20–29 students. Most lab/discussion sessions have 20–29 students. **Majors with Highest Enrollment:** pharmacy (pharmd [usa], pharmd or bs/bpharm [canada]). **Special Study Options:** Accelerated program, cross-registration. **Combined Degree Programs:** BA/JD, Pharm.D./MS, Pharm.D./MBA, BS/Phy Asst. **Disability Services:** Special programs offered to physically disabled students include tutors. **Career Services:** career/job search classes, career assessment

FACILITIES
Housing: Coed dorms, apartments for single students. 100% of campus accessible to physically disabled. **Special Academic Facilities/Equipment:** Throop Pharmaceutical Museum. **Computers:** Students can register for classes online. Administrative functions (other than registration) can be performed online. Undergraduates are required to own a computer.

CAMPUS LIFE
Environment: City. **Activities:** Choral groups, concert band, dance, literary magazine, student government, student newspaper, yearbook, International Student Organization 2 honor societies, 1 religious organizations. **Athletics (Intercollegiate):** *Men:* basketball, soccer. *Women:* basketball, soccer. **On-Campus Highlights:** NEW - ACP Student Center

ADMISSIONS
Freshman Academic Profile: 92.0. 47% in top 10% of high school class, 86% in top 25% of high school class, 99% in top 50% of high school class. % from public high schools. SAT Math middle 50% range 570-650. SAT Critical Reading middle 50% range 530-620. SAT Writing middle 50% range 510-600. ACT middle 50% range 23-28. Minimum paper TOEFL 600. **Basis for Candidate Selection:** *Very important factors considered include:* academic GPA, standardized test scores. *Important factors considered include:* Class rank, rigor of secondary school record. *Other factors considered include:* application essay, recommendation(s), alumni/ae relation, character/personal qualities, extracurricular activities, geographical residence, level of applicant's interest, talent/ability, volunteer work, work experience. **Freshman Admission Requirements:** High school diploma is required and GED is accepted. *Academic units required:* 4 English, 4 mathematics, 3 science, (3 science labs), 4 social studies. *Academic units recommended:* 4 English, 4 mathematics, 3 science, (3 science labs), 4 social studies. **Freshman Admission Statistics:** 1,050 applied, 54% admitted, 43% enrolled. **Transfer Admission Requirements:** college transcript(s), essay or personal statement, statement of good standing from prior institution(s). Minimum college GPA of 3.2 required. Lowest grade transferable B. **General Admission Information:** Application Fee $75. Early decision application deadline 11/1. Regular application deadline 3/1. Regular notification 3/15. Nonfall registration not accepted. Admission may be deferred for a maximum of 1 year. Credit offered for CEEB Advanced Placement tests.

COSTS AND FINANCIAL AID
Required Forms and Deadlines: FAFSA. **Notification of Awards:** Applicants will be notified of awards on a rolling basis beginning 3/25. **Types of Aid:** *Need-based scholarships/grants:* Federal Pell, SEOG, state scholarships/grants, private scholarships, the school's own gift aid. *Loans:* Subsidized Stafford, Unsubsidized Stafford, PLUS, Federal Perkins. **Student Employment:** **Financial Aid Statistics:** 92% freshmen, 80% undergrads receive need-based scholarship or grant aid. 12% freshmen, 6% undergrads receive non-need-based scholarship or grant aid. 84% freshmen, 92% undergrads receive need-based self-help aid. 92% undergrads borrow to pay for school. Average cumulative indebtedness $20,010. **Criteria for awarding institutional aid:** *Non-need-based:* academics, alumni affiliation, leadership.

ALBANY STATE UNIVERSITY

504 College Drive, Albany, GA 31705
Phone: 229-430-4646 • **Financial Aid Phone:** 229-430-4650
E-mail: enrollmentservices@asurams.edu • **CEEB Code:** 5004
Fax: 229-430-4105 • **Website:** www.asurams.edu • **ACT Code:** 782

This public school was founded in 1903. It has a 232-acre campus.

RATINGS
Admissions Selectivity Rating: 87   **Fire Safety Rating:** 80   **Green Rating:** 66

STUDENTS AND FACULTY
Enrollment: 4,173. **Student Body:** 66% female, 34% male, 4% out-of-state, 0% international (22 countries represented). Asian 0%, African American 83%, Caucasian 4%, Hispanic 1%, Native American 0%.
Retention and Graduation: 41% freshmen graduate within 6 years. **Faculty:** Student/faculty ratio 21:1. 164 full-time faculty, 77% hold PhDs, 78% are members of minority groups, 45% are women. 0% of classes are taught by teaching assistants.

ACADEMICS
Degrees: associate, bachelor's, master's, post-master's certificate. **Classes:** Most classes have 20–29 students. **Majors with Highest Enrollment:** business administration and management; early childhood education and teaching; nursing/registered nurse (rn, asn, bsn, msn). **Special Study Options:** cooperative education program, cross-registration, distance learning, double major, dual enrollment, honors program, independent study, internships, liberal arts/career combination, study abroad, teacher certification program, weekend college, 3+2 & 2+2 engineering program with GA Tech. Pre-med, pre-med technology, pre-pharmacy study options. Online degree programs. **Honors Programs:** The Velma Fudge Grant Honors Program represents a commitment made by Albany State University (ASU) to broaden and enrich educational experiences of bright, highly motivated and creative students. Honors Program students are provided opportunities for scholarships, access to special extracurricular programs, a chance to pursue independent projects and research interests, professional experience through internship programs and special service options. Through its specially designed curriculum, the University provides the opportunity for faculty to teach academically talented students in inventive, interdisciplinary, small class settings designed to fulfill core curriculum requirements, as well as in advanced or intensive classes in particular disciplines. The Honors Program is specifically designed for academic scholarship recipients, academically talented students and entering freshman and transfer students with a proven dedication to academic excellence and scholarship. The Honors Program student must reach beyond good grades for success and have the courage to demonstrate superior ethical leadership in his/her chosen field of study. **Disability Services:** Special programs offered to physically disabled students include note-taking services, reader services, tape recorders, tutors. **Career Services:** Alumni network, alumni services, career assessment, internships, regional alumni. Career Services highlights include All opportunities are welcomed to provide experiential learning experiences for ASU students, especially those that result in employment opportunities.

FACILITIES
Housing: Coed dorms, men's dorms, women's dorms, apartments for single students, Upper classmen and graduate halls. 50% of campus accessible to physically disabled. **Computers:** 67% of dorms. have wireless network access.

CAMPUS LIFE
Environment: City. **Activities:** Choral groups, concert band, dance, drama/theater, jazz band, marching band, opera, radio station, student government, student newspaper, television station, Campus Ministries, International Student Organization, Model UN 70 registered organizations, 10 honor societies, 6 fraternities, 4 sororities. **Athletics (Intercollegiate):** *Men:* baseball, basketball, cross-country, football, track/field (outdoor). *Women:* basketball, cross-country, softball, tennis, track/field (outdoor), volleyball. **On-Campus Highlights:** Student Affairs Building, Gymnasium, Housing, Stadium **Environmental Initiatives:** 1. Hazardous Waste Lab 2. Paint shops and carpentry 3. Universal Waste 4. Paperless Initiative 1. Recycling Toner Cartridges 2. Paper and Paper products 3. Used Motor Oil 4. Used cooking oil 1. Automotive operation 2. Pesticide application 3. Containment for elevator reserviors

ADMISSIONS
Freshman Academic Profile: 10% in top 10% of high school class, 30% in top 25% of high school class, 67% in top 50% of high school class. % from public high schools. SAT Math middle 50% range 390-460. SAT Critical Reading middle 50% range 390-450. ACT middle 50% range 16-19. Minimum paper TOEFL 523. **Basis for Candidate Selection:** *Very important factors considered include:* academic GPA, standardized test scores. *Other factors considered include:* interview. **Freshman Admission Requirements:** *Academic units required:* 4 English, 4 mathematics, 3 science, (2 science labs), 2 foreign language, 3 social studies. *Academic units recommended:* 4 English, 4 mathematics, 3 science, (2 science labs), 2 foreign language, 3 social studies. **Freshman Admission Statistics:** 6,554 applied, 29% admitted, 57% enrolled. **Transfer Admission Requirements:** college transcript(s), minimum college GPA of 2.0 required. Lowest grade transferable D. **General Admission Information:** Application Fee $20. Regular application deadline 7/1. Nonfall registration accepted. Admission may be deferred for a maximum of one year.

ALBERTA COLLEGE OF ART & DESIGN

1407 14 Avenue NW, Calgary, AB T2N 4R3
Phone: 403-284-7617 • **Financial Aid Phone:** 403-284-7600
E-mail: admissions@acad.ca
Fax: 403-284-7644 • **Website:** www.acad.ca

This public school was founded in 1926.

RATINGS
Admissions Selectivity Rating: 63   **Fire Safety Rating:** 60*   **Green Rating:** 60*

STUDENTS AND FACULTY
Enrollment: 1,112. **Student Body:** 73% female, 27% male, 11% out-of-state, 5% international (49 countries represented). Asian 0%, African American 0%, Caucasian 0%, Hispanic 0%, Native American 0%.
Retention and Graduation: 64% freshmen return for sophomore year. 38% freshmen graduate within 4 years. **Faculty:** Student/faculty ratio 15:1. 46 full-time faculty.

ACADEMICS
Degrees: bachelor's. **Majors with Highest Enrollment:** drawing; painting; sculpture. **Special Study Options:** cross registration, exchange student program (domestic), internships, study abroad, Mobility and Exchange. **Disability Services:** Special programs offered to physically disabled students include reader services, tutors. **Career Services:**

FACILITIES
Housing: Coed dorms, Assisted off-campus housing search. 100% of campus accessible to physically disabled. **Special Academic Facilities/Equipment:** 2 Art Galleries **Computers:** 100% of classrooms, have wireless network access. Students can register for classes online. Administrative functions (other than registration) can be performed online.

CAMPUS LIFE
Environment: Metropolis. **Activities:** student government. **Athletics (Intercollegiate):** *Men:* basketball, ice hockey, volleyball. *Women:* basketball, volleyball. **On-Campus Highlights:** Facilities, Glass Department, Graffitt Stairwell, Residence

ADMISSIONS
Freshman Academic Profile: Minimum web-based TOEFL 83. Minimum paper TOEFL 560. **Basis for Candidate Selection:** *Very important factors considered include:* application essay, academic GPA, level of applicant's interest, talent/ability. *Other factors considered include:* recommendation(s), standardized test scores, character/personal qualities, extracurricular activities, work experience. **Freshman Admission Requirements:** High school diploma is required and GED is not accepted. *Academic units required:* 4 English. *Academic units recommended:* 4 English. **Freshman Admission Statistics:** 576 applied, 65% admitted, 73% enrolled. **Transfer Admission Requirements:** college transcript(s), essay or personal statement. **General Admission Information:** Application Fee $85. Early decision application deadline 2/1. Regular application deadline 4/1. Regular notification 5/15. Nonfall registration accepted. Credit and/or placement offered for CEEB Advanced Placement tests.

COSTS AND FINANCIAL AID
Annual in-state tuition $4,435. Annual out-of-state tuition $4,435. Room and board $5,904. Required fees $831. Average book expense $3,150. **Required Forms and Deadlines:** FAFSA. **Student Employment:** Off-campus job opportunities are good. **Criteria for awarding institutional aid:** *Non-need-based:* academics, art.

ALBERTUS MAGNUS COLLEGE

700 Prospect Street, New Haven, CT 6511
Phone: 203-773-8501 • **Financial Aid Phone:** 203-773-8508
E-mail: admissions@albertus.edu • **CEEB Code:** 3001
Fax: 203-773-5248 • **Website:** www.albertus.edu • **ACT Code:** 549

This private school, affiliated with the Roman Catholic Church, was founded in 1925. It has a 50-acre campus.

RATINGS
Admissions Selectivity Rating: 68   **Fire Safety Rating:** 74   **Green Rating:** 60*

STUDENTS AND FACULTY
Enrollment: 1,682. **Student Body:** 68% female, 32% male, 15% out-of-state, 0% international. Asian 1%, African American 27%, Caucasian 55%, Hispanic 10%, Native American 0%.
Retention and Graduation: 78% freshmen return for sophomore year. 49% freshmen graduate within 4 years. 62% freshmen graduate within 6 years. **Faculty:** Student/faculty ratio 13:1. 42 full-time faculty, 79% hold PhDs, 43% are women. 0% of classes are taught by teaching assistants.

ACADEMICS
Degrees: associate, bachelor's, certificate, master's. **Classes:** Most classes have 10–19 students. **Majors with Highest Enrollment:** business/commerce; education; psychology. **Special Study Options:** Accelerated program, double major, honors program, independent study, internships, student-designed major, teacher certification program. **Honors Programs:** Students may apply to follow the Honors Program, which involves work in special courses designated each semester as honors courses and the development of individual projects designed in consultation with faculty mentors. Entering qualified students are assigned to special honors courses and returning students interested in such a program should consult, by the spring of their sophomore year or earlier, with their advisor and the Director of the Honors Program. **Disability Services:** Special programs offered to physically disabled students include note-taking services, reader services, tape recorders, tutors. **Career Services:** Alumni network, career/job search classes, career assessment, internships.

FACILITIES
Housing: Coed dorms, women's dorms, Mansion style residence halls. Substance free and quiet halls. 70% of campus accessible to physically disabled.
Special Academic Facilities/Equipment: Margart McDonough Art Gallery.

CAMPUS LIFE
Environment: City. **Activities:** Choral groups, dance, drama/theater, literary magazine, musical theater, student government, yearbook, Campus Ministries 1 honor societies, 1 religious organization. **Athletics (Intercollegiate):** *Men:* baseball, basketball, cross-country, lacrosse, soccer, tennis, volleyball. *Women:* basketball, cross-country, lacrosse, soccer, softball, tennis, volleyball. **On-Campus Highlights:** Center for Science, Art and Technology, Athletic Center, Library, Campus Center, Art Gallery.

ADMISSIONS
Freshman Academic Profile: Average high school GPA 3.0. 10% in top 10% of high school class, 29% in top 25% of high school class, 68% in top 50% of high school class. 70% from public high schools. SAT Math middle 50% range 470-500. SAT Critical Reading middle 50% range 490-560. SAT Writing middle 50% range 430-560. Minimum paper TOEFL 550. **Basis for Candidate Selection:** *Very important factors considered include:* academic GPA, rigor of secondary school record. *Important factors considered include:* recommendation(s), standardized test scores. *Other factors considered include:* Class rank, application essay, alumni/ae relation, character/personal qualities, extracurricular activities, first generation, interview, level of applicant's interest, talent/ability, volunteer work, work experience. **Freshman Admission Requirements:** High school diploma is required and GED is accepted. *Academic units required:* 4 English, 2 mathematics, 2 science, 2 foreign language, 2 social studies, 2 history, 2 academic electives. *Academic units recommended:* 4 English, 2 mathematics, 2 science, 2 foreign language, 2 social studies, 2 history, 2 academic electives. **Freshman Admission Statistics:** 587 applied, 82% admitted, 21% enrolled. **Transfer Admission Requirements:** college transcript(s), minimum college GPA of 2.0 required. Lowest grade transferable C. **General Admission Information:** Application Fee $35. Notification on a rolling basis, beginning on or about 12/1. Nonfall registration accepted. Admission may be deferred for a maximum of 12. Credit offered for CEEB Advanced Placement tests.

COSTS AND FINANCIAL AID
Annual tuition $20,166. Room and board $8,907. Required fees $908. Average book expense $920. **Required Forms and Deadlines:** FAFSA, institution's own financial aid form. **Notification of Awards:** Applicants will be notified of awards on a rolling basis beginning 3/1. **Types of Aid:** *Need-based scholarships/grants:* Federal Pell, SEOG, state scholarships/grants, the school's own gift aid. *Loans:* Direct Subsidized Stafford, Direct Unsubsidized Stafford, Direct PLUS, Subsidized Stafford, Unsubsidized Stafford, PLUS, Federal Perkins. **Student Employment:** Federal Work-Study Program available. **Financial Aid Statistics:** 89% freshmen, 93% undergrads receive need-based scholarship or grant aid. 60% freshmen, 65% undergrads receive non-need-based scholarship or grant aid. 37% freshmen, 39% undergrads receive need-based self-help aid. 87% freshmen, 75% undergrads receive any aid. Average cumulative indebtedness $15,625. **Criteria for awarding institutional aid:** *Non-need-based:* academics, leadership, religious affiliation.

ALBION COLLEGE

611 East Porter, Albion, MI 49224
Phone: 517-629-0321 • **Financial Aid Phone:** 517-629-0440
E-mail: admission@albion.edu • **CEEB Code:** 1007
Fax: 517-629-0569 • **Website:** www.albion.edu • **ACT Code:** 1956

This private school, affiliated with the Methodist Church, was founded in 1835. It has a 585-acre campus.

RATINGS
Admissions Selectivity Rating: 77   **Fire Safety Rating:** 73   **Green Rating:** 77

STUDENTS AND FACULTY
Enrollment: 1,355. **Student Body:** 49% female, 51% male, 9% out-of-state, 4% international (20 countries represented). Asian 1%, African American 4%, Caucasian 81%, Hispanic 3%, Native American 0%.
Retention and Graduation: 73% freshmen return for sophomore year. 62% freshmen graduate within 4 years. 72% freshmen graduate within 6 years. 37% grads go on to further study within 1 year. 20% grads pursue arts and sciences degrees. 5% grads pursue law degrees. 2% grads pursue business degrees. 9% grads pursue medical degrees. **Faculty:** Student/faculty ratio 11:1. 105 full-time faculty, 91% hold PhDs, 9% are members of minority groups, 43% are women. 0% of classes are taught by teaching assistants.

ACADEMICS
Degrees: bachelor's. **Classes:** Most classes have 10–19 students. Most lab/discussion sessions have 10–19 students. **Majors with Highest Enrollment:** biology/biological sciences; economics; psychology. **Special Study Options:** double major, dual enrollment, honors program, independent study, internships, liberal arts/career combination, student-designed major, study abroad, teacher certification program, Environmental Institute, Ford Institute for Public Service, Gerstacker Liberal Arts Program in Professional Management. **Honors Programs:** The Honors Program at Albion was founded in 1976, and in August of 2004 it was renamed The Prentiss M. Brown Honors Institute. We provide an exciting and unique variety of academic experiences for highly motivated and talented students. The Institute's mix of small discussion classes, independent research, academic rigor, and personal attention provides Honors students with special challenges and opportunities for growth. Many of the College's finest teachers and scholars regularly contribute to the Institute's curriculum. **Combined Degree Programs:** BA/MEng. **Disability Services:** Special programs offered to physically disabled students include note-taking services, reader services, tape recorders, tutors. **Career Services:** Alumni network, alumni services, career assessment, internships, regional alumni. Career Services highlights include Our six academic institutes: Professional Management, Environmental, Education, Public Policy & Service, Honors and Pre-Health. All incorporate internships or experiential learning into the curriculum.

FACILITIES
Housing: Coed dorms, special housing for disabled students, women's dorms, fraternity/sorority housing, apartments for married students, cooperative housing, apartments for single students, Special interest annexes available. 90% of campus accessible to physically disabled. **Special Academic Facilities/Equipment:** Visual arts museum, nature center, science complex museum, shark aquarium, greenhouse, geographic information systems/computer-aided mapping lab, observatory. **Computers:** 95% of classrooms, 100% of dorms, 100% of libraries, 100% of dining areas, 100% of student union, 25% of common outdoor areas have wireless network access. Students can register for classes online. Administrative functions (other than registration) can be performed online.

CAMPUS LIFE

Environment: Village. **Activities:** Choral groups, concert band, dance, drama/theater, jazz band, literary magazine, marching band, music ensembles, musical theater, pep band, radio station, student government, symphony orchestra, yearbook, Campus Ministries, International Student Organization, Model UN 122 registered organizations, 17 honor societies, 11 religious organizations. 6 fraternities, 7 sororities. **Athletics (Intercollegiate):** *Men:* baseball, basketball, cross-country, diving, equestrian sports, football, golf, soccer, swimming, tennis, track/field (outdoor), track/field (indoor). *Women:* basketball, cross-country, diving, equestrian sports, golf, soccer, softball, swimming, tennis, track/field (outdoor), track/field (indoor), volleyball. **On-Campus Highlights:** Kellogg Center- Student Center, Dow Recreation Center- Athletic Facility, Quad-Lawn in the center of campus, Baldwin- Dining Hall, Science Center Atrium, Albion is often lauded for the amount of student space available. Whether it's lounge areas, computer classrooms, meeting spaces, or the myriad rooms in the Kellogg Center, Albion students find many areas to congregate socially and academically. **Environmental Initiatives:** Sustainability chosen as a key theme in Albion's new strategic plan. Sustainability was showcased in the inaugural edition of our Theme Year initiative in 2010-11. The Sustainability Theme Year encompasses facilities management and a variety of campus activities including a common reading, named lectures, a film series, career fairs, dining hall meals, and an ongoing lifestyle challenge. The Sustainability Theme will repeat in 2013-14. Development of Center for Sustainability and the Environment, which fosters involvement and projects by students. Examples include establishment of residential E-House (2006-present), E.P.A. P3 grant (2006-07), two National Wildlife Federation Sustainability Fellows (2008), active "Focus the Nation" and "Step it Up" participation (2007-08), and starting a student organic farm (2010). Development of an environmental "category requirement" as a graduation requirement for all students. This has fostered development of over 20 environmental courses spread over the Arts, Humanities, Natural Sciences, and Social Sciences.

ADMISSIONS

Freshman Academic Profile: Average high school GPA 3.4. SAT Math middle 50% range 480-640. SAT Critical Reading middle 50% range 460-620. SAT Writing middle 50% range 490-580. ACT middle 50% range 22-27. Minimum web-based TOEFL 79. Minimum paper TOEFL 550. **Basis for Candidate Selection:** *Very important factors considered include:* application essay, academic GPA, recommendation(s), rigor of secondary school record, standardized test scores, alumni/ae relation, character/personal qualities, extracurricular activities, first generation, geographical residence, level of applicant's interest, state residency, talent/ability, volunteer work, work experience. **Freshman Admission Requirements:** High school diploma is required and GED is accepted. *Academic units required:* 4 English, 3 mathematics, 3 science, (2 science labs), 2 foreign language, 3 social studies, 1 history. *Academic units recommended:* 4 English, 3 mathematics, 3 science, (2 science labs), 2 foreign language, 3 social studies, 1 history. **Freshman Admission Statistics:** 2,383 applied, 70% admitted, 22% enrolled. **Transfer Admission Requirements:** High school transcript, college transcript(s), essay or personal statement, interview, standardized test scores, statement of good standing from prior institution(s). Minimum college GPA of 2.5 required. Lowest grade transferable C. **General Admission Information:** Application Fee $40. Notification on a rolling basis, beginning on or about 11/1. Nonfall registration accepted. Admission may be deferred for a maximum of 1 year. Credit and/or placement offered for CEEB Advanced Placement tests.

COSTS AND FINANCIAL AID

Annual tuition $33,600. Room and board $9,690. Required fees $594. Average book expense $900. **Required Forms and Deadlines:** FAFSA. **Notification of Awards:** Applicants will be notified of awards on a rolling basis beginning 3/15. **Types of Aid:** *Need-based scholarships/grants:* Federal Pell, SEOG, state scholarships/grants, private scholarships, the school's own gift aid. *Loans:* Direct Subsidized Stafford, Direct Unsubsidized Stafford, Direct PLUS, Subsidized Stafford, Unsubsidized Stafford, PLUS, Federal Perkins. **Student Employment:** Federal Work-Study Program available. Institutional employment available. Highest amount earned per year from on-campus jobs $5,330. Off-campus job opportunities are fair. **Financial Aid Statistics:** 100% freshmen, 100% undergrads receive need-based scholarship or grant aid. 88% freshmen, 90% undergrads receive non-need-based scholarship or grant aid. 84% freshmen, 85% undergrads receive need-based self-help aid. 98% freshmen, 98% undergrads receive any aid. 62% undergrads borrow to pay for school. Average cumulative indebtedness $36,029. **Criteria for awarding institutional aid:** *Non-need-based:* academics, alumni affiliation, art, leadership, music/drama.

ALBRIGHT COLLEGE

PO Box 15234, Reading, PA 19612-5234
Phone: 610-921-7799 • **Financial Aid Phone:** 610-921-7515
E-mail: admission@albright.edu • **CEEB Code:** 2004
Fax: 610-921-7729 • **Website:** www.albright.edu • **ACT Code:** 2004

This private school, affiliated with the Methodist Church, was founded in 1856. It has a 118-acre campus.

RATINGS
Admissions Selectivity Rating: 75   **Fire Safety Rating:** 64   **Green Rating:** 60*

STUDENTS AND FACULTY
Enrollment: 2,074. **Student Body:** 58% female, 42% male, 33% out-of-state, 3% international (26 countries represented). Asian 2%, African American 9%, Caucasian 78%, Hispanic 4%, Native American 0%.
Retention and Graduation: 76% freshmen return for sophomore year. 52% freshmen graduate within 4 years. 57% freshmen graduate within 6 years.
Faculty: Student/faculty ratio 14:1. 103 full-time faculty, 83% hold PhDs, 7% are members of minority groups, 46% are women.

ACADEMICS
Degrees: bachelor's, certificate, master's. **Classes:** Most classes have 10–19 students. Most lab/discussion sessions have 10–19 students. **Majors with Highest Enrollment:** business/commerce; sociology. Accelerated program, cross-registration, dual enrollment, English as a Second Language (ESL), exchange student program (domestic), honors program, independent study, internships, liberal arts/career combination, student-designed major, study abroad, teacher certification program, Interdisciplinary.

FACILITIES
Housing: Coed dorms, men's dorms, women's dorms, apartments for single students, Honors-Special Interest-Freshmen Floors vs Dorms. **Special Academic Facilities/Equipment:** Freedman Art Gallery

CAMPUS LIFE
Environment: City. **Activities:** Choral groups, concert band, dance, drama/theater, jazz band, literary magazine, music ensembles, musical theater, pep band, radio station, student government, student newspaper, television station, yearbook 84 registered organizations, 10 honor societies, 3 religious organizations. 4 fraternities, 3 sororities. **Athletics (Intercollegiate):** *Men:* baseball, basketball, cheerleading, cross-country, football, golf, soccer, swimming, tennis, track/field (outdoor), track/field (indoor), wrestling. *Women:* badminton, basketball, cheerleading, cross-country, field hockey, soccer, softball, swimming, tennis, track/field (outdoor), track/field (indoor), volleyball. **On-Campus Highlights:** Student Center, Jake's Place, Wachovia Theatre, Sports Center, Natatorium.

ADMISSIONS
Freshman Academic Profile: Average high school GPA 3.3. 23% in top 10% of high school class, 48% in top 25% of high school class, 79% in top 50% of high school class. 77% from public high schools. SAT Math middle 50% range 460-570. SAT Critical Reading middle 50% range 470-580. **Basis for Candidate Selection:** *Very important factors considered include:* rigor of secondary school record. *Important factors considered include:* Class rank, application essay, academic GPA, recommendation(s), standardized test scores, character/personal qualities. *Other factors considered include:* alumni/ae relation, extracurricular activities, talent/ability, volunteer work, work experience. **Freshman Admission Requirements:** High school diploma is required and GED is accepted. *Academic units required:* 4 English, 2 mathematics, 3 science, (1 science labs), 2 foreign language, 2 social studies, 1 history, 2 academic electives. *Academic units recommended:* 4 English, 2 mathematics, 3 science, (1 science labs), 2 foreign language, 2 social studies, 1 history, 2 academic electives. **Freshman Admission Statistics:** 3,013 applied, 71% admitted, 21% enrolled. **Transfer Admission Requirements:** college transcript(s), essay or personal statement, statement of good standing from prior institution(s). Minimum college GPA of 2.0 required. Lowest grade transferable C-. **General Admission Information:** Application Fee $25. Notification on a rolling basis, beginning on or about 10/1. Nonfall registration accepted. Admission may be deferred for a maximum of 12 months. Credit and/or placement offered for CEEB Advanced Placement tests.

COSTS AND FINANCIAL AID
Annual tuition $25,232. Room and board $7,888. Required fees $800. Average book expense $800. **Required Forms and Deadlines:** FAFSA. **Notification of Awards:** Applicants will be notified of awards on a rolling basis beginning 2/14. **Types of Aid:** *Need-based scholarships/grants:* Federal Pell, SEOG, state scholarships/grants, private scholarships, the school's own gift aid. *Loans:* Subsidized Stafford, Unsubsidized Stafford, PLUS, Federal Perkins, private

educational loans. **Student Employment:** Federal Work-Study Program available. Institutional employment available. Highest amount earned per year from on-campus jobs $1,100. Off-campus job opportunities are good. **Financial Aid Statistics:** 100% freshmen, 96% undergrads receive need-based scholarship or grant aid. 14% freshmen, 13% undergrads receive non-need-based scholarship or grant aid. 84% freshmen, 84% undergrads receive need-based self-help aid. 95% freshmen, 94% undergrads receive any aid. 88% undergrads borrow to pay for school. Average cumulative indebtedness $24,671. **Criteria for awarding institutional aid:** *Non-need-based:* academics, alumni affiliation, art, leadership, minority status, music/drama, religious affiliation, state/district residency.

ALCORN STATE UNIVERSITY

1000 ASU Drive #300, Alcorn State, MS 39096
Phone: 601-877-6147
E-mail: ebarnes@alcorn.edu • **CEEB Code:** 1008
Fax: 601-877-6347 • **Website:** • **ACT Code:** 2176

This public school was founded in 1871. It has a 1756-acre campus.

RATINGS
Admissions Selectivity Rating: 79   **Fire Safety Rating:** 60*   **Green Rating:** 60*

STUDENTS AND FACULTY
Enrollment: 3,208. **Student Body:** 65% female, 35% male, 13% out-of-state, 1% international (14 countries represented). Asian 0%, African American 93%, Caucasian 3%, Hispanic 1%, Native American 0%.
Retention and Graduation: 69% freshmen return for sophomore year. 15% freshmen graduate within 4 years. 32% freshmen graduate within 6 years. 38% grads go on to further study within 1 year. **Faculty:** Student/faculty ratio 18:1. 169 full-time faculty, 65% hold PhDs, 80% are members of minority groups, 47% are women.

ACADEMICS
Degrees: associate, bachelor's, master's, post-master's certificate. **Classes:** Most classes have 20–29 students. Most lab/discussion sessions have fewer than 10 students. **Majors with Highest Enrollment:** biology; elementary education and teaching; liberal arts and sciences/liberal studies. **Special Study Options:** Accelerated program, cooperative education program, distance learning, double major, dual enrollment, honors program, independent study, internships, liberal arts/career combination, study abroad, teacher certification program, Undergrads may take grad level classes (restrictions apply). **Combined Degree Programs:** Cooperative physics program with Howard U. **Career Services:** internships.

FACILITIES
Housing: men's dorms, women's dorms, Honor's Dorm. **Special Academic Facilities/Equipment:** Honor's Resident Hall **Computers:** Students can register for classes online. Administrative functions (other than registration) can be performed online.

CAMPUS LIFE
Environment: Rural. **Activities:** Choral groups, concert band, dance, drama/theater, jazz band, marching band, music ensembles, radio station, student government, student newspaper, television station, yearbook 120 registered organizations, 10 honor societies, 8 religious organizations. 8 fraternities, 7 sororities. **Athletics (Intercollegiate):** *Men:* baseball, basketball, cross-country, football, golf, tennis, track/field (outdoor). *Women:* basketball, cross-country, golf, soccer, softball, tennis, track/field (outdoor), volleyball.

ADMISSIONS
Freshman Academic Profile: Average high school GPA 2.9. 66% in top 50% of high school class. 99% from public high schools. SAT Math middle 50% range 400-500. SAT Critical Reading middle 50% range 390-470. ACT middle 50% range 16-20. Minimum paper TOEFL 525. **Basis for Candidate Selection:** *Very important factors considered include:* Class rank, academic GPA, rigor of secondary school record. *Important factors considered include:* standardized test scores. *Other factors considered include:* recommendation(s), interview. **Freshman Admission Requirements:** High school diploma is required and GED is accepted. *Academic units required:* 4 English, 3 mathematics, 3 science, (2 science labs), 3 social studies, 2 academic electives. *Academic units recommended:* 4 English, 3 mathematics, 3 science, (2 science labs), 3 social studies, 2 academic electives. **Freshman Admission Statistics:** 3,663 applied, 47% admitted, 34% enrolled. **Transfer Admission Requirements:** college transcript(s), statement of good standing from prior institution(s). Minimum college GPA of 2.0 required. Lowest grade transferable C. **General Admission Information:** Nonfall registration accepted. Admission may be deferred for a maximum of na. Credit and/or placement offered for CEEB Advanced Placement tests.

COSTS AND FINANCIAL AID
Annual in-state tuition $5,712. Annual out-of-state tuition $14,064. Room and board $7,999. Average book expense $1,486. **Required Forms and Deadlines:** FAFSA, institution's own financial aid form. **Notification of Awards:** Applicants will be notified of awards on a rolling basis beginning 4/1. **Types of Aid:** *Need-based scholarships/grants:* Federal Pell, SEOG, state scholarships/grants, private scholarships, the school's own gift aid. *Loans:* Direct Subsidized Stafford, Direct Unsubsidized Stafford, Direct PLUS. **Student Employment:** Federal Work-Study Program available. Institutional employment available. Highest amount earned per year from on-campus jobs $500. Off-campus job opportunities are poor. **Financial Aid Statistics:** 95% freshmen, 92% undergrads receive need-based scholarship or grant aid. 31% freshmen, 21% undergrads receive non-need-based scholarship or grant aid. 80% freshmen, 82% undergrads receive need-based self-help aid. 12% freshmen, 8% undergrads receive athletic scholarships. 89% undergrads borrow to pay for school. Average cumulative indebtedness $29,001. **Criteria for awarding institutional aid:** *Non-need-based:* academics, athletics.

ALDERSON-BROADDUS COLLEGE

101 College Hill Drive, Philippi, WV 26416
Phone: 800-263-1549 • **Financial Aid Phone:** 304-457-6354
E-mail: admissions@ab.edu • **CEEB Code:** 5005
Fax: 304-457-6239 • **Website:** www.ab.edu • **ACT Code:** 4508

This private school, affiliated with the American Baptist Church, was founded in 1871. It has a 170-acre campus.

RATINGS
Admissions Selectivity Rating: 72   **Fire Safety Rating:** 71   **Green Rating:** 61

STUDENTS AND FACULTY
Enrollment: 546. **Student Body:** 64% female, 36% male, 20% out-of-state, 2% international (6 countries represented). Asian 1%, African American 3%, Caucasian 90%, Hispanic 2%, Native American 1%.
Retention and Graduation: 65% freshmen return for sophomore year. 29% freshmen graduate within 4 years. 51% freshmen graduate within 6 years. 15% grads go on to further study within 1 year. 19% grads pursue arts and sciences degrees. 4% grads pursue law degrees. 7% grads pursue business degrees. 11% grads pursue medical degrees. **Faculty:** Student/faculty ratio 9:1. 57 full-time faculty, 44% hold PhDs, 12% are members of minority groups, 56% are women. 0% of classes are taught by teaching assistants.

ACADEMICS
Degrees: associate, bachelor's, certificate, master's, post-bachelor's certificate. **Classes:** Most classes have fewer than 10 students. Most lab/discussion sessions have 10–19 students. **Majors with Highest Enrollment:** biology/biological sciences; health services/allied health/health sciences; nursing/registered nurse (rn, asn, bsn, msn). **Special Study Options:** double major, honors program, independent study, internships, liberal arts/career combination, study abroad, teacher certification program, Business Department offers on-line certificate program. **Disability Services:** Special programs offered to physically disabled students include note-taking services, reader services, tape recorders, tutors. **Career Services:** Alumni network, career/job search classes, career assessment, internships.

FACILITIES
Housing: Coed dorms, special housing for disabled students, women's dorms, apartments for married students, apartments for single students, wellness housing 70% of campus accessible to physically disabled. **Special Academic Facilities/Equipment:** Art Gallery in Burbick Hall. Campbell School House **Computers:** 75% of classrooms, 100% of dorms, 90% of libraries, 100% of dining areas, 100% of student union, have wireless network access. Administrative functions (other than registration) can be performed online.

CAMPUS LIFE
Environment: Rural. **Activities:** Choral groups, concert band, drama/theater, jazz band, literary magazine, music ensembles, musical theater, radio station, student government, student newspaper, television station, yearbook, Campus Ministries 49 registered organizations, 2 honor societies, 2 religious organizations. 2 fraternities, 3 sororities. **Athletics (Intercollegiate):** *Men:* baseball, basketball, cross-country, soccer, track/field (outdoor), track/field (indoor). *Women:* basketball, cross-country, soccer, softball, track/field (outdoor), track/field (indoor), volleyball. **On-Campus Highlights:** Cave, Burbick Hall, Rex Pyles Arena, Wilcox Chapel **Environmental Initiatives:** recycling efforts electric maintenance vehicles sustainability survey

ADMISSIONS

Freshman Academic Profile: Average high school GPA 3.3. 25% in top 10% of high school class, 44% in top 25% of high school class, 79% in top 50% of high school class. 97% from public high schools. SAT Math middle 50% range 450-560. SAT Critical Reading middle 50% range 440-570. SAT Writing middle 50% range 420-530. ACT middle 50% range 19-24. Minimum paper TOEFL 500. **Basis for Candidate Selection:** *Very important factors considered include:* academic GPA, rigor of secondary school record, standardized test scores. *Important factors considered include:* application essay. *Other factors considered include:* recommendation(s), alumni/ae relation, first generation, interview, level of applicant's interest, talent/ability. **Freshman Admission Requirements:** High school diploma is required and GED is accepted. *Academic units required:* 4 English, 3 mathematics, 3 science, (1 science labs), 1 social studies, 0 history. *Academic units recommended:* 4 English, 3 mathematics, 3 science, (1 science labs), 1 social studies, 0 history. **Freshman Admission Statistics:** 791 applied, 71% admitted, 24% enrolled. **Transfer Admission Requirements:** High school transcript, college transcript(s), statement of good standing from prior institution(s). Minimum college GPA of 2.0 required. Lowest grade transferable C. **General Admission Information:** Application Fee $25. Nonfall registration accepted. Admission may be deferred for a maximum of 1 year. Placement offered for CEEB Advanced Placement tests.

COSTS AND FINANCIAL AID

Annual tuition $21,994. Room and board $7,222. Required fees $210. Average book expense $800. **Required Forms and Deadlines:** FAFSA, state aid form. **Notification of Awards:** Applicants will be notified of awards on a rolling basis beginning 2/15. **Types of Aid:** *Need-based scholarships/grants:* Federal Pell, SEOG, state scholarships/grants, private scholarships, the school's own gift aid, Federal Nursing Scholarships. , National Health Service Corp, Scholarship for disadvantaged students. *Loans:* Subsidized Stafford, Unsubsidized Stafford, PLUS, Federal Perkins, Federal Nursing, college/university loans from institutional funds. **Student Employment:** Federal Work-Study Program available. Highest amount earned per year from on-campus jobs $1,400. Off-campus job opportunities are fair. **Financial Aid Statistics:** 100% freshmen, 99% undergrads receive need-based scholarship or grant aid. 23% freshmen, 14% undergrads receive non-need-based scholarship or grant aid. 80% freshmen, 87% undergrads receive need-based self-help aid. 2% freshmen, 4% undergrads receive athletic scholarships. 100% freshmen, 99% undergrads receive any aid. 86% undergrads borrow to pay for school. Average cumulative indebtedness $29,362. **Criteria for awarding institutional aid:** *Non-need-based:* academics, athletics, music/drama.

ALFRED UNIVERSITY

Best 378

Alumni Hall, Alfred, NY 14802-1205
Phone: 607-871-2115 • **Financial Aid Phone:** 607-871-2159
E-mail: admissions@alfred.edu • **CEEB Code:** 2005
Fax: 607-871-2198 • **Website:** www.alfred.edu • **ACT Code:** 2666

This private school was founded in 1836. It has a 600-acre campus.

RATINGS

Admissions Selectivity Rating: 75   **Fire Safety Rating:** 64   **Green Rating:** 68

STUDENTS AND FACULTY

Enrollment: 1,918. **Student Body:** 49% female, 51% male, 23% out-of-state, 2% international (18 countries represented). Asian 6%, African American 0%, Caucasian 1%, Hispanic 7%, Native American 0%.
Retention and Graduation: 43% freshmen graduate within 4 years. 60% freshmen graduate within 6 years. 30% grads go on to further study within 1 year. **Faculty:** Student/faculty ratio 13:1. 161 full-time faculty, % hold PhDs, 7% are members of minority groups, 43% are women. 0% of classes are taught by teaching assistants.

ACADEMICS

Degrees: bachelor's, master's, post-master's certificate. **Classes:** Most classes have 10–19 students. Most lab/discussion sessions have fewer than 10 students. **Majors with Highest Enrollment:** business/commerce; ceramic sciences and engineering; fine/studio arts. **Special Study Options:** cooperative education program, cross-registration, double major, English as a Second Language (ESL), exchange student program (domestic), honors program, independent study, internships, liberal arts/career combination, student-designed major, study abroad, teacher certification program. **Honors Programs:** The Alfred

University Honors Program is designed to enrich the lives of exceptional students. It has two components: an honors seminar - meets one evening a week and the senior thesis. **Combined Degree Programs:** 4+1 MBA program for bus, liberal arts and sciences. **Disability Services:** Special programs offered to physically disabled students include note-taking services, tape recorders, tutors. **Career Services:** Alumni network, career assessment, internships Career Services highlights include We are extremely proud of all of the services offered by the staff at the Robert R. McComsey Career Development Center.

FACILITIES

Housing: Coed dorms, apartments for single students, theme housing (i.e. Environmental Studies House, Language House, etc.). 50% of campus accessible to physically disabled. **Special Academic Facilities/Equipment:** Art museums, carillon, language labs, electron microscope, observatory, extensive engineering equipment, performing arts center. **Computers:** 90% of classrooms, 100% of dorms, 100% of libraries, 100% of student union, have wireless network access. Students can register for classes online. Administrative functions (other than registration) can be performed online.

CAMPUS LIFE

Environment: Rural. **Activities:** Choral groups, concert band, dance, drama/theater, literary magazine, music ensembles, musical theater, pep band, radio station, student government, student newspaper, student-run film society, television station, yearbook, Campus Ministries, International Student Organization 90 registered organizations, 13 honor societies, 3 religious organizations. **Athletics (Intercollegiate):** *Men:* basketball, cross-country, diving, equestrian sports, football, lacrosse, skiing (downhill/alpine), soccer, swimming, tennis, track/field (outdoor), track/field (indoor). *Women:* basketball, cross-country, diving, equestrian sports, lacrosse, skiing (downhill/alpine), soccer, softball, swimming, tennis, track/field (outdoor), track/field (indoor), volleyball. **On-Campus Highlights:** Powell Campus Center, Binns Merrill Hall, Schein-Joseph International Museum of Ceramic Art, John L. Stull Observatory, Robert Turner Student Art Gallery. **Environmental Initiatives:** Campus-wide recycling program (paper, glass, plastic, electronics, printer/toner cartridges) Re-usable material exchange (REPO) Tray-less dining.

ADMISSIONS

Freshman Academic Profile: Average high school GPA 3.1. 17% in top 10% of high school class, 43% in top 25% of high school class, 82% in top 50% of high school class. % from public high schools. SAT Math middle 50% range 500-600. SAT Critical Reading middle 50% range 480-580. SAT Writing middle 50% range 460-570. ACT middle 50% range 21-26. Minimum web-based TOEFL 80. Minimum paper TOEFL 550. **Basis for Candidate Selection:** *Very important factors considered include:* Class rank, recommendation(s), rigor of secondary school record, character/personal qualities, extracurricular activities. *Important factors considered include:* application essay, standardized test scores, volunteer work, work experience. *Other factors considered include:* interview, racial/ethnic status, talent/ability. **Freshman Admission Requirements:** High school diploma is required and GED is accepted. *Academic units required:* 4 English, 2 mathematics, 2 science, (2 science labs), 2 social studies. *Academic units recommended:* 4 English, 2 mathematics, 2 science, (2 science labs), 2 social studies. **Freshman Admission Statistics:** 3,025 applied, 72% admitted, 26% enrolled. **Transfer Admission Requirements:** college transcript(s), statement of good standing from prior institution(s). Minimum college GPA of 2.5 required. Lowest grade transferable C. **General Admission Information:** Application Fee $40. Early decision application deadline 12/1. Notification on a rolling basis, beginning on or about 2/15. Nonfall registration accepted. Admission may be deferred for a maximum of 2 years. Credit offered for CEEB Advanced Placement tests.

COSTS AND FINANCIAL AID

Annual tuition $25,974. Room and board $11,498. Required fees $910. Average book expense $1,050. **Required Forms and Deadlines:** FAFSA, institution's own financial aid form, state aid form, noncustodial PROFILE, business/farm supplement. **Notification of Awards:** Applicants will be notified of awards on a rolling basis beginning 2/15. **Types of Aid:** *Need-based scholarships/grants:* Federal Pell, SEOG, state scholarships/grants, private scholarships, the school's own gift aid. *Loans:* Subsidized Stafford, Unsubsidized Stafford, PLUS, Federal Perkins, college/university loans from institutional funds, Private alternative loans. **Student Employment:** Federal Work-Study Program available. Institutional employment available. Off-campus job opportunities are poor. **Financial Aid Statistics:** 100% freshmen, 99% undergrads receive need-based scholarship or grant aid. 54% freshmen, 54% undergrads receive non-need-based scholarship or grant aid. 87% freshmen, 89% undergrads receive need-based self-help aid. 92% freshmen, 90% undergrads receive any aid. 82% undergrads borrow to pay for school. Average cumulative indebtedness $31,159. **Criteria for awarding institutional aid:** *Non-need-based:* academics, art, leadership, music/drama.

ALICE LLOYD COLLEGE

100 Purpose Road, Pippa Passes, KY 41844
Phone: 606-368-6036 • **Financial Aid Phone:**
E-mail: admissions@alc.edu • **CEEB Code:** 1098
Fax: 606-368-6215 • **Website:** www.alc.edu • **ACT Code:** 1502

This private school was founded in 1923. It has a 225-acre campus.

RATINGS
Admissions Selectivity Rating: 81   **Fire Safety Rating:** 92   **Green Rating:** 60*

STUDENTS AND FACULTY
Enrollment: 607. **Student Body:** 51% female, 49% male, 13% out-of-state, 0% international (1 countries represented). Asian 0%, African American 1%, Caucasian 99%, Hispanic 0%, Native American 0%.
Retention and Graduation: 63% freshmen return for sophomore year. 25% freshmen graduate within 4 years. 33% freshmen graduate within 6 years. 55% grads go on to further study within 1 year. 35% grads pursue arts and sciences degrees. 5% grads pursue law degrees. 10% grads pursue business degrees. 5% grads pursue medical degrees. **Faculty:** Student/faculty ratio 18:1. 29 full-time faculty, 59% hold PhDs, 10% are members of minority groups, 41% are women. 0% of classes are taught by teaching assistants.

ACADEMICS
Degrees: bachelor's. **Classes:** Most classes have 20–29 students. **Majors with Highest Enrollment:** biology/biological sciences; business/commerce; education. **Special Study Options:** cooperative education program, double major, honors program, independent study, internships, liberal arts/career combination, study abroad, teacher certification program. **Disability Services:** Special programs offered to physically disabled students include reader services, tutors. **Career Services:** Alumni network, alumni services, career assessment, internships, regional alumni.

FACILITIES
Housing: men's dorms, women's dorms. 90% of campus accessible to physically disabled. **Special Academic Facilities/Equipment:** Photographic archives, oral history museum, Appalachian collection, on-campus day care center, kindergarten, elementary, and secondary school. **Computers:** 100% of classrooms, 50% of dorms, 100% of libraries, 100% of dining areas, 75% of common outdoor areas have wireless network access.

CAMPUS LIFE
Environment: Rural. **Activities:** Choral groups, drama/theater, music ensembles, musical theater, pep band, radio station, student government, student newspaper, yearbook 19 registered organizations, 2 honor societies, 1 religious organizations. **Athletics (Intercollegiate):** *Men:* baseball, basketball, cheerleading, cross-country, golf, tennis. *Women:* basketball, cheerleading, cross-country, golf, softball, tennis. **On-Campus Highlights:** Jerry Davis Student Center, Historical Tour, Grady Nutt Athletic Center, Campbell Arts Center, Cushing Hall.

ADMISSIONS
Freshman Academic Profile: Average high school GPA 3.4. 30% in top 10% of high school class, 58% in top 25% of high school class, 86% in top 50% of high school class. 90% from public high schools. SAT Math middle 50% range 480-570. SAT Critical Reading middle 50% range 440-590. SAT Writing middle 50% range 430-520. ACT middle 50% range 17-23. Minimum paper TOEFL 550. **Basis for Candidate Selection:** *Very important factors considered include:* rigor of secondary school record, standardized test scores, character/personal qualities, geographical residence. *Important factors considered include:* Class rank, recommendation(s), alumni/ae relation, state residency. *Other factors considered include:* application essay, extracurricular activities, interview, talent/ability, volunteer work, work experience. **Freshman Admission Requirements:** High school diploma is required and GED is accepted. *Academic units required:* 4 English, 3 mathematics, 2 science, 2 social studies, 1 history. *Academic units recommended:* 4 English, 3 mathematics, 2 science, 2 social studies, 1 history. **Freshman Admission Statistics:** 994 applied, 56% admitted, 32% enrolled. **Transfer Admission Requirements:** High school transcript, college transcript(s), standardized test scores, statement of good standing from prior institution(s). Minimum college GPA of 2.0 required. Lowest grade transferable C. **General Admission Information:** Regular application deadline 5/1. Nonfall registration accepted. Credit and/or placement offered for CEEB Advanced Placement tests.

COSTS AND FINANCIAL AID
. Room and board $4,250. Required fees $1,300. Average book expense $850. **Required Forms and Deadlines:** FAFSA. **Notification of Awards:** Applicants will be notified of awards on a rolling basis beginning 4/1. **Types of Aid:** *Need-based scholarships/grants:* Federal Pell, SEOG, state scholarships/grants, private scholarships, the school's own gift aid. *Loans:* Subsidized Stafford, Unsubsidized Stafford, PLUS, college/university loans from institutional funds. **Student Employment:** Federal Work-Study Program available. Institutional employment available. Off-campus job opportunities are fair. **Financial Aid Statistics:** 99% freshmen, 99% undergrads receive need-based scholarship or grant aid. 11% freshmen, 16% undergrads receive non-need-based scholarship or grant aid. 89% freshmen, 84% undergrads receive need-based self-help aid. 7% freshmen, 5% undergrads receive athletic scholarships. 100% freshmen, 100% undergrads receive any aid. 33% undergrads borrow to pay for school. Average cumulative indebtedness $4,653. **Criteria for awarding institutional aid:** *Non-need-based:* athletics, minority status, state/district residency.

ALLEGHENY COLLEGE

Allegheny College, Meadville, PA 16335
Phone: 814-332-4351 • **Financial Aid Phone:** 800-835-7780
E-mail: admissions@allegheny.edu • **CEEB Code:** 2006
Fax: 814-337-0431 • **Website:** www.allegheny.edu • **ACT Code:** 3520

This private school was founded in 1815. It has a 565-acre campus.

RATINGS
Admissions Selectivity Rating: 89   **Fire Safety Rating:** 71   **Green Rating:** 84

STUDENTS AND FACULTY
Enrollment: 2,112. **Student Body:** 54% female, 46% male, 44% out-of-state, 1% international (34 countries represented). Asian 3%, African American 5%, Caucasian 82%, Hispanic 5%, Native American 0%.
Retention and Graduation: 89% freshmen return for sophomore year. 70% freshmen graduate within 4 years. 78% freshmen graduate within 6 years. 37% grads go on to further study within 1 year. 10% grads pursue arts and sciences degrees. 3% grads pursue law degrees. 3% grads pursue business degrees. 6% grads pursue medical degrees. **Faculty:** Student/faculty ratio 12:1. 165 full-time faculty, 93% hold PhDs, 15% are members of minority groups, 45% are women. 0% of classes are taught by teaching assistants.

ACADEMICS
Degrees: bachelor's. **Classes:** Most classes have 10–19 students. Most lab/discussion sessions have 10–19 students. **Majors with Highest Enrollment:** biology/biological sciences; economics; psychology. **Special Study Options:** double major, dual enrollment, English as a Second Language (ESL), exchange student program (domestic), independent study, internships, student-designed major, study abroad, Pre-professional programs, teacher preparation partnerships, Combined Degree Programs,experiential learning terms (summer study program), marine biology study program, Washington Semester, medical school partnerships, graduate school partnerships, double minor, domestic off campus semester away study programs, accelerated masters and doctorate degree programs. **Combined Degree Programs:** BA/MA, BA/MEng, Management, public policy, teaching, nursing, occupational & physical therapy, osteopathic medicine, physician's assistant. **Disability Services:** Special programs offered to physically disabled students include note-taking services, tape recorders, tutors. **Career Services:** Alumni network, alumni services, career/job search classes, career assessment, internships, regional alumni. Career Services highlights include Experiential learning connects classroom learning to the wider world, including social issues, international relations, key concepts in leadership development, and ultimately career and life goals. Through internships, community service programs and service learning, off-campus study, and other leadership opportunities students become active participants in the learning process by adapting academic skills and knowledge to meet new challenges. ACCEL, Allegheny College Center for Experiential Learning, unites resources, personnel, and funding sources to create experiential learning initiatives for Allegheny students.

FACILITIES
Housing: Coed dorms, special housing for disabled students, men's dorms, women's dorms, fraternity/sorority housing, apartments for single students, wellness housing, theme housingquiet study floors; townhouses-environmentally-sensitive, low fume material, LEED certified. 35% of campus accessible to physically disabled. **Special Academic Facilities/Equipment:** New Center For Communication Arts with a trap stage and green and blue screen room; radio and television stations; state-of-the-art, nationally acclaimed science complex; videoconference facilities; planetarium; observatory; GIS lab; state-

of-the-art language-learning center; smart classrooms; renovated dance and art studios and performance spaces; art galleries; world's largest solid-volume glass sculpture grouping; 283-acre Environmental Research Reserve; 80-acre protected forest; new alumni center; comprehensive sports and fitness center, seismographic network station, Center for Political Participation, Center for Economic and Environmental Development, environmental roof garden. **Computers:** 50% of classrooms, 100% of dorms, 100% of libraries, 100% of dining areas, 100% of student union, 100% of common outdoor areas have wireless network access. Students can register for classes online. Administrative functions (other than registration) can be performed online.

CAMPUS LIFE

Environment: Town. **Activities:** Choral groups, concert band, dance, drama/theater, jazz band, literary magazine, music ensembles, musical theater, radio station, student government, student newspaper, symphony orchestra, television station, yearbook, Campus Ministries, International Student Organization, Model UN 113 registered organizations, 15 honor societies, 8 religious organizations. 5 fraternities, 5 sororities. **Athletics (Intercollegiate):** *Men:* baseball, basketball, cross-country, diving, football, golf, soccer, swimming, tennis, track/field (outdoor), track/field (indoor). *Women:* basketball, cross-country, diving, golf, lacrosse, soccer, softball, swimming, tennis, track/field (outdoor), track/field (indoor), volleyball. **On-Campus Highlights:** Rustic Bridge, Wise Sport and Fitness Center, Henderson Campus Center, Pelletier Library, World's largest solid-volume glass sculpture group, State-of-the-art, nationally acclaimed science complex dedicated to biology, chemistry and environmental science; Patricia Bush Tippie Alumni Center; seismographic network station; Center for Political Participation; Center for Economic & Environmental Development; radio and TV stations, Grounds For Change Coffeehouse, Vukovich Communication Arts Building Environmental Roof Garden; Robertson athletic fields and recreation area. **Environmental Initiatives:** Climate action plan Energy efficiency through energy audit, retrofits, geothermal wells, education, green building, submetering, dorm competitions; as well as wind energy Composting.

ADMISSIONS

Freshman Academic Profile: Average high school GPA 3.7. 40% in top 10% of high school class, 70% in top 25% of high school class, 93% in top 50% of high school class. 84% from public high schools. SAT Math middle 50% range 560-650. SAT Critical Reading middle 50% range 540-650. SAT Writing middle 50% range 530-640. ACT middle 50% range 24-29. Minimum web-based TOEFL 80. Minimum paper TOEFL 550. **Basis for Candidate Selection:** *Very important factors considered include:* Class rank, academic GPA, rigor of secondary school record. *Important factors considered include:* recommendation(s), standardized test scores, character/personal qualities, extracurricular activities, interview, level of applicant's interest. *Other factors considered include:* application essay, alumni/ae relation, first generation, geographical residence, racial/ethnic status, talent/ability, volunteer work, work experience. **Freshman Admission Requirements:** High school diploma is required and GED is accepted. *Academic units required:* 4 English, 3 mathematics, 3 science, 2 foreign language, 3 social studies, 1 academic electives. *Academic units recommended:* 4 English, 3 mathematics, 3 science, 2 foreign language, 3 social studies, 1 academic electives. **Freshman Admission Statistics:** 4,795 applied, 63% admitted, 19% enrolled. **Transfer Admission Requirements:** High school transcript, college transcript(s), essay or personal statement, standardized test scores, minimum college GPA of 2.5 required. Lowest grade transferable C. **General Admission Information:** Application Fee $35. Early decision application deadline 11/15. Regular application deadline 2/15. Regular notification 4/1. Nonfall registration accepted. Admission may be deferred for a maximum of 1 year. Credit and/or placement offered for CEEB Advanced Placement tests.

COSTS AND FINANCIAL AID

Annual tuition $38,710. Room and board $9,920. Required fees $390. Average book expense $1,000. **Required Forms and Deadlines:** FAFSA. **Notification of Awards:** Applicants will be notified of awards on a rolling basis beginning 3/1. **Types of Aid:** *Need-based scholarships/grants:* Federal Pell, SEOG, state scholarships/grants, private scholarships, the school's own gift aid, Federal Academic Competitiveness Grant, National SMART Grant, Veterans Educational Benefits, Yellow Ribbon Program. *Loans:* Direct Subsidized Stafford, Direct Unsubsidized Stafford, Direct PLUS, Federal Perkins, Private loans from commercial lenders. **Student Employment:** Federal Work-Study Program available. Institutional employment available. Highest amount earned per year from on-campus jobs $8,350. Off-campus job opportunities are excellent. **Financial Aid Statistics:** 100% freshmen, 100% undergrads receive need-based scholarship or grant aid. 16% freshmen, 16% undergrads receive non-need-based scholarship or grant aid. 86% freshmen, 87% undergrads receive need-based self-help aid. 100% freshmen, 99% undergrads receive any aid. **Criteria for awarding institutional aid:** *Non-need-based:* academics, leadership, minority status, state/district residency.

1825 Logan Avenue, Waterloo, IA 50703
Phone: 319-226-2000 • **Financial Aid Phone:** 319-226-2003
E-mail: AllenCollegeAdmissions@ihs.org • **CEEB Code:**
Fax: 319-226-2051 • **Website:** www.allencollege.edu • **ACT Code:** 30691

This private school was founded in 1989.

RATINGS
Admissions Selectivity Rating: 64   **Fire Safety Rating:** 93   **Green Rating:** 60*

STUDENTS AND FACULTY
Enrollment: 385. **Student Body:** 93% female, 7% male, 5% out-of-state, 1% international (2 countries represented). Asian 1%, African American 2%, Caucasian 95%, Hispanic 0%, Native American 0%.
Retention and Graduation: 79% freshmen graduate within 4 years. 82% freshmen graduate within 6 years. 10% grads go on to further study within 1 year. **Faculty:** 28 full-time faculty, 32% hold PhDs, 4% are members of minority groups, 96% are women. 0% of classes are taught by teaching assistants.

ACADEMICS
Degrees: associate, bachelor's, certificate, master's, post-master's certificate. **Classes:** Most classes have fewer than 10 students. Most lab/discussion sessions have fewer than 10 students. **Majors with Highest Enrollment:** family practice nurse/nurse practitioner; health services/allied health/health sciences; nursing/registered nurse (rn, asn, bsn, msn). **Special Study Options:** Accelerated program, cooperative education program, distance learning, honors program, independent study, internships. **Disability Services:** Special programs offered to physically disabled students include tutors.

FACILITIES
Housing: Coed dorms, Housing also available at a cooperating institution. 100% of campus accessible to physically disabled. **Computers:** 100% of classrooms, 100% of dorms, 100% of libraries, 100% of student union, 100% of common outdoor areas have wireless network access. Administrative functions (other than registration) can be performed online.

CAMPUS LIFE
Environment: City. **Activities:** Choral groups, student government, student newspaper, yearbook 4 registered organizations, 1 honor societies, 1 religious organizations.

ADMISSIONS
Freshman Academic Profile: Minimum paper TOEFL 550. **Basis for Candidate Selection:** *Very important factors considered include:* Class rank, academic GPA, rigor of secondary school record, standardized test scores. *Important factors considered include:* application essay, recommendation(s). *Other factors considered include:* character/personal qualities, extracurricular activities, first generation, interview, talent/ability. **Freshman Admission Requirements:** High school diploma is required and GED is accepted. *Academic units required:* 8 English, 6 mathematics, 6 science, 6 social studies. 8 English, 6 mathematics, 6 science, 6 social studies. **Freshman Admission Statistics:** 9 applied, 11% admitted. **Transfer Admission Requirements:** High school transcript, college transcript(s), essay or personal statement, standardized test scores, minimum college GPA of 2.7 required. Lowest grade transferable C. **General Admission Information:** Application Fee $50. Regular application deadline 3/1. Notification on a rolling basis, beginning on or about 3/15. Nonfall registration accepted. Credit offered for CEEB Advanced Placement tests.

COSTS AND FINANCIAL AID
Annual tuition $16,236. Room and board $7,281. Required fees $1,867. Average book expense $1,200. **Required Forms and Deadlines:** FAFSA, institution's own financial aid form. **Notification of Awards:** Applicants will be notified of awards on a rolling basis beginning 4/1. **Types of Aid:** *Need-based scholarships/grants:* Federal Pell, SEOG, state scholarships/grants, private scholarships, the school's own gift aid, Federal Nursing Scholarships. Various funds from HRSA (SDS- Scholarship for Disadvantaged Students, NSP, Nursing Scholarship Program, AENT - Advanced Education Nurse Traineeship. *Loans:* Direct Subsidized Stafford, Direct Unsubsidized Stafford, Direct PLUS, Federal Perkins, Federal Nursing, college/university loans from institutional funds, Alternative Loans. **Student Employment:** Federal Work-Study Program available. Off-campus job opportunities are excellent. **Financial Aid Statistics:** 100% freshmen, 88% undergrads receive need-based scholarship or grant aid. 50% freshmen, 83% undergrads receive need-based self-help aid. 100% freshmen, 99% undergrads receive any aid. 0% undergrads borrow to pay for school. Average cumulative indebtedness $0. **Criteria for awarding institutional aid:** *Non-need-based:* academics, alumni affiliation, leadership, minority status, state/district residency.

ALMA COLLEGE

614 West Superior Street, Alma, MI 48801-1599
Phone: 989-463-7139 • **Financial Aid Phone:** 989-463-7347
E-mail: admissions@alma.edu • **CEEB Code:** 1010
Fax: 989-463-7057 • **Website:** www.alma.edu • **ACT Code:** 1958

This private school, affiliated with the Presbyterian Church, was founded in 1886. It has a 125-acre campus.

RATINGS
Admissions Selectivity Rating: 74   **Fire Safety Rating:** 62   **Green Rating:** 61

STUDENTS AND FACULTY
Enrollment: 1,430. **Student Body:** 54% female, 46% male, 8% out-of-state, 1% international (14 countries represented). Asian 1%, African American 3%, Caucasian 86%, Hispanic 2%, Native American 1%.
Retention and Graduation: 50% freshmen graduate within 4 years. 66% freshmen graduate within 6 years. **Faculty:** Student/faculty ratio 12:1. 95 full-time faculty, 84% hold PhDs, 12% are members of minority groups, 41% are women. 0% of classes are taught by teaching assistants.

ACADEMICS
Degrees: bachelor's. **Classes:** Most classes have 10–19 students. Most lab/discussion sessions have 10–19 students. **Majors with Highest Enrollment:** biological and physical sciences; business/commerce; education. **Special Study Options:** double major, dual enrollment, exchange student program (domestic), honors program, independent study, internships, student-designed major, study abroad, teacher certification program. **Honors Programs:** Students in the Honors Program participate in special seminar opportunities and enroll in courses designed for honors scholars. **Combined Degree Programs:** 3-2 occupational therapy. **Disability Services:** Special programs offered to physically disabled students include note-taking services, reader services, tape recorders, tutors. **Career Services:** alumni services, career assessment, internships.

FACILITIES
Housing: Coed dorms, fraternity/sorority housing, theme housing 75% of campus accessible to physically disabled. **Special Academic Facilities/Equipment:** Music and arts centers, science lab, planetarium, a DNA synthesizer and sequencer, and a multinuclear magnetic resonance spectrometer. **Computers:** 60% of classrooms, 100% of libraries, 100% of dining areas, 100% of student union, have wireless network access. Students can register for classes online.

CAMPUS LIFE
Environment: Village. **Activities:** Choral groups, concert band, dance, drama/theater, jazz band, marching band, music ensembles, radio station, student government, student newspaper, symphony orchestra, yearbook, Campus Ministries, International Student Organization, Model UN 75 registered organizations, 20 honor societies, 4 religious organizations. 6 fraternities, 5 sororities. **Athletics (Intercollegiate):** *Men:* baseball, basketball, cross-country, diving, football, golf, soccer, swimming, tennis, track/field (outdoor). *Women:* basketball, cross-country, diving, golf, soccer, softball, swimming, tennis, track/field (outdoor), volleyball. **On-Campus Highlights:** Joe's Place, Stone Center for Recreation, Library, Remick Heritage Center, Wright Hall (residence hall). **Environmental Initiatives:** Alma's green residence hall, Wright Hall, was completed in January 2005. The modern, 60-bed apartment-style hall features a number of environmentally friendly features, including geothermal heating and cooling, recycled-content ceiling tiles and carpeting, energy-efficient windows, rooftop solar heating panels, energy-efficient showers and washing machines, and a computerized energy monitoring system. The Hogan Center is the first official LEED-certified building for green construction at Alma College and Gratiot County. The renovated Hogan Center and new Art Smith Arena were awarded LEED'® certification at the Silver level by the U.S. Green Building Council (USGBC) and verified by the Green Building Certification Institute (GBCI). LEED is the nation's preeminent program for the design, construction and operation of high performance green buildings. The arena serves as the primary venue for commencement, convocations, major speakers, concerts, athletics and other major events. Alma College and the Pine River Superfund Task Force organized an international conference that examined the impact of DDT on human health and the environment. The Eugene Kenaga International DDT Conference on Environment and Health took place March 14, 2008 at Alma College. It brought together international experts to frame and lead discussions of current knowledge of DDT and other persistent organic pollutants (POPs).

ADMISSIONS
Freshman Academic Profile: Average high school GPA 3.5. 23% in top 10% of high school class, 54% in top 25% of high school class, 84% in top 50% of high school class. 90% from public high schools. SAT Math middle 50% range 450-620. SAT Writing middle 50% range 470-590. ACT middle 50% range 21-26. Minimum web-based TOEFL 69. Minimum paper TOEFL 525. **Basis**

for Candidate Selection: *Very important factors considered include:* academic GPA, standardized test scores. *Important factors considered include:* application essay. *Other factors considered include:* Class rank, recommendation(s), rigor of secondary school record, alumni/ae relation, character/personal qualities, extracurricular activities, geographical residence, interview, level of applicant's interest, state residency, talent/ability, volunteer work, work experience. **Freshman Admission Requirements:** High school diploma is required and GED is accepted. *Academic units required:* 4 English, 3 mathematics, 3 science, 3 social studies. *Academic units recommended:* 4 English, 3 mathematics, 3 science, 3 social studies. **Freshman Admission Statistics:** 2,232 applied, 72% admitted, 27% enrolled. **Transfer Admission Requirements:** High school transcript, college transcript(s), statement of good standing from prior institution(s). Minimum college GPA of 3.0 required. Lowest grade transferable C. **General Admission Information:** Application Fee $25. Notification on a rolling basis, beginning on or about 9/1. Nonfall registration accepted. Admission may be deferred for a maximum of 1 year. Credit and/or placement offered for CEEB Advanced Placement tests.

COSTS AND FINANCIAL AID
Annual tuition $30,700. Room and board $8,990. Required fees $360. Average book expense $926. **Required Forms and Deadlines:** FAFSA. **Notification of Awards:** Applicants will be notified of awards on a rolling basis beginning 3/1. **Types of Aid:** *Need-based scholarships/grants:* Federal Pell, SEOG, state scholarships/grants, the school's own gift aid. *Loans:* Subsidized Stafford, Unsubsidized Stafford, PLUS, Federal Perkins, college/university loans from institutional funds, Alternative loans. **Student Employment:** Federal Work-Study Program available. Institutional employment available. Off-campus job opportunities are good. **Financial Aid Statistics:** 100% freshmen, 100% undergrads receive need-based scholarship or grant aid. 13% freshmen, 13% undergrads receive non-need-based scholarship or grant aid. 86% freshmen, 83% undergrads receive need-based self-help aid. 99% freshmen, 99% undergrads receive any aid. 77% undergrads borrow to pay for school. Average cumulative indebtedness $31,297. **Criteria for awarding institutional aid:** *Non-need-based:* academics, alumni affiliation, art, minority status, music/drama.

ALVERNIA COLLEGE

400 St. Bernardine Street, Reading, PA 19607
Phone: 610-796-8220 • **Financial Aid Phone:** 610-796-8356
E-mail: admissions@alvernia.edu
Fax: 610-796-8336

This private school, affiliated with the Roman Catholic Church, was founded in 1958. It has a 80-acre campus.

RATINGS
Admissions Selectivity Rating: 69   **Fire Safety Rating:** 73   **Green Rating:** 60*

STUDENTS AND FACULTY
Enrollment: 2,019. **Student Body:** 71% female, 29% male, 14% out-of-state, 0% international (9 countries represented). Asian 1%, African American 11%, Caucasian 74%, Hispanic 6%, Native American 0%.
Retention and Graduation: 77% freshmen return for sophomore year. 40% freshmen graduate within 4 years. 46% freshmen graduate within 6 years. **Faculty:** Student/faculty ratio 13:1. 74 full-time faculty, 68% hold PhDs, 7% are members of minority groups, 57% are women. 0% of classes are taught by teaching assistants.

ACADEMICS
Degrees: associate, bachelor's, certificate, master's, post-bachelor's certificate, post-master's certificate. **Classes:** Most classes have 10–19 students. Most lab/discussion sessions have 10–19 students. **Majors with Highest Enrollment:** criminal justice/law enforcement administration; elementary education and teaching; substance abuse/addiction counseling. **Special Study Options:** Accelerated program, cross-registration, double major, dual enrollment, English as a Second Language (ESL), honors program, independent study, internships, student-designed major, study abroad, teacher certification program. **Honors Programs:** Alvernia College Honors Program **Combined Degree Programs:** BA/MA, BS/MS Occupational Therapy. **Disability Services:** Special programs offered to physically disabled students include note-taking services, tape recorders, tutors. **Career Services:** career/job search classes, career assessment, internships Career Services highlights include The Washington Center and many local internship opportunities.

FACILITIES
Housing: Coed dorms, special housing for disabled students, women's dorms-Single-sex suites in townhouses. Single-sex floors in dorms. 90% of campus accessible to physically disabled. **Computers:** Students can register for classes

online. Administrative functions (other than registration) can be performed online.

CAMPUS LIFE

Environment: Village. **Activities:** Choral groups, dance, drama/theater, literary magazine, music ensembles, student government, student newspaper, yearbook 35 registered organizations, 5 honor societies, 5 religious organizations. **Athletics (Intercollegiate):** *Men:* baseball, basketball, cross-country, golf, lacrosse, soccer, tennis. *Women:* basketball, cheerleading, cross-country, field hockey, lacrosse, soccer, softball, tennis, volleyball. **On-Campus Highlights:** Student Center, Crusader Cafe, Library, Gym, Residence Hall Lounge.

ADMISSIONS

Freshman Academic Profile: Average high school GPA 2.9. 8% in top 10% of high school class, 27% in top 25% of high school class, 53% in top 50% of high school class. 74% from public high schools. SAT Math middle 50% range 420-530. SAT Critical Reading middle 50% range 420-520. Minimum paper TOEFL 550. **Basis for Candidate Selection:** *Very important factors considered include:* academic GPA, standardized test scores. *Important factors considered include:* Class rank, application essay, recommendation(s), rigor of secondary school record, character/personal qualities, extracurricular activities, interview, level of applicant's interest, talent/ability, volunteer work, work experience. *Other factors considered include:* religious affiliation/commitment. **Freshman Admission Requirements:** High school diploma is required and GED is accepted. **Freshman Admission Statistics:** 922 applied, 76% admitted, 41% enrolled. **Transfer Admission Requirements:** High school transcript, college transcript(s), essay or personal statement, minimum college GPA of 2.0 required. Lowest grade transferable C. **General Admission Information:** Application Fee $25. Nonfall registration accepted. Admission may be deferred for a maximum of 12 months. Credit and/or placement offered for CEEB Advanced Placement tests.

COSTS AND FINANCIAL AID

Annual tuition $20,220. Room and board $8,220. Required fees $202. Average book expense $1,200. **Required Forms and Deadlines:** FAFSA. **Notification of Awards:** Applicants will be notified of awards on a rolling basis beginning 2/10. **Types of Aid:** *Need-based scholarships/grants:* Federal Pell, SEOG, state scholarships/grants, private scholarships. *Loans:* Subsidized Stafford, Unsubsidized Stafford, PLUS. **Student Employment:** Highest amount earned per year from on-campus jobs $3,886. **Financial Aid Statistics:** 100% freshmen, 100% undergrads receive need-based scholarship or grant aid. 1% freshmen, 12% undergrads receive non-need-based scholarship or grant aid. 95% freshmen, 95% undergrads receive need-based self-help aid. 94% freshmen, 98% undergrads receive any aid. 91% undergrads borrow to pay for school. Average cumulative indebtedness $6,985. **Criteria for awarding institutional aid:** *Non-need-based:* academics, alumni affiliation.

See page 1006.

ALVERNO COLLEGE

3400 South 43rd Street, Milwaukee, WI 53234-3922
Phone: 414-382-6101 • **Financial Aid Phone:** 414-382-6046
E-mail: admissions@alverno.edu • **CEEB Code:** 1012
Fax: 414-382-6055 • **Website:** www.alverno.edu • **ACT Code:** 4558

This private school, affiliated with the Roman Catholic Church, was founded in 1887. It has a 47-acre campus.

RATINGS

Admissions Selectivity Rating: 69 **Fire Safety Rating:** 76 **Green Rating:** 72

STUDENTS AND FACULTY

Enrollment: 1,898. **Student Body:** 100% female, 0% male, 4% out-of-state, 1% international (14 countries represented). Asian 5%, African American 18%, Caucasian 55%, Hispanic 17%, Native American 1%. **Retention and Graduation:** 72% freshmen return for sophomore year. 15% freshmen graduate within 4 years. **Faculty:** Student/faculty ratio 10:1. 119 full-time faculty, 92% hold PhDs, 9% are members of minority groups, 79% are women. 0% of classes are taught by teaching assistants.

ACADEMICS

Degrees: associate, bachelor's, master's, post-bachelor's certificate, post-master's certificate. **Classes:** Most classes have 20–29 students. Most lab/discussion sessions have 20–29 students. **Majors with Highest Enrollment:** business administration and management; education; nursing/registered nurse (rn, asn, bsn, msn). **Special Study Options:** double major, independent study, internships, student-designed major, study abroad, teacher certification program, weekend college. **Disability Services:** Special programs offered to physically disabled

students include note-taking services, reader services, tape recorders, tutors. **Career Services:** alumni services, career/job search classes, career assessment, Career Services highlights include We are proudest of our integration into the Alverno curriculum. Counselors design and teach 3 courses that are required by various disciplines (one at the first-year level and two at the senior level), as well as teach segments in several additional courses. The result is that virtually every student has done in-class work with a career counselor prior to graduation.

FACILITIES

Housing: women's dorms. 95% of campus accessible to physically disabled. **Special Academic Facilities/Equipment:** Art & Culture Gallery, Career Center, Fitness center, Reiman Gymnasium, Nursing Skills Lab, Student centered multi-media production facility, Diagnostic Digital Portfolio, computer center, science labs, theatre venue **Computers:** 35% of classrooms, 100% of dorms, 100% of libraries, 100% of dining areas, 100% of student union, have wireless network access. Students can register for classes online. Administrative functions (other than registration) can be performed online.

CAMPUS LIFE

Environment: Metropolis. **Activities:** Choral groups, dance, drama/theater, literary magazine, music ensembles, student government, student newspaper, Campus Ministries, International Student Organization 37 registered organizations, 1 honor societies, 1 religious organizations. 2 sororities. **Athletics (Intercollegiate):** *Women:* basketball, cross-country, soccer, softball, tennis, volleyball. **On-Campus Highlights:** Teaching, Learning and Technology Center, The Mug Coffee House, Fitness Center, The Pipeline - Activity Center, Reiman Gymnasium. **Environmental Initiatives:** Created sustainability guidelines for construction and renovation (2011). Converting to energy efficient lighting as feasible (i.e., 2011-12 replaced incandescent lighting in chapel with compact fluorescent-88% savings; metal halide in gym with hi-bay fluorescent-66% savings; stairwell lights to T8 fixtures controlled by automatic sensors) Installed new domestic 92% energy-efficient hot water system, replacing 75-80% system.

ADMISSIONS

Freshman Academic Profile: Average high school GPA 2.8. 85% from public high schools. ACT middle 50% range 17-21. Minimum web-based TOEFL 68. Minimum paper TOEFL 520. **Basis for Candidate Selection:** *Very important factors considered include:* academic GPA, standardized test scores. *Important factors considered include:* application essay, rigor of secondary school record. *Other factors considered include:* recommendation(s), character/personal qualities, extracurricular activities, interview, level of applicant's interest, talent/ability, volunteer work, work experience. **Freshman Admission Requirements:** High school diploma is required and GED is accepted. *Academic units required:* 4 English, 3 mathematics, 3 science, 3 social studies, 4 academic electives. *Academic units recommended:* 4 English, 3 mathematics, 3 science, 3 social studies, 4 academic electives. **Freshman Admission Statistics:** 643 applied, 65% admitted, 48% enrolled. **Transfer Admission Requirements:** High school transcript, college transcript(s), essay or personal statement, minimum college GPA of 2.0 required. Lowest grade transferable C. **General Admission Information:** Application Fee $20. Notification on a rolling basis, beginning on or about 9/1. Nonfall registration accepted. Admission may be deferred for a maximum of 1 year. Credit and/or placement offered for CEEB Advanced Placement tests.

COSTS AND FINANCIAL AID

. Required fees. Average book expense $1,056. **Required Forms and Deadlines:** FAFSA, institution's own financial aid form. **Notification of Awards:** Applicants will be notified of awards on a rolling basis beginning 3/15. **Types of Aid:** *Need-based scholarships/grants:* Federal Pell, SEOG, state scholarships/grants, private scholarships, the school's own gift aid, Federal Nursing Scholarships. *Loans:* Subsidized Stafford, Unsubsidized Stafford, PLUS, Federal Perkins, state loans. **Student Employment:** Federal Work-Study Program available. Institutional employment available. Highest amount earned per year from on-campus jobs $8,830. Off-campus job opportunities are good. **Financial Aid Statistics:** 100% freshmen, 99% undergrads receive need-based scholarship or grant aid. 96% freshmen, 84% undergrads receive non-need-based scholarship or grant aid. 90% freshmen, 90% undergrads receive need-based self-help aid. 100% freshmen, 100% undergrads receive any aid. 92% undergrads borrow to pay for school. Average cumulative indebtedness $41,405. **Criteria for awarding institutional aid:** *Non-need-based:* academics, alumni affiliation.

AMERICAN CONSERVATORY OF MUSIC

252 Wildwood Road, Hammond, IN 46324
Phone: 219-931-6000
E-mail: registrar@americanconservatory.edu
Fax: 219-931-6089

This private school, affiliated with the Greek Orthodox Church, was founded in 1886.

RATINGS
Admissions Selectivity Rating: 60*   **Fire Safety Rating:** 60*   **Green Rating:** 60*

STUDENTS AND FACULTY
Faculty: Student/faculty ratio 1:1.

ACADEMICS
Degrees: associate, bachelor's, certificate, diploma, master's. **Classes: Special Study Options:** Accelerated program, distance learning, double major, English as a Second Language (ESL).

FACILITIES
Housing: apartments for married students, apartments for single students. **Computers:** Undergraduates are required to own a computer.

CAMPUS LIFE
Environment: Metropolis. **Activities:** Choral groups, jazz band, music ensembles, opera, symphony orchestra.

ADMISSIONS
Transfer Admission Requirements: High school transcript, college transcript(s), essay or personal statement, interview, statement of good standing from prior institution(s). Minimum college GPA of 2.0 required. Lowest grade transferable C. **General Admission Information:**

COSTS AND FINANCIAL AID
Average book expense $2,400. **Types of Aid:** *Need-based scholarships/grants:* the school's own gift aid. **Criteria for awarding institutional aid:** *Non-need-based:* music/drama.

AMERICAN INDIAN COLLEGE OF THE ASSEMBLIES OF GOD, INC.

10020 North 15th Avenue, Phoenix, AZ 85021
Phone: 602-944-3335
E-mail: aicadm@aicag.edu
Fax: 602-943-8299 • **Website:** www.aicag.edu • **ACT Code:** 6005

This private school, affiliated with the Assemblies of God Church, was founded in 1957. It has a 10-acre campus.

RATINGS
Admissions Selectivity Rating: 63   **Fire Safety Rating:** 60*   **Green Rating:** 60*

STUDENTS AND FACULTY
Enrollment: 70. **Student Body:** 44% female, 56% male, 69% out-of-state, 1% international (2 countries represented). Asian 6%, African American 4%, Caucasian 14%, Hispanic 6%, Native American 69%.
Retention and Graduation: **Faculty:** Student/faculty ratio 5:1. 8 full-time faculty, 88% hold PhDs, 0% are members of minority groups, 38% are women. 0% of classes are taught by teaching assistants.

ACADEMICS
Degrees: associate, bachelor's. **Classes:** Most classes have fewer than 10 students. Most lab/discussion sessions have fewer than 10 students. **Special Study Options:** double major.

FACILITIES
Housing: special housing for disabled students, men's dorms, women's dorms, apartments for married students.

CAMPUS LIFE
Environment: Metropolis. **Activities:** Choral groups, drama/theater, literary magazine, music ensembles, musical theater, student government, student newspaper, yearbook, Campus Ministries. **On-Campus Highlights:** Gymnasium, Cree Student Union, Ramsey Cafeteria, Chapel, Prayer Mountain Trail.

ADMISSIONS
Freshman Academic Profile: Average high school GPA 2.5. 0% in top 10% of high school class, 0% in top 25% of high school class, 60% in top 50% of high school class. Minimum paper TOEFL 500. **Basis for Candidate Selection:** *Very important factors considered include:* Class rank, recommendation(s), rigor of secondary school record, standardized test scores, character/personal qualities, religious affiliation/commitment. *Important factors considered include:* application essay. *Other factors considered include:* extracurricular activities, interview, talent/ability, volunteer work, work experience. **Freshman Admission Requirements:** High school diploma is required and GED is accepted. **Freshman Admission Statistics:** 18 applied, 44% admitted. **Transfer Admission Requirements:** High school transcript, college transcript(s), standardized test scores, minimum college GPA of 2.0 required. Lowest grade transferable C. **General Admission Information:** Nonfall registration accepted.

COSTS AND FINANCIAL AID
Annual tuition $4,950. Room and board $3,850. Required fees $605. Average book expense $500. **Required Forms and Deadlines:** FAFSA, institution's own financial aid form, CSS/Financial Aid PROFILE, state aid form, noncustodial PROFILE, business/farm supplement. **Types of Aid:** *Need-based scholarships/grants:* Federal Pell, SEOG, state scholarships/grants, private scholarships, the school's own gift aid. *Loans:* Subsidized Stafford, Unsubsidized Stafford, PLUS. **Student Employment:** Off-campus job opportunities are fair. **Financial Aid Statistics:** 46% undergrads receive any aid.

AMERICAN INTERNATIONAL COLLEGE

1000 State Street, Springfield, MA 01109-3184
Phone: 413-205-3201 • **Financial Aid Phone:** 413-205-3259
E-mail: inquiry@aic.edu • **CEEB Code:** 3002
Fax: 413-205-3051 • **Website:** www.aic.edu • **ACT Code:** 1772

This private school was founded in 1885. It has a 58-acre campus.

RATINGS
Admissions Selectivity Rating: 67   **Fire Safety Rating:** 86   **Green Rating:** 60*

STUDENTS AND FACULTY
Enrollment: 1,492. **Student Body:** 56% female, 44% male, 37% out-of-state, 2% international (30 countries represented). Asian 1%, African American 24%, Caucasian 41%, Hispanic 9%, Native American 0%.
Retention and Graduation: 61% freshmen return for sophomore year. 20% grads go on to further study within 1 year. 9% grads pursue arts and sciences degrees. 5% grads pursue law degrees. 15% grads pursue business degrees. 2% grads pursue medical degrees. **Faculty:** Student/faculty ratio 14:1. 74 full-time faculty, 51% hold PhDs, 12% are members of minority groups, 61% are women. 0% of classes are taught by teaching assistants.

ACADEMICS
Degrees: associate, bachelor's, master's, post-master's certificate, terminal associate. **Classes:** Most classes have 10–19 students. Most lab/discussion sessions have 10–19 students. **Majors with Highest Enrollment:** criminal justice/safety studies; nursing/registered nurse (rn, asn, bsn, msn); psychology. **Special Study Options:** Accelerated program, cross-registration, distance learning, double major, dual enrollment, English as a Second Language (ESL), honors program, independent study, internships, liberal arts/career combination, study abroad, teacher certification program, weekend college, Off-campus study in Washington, DC; upper division undergrads may take grad level courses. **Honors Programs:** Four Year Honors program open to students in any major with appropriate credentials. **Combined Degree Programs:** BA/MA, 4-1 bachelor's/M.B.A. program. **Disability Services:** Special programs offered to physically disabled students include note-taking services, reader services, tape recorders, tutors. **Career Services:** alumni services, career/job search classes, career assessment, internships.

FACILITIES
Housing: Coed dorms, women's dorms, wellness housing. 75% of campus accessible to physically disabled. **Special Academic Facilities/Equipment:** Centers for child development, cultural arts, and human technology. **Computers:** 100% of classrooms, 90% of dorms, 100% of libraries, 100% of dining areas, 100% of student union, 100% of common outdoor areas have wireless network access. Students can register for classes online. Administrative functions (other than registration) can be performed online.

CAMPUS LIFE
Environment: City. **Activities:** Choral groups, dance, drama/theater, literary magazine, musical theater, pep band, radio station, student government, student newspaper, yearbook, Campus Ministries, International Student Organiza-

tion 45 registered organizations, 5 honor societies, 3 religious organizations. 4 fraternities, 5 sororities. **Athletics (Intercollegiate):** *Men:* baseball, basketball, cheerleading, cross-country, football, golf, ice hockey, lacrosse, soccer, tennis, track/field (outdoor), track/field (indoor), wrestling. *Women:* basketball, cheerleading, cross-country, field hockey, lacrosse, soccer, softball, tennis, track/field (outdoor), track/field (indoor), volleyball. **On-Campus Highlights:** Courniotes Hall - Health Sciences, Karen Sprague Cultural Arts Center, Butova & Metcalf Gymnasiums, WAIC-FM (Radio Station).

ADMISSIONS

Freshman Academic Profile: Average high school GPA 2.6. SAT Math middle 50% range 355-565. SAT Critical Reading middle 50% range 340-530. SAT Writing middle 50% range 315-525. ACT middle 50% range 16-22. Minimum web-based TOEFL 80. Minimum paper TOEFL 550. **Basis for Candidate Selection:** *Important factors considered include:* Class rank, academic GPA, rigor of secondary school record, standardized test scores. *Other factors considered include:* application essay, recommendation(s), alumni/ae relation, character/personal qualities, extracurricular activities, first generation, interview, level of applicant's interest, racial/ethnic status, volunteer work, work experience. **Freshman Admission Requirements:** High school diploma is required and GED is accepted. *Academic units required:* 4 English, 3 mathematics, 2 science, (2 science labs), 1 foreign language, 1 social studies, 2 history, 4 academic electives. *Academic units recommended:* 4 English, 3 mathematics, 2 science, (2 science labs), 1 foreign language, 1 social studies, 2 history, 4 academic electives. **Freshman Admission Statistics:** 1,522 applied, 74% admitted, 27% enrolled. **Transfer Admission Requirements:** High school transcript, college transcript(s), minimum college GPA of 2.0 required. Lowest grade transferable C. **General Admission Information:** Application Fee $25. Notification on a rolling basis, beginning on or about 12/15. Nonfall registration accepted. Admission may be deferred for a maximum of 2 years. Credit and/or placement offered for CEEB Advanced Placement tests.

COSTS AND FINANCIAL AID

Annual tuition $29,015. Room and board $11,710. Average book expense $1,200. **Required Forms and Deadlines:** FAFSA, state aid form. **Notification of Awards:** Applicants will be notified of awards on a rolling basis beginning 3/15. **Types of Aid:** *Need-based scholarships/grants:* Federal Pell, SEOG, state scholarships/grants, private scholarships, the school's own gift aid, Federal Nursing Scholarships. *Loans:* Subsidized Stafford, Unsubsidized Stafford, PLUS, Federal Perkins, college/university loans from institutional funds. **Student Employment:** Federal Work-Study Program available. Institutional employment available. Highest amount earned per year from on-campus jobs $2,200. Off-campus job opportunities are good. **Financial Aid Statistics:** 100% freshmen, 99% undergrads receive need-based scholarship or grant aid. 12% freshmen, 12% undergrads receive non-need-based scholarship or grant aid. 89% freshmen, 88% undergrads receive need-based self-help aid. 12% freshmen, 8% undergrads receive athletic scholarships. 100% freshmen, 85% undergrads receive any aid. 86% undergrads borrow to pay for school. Average cumulative indebtedness $33,170. **Criteria for awarding institutional aid:** *Non-need-based:* academics, alumni affiliation, athletics, leadership.

AMERICAN JEWISH UNIVERSITY

15600 Mulholland Drive, Familian Campus, Bel Air, CA 90077
Phone: 310-440-1247 • **Financial Aid Phone:** 310-440-1252
E-mail: admissions@ajula.edu • **CEEB Code:** 4876
Fax: 310 471 3657 • **Website:** www.ajula.edu • **ACT Code:** 462

This private school, affiliated with the Jewish Church, was founded in 1947. It has a 28-acre campus.

RATINGS
Admissions Selectivity Rating: 66   **Fire Safety Rating:** 68   **Green Rating:** 61

STUDENTS AND FACULTY
Enrollment: 130. **Student Body:** 50% female, 50% male, 24% out-of-state, 5% international (5 countries represented). Asian 2%, African American 2%, Caucasian 52%, Hispanic 4%, Native American 2%.
Retention and Graduation: 91% freshmen return for sophomore year. 38% freshmen graduate within 4 years. 38% freshmen graduate within 6 years.
Faculty: Student/faculty ratio 8:1. 12 full-time faculty, 100% hold PhDs, 0% are members of minority groups, 42% are women. 0% of classes are taught by teaching assistants.

ACADEMICS
Degrees: bachelor's, master's. **Classes:** Most classes have fewer than 10 students. Most lab/discussion sessions have fewer than 10 students. **Majors with Highest Enrollment:** business administration and management; political

science and government; psychology. **Special Study Options:** cross-registration, double major, independent study, internships, student-designed major, study abroad. **Combined Degree Programs:** BA/MA, BA/MBA, BA/MAEd. **Career Services:** career assessment, internships, Career Services highlights include Internships. Our students have had internships with American Jewish Joint Distribution Committee, Anti-Defamation League, Cedars-Sinai Medical Center, Jewish Federation of Greater Los Angeles, Jewish Telegraphic Agency, Jewish Television Network, Los Angeles Holocaust Museum, Museum of Tolerance, New Line Cinema, and the Simon Wiesenthal Center.

FACILITIES

Housing: Coed dorms, special housing for disabled students, apartments for married students, apartments for single students. 90% of campus accessible to physically disabled. **Special Academic Facilities/Equipment:** Art Gallery, Ostrow Library **Computers:** 100% of dorms, 100% of libraries, 100% of student union, 50% of common outdoor areas have wireless network access. Administrative functions (other than registration) can be performed online.

CAMPUS LIFE

Environment: Metropolis. **Activities:** Choral groups, drama/theater, literary magazine, student government, student newspaper, Model UN 17 registered organizations, 1 religious organizations. **On-Campus Highlights:** Residence Halls, Auerbach Student Union, The Berg, our kosher dining hall, Sculpture Garden, Ostrow Library. **Environmental Initiatives:** Energy Management Conserving Water Recycling

ADMISSIONS

Freshman Academic Profile: Average high school GPA 3.3. 50% in top 10% of high school class, 0% in top 25% of high school class, 75% in top 50% of high school class. SAT Math middle 50% range 448-578. SAT Critical Reading middle 50% range 470-605. SAT Writing middle 50% range 490-583. ACT middle 50% range 20-22. Minimum web-based TOEFL 75. Minimum paper TOEFL 530. **Basis for Candidate Selection:** *Very important factors considered include:* application essay, recommendation(s), character/personal qualities, extracurricular activities, interview, talent/ability, volunteer work. *Important factors considered include:* academic GPA, standardized test scores, level of applicant's interest. *Other factors considered include:* Class rank, rigor of secondary school record, alumni/ae relation, geographical residence, religious affiliation/commitment, state residency, work experience. **Freshman Admission Requirements:** High school diploma is required and GED is accepted. **Freshman Admission Statistics:** 39 applied, 95% admitted, 30% enrolled. **Transfer Admission Requirements:** college transcript(s), essay or personal statement, minimum college GPA of N/A required. Lowest grade transferable C. **General Admission Information:** Application Fee $35. Regular application deadline 5/31. Notification on a rolling basis, beginning on or about 9/15. Nonfall registration accepted. Admission may be deferred for a maximum of 1 year. Credit offered for CEEB Advanced Placement tests.

COSTS AND FINANCIAL AID

Annual tuition $24,744. Room and board $12,764. Required fees $1,044. Average book expense $1,656. **Required Forms and Deadlines:** FAFSA, institution's own financial aid form Tax Form, Verification Form. **Notification of Awards:** Applicants will be notified of awards on a rolling basis beginning 1/1. **Types of Aid:** *Need-based scholarships/grants:* Federal Pell, SEOG, state scholarships/grants, private scholarships, the school's own gift aid. *Loans:* Subsidized Stafford, Unsubsidized Stafford, PLUS. **Student Employment:** Federal Work-Study Program available. Institutional employment available. Highest amount earned per year from on-campus jobs $1,000. Off-campus job opportunities are good. **Financial Aid Statistics:** 100% freshmen, 100% undergrads receive need-based scholarship or grant aid. 100% freshmen, 100% undergrads receive non-need-based scholarship or grant aid. 100% freshmen, 100% undergrads receive need-based self-help aid. 100% freshmen, 95% undergrads receive any aid. 33% undergrads borrow to pay for school. **Criteria for awarding institutional aid:** *Non-need-based:* leadership, minority status, music/drama, state/district residency.

AMERICAN UNIVERSITY

Best 378

4400 Massachusetts Ave, NW, Washington, DC 20016-8001
Phone: 202-885-6000 • **Financial Aid Phone:** 202-885-6100
E-mail: admissions@american.edu • **CEEB Code:** 5007
Fax: 202-885-1025 • **Website:** www.american.edu • **ACT Code:** 648

This private school, affiliated with the Methodist Church, was founded in 1893. It has a 84-acre campus.

RATINGS

Admissions Selectivity Rating: 94   **Fire Safety Rating:** 74   **Green Rating:** 99

STUDENTS AND FACULTY

Enrollment: 6,793. **Student Body:** 59% female, 41% male, 84% out-of-state, 7% international (146 countries represented). Asian 6%, African American 5%, Caucasian 57%, Hispanic 8%, Native American 0%.
Retention and Graduation: 74% freshmen graduate within 4 years. 77% freshmen graduate within 6 years. **Faculty:** Student/faculty ratio 12:1. 712 full-time faculty, 94% hold PhDs, 18% are members of minority groups, 46% are women. 0% of classes are taught by teaching assistants.

ACADEMICS

Degrees: associate, bachelor's, certificate, first professional, master's, post-bachelor's certificate. **Classes: Majors with Highest Enrollment:** business/commerce; international relations and affairs; mass communication/media studies. **Special Study Options:** Accelerated program, cooperative education program, cross-registration, double major, exchange student program (domestic), honors program, independent study, internships, student-designed major, study abroad, teacher certification program, weekend college, AU Abroad offers more than 100 study Abroad programs in 33 geographic locations around the world. Earn college credit, learn a foreign language, pursue and internship and gain international experience and contacts. One-semester, full year, alternative spring break, and language immersion options are available. With AU Abroad partner universities in Canada, Mexico, England, Scotland, Ireland, Argentina, Australia, Egypt,the United Arab Emirates and numerous other countries around the world, you have the ability to go almost anywhere. **Honors Programs:** The University Honors Program is designed to promote a continuous learning environment, making optimum use of AU's outstanding faculty, campus facilities and the numerous resources available in the Washington, D.C. area and abroad. Students enjoy small classes, proven instructors, cultural events, a wide range of social activities and the option of living in Honors housing. Members of the University Honors Program can major in any discipline at the university and can also participate in multidisciplinary Honors Colloquia. **Combined Degree Programs:** BA/MA, BS/MS, BA/MPA, BA/MS. **Disability Services:** Special programs offered to physically disabled students include note-taking services, reader services, tape recorders, tutors. **Career Services:** Alumni network, alumni services, career/job search classes, career assessment, internships, regional alumni. For more Career Services highlights: http://www.american.edu/careercenter/SuccessStories/internvideo.html.

FACILITIES

Housing: Coed dorms, special housing for disabled students, special housing for international students, apartments for married students, apartments for single students. 94% of campus accessible to physically disabled. **Special Academic Facilities/Equipment:** Student-run Radio and TV Facilities Watkins Art Gallery Katzen Arts Center Experimental Theatre Greenberg Theatre Friedheim Journalism Center William I Jacobs Fitness Center Language Resource Center Multimedia Center Audiotechnology Lab UNIX and Oracle Labs Kay Spiritual Life Center(interdenominational) **Computers:** 100% of classrooms, 100% of dorms, 100% of libraries, 100% of dining areas, 100% of student union, 100% of common outdoor areas have wireless network access. Students can register for classes online. Administrative functions (other than registration) can be performed online.

CAMPUS LIFE

Environment: Metropolis. **Activities:** Choral groups, dance, drama/theater, jazz band, literary magazine, music ensembles, musical theater, opera, pep band, radio station, student government, student newspaper, student-run film society, symphony orchestra, television station, yearbook, International Student Organization 180 registered organizations, 15 honor societies, 15 religious organizations. 11 fraternities, 12 sororities. **Athletics (Intercollegiate):** *Men:* basketball, cross-country, diving, soccer, swimming, track/field (outdoor), track/field (indoor), wrestling. *Women:* basketball, cross-country, diving, field hockey, lacrosse, soccer, swimming, track/field (outdoor), track/field (indoor), volleyball. **On-Campus Highlights:** Mary Graydon Center, Sports Center Complex and

Jacobs Fitness, Katzen Arts Center, The Quad, Terrace Dining Room. **Environmental Initiatives:** A Climate Action Plan which calls for achieving carbon neutrality by 2020. The certification of 65% of campus buildings to LEED for Existing Buildings, and new buildings to LEED for New Construction. The development of a Zero Waste Policy through which a team has been created to develop a plan for reducing and diverting 100% of the university's waste stream.

ADMISSIONS

Freshman Academic Profile: Average high school GPA 3.8. 45% in top 10% of high school class, 81% in top 25% of high school class, 98% in top 50% of high school class. SAT Math middle 50% range 570-670. SAT Critical Reading middle 50% range 600-700. SAT Writing middle 50% range 580-680. ACT middle 50% range 26-30. Minimum web-based TOEFL 80. Minimum paper TOEFL 550. **Basis for Candidate Selection:** *Very important factors considered include:* academic GPA, rigor of secondary school record, standardized test scores, level of applicant's interest. *Important factors considered include:* application essay, recommendation(s), extracurricular activities, volunteer work. *Other factors considered include:* alumni/ae relation, character/personal qualities, first generation, geographical residence, racial/ethnic status, talent/ability, work experience. **Freshman Admission Requirements:** High school diploma is required and GED is accepted. *Academic units required:* 4 English, 3 mathematics, 3 science, (2 science labs), 2 foreign language, 2 social studies, 3 academic electives. *Academic units recommended:* 4 English, 3 mathematics, 3 science, (2 science labs), 2 foreign language, 2 social studies, 3 academic electives. **Freshman Admission Statistics:** 18,706 applied, 42% admitted, 20% enrolled. **Transfer Admission Requirements:** college transcript(s), essay or personal statement, minimum college GPA of 2.5 required. Lowest grade transferable C. **General Admission Information:** Application Fee $60. Early decision application deadline 11/15. Regular application deadline 1/15. Regular notification 4/1. Nonfall registration accepted. Admission may be deferred for a maximum of 12 months. Credit and/or placement offered for CEEB Advanced Placement tests.

COSTS AND FINANCIAL AID

Annual tuition $44,234. Room and board $15,102. Required fees $492. Average book expense $1,500. **Required Forms and Deadlines:** FAFSA, institution's own financial aid form. **Notification of Awards:** Applicants will be notified of awards on or about 4/1. **Types of Aid:** *Need-based scholarships/grants:* Federal Pell, SEOG, state scholarships/grants, private scholarships, the school's own gift aid, Academic merit scholarships: Presidential Scholarships, Dean's Scholarships, Leadership Scholarships, Phi Theta Kappa Scholarships (transfers only), Tuition Exchange Scholarships, United Methodist Scholarships, and other private/restricted scholarships are awarded by the Undergraduate Admissions Office. Most scholarships do not require a separate application and are renewable for up to three years if certain criteria are met. *Loans:* Direct Subsidized Stafford, Direct Unsubsidized Stafford, Direct PLUS, PLUS, Federal Perkins, college/university loans from institutional funds. **Student Employment:** Federal Work-Study Program available. Institutional employment available. Off-campus job opportunities are excellent. **Financial Aid Statistics:** 52% freshmen, 47% undergrads receive need-based scholarship or grant aid. 46% freshmen, 43% undergrads receive non-need-based scholarship or grant aid. 80% freshmen, 85% undergrads receive need-based self-help aid. 2% freshmen, 3% undergrads receive athletic scholarships. 60% undergrads borrow to pay for school. Average cumulative indebtedness $36,206. **Criteria for awarding institutional aid:** *Non-need-based:* academics, alumni affiliation, athletics, leadership, minority status, music/drama, religious affiliation, state/district residency.

AMERICAN UNIVERSITY IN CAIRO

AUC Avenue, P.O. Box 74 New Cairo 11835,
Phone: 20.2.26151459 • **Financial Aid Phone:** 2.02.26151480
E-mail: enrolauc@aucegypt.edu
Website: www.aucegypt.edu

This private school was founded in 1919. It has a 260-acre campus.

RATINGS

Admissions Selectivity Rating: 90   **Fire Safety Rating:** 73   **Green Rating:** 61

STUDENTS AND FACULTY

Enrollment: 5,329. **Student Body:** 52% female, 48% male.
Retention and Graduation: 89% freshmen return for sophomore year. 29% freshmen graduate within 4 years. **Faculty:** Student/faculty ratio 12:1. 456 full-time faculty, 74% hold PhDs, 44% are women. 0% of classes are taught by teaching assistants.

ACADEMICS

Degrees: bachelor's, diploma, master's. **Classes:** Most classes have 10–19 students. Most lab/discussion sessions have 10–19 students. **Majors with High-**

est Enrollment: business administration, management and operations, other; mechanical engineering; political science and government. **Special Study Options:** double major, English as a Second Language (ESL), independent study, internships, liberal arts/career combination, study abroad. **Career Services:** Alumni network, alumni services, career/job search classes, career assessment, internships Career Services highlights include Job shadwoing and internships to help students explore career options. Online recruitment and Employment Fairs generate employment opportunities.

FACILITIES
Housing: men's dorms, women's dorms, apartments for married students, apartments for single students. 100% of campus accessible to physically disabled. **Computers:** 100% of classrooms, 100% of dorms, 100% of libraries, 100% of dining areas, 100% of student union, 100% of common outdoor areas have wireless network access. Students can register for classes online. Administrative functions (other than registration) can be performed online.

CAMPUS LIFE
Environment: Metropolis. **Activities:** Choral groups, dance, drama/theater, literary magazine, music ensembles, radio station, student government, student newspaper, student-run film society, yearbook, International Student Organization, Model UN 62 registered organizations. **Athletics (Intercollegiate):** Men: basketball, boxing, fencing, football, gymnastics, handball, rugby, soccer, squash, swimming, table tennis, tennis, track/field (outdoor), volleyball, water polo, wrestling. Women: basketball, fencing, football, gymnastics, handball, soccer, squash, swimming, table tennis, tennis, track/field (outdoor), volleyball. **On-Campus Highlights:** Athletic Facility, Food Court, Library, Student Center.

ADMISSIONS
Freshman Academic Profile: SAT Math middle 50% range 540-650. SAT Critical Reading middle 50% range 430-540. SAT Writing middle 50% range 520-610. Minimum web-based TOEFL 83. Minimum paper TOEFL 557. **Basis for Candidate Selection:** Very important factors considered include: academic GPA, recommendation(s), character/personal qualities, level of applicant's interest, religious affiliation/commitment. Important factors considered include: application essay, rigor of secondary school record. Other factors considered include: Class rank, standardized test scores, alumni/ae relation, extracurricular activities, first generation, talent/ability, volunteer work, work experience. **Freshman Admission Requirements:** High school diploma is required and GED is accepted. **Freshman Admission Statistics:** 2,774 applied, 46% admitted, 76% enrolled. **Transfer Admission Requirements:** High school transcript, college transcript(s), essay or personal statement, standardized test scores, statement of good standing from prior institution(s). Minimum college GPA of 2.0 required. Lowest grade transferable C. **General Admission Information:** Application Fee $45. Regular application deadline 8/1. Nonfall registration accepted. Admission may be deferred for a maximum of One year. Credit offered for CEEB Advanced Placement tests.

COSTS AND FINANCIAL AID
Types of Aid: Need-based scholarships/grants: Federal Pell, SEOG, state scholarships/grants, private scholarships, the school's own gift aid, United Negro College Fund. Loans: Subsidized Stafford, Unsubsidized Stafford, PLUS, college/university loans from institutional funds. **Student Employment:** Federal Work-Study Program available. Institutional employment available. Highest amount earned per year from on-campus jobs $5,000. Off-campus job opportunities are good. **Financial Aid Statistics:** 2% freshmen, 2% undergrads receive athletic scholarships. **Criteria for awarding institutional aid:** Non-need-based: alumni affiliation.

THE AMERICAN UNIVERSITY OF PARIS (CO)

US Admissions Office, Denver, CO 80246
Phone: 303-757-6333 • **Financial Aid Phone:** +1 40620720
E-mail: usoffice@aup.edu • **CEEB Code:** 866
Fax: 303-757-6444 • **ACT Code:** 5295

This private school was founded in 1962.

RATINGS
Admissions Selectivity Rating: 82　　**Fire Safety Rating:** 60*　　**Green Rating:** 60*

STUDENTS AND FACULTY
Enrollment: 925. **Student Body:** 67% female, 33% male, 0% international (100 countries represented). Asian 0%, African American 0%, Caucasian 0%, Hispanic 0%, Native American 0%.
Retention and Graduation: 64% freshmen return for sophomore year. 32% freshmen graduate within 4 years. 45% freshmen graduate within 6 years. **Faculty:** Student/faculty ratio 12:1. 56 full-time faculty, 80% hold PhDs, %

are members of minority groups, 46% are women. 0% of classes are taught by teaching assistants.

ACADEMICS
Degrees: bachelor's, master's. **Classes:** Most classes have 10–19 students. Most lab/discussion sessions have 10–19 students. **Special Study Options:** double major, exchange student program (domestic), independent study, internships, study abroad. **Combined Degree Programs:** BA/MA, BA/MA. **Career Services:** Alumni network, alumni services, career assessment, internships.

FACILITIES
Housing: Students are housed in independent rooms or with French families. 60% of campus accessible to physically disabled. **Computers:** Administrative functions (other than registration) can be performed online.

CAMPUS LIFE
Environment: Metropolis. **Activities:** drama/theater, literary magazine, musical theater, student government, student newspaper, yearbook 20 registered organizations. **Athletics (Intercollegiate):** Men: basketball, football, rugby, soccer, swimming, volleyball. Women: basketball, football, soccer, swimming, volleyball.

ADMISSIONS
Freshman Academic Profile: SAT Math middle 50% range 520-640. SAT Critical Reading middle 50% range 550-660. Minimum paper TOEFL 600. **Basis for Candidate Selection:** Very important factors considered include: Class rank, application essay, recommendation(s), rigor of secondary school record. Important factors considered include: academic GPA, standardized test scores, character/personal qualities, extracurricular activities, level of applicant's interest. Other factors considered include: alumni/ae relation, interview, talent/ability, volunteer work, work experience. **Freshman Admission Requirements:** High school diploma is required and GED is accepted. **Freshman Admission Statistics:** 541 applied, 71% admitted, 41% enrolled. **Transfer Admission Requirements:** college transcript(s), essay or personal statement, statement of good standing from prior institution(s). Minimum college GPA of 3.0 required. Lowest grade transferable C. **General Admission Information:** Application Fee $50. Nonfall registration accepted. Admission may be deferred for a maximum of 1 year. Credit and/or placement offered for CEEB Advanced Placement tests.

COSTS AND FINANCIAL AID
Average book expense $1,200. **Required Forms and Deadlines:** FAFSA, institution's own financial aid form. **Types of Aid:** Need-based scholarships/grants: the school's own gift aid. Loans: Subsidized Stafford, Unsubsidized Stafford, PLUS. **Student Employment:** Highest amount earned per year from on-campus jobs $2,500. **Financial Aid Statistics:** 32% freshmen, 32% undergrads receive need-based self-help aid. **Criteria for awarding institutional aid:** Non-need-based: academics, alumni affiliation.

AMERICAN UNIVERSITY OF PUERTO RICO

PO Box 2037, Bayamon, PR 00960-2037
Phone: 787-740-6410
E-mail: mcruz@aupr.edu
Fax: 787-785-7377 • **Website:** www.aupr.edu

This private school was founded in 1963.

RATINGS
Admissions Selectivity Rating: 62　　**Fire Safety Rating:** 60*　　**Green Rating:** 60*

STUDENTS AND FACULTY
Enrollment: 4,060.

ACADEMICS
Degrees: associate, bachelor's, master's. **Special Study Options:** cooperative education program, distance learning, English as a Second Language (ESL), honors program, independent study, liberal arts/career combination, student-designed major. **Career Services:** career/job search classes

CAMPUS LIFE
Activities: dance, drama/theater, literary magazine. **Athletics (Intercollegiate):** Men: baseball, basketball, soccer, tennis, volleyball. Women: baseball, basketball, soccer, tennis, volleyball.

ADMISSIONS
Freshman Academic Profile: Average high school GPA 2.5. 66% from public high schools. **Basis for Candidate Selection:** Very important factors considered include: rigor of secondary school record, standardized test scores. Other

factors considered include: character/personal qualities, interview, talent/ability. **Freshman Admission Requirements:** High school diploma is required and GED is accepted. **Freshman Admission Statistics:** 1,131 applied, 100% admitted, 71% enrolled. **General Admission Information:** Application Fee $15. Nonfall registration accepted.

COSTS AND FINANCIAL AID

Annual tuition $1,740. Required fees $160. Average book expense $160. **Types of Aid:** *Need-based scholarships/grants:* Federal Pell, SEOG, state scholarships/grants. *Loans:* Direct Subsidized Stafford, state loans. **Student Employment:** Federal Work-Study Program available. Off-campus job opportunities are good. **Financial Aid Statistics:** 100% freshmen, 98% undergrads receive need-based scholarship or grant aid. 92% freshmen, 52% undergrads receive need-based self-help aid. 4% freshmen, 3% undergrads receive athletic scholarships. **Criteria for awarding institutional aid:** *Non-need-based:* academics, alumni affiliation, art, athletics, job skills, leadership, minority status, music/drama, religious affiliation, state/district residency.

AMHERST COLLEGE

Campus Box 2231, Amherst, MA 1002
Phone: 413-542-2328 • **Financial Aid Phone:** 413-542-2296
E-mail: admission@amherst.edu • **CEEB Code:** 3003
Fax: 413-542-2040 • **Website:** www.amherst.edu • **ACT Code:** 1774

This private school was founded in 1821. It has a 999-acre campus.

RATINGS
Admissions Selectivity Rating: 99   **Fire Safety Rating:** 70   **Green Rating:** 61

STUDENTS AND FACULTY
Enrollment: 1,791. **Student Body:** 49% female, 51% male, 87% out-of-state, 10% international. Asian 11%, African American 12%, Caucasian 40%, Hispanic 11%, Native American 0%.
Retention and Graduation: 97% freshmen return for sophomore year. 87% freshmen graduate within 4 years. **Faculty:** Student/faculty ratio 8:1. 204 full-time faculty, 99% hold PhDs, 20% are members of minority groups, 43% are women. 0% of classes are taught by teaching assistants.

ACADEMICS
Degrees: bachelor's. **Classes:** Most classes have 10–19 students. Most lab/discussion sessions have fewer than 10 students. **Majors with Highest Enrollment:** economics; political science and government; psychology. **Special Study Options:** cross-registration, double major, exchange student program (domestic), honors program, independent study, student-designed major, study abroad, teacher certification program. **Honors Programs:** Senior Honors Thesis-an opportunity to engage in extensive research with a professor as the student's advisor. **Disability Services:** Special programs offered to physically disabled students include note-taking services, reader services, tape recorders, tutors. **Career Services:** Alumni network, alumni services, career/job search classes, career assessment, internships, regional alumni.

FACILITIES
Housing: Coed dorms, cooperative housing, French/Spanish language house, German/Russian language house, Latino culture house, African American culture house, Health and Wellness house, Arts house, Food Cooperative house and single sex floors for men and women within specific dorms. **Special Academic Facilities/Equipment:** Art, natural history, geology museums, language labs, observatory,planetarium, The Amherst Center for Russian Culture, The Dickinson Homestead **Computers:** Administrative functions (other than registration) can be performed online.

CAMPUS LIFE
Environment: Town. **Activities:** Choral groups, concert band, dance, drama/theater, jazz band, literary magazine, music ensembles, musical theater, opera, radio station, student government, student newspaper, student-run film society, symphony orchestra, yearbook, International Student Organization, Model UN 100 registered organizations, 2 honor societies, 7 religious organizations. **Athletics (Intercollegiate):** *Men:* baseball, basketball, cross-country, diving, football, golf, ice hockey, lacrosse, soccer, squash, swimming, tennis, track/field (outdoor), track/field (indoor). *Women:* basketball, cross-country, diving, field hockey, golf, ice hockey, lacrosse, soccer, softball, squash, swimming, tennis, track/field (outdoor), track/field (indoor), volleyball. **On-Campus Highlights:**

Mead Art Museum, Pratt Museum of Natural History, Russian Cultural Center, Japanese Peace Garden, Observatory.

ADMISSIONS
Freshman Academic Profile: 84% in top 10% of high school class, 97% in top 25% of high school class, 100% in top 50% of high school class. 59% from public high schools. SAT Math middle 50% range 660-770. SAT Critical Reading middle 50% range 660-760. SAT Writing middle 50% range 670-770. ACT middle 50% range 30-34. Minimum web-based TOEFL 100. Minimum paper TOEFL 600. **Basis for Candidate Selection:** *Very important factors considered include:* application essay, academic GPA, recommendation(s), rigor of secondary school record, standardized test scores, character/personal qualities, extracurricular activities, first generation, talent/ability. *Important factors considered include:* Class rank, alumni/ae relation, volunteer work. *Other factors considered include:* geographical residence, state residency, work experience. **Freshman Admission Requirements:** High school diploma or equivalent is not required. **Freshman Admission Statistics:** 8,461 applied, 13% admitted, 41% enrolled. **Transfer Admission Requirements:** High school transcript, college transcript(s), essay or personal statement, statement of good standing from prior institution(s). Minimum college GPA of 3.5 required. Lowest grade transferable C. **General Admission Information:** Application Fee $60. Early decision application deadline 11/15. Regular application deadline 1/1. Regular notification 4/5. Nonfall registration not accepted. Admission may be deferred for a maximum of 2 years. Neither credit nor placement offered for CEEB Advanced Placement tests.

COSTS AND FINANCIAL AID
Annual tuition $42,170. Room and board $11,200. Required fees $728. Average book expense $1,000. **Required Forms and Deadlines:** FAFSA, CSS/Financial Aid PROFILE, noncustodial PROFILE, business/farm supplement. Income documentation submitted through College. **Notification of Awards:** Applicants will be notified of awards on or about 4/1. **Types of Aid:** *Need-based scholarships/grants:* Federal Pell, SEOG, state scholarships/grants, private scholarships, the school's own gift aid. *Loans:* Direct Subsidized Stafford, Direct Unsubsidized Stafford, Direct PLUS, Federal Perkins, college/university loans from institutional funds. **Student Employment:** Federal Work-Study Program available. Institutional employment available. Off-campus job opportunities are excellent. **Financial Aid Statistics:** 90% freshmen, 92% undergrads receive need-based scholarship or grant aid. 78% freshmen, 85% undergrads receive need-based self-help aid. 59% freshmen, 62% undergrads receive any aid. 41% undergrads borrow to pay for school. Average cumulative indebtedness $12,713.

ANDERSON UNIVERSITY (IN)

1100 East Fifth Street, Anderson, IN 46012
Phone: 765-641-4080 • **Financial Aid Phone:** 765-641-4180
E-mail: info@anderson.edu • **CEEB Code:** 1016
Fax: 765-641-4091 • **Website:** www.anderson.edu • **ACT Code:** 1174

This private school, affiliated with the Church of God Church, was founded in 1917. It has a 100-acre campus.

RATINGS
Admissions Selectivity Rating: 84   **Fire Safety Rating:** 72   **Green Rating:** 60*

STUDENTS AND FACULTY
Enrollment: 2,019. **Student Body:** 59% female, 41% male, 25% out-of-state, 3% international (27 countries represented). Asian 0%, African American 6%, Caucasian 81%, Hispanic 3%, Native American 0%.
Retention and Graduation: 75% freshmen return for sophomore year. 46% freshmen graduate within 4 years. 57% freshmen graduate within 6 years. 20% grads go on to further study within 1 year. **Faculty:** Student/faculty ratio 12:1. 135 full-time faculty, 69% hold PhDs, 5% are members of minority groups, 39% are women. 0% of classes are taught by teaching assistants.

ACADEMICS
Degrees: associate, bachelor's, first professional, master's. **Classes:** Most classes have 10–19 students. Most lab/discussion sessions have 10–19 students. **Majors with Highest Enrollment:** business administration and management; elementary education and teaching; nursing/registered nurse (rn, asn, bsn, msn). **Special Study Options:** Accelerated program, cross-registration, double major, honors program, independent study, internships, student-designed major, study abroad, teacher certification program, Summer over seas service program. **Honors Programs:** The Honors Program at Anderson University is devoted to fostering within its honors scholars a passionate dedication to intellectual inquiry and spiritual development so that they may serve as vibrant leaders in their professions and in their communities. **Disability Services:** Special programs offered to physically disabled students include note-taking services, reader services, tape recorders, tutors.

FACILITIES

Housing: Coed dorms, men's dorms, women's dorms, apartments for married students, apartments for single students, one house. 95% of campus accessible to physically disabled. **Special Academic Facilities/Equipment:** Gustav Jeeninga Museum of Bible and Near Eastern Studies, Wilson Galleries, Archives of the Church of God **Computers:** Students can register for classes online. Administrative functions (other than registration) can be performed online.

CAMPUS LIFE

Environment: Town. **Activities:** Choral groups, concert band, dance, drama/theater, jazz band, literary magazine, music ensembles, musical theater, opera, pep band, radio station, student government, student newspaper, symphony orchestra, yearbook 33 registered organizations, 12 honor societies, 15 religious organizations. **Athletics (Intercollegiate):** *Men:* baseball, basketball, cheerleading, cross-country, football, golf, soccer, tennis, track/field (outdoor). *Women:* basketball, cheerleading, cross-country, golf, soccer, softball, tennis, track/field (outdoor), volleyball. **On-Campus Highlights:** Kardatzke Wellness Center, Mocha Joe's in the Olt Student Center, Decker Commons and Cafe Ole, Reardon Auditorium.

ADMISSIONS

Freshman Academic Profile: Average high school GPA 3.4. 22% in top 10% of high school class, 49% in top 25% of high school class, 81% in top 50% of high school class. 96% from public high schools. SAT Math middle 50% range 470-570. SAT Critical Reading middle 50% range 470-570. ACT middle 50% range 21-25. Minimum web-based TOEFL 71. Minimum paper TOEFL 530. **Basis for Candidate Selection:** *Very important factors considered include:* recommendation(s), rigor of secondary school record, religious affiliation/commitment. *Important factors considered include:* Class rank, standardized test scores, character/personal qualities, extracurricular activities, interview, volunteer work. *Other factors considered include:* application essay, alumni/ae relation, first generation, level of applicant's interest, racial/ethnic status, talent/ability. **Freshman Admission Requirements:** High school diploma is required and GED is not accepted. *Academic units required:* 4 English, 3 mathematics, 3 science, (3 science labs), 2 foreign language, 1 social studies, 1 history. *Academic units recommended:* 4 English, 3 mathematics, 3 science, (3 science labs), 2 foreign language, 1 social studies, 1 history. **Freshman Admission Statistics:** 2,894 applied, 54% admitted, 32% enrolled. **Transfer Admission Requirements:** High school transcript, college transcript(s), standardized test scores, statement of good standing from prior institution(s). Minimum college GPA of 2.0 required. Lowest grade transferable C-. **General Admission Information:** Application Fee $25. Regular application deadline 7/1. Notification on a rolling basis, beginning on or about 9/1. Nonfall registration accepted. Admission may be deferred for a maximum of 1 year. Credit and/or placement offered for CEEB Advanced Placement tests.

COSTS AND FINANCIAL AID

Annual tuition $25,400. Room and board $8,860. Required fees $80. Average book expense $1,200. **Required Forms and Deadlines:** FAFSA. **Notification of Awards:** Applicants will be notified of awards on a rolling basis beginning 2/15. **Types of Aid:** *Need-based scholarships/grants:* Federal Pell, SEOG, state scholarships/grants, private scholarships, the school's own gift aid. *Loans:* Subsidized Stafford, Unsubsidized Stafford, PLUS, Federal Perkins, college/university loans from institutional funds. **Student Employment:** Federal Work-Study Program available. **Financial Aid Statistics:** 100% freshmen, 100% undergrads receive need-based scholarship or grant aid. 73% freshmen, 63% undergrads receive non-need-based scholarship or grant aid. 99% freshmen, 99% undergrads receive need-based self-help aid. 76% undergrads borrow to pay for school. Average cumulative indebtedness $17,439. **Criteria for awarding institutional aid:** *Non need based:* academics.

ANDERSON UNIVERSITY (SC)

316 Boulevard, Anderson, SC 29621
Phone: 864-231-5607 • **Financial Aid Phone:** 864-231-2073
E-mail: admission@andersonuniversity.edu • **CEEB Code:** 5008
Fax: 864-231-2033 • **Website:** www.andersonuniversity.edu • **ACT Code:** 3832

This private school, affiliated with the Southern Baptist Church,, affiliated with the South Carolina Baptist Convention Church, was founded in 1911. It has a 56-acre campus.

RATINGS

Admissions Selectivity Rating: 71   **Fire Safety Rating:** 70   **Green Rating:** 60*

STUDENTS AND FACULTY

Enrollment: 2,618. **Student Body:** 65% female, 35% male, 18% out-of-state, 1% international (24 countries represented). Asian 1%, African American 9%, Caucasian 64%, Hispanic 2%, Native American 0%.
Retention and Graduation: 77% freshmen return for sophomore year. 41% freshmen graduate within 4 years. 49% freshmen graduate within 6 years. 15% grads go on to further study within 1 year. **Faculty:** Student/faculty ratio 15:1. 115 full-time faculty, 69% hold PhDs, 48% are women. 0% of classes are taught by teaching assistants.

ACADEMICS

Degrees: bachelor's, master's. **Classes:** Most classes have 20–29 students. Most lab/discussion sessions have 20–29 students. **Majors with Highest Enrollment:** business administration and management; elementary education and teaching; kinesiology and exercise science. **Special Study Options:** Accelerated program, cooperative education program, distance learning, double major, dual enrollment, honors program, independent study, internships, liberal arts/career combination, study abroad, teacher certification program, Washington Semester. **Disability Services:** Special programs offered to physically disabled students include note-taking services, reader services, tape recorders, tutors. **Career Services:** career/job search classes, career assessment, internships.

FACILITIES

Housing: men's dorms, women's dorms. **Special Academic Facilities/Equipment:** Electronic classroom Art galleries Recording studio **Computers:** Students can register for classes online. Administrative functions (other than registration) can be performed online.

CAMPUS LIFE

Environment: Town. **Activities:** Choral groups, concert band, dance, drama/theater, jazz band, literary magazine, music ensembles, musical theater, student government, student newspaper, symphony orchestra, yearbook, Campus Ministries 27 registered organizations, 1 honor societies, 6 religious organizations. **Athletics (Intercollegiate):** *Men:* baseball, basketball, cross-country, equestrian sports, golf, soccer, tennis, track/field (outdoor), wrestling. *Women:* basketball, cheerleading, cross-country, equestrian sports, golf, soccer, softball, tennis, track/field (outdoor), volleyball. **On-Campus Highlights:** Java City, Student Center, Bunton Computer Lab, Thrift Library, Fitness Center.

ADMISSIONS

Freshman Academic Profile: Average high school GPA 3.4. 39% in top 10% of high school class, 61% in top 25% of high school class, 86% in top 50% of high school class. 94% from public high schools. SAT Math middle 50% range 470-580. SAT Critical Reading middle 50% range 470-590. SAT Writing middle 50% range 460-570. ACT middle 50% range 20-25. Minimum paper TOEFL 550. **Basis for Candidate Selection:** *Very important factors considered include:* academic GPA, standardized test scores. *Important factors considered include:* Class rank, rigor of secondary school record. *Other factors considered include:* application essay, recommendation(s), alumni/ae relation, character/personal qualities, first generation, interview, racial/ethnic status, religious affiliation/commitment, talent/ability, volunteer work. **Freshman Admission Requirements:** High school diploma is required and GED is accepted. *Academic units required:* 4 English, 3 mathematics, 3 science, (2 science labs), 2 foreign language, 2 social studies, 2 history, 4 academic electives. *Academic units recommended:* 4 English, 3 mathematics, 3 science, (2 science labs), 2 foreign language, 2 social studies, 2 history, 4 academic electives. **Freshman Admission Statistics:** 1,101 applied, 70% admitted, 46% enrolled. **Transfer Admission Requirements:** College transcript(s), minimum college GPA of 2.0 required. Lowest grade transferable C. **General Admission Information:** Application Fee $25. Notification on a rolling basis, beginning on or about 9/2. Nonfall registration accepted. Admission may be deferred for a maximum of 1 year. Credit and/or placement offered for CEEB Advanced Placement tests.

COSTS AND FINANCIAL AID

Annual tuition $20,020. Room and board $8,282. Required fees $1,710. Average book expense $2,000. **Required Forms and Deadlines:** FAFSA. **Notification of Awards:** Applicants will be notified of awards on a rolling basis beginning 3/15. **Types of Aid:** *Need-based scholarships/grants:* Federal Pell, SEOG, state scholarships/grants, the school's own gift aid. *Loans:* Subsidized Stafford, Unsubsidized Stafford, PLUS, Federal Perkins. **Student Employment: Financial Aid Statistics:** 100% freshmen, 96% undergrads receive need-based scholarship or grant aid. 27% freshmen, 21% undergrads receive non-need-based scholarship or grant aid. 65% freshmen, 72% undergrads receive need-based self-help aid. 5% freshmen, 4% undergrads receive athletic scholarships. 73% undergrads borrow to pay for school. Average cumulative indebtedness $27,187. **Criteria for awarding institutional aid:** *Non-need-based:* academics, alumni affiliation, art, athletics, leadership, minority status, music/drama, religious affiliation, state/district residency.

ANDREWS UNIVERSITY

Office of Admissions, Berrien Springs, MI 49104
Phone: 269-471-6343
E-mail: enroll@andrews.edu • **CEEB Code:** 1030
Fax: 269-471-2670 • **Website:** www.andrews.edu • **ACT Code:** 1992

This private school, affiliated with the Seventh Day Adventist Church, was founded in 1874. It has a 1600-acre campus.

RATINGS
Admissions Selectivity Rating: 65   **Fire Safety Rating:** 60*   **Green Rating:** 60*

STUDENTS AND FACULTY
Enrollment: 1,746. **Student Body:** 56% female, 44% male, 42% out-of-state, 15% international. Asian 10%, African American 21%, Caucasian 52%, Hispanic 8%, Native American 0%.
Retention and Graduation: 69% freshmen return for sophomore year. 24% grads go on to further study within 1 year. 24% grads pursue arts and sciences degrees. **Faculty:** 10% of classes are taught by teaching assistants.

ACADEMICS
Degrees: associate, bachelor's, diploma, first professional, master's. **Special Study Options:** study abroad, Undergrads may take grad level classes. **Combined Degree Programs:** BA/MD, BA/DDS, BA/MEng, Co-op in dental assisting,hygiene; med record admi. **Career Services:** internships.

FACILITIES
Housing: men's dorms, women's dorms, apartments for married students, apartments for single students. **Special Academic Facilities/Equipment:** Audio-visual center, lab school, natural history and archaeological museums, observatory, physical therapy facilities. **Computers:**

CAMPUS LIFE
Environment: Rural. **Activities:** Choral groups, concert band, radio station, student government, student newspaper, yearbook 2 religious organizations.

ADMISSIONS
Freshman Academic Profile: 23% from public high schools. SAT Math middle 50% range 420-600. SAT Critical Reading middle 50% range 440-610. ACT middle 50% range 19-27. **Freshman Admission Requirements:** High school diploma is required and GED is accepted. **Transfer Admission Requirements:** Minimum college GPA of 2.0 required. Lowest grade transferable C. **General Admission Information:** Application Fee $30. Early decision application deadline 1/1. Nonfall registration accepted. Credit offered for CEEB Advanced Placement tests.

COSTS AND FINANCIAL AID
Annual tuition $11,685. Room and board $3,630. Required fees $285. Average book expense $1,128. **Required Forms and Deadlines:** FAFSA, institution's own financial aid form, state aid form. **Types of Aid:** *Need-based scholarships/grants:* state scholarships/grants. *Loans:* Subsidized Stafford, PLUS. **Student Employment:** Federal Work-Study Program available. Institutional employment available. Highest amount earned per year from on-campus jobs $1,200. Off-campus job opportunities are good.

ANGELO STATE UNIVERSITY

ASU Station #11014, San Angelo, TX 76909-1014
Phone: 325-942-2041 • **Financial Aid Phone:** 325-942-2246
E-mail: admissions@angelo.edu • **CEEB Code:** 6644
Fax: 325-942-2078 • **Website:** www.angelo.edu • **ACT Code:** 4164

This public school was founded in 1928. It has a 268-acre campus.

RATINGS
Admissions Selectivity Rating: 65   **Fire Safety Rating:** 93   **Green Rating:** 72

STUDENTS AND FACULTY
Enrollment: 5,859. **Student Body:** 54% female, 46% male, 3% out-of-state, 2% international (24 countries represented). Asian 1%, African American 9%, Caucasian 56%, Hispanic 29%, Native American 1%.

Retention and Graduation: 16% freshmen graduate within 4 years. 31% freshmen graduate within 6 years. 15% grads go on to further study within 1 year. **Faculty:** Student/faculty ratio 20:1. 274 full-time faculty, 77% hold PhDs, 18% are members of minority groups, 43% are women. 3% of classes are taught by teaching assistants.

ACADEMICS
Degrees: associate, bachelor's, master's. **Classes:** Most classes have 20–29 students. Most lab/discussion sessions have 20–29 students. **Majors with Highest Enrollment:** business/commerce; nursing/registered nurse (rn, asn, bsn, msn); psychology. **Special Study Options:** distance learning, double major, dual enrollment, honors program, independent study, internships, study abroad, teacher certification program, 4+1 programs in various disciplines allowing students to complete a bachelor's degree in four years and a master's degree in a related field in one year at Texas Tech University. Also, 3+2 physics/pre-engineering program allowing three years of study in applied physics and two years at an affiliated university for an engineering degree. **Honors Programs:** http://www.angelo.edu/dept/honors/index.htm **Combined Degree Programs:** BBA/MBA. **Disability Services:** Special programs offered to physically disabled students include note-taking services, tutors. **Career Services:** Alumni network, alumni services, career/job search classes, career assessment, internships Career Services highlights include ASU's multiple internship programs have provided exceptional worklife experiences for undergraduates with students interning in positions ranging from the Los Alamos National Labs to Washington, D.C., news services. Additionally, the Career Development Office Career Exploration and Planning classes, which help broaden student understanding of career possibilities and the value of internships.

FACILITIES
Housing: Coed dorms, women's dorms, apartments for single students, theme housingRooms for disabled and Honors students. 99% of campus accessible to physically disabled. **Special Academic Facilities/Equipment:** Planetarium; West Texas Collection; Management, Instruction, and Research (Agricultural) Center; Food Safety and Product Development Lab. **Computers:** 100% of classrooms, 100% of dorms, 100% of libraries, 100% of dining areas, 100% of student union, 100% of common outdoor areas have wireless network access. Students can register for classes online. Administrative functions (other than registration) can be performed online.

CAMPUS LIFE
Environment: City. **Activities:** Choral groups, concert band, dance, drama/theater, jazz band, literary magazine, marching band, music ensembles, musical theater, pep band, radio station, student government, student newspaper, student-run film society, television station, Campus Ministries, International Student Organization 76 registered organizations, 11 honor societies, 9 religious organizations. 4 fraternities, 2 sororities. **Athletics (Intercollegiate):** *Men:* baseball, basketball, cross-country, football, track/field (outdoor). *Women:* basketball, cross-country, golf, soccer, softball, track/field (outdoor), volleyball. **On-Campus Highlights:** Houston Harte University Center, Junell Center/Stephens Arena, ASU Planetarium, ASU Lake House, West Texas Collection, ASU Mall and Student Gathering Areas Porter Henderson Library. **Environmental Initiatives:** LEED Certification initiataives in all new buildings. Recycling programs Utilizing green cleaning products.

ADMISSIONS
Freshman Academic Profile: 10% in top 10% of high school class, 33% in top 25% of high school class, 68% in top 50% of high school class. 96% from public high schools. SAT Math middle 50% range 430-530. SAT Critical Reading middle 50% range 410-500. ACT middle 50% range 18-23. Minimum web-based TOEFL 79. Minimum paper TOEFL 550. **Basis for Candidate Selection:** *Very important factors considered include:* Class rank, rigor of secondary school record, standardized test scores. **Freshman Admission Requirements:** High school diploma is required and GED is accepted. **Freshman Admission Statistics:** 2,588 applied, 90% admitted, 60% enrolled. **Transfer Admission Requirements:** college transcript(s), statement of good standing from prior institution(s). Minimum college GPA of 2.0 required. Lowest grade transferable D. **General Admission Information:** Application Fee $25. Nonfall registration accepted. Credit offered for CEEB Advanced Placement tests.

COSTS AND FINANCIAL AID
Annual in-state tuition $4,994. Annual out-of-state tuition $15,524. Room and board $8,026. Required fees $2,499. Average book expense $1,500. **Required Forms and Deadlines:** FAFSA. **Notification of Awards:** Applicants will be notified of awards on a rolling basis beginning 4/1. **Types of Aid:** *Need-based scholarships/grants:* Federal Pell, SEOG, state scholarships/grants, private scholarships, the school's own gift aid, Federal Nursing Scholarships. *Loans:* Subsidized Stafford, Unsubsidized Stafford, PLUS, Federal Perkins, Federal Nursing, state loans, college/university loans from institutional funds. **Student Employment:** Federal Work-Study Program available. Institutional employment available. Off-campus job opportunities are good. **Financial Aid Statistics:** 75% freshmen, 83% undergrads receive need-based scholarship or

grant aid. 71% freshmen, 43% undergrads receive non-need-based scholarship or grant aid. 69% freshmen, 75% undergrads receive need-based self-help aid. 4% freshmen, 5% undergrads receive athletic scholarships. 89% freshmen, 82% undergrads receive any aid. 57% undergrads borrow to pay for school. Average cumulative indebtedness $21,373. **Criteria for awarding institutional aid:** *Non-need-based:* academics, art, athletics, leadership, music/drama, state/district residency.

ANNA MARIA COLLEGE

50 Sunset Lane, Paxton, MA 01612-1198
Phone: 508-849-3360 • **Financial Aid Phone:** 508-849-3366
E-mail: admission@annamaria.edu • **CEEB Code:** 3005
Fax: 508-849-3362 • **Website:** www.annamaria.edu • **ACT Code:** 3232

This private school, affiliated with the Roman Catholic Church, was founded in 1946. It has a 190-acre campus.

RATINGS
Admissions Selectivity Rating: 64   **Fire Safety Rating:** 72   **Green Rating:** 73

STUDENTS AND FACULTY
Enrollment: 978. **Student Body:** 56% female, 44% male, 12% out-of-state, 1% international. Asian 1%, African American 6%, Caucasian 73%, Hispanic 5%, Native American 0%.
Retention and Graduation: 70% freshmen return for sophomore year. 50% freshmen graduate within 4 years. 59% freshmen graduate within 6 years. 47% grads go on to further study within 1 year. 19% grads pursue arts and sciences degrees. 2% grads pursue law degrees. 1% grads pursue business degrees.
Faculty: Student/faculty ratio 10:1. 50 full-time faculty, 72% hold PhDs, 66% are women. 0% of classes are taught by teaching assistants.

ACADEMICS
Degrees: associate, bachelor's, certificate, master's, post-bachelor's certificate, post-master's certificate. **Classes:** Most classes have 10–19 students. Most lab/discussion sessions have fewer than 10 students. **Majors with Highest Enrollment:** business administration and management; criminal justice/safety studies; fire science/fire-fighting. **Special Study Options:** Accelerated program, cooperative education program, cross-registration, double major, independent study, internships, liberal arts/career combination, student-designed major, study abroad, teacher certification program. **Honors Programs:** The Honors Program at Anna Maria College is designed to intellectually challenge highly motivated scholastic achievers. The Program is now a member of "National Collegiate Honors Programs," the national association of Honors Programs. Each Honors Program participant will have the opportunity to engage directly in foreign culture through interesting study abroad programs, such as a semester abroad experience,or a focused Urban Seminar that meets in a city like Paris, Vienna, Rome or Berlin that is sponsored by the College and supervised by a professor who oversees the program. **Combined Degree Programs:** BA/MA. **Disability Services:** Special programs offered to physically disabled students include note-taking services, reader services, tape recorders, tutors. **Career Services:** alumni services, career assessment, internships.

FACILITIES
Housing: Coed dorms, special housing for disabled students, wellness housing. **Special Academic Facilities/Equipment:** The Mondor-Eagan Library houses Anna Maria College's volumes, stacks, periodicals, study rooms, computer center, resource centers, and language laboratory. Classrooms are located in Trinity Hall, Cardinal Cushing Hall, and Foundress Hall. Foundress Hall houses the Zecco Performing Arts Center. Trinity Hall also houses the learning center. Among the other buildings are Madore Chapel, St. Joseph's Hall for sciences and Miriam Hall for music, performance, and art. **Computers:** 100% of classrooms, 100% of dorms, 100% of libraries, 100% of dining areas, 100% of student union, 100% of common outdoor areas have wireless network access. Administrative functions (other than registration) can be performed online.

CAMPUS LIFE
Environment: Rural. **Activities:** Choral groups, dance, drama/theater, jazz band, pep band, student government, student newspaper, yearbook, Campus Ministries 17 registered organizations, 5 honor societies, 1 religious organizations. **Athletics (Intercollegiate):** *Men:* baseball, basketball, cross-country, football, golf, lacrosse, soccer, tennis. *Women:* basketball, field hockey, lacrosse, soccer, softball, tennis, volleyball. **On-Campus Highlights:** NEW: Residence Hall, NEW: Exercise / Weight Room, New Art Building w/ art gallery, Snack bar / Lounge, Student Center. **Environmental Initiatives:** There is a "Green Committee" that meets regularly to discuss environmental issues and ways that the college can be be more sustainable. Efforts are ongoing in moving to a paperless environment. We have made significant progress in this area.

ADMISSIONS
Freshman Academic Profile: Average high school GPA 2.6. 2% in top 10% of high school class, 13% in top 25% of high school class, 41% in top 50% of high school class. SAT Math middle 50% range 378-480. SAT Critical Reading middle 50% range 378-490. ACT middle 50% range 18-21. Minimum paper TOEFL 500. **Basis for Candidate Selection:** *Very important factors considered include:* academic GPA, standardized test scores. *Other factors considered include:* application essay, recommendation(s), rigor of secondary school record, extracurricular activities, level of applicant's interest, volunteer work, work experience. **Freshman Admission Requirements:** High school diploma is required and GED is accepted. *Academic units required:* 4 English, 3 mathematics, 3 science, (1 science labs), 2 foreign language, 2 social studies, 2 history, 4 academic electives. *Academic units recommended:* 4 English, 3 mathematics, 3 science, (1 science labs), 2 foreign language, 2 social studies, 2 history, 4 academic electives. **Freshman Admission Statistics:** 935 applied, 89% admitted, 30% enrolled. **Transfer Admission Requirements:** High school transcript, college transcript(s), essay or personal statement, statement of good standing from prior institution(s). Minimum college GPA of 2.0 required. Lowest grade transferable C. **General Admission Information:** Application Fee $40. Notification on a rolling basis, beginning on or about 12/1. Nonfall registration accepted. Admission may be deferred for a maximum of 1 year. Credit and/or placement offered for CEEB Advanced Placement tests.

COSTS AND FINANCIAL AID
Annual tuition $23,500. Room and board $9,350. Required fees $2,350. Average book expense $800. **Required Forms and Deadlines:** FAFSA, state aid form. **Notification of Awards:** Applicants will be notified of awards on a rolling basis beginning 4/1. **Types of Aid:** *Need-based scholarships/grants:* Federal Pell, SEOG, state scholarships/grants, private scholarships, the school's own gift aid, United Negro College Fund. *Loans:* Subsidized Stafford, Unsubsidized Stafford, PLUS, Federal Perkins, college/university loans from institutional funds. **Student Employment:** Federal Work-Study Program available. Off-campus job opportunities are good. **Financial Aid Statistics:** 99% freshmen, 98% undergrads receive need-based scholarship or grant aid. 99% freshmen, 98% undergrads receive non-need-based scholarship or grant aid. 92% freshmen, 92% undergrads receive need-based self-help aid. 98% freshmen, 95% undergrads receive any aid. 92% undergrads borrow to pay for school. Average cumulative indebtedness $35,575. **Criteria for awarding institutional aid:** *Non-need-based:* academics, alumni affiliation, music/drama, religious affiliation, state/district residency.

ANTIOCH COLLEGE

795 Livermore Street, Yellow Springs, OH 45387
Phone: 937-769-1100
E-mail: admissions@antioch-college.edu • **CEEB Code:** 1017
Fax: 937-769-1111 • **Website:** www.antioch-college.edu • **ACT Code:** 3232

This private school was founded in 1852. It has a 100-acre campus.

RATINGS
Admissions Selectivity Rating: 87   **Fire Safety Rating:** 60*   **Green Rating:** 60*

STUDENTS AND FACULTY
Enrollment: 120. **Student Body:** 68% female, 33% male, 66% out-of-state. **Retention and Graduation:** 60% freshmen return for sophomore year. 28% freshmen graduate within 4 years. 64% freshmen graduate within 6 years. **Faculty:** Student/faculty ratio 8:1. 45 full-time faculty, 78% hold PhDs, 13% are members of minority groups, 56% are women.

ACADEMICS
Degrees: bachelor's. **Classes:** Most classes have fewer than 10 students. **Special Study Options:** cooperative education program, cross-registration, dual enrollment, independent study, internships, liberal arts/career combination, student-designed major, study abroad. **Disability Services:** Special programs offered to physically disabled students include note-taking services, reader services, tape recorders, tutors. **Career Services:** alumni services, career/job search classes, career assessment, internships.

FACILITIES
Housing: Coed dorms, special housing for disabled students, special housing for international students, Gender specific floors. 25% of campus accessible to physically disabled. **Special Academic Facilities/Equipment:** 1,000-acre nature preserve.

CAMPUS LIFE
Environment: Rural. **Activities:** Choral groups, dance, drama/theater, literary magazine, music ensembles, musical theater, radio station, student government,

student newspaper 16 registered organizations. **On-Campus Highlights:** Herndon Gallery, Glen Hellen Nature Preserve, Japanese Tea Garden, Community Bike Shop, Alternative Library.

ADMISSIONS

Freshman Academic Profile: Average high school GPA 3.3. 14% in top 10% of high school class, 42% in top 25% of high school class, 70% in top 50% of high school class. SAT Math middle 50% range 500-620. SAT Critical Reading middle 50% range 550-690. ACT middle 50% range 22-27. Minimum paper TOEFL 525. **Basis for Candidate Selection:** *Very important factors considered include:* application essay, academic GPA, recommendation(s), rigor of secondary school record, character/personal qualities, interview, level of applicant's interest. *Important factors considered include:* Class rank, volunteer work, work experience. *Other factors considered include:* standardized test scores, alumni/ ae relation, extracurricular activities, first generation, talent/ability. **Freshman Admission Requirements:** High school diploma is required and GED is accepted. *Academic units required:* 4 English. *Academic units recommended:* 4 English. **Freshman Admission Statistics:** 1,204 applied, 60% admitted, 15% enrolled. **Transfer Admission Requirements:** High school transcript, college transcript(s), essay or personal statement, statement of good standing from prior institution(s). **General Admission Information:** Notification on a rolling basis, beginning on or about 1/1. Nonfall registration not accepted. Admission may be deferred for a maximum of 1 year. Credit and/or placement offered for CEEB Advanced Placement tests.

COSTS AND FINANCIAL AID

Annual tuition $27,800. Room and board $7,354. Required fees $750. Average book expense $2,000. **Required Forms and Deadlines:** FAFSA, institution's own financial aid form. **Notification of Awards:** Applicants will be notified of awards on a rolling basis beginning 3/15. **Types of Aid:** *Need-based scholarships/grants:* Federal Pell, SEOG, state scholarships/grants, private scholarships, the school's own gift aid. *Loans:* Direct Subsidized Stafford, Direct Unsubsidized Stafford, Direct PLUS, Subsidized Stafford, Unsubsidized Stafford, PLUS, Federal Perkins. **Student Employment:** Federal Work-Study Program available. Institutional employment available. Off-campus job opportunities are fair. **Financial Aid Statistics:** 79% freshmen, 94% undergrads receive need-based scholarship or grant aid. 100% freshmen receive non-need-based scholarship or grant aid. 81% freshmen, 90% undergrads receive need-based self-help aid. 85% undergrads borrow to pay for school. Average cumulative indebtedness $17,112. **Criteria for awarding institutional aid:** *Non-need-based:* academics.

ANTIOCH SOUTHERN CALIFORNIA/ LOS ANGELES

Office of Admissions, Culver City, CA 90230
Phone: 310-578-1090
E-mail: admissions@atiochla.edu • **CEEB Code:** 1862
Fax: 310-822-4824 • **Website:** www.antiochla.edu

This private school was founded in 1852. It has a 800-acre campus.

RATINGS

Admissions Selectivity Rating: 61   **Fire Safety Rating:** 60*   **Green Rating:** 60*

STUDENTS AND FACULTY

Enrollment: 188. **Student Body:** 100% female, 0% male, 9% out-of-state, 0% international (20 countries represented). Asian 5%, African American 24%, Caucasian 80%, Hispanic 11%, Native American 2%.
Retention and Graduation: 73% grads go on to further study within 1 year. 82% grads pursue arts and sciences degrees. 4% grads pursue law degrees. 12% grads pursue business degrees. **Faculty:** Student/faculty ratio 14:1. 21 full-time faculty, 81% hold PhDs, 24% are members of minority groups, 71% are women. 0% of classes are taught by teaching assistants.

ACADEMICS

Degrees: bachelor's, certificate, diploma, master's, post-bachelor's certificate, post-master's certificate. **Classes:** Most classes have 10–19 students. **Special Study Options:** cross-registration, double major, independent study, internships, teacher certification program, weekend college. **Combined Degree Programs:** BA/MA. **Disability Services:** Special programs offered to physically disabled students include note-taking services, tape recorders. **Career Services:** internships.

FACILITIES

Housing: Coed dorms. 100% of campus accessible to physically disabled.

CAMPUS LIFE

Environment: City. **Activities:** radio station, student government, Campus Ministries 1 registered organizations. **On-Campus Highlights:** Student Lounge, Campus Services, Classrooms, Computer lab, Faculty and Student Services Offices.

ADMISSIONS

Freshman Academic Profile: Minimum paper TOEFL 600. **Transfer Admission Requirements:** college transcript(s), essay or personal statement, Lowest grade transferable C. **General Admission Information:** Application Fee $60. Regular application deadline 8/1. Notification on a rolling basis, beginning on or about 9/1. Nonfall registration not accepted. Admission may be deferred for a maximum of 1 yr. Credit and/or placement offered for CEEB Advanced Placement tests.

COSTS AND FINANCIAL AID

Annual tuition $15,380. Required fees $260. Average book expense $0. **Required Forms and Deadlines:** FAFSA, institution's own financial aid form. **Notification of Awards:** Applicants will be notified of awards on a rolling basis beginning 4/15. **Types of Aid:** *Need-based scholarships/grants:* Federal Pell, SEOG, state scholarships/grants, private scholarships, the school's own gift aid. *Loans:* Subsidized Stafford, Unsubsidized Stafford, PLUS, Federal Perkins. **Student Employment:** Federal Work-Study Program available. Institutional employment available. Off-campus job opportunities are excellent. **Financial Aid Statistics:** 91% undergrads receive need-based scholarship or grant aid. **Criteria for awarding institutional aid:** *Non-need-based:* academics, leadership.

ANTIOCH UNIVERSITY SANTA BARBARA

801 Garden Street, Santa Barbara, CA 93101
Phone: 805-962-8179 • **Financial Aid Phone:** 805-962-8179
E-mail: admissions@antiochsb.edu
Fax: 805-962-4786 • **Website:** www.antiochsb.edu

This private school was founded in 1852.

RATINGS

Admissions Selectivity Rating: 60*   **Fire Safety Rating:** 60*   **Green Rating:** 60*

STUDENTS AND FACULTY

Enrollment: 105. **Student Body:** 75% female, 25% male
Faculty: 16 full-time faculty, 69% are women.

ACADEMICS

Degrees: bachelor's, master's. **Special Study Options:** cross-registration, double major, independent study, internships, liberal arts/career combination, study abroad, teacher certification program, weekend college.

FACILITIES

Computers: Students can register for classes online. Administrative functions (other than registration) can be performed online.

CAMPUS LIFE

Environment: City.

ADMISSIONS

Freshman Admission Requirements: High school diploma is required and GED is accepted. **Transfer Admission Requirements:** High school transcript, college transcript(s), essay or personal statement, interview, statement of good standing from prior institution(s). Minimum college GPA of 2.0 required. Lowest grade transferable C. **General Admission Information:** Application Fee $60. Nonfall registration not accepted.

COSTS AND FINANCIAL AID

Annual tuition $15,375. Required fees $26. **Required Forms and Deadlines:** FAFSA, institution's own financial aid form. **Types of Aid:** *Need-based scholarships/grants:* Federal Pell, SEOG, state scholarships/grants, private scholarships, the school's own gift aid. *Loans:* Subsidized Stafford, Unsubsidized Stafford, PLUS, Federal Perkins. **Financial Aid Statistics:** 54% undergrads receive need-based scholarship or grant aid. 54% undergrads receive need-based self-help aid. 75% undergrads borrow to pay for school. Average cumulative indebtedness $25,000.

APPALACHIAN STATE UNIVERSITY

Office of Admissions, Boone, NC 28608-2004
Phone: 828-262-2120 • **Financial Aid Phone:** 828-262-2190
E-mail: admissions@appstate.edu • **CEEB Code:** 5010
Fax: 828-262-3296 • **Website:** www.appstate.edu • **ACT Code:** 3062

This public school was founded in 1899. It has a 1300-acre campus.

RATINGS
Admissions Selectivity Rating: 83   **Fire Safety Rating:** 83   **Green Rating:** 96

STUDENTS AND FACULTY
Enrollment: 15,527. **Student Body:** 53% female, 47% male, 8% out-of-state, 1% international (61 countries represented). Asian 1%, African American 3%, Caucasian 87%, Hispanic 4%, Native American 0%.
Retention and Graduation: 88% freshmen return for sophomore year. 40% freshmen graduate within 4 years. **Faculty:** Student/faculty ratio 16:1. 898 full-time faculty, 100% hold PhDs, 11% are members of minority groups, 47% are women. 2% of classes are taught by teaching assistants.

ACADEMICS
Degrees: bachelor's, certificate, master's, post-bachelor's certificate, post-master's certificate. **Classes:** Most classes have 20–29 students. Most lab/discussion sessions have 20–29 students. **Majors with Highest Enrollment:** business administration and management; elementary education and teaching; psychology. **Special Study Options:** distance learning, double major, dual enrollment, English as a Second Language (ESL), exchange student program (domestic), honors program, independent study, internships, liberal arts/career combination, student-designed major, study abroad, teacher certification program. **Honors Programs:** Heltzer Honors Program offers promising and highly motivated students opportunities by providing honors classes in many fields. **Disability Services:** Special programs offered to physically disabled students include note-taking services, reader services, tape recorders, tutors. **Career Services:** Alumni network, alumni services, career/job search classes, career assessment, internships, regional alumni.

FACILITIES
Housing: Coed dorms, special housing for disabled students, men's dorms, special housing for international students, women's dorms, apartments for married students, apartments for single students, wellness housing, theme housingSorority housing. 100% of campus accessible to physically disabled. **Special Academic Facilities/Equipment:** Language lab, Dark Sky Observatory http://www.dancaton.physics.appstate.edu/Observatories/DSO/index.htm, meteorological reporting station, art gallery, Living Learning Center, geology museum and rock garden http://www.geology.appstate.edu/museum/museum. htm, wind research site http://www.wind.appstate.edu/swiwind/smallwindsite. php, library Special Collections http://www.library.appstate.edu/collections/sc/index.html **Computers:** 95% of classrooms, 70% of dorms, 90% of libraries, 90% of dining areas, 85% of student union, 5% of common outdoor areas have wireless network access. Students can register for classes online. Administrative functions (other than registration) can be performed online.

CAMPUS LIFE
Environment: Village. **Activities:** Choral groups, concert band, dance, drama/theater, jazz band, literary magazine, marching band, music ensembles, musical theater, opera, pep band, radio station, student government, student newspaper, student-run film society, symphony orchestra, Campus Ministries, International Student Organization, Model UN 270 registered organizations, 20 honor societies, 25 religious organizations. 18 fraternities, 11 sororities. **Athletics (Intercollegiate):** *Men:* baseball, basketball, cross-country, football, golf, soccer, tennis, track/field (outdoor), track/field (indoor), wrestling. *Women:* basketball, cross-country, field hockey, golf, soccer, softball, tennis, track/field (outdoor), track/field (indoor), volleyball. **On-Campus Highlights:** Student Union, Central Dining Hall, Belk Library, Student Recreation Center, Holmes Convocation Center. **Environmental Initiatives:** Signatory of the American College and University Presidents Climate Commitment. On track with the target requirements. Climate Action Plan completed 2010. Climate neutrality date of 2050. Significant recent institutional commitments include establishment of the Office of Sustainability reporting to the Vice Chancellor, creation of 50-member interdisciplinary Sustainability Council co-chaired by the University Sustainability director and a faculty member. ASU has a commitment of zero waste and intends to divert at least 90% of waste. A target date of 2022 is set for this goal.

ADMISSIONS
Freshman Academic Profile: Average high school GPA 4.0. 21% in top 10% of high school class, 56% in top 25% of high school class, 90% in top 50% of high school class. 90% from public high schools. SAT Math middle 50% range 540-620. SAT Critical Reading middle 50% range 520-620. SAT Writing middle 50% range 500-590. ACT middle 50% range 24-28. Minimum web-based TOEFL 75. Minimum paper TOEFL 525. **Basis for Candidate Selection:** *Very important factors considered include:* Class rank, academic GPA, rigor of secondary school record, standardized test scores. *Other factors considered include:* application essay, recommendation(s), character/personal qualities, extracurricular activities, first generation, racial/ethnic status, talent/ability, volunteer work, work experience. **Freshman Admission Requirements:** High school diploma is required and GED is not accepted. *Academic units required:* 4 English, 4 mathematics, 3 science, (1 science labs), 2 foreign language, 1 social studies, 1 history. *Academic units recommended:* 4 English, 4 mathematics, 3 science, (1 science labs), 2 foreign language, 1 social studies, 1 history. **Freshman Admission Statistics:** 12,248 applied, 63% admitted, 39% enrolled. **Transfer Admission Requirements:** High school transcript, college transcript(s), minimum college GPA of 2.0 required. Lowest grade transferable C. **General Admission Information:** Application Fee $50. Nonfall registration accepted. Admission may be deferred for a maximum of 1 yr. Credit and/or placement offered for CEEB Advanced Placement tests.

COSTS AND FINANCIAL AID
Annual in-state tuition $3,542. Annual out-of-state tuition $15,590. Room and board $7,060. Required fees $2,317. Average book expense $700. **Required Forms and Deadlines:** FAFSA. **Notification of Awards:** Applicants will be notified of awards on a rolling basis beginning 4/1. **Types of Aid:** *Need-based scholarships/grants:* Federal Pell, SEOG, state scholarships/grants, private scholarships, the school's own gift aid. *Loans:* Subsidized Stafford, Unsubsidized Stafford, PLUS, Federal Perkins. **Financial Aid Statistics:** 72% freshmen, 75% undergrads receive need-based scholarship or grant aid. 32% freshmen, 33% undergrads receive non-need-based scholarship or grant aid. 78% freshmen, 81% undergrads receive need-based self-help aid. 1% freshmen, 1% undergrads receive athletic scholarships. 67% freshmen, 65% undergrads receive any aid. 54% undergrads borrow to pay for school. Average cumulative indebtedness $17,155. **Criteria for awarding institutional aid:** *Non-need-based:* academics, alumni affiliation, art, athletics, job skills, leadership, minority status, music/drama, religious affiliation, state/district residency.

AQUINAS COLLEGE

1607 Robinson Road SE, Grand Rapids, MI 49506-1799
Phone: 616-632-2900 • **Financial Aid Phone:** 616-632-2893
E-mail: admissions@aquinas.edu • **CEEB Code:** 1018
Fax: 616-732-4469 • **Website:** www.aquinas.edu • **ACT Code:** 1962

This private school was founded in 1886. It has a 107-acre campus.

RATINGS
Admissions Selectivity Rating: 76   **Fire Safety Rating:** 98   **Green Rating:** 89

STUDENTS AND FACULTY
Enrollment: 1,922. **Student Body:** 60% female, 40% male, 6% out-of-state, 0% international (8 countries represented). Asian 1%, African American 3%, Caucasian 86%, Hispanic 6%, Native American 0%.
Retention and Graduation: 34% freshmen graduate within 4 years. 17% grads go on to further study within 1 year. 7% grads pursue arts and sciences degrees. 3% grads pursue law degrees. 3% grads pursue business degrees. 2% grads pursue medical degrees. **Faculty:** Student/faculty ratio 13:1. 88 full-time faculty, 81% hold PhDs, 9% are members of minority groups, 48% are women.

ACADEMICS
Degrees: associate, bachelor's, master's. **Classes:** Most classes have 20–29 students. **Special Study Options:** Accelerated program, cooperative education program, cross-registration, distance learning, double major, dual enrollment, exchange student program (domestic), honors program, independent study, internships, liberal arts/career combination, student-designed major, study abroad, teacher certification program, Service learning experiences in Peru, Haiti, Mexico. Semester abroad in Costa Rica, France, Germany, Spain, Italy, Japan and Ireland. Domestic exchange in California, Florida and Chicago. **Honors Programs:** Insignis Honors Program. **Disability Services:** Special programs offered to physically disabled students include note-taking services, reader services, tape recorders, tutors. **Career Services:** alumni services, career/job search classes, career assessment, internships.

FACILITIES
Housing: Coed dorms, women's dorms, apartments for single students, theme housing 95% of campus accessible to physically disabled. **Special Academic Facilities/Equipment:** Observatory and Jarecki Center for Advanced Learning featuring high-speed, two-way interactive video conferencing for courses and a virtual connection for external experts to interact with classes (sound, video, graphics) using a laptop computer equipped with a camera that is housed in

a self-contained briefcase. The package includes all the technology needed to accomplish the connection through a standard phone jack. This "virtual faculty briefcase" can be shipped to a guest lecturer at another location anywhere in the world and they are able to conduct an interactive lecture or discussion with an Aquinas classroom. **Computers:** 100% of classrooms, 100% of dorms, 100% of libraries, 100% of dining areas, 100% of student union, 80% of common outdoor areas have wireless network access. Administrative functions (other than registration) can be performed online.

CAMPUS LIFE
Environment: Metropolis. **Activities:** Choral groups, concert band, dance, drama/theater, jazz band, literary magazine, music ensembles, radio station, student government, student newspaper, Campus Ministries, Model UN 71 registered organizations, 4 honor societies, 2 religious organizations. **Athletics (Intercollegiate):** *Men:* baseball, basketball, cheerleading, cross-country, golf, lacrosse, soccer, tennis, track/field (outdoor), track/field (indoor). *Women:* basketball, cheerleading, cross-country, golf, lacrosse, soccer, softball, tennis, track/field (outdoor), track/field (indoor), volleyball. **On-Campus Highlights:** Physical Education Building, Jarecki Center, Moose Cafe, Wege Student Center, Performing Arts Center, The new, state-of-the-art, Grace Hauenstein Library located in the Jarecki Center opened in August 2006. With ample parking, many meeting rooms, and the latest technology, it is now the most popular meeting place on the campus. **Environmental Initiatives:** Sustainable Business practices restore environmental quality, promote stable and healthy communities, and increase long-term profitability. The Aquinas Sustainable Business Degree program fosters ecological and social intelligence in all business decisions and is the only undergraduate program of its kind in Michigan and possibly the United States. Aquinas also offers a Master of Sustainable Business. Aquinas has a formal sustainability initiative process for addressing college redesign, consisting of sustainability committees built into the governing document of the college. The Faculty Assembly, the Staff Assembly, and the Student Senate all have such standing sustainability committees, each of which send representatives to a joint committee on sustainability. A number of outcomes have emerged, including increased awareness and utilization of the principles of sustainability by students, staff and faculty. Multiple projects generated from proposed sustainability initiatives are also being implemented. In 2008, Aquinas became a signatory of the American College and University Presidents' Climate Commitment, and set a future goal of carbon neutrality by 2040. A recent update to the carbon footprint report revealed a 10.5% decrease in carbon emissions since the 2009 baseline. The Center for Sustainability at Aquinas College is working diligently to meet our first, short term goals laid out in the Climate Action Plan, and develop a system to better track directly financed outsourced travel.

ADMISSIONS
Freshman Academic Profile: 20% in top 10% of high school class, 48% in top 25% of high school class, 60% in top 50% of high school class. 80% from public high schools. ACT middle 50% range 21-26. **Basis for Candidate Selection:** *Very important factors considered include:* academic GPA, rigor of secondary school record, standardized test scores. *Other factors considered include:* character/personal qualities, extracurricular activities, first generation, talent/ability, volunteer work, work experience. **Freshman Admission Requirements:** High school diploma is required and GED is not accepted. *Academic units required:* 4 English, 4 mathematics, 3 science, 4 social studies. *Academic units recommended:* 4 English, 4 mathematics, 3 science, 4 social studies. **Freshman Admission Statistics:** 2,695 applied, 69% admitted, 24% enrolled. **Transfer Admission Requirements:** High school transcript, college transcript(s), minimum college GPA of 2.0 required. Lowest grade transferable D. **General Admission Information:** Notification on a rolling basis, beginning on or about 9/15. Nonfall registration accepted. Admission may be deferred for a maximum of one year. Credit offered for CEEB Advanced Placement tests.

COSTS AND FINANCIAL AID
Annual tuition $26,280. Room and board $7,810. Required fees $180. Average book expense $800. **Required Forms and Deadlines:** FAFSA. **Notification of Awards:** Applicants will be notified of awards on a rolling basis beginning 3/1. **Types of Aid:** *Need-based scholarships/grants:* Federal Pell, SEOG, state scholarships/grants, private scholarships, the school's own gift aid. *Loans:* Direct Subsidized Stafford, Direct Unsubsidized Stafford, Direct PLUS, Federal Perkins. **Student Employment:** Federal Work-Study Program available. Institutional employment available. Highest amount earned per year from on-campus jobs $13,040. Off-campus job opportunities are good. **Financial Aid Statistics:** 100% freshmen, 100% undergrads receive need-based scholarship or grant aid. 67% freshmen, 29% undergrads receive non-need-based scholarship or grant aid. 68% freshmen, 71% undergrads receive need-based self-help aid. 7% freshmen, 5% undergrads receive athletic scholarships. 95% freshmen, 90% undergrads receive any aid. 78% undergrads borrow to pay for school. Average cumulative indebtedness $20,694. **Criteria for awarding institutional aid:** *Non-need-based:* academics, alumni affiliation, art, athletics, leadership, music/drama.

AQUINAS COLLEGE (TN)

4210 Harding Road, Nashville, TN 37205
Phone: 615-297-7545
E-mail: admissions@aquinas-tn.edu
Fax: 615-297-7970 • **Website:** www.aquinas-tn.edu • **ACT Code:** 3942

This private school, affiliated with the Roman Catholic Church, was founded in 1961. It has a 80-acre campus.

RATINGS
Admissions Selectivity Rating: 62   **Fire Safety Rating:** 60*   **Green Rating:** 60*

STUDENTS AND FACULTY
Enrollment: 329. **Student Body:** 77% female, 23% male, 12% out-of-state
Faculty: Student/faculty ratio 12:1. 21 full-time faculty, 43% hold PhDs, 5% are members of minority groups, 67% are women. 0% of classes are taught by teaching assistants.

ACADEMICS
Degrees: associate, bachelor's, post-bachelor's certificate, terminal associate, transfer associate. **Special Study Options:** liberal arts/career combination, teacher certification program, weekend college. **Career Services:** career/job search classes, career assessment.

FACILITIES
Housing: 70% of campus accessible to physically disabled.

CAMPUS LIFE
Environment: Activities: student government, student newspaper 5 registered organizations. **Athletics (Intercollegiate):** *Men:* baseball, basketball. *Women:* cheerleading.

ADMISSIONS
Freshman Academic Profile: 80% from public high schools. Minimum paper TOEFL 525. **Basis for Candidate Selection:** *Very important factors considered include:* rigor of secondary school record, standardized test scores. *Other factors considered include:* recommendation(s), alumni/ae relation, character/personal qualities, extracurricular activities, interview, work experience. **Freshman Admission Requirements:** High school diploma is required and GED is accepted. **Freshman Admission Statistics:** 329 applied, 73% admitted, 28% enrolled. **Transfer Admission Requirements:** college transcript(s), minimum college GPA of 2.0 required. Lowest grade transferable C. **General Admission Information:** Application Fee $10. Notification on a rolling basis, beginning on or about 10/1. Nonfall registration accepted. Admission may be deferred for a maximum of 1 yr. Credit offered for CEEB Advanced Placement tests.

COSTS AND FINANCIAL AID
Required Forms and Deadlines: FAFSA, institution's own financial aid form. **Notification of Awards:** Applicants will be notified of awards on a rolling basis beginning 3/1. **Types of Aid:** *Need-based scholarships/grants:* Federal Pell, SEOG, state scholarships/grants, private scholarships, the school's own gift aid. *Loans:* Subsidized Stafford, Unsubsidized Stafford, PLUS. **Student Employment:** Federal Work-Study Program available. Off-campus job opportunities are excellent. **Financial Aid Statistics:** 51% freshmen, 38% undergrads receive need-based scholarship or grant aid. 82% freshmen, 59% undergrads receive need-based self-help aid. 2% undergrads receive athletic scholarships. **Criteria for awarding institutional aid:** *Non-need-based:* academics, athletics, leadership, religious affiliation.

ARCADIA UNIVERSITY

450 South Easton Road, Glenside, PA 19038
Phone: 215-572-2910 • **Financial Aid Phone:** 215-572-2980
E-mail: admiss@arcadia.edu • **CEEB Code:** 2039
Fax: 215-572-4049 • **Website:** www.arcadia.edu

This private school, affiliated with the Presbyterian Church, was founded in 1853. It has a 60-acre campus.

RATINGS
Admissions Selectivity Rating: 87   **Fire Safety Rating:** 60*   **Green Rating:** 60*

STUDENTS AND FACULTY
Enrollment: 2,151. **Student Body:** 71% female, 29% male, 38% out-of-state, 1% international (28 countries represented). Asian 4%, African American 7%, Caucasian 67%, Hispanic 5%, Native American 0%.

Retention and Graduation: 78% freshmen return for sophomore year. 52% freshmen graduate within 4 years. 61% freshmen graduate within 6 years. 28% grads go on to further study within 1 year. 24% grads pursue arts and sciences degrees. 2% grads pursue law degrees. 2% grads pursue business degrees. 2% grads pursue medical degrees. **Faculty:** Student/faculty ratio 11:1. 161 full-time faculty. 0% of classes are taught by teaching assistants.

ACADEMICS

Degrees: bachelor's, master's, post-bachelor's certificate, post-master's certificate. **Classes:** Most classes have 10–19 students. Most lab/discussion sessions have 10–19 students. **Majors with Highest Enrollment:** business/commerce; education; psychology. **Special Study Options:** cooperative education program, cross-registration, double major, exchange student program (domestic), honors program, independent study, internships, liberal arts/career combination, student-designed major, study abroad, teacher certification program, Arcadia also offers programs in Washington DC and a Philadelphia Urban Semester. Undergraduate students may also take gradutate courses. The university also offers evening and some weekend classes. **Honors Programs:** Honors program for invited students. **Combined Degree Programs:** BA/MA, 4-2 1/2 PT;4+2 PA, 4+2, FS, 7-yr optometry. **Disability Services:** Special programs offered to physically disabled students include reader services, tape recorders, tutors. **Career Services:** Alumni network, alumni services, career assessment, internships.

FACILITIES

Housing: Coed dorms, special housing for disabled students, women's dorms, apartments for single students, Living Learning Communities. 99% of campus accessible to physically disabled. **Special Academic Facilities/Equipment:** Art gallery, language lab, observatory. **Computers:** Students can register for classes online. Administrative functions (other than registration) can be performed online.

CAMPUS LIFE

Environment: Town. **Activities:** Choral groups, dance, drama/theater, literary magazine, music ensembles, musical theater, radio station, student government, student newspaper, television station, yearbook 40 registered organizations, 8 honor societies, 3 religious organizations. **Athletics (Intercollegiate):** *Men:* baseball, basketball, cheerleading, golf, soccer, swimming, tennis. *Women:* basketball, cheerleading, field hockey, lacrosse, soccer, softball, swimming, tennis, volleyball. **On-Campus Highlights:** Grey Towers Castle, Kuch Center, The Chat, Walk of Pride, Landman Library.

ADMISSIONS

Freshman Academic Profile: Average high school GPA 3.6. 30% in top 10% of high school class, 62% in top 25% of high school class, 90% in top 50% of high school class. 72% from public high schools. SAT Math middle 50% range 510-600. SAT Critical Reading middle 50% range 510-600. SAT Writing middle 50% range 500-600. ACT middle 50% range 22-27. Minimum web-based TOEFL 90. Minimum paper TOEFL 530. **Basis for Candidate Selection:** *Very important factors considered include:* academic GPA, rigor of secondary school record. *Important factors considered include:* Class rank, application essay, recommendation(s), standardized test scores, extracurricular activities. *Other factors considered include:* alumni/ae relation, character/personal qualities, interview, talent/ability, volunteer work, work experience. **Freshman Admission Requirements:** High school diploma is required and GED is accepted. **Freshman Admission Statistics:** 7,673 applied, 54% admitted, 12% enrolled. **Transfer Admission Requirements:** college transcript(s), essay or personal statement, minimum college GPA of 2.5 required. Lowest grade transferable C-. **General Admission Information:** Application Fee $30. Early decision application deadline 10/15. Regular application deadline 8/1. Notification on a rolling basis, beginning on or about 11/1. Nonfall registration accepted. Admission may be deferred for a maximum of 12 months. Credit and/or placement offered for CEEB Advanced Placement tests.

COSTS AND FINANCIAL AID

Annual tuition $33,490. Room and board $11,640. Required fees $660. Average book expense $1,400. **Student Employment:** Off-campus job opportunities are good. **Financial Aid Statistics:** 90% freshmen, 99% undergrads receive need-based scholarship or grant aid. 12% freshmen, 10% undergrads receive non-need-based scholarship or grant aid. 86% freshmen, 88% undergrads receive need-based self-help aid. 97% freshmen, % undergrads receive any aid. 100% undergrads borrow to pay for school. Average cumulative indebtedness $75,875.

See page 1008.

ARIZONA STATE UNIVERSITY

Best 378

PO Box 870112, Tempe, AZ 85287-0112
Phone: 480-965-7788 • **Financial Aid Phone:** 480-965-3355
E-mail: admissions@asu.edu • **CEEB Code:** 4007
Fax: 480-965-3610 • **Website:** www.asu.edu • **ACT Code:** 88

This public school was founded in 1885. It has a 1,963.73-acre campus.

RATINGS

Admissions Selectivity Rating: 74   **Fire Safety Rating:** 87   **Green Rating:** 98

STUDENTS AND FACULTY

Enrollment: 59,183. **Student Body:** 50% female, 50% male, 25% out-of-state, 4% international (118 countries represented). Asian 6%, African American 5%, Caucasian 60%, Hispanic 19%, Native American 2%.
Retention and Graduation: 80% freshmen return for sophomore year. 33% freshmen graduate within 4 years. 57% freshmen graduate within 6 years. 16% grads go on to further study within 1 year. 14% grads pursue arts and sciences degrees. 1% grads pursue business degrees. 1% grads pursue medical degrees. **Faculty:** Student/faculty ratio 23:1. 2546 full-time faculty, 87% hold PhDs, 23% are members of minority groups, 43% are women.

ACADEMICS

Degrees: bachelor's, master's, post-bachelor's certificate, post-master's certificate. **Classes:** Most classes have 10–19 students. Most lab/discussion sessions have 20–29 students. **Majors with Highest Enrollment:** business, management, marketing, and related support services, other; multi-/interdisciplinary studies, other; psychology. **Special Study Options:** Accelerated program, cooperative education program, distance learning, double major, exchange student program (domestic), honors program, independent study, internships, study abroad, teacher certification program, ASU offers internships in many disciplines, study abroad in 60 countries, work-study programs, accelerated degree programs and a variety of interdisciplinary undergraduate programs. Students may participate in educational programs supported by several institutes and centers. Also available are continuing education programs and a summer programs for high school students. **Honors Programs:** The Honors College at ASU, Barrett, is a selective, residential college that educates academically outstanding undergraduates from across the nation. Students enrolled in Barrett are part of both the honors college community and an ASU disciplinary college of their choice. They may major in any field offered at any one of ASU's four campuses. Honors courses are taught by honors faculty within the college and within a variety of departments and programs. **Combined Degree Programs:** BA/MA, MBA/MSE EE; MBA/MHSM; MArch/MBS; MAIS/MBA; JD/MBA; JD/MHSM; MPA/MSW. **Disability Services:** Special programs offered to physically disabled students include note-taking services, reader services, tape recorders, tutors. **Career Services:** Alumni network, alumni services, career/job search classes, career assessment, internships Career Services highlights include ASU Career Services worked with APPLE during the Spring 2009 semester to educate the campus community on a new Summer Customer Support program that is full-time during the Summer and then continues on a part-time basis for the following academic year. ASU was one of only 5 schools selected for this program, and attracted the most students of any of the 5 schools (about 80 students were hired). APPLE will continue recruiting for the 2010 year at ASU because of the coordination support from ASU and the positive results of this program.

FACILITIES

Housing: Coed dorms, fraternity/sorority housing, apartments for married students, apartments for single students, freshmen housing. Please visit - http://www.asu.edu/housing. 99% of campus accessible to physically disabled. **Special Academic Facilities/Equipment:** Art, anthropology, geology, history, and sports museums, early childhood development lab, herbarium, robotics lab, semiconductor clean room, high-resolution electron microscope facility, gamma cell irradiation chamber, solar research facilities, nuclear reactor, biodesign institute, thermal emission imaging system, melikian center, KAET (public television station), KASR 1260 AM, Phoenix urban research laboratory, Arizona biomedical collaborative, altitude chamber, simulator building, planetarium **Computers:** 100% of classrooms, 100% of dorms, 100% of libraries, 100% of dining areas, 100% of student union, 70% of common outdoor areas have wireless network access. Students can register for classes online. Administrative functions (other than registration) can be performed online.

CAMPUS LIFE

Environment: Metropolis. **Activities:** Choral groups, concert band, dance, drama/theater, jazz band, literary magazine, marching band, music ensembles, musical theater, opera, pep band, radio station, student government, student newspaper, student-run film society, symphony orchestra, television station, Campus Ministries, International Student Organization, Model UN 675 registered organizations, 16 honor societies, 51 religious organizations. 32 fraternities, 22 sororities. **Athletics (Intercollegiate):** *Men:* baseball, basketball, cross-country, diving, football, golf, swimming, track/field (outdoor), wrestling. *Women:* basketball, cross-country, diving, golf, gymnastics, soccer, softball, swimming, tennis, track/field (outdoor), volleyball, water polo. **On-Campus Highlights:** ASU Memorial Union - Tempe campus, Grady Gammage Auditorium - Tempe campus, Barrett Honors Complex - Tempe campus, Fletcher Library - West campus, Union - Polytechnic campus, Hayden Library - Tempe campus, Walter Cronkite School of Journalism and Mass Communication - Downtown Phoenix campus, Academic Complex - Polytechnic campus, Las Casas Residence Hall - West campus, Taylor Place - Downtown Phoenix campus. **Environmental Initiatives:** Carbon Neutrality Energy Efficiency/Conservation/Renewable Generation ° Transportation ° Solid Waste ° Misc. Zero Solid Waste and Water Waste Averting and Diverting Solid Waste ° Conserving Water and Reducing Waste Water Active Community Engagement, Principled Practice 82k Potential Change Agents in our ASU Community ° The Campus as a Living Laboratory ° Demonstrating Sustainability Values Through a Productive-Healthy-Quality Work/Learning/LIVING Environment

ADMISSIONS

Freshman Academic Profile: Average high school GPA 3.4. 30% in top 10% of high school class, 59% in top 25% of high school class, 86% in top 50% of high school class. 93% from public high schools. SAT Math middle 50% range 500-630. SAT Critical Reading middle 50% range 480-610. ACT middle 50% range 21-27. Minimum web-based TOEFL 61. Minimum paper TOEFL 500. **Basis for Candidate Selection:** *Very important factors considered include:* Class rank, academic GPA, standardized test scores. *Important factors considered include:* state residency. **Freshman Admission Requirements:** High school diploma is required and GED is accepted. *Academic units required:* 4 English, 4 mathematics, 3 science, (3 science labs), 2 foreign language, 1 social studies, 1 history, 1 Fine Arts. *Academic units recommended:* 4 English, 4 mathematics, 3 science, (3 science labs), 2 foreign language, 1 social studies, 1 history, 1 Fine Arts **Freshman Admission Statistics:** 30,696 applied, 88% admitted, 34% enrolled. **Transfer Admission Requirements:** college transcript(s), standardized test scores, minimum college GPA of 2.0 required. Lowest grade transferable C. **General Admission Information:** Application Fee $50. Regular application deadline 2/1. Nonfall registration accepted. Credit and/or placement offered for CEEB Advanced Placement tests.

COSTS AND FINANCIAL AID

Annual in-state tuition $9,208. Annual out-of-state tuition $22,461. Room and board $9,094. Required fees $516. Average book expense $1,020. **Required Forms and Deadlines:** FAFSA. **Notification of Awards: Types of Aid:** *Need-based scholarships/grants:* Federal Pell, SEOG, state scholarships/grants, private scholarships, the school's own gift aid, Federal Nursing Scholarships. *Loans:* Direct Subsidized Stafford, Direct Unsubsidized Stafford, Direct PLUS, PLUS, Federal Perkins. **Student Employment:** Federal Work-Study Program available. Institutional employment available. Off-campus job opportunities are good. **Financial Aid Statistics:** 95% freshmen, 88% undergrads receive need-based scholarship or grant aid. 9% freshmen, 5% undergrads receive non-need-based scholarship or grant aid. 65% freshmen, 77% undergrads receive need-based self-help aid. 1% undergrads receive athletic scholarships. 89% freshmen, 82% undergrads receive any aid. 55% undergrads borrow to pay for school. Average cumulative indebtedness $18,615.

ARKANSAS STATE UNIVERSITY

PO Box 1630, State University, AR 72467
Phone: 870-972-3024
E-mail: admissions@astate.edu • **CEEB Code:** 6011
Fax: 870-910-8094 • **Website:** www.astate.edu • **ACT Code:** 116

This public school was founded in 1909. It has a 941-acre campus.

RATINGS

Admissions Selectivity Rating: 73   **Fire Safety Rating:** 60*   **Green Rating:** 60*

STUDENTS AND FACULTY

Enrollment: 9,000. **Student Body:** 59% female, 41% male, 10% out-of-state, 1% international (56 countries represented). Asian 1%, African American 15%, Caucasian 82%, Hispanic 1%, Native American 0%. **Retention and Graduation:** 70% freshmen return for sophomore year. 15% freshmen graduate within 4 years. 37% freshmen graduate within 6 years. 3% grads go on to further study within 1 year. 1% grads pursue arts and sciences degrees. 1% grads pursue law degrees. 2% grads pursue business degrees. 1%

grads pursue medical degrees. **Faculty:** Student/faculty ratio 19:1. 446 full-time faculty, 62% hold PhDs, 11% are members of minority groups, 43% are women. 3% of classes are taught by teaching assistants.

ACADEMICS

Degrees: associate, bachelor's, certificate, master's, post-bachelor's certificate, post-master's certificate. **Classes:** Most classes have 20–29 students. Most lab/discussion sessions have fewer than 10 students. **Majors with Highest Enrollment:** business/commerce; data processing and data processing technology/technician; early childhood education. **Special Study Options:** Accelerated program, cooperative education program, distance learning, double major, dual enrollment, English as a Second Language (ESL), exchange student program (domestic), honors program, independent study, internships, study abroad, teacher certification program. **Disability Services:** Special programs offered to physically disabled students include note-taking services, reader services, tape recorders, tutors. **Career Services:** alumni services, career/job search classes, career assessment, internships.

FACILITIES

Housing: men's dorms, women's dorms, fraternity/sorority housing, apartments for married students, apartments for single students, Married and graduate student housing. 95% of campus accessible to physically disabled. **Special Academic Facilities/Equipment:** Art gallery, museum of Native American cultures and Arkansas artifacts. Ecotoxicology research facility, electron microscope facility, geographic information system facility. Equine center. **Computers:** Students can register for classes online. Administrative functions (other than registration) can be performed online.

CAMPUS LIFE

Environment: Town. **Activities:** Choral groups, concert band, dance, drama/theater, jazz band, marching band, music ensembles, musical theater, opera, pep band, radio station, student government, student newspaper, symphony orchestra, television station, yearbook 192 registered organizations, 42 honor societies, 16 religious organizations. 12 fraternities, 9 sororities. **Athletics (Intercollegiate):** *Men:* baseball, basketball, cross-country, football, golf, track/field (outdoor), track/field (indoor). *Women:* basketball, cross-country, golf, soccer, tennis, track/field (outdoor), track/field (indoor), volleyball. **On-Campus Highlights:** New Student Union, Fowler Center for Performing Arts, ASU Convocation Center, Outdoor theatre, ASU Museum.

ADMISSIONS

Freshman Academic Profile: Average high school GPA 3.2. 93% from public high schools. ACT middle 50% range 18-25. Minimum paper TOEFL 500. **Basis for Candidate Selection:** *Very important factors considered include:* rigor of secondary school record, standardized test scores. *Other factors considered include:* Class rank, recommendation(s), talent/ability. **Freshman Admission Requirements:** High school diploma is required and GED is accepted. **Freshman Admission Statistics:** 3,088 applied, 66% admitted, 75% enrolled. **Transfer Admission Requirements:** college transcript(s), minimum college GPA of 2.0 required. Lowest grade transferable C. **General Admission Information:** Application Fee $15. Regular application deadline 8/23. Nonfall registration accepted. Admission may be deferred for a maximum of no maximum. Credit offered for CEEB Advanced Placement tests.

COSTS AND FINANCIAL AID

Annual in-state tuition $3,750. Annual out-of-state tuition $9,660. Room and board $3,640. Required fees $1,060. Average book expense $1,000. **Required Forms and Deadlines:** FAFSA, institution's own financial aid form. **Notification of Awards:** Applicants will be notified of awards on a rolling basis beginning 6/1. **Types of Aid:** *Need-based scholarships/grants:* Federal Pell, SEOG, state scholarships/grants, private scholarships, the school's own gift aid. *Loans:* Subsidized Stafford, Unsubsidized Stafford, PLUS, Federal Perkins. **Student Employment:** Federal Work-Study Program available. Institutional employment available. Highest amount earned per year from on-campus jobs $3,600. Off-campus job opportunities are good. **Financial Aid Statistics:** 90% freshmen, 85% undergrads receive need-based scholarship or grant aid. 24% freshmen, 30% undergrads receive non-need-based scholarship or grant aid. 40% freshmen, 45% undergrads receive need-based self-help aid. 3% freshmen, 3% undergrads receive athletic scholarships. 76% freshmen, 67% undergrads receive any aid. 63% undergrads borrow to pay for school. Average cumulative indebtedness $14,900. **Criteria for awarding institutional aid:** *Non-need-based:* academics, alumni affiliation, art, athletics, leadership, minority status, music/drama, state/district residency.

ARKANSAS TECH UNIVERSITY

Doc Bryan; 1605 Coliseum Dr, Russellville, AR 72801
Phone: 479-968-0343 • **Financial Aid Phone:** 479-968-0399
E-mail: tech.enroll@atu.edu • **CEEB Code:** 6010
Fax: 479-964-0522 • **Website:** www.atu.edu/ • **ACT Code:** 114

This public school was founded in 1909. It has a 541-acre campus.

RATINGS
Admissions Selectivity Rating: 67 **Fire Safety Rating:** 78 **Green Rating:** 60*

STUDENTS AND FACULTY
Enrollment: 8,643. **Student Body:** 56% female, 44% male, 4% out-of-state, 2% international (33 countries represented). Asian 1%, African American 8%, Caucasian 82%, Hispanic 4%, Native American 2%.
Retention and Graduation: 67% freshmen return for sophomore year. 21% freshmen graduate within 4 years. 42% freshmen graduate within 6 years.
Faculty: Student/faculty ratio 20:1. 330 full-time faculty, 61% hold PhDs, 8% are members of minority groups, 48% are women. 1% of classes are taught by teaching assistants.

ACADEMICS
Degrees: associate, bachelor's, certificate, master's, post-master's certificate, terminal associate. **Classes:** Most classes have 20–29 students. Most lab/discussion sessions have 10–19 students. **Majors with Highest Enrollment:** business administration and management; mechanical engineering; nursing/registered nurse (rn, asn, bsn, msn). **Special Study Options:** distance learning, double major, dual enrollment, English as a Second Language (ESL), honors program, independent study, internships, study abroad, teacher certification program. **Disability Services:** Special programs offered to physically disabled students include note-taking services, reader services, tape recorders, tutors. **Career Services:** career assessment, internships

FACILITIES
Housing: Coed dorms, special housing for disabled students, men's dorms, women's dorms, fraternity/sorority housing, apartments for single students. 100% of campus accessible to physically disabled. **Special Academic Facilities/Equipment:** 1. Arkansas Center for Energy, Natural Resources, and Environmental Studies. 2. Crabaugh Communications Center. 3. Museum of Prehistory and History. 4. Technology Center. **Computers:** Students can register for classes online. Administrative functions (other than registration) can be performed online.

CAMPUS LIFE
Environment: Town. **Activities:** Choral groups, concert band, dance, drama/theater, jazz band, literary magazine, marching band, music ensembles, musical theater, pep band, radio station, student government, student newspaper, television station, Campus Ministries, International Student Organization 130 registered organizations, 14 honor societies, 13 religious organizations. 6 fraternities, 4 sororities. **Athletics (Intercollegiate):** *Men:* baseball, basketball, cheerleading, football, golf. *Women:* basketball, cheerleading, cross-country, golf, softball, tennis, volleyball. **On-Campus Highlights:** Ross Pendergraft Library and Technology Center, Tech Fit, Doc's Place, Summit Hall, Tucker Coliseum.

ADMISSIONS
Freshman Academic Profile: Average high school GPA 3.2. 14% in top 10% of high school class, 34% in top 25% of high school class, 64% in top 50% of high school class. SAT Math middle 50% range 450-580. SAT Critical Reading middle 50% range 440-570. ACT middle 50% range 18-25. Minimum web-based TOEFL 61. Minimum paper TOEFL 500. **Basis for Candidate Selection:** *Very important factors considered include:* academic GPA, standardized test scores. *Important factors considered include:* rigor of secondary school record. **Freshman Admission Requirements:** High school diploma is required and GED is accepted. *Academic units required:* 4 mathematics. *Academic units recommended:* 4 mathematics. **Freshman Admission Statistics:** 3,857 applied, 88% admitted, 53% enrolled. **Transfer Admission Requirements:** college transcript(s), minimum college GPA of 2.0 required. Lowest grade transferable D. **General Admission Information:** Nonfall registration accepted. Admission may be deferred for a maximum of 1 semester. Credit and/or placement offered for CEEB Advanced Placement tests.

COSTS AND FINANCIAL AID
Annual in-state tuition $5,610. Annual out-of-state tuition $11,220. Room and board $5,846. Required fees $918. Average book expense $1,410. **Required Forms and Deadlines:** FAFSA, institution's own financial aid form. **Notification of Awards:** Applicants will be notified of awards on a rolling basis beginning 5/1. **Types of Aid:** *Need-based scholarships/grants:* Federal Pell, SEOG, state scholarships/grants, private scholarships. *Loans:* Subsidized Stafford, Unsubsidized Stafford, PLUS, Federal Perkins. **Student Employment:** Federal

Work-Study Program available. Institutional employment available. Off-campus job opportunities are excellent. **Financial Aid Statistics:** 86% freshmen, 84% undergrads receive need-based scholarship or grant aid. 61% freshmen, 40% undergrads receive non-need-based scholarship or grant aid. 60% freshmen, 68% undergrads receive need-based self-help aid. 3% freshmen, 3% undergrads receive athletic scholarships. 57% undergrads borrow to pay for school. Average cumulative indebtedness $22,649. **Criteria for awarding institutional aid:** *Non-need-based:* academics, athletics, leadership, music/drama, state/district residency.

ARLINGTON BAPTIST COLLEGE

Admissions Office, Arlington, TX 76012
Phone: 817-461-8741 • **Financial Aid Phone:** 817-461-8741, ext 110
E-mail: jtaylor@arlingtonbaptistcollege.edu
Fax: 817-274-1138 • **Website:** www.arlingtonbaptistcollege.edu • **ACT Code:** 4163

This private school, affiliated with the Baptist Church, was founded in 1939. It has a 35-acre campus.

RATINGS
Admissions Selectivity Rating: 60* **Fire Safety Rating:** 91 **Green Rating:** 60*

STUDENTS AND FACULTY
Enrollment: 220. **Student Body:** 45% female, 55% male, 17% out-of-state, 1% international (1 country represented). Asian 0%, African American 18%, Caucasian 71%, Hispanic 8%, Native American 2%.
Retention and Graduation: 51% freshmen return for sophomore year. 19% freshmen graduate within 4 years. 41% freshmen graduate within 6 years. 15% grads go on to further study within 1 year. **Faculty:** Student/faculty ratio 16:1. 12 full-time faculty, 17% hold PhDs, % are members of minority groups, 25% are women. % of classes are taught by teaching assistants.

ACADEMICS
Degrees: bachelor's, certificate, diploma, master's. **Classes:** Most classes have fewer than 10 students. Most lab/discussion sessions have 10–19 students. **Majors with Highest Enrollment:** pastoral studies/counseling; religious education; theological and ministerial studies, other. **Special Study Options:** distance learning, double major, dual enrollment, external degree program, teacher certification program.

FACILITIES
Housing: men's dorms, women's dorms, wellness housing. **Special Academic Facilities/Equipment:** Heritage Collection **Computers:** 100% of classrooms, 100% of dorms, 100% of libraries, have wireless network access.

CAMPUS LIFE
Environment: Metropolis. **Activities:** Choral groups, student government, yearbook, Campus Ministries 5 religious organizations. **Athletics (Intercollegiate):** *Men:* baseball, basketball. *Women:* basketball, cheerleading, volleyball. **On-Campus Highlights:** Student Union Building, Library, Heritage Collection.

ADMISSIONS
Freshman Academic Profile: Average high school GPA 2.9. 2% in top 10% of high school class, 21% in top 25% of high school class, 47% in top 50% of high school class. 80% from public high schools. Minimum paper TOEFL 550. **Basis for Candidate Selection:** *Very important factors considered include:* application essay, recommendation(s), religious affiliation/commitment. *Important factors considered include:* interview, level of applicant's interest. *Other factors considered include:* character/personal qualities, extracurricular activities. **Freshman Admission Requirements:** High school diploma is required and GED is accepted. *Academic units required:* 3 English, 2 mathematics, 1 science, 2 social studies. *Academic units recommended:* 3 English, 2 mathematics, 1 science, 2 social studies **Freshman Admission Statistics:** 86 applied, 100% admitted, 63% enrolled. **Transfer Admission Requirements:** High school transcript, college transcript(s), essay or personal statement, Lowest grade transferable C. **General Admission Information:** Application Fee $15. Nonfall registration accepted. Admission may be deferred for a maximum of three semesters. Neither credit nor placement offered for CEEB Advanced Placement tests.

COSTS AND FINANCIAL AID
Annual tuition $7,100. Room and board $4,800. Required fees $740. Average book expense $750. **Required Forms and Deadlines:** FAFSA. **Notification of Awards:** Applicants will be notified of awards on a rolling basis beginning 6/1. **Types of Aid:** *Need-based scholarships/grants:* Federal Pell, SEOG, private scholarships, the school's own gift aid. *Loans:* Subsidized Stafford, Unsubsidized Stafford, PLUS. **Student Employment:** Institutional employ-

ment available. Highest amount earned per year from on-campus jobs $5,600. Off-campus job opportunities are excellent. **Financial Aid Statistics:** 100% freshmen, 100% undergrads receive need-based scholarship or grant aid. 80% freshmen, 80% undergrads receive any aid. 88% undergrads borrow to pay for school. Average cumulative indebtedness $8,825.

ARMSTRONG ATLANTIC STATE UNIVERSITY

11935 Abercorn Street, Savannah, GA 31419-1997
Phone: 912-927-5277
E-mail: adm-info@mail.armstrong.edu • **CEEB Code:** 5012
Fax: 912-927-5462 • **Website:** www.armstrong.edu • **ACT Code:** 786

This public school was founded in 1935. It has a 250-acre campus.

RATINGS
Admissions Selectivity Rating: 76   **Fire Safety Rating:** 67   **Green Rating:** 60*

STUDENTS AND FACULTY
Enrollment: 5,281. **Student Body:** 68% female, 32% male, 8% out-of-state, 2% international (71 countries represented). Asian 3%, African American 22%, Caucasian 65%, Hispanic 3%, Native American 0%.
Faculty: Student/faculty ratio 19:1. 229 full-time faculty, 70% hold PhDs, 16% are members of minority groups, 51% are women. 0% of classes are taught by teaching assistants.

ACADEMICS
Degrees: associate, bachelor's, master's, post-bachelor's certificate, post-master's certificate. **Classes:** Most classes have 20–29 students. Most lab/discussion sessions have fewer than 10 students. **Majors with Highest Enrollment:** early childhood education; liberal arts and sciences/liberal studies; nursing/registered nurse (rn, asn, bsn, msn). **Special Study Options:** cooperative education program, cross-registration, distance learning, double major, dual enrollment, honors program, independent study, internships, study abroad, teacher certification program, weekend college. **Combined Degree Programs:** BSPT/MSPT, BSN/MSN. **Disability Services:** Special programs offered to physically disabled students include note-taking services, reader services, tape recorders, tutors. **Career Services:** alumni services, career/job search classes, career assessment, internships.

FACILITIES
Housing: apartments for single students. 80% of campus accessible to physically disabled. **Special Academic Facilities/Equipment:** Language lab. Criminal justice training center. Sports medicine clinic. Speech/lang. pathology lab **Computers:** Students can register for classes online. Administrative functions (other than registration) can be performed online.

CAMPUS LIFE
Environment: City. **Activities:** Choral groups, concert band, drama/theater, jazz band, literary magazine, music ensembles, musical theater, pep band, student government, student newspaper, symphony orchestra 55 registered organizations, 7 honor societies, 3 religious organizations. 1 fraternities, 1 sororities. **Athletics (Intercollegiate):** *Men:* baseball, basketball, golf, tennis. *Women:* basketball, softball, tennis, volleyball. **On-Campus Highlights:** Library, Main computer lab, Compass Point (on-campus apartments), Gym, Cafeteria.

ADMISSIONS
Freshman Academic Profile: Average high school GPA 3.1. SAT Math middle 50% range 450-550. SAT Critical Reading middle 50% range 470-570. ACT middle 50% range 18-23. Minimum web-based TOEFL. Minimum paper TOEFL 523. **Basis for Candidate Selection:** *Important factors considered include:* rigor of secondary school record, standardized test scores. *Other factors considered include:* extracurricular activities, volunteer work. **Freshman Admission Requirements:** High school diploma is required and GED is accepted. *Academic units required:* 4 English, 4 mathematics, 3 science, (2 science labs), 2 foreign language, 3 social studies. *Academic units recommended:* 4 English, 4 mathematics, 3 science, (2 science labs), 2 foreign language, 3 social studies. **Freshman Admission Statistics:** 1,685 applied, 65% admitted, 75% enrolled. **Transfer Admission Requirements:** college transcript(s), minimum college GPA of 2.0 required. Lowest grade transferable D. **General Admission Information:** Application Fee $20. Regular application deadline 7/1. Notification on a rolling basis, beginning on or about 1/1. Nonfall registration accepted. Admission may be deferred for a maximum of 1 year. Credit and/or placement offered for CEEB Advanced Placement tests.

COSTS AND FINANCIAL AID
Annual in-state tuition $2,212. Annual out-of-state tuition $8,842. Room and board $4,500. Required fees $390. Average book expense $800. **Required**

Forms and Deadlines: FAFSA. **Notification of Awards:** Applicants will be notified of awards on or about 2/1. **Types of Aid:** *Need-based scholarships/grants:* Federal Pell, SEOG, state scholarships/grants, private scholarships, the school's own gift aid, Federal Nursing Scholarships. *Loans:* Subsidized Stafford, Unsubsidized Stafford, PLUS, state loans. **Student Employment:** Federal Work-Study Program available. Institutional employment available. Off-campus job opportunities are excellent. **Financial Aid Statistics:** 34% freshmen, 50% undergrads receive need-based scholarship or grant aid. 40% freshmen, 30% undergrads receive non-need-based scholarship or grant aid. 29% freshmen, 73% undergrads receive need-based self-help aid. 6% freshmen, 3% undergrads receive athletic scholarships. 90% freshmen, 90% undergrads receive any aid. 55% undergrads borrow to pay for school. Average cumulative indebtedness $11,000. **Criteria for awarding institutional aid:** *Non-need-based:* academics, athletics, leadership, minority status, religious affiliation, state/district residency.

ARNOLD AND MARIE SCHWARTZ COLLEGE OF PHARMACY AND HEALTH SCIENCE

Long Island University, Brooklyn, NY 11201
Phone: 718-403-1011
E-mail: admissions@brooklyn.liu.edu
Fax: 718-797-2399 • **Website:** www.liu.edu

This is a private school.

RATINGS
Admissions Selectivity Rating: 60*   **Fire Safety Rating:** 60*   **Green Rating:** 60*

ACADEMICS
Degrees: first professional, master's. **Special Study Options:** honors program.

FACILITIES
Housing: Coed dorms, women's dorms, apartments for single students.

CAMPUS LIFE
Environment: Activities: 3 honor societies, 2 religious organizations. **Athletics (Intercollegiate):** *Men:* basketball, cross-country, softball, tennis, track/field (outdoor), track/field (indoor).

ADMISSIONS
Freshman Academic Profile: Minimum paper TOEFL 500. **Basis for Candidate Selection:** *Very important factors considered include:* rigor of secondary school record, standardized test scores. *Important factors considered include:* character/personal qualities, extracurricular activities, talent/ability. *Other factors considered include:* Class rank, recommendation(s), interview, volunteer work, work experience. **Freshman Admission Requirements:** High school diploma is required and GED is accepted. *Academic units required:* 2 mathematics, 1 science, (1 science labs). *Academic units recommended:* 2 mathematics, 1 science, (1 science labs). **Transfer Admission Requirements:** college transcript(s), minimum college GPA of 3.0 required. Lowest grade transferable C. **General Admission Information:** Application Fee $30. Nonfall registration not accepted.

COSTS AND FINANCIAL AID
Required Forms and Deadlines: FAFSA. **Notification of Awards: Types of Aid:** *Need-based scholarships/grants:* Federal Pell, SEOG, state scholarships/grants, private scholarships, the school's own gift aid. *Loans:* Direct Subsidized Stafford, Direct Unsubsidized Stafford, Direct PLUS, Federal Perkins, Health Professions Student Loan (HPSL). **Student Employment:** Federal Work-Study Program available. **Criteria for awarding institutional aid:** *Non-need-based:* academics.

ART ACADEMY OF CINCINNATI

1212 Jackson Street, Cincinnati, OH 45202
Phone: 513-562-8740 • **Financial Aid Phone:** 513-562-8751
E-mail: admissions@artacademy.edu
Fax: 513-562-8778 • **Website:** www.artacademy.edu • **ACT Code:** 3011

This private school was founded in 1887.

RATINGS
Admissions Selectivity Rating: 80   **Fire Safety Rating:** 61   **Green Rating:** 60*

STUDENTS AND FACULTY

Enrollment: 159. **Student Body:** 64% female, 36% male, % out-of-state, 1% international (2 countries represented). Asian 1%, African American 4%, Caucasian 90%, Hispanic 1%, Native American 0%.
Faculty: Student/faculty ratio 6:1. 14 full-time faculty, 100% hold PhDs, 7% are members of minority groups, 57% are women. 0% of classes are taught by teaching assistants.

ACADEMICS

Degrees: associate, bachelor's, master's. **Majors with Highest Enrollment:** graphic design; illustration; painting. **Special Study Options:** cooperative education program, cross-registration, double major, internships. **Disability Services:** Special programs offered to physically disabled students include note-taking services, tape recorders, tutors.

FACILITIES

Housing: Coed dorms.

CAMPUS LIFE

Environment: Metropolis. **Activities:** literary magazine, student government, student-run film society, yearbook. **On-Campus Highlights:** New Building, Dorms, Student Studios, Student Commons, Three Art Galleries. **Environmental Initiatives:** Received Leadership in Energy and Environmental Design (LEED) Green Building certification by the United States Green Building Council. On-going recycling program.

ADMISSIONS

Freshman Academic Profile: SAT Math middle 50% range 420-570. SAT Critical Reading middle 50% range 480-600. ACT middle 50% range 18-24. Minimum web-based TOEFL 80. Minimum paper TOEFL 550. **Basis for Candidate Selection:** *Very important factors considered include:* rigor of secondary school record, interview, talent/ability. *Important factors considered include:* application essay, academic GPA. *Other factors considered include:* recommendation(s), standardized test scores, character/personal qualities, extracurricular activities. **Freshman Admission Requirements:** High school diploma is required and GED is accepted. **Freshman Admission Statistics:** 541 applied, 21% admitted, 42% enrolled. **Transfer Admission Requirements:** High school transcript, college transcript(s), essay or personal statement, interview, minimum college GPA of 2.0 required. Lowest grade transferable C. **General Admission Information:** Regular application deadline 6/30. Notification on a rolling basis, beginning on or about 9/1. Nonfall registration accepted. Admission may be deferred for a maximum of one year.

COSTS AND FINANCIAL AID

Annual tuition $21,500. Room and board $6,000. Required fees $380. Average book expense $1,200. **Required Forms and Deadlines:** FAFSA, state aid form. **Notification of Awards:** Applicants will be notified of awards on a rolling basis beginning 3/1. *Types of Aid: Need-based scholarships/grants:* Federal Pell, SEOG, state scholarships/grants, private scholarships, the school's own gift aid. *Loans:* Direct Subsidized Stafford, Direct Unsubsidized Stafford, Direct PLUS, Subsidized Stafford, Unsubsidized Stafford, PLUS, Federal Perkins. **Student Employment:** Federal Work-Study Program available. Institutional employment available. Off-campus job opportunities are good. **Financial Aid Statistics:** 95% undergrads receive any aid. **Criteria for awarding institutional aid:** *Non-need-based:* academics, art.

ART CENTER COLLEGE OF DESIGN

1700 Lida Street, Pasadena, CA 91103 1999
Phone: 626-396-2373 • **Financial Aid Phone:** 626-396-2215
E-mail: admissions@artcenter.edu • **CEEB Code:** 4009
Fax: 626-795-0578 • **Website:** www.artcenter.edu • **ACT Code:** 164

This private school was founded in 1930. It has a 175-acre campus.

RATINGS

Admissions Selectivity Rating: 62   **Fire Safety Rating:** 60*   **Green Rating:** 73

STUDENTS AND FACULTY

Enrollment: 1,641. **Student Body:** 48% female, 52% male, % out-of-state, 20% international (45 countries represented). Asian 37%, African American 2%, Caucasian 26%, Hispanic 11%, Native American 0%.
Faculty: Student/faculty ratio 9:1. 93 full-time faculty, 0% of classes are taught by teaching assistants.

ACADEMICS

Degrees: bachelor's, master's. **Classes:** Most classes have 10–19 students. **Majors with Highest Enrollment:** graphic design; illustration; industrial design. **Special Study Options:** cooperative education program, independent

---

study, internships. **Disability Services:** Special programs offered to physically disabled students include note-taking services, tape recorders, tutors. **Career Services:** Alumni network, alumni services, internships.

FACILITIES

Housing: 100% of campus accessible to physically disabled. **Special Academic Facilities/Equipment:** 2 art galleries. **Computers:** Administrative functions (other than registration) can be performed online.

CAMPUS LIFE

Environment: City. **Activities:** student government 12 registered organizations. **On-Campus Highlights:** Student Gallery. **Environmental Initiatives:** 1)Conducted thorough Waste Stream Analysis to evaluate and develop a plan to initiate a long-term Sustainability Initiative to achieve Zero Waste. 2)Replaced all supply of disposables in Café with compostable materials and trash separation and pick up. 3)Built a fenced organic garden on campus, used as a learning and teaching tool. Café will plant and use herbs from garden as well.

ADMISSIONS

Freshman Academic Profile: Average high school GPA 3.3. Minimum web-based TOEFL 80. **Basis for Candidate Selection:** *Very important factors considered include:* application essay, academic GPA, rigor of secondary school record, talent/ability. *Important factors considered include:* Class rank, standardized test scores. *Other factors considered include:* recommendation(s), character/personal qualities, extracurricular activities, interview, racial/ethnic status, volunteer work, work experience. **Freshman Admission Requirements:** High school diploma is required and GED is accepted. **Freshman Admission Statistics:** 525 applied, 70% admitted, 43% enrolled. **Transfer Admission Requirements:** college transcript(s), essay or personal statement, Lowest grade transferable c. **General Admission Information:** Application Fee $50. Notification on a rolling basis, beginning on or about 1/1. Nonfall registration accepted. Admission may be deferred for a maximum of 1 consecutive semest. Credit offered for CEEB Advanced Placement tests.

COSTS AND FINANCIAL AID

Annual tuition $35,052. Required fees $500. **Required Forms and Deadlines:** FAFSA. *Types of Aid: Need-based scholarships/grants:* Federal Pell, SEOG, state scholarships/grants, private scholarships, the school's own gift aid. *Loans:* Direct Subsidized Stafford, Direct Unsubsidized Stafford, Direct PLUS. **Student Employment:** Federal Work-Study Program available. Institutional employment available. **Financial Aid Statistics:** 85% freshmen, 69% undergrads receive need-based self help aid.

THE ART INSTITUTE OF ATLANTA

6600 Peachtree Dunwoody Road, Atlanta, GA 30328
Phone: 770-394-8300 • **Financial Aid Phone:** 770-689-4824
E-mail: aia-admis@aii.edu
Fax: 770-394-0008 • **Website:** www.artinstitutes.edu/atlanta/ • **ACT Code:** 859

This proprietary school was founded in 1949. It has a 7-acre campus.

RATINGS

Admissions Selectivity Rating: 60*   **Fire Safety Rating:** 60*   **Green Rating:** 60*

STUDENTS AND FACULTY

Enrollment: 3,839. **Student Body:** 44% female, 56% male, 0% international (33 countries represented). Asian 0%, African American 22%, Caucasian 19%, Hispanic 2%, Native American 0%.
Retention and Graduation: Faculty: Student/faculty ratio 21:1. 131 full-time faculty, 48% hold PhDs, 21% are members of minority groups, 45% are women.

ACADEMICS

Degrees: associate, bachelor's, certificate, diploma. **Classes:** Most classes have 10–19 students. **Majors with Highest Enrollment:** commercial and advertising art; culinary arts/chef training; interior design. **Special Study Options:** Accelerated program, distance learning, dual enrollment, honors program, independent study, internships, study abroad, weekend college. **Honors Programs:** Design Honors Studio for graphic design students: students work with clients in the community . **Disability Services:** Special programs offered to physically disabled students include note-taking services, reader services, tape recorders, tutors. **Career Services:** Alumni network, alumni services, career/job search classes, internships.

FACILITIES

Housing: Coed dorms. 100% of campus accessible to physically disabled. **Special Academic Facilities/Equipment:** Art gallery, multi-camera video studio with digital and non-linear video editing suites, and an audio studio and control room featuring Protools stations. Professional photography studios with traditional and digital darkroom facilities containing high-end professional equipment such as the Imacon scanner, Cone Piezograph B and W printers, Epson 5500 printer, and Epson 10000 printer. Photographic video editing stations consist of Dual Processor G4s with cinema displays that are color managed with Greytag MacBeth equipment. Culinary facilities with five teaching kitchens and a dining lab. **Computers:** Students can register for classes online.

CAMPUS LIFE

Environment: Metropolis. **Activities:** student government, International Student Organization 16 registered organizations. **On-Campus Highlights:** Gallery, Supply Store, Coffee Bar, Snack Bar, Creations Dining Lab, Entertainers perform in the coffee bar and reduced-price tickets are often available for events in Atlanta. The student affairs department also coordinates college community service programs and quarterly blood drives. Besides being enjoyable, student activities provide opportunities for making new friends and trying new experiences, as well as offering a great way to gain leadership experience.

ADMISSIONS

Freshman Academic Profile: Minimum paper TOEFL 550. **Basis for Candidate Selection:** *Very important factors considered include:* application essay, academic GPA, recommendation(s), standardized test scores. *Important factors considered include:* interview. **Freshman Admission Requirements:** High school diploma is required and GED is accepted. **Transfer Admission Requirements:** High school transcript, college transcript(s), essay or personal statement, interview, standardized test scores, statement of good standing from prior institution(s). Lowest grade transferable C. **General Admission Information:** Application Fee $50. Nonfall registration accepted. Admission may be deferred for a maximum of 4 quarters. Credit and/or placement offered for CEEB Advanced Placement tests.

COSTS AND FINANCIAL AID

Annual tuition $23,535. Room and board $9,984. Average book expense $1,700. **Required Forms and Deadlines:** FAFSA, state aid form. **Notification of Awards:** Applicants will be notified of awards on a rolling basis beginning 3/15. **Types of Aid:** *Need-based scholarships/grants:* Federal Pell, SEOG, state scholarships/grants, private scholarships, the school's own gift aid. *Loans:* Direct Subsidized Stafford, Direct Unsubsidized Stafford, Direct PLUS, Subsidized Stafford, Unsubsidized Stafford, PLUS, Federal Perkins. **Student Employment:** Federal Work-Study Program available. Institutional employment available. Off-campus job opportunities are good. **Financial Aid Statistics:** 52% freshmen, 72% undergrads receive need-based scholarship or grant aid. 39% freshmen, 8% undergrads receive non-need-based scholarship or grant aid. 100% freshmen, 100% undergrads receive need-based self-help aid. 19% freshmen, 81% undergrads receive any aid. 90% undergrads borrow to pay for school. Average cumulative indebtedness $6,375. **Criteria for awarding institutional aid:** *Non-need-based:* academics, art, state/district residency.

THE ART INSTITUTE OF BOSTON AT LESLEY UNIVERSITY

700 Beacon Street, Boston, MA 02215-2598
Phone: 617.585.6710 • **Financial Aid Phone:** 617-349-8710
E-mail: admissions@aiboston.edu • **CEEB Code:** 3777
Fax: 617.585.6720 • **Website:** aiboston.edu • **ACT Code:** 1850

This private school was founded in 1912. It has a 1-acre campus.

RATINGS
Admissions Selectivity Rating: 79   **Fire Safety Rating:** 82   **Green Rating:** 67

STUDENTS AND FACULTY
Enrollment: 1,261. **Student Body:** 75% female, 25% male, 44% out-of-state, 3% international (15 countries represented). Asian 3%, African American 4%, Caucasian 63%, Hispanic 5%, Native American 0%.
Retention and Graduation: 66% freshmen return for sophomore year. 37% freshmen graduate within 4 years. 49% freshmen graduate within 6 years.
Faculty: Student/faculty ratio 10:1. 73 full-time faculty, 68% hold PhDs, 12% are members of minority groups, 55% are women. 0% of classes are taught by teaching assistants.

ACADEMICS
Degrees: associate, bachelor's, master's, post-master's certificate. **Classes:** Most classes have 10–19 students. **Majors with Highest Enrollment:** graphic design; illustration; photography. **Special Study Options:** Accelerated program, cross-registration, distance learning, double major, dual enrollment, exchange student program (domestic), honors program, independent study, internships, liberal arts/career combination, student-designed major, study abroad, teacher certification program, Studio Courses. **Honors Programs:** First year foundation students are eligible for advanced placement, foundation studio exemp-

tions, and enrolling in Honors Studio and Honors English. **Combined Degree Programs:** BFA/M.Ed. **Disability Services:** Special programs offered to physically disabled students include note-taking services, reader services, tape recorders, tutors. **Career Services:** Alumni network, alumni services, career/job search classes, career assessment, internships, regional alumni. Career Services highlights include We are proud of the wide range of services available to our students and alumni through our new online system, Lesley Career Connection, which includes job listings, internships, career fairs, career center workshops, employer directory and more.

FACILITIES

Housing: Coed dorms, women's dorms, Special Interest and themed housing. 90% of campus accessible to physically disabled. **Special Academic Facilities/Equipment:** Art Gallery with regular shows of prominant artists; art library; applied art facilities, including state of the art photo and computer labs, animation studio, ceramics studio, wood shop, metals studio, and printmaking studio. **Computers:** 100% of classrooms, 10% of dorms, 100% of libraries, 100% of dining areas, 100% of student union, 25% of common outdoor areas have wireless network access. Students can register for classes online. Administrative functions (other than registration) can be performed online.

CAMPUS LIFE

Environment: Metropolis. **Activities:** Choral groups, dance, drama/theater, literary magazine, musical theater, student government, student newspaper, Campus Ministries, International Student Organization 25 registered organizations, 2 honor societies, 2 religious organizations. **Athletics (Intercollegiate):** *Men:* basketball, cross-country, soccer, tennis, volleyball. *Women:* basketball, crew/rowing, cross-country, soccer, softball, tennis, volleyball. **On-Campus Highlights:** Gallery, Computer Labs, Animation Studio, Photo Labs, Student Lounge. **Environmental Initiatives:** Continual enhancement of recycling, waste management and composting programs on campus. The formation of sustainability recommendations for faculty, staff and students. Student groups on campus are involved with and sponsor sustainability events.

ADMISSIONS

Freshman Academic Profile: Average high school GPA 3.0. 12% in top 10% of high school class, 38% in top 25% of high school class, 70% in top 50% of high school class. 84% from public high schools. SAT Math middle 50% range 460-560. SAT Critical Reading middle 50% range 490-600. SAT Writing middle 50% range 490-590. ACT middle 50% range 19-26. Minimum web-based TOEFL 61. Minimum paper TOEFL 500. **Basis for Candidate Selection:** *Very important factors considered include:* academic GPA, rigor of secondary school record. *Important factors considered include:* Class rank, application essay, recommendation(s), standardized test scores, character/personal qualities, extracurricular activities, interview, talent/ability. *Other factors considered include:* alumni/ae relation, first generation, geographical residence, level of applicant's interest, racial/ethnic status, volunteer work, work experience. **Freshman Admission Requirements:** High school diploma is required and GED is accepted. *Academic units required:* 4 English. *Academic units recommended:* 4 English. **Freshman Admission Statistics:** 2,523 applied, 65% admitted, 20% enrolled. **Transfer Admission Requirements:** High school transcript, college transcript(s), essay or personal statement, interview, statement of good standing from prior institution(s). Minimum college GPA of 2.0 required. Lowest grade transferable C. **General Admission Information:** Application Fee $50. Notification on a rolling basis, beginning on or about 1/15. Nonfall registration accepted. Admission may be deferred for a maximum of 1 year. Credit and/or placement offered for CEEB Advanced Placement tests.

COSTS AND FINANCIAL AID

Annual tuition $28,000. Room and board $13,250. Required fees $750. Average book expense $1,575. **Required Forms and Deadlines:** FAFSA. **Notification of Awards:** Applicants will be notified of awards on a rolling basis beginning 2/15. **Types of Aid:** *Need-based scholarships/grants:* Federal Pell, SEOG, state scholarships/grants, private scholarships, the school's own gift aid. *Loans:* Direct Subsidized Stafford, Direct Unsubsidized Stafford, Direct PLUS, Subsidized Stafford, Unsubsidized Stafford, PLUS, Federal Perkins, state loans. **Student Employment:** Federal Work-Study Program available. Institutional employment available. Highest amount earned per year from on-campus jobs $1,200. Off-campus job opportunities are excellent. **Financial Aid Statistics:** 98% freshmen, 96% undergrads receive need-based scholarship or grant aid. 19% freshmen, 38% undergrads receive non-need-based scholarship or grant aid. 73% freshmen, 70% undergrads receive need-based self-help aid. 70% freshmen, 70% undergrads receive any aid. 93% undergrads borrow to pay for school. Average cumulative indebtedness $17,000. **Criteria for awarding institutional aid:** *Non-need-based:* academics, art, leadership, minority status, state/district residency.

ART INSTITUTE OF COLORADO

1200 Lincoln St., Denver, CO 80203
Phone: 303-837-0825
E-mail: aicinfo@artinstitutes.edu
Fax: 303-860-8520 • **Website:** www.aic.artinstitutes.edu • **ACT Code:** 495

This proprietary school was founded in 1952.

RATINGS
Admissions Selectivity Rating: 63   **Fire Safety Rating:** 60*   **Green Rating:** 60*

STUDENTS AND FACULTY
Enrollment: 2,320. **Student Body:** 48% female, 52% male. Asian 2%, African American 1%, Caucasian 43%, Hispanic 6%, Native American 1%. **Faculty:** Student/faculty ratio 20:1. 64 full-time faculty, 17% hold PhDs, 11% are members of minority groups, 38% are women.

ACADEMICS
Degrees: associate, bachelor's, certificate, diploma. **Majors with Highest Enrollment:** missions/missionary studies and missiology; pastoral studies/counseling; pre-theology/pre-ministerial studies. **Special Study Options:** independent study, internships, study abroad. **Career Services:** alumni services, career/job search classes, internships.

FACILITIES
Housing: apartments for single students. **Computers:** Administrative functions (other than registration) can be performed online.

CAMPUS LIFE
Environment: Activities: 3 honor societies.

ADMISSIONS
Freshman Academic Profile: Minimum paper TOEFL 480. **Basis for Candidate Selection:** *Important factors considered include:* application essay, standardized test scores, interview. *Other factors considered include:* rigor of secondary school record. **Freshman Admission Requirements:** High school diploma is required and GED is accepted. **Freshman Admission Statistics:** 748 applied, 52% admitted, 96% enrolled. **Transfer Admission Requirements:** High school transcript, essay or personal statement, interview, Lowest grade transferable C. **General Admission Information:** Application Fee $50. Nonfall registration accepted. Admission may be deferred for a maximum of 1 yr. Credit offered for CEEB Advanced Placement tests.

COSTS AND FINANCIAL AID
Annual tuition $14,880. Room and board $6,048. Required fees $50. Average book expense $2,250. **Required Forms and Deadlines:** FAFSA, institution's own financial aid form. **Notification of Awards: Types of Aid:** *Need-based scholarships/grants:* Federal Pell, SEOG, state scholarships/grants, private scholarships, the school's own gift aid. *Loans:* Subsidized Stafford, Unsubsidized Stafford, PLUS, Federal Perkins, state loans. **Student Employment:** Federal Work-Study Program available. Institutional employment available. Off-campus job opportunities are excellent. **Financial Aid Statistics:** 3% undergrads receive non-need-based scholarship or grant aid. 56% undergrads receive need-based self-help aid. 97% undergrads borrow to pay for school. Average cumulative indebtedness $30,000.

THE ART INSTITUTE OF LAS VEGAS

2350 Corporate Circle, Las Vegas, NV 89074
Phone: 702.369.9944
E-mail: ailvadm@aii.edu
Fax: 702.992.8458 • **Website:** www.artinstitutes.edu/lasvegas/

This is a proprietary school. It has a 1.5-acre campus.

RATINGS
Admissions Selectivity Rating: 63   **Fire Safety Rating:** 64   **Green Rating:** 60*

STUDENTS AND FACULTY
Enrollment: 1,301. **Student Body:** 48% female, 52% male, 0% international. Asian 12%, African American 9%, Caucasian 35%, Hispanic 14%, Native American 1%.
Retention and Graduation: 54% freshmen return for sophomore year. **Faculty:** Student/faculty ratio 17:1. 27 full-time faculty, 7% hold PhDs, 22% are women. 0% of classes are taught by teaching assistants.

ACADEMICS
Degrees: associate, bachelor's. **Classes:** Most classes have 10–19 students. **Majors with Highest Enrollment:** culinary arts/chef training; digital communication and media/multimedia. **Special Study Options:** distance learning, independent study, internships, study abroad. **Disability Services:** Special programs offered to physically disabled students include note-taking services, reader services, tape recorders, tutors. **Career Services:** Alumni network, alumni services, career/job search classes, career assessment, internships, regional alumni.

FACILITIES
Housing: apartments for single students, wellness housing.

CAMPUS LIFE
Environment: City. **Activities:** student-run film society. **On-Campus Highlights:** Student Lounge

ADMISSIONS
Freshman Academic Profile: Average high school GPA 2.6. Minimum paper TOEFL 500. **Basis for Candidate Selection:** *Very important factors considered include:* application essay, interview. *Important factors considered include:* level of applicant's interest, talent/ability. *Other factors considered include:* academic GPA, standardized test scores, character/personal qualities. **Freshman Admission Requirements:** High school diploma is required and GED is accepted. **Freshman Admission Statistics:** 436 applied, 68% admitted, 78% enrolled. **Transfer Admission Requirements:** High school transcript, college transcript(s), essay or personal statement, interview, statement of good standing from prior institution(s). Minimum college GPA of 2.0 required. Lowest grade transferable 2. **General Admission Information:** Application Fee $150. Nonfall registration accepted. Admission may be deferred for a maximum of None.

COSTS AND FINANCIAL AID
Annual tuition $21,552. Required fees $450. **Student Employment:** Federal Work-Study Program available.

THE ART INSTITUTE OF PITTSBURGH

420 Blvd. of The Allies, Pittsburgh, PA 15219
Phone: 412-263-6600 • **Financial Aid Phone:** 412-291-6376
E-mail: aip_admissions@aii.edu
Fax: 412-263-6667 • **Website:** www.aip.aii.edu

This proprietary school was founded in 1921.

RATINGS
Admissions Selectivity Rating: 63   **Fire Safety Rating:** 63   **Green Rating:** 60*

STUDENTS AND FACULTY
Enrollment: 4,864. **Student Body:** 55% female, 45% male, 1% out-of-state, 0% international (20 countries represented). Asian 0%, African American 2%, Caucasian 30%, Hispanic 0%, Native American 0%.
Retention and Graduation: Faculty: Student/faculty ratio 20:1. 44 full-time faculty, 50% hold PhDs, 102% are members of minority groups, 70% are women. 0% of classes are taught by teaching assistants.

ACADEMICS
Degrees: associate, bachelor's, diploma, transfer associate. **Special Study Options:** distance learning, English as a Second Language (ESL), internships. **Disability Services:** Special programs offered to physically disabled students include note-taking services, tape recorders, tutors. **Career Services:** alumni services, career/job search classes, internships, regional alumni.

FACILITIES
Housing: 100% of campus accessible to physically disabled.

CAMPUS LIFE
Environment: Activities: student government, student newspaper, student-run film society 21 registered organizations, 2 honor societies, 1 religious organizations.

ADMISSIONS
Basis for Candidate Selection: *Very important factors considered include:* application essay, rigor of secondary school record. *Important factors considered include:* talent/ability. *Other factors considered include:* recommendation(s), extracurricular activities. **Freshman Admission Requirements:** High school diploma is required and GED is accepted. **Freshman Admission Statistics:** 2,177 applied, 46% admitted, 100% enrolled. **Transfer Admission Requirements:** High school transcript, essay or personal statement, interview, Lowest grade transferable C. **General Admission Information:** Application Fee

$150. Nonfall registration accepted. Admission may be deferred for a maximum of 1 year. Neither credit nor placement offered for CEEB Advanced Placement tests.

COSTS AND FINANCIAL AID
Room and board $6,525. Average book expense $900. **Required Forms and Deadlines:** FAFSA, institution's own financial aid form, state aid form. **Types of Aid:** *Need-based scholarships/grants:* Federal Pell, SEOG, state scholarships/grants, private scholarships, the school's own gift aid. *Loans:* Subsidized Stafford, Unsubsidized Stafford, PLUS, Federal Perkins, state loans, college/university loans from institutional funds. **Student Employment:** Federal Work-Study Program available. Institutional employment available. Off-campus job opportunities are excellent.

THE ART INSTITUTES INTERNATIONAL MINNESOTA

15 South 9th Street, Minneapolis, mn 55402
Phone: 612-332-3361 • **Financial Aid Phone:** 612-332-3361
E-mail: aimadm@aii.edu
Fax: 612-332-3934 • **Website:** www.artinstitutes.edu/minneapolis

This proprietary school was founded in 1997.

RATINGS
Admissions Selectivity Rating: 61   **Fire Safety Rating:** 78   **Green Rating:** 60*

STUDENTS AND FACULTY
Enrollment: 1,974. **Student Body:** 61% female, 39% male, 20% out-of-state. **Retention and Graduation:** 60% freshmen return for sophomore year. **Faculty:** Student/faculty ratio 20:1. 56 full-time faculty, 36% are women.

ACADEMICS
Degrees: associate, bachelor's, certificate. **Special Study Options:** distance learning, independent study, internships, study abroad, Evening & Weekend. **Disability Services:** Special programs offered to physically disabled students include note-taking services, tape recorders, tutors. **Career Services:** Alumni network, alumni services, career/job search classes, internships, regional alumni.

FACILITIES
Housing: apartments for single students. 100% of campus accessible to physically disabled. **Computers:** 100% of classrooms, 100% of dorms, 100% of libraries, 100% of dining areas, 100% of student union, have wireless network access. Students can register for classes online. Administrative functions (other than registration) can be performed online.

CAMPUS LIFE
Environment: Metropolis. **Activities:** literary magazine, student newspaper, Campus Ministries, International Student Organization 16 registered organizations, 1 honor societies. **On-Campus Highlights:** School dining lab, Art galleries, Connection to the city's skyway system, New second campus

ADMISSIONS
Basis for Candidate Selection: *Other factors considered include:* state residency. **Transfer Admission Requirements:** High school transcript, college transcript(s). **General Admission Information:** Application Fee $20. Nonfall registration accepted. Admission may be deferred for a maximum of none.

COSTS AND FINANCIAL AID
Annual tuition $22,416.

ASBURY COLLEGE

1 Macklem Drive, Wilmore, KY 40390
Phone: 859-858-3511
E-mail: admissions@asbury.edu • **CEEB Code:** 1019
Fax: 859-858-3921 • **Website:** www.asbury.edu • **ACT Code:** 1486

This private school was founded in 1890. It has a 400-acre campus.

RATINGS
Admissions Selectivity Rating: 79   **Fire Safety Rating:** 60*   **Green Rating:** 60*

STUDENTS AND FACULTY
Enrollment: 1,167. **Student Body:** 58% female, 42% male, 70% out-of-state, 1% international (10 countries represented). Asian 1%, African American 1%, Caucasian 96%, Hispanic 1%, Native American 0%.
Retention and Graduation: 82% freshmen return for sophomore year. 49% freshmen graduate within 4 years. 63% freshmen graduate within 6 years.
Faculty: Student/faculty ratio 11:1. 90 full-time faculty, 78% hold PhDs, 0% are members of minority groups, 27% are women. 0% of classes are taught by teaching assistants.

ACADEMICS
Degrees: bachelor's, master's. **Classes:** Most classes have 10–19 students. **Majors with Highest Enrollment:** communications technologies/technicians and support services, other; elementary education and teaching; psychology. **Special Study Options:** double major, internships, teacher certification program, 3-2 programs in engineering and computer science with the University of Kentucky. **Disability Services:** Special programs offered to physically disabled students include tape recorders, tutors. **Career Services:** alumni services, career/job search classes, career assessment, internships.

FACILITIES
Housing: special housing for disabled students, men's dorms, women's dorms, apartments for married students, apartments for single students, Spanish House. 70% of campus accessible to physically disabled. **Special Academic Facilities/Equipment:** Art gallery, Art Annex, practice rooms, theatre building, Luce Physical Activities Center, TV/radio studios and Mac lab. **Computers:** Administrative functions (other than registration) can be performed online.

CAMPUS LIFE
Environment: Rural. **Activities:** Choral groups, concert band, drama/theater, jazz band, literary magazine, music ensembles, opera, radio station, student government, student newspaper, symphony orchestra, television station, yearbook 41 registered organizations, 6 honor societies, 8 religious organizations. **Athletics (Intercollegiate):** *Men:* baseball, basketball, cross-country, diving, soccer, swimming, tennis, track/field (outdoor). *Women:* basketball, cross-country, diving, soccer, softball, swimming, tennis, track/field (outdoor), volleyball.

ADMISSIONS
Freshman Academic Profile: Average high school GPA 3.6. 30% in top 10% of high school class, 60% in top 25% of high school class, 86% in top 50% of high school class. 65% from public high schools. SAT Math middle 50% range 490-620. SAT Critical Reading middle 50% range 530-650. ACT middle 50% range 21-28. Minimum paper TOEFL 550. **Basis for Candidate Selection:** *Very important factors considered include:* recommendation(s), rigor of secondary school record, standardized test scores, character/personal qualities, racial/ethnic status, religious affiliation/commitment. *Important factors considered include:* Class rank, application essay, volunteer work, work experience. *Other factors considered include:* alumni/ae relation, extracurricular activities, geographical residence, state residency, talent/ability. **Freshman Admission Requirements:** High school diploma is required and GED is accepted. **Freshman Admission Statistics:** 820 applied, 73% admitted, 49% enrolled. **Transfer Admission Requirements:** High school transcript, college transcript(s), essay or personal statement, standardized test scores, minimum college GPA of 2.5 required. Lowest grade transferable C-. **General Admission Information:** Application Fee $30. Nonfall registration accepted. Admission may be deferred for a maximum of 1 year. Neither credit nor placement offered for CEEB Advanced Placement tests.

COSTS AND FINANCIAL AID
Annual tuition $17,660. Room and board $4,494. Required fees $148. Average book expense $600. **Required Forms and Deadlines:** FAFSA, institution's own financial aid form. **Notification of Awards:** Applicants will be notified of awards on a rolling basis beginning 3/1. **Types of Aid:** *Need-based scholarships/grants:* Federal Pell, SEOG, state scholarships/grants, the school's own gift aid. *Loans:* Subsidized Stafford, Unsubsidized Stafford, PLUS, Federal Perkins, college/university loans from institutional funds, Private alternative loans. **Student Employment:** Federal Work-Study Program available. Institutional employment available. Highest amount earned per year from on-campus jobs $1,200. Off-campus job opportunities are good. **Financial Aid Statistics:** 99% freshmen, 99% undergrads receive need-based scholarship or grant aid. 35% freshmen, 3% undergrads receive non-need-based scholarship or grant aid. 94% freshmen, 88% undergrads receive need-based self-help aid. 1% freshmen receive athletic scholarships. 68% undergrads borrow to pay for school. Average cumulative indebtedness $18,885. **Criteria for awarding institutional aid:** *Non-need-based:* academics, alumni affiliation, athletics, leadership, music/drama.

ASHLAND UNIVERSITY

401 College Ave, Ashland, OH 44805
Phone: 419-289-5052 • **Financial Aid Phone:** 419-289-5002
E-mail: enrollme@ashland.edu • **CEEB Code:** 1021
Fax: 419-289-5999 • **Website:** www.ashland.edu • **ACT Code:** 3234

This private school, affiliated with the Church of Brethren Church, was founded in 1878. It has a 12-acre campus.

RATINGS
Admissions Selectivity Rating: 71   **Fire Safety Rating:** 65   **Green Rating:** 61

STUDENTS AND FACULTY
Enrollment: 2,701. **Student Body:** 62% female, 38% male, 8% out-of-state, 2% international (16 countries represented). Asian 1%, African American 4%, Caucasian 85%, Hispanic 2%, Native American 1%.
Retention and Graduation: 69% freshmen return for sophomore year. 43% freshmen graduate within 4 years. 59% freshmen graduate within 6 years. 13% grads go on to further study within 1 year. 2% grads pursue arts and sciences degrees. 1% grads pursue law degrees. 1% grads pursue business degrees. 1% grads pursue medical degrees. **Faculty:** Student/faculty ratio 13:1. 272 full-time faculty, 82% hold PhDs, 7% are members of minority groups, 46% are women. 0% of classes are taught by teaching assistants.

ACADEMICS
Degrees: associate, bachelor's, certificate, diploma, doctoral, master's, terminal associate, transfer associate. **Classes:** Most classes have 10–19 students. Most lab/discussion sessions have 10–19 students. **Majors with Highest Enrollment:** business/commerce; education; psychology. **Special Study Options:** double major, English as a Second Language (ESL), honors program, independent study, internships, student-designed major, study abroad, teacher certification program, weekend college, Ashbrook Center for Public Affairs. **Honors Programs:** Ashland University Honors Program. **Disability Services:** Special programs offered to physically disabled students include note-taking services, reader services, tape recorders, tutors. **Career Services:** Alumni network, alumni services, career/job search classes, career assessment, internships.

FACILITIES
Housing: Coed dorms, special housing for disabled students, men's dorms, women's dorms, fraternity/sorority housing, apartments for single students, theme housing 70% of campus accessible to physically disabled. **Special Academic Facilities/Equipment:** Neumismatic Center, Patterson Technology Center, Coburn Art Gallery, Hugo Young Theatre, Studio Theatre, 33 room Radio/Television Complex, Media Center, Pre-Columbian Art Exhibit, Ashbrook Center. **Computers:** 90% of classrooms, 50% of dorms, 100% of libraries, 50% of dining areas, 100% of student union, 50% of common outdoor areas have wireless network access. Students can register for classes online. Administrative functions (other than registration) can be performed online.

CAMPUS LIFE
Environment: Town. **Activities:** Choral groups, concert band, dance, drama/theater, jazz band, literary magazine, marching band, music ensembles, musical theater, pep band, radio station, student government, student newspaper, symphony orchestra, television station, yearbook, Campus Ministries, International Student Organization 102 registered organizations, 18 honor societies, 9 religious organizations. 4 fraternities, 5 sororities. **Athletics (Intercollegiate):** *Men:* baseball, basketball, cross-country, diving, football, golf, soccer, swimming, track/field (outdoor), track/field (indoor), wrestling. *Women:* basketball, cheerleading, cross-country, diving, golf, soccer, softball, swimming, tennis, track/field (outdoor), track/field (indoor), volleyball. **On-Campus Highlights:** Kettering Science Center, Recreation and Sport Sciences Center, Schar College of Education, Dauch College of Business and Economics, National ranked food service, NCAA Division II Athletics 2009-2010 New football stadium, new soccer complex, new track and field complex.

ADMISSIONS
Freshman Academic Profile: Average high school GPA 3.4. 22% in top 10% of high school class, 49% in top 25% of high school class, 80% in top 50% of high school class. 89% from public high schools. SAT Math middle 50% range 490-580. SAT Critical Reading middle 50% range 460-560. ACT middle 50% range 20-25. Minimum web-based TOEFL 65. Minimum paper TOEFL 500. **Basis for Candidate Selection:** *Very important factors considered include:* rigor of secondary school record, standardized test scores. *Important factors considered include:* Class rank, academic GPA, alumni/ae relation, character/personal qualities, extracurricular activities, interview, level of applicant's interest. *Other factors considered include:* application essay, recommendation(s), geographical residence, religious affiliation/commitment, state residency, talent/ability, volunteer work, work experience. **Freshman Admission Requirements:** High school diploma is required and GED is accepted. *Academic units required:* 3 English, 2 mathematics, 2 science, 2 social studies, 1 history. *Aca-

demic units recommended: 3 English, 2 mathematics, 2 science, 2 social studies, 1 history. **Freshman Admission Statistics:** 3,530 applied, 77% admitted, 25% enrolled. **Transfer Admission Requirements:** college transcript(s), essay or personal statement, minimum college GPA of 2.5 required. Lowest grade transferable C-. **General Admission Information:** Regular application deadline 8/15. Notification on a rolling basis, beginning on or about 10/15. Nonfall registration accepted. Admission may be deferred for a maximum of 1 Semester. Credit and/or placement offered for CEEB Advanced Placement tests.

COSTS AND FINANCIAL AID
Annual tuition $26,566. Room and board $9,352. Required fees $846. Average book expense $900. **Required Forms and Deadlines:** FAFSA. **Notification of Awards:** Applicants will be notified of awards on a rolling basis beginning 3/1. **Types of Aid:** *Need-based scholarships/grants:* Federal Pell, SEOG, state scholarships/grants, private scholarships, the school's own gift aid. *Loans:* Direct Subsidized Stafford, Direct Unsubsidized Stafford, Direct PLUS, Subsidized Stafford, Unsubsidized Stafford, PLUS, Federal Perkins, Federal Nursing, state loans, college/university loans from institutional funds. **Student Employment:** Federal Work-Study Program available. Institutional employment available. Highest amount earned per year from on-campus jobs $2,800. Off-campus job opportunities are good. **Financial Aid Statistics:** 100% freshmen, 100% undergrads receive need-based scholarship or grant aid. 95% undergrads receive non-need-based scholarship or grant aid. 93% freshmen, 93% undergrads receive need-based self-help aid. 3% freshmen, 3% undergrads receive athletic scholarships. 99% freshmen, 98% undergrads receive any aid. 79% undergrads borrow to pay for school. Average cumulative indebtedness $39,399. **Criteria for awarding institutional aid:** *Non-need-based:* academics, alumni affiliation, art, athletics, job skills, leadership, minority status, music/drama, religious affiliation.

ASSUMPTION COLLEGE

500 Salisbury Street, Worcester, MA 01609-1296
Phone: 508-767-7285 • **Financial Aid Phone:** 508-767-7158
E-mail: admiss@assumption.edu • **CEEB Code:** 3009
Fax: 508-799-4412 • **Website:** www.assumption.edu • **ACT Code:** 1782

This private school, affiliated with the Roman Catholic Church, was founded in 1904. It has a 180-acre campus.

RATINGS
Admissions Selectivity Rating: 75   **Fire Safety Rating:** 74   **Green Rating:** 61

STUDENTS AND FACULTY
Enrollment: 2,083. **Student Body:** 60% female, 40% male, 36% out-of-state, 1% international (22 countries represented). Asian 2%, African American 3%, Caucasian 75%, Hispanic 6%, Native American 0%.
Retention and Graduation: 65% freshmen graduate within 4 years. 67% freshmen graduate within 6 years. **Faculty:** Student/faculty ratio 12:1. 147 full-time faculty, 91% hold PhDs, 5% are members of minority groups, 41% are women. 0% of classes are taught by teaching assistants.

ACADEMICS
Degrees: bachelor's, master's, post-master's certificate. **Classes:** Most classes have 20–29 students. Most lab/discussion sessions have 10–19 students. **Majors with Highest Enrollment:** accounting; psychology; rehabilitation and therapeutic professions, other. **Special Study Options:** cross-registration, double major, honors program, independent study, internships, student-designed major, study abroad, teacher certification program. **Honors Programs:** The Assumption College Honors Program is a selective program designed to foster academic engagement inside and outside the classroom. The program promotes intellectual friendship and discourse while providing a common, intensive learning experience in small seminar classes. **Combined Degree Programs:** BA/MA, BA/MAs SP ED, Rehab Couns, School Couns; BA/MBA. **Disability Services:** Special programs offered to physically disabled students include note-taking services, reader services, tape recorders, tutors. **Career Services:** Alumni network, career/job search classes, career assessment, internships, regional alumni.

FACILITIES
Housing: Coed dorms, special housing for disabled students, women's dorms, wellness housing, theme housing, freshmen dorms. 71% of campus accessible to physically disabled. **Special Academic Facilities/Equipment:** French Institute museum, Institute for Social and Rehabilitation Services, language lab, media center Living/Learning Center Testa Science Center Information Technology Center **Computers:** 100% of classrooms, 100% of libraries, 50% of dining areas, 100% of student union, 25% of common outdoor areas have wireless network access. Students can register for classes online. Administrative functions (other than registration) can be performed online.

CAMPUS LIFE

Environment: City. **Activities:** Choral groups, concert band, drama/theater, literary magazine, musical theater, pep band, student government, student newspaper, student-run film society, television station, yearbook, Campus Ministries 50 registered organizations, 12 honor societies, 1 religious organizations. **Athletics (Intercollegiate): Men:** baseball, basketball, cross-country, football, golf, ice hockey, lacrosse, soccer, tennis, track/field (outdoor), track/field (indoor). **Women:** basketball, crew/rowing, cross-country, field hockey, lacrosse, soccer, softball, swimming, tennis, track/field (outdoor), track/field (indoor), volleyball. **On-Campus Highlights:** Testa Science Center, Living Learning Center, Plourde Recreation Center, Charlie's Cafe, D'Alzon Library.

ADMISSIONS

Freshman Academic Profile: Average high school GPA 3.3. 21% in top 10% of high school class, 42% in top 25% of high school class, 82% in top 50% of high school class. SAT Math middle 50% range 500-600. SAT Critical Reading middle 50% range 500-580. ACT middle 50% range 23-27. **Basis for Candidate Selection:** *Very important factors considered include:* application essay, academic GPA. *Important factors considered include:* recommendation(s), rigor of secondary school record, interview, level of applicant's interest, volunteer work. *Other factors considered include:* Class rank, standardized test scores, alumni/ae relation, character/personal qualities, extracurricular activities, first generation, racial/ethnic status, talent/ability. **Freshman Admission Requirements:** High school diploma is required and GED is accepted. *Academic units required:* 4 English, 3 mathematics, 2 science, 2 foreign language, 2 history, 5 academic electives. *Academic units recommended:* 4 English, 3 mathematics, 2 science, 2 foreign language, 2 history, 5 academic electives **Freshman Admission Statistics:** 4,380 applied, 75% admitted, 18% enrolled. **Transfer Admission Requirements:** High school transcript, college transcript(s), essay or personal statement, statement of good standing from prior institution(s). Minimum college GPA of 2.5 required. Lowest grade transferable C. **General Admission Information:** Application Fee $50. Regular application deadline 2/15. Nonfall registration accepted. Admission may be deferred for a maximum of 1 year. Credit and/or placement offered for CEEB Advanced Placement tests.

COSTS AND FINANCIAL AID

Annual tuition $33,390. Room and board $10,590. Required fees $415. Average book expense $1,000. **Required Forms and Deadlines:** FAFSA. **Notification of Awards:** Applicants will be notified of awards on a rolling basis beginning 2/16. **Types of Aid:** *Need-based scholarships/grants:* Federal Pell, SEOG, state scholarships/grants, private scholarships, the school's own gift aid. *Loans:* Direct Subsidized Stafford, Direct Unsubsidized Stafford, Direct PLUS, Unsubsidized Stafford, PLUS. **Student Employment:** Federal Work-Study Program available. Institutional employment available. Highest amount earned per year from on-campus jobs $2,948. Off-campus job opportunities are good. **Financial Aid Statistics:** 99% freshmen, 98% undergrads receive need-based scholarship or grant aid. 14% freshmen, 6% undergrads receive non-need-based scholarship or grant aid. 86% freshmen, 88% undergrads receive need-based self-help aid. 3% freshmen, 3% undergrads receive athletic scholarships. 99% freshmen, 97% undergrads receive any aid. 83% undergrads borrow to pay for school. Average cumulative indebtedness $37,103. **Criteria for awarding institutional aid:** *Non-need-based:* academics, athletics.

See page 1010.

ATHABASCA UNIVERSITY

1 University Drive, Athabasca, AB T9S 3A3
Phone: 780-675-6100 • **Financial Aid Phone:** 780-675-6147
Fax: 780-675-6145 • **Website:** www.athabascau.ca

This public school was founded in 1970.

RATINGS
Admissions Selectivity Rating: 61   **Fire Safety Rating:** 60*   **Green Rating:** 60*

ACADEMICS
Degrees: bachelor's, certificate, diploma, master's, post-bachelor's certificate, post-master's certificate. **Classes: Majors with Highest Enrollment:** criminal justice/safety studies; elementary education and teaching; nursing/registered nurse (rn, asn, bsn, msn). **Special Study Options:** Accelerated program, cross-registration, distance learning, English as a Second Language (ESL), external degree program. **Disability Services:** Special programs offered to physically disabled students include tape recorders, tutors.

FACILITIES
Housing: Coed dorms. **Computers:** Students can register for classes online. Administrative functions (other than registration) can be performed online.

CAMPUS LIFE
Environment: Rural. **Activities:** student government, yearbook.

ADMISSIONS
Transfer Admission Requirements: High school transcript, college transcript(s). **General Admission Information:** Application Fee $56. Nonfall registration accepted. Admission may be deferred for a maximum of 1 year.

COSTS AND FINANCIAL AID
Annual in-state tuition $657. Annual out-of-state tuition $762. Room and board.

ATLANTA CHRISTIAN COLLEGE

Office of Admissions, East Point, GA 30344
Phone: 404-669-3202
E-mail: admissions@acc.edu
Fax: 404-460-2451 • **Website:** www.acc.edu • **ACT Code:** 785

This private school, affiliated with the Christian (Nondenominational) Church, was founded in 1937. It has a 52-acre campus.

RATINGS
Admissions Selectivity Rating: 62   **Fire Safety Rating:** 60*   **Green Rating:** 60*

STUDENTS AND FACULTY

Faculty: Student/faculty ratio 16:1. 0% of classes are taught by teaching assistants.

ACADEMICS
Degrees: associate, bachelor's. **Majors with Highest Enrollment:** bible/biblical studies; elementary education and teaching; social work. **Special Study Options:** double major, dual enrollment, independent study, internships. **Career Services:** alumni services, career/job search classes, internships.

FACILITIES
Housing: men's dorms, women's dorms, apartments for married students, apartments for single students. 95% of campus accessible to physically disabled. **Computers:** Students can register for classes online.

CAMPUS LIFE
Environment: Village. **Activities:** Choral groups, music ensembles, student government, yearbook 2 fraternities, 2 sororities. **Athletics (Intercollegiate):** *Men:* baseball, basketball, golf, soccer. *Women:* basketball, soccer, volleyball.

ADMISSIONS
Freshman Academic Profile: 10% in top 10% of high school class, 15% in top 25% of high school class, 90% in top 50% of high school class. 85% from public high schools. Minimum paper TOEFL 500. **Basis for Candidate Selection:** *Very important factors considered include:* recommendation(s), rigor of secondary school record, standardized test scores. *Important factors considered include:* character/personal qualities. **Freshman Admission Requirements:** High school diploma is required and GED is accepted. **Transfer Admission Requirements:** college transcript(s), statement of good standing from prior institution(s). Minimum college GPA of 2.0 required. Lowest grade transferable C. **General Admission Information:** Application Fee $25. Early decision application deadline 11/15. Regular application deadline 8/1. Notification on a rolling basis, beginning on or about 8/20. Nonfall registration accepted. Admission may be deferred for a maximum of 1 semester. Credit and/or placement offered for CEEB Advanced Placement tests.

COSTS AND FINANCIAL AID
Annual tuition $10,800. Room and board $4,400. Required fees $560. Average book expense $800. **Required Forms and Deadlines: Notification of Awards: Types of Aid:** *Need-based scholarships/grants: Loans:* **Student Employment:** Federal Work-Study Program available. Institutional employment available. Off-campus job opportunities are excellent.

AUBURN UNIVERSITY

Best 378

108 Mary Martin Hall, Auburn, AL 36849-5149
Phone: 334-844-4080 • **Financial Aid Phone:** 334-844-4634
E-mail: admissions@auburn.edu • **CEEB Code:** 1005
Fax: 334-844-6436 • **Website:** www.auburn.edu • **ACT Code:** 11

This public school was founded in 1856. It has a 1875-acre campus.

RATINGS
Admissions Selectivity Rating: 82   **Fire Safety Rating:** 82   **Green Rating:** 83

STUDENTS AND FACULTY
Enrollment: 20,137. **Student Body:** 49% female, 51% male, 38% out-of-state, 1% international (81 countries represented). Asian 2%, African American 7%, Caucasian 85%, Hispanic 3%, Native American 1%.
Retention and Graduation: 90% freshmen return for sophomore year. 38% freshmen graduate within 4 years. 68% freshmen graduate within 6 years. 39% grads go on to further study within 1 year. 6% grads pursue arts and sciences degrees. 9% grads pursue law degrees. 17% grads pursue business degrees. 19% grads pursue medical degrees. **Faculty:** Student/faculty ratio 18:1. 1192 full-time faculty, 88% hold PhDs, 19% are members of minority groups, 35% are women.

ACADEMICS
Degrees: bachelor's, doctoral, master's, post-master's certificate. **Classes:** Most classes have 20–29 students. Most lab/discussion sessions have 20–29 students. **Majors with Highest Enrollment:** business administration and management; mechanical engineering; secondary education and teaching. **Special Study Options:** Accelerated program, cooperative education program, distance learning, double major, dual enrollment, English as a Second Language (ESL), honors program, independent study, internships, liberal arts/career combination, study abroad, teacher certification program. **Honors Programs:** The Auburn University's Honors College offers qualified students a unique academic experience, designed to provide many of the advantages of a small college in the midst of the many diverse opportunities available at a large university. It is designed for students capable of academic excellence. The program selects 200 entering freshmen each year, who may be enrolled in any College or School of the University which has undergraduate programs or offerings. Students already enrolled at Auburn can also qualify for the Honors College. **Combined Degree Programs:** w/ Liberal Arts or Agriculture. **Disability Services:** Special programs offered to physically disabled students include note-taking services, reader services, tape recorders, tutors. **Career Services:** Alumni network, alumni services, career/job search classes, career assessment, internships.

FACILITIES
Housing: Coed dorms, special housing for disabled students, men's dorms, women's dorms, fraternity/sorority housing, apartments for married students, apartments for single students, Housing for students enrolled in Honors College and academic-themed learning communities (i.e. Agriculture Pre-Vet, AT&T Minority Engineering Program, Conservation Biology). 05% of campus accessible to physically disabled. **Special Academic Facilities/Equipment:** Nuclear Science Center; Hybridoma Facility; Freeman Herbarium; Jule Collins Smith Art Museum; Hypervelocity Impact Facility; Advanced Microscopy & Imaging Laboratory; Alabama Microelectronics Science & Technology Center; Alabama Water Resources Research Institute; AU Airport with single/multi-engine aircraft and flight simulators; Center for Forest Sustainability; Center for Governmental Services; Center for Pharmacy Operations & Designs; Drug Information & Learning Resources Center; Economic & Community Development Institute; Fish Molecular Genetics & Biotechnology Laboratory; Forest Policy Center; Forest Products Development Center; Fusion Lab; Harris Early Learning Center; Dept of Psychology Health Behavior Assessment Center; Highway Research Center; Marriage & Family Therapy Center; Microfibrous Materials Manufacturing Center; Dept of Kinesiology Biomechanics Lab, and Motor Behavior Center; Plasma Sciences Lab; Veterinary Medicine Radiology Clinic, Scott-Ritchey Research Center, Southeastern Raptor Rehabilitation Center, Small & Large Animal Health Clinics. **Computers:** 35% of classrooms, 100% of dorms, 95% of libraries, 50% of dining areas, 100% of student union, 30% of common outdoor areas have wireless network access. Students can register for classes online. Administrative functions (other than registration) can be performed online.

CAMPUS LIFE
Environment: Town. **Activities:** Choral groups, concert band, dance, drama/theater, jazz band, literary magazine, marching band, music ensembles, musical theater, opera, pep band, radio station, student government, student newspaper, student-run film society, symphony orchestra, television station, yearbook, International Student Organization 300 registered organizations, 56 honor societies, 15 religious organizations. 30 fraternities, 19 sororities. **Athletics (Intercollegiate):** *Men:* baseball, basketball, cheerleading, cross-country, diving, football, golf, swimming, tennis, track/field (outdoor), track/field (indoor). *Women:* basketball, cheerleading, cross-country, diving, equestrian sports, golf, gymnastics, soccer, softball, swimming, tennis, track/field (outdoor), track/field (indoor), volleyball. **On-Campus Highlights:** Telfair B. Peet Theatre, Student Activity Center, Haley Center Concourse, Library Coffee Shop, War Eagle Dining, Student Center; Arboretum; Agricultural Heritage Park; Forest Ecology Preserve. **Environmental Initiatives:** Incorporation of sustainability initiatives into university curricula, including one of the first truly interdisciplinary sustainability minors in the country. Establishment of campus-wide sustainability policy in December, 2011 2008 University Strategic Plan incorporating commitment to sustainability as guiding concept: "We recognize the importance of sustainability as crucial for this century, and we are integrating this theme into our work."

ADMISSIONS
Freshman Academic Profile: Average high school GPA 3.8. 32% in top 10% of high school class, 63% in top 25% of high school class, 90% in top 50% of high school class. 89% from public high schools. SAT Math middle 50% range 550-650. SAT Critical Reading middle 50% range 530-630. SAT Writing middle 50% range 520-610. ACT middle 50% range 24-30. Minimum web-based TOEFL 79. Minimum paper TOEFL 550. **Basis for Candidate Selection:** *Very important factors considered include:* application essay, academic GPA, standardized test scores. *Important factors considered include:* rigor of secondary school record, alumni/ae relation, character/personal qualities, extracurricular activities, first generation, geographical residence, level of applicant's interest, state residency, talent/ability, volunteer work, work experience. *Other factors considered include:* recommendation(s). **Freshman Admission Requirements:** High school diploma is required and GED is accepted. *Academic units required:* 4 English, 3 mathematics, 2 science, (1 science labs), 3 social studies. *Academic units recommended:* 4 English, 3 mathematics, 2 science, (1 science labs), 3 social studies. **Freshman Admission Statistics:** 17,463 applied, 77% admitted, 42% enrolled. **Transfer Admission Requirements:** college transcript(s), minimum college GPA of 2.5 required. Lowest grade transferable C. **General Admission Information:** Application Fee $40. Regular application deadline 6/1. Regular notification 2/15. Notification on a rolling basis, beginning on or about 10/15. Nonfall registration accepted. Admission may be deferred for a maximum of 1 year. Credit and/or placement offered for CEEB Advanced Placement tests.

COSTS AND FINANCIAL AID
Annual in-state tuition $7,872. Annual out-of-state tuition $23,616. Room and board $10,606. Required fees $1,574. Average book expense $1,100. **Required Forms and Deadlines:** FAFSA. **Notification of Awards:** Applicants will be notified of awards on a rolling basis beginning 10/2. **Types of Aid:** *Need based scholarships/grants:* Federal Pell, SEOG, state scholarships/grants, private scholarships, the school's own gift aid. *Loans:* Direct Subsidized Stafford, Direct Unsubsidized Stafford, Direct PLUS, Federal Perkins, Federal Nursing, college/university loans from institutional funds. **Student Employment:** Federal Work-Study Program available. Institutional employment available. Highest amount earned per year from on-campus jobs $10,920. Off-campus job opportunities are good. **Financial Aid Statistics:** 86% freshmen, 73% undergrads receive need-based scholarship or grant aid. 19% freshmen, 9% undergrads receive non-need-based scholarship or grant aid. 64% freshmen, 80% undergrads receive need-based self-help aid. 2% freshmen, 2% undergrads receive athletic scholarships. 59% freshmen, 48% undergrads receive any aid. 45% undergrads borrow to pay for school. Average cumulative indebtedness $24,903.

AUBURN UNIVERSITY MONTGOMERY

P.O. Box 244023, Montgomery, AL 36124-4023
Phone: 334-244-3615 • **Financial Aid Phone:** 334-244-3571
E-mail: admitme@aum.edu
Fax: 334-244-3795 • **Website:** www.aum.edu • **ACT Code:** 57

This public school was founded in 1967. It has a 500-acre campus.

RATINGS
Admissions Selectivity Rating: 68   **Fire Safety Rating:** 63   **Green Rating:** 71

STUDENTS AND FACULTY
Enrollment: 4,155. **Student Body:** 60% female, 40% male, 6% out-of-state, 4% international. Asian 2%, African American 29%, Caucasian 55%, Hispanic 0%, Native American 1%.

Retention and Graduation: 58% freshmen return for sophomore year. 13% freshmen graduate within 4 years. **Faculty:** Student/faculty ratio 15:1. 223 full-time faculty, 17% are members of minority groups, 46% are women.

ACADEMICS

Degrees: bachelor's, master's, post-master's certificate. **Classes:** Most classes have 20–29 students. Most lab/discussion sessions have 20–29 students. **Majors with Highest Enrollment:** business/commerce; elementary education and teaching; nursing/registered nurse (rn, asn, bsn, msn). **Special Study Options:** Accelerated program, cooperative education program, cross-registration, distance learning, double major, dual enrollment, English as a Second Language (ESL), honors program, independent study, internships, liberal arts/career combination, study abroad, teacher certification program, weekend college, Joint Ph.D.in public administration with Auburn University; Ed.D. in cooperation with Auburn University. **Disability Services:** Special programs offered to physically disabled students include note-taking services, reader services, tape recorders, tutors. **Career Services:** Alumni network, alumni services, career/job search classes, career assessment, internships.

FACILITIES

Housing: Coed dorms, special housing for disabled students, apartments for married students, apartments for single students. 100% of campus accessible to physically disabled. **Computers:** Students can register for classes online. Administrative functions (other than registration) can be performed online.

CAMPUS LIFE

Environment: City. **Activities:** Choral groups, dance, drama/theater, musical theater, student government, student newspaper, student-run film society, Campus Ministries, International Student Organization 50 registered organizations, 10 honor societies, 7 religious organizations. 3 fraternities, 6 sororities. **Athletics (Intercollegiate):** *Men:* baseball, basketball, cheerleading, soccer, tennis. *Women:* basketball, cheerleading, soccer, softball, tennis. **On-Campus Highlights:** Senator's Cafe, Computer Labs, Taylor Center/Student Union, Residence Hall, Athletic Facility. **Environmental Initiatives:** Recycling Campus Beautification - Plant Trees Educating the Campus on Sustainability Initiative.

ADMISSIONS

Freshman Academic Profile: Average high school GPA 3.2. 19% in top 10% of high school class, 43% in top 25% of high school class, 76% in top 50% of high school class. ACT middle 50% range 18-22. Minimum web-based TOEFL 61. Minimum paper TOEFL 500. **Basis for Candidate Selection:** *Very important factors considered include:* Class rank, academic GPA, rigor of secondary school record, standardized test scores. *Other factors considered include:* recommendation(s), alumni/ae relation, extracurricular activities, geographical residence, state residency. **Freshman Admission Requirements:** High school diploma is required and GED is accepted. **Freshman Admission Statistics:** 2,386 applied, 72% admitted, 68% enrolled. **Transfer Admission Requirements:** college transcript(s), minimum college GPA of 2.0 required. Lowest grade transferable D. **General Admission Information:** Application Fee $25. Nonfall registration accepted. Admission may be deferred for a maximum of 1 year. Credit offered for CEEB Advanced Placement tests.

COSTS AND FINANCIAL AID

Annual in-state tuition $7,500. Annual out-of-state tuition $22,500. Room and board $4,470. Required fees $690. Average book expense $1,000. **Required Forms and Deadlines:** FAFSA. **Notification of Awards:** Applicants will be notified of awards on a rolling basis beginning 6/1. **Types of Aid:** *Need-based scholarships/grants:* Federal Pell. *Loans:* Subsidized Stafford, Unsubsidized Stafford, PLUS, Federal Perkins. **Student Employment:** Federal Work-Study Program available. Institutional employment available. **Financial Aid Statistics:** 69% freshmen, 74% undergrads receive need-based self-help aid. **Criteria for awarding institutional aid:** *Non-need-based:* academics, alumni affiliation, art, athletics, job skills, leadership, minority status, music/drama.

AUGSBURG COLLEGE

2211 Riverside Avenue South, Minneapolis, MN 55454
Phone: 612-330-1001 • **Financial Aid Phone:** 612-330-1046
E-mail: admissions@augsburg.edu • **CEEB Code:** 6014
Fax: 612-330-1590 • **Website:** www.augsburg.edu • **ACT Code:** 2080

This private school, affiliated with the Lutheran Church, was founded in 1869. It has a 23-acre campus.

RATINGS

Admissions Selectivity Rating: 88   **Fire Safety Rating:** 75   **Green Rating:** 67

STUDENTS AND FACULTY

Enrollment: 3,014. **Student Body:** 55% female, 45% male, 13% out-of-state, 2% international (24 countries represented). Asian 7%, African American 9%, Caucasian 68%, Hispanic 3%, Native American 2%.
Retention and Graduation: 83% freshmen return for sophomore year. 41% freshmen graduate within 4 years. 62% freshmen graduate within 6 years. 27% grads go on to further study within 1 year. 15% grads pursue arts and sciences degrees. 2% grads pursue law degrees. 4% grads pursue business degrees. 5% grads pursue medical degrees. **Faculty:** Student/faculty ratio 16:1. 195 full-time faculty, 75% hold PhDs, 8% are members of minority groups, 51% are women. 0% of classes are taught by teaching assistants.

ACADEMICS

Degrees: bachelor's, certificate, master's. **Classes:** Most classes have 10–19 students. Most lab/discussion sessions have 10–19 students. **Majors with Highest Enrollment:** business/commerce; education; psychology. **Special Study Options:** cooperative education program, cross-registration, double major, dual enrollment, honors program, independent study, internships, liberal arts/career combination, student-designed major, study abroad, teacher certification program, weekend college. **Honors Programs:** First, the Honors Signature Courses, based on the medieval divisions of knowledge, automatically satisfy all of the College's general education requirements (except health/physical education and modern language) in a simple sequence of challenging courses, created just for Honors students. Second, Student-Created Courses allow students to design their own courses as either a replacement or supplement to the established Honors courses. Students can learn through one-on-one tutoring, small reading groups, or out-of-classroom experiences. Third, Honors Leadership Activities give Honors students access to the The Augsburg Review, Honors Debate League, Faculty/Student Research Collaboration, and the Honors Houses. Through these activities, students can engage in travel abroad, service-learning, social justice activities, political activism, leadership, research, and social gatherings with their friends. **Combined Degree Programs:** BA/MEng. **Disability Services:** Special programs offered to physically disabled students include note-taking services, reader services, tape recorders, tutors. **Career Services:** career/job search classes, internships.

FACILITIES

Housing: Coed dorms, special housing for disabled students, Special housing for Step-Up program students (i.e. Sober student program). 99% of campus accessible to physically disabled. **Special Academic Facilities/Equipment:** Electron microscope, center for atmospheric science research, theatre, pipe organ. **Computers:** Students can register for classes online. Administrative functions (other than registration) can be performed online.

CAMPUS LIFE

Environment: Metropolis. **Activities:** Choral groups, concert band, dance, drama/theater, jazz band, literary magazine, music ensembles, opera, radio station, student government, student newspaper, yearbook, Campus Ministries, International Student Organization 35 registered organizations, 1 honor societies, 1 religious organizations. **Athletics (Intercollegiate):** *Men:* baseball, basketball, cross-country, football, golf, ice hockey, soccer, tennis, track/field (outdoor), track/field (indoor), wrestling. *Women:* basketball, cheerleading, cross-country, golf, ice hockey, soccer, softball, swimming, tennis, track/field (outdoor), track/field (indoor), volleyball. **On-Campus Highlights:** Christensen Center/Starbucks Coffee Shop, Si Melby Athletic Fieldhouse, Lindell Library, Foss Center/Atrium, Gateway Center.

ADMISSIONS

Freshman Academic Profile: Average high school GPA 3.3. 11% in top 10% of high school class, 37% in top 25% of high school class, 69% in top 50% of high school class. SAT Math middle 50% range 500-640. SAT Critical Reading middle 50% range 510-640. SAT Writing middle 50% range 480-600. ACT middle 50% range 19-25. Minimum paper TOEFL 550. **Basis for Candidate Selection:** *Very important factors considered include:* Class rank, application essay, academic GPA, recommendation(s), rigor of secondary school record. *Important factors considered include:* standardized test scores, alumni/ae relation, extracurricular activities, level of applicant's interest. *Other factors considered include:* first generation, interview, talent/ability, volunteer work, work experience. **Freshman Admission Requirements:** High school diploma is required and GED is accepted. *Academic units required:* 4 English, 3 mathematics, 3 science, 2 foreign language, 2 social studies. *Academic units recommended:* 4 English, 3 mathematics, 3 science, 2 foreign language, 2 social studies. **Freshman Admission Statistics:** 2,192 applied, 54% admitted, 35% enrolled. **Transfer Admission Requirements:** college transcript(s), statement of good standing from prior institution(s). Minimum college GPA of 2.5 required. Lowest grade transferable B. **General Admission Information:** Application Fee $25. Regular application deadline 8/15. Notification on a rolling basis, beginning on or about 11/1. Nonfall registration accepted. Admission may be deferred for a maximum of 24 mos. Neither credit nor placement offered for CEEB Advanced Placement tests.

COSTS AND FINANCIAL AID

Annual tuition $29,794. Room and board $8,072. Required fees $624. Average book expense $1,000. **Required Forms and Deadlines:** FAFSA. **Notification of Awards:** Applicants will be notified of awards on a rolling basis beginning 3/1. **Types of Aid:** *Need-based scholarships/grants:* Federal Pell, SEOG, state scholarships/grants, private scholarships, the school's own gift aid. *Loans:* Subsidized Stafford, Unsubsidized Stafford, PLUS, Federal Perkins, Federal Nursing, state loans, Supplemental Loans from Private Lenders. **Student Employment:** Institutional employment available. Highest amount earned per year from on-campus jobs $3,000. Off-campus job opportunities are good. **Financial Aid Statistics:** 99% freshmen, 91% undergrads receive need-based scholarship or grant aid. 19% freshmen, 17% undergrads receive non-need-based scholarship or grant aid. 94% freshmen, 92% undergrads receive need-based self-help aid. 93% freshmen, 86% undergrads receive any aid. 83% undergrads borrow to pay for school. Average cumulative indebtedness $24,311. **Criteria for awarding institutional aid:** *Non-need-based:* academics, alumni affiliation, art, leadership, minority status, music/drama, religious affiliation.

AUGUSTA STATE UNIVERSITY

2500 Walton Way, Augusta, GA 30904-2200
Phone: 706-737-1632 • **Financial Aid Phone:** 706-737-1431
E-mail: admissio@aug.edu • **CEEB Code:** 5336
Fax: 706-667-4355 • **ACT Code:** 796

This public school was founded in 1925. It has a 76-acre campus.

RATINGS

Admissions Selectivity Rating: 78   **Fire Safety Rating:** 70   **Green Rating:** 60*

STUDENTS AND FACULTY

Enrollment: 5,394. **Student Body:** 64% female, 36% male, 9% out-of-state, 1% international (60 countries represented). Asian 3%, African American 28%, Caucasian 59%, Hispanic 3%, Native American 0%.
Retention and Graduation: 69% freshmen return for sophomore year. 4% freshmen graduate within 4 years. 21% freshmen graduate within 6 years. **Faculty:** Student/faculty ratio 18:1. 236 full-time faculty. 64% hold PhDs, 16% are members of minority groups, 51% are women. 0% of classes are taught by teaching assistants.

ACADEMICS

Degrees: associate, bachelor's, master's, post-master's certificate, terminal associate, transfer associate. **Classes:** Most classes have 20–29 students. Most lab/discussion sessions have 20–29 students. **Majors with Highest Enrollment:** biology/biological sciences; elementary education and teaching; psychology. **Special Study Options:** cooperative education program, cross-registration, distance learning, double major, dual enrollment, English as a Second Language (ESL), honors program, independent study, internships, study abroad, teacher certification program, Paralegal Certification. **Honors Programs:** Augusta State University's Honors Program provides about 100 of our best students with special sections of classes in the core curriculum. Those classes are usually smaller, involve much closer interaction with the professor, and encourage more independent and collaborative work than non-honors sections of these courses. In their Junior and Senior years, Honors students take two interdisciplinary courses, prepare, write, and defend a thesis, and conclude their undergraduate program with a Capstone course. **Disability Services:** Special programs offered to physically disabled students include note-taking services, reader services, tape recorders, tutors. **Career Services:** alumni services Career Services highlights include Our outreach to students via the classrooms and appointments for individualized help.

FACILITIES

Housing: apartments for single students. 90% of campus accessible to physically disabled. **Special Academic Facilities/Equipment:** Performing Arts Theatre, Christenberry Field House, Forest Hill Golf Course **Computers:** 95% of classrooms, 5% of dorms, 100% of libraries, 100% of dining areas, 100% of student union, have wireless network access. Students can register for classes online. Administrative functions (other than registration) can be performed online.

CAMPUS LIFE

Environment: City. **Activities:** Choral groups, concert band, drama/theater, jazz band, literary magazine, pep band, radio station, student government, student newspaper 60 registered organizations, 5 honor societies, 5 religious organizations. 3 fraternities, 3 sororities. **Athletics (Intercollegiate):** *Men:* baseball, basketball, golf, tennis. *Women:* basketball, golf, softball, tennis, volleyball. **On-Campus Highlights:** Allgood Hall, Christenberry Field House, University Hall, Jaguar Student Activities Center, Maxwell Performing Arts Theater.

ADMISSIONS

Freshman Academic Profile: Average high school GPA 2.9. 95% from public high schools. SAT Math middle 50% range 430-540. SAT Critical Reading middle 50% range 440-540. ACT middle 50% range 17-21. Minimum web-based TOEFL. Minimum paper TOEFL 500. **Basis for Candidate Selection:** *Important factors considered include:* academic GPA, rigor of secondary school record, standardized test scores. **Freshman Admission Requirements:** High school diploma is required and GED is accepted. *Academic units required:* 4 English, 4 mathematics, 3 science, 2 foreign language, 3 social studies. *Academic units recommended:* 4 English, 4 mathematics, 3 science, 2 foreign language, 3 social studies. **Freshman Admission Statistics:** 2,418 applied, 57% admitted, 68% enrolled. **Transfer Admission Requirements:** college transcript(s), minimum college GPA of 2.0 required. Lowest grade transferable D. **General Admission Information:** Application Fee $20. Nonfall registration accepted. Admission may be deferred for a maximum of Period is not limite. Credit and/or placement offered for CEEB Advanced Placement tests.

COSTS AND FINANCIAL AID

. Average book expense $1,000. **Required Forms and Deadlines:** FAFSA, state aid form. **Notification of Awards:** Applicants will be notified of awards on or about 6/1. **Types of Aid:** *Need-based scholarships/grants:* Federal Pell, SEOG, state scholarships/grants, private scholarships, the school's own gift aid. *Loans:* Subsidized Stafford, Unsubsidized Stafford, PLUS, Federal Perkins, state loans, college/university loans from institutional funds, Alternative loans. **Student Employment:** Highest amount earned per year from on-campus jobs $10,637. **Financial Aid Statistics:** 73% freshmen, 67% undergrads receive need-based scholarship or grant aid. 27% freshmen, 31% undergrads receive non-need-based scholarship or grant aid. 73% freshmen, 70% undergrads receive need-based self-help aid. 2% undergrads receive athletic scholarships. 36% undergrads borrow to pay for school. Average cumulative indebtedness $5,961. **Criteria for awarding institutional aid:** *Non-need-based:* academics, alumni affiliation, art, athletics, job skills, leadership, minority status, music/drama, state/district residency.

AUGUSTANA COLLEGE (IL)

639 38th Street, Rock Island, IL 61201-2296
Phone: 309-794-7341 • **Financial Aid Phone:** 309-794-7207
E-mail: admissions@augustana.edu • **CEEB Code:** 1025
Fax: 309-794-7422 • **Website:** www.augustana.edu • **ACT Code:** 946

This private school, affiliated with the Lutheran Church, was founded in 1860. It has a 115-acre campus.

RATINGS

Admissions Selectivity Rating: 82   **Fire Safety Rating:** 66   **Green Rating:** 75

STUDENTS AND FACULTY

Enrollment: 2,509. **Student Body:** 58% female, 42% male, 13% out-of-state, 1% international (23 countries represented). Asian 2%, African American 2%, Caucasian 80%, Hispanic 3%, Native American 0%.
Retention and Graduation: 88% freshmen return for sophomore year. 72% freshmen graduate within 4 years. 78% freshmen graduate within 6 years. 45% grads go on to further study within 1 year. 25% grads pursue arts and sciences degrees. 3% grads pursue law degrees. 10% grads pursue business degrees. 7% grads pursue medical degrees. **Faculty:** Student/faculty ratio 12:1. 182 full-time faculty, 91% hold PhDs, 23% are members of minority groups, 45% are women. 0% of classes are taught by teaching assistants.

ACADEMICS

Degrees: bachelor's. **Classes:** Most classes have 10–19 students. **Majors with Highest Enrollment:** business/commerce; pre-medicine/pre-medical studies; psychology. **Special Study Options:** Accelerated program, double major, honors program, independent study, internships, liberal arts/career combination, student-designed major, study abroad, teacher certification program. **Honors Programs:** Augustana has two tracks in first-year honors studies, Foundations and Logos. The Foundations program is a challenging interdisciplinary honors curriculum offering an intensive examination of the basic questions that have perplexed humans for centuries, and focuses on integrated learning and the development of critical thinking and writing skills. Logos is a challenging interdisciplinary honors curriculum with a special focus on how science has evolved across the centuries, how science has been used and viewed at particular historical moments, and how we live with the fruits of science today. **Combined Degree Programs:** Env. Mgt., Forestry, Occ. Therapy, Landscape Arch. **Disability Services:** Special programs offered to physically disabled students include reader services, tape recorders, tutors. **Career Services:** Alumni network, alumni services, career/job search classes, career assessment, internships.

FACILITIES

Housing: Coed dorms, men's dorms, women's dorms, apartments for single students. 80% of campus accessible to physically disabled. **Special Academic Facilities/Equipment:** Educational technology building, art gallery, black culture house, Hispanic culture house, geology museum, on-campus preschool, immigration research center, scanning and transmission electron microscopes, nuclear magnetic resonance, atomic absorption, and diode array mass spectro-photometers, planetarium, observatory with celestron telescope, environmental field stations. **Computers:** 50% of classrooms, 30% of dorms, 100% of libraries, 100% of dining areas, 90% of student union, 25% of common outdoor areas have wireless network access. Students can register for classes online. Administrative functions (other than registration) can be performed online.

CAMPUS LIFE

Environment: City. **Activities:** Choral groups, concert band, dance, drama/theater, jazz band, literary magazine, music ensembles, musical theater, opera, pep band, radio station, student government, student newspaper, symphony orchestra, yearbook, Campus Ministries, International Student Organization, Model UN 128 registered organizations, 15 honor societies, 5 religious organizations. 7 fraternities, 6 sororities. **Athletics (Intercollegiate):** *Men:* baseball, basketball, cross-country, diving, football, golf, soccer, swimming, tennis, track/field (outdoor), track/field (indoor), wrestling. *Women:* basketball, cross-country, diving, golf, lacrosse, soccer, softball, swimming, tennis, track/field (outdoor), track/field (indoor), volleyball. **On-Campus Highlights:** Thomas Tredway Library, Pepsico Recreation Center, Java 101-Coffee shop, F.W. Olin Center for Educational Technology, College Center. **Environmental Initiatives:** Recycling Program LEEDS certification for new construction, including geothermal heating for newest housing Farm to Fork Program - Food services practices with partnerships involving local agriculture producers, keeping small-scale and family businesses profitable.

ADMISSIONS

Freshman Academic Profile: Average high school GPA 3.3. 30% in top 10% of high school class, 63% in top 25% of high school class, 89% in top 50% of high school class. 85% from public high schools. ACT middle 50% range 23-28. Minimum paper TOEFL 550. **Basis for Candidate Selection:** *Very important factors considered include:* Class rank, academic GPA, rigor of secondary school record. *Important factors considered include:* application essay, recommendation(s), standardized test scores, character/personal qualities, extracurricular activities, interview, level of applicant's interest, talent/ability. *Other factors considered include:* alumni/ae relation, geographical residence, racial/ethnic status, religious affiliation/commitment, volunteer work, work experience. **Freshman Admission Requirements:** High school diploma is required and GED is accepted. *Academic units required:* 3 English, 3 mathematics, 3 science, (2 science labs), 1 foreign language, 1 social studies, 1 history. *Academic units recommended:* 3 English, 3 mathematics, 3 science, (2 science labs), 1 foreign language, 1 social studies, 1 history. **Freshman Admission Statistics:** 4,067 applied, 66% admitted, 28% enrolled. **Transfer Admission Requirements:** High school transcript, college transcript(s), statement of good standing from prior institution(s). Minimum college GPA of 2.0 required. Lowest grade transferable D. **General Admission Information:** Application Fee $35. Nonfall registration accepted. Credit and/or placement offered for CEEB Advanced Placement tests.

COSTS AND FINANCIAL AID

Annual tuition $34,614. Room and board $8,784. Required fees. Average book expense $1,000. **Required Forms and Deadlines:** FAFSA, institution's own financial aid form. **Notification of Awards: Types of Aid:** *Need-based scholarships/grants:* Federal Pell, SEOG, state scholarships/grants, private scholarships, the school's own gift aid. *Loans:* Subsidized Stafford, Unsubsidized Stafford, PLUS, Federal Perkins. **Student Employment:** Federal Work-Study Program available. Institutional employment available. Highest amount earned per year from on-campus jobs $900. Off-campus job opportunities are excellent. **Financial Aid Statistics:** 98% freshmen, 99% undergrads receive need-based scholarship or grant aid. 19% freshmen, 14% undergrads receive non-need-based scholarship or grant aid. 79% freshmen, 81% undergrads receive need-based self-help aid. % freshmen, % undergrads receive athletic scholarships. 98% freshmen, 98% undergrads receive any aid. % undergrads borrow to pay for school. Average cumulative indebtedness. **Criteria for awarding institutional aid:** *Non-need-based:* academics, alumni affiliation, art, leadership, music/drama, religious affiliation.

AUGUSTANA COLLEGE (SD)

2001 South Summit Avenue, Sioux Falls, SD 57197
Phone: 605-274-5516 • **Financial Aid Phone:** 605-274-5216
E-mail: admissions@augie.edu • **CEEB Code:** 6015
Fax: 605-274-5518 • **Website:** www.augie.edu • **ACT Code:** 3902

This private school, affiliated with the Lutheran Church, was founded in 1860. It has a 100-acre campus.

RATINGS

Admissions Selectivity Rating: 77   **Fire Safety Rating:** 87   **Green Rating:** 67

STUDENTS AND FACULTY

Enrollment: 1,709. **Student Body:** 60% female, 40% male, 54% out-of-state, 6% international (43 countries represented). Asian 1%, African American 1%, Caucasian 90%, Hispanic 1%, Native American 0%.
Retention and Graduation: 52% freshmen graduate within 4 years. 20% grads go on to further study within 1 year. 20% grads pursue arts and sciences degrees. 7% grads pursue law degrees. 2% grads pursue business degrees. 31% grads pursue medical degrees. **Faculty:** Student/faculty ratio 11:1. 134 full-time faculty, 81% hold PhDs, 6% are members of minority groups, 46% are women. 0% of classes are taught by teaching assistants.

ACADEMICS

Degrees: bachelor's, master's. **Classes:** Most classes have 10–19 students. Most lab/discussion sessions have fewer than 10 students. **Majors with Highest Enrollment:** biology/biological sciences; business/commerce; nursing/registered nurse (rn, asn, bsn, msn). **Special Study Options:** cooperative education program, cross-registration, double major, dual enrollment, exchange student program (domestic), external degree program, honors program, independent study, internships, liberal arts/career combination, study abroad, teacher certification program, Metro-Urban Studies through HECUA. January Abroad program through UMAIE. Washington, D.C. Semesters. Study Austrailia through EAN. Dual Degree Program in Engineering. Service-Learning Spring Breaks trips; Faculty-led Spring Breaks Abroad; Honors Courses in Western Civilization, Chemistry, and Religion. Civitas honors program for students with 27 ACT and 3.5 GPA. **Honors Programs:** Our campus-wide, interdisciplinary Honors program is called Civitas (citizenship). Specific majors also offer departmental honors programs for students willing to accept academic challenges that go well beyond those required for graduation. **Disability Services:** Special programs offered to physically disabled students include note-taking services, reader services, tape recorders, tutors. **Career Services:** Alumni network, alumni services, career/job search classes, career assessment, internships, regional alumni. Career Services highlights include The city of Sioux Falls (151,000), along with Augustana alumni and connections, provides excellent opportunities for internships and research opportunities. It is the best laboratory for our students to apply their knowledge.

FACILITIES

Housing: Coed dorms, special housing for disabled students, apartments for married students, apartments for single students, theme housingHousing is available for students with children. 80% of campus accessible to physically disabled. **Special Academic Facilities/Equipment:** Center for Western Studies, Archeology Lab, Eide/Dalrymple Gallery, Center for Liturgical Art. **Computers:** 25% of classrooms, 25% of dorms, 100% of libraries, 100% of dining areas, 75% of student union, have wireless network access. Students can register for classes online. Administrative functions (other than registration) can be performed online.

CAMPUS LIFE

Environment: City. **Activities:** Choral groups, concert band, dance, drama/theater, jazz band, literary magazine, music ensembles, musical theater, opera, pep band, student government, student newspaper, student-run film society, symphony orchestra, yearbook, Campus Ministries, International Student Organization 92 registered organizations, 13 honor societies, 9 religious organizations. **Athletics (Intercollegiate):** *Men:* baseball, basketball, cross-country, football, golf, tennis, track/field (outdoor), track/field (indoor), wrestling. *Women:* basketball, cheerleading, cross-country, golf, soccer, softball, tennis, track/field (outdoor), track/field (indoor), volleyball. **On-Campus Highlights:** Morrison Commons, The Huddle, Mikkelson Library, Elmen Center, Center for Visual Arts, The Madsen Center, home to our social science programs, is also a popular place for students to gather and study, or use the computer lab. With newly renovated and refurbished lounges, our resident halls also serve as gathering areas for students to converse, watch TV, play ping pong or pool. **Environmental Initiatives:** Examples include: Additional recycle bins placed in all campus buildings; Sodexho Dining Services has decreased food and beverage waste by 50% through redesigning of trays and cups. They have also cut back on paper waste by installing high-definition televisions to post announcements and by substituting post-recycled cups and napkins for students on-the-go. "Green bike program" offers students the chance to use bikes for free transportation on and around campus. Student group, Augie Green, has started an Augustana garden and a program called "trash talkers".

ADMISSIONS

Freshman Academic Profile: Average high school GPA 3.7. 35% in top 10% of high school class, 67% in top 25% of high school class, 91% in top 50% of high school class. 84% from public high schools. ACT middle 50% range 23-28. Minimum web-based TOEFL 79. Minimum paper TOEFL 550. **Basis for Candidate Selection:** *Very important factors considered include:* academic GPA, standardized test scores. *Important factors considered include:* Class rank, application essay, recommendation(s), rigor of secondary school record, extracurricular activities. *Other factors considered include:* interview, volunteer work, work experience. **Freshman Admission Requirements:** High school diploma is required and GED is accepted. **Freshman Admission Statistics:** 1,415 applied, 76% admitted, 38% enrolled. **Transfer Admission Requirements:** High school transcript, college transcript(s), essay or personal statement, minimum college GPA of 2.2 required. Lowest grade transferable C-. **General Admission Information:** Notification on a rolling basis, beginning on or about 10/1. Nonfall registration not accepted. Admission may be deferred for a maximum of 1 year. Credit offered for CEEB Advanced Placement tests.

COSTS AND FINANCIAL AID

Annual tuition $27,380. Room and board $6,626. Required fees $400. Average book expense $1,000. **Required Forms and Deadlines:** FAFSA. **Notification of Awards:** Applicants will be notified of awards on a rolling basis beginning 4/1. **Types of Aid:** *Need-based scholarships/grants:* Federal Pell, SEOG, state scholarships/grants, private scholarships, the school's own gift aid. *Loans:* Direct Subsidized Stafford, Direct Unsubsidized Stafford, Direct PLUS, Subsidized Stafford, Unsubsidized Stafford, PLUS, Federal Perkins, Federal Nursing, college/university loans from institutional funds. **Student Employment:** Federal Work-Study Program available. Institutional employment available. Highest amount earned per year from on-campus jobs $1,794. Off-campus job opportunities are excellent. **Financial Aid Statistics:** 100% freshmen, 100% undergrads receive need-based scholarship or grant aid. 98% freshmen, 98% undergrads receive non-need-based scholarship or grant aid. 72% freshmen, 81% undergrads receive need-based self-help aid. 14% freshmen, 11% undergrads receive athletic scholarships. 100% freshmen, 100% undergrads receive any aid. 79% undergrads borrow to pay for school. Average cumulative indebtedness $34,878. **Criteria for awarding institutional aid:** *Non-need-based:* academics, alumni affiliation, art, athletics, leadership, minority status, music/drama, religious affiliation, state/district residency.

AURORA UNIVERSITY

347 South Gladstone Ave, Aurora, IL 60506
Phone: 630-844-5533 • **Financial Aid Phone:** 630-844-6190
E-mail: admission@aurora.edu • **CEEB Code:** 1027
Fax: 630-844-5535 • **Website:** www.aurora.edu • **ACT Code:** 950

This private school was founded in 1893. It has a 30-acre campus.

RATINGS

Admissions Selectivity Rating: 70   **Fire Safety Rating:** 82   **Green Rating:** 61

STUDENTS AND FACULTY

Enrollment: 2,614. **Student Body:** 65% female, 35% male, 8% out-of-state, 0% international (2 countries represented). Asian 3%, African American 8%, Caucasian 71%, Hispanic 14%, Native American 0%.
Retention and Graduation: 74% freshmen return for sophomore year. 42% freshmen graduate within 4 years. 54% freshmen graduate within 6 years.
Faculty: Student/faculty ratio 15:1. 116 full-time faculty, 86% hold PhDs, 9% are members of minority groups, 49% are women. 0% of classes are taught by teaching assistants.

ACADEMICS

Degrees: bachelor's, master's, post-bachelor's certificate, post-master's certificate. **Classes:** Most classes have 10–19 students. Most lab/discussion sessions have 10–19 students. **Majors with Highest Enrollment:** elementary education and teaching; nursing/registered nurse (rn, asn, bsn, msn); social work.
Special Study Options: Accelerated program, cross-registration, double major, honors program, independent study, internships, liberal arts/career combination, student-designed major, study abroad, teacher certification program.
Honors Programs: Honors Program including honors seminars, honors section of some general education courses and a senior honors project. **Disability Services:** Special programs offered to physically disabled students include

note-taking services, reader services, tape recorders, tutors. **Career Services:** Alumni network, alumni services, career/job search classes, career assessment, internships.

FACILITIES

Housing: Coed dorms. 95% of campus accessible to physically disabled.
Special Academic Facilities/Equipment: Schingoethe Center for Native American Culture Downstairs Dunham Gallery Center For Faith And Action Perry Theatre in the Aurora Foundation Center for Community Education.
Computers: 100% of classrooms, 80% of dorms, 100% of libraries, 100% of dining areas, 100% of student union, 90% of common outdoor areas have wireless network access. Administrative functions (other than registration) can be performed online.

CAMPUS LIFE

Environment: City. **Activities:** Choral groups, drama/theater, literary magazine, pep band, radio station, student government, student newspaper, Campus Ministries, Model UN 49 registered organizations, 2 honor societies, 1 religious organizations. 1 fraternities, 4 sororities. **Athletics (Intercollegiate):** *Men:* baseball, basketball, cross-country, football, golf, soccer, tennis, track/field (outdoor), track/field (indoor). *Women:* basketball, cross-country, golf, soccer, softball, tennis, track/field (outdoor), track/field (indoor), volleyball. **On-Campus Highlights:** The Spartan Spot, Fitness Center, The Learning Center, Computer Labs, Vago Stadium. **Environmental Initiatives:** Campus-wide recycling Use of green chemicals for cleaning. Energy conservation audit for campus-wide lighting.

ADMISSIONS

Freshman Academic Profile: Average high school GPA 3.3. 12% in top 10% of high school class, 38% in top 25% of high school class, 73% in top 50% of high school class. 92% from public high schools. SAT Math middle 50% range 440-510. SAT Critical Reading middle 50% range 450-520. ACT middle 50% range 20-24. Minimum web-based TOEFL 79. Minimum paper TOEFL 550. **Basis for Candidate Selection:** *Very important factors considered include:* Class rank, academic GPA, rigor of secondary school record, standardized test scores, interview. *Important factors considered include:* alumni/ae relation, character/personal qualities, extracurricular activities. *Other factors considered include:* application essay, recommendation(s), first generation, level of applicant's interest, talent/ability, volunteer work, work experience. **Freshman Admission Requirements:** High school diploma is required and GED is accepted. *Academic units required:* 4 English, 3 mathematics, 3 science, 3 social studies, 3 academic electives. *Academic units recommended:* 4 English, 3 mathematics, 3 science, 3 social studies, 3 academic electives. **Freshman Admission Statistics:** 1,872 applied, 73% admitted, 37% enrolled. **Transfer Admission Requirements:** college transcript(s), statement of good standing from prior institution(s). Minimum college GPA of 2.0 required. Lowest grade transferable C. **General Admission Information:** Application Fee $25. Regular application deadline 5/1. Notification on a rolling basis, beginning on or about 9/1. Nonfall registration accepted. Admission may be deferred for a maximum of two years. Credit and/or placement offered for CEEB Advanced Placement tests.

COSTS AND FINANCIAL AID

Annual tuition $19,250. Room and board $9,100. Required fees $200. Average book expense $1,000. **Required Forms and Deadlines:** FAFSA. **Notification of Awards:** Applicants will be notified of awards on a rolling basis beginning 3/1. **Types of Aid:** *Need-based scholarships/grants:* Federal Pell, SEOG, state scholarships/grants, private scholarships, the school's own gift aid. *Loans:* Subsidized Stafford, Unsubsidized Stafford, PLUS, Federal Perkins, college/university loans from institutional funds. **Student Employment:** Federal Work-Study Program available. Institutional employment available. Highest amount earned per year from on-campus jobs $4,960. Off-campus job opportunities are excellent. **Financial Aid Statistics:** 78% freshmen, 81% undergrads receive need-based scholarship or grant aid. 100% freshmen, 94% undergrads receive non-need-based scholarship or grant aid. 84% freshmen, 86% undergrads receive need-based self-help aid. 100% freshmen, 98% undergrads receive any aid. 80% undergrads borrow to pay for school. Average cumulative indebtedness $24,083. **Criteria for awarding institutional aid:** *Non-need-based:* academics, alumni affiliation, art, music/drama, religious affiliation, state/district residency.

AUSTIN COLLEGE

900 North Grand Ave, Suite 6N, Sherman, TX 75090-4400
Phone: 903-813-3000 • **Financial Aid Phone:** 903-813-2900
E-mail: admission@austincollege.edu • **CEEB Code:** 6016
Fax: 903-813-3198 • **Website:** www.austincollege.edu • **ACT Code:** 4058

This private school, affiliated with the Presbyterian Church, was founded in 1849. It has a 70-acre campus.

RATINGS
Admissions Selectivity Rating: 89   **Fire Safety Rating:** 72   **Green Rating:** 83

STUDENTS AND FACULTY
Enrollment: 1,242. **Student Body:** 52% female, 48% male, 9% out-of-state, 2% international (9 countries represented). Asian 13%, African American 4%, Caucasian 64%, Hispanic 12%, Native American 0%.
Retention and Graduation: 73% freshmen graduate within 4 years. 36% grads go on to further study within 1 year. 4% grads pursue law degrees. 1% grads pursue business degrees. 12% grads pursue medical degrees. **Faculty:** Student/faculty ratio 12:1. 94 full-time faculty, 97% hold PhDs, 11% are members of minority groups, 31% are women. 0% of classes are taught by teaching assistants.

ACADEMICS
Degrees: bachelor's, master's. **Classes:** Most classes have 10–19 students. Most lab/discussion sessions have fewer than 10 students. **Majors with Highest Enrollment:** biology/biological sciences; business/commerce; psychology. **Special Study Options:** double major, exchange student program (domestic), honors program, independent study, internships, student-designed major, study abroad, teacher certification program, Phi Beta Kappa. **Combined Degree Programs:** 3-2 Program in Engineeri with UT, Dal and Wash Univ. **Disability Services:** Special programs offered to physically disabled students include tutors. **Career Services:** Alumni network, alumni services, career/job search classes, career assessment, internships.

FACILITIES
Housing: Coed dorms, special housing for disabled students, men's dorms, women's dorms, apartments for single students, Jordan Family Language House. 99% of campus accessible to physically disabled. **Special Academic Facilities/Equipment:** Tissue culture facility, high-performance numerics and graphics computing facility. **Computers:** 30% of classrooms, 100% of dorms, 100% of libraries, 100% of dining areas, 100% of student union, 30% of common outdoor areas have wireless network access. Students can register for classes online. Administrative functions (other than registration) can be performed online.

CAMPUS LIFE
Environment: Town. **Activities:** Choral groups, dance, drama/theater, jazz band, literary magazine, music ensembles, musical theater, pep band, student government, student newspaper, symphony orchestra, yearbook, Campus Ministries, International Student Organization, Model UN 52 registered organizations, 15 honor societies, 6 religious organizations. 6 fraternities, 6 sororities. **Athletics (Intercollegiate):** *Men:* baseball, basketball, football, soccer, swimming, tennis. *Women:* basketball, soccer, softball, swimming, tennis, volleyball. **On-Campus Highlights:** Wright Campus Center, Jordan Family Language House, Verde Dickey Fitness Pavilion, Abell Library, Residence hall facilities, Roo Suites, a suite-style residence facility for upperclass students is the favored residential experience. **Environmental Initiatives:** Board approval of Climate Action Plan to reduce emissions to 0 by 2020. Month-long student dorm energy saving competition Construct a new science building to be LEED silver certified.

ADMISSIONS
Freshman Academic Profile: 3.6. 36% in top 10% of high school class, 70% in top 25% of high school class, 96% in top 50% of high school class. 84% from public high schools. SAT Math middle 50% range 570-670. SAT Critical Reading middle 50% range 560-660. SAT Writing middle 50% range 530-650. ACT middle 50% range 23-29. Minimum paper TOEFL 550. **Basis for Candidate Selection:** *Very important factors considered include:* academic GPA, rigor of secondary school record. *Important factors considered include:* Class rank, application essay, recommendation(s), standardized test scores, character/personal qualities, extracurricular activities, talent/ability. *Other factors considered include:* alumni/ae relation, first generation, geographical residence, interview, racial/ethnic status, religious affiliation/commitment, state residency, volunteer

work, work experience. **Freshman Admission Requirements:** High school diploma is required and GED is accepted. *Academic units required:* 4 English, 3 mathematics, 3 science, (2 science labs), 2 foreign language, 2 social studies, 1 visual/performing arts, 1 academic electives. *Academic units recommended:* 4 English, 3 mathematics, 3 science, (2 science labs), 2 foreign language, 2 social studies, 1 visual/performing arts, 1 academic electives. **Freshman Admission Statistics:** 3,003 applied, 59% admitted, 17% enrolled. **Transfer Admission Requirements:** college transcript(s), essay or personal statement, statement of good standing from prior institution(s). Minimum college GPA of 3.0 required. Lowest grade transferable C. **General Admission Information:** Application Fee $35. Regular application deadline 5/1. Notification on a rolling basis, beginning on or about 12/15. Nonfall registration accepted. Admission may be deferred for a maximum of 1 year. Credit and/or placement offered for CEEB Advanced Placement tests.

COSTS AND FINANCIAL AID
Annual tuition $30,820. Room and board $10,078. Required fees $160. Average book expense $1,200. **Required Forms and Deadlines:** FAFSA. **Notification of Awards:** Applicants will be notified of awards on a rolling basis beginning 3/1. **Types of Aid:** *Need-based scholarships/grants:* Federal Pell, SEOG, state scholarships/grants, private scholarships, the school's own gift aid. *Loans:* Subsidized Stafford, Unsubsidized Stafford, PLUS, Federal Perkins, state loans, college/university loans from institutional funds, Alternative loans through various sources. **Student Employment:** Federal Work-Study Program available. Institutional employment available. Highest amount earned per year from on-campus jobs $1,164. Off-campus job opportunities are good. **Financial Aid Statistics:** 100% freshmen, 100% undergrads receive need-based scholarship or grant aid. 20% freshmen, 18% undergrads receive non-need-based scholarship or grant aid. 100% freshmen, 100% undergrads receive need-based self-help aid. 97% freshmen, 98% undergrads receive any aid. **Criteria for awarding institutional aid:** *Non-need-based:* academics, alumni affiliation, art, leadership, music/drama, religious affiliation, state/district residency.

AUSTIN PEAY STATE UNIVERSITY

P.O. Box 4548, Clarksville, TN 37044
Phone: 931-221-7661
E-mail: admissions@apsu.edu • **CEEB Code:** 1028
Fax: 931-221-6168 • **Website:** www.apsu.edu • **ACT Code:** 3944

This public school was founded in 1927. It has a 210-acre campus.

RATINGS
Admissions Selectivity Rating: 67   **Fire Safety Rating:** 60*   **Green Rating:** 60*

STUDENTS AND FACULTY
Enrollment: 9,475. **Student Body:** 60% female, 40% male, 11% out-of-state, 0% international (13 countries represented). Asian 2%, African American 19%, Caucasian 66%, Hispanic 5%, Native American 1%.
Retention and Graduation: 67% freshmen return for sophomore year. 17% freshmen graduate within 4 years. 37% freshmen graduate within 6 years. **Faculty:** Student/faculty ratio 19:1. 350 full-time faculty, 13% are members of minority groups, 47% are women. 0% of classes are taught by teaching assistants.

ACADEMICS
Degrees: associate, bachelor's, certificate, master's, post-bachelor's certificate, post-master's certificate, terminal associate, transfer associate. **Classes:** Most classes have 20–29 students. Most lab/discussion sessions have 20–29 students. **Special Study Options:** Accelerated program, cooperative education program, distance learning, double major, dual enrollment, English as a Second Language (ESL), honors program, independent study, internships, study abroad, teacher certification program, Servicemembers Opportunity College (SOC) for associate and bachelor's degrees. **Disability Services:** Special programs offered to physically disabled students include note-taking services, reader services, tutors. **Career Services:** career/job search classes, career assessment, internships.

FACILITIES
Housing: Coed dorms, special housing for disabled students, men's dorms, women's dorms, fraternity/sorority housing, apartments for married students, apartments for single students, for faculty/staff. 100% of campus accessible to physically disabled. **Special Academic Facilities/Equipment:** Art museum, biology museum, language lab, demonstration farm, 21st century classroom.

CAMPUS LIFE
Environment: Village. **Activities:** Choral groups, concert band, dance, drama/theater, jazz band, literary magazine, marching band, music ensembles, musical theater, opera, pep band, radio station, student government, student newspaper, student-run film society, symphony orchestra, television station, yearbook, Cam-

pus Ministries, International Student Organization 50 registered organizations, 13 honor societies, 10 religious organizations. 8 fraternities, 6 sororities. **Athletics (Intercollegiate):** *Men:* baseball, basketball, cheerleading, cross-country, football, golf, tennis. *Women:* basketball, cheerleading, cross-country, golf, riflery, soccer, softball, tennis, track/field (outdoor), volleyball. **On-Campus Highlights:** University Center, Sundquist Science Complex, Hand Village, Dunn Center.

ADMISSIONS

Freshman Academic Profile: Average high school GPA 3.2. 13% in top 10% of high school class, 34% in top 25% of high school class, 70% in top 50% of high school class. 95% from public high schools. SAT Math middle 50% range 430-560. SAT Critical Reading middle 50% range 430-540. ACT middle 50% range 19-24. Minimum paper TOEFL 500. **Basis for Candidate Selection:** *Very important factors considered include:* academic GPA, standardized test scores. *Other factors considered include:* rigor of secondary school record. **Freshman Admission Requirements:** High school diploma is required and GED is accepted. *Academic units required:* 4 English, 3 mathematics, 2 science, (1 science labs), 2 foreign language, 1 social studies, 1 history, 1 Visual/Performing Arts. *Academic units recommended:* 4 English, 3 mathematics, 2 science, (1 science labs), 2 foreign language, 1 social studies, 1 history, 1 Visual/Performing Arts. **Freshman Admission Statistics:** 3,453 applied, 86% admitted, 51% enrolled. **Transfer Admission Requirements:** college transcript(s), Lowest grade transferable D. **General Admission Information:** Application Fee $15. Regular application deadline 7/29. Nonfall registration accepted. Admission may be deferred for a maximum of 12 months. Credit offered for CEEB Advanced Placement tests.

COSTS AND FINANCIAL AID

Annual in-state tuition $5,424. Annual out-of-state tuition $19,512. Room and board $7,380. Required fees $1,224. Average book expense $1,550. **Required Forms and Deadlines:** FAFSA. **Notification of Awards:** Applicants will be notified of awards on a rolling basis beginning 5/1. **Types of Aid:** *Need-based scholarships/grants:* Federal Pell, SEOG, state scholarships/grants, private scholarships, the school's own gift aid, Corporate. *Loans:* Subsidized Stafford, Unsubsidized Stafford, PLUS, Federal Perkins. **Student Employment:** Federal Work-Study Program available. Institutional employment available. Off-campus job opportunities are good. **Financial Aid Statistics:** 83% freshmen, 87% undergrads receive need-based scholarship or grant aid. 69% freshmen, 45% undergrads receive non-need-based scholarship or grant aid. 54% freshmen, 64% undergrads receive need-based self-help aid. 1% freshmen, 1% undergrads receive athletic scholarships. 59% undergrads borrow to pay for school. Average cumulative indebtedness $26,181. **Criteria for awarding institutional aid:** *Non-need-based:* academics, alumni affiliation, art, athletics, leadership, music/drama, state/district residency.

AVERETT UNIVERSITY

420 West Main Street, Danville, VA 24541
Phone: 434-791-4996 • **Financial Aid Phone:** 434-791-5890
E-mail: admit@averett.edu • **CEEB Code:** 5017
Fax: 434-797-2784 • **Website:** www.averett.edu • **ACT Code:** 4338

This private school was founded in 1859. It has a 19-acre campus.

RATINGS
Admissions Selectivity Rating: 77   **Fire Safety Rating:** 96   **Green Rating:** 71

STUDENTS AND FACULTY
Enrollment: 886. **Student Body:** 48% female, 52% male, 33% out-of-state, 9% international (15 countries represented). Asian 1%, African American 27%, Caucasian 59%, Hispanic 3%, Native American 1%.
Retention and Graduation: 62% freshmen return for sophomore year. 28% freshmen graduate within 4 years. **Faculty:** Student/faculty ratio 11:1. 61 full-time faculty, 75% hold PhDs, 8% are members of minority groups, 51% are women. 0% of classes are taught by teaching assistants.

ACADEMICS
Degrees: associate, bachelor's, master's, transfer associate. **Classes:** Most classes have 10–19 students. Most lab/discussion sessions have 10–19 students. **Majors with Highest Enrollment:** management science; sport and fitness administration/management; teacher education, multiple levels. **Special Study Options:** Accelerated program, cooperative education program, cross-registration, distance learning, double major, dual enrollment, exchange student program (domestic), honors program, independent study, internships, student-designed major, study abroad, teacher certification program, Also offered: Interdisciplinary studies and Leadership studies. Undergraduates may

take grad level classes. Some online courses available. **Honors Programs:** Averett's Honors Program gives students the opportunity to go a step beyond regular classroom study. Honors students explore, in-depth, selected areas of academics. Participation in the Honors Program demonstrates a commitment to scholarship and will give students an edge in graduate study or in the job market. To earn the honors distinction, approximately 20% of all coursework completed must carry honors credit. The program culminates with a senior honors project. Honors Program students may also participate in the Honors Association and attend conferences, social activities and cultural performances. **Disability Services:** Special programs offered to physically disabled students include note-taking services, reader services, tape recorders, tutors. **Career Services:** Alumni network, alumni services, career/job search classes, career assessment, internships, regional alumni.

FACILITIES
Housing: Coed dorms, men's dorms, women's dorms, apartments for single students. 73% of campus accessible to physically disabled. **Special Academic Facilities/Equipment:** Averett's Flight Center located 4 miles from the main campus at Danville Regional Airport has two runways (one with ILS approach), automated weather system, and UNICOM service. Averett's facility houses aircraft, areas for ground instruction, simulator rooms, technology center. Averett's 100-acre Equestrian Center is a 15-minute drive from the main campus. It houses an indoor ring, 40 stalls with removable partitions, 3 tack rooms, wash room for horses and equipment, breeding area, offices, and a laboratory. The outdoor facilities include a round pen, riding ring, jumping area, pastures, and cross-country trails. **Computers:** 100% of libraries, 100% of dining areas, 100% of student union, have wireless network access. Students can register for classes online. Administrative functions (other than registration) can be performed online.

CAMPUS LIFE
Environment: Town. **Activities:** Choral groups, drama/theater, literary magazine, musical theater, student government, student newspaper, International Student Organization 30 registered organizations, 4 honor societies, 4 religious organizations. 1 fraternities, 1 sororities. **Athletics (Intercollegiate):** *Men:* baseball, basketball, cheerleading, cross-country, equestrian sports, football, golf, soccer, tennis. *Women:* basketball, cheerleading, cross-country, equestrian sports, soccer, softball, tennis, volleyball. **On-Campus Highlights:** Student Center, Grant Athletic Center (North Campus), Equestrian Center, Airport Facilities, Jut's Cafe.

ADMISSIONS
Freshman Academic Profile: Average high school GPA 3.2. 8% in top 10% of high school class, 39% in top 25% of high school class, 73% in top 50% of high school class. % from public high schools. SAT Math middle 50% range 420-530. SAT Critical Reading middle 50% range 450-520. ACT middle 50% range 16-21. Minimum web-based TOEFL 61. Minimum paper TOEFL 500. **Basis for Candidate Selection:** *Very important factors considered include:* academic GPA, rigor of secondary school record. *Important factors considered include:* Class rank, standardized test scores. *Other factors considered include:* application essay, recommendation(s), alumni/ae relation, character/personal qualities, extracurricular activities, interview, level of applicant's interest, talent/ability, volunteer work, work experience. **Freshman Admission Requirements:** High school diploma is required and GED is accepted. *Academic units required:* 4 English, 3 mathematics, 3 science, (3 science labs), 3 social studies, 3 academic electives. *Academic units recommended:* 4 English, 3 mathematics, 3 science, (3 science labs), 3 social studies. **Freshman Admission Statistics:** 2,477 applied, 58% admitted, 18% enrolled. **Transfer Admission Requirements:** college transcript(s), statement of good standing from prior institution(s). Minimum college GPA of 2.0 required. Lowest grade transferable C. **General Admission Information:** Regular application deadline 7/15. Nonfall registration accepted. Admission may be deferred for a maximum of 1 year. Credit and/or placement offered for CEEB Advanced Placement tests.

COSTS AND FINANCIAL AID
Annual tuition $25,950. Room and board $8,370. Required fees. Average book expense $1,000. **Required Forms and Deadlines:** FAFSA, state aid form. **Notification of Awards:** Applicants will be notified of awards on a rolling basis beginning 2/15. **Types of Aid:** *Need-based scholarships/grants:* Federal Pell, SEOG, state scholarships/grants, private scholarships, the school's own gift aid. *Loans:* Subsidized Stafford, Unsubsidized Stafford, PLUS, Federal Perkins, state loans, college/university loans from institutional funds, Private. **Student Employment:** Federal Work-Study Program available. Institutional employment available. Highest amount earned per year from on-campus jobs $2,000. Off-campus job opportunities are fair. **Financial Aid Statistics:** 100% freshmen, 99% undergrads receive need-based scholarship or grant aid. 9% freshmen, 11% undergrads receive non-need-based scholarship or grant aid. 86% freshmen, 82% undergrads receive need-based self-help aid. 99% freshmen, 99% undergrads receive any aid. 73% undergrads borrow to pay for school. Average cumulative indebtedness $31,373. **Criteria for awarding institutional aid:** *Non-need-based:* academics, alumni affiliation, art, leadership, minority status, music/drama, state/district residency.

AVILA UNIVERSITY

11901 Wornall Road, Kansas City, MO 64145-1698
Phone: 816-942-8400
E-mail: admissions@mail.avila.edu • **CEEB Code:** 6109
Fax: 816-942-3362 • **Website:** www.avila.edu • **ACT Code:** 2278

This private school, affiliated with the Roman Catholic Church, was founded in 1916. It has a 48-acre campus.

RATINGS
Admissions Selectivity Rating: 86   **Fire Safety Rating:** 60*   **Green Rating:** 60*

STUDENTS AND FACULTY
Enrollment: 1,096. **Student Body:** 64% female, 36% male, 34% out-of-state, 3% international. Asian 1%, African American 18%, Caucasian 70%, Hispanic 4%, Native American 1%.
Retention and Graduation: 69% freshmen return for sophomore year. 30% freshmen graduate within 4 years. 36% freshmen graduate within 6 years. 40% grads go on to further study within 1 year. 20% grads pursue arts and sciences degrees. 2% grads pursue law degrees. 15% grads pursue business degrees. 3% grads pursue medical degrees. **Faculty:** Student/faculty ratio 12:1. 63 full-time faculty, 71% hold PhDs, 3% are members of minority groups, 63% are women. 0% of classes are taught by teaching assistants.

ACADEMICS
Degrees: bachelor's, certificate, master's. **Classes:** Most classes have fewer than 10 students. **Majors with Highest Enrollment:** business/commerce; nursing, other; psychology. **Special Study Options:** Accelerated program, double major, dual enrollment, English as a Second Language (ESL), independent study, internships, study abroad, teacher certification program.

FACILITIES
Housing: Coed dorms.

CAMPUS LIFE
Environment: Metropolis. **Activities:** Choral groups, drama/theater, literary magazine, student government, student newspaper, television station 12 religious organizations. **Athletics (Intercollegiate):** *Men:* baseball, basketball, football, soccer, volleyball. *Women:* basketball, cheerleading, golf, soccer, softball, volleyball.

ADMISSIONS
Freshman Academic Profile: Average high school GPA 3.2. 17% in top 10% of high school class, 39% in top 25% of high school class, 74% in top 50% of high school class. 92% from public high schools. ACT middle 50% range 18-25. Minimum paper TOEFL 550. **Basis for Candidate Selection:** *Very important factors considered include:* rigor of secondary school record, standardized test scores. *Other factors considered include:* Class rank, application essay, recommendation(s), character/personal qualities, extracurricular activities, interview, talent/ability. **Freshman Admission Requirements:** High school diploma is required and GED is accepted. **Freshman Admission Statistics:** 936 applied, 42% admitted, 38% enrolled. **Transfer Admission Requirements:** college transcript(s), minimum college GPA of 2.0 required. Lowest grade transferable C. **General Admission Information:** Notification on a rolling basis, beginning on or about 9/4. Nonfall registration accepted. Admission may be deferred for a maximum of 12 months. Credit and/or placement offered for CEEB Advanced Placement tests.

COSTS AND FINANCIAL AID
Annual tuition $14,700. Room and board $5,300. Required fees $187. Average book expense $800. **Required Forms and Deadlines:** FAFSA, institution's own financial aid form. **Notification of Awards:** Applicants will be notified of awards on a rolling basis beginning 2/15. **Types of Aid:** *Need-based scholarships/grants:* Federal Pell, SEOG, state scholarships/grants. *Loans:* Subsidized Stafford, Unsubsidized Stafford, PLUS, Federal Perkins. **Student Employment:** Federal Work-Study Program available. Institutional employment available. Highest amount earned per year from on-campus jobs $1,500. **Financial Aid Statistics:** 66% freshmen, 70% undergrads receive need-based scholarship or grant aid. 100% freshmen, 80% undergrads receive non-need-based scholarship or grant aid. 100% freshmen, 90% undergrads receive need-based self-help aid. 100% freshmen, 70% undergrads receive athletic scholarships. 75% undergrads borrow to pay for school. Average cumulative indebtedness $20,000. **Criteria for awarding institutional aid:** *Non-need-based:* academics, alumni affiliation, art, athletics, music/drama, religious affiliation, state/district residency.

AZUSA PACIFIC UNIVERSITY

901 East Alosta Avenue, Azusa, CA 91702-7000
Phone: 626-812-3016 • **Financial Aid Phone:** 626-812-3009
E-mail: admissions@apu.edu • **CEEB Code:** 4596
Fax: 626-812-3096 • **Website:** www.apu.edu

This private school, affiliated with the Christian (Nondenominational) Church, was founded in 1899. It has a 103-acre campus.

RATINGS
Admissions Selectivity Rating: 83   **Fire Safety Rating:** 61   **Green Rating:** 60*

STUDENTS AND FACULTY
Enrollment: 4,874. **Student Body:** 64% female, 36% male, 19% out-of-state, 2% international (41 countries represented). Asian 8%, African American 5%, Caucasian 60%, Hispanic 15%, Native American 1%.
Retention and Graduation: 82% freshmen return for sophomore year. 55% freshmen graduate within 4 years. 67% freshmen graduate within 6 years. **Faculty:** Student/faculty ratio 12:1. 339 full-time faculty, 74% hold PhDs, 22% are members of minority groups, 47% are women. 0% of classes are taught by teaching assistants.

ACADEMICS
Degrees: bachelor's, master's. **Classes:** Most classes have 10–19 students. Most lab/discussion sessions have 10–19 students. **Majors with Highest Enrollment:** business, management, marketing, and related support services, other; nursing, other; psychology. **Special Study Options:** Accelerated program, cooperative education program, distance learning, double major, English as a Second Language (ESL), exchange student program (domestic), honors program, independent study, internships, study abroad, teacher certification program. **Combined Degree Programs:** BA/MA. **Career Services:** career/job search classes, career assessment, internships.

FACILITIES
Housing: Coed dorms, men's dorms, women's dorms, apartments for single students. 100% of campus accessible to physically disabled. **Special Academic Facilities/Equipment:** Electron microscope. **Computers:** 100% of classrooms, 100% of dorms, 100% of libraries, 100% of dining areas, 100% of student union, 100% of common outdoor areas have wireless network access. Students can register for classes online. Administrative functions (other than registration) can be performed online.

CAMPUS LIFE
Environment: Town. **Activities:** Choral groups, concert band, drama/theater, jazz band, marching band, music ensembles, musical theater, opera, pep band, radio station, student government, student newspaper, symphony orchestra, television station, yearbook 30 registered organizations, 7 honor societies. **Athletics (Intercollegiate):** *Men:* baseball, basketball, cross-country, football, soccer, tennis, track/field (outdoor), volleyball. *Women:* basketball, cheerleading, cross-country, diving, soccer, softball, swimming, tennis, track/field (outdoor), volleyball, water polo. **On-Campus Highlights:** Coffee Shops, Cougars' Den (Dining Facility), An Athletic Facility, Darling Library, Cougar Dome.

ADMISSIONS
Freshman Academic Profile: Average high school GPA 3.6. 32% in top 10% of high school class, 63% in top 25% of high school class, 86% in top 50% of high school class. SAT Math middle 50% range 480-600. SAT Critical Reading middle 50% range 490-590. SAT Writing middle 50% range 970-1180. ACT middle 50% range 21-27. Minimum paper TOEFL 500. **Basis for Candidate Selection:** *Very important factors considered include:* Class rank, application essay, academic GPA, recommendation(s), standardized test scores. *Important factors considered include:* character/personal qualities, state residency. *Other factors considered include:* rigor of secondary school record, alumni/ae relation, extracurricular activities, first generation, interview, level of applicant's interest, racial/ethnic status, talent/ability, volunteer work, work experience. **Freshman Admission Requirements:** High school diploma is required and GED is accepted. **Freshman Admission Statistics:** 5,262 applied, 59% admitted, 33% enrolled. **Transfer Admission Requirements:** college transcript(s), essay or personal statement, statement of good standing from prior institution(s). Minimum college GPA of 2.2 required. Lowest grade transferable C. **General Admission Information:** Application Fee $45. Regular application deadline 6/1. Regular notification 4/1. Nonfall registration accepted. Credit offered for CEEB Advanced Placement tests.

COSTS AND FINANCIAL AID
Annual tuition $28,000. Room and board $8,206. Required fees $800. Average book expense $1,620. **Required Forms and Deadlines:** FAFSA, institution's own financial aid form. **Notification of Awards:** Applicants will be notified of awards on a rolling basis beginning 3/1. **Types of Aid:** *Need-based scholarships/grants:* Federal Pell, SEOG, state scholarships/grants, private scholarships,

the school's own gift aid, Federal Nursing Scholarships. *Loans:* Subsidized Stafford, Unsubsidized Stafford, PLUS, Federal Perkins, Federal Nursing. **Student Employment:** Federal Work-Study Program available. Institutional employment available. Highest amount earned per year from on-campus jobs $8,000. Off-campus job opportunities are good. **Financial Aid Statistics:** 99% freshmen, 97% undergrads receive need-based scholarship or grant aid. 87% freshmen, 91% undergrads receive non-need-based scholarship or grant aid. 77% freshmen, 83% undergrads receive need-based self-help aid. 2% freshmen, 2% undergrads receive athletic scholarships. 90% undergrads receive any aid. % undergrads borrow to pay for school. Average cumulative indebtedness. **Criteria for awarding institutional aid:** *Non-need-based:* academics, athletics, leadership, minority status, music/drama, religious affiliation.

BABSON COLLEGE

Lunder Hall, Babson Park, MA 2457
Phone: 781-239-5522 • **Financial Aid Phone:** 781-239-4219
E-mail: ugradadmission@babson.edu • **CEEB Code:** 3075
Fax: 781-239-4006 • **Website:** www.babson.edu • **ACT Code:** 1780

This private school was founded in 1919. It has a 370-acre campus.

RATINGS
Admissions Selectivity Rating: 95   **Fire Safety Rating:** 79   **Green Rating:** 91

STUDENTS AND FACULTY
Enrollment: 513. **Student Body:** 47% female, 53% male. 27% international (69 countries represented). Asian 49%, African American 17%, Caucasian 143%, Hispanic 38%, Native American 1%.
Retention and Graduation: 94% freshmen return for sophomore year. 85% freshmen graduate within 4 years. **Faculty:** Student/faculty ratio 15:1. 163 full-time faculty, 87% hold PhDs, 16% are members of minority groups, 35% are women. 0% of classes are taught by teaching assistants.

ACADEMICS
Degrees: bachelor's, master's, post-master's certificate. **Classes:** Most classes have 30–39 students. **Majors with Highest Enrollment:** accounting; entrepreneurial and small business operations, other; finance. **Special Study Options:** cross-registration, exchange student program (domestic), honors program, independent study, internships, liberal arts/career combination, study abroad. We offer 26 concentrations which provide groupings of courses that help students choose a coherent set of courses for academic and external recognition. **Honors Programs:** The Honors Program consists of three components in which participants add to their academic and cocurricular development. These include honors courses, an honors project and an international experience. **Combined Degree Programs:** BS/MS In Accounting. **Disability Services:** Special programs offered to physically disabled students include note-taking services, reader services, tape recorders. **Career Services:** Alumni network, alumni services, career/job search classes, career assessment, internships, regional alumni. Career Services highlights include Coaching for Leadership and Teamwork.

FACILITIES
Housing: Coed dorms, special housing for disabled students, fraternity/sorority housing, substance free, special interest housing. 50% of campus accessible to physically disabled. **Special Academic Facilities/Equipment:** The Babson World Globe, Roger Babson Museum, Isaac Newton Museum, Arthur M. Blank Center for Entrepreneurship **Computers:** 100% of classrooms, 100% of dorms, 100% of libraries, 100% of dining areas, 100% of student union, 100% of common outdoor areas have wireless network access. Students can register for classes online. Administrative functions (other than registration) can be performed online. Undergraduates are required to own a computer.

CAMPUS LIFE
Environment: Village. **Activities:** dance, drama/theater, jazz band, literary magazine, musical theater, radio station, student government, student newspaper, yearbook 78 registered organizations, 3 religious organizations. 4 fraternities, 3 sororities. **Athletics (Intercollegiate):** *Men:* baseball, basketball, cross-country, diving, golf, ice hockey, lacrosse, skiing (downhill/alpine), soccer, swimming, tennis, track/field (outdoor), track/field (indoor). *Women:* basketball, cross-country, diving, field hockey, lacrosse, skiing (downhill/alpine), soccer, softball, swimming, tennis, track/field (outdoor), track/field (indoor), volleyball.

On-Campus Highlights: Sorenson Arts Center, Blank Center for Entrepreneurship, Glavin Family Chapel, Reynolds Student Center, Webster Athletic Center. **Environmental Initiatives:** Babson Joined the American College & University Presidents' Climate Commitment and wrote a Sustainability and Climate Action Plan. In 2010, Babson engaged GreenerU, Inc.—an innovative, higher education-focused energy and sustainability services company—to assist in establishing and operating our first dedicated Sustainability Office. program. This Sustainability Certificate program is a collaborate effort between Babson College (business) Olin College (engineering) and Wellesley College (liberal arts).

ADMISSIONS
Freshman Academic Profile: Average high school GPA 3.6. 53% in top 10% of high school class, 84% in top 25% of high school class, 98% in top 50% of high school class. 50% from public high schools. SAT Math middle 50% range 610-700. SAT Critical Reading middle 50% range 550-640. SAT Writing middle 50% range 580-670. ACT middle 50% range 26-29. Minimum web-based TOEFL 100. Minimum paper TOEFL 600. **Basis for Candidate Selection:** *Very important factors considered include:* application essay, academic GPA, recommendation(s), rigor of secondary school record, standardized test scores, character/personal qualities. *Important factors considered include:* Class rank, extracurricular activities. *Other factors considered include:* alumni/ae relation, first generation, geographical residence, interview, level of applicant's interest, racial/ethnic status, state residency, talent/ability, volunteer work, work experience. **Freshman Admission Requirements:** High school diploma is required and GED is accepted. **Freshman Admission Statistics:** 5,512 applied, 30% admitted, 29% enrolled. **Transfer Admission Requirements:** High school transcript, college transcript(s), essay or personal statement, statement of good standing from prior institution(s). Lowest grade transferable C. **General Admission Information:** Application Fee $65. Early decision application deadline 11/1. Regular application deadline 1/15. Regular notification 4/1. Nonfall registration not accepted. Admission may be deferred for a maximum of 1 year. Credit and/or placement offered for CEEB Advanced Placement tests.

COSTS AND FINANCIAL AID
Annual tuition $43,520. Room and board $14,142. Average book expense $1,020. **Required Forms and Deadlines:** FAFSA, CSS/Financial Aid PROFILE, noncustodial PROFILE, business/farm supplement. Federal tax returns, W-2s, and Verification Worksheet. **Notification of Awards:** Applicants will be notified of awards on or about 4/1. **Types of Aid:** *Need-based scholarships/grants:* Federal Pell, SEOG, state scholarships/grants, the school's own gift aid. *Loans:* Subsidized Stafford, Unsubsidized Stafford, PLUS, Federal Perkins, state loans. **Student Employment:** Federal Work-Study Program available. Institutional employment available. Highest amount earned per year from on-campus jobs $5,400. Off-campus job opportunities are good. **Financial Aid Statistics:** 92% freshmen, 95% undergrads receive need-based scholarship or grant aid. 4% freshmen, 10% undergrads receive non-need-based scholarship or grant aid. 92% freshmen, 85% undergrads receive need-based self-help aid. 48% freshmen, 51% undergrads receive any aid. 48% undergrads borrow to pay for school. Average cumulative indebtedness $31,918. **Criteria for awarding institutional aid:** *Non-need-based:* academics, leadership.

See page 1012.

BAKER UNIVERSITY

P.O. Box 65, Baldwin City, KS 66006
Phone: 785-594-8307 • **Financial Aid Phone:** 785-594-4595
E-mail: admissions@bakeru.edu • **CEEB Code:** 6031
Fax: 785-594-8372 • **Website:** www.bakerU.edu • **ACT Code:** 1386

This private school, affiliated with the Methodist Church, was founded in 1858. It has a 36-acre campus.

RATINGS
Admissions Selectivity Rating: 67   **Fire Safety Rating:** 61   **Green Rating:** 60*

STUDENTS AND FACULTY
Enrollment: 824. **Student Body:** 45% female, 55% male, 25% out-of-state, 2% international (8 countries represented). Asian 1%, African American 10%, Caucasian 74%, Hispanic 4%, Native American 3%.
Retention and Graduation: 75% freshmen return for sophomore year. 39% freshmen graduate within 4 years. 55% freshmen graduate within 6 years. 30% grads go on to further study within 1 year. 17% grads pursue arts and sciences degrees. 2% grads pursue law degrees. 4% grads pursue business degrees. 1% grads pursue medical degrees. **Faculty:** Student/faculty ratio 12:1. 57 full-time faculty, 79% hold PhDs, 4% are members of minority groups, 47% are women. 0% of classes are taught by teaching assistants.

ACADEMICS

Degrees: bachelor's. **Classes:** Most classes have 10–19 students. Most lab/discussion sessions have fewer than 10 students. **Majors with Highest Enrollment:** biology/biological sciences; business/commerce; elementary education and teaching. **Special Study Options:** Accelerated program, double major, honors program, independent study, internships, liberal arts/career combination, student-designed major, study abroad, teacher certification program, Students can transfer to the School of Nursing (located in a clinical setting in Topeka, KS) after completing their first two years of general education and pre-nursing course work. Baker also offers an Interterm program (3 weeks in January), during which students can take classes on campus, pursue travel courses, or work in internships. **Honors Programs:** Honors Program, Bronston Fellows Program **Combined Degree Programs:** 3-2 forestry program with Duke U. **Disability Services:** Special programs offered to physically disabled students include note-taking services, reader services, tape recorders, tutors. **Career Services:** alumni services, career/job search classes, career assessment, internships Career Services highlights include Professional project-based practicum experiences sponsored by local businesses and organizations (facilitated by faculty within the Business and Economics Department).

FACILITIES

Housing: Coed dorms, special housing for disabled students, men's dorms, women's dorms, fraternity/sorority housing, apartments for single students. 85% of campus accessible to physically disabled. **Special Academic Facilities/Equipment:** Old Castle Museum, Quayle Bible Collection **Computers:** 95% of classrooms, 100% of dorms, 100% of libraries, 100% of dining areas, 100% of student union, have wireless network access. Students can register for classes online. Administrative functions (other than registration) can be performed online.

CAMPUS LIFE

Environment: Rural. **Activities:** Choral groups, concert band, dance, drama/theater, jazz band, literary magazine, music ensembles, pep band, radio station, student government, student newspaper, television station, yearbook, International Student Organization 60 registered organizations, 18 honor societies, 2 religious organizations. 5 fraternities, 5 sororities. **Athletics (Intercollegiate):** *Men:* baseball, basketball, cheerleading, cross-country, football, golf, soccer, tennis, track/field (outdoor), track/field (indoor), wrestling. *Women:* basketball, bowling, cheerleading, cross-country, golf, soccer, softball, tennis, track/field (outdoor), track/field (indoor), volleyball. **On-Campus Highlights:** Library, Wildcat Cafe, Osborne Chapel, Fitness Center, Living Learning Center.

ADMISSIONS

Freshman Academic Profile: Average high school GPA 3.5. 20% in top 10% of high school class, 40% in top 25% of high school class, 76% in top 50% of high school class. 95% from public high schools. SAT Math middle 50% range 420-570. SAT Critical Reading middle 50% range 420-525. ACT middle 50% range 21-26. Minimum web-based TOEFL 69. Minimum paper TOEFL 525. **Basis for Candidate Selection:** *Very important factors considered include:* academic GPA, recommendation(s), rigor of secondary school record, standardized test scores, level of applicant's interest. *Important factors considered include:* Class rank. *Other factors considered include:* application essay, alumni/ae relation, character/personal qualities, extracurricular activities, geographical residence, interview, talent/ability, volunteer work, work experience. **Freshman Admission Requirements:** High school diploma is required and GED is accepted. **Freshman Admission Statistics:** 775 applied, 85% admitted, 31% enrolled. **Transfer Admission Requirements:** High school transcript, college transcript(s), standardized test scores, minimum college GPA of 2.3 required. Lowest grade transferable C. **General Admission Information:** Nonfall registration accepted. Admission may be deferred for a maximum of 1 year. Credit and/or placement offered for CEEB Advanced Placement tests.

COSTS AND FINANCIAL AID

Annual tuition $24,470. Room and board $7,660. Average book expense $1,200. **Required Forms and Deadlines:** FAFSA, institution's own financial aid form. **Notification of Awards:** Applicants will be notified of awards on a rolling basis beginning 3/1. **Types of Aid:** *Need-based scholarships/grants:* Federal Pell, SEOG, state scholarships/grants, private scholarships, the school's own gift aid. *Loans:* Subsidized Stafford, Unsubsidized Stafford, PLUS, Federal Perkins. **Student Employment:** Federal Work-Study Program available. Institutional employment available. Off-campus job opportunities are good. **Financial Aid Statistics:** 57% freshmen, 57% undergrads receive need-based scholarship or grant aid. 97% freshmen, 97% undergrads receive non-need-based scholarship or grant aid. 78% freshmen, 74% undergrads receive need-based self-help aid. 10% freshmen, 8% undergrads receive athletic scholarships. **Criteria for awarding institutional aid:** *Non-need-based:* academics, alumni affiliation, art, athletics, leadership, music/drama, religious affiliation.

BALDWIN WALLACE UNIVERSITY

275 Eastland Rd, Berea, OH 44017
Phone: 440-826-2222 • **Financial Aid Phone:** 440-826-2108
E-mail: admission@bw.edu • **CEEB Code:** 1050
Fax: 440-826-3830 • **Website:** www.bw.edu • **ACT Code:** 3236

This private school was founded in 1845. It has a 100-acre campus.

RATINGS

Admissions Selectivity Rating: 77   **Fire Safety Rating:** 66   **Green Rating:** 80

STUDENTS AND FACULTY

Enrollment: 3,428. **Student Body:** 55% female, 45% male, 15% out-of-state, 1% international (25 countries represented). Asian 1%, African American 8%, Caucasian 82%, Hispanic 4%, Native American 0%.
Retention and Graduation: 82% freshmen return for sophomore year. 50% freshmen graduate within 4 years. 68% freshmen graduate within 6 years. 12% grads go on to further study within 1 year. 7% grads pursue arts and sciences degrees. 1% grads pursue law degrees. 2% grads pursue business degrees. 1% grads pursue medical degrees. **Faculty:** Student/faculty ratio 14:1. 169 full-time faculty, 78% hold PhDs, 8% are members of minority groups, 42% are women. 0% of classes are taught by teaching assistants.

ACADEMICS

Degrees: bachelor's, certificate, master's. **Classes:** Most classes have 10–19 students. Most lab/discussion sessions have 20–29 students. **Majors with Highest Enrollment:** accounting; business administration and management; psychology. **Special Study Options:** Accelerated program, cross-registration, distance learning, double major, dual enrollment, English as a Second Language (ESL), exchange student program (domestic), honors program, independent study, internships, liberal arts/career combination, student-designed major, study abroad, teacher certification program, weekend college, 3-2 in Engineering with Case Western Reserve University and Columbia University; 3-2 in Social Work with Case Western Reserve University; 3/2 Accounting MBA, 3/2 Human Resources MBA and 3/2 Computer Science/Info. Systems MBA Programs. **Honors Programs:** Liberal Arts Program. **Combined Degree Programs:** BA/MBA Acct,BA/MBA HR, BS-CompSci/MBA,BS-CompInfoSyst/MBA,BA/MSSASocialWork. **Disability Services:** Special programs offered to physically disabled students include note-taking services, reader services, tutors. **Career Services:** Alumni network, alumni services, career assessment, internships Career Services highlights include It is hard to pick just one of the programs, because part of their strength is the combination of them all: On Campus Recruiting Services, Employer Meet and Greets, Career and Internship Expo (annual job fair) and Career Connections (alumni network and mentor program), Fall Career Week and Spring Career Week that coincide with job fairs.

FACILITIES

Housing: Coed dorms, special housing for disabled students, special housing for international students, women's dorms, fraternity/sorority housing, apartments for single students, theme housing, Carmel Living Learning Center (Education-based), Student-Directed Learning Communities (Sustainability, Art, Women's Christian, Men's Christian), Themed Housing (STEM, Language, Conservatory, SPROUT-for single mothers and children). 80% of campus accessible to physically disabled. **Special Academic Facilities/Equipment:** Art gallery, electron microscope, observatory. **Computers:** 100% of classrooms, 100% of dorms, 100% of libraries, 100% of dining areas, 100% of student union, 100% of common outdoor areas have wireless network access. Students can register for classes online. Administrative functions (other than registration) can be performed online.

CAMPUS LIFE

Environment: Village. **Activities:** Choral groups, concert band, dance, drama/theater, jazz band, literary magazine, marching band, music ensembles, musical theater, opera, pep band, radio station, student government, student newspaper, student-run film society, symphony orchestra, television station, yearbook, Campus Ministries, International Student Organization, Model UN 136 registered organizations, 25 honor societies, 7 religious organizations. 5 fraternities, 5 sororities. **Athletics (Intercollegiate):** *Men:* baseball, basketball, cross-country, diving, football, golf, soccer, swimming, tennis, track/field (outdoor), track/field (indoor), wrestling. *Women:* basketball, cross-country, diving, golf, soccer, softball, swimming, tennis, track/field (outdoor), track/field (indoor), volleyball. **On-Campus Highlights:** CyberCafe, The Hive, The S.A.C. (Student Activities Center), Conservatory/Theatre performances, Recreation Center, The new Lou Higgins Recreation Center features a Fitness Center, Weight Room, Dance Studio, multipurpose basketball, volleyball, badminton courts and racquetball courts, swimming pool, indoor batting cage and second-floor computer lab. The Student Activities Center provides a club-like atmosphere for entertainment programming on campus. It features a pulsating sound and dance light system,

56

The Princeton Review's Complete Book of Colleges

a 10' x 12' video screen, neon lights and snack bar. Comedians, live bands, disc jockeys, multi-media capabilities and special snack foods attracting students to all-campus events. **Environmental Initiatives:** Commitment to geo-thermal energy with all new buildings and major renovations Creation of Ohio's first undergraduate major in Sustainability and MBA in Sustainability Considerable investments in electricity energy conservation and renewable energy sources

ADMISSIONS

Freshman Academic Profile: Average high school GPA 3.5. 28% in top 10% of high school class, 53% in top 25% of high school class, 82% in top 50% of high school class. 81% from public high schools. SAT Math middle 50% range 490-593. SAT Critical Reading middle 50% range 480-610. ACT middle 50% range 20-27. Minimum web-based TOEFL 79. Minimum paper TOEFL 550. **Basis for Candidate Selection:** *Very important factors considered include:* academic GPA, rigor of secondary school record. *Important factors considered include:* Class rank, application essay, character/personal qualities, extracurricular activities, talent/ability. *Other factors considered include:* recommendation(s), standardized test scores, alumni/ae relation, first generation, geographical residence, interview, level of applicant's interest, racial/ethnic status, state residency, volunteer work, work experience. **Freshman Admission Requirements:** High school diploma is required and GED is accepted. *Academic units required:* 4 English, 3 mathematics, 3 science, (2 science labs), 1 foreign language, 2 social studies, 1 history. *Academic units recommended:* 4 English, 3 mathematics, 3 science, (2 science labs), 1 foreign language, 2 social studies, 1 history. **Freshman Admission Statistics:** 3,573 applied, 70% admitted, 28% enrolled. **Transfer Admission Requirements:** High school transcript, college transcript(s), statement of good standing from prior institution(s). Minimum college GPA of 2.5 required. Lowest grade transferable C. **General Admission Information:** Application Fee $25. Notification on a rolling basis, beginning on or about 11/1. Nonfall registration accepted. Admission may be deferred for a maximum of 1 year. Credit and/or placement offered for CEEB Advanced Placement tests.

COSTS AND FINANCIAL AID

Annual tuition $27,060. Room and board $7,520. Average book expense $1,360. **Required Forms and Deadlines:** FAFSA. **Notification of Awards:** Applicants will be notified of awards on a rolling basis beginning 2/14. **Types of Aid:** *Need-based scholarships/grants:* Federal Pell, SEOG, state scholarships/grants, private scholarships, the school's own gift aid. *Loans:* Subsidized Stafford, Unsubsidized Stafford, PLUS, Federal Perkins, college/university loans from institutional funds. **Student Employment:** Federal Work-Study Program available. Institutional employment available. Highest amount earned per year from on-campus jobs $2,400. Off-campus job opportunities are excellent. **Financial Aid Statistics:** 100% freshmen, 100% undergrads receive need-based scholarship or grant aid. 13% freshmen, 21% undergrads receive non-need-based scholarship or grant aid. 91% freshmen, 87% undergrads receive need-based self-help aid. 100% freshmen, 97% undergrads receive any aid. 83% undergrads borrow to pay for school. Average cumulative indebtedness $31,022. **Criteria for awarding institutional aid:** *Non-need-based:* academics, alumni affiliation, minority status, music/drama, religious affiliation, state/district residency.

BALL STATE UNIVERSITY

Office of Admissions, Muncie, IN 47306
Phone: 765-285-8300 • **Financial Aid Phone:** 765-285-5000
E-mail: askus@bsu.edu • **CEEB Code:** 1051
Fax: 765-285-1632 • **Website:** www.bsu.edu • **ACT Code:** 1176

This public school was founded in 1918. It has a 1035-acre campus.

RATINGS
Admissions Selectivity Rating: 80 **Fire Safety Rating:** 79 **Green Rating:** 98

STUDENTS AND FACULTY
Enrollment: 16,323. **Student Body:** 57% female, 43% male, 10% out-of-state, 2% international (44 countries represented). Asian 1%, African American 6%, Caucasian 85%, Hispanic 3%, Native American 0%. **Retention and Graduation:** 77% freshmen return for sophomore year. **Faculty:** Student/faculty ratio 16:1. 959 full-time faculty, 74% hold PhDs, 13% are members of minority groups, 45% are women.

ACADEMICS
Degrees: associate, bachelor's, doctoral, master's, post-bachelor's certificate, post-master's certificate. **Classes:** Most classes have 20–29 students. **Majors with Highest Enrollment:** elementary education and teaching; family and consumer sciences/human sciences; radio and television. **Special Study Options:** Accelerated program, distance learning, double major, dual enrollment,

English as a Second Language (ESL), exchange student program (domestic), external degree program, honors program, independent study, internships, student-designed major, study abroad, teacher certification program. **Honors Programs:** BSU offers an Honors College which has its own curriculum, undergraduate research fellowships and study abroad programs. **Disability Services:** Special programs offered to physically disabled students include note-taking services, reader services, tape recorders, tutors. **Career Services:** alumni services, career assessment, internships, regional alumni. Career Services highlights include The professional skills development programs and services provided by the career center offer the highest level of staff expertise and training methods. Student use of these services has grown an average of 86% over the past three years. Students and alumni use the online resume review program, professional etiquette dinners, and individual appointments for job coaching including video-taped practice interviews to prepare for internships and job searches.

FACILITIES
Housing: Coed dorms, special housing for disabled students, men's dorms, special housing for international students, women's dorms, fraternity/sorority housing, apartments for married students, apartments for single students, wellness housing, theme housing, Living/Learning Communities. 95% of campus accessible to physically disabled. **Special Academic Facilities/Equipment:** Art gallery, museum, on-campus school (K-12), learning center, weather station, physical therapy lab, human performance lab, planetarium/observatory, wildlife and nature preserve. **Computers:** 100% of classrooms, 100% of dorms, 100% of libraries, 100% of dining areas, 100% of student union, 100% of common outdoor areas have wireless network access. Students can register for classes online. Administrative functions (other than registration) can be performed online. Undergraduates are required to own a computer.

CAMPUS LIFE
Environment: City. **Activities:** Choral groups, concert band, dance, drama/theater, jazz band, literary magazine, marching band, music ensembles, musical theater, opera, pep band, radio station, student government, student newspaper, student-run film society, symphony orchestra, television station, Campus Ministries 355 registered organizations, 31 honor societies, 32 religious organizations. 15 fraternities, 12 sororities. **Athletics (Intercollegiate):** *Men:* baseball, basketball, cheerleading, cross-country, diving, football, golf, swimming, tennis, volleyball. *Women:* basketball, cheerleading, cross-country, diving, field hockey, golf, gymnastics, soccer, softball, swimming, tennis, track/field (outdoor), volleyball. **On-Campus Highlights:** Museum of Art, Worthen Arena, Emens Auditorium, Atrium, Letterman Communication & Media Bldg, Emens Auditorium, Music Building/Sursa Hall, Bracken Library. **Environmental Initiatives:** Installing a district-scale ground-source heating and cooling system to serve all 45 campus buildings and eliminate four coal-fired boilers and reduce our GHG emissions by nearly 50%. Creating in 2001 a Council on the environment which represents every constituency group on campus and in the surrounding community which in turn has shepherded creation of unit-level sustainability plans for 102 administrative units on campus. Requiring that all new construction be LEED Silver Certified at minimum and that all renovation and remodeling seek the same performance levels.

ADMISSIONS
Freshman Academic Profile: Average high school GPA 3.4. 18% in top 10% of high school class, 48% in top 25% of high school class, 88% in top 50% of high school class. 93% from public high schools. SAT Math middle 50% range 480-580. SAT Critical Reading middle 50% range 480-580. SAT Writing middle 50% range 470-560. ACT middle 50% range 19-23. Minimum web-based TOEFL 79. Minimum paper TOEFL 550. **Basis for Candidate Selection:** *Very important factors considered include:* academic GPA, rigor of secondary school record, standardized test scores. *Other factors considered include:* Class rank, application essay, recommendation(s), character/personal qualities, extracurricular activities, talent/ability, volunteer work, work experience. **Freshman Admission Requirements:** High school diploma is required and GED is accepted. *Academic units required:* 4 English, 3 mathematics, 3 science, (2 science labs), 3 social studies. *Academic units recommended:* 4 English, 3 mathematics, 3 science, (2 science labs), 3 social studies. **Freshman Admission Statistics:** 16,896 applied, 61% admitted, 34% enrolled. **Transfer Admission Requirements:** college transcript(s), minimum college GPA of 2.0 required. Lowest grade transferable C. **General Admission Information:** Application Fee $25. Regular application deadline 8/15. Nonfall registration accepted. Admission may be deferred for a maximum of one year. Credit and/or placement offered for CEEB Advanced Placement tests.

COSTS AND FINANCIAL AID
Annual in-state tuition $8,318. Annual out-of-state tuition $22,988. Room and board $8,870. Required fees $662. Average book expense $1,020. **Required Forms and Deadlines:** FAFSA. **Notification of Awards:** Applicants will be notified of awards on a rolling basis beginning 4/1. **Types of Aid:** *Need-based scholarships/grants:* Federal Pell, SEOG, state scholarships/grants, private scholarships, the school's own gift aid. *Loans:* Direct Subsidized Stafford, Direct Unsubsidized Stafford, Direct PLUS, Federal Perkins. **Student Employment:**

Federal Work-Study Program available. Institutional employment available. Off-campus job opportunities are good. **Financial Aid Statistics:** 63% freshmen, 59% undergrads receive need-based scholarship or grant aid. 40% freshmen, 35% undergrads receive non-need-based scholarship or grant aid. 94% freshmen, 93% undergrads receive need-based self-help aid. 2% freshmen, 2% undergrads receive athletic scholarships. 82% freshmen, 78% undergrads receive any aid. 72% undergrads borrow to pay for school. Average cumulative indebtedness $27,373. **Criteria for awarding institutional aid:** *Non-need-based:* academics, athletics, leadership, minority status, music/drama, state/district residency.

BALTIMORE HEBREW UNIVERSITY

5800 Park Heights, Baltimore, MD 21215
Phone: 410-578-6967
E-mail: bhu@bhu.edu • **CEEB Code:** 5035
Fax: 410-578-6940 • **Website:** www.bhu.edu • **ACT Code:** 20093

This private school was founded in 1919.

RATINGS
Admissions Selectivity Rating: 60*   **Fire Safety Rating:** 60*   **Green Rating:** 60*

STUDENTS AND FACULTY
Enrollment: 75. **Student Body:** 63% female, 37% male, (4 countries represented).
Retention and Graduation: 67% freshmen return for sophomore year. 33% freshmen graduate within 4 years. 34% freshmen graduate within 6 years. **Faculty:** Student/faculty ratio 8:1.

ACADEMICS
Degrees: associate, bachelor's, certificate, master's. **Special Study Options:** cross-registration, double major, dual enrollment, independent study, internships, study abroad, teacher certification program, English language skills program for non-native speakers. **Disability Services:** Special programs offered to physically disabled students include tape recorders.

FACILITIES
Housing: 65% of campus accessible to physically disabled. **Special Academic Facilities/Equipment:** Joseph Meyerhoff Library Cohen Auditorium.

CAMPUS LIFE
Activities: 2 registered organizations.

ADMISSIONS
Freshman Academic Profile: Minimum paper TOEFL 250. **Basis for Candidate Selection:** *Very important factors considered include:* recommendation(s), interview. *Other factors considered include:* Class rank, rigor of secondary school record, standardized test scores, character/personal qualities. **Freshman Admission Requirements:** High school diploma is required and GED is accepted. **Freshman Admission Statistics:** 6 applied, 100% admitted, 67% enrolled. **Transfer Admission Requirements:** college transcript(s), minimum college GPA of 2.0 required. Lowest grade transferable C. **General Admission Information:** Application Fee $20. Nonfall registration accepted. Admission may be deferred for a maximum of one year.

COSTS AND FINANCIAL AID
Annual tuition $6,400. Required fees $30. Average book expense $600. **Required Forms and Deadlines:** FAFSA. **Types of Aid:** *Need-based scholarships/grants:* Federal Pell, state scholarships/grants, private scholarships, the school's own gift aid. *Loans:* Subsidized Stafford, Unsubsidized Stafford, PLUS. **Student Employment:** Off-campus job opportunities are excellent. **Financial Aid Statistics:** 2% undergrads receive need-based scholarship or grant aid. 2% undergrads receive need-based self-help aid. 0% undergrads borrow to pay for school. **Criteria for awarding institutional aid:** *Non-need-based:* academics.

BAPTIST BIBLE COLLEGE AND SEMINARY

538 Veanrd Rd, Clarks summit, PA 18411
Phone: 570-586-2400 • **Financial Aid Phone:** 570-585-9206
E-mail: admissions@bbc.edu • **CEEB Code:** 2036
Fax: 570-585-9299 • **Website:** www/bbc/edu • **ACT Code:** 3523

This private school, affiliated with the Baptist Church, was founded in 1932. It has a 121-acre campus.

RATINGS
Admissions Selectivity Rating: 70   **Fire Safety Rating:** 62   **Green Rating:** 60*

STUDENTS AND FACULTY
Enrollment: 668. **Student Body:** 59% female, 41% male, 68% out-of-state, 2% international (13 countries represented). Asian 1%, African American 1%, Caucasian 94%, Hispanic 2%, Native American 0%.
Retention and Graduation: 69% freshmen return for sophomore year. **Faculty:** 35 full-time faculty, 57% hold PhDs, 3% are members of minority groups, 29% are women. 0% of classes are taught by teaching assistants.

ACADEMICS
Degrees: associate, bachelor's, certificate, master's. **Classes:** Most classes have fewer than 10 students. **Majors with Highest Enrollment:** counseling psychology; elementary education and teaching; theology and religious vocations, other. **Special Study Options:** distance learning, double major, dual enrollment, independent study, internships, study abroad, teacher certification program. **Career Services:** alumni services, internships.

FACILITIES
Housing: men's dorms, women's dorms. **Computers:** 100% of classrooms, 100% of libraries, 100% of dining areas, 100% of student union, 100% of common outdoor areas have wireless network access. Students can register for classes online. Administrative functions (other than registration) can be performed online.

CAMPUS LIFE
Environment: Town. **Activities:** Choral groups, concert band, drama/theater, music ensembles, student government, yearbook, Campus Ministries. **Athletics (Intercollegiate):** *Men:* baseball, basketball, cross-country, golf, soccer. *Women:* basketball, cross-country, soccer, softball, tennis, volleyball. **On-Campus Highlights:** Underground Cafe, Dorm, Student Center, Classroom building.

ADMISSIONS
Freshman Academic Profile: 40% from public high schools. SAT Math middle 50% range 430-560. SAT Critical Reading middle 50% range 460-570. ACT middle 50% range 20-24. Minimum paper TOEFL 500. **Basis for Candidate Selection:** *Very important factors considered include:* application essay, recommendation(s), rigor of secondary school record, standardized test scores, character/personal qualities, religious affiliation/commitment. *Important factors considered include:* academic GPA. *Other factors considered include:* extracurricular activities, interview, level of applicant's interest, talent/ability, volunteer work, work experience. **Freshman Admission Requirements:** High school diploma is required and GED is accepted. **Freshman Admission Statistics:** 452 applied, 76% admitted, 48% enrolled. **Transfer Admission Requirements:** High school transcript, college transcript(s), essay or personal statement, minimum college GPA of 2 required. Lowest grade transferable 2. **General Admission Information:** Application Fee $30. Regular application deadline 8/15. Nonfall registration accepted. Credit offered for CEEB Advanced Placement tests.

COSTS AND FINANCIAL AID
Annual tuition $6,840. Room and board $5,900. Required fees $468. **Required Forms and Deadlines:** FAFSA, institution's own financial aid form. **Notification of Awards:** Applicants will be notified of awards on a rolling basis beginning 10/1. **Types of Aid:** *Need-based scholarships/grants:* Federal Pell, state scholarships/grants, the school's own gift aid. *Loans:* Direct Unsubsidized Stafford, Subsidized Stafford, Unsubsidized Stafford, PLUS, state loans. **Student Employment:** Federal Work-Study Program available. Institutional employment available. Off-campus job opportunities are excellent. **Financial Aid Statistics:** 100% freshmen, 96% undergrads receive any aid. **Criteria for awarding institutional aid:** *Non-need-based:* academics, leadership.

BAPTIST COLLEGE OF FLORIDA

5400 College Drive, Graceville, FL 32440-1898
Phone: 850-263-3261 • **Financial Aid Phone:** 1-800-328-2660 ext. 461
E-mail: admissions@baptistcollege.edu
Fax: 850-263-9026 • **Website:** www.baptistcollege.edu • **ACT Code:** 6870

This private school, affiliated with the Southern Baptist Church, was founded in 1943. It has a 217-acre campus.

RATINGS
Admissions Selectivity Rating: 91   **Fire Safety Rating:** 72   **Green Rating:** 60*

STUDENTS AND FACULTY
Enrollment: 537. **Student Body:** 38% female, 62% male, 29% out-of-state, 0% international (1 country represented). Asian 0%, African American 5%, Caucasian 79%, Hispanic 3%, Native American 1%.
Retention and Graduation: 82% freshmen return for sophomore year. 13% freshmen graduate within 4 years. 26% freshmen graduate within 6 years. 60% grads go on to further study within 1 year. 60% grads pursue arts and sciences degrees. **Faculty:** Student/faculty ratio 13:1. 23 full-time faculty, 74% hold PhDs, 0% are members of minority groups, 17% are women. 0% of classes are taught by teaching assistants.

ACADEMICS
Degrees: associate, bachelor's, certificate, terminal associate. **Classes:** Most classes have fewer than 10 students. Most lab/discussion sessions have 10–19 students. **Majors with Highest Enrollment:** pastoral studies/counseling; religious education; theology/theological studies. **Special Study Options:** distance learning, double major, independent study, internships, teacher certification program, -Academic Remediation -Advanced Placement Credit -Learning Disabilities Services. **Disability Services:** Special programs offered to physically disabled students include note-taking services, reader services, tape recorders, tutors. **Career Services:** alumni services, internships.

FACILITIES
Housing: special housing for disabled students, men's dorms, women's dorms, apartments for married students 100% of campus accessible to physically disabled. **Special Academic Facilities/Equipment:** Florida Baptist Historical Society; Heritage Village; Weight Rooms in Assembly Center. **Computers:** 100% of classrooms, 100% of dorms, 100% of libraries, 100% of dining areas, 100% of student union, 100% of common outdoor areas have wireless network access. Students can register for classes online. Administrative functions (other than registration) can be performed online.

CAMPUS LIFE
Environment: Rural. **Activities:** Choral groups, concert band, drama/theater, jazz band, music ensembles, radio station, Campus Ministries 3 registered organizations, 2 religious organizations. **Athletics (Intercollegiate):** *Men:* golf. *Women:* volleyball. **On-Campus Highlights:** Athletic Center, Coffee Shop, Courtyard, Student Center, Chapel.

ADMISSIONS
Freshman Academic Profile: 90% from public high schools. SAT Math middle 50% range 390-540. SAT Critical Reading middle 50% range 450-640. ACT middle 50% range 17-22. Minimum paper TOEFL 500. **Basis for Candidate Selection:** *Very important factors considered include:* recommendation(s), character/personal qualities, level of applicant's interest, religious affiliation/commitment. *Important factors considered include:* academic GPA, alumni/ae relation, talent/ability. *Other factors considered include:* Class rank, rigor of secondary school record, standardized test scores, extracurricular activities, interview, volunteer work. **Freshman Admission Requirements:** High school diploma is required and GED is accepted. **Freshman Admission Statistics:** 190 applied, 36% admitted, 65% enrolled. **Transfer Admission Requirements:** High school transcript, college transcript(s), essay or personal statement, minimum college GPA of 2.0 required. Lowest grade transferable C. **General Admission Information:** Application Fee $25. Regular application deadline 8/15. Notification on a rolling basis, beginning on or about 9/1. Nonfall registration accepted. Admission may be deferred for a maximum of 2 semesters. Neither credit nor placement offered for CEEB Advanced Placement tests.

COSTS AND FINANCIAL AID
Annual tuition $9,000. Room and board $4,888. Required fees $350. Average book expense $900. **Required Forms and Deadlines:** FAFSA, institution's own financial aid form, state aid form. **Notification of Awards:** Applicants will be notified of awards on a rolling basis beginning 6/15. **Types of Aid:** *Need-based scholarships/grants:* Federal Pell, SEOG, state scholarships/grants, private scholarships, the school's own gift aid. *Loans:* Subsidized Stafford, Unsubsidized Stafford, PLUS, college/university loans from institutional funds,

Alternative Loans. **Student Employment:** Federal Work-Study Program available. Institutional employment available. Highest amount earned per year from on-campus jobs $7,600. Off-campus job opportunities are good. **Financial Aid Statistics:** 46% freshmen, 62% undergrads receive need-based scholarship or grant aid. 3% freshmen, 2% undergrads receive non-need-based scholarship or grant aid. 52% freshmen, 68% undergrads receive need-based self-help aid. 0% undergrads borrow to pay for school. Average cumulative indebtedness $0. **Criteria for awarding institutional aid:** *Non-need-based:* academics, minority status, music/drama, religious affiliation.

BARBER SCOTIA COLLEGE

145 Cabarrus Avenue, Concord, NC 28025
Phone: 704-789-2901
E-mail: wwhite@b-sc.edu
Fax: 704-789-2624 • **Website:** www.barber-scotia.edu • **ACT Code:** 3060

This private school, affiliated with the Presbyterian Church, was founded in 1867. It has a 40-acre campus.

RATINGS
Admissions Selectivity Rating: 63   **Fire Safety Rating:** 60*   **Green Rating:** 60*

STUDENTS AND FACULTY
Enrollment: 475. **Student Body:** 45% out-of-state, 0% international (2 countries represented). Asian 0%, Caucasian 1%, Hispanic 0%, Native American 0%.
Retention and Graduation: 61% freshmen return for sophomore year. 9% grads go on to further study within 1 year. 7% grads pursue arts and sciences degrees. 2% grads pursue business degrees.

ACADEMICS
Degrees: bachelor's. **Special Study Options:** cooperative education program, double major, dual enrollment, honors program, internships, student-designed major, teacher certification program. **Combined Degree Programs:** BA/JD, BA/BSN. **Disability Services:** Special programs offered to physically disabled students include note-taking services, reader services, tape recorders, tutors. **Career Services:** alumni services, career/job search classes, career assessment, internships.

FACILITIES
Housing: special housing for disabled students, men's dorms, women's dorms, apartments for married students 50% of campus accessible to physically disabled. **Special Academic Facilities/Equipment:** Barber-Scotia's African-American Women's History Collection: This Collection houses one of the largest bodies of documents related to African-American women in the united States. Major areas of interest are the Reconstruction-Jim Crow Era.

CAMPUS LIFE
Environment: Village. **Activities:** Choral groups, dance, pep band, student government, student newspaper, yearbook 18 registered organizations, 2 honor societies, 2 religious organizations. 4 fraternities, 4 sororities. **Athletics (Intercollegiate):** *Men:* basketball, cross-country, track/field (outdoor). *Women:* basketball, cheerleading, cross-country, softball, track/field (outdoor), volleyball.

ADMISSIONS
Freshman Academic Profile: 98% from public high schools. **Basis for Candidate Selection:** *Very important factors considered include:* Class rank, application essay, recommendation(s), interview. *Important factors considered include:* rigor of secondary school record, extracurricular activities, talent/ability, volunteer work. *Other factors considered include:* alumni/ae relation, character/personal qualities, state residency. **Freshman Admission Requirements:** High school diploma is required and GED is accepted. *Academic units required:* 4 English, 3 mathematics, 3 science, 2 social studies, 1 history. *Academic units recommended:* 4 English, 3 mathematics, 3 science, 2 social studies, 1 history. **Freshman Admission Statistics:** 840 applied, 64% admitted, 32% enrolled. **Transfer Admission Requirements:** college transcript(s), minimum college GPA of 2.0 required. Lowest grade transferable C. **General Admission Information:** Application Fee $15. Regular application deadline 7/1. Nonfall registration accepted. Credit and/or placement offered for CEEB Advanced Placement tests.

COSTS AND FINANCIAL AID
Annual tuition $7,400. Room and board $3,500. Required fees $466. Average book expense $250. **Required Forms and Deadlines:** FAFSA. **Notification of Awards:** Applicants will be notified of awards on or about 6/15. **Types of Aid:** *Need-based scholarships/grants:* Federal Pell, SEOG, state scholarships/grants, private scholarships, the school's own gift aid, United Negro College Fund. *Loans:* Direct Subsidized Stafford, Direct Unsubsidized Stafford, Direct PLUS, Subsidized Stafford, Unsubsidized Stafford, PLUS. **Student Employ-**

ment: Federal Work-Study Program available. Institutional employment available. Off-campus job opportunities are excellent. **Financial Aid Statistics:** 94% freshmen, 98% undergrads receive need-based scholarship or grant aid. 8% freshmen, 29% undergrads receive non-need-based scholarship or grant aid. 87% freshmen, 70% undergrads receive need-based self-help aid. 8% freshmen, 10% undergrads receive athletic scholarships. 84% undergrads borrow to pay for school. Average cumulative indebtedness $14,629. **Criteria for awarding institutional aid:** *Non-need-based:* academics, alumni affiliation, athletics, leadership, minority status, music/drama, religious affiliation, state/district residency.

BARD COLLEGE (NY)

Office of Admissions, Annandale-on-Hudson, NY 12504
Phone: 845-758-7472 • **Financial Aid Phone:** 845-758-7526
E-mail: admission@bard.edu • **CEEB Code:** 2037
Fax: 845-758-5208 • **Website:** www.bard.edu • **ACT Code:** 2674

This private school was founded in 1860. It has a 600-acre campus.

RATINGS
Admissions Selectivity Rating: 96   **Fire Safety Rating:** 83   **Green Rating:** 89

STUDENTS AND FACULTY
Enrollment: 1,971. **Student Body:** 56% female, 44% male, 66% out-of-state, 12% international (64 countries represented). Asian 3%, African American 5%, Caucasian 62%, Hispanic 3%, Native American 1%.
Retention and Graduation: 86% freshmen return for sophomore year. 67% freshmen graduate within 4 years. 79% freshmen graduate within 6 years.
Faculty: Student/faculty ratio 10:1. 149 full-time faculty, 95% hold PhDs, 12% are members of minority groups, 42% are women. 0% of classes are taught by teaching assistants.

ACADEMICS
Degrees: associate, bachelor's, doctoral, master's. **Majors with Highest Enrollment:** English language and literature; social sciences; visual and performing arts. **Special Study Options:** cross-registration, double major, dual enrollment, English as a Second Language (ESL), independent study, internships, student-designed major, study abroad, Intensive language studies in Italy, Germany, France, Mexico, Russia, China, program in International Education (Central and Eastern Europe and Southern Africa). **Combined Degree Programs:** BA/MA, BA/MEng, See catalog, pp. 244. **Disability Services:** Special programs offered to physically disabled students include note-taking services, reader services, tape recorders, tutors. **Career Services:** Alumni network, alumni services, career/job search classes, career assessment, internships, regional alumni. The Career Office offers over 30 career information workshops a year.

FACILITIES
Housing: Coed dorms, women's dorms, cooperative housing, wellness housing, theme housing. 70% of campus accessible to physically disabled. **Special Academic Facilities/Equipment:** Performing arts center, gallery, art museum, collection of contemporary art, center for curatorial studies, language lab, nursery school, ecology field station, archaeology field school, economics institute. **Computers:** 5% of classrooms, 50% of dorms, 100% of libraries, 100% of dining areas, 100% of student union, have wireless network access. Students can register for classes online. Administrative functions (other than registration) can be performed online.

CAMPUS LIFE
Environment: Rural. **Activities:** Choral groups, concert band, dance, drama/theater, jazz band, literary magazine, music ensembles, musical theater, opera, radio station, student government, student newspaper, student-run film society, symphony orchestra, Campus Ministries, International Student Organization, Model UN 120 registered organizations, 5 religious organizations. **Athletics (Intercollegiate):** *Men:* basketball, cross-country, soccer, squash, tennis, track/field (outdoor), volleyball. *Women:* basketball, cross-country, soccer, tennis, track/field (outdoor), volleyball. **On-Campus Highlights:** Richard B Fisher Center for the Performing Arts, Stevenson Library, Bertelsmann Campus Center, Museum @ Center for Curatorial Studies, Levy Economics Institute - Blithewood Mansion, A new Center for Science and Computation designed by the renowned firm Rafael Vinoly Architects opened in the fall of 2007.

Environmental Initiatives: Renewable energy (geothermal) installed in new buildings and currently in place in 20 existing buildings. 100% food composting onsite. (#1 in "Food Scrap" category in 2009 Recyclemania). Sustainability literacy of first-year students.

ADMISSIONS
Freshman Academic Profile: Average high school GPA 3.5. 60% in top 10% of high school class, 95% in top 25% of high school class, 97% in top 50% of high school class. 60% from public high schools. SAT Math middle 50% range 600-670. SAT Critical Reading middle 50% range 650-710. Minimum web-based TOEFL 100. Minimum paper TOEFL 600. **Basis for Candidate Selection:** *Very important factors considered include:* application essay, academic GPA, recommendation(s), rigor of secondary school record, character/personal qualities, extracurricular activities, talent/ability. *Important factors considered include:* volunteer work, work experience. *Other factors considered include:* Class rank, standardized test scores, alumni/ae relation, first generation, geographical residence, interview, level of applicant's interest, racial/ethnic status, religious affiliation/commitment, state residency. **Freshman Admission Requirements:** High school diploma is required and GED is accepted. **Freshman Admission Statistics:** 5,410 applied, 35% admitted, 28% enrolled. **Transfer Admission Requirements:** college transcript(s), essay or personal statement, statement of good standing from prior institution(s). Minimum college GPA of 3.0 required. Lowest grade transferable C. **General Admission Information:** Application Fee $50. Regular application deadline 1/15. Regular notification 4/1. Nonfall registration not accepted. Admission may be deferred for a maximum of 12 months. Credit offered for CEEB Advanced Placement tests.

COSTS AND FINANCIAL AID
Annual tuition $44,176. Room and board $12,782. Required fees $622. Average book expense $950. **Required Forms and Deadlines:** FAFSA, CSS/Financial Aid PROFILE, state aid form, noncustodial PROFILE, business/farm supplement. **Notification of Awards:** Applicants will be notified of awards on or about 4/1. **Types of Aid:** *Need-based scholarships/grants:* Federal Pell, SEOG, state scholarships/grants, private scholarships, the school's own gift aid. *Loans:* Subsidized Stafford, Unsubsidized Stafford, PLUS, Federal Perkins, Loans from institutional funds (for international students only). **Student Employment:** Federal Work-Study Program available. Institutional employment available. Highest amount earned per year from on-campus jobs $1,800. Off-campus job opportunities are good. **Financial Aid Statistics:** 97% freshmen, 94% undergrads receive need-based scholarship or grant aid. 87% freshmen, 83% undergrads receive need-based self-help aid. 73% freshmen, 70% undergrads receive any aid. 49% undergrads borrow to pay for school. Average cumulative indebtedness $24,913. **Criteria for awarding institutional aid:** *Non-need-based:* academics.

BARD COLLEGE AT SIMON'S ROCK (MA)

84 Alford Road, Great Barrington, MA 1230
Phone: 413-528-7312 • **Financial Aid Phone:** 413-528-7297
E-mail: admit@simons-rock.edu • **CEEB Code:** 3795
Fax: 413-528-7334 • **Website:** www.simons-rock.edu • **ACT Code:** 1893

This private school was founded in 1964. It has a 275-acre campus.

RATINGS
Admissions Selectivity Rating: 91   **Fire Safety Rating:** 93   **Green Rating:** 60*

STUDENTS AND FACULTY
Enrollment: 343. **Student Body:** 60% female, 40% male, 86% out-of-state, 4% international (16 countries represented). Asian 4%, African American 5%, Caucasian 29%, Hispanic 3%, Native American 0%.
Retention and Graduation: 71% freshmen return for sophomore year. 26% freshmen graduate within 4 years. **Faculty:** Student/faculty ratio 6:1. 26 full-time faculty, 162% hold PhDs, 31% are members of minority groups, 73% are women. 0% of classes are taught by teaching assistants.

ACADEMICS
Degrees: associate, bachelor's. **Classes:** Most classes have 10–19 students. Most lab/discussion sessions have 10–19 students. **Majors with Highest Enrollment:** cell/cellular biology and histology; creative writing; psychology. **Special Study Options:** Accelerated program, cooperative education program,

cross-registration, dual enrollment, exchange student program (domestic), independent study, internships, student-designed major, study abroad, Study Abroad Program(s)within in the last two years: In Hondorus, Spain, England, Germany, Thailand, South Africa, Japan, China. **Combined Degree Programs:** BS Eng from Dartmouth/Washington U/or Columbia. **Disability Services:** Special programs offered to physically disabled students include tape recorders, tutors. **Career Services:** Alumni network, career/job search classes, internships, regional alumni..

FACILITIES

Housing: Coed dorms, men's dorms, women's dorms, apartments for single students. If students propose a plan for cooperative housing it will be considered by Dean of Student Life. 75% of campus accessible to physically disabled. **Special Academic Facilities/Equipment:** Daniel Arts Center, Fisher Science and Academic Center. **Computers:** Administrative functions (other than registration) can be performed online.

CAMPUS LIFE

Environment: Village. **Activities:** Choral groups, dance, drama/theater, jazz band, literary magazine, music ensembles, radio station, student government, student newspaper, student-run film society, yearbook 21 registered organizations, 3 religious organizations. **Athletics (Intercollegiate):** *Men:* basketball, soccer, swimming, tennis. *Women:* basketball, soccer, swimming, tennis. **On-Campus Highlights:** Fisher Science and Academic Center, Daniel Arts Center, Alumni Library, Kellogg Music Center, Kilpatrick Athletic Center, New building coming on line in 2005: Livingston Hall Student Union.

ADMISSIONS

Freshman Academic Profile: Average high school GPA 3.4. 60% in top 10% of high school class, 84% in top 25% of high school class, 94% in top 50% of high school class. 64% from public high schools. SAT Math middle 50% range 580-740. SAT Critical Reading middle 50% range 620-740. SAT Writing middle 50% range 560-670. ACT middle 50% range 28-31. Minimum web-based TOEFL 100. Minimum paper TOEFL 600. **Basis for Candidate Selection:** *Very important factors considered include:* application essay, recommendation(s), rigor of secondary school record, character/personal qualities, interview, talent/ability. *Important factors considered include:* Class rank, academic GPA, level of applicant's interest. *Other factors considered include:* standardized test scores, alumni/ae relation, extracurricular activities, first generation, racial/ethnic status, volunteer work, work experience. **Freshman Admission Requirements:** High school diploma or equivalent is not required. **Freshman Admission Statistics:** 258 applied, 93% admitted, 56% enrolled. **Transfer Admission Requirements:** college transcript(s), essay or personal statement, interview, minimum college GPA of 2.0 required. Lowest grade transferable C. **General Admission Information:** Application Fee $50. Regular application deadline 5/31. Notification on a rolling basis beginning on or about 9/1. Nonfall registration accepted. Admission may be deferred for a maximum of 12 months. Credit and/or placement offered for CEEB Advanced Placement tests.

COSTS AND FINANCIAL AID

Annual tuition $44,075. Room and board $12,260. Required fees $1,050. Average book expense $1,000. **Required Forms and Deadlines:** FAFSA, CSS/Financial Aid PROFILE, business/farm supplement. Parent and Student Federal Taxes/ Federal Verification Worksheet. **Notification of Awards:** Applicants will be notified of awards on a rolling basis beginning 4/15. **Types of Aid:** *Need-based scholarships/grants:* Federal Pell, SEOG, state scholarships/grants, private scholarships, the school's own gift aid. *Loans:* Subsidized Stafford, Unsubsidized Stafford, PLUS, Federal Perkins, state loans, Alternative Educational Loans. **Student Employment:** Federal Work-Study Program available. Institutional employment available. Highest amount earned per year from on-campus jobs $1,300. Off-campus job opportunities are good. **Financial Aid Statistics:** 86% freshmen, 93% undergrads receive need-based scholarship or grant aid. 76% freshmen, 78% undergrads receive non-need-based scholarship or grant aid. 86% freshmen, 93% undergrads receive need-based self-help aid. 94% freshmen, 86% undergrads receive any aid. 68% undergrads borrow to pay for school. Average cumulative indebtedness $30,000. **Criteria for awarding institutional aid:** *Non-need-based:* academics, alumni affiliation, leadership, state/district residency.

BARNARD COLLEGE

3009 Broadway, New York, NY 10027
Phone: 212-854-2014 • **Financial Aid Phone:** 212-854-2154
E-mail: admissions@barnard.edu • **CEEB Code:** 2038
Fax: 212-854-6220 • **Website:** www.barnard.edu • **ACT Code:** 2718

This private school was founded in 1889. It has a 4-acre campus.

RATINGS
Admissions Selectivity Rating: 98   **Fire Safety Rating:** 66   **Green Rating:** 78

STUDENTS AND FACULTY

Enrollment: 2,445. **Student Body:** 66% out-of-state, 6% international (43 countries represented). Asian 17%, African American 5%, Caucasian 63%, Hispanic 9%, Native American 0%.
Retention and Graduation: 94% freshmen return for sophomore year. 22% grads go on to further study within 1 year. 6% grads pursue arts and sciences degrees. 7% grads pursue law degrees. 1% grads pursue business degrees. 5% grads pursue medical degrees. **Faculty:** Student/faculty ratio 10:1. 206 full-time faculty, 88% hold PhDs, 16% are members of minority groups, 61% are women. 0% of classes are taught by teaching assistants.

ACADEMICS

Degrees: bachelor's. **Classes:** Most classes have 10–19 students. Most lab/discussion sessions have 10–19 students. **Majors with Highest Enrollment:** economics, other; English language and literature; psychology. **Special Study Options:** Accelerated program, cross-registration, double major, dual enrollment, exchange student program (domestic), honors program, independent study, internships, liberal arts/career combination, student-designed major, study abroad, teacher certification program, independant scholars program, BA/BS in engineering and applied science. **Honors Programs:** The Barnard Centennial Scholars Program, established in 1984, offers selected students the opportunity to pursue courses of independent study early in their college careers. Working closely with mentors of their choice over a period of several semesters, these young women undertake investigations in areas of personal interest that culminate in projects presented to faculty and peers. The Athena Center for Leadership Studies was launched in September of 2009 and offers a range of academic courses that examines all aspects of women's leadership, sponsored lectures, mentoring and leadership opportunities and a lab which offers a wide range of workshops designed to teach practical elements of leadership to students, alums and other leaders in New York. **Combined Degree Programs:** BA/JD, BA/DDS, BA/MIA or BA/MBA Col. Schl. of Intern. and Public Af. **Disability Services:** Special programs offered to physically disabled students include note-taking services, reader services, tape recorders, tutors. **Career Services:** Alumni network, alumni services, career/job search classes, career assessment, internships, regional alumni. Career Services highlights include Because of our urban setting, our students are exposed to extremely wide range of internship opportunities. Barnard also offers funding for some unpaid internships.

FACILITIES

Housing: Coed dorms, special housing for disabled students, women's dorms, apartments for single students. 100% of campus accessible to physically disabled. **Special Academic Facilities/Equipment:** Black Box theater, infant-toddler center, greenhouse, academic computer center, advanced architecture labs. **Computers:** 60% of classrooms, 80% of dorms, 80% of libraries, 100% of dining areas, 100% of student union, 100% of common outdoor areas have wireless network access. Students can register for classes online. Administrative functions (other than registration) can be performed online.

CAMPUS LIFE

Environment: Metropolis. **Activities:** Choral groups, concert band, dance, drama/theater, jazz band, literary magazine, marching band, music ensembles, musical theater, opera, pep band, radio station, student government, student newspaper, student-run film society, symphony orchestra, television station, yearbook, Campus Ministries 100 registered organizations, 1 honor societies. **Athletics (Intercollegiate):** *Women:* archery, basketball, crew/rowing, cross-country, diving, fencing, field hockey, golf, lacrosse, soccer, softball, swimming, tennis, track/field (outdoor), volleyball. **On-Campus Highlights:** Diana Center, Arthur Ross Greenhouse, Held Auditorium, Smart Media Classrooms, Liz's Place Cafe. **Environmental Initiatives:** Barnard has mandated LEED certification for new buildings. The newest addition to Barnard's campus, The Diana Center, is a LEED Gold building. Barnard is partnered with other New York

City organizations as part of Mayor Bloomberg's "PlanNYC 2030 Challenge" to reduce the City's greenhouse gas footprint and improve the urban infrastructure and environment. In 2008, Barnard purchased and installed LabStats, a program that tracks the hourly activity of the computers in the student labs. Barnard is keeping logs of the use of these computers to help optimize power management in the labs.

ADMISSIONS

Freshman Academic Profile: Average high school GPA 3.8. 84% in top 10% of high school class, 99% in top 25% of high school class, 99% in top 50% of high school class. 48% from public high schools. SAT Math middle 50% range 620-710. SAT Critical Reading middle 50% range 630-730. SAT Writing middle 50% range 650-750. ACT middle 50% range 28-32. Minimum paper TOEFL 600. **Basis for Candidate Selection:** *Very important factors considered include:* academic GPA, recommendation(s), rigor of secondary school record, standardized test scores, character/personal qualities, extracurricular activities. *Important factors considered include:* application essay, talent/ability, volunteer work. *Other factors considered include:* Class rank, alumni/ae relation, first generation, geographical residence, interview, level of applicant's interest, racial/ethnic status, work experience. **Freshman Admission Requirements:** High school diploma or equivalent is not required. **Freshman Admission Statistics:** 5,153 applied, 25% admitted, 48% enrolled. **Transfer Admission Requirements:** High school transcript, college transcript(s), essay or personal statement, standardized test scores, statement of good standing from prior institution(s). Lowest grade transferable C-. **General Admission Information:** Application Fee $55. Early decision application deadline 11/15. Regular application deadline 1/1. Regular notification 4/1. Nonfall registration not accepted. Admission may be deferred for a maximum of 12 months. Credit and/or placement offered for CEEB Advanced Placement tests.

COSTS AND FINANCIAL AID

Annual tuition $41,850. Room and board $13,810. Required fees $1,652. **Required Forms and Deadlines:** FAFSA, institution's own financial aid form, CSS/Financial Aid PROFILE, state aid form, noncustodial PROFILE, business/farm supplement. federal income tax returns. **Notification of Awards:** Applicants will be notified of awards on or about 3/31. **Types of Aid:** *Need-based scholarships/grants:* Federal Pell, SEOG, state scholarships/grants, private scholarships, the school's own gift aid. *Loans:* Subsidized Stafford, Unsubsidized Stafford, PLUS, Federal Perkins, state loans, college/university loans from institutional funds. **Student Employment:** Federal Work-Study Program available. Institutional employment available. Highest amount earned per year from on-campus jobs $8,325. Off-campus job opportunities are excellent. **Financial Aid Statistics:** 96% freshmen, 96% undergrads receive need-based scholarship or grant aid. 100% freshmen, 100% undergrads receive need-based self-help aid. 57% freshmen, 50% undergrads receive any aid. Average cumulative indebtedness $17,360

See page 1014.

BARRY UNIVERSITY

11300 North East Second Avenue, Miami Shores, FL 33161-6695
Phone: 305-899-3100 • **Financial Aid Phone:** 305-899-3673
E-mail: Des-forms@mail.barry.edu • **CEEB Code:** 5053
Fax: 305-899-2971 • **Website:** www.barry.edu • **ACT Code:** 718

This private school, affiliated with the Roman Catholic Church, was founded in 1940. It has a 122-acre campus.

RATINGS
Admissions Selectivity Rating: 80   **Fire Safety Rating:** 60*   **Green Rating:** 60*

STUDENTS AND FACULTY
Enrollment: 4,551. **Student Body:** 63% female, 37% male, 26% out-of-state, 7% international (101 countries represented). Asian 1%, African American 19%, Caucasian 13%, Hispanic 17%, Native American 0%.
Retention and Graduation: 62% freshmen return for sophomore year. **Faculty:** Student/faculty ratio 13:1. 340 full-time faculty, 84% hold PhDs, 26% are members of minority groups, 53% are women.

ACADEMICS
Degrees: bachelor's, first professional, master's, post-bachelor's certificate, post-master's certificate. **Classes:** Most classes have 10–19 students. **Majors with Highest Enrollment:** business/commerce; elementary education and teaching; information science/studies. **Special Study Options:** Accelerated program, double major, English as a Second Language (ESL), honors program, internships, study abroad, teacher certification program. **Combined Degree Programs:** DPM/MBA; JD/MBA; MSN/MBA. **Disability Services:** Special

programs offered to physically disabled students include note-taking services, reader services, tape recorders, tutors. **Career Services:** alumni services.

FACILITIES
Housing: Coed dorms, special housing for disabled students, men's dorms, women's dorms. 82% of campus accessible to physically disabled. **Special Academic Facilities/Equipment:** Human performance lab, broadcasting studio, radio station, athletic training room, cell biology/biotechnology labs, Classroom of Tomorrow, Biomechanics lab, Photogrpahy lab, darkroom, and studio, Language lab, athletic training room. **Computers:** Students can register for classes online. Administrative functions (other than registration) can be performed online.

CAMPUS LIFE
Environment: Village. **Activities:** Choral groups, dance, drama/theater, literary magazine, music ensembles, musical theater, radio station, student government, student newspaper, television station, Campus Ministries, International Student Organization 67 registered organizations, 20 honor societies, 5 religious organizations. 2 fraternities, 2 sororities. **Athletics (Intercollegiate):** *Men:* baseball, basketball, golf, soccer, tennis. *Women:* basketball, crew/rowing, golf, soccer, softball, tennis, volleyball. **On-Campus Highlights:** Thompson Hall-Student Center, Human Performance Leisure Sciences-Athletic Complex, Penaport Pool, Residence Halls, Library.

ADMISSIONS
Freshman Academic Profile: Average high school GPA 3.1. 100% in top 50% of high school class. SAT Math middle 50% range 420-520. SAT Critical Reading middle 50% range 440-520. ACT middle 50% range 18-21. Minimum web-based TOEFL 61. **Basis for Candidate Selection:** *Very important factors considered include:* academic GPA, standardized test scores. *Important factors considered include:* character/personal qualities, interview, talent/ability. *Other factors considered include:* Class rank, application essay, recommendation(s), rigor of secondary school record, extracurricular activities, volunteer work, work experience. **Freshman Admission Requirements:** High school diploma is required and GED is accepted. **Freshman Admission Statistics:** 7,645 applied, 52% admitted, 16% enrolled. **Transfer Admission Requirements:** college transcript(s), minimum college GPA of 2.0 required. Lowest grade transferable C. **General Admission Information:** Application Fee $30. Notification on a rolling basis, beginning on or about 9/8. Nonfall registration accepted. Admission may be deferred for a maximum of 1 year. Credit offered for CEEB Advanced Placement tests.

COSTS AND FINANCIAL AID
Annual tuition $28,160. Room and board $9,300. Average book expense $1,200. **Required Forms and Deadlines:** FAFSA. **Notification of Awards:** Applicants will be notified of awards on a rolling basis beginning 1/25. **Types of Aid:** *Need-based scholarships/grants:* Federal Pell, SEOG, state scholarships/grants, private scholarships, the school's own gift aid, Federal Nursing Scholarships. *Loans:* Subsidized Stafford, Unsubsidized Stafford, PLUS, Federal Perkins, Federal Nursing, college/university loans from institutional funds, Alternative Loans. **Student Employment:** Federal Work-Study Program available. Institutional employment available. Highest amount earned per year from on-campus jobs $7,400. Off-campus job opportunities are good. **Financial Aid Statistics:** 83% freshmen, 71% undergrads receive need-based scholarship or grant aid. 100% freshmen, 98% undergrads receive non-need-based scholarship or grant aid. 96% freshmen, 94% undergrads receive need-based self-help aid. 4% freshmen, 4% undergrads receive athletic scholarships. 98% freshmen, 85% undergrads receive any aid. **Criteria for awarding institutional aid:** *Non-need-based:* academics, art, athletics, music/drama.

BARTON COLLEGE

Box 5000, Wilson, NC 27893-7000
Phone: 252-399-6317 • **Financial Aid Phone:** 252-399-6316
E-mail: enroll@barton.edu • **CEEB Code:** 5016
Fax: 252-399-6572 • **Website:** www.barton.edu • **ACT Code:** 3066

This private school, affiliated with the Disciples of Christ Church, was founded in 1902. It has a 76-acre campus.

RATINGS
Admissions Selectivity Rating: 81   **Fire Safety Rating:** 79   **Green Rating:** 60*

STUDENTS AND FACULTY
Enrollment: 1,149. **Student Body:** 72% female, 28% male, 11% out-of-state, 2% international (8 countries represented). Asian 1%, African American 27%, Caucasian 59%, Hispanic 3%, Native American 0%.
Retention and Graduation: 68% freshmen return for sophomore year. 35%

freshmen graduate within 4 years. 47% freshmen graduate within 6 years. **Faculty:** Student/faculty ratio 12:1. 70 full-time faculty, 66% hold PhDs, 11% are members of minority groups, 50% are women. 0% of classes are taught by teaching assistants.

ACADEMICS

Degrees: bachelor's. **Classes:** Most classes have 10–19 students. Most lab/discussion sessions have fewer than 10 students. **Majors with Highest Enrollment:** business administration and management; elementary education and teaching; nursing/registered nurse (rn, asn, bsn, msn). **Special Study Options:** cooperative education program, double major, honors program, independent study, internships, liberal arts/career combination, study abroad, teacher certification program, weekend college. **Honors Programs:** Three competitive international travel scholarships awarded to entering honors students. **Disability Services:** Special programs offered to physically disabled students include note-taking services, reader services, tape recorders, tutors. **Career Services:** alumni services, career/job search classes, career assessment, internships.

FACILITIES

Housing: Coed dorms, special housing for disabled students, women's dorms, fraternity/sorority housing. 90% of campus accessible to physically disabled. **Special Academic Facilities/Equipment:** TV station, art museum, music recording studio, greenhouse **Computers:** 90% of libraries, 90% of dining areas, have wireless network access. Administrative functions (other than registration) can be performed online.

CAMPUS LIFE

Environment: Town. **Activities:** Choral groups, dance, drama/theater, musical theater, pep band, student government, student newspaper, symphony orchestra, Campus Ministries 51 registered organizations, 7 honor societies, 4 religious organizations. 3 fraternities, 3 sororities. **Athletics (Intercollegiate):** *Men:* baseball, basketball, cross-country, golf, soccer, tennis. *Women:* basketball, cross-country, soccer, softball, tennis, volleyball. **On-Campus Highlights:** Hamlin Student Center, Sam and Marjorie Ragan Writing Center, Kennedy Recreation and Intramural Center, Hackney Library, Barton Art Museum.

ADMISSIONS

Freshman Academic Profile: Average high school GPA 3.0. 7% in top 10% of high school class, 31% in top 25% of high school class, 74% in top 50% of high school class. 87% from public high schools. SAT Math middle 50% range 430-570. SAT Critical Reading middle 50% range 390-540. Minimum paper TOEFL 525. **Basis for Candidate Selection:** *Very important factors considered include:* academic GPA, standardized test scores. *Other factors considered include:* Class rank, recommendation(s), rigor of secondary school record, extracurricular activities, interview, volunteer work, work experience. **Freshman Admission Requirements:** High school diploma is required and GED is accepted. *Academic units required:* 4 English, 3 mathematics, 2 science, (1 science labs), 1 academic electives. *Academic units recommended:* 4 English, 3 mathematics, 2 science, (1 science labs), 1 academic electives. **Freshman Admission Statistics:** 2,598 applied, 52% admitted, 17% enrolled. **Transfer Admission Requirements:** college transcript(s), statement of good standing from prior institution(s). Minimum college GPA of 2.0 required. Lowest grade transferable C. **General Admission Information:** Application Fee $25. Notification on a rolling basis, beginning on or about 8/15. Nonfall registration accepted. Admission may be deferred for a maximum of 1 year. Credit and/or placement offered for CEEB Advanced Placement tests.

COSTS AND FINANCIAL AID

Annual tuition $22,278. Room and board $7,940. Required fees $1,902. Average book expense $1,200. **Required Forms and Deadlines:** FAFSA. **Types of Aid:** *Need-based scholarships/grants:* Federal Pell, SEOG, state scholarships/grants, private scholarships, the school's own gift aid. *Loans:* Subsidized Stafford, Unsubsidized Stafford, PLUS, Federal Perkins. **Student Employment:** Federal Work-Study Program available. Institutional employment available. Highest amount earned per year from on-campus jobs $1,500. Off-campus job opportunities are good. **Financial Aid Statistics:** 99% freshmen, 96% undergrads receive need-based scholarship or grant aid. 10% freshmen, 6% undergrads receive non-need-based scholarship or grant aid. 87% freshmen, 87% undergrads receive need-based self-help aid. 9% freshmen, 6% undergrads receive athletic scholarships. 98% freshmen, 93% undergrads receive any aid. **Criteria for awarding institutional aid:** *Non-need-based:* academics, alumni affiliation, art, athletics, leadership, minority status, music/drama, religious affiliation, state/district residency.

BASTYR UNIVERSITY

14500 Juanita Drive NE, Kenmore, WA 98028
Phone: 425-602-3330 • **Financial Aid Phone:** 425-602-3083
E-mail: admissions@bastyr.edu
Fax: 425-602-3090 • **Website:** www.bastyr.edu

This private school was founded in 1978. It has a 51-acre campus.

RATINGS

Admissions Selectivity Rating: 61   **Fire Safety Rating:** 82   **Green Rating:** 91

STUDENTS AND FACULTY

Enrollment: 207. **Student Body:** 81% female, 19% male, 25% out-of-state, 7% international (31 countries represented). Asian 9%, African American 3%, Caucasian 65%, Hispanic 5%, Native American 1%.
Faculty: 66 full-time faculty, 97% hold PhDs, 18% are members of minority groups, 58% are women. 0% of classes are taught by teaching assistants.

ACADEMICS

Degrees: bachelor's, certificate, master's, post-master's certificate. **Majors with Highest Enrollment:** acupuncture; naturopathic medicine/naturopathy (nd); nutrition sciences. **Special Study Options:** double major, internships, selected tracks within major. **Combined Degree Programs:** naturopathic medicine and acupuncture. **Career Services:** career/job search classes, career assessment, internships.

FACILITIES

Housing: Coed dorms, wellness housing.

CAMPUS LIFE

Environment: Town. **Activities:** Choral groups, student government. **On-Campus Highlights:** Vegetarian cafeteria, Medicinal herb garden, Spacious campus grounds and playfields, Adjacent state park, Bookstore. **Environmental Initiatives:** Our 11-building Student Village has earned LEED Platinum-certification (the first student housing project on the West Coast to receive this honor) and the U.S. Green Building Council's (USGBC) Outstanding Multifamily Project in the 2010 LEED for Homes Awards. The buildings feature "butterfly" roofs to capture rainwater, high efficiency water heaters and gas boilers, energy-efficient appliances and light fixtures, low-flow plumbing, natural ventilation, radiant-heat flooring made of finished concrete, sustainable landscaping, and bicycle storage. Our campus features a rigorous composting and recycling program that allows us to divert 65 percent of waste from landfills. All disposable dishware, cups, silverware and paper towels are compostable. We offer bins for recycling paper, styrofoam, batteries, and light bulbs. A paperless office policy further allows us to reduce paper usage. Our buildings also include automatic lighting and other lighting efficiency, resulting in 14 percent reduced wattage consumption based on 2010 levels. Our dining services and our nutrition curriculum follow a distinctive whole-food philosophy that emphasizes a plant-focused diet and eating a wide variety of foods in unprocessed form. Local, organic, and responsibly-sourced food (both vegetarian and meat) comprise 75 percent of our food expenditures. Our cafeteria is known in the neighboring community for offering restaurant-quality, healthy food, and is frequently mentioned by students as a highlight of the school.

ADMISSIONS

Freshman Academic Profile: Minimum web-based TOEFL 79. Minimum paper TOEFL 550. **Transfer Admission Requirements:** college transcript(s), essay or personal statement, minimum college GPA of 2.25 required. Lowest grade transferable 2. **General Admission Information:** Application Fee $60. Notification on a rolling basis, beginning on or about 4/15.

COSTS AND FINANCIAL AID

Average book expense $2,150. **Required Forms and Deadlines:** FAFSA, institution's own financial aid form. **Notification of Awards:** Applicants will be notified of awards on a rolling basis beginning 5/15. **Types of Aid:** *Need-based scholarships/grants:* Federal Pell, SEOG, state scholarships/grants, private scholarships, the school's own gift aid. *Loans:* Direct Subsidized Stafford, Direct Unsubsidized Stafford, Direct PLUS, Subsidized Stafford, Unsubsidized Stafford, PLUS, Federal Perkins. **Student Employment:** Federal Work-Study Program available. **Financial Aid Statistics:** 80% undergrads receive need-based scholarship or grant aid. 96% undergrads receive need-based self-help aid. 87% undergrads receive any aid. 0% undergrads borrow to pay for school. Average cumulative indebtedness $0. **Criteria for awarding institutional aid:** *Non-need-based:* academics, alumni affiliation.

BATES COLLEGE

23 Campus Avenue, Lewiston, ME 4240
Phone: 207-786-6000 • **Financial Aid Phone:** 207-786-6096
E-mail: admissions@bates.edu • **CEEB Code:** 3076
Fax: 207-786-6025 • **Website:** www.bates.edu • **ACT Code:** 1634

This private school was founded in 1855. It has a 109-acre campus.

RATINGS
Admissions Selectivity Rating: 97   **Fire Safety Rating:** 93   **Green Rating:** 90

STUDENTS AND FACULTY
Enrollment: 1,753. **Student Body:** 89% out-of-state, 6% international (71 countries represented). Asian 4%, African American 4%, Caucasian 74%, Hispanic 5%, Native American 0%.
Retention and Graduation: 95% freshmen return for sophomore year. 85% freshmen graduate within 4 years. 88% freshmen graduate within 6 years.
Faculty: Student/faculty ratio 10:1. 168 full-time faculty, 89% hold PhDs, 15% are members of minority groups, 49% are women. 0% of classes are taught by teaching assistants.

ACADEMICS
Degrees: bachelor's. **Classes:** Most classes have 10–19 students. Most lab/discussion sessions have 10–19 students. **Majors with Highest Enrollment:** economics; political science and government; psychology. **Special Study Options:** Accelerated program, cooperative education program, double major, honors program, independent study, internships, liberal arts/career combination, student-designed major, study abroad, teacher certification program. **Honors Programs:** The Honors Program. **Disability Services:** Special programs offered to physically disabled students include note-taking services, reader services, tape recorders, tutors. **Career Services:** Alumni network, alumni services, career/job search classes, career assessment, internships, regional alumni. Career Services highlights include Finance Boot Camp. A day long introductory workshop presented by alumni working in all facets of the industy. The day provides a soup to nuts look at the industry with class specific small group options and networking opportunities.

FACILITIES
Housing: Coed dorms, men's dorms, women's dorms, Theme houses, quiet/study houses and halls, chem-free and low chem houses and halls. 65% of campus accessible to physically disabled. **Special Academic Facilities/Equipment:** Art gallery, Edmund S. Muskie Archives, language labs, planetarium, 600-acre conservation area on seacoast for environmental studies, scanning electron microscope, Imaging Center. **Computers:** 40% of classrooms, 100% of dorms, 100% of libraries, 100% of dining areas, 100% of student union, 10% of common outdoor areas have wireless network access. Students can register for classes online. Administrative functions (other than registration) can be performed online.

CAMPUS LIFE
Environment: Town. **Activities:** Choral groups, dance, drama/theater, jazz band, literary magazine, music ensembles, pep band, radio station, student government, student newspaper, student-run film society, symphony orchestra, yearbook, Campus Ministries, International Student Organization 99 registered organizations, 3 honor societies, 9 religious organizations. **Athletics (Intercollegiate):** *Men:* baseball, basketball, crew/rowing, cross-country, diving, football, golf, lacrosse, skiing (downhill/alpine), skiingnordiccross-country, soccer, squash, swimming, tennis, track/field (outdoor), track/field (indoor). *Women:* basketball, crew/rowing, cross-country, diving, field hockey, golf, lacrosse, skiing (downhill/alpine), skiingnordiccross-country, soccer, softball, squash, swimming, tennis, track/field (outdoor), track/field (indoor), volleyball. **On-Campus Highlights:** Pettengill Hall, Bates College Museum of Art, Dining Commons, The George and Helen Ladd Library, Merrill Gymnasium/Underhill Arena. **Environmental Initiatives:** Developing sustainable building guidelines and campus energy goals. Developing an environmental leadership course for students. Adopting metrics to measure progress in campus sustainability.

ADMISSIONS
Freshman Academic Profile: 45% in top 10% of high school class, 71% in top 25% of high school class, 94% in top 50% of high school class. 53% from public high schools. SAT Math middle 50% range 630-710. SAT Critical Reading middle 50% range 630-720. SAT Writing middle 50% range 643-720. ACT middle 50% range 30-32. **Basis for Candidate Selection:** *Very important factors considered include:* Class rank, application essay, academic GPA, recommendation(s), rigor of secondary school record, character/personal

qualities, extracurricular activities, interview, level of applicant's interest, talent/ability. *Other factors considered include:* standardized test scores, alumni/ae relation, first generation, geographical residence, racial/ethnic status, state residency, volunteer work, work experience. **Freshman Admission Requirements:** High school diploma is required and GED is not accepted. *Academic units required:* 4 English, 3 mathematics, 3 science, (2 science labs), 2 foreign language, 3 social studies. *Academic units recommended:* 4 English, 3 mathematics, 3 science, (2 science labs), 2 foreign language, 3 social studies. **Freshman Admission Statistics:** 4,906 applied, 27% admitted, 39% enrolled. **Transfer Admission Requirements:** High school transcript, college transcript(s), essay or personal statement, statement of good standing from prior institution(s). Lowest grade transferable C. **General Admission Information:** Application Fee $60. Early decision application deadline 11/15. Regular application deadline 1/1. Regular notification 3/31. Nonfall registration accepted. Admission may be deferred for a maximum of 1 year. Credit and/or placement offered for CEEB Advanced Placement tests.

COSTS AND FINANCIAL AID
Annual tuition $44,040. Room and board $12,935. Required fees $260. Average book expense $1,750. **Required Forms and Deadlines:** FAFSA, CSS/Financial Aid PROFILE, noncustodial PROFILE, business/farm supplement. **Notification of Awards:** Applicants will be notified of awards on or about 4/1. **Types of Aid:** *Need-based scholarships/grants:* Federal Pell, SEOG, state scholarships/grants, private scholarships, the school's own gift aid. *Loans:* Subsidized Stafford, Unsubsidized Stafford, PLUS, Federal Perkins, state loans. **Student Employment:** Federal Work-Study Program available. Institutional employment available. Off-campus job opportunities are good. **Financial Aid Statistics:** 92% freshmen, 91% undergrads receive need-based scholarship or grant aid. 88% freshmen, 95% undergrads receive need-based self-help aid. 42% freshmen, 42% undergrads receive any aid. 40% undergrads borrow to pay for school. Average cumulative indebtedness $24,515.

BAY PATH COLLEGE

588 Longmeadow Street, Longmeadow, MA 01106-2292
Phone: 413-565-1331 • **Financial Aid Phone:** 413-565-1345
E-mail: admiss@baypath.edu • **CEEB Code:** 2122
Fax: 413-565-1105 • **Website:** www.baypath.edu • **ACT Code:** 1785

This private school was founded in 1897. It has a 48-acre campus.

RATINGS
Admissions Selectivity Rating: 77   **Fire Safety Rating:** 99   **Green Rating:** 65

STUDENTS AND FACULTY
Enrollment: 1,556. **Student Body:** 100% female, 0% male, 36% out-of-state, 0% international (11 countries represented). Asian 1%, African American 12%, Caucasian 56%, Hispanic 14%, Native American 0%.
Retention and Graduation: 74% freshmen return for sophomore year. 46% freshmen graduate within 4 years. 34% grads go on to further study within 1 year. **Faculty:** Student/faculty ratio 12:1. 55 full-time faculty, 67% hold PhDs, 15% are members of minority groups, 64% are women. 0% of classes are taught by teaching assistants.

ACADEMICS
Degrees: associate, bachelor's, certificate, master's, post-bachelor's certificate. **Classes:** Most classes have 10–19 students. Most lab/discussion sessions have 10–19 students. **Majors with Highest Enrollment:** business administration and management; forensic science and technology; psychology. **Special Study Options:** Accelerated program, cooperative education program, cross-registration, distance learning, double major, English as a Second Language (ESL), exchange student program (domestic), honors program, independent study, internships, student-designed major, study abroad, teacher certification program, weekend college, Directed study program. **Honors Programs:** The Bay Path Honors Program offers unique learning experiences to the most qualified undergraduate students through honors courses, service projects, on and off campus events and participation in and development of the Bay Path College Honors Program community. The Honors Program at Bay Path provides academically talented and motivated students with uniquely challenging and intellectually stimulating educational opportunities. In the first two years, Honors students take team-taught, interdisciplinary seminars on specific topics, such as Darwin Across the Disciplines. This innovative approach broadens exposure to areas outside the major and provides connections with other Honors students. In the last two years, under the guidance of a faculty mentor, students are immersed in their field of study, and are urged to explore new areas of knowledge with an Honors thesis or creative project. **Disability Services:** Special programs offered to physically disabled students include tutors. **Career Services:** Alumni network, alumni services, career/job search classes, career assessment,

The Princeton Review's Complete Book of Colleges

internships, regional alumni. Career Services highlights include We have a very strong internship program, with all students required in each respective major to perform fieldwork, an internship, student teaching, or experiential learning. Internships are listed in the top 3 important experiences employers wish to see on a college student's resume, aside from major and degree achieved.

FACILITIES

Housing: women's dorms. 50% of campus accessible to physically disabled. **Special Academic Facilities/Equipment:** Blake Student Commons, Bashevkin Academic Development Center, Breck Fitness Center, occupational therapy laboratory, and D'Amour Hall for Business, Communications and Technology. **Computers:** 100% of libraries, 100% of dining areas, 100% of student union, 25% of common outdoor areas have wireless network access. Students can register for classes online. Administrative functions (other than registration) can be performed online.

CAMPUS LIFE

Environment: Village. **Activities:** Choral groups, dance, drama/theater, literary magazine, musical theater, student government, student newspaper, International Student Organization, Model UN 42 registered organizations, 3 honor societies, 1 religious organizations. **Athletics (Intercollegiate):** *Women:* basketball, cross-country, field hockey, soccer, softball, tennis, volleyball. **On-Campus Highlights:** Carpe Diem Cafe, Toner/Helliwell Hearth and Lounge, Game Room, Breck Fitness Center, D'Amour Hall for Business, Communications and Tech.. **Environmental Initiatives:** Recycling program Energy Conservation Efforts conversion of electric heat in student residence hall to gas heat

ADMISSIONS

Freshman Academic Profile: Average high school GPA 3.2. 12% in top 10% of high school class, 41% in top 25% of high school class, 78% in top 50% of high school class. 88% from public high schools. SAT Math middle 50% range 440-540. SAT Critical Reading middle 50% range 440-550. SAT Writing middle 50% range 450-530. ACT middle 50% range 17-25. Minimum web-based TOEFL 71. **Basis for Candidate Selection:** *Very important factors considered include: academic GPA, rigor of secondary school record. Important factors considered include:* standardized test scores. *Other factors considered include:* Class rank, application essay, recommendation(s), alumni/ae relation, character/personal qualities, extracurricular activities, first generation, geographical residence, interview, level of applicant's interest, state residency, talent/ability, volunteer work, work experience. **Freshman Admission Requirements:** High school diploma is required and GED is accepted. *Academic units required:* 4 English, 3 mathematics, 2 science, (2 science labs), 2 social studies, 1 history. *Academic units recommended:* 4 English, 3 mathematics, 2 science, (2 science labs), 2 social studies, 1 history. **Freshman Admission Statistics:** 978 applied, 61% admitted, 26% enrolled. **Transfer Admission Requirements:** college transcript(s), minimum college GPA of 2.0 required. Lowest grade transferable C-. **General Admission Information:** Application Fee $25. Notification on a rolling basis, beginning on or about 9/15. Nonfall registration accepted. Placement offered for CEEB Advanced Placement tests.

COSTS AND FINANCIAL AID

Annual tuition $28,532. Room and board $11,440. Average book expense $975. **Required Forms and Deadlines:** FAFSA, institution's own financial aid form. **Notification of Awards:** Applicants will be notified of awards on a rolling basis beginning 3/1. **Types of Aid:** *Need-based scholarships/grants:* Federal Pell, SEOG, state scholarships/grants, private scholarships, the school's own gift aid. *Loans:* Subsidized Stafford, Unsubsidized Stafford, PLUS, Federal Perkins, state loans. **Student Employment:** Federal Work-Study Program available. Institutional employment available. Highest amount earned per year from on-campus jobs $2,000. **Financial Aid Statistics:** 100% freshmen, 100% undergrads receive need-based scholarship or grant aid. 9% freshmen, 5% undergrads receive non-need-based scholarship or grant aid. 91% freshmen, 95% undergrads receive need-based self-help aid. 94% freshmen, 90% undergrads receive any aid. 91% undergrads borrow to pay for school. Average cumulative indebtedness $31,456. **Criteria for awarding institutional aid:** *Non-need-based:* academics, state/district residency.

BAYLOR UNIVERSITY

One Bear Place #97056, Waco, TX 76798-7056
Phone: 254-710-3435 • **Financial Aid Phone:** 254-710-2611
E-mail: admissions@baylor.edu • **CEEB Code:** 6032
Fax: 254-710-3436 • **Website:** www.baylor.edu • **ACT Code:** 4062

This private school was founded in 1845. It has a 508-acre campus.

RATINGS

Admissions Selectivity Rating: 94   **Fire Safety Rating:** 93   **Green Rating:** 81

STUDENTS AND FACULTY

Enrollment: 12,518. **Student Body:** 58% female, 42% male, 20% out-of-state, 2% international (87 countries represented). Asian 6%, African American 8%, Caucasian 65%, Hispanic 13%, Native American 0%.
Retention and Graduation: 85% freshmen return for sophomore year. 52% freshmen graduate within 4 years. 72% freshmen graduate within 6 years. **Faculty:** Student/faculty ratio 14:1. 886 full-time faculty, 81% hold PhDs, 13% are members of minority groups, 38% are women.

ACADEMICS

Degrees: bachelor's, master's, post-master's certificate. **Classes:** Most classes have 10–19 students. Most lab/discussion sessions have 10–19 students. **Majors with Highest Enrollment:** biology/biological sciences; marketing/marketing management; psychology. **Special Study Options:** Accelerated program, double major, honors program, internships, student-designed major, study abroad, teacher certification program. **Honors Programs:** Honors Program, University Scholars Program, Great Texts Program **Combined Degree Programs:** BBA/MAccounting, BBA/MTax, BSN/MSNursing, BBA/MBA, BSE/MSBE, BSE/ME, ETC. **Disability Services:** Special programs offered to physically disabled students include note-taking services, reader services. **Career Services:** Alumni network, alumni services, career/job search classes, career assessment, internships.

FACILITIES

Housing: special housing for disabled students, men's dorms, special housing for international students, women's dorms, apartments for married students, apartments for single students, theme housing, Living-Learning centers. **Special Academic Facilities/Equipment:** Language and environmental studies labs, natural science museum, high definition television, Armstrong Browning library, Texas Collection Library, Strecker Museum/Bill and Vara Daniel Historical Village, TV Station, Radio Station **Computers:** 98% of classrooms, 10% of dorms, 95% of libraries, 95% of dining areas, 95% of student union, 50% of common outdoor areas have wireless network access. Students can register for classes online. Administrative functions (other than registration) can be performed online.

CAMPUS LIFE

Environment: City. **Activities:** Choral groups, concert band, dance, drama/theater, jazz band, literary magazine, marching band, music ensembles, musical theater, opera, pep band, radio station, student government, student newspaper, student-run film society, symphony orchestra, television station, yearbook, Campus Ministries, International Student Organization, Model UN 222 registered organizations, 32 honor societies, 11 religious organizations. 22 fraternities, 20 sororities. **Athletics (Intercollegiate):** *Men:* baseball, basketball, cheerleading, cross-country, football, golf, tennis, track/field (outdoor), track/field (indoor). *Women:* basketball, cheerleading, cross-country, equestrian sports, golf, soccer, softball, tennis, track/field (outdoor), track/field (indoor), volleyball. **On-Campus Highlights:** Mayborn Museum Complex, Armstrong Browning Library, Baylor Sciences Building, Student Life Center, Chili's Too -- 1st on a University Campus. **Environmental Initiatives:** Campus wide recycling, with over 700 locations on campus to recycle in which to recycle and collaboration with Athletics Department to recycle at all university sporting events. Financing wind power generation facilities through our contract for the next 10 years to finance the construction of wind turbines. 3. Campus wide commitment to energy conservation through campaigns such as Last Out, Lights Out.

ADMISSIONS

Freshman Academic Profile: 39% in top 10% of high school class, 74% in top 25% of high school class, 97% in top 50% of high school class. % from public high schools. SAT Math middle 50% range 570-680. SAT Critical Reading middle 50% range 560-660. SAT Writing middle 50% range 530-640. ACT middle 50% range 24-29. Minimum web-based TOEFL 76. Minimum paper TOEFL 540. **Basis for Candidate Selection:** *Very important factors considered* *include:* Class rank, rigor of secondary school record, standardized test scores. *Important factors considered include:* academic GPA. *Other factors considered include:* application essay, recommendation(s), alumni/ae relation, character/personal qualities, extracurricular activities, first generation, interview, level of applicant's interest, religious affiliation/commitment, talent/ability, volunteer work. **Freshman Admission Requirements:** High school diploma is required and GED is accepted. *Academic units required:* 4 English, 3 mathematics, 3 science, (2 science labs), 2 foreign language, 1 social studies, 1 history. *Academic units recommended:* 4 English, 3 mathematics, 3 science, (2 science labs), 2 foreign language, 1 social studies, 1 history. **Freshman Admission Statistics:** 38,960 applied, 40% admitted, 20% enrolled. **Transfer Admission Requirements:** college transcript(s), minimum college GPA of 2.5 required. Lowest grade transferable C. **General Admission Information:** Application Fee $50. Nonfall registration accepted. Credit and/or placement offered for CEEB Advanced Placement tests.

COSTS AND FINANCIAL AID

Annual tuition $30,586. Room and board $9,422. Required fees $3,130. Average book expense $1,364. **Required Forms and Deadlines:** FAFSAState Residency Affirmation. **Notification of Awards:** Applicants will be notified of awards on a rolling basis beginning 3/1. **Types of Aid:** *Need-based scholarships/grants:* Federal Pell, SEOG, state scholarships/grants, the school's own gift aid. *Loans:* Subsidized Stafford, Unsubsidized Stafford, PLUS, Federal Perkins, Federal Nursing, state loans. **Student Employment:** Federal Work-Study Program available. Institutional employment available. Highest amount earned per year from on-campus jobs $9,325. Off-campus job opportunities are good. **Financial Aid Statistics:** 98% freshmen, 95% undergrads receive need-based scholarship or grant aid. 97% freshmen, 89% undergrads receive non-need-based scholarship or grant aid. 82% freshmen, 81% undergrads receive need-based self-help aid. 3% freshmen, 3% undergrads receive athletic scholarships. 97% freshmen, 93% undergrads receive any aid. % undergrads borrow to pay for school. Average cumulative indebtedness. **Criteria for awarding institutional aid:** *Non-need-based:* academics, art, athletics, job skills, leadership, music/drama.

BEACON COLLEGE

105 E. Main Street, Leesburg, FL 34748
Phone: 352-638-9731 • **Financial Aid Phone:** 352-787-6306
E-mail: admissions@beaconcollege.edu
Fax: 352-787-0721 • **Website:** www.beaconcollege.edu • **ACT Code:** 704

This private school was founded in 1989.

RATINGS
Admissions Selectivity Rating: 61   **Fire Safety Rating:** 93   **Green Rating:** 60*

STUDENTS AND FACULTY
Enrollment: 128. **Student Body:** 80% out-of-state, 0% international (2 countries represented). Asian 2%, African American 10%, Caucasian 85%, Hispanic 3%, Native American 0%. **Retention and Graduation:** 73% freshmen return for sophomore year. 50% freshmen graduate within 4 years. **Faculty:** Student/faculty ratio 714:1. 17 full-time faculty, 65% hold PhDs, 6% are members of minority groups, 59% are women. 0% of classes are taught by teaching assistants.

ACADEMICS
Degrees: associate, bachelor's. **Classes:** Most classes have 10–19 students. **Special Study Options:** cooperative education program, independent study, internships, study abroad. **Honors Programs:** Psi Tau Omega is the academic honor society at Beacon College. **Disability Services:** Special programs offered to physically disabled students include note-taking services, reader services, tape recorders, tutors.

FACILITIES
Housing: special housing for disabled students, apartments for single students, Students enjoy 1, 2, and 3 bedroom apartment style living accommodations. **Computers:** 100% of classrooms, have wireless network access.

CAMPUS LIFE
Environment: Village. **Activities:** Choral groups, drama/theater, literary magazine, student government, student newspaper, yearbook 13 registered organizations, 1 honor societies, 1 fraternities, 1 sororities. **On-Campus Highlights:** New Resident Apartment Complex, Student Center, Stoer Building - Office of Student Services, Beacon College Library, Administration Building.

ADMISSIONS
Freshman Academic Profile: Average high school GPA 2.8. Minimum paper TOEFL 525. **Basis for Candidate Selection:** *Very important factors*

considered include: recommendation(s). *Important factors considered include:* application essay, rigor of secondary school record, standardized test scores, character/personal qualities, talent/ability. *Other factors considered include:* Class rank, academic GPA, extracurricular activities, interview, volunteer work, work experience. **Freshman Admission Requirements:** High school diploma is required and GED is accepted. *Academic units required:* 4 English, 1 mathematics, 1 science, 1 social studies, 2 history, 3 academic electives. *Academic units recommended:* 4 English, 1 mathematics, 1 science, 1 social studies, 2 history, 3 academic electives. **Freshman Admission Statistics:** 53 applied, 92% admitted, 59% enrolled. **Transfer Admission Requirements:** High school transcript, college transcript(s), essay or personal statement, interview, Lowest grade transferable C. **General Admission Information:** Application Fee $50. Regular application deadline 8/1. Notification on a rolling basis, beginning on or about 9/1. Nonfall registration accepted. Credit offered for CEEB Advanced Placement tests.

COSTS AND FINANCIAL AID
Annual tuition $27,000. Room and board $8,150. Required fees $700. Average book expense $900. **Required Forms and Deadlines:** FAFSA, institution's own financial aid form, state aid form. **Notification of Awards:** Applicants will be notified of awards on or about 2/1. **Types of Aid:** *Need-based scholarships/grants:* Federal Pell, SEOG, state scholarships/grants, private scholarships, the school's own gift aid. *Loans:* **Student Employment:** Federal Work-Study Program available. Highest amount earned per year from on-campus jobs $6,000. Off-campus job opportunities are good. **Financial Aid Statistics:** 60% freshmen, 22% undergrads receive need-based scholarship or grant aid. 60% freshmen, 22% undergrads receive need-based self-help aid. 67% undergrads borrow to pay for school. Average cumulative indebtedness $28,000.

BECKER COLLEGE

61 Sever Street, Worcester, MA 01609
Phone: 508-373-9400 • **Financial Aid Phone:** 508-373-9440
E-mail: admissions@becker.edu • **CEEB Code:** 3079
Fax: 508-373-1500 • **Website:** www.becker.edu • **ACT Code:** 1784

RATINGS
Admissions Selectivity Rating: 76   **Fire Safety Rating:** 76   **Green Rating:** 60*

STUDENTS AND FACULTY
Enrollment: 1,787. **Student Body:** 58% female, 42% male, 31% out-of-state, 1% international (19 countries represented). Asian 1%, African American 7%, Caucasian 59%, Hispanic 8%, Native American 0%. **Retention and Graduation:** 65% freshmen return for sophomore year. 18% freshmen graduate within 4 years. 29% freshmen graduate within 6 years. **Faculty:** Student/faculty ratio 16:1. 44 full-time faculty, 61% hold PhDs, 9% are members of minority groups, 61% are women. 0% of classes are taught by teaching assistants.

ADMISSIONS
Freshman Academic Profile: 2.8. 4% in top 10% of high school class, 27% in top 25% of high school class, 62% in top 50% of high school class. 65% from public high schools. SAT Math middle 50% range 440-560. SAT Critical Reading middle 50% range 430-550. SAT Writing middle 50% range 430–520. ACT middle 50% range 18-24. Minimum paper TOEFL 550. **Basis for Candidate Selection:** *Very important factors considered include:* Class rank, academic GPA, standardized test scores. *Important factors considered include:* recommendation(s). *Other factors considered include:* application essay, rigor of secondary school record, alumni/ae relation, character/personal qualities, extracurricular activities, interview, level of applicant's interest, volunteer work, work experience. **Freshman Admission Requirements:** High school diploma is required and GED is accepted. *Academic units required:* 4 English, 3 mathematics, 2 science, (2 science labs), 2 social studies, 1 history, 4 academic electives. *Academic units recommended:* 4 English, 3 mathematics, 2 science, (2 science labs), 2 social studies, 1 history, 4 academic electives. **Freshman Admission Statistics:** 3,350 applied, 62% admitted, 18% enrolled. **Transfer Admission Requirements:** college transcript(s), minimum college GPA of 2.00 required. Lowest grade transferable C. **General Admission Information:** Application Fee $50. Notification on a rolling basis, beginning on or about 11/1. Nonfall registration accepted. Admission may be deferred for a maximum of 1 year. Credit and/or placement offered for CEEB Advanced Placement tests.

COSTS AND FINANCIAL AID

Annual tuition $28,900. Room and board $11,080. Required fees $1,440. Average book expense $1,100. **Required Forms and Deadlines:** FAFSA. **Types of Aid:** *Need-based scholarships/grants:* Federal Pell, SEOG, state scholarships/grants, private scholarships, the school's own gift aid. *Loans:* Subsidized Stafford, Unsubsidized Stafford, PLUS, Federal Perkins. **Student Employment:** Federal Work-Study Program available. Institutional employment available. Off-campus job opportunities are good. **Financial Aid Statistics:** 64% freshmen, 68% undergrads receive need-based scholarship or grant aid. 100% freshmen, 95% undergrads receive non-need-based scholarship or grant aid. 94% freshmen, 95% undergrads receive need-based self-help aid. 100% freshmen, 93% undergrads receive any aid. 95% undergrads borrow to pay for school. Average cumulative indebtedness $41,666. **Criteria for awarding institutional aid:** *Non-need-based:* academics, alumni affiliation, athletics, leadership.

See page 1016.

BELHAVEN COLLEGE

1500 Peachtree Street, Jackson, MS 39202
Phone: 601-968-5940 • **Financial Aid Phone:** 601-968-5933
E-mail: admission@belhaven.edu • **CEEB Code:** 1055
Fax: 601-968-8946 • **Website:** www.belhaven.edu • **ACT Code:** 2180

This private school, affiliated with the Presbyterian Church, was founded in 1883. It has a 42-acre campus.

RATINGS
Admissions Selectivity Rating: 87   **Fire Safety Rating:** 60*   **Green Rating:** 60*

STUDENTS AND FACULTY
Enrollment: 2,443. **Student Body:** 66% female, 34% male, 45% out-of-state, (20 countries represented).
Retention and Graduation: 73% freshmen return for sophomore year. 43% freshmen graduate within 4 years. 54% freshmen graduate within 6 years. **Faculty:** Student/faculty ratio 12:1. 60 full-time faculty, 72% hold PhDs, 38% are women. 0% of classes are taught by teaching assistants.

ACADEMICS
Degrees: associate, bachelor's, certificate, master's. **Classes:** Most classes have fewer than 10 students. Most lab/discussion sessions have fewer than 10 students. **Majors with Highest Enrollment:** business/commerce; dance; elementary education and teaching; history; social sciences. **Special Study Options:** Accelerated program, distance learning, double major, dual enrollment, English as a Second Language (ESL), honors program, independent study, internships, student-designed major, study abroad, teacher certification program. **Honors Programs:** Honors Program: The Honors College at Belhaven College gives academically advanced, highly motivated students a forum in which to deepen and expand their college education, both intellectually and spiritually. Enrollment in the Honors College is limited to students who demonstrate a past record of academic achievement, seriousness about their calling, and enthusiasm for challenging dialogue with students and scholars from a variety of fields. **Combined Degree Programs:** BA/MEng. **Career Services:** internships.

FACILITIES
Housing: men's dorms, women's dorms. **Special Academic Facilities/Equipment:** Bitsy Irby art gallery **Computers:** 100% of dorms, 100% of libraries, 100% of student union, have wireless network access. Students can register for classes online. Administrative functions (other than registration) can be performed online.

CAMPUS LIFE
Environment: City. **Activities:** Choral groups, dance, drama/theater, jazz band, literary magazine, marching band, music ensembles, pep band, student government, student newspaper, yearbook, International Student Organization 29 registered organizations, 5 religious organizations. **Athletics (Intercollegiate):** *Men:* baseball, basketball, cheerleading, cross-country, football, golf, soccer, tennis. *Women:* basketball, cheerleading, cross-country, golf, soccer, softball, tennis, volleyball.

ADMISSIONS
Freshman Academic Profile: Average high school GPA 3.2. 14% in top 10% of high school class, 29% in top 25% of high school class, 64% in top 50% of high school class. % from public high schools. SAT Math middle 50% range 440-560. SAT Critical Reading middle 50% range 450-600. ACT middle 50% range 20-25. Minimum web-based TOEFL 61. Minimum paper TOEFL 500. **Basis for Candidate Selection:** *Very important factors considered include:* academic GPA, standardized test scores. *Other factors considered include:*

application essay, recommendation(s), interview. **Freshman Admission Requirements:** High school diploma is required and GED is accepted. *Academic units required:* 4 English, 2 mathematics, 1 science, 1 history, 8 academic electives. *Academic units recommended:* 4 English, 2 mathematics, 1 science, 1 history, 8 academic electives. **Freshman Admission Statistics:** 1,568 applied, 46% admitted, 26% enrolled. **Transfer Admission Requirements:** college transcript(s), minimum college GPA of 2.0 required. Lowest grade transferable D. **General Admission Information:** Application Fee $25. Nonfall registration accepted. Admission may be deferred for a maximum of 12. Credit and/or placement offered for CEEB Advanced Placement tests.

COSTS AND FINANCIAL AID
Annual tuition $17,700. Room and board $6,500. Average book expense $1,400. **Required Forms and Deadlines:** FAFSA, state aid form. **Notification of Awards:** Applicants will be notified of awards on a rolling basis beginning 2/1. **Types of Aid:** *Need-based scholarships/grants:* Federal Pell, SEOG, state scholarships/grants, private scholarships, the school's own gift aid. *Loans:* Subsidized Stafford, Unsubsidized Stafford, PLUS, Federal Perkins. **Student Employment:** Federal Work-Study Program available. **Financial Aid Statistics:** 99% freshmen, 98% undergrads receive need-based scholarship or grant aid. 9% freshmen, 7% undergrads receive non-need-based scholarship or grant aid. 82% freshmen, 83% undergrads receive need-based self-help aid. 15% freshmen, 9% undergrads receive athletic scholarships. 100% undergrads borrow to pay for school. Average cumulative indebtedness $32,728. **Criteria for awarding institutional aid:** *Non-need-based:* academics, alumni affiliation, art, athletics, music/drama.

BELLARMINE UNIVERSITY

Best 378

2001 Newburg Road, Louisville, KY 40205
Phone: 502-272-8131 • **Financial Aid Phone:** 502-272-8124
E-mail: admissions@bellarmine.edu • **CEEB Code:** 1056
Fax: 502-272-8002 • **Website:** www.bellarmine.edu • **ACT Code:** 1490

This private school, affiliated with the Roman Catholic Church, was founded in 1950. It has a 135-acre campus.

RATINGS
Admissions Selectivity Rating: 81   **Fire Safety Rating:** 90   **Green Rating:** 71

STUDENTS AND FACULTY
Enrollment: 2,440. **Student Body:** 64% female, 36% male, 33% out-of-state, 1% international (31 countries represented). Asian 2%, African American 4%, Caucasian 83%, Hispanic 4%, Native American 0%.
Retention and Graduation: 25% grads go on to further study within 1 year. 5% grads pursue arts and sciences degrees. 5% grads pursue law degrees. 5% grads pursue business degrees. 5% grads pursue medical degrees. **Faculty:** Student/faculty ratio 12:1. 156 full-time faculty, 81% hold PhDs, 10% are members of minority groups, 53% are women. 0% of classes are taught by teaching assistants.

ACADEMICS
Degrees: bachelor's, master's, post-bachelor's certificate. **Classes:** Most classes have 10–19 students. Most lab/discussion sessions have 10–19 students. **Majors with Highest Enrollment:** business/commerce; nursing/registered nurse (rn, asn, bsn, msn); psychology. **Special Study Options:** Accelerated program, cross-registration, double major, dual enrollment, honors program, independent study, internships, liberal arts/career combination, student-designed major, study abroad, teacher certification program. **Honors Programs:** Bellarmine Honors Program Bellarmine Brown Scholars Program **Combined Degree Programs:** Accounting BA and MBA. **Disability Services:** Special programs offered to physically disabled students include note-taking services, reader services, tutors. **Career Services:** Alumni network, alumni services, career/job search classes, career assessment, internships Career Services highlights include 80% of Bellarmine undergraduates will complete an internship or another form of experiential learning before graduating (Source NSSE 2007 BU Seniors).

FACILITIES
Housing: Coed dorms, special housing for disabled students, men's dorms, women's dorms, 4 bedroom or 2 bedroom suites. 85% of campus accessible to physically disabled. **Special Academic Facilities/Equipment:** McGrath Art Gallery; Thomas Merton Center. **Computers:** 50% of classrooms, 100% of dorms, 100% of libraries, 25% of dining areas, 100% of student union, 25% of common outdoor areas have wireless network access. Students can register

for classes online. Administrative functions (other than registration) can be performed online.

CAMPUS LIFE

Environment: Metropolis. **Activities:** Choral groups, concert band, dance, drama/theater, jazz band, literary magazine, music ensembles, musical theater, pep band, radio station, student government, student newspaper, yearbook, Campus Ministries, International Student Organization 70 registered organizations, 3 honor societies, 6 religious organizations. 1 fraternities, 1 sororities. **Athletics (Intercollegiate):** *Men:* baseball, basketball, bowling, cross-country, golf, lacrosse, soccer, tennis, track/field (outdoor). *Women:* basketball, bowling, cheerleading, cross-country, field hockey, golf, soccer, softball, tennis, track/field (outdoor), volleyball. **On-Campus Highlights:** Norton Health Science Center, Our Lady of the Woods Chapel, Siena Halls, Owsley B. Frazier Stadium, The Thomas Merton Center, The $5.1 million Owsley B. Frazier Stadium has taken approximately 18 months to build and will be the new home for Bellarmine's soccer, field hockey, lacrosse, and track teams. The new facility has several outstanding features which are outlined below. *Artificial Turf:* The artificial turf product, called "24/7," was produced and installed by the Motz Group. It has permanent markings for soccer, field hockey, and lacrosse and has an exceptional drainage system to allow for extensive play in all weather conditions. *Lighting:* Lighting has been installed at the field to allow for night play. The Musco Lighting system features redirected lighting which bends spill lighting back on to the field, drastically reducing the amount of light which will fall outside the stadium's perimeter. *Track Surface:* The track is an eight-lane, 400-meter track, featuring three long jump pits, two pole vault areas, a high jump pit, and a steeplechase water jump pit. The surface is a dual-durometer, polyurethane poured surface provided by Beynon Sport Surfaces, the same company which has installed tracks at other top college facilities over the past three years including Illinois, Maryland, and Purdue. *Capacity:* Chairback bench seating is available for 2,000 spectators. *Scoreboard:* A Daktronics scoreboard featuring a 17' x 3' scrolling message board is installed on the three-story clock tower at the south end of the stadium. *Press Box:* The fully enclosed press box features seating for 14 people and wireless internet access. The stadium also has a concession stand, public address system, officials' locker rooms, storage areas, and public restrooms. **Environmental Initiatives:** Development of an on-campus fruit/vegetable garden. Our major geothermal heating/cooling project and improved energy efficiency in new dormitory construction. Establishment of the Center for Regional Environmental Studies in July 2009.

ADMISSIONS

Freshman Academic Profile: Average high school GPA 3.5. 21% in top 10% of high school class, 50% in top 25% of high school class, 84% in top 50% of high school class. 63% from public high schools. SAT Math middle 50% range 490-600. SAT Critical Reading middle 50% range 490-580. ACT middle 50% range 22-27. Minimum web-based TOEFL 80. Minimum paper TOEFL 550. **Basis for Candidate Selection:** *Very important factors considered include:* academic GPA, recommendation(s), rigor of secondary school record, standardized test scores, character/personal qualities, level of applicant's interest. *Important factors considered include:* Class rank, extracurricular activities. *Other factors considered include:* application essay, alumni/ae relation, first generation, geographical residence, interview, racial/ethnic status, state residency, talent/ability, volunteer work, work experience. **Freshman Admission Requirements:** High school diploma is required and GED is accepted. *Academic units required:* 4 English, 3 mathematics, 3 science, (2 science labs), 2 foreign language, 2 social studies, 1 history, 5 academic electives. *Academic units recommended:* 4 English, 3 mathematics, 3 science, (2 science labs), 2 foreign language, 2 social studies, 1 history, 5 academic electives. **Freshman Admission Statistics:** 4,317 applied, 86% admitted, 16% enrolled. **Transfer Admission Requirements:** college transcript(s), minimum college GPA of 2.0 required. Lowest grade transferable D. **General Admission Information:** Application Fee $25. Regular application deadline 8/15. Notification on a rolling basis, beginning on or about 10/1. Nonfall registration accepted. Admission may be deferred for a maximum of 12 months. Credit offered for CEEB Advanced Placement tests.

COSTS AND FINANCIAL AID

Annual tuition $31,990. Room and board $9,770. Required fees $1,280. Average book expense $792. **Required Forms and Deadlines:** FAFSA. **Notification of Awards:** Applicants will be notified of awards on a rolling basis beginning 4/1. **Types of Aid:** *Need-based scholarships/grants:* Federal Pell, SEOG, state scholarships/grants, private scholarships, the school's own gift aid. *Loans:* Subsidized Stafford, Unsubsidized Stafford, PLUS, Federal Perkins, state loans, college/university loans from institutional funds. **Student Employment:** Federal Work-Study Program available. Institutional employment available. Highest amount earned per year from on-campus jobs $2,500. Off-campus job opportunities are excellent. **Financial Aid Statistics:** 100% freshmen, 96% undergrads receive need-based scholarship or grant aid. 30% freshmen, 30% undergrads receive non-need-based scholarship or grant aid. 64% freshmen, 66% undergrads receive need-based self-help aid. 7% freshmen, 7% undergrads receive athletic scholarships. 100% freshmen, 98% undergrads receive any aid.

69% undergrads borrow to pay for school. Average cumulative indebtedness $28,722. **Criteria for awarding institutional aid:** *Non-need-based:* academics, alumni affiliation, art, athletics, leadership, minority status, music/drama, religious affiliation, state/district residency.

BELMONT ABBEY COLLEGE

100 Belmont-Mount Holly Road, Belmont, NC 28012
Phone: 704-461-6665 • **Financial Aid Phone:** 704-461-718
E-mail: admissions@bac.edu • **CEEB Code:** 5055
Fax: 704-461-6220 • **Website:** www.belmontabbeycollege.edu • **ACT Code:** 3070

This private school, affiliated with the Roman Catholic Church, was founded in 1876. It has a 650-acre campus.

RATINGS

Admissions Selectivity Rating: 76   **Fire Safety Rating:** 60*   **Green Rating:** 60*

STUDENTS AND FACULTY

Enrollment: 1,695. **Student Body:** 59% female, 41% male, 28% out-of-state, 3% international (24 countries represented). Asian 1%, African American 27%, Caucasian 35%, Hispanic 2%, Native American 0%.
Retention and Graduation: 63% freshmen return for sophomore year. 34% freshmen graduate within 4 years. 43% freshmen graduate within 6 years.
Faculty: Student/faculty ratio 16:1. 76 full-time faculty, 70% hold PhDs, 1% are members of minority groups, 45% are women. 0% of classes are taught by teaching assistants.

ACADEMICS

Degrees: bachelor's. **Classes:** Most classes have 10–19 students. **Special Study Options:** Accelerated program, cooperative education program, double major, dual enrollment, external degree program, honors program, independent study, internships, liberal arts/career combination, study abroad, teacher certification program, weekend college. **Honors Programs:** Anne Horne Little Honors Program Hintemeyer Scholars Program. **Disability Services:** Special programs offered to physically disabled students include tutors. **Career Services:** Alumni network, alumni services, career/job search classes, career assessment, internships, regional alumni. Career Services highlights include internships.

FACILITIES

Housing: Coed dorms, men's dorms, women's dorms, apartments for single students. **Special Academic Facilities/Equipment:** Museum with rare book collection. **Computers:** 10% of classrooms, 100% of libraries, 100% of dining areas, 100% of student union, have wireless network access.

CAMPUS LIFE

Environment: Village. **Activities:** Choral groups, drama/theater, literary magazine, musical theater, student government, student newspaper, Campus Ministries, International Student Organization 21 registered organizations, 5 honor societies, 3 religious organizations. 5 fraternities, 4 sororities. **Athletics (Intercollegiate):** *Men:* baseball, basketball, cross-country, golf, soccer, tennis, wrestling. *Women:* basketball, cross-country, soccer, softball, tennis, volleyball. **On-Campus Highlights:** Church/Basillica, Weeler Center Athletic Center, Dining hall, Holy Grounds Coffee Shop.

ADMISSIONS

Freshman Academic Profile: Average high school GPA 3.1. 12% in top 10% of high school class, 85% in top 25% of high school class, 65% in top 50% of high school class. 65% from public high schools. SAT Math middle 50% range 450-570. SAT Critical Reading middle 50% range 420-560. ACT middle 50% range 20-24. Minimum paper TOEFL 550. **Basis for Candidate Selection:** *Very important factors considered include:* rigor of secondary school record, standardized test scores, character/personal qualities. *Important factors considered include:* Class rank, alumni/ae relation, extracurricular activities, interview, volunteer work. *Other factors considered include:* application essay, recommendation(s), talent/ability, work experience. **Freshman Admission Requirements:** High school diploma is required and GED is accepted. *Academic units required:* 4 English, 3 mathematics, 2 science, 2 foreign language, 1 social studies, 1 history, 3 academic electives. *Academic units recommended:* 4 English, 3 mathematics, 2 science, 2 foreign language, 1 social studies, 1 history, 3 academic electives. **Freshman Admission Statistics:** 1,842 applied, 64% admitted, 26% enrolled. **Transfer Admission Requirements:** college transcript(s), minimum college GPA of 2.0 required. Lowest grade transferable C. **General Admission Information:** Application Fee $35. Regular application deadline 8/2. Notification on a rolling basis, beginning on or about 9/15. Nonfall registration accepted. Admission may be deferred for a maximum of 1 yr. Credit offered for CEEB Advanced Placement tests.

COSTS AND FINANCIAL AID

Annual tuition $27,622. Room and board $10,403. **Required Forms and Deadlines:** FAFSA. **Notification of Awards:** Applicants will be notified of awards on a rolling basis beginning 3/10. **Types of Aid:** *Need-based scholarships/grants:* Federal Pell, SEOG, state scholarships/grants, private scholarships, the school's own gift aid. *Loans:* Direct Subsidized Stafford, Direct Unsubsidized Stafford, Direct PLUS, Federal Perkins. **Student Employment:** Federal Work-Study Program available. Institutional employment available. Highest amount earned per year from on-campus jobs $1,800. Off-campus job opportunities are fair. **Financial Aid Statistics:** 100% freshmen, 99% undergrads receive need-based scholarship or grant aid. 9% freshmen, 5% undergrads receive non-need-based scholarship or grant aid. 82% freshmen, 94% undergrads receive need-based self-help aid. 4% freshmen, 5% undergrads receive athletic scholarships. 99% freshmen, 96% undergrads receive any aid. 62% undergrads borrow to pay for school. Average cumulative indebtedness $17,004. **Criteria for awarding institutional aid:** *Non-need-based:* academics, athletics, leadership, religious affiliation, state/district residency.

BELMONT UNIVERSITY

1900 Belmont Boulevard, Nashville, TN 37212-3757
Phone: 615-460-6785 • **Financial Aid Phone:** 615-460-6403
E-mail: buadmission@belmont.edu • **CEEB Code:** 1058
Fax: 615-460-5434 • **Website:** www.belmont.edu • **ACT Code:** 3946

This private school, affiliated with the Christian (Nondenominational) Church, was founded in 1860. It has a 66-acre campus.

RATINGS
Admissions Selectivity Rating: 74   **Fire Safety Rating:** 96   **Green Rating:** 73

STUDENTS AND FACULTY
Enrollment: 5,237. **Student Body:** 59% female, 41% male, 63% out-of-state, 1% international (30 countries represented). Asian 1%, African American 4%, Caucasian 85%, Hispanic 4%, Native American 0%.
Retention and Graduation: 81% freshmen return for sophomore year. 55% freshmen graduate within 4 years. 67% freshmen graduate within 6 years. 17% grads go on to further study within 1 year. **Faculty:** Student/faculty ratio 13:1. 306 full-time faculty, 81% hold PhDs, 8% are members of minority groups, 51% are women.

ACADEMICS
Degrees: bachelor's, master's, post-bachelor's certificate, post-master's certificate. **Classes:** Most classes have 10–19 students. Most lab/discussion sessions have 10–19 students. **Majors with Highest Enrollment:** business/commerce; music management and merchandising; music performance. **Special Study Options:** Accelerated program, cooperative education program, distance learning, double major, honors program, independent study, internships, liberal arts/career combination, student-designed major, study abroad, teacher certification program. **Career Services:** Alumni network, alumni services, career/job search classes, career assessment, internships Career Services highlights include Campus-based business program - Our undergraduate students run five campus-based businesses that are collaborations with other programs on campus. This offers experiential learning for students who do not have a business of their own. Three of these businesses are retail oriented - located in 3,400 square feet of prime retail space in our student life building facing the edge of campus, and the other two are service business. These programs involve as many as 60 students at any given time.

FACILITIES
Housing: men's dorms, women's dorms, apartments for single students. 98% of campus accessible to physically disabled. **Special Academic Facilities/Equipment:** Language lab, recording studio, the Belmont Mansion, Little Theatre **Computers:** 100% of classrooms, 100% of dorms, 100% of libraries, 100% of dining areas, 100% of student union, 100% of common outdoor areas have wireless network access. Students can register for classes online. Administrative functions (other than registration) can be performed online.

CAMPUS LIFE
Environment: Metropolis. **Activities:** Choral groups, concert band, dance, drama/theater, jazz band, literary magazine, marching band, music ensembles, musical theater, opera, pep band, radio station, student government, student newspaper, symphony orchestra, television station, Campus Ministries, International Student Organization 80 registered organizations, 17 honor societies, 12 religious organizations. 3 fraternities, 4 sororities. **Athletics (Intercollegiate):** *Men:* baseball, basketball, cross-country, golf, soccer, tennis, track/field (outdoor). *Women:* basketball, cross-country, golf, soccer, softball, tennis, track/field (outdoor), volleyball. **On-Campus Highlights:** Beaman Student Life Center, Curb Event Center, Belmont Mansion, Center for Music Business Recording

Studios, Massey Courtyard. **Environmental Initiatives:** Recycle Composting of all leaves Conservation

ADMISSIONS
Freshman Academic Profile: Average high school GPA 3.5. 35% in top 10% of high school class, 62% in top 25% of high school class, 91% in top 50% of high school class. SAT Math middle 50% range 530-630. SAT Critical Reading middle 50% range 540-640. ACT middle 50% range 24-29. Minimum paper TOEFL 550. **Basis for Candidate Selection:** *Very important factors considered include:* Class rank, academic GPA, rigor of secondary school record, standardized test scores. *Important factors considered include:* application essay, recommendation(s). *Other factors considered include:* alumni/ae relation, character/personal qualities, extracurricular activities, first generation, racial/ethnic status, talent/ability, volunteer work, work experience. **Freshman Admission Requirements:** High school diploma is required and GED is accepted. *Academic units required:* 4 English, 3 mathematics, 3 science, 2 foreign language, 3 social studies, 3 academic electives. *Academic units recommended:* 4 English, 3 mathematics, 3 science, 2 foreign language, 3 social studies, 3 academic electives. **Freshman Admission Statistics:** 4,046 applied, 84% admitted, 37% enrolled. **Transfer Admission Requirements:** High school transcript, college transcript(s), essay or personal statement, standardized test scores, minimum college GPA of 2.0 required. Lowest grade transferable C. **General Admission Information:** Application Fee $50. Regular application deadline 8/1. Notification on a rolling basis, beginning on or about 9/1. Nonfall registration accepted. Admission may be deferred for a maximum of 1 YEAR. Credit and/or placement offered for CEEB Advanced Placement tests.

COSTS AND FINANCIAL AID
Required Forms and Deadlines: FAFSA. **Notification of Awards:** Applicants will be notified of awards on a rolling basis beginning 3/15. **Types of Aid:** *Need-based scholarships/grants:* Federal Pell, SEOG, state scholarships/grants, private scholarships, the school's own gift aid. *Loans:* Direct PLUS, Subsidized Stafford, Unsubsidized Stafford, PLUS, Federal Perkins, college/university loans from institutional funds. **Student Employment:** Federal Work-Study Program available. Highest amount earned per year from on-campus jobs $4,000. Off-campus job opportunities are excellent. **Financial Aid Statistics:** 71% freshmen, 68% undergrads receive need-based scholarship or grant aid. 64% freshmen, 52% undergrads receive non-need-based scholarship or grant aid. 84% freshmen, 87% undergrads receive need-based self-help aid. 2% freshmen, 2% undergrads receive athletic scholarships. 52% undergrads borrow to pay for school. Average cumulative indebtedness $31,079. **Criteria for awarding institutional aid:** *Non-need-based:* academics, art, athletics, leadership, music/drama, religious affiliation, state/district residency.

See page 1018.

BELOIT COLLEGE

Best 378

700 College Street, Beloit, WI 53511
Phone: 608-363-2500 • **Financial Aid Phone:** 608-363-2663
E-mail: admiss@beloit.edu • **CEEB Code:** 1059
Fax: 608-363-2075 • **Website:** www.beloit.edu • **ACT Code:** 4564

This private school was founded in 1846. It has a 75-acre campus.

RATINGS
Admissions Selectivity Rating: 87   **Fire Safety Rating:** 67   **Green Rating:** 65

STUDENTS AND FACULTY
Enrollment: 1,274. **Student Body:** 59% female, 41% male, 80% out-of-state, 10% international (36 countries represented). Asian 2%, African American 3%, Caucasian 71%, Hispanic 8%, Native American 0%.
Retention and Graduation: 91% freshmen return for sophomore year. 68% freshmen graduate within 4 years. 34% grads go on to further study within 1 year. **Faculty:** Student/faculty ratio 11:1. 115 full-time faculty, 98% hold PhDs, 15% are members of minority groups, 51% are women. 0% of classes are taught by teaching assistants.

ACADEMICS
Degrees: bachelor's. **Classes:** Most classes have 10–19 students. **Majors with Highest Enrollment:** anthropology; international relations and affairs; political science and government. **Special Study Options:** double major, English as a Second Language (ESL), exchange student program (domestic), independent

study, internships, liberal arts/career combination, student-designed major, study abroad, teacher certification program, 3-2 Programs in Engineering and Forestry. Over half of our graduates earn credit off-campus for at least a semester through our comprehensive study abroad and "field term" programs. **Combined Degree Programs:** BA/MEng, Rush University - Nursing and Med. Tech. **Disability Services:** Special programs offered to physically disabled students include note-taking services, tape recorders, tutors. **Career Services:** Alumni network, alumni services, career assessment, internships, regional alumni. Career Services highlights include Beloit offers career exploration programs and services that connect students with alumni and other professionals for job shadowing, informational interviews and internships. Programs can be reviewed at http://www.beloit.edu/facs/.

FACILITIES

Housing: Coed dorms, women's dorms, fraternity/sorority housing, cooperative housing, apartments for single students, theme housing, a wide variety of special-interest housing, particularly for languages. See Beloit College's web site for a current list of special-interest housing. 35% of campus accessible to physically disabled. **Special Academic Facilities/Equipment:** Wright Museum of Art Logan Museum of Anthropology Center for Language Study Student Run Market Research Company (BELMARK) Alfred S. Thompson Observatory Center for Entrepreneurial Leadership (CELEB) **Computers:** 80% of classrooms, 10% of dorms, 100% of libraries, 100% of dining areas, 80% of student union, 4% of common outdoor areas have wireless network access. Administrative functions (other than registration) can be performed online.

CAMPUS LIFE

Environment: Town. **Activities:** Choral groups, dance, drama/theater, jazz band, literary magazine, music ensembles, musical theater, radio station, student government, student newspaper, student-run film society, symphony orchestra, television station, yearbook, International Student Organization 95 registered organizations, 6 honor societies, 3 religious organizations. 3 fraternities, 3 sororities. **Athletics (Intercollegiate):** *Men:* baseball, basketball, cross-country, football, golf, soccer, swimming, tennis, track/field (outdoor), track/field (indoor). *Women:* basketball, cross-country, soccer, softball, swimming, tennis, track/field (outdoor), track/field (indoor), volleyball. **On-Campus Highlights:** Logan Museum of Anthropology, Wright Museum of Art, Center for the Sciences, Alfred S. Thompson Observatory, Laura H. Idrich Neese Theatre Complex, Other popular spaces include the Poetry Garden, the Java Joint, Morse Library, Sports Center, and Pearsons Hall. **Environmental Initiatives:** New Science Center has been platinum-level LEED certified, one of only three such buildings in the state Campus-wide recycling program; in 2009 Beloit recycled 72 tons of material, 15% of the total waste stream. Green meal plan for food service is under continuous discussion and development. The introduction of tray-less dining in 2008 has reduced waste by 35%, locally sourced food and produce from the campus vegetable garden are used whenever possible, and two campus dining options have switched to bio-degradable utensils and plates.

ADMISSIONS

Freshman Academic Profile: Average high school GPA 3.5. 34% in top 10% of high school class, 74% in top 25% of high school class, 97% in top 50% of high school class. 76% from public high schools. SAT Math middle 50% range 560-690. SAT Critical Reading middle 50% range 550-710. ACT middle 50% range 24-30. Minimum web-based TOEFL 80. Minimum paper TOEFL 550. **Basis for Candidate Selection:** *Very important factors considered include:* application essay, academic GPA, recommendation(s), rigor of secondary school record. *Important factors considered include:* Class rank, standardized test scores, interview. *Other factors considered include:* alumni/ae relation, character/personal qualities, extracurricular activities, first generation, level of applicant's interest, talent/ability, volunteer work, work experience. **Freshman Admission Requirements:** High school diploma is required and GED is accepted. **Freshman Admission Statistics:** 2,205 applied, 67% admitted, 21% enrolled. **Transfer Admission Requirements:** college transcript(s), essay or personal statement, statement of good standing from prior institution(s). Minimum college GPA of 3.00 required. Lowest grade transferable C. **General Admission Information:** Application Fee $35. Notification on a rolling basis, beginning on or about 2/15. Nonfall registration accepted. Admission may be deferred for a maximum of 12 months. Credit and/or placement offered for CEEB Advanced Placement tests.

COSTS AND FINANCIAL AID

Annual tuition $40,970. Room and board $7,256. Required fees $280. Average book expense $600. **Required Forms and Deadlines:** FAFSA, institution's own financial aid form, state aid form. **Notification of Awards:** Applicants will be notified of awards on a rolling basis beginning 4/1. **Types of Aid:** *Need-based scholarships/grants:* Federal Pell, SEOG, state scholarships/grants, private scholarships, the school's own gift aid. *Loans:* Subsidized Stafford, Unsubsidized Stafford, PLUS, Federal Perkins, college/university loans from institutional funds. **Student Employment:** Federal Work-Study Program available. Institutional employment available. Highest amount earned per year from on-campus jobs $3,000. Off-campus job opportunities are good. **Financial Aid**

Statistics: 100% freshmen, 100% undergrads receive need-based scholarship or grant aid. 20% freshmen, 18% undergrads receive non-need-based scholarship or grant aid. 80% freshmen, 81% undergrads receive need-based self-help aid. 94% freshmen, 93% undergrads receive any aid. 57% undergrads borrow to pay for school. Average cumulative indebtedness $27,981. **Criteria for awarding institutional aid:** *Non-need-based:* academics, leadership, minority status, music/drama.

See page 1020.

BEMIDJI STATE UNIVERSITY

1500 Birchmont Dr. NE, Bemidji, MN 56601
Phone: 218-755-2040 • **Financial Aid Phone:** 218-755-4143
E-mail: admissions@bemidjistate.edu • **CEEB Code:** 6676
Fax: 218-755-2074 • **Website:** www.bemidjistate.edu • **ACT Code:** 2084

This public school was founded in 1919. It has a 90-acre campus.

RATINGS
Admissions Selectivity Rating: 67　　　**Fire Safety Rating:** 65　　　**Green Rating:** 79

STUDENTS AND FACULTY
Enrollment: 4,362. **Student Body:** 52% female, 48% male, 9% out-of-state, (35 countries represented).
Retention and Graduation: 33% freshmen graduate within 4 years. 49% freshmen graduate within 6 years. 34% grads go on to further study within 1 year. 27% grads pursue arts and sciences degrees. 1% grads pursue law degrees. 5% grads pursue business degrees. 1% grads pursue medical degrees. **Faculty:** Student/faculty ratio 19:1. 192 full-time faculty, 60% hold PhDs, 6% are members of minority groups, 40% are women. 5% of classes are taught by teaching assistants.

ACADEMICS
Degrees: associate, bachelor's, master's. **Classes:** Most classes have 10–19 students. Most lab/discussion sessions have 20–29 students. **Majors with Highest Enrollment:** business/commerce; education; industrial production technologies/technicians, other. **Special Study Options:** Accelerated program, cooperative education program, distance learning, double major, dual enrollment, English as a Second Language (ESL), exchange student program (domestic), external degree program, honors program, independent study, internships, liberal arts/career combination, study abroad, teacher certification program, Eurospring Semester, Sino-Summer, Exchange program with other Minnesota state universities; other study-travel. **Disability Services:** Special programs offered to physically disabled students include note-taking services, reader services, tutors. **Career Services:** Alumni network, career/job search classes, career assessment, regional alumni.

FACILITIES
Housing: Coed dorms, men's dorms, special housing for international students, women's dorms, apartments for married students, cooperative housing, apartments for single students, two floors for SOTA (Students Older Than Average age.) Cooperative housing for international students. 95% of campus accessible to physically disabled. **Special Academic Facilities/Equipment:** Aquatics lab. Waterfront. C.V. Hobson Forest. Center for Research and Innovation (CRI). **Computers:** 90% of classrooms, 90% of dorms, 100% of libraries, 100% of student union, have wireless network access. Students can register for classes online. Administrative functions (other than registration) can be performed online.

CAMPUS LIFE
Environment: Village. **Activities:** Choral groups, concert band, dance, drama/theater, jazz band, literary magazine, music ensembles, musical theater, opera, pep band, radio station, student government, student newspaper, student-run film society, symphony orchestra, television station, Campus Ministries, International Student Organization, Model UN 83 registered organizations, 1 honor societies, 8 religious organizations. 2 fraternities, 1 sororities. **Athletics (Intercollegiate):** *Men:* baseball, basketball, cross-country, football, golf, ice hockey, soccer, softball, tennis, track/field (outdoor), track/field (indoor), volleyball. *Women:* basketball, cross-country, golf, ice hockey, soccer, softball, tennis, track/field (outdoor), track/field (indoor), volleyball. **On-Campus Highlights:** Recreation Center, Student Union, Library, Dormitories, Computer labs. **Environmental Initiatives:** Signature theme of Environmental Stewardship ACUPCC signatory Talloires Declaration Signatory.

ADMISSIONS
Freshman Academic Profile: Average high school GPA 3.3. 4% in top 10% of high school class, 27% in top 25% of high school class, 62% in top 50% of

high school class. 95% from public high schools. ACT middle 50% range 19-24. Minimum paper TOEFL 550. **Basis for Candidate Selection:** *Very important factors considered include:* Class rank, standardized test scores. *Important factors considered include:* rigor of secondary school record. *Other factors considered include:* application essay, recommendation(s). **Freshman Admission Requirements:** High school diploma is required and GED is accepted. *Academic units required:* 4 English, 3 mathematics, 3 science, (1 science labs), 2 foreign language, 3 social studies, 1 history, 1 Art/Music/World Culture. *Academic units recommended:* 4 English, 3 mathematics, 3 science, (1 science labs), 2 foreign language, 3 social studies, 1 history, 1 Art/Music/World Culture. **Freshman Admission Statistics:** 2,062 applied, 83% admitted, 45% enrolled. Minimum college GPA of 2.0 required. Lowest grade transferable C. **General Admission Information:** Application Fee $20. Regular application deadline 8/15. Nonfall registration accepted. Admission may be deferred for a maximum of 1 year. Placement offered for CEEB Advanced Placement tests.

COSTS AND FINANCIAL AID
Annual in-state tuition $6,410. Annual out-of-state tuition $6,410. Room and board $6,325. Required fees $950. Average book expense $800. **Required Forms and Deadlines:** institution's own financial aid form. **Notification of Awards:** Applicants will be notified of awards on a rolling basis beginning 5/15. **Types of Aid:** *Need-based scholarships/grants:* Federal Pell, SEOG, state scholarships/grants, private scholarships, the school's own gift aid. *Loans:* Direct Subsidized Stafford, Direct Unsubsidized Stafford, Direct PLUS, Federal Perkins, state loans. **Student Employment:** Federal Work-Study Program available. Institutional employment available. Highest amount earned per year from on-campus jobs $2,700. Off-campus job opportunities are good. **Financial Aid Statistics:** 69% freshmen, 75% undergrads receive need-based scholarship or grant aid. 75% freshmen, 72% undergrads receive non-need-based scholarship or grant aid. 89% freshmen, 88% undergrads receive need-based self-help aid. 13% freshmen, 4% undergrads receive athletic scholarships. 77% freshmen, 77% undergrads receive any aid. 67% undergrads borrow to pay for school. Average cumulative indebtedness $21,931. **Criteria for awarding institutional aid:** *Non-need-based:* academics, alumni affiliation, art, athletics, music/drama.

BENEDICT COLLEGE

1600 Harden St, Columbia, SC 29204
Phone: 803-705-4491
E-mail: thompso@benedict.edu
Fax: 803-253-5167 • **Website:** www.benedict.edu

This private school, affiliated with the Baptist Church, was founded in 1870. It has a 110-acre campus.

RATINGS
Admissions Selectivity Rating: 64   **Fire Safety Rating:** 60*   **Green Rating:** 60*

STUDENTS AND FACULTY
Enrollment: 2,641. **Student Body:** 51% female, 49% male, 40% out-of-state. Asian 0%, African American 99%, Caucasian 0%, Hispanic 1%, Native American 0%.
Retention and Graduation: 53% freshmen return for sophomore year. 11% freshmen graduate within 4 years. 26% freshmen graduate within 6 years. **Faculty:** Student/faculty ratio 19:1. 117 full-time faculty, 65% hold PhDs, 95% are members of minority groups, 58% are women.

ACADEMICS
Degrees: bachelor's. **Classes:** Most classes have fewer than 10 students. Most lab/discussion sessions have fewer than 10 students. **Special Study Options:** Accelerated program, double major, dual enrollment, external degree program, honors program, internships, teacher certification program, weekend college.

FACILITIES
Housing: men's dorms, women's dorms.

CAMPUS LIFE
Environment: City. **Activities:** Choral groups, concert band, marching band, student government, student newspaper, Campus Ministries, International Student Organization.

ADMISSIONS
Freshman Academic Profile: Average high school GPA 2.5. 5% in top 10% of high school class, 15% in top 25% of high school class, 39% in top 50% of high school class. 63% from public high schools. SAT Math middle 50% range 320-430. SAT Critical Reading middle 50% range 320-430. ACT middle 50% range 13-17. Minimum web-based TOEFL 80. Minimum paper TOEFL 550. **Freshman Admission Requirements:** High school diploma is required and GED is accepted. **Freshman Admission Statistics:** 4,624 applied, 83% admitted, 17% enrolled. **Transfer Admission Requirements:** High school transcript, college

transcript(s), statement of good standing from prior institution(s). Minimum college GPA of 2.0 required. Lowest grade transferable C. **General Admission Information:** Application Fee $25. Nonfall registration accepted. Credit offered for CEEB Advanced Placement tests.

COSTS AND FINANCIAL AID
Annual tuition $12,516. Room and board $6,444. Required fees $1,494. Average book expense $1,000. **Required Forms and Deadlines:** FAFSA. **Types of Aid:** *Need-based scholarships/grants:* Federal Pell, SEOG, state scholarships/grants, private scholarships, the school's own gift aid, United Negro College Fund. *Loans:* Direct Subsidized Stafford, Direct Unsubsidized Stafford, Direct PLUS.

BENEDICTINE COLLEGE

1020 North Second Street, Atchison, KS 66002
Phone: 913-360-7476 • **Financial Aid Phone:** 913-360-7480
E-mail: bcadmiss@benedictine.edu • **CEEB Code:** 6056
Fax: 913-367-5462 • **Website:** www.benedictine.edu • **ACT Code:** 1444

This private school, affiliated with the Roman Catholic Church, was founded in 1859. It has a 225-acre campus.

RATINGS
Admissions Selectivity Rating: 84   **Fire Safety Rating:** 64   **Green Rating:** 60*

STUDENTS AND FACULTY
Enrollment: 1,382. **Student Body:** 53% female, 47% male, 44% out-of-state, 2% international (18 countries represented). Asian 1%, African American 4%, Caucasian 81%, Hispanic 5%, Native American 1%.
Retention and Graduation: 76% freshmen return for sophomore year. 43% freshmen graduate within 4 years. 61% freshmen graduate within 6 years. 28% grads go on to further study within 1 year. 20% grads pursue arts and sciences degrees. 1% grads pursue law degrees. 7% grads pursue business degrees. 3% grads pursue medical degrees. **Faculty:** Student/faculty ratio 14:1. 76 full-time faculty, 68% hold PhDs, 7% are members of minority groups, 26% are women. 0% of classes are taught by teaching assistants.

ACADEMICS
Degrees: associate, bachelor's, master's. **Classes:** Most classes have 20–29 students. Most lab/discussion sessions have 10–19 students. **Majors with Highest Enrollment:** business/commerce; elementary education and teaching; religion/religious studies. **Special Study Options:** cooperative education program, double major, dual enrollment, English as a Second Language (ESL), independent study, internships, liberal arts/career combination, student-designed major, study abroad, teacher certification program. **Combined Degree Programs:** BA/MA, BA/MEng, 3-2 occupational therapy with Washington U. **Disability Services:** Special programs offered to physically disabled students include tutors. **Career Services:** alumni services, career/job search classes, career assessment, internships.

FACILITIES
Housing: Coed dorms, men's dorms, women's dorms, Off-campus college-owned housing. 80% of campus accessible to physically disabled. **Special Academic Facilities/Equipment:** Language and special education labs, high tech classroom, stadium, student union. **Computers:** 60% of classrooms, 100% of dorms, 100% of libraries, 100% of dining areas, 100% of student union, 75% of common outdoor areas have wireless network access. Administrative functions (other than registration) can be performed online.

CAMPUS LIFE
Environment: Town. **Activities:** Choral groups, concert band, dance, drama/theater, jazz band, literary magazine, music ensembles, musical theater, pep band, student government, student newspaper, symphony orchestra, yearbook. 38 registered organizations, 14 honor societies, 4 religious organizations. **Athletics (Intercollegiate):** *Men:* baseball, basketball, cheerleading, cross-country, football, golf, soccer, tennis, track/field (outdoor), track/field (indoor). *Women:* basketball, cheerleading, cross-country, golf, soccer, softball, tennis, track/field (outdoor), track/field (indoor), volleyball. **On-Campus Highlights:** Raven Roost, Ferrell Hall, Student Union, Abbey Church, River Lookout.

ADMISSIONS
Freshman Academic Profile: Average high school GPA 3.3. 5% in top 10% of high school class, 15% in top 25% of high school class, 36% in top 50% of high school class. 44% from public high schools. ACT middle 50% range 21-27. Minimum paper TOEFL 535. **Basis for Candidate Selection:** *Very important factors considered include:* Class rank, rigor of secondary school record, standardized test scores. *Other factors considered include:* application essay, recommendation(s), alumni/ae relation, character/personal qualities, extracurricular activities, interview, racial/ethnic status, talent/ability, volunteer work,

work experience. **Freshman Admission Requirements:** High school diploma is required and GED is accepted. *Academic units required:* 4 English, 3 mathematics, 2 science, 2 foreign language, 2 social studies, 1 history, 1 academic electives. *Academic units recommended:* 4 English, 3 mathematics, 2 science, 2 foreign language, 2 social studies, 2 history, 1 academic electives. **Freshman Admission Statistics:** 2,192 applied, 20% admitted, 91% enrolled. **Transfer Admission Requirements:** college transcript(s), minimum college GPA of 2.0 required. Lowest grade transferable C. **General Admission Information:** Application Fee $25. Notification on a rolling basis, beginning on or about 3/1. Nonfall registration accepted. Admission may be deferred for a maximum of 1 year. Credit and/or placement offered for CEEB Advanced Placement tests.

COSTS AND FINANCIAL AID

Annual tuition $18,800. Room and board $6,400. Average book expense $1,000. **Required Forms and Deadlines:** FAFSA. **Notification of Awards:** Applicants will be notified of awards on a rolling basis beginning 2/1. **Types of Aid:** *Need-based scholarships/grants:* Federal Pell, SEOG, state scholarships/grants, private scholarships, the school's own gift aid. *Loans:* Subsidized Stafford, Unsubsidized Stafford, PLUS, Federal Perkins, Alternative Loans. **Student Employment:** Federal Work-Study Program available. Institutional employment available. Off-campus job opportunities are good. **Financial Aid Statistics:** 64% freshmen, 64% undergrads receive need-based scholarship or grant aid. 100% freshmen, 99% undergrads receive non-need-based scholarship or grant aid. 80% freshmen, 85% undergrads receive need-based self-help aid. 35% freshmen, 35% undergrads receive athletic scholarships. 98% freshmen, 77% undergrads receive any aid. 98% undergrads borrow to pay for school. Average cumulative indebtedness $26,000. **Criteria for awarding institutional aid:** *Non-need-based:* academics, alumni affiliation, art, athletics, job skills, leadership, minority status, music/drama, religious affiliation.

BENEDICTINE UNIVERSITY

5700 College Road, Lisle, IL 60532-0900
Phone: 630-829-6300 • **Financial Aid Phone:** 630-829-6100
E-mail: admissions@ben.edu • **CEEB Code:** 1707
Fax: 630-829-6301 • **Website:** www.ben.edu • **ACT Code:** 1132

This private school, affiliated with the Roman Catholic Church, was founded in 1887. It has a 108-acre campus.

RATINGS
Admissions Selectivity Rating: 70   **Fire Safety Rating:** 93   **Green Rating:** 69

STUDENTS AND FACULTY
Enrollment: 3,659. **Student Body:** 61% female, 39% male, 8% out-of-state, 2% international (17 countries represented). Asian 14%, African American 10%, Caucasian 42%, Hispanic 7%, Native American 0%.
Retention and Graduation: 73% freshmen return for sophomore year. **Faculty:** Student/faculty ratio 18:1. 146 full-time faculty, 70% hold PhDs, 13% are members of minority groups, 51% are women. 0% of classes are taught by teaching assistants.

ACADEMICS
Degrees: associate, bachelor's, certificate, master's, post-bachelor's certificate, transfer associate. **Classes:** Most classes have 10–19 students. **Majors with Highest Enrollment:** biology/biological sciences; business administration, management and operations, other; computer science. **Special Study Options:** Accelerated program, cross-registration, distance learning, double major, dual enrollment, English as a Second Language (ESL), honors program, independent study, internships, study abroad, teacher certification program, weekend college, Engineering degree program with Illinois Institute of Technology. **Honors Programs:** University Scholars Program. **Disability Services:** Special programs offered to physically disabled students include note-taking services, reader services, tape recorders, tutors. **Career Services:** Alumni network, alumni services, career/job search classes, career assessment, internships Career Services highlights include Internship program.

FACILITIES
Housing: Coed dorms, men's dorms, women's dorms, apartments for married students, apartments for single students, wellness housing 100% of campus accessible to physically disabled. **Special Academic Facilities/Equipment:** Natural science and history museums,http://www.ben.edu/museum/ Exercise physiology lab. **Computers:** 100% of dorms, 100% of libraries, 100% of student union, have wireless network access. Students can register for classes online. Administrative functions (other than registration) can be performed online.

CAMPUS LIFE
Environment: Town. **Activities:** Choral groups, concert band, dance, drama/theater, jazz band, literary magazine, music ensembles, pep band, student

government, student newspaper, student-run film society, symphony orchestra, television station, Campus Ministries, International Student Organization, Model UN 40 registered organizations, 3 religious organizations. **Athletics (Intercollegiate):** *Men:* baseball, basketball, cross-country, football, golf, soccer, track/field (outdoor), track/field (indoor). *Women:* basketball, cross-country, golf, soccer, softball, tennis, track/field (outdoor), track/field (indoor), volleyball. **On-Campus Highlights:** Jurica Nature Museum, Kindlon Hall and Benedictine Library, Birck Hall of Science, Krasa Center: Chapel, cafeteria, snack bar, The Sports Complex, Coal Ben. **Environmental Initiatives:** Energy reduction Education Recycling.

ADMISSIONS
Freshman Academic Profile: Average high school GPA 3.3. 14% in top 10% of high school class, 39% in top 25% of high school class, 71% in top 50% of high school class. 80% from public high schools. ACT middle 50% range 19-25. Minimum web-based TOEFL 76. Minimum paper TOEFL 550. **Basis for Candidate Selection:** *Very important factors considered include:* Class rank, academic GPA, rigor of secondary school record, standardized test scores. *Other factors considered include:* application essay, recommendation(s), extracurricular activities, interview. **Freshman Admission Requirements:** High school diploma is required and GED is accepted. *Academic units required:* 4 English, 3 mathematics, 2 science, (1 science labs), 2 foreign language, 3 social studies, 1 history. *Academic units recommended:* 4 English, 3 mathematics, 2 science, (1 science labs), 2 foreign language, 3 social studies, 1 history. **Freshman Admission Statistics:** 2,091 applied, 76% admitted, 39% enrolled. **Transfer Admission Requirements:** college transcript(s), statement of good standing from prior institution(s). Minimum college GPA of 2.0 required. Lowest grade transferable D. **General Admission Information:** Application Fee $40. Regular application deadline 8/30. Nonfall registration accepted. Admission may be deferred for a maximum of 4. Credit offered for CEEB Advanced Placement tests.

COSTS AND FINANCIAL AID
Annual tuition $24,850. Room and board $10,900. Required fees $1,000. Average book expense $1,410. **Required Forms and Deadlines:** FAFSA. **Notification of Awards:** Applicants will be notified of awards on a rolling basis beginning 2/15. **Types of Aid:** *Need-based scholarships/grants:* Federal Pell, SEOG, state scholarships/grants, private scholarships, the school's own gift aid. *Loans:* Subsidized Stafford, Unsubsidized Stafford, PLUS, Federal Perkins. **Student Employment:** Federal Work-Study Program available. Institutional employment available. Highest amount earned per year from on-campus jobs $11,506. Off-campus job opportunities are excellent. **Financial Aid Statistics:** 65% freshmen, 63% undergrads receive need-based scholarship or grant aid. 97% freshmen, 83% undergrads receive non-need-based scholarship or grant aid. 75% freshmen, 85% undergrads receive need-based self-help aid. 1% freshmen, 98% freshmen, 92% undergrads receive any aid. 77% undergrads borrow to pay for school. Average cumulative indebtedness $19,560. **Criteria for awarding institutional aid:** *Non-need-based:* academics, alumni affiliation, leadership, music/drama, religious affiliation, state/district residency.

BENNETT COLLEGE

900 East Washington Street, Greensboro, NC 27401
Phone: 336-370-8624 • **Financial Aid Phone:** 336-517-2220
E-mail: admiss@bennett.edu • **CEEB Code:** 5058
Fax: 336-370-8653 • **Website:** www.bennett.edu • **ACT Code:** 3072

This private school, affiliated with the Methodist Church, was founded in 1873. It has a 55-acre campus.

RATINGS
Admissions Selectivity Rating: 68   **Fire Safety Rating:** 71   **Green Rating:** 60*

STUDENTS AND FACULTY
Enrollment: 651. **Student Body:** 62% out-of-state, 0% international (2 countries represented). African American 94%, Caucasian 0%, Hispanic 2%, Native American 0%.
Retention and Graduation: 20% freshmen graduate within 4 years. 34% freshmen graduate within 6 years. **Faculty:** Student/faculty ratio 10:1. 61 full-time faculty, 64% hold PhDs, 70% are members of minority groups, 77% are women. 0% of classes are taught by teaching assistants.

ACADEMICS
Degrees: bachelor's. **Classes:** Most classes have fewer than 10 students. Most lab/discussion sessions have 30–39 students. **Majors with Highest Enrollment:** communication and media studies, other; psychology; social work. **Special Study Options:** Accelerated program, cooperative education program,

cross-registration, double major, dual enrollment, honors program, independent study, internships, student-designed major, study abroad, teacher certification program, Collaborative degree program with Howard University in Nursing (2x2). **Disability Services:** Special programs offered to physically disabled students include tape recorders, tutors. **Career Services:** alumni services, career/job search classes.

FACILITIES

Housing: women's dorms, wellness housing. 21% of campus accessible to physically disabled. **Special Academic Facilities/Equipment:** Children's House, Constance Maiteena collection, college archives, telecommunications satellite dish. **Computers:** Students can register for classes online.

CAMPUS LIFE

Environment: City. **Activities:** Choral groups, dance, drama/theater, literary magazine, music ensembles, student government, student newspaper, Campus Ministries, International Student Organization 34 registered organizations, 5 honor societies, 1 religious organizations. 4 sororities. **Athletics (Intercollegiate):** *Women:* basketball, cheerleading, cross-country, softball, swimming, tennis, track/field (outdoor), volleyball. **On-Campus Highlights:** Student Union, Chapel, Little Theathre, Holgate Library, Lda Goode Gym.

ADMISSIONS

Freshman Academic Profile: 8% in top 10% of high school class, 12% in top 25% of high school class, 50% in top 50% of high school class. SAT Math middle 50% range 350-420. SAT Critical Reading middle 50% range 350-430. **Basis for Candidate Selection:** *Very important factors considered include:* academic GPA, rigor of secondary school record, standardized test scores. *Important factors considered include:* Class rank, application essay, recommendation(s), alumni/ae relation, talent/ability. *Other factors considered include:* character/personal qualities, extracurricular activities, first generation, geographical residence, interview, level of applicant's interest, racial/ethnic status, religious affiliation/commitment, state residency, volunteer work, work experience. **Freshman Admission Requirements:** High school diploma is required and GED is accepted. *Academic units required:* 4 English, 3 mathematics, 2 science, 2 foreign language, 2 social studies, 5 academic electives. *Academic units recommended:* 4 English, 3 mathematics, 2 science, 2 foreign language, 2 social studies, 5 academic electives. **Freshman Admission Statistics:** 1,433 applied, 63% admitted, 18% enrolled. **Transfer Admission Requirements:** college transcript(s), essay or personal statement, minimum college GPA of 2.0 required. Lowest grade transferable C. **General Admission Information:** Application Fee $30. Nonfall registration accepted. Credit offered for CEEB Advanced Placement tests.

COSTS AND FINANCIAL AID

Annual tuition $14,614. Room and board $7,428. Required fees $2,180. Average book expense $1,500. **Required Forms and Deadlines:** FAFSA, institution's own financial aid form. **Notification of Awards:** Applicants will be notified of awards on or about 7/15. **Types of Aid:** *Need-based scholarships/grants:* Federal Pell, SEOG, state scholarships/grants, private scholarships, the school's own gift aid, United Negro College Fund, Federal Nursing Scholarships. *Loans:* Subsidized Stafford, Unsubsidized Stafford, PLUS, Federal Perkins, The College has emergency funds available. **Student Employment:** Federal Work-Study Program available. Institutional employment available. Highest amount earned per year from on-campus jobs $1,500. Off-campus job opportunities are good. **Financial Aid Statistics:** 96% freshmen, 93% undergrads receive need-based scholarship or grant aid. 1% freshmen, 2% undergrads receive non-need-based scholarship or grant aid. 96% freshmen, 94% undergrads receive need-based self-help aid. 94% undergrads borrow to pay for school. Average cumulative indebtedness $45,276. **Criteria for awarding institutional aid:** *Non-need-based:* academics, alumni affiliation, leadership, minority status, religious affiliation, state/district residency.

BENNINGTON COLLEGE

Office of Admissions, Bennington, VT 05201-6003
Phone: 802-440-4312
E-mail: admissions@bennington.edu • **CEEB Code:** 3080
Fax: 802-440-4320 • **Website:** www.bennington.edu • **ACT Code:** 4296

This private school was founded in 1932. It has a 470-acre campus.

RATINGS

Admissions Selectivity Rating: 91   **Fire Safety Rating:** 93   **Green Rating:** 84

STUDENTS AND FACULTY

Enrollment: 688. **Student Body:** 64% female, 36% male, 96% out-of-state, 7% international (35 countries represented). Asian 2%, African American 2%, Caucasian 77%, Hispanic 5%, Native American 0%.
Retention and Graduation: 83% freshmen return for sophomore year. 59% freshmen graduate within 4 years. 64% freshmen graduate within 6 years. 16% grads go on to further study within 1 year. 10% grads pursue arts and sciences degrees. 1% grads pursue law degrees. 1% grads pursue business degrees. 3% grads pursue medical degrees. **Faculty:** Student/faculty ratio 9:1. 64 full-time faculty, 70% hold PhDs, 13% are members of minority groups, 45% are women. 0% of classes are taught by teaching assistants.

ACADEMICS

Degrees: bachelor's, master's, post-bachelor's certificate. **Classes:** Most classes have 10–19 students. Most lab/discussion sessions have 10–19 students. **Majors with Highest Enrollment:** English language and literature; visual and performing arts. **Special Study Options:** Accelerated program, cross-registration, double major, English as a Second Language (ESL), independent study, internships, student-designed major, study abroad, teacher certification program, Postbaccalaureate program in preparation for Medical or Allied Health School Grad Programs. **Combined Degree Programs:** BA/MAT. **Disability Services:** Special programs offered to physically disabled students include note-taking services, reader services, tape recorders. **Career Services:** Alumni network, alumni services, career/job search classes, career assessment, internships Career Services highlights include Each academic year at Bennington College includes a seven-week winter term of field work off campus. During Field Work Term, students take their interests to the world beyond the College, where they work at jobs or internships in fields that complement their studies, clarify their interests, and open possibilities for their future.

FACILITIES

Housing: Coed dorms, cooperative housing, theme housing, off-campus. 78% of campus accessible to physically disabled. **Special Academic Facilities/Equipment:** Observatory; greenhouse; digital arts lab; architecture, drawing, painting, printmaking, and sculpture studios; ceramics studio and kilns; color and black-and-white photography darkrooms; film and video editing studio; fully equipped professional theaters; scripts library; dance studios and archives; electronic music and sound recording studios; music practice rooms and music library **Computers:** 100% of classrooms, 100% of dorms, 100% of libraries, 100% of dining areas, 100% of student union, 75% of common outdoor areas have wireless network access. Administrative functions (other than registration) can be performed online.

CAMPUS LIFE

Environment: Town. **Activities:** Choral groups, dance, drama/theater, literary magazine, music ensembles, musical theater, radio station, student government, student newspaper, International Student Organization 21 registered organizations. **On-Campus Highlights:** Edward Clark Crossett Library, Visual and Performing Arts Center, Student Center, Commons Dining Hall and Lounge, Meyer Recreation Barn, Opening in 2011, the Center for the Advancement of Public Action (CAPA), is a $20-million, state-of-the-art, green, academic facility for Bennington's new citizenship curriculum. It morphs the studio of the artist, the laboratory of a scientist, the workshop of a craftsman, and the think tank of policy work. **Environmental Initiatives:** Converting to a campus-wide biomass heating system New green construction Energy conservation program

ADMISSIONS

Freshman Academic Profile: Average high school GPA 3.5. 35% in top 10% of high school class, 67% in top 25% of high school class, 93% in top 50% of high school class. 57% from public high schools. SAT Math middle 50% range 560-660. SAT Critical Reading middle 50% range 620-720. SAT Writing middle 50% range 610-700. ACT middle 50% range 26-30. Minimum paper TOEFL 577. **Basis for Candidate Selection:** *Very important factors considered include:* Class rank, application essay, academic GPA, recommendation(s), rigor of secondary school record, character/personal qualities, extracurricular activities, interview, talent/ability. *Other factors considered include:* standardized test scores, alumni/ae relation, first generation, geographical residence, level of applicant's interest, racial/ethnic status, volunteer work, work experience. **Freshman Admission Requirements:** High school diploma is required and GED is accepted. **Freshman Admission Statistics:** 1,236 applied, 63% admitted, 25% enrolled. **Transfer Admission Requirements:** High school transcript, college transcript(s), essay or personal statement, statement of good standing from prior institution(s). Lowest grade transferable C. **General Admission Information:** Application Fee $60. Regular application deadline 1/3. Regular notification 4/1. Nonfall registration accepted. Admission may be deferred for a maximum of one year. Neither credit nor placement offered for CEEB Advanced Placement tests.

COSTS AND FINANCIAL AID

Annual tuition $43,070. Room and board $12,770. Required fees $1,150. Average book expense $1,000. **Required Forms and Deadlines:** FAFSA, institution's own financial aid form, CSS/Financial Aid PROFILE, noncustodial

PROFILEStudent and Parent Federal Tax Returns and W-2s. **Notification of Awards:** Applicants will be notified of awards on or about 4/1. **Types of Aid:** *Need-based scholarships/grants:* Federal Pell, SEOG, state scholarships/grants, private scholarships, the school's own gift aid. *Loans:* Direct Subsidized Stafford, Direct Unsubsidized Stafford, Direct PLUS, college/university loans from institutional fundsNOTE: College/university loans from institutional funds for International students only. **Student Employment:** Federal Work-Study Program available. Institutional employment available. Highest amount earned per year from on-campus jobs $1,900. Off-campus job opportunities are good. **Financial Aid Statistics:** 99% freshmen, 98% undergrads receive need-based scholarship or grant aid. 16% freshmen, 8% undergrads receive non-need-based scholarship or grant aid. 81% freshmen, 90% undergrads receive need-based self-help aid. 95% freshmen, 90% undergrads receive any aid. 68% undergrads borrow to pay for school. Average cumulative indebtedness $25,716. **Criteria for awarding institutional aid:** *Non-need-based:* academics.

BENTLEY UNIVERSITY

Best 378

175 Forest Street, Waltham, MA 2452
Phone: 781-891-2244 • **Financial Aid Phone:** 781-891-3441
E-mail: ugadmission@bentley.edu • **CEEB Code:** 3096
Fax: 781-891-3414 • **Website:** www.bentley.edu • **ACT Code:** 1783

This private school was founded in 1917. It has a 163-acre campus.

RATINGS
Admissions Selectivity Rating: 93   **Fire Safety Rating:** 99   **Green Rating:** 92

STUDENTS AND FACULTY
Enrollment: 4,154. **Student Body:** 41% female, 59% male, 52% out-of-state, 12% international (97 countries represented). Asian 7%, African American 3%, Caucasian 61%, Hispanic 7%, Native American 0%.
Retention and Graduation: 94% freshmen return for sophomore year. 81% freshmen graduate within 4 years. 89% freshmen graduate within 6 years. 17% grads go on to further study within 1 year. 1% grads pursue arts and sciences degrees. 1% grads pursue law degrees. 11% grads pursue business degrees.
Faculty: Student/faculty ratio 14:1. 280 full-time faculty, 82% hold PhDs, 12% are members of minority groups, 39% are women.

ACADEMICS
Degrees: associate, bachelor's, doctoral, master's, post-bachelor's certificate, post-master's certificate, terminal associate, transfer associate. **Classes:** Most classes have 30–39 students. **Majors with Highest Enrollment:** accounting and related services, other; business administration and management; marketing/marketing management. **Special Study Options:** Accelerated program, cross-registration, double major, honors program, independent study, internships, liberal arts/career combination, student-designed major, study abroad, 5 year Bachelors/Masters program in Business Administration, Accountancy, Finance, Marketing, Analytics, Info Technology, Financial Planning, Taxation. **Honors Programs:** The Honors Program is a four-year journey that provides special challenge and fulfillment to select Bentley students. Students in approximately the top ten percent of the entering class are invited to participate in this four-year program. **Combined Degree Programs:** BA-MS, BS-MS, BA-MBA, BS-MBA. **Disability Services:** Special programs offered to physically disabled students include note-taking services, reader services, tape recorders, tutors. **Career Services:** Alumni network, alumni services, career/job search classes, career assessment, internships, regional alumni. Career Services highlights include For the past several years, Bentley students have journeyed to Ghana, West Africa, to work on a long-term economic development partnership focused on helping an orphanage become self-sustaining. This effort has expanded to include students who now implement and train Ghanian NGOs in the use of accounting software to allow them to apply for an receive USAID funding.

FACILITIES
Housing: Coed dorms, special housing for disabled students, apartments for single students, wellness housing, theme housing. Three Wellness Houses with an overall health and wellness theme are available. Global living floors with a focus on connecting international and US students are available to residents. 70% of campus accessible to physically disabled. **Special Academic Facilities/Equipment:** Academic Technology Center, Alliance for Ethics and Social Responsibility, Center for Business Ethics, Center for International Students and Scholars, Center for Quantitative Analysis, Art Gallery, Center for Marketing Technology, Center for Languages and International Collaboration, ESOL Cen-

ter, Math Learning Center, Writing Center, Financial Trading Room, Design and Usability Center, Service Learning Center, Cronin International Center, Cyberlaw Center, Enterprise Risk Management Program, Hughey Center for Financial Services, Library, Media & Culture labs and studio, Valente Center for Arts and Sciences, Winer Accounting Center, Women's Leadership Institute, Academic Technology Center, Spiritual Life Center. **Computers:** 100% of classrooms, 100% of dorms, 100% of libraries, 100% of dining areas, 100% of student union, 100% of common outdoor areas have wireless network access. Students can register for classes online. Administrative functions (other than registration) can be performed online. Undergraduates are required to own a computer.

CAMPUS LIFE
Environment: Town. **Activities:** Choral groups, dance, drama/theater, jazz band, literary magazine, music ensembles, pep band, radio station, student government, student newspaper, television station, Campus Ministries, International Student Organization, Model UN 101 registered organizations, 3 honor societies, 4 religious organizations. 5 fraternities, 4 sororities. **Athletics (Intercollegiate):** *Men:* baseball, basketball, cross-country, diving, football, golf, ice hockey, lacrosse, soccer, swimming, tennis, track/field (outdoor), track/field (indoor). *Women:* basketball, cross-country, diving, field hockey, lacrosse, soccer, softball, swimming, tennis, track/field (outdoor), track/field (indoor), volleyball. **On-Campus Highlights:** Student Center, Dana Athletic Center, Currito Burrito, Einstein's Coffee Shop, Library. **Environmental Initiatives:** Continued upgrades of the energy management system (EMS) for greater control and scheduling of heating/cooling systems in campus buildings Achieved a 7% reduction in GHGs in FY2010 as compared to FY2008—the result of sound energy management and energy efficiency upgrades in Bentley's campus buildings Ongoing education, outreach and engagement of the Bentley community (faculty, staff, students) in sustainability intiatives (energy conservation, water conservation, recycling, reuse, etc)

ADMISSIONS
Freshman Academic Profile: 45% in top 10% of high school class, 82% in top 25% of high school class, 98% in top 50% of high school class. 72% from public high schools. SAT Math middle 50% range 600-680. SAT Critical Reading middle 50% range 540-635. SAT Writing middle 50% range 550-650. ACT middle 50% range 25-29. Minimum web-based TOEFL 90. Minimum paper TOEFL 577. **Basis for Candidate Selection:** *Very important factors considered include:* academic GPA, rigor of secondary school record, standardized test scores. *Important factors considered include:* application essay, recommendation(s), character/personal qualities, extracurricular activities, level of applicant's interest, volunteer work. *Other factors considered include:* Class rank, alumni/ae relation, first generation, geographical residence, interview, racial/ethnic status, state residency, talent/ability, work experience. **Freshman Admission Requirements:** High school diploma is required and GED is accepted. **Freshman Admission Statistics:** 6,695 applied, 43% admitted, 31% enrolled. **Transfer Admission Requirements:** High school transcript, college transcript(s), essay or personal statement, statement of good standing from prior institution(s). Lowest grade transferable C. **General Admission Information:** Application Fee $50. Early decision application deadline 11/1. Regular application deadline 1/15. Regular notification 4/1. Nonfall registration accepted. Admission may be deferred for a maximum of 1 year. Credit and/or placement offered for CEEB Advanced Placement tests.

COSTS AND FINANCIAL AID
Annual tuition $38,130. Room and board $12,960. Required fees $1,498. Average book expense $1,150. **Required Forms and Deadlines:** FAFSA, CSS/Financial Aid PROFILE, noncustodial PROFILE, business/farm supplement. Federal Tax Returns, including all schedules for parents and student. **Notification of Awards:** Applicants will be notified of awards on a rolling basis beginning 3/25. **Types of Aid:** *Need-based scholarships/grants:* Federal Pell, SEOG, state scholarships/grants, private scholarships, the school's own gift aid. *Loans:* Subsidized Stafford, Unsubsidized Stafford, PLUS, Federal Perkins, state loans. **Student Employment:** Federal Work-Study Program available. Institutional employment available. Off-campus job opportunities are good. **Financial Aid Statistics:** 87% freshmen, 84% undergrads receive need-based scholarship or grant aid. 32% freshmen, 30% undergrads receive non-need-based scholarship or grant aid. 90% freshmen, 91% undergrads receive need-based self-help aid. 1% freshmen, 1% undergrads receive athletic scholarships. 74% freshmen, 73% undergrads receive any aid. 64% undergrads borrow to pay for school. Average cumulative indebtedness $33,066. **Criteria for awarding institutional aid:** *Non-need-based:* academics, athletics, leadership, minority status.

See page 1022.

BEREA COLLEGE

CPO 2220, Berea, KY 40404
Phone: 859-985-3500 • **Financial Aid Phone:** 859-985-3310
E-mail: admissions@berea.edu • **CEEB Code:** 1060
Fax: 859-985-3512 • **Website:** www.berea.edu • **ACT Code:** 1492

This private school was founded in 1855. It has a 140-acre campus.

RATINGS
Admissions Selectivity Rating: 96 **Fire Safety Rating:** 90 **Green Rating:** 89

STUDENTS AND FACULTY
Enrollment: 1,613. **Student Body:** 57% female, 43% male, 56% out-of-state, 7% international (58 countries represented). Asian 1%, African American 15%, Caucasian 65%, Hispanic 3%, Native American 0%.
Retention and Graduation: 43% freshmen graduate within 4 years. 62% freshmen graduate within 6 years. **Faculty:** Student/faculty ratio 11:1. 124 full-time faculty, 89% hold PhDs, 13% are members of minority groups, 46% are women. 0% of classes are taught by teaching assistants.

ACADEMICS
Degrees: bachelor's. **Classes:** Most classes have 10–19 students. **Majors with Highest Enrollment:** biology/biological sciences; business/commerce; family and consumer sciences/human sciences. **Special Study Options:** double major, English as a Second Language (ESL), exchange student program (domestic), honors program, independent study, internships, student-designed major, study abroad, teacher certification program, 3-2 engineering program with Washington University, St. Louis, and University of Kentucky. **Combined Degree Programs:** at UK or Washington Univ (MO) resulting in BS. **Disability Services:** Special programs offered to physically disabled students include note-taking services, reader services, tape recorders. **Career Services:** Alumni network, alumni services, career/job search classes, career assessment, internships.

FACILITIES
Housing: men's dorms, women's dorms, apartments for married students, apartments for single parents and married students at our Ecovillage (see the following site for more information: http://www.berea.edu/sens/ecovillage/). 75% of campus accessible to physically disabled. **Special Academic Facilities/ Equipment:** Appalachian Gallery, Special Collections and Sound Archives in the Hutchins Library, Planetarium and Observatory, Geology Museum, The Ecovillage, the Child Development Laboratory, extensive acreage of farmland and forestland, and the Monty Saulmon Early Technology Lab. **Computers:** 33% of classrooms, 100% of libraries, 100% of dining areas, 100% of student union, 33% of common outdoor areas have wireless network access. Students can register for classes online. Administrative functions (other than registration) can be performed online. Undergraduates are required to own a computer.

CAMPUS LIFE
Environment: Village. **Activities:** Choral groups, dance, drama/theater, jazz band, literary magazine, music ensembles, pep band, student government, student newspaper, yearbook, Campus Ministries, International Student Organization 75 registered organizations, 14 honor societies, 5 religious organizations. **Athletics (Intercollegiate):** *Men:* baseball, basketball, cross-country, golf, soccer, swimming, tennis, track/field (outdoor). *Women:* basketball, cross-country, soccer, softball, swimming, tennis, track/field (outdoor), volleyball. **On-Campus Highlights:** Carillon (in Draper building tower), EcoVillage (married and single parent housing), Alumni Building (cafeteria, lounge, gameroom), Woods-Penn Complex (post office, cafe, etc), Seabury Center (gym). **Environmental Initiatives:** 1. Sustainability and Environmental Studies academic program 2. Ecological Construction and Renovations (including 1st LEED-certified building in KY and the Ecovillage residential complex for student families). Current residence hall construction expected to be LEED Platinum including organic and sustainable practices on College Farm and increased utilization of College and locally grown products in Dining Services. 3. Local Food Initiative

ADMISSIONS
Freshman Academic Profile: Average high school GPA 3.4. 31% in top 10% of high school class, 73% in top 25% of high school class, 98% in top 50% of high school class. SAT Math middle 50% range 483-588. SAT Critical Reading middle 50% range 495-640. SAT Writing middle 50% range 513-610. ACT middle 50% range 22-27. Minimum web-based TOEFL 61. Minimum paper TOEFL 500. **Basis for Candidate Selection:** *Very important factors considered include:* Class rank, academic GPA, rigor of secondary school record,

standardized test scores, interview. *Important factors considered include:* application essay, character/personal qualities. *Other factors considered include:* recommendation(s), extracurricular activities, first generation, geographical residence, level of applicant's interest, racial/ethnic status, state residency, talent/ability, volunteer work, work experience. **Freshman Admission Requirements:** High school diploma is required and GED is accepted. **Freshman Admission Statistics:** 4,707 applied, 12% admitted. **Transfer Admission Requirements:** High school transcript, college transcript(s), interview, minimum college GPA of 2.0 required. Lowest grade transferable C. **General Admission Information:** Regular application deadline 4/30. Notification on a rolling basis, beginning on or about 11/1. Nonfall registration accepted. Credit offered for CEEB Advanced Placement tests.

COSTS AND FINANCIAL AID
. Room and board $5,966. Required fees $980. Average book expense $700. **Required Forms and Deadlines:** FAFSA. **Notification of Awards:** Applicants will be notified of awards on a rolling basis beginning 4/1. **Types of Aid:** *Need-based scholarships/grants:* Federal Pell, SEOG, state scholarships/grants, private scholarships, the school's own gift aid. *Loans:* Subsidized Stafford, Unsubsidized Stafford, PLUS, Federal Perkins, college/university loans from institutional funds. **Student Employment:** Federal Work-Study Program available. **Financial Aid Statistics:** 100% freshmen, 100% undergrads receive need-based scholarship or grant aid. 100% freshmen, 100% undergrads receive need-based self-help aid. 100% freshmen, 100% undergrads receive any aid. 77% undergrads borrow to pay for school. Average cumulative indebtedness $7,661.

BERKELEY COLLEGE

44 Rifle Camp Road, West Paterson, NJ 7424
Phone: 973-278-5400
E-mail: Info@berkeleycollege.edu • **CEEB Code:** 2061
Fax: 973-278-9141 • **ACT Code:** 2576

This proprietary school was founded in 1931. It has a 25-acre campus.

RATINGS
Admissions Selectivity Rating: 61 **Fire Safety Rating:** 67 **Green Rating:** 60*

STUDENTS AND FACULTY
Enrollment: 2,709. **Student Body:** 72% female, 28% male, 4% out-of-state, 1% international. Asian 5%, African American 20%, Caucasian 35%, Hispanic 35%, Native American 0%.
Retention and Graduation: 53% freshmen return for sophomore year. **Faculty:** Student/faculty ratio 24:1. 54 full-time faculty, 15% are members of minority groups, 54% are women.

ACADEMICS
Degrees: associate, bachelor's, certificate, terminal associate, transfer associate. **Classes: Majors with Highest Enrollment:** accounting; business administration and management; fashion merchandising. **Special Study Options:** Accelerated program, distance learning, internships, study abroad, Academic remediation, Off-campus study at Berkeley College, New York City; Berkeley College, White Plains. **Disability Services:** Special programs offered to physically disabled students include tutors.

FACILITIES
Housing: Coed dorms. **Computers:** Administrative functions (other than registration) can be performed online.

CAMPUS LIFE
Environment: City. **Activities:** Choral groups, literary magazine, student government, student newspaper 8 registered organizations, 1 honor societies.

ADMISSIONS
Freshman Academic Profile: Minimum paper TOEFL 500. **Basis for Candidate Selection:** *Very important factors considered include:* rigor of secondary school record. *Important factors considered include:* standardized test scores. *Other factors considered include:* Class rank, academic GPA, recommendation(s), character/personal qualities, extracurricular activities, talent/ability, volunteer work, work experience. **Freshman Admission Requirements:** High school diploma is required and GED is accepted. **Transfer Admission Requirements:** college transcript(s), Lowest grade transferable C. **General Admission Information:** Application Fee $50. Nonfall registration accepted. Admission may be deferred for a maximum of no time limi. Credit and/or placement offered for CEEB Advanced Placement tests.

COSTS AND FINANCIAL AID
Annual tuition $17,400. Room and board $12,500. Required fees $750. Average book expense $1,200. **Required Forms and Deadlines:** FAFSA, state

aid form. **Notification of Awards:** Applicants will be notified of awards on or about 3/1. **Types of Aid:** *Need-based scholarships/grants:* Federal Pell, SEOG, state scholarships/grants, private scholarships, the school's own gift aid. *Loans:* Subsidized Stafford, Unsubsidized Stafford, PLUS. **Student Employment:** Federal Work-Study Program available. Institutional employment available. Off-campus job opportunities are excellent. **Financial Aid Statistics:** 85% freshmen receive any aid. 88% undergrads borrow to pay for school. Average cumulative indebtedness $5,000. **Criteria for awarding institutional aid:** *Non-need-based:* academics, alumni affiliation.

BERKLEE COLLEGE OF MUSIC

1140 Boylston Street, Boston, MA 02215-3693
Phone: 617-747-2222 • **Financial Aid Phone:** 617-747-2274
E-mail: admissions@berklee.edu • **CEEB Code:** 3107
Fax: 617-747-2047 • **Website:** www.berklee.edu • **ACT Code:** 1789

This private school was founded in 1945.

RATINGS
Admissions Selectivity Rating: 64   **Fire Safety Rating:** 60*   **Green Rating:** 60*

STUDENTS AND FACULTY
Enrollment: 3,846. **Student Body:** 31% female, 69% male, 84% out-of-state, 25% international (70 countries represented). Asian 3%, African American 6%, Caucasian 45%, Hispanic 10%, Native American 0%.
Faculty: Student/faculty ratio 13:1. 240 full-time faculty, 15% hold PhDs, 23% are women.

ACADEMICS
Degrees: bachelor's, diploma. **Classes:** Most classes have fewer than 10 students. **Majors with Highest Enrollment:** music performance; music, other. **Special Study Options:** cooperative education program, cross-registration, distance learning, double major, dual enrollment, English as a Second Language (ESL), independent study, internships, student-designed major, study abroad, teacher certification program, Berkleemusic.com is the online continuing education division of Berklee College of Music. Study is online with Berklee's renowned faculty in areas that include Music Business, Music Production, Guitar, Theory, Harmony & Ear Training, and Songwriting. **Disability Services:** Special programs offered to physically disabled students include reader services, tape recorders, tutors. **Career Services:** alumni services, career/job search classes, internships.

FACILITIES
Housing: Coed dorms. 80% of campus accessible to physically disabled. **Special Academic Facilities/Equipment:** Ensemble library, 10 professional recording studios, film scoring and editing studio, analog and digital music synthesis labs, 1,200-seat performance center, learning center.

CAMPUS LIFE
Environment: Metropolis. **Activities:** Choral groups, concert band, dance, jazz band, literary magazine, music ensembles, musical theater, radio station, student government, student newspaper, student-run film society, International Student Organization 47 registered organizations, 2 honor societies, 4 religious organizations. **On-Campus Highlights:** Student Activities Center, Berklee Performance Center, Practice Rooms, Stan Getz Media Center

ADMISSIONS
Freshman Academic Profile: Minimum paper TOEFL 500. **Basis for Candidate Selection:** *Very important factors considered include:* character/personal qualities, interview, talent/ability. *Important factors considered include:* application essay, academic GPA, rigor of secondary school record. *Other factors considered include:* Class rank, recommendation(s), standardized test scores, alumni/ae relation, extracurricular activities, first generation, level of applicant's interest, volunteer work, work experience. **Freshman Admission Requirements:** High school diploma is required and GED is accepted. **Freshman Admission Statistics:** 5,538 applied, 19% admitted, 84% enrolled. **Transfer Admission Requirements:** High school transcript, college transcript(s), essay or personal statement, interview, Lowest grade transferable C. **General Admission Information:** Application Fee $150. Regular application deadline 1/15. Regular notification 3/31. Nonfall registration accepted. Admission may be deferred for a maximum of 1 year. Credit offered for CEEB Advanced Placement tests.

COSTS AND FINANCIAL AID
. Room and board $17,200. Required fees $3,032. Average book expense $474. **Student Employment:** Federal Work-Study Program available. Highest amount earned per year from on-campus jobs $2,000. Off-campus job opportunities are good. **Financial Aid Statistics:** 50% freshmen, 50% undergrads receive need-based scholarship or grant aid. 48% freshmen, 50% undergrads re-

ceive non-need-based scholarship or grant aid. 98% freshmen, 98% undergrads receive need-based self-help aid. 57% freshmen, 38% undergrads receive any aid.

BERRY COLLEGE

P.O. Box 490159, Mount Berry, GA 30149-0159
Phone: 706-236-2215 • **Financial Aid Phone:** 706-236-1714
E-mail: admissions@berry.edu • **CEEB Code:** 5059
Fax: 706-290-2178 • **Website:** www.berry.edu • **ACT Code:** 798

This private school was founded in 1902. It has a 26000-acre campus.

RATINGS
Admissions Selectivity Rating: 82   **Fire Safety Rating:** 88   **Green Rating:** 84

STUDENTS AND FACULTY
Enrollment: 2,018. **Student Body:** 67% female, 33% male, 27% out-of-state, 1% international (17 countries represented). Asian 2%, African American 4%, Caucasian 84%, Hispanic 5%, Native American 0%.
Retention and Graduation: 75% freshmen return for sophomore year. 51% freshmen graduate within 4 years. 61% freshmen graduate within 6 years. 30% grads go on to further study within 1 year. 11% grads pursue arts and sciences degrees. 1% grads pursue law degrees. 1% grads pursue business degrees. 13% grads pursue medical degrees. **Faculty:** Student/faculty ratio 13:1. 154 full-time faculty, 90% hold PhDs, 6% are members of minority groups, 44% are women.

ACADEMICS
Degrees: bachelor's, master's, post-master's certificate. **Classes:** Most classes have 10–19 students. Most lab/discussion sessions have 20–29 students. **Majors with Highest Enrollment:** animal sciences; communication, journalism, and related programs, other; psychology. **Special Study Options:** cooperative education program, cross-registration, double major, dual enrollment, honors program, independent study, internships, student-designed major, study abroad, teacher certification program, 3-2 nursing with Emory University, 3-2 engineering with Georgia Institute of Technology. **Honors Programs:** The Berry College Honors Program provides students with an opportunity to learn within an intellectually challenging community of peers and instructors. Honors courses familiarize students with works that have been central to our past and contemporary intellectual traditions, while encouraging them to examine issues or themes from multiple and conflicting perspectives. All Honors courses are taught as seminars that provide an ideal environment for the development of effective communication and critical-thinking skills. As part of the Honors program the Oxbridge Lecture Series uses the English model of instruction with public lectures and private tutorials. Students enrolled benefit from small group, intensive student-faculty interaction, and exploratory assignments that stimulate inquiry and intellectual growth. Additionally, the Berry College Honors Program now offers a unique education abroad opportunity in conjunction with the University of Glasgow in Scotland and Berry College International Programs. **Combined Degree Programs:** 3-2 Nursing with Emory University. **Disability Services:** Special programs offered to physically disabled students include note-taking services, reader services, tape recorders, tutors. **Career Services:** Alumni network, alumni services, career/job search classes, career assessment, internships, regional alumni.

FACILITIES
Housing: Coed dorms, men's dorms, women's dorms, apartments for single students, wellness housing. Traditional residence halls are single sex; apartments and townhouses are co-ed by site or apartment. Special-interest houses for women in Math and Science (primarily first-year students). 80% of campus accessible to physically disabled. **Special Academic Facilities/Equipment:** The 131,000-square-foot Steven J. Cage Athletic and Recreation Center, National Historic Site containing Oak Hill and The Martha Berry Museum, 34-foot overshot waterwheel, Georgia wildlife management area and refuge, equine center, dairy and beef cattle research center, on-campus elementary and middle schools, child development center, science center featuring 60-foot Foucault pendulum. **Computers:** 100% of classrooms, 100% of dorms, 100% of libraries, 100% of dining areas, 100% of student union, 10% of common outdoor areas have wireless network access. Students can register for classes online. Administrative functions (other than registration) can be performed online.

CAMPUS LIFE
Environment: Town. **Activities:** Choral groups, concert band, dance, drama/theater, jazz band, literary magazine, music ensembles, musical theater, student government, student newspaper, symphony orchestra, television station, yearbook, Campus Ministries, International Student Organization, Model UN 75 registered organizations, 15 honor societies, 11 religious organizations. **Athletics (Intercollegiate):** *Men:* baseball, basketball, cross-country, diving, golf, lacrosse, soccer, swimming, tennis. *Women:* basketball, cross-country, diving,

equestrian sports, golf, lacrosse, soccer, softball, swimming, tennis, volleyball. **On-Campus Highlights:** Steven J. Cage Athletic & Recreation Ctr, Ford Complex, Science Center, Gunby Equestrian Center (Mountain Campus), The Old Mill (Mountain Campus), The 131,000 square foot Steven J. Cage Athletic and Recreation Center houses an indoor swimming pool, three basketball courts, two racquetball courts, one multi-purpose court and a jogging track. Berry Beanery (Starbucks) in Krannert Student Center. **Environmental Initiatives:** President's Climate Commitment: Sustainability office formed. Energy Star Policy, Recyclemania Environmental Land Management: Carbon Reserve, wetland banking, and EPA Compliance-Peer Audit Berry has an environmental science major

ADMISSIONS

Freshman Academic Profile: Average high school GPA 3.7. 33% in top 10% of high school class, 67% in top 25% of high school class, 91% in top 50% of high school class. 72% from public high schools. SAT Math middle 50% range 520-620. SAT Critical Reading middle 50% range 520-630. SAT Writing middle 50% range 510-620. ACT middle 50% range 24-29. Minimum web-based TOEFL 80. Minimum paper TOEFL 550. **Basis for Candidate Selection:** *Very important factors considered include:* academic GPA, rigor of secondary school record, standardized test scores. *Important factors considered include:* extracurricular activities. *Other factors considered include:* Class rank, application essay, recommendation(s), interview, volunteer work, work experience. **Freshman Admission Requirements:** High school diploma is required and GED is accepted. *Academic units required:* 4 English, 4 mathematics, 3 science, 2 foreign language, 3 social studies. *Academic units recommended:* 4 English, 4 mathematics, 3 science, 2 foreign language, 3 social studies. **Freshman Admission Statistics:** 3,485 applied, 66% admitted, 27% enrolled. **Transfer Admission Requirements:** college transcript(s), statement of good standing from prior institution(s). Minimum college GPA of 2.5 required. Lowest grade transferable C. **General Admission Information:** Application Fee $50. Regular application deadline 7/23. Notification on a rolling basis, beginning on or about 11/1. Nonfall registration accepted. Admission may be deferred for a maximum of Up to one year. Credit and/or placement offered for CEEB Advanced Placement tests.

COSTS AND FINANCIAL AID

Annual tuition $27,450. Room and board $9,679. Required fees $200. Average book expense $1,000. **Required Forms and Deadlines:** FAFSA. **Notification of Awards:** Applicants will be notified of awards on a rolling basis beginning 2/1. **Types of Aid:** *Need-based scholarships/grants:* Federal Pell, SEOG, state scholarships/grants, private scholarships, the school's own gift aid. *Loans:* Subsidized Stafford, Unsubsidized Stafford, PLUS, Federal Perkins, college/university loans from institutional funds. **Student Employment:** Federal Work-Study Program available. Institutional employment available. Highest amount earned per year from on-campus jobs $5,873. Off-campus job opportunities are good. **Financial Aid Statistics:** 100% freshmen, 100% undergrads receive need-based scholarship or grant aid. 19% freshmen, 19% undergrads receive non-need-based scholarship or grant aid. 80% freshmen, 80% undergrads receive need-based self-help aid. 100% freshmen, 99% undergrads receive any aid. 76% undergrads borrow to pay for school. Average cumulative indebtedness $20,611. **Criteria for awarding institutional aid:** *Non-need-based:* academics, art, job skills, leadership, minority status, music/drama, state/district residency.

BETHANY COLLEGE (KS)

335 E Swensson, Lindsborg, KS 67456-1897
Phone: 785-227-3311 • **Financial Aid Phone:** 785-227-3311
E-mail: admissions@bethanylb.edu • **CEEB Code:** 6034
Fax: 785-227-8993 • **Website:** www.bethanylb.edu • **ACT Code:** 1388

This private school, affiliated with the Lutheran Church, was founded in 1881. It has a 62-acre campus.

RATINGS
Admissions Selectivity Rating: 71   **Fire Safety Rating:** 97   **Green Rating:** 60*

STUDENTS AND FACULTY
Enrollment: 569. **Student Body:** 48% female, 52% male, 49% out-of-state, 6% international (29 countries represented). Asian 1%, African American 11%, Caucasian 71%, Hispanic 7%, Native American 1%.
Retention and Graduation: 61% freshmen return for sophomore year. 32% freshmen graduate within 4 years. 40% freshmen graduate within 6 years. 20% grads go on to further study within 1 year. 1% grads pursue law degrees. 3% grads pursue medical degrees. **Faculty:** Student/faculty ratio 9:1. 44 full-time faculty, 57% hold PhDs, 5% are members of minority groups, 36% are women. 0% of classes are taught by teaching assistants.

ACADEMICS
Degrees: bachelor's. **Classes:** Most classes have fewer than 10 students. Most lab/discussion sessions have fewer than 10 students. **Majors with Highest Enrollment:** biology/biological sciences; business administration and management; elementary education and teaching. **Special Study Options:** Accelerated program, cross-registration, double major, dual enrollment, exchange student program (domestic), honors program, independent study, internships, liberal arts/career combination, student-designed major, study abroad, teacher certification program. **Honors Programs:** Honors program offered **Combined Degree Programs:** BA/MEng. **Disability Services:** Special programs offered to physically disabled students include note-taking services, reader services, tape recorders, tutors. **Career Services:** Alumni network, alumni services, career/job search classes, career assessment, internships, regional alumni. Career Services highlights include Experienced Based Education.

FACILITIES
Housing: Coed dorms, women's dorms, apartments for single students, special interest housing- bid on by student groups, community service and house improvements. 80% of campus accessible to physically disabled. **Special Academic Facilities/Equipment:** Mingenback Gallery, Bethany College Archives, Plym Gallery, Sandzen Gallery.

CAMPUS LIFE
Environment: Rural. **Activities:** Choral groups, concert band, dance, drama/theater, jazz band, music ensembles, musical theater, pep band, student government, student newspaper, symphony orchestra, yearbook, Campus Ministries, International Student Organization 49 registered organizations, 8 honor societies, 9 religious organizations. 3 fraternities, 3 sororities. **Athletics (Intercollegiate):** *Men:* baseball, basketball, cheerleading, cross-country, football, golf, soccer, tennis, track/field (outdoor), track/field (indoor). *Women:* basketball, cheerleading, cross-country, golf, soccer, softball, tennis, track/field (outdoor), track/field (indoor), volleyball. **On-Campus Highlights:** Student Union, Walderstadt Library, Mingenback Art Gallery, Residence Halls, Athletic Fields.

ADMISSIONS
Freshman Academic Profile: Average high school GPA 3.3. 15% in top 10% of high school class, 42% in top 25% of high school class, 76% in top 50% of high school class. 97% from public high schools. SAT Math middle 50% range 420-560. SAT Critical Reading middle 50% range 370-500. SAT Writing middle 50% range 380-490. ACT middle 50% range 19-24. Minimum web-based TOEFL 71. Minimum paper TOEFL 525. **Basis for Candidate Selection:** *Very important factors considered include:* academic GPA, rigor of secondary school record, standardized test scores. *Other factors considered include:* application essay, recommendation(s), character/personal qualities, extracurricular activities, racial/ethnic status, talent/ability, volunteer work. **Freshman Admission Requirements:** High school diploma is required and GED is accepted. **Freshman Admission Statistics:** 811 applied, 65% admitted, 34% enrolled. **Transfer Admission Requirements:** college transcript(s), statement of good standing from prior institution(s). Minimum college GPA of 2.3 required. Lowest grade transferable D. **General Admission Information:** Application Fee $20. Regular application deadline 7/1. Notification on a rolling basis, beginning on or about 10/1. Nonfall registration accepted. Neither credit nor placement offered for CEEB Advanced Placement tests.

COSTS AND FINANCIAL AID
Annual tuition $17,824. Room and board $5,650. Required fees $300. Average book expense $1,000. **Required Forms and Deadlines:** FAFSA. **Notification of Awards:** Applicants will be notified of awards on a rolling basis beginning 3/1. **Types of Aid:** *Need-based scholarships/grants:* Federal Pell, SEOG, state scholarships/grants, private scholarships, the school's own gift aid, Federal ACG and Federal SMART and TEACH Grant. *Loans:* Subsidized Stafford, Unsubsidized Stafford, PLUS, Federal Perkins. **Student Employment:** Federal Work-Study Program available. Institutional employment available. Highest amount earned per year from on-campus jobs $1,500. Off-campus job opportunities are good. **Financial Aid Statistics:** 85% freshmen, 84% undergrads receive need-based scholarship or grant aid. 40% freshmen, 32% undergrads receive non-need-based scholarship or grant aid. 76% freshmen, 78% undergrads receive need-based self-help aid. 7% undergrads receive athletic scholarships. 100% freshmen, 98% undergrads receive any aid. 82% undergrads borrow to pay for school. Average cumulative indebtedness $17,161. **Criteria for awarding institutional aid:** *Non-need-based:* academics, alumni affiliation, art, athletics, leadership, music/drama, religious affiliation.

BETHANY COLLEGE (WV)

Office of Admission, Bethany, WV 26032
Phone: 304-829-7611 • **Financial Aid Phone:** 304-829-7141
E-mail: admission@bethanywv.edu • **CEEB Code:** 5060
Fax: 304-829-7142 • **Website:** www.bethanywv.edu • **ACT Code:** 4512

This private school, affiliated with the Disciples of Christ Church, was founded in 1840. It has a 400-acre campus.

RATINGS
Admissions Selectivity Rating: 80   **Fire Safety Rating:** 67   **Green Rating:** 60*

STUDENTS AND FACULTY
Enrollment: 805. **Student Body:** 40% female, 60% male, 79% out-of-state, (5 countries represented). Asian 0%, African American 20%, Caucasian 62%, Hispanic 2%.
Retention and Graduation: 63% freshmen return for sophomore year. 48% freshmen graduate within 6 years. **Faculty:** Student/faculty ratio 14:1. 47 full-time faculty, 81% hold PhDs, 4% are members of minority groups, 36% are women. 0% of classes are taught by teaching assistants.

ACADEMICS
Degrees: bachelor's. **Classes:** Most classes have 10–19 students. Most lab/discussion sessions have 10–19 students. **Majors with Highest Enrollment:** education; mass communication/media studies; psychology. **Special Study Options:** double major, exchange student program (domestic), independent study, internships, liberal arts/career combination, student-designed major, study abroad, teacher certification program, Off Campus Study: Washington, DC. **Combined Degree Programs:** BA/JD, BA/MEng, BA/JD with Duquesne University. **Disability Services:** Special programs offered to physically disabled students include note-taking services, reader services, tape recorders, tutors.

FACILITIES
Housing: Coed dorms, special housing for disabled students, men's dorms, women's dorms, fraternity/sorority housing, apartments for married students, apartments for single students. **Computers:** Administrative functions (other than registration) can be performed online.

CAMPUS LIFE
Environment: Rural. **Activities:** Choral groups, concert band, drama/theater, jazz band, literary magazine, music ensembles, musical theater, pep band, radio station, student government, student newspaper, student-run film society, television station, yearbook 38 registered organizations, 16 honor societies, 3 religious organizations. 6 fraternities, 3 sororities. **Athletics (Intercollegiate):** *Men:* baseball, basketball, cross-country, diving, football, golf, soccer, swimming, tennis, track/field (outdoor), track/field (indoor). *Women:* basketball, cross-country, diving, golf, soccer, softball, swimming, tennis, track/field (outdoor), track/field (indoor), volleyball. **On-Campus Highlights:** Old Main, Bethany House, Athletic Facilities, Campbell Village, Campbell Mansion.

ADMISSIONS
Freshman Academic Profile: Average high school GPA. 8% in top 10% of high school class, 9% in top 25% of high school class, 18% in top 50% of high school class. 75% from public high schools. SAT Math middle 50% range 390-510. SAT Critical Reading middle 50% range 380-480. SAT Writing middle 50% range 360-470. ACT middle 50% range 16-22. Minimum paper TOEFL 500. **Basis for Candidate Selection:** *Very important factors considered include:* Class rank, application essay, recommendation(s), rigor of secondary school record, standardized test scores. *Important factors considered include:* interview. *Other factors considered include:* alumni/ae relation, character/personal qualities, extracurricular activities, talent/ability, volunteer work, work experience. **Freshman Admission Requirements:** High school diploma is required and GED is accepted. *Academic units required:* 4 English, 3 mathematics, 3 science, 2 foreign language, 3 social studies. *Academic units recommended:* 4 English, 3 mathematics, 3 science, 2 foreign language, 3 social studies. **Freshman Admission Statistics:** 1,523 applied, 43% admitted, 40% enrolled. **Transfer Admission Requirements:** college transcript(s), essay or personal statement, statement of good standing from prior institution(s). Minimum college GPA of 2.0 required. Lowest grade transferable D°. **General Admission Information:** Application Fee $25. Notification on a rolling basis, beginning on or about 10/1. Nonfall registration accepted. Admission may be deferred for a maximum of 1 year. Credit and/or placement offered for CEEB Advanced Placement tests.

COSTS AND FINANCIAL AID
Annual tuition $23,880. Room and board $9,546. Required fees $900. Average book expense $1,300. **Required Forms and Deadlines:** FAFSA, institution's own financial aid form. **Notification of Awards:** Applicants will be notified of awards on a rolling basis beginning 3/1. **Types of Aid:** *Need-based scholarships/grants:* Federal Pell, SEOG, state scholarships/grants, private scholarships, the school's own gift aid. *Loans:* Direct Subsidized Stafford, Direct Unsubsidized Stafford, Direct PLUS, Federal Perkins. **Student Employment:** Federal Work-Study Program available. Institutional employment available. Highest amount earned per year from on-campus jobs $1,000. Off-campus job opportunities are fair. **Financial Aid Statistics:** 100% freshmen receive any aid. **Criteria for awarding institutional aid:** *Non-need-based:* academics, alumni affiliation, leadership, music/drama, religious affiliation.

See page 1024.

BETHANY UNIVERSITY

800 Bethany Drive, Scotts Valley, CA 95066
Phone: 831-438-3800
E-mail: info@bethany.edu • **CEEB Code:** 4021
Fax: 831-438-6104

This is a private school.

RATINGS
Admissions Selectivity Rating: 63   **Fire Safety Rating:** 60*   **Green Rating:** 60*

STUDENTS AND FACULTY
Enrollment: 504. **Student Body:** 60% female, 40% male, 20% out-of-state, 2% international. Asian 5%, African American 10%, Caucasian 62%, Hispanic 18%, Native American 1%.
Retention and Graduation: 59% freshmen return for sophomore year. 6% grads go on to further study within 1 year. 6% grads pursue arts and sciences degrees. **Faculty:** Student/faculty ratio 12:1. 25 full-time faculty, 84% hold PhDs, 40% are women.

ACADEMICS
Degrees: associate, bachelor's, certificate, master's, post-bachelor's certificate. **Classes:** Most classes have 10–19 students. Most lab/discussion sessions have fewer than 10 students. **Special Study Options:** Accelerated program, distance learning, double major, external degree program, independent study, internships, teacher certification program, weekend college.

FACILITIES
Housing: Coed dorms, special housing for disabled students, men's dorms, women's dorms, fraternity/sorority housing, apartments for married students, apartments for single students, theme housing. **Computers:**

CAMPUS LIFE
Environment: Activities: Choral groups, concert band, dance, drama/theater, jazz band, literary magazine, marching band, music ensembles, musical theater, opera, pep band, radio station, student government, student newspaper, student-run film society, symphony orchestra, television station, yearbook, Campus Ministries, International Student Organization 1 honor societies, 1 religious organizations. **Athletics (Intercollegiate):** *Men:* basketball, cheerleading, golf. *Women:* basketball, cheerleading, softball, volleyball.

ADMISSIONS
Freshman Academic Profile: 16% in top 10% of high school class, 59% in top 25% of high school class, 75% in top 50% of high school class. Minimum paper TOEFL 500. **Basis for Candidate Selection:** *Very important factors considered include:* application essay, academic GPA, recommendation(s), standardized test scores, religious affiliation/commitment. *Other factors considered include:* Class rank, rigor of secondary school record, character/personal qualities, extracurricular activities, level of applicant's interest. **Freshman Admission Requirements: Freshman Admission Statistics:** 228 applied, 55% admitted, 67% enrolled. **Transfer Admission Requirements:** college transcript(s), essay or personal statement, minimum college GPA of 2.0 required. **General Admission Information:** Application Fee $35. Regular application deadline 7/1. Nonfall registration accepted. Admission may be deferred for a maximum of 2 years.

COSTS AND FINANCIAL AID
Annual tuition $14,300. Room and board $6,320. Required fees $715. Average book expense $500. **Required Forms and Deadlines:** FAFSA, institution's own financial aid form. **Notification of Awards: Types of Aid:** *Need-based scholarships/grants:* Federal Pell, SEOG, state scholarships/grants, private scholarships, the school's own gift aid. *Loans:* Subsidized Stafford, Unsubsidized Stafford, PLUS, Federal Perkins, college/university loans from institutional funds. **Student Employment:** Federal Work-Study Program available.

BETHEL COLLEGE (IN)

1001 W McKinley Avenue, Mishawaka, IN 46545
Phone: 574-257-3339 • **Financial Aid Phone:** 574-257-3316
E-mail: admissions@bethelcollege.edu • **CEEB Code:** 1079
Fax: 574-257-3335 • **Website:** www.bethelcollege.edu • **ACT Code:** 1178

This private school was founded in 1947. It has a 75-acre campus.

RATINGS
Admissions Selectivity Rating: 66   **Fire Safety Rating:** 73   **Green Rating:** 61

STUDENTS AND FACULTY
Enrollment: 1,974. **Student Body:** 34% female, 66% male, 27% out-of-state, 2% international (18 countries represented). Asian 2%, African American 10%, Caucasian 80%, Hispanic 3%, Native American 0%.
Retention and Graduation: 79% freshmen return for sophomore year. 37% freshmen graduate within 4 years. 59% freshmen graduate within 6 years. **Faculty:** Student/faculty ratio 13:1. 97 full-time faculty, 10% are members of minority groups, 43% are women. 0% of classes are taught by teaching assistants.

ACADEMICS
Degrees: associate, bachelor's, master's. **Classes:** Most classes have 10–19 students. Most lab/discussion sessions have fewer than 10 students. **Majors with Highest Enrollment:** business/commerce; elementary education and teaching; nursing/registered nurse (rn, asn, bsn, msn). **Special Study Options:** Accelerated program, cross-registration, double major, English as a Second Language (ESL), exchange student program (domestic), independent study, internships, student-designed major, study abroad, teacher certification program. **Disability Services:** Special programs offered to physically disabled students include note-taking services, reader services, tape recorders, tutors. **Career Services:** alumni services, career/job search classes, career assessment, internships Career Services highlights include Reputation of Career Service Office Usership is up.

FACILITIES
Housing: special housing for disabled students, men's dorms, women's dorms. 90% of campus accessible to physically disabled. **Special Academic Facilities/Equipment:** Bowen Museum Weaver Gallery **Computers:** 25% of classrooms, 100% of dorms, 100% of libraries, 100% of dining areas, 100% of student union, 25% of common outdoor areas have wireless network access. Administrative functions (other than registration) can be performed online.

CAMPUS LIFE
Environment: City. **Activities:** Choral groups, concert band, dance, drama/theater, jazz band, literary magazine, music ensembles, musical theater, pep band, radio station, student government, student newspaper, yearbook 18 registered organizations, 1 honor societies, 5 religious organizations. **Athletics (Intercollegiate):** *Men:* baseball, basketball, cheerleading, cross-country, golf, soccer, tennis, track/field (outdoor), track/field (indoor). *Women:* basketball, cheerleading, cross-country, golf, soccer, softball, tennis, track/field (outdoor), track/field (indoor), volleyball. **On-Campus Highlights:** Acorn Student Center, Everst Rohrer Chapel, Sufficient Grounds Coffee House, Wiekamp Athletic Center, Dining Commons, workout and weight rooms. **Environmental Initiatives:** Recycle trash, working with local community on MS4 program, recycle leaves

ADMISSIONS
Freshman Academic Profile: Average high school GPA 3.0. 15% in top 10% of high school class, 39% in top 25% of high school class, 74% in top 50% of high school class. 70% from public high schools. SAT Math middle 50% range 460-590. SAT Critical Reading middle 50% range 450-570. SAT Writing middle 50% range 435-560. ACT middle 50% range 19-25. Minimum web-based TOEFL 76. Minimum paper TOEFL 540. **Basis for Candidate Selection:** *Important factors considered include:* Class rank, application essay, academic GPA, recommendation(s), rigor of secondary school record, standardized test scores, character/personal qualities, extracurricular activities. *Other factors considered include:* interview, racial/ethnic status, volunteer work. **Freshman Admission Requirements:** High school diploma is required and GED is accepted. **Freshman Admission Statistics:** 645 applied, 91% admitted, 53% enrolled. **Transfer Admission Requirements:** High school transcript, college transcript(s), essay or personal statement, standardized test scores, statement of good standing from prior institution(s). Minimum college GPA of 2.0 required. Lowest grade transferable C-. **General Admission Information:** Application Fee $25. Regular application deadline 8/15. Notification on a rolling basis, beginning on or about 10/1. Nonfall registration accepted. Admission may be deferred for a maximum of 1 year. Credit and/or placement offered for CEEB Advanced Placement tests.

COSTS AND FINANCIAL AID
Annual tuition $17,450. Room and board $5,380. Average book expense $1,600. **Required Forms and Deadlines:** FAFSA. **Notification of Awards:** Applicants will be notified of awards on a rolling basis beginning 4/15. **Types of Aid:** *Need-based scholarships/grants:* Federal Pell, SEOG, state scholarships/grants, private scholarships, the school's own gift aid, Federal Nursing Scholarships. *Loans:* Subsidized Stafford, Unsubsidized Stafford, PLUS, Federal Perkins, college/university loans from institutional funds. **Student Employment:** Federal Work-Study Program available. Institutional employment available. Highest amount earned per year from on-campus jobs $2,500. Off-campus job opportunities are excellent. **Financial Aid Statistics:** 79% freshmen, 73% undergrads receive need-based scholarship or grant aid. 96% freshmen, 88% undergrads receive non-need-based scholarship or grant aid. 96% freshmen, 92% undergrads receive need-based self-help aid. 25% freshmen, 17% undergrads receive athletic scholarships. 76% freshmen, 73% undergrads receive any aid. 83% undergrads borrow to pay for school. Average cumulative indebtedness $15,990. **Criteria for awarding institutional aid:** *Non-need-based:* academics, art, athletics, job skills, leadership, minority status, music/drama, religious affiliation, state/district residency.

BETHEL COLLEGE (KS)

300 E 27th St, North Newton, KS 67117
Phone: 316-284-5230 • **Financial Aid Phone:** 316-284-5232
E-mail: admissions@bethelks.edu • **CEEB Code:** 6037
Fax: 316-284-5870 • **Website:** www.bethelks.edu • **ACT Code:** 1390

This private school was founded in 1887. It has a 60-acre campus.

RATINGS
Admissions Selectivity Rating: 77   **Fire Safety Rating:** 69   **Green Rating:** 60*

STUDENTS AND FACULTY
Enrollment: 472. **Student Body:** 55% female, 45% male, 28% out-of-state, 2% international (13 countries represented). Asian 1%, African American 9%, Caucasian 76%, Hispanic 9%, Native American 0%.
Retention and Graduation: 62% freshmen return for sophomore year. 36% freshmen graduate within 4 years. **Faculty:** Student/faculty ratio 9:1. 37 full-time faculty, 65% hold PhDs, 5% are members of minority groups, 46% are women. 0% of classes are taught by teaching assistants.

ACADEMICS
Degrees: bachelor's, certificate. **Classes:** Most classes have 10–19 students. Most lab/discussion sessions have 10–19 students. **Majors with Highest Enrollment:** biology/biological sciences; business/commerce; nursing/registered nurse (rn, asn, bsn, msn). **Special Study Options:** cross-registration, double major, dual enrollment, independent study, internships, liberal arts/career combination, study abroad, teacher certification program. **Combined Degree Programs:** BA/MEng. **Disability Services:** Special programs offered to physically disabled students include note-taking services, reader services, tape recorders, tutors. **Career Services:** Alumni network, career/job search classes, career assessment, Career Services highlights include The liberal arts program provides students with a foundational, broad understanding of the social and natural world. Focused study in a major field equips students with the intellectual achievement vital to vocational success. Internships are thus an additional, integrated component of a larger academic program that fosters in students a powerful sense of purpose. The skills developed in a liberal education - the ability to speak, read and write correctly, clearly and cogently - are the skills needed in employment. Internship experiences help students understand the relationship of their educational experience to potential careers.

FACILITIES
Housing: Coed dorms, special housing for disabled students, apartments for married students, apartments for single students. 75% of campus accessible to physically disabled. **Special Academic Facilities/Equipment:** Art gallery, natural history and midwestern/Kansas history museums, 80 acre natural history field laboratory for biological studies, Mennonite Historical Library and Archives, Institute for Peace and Conflict Resolution, observatory **Computers:** 25% of classrooms, 75% of libraries, 100% of dining areas, 100% of student union, 50% of common outdoor areas have wireless network access. Administrative functions (other than registration) can be performed online.

CAMPUS LIFE
Environment: Village. **Activities:** Choral groups, concert band, dance, drama/theater, jazz band, literary magazine, music ensembles, musical theater, opera, radio station, student government, student newspaper, symphony orchestra, television station, yearbook, Campus Ministries, International Student Organization 50 registered organizations, 2 religious organizations. **Athletics (Intercollegiate):** *Men:* basketball, cross-country, football, golf, soccer, tennis, track/field (outdoor), track/field (indoor). *Women:* basketball, cross-country, golf, soccer, tennis, track/field (outdoor), track/field (indoor), volleyball. **On-Campus Highlights:** Student Center, Krehbiel Science Center, Athletic Complex, The Green, Warkentine Court.

ADMISSIONS

Freshman Academic Profile: Average high school GPA 3.4. 17% in top 10% of high school class, 42% in top 25% of high school class, 69% in top 50% of high school class. 97% from public high schools. SAT Math middle 50% range 440-640. SAT Critical Reading middle 50% range 460-620. SAT Writing middle 50% range 400-530. ACT middle 50% range 20-27. Minimum web-based TOEFL 76. Minimum paper TOEFL 540. **Basis for Candidate Selection:** *Very important factors considered include:* academic GPA, standardized test scores, level of applicant's interest. *Important factors considered include:* Class rank, alumni/ae relation, character/personal qualities, extracurricular activities. *Other factors considered include:* recommendation(s), rigor of secondary school record. **Freshman Admission Requirements:** High school diploma is required and GED is accepted. **Freshman Admission Statistics:** 521 applied, 65% admitted, 30% enrolled. **Transfer Admission Requirements:** High school transcript, college transcript(s), statement of good standing from prior institution(s). Lowest grade transferable D-. **General Admission Information:** Application Fee $20. Notification on a rolling basis, beginning on or about 9/1. Nonfall registration accepted. Admission may be deferred for a maximum of 1 yr. Credit and/or placement offered for CEEB Advanced Placement tests.

COSTS AND FINANCIAL AID

Annual tuition $22,600. Room and board $7,150. Required fees. Average book expense $900. **Required Forms and Deadlines:** FAFSA. **Notification of Awards:** Applicants will be notified of awards on a rolling basis beginning 2/1. **Types of Aid:** *Need-based scholarships/grants:* Federal Pell, SEOG, state scholarships/grants, private scholarships, the school's own gift aid. *Loans:* Direct Subsidized Stafford, Direct Unsubsidized Stafford, Direct PLUS, Subsidized Stafford, Unsubsidized Stafford, PLUS, Federal Perkins. **Student Employment:** Federal Work-Study Program available. Institutional employment available. Highest amount earned per year from on-campus jobs $9,278. Off-campus job opportunities are good. **Financial Aid Statistics:** 88% freshmen, 86% undergrads receive need-based scholarship or grant aid. 100% freshmen, 99% undergrads receive non-need-based scholarship or grant aid. 90% freshmen, 89% undergrads receive need-based self-help aid. 63% freshmen, 46% undergrads receive athletic scholarships. 100% freshmen, 94% undergrads receive any aid. 78% undergrads borrow to pay for school. Average cumulative indebtedness $20,356. **Criteria for awarding institutional aid:** *Non-need-based:* academics, alumni affiliation, art, athletics, minority status, music/drama, religious affiliation, state/district residency.

BETHEL UNIVERSITY (MN)

Office of Admissions - CAS, Saint Paul, MN 55112
Phone: 651-638-6242 • **Financial Aid Phone:** 651-638-6241
E-mail: BUadmissions-cas@bethel.edu • **CEEB Code:** 6038
Fax: 651-635-1490 • **Website:** www.bethel.edu • **ACT Code:** 2088

This private school was founded in 1871. It has a 247-acre campus.

RATINGS

Admissions Selectivity Rating: 78   **Fire Safety Rating:** 89   **Green Rating:** 62

STUDENTS AND FACULTY

Enrollment: 3,361. **Student Body:** 62% female, 38% male, 20% out-of-state, 0% international (24 countries represented). Asian 3%, African American 5%, Caucasian 85%, Hispanic 2%, Native American 0%.
Retention and Graduation: 83% freshmen return for sophomore year. 62% freshmen graduate within 4 years. 71% freshmen graduate within 6 years. 28% grads go on to further study within 1 year. 6% grads pursue arts and sciences degrees. 1% grads pursue law degrees. 2% grads pursue business degrees. 5% grads pursue medical degrees. **Faculty:** Student/faculty ratio 12:1. 182 full-time faculty, 81% hold PhDs, 5% are members of minority groups, 43% are women. 0% of classes are taught by teaching assistants.

ACADEMICS

Degrees: associate, bachelor's, master's, post-bachelor's certificate, post-master's certificate. **Classes:** Most classes have 10–19 students. Most lab/discussion sessions have 10–19 students. **Majors with Highest Enrollment:** business administration and management; education; nursing/registered nurse (rn, asn, bsn, msn). **Special Study Options:** double major, exchange student program (domestic), honors program, independent study, internships, student-designed major, study abroad, teacher certification program. **Honors Programs:** The program consists of two honors courses in the freshman year, one in the sophomore year and one in the junior year. In their senior year the student will complete an Honors Senior Project. The two courses in the sophomore year and junior year, as well as the Honors Senior Project are geared toward a discipline of the students choosing. This program also consists of other Honors classes

and Honors Forums throughout all four years. **Combined Degree Programs:** Dual degree B.A./B.S. Program in Engineering. **Disability Services:** Special programs offered to physically disabled students include note-taking services, reader services, tape recorders, tutors. **Career Services:** alumni services, career/job search classes, career assessment, internships Career Services highlights include We have a very collaborative network of colleagues around the state and provide high quality job fairs through our joint effort.

FACILITIES

Housing: Coed dorms, special housing for disabled students, apartments for single students. 99% of campus accessible to physically disabled. **Special Academic Facilities/Equipment:** Two Art galleries, media center, closed circuit TV, television studio, and radio station, cadaver lab **Computers:** 100% of classrooms, 50% of dorms, 100% of libraries, 100% of dining areas, 100% of student union, 50% of common outdoor areas have wireless network access. Students can register for classes online. Administrative functions (other than registration) can be performed online.

CAMPUS LIFE

Environment: Metropolis. **Activities:** Choral groups, concert band, dance, drama/theater, jazz band, literary magazine, music ensembles, musical theater, radio station, student government, student newspaper, student-run film society, symphony orchestra, Campus Ministries, International Student Organization 55 registered organizations, 5 honor societies, 20 religious organizations. **Athletics (Intercollegiate):** *Men:* baseball, basketball, cross-country, football, golf, ice hockey, soccer, tennis, track/field (outdoor), track/field (indoor). *Women:* basketball, cross-country, golf, ice hockey, soccer, softball, tennis, track/field (outdoor), track/field (indoor), volleyball. **On-Campus Highlights:** Brushaber Commons (new student facility), SRC-Student Recreation Center, Market Square/Dining Center, Lissner Hall-New Dorm/ Lounges, Ona Orth Athletic Complex, Brushaber Commons: all new student facility. Great Hall: seats 1600 people; location of Chapel services, Vespers, concerts, musicals and large on-campus events. **Environmental Initiatives:** Green Roof and Permeable Pavers for Brushaber Commons Day Lighting Control for Monson Dining Center North Village Composting.

ADMISSIONS

Freshman Academic Profile: Average high school GPA 3.5. 32% in top 10% of high school class, 61% in top 25% of high school class, 84% in top 50% of high school class. 80% from public high schools. ACT middle 50% range 22-28. Minimum web-based TOEFL 70. Minimum paper TOEFL 525. **Basis for Candidate Selection:** *Very important factors considered include:* academic GPA, rigor of secondary school record, standardized test scores, character/personal qualities, religious affiliation/commitment. *Important factors considered include:* Class rank, application essay, extracurricular activities. *Other factors considered include:* recommendation(s), alumni/ae relation, first generation, geographical residence, interview, level of applicant's interest, racial/ethnic status, state residency, talent/ability, volunteer work. **Freshman Admission Requirements:** High school diploma is required and GED is accepted. *Academic units required:* 4 English, 3 mathematics, 3 science, (3 science labs), 4 social studies. *Academic units recommended:* 4 English, 3 mathematics, 3 science, (3 science labs), 4 social studies. **Freshman Admission Statistics:** 2,684 applied, 71% admitted, 32% enrolled. **Transfer Admission Requirements:** college transcript(s), essay or personal statement, minimum college GPA of 2.5 required. Lowest grade transferable C. **General Admission Information:** Notification on a rolling basis, beginning on or about 10/1. Nonfall registration accepted. Admission may be deferred for a maximum of 1 term. Credit and/or placement offered for CEEB Advanced Placement tests.

COSTS AND FINANCIAL AID

Annual tuition $30,700. Room and board $8,900. Required fees $140. Average book expense $1,050. **Required Forms and Deadlines:** FAFSA, institution's own financial aid form. **Notification of Awards:** Applicants will be notified of awards on a rolling basis beginning 3/1. **Types of Aid:** *Need-based scholarships/grants:* Federal Pell, SEOG, state scholarships/grants, private scholarships, the school's own gift aid. *Loans:* Direct Subsidized Stafford, Direct Unsubsidized Stafford, Direct PLUS, Federal Perkins, state loans. **Student Employment:** Federal Work-Study Program available. Institutional employment available. Highest amount earned per year from on-campus jobs $6,500. Off-campus job opportunities are excellent. **Financial Aid Statistics:** 100% freshmen, 100% undergrads receive need-based scholarship or grant aid. 13% freshmen, 10% undergrads receive non-need-based scholarship or grant aid. 84% freshmen, 87% undergrads receive need-based self-help aid. 99% freshmen, 99% undergrads receive any aid. 76% undergrads borrow to pay for school. Average cumulative indebtedness $32,483. **Criteria for awarding institutional aid:** *Non-need-based:* academics, alumni affiliation, art, leadership, music/drama, state/district residency.

BETHUNE-COOKMAN COLLEGE

640 Dr. Mary McLeod Bethune Boulevard, Daytona Beach, FL 32114-3099
Phone: 386-481-2600 • **Financial Aid Phone:** 386-481-2626
E-mail: admissions@cookman.edu • **CEEB Code:** 5061
Fax: 386-481-2601 • **Website:** www.bethune.cookman.edu • **ACT Code:** 720

This private school, affiliated with the Methodist Church, was founded in 1904. It has a 78-acre campus.

RATINGS
Admissions Selectivity Rating: 65   **Fire Safety Rating:** 69   **Green Rating:** 60*

STUDENTS AND FACULTY
Enrollment: 3,093. **Student Body:** 58% female, 42% male, 30% out-of-state, 3% international (25 countries represented). Asian 0%, African American 91%, Caucasian 1%, Hispanic 2%, Native American 0%.
Retention and Graduation: 69% freshmen return for sophomore year. 13% freshmen graduate within 4 years. 33% freshmen graduate within 6 years. 28% grads go on to further study within 1 year. 12% grads pursue arts and sciences degrees. 1% grads pursue law degrees. 14% grads pursue business degrees. 1% grads pursue medical degrees. **Faculty:** Student/faculty ratio 17:1. 161 full-time faculty, 57% hold PhDs, 58% are members of minority groups, 50% are women. 0% of classes are taught by teaching assistants.

ACADEMICS
Degrees: bachelor's, master's. **Classes:** Most classes have 20–29 students. Most lab/discussion sessions have fewer than 10 students. **Majors with Highest Enrollment:** business/commerce; corrections and criminal justice, other; elementary education and teaching. **Special Study Options:** Accelerated program, distance learning, double major, honors program, independent study, internships, study abroad, teacher certification program, weekend college. **Honors Programs:** The Honors program is designed to provide expanded study opportunities for highly motivated and exceptionally qualified students, broaden their intellectual horizons, integrate various areas of knowledge, and explore intensively major fields of study through innovative techniques of individualized learning and independent research, preparing students more adequately for graduate school. **Disability Services:** Special programs offered to physically disabled students include tutors. **Career Services:** internships Career Services highlights include Opportunities in the Teacher Education Internships.

FACILITIES
Housing: men's dorms, women's dorms, Scholarship Housing. 70% of campus accessible to physically disabled. **Special Academic Facilities/Equipment:** Historic archives, founder's home and gravesite (historic landmark), outreach center, telecommunications satellite network, art gallery/studio, audiologic recording studio, observatory. **Computers:** Students can register for classes online. Administrative functions (other than registration) can be performed online.

CAMPUS LIFE
Environment: Town. **Activities:** Choral groups, concert band, drama/theater, jazz band, marching band, music ensembles, radio station, student government, student newspaper, yearbook 40 registered organizations, 9 honor societies, 2 religious organizations. 5 fraternities, 4 sororities. **Athletics (Intercollegiate):** *Men:* baseball, basketball, cross-country, football, golf, tennis, track/field (outdoor), track/field (indoor). *Women:* basketball, cross-country, golf, softball, tennis, track/field (outdoor), track/field (indoor), volleyball. **On-Campus Highlights:** Bethune Foundation (the Founder's Home), Bethune Performing Arts Center, Bethune Fine Arts studio and Gallery, Swisher Library Archives and Exhibit Rooms, Heyn Memorial Chapel (White Hall).

ADMISSIONS
Freshman Academic Profile: Average high school GPA 2.8. 5% in top 10% of high school class, 15% in top 25% of high school class, 48% in top 50% of high school class. 90% from public high schools. SAT Math middle 50% range 360-460. SAT Critical Reading middle 50% range 360-460. ACT middle 50% range 14-18. Minimum paper TOEFL 550. **Basis for Candidate Selection:** *Very important factors considered include:* academic GPA, rigor of secondary school record, standardized test scores. *Important factors considered include:* recommendation(s), character/personal qualities. *Other factors considered include:* Class rank, application essay, alumni/ae relation, extracurricular activities, first generation, interview, level of applicant's interest, talent/ability, volunteer work, work experience. **Freshman Admission Requirements:** High school diploma is required and GED is accepted. *Academic units required:* 4 English, 3 mathematics, 3 science, (1 science labs), 1 social studies, 6 academic electives. *Academic units recommended:* 4 English, 3 mathematics, 3 science, (1 science labs), 1 social studies, 2 history, 6 academic electives. **Freshman Admission Statistics:** 4,129 applied, 78% admitted, 28% enrolled. **Transfer Admission Requirements:** college transcript(s), essay or personal statement, statement of good standing from prior institution(s). Minimum college GPA of 2.2 required. Lowest grade transferable C. **General Admission Information:**

Application Fee $25. Nonfall registration accepted. Admission may be deferred for a maximum of 1 year. Credit offered for CEEB Advanced Placement tests.

COSTS AND FINANCIAL AID
Annual tuition $11,792. Room and board $7,206. Average book expense $850. **Required Forms and Deadlines:** FAFSA. **Notification of Awards:** Applicants will be notified of awards on a rolling basis beginning 4/1. **Types of Aid:** *Need-based scholarships/grants:* Federal Pell, SEOG, state scholarships/grants, private scholarships, the school's own gift aid, United Negro College Fund, Federal Nursing Scholarships. *Loans:* Direct Subsidized Stafford, Direct Unsubsidized Stafford, Direct PLUS, Subsidized Stafford, Unsubsidized Stafford, PLUS. **Student Employment:** Federal Work-Study Program available. Institutional employment available. Highest amount earned per year from on-campus jobs $2,500. Off-campus job opportunities are good. **Financial Aid Statistics:** 78% freshmen, 79% undergrads receive need-based scholarship or grant aid. 11% freshmen, 13% undergrads receive non-need-based scholarship or grant aid. 87% freshmen, 91% undergrads receive need-based self-help aid. 8% freshmen, 9% undergrads receive athletic scholarships. 94% freshmen, 93% undergrads receive any aid. 85% undergrads borrow to pay for school. Average cumulative indebtedness $32,500. **Criteria for awarding institutional aid:** *Non-need-based:* academics, athletics, leadership, music/drama, religious affiliation, state/district residency.

BIOLA UNIVERSITY

13800 Biola Avenue, La Mirada, CA 90639
Phone: 1-800-OK-BIOLA • **Financial Aid Phone:** 562-903-4752 • **CEEB Code:** 4017
Fax: 562-903-4709 • **Website:** www.biola.edu • **ACT Code:** 172

This private school, affiliated with the Christian (Nondenominational) Church, was founded in 1908. It has a 95-acre campus.

RATINGS
Admissions Selectivity Rating: 76   **Fire Safety Rating:** 77   **Green Rating:** 75

STUDENTS AND FACULTY
Enrollment: 4,337. **Student Body:** 61% female, 39% male, 27% out-of-state, 2% international (40 countries represented). Asian 12%, African American 2%, Caucasian 44%, Hispanic 13%, Native American 0%.
Retention and Graduation: 86% freshmen return for sophomore year. 47% freshmen graduate within 4 years. **Faculty:** Student/faculty ratio 16:1. 255 full-time faculty, 74% hold PhDs, 18% are members of minority groups, 35% are women. 0% of classes are taught by teaching assistants.

ACADEMICS
Degrees: bachelor's, first professional, master's, post-master's certificate. **Classes:** Most classes have 10–19 students. Most lab/discussion sessions have 10–19 students. **Majors with Highest Enrollment:** business/commerce; elementary education and teaching; psychology. **Special Study Options:** double major, English as a Second Language (ESL), exchange student program (domestic), honors program, internships, study abroad, teacher certification program. **Disability Services:** Special programs offered to physically disabled students include note-taking services, reader services, tape recorders, tutors. **Career Services:** Alumni network, alumni services, career/job search classes, career assessment, internships, regional alumni. Career Services highlights include Biola University provides internships applicable to a student's major allowing them to gain academic credit and career development.

FACILITIES
Housing: Coed dorms, special housing for disabled students, men's dorms, women's dorms, apartments for married students, apartments for single students, Flex style dorms—separate floors and wings for specific genders, Off Campus Apartments, On Campus Apartments. 70% of campus accessible to physically disabled. **Special Academic Facilities/Equipment:** Art gallery, electron microscope, TV production facility, film editing facility, media center, writing center, Student Ministry Union and tutoring services. **Computers:** 100% of dorms, 100% of libraries, 100% of student union, 75% of common outdoor areas have wireless network access. Students can register for classes online. Administrative functions (other than registration) can be performed online.

CAMPUS LIFE
Environment: Town. **Activities:** Choral groups, concert band, drama/theater, jazz band, music ensembles, musical theater, opera, radio station, student government, student newspaper, student-run film society, symphony orchestra, television station, yearbook 33 registered organizations, 2 honor societies. **Athletics (Intercollegiate):** *Men:* baseball, basketball, cross-country, golf, soccer, swimming, tennis, track/field (outdoor). *Women:* basketball, cross-country, golf, soccer, softball, swimming, tennis, track/field (outdoor), volleyball. **On-Campus**

Highlights: Common Grounds, The Eagle's Nest, Art Gallery, McNally Field, The Sub (Student Union Building). **Environmental Initiatives:** *Cogen*: We produce clean power on campus and use clean waste heat. A certain percentage of this is also used towards cooling purposes. We use 85% all green cleaning chemicals for janitorial purposes. *Recycling*: We have an intense recycling system on campus where we can divert a great amount of waste by use of our cardboard baler on campus as well as other recycling stations.

ADMISSIONS

Freshman Academic Profile: Average high school GPA 3.5. 34% in top 10% of high school class, 64% in top 25% of high school class, 88% in top 50% of high school class. 59% from public high schools. SAT Math middle 50% range 490-610. SAT Critical Reading middle 50% range 500-620. SAT Writing middle 50% range 510-610. ACT middle 50% range 21-27. Minimum web-based TOEFL 100. Minimum paper TOEFL 600. **Basis for Candidate Selection:** *Very important factors considered include:* application essay, academic GPA, recommendation(s), standardized test scores, character/personal qualities, religious affiliation/commitment. *Important factors considered include:* rigor of secondary school record, extracurricular activities, interview. *Other factors considered include:* Class rank, alumni/ae relation, first generation, geographical residence, level of applicant's interest, state residency, volunteer work, work experience. **Freshman Admission Requirements:** High school diploma is required and GED is accepted. **Freshman Admission Statistics:** 3,528 applied, 75% admitted, 35% enrolled. **Transfer Admission Requirements:** High school transcript, college transcript(s), essay or personal statement, statement of good standing from prior institution(s). Minimum college GPA of 2.0 required. Lowest grade transferable C. **General Admission Information:** Application Fee $45. Regular application deadline 3/1. Regular notification 4/1. Nonfall registration not accepted. Admission may be deferred for a maximum of 2 years. Credit offered for CEEB Advanced Placement tests.

COSTS AND FINANCIAL AID

Annual tuition $31,004. Room and board $9,316. Average book expense $1,665. **Required Forms and Deadlines:** FAFSA, state aid form. **Notification of Awards:** Applicants will be notified of awards on a rolling basis beginning 3/1. **Types of Aid:** *Need-based scholarships/grants:* Federal Pell, SEOG, state scholarships/grants, private scholarships, the school's own gift aid. *Loans:* Subsidized Stafford, Unsubsidized Stafford, PLUS, Federal Perkins, Federal Nursing, college/university loans from institutional funds. **Student Employment:** Highest amount earned per year from on-campus jobs $2,000. Off-campus job opportunities are good. **Financial Aid Statistics:** 98% freshmen, 95% undergrads receive need-based scholarship or grant aid. 3% freshmen, 2% undergrads receive non-need-based scholarship or grant aid. 80% freshmen, 86% undergrads receive need-based self-help aid. 2% freshmen, 2% undergrads receive athletic scholarships. 87% freshmen, 91% undergrads receive any aid. 73% undergrads borrow to pay for school. Average cumulative indebtedness $34,587. **Criteria for awarding institutional aid:** *Non-need-based:* academics, alumni affiliation, art, athletics, leadership, minority status, music/drama.

BIRMINGHAM-SOUTHERN COLLEGE

Box 549008, Birmingham, AL 35254
Phone: 205-226-4696 • **Financial Aid Phone:** 205-226-4688
E-mail: admission@bsc.edu • **CEEB Code:** 1064
Fax: 205-226-3074 • **Website:** www.bsc.edu • **ACT Code:** 1012

This private school, affiliated with the Methodist Church, was founded in 1856. It has a 196-acre campus.

RATINGS

Admissions Selectivity Rating: 82   Fire Safety Rating: 76   Green Rating: 71

STUDENTS AND FACULTY

Enrollment: 1,305. **Student Body:** 49% female, 51% male, 38% out-of-state, 0% international (12 countries represented). Asian 5%, African American 7%, Caucasian 82%, Hispanic 3%, Native American 1%. **Retention and Graduation:** 79% freshmen return for sophomore year. 61% freshmen graduate within 6 years. 42% grads go on to further study within 1 year. 27% grads pursue arts and sciences degrees. 17% grads pursue law degrees. 13% grads pursue business degrees. 24% grads pursue medical degrees. **Faculty:** Student/faculty ratio 13:1. 81 full-time faculty, 99% hold PhDs, 0% are members of minority groups, 37% are women. 0% of classes are taught by teaching assistants.

ACADEMICS

Degrees: bachelor's, master's. **Classes:** Most classes have 10–19 students. Most lab/discussion sessions have 10–19 students. **Majors with Highest Enrollment:** business/commerce; English language and literature; psychology. **Spe-**cial Study Options:** cooperative education program, cross-registration, double major, dual enrollment, exchange student program (domestic), honors program, independent study, internships, liberal arts/career combination, student-designed major, study abroad, teacher certification program. **Honors Programs:** The Honors Program at Birmingham-Southern is designed to engage students' intellectual curiosity, enhance their oral and written communications skills, and further develop their ability to think and study independently. The importance of viewing issues from interdisciplinary perspectives and of integrating, as well as analyzing, knowledge is a special focus of the program's courses and requirements. The program addresses its mission through small, interdisciplinary seminars developed specifically for Honors students and through upper-level courses with an interdisciplinary focus. The Honors Program serves as a complementary approach to fulfilling the requirements of the College's Foundations Plan for General Education. "Honors students are open to new ideas, aware of expanding horizons, and willing to change their own ideas to make room for the knowledge that they gain. They incorporate, embrace, and encourage differences. 'Honors' is not synonymous with straight A's and valedictorians. Ideal Honors students would participate in the program even if it did not appear on their transcripts." —Excerpted from "The Ideal Student in the Honors Program" as adopted by the Honors Committee 2002. The Honors Program component of Honors student's general education consists of five units of Honors seminars and one unit of independent study, known as the Honors Project. The specific general education requirements met by Honors courses and those met by regular courses will vary from student to student, depending on which Honors courses the student elects to take. Students may take one January Interim Term Honors project which will count toward the five units of Honors seminars. Students who participate in study abroad programs that include interdisciplinary courses also may petition to count one such course toward their Honors requirements. Honors students' remaining general education coursework is completed in the regular curriculum of the College. The student's sixth unit in independent study is typically taken over two terms. One-half unit is taken while the project is being designed by the student, the program director, and a faculty sponsor. The project must be interdisciplinary in nature and outside the student's major. Once approved by the Honors Program Committee, the independent study is completed the next term, giving the second half-unit of credit. All Honors Senior, or independent study, projects are presented publicly as part of the program's requirements. **Combined Degree Programs:** BA/MEng, BS/MSN (with Vanderbilt University; BS/MF or BS/MEM (with Duke Univ.). **Career Services:** Alumni network, alumni services, career/job search classes, career assessment, internships, regional alumni. Career Services highlights include The Mentor Program is a unique job shadowing program that matches students with local successful professionals in the student's field of interest.

FACILITIES

Housing: special housing for disabled students, men's dorms, special housing for international students, women's dorms, fraternity/sorority housing, apartments for married students, apartments for single students, wellness housing, theme housing, "Honors" floors in residence halls. 90% of campus accessible to physically disabled. **Special Academic Facilities/Equipment:** Theatre planetarium Environmental Center Urban Environmental Park Kennedy Art Center Ropes Course for Leadership Training **Computers:** 100% of classrooms, 100% of dorms, 100% of libraries, 100% of dining areas, 100% of student union, 90% of common outdoor areas have wireless network access. Students can register for classes online. Administrative functions (other than registration) can be performed online.

CAMPUS LIFE

Environment: Metropolis. **Activities:** Choral groups, dance, drama/theater, jazz band, literary magazine, musical theater, opera, pep band, student government, student newspaper, yearbook, Campus Ministries, International Student Organization 70 registered organizations, 18 honor societies, 5 religious organizations. 6 fraternities, 6 sororities. **Athletics (Intercollegiate):** *Men:* baseball, basketball, cheerleading, cross-country, football, golf, lacrosse, soccer, tennis, track/field (outdoor), track/field (indoor). *Women:* basketball, cheerleading, cross-country, golf, lacrosse, riflery, soccer, softball, tennis, track/field (outdoor), track/field (indoor), volleyball. **On-Campus Highlights:** Urban Environmental Park, Striplin Physical Fitness Center, The Cellar - Coffee House, The Court **Environmental Initiatives:** 10 compressed natural gas operations vehicles will come on line this spring. Campus police vehicles are hybrids. The Southern Environmental Center (SEC) is the largest educational facility of its kind in Alabama. In addition to its award winning interactive museum and Ecoscape Gardens, the SEC is also active in the community. Annually, 15,000 school children visit the center. An Urban Environmental Park, which opened in the fall of 2009, serves as both a place of recreation for students, as well as an academic laboratory for the study of environmental issues.

ADMISSIONS

Freshman Academic Profile: Average high school GPA 3.4. 31% in top 10% of high school class, 57% in top 25% of high school class, 86% in top 50% of high school class. 65% from public high schools. SAT Math middle 50% range

490-630. SAT Critical Reading middle 50% range 500-620. SAT Writing middle 50% range 490-630. ACT middle 50% range 23-29. Minimum web-based TOEFL 61. Minimum paper TOEFL 500. **Basis for Candidate Selection:** *Very important factors considered include:* application essay, academic GPA, recommendation(s), rigor of secondary school record, standardized test scores. *Important factors considered include:* character/personal qualities. *Other factors considered include:* extracurricular activities, interview, level of applicant's interest, talent/ability, work experience. **Freshman Admission Requirements:** High school diploma is required and GED is accepted. *Academic units required:* 4 English. *Academic units recommended:* 4 English. **Freshman Admission Statistics:** 1,798 applied, 64% admitted, 24% enrolled. **Transfer Admission Requirements:** High school transcript, college transcript(s), essay or personal statement, standardized test scores, statement of good standing from prior institution(s). Minimum college GPA of 2.0 required. Lowest grade transferable D. **General Admission Information:** Application Fee $40. Notification on a rolling basis, beginning on or about 7/1. Nonfall registration accepted. Admission may be deferred for a maximum of 1 year. Credit and/or placement offered for CEEB Advanced Placement tests.

COSTS AND FINANCIAL AID

Annual tuition $28,250. Room and board $9,620. Required fees $1,040. Average book expense $1,260. **Required Forms and Deadlines:** FAFSA. **Notification of Awards:** Applicants will be notified of awards on a rolling basis beginning 3/1. **Types of Aid:** *Need-based scholarships/grants:* Federal Pell, SEOG, state scholarships/grants, private scholarships, the school's own gift aid, United Negro College Fund. *Loans:* Subsidized Stafford, Unsubsidized Stafford, PLUS, Federal Perkins. **Student Employment:** Federal Work-Study Program available. Institutional employment available. Highest amount earned per year from on-campus jobs $1,800. Off-campus job opportunities are excellent. **Financial Aid Statistics:** 83% freshmen, 81% undergrads receive need-based scholarship or grant aid. 77% freshmen, 85% undergrads receive non-need-based scholarship or grant aid. 77% freshmen, 78% undergrads receive need-based self-help aid. 99% freshmen, 98% undergrads receive any aid. 31% undergrads borrow to pay for school. Average cumulative indebtedness $27,463. **Criteria for awarding institutional aid:** *Non-need-based:* academics, alumni affiliation, art, leadership, minority status, music/drama, religious affiliation.

BISHOP'S UNIVERSITY

2600 College Street, Sherbrooke, QC J1M0C8
Phone: 819-822-9600
E-mail: admissio@ubishops.ca
Fax: 819-822-9616 • **Website:** www.ubishops.ca

This public school was founded in 1843. It has a 550-acre campus.

RATINGS

Admissions Selectivity Rating: 60*   **Fire Safety Rating:** 60*   **Green Rating:** 60*

STUDENTS AND FACULTY

Retention and Graduation: 78% freshmen return for sophomore year. 57% freshmen graduate within 4 years. 69% freshmen graduate within 6 years. 50% grads go on to further study within 1 year. **Faculty:** Student/faculty ratio 12:1. 120 full-time faculty, 68% hold PhDs, % are members of minority groups, 30% are women. 0% of classes are taught by teaching assistants.

ACADEMICS

Degrees: bachelor's, certificate, master's. **Classes:** Most classes have 10–19 students. Most lab/discussion sessions have 10–19 students. **Majors with Highest Enrollment:** biology; business/commerce; education. **Special Study Options:** double major, English as a Second Language (ESL), exchange student program (domestic), honors program, independent study, liberal arts/career combination, student-designed major, study abroad, teacher certification program. **Disability Services:** Special programs offered to physically disabled students include note-taking services, reader services, tape recorders, tutors. **Career Services:** alumni services, career/job search classes, career assessment.

FACILITIES

Housing: Coed dorms, special housing for disabled students, women's dorms. 75% of campus accessible to physically disabled. **Special Academic Facilities/Equipment:** Eastern Townships Research Centre Cormier Economics Centre Dobson-Lagasse Entreprenneurship Centre Molson Fine Arts Building Art .

CAMPUS LIFE

Environment: Rural. **Activities:** Choral groups, concert band, dance, drama/theater, jazz band, literary magazine, music ensembles, musical theater, radio station, student government, student newspaper, yearbook 60 registered organizations, 2 religious organizations. **Athletics (Intercollegiate):** *Men:* basketball,

football, golf, rugby, skiing (downhill/alpine). *Women:* basketball, rugby, skiing (downhill/alpine), soccer.

ADMISSIONS

Freshman Academic Profile: Minimum paper TOEFL 550. **Basis for Candidate Selection:** *Very important factors considered include:* rigor of secondary school record. *Important factors considered include:* standardized test scores. *Other factors considered include:* Class rank, application essay, recommendation(s), character/personal qualities, extracurricular activities, talent/ability, volunteer work. **Freshman Admission Requirements:** High school diploma is required and GED is accepted. **Transfer Admission Requirements:** college transcript(s). **General Admission Information:** Application Fee $55. Notification on a rolling basis, beginning on or about 2/1. Nonfall registration accepted. Admission may be deferred for a maximum of 1 year. Credit offered for CEEB Advanced Placement tests.

COSTS AND FINANCIAL AID

Annual in-state tuition $1,668. Annual out-of-state tuition $3,438. Room and board $4,000. Required fees $525. Average book expense $625. **Required Forms and Deadlines:** state aid form. **Notification of Awards: Types of Aid:** *Need-based scholarships/grants: Loans:* Direct Subsidized Stafford, Direct Unsubsidized Stafford, Subsidized Stafford, Unsubsidized Stafford, state loans. **Student Employment:** Off-campus job opportunities are good. **Financial Aid Statistics:** 33% undergrads borrow to pay for school.

BLACK HILLS STATE UNIVERSITY

1200 University Street Unit 9502, Spearfish, SD 57799-9502
Phone: 605-642-6343
E-mail: admissions@bhsu.edu • **CEEB Code:** 6042
Fax: 605-642-6254 • **ACT Code:** 3904

This public school was founded in 1883. It has a 123-acre campus.

RATINGS

Admissions Selectivity Rating: 65   **Fire Safety Rating:** 61   **Green Rating:** 60*

STUDENTS AND FACULTY

Enrollment: 3,138. **Student Body:** 63% female, 37% male, 21% out-of-state, 1% international (6 countries represented). Asian 1%, African American 1%, Caucasian 87%, Hispanic 2%, Native American 4%. **Retention and Graduation:** 55% freshmen return for sophomore year. 10% freshmen graduate within 4 years. 22% freshmen graduate within 6 years. 20% grads go on to further study within 1 year. 1% grads pursue arts and sciences degrees. 2% grads pursue law degrees. 2% grads pursue business degrees. 2% grads pursue medical degrees. **Faculty:** Student/faculty ratio 21:1. 117 full-time faculty, 71% hold PhDs, 8% are members of minority groups, 39% are women. 0% of classes are taught by teaching assistants.

ACADEMICS

Degrees: associate, bachelor's, master's, post-bachelor's certificate. **Classes:** Most classes have 20–29 students. Most lab/discussion sessions have 20–29 students. **Special Study Options:** cooperative education program, distance learning, double major, dual enrollment, honors program, independent study, internships, study abroad, teacher certification program. **Disability Services:** Special programs offered to physically disabled students include note-taking services, reader services, tape recorders, tutors.

FACILITIES

Housing: Coed dorms, men's dorms, women's dorms, apartments for married students, apartments for single students. **Special Academic Facilities/Equipment:** Art galleries, museum collections, western historical studies library, center for Indian studies, center for advancement and study of tourism, small business institute, center of excellence for math and science education. **Computers:** Students can register for classes online.

CAMPUS LIFE

Environment: Village. **Activities:** Choral groups, concert band, drama/theater, jazz band, music ensembles, pep band, radio station, student government, student newspaper, television station 60 registered organizations, 5 honor societies, 3 religious organizations. 1 fraternities, 1 sororities. **Athletics (Intercollegiate):** *Men:* basketball, cross-country, football, track/field (outdoor), track/field (indoor). *Women:* basketball, cross-country, track/field (outdoor), track/field (indoor), volleyball. **On-Campus Highlights:** Clare and Josef Meier Hall, Donald E. Young Sports and Fitness Center, David B. Miller Yellow Jacket Student Union, Woodburn Hall, Jonas Hall.

ADMISSIONS

Freshman Academic Profile: Average high school GPA 3.1. 6% in top 10% of high school class, 24% in top 25% of high school class, 60% in top 50% of

high school class. ACT middle 50% range 18-23. Minimum paper TOEFL 520. **Basis for Candidate Selection:** *Very important factors considered include:* Class rank, rigor of secondary school record, standardized test scores. *Other factors considered include:* character/personal qualities, extracurricular activities, talent/ability. **Freshman Admission Requirements:** High school diploma is required and GED is accepted. *Academic units required:* 4 English, 3 mathematics, 3 science, (3 science labs), 3 social studies, 1 Fine Arts. *Academic units recommended:* 4 English, 3 mathematics, 3 science, (3 science labs), 3 social studies, 1 Fine Arts **Freshman Admission Statistics:** 1,341 applied, 93% admitted, 52% enrolled. **Transfer Admission Requirements:** High school transcript, college transcript(s), minimum college GPA of 2.0 required. Lowest grade transferable D. **General Admission Information:** Application Fee $20. Nonfall registration accepted. Credit and/or placement offered for CEEB Advanced Placement tests.

COSTS AND FINANCIAL AID

Annual in-state tuition $2,382. Annual out-of-state tuition $8,074. Room and board $4,667. Required fees $2,619. Average book expense $800. **Required Forms and Deadlines:** FAFSA. **Notification of Awards:** Applicants will be notified of awards on or about 5/15. **Types of Aid:** *Need-based scholarships/grants:* Federal Pell, SEOG, state scholarships/grants, private scholarships, the school's own gift aid. *Loans:* Subsidized Stafford, Unsubsidized Stafford, PLUS, Federal Perkins. **Student Employment:** Highest amount earned per year from on-campus jobs $1,700. **Financial Aid Statistics:** 75% undergrads borrow to pay for school. Average cumulative indebtedness $12,701. **Criteria for awarding institutional aid:** *Non-need-based:* academics, art, athletics.

BLACKBURN COLLEGE

700 College Ave., Carlinville, il 62626
Phone: 217-854-3231
E-mail: admit@blackburn.edu
Fax: 217-854-3713 • **Website:** www.blackburn.edu • **ACT Code:** 958

This private school, affiliated with the Presbyterian Church, was founded in 1837. It has a 80-acre campus.

RATINGS

Admissions Selectivity Rating: 63 | **Fire Safety Rating:** 60* | **Green Rating:** 60*

STUDENTS AND FACULTY

Enrollment: 603. **Student Body:** 59% female, 41% male.
Retention and Graduation: **Faculty:** Student/faculty ratio 17:1. 31 full-time faculty, 6% are members of minority groups, 35% are women.

ACADEMICS

Degrees: bachelor's. **Special Study Options:** double major, exchange student program (domestic), honors program, independent study, internships, liberal arts/career combination, student-designed major, study abroad, teacher certification program.

FACILITIES

Housing: Coed dorms, men's dorms, women's dorms, theme housing. **Computers:**

CAMPUS LIFE

Environment: Village. **Activities:** Choral groups, dance, drama/theater, jazz band, literary magazine, music ensembles, musical theater, radio station, student government, student newspaper, student-run film society, yearbook, Campus Ministries, International Student Organization.

ADMISSIONS

Freshman Academic Profile: Average high school GPA 3.5. 16% in top 10% of high school class, 22% in top 25% of high school class, 37% in top 50% of high school class. 80% from public high schools. Minimum web-based TOEFL 70. Minimum paper TOEFL 525. **Basis for Candidate Selection:** *Very important factors considered include:* academic GPA, rigor of secondary school record, standardized test scores. *Important factors considered include:* Class rank, level of applicant's interest. *Other factors considered include:* application essay, recommendation(s), alumni/ae relation, character/personal qualities, extracurricular activities, talent/ability, volunteer work, work experience. **Freshman Admission Requirements:** High school diploma is required and GED is accepted. **Freshman Admission Statistics:** 893 applied, 64% admitted, 26% enrolled. **Transfer Admission Requirements:** High school transcript, college transcript(s), standardized test scores, minimum college GPA of 2.0 required. Lowest grade transferable C. **General Admission Information:** Nonfall registration accepted. Credit and/or placement offered for CEEB Advanced Placement tests.

BLESSING-RIEMAN COLLEGE OF NURSING

Broadway at 11th Street, Quincy, IL 62305-7005
Phone: 217-228-5520
E-mail: hmutter@blessinghospital.com
Fax: 217-223-4661 • **Website:** www.brcn.edu • **ACT Code:** 956

This private school was founded in 1891. It has a 1-acre campus.

RATINGS

Admissions Selectivity Rating: 88 | **Fire Safety Rating:** 60* | **Green Rating:** 60*

STUDENTS AND FACULTY

Enrollment: 177. **Student Body:** 97% female, 3% male, 28% out-of-state, 0% international. Asian 0%, African American 2%, Caucasian 84%, Hispanic 1%, Native American 1%.
Retention and Graduation: 76% freshmen return for sophomore year. 47% freshmen graduate within 4 years. 53% freshmen graduate within 6 years. **Faculty:** Student/faculty ratio 9:1. 13 full-time faculty, 31% hold PhDs, 0% are members of minority groups, 100% are women.

ACADEMICS

Degrees: bachelor's. **Classes:** Most classes have 10–19 students. Most lab/discussion sessions have fewer than 10 students. **Special Study Options:** double major.

FACILITIES

Housing: apartments for single students, Men's and Women's dormitories available at Culver-Stockton College and Quincy University. 100% of campus accessible to physically disabled. **Computers:** Students can register for classes online. Administrative functions (other than registration) can be performed online.

CAMPUS LIFE

Activities: student government 1 registered organizations, 1 honor societies.

ADMISSIONS

Freshman Academic Profile: Average high school GPA 3.6. 20% in top 10% of high school class, 97% in top 25% of high school class, 100% in top 50% of high school class. 89% from public high schools. Minimum paper TOEFL 550. **Basis for Candidate Selection:** *Very important factors considered include:* Class rank, rigor of secondary school record, standardized test scores. **Freshman Admission Requirements:** High school diploma is required and GED is accepted. *Academic units required:* 4 English, 2 mathematics, 3 science, (2 science labs), 3 social studies. *Academic units recommended:* 4 English, 2 mathematics, 3 science, (2 science labs), 3 social studies. **Freshman Admission Statistics:** 153 applied, 50% admitted, 34% enrolled. **Transfer Admission Requirements:** High school transcript, college transcript(s), minimum college GPA of 2.0 required. Lowest grade transferable C. **General Admission Information:** Notification on a rolling basis, beginning on or about 9/1. Nonfall registration accepted.

COSTS AND FINANCIAL AID

Annual tuition $11,200. Room and board $4,975. Required fees $300. Average book expense $800. **Required Forms and Deadlines:** FAFSA. **Notification of Awards:** Applicants will be notified of awards on a rolling basis beginning 9/1. **Types of Aid:** *Need-based scholarships/grants:* Federal Pell, state scholarships/grants, Federal Nursing Scholarships. *Loans:* Subsidized Stafford, Unsubsidized Stafford, PLUS, Federal Nursing, college/university loans from institutional funds. **Student Employment:** Institutional employment available. Off-campus job opportunities are excellent. **Financial Aid Statistics:** 100% undergrads receive need-based scholarship or grant aid. 43% undergrads receive need-based self-help aid. 75% undergrads borrow to pay for school. Average cumulative indebtedness $20,000.

BLOOMFIELD COLLEGE

1 Park Place, Bloomfield, NJ 7003
Phone: 973-748-9000 x230- • **Financial Aid Phone:** 973-748-9000 x212
E-mail: admission@bloomfield.edu • **CEEB Code:** 2044
Fax: 973-748-0916 • **Website:** www.bloomfield.edu • **ACT Code:** 2540

This private school, affiliated with the Presbyterian Church, was founded in 1868. It has a 12.5-acre campus.

RATINGS

Admissions Selectivity Rating: 76 | **Fire Safety Rating:** 90 | **Green Rating:** 68

STUDENTS AND FACULTY

Enrollment: 2,123. **Student Body:** 64% female, 36% male, 5% out-of-state, 2% international (36 countries represented). Asian 3%, African American 52%, Caucasian 14%, Hispanic 18%, Native American 0%. **Retention and Graduation:** 17% freshmen graduate within 4 years. 14% grads go on to further study within 1 year. **Faculty:** Student/faculty ratio 15:1. 70 full-time faculty, 73% hold PhDs, 24% are members of minority groups, 59% are women. 0% of classes are taught by teaching assistants.

ACADEMICS

Degrees: bachelor's, certificate, post-bachelor's certificate. **Classes:** Most classes have 10–19 students. Most lab/discussion sessions have 10–19 students. **Majors with Highest Enrollment:** nursing/registered nurse (rn, asn, bsn, msn); psychology; sociology. **Special Study Options:** Accelerated program, distance learning, double major, dual enrollment, English as a Second Language (ESL), honors program, independent study, internships, liberal arts/career combination, student-designed major, study abroad, teacher certification program, Four-year clinical laboratory science program and allied health technologies major offered in conjunction with University of Medicine and Dentistry of New Jersey. Joint BS/MS in computer information systems program offered with NJIT. Special programs offered by the Institute of Technology and Professional Studies. **Honors Programs:** Honors program open to new and enrolled students consisting of interdisciplinary courses, honors seminars in the arts and sciences, special courses, and honors projects. **Combined Degree Programs:** BA/MA, Joint BS/MS Comp Inform Sys Dgr with NJ Inst Tech. **Disability Services:** Special programs offered to physically disabled students include note-taking services, reader services, tape recorders, tutors. **Career Services:** Alumni network, alumni services, career/job search classes, career assessment, internships, regional alumni. Career Services highlights include Personalized career counseling to indentify individual skills and abilities as the relate to career options and internship opportunities.

FACILITIES

Housing: Coed dorms, theme housing. 55% of campus accessible to physically disabled. **Special Academic Facilities/Equipment:** Westminster Theatre, Art Gallery, State-of-the-Art Library **Computers:** 20% of classrooms, 100% of dorms, 100% of libraries, 100% of dining areas, 100% of student union, have wireless network access. Administrative functions (other than registration) can be performed online.

CAMPUS LIFE

Environment: Town. **Activities:** dance, drama/theater, radio station, student government, Campus Ministries, International Student Organization 40 registered organizations, 4 honor societies, 1 religious organizations. 6 fraternities, 6 sororities. **Athletics (Intercollegiate):** *Men:* baseball, basketball, cross-country, soccer, tennis. *Women:* basketball, cross-country, soccer, softball, volleyball. **On-Campus Highlights:** Library, Art Gallery, College Center, Deacons Den, Gymnasium, Quad. **Environmental Initiatives:** Campus-wide recycling program E-waste recycling Continued upgrading of newer, more efficient heating systems.

ADMISSIONS

Freshman Academic Profile: Average high school GPA 2.6. 9% in top 10% of high school class, 32% in top 25% of high school class, 60% in top 50% of high school class. 80% from public high schools. SAT Math middle 50% range 390-470. SAT Critical Reading middle 50% range 380-470. Minimum web-based TOEFL 79. Minimum paper TOEFL 550. **Basis for Candidate Selection:** *Very important factors considered include:* application essay, academic GPA, recommendation(s), rigor of secondary school record, standardized test scores. *Important factors considered include:* Class rank, extracurricular activities, interview, talent/ability, volunteer work. *Other factors considered include:* alumni/ae relation, work experience. **Freshman Admission Requirements:** Freshman Admission Statistics: 3,673 applied, 50% admitted, 21% enrolled. **Transfer Admission Requirements:** college transcript(s), minimum college GPA of 2.0 required. Lowest grade transferable 2. **General Admission Information:** Application Fee $40. Regular application deadline 8/1. Notification on a rolling basis, beginning on or about 10/1. Nonfall registration accepted. Admission may be deferred for a maximum of 1 Year. Credit and/or placement offered for CEEB Advanced Placement tests.

COSTS AND FINANCIAL AID

Average book expense $1,000. **Required Forms and Deadlines:** FAFSA. **Notification of Awards:** Applicants will be notified of awards on a rolling basis beginning 3/15. **Types of Aid:** *Need-based scholarships/grants:* Federal Pell, SEOG, state scholarships/grants, private scholarships, the school's own gift aid. *Loans:* Subsidized Stafford, Unsubsidized Stafford, PLUS. **Student Employment:** Federal Work-Study Program available. Institutional employment available. Highest amount earned per year from on-campus jobs $2,400. Off-campus job opportunities are good. **Financial Aid Statistics:** 95% freshmen, 95% undergrads receive need-based scholarship or grant aid. 32% freshmen, 36% undergrads receive non-need-based scholarship or grant aid. 47% freshmen,

34% undergrads receive need-based self-help aid. 1% undergrads receive athletic scholarships. 98% freshmen, 93% undergrads receive any aid. 92% undergrads borrow to pay for school. Average cumulative indebtedness $32,698. **Criteria for awarding institutional aid:** *Non-need-based:* academics, alumni affiliation, athletics, music/drama, religious affiliation.

BLOOMSBURG UNIVERSITY OF PENNSYLVANIA

104 Student Services Center, Bloomsburg, PA 17815
Phone: 570-389-4316 • **Financial Aid Phone:** 570-389-4279
E-mail: www.bloomu.edu/admissions • **CEEB Code:** 2646
Fax: 570-389-4741 • **Website:** www.bloomu.edu • **ACT Code:** 3692

This public school was founded in 1839. It has a 282-acre campus.

RATINGS

Admissions Selectivity Rating: 73   **Fire Safety Rating:** 95   **Green Rating:** 61

STUDENTS AND FACULTY

Enrollment: 9,044. **Student Body:** 56% female, 44% male, 11% out-of-state, 2% international (27 countries represented). Asian 1%, African American 7%, Caucasian 82%, Hispanic 4%, Native American 0%. **Retention and Graduation:** 78% freshmen return for sophomore year. 43% freshmen graduate within 4 years. 64% freshmen graduate within 6 years. 24% grads go on to further study within 1 year. **Faculty:** Student/faculty ratio 21:1. 414 full-time faculty, 80% hold PhDs, 13% are members of minority groups, 43% are women. 0% of classes are taught by teaching assistants.

ACADEMICS

Degrees: bachelor's, certificate, master's, post-bachelor's certificate, post-master's certificate. **Classes:** Most classes have 20–29 students. Most lab/discussion sessions have 10–19 students. **Majors with Highest Enrollment:** business administration and management; elementary education and teaching; special education and teaching. **Special Study Options:** cooperative education program, cross-registration, distance learning, double major, dual enrollment, English as a Second Language (ESL), exchange student program (domestic), honors program, independent study, internships, liberal arts/career combination, study abroad, teacher certification program. **Honors Programs:** The Honors Program's goals are: to challenge students to perform at the highest level of excellence to encourage independent thinking and learning; to create a supportive environment that encourages the aspirations and achievements of students and fosters their dignity, self esteem and sense of initiative; to encourage creativity, intellectual independence, analytical thinking and problem solving and the growth of communication skills through a strong emphasis on reading, writing and research; to provide opportunities for students to develop a broader perspective on national and global issues; to provide forums for symposia, experiential learning and independent study; to create a meaningful learning community; to develop students' leadership potential; to enable students to engage in a rigorous, coherent, integrated academic experience with a high degree of student-faculty interaction. **Disability Services:** Special programs offered to physically disabled students include note-taking services, reader services, tape recorders, tutors. **Career Services:** career/job search classes, career assessment Career Services highlights include http://internships.bloomu.edu/.

FACILITIES

Housing: Coed dorms, apartments for single students, Affiliated off-campus apartments operated by the Community Government Association. 100% of campus accessible to physically disabled. **Special Academic Facilities/Equipment:** Art gallery, language lab, TV studio, radio station. **Computers:** 100% of classrooms, 100% of libraries, 100% of student union, 50% of common outdoor areas have wireless network access. Students can register for classes online. Administrative functions (other than registration) can be performed online.

CAMPUS LIFE

Environment: Village. **Activities:** Choral groups, concert band, dance, drama/theater, literary magazine, marching band, music ensembles, pep band, radio station, student government, student newspaper, television station, yearbook, Campus Ministries, International Student Organization, Model UN 195 registered organizations, 19 honor societies, 8 religious organizations. 15 fraternities, 13 sororities. **Athletics (Intercollegiate):** *Men:* baseball, basketball, cheerleading, cross-country, football, soccer, swimming, tennis, track/field (outdoor), track/field (indoor), wrestling. *Women:* basketball, cheerleading, cross-country, field hockey, lacrosse, soccer, softball, swimming, tennis, track/field (outdoor), track/field (indoor). **On-Campus Highlights:** Kehr Student Union, Dining Hall/Food Court, Climbing Wall, Recreation Center, Redman Stadium, Starbucks. **Environmental Initiatives:** Biofuel bus. One of Bloomsburg's shuttle buses uses carbon neutral B100 fuel processed from dining services' used cooking oil during fall and spring. Two 1951 vintage coal boilers have been replaced with a biomass (wood chip) boiler and a natural gas boiler to reduce emissions at Bloomsburg's heating plant. 1,500 gallons of water are saved by going trayless each Tuesday at the campus dining hall. Food waste is reduced as well. Possibly completely trayless in near future.

ADMISSIONS
Freshman Academic Profile: Average high school GPA. 9% in top 10% of high school class, 28% in top 25% of high school class, 68% in top 50% of high school class. 88% from public high schools. SAT Math middle 50% range 460-550. SAT Critical Reading middle 50% range 440-530. SAT Writing middle 50% range 430-530. ACT middle 50% range 19-23. Minimum web-based TOEFL. Minimum paper TOEFL 550. **Basis for Candidate Selection:** *Very important factors considered include:* Class rank, academic GPA, rigor of secondary school record, standardized test scores. *Other factors considered include:* application essay, recommendation(s), character/personal qualities, extracurricular activities, geographical residence, interview, state residency, talent/ability, volunteer work, work experience. **Freshman Admission Requirements:** High school diploma is required and GED is accepted. *Academic units required:* 4 English, 3 mathematics, 3 science, 2 social studies, 2 history, 2 academic electives. *Academic units recommended:* 4 English, 3 mathematics, 3 science, 2 social studies, 2 history, 2 academic electives. **Freshman Admission Statistics:** 10,379 applied, 68% admitted, 27% enrolled. **Transfer Admission Requirements:** High school transcript, college transcript(s), minimum college GPA of 2.0 required. Lowest grade transferable C. **General Admission Information:** Application Fee $30. Notification on a rolling basis, beginning on or about 9/18. Nonfall registration accepted. Admission may be deferred for a maximum of 1 year. Credit and/or placement offered for CEEB Advanced Placement tests.

COSTS AND FINANCIAL AID
Annual in-state tuition $6,428. Annual out-of-state tuition $16,070. Room and board $7,498. Required fees $1,916. Average book expense $1,200. **Required Forms and Deadlines:** FAFSA. **Notification of Awards:** Applicants will be notified of awards on a rolling basis beginning 4/1. **Types of Aid:** *Need-based scholarships/grants:* Federal Pell, SEOG, state scholarships/grants, private scholarships, the school's own gift aid, Federal ACG and Federal Smart Grants. *Loans:* Subsidized Stafford, Unsubsidized Stafford, PLUS, Federal Perkins, state loans, Alternative Loans. **Student Employment:** Federal Work-Study Program available. Institutional employment available. Highest amount earned per year from on-campus jobs $4,640. **Financial Aid Statistics:** 59% freshmen, 60% undergrads receive need-based scholarship or grant aid. 22% freshmen, 14% undergrads receive non-need-based scholarship or grant aid. 93% freshmen, 92% undergrads receive need-based self-help aid. 3% freshmen, 2% undergrads receive athletic scholarships. 77% freshmen, % undergrads receive any aid. 71% undergrads borrow to pay for school. Average cumulative indebtedness $27,223. **Criteria for awarding institutional aid:** *Non-need-based:* academics, art, athletics, job skills, leadership, minority status, music/drama, state/district residency.

BLUE MOUNTAIN COLLEGE

PO Box 160, Blue Mountain, MS 38610
Phone: 662-685-4771 • **Financial Aid Phone:** 662-685-4771
E-mail: admissions@bmc.edu
Fax: 662-685-4776 • **Website:** bmc.edu

This private school, affiliated with the Baptist Church, was founded in 1873. It has a 44-acre campus.

RATINGS
Admissions Selectivity Rating: 79   **Fire Safety Rating:** 64   **Green Rating:** 60*

STUDENTS AND FACULTY
Enrollment: 406. **Student Body:** 64% female, 36% male, 12% out-of-state, 0% international (1 countries represented). Asian 0%, African American 12%, Caucasian 87%, Hispanic 0%, Native American 0%.
Retention and Graduation: 72% freshmen return for sophomore year. 31% freshmen graduate within 4 years. 58% freshmen graduate within 6 years. 14% grads go on to further study within 1 year. 14% grads pursue arts and sciences degrees. 1% grads pursue business degrees. 2% grads pursue medical degrees. **Faculty:** Student/faculty ratio 13:1. 24 full-time faculty, 67% hold PhDs, 0% are members of minority groups, 54% are women. 0% of classes are taught by teaching assistants.

ACADEMICS
Degrees: bachelor's, master's. **Classes:** Most classes have 10–19 students. Most lab/discussion sessions have 10–19 students. **Majors with Highest Enrollment:** bible/biblical studies; elementary education and teaching; psychology. **Special Study Options:** double major, honors program, internships, teacher

certification program. **Honors Programs:** Academic Honors Program. **Disability Services:** Special programs offered to physically disabled students include note-taking services, tutors.

FACILITIES
Housing: men's dorms, women's dorms, 50% of campus accessible to physically disabled. **Special Academic Facilities/Equipment:** 1 **Computers:**

CAMPUS LIFE
Environment: Rural. **Activities:** Choral groups, drama/theater, literary magazine, musical theater, student government, yearbook 28 registered organizations, 4 honor societies, 2 religious organizations. **Athletics (Intercollegiate):** *Women:* basketball, tennis. **On-Campus Highlights:** Johnnie Armstrong Galry, Student Union Building, Tyler Gymnasium, Broach Hall, Fisher-Washburn Hall.

ADMISSIONS
Freshman Academic Profile: Average high school GPA 3.3. 19% in top 10% of high school class, 50% in top 25% of high school class, 86% in top 50% of high school class. 73% from public high schools. ACT middle 50% range 18-23. Minimum paper TOEFL 500. **Basis for Candidate Selection:** *Important factors considered include:* Class rank, academic GPA, rigor of secondary school record, standardized test scores. *Other factors considered include:* recommendation(s), alumni/ae relation, character/personal qualities. **Freshman Admission Requirements:** High school diploma is required and GED is accepted. *Academic units required:* 4 English, 3 mathematics, 3 science, (2 science labs), 2 foreign language, 1 social studies, 2 history. *Academic units recommended:* 4 English, 3 mathematics, 3 science, (2 science labs), 2 foreign language, 1 social studies, 2 history. **Freshman Admission Statistics:** 197 applied, 50% admitted, 60% enrolled. **Transfer Admission Requirements:** college transcript(s), Lowest grade transferable C. **General Admission Information:** Application Fee $10. Notification on a rolling basis, beginning on or about 10/1. Nonfall registration accepted. Admission may be deferred for a maximum of semester. Credit offered for CEEB Advanced Placement tests.

COSTS AND FINANCIAL AID
Annual tuition $6,900. Room and board $3,766. Required fees $540. Average book expense $650. **Required Forms and Deadlines:** FAFSA, institution's own financial aid form. **Notification of Awards:** Applicants will be notified of awards on a rolling basis beginning 4/1. **Types of Aid:** *Need-based scholarships/grants:* Federal Pell, SEOG, state scholarships/grants, private scholarships. *Loans:* Subsidized Stafford, Unsubsidized Stafford, PLUS, Federal Perkins. **Student Employment:** Federal Work-Study Program available. Institutional employment available. Highest amount earned per year from on-campus jobs $1,400. Off-campus job opportunities are good. **Financial Aid Statistics:** 81% freshmen, 64% undergrads receive need-based scholarship or grant aid. 81% freshmen, 100% undergrads receive non-need-based scholarship or grant aid. 62% freshmen, 18% undergrads receive need-based self-help aid. 8% freshmen, 6% undergrads receive athletic scholarships. 95% freshmen, 96% undergrads receive any aid. 83% undergrads borrow to pay for school. Average cumulative indebtedness $11,484. **Criteria for awarding institutional aid:** *Non-need-based:* academics, alumni affiliation, athletics, religious affiliation, state/district residency.

BLUEFIELD COLLEGE

3000 College Drive, Bluefield, VA 24605
Phone: 540-326-4214 • **Financial Aid Phone:** 800-872-0175
E-mail: thavens@mail.bluefield.edu • **CEEB Code:** 5063
Fax: 540-326-4288 • **Website:** www.bluefield.edu • **ACT Code:** 4340

This private school, affiliated with the Baptist Church, was founded in 1922.

RATINGS
Admissions Selectivity Rating: 82   **Fire Safety Rating:** 60*   **Green Rating:** 60*

STUDENTS AND FACULTY
Enrollment: 776. **Student Body:** 60% female, 40% male, 22% out-of-state, 0% international. Asian 1%, African American 18%, Caucasian 78%, Hispanic 1%, Native American 0%.
Retention and Graduation: 66% freshmen return for sophomore year. 36% freshmen graduate within 4 years. 47% freshmen graduate within 6 years. 23% grads go on to further study within 1 year. 10% grads pursue arts and sciences degrees. 3% grads pursue law degrees. 8% grads pursue business degrees. 2% grads pursue medical degrees. **Faculty:** Student/faculty ratio 12:1. 33 full-time faculty, 64% hold PhDs, 0% are members of minority groups, 30% are women. 0% of classes are taught by teaching assistants.

ACADEMICS

Degrees: bachelor's. **Classes:** Most classes have fewer than 10 students. Most lab/discussion sessions have 10–19 students. **Majors with Highest Enrollment:** business/commerce; christian studies; criminal justice/law enforcement administration. **Special Study Options:** Accelerated program, double major, dual enrollment, honors program, internships, student-designed major, study abroad, teacher certification program, weekend college. **Disability Services:** Special programs offered to physically disabled students include tape recorders, tutors. **Career Services:** Alumni network, alumni services, career/job search classes, internships.

FACILITIES

Housing: Coed dorms, men's dorms, women's dorms, 50% of campus accessible to physically disabled. **Special Academic Facilities/Equipment:** Art center.

CAMPUS LIFE

Environment: Rural. **Activities:** Choral groups, drama/theater, literary magazine, music ensembles, student government, student newspaper, yearbook 18 registered organizations, 7 honor societies, 6 religious organizations. 2 fraternities, 2 sororities. **Athletics (Intercollegiate):** Men: baseball, basketball, golf, soccer, tennis. Women: basketball, soccer, softball, tennis, volleyball.

ADMISSIONS

Freshman Academic Profile: Average high school GPA 3.2. 23% in top 10% of high school class, 44% in top 25% of high school class, 83% in top 50% of high school class. 95% from public high schools. SAT Math middle 50% range 420-520. SAT Critical Reading middle 50% range 440-530. ACT middle 50% range 19-24. **Basis for Candidate Selection:** Very important factors considered include: rigor of secondary school record, standardized test scores, character/personal qualities. Important factors considered include: Class rank, interview. Other factors considered include: application essay, recommendation(s), alumni/ae relation, extracurricular activities, talent/ability, volunteer work, work experience. **Freshman Admission Requirements:** High school diploma is required and GED is accepted. Academic units required: 4 English, 3 mathematics, 3 science, (1 science labs), 3 social studies, 6 academic electives. Academic units recommended: 4 English, 3 mathematics, 3 science, (1 science labs), 3 social studies, 6 academic electives. **Freshman Admission Statistics:** 537 applied, 50% admitted, 40% enrolled. **Transfer Admission Requirements:** college transcript(s), minimum college GPA of 2.0 required. Lowest grade transferable D. **General Admission Information:** Application Fee $30. Notification on a rolling basis, beginning on or about 9/1. Nonfall registration accepted. Admission may be deferred for a maximum of semester.

COSTS AND FINANCIAL AID

Annual tuition $6,900. Room and board $4,890. Average book expense $900. **Required Forms and Deadlines:** FAFSA, institution's own financial aid form, state aid form. **Notification of Awards:** Applicants will be notified of awards on a rolling basis beginning 3/10. **Types of Aid:** Need-based scholarships/grants: Federal Pell, SEOG, state scholarships/grants, private scholarships, the school's own gift aid. Loans: Subsidized Stafford, Unsubsidized Stafford, PLUS, Keesee Foundation. **Student Employment:** Highest amount earned per year from on-campus jobs $700. Off-campus job opportunities are good. **Financial Aid Statistics:** 99% freshmen, 95% undergrads receive need-based scholarship or grant aid. 16% freshmen, 12% undergrads receive non-need-based scholarship or grant aid. 73% freshmen, 82% undergrads receive need-based self-help aid. 80% undergrads borrow to pay for school. Average cumulative indebtedness $12,177. **Criteria for awarding institutional aid:** Non-need-based: academics, art, athletics, leadership, minority status, music/drama, religious affiliation, state/district residency.

BLUEFIELD STATE COLLEGE

219 Rock Street, Bluefield, WV 24701
Phone: 304-327-4065
E-mail: bscadmit@bluefieldstate.edu • **CEEB Code:** 5064
Fax: 304-325-7747 • **Website:** www.bluefieldstate.edu • **ACT Code:** 4514

This public school was founded in 1895. It has a 40-acre campus.

RATINGS

Admissions Selectivity Rating: 64   **Fire Safety Rating:** 60*   **Green Rating:** 60*

STUDENTS AND FACULTY

Enrollment: 3,092. **Student Body:** 65% female, 35% male, 5% out-of-state, 0% international (15 countries represented). Asian 0%, African American 11%, Caucasian 100%, Hispanic 1%, Native American 0%.
Retention and Graduation: 76% freshmen return for sophomore year. 24% freshmen graduate within 4 years. 45% freshmen graduate within 6 years. 9%

grads go on to further study within 1 year. 4% grads pursue arts and sciences degrees. 1% grads pursue law degrees. 3% grads pursue business degrees. 1% grads pursue medical degrees. **Faculty:** Student/faculty ratio 17:1. 92 full-time faculty, 40% hold PhDs, 9% are members of minority groups, 55% are women. 0% of classes are taught by teaching assistants.

ACADEMICS

Degrees: associate, bachelor's, certificate, terminal associate, transfer associate. **Classes:** Most classes have 10–19 students. Most lab/discussion sessions have 10–19 students. **Majors with Highest Enrollment:** business/commerce; elementary education and teaching; nursing/registered nurse (rn, asn, bsn, msn). **Special Study Options:** distance learning, dual enrollment, honors program, internships, student-designed major, teacher certification program. **Honors Programs:** Bluefield State College Honors Program. **Disability Services:** Special programs offered to physically disabled students include note-taking services, reader services, tape recorders, tutors. **Career Services:** career/job search classes

FACILITIES

Housing: Off-campus housing services provided, including referrals and resources. 100% of campus accessible to physically disabled. **Computers:** Students can register for classes online. Administrative functions (other than registration) can be performed online.

CAMPUS LIFE

Environment: Village. **Activities:** Choral groups, student government, student newspaper, yearbook 28 registered organizations, 6 honor societies, 1 religious organizations. 3 fraternities, 4 sororities. **Athletics (Intercollegiate):** Men: baseball, basketball, cross-country, golf, tennis. Women: basketball, cheerleading, cross-country, softball, tennis, volleyball.

ADMISSIONS

Freshman Academic Profile: Average high school GPA 3.2. 10% in top 10% of high school class, 27% in top 25% of high school class, 73% in top 50% of high school class. 98% from public high schools. ACT middle 50% range 21-16. Minimum paper TOEFL 550. **Basis for Candidate Selection:** Important factors considered include: rigor of secondary school record, standardized test scores. **Freshman Admission Requirements:** High school diploma is required and GED is accepted. Academic units required: 4 English, 3 mathematics, 3 science, (2 science labs), 3 social studies, 1 history, 1 academic electives. Academic units recommended: 4 English, 3 mathematics, 3 science, (2 science labs), 3 social studies, 1 history, 1 academic electives. **Freshman Admission Statistics:** 1,135 applied, 98% admitted, 53% enrolled. **Transfer Admission Requirements:** college transcript(s), Lowest grade transferable D. **General Admission Information:** Nonfall registration accepted. Admission may be deferred for a maximum of 1 semester. Credit and/or placement offered for CEEB Advanced Placement tests.

COSTS AND FINANCIAL AID

Annual in-state tuition $3,114. Annual out-of-state tuition $6,894. Required fees. Average book expense $1,200. **Required Forms and Deadlines:** FAFSA, institution's own financial aid form, state aid form. **Notification of Awards:** Applicants will be notified of awards on a rolling basis beginning 6/1. **Types of Aid:** Need-based scholarships/grants: Federal Pell, SEOG, state scholarships/grants, private scholarships, the school's own gift aid. Loans: Direct Subsidized Stafford, Direct Unsubsidized Stafford, Direct PLUS, Federal Perkins. **Student Employment:** Highest amount earned per year from on-campus jobs $1,500. **Financial Aid Statistics:** 100% freshmen, 100% undergrads receive need-based scholarship or grant aid. 16% freshmen, 18% undergrads receive non-need-based scholarship or grant aid. 80% freshmen, 78% undergrads receive need-based self-help aid. 5% freshmen, 5% undergrads receive athletic scholarships. 50% undergrads borrow to pay for school. Average cumulative indebtedness $10,500. **Criteria for awarding institutional aid:** Non-need-based: academics, alumni affiliation, athletics, leadership, minority status, state/district residency.

BLUFFTON UNIVERSITY

Office of Admissions, Bluffton, OH 45817
Phone: 419-358-3257
E-mail: admissions@bluffton.edu • **CEEB Code:** 1067
Fax: 419-358-3081 • **Website:** www.bluffton.edu • **ACT Code:** 3238

This private school, affiliated with the Mennonite Church, was founded in 1899. It has a 65-acre campus.

RATINGS

Admissions Selectivity Rating: 76   **Fire Safety Rating:** 60*   **Green Rating:** 60*

STUDENTS AND FACULTY

Enrollment: 943. **Student Body:** 51% female, 49% male, 12% out-of-state, 2% international. Asian 1%, African American 7%, Caucasian 85%, Hispanic 2%, Native American 0%.
Retention and Graduation: 75% freshmen return for sophomore year. 56% freshmen graduate within 4 years. 64% freshmen graduate within 6 years. 9% grads go on to further study within 1 year. 9% grads pursue arts and sciences degrees. 1% grads pursue law degrees. 1% grads pursue medical degrees.
Faculty: Student/faculty ratio 13:1. 62 full-time faculty, 73% hold PhDs, 2% are members of minority groups, 34% are women. 0% of classes are taught by teaching assistants.

ACADEMICS

Degrees: bachelor's, master's. **Classes:** Most classes have 10–19 students. Most lab/discussion sessions have 10–19 students. **Special Study Options:** distance learning, double major, dual enrollment, English as a Second Language (ESL), honors program, independent study, internships, student-designed major, study abroad, teacher certification program. **Disability Services:** Special programs offered to physically disabled students include reader services, tape recorders, tutors. **Career Services:** alumni services, career/job search classes.

FACILITIES

Housing: Coed dorms, men's dorms, women's dorms, theme housing. 99% of campus accessible to physically disabled. **Special Academic Facilities/Equipment:** Mennonite historical library, peace arts center, nature preserve.

CAMPUS LIFE

Environment: Rural. **Activities:** Choral groups, concert band, dance, drama/theater, jazz band, literary magazine, music ensembles, musical theater, pep band, radio station, student government, Campus Ministries, International Student Organization 50 registered organizations, 19 honor societies, 10 religious organizations. **Athletics (Intercollegiate):** *Men:* baseball, basketball, cheerleading, cross-country, football, golf, soccer, tennis, track/field (outdoor), track/field (indoor). *Women:* basketball, cheerleading, cross-country, golf, soccer, softball, tennis, track/field (outdoor), track/field (indoor), volleyball. **On-Campus Highlights:** Centennial Hall-academic center, Marbeck Center-student union, College Hall-administrative/classroom building, Salzman Stadium-Football Stadium, Founders Hall-gymnasium.

ADMISSIONS

Freshman Academic Profile: Average high school GPA 3.2. 14% in top 10% of high school class, 33% in top 25% of high school class, 67% in top 50% of high school class. 98% from public high schools. SAT Math middle 50% range 450-600. SAT Critical Reading middle 50% range 420-570. ACT middle 50% range 19-24. Minimum paper TOEFL 500. **Basis for Candidate Selection:** *Very important factors considered include:* Class rank, academic GPA, standardized test scores. *Important factors considered include:* recommendation(s). *Other factors considered include:* application essay, rigor of secondary school record, character/personal qualities, religious affiliation/commitment, talent/ability, volunteer work. **Freshman Admission Requirements:** High school diploma is required and GED is accepted. **Freshman Admission Statistics:** 1,674 applied, 66% admitted, 23% enrolled. **Transfer Admission Requirements:** High school transcript, college transcript(s), statement of good standing from prior institution. Minimum college GPA of 2.0 required. Lowest grade transferable C-. **General Admission Information:** Application Fee $20. Regular application deadline 8/15. Nonfall registration accepted. Admission may be deferred for a maximum of two years. Credit and/or placement offered for CEEB Advanced Placement tests.

COSTS AND FINANCIAL AID

Annual tuition $23,594. Room and board $8,170. Required fees $450. Average book expense $1,400. **Required Forms and Deadlines:** FAFSA. **Notification of Awards:** Applicants will be notified of awards on a rolling basis beginning 3/1. **Types of Aid:** *Need-based scholarships/grants:* Federal Pell, SEOG, state scholarships/grants, private scholarships, the school's own gift aid. *Loans:* Subsidized Stafford, Unsubsidized Stafford, PLUS, Federal Perkins. **Student Employment:** Federal Work-Study Program available. Institutional employment available. Highest amount earned per year from on-campus jobs $1,350. Off-campus job opportunities are good. **Financial Aid Statistics:** 100% freshmen, 98% undergrads receive need-based scholarship or grant aid. 1% freshmen, 5% undergrads receive non-need-based scholarship or grant aid. 94% freshmen, 93% undergrads receive need-based self-help aid. 88% undergrads borrow to pay for school. Average cumulative indebtedness $26,896. **Criteria for awarding institutional aid:** *Non-need-based:* academics, art, job skills, leadership, minority status, music/drama, religious affiliation, state/district residency.

BOB JONES UNIVERSITY

1700 Wade Hampton Blvd, Greenville, SC 29614
Phone: 800-252-6363 • **Financial Aid Phone:** 864-242-5100 Ext 3040
E-mail: admission@bju.edu • **CEEB Code:** 5065
Fax: 800-232-9258 • **Website:** www.bju.edu • **ACT Code:** 3836

This proprietary school was founded in 1927. It has a 225-acre campus.

RATINGS

Admissions Selectivity Rating: 72   **Fire Safety Rating:** 79   **Green Rating:** 60*

STUDENTS AND FACULTY

Enrollment: 2,859. **Student Body:** 57% female, 43% male, 69% out-of-state, 5% international (47 countries represented). Asian 2%, African American 1%, Caucasian 80%, Hispanic 2%, Native American 0%.
Retention and Graduation: 83% freshmen return for sophomore year. 46% freshmen graduate within 4 years. 64% freshmen graduate within 6 years. 18% grads go on to further study within 1 year. 1% grads pursue arts and sciences degrees. 1% grads pursue law degrees. 2% grads pursue business degrees. 3% grads pursue medical degrees. **Faculty:** Student/faculty ratio 15:1. 198 full-time faculty, 50% hold PhDs, 8% are members of minority groups, 39% are women.

ACADEMICS

Degrees: associate, bachelor's, certificate, doctoral, master's, transfer associate. **Classes:** Most classes have fewer than 10 students. Most lab/discussion sessions have fewer than 10 students. **Majors with Highest Enrollment:** accounting; elementary education and teaching; nursing/registered nurse (rn, asn, bsn, msn). **Special Study Options:** Accelerated program, distance learning, English as a Second Language (ESL), internships, teacher certification program. **Disability Services:** Special programs offered to physically disabled students include note-taking services, reader services, tape recorders, tutors. **Career Services:** alumni services, career/job search classes, career assessment.

FACILITIES

Housing: special housing for disabled students, men's dorms, women's dorms, apartments for married students, apartments for single students. 90% of campus accessible to physically disabled. **Special Academic Facilities/Equipment:** Museum & Gallery Davis Field House Rodeheaver Auditorium Bob Jones Jr. Memorial Seminary & Evangelism Center. **Computers:** 85% of classrooms, 100% of dorms, 100% of libraries, 20% of dining areas, 100% of student union, 70% of common outdoor areas have wireless network access. Students can register for classes online. Administrative functions (other than registration) can be performed online.

CAMPUS LIFE

Environment: City. **Activities:** Choral groups, concert band, drama/theater, music ensembles, opera, radio station, student government, student newspaper, symphony orchestra, television station, yearbook, Campus Ministries 31 registered organizations, 18 religious organizations. **On-Campus Highlights:** University Student Center, Davis Field House, Cuppa Jones coffee shop, Fast Break lunch area, BJU Museum & Gallery.

ADMISSIONS

Freshman Academic Profile: Average high school GPA 3.4. 17% in top 25% of high school class, 36% in top 50% of high school class. 11% from public high schools. ACT middle 50% range 20-26. Minimum web-based TOEFL 61. Minimum paper TOEFL 500. **Basis for Candidate Selection:** *Important factors considered include:* academic GPA, rigor of secondary school record, standardized test scores. *Other factors considered include:* recommendation(s), state residency. **Freshman Admission Requirements:** High school diploma is required and GED is accepted. *Academic units required:* 4 English, 3 mathematics, 2 science, (2 science labs), 2 foreign language, 1 social studies, 1 history, 1 visual/performing arts, 1 academic electives. *Academic units recommended:* 4 English, 3 mathematics, 2 science, (2 science labs), 2 foreign language, 1 social studies, 1 history, 1 visual/performing arts, 1 academic electives. **Freshman Admission Statistics:** 1,437 applied, 73% admitted, 66% enrolled. **Transfer Admission Requirements:** college transcript(s), minimum college GPA of 2.0 required. Lowest grade transferable D-. **General Admission Information:** Application Fee $55. Regular application deadline 11/30. Notification on a rolling basis, beginning on or about 10/2. Nonfall registration accepted. Admission may be deferred for a maximum of 1 semester. Credit and/or placement offered for CEEB Advanced Placement tests.

COSTS AND FINANCIAL AID

Annual tuition $12,480. Room and board $5,430. Required fees $610. Average book expense $1,398. **Required Forms and Deadlines:** FAFSA, state aid form. **Notification of Awards:** Applicants will be notified of awards on or about 3/1. **Types of Aid:** *Need-based scholarships/grants:* Federal Pell, SEOG, state scholarships/grants, private scholarships, the school's own gift aid. *Loans:* Direct Subsidized Stafford, Direct Unsubsidized Stafford, Direct

The Princeton Review's Complete Book of Colleges

PLUS, Subsidized Stafford, Unsubsidized Stafford, PLUS, Federal Perkins. **Student Employment:** Federal Work-Study Program available. Institutional employment available. Highest amount earned per year from on-campus jobs $12,914. Off-campus job opportunities are good. **Financial Aid Statistics:** 88% freshmen, 84% undergrads receive need-based scholarship or grant aid. 7% freshmen, 12% undergrads receive non-need-based scholarship or grant aid. 44% freshmen, 56% undergrads receive need-based self-help aid. 60% freshmen, 61% undergrads receive any aid. **Criteria for awarding institutional aid:** *Non-need-based:* academics, alumni affiliation, athletics, leadership, state/district residency.

BOISE BIBLE COLLEGE

8695 W Marigold Street, Boise, ID 83714-1220
Phone: 208-376-7731
E-mail: boisebible@boisebible.edu • **CEEB Code:** 891
Fax: 208-376-7743 • **ACT Code:** 917

This private school, affiliated with the Christian (Nondenominational) Church, was founded in 1945. It has a 16-acre campus.

RATINGS
Admissions Selectivity Rating: 65   **Fire Safety Rating:** 60*   **Green Rating:** 60*

STUDENTS AND FACULTY
Enrollment: 175. **Student Body:** 50% female, 50% male, 55% out-of-state, 2% international (3 countries represented). Asian 2%, African American 1%, Caucasian 89%, Hispanic 3%, Native American 1%.
Retention and Graduation: 60% freshmen return for sophomore year.
Faculty: Student/faculty ratio 16:1. 8 full-time faculty, 13% hold PhDs, 0% are members of minority groups, 13% are women.

ACADEMICS
Degrees: associate, bachelor's, certificate. **Classes: Majors with Highest Enrollment:** pastoral studies/counseling; religious education; theological and ministerial studies, other. **Special Study Options:** double major, internships, teacher certification program.

FACILITIES
Housing: men's dorms, women's dorms.

CAMPUS LIFE
Environment: Village. **Activities:** Choral groups, music ensembles, student government.

ADMISSIONS
Freshman Academic Profile: Average high school GPA 3.2. 8% in top 10% of high school class, 40% in top 25% of high school class, 70% in top 50% of high school class. SAT Math middle 50% range 410-540. SAT Critical Reading middle 50% range 460-550. ACT middle 50% range 16-21. Minimum paper TOEFL 500. **Basis for Candidate Selection:** *Important factors considered include:* Class rank, application essay, academic GPA, recommendation(s), standardized test scores, character/personal qualities, religious affiliation/commitment. *Other factors considered include:* interview, level of applicant's interest. **Freshman Admission Requirements:** High school diploma is required and GED is accepted. **Freshman Admission Statistics:** 80 applied, 99% admitted, 75% enrolled. **Transfer Admission Requirements:** college transcript(s), essay or personal statement, statement of good standing from prior institution(s). Minimum college GPA of 2.0 required. Lowest grade transferable C. **General Admission Information:** Application Fee $25. Regular application deadline 8/15. Notification on a rolling basis, beginning on or about 2/15. Nonfall registration accepted. Admission may be deferred for a maximum of 1 year. Credit offered for CEEB Advanced Placement tests.

COSTS AND FINANCIAL AID
Annual tuition $6,840. Room and board $4,800. Required fees $49. Average book expense $450. **Required Forms and Deadlines:** FAFSA, institution's own financial aid form. **Notification of Awards: Types of Aid:** *Need-based scholarships/grants:* Federal Pell, SEOG, private scholarships. *Loans:* Direct Subsidized Stafford, Direct Unsubsidized Stafford, Direct PLUS. **Student Employment:** Federal Work-Study Program available. **Criteria for awarding institutional aid:** *Non-need-based:* academics, leadership, music/drama.

BOISE STATE UNIVERSITY

1910 University Drive, Boise, ID 83725
Phone: 208-426-1156 • **Financial Aid Phone:** 208-426-1664
E-mail: bsuinfo@boisestate.edu • **CEEB Code:** 4018
Fax: 208-426-3765 • **Website:** • **ACT Code:** 914

This public school was founded in 1932. It has a 150-acre campus.

RATINGS
Admissions Selectivity Rating: 69   **Fire Safety Rating:** 67   **Green Rating:** 61

STUDENTS AND FACULTY
Enrollment: 17,069. **Student Body:** 53% female, 47% male, 20% out-of-state, 3% international (73 countries represented). Asian 2%, African American 2%, Caucasian 77%, Hispanic 8%, Native American 1%.
Retention and Graduation: 72% freshmen return for sophomore year. 7% freshmen graduate within 4 years. 30% freshmen graduate within 6 years. 15% grads go on to further study within 1 year. 4% grads pursue arts and sciences degrees. 1% grads pursue law degrees. 2% grads pursue business degrees. 1% grads pursue medical degrees. **Faculty:** Student/faculty ratio 20:1. 615 full-time faculty, 67% hold PhDs, 8% are members of minority groups, 47% are women. 1% of classes are taught by teaching assistants.

ACADEMICS
Degrees: associate, bachelor's, doctoral, master's, post-bachelor's certificate. **Classes:** Most classes have 20–29 students. Most lab/discussion sessions have 20–29 students. **Majors with Highest Enrollment:** communication studies/speech communication and rhetoric; computer science; information science/studies. **Special Study Options:** cooperative education program, distance learning, double major, dual enrollment, English as a Second Language (ESL), exchange student program (domestic), honors program, independent study, internships, liberal arts/career combination, study abroad, teacher certification program, weekend college. **Disability Services:** Special programs offered to physically disabled students include note-taking services, reader services, tape recorders, tutors. **Career Services:** Alumni network, alumni services, career assessment, internships Career Services highlights include One of the larger intrnship programs in the Northwest.

FACILITIES
Housing: Coed dorms, special housing for disabled students, men's dorms, women's dorms, fraternity/sorority housing, apartments for married students, apartments for single students. 95% of campus accessible to physically disabled. **Computers:** Students can register for classes online. Administrative functions (other than registration) can be performed online.

CAMPUS LIFE
Environment: City. **Activities:** Choral groups, drama/theater, literary magazine, marching band, music ensembles, musical theater, pep band, radio station, student government, student newspaper, student-run film society, International Student Organization 180 registered organizations, 4 fraternities, 3 sororities. **Athletics (Intercollegiate):** *Men:* basketball, cheerleading, cross-country, football, golf, tennis, track/field (outdoor), track/field (indoor), wrestling. *Women:* basketball, cheerleading, cross-country, golf, gymnastics, skiing (downhill/alpine), soccer, tennis, track/field (outdoor), track/field (indoor), volleyball.

ADMISSIONS
Freshman Academic Profile: Average high school GPA 3.4. 14% in top 10% of high school class, 38% in top 25% of high school class, 73% in top 50% of high school class. 89% from public high schools. SAT Math middle 50% range 480-600. SAT Critical Reading middle 50% range 470-580. SAT Writing middle 50% range 450-560. ACT middle 50% range 20-25. Minimum paper TOEFL 500. **Basis for Candidate Selection:** *Very important factors considered include:* academic GPA, rigor of secondary school record, standardized test scores. *Other factors considered include:* Class rank, extracurricular activities, first generation, racial/ethnic status, talent/ability. **Freshman Admission Requirements:** High school diploma is required and GED is accepted. *Academic units required:* 4 English, 3 mathematics, 3 science, 1 foreign language, 2 social studies, 1 academic electives. *Academic units recommended:* 4 English, 3 mathematics, 3 science, 1 foreign language, 2 social studies, 1 academic electives. **Freshman Admission Statistics:** 5,184 applied, 85% admitted, 54% enrolled. **Transfer Admission Requirements:** college transcript(s), minimum college GPA of 2.0 required. Lowest grade transferable c. **General Admission Information:** Application Fee $50. Regular application deadline 6/30. Notification on a rolling basis, beginning on or about 4/1. Nonfall registration accepted. Credit offered for CEEB Advanced Placement tests.

COSTS AND FINANCIAL AID
Annual in-state tuition $3,991. Annual out-of-state tuition $15,431. Required fees $1,893. Average book expense $1,200. **Required Forms and Deadlines:** FAFSA. **Notification of Awards:** Applicants will be notified of awards on a rolling basis beginning 4/1. **Types of Aid:** *Need-based scholarships/grants:*

Federal Pell, SEOG, state scholarships/grants, private scholarships, the school's own gift aid. *Loans:* Direct Subsidized Stafford, Direct Unsubsidized Stafford, Direct PLUS, Federal Perkins, college/university loans from institutional funds. **Student Employment:** Federal Work-Study Program available. Institutional employment available. Highest amount earned per year from on-campus jobs $10,000. Off-campus job opportunities are excellent. **Financial Aid Statistics:** 81% freshmen, 77% undergrads receive need-based scholarship or grant aid. 15% freshmen, 6% undergrads receive non-need-based scholarship or grant aid. 84% freshmen, 92% undergrads receive need-based self-help aid. 1% undergrads receive athletic scholarships. 70% freshmen, 80% undergrads receive any aid. 64% undergrads borrow to pay for school. Average cumulative indebtedness $27,369. **Criteria for awarding institutional aid:** *Non-need-based:* academics, art, athletics, music/drama.

BOSTON ARCHITECTURAL COLLEGE

320 Newbury Street, Boston, MA 02115-2703
Phone: 617-585-0123
E-mail: admissions@the-bac.edu • **CEEB Code:** 1168
Fax: 617-585-0121 • **Website:** www.the-bac.edu

This private school was founded in 1889.

RATINGS
Admissions Selectivity Rating: 61   **Fire Safety Rating:** 60*   **Green Rating:** 60*

STUDENTS AND FACULTY
Faculty: Student/faculty ratio 15:1.

ACADEMICS
Degrees: bachelor's, certificate, first professional, master's. **Majors with Highest Enrollment:** computer and information sciences; elementary education and teaching; psychology. **Special Study Options:** cross-registration, distance learning, study abroad, Concurrent academic and practice-based learning. **Career Services:** career/job search classes, internships.

FACILITIES
Housing: 100% of campus accessible to physically disabled. **Special Academic Facilities/Equipment:** McCormick Gallery.

CAMPUS LIFE
Activities: student newspaper 2 registered organizations.

ADMISSIONS
Freshman Academic Profile: Minimum paper TOEFL 550. **Freshman Admission Requirements:** High school diploma is required and GED is accepted. **Freshman Admission Statistics:** 368 applied, 94% admitted, 32% enrolled. **Transfer Admission Requirements:** High school transcript, college transcript(s), Lowest grade transferable C. **General Admission Information:** Application Fee $50. Nonfall registration accepted. Admission may be deferred for a maximum of 1 Semester. Credit and/or placement offered for CEEB Advanced Placement tests.

COSTS AND FINANCIAL AID
Annual tuition $7,438. Required fees $150. Average book expense $1,105. **Required Forms and Deadlines:** FAFSA, institution's own financial aid form. **Notification of Awards:** Applicants will be notified of awards on a rolling basis beginning 4/30. **Types of Aid:** *Need-based scholarships/grants:* Federal Pell, state scholarships/grants, private scholarships. *Loans:* Subsidized Stafford, Unsubsidized Stafford, PLUS, state loans. **Student Employment:** Off-campus job opportunities are excellent. **Financial Aid Statistics:** 50% undergrads borrow to pay for school. Average cumulative indebtedness $40,000. **Criteria for awarding institutional aid:** *Non-need-based:* academics, job skills.

BOSTON COLLEGE

140 Commonwealth Avenue, Chestnut Hill, MA 02467-3809
Phone: 617-552-3100 • **Financial Aid Phone:** 617-552-3300 • **CEEB Code:** 3083
Fax: 617-552-0798 • **Website:** www.bc.edu • **ACT Code:** 1788

This private school, affiliated with the Roman Catholic Church, was founded in 1863. It has a 386.1-acre campus.

RATINGS
Admissions Selectivity Rating: 97   **Fire Safety Rating:** 88   **Green Rating:** 83

STUDENTS AND FACULTY
Enrollment: 9,110. **Student Body:** 74% out-of-state, 4% international (94 countries represented). Asian 10%, African American 4%, Caucasian 60%, Hispanic 11%, Native American 0%.
Retention and Graduation: 95% freshmen return for sophomore year. 21% grads go on to further study within 1 year. 6% grads pursue arts and sciences degrees. 5% grads pursue law degrees. 1% grads pursue business degrees. 3% grads pursue medical degrees. **Faculty:** Student/faculty ratio 14:1. 752 full-time faculty, 95% hold PhDs, 15% are members of minority groups, 39% are women.

ACADEMICS
Degrees: bachelor's, doctoral, master's, post-master's certificate. **Classes:** Most classes have 10–19 students. **Majors with Highest Enrollment:** communication and media studies, other; English language and literature; finance. **Special Study Options:** Accelerated program, cross-registration, distance learning, double major, English as a Second Language (ESL), exchange student program (domestic), honors program, independent study, internships, liberal arts/career combination, student-designed major, study abroad, teacher certification program. **Honors Programs:** Multiple Honors Programs in various Schools and Departments, along with a Presidential Scholars Program. **Combined Degree Programs:** BA/MD, BA/MA, MD with Tufts Medical School. **Disability Services:** Special programs offered to physically disabled students include note-taking services, reader services, tape recorders, tutors. **Career Services:** Alumni network, alumni services, career/job search classes, career assessment, internships, regional alumni. Career Services highlights include Internships.

FACILITIES
Housing: Coed dorms, special housing for disabled students, women's dorms, Greycliff Honors House, multicultural and intercultural floors, a quiet floor, social justice floor, a community living floor, and a leadership house. Also apartment style housing and Townhouse apartments. 95% of campus accessible to physically disabled. **Special Academic Facilities/Equipment:** Art museum, theatre arts center, on-campus school for multihandicapped students, athletic facility, state-of-the-art science facilities. **Computers:** 100% of classrooms, 100% of dorms, 100% of libraries, 100% of dining areas, 100% of student union, 100% of common outdoor areas have wireless network access. Students can register for classes online. Administrative functions (other than registration) can be performed online.

CAMPUS LIFE
Environment: City. **Activities:** Choral groups, concert band, dance, drama/theater, jazz band, literary magazine, marching band, music ensembles, musical theater, pep band, radio station, student government, student newspaper, student-run film society, symphony orchestra, television station, yearbook, Campus Ministries, International Student Organization 225 registered organizations, 12 honor societies, 14 religious organizations. **Athletics (Intercollegiate):** *Men:* baseball, basketball, cross-country, diving, fencing, football, golf, ice hockey, lacrosse, sailing, skiing (downhill/alpine), soccer, swimming, tennis, track/field (outdoor), track/field (indoor). *Women:* basketball, crew/rowing, cross-country, diving, fencing, field hockey, golf, ice hockey, lacrosse, sailing, skiing (downhill/alpine), soccer, softball, swimming, tennis, track/field (outdoor), track/field (indoor), volleyball. **On-Campus Highlights:** McMullen Museum of Art, Alumni Stadium/Conte Forum, Robsham Theater, Bapst Library, McElroy Commons/Bookstore. **Environmental Initiatives:** 180K SF Building Registered for LEED Silver; 4 Buildings - LEED Certified Platinum; 1 Building - Anticipate LEED Gold Enerergy Conservation program metering 75% of buildings. Carbon footprint is completed. Setting new goals.

ADMISSIONS
Freshman Academic Profile: 81% in top 10% of high school class, 96% in top 25% of high school class, 99% in top 50% of high school class. 48% from public high schools. SAT Math middle 50% range 640-740. SAT Critical Reading middle 50% range 620-710. SAT Writing middle 50% range 640-730. ACT

middle 50% range 29-32. Minimum web-based TOEFL 100. Minimum paper TOEFL 600. **Basis for Candidate Selection:** *Very important factors considered include:* academic GPA, rigor of secondary school record, standardized test scores. *Important factors considered include:* Class rank, application essay, recommendation(s), alumni/ae relation, character/personal qualities, extracurricular activities, religious affiliation/commitment, talent/ability, volunteer work. *Other factors considered include:* first generation, racial/ethnic status, work experience. **Freshman Admission Requirements:** High school diploma is required and GED is accepted. **Freshman Admission Statistics:** 34,061 applied, 29% admitted, 25% enrolled. **Transfer Admission Requirements:** High school transcript, college transcript(s), essay or personal statement, standardized test scores, statement of good standing from prior institution(s). Minimum college GPA of 3.0 required. Lowest grade transferable C. **General Admission Information:** Application Fee $70. Regular application deadline 1/1. Regular notification 4/15. Nonfall registration accepted. Admission may be deferred for a maximum of 2 years. Placement offered for CEEB Advanced Placement tests.

COSTS AND FINANCIAL AID
Annual tuition $43,140. Room and board $12,608. Required fees $738. Average book expense $1,000. **Required Forms and Deadlines:** FAFSA, CSS/Financial Aid PROFILE, noncustodial PROFILE, business/farm supplement. **Notification of Awards:** Applicants will be notified of awards on or about 4/1. **Types of Aid:** *Need-based scholarships/grants:* Federal Pell, SEOG, state scholarships/grants, private scholarships, the school's own gift aid. *Loans:* Subsidized Stafford, Unsubsidized Stafford, PLUS, Federal Perkins, Federal Nursing, state loans. **Student Employment:** Federal Work-Study Program available. Institutional employment available. Highest amount earned per year from on-campus jobs $2,400. Off-campus job opportunities are good. **Financial Aid Statistics:** 89% freshmen, 89% undergrads receive need-based scholarship or grant aid. 2% freshmen, 2% undergrads receive non-need-based scholarship or grant aid. 93% freshmen, 94% undergrads receive need-based self-help aid. 3% freshmen, 3% undergrads receive athletic scholarships. 63% freshmen, 68% undergrads receive any aid. 52% undergrads borrow to pay for school. Average cumulative indebtedness $20,975. **Criteria for awarding institutional aid:** *Non-need-based:* academics, athletics, leadership.

BOSTON CONSERVATORY

8 The Fenway, Boston, MA 2215
Phone: 617-912-9153
E-mail: admissions@bostonconservatory.edu • **CEEB Code:** 3084
Fax: 617-247-3159 • **Website:** www.bostonconservatory.edu • **ACT Code:** 1790

This private school was founded in 1867.

RATINGS
Admissions Selectivity Rating: 63   **Fire Safety Rating:** 60*   **Green Rating:** 60*

STUDENTS AND FACULTY
Enrollment: 450. **Student Body:** 63% female, 37% male, 60% out-of-state, (26 countries represented).
Retention and Graduation: 68% freshmen return for sophomore year. 35% freshmen graduate within 4 years. 72% freshmen graduate within 6 years. **Faculty:** Student/faculty ratio 4:1. 44 full-time faculty, % hold PhDs, 0% are members of minority groups, 59% are women. 0% of classes are taught by teaching assistants.

ACADEMICS
Degrees: bachelor's, diploma, master's, post-bachelor's certificate, post-master's certificate. **Classes:** Most classes have fewer than 10 students. **Special Study Options:** cross-registration, double major, English as a Second Language (ESL), independent study, teacher certification program. **Career Services:** alumni services, career/job search classes, career assessment, internships.

FACILITIES
Housing: Coed dorms, women's dorms, Graduate house.

CAMPUS LIFE
Environment: Activities: literary magazine, student government, student newspaper 11 registered organizations, 1 honor societies, 1 religious organizations.

ADMISSIONS
Freshman Academic Profile: 90% from public high schools. **Basis for Candidate Selection:** *Very important factors considered include:* recommendation(s), character/personal qualities, talent/ability. *Important factors considered include:* Class rank, application essay, rigor of secondary school record, interview. *Other factors considered include:* extracurricular activities.

Freshman Admission Requirements: High school diploma is required and GED is accepted. *Academic units required:* 4 English, 3 mathematics, 2 science, 2 foreign language, 2 social studies, 2 history. *Academic units recommended:* 4 English, 3 mathematics, 2 science, 2 foreign language, 2 social studies, 2 history. **Freshman Admission Statistics:** 989 applied, 43% admitted, 28% enrolled. **Transfer Admission Requirements:** High school transcript, college transcript(s), essay or personal statement, minimum college GPA of 2.5 required. Lowest grade transferable C. **General Admission Information:** Application Fee $100. Regular notification 4/1. Nonfall registration accepted. Admission may be deferred for a maximum of 12. Credit offered for CEEB Advanced Placement tests.

COSTS AND FINANCIAL AID
Room and board $15,640. Required fees $2,690. Average book expense $0. **Required Forms and Deadlines:** FAFSA, institution's own financial aid form. **Notification of Awards:** Applicants will be notified of awards on or about 4/1. **Types of Aid:** *Need-based scholarships/grants:* Federal Pell, SEOG, state scholarships/grants, private scholarships, the school's own gift aid. *Loans:* Subsidized Stafford, Unsubsidized Stafford, PLUS, college/university loans from institutional funds, Private Educational Loans. **Student Employment:** Federal Work-Study Program available. Institutional employment available. Highest amount earned per year from on-campus jobs $830. Off-campus job opportunities are excellent. **Financial Aid Statistics:** 22% freshmen, 25% undergrads receive need-based scholarship or grant aid. 73% freshmen, 72% undergrads receive non-need-based scholarship or grant aid. 94% freshmen, 82% undergrads receive need-based self-help aid. 76% undergrads borrow to pay for school. Average cumulative indebtedness $15,000. **Criteria for awarding institutional aid:** *Non-need-based:* music/drama.

BOSTON UNIVERSITY

121 Bay State Road, Boston, MA 2215
Phone: 617-353-2300 • **Financial Aid Phone:** 617-353-4176
E-mail: admissions@bu.edu • **CEEB Code:** 3087
Fax: 617-353-9695 • **Website:** www.bu.edu • **ACT Code:** 1794

This private school was founded in 1839. It has a 132-acre campus.

RATINGS
Admissions Selectivity Rating: 95   **Fire Safety Rating:** 61   **Green Rating:** 86

STUDENTS AND FACULTY
Enrollment: 16,466. **Student Body:** 60% female, 40% male, 77% out-of-state, 13% international (133 countries represented). Asian 14%, African American 3%, Caucasian 49%, Hispanic 9%, Native American 0%.
Retention and Graduation: 92% freshmen return for sophomore year. 79% freshmen graduate within 4 years. 27% grads go on to further study within 1 year. **Faculty:** Student/faculty ratio 13:1. 1632 full-time faculty, 86% hold PhDs, 18% are members of minority groups, 38% are women. 6% of classes are taught by teaching assistants.

ACADEMICS
Degrees: bachelor's, first professional, first professional certificate, master's, post-bachelor's certificate, post-master's certificate. **Classes:** Most classes have 10–19 students. Most lab/discussion sessions have 20–29 students. **Majors with Highest Enrollment:** business/commerce; international relations and affairs; psychology. **Special Study Options:** Accelerated program, cooperative education program, cross-registration, distance learning, double major, dual enrollment, English as a Second Language (ESL), honors program, independent study, internships, liberal arts/career combination, student-designed major, study abroad, teacher certification program, weekend college, Field study in Marine Science at the Woods Hole Institute and in Environmental/Ecological Science in Ecuador at the Biodiversity Station in the tropical rain forest. The Photonics Center. **Honors Programs:** Honors Programs are offered in the College of Arts and Sciences and the School of Management **Combined Degree Programs:** BA/MD, BA/MA, BA/DMD, BS/MS, BA/MD,BS/MSOT,BS/DPT. **Disability Services:** Special programs offered to physically disabled students include note-taking services, reader services, tape recorders, tutors. **Career Services:** Alumni network, alumni services, career/job search classes, career assessment, internships, regional alumni. Career Services highlights include Our internship program provides opportunities for student to work with early stage companies at the BU incubators, as well as in the community. One particularly unusual aspect of the program is that we provide opportunities for non-business

students to "intern" with startups our business students are creating. One such program this year had Graphic Design students working with MBA student entrepreneurs to develop corporate identity programs for them.

FACILITIES

Housing: Coed dorms, special housing for disabled students, women's dorms, apartments for married students, cooperative housing, apartments for single students, Specialty dorms/floors for groups of students with a common interest or academic major. 90% of campus accessible to physically disabled. **Special Academic Facilities/Equipment:** Center for Computational Science, Center for Advanced Biotechnology, Center for Photonics Research, art galleries, planetarium, commercial TV station, National Public Radio station, 20th century archives, professional theatre and theatre company, Center for Remote Sensing, Geddes Language Labratory, speech, language and hearing clinic, Culinary Center, Metcalf Center for Science and Engineering, Tsai Performance Center, and College of Communication Multimedia Lab. **Computers:** Students can register for classes online. Administrative functions (other than registration) can be performed online.

CAMPUS LIFE

Environment: Metropolis. **Activities:** Choral groups, concert band, dance, drama/theater, jazz band, literary magazine, marching band, music ensembles, musical theater, opera, radio station, student government, student newspaper, student-run film society, symphony orchestra, yearbook, International Student Organization 400 registered organizations, 11 honor societies, 26 religious organizations. 9 fraternities, 9 sororities. **Athletics (Intercollegiate):** *Men:* basketball, crew/rowing, cross-country, diving, golf, ice hockey, soccer, swimming, tennis, track/field (outdoor), track/field (indoor), wrestling. *Women:* basketball, crew/rowing, cross-country, diving, field hockey, golf, ice hockey, lacrosse, soccer, softball, swimming, tennis, track/field (outdoor), track/field (indoor). **On-Campus Highlights:** Marsh Chapel Plaza, Mugar Memorial Library, special collections, DeWolfe Boathouse, George Sherman Student Union, The Photonics Center. **Environmental Initiatives:** Energy Efficiency Retrofits Recycling Program Green building practices

ADMISSIONS

Freshman Academic Profile: Average high school GPA 3.6. 57% in top 10% of high school class, 87% in top 25% of high school class, 99% in top 50% of high school class. 68% from public high schools. SAT Math middle 50% range 610-720. SAT Critical Reading middle 50% range 570-670. SAT Writing middle 50% range 600-690. ACT middle 50% range 26-30. **Basis for Candidate Selection:** *Very important factors considered include:* rigor of secondary school record. *Important factors considered include:* Class rank, application essay, academic GPA, recommendation(s), standardized test scores. *Other factors considered include:* alumni/ae relation, character/personal qualities, extracurricular activities, first generation, geographical residence, level of applicant's interest, racial/ethnic status, state residency, volunteer work, work experience. **Freshman Admission Requirements:** High school diploma is required and GED is accepted. *Academic units required:* 4 English, 3 mathematics, 3 science, (3 science lab), 2 foreign language, 3 social studies, 0 academic electives. *Academic units recommended:* 4 English, 3 mathematics, 3 science, (3 science labs), 2 foreign language, 3 social studies. **Freshman Admission Statistics:** 44,006 applied, 46% admitted, 19% enrolled. **Transfer Admission Requirements:** High school transcript, college transcript(s), essay or personal statement, standardized test scores, statement of good standing from prior institution(s). Minimum college GPA of 3.5 required. Lowest grade transferable C. **General Admission Information:** Application Fee $75. Early decision application deadline 11/1. Regular application deadline 1/1. Nonfall registration accepted. Admission may be deferred for a maximum of 1 year. Credit and/or placement offered for CEEB Advanced Placement tests.

COSTS AND FINANCIAL AID

Annual tuition $42,400. Room and board $13,190. Required fees $594. Average book expense $1,000. **Required Forms and Deadlines:** FAFSA, CSS/Financial Aid PROFILE, state aid form, noncustodial PROFILE, business/farm supplement. **Notification of Awards:** Applicants will be notified of awards on a rolling basis beginning 3/15. **Types of Aid:** *Need-based scholarships/grants:* Federal Pell, SEOG, state scholarships/grants, private scholarships, the school's own gift aid. *Loans:* Direct Subsidized Stafford, Direct Unsubsidized Stafford, Direct PLUS, Federal Perkins, state loans. **Student Employment:** Federal Work-Study Program available. Institutional employment available. Off-campus job opportunities are excellent. **Financial Aid Statistics:** 94% freshmen, 95% undergrads receive need-based scholarship or grant aid. 37% freshmen, 25% undergrads receive non-need-based scholarship or grant aid. 88% freshmen, 91% undergrads receive need-based self-help aid. 2% freshmen, 2% undergrads receive athletic scholarships. 61% freshmen, 61% undergrads receive any aid. 59% undergrads borrow to pay for school. Average cumulative indebtedness $21,149. **Criteria for awarding institutional aid:** *Non-need-based:* academics, alumni affiliation, art, athletics, leadership, music/drama, religious affiliation, state/district residency.

See page 1026.

BOWDOIN COLLEGE

5000 College Station, Brunswick, ME 04011-8441
Phone: 207-725-3100 • **Financial Aid Phone:** 207-725-3273
E-mail: admissions@bowdoin.edu • **CEEB Code:** 3089
Fax: 207-725-3101 • **Website:** www.bowdoin.edu • **ACT Code:** 1636

This private school was founded in 1794. It has a 205-acre campus.

RATINGS

Admissions Selectivity Rating: 99   **Fire Safety Rating:** 88   **Green Rating:** 87

STUDENTS AND FACULTY

Enrollment: 1,831. **Student Body:** 50% female, 50% male, 87% out-of-state, 4% international (27 countries represented). Asian 7%, African American 5%, Caucasian 65%, Hispanic 13%, Native American 0%.
Retention and Graduation: 97% freshmen return for sophomore year. 91% freshmen graduate within 4 years. 95% freshmen graduate within 6 years. 15% grads go on to further study within 1 year. 9% grads pursue arts and sciences degrees. 2% grads pursue law degrees. 1% grads pursue business degrees. 2% grads pursue medical degrees. **Faculty:** Student/faculty ratio 9:1. 186 full-time faculty, 100% hold PhDs, 15% are members of minority groups, 48% are women. 0% of classes are taught by teaching assistants.

ACADEMICS

Degrees: bachelor's. **Classes:** Most classes have 10–19 students. Most lab/discussion sessions have 10–19 students. **Majors with Highest Enrollment:** biology/biological sciences; economics; political science and government. **Special Study Options:** Accelerated program, double major, exchange student program (domestic), independent study, liberal arts/career combination, student-designed major, study abroad, teacher certification program, 3-2 or 4-2 Engineering Degree Programs with Dartmouth College, California Institute of Technology, Columbia University and the University of Maine; and 3-3 Legal Studies Degree Program with Columbia University Law School. Pass/Fail grading options are available. **Combined Degree Programs:** BA/JD, BA/MEng, 3-3 Law - Columbia University Law. **Disability Services:** Special programs offered to physically disabled students include note-taking services, reader services, tape recorders, tutors. **Career Services:** Alumni network, alumni services, career/job search classes, career assessment, internships, regional alumni. Career Services highlights include Paid internship opportunities through the generosity of donors. Many of these internships serve the needs of underserved and disadvantaged populations.

FACILITIES

Housing: Coed dorms, special housing for disabled students, apartments for single students, wellness housing, three small college houses and 8 college house system houses. 70% of campus accessible to physically disabled. **Special Academic Facilities/Equipment:** Art Museum; Arctic Museum; Arctic Studies Center; coastal marine biology and ornithology research facility on Orr's Island; scientific station on Kent Island; black box theater; Pickard Theater; Baldwin Center for Learning and Teaching; Outdoor Leadership Center; Visual Arts Center; Crafts Center; 8 specialized libraries, including the Language Media Center; Coleman Farm; Quantitative Skills Program; The Writing Project; Gibson Hall of Music; Recital Hall; Educational Technology Center; Environmental Studies Center; Russwurm African-American Center; Women's Resource Center; Off-Campus Study Office; Office of Health Professions Advising; Pre-Law Advising Office; Career Planning Center; Community Service Resource Center; Electronic Classroom; Recording Studio; and a state-of-the-art science facility. **Computers:** 100% of classrooms, 100% of dorms, 100% of libraries, 100% of dining areas, 100% of student union, 100% of common outdoor areas have wireless network access. Administrative functions (other than registration) can be performed online.

CAMPUS LIFE

Environment: Village. **Activities:** Choral groups, concert band, dance, drama/theater, jazz band, literary magazine, music ensembles, musical theater, radio station, student government, student newspaper, student-run film society, symphony orchestra, television station, yearbook, International Student Organization 109 registered organizations, 1 honor societies, 4 religious organizations. **Athletics (Intercollegiate):** *Men:* baseball, basketball, cross-country, diving, football, golf, ice hockey, lacrosse, sailing, skiingnordiccross-country, soccer, squash, swimming, tennis, track/field (outdoor), track/field (indoor). *Women:* basketball, cross-country, diving, field hockey, golf, ice hockey, lacrosse, rugby, sailing, skiingnordiccross-country, soccer, softball, squash, swimming, tennis, track/field (outdoor), track/field (indoor), volleyball. **On-Campus Highlights:** Bowdoin College Museum of Art, Druckenmiller Science Building, Studzinski Recital Hall, Schwartz Outdoor Leadership Center, Wish / Pickard Theater, Peary MacMillan Arctic Museum; Visual Arts Center and McLellan art studios; Hawthorne-Longfellow Library; Smith Student Union; Thorne Dining Hall; top of Coles Tower (for birds-eye view); athletic facilities and playing fields/trails; walk the Bowdoin Quad and the Bowdoin Pines. **Environmental Initiatives:** Bowdoin has committed to becoming a carbon-neutral campus by 2020 and provided a detailed Climate Action Plan to help achieve the goal. Bowdoin implemented a co-generation system at its campus steam plant this summer, along with a 1,920-square-foot solar hot water system. The Co-Gen system will reduce the College's net 2008 emissions by 18%. Bowdoin maintains a Building Dashboard system on 49 campus buildings that allows the campus community to track the electricity use of its buildings in real-time. Bowdoin has established a campus-managed, certified organic garden that provides produce to the dining halls, a year-round composting program, a small hoop house, academic and co-curricular opportunities for students and bicycle delivery carts to provide carbon-neutral produce. Bowdoin has implemented a comprehensive approach to alternative transportation on campus that includes a bike sharing program, Zipcars, a free campus shuttle for students, promotions for faculty and staff who carpool, bike and walk to work as well as reserved parking for carpoolers and low-emitting, fuel-efficient vehicles and increased emphasis on biking infrastructure on campus.

ADMISSIONS

Freshman Academic Profile: Average high school GPA 3.8. 86% in top 10% of high school class, 98% in top 25% of high school class, 100% in top 50% of high school class. 53% from public high schools. SAT Math middle 50% range 670-760. SAT Critical Reading middle 50% range 670-760. SAT Writing middle 50% range 670-760. ACT middle 50% range 31-33. Minimum web-based TOEFL 100. Minimum paper TOEFL 600. **Basis for Candidate Selection:** *Very important factors considered include:* Class rank, application essay, academic GPA, recommendation(s), rigor of secondary school record, character/personal qualities, extracurricular activities, talent/ability. *Important factors considered include:* standardized test scores, alumni/ae relation, first generation. *Other factors considered include:* geographical residence, interview, racial/ethnic status, state residency. **Freshman Admission Requirements:** High school diploma is required and GED is not accepted. **Freshman Admission Statistics:** 6,716 applied, 16% admitted, 46% enrolled. **Transfer Admission Requirements:** High school transcript, college transcript(s), essay or personal statement, statement of good standing from prior institution(s). Minimum college GPA of 3.0 required. Lowest grade transferable C-. **General Admission Information:** Application Fee $60. Early decision application deadline 11/15. Regular application deadline 1/1. Regular notification 4/5. Nonfall registration not accepted. Admission may be deferred for a maximum of 12 months. Credit and/or placement offered for CEEB Advanced Placement tests.

COSTS AND FINANCIAL AID

Annual tuition $43,676. Room and board $12,010. Required fees $442. Average book expense $822. **Required Forms and Deadlines:** FAFSA, CSS/Financial Aid PROFILE, noncustodial PROFILE, business/farm supplement. **Notification of Awards:** Applicants will be notified of awards on or about 4/5. **Types of Aid:** *Need-based scholarships/grants:* Federal Pell, SEOG, state scholarships/grants, private scholarships, the school's own gift aid. *Loans:* Subsidized Stafford, Unsubsidized Stafford, PLUS, Federal Perkins, state loans. **Student Employment:** Federal Work-Study Program available. Institutional employment available. Highest amount earned per year from on-campus jobs $2,000. Off-campus job opportunities are good. **Financial Aid Statistics:** 100% freshmen, 100% undergrads receive need-based scholarship or grant aid. 97% freshmen, 90% undergrads receive need-based self-help aid. 48% freshmen, 47% undergrads receive any aid. 33% undergrads borrow to pay for school. Average cumulative indebtedness $23,092. **Criteria for awarding institutional aid:** *Non-need-based:* academics, leadership.

BOWIE STATE UNIVERSITY

14000 Jericho Park Road, Bowie, MD 20715
Phone: 301-860-3415 • **Financial Aid Phone:** 301-860-3543
E-mail: dkiah@bowiestate.edu • **CEEB Code:** 5401
Fax: 301-860-3438 • **Website:** www.bowiestate.edu • **ACT Code:**

This public school was founded in 1865. It has a 312-acre campus.

STUDENTS AND FACULTY

Enrollment: 3,953. **Student Body:** 64% female, 36% male, 8% out-of-state, 1% international (48 countries represented). Asian 1%, African American 74%, Caucasian 5%, Hispanic 1%, Native American 0%.
Retention and Graduation: 72% freshmen return for sophomore year. 11% freshmen graduate within 4 years. 36% freshmen graduate within 6 years. 30% grads go on to further study within 1 year. **Faculty:** Student/faculty ratio 19:1. 191 full-time faculty, 68% hold PhDs, 73% are members of minority groups, 45% are women. 0% of classes are taught by teaching assistants.

ACADEMICS

Degrees: bachelor's, certificate, master's, post-bachelor's certificate, post-master's certificate. **Classes:** Most classes have 20–29 students. **Special Study Options:** cooperative education program, cross-registration, distance learning, double major, dual enrollment, exchange student program (domestic), honors program, independent study, internships, liberal arts/career combination, study abroad, teacher certification program, Dual degree Mathematics/Engineering Program. **Combined Degree Programs:** BA/MEng. **Disability Services:** Special programs offered to physically disabled students include note-taking services, reader services, tape recorders, tutors. **Career Services:** career/job search classes, internships.

FACILITIES

Housing: Coed dorms, men's dorms, women's dorms, apartments for single students, Honors' Residence available; Special interest floors. 100% of campus accessible to physically disabled. **Special Academic Facilities/Equipment:** Science and math labs, computer academy, art galleries. **Computers:** Students can register for classes online. Administrative functions (other than registration) can be performed online.

CAMPUS LIFE

Environment: Town. **Activities:** Choral groups, concert band, dance, drama/theater, jazz band, literary magazine, marching band, music ensembles, musical theater, pep band, radio station, student government, student newspaper, television station, yearbook 71 registered organizations, 17 honor societies, 2 religious organizations. 4 fraternities, 4 sororities. **Athletics (Intercollegiate):** *Men:* basketball, cross-country, football, track/field (outdoor). *Women:* basketball, cross-country, softball, tennis, track/field (outdoor), volleyball. **On-Campus Highlights:** New Science Bldg, The Jazz man Coffee Shop.

ADMISSIONS

Freshman Academic Profile: Average high school GPA 3.1. 88% from public high schools. SAT Math middle 50% range 400-480. SAT Critical Reading middle 50% range 400-490. Minimum paper TOEFL 500. **Basis for Candidate Selection:** *Very important factors considered include:* rigor of secondary school record, standardized test scores. *Other factors considered include:* application essay, recommendation(s), extracurricular activities, interview. **Freshman Admission Requirements:** High school diploma is required and GED is accepted. *Academic units required:* 4 English, 3 mathematics, 3 science, 2 foreign language, 1 social studies, 2 history. *Academic units recommended:* 4 English, 3 mathematics, 3 science, 2 foreign language, 1 social studies, 2 history. **Freshman Admission Statistics:** 2,826 applied, 52% admitted, 44% enrolled. **Transfer Admission Requirements:** college transcript(s), minimum college GPA of 2.0 required. Lowest grade transferable C. **General Admission Information:** Application Fee $40. Notification on a rolling basis, beginning on or about 4/3. Nonfall registration accepted. Admission may be deferred for a maximum of 1 year. Credit and/or placement offered for CEEB Advanced Placement tests.

COSTS AND FINANCIAL AID

Annual in-state tuition $4,286. Annual out-of-state tuition $13,591. Room and board $6,823. Required fees $1,195. Average book expense $1,388. **Required Forms and Deadlines:** FAFSA. **Notification of Awards: Types of Aid:** *Need-based scholarships/grants:* Federal Pell, SEOG, state scholarships/grants, private scholarships, the school's own gift aid. *Loans:* Direct Subsidized Stafford, Direct Unsubsidized Stafford, Direct PLUS, Federal Perkins. **Student Employment:** Federal Work-Study Program available. **Financial Aid Statistics:** 71% freshmen, 73% undergrads receive need-based scholarship or grant aid. 53% freshmen, 55% undergrads receive non-need-based scholarship or grant aid. 62% freshmen, 74% undergrads receive need-based self-help aid. 7% freshmen, 8% undergrads receive athletic scholarships. 34% undergrads borrow to pay for school. Average cumulative indebtedness $10,842. **Criteria for awarding institutional aid:** *Non-need-based:* academics, art, athletics, music/drama, state/district residency.

RATINGS

Admissions Selectivity Rating: 77   **Fire Safety Rating:** 07   **Green Rating:** 60*

BOWLING GREEN STATE UNIVERSITY

110 McFall Center, Bowling Green, OH 43403-0085
Phone: 419-372-BGSU • **Financial Aid Phone:** 419-372-2651
E-mail: choosebgsu@bgsu.edu • **CEEB Code:** 1069
Fax: 419-372-6955 • **Website:** www.bgsu.edu • **ACT Code:** 3240

This public school was founded in 1910. It has a 1250-acre campus.

RATINGS
Admissions Selectivity Rating: 71   **Fire Safety Rating:** 74   **Green Rating:** 83

STUDENTS AND FACULTY
Enrollment: 14,514. **Student Body:** 56% female, 44% male, 12% out-of-state, 2% international (76 countries represented). Asian 1%, African American 11%, Caucasian 78%, Hispanic 4%, Native American 0%.
Retention and Graduation: 69% freshmen return for sophomore year. 36% freshmen graduate within 4 years. 58% freshmen graduate within 6 years. **Faculty:** Student/faculty ratio 18:1. 814 full-time faculty, 78% hold PhDs, 14% are members of minority groups, 47% are women. 10% of classes are taught by teaching assistants.

ACADEMICS
Degrees: bachelor's, doctoral, master's, post-master's certificate. **Classes:** Most classes have 20–29 students. **Majors with Highest Enrollment:** biology/biological sciences; sport and fitness administration/management; teacher education, multiple levels. **Special Study Options:** Accelerated program, cooperative education program, cross-registration, distance learning, double major, dual enrollment, English as a Second Language (ESL), exchange student program (domestic), honors program, independent study, internships, liberal arts/career combination, student-designed major, study abroad, teacher certification program. **Honors Programs:** http://www.bgsu.edu/offices/honors/. **Disability Services:** Special programs offered to physically disabled students include note-taking services, reader services, tape recorders, tutors. **Career Services:** Alumni network, alumni services, career/job search classes, career assessment, internships, regional alumni. Career Services highlights include http://www.bgsu.edu/offices/sa/career/.

FACILITIES
Housing: Coed dorms, fraternity/sorority housing, wellness housing, theme housing, residental learning communities (including Wellness Community), no-alcohol wings. **Special Academic Facilities/Equipment:** http://go2.bgsu.edu/choose/campus/tour/ http://www.bgsu.edu/map/buildings/ **Computers:** 99% of classrooms, 64% of dorms, 100% of libraries, 100% of dining areas, 100% of student union, 40% of common outdoor areas have wireless network access. Students can register for classes online. Administrative functions (other than registration) can be performed online.

CAMPUS LIFE
Environment: Town. **Activities:** Choral groups, concert band, dance, drama/theater, jazz band, literary magazine, marching band, music ensembles, musical theater, radio station, student government, student newspaper, student-run film society, symphony orchestra, television station, yearbook, International Student Organization 20 honor societies, 24 fraternities, 19 sororities. **Athletics (Intercollegiate):** *Men:* baseball, basketball, cross-country, football, golf, ice hockey, soccer. *Women:* basketball, cross-country, golf, gymnastics, soccer, softball, swimming, tennis, track/field (outdoor), track/field (indoor), volleyball. **On-Campus Highlights:** Bowen Thompson Student Union, Jerome Library, McFall Center, College of Business Administration, Residence Halls, http://go2.bgsu.edu/choose/campus/tour/. **Environmental Initiatives:** Recent completion and current certification process for 4 new minimum LEED certified buildings (Current points indicate one gold; two silver, and one LEED certified) Moving forward on becoming a part of the ACUPCC with formation of University-wide committee Funding of a dozen sustainability projects with student fee monies procured through Student Green Initiatives Fund, approved by student body which projects were conceived by and submitted by students, and the approval of which was provided by a committee composed of students

ADMISSIONS
Freshman Academic Profile: Average high school GPA 3.2. 12% in top 10% of high school class, 36% in top 25% of high school class, 70% in top 50% of high school class. 89% from public high schools. SAT Math middle 50% range 440-570. SAT Critical Reading middle 50% range 450-560. SAT Writing middle 50% range 420-540. ACT middle 50% range 19-24. Minimum web-based TOEFL 61. Minimum paper TOEFL 500. **Basis for Candidate Selection:** *Very important factors considered include:* academic GPA, rigor of secondary school record, standardized test scores. *Important factors considered include:* Class rank, talent/ability. *Other factors considered include:* application essay, recommendation(s), alumni/ae relation, character/personal qualities, extra-

curricular activities, first generation, interview, level of applicant's interest, racial/ethnic status, volunteer work, work experience. **Freshman Admission Requirements:** High school diploma is required and GED is accepted. *Academic units required:* 4 English, 3 mathematics, 3 science, (2 science labs), 2 foreign language, 3 social studies, 1 visual/performing arts. *Academic units recommended:* 4 English, 3 mathematics, 3 science, (2 science labs), 2 foreign language, 3 social studies, 1 visual/performing arts. **Freshman Admission Statistics:** 16,108 applied, 74% admitted, 31% enrolled. Minimum college GPA of 2.5 required. Lowest grade transferable C. **General Admission Information:** Application Fee $40. Regular application deadline 7/15. Notification on a rolling basis, beginning on or about 10/1. Nonfall registration accepted. Admission may be deferred for a maximum of 12 months. Credit and/or placement offered for CEEB Advanced Placement tests.

COSTS AND FINANCIAL AID
Annual in-state tuition $8,914. Annual out-of-state tuition $16,222. Room and board $8,064. Required fees $1,600. Average book expense $1,194. **Required Forms and Deadlines:** FAFSA. **Notification of Awards:** Applicants will be notified of awards on a rolling basis beginning 4/15. **Types of Aid:** *Need-based scholarships/grants:* Federal Pell, SEOG, state scholarships/grants, private scholarships, the school's own gift aid. *Loans:* Direct Subsidized Stafford, Direct Unsubsidized Stafford, Direct PLUS, Federal Perkins, Federal Nursing, state loans, college/university loans from institutional funds. **Student Employment:** Federal Work-Study Program available. Institutional employment available. Highest amount earned per year from on-campus jobs $13,544. Off-campus job opportunities are good. **Financial Aid Statistics:** 96% freshmen, 91% undergrads receive any aid. **Criteria for awarding institutional aid:** *Non-need-based:* academics, alumni affiliation, art, athletics, leadership, minority status, music/drama, state/district residency.

BRADLEY UNIVERSITY

1501 West Bradley Avenue, Peoria, IL 61625
Phone: 309-677-1000 • **Financial Aid Phone:** 309-677-3089
E-mail: admissions@bradley.edu • **CEEB Code:** 1070
Fax: 309-677-2797 • **Website:** www.bradley.edu • **ACT Code:** 960

This private school was founded in 1897. It has a 85-acre campus.

RATINGS
Admissions Selectivity Rating: 85   **Fire Safety Rating:** 82   **Green Rating:** 60*

STUDENTS AND FACULTY
Enrollment: 4,872. **Student Body:** 53% female, 47% male, 12% out-of-state, 1% international (34 countries represented). Asian 4%, African American 7%, Caucasian 80%, Hispanic 6%, Native American 0%.
Retention and Graduation: 10% grads go on to further study within 1 year. 6% grads pursue arts and sciences degrees. 1% grads pursue law degrees. 1% grads pursue business degrees. 1% grads pursue medical degrees. **Faculty:** Student/faculty ratio 12:1. 352 full-time faculty, 84% hold PhDs, 17% are members of minority groups, 61% are women. 0% of classes are taught by teaching assistants.

ACADEMICS
Degrees: bachelor's, master's. **Classes:** Most classes have 20–29 students. **Majors with Highest Enrollment:** mechanical engineering; nursing/registered nurse (rn, asn, bsn, msn); organizational communication. **Special Study Options:** Accelerated program, cooperative education program, distance learning, double major, honors program, independent study, internships, liberal arts/career combination, student-designed major, study abroad, teacher certification program, Limited distance learning courses available. Collaborative classes with other institutions taught through Internet2. **Honors Programs:** The Honors Program is structured so that students majoring in any department are eligible to participate. The programs builds progressively through a student's four years, beginning with special honors sections of General Education courses and leading to interdisciplinary seminars and possibilities for independent research. **Combined Degree Programs:** BA/MSA. **Disability Services:** Special programs offered to physically disabled students include tutors. **Career Services:** Alumni network, alumni services, career/job search classes, career assessment, internships, regional alumni. Career Services highlights include Bradley recently established the Marjorie and Bill Springer Center for Excellence in Internships. The Center will focus on five areas: expanding opportunities for stu-

dents to gain career-related experience; generating more student participation in the cooperative education and internship program; increasing awareness of international internship opportunities; enhancing activities that assist students in conducting their job searches and preparing them for on-the-job success; and providing continuous evaluation and improvement of the cooperative education and internship program policies, procedures, and data collected.

FACILITIES

Housing: Coed dorms, fraternity/sorority housing, apartments for single students, wellness housing, Service and leadership floor. 75% of campus accessible to physically disabled. **Special Academic Facilities/Equipment:** Caterpillar Global Communication Center, two art galleries on campus. **Computers:** 95% of classrooms, 5% of dorms, 100% of libraries, 80% of dining areas, 100% of student union, 30% of common outdoor areas have wireless network access. Students can register for classes online. Administrative functions (other than registration) can be performed online.

CAMPUS LIFE

Environment: City. **Activities:** Choral groups, concert band, dance, drama/theater, jazz band, literary magazine, music ensembles, musical theater, pep band, radio station, student government, student newspaper, student-run film society, symphony orchestra, television station, yearbook, Campus Ministries, International Student Organization, Model UN 220 registered organizations, 31 honor societies, 17 religious organizations. 16 fraternities, 11 sororities. **Athletics (Intercollegiate):** *Men:* baseball, basketball, cross-country, golf, soccer, tennis. *Women:* basketball, cross-country, golf, softball, tennis, track/field (outdoor), track/field (indoor), volleyball. **On-Campus Highlights:** Markin Family Student Recreation Center, Caterpillar Global Communications Center, Olin Hall of Science, Michel Student Center, Cullom-Davis Library, Bradley's 85 acre campus, is the heart of a residential neighborhood just 1 mile from downtown. Peoria is the largest metropolitan area in Illinois south of Chicago.

ADMISSIONS

Freshman Academic Profile: Average high school GPA 3.7. 35% in top 10% of high school class, 69% in top 25% of high school class, 94% in top 50% of high school class. 82% from public high schools. SAT Math middle 50% range 510-650. SAT Critical Reading middle 50% range 520-660. SAT Writing middle 50% range 520-620. ACT middle 50% range 23-28. Minimum web-based TOEFL 79. Minimum paper TOEFL 550. **Basis for Candidate Selection:** *Very important factors considered include:* academic GPA, rigor of secondary school record. *Important factors considered include:* Class rank, standardized test scores. *Other factors considered include:* application essay, recommendation(s), alumni/ae relation, character/personal qualities, extracurricular activities, geographical residence, interview, level of applicant's interest, racial/ethnic status, talent/ability, volunteer work, work experience. **Freshman Admission Requirements:** High school diploma is required and GED is accepted. *Academic units required:* 4 English, 3 mathematics, 2 science, (2 science labs), 2 social studies. *Academic units recommended:* 4 English, 3 mathematics, 2 science, (2 science labs), 2 social studies. **Freshman Admission Statistics:** 7,562 applied, 63% admitted, 21% enrolled. **Transfer Admission Requirements:** college transcript(s), statement of good standing from prior institution(s). Minimum college GPA of 2.0 required. Lowest grade transferable C. **General Admission Information:** Application Fee $35. Notification on a rolling basis, beginning on or about 9/15. Nonfall registration accepted. Admission may be deferred for a maximum of 12 months. Credit and/or placement offered for CEEB Advanced Placement tests.

COSTS AND FINANCIAL AID

Annual tuition $27,920. Room and board $8,700. Required fees $344. Average book expense $1,200. **Required Forms and Deadlines:** FAFSA. **Notification of Awards: Types of Aid:** *Need-based scholarships/grants:* Federal Pell, SEOG, state scholarships/grants, private scholarships, the school's own gift aid. *Loans:* Direct Subsidized Stafford, Direct Unsubsidized Stafford, Direct PLUS, PLUS, Federal Perkins, Federal Nursing. **Student Employment:** Federal Work-Study Program available. Institutional employment available. **Financial Aid Statistics:** 97% freshmen, 95% undergrads receive need-based scholarship or grant aid. 10% freshmen, 8% undergrads receive non-need-based scholarship or grant aid. 100% freshmen, 99% undergrads receive need-based self-help aid. 4% freshmen, 3% undergrads receive athletic scholarships. 97% freshmen, 94% undergrads receive any aid. **Criteria for awarding institutional aid:** *Non-need-based:* academics, alumni affiliation, art, athletics, leadership, music/drama, state/district residency.

BRANDEIS UNIVERSITY

415 South St., Waltham, MA 02454-9110
Phone: 781-736-3500 • **Financial Aid Phone:** 781-736-3700
E-mail: admissions@brandeis.edu • **CEEB Code:** 3092
Fax: 781-736-3536 • **Website:** www.brandeis.edu/ • **ACT Code:** 1802

This private school was founded in 1948. It has a 235-acre campus.

RATINGS

Admissions Selectivity Rating: 97 **Fire Safety Rating:** 93 **Green Rating:** 85

STUDENTS AND FACULTY

Enrollment: 3,570. **Student Body:** 57% female, 43% male, 72% out-of-state, 14% international (97 countries represented). Asian 13%, African American 4%, Caucasian 50%, Hispanic 6%, Native American 0%. **Retention and Graduation:** 95% freshmen return for sophomore year. 86% freshmen graduate within 4 years. 30% grads go on to further study within 1 year. 15% grads pursue arts and sciences degrees. 5% grads pursue law degrees. 1% grads pursue business degrees. 5% grads pursue medical degrees. **Faculty:** Student/faculty ratio 10:1. 362 full-time faculty, 95% hold PhDs, 13% are members of minority groups, 42% are women.

ACADEMICS

Degrees: bachelor's, doctoral, master's, post-bachelor's certificate. **Classes:** Most classes have 10–19 students. **Majors with Highest Enrollment:** biology/biological sciences; economics; psychology. **Special Study Options:** cross-registration, double major, independent study, internships, student-designed major, study abroad. **Combined Degree Programs:** BA/MA, Early admission to Mt. Sinai;Tufts medical schools. **Disability Services:** Special programs offered to physically disabled students include note-taking services, tape recorders. **Career Services:** Alumni network, alumni services, career/job search classes, career assessment, internships, regional alumni.

FACILITIES

Housing: Coed dorms, men's dorms, women's dorms, apartments for single students, Thematic Learning Communities. 78% of campus accessible to physically disabled. **Special Academic Facilities/Equipment:** Art museum, multicultural library, intercultural center, theater arts complex, language lab, spatial orientation lab, research centers on aging, basic medical sciences, complex systems, family/children's policy, health policy, mental retardation, public policy, study of European Jewry, student leadership Development Room. **Computers:** 100% of classrooms, 100% of dorms, 100% of libraries, 100% of dining areas, 100% of student union, 100% of common outdoor areas have wireless network access. Students can register for classes online. Administrative functions (other than registration) can be performed online.

CAMPUS LIFE

Environment: City. **Activities:** Choral groups, concert band, dance, drama/theater, jazz band, literary magazine, music ensembles, musical theater, radio station, student government, student newspaper, student-run film society, symphony orchestra, television station, yearbook, Campus Ministries, International Student Organization 253 registered organizations, 4 honor societies, 19 religious organizations. **Athletics (Intercollegiate):** *Men:* baseball, basketball, cross-country, diving, fencing, soccer, tennis, track/field (outdoor), track/field (indoor), wrestling. *Women:* basketball, cheerleading, cross-country, diving, fencing, soccer, softball, tennis, track/field (outdoor), track/field (indoor), volleyball, wrestling. **On-Campus Highlights:** Shapiro Science Center, Spingold Theater, Usen Castle, Shapiro Campus Center, Rapaporte Treasure Hall. **Environmental Initiatives:** The Brandeis University Climate Action Plan was completed in Fall of 2009. This plan sets aggressive goals for future energy and climate impact reductions. Brandeis has invested significantly since 2005 in energy reduction efforts- realizing an over 10% drop in campus energy use. The Climate Action Plan builds on these past successes to further reduce cost and environmental impact A 277 kW sized Solar Photovolatic Array, was installed on the Gosman Sports Center. The solar array is one of the larges in Massachusetts. This system is owned by a for profit business, while Brandeis essentially rents the power affordably. This innovative financing structure has allowed Brandeis to support the renewable energy industry, educate students about a growing technology, and reduce world wide carbon impact. To be clear, as the array is not currently owned by the University we can not claim the % of solar energy generated in other questions on this survey because of federal marketing regulations. However, the solar generated at Brandeis is improving air quality for the region. Brandeis is proud of the active student engagement in activism and education on environmental issues. Students are involved in Eco-Reps, where each residential building as a environmental peer educator. Many other accomplishments for sustainability have been brought about through student innovation and education. Brandeis Students voted to create the Brandeis Sustainability Fund creating $50,000 of funded projects for sustainability.

ADMISSIONS

Freshman Academic Profile: Average high school GPA 3.8. 66% in top 10% of high school class, 93% in top 25% of high school class, 98% in top 50% of high school class. 72% from public high schools. SAT Math middle 50% range 620-740. SAT Critical Reading middle 50% range 610-710. SAT Writing middle 50% range 620-710. ACT middle 50% range 28-32. Minimum web-based TOEFL 100. Minimum paper TOEFL 600. **Basis for Candidate Selection:** *Very important factors considered include:* Class rank, academic GPA, rigor of secondary school record, standardized test scores, character/personal qualities. *Important factors considered include:* application essay, recommendation(s), extracurricular activities, level of applicant's interest, talent/ability, volunteer work, work experience. *Other factors considered include:* alumni/ae relation, first generation, geographical residence, interview, racial/ethnic status. **Freshman Admission Requirements:** High school diploma is required and GED is accepted. **Freshman Admission Statistics:** 8,380 applied, 39% admitted, 25% enrolled. **Transfer Admission Requirements:** High school transcript, college transcript(s), essay or personal statement, standardized test scores, statement of good standing from prior institution(s). Minimum college GPA of 3.20 required. Lowest grade transferable C-. **General Admission Information:** Application Fee $55. Early decision application deadline 11/15. Regular application deadline 1/15. Regular notification 4/1. Nonfall registration accepted. Admission may be deferred for a maximum of 1 year. Credit and/or placement offered for CEEB Advanced Placement tests.

COSTS AND FINANCIAL AID

Annual tuition $42,296. Room and board $12,422. Required fees $1,412. Average book expense $1,000. **Required Forms and Deadlines:** FAFSA, CSS/Financial Aid PROFILE, noncustodial PROFILE, business/farm supplement. **Notification of Awards: Types of Aid:** *Need-based scholarships/grants:* Federal Pell, SEOG, state scholarships/grants, private scholarships, the school's own gift aid. *Loans:* Direct Subsidized Stafford, Direct Unsubsidized Stafford, Direct PLUS, Federal Perkins, state loans, college/university loans from institutional funds. **Student Employment:** Federal Work-Study Program available. Institutional employment available. Off-campus job opportunities are fair. **Financial Aid Statistics:** 97% freshmen, 96% undergrads receive need-based scholarship or grant aid. 7% freshmen, 7% undergrads receive non-need-based scholarship or grant aid. 90% freshmen, 91% undergrads receive need-based self-help aid. 69% freshmen, 68% undergrads receive any aid. 56% undergrads borrow to pay for school. Average cumulative indebtedness $27,906. **Criteria for awarding institutional aid:** *Non-need-based:* academics.

BRANDON UNIVERSITY

270-18TH Street, Brandon, MB R7A 6A9
Phone: 204-727-9784
E-mail: admission@brandonu.ca
Fax: 204-728-3221 • **Website:** www.brandonu.ca

This public school was founded in 1899. It has a 3-acre campus.

RATINGS
Admissions Selectivity Rating: 61 **Fire Safety Rating:** 60* **Green Rating:** 60*

STUDENTS AND FACULTY
Enrollment: 3,097. **Student Body:** 68% female, 32% male, 55% out-of-state, 0% international (30 countries represented). Asian 0%, African American 0%, Caucasian 0%, Hispanic 0%, Native American 0%.
Retention and Graduation: 65% freshmen return for sophomore year. **Faculty:** Student/faculty ratio 11:1. 215 full-time faculty.

ACADEMICS
Degrees: bachelor's, certificate, master's. **Classes:** Most classes have fewer than 10 students. **Majors with Highest Enrollment:** pharmacy (pharmd [usa], pharmd or bs/bpharm [canada]). **Special Study Options:** distance learning, double major, English as a Second Language (ESL), teacher certification program. **Combined Degree Programs:** BMus/BEd (AD). **Disability Services:** Special programs offered to physically disabled students include note-taking services, reader services, tape recorders, tutors.

FACILITIES
Housing: men's dorms, women's dorms. 80% of campus accessible to physically disabled. **Special Academic Facilities/Equipment:** B.J. Hales Museum **Computers:** Administrative functions (other than registration) can be performed online.

CAMPUS LIFE
Environment: Town. **Activities:** Choral groups, music ensembles, student government. **Athletics (Intercollegiate):** *Men:* basketball, volleyball. *Women:* basketball, volleyball.

ADMISSIONS
Freshman Academic Profile: Minimum paper TOEFL 550. **Basis for Candidate Selection:** *Very important factors considered include:* academic GPA, rigor of secondary school record. **Freshman Admission Requirements:** High school diploma is required and GED is accepted. **Transfer Admission Requirements:** college transcript(s), statement of good standing from prior institution(s). **General Admission Information:** Application Fee $125. Notification on a rolling basis, beginning on or about 11/1. Nonfall registration accepted. Admission may be deferred for a maximum of nil.

COSTS AND FINANCIAL AID
Annual in-state tuition $3,354. Annual out-of-state tuition $3,354. Room and board $6,270. Required fees $345. Average book expense $1,000. **Required Forms and Deadlines:** institution's own financial aid form.

BRENAU UNIVERSITY—THE WOMEN'S COLLEGE

500 Washington St SE, Gainesville, GA 30501
Phone: 770-534-6100 • **Financial Aid Phone:** 770-534-6152
E-mail: admissions@brenau.edu • **CEEB Code:** 5066
Fax: 770-538-4306 • **Website:** www.brenau.edu • **ACT Code:** 800

This private school was founded in 1878. It has a 56-acre campus.

RATINGS
Admissions Selectivity Rating: 77 **Fire Safety Rating:** 93 **Green Rating:** 60*

STUDENTS AND FACULTY
Enrollment: 772. **Student Body:** 100% female, 0% male, 7% out-of-state, 4% international. Asian 3%, African American 23%, Caucasian 55%, Hispanic 7%, Native American 0%.
Retention and Graduation: 66% freshmen return for sophomore year. 33% freshmen graduate within 4 years. **Faculty:** Student/faculty ratio 8:1. 88 full-time faculty, 74% hold PhDs, 10% are members of minority groups, 66% are women. 0% of classes are taught by teaching assistants.

ACADEMICS
Degrees: bachelor's, master's. **Classes:** Most classes have 10–19 students. Most lab/discussion sessions have 10–19 students. **Majors with Highest Enrollment:** nursing/registered nurse (rn, asn, bsn, msn); psychology. **Special Study Options:** cross-registration, distance learning, double major, dual enrollment, English as a Second Language (ESL), honors program, independent study, internships, student-designed major, study abroad, teacher certification program, weekend college. **Honors Programs:** The Honors Program at the Women's College of Brenau University begins in the freshman year and is followed throughout the student's entire college career at Brenau. Special classes reserved for honors students are taught in an enriched manner, affording these students an approach to their general education courses which enables them to study these subjects at an advanced level. **Combined Degree Programs:** B.S/MS in Occupational Therapy. **Disability Services:** Special programs offered to physically disabled students include note-taking services, tape recorders, tutors.

FACILITIES
Housing: special housing for disabled students, special housing for international students, women's dorms, fraternity/sorority housing, cooperative housing, apartments for single students. 90% of campus accessible to physically disabled. **Special Academic Facilities/Equipment:** Simmons Art Gallery, Wages House, Whitepath House, Natatorium Physical Fitness Center, Leo Castelli Art Gallery **Computers:** Students can register for classes online. Administrative functions (other than registration) can be performed online.

CAMPUS LIFE
Environment: Town. **Activities:** Choral groups, dance, drama/theater, literary magazine, music ensembles, musical theater, radio station, student government, student newspaper, television station, yearbook, Campus Ministries, International Student Organization 54 registered organizations, 12 honor societies, 2 religious organizations. 8 sororities. **Athletics (Intercollegiate):** *Women:* basketball, cross-country, soccer, softball, swimming, tennis, volleyball. **On-Campus Highlights:** Pearce Auditorium, Burd Center for Performing Arts, Fitness Center, Dining Hall and Tea Room, Northeast Georgia History Center.

ADMISSIONS
Freshman Academic Profile: SAT Math middle 50% range 430-520. SAT Critical Reading middle 50% range 450-540. SAT Writing middle 50% range 440-530. Minimum web-based TOEFL 61. Minimum paper TOEFL 500. **Basis

for Candidate Selection: *Important factors considered include:* academic GPA, rigor of secondary school record, standardized test scores. *Other factors considered include:* Class rank, character/personal qualities, extracurricular activities, first generation, interview, level of applicant's interest, talent/ability, volunteer work, work experience. **Freshman Admission Requirements:** High school diploma is required and GED is accepted. **Freshman Admission Statistics:** 4,525 applied, 30% admitted, 13% enrolled. **Transfer Admission Requirements:** college transcript(s), minimum college GPA of 2.0 required. Lowest grade transferable C. **General Admission Information:** Application Fee $35. Notification on a rolling basis, beginning on or about 10/1. Nonfall registration accepted. Credit and/or placement offered for CEEB Advanced Placement tests.

COSTS AND FINANCIAL AID
Annual tuition $2,108. Room and board $10,884. Required fees $330. **Required Forms and Deadlines:** FAFSA, state aid form. **Notification of Awards:** Applicants will be notified of awards on a rolling basis beginning 3/1. **Types of Aid:** *Need-based scholarships/grants:* Federal Pell, SEOG, state scholarships/grants, private scholarships, the school's own gift aid, National Smart Grant. *Loans:* Subsidized Stafford, Unsubsidized Stafford, PLUS, Federal Perkins, state loans, Private Alternative Loans. **Student Employment:** Off-campus job opportunities are excellent. **Financial Aid Statistics:** 100% freshmen, 99% undergrads receive need-based scholarship or grant aid. 17% freshmen, 13% undergrads receive non-need-based scholarship or grant aid. 65% freshmen, 76% undergrads receive need-based self-help aid. 3% freshmen, 5% undergrads receive athletic scholarships. 80% undergrads borrow to pay for school. Average cumulative indebtedness $21,748. **Criteria for awarding institutional aid:** *Non-need-based:* academics, art, athletics, leadership, minority status, music/drama.

BRESCIA UNIVERSITY

717 Frederica Street, Owensboro, KY 42301-3023
Phone: 270-686-4241 • **Financial Aid Phone:** 1-877-BRESCIA
E-mail: admissions@brescia.edu • **CEEB Code:** 1071
Fax: 270-686-4314 • **Website:** www.brescia.edu • **ACT Code:** 14980

This private school, affiliated with the Roman Catholic Church, was founded in 1950. It has a 9-acre campus.

RATINGS
Admissions Selectivity Rating: 86   **Fire Safety Rating:** 91   **Green Rating:** 60+

STUDENTS AND FACULTY
Enrollment: 801. **Student Body:** 72% female, 28% male, 29% out-of-state, 1% international (17 countries represented). Asian 0%, African American 12%, Caucasian 73%, Hispanic 4%, Native American 0%.
Retention and Graduation: 57% freshmen return for sophomore year.
Faculty: Student/faculty ratio 13:1. 37 full-time faculty, 70% hold PhDs, 16% are members of minority groups, 51% are women. 0% of classes are taught by teaching assistants.

ACADEMICS
Degrees: associate, bachelor's, master's, post-bachelor's certificate. **Classes:** Most classes have fewer than 10 students. Most lab/discussion sessions have fewer than 10 students. **Majors with Highest Enrollment:** elementary education and teaching; general studies; social work, other. **Special Study Options:** Accelerated program, cross-registration, distance learning, double major, English as a Second Language (ESL), exchange student program (domestic), honors program, independent study, internships, liberal arts/career combination, student-designed major, teacher certification program, weekend college. **Disability Services:** Special programs offered to physically disabled students include note-taking services, tape recorders, tutors. **Career Services:** alumni services, career/job search classes, career assessment, internships.

FACILITIES
Housing: Coed dorms, special housing for disabled students, men's dorms, women's dorms, apartments for single students, theme housing **Special Academic Facilities/Equipment:** Art Gallery, computer labs, campus center, greenhouse, observatory, science building. **Computers:** 100% of classrooms, 100% of dorms, 100% of libraries, 100% of dining areas, 100% of common outdoor areas have wireless network access. Administrative functions (other than registration) can be performed online.

CAMPUS LIFE
Environment: City. **Activities:** Choral groups, dance, drama/theater, literary magazine, pep band, student government, student newspaper, Campus Ministries, International Student Organization 22 registered organizations, 3 honor

societies, 2 religious organizations. **Athletics (Intercollegiate):** *Men:* baseball, basketball, cross-country, golf, soccer, tennis, track/field (outdoor). *Women:* basketball, cross-country, golf, soccer, softball, tennis, track/field (outdoor), volleyball. **Environmental Initiatives:** Recycling Purchasing more energy efficient windows Purchasing more energy efficient equipment when needed.

ADMISSIONS
Freshman Academic Profile: Average high school GPA 3.3. 61% from public high schools. SAT Math middle 50% range 410-510. ACT middle 50% range 19-25. Minimum paper TOEFL 550. **Basis for Candidate Selection:** *Very important factors considered include:* academic GPA, standardized test scores. **Freshman Admission Requirements:** High school diploma is required and GED is accepted. **Freshman Admission Statistics:** 5,798 applied, 21% admitted, 14% enrolled. **Transfer Admission Requirements:** High school transcript, college transcript(s), minimum college GPA of 2.0 required. Lowest grade transferable C. **General Admission Information:** Application Fee $25. Notification on a rolling basis, beginning on or about 9/1. Nonfall registration accepted. Admission may be deferred for a maximum of 1 year. Credit and/or placement offered for CEEB Advanced Placement tests.

COSTS AND FINANCIAL AID
Annual tuition $18,500. Room and board $8,000. Required fees $440. Average book expense. **Required Forms and Deadlines:** FAFSA. **Notification of Awards:** Applicants will be notified of awards on a rolling basis beginning 3/1. **Types of Aid:** *Need-based scholarships/grants:* Federal Pell, SEOG, state scholarships/grants, private scholarships, the school's own gift aid. *Loans:* Direct Subsidized Stafford, Direct Unsubsidized Stafford, Direct PLUS, Subsidized Stafford, Unsubsidized Stafford, PLUS, Federal Perkins, college/university loans from institutional funds. **Student Employment:** Federal Work-Study Program available. Institutional employment available. Highest amount earned per year from on-campus jobs $1,236. Off-campus job opportunities are excellent. **Financial Aid Statistics:** 99% freshmen, 98% undergrads receive any aid. **Criteria for awarding institutional aid:** *Non-need-based:* academics, alumni affiliation, art, athletics, minority status, music/drama, religious affiliation, state/district residency.

BREVARD COLLEGE

One Brevard College Drive, Brevard, NC 28712
Phone: 828-884-8300 • **Financial Aid Phone:** 828-884-8287
E-mail: admissions@brevard.edu • **CEEB Code:** 5067
Fax: 828-884-3790 • **ACT Code:** 3074

This private school, affiliated with the Methodist Church, was founded in 1853. It has a 120-acre campus.

RATINGS
Admissions Selectivity Rating: 81   **Fire Safety Rating:** 68   **Green Rating:** 75

STUDENTS AND FACULTY
Enrollment: 630. **Student Body:** 41% female, 59% male, 42% out-of-state, 5% international (13 countries represented). Asian 1%, African American 11%, Caucasian 73%, Hispanic 0%, Native American 1%.
Retention and Graduation: 52% freshmen return for sophomore year. 26% freshmen graduate within 4 years. 32% freshmen graduate within 6 years.
Faculty: Student/faculty ratio 10:1. 52 full-time faculty, 71% hold PhDs, 0% are members of minority groups, 40% are women. 0% of classes are taught by teaching assistants.

ACADEMICS
Degrees: bachelor's. **Classes:** Most classes have 10–19 students. Most lab/discussion sessions have 10–19 students. **Majors with Highest Enrollment:** business administration and management; music; parks, recreation and leisure studies. **Special Study Options:** double major, dual enrollment, honors program, independent study, internships, student-designed major, study abroad, teacher certification program. **Honors Programs:** To complete the Honors Program, students must take a minimum of 19 s.h. in honors courses during the typical 4-year period of their enrollment at Brevard College. These hours include honors enrichment seminar courses, honors-designated sections of courses, and a senior project. The only coursework of these 19 hours that is not directly attributable to core or major requirements is 4 s.h. of ENR (Enrichment) seminars. **Disability Services:** Special programs offered to physically disabled students include note-taking services, reader services, tape recorders, tutors. **Career Services:** career/job search classes, career assessment, internships.

FACILITIES
Housing: Coed dorms, special housing for disabled students, men's dorms, women's dorms, Coed upper classperson dorm. 100% of campus accessible to

physically disabled. **Special Academic Facilities/Equipment:** Porter Center for Performing Arts; Sims Art Center; Morrison Playhouse; Fitness Appraisal Laboratory; Academic Enrichment Center; Center for Career, Service, and Learning; Medical Services Building; Stamey Counseling Center; 24-hour computer lab; Library with wireless connection; Moore Science Annex Building **Computers:** 25% of dorms, 100% of libraries, 100% of dining areas, 100% of student union, have wireless network access. Administrative functions (other than registration) can be performed online.

CAMPUS LIFE

Environment: Village. **Activities:** Choral groups, concert band, dance, drama/theater, jazz band, literary magazine, music ensembles, musical theater, opera, pep band, student government, student newspaper, yearbook, Campus Ministries 32 registered organizations, 3 honor societies, 1 religious organizations. **Athletics (Intercollegiate):** *Men:* baseball, basketball, cheerleading, cross-country, cycling, football, golf, soccer, tennis, track/field (outdoor). *Women:* basketball, cheerleading, cross-country, cycling, golf, soccer, softball, tennis, track/field (outdoor), volleyball. **On-Campus Highlights:** Food Court & Dining Hall, Porter Center for Performing Arts, The Village, MG Super Lab, Moore Science Annex Building, Academic Enrichment Center. **Environmental Initiatives:** Campus-wide recycling program HVAC renovations to increase energy efficiency Master landscaping plan that focuses on native vegetation

ADMISSIONS

Freshman Academic Profile: Average high school GPA 2.9. 9% in top 10% of high school class, 28% in top 25% of high school class, 60% in top 50% of high school class. 77% from public high schools. SAT Math middle 50% range 450-540. SAT Critical Reading middle 50% range 440-530. ACT middle 50% range 17-22. Minimum paper TOEFL 537. **Basis for Candidate Selection:** *Very important factors considered include:* academic GPA, rigor of secondary school record, standardized test scores, level of applicant's interest. *Important factors considered include:* Class rank, application essay, character/personal qualities, extracurricular activities, interview, talent/ability, volunteer work. *Other factors considered include:* recommendation(s), alumni/ae relation, work experience. **Freshman Admission Requirements:** High school diploma is required and GED is accepted. **Freshman Admission Statistics:** 1,591 applied, 54% admitted, 26% enrolled. **Transfer Admission Requirements:** High school transcript, college transcript(s), essay or personal statement, standardized test scores, statement of good standing from prior institution(s). Minimum college GPA of 2.0 required. Lowest grade transferable C-. **General Admission Information:** Application Fee $30. Notification on a rolling basis, beginning on or about 7/1. Nonfall registration accepted. Admission may be deferred for a maximum of one semester. Credit and/or placement offered for CEEB Advanced Placement tests.

COSTS AND FINANCIAL AID

Annual tuition $23,900. Room and board $8,200. Average book expense $1,000. **Required Forms and Deadlines:** FAFSA, state aid form. **Notification of Awards:** Applicants will be notified of awards on a rolling basis beginning 2/1. **Types of Aid:** *Need-based scholarships/grants:* Federal Pell, SEOG, state scholarships/grants, private scholarships, the school's own gift aid. *Loans:* Direct Subsidized Stafford, Direct Unsubsidized Stafford, Direct PLUS, Subsidized Stafford, Unsubsidized Stafford, PLUS, Federal Perkins, state loans. **Student Employment:** Federal Work-Study Program available. Institutional employment available. Highest amount earned per year from on-campus jobs $1,860. Off-campus job opportunities are fair. **Financial Aid Statistics:** 99% freshmen, 100% undergrads receive need-based scholarship or grant aid. 79% freshmen, 11% undergrads receive non-need-based scholarship or grant aid. 100% freshmen, 100% undergrads receive need-based self-help aid. 9% freshmen, 11% undergrads receive athletic scholarships. 0% freshmen, 0% undergrads receive any aid. 52% undergrads borrow to pay for school. Average cumulative indebtedness $29,002. **Criteria for awarding institutional aid:** *Non-need-based:* academics, art, athletics, job skills, leadership, minority status, music/drama, religious affiliation, state/district residency.

BREWTON-PARKER COLLEGE

P.O. Box 2011, Mt. Vernon, GA 30445
Phone: 912-583-3265
E-mail: admissions@bpc.edu
Fax: 912-583-3598 • **Website:** www.bpc.edu

This private school, affiliated with the Baptist Church, was founded in 1904. It has a 270-acre campus.

RATINGS
Admissions Selectivity Rating: 79   **Fire Safety Rating:** 63   **Green Rating:** 60*

STUDENTS AND FACULTY
Enrollment: 1,124. **Student Body:** 64% female, 36% male, 5% out-of-state, 2% international (19 countries represented). Asian 0%, African American 20%, Caucasian 65%, Hispanic 2%, Native American 0%.
Retention and Graduation: 59% freshmen return for sophomore year. 8% freshmen graduate within 4 years. 18% freshmen graduate within 6 years. 10% grads go on to further study within 1 year. **Faculty:** Student/faculty ratio 9:1. 52 full-time faculty, 73% hold PhDs, % are members of minority groups, 38% are women. 0% of classes are taught by teaching assistants.

ACADEMICS
Degrees: associate, bachelor's. **Classes:** Most classes have fewer than 10 students. **Majors with Highest Enrollment:** business/commerce; education; psychology. **Special Study Options:** double major, dual enrollment, exchange student program (domestic), honors program, independent study, internships, teacher certification program, weekend college. **Disability Services:** Special programs offered to physically disabled students include note-taking services, reader services, tape recorders, tutors. **Career Services:** alumni services, career assessment, internships.

FACILITIES
Housing: men's dorms, women's dorms. 80% of campus accessible to physically disabled. **Special Academic Facilities/Equipment:** Library **Computers:** Students can register for classes online.

CAMPUS LIFE
Environment: Rural. **Activities:** Choral groups, concert band, drama/theater, jazz band, literary magazine, music ensembles, musical theater, student government, student newspaper, yearbook 24 registered organizations, 1 honor societies, 5 religious organizations. 3 fraternities, 3 sororities. **Athletics (Intercollegiate):** *Men:* baseball, basketball, cheerleading, soccer. *Women:* basketball, cheerleading, soccer, softball, volleyball. **On-Campus Highlights:** New Student Activities Center, Upstairs Cafe, Phillips Student Center Lobby, McAllister Lobby, Baseball/Softball Field.

ADMISSIONS
Freshman Academic Profile: 12% in top 10% of high school class, 26% in top 25% of high school class, 62% in top 50% of high school class. 80% from public high schools. SAT Math middle 50% range 400-500. SAT Critical Reading middle 50% range 390-510. ACT middle 50% range 17-21. **Basis for Candidate Selection:** *Very important factors considered include:* standardized test scores. *Important factors considered include:* Class rank, rigor of secondary school record. **Freshman Admission Requirements:** High school diploma is required and GED is accepted. *Academic units required:* 4 English, 3 mathematics, 3 science, 3 social studies. *Academic units recommended:* 4 English, 3 mathematics, 3 science, 3 social studies. **Freshman Admission Statistics:** 498 applied, 48% admitted, 49% enrolled. **Transfer Admission Requirements:** college transcript(s), statement of good standing from prior institution(s). Minimum college GPA of 2.0 required. Lowest grade transferable D. **General Admission Information:** Application Fee $25. Regular notification 1/1. Nonfall registration accepted. Admission may be deferred for a maximum of 1 year.

COSTS AND FINANCIAL AID
Annual tuition $11,500. Room and board $5,200. Required fees $1,100. Average book expense $1,000. **Required Forms and Deadlines:** FAFSA, state aid formCertification Statement. **Notification of Awards:** Applicants will be notified of awards on a rolling basis beginning 2/1. **Types of Aid:** *Need-based scholarships/grants:* Federal Pell, SEOG, state scholarships/grants, private scholarships, the school's own gift aid, Georgia Baptist Funds. *Loans:* Subsidized Stafford, Unsubsidized Stafford, PLUS, Federal Perkins, state loans, college/university loans from institutional funds. **Student Employment:** Federal Work-Study Program available. Institutional employment available. Highest amount earned per year from on-campus jobs $1,235. Off-campus job opportunities are fair. **Financial Aid Statistics:** 100% freshmen, 100% undergrads receive need-based scholarship or grant aid. 9% freshmen, 8% undergrads receive non-need-based scholarship or grant aid. 70% freshmen, 75% undergrads receive need-based self-help aid. 6% freshmen, 6% undergrads receive athletic scholarships. 82% undergrads borrow to pay for school. Average cumulative indebtedness $21,169. **Criteria for awarding institutional aid:** *Non-need-based:* academics, art, athletics, leadership, music/drama, religious affiliation, state/district residency.

BRIAR CLIFF UNIVERSITY

Admissions Office, Sioux City, IA 51104-0100
Phone: 712-279-5200 • **Financial Aid Phone:** 712-279-5239
E-mail: admissions@briarcliff.edu • **CEEB Code:** 1846
Fax: 712-279-1632 • **Website:** www.briarcliff.edu • **ACT Code:** 1276

This private school, affiliated with the Roman Catholic Church, was founded in 1930. It has a 70-acre campus.

RATINGS

Admissions Selectivity Rating: 75   **Fire Safety Rating:** 77   **Green Rating:** 61

STUDENTS AND FACULTY

Enrollment: 978. **Student Body:** 54% female, 46% male, 42% out-of-state, 1% international (11 countries represented). Asian 2%, African American 7%, Caucasian 78%, Hispanic 9%, Native American 2%.
Retention and Graduation: 68% freshmen return for sophomore year. 43% freshmen graduate within 4 years. 55% freshmen graduate within 6 years. 37% grads go on to further study within 1 year. 3% grads pursue arts and sciences degrees. 3% grads pursue law degrees. 4% grads pursue business degrees. 11% grads pursue medical degrees. **Faculty:** Student/faculty ratio 13:1. 61 full-time faculty, 75% hold PhDs, 2% are members of minority groups, 54% are women. 0% of classes are taught by teaching assistants.

ACADEMICS

Degrees: associate, bachelor's, master's, post-bachelor's certificate, post-master's certificate. **Classes:** Most classes have 10–19 students. Most lab/discussion sessions have fewer than 10 students. **Majors with Highest Enrollment:** business/commerce; elementary education and teaching; nursing/registered nurse (rn, asn, bsn, msn). **Special Study Options:** Accelerated program, cross-registration, distance learning, double major, dual enrollment, honors program, independent study, internships, liberal arts/career combination, student-designed major, study abroad, teacher certification program, weekend college. **Honors Programs:** Briar Cliff's Honor Program involves elements of leadership, service and character as well as academics, and is led by the Student Honors Executive Board. In addition to talking Honors courses with small enrollments, Honors students perform individual research work with faculty at the upper levels. **Disability Services:** Special programs offered to physically disabled students include note-taking services, reader services, tape recorders, tutors. **Career Services:** alumni services, career/job search classes, career assessment, internships Career Services highlights include The Chicago Semester allows students from any major field of study to work, study, and live in Chicago for a semester.

FACILITIES

Housing: Coed dorms, men's dorms, women's dorms, apartments for single students. 90% of campus accessible to physically disabled. **Special Academic Facilities/Equipment:** Nursing Simulation Lab Integrated Multimedia Center Human Anatomy Lab Clausen Art Gallery **Computers:** 100% of classrooms, 100% of libraries, 100% of dining areas, 100% of student union, have wireless network access. Administrative functions (other than registration) can be performed online.

CAMPUS LIFE

Environment: City. **Activities:** Choral groups, drama/theater, jazz band, literary magazine, music ensembles, musical theater, opera, radio station, student government, student newspaper, Campus Ministries 36 registered organizations, 2 honor societies, 3 religious organizations. **Athletics (Intercollegiate):** *Men:* baseball, basketball, cross-country, football, golf, soccer, tennis, track/field (outdoor), track/field (indoor), wrestling. *Women:* basketball, cross-country, golf, soccer, softball, tennis, track/field (outdoor), track/field (indoor), volleyball.
On-Campus Highlights: Java City, Stark Student Center, Newman Flanagan Athletic Center, Game Room, tunnels, The McCoy Arnold Athletic Facility was completed in 2004. This multi-use athletic facility provides additional facilities for students to work on personal training and fitness. **Environmental Initiatives:** Recycling Prairie Restoration Trayless dining.

ADMISSIONS

Freshman Academic Profile: Average high school GPA 3.1. 11% in top 10% of high school class, 32% in top 25% of high school class, 68% in top 50% of high school class. 82% from public high schools. ACT middle 50% range 18-23. Minimum web-based TOEFL 70. Minimum paper TOEFL 525. **Basis for Candidate Selection:** *Very important factors considered include:* academic GPA, rigor of secondary school record, standardized test scores. *Other factors considered include:* Class rank, application essay, recommendation(s), alumni/ae relation, character/personal qualities, extracurricular activities, first generation, interview, talent/ability. **Freshman Admission Requirements:** High school diploma is required and GED is accepted. **Freshman Admission Statistics:**

1,774 applied, 58% admitted, 23% enrolled. **Transfer Admission Requirements:** High school transcript, college transcript(s), statement of good standing from prior institution(s). Minimum college GPA of 2.0 required. Lowest grade transferable D. **General Admission Information:** Application Fee $20. Non-fall registration accepted. Admission may be deferred for a maximum of One year. Credit offered for CEEB Advanced Placement tests.

COSTS AND FINANCIAL AID

Annual tuition $22,719. Room and board $7,290. Required fees $699. Average book expense $1,050. **Required Forms and Deadlines:** FAFSA. **Notification of Awards: Types of Aid:** *Need-based scholarships/grants:* Federal Pell, SEOG, state scholarships/grants, private scholarships, the school's own gift aid. *Loans:* Subsidized Stafford, Unsubsidized Stafford, PLUS, Federal Perkins, state loans. **Student Employment:** Federal Work-Study Program available. Institutional employment available. Highest amount earned per year from on-campus jobs $2,500. Off-campus job opportunities are excellent. **Financial Aid Statistics:** 100% freshmen, 100% undergrads receive need-based scholarship or grant aid. 100% freshmen, 100% undergrads receive non-need-based scholarship or grant aid. 100% freshmen, 100% undergrads receive need-based self-help aid. 61% freshmen, 47% undergrads receive athletic scholarships. 100% freshmen, 97% undergrads receive any aid. 89% undergrads borrow to pay for school. Average cumulative indebtedness $30,865. **Criteria for awarding institutional aid:** *Non-need-based:* academics, alumni affiliation, art, athletics, leadership, music/drama, religious affiliation, state/district residency.

BRIDGEWATER COLLEGE

402 East College Street, Bridgewater, VA 22812-1599
Phone: 540-828-5375 • **Financial Aid Phone:** 540-828-5376
E-mail: admissions@bridgewater.edu • **CEEB Code:** 5069
Fax: 540-828-5481 • **Website:** www.bridgewater.edu • **ACT Code:** 4342

This private school, affiliated with the Church of Brethren Church, was founded in 1880. It has a 190-acre campus.

RATINGS

Admissions Selectivity Rating: 83   **Fire Safety Rating:** 69   **Green Rating:** 69

STUDENTS AND FACULTY

Enrollment: 1,749. **Student Body:** 56% female, 44% male, 22% out-of-state, 1% international (5 countries represented). Asian 1%, African American 8%, Caucasian 81%, Hispanic 3%, Native American 0%.
Retention and Graduation: 77% freshmen return for sophomore year. 49% freshmen graduate within 4 years. 57% freshmen graduate within 6 years. **Faculty:** Student/faculty ratio 15:1. 106 full-time faculty, 81% hold PhDs, 6% are members of minority groups, 42% are women. 0% of classes are taught by teaching assistants.

ACADEMICS

Degrees: bachelor's. **Classes:** Most classes have 10–19 students. Most lab/discussion sessions have 10–19 students. **Majors with Highest Enrollment:** biology/biological sciences; business administration and management; liberal arts and sciences/liberal studies. **Special Study Options:** double major, honors program, independent study, internships, liberal arts/career combination, study abroad, teacher certification program, Dual Degree Programs: 3-2 Engineering Program with George Washington University(BA/BA) 3-2 Engineering Program with Virginia Tech (BA/BA) 3-2 Nursing Program with Vanderbilt University (BA/MN) 3-4 Veterinary Science Program with Virginia Tech (BA/DVM) 3-4 Physical Therapy Program with Shenandoah University (BA/DPT) Pre Professional Programs in Dentistry, Engineering, Law, Medicine, Ministry, Nursing, Occupational Therapy, Pharmacy, Physical Therapy, and Veterinary Science. **Honors Programs:** The Honors Program is designed to provide additional challenges and opportunities for outstanding students. Honors courses are taught as smaller classes and provide opportunities for different types of student learning and faculty teaching--greater independence, research, and discussion formats. An Honors Project is one in which a student researches a subject, by examination of relevant literature or by experimentation or both; the student reports the results in an accurately documented and well-written paper or appropriate representation of the work. **Combined Degree Programs:** BA/MA, Vet. Science, Physical Therapy, Nursing. **Disability Services:** Special programs offered to physically disabled students include note-taking services, reader services, tape recorders, tutors. **Career Services:** alumni services, career/job search classes, career assessment, internships Career Services highlights include The internship program promotes student participation and establishes new opportunities/sites for internships within the local, regional, and distant communities.

FACILITIES

Housing: Coed dorms, special housing for disabled students, men's dorms, women's dorms, apartments for single students, wellness housing, theme housingHonor Housing. 95% of campus accessible to physically disabled. **Special Academic Facilities/Equipment:** Museum of Shenandoah region and Brethren history. **Computers:** 5% of classrooms, 10% of dorms, 75% of libraries, 100% of dining areas, 100% of student union, have wireless network access. Students can register for classes online. Administrative functions (other than registration) can be performed online.

CAMPUS LIFE

Environment: Village. **Activities:** Choral groups, concert band, dance, drama/theater, jazz band, literary magazine, music ensembles, musical theater, pep band, radio station, student government, student newspaper, yearbook, Campus Ministries, International Student Organization 74 registered organizations, 8 honor societies, 9 religious organizations. **Athletics (Intercollegiate):** *Men:* baseball, basketball, cross-country, equestrian sports, football, golf, soccer, tennis, track/field (outdoor), track/field (indoor). *Women:* basketball, cross-country, equestrian sports, field hockey, lacrosse, soccer, softball, swimming, tennis, track/field (outdoor), track/field (indoor), volleyball. **On-Campus Highlights:** McKinney Center for Science and Mathematics, Kline Campus Center, Funkhouser Center for Health and Wellness, Carter Center for Worship and Music, Eagle's Nest (snack shop). **Environmental Initiatives:** Energy and water conservation 3R's - Reduce, Reuse and Recycle Food Services: trayless operation, use of local produce, and project clean plate.

ADMISSIONS

Freshman Academic Profile: Average high school GPA 2.4. 17% in top 10% of high school class, 49% in top 25% of high school class, 82% in top 50% of high school class. 91% from public high schools. SAT Math middle 50% range 470-580. SAT Critical Reading middle 50% range 460-570. SAT Writing middle 50% range 450-550. ACT middle 50% range 19-22. Minimum web-based TOEFL 65. Minimum paper TOEFL 500. **Basis for Candidate Selection:** *Very important factors considered include:* academic GPA, rigor of secondary school record, standardized test scores. *Important factors considered include:* Class rank, recommendation(s), character/personal qualities, extracurricular activities, interview, talent/ability. *Other factors considered include:* geographical residence, level of applicant's interest, state residency, volunteer work, work experience. **Freshman Admission Requirements:** High school diploma is required and GED is accepted. *Academic units required:* 4 English, 3 mathematics, 2 science, (2 science labs), 4 academic electives, 2 social studies and history. *Academic units recommended:* 4 English, 3 mathematics, 2 science, (2 science labs), 4 academic electives, 2 social studies and history. **Freshman Admission Statistics:** 6,079 applied, 54% admitted, 17% enrolled. **Transfer Admission Requirements:** High school transcript, college transcript(s), standardized test scores, statement of good standing from prior institution(s). Minimum college GPA of 2.2 required. Lowest grade transferable C. **General Admission Information:** Application Fee $30. Notification on a rolling basis, beginning on or about 9/1. Nonfall registration accepted. Admission may be deferred for a maximum of 1 year. Credit and/or placement offered for CEEB Advanced Placement tests.

COSTS AND FINANCIAL AID

Annual tuition $28,500. Room and board $10,790. Required fees $590. Average book expense $1,150. **Required Forms and Deadlines:** FAFSA, state aid form. **Notification of Awards:** Applicants will be notified of awards on a rolling basis beginning 3/16. **Types of Aid:** *Need-based scholarships/grants:* Federal Pell, SEOG, state scholarships/grants, private scholarships, the school's own gift aid. *Loans:* Subsidized Stafford, Unsubsidized Stafford, PLUS, Federal Perkins. **Student Employment:** Federal Work-Study Program available. Institutional employment available. Highest amount earned per year from on-campus jobs $1,947. Off-campus job opportunities are good. **Financial Aid Statistics:** 100% freshmen, 100% undergrads receive need-based scholarship or grant aid. 98% freshmen, 97% undergrads receive non-need-based scholarship or grant aid. 69% freshmen, 72% undergrads receive need-based self-help aid. 99% freshmen, 99% undergrads receive any aid. 78% undergrads borrow to pay for school. Average cumulative indebtedness $31,153. **Criteria for awarding institutional aid:** *Non-need-based:* academics, music/drama, religious affiliation.

BRIDGEWATER STATE COLLEGE

Gates House, Bridgewater State College, Bridgewater, MA 2325
Phone: 508-531-1237 • **Financial Aid Phone:** 508-531-1341
E-mail: admission@bridgew.edu • **CEEB Code:** 3517
Fax: 508-531-1746 • **Website:** www.bridgew.edu • **ACT Code:** 1900

This public school was founded in 1840. It has a 235-acre campus.

RATINGS

Admissions Selectivity Rating: 73   **Fire Safety Rating:** 60*   **Green Rating:** 61

STUDENTS AND FACULTY

Enrollment: 8,310. **Student Body:** 60% female, 40% male, 5% out-of-state, 1% international (52 countries represented). Asian 2%, African American 6%, Caucasian 81%, Hispanic 2%, Native American 0%.
Retention and Graduation: 80% freshmen return for sophomore year. 22% freshmen graduate within 4 years. 51% freshmen graduate within 6 years. 16% grads go on to further study within 1 year. 2% grads pursue law degrees. 1% grads pursue business degrees. **Faculty:** Student/faculty ratio 19:1. 306 full-time faculty, 90% hold PhDs, 11% are members of minority groups, 48% are women. 0% of classes are taught by teaching assistants.

ACADEMICS

Degrees: bachelor's, master's, post-bachelor's certificate, post-master's certificate. **Classes:** Most classes have 20–29 students. Most lab/discussion sessions have 10–19 students. **Majors with Highest Enrollment:** business/commerce; elementary education and teaching; psychology. **Special Study Options:** Accelerated program, cross-registration, distance learning, double major, dual enrollment, English as a Second Language (ESL), exchange student program (domestic), honors program, independent study, internships, study abroad, teacher certification program. **Combined Degree Programs:** BS/MSM in Management, BSE/M.Ed in Elem/Spec. Ed. **Disability Services:** Special programs offered to physically disabled students include note-taking services, reader services, tape recorders, tutors. **Career Services:** alumni services, career/job search classes, career assessment, internships.

FACILITIES

Housing: Coed dorms, special housing for disabled students, apartments for single students, break housing for athletes, student teachers, international students, visiting lecturers. 95% of campus accessible to physically disabled. **Special Academic Facilities/Equipment:** On-campus school, children's physical development clinic, human performance lab, TV studio, observatory, flight simulators, electron microscope, Moakley Technology Center **Computers:** Students can register for classes online. Administrative functions (other than registration) can be performed online. Undergraduates are required to own a computer.

CAMPUS LIFE

Environment: Village. **Activities:** Choral groups, concert band, dance, drama/theater, jazz band, literary magazine, marching band, music ensembles, musical theater, radio station, student government, student newspaper, yearbook, Campus Ministries, International Student Organization 67 registered organizations, 11 honor societies, 1 religious organizations. **Athletics (Intercollegiate):** *Men:* baseball, basketball, cross-country, football, soccer, swimming, tennis, track/field (outdoor), wrestling. *Women:* basketball, cross-country, field hockey, lacrosse, soccer, softball, swimming, tennis, track/field (outdoor), volleyball.

ADMISSIONS

Freshman Academic Profile: Average high school GPA 3.0. 8% in top 10% of high school class, 32% in top 25% of high school class, 77% in top 50% of high school class. % from public high schools. SAT Math middle 50% range 470-560. SAT Critical Reading middle 50% range 460-560. ACT middle 50% range 19-23. Minimum paper TOEFL 500. **Basis for Candidate Selection:** *Very important factors considered include:* academic GPA, rigor of secondary school record. *Important factors considered include:* Class rank, standardized test scores. *Other factors considered include:* application essay, recommendation(s), alumni/ae relation, character/personal qualities, extracurricular activities, racial/ethnic status, talent/ability, volunteer work, work experience. **Freshman Admission Requirements:** High school diploma is required and GED is accepted. *Academic units required:* 4 English, 3 mathematics, 3 science, (2 science labs), 2 foreign language, 1 social studies, 1 history, 2 academic electives. *Academic units recommended:* 4 English, 3 mathematics, 3 science, (2 science labs), 2 foreign language, 1 social studies, 1 history, 2 academic electives. **Freshman Admission Statistics:** 6,226 applied, 72% admitted, 33% enrolled. **Transfer Admission Requirements:** college transcript(s), essay or personal statement, minimum college GPA of 2.0 required. Lowest grade transferable C-. **General Admission Information:** Notification on a rolling basis, beginning on or about 12/15. Nonfall registration accepted. Credit and/or placement offered for CEEB Advanced Placement tests.

COSTS AND FINANCIAL AID

Annual in-state tuition $910. Annual out-of-state tuition $7,050. Room and board $6,852. Required fees $532,700. Average book expense $1,000. **Required Forms and Deadlines:** FAFSA. **Notification of Awards: Types of Aid:** *Need-based scholarships/grants:* Federal Pell, SEOG, state scholarships/grants, private scholarships, the school's own gift aid. *Loans:* Direct Subsidized Stafford, Direct Unsubsidized Stafford, Direct PLUS, Federal Perkins, state loans. **Student Employment:** Federal Work-Study Program available. Institutional employment available. Highest amount earned per year from on-campus jobs $4,000. Off-campus job opportunities are good. **Financial Aid Statistics:** 83% freshmen, 83% undergrads receive need-based scholarship or grant aid. 24% freshmen, 10% undergrads receive non-need-based scholarship or grant aid. 97% freshmen, 100% undergrads receive need-based self-help aid. Average cumulative indebtedness $21,399. **Criteria for awarding institutional aid:** *Non-need-based:* academics, leadership, minority status, state/district residency.

BRIERCREST COLLEGE AND SEMINARY

510 College Drive, Caronport, SK S0H 0S0
Phone: 1-800-667-5199
E-mail: admissions@briercrest.ca
Fax: 800-667-5500 • **Website:** www.briercrest.ca

This private school was founded in 1935. It has a 160-acre campus.

RATINGS
Admissions Selectivity Rating: 61 **Fire Safety Rating:** 60* **Green Rating:** 60*

STUDENTS AND FACULTY
Faculty: Student/faculty ratio 18:1. 31 full-time faculty.

ACADEMICS
Degrees: associate, bachelor's, certificate, master's, post-bachelor's certificate. **Special Study Options:** distance learning, double major, English as a Second Language (ESL), independent study, internships, study abroad. **Career Services:** alumni services, career assessment

FACILITIES
Housing: Coed dorms, special housing for disabled students, Suite, corridor, singles, smoke-free, over 21 yrs, over 24 yrs, wellness living, quiet study, same curriculum housing, baccalaureate, single room options, and computer life style New upperclassmen apartment suite complex. **Computers:** Students can register for classes online.

CAMPUS LIFE
Environment: Rural. **Activities:** Choral groups, concert band, drama/theater, jazz band, literary magazine, music ensembles, musical theater, radio station, student government, student newspaper, symphony orchestra, yearbook. **Athletics (Intercollegiate):** *Men:* basketball, ice hockey, volleyball. *Women:* basketball, volleyball.

ADMISSIONS
Transfer Admission Requirements: High school transcript, college transcript(s), essay or personal statement. **General Admission Information:** Nonfall registration accepted.

COSTS AND FINANCIAL AID
Annual tuition $7,470. Room and board $2,515. Required fees $250. Average book expense $500.

BRIGHAM YOUNG UNIVERSITY (UT)

Best 378

A-153 ASB, Provo, UT 84602-1110
Phone: 801-422-2507 • **Financial Aid Phone:** 801-378-4104
E-mail: admissions@byu.edu • **CEEB Code:** 4019
Fax: 801-422-0005 • **Website:** www.byu.edu • **ACT Code:** 4266

This private school, affiliated with the Church of Jesus Christ of Latt Church, was founded in 1875. It has a 557-acre campus.

RATINGS
Admissions Selectivity Rating: 93 **Fire Safety Rating:** 64 **Green Rating:** 60*

STUDENTS AND FACULTY
Enrollment: 30,684. **Student Body:** 49% female, 51% male, 65% out-of-state, 4% international (121 countries represented). Asian 1%, African American 0%, Caucasian 66%, Hispanic 4%, Native American 0%.
Retention and Graduation: 87% freshmen return for sophomore year. 31% freshmen graduate within 4 years. 78% freshmen graduate within 6 years. **Faculty:** Student/faculty ratio 21:1. 1216 full-time faculty, 93% hold PhDs, 4% are members of minority groups, 21% are women.

ACADEMICS
Degrees: bachelor's, master's. **Classes:** Most classes have 10–19 students. **Majors with Highest Enrollment:** business/commerce; elementary education and teaching; exercise physiology. **Special Study Options:** Accelerated program, cooperative education program, cross-registration, distance learning, double major, English as a Second Language (ESL), external degree program, honors program, independent study, internships, liberal arts/career combination, study abroad, teacher certification program. **Honors Programs:** The Honors Program, participation in which is open to all BYU students, complements the university's expansive educational agenda by providing the benefits of a small liberal arts learning community. These benefits include offering small classes with high-quality teaching and learning that challenge students to reach their highest potential; fostering a spirit of ongoing inquiry that includes undergraduate research in a mentored environment; and underscoring the importance of combining personal excellence, faithful discipleship, and meaningful service. **Combined Degree Programs:** BA/JD, BA/MA, BA/Macc, BS/MS. **Disability Services:** Special programs offered to physically disabled students include note-taking services, reader services, tape recorders, tutors.

FACILITIES
Housing: special housing for disabled students, men's dorms, women's dorms, apartments for married students, apartments for single students, Language houses are available. 97% of campus accessible to physically disabled. **Special Academic Facilities/Equipment:** Art, peoples/cultures, life science, and earth science museums, film studio, on-campus nursery school, language research center, seismography equipment, electron microscope. **Computers:** 10% of classrooms, 100% of libraries, 100% of dining areas, 100% of student union, have wireless network access. Students can register for classes online. Administrative functions (other than registration) can be performed online.

CAMPUS LIFE
Environment: City. **Activities:** Choral groups, concert band, dance, drama/theater, jazz band, literary magazine, marching band, music ensembles, musical theater, opera, pep band, radio station, student government, student newspaper, student-run film society, symphony orchestra, television station 390 registered organizations, 22 honor societies, 25 religious organizations. **Athletics (Intercollegiate):** *Men:* baseball, basketball, cheerleading, cross-country, diving, football, golf, swimming, tennis, track/field (outdoor), track/field (indoor), volleyball. *Women:* basketball, cheerleading, cross-country, diving, golf, gymnastics, soccer, softball, swimming, tennis, track/field (outdoor), track/field (indoor), volleyball. **On-Campus Highlights:** Monte L. Bean Life Science Museum, The Museum of Art, Gordon B. Hinckley Alumni & Visitors Cen, Harold B. Lee Library, Wilkinson Student Center, Some of the popular places on campus are the HFAC theatres and music halls, the Creamery on 9th, and the Marriott Center (where weekly devotionals and forums as well as sports events are held). Campus highlights also include BYU's new Student Athlete Building houses the impressive Legacy Hall (BYU sports Hall of Fame) and the popular Legends Grille, the very large (athletic teams')Indoor Practice Facility is completed, the newly remodeled Brimhall Building is housing the Communications Department, and the new Joseph F. Smith Building (which replaced the Smith Family Living Center) has been completed and now houses the College of Family, Home and Social Sciences.

ADMISSIONS

Freshman Academic Profile: Average high school GPA 3.8. 53% in top 10% of high school class, 84% in top 25% of high school class, 98% in top 50% of high school class. SAT Math middle 50% range 580-680. SAT Critical Reading middle 50% range 570-680. SAT Writing middle 50% range 540-650. ACT middle 50% range 26-30. Minimum paper TOEFL 500. **Basis for Candidate Selection:** *Very important factors considered include:* academic GPA, rigor of secondary school record, standardized test scores, character/personal qualities, interview, religious affiliation/commitment. *Important factors considered include:* application essay, recommendation(s), extracurricular activities, racial/ethnic status, volunteer work. *Other factors considered include:* first generation, talent/ability, work experience. **Freshman Admission Requirements:** High school diploma is required and GED is accepted. *Academic units required:* 4 English, 3 mathematics, 2 science, (2 science labs), 2 foreign language, 2 history, 2 literature or writing. *Academic units recommended:* 4 English, 3 mathematics, 2 science, (2 science labs), 2 foreign language, 2 history, 2 literature or writing. **Freshman Admission Statistics:** 11,238 applied, 63% admitted, 80% enrolled. **Transfer Admission Requirements:** college transcript(s), essay or personal statement, interview, minimum college GPA of 3.0 required. Lowest grade transferable C-. **General Admission Information:** Application Fee $30. Regular application deadline 2/1. Nonfall registration accepted. Admission may be deferred for a maximum of 2 years. Credit and/or placement offered for CEEB Advanced Placement tests.

COSTS AND FINANCIAL AID

Annual tuition $4,710. Room and board $7,200. Average book expense $932. **Required Forms and Deadlines:** FAFSAInstitutional Application for Financial Aid. **Notification of Awards:** Applicants will be notified of awards on a rolling basis beginning 5/1. **Types of Aid:** *Need-based scholarships/grants:* Federal Pell, state scholarships/grants, private scholarships, the school's own gift aid. *Loans:* Subsidized Stafford, Unsubsidized Stafford, PLUS. **Student Employment: Financial Aid Statistics:** 55% freshmen, 79% undergrads receive need-based scholarship or grant aid. 80% freshmen, 49% undergrads receive non-need-based scholarship or grant aid. 31% freshmen, 35% undergrads receive need-based self-help aid. 2% freshmen, 2% undergrads receive athletic scholarships. 53% freshmen, 64% undergrads receive any aid. 32% undergrads borrow to pay for school. Average cumulative indebtedness $14,320. **Criteria for awarding institutional aid:** *Non-need-based:* academics, art, athletics, leadership, minority status, music/drama, religious affiliation, state/district residency.

BRIGHAM YOUNG UNIVERSITY—HAWAII

BYU- Hawaii # 1973, Laie, HI 96762
Phone: 808-675- 3738 • **Financial Aid Phone:** 808-293-3530
E-mail: admissions@byuh.edu • **CEEB Code:** 4106
Fax: 808-675-3741 • **ACT Code:** 899

This private school, affiliated with the Church of Jesus Christ of Latt Church, was founded in 1955. It has a 60-acre campus.

RATINGS

Admissions Selectivity Rating: 88   **Fire Safety Rating:** 65   **Green Rating:** 60*

STUDENTS AND FACULTY

Enrollment: 2,312. **Student Body:** 56% female, 44% male, 68% out-of-state, 44% international (67 countries represented). Asian 22%, African American 1%, Caucasian 29%, Hispanic 2%, Native American 1%.
Retention and Graduation: 57% freshmen return for sophomore year. 25% freshmen graduate within 4 years. 39% freshmen graduate within 6 years.
Faculty: Student/faculty ratio 14:1. 122 full-time faculty, 80% hold PhDs, 23% are members of minority groups, 21% are women. 0% of classes are taught by teaching assistants.

ACADEMICS

Degrees: bachelor's. **Classes:** Most classes have 10–19 students. Most lab/discussion sessions have 10–19 students. **Majors with Highest Enrollment:** information science/studies; intercultural/multicultural and diversity studies; international business/trade/commerce. **Special Study Options:** Accelerated program, cooperative education program, distance learning, English as a Second Language (ESL), exchange student program (domestic), honors program, independent study, internships, student-designed major, teacher certification program. **Honors Programs:** The University Honors Program is open to all interested students who feel they are capable of accepting the challenge of an Honors Education. You will have the opportunity to participate in a stimulating class environment with other top students and the best professors. **Disability Services:** Special programs offered to physically disabled students include note-taking services, reader services, tape recorders, tutors.

FACILITIES

Housing: men's dorms, women's dorms, apartments for married students 90% of campus accessible to physically disabled. **Special Academic Facilities/Equipment:** Museum of Natural History Media Lab **Computers:** 100% of classrooms, 100% of libraries, 100% of dining areas, 100% of student union, 100% of common outdoor areas have wireless network access. Students can register for classes online. Administrative functions (other than registration) can be performed online.

CAMPUS LIFE

Environment: Village. **Activities:** Choral groups, concert band, dance, jazz band, literary magazine, music ensembles, pep band, student government, student newspaper, student-run film society 52 registered organizations, 3 honor societies. **Athletics (Intercollegiate):** *Men:* basketball, cross-country, golf, soccer, tennis. *Women:* basketball, cross-country, soccer, softball, tennis, volleyball. **On-Campus Highlights:** Joseph F. Smith Library, Cannon Activities Center, The Club Cafe, The Seasider Snackbar, Aloha Center.

ADMISSIONS

Freshman Academic Profile: Average high school GPA 3.4. SAT Math middle 50% range 480-600. SAT Critical Reading middle 50% range 460-580. ACT middle 50% range 20-27. Minimum paper TOEFL 475. **Basis for Candidate Selection:** *Very important factors considered include:* application essay, recommendation(s), rigor of secondary school record, standardized test scores, character/personal qualities, extracurricular activities, geographical residence, interview, religious affiliation/commitment. *Important factors considered include:* Class rank, alumni/ae relation, talent/ability, volunteer work, work experience. *Other factors considered include:* state residency. **Freshman Admission Requirements:** High school diploma is required and GED is not accepted. **Freshman Admission Statistics:** 1,268 applied, 48% admitted, 49% enrolled. **Transfer Admission Requirements:** college transcript(s), essay or personal statement, statement of good standing from prior institution(s). Minimum college GPA of 3.0 required. Lowest grade transferable C-. **General Admission Information:** Application Fee $30. Regular application deadline 2/15. Regular notification 4/1. Nonfall registration accepted. Admission may be deferred for a maximum of 1 semester. Credit offered for CEEB Advanced Placement tests.

COSTS AND FINANCIAL AID

Annual tuition $3,600. Room and board $5,568. Required fees. Average book expense $900. **Required Forms and Deadlines:** FAFSA, institution's own financial aid form. **Notification of Awards:** Applicants will be notified of awards on or about 6/30. **Types of Aid:** *Need-based scholarships/grants:* Federal Pell, private scholarships, the school's own gift aid. *Loans:* Subsidized Stafford, Unsubsidized Stafford, PLUS, college/university loans from institutional funds. **Student Employment:** Institutional employment available. Highest amount earned per year from on-campus jobs $4,500. Off-campus job opportunities are fair. **Financial Aid Statistics:** 88% freshmen, 64% undergrads receive need-based scholarship or grant aid. 24% freshmen, 45% undergrads receive non-need-based scholarship or grant aid. 73% freshmen, 45% undergrads receive need-based self-help aid. 13% freshmen, 7% undergrads receive athletic scholarships. 70% freshmen, 72% undergrads receive any aid. 36% undergrads borrow to pay for school. Average cumulative indebtedness $12,418. **Criteria for awarding institutional aid:** *Non-need-based:* academics, art, athletics, leadership, music/drama, state/district residency.

BROCK UNIVERSITY

500 Glenridge Avenue, St. Catharines, ON L2S 3A1
Phone: 905-688-5550
E-mail: admissns@brocku.ca
Fax: 905-988-5488 • **Website:** www.brocku.ca

This public school was founded in 1964. It has a 457-acre campus.

RATINGS

Admissions Selectivity Rating: 61   **Fire Safety Rating:** 78   **Green Rating:** 69

STUDENTS AND FACULTY

Student Body: 8% out-of-state, (80 countries represented).
Retention and Graduation: 52% freshmen graduate within 4 years. **Faculty:** Student/faculty ratio 27:1. 577 full-time faculty, 43% are women. 0% of classes are taught by teaching assistants.

ACADEMICS

Degrees: bachelor's, certificate, master's. **Majors with Highest Enrollment:** business/commerce; education; health professions and related clinical sciences, other. **Special Study Options:** cooperative education program, double major, English as a Second Language (ESL), exchange student program (domestic), honors program, internships, liberal arts/career combination, student-designed major, study abroad, teacher certification program, Liberal arts/career combination: Students may choose from 7 Concurrent Education programs, combining their undergraduate degree and Bachelor of Education degree. **Combined Degree Programs:** BA/BEd; BSc/BEd; BPHEd/BEd. **Disability Services:** Special programs offered to physically disabled students include note-taking services, reader services, tape recorders, tutors. **Career Services:** career/job search classes, internships Career Services highlights include Brock offers the third largest selection of Co-op programs in Ontario. A variety of additional experiential learning opportunities are built into virtually all of our programs.

FACILITIES

Housing: Coed dorms, special housing for disabled students, women's dorms, Village Residence and Quarry View Residence (Townhouses). 100% of campus accessible to physically disabled. **Special Academic Facilities/Equipment:** Cool Climate Oenology and Viticulture Institute Map Library Intructional Resource Centre Rodman Hall Arts Centre Cypriote Museum. **Computers:** 100% of classrooms, 100% of libraries, 100% of student union, have wireless network access. Students can register for classes online. Administrative functions (other than registration) can be performed online.

CAMPUS LIFE

Environment: City. **Activities:** Choral groups, concert band, dance, drama/theater, literary magazine, music ensembles, musical theater, radio station, student government, student newspaper, student-run film society, symphony orchestra, television station, yearbook, Campus Ministries 40 registered organizations, 6 religious organizations. **Athletics (Intercollegiate):** *Men:* baseball, basketball, cheerleading, crew/rowing, cross-country, curling, fencing, ice hockey, lacrosse, rugby, soccer, squash, swimming, wrestling. *Women:* basketball, cheerleading, crew/rowing, cross-country, curling, fencing, ice hockey, rugby, soccer, swimming, volleyball, wrestling. **On-Campus Highlights:** Residences, Walker Complex - athletic facility, Computer Commons, Isaacs, Plaza Building. **Environmental Initiatives:** Our newest building earned LEED Silver Certification. The energy cost performance is almost 43 per cent better than the Model National Energy Code. Brock's campus has been designated as a UNESCO Biosphere Reserve.

ADMISSIONS

Freshman Academic Profile: Minimum web-based TOEFL 88. **Basis for Candidate Selection:** *Very important factors considered include:* academic GPA, rigor of secondary school record. *Important factors considered include:* standardized test scores. *Other factors considered include:* Class rank, recommendation(s), talent/ability. **Freshman Admission Requirements:** High school diploma is required and GED is accepted. **Transfer Admission Requirements:** High school transcript, college transcript(s). **General Admission Information:** Application Fee $155. Regular application deadline 4/1. Notification on a rolling basis, beginning on or about 1/1. Nonfall registration not accepted. Neither credit nor placement offered for CEEB Advanced Placement tests

COSTS AND FINANCIAL AID

Annual in-state tuition $4,852. Room and board $8,215. Required fees. Average book expense $900. **Required Forms and Deadlines:** institution's own financial aid formOntario Student Assistance Program. **Types of Aid:** *Need-based scholarships/grants:* the school's own gift aid. *Loans:* Ontario Student Assistance Program. **Student Employment:** Federal Work-Study Program available. Institutional employment available. Off-campus job opportunities are good. **Financial Aid Statistics:** 29% undergrads receive need-based scholarship or grant aid. 39% undergrads receive any aid. **Criteria for awarding institutional aid:** *Non-need-based:* academics, athletics, leadership.

BROWN UNIVERSITY

Best 378

Box 1876, Providence, RI 2912
Phone: 401-863-2378 • **Financial Aid Phone:** 401-863-2721
E-mail: admission_undergraduate@brown.edu • **CEEB Code:** 3094
Fax: 401-863-9300 • **Website:** www.brown.edu • **ACT Code:** 3800

This private school was founded in 1764. It has a 146-acre campus.

RATINGS

Admissions Selectivity Rating: 99   **Fire Safety Rating:** 81   **Green Rating:** 89

STUDENTS AND FACULTY

Enrollment: 6,133. **Student Body:** 52% female, 48% male, 95% out-of-state, 11% international (105 countries represented). Asian 12%, African American 6%, Caucasian 45%, Hispanic 10%, Native American 0%.

Retention and Graduation: 97% freshmen return for sophomore year. 83% freshmen graduate within 4 years. 95% freshmen graduate within 6 years. 23% grads go on to further study within 1 year. **Faculty:** Student/faculty ratio 9:1. 813 full-time faculty, 93% hold PhDs, 17% are members of minority groups, 36% are women.

ACADEMICS

Degrees: bachelor's, master's. **Classes:** Most classes have 10–19 students. **Majors with Highest Enrollment:** biology/biological sciences; economics; international relations and affairs. **Special Study Options:** cross-registration, double major, exchange student program (domestic), honors program, independent study, internships, student-designed major, study abroad, teacher certification program, 8-Year medical program (AB or SCB plus MD) 5-year degree program (AB and SCB). **Combined Degree Programs:** BA/MD, BA/MA, BS/MD, BS/MS, BA/BS. **Disability Services:** Special programs offered to physically disabled students include note-taking services, reader services, tape recorders, tutors. **Career Services:** Alumni network, career/job search classes, career assessment, internships, regional alumni. Career Services highlights include Each year, hundreds of brown students receive funding to pursue independent research, internships, projects, or faculty collaborations to deepen and connect their learning and experience. The Brown Internship Award Program provides funding on a competitive basis for students pursuing unpaid or low-paying summer internships. The program has two components, a living stipend and, for students on financial aid, the opportunity to have their summer earnings requirement waived. The Royce Fellowship is one of several Brown fellowships which invite proposals for summer projects of students' own design. They Royce provides not only a financial award for research projects but ongoing seminars and programs for fellows in the academic year following their award. Each of the fellowships has a particular focus: research, international service, social entrepreneurship, public interest law, sports and human rights, etc. The Undergraduate Teaching and Research Award supports nearly 300 students each year to collaborate with a Brown faculty member on course development or research. More information on these programs can be found at http://www.brown.edu/Administration/Dean_of_the_College/fellowships/.

FACILITIES

Housing: Coed dorms, special housing for disabled students, fraternity/sorority housing, cooperative housing, apartments for single students, wellness housing, theme housing. **Special Academic Facilities/Equipment:** Art gallery, anthropology museum, language lab, information technology center, NASA research center, center for modern culture/media. **Computers:** 50% of classrooms, 100% of dorms, 100% of libraries, 100% of dining areas, 100% of student union, 50% of common outdoor areas have wireless network access. Students can register for classes online. Administrative functions (other than registration) can be performed online.

CAMPUS LIFE

Environment: City. **Activities:** Choral groups, concert band, dance, drama/theater, jazz band, literary magazine, marching band, music ensembles, musical theater, opera, pep band, radio station, student government, student newspaper, student-run film society, symphony orchestra, television station, yearbook, Campus Ministries, International Student Organization, Model UN 400 registered organizations, 3 honor societies, 20 religious organizations. 8 fraternities, 2 sororities. **Athletics (Intercollegiate):** *Men:* baseball, basketball, crew/rowing, cross-country, diving, fencing, football, golf, ice hockey, lacrosse, soccer, squash, swimming, tennis, track/field (outdoor), track/field (indoor), water polo, wrestling. *Women:* basketball, crew/rowing, cross-country, diving, equestrian sports, fencing, field hockey, golf, gymnastics, ice hockey, lacrosse, skiing (downhill/alpine), soccer, softball, squash, swimming, tennis, track/field (outdoor), track/field (indoor), volleyball, water polo. **On-Campus Highlights:** The College Green, Bell Gallery, Libraries - Jon Hay, John Carter Brown, Watson Institute, Lyman Hall & Dill Center. **Environmental Initiatives:** Reduce GHG emissions to 42% (15% below 1990) below 2007 for existing buildings by 2020 Reduce GHG emissions for all newly constructed facilities between 25% and 50% below code requirements Reduce GHG emissions for all newly acquired facilities by a minimum of 15% and as much as 30%.

ADMISSIONS

Freshman Academic Profile: 94% in top 10% of high school class, 99% in top 25% of high school class, 100% in top 50% of high school class. 63% from public high schools. SAT Math middle 50% range 660-770. SAT Critical Reading middle 50% range 660-760. SAT Writing middle 50% range 670-780. ACT middle 50% range 29-34. Minimum web-based TOEFL 100. Minimum paper TOEFL 600. **Basis for Candidate Selection:** *Very important factors considered include:* rigor of secondary school record, character/personal qualities, level of applicant's interest, talent/ability. *Important factors considered include:* Class rank, application essay, academic GPA, recommendation(s), standardized test scores, extracurricular activities. *Other factors considered include:* alumni/ae relation, first generation, geographical residence, interview, racial/ethnic status, state residency, volunteer work, work experience. **Freshman Admission Requirements:** High school diploma is required and GED is not accepted.

Academic units required: 4 English, 3 mathematics, 3 science, (2 science labs), 3 foreign language, 2 history, 1 academic electives. *Academic units recommended:* 4 English, 3 mathematics, 3 science, (2 science labs), 3 foreign language, 2 history, 1 academic electives. **Freshman Admission Statistics:** 28,742 applied, 10% admitted, 56% enrolled. **Transfer Admission Requirements:** High school transcript, college transcript(s), essay or personal statement, standardized test scores, statement of good standing from prior institution(s). Lowest grade transferable C. **General Admission Information:** Application Fee $75. Early decision application deadline 11/1. Regular application deadline 1/1. Regular notification 4/1. Nonfall registration not accepted. Admission may be deferred for a maximum of 1 year. Placement offered for CEEB Advanced Placement tests.

COSTS AND FINANCIAL AID

Annual tuition $42,808. Room and board $11,258. Required fees $950. Average book expense $1,360. **Required Forms and Deadlines:** FAFSA, CSS/Financial Aid PROFILE, noncustodial PROFILE. **Notification of Awards:** Applicants will be notified of awards on or about 4/1. **Types of Aid:** *Need-based scholarships/grants:* Federal Pell, SEOG, state scholarships/grants, private scholarships, the school's own gift aid. *Loans:* Direct Subsidized Stafford, Direct Unsubsidized Stafford, Direct PLUS, Federal Perkins, college/university loans from institutional funds. **Student Employment:** Federal Work-Study Program available. Institutional employment available. Off-campus job opportunities are excellent. **Financial Aid Statistics:** 96% freshmen, 95% undergrads receive need-based scholarship or grant aid. 85% freshmen, 90% undergrads receive need-based self-help aid. 62% freshmen, 57% undergrads receive any aid. 36% undergrads borrow to pay for school. Average cumulative indebtedness $23,521.

BRYAN COLLEGE

The Office of Admissions, Dayton, TN 37321
Phone: 423-775-7204 • **Financial Aid Phone:** 423-775-7339
E-mail: admissions@bryan.edu • **CEEB Code:** 1908
Fax: 423-775-7199 • **Website:** www.bryan.edu • **ACT Code:** 4038

This private school was founded in 1930. It has a 125-acre campus.

RATINGS
Admissions Selectivity Rating: 86 **Fire Safety Rating:** 60* **Green Rating:** 60*

STUDENTS AND FACULTY
Enrollment: 1,120. **Student Body:** 53% female, 47% male, 61% out-of-state, 2% international. Asian 0%, African American 5%, Caucasian 88%, Hispanic 2%, Native American 0%.
Retention and Graduation: 71% freshmen return for sophomore year. 47% freshmen graduate within 4 years. 56% freshmen graduate within 6 years.
Faculty: Student/faculty ratio 17:1. 43 full-time faculty, 79% hold PhDs, 0% are members of minority groups, 19% are women. 0% of classes are taught by teaching assistants.

ACADEMICS
Degrees: associate, bachelor's, master's. **Classes:** Most classes have 10–19 students. **Majors with Highest Enrollment:** business administration and management; communication studies/speech communication and rhetoric; English language and literature. **Special Study Options:** distance learning, dual enrollment, honors program, independent study, internships, study abroad. **Disability Services:** Special programs offered to physically disabled students include note-taking services, reader services, tape recorders, tutors. **Career Services:** Alumni network, alumni services, career/job search classes, career assessment, internships.

FACILITIES
Housing: men's dorms, women's dorms, apartments for married students, apartments for single students. **Special Academic Facilities/Equipment:** Willard Henning Natural History Museum **Computers:** 100% of classrooms, 100% of dorms, 100% of libraries, 100% of dining areas, 100% of student union, 80% of common outdoor areas have wireless network access. Administrative functions (other than registration) can be performed online.

CAMPUS LIFE
Environment: Town. **Activities:** Choral groups, drama/theater, musical theater, radio station, student government, student newspaper, yearbook, Campus Ministries. **Athletics (Intercollegiate):** *Men:* baseball, basketball, cross-country, golf, soccer, track/field (outdoor), track/field (indoor). *Women:* basketball, cross-country, golf, soccer, softball, track/field (outdoor), track/field (indoor). **On-Campus Highlights:** Student Center, Library, The "Grassy Bowl", The Commons.

ADMISSIONS
Freshman Academic Profile: Average high school GPA 3.6. 20% in top 10% of high school class, 48% in top 25% of high school class, 80% in top 50% of high school class. 42% from public high schools. SAT Math middle 50% range 470-600. SAT Critical Reading middle 50% range 500-670. SAT Writing middle 50% range 460-640. ACT middle 50% range 20-26. Minimum web-based TOEFL 76. Minimum paper TOEFL 540. **Basis for Candidate Selection:** *Very important factors considered include:* application essay, academic GPA, rigor of secondary school record, standardized test scores. *Important factors considered include:* character/personal qualities, level of applicant's interest, religious affiliation/commitment. *Other factors considered include:* Class rank, recommendation(s), alumni/ae relation, extracurricular activities, interview, talent/ability, volunteer work. **Freshman Admission Requirements:** High school diploma is required and GED is accepted. *Academic units required:* 4 English, 3 mathematics, 3 science, 2 foreign language, 3 social studies. *Academic units recommended:* 4 English, 3 mathematics, 3 science, 2 foreign language, 3 social studies. **Freshman Admission Statistics:** 846 applied, 57% admitted, 48% enrolled. **Transfer Admission Requirements:** college transcript(s), essay or personal statement, standardized test scores, minimum college GPA of 2.75 required. Lowest grade transferable 2. **General Admission Information:** Application Fee $35. Nonfall registration accepted. Credit offered for CEEB Advanced Placement tests.

COSTS AND FINANCIAL AID
Annual tuition $20,150. Room and board $5,950. Required fees $120. Average book expense $1,400. **Required Forms and Deadlines:** FAFSA. **Notification of Awards:** Applicants will be notified of awards on a rolling basis beginning 2/15. **Types of Aid:** *Need-based scholarships/grants:* Federal Pell, SEOG, state scholarships/grants, private scholarships, the school's own gift aid. *Loans:* Direct Subsidized Stafford, Direct Unsubsidized Stafford, Direct PLUS, Subsidized Stafford, Unsubsidized Stafford, PLUS, Federal Perkins, college/university loans from institutional funds. **Student Employment:** Federal Work-Study Program available. Institutional employment available. Off-campus job opportunities are fair. **Financial Aid Statistics:** 79% freshmen, 75% undergrads receive any aid. **Criteria for awarding institutional aid:** *Non-need-based:* academics, alumni affiliation, athletics, leadership, minority status, music/drama, state/district residency.

BRYANT UNIVERSITY

Best 378

Office of Admission; 1150 Douglas Pike, Smithfield, RI 02917-1291
Phone: 401-232-6100 • **Financial Aid Phone:** 401-232-6020
E-mail: admission@bryant.edu • **CEEB Code:** 3095
Fax: 401-232-6731 • **Website:** www.bryant.edu • **ACT Code:** 3802

This private school was founded in 1863. It has a 420-acre campus.

RATINGS
Admissions Selectivity Rating: 84 **Fire Safety Rating:** 89 **Green Rating:** 76

STUDENTS AND FACULTY
Enrollment: 3,157. **Student Body:** 42% female, 58% male, 87% out-of-state, 8% international (68 countries represented). Asian 4%, African American 4%, Caucasian 75%, Hispanic 5%, Native American 0%.
Retention and Graduation: 88% freshmen return for sophomore year. 77% freshmen graduate within 4 years. 23% grads go on to further study within 1 year. 2% grads pursue arts and sciences degrees. 2% grads pursue law degrees. 17% grads pursue business degrees. **Faculty:** Student/faculty ratio 15:1. 168 full-time faculty, 82% hold PhDs, 19% are members of minority groups, 40% are women. 0% of classes are taught by teaching assistants.

ACADEMICS
Degrees: bachelor's, master's. **Classes:** Most classes have 30–39 students. Most lab/discussion sessions have fewer than 10 students. **Majors with Highest Enrollment:** accounting; finance; marketing/marketing management. **Special Study Options:** double major, English as a Second Language (ESL), honors program, independent study, internships, study abroad. **Honors Programs:** The Bryant University Honors Program offers its members a personalized, distinctive experience that enriches their academic, social, cultural and professional talents in a mentor-oriented environment. The Program offers its members a different experience to develop the unique talents of exceptionally prepared and focused individuals. Designated courses in the Honors Program are

organized to encourage in-depth classroom discussions and application of business and liberal arts disciplines with reduced class sizes. **Disability Services:** Special programs offered to physically disabled students include note-taking services, tape recorders, tutors. **Career Services:** Alumni network, alumni services, career/job search classes, career assessment, internships, regional alumni. Career Services highlights include In 2008, 343 companies participated in the Corporate Recruiting Program.

FACILITIES

Housing: Coed dorms, special housing for disabled students, women's dorms, apartments for single students, Honors, International Business. 90% of campus accessible to physically disabled. **Special Academic Facilities/Equipment:** George E. Bello Center for Information and Technology, Koffler Technology Center and Communications Complex, John H. Chafee Center for International Business, Koffler Television Studio, C.V. Starr Financial Markets Center, Learning and Language Lab **Computers:** 100% of classrooms, 100% of dorms, 100% of libraries, 100% of dining areas, 100% of student union, 100% of common outdoor areas have wireless network access. Students can register for classes online. Administrative functions (other than registration) can be performed online. Undergraduates are required to own a computer.

CAMPUS LIFE

Environment: Village. **Activities:** Choral groups, dance, drama/theater, jazz band, literary magazine, music ensembles, musical theater, pep band, radio station, student government, student newspaper, television station, yearbook, Campus Ministries, International Student Organization 87 registered organizations, 6 honor societies, 5 religious organizations. 6 fraternities, 2 sororities. **Athletics (Intercollegiate):** *Men:* baseball, basketball, cross-country, football, golf, lacrosse, soccer, swimming, tennis, track/field (outdoor), track/field (indoor). *Women:* basketball, cross-country, field hockey, lacrosse, soccer, softball, swimming, tennis, track/field (outdoor), track/field (indoor), volleyball. **On-Campus Highlights:** Bello Center for Information andTechnolo, Chase Athletics and Wellness Center, Unistructure Rotunda, Koffler Technology and Communications Co, Bryant Center, The Bello Center for Information & Technology houses the Douglas & Judith Krupp Library, the Stepan Grand Hall, and the C.V. Starr Financial Markets Center (FMC) featuring real-time stock market data and Reuters 3000. The Wellness Center features a fitness center modeled after private health clubs and a six-lane, 25-yard swimming pool. The Bryant Center houses offices for student organizations around campus including The Archway, the student newspaper, as well as dining options including Subway, South Side Deli, the Scoop, South Cafe, and the Sky Ranch Grill. The Rotunda is a hub of student activity located in the main classroom building, the Unistructure. The Communication Complex houses the all-digital television studio and radio station, WJMF, as well as advanced multimedia editing rooms for use with AVID software. WJMF streams live over the internet and offers podcasts on its website, http://www.wjmf887.com. **Environmental Initiatives:** Recycling Program Green Data Center Purchasing renewable energy credits

ADMISSIONS

Freshman Academic Profile: Average high school GPA 3.3. 18% in top 10% of high school class, 53% in top 25% of high school class, 88% in top 50% of high school class. 70% from public high schools. SAT Math middle 50% range 540-635. SAT Critical Reading middle 50% range 510-600. SAT Writing middle 50% range 510-600. ACT middle 50% range 23-27. Minimum web-based TOEFL 80. Minimum paper TOEFL 550. **Basis for Candidate Selection:** *Very important factors considered include:* academic GPA, rigor of secondary school record. *Important factors considered include.* Class rank, application essay, recommendation(s), standardized test scores. *Other factors considered include:* alumni/ae relation, character/personal qualities, extracurricular activities, first generation, geographical residence, interview, level of applicant's interest, racial/ethnic status, state residency, talent/ability, volunteer work, work experience. **Freshman Admission Requirements:** High school diploma is required and GED is accepted. *Academic units required:* 4 English, 4 mathematics, 2 science, (2 science labs), 2 foreign language, 2 history. *Academic units recommended:* 4 English, 4 mathematics, 2 science, (2 science labs), 2 foreign language, 2 history. **Freshman Admission Statistics:** 5,997 applied, 62% admitted, 21% enrolled. **Transfer Admission Requirements:** High school transcript, college transcript(s), essay or personal statement, minimum college GPA of 2.5 required. Lowest grade transferable C. **General Admission Information:** Application Fee $50. Early decision application deadline 11/16. Regular application deadline 2/1. Regular notification 3/21. Nonfall registration accepted. Admission may be deferred for a maximum of 1 year. Credit and/or placement offered for CEEB Advanced Placement tests.

COSTS AND FINANCIAL AID

Annual tuition $35,591. Room and board $13,240. Required fees $349. Average book expense $1,300. **Required Forms and Deadlines:** FAFSA. **Notification of Awards:** Applicants will be notified of awards on or about 3/24. **Types of Aid:** *Need-based scholarships/grants:* Federal Pell, SEOG, state scholarships/grants, private scholarships, the school's own gift aid. *Loans:* Direct Subsidized Stafford, Direct Unsubsidized Stafford, PLUS, Federal Perkins, privately funded education loans. **Student Employment:** Federal Work-Study Program

available. Institutional employment available. Highest amount earned per year from on-campus jobs $7,378. Off-campus job opportunities are fair. **Financial Aid Statistics:** 81% freshmen, 83% undergrads receive need-based scholarship or grant aid. 46% freshmen, 37% undergrads receive non-need-based scholarship or grant aid. 87% freshmen, 90% undergrads receive need-based self-help aid. 13% freshmen, 10% undergrads receive athletic scholarships. 81% freshmen, 79% undergrads receive any aid. 65% undergrads borrow to pay for school. Average cumulative indebtedness $39,490. **Criteria for awarding institutional aid:** *Non-need-based:* academics, athletics, minority status.

See page 1028.

BRYN ATHYN COLLEGE OF THE NEW CHURCH

P.O. Box 462, Bryn Athyn, PA 19009
Phone: 267-502-6000 • **Financial Aid Phone:** 267-502-2493
E-mail: admissions@brynathyn.edu • **CEEB Code:** 2002
Fax: 267-502-2593 • **Website:** www.brynathyn.edu • **ACT Code:** 3228

This private school was founded in 1877. It has a 130-acre campus.

RATINGS

Admissions Selectivity Rating: 85   **Fire Safety Rating:** 79   **Green Rating:** 60*

STUDENTS AND FACULTY

Enrollment: 232. **Student Body:** 59% female, 41% male, 41% out-of-state, 13% international (12 countries represented). Asian 1%, African American 12%, Caucasian 69%, Hispanic 3%, Native American 0%.
Retention and Graduation: 71% freshmen return for sophomore year. 14% freshmen graduate within 4 years. 25% freshmen graduate within 6 years. **Faculty:** Student/faculty ratio 7:1. 26 full-time faculty, 58% hold PhDs, 0% are members of minority groups, 46% are women. 0% of classes are taught by teaching assistants.

ACADEMICS

Degrees: associate, bachelor's, master's. **Classes:** Most classes have 10–19 students. **Majors with Highest Enrollment:** elementary education and teaching; English language and literature; multi-/interdisciplinary studies, other. **Special Study Options:** Accelerated program, cooperative education program, cross-registration, distance learning, English as a Second Language (ESL), independent study, internships, student-designed major, study abroad, teacher certification program. **Disability Services:** Special programs offered to physically disabled students include tape recorders, tutors. **Career Services:** Alumni network, internships, Career Services highlights include Internships at Bryn Athyn College are developed on an individual basis, and occur in places around the world. Opportunities can be arranged as early as the first year, founded on the belief that this applied learning can help new first-year students chart their academic programs of study.

FACILITIES

Housing: men's dorms, women's dorms, On-campus cottages for upperclassmen. 65% of campus accessible to physically disabled. **Special Academic Facilities/Equipment:** Glencairn Museum Swedenborg Library Swedenborgiana Academy of the New Church Archives John Pitcairn Archives Raymond and Mildred Pitcairn Archives. **Computers:** 100% of classrooms, 100% of dorms, 100% of libraries, 75% of common outdoor areas have wireless network access.

CAMPUS LIFE

Environment: Village. **Activities:** Choral groups, concert band, dance, drama/theater, music ensembles, student government, student newspaper, International Student Organization 15 registered organizations. **On-Campus Highlights:** College Grounds Cafe, Swedenborg Library, Brickman Center for Student Life, Asplundh Field House, Glencairn Museum. **Environmental Initiatives:** Chemical purchase, storage and disposal plan, Recycling program for glass and paper in all buildings. LEED certified construction. Bryn Athyn College Garden, and recycled bike program.

ADMISSIONS

Freshman Academic Profile: 3.2. SAT Math middle 50% range 430-570. SAT Critical Reading middle 50% range 430-550. SAT Writing middle 50% range 420-550. ACT middle 50% range 19-32. Minimum web-based TOEFL 70. Minimum paper TOEFL 520. **Basis for Candidate Selection:** *Very important factors considered include:* application essay, academic GPA, recommendation(s), rigor of secondary school record, standardized test scores, level of applicant's interest. *Important factors considered include:* character/personal qualities, religious affiliation/commitment, talent/ability. *Other factors considered include:* Class rank, alumni/ae relation, extracurricular activities, interview, volunteer work, work experience. **Freshman Admission Requirements:** High school diploma is required and GED is accepted. *Academic units required:* 4 English, 3 mathematics, 3 science, 2 foreign language, 3 social studies or history. *Academic units recommended:* 4 English, 3 mathematics, 3 science, 2 foreign language, 3 social studies or history. **Freshman Admission Statistics:** 456 applied, 45% admitted, 27% enrolled. **Transfer Admission Requirements:** High school transcript, college transcript(s), essay or personal statement, minimum college GPA of 2.0 required. Lowest grade transferable C. **General Admission Information:** Regular application deadline 7/1. Notification on a rolling basis, beginning on or about 12/1. Nonfall registration accepted. Credit and/or placement offered for CEEB Advanced Placement tests.

COSTS AND FINANCIAL AID

Average book expense $750. **Required Forms and Deadlines:** FAFSA, institution's own financial aid formFederal income tax forms (1040 or equivalent). **Notification of Awards:** Applicants will be notified of awards on a rolling basis beginning 4/1. **Types of Aid:** *Need-based scholarships/grants:* Federal Pell, SEOG, state scholarships/grants, private scholarships, the school's own gift aid. *Loans:* Direct Subsidized Stafford, Direct Unsubsidized Stafford, Direct PLUS, Subsidized Stafford, Unsubsidized Stafford, PLUS, college/university loans from institutional funds. **Student Employment:** Institutional employment available. Highest amount earned per year from on-campus jobs $13,780. Off-campus job opportunities are good. **Financial Aid Statistics:** 100% freshmen, 100% undergrads receive need-based scholarship or grant aid. 80% freshmen, 58% undergrads receive non-need-based scholarship or grant aid. 100% freshmen, 100% undergrads receive need-based self-help aid. 71% freshmen, 65% undergrads receive any aid. 45% undergrads borrow to pay for school. Average cumulative indebtedness $8,100. **Criteria for awarding institutional aid:** *Non-need-based:* academics, leadership, religious affiliation.

BRYN MAWR COLLEGE

Best 378

101 North Merion Avenue, Bryn Mawr, PA 19010-2859
Phone: 610-526-5152 • **Financial Aid Phone:** 610-526-5245
E-mail: admissions@brynmawr.edu • **CEEB Code:** 2049
Fax: 610-526-7471 • **Website:** www.brynmawr.edu • **ACT Code:** 3526

This private school was founded in 1885. It has a 135-acre campus.

RATINGS

Admissions Selectivity Rating: 94   **Fire Safety Rating:** 71   **Green Rating:** 73

STUDENTS AND FACULTY

Enrollment: 1,309. **Student Body:** 100% female, 0% male, 82% out-of-state, 19% international (63 countries represented). Asian 13%, African American 6%, Caucasian 35%, Hispanic 9%, Native American 0%. **Retention and Graduation:** 90% freshmen return for sophomore year. 78% freshmen graduate within 4 years. 26% grads go on to further study within 1 year. 19% grads pursue arts and sciences degrees. 2% grads pursue law degrees. 1% grads pursue business degrees. 3% grads pursue medical degrees. **Faculty:** Student/faculty ratio 8:1. 163 full-time faculty, 96% hold PhDs, 17% are members of minority groups, 54% are women. 0% of classes are taught by teaching assistants.

ACADEMICS

Degrees: bachelor's, master's, post-bachelor's certificate. **Classes:** Most classes have 10–19 students. **Majors with Highest Enrollment:** English language and literature; mathematics; psychology. **Special Study Options:** Accelerated program, cross-registration, double major, dual enrollment, exchange student program (domestic), independent study, internships, liberal arts/career combination, student-designed major, study abroad, teacher certification program, A.B./M.A. City Planning 3-2 Program in City and Regional Planning offered with the University of Pennsylvania. A.B./B.S. 3-2 engineering programs with Cal Tech. **Combined Degree Programs:** BA/MA, 3-2 progam in city planning w/U Penn. **Disability Services:** Special programs offered to physically disabled students include note-taking services, reader services, tape recorders, tutors. **Career Services:** Alumni network, alumni services, career/job search classes, career assessment, internships, regional alumni. Career Services highlights include Praxis I for 3 hours per week, Praxis II for 6 - 8 hours per week and Praxis III as a supervised independent study involving 10 - 12 hours per week in the field. These are courses for full credit.

FACILITIES

Housing: Coed dorms, women's dorms, cooperative housing, apartments for single students, Students may live at Haverford. Foreign language houses

available to students studying Chinese, French, German, Hebrew, Italian, Russsian or Spanish. Coed housing is available. Special housing available for non-traditional-aged students. Co-ops, such as Vegan House, are available as well. **Special Academic Facilities/Equipment:** Museum of classical and Near Eastern archaeology, mineral collection, Child Study Institute, on-campus nursery school, Newfeld Collection of African Art, Language Learning Center. **Computers:** 60% of classrooms, 10% of dorms, 25% of libraries, 10% of dining areas, 100% of student union, 10% of common outdoor areas have wireless network access. Students can register for classes online. Administrative functions (other than registration) can be performed online.

CAMPUS LIFE

Environment: Metropolis. **Activities:** Choral groups, dance, drama/theater, jazz band, literary magazine, marching band, music ensembles, musical theater, radio station, student government, student newspaper, student-run film society, yearbook 94 registered organizations, 10 religious organizations. **Athletics (Intercollegiate):** *Women:* badminton, basketball, crew/rowing, cross-country, field hockey, lacrosse, soccer, swimming, tennis, track/field (outdoor), track/field (indoor), volleyball. **On-Campus Highlights:** Thomas Hall (on National Historic Landma, Erdman Hall (designed by famed architect, The Cloister and Great Hall, Taft Garden, Rhys Carpenter Library, Goodhart Theater. **Environmental Initiatives:** We have received two Pennsylvania Growing Greener Grants for watershed improvements under the Environmental improvement and Watershed Protection Act. We are committed to being good steward's of the waterway that pass through our campus. We currently removing all incandescent light bulbs from Campus. We are committed to reducing our consumption of electricity through the use of technology. All capital projects are required to be designed using the appropriate LEED checklist archiving a minimum of 26 points. We are committed to designing sustainability into the renovations of our buildings.

ADMISSIONS

Freshman Academic Profile: 68% in top 10% of high school class, 93% in top 25% of high school class, 100% in top 50% of high school class. 63% from public high schools. SAT Math middle 50% range 590-720. SAT Critical Reading middle 50% range 600-710. SAT Writing middle 50% range 610-710. ACT middle 50% range 26-30. Minimum web-based TOEFL 90. Minimum paper TOEFL 600. **Basis for Candidate Selection:** *Very important factors considered include:* recommendation(s), rigor of secondary school record. *Important factors considered include:* application essay, academic GPA, character/personal qualities, extracurricular activities. *Other factors considered include:* Class rank, standardized test scores, alumni/ae relation, first generation, geographical residence, interview, racial/ethnic status, talent/ability, volunteer work, work experience. **Freshman Admission Requirements:** High school diploma is required and GED is accepted. *Academic units required:* 2 academic electives. *Academic units recommended:* 2 academic electives. **Freshman Admission Statistics:** 2,626 applied, 41% admitted, 34% enrolled. **Transfer Admission Requirements:** High school transcript, college transcript(s), essay or personal statement, standardized test scores, statement of good standing from prior institution(s). Lowest grade transferable C. **General Admission Information:** Application Fee $50. Early decision application deadline 11/15. Regular application deadline 1/15. Regular notification 4/1. Nonfall registration not accepted. Admission may be deferred for a maximum of 12 months. Credit and/or placement offered for CEEB Advanced Placement tests.

COSTS AND FINANCIAL AID

Annual tuition $41,260. Room and board $13,340. Average book expense $1,000. **Required Forms and Deadlines:** FAFSA, CSS/Financial Aid PROFILE, business/farm supplement. Statement of earnings from parents' employer. **Notification of Awards:** Applicants will be notified of awards on or about 3/23. **Types of Aid:** *Need-based scholarships/grants:* Federal Pell, SEOG, state scholarships/grants, the school's own gift aid, Federal Academic Competitiveness Grant (ACG), Federal National Science and Mathematics to Retain Talent Grant (SMART). *Loans:* Subsidized Stafford, Unsubsidized Stafford, PLUS, Federal Perkins. **Student Employment:** Highest amount earned per year from on-campus jobs $2,000. **Financial Aid Statistics:** 100% freshmen, 99% undergrads receive need-based scholarship or grant aid. 6% freshmen, 3% undergrads receive non-need-based scholarship or grant aid. 93% freshmen, 94% undergrads receive need-based self-help aid. 81% freshmen, 72% undergrads receive any aid. 52% undergrads borrow to pay for school. Average cumulative indebtedness $23,579. **Criteria for awarding institutional aid:** *Non-need-based:* academics, leadership.

BUCKNELL UNIVERSITY

Best 378

Freas Hall, Lewisburg, PA 17837
Phone: 570-577-1101 • **Financial Aid Phone:** 570-577-1331
E-mail: admissions@bucknell.edu • **CEEB Code:** 2050
Fax: 570-577-3538 • **Website:** www.bucknell.edu • **ACT Code:** 3528

This private school was founded in 1846. It has a 446-acre campus.

RATINGS

Admissions Selectivity Rating: 97   **Fire Safety Rating:** 85   **Green Rating:** 97

STUDENTS AND FACULTY

Enrollment: 3,502. **Student Body:** 52% female, 48% male, 76% out-of-state, 5% international (63 countries represented). Asian 3%, African American 3%, Caucasian 80%, Hispanic 5%, Native American 0%.
Retention and Graduation: 95% freshmen return for sophomore year. 86% freshmen graduate within 4 years. 90% freshmen graduate within 6 years. 21% grads go on to further study within 1 year. 9% grads pursue arts and sciences degrees. 3% grads pursue law degrees. 3% grads pursue medical degrees.
Faculty: Student/faculty ratio 10:1. 361 full-time faculty, 98% hold PhDs, 17% are members of minority groups, 40% are women. 0% of classes are taught by teaching assistants.

ACADEMICS

Degrees: bachelor's, master's. **Classes:** Most classes have 10–19 students. Most lab/discussion sessions have 10–19 students. **Majors with Highest Enrollment:** business administration and management; economics; English language and literature. **Special Study Options:** double major, dual enrollment, honors program, independent study, internships, liberal arts/career combination, student-designed major, study abroad, teacher certification program. **Combined Degree Programs:** BS/MS 5-yr. program in biology, chem, math, eng. **Disability Services:** Special programs offered to physically disabled students include tape recorders, tutors. **Career Services:** Alumni network, alumni services, career/job search classes, career assessment, internships, regional alumni. Career Services highlights include Bucknell's Institute for Leadership in Technology and Management (ILTM) was founded in 1993 to offer Bucknell students a unique learning experience that bridges the disciplines of engineering and management. Consisting of a two-summer sequence of programs, the ILTM brings together in the first summer 18 of the best and most highly motivated rising juniors in engineering and management to engage in an extremely intensive, six-week, on-campus program that focuses on globalization, ethics, communication skills, critical thinking, teamwork, and leadership.

FACILITIES

Housing: Coed dorms, special housing for disabled students, men's dorms, special housing for international students, women's dorms, fraternity/sorority housing, cooperative housing, apartments for single students, wellness housing, theme housing. 70% of campus accessible to physically disabled. **Special Academic Facilities/Equipment:** Art gallery, center for performing arts, poetry center, photography lab, observatory, 63-acre nature site, greenhouse, primate facility, gas chromatograph/mass spectrometer, electron microscope, herbarium, crafts center, engineering structural test lab, nuclear magnetic resonance spectrometer, 18-hole golf course, conference center, high ropes course **Computers:** 100% of classrooms, 100% of dorms, 100% of libraries, 100% of dining areas, 100% of student union, 95% of common outdoor areas have wireless network access. Students can register for classes online. Administrative functions (other than registration) can be performed online.

CAMPUS LIFE

Environment: Village. **Activities:** Choral groups, concert band, dance, drama/theater, jazz band, literary magazine, music ensembles, musical theater, opera, pep band, radio station, student government, student newspaper, student-run film society, symphony orchestra, yearbook, Campus Ministries, International Student Organization, Model UN 150 registered organizations, 23 honor societies, 13 religious organizations. 12 fraternities, 8 sororities. **Athletics (Intercollegiate):** *Men:* baseball, basketball, cross-country, diving, football, golf, lacrosse, soccer, swimming, tennis, track/field (outdoor), track/field (indoor), water polo, wrestling. *Women:* basketball, crew/rowing, cross-country, diving, field hockey, golf, lacrosse, soccer, softball, swimming, tennis, track/field (outdoor), track/field (indoor), volleyball, water polo. **On-Campus Highlights:** Weis Center for the Performing Arts, Outdoor Primate Facilities, Uptown Night Club, Stadler Poetry Center, Library with Technology and Media Commons, Bertrand Library, Seventh Street Cafe, Elaine Langone Center (student center), Bucknell Observatory, Environmental Center, Samek Art Gallery. **Environmental Initiatives:** In May 2009, the Bucknell University Environmental Center (BUEC) completed a campus-wide environmental assessment of the university's operations, involving over 70 faculty, students, staff, and community members in a highly educational and collaborative project. Teams conducted research on ten indicators of sustainability, including administration/policy, education, energy, water, solid waste, hazardous materials, purchasing, dining, built environment, and landscape. Environmental Connections Requirement: In 2009 the faculty overwhelmingly passed an ammendment to the curriculum that requires all Arts and Sciences students to complete an environmental course before graduating. Energy conservation initiatives: In 1998 Bucknell University transitioned from a conventional coal-burning power plant to a highly efficient co-generation power plant fueled by cleaner-burning natural gas. The new power plant has allowed Bucknell to reduce its greenhouse gas emissions by 40% compared to pre-1998 levels, a fact that was established through the completion of the university's first greenhouse gas inventory in 2006. In 2011 Bucknell hired a full-time energy manager dedicated to indentifying and implementing energy conservation measures on campus.

ADMISSIONS

Freshman Academic Profile: Average high school GPA 3.5. 66% in top 10% of high school class, 89% in top 25% of high school class, 99% in top 50% of high school class. 62% from public high schools. SAT Math middle 50% range 620-710. SAT Critical Reading middle 50% range 580-680. SAT Writing middle 50% range 590-690. ACT middle 50% range 27-31. Minimum web-based TOEFL 85. Minimum paper TOEFL 600. **Basis for Candidate Selection:** *Very important factors considered include:* Class rank, application essay, academic GPA, rigor of secondary school record, standardized test scores, character/personal qualities, talent/ability. *Important factors considered include:* recommendation(s), extracurricular activities, level of applicant's interest, volunteer work, work experience. *Other factors considered include:* alumni/ae relation, first generation, geographical residence, racial/ethnic status, religious affiliation/commitment. **Freshman Admission Requirements:** High school diploma is required and GED is accepted. *Academic units required:* 4 English, 3 mathematics, 2 science, 2 foreign language, 2 social studies, 2 history, 1 academic electives. *Academic units recommended:* 4 English, 3 mathematics, 2 science, 2 foreign language, 2 social studies, 2 history, 1 academic electives. **Freshman Admission Statistics:** 8,291 applied, 27% admitted, 41% enrolled. **Transfer Admission Requirements:** High school transcript, college transcript(s), essay or personal statement, standardized test scores, statement of good standing from prior institution(s). Minimum college GPA of 2.5 required. Lowest grade transferable C. **General Admission Information:** Application Fee $60. Early decision application deadline 11/15. Regular application deadline 1/15. Regular notification 4/1. Nonfall registration not accepted. Admission may be deferred for a maximum of 2 years. Credit and/or placement offered for CEEB Advanced Placement tests.

COSTS AND FINANCIAL AID

Annual tuition $45,132. Room and board $10,812. Required fees $246. Average book expense $900. **Required Forms and Deadlines:** FAFSA, CSS/Financial Aid PROFILE, noncustodial PROFILE. **Notification of Awards:** Applicants will be notified of awards on or about 4/1. **Types of Aid:** *Need-based scholarships/grants:* Federal Pell, SEOG, state scholarships/grants, private scholarships, the school's own gift aid, Federal ACG Grant, Federal SMART. *Loans:* Subsidized Stafford, Unsubsidized Stafford, PLUS, Federal Perkins. **Student Employment:** Federal Work-Study Program available. Institutional employment available. Highest amount earned per year from on-campus jobs $1,500. Off-campus job opportunities are poor. **Financial Aid Statistics:** 100% freshmen, 97% undergrads receive need-based scholarship or grant aid. 14% freshmen, 13% undergrads receive non-need-based scholarship or grant aid. 100% freshmen, 100% undergrads receive need-based self help aid. 3% freshmen, 2% undergrads receive athletic scholarships. 56% freshmen, 61% undergrads receive any aid. 55% undergrads borrow to pay for school. Average cumulative indebtedness $21,163. **Criteria for awarding institutional aid:** *Non-need-based:* academics, art, athletics, leadership, music/drama.

See page 1030.

BUENA VISTA UNIVERSITY

610 West Fourth Street, Storm Lake, IA 50588-1798
Phone: 712-749-2235 • **Financial Aid Phone:** 712-749-2164
E-mail: admissions@bvu.edu • **CEEB Code:** 6047
Fax: 712-749-1459 • **Website:** www.bvu.edu • **ACT Code:** 1278

This private school, affiliated with the Presbyterian Church, was founded in 1891. It has a 60-acre campus.

RATINGS
Admissions Selectivity Rating: 72   **Fire Safety Rating:** 62   **Green Rating:** 67

STUDENTS AND FACULTY
Enrollment: 886. **Student Body:** 51% female, 49% male, 21% out-of-state, 4% international (9 countries represented). Asian 1%, African American 3%, Caucasian 79%, Hispanic 7%, Native American 0%.
Retention and Graduation: 77% freshmen return for sophomore year. 42% freshmen graduate within 4 years. 51% freshmen graduate within 6 years. 23% grads go on to further study within 1 year. **Faculty:** Student/faculty ratio 9:1. 88 full-time faculty, 73% hold PhDs, 10% are members of minority groups, 47% are women. 0% of classes are taught by teaching assistants.

ACADEMICS
Degrees: bachelor's, master's. **Classes:** Most classes have 10–19 students. Most lab/discussion sessions have 10–19 students. **Majors with Highest Enrollment:** biology/biological sciences; elementary education and teaching; management science. **Special Study Options:** distance learning, double major, dual enrollment, English as a Second Language (ESL), external degree program, honors program, independent study, internships, student-designed major, study abroad, teacher certification program, Off-Campus Study:Other semester-away programs available. Academic and cultural events series brings national and world leaders and performers to campus; students earn credits for attendance. **Combined Degree Programs:** BA/MEng. **Disability Services:** Special programs offered to physically disabled students include note-taking services, reader services, tape recorders, tutors. **Career Services:** Alumni network, alumni services, career/job search classes, career assessment, internships.

FACILITIES
Housing: Coed dorms, men's dorms, women's dorms. **Special Academic Facilities/Equipment:** Art gallery, language lab, television station, radio station, satellite telecommunications system, computer labs/centers, electron microscope. **Computers:** 100% of classrooms, 100% of dorms, 100% of libraries, 100% of dining areas, 100% of common outdoor areas have wireless network access. Students can register for classes online. Administrative functions (other than registration) can be performed online.

CAMPUS LIFE
Environment: Village. **Activities:** Choral groups, concert band, dance, drama/theater, jazz band, music ensembles, musical theater, pep band, radio station, student government, student newspaper, television station, Campus Ministries, International Student Organization 65 registered organizations, 5 honor societies, 3 religious organizations. **Athletics (Intercollegiate):** *Men:* baseball, basketball, cross-country, football, golf, soccer, tennis, track/field (outdoor), track/field (indoor), wrestling. *Women:* basketball, cross-country, golf, soccer, softball, tennis, track/field (outdoor), track/field (indoor), volleyball. **On-Campus Highlights:**

ADMISSIONS
Freshman Academic Profile: Average high school GPA 3.4. 17% in top 10% of high school class, 42% in top 25% of high school class, 80% in top 50% of high school class. 85% from public high schools. ACT middle 50% range 20-25. Minimum web-based TOEFL 60. Minimum paper TOEFL 475. **Basis for Candidate Selection:** *Very important factors considered include:* Class rank, academic GPA, recommendation(s), rigor of secondary school record, standardized test scores. *Other factors considered include:* application essay, alumni/ae relation, character/personal qualities, extracurricular activities, first generation, interview, talent/ability, volunteer work, work experience. **Freshman Admission Requirements:** High school diploma is required and GED is accepted. *Academic units required:* 4 English, 2 science, 2 social studies. *Academic units recommended:* 4 English, 2 science, 2 social studies. **Freshman Admission Statistics:** 1,223 applied, 71% admitted, 26% enrolled. **Transfer Admission Requirements:** college transcript(s), statement of good standing from prior institution(s). Minimum college GPA of 2.0 required. Lowest grade transferable D. **General Admission Information:** Nonfall registration accepted. Admission may be deferred for a maximum of 1 year. Credit and/or placement offered for CEEB Advanced Placement tests.

COSTS AND FINANCIAL AID
Annual tuition $28,314. Room and board $8,180. Required fees. Average book expense $885. **Required Forms and Deadlines:** FAFSA. **Notification of Awards:** Applicants will be notified of awards on a rolling basis beginning 2/15. **Types of Aid:** *Need-based scholarships/grants:* Federal Pell, SEOG, state scholarships/grants, private scholarships, the school's own gift aid. *Loans:* Subsidized Stafford, Unsubsidized Stafford, PLUS, Federal Perkins, college/university loans from institutional funds. **Student Employment:** Federal Work-Study Program available. Institutional employment available. Off-campus job opportunities are excellent. **Financial Aid Statistics:** 100% freshmen, 99% undergrads receive need-based scholarship or grant aid. 53% freshmen, 32% undergrads receive non-need-based scholarship or grant aid. 82% freshmen, 84% undergrads receive need-based self-help aid. 99% freshmen, 98% undergrads receive any aid. Average cumulative indebtedness. **Criteria for awarding institutional aid:** *Non-need-based:* academics, art, minority status, music/drama, religious affiliation.

BURLINGTON COLLEGE

351 North Ave, Burlington, VT 5401
Phone: 802-862-9616 x104 • **Financial Aid Phone:** 802-862-9616 ext 110
E-mail: admissions@burlington.edu • **CEEB Code:** 1119
Fax: 802-660-4331 • **Website:** www.burlington.edu • **ACT Code:** 4329

This private school was founded in 1972. It has a 1-acre campus.

RATINGS
Admissions Selectivity Rating: 67   **Fire Safety Rating:** 63   **Green Rating:** 60*

STUDENTS AND FACULTY
Enrollment: 178. **Student Body:** 48% female, 52% male, 46% out-of-state, 2% international (5 countries represented). Asian 1%, African American 1%, Caucasian 83%, Hispanic 2%, Native American 1%.
Retention and Graduation: 40% freshmen return for sophomore year. 16% grads go on to further study within 1 year. 10% grads pursue arts and sciences degrees. 5% grads pursue law degrees. **Faculty:** Student/faculty ratio 6:1. 5 full-time faculty, 60% hold PhDs, 60% are women. 0% of classes are taught by teaching assistants.

ACADEMICS
Degrees: associate, bachelor's, certificate. **Classes:** Most classes have fewer than 10 students. **Majors with Highest Enrollment:** film/cinema studies; multi-/interdisciplinary studies, other; psychology, other. **Special Study Options:** cross-registration, distance learning, double major, dual enrollment, external degree program, independent study, internships, liberal arts/career combination, student-designed major, study abroad, Flexible, self-designed degree program, independent study option. **Honors Programs:** A capstone Degree Project, equivalent to a graduate thesis, is required of all BA candidates. **Disability Services:** Special programs offered to physically disabled students include note-taking services, reader services, tape recorders, tutors. **Career Services:** career/job search classes, internships, Career Services highlights include Action Learning/Internship. There is an internship requirement for each major carrying a minimum of 3 academic credits (96 on-site hours). For each credit, the student must complete 32 hrs of field-supervised, hands-on experience and attend a concurrent seminar which provides guidance and support.

FACILITIES
Housing: cooperative housing, apartments for single students. 100% of campus accessible to physically disabled. **Special Academic Facilities/Equipment:** The main campus houses classrooms, film and video editing labs, a photography darkroom, a college-operated gallery and a community garden. We are within walking distance from the ECHO lake aquarium and science center, the Waterfront Blackbox Theatre and Cinema, the Community Sailing Center, the YMCA, and the Flynn Theatre. As Burlington's College, our downtown location also allows us to utilize multiple local art galleries and music venues for showcasing students arts and talents. **Computers:** 100% of classrooms, 100% of dorms, 100% of libraries, 100% of student union, have wireless network access.

CAMPUS LIFE
Environment: Town. **Activities:** literary magazine, student government, student-run film society 1 registered organizations. **On-Campus Highlights:** Burlington College Community Gallery, Miller Studio, Photography Darkroom **Environmental Initiatives:** New lighting with motion sensors New air handling system New pump system

ADMISSIONS
Freshman Academic Profile: Average high school GPA 2.9. 5% in top 10% of high school class, 19% in top 25% of high school class, 38% in top 50% of high school class. 72% from public high schools. SAT Math middle 50% range

The Princeton Review's Complete Book of Colleges

425-530. SAT Critical Reading middle 50% range 440-575. SAT Writing middle 50% range 420-565. ACT middle 50% range 18-26. Minimum web-based TOEFL 79. Minimum paper TOEFL 550. **Basis for Candidate Selection:** *Very important factors considered include:* application essay, character/personal qualities, interview, level of applicant's interest. *Important factors considered include:* recommendation(s), talent/ability, volunteer work. *Other factors considered include:* academic GPA, rigor of secondary school record, standardized test scores, alumni/ae relation, extracurricular activities, first generation, work experience. **Freshman Admission Requirements:** High school diploma is required and GED is accepted. **Freshman Admission Statistics:** 180 applied, 86% admitted, 25% enrolled. **Transfer Admission Requirements:** High school transcript, college transcript(s), essay or personal statement, Lowest grade transferable C. **General Admission Information:** Application Fee $50. Regular application deadline 8/15. Nonfall registration accepted. Admission may be deferred for a maximum of 2 semesters. Credit and/or placement offered for CEEB Advanced Placement tests.

COSTS AND FINANCIAL AID

Annual tuition $22,410. Room and board $6,670. Required fees $135. Average book expense $1,064. **Required Forms and Deadlines:** FAFSA, state aid form. **Notification of Awards:** Applicants will be notified of awards on a rolling basis beginning 3/15. **Types of Aid:** *Need-based scholarships/grants:* Federal Pell, SEOG, state scholarships/grants, private scholarships, the school's own gift aid. *Loans:* Subsidized Stafford, Unsubsidized Stafford, PLUS, Federal Perkins. **Student Employment:** Federal Work-Study Program available. Off-campus job opportunities are good. **Financial Aid Statistics:** 100% freshmen, 95% undergrads receive need-based scholarship or grant aid. 86% freshmen, 96% undergrads receive need-based self-help aid. 75% freshmen, 76% undergrads receive any aid. 90% undergrads borrow to pay for school. Average cumulative indebtedness $55,240. **Criteria for awarding institutional aid:** *Non-need-based:* academics, leadership.

BUTLER UNIVERSITY

4600 Sunset Avenue, Indianapolis, IN 46208
Phone: 317-940-8100 • **Financial Aid Phone:** 317-940-8200
E-mail: admission@butler.edu • **CEEB Code:** 1073
Fax: 317-940-8150 • **Website:** www.butler.edu • **ACT Code:** 1180

This private school was founded in 1855. It has a 290-acre campus.

RATINGS

Admissions Selectivity Rating: 84   **Fire Safety Rating:** 71   **Green Rating:** 69

STUDENTS AND FACULTY

Enrollment: 3,970. **Student Body:** 60% female, 40% male, 48% out-of-state, 2% international (19 countries represented). Asian 3%, African American 3%, Caucasian 83%, Hispanic 3%, Native American 0%.
Retention and Graduation: 91% freshmen return for sophomore year. 55% freshmen graduate within 4 years. 23% grads go on to further study within 1 year. 4% grads pursue arts and sciences degrees. 5% grads pursue law degrees. 3% grads pursue business degrees. 7% grads pursue medical degrees. **Faculty:** Student/faculty ratio 11:1. 341 full-time faculty, 79% hold PhDs, 12% are members of minority groups, 46% are women. 0% of classes are taught by teaching assistants.

ACADEMICS

Degrees: associate, bachelor's, master's. **Classes:** Most classes have 10–19 students. Most lab/discussion sessions have 20–29 students. **Majors with Highest Enrollment:** biology/biological sciences; marketing/marketing management; pharmacy (pharmd [usa], pharmd or bs/bpharm [canada]). **Special Study Options:** cross-registration, double major, dual enrollment, exchange student program (domestic), honors program, independent study, internships, student-designed major, study abroad, teacher certification program, Cooperative program in Business only. **Honors Programs:** The Butler University Honors Program exists to meet the expectations of academically outstanding students in all colleges and majors who wish to develop their talents and potential to the fullest. Through a combination of honors courses, cultural events, independent study, creative activity and research, it is designed to foster a diverse and challenging intellectual environment for honors students and to enhance our academic community by adding a distinctive note of innovative thinking and interdisciplinary dialogue. **Combined Degree Programs:** BA/MEng. **Disability Services:** Special programs offered to physically disabled students include note-taking services, reader services. **Career Services:** Alumni network, alumni services, career/job search classes, career assessment, internships, regional alumni. Career Services highlights include College of Business assigns each student a career mentor and requires two internships for each of their majors; 75% of Butler undergraduates participate in some form of experiential learning.

FACILITIES

Housing: Coed dorms, women's dorms, fraternity/sorority housing, apartments for single students. 90% of campus accessible to physically disabled. **Special Academic Facilities/Equipment:** Holcomb Observatory, Clowes Memorial Hall (performing arts theatre) **Computers:** 100% of classrooms, 100% of dorms, 100% of libraries, 100% of dining areas, 100% of student union, have wireless network access. Students can register for classes online. Administrative functions (other than registration) can be performed online.

CAMPUS LIFE

Environment: Metropolis. **Activities:** Choral groups, concert band, dance, drama/theater, jazz band, literary magazine, marching band, music ensembles, musical theater, opera, pep band, student government, student newspaper, symphony orchestra, television station, yearbook, Campus Ministries, International Student Organization, Model UN 135 registered organizations, 8 honor societies, 6 religious organizations. 7 fraternities, 9 sororities. **Athletics (Intercollegiate):** *Men:* baseball, basketball, cross-country, football, golf, soccer, tennis, track/field (outdoor), track/field (indoor). *Women:* basketball, cross-country, golf, soccer, softball, swimming, tennis, track/field (outdoor), track/field (indoor), volleyball. **On-Campus Highlights:** Starbucks in the Union, Carillon on Lake Road, Holcomb Gardens, Fairbanks Center, Lilly Music Hall (newly renovated). **Environmental Initiatives:** College of Pharmacy and Health Sciences building will be "Leed Certified-Silver" IDEM grant for campus recycling, $25,000. Completely Green cleaning operations for our custodial operation.

ADMISSIONS

Freshman Academic Profile: Average high school GPA 3.8. 52% in top 10% of high school class, 77% in top 25% of high school class, 97% in top 50% of high school class. SAT Math middle 50% range 540-650. SAT Critical Reading middle 50% range 530-630. SAT Writing middle 50% range 510-620. ACT middle 50% range 25-30. Minimum web-based TOEFL 79. Minimum paper TOEFL 550. **Basis for Candidate Selection:** *Very important factors considered include:* application essay, academic GPA, rigor of secondary school record, standardized test scores. *Important factors considered include:* Class rank, extracurricular activities, talent/ability. *Other factors considered include:* recommendation(s), alumni/ae relation, character/personal qualities, volunteer work, work experience. **Freshman Admission Requirements:** High school diploma is required and GED is accepted. *Academic units required:* 4 English, 3 mathematics, 3 science, (2 science labs), 2 foreign language, 2 social studies, 2 history. *Academic units recommended:* 4 English, 3 mathematics, 3 science, (2 science labs), 2 foreign language, 2 social studies, 2 history. **Freshman Admission Statistics:** 9,682 applied, 66% admitted, 17% enrolled. **Transfer Admission Requirements:** college transcript(s), essay or personal statement, statement of good standing from prior institution(s). Minimum college GPA of 2.0 required. Lowest grade transferable C. **General Admission Information:** Application Fee $35. Regular application deadline 8/1. Notification on a rolling basis, beginning on or about 3/6. Nonfall registration accepted. Admission may be deferred for a maximum of 1 year. Credit offered for CEEB Advanced Placement tests.

COSTS AND FINANCIAL AID

Annual tuition $32,280. Room and board $11,110. Required fees $858. Average book expense $1,000. **Required Forms and Deadlines:** FAFSA. **Notification of Awards:** Applicants will be notified of awards on a rolling basis beginning 3/15. **Types of Aid:** *Need-based scholarships/grants:* Federal Pell, SEOG, state scholarships/grants, the school's own gift aid. *Loans:* Subsidized Stafford, Unsubsidized Stafford, PLUS, Federal Perkins. **Student Employment:** Federal Work-Study Program available. Institutional employment available. Highest amount earned per year from on-campus jobs $3,000. Off-campus job opportunities are excellent. **Financial Aid Statistics:** 99% freshmen, 96% undergrads receive need-based scholarship or grant aid. 14% freshmen, 13% undergrads receive non-need-based scholarship or grant aid. 79% freshmen, 81% undergrads receive need-based self-help aid. 2% freshmen, 2% undergrads receive athletic scholarships. 64% undergrads borrow to pay for school. Average cumulative indebtedness $35,210. **Criteria for awarding institutional aid:** *Non-need-based:* academics, athletics, music/drama.

CABRINI COLLEGE

610 King of Prussia Road, Radnor, PA 19087-3698
Phone: 610-902-8552 • **Financial Aid Phone:** 610-902-8420
E-mail: admit@cabrini.edu • **CEEB Code:** 2071
Fax: 610-902-8508 • **Website:** www.cabrini.edu • **ACT Code:** 3532

This private school, affiliated with the Roman Catholic Church, was founded in 1957. It has a 112-acre campus.

RATINGS
Admissions Selectivity Rating: 69   **Fire Safety Rating:** 88   **Green Rating:** 60*

STUDENTS AND FACULTY
Enrollment: 1,820. **Student Body:** 66% female, 34% male, 34% out-of-state, 1% international (34 countries represented). Asian 2%, African American 6%, Caucasian 83%, Hispanic 3%, Native American 0%.
Retention and Graduation: 66% freshmen return for sophomore year. 46% freshmen graduate within 4 years. 59% freshmen graduate within 6 years. 21% grads go on to further study within 1 year. 16% grads pursue arts and sciences degrees. 1% grads pursue law degrees. 3% grads pursue business degrees. 1% grads pursue medical degrees. **Faculty:** Student/faculty ratio 16:1. 64 full-time faculty, 80% hold PhDs, 5% are members of minority groups, 55% are women. 0% of classes are taught by teaching assistants.

ACADEMICS
Degrees: bachelor's, certificate, master's, post-bachelor's certificate. **Classes:** Most classes have 20–29 students. Most lab/discussion sessions have 10–19 students. **Majors with Highest Enrollment:** business, management, marketing, and related support services, other; elementary education and teaching. **Special Study Options:** Accelerated program, cooperative education program, cross-registration, double major, honors program, independent study, internships, liberal arts/career combination, student-designed major, study abroad, teacher certification program. **Honors Programs:** Cabrini College Honors Program; Honors in the major. **Disability Services:** Special programs offered to physically disabled students include note-taking services, reader services, tape recorders, tutors. **Career Services:** Alumni network, alumni services, career/job search classes, career assessment, internships Career Services highlights include Parallel cooperative education program semester to semester.

FACILITIES
Housing: Coed dorms, special housing for disabled students, women's dorms, Special Interest Housing is available. 97% of campus accessible to physically disabled. **Special Academic Facilities/Equipment:** Exercise Science Lab, Communications center (includes a graphic design lab, radio station, newsroom, and television studio.) Science Education and Technology building with state-of-the-art biology, chemistry, and physics labs, Instructional Technology labs, and research space. **Computers:** 100% of classrooms, 95% of dorms, 100% of libraries, 100% of dining areas, 100% of student union, 95% of common outdoor areas have wireless network access. Students can register for classes online. Administrative functions (other than registration) can be performed online.

CAMPUS LIFE
Environment: Town. **Activities:** Choral groups, dance, drama/theater, literary magazine, radio station, student government, student newspaper, student-run film society, television station, yearbook, Campus Ministries, International Student Organization 32 registered organizations, 18 honor societies, 1 religious organizations. **Athletics (Intercollegiate):** *Men:* basketball, cross-country, golf, lacrosse, soccer, swimming, tennis, track/field (outdoor). *Women:* basketball, cross-country, field hockey, lacrosse, soccer, softball, swimming, tennis, track/field (outdoor), volleyball. **On-Campus Highlights:** Dixon Center- Athletic/Recreation facility, Jazzman's Cafe, Holy Spirit Library, Mansion, Science Technology Education Building, The College also has a Communications Center with a radio station, newsroom, graphic design lab, and a television studio.

ADMISSIONS
Freshman Academic Profile: Average high school GPA 3.1. 6% in top 10% of high school class, 20% in top 25% of high school class, 49% in top 50% of high school class. 56% from public high schools. SAT Math middle 50% range 430-520. SAT Critical Reading middle 50% range 440-530. Minimum paper TOEFL 500. **Basis for Candidate Selection:** *Very important factors considered include:* academic GPA, standardized test scores. *Important factors considered include:* level of applicant's interest. *Other factors considered include:* Class rank, application essay, recommendation(s), rigor of secondary school record, alumni/ae relation, character/personal qualities, extracurricular activities, interview, talent/ability, volunteer work, work experience. **Freshman Admission Requirements:** High school diploma is required and GED is accepted. *Academic units required:* 4 English, 3 mathematics, 3 science, 2 foreign language, 3 social studies, 3 history. *Academic units recommended:* 4 English, 3 mathematics, 3 science, 2 foreign language, 3 social studies, 3 history. **Freshman Admission**

Statistics: 4,015 applied, 75% admitted, 17% enrolled. **Transfer Admission Requirements:** college transcript(s), minimum college GPA of 2.2 required. Lowest grade transferable C-. **General Admission Information:** Application Fee $35. Notification on a rolling basis, beginning on or about 8/1. Nonfall registration accepted. Admission may be deferred for a maximum of One year. Credit and/or placement offered for CEEB Advanced Placement tests.

COSTS AND FINANCIAL AID
Average book expense $960. **Required Forms and Deadlines:** FAFSA. **Notification of Awards:** Applicants will be notified of awards on a rolling basis beginning 2/20. **Types of Aid:** *Need-based scholarships/grants:* Federal Pell, SEOG, state scholarships/grants, private scholarships, the school's own gift aid. *Loans:* Subsidized Stafford, Unsubsidized Stafford, PLUS, Federal Perkins. **Student Employment:** Highest amount earned per year from on-campus jobs $4,160. Off-campus job opportunities are good. **Financial Aid Statistics:** 81% freshmen, 78% undergrads receive need-based scholarship or grant aid. 92% freshmen, 94% undergrads receive non-need-based scholarship or grant aid. 80% freshmen, 84% undergrads receive need-based self-help aid. 98% freshmen, 97% undergrads receive any aid. 77% undergrads borrow to pay for school. Average cumulative indebtedness $22,700. **Criteria for awarding institutional aid:** *Non-need-based:* academics, alumni affiliation.

See page 1032.

CAIRN UNIVERSITY

200 Manor Avenue, Langhorne, PA 19047
Phone: 215-702-4235 • **Financial Aid Phone:** 215-702-4246
E-mail: admissions@pbu.edu
Fax: 215-702-4248 • **Website:** www.pbu.edu • **ACT Code:** 3658

This private school, affiliated with the Protestant Church, was founded in 1913. It has a 114-acre campus.

RATINGS
Admissions Selectivity Rating: 73   **Fire Safety Rating:** 74   **Green Rating:** 61

STUDENTS AND FACULTY
Enrollment: 937. **Student Body:** 53% female, 47% male, 44% out-of-state, 2% international (31 countries represented). Asian 4%, African American 14%, Caucasian 72%, Hispanic 5%, Native American 1%.
Retention and Graduation: 78% freshmen return for sophomore year. 20% freshmen graduate within 4 years. 40% grads go on to further study within 1 year. **Faculty:** Student/faculty ratio 13:1. 50 full-time faculty, 70% hold PhDs, 18% are members of minority groups, 30% are women. 0% of classes are taught by teaching assistants.

ACADEMICS
Degrees: bachelor's, certificate, master's. **Classes:** Most classes have 10–19 students. **Majors with Highest Enrollment:** bible/biblical studies; elementary education and teaching; social work. **Special Study Options:** Accelerated program, double major, honors program, internships, study abroad, teacher certification program. **Combined Degree Programs:** BS in Bible+ MS in Chr Counseling or MS in Education or MS in Org. Leader. **Disability Services:** Special programs offered to physically disabled students include reader services, tutors. **Career Services:** alumni services, career/job search classes, career assessment.

FACILITIES
Housing: special housing for disabled students, men's dorms, special housing for international students, women's dorms, apartments for married students, apartments for single students. 99% of campus accessible to physically disabled. **Special Academic Facilities/Equipment:** Biblical Learning Center Museum area **Computers:** 59% of classrooms, 62% of dorms, 90% of libraries, 100% of dining areas, 100% of student union, 15% of common outdoor areas have wireless network access. Students can register for classes online. Administrative functions (other than registration) can be performed online.

CAMPUS LIFE
Environment: Village. **Activities:** Choral groups, concert band, drama/theater, music ensembles, musical theater, opera, student government, student newspaper, symphony orchestra, yearbook, Campus Ministries, International Student Organization 25 registered organizations, 4 honor societies, 3 religious organizations. **Athletics (Intercollegiate):** *Men:* baseball, basketball, cross-country, golf, soccer, volleyball. *Women:* basketball, cross-country, soccer, softball, tennis, volleyball. **On-Campus Highlights:** Eagle's Nest grill & cafe, Student Lounge, Campus Walkway, Sports Fields, Heritage Hall Lounge.

ADMISSIONS

Freshman Academic Profile: Average high school GPA 3.3. 18% in top 10% of high school class, 39% in top 25% of high school class, 17% in top 50% of high school class. 60% from public high schools. SAT Math middle 50% range 450-580. SAT Critical Reading middle 50% range 470-590. ACT middle 50% range 17-24. Minimum paper TOEFL 520. **Basis for Candidate Selection:** *Very important factors considered include:* academic GPA, standardized test scores, religious affiliation/commitment. *Important factors considered include:* application essay, rigor of secondary school record, character/personal qualities, interview. *Other factors considered include:* Class rank, recommendation(s), extracurricular activities, level of applicant's interest. **Freshman Admission Requirements:** High school diploma is required and GED is accepted. **Freshman Admission Statistics:** 482 applied, 74% admitted, 41% enrolled. **Transfer Admission Requirements:** college transcript(s), essay or personal statement, interview, minimum college GPA of 2.2 required. Lowest grade transferable C. **General Admission Information:** Application Fee $25. Notification on a rolling basis, beginning on or about 7/1. Nonfall registration accepted. Admission may be deferred for a maximum of 1 year. Credit and/or placement offered for CEEB Advanced Placement tests.

COSTS AND FINANCIAL AID

Annual tuition $21,500. Room and board $8,525. Required fees $205. Average book expense $1,200. **Required Forms and Deadlines:** FAFSA. **Notification of Awards:** Applicants will be notified of awards on a rolling basis beginning 2/15. **Types of Aid:** *Need-based scholarships/grants:* Federal Pell, SEOG, state scholarships/grants, private scholarships, the school's own gift aid. *Loans:* Direct Subsidized Stafford, Direct Unsubsidized Stafford, Direct PLUS, Subsidized Stafford, Unsubsidized Stafford, PLUS, state loans. **Student Employment:** Federal Work-Study Program available. Institutional employment available. Off-campus job opportunities are excellent. **Financial Aid Statistics:** 99% freshmen, 96% undergrads receive need-based scholarship or grant aid. 6% freshmen, 6% undergrads receive non-need-based scholarship or grant aid. 98% freshmen, 96% undergrads receive need-based self-help aid. 84% freshmen, 82% undergrads receive any aid. 82% undergrads borrow to pay for school. Average cumulative indebtedness $32,725. **Criteria for awarding institutional aid:** *Non-need-based:* academics, leadership, minority status.

CALDWELL COLLEGE

9 Ryerson Avenue, Caldwell, NJ 07006-6195
Phone: 973-618-3500
E-mail: admissions@caldwell.edu • **CEEB Code:** 2072
Fax: 973-618-3600 • **Website:** www.caldwell.edu • **ACT Code:** 2542

This private school, affiliated with the Roman Catholic Church, was founded in 1939. It has a 80-acre campus.

RATINGS

Admissions Selectivity Rating: 73   **Fire Safety Rating:** 70   **Green Rating:** 60*

STUDENTS AND FACULTY

Enrollment: 1,563. **Student Body:** 67% female, 33% male, 14% out-of-state, 5% international (26 countries represented). Asian 2%, African American 16%, Caucasian 61%, Hispanic 12%, Native American 0%.
Retention and Graduation: 73% freshmen return for sophomore year. 45% freshmen graduate within 4 years. 52% freshmen graduate within 6 years. **Faculty:** Student/faculty ratio 12:1. 80 full-time faculty, 83% hold PhDs, % are members of minority groups, 63% are women. 0% of classes are taught by teaching assistants.

ACADEMICS

Degrees: bachelor's, certificate, master's, post-bachelor's certificate, post-master's certificate. **Majors with Highest Enrollment:** business/commerce; elementary education and teaching; psychology. **Special Study Options:** Accelerated program, cooperative education program, distance learning, double major, English as a Second Language (ESL), external degree program, honors program, independent study, internships, liberal arts/career combination, student-designed major, study abroad, teacher certification program, weekend college. **Disability Services:** Special programs offered to physically disabled students include note-taking services, reader services, tape recorders, tutors. **Career Services:** alumni services, career/job search classes, career assessment, internships.

FACILITIES

Housing: Coed dorms. 85% of campus accessible to physically disabled. **Special Academic Facilities/Equipment:** Art gallery, theatre, library with media center, TV studio, state of the art technology building with Interactive Television Classroom, new student center. **Computers:** Students can register

for classes online. Administrative functions (other than registration) can be performed online.

CAMPUS LIFE

Environment: Village. **Activities:** Choral groups, drama/theater, jazz band, literary magazine, music ensembles, musical theater, pep band, student government, student newspaper, yearbook 20 registered organizations, 15 honor societies, 1 religious organizations. **Athletics (Intercollegiate):** *Men:* baseball, basketball, golf, soccer, tennis. *Women:* basketball, golf, soccer, softball, tennis. **On-Campus Highlights:** Newly opened 60,000 square-foot Recreation Center, Completed renovated Science Labs, Brand new Fitness Center, Radio and TV Studios, Art Department Galleries.

ADMISSIONS

Freshman Academic Profile: Average high school GPA 3.0. 7% in top 10% of high school class, 14% in top 25% of high school class, 47% in top 50% of high school class. 67% from public high schools. SAT Math middle 50% range 430-530. SAT Critical Reading middle 50% range 440-520. Minimum paper TOEFL 500. **Basis for Candidate Selection:** *Very important factors considered include:* rigor of secondary school record, extracurricular activities. *Important factors considered include:* Class rank, academic GPA, standardized test scores, talent/ability. *Other factors considered include:* application essay, recommendation(s), alumni/ae relation, character/personal qualities, interview, volunteer work, work experience. **Freshman Admission Requirements:** High school diploma is required and GED is accepted. *Academic units required:* 4 English, 2 mathematics, 2 science, (1 science labs), 2 foreign language, 1 history, 5 academic electives. *Academic units recommended:* 4 English, 2 mathematics, 2 science, (1 science labs), 2 foreign language, 1 history, 5 academic electives. **Freshman Admission Statistics:** 1,442 applied, 66% admitted, 30% enrolled. **Transfer Admission Requirements:** High school transcript, college transcript(s), minimum college GPA of 2.0 required. Lowest grade transferable c. **General Admission Information:** Application Fee $40. Regular application deadline 4/1. Nonfall registration accepted. Admission may be deferred for a maximum of 1 semester. Credit and/or placement offered for CEEB Advanced Placement tests.

COSTS AND FINANCIAL AID

Room and board $7,000. Required fees $100. Average book expense $800. **Required Forms and Deadlines:** FAFSA, institution's own financial aid form. **Notification of Awards:** Applicants will be notified of awards on a rolling basis beginning 3/1. **Types of Aid:** *Need-based scholarships/grants:* Federal Pell, SEOG, state scholarships/grants, private scholarships, the school's own gift aid. *Loans:* Subsidized Stafford, Unsubsidized Stafford, PLUS, state loans, Alternative Loans, such as Key, TERI, Signature. **Student Employment:** Federal Work-Study Program available. Institutional employment available. Highest amount earned per year from on-campus jobs $1,000. Off-campus job opportunities are excellent. **Financial Aid Statistics:** 83% freshmen, 83% undergrads receive need-based scholarship or grant aid. 73% freshmen, 63% undergrads receive need-based self-help aid. 79% undergrads borrow to pay for school. Average cumulative indebtedness $15,125. **Criteria for awarding institutional aid:** *Non-need-based:* academics, alumni affiliation, art, athletics, leadership, music/drama, religious affiliation.

CALIFORNIA BAPTIST UNIVERSITY

8432 Magnolia Ave, Riverside, CA 92504
Phone: 951-343-4212 • **Financial Aid Phone:** 951-343-4236
E-mail: admissions@calbaptist.edu • **CEEB Code:** 4094
Fax: 951-343-4525 • **Website:** • **ACT Code:** 4094

This private school, affiliated with the Southern Baptist Church, was founded in 1950. It has a 103-acre campus.

RATINGS

Admissions Selectivity Rating: 70   **Fire Safety Rating:** 72   **Green Rating:** 60*

STUDENTS AND FACULTY

Enrollment: 4,954. **Student Body:** 63% female, 37% male, 5% out-of-state, 2% international (29 countries represented). Asian 5%, African American 9%, Caucasian 47%, Hispanic 27%, Native American 1%.
Retention and Graduation: 78% freshmen return for sophomore year. 49% freshmen graduate within 4 years. **Faculty:** Student/faculty ratio 17:1. 227 full-time faculty, 68% hold PhDs, 22% are members of minority groups, 44% are women. 0% of classes are taught by teaching assistants.

ACADEMICS

Degrees: bachelor's, master's. **Classes:** Most classes have 10–19 students. Most lab/discussion sessions have 10–19 students. **Majors with Highest Enrollment:** business/commerce; liberal arts and sciences/liberal studies; psychology.

Special Study Options: Accelerated program, distance learning, double major, English as a Second Language (ESL), exchange student program (domestic), honors program, internships, liberal arts/career combination, study abroad, teacher certification program, weekend college. **Honors Programs:** The Honors program offers students from all major areas of study the opportunity to participate in rigorous study, requiring diligence in reading primary sources and writing original essays thorugh 8 intensive seminars. Honors students progressively investigate a single generative idea using primary texts, drawing upon the expertise of leading faculty. These seminars may be used to fulfill elective unit requirements and specially selected general education requirements. Successful completion of the Honors Program will be posted on the academic transcript and students will be designated as Honors Program graduates at commencement. **Disability Services:** Special programs offered to physically disabled students include note-taking services, tutors. **Career Services:** alumni services, career/job search classes, internships Career Services highlights include Internship elective credit is available for students in all academic disciplines. In addition, a RE-FOCUS program is available which seeks to prepare students in their transition from the academic culture of the university to a professional culture. The program is designed for Juniors and Seniors and offers interactive workshops such as mock interviews hosted by a national employer, business etiquette dinners, resume and interview skills workshops and graduate school information sessions.

FACILITIES
Housing: men's dorms, women's dorms, cooperative housing, apartments for single students. 95% of campus accessible to physically disabled. **Special Academic Facilities/Equipment:** Metcalf Art Gallery, Annie Gabriel Library, Wallace Theater, P. Boyd Smith Hymnology Collection, School of Music Performance and Recording Studios, Nie Wieder! Collection, Lancer Sports Complex and Aquatic Center **Computers:** 40% of classrooms, 10% of dorms, 100% of libraries, 100% of dining areas, 100% of student union, 25% of common outdoor areas have wireless network access. Students can register for classes online. Administrative functions (other than registration) can be performed online.

CAMPUS LIFE
Environment: City. **Activities:** Choral groups, concert band, drama/theater, jazz band, music ensembles, musical theater, pep band, student government, student newspaper, symphony orchestra, yearbook, Campus Ministries, International Student Organization 30 registered organizations, 2 honor societies, 6 religious organizations. **Athletics (Intercollegiate):** Men: baseball, basketball, cheerleading, cross-country, diving, golf, soccer, swimming, volleyball, water polo, wrestling. Women: basketball, cheerleading, cross-country, diving, golf, soccer, softball, swimming, volleyball, water polo. **On-Campus Highlights:** Alumni Dining Commons, Student Activity Center, Wanda's (Coffee Shop), Van Dyne Gymnasium, Aquatic Center. **Environmental Initiatives:** Energy Efficient Lighting HVAC Regulators Strategic Landscaping Considerations.

ADMISSIONS
Freshman Academic Profile: Average high school GPA 3.3. 18% in top 10% of high school class, 49% in top 25% of high school class, 82% in top 50% of high school class. 78% from public high schools. SAT Math middle 50% range 420-550. SAT Critical Reading middle 50% range 420-540. SAT Writing middle 50% range 420-530. ACT middle 50% range 18-23. Minimum web-based TOEFL 71. Minimum paper TOEFL 527. **Basis for Candidate Selection:** Very important factors considered include: application essay, academic GPA, recommendation(s), rigor of secondary school record, standardized test scores, character/personal qualities. Important factors considered include: level of applicant's interest. Other factors considered include: Class rank, extracurricular activities, talent/ability, volunteer work. **Freshman Admission Requirements:** High school diploma is required and GED is accepted. Academic units required: 4 English, 3 mathematics, 1 science, (1 science labs), 2 foreign language, 2 social studies, 2 history. Academic units recommended: 4 English, 3 mathematics, 1 science, (1 science labs), 2 foreign language, 2 social studies, 2 history. **Freshman Admission Statistics:** 2,916 applied, 73% admitted, 43% enrolled. **Transfer Admission Requirements:** college transcript(s), essay or personal statement, statement of good standing from prior institution(s). Minimum college GPA of 2.0 required. Lowest grade transferable C. **General Admission Information:** Application Fee $45. Notification on a rolling basis, beginning on or about 11/9. Nonfall registration accepted. Admission may be deferred for a maximum of 1 year. Credit and/or placement offered for CEEB Advanced Placement tests.

COSTS AND FINANCIAL AID
Annual tuition $25,090. Room and board $8,990. Required fees $1,810. Average book expense $1,664. **Required Forms and Deadlines:** FAFSA, state aid form. **Notification of Awards:** Applicants will be notified of awards on a rolling basis beginning 3/2. **Types of Aid:** Need-based scholarships/grants: Federal Pell, SEOG, state scholarships/grants, private scholarships, the school's own gift aid, Federal Nursing Scholarships. Loans: Subsidized Stafford, Unsubsidized Stafford, PLUS, Federal Perkins, Federal Nursing, Alternative Loans. **Student Employment:** Federal Work-Study Program available. Institutional employment available. Highest amount earned per year from on-campus jobs $1,900. Off-campus job opportunities are good. **Financial Aid Statistics:** 98%

freshmen, 98% undergrads receive need-based scholarship or grant aid. 64% freshmen, 60% undergrads receive non-need-based scholarship or grant aid. 83% freshmen, 83% undergrads receive need-based self-help aid. 1% freshmen, 1% undergrads receive athletic scholarships. 93% freshmen, 87% undergrads receive any aid. 82% undergrads borrow to pay for school. Average cumulative indebtedness $33,807. **Criteria for awarding institutional aid:** Non-need-based: academics, art, athletics, music/drama, religious affiliation.

CALIFORNIA COLLEGE FOR HEALTH SCIENCES

2423 Hoover Avenue, National City, CA 91950
Phone: 619-477-4800
E-mail: admissns@cchs.edu
Fax: 619-477-4360 • **Website:** www.cchs.edu

This proprietary school was founded in 1978. It has a 1-acre campus.

RATINGS
Admissions Selectivity Rating: 60*   **Fire Safety Rating:** 60*   **Green Rating:** 60*

STUDENTS AND FACULTY
Faculty: Student/faculty ratio 17:1. 5 full-time faculty.

ACADEMICS
Degrees: associate, bachelor's, master's. **Special Study Options:** distance learning.

CAMPUS LIFE
Environment: Metropolis. **Activities:** 2 honor societies.

ADMISSIONS
Freshman Admission Requirements: High school diploma is required and GED is accepted. **Transfer Admission Requirements:** college transcript(s), Lowest grade transferable C. **General Admission Information:** Application Fee $35. Notification on a rolling basis, beginning on or about 11/11. Nonfall registration accepted. Admission may be deferred for a maximum of 11 months. Neither credit nor placement offered for CEEB Advanced Placement tests.

COSTS AND FINANCIAL AID
Room and board $7,482. Required fees $1,858. Average book expense $1,300.

CALIFORNIA COLLEGE OF THE ARTS

1111 Eighth Street, San Francisco, CA 94107
Phone: 415-703-9523 • **Financial Aid Phone:** 415-703-9528
E-mail: enroll@cca.edu • **CEEB Code:** 4031
Fax: 415-703-9539 • **Website:** www.cca.edu • **ACT Code:** 176

This private school was founded in 1907. It has a 4-acre campus.

RATINGS
Admissions Selectivity Rating: 67   **Fire Safety Rating:** 85   **Green Rating:** 80

STUDENTS AND FACULTY
Enrollment: 1,450. **Student Body:** 61% female, 39% male, 33% out-of-state, 19% international (47 countries represented). Asian 16%, African American 5%, Caucasian 36%, Hispanic 13%, Native American 0%.
Retention and Graduation: 78% freshmen return for sophomore year. 28% freshmen graduate within 4 years. 44% freshmen graduate within 6 years.
Faculty: Student/faculty ratio 10:1. 81 full-time faculty, 79% hold PhDs, 26% are members of minority groups, 48% are women. 0% of classes are taught by teaching assistants.

ACADEMICS
Degrees: bachelor's, master's. **Classes:** Most classes have 10–19 students. **Majors with Highest Enrollment:** architecture (barch, ba/bs, march, ma/ms, phd); graphic design; illustration. **Special Study Options:** cross-registration, double major, English as a Second Language (ESL), exchange student program (domestic), independent study, internships, student-designed major, study abroad, Sponsored studios and project-based learning with community engagement courses integrated in the curriculum. Learning disability services also offered. **Combined Degree Programs:** MFA/MA, MFA/MBA. **Disability Services:** Special programs offered to physically disabled students include note-taking services, reader services, tape recorders, tutors. **Career Services:** Alumni network, alumni services, career/job search classes, career assess-

ment, internships Career Services highlights include Engage at CCA combines project-based learning with community engagement throughout the curriculum of CCA's diverse programs. An example of an Engage course includes a furniture design class working with Lighthouse Community Charter School to create tables for the school's courtyard atrium.

FACILITIES

Housing: Coed dorms, special housing for disabled students, apartments for single students, theme housingThemed communities and living-learning communities. 80% of campus accessible to physically disabled. **Special Academic Facilities/Equipment:** Logan Gallery on the San Francisco Campus, Wattis Institute for Contemporary Art. **Computers:** 100% of classrooms, 60% of dorms, 100% of libraries, 100% of dining areas, 90% of common outdoor areas have wireless network access. Students can register for classes online. Administrative functions (other than registration) can be performed online.

CAMPUS LIFE

Environment: Metropolis. **Activities:** literary magazine, student government, student-run film society, International Student Organization 10 registered organizations, 1 fraternities. **On-Campus Highlights:** The Nave- San Francisco campus, The Foundry - Oakland campus, Individualized Painting Studios - SF, North/South Student Galleries - Oakland, Wattis Institute for Contemporary Art, Students learn from individuals, the inter-cultural community, and the myriad events and activities sponsored by the Center for Art and Public Life, the CCA Wattis Institute, and the Student Affairs Office. Activities range from social events, yoga classes, exhibition receptions, workshops, and topical forums to programs designed to engage the public and the academic community in a dialogue about the nature of arts and culture. Readings, lectures, performances, issue-based symposia, and panel discussions on the arts, architecture, design, and humanities are offered throughout the year. **Environmental Initiatives:** Largest solar heated facility in San Francisco, named Top Ten Green Building on Earth Day 2001. Curricular content commitment to sustainability with national experts teaching. Ongoing partnerships with Pacific Energy Center, Sustainable Cotton Project, IDSA's Okala curriculum standards, etc.

ADMISSIONS

Freshman Academic Profile: Average high school GPA 3.2. 62% from public high schools. SAT Math middle 50% range 470-610. SAT Critical Reading middle 50% range 450-590. SAT Writing middle 50% range 460-580. ACT middle 50% range 19-27. Minimum web-based TOEFL 79. Minimum paper TOEFL 550. **Basis for Candidate Selection:** *Very important factors considered include:* application essay, academic GPA, talent/ability. *Important factors considered include:* recommendation(s). *Other factors considered include:* rigor of secondary school record, standardized test scores, alumni/ae relation, character/personal qualities, extracurricular activities, first generation, interview, level of applicant's interest, racial/ethnic status, volunteer work, work experience. **Freshman Admission Requirements:** High school diploma is required and GED is accepted. **Freshman Admission Statistics:** 1,231 applied, 90% admitted, 21% enrolled. **Transfer Admission Requirements:** college transcript(s), essay or personal statement, minimum college GPA of 2.0 required. Lowest grade transferable C. **General Admission Information:** Application Fee $60. Notification on a rolling basis, beginning on or about 1/15. Nonfall registration accepted. Admission may be deferred for a maximum of one semester. Credit and/or placement offered for CEEB Advanced Placement tests.

COSTS AND FINANCIAL AID

Annual tuition $38,448. Room and board $7,700. Required fees $350. Average book expense $1,500. **Required Forms and Deadlines:** FAFSA. **Notification of Awards:** Applicants will be notified of awards on a rolling basis beginning 3/15. **Types of Aid:** *Need-based scholarships/grants:* Federal Pell, SEOG, state scholarships/grants, private scholarships, the school's own gift aid, Various. *Loans:* Subsidized Stafford, Unsubsidized Stafford, PLUS, Federal Perkins, state loans. **Student Employment:** Federal Work-Study Program available. Institutional employment available. Highest amount earned per year from on-campus jobs $1,800. Off-campus job opportunities are good. **Financial Aid Statistics:** 94% freshmen, 93% undergrads receive need-based scholarship or grant aid. 79% freshmen, 54% undergrads receive non-need-based scholarship or grant aid. 97% freshmen, 97% undergrads receive need-based self-help aid. 85% freshmen, 84% undergrads receive any aid. 57% undergrads borrow to pay for school. Average cumulative indebtedness $36,690. **Criteria for awarding institutional aid:** *Non-need-based:* academics, art.

See page 1034.

CALIFORNIA INSTITUTE OF INTEGRAL STUDIES

1453 Mission St., San Francisco, CA 94103
Phone: 415-575-6154 • **Financial Aid Phone:** 415-575-6122
E-mail: admissions@ciis.edu
Fax: 415-575-1268 • **Website:** www.ciis.edu

This private school was founded in 1968. It has a 1-acre campus.

RATINGS

Admissions Selectivity Rating: 61   **Fire Safety Rating:** 60*   **Green Rating:** 64

STUDENTS AND FACULTY

Student Body: 10% out-of-state, (42 countries represented).
Faculty: Student/faculty ratio 11:1. 62 full-time faculty, 48% are women. 0% of classes are taught by teaching assistants.

ACADEMICS

Degrees: bachelor's, certificate, master's. **Majors with Highest Enrollment:** dance therapy/therapist; marriage and family therapy/counseling; psychiatry. **Special Study Options:** distance learning, dual enrollment, student-designed major, weekend college. **Combined Degree Programs:** BA/MA. **Disability Services:** Special programs offered to physically disabled students include note-taking services, reader services, tape recorders.

FACILITIES

Housing: 100% of campus accessible to physically disabled. **Computers:** 100% of classrooms, 100% of libraries, 100% of dining areas, 100% of student union, 100% of common outdoor areas have wireless network access. Students can register for classes online. Administrative functions (other than registration) can be performed online.

CAMPUS LIFE

Environment: Metropolis. **Activities:** student government, International Student Organization. **On-Campus Highlights:** CIIS Cafe, Meditation Room, Roof Top Garden, Library, Bookstore.

ADMISSIONS

Freshman Academic Profile: Minimum web-based TOEFL 80. Minimum paper TOEFL 550. **Transfer Admission Requirements:** college transcript(s), essay or personal statement, minimum college GPA of 3.0 required. Lowest grade transferable C.

COSTS AND FINANCIAL AID

Annual tuition $21,285. Required fees $21,285. Average book expense.

CALIFORNIA INSTITUTE OF TECHNOLOGY

1200 East California Boulevard, Pasadena, CA 91125
Phone: 626-395-6341 • **Financial Aid Phone:** 626-395-6280
E-mail: ugadmissions@caltech.edu • **CEEB Code:** 4034
Fax: 626-683-3026 • **Website:** admissions.caltech.edu • **ACT Code:** 182

This private school was founded in 1891. It has a 124-acre campus.

RATINGS

Admissions Selectivity Rating: 99   **Fire Safety Rating:** 65   **Green Rating:** 97

STUDENTS AND FACULTY

Enrollment: 978. **Student Body:** 9% international (32 countries represented). Asian 30%, African American 1%, Caucasian 28%, Hispanic 5%, Native American 0%.
Retention and Graduation: 98% freshmen return for sophomore year. 76% freshmen graduate within 4 years. 53% grads go on to further study within 1 year. 40% grads pursue arts and sciences degrees. 1% grads pursue law degrees. 3% grads pursue medical degrees. **Faculty:** Student/faculty ratio 3:1. 332 full-time faculty, 95% hold PhDs, 17% are members of minority groups, 18% are women. 0% of classes are taught by teaching assistants.

ACADEMICS

Degrees: bachelor's, master's, post-master's certificate. **Classes:** Most classes have fewer than 10 students. Most lab/discussion sessions have 20–29 students. **Majors with Highest Enrollment:** mathematics; mechanical engineering; physics; physics. **Special Study Options:** cooperative education program, cross-registration, double major, English as a Second Language (ESL), exchange student program (domestic), independent study, liberal arts/career combination, student-designed major, study abroad, "Remedial services" are not formally offered. However, remediation is available for students who are deficient in basic scientific knowledge or technical skills. **Combined Degree Programs:** Caltech-UCSD Medical Scholars Program. **Disability Services:** Special programs offered to physically disabled students include note-taking services, reader services, tape recorders, tutors.

FACILITIES
Housing: Coed dorms, special housing for disabled students, apartments for married students, single-unit houses. 95% of campus accessible to physically disabled. **Special Academic Facilities/Equipment:** Jet Propulsion Laboratory, Palomar Observatory, Seismological Laboratory, Beckman Institute for Fundamental Research in Biology and Chemistry, Mead Chemistry Laboratory, Moore Laboratory. **Computers:** 50% of classrooms, 50% of dorms, 100% of libraries, 50% of dining areas, 100% of student union, 50% of common outdoor areas have wireless network access. Students can register for classes online. Administrative functions (other than registration) can be performed online.

CAMPUS LIFE
Environment: Metropolis. **Activities:** Choral groups, concert band, dance, drama/theater, jazz band, literary magazine, music ensembles, musical theater, opera, pep band, student government, student newspaper, student-run film society, symphony orchestra, yearbook 148 registered organizations, 2 honor societies, 6 religious organizations. **Athletics (Intercollegiate):** *Men:* baseball, basketball, cross-country, diving, fencing, soccer, swimming, tennis, track/field (outdoor), water polo. *Women:* basketball, cross-country, diving, fencing, swimming, tennis, track/field (outdoor), volleyball, water polo. **On-Campus Highlights:** Caltech Bookstore, Moore Laboratory, Mead Chemistry Laboratory, Broad Center for the Biological Sciences, Red Door Cafe. **Environmental Initiatives:** Energy efficiency and retro-commissioning programs finances through the use of a green revolving loan fund Greenhouse gas mitigation program and AB 32 cap-and-trade compliance Sustainability focused research: Joint Center for Artificial Photosynthesis, Linde Center for Global Environmental Science, Resnick Institute.

ADMISSIONS
Freshman Academic Profile: 97% in top 10% of high school class, 100% in top 25% of high school class, 100% in top 50% of high school class. 70% from public high schools. SAT Math middle 50% range 760-800. SAT Critical Reading middle 50% range 700-790. SAT Writing middle 50% range 700-790. ACT middle 50% range 33-35. **Basis for Candidate Selection:** *Very important factors considered include:* rigor of secondary school record. *Important factors considered include:* Class rank, application essay, academic GPA, recommendation(s), standardized test scores, character/personal qualities, extracurricular activities. *Other factors considered include:* alumni/ae relation, first generation, racial/ethnic status, talent/ability, volunteer work, work experience. **Freshman Admission Requirements:** High school diploma or equivalent is not required. *Academic units required:* 3 English, 4 mathematics, 2 science, (1 science labs), 1 social studies, 1 history. *Academic units recommended:* 3 English, 4 mathematics, 2 science, (1 science labs), 1 social studies, 1 history. **Freshman Admission Statistics:** 5,225 applied, 13% admitted, 37% enrolled. **Transfer Admission Requirements:** High school transcript, college transcript(s), essay or personal statement, statement of good standing from prior institution(s). **General Admission Information:** Application Fee $60. Regular application deadline 1/1. Regular notification 4/1. Nonfall registration not accepted. Admission may be deferred for a maximum of 1 year. Neither credit nor placement offered for CEEB Advanced Placement tests.

COSTS AND FINANCIAL AID
Annual tuition $38,085. Room and board $12,084. Required fees $1,503. Average book expense $1,323. **Required Forms and Deadlines:** FAFSA, institution's own financial aid form, CSS/Financial Aid PROFILE, state aid form, noncustodial PROFILE, business/farm supplement. **Notification of Awards:** Applicants will be notified of awards on or about 4/15. **Types of Aid:** *Need-based scholarships/grants:* Federal Pell, SEOG, state scholarships/grants, private scholarships. *Loans:* Direct Subsidized Stafford, Direct Unsubsidized Stafford, Direct PLUS, Federal Perkins, college/university loans from institutional funds. **Student Employment:** Federal Work-Study Program available. Institutional employment available. **Financial Aid Statistics:** 100% freshmen, 100% undergrads receive need-based scholarship or grant aid. 3% freshmen, 6% undergrads receive non-need-based scholarship or grant aid. 61% freshmen, 79% undergrads receive need-based self-help aid. 60% freshmen, 60% undergrads receive any aid. 43% undergrads borrow to pay for school. Average cumulative indebtedness $13,442. **Criteria for awarding institutional aid:** *Non-need-based:* academics.

CALIFORNIA INSTITUTE OF THE ARTS

24700 McBean Parkway, Valencia, CA 91355
Phone: 661-255-1050 • **Financial Aid Phone:** 661-253-7869
E-mail: admissions@calarts.edu • **CEEB Code:** 4049
Fax: 661-253-7710 • **Website:** www.calarts.edu • **ACT Code:** 121

This private school was founded in 1961. It has a 60-acre campus.

RATINGS
Admissions Selectivity Rating: 63   **Fire Safety Rating:** 63   **Green Rating:** 61

STUDENTS AND FACULTY
Enrollment: 888. **Student Body:** 49% female, 51% male, 49% out-of-state, 8% international (34 countries represented). Asian 12%, African American 8%, Caucasian 58%, Hispanic 12%, Native American 1%.
Retention and Graduation: 75% freshmen return for sophomore year. 57% freshmen graduate within 6 years. **Faculty:** Student/faculty ratio 7:1. 160 full-time faculty, 100% hold PhDs, 18% are members of minority groups, 44% are women. 0% of classes are taught by teaching assistants.

ACADEMICS
Degrees: bachelor's, certificate, doctoral, master's, post-bachelor's certificate. **Classes:** Most classes have fewer than 10 students. **Majors with Highest Enrollment:** music performance. **Special Study Options:** independent study, internships, student-designed major, study abroad. **Disability Services:** Special programs offered to physically disabled students include note-taking services, reader services, tape recorders, tutors. **Career Services:** career/job search classes, career assessment, internships Career Services highlights include The new career mentorship program "Arts In The world Coaching".

FACILITIES
Housing: Coed dorms, special housing for disabled students, apartments for single students. 98% of campus accessible to physically disabled. **Special Academic Facilities/Equipment:** 7 Art galleries, TV studio, Walt Disney Theater, Roy Disney Music Hall, Sharon Disney Lund Dance Theater, Bijou Film Theater **Computers:** 20% of classrooms, 100% of libraries, 100% of dining areas, 20% of common outdoor areas have wireless network access. Students can register for classes online. Administrative functions (other than registration) can be performed online.

CAMPUS LIFE
Environment: City. **Activities:** Choral groups, dance, drama/theater, jazz band, literary magazine, music ensembles, opera, radio station, student government, student newspaper, student-run film society, symphony orchestra, television station 5 registered organizations. **On-Campus Highlights:** Modular Theater, Permanent Set, Gamelan Room, Main Gallery, Lund Dance Theater, Roy O. Disney Music Hall, Bijou Theater. **Environmental Initiatives:** Recycling Program Boiler Modernization White Energy Efficient Roofing in Ahmanson Building.

ADMISSIONS
Freshman Academic Profile: Minimum web-based TOEFL 80. Minimum paper TOEFL 550. **Basis for Candidate Selection:** *Very important factors considered include:* application essay, talent/ability. *Important factors considered include:* recommendation(s), extracurricular activities. *Other factors considered include:* academic GPA, rigor of secondary school record, character/personal qualities, interview, level of applicant's interest. **Freshman Admission Requirements:** High school diploma is required and GED is accepted. **Freshman Admission Statistics:** 1,186 applied, 33% admitted, 40% enrolled. **Transfer Admission Requirements:** High school transcript, college transcript(s), essay or personal statement, Lowest grade transferable C. **General Admission Information:** Application Fee $70. Regular application deadline 1/5. Notification on a rolling basis, beginning on or about 4/1. Nonfall registration accepted. Credit offered for CEEB Advanced Placement tests.

COSTS AND FINANCIAL AID
Annual tuition $36,166. Room and board $9,293. Required fees $576. Average book expense $1,500. **Required Forms and Deadlines:** FAFSA. **Notification of Awards:** Applicants will be notified of awards on a rolling basis beginning 4/1. **Types of Aid:** *Need-based scholarships/grants:* Federal Pell, SEOG, state scholarships/grants, private scholarships, the school's own gift aid. *Loans:* Subsidized Stafford, Unsubsidized Stafford, PLUS, Federal Perkins, college/university loans from institutional funds, Private/Alternative Loans. **Student Employment:** Federal Work-Study Program available. Institutional employment available. Highest amount earned per year from on-campus jobs $3,222. Off-campus job opportunities are good. **Financial Aid Statistics:** 92% freshmen, 93% undergrads receive need-based scholarship or grant aid. % freshmen, % undergrads receive non-need-based scholarship or grant aid. 88% freshmen, 91% undergrads receive need-based self-help aid. % freshmen, % undergrads

receive athletic scholarships. 71% freshmen, 77% undergrads receive any aid. 67% undergrads borrow to pay for school. Average cumulative indebtedness $39,286. **Criteria for awarding institutional aid:** *Non-need-based:* art, minority status, music/drama.

CALIFORNIA LUTHERAN UNIVERSITY

60 West Olsen Road, Thousand Oaks, CA 91360
Phone: 805-493-3135
E-mail: admissions@callutheran.edu • **CEEB Code:** 4088
Fax: 805-493-3645 • **Website:** www.callutheran.edu • **ACT Code:** 183

This private school, affiliated with the Lutheran Church, was founded in 1959. It has a 290-acre campus.

RATINGS
Admissions Selectivity Rating: 84   **Fire Safety Rating:** 61   **Green Rating:** 60*

STUDENTS AND FACULTY
Enrollment: 2,788. **Student Body:** 56% female, 44% male, 12% out-of-state, 4% international (39 countries represented). Asian 6%, African American 4%, Caucasian 54%, Hispanic 23%, Native American 1%.
Retention and Graduation: 83% freshmen return for sophomore year. 51% freshmen graduate within 4 years. 66% grads go on to further study within 1 year. 46% grads pursue arts and sciences degrees. 5% grads pursue law degree. 12% grads pursue business degrees. 4% grads pursue medical degrees. **Faculty:** Student/faculty ratio 15:1. 166 full-time faculty, 86% hold PhDs, 20% are members of minority groups, 46% are women. 0% of classes are taught by teaching assistants.

ACADEMICS
Degrees: bachelor's, master's, post-bachelor's certificate, post-master's certificate. **Classes:** Most classes have 20–29 students. Most lab/discussion sessions have 10–19 students. **Majors with Highest Enrollment:** biology; business/commerce; liberal arts and sciences/liberal studies. **Special Study Options:** Accelerated program, cooperative education program, double major, dual enrollment, exchange student program (domestic), honors program, independent study, internships, student-designed major, study abroad, teacher certification program. **Honors Programs:** Honors Program **Combined Degree Programs:** 3-2 with Washington University. **Disability Services:** Special programs offered to physically disabled students include note-taking services, reader services, tape recorders, tutors. **Career Services:** career/job search classes, career assessment, internships.

FACILITIES
Housing: Coed dorms, special housing for disabled students, apartments for single students. 90% of campus accessible to physically disabled. **Special Academic Facilities/Equipment:** On-campus pre-school, hypermedia lab, multimedia center and program,film studio, Kwan Fong Art Gallary, Scandinavian Center, Educational Technology Center. **Computers:** Students can register for classes online. Administrative functions (other than registration) can be performed online.

CAMPUS LIFE
Environment: Town. **Activities:** Choral groups, concert band, dance, drama/theater, jazz band, literary magazine, music ensembles, musical theater, pep band, radio station, student government, student newspaper, symphony orchestra, television station, yearbook 75 registered organizations, 11 honor societies, 3 religious organizations. **Athletics (Intercollegiate):** *Men:* baseball, basketball, cheerleading, cross-country, diving, football, golf, soccer, swimming, tennis, track/field (outdoor), water polo. *Women:* basketball, cheerleading, cross-country, diving, soccer, softball, swimming, tennis, track/field (outdoor), volleyball, water polo. **On-Campus Highlights:** Education and Technology Building, Soland Humanities Center, The Apartments, Kingsmen Park, Samuelson Chapel, Will begin construction on a new athletics complex and lab facilities for sports medicine in January 2004.

ADMISSIONS
Freshman Academic Profile: Average high school GPA 3.7. 42% in top 10% of high school class, 76% in top 25% of high school class, 96% in top 50% of high school class. SAT Math middle 50% range 520-610. SAT Critical Reading middle 50% range 500-600. ACT middle 50% range 22-7. **Basis for Candidate Selection:** *Very important factors considered include:* recommendation(s), rigor of secondary school record, standardized test scores. *Important factors considered include:* application essay, extracurricular activities, talent/ability, volunteer work, work experience. *Other factors considered include:* Class rank, alumni/ae relation, character/personal qualities, geographical residence, interview, racial/ethnic status, religious affiliation/commitment, state residency. **Freshman Admission Requirements:** High school diploma is required

and GED is accepted. *Academic units required:* 4 English, 3 mathematics, 3 science, 2 foreign language, 2 social studies, 1 history, 2 humanities. *Academic units recommended:* 4 English, 3 mathematics, 3 science, 2 foreign language, 2 social studies, 1 history, 2 humanities. **Freshman Admission Statistics:** 6,759 applied, 47% admitted, 17% enrolled. **Transfer Admission Requirements:** college transcript(s), essay or personal statement, statement of good standing from prior institution(s). Minimum college GPA of 2.8 required. Lowest grade transferable D. **General Admission Information:** Application Fee $45. Notification on a rolling basis, beginning on or about 12/1. Nonfall registration accepted. Admission may be deferred for a maximum of 1 year. Credit and/or placement offered for CEEB Advanced Placement tests.

COSTS AND FINANCIAL AID
Annual tuition $33,910. Room and board $11,510. Required fees $450. Average book expense $1,665. **Required Forms and Deadlines:** FAFSAStudent Request Form. **Notification of Awards:** Applicants will be notified of awards on a rolling basis beginning 4/1. **Types of Aid:** *Need-based scholarships/grants:* Federal Pell, SEOG, state scholarships/grants, private scholarships, the school's own gift aid. *Loans:* Subsidized Stafford, Unsubsidized Stafford, PLUS, Federal Perkins, Opportunity Loans From Loan Servicer. **Student Employment:** Federal Work-Study Program available. Institutional employment available. Highest amount earned per year from on-campus jobs $1,200. Off-campus job opportunities are good. **Financial Aid Statistics:** 100% freshmen, 99% undergrads receive need-based scholarship or grant aid. 4% freshmen, 4% undergrads receive non-need-based scholarship or grant aid. 81% freshmen, 83% undergrads receive need-based self-help aid. 70% freshmen, 67% undergrads receive any aid. 76% undergrads borrow to pay for school. Average cumulative indebtedness $26,610. **Criteria for awarding institutional aid:** *Non-need-based:* academics, art, leadership, music/drama, religious affiliation.

CALIFORNIA MARITIME ACADEMY OF CALIFORNIA STATE UNIVERSITY

200 Maritime Academy, Vallejo, CA 94590-0644
Phone: 707-654-1330 • **Financial Aid Phone:** 707-654-1276
E-mail: admission@csum.edu • **CEEB Code:** 4035
Fax: 707-654-1336 • **Website:** www.csum.edu • **ACT Code:** 184

This public school was founded in 1929. It has a 67-acre campus.

RATINGS
Admissions Selectivity Rating: 62   **Fire Safety Rating:** 60*   **Green Rating:** 60*

STUDENTS AND FACULTY
Enrollment: 974. **Student Body:** 13% female, 87% male, 15% out-of-state. Asian 0%, African American 1%, Caucasian 4%, Hispanic 15%.
Retention and Graduation: 82% freshmen return for sophomore year. **Faculty:** 0% of classes are taught by teaching assistants.

ACADEMICS
Degrees: bachelor's. **Majors with Highest Enrollment:** heating, air conditioning and refrigeration technology/technician (ach/acr/achr/hrac/hvac/ac technology); international business/trade/commerce; logistics and materials management; mechanical engineering. **Special Study Options:** cooperative education program, distance learning, double major, internships, all students participate in at least one 2-month training cruise around the pacific rim over the summer on The GOLDEN BEAR. **Disability Services:** Special programs offered to physically disabled students include tutors. **Career Services:** alumni services, career/job search classes, internships.

FACILITIES
Housing: Coed dorms. 70% of campus accessible to physically disabled. **Special Academic Facilities/Equipment:** Bookstore, Library, Gym, Swimming Pool.

CAMPUS LIFE
Environment: Activities: student government 16 registered organizations. **Athletics (Intercollegiate):** *Men:* basketball, crew/rowing, golf, sailing, soccer, water polo. *Women:* crew/rowing, sailing, volleyball.

ADMISSIONS
Freshman Academic Profile: Average high school GPA 3.1. 80% from public high schools. Minimum paper TOEFL 550. **Basis for Candidate Selection:** *Very important factors considered include:* rigor of secondary school record, standardized test scores. *Other factors considered include:* application essay, recommendation(s), alumni/ae relation, character/personal qualities, extracurricular activities, geographical residence, interview, state residency, talent/ability, volunteer work, work experience. **Freshman Admission Require-**

ments: High school diploma is required and GED is accepted. *Academic units required:* 4 English, 3 mathematics, 2 science, (2 science labs), 2 foreign language, 1 social studies, 1 history, 1 visual/performing arts, 1 academic electives. *Academic units recommended:* 4 English, 3 mathematics, 2 science, (2 science labs), 2 foreign language, 1 social studies, 1 history, 1 visual/performing arts, 1 academic electives. **Freshman Admission Statistics:** 893 applied, 75% admitted, 30% enrolled. **Transfer Admission Requirements:** college transcript(s), statement of good standing from prior institution(s). Minimum college GPA of 2.0 required. Lowest grade transferable C. **General Admission Information:** Application Fee $55. Regular application deadline 5/1. Regular notification 5/1. Notification on a rolling basis, beginning on or about 11/30. Nonfall registration not accepted.

COSTS AND FINANCIAL AID
Annual in-state tuition $5,472. Room and board $10,544. Required fees $2,270. Average book expense $1,262. **Required Forms and Deadlines:** FAFSA. **Notification of Awards:** Applicants will be notified of awards on a rolling basis beginning 4/15. **Types of Aid:** *Need-based scholarships/grants:* Federal Pell, SEOG, state scholarships/grants, private scholarships, the school's own gift aid. *Loans:* Subsidized Stafford, Unsubsidized Stafford, PLUS, Federal Perkins. **Student Employment:** Federal Work-Study Program available. Highest amount earned per year from on-campus jobs $750. Off-campus job opportunities are fair.

CALIFORNIA POLYTECHNIC STATE UNIVERSITY, SAN LUIS OBISPO

Admissions Office, San Luis Obispo, CA 93407-0031
Phone: 805-756-2311 • **Financial Aid Phone:** 805-756-2927
E-mail: admissions@calpoly.edu • **CEEB Code:** 4038
Fax: 805-756-5400 • **Website:** www.calpoly.edu • **ACT Code:** 188

This public school was founded in 1901. It has a 9678-acre campus.

RATINGS
Admissions Selectivity Rating: 94   **Fire Safety Rating:** 64   **Green Rating:** 60*

STUDENTS AND FACULTY
Enrollment: 17,652. **Student Body:** 45% female, 55% male, 8% out-of-state, 1% international. Asian 11%, African American 1%, Caucasian 63%, Hispanic 13%, Native American 0%.
Retention and Graduation: 93% freshmen return for sophomore year. 31% freshmen graduate within 4 years. 76% freshmen graduate within 6 years. **Faculty:** Student/faculty ratio 19:1. 800 full-time faculty, 80% hold PhDs, 33% are women.

ACADEMICS
Degrees: bachelor's, master's. **Classes:** Most classes have 20–29 students. Most lab/discussion sessions have 20–29 students. **Special Study Options:** cooperative education program, distance learning, double major, English as a Second Language (ESL), exchange student program (domestic), honors program, internships, liberal arts/career combination, study abroad, teacher certification program. **Combined Degree Programs:** BS/MS. **Disability Services:** Special programs offered to physically disabled students include note-taking services, reader services, tape recorders, tutors. **Career Services:** Alumni network, alumni services, career/job search classes, career assessment, internships, regional alumni. Career Services highlights include Cooperative Education Program.

FACILITIES
Housing: Coed dorms, special housing for disabled students, special housing for international students, apartments for single students, theme housing **Special Academic Facilities/Equipment:** Dairy, veterinary clinic, printing museum, art gallery **Computers:** 100% of classrooms, 5% of dorms, 100% of libraries, 100% of dining areas, 100% of student union, 5% of common outdoor areas have wireless network access. Students can register for classes online. Administrative functions (other than registration) can be performed online.

CAMPUS LIFE
Environment: Town. **Activities:** Choral groups, concert band, dance, drama/theater, jazz band, literary magazine, marching band, music ensembles, musical theater, opera, pep band, radio station, student government, student newspaper, symphony orchestra, television station, Campus Ministries, International Student Organization, Model UN 400 registered organizations, 14 religious organizations. 25 fraternities, 14 sororities. **Athletics (Intercollegiate):** *Men:* baseball, basketball, cross-country, football, golf, soccer, swimming, tennis, track/field (outdoor), wrestling. *Women:* basketball, cross-country, golf, soccer,

softball, swimming, tennis, track/field (outdoor), track/field (indoor), volleyball.
On-Campus Highlights: Performing Arts Center, Recreation Center, Julian's Coffee Shop, Spanos Stadium, University Union, El Corral Bookstore.

ADMISSIONS
Freshman Academic Profile: Average high school GPA 3.8. 46% in top 10% of high school class, 83% in top 25% of high school class, 98% in top 50% of high school class. SAT Math middle 50% range 580-690. SAT Critical Reading middle 50% range 540-640. ACT middle 50% range 25-29. Minimum web-based TOEFL 80. Minimum paper TOEFL 550. **Basis for Candidate Selection:** *Very important factors considered include:* academic GPA, rigor of secondary school record, standardized test scores. *Other factors considered include:* extracurricular activities, first generation, geographical residence, talent/ability, volunteer work, work experience. **Freshman Admission Requirements:** High school diploma is required and GED is accepted. *Academic units required:* 4 English, 3 mathematics, 3 science, (1 science labs), 2 foreign language, 2 social studies, 1 history, 1 visual/performing arts, 1 academic electives. *Academic units recommended:* 4 English, 3 mathematics, 3 science, (1 science labs), 2 foreign language, 2 social studies, 1 history, 1 visual/performing arts, 1 academic electives. **Freshman Admission Statistics:** 33,001 applied, 37% admitted, 35% enrolled. **Transfer Admission Requirements:** college transcript(s), minimum college GPA of 2.0 required. Lowest grade transferable D. **General Admission Information:** Application Fee $55. Early decision application deadline 10/31. Regular application deadline 11/30. Regular notification 4/1. Nonfall registration not accepted. Credit offered for CEEB Advanced Placement tests.

COSTS AND FINANCIAL AID
Annual in-state tuition $5,970. Room and board $10,679. Required fees $3,051. Average book expense $1,737. **Required Forms and Deadlines:** FAFSA. **Notification of Awards:** Applicants will be notified of awards on a rolling basis beginning 4/1. **Types of Aid:** *Need-based scholarships/grants:* Federal Pell, SEOG, state scholarships/grants, private scholarships, the school's own gift aid, Federal TEACH Grant. *Loans:* Direct Subsidized Stafford, Direct Unsubsidized Stafford, Direct PLUS, Federal Perkins, college/university loans from institutional funds, Alternative loans. **Student Employment:** Federal Work-Study Program available. Institutional employment available. Off-campus job opportunities are fair. **Financial Aid Statistics:** 71% freshmen, 67% undergrads receive need-based scholarship or grant aid. 3% freshmen, 1% undergrads receive non-need-based scholarship or grant aid. 73% freshmen, 75% undergrads receive need-based self-help aid. 2% freshmen, 2% undergrads receive athletic scholarships. **Criteria for awarding institutional aid:** *Non-need-based:* academics, alumni affiliation, art, athletics, job skills, leadership, music/drama, state/district residency.

CALIFORNIA STATE POLYTECHNIC UNIVERSITY, POMONA

3801 West Temple Avenue, Pomona, CA 91768
Phone: 909-869-3210 • **Financial Aid Phone:** 909-869-3700
E-mail: admissions@csupomona.edu • **CEEB Code:** 4082
Fax: 909-869-4529 • **Website:** www.csupomona.edu/ • **ACT Code:** 4048

This public school was founded in 1938. It has a 1437-acre campus.

RATINGS
Admissions Selectivity Rating: 85   **Fire Safety Rating:** 82   **Green Rating:** 91

STUDENTS AND FACULTY
Enrollment: 20,461. **Student Body:** 43% female, 57% male, 1% out-of-state, 4% international (95 countries represented). Asian 25%, African American 3%, Caucasian 23%, Hispanic 35%, Native American 0%.
Retention and Graduation: 92% freshmen return for sophomore year. 11% freshmen graduate within 4 years. 51% freshmen graduate within 6 years. **Faculty:** Student/faculty ratio 25:1. 532 full-time faculty, 80% hold PhDs, 33% are members of minority groups, 40% are women. 3% of classes are taught by teaching assistants.

ACADEMICS
Degrees: bachelor's, master's. **Classes:** Most classes have 30–39 students. Most lab/discussion sessions have 20–29 students. **Majors with Highest Enrollment:** business administration and management; civil engineering; mechanical engineering. **Special Study Options:** cooperative education program, cross-registration, distance learning, double major, dual enrollment, English as a Second Language (ESL), exchange student program (domestic), external degree program, honors program, internships, study abroad, teacher certification program, Ocean Studies Institute Desert Studies Consortium. **Honors**

Programs: See web site for complete information about The Kellogg Honors College: http://www.csupomona.edu/~honorscollege/. **Disability Services:** Special programs offered to physically disabled students include note-taking services, reader services, tutors. **Career Services:** Alumni network, alumni services, career/job search classes, career assessment, internships, regional alumni. Career Services highlights include Career Development/Counseling: The Career Center assists all students in selecting or changing their major, as well as, what students can do with their major. Students are offered a number of career assessment inventories to assist with career development. The Career Center at Cal Poly Pomona has one of the largest number of organizations recruiting Cal Poly Pomona students in the State of California.

FACILITIES

Housing: Coed dorms, apartments for single students. 95% of campus accessible to physically disabled. **Special Academic Facilities/Equipment:** Center for hospitality management, art gallery, center for regenerative studies, citrus-packing house, meat-processing building, poultry plant, feed mill, beef, sheep, swine, Arabian horse units, horse show arena, and aerospace wind tunnel. **Computers:** 10% of classrooms, 10% of dorms, 100% of libraries, 100% of dining areas, 100% of student union, 60% of common outdoor areas have wireless network access. Students can register for classes online. Administrative functions (other than registration) can be performed online.

CAMPUS LIFE

Environment: City. **Activities:** Choral groups, concert band, dance, drama/theater, jazz band, literary magazine, music ensembles, musical theater, opera, pep band, student government, student newspaper, symphony orchestra, yearbook, Campus Ministries, International Student Organization 280 registered organizations, 26 honor societies, 10 religious organizations. 12 fraternities, 8 sororities. **Athletics (Intercollegiate):** Men: baseball, basketball, cheerleading, cross-country, soccer, tennis, track/field (outdoor). Women: basketball, cheerleading, cross-country, soccer, tennis, track/field (outdoor), volleyball. **On-Campus Highlights:** The Farmstore at Kellogg Ranch, Rain Bird Aquatic,Ethnobotony&Rainforest, W. K. Kellogg Arabian Horse Center, Kellogg House Pomona, John T. Lyle Center for Regenerative Studies, Full name for #2 above:The Rain Bird Aquatic, Ethnobotany & Rainforest Learning Centers Cal Poly Pomona is located on the eastern edge of Southern California's San Gabriel Valley. The University's 1,400-acre campus features lush rolling hills; flowers, plants and trees from all seven continents; a rose garden personally built by W.K. Kellogg; and a beautifully landscaped Japanese garden. The university's aesthetic qualities are one of its best kept secrets. Some of the world's finest architects and landscape architects designed and built the ranch '– a hybrid of architecture, which combined the formal courtyards, gardens and elements of Spanish, Italian and Islamic architecture with the informality of a growing nouveau-riche society. Pasadena architect Myron Hunt (Rose Bowl, Huntington Library) designed W.K. Kellogg's main house. Charles Gibbs Adams whose work included the Hearst Castle Gardens in San Simeon, California was selected to landscape the grounds. Later, the landscape was completed by Florence Yoch and Lucile Council, widely recognized as two of the finest garden designers and landscape architects in California. More recently, Antoine Predock designed the University's administration building with a desert theme. **Environmental Initiatives:** Completed baseline inventory and updated GHG inventory for 2009. Established LEED Silver Standard or Equivalent on all new buildings. Established Energy Star Policy on Purchase of Office Equipment and Appliances.

ADMISSIONS

Freshman Academic Profile: Average high school GPA 3.4. 86% from public high schools. SAT Math middle 50% range 490-620. SAT Critical Reading middle 50% range 450-570. ACT middle 50% range 20-26. Minimum paper TOEFL 525. **Basis for Candidate Selection:** Very important factors considered include: academic GPA, rigor of secondary school record, standardized test scores. **Freshman Admission Requirements:** High school diploma is required and GED is accepted. Academic units required: 4 English, 3 mathematics, 2 science, (2 science labs), 2 foreign language, 1 social studies, 1 history, 1 visual/performing arts, 1 academic electives. Academic units recommended: 4 English, 3 mathematics, 2 science, (2 science labs), 2 foreign language, 1 social studies, 1 history, 1 visual/performing arts, 1 academic electives. **Freshman Admission Statistics:** 40,456 applied, 54% admitted, 14% enrolled. **Transfer Admission Requirements:** college transcript(s), statement of good standing from prior institution(s). Minimum college GPA of 2.0 required. **General Admission Information:** Application Fee $55. Regular application deadline 11/30. Notification on a rolling basis, beginning on or about 10/2. Nonfall registration not accepted. Credit and/or placement offered for CEEB Advanced Placement tests.

COSTS AND FINANCIAL AID

Annual in-state tuition $5,970. Annual out-of-state tuition $17,130. Room and board $11,615. Required fees $653. Average book expense $1,500. **Required Forms and Deadlines:** FAFSA. **Notification of Awards:** Applicants will be notified of awards on a rolling basis beginning 4/1. **Types of Aid:** Need-based scholarships/grants: Federal Pell, SEOG, state scholarships/grants, private

scholarships, the school's own gift aid. Loans: Subsidized Stafford, Unsubsidized Stafford, PLUS, Federal Perkins, college/university loans from institutional funds. **Student Employment:** Federal Work-Study Program available. Institutional employment available. Off-campus job opportunities are good. **Financial Aid Statistics:** 71% freshmen, 75% undergrads receive need-based scholarship or grant aid. 7% freshmen, 6% undergrads receive non-need-based scholarship or grant aid. 97% freshmen, 96% undergrads receive need-based self-help aid. 69% freshmen, 66% undergrads receive any aid. 45% undergrads borrow to pay for school. Average cumulative indebtedness $18,659. **Criteria for awarding institutional aid:** Non-need-based: academics, alumni affiliation, athletics, leadership, state/district residency.

CALIFORNIA STATE UNIVERSITY, BAKERSFIELD

9001 Stockdale Highway, Bakersfield, CA 93311
Phone: 661-664-3036 • **Financial Aid Phone:**
E-mail: swatkin@csub.edu • **CEEB Code:** 4110
Fax: 661-664-3389 • **Website:** www.csub.edu • **ACT Code:**

This public school was founded in 1970. It has a 375-acre campus.

RATINGS

Admissions Selectivity Rating: 61 **Fire Safety Rating:** 60* **Green Rating:** 60*

STUDENTS AND FACULTY

Retention and Graduation: 20% grads go on to further study within 1 year. 10% grads pursue arts and sciences degrees. 10% grads pursue business degrees. **Faculty:** Student/faculty ratio 19:1.

ACADEMICS

Degrees: bachelor's, master's. **Majors with Highest Enrollment:** business, management, marketing, and related support services, other, liberal arts and sciences/liberal studies; psychology. **Special Study Options:** Accelerated program, cooperative education program, cross-registration, distance learning, double major, dual enrollment, English as a Second Language (ESL), exchange student program (domestic), external degree program, honors program, independent study, internships, liberal arts/career combination, student-designed major, study abroad, teacher certification program. **Disability Services:** Special programs offered to physically disabled students include note-taking services, reader services, tape recorders, tutors. **Career Services:** alumni services, career/job search classes, career assessment, internships.

FACILITIES

Housing: Coed dorms, women's dorms. 100% of campus accessible to physically disabled. **Special Academic Facilities/Equipment:** Todd Madigan Art Gallery Frances Dor Theater Calif. Well Sample Repository Geotechnology Training Center Family Business Institute **Computers:** Students can register for classes online.

CAMPUS LIFE

Environment: Village. **Activities:** Choral groups, concert band, drama/theater, jazz band, literary magazine, music ensembles, musical theater, opera, pep band, student government, student newspaper 71 registered organizations, 1 honor societies, 2 religious organizations. 2 fraternities, 2 sororities. **Athletics (Intercollegiate):** Men: basketball, diving, golf, soccer, swimming, track/field (outdoor), wrestling. Women: basketball, cross-country, diving, soccer, softball, swimming, tennis, track/field (outdoor), volleyball, water polo.

ADMISSIONS

Freshman Academic Profile: Minimum paper TOEFL 550. **Freshman Admission Requirements:** High school diploma is required and GED is accepted. Academic units required: 4 English, 3 mathematics, 1 science, (2 science labs), 2 foreign language, 2 history, 1 academic electives, 1 Visual/Performing Arts. Academic units recommended: 4 English, 3 mathematics, 1 science, (2 science labs), 2 foreign language, 2 history, 1 academic electives, 1 Visual/Performing Arts. **Transfer Admission Requirements:** college transcript(s), minimum college GPA of 2.0 required. Lowest grade transferable D. **General Admission Information:** Application Fee $55. Nonfall registration accepted. Admission may be deferred for a maximum of N/A. Credit and/or placement offered for CEEB Advanced Placement tests.

COSTS AND FINANCIAL AID

Required Forms and Deadlines: FAFSA, state aid form. **Notification of Awards: Types of Aid:** Need-based scholarships/grants: Federal Pell, SEOG, state scholarships/grants, private scholarships, the school's own gift aid, United Negro College Fund, Federal Nursing Scholarships. Loans: Direct Subsidized Stafford, Subsidized Stafford, Federal Perkins, Federal Nursing, state loans, college/university loans from institutional funds. **Student Employment:** Federal Work-Study Program available. Institutional employment available.

Highest amount earned per year from on-campus jobs $3,916. Off-campus job opportunities are good. **Financial Aid Statistics:** 85% freshmen, 83% undergrads receive need-based scholarship or grant aid. 72% undergrads borrow to pay for school.

CALIFORNIA STATE UNIVERSITY, CHICO

400 West First Street, Chico, CA 95929-0722
Phone: 530-898-4428 • **Financial Aid Phone:** 530-898-6451
E-mail: info@csuchico.edu • **CEEB Code:** 4048
Fax: 530-898-6456 • **Website:** www.csuchico.edu • **ACT Code:** 212

This public school was founded in 1887. It has a 130-acre campus.

RATINGS
Admissions Selectivity Rating: 70   **Fire Safety Rating:** 65   **Green Rating:** 99

STUDENTS AND FACULTY
Enrollment: 15,316. **Student Body:** 52% female, 48% male, 1% out-of-state, 4% international (46 countries represented). Asian 6%, African American 2%, Caucasian 55%, Hispanic 20%, Native American 1%.
Retention and Graduation: 86% freshmen return for sophomore year.
Faculty: Student/faculty ratio 25:1. 451 full-time faculty, 84% hold PhDs, 17% are members of minority groups, 41% are women. 1% of classes are taught by teaching assistants.

ACADEMICS
Degrees: bachelor's, certificate, master's, post-bachelor's certificate, post-master's certificate. **Classes:** Most classes have 20–29 students. Most lab/discussion sessions have 20–29 students. **Majors with Highest Enrollment:** business administration, management and operations, other; liberal arts and sciences/liberal studies; psychology. **Special Study Options:** cooperative education program, cross-registration, distance learning, double major, dual enrollment, English as a Second Language (ESL), exchange student program (domestic), external degree program, honors program, independent study, internships, student-designed major, study abroad, teacher certification program. **Honors Programs:** Honors in General Education (HGE) Honors in the Major (HIM) **Combined Degree Programs:** We currently offer BA or BS combined with a post-bac credential. **Disability Services:** Special programs offered to physically disabled students include note-taking services, reader services, tape recorders, tutors. **Career Services:** Alumni network, career assessment, internships Career Services highlights include We are most proud of the experiential learning that we afford our students. Typical of the types of projects our entrepreneurship students engage in is the collaboration between teams of students associated with our Center for Entrepreneurship (CFE) and teams of students enrolled in the College of Engineering's Manufacturing Technology Program. This collaboration takes these student teams out of the classroom and into the middle of one of the most important industries (rice) in the University's service region. In March 2007, Chico State Manufacturing Technology Program (MFP) students won the Grand Prize in the prestigious WESTEC (Western Tool Exposition and Conference) Manufacturing Challenge for building a bio-diesel reactor unit that they redesigned from an existing manually operated home bio-diesel kit. The bio diesel reactor unit was originally designed to reduce, reuse and recycle the used vegetable oil and animal fat from Chico State's residence hall kitchen. The project team also considered use of animal renderings from the university farm as a potential feedstock for bio-diesel fuel. While the Chico State bio-diesel reactor unit was built more for research than for commercial production, conversations between our CFE Director and the MFP Director led to a CFE-initiated assessment of the feasibility of alternative feed stock products from which bio-diesel could be produced. A study conducted by the interdisciplinary team of students led to the discovery that rice processing provides an effective feedstock for the production of bio-diesel. The study demonstrated that rice producing areas in Butte and Glenn counties may be capable of producing sufficient bio diesel from rice bran to substantially impact the amount of petroleum-based diesel fuel needed for the industry's production processes. The study concluded that feedstock within the university's 12-county service region would be plentiful, thereby creating new revenue sources for the local agricultural business community and facilitating new opportunities in the area of sustainable farming. This and other types of experiential learning projects that we make available for our students aligns perfectly with the college's vision for a world-class Center for Entrepreneurship at California State University, Chico. It also supports the University's strong commitment and unique competencies in the area of sustainability, it furthers our commitment to provide students with experiential learning opportunities, and it helps us mobilize campus resources that can contribute to the vibrancy of the local economy.

FACILITIES
Housing: Coed dorms, special housing for disabled students, special housing for international students, fraternity/sorority housing, apartments for single students, Thematic housing for honors, engineering, minorities in engineering and science, business, and math. Theme floors include community service, recreational sports, leadership, and Adventure Outings. 95% of campus accessible to physically disabled. **Special Academic Facilities/Equipment:** Anthropology museum, center for intercultural studies, satellite communication dishes, biological field station, university farm, electron microscope. **Computers:** 100% of classrooms, 100% of dorms, 100% of libraries, 100% of dining areas, 100% of student union, 25% of common outdoor areas have wireless network access. Students can register for classes online. Administrative functions (other than registration) can be performed online.

CAMPUS LIFE
Environment: City. **Activities:** Choral groups, concert band, dance, drama/theater, jazz band, literary magazine, music ensembles, musical theater, opera, pep band, radio station, student government, student newspaper, student-run film society, symphony orchestra, yearbook 192 registered organizations, 18 honor societies, 12 religious organizations. 15 fraternities, 14 sororities. **Athletics (Intercollegiate):** *Men:* baseball, basketball, cross-country, golf, soccer, track/field (outdoor). *Women:* basketball, cross-country, golf, soccer, softball, track/field (outdoor), volleyball. **On-Campus Highlights:** Bell Memorial Union, Meriam Library, Turner Print Museum, Humanities Gallery/University Gallery, Wildcat Recreation Center, Nettleton Stadium; on-campus housing facilities; athletic facilities; recording arts studio. **Environmental Initiatives:** This Way to Sustainability Conference AASHE STARS Pilot Project ACUPCC.

ADMISSIONS
Freshman Academic Profile: Average high school GPA 3.2. 35% in top 10% of high school class, 76% in top 25% of high school class, 100% in top 50% of high school class. 87% from public high schools. SAT Math middle 50% range 460-570. SAT Critical Reading middle 50% range 450-550. ACT middle 50% range 19-24. Minimum web-based TOEFL 79. Minimum paper TOEFL 500. **Basis for Candidate Selection:** *Very important factors considered include:* academic GPA, standardized test scores. *Important factors considered include:* geographical residence state residency. **Freshman Admission Requirements:** High school diploma is required and GED is accepted. *Academic units required:* 4 English, 3 mathematics, 2 science, (2 science labs), 2 foreign language, 2 social studies, 1 visual/performing arts, 1 academic electives. *Academic units recommended:* 4 English, 3 mathematics, 2 science, (2 science labs), 2 foreign language, 2 social studies, 1 visual/performing arts, 1 academic electives. **Freshman Admission Statistics:** 15,568 applied, 79% admitted, 22% enrolled. **Transfer Admission Requirements:** college transcript(s), statement of good standing from prior institution(s). Minimum college GPA of 2.0 required. Lowest grade transferable D. **General Admission Information:** Application Fee $55. Regular application deadline 11/30. Regular notification 3/1. Nonfall registration accepted. Admission may be deferred for a maximum of 1 year. Credit offered for CEEB Advanced Placement tests.

COSTS AND FINANCIAL AID
Annual in-state tuition $7,438. Annual out-of-state tuition $18,598. Room and board $10,414. Required fees $1,468. Average book expense $1,666. **Required Forms and Deadlines:** FAFSA, Scholarship Application Form. **Notification of Awards:** Applicants will be notified of awards on a rolling basis beginning 3/2. **Types of Aid:** *Need-based scholarships/grants:* Federal Pell, SEOG, state scholarships/grants, private scholarships, the school's own gift aid. *Loans:* Direct Subsidized Stafford, Direct Unsubsidized Stafford, Direct PLUS, Federal Perkins, college/university loans from institutional funds. **Student Employment:** Federal Work-Study Program available. Institutional employment available. Off-campus job opportunities are fair. **Financial Aid Statistics:** 67% freshmen, 72% undergrads receive need-based scholarship or grant aid. 23% freshmen, 14% undergrads receive non-need-based scholarship or grant aid. 70% freshmen, 74% undergrads receive need-based self-help aid. 1% freshmen receive athletic scholarships. 80% freshmen, 84% undergrads receive any aid. **Criteria for awarding institutional aid:** *Non-need-based:* academics, art, athletics, leadership, minority status, music/drama, religious affiliation.

CALIFORNIA STATE UNIVERSITY, DOMINGUEZ HILLS

100 East Victoria Street, Carson, CA 90747
Phone: 310-243-3600
E-mail: lwise@csudh.edu • **CEEB Code:** 4098
Fax: 310-516-3609 • **Website:** www.csudh.edu

This public school was founded in 1960. It has a 346-acre campus.

RATINGS
Admissions Selectivity Rating: 85   **Fire Safety Rating:** 63   **Green Rating:** 60*

STUDENTS AND FACULTY
Enrollment: 8,698. **Student Body:** 69% female, 31% male, 1% out-of-state, 2% international. Asian 9%, African American 27%, Caucasian 13%, Hispanic 36%, Native American 1%.
Retention and Graduation: 67% freshmen return for sophomore year. 5% freshmen graduate within 4 years. 33% freshmen graduate within 6 years. **Faculty:** Student/faculty ratio 22:1. 252 full-time faculty, 76% hold PhDs, 33% are members of minority groups, 48% are women.

ACADEMICS
Degrees: bachelor's, certificate, master's, post-bachelor's certificate. **Classes:** Most classes have 20–29 students. Most lab/discussion sessions have 20–29 students. **Special Study Options:** cooperative education program, cross-registration, distance learning, double major, dual enrollment, external degree program, honors program, independent study, internships, study abroad, teacher certification program, weekend college. **Disability Services:** Special programs offered to physically disabled students include note-taking services, reader services, tape recorders, tutors.

FACILITIES
Housing: apartments for married students, apartments for single students. 100% of campus accessible to physically disabled. **Special Academic Facilities/Equipment:** University Art Gallery. Olympic Velodrome University.

CAMPUS LIFE
Environment: City. **Activities:** Choral groups, concert band, dance, drama/theater, jazz band, music ensembles, student government, student newspaper, symphony orchestra 65 registered organizations, 6 honor societies, 3 religious organizations. 4 fraternities, 4 sororities. **Athletics (Intercollegiate):** *Men:* baseball, basketball, golf, soccer. *Women:* basketball, cross-country, soccer, softball, tennis, track/field (outdoor), volleyball. **On-Campus Highlights:** Welch Hall, Student Union, Library, Athletic Fields/Home Depot Center, Sculpture Garden.

ADMISSIONS
Freshman Academic Profile: Average high school GPA 3.0. 50% in top 50% of high school class. 84% from public high schools. SAT Math middle 50% range 370-480. SAT Critical Reading middle 50% range 360-470. ACT middle 50% range 13-19. Minimum paper TOEFL 550. **Basis for Candidate Selection:** *Other factors considered include:* recommendation(s), geographical residence, state residency. **Freshman Admission Requirements:** High school diploma is required and GED is accepted. *Academic units required:* 4 English, 3 mathematics, 2 science, (2 science labs), 2 foreign language, 2 social studies, 1 history, 1 academic electives, 1 Visual/Performing Arts *Academic units recommended:* 4 English, 3 mathematics, 2 science, (2 science labs), 2 foreign language, 2 social studies, 1 history, 1 academic electives, 1 Visual/Performing Arts **Freshman Admission Statistics:** 6,486 applied, 15% admitted, 75% enrolled. **Transfer Admission Requirements:** High school transcript, college transcript(s), minimum college GPA of 2.0 required. Lowest grade transferable c. **General Admission Information:** Application Fee $55. Regular application deadline 6/1. Nonfall registration accepted. Credit offered for CEEB Advanced Placement tests.

COSTS AND FINANCIAL AID
Annual in-state tuition $1,815. Annual out-of-state tuition $7,380. Room and board $5,801. Required fees $300. Average book expense $630. **Required Forms and Deadlines:** FAFSA, institution's own financial aid form, state aid form. **Notification of Awards:** Applicants will be notified of awards on a rolling basis beginning 2/28. **Types of Aid:** *Need-based scholarships/grants:* Federal Pell, state scholarships/grants. *Loans:* Direct Subsidized Stafford, Direct Unsubsidized Stafford, PLUS, Federal Perkins. **Student Employment:** Highest amount earned per year from on-campus jobs $3,000. **Financial Aid Statistics:** 94% freshmen, 93% undergrads receive need-based scholarship or grant aid. 23% freshmen, 8% undergrads receive non-need-based scholarship or grant aid. 30% freshmen, 52% undergrads receive need-based self-help aid. 55% undergrads borrow to pay for school. Average cumulative indebtedness $15,112.

CALIFORNIA STATE UNIVERSITY, EAST BAY

25800 Carlos Bee Blvd., Hayward, CA 94542-3035
Phone: 510-885-2784 • **Financial Aid Phone:** 510-885-2784
E-mail: admissions@csueastbay.edu • **CEEB Code:** 4011
Fax: 510-885-3505 • **Website:** www.csueastbay.edu • **ACT Code:** 154

This public school was founded in 1957. It has a 342-acre campus.

RATINGS
Admissions Selectivity Rating: 87   **Fire Safety Rating:** 67   **Green Rating:** 60*

STUDENTS AND FACULTY
Enrollment: 9,788. **Student Body:** 60% female, 40% male, 1% out-of-state, 8% international (86 countries represented). Asian 20%, African American 10%, Caucasian 22%, Hispanic 19%, Native American 0%.
Retention and Graduation: 16% freshmen graduate within 4 years. 43% freshmen graduate within 6 years. **Faculty:** Student/faculty ratio 26:1. 322 full-time faculty, 34% are members of minority groups, 49% are women. 5% of classes are taught by teaching assistants.

ACADEMICS
Degrees: bachelor's, certificate, master's, post-bachelor's certificate, post-master's certificate. **Classes: Special Study Options:** cooperative education program, cross-registration, distance learning, double major, dual enrollment, English as a Second Language (ESL), exchange student program (domestic), external degree program, honors program, independent study, liberal arts/career combination, student-designed major, study abroad, teacher certification program, weekend college, Year round operation with state supported summer quarter. Joint Master's Degree in Marine Science offered at Moss Landing Marine Lab. Joint MFA in Creative Writing in summer. Overseas MBA programs in Hong Kong, Moscow, Singapore, and Vienna. **Disability Services:** Special programs offered to physically disabled students include note-taking services, reader services, tape recorders, tutors. **Career Services:** alumni services, career/job search classes, career assessment, internships.

FACILITIES
Housing: apartments for single students, 95% of campus accessible to physically disabled. **Special Academic Facilities/Equipment:** Anthropology museum, art gallery, scanning electron microscope facility, marine lab, ecological field station, geology summer camp. **Computers:** Students can register for classes online. Administrative functions (other than registration) can be performed online.

CAMPUS LIFE
Environment: City. **Activities:** Choral groups, concert band, dance, drama/theater, jazz band, literary magazine, music ensembles, musical theater, opera, pep band, radio station, student government, student newspaper, symphony orchestra, television station 100 registered organizations, 2 honor societies, 2 religious organizations. 7 fraternities, 7 sororities. **Athletics (Intercollegiate):** *Men:* baseball, basketball, cross country, golf, soccer. *Women:* basketball, cross-country, golf, soccer, softball, swimming, volleyball, water polo. **On-Campus Highlights:** University Union, Gymnasium/Pools, Warren Hall /Administration, University Theatre, University Art Gallery.

ADMISSIONS
Freshman Academic Profile: Average high school GPA 3.1. SAT Math middle 50% range 400-510. SAT Critical Reading middle 50% range 400-500. SAT Writing middle 50% range 410-500. ACT middle 50% range 16-21. Minimum paper TOEFL 525. **Basis for Candidate Selection:** *Very important factors considered include:* academic GPA, rigor of secondary school record, standardized test scores. *Other factors considered include:* recommendation(s), state residency. **Freshman Admission Requirements:** High school diploma is required and GED is accepted. *Academic units required:* 4 English, 3 mathematics, 2 science, (2 science labs), 2 foreign language, 1 social studies, 1 history, 1 academic electives, 1 Visual/Performing Arts. *Academic units recommended:* 4 English, 3 mathematics, 2 science, (2 science labs), 2 foreign language, 1 social studies, 1 history, 1 academic electives, 1 Visual/Performing Arts **Freshman Admission Statistics:** 10,749 applied, 36% admitted, 32% enrolled. **Transfer Admission Requirements:** college transcript(s), statement of good standing from prior institution(s). Minimum college GPA of 2.0 required. Lowest grade transferable D. **General Admission Information:** Application Fee $55. Early decision application deadline 3/15. Regular application deadline 6/30. Notification on a rolling basis, beginning on or about 3/15. Nonfall registration accepted. Admission may be deferred for a maximum of 2 quarters. Credit and/or placement offered for CEEB Advanced Placement tests.

COSTS AND FINANCIAL AID
Annual in-state tuition $5,091. Annual out-of-state tuition $14,019. Room and board $11,042. Required fees. Average book expense $1,734. **Required Forms and Deadlines:** FAFSA. **Notification of Awards:** Applicants will be

notified of awards on a rolling basis beginning 3/15. **Types of Aid:** *Need-based scholarships/grants:* Federal Pell, SEOG, state scholarships/grants, private scholarships, the school's own gift aid. *Loans:* Subsidized Stafford, Unsubsidized Stafford, PLUS, Federal Perkins. **Student Employment:** Federal Work-Study Program available. Institutional employment available. Off-campus job opportunities are excellent. **Financial Aid Statistics:** 83% freshmen, 83% undergrads receive need-based scholarship or grant aid. 63% freshmen, 62% undergrads receive need-based self-help aid. 43% freshmen, 42% undergrads receive any aid. 34% undergrads borrow to pay for school. Average cumulative indebtedness $11,643. **Criteria for awarding institutional aid:** *Non-need-based:* academics.

CALIFORNIA STATE UNIVERSITY, FRESNO

5150 North Maple Ave. M/S JA 57, Fresno, CA 93740-8026
Phone: 559-278-2261 • **Financial Aid Phone:** 559-278-2182
E-mail: admissions@csufresno.edu • **CEEB Code:** 4312
Fax: 559-278-4812 • **Website:** www.csufresno.edu • **ACT Code:** 266

This public school was founded in 1911. It has a 388-acre campus.

RATINGS
Admissions Selectivity Rating: 74   **Fire Safety Rating:** 68   **Green Rating:** 86

STUDENTS AND FACULTY
Enrollment: 18,784. **Student Body:** 57% female, 43% male, 0% out-of-state, 3% international (116 countries represented). Asian 15%, African American 5%, Caucasian 30%, Hispanic 38%, Native American 1%.
Retention and Graduation: 14% freshmen graduate within 4 years. 49% freshmen graduate within 6 years. **Faculty:** Student/faculty ratio 22:1. 624 full-time faculty, 95% hold PhDs, 29% are members of minority groups, 42% are women. 8% of classes are taught by teaching assistants.

ACADEMICS
Degrees: bachelor's, master's. **Classes:** Most classes have 20–29 students. Most lab/discussion sessions have 20–29 students. **Majors with Highest Enrollment:** health services/allied health/health sciences; liberal arts and sciences/liberal studies. **Special Study Options:** Accelerated program, cooperative education program, cross-registration, distance learning, double major, dual enrollment, English as a Second Language (ESL), exchange student program (domestic), honors program, independent study, internships, student-designed major, study abroad, teacher certification program. **Disability Services:** Special programs offered to physically disabled students include note-taking services, reader services, tape recorders, tutors.

FACILITIES
Housing: Coed dorms, men's dorms, women's dorms, fraternity/sorority housing. 100% of campus accessible to physically disabled. **Special Academic Facilities/Equipment:** Marine lab, Downing Planeterium. **Computers:** 100% of classrooms, 100% of dorms, 100% of libraries, 100% of dining areas, 100% of student union, 20% of common outdoor areas have wireless network access. Students can register for classes online. Administrative functions (other than registration) can be performed online. Undergraduates are required to own a computer.

CAMPUS LIFE
Environment: Metropolis. **Activities:** Choral groups, concert band, dance, drama/theater, jazz band, marching band, music ensembles, musical theater, radio station, student government, student newspaper, symphony orchestra, television station, International Student Organization 250 registered organizations, 21 honor societies, 11 religious organizations. 19 fraternities, 13 sororities. **Athletics (Intercollegiate):** *Men:* baseball, basketball, cheerleading, cross-country, football, golf, tennis, track/field (outdoor). *Women:* basketball, cheerleading, cross-country, diving, equestrian sports, golf, lacrosse, light weight football, soccer, softball, swimming, tennis, track/field (outdoor), volleyball. **On-Campus Highlights:** Savemart Events Center, Downing Planetarium, Kennel Bookstore, New Ciminology Center, Henry Madden Library, Please check out our website for more inforamtion: www.gotofresnostate.com. **Environmental Initiatives:** Solar Photovoltaic Canopy Parking Structure (Lot V) This structure is a 1.1 megawatt solar system, making it the largest photovoltaic paneled parting installation at a U.S. university. Completed in the fall of 2007, the structure was estimated to provide 20% of the core campus power. The system offsets approximately 950 metric tons of carbon monoxide emissions " that is equivalent to planting over 24,300 trees or eliminating from our road systems over 200 vehicles a year! On February 20, 2009, students, faculty and members of the community were in attendance of the long-awaited opening of the new Henry Madden Library. With the wide range of attractive features such as electronic compact bookshelves, hi-definition flat screens, comfortably furnished study

rooms, and of course the ever-popular Starbucks café, its no wonder why the library has become the new focal point of Fresno State. However, many people are still unaware of the sustainable features of the Henry Madden Library that, despite the structure's size, make it the most environmentally friendly building on campus. These features include: One of the largest collections of movable stacks in the country, which helps to minimize the overall carbon footprint of the library Highest standards of energy efficient insulation Centralized HVAC which controls air handling areas of the library Thermal comfort managed using fresh, outdoor air rather than conditioned air when appropriate Ubiquitous compact fluorescent lighting Motion sensor activated lighting system in conference and private study rooms North side made entirely of class providing year-round natural lighting, thus lowering energy usage and costs Recycling of the old building materials during demolition Furniture made from recycled materials Carpet tiles designed, produced and disposed of in a cradle-to-cradle process Building materials that were sourced from local manufacturers (i.e. granite and wood used to furnish the library) Newly renovated Peace Garden, which contains native species that require no irrigation and help to manage storm water, thus maximizing efficiency of water use! The University understands the importance of water as a finite resource and has been taking a leadership role in developing ways to utilize water more efficiently by establishing the International Center for Water Technology (ICWT). In 2007, the campus reduced the amount of water used to irrigate the 380-acre academic core of campus by an estimated 33%. This was done through alternative watering schedules, repairs to failing irrigation lines and the installation of better controls. Phase II of the planned Campus Utility Infrastructure Replacement will include new water mains that will provide non-potable water to campus irrigation systems.

ADMISSIONS
Freshman Academic Profile: Average high school GPA 3.3. 15% in top 10% of high school class, 80% in top 25% of high school class, 100% in top 50% of high school class. 99% from public high schools. SAT Math middle 50% range 410-530. SAT Critical Reading middle 50% range 400-510. SAT Writing middle 50% range 400-510. ACT middle 50% range 16-22. Minimum web-based TOEFL 61. Minimum paper TOEFL 500. **Basis for Candidate Selection:** *Very important factors considered include:* academic GPA, rigor of secondary school record, standardized test scores. **Freshman Admission Requirements:** High school diploma is required and GED is accepted. *Academic units required:* 4 English, 3 mathematics, 1 science, (1 science labs), 2 foreign language, 1 social studies, 1 history, 1 visual/performing arts, 1 academic electives. *Academic units recommended:* 4 English, 3 mathematics, 1 science, (1 science labs), 2 foreign language, 1 social studies, 1 history, 1 visual/performing arts, 1 academic electives. **Freshman Admission Statistics:** 15,482 applied, 60% admitted, 31% enrolled. **Transfer Admission Requirements:** college transcript(s), minimum college GPA of 2.4 required. Lowest grade transferable D. **General Admission Information:** Application Fee $55. Regular application deadline 11/30. Notification on a rolling basis, beginning on or about 8/1. Nonfall registration accepted. Credit offered for CEEB Advanced Placement tests.

COSTS AND FINANCIAL AID
Annual in-state tuition $5,472. Annual out-of-state tuition $11,160. Room and board $10,550. Required fees $790. Average book expense $1,256. **Required Forms and Deadlines:** FAFSA. **Notification of Awards:** Applicants will be notified of awards on a rolling basis beginning 4/1. **Types of Aid:** *Need-based scholarships/grants:* Federal Pell, SEOG, state scholarships/grants, private scholarships, the school's own gift aid. *Loans:* Subsidized Stafford, Unsubsidized Stafford, PLUS, Federal Perkins, Federal Nursing, college/university loans from institutional funds. **Student Employment:** Federal Work-Study Program available. Institutional employment available. Off-campus job opportunities are good. **Financial Aid Statistics:** 83% freshmen, 80% undergrads receive need-based scholarship or grant aid. 2% freshmen, 9% undergrads receive non-need-based scholarship or grant aid. 69% freshmen, 82% undergrads receive need-based self-help aid. 3% freshmen, 2% undergrads receive athletic scholarships. 76% freshmen, 78% undergrads receive any aid. 79% undergrads borrow to pay for school. Average cumulative indebtedness $11,349. **Criteria for awarding institutional aid:** *Non-need-based:* academics, art, athletics, leadership, music/drama, state/district residency.

CALIFORNIA STATE UNIVERSITY, FULLERTON

800 North State College Boulevard, Fullerton, CA 92834-6900
Phone: 657-278-2370 • **Financial Aid Phone:** 657-278-3125
E-mail: admissions@fullerton.edu • **CEEB Code:** 4589
Fax: 657-278-2356 • **Website:** www.fullerton.edu • **ACT Code:** 355

This public school was founded in 1957. It has a 225-acre campus.

RATINGS
Admissions Selectivity Rating: 87   **Fire Safety Rating:** 77   **Green Rating:** 60*

STUDENTS AND FACULTY
Enrollment: 32,278. **Student Body:** 56% female, 44% male, 1% out-of-state, 4% international (75 countries represented). Asian 22%, African American 2%, Caucasian 28%, Hispanic 36%, Native American 0%.
Retention and Graduation: 88% freshmen return for sophomore year. 13% freshmen graduate within 4 years. **Faculty:** Student/faculty ratio 25:1. 880 full-time faculty, 87% hold PhDs, 26% are members of minority groups, 48% are women. 0% of classes are taught by teaching assistants.

ACADEMICS
Degrees: bachelor's, master's. **Classes:** Most classes have 20–29 students. Most lab/discussion sessions have 20–29 students. **Special Study Options:** cooperative education program, double major, honors program, independent study, internships, student-designed major, study abroad. **Disability Services:** Special programs offered to physically disabled students include note-taking services, reader services, tape recorders. **Career Services:** alumni services, career/job search classes, career assessment, internships.

FACILITIES
Housing: fraternity/sorority housing, apartments for single students. 90% of campus accessible to physically disabled. **Computers:** Students can register for classes online. Administrative functions (other than registration) can be performed online.

CAMPUS LIFE
Environment: Activities: Choral groups, concert band, dance, drama/theater, jazz band, music ensembles, musical theater, radio station, student government, student newspaper. **Athletics (Intercollegiate):** *Men:* baseball, basketball, cross-country, fencing, soccer, track/field (outdoor), wrestling. *Women:* basketball, cross-country, fencing, gymnastics, soccer, softball, tennis, track/field (outdoor), volleyball. **On-Campus Highlights:** Fullerton Arboretum, 5 Starbucks Coffee shops, Titan Student Union Underground

ADMISSIONS
Freshman Academic Profile: Average high school GPA 3.4. 19% in top 10% of high school class, 60% in top 25% of high school class, 92% in top 50% of high school class. 89% from public high schools. SAT Math middle 50% range 470-580. SAT Critical Reading middle 50% range 450-550. ACT middle 50% range 19-24. Minimum web-based TOEFL 61. Minimum paper TOEFL 500. **Basis for Candidate Selection:** *Very important factors considered include:* rigor of secondary school record, standardized test scores. *Other factors considered include:* state residency. **Freshman Admission Requirements:** High school diploma is required and GED is accepted. *Academic units required:* 2 science, (2 science labs), 2 history, 1 academic electives, 1 Visual/Performing Arts. 2 science, (2 science labs), 2 history, 1 academic electives, 1 Visual/Performing Arts **Freshman Admission Statistics:** 38,900 applied, 46% admitted, 25% enrolled. **Transfer Admission Requirements:** college transcript(s), statement of good standing from prior institution(s). Minimum college GPA of 2.0 required. Lowest grade transferable C. **General Admission Information:** Application Fee $55. Regular application deadline 4/15. Notification on a rolling basis, beginning on or about 1/1. Nonfall registration accepted. Credit and/or placement offered for CEEB Advanced Placement tests.

COSTS AND FINANCIAL AID
Annual in-state tuition $6,182. Annual out-of-state tuition $17,342. Room and board $12,096. Required fees. Average book expense $1,720. **Required Forms and Deadlines:** FAFSA, state aid form. **Notification of Awards:** Applicants will be notified of awards on a rolling basis beginning 3/1. **Types of Aid:** *Need-based scholarships/grants:* Federal Pell, SEOG, state scholarships/grants, private scholarships, the school's own gift aid. *Loans:* Subsidized Stafford, Unsubsidized Stafford, PLUS, Federal Perkins, college/university loans from institutional funds. **Student Employment:** Federal Work-Study Program available. Institutional employment available. Off-campus job opportunities are good. **Financial Aid Statistics:** 80% freshmen, 81% undergrads receive need-based scholarship or grant aid. 15% freshmen, 8% undergrads receive non-need-based scholarship or grant aid. 44% freshmen, 46% undergrads receive need-based self-help aid. 1% freshmen, 1% undergrads receive athletic scholarships. 60% freshmen, 55% undergrads receive any aid. 40% undergrads borrow to pay

for school. Average cumulative indebtedness $14,904. **Criteria for awarding institutional aid:** *Non-need-based:* academics.

CALIFORNIA STATE UNIVERSITY, LONG BEACH

1250 Bellflower Boulevard, Long Beach, CA 90840
Phone: 562-985-5471
E-mail: eslb@csulb.edu • **CEEB Code:** 4389
Fax: 562-985-4973 • **Website:** www.csulb.edu

This public school was founded in 1949. It has a 322-acre campus.

RATINGS
Admissions Selectivity Rating: 92   **Fire Safety Rating:** 62   **Green Rating:** 60*

STUDENTS AND FACULTY
Enrollment: 30,931. **Student Body:** 57% female, 43% male, 1% out-of-state, 5% international. Asian 22%, African American 4%, Caucasian 23%, Hispanic 35%, Native American 1%.
Retention and Graduation: 88% freshmen return for sophomore year. 12% freshmen graduate within 4 years. 57% freshmen graduate within 6 years. **Faculty:** Student/faculty ratio 22:1. 917 full-time faculty, 87% hold PhDs, 31% are members of minority groups, 46% are women. 8% of classes are taught by teaching assistants.

ACADEMICS
Degrees: bachelor's, master's, post-bachelor's certificate. **Classes:** Most classes have 20–29 students. Most lab/discussion sessions have 20–29 students. **Majors with Highest Enrollment:** corrections and criminal justice, other; management information systems; psychology. **Special Study Options:** Accelerated program, cross-registration, distance learning, double major, dual enrollment, English as a Second Language (ESL), honors program, independent study, internships, student-designed major, study abroad, teacher certification program. **Disability Services:** Special programs offered to physically disabled students include note-taking services, reader services, career assessment, internships.

FACILITIES
Housing: Coed dorms, special housing for international students 98% of campus accessible to physically disabled. **Special Academic Facilities/Equipment:** Art and science museums, Japanese garden, special events arena with meeting facilities.

CAMPUS LIFE
Environment: Activities: Choral groups, concert band, dance, drama/theater, jazz band, literary magazine, music ensembles, musical theater, opera, radio station, student government, student newspaper, student-run film society, symphony orchestra, television station, yearbook 300 registered organizations, 25 honor societies, 20 religious organizations. 16 fraternities, 15 sororities. **Athletics (Intercollegiate):** *Men:* baseball, basketball, cross-country, golf, track/field (outdoor), volleyball, water polo. *Women:* basketball, cross-country, golf, soccer, softball, tennis, track/field (outdoor), volleyball, water polo.

ADMISSIONS
Freshman Academic Profile: Average high school GPA 3.4. 84% in top 25% of high school class, 100% in top 50% of high school class. 82% from public high schools. SAT Math middle 50% range 460-590. SAT Critical Reading middle 50% range 440-560. ACT middle 50% range 18-24. Minimum web-based TOEFL. Minimum paper TOEFL 525. **Basis for Candidate Selection:** *Very important factors considered include:* academic GPA, standardized test scores, geographical residence, state residency. *Important factors considered include:* talent/ability. *Other factors considered include:* application essay, recommendation(s), rigor of secondary school record, character/personal qualities, extracurricular activities, volunteer work, work experience. **Freshman Admission Requirements:** High school diploma is required and GED is accepted. *Academic units required:* 4 English, 3 mathematics, 2 science, (2 science labs), 2 foreign language, 1 social studies, 1 history, 1 academic electives, 1 Fine Arts. *Academic units recommended:* 4 English, 3 mathematics, 2 science, (2 science labs), 2 foreign language, 1 social studies, 1 history, 1 academic electives, 1 Fine Arts **Freshman Admission Statistics:** 54,970 applied, 31% admitted, 25% enrolled. **Transfer Admission Requirements:** college transcript(s), minimum college GPA of 2.0 required. Lowest grade transferable C. **General Admission Information:** Application Fee $55. Regular application deadline 11/30. Notification on a rolling basis, beginning on or about 12/1. Nonfall registration accepted. Credit offered for CEEB Advanced Placement tests.

COSTS AND FINANCIAL AID
Annual. Annual out-of-state tuition $11,160. Room and board $11,300. Required fees $6,240. Average book expense $1,788. **Required Forms and**

Deadlines: FAFSA. **Notification of Awards:** Applicants will be notified of awards on a rolling basis beginning 3/30. **Types of Aid:** *Need-based scholarships/grants:* Federal Pell, SEOG, state scholarships/grants, private scholarships, the school's own gift aid. *Loans:* Direct Subsidized Stafford, Direct Unsubsidized Stafford, Direct PLUS, Federal Perkins. **Student Employment:** Federal Work-Study Program available. Institutional employment available. Highest amount earned per year from on-campus jobs $3,000. Off-campus job opportunities are good. **Financial Aid Statistics:** 77% freshmen, 75% undergrads receive need-based scholarship or grant aid. 12% freshmen, 14% undergrads receive non-need-based scholarship or grant aid. 79% freshmen, 86% undergrads receive need-based self-help aid. 39% undergrads borrow to pay for school. Average cumulative indebtedness $13,312. **Criteria for awarding institutional aid:** *Non-need-based:* academics, art, athletics, music/drama.

CALIFORNIA STATE UNIVERSITY, LOS ANGELES

5151 State University Drive, Los Angeles, CA 90032
Phone: 323-343-3901 • **Financial Aid Phone:** 323-343-6260
E-mail: admission@calstatela.edu • **CEEB Code:** 4399
Fax: 323-343-6306 • **Website:** • **ACT Code:** 320

This public school was founded in 1947. It has a 175-acre campus.

RATINGS
Admissions Selectivity Rating: 70   **Fire Safety Rating:** 68   **Green Rating:** 60*

STUDENTS AND FACULTY
Enrollment: 18,074. **Student Body:** 59% female, 41% male, 0% out-of-state, 4% international (121 countries represented). Asian 17%, African American 5%, Caucasian 8%, Hispanic 58%, Native American 0%.
Retention and Graduation: 81% freshmen return for sophomore year. 7% freshmen graduate within 4 years. 37% freshmen graduate within 6 years. **Faculty:** Student/faculty ratio 25:1. 533 full-time faculty, 46% hold PhDs, 44% are members of minority groups, 47% are women. 14% of classes are taught by teaching assistants.

ACADEMICS
Degrees: bachelor's, certificate, master's, post-bachelor's certificate. **Classes:** Most classes have 20–29 students. **Majors with Highest Enrollment:** business administration and management; criminal justice/law enforcement administration; psychology. **Special Study Options:** Accelerated program, cooperative education program, cross-registration, distance learning, double major, dual enrollment, English as a Second Language (ESL), exchange student program (domestic), honors program, independent study, internships, student-designed major, study abroad, teacher certification program. **Disability Services:** Special programs offered to physically disabled students include note-taking services, reader services. **Career Services:** career/job search classes, internships.

FACILITIES
Housing: Coed dorms, special housing for international students, fraternity/sorority housing, apartments for single students, wellness housing, theme housing(Special Interest Housing) First Year House Quite House ACLP/International House The Neighborhood Wellness/Substance Free House The Village Quiet House. **Special Academic Facilities/Equipment:** Baroque pipe organ, bilingual center, entrepreneurship and small business institutes, center for study of armament and disarmament, Van de Graaff accelerator. **Computers:** Administrative functions (other than registration) can be performed online.

CAMPUS LIFE
Environment: Metropolis. **Activities:** Choral groups, dance, drama/theater, jazz band, literary magazine, music ensembles, musical theater, opera, radio station, student government, student newspaper, symphony orchestra, yearbook 130 registered organizations, 3 religious organizations. 7 fraternities, 4 sororities. **Athletics (Intercollegiate):** *Men:* baseball, basketball, cross-country, soccer, track/field (outdoor). *Women:* basketball, cross-country, soccer, tennis, track/field (outdoor), volleyball.

ADMISSIONS
Freshman Academic Profile: Average high school GPA 3.2. SAT Math middle 50% range 390-510. SAT Critical Reading middle 50% range 380-480. SAT Writing middle 50% range 930-450. ACT middle 50% range 15-20. Minimum paper TOEFL 550. **Basis for Candidate Selection:** *Very important factors considered include:* academic GPA, rigor of secondary school record, standardized test scores. *Other factors considered include:* state residency. **Freshman Admission Requirements:** High school diploma is required and GED is accepted. *Academic units required:* 4 English, 3 mathematics, 2 science, (2 science labs), 2 foreign language, 1 social studies, 1 history, 1 academic electives, 1 Visual and Performing Arts. *Academic units recommended:* 4 English, 3 mathematics, 2 science, (2 science labs), 2 foreign language, 1 social studies, 1 his-

tory, 1 academic electives, 1 Visual and Performing Arts **Freshman Admission Statistics:** 27,321 applied, 65% admitted, 16% enrolled. **Transfer Admission Requirements:** college transcript(s), minimum college GPA of 2.0 required. Lowest grade transferable C. **General Admission Information:** Application Fee $55. Regular application deadline 6/15. Nonfall registration accepted. Credit and/or placement offered for CEEB Advanced Placement tests.

COSTS AND FINANCIAL AID
Annual in-state tuition $6,101. Annual out-of-state tuition $17,759. Room and board $9,728. Required fees. Average book expense $1,665. **Required Forms and Deadlines:** FAFSAVerification/Household Size. **Notification of Awards: Types of Aid:** *Need-based scholarships/grants:* Federal Pell, SEOG, state scholarships/grants, private scholarships, the school's own gift aid, Federal and State Work Study. *Loans:* Direct Subsidized Stafford, Direct Unsubsidized Stafford, PLUS, Federal Perkins, Federal Nursing. **Student Employment:** Federal Work-Study Program available. Institutional employment available. Off-campus job opportunities are good. **Financial Aid Statistics:** 88% freshmen, 88% undergrads receive need-based scholarship or grant aid. 66% freshmen, 81% undergrads receive need-based self-help aid. 76% freshmen, 77% undergrads receive any aid.

CALIFORNIA STATE UNIVERSITY, MONTEREY BAY

100 Campus Center, Seaside, CA 93955
Phone: 831-582-3738 • **Financial Aid Phone:** 831-582-5100
E-mail: admissions@csumb.edu • **CEEB Code:** 1945
Fax: 831-582-3783 • **Website:** csumb.edu • **ACT Code:** 321

This public school was founded in 1994. It has a 1387-acre campus.

RATINGS
Admissions Selectivity Rating: 84   **Fire Safety Rating:** 68   **Green Rating:** 90

STUDENTS AND FACULTY
Enrollment: 4,814. **Student Body:** 61% female, 39% male, 2% out-of-state, 1% international (19 countries represented). Asian 5%, African American 5%, Caucasian 44%, Hispanic 32%, Native American 1%.
Retention and Graduation: 79% freshmen return for sophomore year. 10% freshmen graduate within 4 years. **Faculty:** Student/faculty ratio 26:1. 124 full-time faculty, 91% hold PhDs, 44% are members of minority groups, 47% are women. 0% of classes are taught by teaching assistants.

ACADEMICS
Degrees: bachelor's, master's. **Classes:** Most classes have 20–29 students. Most lab/discussion sessions have 20–29 students. **Majors with Highest Enrollment:** biology/biological sciences; business administration and management; humanities/humanistic studies; liberal arts and sciences/liberal studies. **Special Study Options:** cross-registration, distance learning, double major, exchange student program (domestic), independent study, internships, student-designed major, study abroad, teacher certification program, service learning. **Disability Services:** Special programs offered to physically disabled students include note-taking services, reader services, tape recorders. **Career Services:** alumni services, career/job search classes, career assessment, internships, Career Services highlights include Annual career conference that brings together students, alumni and other working professionals together for a day of networking and learning was featured in the "Good Ideas" section of Campus Career Counselor magazine.

FACILITIES
Housing: Coed dorms, special housing for disabled students, special housing for international students, apartments for married students, apartments for single students, wellness housing, theme housing, six-person suite-style living with living areas and kitchenette; substance-free residence hall. 75% of campus accessible to physically disabled. **Special Academic Facilities/Equipment:** Panetta Institute, Tanimura & Antle Family Memorial Library **Computers:** 100% of classrooms, 100% of dorms, 100% of libraries, 100% of dining areas, 100% of student union, 25% of common outdoor areas have wireless network access. Students can register for classes online. Administrative functions (other than registration) can be performed online.

CAMPUS LIFE
Environment: Village. **Activities:** Choral groups, concert band, dance, drama/theater, jazz band, music ensembles, radio station, student government, student newspaper, Campus Ministries, International Student Organization, Model UN 71 registered organizations, 4 religious organizations. 5 fraternities, 8 sororities. **Athletics (Intercollegiate):** *Men:* baseball, basketball, cross-country, golf,

sailing, soccer. *Women:* basketball, cross-country, golf, sailing, soccer, softball, volleyball, water polo. **On-Campus Highlights:** Black Box Cabaret, University Center, Student Center, Tanimura & Antle Library, Chapman Science Academic Center. **Environmental Initiatives:** We are an early signatory to the Presidents Climate Commitment We have completed a one megawatt PV Solar Array that provides 16% of our electrical load. Our Food Service operations has a high commitment to organic foods, compostable packaging and serving products, and new programming, such as meatless Mondays.

ADMISSIONS

Freshman Academic Profile: Average high school GPA 3.2. 11% in top 10% of high school class, 45% in top 25% of high school class, 85% in top 50% of high school class. 88% from public high schools. SAT Math middle 50% range 430-550. SAT Critical Reading middle 50% range 430-540. SAT Writing middle 50% range 430-530. ACT middle 50% range 18-23. Minimum web-based TOEFL 61. Minimum paper TOEFL 500. **Basis for Candidate Selection:** *Very important factors considered include:* academic GPA, standardized test scores. *Important factors considered include:* application essay, recommendation(s), interview, level of applicant's interest, work experience. *Other factors considered include:* Class rank, rigor of secondary school record, character/personal qualities, extracurricular activities, talent/ability, volunteer work. **Freshman Admission Requirements:** High school diploma is required and GED is accepted. **Freshman Admission Statistics:** 11,607 applied, 47% admitted, 16% enrolled. **Transfer Admission Requirements:** High school transcript, essay or personal statement, standardized test scores, minimum college GPA of 2.5 required. Lowest grade transferable C. **General Admission Information:** Application Fee $35. Nonfall registration accepted. Admission may be deferred for a maximum of 1 year.

COSTS AND FINANCIAL AID

Annual. Annual out-of-state tuition $11,160. Room and board $9,152. Required fees $5,963. Average book expense $1,386. **Required Forms and Deadlines:** FAFSA, institution's own financial aid form. **Notification of Awards: Types of Aid:** *Need-based scholarships/grants:* Federal Pell, SEOG, private scholarships, the school's own gift aid. *Loans:* Subsidized Stafford, Unsubsidized Stafford, PLUS, college/university loans from institutional funds. **Student Employment: Financial Aid Statistics:** 75% freshmen, 76% undergrads receive need-based scholarship or grant aid. 15% freshmen, 7% undergrads receive non-need-based scholarship or grant aid. 69% freshmen, 69% undergrads receive need-based self-help aid. 4% freshmen, 3% undergrads receive athletic scholarships. 80% freshmen, 73% undergrads receive any aid. 71% undergrads borrow to pay for school. Average cumulative indebtedness $16,556. **Criteria for awarding institutional aid:** *Non-need-based:* academics.

CALIFORNIA STATE UNIVERSITY, NORTHRIDGE

Admissions and Records, CSU Northridge, Northridge, CA 91330-8207
Phone: 818-677-3700
E-mail: admissions.records@csun.edu • **CEEB Code:** 4707
Fax: 818-677-3766 • **Website:** www.csun.edu • **ACT Code:** 400

This public school was founded in 1956. It has a 350-acre campus.

RATINGS
Admissions Selectivity Rating: 62   **Fire Safety Rating:** 60*   **Green Rating:** 60*

STUDENTS AND FACULTY
Enrollment: 31,119. **Student Body:** 55% female, 45% male, 1% out-of-state, 7% international. Asian 11%, African American 7%, Caucasian 28%, Hispanic 38%, Native American 0%.
Retention and Graduation: 4% freshmen graduate within 4 years. 28% freshmen graduate within 6 years.

ACADEMICS
Degrees: bachelor's, master's. **Special Study Options:** Accelerated program, English as a Second Language (ESL), honors program, student-designed major, study abroad. **Disability Services:** Special programs offered to physically disabled students include note-taking services, reader services, tape recorders, tutors. **Career Services:** alumni services, career/job search classes

FACILITIES
Housing: Coed dorms, special housing for international students, fraternity/sorority housing, apartments for married students, apartments for single students. **Special Academic Facilities/Equipment:** Anthropology museum, art galleries, deafness center, urban archives, map library, cancer research/developmental biology center, planetarium, observatory.

CAMPUS LIFE
Environment: Activities: Choral groups, concert band, drama/theater, jazz band, literary magazine, marching band, music ensembles, musical theater,

---

radio station, student government, student newspaper, yearbook 267 registered organizations, 18 honor societies, 13 religious organizations. 24 fraternities, 12 sororities. **Athletics (Intercollegiate):** *Men:* baseball, basketball, cross-country, diving, football, golf, soccer, swimming, track/field (outdoor), track/field (indoor), volleyball. *Women:* basketball, cross-country, diving, football, golf, soccer, softball, swimming, tennis, track/field (outdoor), track/field (indoor), volleyball.

ADMISSIONS

Freshman Academic Profile: 81% from public high schools. Minimum paper TOEFL 500. **Basis for Candidate Selection:** *Very important factors considered include:* standardized test scores. **Freshman Admission Requirements:** High school diploma is required and GED is accepted.High school diploma is required and GED is not accepted. *Academic units required:* 4 English, 3 mathematics, 1 science, (2 science labs), 2 foreign language, 2 history, 1 academic electives, 1 Visual/Performing Arts. *Academic units recommended:* 4 English, 3 mathematics, 1 science, (2 science labs), 2 foreign language, 2 history, 1 academic electives, 1 Visual/Performing Arts **Freshman Admission Statistics:** 7,931 applied, 78% admitted, 38% enrolled. Lowest grade transferable D. **General Admission Information:** Application Fee $55. Notification on a rolling basis, beginning on or about 11/30. Nonfall registration accepted. Credit and/or placement offered for CEEB Advanced Placement tests.

COSTS AND FINANCIAL AID

Annual in-state tuition $6,504. Room and board $4,402. Average book expense $1,754. **Required Forms and Deadlines:** institution's own financial aid form. **Notification of Awards: Types of Aid:** *Need-based scholarships/grants:* Federal Pell, SEOG, state scholarships/grants, private scholarships, the school's own gift aid, Federal Nursing Scholarships. *Loans:* Subsidized Stafford, Unsubsidized Stafford, PLUS, Federal Perkins, Federal Nursing, college/university loans from institutional funds. **Student Employment:** Federal Work-Study Program available. Institutional employment available. Highest amount earned per year from on-campus jobs $3,000. Off-campus job opportunities are good.

CALIFORNIA STATE UNIVERSITY, SACRAMENTO

6000 J Street, Sacramento, CA 95819-2694
Phone: 916-278-7766 • **Financial Aid Phone:** 916-278-6554
E-mail: admissions@csus.edu • **CEEB Code:** 4671
Fax: 916-278-5603 • **Website:** www.csus.edu • **ACT Code:** 382

This public school was founded in 1947. It has a 300-acre campus.

RATINGS
Admissions Selectivity Rating: 71   **Fire Safety Rating:** 67   **Green Rating:** 60*

STUDENTS AND FACULTY
Enrollment: 25,457. **Student Body:** 57% female, 43% male, 1% out-of-state, 1% international (122 countries represented). Asian 21%, African American 6%, Caucasian 39%, Hispanic 19%, Native American 1%.
Retention and Graduation: 10% freshmen graduate within 4 years. 41% freshmen graduate within 6 years. **Faculty:** Student/faculty ratio 28:1. 558 full-time faculty, 87% hold PhDs, 31% are members of minority groups, 47% are women. 0% of classes are taught by teaching assistants.

ACADEMICS
Degrees: bachelor's, master's. **Classes:** Most classes have 20–29 students. Most lab/discussion sessions have 10–19 students. **Majors with Highest Enrollment:** business/commerce; criminal justice/law enforcement administration; nursing/registered nurse (rn, asn, bsn, msn). **Special Study Options:** Accelerated program, cooperative education program, cross-registration, distance learning, double major, dual enrollment, English as a Second Language (ESL), honors program, independent study, internships, student-designed major, study abroad, teacher certification program. **Combined Degree Programs:** BA/MA. **Disability Services:** Special programs offered to physically disabled students include note-taking services, reader services, tape recorders, tutors. **Career Services:** Alumni network, alumni services, career assessment, internships, regional alumni.

FACILITIES
Housing: Coed dorms. 95% of campus accessible to physically disabled. **Special Academic Facilities/Equipment:** CSUS Museum of Anthropology University Library Gallery (Art) Else Gallery (Art) Witt Gallery (Art) **Computers:** Students can register for classes online. Administrative functions (other than registration) can be performed online.

CAMPUS LIFE
Environment: Metropolis. **Activities:** Choral groups, concert band, dance, drama/theater, jazz band, marching band, music ensembles, musical theater, opera, pep band, radio station, student government, student newspaper, symphony

orchestra 222 registered organizations, 7 honor societies, 13 religious organizations. 19 fraternities, 20 sororities. **Athletics (Intercollegiate):** *Men:* baseball, basketball, cheerleading, cross-country, football, golf, soccer, tennis, track/field (outdoor). *Women:* basketball, cheerleading, crew/rowing, cross-country, golf, gymnastics, soccer, softball, tennis, track/field (outdoor), volleyball. **On-Campus Highlights:** University Union, River Front Center, Guy West Bridge, Mariposa Hall, Hornet Stadium.

ADMISSIONS

Freshman Academic Profile: Average high school GPA 3.3. 89% from public high schools. SAT Math middle 50% range 430-540. SAT Critical Reading middle 50% range 410-520. ACT middle 50% range 17-22. Minimum paper TOEFL 510. **Basis for Candidate Selection:** *Very important factors considered include:* rigor of secondary school record, standardized test scores. *Important factors considered include:* state residency. *Other factors considered include:* recommendation(s), extracurricular activities, geographical residence, interview, talent/ability. **Freshman Admission Requirements:** High school diploma is required and GED is accepted. *Academic units required:* 4 English, 3 mathematics, 2 science, (2 science labs), 2 foreign language, 1 social studies, 1 history, 1 academic electives, 1 visual/performing arts. *Academic units recommended:* 4 English, 3 mathematics, 2 science, (2 science labs), 2 foreign language, 1 social studies, 1 history, 1 academic electives, 1 visual/performing arts **Freshman Admission Statistics:** 19,702 applied, 70% admitted, 23% enrolled. **Transfer Admission Requirements:** college transcript(s), statement of good standing from prior institution(s). Minimum college GPA of 2.0 required. Lowest grade transferable D. **General Admission Information:** Application Fee $55. Regular application deadline 11/30. Notification on a rolling basis, beginning on or about 11/1. Nonfall registration accepted. Admission may be deferred for a maximum of one semester. Credit and/or placement offered for CEEB Advanced Placement tests.

COSTS AND FINANCIAL AID

Annual in-state tuition $5,472. Annual out-of-state tuition $16,632. Room and board $10,370. Required fees $1,130. Average book expense $1,754. **Required Forms and Deadlines:** FAFSA. **Notification of Awards:** Applicants will be notified of awards on a rolling basis beginning 4/1. **Types of Aid:** *Need-based scholarships/grants:* Federal Pell, SEOG, state scholarships/grants, private scholarships, Federal Nursing Scholarships. *Loans:* Direct Subsidized Stafford, Direct Unsubsidized Stafford, Direct PLUS, Federal Perkins, Federal Nursing. **Student Employment:** Federal Work-Study Program available. Institutional employment available. Off-campus job opportunities are fair. **Financial Aid Statistics:** 77% freshmen, 78% undergrads receive need-based scholarship or grant aid. 16% freshmen, 7% undergrads receive non-need-based scholarship or grant aid. 100% freshmen, 99% undergrads receive need-based self-help aid. 50% undergrads receive any aid. 43% undergrads borrow to pay for school. Average cumulative indebtedness $4,456.

CALIFORNIA STATE UNIVERSITY, SAN BERNARDINO

5500 University Parkway, San Bernardino, CA 92407-2397
Phone: 909-537-5188 • **Financial Aid Phone:** 909-537-7800
E-mail: moreinfo@mail.csusb.edu • **CEEB Code:** 4099
Fax: 909-537-7034 • **Website:** www.csusb.edu • **ACT Code:** 205

This public school was founded in 1965. It has a 430-acre campus.

RATINGS

Admissions Selectivity Rating: 74   **Fire Safety Rating:** 68   **Green Rating:** 60*

STUDENTS AND FACULTY

Enrollment: 15,885. **Student Body:** 62% female, 38% male, 1% out-of-state, 5% international (62 countries represented). Asian 6%, African American 8%, Caucasian 20%, Hispanic 53%, Native American 0%. **Retention and Graduation:** 88% freshmen return for sophomore year. 10% freshmen graduate within 4 years. 46% freshmen graduate within 6 years. **Faculty:** Student/faculty ratio 26:1. 430 full-time faculty, 66% hold PhDs, 34% are members of minority groups, 48% are women.

ACADEMICS

Degrees: bachelor's, doctoral, master's. **Classes:** Most classes have 20–29 students. Most lab/discussion sessions have 20–29 students. **Majors with Highest Enrollment:** business/commerce; liberal arts and sciences/liberal studies; psychology. **Special Study Options:** Accelerated program, cooperative education program, cross-registration, distance learning, double major, dual enrollment, exchange student program (domestic), honors program, independent study, internships, study abroad, teacher certification program, School of Social

---

and Behavioral Sciences offers Master's in National Security Studies. **Disability Services:** Special programs offered to physically disabled students include note-taking services, reader services, tape recorders.

FACILITIES

Housing: Coed dorms, women's dorms, apartments for single students, wellness housing. **Special Academic Facilities/Equipment:** Simulation labs, electronic music studios, language lab, desert studies center. Robert V. Fullerton Art Museum. Anthropology Museum. **Computers:** Students can register for classes online. Administrative functions (other than registration) can be performed online.

CAMPUS LIFE

Environment: City. **Activities:** Choral groups, dance, drama/theater, jazz band, music ensembles, musical theater, radio station, student government, student newspaper, television station, Campus Ministries, International Student Organization, Model UN 97 registered organizations, 3 religious organizations. 9 fraternities, 6 sororities. **Athletics (Intercollegiate):** *Men:* baseball, basketball, golf, soccer, swimming, water polo. *Women:* basketball, cross-country, soccer, softball, swimming, tennis, volleyball, water polo. **On-Campus Highlights:** Coussoulis Arena, Robert V. Fullerton Art Museum, Social and Behavorial Sciences Building, Santos Manuel Student Union, Pfau Library.

ADMISSIONS

Freshman Academic Profile: Average high school GPA 3.2. 87% from public high schools. SAT Math middle 50% range 400-510. SAT Critical Reading middle 50% range 390-490. SAT Writing middle 50% range 400-490. ACT middle 50% range 16-20. Minimum paper TOEFL 500. **Basis for Candidate Selection:** *Very important factors considered include:* academic GPA, recommendation(s), standardized test scores. *Other factors considered include:* geographical residence. **Freshman Admission Requirements:** High school diploma is required and GED is accepted. *Academic units required:* 4 English, 3 mathematics, 2 science, (2 science labs), 2 foreign language, 1 social studies, 1 history, 1 visual/performing arts. *Academic units recommended:* 4 English, 3 mathematics, 2 science, (2 science labs), 2 foreign language, 1 social studies, 1 history, 1 visual/performing arts. **Freshman Admission Statistics:** 12,241 applied, 58% admitted, 34% enrolled. **Transfer Admission Requirements:** college transcript(s), minimum college GPA of 2.0 required. Lowest grade transferable C. **General Admission Information:** Application Fee $55. Nonfall registration accepted. Credit and/or placement offered for CEEB Advanced Placement tests.

COSTS AND FINANCIAL AID

Annual. Annual out-of-state tuition $11,160. Room and board $9,972. Required fees $1,077. Average book expense $1,572. **Required Forms and Deadlines:** FAFSA. **Notification of Awards:** Applicants will be notified of awards on a rolling basis beginning 4/1. **Types of Aid:** *Need-based scholarships/grants:* Federal Pell, SEOG, state scholarships/grants, private scholarships, the school's own gift aid. *Loans:* Direct Subsidized Stafford, Direct Unsubsidized Stafford, Direct PLUS, Federal Perkins. **Student Employment:** Federal Work-Study Program available. Institutional employment available. Off-campus job opportunities are fair. **Financial Aid Statistics:** 83% freshmen, 83% undergrads receive need-based scholarship or grant aid. 8% freshmen, 6% undergrads receive non-need-based scholarship or grant aid. 74% freshmen, 82% undergrads receive need-based self-help aid. 1% freshmen receive athletic scholarships. 66% freshmen, 67% undergrads receive any aid. 61% undergrads borrow to pay for school. Average cumulative indebtedness $21,787. **Criteria for awarding institutional aid:** *Non-need-based:* academics, alumni affiliation, art, athletics, leadership, music/drama, state/district residency.

CALIFORNIA STATE UNIVERSITY, SAN MARCOS

, San Marcos, CA 92096-0001
Phone: 760-750-4848 • **Financial Aid Phone:** 760-750-4850
E-mail: apply@csusm.edu • **CEEB Code:** 5677
Fax: 760-750-3248 • **Website:** www.csusm.edu

This public school was founded in 1989. It has a 304-acre campus.

RATINGS

Admissions Selectivity Rating: 64   **Fire Safety Rating:** 60*   **Green Rating:** 60*

STUDENTS AND FACULTY

Enrollment: 8,686. **Student Body:** 61% female, 39% male, 1% out-of-state. **Retention and Graduation:** 74% freshmen return for sophomore year. 14% freshmen graduate within 4 years. 46% freshmen graduate within 6 years. **Faculty:** Student/faculty ratio 25:1. 202 full-time faculty.

ACADEMICS

Degrees: bachelor's, master's. **Classes:** Most classes have 30–39 students. **Special Study Options:** Accelerated program, cross-registration, distance learning, double major, dual enrollment, English as a Second Language (ESL), independent study, internships, student-designed major, study abroad, teacher certification program, weekend college, Evening degree program, Program for Adult College Education (PACE), Saturday classes, Air Force ROTC, extended studies, open university, special sessions, including winter. **Disability Services:** Special programs offered to physically disabled students include note-taking services, reader services, tape recorders, tutors. **Career Services:** alumni services, career assessment, internships.

FACILITIES

Housing: special housing for disabled students, special housing for international students, apartments for single students, Our housing is privatized and operated by Allen and O'Hara. **Computers:** Students can register for classes online.

CAMPUS LIFE

Environment: Town. **Activities:** Choral groups, drama/theater, music ensembles, student newspaper 70 registered organizations, 5 honor societies, 2 religious organizations. 2 fraternities, 2 sororities. **Athletics (Intercollegiate):** *Men:* baseball, cross-country, golf, soccer, track/field (outdoor). *Women:* cross-country, golf, soccer, softball, track/field (outdoor).

ADMISSIONS

Freshman Academic Profile: Average high school GPA 3.2SAT Math middle 50% range 430-540. SAT Critical Reading middle 50% range 430-530. Minimum paper TOEFL 550. **Basis for Candidate Selection:** *Very important factors considered include:* rigor of secondary school record, standardized test scores. *Other factors considered include:* geographical residence, state residency. **Freshman Admission Requirements:** High school diploma is required and GED is accepted. *Academic units required:* 4 English, 3 mathematics, 2 science, (2 science labs), 2 foreign language, 2 social studies, 1 academic electives, 1 Visual Performing Arts. *Academic units recommended:* 4 English, 3 mathematics, 2 science, (2 science labs), 2 foreign language, 2 social studies, 1 academic electives, 1 Visual Performing Arts **Transfer Admission Requirements:** college transcript(s), minimum college GPA of 2.0 required. Lowest grade transferable C. **General Admission Information:** Application Fee $55. Notification on a rolling basis, beginning on or about 12/1. Nonfall registration not accepted. Credit and/or placement offered for CEEB Advanced Placement tests.

COSTS AND FINANCIAL AID

Annual out of state tuition $8,136, Room and board $6,250. Required fees $3,650. Average book expense $1,386. **Required Forms and Deadlines:** FAFSA. **Notification of Awards:** Applicants will be notified of awards on or about 4/15. **Types of Aid:** *Need-based scholarships/grants:* Federal Pell, SEOG, state scholarships/grants, private scholarships, the school's own gift aid. *Loans:* Direct Subsidized Stafford, Direct Unsubsidized Stafford, Direct PLUS, PLUS, Federal Perkins, college/university loans from institutional funds. **Criteria for awarding institutional aid:** *Non-need-based:* academics, athletics, leadership, state/district residency.

CALIFORNIA STATE UNIVERSITY, STANISLAUS

One University Circle, Turlock, CA 95382
Phone: 209-667-3070 • **Financial Aid Phone:** 209-667-3336
E-mail: Outreach_Help_Desk@csustan.edu • **CEEB Code:** 4713
Fax: 209-667-3788 • **Website:** www.csustan.edu • **ACT Code:** 435

This public school was founded in 1957. It has a 228-acre campus.

RATINGS

Admissions Selectivity Rating: 71   **Fire Safety Rating:** 94   **Green Rating:** 83

STUDENTS AND FACULTY

Enrollment: 7,619. **Student Body:** 64% female, 36% male, 1% out-of-state, 1% international (22 countries represented). Asian 11%, African American 3%, Caucasian 30%, Hispanic 42%, Native American 0%.
Retention and Graduation: 83% freshmen return for sophomore year. 18% freshmen graduate within 4 years. 49% freshmen graduate within 6 years. **Faculty:** Student/faculty ratio 23:1. 258 full-time faculty, 87% hold PhDs, 27% are members of minority groups, 46% are women.

ACADEMICS

Degrees: bachelor's, master's, post-bachelor's certificate, post-master's certificate. **Classes:** Most classes have 20–29 students. Most lab/discussion sessions have 20–29 students. **Majors with Highest Enrollment:** business/commerce; liberal arts and sciences/liberal studies; psychology. **Special Study Options:** cooperative education program, distance learning, double major, dual enrollment, English as a Second Language (ESL), exchange student program (domestic), honors program, independent study, internships, liberal arts/career combination, student-designed major, study abroad, teacher certification program. **Honors Programs:** University Honors Program. **Disability Services:** Special programs offered to physically disabled students include note-taking services, reader services, tape recorders, tutors. **Career Services:** Alumni network, alumni services, career/job search classes, career assessment, internships, regional alumni. Career Services highlights include Our Internship Program is exceptional. We work with employers to develop internship and coop opportunities, post information online for students to help them connect with their college department internship coordinator for course credit, and post internship information in the Career Services Center to help students identify appropriate opportunities related to their major course of study.

FACILITIES

Housing: Coed dorms, apartments for single students, housing available in the summer months. ADA compliant units available. 99% of campus accessible to physically disabled. **Special Academic Facilities/Equipment:** Marine sciences station, laser lab, greenhouse, art gallery, mainstage theatre, recital hall, observatory, science building, art complex, distance learning studios, BioAg Eco building. **Computers:** 100% of classrooms, 100% of dorms, 100% of libraries, 100% of dining areas, 100% of student union, 10% of common outdoor areas have wireless network access. Students can register for classes online. Administrative functions (other than registration) can be performed online.

CAMPUS LIFE

Environment: Town. **Activities:** Choral groups, concert band, dance, drama/theater, jazz band, music ensembles, musical theater, opera, radio station, student government, student newspaper, symphony orchestra, television station, International Student Organization 76 registered organizations, 11 honor societies, 4 religious organizations. 7 fraternities, 9 sororities. **Athletics (Intercollegiate):** *Men:* baseball, basketball, cross-country, golf, soccer, track/field (outdoor), track/field (indoor). *Women:* basketball, cross-country, soccer, softball, tennis, track/field (outdoor), track/field (indoor), volleyball. **On-Campus Highlights:** Naraghi Hall of Science, MSR Educational Services Gateway Building, JFR Faculty Development Center, CSU Stanislaus University Art Gallery, Cafeteria and adjoining room, Student Union recently renovated, game room. **Environmental Initiatives:** The campus has replaced ten building air handler units in three major buildings. These new air handler units are more energy efficient and have also improved the air quality of the conditioned spaces. Project cost $1.6 million. Scheduled to have solar-generating (photovoltaic) equipment installed that will deliver zero-emission energy directly to the campus at economical costs. Installation date TBD The campus, in fiscal year 2009/10, reset building thermostats to 78 degrees during the summer months to conserve energy. During this time, Science Building I was shutdown completely to conserve energy.

ADMISSIONS

Freshman Academic Profile: Average high school GPA 3.3. 95% from public high schools. SAT Math middle 50% range 410-520. SAT Critical Reading middle 50% range 400-510. SAT Writing middle 50% range 410-500. ACT middle 50% range 16-22. Minimum web-based TOEFL 61. Minimum paper TOEFL 500. **Basis for Candidate Selection:** *Very important factors considered include:* academic GPA, rigor of secondary school record, standardized test scores. *Important factors considered include:* Class rank. **Freshman Admission Requirements:** High school diploma is required and GED is accepted. *Academic units required:* 4 English, 3 mathematics, 2 science, (2 science labs), 2 foreign language, 1 social studies, 1 history, 1 visual/performing arts, 1 academic electives. *Academic units recommended:* 4 English, 3 mathematics, 2 science, (2 science labs), 2 foreign language, 1 social studies, 1 history, 1 visual/performing arts, 1 academic electives. **Freshman Admission Statistics:** 5,763 applied, 72% admitted, 27% enrolled. **Transfer Admission Requirements:** college transcript(s), statement of good standing from prior institution(s). Minimum college GPA of 2.0 required. Lowest grade transferable D. **General Admission Information:** Application Fee $55. Regular application deadline 3/1. Notification on a rolling basis, beginning on or about 10/1. Nonfall registration accepted. Credit offered for CEEB Advanced Placement tests.

COSTS AND FINANCIAL AID

Required Forms and Deadlines: FAFSA. **Notification of Awards:** Applicants will be notified of awards on a rolling basis beginning 3/15. **Types of Aid:** *Need-based scholarships/grants:* Federal Pell, SEOG, state scholarships/grants, private scholarships, the school's own gift aid, Federal Nursing Scholarships. *Loans:* Subsidized Stafford, Unsubsidized Stafford, PLUS, Federal Perkins, college/university loans from institutional funds. **Student Employment:** Federal Work-Study Program available. Institutional employment available. Highest amount earned per year from on-campus jobs $17,680. Off-campus job opportunities are good. **Criteria for awarding institutional aid:** *Non-need-based:* academics, alumni affiliation, art, athletics, leadership, minority status, music/drama, state/district residency.

CALIFORNIA UNIVERSITY OF PENNSYLVANIA

250 University Avenue, California, PA 15419
Phone: 724-938-4404 • **Financial Aid Phone:** 724-938-4415
E-mail: inquiry@cup.edu • **CEEB Code:** 2647
Fax: 724-938-4564 • **Website:** www.cup.edu • **ACT Code:** 3694

This public school was founded in 1852. It has a 188-acre campus.

RATINGS
Admissions Selectivity Rating: 74   **Fire Safety Rating:** 97   **Green Rating:** 95

STUDENTS AND FACULTY
Enrollment: 6,199. **Student Body:** 52% female, 48% male, 6% out-of-state, 1% international (18 countries represented). Asian 0%, African American 6%, Caucasian 67%, Hispanic 1%, Native American 0%.
Retention and Graduation: 74% freshmen return for sophomore year. 25% freshmen graduate within 4 years. 52% freshmen graduate within 6 years. 16% grads go on to further study within 1 year. **Faculty:** Student/faculty ratio 19:1. 298 full-time faculty, 65% hold PhDs, 12% are members of minority groups, 43% are women. 0% of classes are taught by teaching assistants.

ACADEMICS
Degrees: associate, bachelor's, certificate, master's, post-bachelor's certificate, post-master's certificate, terminal associate. **Classes:** Most classes have 20–29 students. Most lab/discussion sessions have 20–29 students. **Majors with Highest Enrollment:** business administration and management; criminal justice/safety studies; elementary education and teaching. **Special Study Options:** Accelerated program, cooperative education program, distance learning, double major, dual enrollment, exchange student program (domestic), honors program, independent study, internships, liberal arts/career combination, student-designed major, study abroad, teacher certification program, weekend college, Undergrads may take grad classes. **Disability Services:** Special programs offered to physically disabled students include note-taking services, reader services, tape recorders, tutors. **Career Services:** Alumni network, alumni services, career/job search classes, career assessment, internships, regional alumni. Career Services highlights include Extensive programs in Internships and training.

FACILITIES
Housing: Coed dorms, special housing for disabled students, men's dorms, special housing for international students, women's dorms, fraternity/sorority housing, cooperative housing, wellness housing, theme housing, Jefferson Apartments, Garden style with outdoor pool/sandlot volleyball court and extensive gym. 90% of campus accessible to physically disabled. **Special Academic Facilities/Equipment:** Manderino Gallery of Fine Arts, hosts top 40 corporate art collection sin the world. **Computers:** Students can register for classes online. Administrative functions (other than registration) can be performed online.

CAMPUS LIFE
Environment: Village. **Activities:** Choral groups, concert band, dance, drama/theater, jazz band, literary magazine, marching band, music ensembles, musical theater, opera, pep band, radio station, student government, student newspaper, symphony orchestra, television station, yearbook, Campus Ministries, International Student Organization 25 honor societies, 1 religious organizations. 6 fraternities, 7 sororities. **Athletics (Intercollegiate):** *Men:* baseball, basketball, cheerleading, cross-country, football, golf, rugby, soccer, softball, track/field (outdoor), track/field (indoor), volleyball. *Women:* basketball, cheerleading, cross-country, diving, golf, rugby, soccer, softball, swimming, tennis, track/field (outdoor), track/field (indoor), volleyball. **On-Campus Highlights:** Residence Halls, Student Union, Classrooms, Herron Rec Center, Library. **Environmental Initiatives:** Multimillion Dollar Geothermal project plus replacing ALL residence halls in less than 5 years with Green buildings. Massive implementation of Johnson Controls systems to reduce our carbon footprint and energy usage. Campus wide sustainability awareness programs

ADMISSIONS
Freshman Academic Profile: Average high school GPA 3.3. 7% in top 10% of high school class, 28% in top 25% of high school class, 65% in top 50% of high school class. 80% from public high schools. SAT Math middle 50% range 460-540. SAT Critical Reading middle 50% range 460-536. Minimum paper TOEFL 450. **Basis for Candidate Selection:** *Very important factors considered include:* Class rank, rigor of secondary school record, standardized test scores. *Other factors considered include:* application essay, recommendation(s), extracurricular activities, interview, talent/ability, work experience. **Fresh-**

man **Admission Requirements:** High school diploma is required and GED is accepted. *Academic units required:* 4 English, 3 mathematics, 1 science, (1 science labs), 2 social studies, 2 history, 6 academic electives, 1 Arts and Humanities. *Academic units recommended:* 4 English, 3 mathematics, 1 science, (1 science labs), 2 social studies, 2 history, 6 academic electives, 1 Arts and Humanities **Freshman Admission Statistics:** 3,849 applied, 68% admitted, 51% enrolled. **Transfer Admission Requirements:** High school transcript, college transcript(s), statement of good standing from prior institution(s). Minimum college GPA of 2.3 required. Lowest grade transferable C. **General Admission Information:** Application Fee $25. Nonfall registration accepted. Admission may be deferred for a maximum of one semester. Credit offered for CEEB Advanced Placement tests.

COSTS AND FINANCIAL AID
Annual in-state tuition $5,804. Annual out-of-state tuition $9,288. Room and board $9,684. Required fees $2,208. Average book expense $1,000. **Required Forms and Deadlines:** FAFSA. **Notification of Awards:** Applicants will be notified of awards on a rolling basis beginning 4/1. **Types of Aid:** *Need-based scholarships/grants:* Federal Pell, SEOG, state scholarships/grants, private scholarships, the school's own gift aid. *Loans:* Subsidized Stafford, Unsubsidized Stafford, PLUS, Federal Perkins. **Student Employment:** Federal Work-Study Program available. Institutional employment available. Off-campus job opportunities are good. **Financial Aid Statistics:** 72% freshmen, 69% undergrads receive need-based scholarship or grant aid. 26% freshmen, 14% undergrads receive non-need-based scholarship or grant aid. 92% freshmen, 90% undergrads receive need-based self-help aid. 3% freshmen, 4% undergrads receive athletic scholarships. 76% freshmen, 72% undergrads receive any aid. 81% undergrads borrow to pay for school. Average cumulative indebtedness $21,475. **Criteria for awarding institutional aid:** *Non-need-based:* academics, athletics, leadership, minority status, music/drama, state/district residency.

See page 1036.

CALVARY BIBLE COLLEGE
AND THEOLOGICAL SEMINARY

15800 Calvary Rd., Kansas City, MO 64147
Phone: 816-322-3960 • **Financial Aid Phone:** 816-322-0110
E-mail: admissions@calvary.edu
Fax: 816-331-4474 • **Website:** www.college.calvary.edu/ • **ACT Code:** 2312

This private school was founded in 1961. It has a 55-acre campus.

RATINGS
Admissions Selectivity Rating: 66   **Fire Safety Rating:** 73   **Green Rating:** 60*

STUDENTS AND FACULTY
Enrollment: 265. **Student Body:** 48% female, 52% male, 56% out-of-state, 1% international (2 countries represented). Asian 1%, African American 10%, Caucasian 82%, Hispanic 4%, Native American 1%.
Retention and Graduation: 74% freshmen return for sophomore year. 33% freshmen graduate within 4 years. **Faculty:** Student/faculty ratio 8:1. 21 full-time faculty, 29% hold PhDs, 5% are members of minority groups, 29% are women. 0% of classes are taught by teaching assistants.

ACADEMICS
Degrees: associate, bachelor's, certificate, first professional, master's, terminal associate, transfer associate. **Majors with Highest Enrollment:** bible/biblical studies; elementary education and teaching; pastoral studies/counseling. **Special Study Options:** cooperative education program, double major, independent study, internships, student-designed major, teacher certification program.

FACILITIES
Housing: men's dorms, women's dorms, apartments for married students, apartments for single students, Single students required to live in college housing unless living with parents or at least 23 years of age. Duplexes available for married students. **Computers:** 100% of dorms, 100% of libraries, 100% of student union, have wireless network access. Students can register for classes online.

CAMPUS LIFE
Environment: Village. **Activities:** Choral groups, drama/theater, music ensembles, musical theater, pep band, radio station, student government, yearbook. **Athletics (Intercollegiate):** *Men:* basketball, soccer. *Women:* basketball, volleyball. **On-Campus Highlights:** Student Lounge, The Point, Gymnasium

ADMISSIONS
Freshman Academic Profile: ACT middle 50% range 18-22. Minimum paper TOEFL 525. **Basis for Candidate Selection:** *Very important factors*

considered include: academic GPA, recommendation(s), standardized test scores, religious affiliation/commitment. *Important factors considered include:* character/personal qualities. *Other factors considered include:* application essay. **Freshman Admission Requirements:** High school diploma is required and GED is accepted. **Freshman Admission Statistics:** 52 applied, 83% admitted, 77% enrolled. **Transfer Admission Requirements:** college transcript(s), essay or personal statement, minimum college GPA of 2.0 required. Lowest grade transferable C-. **General Admission Information:** Application Fee $25. Regular application deadline 7/15. Nonfall registration accepted. Admission may be deferred for a maximum of 2 Semesters.

COSTS AND FINANCIAL AID

Annual tuition $9,300. Room and board $4,800. Required fees $816. Average book expense $532. **Required Forms and Deadlines:** FAFSA, institution's own financial aid form. **Notification of Awards:** Applicants will be notified of awards on a rolling basis beginning 5/1. **Types of Aid:** *Need-based scholarships/grants:* Federal Pell, SEOG, private scholarships, the school's own gift aid. *Loans:* Subsidized Stafford, Unsubsidized Stafford, PLUS. **Student Employment:** Federal Work-Study Program available. Institutional employment available. Off-campus job opportunities are good. **Criteria for awarding institutional aid:** *Non-need-based:* academics, alumni affiliation, job skills, music/drama, religious affiliation.

CALVIN COLLEGE

Best 378

3201 Burton Street S.E., Grand Rapids, MI 49546
Phone: 616-526-6106 • **Financial Aid Phone:** 800-688-0122
E-mail: admissions@calvin.edu • **CEEB Code:** 1095
Fax: 616-526-6777 • **Website:** www.calvin.edu • **ACT Code:** 1968

This private school, affiliated with the Christian Reformed Church, was founded in 1876. It has a 400-acre campus.

RATINGS

Admissions Selectivity Rating: 80   **Fire Safety Rating:** 68   **Green Rating:** 69

STUDENTS AND FACULTY

Enrollment: 3,838. **Student Body:** 53% female, 47% male, 42% out-of-state, 10% international (57 countries represented). Asian 4%, African American 3%, Caucasian 76%, Hispanic 3%, Native American 0%. **Retention and Graduation:** 86% freshmen return for sophomore year. 60% freshmen graduate within 4 years. 23% grads go on to further study within 1 year. 18% grads pursue arts and sciences degrees. 1% grads pursue law degrees. 1% grads pursue business degrees. 2% grads pursue medical degrees. **Faculty:** Student/faculty ratio 12:1. 302 full-time faculty, 83% hold PhDs, 10% are members of minority groups, 35% are women, 0% of classes are taught by teaching assistants.

ACADEMICS

Degrees: bachelor's, master's, post-bachelor's certificate. **Classes:** Most classes have 20–29 students. Most lab/discussion sessions have 10–19 students. **Majors with Highest Enrollment:** business/commerce; engineering; nursing/registered nurse (rn, asn, bsn, msn). **Special Study Options:** Accelerated program, double major, dual enrollment, honors program, independent study, internships, student-designed major, study abroad, teacher certification program, Academically-based Service-learning. **Honors Programs:** For almost forty years Calvin College has challenged its best students with a campus-wide Honors Program--part of our overall mission to encourage academic excellence in a Christ-centered environment. The McGregor Sophomore Scholars Program develops targeted programming for sophomores in the Honors Program, such as one-on-one mentoring with faculty and program leaders and special events. **Disability Services:** Special programs offered to physically disabled students include note-taking services, reader services, tape recorders, tutors. **Career Services:** Alumni network, alumni services, career/job search classes, career assessment, internships, regional alumni.

FACILITIES

Housing: men's dorms, women's dorms, apartments for single students, theme housing, Project Neighborhood Houses. 95% of campus accessible to physically disabled. **Special Academic Facilities/Equipment:** Art gallery, observatory, ecosystem preserve, electron microscope, seismograph lab. **Computers:** 40% of classrooms, 100% of dorms, 100% of libraries, 75% of dining areas, 20% of

student union, 10% of common outdoor areas have wireless network access. Students can register for classes online. Administrative functions (other than registration) can be performed online.

CAMPUS LIFE

Environment: City. **Activities:** Choral groups, concert band, dance, drama/theater, jazz band, literary magazine, music ensembles, musical theater, pep band, student government, student newspaper, student-run film society, symphony orchestra, yearbook, Campus Ministries, International Student Organization, Model UN 60 registered organizations, 6 honor societies, 5 religious organizations. **Athletics (Intercollegiate):** *Men:* baseball, basketball, cross-country, diving, golf, soccer, swimming, tennis, track/field (outdoor). *Women:* basketball, cross-country, diving, golf, soccer, softball, swimming, tennis, track/field (outdoor), volleyball. **On-Campus Highlights:** Field House, Johnny's Cafe, Heckman Library, DeVos Communications Building, Engineering Projects and Design Building. **Environmental Initiatives:** The Calvin Energy Recovery Fund, a green revolving fund The Calvin College Ecosystem Preserve and the Bunker Interpretive Center The Calvin Sustainability Summit in 2011.

ADMISSIONS

Freshman Academic Profile: Average high school GPA 3.7. 34% in top 10% of high school class, 60% in top 25% of high school class, 85% in top 50% of high school class. 45% from public high schools. SAT Math middle 50% range 540-690. SAT Critical Reading middle 50% range 520-670. ACT middle 50% range 24-30. Minimum web-based TOEFL 80. Minimum paper TOEFL 550. **Basis for Candidate Selection:** *Very important factors considered include:* academic GPA, rigor of secondary school record, standardized test scores, religious affiliation/commitment. *Important factors considered include:* application essay, recommendation(s), character/personal qualities, extracurricular activities. *Other factors considered include:* Class rank, level of applicant's interest, volunteer work, work experience. **Freshman Admission Requirements:** High school diploma is required and GED is accepted. *Academic units required:* 3 English, 3 mathematics, 2 science, 2 social studies, 3 academic electives. *Academic units recommended:* 3 English, 3 mathematics, 2 science, 2 social studies, 3 academic electives. **Freshman Admission Statistics:** 3,284 applied, 75% admitted, 39% enrolled. **Transfer Admission Requirements:** High school transcript, college transcript(s), essay or personal statement, statement of good standing from prior institution(s). Minimum college GPA of 2.5 required. Lowest grade transferable C. **General Admission Information:** Application Fee $35. Regular application deadline 8/15. Notification on a rolling basis, beginning on or about 11/1. Nonfall registration accepted. Admission may be deferred for a maximum of 1 year. Credit and/or placement offered for CEEB Advanced Placement tests.

COSTS AND FINANCIAL AID

Annual tuition $26,480. Room and board $9,110. Required fees $225. Average book expense $1,030. **Required Forms and Deadlines:** FAFSA. **Notification of Awards:** Applicants will be notified of awards on a rolling basis beginning 3/15. **Types of Aid:** *Need-based scholarships/grants:* Federal Pell, SEOG, state scholarships/grants, private scholarships, the school's own gift aid. *Loans:* Direct Subsidized Stafford, Direct Unsubsidized Stafford, Direct PLUS, Federal Perkins, state loans, college/university loans from institutional funds, Alternative Educational Loans. **Student Employment:** Federal Work-Study Program available. Institutional employment available. Highest amount earned per year from on-campus jobs $5,000. Off-campus job opportunities are excellent. **Financial Aid Statistics:** 100% freshmen, 99% undergrads receive need-based scholarship or grant aid. 11% freshmen, 10% undergrads receive non-need-based scholarship or grant aid. 88% freshmen, 91% undergrads receive need based self-help aid. 97% freshmen, 95% undergrads receive any aid. 63% undergrads borrow to pay for school. Average cumulative indebtedness $32,957. **Criteria for awarding institutional aid:** *Non-need-based:* academics, alumni affiliation, art, leadership, minority status, music/drama, religious affiliation, state/district residency.

CAMERON UNIVERSITY

2800 West Gore Boulevard, Lawton, OK 73505
Phone: 580-581-2230 • **Financial Aid Phone:** 580-581-2293
E-mail: admiss@cua.cameron.edu • **CEEB Code:** 6080
Fax: 580-581-5514 • **ACT Code:** 3386

This public school was founded in 1908. It has a 369-acre campus.

RATINGS

Admissions Selectivity Rating: 64   **Fire Safety Rating:** 83   **Green Rating:** 60*

STUDENTS AND FACULTY

Enrollment: 5,076. **Student Body:** 60% female, 40% male, 1% out-of-state, 3% international (50 countries represented). Asian 3%, African American 19%, Caucasian 58%, Hispanic 9%, Native American 8%.
Retention and Graduation: 56% freshmen return for sophomore year. 24% freshmen graduate within 4 years. 29% freshmen graduate within 6 years.
Faculty: Student/faculty ratio 17:1. 180 full-time faculty, 69% hold PhDs, 14% are members of minority groups, 36% are women. 0% of classes are taught by teaching assistants.

ACADEMICS

Degrees: associate, bachelor's, master's. **Classes:** Most classes have 20–29 students. Most lab/discussion sessions have 10–19 students. **Special Study Options:** Accelerated program, distance learning, double major, dual enrollment, honors program, independent study, internships, liberal arts/career combination, teacher certification program, Undergrads may take grad classes. Evening and saturday classes offered; extension study possible. **Honors Programs:** Honors programs have been created for exceptional scholors. This includes studies in Europe and travel to scholorly programs in the U.S.A. Courses and programs providechallinging multidisciplinary activities. **Combined Degree Programs:** BA/MD. **Disability Services:** Special programs offered to physically disabled students include note-taking services, reader services, tape recorders, tutors.

FACILITIES

Housing: men's dorms, women's dorms, quiet and wellness (non-smoking) areas available. 88% of campus accessible to physically disabled. **Special Academic Facilities/Equipment:** Satellite labs **Computers:** Administrative functions (other than registration) can be performed online.

CAMPUS LIFE

Environment: City. **Activities:** Choral groups, concert band, dance, drama/theater, jazz band, literary magazine, music ensembles, musical theater, pep band, radio station, student government, student newspaper, symphony orchestra, television station, yearbook 66 registered organizations, 19 honor societies, 4 religious organizations. 2 fraternities, 3 sororities. **Athletics (Intercollegiate):** *Men:* baseball, basketball, cross-country, golf, tennis. *Women:* basketball, golf, softball, tennis, volleyball. **On-Campus Highlights:** Student Union, Cameron Village, Moody Blue, Student Activities Building, Fitness Center.

ADMISSIONS

Freshman Academic Profile: 8% in top 10% of high school class, 28% in top 25% of high school class, 62% in top 50% of high school class. 99% from public high schools. ACT middle 50% range 16-22. Minimum paper TOEFL 500. **Basis for Candidate Selection:** *Important factors considered include:* Class rank, academic GPA, standardized test scores, geographical residence, state residency. **Freshman Admission Requirements:** High school diploma is required and GED is accepted. *Academic units required:* 4 English, 3 mathematics, 2 science, (2 science labs), 2 history, 3 academic electives. *Academic units recommended:* 4 English, 3 mathematics, 2 science, (2 science labs), 2 history, 3 academic electives. **Freshman Admission Statistics:** 1,357 applied, 100% admitted, 70% enrolled. **Transfer Admission Requirements:** college transcript(s), minimum college GPA of 2.0 required. Lowest grade transferable D. **General Admission Information:** Application Fee $15. Nonfall registration accepted. Admission may be deferred for a maximum of 12. Credit and/or placement offered for CEEB Advanced Placement tests.

COSTS AND FINANCIAL AID

Average book expense $1,050. **Required Forms and Deadlines:** FAFSA. **Notification of Awards:** Applicants will be notified of awards on a rolling basis beginning 4/1. **Types of Aid:** *Need-based scholarships/grants:* Federal Pell, SEOG, state scholarships/grants, private scholarships, the school's own gift aid. *Loans:* Subsidized Stafford, Unsubsidized Stafford, PLUS. **Student Employment: Financial Aid Statistics:** 94% freshmen, 75% undergrads receive need-based scholarship or grant aid. 63% freshmen, 41% undergrads receive non-need-based scholarship or grant aid. 79% freshmen, 54% undergrads receive need-based self-help aid. 1% undergrads receive athletic scholarships. 36% freshmen, 26% undergrads receive any aid. 30% undergrads borrow to pay for school. Average cumulative indebtedness $7,500. **Criteria for awarding institutional aid:** *Non-need-based:* academics, alumni affiliation, art, athletics, leadership, music/drama.

CAMPBELL UNIVERSITY

Post Office Box 546, Buies Creek, NC 27506
Phone: 910-893-1290
E-mail: adm@mailcenter.campbell.edu • **CEEB Code:** 5100
Fax: 910-893-1288 • **Website:** www.campbell.edu • **ACT Code:** 3076

This private school, affiliated with the Southern Baptist Church, was founded in 1887. It has a 850-acre campus.

RATINGS

Admissions Selectivity Rating: 63 **Fire Safety Rating:** 67 **Green Rating:** 60*

STUDENTS AND FACULTY

Enrollment: 2,806. **Student Body:** 52% female, 48% male, 22% out-of-state, 3% international. Asian 0%, African American 8%, Caucasian 56%, Hispanic 2%, Native American 1%.
Retention and Graduation: 71% freshmen return for sophomore year. 23% grads go on to further study within 1 year. 5% grads pursue arts and sciences degrees. 4% grads pursue law degrees. 7% grads pursue business degrees.
Faculty: Student/faculty ratio 14:1. 196 full-time faculty, 91% hold PhDs, 33% are women. 0% of classes are taught by teaching assistants.

ACADEMICS

Degrees: associate, bachelor's, first professional, master's. **Classes:** Most classes have fewer than 10 students. **Special Study Options:** Accelerated program, cooperative education program, distance learning, double major, dual enrollment, exchange student program (domestic), honors program, independent study, internships, liberal arts/career combination, study abroad, teacher certification program. **Combined Degree Programs:** BA/JD, BA/MA, BA/MBA PHD/MBA. **Disability Services:** Special programs offered to physically disabled students include note-taking services, tape recorders. **Career Services:** career/job search classes, career assessment, internships.

FACILITIES

Housing: special housing for disabled students, men's dorms, women's dorms, apartments for married students, apartments for single students, Student apartments and suites for sophomores, juniors and seniors; also graduate apartments. All off-campus housing must be approved by the Office of Residence Life. 75% of campus accessible to physically disabled. **Special Academic Facilities/Equipment:** Taylor Bott-Rogers Fine Arts Bldg. Lundy-Fetterman School of Business museum and exhibit hall School of Pharmacy Clinical Research Facility **Computers:**

CAMPUS LIFE

Environment: Rural. **Activities:** Choral groups, concert band, drama/theater, jazz band, literary magazine, music ensembles, musical theater, pep band, radio station, student government, student newspaper, yearbook, Campus Ministries, International Student Organization 44 registered organizations, 14 honor societies, 20 religious organizations. **Athletics (Intercollegiate):** *Men:* baseball, basketball, cross-country, golf, soccer, tennis, track/field (outdoor), wrestling. *Women:* basketball, cheerleading, cross-country, golf, soccer, softball, swimming, tennis, track/field (outdoor), volleyball. **On-Campus Highlights:** Lundy-Fetterman School of Business, Wallace Student Center/Oasis Grill/Starbucks, Keith Hills Country Club and Golf Course, Eakes Sports Complex, D. Rich Memorial Hall, Saylor Park.

ADMISSIONS

Freshman Academic Profile: Average high school GPA 3.4. 38% in top 10% of high school class, 80% in top 25% of high school class, 92% in top 50% of high school class. 85% from public high schools. Minimum paper TOEFL 500. **Basis for Candidate Selection:** *Very important factors considered include:* academic GPA, rigor of secondary school record, standardized test scores. *Important factors considered include:* Class rank, interview, talent/ability. *Other factors considered include:* application essay, recommendation(s), alumni/ae relation, character/personal qualities, extracurricular activities, level of applicant's interest, volunteer work, work experience. **Freshman Admission Requirements:** High school diploma is required and GED is accepted. *Academic units required:* 4 English, 3 mathematics, 2 science, (1 science labs), 2 foreign language, 2 social science. *Academic units recommended:* 4 English, 3 mathematics, 2 science, (1 science labs), 2 foreign language, 2 social science **Freshman Admission Statistics:** 3,348 applied, 60% admitted, 45% enrolled. **Transfer Admission Requirements:** High school transcript, college transcript(s), standardized test scores, statement of good standing from prior institution(s). Minimum college GPA of 2.5 required. Lowest grade transferable C. **General Admission Information:** Application Fee $35. Regular application deadline 8/19. Notification on a rolling basis, beginning on or about 9/1. Nonfall registration accepted. Admission may be deferred for a maximum of 12. Credit and/or placement offered for CEEB Advanced Placement tests.

COSTS AND FINANCIAL AID

Annual tuition $19,650. Room and board $6,830. Required fees $700. Average book expense $1,100. **Required Forms and Deadlines:** FAFSA. **Notification of Awards:** Applicants will be notified of awards on a rolling basis beginning 3/1. **Types of Aid:** *Need-based scholarships/grants:* Federal Pell, SEOG, state scholarships/grants, private scholarships, the school's own gift aid. *Loans:* Subsidized Stafford, Unsubsidized Stafford, PLUS, Federal Perkins, state loans, college/university loans from institutional funds. **Student Employment:** Federal Work-Study Program available. Institutional employment available. Highest amount earned per year from on-campus jobs $600. Off-campus job opportunities are good. **Financial Aid Statistics:** 72% freshmen, 72% undergrads receive need-based scholarship or grant aid. 96% freshmen receive non-need-based scholarship or grant aid. 85% freshmen, 89% undergrads receive need-based self-help aid. 7% freshmen, 6% undergrads receive athletic scholarships. 97% freshmen, 92% undergrads receive any aid. 75% undergrads borrow to pay for school. Average cumulative indebtedness $21,703. **Criteria for awarding institutional aid:** *Non-need-based:* academics, athletics, music/drama, religious affiliation, state/district residency.

CAMPBELLSVILLE UNIVERSITY

1 University Drive, Campbellsville, KY 42718-2799
Phone: 270-789-5220 • **Financial Aid Phone:** 270-789-5013
E-mail: admissions@campbellsville.edu • **CEEB Code:** 1097
Fax: 270-789-5071 • **ACT Code:** 1500

This private school, affiliated with the Baptist Church, was founded in 1906. It has a 90-acre campus.

RATINGS

Admissions Selectivity Rating: 74   **Fire Safety Rating:** 66   **Green Rating:** 60*

STUDENTS AND FACULTY

Enrollment: 2,250. **Student Body:** 58% female, 42% male, 12% out-of-state, 7% international. Asian 0%, African American 15%, Caucasian 74%, Hispanic 1%, Native American 0%.
Retention and Graduation: 65% freshmen return for sophomore year. 26% freshmen graduate within 4 years. 41% freshmen graduate within 6 years. 20% grads go on to further study within 1 year. 25% grads pursue arts and sciences degrees. 1% grads pursue law degrees. 15% grads pursue business degrees. 1% grads pursue medical degrees. **Faculty:** Student/faculty ratio 13:1. 146 full-time faculty, 62% hold PhDs, 10% are members of minority groups, 49% are women. 0% of classes are taught by teaching assistants.

ACADEMICS

Degrees: associate, bachelor's, master's. **Classes:** Most classes have fewer than 10 students. **Majors with Highest Enrollment:** accounting; business, management, marketing, and related support services, other; junior high/intermediate/middle school education and teaching. **Special Study Options:** cooperative education program, distance learning, double major, dual enrollment, English as a Second Language (ESL), honors program, independent study, internships, liberal arts/career combination, study abroad, teacher certification program, weekend college. **Disability Services:** Special programs offered to physically disabled students include tutors. **Career Services:** alumni services, career assessment, internships.

FACILITIES

Housing: men's dorms, women's dorms, apartments for married students, apartments for single students. 70% of campus accessible to physically disabled. **Special Academic Facilities/Equipment:** Computer labs: Technology lab **Computers:** Students can register for classes online. Administrative functions (other than registration) can be performed online.

CAMPUS LIFE

Environment: Rural. **Activities:** Choral groups, concert band, dance, drama/theater, jazz band, literary magazine, marching band, music ensembles, musical theater, pep band, radio station, student government, student newspaper, television station, yearbook, Campus Ministries, International Student Organization 49 registered organizations, 1 honor societies, 7 religious organizations. **Athletics (Intercollegiate):** *Men:* baseball, basketball, bowling, cheerleading, cross-country, football, golf, soccer, tennis, track/field (outdoor), wrestling. *Women:* basketball, bowling, cheerleading, cross-country, golf, soccer, softball, swimming, tennis, track/field (outdoor), volleyball. **On-Campus Highlights:** Technology Center, Athletic Center, New Resident Village, Library, Fine Arts Center.

ADMISSIONS

Freshman Academic Profile: Average high school GPA 3.2. 17% in top 10% of high school class, 38% in top 25% of high school class, 69% in top 50% of

high school class. 90% from public high schools. SAT Math middle 50% range 430-580. SAT Critical Reading middle 50% range 420-590. SAT Writing middle 50% range 410-540. ACT middle 50% range 18-23. Minimum paper TOEFL 500. **Basis for Candidate Selection:** *Very important factors considered include:* rigor of secondary school record. *Important factors considered include:* Class rank, recommendation(s), standardized test scores, character/personal qualities, interview. *Other factors considered include:* application essay, alumni/ae relation, extracurricular activities, religious affiliation/commitment, talent/ability, volunteer work, work experience. **Freshman Admission Requirements:** High school diploma is required and GED is accepted. **Freshman Admission Statistics:** 2,477 applied, 67% admitted, 35% enrolled. **Transfer Admission Requirements:** college transcript(s), Lowest grade transferable C. **General Admission Information:** Application Fee $20. Regular application deadline 8/15. Notification on a rolling basis, beginning on or about 9/1. Nonfall registration accepted. Admission may be deferred for a maximum of 12. Credit and/or placement offered for CEEB Advanced Placement tests.

COSTS AND FINANCIAL AID

Annual tuition $21,100. Room and board $7,120. Required fees $500. Average book expense $1,000. **Required Forms and Deadlines:** FAFSA. **Notification of Awards:** Applicants will be notified of awards on a rolling basis beginning 2/15. **Types of Aid:** *Need-based scholarships/grants:* Federal Pell, SEOG, state scholarships/grants, private scholarships, the school's own gift aid. *Loans:* Subsidized Stafford, Unsubsidized Stafford, PLUS, Federal Perkins, college/university loans from institutional funds. **Student Employment:** Federal Work-Study Program available. Institutional employment available. Highest amount earned per year from on-campus jobs $2,000. Off-campus job opportunities are good. **Financial Aid Statistics:** 100% freshmen, 97% undergrads receive need-based scholarship or grant aid. 14% freshmen, 11% undergrads receive non-need-based scholarship or grant aid. 74% freshmen, 78% undergrads receive need-based self-help aid. 5% freshmen, 6% undergrads receive athletic scholarships. 95% freshmen, 92% undergrads receive any aid. 90% undergrads borrow to pay for school. Average cumulative indebtedness $21,500. **Criteria for awarding institutional aid:** *Non-need-based:* academics, art, athletics, leadership, minority status, music/drama, religious affiliation, state/district residency.

CANISIUS COLLEGE

2001 Main Street, Buffalo, NY 14208
Phone: 716-888-2200 • **Financial Aid Phone:** 716-888-2300
E-mail: admissions@canisius.edu • **CEEB Code:** 2073
Fax: 716-888-3230 • **Website:** www.canisius.edu • **ACT Code:** 2690

This private school, affiliated with the Roman Catholic-Jesuit Church, was founded in 1870. It has a 32-acre campus.

RATINGS

Admissions Selectivity Rating: 75   **Fire Safety Rating:** 75   **Green Rating:** 65

STUDENTS AND FACULTY

Enrollment: 2,992. **Student Body:** 53% female, 47% male, 8% out-of-state, 4% international (27 countries represented). Asian 2%, African American 7%, Caucasian 75%, Hispanic 3%, Native American 0%.
Retention and Graduation: 58% freshmen graduate within 4 years. 68% freshmen graduate within 6 years. 32% grads go on to further study within 1 year. 2% grads pursue law degrees. 4% grads pursue business degrees. 2% grads pursue medical degrees. **Faculty:** Student/faculty ratio 11:1. 225 full-time faculty, 96% hold PhDs, 7% are members of minority groups, 41% are women. 0% of classes are taught by teaching assistants.

ACADEMICS

Degrees: associate, bachelor's, master's, post-bachelor's certificate, post-master's certificate. **Classes:** Most classes have 20–29 students. Most lab/discussion sessions have 20–29 students. **Majors with Highest Enrollment:** business administration and management; political science and government; psychology. **Special Study Options:** cooperative education program, cross-registration, distance learning, double major, dual enrollment, English as a Second Language (ESL), exchange student program (domestic), honors program, independent study, internships, study abroad, teacher certification program, 4 + 1 BS/MBA 3 + 4 BS/DD (Bio and Dentistry)-Early Assurance guaranteed Medical School Admission). **Honors Programs:** The All College Honors Program offers outstanding students the opportunity for a highly demanding and rewarding experience of the core curriculum. Students study under the college's most distinguished faculty, participate in educational travel, write a senior thesis and compete for special awards and honors. **Combined Degree Programs:** BA/DDS, BA/BS-MBA, BA/BS-MBAPA. **Disability Services:** Special programs offered to physically disabled students include note taking services, reader services, tape recorders, tutors. **Career Services:** Alumni network, alumni services, career/job search classes, career assessment, internships, regional alumni.

FACILITIES

Housing: Coed dorms, special housing for disabled students, special housing for international students, apartments for single students, Honors Student Housing ° All college owned housing is handicapped accessible. 95% of campus accessible to physically disabled. **Special Academic Facilities/Equipment:** TV studio, electron microscope, seismograph, language lab, digital lab, human performance lab, molecular biology and physics labs, mini-planetarium. **Computers:** 100% of classrooms, 100% of dorms, 100% of libraries, 100% of dining areas, 100% of student union, 100% of common outdoor areas have wireless network access. Students can register for classes online. Administrative functions (other than registration) can be performed online.

CAMPUS LIFE

Environment: Metropolis. **Activities:** Choral groups, concert band, dance, drama/theater, jazz band, literary magazine, music ensembles, musical theater, pep band, radio station, student government, student newspaper, student-run film society, television station, yearbook, Campus Ministries, International Student Organization, Model UN 102 registered organizations, 16 honor societies, 2 religious organizations. 1 fraternities, 1 sororities. **Athletics (Intercollegiate):** *Men:* baseball, basketball, cross-country, diving, golf, ice hockey, lacrosse, soccer, swimming. *Women:* basketball, cross-country, diving, lacrosse, soccer, softball, swimming, synchronized swimming, volleyball. **On-Campus Highlights:** Montante Cultural Center, Delavan Townhouses, Palisano Pavillion, Koessler Athletic Center, Richard E. Winter Student Center, Canisius College sponsors a variety of on-campus entertainment to keep students busy throughout the year. Our highly popular Java Jams is a weekly coffee-style event offering entertainment in the Palisano Pavilion. **Environmental Initiatives:** Canisius College is deeply committed to utility conservation and the sustainability of our natural resources. This is accomplished in part through our development of policies and practices which are designed to promote sound energy management, and the economic, social and environmental well-being of our students and staff. Canisius College is working with Ecology and Environment, Inc. (E & E) to develop and implement an energy conservation program. The overall goal of the program is to reduce the college's annual electric consumption by five percent, based on historical consumption during the last three academic years. A web page is being designed to explain how Canisius College conserves and supports sustainable use of our natural resources Canisius College has made major strides towards decreasing our environmental footprint by changing the way we operate, maintain, and construct our facilities. Future design and construction will be weighed against environmentally friendly LEED° recommended practices to ensure the responsible use of our natural resources. Canisius has also made a significant investment in energy conservation measures and software that reduces our consumption of utilities. Topics such as Sustainability, Carbon inventory, Ongoing Conservation Efforts, Green Building Design Strategies, Green Computing, Heating and Cooling Standards, Recycling, Renewable Energy, Smart Energy Behaviors and Awareness and Promotional Campaigns will be introduced and explained in future web issues.

ADMISSIONS

Freshman Academic Profile: 90.3. 25% in top 10% of high school class, 55% in top 25% of high school class, 86% in top 50% of high school class. 71% from public high schools. SAT Math middle 50% range 500-600. SAT Critical Reading middle 50% range 490-590. ACT middle 50% range 22-28. Minimum web-based TOEFL 65. Minimum paper TOEFL 500. **Basis for Candidate Selection:** *Very important factors considered include:* academic GPA, rigor of secondary school record. *Important factors considered include:* application essay, recommendation(s), standardized test scores. *Other factors considered include:* Class rank, alumni/ae relation, character/personal qualities, extracurricular activities, first generation, interview, talent/ability, volunteer work, work experience. **Freshman Admission Requirements:** High school diploma is required and GED is accepted. *Academic units required:* 4 English, 3 mathematics, 2 science, (2 science labs) 2 foreign language, 4 social studies. *Academic units recommended:* 4 English, 3 mathematics, 2 science, (2 science labs), 2 foreign language, 4 social studies. **Freshman Admission Statistics:** 4,361 applied, 74% admitted, 22% enrolled. **Transfer Admission Requirements:** college transcript(s), statement of good standing from prior institution(s). Minimum college GPA of 2.0 required. Lowest grade transferable C. **General Admission Information:** Application Fee $40. Regular application deadline 5/1. Notification on a rolling basis, beginning on or about 12/15. Nonfall registration accepted. Admission may be deferred for a maximum of 1 year. Credit and/or placement offered for CEEB Advanced Placement tests.

COSTS AND FINANCIAL AID

Annual tuition $30,780. Room and board $11,820. Required fees $1,250. Average book expense $700. **Required Forms and Deadlines:** FAFSA, state aid form. **Notification of Awards:** Applicants will be notified of awards on a rolling basis beginning 3/1. **Types of Aid:** *Need-based scholarships/grants:* Federal Pell, SEOG, state scholarships/grants, private scholarships, the school's own gift aid. *Loans:* Subsidized Stafford, Unsubsidized Stafford, PLUS, Federal Perkins.

Student Employment: Federal Work-Study Program available. Institutional employment available. Highest amount earned per year from on-campus jobs $2,175. Off-campus job opportunities are excellent. **Financial Aid Statistics:** 100% freshmen, 99% undergrads receive need-based scholarship or grant aid. 22% freshmen, 19% undergrads receive non-need-based scholarship or grant aid. 80% freshmen, 80% undergrads receive need-based self-help aid. 3% freshmen, 3% undergrads receive athletic scholarships. 98% freshmen, 97% undergrads receive any aid. 72% undergrads borrow to pay for school. Average cumulative indebtedness $36,383. **Criteria for awarding institutional aid:** *Non-need-based:* academics, alumni affiliation, art, athletics, job skills, music/drama, religious affiliation.

CAPE BRETON UNIVERSITY

PO Box 5300, Sydney, NS B1P 6L2
Phone: 902-563-1117 • **Financial Aid Phone:** 902-563-1420
E-mail: registrar@uccb.ns.ca
Fax: 902-563-1371 • **Website:** www.cbu.ca

This public school was founded in 1974. It has a 140-acre campus.

RATINGS

Admissions Selectivity Rating: 62   **Fire Safety Rating:** 60*   **Green Rating:** 60*

STUDENTS AND FACULTY

Enrollment: 2,702. **Student Body:** 58% female, 42% male, (40 countries represented).
Retention and Graduation: 55% freshmen return for sophomore year. 54% freshmen graduate within 4 years. 96% freshmen graduate within 6 years. **Faculty:** Student/faculty ratio 15:1. 189 full-time faculty, 41% hold PhDs, 25% are women. 0% of classes are taught by teaching assistants.

ACADEMICS

Degrees: bachelor's, certificate, diploma, master's, post-bachelor's certificate. **Classes:** Most classes have fewer than 10 students. **Majors with Highest Enrollment:** early childhood education and teaching; education; mathematics and computer science. **Special Study Options:** cooperative education program, distance learning, double major, honors program, independent study, internships, liberal arts/career combination, study abroad. **Combined Degree Programs:** BBA/BACS. **Disability Services:** Special programs offered to physically disabled students include note-taking services, reader services, tape recorders, tutors.

FACILITIES

Housing: Coed dorms. 100% of campus accessible to physically disabled. **Special Academic Facilities/Equipment:** Art Gallery Boardmore Playhouse CAPR Radio **Computers:** Students can register for classes online. Administrative functions (other than registration) can be performed online.

CAMPUS LIFE

Environment: Town. **Activities:** drama/theater, literary magazine, radio station, student government, student newspaper, yearbook 72 registered organizations, 1 honor societies. **Athletics (Intercollegiate):** *Men:* basketball, soccer. *Women:* basketball, soccer, volleyball. **On-Campus Highlights:** Pit Lounge, Sullivan Field House Athletic Centre, Great Hall, Boardmore Playhouse, Centre for Cape Breton Studies.

ADMISSIONS

Freshman Academic Profile: 80% from public high schools. Minimum paper TOEFL 550. **Basis for Candidate Selection:** *Important factors considered include:* rigor of secondary school record. **Freshman Admission Requirements:** High school diploma is required and GED is not accepted. *Academic units required:* 3 English, 2 mathematics. *Academic units recommended:* 3 English, 2 mathematics. **Freshman Admission Statistics:** 1,679 applied, 89% admitted, 85% enrolled. **Transfer Admission Requirements:** college transcript(s). **General Admission Information:** Application Fee $20. Regular application deadline 8/1. Notification on a rolling basis, beginning on or about 3/1. Nonfall registration accepted. Admission may be deferred for a maximum of 1 year.

COSTS AND FINANCIAL AID

Annual in-state tuition $3,887. **Student Employment:** Institutional employment available. Off-campus job opportunities are good.

CAPITAL UNIVERSITY

Admission Office, Columbus, OH 43209
Phone: 614-236-6101 • **Financial Aid Phone:** 614-236-6511
E-mail: admissions@capital.edu • **CEEB Code:** 1099
Fax: 614-236-6926 • **Website:** www.capital.edu • **ACT Code:** 3242

This private school, affiliated with the Lutheran Church, was founded in 1830. It has a 48-acre campus.

RATINGS
Admissions Selectivity Rating: 73   **Fire Safety Rating:** 62   **Green Rating:** 68

STUDENTS AND FACULTY
Enrollment: 2,606. **Student Body:** 57% female, 43% male, 10% out-of-state, 1% international (16 countries represented). Asian 1%, African American 10%, Caucasian 80%, Hispanic 3%, Native American 0%.
Retention and Graduation: 75% freshmen return for sophomore year. 50% freshmen graduate within 4 years. 59% freshmen graduate within 6 years.
Faculty: Student/faculty ratio 11:1. 182 full-time faculty, 77% hold PhDs, 12% are members of minority groups, 48% are women. 0% of classes are taught by teaching assistants.

ACADEMICS
Degrees: bachelor's, first professional, master's. **Classes:** Most classes have 10–19 students. Most lab/discussion sessions have 20–29 students. **Majors with Highest Enrollment:** education; multi-/interdisciplinary studies, other; nursing/registered nurse (rn, asn, bsn, msn). **Special Study Options:** Accelerated program, cooperative education program, cross-registration, double major, English as a Second Language (ESL), exchange student program (domestic), honors program, independent study, internships, liberal arts/career combination, student-designed major, study abroad, teacher certification program. **Honors Programs:** Capital University Honors Program. **Combined Degree Programs:** MSN/JD, MSN/MBA, MSN/Master's of Lay Ministry. **Disability Services:** Special programs offered to physically disabled students include tape recorders, tutors. **Career Services:** Alumni network, alumni services, career/job search classes, career assessment, internships.

FACILITIES
Housing: Coed dorms, special housing for disabled students, special housing for international students, fraternity/sorority housing, apartments for single students, Student organization and special interest housing. 100% of campus accessible to physically disabled. **Special Academic Facilities/Equipment:** Art gallery, Conservatory of Music **Computers:** Students can register for classes online. Administrative functions (other than registration) can be performed online.

CAMPUS LIFE
Environment: Metropolis. **Activities:** Choral groups, concert band, dance, drama/theater, jazz band, literary magazine, music ensembles, musical theater, radio station, student government, student newspaper, symphony orchestra, television station, yearbook, Campus Ministries, International Student Organization 63 registered organizations, 16 honor societies, 5 religious organizations. 5 fraternities, 5 sororities. **Athletics (Intercollegiate):** *Men:* baseball, basketball, cross-country, football, golf, soccer, tennis, track/field (outdoor), track/field (indoor). *Women:* basketball, cross-country, golf, soccer, softball, tennis, track/field (outdoor), track/field (indoor), volleyball. **On-Campus Highlights:** Capital Center, College Avenue Residence Hall, Schumacher Gallery **Environmental Initiatives:** Energy management Solid waste recycling Behavior modification

ADMISSIONS
Freshman Academic Profile: Average high school GPA 3.4. 21% in top 10% of high school class, 49% in top 25% of high school class, 82% in top 50% of high school class. 92% from public high schools. SAT Math middle 50% range 470-600. SAT Critical Reading middle 50% range 470-600. SAT Writing middle 50% range 450-580. ACT middle 50% range 21-27. Minimum paper TOEFL 500. **Basis for Candidate Selection:** *Very important factors considered include:* academic GPA, rigor of secondary school record, standardized test scores. *Important factors considered include:* Class rank, extracurricular activities, interview. *Other factors considered include:* recommendation(s), alumni/ae relation, character/personal qualities, level of applicant's interest, racial/ethnic status, religious affiliation/commitment, talent/ability. **Freshman Admission Requirements:** High school diploma is required and GED is accepted. *Academic units required:* 4 English, 3 mathematics, 3 science, (2 science labs), 2 foreign language, 3 social studies, 1 academic electives. *Academic units recommended:* 4 English, 3 mathematics, 3 science, (2 science labs), 2 foreign language, 3 social studies, 1 academic electives. **Freshman Admission Statistics:** 3,844 applied, 75% admitted, 23% enrolled. **Transfer Admission Requirements:** college transcript(s), minimum college GPA of 2.5 required. Lowest grade transferable C-. **General Admission Information:** Application Fee $25. Notification on a

rolling basis, beginning on or about 9/15. Nonfall registration accepted. Admission may be deferred for a maximum of 1 year. Credit and/or placement offered for CEEB Advanced Placement tests.

COSTS AND FINANCIAL AID
Annual tuition $31,364. Room and board $8,460. Average book expense $1,000. **Required Forms and Deadlines:** FAFSA. **Notification of Awards:** Applicants will be notified of awards on a rolling basis beginning 3/1. **Types of Aid:** *Need-based scholarships/grants:* Federal Pell, SEOG, state scholarships/grants, private scholarships, the school's own gift aid. *Loans:* Subsidized Stafford, Unsubsidized Stafford, PLUS, Federal Perkins, Federal Nursing, state loans, college/university loans from institutional funds. **Student Employment:** Federal Work-Study Program available. Institutional employment available. Off-campus job opportunities are good. **Financial Aid Statistics:** 98% freshmen, 94% undergrads receive need-based scholarship or grant aid. 97% freshmen, 95% undergrads receive non-need-based scholarship or grant aid. 81% freshmen, 81% undergrads receive need-based self-help aid. 99% freshmen receive any aid. 79% undergrads borrow to pay for school. Average cumulative indebtedness $33,200.

CAPITOL COLLEGE

11301 Springfield Road, Laurel, MD 20708
Phone: 800-950-1992
E-mail: admissions@capitol-college.edu
Fax: 301-953-1442 • **Website:** www.capitol-college.edu

This is a private school.

RATINGS
Admissions Selectivity Rating: 66   **Fire Safety Rating:** 60*   **Green Rating:** 60*

STUDENTS AND FACULTY
Enrollment: 452. **Student Body:** 22% female, 78% male, 14% out-of-state, 4% international. Asian 7%, African American 36%, Caucasian 48%, Hispanic 2%, Native American 0%.
Retention and Graduation: 60% freshmen return for sophomore year. 5% freshmen graduate within 4 years. 36% freshmen graduate within 6 years. 10% grads go on to further study within 1 year. 10% grads pursue arts and sciences degrees. **Faculty:** Student/faculty ratio 12:1. 21 full-time faculty, 33% hold PhDs, 14% are members of minority groups, 29% are women.

ACADEMICS
Degrees: associate, bachelor's, certificate, master's, post-bachelor's certificate, transfer associate. **Classes:** Most classes have 10-19 students. Most lab/discussion sessions have fewer than 10 students. **Majors with Highest Enrollment:** aerospace, aeronautical and astronautical engineering; computer engineering; electrical, electronics and communications engineering. **Special Study Options:** cooperative education program, distance learning, double major, independent study, internships, weekend college. **Disability Services:** Special programs offered to physically disabled students include note-taking services, tape recorders, tutors. **Career Services:** alumni services, career/job search classes, career assessment, internships.

FACILITIES
Housing: men's dorms, women's dorms, apartments for single students. 99% of campus accessible to physically disabled. **Computers:**

CAMPUS LIFE
Environment: Activities: dance, drama/theater, literary magazine, radio station, student government, student newspaper 10 registered organizations, 3 honor societies.

ADMISSIONS
Freshman Academic Profile: 85% from public high schools. SAT Math middle 50% range 350-590. SAT Critical Reading middle 50% range 400-520. Minimum paper TOEFL 500. **Basis for Candidate Selection:** *Very important factors considered include:* rigor of secondary school record. *Important factors considered include:* application essay, standardized test scores. *Other factors considered include:* recommendation(s), alumni/ae relation, character/personal qualities, extracurricular activities, interview, talent/ability, volunteer work, work experience. **Freshman Admission Requirements:** High school diploma is required and GED is accepted. *Academic units required:* 4 English, 3 mathematics, 3 science, (2 science labs), 0 history. *Academic units recommended:* 4 English, 3 mathematics, 3 science, (2 science labs), 0 history. **Freshman Admission Statistics:** 190 applied, 86% admitted, 21% enrolled. **Transfer Admission Requirements:** college transcript(s), essay or personal statement, minimum college GPA of 2.0 required. Lowest grade transferable c. **General Admission Information:** Application Fee $25. Notification on a rolling basis,

beginning on or about 11/15. Nonfall registration accepted. Admission may be deferred for a maximum of 1. Credit and/or placement offered for CEEB Advanced Placement tests.

COSTS AND FINANCIAL AID
Annual tuition $16,500. Room and board $3,710. Required fees $600. Average book expense $800. **Required Forms and Deadlines:** FAFSA, institution's own financial aid form. **Notification of Awards:** Applicants will be notified of awards on a rolling basis beginning 6/30. **Types of Aid:** *Need-based scholarships/grants:* Federal Pell, SEOG, state scholarships/grants, private scholarships, the school's own gift aid. *Loans:* Subsidized Stafford, Unsubsidized Stafford, PLUS, Federal Perkins. **Student Employment:** Federal Work-Study Program available. Institutional employment available. Highest amount earned per year from on-campus jobs $2,000. Off-campus job opportunities are excellent. **Financial Aid Statistics:** 83% undergrads receive need-based scholarship or grant aid. 3% undergrads receive non-need-based scholarship or grant aid. 47% freshmen, 69% undergrads receive need-based self-help aid. 89% undergrads borrow to pay for school. Average cumulative indebtedness $18,000. **Criteria for awarding institutional aid:** *Non-need-based:* academics, alumni affiliation, leadership, minority status.

CARLETON COLLEGE

100 South College Street, Northfield, MN 55057
Phone: 507-222-4190 • **Financial Aid Phone:** 507-222-4138
E-mail: admissions@carleton.edu • **CEEB Code:** 6081
Fax: 507-222-4526 • **Website:** www.carleton.edu • **ACT Code:** 2092

This private school was founded in 1866. It has a 955-acre campus.

RATINGS
Admissions Selectivity Rating: 97   **Fire Safety Rating:** 65   **Green Rating:** 90

STUDENTS AND FACULTY
Enrollment: 2,035. **Student Body:** 53% female, 47% male, 78% out-of-state, 8% international (42 countries represented). Asian 8%, African American 3%, Caucasian 67%, Hispanic 6%, Native American 0%.
Retention and Graduation: 98% freshmen return for sophomore year. 91% freshmen graduate within 4 years. 26% grads go on to further study within 1 year. 12% grads pursue arts and sciences degrees. 3% grads pursue law degrees. 2% grads pursue medical degrees. **Faculty:** Student/faculty ratio 9:1. 220 full-time faculty, 97% hold PhDs, 22% are members of minority groups, 47% are women. 0% of classes are taught by teaching assistants.

ACADEMICS
Degrees: bachelor's. **Classes:** Most classes have 10–19 students. Most lab/discussion sessions have 10–19 students. **Majors with Highest Enrollment:** biology/biological sciences; economics; political science and government. **Special Study Options:** Accelerated program, cross-registration, double major, dual enrollment, independent study, internships, student-designed major, study abroad, teacher certification program. **Combined Degree Programs:** BA/JD, 3-2 Nursing, Elementary Education. **Disability Services:** Special programs offered to physically disabled students include note-taking services, reader services, tape recorders, tutors. **Career Services:** Alumni network, regional alumni.

FACILITIES
Housing: Coed dorms, special housing for disabled students, apartments for single students, 25 college-owned houses within 2 blocks of campus with varying meal plan options. Some are designated as special interest houses (ex: Green House, Culinary House). 28% of campus accessible to physically disabled. **Special Academic Facilities/Equipment:** Arboretum, greenhouse, observatory, scanning and transmission electron microscopes, refractor and reflector telescopes, nuclear magnetic resonance spectrometer, art gallery. **Computers:** 45% of classrooms, 15% of dorms, 85% of libraries, 50% of dining areas, 100% of student union, 15% of common outdoor areas have wireless network access. Students can register for classes online.

CAMPUS LIFE
Environment: Village. **Activities:** Choral groups, concert band, dance, drama/theater, jazz band, literary magazine, music ensembles, musical theater, radio station, student government, student newspaper, student-run film society, symphony orchestra, yearbook, Campus Ministries, International Student Organization, Model UN 132 registered organizations, 3 honor societies, 17

religious organizations. **Athletics (Intercollegiate):** *Men:* baseball, basketball, cross-country, diving, football, golf, soccer, swimming, tennis, track/field (outdoor), track/field (indoor). *Women:* basketball, cross-country, diving, golf, soccer, softball, swimming, synchronized swimming, tennis, track/field (outdoor), track/field (indoor), volleyball. **On-Campus Highlights:** Cowling Arboretum, Art Gallery, Historic Goodsell Observatory, Japanese Garden, Recreation Center, Sayles Campus Center, Library. **Environmental Initiatives:** 2nd Wind Turbine provided power directly to the campus grid Completed climate action plan Hiring a manager of Campus Energy and Sustainability and five student sustainability assistants (STA's)

ADMISSIONS
Freshman Academic Profile: 78% in top 10% of high school class, 98% in top 25% of high school class, 100% in top 50% of high school class. 60% from public high schools. SAT Math middle 50% range 660-760. SAT Critical Reading middle 50% range 660-750. SAT Writing middle 50% range 660-750. ACT middle 50% range 29-33. Minimum paper TOEFL 600. **Basis for Candidate Selection:** *Very important factors considered include:* Class rank, academic GPA, rigor of secondary school record. *Important factors considered include:* application essay, recommendation(s), standardized test scores, alumni/ae relation, character/personal qualities, extracurricular activities, racial/ethnic status, talent/ability, volunteer work, work experience. *Other factors considered include:* first generation, geographical residence, interview, state residency. **Freshman Admission Requirements:** High school diploma is required and GED is accepted. **Freshman Admission Statistics:** 4,988 applied, 31% admitted, 34% enrolled. **Transfer Admission Requirements:** High school transcript, college transcript(s), essay or personal statement, standardized test scores, statement of good standing from prior institution(s). Minimum college GPA of 2.0 required. Lowest grade transferable C-. **General Admission Information:** Application Fee $30. Early decision application deadline 11/15. Regular application deadline 1/15. Regular notification 4/15. Nonfall registration not accepted. Admission may be deferred for a maximum of 1 year. Credit and/or placement offered for CEEB Advanced Placement tests.

COSTS AND FINANCIAL AID
Annual tuition $44,184. Room and board $11,553. Required fees $261. Average book expense $1,460. **Required Forms and Deadlines:** FAFSA, CSS/Financial Aid PROFILE, noncustodial PROFILE, business/farm supplement. Prior year tax forms. **Notification of Awards:** Applicants will be notified of awards on or about 4/1. **Types of Aid:** *Need-based scholarships/grants:* Federal Pell, SEOG, state scholarships/grants, private scholarships, the school's own gift aid. *Loans:* Subsidized Stafford, Unsubsidized Stafford, PLUS, Federal Perkins, state loans, college/university loans from institutional funds, Minnesota SELF Loan program. **Student Employment:** Federal Work-Study Program available. **Financial Aid Statistics:** 100% freshmen, 100% undergrads receive need-based scholarship or grant aid. 16% freshmen, 18% undergrads receive non-need-based scholarship or grant aid. 97% freshmen, 98% undergrads receive need-based self-help aid. 55% freshmen, 55% undergrads receive any aid. 45% undergrads borrow to pay for school. Average cumulative indebtedness $19,341. **Criteria for awarding institutional aid:** *Non-need-based:* academics.

CARLOS ALBIZU UNIVERSITY—CAU

2173 NW 99 Ave, Miami, FL 33172
Phone: 800-672-3246
E-mail: admissions@albizu.edu
Fax: 305-593-1854 • **Website:** www.mia.albizu.edu

This private school was founded in 1966. It has a 18-acre campus.

RATINGS
Admissions Selectivity Rating: 63   **Fire Safety Rating:** 60*   **Green Rating:** 60*

STUDENTS AND FACULTY
Enrollment: 563. **Student Body:** 74% female, 26% male, % out-of-state, 2% international. Asian 0%, African American 17%, Caucasian 6%, Hispanic 137%, Native American 0%.
Retention and Graduation: 60% grads go on to further study within 1 year. 85% grads pursue arts and sciences degrees. **Faculty:** Student/faculty ratio 13:1. 4 full-time faculty, 100% hold PhDs, 25% are members of minority groups, 50% are women.

ACADEMICS
Degrees: bachelor's, diploma, master's. **Special Study Options:** Accelerated program, cooperative education program, cross-registration, double major, dual enrollment, English as a Second Language (ESL), independent study, internships, teacher certification program, weekend college.

CAMPUS LIFE

Environment: Activities: student government, student newspaper 3 registered organizations, 1 honor societies.

ADMISSIONS

Basis for Candidate Selection: *Very important factors considered include:* rigor of secondary school record. **Freshman Admission Requirements:** High school diploma is required and GED is accepted. **Freshman Admission Statistics:** 185 applied, 64% admitted, 54% enrolled. Minimum college GPA of 2.0 required. Lowest grade transferable C. **General Admission Information:** Application Fee $25. Nonfall registration accepted. Admission may be deferred for a maximum of 1 year.

COSTS AND FINANCIAL AID

Annual tuition $8,250. Average book expense $690. **Required Forms and Deadlines:** FAFSA, institution's own financial aid form. **Notification of Awards:** Applicants will be notified of awards on a rolling basis beginning 2/1. **Types of Aid:** *Need-based scholarships/grants: Loans:* **Student Employment:** Off-campus job opportunities are good. **Financial Aid Statistics:** 83% freshmen, 90% undergrads receive need-based scholarship or grant aid. 3% undergrads receive non-need-based scholarship or grant aid. 96% freshmen, 97% undergrads receive need-based self-help aid. 85% undergrads borrow to pay for school. Average cumulative indebtedness $23,500. **Criteria for awarding institutional aid:** *Non-need-based:* academics.

CARLOW UNIVERSITY

3333 Fifth Avenue, Pittsburgh, PA 15213-3165
Phone: 412-578-6059
E-mail: admissions@carlow.edu • **CEEB Code:** 2421
Fax: 412-578-6668 • **Website:** www.carlow.edu • **ACT Code:** 2421

This private school, affiliated with the Roman Catholic Church, was founded in 1929. It has a 15-acre campus.

RATINGS

Admissions Selectivity Rating: 74   **Fire Safety Rating:** 62   **Green Rating:** 60*

STUDENTS AND FACULTY

Enrollment: 1,373. **Student Body:** 92% female, 8% male, 4% out-of-state, 0% international (14 countries represented). Asian 1%, African American 19%, Caucasian 56%, Hispanic 2%, Native American 1%. **Retention and Graduation:** 70% freshmen return for sophomore year. 44% freshmen graduate within 4 years. **Faculty:** Student/faculty ratio 11:1. 98 full-time faculty, 76% hold PhDs, 8% are members of minority groups, 92% are women. 0% of classes are taught by teaching assistants.

ACADEMICS

Degrees: bachelor's, master's, post-bachelor's certificate, post-master's certificate. **Classes:** Most classes have 10–19 students. **Majors with Highest Enrollment:** business/commerce; elementary education and teaching; nursing, other. **Special Study Options:** Accelerated program, cross-registration, distance learning, double major, dual enrollment, honors program, independent study, internships, liberal arts/career combination, student-designed major, study abroad, teacher certification program, weekend college, 3/2 programs with Carnegie Mellon for Chem. Engineering, Environmental Engineering, Mechanical Engineering. Other programs with Duquesne U. in Environmental Science and Mgt.(3/2), several programs with Art Institute of Pittsburgh. **Career Services:** Alumni network, career/job search classes

FACILITIES

Housing: women's dorms. **Special Academic Facilities/Equipment:** The A.J. Palumbo Hall of Science and Technology. features research labs, as well as a greenhouse, darkroom, biochamber, an on-site reference library and specially designed study and work zones on every floor to encourage team research. The building incorporates more than 1000 outlets for internet access. Also,on-campus preschool and elementary school. **Computers:** 100% of classrooms, 100% of dorms, 100% of libraries, 100% of dining areas, 100% of student union, have wireless network access. Students can register for classes online.

CAMPUS LIFE

Environment: City. **Activities:** Choral groups, drama/theater, literary magazine, student government, student newspaper, yearbook, Campus Ministries, International Student Organization 28 registered organizations, 5 honor societies, 1 religious organizations. **Athletics (Intercollegiate):** *Women:* basketball, soccer, softball, tennis, volleyball.

ADMISSIONS

Freshman Academic Profile: Average high school GPA 3.6. 16% in top 10% of high school class, 39% in top 25% of high school class, 78% in top 50% of

high school class. SAT Math middle 50% range 420-520. SAT Critical Reading middle 50% range 418-520. SAT Writing middle 50% range 410-510. ACT middle 50% range 17-22. **Basis for Candidate Selection:** *Very important factors considered include:* academic GPA, rigor of secondary school record, standardized test scores. *Important factors considered include:* Class rank. *Other factors considered include:* application essay, recommendation(s), alumni/ae relation, character/personal qualities, extracurricular activities, first generation, interview, level of applicant's interest, talent/ability, volunteer work, work experience. **Freshman Admission Requirements:** High school diploma is required and GED is accepted. *Academic units required:* 4 English, 3 mathematics, 3 science, 2 social studies, 2 history, 4 academic electives. *Academic units recommended:* 4 English, 3 mathematics, 3 science, 2 social studies, 2 history, 4 academic electives. **Freshman Admission Statistics:** 1,169 applied, 61% admitted, 31% enrolled. **Transfer Admission Requirements:** college transcript(s), minimum college GPA of 2.0 required. Lowest grade transferable C. **General Admission Information:** Application Fee $20. Nonfall registration accepted. Credit and/or placement offered for CEEB Advanced Placement tests.

COSTS AND FINANCIAL AID

Annual tuition $24,230. Room and board $9,630. Required fees $208. Average book expense $1,020. **Required Forms and Deadlines:** FAFSA. **Notification of Awards:** Applicants will be notified of awards on a rolling basis beginning 2/15. **Types of Aid:** *Need-based scholarships/grants:* Federal Pell, SEOG, state scholarships/grants, private scholarships, the school's own gift aid. *Loans:* Subsidized Stafford, Unsubsidized Stafford, PLUS, Federal Perkins, Federal Nursing. **Student Employment: Financial Aid Statistics:** 100% freshmen, 100% undergrads receive need-based scholarship or grant aid. 26% freshmen, 36% undergrads receive non-need-based scholarship or grant aid. 65% freshmen, 95% undergrads receive need-based self-help aid. 1% undergrads receive athletic scholarships. 97% undergrads borrow to pay for school. Average cumulative indebtedness $36,776. **Criteria for awarding institutional aid:** *Non-need-based:* academics, athletics, leadership.

CARNEGIE MELLON UNIVERSITY

Best 378

5000 Forbes Avenue, Pittsburgh, PA 15213
Phone: 412-268-2082 • **Financial Aid Phone:** 412-268-8186
E-mail: undergraduate-admissions@andrew.cmu.edu • **CEEB Code:** 2074
Fax: 412-268-7838 • **Website:** www.cmu.edu • **ACT Code:** 3534

This private school was founded in 1900. It has a 136-acre campus.

RATINGS

Admissions Selectivity Rating: 98   **Fire Safety Rating:** 92   **Green Rating:** 95

STUDENTS AND FACULTY

Enrollment: 6,203. **Student Body:** 43% female, 57% male, 82% out-of-state, 16% international (116 countries represented). Asian 22%, African American 5%, Caucasian 39%, Hispanic 7%, Native American 0%. **Retention and Graduation:** 95% freshmen return for sophomore year. 73% freshmen graduate within 4 years. 87% freshmen graduate within 6 years. 29% grads go on to further study within 1 year. 15% grads pursue arts and sciences degrees. 1% grads pursue law degrees. 1% grads pursue business degrees. 1% grads pursue medical degrees.

ACADEMICS

Degrees: bachelor's, master's, post-master's certificate. **Classes:** Most classes have fewer than 10 students. Most lab/discussion sessions have 20–29 students. **Majors with Highest Enrollment:** computer science. **Special Study Options:** cooperative education program, cross-registration, distance learning, double major, dual enrollment, exchange student program (domestic), independent study, internships, liberal arts/career combination, student-designed major, study abroad, teacher certification program. **Combined Degree Programs:** BA/MA, BA/MEng, BS/MBA Industrial Admin; BS/MPM Public Management. **Disability Services:** Special programs offered to physically disabled students include note-taking services, reader services, tape recorders, tutors. **Career Services:** Alumni network, alumni services, career/job search classes, career assessment, internships, regional alumni. Career Services highlights include INTERNSHIPS. Our mission: °Students who value experiential learning and who have participated in internships; campus, summer, part-time employment; and/or community service opportunities. °An energized and expanding employer base (artistic, corporate, public, service, campus) committed to long term relationships with Carnegie Mellon (and the Career Center) founded on the continual enhancement and development of employer relationships. Internship Development and Placement Programs: -Student Employment-Experiential and Professional Development -Pittsburgh Funded Internships (provide funds for students to stay in Pittsburgh for a summer position) -Employment Opportunities Conference (Job Fair) -On-Campus Recruiting -Networking Events-New York, DC, Boston, Chicago, Silicon Valley, Pittsburgh, Baltimore -Internship Search Workshop Series.

FACILITIES

Housing: Coed dorms, special housing for disabled students, men's dorms, women's dorms, fraternity/sorority housing, apartments for single students, Special interest housing. 95% of campus accessible to physically disabled. **Special Academic Facilities/Equipment:** Rare books collection, Entertainment Technology Center, Art galleries, Theatres, Botanical Institute, Extensive lab facilities and equipment, Recording studio, Robotics Institute, Design studios, Photo shoot studio and darkrooms, Radio station, Collaborative Innovation Center, LEED-certified green residence hall, Campo Garden, Observatory, Wood shops **Computers:** 100% of classrooms, 100% of dorms, 100% of libraries, 100% of dining areas, 100% of student union, 100% of common outdoor areas have wireless network access. Students can register for classes online. Administrative functions (other than registration) can be performed online.

CAMPUS LIFE

Environment: Metropolis. **Activities:** Choral groups, concert band, dance, drama/theater, literary magazine, marching band, music ensembles, musical theater, pep band, radio station, student government, student newspaper, student-run film society, symphony orchestra, television station, yearbook, Campus Ministries, International Student Organization 225 registered organizations, 18 religious organizations. 16 fraternities, 7 sororities. **Athletics (Intercollegiate):** *Men:* basketball, cheerleading, cross-country, diving, football, golf, soccer, swimming, tennis, track/field (outdoor). *Women:* basketball, cheerleading, cross-country, diving, soccer, swimming, tennis, track/field (outdoor), volleyball. **On-Campus Highlights:** Hunt Library, Skibo Coffee House, The Cut, The Underground, University Center Building - Student Center. **Environmental Initiatives:** PRACTICE: Bellfield Boiler Plant now using Natural Gas instead of Coal as fuel to produce steam, the purchase of 100% renewable electricity for campus electricity needs and, at minimum, USGBC LEED Silver guidelines required for all building projects and most renovations. EDUCATION - We strive to make every student a steward of the environment through both formal and informal education. Carnegie Mellon offers many courses in the realm of environment and sustainability, including a weekend long immersion course, Environment Today, which is a student driven course focusing on a different sustainability topic each year. CMU offers graduate programs in Civil and Environmental Enginnering, Sustainable Design Engineering and Public Policy and Energy, Science, Technology and Policy. Undergraduate majors are available in Civil and Environmental Enginerering and Environmental Policy, with minors available in Environmental Studies and Environmental Science. Informal education is delivered through our campus operations and promoted by our Green Practices Committee as well as our many student groups. RESEARCH: At Carnegie Mellon we are building a path to an environmentally sustainable society by promoting a culture of interdisciplinary, collaborative research in the realm of science, trechnology, policy, culture and community. The Steinbrenner Institute for Environmental Education and Research, formed in 2004 to promote Carnegie Mellon's strategic goal of "transitioning towards an environmentally sustainable society" coordinates and advances the research done by 20 centers that are spread among all seven colleges at the Univesity. Research Centers include; Climate Decision Making Center, The Green Design Institute, WaterQUEST, and the STUDIO for Creative Inquiry.

ADMISSIONS

Freshman Academic Profile: Average high school GPA 3.7. 76% in top 10% of high school class, 93% in top 25% of high school class, 99% in top 50% of high school class. SAT Math middle 50% range 690-790. SAT Critical Reading middle 50% range 630-730. SAT Writing middle 50% range 650-740. ACT middle 50% range 29-33. Minimum paper TOEFL 600. **Basis for Candidate Selection:** *Very important factors considered include:* Class rank, academic GPA, rigor of secondary school record, standardized test scores. *Important factors considered include:* application essay, recommendation(s), alumni/ae relation, character/personal qualities, extracurricular activities, first generation, interview, level of applicant's interest, racial/ethnic status, talent/ability, volunteer work, work experience. **Freshman Admission Requirements:** High school diploma is required and GED is accepted. *Academic units required:* 4 English, 4 mathematics, 3 science, (3 science labs), 2 foreign language, 3 academic electives. *Academic units recommended:* 4 English, 4 mathematics, 3 science, (3 science labs), 2 foreign language, 3 academic electives. **Freshman Admission Statistics:** 17,313 applied, 28% admitted, 29% enrolled. **Transfer Admission Requirements:** High school transcript, college transcript(s), essay or personal statement, standardized test scores, statement of good standing from prior institution(s). **General Admission Information:** Application Fee $70. Early decision application deadline 11/1. Regular application deadline 1/1. Regular

notification 4/15. Nonfall registration not accepted. Admission may be deferred for a maximum of 1 year. Credit offered for CEEB Advanced Placement tests.

COSTS AND FINANCIAL AID

Annual tuition $46,220. Room and board $11,680. Required fees $742. Average book expense $2,400. **Required Forms and Deadlines:** FAFSA, institution's own financial aid formParent and student Federal Tax Returns. Parent W2 Forms. **Notification of Awards:** Applicants will be notified of awards on or about 3/15. **Types of Aid:** *Need-based scholarships/grants:* Federal Pell, SEOG, state scholarships/grants, private scholarships, the school's own gift aid. *Loans:* Subsidized Stafford, Unsubsidized Stafford, PLUS, Federal Perkins. **Student Employment:** Federal Work-Study Program available. Institutional employment available. Off-campus job opportunities are good. **Financial Aid Statistics:** 95% freshmen, 93% undergrads receive need-based scholarship or grant aid. 35% freshmen, 38% undergrads receive non-need-based scholarship or grant aid. 96% freshmen, 97% undergrads receive need-based self-help aid. 53% freshmen, 47% undergrads receive any aid. 45% undergrads borrow to pay for school. Average cumulative indebtedness $31,747. **Criteria for awarding institutional aid:** *Non-need-based:* academics, art, leadership, minority status, music/drama, state/district residency.

CARROLL COLLEGE (MT)

1601 North Benton Avenue, Helena, MT 59625
Phone: 406-447-4384 • **Financial Aid Phone:** 406-447-5423
E-mail: admission@carroll.edu • **CEEB Code:** 4041
Fax: 406-447-4533 • **Website:** www.carroll.edu • **ACT Code:** 2408

This private school, affiliated with the Roman Catholic Church, was founded in 1909. It has a 63-acre campus.

RATINGS

Admissions Selectivity Rating: 73   **Fire Safety Rating:** 62   **Green Rating:** 60*

STUDENTS AND FACULTY

Enrollment: 1,311. **Student Body:** 56% female, 44% male, 40% out-of-state, 1% international (15 countries represented). Asian 1%, African American 1%, Caucasian 83%, Hispanic 2%, Native American 1%.
Retention and Graduation: 80% freshmen return for sophomore year. 46% freshmen graduate within 4 years. 62% freshmen graduate within 6 years. 22% grads go on to further study within 1 year. **Faculty:** Student/faculty ratio 13:1. 80 full-time faculty, 70% hold PhDs, 3% are members of minority groups, 36% are women. 0% of classes are taught by teaching assistants.

ACADEMICS

Degrees: associate, bachelor's, certificate, transfer associate. **Classes:** Most classes have 10–19 students. Most lab/discussion sessions have 20–29 students. **Majors with Highest Enrollment:** business/commerce; nursing/registered nurse (rn, asn, bsn, msn); psychology. **Special Study Options:** Accelerated program, cooperative education program, double major, dual enrollment, English as a Second Language (ESL), exchange student program (domestic), honors program, independent study, internships, liberal arts/career combination, student-designed major, study abroad, teacher certification program. **Disability Services:** Special programs offered to physically disabled students include tutors. **Career Services:** career/job search classes, career assessment, internships.

FACILITIES

Housing: Coed dorms, apartments for single students, theme housing. 75% of campus accessible to physically disabled. **Special Academic Facilities/Equipment:** Arts lab, observatory, seismograph station, engineering lab.

CAMPUS LIFE

Environment: Village. **Activities:** Choral groups, dance, drama/theater, literary magazine, music ensembles, musical theater, pep band, radio station, student government, student newspaper, student-run film society, yearbook, Campus Ministries, International Student Organization 34 registered organizations, 10 honor societies, 4 religious organizations. **Athletics (Intercollegiate):** *Men:* basketball, cheerleading, football, golf. *Women:* basketball, cheerleading, golf, soccer, volleyball. **On-Campus Highlights:** Science and Technology Center, Nelson Stadium, Campus Center, St. Charles Chapel, Fitness Center.

ADMISSIONS

Freshman Academic Profile: Average high school GPA 3.5. 26% in top 10% of high school class, 59% in top 25% of high school class, 87% in top 50% of high school class. 82% from public high schools. SAT Math middle 50% range 500-610. SAT Critical Reading middle 50% range 490-590. SAT Writing middle 50% range 480-580. ACT middle 50% range 21-26. **Basis for Candidate**

Selection: *Very important factors considered include:* rigor of secondary school record, standardized test scores. *Important factors considered include:* Class rank, application essay, academic GPA, recommendation(s), character/personal qualities. *Other factors considered include:* alumni/ae relation, extracurricular activities, interview, level of applicant's interest, religious affiliation/commitment, talent/ability, volunteer work, work experience. **Freshman Admission Requirements:** High school diploma is required and GED is accepted. **Freshman Admission Statistics:** 1,174 applied, 76% admitted, 39% enrolled. **Transfer Admission Requirements:** college transcript(s), essay or personal statement, statement of good standing from prior institution(s). Minimum college GPA of 2.5 required. Lowest grade transferable C. **General Admission Information:** Application Fee $35. Regular application deadline 6/1. Notification on a rolling basis, beginning on or about 9/10. Nonfall registration accepted. Admission may be deferred for a maximum of 1 year. Credit and/or placement offered for CEEB Advanced Placement tests.

COSTS AND FINANCIAL AID

Annual tuition $22,252. Room and board $7,118. Required fees $340. Average book expense $800. **Required Forms and Deadlines:** FAFSA. **Notification of Awards:** Applicants will be notified of awards on a rolling basis beginning 3/1. **Types of Aid:** *Need-based scholarships/grants:* Federal Pell, SEOG, state scholarships/grants, private scholarships, the school's own gift aid. *Loans:* Subsidized Stafford, Unsubsidized Stafford, PLUS, Federal Perkins, private loans. **Student Employment:** Federal Work-Study Program available. Institutional employment available. Off-campus job opportunities are good. **Financial Aid Statistics:** 83% freshmen, 89% undergrads receive need-based scholarship or grant aid. 19% freshmen, 13% undergrads receive non-need-based scholarship or grant aid. 56% freshmen, 56% undergrads receive need-based self-help aid. 4% freshmen, 3% undergrads receive athletic scholarships. 67% freshmen, 67% undergrads receive any aid. 71% undergrads borrow to pay for school. Average cumulative indebtedness $25,246. **Criteria for awarding institutional aid:** *Non-need-based:* academics, art, athletics, leadership, minority status, music/drama, religious affiliation.

CARROLL COLLEGE (WI)

100 North East Avenue, Waukesha, WI 53186
Phone: 262-524-7220 • **Financial Aid Phone:** 262-524-7297
E-mail: ccinfo@ccadmin.cc.edu • **CEEB Code:** 1101
Fax: 262-951-3037 • **Website:** www.cc.edu • **ACT Code:** 4570

This private school, affiliated with the Presbyterian Church, was founded in 1846. It has a 52-acre campus.

RATINGS
Admissions Selectivity Rating: 72   **Fire Safety Rating:** 69   **Green Rating:** 60*

STUDENTS AND FACULTY
Enrollment: 2,925. **Student Body:** 68% female, 32% male, 20% out-of-state, 2% international (39 countries represented). Asian 1%, African American 2%, Caucasian 87%, Hispanic 3%, Native American 0%. **Retention and Graduation:** 74% freshmen return for sophomore year. 41% freshmen graduate within 4 years. 53% freshmen graduate within 6 years. 13% grads go on to further study within 1 year. **Faculty:** Student/faculty ratio 16:1. 121 full-time faculty, 63% hold PhDs, 2% are members of minority groups, 46% are women. 0% of classes are taught by teaching assistants.

ACADEMICS
Degrees: bachelor's, master's, post-bachelor's certificate. **Classes:** Most classes have 10–19 students. Most lab/discussion sessions have 10–19 students. **Majors with Highest Enrollment:** business/commerce; education; nursing/registered nurse (rn, asn, bsn, msn). **Special Study Options:** distance learning, double major, exchange student program (domestic), honors program, independent study, internships, liberal arts/career combination, student-designed major, study abroad, teacher certification program. **Disability Services:** Special programs offered to physically disabled students include note-taking services, tape recorders, tutors. **Career Services:** Alumni network, career/job search classes, career assessment, internships.

FACILITIES
Housing: Coed dorms, women's dorms, apartments for single students. 50% of campus accessible to physically disabled. **Special Academic Facilities/Equipment:** A 60 acre scientific study and conservancy area with a class 1 trout stream and associated wetland and upland habitats. **Computers:** 80% of classrooms, 100% of dorms, 100% of libraries, 100% of dining areas, 100% of student union, 90% of common outdoor areas have wireless network access. Students can register for classes online. Administrative functions (other than registration) can be performed online.

CAMPUS LIFE
Environment: Town. **Activities:** Choral groups, concert band, dance, drama/theater, jazz band, literary magazine, music ensembles, pep band, radio station, student government, student newspaper, International Student Organization 40 registered organizations, 2 religious organizations. 2 fraternities, 4 sororities. **Athletics (Intercollegiate):** *Men:* baseball, basketball, cross-country, football, golf, soccer, swimming, tennis, track/field (outdoor), track/field (indoor). *Women:* basketball, cross-country, golf, soccer, softball, swimming, tennis, track/field (outdoor), track/field (indoor), volleyball. **On-Campus Highlights:** Main Hall, Van Male Fieldhouse, Campus Center, Shattuck, Physical Therapy Building.

ADMISSIONS
Freshman Academic Profile: 21% in top 10% of high school class, 55% in top 25% of high school class, 83% in top 50% of high school class. 87% from public high schools. ACT middle 50% range 20–25. Minimum paper TOEFL 550. **Basis for Candidate Selection:** *Very important factors considered include:* Class rank, academic GPA, rigor of secondary school record. *Important factors considered include:* standardized test scores. *Other factors considered include:* application essay, recommendation(s), alumni/ae relation, character/personal qualities, extracurricular activities, geographical residence, interview, racial/ethnic status, state residency, talent/ability, work experience. **Freshman Admission Requirements:** High school diploma is required and GED is accepted. **Freshman Admission Statistics:** 2,728 applied, 72% admitted, 34% enrolled. **Transfer Admission Requirements:** High school transcript, college transcript(s), minimum college GPA of 2.0 required. Lowest grade transferable C. **General Admission Information:** Nonfall registration accepted. Credit and/or placement offered for CEEB Advanced Placement tests.

COSTS AND FINANCIAL AID
Annual tuition $20,400. Room and board $6,350. Required fees $430. Average book expense $1,060. **Required Forms and Deadlines:** FAFSA. **Notification of Awards:** Applicants will be notified of awards on a rolling basis beginning 2/15. **Types of Aid:** *Need-based scholarships/grants:* Federal Pell, SEOG, state scholarships/grants, private scholarships, the school's own gift aid, Federal Nursing Scholarships. *Loans:* Unsubsidized Stafford, PLUS, Federal Perkins, state loans. **Student Employment:** Federal Work-Study Program available. Institutional employment available. Highest amount earned per year from on-campus jobs $4,270. **Financial Aid Statistics:** 100% freshmen, 100% undergrads receive need-based scholarship or grant aid. 91% freshmen, 91% undergrads receive non-need-based scholarship or grant aid. 73% freshmen, 79% undergrads receive need-based self-help aid. 98% freshmen, 98% undergrads receive any aid. 73% undergrads borrow to pay for school. Average cumulative indebtedness $21,794. **Criteria for awarding institutional aid:** *Non-need-based:* academics, alumni affiliation, art, leadership, minority status, religious affiliation.

CARSON-NEWMAN COLLEGE

1646 Russell Avenue, Jefferson City, TN 37760
Phone: 865-471-3223
E-mail: admitme@.cn.edu • **CEEB Code:** 1102
Fax: 865-471-3502 • **Website:** www.cn.edu • **ACT Code:** 3950

This private school, affiliated with the Baptist Church, was founded in 1851. It has a 90-acre campus.

RATINGS
Admissions Selectivity Rating: 75   **Fire Safety Rating:** 60*   **Green Rating:** 60*

STUDENTS AND FACULTY
Enrollment: 1,655. **Student Body:** 54% female, 46% male, 31% out-of-state, 2% international. Asian 0%, African American 9%, Caucasian 84%, Hispanic 2%, Native American 0%. **Retention and Graduation:** 64% freshmen return for sophomore year. 30% freshmen graduate within 4 years. 45% freshmen graduate within 6 years. 25% grads go on to further study within 1 year. 20% grads pursue arts and sciences degrees. 3% grads pursue law degrees. 1% grads pursue business degrees. 2% grads pursue medical degrees. **Faculty:** Student/faculty ratio 12:1. 123 full-time faculty, 77% hold PhDs, 2% are members of minority groups, 53% are women. 0% of classes are taught by teaching assistants.

ACADEMICS
Degrees: associate, bachelor's, master's. **Classes:** Most classes have 10–19 students. Most lab/discussion sessions have 10–19 students. **Special Study Options:** cooperative education program, double major, dual enrollment, English as a Second Language (ESL), honors program, independent study, internships, student-designed major, study abroad, teacher certification program. **Disability Services:** Special programs offered to physically disabled students include

note-taking services, reader services, tape recorders, tutors. **Career Services:** alumni services, career/job search classes, career assessment.

FACILITIES

Housing: men's dorms, women's dorms, apartments for married students, apartments for single students. 80% of campus accessible to physically disabled. **Special Academic Facilities/Equipment:** Art galleries, Appalachian history museum, home management house, language lab.

CAMPUS LIFE

Environment: Rural. **Activities:** Choral groups, concert band, dance, drama/theater, jazz band, literary magazine, marching band, music ensembles, musical theater, opera, pep band, student government, student newspaper, television station, yearbook 45 registered organizations, 10 honor societies, 5 religious organizations. 2 fraternities, 2 sororities. **Athletics (Intercollegiate):** *Men:* baseball, basketball, cheerleading, cross-country, football, golf, soccer, tennis, track/field (outdoor), wrestling. *Women:* basketball, cheerleading, cross-country, soccer, softball, tennis, track/field (outdoor), volleyball. **On-Campus Highlights:** Maddox Student Activities Center, Coffee House (in MSAC) and TV lounge, Workout/Weight Rooms (in MSAC), Cafeteria, Swann Field (Intramurals).

ADMISSIONS

Freshman Academic Profile: Average high school GPA 3.4. 27% in top 10% of high school class, 47% in top 25% of high school class, 73% in top 50% of high school class. 87% from public high schools. ACT middle 50% range 20-26. Minimum paper TOEFL 550. **Basis for Candidate Selection:** *Very important factors considered include:* rigor of secondary school record, standardized test scores. *Important factors considered include:* Class rank. *Other factors considered include:* application essay, recommendation(s), alumni/ae relation, character/personal qualities, extracurricular activities, interview, religious affiliation/commitment, talent/ability, volunteer work, work experience. **Freshman Admission Requirements:** High school diploma is required and GED is accepted. *Academic units required:* 4 English, 2 mathematics, 2 science, (1 science labs), 1 social studies, 1 history, 4 academic electives. *Academic units recommended:* 4 English, 2 mathematics, 2 science, (1 science labs), 1 social studies, 1 history, 4 academic electives. **Freshman Admission Statistics:** 3,174 applied, 69% admitted, 20% enrolled. **Transfer Admission Requirements:** college transcript(s), minimum college GPA of 2.0 required. Lowest grade transferable d. **General Admission Information:** Application Fee $25. Notification on a rolling basis, beginning on or about 6/1. Nonfall registration accepted. Admission may be deferred for a maximum of 2 years. Credit and/or placement offered for CEEB Advanced Placement tests.

COSTS AND FINANCIAL AID

Annual tuition $21,660. Room and board $6,406. Required fees $992. Average book expense $1,400. **Required Forms and Deadlines:** FAFSA, institution's own financial aid form. **Notification of Awards: Types of Aid:** *Need-based scholarships/grants:* Federal Pell, SEOG, state scholarships/grants, private scholarships, the school's own gift aid. *Loans:* Direct Subsidized Stafford, Direct Unsubsidized Stafford, Direct PLUS, Federal Perkins, Federal Nursing. **Student Employment:** Federal Work-Study Program available. Institutional employment available. Highest amount earned per year from on-campus jobs $900. Off-campus job opportunities are good. **Financial Aid Statistics:** 99% freshmen, 98% undergrads receive need-based scholarship or grant aid. 98% freshmen, 96% undergrads receive non-need-based scholarship or grant aid. 76% freshmen, 79% undergrads receive need-based self-help aid. 4% freshmen, 5% undergrads receive athletic scholarships. 65% undergrads borrow to pay for school. Average cumulative indebtedness $22,306. **Criteria for awarding institutional aid:** *Non-need-based:* academics, art, athletics, leadership, minority status, music/drama, religious affiliation.

CARTHAGE COLLEGE

2001 Alford Park Drive, Kenosha, WI 53140-1994
Phone: 262-551-6000 • **Financial Aid Phone:** 262-551-6001
E-mail: admissions@carthage.edu • **CEEB Code:** 1103
Fax: 262-551-5762 • **Website:** www.carthage.edu • **ACT Code:** 4571

This private school, affiliated with the Lutheran Church, was founded in 1847. It has a 95-acre campus.

RATINGS
Admissions Selectivity Rating: 74   **Fire Safety Rating:** 73   **Green Rating:** 60*

STUDENTS AND FACULTY
Enrollment: 2,456. **Student Body:** 58% female, 42% male, 70% out-of-state, 0% international (16 countries represented). Asian 0%, African American 0%, Caucasian 0%, Hispanic 0%, Native American 0%.

Retention and Graduation: 75% freshmen return for sophomore year. 46% freshmen graduate within 4 years. 56% freshmen graduate within 6 years. 16% grads go on to further study within 1 year. 4% grads pursue arts and sciences degrees. 2% grads pursue law degrees. 1% grads pursue business degrees. 1% grads pursue medical degrees. **Faculty:** Student/faculty ratio 16:1. 126 full-time faculty, 87% hold PhDs, 6% are members of minority groups, 32% are women. 0% of classes are taught by teaching assistants.

ACADEMICS

Degrees: bachelor's, certificate, master's. **Classes:** Most classes have 20–29 students. **Majors with Highest Enrollment:** biology/biological sciences; business administration and management; elementary education and teaching. **Special Study Options:** Accelerated program, cross-registration, double major, honors program, independent study, internships, student-designed major, study abroad, teacher certification program. **Honors Programs:** We offer All College Honors as well as Honors in the Major. **Combined Degree Programs:** BA/MA, Occupational Therapy at Wash Univ - St. Louis. **Disability Services:** Special programs offered to physically disabled students include note-taking services, reader services, tape recorders, tutors. **Career Services:** career/job search classes, career assessment, internships.

FACILITIES

Housing: Coed dorms, men's dorms, women's dorms, fraternity/sorority housing, Best Western Harborside through Carthage. 99% of campus accessible to physically disabled. **Special Academic Facilities/Equipment:** H.F. Johnson Art Gallery, Center for CHildren's Literature, planetarium, undergraduate science research lab, graphic design lab, greenhouse, computer/math research lab, physics research lab, ScienceWorks lab, A.W. Clausen Center Boardroom **Computers:** Students can register for classes online. Administrative functions (other than registration) can be performed online.

CAMPUS LIFE

Environment: City. **Activities:** Choral groups, concert band, dance, drama/theater, jazz band, literary magazine, music ensembles, musical theater, opera, pep band, radio station, student government, student newspaper, student-run film society, symphony orchestra, yearbook 90 registered organizations, 20 honor societies, 7 religious organizations. 8 fraternities, 7 sororities. **Athletics (Intercollegiate):** *Men:* baseball, basketball, cross-country, football, golf, soccer, swimming, tennis, track/field (outdoor), track/field (indoor), volleyball. *Women:* basketball, cross-country, golf, soccer, softball, swimming, tennis, track/field (outdoor), track/field (indoor), volleyball, water polo. **On-Campus Highlights:** Tarble Athletic and Recreation Center, Hedberg Library, A.W. Clausen Center for World Business, Oaks Residence Halls, Lake Michigan, Located midway between Chicago and Milwaukee, Carthage is easily accessible by car, airplane and train. Our 95 acre, park-like campus is on the shore of Lake Michigan.

ADMISSIONS

Freshman Academic Profile: Average high school GPA 3.2. 19% in top 10% of high school class, 43% in top 25% of high school class, 75% in top 50% of high school class. 91% from public high schools. SAT Math middle 50% range 490-620. SAT Critical Reading middle 50% range 470-630. ACT middle 50% range 21-26. Minimum paper TOEFL 500. **Basis for Candidate Selection:** *Very important factors considered include:* academic GPA, rigor of secondary school record, standardized test scores. *Other factors considered include:* Class rank, application essay, recommendation(s), character/personal qualities, extracurricular activities, interview, talent/ability, volunteer work, work experience. **Freshman Admission Requirements:** High school diploma is required and GED is accepted. **Freshman Admission Statistics:** 4,495 applied, 77% admitted, 19% enrolled. **Transfer Admission Requirements:** college transcript(s), statement of good standing from prior institution(s). Minimum college GPA of 2.0 required. Lowest grade transferable C-. **General Admission Information:** Application Fee $25. Notification on a rolling basis, beginning on or about 9/15. Nonfall registration accepted. Admission may be deferred for a maximum of one year. Credit and/or placement offered for CEEB Advanced Placement tests.

COSTS AND FINANCIAL AID

Annual tuition $25,000. Room and board $7,000. Average book expense $1,200. **Required Forms and Deadlines:** FAFSA. **Notification of Awards:** Applicants will be notified of awards on a rolling basis beginning 3/1. **Types of Aid:** *Need-based scholarships/grants:* Federal Pell, SEOG, state scholarships/grants, private scholarships, the school's own gift aid. *Loans:* Subsidized Stafford, Unsubsidized Stafford, PLUS, Federal Perkins, state loans, college/university loans from institutional funds. **Student Employment:** Highest amount earned per year from on-campus jobs $1,000. **Financial Aid Statistics:** 100% freshmen, 99% undergrads receive need-based scholarship or grant aid. 15% freshmen, 14% undergrads receive non-need-based scholarship or grant aid. 80% freshmen, 81% undergrads receive need-based self-help aid. 97% freshmen, 97% undergrads receive any aid. **Criteria for awarding institutional aid:** *Non-need-based:* academics, alumni affiliation, art, leadership, minority status, music/drama, religious affiliation.

CASCADE COLLEGE

9101 East Burnside Street, Portland, OR 97216-1515
Phone: 503-257-1202 • **Financial Aid Phone:** 503-257-1241
E-mail: admissions@cascade.edu
Fax: 503-257-1222 • **Website:** www.cascade.edu • **ACT Code:** 3459

This private school, affiliated with the Church of Christ Church, was founded in 1993. It has a 12-acre campus.

RATINGS
Admissions Selectivity Rating: 63   **Fire Safety Rating:** 62   **Green Rating:** 60*

STUDENTS AND FACULTY
Enrollment: 262. **Student Body:** 59% female, 41% male, 64% out-of-state, 1% international (8 countries represented). Asian 3%, African American 5%, Caucasian 26%, Hispanic 5%, Native American 0%.
Retention and Graduation: 46% freshmen return for sophomore year. 23% freshmen graduate within 4 years. 30% freshmen graduate within 6 years. 15% grads go on to further study within 1 year. 10% grads pursue arts and sciences degrees. 2% grads pursue law degrees. 1% grads pursue business degrees.
Faculty: Student/faculty ratio 12:1. 15 full-time faculty, 60% hold PhDs, 13% are members of minority groups, 27% are women. 0% of classes are taught by teaching assistants.

ACADEMICS
Degrees: bachelor's. **Classes:** Most classes have 10–19 students. Most lab/discussion sessions have fewer than 10 students. **Majors with Highest Enrollment:** business/commerce; psychology; teacher education, multiple levels.
Special Study Options: double major, dual enrollment, independent study, internships, student-designed major, study abroad, teacher certification program. **Disability Services:** Special programs offered to physically disabled students include note-taking services, reader services, tutors. Career Services highlights include Most majors provide an opportunity for students to participate in an internship or practicum in the area of the major giving most graduates hand-on experience and an opportunity to experience a career in the major.

FACILITIES
Housing: special housing for disabled students, men's dorms, women's dorms, apartments for married students 70% of campus accessible to physically disabled. **Computers:** 100% of classrooms, 100% of dorms, 100% of libraries, 100% of dining areas, 100% of student union, 100% of common outdoor areas have wireless network access. Administrative functions (other than registration) can be performed online.

CAMPUS LIFE
Environment: Metropolis. **Activities:** Choral groups, drama/theater, jazz band, literary magazine, music ensembles, musical theater, student government, yearbook 16 registered organizations, 2 honor societies. **Athletics (Intercollegiate):** *Men:* basketball, cross-country, soccer, track/field (outdoor), track/field (indoor). *Women:* basketball, cross-country, soccer, track/field (outdoor), track/field (indoor), volleyball. **On-Campus Highlights:** Classrooms, Student Center, The Cabin (coffee shop), Weight room, Womack and Hamstreet Fountains.

ADMISSIONS
Freshman Academic Profile: Average high school GPA 3.0. 85% from public high schools. Minimum paper TOEFL 500. **Basis for Candidate Selection:** *Other factors considered include:* academic GPA, recommendation(s), standardized test scores. **Freshman Admission Requirements:** High school diploma is required and GED is accepted. **Transfer Admission Requirements:** High school transcript, college transcript(s), minimum college GPA of 2.0 required. Lowest grade transferable D. **General Admission Information:** Application Fee $25. Nonfall registration accepted. Admission may be deferred for a maximum of 1 year. Credit offered for CEEB Advanced Placement tests.

COSTS AND FINANCIAL AID
Average book expense $900. **Required Forms and Deadlines:** FAFSA, institution's own financial aid formPayment Plan Form FERPA Release Form. **Notification of Awards:** Applicants will be notified of awards on a rolling basis beginning 2/15. **Types of Aid:** *Need-based scholarships/grants:* Federal Pell, SEOG, private scholarships, the school's own gift aid. *Loans:* Subsidized Stafford, Unsubsidized Stafford, PLUS, Private Loans. **Student Employment:** Federal Work-Study Program available. Institutional employment available. Highest amount earned per year from on-campus jobs $2,000. Off-campus job opportunities are excellent. **Financial Aid Statistics:** 100% freshmen, 63% undergrads receive need-based scholarship or grant aid. 19% freshmen, 92% undergrads receive non-need-based scholarship or grant aid. 87% freshmen, 84% undergrads receive need-based self-help aid. 48% freshmen, 36% undergrads receive athletic scholarships. 100% freshmen, 99% undergrads receive any aid. 84% undergrads borrow to pay for school. Average cumulative indebtedness $24,988. **Criteria for awarding institutional aid:** *Non-need-*

based: academics, athletics, leadership, music/drama, religious affiliation, state/district residency.

CASE WESTERN RESERVE UNIVERSITY

Best 378

Wolstein Hall, Cleveland, OH 44106-7055
Phone: 216-368-4450 • **Financial Aid Phone:** 216-368-4530
E-mail: admission@case.edu • **CEEB Code:** 1105
Fax: 216-368-5111 • **Website:** www.case.edu • **ACT Code:** 3244

This private school was founded in 1826. It has a 155-acre campus.

RATINGS
Admissions Selectivity Rating: 93   **Fire Safety Rating:** 74   **Green Rating:** 89

STUDENTS AND FACULTY
Enrollment: 4,278. **Student Body:** 44% female, 56% male, 55% out-of-state, 7% international (30 countries represented). Asian 19%, African American 4%, Caucasian 54%, Hispanic 5%, Native American 0%.
Retention and Graduation: 92% freshmen return for sophomore year. 63% freshmen graduate within 4 years. 41% grads go on to further study within 1 year. 16% grads pursue arts and sciences degrees. 2% grads pursue law degrees. 3% grads pursue business degrees. 6% grads pursue medical degrees. **Faculty:** Student/faculty ratio 10:1. 755 full-time faculty, 91% hold PhDs, 17% are members of minority groups, 41% are women. 6% of classes are taught by teaching assistants.

ACADEMICS
Degrees: bachelor's, doctoral, master's, post-bachelor's certificate. **Classes:** Most classes have 10–19 students. Most lab/discussion sessions have 20–29 students. **Majors with Highest Enrollment:** biology/biological sciences; biomedical/medical engineering; psychology. **Special Study Options:** Accelerated program, cooperative education program, cross-registration, double major, dual enrollment, English as a Second Language (ESL), exchange student program (domestic), honors program, independent study, internships, liberal arts/career combination, student-designed major, study abroad, teacher certification program, Washington Semester. **Honors Programs:** The College Scholars Program is a three-year honors program for a small group of students interested in exploring how academic learning can address larger world concerns. **Combined Degree Programs:** BA/MA, BA/DDS, BA/MEng, BS/MS, BS/MBA, BS/MAcc, BA/MPH, Sr Yr Prof Studies. **Disability Services:** Special programs offered to physically disabled students include note-taking services, reader services, tape recorders, tutors. **Career Services:** Alumni network, alumni services, career/job search classes, career assessment, internships, regional alumni. Career Services highlights include Case's experiential learning options come in many forms. More than 83% of our undergraduate students participate in opportunities for research, cultural immersion through study abroad programs, clinical work in nursing, and internship and co-op programs, or garner valuable leadership experiences through campus, club, and community interactions.

FACILITIES
Housing: Coed dorms, fraternity/sorority housing, apartments for single students, wellness housing, secured women-only floor available. Special-interest housing available. Residential Colleges for first-year students. 90% of campus accessible to physically disabled. **Special Academic Facilities/Equipment:** Art, natural history, and auto-aviation museums, historical society, botanical garden, biology field stations, observatory. **Computers:** 100% of classrooms, 100% of dorms, 100% of libraries, 100% of dining areas, 100% of student union, 100% of common outdoor areas have wireless network access. Students can register for classes online. Administrative functions (other than registration) can be performed online.

CAMPUS LIFE
Environment: Metropolis. **Activities:** Choral groups, concert band, dance, drama/theater, jazz band, literary magazine, marching band, music ensembles, musical theater, pep band, radio station, student government, student newspaper, student-run film society, symphony orchestra, yearbook, Campus Ministries, International Student Organization, Model UN 150 registered organizations, 8 honor societies, 4 religious organizations. 16 fraternities, 8 sororities. **Athletics (Intercollegiate):** *Men:* baseball, basketball, cross-country, football, soccer, swimming, tennis, track/field (outdoor), track/field (indoor), wrestling. *Women:* basketball, cross country, soccer, softball, swimming, tennis, track/field (outdoor), track/field (indoor), volleyball. **On-Campus Highlights:** North Residential Village, Peter B. Lewis Building, Kelvin Smith Library, Veale Convoca-

tion and Athletic Center, Turning Point Sculpture Garden. **Environmental Initiatives:** Signatory to the American College and University President's Climate Commitment. Ongoing comprehensive energy reduction program. Climate Action Plan completed January 2011. Joined Ohio Solar Cooperative which will facilitate installation of PV arrays on campus buildings. Campus food service (Bon Appetit) purchasing bulk of fresh food and supplies from local farms and food producers. Organic, seasonal, local (low carbon footprint), and delicious! And composting kitchen waste, decreasing food waste stream by 35%.

ADMISSIONS

Freshman Academic Profile: 74% in top 10% of high school class, 94% in top 25% of high school class, 100% in top 50% of high school class. 70% from public high schools. SAT Math middle 50% range 660-760. SAT Critical Reading middle 50% range 600-720. SAT Writing middle 50% range 600-700. ACT middle 50% range 29-33. Minimum web-based TOEFL 90. Minimum paper TOEFL 577. **Basis for Candidate Selection:** *Very important factors considered include:* Class rank, academic GPA, rigor of secondary school record, standardized test scores, extracurricular activities. *Important factors considered include:* application essay, recommendation(s), character/personal qualities, interview, level of applicant's interest, talent/ability, volunteer work, work experience. *Other factors considered include:* alumni/ae relation, first generation, racial/ethnic status. **Freshman Admission Requirements:** High school diploma is required and GED is accepted. *Academic units required:* 4 English, 3 mathematics, 3 science, (2 science labs), 2 foreign language, 3 social studies. *Academic units recommended:* 4 English, 3 mathematics, 3 science, (2 science labs), 2 foreign language, 3 social studies. **Freshman Admission Statistics:** 14,778 applied, 54% admitted, 17% enrolled. **Transfer Admission Requirements:** High school transcript, college transcript(s), essay or personal statement, statement of good standing from prior institution(s). Minimum college GPA of 3.2 required. Lowest grade transferable C. **General Admission Information:** Regular application deadline 1/15. Regular notification 4/1. Nonfall registration accepted. Admission may be deferred for a maximum of 1 year. Credit and/or placement offered for CEEB Advanced Placement tests.

COSTS AND FINANCIAL AID

Required Forms and Deadlines: FAFSA, institution's own financial aid form, business/farm supplement. Parent and student income tax returns and W-2 forms. **Notification of Awards:** Applicants will be notified of awards on a rolling basis beginning 3/15. **Types of Aid:** *Need-based scholarships/grants:* Federal Pell, SEOG, state scholarships/grants, private scholarships, the school's own gift aid. *Loans:* Subsidized Stafford, Unsubsidized Stafford, PLUS, Federal Perkins, Federal Nursing, state loans, college/university loans from institutional funds, Alternative loans. **Student Employment:** Federal Work-Study Program available. Institutional employment available. Highest amount earned per year from on-campus jobs $3,200. Off-campus job opportunities are excellent. **Financial Aid Statistics:** 100% freshmen, 99% undergrads receive need-based scholarship or grant aid. 100% undergrads receive non-need-based scholarship or grant aid. 76% freshmen, 82% undergrads receive need-based self-help aid. 91% freshmen, 86% undergrads receive any aid. 52% undergrads borrow to pay for school. Average cumulative indebtedness $39,886. **Criteria for awarding institutional aid:** *Non-need-based:* academics, art, leadership, music/drama.

CASTLETON STATE COLLEGE

Office of Admissions, Castleton, VT 5735
Phone: 802-468-1213 • **Financial Aid Phone:** 802-468-6070
E-mail: info@castleton.edu • **CEEB Code:** 3765
Fax: 802-468-1476 • **ACT Code:** 4314

This public school was founded in 1787. It has a 165-acre campus.

RATINGS
Admissions Selectivity Rating: 70   **Fire Safety Rating:** 73   **Green Rating:** 73

STUDENTS AND FACULTY
Enrollment: 2,017. **Student Body:** 51% female, 49% male, 36% out-of-state, 1% international (16 countries represented). Asian 1%, African American 1%, Caucasian 88%, Hispanic 2%, Native American 1%.
Retention and Graduation: 25% freshmen graduate within 4 years. 41% freshmen graduate within 6 years. **Faculty:** Student/faculty ratio 14:1. 94 full-time faculty, 96% hold PhDs, 6% are members of minority groups, 48% are women. 0% of classes are taught by teaching assistants.

ACADEMICS
Degrees: associate, bachelor's, master's, post-bachelor's certificate, post-master's certificate. **Classes:** Most classes have 10–19 students. Most lab/discussion sessions have 10–19 students. **Majors with Highest Enrollment:** business/commerce; psychology. **Special Study Options:** cooperative education

program, double major, dual enrollment, honors program, independent study, internships, liberal arts/career combination, student-designed major, study abroad, teacher certification program. **Combined Degree Programs:** BA/MA, 4-1 M.B.A. ; 4 + 3 Phys. Therapy; 4 + 2. **Disability Services:** Special programs offered to physically disabled students include note-taking services, reader services, tape recorders, tutors.

FACILITIES
Housing: Coed dorms. 100% of campus accessible to physically disabled. **Special Academic Facilities/Equipment:** Historical/medical museum. **Computers:** 25% of classrooms, 100% of dorms, 100% of libraries, 100% of dining areas, 100% of student union, have wireless network access.

CAMPUS LIFE
Environment: Rural. **Activities:** Choral groups, dance, drama/theater, jazz band, literary magazine, music ensembles, musical theater, radio station, student government, student newspaper, student-run film society, television station, yearbook 40 registered organizations, 7 honor societies, 1 religious organizations. **Athletics (Intercollegiate):** *Men:* baseball, basketball, cross-country, football, ice hockey, lacrosse, skiing (downhill/alpine), soccer, tennis. *Women:* basketball, cross-country, field hockey, ice hockey, lacrosse, skiing (downhill/alpine), soccer, softball, tennis. **On-Campus Highlights:** Fireside Cafe, Coffee Cottage, Fitness center, Library **Environmental Initiatives:** Student-driven recycling effort New construction is significantly green Purchasing is significantly green.

ADMISSIONS
Freshman Academic Profile: Average high school GPA 2.9. 5% in top 10% of high school class, 21% in top 25% of high school class, 61% in top 50% of high school class. SAT Math middle 50% range 440-560. SAT Critical Reading middle 50% range 430-550. SAT Writing middle 50% range 420-530. ACT middle 50% range 17-23. Minimum paper TOEFL 500. **Basis for Candidate Selection:** *Very important factors considered include:* Class rank, application essay, academic GPA, recommendation(s), rigor of secondary school record, character/personal qualities. *Important factors considered include:* standardized test scores. *Other factors considered include:* extracurricular activities, interview, level of applicant's interest, volunteer work, work experience. **Freshman Admission Requirements:** High school diploma is required and GED is accepted. *Academic units required:* 4 English, 3 mathematics, 2 science, (2 science labs), 3 social studies, 3 history. *Academic units recommended:* 4 English, 3 mathematics, 2 science, (2 science labs), 3 social studies, 3 history. **Freshman Admission Statistics:** 2,737 applied, 76% admitted, 23% enrolled. **Transfer Admission Requirements:** college transcript(s), essay or personal statement, minimum college GPA of 2.0 required. Lowest grade transferable C-. **General Admission Information:** Application Fee $35. Notification on a rolling basis, beginning on or about 12/15. Nonfall registration accepted. Admission may be deferred for a maximum of 1 year. Credit and/or placement offered for CEEB Advanced Placement tests.

COSTS AND FINANCIAL AID
Annual in-state tuition $8,568. Annual out-of-state tuition $20,112. Room and board $8,446. Required fees $900. Average book expense $1,000. **Required Forms and Deadlines:** FAFSA. **Notification of Awards:** Applicants will be notified of awards on a rolling basis beginning 2/15. **Types of Aid:** *Need-based scholarships/grants:* Federal Pell, SEOG, state scholarships/grants, private scholarships, the school's own gift aid. *Loans:* Subsidized Stafford, Unsubsidized Stafford, PLUS, Federal Perkins, Federal Nursing. **Student Employment:** Federal Work-Study Program available. Institutional employment available. Off-campus job opportunities are good. **Financial Aid Statistics:** 67% freshmen, 68% undergrads receive need-based scholarship or grant aid. 1% freshmen receive non-need-based scholarship or grant aid. 93% freshmen, 93% undergrads receive need-based self-help aid. 66% freshmen, 66% undergrads receive any aid. 84% undergrads borrow to pay for school. Average cumulative indebtedness $25,474. **Criteria for awarding institutional aid:** *Non-need-based:* academics, alumni affiliation, art, leadership, music/drama, state/district residency.

CATAWBA COLLEGE

Best 378

2300 West Innes Street, Salisbury, NC 28144
Phone: 704-637-4402 • **Financial Aid Phone:** 704-637-4416
E-mail: admission@catawba.edu • **CEEB Code:** 5103
Fax: 704-637-4222 • **Website:** www.catawba.edu • **ACT Code:** 3080

This private school, affiliated with the United Church of Christ Church, was founded in 1851. It has a 276-acre campus.

RATINGS
Admissions Selectivity Rating: 84   **Fire Safety Rating:** 80   **Green Rating:** 95

STUDENTS AND FACULTY
Enrollment: 1,279. **Student Body:** 52% female, 48% male, 24% out-of-state, 3% international (13 countries represented). Asian 1%, African American 18%, Caucasian 72%, Hispanic 3%, Native American 1%.
Retention and Graduation: 37% freshmen graduate within 4 years. 13% grads go on to further study within 1 year. 4% grads pursue arts and sciences degrees. 2% grads pursue law degrees. 4% grads pursue business degrees. 1% grads pursue medical degrees. **Faculty:** Student/faculty ratio 15:1. 65 full-time faculty, 86% hold PhDs, 6% are members of minority groups, 42% are women. 0% of classes are taught by teaching assistants.

ACADEMICS
Degrees: bachelor's, master's. **Classes:** Most classes have 10–19 students. Most lab/discussion sessions have 20–29 students. **Majors with Highest Enrollment:** business/commerce; drama and dramatics/theatre arts; elementary education and teaching. **Special Study Options:** cross-registration, double major, dual enrollment, honors program, independent study, internships, liberal arts/career combination, student-designed major, study abroad, teacher certification program. **Disability Services:** Special programs offered to physically disabled students include note-taking services, tape recorders, tutors. **Career Services:** career/job search classes, career assessment. Career Services highlights include Food Lion (Delhaize Group) offers limited internships in Brussels, Belgium.

FACILITIES
Housing: Coed dorms, men's dorms, women's dorms, Substance free housing. 90% of campus accessible to physically disabled. **Special Academic Facilities/Equipment:** Ecology preserve (183 acres). Wildlife preserve (300 acres). **Computers:** 90% of classrooms, 95% of dorms, 100% of libraries, 25% of dining areas, 80% of student union, 10% of common outdoor areas have wireless network access. Administrative functions (other than registration) can be performed online.

CAMPUS LIFE
Environment: Town. **Activities:** Choral groups, concert band, dance, drama/theater, jazz band, literary magazine, music ensembles, musical theater, pep band, student government, student newspaper, symphony orchestra, yearbook, Campus Ministries 38 registered organizations, 9 honor societies, 4 religious organizations. **Athletics (Intercollegiate):** *Men:* baseball, basketball, cheerleading, cross-country, football, golf, lacrosse, soccer, swimming, tennis. *Women:* basketball, cheerleading, cross-country, golf, soccer, softball, swimming, tennis, volleyball. **On-Campus Highlights:** Center for the Environment, Cannon Field House, Robertson College Community Center, Ketner Hall, Cannon Student Center. **Environmental Initiatives:** our Center for the Environment, along with its national, regional, and community environmental outreach Office of Waste & Recycling and its various efforts on campus LEED certified residence halls, and LEED certification-pending Center for the Environment building.

ADMISSIONS
Freshman Academic Profile: Average high school GPA 3.3. 9% in top 10% of high school class, 29% in top 25% of high school class, 63% in top 50% of high school class. 80% from public high schools. SAT Math middle 50% range 450-550. SAT Critical Reading middle 50% range 430-540. ACT middle 50% range 18-25. Minimum web-based TOEFL 69. Minimum paper TOEFL. **Basis for Candidate Selection:** *Very important factors considered include:* Class rank, application essay, academic GPA, recommendation(s), standardized test scores. *Important factors considered include:* rigor of secondary school record, character/personal qualities, extracurricular activities, interview, level of applicant's interest, talent/ability. *Other factors considered include:* volunteer work. **Freshman Admission Requirements:** High school diploma is required and GED is accepted. **Freshman Admission Statistics:** 3,448 applied, 45% admitted, 19% enrolled. **Transfer Admission Requirements:** High school transcript, college transcript(s), essay or personal statement, statement of good standing from prior institution(s). Minimum college GPA of 2.0 required. Lowest grade transferable C. **General Admission Information:** Application Fee $25. Notification on a rolling basis, beginning on or about 10/1. Nonfall registration accepted. Admission may be deferred for a maximum of 1 Year. Credit and/or placement offered for CEEB Advanced Placement tests.

COSTS AND FINANCIAL AID
Annual tuition $26,820. Room and board $9,410. Average book expense $1,400. **Required Forms and Deadlines:** FAFSA, state aid form. **Notification of Awards:** Applicants will be notified of awards on a rolling basis beginning 2/15. **Types of Aid:** *Need-based scholarships/grants:* Federal Pell, SEOG, state scholarships/grants, private scholarships, the school's own gift aid. *Loans:* Unsubsidized Stafford, PLUS, Federal Perkins, college/university loans from institutional funds, TERI Loans, Nellie Mae Loans, Advantage Loans, Alternative Loans. **Student Employment:** Federal Work-Study Program available. Institutional employment available. Highest amount earned per year from on-campus jobs $2,000. Off-campus job opportunities are good. **Financial Aid Statistics:** 83% freshmen, 81% undergrads receive need-based scholarship or grant aid. 100% freshmen receive non-need-based scholarship or grant aid. 82% freshmen, 84% undergrads receive need-based self-help aid. 23% freshmen, 23% undergrads receive athletic scholarships. 99% freshmen, 99% undergrads receive any aid. 86% undergrads borrow to pay for school. Average cumulative indebtedness $31,966. **Criteria for awarding institutional aid:** *Non-need-based:* academics, athletics, leadership, music/drama, state/district residency.

THE CATHOLIC UNIVERSITY OF AMERICA

Best 378

Office of Undergraduate Admissions, Washington, DC 20064
Phone: 202-319-5305 • **Financial Aid Phone:** 202-319-5307
E-mail: cua-admissions@cua.edu • **CEEB Code:** 5104
Fax: 202-319-6533 • **Website:** www.cua.edu • **ACT Code:** 654

This private school, affiliated with the Roman Catholic Church, was founded in 1887. It has a 193-acre campus.

RATINGS
Admissions Selectivity Rating: 80   **Fire Safety Rating:** 86   **Green Rating:** 78

STUDENTS AND FACULTY
Enrollment: 3,629. **Student Body:** 55% female, 45% male, 96% out-of-state, 4% international (85 countries represented). Asian 3%, African American 5%, Caucasian 62%, Hispanic 9%, Native American 0%.
Retention and Graduation: 84% freshmen return for sophomore year. 62% freshmen graduate within 4 years. 32% grads go on to further study within 1 year. 15% grads pursue law degrees. 5% grads pursue medical degrees. **Faculty:** Student/faculty ratio 9:1. 398 full-time faculty, 96% hold PhDs, 11% are members of minority groups, 39% are women. 14% of classes are taught by teaching assistants.

ACADEMICS
Degrees: associate, bachelor's, doctoral, master's, post-bachelor's certificate, post-master's certificate. **Classes:** Most classes have 10–19 students. Most lab/discussion sessions have 10–19 students. **Majors with Highest Enrollment:** architecture (barch, ba/bs, march, ma/ms, phd); nursing/registered nurse (rn, asn, bsn, msn); political science and government. **Special Study Options:** Accelerated program, cross-registration, distance learning, double major, dual enrollment, English as a Second Language (ESL), honors program, independent study, internships, study abroad, teacher certification program. **Honors Programs:** The University Honors Program offers classes in the classical liberal arts and contemporary social and environmental sciences to compliment students' major studies. Students take small, rigorous, discussion-based courses from offerings in philosophy, theology, history and literature, social science, environmental science, and media studies. Students completing any of these six tracks receive distinction at graduation; students completing three tracks and a senior seminar are designated University Scholars. Special lectures, symposia, social events, and trips are organized for students in the program. **Combined Degree Programs:** BA/MA, BS/MS; BSN/MSN. **Disability Services:** Special programs offered to physically disabled students include note-taking services, reader services, tape recorders, tutors. **Career Services:** Alumni network, alumni services, career assessment, internships, regional alumni. Career Services highlights include Through Cardinal Connection (Jobs and Internships

Online), we share with students the amazing variety and quality of experiential opportunities available to them. Each year hundreds of organizations in the Washington, D.C. area and nationwide list internships that give students a chance to become involved in a range of responsibilities in politics, research, marketing, accounting, finance, public relations, computer science, engineering, architecture and arts management, to name a few. These experiences not only complement students' classroom education, they often lead to offers of full-time employment upon graduation from CUA.

FACILITIES

Housing: Coed dorms, special housing for disabled students, men's dorms, women's dorms, apartments for single students, wellness housing, theme housing, Residential college, honors community, politics and current events community, living as leaders community and social justice community. 85% of campus accessible to physically disabled. **Special Academic Facilities/Equipment:** Facilities available on the university campus include an art department gallery; the John K. Mullen of Denver Memorial Library, which features a rare book collection containing 65,000 volumes that range from medieval documents to first editions of 20th-century authors; the university archives, which has nearly 9,000 feet of records and manuscripts; the Vitreous State Laboratory, which engages some of the world's leading glass scientists to help research and develop methods for safe containment of disposed radioactive materials, primarily by converting nuclear waste into solid glass using vitrification techniques. In 2008, the university dedicated Opus Hall, the first LEED (Leadership in Energy and Environmental Design)-compliant residence hall among colleges and universities in Washington, D.C. The Edward J. Pryzbyla University Center includes nine meeting spaces, two separate dining facilities, a convenience store, the campus bookstore, offices, various atrium and lounge spaces and a 7,500-square-foot great room, where Pope Benedict XVI delivered a speech in April 2008. Adjacent to the campus is the Roman Catholic Basilica of the National Shrine of the Immaculate Conception, the largest church in the Western hemisphere. University Masses and commencement are held every year at the National Shrine. Directly across the street from the university is the Pope John Paul II Cultural Center, a major Catholic museum. **Computers:** 40% of classrooms, 90% of dorms, 100% of libraries, 100% of dining areas, 100% of student union, 20% of common outdoor areas have wireless network access. Students can register for classes online. Administrative functions (other than registration) can be performed online.

CAMPUS LIFE

Environment: Metropolis. **Activities:** Choral groups, dance, drama/theater, jazz band, literary magazine, music ensembles, musical theater, opera, radio station, student government, student newspaper, student-run film society, symphony orchestra, yearbook, Campus Ministries, International Student Organization 87 registered organizations, 16 honor societies, 4 religious organizations. 1 fraternities, 1 sororities. **Athletics (Intercollegiate):** *Men:* baseball, basketball, cross-country, football, lacrosse, soccer, swimming, tennis, track/field (outdoor), track/field (indoor). *Women:* basketball, cross-country, field hockey, lacrosse, soccer, softball, swimming, tennis, track/field (outdoor), track/field (indoor), volleyball. **On-Campus Highlights:** Edward J. Pryzbyla University Center, Eugene I. Kane Fitness Center, St. Vincent de Paul Chapel, Raymond A. Dufour (athletic) Center, John K. Mullen of Denver Memorial Library, Catholic University's 193 acre campus is the largest among universities in Washington, D.C. Its spacious campus setting is adjacent to a Washington Metrorail and has several campus malls for frisbee, football, softball, picnicking and sunning. **Environmental Initiatives:** LEED-NC Certified, 402 Bed Student Dormitory Alternative energy purchasing at 100% of electricity consumption. The University just installed 1505 solar panels on 4 campus buildings. Thes solar panels will produce 720,000 kwh of clean electrical energy on an annual basis. This is the largest solar installation in DC. CUA Beautification Day - On campus planting of 185 trees (large canopy type) donated by Casey Tree, Washington DC with continued collaboration over past three years.

ADMISSIONS

Freshman Academic Profile: Average high school GPA 3.4. 54% from public high schools. SAT Math middle 50% range 500-610. SAT Critical Reading middle 50% range 510-610. ACT middle 50% range 22-27. Minimum web-based TOEFL 80. Minimum paper TOEFL 550. **Basis for Candidate Selection:** *Very important factors considered include:* academic GPA, recommendation(s), rigor of secondary school record, standardized test scores, character/personal qualities, level of applicant's interest, volunteer work. *Important factors considered include:* application essay, extracurricular activities, first generation, interview, talent/ability. *Other factors considered include:* Class rank, alumni/ae relation, racial/ethnic status, work experience. **Freshman Admission Requirements:** High school diploma is required and GED is accepted. **Freshman Admission Statistics:** 6,361 applied, 63% admitted, 22% enrolled. **Transfer Admission Requirements:** High school transcript, college transcript(s), essay or personal statement, standardized test scores, minimum college GPA of 2.8 required. Lowest grade transferable C. **General Admission Information:** Application Fee $55. Regular application deadline 2/15. Notification on a rolling

basis, beginning on or about 3/15. Nonfall registration accepted. Admission may be deferred for a maximum of 1 year. Credit and/or placement offered for CEEB Advanced Placement tests.

COSTS AND FINANCIAL AID

Annual tuition $36,320. Room and board $14,274. Required fees $500. Average book expense $1,440. **Required Forms and Deadlines:** FAFSAAlumni and Parish Scholarship Applications if appropriate. **Notification of Awards:** Applicants will be notified of awards on a rolling basis beginning 4/1. **Types of Aid:** *Need-based scholarships/grants:* Federal Pell, SEOG, state scholarships/grants, private scholarships, the school's own gift aid. *Loans:* Direct Subsidized Stafford, Direct Unsubsidized Stafford, Direct PLUS, Commericial Loans. **Student Employment:** Federal Work-Study Program available. Institutional employment available. Off-campus job opportunities are good. **Financial Aid Statistics:** 99% freshmen, 97% undergrads receive need-based scholarship or grant aid. 87% freshmen, 87% undergrads receive need-based self-help aid. 94% freshmen, 90% undergrads receive any aid. **Criteria for awarding institutional aid:** *Non-need-based:* academics, alumni affiliation, music/drama, religious affiliation.

CAZENOVIA COLLEGE

3 Sullivan Street, Cazenovia, NY 13035
Phone: 315-655-7208 • **Financial Aid Phone:** 315-655-7887
E-mail: admission@cazenovia.edu
Fax: 315-655-4860

This private school was founded in 1824.

RATINGS
Admissions Selectivity Rating: 70   **Fire Safety Rating:** 98   **Green Rating:** 71

STUDENTS AND FACULTY
Enrollment: 980. **Student Body:** 74% female, 26% male, 16% out-of-state, 0% international. Asian 2%, African American 10%, Caucasian 78%, Hispanic 7%, Native American 2%.
Retention and Graduation: 68% freshmen return for sophomore year. 41% freshmen graduate within 4 years. 46% freshmen graduate within 6 years.
Faculty: Student/faculty ratio 11:1. 59 full-time faculty, 80% hold PhDs, 5% are members of minority groups, 68% are women. 0% of classes are taught by teaching assistants.

ACADEMICS
Degrees: associate, bachelor's, certificate. **Classes:** Most classes have 10–19 students. **Majors with Highest Enrollment:** business administration, management and operations, other; fine/studio arts; interior design. **Special Study Options:** Accelerated program, double major, exchange student program (domestic), honors program, independent study, internships, student-designed major, study abroad, teacher certification program. **Honors Programs:** The All-College Honors Program at Cazenovia College offers to outstanding students in all majors (in the liberal arts and in the professional studies) a stimulating learning environment beyond that found in standard classroom coursework, and fosters their exceptional academic talents and intellectual curiosity. Demanding curriculum, independent research opportunities and co-curricular activities challenge students to achieve their full educational potential not only through encouraging academic excellence but also through promoting social responsibilities in the global community. An honors degree certifies that students have produced academic work that meets the highest standards of academic rigor in both general education and in their career field. **Disability Services:** Special programs offered to physically disabled students include note-taking services, reader services, tape recorders, tutors. **Career Services:** Alumni network, alumni services, career/job search classes, career assessment, internships, regional alumni. Career Services highlights include The College's academic programs provide students the opportunity to participate in off-campus internships, often as a graduation requirement. Internships generally provide students with one of three types of experience: ° A continuation of work in a familiar field to increase student knowledge by performing tasks beyond those already mastered in this career area ° An experience intended to broaden student expertise within a career area by working in an area of that profession not previously experienced; and ° A shadowing or observational experience of a professional in a specific career field as a means of exploring a possible new career interest. Regardless of the type of experience, internships make valuable connections between the world of work and the student's academic study. Each academic program has specific eligibility requirements for internships that can be checked in the College Catalog or by contacting either the Program Director or the Director of Career Services.

FACILITIES

Housing: Coed dorms, special housing for disabled students, women's dorms, Single room suites. **Special Academic Facilities/Equipment:** Reisman Hall is a state-of-the-art Art and Design facility and gallery; 243-acre Equine Education Center; historic Catherine Cummings Theatre **Computers:** Administrative functions (other than registration) can be performed online.

CAMPUS LIFE

Environment: Rural. **Activities:** Choral groups, dance, drama/theater, jazz band, musical theater, radio station, student government, student newspaper, student-run film society, yearbook, Campus Ministries 54 registered organizations, 5 honor societies, 1 religious organizations. **Athletics (Intercollegiate):** *Men:* baseball, basketball, cheerleading, crew/rowing, cross-country, equestrian sports, golf, horseback riding, lacrosse, soccer, swimming. *Women:* basketball, cheerleading, crew/rowing, cross-country, equestrian sports, horseback riding, lacrosse, soccer, softball, swimming, volleyball. **On-Campus Highlights:** Residence Halls, Academic Facilities - Art and Design Building, Equestrian Center, Athletic Facilities / Pool, Dining Hall. **Environmental Initiatives:** Environmental Studies education programs; Look Again program - sustainability in fashion Sustainability is a goal in the institution's Strategic Plan and a study of our institutional carbon footprint is underway, use all biodegradable corn based products in place of foam and paper products in dining halls and kitchens, all green chemicals used in dining halls and kitchens, Apex system in use, and solar panels in use in two buildings on campus; contract with gas and electric energy providers that guarantee a minimum of 5% of energy comes from renewable sources Cazenovia College hosts the Annual Symposium on Energy in the 21st Century: Seeking Environmental Solutions Through Partnerships.

ADMISSIONS

Freshman Academic Profile: Average high school GPA 3.2. 12% in top 10% of high school class, 38% in top 25% of high school class, 71% in top 50% of high school class. SAT Math middle 50% range 440-550. SAT Critical Reading middle 50% range 423-540. ACT middle 50% range 19-24. Minimum paper TOEFL 550. **Basis for Candidate Selection:** *Very important factors considered include:* rigor of secondary school record, extracurricular activities. *Important factors considered include:* Class rank, academic GPA, recommendation(s), standardized test scores, character/personal qualities, interview, talent/ability. *Other factors considered include:* application essay, level of applicant's interest, volunteer work, work experience. **Freshman Admission Requirements:** High school diploma is required and GED is accepted. **Freshman Admission Statistics:** 2,322 applied, 74% admitted, 16% enrolled. **Transfer Admission Requirements:** High school transcript, college transcript(s), minimum college GPA of 2.0 required. Lowest grade transferable C. **General Admission Information:** Application Fee $30. Notification on a rolling basis, beginning on or about 11/1. Nonfall registration accepted. Admission may be deferred for a maximum of 1 year. Credit and/or placement offered for CEEB Advanced Placement tests.

COSTS AND FINANCIAL AID

Annual tuition $27,550. Room and board $11,398. Required fees $472. Average book expense $1,000 **Required Forms and Deadlines:** FAFSA, state aid form. **Notification of Awards:** Applicants will be notified of awards on a rolling basis beginning 11/1. **Types of Aid:** *Need-based scholarships/grants:* Federal Pell, SEOG, state scholarships/grants, private scholarships, the school's own gift aid. *Loans:* Direct Subsidized Stafford, Direct Unsubsidized Stafford, Direct PLUS. **Student Employment:** Federal Work-Study Program available. **Financial Aid Statistics:** 100% freshmen, 99% undergrads receive need-based scholarship or grant aid. 17% freshmen, 9% undergrads receive non-need-based scholarship or grant aid. 84% freshmen, 85% undergrads receive need-based self-help aid. 86% freshmen, 85% undergrads receive any aid. 82% undergrads borrow to pay for school. **Criteria for awarding institutional aid:** *Non-need-based:* academics.

CEDAR CREST COLLEGE

100 College Drive, Allentown, PA 18104
Phone: 610-740-3780 • **Financial Aid Phone:** 610-606-4602
E-mail: cccadmis@cedarcrest.edu • **CEEB Code:** 2079
Fax: 610-606-4647 • **Website:** www.cedarcrest.edu • **ACT Code:** 3536

This private school was founded in 1867. It has a 84-acre campus.

RATINGS

Admissions Selectivity Rating: 77   **Fire Safety Rating:** 72   **Green Rating:** 77

STUDENTS AND FACULTY

Enrollment: 1,310. **Student Body:** 95% female, 5% male, 14% out-of-state, 1% international (58 countries represented). Asian 3%, African American 10%, Caucasian 77%, Hispanic 11%, Native American 0%.

Retention and Graduation: 70% freshmen return for sophomore year. 49% freshmen graduate within 4 years. 61% freshmen graduate within 6 years. 25% grads go on to further study within 1 year. 15% grads pursue arts and sciences degrees. 1% grads pursue law degrees. 3% grads pursue business degrees. 2% grads pursue medical degrees. **Faculty:** Student/faculty ratio 10:1. 74 full-time faculty, 76% hold PhDs, 5% are members of minority groups, 69% are women. 0% of classes are taught by teaching assistants.

ACADEMICS

Degrees: bachelor's, master's, post-bachelor's certificate, post-master's certificate. **Classes:** Most classes have 10–19 students. Most lab/discussion sessions have 10–19 students. **Majors with Highest Enrollment:** nursing/registered nurse (rn, asn, bsn, msn); physical sciences, other; social work. **Special Study Options:** cross-registration, distance learning, double major, honors program, independent study, internships, liberal arts/career combination, student-designed major, study abroad, teacher certification program, Ethics. **Honors Programs:** Special courses reserved for Honors Students, undergraduate research opportunities, including Honors Thesis. **Disability Services:** Special programs offered to physically disabled students include note-taking services, reader services, tape recorders, tutors. **Career Services:** Alumni network, alumni services, career/job search classes, career assessment, internships, regional alumni. Career Services highlights include Our Marketing Practicum course has worked with employers such as Just Born, Crayola and the PA Liquor Control Board to provide internship opportunities for students and hands-on experience.

FACILITIES

Housing: special housing for disabled students, women's dorms. 90% of campus accessible to physically disabled. **Special Academic Facilities/Equipment:** Alumnae Museum **Computers:** 75% of classrooms, 85% of dorms, 100% of libraries, 85% of dining areas, 85% of student union, 50% of common outdoor areas have wireless network access. Students can register for classes online. Administrative functions (other than registration) can be performed online.

CAMPUS LIFE

Environment: City. **Activities:** Choral groups, dance, drama/theater, literary magazine, music ensembles, musical theater, radio station, student government, student newspaper, yearbook, Campus Ministries, International Student Organization 18 honor societies, 4 religious organizations. **Athletics (Intercollegiate):** *Women:* basketball, cross-country, field hockey, lacrosse, soccer, softball, tennis, volleyball. **On-Campus Highlights:** Bistro, College Center, Fitness Center, Rodale Aquatic Center **Environmental Initiatives:** Recycling: participating in national Recyclemania Decentralized heat plant Install CFL'S & electronic ballasts & started upgrading exterior lighting to LED's

ADMISSIONS

Freshman Academic Profile: Average high school GPA 3.3. 16% in top 10% of high school class, 52% in top 25% of high school class, 85% in top 50% of high school class. 92% from public high schools. SAT Math middle 50% range 440-560. SAT Critical Reading middle 50% range 430-550. SAT Writing middle 50% range 420-550. ACT middle 50% range 20-23. Minimum web-based TOEFL 61. Minimum paper TOEFL 500. **Basis for Candidate Selection:** *Very important factors considered include:* Class rank, application essay, academic GPA, recommendation(s), rigor of secondary school record, standardized test scores. *Other factors considered include:* alumni/ae relation, extracurricular activities, interview, volunteer work, work experience. **Freshman Admission Requirements:** High school diploma is required and GED is accepted. *Academic units required:* 4 English, 3 mathematics, 2 science, (2 science labs), 2 foreign language, 3 social studies, 0 computer science. *Academic units recommended:* 4 English, 3 mathematics, 2 science, (2 science labs), 2 foreign language, 3 social studies, 0 computer science. **Freshman Admission Statistics:** 1,155 applied, 61% admitted, 21% enrolled. **Transfer Admission Requirements:** High school transcript, college transcript(s), minimum college GPA of 2.00 required. Lowest grade transferable C. **General Admission Information:** Application Fee $30. Notification on a rolling basis, beginning on or about 9/15. Nonfall registration accepted. Credit and/or placement offered for CEEB Advanced Placement tests.

COSTS AND FINANCIAL AID

Required Forms and Deadlines: FAFSA. **Notification of Awards:** Applicants will be notified of awards on a rolling basis beginning 1/1. **Types of Aid:** *Need-based scholarships/grants:* Federal Pell, SEOG, state scholarships/grants, private scholarships, the school's own gift aid, Federal Nursing Scholarships. *Loans:* Direct Subsidized Stafford, Direct Unsubsidized Stafford, Direct PLUS, Federal Perkins, Federal Nursing. **Student Employment:** Federal Work-Study Program available. Institutional employment available. Highest amount earned per year from on-campus jobs $2,200. Off-campus job opportunities are fair. **Financial Aid Statistics:** 100% freshmen, 100% undergrads receive need-based scholarship or grant aid. 9% freshmen, 6% undergrads receive non-need-based scholarship or grant aid. 89% freshmen, 89% undergrads receive need-based self-help aid. 97% freshmen, 99% undergrads receive any aid. 92% undergrads borrow to pay for school. Average cumulative indebtedness $31,933. **Criteria for awarding institutional aid:** *Non-need-based:* academics, alumni affiliation, art, leadership, music/drama.

CEDARVILLE UNIVERSITY

251 N.Main Street, Cedarville, OH 45314
Phone: 937-766-7700 • **Financial Aid Phone:** 937-766-4969
E-mail: admissions@cedarville.edu
Fax: 937-766-7575 • **Website:** www.cedarville.edu • **ACT Code:** 3245

This private school, affiliated with the Baptist Church, was founded in 1887. It has a 400-acre campus.

RATINGS
Admissions Selectivity Rating: 79   **Fire Safety Rating:** 91   **Green Rating:** 60*

STUDENTS AND FACULTY
Enrollment: 3,111. **Student Body:** 54% female, 46% male, 64% out-of-state, 1% international (16 countries represented): Asian 1%, African American 2%, Caucasian 89%, Hispanic 2%, Native American 0%.
Retention and Graduation: 56% freshmen graduate within 4 years. 68% freshmen graduate within 6 years. 17% grads go on to further study within 1 year. 13% grads pursue arts and sciences degrees. 1% grads pursue law degrees. 1% grads pursue business degrees. 1% grads pursue medical degrees. **Faculty:** Student/faculty ratio 13:1. 214 full-time faculty, 68% hold PhDs, 8% are members of minority groups, 34% are women. 0% of classes are taught by teaching assistants.

ACADEMICS
Degrees: bachelor's, certificate, master's. **Classes:** Most classes have 10–19 students. Most lab/discussion sessions have 10–19 students. **Majors with Highest Enrollment:** elementary education and teaching; mechanical engineering; nursing/registered nurse (rn, asn, bsn, msn). **Special Study Options:** Accelerated program, distance learning, double major, dual enrollment, honors program, independent study, internships, student-designed major, study abroad, teacher certification program. **Disability Services:** Special programs offered to physically disabled students include reader services, tape recorders, tutors. **Career Services:** Alumni network, alumni services, career/job search classes, internships, regional alumni.

FACILITIES
Housing: men's dorms, women's dorms, apartments for married students. **Computers:** 100% of classrooms, 100% of dorms, 100% of libraries, 100% of dining areas, 100% of student union, 80% of common outdoor areas have wireless network access. Students can register for classes online. Administrative functions (other than registration) can be performed online.

CAMPUS LIFE
Environment: Rural. **Activities:** Choral groups, concert band, drama/theater, jazz band, music ensembles, musical theater, pep band, radio station, student government, student newspaper, symphony orchestra, yearbook 74 registered organizations, 4 honor societies. **Athletics (Intercollegiate):** *Men:* baseball, basketball, cheerleading, cross-country, golf, soccer, tennis, track/field (outdoor), track/field (indoor). *Women:* basketball, cheerleading, cross-country, soccer, softball, tennis, track/field (outdoor), track/field (indoor), volleyball. **On-Campus Highlights:** Fitness and Recreation Center, The Hive - student snack shop, Dixon Ministry Center - daily chapel and concerts, Chucks - student cafeteria (popular hangout), Callan Athletic Center.

ADMISSIONS
Freshman Academic Profile: Average high school GPA 3.6. 33% in top 10% of high school class, 65% in top 25% of high school class, 89% in top 50% of high school class. 53% from public high schools. SAT Math middle 50% range 530-640. SAT Critical Reading middle 50% range 540-650. SAT Writing middle 50% range 510-640. ACT middle 50% range 23-28. Minimum web-based TOEFL 80. Minimum paper TOEFL 550. **Basis for Candidate Selection:** *Very important factors considered include:* application essay, academic GPA, rigor of secondary school record, standardized test scores, character/personal qualities, religious affiliation/commitment. *Important factors considered include:* recommendation(s), racial/ethnic status. *Other factors considered include:* Class rank, alumni/ae relation, extracurricular activities, interview, talent/ability, volunteer work. **Freshman Admission Requirements:** High school diploma is required and GED is accepted. **Freshman Admission Statistics:** 3,143 applied, 75% admitted, 36% enrolled. **Transfer Admission Requirements:** High school transcript, college transcript(s), essay or personal statement, statement of good standing from prior institution(s). Minimum college GPA of 3.0 required. Lowest grade transferable C-. **General Admission Information:** Application Fee $30. Notification on a rolling basis, beginning on or about 8/1. Nonfall registration accepted. Admission may be deferred for a maximum of 12 months/1 year. Credit and/or placement offered for CEEB Advanced Placement tests.

COSTS AND FINANCIAL AID
Annual tuition $25,496. Room and board $5,540. Required fees $30. Average book expense $1,100. **Required Forms and Deadlines:** FAFSA. **Notification of Awards:** Applicants will be notified of awards on a rolling basis beginning 3/1. **Types of Aid:** *Need-based scholarships/grants:* Federal Pell, SEOG, state scholarships/grants, private scholarships, the school's own gift aid. *Loans:* Subsidized Stafford, Unsubsidized Stafford, PLUS, Federal Perkins, Federal Nursing, state loans, college/university loans from institutional funds. **Student Employment:** Highest amount earned per year from on-campus jobs $5,238. **Financial Aid Statistics:** 85% freshmen, 81% undergrads receive need-based scholarship or grant aid. 83% freshmen, 80% undergrads receive non-need-based scholarship or grant aid. 85% freshmen, 86% undergrads receive need-based self-help aid. 6% freshmen, 5% undergrads receive athletic scholarships. 94% freshmen, 85% undergrads receive any aid. 67% undergrads borrow to pay for school. Average cumulative indebtedness $27,279. **Criteria for awarding institutional aid:** *Non-need-based:* academics, alumni affiliation, athletics, leadership, minority status, music/drama, state/district residency.

CENTENARY COLLEGE

400 Jefferson Street, Hackettstown, NJ 7840
Phone: 800-236-8679 • **Financial Aid Phone:** 1-800-236-8679
E-mail: admissions@centenarycollege.edu • **CEEB Code:** 2080
Fax: 908-852-3454 • **Website:** www.centenarycollege.edu • **ACT Code:** 2544

This private school, affiliated with the Methodist Church, was founded in 1867. It has a 42-acre campus.

RATINGS
Admissions Selectivity Rating: 65   **Fire Safety Rating:** 60*   **Green Rating:** 60*

STUDENTS AND FACULTY
Enrollment: 1,915. **Student Body:** 62% female, 38% male, 16% out-of-state, 2% international (17 countries represented). Asian 1%, African American 6%, Caucasian 47%, Hispanic 7%, Native American 0%.
Retention and Graduation: 76% freshmen return for sophomore year. 49% freshmen graduate within 4 years. 50% freshmen graduate within 6 years. 25% grads go on to further study within 1 year. 8% grads pursue arts and sciences degrees. 8% grads pursue business degrees. **Faculty:** Student/faculty ratio 19:1. 75 full-time faculty, 53% hold PhDs, 7% are members of minority groups, 56% are women. 0% of classes are taught by teaching assistants.

ACADEMICS
Degrees: associate, bachelor's, master's, post-bachelor's certificate, terminal associate, transfer associate. **Classes:** Most classes have 10–19 students. Most lab/discussion sessions have 10–19 students. **Majors with Highest Enrollment:** business administration and management; criminal justice/police science; elementary education and teaching. **Special Study Options:** Accelerated program, cross-registration, distance learning, double major, dual enrollment, English as a Second Language (ESL), exchange student program (domestic), honors program, independent study, internships, liberal arts/career combination, student-designed major, study abroad, teacher certification program, weekend college. **Disability Services:** Special programs offered to physically disabled students include note-taking services, reader services, tutors. **Career Services:** Alumni network, alumni services, career/job search classes, career assessment, internships, regional alumni.

FACILITIES
Housing: Coed dorms, apartments for single students. 60% of campus accessible to physically disabled. **Special Academic Facilities/Equipment:** Art gallery, radio station WNTI 91.9FM, equity-status theater, equestrian center. **Computers:** 100% of classrooms, 100% of dorms, 100% of libraries, 100% of dining areas, 100% of student union, 100% of common outdoor areas have wireless network access. Students can register for classes online. Administrative functions (other than registration) can be performed online. Undergraduates are required to own a computer.

CAMPUS LIFE
Environment: Town. **Activities:** Choral groups, dance, drama/theater, literary magazine, music ensembles, musical theater, radio station, student government, student newspaper, student-run film society, television station, yearbook, Campus Ministries, International Student Organization, Model UN 30 registered organizations, 2 honor societies, 2 fraternities, 3 sororities. **Athletics (Intercollegiate):** *Men:* baseball, basketball, cross-country, golf, lacrosse, soccer, wrestling. *Women:* basketball, cross-country, golf, lacrosse, soccer, softball, volleyball. **On-Campus Highlights:** Reeves Atheltic Facility, Bennett Smith Dormitory, Tilly's Cafe, Library Cyber Cafe.

ADMISSIONS

Freshman Academic Profile: Average high school GPA 2.7. 11% in top 10% of high school class, 28% in top 25% of high school class, 55% in top 50% of high school class. 85% from public high schools. SAT Math middle 50% range 410-500. SAT Critical Reading middle 50% range 410-500. SAT Writing middle 50% range 410-540. ACT middle 50% range 16-21. Minimum paper TOEFL 450. **Basis for Candidate Selection:** *Very important factors considered include:* application essay, academic GPA, standardized test scores, interview. *Important factors considered include:* recommendation(s), rigor of secondary school record, character/personal qualities, extracurricular activities, talent/ability, volunteer work. *Other factors considered include:* Class rank, alumni/ae relation, level of applicant's interest, religious affiliation/commitment, work experience. **Freshman Admission Requirements:** High school diploma is required and GED is accepted. *Academic units required:* 4 English, 3 mathematics, 2 science, (1 science labs), 0 academic electives. *Academic units recommended:* 4 English, 3 mathematics, 2 science, (1 science labs), 0 academic electives. **Freshman Admission Statistics:** 1,060 applied, 88% admitted, 31% enrolled. **Transfer Admission Requirements:** High school transcript, college transcript(s), essay or personal statement, minimum college GPA of 2.0 required. Lowest grade transferable C-. **General Admission Information:** Application Fee $30. Notification on a rolling basis, beginning on or about 12/15. Nonfall registration accepted. Admission may be deferred for a maximum of 1 semester. Credit offered for CEEB Advanced Placement tests.

COSTS AND FINANCIAL AID

Annual tuition $15,700. Room and board $6,850. Required fees $1,100. Average book expense $666. **Required Forms and Deadlines:** FAFSA. **Notification of Awards:** Applicants will be notified of awards on a rolling basis beginning 3/15. **Types of Aid:** *Need-based scholarships/grants:* Federal Pell, SEOG, state scholarships/grants, private scholarships, the school's own gift aid. *Loans:* Subsidized Stafford, Unsubsidized Stafford, PLUS, Federal Perkins, state loans, Alternative. **Student Employment:** Off-campus job opportunities are excellent. **Financial Aid Statistics:** 100% freshmen, 98% undergrads receive need-based scholarship or grant aid. 12% freshmen, 8% undergrads receive non-need-based scholarship or grant aid. 83% freshmen, 86% undergrads receive need-based self-help aid. 83% freshmen, 86% undergrads receive any aid. 83% undergrads borrow to pay for school. Average cumulative indebtedness $28,104. **Criteria for awarding institutional aid:** *Non-need-based:* academics, alumni affiliation, art, leadership, minority status, music/drama, religious affiliation, state/district residency.

CENTENARY COLLEGE OF LOUISIANA

P.O. Box 41188, Shreveport, LA 71134-1188
Phone: 318-869-5131 • **Financial Aid Phone:** 318-869-5137
E-mail: admissions@centenary.edu • **CEEB Code:** 6082
Fax: 318-869-5005 • **Website:** www.centenary.edu • **ACT Code:** 1576

This private school, affiliated with the Methodist Church, was founded in 1825. It has a 68-acre campus.

RATINGS

Admissions Selectivity Rating: 84   **Fire Safety Rating:** 69   **Green Rating:** 60*

STUDENTS AND FACULTY

Enrollment: 689. **Student Body:** 56% female, 44% male, 34% out-of-state, 3% international (12 countries represented). Asian 3%, African American 13%, Caucasian 72%, Hispanic 5%, Native American 1%.
Retention and Graduation: 69% freshmen return for sophomore year. 43% freshmen graduate within 4 years. 56% freshmen graduate within 6 years. **Faculty:** Student/faculty ratio 9:1. 58 full-time faculty, 90% hold PhDs, 5% are members of minority groups, 33% are women. 0% of classes are taught by teaching assistants.

ACADEMICS

Degrees: bachelor's, master's. **Classes:** Most classes have 10–19 students. **Majors with Highest Enrollment:** biology/biological sciences; business/commerce; mass communication/media studies. **Special Study Options:** cross-registration, double major, dual enrollment, exchange student program (domestic), honors program, independent study, internships, liberal arts/career combination, student-designed major, study abroad, teacher certification program, weekend college, 3/2 Dual Degree (Liberal Arts/Engineering) program in cooperation with Case Western Reserve University, Columbia University, Texas

A and M University, University of Southern California, and Washington University in St. Louis; Mathematics/Computer Science double degree program with Southern Methodist University; Semester in Washington D.C.; British Studies at Oxford summer program. **Disability Services:** Special programs offered to physically disabled students include note-taking services, reader services, tape recorders, tutors. **Career Services:** alumni services, career/job search classes, career assessment, internships Career Services highlights include Both Service Learning and Intercultural Experience expose students to people and places quite different from their own and help them appreciate and understand human diversity.

FACILITIES

Housing: Coed dorms, women's dorms, fraternity/sorority housing. 95% of campus accessible to physically disabled. **Special Academic Facilities/Equipment:** Art museum, Art Center, art studios, theatre, performance and practice organs, piano lab, language lab, School of Music recording studio, Science Hall multimedia auditorium **Computers:** 50% of classrooms, 25% of dorms, 50% of libraries, 100% of dining areas, 50% of student union, 10% of common outdoor areas have wireless network access. Students can register for classes online. Administrative functions (other than registration) can be performed online.

CAMPUS LIFE

Environment: Metropolis. **Activities:** Choral groups, concert band, dance, drama/theater, jazz band, literary magazine, music ensembles, musical theater, opera, radio station, student government, student newspaper, student-run film society, yearbook, Campus Ministries, International Student Organization 58 registered organizations, 15 honor societies, 8 religious organizations. 5 fraternities, 2 sororities. **Athletics (Intercollegiate):** *Men:* baseball, basketball, cross-country, golf, soccer, swimming, tennis. *Women:* basketball, cross-country, golf, gymnastics, soccer, softball, swimming, tennis, volleyball. **On-Campus Highlights:** Fitness Center, Jones-Rice Field, Student Union Building, Anderson Choral Building, Gold Dome, Peavy Climbing Tower Anderson Choral Building Crumley Gardens Aboretum Feazel Instrumental Hall.

ADMISSIONS

Freshman Academic Profile: 3.5. 32% in top 10% of high school class, 89% in top 25% of high school class, 97% in top 50% of high school class. SAT Math middle 50% range 430-780. SAT Critical Reading middle 50% range 490-620. ACT middle 50% range 23-28. Minimum paper TOEFL 550. **Basis for Candidate Selection:** *Very important factors considered include:* academic GPA, rigor of secondary school record. *Important factors considered include:* Class rank, application essay, recommendation(s), standardized test scores, alumni/ae relation, character/personal qualities, extracurricular activities, interview, level of applicant's interest, talent/ability, volunteer work, work experience. *Other factors considered include:* first generation, geographical residence, racial/ethnic status, religious affiliation/commitment. **Freshman Admission Requirements:** High school diploma is required and GED is accepted. **Freshman Admission Statistics:** 933 applied, 64% admitted, 26% enrolled. **Transfer Admission Requirements:** High school transcript, college transcript(s), essay or personal statement, statement of good standing from prior institution(s). Minimum college GPA of 2.0 required. Lowest grade transferable C. **General Admission Information:** Application Fee $30. Regular application deadline 8/1. Notification on a rolling basis, beginning on or about 10/1. Nonfall registration accepted. Admission may be deferred for a maximum of 1 year. Credit and/or placement offered for CEEB Advanced Placement tests.

COSTS AND FINANCIAL AID

Annual tuition $29,500. Room and board $9,320. Average book expense $1,200. **Required Forms and Deadlines:** FAFSA, institution's own financial aid form. **Notification of Awards:** Applicants will be notified of awards on or about 3/15. **Types of Aid:** *Need-based scholarships/grants:* Federal Pell, SEOG, state scholarships/grants, private scholarships, the school's own gift aid. *Loans:* Subsidized Stafford, Unsubsidized Stafford, PLUS, Federal Perkins. **Student Employment:** Federal Work-Study Program available. Institutional employment available. Highest amount earned per year from on-campus jobs $4,000. Off-campus job opportunities are good. **Financial Aid Statistics:** 100% freshmen, 99% undergrads receive need-based scholarship or grant aid. 27% freshmen, 20% undergrads receive non-need-based scholarship or grant aid. 73% freshmen, 74% undergrads receive need-based self-help aid1% undergrads receive athletic scholarships. 50% undergrads borrow to pay for school. Average cumulative indebtedness $21,820. **Criteria for awarding institutional aid:** *Non-need-based:* academics, art, athletics, music/drama, religious affiliation, state/district residency.

CENTRAL BAPTIST COLLEGE

1501 College Avenue, Conway, AR 72034
Phone: 501-329-6872
E-mail: ccalhoun@cbc.edu and lwatson@cbc.edu
Fax: 501-329-2941 • **Website:** www.cbc.edu • **ACT Code:** 119

This private school, affiliated with the Baptist Church, was founded in 1952. It has a 13-acre campus.

RATINGS
Admissions Selectivity Rating: 62   **Fire Safety Rating:** 60*   **Green Rating:** 60*

STUDENTS AND FACULTY
Enrollment: 394. **Student Body:** 46% female, 54% male, 11% out-of-state, 1% international. Asian 1%, African American 9%, Caucasian 92%, Hispanic 2%, Native American 1%.
Faculty: Student/faculty ratio 17:1. 16 full-time faculty, 44% hold PhDs, 38% are women. 0% of classes are taught by teaching assistants.

ACADEMICS
Degrees: associate, bachelor's. **Classes: Majors with Highest Enrollment:** elementary education and teaching; psychology; theology and religious vocations, other.

FACILITIES
Housing: men's dorms, women's dorms.

CAMPUS LIFE
Environment: Rural. **Activities:** Choral groups, music ensembles, musical theater, student government, yearbook. **Athletics (Intercollegiate):** *Men:* baseball, basketball. *Women:* basketball, volleyball.

ADMISSIONS
Freshman Academic Profile: Average high school GPA 3.1. 11% in top 10% of high school class, 29% in top 25% of high school class, 66% in top 50% of high school class. Minimum paper TOEFL 500. **Basis for Candidate Selection:** *Very important factors considered include:* Class rank, recommendation(s), rigor of secondary school record, standardized test scores, character/personal qualities. *Important factors considered include:* religious affiliation/commitment. *Other factors considered include:* extracurricular activities, talent/ability. **Freshman Admission Requirements:** High school diploma is required and GED is accepted. **Freshman Admission Statistics:** 164 applied, 84% admitted, 75% enrolled. **Transfer Admission Requirements:** college transcript(s), essay or personal statement, standardized test scores, minimum college GPA of 2.0 required. Lowest grade transferable c. **General Admission Information:** Application Fee $25. Regular application deadline 8/15. Nonfall registration accepted. Admission may be deferred for a maximum of 12.

COSTS AND FINANCIAL AID
. Average book expense $700. **Required Forms and Deadlines:** FAFSA. **Notification of Awards: Types of Aid:** *Need-based scholarships/grants:* Federal Pell, SEOG, state scholarships/grants, private scholarships. *Loans:* Subsidized Stafford, Unsubsidized Stafford, PLUS. **Student Employment:** Federal Work-Study Program available. Off-campus job opportunities are good. **Criteria for awarding institutional aid:** *Non-need-based:* academics, alumni affiliation, leadership, music/drama, religious affiliation.

CENTRAL COLLEGE

812 University Street, Pella, IA 50219-1999
Phone: 641-628-5286 • **Financial Aid Phone:** 641-628-5336
E-mail: admission@central.edu • **CEEB Code:** 6087
Fax: 641-628-5983 • **Website:** www.central.edu • **ACT Code:** 1284

This private school, affiliated with the Reformed Church Church, was founded in 1853. It has a 133-acre campus.

RATINGS
Admissions Selectivity Rating: 77   **Fire Safety Rating:** 77   **Green Rating:** 82

STUDENTS AND FACULTY
Enrollment: 1,417. **Student Body:** 53% female, 47% male, 19% out-of-state, 0% international (12 countries represented). Asian 1%, African American 2%, Caucasian 89%, Hispanic 3%, Native American 0%.
Retention and Graduation: 83% freshmen return for sophomore year. 62% freshmen graduate within 4 years. 19% grads go on to further study within 1 year. 5% grads pursue arts and sciences degrees. 1% grads pursue law degrees. 1% grads pursue business degrees. 2% grads pursue medical degrees. **Faculty:** Student/faculty ratio 13:1. 98 full-time faculty, 84% hold PhDs, 9% are members of minority groups, 42% are women. 0% of classes are taught by teaching assistants.

ACADEMICS
Degrees: bachelor's. **Classes:** Most classes have 10–19 students. Most lab/discussion sessions have 10–19 students. **Majors with Highest Enrollment:** business/commerce; education; kinesiology and exercise science. **Special Study Options:** double major, English as a Second Language (ESL), honors program, independent study, internships, liberal arts/career combination, student-designed major, study abroad, teacher certification program, Off-Campus Study: Washington, DC,Chicago Metro Program. Study abroad in nine countries. Exploring Student Program encourages two years of multidisciplinary study before selecting a major. **Honors Programs:** The entire 4-year Honors program is outstanding **Combined Degree Programs:** BA/MEng, 3-4 architecture program with Washington U. **Disability Services:** Special programs offered to physically disabled students include note-taking services, reader services, tape recorders, tutors.

FACILITIES
Housing: Coed dorms, special housing for disabled students, men's dorms, special housing for international students, women's dorms, fraternity/sorority housing, apartments for married students, apartments for single students. 95% of campus accessible to physically disabled. **Special Academic Facilities/Equipment:** Art gallery, center for communication and theatre, music center, language lab, glass-blowing studio. **Computers:** Students can register for classes online. Administrative functions (other than registration) can be performed online.

CAMPUS LIFE
Environment: Village. **Activities:** Choral groups, concert band, drama/theater, jazz band, literary magazine, music ensembles, musical theater, radio station, student government, student newspaper, symphony orchestra, yearbook 50 registered organizations, 4 religious organizations. 4 fraternities, 2 sororities. **Athletics (Intercollegiate):** *Men:* baseball, basketball, football, golf, soccer, tennis, track/field (outdoor), track/field (indoor), wrestling. *Women:* basketball, cross-country, golf, softball, tennis, track/field (outdoor), track/field (indoor), volleyball. **Environmental Initiatives:** Sustainability Across the Curriculum: Global Sustainability core curriculum graduation requirement (since 2010)for all students, satisfied by a wide variety of sustainability designated courses from across the curriculum; an interdisciplinary minor in Global Sustainability (2011) LEED-rated buildings: Iowa's first LEED-Silver building (2003) Vermeer Science Center; a LEED Gold rated student residence hall (McKee Hall) and a LEED Platinum rated academic building (2010) A commitment to community outreach, particularly working with community partners in the central Iowa(Des Moines) area in the social justice and human rights aspects of sustainmability; extending and connected community-based learning with sustainability education professional training and development for area educators and community partners.

ADMISSIONS
Freshman Academic Profile: Average high school GPA 3.6. 25% in top 10% of high school class, 58% in top 25% of high school class, 89% in top 50% of high school class. 95% from public high schools. SAT Math middle 50% range 470-570. SAT Critical Reading middle 50% range 460-550. ACT middle 50% range 21-26. Minimum web-based TOEFL 71. Minimum paper TOEFL 530. **Basis for Candidate Selection:** *Very important factors considered include:* academic GPA, rigor of secondary school record, standardized test scores. *Important factors considered include:* Class rank. *Other factors considered include:* application essay, recommendation(s), alumni/ae relation, character/personal qualities, extracurricular activities, first generation, interview, talent/ability, volunteer work, work experience. **Freshman Admission Requirements:** High school diploma is required and GED is accepted. *Academic units required:* 4 English, 2 mathematics, 2 science, (2 science labs), 3 social studies, 2 history. *Academic units recommended:* 4 English, 2 mathematics, 2 science, (2 science labs), 3 social studies, 2 history. **Freshman Admission Statistics:** 2,471 applied, 65% admitted, 20% enrolled. **Transfer Admission Requirements:** High school transcript, college transcript(s), standardized test scores, statement of good standing from prior institution(s). Minimum college GPA of 2.5 required. Lowest grade transferable C-. **General Admission Information:** Application Fee $25. Notification on a rolling basis, beginning on or about 9/15. Nonfall registration accepted. Admission may be deferred for a maximum of 1 yr. Credit and/or placement offered for CEEB Advanced Placement tests.

COSTS AND FINANCIAL AID
Required Forms and Deadlines: FAFSA. **Notification of Awards:** Applicants will be notified of awards on a rolling basis beginning 3/15. **Types of Aid:** *Need-based scholarships/grants:* Federal Pell, SEOG, state scholarships/grants, private scholarships, the school's own gift aid. *Loans:* Direct Subsidized

Stafford, Direct Unsubsidized Stafford, Direct PLUS, Federal Perkins, college/university loans from institutional funds, Private Alternative Loans. **Student Employment:** Highest amount earned per year from on-campus jobs $2,600. **Financial Aid Statistics:** 100% freshmen, 100% undergrads receive need-based scholarship or grant aid. 25% freshmen, 10% undergrads receive non-need-based scholarship or grant aid. 83% freshmen, 86% undergrads receive need-based self-help aid. 100% freshmen, 99% undergrads receive any aid. 85% undergrads borrow to pay for school. Average cumulative indebtedness $27,990. **Criteria for awarding institutional aid:** *Non-need-based:* academics, alumni affiliation, art, minority status, music/drama, religious affiliation, state/district residency.

CENTRAL CONNECTICUT STATE UNIVERSITY

1615 Stanley Street, New Britain, CT 6050
Phone: 860-832-2278 • **Financial Aid Phone:** 860-832-2200
E-mail: admissions@ccsu.edu • **CEEB Code:** 3898
Fax: 862-832-2295 • **Website:** www.ccsu.edu • **ACT Code:** 596

This public school was founded in 1849. It has a 294-acre campus.

RATINGS
Admissions Selectivity Rating: 76   **Fire Safety Rating:** 86   **Green Rating:** 74

STUDENTS AND FACULTY
Enrollment: 9,630. **Student Body:** 48% female, 52% male, 3% out-of-state, 1% international (41 countries represented). Asian 3%, African American 10%, Caucasian 70%, Hispanic 11%, Native American 0%.
Retention and Graduation: 76% freshmen return for sophomore year. 17% freshmen graduate within 4 years. 52% freshmen graduate within 6 years. **Faculty:** Student/faculty ratio 16:1. 441 full-time faculty, 84% hold PhDs, 20% are members of minority groups, 43% are women. 0% of classes are taught by teaching assistants.

ACADEMICS
Degrees: bachelor's, master's, post-bachelor's certificate, post-master's certificate. **Classes:** Most classes have 20–29 students. Most lab/discussion sessions have fewer than 10 students. **Majors with Highest Enrollment:** accounting; criminology; psychology. **Special Study Options:** cooperative education program, cross-registration, distance learning, double major, dual enrollment, English as a Second Language (ESL), exchange student program (domestic), honors program, independent study, internships, student-designed major, study abroad, teacher certification program. Undergrads may take grad classes. Co-Op programs: Arts, Business, Computer Science, Education, Humanities, Natural Science, Social/Behavioral Science, Technologies. **Honors Programs:** Interdisciplinary writing/reading program for undergraduates with strong academic skills. Areas of study: Western Culture, Science and Society, and World Culture, capstone honors thesis in junior year. Scholarship available. **Combined Degree Programs:** BA/MEng. **Disability Services:** Special programs offered to physically disabled students include note-taking services, reader services, tape recorders, tutors. **Career Services:** alumni services, career/job search classes, career assessment, internships Career Services highlights include Cooperative learning in the form of cooperative education.

FACILITIES
Housing: Coed dorms, women's dorms. 95% of campus accessible to physically disabled. **Special Academic Facilities/Equipment:** Art gallery, language lab, childhood center, planetarium and space science center, center for economic education, TV studio. **Computers:** 50% of classrooms, 100% of libraries, 100% of dining areas, 100% of student union, 50% of common outdoor areas have wireless network access. Students can register for classes online. Administrative functions (other than registration) can be performed online.

CAMPUS LIFE
Environment: Town. **Activities:** Choral groups, concert band, dance, drama/theater, jazz band, literary magazine, music ensembles, musical theater, radio station, student government, student newspaper, student-run film society, television station, yearbook, International Student Organization 101 registered organizations, 18 honor societies, 5 religious organizations. 1 sororities. **Athletics (Intercollegiate):** *Men:* baseball, basketball, cross-country, football, golf, soccer, track/field (outdoor), track/field (indoor). *Women:* basketball, cross-country, diving, golf, lacrosse, soccer, softball, swimming, track/field (outdoor), track/field (indoor), volleyball. **On-Campus Highlights:** Student Center, Cafeteria, Memorial Hall, Torp Theatre, Davidson Hall, Vance Academic Center, Vance Hall, James Hall (Residence Hall), Semesters, Student Center. **Environmental Initiatives:** Fuel cell Class schedule for carpool ease Building use in summer On-campus education and programs for more sustainable practices providing non-fossil fuel programs for campus stakeholders to change practices Reducing solid waste production and promoting recycling

ADMISSIONS
Freshman Academic Profile: Average high school GPA 3.0. 10% in top 10% of high school class, 22% in top 25% of high school class, 72% in top 50% of high school class. 95% from public high schools. SAT Math middle 50% range 460-560. SAT Critical Reading middle 50% range 450-550. SAT Writing middle 50% range 450-550. Minimum paper TOEFL 500. **Basis for Candidate Selection:** *Very important factors considered include:* rigor of secondary school record. *Important factors considered include:* Class rank, academic GPA, standardized test scores. *Other factors considered include:* application essay, recommendation(s), extracurricular activities, geographical residence, interview, racial/ethnic status, talent/ability. **Freshman Admission Requirements:** High school diploma is required and GED is accepted. *Academic units required:* 4 English, 3 mathematics, 2 science, (1 science labs), 2 social studies, 1 history. *Academic units recommended:* 4 English, 3 mathematics, 2 science, (1 science labs), 2 social studies, 1 history. **Freshman Admission Statistics:** 5,656 applied, 64% admitted, 37% enrolled. **Transfer Admission Requirements:** High school transcript, college transcript(s), statement of good standing from prior institution(s). Minimum college GPA of 2.0 required. Lowest grade transferable C. **General Admission Information:** Application Fee $50. Regular application deadline 6/1. Notification on a rolling basis, beginning on or about 12/1. Nonfall registration accepted. Admission may be deferred for a maximum of n/a. Credit offered for CEEB Advanced Placement tests.

COSTS AND FINANCIAL AID
Annual in-state tuition $4,285. Annual out-of-state tuition $13,866. Room and board $10,056. Required fees $5,487. Average book expense $1,200. **Required Forms and Deadlines:** FAFSA, business/farm supplement. **Notification of Awards:** Applicants will be notified of awards on a rolling basis beginning 3/15. **Types of Aid:** *Need-based scholarships/grants:* Federal Pell, SEOG, state scholarships/grants, the school's own gift aid. *Loans:* Direct Subsidized Stafford, Direct Unsubsidized Stafford, Direct PLUS, PLUS, Federal Perkins. **Student Employment:** Federal Work-Study Program available. Institutional employment available. Highest amount earned per year from on-campus jobs $5,000. Off-campus job opportunities are good. **Financial Aid Statistics:** 84% freshmen, 73% undergrads receive need-based scholarship or grant aid. 19% freshmen, 18% undergrads receive non-need-based scholarship or grant aid. 81% freshmen, 85% undergrads receive need-based self-help aid. 1% freshmen, 3% undergrads receive athletic scholarships. 71% freshmen, 61% undergrads receive any aid. 54% undergrads borrow to pay for school. Average cumulative indebtedness $22,171. **Criteria for awarding institutional aid:** *Non-need-based:* academics, athletics, minority status.

See page 1038.

CENTRAL METHODIST UNIVERSITY

411 Central Methodist Square, Fayette, MO 65248
Phone: 660-248-6251
E-mail: admissions@centralmethodist.edu • **CEEB Code:** 6089
Fax: 660-248-1872 • **Website:** www.centralmethodist.edu • **ACT Code:** 2270

This private school, affiliated with the Methodist Church, was founded in 1854. It has a 90-acre campus.

RATINGS
Admissions Selectivity Rating: 69   **Fire Safety Rating:** 60*   **Green Rating:** 60*

STUDENTS AND FACULTY
Enrollment: 1,143. **Student Body:** 50% female, 50% male, 10% out-of-state, 2% international (15 countries represented). Asian 0%, African American 5%, Caucasian 62%, Hispanic 1%, Native American 0%.
Retention and Graduation: 57% freshmen return for sophomore year. 30% freshmen graduate within 4 years. 41% freshmen graduate within 6 years. 15% grads go on to further study within 1 year. 15% grads pursue arts and sciences degrees. 5% grads pursue law degrees. 5% grads pursue business degrees. 4% grads pursue medical degrees. **Faculty:** Student/faculty ratio 14:1. 54 full-time faculty, 65% hold PhDs, 4% are members of minority groups, 43% are women. 0% of classes are taught by teaching assistants.

ACADEMICS
Degrees: associate, bachelor's, master's. **Classes:** Most classes have fewer than 10 students. **Majors with Highest Enrollment:** business/commerce; early childhood education; elementary education and teaching. **Special Study Options:** Accelerated program, distance learning, double major, dual enrollment, honors program, independent study, internships, liberal arts/career combination, student-designed major, study abroad, teacher certification program. **Career Services:** career/job search classes, career assessment, internships.

FACILITIES

Housing: Coed dorms, men's dorms, women's dorms, apartments for married students, apartments for single students. 39% of campus accessible to physically disabled. **Special Academic Facilities/Equipment:** 2 museums. Telecommunity Technology Center, computer lab in Residence halls.

CAMPUS LIFE

Environment: Rural. **Activities:** Choral groups, concert band, drama/theater, jazz band, literary magazine, marching band, music ensembles, musical theater, radio station, student government, student newspaper, symphony orchestra, television station, yearbook 41 registered organizations, 13 honor societies, 2 religious organizations. 6 fraternities, 4 sororities. **Athletics (Intercollegiate):** *Men:* baseball, basketball, cheerleading, cross-country, football, golf, soccer, track/field (outdoor). *Women:* basketball, cheerleading, cross-country, golf, soccer, softball, track/field (outdoor), volleyball.

ADMISSIONS

Freshman Academic Profile: Average high school GPA 3.2. 7% in top 10% of high school class, 34% in top 25% of high school class, 70% in top 50% of high school class. ACT middle 50% range 19-23. Minimum paper TOEFL 500. **Basis for Candidate Selection:** *Very important factors considered include:* Class rank, rigor of secondary school record, standardized test scores, extracurricular activities. *Important factors considered include:* alumni/ae relation, character/personal qualities, racial/ethnic status, religious affiliation/commitment, talent/ability, volunteer work, work experience. *Other factors considered include:* recommendation(s), geographical residence, interview, state residency. **Freshman Admission Requirements:** High school diploma is required and GED is accepted. **Freshman Admission Statistics:** 1,033 applied, 73% admitted, 30% enrolled. **Transfer Admission Requirements:** High school transcript, college transcript(s), standardized test scores, statement of good standing from prior institution(s). Minimum college GPA of 2.0 required. Lowest grade transferable D. **General Admission Information:** Regular application deadline 8/1. Nonfall registration accepted. Admission may be deferred for a maximum of None. Credit offered for CEEB Advanced Placement tests.

COSTS AND FINANCIAL AID

Required Forms and Deadlines: FAFSA. **Notification of Awards:** Applicants will be notified of awards on a rolling basis beginning 1/30. **Types of Aid:** *Need-based scholarships/grants:* Federal Pell, SEOG, state scholarships/grants, private scholarships, the school's own gift aid. *Loans:* Subsidized Stafford, Unsubsidized Stafford, PLUS, Federal Perkins, college/university loans from institutional funds. **Student Employment:** Federal Work-Study Program available. Off-campus job opportunities are good. **Financial Aid Statistics:** 100% freshmen, 100% undergrads receive need-based scholarship or grant aid. 100% freshmen, 99% undergrads receive non-need-based scholarship or grant aid. 89% freshmen, 81% undergrads receive need-based self-help aid. 2% freshmen, 1% undergrads receive athletic scholarships. 66% undergrads borrow to pay for school. Average cumulative indebtedness $17,037. **Criteria for awarding institutional aid:** *Non-need-based:* academics, alumni affiliation, athletics, leadership, music/drama, religious affiliation.

CENTRAL MICHIGAN UNIVERSITY

102 Warriner Hall, Mount Pleasant, MI 48859
Phone: 989-774-3076 • **Financial Aid Phone:** 888-392-0007
E-mail: cmuadmit@cmich.edu • **CEEB Code:** 1106
Fax: 989-774-7267 • **Website:** www.cmich.edu • **ACT Code:** 1972

This public school was founded in 1892. It has a 854-acre campus.

RATINGS

Admissions Selectivity Rating: 75   **Fire Safety Rating:** 89   **Green Rating:** 88

STUDENTS AND FACULTY

Enrollment: 21,232. **Student Body:** 55% female, 45% male, 3% out-of-state, 1% international (56 countries represented). Asian 1%, African American 6%, Caucasian 80%, Hispanic 2%, Native American 1%.
Retention and Graduation: 76% freshmen return for sophomore year. 18% freshmen graduate within 4 years. 54% freshmen graduate within 6 years. 18% grads go on to further study within 1 year. 26% grads pursue arts and sciences degrees. 5% grads pursue business degrees. **Faculty:** Student/faculty ratio 23:1. 751 full-time faculty, 81% hold PhDs, 18% are members of minority groups, 41% are women. 5% of classes are taught by teaching assistants.

ACADEMICS

Degrees: bachelor's, doctoral, master's, post-bachelor's certificate, post-master's certificate. **Classes:** Most classes have 20–29 students. Most lab/discussion sessions have 10–19 students. **Majors with Highest Enrollment:** account-

ing; kinesiology and exercise science; psychology. **Special Study Options:** Accelerated program, distance learning, double major, dual enrollment, English as a Second Language (ESL), honors program, independent study, internships, student-designed major, study abroad, teacher certification program, Leadership Institute: The Central Michigan University Leadership Institute, which features a four-year leadership development program, an academic minor, and a scholarship cohort that includes a residential experience, s the premier center for leadership education, training, and development in the Midwest. **Honors Programs:** The Honors Program, Centralis Program **Combined Degree Programs:** BA/MA, 8 Accelerated Masters Degree Programs. **Disability Services:** Special programs offered to physically disabled students include note-taking services, reader services, tape recorders, tutors. **Career Services:** Alumni network, alumni services, career/job search classes, career assessment, internships, regional alumni. Career Services highlights include 100% of undergraduates complete internships.

FACILITIES

Housing: Coed dorms, special housing for disabled students, men's dorms, special housing for international students, women's dorms, fraternity/sorority housing, apartments for married students, apartments for single students, theme housing, Residential Colleges: areas of residence halls designated for students with the same majors or academic interests. 95% of campus accessible to physically disabled. **Special Academic Facilities/Equipment:** Clarke Historical Library, Central Michigan University Museum of Cultural and Natural History, Gerald L. Poor School Museum, Brooks Astronomical Observatory, University Art Gallery, University Theater, Public Broadcasting, Student Activity Center, Charles V. Park Library, body scanner **Computers:** 100% of classrooms, 100% of dorms, 100% of libraries, 100% of dining areas, 100% of student union, have wireless network access. Students can register for classes online. Administrative functions (other than registration) can be performed online.

CAMPUS LIFE

Environment: Town. **Activities:** Choral groups, concert band, dance, drama/theater, jazz band, literary magazine, marching band, music ensembles, musical theater, pep band, radio station, student government, student newspaper, student-run film society, television station, yearbook, Campus Ministries, International Student Organization 150 registered organizations, 6 honor societies, 12 religious organizations. 15 fraternities, 15 sororities. **Athletics (Intercollegiate):** *Men:* baseball, basketball, cross-country, football, track/field (outdoor), track/field (indoor), wrestling. *Women:* basketball, cross-country, field hockey, gymnastics, soccer, softball, track/field (outdoor), track/field (indoor), volleyball. **On-Campus Highlights:** Education Building (2009), Student Activity Center, Bovee University Center, Park Library, Academic Buildings. **Environmental Initiatives:** Campus Sustainability Advisory Committee 1. FTE Energy Optimization 2. FTE Retro-Commissioning Achieving LEED certification on all new buildings, additions and major renovations.

ADMISSIONS

Freshman Academic Profile: Average high school GPA 3.3. 14% in top 10% of high school class, 40% in top 25% of high school class, 76% in top 50% of high school class. 88% from public high schools. SAT Math middle 50% range 450-595. SAT Critical Reading middle 50% range 450-568. ACT middle 50% range 20-25. **Basis for Candidate Selection:** *Very important factors considered include:* academic GPA, rigor of secondary school record, standardized test scores. *Important factors considered include:* Class rank, talent/ability. *Other factors considered include:* application essay, recommendation(s), alumni/ae relation, character/personal qualities, extracurricular activities, geographical residence, interview, level of applicant's interest, volunteer work, work experience. **Freshman Admission Requirements:** High school diploma is required and GED is accepted. **Freshman Admission Statistics:** 18,509 applied, 68% admitted, 30% enrolled. **Transfer Admission Requirements:** college transcript(s), statement of good standing from prior institution(s). Minimum college GPA of 2.00 required. Lowest grade transferable C-. **General Admission Information:** Application Fee $35. Regular application deadline 7/1. Nonfall registration accepted. Admission may be deferred for a maximum of 1 semester. Credit and/or placement offered for CEEB Advanced Placement tests.

COSTS AND FINANCIAL AID

Annual in-state tuition $10,950. Annual out-of-state tuition $23,670. Room and board $8,368. Average book expense $1,000. **Required Forms and Deadlines:** FAFSA. **Notification of Awards:** Applicants will be notified of awards on a rolling basis beginning 4/1. **Types of Aid:** *Need-based scholarships/grants:* Federal Pell, SEOG, state scholarships/grants, private scholarships, the school's own gift aid. *Loans:* Direct Subsidized Stafford, Direct Unsubsidized Stafford, Direct PLUS, Federal Perkins, state loans, alternative loans. **Student Employment:** Federal Work-Study Program available. Institutional employment available. Highest amount earned per year from on-campus jobs $3,500. Off-campus job opportunities are good. **Financial Aid Statistics:** 84% freshmen, 77% undergrads receive need-based scholarship or grant aid. 8% freshmen, 4% undergrads receive non-need-based scholarship or grant aid. 85% freshmen,

91% undergrads receive need-based self-help aid. 1% freshmen, 1% undergrads receive athletic scholarships. 89% freshmen, 84% undergrads receive any aid. 73% undergrads borrow to pay for school. Average cumulative indebtedness $29,388. **Criteria for awarding institutional aid:** *Non-need-based:* academics, alumni affiliation, art, athletics, leadership, minority status, music/drama, state/district residency.

CENTRAL STATE UNIVERSITY

PO Box 1004, Wilberforce, OH 45384
Phone: 937-376-6348
E-mail: admissions@centralstate.edu • **CEEB Code:** 1107
Fax: 937-376-6648 • **Website:** www.centralstate.edu • **ACT Code:** 3246

This public school was founded in 1887. It has a 60-acre campus.

RATINGS
Admissions Selectivity Rating: 87   **Fire Safety Rating:** 60*   **Green Rating:** 60*

STUDENTS AND FACULTY
Enrollment: 2,419. **Student Body:** 51% female, 49% male, 42% out-of-state, 0% international. Asian 0%, African American 95%, Caucasian 2%, Hispanic 1%, Native American 0%.
Retention and Graduation: 55% freshmen return for sophomore year. 9% freshmen graduate within 4 years. 24% freshmen graduate within 6 years. 32% grads go on to further study within 1 year. 50% grads pursue arts and sciences degrees. 7% grads pursue law degrees. 29% grads pursue business degrees. **Faculty:** Student/faculty ratio 16:1. 109 full-time faculty, 69% hold PhDs, 72% are members of minority groups, 39% are women.

ACADEMICS
Degrees: bachelor's, master's. **Classes:** Most classes have 20–29 students. Most lab/discussion sessions have 10–19 students. **Majors with Highest Enrollment:** biology; business/commerce; early childhood education. **Special Study Options:** cooperative education program, cross-registration, double major, honors program, independent study, internships, study abroad, teacher certification program. **Disability Services:** Special programs offered to physically disabled students include note-taking services, reader services, tape recorders, tutors. **Career Services:** alumni services, career/job search classes, career assessment, internships, regional alumni

FACILITIES
Housing: Coed dorms, men's dorms, women's dorms, 1% of campus accessible to physically disabled. **Special Academic Facilities/Equipment:** National Afro-American Museum and Cultural Center; CJ McLin International Center for Water Resources Management; Center for Integrated Manufacturing Protocols Architectures and Logistics Laboratory; Biology Technique Laboratory; Electrochemistry Research Laboratory; Cosby Mass Communication Center; Paul Robeson Cultural and Performing Arts Center **Computers:** Administrative functions (other than registration) can be performed online.

CAMPUS LIFE
Environment: Rural. **Activities:** Choral groups, concert band, dance, drama/theater, jazz band, marching band, music ensembles, pep band, radio station, student government, student newspaper, television station, Campus Ministries 30 registered organizations, 3 honor societies, 4 religious organizations. 1 fraternities, 3 sororities. **Athletics (Intercollegiate):** *Men:* basketball, cheerleading, cross-country, golf, track/field (outdoor). *Women:* basketball, cheerleading, cross-country, golf, track/field (outdoor), volleyball.

ADMISSIONS
Freshman Academic Profile: Average high school GPA 2.4. 8% in top 10% of high school class, 19% in top 25% of high school class, 39% in top 50% of high school class. SAT Math middle 50% range 320-430. SAT Critical Reading middle 50% range 330-430. ACT middle 50% range 14-18. Minimum paper TOEFL 500. **Basis for Candidate Selection:** *Very important factors considered include:* academic GPA, rigor of secondary school record, standardized test scores. *Important factors considered include:* Class rank, application essay, character/personal qualities, geographical residence, state residency. *Other factors considered include:* recommendation(s), extracurricular activities, interview, talent/ability. **Freshman Admission Requirements:** High school diploma is required and GED is accepted. **Freshman Admission Statistics:** 8,637 applied, 22% admitted, 31% enrolled. **Transfer Admission Requirements:** college transcript(s), statement of good standing from prior institution(s). Minimum college GPA of 2.0 required. Lowest grade transferable D. **General Admission Information:** Application Fee $20. Nonfall registration accepted. Admission may be deferred for a maximum of none. Credit and/or placement offered for CEEB Advanced Placement tests.

COSTS AND FINANCIAL AID
Annual in-state tuition $3,430. Annual out-of-state tuition $10,406. Room and board $8,484. Required fees $2,242. Average book expense $1,200. **Required Forms and Deadlines:** FAFSA, institution's own financial aid form. **Notification of Awards:** Applicants will be notified of awards on a rolling basis beginning 5/1. **Types of Aid:** *Need-based scholarships/grants:* Federal Pell, SEOG, state scholarships/grants, private scholarships, the school's own gift aid, United Negro College Fund. *Loans:* Direct Subsidized Stafford, Direct Unsubsidized Stafford, Direct PLUS, college/university loans from institutional funds. **Student Employment:** Federal Work-Study Program available. Institutional employment available. Off-campus job opportunities are fair. **Financial Aid Statistics:** 91% freshmen, 93% undergrads receive need-based scholarship or grant aid. 82% freshmen, 41% undergrads receive non-need-based scholarship or grant aid. 99% freshmen, 100% undergrads receive need-based self-help aid. 98% undergrads borrow to pay for school. Average cumulative indebtedness $5,500. **Criteria for awarding institutional aid:** *Non-need-based:* academics, alumni affiliation, art, athletics, leadership, music/drama, religious affiliation, state/district residency.

CENTRAL WASHINGTON UNIVERSITY

Admissions Office, Ellensburg, WA 98926-7463
Phone: 509-963-1211 • **Financial Aid Phone:** 509-963-1611
E-mail: cwuadmis@cwu.edu • **CEEB Code:** 4044
Fax: 509-963-3022 • **Website:** www.cwu.edu • **ACT Code:** 4444

This public school was founded in 1891. It has a 350-acre campus.

RATINGS
Admissions Selectivity Rating: 69   **Fire Safety Rating:** 67   **Green Rating:** 84

STUDENTS AND FACULTY
Enrollment: 9,688. **Student Body:** 51% female, 49% male, 2% out-of-state, 2% international (60 countries represented). Asian 7%, African American 3%, Caucasian 75%, Hispanic 8%, Native American 3%.
Retention and Graduation: 26% freshmen graduate within 4 years. 55% freshmen graduate within 6 years. **Faculty:** Student/faculty ratio 20:1. 432 full-time faculty, 12% are members of minority groups, 39% are women. 3% of classes are taught by teaching assistants.

ACADEMICS
Degrees: bachelor's, master's, post-bachelor's certificate. **Classes:** Most classes have 20–29 students. Most lab/discussion sessions have 10–19 students. **Majors with Highest Enrollment:** business/commerce; elementary education and teaching; social sciences. **Special Study Options:** cooperative education program, distance learning, double major, dual enrollment, English as a Second Language (ESL), exchange student program (domestic), honors program, independent study, internships, liberal arts/career combination, student-designed major, study abroad, teacher certification program. **Honors Programs:** The Douglas Honors College student is expected to maintain a grade point average above 3.0. A student will be placed on probation if the grade point average falls below 3.0, and will be dismissed from the Douglas Honors College if the cumulative grade point average is below 3.0 for two consecutive quarters. This policy does not affect academic standing as a student of Central Washington University. **Disability Services:** Special programs offered to physically disabled students include note-taking services, reader services, tape recorders, tutors. **Career Services:** Alumni network, alumni services, career/job search classes, career assessment, internships, regional alumni.

FACILITIES
Housing: Coed dorms, special housing for disabled students, special housing for international students, women's dorms, apartments for married students, apartments for single students, theme housing, Upperclassmen and 21 years and older. 100% of campus accessible to physically disabled. **Special Academic Facilities/Equipment:** -Chimpanzee and Human Communication Institute -Geodesy Laboratory, a data analysis facility of the Pacific Northwest Geodetic Array -Educational Technology Center -Museum collection of NW Native Amer and Circum-Pacific artifacts for teaching and research. -regional site of the National Consortium for Rural Geospatial Innovations -Sarah Spugeon Art Gallery -Science Facility Building **Computers:** 100% of libraries, 100% of dining areas, 100% of student union, 100% of common outdoor areas have wireless network access. Students can register for classes online. Administrative functions (other than registration) can be performed online.

CAMPUS LIFE
Environment: Village. **Activities:** Choral groups, concert band, dance, drama/theater, jazz band, literary magazine, marching band, music ensembles, musical theater, opera, pep band, radio station, student government, student newspaper, student-run film society, symphony orchestra, television station, Campus Min-

istries, International Student Organization 96 registered organizations, 3 honor societies, 9 religious organizations. **Athletics (Intercollegiate):** *Men:* baseball, basketball, cheerleading, cross-country, football, track/field (outdoor), track/field (indoor). *Women:* basketball, cheerleading, cross-country, soccer, softball, track/field (outdoor), track/field (indoor), volleyball. **On-Campus Highlights:** Award-winning Student Union Recreation Center, Japanese Garden, Nicholson Pavilion Athletic Facilities, Chimpanzee and Human Communication Institute, Performing Arts Center, Presidential Speaker Series. **Environmental Initiatives:** Carbon Reduction Sustainability as defined by our "Sphere of Distinction" Energy Conservation.

ADMISSIONS

Freshman Academic Profile: Average high school GPA 3.2. 4% in top 10% of high school class, 23% in top 25% of high school class, 65% in top 50% of high school class. SAT Math middle 50% range 440-550. SAT Critical Reading middle 50% range 440-540. ACT middle 50% range 18-23. Minimum web-based TOEFL. Minimum paper TOEFL 525. **Basis for Candidate Selection:** *Very important factors considered include:* academic GPA, rigor of secondary school record. *Important factors considered include:* application essay, standardized test scores. *Other factors considered include:* Class rank, recommendation(s), character/personal qualities, extracurricular activities, first generation, interview, level of applicant's interest, talent/ability, volunteer work, work experience. **Freshman Admission Requirements:** High school diploma is required and GED is accepted. *Academic units required:* 4 English, 3 mathematics, 2 science, (1 science labs), 2 foreign language, 3 social studies. *Academic units recommended:* 4 English, 3 mathematics, 2 science, (1 science labs), 2 foreign language, 3 social studies. **Freshman Admission Statistics:** 5,013 applied, 79% admitted, 40% enrolled. **Transfer Admission Requirements:** college transcript(s), statement of good standing from prior institution(s). Minimum college GPA of 2.5 required. Lowest grade transferable D-. **General Admission Information:** Application Fee $55. Regular application deadline 4/1. Notification on a rolling basis, beginning on or about 11/1. Nonfall registration accepted. Credit and/or placement offered for CEEB Advanced Placement tests.

COSTS AND FINANCIAL AID

Annual in-state tuition $4,842. Annual out-of-state tuition $14,013. Room and board $8,052. Required fees $882. Average book expense $924. **Required Forms and Deadlines:** FAFSA. **Notification of Awards:** Applicants will be notified of awards on a rolling basis beginning 4/15. **Types of Aid:** *Need-based scholarships/grants:* Federal Pell, SEOG, state scholarships/grants, private scholarships, the school's own gift aid. *Loans:* Direct Subsidized Stafford, Direct Unsubsidized Stafford, Direct PLUS, Federal Perkins, state loans, college/university loans from institutional funds. **Student Employment:** Highest amount earned per year from on-campus jobs $10,166. **Financial Aid Statistics:** 68% undergrads receive any aid. **Criteria for awarding institutional aid:** *Non-need-based:* academics, alumni affiliation, art, athletics, job skills, leadership, minority status, music/drama, religious affiliation, state/district residency.

CENTRAL WYOMING COLLEGE

2660 Peck Avenue, Riverton, WY 82501
Phone: 307-855-2119 • **Financial Aid Phone:** 307-855-2150
E-mail: admit@cwc.edu • **CEEB Code:** 4115
Fax: 307-855-2093 • **Website:** www.cwc.edu • **ACT Code:** 514999

This public school was founded in 1966. It has a 200-acre campus.

RATINGS

Admissions Selectivity Rating: 64   **Fire Safety Rating:** 76   **Green Rating:** 61

STUDENTS AND FACULTY

Enrollment: 1,484. **Student Body:** 61% female, 39% male, 15% out-of-state, 1% international (9 countries represented). Asian 1%, African American 1%, Caucasian 73%, Hispanic 7%, Native American 13%.
Retention and Graduation: 54% freshmen return for sophomore year.
Faculty: Student/faculty ratio 16:1. 49 full-time faculty, 73% hold PhDs, 8% are members of minority groups, 37% are women. 0% of classes are taught by teaching assistants.

ACADEMICS

Degrees: associate, certificate, diploma, terminal associate, transfer associate. **Classes:** Most classes have fewer than 10 students. **Majors with Highest Enrollment:** general studies; nursing/registered nurse (rn, asn, bsn, msn); parks, recreation and leisure facilities management. **Special Study Options:** cooperative education program, cross-registration, distance learning, double major, dual enrollment, external degree program, honors program, independent study, student-designed major, teacher certification program. **Disability Services:**

Special programs offered to physically disabled students include note-taking services, reader services, tape recorders, tutors. **Career Services:** career/job search classes, career assessment, internships Career Services highlights include Experiential Learning.

FACILITIES

Housing: Coed dorms, apartments for married students, apartments for single students. 100% of campus accessible to physically disabled. **Special Academic Facilities/Equipment:** Fine Arts Center, Microsoft training lab, Cisco training lab, Wyoming Public Television Station and Radio station, Stewart Collection (Native American Artifacts), Sinks Canyon Center, Rodeo Arena, Library, Arts Gallery. **Computers:** Students can register for classes online. Administrative functions (other than registration) can be performed online.

CAMPUS LIFE

Environment: Village. **Activities:** Choral groups, concert band, dance, drama/theater, jazz band, music ensembles, musical theater, radio station, student government, television station, International Student Organization 16 registered organizations, 2 honor societies, 2 religious organizations. **Athletics (Intercollegiate):** *Men:* basketball, rodeo. *Women:* basketball, rodeo, volleyball. **On-Campus Highlights:** Arts Center, Stewart Collection, Student Center, Food Court, The Underground, Others depend on the students interests. For instance, if they are interested in our equine program we would take them to our equine facilities.

ADMISSIONS

Freshman Academic Profile: Average high school GPA 2.9. 8% in top 10% of high school class, 26% in top 25% of high school class, 55% in top 50% of high school class. 89% from public high schools. SAT Math middle 50% range 400-500. SAT Critical Reading middle 50% range 400-500. ACT middle 50% range 17-22. Minimum paper TOEFL 500. **Basis for Candidate Selection:** . **Freshman Admission Requirements:** High school diploma is required and GED is accepted. **Freshman Admission Statistics:** 642 applied, 100% admitted, 59% enrolled. **General Admission Information:** Application Fee $20.

COSTS AND FINANCIAL AID

Average book expense $1,000. **Financial Aid Statistics:** 78% freshmen, 82% undergrads receive need-based scholarship or grant aid. 81% freshmen, 77% undergrads receive non-need-based scholarship or grant aid. 10% freshmen, 12% undergrads receive need-based self-help aid. 43% freshmen, 53% undergrads receive any aid.

CENTRE COLLEGE

600 West Walnut Street, Danville, KY 40422
Phone: 859-238-5350
E-mail: admission@centre.edu • **CEEB Code:** 1109
Fax: 859-238-5373 • **Website:** www.centre.edu • **ACT Code:** 1506

This private school, affiliated with the Presbyterian Church, was founded in 1819. It has a 115-acre campus.

RATINGS

Admissions Selectivity Rating: 91   **Fire Safety Rating:** 60*   **Green Rating:** 80

STUDENTS AND FACULTY

Enrollment: 1,337. **Student Body:** 53% female, 47% male, 43% out-of-state, 3% international (12 countries represented). Asian 3%, African American 5%, Caucasian 85%, Hispanic 2%, Native American 0%.
Retention and Graduation: 91% freshmen return for sophomore year. 87% freshmen graduate within 4 years. 41% grads go on to further study within 1 year. 35% grads pursue arts and sciences degrees. 21% grads pursue law degrees. 3% grads pursue business degrees. 13% grads pursue medical degrees. **Faculty:** Student/faculty ratio 11:1. 117 full-time faculty, 95% hold PhDs, 10% are members of minority groups, 39% are women. 0% of classes are taught by teaching assistants.

ACADEMICS

Degrees: bachelor's. **Classes:** Most classes have 10–19 students. Most lab/discussion sessions have 10–19 students. **Majors with Highest Enrollment:** economics; English language and literature; history. **Special Study Options:** cross-registration, double major, honors program, independent study, internships, student-designed major, study abroad, teacher certification program. **Disability Services:** Special programs offered to physically disabled students include note-taking services, reader services, tape recorders, tutors. **Career Services:** Alumni network, alumni services, career/job search classes, career assessment, internships, regional alumni. Career Services highlights include We provide a college-wide comprehensive internship program. We also provide a unique program of career counseling called "Centre Futures.".

FACILITIES

Housing: Coed dorms, special housing for disabled students, men's dorms, fraternity/sorority housing, apartments for single students, wellness housing, theme housing, 80% of campus accessible to physically disabled. **Special Academic Facilities/Equipment:** Arts center, physical science and math facility, electron microscope, visible and infrared mass spectroscopy equipment, visual arts center. **Computers:** Administrative functions (other than registration) can be performed online.

CAMPUS LIFE

Environment: Village. **Activities:** Choral groups, dance, drama/theater, jazz band, literary magazine, music ensembles, musical theater, opera, pep band, radio station, student government, student newspaper, symphony orchestra, television station, Campus Ministries, International Student Organization 70 registered organizations, 12 honor societies, 6 religious organizations. 4 fraternities, 4 sororities. **Athletics (Intercollegiate):** *Men:* baseball, basketball, cheerleading, cross-country, diving, football, golf, soccer, swimming, tennis, track/field (outdoor). *Women:* basketball, cheerleading, cross-country, diving, field hockey, golf, soccer, softball, swimming, tennis, track/field (outdoor), volleyball. **On-Campus Highlights:** Norton Center for the Arts, College Centre, athletic and library, Combs Center, student center, 21 campus buildings on National Register, Jazzman's Cafe. **Environmental Initiatives:** All new buildings and major renovations will be designed and built to conserve energy and enhance the human environment as evaluated by LEED silver standards or equivalent. Certification through U.S.G.B.C. will be pursued as appropriate. Energy consumption and life-cycle costs will be considered in purchases of all equipment and appliances. The intention will be to purchase E.P.A. Energy Star products in all areas for which such ratings exist. Waste minimization will be promoted and pursued by policy and practice. Specific activities will depend upon technical and economic opportunities. Current efforts include participation in the Waste minimization component of the Recyclemania competition.

ADMISSIONS

Freshman Academic Profile: Average high school GPA 3.7. 49% in top 10% of high school class, 79% in top 25% of high school class, 95% in top 50% of high school class. 79% from public high schools. SAT Math middle 50% range 580-700. SAT Critical Reading middle 50% range 560-690. SAT Writing middle 50% range 560-680. ACT middle 50% range 26-31. Minimum paper TOEFL 580. **Basis for Candidate Selection:** *Very important factors considered include:* academic GPA, rigor of secondary school record. *Important factors considered include:* Class rank, application essay, recommendation(s), standardized test scores. *Other factors considered include:* alumni/ae relation, character/personal qualities, extracurricular activities, first generation, geographical residence, interview, racial/ethnic status, talent/ability, volunteer work, work experience. **Freshman Admission Requirements:** High school diploma or equivalent is not required. *Academic units required:* 4 English, 3 mathematics, 2 science, (2 science labs), 2 foreign language, 1 social studies, 1 history. *Academic units recommended:* 4 English, 3 mathematics, 2 science, (2 science labs), 2 foreign language, 1 social studies, 1 history. **Freshman Admission Statistics:** 2,539 applied, 70% admitted, 20% enrolled. **Transfer Admission Requirements:** High school transcript, college transcript(s), essay or personal statement, standardized test scores, statement of good standing from prior institution(s). Lowest grade transferable C. **General Admission Information:** Application Fee $40. Regular application deadline 2/1. Regular notification 3/15. Nonfall registration not accepted. Admission may be deferred for a maximum of 1 year. Credit and/or placement offered for CEEB Advanced Placement tests.

COSTS AND FINANCIAL AID

Annual tuition $36,000. Room and board $9,100. Average book expense $1,400. **Required Forms and Deadlines:** FAFSA, institution's own financial aid form. **Notification of Awards:** Applicants will be notified of awards on or about 4/1. **Types of Aid:** *Need-based scholarships/grants:* Federal Pell, SEOG, state scholarships/grants, private scholarships, the school's own gift aid, Federal ACG Federal SMART + Federal TEACH. *Loans:* Subsidized Stafford, Unsubsidized Stafford, PLUS, Federal Perkins, college/university loans from institutional funds. **Student Employment:** Federal Work-Study Program available. Institutional employment available. Off-campus job opportunities are fair. **Financial Aid Statistics:** 100% freshmen, 100% undergrads receive need-based scholarship or grant aid. 63% freshmen, 68% undergrads receive need-based self-help aid. 53% undergrads borrow to pay for school. Average cumulative indebtedness. **Criteria for awarding institutional aid:** *Non-need-based:* academics, alumni affiliation, music/drama.

CHADRON STATE COLLEGE

1000 Main Street, Chadron, NE 69337
Phone: 308-432-6263 • **Financial Aid Phone:** 308-432-6230
E-mail: inquire@csc.edu • **CEEB Code:** 6466
Fax: 308-432-6229 • **Website:** www.csc.edu • **ACT Code:** 2466

This public school was founded in 1911. It has a 281-acre campus.

RATINGS
Admissions Selectivity Rating: 60*   **Fire Safety Rating:** 66   **Green Rating:** 60*

STUDENTS AND FACULTY
Enrollment: 2,152. **Student Body:** 57% female, 43% male, 32% out-of-state, 1% international (16 countries represented). Asian 1%, African American 1%, Caucasian 73%, Hispanic 2%, Native American 2%.
Retention and Graduation: 70% freshmen return for sophomore year. 17% freshmen graduate within 4 years. 43% freshmen graduate within 6 years. 41% grads go on to further study within 1 year. 25% grads pursue arts and sciences degrees. 3% grads pursue law degrees. 10% grads pursue business degrees. 3% grads pursue medical degrees. **Faculty:** Student/faculty ratio 19:1. 101 full-time faculty, 57% hold PhDs, 4% are members of minority groups, 36% are women. 0% of classes are taught by teaching assistants.

ACADEMICS
Degrees: bachelor's, master's, post-master's certificate. **Classes:** Most classes have fewer than 10 students. **Majors with Highest Enrollment:** business/commerce; criminal justice/law enforcement administration; elementary education and teaching. **Special Study Options:** Accelerated program, cooperative education program, cross-registration, distance learning, double major, dual enrollment, honors program, independent study, internships, student-designed major, study abroad, teacher certification program. **Disability Services:** Special programs offered to physically disabled students include note-taking services, tape recorders, tutors. **Career Services:** career/job search classes

FACILITIES
Housing: Coed dorms, men's dorms, women's dorms, apartments for married students, apartments for single students. 100% of campus accessible to physically disabled. **Special Academic Facilities/Equipment:** Planetarium, herbarium, geology museum, Mari Sandoz Center **Computers:** Students can register for classes online. Administrative functions (other than registration) can be performed online.

CAMPUS LIFE
Environment: Rural. **Activities:** Choral groups, concert band, dance, drama/theater, jazz band, literary magazine, music ensembles, musical theater, pep band, radio station, student government, student newspaper, yearbook 65 registered organizations, 14 honor societies, 5 religious organizations. **Athletics (Intercollegiate):** *Men:* basketball, football, track/field (outdoor), track/field (indoor), wrestling. *Women:* basketball, golf, track/field (outdoor), track/field (indoor), volleyball. **On-Campus Highlights:** Mari Sandoz Heritage Center, Educational Facility, Laboratories, Student Center.

ADMISSIONS
Freshman Academic Profile: Average high school GPA 3.1. 11% in top 10% of high school class, 33% in top 25% of high school class, 65% in top 50% of high school class. 83% from public high schools. Minimum paper TOEFL 550. **Basis for Candidate Selection:** *Other factors considered include:* academic GPA. **Freshman Admission Requirements:** High school diploma is required and GED is accepted. **Transfer Admission Requirements:** college transcript(s), minimum college GPA of 2.0 required. Lowest grade transferable D. **General Admission Information:** Application Fee $15. Nonfall registration accepted. Credit and/or placement offered for CEEB Advanced Placement tests.

COSTS AND FINANCIAL AID
Annual in-state tuition $2,933. Annual out-of-state tuition $5,865. Room and board $4,074. Required fees $730. **Required Forms and Deadlines:** FAFSA, institution's own financial aid form. **Notification of Awards:** Applicants will be notified of awards on a rolling basis beginning 4/1. **Types of Aid:** *Need-based scholarships/grants:* Federal Pell, SEOG, state scholarships/grants, private scholarships, the school's own gift aid. *Loans:* Direct Subsidized Stafford, Direct Unsubsidized Stafford, Direct PLUS, Subsidized Stafford, Unsubsidized Stafford, PLUS, Federal Perkins. **Student Employment:** Federal Work-Study Program available. Institutional employment available. **Financial Aid Statistics:** 91% freshmen, 81% undergrads receive need-based scholarship or grant aid. 65% freshmen, 73% undergrads receive need-based self-help aid. **Criteria for awarding institutional aid:** *Non-need-based:* academics, alumni affiliation, art, athletics, leadership, minority status, music/drama, state/district residency.

CHAMINADE UNIVERSITY OF HONOLULU

3140 Waialae Avenue, Honolulu, HI 96816-1578
Phone: 808-735-4735 • Financial Aid Phone: 808-735-4780
E-mail: admissions@chaminade.edu • CEEB Code: 4105
Fax: 808-739-4647 • Website: www.chaminade.edu • ACT Code: 898

This private school, affiliated with the Roman Catholic Church, was founded in 1955. It has a 67-acre campus.

RATINGS
Admissions Selectivity Rating: 65   **Fire Safety Rating:** 61   **Green Rating:** 60*

STUDENTS AND FACULTY
Enrollment: 1,223. **Student Body:** 68% female, 32% male, 41% out-of-state, 2% international (12 countries represented). Asian 28%, African American 4%, Caucasian 17%, Hispanic 6%, Native American 1%.
Retention and Graduation: 72% freshmen return for sophomore year. 20% freshmen graduate within 4 years. **Faculty:** Student/faculty ratio 12:1. 70 full-time faculty, 71% hold PhDs, 40% are members of minority groups, 37% are women. 0% of classes are taught by teaching assistants.

ACADEMICS
Degrees: associate, bachelor's, master's, post-bachelor's certificate, post-master's certificate. **Classes:** Most classes have 10–19 students. Most lab/discussion sessions have 10–19 students. **Majors with Highest Enrollment:** business/commerce; criminal justice/safety studies; psychology. **Special Study Options:** Accelerated program, distance learning, double major, exchange student program (domestic), independent study, internships, student-designed major, study abroad, teacher certification program. **Disability Services:** Special programs offered to physically disabled students include note-taking services, reader services, tape recorders. **Career Services:** career/job search classes, career assessment, internships.

FACILITIES
Housing: Coed dorms, women's dorms, apartments for single students. 75% of campus accessible to physically disabled. **Special Academic Facilities/Equipment:** Montessori lab school, observatory, black box theatre. **Computers:** Students can register for classes online. Administrative functions (other than registration) can be performed online.

CAMPUS LIFE
Environment: Metropolis. **Activities:** Choral groups, drama/theater, literary magazine, musical theater, student government, student newspaper, symphony orchestra, yearbook, Campus Ministries 38 registered organizations, 7 honor societies, 1 religious organizations. **Athletics (Intercollegiate):** *Men:* basketball, cross-country, golf, tennis, water polo. *Women:* cross-country, golf, softball, tennis, volleyball. **On-Campus Highlights:** Jean E. Rolles Sculoture Center, Henry Hall Courtyard Cafe, Brother's Brew Cafe, Weigand Observatory, Vi and Paul Loo Student Center.

ADMISSIONS
Freshman Academic Profile: Average high school GPA 3.2. 9% in top 10% of high school class, 34% in top 25% of high school class, 75% in top 50% of high school class. SAT Math middle 50% range 420-520. SAT Critical Reading middle 50% range 420-520. SAT Writing middle 50% range 410-510. ACT middle 50% range 18-22. Minimum paper TOEFL 450. **Basis for Candidate Selection:** *Very important factors considered include:* academic GPA, standardized test scores. *Important factors considered include:* application essay, character/personal qualities, extracurricular activities, interview, talent/ability, volunteer work. *Other factors considered include:* recommendation(s), rigor of secondary school record, work experience. **Freshman Admission Requirements:** High school diploma is required and GED is accepted. **Freshman Admission Statistics:** 1,008 applied, 90% admitted, 33% enrolled. **Transfer Admission Requirements:** college transcript(s), essay or personal statement, statement of good standing from prior institution(s). Minimum college GPA of 2.0 required. Lowest grade transferable C. **General Admission Information:** Application Fee $50. Nonfall registration accepted. Admission may be deferred for a maximum of 1 year. Credit and/or placement offered for CEEB Advanced Placement tests.

COSTS AND FINANCIAL AID
Annual tuition $19,200. Required fees $140. Average book expense $1,200. **Required Forms and Deadlines:** FAFSA. **Notification of Awards:** Applicants will be notified of awards on a rolling basis beginning 3/1. **Types of Aid:** *Need-based scholarships/grants:* Federal Pell, SEOG, private scholarships, the school's own gift aid, LEAP, ASG, SMART, TEACH. *Loans:* Subsidized Stafford, Unsubsidized Stafford, PLUS, Federal Perkins, CitiAssist Loans, Sallie Mae Signature Education Loan Program. **Student Employment:** Federal Work-Study Program available. Institutional employment available. Highest

amount earned per year from on-campus jobs $8,056. Off-campus job opportunities are fair. **Financial Aid Statistics:** 99% freshmen, 96% undergrads receive any aid. **Criteria for awarding institutional aid:** *Non-need-based:* academics, art, athletics, leadership, religious affiliation.

CHAMPLAIN COLLEGE

163 South Willard Street Box 670, Burlington, VT 05402-0670
Phone: 802-860-2727 • Financial Aid Phone: 802-860-2730
E-mail: admission@champlain.edu • CEEB Code: 3291
Fax: 802-860-2767 • Website: www.champlain.edu/ • ACT Code: 3291

This private school was founded in 1878. It has a 19-acre campus.

RATINGS
Admissions Selectivity Rating: 70   **Fire Safety Rating:** 95   **Green Rating:** 92

STUDENTS AND FACULTY
Enrollment: 2,067. **Student Body:** 39% female, 61% male, 70% out-of-state, 0% international (23 countries represented). Asian 2%, African American 1%, Caucasian 69%, Hispanic 2%, Native American 0%.
Retention and Graduation: 76% freshmen return for sophomore year. 52% freshmen graduate within 4 years. 10% grads go on to further study within 1 year. 3% grads pursue arts and sciences degrees. 1% grads pursue law degrees. 6% grads pursue business degrees. **Faculty:** Student/faculty ratio 14:1. 96 full-time faculty, 56% hold PhDs, 7% are members of minority groups, 30% are women. 0% of classes are taught by teaching assistants.

ACADEMICS
Degrees: associate, bachelor's, certificate, master's, terminal associate, transfer associate. **Classes:** Most classes have 10–19 students. Most lab/discussion sessions have fewer than 10 students. **Majors with Highest Enrollment:** business/commerce; intermedia/multimedia; liberal arts and sciences/liberal studies. **Special Study Options:** Accelerated program, cross-registration, distance learning, double major, honors program, independent study, internships, liberal arts/career combination, study abroad, teacher certification program. **Honors Programs:** Honors Program invitation based on high school gpa and SAT/ACT scores. **Combined Degree Programs:** 4+1 MBA offered with Clarkson and SNHU. **Disability Services:** Special programs offered to physically disabled students include note-taking services, reader services, tape recorders, tutors. **Career Services:** career/job search classes, internships.

FACILITIES
Housing: Coed dorms, special housing for international students, women's dorms, Wellness, Performing Arts, International dorm. Suites style singles with common living room and kitchenette (for selected sophomores, juniors and seniors. 50% of campus accessible to physically disabled. **Computers:** Students can register for classes online. Administrative functions (other than registration) can be performed online.

CAMPUS LIFE
Environment: Town. **Activities:** Choral groups, dance, drama/theater, literary magazine, musical theater, radio station, student government, student newspaper, television station 40 registered organizations, 2 honor societies, 1 religious organizations. **On-Campus Highlights:** Center for Global Technology, The View, Hauke Family Center, Student Life Center, Main Street Suites, Miller Information Commons. **Environmental Initiatives:** Green Buildings (Master Plan) Waste Reduction (Recycling & Composting). New Environmental Policy Academic Program

ADMISSIONS
Freshman Academic Profile: 11% in top 10% of high school class, 35% in top 25% of high school class, 70% in top 50% of high school class. 85% from public high schools. SAT Math middle 50% range 490-590. SAT Critical Reading middle 50% range 500-610. ACT middle 50% range 20-25. Minimum web-based TOEFL 61. Minimum paper TOEFL 500. **Basis for Candidate Selection:** *Very important factors considered include:* application essay, academic GPA, rigor of secondary school record. *Important factors considered include:* Class rank, recommendation(s), standardized test scores, first generation, interview. *Other factors considered include:* alumni/ae relation, character/personal qualities, extracurricular activities, level of applicant's interest, talent/ability, volunteer work, work experience. **Freshman Admission Requirements:** High school diploma is required and GED is accepted. *Academic units required:* 4 English, 3 mathematics, 3 science, (2 science labs), 4 history, 4

academic electives. *Academic units recommended:* 4 English, 3 mathematics, 3 science, (2 science labs), 4 history, 4 academic electives. **Freshman Admission Statistics:** 3,077 applied, 85% admitted, 25% enrolled. **Transfer Admission Requirements:** High school transcript, college transcript(s), essay or personal statement, minimum college GPA of 2.0 required. Lowest grade transferable C. **General Admission Information:** Application Fee $40. Early decision application deadline 11/15. Regular application deadline 1/31. Regular notification 3/25. Nonfall registration accepted. Admission may be deferred for a maximum of 1 yr w no tr. Credit offered for CEEB Advanced Placement tests.

COSTS AND FINANCIAL AID

Annual tuition $28,350. Room and board $12,520. Required fees $50. Average book expense $1,000. **Required Forms and Deadlines:** FAFSA, institution's own financial aid form, state aid form, noncustodial PROFILE. **Notification of Awards:** Applicants will be notified of awards on a rolling basis beginning 3/1. **Types of Aid:** *Need-based scholarships/grants:* Federal Pell, SEOG, state scholarships/grants, private scholarships, the school's own gift aid. *Loans:* Subsidized Stafford, Unsubsidized Stafford, PLUS, Federal Perkins. **Student Employment:** Highest amount earned per year from on-campus jobs $2,211. **Financial Aid Statistics:** 74% freshmen, 74% undergrads receive need-based scholarship or grant aid. 2% freshmen, 2% undergrads receive non-need-based scholarship or grant aid. 96% freshmen, 95% undergrads receive need-based self-help aid. 90% freshmen, 83% undergrads receive any aid. **Criteria for awarding institutional aid:** *Non-need-based:* academics, leadership.

CHAPMAN UNIVERSITY

Best 378

One University Drive, Orange, CA 92866
Phone: 714-997-6711 • **Financial Aid Phone:** 714-997-6741
E-mail: admit@chapman.edu • **CEEB Code:** 4047
Fax: 714-997-6713 • **Website:** www.chapman.edu • **ACT Code:** 210

This private school, affiliated with the Disciples of Christ Church, was founded in 1861. It has a 75-acre campus.

RATINGS

Admissions Selectivity Rating: 93   **Fire Safety Rating:** 81   **Green Rating:** 68

STUDENTS AND FACULTY

Enrollment: 5,264. **Student Body:** 57% female, 43% male, 27% out-of-state, 3% international (72 countries represented). Asian 9%, African American 2%, Caucasian 60%, Hispanic 13%, Native American 0%.
Retention and Graduation: 91% freshmen return for sophomore year. 53% freshmen graduate within 4 years. 72% freshmen graduate within 6 years.
Faculty: Student/faculty ratio 14:1. 379 full-time faculty, 87% hold PhDs, 14% are members of minority groups, 42% are women. 0% of classes are taught by teaching assistants.

ACADEMICS

Degrees: bachelor's, master's, post-bachelor's certificate. **Classes:** Most classes have 20–29 students. Most lab/discussion sessions have 10–19 students. **Majors with Highest Enrollment:** business administration and management; cinematography and film/video production; public relations/image management. **Special Study Options:** distance learning, double major, English as a Second Language (ESL), honors program, independent study, internships, liberal arts/career combination, student-designed major, study abroad, teacher certification program. **Honors Programs:** University Honors Program **Combined Degree Programs:** BS/MBA. **Disability Services:** Special programs offered to physically disabled students include note-taking services, reader services, tape recorders, tutors. **Career Services:** alumni services, career/job search classes, career assessment, internships Career Services highlights include We are particularly proud of our Internship Program, which strengthens the link between classroom learning and the work world. Chapman's Program allows students to earn academic credit through faculty and site supervisor advisement. Internships offer students the opportunity to increase their understanding of career fields, gain hands-on work experience and learn job skills, build self-confidence, and gain a new perspective. This "real world" experience gives our graduates an edge when they join the work force.

FACILITIES

Housing: Coed dorms, special housing for disabled students, apartments for married students, apartments for single students, houses for married, single, and students with dependents. **Special Academic Facilities/Equipment:** Anderson Center for Economic Research, Leatherby Center for Entrepre-

neurship and Business Ethics, Schmid Center for International Business, Law and organizational Economics Center, Center for Cold War Studies, Henley Social Science Research Laboratory, Guggenhiem Art gallery, TV studio, film and television production and digital editing studios, Waltmer Theatre, Albert Schweitzer Collection **Computers:** 100% of classrooms, 100% of dorms, 100% of libraries, 100% of dining areas, 100% of common outdoor areas have wireless network access. Students can register for classes online. Administrative functions (other than registration) can be performed online.

CAMPUS LIFE

Environment: Metropolis. **Activities:** Choral groups, concert band, dance, drama/theater, jazz band, literary magazine, music ensembles, musical theater, opera, pep band, radio station, student government, student newspaper, student-run film society, symphony orchestra, yearbook, Campus Ministries, International Student Organization, Model UN 84 registered organizations, 8 honor societies, 8 religious organizations. 6 fraternities, 6 sororities. **Athletics (Intercollegiate):** *Men:* baseball, basketball, cross-country, football, golf, soccer, tennis, water polo. *Women:* basketball, crew/rowing, cross-country, soccer, softball, swimming, tennis, track/field (outdoor), volleyball, water polo. **On-Campus Highlights:** Marion Knott Film Studios, Leatherby Libraries, Liberty Plaza, Beckman Hall, All-Faiths Chapel. **Environmental Initiatives:** Adoption of LEED standards in new building projects. Expanded commitment to reduce use and increase recycling of paper. Investment in energy-saving devices and new requirement of energy-star rating on newly purchased electronic devices and appliances.

ADMISSIONS

Freshman Academic Profile: Average high school GPA 3.7. 49% in top 10% of high school class, 91% in top 25% of high school class, 99% in top 50% of high school class. 70% from public high schools. SAT Math middle 50% range 560-660. SAT Critical Reading middle 50% range 550-650. SAT Writing middle 50% range 570-660. ACT middle 50% range 24-29. Minimum paper TOEFL 550. **Basis for Candidate Selection:** *Very important factors considered include:* Class rank, application essay, academic GPA, rigor of secondary school record, standardized test scores, character/personal qualities. *Important factors considered include:* extracurricular activities, talent/ability, volunteer work. *Other factors considered include:* recommendation(s), alumni/ae relation, first generation, geographical residence, racial/ethnic status, state residency, work experience. **Freshman Admission Requirements:** High school diploma is required and GED is accepted. *Academic units required:* 2 English, 2 mathematics, 2 science, (1 science labs), 2 foreign language, 3 social studies. *Academic units recommended:* 2 English, 2 mathematics, 2 science, (1 science labs), 2 foreign language, 3 social studies. **Freshman Admission Statistics:** 9,616 applied, 45% admitted, 29% enrolled. **Transfer Admission Requirements:** college transcript(s), essay or personal statement, minimum college GPA of 2.5 required. Lowest grade transferable C-. **General Admission Information:** Application Fee $55. Regular application deadline 1/15. Notification on a rolling basis, beginning on or about 3/15. Nonfall registration accepted. Credit and/or placement offered for CEEB Advanced Placement tests.

COSTS AND FINANCIAL AID

Annual tuition $41,040. Room and board $12,204. Required fees $1,044. Average book expense $1,450. **Required Forms and Deadlines:** FAFSA, state aid form. **Notification of Awards:** Applicants will be notified of awards on a rolling basis beginning 3/15. **Types of Aid:** *Need-based scholarships/grants:* Federal Pell, SEOG, state scholarships/grants, private scholarships, the school's own gift aid, Academic Competitiveness Grants. *Loans:* Subsidized Stafford, Unsubsidized Stafford, PLUS, Federal Perkins. **Student Employment:** Federal Work-Study Program available. Institutional employment available. Off-campus job opportunities are excellent. **Financial Aid Statistics:** 81% freshmen, 86% undergrads receive need-based scholarship or grant aid. 69% freshmen, 62% undergrads receive non-need-based scholarship or grant aid. 87% freshmen, 91% undergrads receive need-based self-help aid. 83% freshmen, 81% undergrads receive any aid. 64% undergrads borrow to pay for school. Average cumulative indebtedness $26,446. **Criteria for awarding institutional aid:** *Non-need-based:* academics, alumni affiliation, art, music/drama, religious affiliation.

See page 1040.

CHARLESTON SOUTHERN UNIVERSITY

Enrollment Services, Charleston, SC 29423
Phone: 843-863-7050 • **Financial Aid Phone:** 843-863-7050
E-mail: enroll@csuniv.edu • **CEEB Code:** 5079
Fax: 843-863-7070 • **Website:** www.charlestonsouthern.edu • **ACT Code:** 3833

This private school, affiliated with the Southern Baptist Church, was founded in 1964. It has a 300-acre campus.

RATINGS
Admissions Selectivity Rating: 75   **Fire Safety Rating:** 60*   **Green Rating:** 60*

STUDENTS AND FACULTY
Enrollment: 2,473. **Student Body:** 61% female, 39% male, 18% out-of-state, 2% international (30 countries represented). Asian 2%, African American 27%, Caucasian 55%, Hispanic 1%, Native American 1%.
Retention and Graduation: 60% freshmen return for sophomore year. 22% freshmen graduate within 4 years. 36% freshmen graduate within 6 years. 14% grads go on to further study within 1 year. **Faculty:** Student/faculty ratio 18:1. 107 full-time faculty, 63% hold PhDs, 2% are members of minority groups, 45% are women. 0% of classes are taught by teaching assistants.

ACADEMICS
Degrees: bachelor's, master's. **Classes:** Most classes have 20–29 students. Most lab/discussion sessions have 20–29 students. **Majors with Highest Enrollment:** business/commerce; elementary education and teaching; psychology. **Special Study Options:** Accelerated program, cooperative education program, cross-registration, distance learning, double major, dual enrollment, honors program, internships, study abroad, teacher certification program, Other Special Programs: Evening Division. **Honors Programs:** SAT 1200 or higher or ACT 27 or higher and High School GPA of 3.50 or higher. **Combined Degree Programs:** BA/MD, Allied health tech with Medical U of S. Carolina. **Disability Services:** Special programs offered to physically disabled students include note-taking services, reader services, tape recorders, tutors. **Career Services:** career assessment, internships Career Services highlights include Applied Learning internships for credit.

FACILITIES
Housing: men's dorms, women's dorms. 80% of campus accessible to physically disabled. **Special Academic Facilities/Equipment:** Earthquake Education Center; computer labs w/ wireless internet; nursing clinical lab, specialized music rehearsal modules and advanced music keyboard technology. **Computers:** Students can register for classes online. Administrative functions (other than registration) can be performed online.

CAMPUS LIFE
Environment: Metropolis. **Activities:** Choral groups, concert band, dance, drama/theater, jazz band, literary magazine, marching band, music ensembles, musical theater, pep band, student government, student newspaper, yearbook 22 registered organizations, 3 honor societies, 4 religious organizations. **Athletics (Intercollegiate):** *Men:* baseball, basketball, cross-country, football, golf, tennis, track/field (outdoor), track/field (indoor). *Women:* basketball, cross-country, golf, soccer, softball, tennis, track/field (outdoor), track/field (indoor), volleyball.

ADMISSIONS
Freshman Academic Profile: Average high school GPA 3.3. 18% in top 10% of high school class, 47% in top 25% of high school class, 80% in top 50% of high school class. 81% from public high schools. SAT Math middle 50% range 480-570. SAT Critical Reading middle 50% range 490-570. ACT middle 50% range 20-24. Minimum paper TOEFL 550. **Basis for Candidate Selection:** *Very important factors considered include:* rigor of secondary school record, standardized test scores. *Important factors considered include:* Class rank. *Other factors considered include:* application essay, recommendation(s), character/personal qualities, extracurricular activities, interview, religious affiliation/commitment, talent/ability, work experience. **Freshman Admission Requirements:** High school diploma is required and GED is accepted. *Academic units required:* 4 English, 3 mathematics, 3 science, (2 science labs), 3 history, 3 academic electives. *Academic units recommended:* 4 English, 3 mathematics, 3 science, (2 science labs), 3 history, 3 academic electives. **Freshman Admission Statistics:** 2,283 applied, 72% admitted, 77% enrolled. **Transfer Admission Requirements:** college transcript(s), statement of good standing from prior institution(s). Minimum college GPA of 2.0 required. Lowest grade transferable C. **General Admission Information:** Application Fee $30. Nonfall registration accepted. Credit and/or placement offered for CEEB Advanced Placement tests.

COSTS AND FINANCIAL AID
Average book expense $1,000. **Required Forms and Deadlines:** FAFSA. **Notification of Awards:** Applicants will be notified of awards on a rolling basis

beginning 2/1. **Types of Aid:** *Need-based scholarships/grants:* Federal Pell, SEOG, state scholarships/grants, private scholarships, the school's own gift aid. *Loans:* Direct Subsidized Stafford, Direct Unsubsidized Stafford, Direct PLUS, Subsidized Stafford, PLUS, Federal Perkins, state loans. **Student Employment:** Highest amount earned per year from on-campus jobs $2,000. **Financial Aid Statistics:** 100% freshmen, 99% undergrads receive need-based scholarship or grant aid. 15% freshmen, 14% undergrads receive non-need-based scholarship or grant aid. 81% freshmen, 80% undergrads receive need-based self-help aid. 4% freshmen, 4% undergrads receive athletic scholarships. **Criteria for awarding institutional aid:** *Non-need-based:* academics, alumni affiliation, art, athletics, leadership, music/drama, religious affiliation, state/district residency.

CHARTER OAK STATE COLLEGE

55 Paul J. Manafort Drive, New Britain, CT 06053-2142
Phone: 860-832-3800 • **Financial Aid Phone:** 860-832-3872
E-mail: info@charteroak.edu
Fax: 860-832-3800

This public school was founded in 1973.

RATINGS
Admissions Selectivity Rating: 61   **Fire Safety Rating:** 60*   **Green Rating:** 60*

STUDENTS AND FACULTY
Enrollment: 1,477. **Student Body:** 67% female, 33% male, 25% out-of-state, 0% international. Asian 2%, African American 17%, Caucasian 62%, Hispanic 11%, Native American 0%.
Faculty: Student/faculty ratio 14:1.

ACADEMICS
Degrees: associate, bachelor's, transfer associate. **Special Study Options:** distance learning, external degree program, independent study, liberal arts/career combination, student-designed major.

FACILITIES
Housing: 100% of campus accessible to physically disabled. **Computers:** Students can register for classes online. Administrative functions (other than registration) can be performed online.

CAMPUS LIFE
Environment: Village.

ADMISSIONS
Freshman Admission Requirements: High school diploma is required and GED is accepted. **Transfer Admission Requirements:** college transcript(s), Lowest grade transferable D. **General Admission Information:** Application Fee $75. Nonfall registration not accepted. Admission may be deferred for a maximum of 12 months. Credit offered for CEEB Advanced Placement tests.

COSTS AND FINANCIAL AID
Required Forms and Deadlines: FAFSA, institution's own financial aid form, Contractual Consortium Agreement form and course approval form, if applicable. **Notification of Awards:** Applicants will be notified of awards on a rolling basis beginning 8/15. **Types of Aid:** *Need-based scholarships/grants:* Federal Pell, state scholarships/grants, private scholarships, the school's own gift aid. *Loans:* Subsidized Stafford, Unsubsidized Stafford, PLUS..

CHATHAM UNIVERSITY

Woodland Road, Pittsburgh, PA 15232
Phone: 412-365-1290 • **Financial Aid Phone:** 412-365-2797
E-mail: admissions@chatham.edu • **CEEB Code:** 2081
Fax: 412-365-1609 • **Website:** www.chatham.edu • **ACT Code:** 3538

This private school was founded in 1869. It has a 39388-acre campus.

RATINGS
Admissions Selectivity Rating: 82   **Fire Safety Rating:** 71   **Green Rating:** 98

STUDENTS AND FACULTY
Enrollment: 677. **Student Body:** 98% female, 2% male, 19% out-of-state, 7% international (34 countries represented). Asian 2%, African American 13%, Caucasian 67%, Hispanic 3%, Native American 0%.

Retention and Graduation: 51% freshmen graduate within 4 years. 59% freshmen graduate within 6 years. **Faculty:** Student/faculty ratio 10:1. 101 full-time faculty, 91% hold PhDs, 5% are members of minority groups, 62% are women. 0% of classes are taught by teaching assistants.

ACADEMICS

Degrees: bachelor's, master's, post-bachelor's certificate, post-master's certificate. **Classes:** Most classes have 10–19 students. Most lab/discussion sessions have 10–19 students. **Majors with Highest Enrollment:** biology/biological sciences; English language and literature; psychology. **Special Study Options:** Accelerated program, cooperative education program, cross-registration, distance learning, double major, dual enrollment, English as a Second Language (ESL), exchange student program (domestic), honors program, independent study, internships, liberal arts/career combination, student-designed major, study abroad, teacher certification program, Five-year bachelors/masters programs; five-year bachelors/masters programs also available with Carnegie Mellon (e.g. engineering, public policy) and other institutions. **Honors Programs:** The Chatham Scholars Program offers students a challenging, integrated curriculum with special opportunities for enrichment, mentoring, and networking. **Combined Degree Programs:** BA/MA, 3-2 b/m in 9 fields and 4-2 b/doctorate in Phys Ther. **Disability Services:** Special programs offered to physically disabled students include note-taking services, reader services, tape recorders, tutors. **Career Services:** Alumni network, alumni services, career/job search classes, career assessment, internships.

FACILITIES

Housing: women's dorms, apartments for married students, apartments for single students, theme housing. 75% of campus accessible to physically disabled. **Special Academic Facilities/Equipment:** Athletic and Fitness Center; Art and Design Center; broadcast studio; art gallery, classroom space, and coffee shop; campus arboretum and greenhouse; proscenium theater. **Computers:** 100% of classrooms, 20% of dorms, 100% of libraries, 100% of dining areas, 100% of student union, 75% of common outdoor areas have wireless network access. Students can register for classes online. Administrative functions (other than registration) can be performed online. Undergraduates are required to own a computer.

CAMPUS LIFE

Environment: Metropolis. **Activities:** Choral groups, dance, drama/theater, literary magazine, music ensembles, musical theater, student government, student newspaper, yearbook 25 registered organizations, 10 honor societies, 6 religious organizations. **Athletics (Intercollegiate):** *Women:* basketball, cross-country, ice hockey, soccer, softball, swimming, tennis, volleyball, water polo. **On-Campus Highlights:** New coffee shop and art gallery (2005), Athletic and Fitness Center (2004), Art and Design Center (2004), Science Complex (2001), Campus Arboretum, Many of the campus residence halls are renovated historic mansions. The campus also features an outdoor meditation labyrinth, the largest in Pittsburgh. The Shadyside Campus on Woodland Road is a registered arboretum, with over 120 distinct tree species. **Environmental Initiatives:** The creation of the School of Sustainability and the Environment, and the hiring of the founding Dean. The new School will provide innovative, interdisciplinary education and research opportunities for undergraduate, graduate and professional students to better prepare them to identify and solve challenges related to the environment and sustainability. The school will be located at Eden Hall Campus, on a 300-acre farm with forest. The campus is in the master planning stage, and is intended as a net zero energy campus. Installation of cutting-edge micro-channel solar hot water systems on our two largest residence halls, in use year round. An interactive demonstration and teaching unit has been installed on our research greenhouse. The systems will provide approximately 75% of total hot water use for the buildings over a year, and during the sunier months, we expect it will be able to provide 100% of hot water needs with no combustion required. Our environmentally-friendly transportation initiatives continue. This year Chatham BikeWorks, a bike repair shop, is open and beginning program delivery in the Spring. Bikeworks will teach bike repair and maintenance, as well as provide bike rides, bike commuting info and a possible bikeshare program by summer 2011. Our regular transportation programs continue, including Zipcars on campus, public transit pass full subsidy, biofuel shuttle fleet for inter-campus travel.

ADMISSIONS

Freshman Academic Profile: Average high school GPA 3.6. 24% in top 10% of high school class, 53% in top 25% of high school class, 83% in top 50% of high school class. SAT Math middle 50% range 460-580. SAT Critical Reading middle 50% range 510-590. SAT Writing middle 50% range 480-570. ACT middle 50% range 23-28. Minimum web-based TOEFL 79. Minimum paper TOEFL 550. **Basis for Candidate Selection:** *Very important factors considered include:* rigor of secondary school record. *Important factors considered include:* application essay, academic GPA. *Other factors considered include:* Class rank, recommendation(s), standardized test scores, alumni/ae relation, character/personal qualities, extracurricular activities, interview, level of applicant's interest, talent/ability, volunteer work, work experience. **Freshman Admission Requirements:** High school diploma is required and GED is ac-

cepted. *Academic units required:* 4 English, 2 mathematics, 2 science, 3 Social Science. *Academic units recommended:* 4 English, 2 mathematics, 2 science, 3 Social Science **Freshman Admission Statistics:** 727 applied, 60% admitted, 27% enrolled. **Transfer Admission Requirements:** college transcript(s), essay or personal statement, minimum college GPA of 2.0 required. Lowest grade transferable C-. **General Admission Information:** Application Fee $35. Regular application deadline 8/1. Notification on a rolling basis, beginning on or about 10/15. Nonfall registration accepted. Admission may be deferred for a maximum of 1 year. Credit offered for CEEB Advanced Placement tests.

COSTS AND FINANCIAL AID

Annual tuition $31,294. Room and board $9,692. Required fees $1,160. Average book expense $860. **Required Forms and Deadlines:** FAFSA. **Notification of Awards:** Applicants will be notified of awards on a rolling basis beginning 2/15. **Types of Aid:** *Need-based scholarships/grants:* Federal Pell, SEOG, state scholarships/grants, private scholarships, the school's own gift aid, United Negro College Fund. *Loans:* Subsidized Stafford, Unsubsidized Stafford, PLUS, Federal Perkins. **Student Employment:** Federal Work-Study Program available. Institutional employment available. Highest amount earned per year from on-campus jobs $2,200. Off-campus job opportunities are good. **Financial Aid Statistics:** 96% freshmen, 80% undergrads receive need-based scholarship or grant aid. 100% freshmen, 90% undergrads receive non-need-based scholarship or grant aid. 94% freshmen, 87% undergrads receive need-based self-help aid. 76% freshmen, 62% undergrads receive any aid. 85% undergrads borrow to pay for school. Average cumulative indebtedness $39,176. **Criteria for awarding institutional aid:** *Non-need-based:* academics, alumni affiliation, leadership, minority status.

CHESTNUT HILL COLLEGE

9601 Germantown Avenue, Philadelphia, PA 19118-2693
Phone: 215-248-7001 • **Financial Aid Phone:** 215-248-7182
E-mail: chcapply@chc.edu • **CEEB Code:** 2082
Fax: 215-248-7082 • **Website:** www.chc.edu • **ACT Code:** 3540

This private school, affiliated with the Roman Catholic Church, was founded in 1924. It has a 75-acre campus.

RATINGS

Admissions Selectivity Rating: 66   **Fire Safety Rating:** 82   **Green Rating:** 63

STUDENTS AND FACULTY

Enrollment: 1,556. **Student Body:** 70% female, 30% male, 23% out-of-state, 2% international (43 countries represented). Asian 1%, African American 36%, Caucasian 44%, Hispanic 7%, Native American 0%.
Retention and Graduation: 74% freshmen return for sophomore year. 37% freshmen graduate within 4 years. 22% grads go on to further study within 1 year. 7% grads pursue arts and sciences degrees. 5% grads pursue business degrees. **Faculty:** Student/faculty ratio 9:1. 87 full-time faculty, 83% hold PhDs, 7% are members of minority groups, 71% are women. 0% of classes are taught by teaching assistants.

ACADEMICS

Degrees: associate, bachelor's, certificate, master's, post-bachelor's certificate, post-master's certificate, transfer associate. **Classes:** Most classes have 10–19 students. Most lab/discussion sessions have 10–19 students. **Majors with Highest Enrollment:** business administration and management; elementary education and teaching; human services. **Special Study Options:** cooperative education program, cross-registration, double major, dual enrollment, English as a Second Language (ESL), exchange student program (domestic), honors program, independent study, internships, student-designed major, study abroad, teacher certification program, Upperclass undergraduates may take graduate classes. **Honors Programs:** Interdisciplinary Honors Program for outstanding incoming first year students offers team-taught interdisciplinary seminars emphaisizing discussion and writing which satisfy general education requirements. Departmental Honors challenges students in the junior and senior year to complete an independent research project in their major field. **Combined Degree Programs:** BA/MA, BS/MEd, MA/PsyD, BS/DPM, BS/BS med tech, BS/MS Human Services. **Disability Services:** Special programs offered to physically disabled students include reader services, tutors. **Career Services:** Alumni network, career/job search classes, career assessment, internships, Career Services highlights include Chestnut Hill College encourages all students to participate in some form of experiential learning. Internships are available in a large number of majors and work areas.

FACILITIES

Housing: Coed dormsOn-campus housing includes singles, doubles, suites, and apartment-like units. A new main campus residence hall opened in Fall 2006 and a renovated building opened as a residence hall on the SugarLoaf

Hill campus in 2008. 80% of campus accessible to physically disabled. **Special Academic Facilities/Equipment:** Rare book collection, Irish literature collection, observatory, planetarium. **Computers:** 40% of classrooms, 100% of dorms, 100% of libraries, have wireless network access. Students can register for classes online. Undergraduates are required to own a computer.

CAMPUS LIFE

Environment: Metropolis. **Activities:** Choral groups, drama/theater, jazz band, literary magazine, music ensembles, musical theater, opera, student government, student newspaper, symphony orchestra, television station, yearbook, Campus Ministries, International Student Organization 19 registered organizations, 14 honor societies, 1 religious organizations. **Athletics (Intercollegiate):** *Men:* baseball, basketball, cross-country, golf, lacrosse, soccer, tennis. *Women:* basketball, cross-country, golf, lacrosse, soccer, softball, tennis, volleyball. **On-Campus Highlights:** Martino Hall (smart classrooms, gym), Griffin's Den, Fitzsimmons Hall (new residence hall), Dining Hall, Rotunda of Saint Joseph Hall, SugarLoaf Hill, a 32-acre recent addition to campus, will soon provide additional space for many campus activities. **Environmental Initiatives:** Recycling program Go Green Committee

ADMISSIONS

Freshman Academic Profile: Average high school GPA 3.2. 13% in top 10% of high school class, 35% in top 25% of high school class, 65% in top 50% of high school class. 60% from public high schools. SAT Math middle 50% range 430-540. SAT Critical Reading middle 50% range 440-550. SAT Writing middle 50% range 430-550. ACT middle 50% range 19-23. Minimum web-based TOEFL 79. Minimum paper TOEFL 550. **Basis for Candidate Selection:** *Very important factors considered include:* application essay, rigor of secondary school record. *Important factors considered include:* academic GPA, recommendation(s), standardized test scores, character/personal qualities, extracurricular activities, interview. *Other factors considered include:* Class rank, alumni/ae relation, level of applicant's interest, talent/ability, volunteer work, work experience. **Freshman Admission Requirements:** High school diploma is required and GED is accepted. **Freshman Admission Statistics:** 1,599 applied, 90% admitted, 15% enrolled. **Transfer Admission Requirements:** college transcript(s), essay or personal statement, minimum college GPA of 2.0 required. Lowest grade transferable C. **General Admission Information:** Application Fee $35. Early decision application deadline 12/10. Notification on a rolling basis, beginning on or about 9/1. Nonfall registration accepted. Admission may be deferred for a maximum of 1 year. Credit and/or placement offered for CEEB Advanced Placement tests.

COSTS AND FINANCIAL AID

Annual tuition $31,000. Room and board $9,008. Required fees $170. Average book expense $1,100. **Required Forms and Deadlines:** FAFSA. **Notification of Awards:** Applicants will be notified of awards on a rolling basis beginning 1/31. **Types of Aid:** *Need-based scholarships/grants:* Federal Pell, SEOG, state scholarships/grants, private scholarships, the school's own gift aid. *Loans:* Subsidized Stafford, Unsubsidized Stafford, PLUS, Federal Perkins. **Student Employment:** Federal Work-Study Program available. Highest amount earned per year from on-campus jobs $1,500. Off-campus job opportunities are good. **Financial Aid Statistics:** 96% freshmen, 94% undergrads receive need-based scholarship or grant aid. % freshmen, 3% undergrads receive non-need-based scholarship or grant aid. 89% freshmen, 79% undergrads receive need-based self-help aid. 15% freshmen, 14% undergrads receive athletic scholarships. 97% freshmen, 96% undergrads receive any aid. 80% undergrads borrow to pay for school. Average cumulative indebtedness. **Criteria for awarding institutional aid:** *Non-need-based:* academics, alumni affiliation, athletics, leadership, religious affiliation.

See page 1042.

CHEYNEY UNIVERSITY OF PENNSYLVANIA

1837 University Circle, Cheyney, PA 19319
Phone: 610-399-2275 • **Financial Aid Phone:** 610-399-2302
E-mail: abrown@cheyney.edu • **CEEB Code:** 2648
Fax: 610-399-2099 • **Website:** www.cheyney.edu

This public school was founded in 1837. It has a 275-acre campus.

RATINGS
Admissions Selectivity Rating: 71   **Fire Safety Rating:** 93   **Green Rating:** 83

STUDENTS AND FACULTY
Enrollment: 1,339. **Student Body:** 53% female, 47% male, 22% out-of-state, 0% international (4 countries represented). Asian 0%, African American 92%, Caucasian 1%, Hispanic 1%, Native American 0%.

Retention and Graduation: 60% freshmen return for sophomore year. **Faculty:** Student/faculty ratio 15:1. 75 full-time faculty, % hold PhDs, 79% are members of minority groups, 48% are women. 0% of classes are taught by teaching assistants.

ACADEMICS

Degrees: associate, bachelor's, master's, post-bachelor's certificate. **Classes: Majors with Highest Enrollment:** business administration and management; communication studies/speech communication and rhetoric; social sciences. **Special Study Options:** cooperative education program, cross-registration, distance learning, double major, honors program, independent study, internships, study abroad, teacher certification program. **Honors Programs:** Keystone Honors Program. **Disability Services:** Special programs offered to physically disabled students include note-taking services, tape recorders, tutors. **Career Services:** alumni services, career/job search classes, internships.

FACILITIES

Housing: Coed dorms, men's dorms, women's dorms, Honors dorm. 60% of campus accessible to physically disabled. **Special Academic Facilities/Equipment:** Afro-American history/culture collection, planetarium, weather station, satellite communication network. **Computers:** 60% of classrooms, 100% of libraries, 100% of student union, 20% of common outdoor areas have wireless network access. Students can register for classes online. Administrative functions (other than registration) can be performed online.

CAMPUS LIFE

Environment: Village. **Activities:** Choral groups, drama/theater, jazz band, marching band, music ensembles, radio station, student government, student newspaper, student-run film society, television station, yearbook 30 registered organizations, 12 honor societies, 1 religious organizations. 5 fraternities, 4 sororities. **Athletics (Intercollegiate):** *Men:* basketball, cross-country, football, tennis, track/field (outdoor), wrestling. *Women:* basketball, bowling, cross-country, tennis, track/field (outdoor), volleyball. **On-Campus Highlights:** Athletics, Culinary Arts, Communication Arts, Dorms, Bookstore. **Environmental Initiatives:** Re-cycling Oils Conversion-Biofuels Energy Consonvation-Electric Power.

ADMISSIONS

Freshman Academic Profile: Average high school GPA 2.4. 6% in top 10% of high school class, 15% in top 25% of high school class, 46% in top 50% of high school class. % from public high schools. SAT Math middle 50% range 320-410. SAT Critical Reading middle 50% range 330-420. SAT Writing middle 50% range 320-405. ACT middle 50% range 14-21. Minimum paper TOEFL 500. **Basis for Candidate Selection:** *Very important factors considered include:* recommendation(s), rigor of secondary school record. *Important factors considered include:* Class rank, application essay, standardized test scores, extracurricular activities, interview, state residency. *Other factors considered include:* racial/ethnic status, talent/ability. **Freshman Admission Requirements:** High school diploma is required and GED is accepted. *Academic units required:* 4 English, 3 mathematics, 2 science, 2 foreign language, 2 history. *Academic units recommended:* 4 English, 3 mathematics, 2 science, 2 foreign language, 2 history. **Freshman Admission Statistics:** 3,298 applied, 50% admitted, 37% enrolled. **Transfer Admission Requirements:** college transcript(s), interview, statement of good standing from prior institution(s). Minimum college GPA of 2.0 required. Lowest grade transferable C. **General Admission Information:** Application Fee $20. Regular application deadline 3/31. Nonfall registration accepted. Admission may be deferred for a maximum of 1 year. Placement offered for CEEB Advanced Placement tests.

COSTS AND FINANCIAL AID

Required fees. Average book expense. **Required Forms and Deadlines:** FAFSA. **Notification of Awards:** Applicants will be notified of awards on a rolling basis beginning 3/15. **Types of Aid:** *Need-based scholarships/grants:* Federal Pell, SEOG, state scholarships/grants, private scholarships, the school's own gift aid. *Loans:* Subsidized Stafford, Unsubsidized Stafford, PLUS, Federal Perkins. **Student Employment:** Federal Work-Study Program available. Institutional employment available. Off-campus job opportunities are good. **Financial Aid Statistics:** 82% freshmen, 94% undergrads receive need-based scholarship or grant aid. 32% freshmen, 39% undergrads receive non-need-based scholarship or grant aid. 84% freshmen, 99% undergrads receive need-based self-help aid. 96% undergrads borrow to pay for school. Average cumulative indebtedness $27,000. **Criteria for awarding institutional aid:** *Non-need-based:* academics, alumni affiliation, athletics, minority status.

CHICAGO STATE UNIVERSITY

9501 South Street King Drive, Chicago, IL 60628
Phone: 773-995-2513
E-mail: ug-Admissions@csu.edu
Fax: 773-995-3820 • **Website:** www.csu.edu • **ACT Code:** 1694

This public school was founded in 1867. It has a 161-acre campus.

RATINGS
Admissions Selectivity Rating: 70   **Fire Safety Rating:** 60*   **Green Rating:** 60*

STUDENTS AND FACULTY
Enrollment: 4,818. **Student Body:** 73% female, 27% male, 2% out-of-state, 0% international. Asian 1%, African American 87%, Caucasian 3%, Hispanic 6%, Native American 0%.
Faculty: Student/faculty ratio 13:1. 322 full-time faculty, 61% are members of minority groups, 51% are women.

ACADEMICS
Degrees: bachelor's, master's, post-bachelor's certificate. **Classes:** Most classes have 20–29 students. **Majors with Highest Enrollment:** elementary education and teaching; liberal arts and sciences/liberal studies; nursing/registered nurse (rn, asn, bsn, msn). **Special Study Options:** cooperative education program, distance learning, double major, English as a Second Language (ESL), honors program, independent study, internships, student-designed major, study abroad, teacher certification program, Programs for mature adults (University Without Walls, Individual Curriculum, and Board of Governors degree program). **Disability Services:** Special programs offered to physically disabled students include note-taking services, reader services, tape recorders, tutors. **Career Services:** alumni services, career/job search classes, career assessment, internships.

FACILITIES
Housing: Coed dorms. 51% of campus accessible to physically disabled. **Special Academic Facilities/Equipment:** Art Gallery; Electron microscopes; Greenhouse **Computers:** Students can register for classes online.

CAMPUS LIFE
Environment: Activities: Choral groups, concert band, dance, drama/theater, jazz band, literary magazine, music ensembles, radio station, student government, student newspaper, television station 47 registered organizations, 30 honor societies, 4 religious organizations. 4 fraternities, 4 sororities. **Athletics (Intercollegiate):** *Men:* baseball, basketball, cross-country, golf, tennis, track/field (outdoor), track/field (indoor). *Women:* basketball, cross-country, golf, tennis, track/field (outdoor), track/field (indoor), volleyball.

ADMISSIONS
Freshman Academic Profile: Average high school GPA 2.7. 13% in top 10% of high school class, 35% in top 25% of high school class, 64% in top 50% of high school class. 80% from public high schools. ACT middle 50% range 16-19. Minimum paper TOEFL 500. **Basis for Candidate Selection:** *Very important factors considered include:* rigor of secondary school record, standardized test scores. **Freshman Admission Requirements:** High school diploma is required and GED is accepted. *Academic units required:* 4 English, 3 mathematics, 3 science, 3 social studies, 2 academic electives. *Academic units recommended:* 4 English, 3 mathematics, 3 science, 3 social studies, 2 academic electives. **Freshman Admission Statistics:** 3,949 applied, 56% admitted, 25% enrolled. **Transfer Admission Requirements:** college transcript(s), minimum college GPA of 2.0 required. Lowest grade transferable D. **General Admission Information:** Application Fee $25. Regular application deadline 7/15. Nonfall registration accepted. Admission may be deferred for a maximum of 1 Semester. Credit and/or placement offered for CEEB Advanced Placement tests.

COSTS AND FINANCIAL AID
Annual in-state tuition $3,762. Annual out-of-state tuition $8,448. Room and board $5,700. Required fees $1,060. Average book expense $1,400. **Required Forms and Deadlines:** FAFSA, institution's own financial aid form. **Notification of Awards:** Applicants will be notified of awards on a rolling basis beginning 3/1. **Types of Aid:** *Need-based scholarships/grants:* Federal Pell, SEOG, state scholarships/grants, private scholarships, the school's own gift aid. *Loans:* Subsidized Stafford, Unsubsidized Stafford, PLUS, Federal Perkins. **Student Employment:** Federal Work-Study Program available. Institutional employment available. Highest amount earned per year from on-campus jobs $2,000. Off-campus job opportunities are good. **Financial Aid Statistics:** 82% freshmen, 93% undergrads receive need-based scholarship or grant aid. 2% undergrads receive non-need-based scholarship or grant aid. 30% freshmen, 52% undergrads receive need-based self-help aid. **Criteria for awarding institutional aid:** *Non-need-based:* academics, athletics, state/district residency.

CHOWAN UNIVERSITY

One University Place, Murfreesboro, NC 27855
Phone: 252-398-1236 • **Financial Aid Phone:** 252-398-6513
E-mail: admissions@chowan.edu
Fax: 252-398-1190 • **Website:** www.chowan.edu

This is a private school.

RATINGS
Admissions Selectivity Rating: 71   **Fire Safety Rating:** 64   **Green Rating:** 60*

STUDENTS AND FACULTY
Enrollment: 886. **Student Body:** 46% female, 54% male, 48% out-of-state.
Retention and Graduation: 54% freshmen return for sophomore year. 18% freshmen graduate within 4 years. 26% freshmen graduate within 6 years. 5% grads go on to further study within 1 year. 2% grads pursue arts and sciences degrees. 1% grads pursue law degrees. 1% grads pursue business degrees. 1% grads pursue medical degrees. **Faculty:** Student/faculty ratio 16:1. 47 full-time faculty, 64% hold PhDs, 11% are members of minority groups, 43% are women. 0% of classes are taught by teaching assistants.

ACADEMICS
Degrees: associate, bachelor's, terminal associate. **Classes:** Most classes have fewer than 10 students. **Majors with Highest Enrollment:** business/commerce; graphic communications; health services/allied health/health sciences. **Special Study Options:** distance learning, double major, dual enrollment, honors program, independent study, internships, liberal arts/career combination, study abroad, teacher certification program. **Honors Programs:** Honors College. **Disability Services:** Special programs offered to physically disabled students include note-taking services, reader services, tape recorders, tutors. **Career Services:** internships Career Services highlights include Business Administration internships.

FACILITIES
Housing: special housing for disabled students, men's dorms, women's dorms. 80% of campus accessible to physically disabled. **Special Academic Facilities/Equipment:** Antiquities Room in Whitaker Library Ward Parlor in McDowell Columns Building Green Hall Art Gallery Daniel Hall Recital Hall **Computers:** Students can register for classes online. Administrative functions (other than registration) can be performed online.

CAMPUS LIFE
Environment: Activities: Choral groups, concert band, drama/theater, jazz band, literary magazine, music ensembles, pep band, student government, yearbook 52 registered organizations, 5 honor societies, 2 religious organizations. 2 fraternities, 2 sororities. **Athletics (Intercollegiate):** *Men:* baseball, basketball, cheerleading, football, golf, soccer, tennis. *Women:* basketball, cheerleading, cross-country, golf, soccer, softball, tennis, volleyball. **On-Campus Highlights:** McDowell Columns Building (historic landmark), Jesse Helms Athletic Center, Jenkins Center for Health, Whitaker Library, McSweeney Computer Center.

ADMISSIONS
Freshman Academic Profile: Average high school GPA 2.6. 4% in top 10% of high school class, 35% in top 50% of high school class. 95% from public high schools. SAT Math middle 50% range 380-490. SAT Critical Reading middle 50% range 380-480. ACT middle 50% range 15-19. Minimum paper TOEFL 450. **Basis for Candidate Selection:** *Very important factors considered include:* academic GPA, rigor of secondary school record, standardized test scores. *Other factors considered include:* Class rank, application essay, recommendation(s), alumni/ae relation, character/personal qualities, extracurricular activities, interview, level of applicant's interest, talent/ability, volunteer work, work experience. **Freshman Admission Requirements:** High school diploma is required and GED is accepted. **Freshman Admission Statistics:** 2,385 applied, 61% admitted, 24% enrolled. **Transfer Admission Requirements:** High school transcript, college transcript(s), statement of good standing from prior institution(s). Minimum college GPA of 2.0 required. Lowest grade transferable C. **General Admission Information:** Application Fee $20. Notification on a rolling basis, beginning on or about 3/1. Nonfall registration accepted. Admission may be deferred for a maximum of 1 year. Credit and/or placement offered for CEEB Advanced Placement tests.

COSTS AND FINANCIAL AID
Annual tuition $15,800. Room and board $6,800. Required fees $240. Average book expense $885. **Required Forms and Deadlines:** FAFSA. **Notification of Awards:** Applicants will be notified of awards on a rolling basis beginning 3/1. **Types of Aid:** *Need-based scholarships/grants:* SEOG, state scholarships/grants, private scholarships, the school's own gift aid. *Loans:* Unsubsidized Stafford, PLUS, college/university loans from institutional funds, Alternative Loans. **Student Employment:** Federal Work-Study Program available. Institutional

employment available. Highest amount earned per year from on-campus jobs $700. Off-campus job opportunities are fair. **Financial Aid Statistics:** 95% freshmen, 97% undergrads receive need-based scholarship or grant aid. 7% freshmen, 8% undergrads receive non-need-based scholarship or grant aid. 90% freshmen, 88% undergrads receive need-based self-help aid. 86% freshmen, 86% undergrads receive any aid. 80% undergrads borrow to pay for school. Average cumulative indebtedness $17,275. **Criteria for awarding institutional aid:** *Non-need-based:* academics, leadership, music/drama, religious affiliation, state/district residency.

CHRISTENDOM COLLEGE

134 Christendom Drive, Front Royal, VA 22630
Phone: 540-636-2900 • **Financial Aid Phone:** 800-877-5456
E-mail: admissions@christendom.edu • **CEEB Code:** 5691
Fax: 540-636-1655 • **Website:** www.christendom.edu • **ACT Code:** 4339

This private school, affiliated with the Roman Catholic Church, was founded in 1977. It has a 100-acre campus.

RATINGS
Admissions Selectivity Rating: 74   **Fire Safety Rating:** 61   **Green Rating:** 60*

STUDENTS AND FACULTY
Enrollment: 421. **Student Body:** 54% female, 46% male, 78% out-of-state, 4% international (3 countries represented). Asian 2%, African American 0%, Caucasian 92%, Hispanic 2%, Native American 0%.
Retention and Graduation: 91% freshmen return for sophomore year. 74% freshmen graduate within 4 years. 77% freshmen graduate within 6 years. 25% grads go on to further study within 1 year. 15% grads pursue arts and sciences degrees. 5% grads pursue law degrees. 5% grads pursue business degrees. **Faculty:** Student/faculty ratio 12:1. 23 full-time faculty, 78% hold PhDs, 0% are members of minority groups, 9% are women. 0% of classes are taught by teaching assistants.

ACADEMICS
Degrees: associate, bachelor's, master's. **Classes:** Most classes have 10–19 students. **Majors with Highest Enrollment:** history; philosophy; political science and government. **Special Study Options:** double major, honors program, independent study, internships, study abroad, Semester in Rome.

FACILITIES
Housing: men's dorms, women's dorms.

CAMPUS LIFE
Environment: Rural. **Activities:** Choral groups, dance, drama/theater, literary magazine, musical theater, student government, student newspaper, student-run film society, yearbook 5 registered organizations, 4 religious organizations. **Athletics (Intercollegiate): Men:** baseball, basketball, soccer. **Women:** basketball, soccer, softball, volleyball. **On-Campus Highlights:** St. John the Evangelist Library, Chapel of Christ the King, Regina Coeli Building, John Paul II Student Center

ADMISSIONS
Freshman Academic Profile: Average high school GPA 3.5. 40% in top 10% of high school class, 63% in top 25% of high school class, 100% in top 50% of high school class. 20% from public high schools. SAT Math middle 50% range 520-630. SAT Critical Reading middle 50% range 570-700. SAT Writing middle 50% range 560-690. ACT middle 50% range 23-28. Minimum paper TOEFL 550. **Basis for Candidate Selection:** *Very important factors considered include:* application essay, standardized test scores, character/personal qualities, level of applicant's interest, religious affiliation/commitment. *Important factors considered include:* recommendation(s), rigor of secondary school record, interview. *Other factors considered include:* Class rank, academic GPA, alumni/ae relation, extracurricular activities, first generation, talent/ability, volunteer work, work experience. **Freshman Admission Requirements:** High school diploma or equivalent is not required. **Freshman Admission Statistics:** 271 applied, 88% admitted, 52% enrolled. **Transfer Admission Requirements:** college transcript(s), essay or personal statement, minimum college GPA of 2.8 required. Lowest grade transferable C. **General Admission Information:** Application Fee $25. Regular application deadline 3/1. Regular notification 4/1. Nonfall registration not accepted. Credit offered for CEEB Advanced Placement tests.

COSTS AND FINANCIAL AID
Annual tuition $16,290. Room and board $6,066. Required fees $540. Average book expense $450. **Required Forms and Deadlines:** institution's own financial aid form. **Notification of Awards:** Applicants will be notified of awards on a rolling basis beginning 2/1. **Types of Aid:** *Need-based scholarships/*

grants: private scholarships, the school's own gift aid. *Loans:* college/university loans from institutional funds. **Student Employment:** Institutional employment available. Highest amount earned per year from on-campus jobs $1,850. Off-campus job opportunities are fair. **Financial Aid Statistics:** 95% freshmen, 97% undergrads receive need-based scholarship or grant aid. 30% freshmen, 25% undergrads receive non-need-based scholarship or grant aid. 100% freshmen, 100% undergrads receive need-based self-help aid. 80% freshmen, 65% undergrads receive any aid. 60% undergrads borrow to pay for school. Average cumulative indebtedness $22,000. **Criteria for awarding institutional aid:** *Non-need-based:* academics.

CHRISTIAN BROTHERS UNIVERSITY

Admissions, Box T-6, Memphis, TN 38104-5519
Phone: 901-321-3205 • **Financial Aid Phone:** 901-321-3306
E-mail: admissions@cbu.edu • **CEEB Code:** 1121
Fax: 901-321-3202 • **Website:** www.cbu.edu • **ACT Code:** 3952

This private school, affiliated with the Roman Catholic Church, was founded in 1871. It has a 75-acre campus.

RATINGS
Admissions Selectivity Rating: 88   **Fire Safety Rating:** 65   **Green Rating:** 67

STUDENTS AND FACULTY
Enrollment: 1,327. **Student Body:** 55% female, 45% male, 18% out-of-state, 3% international (21 countries represented). Asian 5%, African American 36%, Caucasian 48%, Hispanic 5%, Native American 0%.
Retention and Graduation: 42% freshmen graduate within 4 years. 57% freshmen graduate within 6 years. **Faculty:** Student/faculty ratio 13:1. 106 full-time faculty, 87% hold PhDs, 14% are members of minority groups, 33% are women. 0% of classes are taught by teaching assistants.

ACADEMICS
Degrees: bachelor's, master's, post-bachelor's certificate. **Classes:** Most classes have 10–19 students. **Majors with Highest Enrollment:** biology/biological sciences; business/commerce; psychology. **Special Study Options:** Accelerated program, distance learning, double major, dual enrollment, honors program, independent study, internships, liberal arts/career combination, study abroad, teacher certification program. **Honors Programs:** The Honors Program at Christian Brothers University is designed to serve the capacities and needs of students with proven academic abilities who seek a more intensive and challenging educational experience. Students accepted into the Honors Program will be allowed each semester to take at least one special-topics course offered only to a limited number of Honors students by an instructor carefully chosen for his or her teaching expertise. These Honors courses will explore important topics in depth, often through a multi-disciplinary approach, and while the pace and the workload will demand self-motivated students, the small size of each Honors class will insure ample group discussion and individual interaction with the instructor. Besides taking honors classes, members of the Honors Program will participate in various extra-curricular activities, including outings to cultural events and regional honors conferences. **Disability Services:** Special programs offered to physically disabled students include note-taking services, reader services, tape recorders, tutors. **Career Services:** alumni services, career assessment, internships Career Services highlights include Internships.

FACILITIES
Housing: men's dorms, women's dorms, apartments for single students, theme housing, Juniors and seniors may live in on-campus apartments. All freshmen and sophomores whose permanent address is beyond a 30 mile radius are required to live on campus. Some houses are available. A private quiet study facility is available. **Special Academic Facilities/Equipment:** Art exhibits, audiovisual lab, MAC graphics lab, engineering graphics lab, Ghandi institute for nonviolence, Facing History. **Computers:** 90% of classrooms, 100% of libraries, 100% of dining areas, 25% of common outdoor areas have wireless network access. Students can register for classes online. Administrative functions (other than registration) can be performed online.

CAMPUS LIFE
Environment: Metropolis. **Activities:** Choral groups, drama/theater, literary magazine, radio station, student government, yearbook, Campus Ministries 37 registered organizations, 10 honor societies, 3 religious organizations. 5 fraternities, 6 sororities. **Athletics (Intercollegiate): Men:** baseball, basketball, cross-country, golf, soccer, tennis. **Women:** basketball, cross-country, golf, soccer, softball, tennis, volleyball. **On-Campus Highlights:** Thomas Center (cafeteria, coffee shop/grill gather, Canale Arena Gymnasium, Computer Center, Canale Outdoor Pool, Art Gallery in library. **Environmental Initiatives:** Building a new "green" dorm that has 90+ beds Joining AASHE

ADMISSIONS

Freshman Academic Profile: Average high school GPA 3.6. 29% in top 10% of high school class, 60% in top 25% of high school class, 89% in top 50% of high school class. 70% from public high schools. ACT middle 50% range 21-26. Minimum paper TOEFL 500. **Basis for Candidate Selection:** *Very important factors considered include:* academic GPA, rigor of secondary school record, standardized test scores. *Important factors considered include:* Class rank, application essay, recommendation(s), alumni/ae relation, extracurricular activities, interview, talent/ability, volunteer work, work experience. **Freshman Admission Requirements:** High school diploma is required and GED is accepted. **Freshman Admission Statistics:** 2,130 applied, 46% admitted, 31% enrolled. **Transfer Admission Requirements:** college transcript(s), minimum college GPA of 2.5 required. Lowest grade transferable C. **General Admission Information:** Application Fee $25. Regular application deadline 8/1. Notification on a rolling basis, beginning on or about 12/1. Nonfall registration accepted. Admission may be deferred for a maximum of 1 year. Credit and/or placement offered for CEEB Advanced Placement tests.

COSTS AND FINANCIAL AID

Annual tuition $25,520. Room and board $6,970. Required fees $590. **Required Forms and Deadlines:** FAFSA. **Notification of Awards:** Applicants will be notified of awards on a rolling basis beginning 3/1. **Types of Aid:** *Need-based scholarships/grants:* Federal Pell, SEOG, state scholarships/grants, private scholarships, the school's own gift aid. *Loans:* Subsidized Stafford, Unsubsidized Stafford, PLUS, Federal Perkins, state loans. **Student Employment:** Federal Work-Study Program available. Off-campus job opportunities are good. **Financial Aid Statistics:** 65% freshmen, 62% undergrads receive need-based scholarship or grant aid. 100% freshmen, 88% undergrads receive non-need-based scholarship or grant aid. 59% freshmen, 68% undergrads receive need-based self-help aid. 11% freshmen, 12% undergrads receive athletic scholarships. 69% undergrads borrow to pay for school. Average cumulative indebtedness $29,207. **Criteria for awarding institutional aid:** *Non-need-based:* academics, alumni affiliation, athletics, leadership, music/drama, religious affiliation, state/district residency.

CHRISTOPHER NEWPORT UNIVERSITY

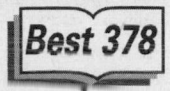

1 University Place, Newport News, VA 23606-2998
Phone: 757-594-7015 • **Financial Aid Phone:** 757-594-7170
E-mail: admit@cnu.edu • **CEEB Code:** 5128
Fax: 757-594-7333 • **Website:** www.cnu.edu • **ACT Code:** 4345

This public school was founded in 1960. It has a 260-acre campus.

RATINGS

Admissions Selectivity Rating: 84   **Fire Safety Rating:** 91   **Green Rating:** 73

STUDENTS AND FACULTY

Enrollment: 5,036. **Student Body:** 57% female, 43% male, 6% out-of-state, 0% international (38 countries represented). Asian 2%, African American 8%, Caucasian 77%, Hispanic 5%, Native American 0%.
Retention and Graduation: 85% freshmen return for sophomore year. 51% freshmen graduate within 4 years. 67% freshmen graduate within 6 years.
Faculty: Student/faculty ratio 17:1. 258 full-time faculty, 86% hold PhDs, 11% are members of minority groups, 45% are women. 0% of classes are taught by teaching assistants.

ACADEMICS

Degrees: bachelor's, master's. **Classes:** Most classes have 20–29 students.
Majors with Highest Enrollment: biology/biological sciences; business administration and management; communication studies/speech communication and rhetoric. **Special Study Options:** cross-registration, double major, dual enrollment, honors program, independent study, internships, student-designed major, study abroad, Member of the Virginia Tidewater Consortium. **Freshman** Learning Communities. **Honors Programs:** CNU Honors Program provides enriched educational experience for academically talented students motivated to participate in challenging courses and cultural and intellectual activities. **Disability Services:** Special programs offered to physically disabled students include note-taking services, tape recorders. **Career Services:** career/job search classes, career assessment, internships Career Services highlights include A new initiative—Freshman Academic Success Program (incorporation of study skills, major choices, and career opportunities).

FACILITIES

Housing: Coed dorms, fraternity/sorority housing, apartments for single students, theme housing. 96% of campus accessible to physically disabled. **Special Academic Facilities/Equipment:** Falk Art Gallery, The Freeman Center, The Ferguson Center for the Arts, Trible Library houses the Mariners Museum Collection. **Computers:** 10% of classrooms, 10% of dorms, 100% of libraries, 100% of dining areas, 100% of student union, 100% of common outdoor areas have wireless network access. Students can register for classes online. Administrative functions (other than registration) can be performed online.

CAMPUS LIFE

Environment: City. **Activities:** Choral groups, concert band, dance, drama/theater, jazz band, literary magazine, marching band, music ensembles, musical theater, opera, pep band, radio station, student government, student newspaper, student-run film society, symphony orchestra, television station, Campus Ministries, International Student Organization, Model UN 139 registered organizations, 23 honor societies, 12 religious organizations. 7 fraternities, 7 sororities. **Athletics (Intercollegiate):** *Men:* baseball, basketball, cheerleading, cross-country, football, golf, lacrosse, sailing, soccer, tennis, track/field (outdoor), track/field (indoor). *Women:* basketball, cheerleading, cross-country, field hockey, lacrosse, sailing, soccer, softball, tennis, track/field (outdoor), track/field (indoor), volleyball. **On-Campus Highlights:** Trible Library, Freeman Athletic Center, Ferguson Center for the Arts, McMurran Classroom Building, David Student Union, CNU Village for upper class students.

ADMISSIONS

Freshman Academic Profile: Average high school GPA 3.7. 18% in top 10% of high school class, 51% in top 25% of high school class, 92% in top 50% of high school class. 15% from public high schools. SAT Math middle 50% range 540-610. SAT Critical Reading middle 50% range 530-630. ACT middle 50% range 21-26. Minimum web-based TOEFL 71. Minimum paper TOEFL 530. **Basis for Candidate Selection:** *Very important factors considered include:* academic GPA, rigor of secondary school record. *Important factors considered include:* recommendation(s), alumni/ae relation, first generation. *Other factors considered include:* application essay, standardized test scores, character/personal qualities, extracurricular activities, level of applicant's interest, talent/ability, volunteer work, work experience. **Freshman Admission Requirements:** High school diploma is required and GED is accepted. *Academic units required:* 4 English, 4 mathematics, 3 science, 3 foreign language, 3 history. *Academic units recommended:* 4 English, 4 mathematics, 3 science, 3 foreign language, 3 history. **Freshman Admission Statistics:** 6,831 applied, 65% admitted, 31% enrolled. **Transfer Admission Requirements:** High school transcript, college transcript(s), statement of good standing from prior institution(s). Minimum college GPA of 3.0 required. Lowest grade transferable C. **General Admission Information:** Application Fee $45. Regular application deadline 2/1. Notification on a rolling basis, beginning on or about 12/1. Nonfall registration accepted. Admission may be deferred for a maximum of 12 Months. Credit and/or placement offered for CEEB Advanced Placement tests.

COSTS AND FINANCIAL AID

Annual in-state tuition $6,210. Annual out-of-state tuition $15,364. Room and board $9,728. Required fees $4,362. Average book expense $1,141. **Required Forms and Deadlines:** FAFSA. **Notification of Awards:** Applicants will be notified of awards on a rolling basis beginning 2/21. **Types of Aid:** *Need-based scholarships/grants:* Federal Pell, SEOG, state scholarships/grants, private scholarships, the school's own gift aid. *Loans:* Subsidized Stafford, Unsubsidized Stafford, PLUS. **Student Employment:** Federal Work-Study Program available. Institutional employment available. Off-campus job opportunities are good. **Financial Aid Statistics:** 67% freshmen, 66% undergrads receive need-based scholarship or grant aid. 48% freshmen, 31% undergrads receive non-need-based scholarship or grant aid. 86% freshmen, 88% undergrads receive need-based self-help aid. 81% freshmen, 70% undergrads receive any aid. 55% undergrads borrow to pay for school. Average cumulative indebtedness $23,250. **Criteria for awarding institutional aid:** *Non-need-based:* academics, art, leadership, music/drama, state/district residency.

CIRCLEVILLE BIBLE COLLEGE

1476 Lancaster Pike, Circleville, OH 43113-9487
Phone: 740-477-7701
E-mail: enroll@biblecollege.edu
Fax: 740-477-7755 • **Website:** www.biblecollege.edu • **ACT Code:** 3030

This private school was founded in 1948.

RATINGS

Admissions Selectivity Rating: 69   **Fire Safety Rating:** 60*   **Green Rating:** 60*

STUDENTS AND FACULTY

Enrollment: 349. **Student Body:** 24% out-of-state, 0% international. Asian 1%, African American 6%, Caucasian 91%, Hispanic 2%, Native American 1%. **Retention and Graduation:** 58% freshmen return for sophomore year. 20% freshmen graduate within 6 years. **Faculty:** Student/faculty ratio 13:1. 14 full-time faculty, 64% hold PhDs, 14% are women.

ACADEMICS

Degrees: associate, bachelor's, terminal associate, transfer associate. **Classes:** Most classes have 10–19 students. **Special Study Options:** double major, independent study, internships, liberal arts/career combination, student-designed major. **Disability Services:** Special programs offered to physically disabled students include note-taking services, reader services, tape recorders, tutors. **Career Services:**

FACILITIES

Housing: men's dorms, special housing for international students, women's dorms, apartments for married students

CAMPUS LIFE

Environment: Rural. **Activities:** Choral groups, drama/theater, music ensembles, student government, yearbook. **Athletics (Intercollegiate):** *Men:* baseball, basketball. *Women:* basketball, volleyball.

ADMISSIONS

Freshman Academic Profile: Average high school GPA 2.9. 21% in top 10% of high school class, 24% in top 25% of high school class, 32% in top 50% of high school class, ACT middle 50% range 17-23. **Basis for Candidate Selection:** *Very important factors considered include:* Class rank, recommendation(s), rigor of secondary school record, standardized test scores, religious affiliation/commitment. *Important factors considered include:* application essay, character/personal qualities. *Other factors considered include:* interview. **Freshman Admission Requirements:** High school diploma is required and GED is accepted. **Freshman Admission Statistics:** 138 applied, 69% admitted, 75% enrolled. **Transfer Admission Requirements:** High school transcript, college transcript(s), essay or personal statement, standardized test scores, statement of good standing from prior institution(s). Minimum college GPA of 2.0 required. Lowest grade transferable C. **General Admission Information:** Application Fee $25. Nonfall registration accepted. Admission may be deferred for a maximum of one year.

COSTS AND FINANCIAL AID

Annual tuition $7,950. Room and board $5,200. Required fees $850. Average book expense $500. **Required Forms and Deadlines:** FAFSA, institution's own financial aid form, CSS/Financial Aid PROFILE. **Notification of Awards:** Applicants will be notified of awards on or about 6/1. **Student Employment:** Federal Work-Study Program available. Off-campus job opportunities are excellent. **Financial Aid Statistics:** 28% freshmen, 32% undergrads receive need-based scholarship or grant aid. 28% freshmen, 32% undergrads receive non-need-based scholarship or grant aid. 28% freshmen, 32% undergrads receive need-based self-help aid.

THE CITADEL—THE MILITARY COLLEGE OF SOUTH CAROLINA

171 Moultrie Street, Charleston, SC 29409
Phone: 843-953-5230 • **Financial Aid Phone:** 843-953-5187
E-mail: admissions@citadel.edu
Fax: 843-953-7036 • **Website:** www.citadel.edu • **ACT Code:** 3838

This public school was founded in 1842. It has a 300-acre campus.

RATINGS

Admissions Selectivity Rating: 72   **Fire Safety Rating:** 98   **Green Rating:** 65

STUDENTS AND FACULTY

Enrollment: 2,555. **Student Body:** 8% female, 92% male, 47% out-of-state, 1% international (8 countries represented). Asian 2%, African American 6%, Caucasian 59%, Hispanic 4%, Native American 1%. **Retention and Graduation:** 84% freshmen return for sophomore year. 16% grads go on to further study within 1 year. 2% grads pursue arts and sciences degrees. 5% grads pursue law degrees. 5% grads pursue business degrees. 2% grads pursue medical degrees. **Faculty:** Student/faculty ratio 13:1. 182 full-time faculty, 91% hold PhDs, 15% are members of minority groups, 35% are women. 0% of classes are taught by teaching assistants.

ACADEMICS

Degrees: bachelor's, master's, post-master's certificate. **Classes:** Most classes have 20–29 students. Most lab/discussion sessions have 10–19 students. **Majors with Highest Enrollment:** business administration and management; civil engineering; criminal justice/law enforcement administration. **Special Study Options:** cooperative education program, distance learning, double major, English as a Second Language (ESL), honors program, independent study, internships, study abroad, teacher certification program. **Honors Programs:** The Citadel's Honors Program is a specially designed educational experience meeting the needs of students with an outstanding record of academic achievement and a sense of intellectual adventure. While pursuing any one of seventeen degree programs offered by The Citadel, Honors Students take a series of Core Curriculum Honors courses--for example, studies based in literature and writing, history, and mathematics,--concentrated in their first two years, and an occasional Honors Seminar in their third and fourth years. For the qualified student, advantages of the Honors Program are clear: special program of pre-professional counseling, small classes, discussion-style teaching, tutorial session, special curriculum, fellow honors students, student advisory committee, honors faculty, special diploma seal and transcript, and emphasis on leadership. **Career Services:** Alumni network, alumni services, career/job search classes, career assessment, internships.

FACILITIES

Housing: Coed dorms. **Special Academic Facilities/Equipment:** Archives and Museum. **Computers:** 5% of classrooms, 20% of dorms, 100% of libraries, 75% of student union, 10% of common outdoor areas have wireless network access. Students can register for classes online. Administrative functions (other than registration) can be performed online.

CAMPUS LIFE

Environment: City. **Activities:** Choral groups, concert band, jazz band, literary magazine, marching band, pep band, student government, student newspaper, yearbook, Campus Ministries 79 registered organizations, 12 honor societies, 16 religious organizations. **Athletics (Intercollegiate):** *Men:* baseball, basketball, cross-country, football, riflery, tennis, track/field (outdoor), track/field (indoor), wrestling. *Women:* cross-country, golf, riflery, soccer, track/field (outdoor), track/field (indoor), volleyball. **On-Campus Highlights:** Summerall Chapel, Mark Clark Hall, Daniel Library, Citadel Museum, McAlister Field House. **Environmental Initiatives:** $5 Million Energy Performance Contract Expanding Energy Management System to nearly 100% of campus. Expanding recycling and waste reduction to 100% of campus.

ADMISSIONS

Freshman Academic Profile: Average high school GPA 3.5. 12% in top 10% of high school class, 33% in top 25% of high school class, 71% in top 50% of high school class. SAT Math middle 50% range 500-600. SAT Critical Reading middle 50% range 480-590. ACT middle 50% range 21-25. Minimum web-based TOEFL 79. Minimum paper TOEFL 550. **Basis for Candidate Selection:** *Very important factors considered include:* academic GPA, standardized test scores, level of applicant's interest. *Important factors considered include:* rigor of secondary school record, character/personal qualities, extracurricular activities, state residency, talent/ability. *Other factors considered include:* Class rank, recommendation(s), alumni/ae relation, first generation, geographical residence, interview, volunteer work. **Freshman Admission Requirements:** High school diploma is required and GED is accepted. *Academic units required:* 4 English, 3 mathematics, 3 science, (3 science labs), 2 foreign language, 2 social studies, 1 history, 4 academic electives, 1 PE or ROTC. *Academic units recommended:* 4 English, 3 mathematics, 3 science, (3 science labs), 2 foreign language, 2 social studies, 1 history, 4 academic electives, 1 PE or ROTC **Freshman Admission Statistics:** 2,557 applied, 80% admitted, 33% enrolled. **Transfer Admission Requirements:** High school transcript, college transcript(s), standardized test scores, statement of good standing from prior institution(s). Minimum college GPA of 2.0 required. Lowest grade transferable C. **General Admission Information:** Application Fee $40. Early decision application deadline 10/26. Notification on a rolling basis, beginning on or about 7/15. Nonfall registration not accepted. Credit and/or placement offered for CEEB Advanced Placement tests.

COSTS AND FINANCIAL AID

Annual in-state tuition $10,523. Annual out-of-state tuition $28,776. Room and board $6,115. Required fees $1,249. Average book expense $6,940. **Required Forms and Deadlines:** FAFSA, institution's own financial aid form. **Notification of Awards:** Applicants will be notified of awards on a rolling basis beginning 4/1. **Types of Aid:** *Need-based scholarships/grants:* Federal Pell, SEOG, state scholarships/grants, the school's own gift aid. *Loans:* Direct Subsidized Stafford, Direct Unsubsidized Stafford, Direct PLUS, Federal Perkins. **Student Employment:** Federal Work-Study Program available. **Financial Aid Statistics:** 75% freshmen, 76% undergrads receive need-based scholarship or grant aid. 14% freshmen, 16% undergrads receive non-need-based scholarship or grant aid. 78% freshmen, 81% undergrads receive need-based self-help aid. 11% freshmen, 12% undergrads receive athletic scholarships. 83% freshmen,

85% undergrads receive any aid. 52% undergrads borrow to pay for school. Average cumulative indebtedness $31,217. **Criteria for awarding institutional aid:** *Non-need-based:* academics, alumni affiliation, athletics, leadership, state/district residency.

CITY UNIVERSITY

11900 NE First Street, Bellevue, WA 98005
Phone: 425-637-1010 • **Financial Aid Phone:** 425-709-5251
E-mail: info@cityu.edu
Fax: 425-709-5361 • **Website:** www.cityu.edu

This private school was founded in 1973. It has a 5-acre campus.

RATINGS
Admissions Selectivity Rating: 61   **Fire Safety Rating:** 60*   **Green Rating:** 60*

STUDENTS AND FACULTY
Enrollment: 1,848. **Student Body:** 55% female, 45% male, 1% out-of-state, 5% international. Asian 6%, African American 5%, Caucasian 66%, Hispanic 3%, Native American 1%.
Retention and Graduation: **Faculty:** Student/faculty ratio 20:1. 36 full-time faculty, 25% hold PhDs, 19% are members of minority groups, 47% are women.

ACADEMICS
Degrees: associate, bachelor's, certificate, master's, transfer associate. **Classes:** **Majors with Highest Enrollment:** business administration and management; computer and information sciences and support services, other; elementary education and teaching. **Special Study Options:** Accelerated program, distance learning, double major, dual enrollment, English as a Second Language (ESL), internships, student-designed major, teacher certification program, weekend college.

FACILITIES
Computers: Students can register for classes online. Administrative functions (other than registration) can be performed online.

CAMPUS LIFE
Environment: Metropolis. **Activities:** Choral groups, drama/theater, music ensembles, student government, student newspaper.

ADMISSIONS
Freshman Academic Profile: Minimum paper TOEFL 540. **Freshman Admission Requirements:** High school diploma is required and GED is accepted. **Freshman Admission Statistics:** 15 applied, 100% admitted. **Transfer Admission Requirements:** High school transcript, college transcript(s), Lowest grade transferable C. **General Admission Information:** Application Fee $80. Nonfall registration accepted. Admission may be deferred for a maximum of Undetermined.

COSTS AND FINANCIAL AID
Annual tuition $9,320. Required fees $120. Average book expense $500.
Required Forms and Deadlines: Notification of Awards: Types of Aid: *Need-based scholarships/grants: Loans:* **Student Employment:** Federal Work-Study Program available. **Financial Aid Statistics:** 27% freshmen, 29% undergrads receive any aid.

CITY UNIVERSITY OF NEW YORK— BARUCH COLLEGE

Undergraduate Admissions, 151 E 25th St, New York, NY 10010
Phone: 646-312-1400 • **Financial Aid Phone:** 646-312-1360
E-mail: admissions@baruch.cuny.edu • **CEEB Code:** 2034
Fax: 646-312-1363 • **Website:** www.baruch.cuny.edu • **ACT Code:**

This public school was founded in 1968.

RATINGS
Admissions Selectivity Rating: 95   **Fire Safety Rating:** 60*   **Green Rating:** 61

STUDENTS AND FACULTY
Enrollment: 13,584. **Student Body:** 48% female, 52% male, 4% out-of-state, 12% international (166 countries represented). Asian 34%, African American 10%, Caucasian 30%, Hispanic 14%, Native American 0%.
Retention and Graduation: 33% freshmen graduate within 4 years. 63% freshmen graduate within 6 years. **Faculty:** Student/faculty ratio 18:1. 473 full-time faculty, 93% hold PhDs, 27% are members of minority groups, 38% are women. 1% of classes are taught by teaching assistants.

ACADEMICS
Degrees: bachelor's, master's, post-master's certificate. **Classes:** Most classes have 20–29 students. Most lab/discussion sessions have 20–29 students. **Majors with Highest Enrollment:** accounting; finance. **Special Study Options:** Accelerated program, cross-registration, distance learning, double major, English as a Second Language (ESL), exchange student program (domestic), honors program, independent study, internships, liberal arts/career combination, student-designed major, study abroad. **Honors Programs:** CUNY Honors Program **Combined Degree Programs:** BA/MA. **Disability Services:** Special programs offered to physically disabled students include note-taking services, reader services, tape recorders, tutors. **Career Services:** Alumni network, alumni services, career/job search classes, career assessment, internships Career Services highlights include The Lawrence N. Field Center for Entrepreneurship is the jewel of our programs. The Field Center is a model of entrepreneurship education built around the collaboration of an institution of higher education, government, and the private sector. Faculty and students from Baruch's Zicklin School of Business, Baruch's Small Business Development Center (SBDC) Business Advisors, alumni and volunteers are brought together to support the entrepreneurial endeavors of start-up and established businesses and the college's constituents. The Center's vision reflects the College's overarching principles of research, teaching, and service. Specifically, are founding vision was to: ° Develop a strong, research-based, academic program. ° Build a strong program at the BBA and MBA level. ° Create an outreach program that made the College's expertise available to operating small businesses and aspiring entrepreneurs. Accomplishing these goals requires that we serve our constituencies via various activities: ° Faculty '– through research opportunities, interfacing and learning from real-world entrepreneurs, and course instruction. ° Students '– through courses, internship opportunities, exposure to networks, and other programs such as the business plan competition. ° Entrepreneurs '– through training, counseling, access to capital, and exposure to networks. The Field Center recently celebrated its 15 year anniversary which comes at the heel of the continuing generosity of Lawrence N. Field ('52) and his family. In 2008 the Eris and Larry Field Foundation endowed the Field Center with a $10 million gift (previously Larry Field endowed the Center with a $3 million gift). In 2008 and worldwide, approximately 2,300 out of 3,000 institutions of higher education teach entrepreneurship. Of these institutions, only 100 institutions have significant endowments devoted to Entrepreneurship. Therefore, our recent $10 million gift from Lawrence N. Field garners us an elite national presence within this select group of institutions with endowed programs. Among these 100 institutions, there are only a few which have a $50 million or greater endowment and about a dozen which have endowments at $30 million. This Lawrence N. Field gift places us among the top 5 percent of institutions globally with significant endowments devoted to Entrepreneurship.

FACILITIES
Housing: 100% of campus accessible to physically disabled. **Special Academic Facilities/Equipment:** Art gallery, Subotnik Financial Services Center and Wasserman Trading Floor **Computers:** 25% of classrooms, 100% of libraries, 100% of dining areas, 100% of student union, 100% of common outdoor areas have wireless network access. Students can register for classes online. Administrative functions (other than registration) can be performed online.

CAMPUS LIFE
Environment: Metropolis. **Activities:** Choral groups, dance, drama/theater, literary magazine, musical theater, radio station, student government, student newspaper, yearbook, Campus Ministries, Model UN 172 registered organizations, 9 honor societies, 7 religious organizations. 9 fraternities, 7 sororities. **Athletics (Intercollegiate):** *Men:* baseball, basketball, cross-country, soccer, swimming, tennis, volleyball. *Women:* basketball, cheerleading, cross-country, softball, swimming, tennis, volleyball. **On-Campus Highlights:** Student Club Area- Vertical Campus Build, NewMan Library, Lobby- 23 St. Building, Food Court- Vertical Campus Building, College Fitness Center-Vertical Campus.

ADMISSIONS
Freshman Academic Profile: Average high school GPA 3.1. 37% in top 10% of high school class, 63% in top 25% of high school class, 86% in top 50% of high school class. 86% from public high schools. SAT Math middle 50% range 580-680. SAT Critical Reading middle 50% range 500-600. Minimum web-based TOEFL 95. Minimum paper TOEFL 587. **Basis for Candidate Selection:** *Very important factors considered include:* academic GPA, rigor of secondary school record, standardized test scores. *Important factors considered include:* application essay, recommendation(s). *Other factors considered include:* Class rank, alumni/ae relation, character/personal qualities, extracur-

ricular activities, interview, talent/ability, work experience. **Freshman Admission Requirements:** High school diploma is required and GED is accepted. *Academic units required:* 4 English, 3 mathematics, 2 science, (2 science labs), 2 foreign language, 4 social studies, 0 Fine Arts. *Academic units recommended:* 4 English, 3 mathematics, 2 science, (2 science labs), 2 foreign language, 4 social studies, 0 Fine Arts **Freshman Admission Statistics:** 19,283 applied, 22% admitted, 30% enrolled. **Transfer Admission Requirements:** High school transcript, college transcript(s), statement of good standing from prior institution(s). Minimum college GPA of 2.7 required. Lowest grade transferable C. **General Admission Information:** Application Fee $65. Early decision application deadline 12/13. Regular application deadline 2/1. Regular notification 5/15. Notification on a rolling basis, beginning on or about 2/1. Nonfall registration accepted. Admission may be deferred for a maximum of Six months. Credit and/or placement offered for CEEB Advanced Placement tests.

COSTS AND FINANCIAL AID
Annual in-state tuition $5,430. Annual out-of-state tuition $14,550. Room and board $11,590. Required fees $480. Average book expense $1,248. **Required Forms and Deadlines:** FAFSA, state aid form. **Notification of Awards:** Applicants will be notified of awards on a rolling basis beginning 4/1. **Types of Aid:** *Need-based scholarships/grants:* Federal Pell, SEOG, state scholarships/ grants, the school's own gift aid, City merit scholarships. *Loans:* Direct Subsidized Stafford, Direct Unsubsidized Stafford, Direct PLUS, Federal Perkins. **Student Employment:** Federal Work-Study Program available. Institutional employment available. Off-campus job opportunities are excellent. **Financial Aid Statistics:** 23% freshmen, 37% undergrads receive need-based scholarship or grant aid. 3% freshmen, 1% undergrads receive non-need-based scholarship or grant aid. 48% freshmen, 46% undergrads receive need-based self-help aid. 51% freshmen, 53% undergrads receive any aid. 43% undergrads borrow to pay for school. Average cumulative indebtedness $15,822. **Criteria for awarding institutional aid:** *Non-need-based:* academics, alumni affiliation, state/district residency.

CITY UNIVERSITY OF NEW YORK—BOROUGH OF MANHATTAN COMMUNITY COLLEGE

199 Chambers Street, New York, NY 10007-1097
Phone: 212-220-1265
E-mail: ebarrios@bmcc.cuny.edu
Fax: 212-346-8110

This public school was founded in 1964. It has a 5-acre campus.

RATINGS
Admissions Selectivity Rating: 62   **Fire Safety Rating:** 60*   **Green Rating:** 60*

STUDENTS AND FACULTY
Enrollment: 16,732. **Student Body:** 64% female, 36% male, % out-of-state, 12% international. Asian 10%, African American 37%, Caucasian 11%, Hispanic 30%, Native American 0%.
Retention and Graduation: 40% grads go on to further study within 1 year. **Faculty:** Student/faculty ratio 21:1. 315 full-time faculty.

ACADEMICS
Degrees: associate, certificate, terminal associate, transfer associate. **Classes: Special Study Options:** cooperative education program, distance learning, English as a Second Language (ESL), honors program, independent study, internships, study abroad, weekend college. **Disability Services:** Special programs offered to physically disabled students include note-taking services, reader services, tape recorders, tutors. **Career Services:** alumni services, career/job search classes, career assessment, internships.

FACILITIES
Housing: special housing for disabled students, men's dorms, special housing for international students, women's dorms, apartments for single students. 100% of campus accessible to physically disabled. **Computers:** Students can register for classes online.

CAMPUS LIFE
Environment: Activities: Choral groups, concert band, dance, drama/theater, jazz band, music ensembles, pep band, student government, student newspaper, yearbook.

ADMISSIONS
Freshman Admission Requirements: High school diploma is required and GED is accepted. **Freshman Admission Statistics:** 6,374 applied, 85% admitted, 60% enrolled. **Transfer Admission Requirements:** college transcript(s).

General Admission Information: Application Fee $40. Nonfall registration not accepted.

COSTS AND FINANCIAL AID
Annual in-state tuition $2,500. Annual out-of-state tuition $3,076. Required fees $80. Average book expense $350. **Student Employment:** Federal Work-Study Program available.

CITY UNIVERSITY OF NEW YORK— BROOKLYN COLLEGE

2900 Bedford Avenue, Brooklyn, NY 11210
Phone: 718-951-5001 • **Financial Aid Phone:** 718-951-51
Fax: 718-951-4506 • **Website:** www.brooklyn.cuny.edu • **ACT Code:** 20169

This public school was founded in 1930. It has a 26-acre campus.

RATINGS
Admissions Selectivity Rating: 93   **Fire Safety Rating:** 60*   **Green Rating:** 86

STUDENTS AND FACULTY
Enrollment: 12,125. **Student Body:** 59% female, 41% male, 1% out-of-state, 4% international. Asian 18%, African American 24%, Caucasian 42%, Hispanic 12%, Native American 0%.
Retention and Graduation: 27% freshmen graduate within 4 years. 52% freshmen graduate within 6 years. **Faculty:** Student/faculty ratio 15:1. 531 full-time faculty, 92% hold PhDs, 26% are members of minority groups, 45% are women.

ACADEMICS
Degrees: bachelor's, certificate, master's, post-bachelor's certificate, post-master's certificate. **Classes:** Most classes have 20–29 students. **Special Study Options:** distance learning, double major, dual enrollment, English as a Second Language (ESL), honors program, independent study, internships, study abroad, teacher certification program, weekend college. **Honors Programs:** See the URL below for more information: http://www.brooklyn.cuny.edu/ pub/1654.htm **Combined Degree Programs:** BA/MD. **Disability Services:** Special programs offered to physically disabled students include note-taking services, reader services, tutors. **Career Services:** Alumni network, alumni services, career/job search classes, career assessment, internships.

FACILITIES
Housing: 100% of campus accessible to physically disabled. **Special Academic Facilities/Equipment:** Art museum. language lab, TV studios, speech clinic, research centers and institutes, particle accelerator. **Computers:** 2% of classrooms, 90% of libraries, 100% of dining areas, 75% of student union, 75% of common outdoor areas have wireless network access. Students can register for classes online. Administrative functions (other than registration) can be performed online.

CAMPUS LIFE
Environment: Metropolis. **Activities:** dance, drama/theater, literary magazine, music ensembles, musical theater, radio station, student government, student newspaper, television station, yearbook, International Student Organization 171 registered organizations, 7 honor societies, 7 fraternities, 9 sororities. **Athletics (Intercollegiate):** *Men:* basketball, cross-country, soccer, tennis, track/field (outdoor), track/field (indoor), volleyball. *Women:* basketball, cross-country, softball, tennis, track/field (outdoor), track/field (indoor), volleyball. **On-Campus Highlights:** Library, Student Center, Lily Pond, Library Cafe, Cafeteria, Dining Hall, Magner Center, James Hall. **Environmental Initiatives:** Reduce material consumption/waste, increase awareness/education, reduce energy use.

ADMISSIONS
Freshman Academic Profile: Average high school GPA 3.3. 18% in top 10% of high school class, 52% in top 25% of high school class, 79% in top 50% of high school class. SAT Math middle 50% range 520-620. SAT Critical Reading middle 50% range 480-580. Minimum paper TOEFL 500. **Basis for Candidate Selection:** *Very important factors considered include:* academic GPA, rigor of secondary school record, standardized test scores. **Freshman Admission Requirements:** High school diploma is required and GED is accepted. **Freshman Admission Statistics:** 19,843 applied, 32% admitted, 18% enrolled. **Transfer Admission Requirements:** college transcript(s), minimum college

GPA of 2.3 required. Lowest grade transferable C-. **General Admission Information:** Application Fee $65. Notification on a rolling basis, beginning on or about 2/1. Nonfall registration accepted. Credit and/or placement offered for CEEB Advanced Placement tests.

COSTS AND FINANCIAL AID
Annual in-state tuition $5,430. Annual out-of-state tuition $14,550. Required fees $454. **Required Forms and Deadlines:** FAFSA, state aid form. **Notification of Awards:** Applicants will be notified of awards on a rolling basis beginning 5/1. **Types of Aid:** *Need-based scholarships/grants:* Federal Pell, SEOG, state scholarships/grants, private scholarships, the school's own gift aid. *Loans:* Direct Subsidized Stafford, Direct Unsubsidized Stafford, Direct PLUS, Federal Perkins. **Student Employment:** Federal Work-Study Program available. Institutional employment available. Off-campus job opportunities are excellent. **Financial Aid Statistics:** 82% freshmen, 87% undergrads receive need-based scholarship or grant aid. 37% freshmen, 29% undergrads receive non-need-based scholarship or grant aid. 86% freshmen, 93% undergrads receive need-based self-help aid. 48% undergrads borrow to pay for school. Average cumulative indebtedness $12,200. **Criteria for awarding institutional aid:** *Non-need-based:* academics, art, leadership, music/drama, state/district residency.

CITY UNIVERSITY OF NEW YORK— CITY COLLEGE

160 Convent Avenue, Wille Admin. Bldg., New York, NY 10031
Phone: 212 650 6977 • **Financial Aid Phone:** 212 650 5819
E-mail: admissions@ccny.cuny.edu • **CEEB Code:** 2083
Fax: 212 650 6417 • **Website:** www.ccny.cuny.edu • **ACT Code:** 2950

This public school was founded in 1847. It has a 36-acre campus.

RATINGS
Admissions Selectivity Rating: 85   **Fire Safety Rating:** 98   **Green Rating:** 96

STUDENTS AND FACULTY
Enrollment: 12,276. **Student Body:** 51% female, 49% male, 8% international (100 countries represented). Asian 23%, African American 20%, Caucasian 18%, Hispanic 30%, Native American 0%.
Retention and Graduation: 7% freshmen graduate within 4 years. 41% freshmen graduate within 6 years. 18% grads go on to further study within 1 year. 1% grads pursue law degrees. 2% grads pursue business degrees. 27% grads pursue medical degrees. **Faculty:** Student/faculty ratio 13:1. 520 full-time faculty, 77% hold PhDs, 19% are members of minority groups, 40% are women.

ACADEMICS
Degrees: bachelor's, master's, post-master's certificate. **Classes:** Most classes have 20–29 students. **Majors with Highest Enrollment:** communication and media studies, other; electrical, electronics and communications engineering; psychology. **Special Study Options:** Accelerated program, cross-registration, double major, English as a Second Language (ESL), honors program, independent study, internships, study abroad, teacher certification program, Adult program called The Center for Worker Education which offers a evening and weekend program in liberal arts. **Honors Programs:** CUNY Macauley College and City College Honors Program. **Combined Degree Programs:** BA/MD, BA/MA. **Disability Services:** Special programs offered to physically disabled students include note-taking services, reader services, tape recorders, tutors. **Career Services:** Alumni network, alumni services, career/job search classes, career assessment, internships.

FACILITIES
Housing: The Towers new residence hall with apartment style quarter. **Special Academic Facilities/Equipment:** Planetarium, NYC Structural Biological Center, Aaron Davis Hall/Harlem Stage Gatehouse, Landmarked Gothic orignaial campus buildings. **Computers:** 100% of classrooms, 100% of libraries, 100% of dining areas, 100% of common outdoor areas have wireless network access. Students can register for classes online. Administrative functions (other than registration) can be performed online.

CAMPUS LIFE
Environment: Metropolis. **Activities:** Choral groups, concert band, dance, drama/theater, jazz band, literary magazine, radio station, student government, student newspaper, student-run film society, yearbook, International Student Organization, Model UN 145 registered organizations, 8 religious organizations. 2 fraternities, 1 sororities. **Athletics (Intercollegiate):** *Men:* baseball, basketball, cross-country, soccer, tennis, track/field (outdoor), track/field (indoor), volleyball. *Women:* basketball, fencing, soccer, tennis, track/field (outdoor), track/field (indoor), volleyball. **On-Campus Highlights:** NAC Rotunda and Plaza, Spitzer School of Archtecture, Wingate Hall Athletic Center, North Campus Quad in warm weather, The Towers -Residence Hall. **Environmental Initiatives:** Signed on to ACUPCC and NYC Mayor's Campus 30in10 Challenge to reduce GHG emissions Task Force to place sustainability at forefront in all operations, outreach and educational mission Undergraduate and Graduate programs in sustainability, interdisciplinary with Science, Engineering, Architecture and Economics.

ADMISSIONS
Freshman Academic Profile: Average high school GPA 87.7. 85% from public high schools. SAT Math middle 50% range 520-640. SAT Critical Reading middle 50% range 460-580. Minimum web-based TOEFL 61. Minimum paper TOEFL 500. **Basis for Candidate Selection:** *Very important factors considered include:* academic GPA, rigor of secondary school record. *Important factors considered include:* standardized test scores. *Other factors considered include:* application essay, recommendation(s). **Freshman Admission Requirements:** High school diploma is required and GED is accepted. **Freshman Admission Statistics:** 28,183 applied, 33% admitted, 15% enrolled. **Transfer Admission Requirements:** college transcript(s), minimum college GPA of 2.0 required. Lowest grade transferable c. **General Admission Information:** Application Fee $65. Notification on a rolling basis, beginning on or about 2/1. Nonfall registration accepted. Credit offered for CEEB Advanced Placement tests.

COSTS AND FINANCIAL AID
Annual in-state tuition $5,430. Annual out-of-state tuition $11,640. Room and board $12,788. Required fees $358. Average book expense $1,248. **Required Forms and Deadlines:** FAFSA. **Notification of Awards:** Applicants will be notified of awards on a rolling basis beginning 4/1. **Types of Aid:** *Need-based scholarships/grants:* Federal Pell, SEOG, state scholarships/grants, the school's own gift aid. *Loans:* Direct Subsidized Stafford, Direct Unsubsidized Stafford, Direct PLUS. **Student Employment:** Federal Work-Study Program available. Institutional employment available. Highest amount earned per year from on-campus jobs $7,200. Off-campus job opportunities are fair. **Financial Aid Statistics:** 91% freshmen, 94% undergrads receive need-based scholarship or grant aid. 57% freshmen, 12% undergrads receive non-need-based scholarship or grant aid. 31% freshmen, 97% undergrads receive need-based self-help aid. 84% freshmen, 84% undergrads receive any aid. 22% undergrads borrow to pay for school. Average cumulative indebtedness $16,944. **Criteria for awarding institutional aid:** *Non-need-based:* academics, alumni affiliation, art, leadership, minority status, music/drama.

See page 1044.

CITY UNIVERSITY OF NEW YORK— THE COLLEGE OF STATEN ISLAND

2800 Victory Boulevard, Staten Island, NY 10314
Phone: 718-982-2010 • **Financial Aid Phone:** 718-982-2030
E-mail: admissions@csi.cuny.edu • **CEEB Code:** 2778
Fax: 718-982-2500 • **Website:** www.csi.cuny.edu • **ACT Code:** 2950

This public school was founded in 1955. It has a 204-acre campus.

RATINGS
Admissions Selectivity Rating: 64   **Fire Safety Rating:** 60*   **Green Rating:** 74

STUDENTS AND FACULTY
Enrollment: 12,977. **Student Body:** 55% female, 45% male, 1% out-of-state, 3% international (114 countries represented). Asian 9%, African American 9%, Caucasian 40%, Hispanic 15%, Native American 0%.
Retention and Graduation: 84% freshmen return for sophomore year. 24% freshmen graduate within 4 years. 47% freshmen graduate within 6 years. 37% grads go on to further study within 1 year. **Faculty:** Student/faculty ratio 18:1. 331 full-time faculty, 84% hold PhDs, 24% are members of minority groups, 45% are women. 0% of classes are taught by teaching assistants.

ACADEMICS
Degrees: associate, bachelor's, certificate, master's, post-master's certificate, terminal associate. **Classes:** Most classes have 30–39 students. Most lab/discussion sessions have 30–39 students. **Majors with Highest Enrollment:**

business/commerce; liberal arts and sciences/liberal studies; psychology. **Special Study Options:** Accelerated program, cooperative education program, cross-registration, distance learning, double major, dual enrollment, English as a Second Language (ESL), exchange student program (domestic), honors program, independent study, internships, liberal arts/career combination, study abroad, teacher certification program, weekend college. **Honors Programs:** CSI is one of seven campuses within CUNY that participates in the William E. Macaulay Honors College. **Disability Services:** Special programs offered to physically disabled students include note-taking services, reader services, tape recorders, tutors. **Career Services:** alumni services, career/job search classes, career assessment, internships Career Services highlights include internships On Campus Recruitment Program.

FACILITIES

Housing: 95% of campus accessible to physically disabled. **Special Academic Facilities/Equipment:** Astrophysical Observatory, Archives and Special Collections, Center for the Arts, Center for Engineered Polymeric Materials, Center for Environmental Science, Center for Developmental Neuroscience and Developmental Disabilities, and the CSI Art Gallery. **Computers:** 97% of classrooms, 100% of libraries, 100% of dining areas, 100% of student union, 100% of common outdoor areas have wireless network access. Students can register for classes online. Administrative functions (other than registration) can be performed online.

CAMPUS LIFE

Environment: Metropolis. **Activities:** Choral groups, dance, drama/theater, jazz band, literary magazine, music ensembles, radio station, student government, student newspaper, student-run film society, yearbook, Campus Ministries, International Student Organization 47 registered organizations, 2 honor societies, 4 religious organizations. **Athletics (Intercollegiate):** *Men:* baseball, basketball, cross-country, diving, soccer, swimming, tennis. *Women:* basketball, cross-country, diving, soccer, softball, swimming, tennis, volleyball. **On-Campus Highlights:** Campus Center Rotunda, Center for the Performing Arts, Library, Sports and Recreation Center, Campus Center Game Room, The Student Lounges are also a popular site on campus for students. **Environmental Initiatives:** Developed paper/cans, bottles, glass/waste minirecycling deposit centers on all floors of all buildings on campus. Experimenting with a biodiesel kit to convert used cooking oil from our cafeteria to biodiesel fuel for equipment. Recently registered to participate in recycle-mania. We are currently recruiting student ambassadors.

ADMISSIONS

Freshman Academic Profile: Average high school GPA 3.0. 67% from public high schools. SAT Math middle 50% range 470-560. SAT Critical Reading middle 50% range 440-530. SAT Writing middle 50% range 430-520. Minimum web-based TOEFL 45. Minimum paper TOEFL 450. **Basis for Candidate Selection:** *Very important factors considered include:* rigor of secondary school record. *Important factors considered include:* academic GPA, standardized test scores. **Freshman Admission Requirements:** High school diploma is required and GED is accepted. *Academic units required:* 4 English, 2 mathematics, 2 science, 2 foreign language, 4 social studies. *Academic units recommended:* 4 English, 2 mathematics, 2 science, 2 foreign language, 4 social studies. **Freshman Admission Statistics:** 11,630 applied, 100% admitted, 22% enrolled. **Transfer Admission Requirements:** college transcript(s), minimum college GPA of 2.0 required. Lowest grade transferable C. **General Admission Information:** Application Fee $65. Notification on a rolling basis, beginning on or about 12/15. Nonfall registration accepted. Admission may be deferred for a maximum of 1 semester. Credit and/or placement offered for CEEB Advanced Placement tests.

COSTS AND FINANCIAL AID

Annual in-state tuition $5,430. Annual out-of-state tuition $14,550. Required fees $428. Average book expense. **Required Forms and Deadlines:** FAFSA. **Notification of Awards: Types of Aid:** *Need-based scholarships/grants:* Federal Pell, SEOG, state scholarships/grants, private scholarships, the school's own gift aid. *Loans:* Direct Subsidized Stafford, Direct Unsubsidized Stafford, Direct PLUS, Federal Perkins, Alternative Proprietary Loans. **Student Employment:** Federal Work-Study Program available. Institutional employment available. Off-campus job opportunities are good. **Financial Aid Statistics:** 89% freshmen, 91% undergrads receive need-based scholarship or grant aid. 80% freshmen, 80% undergrads receive non-need-based scholarship or grant aid. 27% freshmen, 30% undergrads receive need-based self-help aid. **Criteria for awarding institutional aid:** *Non-need-based:* academics, art, leadership, minority status, music/drama, state/district residency.

CITY UNIVERSITY OF NEW YORK— HUNTER COLLEGE

695 Park Ave, Room N203, New York, NY 10065
Phone: 212-772-4490 • **Financial Aid Phone:** 212-772-4820
E-mail: admissions@hunter.cuny.edu • **CEEB Code:** 2301
Fax: 212-650-3472 • **Website:** www.hunter.cuny.edu

This public school was founded in 1870.

RATINGS

Admissions Selectivity Rating: 87   **Fire Safety Rating:** 99   **Green Rating:** 87

STUDENTS AND FACULTY

Enrollment: 15,789. **Student Body:** 66% female, 34% male, 4% out-of-state, 7% international. Asian 25%, African American 11%, Caucasian 38%, Hispanic 18%, Native American 0%. **Retention and Graduation:** 19% freshmen graduate within 4 years. 45% freshmen graduate within 6 years. **Faculty:** Student/faculty ratio 15:1. 710 full-time faculty, 80% hold PhDs, 18% are members of minority groups, 50% are women.

ACADEMICS

Degrees: bachelor's, master's, post-master's certificate. **Classes:** Most classes have 20–29 students. **Majors with Highest Enrollment:** accounting; English literature (british and commonwealth); psychology. **Special Study Options:** Accelerated program, cross-registration, distance learning, double major, dual enrollment, exchange student program (domestic), honors program, independent study, internships, liberal arts/career combination, student-designed major, study abroad, teacher certification program. **Combined Degree Programs:** BA/MA, BA/MS. **Disability Services:** Special programs offered to physically disabled students include note-taking services, reader services, tape recorders, tutors. **Career Services:** Alumni network, alumni services, career/job search classes, internships.

FACILITIES

Housing: Coed dorms. 100% of campus accessible to physically disabled. **Special Academic Facilities/Equipment:** Art Gallery, theatre, geology club, on-campus elementary and secondary schools. **Computers:** 70% of classrooms have wireless network access. Students can register for classes online.

CAMPUS LIFE

Environment: Metropolis. **Activities:** Choral groups, concert band, dance, drama/theater, jazz band, literary magazine, music ensembles, musical theater, radio station, student government, student newspaper, student-run film society, symphony orchestra, television station, yearbook 150 registered organizations, 20 honor societies, 2 fraternities, 2 sororities. **Athletics (Intercollegiate):** *Men:* basketball, cross-country, fencing, soccer, tennis, track/field (outdoor), track/field (indoor), volleyball, wrestling. *Women:* basketball, cross-country, diving, fencing, softball, swimming, tennis, track/field (outdoor), track/field (indoor), volleyball. **On-Campus Highlights:** Over 100 Campus Clubs, CARSI Geography Lab, Television Studio, Learning Center and Computer Lab, Sports Complex. **Environmental Initiatives:** Hunter has an extensive program for recycling paper, metal, glass, plastic, e-waste, and household batteries. This program is continuously being expanded. Thomas Hunter Hall is currently undergoing a multi-year, multimillion-dollar renovation to its facade, roof and windows which is expected to translate into substantial heating and cooling efficiencies. Approximately 350 single-paned windows that are original to this 100-year-old building are being replaced by energy-efficient, double-glazed windows. Hunter's newly-completed East Harlem campus, which houses the Silberman School of Social Work and the CUNY School of Public Health, was recently awarded LEED Certification.

ADMISSIONS

Freshman Academic Profile: 70% from public high schools. SAT Math middle 50% range 540-640. SAT Critical Reading middle 50% range 520-620. Minimum paper TOEFL 500. **Basis for Candidate Selection:** *Very important factors considered include:* application essay, academic GPA, rigor of secondary school record, standardized test scores. **Freshman Admission Requirements:** High school diploma is required and GED is accepted. *Academic units required:* 2 English, 2 mathematics, 1 science, (1 science labs). *Academic units recommended:* 2 English, 2 mathematics, 1 science, (1 science labs). **Freshman Admission Statistics:** 30,758 applied, 30% admitted, 22% enrolled. **Transfer**

Admission Requirements: college transcript(s), minimum college GPA of 2.3 required. Lowest grade transferable C. **General Admission Information:** Application Fee $65. Regular application deadline 3/15. Notification on a rolling basis, beginning on or about 1/15. Nonfall registration accepted. Credit and/or placement offered for CEEB Advanced Placement tests.

COSTS AND FINANCIAL AID

Annual in-state tuition $5,430. Annual out-of-state tuition $14,550. Room and board $4,877. Required fees $399. **Required Forms and Deadlines:** FAFSA, state aid form. **Notification of Awards:** Applicants will be notified of awards on a rolling basis beginning 5/15. **Types of Aid:** *Need-based scholarships/ grants:* Federal Pell, state scholarships/grants, the school's own gift aid. *Loans:* Direct Subsidized Stafford, Direct Unsubsidized Stafford, Direct PLUS, Federal Perkins, state loans, college/university loans from institutional fundsCUNY Student Assistance Program(CUSTA), Aide for Part-Time-Study (APTS), SEEK. **Student Employment:** Federal Work-Study Program available. Institutional employment available. Off-campus job opportunities are fair. **Financial Aid Statistics:** 94% freshmen, 95% undergrads receive need-based scholarship or grant aid. 82% freshmen, 81% undergrads receive non-need-based scholarship or grant aid. 14% freshmen, 19% undergrads receive need-based self-help aid. 91% freshmen, 94% undergrads receive any aid. 62% undergrads borrow to pay for school. Average cumulative indebtedness $11,000. **Criteria for awarding institutional aid:** *Non-need-based:* academics.

See page 1102.

CITY UNIVERSITY OF NEW YORK—JOHN JAY COLLEGE OF CRIMINAL JUSTICE

899 Tenth Avenue, New York, NY 10019
Phone: 212-237-8869
E-mail: admissions@jjay.cuny.edu • **CEEB Code:** 2115
Fax: 212-237-8777 • **Website:** www.jjay.cuny.edu

This public school was founded in 1964.

RATINGS
Admissions Selectivity Rating: 60*   **Fire Safety Rating:** 60*   **Green Rating:** 60*

ACADEMICS
Degrees: associate, bachelor's, certificate, master's, transfer associate. **Special Study Options:** cooperative education program, distance learning, English as a Second Language (ESL), exchange student program (domestic), study abroad, weekend college, Undergrads may take grad level classes. Off-Campus Study: Albany Internship Program. Co-Op Programs: Public Service. **Combined Degree Programs:** BA/MA. **Disability Services:** Special programs offered to physically disabled students include note-taking services, reader services, tape recorders, tutors. **Career Services:** alumni services, career/job search classes, career assessment.

FACILITIES
Housing: List of possible housing arrangements can be obtained from Student Activities (212) 237-8698 **Special Academic Facilities/Equipment:** Criminal justice center, center for violence/human survival, toxicology research/training center, fire science institute, institute for criminal justice ethics, institute for the study of genocide, and institute on alcohol/substance abuse. **Computers:** Students can register for classes online.

CAMPUS LIFE
Environment: Metropolis. **Activities:** Choral groups, dance, drama/theater, musical theater, radio station, student government, student newspaper, yearbook. **Athletics (Intercollegiate):** *Men:* basketball, cross-country, riflery, soccer. *Women:* cross-country, riflery, softball, tennis, volleyball.

ADMISSIONS
Freshman Academic Profile: Minimum paper TOEFL 500. **Freshman Admission Requirements:** High school diploma is required and GED is accepted. High school diploma is required and GED is not accepted. **Transfer Admission Requirements:** Minimum college GPA of 2.0 required. Lowest grade transferable C. **General Admission Information:** Application Fee $50. Regular application deadline 3/15. Nonfall registration accepted. Credit offered for CEEB Advanced Placement tests.

COSTS AND FINANCIAL AID
Annual in-state tuition $4,000. Annual out-of-state tuition $5,440. Room and board $1,802. Required fees $100. Average book expense $500. **Required Forms and Deadlines:** FAFSA. **Notification of Awards: Types of Aid:** *Need-based scholarships/grants:* Federal Pell, SEOG, state scholarships/grants, private scholarships, the school's own gift aid. *Loans:* Subsidized Stafford,

Unsubsidized Stafford, PLUS, Federal Perkins, college/university loans from institutional funds. **Student Employment:** Federal Work-Study Program available. Institutional employment available. Highest amount earned per year from on-campus jobs $2,500. Off-campus job opportunities are good.

CITY UNIVERSITY OF NEW YORK— KINGSBOROUGH COMMUNITY COLLEGE

2001 Oriental Blvd., Brooklyn, NY 11235
Phone: 718-368-4600 • **Financial Aid Phone:** 718-368-4644
E-mail: info@kbcc.cuny.edu
Fax: 718-368-5356

This is a public school.

RATINGS
Admissions Selectivity Rating: 60*   **Fire Safety Rating:** 60*   **Green Rating:** 60*

STUDENTS AND FACULTY
Enrollment: 14,997. **Student Body:** 56% female, 44% male, % out-of-state, 4% international (137 countries represented). Asian 12%, African American 35%, Caucasian 33%, Hispanic 16%, Native American 0%.
Faculty: Student/faculty ratio 23:1. 354 full-time faculty, 54% hold PhDs, 26% are members of minority groups, 52% are women. 0% of classes are taught by teaching assistants.

ACADEMICS
Degrees: associate, certificate, terminal associate, transfer associate. **Classes:** Most classes have 20–29 students. **Special Study Options:** Accelerated program, cross-registration, dual enrollment, English as a Second Language (ESL), honors program, independent study, internships, My Turn Program for senior citizens. New Start Program for students academically dismissed from 4-year institutions.

ADMISSIONS
Freshman Academic Profile: Minimum paper TOEFL 475. **Basis for Candidate Selection:** *Very important factors considered include:* interview. *Important factors considered include:* application essay. *Other factors considered include:* Class rank, recommendation(s), rigor of secondary school record, standardized test scores, alumni/ae relation, character/personal qualities, extracurricular activities, geographical residence, racial/ethnic status, religious affiliation/commitment, state residency, talent/ability, volunteer work, work experience. **Freshman Admission Requirements:** High school diploma or equivalent is not required. **Freshman Admission Statistics:** 0 applied, % admitted, % enrolled. **Transfer Admission Requirements:** college transcript(s), essay or personal statement, interview, Lowest grade transferable C. **General Admission Information:** Application Fee $35. Nonfall registration accepted.

COSTS AND FINANCIAL AID
Annual in-state tuition $3,610. Annual out-of-state tuition $7,200. Required fees $350. Average book expense. **Required Forms and Deadlines:** FAFSA. **Notification of Awards:** Applicants will be notified of awards on or about 7/1. **Types of Aid:** *Need-based scholarships/grants:* Federal Pell, the school's own gift aid. *Loans:* Direct Subsidized Stafford, Direct Unsubsidized Stafford, Direct PLUS.

CITY UNIVERSITY OF NEW YORK— LEHMAN COLLEGE

250 Bedford Park Boulevard West, Bronx, NY 10468
Phone: 718-960-8000 • **Financial Aid Phone:** 718-960-8545
E-mail: wilkes@alpha.lehman.cuny.edu • **CEEB Code:** 2950
Fax: 718-960-8712

This public school was founded in 1968. It has a 38-acre campus.

RATINGS
Admissions Selectivity Rating: 88   **Fire Safety Rating:** 60*   **Green Rating:** 60*

STUDENTS AND FACULTY
Enrollment: 8,236. **Student Body:** 71% female, 29% male, 1% out-of-state, 5% international (123 countries represented). Asian 4%, African American 32%, Caucasian 10%, Hispanic 49%, Native American 0%.

Retention and Graduation: 77% freshmen return for sophomore year. 12% freshmen graduate within 4 years. 33% freshmen graduate within 6 years. **Faculty:** Student/faculty ratio 15:1. 368 full-time faculty, 75% hold PhDs, 27% are members of minority groups, 52% are women.

ACADEMICS

Degrees: bachelor's, certificate, diploma, master's. **Classes:** Most classes have 20–29 students. **Majors with Highest Enrollment:** nursing/registered nurse (rn, asn, bsn, msn); social work; sociology. **Special Study Options:** Accelerated program, cooperative education program, cross-registration, distance learning, double major, dual enrollment, English as a Second Language (ESL), exchange student program (domestic), honors program, independent study, internships, student-designed major, study abroad, teacher certification program, weekend college, bilingual liberal arts (first 2 years may be taken in Spanish), professional writing concentration, 3-2 engineering program with City College. **Honors Programs:** Lehman Scholars Program. Students receive full tuition, stipends, an expense account to use for academically enriching experiences and a laptop computer. **Combined Degree Programs:** BA/MA. **Disability Services:** Special programs offered to physically disabled students include note-taking services, reader services, tape recorders, tutors.

FACILITIES

Housing: 80% of campus accessible to physically disabled. **Special Academic Facilities/Equipment:** Art gallery, concert hall, sports complex. **Computers:** Students can register for classes online. Administrative functions (other than registration) can be performed online.

CAMPUS LIFE

Environment: Metropolis. **Activities:** Choral groups, concert band, dance, drama/theater, jazz band, literary magazine, music ensembles, musical theater, opera, radio station, student government, student newspaper, student-run film society, symphony orchestra, television station, yearbook, International Student Organization 3 honor societies, 1 religious organizations. 1 fraternities, 1 sororities. **Athletics (Intercollegiate):** *Men:* badminton, baseball, basketball, cross-country, diving, swimming, tennis, track/field (outdoor), volleyball. *Women:* badminton, basketball, cross-country, diving, softball, swimming, tennis, track/field (outdoor), volleyball. **On-Campus Highlights:** APEX athletic facility, Cyber Cafe, Art Gallery, Concert Hall, Information Technology Center.

ADMISSIONS

Freshman Academic Profile: Average high school GPA 2.7. 74% from public high schools. SAT Math middle 50% range 400-500. SAT Critical Reading middle 50% range 400-490. Minimum paper TOEFL 500. **Basis for Candidate Selection:** *Very important factors considered include:* rigor of secondary school record, standardized test scores. *Important factors considered include:* academic GPA. *Other factors considered include:* application essay, recommendation(s), extracurricular activities, interview, talent/ability. **Freshman Admission Requirements:** High school diploma is required and GED is accepted. *Academic units required:* 4 English, 2 mathematics, 2 science, (1 science labs), 2 foreign language, 1 social studies, 1 history. *Academic units recommended:* 4 English, 2 mathematics, 2 science, (1 science labs), 2 foreign language, 1 social studies, 1 history. **Freshman Admission Statistics:** 14,155 applied, 32% admitted, 58% enrolled. **Transfer Admission Requirements:** college transcript(s), minimum college GPA of 2 required. Lowest grade transferable C. **General Admission Information:** Application Fee $65. Regular application deadline 8/15. Nonfall registration accepted. Admission may be deferred for a maximum of 1 semester. Credit offered for CEEB Advanced Placement tests.

COSTS AND FINANCIAL AID

Annual in-state tuition $4,000. Annual out-of-state tuition $10,800. Room and board $0. Required fees $290. Average book expense $938. **Required Forms and Deadlines:** FAFSA, state aid form. **Notification of Awards:** Applicants will be notified of awards on a rolling basis beginning 3/1. **Types of Aid:** *Need-based scholarships/grants:* Federal Pell, SEOG, state scholarships/grants, private scholarships, the school's own gift aid, MARC,NBRS. *Loans:* Direct Subsidized Stafford, Direct Unsubsidized Stafford, Direct PLUS, Federal Perkins, state loans, college/university loans from institutional funds. **Student Employment:** Federal Work-Study Program available. Institutional employment available. Off-campus job opportunities are excellent. **Financial Aid Statistics:** 88% freshmen, 90% undergrads receive need-based scholarship or grant aid. 42% freshmen, 15% undergrads receive non-need-based scholarship or grant aid. 19% freshmen, 44% undergrads receive need-based self-help aid. 83% freshmen, 80% undergrads receive any aid. 34% undergrads borrow to pay for school. Average cumulative indebtedness $11,500. **Criteria for awarding institutional aid:** *Non-need-based:* academics.

CITY UNIVERSITY OF NEW YORK— MEDGAR EVERS COLLEGE

1665 Bedford Avenue, Brooklyn, NY 11225
Phone: 718-270-6024 • **Financial Aid Phone:** 718-270-6139
E-mail: applytomec@mec.cuny.edu
Fax: 718-270-6411

This public school was founded in 1969. It has a 7-acre campus.

RATINGS
Admissions Selectivity Rating: 63   **Fire Safety Rating:** 60*   **Green Rating:** 61

STUDENTS AND FACULTY
Enrollment: 6,582. **Student Body:** 74% female, 26% male, 0% out-of-state, 1% international. Asian 2%, African American 85%, Caucasian 1%, Hispanic 9%, Native American 0%.
Retention and Graduation: 20% freshmen graduate within 6 years. **Faculty:** Student/faculty ratio 19:1. 177 full-time faculty, 59% hold PhDs, 81% are members of minority groups, 47% are women. 0% of classes are taught by teaching assistants.

ACADEMICS
Degrees: associate, bachelor's, certificate. **Classes:** Most classes have 30–39 students. Most lab/discussion sessions have 10–19 students. **Majors with Highest Enrollment:** biology/biological sciences; business administration and management; liberal arts and sciences/liberal studies. **Special Study Options:** cross-registration, distance learning, English as a Second Language (ESL), honors program, independent study, internships, study abroad, teacher certification program. **Disability Services:** Special programs offered to physically disabled students include note-taking services, reader services, tape recorders, tutors. **Career Services:** alumni services, career/job search classes, career assessment, internships Career Services highlights include Career Job Search classes Business Etiquette Series Interviewing Skills.

FACILITIES
Housing: 100% of campus accessible to physically disabled. **Computers:** 90% of classrooms, 100% of libraries, have wireless network access. Students can register for classes online. Administrative functions (other than registration) can be performed online.

CAMPUS LIFE
Environment: Metropolis. **Activities:** Choral groups, dance, drama/theater, jazz band, literary magazine, musical theater, radio station, student government, student newspaper, television station, yearbook, International Student Organization 32 registered organizations, 4 honor societies, 2 religious organizations. **Athletics (Intercollegiate):** *Men:* basketball, cross-country, soccer, swimming, track/field (outdoor), track/field (indoor), volleyball. *Women:* basketball, cheerleading, cross-country, soccer, softball, swimming, tennis, track/field (outdoor), track/field (indoor), volleyball. **On-Campus Highlights:** Amphitheater, NASA Space Center Lab, Library, Departments, New Building.

ADMISSIONS
Freshman Academic Profile: SAT Math middle 50% range 340-440. SAT Critical Reading middle 50% range 350-430. SAT Writing middle 50% range 340-430. Minimum paper TOEFL 475. **Basis for Candidate Selection:** *Other factors considered include:* academic GPA, rigor of secondary school record, standardized test scores. **Freshman Admission Requirements:** High school diploma is required and GED is accepted. **Freshman Admission Statistics:** 8,042 applied, 100% admitted, 15% enrolled. **Transfer Admission Requirements:** college transcript(s), minimum college GPA of 2.0 required. Lowest grade transferable C. **General Admission Information:** Application Fee $65. Nonfall registration accepted. Admission may be deferred for a maximum of one semester.

COSTS AND FINANCIAL AID
Annual in-state tuition $5,130. Annual out-of-state tuition $13,800. Required fees $302. Average book expense $1,179. **Required Forms and Deadlines:** FAFSA, state aid form. **Notification of Awards:** Applicants will be notified of awards on a rolling basis beginning 5/1. **Types of Aid:** *Need-based scholarships/grants:* Federal Pell, SEOG, state scholarships/grants. *Loans:* Direct Subsidized Stafford, Direct Unsubsidized Stafford, Direct PLUS, Federal Perkins. **Student Employment:** Federal Work-Study Program available. Institutional employment available. Highest amount earned per year from on-campus jobs $1,300. Off-campus job opportunities are good. **Financial Aid Statistics:** 18% freshmen, 26% undergrads receive need-based self-help aid. **Criteria for awarding institutional aid:** *Non-need-based:* academics, leadership.

CITY UNIVERSITY OF NEW YORK—NEW YORK CITY COLLEGE OF TECHNOLOGY

300 Jay Street, Brooklyn, NY 11201
Phone: 718-260-5500 • **Financial Aid Phone:** 718-260-5700
E-mail: admissions@citytech.cuny.edu • **CEEB Code:** 2550
Fax: 718-260-5504 • **Website:** www.citytech.cuny.edu/ • **ACT Code:** 2950

This public school was founded in 1946. It has a 3-acre campus.

RATINGS
Admissions Selectivity Rating: 62 **Fire Safety Rating:** 60* **Green Rating:** 74

STUDENTS AND FACULTY
Enrollment: 15,303. **Student Body:** 44% female, 56% male, 1% out-of-state, 5% international (138 countries represented). Asian 16%, African American 34%, Caucasian 14%, Hispanic 29%, Native American 0%. **Retention and Graduation:** 77% freshmen return for sophomore year. **Faculty:** Student/faculty ratio 16:1. 433 full-time faculty, 45% are members of minority groups, 48% are women. 0% of classes are taught by teaching assistants.

ACADEMICS
Degrees: associate, bachelor's, certificate. **Classes:** Most classes have 20–29 students. Most lab/discussion sessions have 20–29 students. **Majors with Highest Enrollment:** computer technology/computer systems technology; hospitality administration/management; human services. **Special Study Options:** distance learning, dual enrollment, English as a Second Language (ESL), honors program, independent study, internships, study abroad, teacher certification program, Bridge programs to higher education or careers in engineering technology, alternate format program for those out of high school 5 years with or without diploma. **Disability Services:** Special programs offered to physically disabled students include note-taking services, reader services, tape recorders, tutors. **Career Services:** career assessment, internships.

FACILITIES
Housing: Some housing avilable at nearby university. 100% of campus accessible to physically disabled. **Computers:** Students can register for classes online. Administrative functions (other than registration) can be performed online.

CAMPUS LIFE
Environment: Metropolis. **Activities:** dance, drama/theater, musical theater, student government, student newspaper 60 registered organizations. **Athletics (Intercollegiate):** Men: basketball, tennis, track/field (outdoor). Women: basketball, tennis, track/field (outdoor). **Environmental Initiatives:** reducing the amount of waste produced by our purchasing and procurement system

ADMISSIONS
Freshman Academic Profile: Minimum web-based TOEFL 61. Minimum paper TOEFL 500. **Basis for Candidate Selection:** *Important factors considered include:* academic GPA, rigor of secondary school record. *Other factors considered include:* Class rank, application essay, recommendation(s), standardized test scores. **Freshman Admission Requirements:** High school diploma is required and GED is accepted. *Academic units required:* 4 English, 3 mathematics, 2 science, (2 science labs), 2 foreign language, 3 social studies, 1 academic electives, 1 Fine Arts. *Academic units recommended:* 4 English, 3 mathematics, 2 science, (2 science labs), 2 foreign language, 3 social studies, 1 academic electives, 1 Fine Arts **Freshman Admission Statistics:** 16,870 applied, 77% admitted, 22% enrolled. **Transfer Admission Requirements:** High school transcript, college transcript(s), statement of good standing from prior institution(s). Minimum college GPA of 2.0 required. Lowest grade transferable C. **General Admission Information:** Application Fee $65. Notification on a rolling basis, beginning on or about 1/15. Nonfall registration accepted. Admission may be deferred for a maximum of 1 semester. Credit and/or placement offered for CEEB Advanced Placement tests.

COSTS AND FINANCIAL AID
Annual in-state tuition $5,430. Annual out-of-state tuition $12,450. Required fees $339. **Required Forms and Deadlines:** FAFSA. **Notification of Awards: Types of Aid:** *Need-based scholarships/grants:* Federal Pell, SEOG, state scholarships/grants, Federal Nursing Scholarships. *Loans:* Direct Subsidized Stafford, Direct Unsubsidized Stafford, Direct PLUS, Federal Perkins. **Student Employment:** Federal Work-Study Program available. Institutional employment available. Off-campus job opportunities are fair. **Financial Aid Statistics:** 96% freshmen, 96% undergrads receive need-based scholarship or grant aid. 86% freshmen, 83% undergrads receive non-need-based scholarship or grant aid. 24% freshmen, 26% undergrads receive need-based self-help aid. **Criteria for awarding institutional aid:** *Non-need-based:* state/district residency.

CITY UNIVERSITY OF NEW YORK— QUEENS COLLEGE

6530 Kissena Blvd, Flushing, NY 11367
Phone: 718-997-5600 • **Financial Aid Phone:** 7189975123
E-mail: vincent.angrisani@qc.cuny.edu • **CEEB Code:** 2750
Fax: 7189975617 • **Website:** www.qc.cuny.edu • **ACT Code:** 20173

This public school was founded in 1937. It has a 76-acre campus.

RATINGS
Admissions Selectivity Rating: 81 **Fire Safety Rating:** 99 **Green Rating:** 92

STUDENTS AND FACULTY
Enrollment: 15,257. **Student Body:** 57% female, 43% male, 1% out-of-state, 5% international (173 countries represented). Asian 24%, African American 8%, Caucasian 46%, Hispanic 18%, Native American 0%. **Retention and Graduation:** 26% freshmen graduate within 4 years. 54% freshmen graduate within 6 years. 35% grads go on to further study within 1 year. 10% grads pursue arts and sciences degrees. 2% grads pursue law degrees. 1% grads pursue business degrees. 1% grads pursue medical degrees. **Faculty:** Student/faculty ratio 16:1. 606 full-time faculty, 89% hold PhDs, 21% are members of minority groups, 44% are women. 1% of classes are taught by teaching assistants.

ACADEMICS
Degrees: bachelor's, master's, post-bachelor's certificate, post-master's certificate. **Classes:** Most classes have 20–29 students. **Majors with Highest Enrollment:** accounting; psychology; sociology. **Special Study Options:** Accelerated program, cross-registration, double major, dual enrollment, English as a Second Language (ESL), honors program, independent study, internships, liberal arts/career combination, student-designed major, study abroad, teacher certification program, weekend college, Courses offered through Blackboard. **Honors Programs:** Queens College participates in the CUNY Honors College - a highly selective program that offers a challenging curriculum and a full tuition scholarship plus other financial support. The program accepts first-time freshmen in the fall semester only. **Combined Degree Programs:** BA/MA. **Disability Services:** Special programs offered to physically disabled students include note-taking services, reader services, tape recorders, tutors. **Career Services:** career/job search classes, career assessment, internships Career Services highlights include Career Fair - over 70 employers from various fields (Accounting, Banking, Finance, Human Services, Publishing, Media, Government, Technology, etc) come to the campus to interview and meet with students.

FACILITIES
Housing: Coed dorms. 100% of campus accessible to physically disabled. **Special Academic Facilities/Equipment:** Godwin-Ternbach Museum, Louis Armstrong House Museum & Archieves, Colden Auditorium, Kupferberg Center for the Performing Arts, Art Library **Computers:** 100% of classrooms, 100% of dorms, 100% of libraries, 100% of dining areas, 100% of student union, 100% of common outdoor areas have wireless network access. Students can register for classes online. Administrative functions (other than registration) can be performed online.

CAMPUS LIFE
Environment: Metropolis. **Activities:** Choral groups, concert band, dance, drama/theater, jazz band, literary magazine, music ensembles, musical theater, radio station, student government, student newspaper, student-run film society, symphony orchestra, television station, yearbook, International Student Organization 114 registered organizations, 5 honor societies, 12 religious organizations. 4 fraternities, 3 sororities. **Athletics (Intercollegiate):** Men: baseball, basketball, cross-country, diving, soccer, swimming, tennis, track/field (outdoor), water polo. Women: basketball, cross-country, diving, fencing, lacrosse, soccer, softball, swimming, tennis, track/field (outdoor), volleyball, water polo. **On-Campus Highlights:** Rosenthal Library, Student Union, Athletic Center, Dining Hall, Classrooms and Laboratory Facilities, Cafes around campus. **Environmental Initiatives:** Student Residence Hall (Summit) LEED Gold Energy audit for all buildings; implementation of recommendations New capital projects will all have energy use reduction as part of plan.

ADMISSIONS

Freshman Academic Profile: SAT Math middle 50% range 540-610. SAT Critical Reading middle 50% range 477-570. SAT Writing middle 50% range 460-570. Minimum web-based TOEFL 62. Minimum paper TOEFL 500. **Basis for Candidate Selection:** *Very important factors considered include:* academic GPA, rigor of secondary school record, standardized test scores. **Freshman Admission Requirements:** High school diploma is required and GED is accepted. *Academic units required:* 4 English, 3 mathematics, 2 science, (2 science labs), 3 foreign language, 4 social studies. *Academic units recommended:* 4 English, 3 mathematics, 2 science, (2 science labs), 3 foreign language, 4 social studies. **Freshman Admission Statistics:** 19,032 applied, 37% admitted, 21% enrolled. **Transfer Admission Requirements:** High school transcript, college transcript(s), standardized test scores, minimum college GPA of 2.25 required. Lowest grade transferable 2. **General Admission Information:** Application Fee $65. Notification on a rolling basis, beginning on or about 1/15. Nonfall registration accepted. Admission may be deferred for a maximum of 1 semester. Credit offered for CEEB Advanced Placement tests.

COSTS AND FINANCIAL AID

Annual in-state tuition $5,430. Annual out-of-state tuition $14,550. Required fees $477. Average book expense $1,248. **Required Forms and Deadlines:** FAFSA, institution's own financial aid form, state aid form. **Notification of Awards:** Applicants will be notified of awards on a rolling basis beginning 3/1. **Types of Aid:** *Need-based scholarships/grants:* Federal Pell, SEOG, state scholarships/grants, private scholarships, the school's own gift aid. *Loans:* Direct Subsidized Stafford, Direct Unsubsidized Stafford, Direct PLUS, Federal Perkins. **Student Employment:** Federal Work-Study Program available. Institutional employment available. Off-campus job opportunities are good. **Financial Aid Statistics:** 79% freshmen, 82% undergrads receive need-based scholarship or grant aid. 38% freshmen, 16% undergrads receive non-need-based scholarship or grant aid. 26% freshmen, 36% undergrads receive need-based self-help aid. 2% freshmen, 1% undergrads receive athletic scholarships. 69% freshmen, 48% undergrads receive any aid. 45% undergrads borrow to pay for school. Average cumulative indebtedness $17,700. **Criteria for awarding institutional aid:** *Non-need-based:* academics, athletics.

CITY UNIVERSITY OF NEW YORK— QUEENSBOROUGH COMMUNITY COLLEGE

222-05 56th Ave, A-210, Queens, NY 11364
Phone: 718-631-6236
E-mail: wyarde@qcc.cuny.edu • **CEEB Code:** 2751
Fax: 718-281-5208

This public school was founded in 1967. It has a 34-acre campus.

RATINGS

Admissions Selectivity Rating: 61   **Fire Safety Rating:** 60*   **Green Rating:** 60*

STUDENTS AND FACULTY

Enrollment: 10,955. **Student Body:** 57% female, 43% male, 1% out-of-state, 12% international (132 countries represented). Asian 18%, African American 25%, Caucasian 24%, Hispanic 21%, Native American 0%.
Faculty: Student/faculty ratio 15:1. 289 full-time faculty. 0% of classes are taught by teaching assistants.

ACADEMICS

Degrees: associate, certificate, terminal associate, transfer associate. **Special Study Options:** cooperative education program, distance learning, double major, dual enrollment, English as a Second Language (ESL), honors program, independent study, internships, liberal arts/career combination, study abroad, weekend college, external education for homebound students, honors program for high school seniors. **Honors Programs:** Honors program that has smaller class size and enriched course material and activities. **Disability Services:** Special programs offered to physically disabled students include note-taking services, reader services, tape recorders, tutors. **Career Services:** alumni services, career/job search classes, career assessment, internships.

FACILITIES

Housing: Coed dorms, special housing for disabled students, men's dorms, special housing for international students, women's dorms, fraternity/sorority housing, apartments for married students, cooperative housing, apartments for single students, 85% of campus accessible to physically disabled. **Special Academic Facilities/Equipment:** Oakland Art Gallery, Performing Arts Center, The Holocaust Center. **Computers:** Students can register for classes online. Administrative functions (other than registration) can be performed online.

CAMPUS LIFE

Environment: Metropolis. **Activities:** 37 registered organizations, 3 honor societies. **Athletics (Intercollegiate):** *Men:* baseball, basketball, cross-country, soccer, swimming, tennis, track/field (indoor), volleyball. *Women:* basketball, cross-country, softball, swimming, tennis, volleyball. **On-Campus Highlights:** Holecaust Resources Center and Archives, Student Union, Instructional Support Services Center, Registration Center, Library.

ADMISSIONS

Freshman Academic Profile: 10% in top 50% of high school class. 80% from public high schools. Minimum paper TOEFL 475. **Basis for Candidate Selection:** *Other factors considered include:* academic GPA, standardized test scores. **Freshman Admission Requirements:** High school diploma is required and GED is accepted. **Freshman Admission Statistics:** 7,471 applied, 99% admitted, 35% enrolled. **Transfer Admission Requirements:** High school transcript, college transcript(s), minimum college GPA of 2.0 required. Lowest grade transferable D. **General Admission Information:** Application Fee $50. Notification on a rolling basis, beginning on or about 12/1. Nonfall registration accepted. Credit offered for CEEB Advanced Placement tests.

COSTS AND FINANCIAL AID

Annual in-state tuition $2,800. Annual out-of-state tuition $4,560. Required fees $284. **Required Forms and Deadlines:** FAFSA, institution's own financial aid form. **Notification of Awards:** Applicants will be notified of awards on a rolling basis beginning 7/15. **Types of Aid:** *Need-based scholarships/grants:* Federal Pell, SEOG, state scholarships/grants, the school's own gift aid. *Loans:* Direct Subsidized Stafford, Direct Unsubsidized Stafford, Direct PLUS. **Student Employment:** Federal Work-Study Program available. Institutional employment available. Off-campus job opportunities are good.

CITY UNIVERSITY OF NEW YORK— YORK COLLEGE

94-20 Guy R Brewer Boulevard, Jamaica, NY 11451
Phone: 718-262-2165
E-mail: admissions@york.cuny.edu • **CEEB Code:** 2992
Fax: 718-262-2601 • **Website:** www.york.cuny.edu • **ACT Code:** 20175

This public school was founded in 1968. It has a 50-acre campus.

RATINGS

Admissions Selectivity Rating: 86   **Fire Safety Rating:** 60*   **Green Rating:** 60*

STUDENTS AND FACULTY

Enrollment: 5,311. **Student Body:** 71% female, 29% male, 0% out-of-state, 7% international (113 countries represented). Asian 8%, African American 44%, Caucasian 4%, Hispanic 14%, Native American 0%.
Retention and Graduation: 77% freshmen return for sophomore year. 9% freshmen graduate within 4 years. 28% freshmen graduate within 6 years.
Faculty: Student/faculty ratio 15:1. 166 full-time faculty, 73% hold PhDs, 39% are members of minority groups, 46% are women. 0% of classes are taught by teaching assistants.

ACADEMICS

Degrees: bachelor's. **Classes: Majors with Highest Enrollment:** accounting; psychology; sociology. **Special Study Options:** cooperative education program, double major, dual enrollment, English as a Second Language (ESL), honors program, independent study, internships, teacher certification program, Co-Op programs: Business, Computer Science, Health Professions. **Disability Services:** Special programs offered to physically disabled students include note-taking services, reader services, tape recorders, tutors. **Career Services:** alumni services, career/job search classes, internships.

FACILITIES

Housing: 100% of campus accessible to physically disabled. **Special Academic Facilities/Equipment:** Center for educational technology. State-of-the-art cardio-pneumo-simulator **Computers:** Students can register for classes online. Administrative functions (other than registration) can be performed online.

CAMPUS LIFE

Environment: Activities: Choral groups, drama/theater, jazz band, literary magazine, student government, student newspaper, student-run film society, television station, yearbook 50 registered organizations, 1 honor societies, 2 religious organizations. **Athletics (Intercollegiate):** *Men:* basketball, cheerleading, cross-country, soccer, swimming, tennis, track/field (outdoor), volleyball. *Women:* basketball, cheerleading, cross-country, softball, swimming, track/field (outdoor), volleyball.

ADMISSIONS

Freshman Academic Profile: 68% from public high schools. SAT Math middle 50% range 390–470. SAT Critical Reading middle 50% range 363–460. Minimum paper TOEFL 470. **Basis for Candidate Selection:** *Very important factors considered include:* rigor of secondary school record, standardized test scores. **Freshman Admission Requirements:** High school diploma is required and GED is accepted. *Academic units required:* 3 English, 2 mathematics, 10 academic electives. *Academic units recommended:* 3 English, 2 mathematics, 10 academic electives. **Freshman Admission Statistics:** 2,389 applied, 31% admitted, 80% enrolled. **Transfer Admission Requirements:** High school transcript, college transcript(s), standardized test scores, minimum college GPA of 2.0 required. Lowest grade transferable C. **General Admission Information:** Application Fee $40. Notification on a rolling basis, beginning on or about 2/16. Nonfall registration accepted. Admission may be deferred for a maximum of 1 semester. Placement offered for CEEB Advanced Placement tests.

COSTS AND FINANCIAL AID

Annual in-state tuition $3,200. Annual out-of-state tuition $6,800. Required fees $242. Average book expense $692. **Required Forms and Deadlines:** FAFSA, state aid form. **Notification of Awards:** Applicants will be notified of awards on a rolling basis beginning 3/1. **Types of Aid:** *Need-based scholarships/grants:* Federal Pell, SEOG, state scholarships/grants, private scholarships. *Loans:* Direct Subsidized Stafford, Direct Unsubsidized Stafford, Direct PLUS, Federal Perkins, college/university loans from institutional funds. **Student Employment:** Federal Work-Study Program available.

CLAFLIN UNIVERSITY

400 Magnolia Street, Orangeburg, SC 29115
Phone: 803-535-5340 • **Financial Aid Phone:** 803-535-5720
E-mail: admissions@claflin.edu • **CEEB Code:** 5109
Fax: 803-535-5387 • **ACT Code:** 3840

This private school, affiliated with the Methodist Church, was founded in 1869. It has a 43-acre campus.

RATINGS
Admissions Selectivity Rating: 76   **Fire Safety Rating:** 77   **Green Rating:** 61

STUDENTS AND FACULTY

Enrollment: 1,850. **Student Body:** 65% female, 35% male, 19% out-of-state, 3% international (15 countries represented). Asian 0%, African American 92%, Caucasian 1%, Hispanic 2%, Native American 0%.
Retention and Graduation: 74% freshmen return for sophomore year. 26% freshmen graduate within 4 years. 44% freshmen graduate within 6 years. **Faculty:** Student/faculty ratio 14:1. 121 full-time faculty, 80% hold PhDs, 56% are members of minority groups, 43% are women.

ACADEMICS

Degrees: bachelor's, master's. **Classes:** Most classes have 20–29 students. Most lab/discussion sessions have 10–19 students. **Majors with Highest Enrollment:** biology/biological sciences; business administration and management; sociology. **Special Study Options:** Accelerated program, cooperative education program, cross-registration, double major, dual enrollment, English as a Second Language (ESL), honors program, independent study, internships, study abroad, teacher certification program, weekend college, (3+2) BS Mathematics(Applied Mathematics Track)/Claflin + BS Engineering/Clemson (3+2) BS Mathematics(Applied Mathematics Track)/Claflin + BS Engineering Technology/South Carolina State University (2+2) Associates Degree/ Orangeburg-Calhoun Technical College + BS Biotechnology/Claflin University. **Honors Programs:** The Alice Carson Tisdale Honors College **Combined Degree Programs:** Dual-degree(2+2) in Biotechnology. **Disability Services:** Special programs offered to physically disabled students include note-taking services. **Career Services:** career/job search classes, career assessment, internships.

FACILITIES

Housing: men's dorms, women's dorms. 90% of campus accessible to physically disabled. **Special Academic Facilities/Equipment:** T.V. studio, NMR Wilbur R. Gregg collection, Aruther Rose Museum. **Computers:** 33% of classrooms, 100% of libraries, 100% of dining areas, have wireless network access. Students can register for classes online. Administrative functions (other than registration) can be performed online.

CAMPUS LIFE

Environment: Village. **Activities:** Choral groups, concert band, dance, drama/theater, jazz band, literary magazine, music ensembles, radio station, student government, student newspaper, student-run film society, television station,

yearbook, International Student Organization 3 honor societies, 4 fraternities, 4 sororities. **Athletics (Intercollegiate):** *Men:* baseball, basketball, cross-country, track/field (outdoor), track/field (indoor). *Women:* basketball, cross-country, softball, track/field (outdoor), track/field (indoor), volleyball. **On-Campus Highlights:** Student Life Center, Computer Labs, SOAR Center, Center for Vocational Reflections, Arthur Rose Museum, 6.JONAS T. KENNEDY HEALTH AND PHYSICAL EDUCATION CENTER.

ADMISSIONS

Freshman Academic Profile: Average high school GPA 3.0. 13% in top 10% of high school class, 31% in top 25% of high school class, 66% in top 50% of high school class. SAT Math middle 50% range 380–510. SAT Critical Reading middle 50% range 380–490. **Basis for Candidate Selection:** *Very important factors considered include:* Class rank, academic GPA, rigor of secondary school record, standardized test scores, character/personal qualities, first generation. *Important factors considered include:* application essay, alumni/ae relation, extracurricular activities, level of applicant's interest, talent/ability. *Other factors considered include:* recommendation(s), state residency, volunteer work, work experience. **Freshman Admission Requirements:** High school diploma is required and GED is accepted. *Academic units required:* 4 English, 3 mathematics, 2 science, (1 science labs), 2 social studies, 1 history, 7 academic electives, 0 social studies unit includes history. *Academic units recommended:* 4 English, 3 mathematics, 2 science, (1 science labs), 2 social studies, 1 history, 7 academic electives, 0 social studies unit includes history **Freshman Admission Statistics:** 4,394 applied, 53% admitted, 19% enrolled. **Transfer Admission Requirements:** college transcript(s), statement of good standing from prior institution(s). Minimum college GPA of 2.0 required. Lowest grade transferable C. **General Admission Information:** Application Fee $20. Regular application deadline 7/15. Notification on a rolling basis, beginning on or about 10/1. Nonfall registration accepted. Admission may be deferred for a maximum of 12. Credit and/or placement offered for CEEB Advanced Placement tests.

COSTS AND FINANCIAL AID

Annual tuition $13,968. Room and board $8,040. Required fees $360. Average book expense $1,500. **Required Forms and Deadlines:** FAFSA, institution's own financial aid form. **Notification of Awards:** Applicants will be notified of awards on a rolling basis beginning 5/15. **Types of Aid:** *Need-based scholarships/grants:* Federal Pell, SEOG, state scholarships/grants, private scholarships, the school's own gift aid, United Negro College Fund. *Loans:* Subsidized Stafford, Unsubsidized Stafford, PLUS, Federal Perkins. **Student Employment:** Federal Work-Study Program available. Institutional employment available. Highest amount earned per year from on-campus jobs $1,600. **Financial Aid Statistics:** 88% freshmen, 95% undergrads receive need-based scholarship or grant aid. 7% freshmen, 6% undergrads receive non-need-based scholarship or grant aid. 75% freshmen receive need-based self-help aid. 90% undergrads borrow to pay for school. Average cumulative indebtedness $31,377.

CLAREMONT MCKENNA COLLEGE

Best 378

888 Columbia Avenue, Claremont, CA 91711
Phone: 909-621-8088 • **Financial Aid Phone:** 909-621-8356
E-mail: admission@cmc.edu • **CEEB Code:** 4054
Fax: 909-621-8516 • **Website:** www.cmc.edu • **ACT Code:** 224

This private school was founded in 1946. It has a 56-acre campus.

RATINGS
Admissions Selectivity Rating: 98   **Fire Safety Rating:** 74   **Green Rating:** 78

STUDENTS AND FACULTY

Enrollment: 1,254. **Student Body:** 48% female, 52% male, 56% out-of-state, 12% international. Asian 11%, African American 3%, Caucasian 45%, Hispanic 9%, Native American 0%.
Retention and Graduation: 95% freshmen return for sophomore year. 87% freshmen graduate within 4 years. **Faculty:** Student/faculty ratio 8:1. 138 full-time faculty, 96% hold PhDs, 17% are members of minority groups, 33% are women. 0% of classes are taught by teaching assistants.

ACADEMICS

Degrees: bachelor's, master's. **Classes:** Most classes have 10–19 students. **Majors with Highest Enrollment:** economics; international relations and affairs; political science and government. **Special Study Options:** cross-registration, double major, English as a Second Language (ESL), exchange student program (domestic), independent study, internships, student-designed major, study abroad. **Combined Degree Programs:** BA/JD, BA/MA, BA/MEng, BA/MBA. **Disability Services:** Special programs offered to physically disabled students include note-taking services, reader services, tape recorders, tutors. **Career Services:** Alumni network, alumni services, career/job search classes, career assessment, internships, regional alumni. Career Services highlights include School sponsored grants to cover political, community service, and international-based internships.

FACILITIES

Housing: Coed dorms, special housing for disabled students, apartments for single students. 95% of campus accessible to physically disabled. **Special Academic Facilities/Equipment:** Art galleries, athenaeum complex, centers for Black and Chicano studies, computer lab, leadership lab, science center. **Computers:** 100% of classrooms, 100% of dorms, 100% of libraries, 100% of dining areas, 100% of student union, 100% of common outdoor areas have wireless network access. Administrative functions (other than registration) can be performed online.

CAMPUS LIFE

Environment: Town. **Activities:** Choral groups, dance, drama/theater, music ensembles, pep band, radio station, student government, student newspaper, symphony orchestra, yearbook, Campus Ministries, International Student Organization, Model UN 280 registered organizations, 7 honor societies, 5 religious organizations. **Athletics (Intercollegiate):** *Men:* baseball, basketball, cross-country, diving, football, golf, soccer, swimming, tennis, track/field (outdoor), water polo. *Women:* basketball, cross-country, diving, golf, lacrosse, soccer, softball, swimming, tennis, track/field (outdoor), volleyball, water polo. **On-Campus Highlights:** Marian Miner Cook Athenaeum, Athletic/Aquatics Center, Emett Student Center/The Hub, The Research Institutes, Keck Science Center, 11 of our 13 dorms. have either been recently built or remodelled. Our newest dorm, Claremont Hall, finished construction last summer and is LEED certified Silver.

ADMISSIONS

Freshman Academic Profile: 63% in top 10% of high school class, 93% in top 25% of high school class, 100% in top 50% of high school class. SAT Math middle 50% range 660-760. SAT Critical Reading middle 50% range 650-750. SAT Writing middle 50% range 660-740. ACT middle 50% range 29-32. Minimum web-based TOEFL 100. Minimum paper TOEFL 600. **Basis for Candidate Selection:** *Very important factors considered include:* rigor of secondary school record, standardized test scores, extracurricular activities. *Important factors considered include:* application essay, recommendation(s). *Other factors considered include:* academic GPA, alumni/ae relation, character/personal qualities, first generation, geographical residence, interview, racial/ethnic status, talent/ability, volunteer work, work experience. **Freshman Admission Requirements:** High school diploma is required and GED is accepted. *Academic units required:* 4 English, 3 mathematics, 2 science, (2 science labs), 3 foreign language, 1 social studies, 1 history. *Academic units recommended:* 4 English, 3 mathematics, 2 science, (2 science labs), 3 foreign language, 1 social studies, 1 history. **Freshman Admission Statistics:** 5,058 applied, 14% admitted, 42% enrolled. **Transfer Admission Requirements:** High school transcript, college transcript(s), essay or personal statement, statement of good standing from prior institution(s). Lowest grade transferable C. **General Admission Information:** Application Fee $60. Early decision application deadline 11/15. Regular application deadline 1/2. Regular notification 4/1. Nonfall registration not accepted. Admission may be deferred for a maximum of 1 year. Credit and/or placement offered for CEEB Advanced Placement tests.

COSTS AND FINANCIAL AID

Required Forms and Deadlines: FAFSA, CSS/Financial Aid PROFILE, noncustodial PROFILE, business/farm supplement. **Notification of Awards:** **Types of Aid:** *Need-based scholarships/grants:* Federal Pell, SEOG, state scholarships/grants, private scholarships, the school's own gift aid, United Negro College Fund. *Loans:* Direct Subsidized Stafford, Direct Unsubsidized Stafford, Direct PLUS, Subsidized Stafford, Unsubsidized Stafford, PLUS, Federal Perkins, college/university loans from institutional funds. **Student Employment:** Federal Work-Study Program available. Institutional employment available. Off-campus job opportunities are excellent. **Financial Aid Statistics:** 100% freshmen, 100% undergrads receive need-based scholarship or grant aid. 11% freshmen, 9% undergrads receive non-need-based scholarship or grant aid. 87% freshmen, 79% undergrads receive need-based self-help aid. 31% undergrads borrow to pay for school. Average cumulative indebtedness $23,179. **Criteria for awarding institutional aid:** *Non-need-based:* academics, leadership.

CLARION UNIVERSITY OF PA

Admissions Office, Clarion, PA 16214
Phone: 814-393-2306 • **Financial Aid Phone:** 814-393-2315
E-mail: admissions@clarion.edu • **CEEB Code:** 2649
Fax: 814-393-2030 • **Website:** www.clarion.edu • **ACT Code:** 3698

This public school was founded in 1867. It has a 192-acre campus.

RATINGS

Admissions Selectivity Rating: 68   **Fire Safety Rating:** 85   **Green Rating:** 73

STUDENTS AND FACULTY

Enrollment: 5,335. **Student Body:** 62% female, 38% male, 5% out-of-state, 1% international (35 countries represented). Asian 0%, African American 6%, Caucasian 88%, Hispanic 1%, Native American 0%.
Retention and Graduation: 70% freshmen return for sophomore year. 29% freshmen graduate within 4 years. **Faculty:** Student/faculty ratio 17:1. 273 full-time faculty, 11% are members of minority groups, 51% are women. 0% of classes are taught by teaching assistants.

ACADEMICS

Degrees: associate, bachelor's, certificate, master's, post-bachelor's certificate, post-master's certificate. **Classes:** Most classes have 20–29 students. Most lab/discussion sessions have 10–19 students. **Majors with Highest Enrollment:** business administration and management; elementary education and teaching. **Special Study Options:** Accelerated program, cooperative education program, distance learning, double major, dual enrollment, honors program, independent study, internships, liberal arts/career combination, student-designed major, study abroad, teacher certification program, weekend college. **Honors Programs:** Clarion University's Honors Program is a close-knit group of talented students preparing for the future. Honors courses satisfy general educational requirements and include field experiences. The 21-credit curriculum promotes development of essential life skills targeted for successful career outcomes. The Honors experience extends beyond the walls of the traditional classroom. Students may spend time with archaeologists in Italy, with anthropologists at a primate center, with large corporate firms and in small businesses, and with molecular biologists in laboratories. Studies have included 20th-century music, learning the art of problem solving, and pondered the ethical implications of research. Co-curricular themes prepare Honors Program students to assume leadership roles. The Honors Program is not for all students--only those individuals who desire professional success, demand academic excellence, and expect to create the future. Each year 50 freshmen are selected for the Honors Program. Courses are taught as special topics and faculty instructors are recruited for their scholarly expertise. Honors students major in every department within the university and receive pre-professional advisement. Students take a six-credit linked English and Speech class and a three-credit Humanities course in the Freshman year. In the sophomore year, students take a three-credit mathematics or science class and a three-credit social sciences course. As juniors, students take a Junior Seminar that culminates in a project prospectus for the capstone experience. Honors 450 is the Senior Presentation delivered in a university-wide presentation. The following program standards must be maintained at the end of each academic year: Freshman Year 3.0 QPA 9 program credits Sophomore Year 3.25 QPA 15 program credits Junior Year 3.4 QPA 18 program credits Senior Year 3.4 QPA 21 program credits To be considered for Honors Program admission, entering freshman must have a minimum SAT score of 1150 or equivalent ACT scores, graduate in the top 15 percent of high school class, and successful completion of an interview. Undergraduate students already enrolled or transfer students may also apply. If a student should fail to residence at Clarion University. Candidates for graduation with an associate degree must complete a minimum of 30 credit hours in residence at the Venango Campus in Oil City, Pennsylvania. maintain the required QPA and course progression, the student will be placed on probation and have one semester to meet the requirements. A student who fails to achieve the required QPA and course progression by the end of the probationary semester will not be allowed to continue in the Honors Program or to continue to receive an Honors scholarship. **Disability Services:** Special programs offered to physically disabled students include note-taking services, reader services, tape recorders, tutors. **Career Services:** career/job search classes, career assessment, internships.

FACILITIES

Housing: Coed dorms, men's dorms, women's dorms, fraternity/sorority housing, apartments for single students, Sororities occupy floors of residence halls. 98% of campus accessible to physically disabled. **Special Academic Facilities/Equipment:** Planetarium. Art Gallery. **Computers:** 40% of classrooms, 100% of libraries, 50% of dining areas, 90% of student union, 10% of common outdoor areas have wireless network access. Students can register for classes online. Administrative functions (other than registration) can be performed online.

CAMPUS LIFE

Environment: Village. **Activities:** Choral groups, concert band, dance, drama/theater, jazz band, literary magazine, marching band, music ensembles, musical theater, pep band, radio station, student government, student newspaper, television station, Campus Ministries, International Student Organization 150 registered organizations, 17 honor societies, 4 religious organizations. 5 fraternities, 8 sororities. **Athletics (Intercollegiate):** *Men:* baseball, basketball, diving, football, golf, swimming, wrestling. *Women:* basketball, cross-country, diving, soccer, softball, swimming, tennis, track/field (outdoor), volleyball. **On-Campus Highlights:** Recreation Center, Carlson Library/Art Gallery, Student Center, Athletic Field, Tippin Gymnasium.

ADMISSIONS

Freshman Academic Profile: Average high school GPA 3.2. 9% in top 10% of high school class, 25% in top 25% of high school class, 16% in top 50% of high school class. 87% from public high schools. SAT Math middle 50% range 440-550. SAT Critical Reading middle 50% range 420-530. SAT Writing middle 50% range 410-510. ACT middle 50% range 17-22. Minimum paper TOEFL 500. **Basis for Candidate Selection:** *Very important factors considered include:* Class rank, academic GPA, rigor of secondary school record, standardized test scores. *Important factors considered include:* application essay, recommendation(s). *Other factors considered include:* character/personal qualities, extracurricular activities, interview, level of applicant's interest, talent/ability, volunteer work, work experience. **Freshman Admission Requirements:** High school diploma is required and GED is accepted. *Academic units required:* 4 English, 3 mathematics, 3 science, 3 social studies, 0 academic electives. *Academic units recommended:* 4 English, 3 mathematics, 3 science, 3 social studies, 0 academic electives. **Freshman Admission Statistics:** 3,408 applied, 77% admitted, 43% enrolled. **Transfer Admission Requirements:** High school transcript, college transcript(s), statement of good standing from prior institution(s). Minimum college GPA of 2.0 required. Lowest grade transferable C. **General Admission Information:** Notification on a rolling basis, beginning on or about 9/1. Nonfall registration accepted. Credit offered for CEEB Advanced Placement tests.

COSTS AND FINANCIAL AID

Annual in-state tuition $5,554. Annual out-of-state tuition $11,108. Room and board $6,390. Required fees $1,826. Average book expense $900. **Required Forms and Deadlines:** FAFSA. **Notification of Awards:** Applicants will be notified of awards on a rolling basis beginning 3/1. **Types of Aid:** *Need-based scholarships/grants.* Federal Pell, SEOG, state scholarships/grants, private scholarships, the school's own gift aid, United Negro College Fund, Federal Nursing Scholarships. *Loans:* Direct Subsidized Stafford, Direct Unsubsidized Stafford, Direct PLUS, PLUS. **Student Employment:** Federal Work-Study Program available. Institutional employment available. Highest amount earned per year from on-campus jobs $12,000. Off-campus job opportunities are fair. **Financial Aid Statistics:** 79% freshmen, 74% undergrads receive need-based scholarship or grant aid. 32% freshmen, 24% undergrads receive non-need-based scholarship or grant aid. 95% freshmen, 95% undergrads receive need-based self-help aid. 1% freshmen, 1% undergrads receive athletic scholarships. 78% freshmen, 75% undergrads receive any aid. 81% undergrads borrow to pay for school. Average cumulative indebtedness $29,410. **Criteria for awarding institutional aid:** *Non-need-based:* academics, art, athletics, leadership, minority status, music/drama, state/district residency.

CLARK ATLANTA UNIVERSITY

223 James P. Brawley Dr., SW, Atlanta, GA 30314-4391
Phone: 404-880-8784 • **Financial Aid Phone:** 404-880-8992
E-mail: cauadmissions@cau.edu • **CEEB Code:** 5110
Fax: 404-880-6605 • **Website:** www.cau.edu • **ACT Code:** 804

This private school, affiliated with the Methodist Church, was founded in 1988. It has a 126-acre campus.

RATINGS

Admissions Selectivity Rating: 69   **Fire Safety Rating:** 94   **Green Rating:** 74

STUDENTS AND FACULTY

Enrollment: 2,632. **Student Body:** 75% female, 25% male, 63% out-of-state, 1% international (10 countries represented). Asian 0%, African American 90%, Caucasian 0%, Hispanic 0%, Native American 0%.
Retention and Graduation: 61% freshmen return for sophomore year. 24% freshmen graduate within 4 years. 39% freshmen graduate within 6 years. 26% grads go on to further study within 1 year, 19% grads pursue arts and sciences degrees. 1% grads pursue law degrees. 3% grads pursue business degrees. 1% grads pursue medical degrees. **Faculty:** Student/faculty ratio 15:1. 170 full-time

faculty, 79% hold PhDs, 89% are members of minority groups, 42% are women. 0% of classes are taught by teaching assistants.

ACADEMICS

Degrees: bachelor's, master's, post-bachelor's certificate, post-master's certificate. **Classes:** Most classes have 20–29 students. Most lab/discussion sessions have fewer than 10 students. **Majors with Highest Enrollment:** biology/biological sciences; business administration and management; radio, television, and digital communication, other. **Special Study Options:** Accelerated program, cooperative education program, cross-registration, double major, dual enrollment, exchange student program (domestic), honors program, independent study, internships, study abroad, teacher certification program, weekend college. **Combined Degree Programs:** BA/MA, BA/MEng. **Disability Services:** Special programs offered to physically disabled students include note-taking services, reader services, tape recorders, tutors. **Career Services:** career/job search classes, career assessment, internships.

FACILITIES

Housing: Coed dorms, men's dorms, women's dorms, apartments for single students. 80% of campus accessible to physically disabled. **Computers:** 100% of classrooms, 5% of dorms, 100% of libraries, 100% of dining areas, 100% of student union, 80% of common outdoor areas have wireless network access. Students can register for classes online. Administrative functions (other than registration) can be performed online.

CAMPUS LIFE

Environment: Metropolis. **Activities:** Choral groups, concert band, dance, drama/theater, marching band, music ensembles, musical theater, opera, pep band, radio station, student government, student newspaper, student-run film society, symphony orchestra, television station, yearbook, Campus Ministries, International Student Organization 80 registered organizations, 12 honor societies, 5 religious organizations. 4 fraternities, 4 sororities. **Athletics (Intercollegiate):** *Men:* baseball, basketball, cross-country, football, track/field (outdoor). *Women:* basketball, cross-country, softball, tennis, track/field (outdoor), volleyball. **On-Campus Highlights:** Robert W. Woodruff Library, CAU Radio & Television Station, CAU Art Galleries, Heritage Commons Residence Hall, Henderson Student Center.

ADMISSIONS

Freshman Academic Profile: Average high school GPA 3.1. 11% in top 10% of high school class, 29% in top 25% of high school class, 68% in top 50% of high school class. 90% from public high schools. SAT Math middle 50% range 400-470. SAT Critical Reading middle 50% range 410-480. ACT middle 50% range 17-21. Minimum paper TOEFL 500. **Basis for Candidate Selection:** *Very important factors considered include:* academic GPA, rigor of secondary school record, standardized test scores, character/personal qualities. *Important factors considered include:* application essay, recommendation(s), talent/ability. *Other factors considered include:* alumni/ae relation, level of applicant's interest, work experience. **Freshman Admission Requirements:** High school diploma is required and GED is accepted. *Academic units required:* 4 English, 3 mathematics, 3 science, (1 science labs), 2 foreign language, 3 social studies, 3 academic electives. *Academic units recommended:* 4 English, 3 mathematics, 3 science, (1 science labs), 2 foreign language, 3 social studies, 3 academic electives. **Freshman Admission Statistics:** 5,801 applied, 69% admitted, 16% enrolled. **Transfer Admission Requirements:** college transcript(s), statement of good standing from prior institution(s). Minimum college GPA of 2.5 required. Lowest grade transferable C. **General Admission Information:** Application Fee $35. Regular application deadline 6/1. Notification on a rolling basis, beginning on or about 1/1. Nonfall registration accepted. Admission may be deferred for a maximum of One Year. Credit and/or placement offered for CEEB Advanced Placement tests.

COSTS AND FINANCIAL AID

Annual tuition $19,012. Room and board $8,906. Required fees $818. Average book expense $2,000. **Required Forms and Deadlines:** FAFSA, state aid form. **Notification of Awards:** Applicants will be notified of awards on a rolling basis beginning 4/1. **Types of Aid:** *Need-based scholarships/grants:* Federal Pell, SEOG, state scholarships/grants, private scholarships, the school's own gift aid, United Negro College Fund. *Loans:* Subsidized Stafford, Unsubsidized Stafford, PLUS, Federal Perkins, state loans, Private Loans. **Student Employment:** Federal Work-Study Program available. Institutional employment available. Highest amount earned per year from on-campus jobs $8,500. Off-campus job opportunities are fair. **Financial Aid Statistics:** 87% freshmen, 88% undergrads receive need-based scholarship or grant aid. 24% freshmen, 19% undergrads receive non-need-based scholarship or grant aid. 92% freshmen, 95% undergrads receive need-based self-help aid. 95% freshmen, 95% undergrads receive any aid. 93% undergrads borrow to pay for school. Average cumulative indebtedness $43,727. **Criteria for awarding institutional aid:** *Non-need-based:* academics, art, athletics, leadership, minority status, music/drama, religious affiliation, state/district residency.

CLARK UNIVERSITY

Best 378

950 Main Street, Worcester, MA 01610-1477
Phone: 508-793-7431 • **Financial Aid Phone:** 508-793-7478
E-mail: admissions@clarku.edu • **CEEB Code:** 3279
Fax: 508-793-8821 • **Website:** www.clarku.edu • **ACT Code:** 1808

This private school was founded in 1887. It has a 50-acre campus.

RATINGS
Admissions Selectivity Rating: 86   **Fire Safety Rating:** 94   **Green Rating:** 85

STUDENTS AND FACULTY
Enrollment: 2,240. **Student Body:** 58% female, 42% male, 59% out-of-state, 9% international (104 countries represented). Asian 5%, African American 4%, Caucasian 69%, Hispanic 6%, Native American 0%.
Retention and Graduation: 87% freshmen return for sophomore year. 76% freshmen graduate within 4 years. 80% freshmen graduate within 6 years. 55% grads go on to further study within 1 year. 25% grads pursue arts and sciences degrees. 2% grads pursue law degrees. 7% grads pursue business degrees. 1% grads pursue medical degrees. **Faculty:** Student/faculty ratio 10:1. 197 full-time faculty, 96% hold PhDs, 20% are members of minority groups, 46% are women. 0% of classes are taught by teaching assistants.

ACADEMICS
Degrees: bachelor's, master's, post-bachelor's certificate, post-master's certificate. **Classes:** Most classes have 10–19 students. Most lab/discussion sessions have 10–19 students. **Majors with Highest Enrollment:** biology/biological sciences; political science and government; psychology. **Special Study Options:** cross-registration, double major, English as a Second Language (ESL), independent study, internships, liberal arts/career combination, student-designed major, study abroad, teacher certification program. **Combined Degree Programs:** BA/MA, BA/MA BAMAT BA/MBA BA/MSF BA/MSPC. **Disability Services:** Special programs offered to physically disabled students include note-taking services, tutors. **Career Services:** Alumni network, alumni services, career/job search classes, career assessment, internships, regional alumni.

FACILITIES
Housing: Coed dorms, special housing for disabled students, women's dorms, apartments for single students, wellness housing. 95% of campus accessible to physically disabled. **Special Academic Facilities/Equipment:** Galleries, theatres, Robert H. Goddard historical exhibition, rare book room, craft center, music center, map library, arboretum, herbarium, extensive darkroom facilities, satellite dish for international program reception, electron microscope, nuclear magnetic resonance spectrometer. **Computers:** 100% of classrooms, 15% of dorms, 100% of libraries, 100% of dining areas, 100% of student union, 15% of common outdoor areas have wireless network access. Students can register for classes online. Administrative functions (other than registration) can be performed online.

CAMPUS LIFE
Environment: City. **Activities:** Choral groups, concert band, dance, drama/theater, jazz band, literary magazine, marching band, music ensembles, musical theater, pep band, radio station, student government, student newspaper, student-run film society, symphony orchestra, television station, yearbook, Campus Ministries, International Student Organization, Model UN 110 registered organizations, 10 honor societies, 7 religious organizations. **Athletics (Intercollegiate):** *Men:* baseball, basketball, crew/rowing, cross-country, diving, lacrosse, soccer, swimming, tennis. *Women:* basketball, crew/rowing, cross-country, diving, field hockey, soccer, softball, swimming, tennis, volleyball. **On-Campus Highlights:** Larger than life statue of Freud, Rare book room, Goddard Library, Traina Center for the Arts, New: Dolan Field House and updated fields, The Green on a warm spring day. **Environmental Initiatives:** Becoming Climate Neutral Clark University has operated an on-campus cogeneration facility since 1982 Clark University Sustainability Task Force

ADMISSIONS
Freshman Academic Profile: Average high school GPA 3.5. 30% in top 10% of high school class, 73% in top 25% of high school class, 95% in top 50% of high school class. 75% from public high schools. SAT Math middle 50% range 540-650. SAT Critical Reading middle 50% range 540-660. SAT Writing middle 50% range 540-650. ACT middle 50% range 23-29. Minimum paper TOEFL 550. **Basis for Candidate Selection:** *Very important factors considered include:* academic GPA, recommendation(s), rigor of secondary school record, standardized test scores, character/personal qualities. *Important factors consid-*

ered include: application essay, extracurricular activities, talent/ability, volunteer work. *Other factors considered include:* Class rank, alumni/ae relation, first generation, geographical residence, interview, level of applicant's interest, racial/ethnic status, work experience. **Freshman Admission Requirements:** High school diploma is required and GED is accepted. **Freshman Admission Statistics:** 4,127 applied, 68% admitted, 19% enrolled. **Transfer Admission Requirements:** High school transcript, college transcript(s), essay or personal statement, standardized test scores, statement of good standing from prior institution(s). Minimum college GPA of 2.8 required. **General Admission Information:** Application Fee $55. Early decision application deadline 11/15. Regular application deadline 1/15. Regular notification 4/1. Nonfall registration accepted. Admission may be deferred for a maximum of 1 year. Credit and/or placement offered for CEEB Advanced Placement tests.

COSTS AND FINANCIAL AID
Annual tuition $38,100. Room and board $7,320. Required fees $350. Average book expense $800. **Required Forms and Deadlines:** FAFSA, CSS/Financial Aid PROFILE, noncustodial PROFILE. **Notification of Awards:** Applicants will be notified of awards on or about 3/31. **Types of Aid:** *Need-based scholarships/grants:* Federal Pell, SEOG, state scholarships/grants, the school's own gift aid. *Loans:* Direct Subsidized Stafford, Direct Unsubsidized Stafford, Direct PLUS, Federal Perkins, state loans. **Student Employment:** Federal Work-Study Program available. Institutional employment available. Highest amount earned per year from on-campus jobs $2,500. Off-campus job opportunities are good. **Financial Aid Statistics:** 99% freshmen, 99% undergrads receive need-based scholarship or grant aid. 36% freshmen, 36% undergrads receive non-need-based scholarship or grant aid. 88% freshmen, 87% undergrads receive need-based self-help aid. 94% freshmen, 89% undergrads receive any aid. 92% undergrads borrow to pay for school. Average cumulative indebtedness $27,600. **Criteria for awarding institutional aid:** *Non-need-based:* academics, leadership.

CLARKE COLLEGE

1550 Clarke Drive, Dubuque, IA 52001-3198
Phone: 563-588-6316
E-mail: admissions@clarke.edu • **CEEB Code:** 6099
Fax: 563-588-6789 • **Website:** www.clarke.edu • **ACT Code:** 1290

This private school, affiliated with the Roman Catholic Church, was founded in 1843. It has a 55-acre campus.

RATINGS
Admissions Selectivity Rating: 71   **Fire Safety Rating:** 60*   **Green Rating:** 60*

STUDENTS AND FACULTY
Enrollment: 958. **Student Body:** 67% female, 33% male, 39% out-of-state, 1% international (8 countries represented). Asian 1%, African American 3%, Caucasian 92%, Hispanic 2%, Native American 0%.
Retention and Graduation: 81% freshmen return for sophomore year. 49% freshmen graduate within 4 years. 63% freshmen graduate within 6 years. 25% grads go on to further study within 1 year. 23% grads pursue arts and sciences degrees. 2% grads pursue business degrees. **Faculty:** Student/faculty ratio 10:1. 84 full-time faculty, 65% hold PhDs, 1% are members of minority groups, 68% are women. 0% of classes are taught by teaching assistants.

ACADEMICS
Degrees: associate, bachelor's, master's, terminal associate. **Classes:** Most classes have fewer than 10 students. Most lab/discussion sessions have fewer than 10 students. **Majors with Highest Enrollment:** business/commerce; nursing/registered nurse (rn, asn, bsn, msn); psychology. **Special Study Options:** Accelerated program, cross-registration, distance learning, double major, honors program, independent study, internships, student-designed major, study abroad, teacher certification program. **Combined Degree Programs:** BS/MS in Physical Therapy. **Disability Services:** Special programs offered to physically disabled students include note-taking services, reader services, tape recorders, tutors. **Career Services:** alumni services, career/job search classes, career assessment, internships.

FACILITIES
Housing: Coed dorms, men's dorms, women's dorms, apartments for single students. 90% of campus accessible to physically disabled. **Special Academic Facilities/Equipment:** Art gallery, computer classrooms for math, biology, and computer science, computer-interfaced chemistry lab, human gross anatomy and nursing labs, electron microscope, music performance hall, foreign language lab, distance learning classroom **Computers:** Students can register for classes online. Administrative functions (other than registration) can be performed online.

CAMPUS LIFE

Environment: Town. **Activities:** Choral groups, concert band, dance, drama/theater, jazz band, literary magazine, music ensembles, musical theater, radio station, student government, student newspaper, yearbook 48 registered organizations, 5 honor societies, 1 religious organizations. **Athletics (Intercollegiate):** *Men:* baseball, basketball, cheerleading, cross-country, golf, soccer, tennis, volleyball. *Women:* basketball, cheerleading, cross-country, golf, soccer, softball, tennis, volleyball.

ADMISSIONS

Freshman Academic Profile: Average high school GPA 3.5. 23% in top 10% of high school class, 45% in top 25% of high school class, 82% in top 50% of high school class. 81% from public high schools. ACT middle 50% range 20-25. Minimum paper TOEFL 527. **Basis for Candidate Selection:** *Very important factors considered include:* academic GPA, rigor of secondary school record, standardized test scores, talent/ability. *Important factors considered include:* Class rank. *Other factors considered include:* extracurricular activities, interview, racial/ethnic status, volunteer work. **Freshman Admission Requirements:** High school diploma is required and GED is accepted. *Academic units required:* 4 English, 3 mathematics, 3 science, (2 science labs), 2 foreign language, 2 social studies, 4 academic electives. *Academic units recommended:* 4 English, 3 mathematics, 3 science, (2 science labs), 2 foreign language, 2 social studies, 4 academic electives. **Freshman Admission Statistics:** 1,034 applied, 74% admitted, 20% enrolled. **Transfer Admission Requirements:** High school transcript, college transcript(s), standardized test scores, statement of good standing from prior institution(s). Minimum college GPA of 2.0 required. Lowest grade transferable C. **General Admission Information:** Application Fee $25. Notification on a rolling basis, beginning on or about 1/15. Nonfall registration accepted. Admission may be deferred for a maximum of 12 months. Credit and/or placement offered for CEEB Advanced Placement tests.

COSTS AND FINANCIAL AID

Annual tuition $26,100. Room and board $8,140. Required fees $850. Average book expense $1,040. **Required Forms and Deadlines:** verification worksheets, if required. **Notification of Awards:** Applicants will be notified of awards on a rolling basis beginning 3/1. **Types of Aid:** *Need-based scholarships/grants:* Federal Pell, SEOG, state scholarships/grants, private scholarships, the school's own gift aid. *Loans:* Subsidized Stafford, Unsubsidized Stafford, PLUS, Federal Perkins, Federal Nursing, state loans, college/university loans from institutional funds, alternative and private loans. **Student Employment:** Federal Work-Study Program available. Institutional employment available. Highest amount earned per year from on-campus jobs $1,422. Off-campus job opportunities are excellent. **Financial Aid Statistics:** 99% freshmen, 99% undergrads receive need-based scholarship or grant aid. 99% freshmen, 92% undergrads receive non-need-based scholarship or grant aid. 88% freshmen, 88% undergrads receive need-based self-help aid. 44% freshmen, 31% undergrads receive athletic scholarships. 87% undergrads borrow to pay for school. Average cumulative indebtedness $29,126. **Criteria for awarding institutional aid:** *Non-need-based:* academics, alumni affiliation, art, athletics, leadership, minority status, music/drama, religious affiliation, state/district residency.

CLARKSON UNIVERSITY

Holcroft House, Potsdam, NY 13699
Phone: 315-268-6480 • **Financial Aid Phone:** 315-268-6480
E-mail: admission@clarkson.edu • **CEEB Code:** 2084
Fax: 315-268-7647 • **Website:** www.clarkson.edu • **ACT Code:**

This private school was founded in 1896. It has a 640-acre campus.

RATINGS

Admissions Selectivity Rating: 83   **Fire Safety Rating:** 92   **Green Rating:** 88

STUDENTS AND FACULTY

Enrollment: 3,014. **Student Body:** 28% female, 72% male, 26% out-of-state, 3% international (49 countries represented). Asian 3%, African American 3%, Caucasian 84%, Hispanic 4%, Native American 0%.
Retention and Graduation: 56% freshmen graduate within 4 years. 72% freshmen graduate within 6 years. 24% grads go on to further study within 1 year. 3% grads pursue arts and sciences degrees. 1% grads pursue law degrees. 3% grads pursue business degrees. 2% grads pursue medical degrees. **Faculty:** Student/faculty ratio 15:1. 220 full-time faculty, 87% hold PhDs, 21% are members of minority groups, 26% are women. 0% of classes are taught by teaching assistants.

ACADEMICS

Degrees: bachelor's, master's. **Classes:** Most classes have 10–19 students. Most lab/discussion sessions have 20–29 students. **Majors with Highest Enrollment:** business/commerce; civil engineering; mechanical engineering. **Special Study Options:** Accelerated program, cooperative education program, cross-registration, distance learning, double major, dual enrollment, English as a Second Language (ESL), honors program, independent study, liberal arts/career combination, student-designed major, study abroad, Women In Science and Engineering (WISE) Living/Learning Community; interdisciplinary degree programs that combine Engineering and Business, Business and Liberal Arts, and Environmental Science and Policy; a large number of 3+2 and 2+2 articulation agreements that facilitate transfer to Clarkson from community colleges and other baccalaureate institutions; business students experience a unique introduction to entrepreneurship through working with the Shipley Center for Innovation, the Clarkson Entrepreneurs Organization (CEO) and the Clarkson Center for Global Competitiveness. **Honors Programs:** Built upon current and emerging problems in science, technology and society, the Clarkson University Honors Program offers unique academic challenges and opportunities for Clarkson's most promising students. The program is a gateway to a multitude of opportunities that include internships, research experience, fellowships, graduate schools, study abroad, and jobs. **Combined Degree Programs:** Business/Liberal Studies. **Disability Services:** Special programs offered to physically disabled students include note-taking services, reader services, tape recorders, tutors. **Career Services:** Alumni network, alumni services, career/job search classes, career assessment, internships, regional alumni. Career Services highlights include The Clarkson University School of Business requires that all students complete an internship as part of their degree requirements. The commitment form the University to coordinate and facilitate placement of all students has resulted in tremendous placement outcomes a well as increased experiential application in the classroom.

FACILITIES

Housing: Coed dorms, special housing for disabled students, men's dorms, special housing for international students, women's dorms, fraternity/sorority housing, apartments for single students, wellness housing, theme housing. 85% of campus accessible to physically disabled. **Special Academic Facilities/Equipment:** The Center for Advanced Materials Processing (CAMP) is dedicated to developing innovations in advanced materials processing and to transfer this technology to business and industry, and is built on Clarkson's recognized expertise in colloid and surface science and fine particle technology. The Center for the Environment facilitates the development, promotion and operation of environmental activities within the University and among its partners. The Center for Rehabilitative Science and Technology (CREST). **Computers:** 100% of classrooms, 100% of libraries, 100% of dining areas, 100% of student union, 20% of common outdoor areas have wireless network access. Students can register for classes online. Administrative functions (other than registration) can be performed online.

CAMPUS LIFE

Environment: Village. **Activities:** Choral groups, drama/theater, jazz band, literary magazine, musical theater, pep band, radio station, student government, student newspaper, symphony orchestra, television station, yearbook, International Student Organization 117 registered organizations, 7 honor societies, 3 religious organizations. 11 fraternities, 3 sororities. **Athletics (Intercollegiate):** *Men:* baseball, basketball, cross-country, diving, golf, ice hockey, lacrosse, skiing (downhill/alpine), skiingnordiccross-country, soccer, swimming. *Women:* basketball, cross-country, diving, ice hockey, lacrosse, skiing (downhill/alpine), skiing(cross-country), soccer, swimming, volleyball. **On-Campus Highlights:** Snell Hall Shipley Center for Innovation, Adirondack Lodge, Cheel Campus Center Club 99, CAMP Building SPEED Labs, Java City/Library, Fitness Center. **Environmental Initiatives:** All new construction is designed to meet at least Silver LEED certification. Significant heat and lighting upgrades are included in all renovations. Clarkson offers a wide breadth of environmentally-related academic majors and minors. Recent introductions include an Environmental MBA and a Master's of Science in Environmental Policy & Governance. Clarkson's mission, vision and values statements were recently revised to weave sustainability philosophies throughout (internal approval is complete, pending Board of Trustee confirmation).

ADMISSIONS

Freshman Academic Profile: Average high school GPA 3.6. 38% in top 10% of high school class, 74% in top 25% of high school class, 93% in top 50% of high school class. 85% from public high schools. SAT Math middle 50% range 560-660. SAT Critical Reading middle 50% range 500-610. SAT Writing middle 50% range 480-590. ACT middle 50% range 23-28. Minimum web-based TOEFL 80. Minimum paper TOEFL 550. **Basis for Candidate Selection:** *Very important factors considered include:* academic GPA, rigor of secondary school record. *Important factors considered include:* Class rank, recommendation(s), standardized test scores, extracurricular activities, volunteer work. *Other factors considered include:* application essay, alumni/ae relation, character/personal qualities, first generation, level of applicant's interest, talent/ability, work experience. **Freshman Admission Requirements:** High school diploma is required and GED is accepted. *Academic units required:* 4 English, 3 mathematics, 3 science. *Academic units recommended:* 4 English, 3 mathematics, 3 science. **Freshman Admission Statistics:** 4,199 applied, 76% admitted, 24% enrolled. **Transfer Admission Requirements:** college transcript(s), minimum college GPA of 2.75 required. Lowest grade transferable 2. **General Admission Information:** Application Fee $50. Early decision application deadline 12/1. Regular application deadline 1/15. Notification on a rolling basis, beginning on or about 2/1. Nonfall registration accepted. Admission may be deferred for a maximum of 12 months. Credit offered for CEEB Advanced Placement tests.

COSTS AND FINANCIAL AID
Annual tuition $37,770. Room and board $12,794. Required fees $840. Average book expense $1,322. **Required Forms and Deadlines:** FAFSA, state aid form. **Notification of Awards:** Applicants will be notified of awards on a rolling basis beginning 3/19. **Types of Aid:** *Need-based scholarships/grants:* Federal Pell, SEOG, state scholarships/grants, private scholarships, the school's own gift aid, HEOP. *Loans:* Direct Subsidized Stafford, Direct Unsubsidized Stafford, Direct PLUS, Subsidized Stafford, Unsubsidized Stafford, PLUS, Federal Perkins, college/university loans from institutional funds, Private/alternative loans. **Student Employment:** Federal Work-Study Program available. Institutional employment available. Off-campus job opportunities are excellent. **Financial Aid Statistics:** 99% freshmen, 99% undergrads receive need-based scholarship or grant aid. 11% freshmen, 10% undergrads receive non-need-based scholarship or grant aid. 88% freshmen, 87% undergrads receive need-based self-help aid. 2% freshmen, 1% undergrads receive athletic scholarships. 98% freshmen, 98% undergrads receive any aid. 80% undergrads borrow to pay for school. Average cumulative indebtedness $27,866. **Criteria for awarding institutional aid:** *Non-need-based:* academics, alumni affiliation, leadership, minority status.

CLAYTON COLLEGE & STATE UNIVERSITY

2000 Clayton State Blvd., Morrow, GA 30206-0285
Phone: 678-466-4115
E-mail: ccsu-info@mail.clayton.edu
Fax: 678-466-4149 • **Website:** www.clayton.edu

This is a public school.

RATINGS
Admissions Selectivity Rating: 72   **Fire Safety Rating:** 60*   **Green Rating:** 60*

STUDENTS AND FACULTY
Enrollment: 5,661. **Student Body:** 69% female, 31% male, 5% out-of-state, 2% international. Asian 4%, African American 48%, Caucasian 43%, Hispanic 3%, Native American 1%.
Retention and Graduation: 61% freshmen return for sophomore year. **Faculty:** Student/faculty ratio 28:1. 157 full-time faculty, 57% hold PhDs, 15% are members of minority groups, 59% are women.

ACADEMICS
Degrees: associate, bachelor's, certificate, master's, terminal associate, transfer associate. **Classes:** Most classes have 20–29 students. Most lab/discussion sessions have fewer than 10 students. **Special Study Options:** cooperative education program, cross-registration, distance learning, double major, dual enrollment, exchange student program (domestic), honors program, independent study, internships, liberal arts/career combination, study abroad, teacher certification program.

FACILITIES
Housing: apartments for single studentsLocal Private Apartment Living. **Computers:**

CAMPUS LIFE
Environment: Activities: Choral groups, drama/theater, jazz band, literary magazine, music ensembles, musical theater, opera, pep band, student government, student newspaper.

ADMISSIONS
Freshman Academic Profile: Average high school GPA 2.9. SAT Math middle 50% range 440-550. SAT Critical Reading middle 50% range 450-550. ACT middle 50% range 17-21. **Basis for Candidate Selection:** *Very important factors considered include:* academic GPA, rigor of secondary school record, standardized test scores. *Other factors considered include:* Class rank, extracurricular activities, talent/ability. **Freshman Admission Requirements:** High school diploma is required and GED is not accepted. *Academic units required:* 4 English, 4 mathematics, 3 science, 2 foreign language, 3 social studies. *Academic units recommended:* 4 English, 4 mathematics, 3 science, 2 foreign

language, 3 social studies. **Freshman Admission Statistics:** 2,920 applied, 71% admitted, 63% enrolled. **Transfer Admission Requirements:** college transcript(s), statement of good standing from prior institution(s). Minimum college GPA of 2.0 required. Lowest grade transferable D. **General Admission Information:** Application Fee $40. Regular application deadline 7/1. Notification on a rolling basis, beginning on or about 1/1. Nonfall registration accepted.

COSTS AND FINANCIAL AID
Annual in-state tuition $2,212. Annual out-of-state tuition $8,848. Average book expense $1,000. **Required Forms and Deadlines:** FAFSA, state aid form. **Notification of Awards: Types of Aid:** *Need-based scholarships/grants:* Federal Pell, SEOG, state scholarships/grants, private scholarships, the school's own gift aid, Federal Nursing Scholarships. *Loans:* Subsidized Stafford, Unsubsidized Stafford, PLUS, state loans. **Student Employment: Financial Aid Statistics:** 65% freshmen, 67% undergrads receive need-based scholarship or grant aid. 76% freshmen, 45% undergrads receive non-need-based scholarship or grant aid. 45% freshmen, 64% undergrads receive need-based self-help aid. 1% freshmen, 3% undergrads receive athletic scholarships. **Criteria for awarding institutional aid:** *Non-need-based:* academics.

CLEAR CREEK BAPTIST BIBLE COLLEGE

300 Clear Creek Road, Pineville, KY 40977-9754
Phone: 606-337-3196 • **Financial Aid Phone:** 606-337-1457
E-mail: ccbbc@ccbbc.edu
Fax: 606-337-2372 • **Website:** www.ccbbc.edu

This private school, affiliated with the Southern Baptist Church, was founded in 1926. It has a 700-acre campus.

RATINGS
Admissions Selectivity Rating: 61   **Fire Safety Rating:** 64   **Green Rating:** 60*

STUDENTS AND FACULTY
Enrollment: 160. **Student Body:** 22% female, 78% male, 60% out-of-state, 0% international (0 countries represented). Asian 1%, African American 1%, Caucasian 103%, Hispanic 3%, Native American 0%.
Retention and Graduation: 93% freshmen return for sophomore year. 25% freshmen graduate within 4 years. 30% grads go on to further study within 1 year. **Faculty:** Student/faculty ratio 10:1. 6 full-time faculty, 83% hold PhDs, 0% are members of minority groups, 0% are women.

ACADEMICS
Degrees: associate, bachelor's, certificate, diploma. **Classes:** Most classes have 10–19 students. Most lab/discussion sessions have 10–19 students. **Majors with Highest Enrollment:** bible/biblical studies. **Special Study Options:** distance learning, double major, independent study, internships. **Career Services:** Alumni network

FACILITIES
Housing: men's dorms, women's dorms, apartments for married students, apartments for single students, wellness housing. 95% of campus accessible to physically disabled. **Special Academic Facilities/Equipment:** Jerusalem model **Computers:** 10% of dorms, 100% of libraries, 5% of common outdoor areas have wireless network access. Students can register for classes online.

CAMPUS LIFE
Environment: Rural. **Activities:** Choral groups, music ensembles, radio station, student government, student newspaper, Campus Ministries. **On-Campus Highlights:** Kelly Hall, Jerusalem model, Family Life Center, Creek and walking trails, Carolyn Boatman Brooks Memorial Library.

ADMISSIONS
Freshman Academic Profile: 95% from public high schools. Minimum paper TOEFL 550. **Basis for Candidate Selection:** *Very important factors considered include:* application essay, recommendation(s), character/personal qualities, religious affiliation/commitment. *Other factors considered include:* alumni/ae relation, interview, level of applicant's interest, talent/ability. **Freshman Admission Requirements:** High school diploma is required and GED is accepted. **Freshman Admission Statistics:** 14 applied, 93% admitted, 85% enrolled. **Transfer Admission Requirements:** High school transcript, college transcript(s), essay or personal statement, interview, minimum college GPA of 2.0 required. Lowest grade transferable C. **General Admission Information:** Application Fee $40. Regular application deadline 8/2. Notification on a rolling basis, beginning on or about 4/1. Nonfall registration accepted. Admission may be deferred for a maximum of 2 years. Neither credit nor placement offered for CEEB Advanced Placement tests.

COSTS AND FINANCIAL AID

Annual tuition $5,482. Room and board $3,470. Required fees $400. Average book expense $1,200. **Required Forms and Deadlines:** FAFSA, institution's own financial aid form. **Notification of Awards:** Applicants will be notified of awards on a rolling basis beginning 5/1. **Types of Aid:** *Need-based scholarships/grants:* Federal Pell, SEOG, private scholarships, the school's own gift aid. *Loans:* **Student Employment:** Federal Work-Study Program available. Institutional employment available. Highest amount earned per year from on-campus jobs $7,000. Off-campus job opportunities are fair. **Financial Aid Statistics:** 100% freshmen, 100% undergrads receive need-based scholarship or grant aid. 22% freshmen, 42% undergrads receive non-need-based scholarship or grant aid. 33% freshmen, 37% undergrads receive need-based self-help aid. 81% freshmen, 75% undergrads receive any aid. 0% undergrads borrow to pay for school. Average cumulative indebtedness $0. **Criteria for awarding institutional aid:** *Non-need-based:* academics, leadership, religious affiliation, state/district residency.

CLEARWATER CHRISTIAN COLLEGE

3400 Gulf-to-Bay Boulevard, Clearwater, FL 33759-4595
Phone: 727-726-1153 • **Financial Aid Phone:** 727-726-1153
E-mail: admissions@clearwater.edu
Fax: 727-726-8597 • **Website:** www.clearwater.edu • **ACT Code:** 715

This private school, affiliated with the Christian (Nondenominational) Church, was founded in 1966. It has a 138-acre campus.

RATINGS
Admissions Selectivity Rating: 65   **Fire Safety Rating:** 95   **Green Rating:** 60*

STUDENTS AND FACULTY

Enrollment: 546. **Student Body:** 50% female, 50% male, 52% out-of-state, 0% international (2 countries represented). Asian 1%, African American 5%, Caucasian 82%, Hispanic 4%, Native American 0%.
Retention and Graduation: 70% freshmen return for sophomore year. 34% freshmen graduate within 4 years. 42% freshmen graduate within 6 years. 26% grads go on to further study within 1 year. 16% grads pursue arts and sciences degrees. 1% grads pursue law degrees. 2% grads pursue business degrees. 4% grads pursue medical degrees. **Faculty:** Student/faculty ratio 175:1. 28 full-time faculty, 68% hold PhDs, 4% are members of minority groups, 32% are women. 0% of classes are taught by teaching assistants.

ACADEMICS

Degrees: associate, bachelor's, certificate, master's. **Classes:** Most classes have fewer than 10 students. **Majors with Highest Enrollment:** business administration and management; elementary education and teaching; general studies. **Special Study Options:** cooperative education program, distance learning, double major, dual enrollment, honors program, independent study, internships, liberal arts/career combination, student-designed major, study abroad, teacher certification program, Semester in Washington, DC. **Honors Programs:** Interdisciplinary Studies, a self-designed multidisciplinary program for students with exceptional ability and focus. **Disability Services:** Special programs offered to physically disabled students include tape recorders, tutors. **Career Services:** alumni services, career/job search classes, internships Career Services highlights include During an education student's last semester, the director of clinical field experiences places the student in Hillsborough and Pinellas County public and private schools for a 14-week teaching internship.

FACILITIES

Housing: men's dorms, women's dorms. **Computers:** 100% of classrooms, 100% of dorms, 100% of libraries, 100% of dining areas, have wireless network access. Administrative functions (other than registration) can be performed online.

CAMPUS LIFE

Environment: City. **Activities:** Choral groups, concert band, drama/theater, music ensembles, pep band, student government, student newspaper, student-run film society, symphony orchestra, yearbook, Campus Ministries 17 registered organizations, 1 honor societies, 1 religious organizations. 5 fraternities, 6 sororities. **Athletics (Intercollegiate):** *Men:* baseball, basketball, golf, soccer. *Women:* basketball, golf, soccer, softball, volleyball. **On-Campus Highlights:** Centre Court Cafe, Gymnasium, Cathcart Hall Cafeteria, Easter Library

ADMISSIONS

Freshman Academic Profile: 30% from public high schools. SAT Math middle 50% range 450-530. SAT Critical Reading middle 50% range 470-560. ACT middle 50% range 21-23. Minimum web-based TOEFL 84. Minimum paper TOEFL 500. **Basis for Candidate Selection:** *Very important factors considered include:* application essay, recommendation(s), standardized test

scores, character/personal qualities, religious affiliation/commitment. *Important factors considered include:* academic GPA, rigor of secondary school record, interview. *Other factors considered include:* alumni/ae relation, level of applicant's interest, volunteer work. **Freshman Admission Requirements:** High school diploma is required and GED is accepted. *Academic units required:* 4 English, 3 mathematics, 3 science, 2 foreign language, 3 social studies. *Academic units recommended:* 4 English, 3 mathematics, 3 science, 2 foreign language, 3 social studies. **Transfer Admission Requirements:** High school transcript, college transcript(s), essay or personal statement, standardized test scores, statement of good standing from prior institution(s). Minimum college GPA of 2.0 required. Lowest grade transferable C-. **General Admission Information:** Application Fee $35. Regular application deadline 8/1. Nonfall registration not accepted. Admission may be deferred for a maximum of 1 year. Credit offered for CEEB Advanced Placement tests.

COSTS AND FINANCIAL AID

Annual tuition $16,250. Room and board $7,470. Required fees $95. Average book expense $1,000. **Required Forms and Deadlines:** FAFSA, institution's own financial aid form, state aid form. **Notification of Awards: Types of Aid:** *Need-based scholarships/grants:* Federal Pell, SEOG, state scholarships/grants, private scholarships, the school's own gift aid, Additional scholarships available for students who are considered first generation, international, or whose parents are involved in Christian ministry. *Loans:* Direct Subsidized Stafford, Direct Unsubsidized Stafford, Direct PLUS, Subsidized Stafford, Unsubsidized Stafford, PLUS, state loans. **Student Employment:** Federal Work-Study Program available. Institutional employment available. Off-campus job opportunities are excellent. **Financial Aid Statistics:** 100% freshmen, 99% undergrads receive need-based scholarship or grant aid. 9% freshmen, 9% undergrads receive non-need-based scholarship or grant aid. 63% freshmen, 64% undergrads receive need-based self-help aid. 97% freshmen, 94% undergrads receive any aid. 51% undergrads borrow to pay for school. Average cumulative indebtedness $6,365. **Criteria for awarding institutional aid:** *Non-need-based:* academics, alumni affiliation, leadership, music/drama, religious affiliation.

CLEARY UNIVERSITY

3750 Cleary Drive, Howell, MI 48843
Phone: 517-548-3670
E-mail: admissions@cleary.edu • **CEEB Code:** 1123
Fax: 517-552-7805 • **Website:** www.cleary.edu • **ACT Code:** 1974

This private school was founded in 1883. It has a 32-acre campus.

RATINGS
Admissions Selectivity Rating: 62   **Fire Safety Rating:** 60*   **Green Rating:** 60*

STUDENTS AND FACULTY

Enrollment: 626. **Student Body:** 54% female, 46% male, 0% out-of-state, 1% international (5 countries represented). Asian 1%, African American 6%, Caucasian 77%, Hispanic 1%, Native American 1%.
Retention and Graduation: 75% freshmen return for sophomore year. **Faculty:** Student/faculty ratio 10:1. 8 full-time faculty, 25% hold PhDs, 13% are members of minority groups, 63% are women. 0% of classes are taught by teaching assistants.

ACADEMICS

Degrees: associate, bachelor's, certificate, master's, terminal associate, transfer associate. **Classes:** Most classes have 10–19 students. Most lab/discussion sessions have 10–19 students. **Majors with Highest Enrollment:** accounting; business/commerce; management information systems. **Special Study Options:** Accelerated program, cooperative education program, distance learning, dual enrollment, independent study, internships. **Disability Services:** Special programs offered to physically disabled students include tutors. **Career Services:** Alumni network, alumni services, career/job search classes, internships.

FACILITIES

Housing: 90% of campus accessible to physically disabled. **Special Academic Facilities/Equipment:** Center for Quality, Quality Resource Collection, Center for Business Ethics and Leadership **Computers:** Administrative functions (other than registration) can be performed online. Undergraduates are required to own a computer.

CAMPUS LIFE

Environment: Town. **Activities:** 1 registered organizations. **On-Campus Highlights:** Internet Cafe, Nature Trail, Computer Lab

ADMISSIONS

Freshman Academic Profile: Average high school GPA 3.0. 85% from public high schools. Minimum paper TOEFL 600. **Basis for Candidate Selection:**

Very important factors considered include: rigor of secondary school record. *Important factors considered include:* standardized test scores, interview. *Other factors considered include:* application essay, recommendation(s). **Freshman Admission Requirements:** High school diploma is required and GED is accepted. **Transfer Admission Requirements:** High school transcript, college transcript(s), statement of good standing from prior institution(s). Minimum college GPA of 2.5 required. Lowest grade transferable D. **General Admission Information:** Application Fee $25. Regular application deadline 8/15. Nonfall registration not accepted. Admission may be deferred for a maximum of 1 year. Credit and/or placement offered for CEEB Advanced Placement tests.

COSTS AND FINANCIAL AID

Annual tuition $13,680. Average book expense $0. **Required Forms and Deadlines:** FAFSA, institution's own financial aid form. **Notification of Awards: Types of Aid:** *Need-based scholarships/grants:* Federal Pell, SEOG, state scholarships/grants, private scholarships, the school's own gift aid. *Loans:* Subsidized Stafford, Unsubsidized Stafford, PLUS. **Student Employment: Financial Aid Statistics:** 79% freshmen, 67% undergrads receive need-based scholarship or grant aid. 15% freshmen, 4% undergrads receive non-need-based scholarship or grant aid. 79% freshmen, 92% undergrads receive need-based self-help aid. 75% freshmen, 48% undergrads receive any aid. 36% undergrads borrow to pay for school. Average cumulative indebtedness $10,500. **Criteria for awarding institutional aid:** *Non-need-based:* academics.

CLEMSON UNIVERSITY

105 Sikes Hall, Clemson, SC 29634-5124
Phone: 864-656-2287 • **Financial Aid Phone:** 864-656-2280
E-mail: cuadmissions@clemson.edu • **CEEB Code:** 5111
Fax: 864-656-2464 • **Website:** www.clemson.edu • **ACT Code:** 3842

This public school was founded in 1889.

RATINGS

Admissions Selectivity Rating: 90 **Fire Safety Rating:** 91 **Green Rating:** 83

STUDENTS AND FACULTY

Enrollment: 15,697. **Student Body:** 46% female, 54% male, 29% out-of-state, 1% international (84 countries represented). Asian 2%, African American 6%, Caucasian 84%, Hispanic 2%, Native American 0%.
Retention and Graduation: 54% freshmen graduate within 4 years. 80% freshmen graduate within 6 years. 28% grads go on to further study within 1 year. 25% grads pursue arts and sciences degrees. 5% grads pursue law degrees. 21% grads pursue business degrees. 8% grads pursue medical degrees. **Faculty:** Student/faculty ratio 18:1. 1013 full-time faculty, 88% hold PhDs, 15% are members of minority groups, 34% are women. 7% of classes are taught by teaching assistants.

ACADEMICS

Degrees: bachelor's, master's, post-master's certificate. **Classes:** Most classes have 10–19 students. Most lab/discussion sessions have 20–29 students. **Majors with Highest Enrollment:** biology/biological sciences; business/commerce; engineering. **Special Study Options:** cooperative education program, distance learning, double major, exchange student program (domestic), honors program, independent study, internships, study abroad, teacher certification program, We have an RN to BSN program located in Greenville, SC. This is an off-campus degree program for students that have a 2 year degree in Nursing and an RN. **Honors Programs:** The National Scholars Program. Please visit: http://www.clemson.edu/national_scholars/ **Combined Degree Programs:** BA/MEng, Rn to BSN program. **Disability Services:** Special programs offered to physically disabled students include note-taking services, reader services, tape recorders, tutors. **Career Services:** Alumni network, alumni services, career/job search classes, career assessment, internships, Career Services highlights include Our alumni network has grown in both strength and number over the past few years. Current alumni recognize that today's Clemson graduates are significantly better prepared to enter the job market, if they choose to delay graduate school. Assisting other members of the "Clemson Family" is a natural bond ingrained as one prepares to leave the campus-- as hard as that may be!

FACILITIES

Housing: Coed dorms, men's dorms, special housing for international students, women's dorms, fraternity/sorority housing, apartments for single students, wellness wousing, theme housing, learning- living communities. **Special Academic Facilities/Equipment:** The South Carolina Botanical Gardens, the Campbell Geology Museum, the Brooks Center for the Performing Arts, the Rudolph Lee Art Gallery, The Garrison Livestock Arena, The John C. Calhoun Home **Computers:** 75% of classrooms, 25% of dorms, 100% of libraries, 100% of dining areas, 100% of student union, 40% of common outdoor areas have wireless network access. Students can register for classes online. Administrative functions (other than registration) can be performed online. Undergraduates are required to own a computer.

CAMPUS LIFE

Environment: Village. **Activities:** Choral groups, concert band, dance, drama/theater, jazz band, literary magazine, marching band, music ensembles, pep band, radio station, student government, student newspaper, television station, yearbook 292 registered organizations, 23 honor societies, 24 religious organizations. 26 fraternities, 17 sororities. **Athletics (Intercollegiate):** *Men:* baseball, basketball, cheerleading, cross-country, diving, football, golf, soccer, swimming, tennis, track/field (outdoor), track/field (indoor). *Women:* basketball, cheerleading, crew/rowing, cross-country, diving, soccer, swimming, tennis, track/field (outdoor), track/field (indoor), volleyball. **On-Campus Highlights:** SC Botanical Garden/ Discovery Center/Geology Muse, Hendrix Student Center - Clemson Ice Cream, Conference Center and Inn at Clemson/Walker Golf C, Fort Hill - John C. Calhoun House, Lee Art Gallery, Please visit: http://www.clemson.edu/visitors/index.html. **Environmental Initiatives:** LEED Energy Conservation policy President's Commission on Sustainability.

ADMISSIONS

Freshman Academic Profile: Average high school GPA 4.2. 48% in top 10% of high school class, 80% in top 25% of high school class, 97% in top 50% of high school class. 89% from public high schools. SAT Math middle 50% range 590-680. SAT Critical Reading middle 50% range 550-650. ACT middle 50% range 25-30. Minimum paper TOEFL 550. **Basis for Candidate Selection:** *Very important factors considered include:* Class rank, academic GPA, rigor of secondary school record, standardized test scores, state residency. *Important factors considered include:* alumni/ae relation. *Other factors considered include:* application essay, recommendation(s), extracurricular activities, talent/ability. **Freshman Admission Requirements:** High school diploma is required and GED is accepted. *Academic units required:* 4 English, 3 mathematics, 3 science, (3 science labs), 3 foreign language, 3 social studies, 1 history, 2 academic electives, 1 PE or ROTC. *Academic units recommended:* 4 English, 3 mathematics, 3 science, (3 science labs), 3 foreign language, 3 social studies, 1 history, 2 academic electives, 1 PE or ROTC **Freshman Admission Statistics:** 17,016 applied, 60% admitted, 29% enrolled. **Transfer Admission Requirements:** college transcript(s), minimum college GPA of 2.5 required. Lowest grade transferable C. **General Admission Information:** Application Fee $60. Regular application deadline 5/1. Notification on a rolling basis, beginning on or about 2/15. Nonfall registration accepted. Credit and/or placement offered for CEEB Advanced Placement tests.

COSTS AND FINANCIAL AID

Annual in-state tuition $12,688. Annual out-of-state tuition $28,826. Room and board $7,228. Required fees $780. Average book expense $1,090. **Required Forms and Deadlines:** FAFSA. **Notification of Awards:** Applicants will be notified of awards on a rolling basis beginning 4/1. **Types of Aid:** *Need-based scholarships/grants:* Federal Pell, SEOG, state scholarships/grants, private scholarships, the school's own gift aid, Federal Nursing Scholarships. *Loans:* Direct Subsidized Stafford, Direct Unsubsidized Stafford, Direct PLUS, Subsidized Stafford, Unsubsidized Stafford, PLUS, Federal Perkins, state loans, college/university loans from institutional funds. **Student Employment:** Federal Work-Study Program available. Institutional employment available. Highest amount earned per year from on-campus jobs $3,500. Off-campus job opportunities are fair. **Financial Aid Statistics:** 35% freshmen, 42% undergrads receive need-based scholarship or grant aid. 89% freshmen, 69% undergrads receive non-need-based scholarship or grant aid. 63% freshmen, 74% undergrads receive need-based self-help aid. 3% freshmen, 2% undergrads receive athletic scholarships. 87% freshmen, 71% undergrads receive any aid. 50% undergrads borrow to pay for school. Average cumulative indebtedness $25,826. **Criteria for awarding institutional aid:** *Non-need-based:* academics, art, athletics, leadership, minority status, music/drama, state/district residency.

See page 1046.

THE CLEVELAND INSTITUTE OF ART

11141 East Boulevard, Cleveland, OH 44106
Phone: 216-421-7418 • **Financial Aid Phone:** 216-421-7425
E-mail: admissions@cia.edu • **CEEB Code:** 1152
Fax: 216-754-3634 • **Website:** www.cia.edu • **ACT Code:** 3243

This private school was founded in 1882. It has a 488-acre campus.

RATINGS
Admissions Selectivity Rating: 75   **Fire Safety Rating:** 79   **Green Rating:** 65

STUDENTS AND FACULTY
Enrollment: 536. **Student Body:** 54% female, 46% male, 31% out-of-state, 2% international. Asian 4%, African American 10%, Caucasian 77%, Hispanic 3%, Native American 0%.
Retention and Graduation: 79% freshmen return for sophomore year. 30% freshmen graduate within 4 years. 59% freshmen graduate within 6 years. 4% grads go on to further study within 1 year. 4% grads pursue arts and sciences degrees. **Faculty:** Student/faculty ratio 8:1. 51 full-time faculty, 78% hold PhDs, 10% are members of minority groups, 37% are women. 0% of classes are taught by teaching assistants.

ACADEMICS
Degrees: bachelor's. **Classes:** Most classes have 10–19 students. Most lab/discussion sessions have 10–19 students. **Majors with Highest Enrollment:** illustration; industrial design; intermedia/multimedia. **Special Study Options:** cooperative education program, cross-registration, exchange student program (domestic), honors program, independent study, internships, study abroad, Study for up to 2 semesters at an Alliance of Independent Colleges of Art and Design. **Disability Services:** Special programs offered to physically disabled students include note-taking services, tape recorders, tutors. **Career Services:** Alumni network, alumni services, career/job search classes, career assessment, internships.

FACILITIES
Housing: Coed dorms, fraternity/sorority housing, apartments for single students. **Special Academic Facilities/Equipment:** The Reinberger Galleries. **Computers:** 40% of classrooms, 100% of dorms, 100% of libraries, have wireless network access. Students can register for classes online. Administrative functions (other than registration) can be performed online.

CAMPUS LIFE
Environment: Metropolis. **Activities:** marching band, student government, student newspaper, student-run film society, Campus Ministries 7 registered organizations, 2 religious organizations. **On-Campus Highlights:** Arabica Coffee Shop, Frank Gehry and Peter B. Lewis Building, Live music at Barking Spider, Cleveland Museum of Art, Reinberger Galleries. **Environmental Initiatives:** Recycling Energy Management Purchase of Energy Efficient Equipment

ADMISSIONS
Freshman Academic Profile: Average high school GPA 3.1. 15% in top 10% of high school class, 27% in top 25% of high school class, 63% in top 50% of high school class. SAT Math middle 50% range 440-570. SAT Critical Reading middle 50% range 460-610. ACT middle 50% range 18-25. Minimum paper TOEFL 525. **Basis for Candidate Selection:** *Very important factors considered include:* rigor of secondary school record, talent/ability. *Important factors considered include:* application essay, academic GPA, recommendation(s), standardized test scores, character/personal qualities, interview. *Other factors considered include:* extracurricular activities, level of applicant's interest. **Freshman Admission Requirements:** High school diploma is required and GED is accepted. **Freshman Admission Statistics:** 615 applied, 71% admitted, 29% enrolled. **Transfer Admission Requirements:** college transcript(s), essay or personal statement, minimum college GPA of 2.0 required. Lowest grade transferable C. **General Admission Information:** Application Fee $30. Notification on a rolling basis, beginning on or about 10/1. Nonfall registration not accepted. Admission may be deferred for a maximum of 1 year. Credit offered for CEEB Advanced Placement tests.

COSTS AND FINANCIAL AID
Annual tuition $31,760. Room and board $11,354. Required fees $2,122. Average book expense $2,050. **Required Forms and Deadlines:** FAFSA, institution's own financial aid form. **Notification of Awards:** Applicants will be notified of awards on a rolling basis beginning 3/15. **Types of Aid:** *Need-based scholarships/grants:* Federal Pell, SEOG, state scholarships/grants, private scholarships, the school's own gift aid, Academic Merit scholarships/grants (institutional funds). *Loans:* Subsidized Stafford, Unsubsidized Stafford, PLUS, Federal Perkins. **Student Employment:** Federal Work-Study Program available. Off-campus job opportunities are good. **Financial Aid Statistics:** 100% freshmen, 100% undergrads receive need-based scholarship or grant aid. 7% freshmen, 6% undergrads receive non-need-based scholarship or grant aid. 93% freshmen, 93% undergrads receive need-based self-help aid. 95% freshmen, 95% undergrads receive any aid. 83% undergrads borrow to pay for school. Average cumulative indebtedness $37,618. **Criteria for awarding institutional aid:** *Non-need-based:* academics, art.

CLEVELAND STATE UNIVERSITY

2121 Euclid Avenue, Cleveland, OH 44115
Phone: 216-687-5411 • **Financial Aid Phone:** 216-687-5411
E-mail: admissions@csuohio.edu • **CEEB Code:** 3032
Fax: 216-687-5501 • **Website:** www.csuohio.edu • **ACT Code:** 1221

This public school was founded in 1964. It has a 82-acre campus.

RATINGS
Admissions Selectivity Rating: 78   **Fire Safety Rating:** 60*   **Green Rating:** 61

STUDENTS AND FACULTY
Enrollment: 11,170. **Student Body:** 55% female, 45% male, 3% out-of-state, 4% international (85 countries represented). Asian 2%, African American 21%, Caucasian 62%, Hispanic 4%, Native American 0%.
Retention and Graduation: 65% freshmen return for sophomore year. **Faculty:** Student/faculty ratio 19:1. 520 full-time faculty, 89% hold PhDs, 24% are members of minority groups, 40% are women. 1% of classes are taught by teaching assistants.

ACADEMICS
Degrees: bachelor's, doctoral, master's, post-bachelor's certificate, post-master's certificate. **Classes:** Most classes have 20–29 students. **Majors with Highest Enrollment:** accounting; business administration, management and operations, other; psychology. **Special Study Options:** Accelerated program, cooperative education program, cross-registration, distance learning, double major, dual enrollment, English as a Second Language (ESL), exchange student program (domestic), honors program, independent study, internships, liberal arts/career combination, student-designed major, study abroad, teacher certification program, weekend college. **Honors Programs:** CSU's Honors Program was established in 2004 to serve the needs of academically talented students. Each year, it accepts approximately 40 first-year students and 20-25 juniors who have demonstrated superior academic achievement through their coursework and results on tests such as the ACT and SAT. Honors students at CSU receive a scholarship that covers full tuition as well as all academic fees and the cost of books required for their classes. Honors students in good standing receive this support throughout their four-year undergraduate academic career. **Combined Degree Programs:** JD/MBA. **Disability Services:** Special programs offered to physically disabled students include note-taking services, reader services, tape recorders, tutors. **Career Services:** alumni services, career/job search classes, career assessment, internships.

FACILITIES
Housing: Coed dorms, special housing for disabled students, fraternity/sorority housing. 90% of campus accessible to physically disabled. **Computers:** Students can register for classes online. Administrative functions (other than registration) can be performed online.

CAMPUS LIFE
Environment: Metropolis. **Activities:** Choral groups, concert band, dance, drama/theater, jazz band, literary magazine, musical theater, opera, pep band, radio station, student government, student newspaper, student-run film society, symphony orchestra, International Student Organization 10 religious organizations. 8 fraternities, 7 sororities. **Athletics (Intercollegiate):** *Men:* baseball, basketball, fencing, golf, soccer, swimming, wrestling. *Women:* basketball, cross-country, fencing, softball, swimming, tennis, track/field (outdoor), track/field (indoor), volleyball. **On-Campus Highlights:** Recreation Center, Main Classroom Atrium, Michael Schwartz Library, The Green Room, Farmer's Market.

ADMISSIONS
Freshman Academic Profile: Average high school GPA 3.2. 12% in top 10% of high school class, 38% in top 25% of high school class, 74% in top 50% of high school class. SAT Math middle 50% range 450-580. SAT Critical Reading middle 50% range 440-570. ACT middle 50% range 19-24. Minimum paper TOEFL 525. **Basis for Candidate Selection:** *Very important factors considered include:* academic GPA, rigor of secondary school record, standardized test scores. *Important factors considered include:* Class rank. **Freshman Admission Requirements:** High school diploma is required and GED is accepted. *Academic units required:* 4 English, 3 mathematics, 3 science, 3 social studies. *Academic units recommended:* 4 English, 3 mathematics, 3 science, 3 social

studies. **Freshman Admission Statistics:** 5,938 applied, 63% admitted, 42% enrolled. **Transfer Admission Requirements:** college transcript(s), minimum college GPA of 2.0 required. Lowest grade transferable D. **General Admission Information:** Application Fee $30. Regular application deadline 8/15. Notification on a rolling basis, beginning on or about 9/1. Nonfall registration accepted. Admission may be deferred for a maximum of 1 year. Credit and/or placement offered for CEEB Advanced Placement tests.

COSTS AND FINANCIAL AID

Annual in-state tuition $9,264. Annual out-of-state tuition $12,386. Room and board $11,662. Average book expense $800. **Required Forms and Deadlines:** FAFSA, Tax forms(for base tax year),if selected for verification by Department of Education or the institution; verification documents. **Notification of Awards:** Applicants will be notified of awards on a rolling basis beginning 3/15. **Types of Aid:** *Need-based scholarships/grants:* Federal Pell, SEOG, state scholarships/grants, private scholarships, the school's own gift aid. *Loans:* Subsidized Stafford, Unsubsidized Stafford, PLUS, Federal Perkins, state loans, Alternative. **Student Employment:** Federal Work-Study Program available. Institutional employment available. Off-campus job opportunities are excellent. **Financial Aid Statistics:** 86% freshmen, 78% undergrads receive need-based scholarship or grant aid. 4% freshmen, 3% undergrads receive non-need-based scholarship or grant aid. 84% freshmen, 87% undergrads receive need-based self-help aid. 1% freshmen, 2% undergrads receive athletic scholarships. 57% undergrads borrow to pay for school. Average cumulative indebtedness $23,436. **Criteria for awarding institutional aid:** *Non-need-based:* academics, alumni affiliation, art, athletics, leadership, minority status, music/drama, religious affiliation.

COASTAL CAROLINA UNIVERSITY

PO Box 261954, Conway, SC 29528-6054
Phone: 843-349-2170 • **Financial Aid Phone:** 843-349-2313
E-mail: admissions@coastal.edu • **CEEB Code:** 5837
Fax: 843-349-2127 • **ACT Code:** 3843

This public school was founded in 1954. It has a 302-acre campus.

RATINGS
Admissions Selectivity Rating: 71   **Fire Safety Rating:** 82   **Green Rating:** 85

STUDENTS AND FACULTY
Enrollment: 8,466. **Student Body:** 53% female, 47% male, 47% out-of-state, 1% international (51 countries represented). Asian 1%, African American 20%, Caucasian 71%, Hispanic 4%, Native American 0%.
Retention and Graduation: 60% freshmen return for sophomore year. 29% freshmen graduate within 4 years. 47% freshmen graduate within 6 years.
Faculty: Student/faculty ratio 17:1. 378 full-time faculty, 79% hold PhDs, 12% are members of minority groups, 44% are women. 0% of classes are taught by teaching assistants.

ACADEMICS
Degrees: bachelor's, master's, post-bachelor's certificate. **Classes:** Most classes have 20–29 students. Most lab/discussion sessions have 10–19 students. **Majors with Highest Enrollment:** biology/biological sciences; business administration and management; marine biology and biological oceanography. **Special Study Options:** Accelerated program, cooperative education program, distance learning, double major, dual enrollment, honors program, independent study, internships, student-designed major, study abroad, teacher certification program. **Disability Services:** Special programs offered to physically disabled students include note-taking services, reader services, tape recorders, tutors. **Career Services:** Alumni network, alumni services, career/job search classes, career assessment, internships Career Services highlights include Career Assessment Program which is an integral part of University 110 and is required of all freshmen.

FACILITIES
Housing: Coed dorms, special housing for disabled students 98% of campus accessible to physically disabled. **Computers:** 100% of classrooms, 100% of libraries, 100% of dining areas, 100% of student union, 83% of common outdoor areas have wireless network access. Students can register for classes online. Administrative functions (other than registration) can be performed online.

CAMPUS LIFE
Environment: Town. **Activities:** Choral groups, concert band, dance, drama/theater, jazz band, literary magazine, marching band, music ensembles, musical theater, pep band, radio station, student government, student newspaper, Campus Ministries, International Student Organization 91 registered organizations, 32 honor societies, 13 religious organizations. 9 fraternities, 7 sororities.
Athletics (Intercollegiate): *Men:* baseball, basketball, cheerleading, cross-

country, football, golf, soccer, tennis, track/field (outdoor). *Women:* basketball, cheerleading, cross-country, golf, soccer, softball, tennis, track/field (outdoor), volleyball. **On-Campus Highlights:** Humanities and Fine Arts Building, Brooks Stadium, CINO Grille / Student Center, Recreation Center, Java City Cafe. **Environmental Initiatives:** Adkins Field House - 1st LEED certified building, LEED Gold Green Power, including on-site solar and electric vehicle charging stations Establishment of CCU Green Fund for Student Sustainability Projects.

ADMISSIONS
Freshman Academic Profile: Average high school GPA 3.3. 8% in top 10% of high school class, 28% in top 25% of high school class, 66% in top 50% of high school class. 88% from public high schools. SAT Math middle 50% range 460-550. SAT Critical Reading middle 50% range 450-530. ACT middle 50% range 19-23. Minimum web-based TOEFL 71. Minimum paper TOEFL 527. **Basis for Candidate Selection:** *Very important factors considered include:* academic GPA, rigor of secondary school record, standardized test scores. *Important factors considered include:* Class rank. *Other factors considered include:* application essay, recommendation(s), character/personal qualities, extracurricular activities, first generation, geographical residence, interview, level of applicant's interest, state residency, talent/ability, work experience. **Freshman Admission Requirements:** High school diploma is required and GED is accepted. *Academic units required:* 4 English, 3 mathematics, 3 science, (3 science labs), 2 foreign language, 2 social studies, 1 history, 4 academic electives, 1 PE or ROTC. *Academic units recommended:* 4 English, 3 mathematics, 3 science, (3 science labs), 2 foreign language, 2 social studies, 1 history, 4 academic electives, 1 PE or ROTC **Freshman Admission Statistics:** 10,993 applied, 74% admitted, 27% enrolled. **Transfer Admission Requirements:** college transcript(s), statement of good standing from prior institution(s). Minimum college GPA of 2.0 required. Lowest grade transferable C–. **General Admission Information:** Application Fee $45. Regular application deadline 8/15. Notification on a rolling basis, beginning on or about 9/15. Nonfall registration accepted. Admission may be deferred for a maximum of 1 year. Credit and/or placement offered for CEEB Advanced Placement tests.

COSTS AND FINANCIAL AID
Annual in-state tuition $9,680. Annual out-of-state tuition $21,970. Room and board $7,700. Required fees $80. Average book expense $1,096. **Required Forms and Deadlines:** FAFSA. **Notification of Awards:** Applicants will be notified of awards on a rolling basis beginning 3/1. **Types of Aid:** *Need-based scholarships/grants:* Federal Pell, SEOG, state scholarships/grants, private scholarships, the school's own gift aid, ACG/SMART. *Loans:* Subsidized Stafford, Unsubsidized Stafford, PLUS, Federal Perkins, state loans. **Student Employment:** Federal Work-Study Program available. Institutional employment available. Highest amount earned per year from on-campus jobs $20,030. Off-campus job opportunities are excellent. **Financial Aid Statistics:** 51% freshmen, 55% undergrads receive need-based scholarship or grant aid. 43% freshmen, 30% undergrads receive non-need-based scholarship or grant aid. 95% freshmen, 94% undergrads receive need-based self-help aid. 4% undergrads, 5% undergrads receive athletic scholarships. 98% freshmen, 94% undergrads receive any aid. 72% undergrads borrow to pay for school. Average cumulative indebtedness $34,040. **Criteria for awarding institutional aid:** *Non-need-based:* academics, art, athletics, leadership, music/drama, state/district residency.

COE COLLEGE

1220 First Avenue NE, Cedar Rapids, IA 52402
Phone: 319-399-8500 • **Financial Aid Phone:** 319-399-8540
E-mail: admission@coe.edu • **CEEB Code:** 6101
Fax: 319-399-8816 • **Website:** www.coe.edu • **ACT Code:** 1294

This private school, affiliated with the Presbyterian Church, was founded in 1851. It has a 53-acre campus.

RATINGS
Admissions Selectivity Rating: 81   **Fire Safety Rating:** 72   **Green Rating:** 60*

STUDENTS AND FACULTY
Enrollment: 1,320. **Student Body:** 53% female, 47% male, 43% out-of-state, 2% international (15 countries represented). Asian 3%, African American 4%, Caucasian 79%, Hispanic 4%, Native American 0%.
Retention and Graduation: 81% freshmen return for sophomore year. 60% freshmen graduate within 4 years. 70% freshmen graduate within 6 years.
Faculty: Student/faculty ratio 11:1. 92 full-time faculty, 92% hold PhDs, 9% are members of minority groups, 39% are women. 0% of classes are taught by teaching assistants.

ACADEMICS

Degrees: bachelor's, master's. **Classes:** Most classes have 10–19 students. Most lab/discussion sessions have 10–19 students. **Majors with Highest Enrollment:** biology/biological sciences; business administration and management; psychology. **Special Study Options:** Accelerated program, cross-registration, double major, dual enrollment, English as a Second Language (ESL), exchange student program (domestic), honors program, independent study, internships, student-designed major, study abroad, teacher certification program. **Honors Programs:** College honors program consisting of five honors seminars and an honors project or thesis. **Combined Degree Programs:** BA/MArch Washington University. **Disability Services:** Special programs offered to physically disabled students include note-taking services, tape recorders, tutors. **Career Services:** Alumni network, career/job search classes, career assessment, internships, regional alumni. Career Services highlights include The Coe Plan requires all students to complete an internship, research, study abroad, or other "out of the classroom" experience during their junior year.

FACILITIES

Housing: Coed dorms, men's dorms, women's dorms, fraternity/sorority housing, apartments for single students, wellness housing, theme housing. 70% of campus accessible to physically disabled. **Special Academic Facilities/Equipment:** Ornithological museum, writing lab, theatre. **Computers:** 70% of classrooms, 10% of dorms, 100% of libraries, 100% of dining areas, 100% of student union, 80% of common outdoor areas have wireless network access. Students can register for classes online.

CAMPUS LIFE

Environment: City. **Activities:** Choral groups, concert band, dance, drama/theater, jazz band, literary magazine, music ensembles, musical theater, pep band, radio station, student government, student newspaper, symphony orchestra, television station, yearbook, Campus Ministries, International Student Organization 60 registered organizations, 8 honor societies, 4 religious organizations. 5 fraternities, 3 sororities. **Athletics (Intercollegiate):** *Men:* baseball, basketball, cross-country, diving, football, golf, soccer, swimming, tennis, track/field (outdoor), track/field (indoor), wrestling. *Women:* basketball, cheerleading, cross-country, diving, golf, soccer, softball, swimming, tennis, track/field (outdoor), track/field (indoor), volleyball. **On-Campus Highlights:** Student Union/Coffee Shop, Dows Theatre, Library/Art Galleries, Fitness Center, Racquet Center.

ADMISSIONS

Freshman Academic Profile: Average high school GPA 3.6. 27% in top 10% of high school class, 62% in top 25% of high school class, 89% in top 50% of high school class. 90% from public high schools. SAT Math middle 50% range 500-655. SAT Critical Reading middle 50% range 495-610. SAT Writing middle 50% range 490-615. ACT middle 50% range 23-28. Minimum paper TOEFL 500. **Basis for Candidate Selection:** *Very important factors considered include:* academic GPA, standardized test scores. *Important factors considered include:* Class rank, application essay, recommendation(s). *Other factors considered include:* rigor of secondary school record, alumni/ae relation, character/personal qualities, extracurricular activities, first generation, interview, level of applicant's interest, racial/ethnic status, talent/ability, volunteer work. **Freshman Admission Requirements:** High school diploma is required and GED is accepted. **Freshman Admission Statistics:** 2,509 applied, 67% admitted, 22% enrolled. **Transfer Admission Requirements:** High school transcript, college transcript(s), essay or personal statement, statement of good standing from prior institution(s). Minimum college GPA of 2.5 required. Lowest grade transferable C. **General Admission Information:** Application Fee $30. Regular application deadline 3/1. Regular notification 3/15. Notification on a rolling basis, beginning on or about 10/1. Nonfall registration accepted. Admission may be deferred for a maximum of 2 years. Credit and/or placement offered for CEEB Advanced Placement tests.

COSTS AND FINANCIAL AID

Annual tuition $35,400. Room and board $7,750. Required fees $330. Average book expense $1,000. **Required Forms and Deadlines:** FAFSA. **Notification of Awards:** Applicants will be notified of awards on a rolling basis beginning 3/15. **Types of Aid:** *Need-based scholarships/grants:* Federal Pell, SEOG, state scholarships/grants, private scholarships, the school's own gift aid. *Loans:* Direct Subsidized Stafford, Direct Unsubsidized Stafford, Direct PLUS, Federal Perkins, college/university loans from institutional funds. **Student Employment:** Federal Work-Study Program available. Institutional employment available. Highest amount earned per year from on-campus jobs $500. Off-campus job opportunities are excellent. **Financial Aid Statistics:** 100% freshmen, 100% undergrads receive need-based scholarship or grant aid. 12% freshmen, 14% undergrads receive non-need-based scholarship or grant aid. 85% freshmen, 83% undergrads receive need-based self-help aid. 99% freshmen, 96% undergrads receive any aid. 80% undergrads borrow to pay for school. Average cumulative indebtedness $29,500. **Criteria for awarding institutional aid:** *Non-need-based:* academics, alumni affiliation, art, music/drama.

COGSWELL COLLEGE

1175 Bordeaux Drive, Sunnyvale, CA 94089-1299
Phone: 408-541-0100 • **Financial Aid Phone:** 408-498-5107
E-mail: admissions@cogswell.edu • **CEEB Code:** 1177
Fax: 408-747-0764 • **ACT Code:** 1177

This private school was founded in 1887. It has a 5-acre campus.

RATINGS

Admissions Selectivity Rating: 89   **Fire Safety Rating:** 97   **Green Rating:** 61

STUDENTS AND FACULTY

Enrollment: 388. **Student Body:** 20% female, 80% male, 13% out-of-state, 2% international (13 countries represented). Asian 8%, African American 5%, Caucasian 46%, Hispanic 13%, Native American 1%. **Retention and Graduation:** 68% freshmen return for sophomore year. 19% freshmen graduate within 4 years. 56% freshmen graduate within 6 years. 1% grads pursue business degrees. **Faculty:** Student/faculty ratio 9:1. 16 full-time faculty, 69% hold PhDs, 0% are members of minority groups, 25% are women. 0% of classes are taught by teaching assistants.

ACADEMICS

Degrees: bachelor's. **Classes:** Most classes have fewer than 10 students. **Majors with Highest Enrollment:** animation, interactive technology, video graphics and special effects; fire protection and safety technology/technician; recording arts technology/technician. **Special Study Options:** cooperative education program, distance learning, double major, exchange student program (domestic), internships, student-designed major, study abroad. **Combined Degree Programs:** Digital art and animation, Digital Audio Technology. **Career Services:** Alumni network, career/job search classes.

FACILITIES

Housing: apartments for single students. 100% of campus accessible to physically disabled. **Special Academic Facilities/Equipment:** The Gallery at Cogswell **Computers:** 100% of classrooms, 100% of libraries, 100% of dining areas, 100% of student union, have wireless network access. Students can register for classes online. Administrative functions (other than registration) can be performed online. Undergraduates are required to own a computer.

CAMPUS LIFE

Environment: Village. **Activities:** drama/theater, radio station, student government 5 registered organizations. **On-Campus Highlights:** Gallery, Library, Smart Lab, Dragon's Den, Audio Recording Studio. **Environmental Initiatives:** saving energy recycling saving water

ADMISSIONS

Freshman Academic Profile: SAT Math middle 50% range 460-640. SAT Critical Reading middle 50% range 460-640. SAT Writing middle 50% range 510-630. ACT middle 50% range 19-30. Minimum paper TOEFL 525. **Basis for Candidate Selection:** *Very important factors considered include:* academic GPA, talent/ability. *Important factors considered include:* application essay, recommendation(s). *Other factors considered include:* extracurricular activities, interview, level of applicant's interest, volunteer work. **Freshman Admission Requirements:** High school diploma is required and GED is accepted. *Academic units required:* 3 English, 3 mathematics, 1 science, (1 science labs). *Academic units recommended:* 3 English, 3 mathematics, 1 science, (1 science labs). **Freshman Admission Statistics:** 162 applied, 49% admitted, 78% enrolled. **Transfer Admission Requirements:** High school transcript, college transcript(s), essay or personal statement, minimum college GPA of 2.5 required. Lowest grade transferable C. **General Admission Information:** Application Fee $55. Regular application deadline 3/1. Nonfall registration accepted. Admission may be deferred for a maximum of 1 year. Credit and/or placement offered for CEEB Advanced Placement tests.

COSTS AND FINANCIAL AID

Annual tuition $24,360. Room and board $6,000. Required fees $180. Average book expense $1,665. **Required Forms and Deadlines:** FAFSA, state aid form. **Notification of Awards:** Applicants will be notified of awards on a rolling basis beginning 3/15. **Types of Aid:** *Need-based scholarships/grants:* Federal Pell, SEOG, state scholarships/grants, private scholarships, the school's own gift aid. *Loans:* Subsidized Stafford, Unsubsidized Stafford, PLUS. **Student Employment:** Federal Work-Study Program available. Institutional employment available. Off-campus job opportunities are good. **Financial Aid Statistics:** 76% freshmen, 68% undergrads receive need-based scholarship or grant aid. 87% undergrads receive non-need-based scholarship or grant aid. 90% freshmen, 80% undergrads receive any aid. 75% undergrads borrow to pay for school. Average cumulative indebtedness $45,000. **Criteria for awarding institutional aid:** *Non-need-based:* academics, art, music/drama.

COKER COLLEGE

300 East College Avenue, Hartsville, SC 29550
Phone: 843-383-8050
E-mail: admissions@coker.edu
Fax: 843-383-8056 • **Website:** www.coker.edu

This is a private school.

RATINGS
Admissions Selectivity Rating: 80   **Fire Safety Rating:** 60*   **Green Rating:** 60*

STUDENTS AND FACULTY
Enrollment: 674. **Student Body:** 63% female, 37% male, 19% out-of-state, 3% international. Asian 0%, African American 27%, Caucasian 67%, Hispanic 2%, Native American 1%.
Retention and Graduation: 71% freshmen return for sophomore year. 48% freshmen graduate within 4 years. 60% freshmen graduate within 6 years.
Faculty: Student/faculty ratio 10:1. 58 full-time faculty, 81% hold PhDs, 12% are members of minority groups, 47% are women. 0% of classes are taught by teaching assistants.

ACADEMICS
Degrees: bachelor's. **Classes:** Most classes have 10–19 students. Most lab/discussion sessions have 10–19 students. **Majors with Highest Enrollment:** business/commerce; graphic design; psychology. **Special Study Options:** double major, dual enrollment, honors program, independent study, internships, student-designed major, study abroad, teacher certification program. **Disability Services:** Special programs offered to physically disabled students include tape recorders, tutors. **Career Services:** career/job search classes, career assessment, internships, Career Services highlights include With our internships students have the opportunity to receive hands-on experience in their field, which gives them a competitive edge in today's job market.

FACILITIES
Housing: Coed dorms, special housing for international students 80% of campus accessible to physically disabled. **Special Academic Facilities/Equipment:** Art gallery, state-of-the-art performing arts center, dark rooms, botanical gardens, graduate-level science equipment. **Computers:** Administrative functions (other than registration) can be performed online.

CAMPUS LIFE
Environment: Activities: Choral groups, dance, drama/theater, literary magazine, music ensembles, musical theater, student government, student newspaper, Campus Ministries, International Student Organization 27 registered organizations, 4 honor societies, 2 religious organizations. **Athletics (Intercollegiate):** *Men:* baseball, basketball, cheerleading, cross-country, golf, soccer, tennis. *Women:* basketball, cheerleading, cross-country, soccer, softball, tennis, volleyball. **On-Campus Highlights:** The Cobra Den, The Cobra Caf, The Student Center, The Performing Arts Center, Outdoor Volleyball Courts, The Cobra Den includes a coffee area, dance floor, and a game room.

ADMISSIONS
Freshman Academic Profile: Average high school GPA 3.4. 1% in top 10% of high school class, 28% in top 25% of high school class, 70% in top 50% of high school class. SAT Math middle 50% range 440–570. SAT Critical Reading middle 50% range 420–570. ACT middle 50% range 17–22. Minimum paper TOEFL 500. **Basis for Candidate Selection:** *Very important factors considered include:* academic GPA, standardized test scores. *Important factors considered include:* Class rank, rigor of secondary school record, level of applicant's interest. *Other factors considered include:* application essay, recommendation(s), alumni/ae relation, character/personal qualities, extracurricular activities, interview, talent/ability, volunteer work, work experience. **Freshman Admission Requirements:** High school diploma is required and GED is accepted. *Academic units required:* 4 English, 3 mathematics, 3 science, (1 science labs), 2 foreign language, 3 social studies. 4 English, 3 mathematics, 3 science, (1 science labs), 2 foreign language, 3 social studies. **Freshman Admission Statistics:** 1,112 applied, 56% admitted, 25% enrolled. **Transfer Admission Requirements:** High school transcript, college transcript(s), statement of good standing from prior institution(s). Minimum college GPA of 2.0 required. Lowest grade transferable C. **General Admission Information:** Application Fee $15. Regular application deadline 8/1. Notification on a rolling basis, beginning on or about 9/1. Nonfall registration accepted. Admission may be deferred for a maximum of 1 year. Credit and/or placement offered for CEEB Advanced Placement tests.

COSTS AND FINANCIAL AID
Annual tuition $22,200. Room and board $6,950. Average book expense $1,500. **Required Forms and Deadlines:** FAFSA. **Notification of Awards:** Applicants will be notified of awards on a rolling basis beginning 3/1. **Types of Aid:**

Need-based scholarships/grants: Federal Pell, SEOG, state scholarships/grants, private scholarships, the school's own gift aid. *Loans:* Subsidized Stafford, Unsubsidized Stafford, PLUS, Federal Perkins, state loans, Private Source Loans. **Student Employment:** Federal Work-Study Program available. Institutional employment available. Highest amount earned per year from on-campus jobs $1,072. Off-campus job opportunities are good. **Financial Aid Statistics:** 96% freshmen, 96% undergrads receive need-based scholarship or grant aid. 100% freshmen, 93% undergrads receive non-need-based scholarship or grant aid. 78% freshmen, 80% undergrads receive need-based self-help aid. 5% freshmen, 6% undergrads receive athletic scholarships. 100% freshmen, 100% undergrads receive any aid. 81% undergrads borrow to pay for school. Average cumulative indebtedness $25,593. **Criteria for awarding institutional aid:** *Non-need-based:* academics, alumni affiliation, art, athletics, job skills, leadership, minority status, music/drama, religious affiliation, state/district residency.

COLBY COLLEGE

4000 Mayflower Hill, Waterville, ME 04901-8848
Phone: 207-859-4800 • **Financial Aid Phone:** 207-859-4832
E-mail: admissions@colby.edu • **CEEB Code:** 3280
Fax: 207-859-4828 • **Website:** www.colby.edu • **ACT Code:** 1638

This private school was founded in 1813. It has a 714-acre campus.

RATINGS
Admissions Selectivity Rating: 96   **Fire Safety Rating:** 91   **Green Rating:** 93

STUDENTS AND FACULTY
Enrollment: 1,863. **Student Body:** 55% female, 45% male, 87% out-of-state, 6% international (76 countries represented). Asian 6%, African American 3%, Caucasian 60%, Hispanic 5%, Native American 0%.
Retention and Graduation: 95% freshmen return for sophomore year. 86% freshmen graduate within 4 years. 32% grads go on to further study within 1 year. 18% grads pursue arts and sciences degrees. 5% grads pursue law degrees. 1% grads pursue business degrees. 5% grads pursue medical degrees. **Faculty:** Student/faculty ratio 10:1. 166 full-time faculty, 98% hold PhDs, 14% are members of minority groups, 42% are women. 0% of classes are taught by teaching assistants.

ACADEMICS
Degrees: bachelor's. **Classes:** Most classes have 10–19 students. Most lab/discussion sessions have 10–19 students. **Majors with Highest Enrollment:** biology/biological sciences; economics; political science and government. **Special Study Options:** cross-registration, double major, exchange student program (domestic), honors program, independent study, internships, student-designed major, study abroad, teacher certification program, Summer research assistantships; Colby has coordinated 3-2 engineering programs with Dartmouth; Colby offers junior-year abroad programs in France, Spain, and Russia. **Disability Services:** Special programs offered to physically disabled students include note-taking services, reader services, tape recorders, tutors. **Career Services:** Alumni network, alumni services, career/job search classes, career assessment, internships, regional alumni. Career Services highlights include Colby Connect (see website for details) http://www.colby.edu/academics_cs/resources/offices/careerservices/index.cfm.

FACILITIES
Housing: Coed dorms, wellness housing, theme housing, quiet halls, chem-free halls, apartments for seniors only, student interest halls. 92% of campus accessible to physically disabled. **Special Academic Facilities/Equipment:** 28,000 square foot art museum, completely renovated student center (Pulver Pavilion), arboretum, electronic microscopes, greenhouse, astronomical observatory, writer's center, cross-country ski trails, Goldfarb Center for Public Affairs and Civic Engagement, multicultural center, rare books and archives library, computer research classroom, language lab. **Computers:** 100% of classrooms, 100% of dorms, 100% of libraries, 100% of dining areas, 100% of student union, 10% of common outdoor areas have wireless network access. Students can register for classes online. Administrative functions (other than registration) can be performed online.

CAMPUS LIFE
Environment: Village. **Activities:** Choral groups, concert band, dance, drama/theater, jazz band, literary magazine, music ensembles, musical theater, radio station, student government, student newspaper, student-run film society, symphony orchestra, yearbook, International Student Organization 91 registered

organizations, 9 honor societies, 6 religious organizations. **Athletics (Intercollegiate):** *Men:* baseball, basketball, crew/rowing, cross-country, diving, football, golf, ice hockey, lacrosse, skiing (downhill/alpine), skiingnordiccross-country, soccer, squash, swimming, tennis, track/field (outdoor), track/field (indoor). *Women:* basketball, crew/rowing, cross-country, diving, field hockey, golf, ice hockey, lacrosse, skiing (downhill/alpine), skiingnordiccross-country, soccer, softball, squash, swimming, tennis, track/field (outdoor), track/field (indoor), volleyball. **On-Campus Highlights:** Pulver Pavillion, Colby College Museum of Art, Johnson Pond, Perkins Arboretum trails (running, cross **Environmental Initiatives:** Since October 2003 Colby used electricity only from 100-percent renewable sources. A biomass plant heating plant - burning fuel certified by the Sustainable Forestry Initiative was completed in early 2012, replacing 90 percent (about 1 millon gallons) of heating oil annually. It is a major component of the commitment to carbon-neutrality by 2015. Colby seeks LEED certification for new construction and renovation projects. At the end of 2011 Colby had six LEED-certified buildings, including three certified at the gold level.

ADMISSIONS
Freshman Academic Profile: 65% in top 10% of high school class, 88% in top 25% of high school class, 99% in top 50% of high school class. 53% from public high schools. SAT Math middle 50% range 630-720. SAT Critical Reading middle 50% range 610-710. SAT Writing middle 50% range 610-710. ACT middle 50% range 29-32. Minimum web-based TOEFL 100. **Basis for Candidate Selection:** *Very important factors considered include:* rigor of secondary school record, character/personal qualities. *Important factors considered include:* Class rank, application essay, academic GPA, recommendation(s), standardized test scores, extracurricular activities, racial/ethnic status, talent/ability. *Other factors considered include:* alumni/ae relation, first generation, geographical residence, interview, level of applicant's interest, state residency, volunteer work, work experience. **Freshman Admission Requirements:** High school diploma or equivalent is not required. **Freshman Admission Statistics:** 5,234 applied, 20% admitted, 32% enrolled. **Transfer Admission Requirements:** High school transcript, college transcript(s), essay or personal statement, standardized test scores, statement of good standing from prior institution(s). Minimum college GPA of 3.0 required. Lowest grade transferable C. **General Admission Information:** Application Fee $65. Early decision application deadline 11/15. Regular application deadline 1/1. Regular notification 4/1. Nonfall registration accepted. Admission may be deferred for a maximum of 1 year. Credit and/or placement offered for CEEB Advanced Placement tests.

COSTS AND FINANCIAL AID
Average book expense $700. **Required Forms and Deadlines:** FAFSA, CSS/Financial Aid PROFILE, business/farm supplement. Either CSS Profile or institutional application, and tax returns to finalize aid offers. **Notification of Awards:** Applicants will be notified of awards on or about 4/1. **Types of Aid:** *Need-based scholarships/grants:* Federal Pell, SEOG, state scholarships/grants, private scholarships, the school's own gift aid. *Loans:* Direct Subsidized Stafford, Direct Unsubsidized Stafford, Direct PLUS, Subsidized Stafford, Unsubsidized Stafford, PLUS, Federal Perkins, state loans, college/university loans from institutional funds, Alternative Loans. **Student Employment:** Federal Work-Study Program available. Institutional employment available. Highest amount earned per year from on-campus jobs $5,600. Off-campus job opportunities are poor. **Financial Aid Statistics:** 100% freshmen, 99% undergrads receive need-based scholarship or grant aid. 2% freshmen, 3% undergrads receive non-need-based scholarship or grant aid. 76% freshmen, 80% undergrads receive need-based self help aid. 44% freshmen, 42% undergrads receive any aid. 35% undergrads borrow to pay for school. Average cumulative indebtedness $22,367.

COLBY-SAWYER COLLEGE

541Main Street, New London, NH 03257-7835
Phone: 603-526-3700 • **Financial Aid Phone:** 603-526-3717
E-mail: admissions@colbysawyer.edu • **CEEB Code:** 3281
Fax: 603-526-3452 • **Website:** www.colby-sawyer.edu • **ACT Code:** 2506

This private school was founded in 1837. It has a 200-acre campus.

RATINGS
Admissions Selectivity Rating: 66   **Fire Safety Rating:** 67   **Green Rating:** 60*

STUDENTS AND FACULTY
Enrollment: 942. **Student Body:** 65% female, 35% male, 68% out-of-state, 1% international (11 countries represented). Asian 1%, African American 1%, Caucasian 90%, Hispanic 1%, Native American 0%.
Retention and Graduation: 51% freshmen graduate within 4 years. 60% freshmen graduate within 6 years. **Faculty:** Student/faculty ratio 11:1. 60 full-time faculty, 73% hold PhDs, 2% are members of minority groups, 52% are women. 0% of classes are taught by teaching assistants.

ACADEMICS
Degrees: associate, bachelor's, transfer associate. **Classes:** Most classes have 10–19 students. Most lab/discussion sessions have 10–19 students. **Majors with Highest Enrollment:** business administration and management; nursing/registered nurse (rn, asn, bsn, msn); sport and fitness administration/management. **Special Study Options:** Accelerated program, cross-registration, double major, dual enrollment, English as a Second Language (ESL), exchange student program (domestic), honors program, independent study, internships, student-designed major, study abroad, teacher certification program. **Honors Programs:** The Wesson Honors Program is designed to provide highly motivated students with an optional intensive experience in the liberal arts. By creating academic, cultural, and social opportunities for integrative and interdisciplinary intellectual discovery, the program challenges students not only to widen their own avenues of intellectual exploration, but to take leadership in a community of scholars and participate as catalysts for inquiry and discussion across the college. **Disability Services:** Special programs offered to physically disabled students include tape recorders, tutors.

FACILITIES
Housing: Coed dorms, special housing for disabled students, women's dorms, Substance-free Residence Hall. 50% of campus accessible to physically disabled. **Special Academic Facilities/Equipment:** Sawyer Fine Arts Center, Windy Hill School (pre-school- grade 3 laboratory school), Ivey Science Center, Hogan Sports Center, Video Studio and Editing Room, Radio Station (WSCS 90.9 FM).

CAMPUS LIFE
Environment: Rural. **Activities:** Choral groups, dance, drama/theater, literary magazine, musical theater, radio station, student government, student newspaper, yearbook 40 registered organizations, 5 honor societies, 1 religious organizations. **Athletics (Intercollegiate):** *Men:* baseball, basketball, diving, equestrian sports, skiing (downhill/alpine), soccer, swimming, tennis, track/field (outdoor). *Women:* basketball, diving, equestrian sports, lacrosse, skiing (downhill/alpine), soccer, swimming, tennis, track/field (outdoor), volleyball. **On-Campus Highlights:** Dan and Kathleen Hogan Sports Center, Susan Colgate Cleveland Library/Learning Center, Lethbridge Lodge, Thornton Livingroom, Rooke Hall.

ADMISSIONS
Freshman Academic Profile: Average high school GPA 3.0. 83% from public high schools. SAT Math middle 50% range 440-530. SAT Critical Reading middle 50% range 440-540. ACT middle 50% range 18-22. Minimum paper TOEFL 500. **Basis for Candidate Selection:** *Very important factors considered include:* academic GPA, rigor of secondary school record, interview. *Important factors considered include:* Class rank, application essay, recommendation(s), standardized test scores, alumni/ae relation, extracurricular activities, level of applicant's interest, talent/ability, volunteer work, work experience. *Other factors considered include:* first generation, geographical residence, state residency. **Freshman Admission Requirements:** High school diploma is required and GED is accepted. **Freshman Admission Statistics:** 1,672 applied, 87% admitted, 24% enrolled. **Transfer Admission Requirements:** college transcript(s), essay or personal statement, minimum college GPA of 2.0 required. Lowest grade transferable C. **General Admission Information:** Application Fee $45. Early decision application deadline 12/1. Regular application deadline 4/1. Notification on a rolling basis, beginning on or about 1/1. Nonfall registration accepted. Admission may be deferred for a maximum of 1 YEAR. Credit and/or placement offered for CEEB Advanced Placement tests.

COSTS AND FINANCIAL AID
Annual tuition $29,620. Room and board $10,340. Average book expense $750. **Required Forms and Deadlines:** FAFSA. **Notification of Awards:** Applicants will be notified of awards on a rolling basis beginning 3/1. **Types of Aid:** *Need-based scholarships/grants:* Federal Pell, SEOG, state scholarships/grants, private scholarships, the school's own gift aid. *Loans:* Subsidized Stafford, Unsubsidized Stafford, PLUS, Federal Perkins, state loans, college/university loans from institutional funds. **Student Employment:** Federal Work-Study Program available. Institutional employment available. Off-campus job opportunities are good. **Financial Aid Statistics:** 100% freshmen, 95% undergrads receive need-based scholarship or grant aid. 4% freshmen, 6% undergrads receive non-need-based scholarship or grant aid. 93% freshmen, 99% undergrads receive need-based self-help aid. 83% freshmen, 83% undergrads receive any aid. 77% undergrads borrow to pay for school. Average cumulative indebtedness $18,306. **Criteria for awarding institutional aid:** *Non-need-based:* academics, alumni affiliation, art, leadership, music/drama.

COLGATE UNIVERSITY

13 Oak Drive, Hamilton, NY 13346
Phone: 315-228-7401 • **Financial Aid Phone:** 315-228-7431
E-mail: admission@colgate.edu • **CEEB Code:** 2086
Fax: 315-228-7544 • **Website:** www.colgate.edu • **ACT Code:** 2702

This private school was founded in 1819. It has a 515-acre campus.

RATINGS

Admissions Selectivity Rating: 97   **Fire Safety Rating:** 86   **Green Rating:** 94

STUDENTS AND FACULTY

Enrollment: 2,850. **Student Body:** 54% female, 46% male, 73% out-of-state, 8% international (41 countries represented). Asian 4%, African American 4%, Caucasian 69%, Hispanic 8%, Native American 0%.
Retention and Graduation: 85% freshmen graduate within 4 years. 18% grads go on to further study within 1 year. 10% grads pursue arts and sciences degrees. 4% grads pursue law degrees. 1% grads pursue business degrees. 3% grads pursue medical degrees. **Faculty:** Student/faculty ratio 9:1. 294 full-time faculty, 99% hold PhDs, 22% are members of minority groups, 42% are women. 0% of classes are taught by teaching assistants.

ACADEMICS

Degrees: bachelor's, master's. **Classes:** Most classes have 10–19 students. Most lab/discussion sessions have 10–19 students. **Majors with Highest Enrollment:** economics; English language and literature; history. **Special Study Options:** cross-registration, double major, honors program, independent study, internships, liberal arts/career combination, student-designed major, study abroad, teacher certification program, Extended study program allows students to further academic work with a 3-5 week off campus experience during the winter or summer break. Recent trips have travelled to 13 locations around the world including South Africa, Ireland, and China. **Honors Programs:** Each year, Colgate honors its top (approximately) 200 accepted students as Alumni Memorial Scholars. This recognition is the highest honor within the admission process, and an indication of an excellent match, both academically and personally, with Colgate. **Combined Degree Programs:** Pre-Engineering: BA/MS in Architecture. **Disability Services:** Special programs offered to physically disabled students include note-taking services, reader services, tape recorders, tutors. **Career Services:** Alumni network, alumni services, career assessment, internships Career Services highlights include Colgate alumni are a valuable resource for students who are exploring their career options. Recently, more than 350 alumni helped currenst students in career exploration. Approximately 4,000 alumni are registered with Career Services to aid students in internship and job searches.

FACILITIES

Housing: Coed dorms, special housing for disabled students, fraternity/sorority housing, cooperative housing, apartments for single students, wellness housing, theme housing: Peace Studies, La Casa Pan Latina, Harlem Reniassance Center, French-Italian House, etc. Accomodations for students with special needs. Townhouses for small groups of students. 20% of campus accessible to physically disabled. **Special Academic Facilities/Equipment:** Art galleries, anthropology museum, language lab, cable TV station, life sciences complex, geology/fossil collection, observatory, electron microscopes, laser lab, weather lab. **Computers:** Students can register for classes online. Administrative functions (other than registration) can be performed online.

CAMPUS LIFE

Environment: Rural. **Activities:** Choral groups, concert band, dance, drama/theater, jazz band, literary magazine, music ensembles, musical theater, pep band, radio station, student government, student newspaper, student-run film society, symphony orchestra, television station, yearbook, Campus Ministries, International Student Organization, Model UN 160 registered organizations, 4 honor societies, 8 religious organizations. 6 fraternities, 3 sororities. **Athletics (Intercollegiate):** *Men:* basketball, crew/rowing, cross-country, diving, football, golf, ice hockey, lacrosse, soccer, swimming, tennis, track/field (outdoor). *Women:* basketball, crew/rowing, cross-country, diving, field hockey, ice hockey, lacrosse, soccer, softball, swimming, tennis, track/field (outdoor), volleyball. **On-Campus Highlights:** Picker Art Gallery, Case-Geyer Library, ALANA Culture Center, Ho Science Center, O'Connor Campus Center (The Coop), Two recently completed building projects: $52 million renovation to the Case Library and The Robert H.N. Ho Science Center. **Environmental Initiatives:** All electricity used on campus is hydroelectric, with some supplemental nuclear power. Colgate's wood-chip-burning heating plant utilizes a renewable energy source to provide about 70 percent of our total requirement. Colgate signed an agreement with Clean Air-Cool Planet in 2004, agreeing to complete a campuswide greenhouse gas emissions inventory, raise awareness about the importance of addressing climate change within the campus community, adopt a greenhouse gas emissions reduction target, and develop and implement a strategic plan to meet established targets and monitor progress over time. Colgate routinely builds and renovates to LEED silver standards. Architectural consultants are required to be LEED certified and to provide a rigorous analysis of sustainable features for each major design and construction project.

ADMISSIONS

Freshman Academic Profile: Average high school GPA 3.6. 68% in top 10% of high school class, 60% from public high schools. SAT Math middle 50% range 640-720. SAT Critical Reading middle 50% range 630-730. ACT middle 50% range 30-32. **Basis for Candidate Selection:** *Very important factors considered include:* Class rank, academic GPA, rigor of secondary school record. *Important factors considered include:* application essay, recommendation(s), standardized test scores, character/personal qualities, extracurricular activities, talent/ability. *Other factors considered include:* alumni/ae relation, first generation, geographical residence, racial/ethnic status, volunteer work, work experience. **Freshman Admission Requirements:** High school diploma is required and GED is accepted. *Academic units required:* 4 English, 3 mathematics, 3 science, (2 science labs), 3 foreign language, 3 social studies. *Academic units recommended:* 4 English, 3 mathematics, 3 science, (2 science labs), 3 foreign language, 3 social studies. **Freshman Admission Statistics:** 7,798 applied, 29% admitted, 33% enrolled. **Transfer Admission Requirements:** High school transcript, college transcript(s), essay or personal statement, standardized test scores, statement of good standing from prior institution(s). Minimum college GPA of 3.00 required. Lowest grade transferable C. **General Admission Information:** Application Fee $55. Early decision application deadline 11/15. Regular application deadline 1/15. Regular notification 4/1. Nonfall registration not accepted. Admission may be deferred for a maximum of 1 year. Credit and/or placement offered for CEEB Advanced Placement tests.

COSTS AND FINANCIAL AID

Required Forms and Deadlines: CSS/Financial Aid PROFILE, noncustodial PROFILE. **Notification of Awards:** Applicants will be notified of awards on or about 4/1. **Types of Aid:** *Need-based scholarships/grants:* Federal Pell, SEOG, state scholarships/grants, private scholarships, the school's own gift aid. *Loans:* Subsidized Stafford, Unsubsidized Stafford, PLUS, Federal Perkins. **Student Employment:** Federal Work-Study Program available. Institutional employment available. Highest amount earned per year from on-campus jobs $1,600. Off-campus job opportunities are fair. **Financial Aid Statistics:** 100% freshmen, 99% undergrads receive need-based scholarship or grant aid. 78% undergrads receive non-need-based scholarship or grant aid. 75% freshmen, 78% undergrads receive need-based self-help aid. 7% freshmen, 7% undergrads receive athletic scholarships. 40% freshmen, 41% undergrads receive any aid. 34% undergrads borrow to pay for school. Average cumulative indebtedness $20,751. **Criteria for awarding institutional aid:** *Non-need-based:* athletics.

COLLEGE OF THE ATLANTIC

105 Eden Street, Bar Harbor, ME 4609
Phone: 207-288-5015 • **Financial Aid Phone:** 207-288-5015
E-mail: inquiry@coa.edu • **CEEB Code:** 3305
Fax: 207-288-4126 • **Website:** www.coa.edu • **ACT Code:** 1637

This private school was founded in 1969. It has a 35-acre campus.

RATINGS

Admissions Selectivity Rating: 91   **Fire Safety Rating:** 97   **Green Rating:** 99

STUDENTS AND FACULTY

Enrollment: 340. **Student Body:** 72% female, 28% male, 80% out-of-state, 17% international (36 countries represented). Asian 1%, African American 1%, Caucasian 68%, Hispanic 2%, Native American 0%.
Retention and Graduation: 86% freshmen return for sophomore year. 58% freshmen graduate within 4 years. 71% freshmen graduate within 6 years. 3% grads go on to further study within 1 year. 3% grads pursue arts and sciences degrees. **Faculty:** Student/faculty ratio 11:1. 28 full-time faculty, 86% hold PhDs, 7% are members of minority groups, 32% are women. 0% of classes are taught by teaching assistants.

ACADEMICS

Degrees: bachelor's, master's. **Classes:** Most classes have 10–19 students. Most lab/discussion sessions have 10–19 students. **Majors with Highest Enrollment:** biology/biological sciences; ecology; education. **Special Study Options:** cross-registration, exchange student program (domestic), independent study, internships, liberal arts/career combination, student-designed major, study abroad, teacher certification program, Winter term program in Yucatan, Mexico. EcoLeague - consortium agreement with five other colleges for student exchanges (Alaska Pacific University, Antioch College, Green Mountain College, Northland College, Prescott College. Exchange program with Olin College of Engineering and University of Maine at Orono. **Honors Programs:** We consider all our students to be capable of honors work, which is why all students finish their time at COA with a term-long capstone, or senior project. **Combined Degree Programs:** n/a. **Disability Services:** Special programs offered to physically disabled students include note-taking services, reader services, tape recorders, tutors. **Career Services:** Alumni network, alumni services, career assessment, internships, regional alumni. Career Services highlights include Internships are required for graduation and allow students to apply their classroom knowledge to the world of work over ten weeks and 400 hours.

FACILITIES

Housing: Coed dorms, special housing for disabled students, Substance-free housing; green (environmentally conscious) housing. 70% of campus accessible to physically disabled. **Special Academic Facilities/Equipment:** Natural history museum, pottery studio, greenhouse, Geographic Information Systems lab, Green Graphics Studio Deering Common Campus Center, organic community garden, Blum Gallery, outdoor equipment, two boats: Indigo and Borealis, off-site organic farm and two island research stations **Computers:** 100% of classrooms, 100% of dorms, 100% of libraries, 100% of dining areas, 100% of student union, 25% of common outdoor areas have wireless network access. Students can register for classes online. Administrative functions (other than registration) can be performed online.

CAMPUS LIFE

Environment: Rural. **Activities:** Choral groups, dance, drama/theater, jazz band, literary magazine, music ensembles, student government, student newspaper, yearbook. **On-Campus Highlights:** George B. Dorr Museum of Natural History, Blum Art Gallery, The pier, Turrets, Take-A-Break, College of the Atlantic has recently completed state-of-the-art sustainable dorms. and a creative restoration of an historic building into a similarly sustainable campus center. These are also very popular places to visit. **Environmental Initiatives:** Carbon NetZero Initiative - COA set as its goal to be carbon net zero by the end of 2007 and achieved this goal by offsetting all of its carbon emissions that it could not avoid or reduce. We are currently re-evaluating the commitment to use carbon offsets to attain carbon neutrality. Meanwhile we are working on an electric/solar charging system for our vehicles, with charging stations on our farms to assist non-emitting local transportation. Energy conservation through renewables and campus audits: COA's new student residences have space heating and hot water provided by a wood pellet boiler, the buildings are super-insulated, have triple-pane windows and composting toilets. The building renovated to serve as the campus center received numerous energy efficient improvements and is also heated by the same wood pellet boiler system. Working with an energy services company, COA completed an energy audit of the campus and implemented recommendations to make existing buildings more energy efficient. Retrofits and upgrades to buildings were completed in 2008. Local and organic food: COA has its own organic farm and hosts an organic community garden on its campus. Both sites supply the college cafeteria with local, organic food when possible given the northern growing season. A good percentage of what the farm can't supply is still local and organic. ALL food waste is composted, with food waste bins in all dorms. as well as the cafeteria. COA alumni, working with the organic farm, have been instrumental in creating a farm to school program for local elementary schools. The college has now initiated a Sustainable Food Systems Program to tie together its work in organic agriculture and larger food systems issues. In 2010, we were donated 125 acres of additional farm property - the Peggy Rockefeller Farms within a few miles of the campus. The use of this new farm property is being planned by a task force of stakeholders. Additionally, we've been tray-less for about 3 years in our cafeteria and have had a policy of no bottled water on campus, or even for off-campus college-related activities for more then two years.

ADMISSIONS

Freshman Academic Profile: Average high school GPA 3.6. 24% in top 10% of high school class, 72% in top 25% of high school class, 96% in top 50% of high school class. 61% from public high schools. SAT Math middle 50% range 570-660. SAT Critical Reading middle 50% range 610-700. SAT Writing middle 50% range 570-670. ACT middle 50% range 29-30. Minimum web-based TOEFL 86. Minimum paper TOEFL 567. **Basis for Candidate Selection:** *Very important factors considered include:* application essay, recommendation(s), rigor of secondary school record. *Important factors considered include:* Class rank, academic GPA, character/personal qualities, extracurricular activities, interview, talent/ability, volunteer work, work experience. *Other factors considered include:* standardized test scores, alumni/ae rela-

tion, first generation, geographical residence, level of applicant's interest, racial/ethnic status, state residency. **Freshman Admission Requirements:** High school diploma is required and GED is accepted. *Academic units required:* 4 English, 3 mathematics, 2 science, (2 science labs), 2 social studies. *Academic units recommended:* 4 English, 3 mathematics, 2 science, (2 science labs), 2 social studies. **Freshman Admission Statistics:** 400 applied, 58% admitted, 33% enrolled. **Transfer Admission Requirements:** High school transcript, college transcript(s), essay or personal statement, minimum college GPA of 3.0 required. Lowest grade transferable C. **General Admission Information:** Application Fee $45. Early decision application deadline 12/1. Regular application deadline 2/15. Regular notification 4/1. Nonfall registration accepted. Admission may be deferred for a maximum of 1 year. Credit and/or placement offered for CEEB Advanced Placement tests.

COSTS AND FINANCIAL AID

Annual tuition $37,152. Room and board $9,258. Required fees $549. Average book expense $600. **Required Forms and Deadlines:** FAFSA, institution's own financial aid form, noncustodial PROFILE, business/farm supplement. **Notification of Awards:** Applicants will be notified of awards on or about 4/1. **Types of Aid:** *Need-based scholarships/grants:* Federal Pell, SEOG, state scholarships/grants, private scholarships, the school's own gift aid. *Loans:* Subsidized Stafford, Unsubsidized Stafford, PLUS, Federal Perkins. **Student Employment:** Federal Work-Study Program available. Off-campus job opportunities are good. **Financial Aid Statistics:** 100% freshmen, 97% undergrads receive need-based scholarship or grant aid. 12% freshmen, 4% undergrads receive non-need-based scholarship or grant aid. 97% freshmen, 94% undergrads receive need-based self-help aid. 87% freshmen, 85% undergrads receive any aid. 69% undergrads borrow to pay for school. Average cumulative indebtedness $20,858. **Criteria for awarding institutional aid:** *Non-need-based:* academics.

COLLEGE FOR CREATIVE STUDIES

201 East Kirby, Detroit, MI 48202
Phone: 313-664-7425 • **Financial Aid Phone:** 313-664-7495
E-mail: admissions@ccscad.edu
Fax: 313-872-2739 • **Website:** www.ccscad.edu

This private school was founded in 1906. It has a 11-acre campus.

RATINGS

Admissions Selectivity Rating: 85   **Fire Safety Rating:** 80   **Green Rating:** 60*

STUDENTS AND FACULTY

Retention and Graduation: 73% freshmen return for sophomore year. **Faculty:** Student/faculty ratio 8:1. 51 full-time faculty, 61% hold PhDs, 14% are members of minority groups, 31% are women. 0% of classes are taught by teaching assistants.

ACADEMICS

Degrees: bachelor's, post-bachelor's certificate. **Majors with Highest Enrollment:** commercial and advertising art; film/video and photographic arts; other; industrial design. **Special Study Options:** cooperative education program, double major, dual enrollment, English as a Second Language (ESL), exchange student program (domestic), independent study, internships, study abroad, teacher certification program. **Disability Services:** Special programs offered to physically disabled students include reader services, tape recorders, tutors. **Career Services:** Alumni network, alumni services, career/job search classes, career assessment, internships, regional alumni. Career Services highlights include All seniors take part in a practicum class that allows students to work with and for outside companies, such as Ford Motor Company, Pixar, DaimlerChrysler and various companies.

FACILITIES

Housing: Coed dorms. 95% of campus accessible to physically disabled. **Special Academic Facilities/Equipment:** Top-of-the-line technology for design, animation and audiovisual editing. Wood and Metal shops, hot glass studio, gallery, private studios.

CAMPUS LIFE

Environment: Metropolis. **Activities:** student government 5 registered organizations. **On-Campus Highlights:** Center Galleries, U245 Student Art Gallery, Jazzman's Cafe.

ADMISSIONS

Freshman Academic Profile: ACT middle 50% range 18-23. Minimum paper TOEFL 525. **Basis for Candidate Selection:** *Very important factors considered include:* talent/ability. *Important factors considered include:* academic GPA, standardized test scores. *Other factors considered include:* level of applicant's interest. **Freshman Admission Requirements:** High school diploma is required and GED is accepted. **Freshman Admission Statistics:** 1,260 applied, 39% admitted, 51% enrolled. **Transfer Admission Requirements:** High school transcript, college transcript(s), minimum college GPA of 2.0 required. Lowest grade transferable C. **General Admission Information:** Application Fee $35. Regular application deadline 8/1. Notification on a rolling basis, beginning on or about 9/15. Nonfall registration accepted. Admission may be deferred for a maximum of 4 semesters. Credit offered for CEEB Advanced Placement tests.

COSTS AND FINANCIAL AID

Annual tuition $27,090. Room and board $4,300. Required fees $1,185. Average book expense $2,500. **Required Forms and Deadlines:** FAFSA. **Notification of Awards:** Applicants will be notified of awards on a rolling basis beginning 3/15. **Types of Aid:** *Need-based scholarships/grants:* Federal Pell, SEOG, state scholarships/grants, private scholarships, the school's own gift aid. *Loans:* Subsidized Stafford, Unsubsidized Stafford, PLUS, Alternative loans. **Student Employment:** Highest amount earned per year from on-campus jobs $1,000. **Financial Aid Statistics:** 74% undergrads borrow to pay for school. Average cumulative indebtedness $57,980. **Criteria for awarding institutional aid:** *Non-need-based:* academics, art, minority status.

COLLEGE OF CHARLESTON

Best 378

66 George Street, Charleston, SC 29424
Phone: 843-953-5670 • **Financial Aid Phone:** 843-953-5540
E-mail: admissions@cofc.edu • **CEEB Code:** 5113
Fax: 843-953-6322 • **Website:** www.cofc.edu • **ACT Code:** 3846

This public school was founded in 1770. It has a 52-acre campus.

RATINGS
Admissions Selectivity Rating: 85   **Fire Safety Rating:** 94   **Green Rating:** 89

STUDENTS AND FACULTY
Enrollment: 10,206. **Student Body:** 63% female, 37% male, 38% out-of-state, 1% international (63 countries represented). Asian 2%, African American 6%, Caucasian 83%, Hispanic 4%, Native American 0%.
Retention and Graduation: 58% freshmen graduate within 4 years. 69% freshmen graduate within 6 years. 40% grads go on to further study within 1 year. 31% grads pursue arts and sciences degrees. 1% grads pursue law degrees. 19% grads pursue business degrees. 2% grads pursue medical degrees.
Faculty: Student/faculty ratio 16:1. 541 full-time faculty, 89% hold PhDs, 12% are members of minority groups, 43% are women. 4% of classes are taught by teaching assistants.

ACADEMICS
Degrees: bachelor's, master's, post-bachelor's certificate. **Classes:** Most classes have 20–29 students. Most lab/discussion sessions have 20–29 students. **Majors with Highest Enrollment:** biology/biological sciences; business administration and management; communication studies/speech communication and rhetoric. **Special Study Options:** Accelerated program, cooperative education program, cross-registration, distance learning, double major, dual enrollment, English as a Second Language (ESL), exchange student program (domestic), honors program, independent study, internships, liberal arts/career combination, study abroad, teacher certification program, Semester at Sea. **Honors Programs:** The Honors College at the College of Charleston began as an Honors Program in 1978 to provide a program and a community for talented and motivated students who enjoy active participation in small stimulating classes and want to be involved in a meaningful way in undergraduate research. In order to better serve the needs of the students, it became an Honors College in 2005, with new positions to provide academic advising and assistance in applying for postgraduate fellowships and additional funding to support its mission. The Honors College is dedicated to providing these students with a place where they can flourish and grow, a true learning community of teachers and students. In addition to receiving exciting and unique educational experiences, students can participate with their fellow Honors students in social, cultural, and intellectual events on the campus and in historic Charleston, SC. The Honors College challenges intellectually talented students to make the most of the opportunities available to them, to become actively involved in their own education, and to prepare themselves to excel in graduate programs, medical or law school, or in whatever comes after they complete their undergraduate education. In Honors classes, students take responsibility for their own learning through class discussions,

through interaction with faculty and fellow students, and through independent research. Honors students are advised by a full time Honors academic advisor and specially chosen faculty mentors, receive priority registration, and have the opportunity to room with other Honors students in special Honors residence halls. Classes, seminars, and student gatherings are held in the Honors Center, the historic William Aiken House built by Governor William Aiken in 1839. **Disability Services:** Special programs offered to physically disabled students include note-taking services, reader services, tape recorders, tutors. **Career Services:** Alumni network, alumni services, career/job search classes, career assessment, internships, regional alumni. Career Services highlights include Internships. Most academic departments offer internships for credit and the career center offers a certificate/no-credit option. A large number of students do these each year.

FACILITIES
Housing: Coed dorms, men's dorms, women's dorms, fraternity/sorority housing, apartments for single students, theme housing, restored old Charleston houses used as residence halls, some with kitchen facilities in suites. 80% of campus accessible to physically disabled. **Special Academic Facilities/Equipment:** Halsey Institute of Contemporary Art, sculpture facility, Rivers Communications Museum, Miles Early Childhood Development Center, Avery Institute for African-American History and Culture, physics and astronomy observatory, Grice Marine Laboratory, Patriots Point Athletics Complex (includes softball, baseball, tennis, soccer and sailing) **Computers:** 75% of classrooms, 100% of dorms, 100% of libraries, 100% of dining areas, 100% of student union, 80% of common outdoor areas have wireless network access. Students can register for classes online. Administrative functions (other than registration) can be performed online.

CAMPUS LIFE
Environment: City. **Activities:** Choral groups, dance, drama/theater, jazz band, literary magazine, music ensembles, musical theater, pep band, radio station, student government, student newspaper, symphony orchestra, yearbook, Campus Ministries, International Student Organization 120 registered organizations, 19 honor societies, 16 religious organizations. 13 fraternities, 12 sororities. **Athletics (Intercollegiate):** *Men:* baseball, basketball, cross-country, diving, golf, sailing, soccer, swimming, tennis. *Women:* basketball, cross-country, diving, equestrian sports, golf, sailing, soccer, softball, swimming, tennis, track/field (outdoor), track/field (indoor), volleyball. **On-Campus Highlights:** The Cistern Yard, Carolina First Arena, Fresh Food Company, Addlestone Library, Cougar Plaza, The College opened two new facilities in January 2010: The The Marion and Wayland H. Cato Jr. Center for the Arts and a second building for the School of Sciences and Mathematics. Their completion is part of a significant transformation of the College's facilities, providing students with the best and most effective learning and recreational opportunities. Six new facilities were completed in 2007, and several others were finished in 2008. Patriots Point Athletics Complex is located just across the Ravenel Bridge in Mt. Pleasant. Recently renovated, this 35-acre complex is home to baseball, soccer, softball, sailing and tennis. **Environmental Initiatives:** Completed the campus' first GHG Inventory 2011. Created formally the "Office of Sustainability" and hired a Director. Building a decentralized network of governance on sustainability issues that builds on relationships and connections as foundation for campus sustainability.

ADMISSIONS
Freshman Academic Profile: Average high school GPA 3.9. 31% in top 10% of high school class, 67% in top 25% of high school class, 94% in top 50% of high school class. 43% from public high schools. SAT Math middle 50% range 560-650. SAT Critical Reading middle 50% range 550-650. ACT middle 50% range 23-27. Minimum web-based TOEFL 80. Minimum paper TOEFL 570. **Basis for Candidate Selection:** *Very important factors considered include:* academic GPA, rigor of secondary school record, standardized test scores, state residency. *Important factors considered include:* Class rank, character/personal qualities, first generation, talent/ability. *Other factors considered include:* application essay, recommendation(s), extracurricular activities, racial/ethnic status, volunteer work, work experience. **Freshman Admission Requirements:** High school diploma is required and GED is accepted. *Academic units required:* 4 English, 3 mathematics, 3 science, (3 science labs), 3 foreign language, 3 social studies, 4 academic electives. *Academic units recommended:* 4 English, 3 mathematics, 3 science, (3 science labs), 3 foreign language, 3 social studies, 4 academic electives. **Freshman Admission Statistics:** 11,962 applied, 68% admitted, 26% enrolled. **Transfer Admission Requirements:** college transcript(s), minimum college GPA of 2.6 required. Lowest grade transferable C. **General Admission Information:** Application Fee $50. Regular application deadline 2/1. Nonfall registration accepted. Admission may be deferred for a maximum of 1or2semester. Credit and/or placement offered for CEEB Advanced Placement tests.

COSTS AND FINANCIAL AID
Annual in-state tuition $9,918. Annual out-of-state tuition $25,304. Room and board $10,461. Average book expense $1,167. **Required Forms and Deadlines:** FAFSA. **Notification of Awards:** Applicants will be notified of awards

on a rolling basis beginning 4/10. **Types of Aid:** *Need-based scholarships/ grants:* Federal Pell, SEOG, state scholarships/grants, private scholarships, the school's own gift aid. *Loans:* Direct Subsidized Stafford, Direct Unsubsidized Stafford, Direct PLUS, Federal Perkins. **Student Employment:** Federal Work-Study Program available. Institutional employment available. Highest amount earned per year from on-campus jobs $9,400. Off-campus job opportunities are fair. **Financial Aid Statistics:** 68% freshmen, 67% undergrads receive need-based scholarship or grant aid. 72% freshmen, 44% undergrads receive non-need-based scholarship or grant aid. 77% freshmen, 82% undergrads receive need-based self-help aid. 2% freshmen, 2% undergrads receive athletic scholarships. 50% freshmen, 47% undergrads receive any aid. 45% undergrads borrow to pay for school. Average cumulative indebtedness $26,024. **Criteria for awarding institutional aid:** *Non-need-based:* academics, alumni affiliation, art, athletics, music/drama.

COLLEGE OF THE HOLY CROSS

1 College Street, Worcester, MA 01610-2395
Phone: 508-793-2443 • **Financial Aid Phone:** 508-793-2265
E-mail: admissions@holycross.edu • **CEEB Code:** 3282
Fax: 508-793-3888 • **Website:** www.holycross.edu • **ACT Code:** 1810

This private school, affiliated with the Roman Catholic Church, was founded in 1843. It has a 174-acre campus.

RATINGS

Admissions Selectivity Rating: 96   **Fire Safety Rating:** 94   **Green Rating:** 92

STUDENTS AND FACULTY

Enrollment: 2,891. **Student Body:** 51% female, 49% male, 63% out-of-state, 1% international (21 countries represented). Asian 5%, African American 5%, Caucasian 69%, Hispanic 10%, Native American 0%.
Retention and Graduation: 95% freshmen return for sophomore year. 90% freshmen graduate within 4 years. 93% freshmen graduate within 6 years. 20% grads go on to further study within 1 year. 8% grads pursue arts and sciences degrees. 6% grads pursue law degrees. 1% grads pursue medical degrees. **Faculty:** Student/faculty ratio 10:1. 272 full-time faculty, 97% hold PhDs, 13% are members of minority groups, 45% are women. 0% of classes are taught by teaching assistants.

ACADEMICS

Degrees: bachelor's. **Classes:** Most classes have 10–19 students. Most lab/ discussion sessions have 10–19 students. **Majors with Highest Enrollment:** economics; English language and literature; political science and government. **Special Study Options:** Accelerated program, cross-registration, double major, dual enrollment, exchange student program (domestic), honors program, independent study, internships, liberal arts/career combination, student-designed major, study abroad, teacher certification program, First-year integrated living and learning program ("Montserrat"). **Honors Programs:** Fenwick Scholar Program. **Disability Services:** Special programs offered to physically disabled students include note-taking services, reader services, tutors. **Career Services:** Alumni network, career/job search classes, internships, regional alumni. Career Services highlights include Summer Internship Program.

FACILITIES

Housing: Coed dorms, special housing for disabled students, apartments for single students, Suites on campus available for juniors and seniors. Substance-free housing also available. 85% of campus accessible to physically disabled. **Special Academic Facilities/Equipment:** Art gallery, Concert Hall, Taylor and Boody tracker organ, O'Callahan Science Library, Rehm Library, Multimedia Resource Center, Wellness Center; scientific equipment on par with the best research universities **Computers:** 100% of classrooms, 100% of dorms, 100% of libraries, 100% of dining areas, 100% of student union, 60% of common outdoor areas have wireless network access. Students can register for classes online. Administrative functions (other than registration) can be performed online.

CAMPUS LIFE

Environment: City. **Activities:** Choral groups, concert band, dance, drama/ theater, jazz band, literary magazine, marching band, music ensembles, musical theater, pep band, radio station, student government, student newspaper, year book, Campus Ministries, International Student Organization 105 registered organizations, 20 honor societies, 4 religious organizations. **Athletics (Intercol-**

legiate): *Men:* baseball, basketball, crew/rowing, cross-country, diving, football, golf, ice hockey, lacrosse, soccer, swimming, tennis, track/field (outdoor), track/ field (indoor). *Women:* basketball, crew/rowing, cross-country, diving, field hockey, golf, ice hockey, lacrosse, soccer, softball, swimming, tennis, track/field (outdoor), track/field (indoor), volleyball. **On-Campus Highlights:** Library, Smith Hall, St. Joseph Chapel, Hart Recreation Center, Hogan Campus Center. **Environmental Initiatives:** College has committed to a 20% carbon reduction by 2015 and Carbon Neutrality. The College has already achieved a 28% reduction in carbon emissions. The College achieved LEED Gold for a science complex addition and renovation project. College is continuously updating energy consuming equipment and fixtures. This includes solar lighting, LED lighting, HVAC systems & controls and underground steam lines.

ADMISSIONS

Freshman Academic Profile: Average high school GPA 3.9. 60% in top 10% of high school class, 95% in top 25% of high school class, 100% in top 50% of high school class. 49% from public high schools. SAT Math middle 50% range 620-680. SAT Critical Reading middle 50% range 600-700. SAT Writing middle 50% range 610-700. ACT middle 50% range 27-30. Minimum web-based TOEFL 79. Minimum paper TOEFL 550. **Basis for Candidate Selection:** *Very important factors considered include:* Class rank, academic GPA, recommendation(s), rigor of secondary school record, interview. *Important factors considered include:* application essay, character/personal qualities, extracurricular activities, level of applicant's interest. *Other factors considered include:* standardized test scores, alumni/ae relation, first generation, geographical residence, racial/ethnic status, talent/ability, volunteer work, work experience. **Freshman Admission Requirements:** High school diploma is required and GED is accepted. **Freshman Admission Statistics:** 7,228 applied, 34% admitted, 31% enrolled. **Transfer Admission Requirements:** High school transcript, college transcript(s), essay or personal statement, statement of good standing from prior institution(s). Lowest grade transferable C. **General Admission Information:** Application Fee $60. Early decision application deadline 12/15. Regular application deadline 1/15. Nonfall registration not accepted. Admission may be deferred for a maximum of 12 months. Credit offered for CEEB Advanced Placement tests.

COSTS AND FINANCIAL AID

Annual tuition $43,660. Room and board $11,960. Required fees $612. Average book expense $700. **Required Forms and Deadlines:** FAFSA, CSS/Financial Aid PROFILE, noncustodial PROFILE, business/farm supplement. Parent and student federal tax returns. **Notification of Awards:** Applicants will be notified of awards on or about 4/1. **Types of Aid:** *Need-based scholarships/grants:* Federal Pell, SEOG, state scholarships/grants, private scholarships, the school's own gift aid. *Loans:* Direct Subsidized Stafford, Direct Unsubsidized Stafford, Direct PLUS, Federal Perkins, MEFA. **Student Employment:** Federal Work-Study Program available. Institutional employment available. Highest amount earned per year from on-campus jobs $1,604. Off-campus job opportunities are fair. **Financial Aid Statistics:** 76% freshmen, 78% undergrads receive need-based scholarship or grant aid. 2% freshmen, 2% undergrads receive non-need-based scholarship or grant aid. 82% freshmen, 82% undergrads receive need-based self-help aid. 2% freshmen, 2% undergrads receive athletic scholarships. 68% freshmen, 62% undergrads receive any aid. 55% undergrads borrow to pay for school. Average cumulative indebtedness $26,567. **Criteria for awarding institutional aid:** *Non-need-based:* academics, athletics.

THE COLLEGE OF IDAHO

2112 Cleveland Boulevard, Caldwell, ID 83605-4432
Phone: 208-459-5305 • **Financial Aid Phone:** 208-459-5307
E-mail: admission@collegeofidaho.edu • **CEEB Code:** 4060
Fax: 208-459-5757 • **Website:** www.collegeofidaho.edu • **ACT Code:** 916

This private school was founded in 1891. It has a 50-acre campus.

RATINGS

Admissions Selectivity Rating: 79   **Fire Safety Rating:** 79   **Green Rating:** 75

STUDENTS AND FACULTY

Enrollment: 1,030. **Student Body:** 58% female, 42% male, 15% out-of-state, 10% international (46 countries represented). Asian 3%, African American 1%, Caucasian 55%, Hispanic 14%, Native American 1%.
Retention and Graduation: 50% freshmen graduate within 4 years. **Faculty:** Student/faculty ratio 12:1. 75 full-time faculty, 85% hold PhDs, 7% are mem-

bers of minority groups, 41% are women. 0% of classes are taught by teaching assistants.

ACADEMICS

Degrees: bachelor's, master's. **Classes:** Most classes have fewer than 10 students. **Majors with Highest Enrollment:** biology/biological sciences; business/commerce; psychology. **Special Study Options:** cross-registration, double major, dual enrollment, exchange student program (domestic), honors program, independent study, internships, liberal arts/career combination, student-designed major, study abroad, teacher certification program. **Honors Programs:** Heritage Scholars Program, Gipson Honors Program; Kathryn Albertson Scholars Program; Davis United World Scholars **Combined Degree Programs:** BA/JD, MBA (Gonzaga, BSU), MNR (U of ID), Nursing (ISU). **Disability Services:** Special programs offered to physically disabled students include note-taking services, reader services, tape recorders. **Career Services:** Alumni network, alumni services, career assessment, internships, regional alumni. Career Services highlights include Internship program - students are required to connect their internship with the academic coursework though writing.

FACILITIES

Housing: Coed dorms, special housing for disabled students, fraternity/sorority housing, apartments for single students, College owned houses; dorms. for Healthy/Quiet Lifestyle, Academic Honor, First Year Community, Honor Code. 80% of campus accessible to physically disabled. **Special Academic Facilities/Equipment:** Art and natural history museums, gem and mineral collections, observatory, planetarium, nuclear magnetic resonance spectrometer, gas chromatograph, gamma camera, graphic computer, art gallery, Robert E. Smylie Archives. **Computers:** 100% of classrooms, 100% of dorms, 100% of libraries, 100% of dining areas, 100% of student union, 100% of common outdoor areas have wireless network access. Administrative functions (other than registration) can be performed online.

CAMPUS LIFE

Environment: Town. **Activities:** Choral groups, concert band, dance, drama/theater, jazz band, literary magazine, music ensembles, musical theater, opera, pep band, radio station, student government, student newspaper, student-run film society, symphony orchestra, yearbook, Campus Ministries, International Student Organization, Model UN 55 registered organizations, 4 honor societies, 3 religious organizations. 3 fraternities, 4 sororities. **Athletics (Intercollegiate):** *Men:* baseball, cheerleading, cross-country, golf, skiing (downhill/alpine), skiingnordiccross-country, snowboarding, soccer, swimming, tennis, track/field (outdoor). *Women:* basketball, cheerleading, cross-country, golf, skiing (downhill/alpine), skiingnordiccross-country, snowboarding, soccer, softball, swimming, tennis, track/field (outdoor), volleyball. **On-Campus Highlights:** J.A. Albertson Activity Center, McCain Student Center, Langroise Center for Performing and Fine Arts, Centennial Amphitheater, Dorms. **Environmental Initiatives:** Campus Sustainability council Comprehensive recycling program and TERRA organization Boone Science Hall recognized for commitment to energy efficiency by Idaho Power recognition

ADMISSIONS

Freshman Academic Profile: Average high school GPA 3.6. 25% in top 10% of high school class, 56% in top 25% of high school class, 88% in top 50% of high school class. SAT Math middle 50% range 480-600. SAT Critical Reading middle 50% range 470-630. SAT Writing middle 50% range 460-600. ACT middle 50% range 22-27. Minimum web-based TOEFL 79. Minimum paper TOEFL 550. **Basis for Candidate Selection:** *Very important factors considered include:* application essay, academic GPA, recommendation(s), rigor of secondary school record, standardized test scores, character/personal qualities, extracurricular activities, level of applicant's interest. *Important factors considered include:* Class rank, interview. *Other factors considered include:* alumni/ae relation, first generation, geographical residence, talent/ability, volunteer work. **Freshman Admission Requirements:** High school diploma is required and GED is accepted. *Academic units required:* 3 English, 2 mathematics, 3 social studies, 3 history, 3 academic electives. *Academic units recommended:* 3 English, 2 mathematics, 3 social studies, 3 history, 3 academic electives. **Freshman Admission Statistics:** 1,388 applied, 65% admitted, 32% enrolled. **Transfer Admission Requirements:** college transcript(s), essay or personal statement, minimum college GPA of 2.2 required. Lowest grade transferable D-. **General Admission Information:** Regular application deadline 8/1. Notification on a rolling basis, beginning on or about 10/15. Nonfall registration accepted. Admission may be deferred for a maximum of one year. Credit and/or placement offered for CEEB Advanced Placement tests.

COSTS AND FINANCIAL AID

Annual tuition $22,600. Room and board $8,646. Required fees $400. Average book expense $1,200. **Required Forms and Deadlines:** FAFSA, institution's own financial aid form. **Notification of Awards:** Applicants will be notified of awards on a rolling basis beginning 2/1. **Types of Aid:** *Need-based scholarships/grants:* Federal Pell, SEOG, state scholarships/grants, private scholarships, the school's own gift aid. *Loans:* Subsidized Stafford, Unsubsidized Stafford, PLUS, Federal Perkins, Alternative Education Loans. **Student Employment:** Federal Work-Study Program available. Highest amount earned per year from

on-campus jobs $77,073. Off-campus job opportunities are good. **Financial Aid Statistics:** 100% freshmen, 100% undergrads receive need-based scholarship or grant aid. 100% freshmen, 100% undergrads receive non-need-based scholarship or grant aid. 81% freshmen, 81% undergrads receive need-based self-help aid. 21% freshmen, 19% undergrads receive athletic scholarships. 98% freshmen, 96% undergrads receive any aid. 55% undergrads borrow to pay for school. Average cumulative indebtedness $27,008. **Criteria for awarding institutional aid:** *Non-need-based:* academics, alumni affiliation, art, athletics, leadership, minority status, music/drama, religious affiliation, state/district residency.

COLLEGE OF MOUNT SAINT VINCENT

6301 Riverdale Avenue, Riverdale, NY 10471
Phone: 718-405-3267 • **Financial Aid Phone:** 718-405-3349
E-mail: admissions@mountsaintvincent.edu • **CEEB Code:** 2088
Fax: 718-549-7945 • **Website:** www.mountsaintvincent.edu

This private school, affiliated with the Roman Catholic Church, was founded in 1847. It has a 70-acre campus.

RATINGS

Admissions Selectivity Rating: 65   **Fire Safety Rating:** 69   **Green Rating:** 60*

STUDENTS AND FACULTY

Enrollment: 1,655. **Student Body:** 72% female, 28% male, 9% out-of-state, 1% international (6 countries represented). Asian 8%, African American 16%, Caucasian 27%, Hispanic 36%, Native American 0%.
Retention and Graduation: 71% freshmen return for sophomore year. 41% freshmen graduate within 4 years. 57% freshmen graduate within 6 years. 39% grads go on to further study within 1 year. 9% grads pursue arts and sciences degrees. 1% grads pursue law degrees. 1% grads pursue business degrees. **Faculty:** Student/faculty ratio 12:1. 0% of classes are taught by teaching assistants.

ACADEMICS

Degrees: associate, bachelor's, master's, post-master's certificate. **Classes:** Most classes have 20–29 students. Most lab/discussion sessions have 10–19 students. **Majors with Highest Enrollment:** business/commerce; nursing/registered nurse (rn, asn, bsn, msn); psychology. **Special Study Options:** Accelerated program, double major, honors program, independent study, internships, liberal arts/career combination, study abroad, teacher certification program. **Honors Programs:** At present, the Honors Program reflects several distinctive dimensions and provides gifted students with the opportunity to develop critical thinking skills, an affirmative acknowledgement of the human dignity of self and others, and a commitment to realize one's intellectual potential, through participation in enhanced learning experiences both in and out of the classroom. Freshman and sophomore honors students are required to complete six of eight paired Honors Sections of the college's Core Curriculum courses. Specifically, in freshman year, literature is paired with psychology and fine arts with history; sociology is paired with economics and philosophy with religious studies in sophomore year. Juniors and seniors are challenged to enrich themselves through involvement in research projects that are faculty-mentored and through engaging themselves in reflective extra-curricular events (e.g., attending lectures, conferences, or cultural event) with faculty assistance and support. At the same time, the college has initiated a process to further develop and restructure the honors experience by the development of courses that are more inter-disciplinary in nature, utilize more diversified pedagogical styles, and, consistent with the college's mission, provide the opportunity for community service and learning. Through its honors program, the college seeks to develop informed, critically reflective, and value-oriented young men and women who will successfully pursue higher educational opportunities and make meaningful contributions to society both professionally and in their personal lives. **Disability Services:** Special programs offered to physically disabled students include note-taking services, tape recorders, tutors. **Career Services:** career/job search classes, career assessment, internships, regional alumni.

FACILITIES

Housing: Coed dorms, special housing for disabled students, women's dorms. 90% of campus accessible to physically disabled. **Special Academic Facilities/Equipment:** Newly renovated Maryvale Hall, with newly constructed wing, for Communications and Fine Arts Departments; Nursing lab, TV studio, radio station, Elizabeth Seton Travelling Museum, Forensic Laboratory equipment **Computers:** Students can register for classes online. Administrative functions (other than registration) can be performed online.

CAMPUS LIFE

Environment: Metropolis. **Activities:** dance, drama/theater, literary magazine, musical theater, radio station, student government, student newspaper, television station, yearbook, Campus Ministries 30 registered organizations, 15 honor societies, 2 religious organizations. **Athletics (Intercollegiate):** *Men:* baseball, basketball, cross-country, lacrosse, soccer, swimming, tennis, volleyball. *Women:* basketball, cross-country, lacrosse, soccer, softball, swimming, tennis, track/field (outdoor), volleyball. **On-Campus Highlights:** Crossroads (Student Lounge), Maryvale(new Communication/Art building), Fitness Center (includes swimming pool), Benedict's Cafe **Environmental Initiatives:** Recycling "Green" cleaning products "Green" construction

ADMISSIONS

Freshman Academic Profile: Average high school GPA 3.3. 3% in top 10% of high school class, 17% in top 25% of high school class, 44% in top 50% of high school class. 46% from public high schools. SAT Math middle 50% range 400-490. SAT Critical Reading middle 50% range 410-500. SAT Writing middle 50% range 410-490. ACT middle 50% range 16-21. Minimum paper TOEFL 550. **Basis for Candidate Selection:** *Very important factors considered include:* academic GPA, rigor of secondary school record. *Important factors considered include:* application essay, recommendation(s), standardized test scores, character/personal qualities, extracurricular activities, interview. *Other factors considered include:* Class rank, alumni/ae relation, first generation, geographical residence, religious affiliation/commitment, state residency, volunteer work, work experience. **Freshman Admission Requirements:** High school diploma is required and GED is accepted. *Academic units required:* 4 English, 2 mathematics, 2 science, 2 foreign language, 3 social studies, 3 academic electives. *Academic units recommended:* 4 English, 2 mathematics, 2 science, 2 foreign language, 3 social studies, 3 academic electives. **Freshman Admission Statistics:** 2,637 applied, 92% admitted, 20% enrolled. **Transfer Admission Requirements:** college transcript(s), essay or personal statement, minimum college GPA of 2.0 required. Lowest grade transferable C. **General Admission Information:** Application Fee $35. Notification on a rolling basis, beginning on or about 2/1. Nonfall registration accepted. Admission may be deferred for a maximum of 1 year. Credit and/or placement offered for CEEB Advanced Placement tests.

COSTS AND FINANCIAL AID

Annual tuition $28,980. Room and board $12,060. Required fees $1,310. Average book expense $1,185. **Required Forms and Deadlines:** FAFSA, state aid form. **Notification of Awards:** Applicants will be notified of awards on a rolling basis beginning 3/1. **Types of Aid:** *Need-based scholarships/grants:* Federal Pell, SEOG, state scholarships/grants, private scholarships, the school's own gift aid. *Loans:* Subsidized Stafford, Unsubsidized Stafford, PLUS, Federal Perkins. **Student Employment:** Federal Work-Study Program available. Institutional employment available. Off-campus job opportunities are good. **Financial Aid Statistics:** 100% freshmen, 100% undergrads receive need-based scholarship or grant aid. 100% freshmen, 100% undergrads receive need-based self-help aid. %87% freshmen, 86% undergrads receive any aid. 80% undergrads borrow to pay for school. Average cumulative indebtedness $17,000. **Criteria for awarding institutional aid:** *Non-need-based:* academics, alumni affiliation, leadership.

COLLEGE OF MOUNT ST. JOSEPH

5701 Delhi Road, Cincinnati, OH 45233
Phone: 513-244-4531 • **Financial Aid Phone:** 513-244-4418
E-mail: admissions@mail.msj.edu • **CEEB Code:** 1129
Fax: 513-244-4629 • **Website:** www.msj.edu • **ACT Code:** 3254

This private school, affiliated with the Roman Catholic Church, was founded in 1920. It has a 92-acre campus.

RATINGS

Admissions Selectivity Rating: 71   **Fire Safety Rating:** 99   **Green Rating:** 65

STUDENTS AND FACULTY

Enrollment: 1,690. **Student Body:** 62% female, 38% male, 18% out-of-state, 0% international (3 countries represented). Asian 0%, African American 9%, Caucasian 84%, Hispanic 3%, Native American 0%.
Retention and Graduation: 77% freshmen return for sophomore year. 42% freshmen graduate within 4 years. 57% freshmen graduate within 6 years. 15% grads go on to further study within 1 year. 15% grads pursue arts and sciences degrees. **Faculty:** Student/faculty ratio 11:1. 118 full-time faculty, 76% hold PhDs, 3% are members of minority groups, 60% are women. 0% of classes are taught by teaching assistants.

ACADEMICS

Degrees: associate, bachelor's, certificate, master's, post-bachelor's certificate.
Classes: Most classes have 10–19 students. Most lab/discussion sessions have 10–19 students. **Majors with Highest Enrollment:** business administration

and management; nursing/registered nurse (rn, asn, bsn, msn); sport and fitness administration/management. **Special Study Options:** Accelerated program, cooperative education program, cross-registration, distance learning, double major, dual enrollment, honors program, independent study, internships, liberal arts/career combination, study abroad, teacher certification program. **Honors Programs:** Honors program--designed to meet the interests of highly motivated students who are able to take responsibility for their own learning under the guidance of experienced faculty members. **Disability Services:** Special programs offered to physically disabled students include note-taking services, reader services, tape recorders, tutors. **Career Services:** alumni services, career/job search classes, career assessment, internships Career Services highlights include Qualified students have the opportunity to gain career related, paid work experience. Co-ops earn academic credit that will complement classroom training by integrating theory and practice.

FACILITIES

Housing: Coed dorms, special housing for disabled students. 95% of campus accessible to physically disabled. **Special Academic Facilities/Equipment:** Art studio/gallery, Student Scholar Center, Computer Labs, Theatre. **Computers:** 100% of classrooms, 100% of dorms, 100% of libraries, 100% of dining areas, 100% of common outdoor areas have wireless network access. Students can register for classes online. Administrative functions (other than registration) can be performed online.

CAMPUS LIFE

Environment: Metropolis. **Activities:** Choral groups, concert band, dance, drama/theater, jazz band, literary magazine, music ensembles, musical theater, pep band, student government, student newspaper, Campus Ministries, International Student Organization 35 registered organizations, 10 honor societies, 1 religious organizations. **Athletics (Intercollegiate):** *Men:* baseball, basketball, cross-country, football, golf, lacrosse, soccer, tennis, track/field (outdoor), track/field (indoor), volleyball, wrestling. *Women:* basketball, cheerleading, cross-country, golf, lacrosse, soccer, softball, tennis, track/field (outdoor), track/field (indoor), volleyball. **On-Campus Highlights:** Harrington Student Center/Sports Complex, Starbucks Gallery, Residential Suites, Computer Learning Center, Project EXCEL. **Environmental Initiatives:** New green roof installed on Library (2008) Switch to trayless dining in cafeteria (2008) - less food waste (450 lbs/day), water conservation (250 gallons/day) Recycling across campus and increased amounts/types of materials

ADMISSIONS

Freshman Academic Profile: Average high school GPA 3.2. 16% in top 10% of high school class, 39% in top 25% of high school class, 73% in top 50% of high school class. 76% from public high schools. SAT Math middle 50% range 430-540. SAT Critical Reading middle 50% range 430-520. ACT middle 50% range 20-24. Minimum web-based TOEFL 64. Minimum paper TOEFL 510. **Basis for Candidate Selection:** *Very important factors considered include:* academic GPA, rigor of secondary school record, standardized test scores. *Other factors considered include:* application essay, recommendation(s), alumni/ae relation, character/personal qualities, extracurricular activities, first generation, geographical residence, interview, level of applicant's interest, racial/ethnic status, religious affiliation/commitment, state residency, talent/ability, volunteer work, work experience. **Freshman Admission Requirements:** High school diploma is required and GED is accepted. *Academic units required:* 4 English, 3 mathematics, 3 science, (1 science labs), 2 foreign language, 1 social studies, 1 history, 1 visual/performing arts, 1 academic electives, 1 academic elective. *Academic units recommended:* 4 English, 3 mathematics, 3 science, (1 science labs), 2 foreign language, 1 social studies, 1 history, 1 visual/performing arts, 1 academic electives, 1 academic elective. **Freshman Admission Statistics:** 1,235 applied, 70% admitted, 33% enrolled. **Transfer Admission Requirements:** college transcript(s), minimum college GPA of 2.0 required. Lowest grade transferable C. **General Admission Information:** Application Fee $25. Regular application deadline 8/15. Notification on a rolling basis, beginning on or about 10/1. Nonfall registration accepted. Admission may be deferred for a maximum of 12 months. Credit and/or placement offered for CEEB Advanced Placement tests.

COSTS AND FINANCIAL AID

Annual tuition $24,200. Room and board $7,860. Required fees $900. Average book expense $800. **Required Forms and Deadlines:** FAFSA. **Notification of Awards:** Applicants will be notified of awards on a rolling basis beginning 1/31. **Types of Aid:** *Need-based scholarships/grants:* Federal Pell, SEOG, state scholarships/grants, private scholarships, the school's own gift aid. *Loans:* Subsidized Stafford, Unsubsidized Stafford, PLUS, Federal Perkins, Federal Nursing, state loans. **Student Employment:** Federal Work-Study Program available. Institutional employment available. Highest amount earned per year from on-campus jobs $1,500. Off-campus job opportunities are good. **Financial Aid Statistics:** 98% freshmen, 97% undergrads receive need-based scholarship or grant aid. 11% freshmen, 11% undergrads receive non-need-based scholarship or grant aid. 96% freshmen, 95% undergrads receive need-based self-help aid. 100% freshmen, 80% undergrads receive any aid. **Criteria for awarding** institutional aid: *Non-need-based:* academics, alumni affiliation, art, leadership, music/drama, state/district residency.

THE COLLEGE OF NEW JERSEY

PO Box 7718, Ewing, NJ 08628-0718
Phone: 609-771-2131 • **Financial Aid Phone:** 609-771-2211
E-mail: tcnjinfo@tcnj.edu • **CEEB Code:** 2519
Fax: 609-637-5174 • **Website:** www.tcnj.edu • **ACT Code:** 2614

This public school was founded in 1855. It has a 289-acre campus.

RATINGS
Admissions Selectivity Rating: 93   **Fire Safety Rating:** 95   **Green Rating:** 83

STUDENTS AND FACULTY
Enrollment: 6,434. **Student Body:** 56% female, 44% male, 6% out-of-state, 0% international (30 countries represented). Asian 9%, African American 6%, Caucasian 66%, Hispanic 10%, Native American 0%.
Retention and Graduation: 94% freshmen return for sophomore year. 73% freshmen graduate within 4 years. 88% freshmen graduate within 6 years. 25% grads go on to further study within 1 year. 16% grads pursue arts and sciences degrees. 3% grads pursue law degrees. 3% grads pursue medical degrees.
Faculty: Student/faculty ratio 13:1. 349 full-time faculty, 88% hold PhDs, 22% are members of minority groups, 50% are women. 0% of classes are taught by teaching assistants.

ACADEMICS
Degrees: bachelor's, master's, post-bachelor's certificate, post-master's certificate. **Classes:** Most classes have 20–29 students. Most lab/discussion sessions have 10–19 students. **Majors with Highest Enrollment:** biology/biological sciences; business administration and management; psychology. **Special Study Options:** Accelerated program, double major, dual enrollment, exchange student program (domestic), honors program, independent study, internships, liberal arts/career combination, student-designed major, study abroad, teacher certification program, 7 year medical program with UMDNJ, 7 year BS/OD program with SUNY, Mentored undergraduate summer research program. **Combined Degree Programs:** BA/MD, BS/MD, BS/OD, BS/MAT. **Disability Services:** Special programs offered to physically disabled students include note-taking services, reader services, tape recorders, tutors. **Career Services:** alumni services, career/job search classes, career assessment, internships Career Services highlights include Education Interview Days Each Spring TCNJ hosts up to 150 school district interview visits. The districts send administrators to conduct 30 minute interviews on-campus. Over the four days the visits are scheduled more than 1500 first-round interviews are conducted. Though the school districts are primarily from New Jersey and the surrounding area, we attract school districts from throughout the nation, including as far away as Hawaii. Students and employers both report that this is a highly successful program for meeting their recruitment needs.

FACILITIES
Housing: Coed dorms, special housing for disabled students, special housing for international students, women's dorms, apartments for single students, wellness housing. Faculty and students have the opportunity to develop their own special interest learning communities on campus. 90% of campus accessible to physically disabled. **Special Academic Facilities/Equipment:** Art gallery, concert hall, greenhouse, observatory, planetarium, nuclear magnetic resonance lab, optical spectroscopy lab, scanning and transmission electron microscopes. **Computers:** 22% of classrooms, 5% of dorms, 100% of libraries, 85% of dining areas, 70% of student union, 5% of common outdoor areas have wireless network access. Students can register for classes online. Administrative functions (other than registration) can be performed online.

CAMPUS LIFE
Environment: Village. **Activities:** Choral groups, concert band, dance, drama/theater, jazz band, literary magazine, music ensembles, musical theater, opera, pep band, radio station, student government, student newspaper, symphony orchestra, television station, yearbook, Campus Ministries, International Student Organization, Model UN 205 registered organizations, 16 honor societies, 11 religious organizations. 12 fraternities, 16 sororities. **Athletics (Intercollegiate):** *Men:* baseball, basketball, cross-country, diving, football, soccer, swimming, tennis, track/field (outdoor), track/field (indoor). *Women:* basketball, cross-country, diving, field hockey, lacrosse, soccer, softball, swimming, tennis, track/field (outdoor), track/field (indoor). **On-Campus Highlights:** New Library,

New Science Complex, New Arts and Multimedia Building, Student Center, Athletic Center. **Environmental Initiatives:** Commitment to sustainability being incorporated into the curriculum at TCNJ. This may include Freshman seminars, liberal learning programs, research and possible new minor or major degrees. The College's Municipal Land Use Center is authoring the State's sustainabilty and climate neutrality plans. Development of a plan to achieve climate neutrality. Consultant was hired to prepare a comprehensive sustainability and climate neutrality plan for the College. That plan outlines potential projects and initiatives to bring the College to neutrality by 2040. The College has committed to offsetting greenhouse gas produced by faculty and staff travel on an annual basis through the purchase of carbon offsets.

ADMISSIONS
Freshman Academic Profile: 58% in top 10% of high school class, 93% in top 25% of high school class, 99% in top 50% of high school class. 70% from public high schools. SAT Math middle 50% range 580-680. SAT Critical Reading middle 50% range 550-650. SAT Writing middle 50% range 560-680. Minimum web-based TOEFL 90. Minimum paper TOEFL 550. **Basis for Candidate Selection:** *Very important factors considered include:* Class rank, rigor of secondary school record, standardized test scores, extracurricular activities, volunteer work. *Important factors considered include:* application essay, recommendation(s), character/personal qualities, geographical residence, state residency, talent/ability. *Other factors considered include:* academic GPA, alumni/ae relation, first generation, level of applicant's interest, racial/ethnic status, work experience. **Freshman Admission Requirements:** High school diploma is required and GED is accepted. *Academic units required:* 4 English, 3 mathematics, 3 science, (2 science labs), 2 foreign language, 2 social studies. *Academic units recommended:* 4 English, 3 mathematics, 3 science, (2 science labs), 2 foreign language, 2 social studies. **Freshman Admission Statistics:** 10,295 applied, 46% admitted, 29% enrolled. **Transfer Admission Requirements:** High school transcript, college transcript(s), essay or personal statement, standardized test scores, statement of good standing from prior institution(s). Minimum college GPA of 2.5 required. Lowest grade transferable C. **General Admission Information:** Application Fee $70. Early decision application deadline 11/15. Regular application deadline 1/15. Notification on a rolling basis, beginning on or about 1/15. Nonfall registration accepted. Admission may be deferred for a maximum of 2 semesters. Credit and/or placement offered for CEEB Advanced Placement tests.

COSTS AND FINANCIAL AID
Annual in-state tuition $10,102. Annual out-of-state tuition $20,254. Room and board $10,998. Required fees $4,276. Average book expense $1,200. **Required Forms and Deadlines:** FAFSA. **Notification of Awards:** Applicants will be notified of awards on a rolling basis beginning 6/1. **Types of Aid:** *Need-based scholarships/grants:* Federal Pell, SEOG, state scholarships/grants, private scholarships, the school's own gift aid. *Loans:* Subsidized Stafford, Unsubsidized Stafford, PLUS, Federal Perkins, Federal Nursing. **Student Employment:** Federal Work-Study Program available. Institutional employment available. Highest amount earned per year from on-campus jobs $9,329. Off-campus job opportunities are excellent. **Financial Aid Statistics:** 37% freshmen, 39% undergrads receive need-based scholarship or grant aid. 49% freshmen, 40% undergrads receive non-need-based scholarship or grant aid. 69% freshmen, 77% undergrads receive need-based self-help aid. 70% freshmen, 62% undergrads receive any aid. 60% undergrads borrow to pay for school. Average cumulative indebtedness $33,889. **Criteria for awarding institutional aid:** *Non-need-based:* academics.

See page 1048.

THE COLLEGE OF NEW ROCHELLE

29 Castle Place, New Rochelle, NY 10805-2339
Phone: 914-654-5452
E-mail: admission@cnr.edu • **CEEB Code:** 2089
Fax: 914-654-5464 • **ACT Code:** 2712

This private school, affiliated with the Roman Catholic Church, was founded in 1904. It has a 20-acre campus.

RATINGS
Admissions Selectivity Rating: 64   **Fire Safety Rating:** 60*   **Green Rating:** 60*

STUDENTS AND FACULTY
Enrollment: 1,003. **Student Body:** 95% female, 5% male, 10% out-of-state, 1% international (6 countries represented). Asian 6%, African American 39%, Caucasian 14%, Hispanic 13%, Native American 0%.
Retention and Graduation: 70% freshmen return for sophomore year. 41% freshmen graduate within 4 years. 15% grads go on to further study within 1 year. **Faculty:** Student/faculty ratio :1. 85 full-time faculty, 84% hold PhDs,

12% are members of minority groups, 71% are women. 0% of classes are taught by teaching assistants.

ACADEMICS

Degrees: bachelor's, master's, post-bachelor's certificate, post-master's certificate. **Classes:** Most classes have 10–19 students. Most lab/discussion sessions have fewer than 10 students. **Majors with Highest Enrollment:** mass communication/media studies; nursing/registered nurse (rn, asn, bsn, msn); psychology. **Special Study Options:** Accelerated program, cooperative education program, cross-registration, double major, exchange student program (domestic), honors program, independent study, internships, liberal arts/career combination, student-designed major, study abroad, teacher certification program. **Combined Degree Programs:** BA/MA. **Disability Services:** Special programs offered to physically disabled students include tape recorders, tutors. **Career Services:** alumni services, career/job search classes, career assessment, internships.

FACILITIES

Housing: women's dorms. 25% of campus accessible to physically disabled. **Special Academic Facilities/Equipment:** Art gallery, multimedia theatre/teleconference center, language lab, centers for media, computer studies, TV studio, Learning Center for Women, Learning Center for Nursing. **Computers:** Students can register for classes online. Administrative functions (other than registration) can be performed online.

CAMPUS LIFE

Environment: Village. **Activities:** Choral groups, dance, drama/theater, literary magazine, musical theater, student government, student newspaper, yearbook 26 registered organizations, 2 honor societies, 1 religious organizations. **Athletics (Intercollegiate):** *Women:* basketball, cross-country, softball, swimming, tennis, volleyball.

ADMISSIONS

Freshman Academic Profile: 15% in top 10% of high school class, 46% in top 25% of high school class, 82% in top 50% of high school class. 76% from public high schools. SAT Math middle 50% range 440-530. SAT Critical Reading middle 50% range 440-530. ACT middle 50% range 16-22. Minimum paper TOEFL 550. **Basis for Candidate Selection:** *Very important factors considered include:* rigor of secondary school record. *Important factors considered include:* Class rank, application essay, standardized test scores. *Other factors considered include:* recommendation(s), alumni/ae relation, character/personal qualities, extracurricular activities, interview, talent/ability, volunteer work, work experience. **Freshman Admission Requirements:** High school diploma is required and GED is accepted. **Transfer Admission Requirements:** High school transcript, college transcript(s), Lowest grade transferable C–. **General Admission Information:** Application Fee $20. Early decision application deadline 11/1. Notification on a rolling basis, beginning on or about 11/1. Nonfall registration accepted. Admission may be deferred for a maximum of 1 year. Credit and/or placement offered for CEEB Advanced Placement tests.

COSTS AND FINANCIAL AID

Annual tuition $23,200. Room and board $9,700. Required fees $500. Average book expense $600. **Required Forms and Deadlines:** FAFSA, institution's own financial aid formfederal income tax form(s). **Notification of Awards:** Applicants will be notified of awards on a rolling basis beginning 1/1. **Types of Aid:** *Need-based scholarships/grants:* Federal Pell, SEOG, state scholarships/grants, private scholarships, the school's own gift aid. *Loans:* Direct Subsidized Stafford, Direct Unsubsidized Stafford, PLUS, Federal Perkins, Federal Nursing. **Student Employment:** Federal Work-Study Program available. Institutional employment available. Highest amount earned per year from on-campus jobs $1,500. Off-campus job opportunities are excellent. **Financial Aid Statistics:** 97% freshmen, 93% undergrads receive need-based scholarship or grant aid. 55% freshmen, 57% undergrads receive non-need-based scholarship or grant aid. 84% freshmen, 85% undergrads receive need-based self-help aid. **Criteria for awarding institutional aid:** *Non-need-based:* academics, art, leadership.

COLLEGE OF NOTRE DAME OF MARYLAND

4701 North Charles Street, Baltimore, MD 21210
Phone: 410-532-5330 • **Financial Aid Phone:** 410-532-5369
E-mail: admiss@ndm.edu • **CEEB Code:** 5114
Fax: 410-532-6287 • **Website:** www.ndm.edu • **ACT Code:** 1727

This private school, affiliated with the Roman Catholic Church, was founded in 1896. It has a 58-acre campus.

RATINGS

Admissions Selectivity Rating: 73   **Fire Safety Rating:** 60*   **Green Rating:** 60*

STUDENTS AND FACULTY

Enrollment: 1,686. **Student Body:** Asian 3%, African American 26%, Caucasian 66%, Hispanic 3%, Native American 0%.
Retention and Graduation: 87% freshmen return for sophomore year. 49% freshmen graduate within 4 years. 66% freshmen graduate within 6 years.
Faculty: Student/faculty ratio 13:1. 83 full-time faculty, 78% hold PhDs, 4% are members of minority groups, 65% are women. 0% of classes are taught by teaching assistants.

ACADEMICS

Degrees: bachelor's, master's, post-master's certificate. **Classes:** Most classes have 20–29 students. **Majors with Highest Enrollment:** business, management, marketing, and related support services, other; liberal arts and sciences/liberal studies; nursing/registered nurse (rn, asn, bsn, msn). **Special Study Options:** Accelerated program, cross-registration, double major, dual enrollment, English as a Second Language (ESL), exchange student program (domestic), honors program, independent study, internships, liberal arts/career combination, student-designed major, study abroad, teacher certification program, weekend college, Orientation program for all new students to college which includes a first semester seminar course for entering freshman. Also a Career Action Plan for all students and an academic consortium with seven local colleges and universities. **Honors Programs:** Exceptionally motivated students with outstanding academic ability may be invited to become a Morrissy Scholar. Students take selected interdisciplinary courses throughout their academic program and must complete 18 credits in the program to graduate as a Morrissy Scholar. The students are engaged in various activities on campus, off campus - nationally and internationally. The group selected each year to join the program is approximately 10-12% of the entering class. **Combined Degree Programs:** BA/MA, BA/MAT; dual degree BA/BS; BA/MA in Business. **Disability Services:** Special programs offered to physically disabled students include note-taking services, reader services, tutors. **Career Services:** Alumni network, alumni services, career/job search classes, career assessment, internships, regional alumni., Career Services highlights include Approximately 90% or more of all graduating students from the Women's College have at least on internship experience upon graduating. This takes the liberal arts in-classroom learning and ties it directly to practical experience - best of all worlds.

FACILITIES

Housing: women's dorms. **Special Academic Facilities/Equipment:** Art gallery, photo labs, language labs, child care center, fitness center, television and radio studios, music practice labs, planetarium. **Computers:** Administrative functions (other than registration) can be performed online.

CAMPUS LIFE

Environment: Metropolis. **Activities:** Choral groups, dance, drama/theater, literary magazine, music ensembles, radio station, student government, student newspaper, student-run film society, television station, yearbook 24 registered organizations, 7 honor societies. **Athletics (Intercollegiate):** *Women:* basketball, field hockey, lacrosse, soccer, swimming, tennis, volleyball. **On-Campus Highlights:** Gator Alley - pub-like eatery, MBK Sports and Activities center (fitness center), Loyola/Notre Dame library, Doyle Hall- residence hall, student activity area, Marikle Chapel.

ADMISSIONS

Freshman Academic Profile: Average high school GPA 3.4. 15% in top 10% of high school class, 43% in top 25% of high school class, 80% in top 50% of high school class. 71% from public high schools. SAT Math middle 50% range 450-560. SAT Critical Reading middle 50% range 490-580. ACT middle 50% range -. Minimum paper TOEFL. **Basis for Candidate Selection:** *Very important factors considered include:* application essay, recommendation(s), rigor of secondary school record, standardized test scores, interview. *Important factors considered include:* extracurricular activities, volunteer work. *Other factors considered include:* Class rank, alumni/ae relation, character/personal qualities, talent/ability, work experience. **Freshman Admission Requirements:** High school diploma is required and GED is accepted. *Academic units required:* 4 English, 3 mathematics, 2 science, (2 science labs), 3 foreign language, 2 history, 4 academic electives. 4 English, 3 mathematics, 2 science, (2 science labs), 3 foreign language, 2 history, 4 academic electives. **Freshman Admission Statistics:** 450 applied, 72% admitted, 46% enrolled. **Transfer Admission Requirements:** college transcript(s), essay or personal statement, minimum college GPA of 2.5 required. Lowest grade transferable C. **General Admission Information:** Application Fee $40. Notification on a rolling basis, beginning on or about 10/1. Nonfall registration accepted. Admission may be deferred for a maximum of 12 months. Credit and/or placement offered for CEEB Advanced Placement tests.

COSTS AND FINANCIAL AID

Annual tuition $19,900. Room and board $7,800. Required fees $400. Average book expense $800. **Required Forms and Deadlines:** FAFSA. **Notification of Awards:** Applicants will be notified of awards on a rolling basis beginning 3/1. **Types of Aid:** *Need-based scholarships/grants:* Federal Pell, SEOG, state scholarships/grants. *Loans:* Direct Subsidized Stafford, Direct Unsubsidized

Stafford, Direct PLUS, Federal Perkins. **Student Employment:** Federal Work-Study Program available. Institutional employment available. Off-campus job opportunities are good. **Financial Aid Statistics:** 97% freshmen, 86% undergrads receive need-based scholarship or grant aid. 88% freshmen, 90% undergrads receive non-need-based scholarship or grant aid. 74% freshmen, 82% undergrads receive need-based self-help aid. Average cumulative indebtedness $16,000. **Criteria for awarding institutional aid:** *Non-need-based:* academics, alumni affiliation, art, leadership, music/drama.

COLLEGE OF THE OZARKS

Best 378

Office of Admissions, Point Lookout, MO 65726
Phone: 417-690-2636 • **Financial Aid Phone:** 417-690-3292
E-mail: admiss4@cofo.edu • **CEEB Code:** 6713
Fax: 417-335-2618 • **Website:** www.cofo.edu • **ACT Code:** 2364

This private school was founded in 1906. It has a 1000-acre campus.

RATINGS
Admissions Selectivity Rating: 95   **Fire Safety Rating:** 76   **Green Rating:** 69

STUDENTS AND FACULTY
Enrollment: 1,376. **Student Body:** 57% female, 43% male, 21% out-of-state, 2% international (22 countries represented). Asian 0%, African American 1%, Caucasian 91%, Hispanic 2%, Native American 0%.
Retention and Graduation: 87% freshmen return for sophomore year. 18% grads go on to further study within 1 year. 8% grads pursue arts and sciences degrees. 1% grads pursue law degrees. 4% grads pursue business degrees. 1% grads pursue medical degrees. **Faculty:** Student/faculty ratio 14:1. 83 full-time faculty, 54% hold PhDs, 2% are members of minority groups, 39% are women. 0% of classes are taught by teaching assistants.

ACADEMICS
Degrees: bachelor's. **Classes:** Most classes have 10–19 students. Most lab/discussion sessions have 10–19 students. **Majors with Highest Enrollment:** business administration and management; communication studies/speech communication and rhetoric; elementary education and teaching. **Special Study Options:** Accelerated program, double major, dual enrollment, independent study, internships, student-designed major, teacher certification program. **Combined Degree Programs:** BA/JD, BA/MEng. **Disability Services:** Special programs offered to physically disabled students include note-taking services, reader services, tape recorders, tutors. **Career Services:** Alumni network, alumni services, career/job search classes, career assessment, internships Career Services highlights include Outstanding internships that offer graduates opportunities for phenomenal careers.

FACILITIES
Housing: men's dorms, women's dorms, wellness housing. All full-time students must live in residence halls unless they meet one of the following criteria: 21 years of age or older, married, living with parents, or veteran of the armed forces. 75% of campus accessible to physically disabled. **Special Academic Facilities/Equipment:** Ralph Foster Museum Edwards Mill The Keeter Center Fruitcake and Jelly Kitchen Greenhouses **Computers:** 100% of dorms, 100% of libraries, 100% of dining areas, 100% of student union, have wireless network access. Students can register for classes online. Administrative functions (other than registration) can be performed online.

CAMPUS LIFE
Environment: Rural. **Activities:** Choral groups, concert band, drama/theater, jazz band, literary magazine, music ensembles, musical theater, pep band, radio station, student government, student newspaper, student-run film society, yearbook, Campus Ministries 45 registered organizations, 6 honor societies, 10 religious organizations. **Athletics (Intercollegiate):** *Men:* baseball, basketball, cheerleading. *Women:* basketball, cheerleading, volleyball. **On-Campus Highlights:** Memorial Fieldhouse and Keeter Gymnasium, Ralph Foster Museum, Williams Memorial Chapel, The Keeter Center, Agriculture, Edwards Mill, Fruitcake and Jelly Kitchen. **Environmental Initiatives:** 1. The College ensures proper management of hazardous, special and universal waste. There is campus- wide recycling: plastic bottles, corrugated cardboard, aluminum cans, tin cans, batteries, tires, light bulbs and electronic products. Light bulb reclamation (recycle of bulbs) and energy efficient lights Agricultural Livestock Waste Containment program (protects area lakes) Many campus buildings have cooling systems that utilize 48 degree lake water and save energy.Ground source heating and cooling pumps.

ADMISSIONS
Freshman Academic Profile: Average high school GPA 3.6. 19% in top 10% of high school class, 50% in top 25% of high school class, 87% in top 50% of high school class. 76% from public high schools. SAT Math middle 50% range 440-560. SAT Critical Reading middle 50% range 510-610. SAT Writing middle 50% range 430-530. ACT middle 50% range 21-25. Minimum web-based TOEFL 79. Minimum paper TOEFL 550. **Basis for Candidate Selection:** *Very important factors considered include:* Class rank, rigor of secondary school record, character/personal qualities, interview. *Important factors considered include:* academic GPA, recommendation(s), standardized test scores, geographical residence, level of applicant's interest, volunteer work, work experience. *Other factors considered include:* alumni/ae relation, extracurricular activities, first generation, religious affiliation/commitment, state residency, talent/ability. **Freshman Admission Requirements:** High school diploma is required and GED is accepted. **Freshman Admission Statistics:** 3,048 applied, 9% admitted, 85% enrolled. **Transfer Admission Requirements:** college transcript(s), interview, statement of good standing from prior institution(s). Minimum college GPA of 3.0 required. Lowest grade transferable D-. **General Admission Information:** Regular application deadline 2/15. Notification on a rolling basis, beginning on or about 3/1. Nonfall registration accepted. Credit offered for CEEB Advanced Placement tests.

COSTS AND FINANCIAL AID
Room and board $5,900. Required fees $430. Average book expense $800. **Required Forms and Deadlines:** FAFSA. **Notification of Awards:** Applicants will be notified of awards on or about 7/1. **Types of Aid:** *Need-based scholarships/grants:* Federal Pell, SEOG, state scholarships/grants, private scholarships, the school's own gift aid. *Loans:* **Student Employment:** Federal Work-Study Program available. Off-campus job opportunities are excellent. **Financial Aid Statistics:** 100% freshmen, 100% undergrads receive need-based scholarship or grant aid. 9% freshmen, 13% undergrads receive non-need-based scholarship or grant aid. 90% freshmen, 87% undergrads receive need-based self-help aid. 3% freshmen, 3% undergrads receive athletic scholarships. 100% freshmen, 100% undergrads receive any aid. 11% undergrads borrow to pay for school. Average cumulative indebtedness $8,915. **Criteria for awarding institutional aid:** *Non-need-based:* academics, art, athletics, leadership, minority status, music/drama, state/district residency.

COLLEGE OF SAINT BENEDICT/
SAINT JOHN'S UNIVERSITY

PO Box 7155, Collegeville, MN 56321-7155
Phone: 320-363-2196 • **Financial Aid Phone:** 320-363-5452
E-mail: admissions@csbsju.edu • **CEEB Code:** 6624
Fax: 320-363-2750 • **Website:** www.csbsju.edu • **ACT Code:** 2140

This private school, affiliated with the Roman Catholic Church, was founded in 1857. It has a 2400-acre campus.

RATINGS
Admissions Selectivity Rating: 71   **Fire Safety Rating:** 90   **Green Rating:** 91

STUDENTS AND FACULTY
Enrollment: 3,924. **Student Body:** 53% female, 47% male, 17% out-of-state, 6% international (36 countries represented). Asian 5%, African American 2%, Caucasian 82%, Hispanic 4%, Native American 1%.
Retention and Graduation: 89% freshmen return for sophomore year. 71% freshmen graduate within 4 years. 79% freshmen graduate within 6 years. 15% grads go on to further study within 1 year. **Faculty:** Student/faculty ratio 12:1. 284 full-time faculty, 85% hold PhDs, 10% are members of minority groups, 51% are women. 0% of classes are taught by teaching assistants.

ACADEMICS
Degrees: bachelor's, first professional, master's. **Classes:** Most classes have 20–29 students. Most lab/discussion sessions have 10–19 students. **Majors with Highest Enrollment:** biology/biological sciences; business administration and management; speech and rhetorical studies. **Special Study Options:** cross-registration, double major, dual enrollment, English as a Second Language (ESL), exchange student program (domestic), honors program, independent study, internships, student-designed major, study abroad, teacher certification program. **Honors Programs:** All departments may contribute courses to our honors program. Students in all majors may participate in the Honors Program and receive honors distinction inside the major. **Combined Degree Programs:** 3/2 program in engineering with U of MN-TC. **Disability Services:** Special programs offered to physically disabled students include note-taking services, tape recorders, tutors. **Career Services:** Alumni network, alumni services, career/job search classes, career assessment, internships, regional alumni. Career

Services highlights include At CSB/SJU academic internships have tripled in the last decade. Currently 8% of our total student body engage in internships with a credit requirement attached. In any given semester students in 20 different majors receive individual guidance from faculty, so that intentional learning and reflection are integrated into the experience. Internship opportunities exist, not only for business-related majors in the private sector, but also for a variety of humanities and social science majors (Communication, Psychology, Political Science, Environmental Studies, Peace Studies to name a few) in government, education and the non profit sector. Within the last three years 53% of the total internships at CSB/SJU were completed in the private sector by business majors while 47% were service-related internships completed by non business majors.

FACILITIES

Housing: special housing for disabled students, men's dorms, special housing for international students, women's dorms, apartments for single students, Health and Wellness floor, Global Initiative Group house, ROTC housing. 90% of campus accessible to physically disabled. **Special Academic Facilities/Equipment:** Hill Museum and Manuscript Library, art galleries, natural science museum, arboretum, Benedicta Arts Center, Sommers Digital Lab **Computers:** 100% of classrooms, 20% of dorms, 100% of libraries, 100% of dining areas, 100% of student union, 100% of common outdoor areas have wireless network access. Students can register for classes online. Administrative functions (other than registration) can be performed online.

CAMPUS LIFE

Environment: Village. **Activities:** Choral groups, concert band, dance, drama/theater, jazz band, literary magazine, music ensembles, musical theater, opera, pep band, radio station, student government, student newspaper, symphony orchestra, Campus Ministries, International Student Organization, Model UN 85 registered organizations, 3 honor societies, 4 religious organizations. **Athletics (Intercollegiate):** *Men:* baseball, basketball, cross-country, diving, football, golf, ice hockey, skiingnordiccross-country, soccer, swimming, tennis, track/field (outdoor), track/field (indoor), wrestling. *Women:* basketball, cross-country, diving, golf, ice hockey, skiingnordiccross-country, soccer, softball, swimming, tennis, track/field (outdoor), track/field (indoor), volleyball. **On-Campus Highlights:** Gorecki Dining Center, Benedicta Ars Center, Warner Palaestra/Clemens Field House, Lake Sagatagan/Stell Maris Chapel, Brother Willie's Pub/O'Connell's Coffee, Abbey Church/Sacred Heart Chapel; Hill Museum and Manuscript Library; 15 KM hiking trails. **Environmental Initiatives:** ACUPCC signatory process SJU arboretum CSB Green building policy

ADMISSIONS

Freshman Academic Profile: Average high school GPA 3.6. 30% in top 10% of high school class, 65% in top 25% of high school class, 91% in top 50% of high school class. 71% from public high schools. SAT Math middle 50% range 478-540. SAT Critical Reading middle 50% range 478-540. ACT middle 50% range 23-28. Minimum web-based TOEFL 70. Minimum paper TOEFL 500. **Basis for Candidate Selection:** *Very important factors considered include:* application essay, academic GPA, rigor of secondary school record, standardized test scores. *Important factors considered include:* recommendation(s), extracurricular activities. *Other factors considered include:* Class rank, alumni/ae relation, character/personal qualities, first generation, geographical residence, interview, racial/ethnic status, talent/ability, volunteer work, work experience. **Freshman Admission Requirements:** High school diploma is required and GED is accepted. *Academic units required:* 4 English, 3 mathematics, 2 science, (2 science labs), 2 social studies, 4 academic electives. *Academic units recommended:* 4 English, 3 mathematics, 2 science, (2 science labs), 2 social studies, 4 academic electives. **Freshman Admission Statistics:** 3,533 applied, 76% admitted, 35% enrolled. **Transfer Admission Requirements:** High school transcript, college transcript(s), essay or personal statement, statement of good standing from prior institution(s). Minimum college GPA of 2.75 required. Lowest grade transferable C. **General Admission Information:** Nonfall registration accepted. Admission may be deferred for a maximum of one year. Credit and/or placement offered for CEEB Advanced Placement tests.

COSTS AND FINANCIAL AID

Annual tuition $35,298. Room and board $9,270. Required fees $920. Average book expense $1,000. **Required Forms and Deadlines:** FAFSA, institution's own financial aid form. **Notification of Awards:** Applicants will be notified of awards on a rolling basis beginning 3/15. **Types of Aid:** *Need-based scholarships/grants:* Federal Pell, SEOG, state scholarships/grants, private scholarships, the school's own gift aid. *Loans:* Subsidized Stafford, Unsubsidized Stafford, PLUS, Federal Perkins, state loans, Various private education loans. **Student Employment:** Federal Work-Study Program available. Institutional employment available. Highest amount earned per year from on-campus jobs $6,870. Off-campus job opportunities are fair. **Financial Aid Statistics:** 99% freshmen, 97% undergrads receive need-based scholarship or grant aid. 97% freshmen, 94% undergrads receive non-need-based scholarship or grant aid. 91% freshmen, 93% undergrads receive need-based self-help aid. 95% freshmen, 93% undergrads receive any aid. 72% undergrads borrow to pay for school. Average cumulative indebtedness $37,460. **Criteria for awarding institutional aid:** *Non-need-based:* academics, art, leadership, music/drama.

COLLEGE OF SAINT ELIZABETH

Admissions Office, Morristown, NJ 07960-6989
Phone: 973-290-4700 • **Financial Aid Phone:** 973-290-4445
E-mail: apply@cse.edu • **CEEB Code:** 2090
Fax: 973-290-4710 • **Website:** • **ACT Code:**

This private school, affiliated with the Roman Catholic Church, was founded in 1899. It has a 200-acre campus.

RATINGS
Admissions Selectivity Rating: 74   **Fire Safety Rating:** 98   **Green Rating:** 60*

STUDENTS AND FACULTY
Enrollment: 1,122. **Student Body:** 91% female, 9% male, 3% out-of-state, 4% international (47 countries represented). Asian 5%, African American 22%, Caucasian 41%, Hispanic 16%, Native American 0%.
Retention and Graduation: 64% freshmen return for sophomore year. 50% freshmen graduate within 4 years. 58% freshmen graduate within 6 years.
Faculty: Student/faculty ratio 9:1. 72 full-time faculty, 83% hold PhDs, 4% are members of minority groups, 68% are women. 0% of classes are taught by teaching assistants.

ACADEMICS
Degrees: bachelor's, certificate, master's, post-bachelor's certificate, post-master's certificate. **Classes:** Most classes have 10–19 students. **Majors with Highest Enrollment:** business/commerce; nursing/registered nurse (rn, asn, bsn, msn); teacher education, multiple levels. **Special Study Options:** Accelerated program, cross-registration, distance learning, double major, dual enrollment, English as a Second Language (ESL), exchange student program (domestic), honors program, independent study, internships, student-designed major, study abroad, teacher certification program, weekend college. **Combined Degree Programs:** BA/MA, BS/MS. **Disability Services:** Special programs offered to physically disabled students include note-taking services, reader services, tape recorders, tutors. **Career Services:** Alumni network, career/job search classes, career assessment, internships Career Services highlights include Partnerships with employers such as American Red Cross, MEDCO Solutions, Verizon Wireless & the Department of Human Services have fortified our students with practical opportunities for development. An example of this is a collaborative venture between Career Services, the Communications and Business departments and the Business Club. Students are scheduled to spend a half day at Verizon, experiencing corporate culture and attend workshops lead by Verizon Human Resources staff on topics such as "'Group Interviewing'".

FACILITIES
Housing: women's dorms. 85% of campus accessible to physically disabled. **Computers:** 100% of classrooms, 100% of dorms, 100% of libraries, 100% of dining areas, 100% of student union, 5% of common outdoor areas have wireless network access.

CAMPUS LIFE
Environment: Village. **Activities:** Choral groups, dance, drama/theater, literary magazine, music ensembles, student government, student newspaper, yearbook, Campus Ministries, International Student Organization 28 registered organizations, 9 honor societies, 1 religious organizations. **Athletics (Intercollegiate):** *Women:* basketball, equestrian sports, soccer, softball, swimming, tennis. **On-Campus Highlights:** St. Joesph's Hall-Student Center, Henderson Hall-Classroom Building, O'Connor Hall-Residence Hall, Santa Rita Hall-Administration Building, Mahoney Library.

ADMISSIONS
Freshman Academic Profile: 11% in top 10% of high school class, 27% in top 25% of high school class, 52% in top 50% of high school class. 81% from public high schools. SAT Math middle 50% range 370-470. SAT Critical Reading middle 50% range 360-470. SAT Writing middle 50% range 380-470. Minimum paper TOEFL 500. **Basis for Candidate Selection:** *Very important factors considered include:* Class rank, academic GPA, recommendation(s), rigor of secondary school record, standardized test scores. *Important factors considered include:* application essay, character/personal qualities. *Other factors considered include:* alumni/ae relation, extracurricular activities, first generation, geographical residence, interview, level of applicant's interest, talent/ability, volunteer work, work experience. **Freshman Admission Requirements:** High school diploma is required and GED is accepted. *Academic units required:* 3 English, 2 mathematics, 1 science, (1 science labs), 2 foreign language, 1 history, 7 academic electives. *Academic units recommended:* 3 English, 2 mathematics, 1 science, (1 science labs), 2 foreign language, 1 history, 7 academic electives. **Freshman Admission Statistics:** 1,486 applied, 53% admitted, 23% enrolled. **Transfer Admission Requirements:** college transcript(s), essay or personal statement, minimum college GPA of 2.0 required. Lowest grade transferable C.

General Admission Information: Application Fee $35. Regular application deadline 8/15. Notification on a rolling basis, beginning on or about 11/15. Non-fall registration accepted. Admission may be deferred for a maximum of 1 year. Credit and/or placement offered for CEEB Advanced Placement tests.

COSTS AND FINANCIAL AID

Required Forms and Deadlines: FAFSA. **Notification of Awards:** Applicants will be notified of awards on a rolling basis beginning 11/15. **Types of Aid:** *Need-based scholarships/grants:* Federal Pell, SEOG, state scholarships/grants, private scholarships, the school's own gift aid. *Loans:* Subsidized Stafford, Unsubsidized Stafford, PLUS, Federal Perkins, state loans. **Student Employment:** Federal Work-Study Program available. Institutional employment available. Highest amount earned per year from on-campus jobs $4,350. Off-campus job opportunities are good. **Financial Aid Statistics:** 82% freshmen, 74% undergrads receive need-based scholarship or grant aid. 54% freshmen, 55% undergrads receive non-need-based scholarship or grant aid. 81% freshmen, 75% undergrads receive need-based self-help aid. 98% freshmen, 54% undergrads receive any aid. 16% undergrads borrow to pay for school. Average cumulative indebtedness $7,746. **Criteria for awarding institutional aid:** *Non-need-based:* academics, alumni affiliation, art, leadership, religious affiliation, state/district residency.

COLLEGE OF SAINT JOSEPH IN VERMONT

71 Clement Road, Rutland, VT 5701
Phone: 802-776-5286 • **Financial Aid Phone:** 802-776-5218
E-mail: admissions@csj.edu • **CEEB Code:** 3297
Fax: 802-776-5258 • **Website:** www.csj.edu

This private school, affiliated with the Roman Catholic Church, was founded in 1956. It has a 116-acre campus.

RATINGS
Admissions Selectivity Rating: 65   **Fire Safety Rating:** 65   **Green Rating:** 60*

STUDENTS AND FACULTY
Enrollment: 208. **Student Body:** 55% female, 45% male, 42% out-of-state, 0% international (6 countries represented). Asian 1%, African American 4%, Caucasian 89%, Hispanic 5%, Native American 1%.
Retention and Graduation: 83% freshmen return for sophomore year. 40% freshmen graduate within 4 years. 45% freshmen graduate within 6 years. **Faculty:** Student/faculty ratio 11:1. 15 full-time faculty, 47% hold PhDs, 0% are members of minority groups, 40% are women. 0% of classes are taught by teaching assistants.

ACADEMICS
Degrees: associate, bachelor's, master's. **Classes:** Most classes have fewer than 10 students. **Majors with Highest Enrollment:** business, management, marketing, and related support services, other; elementary education and teaching; psychology. **Special Study Options:** Accelerated program, double major, dual enrollment, independent study, internships, liberal arts/career combination, teacher certification program. **Disability Services:** Special programs offered to physically disabled students include note-taking services, reader services, tape recorders, tutors. **Career Services:** alumni services, career/job search classes, career assessment, internships, Career Services highlights include Variety of internships available.

FACILITIES
Housing: men's dorms, women's dorms. 100% of campus accessible to physically disabled. **Special Academic Facilities/Equipment:** Theater and Athletic Center **Computers:** 100% of libraries, have wireless network access.

CAMPUS LIFE
Environment: Village. **Activities:** Choral groups, drama/theater, literary magazine, student government, Campus Ministries 20 registered organizations, 6 honor societies, 1 religious organizations. **Athletics (Intercollegiate):** *Men:* baseball, basketball, soccer. *Women:* basketball, soccer, softball. **On-Campus Highlights:** Tuttle Hall-Student Center, Athletic Center, Theater, Giorgetti Library, St. Joseph Hall.

ADMISSIONS
Freshman Academic Profile: Average high school GPA 2.6. 0% in top 10% of high school class, 3% in top 25% of high school class, 36% in top 50% of high school class. 75% from public high schools. SAT Math middle 50% range 390-490. SAT Critical Reading middle 50% range 410-530. ACT middle 50% range 17-23. Minimum web-based TOEFL 79. Minimum paper TOEFL 550. **Basis for Candidate Selection:** *Very important factors considered:* academic GPA, recommendation(s), rigor of secondary school record. *Important factors considered include:* application essay, standardized test scores, character/per-

sonal qualities, interview. *Other factors considered include:* Class rank, alumni/ae relation, extracurricular activities, level of applicant's interest, talent/ability, volunteer work. **Freshman Admission Requirements:** High school diploma is required and GED is not accepted. *Academic units required:* 4 English, 3 mathematics, 2 science, 2 social studies, 2 history, 5 academic electives. *Academic units recommended:* 4 English, 3 mathematics, 2 science, 2 social studies, 2 history, 5 academic electives. **Freshman Admission Statistics:** 101 applied, 88% admitted, 37% enrolled. **Transfer Admission Requirements:** High school transcript, college transcript(s), essay or personal statement, minimum college GPA of 2.0 required. Lowest grade transferable C. **General Admission Information:** Application Fee $25. Notification on a rolling basis, beginning on or about 10/1. Nonfall registration accepted. Admission may be deferred for a maximum of 1 year. Credit and/or placement offered for CEEB Advanced Placement tests.

COSTS AND FINANCIAL AID
Annual tuition $15,500. Room and board $7,600. Required fees $260. Average book expense $1,000. Required Forms and Deadlines: FAFSA, institution's own financial aid form. Notification of Awards: Applicants will be notified of awards on a rolling basis beginning 3/15. Types of Aid: Need-based scholarships/grants: Federal Pell, SEOG, state scholarships/grants, private scholarships, the school's own gift aid. Loans: Subsidized Stafford, Unsubsidized Stafford, PLUS, Federal Perkins. Student Employment: Federal Work-Study Program available. Institutional employment available. Highest amount earned per year from on-campus jobs $1,317. Off-campus job opportunities are good. Financial Aid Statistics: 100% freshmen, 98% undergrads receive need-based scholarship or grant aid. 3% undergrads receive non-need-based scholarship or grant aid. 96% freshmen, 94% undergrads receive need-based self-help aid. 91% freshmen, 88% undergrads receive any aid. 100% undergrads borrow to pay for school. Average cumulative indebtedness $24,402. Criteria for awarding institutional aid: Non-need-based: academics, music/drama.

COLLEGE OF SAINT MARY

7000 Mercy Rd., Omaha, NE 68106
Phone: 402-399-2355 • **Financial Aid Phone:** 402-399-2415
E-mail: enroll@csm.edu • **CEEB Code:** 6106
Fax: 402-399-2412 • **Website:** www.csm.edu • **ACT Code:** 2440

This private school, affiliated with the Roman Catholic Church, was founded in 1923. It has a 25-acre campus.

RATINGS
Admissions Selectivity Rating: 80   **Fire Safety Rating:** 98   **Green Rating:** 73

STUDENTS AND FACULTY
Enrollment: 697. **Student Body:** % female, % male, 15% out-of-state, 0% international (7 countries represented). Asian 1%, African American 7%, Caucasian 77%, Hispanic 11%, Native American 0%.
Retention and Graduation: 69% freshmen return for sophomore year. 29% freshmen graduate within 4 years. 36% freshmen graduate within 6 years. 51% grads go on to further study within 1 year. **Faculty:** Student/faculty ratio 9:1. 61 full-time faculty, 66% hold PhDs, 11% are members of minority groups, 77% are women. 0% of classes are taught by teaching assistants.

ACADEMICS
Degrees: associate, bachelor's, certificate, doctoral, master's, post-bachelor's certificate, terminal associate. **Classes:** Most classes have fewer than 10 students. Most lab/discussion sessions have fewer than 10 students. **Majors with Highest Enrollment:** business, management, marketing, and related support services, other; elementary education and teaching; nursing/registered nurse (rn, asn, bsn, msn). **Special Study Options:** Accelerated program, cooperative education program, distance learning, double major, dual enrollment, honors program, independent study, internships, study abroad, teacher certification program, weekend college. **Honors Programs:** Honors Program **Combined Degree Programs:** BS/Eng. **Disability Services:** Special programs offered to physically disabled students include note-taking services, reader services, tape recorders, tutors. **Career Services:** alumni services, career/job search classes, career assessment, internships Career Services highlights include Service learning projects are an integral part of classes.

FACILITIES
Housing: special housing for disabled students, women's dorms, Women with children housing. 100% of campus accessible to physically disabled. **Special Academic Facilities/Equipment:** Hillmer Art Gallery Gross Auditorium **Computers:** 100% of classrooms, 100% of dorms, 100% of libraries, 100% of dining areas, 100% of student union, 100% of common outdoor areas have wireless network access. Students can register for classes online. Administrative functions (other than registration) can be performed online.

CAMPUS LIFE

Environment: Metropolis. **Activities:** Choral groups, music ensembles, student government, Campus Ministries 20 registered organizations, 2 honor societies, 1 religious organizations. **Athletics (Intercollegiate):** *Women:* basketball, cross-country, soccer, softball, swimming, volleyball. **On-Campus Highlights:** Hillmer Art Gallery - Year round exhibits, Gross Theater, Hixson-Lied Commons - Student Center, Library, Lied Fitness Center - gym, weight rm, pool, tennis, Our Lady of Mercy Chapel - Daily Mass offered, Our residence halls include computer labs, lounge areas, a prayer and reflection room, and study area/small group meeting rooms. **Environmental Initiatives:** Reuseable to-go containers in dining hall. Going tray-less in the dining hall. Recycle receptacles located across campus.

ADMISSIONS

Freshman Academic Profile: Average high school GPA 3.4. 19% in top 10% of high school class, 45% in top 25% of high school class, 78% in top 50% of high school class. 80% from public high schools. ACT middle 50% range 19-24. Minimum web-based TOEFL 80. Minimum paper TOEFL 550. **Basis for Candidate Selection:** *Very important factors considered include:* Class rank, academic GPA, standardized test scores. *Other factors considered include:* application essay, recommendation(s), rigor of secondary school record, alumni/ae relation, character/personal qualities, extracurricular activities, interview, level of applicant's interest, talent/ability. **Freshman Admission Requirements:** High school diploma is required and GED is accepted. *Academic units required:* 4 English, 2 mathematics, 2 science, 2 social studies. *Academic units recommended:* 4 English, 2 mathematics, 2 science, 2 social studies. **Freshman Admission Statistics:** 402 applied, 52% admitted, 44% enrolled. **Transfer Admission Requirements:** High school transcript, college transcript(s), minimum college GPA of 2.0 required. Lowest grade transferable C. **General Admission Information:** Application Fee $30. Nonfall registration accepted. Admission may be deferred for a maximum of 12 months. Credit and/or placement offered for CEEB Advanced Placement tests.

COSTS AND FINANCIAL AID

Annual tuition $24,830. Room and board $6,800. Required fees $480. Average book expense $1,280. **Required Forms and Deadlines:** FAFSA. **Notification of Awards:** Applicants will be notified of awards on a rolling basis beginning 3/15. **Types of Aid:** *Need-based scholarships/grants:* Federal Pell, SEOG, state scholarships/grants, private scholarships, the school's own gift aid, Federal Nursing Scholarships. *Loans:* Direct Subsidized Stafford, Direct Unsubsidized Stafford, Direct PLUS, Federal Perkins, Federal Nursing. **Student Employment:** Federal Work-Study Program available. Highest amount earned per year from on-campus jobs $1,800. Off-campus job opportunities are fair. **Financial Aid Statistics:** 100% freshmen, 97% undergrads receive need-based scholarship or grant aid. 17% freshmen, 6% undergrads receive non-need-based scholarship or grant aid. 78% freshmen, 90% undergrads receive need-based self-help aid. 16% freshmen, 5% undergrads receive athletic scholarships. 94% freshmen, 92% undergrads receive any aid. 77% undergrads borrow to pay for school. Average cumulative indebtedness $31,522. **Criteria for awarding institutional aid:** *Non-need-based:* academics, art, athletics, leadership, music/drama.

THE COLLEGE OF SAINT ROSE

432 Western Avenue, Albany, NY 12203
Phone: 800-637-8556
E-mail: admit@strose.edu • **CEEB Code:** 2091
Fax: 518-454-2013 • **Website:** www.strose.edu • **ACT Code:** 2714

This private school, affiliated with the Roman Catholic Church, was founded in 1920. It has a 28-acre campus.

RATINGS

Admissions Selectivity Rating: 78   **Fire Safety Rating:** 96   **Green Rating:** 60*

STUDENTS AND FACULTY

Enrollment: 3,165. **Student Body:** 71% female, 29% male, 7% out-of-state, 0% international (20 countries represented). Asian 1%, African American 3%, Caucasian 78%, Hispanic 4%, Native American 0%.
Retention and Graduation: 82% freshmen return for sophomore year. 49% freshmen graduate within 4 years. 68% freshmen graduate within 6 years. **Faculty:** Student/faculty ratio 14:1. 198 full-time faculty, 82% hold PhDs, 11% are members of minority groups, 55% are women. 0% of classes are taught by teaching assistants.

ACADEMICS

Degrees: bachelor's, master's, post-bachelor's certificate, post-master's certificate. **Classes:** Most classes have 20–29 students. Most lab/discussion sessions have 10–19 students. **Special Study Options:** Accelerated program, cross-registration, double major, exchange student program (domestic), independent study, internships, liberal arts/career combination, student-designed major, study abroad, teacher certification program. **Combined Degree Programs:** BA/JD, BA/MA, MBA/JD graduate degree. **Disability Services:** Special programs offered to physically disabled students include note-taking services, reader services, tape recorders, tutors.

FACILITIES

Housing: Coed dorms, men's dorms, women's dorms, apartments for single students. 90% of campus accessible to physically disabled. **Special Academic Facilities/Equipment:** The Center for Art and Design houses the Saint Rose Art Gallery, the venue for student art shows and exhibits by acclaimed visiting artists, in addition to one of the largest screen printing facilities in the state of New York. The College's full-scale television studio is where communications students produce three 30-minute weekly television shows aired on Time Warner Cable. The Music Center features the Saints and Sinners Sound Studio, a 16-track professional recording studio, in addition to a music library. Athletic Facilities include the College's new Fitness Center, competition-size pool, weight room, and regulation NCAA basketball court. The Hubbard Interfaith Sanctuary is home to Campus Ministry and hosts a variety of interfaith lectures, concerts and poetry readings. With private meditation rooms and an indoor garden, this interreligious space provides a place to escape for a few minutes of quiet prayer. The Center for Cultural Diversity provides academic, social, and cultural support in an effort to enhance the quality of experiences for our diverse student population. **Computers:** 98% of classrooms, 90% of dorms, 100% of libraries, 100% of dining areas, 100% of student union, 80% of common outdoor areas have wireless network access. Students can register for classes online. Administrative functions (other than registration) can be performed online.

CAMPUS LIFE

Environment: City. **Activities:** Choral groups, concert band, dance, drama/theater, jazz band, literary magazine, music ensembles, musical theater, radio station, student government, student newspaper, symphony orchestra, television station, yearbook, Campus Ministries, International Student Organization 38 registered organizations, 6 honor societies, 2 religious organizations. **Athletics (Intercollegiate):** *Men:* baseball, basketball, cross-country, golf, soccer, swimming, track/field (outdoor). *Women:* basketball, cross-country, soccer, softball, swimming, tennis, track/field (outdoor), volleyball. **On-Campus Highlights:** Lally School of Education, Massry Center for the Fine Arts/Center for Art and D, Events and Athletic Center, Quiznos and Starbucks, Student Solution Center, Completely renovated (all) classrooms.

ADMISSIONS

Freshman Academic Profile: Average high school GPA 3.6. 19% in top 10% of high school class, 48% in top 25% of high school class, 86% in top 50% of high school class. 82% from public high schools. SAT Math middle 50% range 480-580. SAT Critical Reading middle 50% range 480-580. ACT middle 50% range 21-27. Minimum web-based TOEFL 83. Minimum paper TOEFL 500. **Basis for Candidate Selection:** *Very important factors considered include:* academic GPA, rigor of secondary school record, interview, level of applicant's interest, talent/ability, work experience. *Important factors considered include:* standardized test scores, extracurricular activities, geographical residence, volunteer work. *Other factors considered include:* Class rank, application essay, alumni/ae relation, racial/ethnic status, state residency. **Freshman Admission Requirements:** High school diploma is required and GED is accepted. *Academic units required:* 4 English, 4 mathematics, 4 science, (2 science labs), 3 foreign language, 4 social studies, 4 history, 22. *Academic units recommended:* 4 English, 4 mathematics, 4 science, (2 science labs), 3 foreign language, 4 social studies, 4 history, 22 **Freshman Admission Statistics:** 3,842 applied, 67% admitted, 24% enrolled. **Transfer Admission Requirements:** High school transcript, college transcript(s), statement of good standing from prior institution(s). Minimum college GPA of 2.5 required. Lowest grade transferable C–. **General Admission Information:** Application Fee $35. Regular application deadline 2/1. Notification on a rolling basis, beginning on or about 12/1. Nonfall registration accepted. Admission may be deferred for a maximum of 1 year. Credit and/or placement offered for CEEB Advanced Placement tests.

COSTS AND FINANCIAL AID

Required Forms and Deadlines: FAFSA. **Notification of Awards:** Applicants will be notified of awards on a rolling basis beginning 3/15. **Types of Aid:** *Need-based scholarships/grants:* Federal Pell, SEOG, state scholarships/grants, private scholarships, the school's own gift aid. *Loans:* Subsidized Stafford, Unsubsidized Stafford, PLUS, Federal Perkins. **Student Employment:** **Financial Aid Statistics:** 88% freshmen, 93% undergrads receive need-based scholarship or grant aid. 96% freshmen, 96% undergrads receive need-based self-help aid. 2% freshmen, 2% undergrads receive athletic scholarships. 85% undergrads borrow to pay for school. Average cumulative indebtedness $24,920. **Criteria for awarding institutional aid:** *Non-need-based:* academics, alumni affiliation, art, athletics, minority status, music/drama.

THE COLLEGE OF SAINT SCHOLASTICA

1200 Kenwood Avenue, Duluth, MN 55811-4199
Phone: 218-723-6046 • **Financial Aid Phone:** 218-723-6047
E-mail: admissions@css.edu • **CEEB Code:** 6107
Fax: 218-723-5991 • **Website:** www.css.edu • **ACT Code:** 2098

This private school, affiliated with the Roman Catholic Church, was founded in 1912. It has a 186-acre campus.

RATINGS
Admissions Selectivity Rating: 73 **Fire Safety Rating:** 72 **Green Rating:** 60*

STUDENTS AND FACULTY
Enrollment: 2,843. **Student Body:** 68% female, 32% male, 14% out-of-state, 4% international (34 countries represented). Asian 1%, African American 2%, Caucasian 80%, Hispanic 2%, Native American 2%.
Retention and Graduation: 81% freshmen return for sophomore year. 57% freshmen graduate within 4 years. 65% freshmen graduate within 6 years. 29% grads go on to further study within 1 year. **Faculty:** Student/faculty ratio 13:1. 172 full-time faculty, 56% hold PhDs, 7% are members of minority groups, 60% are women. 0% of classes are taught by teaching assistants.

ACADEMICS
Degrees: bachelor's, certificate, master's, post-bachelor's certificate, post-master's certificate. **Classes:** Most classes have 20–29 students. Most lab/discussion sessions have 20–29 students. **Majors with Highest Enrollment:** business administration and management; computer and information sciences; nursing/registered nurse (rn, asn, bsn, msn). **Special Study Options:** Accelerated program, cross-registration, distance learning, double major, dual enrollment, external degree program, honors program, independent study, internships, liberal arts/career combination, student-designed major, study abroad, teacher certification program. **Honors Programs:** The Honors Program at The College of St. Scholastica was created to give honors students enriched learning experiences and to provide a community of support for learners devoted to a vigorous life of the mind. **Combined Degree Programs:** BA/MA, BA/Doctor of Physical Therapy. **Disability Services:** Special programs offered to physically disabled students include note-taking services, reader services, tape recorders, tutors. **Career Services:** Alumni network, alumni services, career/job search classes, career assessment, internships Career Services highlights include Semester abroad in Mexico: an international service learning program devoted to educating students about social justice issues and the life of the poor in Mexico.

FACILITIES
Housing: Coed dorms, special housing for disabled students, special housing for international students, apartments for single students, wellness housing, apartments for students with dependent children. Quiet or study wings available. 95% of campus accessible to physically disabled. **Computers:** Students can register for classes online. Administrative functions (other than registration) can be performed online.

CAMPUS LIFE
Environment: City. **Activities:** Choral groups, concert band, dance, drama/theater, jazz band, literary magazine, music ensembles, pep band, student government, student newspaper, television station, Campus Ministries, International Student Organization 67 registered organizations, 2 honor societies, 7 religious organizations. **Athletics (Intercollegiate):** *Men:* baseball, basketball, cross-country, ice hockey, skiingnordiccross-country, soccer, tennis, track/field (outdoor), track/field (indoor). *Women:* basketball, cross-country, skiingnordic-cross-country, soccer, softball, tennis, track/field (outdoor), track/field (indoor), volleyball. **On-Campus Highlights:** Wellness Center, Student Union, Storm's Den, Cedar Hall

ADMISSIONS
Freshman Academic Profile: Average high school GPA 3.5. 20% in top 10% of high school class, 42% in top 25% of high school class, 86% in top 50% of high school class. SAT Math middle 50% range 500-640. SAT Critical Reading middle 50% range 430-660. SAT Writing middle 50% range 420-640. ACT middle 50% range 21-26. Minimum web-based TOEFL 79. Minimum paper TOEFL 550. **Basis for Candidate Selection:** *Very important factors considered include:* academic GPA, standardized test scores. *Important factors considered include:* Class rank, rigor of secondary school record. *Other factors considered include:* application essay, recommendation(s), interview. **Freshman Admission Requirements:** High school diploma is required and GED is accepted. **Freshman Admission Statistics:** 1,833 applied, 78% admitted, 33% enrolled. **Transfer Admission Requirements:** college transcript(s), minimum college GPA of 1.5 required. Lowest grade transferable C. **General Admission Information:** Application Fee $25. Notification on a rolling basis, beginning on or about 9/1. Nonfall registration accepted. Admission may be deferred for a maximum of 1 year. Credit and/or placement offered for CEEB Advanced Placement tests.

COSTS AND FINANCIAL AID
Annual tuition $30,208. Room and board $8,040. Required fees $190. Average book expense $1,150. **Required Forms and Deadlines:** FAFSA. **Notification of Awards:** Applicants will be notified of awards on a rolling basis beginning 3/1. **Types of Aid:** *Need-based scholarships/grants:* Federal Pell, SEOG, state scholarships/grants, private scholarships, the school's own gift aid. *Loans:* Direct Subsidized Stafford, Direct Unsubsidized Stafford, Direct PLUS, Federal Perkins, Federal Nursing, state loans, Private supplemental loans. **Student Employment:** Federal Work-Study Program available. Institutional employment available. Highest amount earned per year from on-campus jobs $4,688. Off-campus job opportunities are good. **Financial Aid Statistics:** 83% freshmen, 80% undergrads receive need-based scholarship or grant aid. 97% freshmen, 81% undergrads receive non-need-based scholarship or grant aid. 73% freshmen, 77% undergrads receive need-based self-help aid. 75% freshmen, 98% undergrads receive any aid. 75% undergrads borrow to pay for school. Average cumulative indebtedness $39,918. **Criteria for awarding institutional aid:** *Non-need-based:* academics, alumni affiliation, music/drama, religious affiliation, state/district residency.

COLLEGE OF ST. CATHERINE

2004 Randolph Avenue, Saint Paul, MN 55105
Phone: 651-690-8850 • **Financial Aid Phone:** 651-690-6540
E-mail: admissions@stkate.edu • **CEEB Code:** 6105
Fax: 651-690-8868 • **Website:** www.stkate.edu • **ACT Code:** 2096

This private school, affiliated with the Roman Catholic Church, was founded in 1905. It has a 110-acre campus.

RATINGS
Admissions Selectivity Rating: 87 **Fire Safety Rating:** 83 **Green Rating:** 60*

STUDENTS AND FACULTY
Enrollment: 3,734. **Student Body:** 97% female, 3% male, 10% out-of-state, 1% international (34 countries represented). Asian 11%, African American 11%, Caucasian 67%, Hispanic 4%, Native American 1%.
Retention and Graduation: 84% freshmen return for sophomore year. 44% freshmen graduate within 4 years. 66% freshmen graduate within 6 years. 28% grads go on to further study within 1 year. 2% grads pursue arts and sciences degrees. 4% grads pursue law degrees. 10% grads pursue business degrees. 2% grads pursue medical degrees. **Faculty:** Student/faculty ratio 12:1. 292 full-time faculty, 10% are members of minority groups, 81% are women. 0% of classes are taught by teaching assistants.

ACADEMICS
Degrees: associate, bachelor's, certificate, master's, post-bachelor's certificate, post-master's certificate, terminal associate, transfer associate. **Classes:** Most classes have 10–19 students. Most lab/discussion sessions have 10–19 students. **Majors with Highest Enrollment:** elementary education and teaching; nursing/registered nurse (rn, asn, bsn, msn); occupational therapy/therapist. **Special Study Options:** cross-registration, double major, dual enrollment, exchange student program (domestic), honors program, independent study, internships, student-designed major, study abroad, weekend college. **Honors Programs:** Antonian Scholars are students who exhibit exceptional academic performance in the University and who show promise as learners, researchers, writers, performers, campus or community leaders, and/or creative thinkers. Scholars possess both creativity and love of learning. Scholars are inquisitive and hard working. They love challenges. Scholars are also students who want to take an active role in '"tailoring'" their college experiences to their needs, interests and passions. Scholars complete a five-component program that includes interdisciplinary seminars, as well as optional honors sections of TRW and/or GSJ, optional study abroad experiences, and a required Senior Honors Project. Scholars participate in at least two and up to four Honors seminars specifically designed for their learning needs and offered in an interdisciplinary format with two professors. All scholars as seniors are required to enroll in a four-credit independent study course in which they develop a senior project based on an interest, curiosity, or passion. Senior projects are completed with a faculty advisor and an interdisciplinary faculty committee who provide guidance and feedback on the project. Other privileges of membership in the Antonian Scholars Honors Program includes priority registration for courses each semester, special diplomas and commencement recognition, and leadership opportunities in the Honors Program Student Organization. Scholars also have opportunities on a regular basis to socialize, network, and converse with others in the Honors Program. Scholars have access to the Honor's Hub in Coeur de Catherine. The Hub is a quiet place to study when you need one and also a place where Scholars may gather for special activities or conversation. **Combined Degree Programs:** BA/DPT, BA/MA (Occupational Therapy). **Disability Services:** Special programs offered to physically disabled students include note-taking

services, reader services, tape recorders, tutors. **Career Services:** Alumni network, alumni services, career/job search classes, career assessment, internships.

FACILITIES

Housing: women's dorms, apartments for single students, theme housing, housing for student-parents. 90% of campus accessible to physically disabled. **Special Academic Facilities/Equipment:** Art gallery, theatre, recital hall, experimental psychology lab, language lab, observatory. **Computers:** Students can register for classes online. Administrative functions (other than registration) can be performed online.

CAMPUS LIFE

Environment: Metropolis. **Activities:** Choral groups, drama/theater, literary magazine, music ensembles, musical theater, student government, student newspaper, Campus Ministries 40 registered organizations, 24 honor societies, 4 religious organizations. 1 sororities. **Athletics (Intercollegiate):** *Women:* basketball, cross-country, diving, ice hockey, soccer, softball, swimming, tennis, track/field (outdoor), track/field (indoor), volleyball. **On-Campus Highlights:** Coeur de Catherine, English garden, Butler Center, Dew Drop Pond, Art Gallery. **Environmental Initiatives:** Retrofitted older building with green roof energy-efficient design in new residence halls sustainable landscaping

ADMISSIONS

Freshman Academic Profile: Average high school GPA 3.6. 26% in top 10% of high school class, 63% in top 25% of high school class, 91% in top 50% of high school class. 86% from public high schools. ACT middle 50% range 22-26. Minimum paper TOEFL 500. **Basis for Candidate Selection:** *Very important factors considered include:* academic GPA, rigor of secondary school record. *Important factors considered include:* Class rank, application essay, recommendation(s), standardized test scores. *Other factors considered include:* interview. **Freshman Admission Requirements:** High school diploma is required and GED is accepted. **Freshman Admission Statistics:** 2,808 applied, 52% admitted, 25% enrolled. **Transfer Admission Requirements:** High school transcript, college transcript(s), statement of good standing from prior institution(s). Minimum college GPA of 2.0 required. Lowest grade transferable C–. **General Admission Information:** Credit offered for CEEB Advanced Placement tests.

COSTS AND FINANCIAL AID

Annual tuition $29,400. Room and board $7,402. Required fees $280. Average book expense $1,000. **Required Forms and Deadlines:** FAFSA, institution's own financial aid form. **Notification of Awards:** Applicants will be notified of awards on a rolling basis beginning 3/15. **Types of Aid:** *Need-based scholarships/grants:* Federal Pell, SEOG, state scholarships/grants, private scholarships, the school's own gift aid. *Loans:* Direct Subsidized Stafford, Direct Unsubsidized Stafford, Direct PLUS, Federal Perkins, Federal Nursing, state loans. **Student Employment:** Federal Work-Study Program available. Institutional employment available. Highest amount earned per year from on-campus jobs $2,158. Off-campus job opportunities are excellent. **Financial Aid Statistics:** 89% freshmen, 87% undergrads receive need-based scholarship or grant aid. 87% freshmen, 73% undergrads receive non-need-based scholarship or grant aid. 80% freshmen, 84% undergrads receive need-based self-help aid. 94% freshmen, 93% undergrads receive any aid. 85% undergrads borrow to pay for school. Average cumulative indebtedness $35,237. **Criteria for awarding institutional aid:** *Non-need-based:* academics, alumni affiliation, leadership, minority status, state/district residency.

THE COLLEGE OF WILLIAM AND MARY

Office of Admissions, P.O. Box 8795, Williamsburg, VA 23187-8795
Phone: 757-221-4223 • **Financial Aid Phone:** 757-221-2420
E-mail: admission@wm.edu • **CEEB Code:** 5115
Fax: 757-221-1242 • **Website:** www.wm.edu • **ACT Code:** 4344

This public school was founded in 1693. It has a 1200-acre campus.

RATINGS

Admissions Selectivity Rating: 97   **Fire Safety Rating:** 75   **Green Rating:** 88

STUDENTS AND FACULTY

Enrollment: 6,129. **Student Body:** 55% female, 45% male, 32% out-of-state, 4% international (54 countries represented). Asian 6%, African American 7%, Caucasian 59%, Hispanic 9%, Native American 0%.

Retention and Graduation: 96% freshmen return for sophomore year. **Faculty:** Student/faculty ratio 12:1. 592 full-time faculty, 92% hold PhDs, 13% are members of minority groups, 38% are women. 1% of classes are taught by teaching assistants.

ACADEMICS

Degrees: bachelor's, doctoral, master's, post-master's certificate. **Classes:** Most classes have 10–19 students. Most lab/discussion sessions have 10–19 students. **Special Study Options:** Accelerated program, double major, dual enrollment, honors program, independent study, internships, student-designed major, study abroad, teacher certification program. **Honors Programs:** Monroe Scholars; Sharpe Scholars; Murray Scholars; William and Mary Scholar Award; Alpha Lambda Delta and Phi Eta Sigma Honor Societies for Freshman. **Combined Degree Programs:** BA/MEng, Bachelor's/Master of Forestry or Master of Env. Management from Duke Univ. **Disability Services:** Special programs offered to physically disabled students include note-taking services, reader services, tape recorders, tutors. **Career Services:** Alumni network, alumni services, career/job search classes, career assessment, internships Career Services highlights include The Alumni Mentoring Program provides valuable and searchable information for students and alumni alike to connect for the purposes of seeking career advice, support, and referral. The synergy of this networking program simultaneously strengthens the College community.

FACILITIES

Housing: Coed dorms, special housing for disabled students, special housing for international students, fraternity/sorority housing, apartments for single students, wellness housing, theme housing, International Studies hall, Eco-House, Community Scholars House, Africana House, Multicultural Unit, and 8 language houses (Arabic, Chinese, French, German, Italian, Japanese, Russian, Spanish). 80% of campus accessible to physically disabled. **Special Academic Facilities/Equipment:** observatory, continuous beam accelerator, 3 interdisciplinary centers in humanities, international studies, writing resources, marine science institute, materials processes research center, public policy research center. **Computers:** 100% of classrooms, 100% of dorms, 100% of libraries, 100% of dining areas, 100% of student union, 33% of common outdoor areas have wireless network access. Students can register for classes online. Administrative functions (other than registration) can be performed online. Undergraduates are required to own a computer.

CAMPUS LIFE

Environment: Village. **Activities:** Choral groups, concert band, dance, drama/theater, jazz band, literary magazine, music ensembles, musical theater, opera, pep band, radio station, student government, student newspaper, student-run film society, symphony orchestra, television station, yearbook, Campus Ministries, International Student Organization, Model UN 375 registered organizations, 32 honor societies, 32 religious organizations. 18 fraternities, 11 sororities. **Athletics (Intercollegiate):** *Men:* baseball, basketball, cheerleading, cross-country, diving, football, golf, gymnastics, soccer, swimming, tennis, track/field (outdoor), track/field (indoor). *Women:* basketball, cheerleading, cross-country, diving, field hockey, golf, gymnastics, lacrosse, soccer, swimming, tennis, track/field (outdoor), track/field (indoor), volleyball. **On-Campus Highlights:** Wren Building (oldest academic building), Muscarelle Museum of Art, Lake Matoaka/College Woods, Crim Dell Bridge, Sunken Garden. **Environmental Initiatives:** Adhere to LEED construction guidelines in all new construction and renovations. Three buildings have been LEED certified to date and two are in progress. Retrofit of systems to improve energy consumption and reduce consumption. Participated in major ESCO contract for Athletic Center. Purchase of environmentally sustainable materials. Develop a sustainable procurement manual. Provide leadership in providing state-wide sustainable procurement guidelines in higher education.

ADMISSIONS

Freshman Academic Profile: Average high school GPA 4.0. 79% in top 10% of high school class, 97% in top 25% of high school class, 100% in top 50% of high school class. ~70% from public high schools. SAT Math middle 50% range 620-720. SAT Critical Reading middle 50% range 630-740. SAT Writing middle 50% range 620-720. ACT middle 50% range 28-32. Minimum web-based TOEFL 100. Minimum paper TOEFL 600. **Basis for Candidate Selection:** *Very important factors considered include:* Class rank, application essay, academic GPA, recommendation(s), rigor of secondary school record, standardized test scores, character/personal qualities, extracurricular activities, state residency, talent/ability, volunteer work, work experience. *Other factors considered include:* alumni/ae relation, first generation, geographical residence, interview, racial/ethnic status. **Freshman Admission Requirements:** High school diploma or equivalent is not required. **Freshman Admission Statistics:** 13,660 applied, 32% admitted, 33% enrolled. **Transfer Admission Requirements:** High school transcript, college transcript(s), essay or personal statement, statement of good standing from prior institution(s). Minimum college GPA of 3.00 required. Lowest grade transferable C. **General Admission Information:** Application Fee $60. Early decision application deadline 11/1. Regular application deadline 1/1. Regular notification 4/1. Nonfall registration not accepted. Admission may be deferred for a maximum of 1 year. Credit and/or placement offered for CEEB Advanced Placement tests.

COSTS AND FINANCIAL AID

Annual in-state tuition $8,677. Annual out-of-state tuition $31,860. Room and board $9,180. Required fees $4,893. Average book expense $1,200. **Required Forms and Deadlines:** FAFSA. **Notification of Awards:** Applicants will be notified of awards on a rolling basis beginning 3/15. **Types of Aid:** *Need-based scholarships/grants:* Federal Pell, SEOG, state scholarships/grants, private scholarships, the school's own gift aid. *Loans:* Subsidized Stafford, Unsubsidized Stafford, PLUS, Federal Perkins. **Student Employment:** Federal Work-Study Program available. Institutional employment available. Highest amount earned per year from on-campus jobs $1,400. Off-campus job opportunities are excellent. **Financial Aid Statistics:** 68% freshmen, 75% undergrads receive need-based scholarship or grant aid. 48% freshmen, 37% undergrads receive non-need-based scholarship or grant aid. 66% freshmen, 67% undergrads receive need-based self-help aid. 5% freshmen, 5% undergrads receive athletic scholarships. 54% freshmen, 53% undergrads receive any aid. 3418% undergrads borrow to pay for school. Average cumulative indebtedness $20,835. **Criteria for awarding institutional aid:** *Non-need-based:* academics, art, athletics, leadership, music/drama, state/district residency.

THE COLLEGE OF WOOSTER

 Best 378

847 College Avenue, Wooster, OH 44691
Phone: 330-263-2322 • **Financial Aid Phone:** 800-877-3688
E-mail: admissions@wooster.edu • **CEEB Code:** 1134
Fax: 330-263-2621 • **Website:** www.wooster.edu • **ACT Code:** 3260

This private school was founded in 1866. It has a 240-acre campus.

RATINGS
Admissions Selectivity Rating: 89   **Fire Safety Rating:** 73   **Green Rating:** 90

STUDENTS AND FACULTY

Enrollment: 2,038. **Student Body:** 55% female, 45% male, 62% out-of-state, 6% international (40 countries represented). Asian 3%, African American 9%, Caucasian 71%, Hispanic 4%, Native American 1%.
Retention and Graduation: 90% freshmen return for sophomore year. 70% freshmen graduate within 4 years. 76% freshmen graduate within 6 years. 28% grads go on to further study within 1 year. 63% grads pursue arts and sciences degrees. 21% grads pursue law degrees. 7% grads pursue medical degrees. **Faculty:** Student/faculty ratio 11:1. 173 full-time faculty, 95% hold PhDs, 15% are members of minority groups, 51% are women. 0% of classes are taught by teaching assistants.

ACADEMICS

Degrees: bachelor's. **Classes:** Most classes have 10–19 students. Most lab/discussion sessions have 10–19 students. **Majors with Highest Enrollment:** English language and literature; history; psychology. **Special Study Options:** cooperative education program, double major, dual enrollment, exchange student program (domestic), independent study, internships, student-designed major, study abroad, teacher certification program. **Combined Degree Programs:** BA/MA, BA/DDS, BA/MEng, many combined programs with other institutions. **Disability Services:** Special programs offered to physically disabled students include note-taking services, reader services, tape recorders, tutors. **Career Services:** Alumni network, alumni services, career/job search classes, career assessment, internships, regional alumni.

FACILITIES

Housing: Coed dorms, special housing for international students, women's dorms, fraternity/sorority housing, apartments for single students, theme housing, special housing for students participating in volunteer programs. 95% of campus accessible to physically disabled. **Special Academic Facilities/Equipment:** Art museum, language lab, on-campus nursery school, science library. **Computers:** 100% of classrooms, 95% of dorms, 100% of libraries, 100% of dining areas, 100% of student union, 50% of common outdoor areas have wireless network access. Students can register for classes online. Administrative functions (other than registration) can be performed online.

CAMPUS LIFE

Environment: Town. **Activities:** Choral groups, concert band, dance, drama/theater, jazz band, literary magazine, marching band, music ensembles, musical theater, pep band, radio station, student government, student newspaper,

student-run film society, symphony orchestra, yearbook, Campus Ministries, International Student Organization, Model UN 100 registered organizations, 6 honor societies, 9 religious organizations. 5 fraternities, 6 sororities. **Athletics (Intercollegiate): Men:** baseball, basketball, cross-country, diving, football, golf, lacrosse, soccer, swimming, tennis, track/field (outdoor), track/field (indoor). *Women:* basketball, cross-country, diving, field hockey, lacrosse, soccer, softball, swimming, tennis, track/field (outdoor), track/field (indoor), volleyball. **On-Campus Highlights:** Kauke Hall, Severance Hall Chemistry Bldg., Timken Science Library, Ebert Art Center, Burton D. Morgan Hall, Gault Manor (residence hall). **Environmental Initiatives:** campus food service: reducing the use of disposable items and their environmental impact across all operations Local foods initiative. We buy locally grown, seasonal produce as well as baked goods, dairy, eggs, and other food items that are locally produced. Recently we started purchasing biodegradable containers (Stalkmarket brand) and cutlery (Jaya brand) made from sustainable crops such as sugar cane stalks and corn. We have a longstanding and comprehensive recycling policy, which includes not only the usual paper etc. but also recycling computers (through Apple) and recycling yard waste (to use as mulch). Building debris is recycled wherever possible. Parking blocks are made of recycled materials.

ADMISSIONS

Freshman Academic Profile: Average high school GPA 3.6. 41% in top 10% of high school class, 76% in top 25% of high school class, 96% in top 50% of high school class. 70% from public high schools. SAT Math middle 50% range 540-660. SAT Critical Reading middle 50% range 540-660. SAT Writing middle 50% range 540-660. ACT middle 50% range 25-30. Minimum web-based TOEFL 81. **Basis for Candidate Selection:** *Very important factors considered include:* Class rank, academic GPA, rigor of secondary school record. *Important factors considered include:* application essay, recommendation(s), standardized test scores, character/personal qualities, talent/ability. *Other factors considered include:* alumni/ae relation, extracurricular activities, geographical residence, interview, racial/ethnic status, state residency, volunteer work, work experience. **Freshman Admission Requirements:** High school diploma is required and GED is accepted. *Academic units required:* 4 English, 3 mathematics, 3 science, 2 foreign language, 3 social studies, 2 academic electives. *Academic units recommended:* 4 English, 3 mathematics, 3 science, 2 foreign language, 3 social studies, 2 academic electives. **Freshman Admission Statistics:** 5,208 applied, 58% admitted, 19% enrolled. **Transfer Admission Requirements:** High school transcript, college transcript(s), essay or personal statement, standardized test scores, statement of good standing from prior institution(s). Minimum college GPA of 2.5 required. Lowest grade transferable C. **General Admission Information:** Application Fee $40. Early decision application deadline 12/1. Regular application deadline 2/15. Nonfall registration accepted. Admission may be deferred for a maximum of 1 year. Credit and/or placement offered for CEEB Advanced Placement tests.

COSTS AND FINANCIAL AID

Annual tuition $39,500. Room and board $9,590. Required fees $310. Average book expense $1,000. **Required Forms and Deadlines:** FAFSA, institution's own financial aid form, CSS/Financial Aid PROFILE. **Notification of Awards:** Applicants will be notified of awards on or about 4/1. **Types of Aid:** *Need-based scholarships/grants:* Federal Pell, SEOG, state scholarships/grants, private scholarships, the school's own gift aid. *Loans:* Direct Subsidized Stafford, Direct Unsubsidized Stafford, Direct PLUS, Federal Perkins, college/university loans from institutional funds. **Student Employment:** Federal Work-Study Program available. Institutional employment available. Off-campus job opportunities are good. **Financial Aid Statistics:** 98% freshmen, 98% undergrads receive need-based scholarship or grant aid. 13% freshmen, 11% undergrads receive non-need-based scholarship or grant aid. 85% freshmen, 87% undergrads receive need-based self-help aid. 99% freshmen, 99% undergrads receive any aid. 49% undergrads borrow to pay for school. Average cumulative indebtedness $26,750. **Criteria for awarding institutional aid:** *Non-need-based:* academics, leadership, minority status, music/drama, religious affiliation, state/district residency.

COLORADO CHRISTIAN UNIVERSITY

8787 W. Alameda Ave., Lakewood, CO 80226
Phone: 303-963-3200 • **Financial Aid Phone:** 303-963-3233
E-mail: ccuadmissions@ccu.edu • **CEEB Code:** 4659
Fax: 303-963-3201 • **Website:** www.ccu.edu • **ACT Code:** 523

This private school, affiliated with the Christian (Nondenominational) Church, was founded in 1914. It has a 26-acre campus.

RATINGS
Admissions Selectivity Rating: 74   **Fire Safety Rating:** 61   **Green Rating:** 60*

STUDENTS AND FACULTY

Enrollment: 1,849. **Student Body:** 60% female, 40% male, 56% out-of-state, 0% international. Asian 1%, African American 3%, Caucasian 69%, Hispanic 8%, Native American 1%.
Retention and Graduation: 86% freshmen return for sophomore year. 34% freshmen graduate within 4 years. 44% freshmen graduate within 6 years.
Faculty: Student/faculty ratio 21:1. 41 full-time faculty, 68% hold PhDs, 5% are members of minority groups, 46% are women. 0% of classes are taught by teaching assistants.

ACADEMICS

Degrees: associate, bachelor's, master's. **Classes:** Most classes have fewer than 10 students. Most lab/discussion sessions have 10–19 students. **Majors with Highest Enrollment:** computer/information technology services administration and management, other; liberal arts and sciences/liberal studies; management information systems. **Special Study Options:** Accelerated program, co-operative education program, distance learning, double major, honors program, independent study, internships, student-designed major, study abroad, teacher certification program, weekend college, American Studies Program (Washington DC); Host University for Institute for Family Studies; China Studies Program (various sites in China); Latin American Studies Program (Costa Rica); Los Angeles Film Studies Center; Middle East Studies (Cairo, Egypt); Oxford Honors Program (University of Oxford, England); Russian Studies Program (various sites in Russia); Summer Institute of Journalism (Washington DC).
Disability Services: Special programs offered to physically disabled students include tutors. **Career Services:** alumni services, career/job search classes, career assessment, internships.

FACILITIES

Housing: Coed dorms, special housing for disabled students, men's dorms, women's dorms, apartments for single students, theme housing. 85% of campus accessible to physically disabled. **Special Academic Facilities/Equipment:** Music recording studio, electron microscope. **Computers:** 100% of classrooms, 100% of dorms, 100% of student union, have wireless network access. Students can register for classes online. Administrative functions (other than registration) can be performed online.

CAMPUS LIFE

Environment: Activities: Choral groups, concert band, drama/theater, jazz band, literary magazine, music ensembles, musical theater, student government, student newspaper, symphony orchestra 21 registered organizations, 3 honor societies, 14 religious organizations. **Athletics (Intercollegiate):** *Men:* basketball, cross-country, golf, soccer, tennis. *Women:* basketball, cross-country, soccer, tennis, volleyball.

ADMISSIONS

Freshman Academic Profile: Average high school GPA 3.4. 22% in top 10% of high school class, 46% in top 25% of high school class, 79% in top 50% of high school class. SAT Math middle 50% range 480-590. SAT Critical Reading middle 50% range 510-630. ACT middle 50% range 20-26. Minimum paper TOEFL 500. **Basis for Candidate Selection:** *Very important factors considered include:* application essay, rigor of secondary school record, standardized test scores, character/personal qualities, first generation, religious affiliation/commitment, talent/ability. *Important factors considered include:* Class rank, academic GPA, recommendation(s), extracurricular activities, level of applicant's interest, racial/ethnic status, volunteer work. *Other factors considered include:* alumni/ae relation, interview, work experience. **Freshman Admission Requirements:** High school diploma is required and GED is accepted. **Freshman Admission Statistics:** 946 applied, 77% admitted, 33% enrolled. **Transfer Admission Requirements:** college transcript(s), essay or personal statement, statement of good standing from prior institution(s). Minimum college GPA of 2.0 required. Lowest grade transferable C. **General Admission Information:** Application Fee $50. Regular application deadline 8/21. Notification on a rolling basis, beginning on or about 11/1. Nonfall registration accepted. Admission may be deferred for a maximum of 1 YEAR. Credit and/or placement offered for CEEB Advanced Placement tests.

COSTS AND FINANCIAL AID

Annual tuition $18,850. Room and board $6,682. Required fees $150. Average book expense $1,188. **Required Forms and Deadlines:** FAFSA. **Notification of Awards:** Applicants will be notified of awards on a rolling basis beginning 4/1. **Types of Aid:** *Need-based scholarships/grants:* Federal Pell, SEOG, private scholarships, the school's own gift aid. *Loans:* Subsidized Stafford, Unsubsidized Stafford, PLUS, Federal Perkins. **Student Employment:** Federal Work-Study Program available. Institutional employment available. Off-campus job opportunities are good. **Financial Aid Statistics:** 97% freshmen, 88% undergrads receive need-based scholarship or grant aid. 88% freshmen, 82% undergrads receive non-need-based scholarship or grant aid. 100% freshmen, 100% undergrads receive need-based self-help aid. 14% freshmen, 7% undergrads receive athletic scholarships. 61% undergrads borrow to pay for school. Average cumulative indebtedness $17,275. **Criteria for awarding institutional aid:** *Non-need-based:* academics, athletics, leadership, minority status.

COLORADO COLLEGE

14 East Cache la Poudre Street, Colorado Springs, CO 80903
Phone: 719-389-6344 • **Financial Aid Phone:** 719-389-6651
E-mail: admission@coloradocollege.edu • **CEEB Code:** 4072
Fax: 719-389-6816 • **Website:** www.coloradocollege.edu • **ACT Code:** 498

This private school was founded in 1874. It has a 90-acre campus.

RATINGS

Admissions Selectivity Rating: 97   **Fire Safety Rating:** 90   **Green Rating:** 94

STUDENTS AND FACULTY

Enrollment: 1,983. **Student Body:** 54% female, 46% male, 80% out-of-state, 5% international (58 countries represented). Asian 4%, African American 2%, Caucasian 73%, Hispanic 7%, Native American 0%.
Retention and Graduation: 95% freshmen return for sophomore year. 83% freshmen graduate within 4 years. 90% freshmen graduate within 6 years.
Faculty: Student/faculty ratio 10:1. 167 full-time faculty, 99% hold PhDs, 16% are members of minority groups, 43% are women. 0% of classes are taught by teaching assistants.

ACADEMICS

Degrees: bachelor's, master's. **Classes:** Most classes have 20–29 students. **Majors with Highest Enrollment:** biology/biological sciences; economics; political science and government. **Special Study Options:** double major, English as a Second Language (ESL), independent study, internships, liberal arts/career combination, student-designed major, study abroad, Teacher licensure program; Cooperative 3/2 program. **Combined Degree Programs:** BA/JD, BA/MEng, Columbia University School of Law. **Disability Services:** Special programs offered to physically disabled students include note-taking services, tutors. **Career Services:** Alumni network, alumni services, career assessment, internships.

FACILITIES

Housing: Coed dorms, men's dorms, women's dorms, fraternity/sorority housing, apartments for single students, theme housing. **Special Academic Facilities/Equipment:** Electronic music studio, telescope dome, multimedia computer laboratory, Balinese orchestras, The Colorado Electronic music studio, Observatory, Extensive herbarium collection 4 greenhouses Environmental Science van equipped for field research Fourier transform nuclear magnetic resonance spectrometer Packard Hall, 300 seat concert/lecture hall Photography darkrooms Drama/Dance: Armstrong Theatre, 740 seat proscenium theatre Armstrong 32, 100 seat experimental theatre 4 dance studios w/Marley, variable speed cd players Drama computer lab Geology: Petrographic microscopes X ray diffractometer Sedimentology lab El Pomar Sports Center: Metabolic Equipment (COSMED Quark PFT Ergo) Hydrostatic Weighing Equipment Cadaver study in Sports Science Biology: Scanning electron microscope Transmission electron microscope **Computers:** 100% of classrooms, 100% of dorms, 100% of libraries, 100% of dining areas, 100% of student union, 80% of common outdoor areas have wireless network access. Students can register for classes online. Administrative functions (other than registration) can be performed online.

CAMPUS LIFE

Environment: Metropolis. **Activities:** Choral groups, concert band, dance, drama/theater, jazz band, literary magazine, music ensembles, musical theater, radio station, student government, student newspaper, student-run film society, yearbook, Campus Ministries, International Student Organization 147 registered organizations, 13 honor societies, 20 religious organizations. 1 fraternities, 3 sororities. **Athletics (Intercollegiate):** *Men:* basketball, cross-country, ice hockey, lacrosse, soccer, swimming, tennis, track/field (outdoor). *Women:* basketball, cross-country, lacrosse, soccer, swimming, tennis, track/field (outdoor), track/field (indoor), volleyball. **On-Campus Highlights:** Worner Student Center, Palmer Hall, Shove Chapel, Cutler Hall - Admission, View of Pikes Peak. **Environmental Initiatives:** The College is committed to achieving carbon neutrality by 2020. The plan includes an efficiency target in all campus buildings that will reduce energy intensity by 30%, along with a 20% reduction target through behavior change and conservation, and a strategy to derive 100% of electricity from renewable sources. The College has a comprehensive waste minimization plan that includes single stream recycling, composting in all major dining halls, and the phase-out of single use plastic bags and bottled water. Colorado College President Richard Celeste has joined local government, business and non-profit leaders in signing a statement of commitment to pursue a cooperative approach to sustainability in the Pikes Peak region. This commitment will initiate a regional sustainability planning process.

ADMISSIONS

Freshman Academic Profile: 62% in top 10% of high school class, 90% in top 25% of high school class, 98% in top 50% of high school class. 54% from public high schools. SAT Math middle 50% range 610-710. SAT Critical Reading middle 50% range 630-720. SAT Writing middle 50% range 620-720. ACT middle 50% range 28-32. Minimum paper TOEFL. **Basis for Candidate Selection:** *Very important factors considered include:* rigor of secondary school record. *Important factors considered include:* Class rank, application essay, academic GPA, recommendation(s), standardized test scores, extracurricular activities, interview. *Other factors considered include:* alumni/ae relation, character/personal qualities, first generation, level of applicant's interest, racial/ethnic status, religious affiliation/commitment, talent/ability, volunteer work, work experience. **Freshman Admission Requirements:** High school diploma or equivalent is not required. *Academic units required:* 4 English. *Academic units recommended:* 4 English. **Freshman Admission Statistics:** 40% enrolled. **Transfer Admission Requirements:** High school transcript, college transcript(s), essay or personal statement, standardized test scores, statement of good standing from prior institution(s). Lowest grade transferable C. **General Admission Information:** Application Fee $50. Early decision application deadline 11/15. Regular application deadline 1/15. Regular notification 4/1. Nonfall registration accepted. Admission may be deferred for a maximum of 1 year. Credit and/or placement offered for CEEB Advanced Placement tests.

COSTS AND FINANCIAL AID

Annual tuition $41,742. Room and board $9,728. Average book expense $1,214. **Required Forms and Deadlines:** FAFSA, CSS/Financial Aid PROFILE, noncustodial PROFILE, Federal 1040 parent and student tax returns and parent W-2 forms. **Notification of Awards:** Applicants will be notified of awards on or about 3/20. *Types of Aid: Need-based scholarships/grants:* Federal Pell, SEOG, state scholarships/grants, private scholarships, Federal ACG and SMART grants. *Loans:* Direct Subsidized Stafford, Direct Unsubsidized Stafford, Direct PLUS, Federal Perkins. **Student Employment:** Federal Work-Study Program available. Institutional employment available. Off-campus job opportunities are good. **Financial Aid Statistics:** 97% freshmen, 99% undergrads receive need-based scholarship or grant aid. 58% freshmen, 54% undergrads receive non-need-based scholarship or grant aid. 95% freshmen, 75% undergrads receive need-based self-help aid. 1% freshmen, 2% undergrads receive athletic scholarships. 57% freshmen, 58% undergrads receive any aid. 31% undergrads borrow to pay for school. Average cumulative indebtedness $19,230. **Criteria for awarding institutional aid:** *Non-need-based:* academics, athletics.

COLORADO SCHOOL OF MINES

1600 Maple Street, Golden, CO 80401
Phone: 303-273-3220 • **Financial Aid Phone:** 303-273-3220
E-mail: admit@mines.edu • **CEEB Code:** 4073
Fax: 303-273-3509 • **Website:** www.mines.edu • **ACT Code:** 500

This public school was founded in 1874. It has a 373-acre campus.

RATINGS

Admissions Selectivity Rating: 95   **Fire Safety Rating:** 68   **Green Rating:** 63

STUDENTS AND FACULTY

Enrollment: 4,075. **Student Body:** 27% female, 73% male, 30% out-of-state, 4% international (79 countries represented). Asian 5%, African American 1%, Caucasian 76%, Hispanic 8%, Native American 0%.
Retention and Graduation: 89% freshmen return for sophomore year. 35% freshmen graduate within 4 years. 67% freshmen graduate within 6 years. 14% grads go on to further study within 1 year. 4% grads pursue arts and sciences degrees. 1% grads pursue law degrees. 2% grads pursue business degrees. 1% grads pursue medical degrees. **Faculty:** Student/faculty ratio 16:1. 251 full-time faculty, 92% hold PhDs, 16% are members of minority groups, 25% are women. 3% of classes are taught by teaching assistants.

ACADEMICS

Degrees: bachelor's, master's, post-master's certificate. **Classes:** Most classes have 10–19 students. Most lab/discussion sessions have 20–29 students. **Majors with Highest Enrollment:** chemical engineering; mechanical engineering; petroleum engineering. **Special Study Options:** Accelerated program, cooperative education program, double major, dual enrollment, English as a Second Language (ESL), exchange student program (domestic), honors program, independent study, internships, study abroad. **Honors Programs:** McBride Honors Program - The McBride Honors Program, instituted in 1978 through a grant from the National Endowment for the Humanities, is a 24 semester-hour program of seminars and off-campus activities that has as its primary goal:

To provide a select community of CSM students the enhanced opportunity to explore the interfaces between their areas of technical expertise and the humanities and social sciences; to gain the sensitivity to project and test the moral and social implications of their future professional judgments and activities; and to foster their leadership abilities in preparation for managing change and promoting the general welfare in an evolving technological and global context. To achieve this goal, the program seeks to bring themes from the humanities and the social sciences into the engineering curriculum that will encourage in students the habits of thought necessary for effective management and enlightened leadership. **Combined Degree Programs:** BS/MS. **Disability Services:** Special programs offered to physically disabled students include note-taking services, reader services, tape recorders, tutors. **Career Services:** alumni services, career/job search classes, career assessment, internships Career Services highlights include One of the newest opportunities is through the Renewable Energy Materials Research Science and Engineering Center: The Center focuses on preparing undergraduate and graduate students to embark on careers in renewable fields by providing a multitude of research and classroom experiences in renewable energy. REMRSEC offers a coordinated approach from K to gray in renewable energy education, outreach, and work force development founded on research proven best practices. National Renewable Energy Laboratory(NREL) NREL will be a principle partner in the Colorado School of Mines (CSM) Renewable Energy Materials Research Science and Engineering Center (REMRSEC), building upon and strengthening the existing relationship between CSM and NREL. The goals of this partnership are to provide a convenient avenue to transition basic research and engineering discoveries into more applied projects and ultimately into the market place using NREL's strengths, to facilitate the training of future scientists and engineers by providing access to world class researchers and equipment at NREL, and to greatly augment the outreach efforts of the Center by coupling with the superb outreach efforts at NREL. http://remrsec.mines.edu/educationoutreach.htm.

FACILITIES

Housing: Coed dorms, fraternity/sorority housing, apartments for married students, apartments for single students. 100% of campus accessible to physically disabled. **Special Academic Facilities/Equipment:** Geology Museum, US Geological Survey & Earthquake Center, Edgar Experimental Mine, Graduate Research Laboratory (GRL), Center for Technology & Learning Media which houses supercomputer "'Ra,'" - high performance computing (HPC) cluster that aims to be a national hub for computational inquiries aimed at the discovery of new ways to meet the world's energy demands. Estimated peak performance will be approximately 20 teraflops'—This places the machine well within the top-100 fastest computers in the world. The new facility, administered by the Golden Energy Computing Organization (GECO), is dedicated to advancing energy-related science. **Computers:** 100% of classrooms, 100% of dorms, 100% of libraries, 100% of dining areas, 100% of student union, 80% of common outdoor areas have wireless network access. Students can register for classes online. Administrative functions (other than registration) can be performed online.

CAMPUS LIFE

Environment: Metropolis. **Activities:** Choral groups, concert band, dance, drama/theater, jazz band, literary magazine, marching band, music ensembles, musical theater, pep band, radio station, student government, student newspaper, symphony orchestra, yearbook, Campus Ministries, International Student Organization 148 registered organizations, 9 honor societies, 7 religious organizations. 7 fraternities, 3 sororities. **Athletics (Intercollegiate):** *Men:* baseball, basketball, cross-country, diving, football, golf, soccer, swimming, track/field (outdoor), track/field (indoor), wrestling. *Women:* basketball, cross-country, diving, soccer, softball, swimming, track/field (outdoor), track/field (indoor), volleyball. **On-Campus Highlights:** Student Recreation Center, Outdoor Recreation Center, Geology Museum, National Earthquake Center, Computer Commons at the CTLM.

ADMISSIONS

Freshman Academic Profile: Average high school GPA 3.8. 60% in top 10% of high school class, 91% in top 25% of high school class, 100% in top 50% of high school class. 90% from public high schools. SAT Math middle 50% range 630-720. SAT Critical Reading middle 50% range 570-670. SAT Writing middle 50% range 550-650. ACT middle 50% range 27-31. Minimum web-based TOEFL 79. Minimum paper TOEFL 550. **Basis for Candidate Selection:** *Very important factors considered include:* Class rank, academic GPA, rigor of secondary school record. *Important factors considered include:* standardized test scores. *Other factors considered include:* application essay, recommendation(s), alumni/ae relation, character/personal qualities, extracurricular activities, geographical residence, interview, level of applicant's interest, state residency, talent/ability. **Freshman Admission Requirements:** High school diploma is required and GED is accepted. *Academic units required:* 4 English, 4 mathematics, 3 science, (3 science labs), 3 social studies, 2 academic electives. *Academic units recommended:* 4 English, 4 mathematics, 3 science, (3 science labs), 3 social studies, 2 academic electives. **Freshman Admission Statistics:** 11,682 applied, 37% admitted, 22% enrolled. **Transfer Admission**

Requirements: High school transcript, college transcript(s), statement of good standing from prior institution(s). Minimum college GPA of 2.75 required. Lowest grade transferable C. **General Admission Information:** Application Fee $45. Regular application deadline 5/1. Notification on a rolling basis, beginning on or about 10/1. Nonfall registration accepted. Admission may be deferred for a maximum of 12 months. Credit and/or placement offered for CEEB Advanced Placement tests.

COSTS AND FINANCIAL AID

Annual in-state tuition $13,590. Annual out-of-state tuition $28,620. Room and board $9,922. Required fees $2,064. Average book expense $1,500. **Required Forms and Deadlines:** FAFSA. **Notification of Awards:** Applicants will be notified of awards on a rolling basis beginning 3/15. **Types of Aid:** *Need-based scholarships/grants:* Federal Pell, SEOG, state scholarships/grants, private scholarships, the school's own gift aid. *Loans:* Subsidized Stafford, Unsubsidized Stafford, PLUS, Federal Perkins, college/university loans from institutional funds. **Student Employment:** Federal Work-Study Program available. Institutional employment available. Highest amount earned per year from on-campus jobs $3,000. Off-campus job opportunities are good. **Financial Aid Statistics:** 56% freshmen, 60% undergrads receive need-based scholarship or grant aid. 77% freshmen, 63% undergrads receive non-need-based scholarship or grant aid. 92% freshmen, 92% undergrads receive need-based self-help aid. 4% freshmen, 4% undergrads receive athletic scholarships. 85% freshmen, 85% undergrads receive any aid. 51% undergrads borrow to pay for school. Average cumulative indebtedness $33,209. **Criteria for awarding institutional aid:** *Non-need-based:* academics, athletics, music/drama.

COLORADO STATE UNIVERSITY

1062 Campus Delivery, Fort Collins, CO 80523-1062
Phone: 970-491-6909 • **Financial Aid Phone:** 970-491-6321
E-mail: admissions@colostate.edu • **CEEB Code:** 4075
Fax: 970-491-7799 • **Website:** www.colostate.edu/ • **ACT Code:** 504

This public school was founded in 1870. It has a 582-acre campus.

RATINGS

Admissions Selectivity Rating: 77   **Fire Safety Rating:** 75   **Green Rating:** 97

STUDENTS AND FACULTY

Enrollment: 22,412. **Student Body:** 51% female, 49% male, 18% out-of-state, 2% international (86 countries represented). Asian 2%, African American 2%, Caucasian 76%, Hispanic 9%, Native American 0%.
Retention and Graduation: 84% freshmen return for sophomore year. 38% freshmen graduate within 4 years, 64% freshmen graduate within 6 years. 26% grads go on to further study within 1 year. 1% grads pursue arts and sciences degrees. 1% grads pursue law degrees. 1% grads pursue business degrees. **Faculty:** Student/faculty ratio 19:1. 940 full-time faculty, 99% hold PhDs, 17% are members of minority groups, 34% are women. 8% of classes are taught by teaching assistants.

ACADEMICS

Degrees: bachelor's, doctoral, master's. **Classes:** Most classes have 10–19 students. Most lab/discussion sessions have 20–29 students. **Majors with Highest Enrollment:** construction management; human development and family studies; psychology. **Special Study Options:** Accelerated program, cooperative education program, cross-registration, distance learning, double major, dual enrollment, English as a Second Language (ESL), exchange student program (domestic), honors program, independent study, internships, liberal arts/career combination, study abroad, teacher certification program. **Honors Programs:** University Honors Program. **Combined Degree Programs:** MS/DVM, MBA/DVM, PhD/DVM, MS of Public Health/DVM, BS/MS. **Disability Services:** Special programs offered to physically disabled students include note-taking services, reader services, tape recorders, tutors. **Career Services:** Alumni network, alumni services, career/job search classes, career assessment, internships.

FACILITIES

Housing: Coed dorms, special housing for disabled students, apartments for married students, apartments for single students, wellness housing, theme housing. Non college-owned fraternity/sorority housing, is available. Also available are Living-Learning Communities, and special interest floors. 97% of campus accessible to physically disabled. **Special Academic Facilities/Equipment:**

International Poster collection Gustafson Gallery--historic clothing Curfman Gallery-- Art Student Recreation Center Ropes Course University Center for the Arts (performance hall, thrust theater,art museum) Avenir Museum of Design and Merchandising (Costumes, Textiles, Interior Artifacts) **Computers:** 100% of classrooms, 100% of dorms, 100% of libraries, 100% of dining areas, 100% of student union, 60% of common outdoor areas have wireless network access. Students can register for classes online. Administrative functions (other than registration) can be performed online.

CAMPUS LIFE

Environment: City. **Activities:** Choral groups, concert band, dance, drama/theater, jazz band, literary magazine, marching band, music ensembles, musical theater, opera, pep band, radio station, student government, student newspaper, symphony orchestra, television station, Campus Ministries, International Student Organization 350 registered organizations, 35 honor societies, 28 religious organizations. 21 fraternities, 14 sororities. **Athletics (Intercollegiate):** *Men:* basketball, cross-country, football, golf, track/field (outdoor), track/field (indoor). *Women:* basketball, cross-country, diving, golf, softball, swimming, tennis, track/field (outdoor), track/field (indoor), volleyball, water polo. **On-Campus Highlights:** Lory Student Center, Student Recreation Center, Library, University Center For the Arts, Moby Arena, The University Center for the Arts is complete, featuring the newly-constructed University Art Museum. Also housed at the UCA is the Griffin Concert Hall, Bohemian Complex with 317 seat thrust theatre, Casavant Organ Recital Hall, and other world-class student resources. **Environmental Initiatives:** Several renewable energy sources went live in the year 2010 including: a second phase of a large solar array that now totals 5,300 kilowatts on the Foothills Campus, an 18.9 kW solar array on the roof of the Engineering building, and a 12.6 kW solar array at the Academic Village residence hall, 133 kW solar array on the roof of the Lake Street Parking Garage, a 15.8 kW on the Behavioral Sciences Building and a 54 kW solar array at the Research Innovation Center. The five smaller arrays are owned and operated by the University, the larger array is owned by a third party and Colorado State serves as a site host and purchases the power produced by the panels. In addition to solar power, CSU's Foothills Campus is also home to a biomass heating plant on the Foothills Campus. This plant burns wood chips to produce hot water for building heat and displaces natural gas use. Campaigns to engage campus faculty staff and students have launched in 2009 to advance sustainability efforts on campus. The faculty campaign, Green is Gold is intended to encourage environmentally friendly habits in the workplace. More information can be found at http://www.green.colostate.edu/gold/. The "Green Warrior Campaign" aims to engage students in creating a climate of sustainability at CSU. The student campaign provides incentives for students to live more sustainably. Colorado State has constructed eight new buildings on campus in the past year. All of these buildings have achieved LEED Gold certification. The university has embraced the green building concept and is getting creative on how to build and renovate buildings more sustainably. Some of the green features on these buildings involve collaboration with researchers on campus in order to further the value of the green buildings. For example, a greywater research project at the new residence hall will study the effects and feasibility of using greywater for irrigation on campus.

ADMISSIONS

Freshman Academic Profile: Average high school GPA 3.6. 22% in top 10% of high school class, 51% in top 25% of high school class, 88% in top 50% of high school class. SAT Math middle 50% range 520-640. SAT Critical Reading middle 50% range 500-620. ACT middle 50% range 22-27. Minimum web-based TOEFL 45. Minimum paper TOEFL 450. **Basis for Candidate Selection:** *Very important factors considered include:* Class rank, academic GPA, rigor of secondary school record. *Important factors considered include:* application essay, recommendation(s), standardized test scores, character/personal qualities, extracurricular activities, talent/ability, volunteer work. *Other factors considered include:* alumni/ae relation, first generation, geographical residence, interview, level of applicant's interest, state residency, work experience. **Freshman Admission Requirements:** High school diploma is required and GED is accepted. *Academic units required:* 4 English, 4 mathematics, 3 science, (2 science labs), 1 foreign language, 2 social studies, 1 history, 2 academic electives. *Academic units recommended:* 4 English, 4 mathematics, 3 science, (2 science labs), 1 foreign language, 2 social studies, 1 history, 2 academic electives. **Freshman Admission Statistics:** 17,929 applied, 75% admitted, 34% enrolled. **Transfer Admission Requirements:** college transcript(s), essay or personal statement, minimum college GPA of 2.0 required. Lowest grade transferable C–. **General Admission Information:** Application Fee $50. Regular application deadline 2/1. Notification on a rolling basis, beginning on or about 10/1. Nonfall registration accepted. Admission may be deferred for a maximum of 1 year. Credit and/or placement offered for CEEB Advanced Placement tests.

COSTS AND FINANCIAL AID

Annual in-state tuition $6,875. Annual out-of-state tuition $22,667. Room and board $10,278. Required fees $1,774. Average book expense $1,126. **Required Forms and Deadlines:** FAFSA. **Notification of Awards:** Applicants will be notified of awards on a rolling basis beginning 3/1. **Types of Aid:** *Need-based scholarships/grants:* Federal Pell, SEOG, state scholarships/grants, private scholarships, the school's own gift aid. *Loans:* Direct Subsidized Stafford, Direct Unsubsidized Stafford, Direct PLUS, Federal Perkins, college/university loans from institutional funds, Alternative Loans. **Student Employment:** Federal Work-Study Program available. Institutional employment available. Highest amount earned per year from on-campus jobs $2,500. Off-campus job opportunities are excellent. **Financial Aid Statistics:** 71% freshmen, 69% undergrads receive need-based scholarship or grant aid. 71% freshmen, 77% undergrads receive need-based self-help aid. 1% freshmen, 1% undergrads receive athletic scholarships. 72% freshmen, 70% undergrads receive any aid. 63% undergrads borrow to pay for school. Average cumulative indebtedness $22,039. **Criteria for awarding institutional aid:** *Non-need-based:* academics, art, athletics, leadership, music/drama, state/district residency.

COLORADO STATE UNIVERSITY—PUEBLO

Admissions, Pueblo, CO 81001
Phone: 719-549-2461 • **Financial Aid Phone:** 719-549-2178
E-mail: info@colostate-pueblo.edu • **CEEB Code:** 4611
Fax: 719-549-2419 • **Website:** www.colostate-pueblo.edu • **ACT Code:** 524

This public school was founded in 1933. It has a 275-acre campus.

RATINGS
Admissions Selectivity Rating: 65   **Fire Safety Rating:** 66   **Green Rating:** 60*

STUDENTS AND FACULTY
Enrollment: 3,947. **Student Body:** 57% female, 43% male, 7% out-of-state, 2% international (27 countries represented). Asian 3%, African American 6%, Caucasian 55%, Hispanic 25%, Native American 2%.
Retention and Graduation: 63% freshmen return for sophomore year. **Faculty:** Student/faculty ratio 17:1. 155 full-time faculty, % hold PhDs, 17% are members of minority groups, 47% are women. 0% of classes are taught by teaching assistants.

ACADEMICS
Degrees: bachelor's, master's. **Classes:** Most classes have 10–19 students. Most lab/discussion sessions have 10–19 students. **Majors with Highest Enrollment:** biology/biological sciences; liberal arts and sciences/liberal studies; mass communication/media studies. **Special Study Options:** Accelerated program, cooperative education program, distance learning, double major, dual enrollment, English as a Second Language (ESL), external degree program, independent study, internships, liberal arts/career combination, study abroad, teacher certification program, weekend college. **Honors Programs:** We do not have an Honor Program, however, we offer several undergraduate honor courses. **Combined Degree Programs:** BSBA/MBA, BS/MS. **Disability Services:** Special programs offered to physically disabled students include note-taking services, reader services, tape recorders, tutors.

FACILITIES
Housing: Coed dorms, special housing for disabled students, apartments for single students. 100% of campus accessible to physically disabled. **Special Academic Facilities/Equipment:** Recital hall, public television and radio station. **Computers:** Students can register for classes online. Administrative functions (other than registration) can be performed online.

CAMPUS LIFE
Environment: City. **Activities:** Choral groups, concert band, dance, jazz band, literary magazine, music ensembles, pep band, student government, student newspaper, symphony orchestra, television station 24 registered organizations, 6 honor societies, 4 religious organizations. 2 fraternities, 1 sororities. **Athletics (Intercollegiate):** *Men:* baseball, basketball, golf, soccer, tennis. *Women:* basketball, cross-country, golf, soccer, softball, tennis, volleyball. **On-Campus Highlights:** University Library, Occhiato University Center - La Cantina, Occhiato University Center - The Undergroundn, The Pavillion, The Wall.

ADMISSIONS
Freshman Academic Profile: Average high school GPA 3.1. 2% in top 10% of high school class, 8% in top 25% of high school class, 36% in top 50% of high school class. 85% from public high schools. SAT Math middle 50% range 420-550. SAT Critical Reading middle 50% range 420-530. ACT middle 50% range 18-22. Minimum paper TOEFL 500. **Basis for Candidate Selection:** *Very important factors considered include:* academic GPA, rigor of secondary school record, standardized test scores. *Important factors considered include:* Class rank. *Other factors considered include:* application essay, recommendation(s), character/personal qualities, interview, level of applicant's interest, talent/ability,

volunteer work, work experience. **Freshman Admission Requirements:** High school diploma is required and GED is accepted. *Academic units required:* 4 English, 3 mathematics, 3 science, (2 science labs), 2 foreign language, 2 social studies, 1 history. *Academic units recommended:* 4 English, 3 mathematics, 3 science, (2 science labs), 2 foreign language, 2 social studies, 1 history. **Freshman Admission Statistics:** 1,485 applied, 94% admitted, 46% enrolled. **Transfer Admission Requirements:** college transcript(s), minimum college GPA of 2.3 required. Lowest grade transferable C–. **General Admission Information:** Application Fee $25. Regular application deadline 8/1. Notification on a rolling basis, beginning on or about 8/1. Nonfall registration accepted. Admission may be deferred for a maximum of 1 semester. Credit offered for CEEB Advanced Placement tests.

COSTS AND FINANCIAL AID
Annual in-state tuition $3,422. Annual out-of-state tuition $13,543. Room and board $6,300. Required fees $996. Average book expense $1,698. **Required Forms and Deadlines:** FAFSA, institution's own financial aid form. **Notification of Awards:** Applicants will be notified of awards on a rolling basis beginning 3/15. **Types of Aid:** *Need-based scholarships/grants:* Federal Pell, SEOG, state scholarships/grants, private scholarships, the school's own gift aid, Academic Competitiveness Grant and National SMART Grant. *Loans:* Subsidized Stafford, Unsubsidized Stafford, PLUS, Federal Perkins. **Student Employment:** Highest amount earned per year from on-campus jobs $8,000. **Financial Aid Statistics:** 81% freshmen, 80% undergrads receive need-based scholarship or grant aid. 7% freshmen, 4% undergrads receive non-need-based scholarship or grant aid. 78% freshmen, 87% undergrads receive need-based self-help aid. 3% freshmen, 4% undergrads receive athletic scholarships. 81% freshmen, 86% undergrads receive any aid. 54% undergrads borrow to pay for school. Average cumulative indebtedness $16,481. **Criteria for awarding institutional aid:** *Non-need-based:* academics, alumni affiliation, art, athletics, leadership, minority status, music/drama, state/district residency.

COLORADO TECHNICAL UNIVERSITY

4435 North Chestnut Street, Colorado Springs, CO 80907-3740
Phone: 719-598-0200
E-mail: cosadmissions@coloradotech.edu • **Website:** www.coloradotech.edu/

This is a proprietary school.

RATINGS
Admissions Selectivity Rating: 60*   **Fire Safety Rating:** 60*   **Green Rating:** 60*

STUDENTS AND FACULTY
Faculty: Student/faculty ratio 25:1. 31 full-time faculty, 52% hold PhDs, 13% are members of minority groups, 35% are women.

ACADEMICS
Degrees: associate, bachelor's, certificate, master's, transfer associate. **Classes:** Most classes have 10–19 students. **Special Study Options:** Accelerated program, double major, independent study, internships, weekend college, Sixteen and 1/2 month M.S. degree programs and 2-year doctoral programs.

ADMISSIONS
Basis for Candidate Selection: *Other factors considered include:* Class rank, recommendation(s), rigor of secondary school record, standardized test scores, alumni/ae relation, character/personal qualities, interview, work experience. **Freshman Admission Requirements:** *Academic units required:* 1 English, 1 mathematics, 1 science, (1 science labs). *Academic units recommended:* 1 English, 1 mathematics, 1 science, (1 science labs). **Transfer Admission Requirements:** college transcript(s), statement of good standing from prior institution(s). Lowest grade transferable C. **General Admission Information:** Application Fee $50. Regular application deadline 10/2. Nonfall registration accepted.

COSTS AND FINANCIAL AID
Required fees $171. Average book expense $1,000. **Required Forms and Deadlines:** FAFSA, institution's own financial aid form, state aid form. **Notification of Awards:** Applicants will be notified of awards on a rolling basis beginning 2/1. **Types of Aid:** *Need-based scholarships/grants: Loans:* Subsidized Stafford, Unsubsidized Stafford, PLUS, Federal Perkins.

COLUMBIA COLLEGE (MO)

1001 Rogers St., Columbia, MO 65216
Phone: 573-875-7352 • **Financial Aid Phone:** 573-875-7390
E-mail: admissions@ccis.edu • **CEEB Code:** 6095
Fax: 573-875-7506 • **Website:** www.ccis.edu • **ACT Code:** 2276

This private school, affiliated with the Disciples of Christ Church, was founded in 1851. It has a 33-acre campus.

RATINGS
Admissions Selectivity Rating: 74   **Fire Safety Rating:** 83   **Green Rating:** 65

STUDENTS AND FACULTY
Enrollment: 903. **Student Body:** 58% female, 42% male, 12% out-of-state, 10% international (27 countries represented). Asian 1%, African American 5%, Caucasian 73%, Hispanic 3%, Native American 1%.
Retention and Graduation: 67% freshmen return for sophomore year. 33% freshmen graduate within 4 years. 43% freshmen graduate within 6 years. 13% grads go on to further study within 1 year. 1% grads pursue law degrees. 8% grads pursue business degrees. 1% grads pursue medical degrees. **Faculty:** Student/faculty ratio 11:1. 68 full-time faculty, 72% hold PhDs, 7% are members of minority groups, 49% are women. 0% of classes are taught by teaching assistants.

ACADEMICS
Degrees: associate, bachelor's, certificate, master's, post-bachelor's certificate. **Classes:** Most classes have 10–19 students. Most lab/discussion sessions have 10–19 students. **Majors with Highest Enrollment:** biology/biological sciences; business administration and management; psychology. **Special Study Options:** cross-registration, distance learning, double major, dual enrollment, English as a Second Language (ESL), honors program, independent study, internships, student-designed major, study abroad, teacher certification program. **Honors Programs:** The Honors Program is designed for high achieving students who are philosophers in the literal sense, i.e., lovers of wisdom. The goal of the program is to promote genuine inquiry and collaborative learning, emphasizing the dialogic nature of academic work and intellectual discovery. **Disability Services:** Special programs offered to physically disabled students include note-taking services, tutors. **Career Services:** Alumni network, alumni services, career/job search classes, internships, regional alumni. Career Services highlights include ***** All of our Career Services that are offered to our regular students are offered to Alumni and they are FREE.

FACILITIES
Housing: Coed dorms, special housing for disabled students, special housing for international students, women's dorms, apartments for single students, wellness housing, 97% of campus accessible to physically disabled. **Special Academic Facilities/Equipment:** Most classrooms are multimedia with SmartBoards, new student commons building, arts center, Larson Gallery, Jane Froman Archive **Computers:** 100% of classrooms, 100% of dorms, 100% of libraries, 100% of dining areas, 100% of student union, have wireless network access. Students can register for classes online. Administrative functions (other than registration) can be performed online.

CAMPUS LIFE
Environment: City. **Activities:** Choral groups, dance, drama/theater, literary magazine, music ensembles, musical theater, student government, student newspaper, Campus Ministries, International Student Organization, Model UN 42 registered organizations, 16 honor societies, 2 religious organizations. **Athletics (Intercollegiate):** *Men:* basketball, soccer. *Women:* basketball, softball, volleyball. **On-Campus Highlights:** Larson Art Gallery, The newly expanded Southwell Athletic Complex, New Atkins-Holman Student Commons building, Stafford Library **Environmental Initiatives:** 77% of campus building square footage is on highly efficient ground source water heat pump system. We have in place a fairly substantial recycling program. We have in place a lighting retro-fit program replacing ineffient lights with more efficient ones.

ADMISSIONS
Freshman Academic Profile: Average high school GPA 3.4. 20% in top 10% of high school class, 23% in top 25% of high school class, 78% in top 50% of high school class. 89% from public high schools. SAT Math middle 50% range 470-600. SAT Critical Reading middle 50% range 440-510. ACT middle 50% range 20-26. Minimum web-based TOEFL 61. Minimum paper TOEFL 500. **Basis for Candidate Selection:** *Very important factors considered include:* Class rank, academic GPA, standardized test scores. *Other factors considered include:* rigor of secondary school record, character/personal qualities. **Freshman Admission Requirements:** High school diploma is required and GED is accepted. **Freshman Admission Statistics:** 571 applied, 69% admitted, 38% enrolled. **Transfer Admission Requirements:** college transcript(s), statement of good standing from prior institution(s). Minimum college GPA of

2.0 required. Lowest grade transferable 2. **General Admission Information:** Regular application deadline 8/14. Notification on a rolling basis, beginning on or about 9/15. Nonfall registration accepted. Admission may be deferred for a maximum of 1 year. Credit and/or placement offered for CEEB Advanced Placement tests.

COSTS AND FINANCIAL AID
Annual tuition $17,950. Room and board $6,254. Average book expense $936. **Required Forms and Deadlines:** FAFSA. **Notification of Awards:** Applicants will be notified of awards on a rolling basis beginning 3/1. **Types of Aid:** *Need-based scholarships/grants:* Federal Pell, SEOG, state scholarships/grants, private scholarships. *Loans:* Direct Subsidized Stafford, Direct Unsubsidized Stafford, Direct PLUS. **Student Employment:** Federal Work-Study Program available. Institutional employment available. Highest amount earned per year from on-campus jobs $5,982. Off-campus job opportunities are excellent. **Financial Aid Statistics:** 55% freshmen, 64% undergrads receive need-based scholarship or grant aid. 1% freshmen, 47% undergrads receive non-need-based scholarship or grant aid. 1% freshmen, 75% undergrads receive need-based self-help aid. 3% freshmen, 3% undergrads receive athletic scholarships. 84% freshmen, 78% undergrads receive any aid. 53% undergrads borrow to pay for school. Average cumulative indebtedness $11,726. **Criteria for awarding institutional aid:** *Non-need-based:* academics, alumni affiliation, art, athletics, job skills, leadership, music/drama, religious affiliation, state/district residency.

See page 1050.

COLUMBIA COLLEGE (SC)

1301 Columbia College Drive, Columbia, SC 29203
Phone: 803-786-3871 • **Financial Aid Phone:** 803-786-3612
E-mail: admissions@columbiasc.edu • **CEEB Code:** 5117
Fax: 803-786-3674 • **Website:** www.columbiacollegesc.edu • **ACT Code:** 3850

This private school, affiliated with the Methodist Church, was founded in 1854. It has a 33-acre campus.

RATINGS
Admissions Selectivity Rating: 70   **Fire Safety Rating:** 86   **Green Rating:** 60*

STUDENTS AND FACULTY
Enrollment: 1,225. **Student Body:** 97% female, 3% male, 6% out-of-state, 0% international (14 countries represented). Asian 1%, African American 44%, Caucasian 47%, Hispanic 2%, Native American 2%.
Retention and Graduation: 62% freshmen return for sophomore year. 39% freshmen graduate within 4 years. 47% freshmen graduate within 6 years. **Faculty:** Student/faculty ratio 10:1. 87 full-time faculty, 75% hold PhDs, 11% are members of minority groups, 68% are women. 0% of classes are taught by teaching assistants

ACADEMICS
Degrees: bachelor's, master's, post-bachelor's certificate. **Classes:** Most classes have 10–19 students. **Majors with Highest Enrollment:** business administration and management; elementary education and teaching; human development, family studies, and related services, other. **Special Study Options:** distance learning, double major, dual enrollment, honors program, independent study, internships, student-designed major, study abroad, teacher certification program. **Honors Programs:** The Columbia College Honors Program provides enriched academic and co-curricular experiences for outstanding, motivated students committed to excellence. Offering a variety of opportunities for superior, engaged learning both within and outside the classroom, honors challenges students to reach their highest potential as scholars, individual thinkers, and leaders by emphasizing rigorous intellectual standards, risk, creativity, integrity, and dedication to service and leadership. The program is deeply active in the National Collegiate Honors Council and its regional association, regularly sponsoring numerous faculty and students at annual conferences and in executive leadership positions; honors has also earned special recognition through national and regional awards for honors faculty and students. To complete honors, students take 24 semester hours across disciplines in honors courses, including the 3 hour interdisciplinary senior seminar and the 3 - 4 hour mentored independent project. Students must maintain at least a 3.4 cumulative GPA to remain in honors. **Career Services:** career/job search classes, career assessment, internships.

FACILITIES
Housing: women's dorms, Special programs: Leadership; Honors Program. 75% of campus accessible to physically disabled. **Special Academic Facilities/Equipment:** Language lab, Alumnae Hall, Barbara Bush Center for Science and Technology, Breed Leadership Center for Women. **Computers:** 50% of libraries, 100% of dining areas, 100% of student union, 30% of common outdoor

areas have wireless network access. Students can register for classes online. Administrative functions (other than registration) can be performed online.

CAMPUS LIFE

Environment: Metropolis. **Activities:** Choral groups, concert band, dance, drama/theater, literary magazine, music ensembles, musical theater, opera, student government, student newspaper, yearbook, Campus Ministries, International Student Organization 53 registered organizations, 10 honor societies, 7 religious organizations. **Athletics (Intercollegiate):** *Women:* basketball, soccer, softball, tennis, volleyball. **On-Campus Highlights:** Leadership Center, Terrace Cafe, Student Union, Cottingham Performance Theatre, Bush Science Center. **Environmental Initiatives:** Student-sponsored and initiated recycling program

ADMISSIONS

Freshman Academic Profile: Average high school GPA 3.5. 19% in top 10% of high school class, 45% in top 25% of high school class, 78% in top 50% of high school class. SAT Math middle 50% range 450-550. SAT Critical Reading middle 50% range 450-570. SAT Writing middle 50% range 440-560. ACT middle 50% range 18-24. Minimum paper TOEFL 550. **Basis for Candidate Selection:** *Very important factors considered include:* recommendation(s), rigor of secondary school record, standardized test scores. *Important factors considered include:* Class rank, character/personal qualities. *Other factors considered include:* application essay, alumni/ae relation, extracurricular activities, talent/ability, volunteer work. **Freshman Admission Requirements:** High school diploma is required and GED is accepted. **Freshman Admission Statistics:** 1,078 applied, 76% admitted, 34% enrolled. **Transfer Admission Requirements:** High school transcript, college transcript(s), standardized test scores, statement of good standing from prior institution(s). Minimum college GPA of 2.0 required. Lowest grade transferable C. **General Admission Information:** Application Fee $25. Regular application deadline 8/1. Notification on a rolling basis, beginning on or about 10/1. Nonfall registration accepted. Admission may be deferred for a maximum of 1 year. Credit offered for CEEB Advanced Placement tests.

COSTS AND FINANCIAL AID

Annual tuition $22,580. Room and board $6,450. Required fees $450. Required **Forms and Deadlines:** FAFSA. **Notification of Awards:** Applicants will be notified of awards on a rolling basis beginning 3/1. **Types of Aid:** *Need-based scholarships/grants:* Federal Pell, SEOG, state scholarships/grants, private scholarships, the school's own gift aid, United Negro College Fund. *Loans:* Subsidized Stafford, Unsubsidized Stafford, PLUS, Federal Perkins, state loans, signature student loan. **Student Employment:** Federal Work-Study Program available. Institutional employment available. Highest amount earned per year from on-campus jobs $1,000. Off-campus job opportunities are excellent. **Financial Aid Statistics:** 98% freshmen, 95% undergrads receive need-based scholarship or grant aid. 85% freshmen, 76% undergrads receive non-need-based scholarship or grant aid. 83% freshmen, 85% undergrads receive need-based self-help aid. 2% freshmen, 3% undergrads receive athletic scholarships. 99% freshmen, 92% undergrads receive any aid. 94% undergrads borrow to pay for school. Average cumulative indebtedness $16,976. **Criteria for awarding institutional aid:** *Non-need-based:* academics, alumni affiliation, art, athletics, leadership, music/drama.

COLUMBIA COLLEGE CHICAGO (IL)

600 South Michigan Avenue, Chicago, IL 60605-1996
Phone: 312-369-7130 • **Financial Aid Phone:** 312-369-7140
E-mail: admissions@colum.edu • **CEEB Code:** 1135
Fax: 312-369-8024 • **Website:** www.colum.edu • **ACT Code:** 1002

This private school was founded in 1890.

RATINGS

Admissions Selectivity Rating: 68   **Fire Safety Rating:** 73   **Green Rating:** 65

STUDENTS AND FACULTY

Enrollment: 10,208. **Student Body:** 53% female, 47% male, 37% out-of-state, 2% international (48 countries represented). Asian 3%, African American 17%, Caucasian 57%, Hispanic 13%, Native American 0%.
Retention and Graduation: 64% freshmen return for sophomore year. 26% freshmen graduate within 4 years. 40% freshmen graduate within 6 years. 9% grads go on to further study within 1 year. 10% grads pursue arts and sciences degrees. **Faculty:** Student/faculty ratio 11:1. 380 full-time faculty, 0% hold PhDs, 15% are members of minority groups, 47% are women. 0% of classes are taught by teaching assistants.

ACADEMICS

Degrees: bachelor's, master's, post-bachelor's certificate, post-master's certificate. **Classes:** Most classes have 10–19 students. **Majors with Highest Enrollment:** arts management; cinematography and film/video production; fine/studio arts. **Special Study Options:** cross-registration, exchange student program (domestic), honors program, independent study, internships, student-designed major, study abroad, teacher certification program. **Disability Services:** Special programs offered to physically disabled students include note-taking services, reader services, tape recorders, tutors.

FACILITIES

Housing: Coed dorms, apartments for single students. 90% of campus accessible to physically disabled. **Special Academic Facilities/Equipment:** Art galleries, center for black music research, contemporary photography museum, dance center. **Computers:** Students can register for classes online. Administrative functions (other than registration) can be performed online.

CAMPUS LIFE

Environment: Metropolis. **Activities:** Choral groups, concert band, dance, drama/theater, jazz band, literary magazine, music ensembles, musical theater, opera, radio station, student government, student newspaper, student-run film society, television station, Campus Ministries, International Student Organization 64 registered organizations. **On-Campus Highlights:** Museum of Contemporary Photography, Center for Black Music Research, Hokin Annex and Gallery **Environmental Initiatives:** Campus-wide recycling Sustainable materials in capital construction projects LEED cerfitication in capital construction projects

ADMISSIONS

Freshman Academic Profile: 8% in top 10% of high school class, 24% in top 25% of high school class, 54% in top 50% of high school class. SAT Math middle 50% range 440-550. SAT Critical Reading middle 50% range 460-590. SAT Writing middle 50% range 450-560. ACT middle 50% range 19-25. Minimum web-based TOEFL 80. Minimum paper TOEFL 533. **Basis for Candidate Selection:** *Important factors considered include:* application essay, academic GPA, recommendation(s), character/personal qualities, talent/ability. *Other factors considered include:* rigor of secondary school record, standardized test scores, extracurricular activities, interview, volunteer work, work experience. **Freshman Admission Requirements:** High school diploma is required and GED is accepted. **Freshman Admission Statistics:** 7,416 applied, 85% admitted, 33% enrolled. **Transfer Admission Requirements:** High school transcript, college transcript(s), essay or personal statement, Lowest grade transferable C. **General Admission Information:** Application Fee $35. Nonfall registration accepted. Admission may be deferred for a maximum of 1 year. Credit and/or placement offered for CEEB Advanced Placement tests.

COSTS AND FINANCIAL AID

Annual tuition $21,200. Room and board $11,920. Required fees $1,190. Average book expense $1,654. **Required Forms and Deadlines:** FAFSA. **Notification of Awards: Types of Aid:** *Need-based scholarships/grants:* Federal Pell, SEOG, state scholarships/grants, private scholarships, the school's own gift aid. *Loans:* Direct Subsidized Stafford, Direct Unsubsidized Stafford, Direct PLUS. **Student Employment:** Federal Work-Study Program available. **Financial Aid Statistics:** 79% freshmen, 77% undergrads receive any aid.

See page 1052.

COLUMBIA COLLEGE—HOLLYWOOD

18618 Oxnard St., Tarzana, CA 91356
Phone: 818-345-8414
E-mail: admissions@columbiacollege.edu • **CEEB Code:** 7213
Fax: 818-345-9053 • **Website:** www.columbiacollege.edu

This private school was founded in 1952.

RATINGS

Admissions Selectivity Rating: 62   **Fire Safety Rating:** 60*   **Green Rating:** 60*

STUDENTS AND FACULTY

Enrollment: 150. **Student Body:** 31% female, 69% male, 10% international (24 countries represented). Asian 5%, African American 9%, Caucasian 60%, Hispanic 14%, Native American 1%.
Retention and Graduation: 47% freshmen return for sophomore year. 36% freshmen graduate within 4 years. 5% grads go on to further study within 1 year. **Faculty:** Student/faculty ratio 6:1. 0% of classes are taught by teaching assistants.

ACADEMICS

Degrees: associate, bachelor's. **Majors with Highest Enrollment:** cinematography and film/video production; film/cinema studies. **Special Study Options:** Accelerated program, double major, internships, liberal arts/career combination. **Combined Degree Programs:** Combined BA degree in Cinema and Video/TV. **Career Services:** Alumni network, career assessment, internships Career Services highlights include All students are strongly encouraged to meet with the Placement Advisor upon enrollment. Employment is not guaranteed but CCH offers career counseling and guidance that prepares students to meet the challenges of the highly competitive entertainment industry. For-pay and for-college credit internships at entertainment production companies are available year round. The Placement Advisor assists students in selecting internships, drafting resumes, and preparing for interviews. In addition, the Faculty Association mentors students with senior status. Each student is matched with a faculty advisor in his or her chosen field of study. The advisor offers one-on-one counseling. Many faculty members are industry insiders with invaluable insight into the craft and the business of movie and television production.

FACILITIES

Housing: CCH does not offer housing, but our staff does assist students in trying to find apartments and potential roommates.

CAMPUS LIFE

Environment: Metropolis. **Activities:** student government 1 registered organizations, 3 honor societies.

ADMISSIONS

Freshman Academic Profile: Average high school GPA 3.3. 50% from public high schools. Minimum paper TOEFL 550. **Basis for Candidate Selection:** *Very important factors considered include:* application essay, recommendation(s), rigor of secondary school record. *Other factors considered include:* standardized test scores, character/personal qualities, extracurricular activities, interview, talent/ability. **Freshman Admission Requirements:** High school diploma is required and GED is accepted. **Freshman Admission Statistics:** 87 applied, 77% admitted, 90% enrolled. **Transfer Admission Requirements:** High school transcript, college transcript(s), essay or personal statement, minimum college GPA of 2.0 required. Lowest grade transferable C. **General Admission Information:** Application Fee $50. Nonfall registration accepted. Admission may be deferred for a maximum of 12 months. Neither credit nor placement offered for CEEB Advanced Placement tests.

COSTS AND FINANCIAL AID

Annual tuition $11,400. Required fees $225. Average book expense $400. **Required Forms and Deadlines:** FAFSA, institution's own financial aid formC. **Notification of Awards: Types of Aid:** *Need-based scholarships/grants:* Federal Pell, SEOG, state scholarships/grants. *Loans:* Subsidized Stafford, Unsubsidized Stafford, PLUS. **Student Employment:** Federal Work-Study Program available. Off-campus job opportunities are excellent. **Financial Aid Statistics:** 63% freshmen, 74% undergrads receive need-based scholarship or grant aid. 78% freshmen, 75% undergrads receive any aid. 95% undergrads borrow to pay for school. Average cumulative indebtedness $35,125.

COLUMBIA INTERNATIONAL UNIVERSITY

PO Box 3122, Columbia, SC 29230-3122
Phone: 803-754-4100
E-mail: yesciu@ciu.edu
Fax: 803-786-4041 • **Website:** www.ciu.edu • **ACT Code:** 5016

This private school was founded in 1923. It has a 400-acre campus.

RATINGS

Admissions Selectivity Rating: 67   **Fire Safety Rating:** 60*   **Green Rating:** 60*

STUDENTS AND FACULTY

Enrollment: 568. **Student Body:** 54% female, 46% male, 56% out-of-state, 0% international. Asian 0%, African American 0%, Caucasian 0%, Hispanic 0%, Native American 0%.
Retention and Graduation: 77% freshmen return for sophomore year. 35% freshmen graduate within 4 years. **Faculty:** Student/faculty ratio 19:1. 19 full-time faculty, 58% hold PhDs, 11% are members of minority groups, 21% are women.

ACADEMICS

Degrees: associate, bachelor's, certificate, first professional, master's, post-bachelor's certificate, terminal associate, transfer associate. **Special Study Options:** cross-registration, distance learning, double major, dual enrollment, English as a Second Language (ESL), independent study, internships, liberal

---

arts/career combination, study abroad, Cooperative studies with Midlands Technical College. **Disability Services:** Special programs offered to physically disabled students include note-taking services, reader services, tape recorders, tutors. **Career Services:** alumni services.

FACILITIES

Housing: men's dorms, women's dorms, apartments for single students, mobile home park for married students.

CAMPUS LIFE

Environment: Village. **Activities:** Choral groups, concert band, drama/theater, music ensembles, student government, symphony orchestra, yearbook 4 religious organizations.

ADMISSIONS

Freshman Academic Profile: Average high school GPA 3.9. 27% in top 10% of high school class, 47% in top 25% of high school class, 75% in top 50% of high school class. SAT Math middle 50% range 490-580. SAT Critical Reading middle 50% range 530-630. SAT Writing middle 50% range 490-600. ACT middle 50% range 20-26. Minimum paper TOEFL 525. **Basis for Candidate Selection:** *Very important factors considered include:* rigor of secondary school record, character/personal qualities, religious affiliation/commitment. *Important factors considered include:* application essay, recommendation(s), standardized test scores, volunteer work. *Other factors considered include:* Class rank, extracurricular activities, interview, talent/ability. **Freshman Admission Requirements:** High school diploma is required and GED is accepted. **Freshman Admission Statistics:** 163 applied, 99% admitted, 52% enrolled. **Transfer Admission Requirements:** college transcript(s), essay or personal statement, statement of good standing from prior institution(s). Minimum college GPA of 2.0 required. Lowest grade transferable C. **General Admission Information:** Application Fee $25. Notification on a rolling basis, beginning on or about 9/1. Nonfall registration accepted. Admission may be deferred for a maximum of n/a.

COSTS AND FINANCIAL AID

Annual tuition $8,980. Room and board $4,520. Required fees $160. Average book expense $800. **Required Forms and Deadlines:** FAFSA. **Notification of Awards: Types of Aid:** *Need-based scholarships/grants:* Federal Pell, SEOG, state scholarships/grants, private scholarships, the school's own gift aid. *Loans:* Subsidized Stafford, Unsubsidized Stafford, PLUS, college/university loans from institutional funds. **Student Employment:** Federal Work-Study Program available. Highest amount earned per year from on-campus jobs $1,200. Off-campus job opportunities are good. **Financial Aid Statistics:** 75% freshmen, 78% undergrads receive need-based scholarship or grant aid. 58% undergrads borrow to pay for school. Average cumulative indebtedness $12,400.

COLUMBIA UNION COLLEGE

7600 Flower Avenue, Takoma Park, MD 20912
Phone: 301-891-4080 • **Financial Aid Phone:** 301-891-4005
E-mail: enroll@wau.edu • **CEEB Code:** 5890
Fax: 301-891-4230 • **ACT Code:** 1687

This private school, affiliated with the Seventh Day Adventist Church, was founded in 1904. It has a 19-acre campus.

RATINGS

Admissions Selectivity Rating: 61   **Fire Safety Rating:** 60*   **Green Rating:** 60*

STUDENTS AND FACULTY

Enrollment: 986. **Student Body:** 65% female, 35% male, 57% out-of-state, (47 countries represented). Asian 6%, African American 52%, Caucasian 11%, Hispanic 11%, Native American 0%.
Retention and Graduation: 13% freshmen graduate within 4 years. **Faculty:** Student/faculty ratio 14:1. 41 full-time faculty, 51% hold PhDs, 44% are members of minority groups, 51% are women. 0% of classes are taught by teaching assistants.

ACADEMICS

Degrees: associate, bachelor's, master's. **Classes:** Most classes have fewer than 10 students. **Majors with Highest Enrollment:** business/commerce; communication and media studies, other; nursing/registered nurse (rn, asn, bsn, msn). **Special Study Options:** Accelerated program, cooperative education program, cross-registration, distance learning, double major, dual enrollment, English as a Second Language (ESL), external degree program, honors program, independent study, internships, student-designed major, study abroad, teacher certification program, Co-Op Programs: Business, Biochemistry, Communication/Journalism, Computer Science, English. Other Special Programs: Adult education and external degree programs. **Honors Programs:** The

Honors Program at CUC strives to provide academically talented students the opportunity to engage and explore subject material in greater depth. This does not mean more work, it means a different kind of work, with more individual attention. The honors classes are different in design as each class explores the topic from an interdisciplinary perspective, where areas of study are combined into one course. **Combined Degree Programs:** Liberal Studies - Combination of bachelors programs designed by students. **Disability Services:** Special programs offered to physically disabled students include reader services, tutors. **Career Services:** career assessment, internships Career Services highlights include Internships on Capitol Hill NASA Cooperative Learning Experiences White House Internships NOAA Internships.

FACILITIES

Housing: men's dorms, women's dorms, apartments for married students, apartments for single students. 30% of campus accessible to physically disabled. **Special Academic Facilities/Equipment:** Hospital adjacent to campus for students in health fields, performing arts at adfacent large church auditorium, learning center, radio station, playing fields and gymnasium. **Computers:** 100% of classrooms, 100% of dorms, 100% of libraries, 100% of dining areas, 100% of student union, 100% of common outdoor areas have wireless network access. Students can register for classes online. Administrative functions (other than registration) can be performed online.

CAMPUS LIFE

Environment: Metropolis. **Activities:** Choral groups, concert band, literary magazine, music ensembles, musical theater, radio station, student government, student newspaper, symphony orchestra, yearbook, Campus Ministries, International Student Organization 6 honor societies. **Athletics (Intercollegiate):** *Men:* baseball, basketball, cross-country, soccer, track/field (outdoor). *Women:* basketball, cross-country, soccer, softball, track/field (outdoor).

ADMISSIONS

Freshman Academic Profile: 53% from public high schools. Minimum paper TOEFL 550. **Basis for Candidate Selection:** *Very important factors considered include:* academic GPA, rigor of secondary school record, standardized test scores. *Important factors considered include:* recommendation(s), character/personal qualities, religious affiliation/commitment, talent/ability. *Other factors considered include:* application essay, extracurricular activities, volunteer work, work experience. **Freshman Admission Requirements:** High school diploma is required and GED is accepted. *Academic units required:* 4 English, 2 mathematics, 2 science, (2 science labs), 2 history, 4 academic electives. 4 English, 2 mathematics, 2 science, (2 science labs), 2 history, 4 academic electives. **Transfer Admission Requirements:** college transcript(s), minimum college GPA of 2.0 required. Lowest grade transferable C. **General Admission Information:** Application Fee $25. Regular application deadline 8/1. Nonfall registration accepted. Admission may be deferred for a maximum of 1 year. Credit and/or placement offered for CEEB Advanced Placement tests.

COSTS AND FINANCIAL AID

Annual tuition $18,200. Room and board $7,200. Required fees $1,280. Average book expense $1,200. **Required Forms and Deadlines:** FAFSA, state aid form. **Notification of Awards:** Applicants will be notified of awards on a rolling basis beginning 5/1. **Types of Aid:** *Need-based scholarships/grants:* Federal Pell, SEOG, state scholarships/grants, private scholarships. *Loans:* Direct Subsidized Stafford, Direct Unsubsidized Stafford, Direct PLUS, Subsidized Stafford, PLUS, Federal Perkins. **Student Employment:** Federal Work-Study Program available. Institutional employment available. Off-campus job opportunities are excellent. **Criteria for awarding institutional aid:** *Non-need-based:* academics, athletics, music/drama.

COLUMBIA UNIVERSITY

212 Hamilton Hall MC 2807, New York, NY 10027
Phone: 212-854-2522 • **CEEB Code:** 2116
Fax: 212-894-1209 • **Website:** studentaffairs.columbia.edu/admissions
ACT Code: 2717

This private school was founded in 1754. It has a 36-acre campus.

RATINGS
Admissions Selectivity Rating: 99   **Fire Safety Rating:** 61   **Green Rating:** 99

STUDENTS AND FACULTY
Enrollment: 6,068. **Student Body:** 73% out-of-state, 12% international (87 countries represented). Asian 20%, African American 12%, Caucasian 34%, Hispanic 15%, Native American 2%.
Retention and Graduation: 99% freshmen return for sophomore year. 91% freshmen graduate within 4 years. 98% freshmen graduate within 6 years. **Faculty:** 0% of classes are taught by teaching assistants.

ACADEMICS
Degrees: bachelor's, master's. **Classes:** Most classes have 10–19 students. **Majors with Highest Enrollment:** engineering; English language and literature; political science and government. **Special Study Options:** Accelerated program, cooperative education program, cross-registration, double major, dual enrollment, English as a Second Language (ESL), exchange student program (domestic), independent study, internships, liberal arts/career combination, student-designed major, study abroad, teacher certification program, Combined 3-2 program. **Combined Degree Programs:** BA/JD, BA/MIA and BA/MPA (programs with SIPA). **Disability Services:** Special programs offered to physically disabled students include note-taking services, reader services, tape recorders, tutors. **Career Services:** Alumni network, alumni services, career/job search classes, career assessment, internships.

FACILITIES
Housing: Coed dorms, special housing for disabled students, fraternity/sorority housing, Special Interest Housing: Single-Sex First-Year Floor available. 95% of campus accessible to physically disabled. **Special Academic Facilities/Equipment:** Art and Architecture Galleries; Theatres, Cinema, Observatory **Computers:** Students can register for classes online. Administrative functions (other than registration) can be performed online.

CAMPUS LIFE
Environment: Metropolis. **Activities:** Choral groups, concert band, dance, drama/theater, jazz band, literary magazine, marching band, music ensembles, musical theater, opera, pep band, radio station, student government, student newspaper, student-run film society, symphony orchestra, television station, yearbook, Campus Ministries, International Student Organization, Model UN 300 registered organizations, 17 religious organizations. 17 fraternities, 11 sororities. **Athletics (Intercollegiate):** *Men:* baseball, basketball, crew/rowing, cross-country, diving, fencing, football, golf, soccer, swimming, tennis, track/field (outdoor), track/field (indoor), wrestling. *Women:* archery, basketball, crew/rowing, cross-country, diving, fencing, field hockey, golf, lacrosse, soccer, softball, swimming, tennis, track/field (outdoor), track/field (indoor), volleyball. **On-Campus Highlights:** Low Library and Plaza, Butler Library, Postcrypt Coffee House, Ferris Booth Commons, Levian Gym, www.studentaffairs.columbia.edu/admissions/virtualvisit/. **Environmental Initiatives:** Greenhouse gas reduction program targeted to meet a 30% reduction by 2017 and clean heat initiative to improve air quality and asthma rates by phasing out the use of heavy heating oils to cleaner fuels like natural gas and low-sulfur #2 oil. Columbia has also converted its entire 14 car public safety fleet to hybrid vehicles. As part of our energy efficiency initiatives, 45% of all food purchased is local and/ororganic. All honey and apples are purchased through vendors at the on-campus green market from NY farmers. Annually Dining Services contracts with a local NY farmer and canner to make all the salsa and strawberry jam for the year. In addition all milk is local and hormone free. Liquid eggs are certified humane. All coffee is roasted locally and is fair-trade, organic, shade grown and bird friendly. Tomatoes are also fair trade. All bakery items and grab and go sandwiches are purchased from local vendors. 50% of daily meals served in the dining halls are vegetarian and Meatless Mondays are run every Monday. Green building and construction commitment: LEED Silver baseline commitment for all new construction that includes 4 LEED Gold Buildings; LEED for Neighborhood Development pilot program for 17 acre campus expansion. Columbia's robust surplus reuse program diverts furniture and equipment from landfill as well as achieves a 90% construction recycling rate for recent LEED projects. The model clean construction program has significantly reduced particulates and other pollutants that are a contributor to Harlem's high asthma rates. Columbia is the leading U.S. research and educational institution on the environment and climate change. Twenty-four environmental degree granting programs including a sustainable development major; 33 environmental research centers, home of the Earth Institute and the Lamont Doherty Earth Observatory, also NASA/GISS -- Columbia University is one of the world's leading research institutions on climate and earth systems; The term global warming was coined at Columbia and the phenomanom of El Nino was discovered here.

ADMISSIONS
Freshman Academic Profile: 57% from public high schools. SAT Math middle 50% range 700-790. SAT Critical Reading middle 50% range 690-780. SAT Writing middle 50% range 690-780. ACT middle 50% range 31-34. Minimum paper TOEFL 600. **Basis for Candidate Selection:** *Very important factors considered include:* Class rank, application essay, academic GPA, recommendation(s), rigor of secondary school record, standardized test scores, character/personal qualities. *Important factors considered include:* extracurricular activities, talent/ability. *Other factors considered include:* alumni/ae relation,

geographical residence, interview, racial/ethnic status, volunteer work, work experience. **Freshman Admission Requirements:** High school diploma is required and GED is accepted. **Freshman Admission Statistics:** 31,851 applied, 7% admitted, 60% enrolled. **Transfer Admission Requirements:** High school transcript, college transcript(s), essay or personal statement, standardized test scores, statement of good standing from prior institution(s). Lowest grade transferable C. **General Admission Information:** Application Fee $70. Early decision application deadline 11/1. Regular application deadline 1/2. Regular notification 4/1. Nonfall registration not accepted. Admission may be deferred for a maximum of 2 years. Credit and/or placement offered for CEEB Advanced Placement tests.

COSTS AND FINANCIAL AID
Annual tuition $45,028. Room and board $11,496. Required fees $2,218. Average book expense $1,040. **Required Forms and Deadlines:** FAFSA, CSS/Financial Aid PROFILE, noncustodial PROFILE, Parent and student income tax forms. **Notification of Awards:** Applicants will be notified of awards on or about 4/1. **Types of Aid:** *Need-based scholarships/grants:* Federal Pell, SEOG, state scholarships/grants, private scholarships, the school's own gift aid. *Loans:* Subsidized Stafford, Unsubsidized Stafford, PLUS, Federal Perkins, Alternative loans. **Student Employment:** Federal Work-Study Program available. Institutional employment available. Off-campus job opportunities are excellent. **Financial Aid Statistics:** 55% freshmen, 60% undergrads receive any aid. % undergrads borrow to pay for school.

COLUMBIA UNIVERSITY SCHOOL OF GENERAL STUDIES

408 Lewisohn Hall, Mail Code 4101, New York, NY 10027
Phone: 212)854-2772 • **Financial Aid Phone:** 212-854-2772
E-mail: gsdegree@columbia.edu • **CEEB Code:** 2095
Fax: 212-854-6316 • **Website:** www.gs.columbia.edu • **ACT Code:** 2716

This private school was founded in 1947. It has a 36-acre campus.

RATINGS
Admissions Selectivity Rating: 63   **Fire Safety Rating:** 74   **Green Rating:** 94

STUDENTS AND FACULTY
Enrollment: 1,632. **Student Body:** 43% female, 57% male, 45% out-of-state, 16% international (80 countries represented). Asian 7%, African American 5%, Caucasian 52%, Hispanic 10%, Native American 0%.

ACADEMICS
Degrees: bachelor's, post-bachelor's certificate. **Majors with Highest Enrollment:** economics; English language and literature; political science and government. **Special Study Options:** Accelerated program, cross-registration, double major, dual enrollment, exchange student program (domestic), honors program, independent study, internships, student-designed major, study abroad, teacher certification program. **Honors Programs:** Honor Society of School of General Studies **Combined Degree Programs:** BA/JD, BA/MA, BA/DDS, BA/MEng, Joint Programs. **Disability Services:** Special programs offered to physically disabled students include note-taking services, reader services, tape recorders, tutors. **Career Services:** Alumni network, alumni services, career/job search classes, career assessment, internships, regional alumni.

FACILITIES
Housing: Coed dorms, special housing for international students, fraternity/sorority housing, apartments for married students, cooperative housing, apartments for single students, theme housing. 100% of campus accessible to physically disabled. **Special Academic Facilities/Equipment:** Earth Institute, Lamont-Doherty Earth Observatory University Art Collection Miller Theatre Low Memorial Library Rotunda LeRoy Neiman Center for Print Studies Music at St. Paul's Postcrypt Coffeehouse Miriam and Ira D. Wallach Art Gallery Language Houses **Computers:** 50% of classrooms, 10% of dorms, 64% of libraries, 50% of dining areas, 90% of student union, 25% of common outdoor areas have wireless network access. Students can register for classes online. Administrative functions (other than registration) can be performed online.

CAMPUS LIFE
Environment: Metropolis. **Activities:** Choral groups, concert band, dance, drama/theater, jazz band, literary magazine, marching band, music ensembles, musical theater, opera, radio station, student government, student newspaper, student-run film society, symphony orchestra, television station, yearbook, Campus Ministries, International Student Organization, Model UN 250 registered organizations, 2 honor societies, 21 religious organizations. **Athletics (Intercollegiate):** *Men:* baseball, basketball, crew/rowing, cross-country, diving, fencing,

football, golf, soccer, swimming, track/field (outdoor), track/field (indoor). *Women:* archery, basketball, crew/rowing, cross-country, diving, fencing, field hockey, golf, lacrosse, soccer, softball, swimming, track/field (outdoor), track/field (indoor), volleyball. **On-Campus Highlights:** Low Library, Lerner Hall, Butler Library, Miller Theater, College Walk, Low Plaza. **Environmental Initiatives:** Greenhouse gas reduction program targeted to meet a 30% reduction by 2017 and clean heat initiative to improve air quality and asthma rates by phasing out the use of heavy heating oils to cleaner fuels like natural gas and low-sulfur #2 oil. Columbia has also converted its entire 14 car public safety fleet to hybrid vehicles. As part of our energy efficiency initiatives, 45% of all food purchased is local and/ororganic. All honey and apples are purchased through vendors at the on-campus green market from NY farmers. Annually Dining Services contracts with a local NY farmer and canner to make all the salsa and strawberry jam for the year. In addition all milk is local and hormone free. Liquid eggs are certified humane. All coffee is roasted locally and is fair-trade, organic, shade grown and bird friendly. Tomatoes are also fair trade. All bakery items and grab and go sandwiches are purchased from local vendors. 50% of daily meals served in the dining halls are vegetarian and Meatless Mondays are run every Monday. Green building and construction commitment: LEED Silver baseline commitment for all new construction that includes 4 LEED Gold Buildings; LEED for Neighborhood Development pilot program for 17 acre campus expansion. Columbia's robust surplus reuse program diverts furniture and equipment from landfill as well as achieves a 90% construction recycling rate for recent LEED projects. The model clean construction program has significantly reduced particulates and other pollutants that are a contributor to Harlem's high asthma rates. Columbia is the leading U.S. research and educational institution on the environment and climate change. Twenty-four environmental degree granting programs including a sustainable development major; 33 environmental research centers, home of the Earth Institute and the Lamont Doherty Earth Observatory, also NASA/GISS -- Columbia University is one of the world's leading research institutions on climate and earth systems; The term global warming was coined at Columbia and the phenomanom of El Nino was discovered here.

ADMISSIONS
Freshman Academic Profile: Minimum paper TOEFL 600. **Basis for Candidate Selection:** *Very important factors considered include:* Class rank, academic GPA, rigor of secondary school record, standardized test scores. *Important factors considered include:* application essay, recommendation(s). *Other factors considered include:* alumni/ae relation, extracurricular activities, talent/ability. **Freshman Admission Requirements:** High school diploma is required and GED is accepted. *Academic units required:* 4 English, 3 mathematics, 2 science, (2 science labs), 2 foreign language, 2 history, 1 academic electives. 4 English, 3 mathematics, 2 science, (2 science labs), 2 foreign language, 2 history, 1 academic electives. **Freshman Admission Statistics:** 601 applied, 34% admitted, 56% enrolled. **Transfer Admission Requirements:** High school transcript, college transcript(s), Lowest grade transferable C. **General Admission Information:** Application Fee $20. Nonfall registration accepted.

COSTS AND FINANCIAL AID
Annual tuition $43,620. Room and board $11,070. Required fees $1,974. Average book expense $1,390. **Required Forms and Deadlines: Notification of Awards:** Applicants will be notified of awards on a rolling basis beginning 5/1. **Types of Aid:** *Need-based scholarships/grants:* Federal Pell, SEOG, state scholarships/grants, private scholarships. *Loans:* Direct Subsidized Stafford, Direct Unsubsidized Stafford, Direct PLUS, Subsidized Stafford, Unsubsidized Stafford, PLUS, Federal Perkins. **Student Employment: Financial Aid Statistics:** 70% undergrads receive any aid. **Criteria for awarding institutional aid:** *Non-need-based:* academics, alumni affiliation, art, athletics, leadership, music/drama, state/district residency.

See page 1054.

COLUMBUS COLLEGE OF ART & DESIGN

107 North Ninth Street, Columbus, OH 43215-3875
Phone: 614-222-3261
E-mail: admissions@ccad.edu • **CEEB Code:** 1085
Fax: 614-232-8344 • **Website:** www.ccad.edu • **ACT Code:** 3281

This private school was founded in 1879. It has a 17-acre campus.

RATINGS
Admissions Selectivity Rating: 65   **Fire Safety Rating:** 60*   **Green Rating:** 60*

STUDENTS AND FACULTY
Enrollment: 1,359. **Student Body:** 48% female, 52% male, 28% out-of-state, 5% international (29 countries represented). Asian 4%, African American 6%, Caucasian 83%, Hispanic 2%, Native American 0%.

Retention and Graduation: 79% freshmen return for sophomore year. 32% freshmen graduate within 4 years. 41% freshmen graduate within 6 years. 12% grads go on to further study within 1 year. 12% grads pursue arts and sciences degrees. **Faculty:** Student/faculty ratio 12:1. 72 full-time faculty, 56% hold PhDs, 8% are members of minority groups, 29% are women. 0% of classes are taught by teaching assistants.

ACADEMICS

Degrees: bachelor's. **Special Study Options:** cooperative education program, cross-registration, internships, study abroad, Undergrads may take grad level classes. Other Special Programs: Evening classes for credit. Saturday School (ages 6-18). **Career Services:** career/job search classes, internships.

FACILITIES

Housing: Coed dorms. **Special Academic Facilities/Equipment:** Student art exhibition hall, gallery, auditorium, recreation center.

CAMPUS LIFE

Environment: Activities: literary magazine, student government, student newspaper 2 registered organizations, 1 religious organizations.

ADMISSIONS

Freshman Academic Profile: Average high school GPA 2.9. 10% in top 10% of high school class, 30% in top 25% of high school class, 61% in top 50% of high school class. % from public high schools. SAT Math middle 50% range 433-550. SAT Critical Reading middle 50% range 433-580. ACT middle 50% range 18-23. Minimum paper TOEFL 500. **Basis for Candidate Selection:** *Very important factors considered include:* rigor of secondary school record, talent/ability. *Important factors considered include:* application essay, recommendation(s), standardized test scores, character/personal qualities, interview. *Other factors considered include:* Class rank, extracurricular activities. **Freshman Admission Requirements:** High school diploma is required and GED is accepted. **Transfer Admission Requirements:** High school transcript, college transcript(s), essay or personal statement, minimum college GPA of 2.0 required. Lowest grade transferable C. **General Admission Information:** Application Fee $25. Nonfall registration accepted. Admission may be deferred for a maximum of 1 year. Credit and/or placement offered for CEEB Advanced Placement tests.

COSTS AND FINANCIAL AID

Annual tuition $17,880. Room and board $6,300. Required fees $390. Average book expense $1,800. **Required Forms and Deadlines:** FAFSA. **Notification of Awards:** Applicants will be notified of awards on or about 6/15. **Types of Aid:** *Need-based scholarships/grants:* Federal Pell, SEOG, state scholarships/grants, private scholarships, the school's own gift aid. *Loans:* Subsidized Stafford, Unsubsidized Stafford, PLUS, Federal Perkins, state loans. **Student Employment:** Federal Work-Study Program available. Institutional employment available. Highest amount earned per year from on-campus jobs $2,500. Off-campus job opportunities are excellent. **Financial Aid Statistics:** 99% freshmen, 97% undergrads receive need-based scholarship or grant aid. 10% freshmen, 10% undergrads receive non-need-based scholarship or grant aid. 76% freshmen, 80% undergrads receive need-based self-help aid. 86% undergrads borrow to pay for school. Average cumulative indebtedness $21,700. **Criteria for awarding institutional aid:** *Non-need-based:* academics, art.

COLUMBUS STATE UNIVERSITY

4225 University Avenue, Columbus, GA 31907-5645
Phone: 706-568-2035 • **Financial Aid Phone:** 706-507-8800
E-mail: admissions@colstate.edu
Fax: 706-568-5091 • **Website:** www.columbusstate.edu • **ACT Code:**

This public school was founded in 1958. It has a 150-acre campus.

RATINGS
Admissions Selectivity Rating: 76   **Fire Safety Rating:** 78   **Green Rating:** 71

STUDENTS AND FACULTY
Enrollment: 6,890. **Student Body:** 60% female, 40% male, 14% out-of-state, 1% international (67 countries represented). Asian 2%, African American 35%, Caucasian 55%, Hispanic 4%, Native American 1%.
Retention and Graduation: 69% freshmen return for sophomore year. 12% freshmen graduate within 4 years. **Faculty:** Student/faculty ratio 18:1. 279 full-time faculty, 78% hold PhDs, 23% are members of minority groups, 43% are women. 0% of classes are taught by teaching assistants.

ACADEMICS
Degrees: bachelor's, certificate, doctoral, master's, post-master's certificate, terminal associate, transfer associate. **Classes:** Most classes have 20–29 students. Most lab/discussion sessions have 10–19 students. **Majors with Highest En-**

rollment: business/commerce; early childhood education and teaching; nursing/registered nurse (rn, asn, bsn, msn). **Special Study Options:** Accelerated program, cooperative education program, distance learning, double major, dual enrollment, English as a Second Language (ESL), honors program, independent study, internships, liberal arts/career combination, study abroad, teacher certification program. **Honors Programs:** Honors Program Servant Leadership Program. **Disability Services:** Special programs offered to physically disabled students include note-taking services, reader services, tape recorders, tutors. **Career Services:** Alumni network, alumni services, career/job search classes, career assessment, internships, regional alumni. Career Services highlights include Internships and experiential learning via volunteer placements in the community.

FACILITIES
Housing: special housing for disabled students, special housing for international students, apartments for married students, apartments for single students, theme housing..100% of campus accessible to physically disabled. **Computers:** 80% of classrooms, 100% of libraries, 100% of dining areas, 100% of student union, 25% of common outdoor areas have wireless network access. Students can register for classes online. Administrative functions (other than registration) can be performed online.

CAMPUS LIFE
Environment: City. **Activities:** Choral groups, concert band, dance, drama/theater, jazz band, literary magazine, music ensembles, musical theater, pep band, student government, student newspaper, symphony orchestra, Campus Ministries, International Student Organization, Model UN 90 registered organizations, 22 honor societies, 10 religious organizations. 7 fraternities, 6 sororities. **Athletics (Intercollegiate):** *Men:* baseball, basketball, cheerleading, cross-country, golf, riflery, tennis. *Women:* basketball, cheerleading, cross-country, golf, riflery, soccer, softball, tennis. **On-Campus Highlights:** Einstein Bos. Bagels, RiverPark Campus, Davidson Student Center, Lumpkin Center, Coca Cola Space Science Center. **Environmental Initiatives:** Green Seal Cleaning Products Recycling of paper, plastic, & aluminum cans Energy efficient equipment upgrades throughout campus

ADMISSIONS
Freshman Academic Profile: Average high school GPA 3.0. SAT Math middle 50% range 420-540. SAT Critical Reading middle 50% range 430-550. SAT Writing middle 50% range 420-530. ACT middle 50% range 17-22. Minimum web-based TOEFL 79. Minimum paper TOEFL 550. **Basis for Candidate Selection:** *Very important factors considered include:* rigor of secondary school record. *Important factors considered include:* academic GPA, standardized test scores. *Other factors considered include:* extracurricular activities, geographical residence, interview, talent/ability. **Freshman Admission Requirements:** High school diploma is required and GED is not accepted. *Academic units required:* 4 English, 4 mathematics, 3 science, (2 science labs), 2 foreign language, 3 social studies. 4 English, 4 mathematics, 3 science, (2 science labs), 2 foreign language, 3 social studies. **Freshman Admission Statistics:** 3,454 applied, 60% admitted, 60% enrolled. **Transfer Admission Requirements:** college transcript(s), statement of good standing from prior institution(s). Minimum college GPA of 2.00 required. Lowest grade transferable D. **General Admission Information:** Application Fee $30. Regular application deadline 6/30. Notification on a rolling basis, beginning on or about 9/1. Nonfall registration accepted. Admission may be deferred for a maximum of One year. Credit and/or placement offered for CEEB Advanced Placement tests.

COSTS AND FINANCIAL AID
Annual in-state tuition $3,281. Annual out-of-state tuition $12,669. Room and board $7,280. Required fees $1,300. Average book expense $1,072. **Required Forms and Deadlines:** FAFSA. **Notification of Awards:** Applicants will be notified of awards on a rolling basis beginning 5/15. **Types of Aid:** *Need-based scholarships/grants:* Federal Pell, SEOG, state scholarships/grants, private scholarships, the school's own gift aid. *Loans:* Direct Subsidized Stafford, Direct Unsubsidized Stafford, Direct PLUS, Federal Perkins, Federal Nursing, state loans, college/university loans from institutional funds. **Student Employment:** Federal Work-Study Program available. Institutional employment available. Off-campus job opportunities are good. **Financial Aid Statistics:** 71% freshmen, 72% undergrads receive need-based scholarship or grant aid. 51% freshmen, 34% undergrads receive non-need-based scholarship or grant aid. 66% freshmen, 73% undergrads receive need-based self-help aid. 4% freshmen, 4% undergrads receive athletic scholarships. 87% freshmen, 78% undergrads receive any aid. 63% undergrads borrow to pay for school. Average cumulative indebtedness $21,486. **Criteria for awarding institutional aid:** *Non-need-based:* academics, alumni affiliation, art, athletics, job skills, leadership, minority status, music/drama.

CONCEPTION SEMINARY COLLEGE

P.O. Box 502, Conception, MO 64433
Phone: 660-944-2886
E-mail: vocations@conception.edu
Fax: 660-944-2829 • **Website:** www.conception.edu • **ACT Code:** 2280

This private school, affiliated with the Roman Catholic Church, was founded in 1886. It has a 30-acre campus.

RATINGS
Admissions Selectivity Rating: 64   **Fire Safety Rating:** 60*   **Green Rating:** 60*

STUDENTS AND FACULTY
Enrollment: 96. **Student Body:** 73% out-of-state, 5% international. Asian 10%, African American 0%, Caucasian 56%, Hispanic 2%, Native American 0%. **Retention and Graduation:** 50% freshmen return for sophomore year. 60% grads go on to further study within 1 year. **Faculty:** Student/faculty ratio 4:1. 20 full-time faculty, 85% hold PhDs, 10% are members of minority groups, 15% are women. 0% of classes are taught by teaching assistants.

ACADEMICS
Degrees: bachelor's, certificate. **Special Study Options:** double major, English as a Second Language (ESL), independent study.

FACILITIES
Housing: men's dorms. **Computers:** Administrative functions (other than registration) can be performed online.

CAMPUS LIFE
Environment: Rural. **Activities:** drama/theater, music ensembles, student government, student newspaper, yearbook 12 registered organizations. **Athletics (Intercollegiate):** *Men:* soccer, volleyball.

ADMISSIONS
Freshman Academic Profile: ACT middle 50% range 12-29. **Basis for Candidate Selection:** *Very important factors considered include:* application essay, recommendation(s), religious affiliation/commitment. *Important factors considered include:* rigor of secondary school record, standardized test scores, character/personal qualities, talent/ability. *Other factors considered include:* Class rank, extracurricular activities, interview, volunteer work, work experience. **Freshman Admission Requirements:** High school diploma is required and GED is accepted. *Academic units required:* 4 English, 4 science, 4 social studies. 4 English, 4 science, 4 social studies. **Freshman Admission Statistics:** 17 applied, 100% admitted, 100% enrolled. **Transfer Admission Requirements:** college transcript(s), essay or personal statement, minimum college GPA of 2.0 required. Lowest grade transferable C. **General Admission Information:** Regular application deadline 8/15. Notification on a rolling basis, beginning on or about 1/1. Nonfall registration accepted. Admission may be deferred for a maximum of 1 year.

COSTS AND FINANCIAL AID
Required Forms and Deadlines: FAFSA. **Notification of Awards: Types of Aid:** *Need-based scholarships/grants: Loans:* **Student Employment: Financial Aid Statistics:** 73% freshmen, 81% undergrads receive need-based scholarship or grant aid. 27% freshmen, 47% undergrads receive non-need-based scholarship or grant aid. 27% freshmen, 49% undergrads receive need-based self-help aid. 33% undergrads borrow to pay for school. Average cumulative indebtedness $11,302. **Criteria for awarding institutional aid:** *Non-need-based:* academics.

CONCORD UNIVERSITY

1000 Vermillion Street, Athens, WV 24712
Phone: 304-384-5248 • **Financial Aid Phone:** 304-384-6069
E-mail: admissions@concord.edu • **CEEB Code:** 5120
Fax: 304-384-9044 • **Website:** www.concord.edu • **ACT Code:** 3810

This public school was founded in 1872. It has a 123-acre campus.

RATINGS
Admissions Selectivity Rating: 75   **Fire Safety Rating:** 80   **Green Rating:** 60*

STUDENTS AND FACULTY
Enrollment: 2,611. **Student Body:** 55% female, 45% male, 18% out-of-state, 0% international (16 countries represented). Asian 2%, African American 7%, Caucasian 100%, Hispanic 1%, Native American 0%.

Retention and Graduation: 65% freshmen return for sophomore year. 15% freshmen graduate within 4 years. 39% freshmen graduate within 6 years. 33% grads go on to further study within 1 year. 8% grads pursue arts and sciences degrees. 2% grads pursue law degrees. 10% grads pursue business degrees. 3% grads pursue medical degrees. **Faculty:** Student/faculty ratio 23:1. 121 full-time faculty, 64% hold PhDs, 3% are members of minority groups, 41% are women.

ACADEMICS
Degrees: associate, bachelor's, master's, terminal associate. **Classes:** Most classes have fewer than 10 students. Most lab/discussion sessions have 10–19 students. **Majors with Highest Enrollment:** business administration and management; education; social sciences. **Special Study Options:** cooperative education program, double major, dual enrollment, English as a Second Language (ESL), honors program, student-designed major, teacher certification program. **Career Services:** alumni services, career/job search classes, career assessment, internships.

FACILITIES
Housing: Coed dorms, special housing for disabled students, men's dorms, special housing for international students, women's dorms, apartments for married students 100% of campus accessible to physically disabled. **Computers:** 50% of classrooms, 20% of dorms, 100% of libraries, 100% of dining areas, 100% of student union, 50% of common outdoor areas have wireless network access. Students can register for classes online. Administrative functions (other than registration) can be performed online.

CAMPUS LIFE
Environment: Rural. **Activities:** Choral groups, concert band, drama/theater, jazz band, pep band, radio station, student government, student newspaper, student-run film society, television station, yearbook 57 registered organizations, 1 honor societies, 2 religious organizations. 6 fraternities, 4 sororities. **Athletics (Intercollegiate):** *Men:* baseball, basketball, cheerleading, cross-country, football, golf, soccer, tennis, track/field (outdoor). *Women:* basketball, cheerleading, cross-country, golf, soccer, softball, tennis, track/field (outdoor), volleyball. **On-Campus Highlights:** Rahall Technology Ctr, 48 Bell Carillon, University Point, Beasley Student Ctr., Callaghan Stadium.

ADMISSIONS
Freshman Academic Profile: Average high school GPA 3.2. 18% in top 10% of high school class, 45% in top 25% of high school class, 73% in top 50% of high school class. 95% from public high schools. SAT Math middle 50% range 420-520. SAT Critical Reading middle 50% range 420-540. ACT middle 50% range 17-25. Minimum paper TOEFL 500. **Basis for Candidate Selection:** *Very important factors considered include:* rigor of secondary school record. *Important factors considered include:* Class rank; standardized test scores, extracurricular activities. *Other factors considered include:* application essay, recommendation(s), alumni/ae relation, character/personal qualities, geographical residence, interview, racial/ethnic status, talent/ability, volunteer work, work experience. **Freshman Admission Requirements:** High school diploma is required and GED is accepted. *Academic units required:* 4 English, 2 mathematics, 2 science, (2 science labs), 2 social studies, 1 history, 6 academic electives. *Academic units recommended:* 4 English, 2 mathematics, 2 science, (2 science labs), 2 social studies, 1 history, 6 academic electives. **Freshman Admission Statistics:** 2,290 applied, 61% admitted, 41% enrolled. **Transfer Admission Requirements:** college transcript(s), Lowest grade transferable D. **General Admission Information:** Notification on a rolling basis, beginning on or about 9/1. Nonfall registration accepted. Admission may be deferred for a maximum of 1 YEAR. Credit and/or placement offered for CEEB Advanced Placement tests.

COSTS AND FINANCIAL AID
Annual in-state tuition $4,974. Annual out-of-state tuition $11,050. Room and board $6,962. Average book expense $1,100. **Required Forms and Deadlines:** FAFSA, institution's own financial aid formVerification worksheet. **Notification of Awards:** Applicants will be notified of awards on a rolling basis beginning 3/1. **Types of Aid:** *Need-based scholarships/grants:* Federal Pell, SEOG, state scholarships/grants, the school's own gift aid. *Loans:* Subsidized Stafford, Unsubsidized Stafford, PLUS, Federal Perkins. **Student Employment:** Federal Work-Study Program available. Institutional employment available. Highest amount earned per year from on-campus jobs $1,343. Off-campus job opportunities are excellent. **Financial Aid Statistics:** 84% freshmen, 83% undergrads receive need-based scholarship or grant aid. 52% freshmen, 36% undergrads receive non-need-based scholarship or grant aid. 74% freshmen, 75% undergrads receive need-based self-help aid. 5% freshmen, 4% undergrads receive athletic scholarships. 90% freshmen, 77% undergrads receive any aid. 85% undergrads borrow to pay for school. Average cumulative indebtedness $16,296. **Criteria for awarding institutional aid:** *Non-need-based:* academics, alumni affiliation, art, athletics, job skills, leadership, minority status, music/drama, state/district residency.

CONCORDIA COLLEGE (MOORHEAD- MN)

901 Eighth Street South, Moorhead, MN 56562
Phone: 218-299-3004
E-mail: admissions@cord.edu • **CEEB Code:** 6113
Fax: 218-299-4720 • **Website:** www.goconcordia.com • **ACT Code:** 2104

This private school, affiliated with the Lutheran Church, was founded in 1891. It has a 120-acre campus.

RATINGS
Admissions Selectivity Rating: 72   **Fire Safety Rating:** 62   **Green Rating:** 60*

STUDENTS AND FACULTY
Enrollment: 2,793. **Student Body:** 63% female, 37% male, 33% out-of-state, 6% international (42 countries represented). Asian 2%, African American 1%, Caucasian 92%, Hispanic 1%, Native American 0%.
Retention and Graduation: 80% freshmen return for sophomore year. 57% freshmen graduate within 4 years. 66% freshmen graduate within 6 years. 20% grads go on to further study within 1 year. 9% grads pursue arts and sciences degrees. 4% grads pursue law degrees. 3% grads pursue business degrees. 4% grads pursue medical degrees. **Faculty:** Student/faculty ratio 14:1. 175 full-time faculty, 78% hold PhDs, 3% are members of minority groups, 45% are women. 0% of classes are taught by teaching assistants.

ACADEMICS
Degrees: bachelor's, master's. **Classes:** Most classes have 20–29 students. **Special Study Options:** cooperative education program, double major, exchange student program (domestic), honors program, independent study, internships, liberal arts/career combination, study abroad, teacher certification program. **Combined Degree Programs:** BA/BS Engineering NOSU, U of Minnesota Institute o. **Disability Services:** Special programs offered to physically disabled students include note-taking services, reader services, tape recorders, tutors. **Career Services:** Alumni network, alumni services, career/job search classes, career assessment, internships.

FACILITIES
Housing: Coed dorms, special housing for disabled students, men's dorms, women's dorms, apartments for single students, French, German, and Spanish language houses. 95% of campus accessible to physically disabled. **Special Academic Facilities/Equipment:** Cyrus M. Running Gallery. **Computers:** Administrative functions (other than registration) can be performed online.

CAMPUS LIFE
Environment: City. **Activities:** Choral groups, concert band, dance, drama/theater, jazz band, literary magazine, music ensembles, musical theater, pep band, radio station, student government, student newspaper, symphony orchestra, television station, yearbook 80 registered organizations, 22 honor societies, 12 religious organizations. 2 fraternities, 2 sororities. **Athletics (Intercollegiate):** *Men:* baseball, basketball, cross-country, football, golf, ice hockey, soccer, tennis, track/field (outdoor), track/field (indoor), wrestling. *Women:* basketball, cross-country, diving, golf, ice hockey, soccer, softball, swimming, tennis, track/field (outdoor), track/field (indoor), volleyball.

ADMISSIONS
Freshman Academic Profile: 31% in top 10% of high school class, 62% in top 25% of high school class, 89% in top 50% of high school class. SAT Math middle 50% range 520-630. SAT Critical Reading middle 50% range 530-650. ACT middle 50% range 21-27. Minimum paper TOEFL 550. **Basis for Candidate Selection:** *Very important factors considered include:* rigor of secondary school record. *Important factors considered include:* Class rank, recommendation(s). *Other factors considered include:* standardized test scores, alumni/ae relation, character/personal qualities, extracurricular activities, racial/ethnic status, talent/ability, volunteer work. **Freshman Admission Requirements:** High school diploma is required and GED is accepted. **Freshman Admission Statistics:** 2,444 applied, 86% admitted, 37% enrolled. **Transfer Admission Requirements:** college transcript(s), minimum college GPA of 2.0 required. Lowest grade transferable C–. **General Admission Information:** Application Fee $20. Nonfall registration accepted. Admission may be deferred for a maximum of 1. Credit and/or placement offered for CEEB Advanced Placement tests.

COSTS AND FINANCIAL AID
Annual tuition $17,620. Room and board $4,690. Required fees $150. Average book expense $700. **Student Employment:** Federal Work-Study Program available. Institutional employment available. Off-campus job opportunities are excellent. **Financial Aid Statistics:** 97% freshmen, 94% undergrads receive any aid.

CONCORDIA COLLEGE (NY)

171 White Plains Road, Bronxville, NY 10708
Phone: 914-337-9300
E-mail: admission@concordia-ny.edu • **CEEB Code:** 2096
Fax: 914-395-4636 • **Website:** www.concordia-ny.edu • **ACT Code:** 2722

This private school, affiliated with the Lutheran Church, was founded in 1881. It has a 33-acre campus.

RATINGS
Admissions Selectivity Rating: 70   **Fire Safety Rating:** 60*   **Green Rating:** 60*

STUDENTS AND FACULTY
Enrollment: 587. **Student Body:** 58% female, 42% male, 27% out-of-state, 0% international (36 countries represented). Asian 7%, African American 14%, Caucasian 63%, Hispanic 10%, Native American 1%.
Retention and Graduation: 76% freshmen return for sophomore year. 23% freshmen graduate within 4 years. 60% freshmen graduate within 6 years. 40% grads go on to further study within 1 year. 30% grads pursue arts and sciences degrees. 2% grads pursue law degrees. 30% grads pursue business degrees. 10% grads pursue medical degrees. **Faculty:** Student/faculty ratio 16:1. 33 full-time faculty, 67% hold PhDs, 18% are members of minority groups, 45% are women. 0% of classes are taught by teaching assistants.

ACADEMICS
Degrees: associate, bachelor's. **Classes:** Most classes have 10–19 students. Most lab/discussion sessions have 10–19 students. **Majors with Highest Enrollment:** business/commerce; education; social sciences. **Special Study Options:** Accelerated program, cooperative education program, cross-registration, double major, English as a Second Language (ESL), exchange student program (domestic), honors program, independent study, internships, liberal arts/career combination, student-designed major, study abroad, teacher certification program. **Disability Services:** Special programs offered to physically disabled students include reader services, tutors. **Career Services:** career/job search classes, career assessment, internships.

FACILITIES
Housing: men's dorms, women's dorms. 50% of campus accessible to physically disabled. **Special Academic Facilities/Equipment:** Art gallery, center for worship and performing arts, English language center, distance learning classroom.

CAMPUS LIFE
Environment: Village. **Activities:** Choral groups, concert band, drama/theater, jazz band, literary magazine, music ensembles, musical theater, student government, student newspaper, yearbook 35 registered organizations, 1 honor societies, 3 religious organizations. **Athletics (Intercollegiate):** *Men:* baseball, basketball, soccer, tennis, volleyball. *Women:* basketball, soccer, softball, tennis, volleyball.

ADMISSIONS
Freshman Academic Profile: Average high school GPA 2.7. 9% in top 10% of high school class, 20% in top 25% of high school class, 59% in top 50% of high school class. 60% from public high schools. SAT Math middle 50% range 410-530. SAT Critical Reading middle 50% range 420-520. ACT middle 50% range 17-22. Minimum paper TOEFL 550. **Basis for Candidate Selection:** *Very important factors considered include:* rigor of secondary school record. *Important factors considered include:* Class rank, standardized test scores, character/personal qualities, interview. *Other factors considered include:* application essay, recommendation(s), alumni/ae relation, extracurricular activities, religious affiliation/commitment, talent/ability, volunteer work, work experience. **Freshman Admission Requirements:** High school diploma is required and GED is accepted. *Academic units required:* 4 English, 3 mathematics, 2 science, (2 science labs), 2 foreign language, 2 social studies, 2 history. 4 English, 3 mathematics, 2 science, (2 science labs), 2 foreign language, 2 social studies, 2 history. **Freshman Admission Statistics:** 684 applied, 70% admitted, 37% enrolled. **Transfer Admission Requirements:** High school transcript, college transcript(s), statement of good standing from prior institution(s). Minimum college GPA of 2.0 required. Lowest grade transferable C. **General Admission Information:** Application Fee $40. Regular application deadline 3/15. Notification on a rolling basis, beginning on or about 1/15. Nonfall registration accepted. Admission may be deferred for a maximum of 12. Credit and/or placement offered for CEEB Advanced Placement tests.

COSTS AND FINANCIAL AID
Annual tuition $20,700. Room and board $8,230. Required fees $150. Average book expense $750. **Student Employment:** Federal Work-Study Program available. Institutional employment available. Highest amount earned per year from on-campus jobs $2,000. Off-campus job opportunities are excellent.

CONCORDIA UNIVERSITY—ST PAUL

275 Syndicate Street N, Saint Paul, MN 55104-5494
Phone: 651-641-8230 • **Financial Aid Phone:** 651-603-6300
E-mail: admission@csp.edu • **CEEB Code:** 6114
Fax: 651-603-6320 • **ACT Code:** 2106

This private school, affiliated with the Lutheran Church, was founded in 1893. It has a 37-acre campus.

RATINGS
Admissions Selectivity Rating: 73   **Fire Safety Rating:** 72   **Green Rating:** 69

STUDENTS AND FACULTY
Enrollment: 1,515. **Student Body:** 60% female, 40% male, 16% out-of-state, 0% international (5 countries represented). Asian 6%, African American 11%, Caucasian 68%, Hispanic 5%, Native American 1%.
Retention and Graduation: 71% freshmen return for sophomore year. 30% freshmen graduate within 4 years. 46% freshmen graduate within 6 years. **Faculty:** Student/faculty ratio 15:1. 82 full-time faculty, 66% hold PhDs, 12% are members of minority groups, 46% are women. 0% of classes are taught by teaching assistants.

ACADEMICS
Degrees: associate, bachelor's, certificate, master's, post-bachelor's certificate. **Classes:** Most classes have 10–19 students. **Special Study Options:** Accelerated program, cross-registration, distance learning, double major, dual enrollment, exchange student program (domestic), honors program, independent study, internships, student-designed major, study abroad, teacher certification program. **Disability Services:** Special programs offered to physically disabled students include note-taking services, reader services, tape recorders, tutors. **Career Services:** career assessment, internships.

FACILITIES
Housing: Coed dorms, men's dorms, women's dorms, apartments for married students, apartments for single students. 75% of campus accessible to physically disabled. **Computers:** Students can register for classes online. Administrative functions (other than registration) can be performed online.

CAMPUS LIFE
Environment: Metropolis. **Activities:** Choral groups, concert band, drama/theater, jazz band, music ensembles, musical theater, student government, student newspaper, television station, Campus Ministries. **Athletics (Intercollegiate):** *Men:* baseball, basketball, cross-country, football, golf, track/field (outdoor), track/field (indoor). *Women:* basketball, cross-country, golf, soccer, softball, track/field (outdoor), track/field (indoor), volleyball. **On-Campus Highlights:** Residence Life Center, Library Technology Center, Graebner Memorial Chapel, Gangelhoff Athletic Center, Pearson Theater.

ADMISSIONS
Freshman Academic Profile: Average high school GPA 3.2. 14% in top 10% of high school class, 35% in top 25% of high school class, 67% in top 50% of high school class. 90% from public high schools. ACT middle 50% range 19-24. Minimum paper TOEFL 500. **Basis for Candidate Selection:** *Very important factors considered include:* academic GPA, recommendation(s), standardized test scores. *Important factors considered include:* rigor of secondary school record, character/personal qualities, talent/ability. *Other factors considered include:* application essay, extracurricular activities, level of applicant's interest. **Freshman Admission Requirements:** High school diploma is required and GED is accepted. *Academic units required:* 4 English, 2 mathematics, 2 science, (2 science labs), 1 social studies, 1 history, 2 fine arts and 1 health/P.E. *Academic units recommended:* 4 English, 2 mathematics, 2 science, (2 science labs), 1 social studies, 1 history, 2 fine arts and 1 health/P.E. **Freshman Admission Statistics:** 935 applied, 65% admitted, 30% enrolled. **Transfer Admission Requirements:** college transcript(s), statement of good standing from prior institution(s). Minimum college GPA of 2.0 required. Lowest grade transferable D. **General Admission Information:** Application Fee $30. Regular application deadline 8/1. Nonfall registration accepted. Admission may be deferred for a maximum of 1 year. Credit and/or placement offered for CEEB Advanced Placement tests.

COSTS AND FINANCIAL AID
Annual tuition $19,700. Room and board $7,750. Average book expense $1,400. **Required Forms and Deadlines:** FAFSA, institution's own financial aid form. **Notification of Awards:** Applicants will be notified of awards on a rolling basis beginning 3/15. **Types of Aid:** *Need-based scholarships/grants:* Federal Pell, SEOG, state scholarships/grants, private scholarships, the school's own gift aid. *Loans:* Subsidized Stafford, Unsubsidized Stafford, PLUS, Federal Perkins, state loans. **Student Employment:** Federal Work-Study Program available. Institutional employment available. Off-campus job opportunities are fair. **Financial Aid Statistics:** 99% freshmen, 95% undergrads receive need-based

scholarship or grant aid. 9% freshmen, 11% undergrads receive non-need-based scholarship or grant aid. 77% freshmen, 80% undergrads receive need-based self-help aid. 99% freshmen receive any aid. 87% undergrads borrow to pay for school. Average cumulative indebtedness $42,020. **Criteria for awarding institutional aid:** *Non-need-based:* academics, art, athletics, minority status, music/drama, religious affiliation.

CONCORDIA UNIVERSITY (OR)

2811 NE Holman St, Portland, OR 97211-6099
Phone: 503-280-8501 • **Financial Aid Phone:** 800-321-9371
E-mail: admissions@cu-portland.edu • **CEEB Code:** 4078
Fax: 503-280-8531 • **Website:** www.cu-portland.edu • **ACT Code:** 3458

This private school, affiliated with the Lutheran Church, was founded in 1905. It has a 12-acre campus.

RATINGS
Admissions Selectivity Rating: 79   **Fire Safety Rating:** 60*   **Green Rating:** 60*

STUDENTS AND FACULTY
Enrollment: 1,073. **Student Body:** 64% female, 36% male, 41% out-of-state, 1% international. Asian 6%, African American 7%, Caucasian 65%, Hispanic 6%, Native American 1%.
Retention and Graduation: 74% freshmen return for sophomore year. 41% freshmen graduate within 6 years. **Faculty:** Student/faculty ratio 18:1. 52 full-time faculty, 67% hold PhDs, 4% are members of minority groups, 48% are women. 0% of classes are taught by teaching assistants.

ACADEMICS
Degrees: bachelor's, certificate, master's, post-bachelor's certificate, terminal associate. **Classes:** Most classes have 10–19 students. **Special Study Options:** Accelerated program, cross-registration, distance learning, dual enrollment, English as a Second Language (ESL), honors program, independent study, internships, study abroad, teacher certification program. **Honors Programs:** Honors program features limited enrollment to 25 students create greater intellectual opportunity. **Career Services:** alumni services, career assessment, internships, regional alumni., Career Services highlights include Concordia Committment offers students who complete the 4-year program partial tuition reimbursement if they are not employed in the field of their choice 6 months after graduation.

FACILITIES
Housing: Coed dorms, apartments for single students. **Computers:** Administrative functions (other than registration) can be performed online.

CAMPUS LIFE
Environment: Metropolis. **Activities:** Choral groups, drama/theater, literary magazine, music ensembles, student government, student newspaper, Campus Ministries, International Student Organization 10 registered organizations, 2 honor societies, 1 religious organizations. **Athletics (Intercollegiate):** *Men:* baseball, basketball, cross-country, golf, soccer, track/field (outdoor), track/field (indoor). *Women:* basketball, cross-country, golf, soccer, softball, track/field (outdoor), track/field (indoor), volleyball.

ADMISSIONS
Freshman Academic Profile: Average high school GPA 3.4. 19% in top 10% of high school class, 45% in top 25% of high school class, 76% in top 50% of high school class. SAT Math middle 50% range 460-560. SAT Critical Reading middle 50% range 450-570. ACT middle 50% range 18-24. Minimum paper TOEFL 500. **Basis for Candidate Selection:** *Very important factors considered include:* recommendation(s), rigor of secondary school record, standardized test scores. *Other factors considered include:* Class rank, application essay, academic GPA, character/personal qualities, interview. **Freshman Admission Requirements:** High school diploma is required and GED is accepted. **Freshman Admission Statistics:** 1,002 applied, 59% admitted, 32% enrolled. **Transfer Admission Requirements:** college transcript(s), statement of good standing from prior institution(s). Minimum college GPA of 2.0 required. Lowest grade transferable D. **General Admission Information:** Application Fee $20. Regular application deadline 7/1. Notification on a rolling basis, beginning on or about 1/1. Nonfall registration accepted. Admission may be deferred for a maximum of 1.

COSTS AND FINANCIAL AID
Annual tuition $20,900. Room and board $6,270. Required fees $210. Average book expense $800. **Required Forms and Deadlines:** FAFSA. **Notification of Awards:** Applicants will be notified of awards on a rolling basis beginning 3/15. **Types of Aid:** *Need-based scholarships/grants:* Federal Pell, SEOG, state scholarships/grants, the school's own gift aid. *Loans:* Subsidized Stafford, Un-

subsidized Stafford, PLUS, Federal Perkins. **Student Employment:** Federal Work-Study Program available. Institutional employment available. Off-campus job opportunities are good. **Financial Aid Statistics:** 83% freshmen, 81% undergrads receive need-based scholarship or grant aid. 91% freshmen, 88% undergrads receive non-need-based scholarship or grant aid. 77% freshmen, 78% undergrads receive need-based self-help aid. 28% freshmen, 27% undergrads receive athletic scholarships. 95% freshmen receive any aid. 78% undergrads borrow to pay for school. Average cumulative indebtedness $23,966. **Criteria for awarding institutional aid:** *Non-need-based:* academics, athletics, leadership, music/drama, religious affiliation.

CONCORDIA UNIVERSITY AT AUSTIN

3400 I-35 N, Austin, TX 78705
Phone: 512-486-1106 • **Financial Aid Phone:** 512-486-2000
E-mail: admissions@concordia.edu • **CEEB Code:** 6127
Fax: 512-486-1350 • **Website:** www.concordia.edu • **ACT Code:** 4124

This private school, affiliated with the Lutheran Church, was founded in 1926. It has a 23-acre campus.

RATINGS
Admissions Selectivity Rating: 69   **Fire Safety Rating:** 61   **Green Rating:** 60*

STUDENTS AND FACULTY
Enrollment: 966. **Student Body:** 56% female, 44% male, 7% out-of-state, 1% international (10 countries represented). Asian 2%, African American 9%, Caucasian 67%, Hispanic 14%, Native American 1%.
Retention and Graduation: 56% freshmen return for sophomore year. 12% freshmen graduate within 4 years. 22% freshmen graduate within 6 years. 12% grads go on to further study within 1 year. 9% grads pursue arts and sciences degrees. 1% grads pursue law degrees. 2% grads pursue business degrees. **Faculty:** Student/faculty ratio 19:1. 33 full-time faculty, 70% hold PhDs, 6% are members of minority groups, 36% are women. 0% of classes are taught by teaching assistants.

ACADEMICS
Degrees: associate, bachelor's, certificate, diploma, master's, post-bachelor's certificate. **Classes:** Most classes have 10–19 students. Most lab/discussion sessions have 20–29 students. **Majors with Highest Enrollment:** biology; elementary education and teaching. **Special Study Options:** Accelerated program, cooperative education program, cross-registration, distance learning, double major, dual enrollment, exchange student program (domestic), external degree program, honors program, independent study, internships, study abroad, teacher certification program. **Honors Programs:** Honors Program. **Career Services:**

FACILITIES
Housing: Coed dorms, men's dorms, women's dorms. 95% of campus accessible to physically disabled.

CAMPUS LIFE
Environment: Metropolis. **Activities:** Choral groups, drama/theater, jazz band, literary magazine, music ensembles, student government, yearbook 20 registered organizations, 4 honor societies, 5 religious organizations. **Athletics (Intercollegiate):** *Men:* baseball, basketball, cross-country, golf, rugby, soccer, tennis. *Women:* basketball, cross-country, golf, soccer, softball, tennis, volleyball. **On-Campus Highlights:** Oliver R. Harms Residential Suites (opened in 2001), Bokenkamp Student Center, Louise T Peter Center-communication and Fine Arts, Woltman Activity Center-Gymnasium, Texas Hall-Dining Facility.

ADMISSIONS
Freshman Academic Profile: Average high school GPA 3.1. 8% in top 10% of high school class, 26% in top 25% of high school class, 60% in top 50% of high school class. 86% from public high schools. SAT Math middle 50% range 450-550. SAT Critical Reading middle 50% range 430-500. ACT middle 50% range 18-24. **Basis for Candidate Selection:** *Very important factors considered include:* rigor of secondary school record, standardized test scores. *Other factors considered include:* Class rank, application essay, recommendation(s). **Freshman Admission Requirements:** High school diploma is required and GED is accepted. **Freshman Admission Statistics:** 523 applied, 76% admitted, 40% enrolled. **Transfer Admission Requirements:** college transcript(s), minimum college GPA of 2.0 required. Lowest grade transferable C. **General Admission Information:** Application Fee $25. Nonfall registration accepted. Credit offered for CEEB Advanced Placement tests.

COSTS AND FINANCIAL AID
Required Forms and Deadlines: FAFSA, institution's own financial aid form. **Notification of Awards:** Applicants will be notified of awards on a rolling basis

beginning 2/1. **Types of Aid:** *Need-based scholarships/grants:* Federal Pell, SEOG, state scholarships/grants, the school's own gift aid. *Loans:* Subsidized Stafford, Unsubsidized Stafford, PLUS, state loans. **Student Employment:** Federal Work-Study Program available. Highest amount earned per year from on-campus jobs $1,000. Off-campus job opportunities are excellent. **Financial Aid Statistics:** 83% freshmen, 83% undergrads receive need-based scholarship or grant aid. 81% freshmen, 57% undergrads receive non-need-based scholarship or grant aid. 75% freshmen, 75% undergrads receive need-based self-help aid. 85% undergrads receive any aid. 54% undergrads borrow to pay for school. Average cumulative indebtedness $29,449. **Criteria for awarding institutional aid:** *Non-need-based:* academics, leadership, music/drama, religious affiliation.

CONCORDIA UNIVERSITY CHICAGO

7400 Augusta Street, River Forest, IL 60305-1499
Phone: 708-209-3100 • **Financial Aid Phone:** 708-209-3113
E-mail: admission@cuchicago.edu • **CEEB Code:** 1140
Fax: 708-209-3473 • **Website:** www.CUChicago.edu • **ACT Code:** 1004

This private school, affiliated with the Lutheran Church, was founded in 1864. It has a 40-acre campus.

RATINGS
Admissions Selectivity Rating: 76   **Fire Safety Rating:** 66   **Green Rating:** 60*

STUDENTS AND FACULTY
Enrollment: 1,011. **Student Body:** 62% female, 38% male, 0% international (1 countries represented). Asian 1%, African American 13%, Caucasian 70%, Hispanic 9%, Native American 0%.
Retention and Graduation: 79% freshmen return for sophomore year. 23% grads go on to further study within 1 year. **Faculty:** Student/faculty ratio 17:1. 99 full-time faculty. 0% of classes are taught by teaching assistants.

ACADEMICS
Degrees: bachelor's, master's, post-master's certificate. **Classes:** Most classes have 10–19 students. **Majors with Highest Enrollment:** business/commerce; elementary education and teaching; kinesiology and exercise science. **Special Study Options:** double major, exchange student program (domestic), honors program, independent study, internships, study abroad, teacher certification program. **Honors Programs:** Honors Program. **Disability Services:** Special programs offered to physically disabled students include note-taking services, reader services, tape recorders, tutors. **Career Services:** alumni services, career/job search classes, career assessment, internships.

FACILITIES
Housing: Coed dorms, special housing for disabled students, men's dorms, women's dorms. 74% of campus accessible to physically disabled. **Special Academic Facilities/Equipment:** Art museum, zoology exhibit, human performance lab, early childhood education lab school, TV studio, weather station, radio station. **Computers:** Students can register for classes online. Administrative functions (other than registration) can be performed online.

CAMPUS LIFE
Environment: Metropolis. **Activities:** Choral groups, concert band, dance, drama/theater, jazz band, literary magazine, music ensembles, musical theater, pep band, radio station, student government, student newspaper, television station, yearbook 15 registered organizations, 3 honor societies, 5 religious organizations. **Athletics (Intercollegiate):** *Men:* baseball, basketball, cheerleading, cross-country, football, soccer, tennis, track/field (outdoor). *Women:* basketball, cheerleading, cross-country, soccer, softball, tennis, track/field (outdoor), volleyball. **On-Campus Highlights:** Fitness center, Soccer, football and track stadium, Library Cafe, Triangle, Chapel of our Lord.

ADMISSIONS
Freshman Academic Profile: Average high school GPA 3.1. 18% in top 10% of high school class, 41% in top 25% of high school class, 67% in top 50% of high school class. ACT middle 50% range 19-26. Minimum paper TOEFL 500. **Basis for Candidate Selection:** *Important factors considered include:* Class rank, academic GPA, rigor of secondary school record, standardized test scores. *Other factors considered include:* application essay, recommendation(s), character/personal qualities, extracurricular activities, interview. **Freshman Admission Requirements:** High school diploma is required and GED is accepted. *Academic units required:* 4 English, 3 mathematics, 2 science, (1 science labs), 2 social studies. *Academic units recommended:* 4 English, 3 mathematics, 2 science, (1 science labs), 2 social studies. **Freshman Admission Statistics:** 1,092 applied, 65% admitted, 30% enrolled. **Transfer Admission Requirements:** college transcript(s), statement of good standing from prior institution(s).

Minimum college GPA of 2.0 required. Lowest grade transferable C. **General Admission Information:** Notification on a rolling basis, beginning on or about 9/4. Nonfall registration accepted. Admission may be deferred for a maximum of 1. Credit and/or placement offered for CEEB Advanced Placement tests.

COSTS AND FINANCIAL AID
Annual tuition $20,900. Room and board $6,992. Required fees $420. Average book expense $600. **Required Forms and Deadlines: Notification of Awards: Types of Aid:** *Need-based scholarships/grants: Loans:* **Student Employment:** Federal Work-Study Program available. Institutional employment available. Highest amount earned per year from on-campus jobs $17,000. Off-campus job opportunities are good. **Financial Aid Statistics:** 81% freshmen, 77% undergrads receive any aid.

CONCORDIA UNIVERSITY IRVINE

1530 Concordia West, Irvine, CA 92612-3299
Phone: 949-854-8002 • **Financial Aid Phone:** 949-854-8002
E-mail: admission@cui.edu
Fax: 949-854-6894 • **Website:** www.cui.edu • **ACT Code:** 227

This private school, affiliated with the Lutheran Church, was founded in 1976. It has a 70-acre campus.

RATINGS
Admissions Selectivity Rating: 75   **Fire Safety Rating:** 93   **Green Rating:** 60*

STUDENTS AND FACULTY
Enrollment: 1,203. **Student Body:** 61% female, 39% male, 17% out-of-state, 2% international (18 countries represented). Asian 4%, African American 4%, Caucasian 68%, Hispanic 13%, Native American 1%.
Retention and Graduation: 73% freshmen return for sophomore year. 56% freshmen graduate within 4 years. 62% freshmen graduate within 6 years. **Faculty:** Student/faculty ratio 14:1. 91 full-time faculty, 67% hold PhDs, 37% are women. 0% of classes are taught by teaching assistants.

ACADEMICS
Degrees: associate, bachelor's, master's, post-bachelor's certificate. **Classes:** Most classes have 10–19 students. **Majors with Highest Enrollment:** business/commerce; liberal arts and sciences/liberal studies; psychology. **Special Study Options:** Accelerated program, cross-registration, distance learning, double major, dual enrollment, English as a Second Language (ESL), exchange student program (domestic), honors program, independent study, internships, liberal arts/career combination, student-designed major, study abroad, teacher certification program. **Honors Programs:** General Education Honor Programs **Combined Degree Programs:** BA/MA. **Disability Services:** Special programs offered to physically disabled students include tutors. **Career Services:** Career Services highlights include We are proud of all the programs offered by Concordia University.

FACILITIES
Housing: special housing for disabled students, men's dorms, women's dorms. 75% of campus accessible to physically disabled. **Special Academic Facilities/Equipment:** A hi-tech Educational/Business/Technology building, which was recently completed, houses also an art gallery. **Computers:** 60% of classrooms, 100% of dorms, 95% of libraries, 70% of dining areas, 100% of student union, 10% of common outdoor areas have wireless network access. Students can register for classes online.

CAMPUS LIFE
Environment: City. **Activities:** Choral groups, concert band, dance, drama/theater, literary magazine, music ensembles, musical theater, pep band, radio station, student government, student newspaper, student-run film society, yearbook, Campus Ministries 18 registered organizations, 5 honor societies, 8 religious organizations. **Athletics (Intercollegiate):** *Men:* baseball, basketball, cross-country, golf, soccer, swimming, tennis, track/field (outdoor), water polo. *Women:* basketball, cross-country, golf, soccer, softball, swimming, tennis, track/field (outdoor), volleyball, water polo. **On-Campus Highlights:** The Gym, Student Life Center (Lounge and computer resource), Library, CU Center (Worship Center), Student Union (cafeteria).

ADMISSIONS
Freshman Academic Profile: Average high school GPA 3.5. 20% in top 10% of high school class, 54% in top 25% of high school class, 84% in top 50% of high school class. SAT Math middle 50% range 450-570. SAT Critical Reading middle 50% range 450-570. ACT middle 50% range 20-24. Minimum paper TOEFL 550. **Basis for Candidate Selection:** *Very important factors considered include:* Class rank, academic GPA, rigor of secondary school record, standardized test scores, character/personal qualities. *Important factors*

considered include: recommendation(s), religious affiliation/commitment. *Other factors considered include:* application essay, alumni/ae relation, extracurricular activities, interview, level of applicant's interest, racial/ethnic status, talent/ability, volunteer work, work experience. **Freshman Admission Requirements:** High school diploma is required and GED is accepted. *Academic units required:* 4 English, 3 mathematics, 3 science, 2 foreign language, 2 social studies. 4 English, 3 mathematics, 3 science, 2 foreign language, 2 social studies. **Freshman Admission Statistics:** 827 applied, 67% admitted, 41% enrolled. **Transfer Admission Requirements:** High school transcript, college transcript(s), statement of good standing from prior institution(s). Minimum college GPA of 2.3 required. Lowest grade transferable D. **General Admission Information:** Application Fee $50. Nonfall registration accepted. Admission may be deferred for a maximum of 12 months. Credit and/or placement offered for CEEB Advanced Placement tests.

COSTS AND FINANCIAL AID
Annual tuition $23,400. Room and board $7,650. Required fees $300. **Required Forms and Deadlines:** FAFSA, institution's own financial aid form, state aid formState aid form: GPA Verification Form. **Notification of Awards:** Applicants will be notified of awards on a rolling basis beginning 2/1. **Types of Aid:** *Need-based scholarships/grants:* Federal Pell, SEOG, state scholarships/grants, private scholarships, the school's own gift aid. *Loans:* Subsidized Stafford, Unsubsidized Stafford, PLUS. **Student Employment:** Highest amount earned per year from on-campus jobs $2,000. Off-campus job opportunities are good. **Financial Aid Statistics:** 95% freshmen, 92% undergrads receive need-based scholarship or grant aid. 18% freshmen, 13% undergrads receive non-need-based scholarship or grant aid. 71% freshmen, 77% undergrads receive need-based self-help aid. 10% freshmen, 7% undergrads receive athletic scholarships. 74% freshmen, 71% undergrads receive any aid. 67% undergrads borrow to pay for school. Average cumulative indebtedness $20,254. **Criteria for awarding institutional aid:** *Non-need-based:* academics, art, athletics, leadership, music/drama, religious affiliation.

CONCORDIA UNIVERSITY WISCONSIN

12800 North Lake Shore Drive, Mequon, WI 53097
Phone: 262-243-5700 • **Financial Aid Phone:** 262-243-4392
E-mail: admissions@cuw.edu • **CEEB Code:** 1139
Fax: 262-243-4545 • **Website:** www.cuw.edu • **ACT Code:** 4574

This private school, affiliated with the Lutheran Church, was founded in 1881. It has a 192-acre campus.

RATINGS
Admissions Selectivity Rating: 74   **Fire Safety Rating:** 60*   **Green Rating:** 67

STUDENTS AND FACULTY
Enrollment: 4,177. **Student Body:** 66% female, 34% male, 20% out of state, 1% international (23 countries represented). Asian 1%, African American 18%, Caucasian 65%, Hispanic 2%, Native American 1%.
Retention and Graduation: 75% freshmen return for sophomore year. 28% grads go on to further study within 1 year. **Faculty:** Student/faculty ratio 14:1. 151 full-time faculty, 74% hold PhDs, 5% are members of minority groups, 47% are women. 0% of classes are taught by teaching assistants.

ACADEMICS
Degrees: associate, bachelor's, certificate, master's, post-bachelor's certificate. **Classes:** Most classes have 10–19 students. Most lab/discussion sessions have 10–19 students. **Majors with Highest Enrollment:** business/commerce; education; health services/allied health/health sciences. **Special Study Options:** Accelerated program, cross-registration, distance learning, double major, dual enrollment, English as a Second Language (ESL), exchange student program (domestic), independent study, internships, liberal arts/career combination, student-designed major, study abroad, teacher certification program, CUW offers cooperative programs with Cardinal Stritch University, Marquette University, Milwaukee Institute of Art and Design and Alverno College. **Combined Degree Programs:** 2-2 interior design program. **Disability Services:** Special programs offered to physically disabled students include note-taking services, reader services, tape recorders, tutors. **Career Services:** Alumni network, alumni services, career/job search classes, career assessment, internships, regional alumni.

FACILITIES
Housing: men's dorms, women's dorms.

CAMPUS LIFE
Environment: Village. **Activities:** Choral groups, concert band, dance, drama/theater, jazz band, music ensembles, musical theater, pep band, radio station,

student government, student newspaper, Campus Ministries, International Student Organization. **Athletics (Intercollegiate):** *Men:* baseball, basketball, cross-country, football, ice hockey, soccer, tennis, track/field (outdoor), volleyball, wrestling. *Women:* basketball, cross-country, ice hockey, soccer, softball, tennis, track/field (outdoor), volleyball. **On-Campus Highlights:** Coberg Residence Hall - new, Sports and Fitness Center, Field House **Environmental Initiatives:** Construction of environmental education center with LEED status

ADMISSIONS

Freshman Academic Profile: Average high school GPA 3.4. 17% in top 10% of high school class, 43% in top 25% of high school class, 73% in top 50% of high school class. SAT Math middle 50% range 450-550. SAT Critical Reading middle 50% range 420-560. SAT Writing middle 50% range 440-530. ACT middle 50% range 20-26. Minimum paper TOEFL 500. **Basis for Candidate Selection:** *Very important factors considered include:* application essay, academic GPA, rigor of secondary school record. *Important factors considered include:* character/personal qualities, work experience. *Other factors considered include:* Class rank, recommendation(s), standardized test scores, alumni/ae relation, extracurricular activities, interview, racial/ethnic status, religious affiliation/commitment, state residency, talent/ability, volunteer work. **Freshman Admission Requirements:** High school diploma is required and GED is accepted. *Academic units required:* 3 English, 2 mathematics, 2 science, 2 social studies, 5 academic electives. *Academic units recommended:* 3 English, 2 mathematics, 2 science, 2 social studies, 5 academic electives. **Freshman Admission Statistics:** 2,639 applied, 66% admitted, 32% enrolled. **Transfer Admission Requirements:** college transcript(s), statement of good standing from prior institution(s). Minimum college GPA of 2.0 required. Lowest grade transferable C. **General Admission Information:** Application Fee $35. Regular application deadline 8/15. Notification on a rolling basis, beginning on or about 10/15. Nonfall registration accepted.

COSTS AND FINANCIAL AID

Required Forms and Deadlines: FAFSA. **Notification of Awards:** Applicants will be notified of awards on a rolling basis beginning 2/1. **Types of Aid:** *Need-based scholarships/grants:* Federal Pell, SEOG, state scholarships/grants, private scholarships, the school's own gift aid. *Loans:* Direct Subsidized Stafford, Direct Unsubsidized Stafford, Direct PLUS. **Student Employment:** Off-campus job opportunities are excellent. **Financial Aid Statistics:** 97% freshmen, 95% undergrads receive need-based scholarship or grant aid. 25% freshmen, 19% undergrads receive non-need-based scholarship or grant aid. 82% freshmen, 83% undergrads receive need-based self-help aid. 95% freshmen receive any aid. 82% undergrads borrow to pay for school. Average cumulative indebtedness $30,879.

CONCORDIA UNIVERSITY, NEBRASKA

800 North Columbia Avenue, Seward, NE 68434-1556
Phone: 800-535-5494 • **Financial Aid Phone:** 800 535-5494
E-mail: admiss@cune.edu • **CEEB Code:** 6116
Fax: 402-643-4073 • **Website:** www.cune.edu • **ACT Code:** 2442

This private school, affiliated with the Lutheran Church, was founded in 1894. It has a 120-acre campus.

RATINGS

Admissions Selectivity Rating: 78   **Fire Safety Rating:** 75   **Green Rating:** 61

STUDENTS AND FACULTY

Enrollment: 1,213. **Student Body:** 51% female, 49% male, 53% out-of-state, 1% international (8 countries represented). Asian 0%, African American 3%, Caucasian 89%, Hispanic 2%, Native American 0%.
Retention and Graduation: 81% freshmen return for sophomore year. 41% freshmen graduate within 4 years. 55% freshmen graduate within 6 years. 25% grads go on to further study within 1 year. 12% grads pursue arts and sciences degrees. 3% grads pursue law degrees. 8% grads pursue business degrees. 10% grads pursue medical degrees. **Faculty:** Student/faculty ratio 14:1. 58 full-time faculty, 71% hold PhDs, 3% are members of minority groups, 29% are women. 0% of classes are taught by teaching assistants.

ACADEMICS

Degrees: bachelor's, master's, post-bachelor's certificate. **Classes:** Most classes have 20–29 students. Most lab/discussion sessions have 10–19 students. **Majors with Highest Enrollment:** biology/biological sciences; business/commerce; education. **Special Study Options:** Accelerated program, distance learning, double major, dual enrollment, English as a Second Language (ESL), exchange student program (domestic), independent study, internships, study abroad, teacher certification program, Undergradate students may take graduate level classes. **Disability Services:** Special programs offered to physically disabled

students include note-taking services, reader services, tape recorders, tutors. **Career Services:** Alumni network, alumni services, career/job search classes, career assessment, internships, regional alumni. Career Services highlights include Intentional "4 year plan" to serve students prior to graduation.

FACILITIES

Housing: special housing for disabled students, men's dorms, women's dorms, apartments for married students, apartments for single students. 60% of campus accessible to physically disabled. **Special Academic Facilities/Equipment:** Art gallery, Bartels rock museum, observatory, arboretum **Computers:** 40% of classrooms, 100% of dorms, 100% of libraries, 100% of student union, have wireless network access. Students can register for classes online. Administrative functions (other than registration) can be performed online.

CAMPUS LIFE

Environment: Village. **Activities:** Choral groups, concert band, dance, drama/theater, jazz band, literary magazine, music ensembles, musical theater, pep band, student government, student newspaper, symphony orchestra, yearbook, Campus Ministries 33 registered organizations, 1 honor societies, 5 religious organizations. **Athletics (Intercollegiate):** *Men:* baseball, basketball, cross-country, football, golf, soccer, tennis, track/field (outdoor), track/field (indoor), wrestling. *Women:* basketball, cross-country, golf, soccer, softball, tennis, track/field (outdoor), track/field (indoor), volleyball. **On-Campus Highlights:** Student Center / Game Room, Coffee Shop, Marxhausen Art Gallery, Osten Observatory, Physical Education Building. **Environmental Initiatives:** The committee is charged with outlining short-term and long-term plans that will render the university carbon neutral as soon as is feasible and to report progress periodically. Specific plans have not yet been formulated. Purchasing "Energy Star" equipment. Incorporating sustainability in new construction and renovation projects.

ADMISSIONS

Freshman Academic Profile: Average high school GPA 3.5. 20% in top 10% of high school class, 48% in top 25% of high school class, 76% in top 50% of high school class. SAT Math middle 50% range 490-610. SAT Critical Reading middle 50% range 480-590. ACT middle 50% range 21-27. Minimum paper TOEFL 500. **Basis for Candidate Selection:** *Very important factors considered include:* academic GPA, standardized test scores. *Important factors considered include:* Class rank, rigor of secondary school record, character/personal qualities. *Other factors considered include:* recommendation(s), alumni/ae relation, extracurricular activities, interview, religious affiliation/commitment. **Freshman Admission Requirements:** High school diploma is required and GED is accepted. **Freshman Admission Statistics:** 1,397 applied, 69% admitted, 33% enrolled. **Transfer Admission Requirements:** High school transcript, college transcript(s), minimum college GPA of 2.0 required. Lowest grade transferable D. **General Admission Information:** Regular application deadline 8/1. Notification on a rolling basis, beginning on or about 9/1. Nonfall registration accepted. Admission may be deferred for a maximum of 1 year. Credit and/or placement offered for CEEB Advanced Placement tests.

COSTS AND FINANCIAL AID

Annual tuition $23,550. Room and board $6,440. Required fees $250. Average book expense $900. **Required Forms and Deadlines:** FAFSA. **Notification of Awards:** Applicants will be notified of awards on a rolling basis beginning 3/1. **Types of Aid:** *Need-based scholarships/grants:* Federal Pell, SEOG, state scholarships/grants, private scholarships, the school's own gift aid. *Loans:* Subsidized Stafford, Unsubsidized Stafford, PLUS, Federal Perkins. **Student Employment:** Federal Work-Study Program available. Institutional employment available. Highest amount earned per year from on-campus jobs $3,500. Off-campus job opportunities are good. **Financial Aid Statistics:** 100% freshmen, 99% undergrads receive need-based scholarship or grant aid. 19% freshmen, 16% undergrads receive non-need-based scholarship or grant aid. 66% freshmen, 72% undergrads receive need-based self-help aid. 17% freshmen, 12% undergrads receive athletic scholarships. 100% freshmen, 99% undergrads receive any aid. 80% undergrads borrow to pay for school. Average cumulative indebtedness $27,387. **Criteria for awarding institutional aid:** *Non-need-based:* academics, alumni affiliation, art, athletics, leadership, music/drama, religious affiliation.

CONNECTICUT COLLEGE

270 Mohegan Avenue, New London, CT 6320
Phone: 860-439-2200 • **Financial Aid Phone:** 860-439-2058
E-mail: admission@conncoll.edu • **CEEB Code:** 3284
Fax: 860-439-4301 • **Website:** www.connecticutcollege.edu • **ACT Code:** 556

This private school was founded in 1911. It has a 750-acre campus.

RATINGS
Admissions Selectivity Rating: 96   **Fire Safety Rating:** 76   **Green Rating:** 84

STUDENTS AND FACULTY
Enrollment: 1,781. **Student Body:** 61% female, 39% male, 82% out-of-state, 4% international (74 countries represented). Asian 3%, African American 4%, Caucasian 74%, Hispanic 7%, Native American 0%.
Retention and Graduation: 80% freshmen graduate within 4 years. 25% grads go on to further study within 1 year. **Faculty:** Student/faculty ratio 9:1. 178 full-time faculty, 92% hold PhDs, 24% are members of minority groups, 48% are women. 0% of classes are taught by teaching assistants.

ACADEMICS
Degrees: bachelor's, master's. **Classes:** Most classes have 10–19 students. Most lab/discussion sessions have 10–19 students. **Majors with Highest Enrollment:** economics; English language and literature; political science and government. **Special Study Options:** cross-registration, double major, exchange student program (domestic), independent study, internships, student-designed major, study abroad, teacher certification program, Cross-registration with the U.S. Coast Guard Academy, Trinity College, and Wesleyan University; 3-2 Program with Washington University or Boston University for a five-year BA/BS degree; Exchange Student Program; 12 Exchanges. **Combined Degree Programs:** BA/MA. **Disability Services:** Special programs offered to physically disabled students include note-taking services, reader services, tape recorders, tutors. **Career Services:** Alumni network, alumni services, career/job search classes, career assessment, internships, regional alumni. Career Services highlights include Our Career-Enhancing Life Skills (CELS) office administers a program that facilitates College-funded internships for students who complete a series of preparatory seminars and workshops.

FACILITIES
Housing: Coed dorms, special housing for disabled students, wellness housing, theme housing. (environmentalism, foreign language, substance-free housing, etc.), men's floors, women's floors, living and learning arrangements. **Special Academic Facilities/Equipment:** Children's Program used as "lab school" for human development program, language lab, 750-acre arboretum, botanic garden, greenhouse, environment control labs, transmission and scanning electron microscope, ion accelerator, GIS lab, refracting telescope, observatory. **Computers:** 75% of classrooms, 100% of dorms, 100% of libraries, 100% of dining areas, 100% of student union, 70% of common outdoor areas have wireless network access. Students can register for classes online. Administrative functions (other than registration) can be performed online.

CAMPUS LIFE
Environment: Town. **Activities:** Choral groups, concert band, dance, drama/theater, jazz band, literary magazine, music ensembles, radio station, student government, student newspaper, student-run film society, symphony orchestra, yearbook, Campus Ministries, International Student Organization 60 registered organizations, 5 honor societies, 6 religious organizations. **Athletics (Intercollegiate):** *Men:* basketball, crew/rowing, cross-country, diving, ice hockey, lacrosse, sailing, soccer, squash, swimming, tennis, track/field (outdoor), track/field (indoor), water polo. *Women:* basketball, crew/rowing, cross-country, diving, field hockey, ice hockey, lacrosse, sailing, soccer, squash, swimming, tennis, track/field (outdoor), track/field (indoor), volleyball, water polo. **On-Campus Highlights:** College Center (Crozier-Williams), Connecticut College Arboretum, Blue Camel Cafe (in library), Athletics Center, Coffee Grounds. **Environmental Initiatives:** Signatory of the American College and University President's Climate Commitment Signatory of the Talloires Declaration U.S. Environmental Protection Agency Green Power Partner

ADMISSIONS
Freshman Academic Profile: 55% in top 10% of high school class, 91% in top 25% of high school class, 98% in top 50% of high school class. 55% from public high schools. SAT Math middle 50% range 630-700. SAT Critical Reading middle 50% range 620-710. SAT Writing middle 50% range 630-720. ACT middle 50% range 27-32. Minimum web-based TOEFL 100. Minimum paper TOEFL 600. **Basis for Candidate Selection:** *Very important factors considered include:* Class rank, academic GPA, rigor of secondary school record, character/personal qualities. *Important factors considered include:* application essay, recommendation(s), extracurricular activities, interview, racial/ethnic status, talent/ability, volunteer work, work experience. *Other factors considered include:* standardized test scores, alumni/ae relation, first generation, geographical residence, level of applicant's interest, religious affiliation/commitment, state residency. **Freshman Admission Requirements:** High school diploma is required and GED is accepted. **Freshman Admission Statistics:** 5,241 applied, 34% admitted, 28% enrolled. **Transfer Admission Requirements:** High school transcript, college transcript(s), essay or personal statement, statement of good standing from prior institution(s). Lowest grade transferable C. **General Admission Information:** Application Fee $60. Early decision application deadline 11/15. Regular application deadline 1/1. Regular notification 3/31. Nonfall registration not accepted. Admission may be deferred for a maximum of 1 year. Credit and/or placement offered for CEEB Advanced Placement tests.

COSTS AND FINANCIAL AID
Annual tuition $44,890. Room and board $11,900. Average book expense $1,000. **Required Forms and Deadlines:** FAFSA, CSS/Financial Aid PROFILE, noncustodial PROFILE, business/farm supplement. Federal tax returns; personal, partnership, and Federal W2 statements. **Notification of Awards:** Applicants will be notified of awards on or about 4/1. **Types of Aid:** *Need-based scholarships/grants:* Federal Pell, SEOG, state scholarships/grants, the school's own gift aid. *Loans:* Direct Subsidized Stafford, Direct Unsubsidized Stafford, Direct PLUS, Subsidized Stafford, Unsubsidized Stafford, PLUS, Federal Perkins. **Student Employment:** Federal Work-Study Program available. Institutional employment available. Off-campus job opportunities are good. **Financial Aid Statistics:** 94% freshmen, 93% undergrads receive need-based scholarship or grant aid. 89% freshmen, 89% undergrads receive need-based self-help aid. 41% freshmen receive any aid. 38% undergrads borrow to pay for school. Average cumulative indebtedness $30,505.

See page 1056.

CONVERSE COLLEGE

580 East Main Street, Spartanburg, SC 29302
Phone: 864-596-9040 • **Financial Aid Phone:** 864-596-9019
E-mail: admissions@converse.edu • **CEEB Code:** 5121
Fax: 864-596-9225 • **Website:** www.converse.edu • **ACT Code:** 3852

This private school was founded in 1889. It has a 70-acre campus.

RATINGS
Admissions Selectivity Rating: 86   **Fire Safety Rating:** 70   **Green Rating:** 67

STUDENTS AND FACULTY
Enrollment: 687. **Student Body:** 100% female, 0% male, 23% out-of-state, 1% international. Asian 1%, African American 8%, Caucasian 46%, Hispanic 3%, Native American 0%.
Retention and Graduation: 76% freshmen return for sophomore year. 56% freshmen graduate within 4 years. 57% freshmen graduate within 6 years. 37% grads go on to further study within 1 year. **Faculty:** Student/faculty ratio 11:1. 76 full-time faculty, 91% hold PhDs, 7% are members of minority groups, 59% are women. 0% of classes are taught by teaching assistants.

ACADEMICS
Degrees: bachelor's, master's, post-master's certificate. **Classes:** Most classes have fewer than 10 students. Most lab/discussion sessions have fewer than 10 students. **Majors with Highest Enrollment:** business/commerce; education; psychology. **Special Study Options:** cross-registration, double major, English as a Second Language (ESL), honors program, independent study, internships, liberal arts/career combination, student-designed major, study abroad, teacher certification program, Undergrads may take grad level classes. **Honors Programs:** Nisbet Honors Program. **Disability Services:** Special programs offered to physically disabled students include note-taking services, tape recorders, tutors. **Career Services:** Alumni network, alumni services, career/job search classes, career assessment, internships, regional alumni. Every undergraduate student at Converse is guaranteed an internship.

FACILITIES
Housing: women's dorms. **Special Academic Facilities/Equipment:** Language lab. Phifer Science Building, Blackman Auditorium (Music), DNA sequencer and lab. **Computers:** Students can register for classes online. Administrative functions (other than registration) can be performed online.

CAMPUS LIFE

Environment: City. **Activities:** Choral groups, concert band, dance, drama/theater, literary magazine, music ensembles, musical theater, opera, student government, student newspaper, symphony orchestra, yearbook 60 registered organizations, 16 honor societies, 7 religious organizations. **Athletics (Intercollegiate):** *Women:* basketball, cross-country, lacrosse, soccer, swimming, tennis, volleyball. **On-Campus Highlights:** Montgomery Student Life Center, Weisiger Physical Activity Complex, Phifer Science Complex, Petrie School of Music- Twichell Auditorium, Outdoor Quad area for studying and relaxing. **Environmental Initiatives:** LEED Certified new construction Sustainable foodstuffs bought and used by Dining Services Student Environmental Group - WISE

ADMISSIONS

Freshman Academic Profile: 18% in top 10% of high school class, 43% in top 25% of high school class, 80% in top 50% of high school class. 80% from public high schools. SAT Math middle 50% range 460-570. SAT Critical Reading middle 50% range 470-600. ACT middle 50% range 20-26. Minimum web-based TOEFL 79. Minimum paper TOEFL 550. **Basis for Candidate Selection:** *Very important factors considered include:* academic GPA, rigor of secondary school record. *Important factors considered include:* Class rank, application essay, recommendation(s), standardized test scores, character/personal qualities, extracurricular activities, talent/ability. *Other factors considered include:* alumni/ae relation, first generation, interview, level of applicant's interest, racial/ethnic status, volunteer work, work experience. **Freshman Admission Requirements:** High school diploma is required and GED is accepted. **Freshman Admission Statistics:** 1,383 applied, 51% admitted, 26% enrolled. **Transfer Admission Requirements:** college transcript(s), statement of good standing from prior institution(s). Minimum college GPA of 2.0 required. Lowest grade transferable C. **General Admission Information:** Notification on a rolling basis, beginning on or about 10/1. Nonfall registration accepted. Admission may be deferred for a maximum of 1 year. Credit offered for CEEB Advanced Placement tests.

COSTS AND FINANCIAL AID

Annual tuition $27,276. Room and board $8,854. Required fees $1,000. Average book expense $1,000. **Required Forms and Deadlines:** FAFSA. **Notification of Awards:** Applicants will be notified of awards on a rolling basis beginning 3/1. **Types of Aid:** *Need-based scholarships/grants:* Federal Pell, SEOG, state scholarships/grants, private scholarships, the school's own gift aid. *Loans:* Subsidized Stafford, Unsubsidized Stafford, PLUS, Federal Perkins, state loans. **Student Employment:** Federal Work-Study Program available. Institutional employment available. Off-campus job opportunities are good. **Financial Aid Statistics:** 100% freshmen, 98% undergrads receive need-based scholarship or grant aid. 18% freshmen, 17% undergrads receive non-need-based scholarship or grant aid. 79% freshmen, 77% undergrads receive need-based self-help aid. 14% freshmen, 8% undergrads receive athletic scholarships. 95% freshmen, 93% undergrads receive any aid. Average cumulative indebtedness $28,986. **Criteria for awarding institutional aid:** *Non-need-based:* academics, alumni affiliation, art, athletics, leadership, music/drama, state/district residency.

THE COOPER UNION FOR THE ADVANCEMENT OF SCIENCE AND ART

Best 378

30 Cooper Square, New York, NY 10003
Phone: 212-353-4120 • **Financial Aid Phone:** 212-353-4130
E-mail: admissions@cooper.edu • **CEEB Code:** 2097
Fax: 212-353-4342 • **Website:** www.cooper.edu • **ACT Code:** 2724

This private school was founded in 1859.

RATINGS

Admissions Selectivity Rating: 98   **Fire Safety Rating:** 99   **Green Rating:** 78

STUDENTS AND FACULTY

Enrollment: 855. **Student Body:** 36% female, 64% male, 40% out-of-state, 9% international. Asian 14%, African American 5%, Caucasian 29%, Hispanic 7%, Native American 1%.
Retention and Graduation: 90% freshmen return for sophomore year. 65% freshmen graduate within 4 years. 81% freshmen graduate within 6 years. 60% grads go on to further study within 1 year. 15% grads pursue arts and sciences

degrees. 6% grads pursue law degrees. 10% grads pursue business degrees. 3% grads pursue medical degrees. **Faculty:** Student/faculty ratio 8:1. 50 full-time faculty, 90% hold PhDs, 12% are members of minority groups, 28% are women. 0% of classes are taught by teaching assistants.

ACADEMICS

Degrees: bachelor's, certificate, master's. **Classes:** Most classes have 10–19 students. Most lab/discussion sessions have greater than 100 students. **Majors with Highest Enrollment:** electrical, electronics and communications engineering; fine arts and art studies, other; mechanical engineering. **Special Study Options:** cross-registration, exchange student program (domestic), independent study, internships, student-designed major, study abroad, Cooper Union is indeed an all-honors college. Research opportunities available. Students may take up to one year off during their studies with us to pursue other interests. **Honors Programs:** Cooper Union is an all-honors college **Combined Degree Programs:** MEng/MD. **Disability Services:** Special programs offered to physically disabled students include reader services, tape recorders, tutors. **Career Services:** Alumni network, alumni services, career/job search classes, career assessment, internships, regional alumni. Career Services highlights include Cooper Union Professional Internship Program-provides funding for students to learn through an internship that normally doesn't pay.

FACILITIES

Housing: Coed dorms. 75% of campus accessible to physically disabled. The Great Hall; Houghton Gallery; The Brooks Lab, Prototyping Lab, Bio-Medical Engineering Lab, Tissue Engineering Lab, Center for Sustainable Design, Center for Infrastructure and Urban Systems, Center for Signal Processing Communications and Computer Engineering Research, **Computers:** 85% of classrooms, have wireless network access. Administrative functions (other than registration) can be performed online.

CAMPUS LIFE

Environment: Metropolis. **Activities:** Choral groups, concert band, dance, drama/theater, jazz band, literary magazine, music ensembles, student government, student newspaper, student-run film society, symphony orchestra, yearbook 90 registered organizations, 18 honor societies, 8 religious organizations. 2 fraternities, 1 sororities. **Athletics (Intercollegiate):** *Men:* baseball, basketball, cross-country, soccer, tennis, volleyball. *Women:* basketball, cross-country, soccer, tennis, volleyball. **On-Campus Highlights:** Great Hall, 41 Cooper Square, Foundation Building, Houghton Gallery, 41 Cooper Square Gallery, 41 Cooper Square-our newest building, Opened in September of 2009 to critical acclaim. Designed by Pritzker Prize winning architect, Thom Mayne, this building has many green features and is targeted to earn Platinum LEED certification. **Environmental Initiatives:** New Academic Building please see: cooper.edu http://cooper.edu/the-cooper-union-honored-at-the-global-green-sustainable-design-awards/

ADMISSIONS

Freshman Academic Profile: Average high school GPA 3.6. 90% in top 10% of high school class, 95% in top 25% of high school class, 96% in top 50% of high school class. 65% from public high schools. SAT Math middle 50% range 610-770. SAT Critical Reading middle 50% range 620-710. SAT Writing middle 50% range 590-740. ACT middle 50% range 28-33. Minimum web-based TOEFL 100. Minimum paper TOEFL 600. **Basis for Candidate Selection:** *Very important factors considered include:* academic GPA, rigor of secondary school record, standardized test scores, level of applicant's interest, talent/ability. *Important factors considered include:* application essay, character/personal qualities, extracurricular activities. *Other factors considered include:* Class rank, recommendation(s), first generation, interview, racial/ethnic status, volunteer work, work experience. **Freshman Admission Requirements:** High school diploma is required and GED is accepted. *Academic units required:* 4 English, 1 mathematics, 1 science, 1 social studies, 1 history, 8 academic electives. *Academic units recommended:* 4 English, 1 mathematics, 1 science, 1 social studies, 1 history, 8 academic electives. **Freshman Admission Statistics:** 3,573 applied, 7% admitted, 76% enrolled. **Transfer Admission Requirements:** High school transcript, college transcript(s), essay or personal statement, standardized test scores, statement of good standing from prior institution(s). Minimum college GPA of 3.0 required. Lowest grade transferable B. **General Admission Information:** Application Fee $65. Early decision application deadline 12/1. Regular application deadline 1/1. Regular notification 4/1. Nonfall registration not accepted. Admission may be deferred for a maximum of 1 year. Credit and/or placement offered for CEEB Advanced Placement tests.

COSTS AND FINANCIAL AID

Annual tuition $38,550. Room and board $13,970. Required fees $1,700. Average book expense $1,800. **Required Forms and Deadlines:** FAFSA, CSS/Financial Aid PROFILE. **Notification of Awards:** Applicants will be notified of awards on or about 6/1. **Types of Aid:** *Need-based scholarships/grants:* Federal Pell, SEOG, state scholarships/grants, private scholarships, the school's own gift aid. *Loans:* Subsidized Stafford, Unsubsidized Stafford, PLUS, Federal Perkins, college/university loans from institutional funds. **Student Employment:** Federal Work-Study Program available. Institutional employment available. Off-campus job opportunities are excellent. **Financial Aid Statistics:** 100% freshmen, 100% undergrads receive need-based scholarship or grant aid. 100% freshmen, 100% undergrads receive non-need-based scholarship or grant aid. 52% freshmen, 66% undergrads receive need-based self-help aid. 100% freshmen, 100% undergrads receive any aid. 23% undergrads borrow to pay for school. Average cumulative indebtedness $15,864. **Criteria for awarding institutional aid:** *Non-need-based:* academics.

COPPIN STATE UNIVERSITY

2500 West North Avenue, Baltimore, MD 21216
Phone: 410-951-3600 • **Financial Aid Phone:** 410-951-3636
E-mail: admissions@coppin.edu • **CEEB Code:** 5122
Fax: 410-523-7351 • **Website:** WWW.COPPIN.EDU • **ACT Code:** 1688

This public school was founded in 1900. It has a 52-acre campus.

RATINGS
Admissions Selectivity Rating: 77   **Fire Safety Rating:** 74   **Green Rating:** 60*

STUDENTS AND FACULTY
Enrollment: 3,185. **Student Body:** 77% female, 23% male, 8% out-of-state, 3% international. Asian 0%, African American 95%, Caucasian 2%, Hispanic 0%, Native American 0%.
Retention and Graduation: 65% freshmen return for sophomore year. 7% freshmen graduate within 4 years. 53% freshmen graduate within 6 years. **Faculty:** Student/faculty ratio 19:1. 130 full-time faculty, 59% hold PhDs, 82% are members of minority groups, 49% are women. 0% of classes are taught by teaching assistants.

ACADEMICS
Degrees: bachelor's, master's, post-master's certificate. **Classes: Majors with Highest Enrollment:** criminal justice/law enforcement administration; management science; nursing/registered nurse (rn, asn, bsn, msn). **Special Study Options:** Accelerated program, cooperative education program, distance learning, double major, dual enrollment, external degree program, honors program, independent study, internships, liberal arts/career combination, study abroad, teacher certification program, weekend college, 3-2 programs in Engineering; Pharmacy; Denistry; Physical Therapy. **Honors Programs:** Honors Program and McNair Program. **Combined Degree Programs:** BA/MA, Dental and Pharmacy. **Disability Services:** Special programs offered to physically disabled students include reader services, tutors. **Career Services:** alumni services, career/job search classes, career assessment, internships Career Services highlights include Cooperative Education Program.

FACILITIES
Housing: Coed dorms, special housing for disabled students 75% of campus accessible to physically disabled. **Special Academic Facilities/Equipment:** Language lab, school of special education, TV studio. **Computers:** Students can register for classes online. Administrative functions (other than registration) can be performed online.

CAMPUS LIFE
Environment: City. **Activities:** Choral groups, concert band, dance, drama/theater, music ensembles, radio station, student government, student newspaper, student-run film society, television station, yearbook 28 registered organizations, 1 honor societies, 1 religious organizations. 3 fraternities, 4 sororities. **Athletics (Intercollegiate):** *Men:* baseball, basketball, cross-country, tennis, track/field (outdoor), track/field (indoor). *Women:* basketball, bowling, cheerleading, cross-country, golf, softball, tennis, track/field (outdoor), track/field (indoor), volleyball. **On-Campus Highlights:** New Dining Facility (no official naming), Tawes Building (Student Building), Greek Row (located in front of Dorms), Coppin Center (Athletic Facility)

ADMISSIONS
Freshman Academic Profile: Average high school GPA 2.8. SAT Math middle 50% range 370-450. SAT Critical Reading middle 50% range 380-460. Minimum paper TOEFL 500. **Basis for Candidate Selection:** *Very important factors considered include:* rigor of secondary school record. *Important factors considered include:* recommendation(s), standardized test scores, talent/ability. *Other factors considered include:* Class rank, application essay, alumni/ae relation, character/personal qualities, extracurricular activities, geographical residence, interview, racial/ethnic status, state residency, volunteer work, work experience. **Freshman Admission Requirements:** High school diploma is required and GED is accepted. *Academic units required:* 4 English, 3 mathematics, 2 science, (2 science labs), 2 foreign language, 3 social studies, 2 Advanced Tech Prep (alternative to Foreign language requirement. 4 English, 3 mathematics, 2 science, (2 science labs), 2 foreign language, 3 social studies, 2

Advanced Tech Prep (alternative to Foreign language requirement **Freshman Admission Statistics:** 3,075 applied, 46% admitted, 44% enrolled. **Transfer Admission Requirements:** college transcript(s), minimum college GPA of 2.0 required. Lowest grade transferable C. **General Admission Information:** Application Fee $35. Regular application deadline 7/15. Notification on a rolling basis, beginning on or about 3/15. Nonfall registration accepted. Admission may be deferred for a maximum of 1 semester. Credit and/or placement offered for CEEB Advanced Placement tests.

COSTS AND FINANCIAL AID
Required Forms and Deadlines: FAFSA. **Notification of Awards:** Applicants will be notified of awards on a rolling basis beginning 4/15. **Types of Aid:** *Need-based scholarships/grants:* Federal Pell, SEOG, state scholarships/grants, private scholarships, the school's own gift aid, United Negro College Fund, Federal Nursing Scholarships. *Loans:* Direct Subsidized Stafford, Direct Unsubsidized Stafford, Direct PLUS, PLUS, Federal Perkins, college/university loans from institutional funds, Sallie Mae's Signature Loans and Key Alternative Loan. **Student Employment:** Federal Work-Study Program available. Institutional employment available. Off-campus job opportunities are excellent. **Financial Aid Statistics:** 61% freshmen, 86% undergrads receive need-based scholarship or grant aid. 16% freshmen, 20% undergrads receive non-need-based scholarship or grant aid. 80% freshmen, 85% undergrads receive need-based self-help aid. 5% freshmen, 5% undergrads receive athletic scholarships. 90% undergrads borrow to pay for school. Average cumulative indebtedness $17,844. **Criteria for awarding institutional aid:** *Non-need-based:* academics, alumni affiliation, athletics, state/district residency.

CORBAN COLLEGE

5000 Deer Park Drive Southeast, Salem, OR 97317
Phone: 503-375-7005 • **Financial Aid Phone:** 503-375-7007
E-mail: admissions@corban.edu
Fax: 503-585-4316 • **Website:** www.corban.edu • **ACT Code:** 477

This private school, affiliated with the Baptist Church, was founded in 1935. It has a 145-acre campus.

RATINGS
Admissions Selectivity Rating: 90   **Fire Safety Rating:** 77   **Green Rating:** 60*

STUDENTS AND FACULTY
Enrollment: 983. **Student Body:** 63% female, 37% male, 42% out-of-state, 2% international (6 countries represented). Asian 3%, African American 2%, Caucasian 71%, Hispanic 5%, Native American 2%.
Retention and Graduation: 77% freshmen return for sophomore year. 42% freshmen graduate within 4 years. **Faculty:** Student/faculty ratio 14:1. 47 full-time faculty, 55% hold PhDs, 2% are members of minority groups, 26% are women. 0% of classes are taught by teaching assistants.

ACADEMICS
Degrees: associate, bachelor's, master's. **Classes:** Most classes have 10–19 students. Most lab/discussion sessions have 10–19 students. **Majors with Highest Enrollment:** business/commerce; education; psychology. **Special Study Options:** Accelerated program, cross-registration, distance learning, double major, dual enrollment, honors program, independent study, internships, liberal arts/career combination, study abroad, teacher certification program, weekend college. **Combined Degree Programs:** BA/MA, Education. **Disability Services:** Special programs offered to physically disabled students include note-taking services, reader services, tape recorders, tutors. **Career Services:** Career Services highlights include Students in business program work with local business and agencies on various projects beneficial to both.

FACILITIES
Housing: men's dorms, women's dorms, apartments for married students, apartments for single students. 80% of campus accessible to physically disabled. **Special Academic Facilities/Equipment:** Prewitt-Allen Archeological Museum. Psalms Performing Arts Center. **Computers:** Students can register for classes online.

CAMPUS LIFE
Environment: City. **Activities:** Choral groups, concert band, drama/theater, jazz band, music ensembles, student government, student newspaper, yearbook, Campus Ministries 1 honor societies, 10 religious organizations. **Athletics (Intercollegiate):** *Men:* baseball, basketball, cross-country, golf, soccer, track/field (outdoor). *Women:* basketball, cross-country, golf, soccer, softball, track/field (outdoor), volleyball. **On-Campus Highlights:** Common Grounds Coffee Shop, Dining Hall, Gymnasium and Athletic Fields, Computer Lab, Book Store, 6. Archaeological Museum, 7. Psalms Performing Arts Center.

ADMISSIONS

Freshman Academic Profile: Average high school GPA 3.6. 33% in top 10% of high school class, 60% in top 25% of high school class, 88% in top 50% of high school class. 60% from public high schools. SAT Math middle 50% range 460–580. SAT Critical Reading middle 50% range 488–610. SAT Writing middle 50% range 468–580. ACT middle 50% range 20–26. Minimum paper TOEFL 500. **Basis for Candidate Selection:** *Very important factors considered include:* application essay, academic GPA, recommendation(s), religious affiliation/commitment. *Important factors considered include:* rigor of secondary school record, standardized test scores, character/personal qualities, level of applicant's interest. *Other factors considered include:* Class rank, alumni/ae relation, extracurricular activities, interview. **Freshman Admission Requirements:** High school diploma is required and GED is accepted. **Freshman Admission Statistics:** 2,551 applied, 43% admitted, 25% enrolled. **Transfer Admission Requirements:** High school transcript, college transcript(s), essay or personal statement, minimum college GPA of 2.00 required. Lowest grade transferable C–. **General Admission Information:** Application Fee $40. Regular application deadline 8/1. Notification on a rolling basis, beginning on or about 12/1. Nonfall registration accepted. Credit offered for CEEB Advanced Placement tests.

COSTS AND FINANCIAL AID

Annual tuition $24,975. Room and board $7,980. Required fees $430. Average book expense $900. **Required Forms and Deadlines:** FAFSA. **Notification of Awards:** Applicants will be notified of awards on a rolling basis beginning 3/1. **Types of Aid:** *Need-based scholarships/grants:* Federal Pell, SEOG, state scholarships/grants, private scholarships, the school's own gift aid. *Loans:* Direct Subsidized Stafford, Direct Unsubsidized Stafford, Direct PLUS, Federal Perkins, state loans. **Student Employment:** Federal Work-Study Program available. Institutional employment available. Highest amount earned per year from on-campus jobs $1,000. Off-campus job opportunities are fair. **Financial Aid Statistics:** 100% freshmen, 100% undergrads receive need-based scholarship or grant aid. 6% freshmen, 6% undergrads receive non-need-based scholarship or grant aid. 83% freshmen, 78% undergrads receive need-based self-help aid. 5% freshmen, 5% undergrads receive athletic scholarships. 97% freshmen, 97% undergrads receive any aid. 85% undergrads borrow to pay for school. Average cumulative indebtedness $27,756. **Criteria for awarding institutional aid:** *Non-need-based:* academics, alumni affiliation, athletics, leadership, music/drama.

CORCORAN COLLEGE OF ART AND DESIGN

500 17th Street NW, Washington, DC 20006-4804
Phone: 202-639-1814 • **Financial Aid Phone:** 202-639-1816
E-mail: admissions@corcoran.org • **CEEB Code:** 5705
Fax: 202-639-1830 • **Website:** www.corcoran.edu • **ACT Code:** 671

This private school was founded in 1890. It has a 7-acre campus.

RATINGS

Admissions Selectivity Rating: 66   Fire Safety Rating: 63   Green Rating: 60*

STUDENTS AND FACULTY

Enrollment: 352. **Student Body:** 64% female, 36% male, 73% out-of-state, 11% international (20 countries represented). Asian 6%, African American 7%, Caucasian 51%, Hispanic 5%, Native American 0%. **Retention and Graduation:** 64% freshmen return for sophomore year. 23% freshmen graduate within 6 years. **Faculty:** Student/faculty ratio 4:1. 31 full-time faculty, 42% hold PhDs, 48% are women. 0% of classes are taught by teaching assistants.

ACADEMICS

Degrees: associate, bachelor's, certificate, master's. **Classes:** Most classes have fewer than 10 students. **Majors with Highest Enrollment:** fine/studio arts; graphic design; photography. **Special Study Options:** cross-registration, exchange student program (domestic), internships, study abroad. **Combined Degree Programs:** BA/MA. **Disability Services:** Special programs offered to physically disabled students include note-taking services, reader services, tape recorders, tutors. **Career Services:** Alumni network, alumni services, career/job search classes, internships.

FACILITIES

Housing: Corcoran Leased Apartments and assistance in finding area housing. 70% of campus accessible to physically disabled. **Special Academic Facilities/Equipment:** Art gallery. Student exhibition spaces **Computers:** Administrative functions (other than registration) can be performed online. Undergraduates are required to own a computer.

CAMPUS LIFE

Environment: Metropolis. **Activities:** student government, student-run film society. **On-Campus Highlights:** Corcoran Gallery, Corcoran Studios, Corcoran Cafe des Artistes.

ADMISSIONS

Freshman Academic Profile: Average high school GPA 3.2. 11% in top 10% of high school class, 50% in top 25% of high school class, 83% in top 50% of high school class. SAT Math middle 50% range 410–530. SAT Critical Reading middle 50% range 460–585. SAT Writing middle 50% range 430–540. ACT middle 50% range 16–28. Minimum paper TOEFL 550. **Basis for Candidate Selection:** *Very important factors considered include:* academic GPA, rigor of secondary school record, interview, talent/ability. *Important factors considered include:* Class rank, application essay, recommendation(s), standardized test scores. *Other factors considered include:* alumni/ae relation, character/personal qualities, extracurricular activities, volunteer work, work experience. **Freshman Admission Requirements:** High school diploma is required and GED is accepted. **Freshman Admission Statistics:** 167 applied, 90% admitted, 26% enrolled. **Transfer Admission Requirements:** High school transcript, college transcript(s), minimum college GPA of 2.5 required. Lowest grade transferable C. **General Admission Information:** Application Fee $40. Notification on a rolling basis, beginning on or about 1/1. Nonfall registration accepted. Admission may be deferred for a maximum of 1 year. Credit and/or placement offered for CEEB Advanced Placement tests.

COSTS AND FINANCIAL AID

Annual tuition $24,289. Room and board $10,795. Required fees $200. Average book expense $2,500. **Required Forms and Deadlines:** FAFSA, institution's own financial aid form. **Notification of Awards:** Applicants will be notified of awards on a rolling basis beginning 4/1. **Types of Aid:** *Need-based scholarships/grants:* Federal Pell, SEOG, state scholarships/grants, the school's own gift aid. *Loans:* Direct Subsidized Stafford, Direct Unsubsidized Stafford, Direct PLUS, Subsidized Stafford, Unsubsidized Stafford, PLUS, Federal Perkins, Alternative loans, ie: PLATO, Signature Loans. **Student Employment:** Federal Work-Study Program available. Institutional employment available. Off-campus job opportunities are excellent. **Financial Aid Statistics:** 88% freshmen, 75% undergrads receive need-based scholarship or grant aid. 92% freshmen, 52% undergrads receive non-need-based scholarship or grant aid. 100% freshmen, 92% undergrads receive need-based self-help aid. 76% undergrads borrow to pay for school. Average cumulative indebtedness $31,541. **Criteria for awarding institutional aid:** *Non-need-based:* academics, art.

CORNELL COLLEGE

600 First Street South West, Mount Vernon, IA 52314-1098
Phone: 319-895-4215 • **Financial Aid Phone:** 319-895-4216
E-mail: admissions@cornellcollege.edu • **CEEB Code:** 6119
Fax: 319-895-4451 • **Website:** www.cornellcollege.edu • **ACT Code:** 1296

This private school, affiliated with the Methodist Church, was founded in 1853. It has a 129-acre campus.

RATINGS

Admissions Selectivity Rating: 91   Fire Safety Rating: 71   Green Rating: 73

STUDENTS AND FACULTY

Enrollment: 1,174. **Student Body:** 55% female, 45% male, 83% out-of-state, 6% international (19 countries represented). Asian 4%, African American 5%, Caucasian 65%, Hispanic 11%, Native American 1%. **Retention and Graduation:** 84% freshmen return for sophomore year. 68% freshmen graduate within 4 years. 70% freshmen graduate within 6 years. **Faculty:** Student/faculty ratio 12:1. 89 full-time faculty, 96% hold PhDs, 7% are members of minority groups, 49% are women. 0% of classes are taught by teaching assistants.

ACADEMICS

Degrees: bachelor's. **Classes:** Most classes have 10–19 students. **Majors with Highest Enrollment:** economics; history; psychology. **Special Study Options:** Accelerated program, double major, English as a Second Language (ESL), exchange student program (domestic), independent study, internships, liberal arts/career combination, student-designed major, study abroad, teacher certification program. **Combined Degree Programs:** BA/MA, Engineering; Forestry and Environmental Management, Duke Universi. **Disability Services:** Special programs offered to physically disabled students include tape recorders, tutors.

Career Services: Alumni network, alumni services, career/job search classes, career assessment, internships, regional alumni. Career Services highlights include Fellowships with premier internship programs. Externship Program, 3-5 day job shadowing opportunites.

FACILITIES

Housing: Coed dorms, men's dorms, women's dorms, apartments for single students. Our first year students live on first- year only floors and/or in first-year only residence halls. 47% of campus accessible to physically disabled. **Special Academic Facilities/Equipment:** Geology center and museum, MNR machine in West Sc. Building, Luce Art Gallery. **Computers:** 100% of classrooms, 20% of dorms, 100% of libraries, 100% of dining areas, 100% of student union, 10% of common outdoor areas have wireless network access. Administrative functions (other than registration) can be performed online.

CAMPUS LIFE

Environment: Rural. **Activities:** Choral groups, concert band, dance, drama/theater, jazz band, literary magazine, music ensembles, musical theater, opera, radio station, student government, student newspaper, symphony orchestra, yearbook, Campus Ministries, International Student Organization 90 registered organizations, 11 honor societies, 11 religious organizations. 8 fraternities, 7 sororities. **Athletics (Intercollegiate):** *Men:* baseball, basketball, cross-country, football, golf, soccer, tennis, track/field (outdoor), track/field (indoor), wrestling. *Women:* basketball, cross-country, golf, soccer, softball, tennis, track/field (outdoor), track/field (indoor), volleyball. **On-Campus Highlights:** Commons - Orange Carpet - student center, Cole Library, Small Multi-Sports Center, Kimmel Theatre - new state of the art theatre, McWethy Hall - newly renovated art building, Most prodominant features on campus are our beautiful King Chapel. A newly renovated Armstrong Hall of Fine Arts. A new pedestrian mall [with outdoor ampitheatre]that connects the entire campus. **Environmental Initiatives:** Engineering study on costs of replacing current campus-side steam heat network, including specific costs and energy savings payback times for each building. Implementation of plan in two building remodels and designed into two upcoming remodel projects. Wrote and received grant for recycling facility construction and negotiating contract with cleaning service for nightly collection of recyclable categories possible in our area. Currently spec'ing biodiesel refinery to convert food service discarded oils into fuel for college equipment.

ADMISSIONS

Freshman Academic Profile: Average high school GPA 3.5. 38% in top 10% of high school class, 66% in top 25% of high school class, 91% in top 50% of high school class. SAT Math middle 50% range 540-690. SAT Critical Reading middle 50% range 535-685. SAT Writing middle 50% range 520-660. ACT middle 50% range 24-60. Minimum web-based TOEFL 79. Minimum paper TOEFL 550. **Basis for Candidate Selection:** *Very important factors considered include:* application essay, academic GPA, recommendation(s), rigor of secondary school record. *Important factors considered include:* Class rank, standardized test scores, character/personal qualities, extracurricular activities, first generation, interview, level of applicant's interest, talent/ability, volunteer work, work experience. *Other factors considered include:* alumni/ac relation, geographical residence, racial/ethnic status, state residency. **Freshman Admission Requirements:** High school diploma is required and GED is accepted. **Freshman Admission Statistics:** 2,718 applied, 53% admitted, 21% enrolled. **Transfer Admission Requirements:** college transcript(s), essay or personal statement, statement of good standing from prior institution(s). Lowest grade transferable C. **General Admission Information:** Application Fee $30. Regular application deadline 2/1. Regular notification 3/20. Nonfall registration accepted. Admission may be deferred for a maximum of 1 year. Credit and/or placement offered for CEEB Advanced Placement tests.

COSTS AND FINANCIAL AID

Annual tuition $34,480. Room and board $7,900. Required fees $225. Average book expense $800. **Required Forms and Deadlines:** FAFSA, institution's own financial aid formNoncustodial (Divorced/Separated) Parent's Statement. **Notification of Awards:** Applicants will be notified of awards on a rolling basis beginning 3/1. **Types of Aid:** *Need-based scholarships/grants:* Federal Pell, SEOG, state scholarships/grants, private scholarships, the school's own gift aid, AC, SMART, and TEACH Grants. *Loans:* Direct Subsidized Stafford, Direct Unsubsidized Stafford, Direct PLUS, Sherman Loan, United Methodist Loan. **Student Employment:** Federal Work-Study Program available. Institutional employment available. Highest amount earned per year from on-campus jobs $350. Off-campus job opportunities are fair. **Financial Aid Statistics:** 100% freshmen, 100% undergrads receive need-based scholarship or grant aid. 92% freshmen, 88% undergrads receive non-need-based scholarship or grant aid. 83% freshmen, 88% undergrads receive need-based self-help aid. 96% freshmen, 95% undergrads receive any aid. 81% undergrads borrow to pay for school. Average cumulative indebtedness $27,227. **Criteria for awarding institutional aid:** *Non-need-based:* academics, art, leadership, minority status, music/drama, religious affiliation, state/district residency.

CORNELL UNIVERSITY

Undergraduate Admissions, Ithaca, NY 14850
Phone: 607-255-5241 • **Financial Aid Phone:** 607-255-5147
E-mail: admissions@cornell.edu • **CEEB Code:** 2098
Fax: 607-255-0659 • **Website:** www.cornell.edu • **ACT Code:** 2726

This private school was founded in 1865. It has a 745-acre campus.

RATINGS
Admissions Selectivity Rating: 98 **Fire Safety Rating:** 76 **Green Rating:** 99

STUDENTS AND FACULTY
Enrollment: 14,108. **Student Body:** 50% female, 50% male, 65% out-of-state, 9% international (77 countries represented). Asian 16%, African American 6%, Caucasian 46%, Hispanic 9%, Native American 0%.
Retention and Graduation: 97% freshmen return for sophomore year. 87% freshmen graduate within 4 years. **Faculty:** Student/faculty ratio 9:1. 1646 full-time faculty, 93% hold PhDs, 17% are members of minority groups, 32% are women.

ACADEMICS
Degrees: bachelor's, master's. **Classes:** Most classes have 10–19 students. Most lab/discussion sessions have 10–19 students. **Majors with Highest Enrollment:** biology/biological sciences; hotel/motel administration/management; labor and industrial relations. **Special Study Options:** Accelerated program, cooperative education program, cross-registration, distance learning, double major, English as a Second Language (ESL), exchange student program (domestic), honors program, independent study, internships, liberal arts/career combination, student-designed major, study abroad, teacher certification program. **Disability Services:** Special programs offered to physically disabled students include note-taking services, reader services, tape recorders, tutors. **Career Services:** Alumni network, alumni services, career/job search classes, career assessment, internships, regional alumni. Career Services highlights include Two of our stellar programs, the Extern Program and FRESH, provide students the opportunity to shadow and work with alumni. This gives students a chance to broaden their horizons by exploring unfamiliar career fields or to deepen their knowledge of a career field through hands-on exposure. Either way, the programs build networking skills in students and foster positive alumni connections with the University.

FACILITIES
Housing: Coed dorms, special housing for disabled students, men's dorms, special housing for international students, women's dorms, fraternity/sorority housing, apartments for married students, cooperative housing, apartments for single students, theme housing. See http://www.campuslife.cornell.edu/campuslife/housing. **Special Academic Facilities/Equipment:** Biotechnology institute, a woods sanctuary, 4 designated national resource centers, 2 local optical observatories, Africana studies and research center, arboretum, particle accelerator, supercomputer, national research centers, performing arts center, art museum, lab of ornithology, vertebrates museum, living and learning communities, campus orchard, dairy pilot plant, mineralogical museum, animal teaching hospital, 2 agricultural experiment stations, and marine laboratory. **Computers:** 20% of classrooms, 100% of dorms, 100% of libraries, 100% of dining areas, 75% of student union, 20% of common outdoor areas have wireless network access. Students can register for classes online. Administrative functions (other than registration) can be performed online.

CAMPUS LIFE
Environment: Town. **Activities:** Choral groups, concert band, dance, drama/theater, jazz band, literary magazine, marching band, music ensembles, musical theater, pep band, radio station, student government, student newspaper, student-run film society, symphony orchestra, television station, yearbook, Campus Ministries, International Student Organization, Model UN 841 registered organizations, 22 honor societies, 61 religious organizations. 50 fraternities, 19 sororities. **Athletics (Intercollegiate):** *Men:* baseball, basketball, crew/rowing, cross-country, diving, football, golf, ice hockey, lacrosse, polo, soccer, squash, swimming, tennis, track/field (outdoor), track/field (indoor), wrestling. *Women:* basketball, crew/rowing, cross-country, diving, equestrian sports, fencing, field hockey, gymnastics, ice hockey, lacrosse, polo, soccer, softball, squash, swimming, tennis, track/field (outdoor), track/field (indoor), volleyball. **On-Campus Highlights:** Johnson Art Museum, Gorges and waterfalls bordering campus, Center for Theater Arts, Cornell Plantations, including Beebe Lak, Willard Straight Hall, http://explore.cornell.edu/. **Environmental Initiatives:** $80

million endowment of the Atkinson Center for a Sustainable Future Climate Neutrality by 2050(www.sustainablecampus.cornell.edu/climate); Energy conservation behavior-change projects led by staff.

ADMISSIONS

Freshman Academic Profile: 89% in top 10% of high school class, 98% in top 25% of high school class, 99% in top 50% of high school class. SAT Math middle 50% range 670-770. SAT Critical Reading middle 50% range 630-730. ACT middle 50% range 29-33. Minimum web-based TOEFL 100. Minimum paper TOEFL 600. **Basis for Candidate Selection:** *Very important factors considered include:* application essay, academic GPA, recommendation(s), rigor of secondary school record, standardized test scores, extracurricular activities, talent/ability. *Important factors considered include:* Class rank. *Other factors considered include:* alumni/ae relation, character/personal qualities, first generation, geographical residence, interview, racial/ethnic status, state residency, volunteer work, work experience. **Freshman Admission Requirements:** High school diploma or equivalent is not required. *Academic units required:* 4 English, 3 mathematics. *Academic units recommended:* 4 English, 3 mathematics. **Freshman Admission Statistics:** 36,387 applied, 18% admitted, 51% enrolled. **Transfer Admission Requirements:** High school transcript, college transcript(s), essay or personal statement, statement of good standing from prior institution(s). Lowest grade transferable C. **General Admission Information:** Application Fee $70. Early decision application deadline 11/1. Regular application deadline 1/2. Regular notification 4/1. Nonfall registration not accepted. Credit and/or placement offered for CEEB Advanced Placement tests.

COSTS AND FINANCIAL AID

Annual tuition $43,185. Room and board $13,678. Required fees $228. Average book expense $820. **Required Forms and Deadlines:** FAFSA, institution's own financial aid form, CSS/Financial Aid PROFILE, noncustodial PROFILE, business/farm supplement. Prior Year Tax Forms. **Notification of Awards:** Applicants will be notified of awards on or about 4/1. **Types of Aid:** *Need-based scholarships/grants:* Federal Pell, SEOG, state scholarships/grants, private scholarships, the school's own gift aid. *Loans:* Direct Subsidized Stafford, Direct Unsubsidized Stafford, Direct PLUS, Subsidized Stafford, Unsubsidized Stafford, PLUS, Federal Perkins, college/university loans from institutional funds. **Student Employment:** Federal Work-Study Program available. Institutional employment available. Highest amount earned per year from on-campus jobs $2,500. Off-campus job opportunities are fair. **Financial Aid Statistics:** 98% freshmen, 98% undergrads receive need-based scholarship or grant aid. 86% freshmen, 92% undergrads receive need-based self-help aid. 48% freshmen, 50% undergrads receive any aid. 50% undergrads borrow to pay for school. Average cumulative indebtedness $19,180.

CORNERSTONE UNIVERSITY

1001 East Beltline Avenue, NE, Grand Rapids, MI 49525-5897
Phone: 616-222-1418 • **Financial Aid Phone:** 616-949-5300
E-mail: admissions@cornerstone.edu
Fax: 616-222-1418 • **Website:** www.cornerstone.edu • **ACT Code:** 2002

This private school, affiliated with the Christian (Nondenominational) Church, was founded in 1941. It has a 130-acre campus.

RATINGS

Admissions Selectivity Rating: 70   Fire Safety Rating: 96   Green Rating: 68

STUDENTS AND FACULTY

Enrollment: 1,741. **Student Body:** 59% female, 41% male, 16% out-of-state, 1% international (15 countries represented). Asian 1%, African American 11%, Caucasian 83%, Hispanic 4%, Native American 0%.
Retention and Graduation: 69% freshmen return for sophomore year. 15% grads go on to further study within 1 year. 10% grads pursue arts and sciences degrees. 1% grads pursue law degrees. 3% grads pursue business degrees. 1% grads pursue medical degrees. **Faculty:** Student/faculty ratio 13:1. 62 full-time faculty, 50% hold PhDs, 5% are members of minority groups, 32% are women. 0% of classes are taught by teaching assistants.

ACADEMICS

Degrees: associate, bachelor's, certificate, diploma, first professional, master's, terminal associate. **Classes:** Most classes have 10–19 students. **Majors with Highest Enrollment:** elementary education and teaching; mass communication/media studies; youth ministry. **Special Study Options:** Accelerated program, distance learning, double major, dual enrollment, English as a Second Language (ESL), honors program, independent study, internships, liberal arts/career combination, study abroad, teacher certification program, weekend college. **Honors Programs:** Honors Program based on a "great books" cur-

riculum. **Disability Services:** Special programs offered to physically disabled students include note-taking services, reader services, tape recorders, tutors. **Career Services:** career/job search classes, career assessment, internships Career Services highlights include The required internship of all students as part of the graduation requirements.

FACILITIES

Housing: special housing for disabled students, men's dorms, women's dorms, apartments for married students, apartments for single students, theme housing, 100% of campus accessible to physically disabled. **Computers:** 100% of classrooms, 100% of dorms, 100% of libraries, 100% of dining areas, 100% of student union, 100% of common outdoor areas have wireless network access. Students can register for classes online. Administrative functions (other than registration) can be performed online.

CAMPUS LIFE

Environment: City. **Activities:** Choral groups, concert band, dance, drama/theater, jazz band, literary magazine, music ensembles, musical theater, opera, pep band, radio station, student government, student newspaper, student-run film society, Campus Ministries, International Student Organization 11 registered organizations, 2 honor societies, 1 religious organizations. **Athletics (Intercollegiate):** *Men:* basketball, cross-country, golf, soccer, track/field (outdoor), track/field (indoor). *Women:* basketball, cross-country, golf, soccer, softball, track/field (outdoor), track/field (indoor), volleyball. **On-Campus Highlights:** Corum Student Union, Bernice Hansen Athletic Center, Campus Bookstore Atrium, Faber Hall Seating Area, Gordon Music Hall. **Environmental Initiatives:** On campus dialogue and focus on sustainability issues, joining a community organization.

ADMISSIONS

Freshman Academic Profile: Average high school GPA 3.3. 60% from public high schools. SAT Math middle 50% range 440-540. SAT Critical Reading middle 50% range 360-580. SAT Writing middle 50% range 480-500. ACT middle 50% range 20-25. Minimum paper TOEFL 500. **Basis for Candidate Selection:** *Very important factors considered include:* application essay, academic GPA, recommendation(s), standardized test scores, character/personal qualities, religious affiliation/commitment. *Important factors considered include:* Class rank, rigor of secondary school record. *Other factors considered include:* level of applicant's interest. **Freshman Admission Requirements:** High school diploma is required and GED is accepted. **Freshman Admission Statistics:** 939 applied, 75% admitted, 31% enrolled. **Transfer Admission Requirements:** High school transcript, college transcript(s), essay or personal statement, minimum college GPA of 2.0 required. Lowest grade transferable C–. **General Admission Information:** Application Fee $25. Nonfall registration accepted. Credit and/or placement offered for CEEB Advanced Placement tests.

COSTS AND FINANCIAL AID

Annual tuition $19,190. Room and board $6,500. Required fees $340. Average book expense $1,000. **Required Forms and Deadlines:** FAFSA. **Notification of Awards:** Applicants will be notified on a rolling basis beginning 2/15. **Types of Aid:** *Need-based scholarships/grants:* Federal Pell, SEOG, state scholarships/grants, private scholarships, the school's own gift aid. *Loans:* Subsidized Stafford, Unsubsidized Stafford, PLUS, Federal Perkins. **Student Employment:** Federal Work-Study Program available. Highest amount earned per year from on-campus jobs $5,500. Off-campus job opportunities are good. **Financial Aid Statistics:** 100% freshmen, 99% undergrads receive need-based scholarship or grant aid. 100% freshmen, 94% undergrads receive non-need-based scholarship or grant aid. 81% freshmen, 79% undergrads receive need-based self-help aid. 23% freshmen, 15% undergrads receive athletic scholarships. 100% freshmen, 98% undergrads receive any aid. 77% undergrads borrow to pay for school. Average cumulative indebtedness $28,074. **Criteria for awarding institutional aid:** *Non-need-based:* academics, athletics, leadership, music/drama, state/district residency.

CORNISH COLLEGE OF THE ARTS

1000 Lenora Street, Seattle, WA 98121
Phone: 206-726-5016 • **Financial Aid Phone:** 206-726-5013
E-mail: admissions@cornish.edu • **CEEB Code:** 58
Fax: 206-720-1011 • **Website:** www.cornish.edu • **ACT Code:** 4801

This private school was founded in 1914. It has a 4-acre campus.

RATINGS

Admissions Selectivity Rating: 62   Fire Safety Rating: 60*   Green Rating: 60*

STUDENTS AND FACULTY

Enrollment: 788. **Student Body:** 62% female, 38% male, 46% out-of-state, 3% international (6 countries represented). Asian 6%, African American 3%, Caucasian 67%, Hispanic 8%, Native American 1%.
Retention and Graduation: 65% freshmen return for sophomore year. 41% freshmen graduate within 4 years. 12% grads go on to further study within 1 year. 5% grads pursue arts and sciences degrees. **Faculty:** Student/faculty ratio 8:1. full-time faculty.

ACADEMICS

Degrees: bachelor's. **Classes:** Most classes have 10–19 students. **Majors with Highest Enrollment:** design and visual communications; drama and dramatics/theatre arts; fine/studio arts. **Special Study Options:** cooperative education program, independent study, internships, study abroad. **Disability Services:** Special programs offered to physically disabled students include note-taking services, tape recorders. **Career Services:** internships.

FACILITIES

Housing: 50% of campus accessible to physically disabled. **Special Academic Facilities/Equipment:** Art galleries, extensive art studio space, theatres, electronic music studio, dance studio, concert hall.

CAMPUS LIFE

Environment: Metropolis. **Activities:** Choral groups, concert band, dance, drama/theater, jazz band, literary magazine, music ensembles, musical theater, opera, student government, student newspaper, student-run film society 18 registered organizations, 6 honor societies, 1 religious organizations. **On-Campus Highlights:** Raisbeck Performance Hall, Cornsh Gallery, Nellie's Cafe.

ADMISSIONS

Freshman Academic Profile: Average high school GPA 3.1. 75% from public high schools. ACT middle 50% range 122-999. Minimum paper TOEFL 525. **Basis for Candidate Selection:** *Very important factors considered include:* talent/ability. *Important factors considered include:* application essay, rigor of secondary school record. *Other factors considered include:* recommendation(s), standardized test scores, extracurricular activities, interview. **Freshman Admission Requirements:** High school diploma is required and GED is accepted. **Freshman Admission Statistics:** 602 applied, 81% admitted, 51% enrolled. **Transfer Admission Requirements:** High school transcript, college transcript(s), essay or personal statement, interview, minimum college GPA of 2.0 required. Lowest grade transferable C. **General Admission Information:** Application Fee $35. Regular application deadline 2/15. Notification on a rolling basis, beginning on or about 1/1. Nonfall registration not accepted. Admission may be deferred for a maximum of 12 months. Credit offered for CEEB Advanced Placement tests.

COSTS AND FINANCIAL AID

Annual tuition $31,980. Room and board $0. **Required Forms and Deadlines:** FAFSA, institution's own financial aid form. **Notification of Awards:** Applicants will be notified of awards on or about 5/15. **Types of Aid:** *Need-based scholarships/grants:* Federal Pell, SEOG, state scholarships/grants, Merit scholarships based on artistic merit and merit w/need scholarships Both are institutional money. *Loans:* Subsidized Stafford, Unsubsidized Stafford, PLUS, Federal Perkins. **Student Employment:** Federal Work-Study Program available. Highest amount earned per year from on-campus jobs $3,000. Off-campus job opportunities are excellent. **Financial Aid Statistics:** 84% undergrads receive need-based scholarship or grant aid. 100% undergrads receive non-need-based scholarship or grant aid. 84% undergrads receive need-based self-help aid. Average cumulative indebtedness $23,000. **Criteria for awarding institutional aid:** *Non-need-based:* academics, art, music/drama.

COVENANT COLLEGE

14049 Scenic Highway, Lookout Mtn., GA 30750
Phone: 706-820-2398 • **Financial Aid Phone:** 706-419-1126
E-mail: admissions@covenant.edu • **CEEB Code:** 6124
Fax: 706-820-0893 • **Website:** www.covenant.edu • **ACT Code:** 3951

This private school was founded in 1955. It has a 300-acre campus.

RATINGS

Admissions Selectivity Rating: 89   **Fire Safety Rating:** 79   **Green Rating:** 60*

STUDENTS AND FACULTY

Enrollment: 1,027. **Student Body:** 57% female, 43% male, 76% out-of-state, 2% international (21 countries represented). Asian 2%, African American 3%, Caucasian 89%, Hispanic 2%, Native American 0%.

Retention and Graduation: 87% freshmen return for sophomore year. 55% freshmen graduate within 4 years. 61% freshmen graduate within 6 years. 28% grads go on to further study within 1 year. 10% grads pursue arts and sciences degrees. 1% grads pursue law degrees. 2% grads pursue business degrees. 1% grads pursue medical degrees. **Faculty:** Student/faculty ratio 13:1. 67 full-time faculty, 88% hold PhDs, 9% are members of minority groups, 19% are women. 0% of classes are taught by teaching assistants.

ACADEMICS

Degrees: associate, bachelor's, master's. **Classes:** Most classes have 10–19 students. Most lab/discussion sessions have 20–29 students. **Majors with Highest Enrollment:** elementary education and teaching; English language and literature; sociology. **Special Study Options:** double major, dual enrollment, exchange student program (domestic), independent study, internships, student-designed major, study abroad, teacher certification program, Dual-engineering degree with Georgia Tech; cooperative nursing program with Emory University and Chattanooga State; bridge program for MSN with Vanderbilt University. **Disability Services:** Special programs offered to physically disabled students include note-taking services, tape recorders. **Career Services:** Alumni network, alumni services, career assessment, internships, Career Services highlights include Internship program.

FACILITIES

Housing: men's dorms, women's dorms, apartments for single students. 95% of campus accessible to physically disabled. **Computers:** 100% of classrooms, 100% of dorms, 100% of libraries, 100% of dining areas, NA% of student union, 100% of common outdoor areas have wireless network access. Students can register for classes online. Administrative functions (other than registration) can be performed online.

CAMPUS LIFE

Environment: City. **Activities:** Choral groups, concert band, drama/theater, jazz band, literary magazine, music ensembles, radio station, student government, student newspaper, yearbook 40 registered organizations, 4 honor societies, 1 religious organizations. **Athletics (Intercollegiate):** *Men:* baseball, basketball, cross-country, golf, soccer, tennis. *Women:* basketball, cross-country, golf, soccer, softball, tennis, volleyball. **On-Campus Highlights:** Probasco Visitor's Center, Carter Hall, The Overlook, The Chapel, Ashe Gym, The campus is located on top of Lookout Mountain in Georgia, providing a backdrop of scenic beauty.

ADMISSIONS

Freshman Academic Profile: Average high school GPA 3.6. 31% in top 10% of high school class, 47% in top 25% of high school class, 84% in top 50% of high school class. 42% from public high schools. SAT Math middle 50% range 530-630. SAT Critical Reading middle 50% range 530-670. SAT Writing middle 50% range 530-650. ACT middle 50% range 23-28. Minimum web-based TOEFL 76. Minimum paper TOEFL 540. **Basis for Candidate Selection:** *Very important factors considered include:* application essay, academic GPA, recommendation(s), rigor of secondary school record, standardized test scores, character/personal qualities. *Important factors considered include:* interview. *Other factors considered include:* Class rank, alumni/ae relation, extracurricular activities, first generation, level of applicant's interest, racial/ethnic status, religious affiliation/commitment, volunteer work. **Freshman Admission Requirements:** High school diploma is required and GED is accepted. *Academic units required:* 4 English, 3 mathematics, 2 science, 2 social studies, 3 academic electives. *Academic units recommended:* 4 English, 3 mathematics, 2 science, 2 social studies, 3 academic electives. **Freshman Admission Statistics:** 1,129 applied, 57% admitted, 42% enrolled. **Transfer Admission Requirements:** High school transcript, college transcript(s), essay or personal statement, interview, standardized test scores, statement of good standing from prior institution(s). Minimum college GPA of 2.0 required. Lowest grade transferable C-. **General Admission Information:** Application Fee $35. Notification on a rolling basis, beginning on or about 8/1. Nonfall registration accepted. Admission may be deferred for a maximum of 1 year. Credit offered for CEEB Advanced Placement tests.

COSTS AND FINANCIAL AID

Annual tuition $27,500. Room and board $8,040. Required fees $770. Average book expense $1,000. **Required Forms and Deadlines:** FAFSA, state aid form. **Notification of Awards:** Applicants will be notified of awards on a rolling basis beginning 2/1. **Types of Aid:** *Need-based scholarships/grants:* Federal Pell, SEOG, state scholarships/grants, private scholarships, the school's own gift aid. *Loans:* Subsidized Stafford, Unsubsidized Stafford, PLUS, Federal Perkins, state loans, college/university loans from institutional funds. **Student Employment:** Federal Work-Study Program available. Institutional employment available. Highest amount earned per year from on-campus jobs $3,840. Off-campus job opportunities are good. **Financial Aid Statistics:** 99% freshmen, 99% undergrads receive need-based scholarship or grant aid. 89% freshmen, 89% undergrads receive need-based self-help aid. 100% freshmen, 99% undergrads receive any aid. 66% undergrads borrow to pay for school. Average cumulative indebtedness $22,861. **Criteria for awarding institutional aid:** *Non-need-based:* academics, alumni affiliation, art, athletics, job skills, leadership, minority status, music/drama, religious affiliation, state/district residency.

CREIGHTON UNIVERSITY

2500 California Plaza, Omaha, NE 68178
Phone: 402-280-2703 • **Financial Aid Phone:** 402-280-2731
E-mail: admissions@creighton.edu • **CEEB Code:** 6121
Fax: 402-280-2685 • **Website:** www.creighton.edu • **ACT Code:** 2444

This private school, affiliated with the Roman Catholic Church, was founded in 1878. It has a 130-acre campus.

RATINGS
Admissions Selectivity Rating: 87   Fire Safety Rating: 89   Green Rating: 84

STUDENTS AND FACULTY
Enrollment: 4,032. **Student Body:** 59% female, 41% male, 68% out-of-state, 2% international (42 countries represented). Asian 10%, African American 3%, Caucasian 74%, Hispanic 6%, Native American 0%.
Retention and Graduation: 90% freshmen return for sophomore year. 68% freshmen graduate within 4 years. 74% freshmen graduate within 6 years. 36% grads go on to further study within 1 year. 10% grads pursue arts and sciences degrees. 9% grads pursue law degrees. 9% grads pursue business degrees. 13% grads pursue medical degrees. **Faculty:** Student/faculty ratio 12:1. 534 full-time faculty, 91% hold PhDs, 13% are members of minority groups, 41% are women. 0% of classes are taught by teaching assistants.

ACADEMICS
Degrees: associate, bachelor's, certificate, master's. **Classes:** Most classes have 20–29 students. Most lab/discussion sessions have 10–19 students. **Majors with Highest Enrollment:** business/commerce; health/medical preparatory programs, other; psychology. **Special Study Options:** Accelerated program, cross-registration, distance learning, double major, dual enrollment, English as a Second Language (ESL), exchange student program (domestic), honors program, independent study, internships, liberal arts/career combination, study abroad, teacher certification program, 3-3 Engineering Program with University of Detroit Mercy; 3-3 Law Program within Creighton University. **Honors Programs:** Designed for talented, imaginative students desirous of participation in small, iscussion-oriented classes and in courses on interdisciplinary and topical issues. **Combined Degree Programs:** BA/JD, BA/DDS, BA/MEng. **Disability Services:** Special programs offered to physically disabled students include note-taking services, reader services, tape recorders, tutors. **Career Services:** Alumni network, alumni services, career/job search classes, career assessment, internships, regional alumni. Career Services highlights include Intership web site: http://www2.creighton.edu/careercenter/internships/internshipsearchsites/index.php.

FACILITIES
Housing: Coed dorms, special housing for disabled students, women's dorms, apartments for married students, apartments for single students, Honors. Freshman Leadership. 97% of campus accessible to physically disabled. **Special Academic Facilities/Equipment:** Fine arts/performing center, health science and research complex, hospital. **Computers:** 100% of classrooms, 100% of dorms, 100% of libraries, 100% of dining areas, 100% of student union, 100% of common outdoor areas have wireless network access. Students can register for classes online. Administrative functions (other than registration) can be performed online.

CAMPUS LIFE
Environment: Metropolis. **Activities:** Choral groups, concert band, dance, drama/theater, jazz band, literary magazine, music ensembles, musical theater, pep band, student government, student newspaper, symphony orchestra, television station, yearbook, Campus Ministries, International Student Organization, Model UN 182 registered organizations, 11 honor societies, 6 religious organizations. 5 fraternities, 8 sororities. **Athletics (Intercollegiate):** *Men:* baseball, basketball, cross-country, golf, soccer, tennis. *Women:* basketball, crew/rowing, cross-country, golf, soccer, softball, tennis, volleyball. **On-Campus Highlights:** Harper Living Learning Center, Campus Mall and green in front of Studen, Hixson-Lied Science Building, Morrison Soccer stadium, Jesuit Gardens, Ryan Athletics Center and D.J. Sokol Auditorium completed Fall 2009. **Environ-

mental Initiatives:** The University has continued to expand renewable energy sources including the solar array in Nebraska, four wind turbines designed for urban environments, geothermal hearing, low volateg lighting and solar hot water. The enhanced recycling program is directed toward a single stream of recycle commodity collection. This includes entry in Recyclemania. We are actively involved in promoting sustainability in our community. The university started a forum of like-minded universities across the region; we hold these meetings quarterly. Not only do we have a community garden for faculty, staff and students bu we provide land to a local neighborhood association to host their community garden.

ADMISSIONS
Freshman Academic Profile: Average high school GPA 3.8. 40% in top 10% of high school class, 72% in top 25% of high school class, 93% in top 50% of high school class. 52% from public high schools. SAT Math middle 50% range 540-660. SAT Critical Reading middle 50% range 530-630. SAT Writing middle 50% range 520-630. ACT middle 50% range 24-29. Minimum web-based TOEFL 80. **Basis for Candidate Selection:** *Very important factors considered include:* academic GPA, rigor of secondary school record. *Important factors considered include:* application essay, standardized test scores. *Other factors considered include:* Class rank, recommendation(s), character/personal qualities, extracurricular activities, first generation, level of applicant's interest, racial/ethnic status, talent/ability, volunteer work. **Freshman Admission Requirements:** High school diploma is required and GED is accepted. *Academic units required:* 4 English, 3 mathematics, 2 science, 2 foreign language, 2 social studies, 3 academic electives. *Academic units recommended:* 4 English, 3 mathematics, 2 science, 2 foreign language, 2 social studies, 3 academic electives. **Freshman Admission Statistics:** 5,361 applied, 78% admitted, 23% enrolled. **Transfer Admission Requirements:** High school transcript, college transcript(s), statement of good standing from prior institution(s). Minimum college GPA of 2.50 required. Lowest grade transferable C. **General Admission Information:** Application Fee $40. Regular application deadline 2/15. Notification on a rolling basis, beginning on or about 12/15. Nonfall registration accepted. Admission may be deferred for a maximum of 12 months. Credit and/or placement offered for CEEB Advanced Placement tests.

COSTS AND FINANCIAL AID
Room and board $9,446. Required fees $1,474. Average book expense $1,200. **Required Forms and Deadlines:** FAFSA, institution's own financial aid form. **Notification of Awards:** Applicants will be notified of awards on a rolling basis beginning 3/15. **Types of Aid:** *Need-based scholarships/grants:* Federal Pell, SEOG, state scholarships/grants, private scholarships, the school's own gift aid. *Loans:* Subsidized Stafford, Unsubsidized Stafford, PLUS, Federal Perkins, Federal Nursing. **Student Employment:** Federal Work-Study Program available. Institutional employment available. Highest amount earned per year from on-campus jobs $1,400. Off-campus job opportunities are excellent. **Financial Aid Statistics:** 100% freshmen, 98% undergrads receive need-based scholarship or grant aid. 94% freshmen, 76% undergrads receive non-need-based scholarship or grant aid. 75% freshmen, 76% undergrads receive need-based self-help aid. 6% freshmen, 5% undergrads receive athletic scholarships. 95% freshmen, 89% undergrads receive any aid. 61% undergrads borrow to pay for school. Average cumulative indebtedness $36,333. **Criteria for awarding institutional aid:** *Non-need-based:* academics, alumni affiliation, art, athletics, leadership, minority status, music/drama.

CROWN COLLEGE

8700 College View Drive, St. Bonifacius, MN 55375-9001
Phone: 952-446-4142 • **Financial Aid Phone:** 952-446-4175
E-mail: info@crown.edu
Fax: 952-446-4149 • **Website:** www.crown.edu • **ACT Code:** 2152

This private school, affiliated with the Christian & Missionary Alliance Church, was founded in 1916. It has a 215-acre campus.

RATINGS
Admissions Selectivity Rating: 74   Fire Safety Rating: 65   Green Rating: 60*

STUDENTS AND FACULTY
Enrollment: 1,017. **Student Body:** 57% female, 43% male, 31% out-of-state, 1% international (21 countries represented). Asian 7%, African American 4%, Caucasian 78%, Hispanic 2%, Native American 1%.
Retention and Graduation: 63% freshmen return for sophomore year. 40% freshmen graduate within 4 years. 52% freshmen graduate within 6 years.
Faculty: Student/faculty ratio 14:1. 34 full-time faculty, 47% hold PhDs, 6% are members of minority groups, 26% are women. 0% of classes are taught by teaching assistants.

ACADEMICS

Degrees: associate, bachelor's, certificate, master's, post-bachelor's certificate.
Classes: Most classes have 10–19 students. Most lab/discussion sessions have 20–29 students. **Majors with Highest Enrollment:** elementary education and teaching; nursing/registered nurse (rn, asn, bsn, msn); religious education.
Special Study Options: Accelerated program, distance learning, double major, dual enrollment, English as a Second Language (ESL), honors program, independent study, internships, study abroad, teacher certification program, weekend college, 2-2 with non-accredited Bible colleges. **Honors Programs:** The Honors Program. **Disability Services:** Special programs offered to physically disabled students include note-taking services, reader services, tape recorders, tutors. **Career Services:** alumni services, career/job search classes, career assessment, internships Career Services highlights include We are very excited about the number of opportunities that students have to engage in practical hands-on learning activities through the SIFE and practicum programs.

FACILITIES

Housing: special housing for disabled students, men's dorms, women's dorms, apartments for married students, apartments for single students, apartments for students with dependent children. 95% of campus accessible to physically disabled. **Special Academic Facilities/Equipment:** Peter Watne Memorial Library **Computers:** 100% of classrooms, 20% of dorms, 100% of libraries, 100% of dining areas, 100% of student union, 10% of common outdoor areas have wireless network access. Administrative functions (other than registration) can be performed online.

CAMPUS LIFE

Environment: Rural. **Activities:** Choral groups, concert band, drama/theater, jazz band, literary magazine, music ensembles, musical theater, pep band, radio station, student government, student newspaper, student-run film society, yearbook, Campus Ministries, International Student Organization 19 registered organizations, 1 honor societies, 6 religious organizations. **Athletics (Intercollegiate):** *Men:* baseball, basketball, cross-country, football, golf, soccer. *Women:* basketball, cross-country, golf, soccer, softball, volleyball. **On-Campus Highlights:** Student Center, Coffee Shoppe and Climbing Wall, Storm Cafe/student union, Wild Athletic Center/Weight Room, Life Fitness Center. **Environmental Initiatives:** The College recycles all cardboard and provides co-mingled recycling containers in all common areas, each classroom, and in each office. We post recycling program notes on our website from time to time and also posters throughout the building quarterly. Large amounts of metals, plastics, light bulbs, electronics, etc. are recycled each month by facilities mgmt. Low flow toilets are used to replace older units as needed and all water fixtures are being replaced with low flow units. All water heaters and HVAC components are being replaced (both planned and unplanned) with high-efficiency units Appliance replacement cycles utilize high-efficiency appliances (stoves, refrigerators, etc). We are working to integrate all campus building systems to one central control system in order to decrease our energy footprint.

ADMISSIONS

Freshman Academic Profile: Average high school GPA 3.4. 13% in top 10% of high school class, 38% in top 25% of high school class, 79% in top 50% of high school class. SAT Math middle 50% range 475-598. SAT Critical Reading middle 50% range 508-600. SAT Writing middle 50% range 533-618. ACT middle 50% range 21-25. Minimum web-based TOEFL 75. Minimum paper TOEFL 500. **Basis for Candidate Selection:** *Very important factors considered include:* application essay, academic GPA, recommendation(s), rigor of secondary school record, standardized test scores, religious affiliation/commitment. *Important factors considered include:* Class rank, character/personal qualities. *Other factors considered include:* extracurricular activities, interview, level of applicant's interest, talent/ability, volunteer work, work experience. **Freshman Admission Requirements:** High school diploma is required and GED is accepted. **Freshman Admission Statistics:** 453 applied, 78% admitted, 42% enrolled. **Transfer Admission Requirements:** High school transcript, college transcript(s), essay or personal statement, minimum college GPA of 2.0 required. Lowest grade transferable C. **General Admission Information:** Application Fee $35. Regular application deadline 8/20. Nonfall registration accepted. Admission may be deferred for a maximum of 1 year. Credit offered for CEEB Advanced Placement tests.

COSTS AND FINANCIAL AID

Annual tuition $22,100. Room and board $7,480. Average book expense $1,140. **Required Forms and Deadlines:** FAFSA, institution's own financial aid form. **Notification of Awards:** Applicants will be notified of awards on a rolling basis beginning 4/1. **Types of Aid:** *Need-based scholarships/grants:* Federal Pell, SEOG, state scholarships/grants, private scholarships, the school's own gift aid. *Loans:* Subsidized Stafford, Unsubsidized Stafford, PLUS, Federal Perkins, state loans, US Bank No Fee Education loans, CitiAssist loans, Signature loans, Wells Fargo Collegiate Loan. **Student Employment:** Federal Work-Study Program available. Off-campus job opportunities are good. **Financial Aid Statistics:** 84% freshmen, 83% undergrads receive any aid. 82% undergrads borrow to pay for school. Average cumulative indebtedness $35,356. **Criteria**

for awarding institutional aid: Non-need-based: academics, alumni affiliation, leadership, minority status, music/drama, religious affiliation.

CULVER-STOCKTON COLLEGE

One College Hill, Canton, MO 63435
Phone: 573-288-6331 • **Financial Aid Phone:** 573-288-6307
E-mail: admissions@culver.edu • **CEEB Code:** 6123
Fax: 573-288-6618 • **ACT Code:** 2290

This private school, affiliated with the Disciples of Christ Church, was founded in 1853. It has a 139-acre campus.

RATINGS

Admissions Selectivity Rating: 72   **Fire Safety Rating:** 64   **Green Rating:** 60*

STUDENTS AND FACULTY

Enrollment: 749. **Student Body:** 47% female, 53% male, 46% out-of-state, 2% international (13 countries represented). Asian 0%, African American 12%, Caucasian 80%, Hispanic 4%, Native American 1%.
Retention and Graduation: 68% freshmen return for sophomore year. 42% freshmen graduate within 4 years. 16% grads go on to further study within 1 year. 6% grads pursue arts and sciences degrees. 2% grads pursue law degrees. 4% grads pursue business degrees. 1% grads pursue medical degrees. **Faculty:** Student/faculty ratio 12:1. 49 full-time faculty, 69% hold PhDs, 4% are members of minority groups, 45% are women. 0% of classes are taught by teaching assistants.

ACADEMICS

Degrees: bachelor's. **Classes:** Most classes have 10–19 students. Most lab/discussion sessions have 10–19 students. **Majors with Highest Enrollment:** business administration and management; elementary education and teaching; nursing/registered nurse (rn, asn, bsn, msn). **Special Study Options:** Accelerated program, distance learning, double major, dual enrollment, honors program, independent study, internships, liberal arts/career combination, student-designed major, study abroad, teacher certification program. **Honors Programs:** Honors Scholars are expected to complete both an academic and enrollment requirement. **Combined Degree Programs:** BA/MA, Washington University-OT program. **Disability Services:** Special programs offered to physically disabled students include note-taking services, reader services, tape recorders, tutors. **Career Services:** Alumni network, alumni services, career/job search classes, career assessment, internships, regional alumni. Career Services highlights include All students participate in experiential learning since fall 2008 as part of the new CSC@EXP curriculum.

FACILITIES

Housing: Coed dorms, fraternity/sorority housing. 40% of campus accessible to physically disabled. **Special Academic Facilities/Equipment:** Art gallery, performing arts center. **Computers:** 100% of classrooms, 100% of dorms, 100% of libraries, 100% of dining areas, 100% of student union, 100% of common outdoor areas have wireless network access. Students can register for classes online. Administrative functions (other than registration) can be performed online.

CAMPUS LIFE

Environment: Rural. **Activities:** Choral groups, concert band, dance, drama/theater, jazz band, literary magazine, music ensembles, musical theater, pep band, radio station, student government, student newspaper, Campus Ministries, International Student Organization, Model UN 44 registered organizations, 11 honor societies, 4 religious organizations. 4 fraternities, 3 sororities. **Athletics (Intercollegiate):** *Men:* baseball, basketball, cheerleading, cross-country, football, golf, soccer, track/field (outdoor), track/field (indoor). *Women:* basketball, cheerleading, cross-country, golf, soccer, softball, track/field (outdoor), track/field (indoor), volleyball. **On-Campus Highlights:** Computer labs, Cat's 'Pause', Cafeteria, Joe Charles Field House, Activity & Recreation Center. **Environmental Initiatives:** Thermostat control Sustainability focus group Limited use of disposable containers and removal of cafeteria trays

ADMISSIONS

Freshman Academic Profile: Average high school GPA 3.2. 10% in top 10% of high school class, 29% in top 25% of high school class, 66% in top 50% of high school class. 89% from public high schools. SAT Math middle 50% range 390-500. SAT Critical Reading middle 50% range 380-510. ACT middle 50% range 18-23. Minimum web-based TOEFL 79. Minimum paper TOEFL 550. **Basis for Candidate Selection:** *Very important factors considered include:* academic GPA, standardized test scores. *Important factors considered include:* rigor of secondary school record. *Other factors considered include:* application essay, recommendation(s), alumni/ae relation. **Freshman Admission Requirements:** High school diploma is required and GED is accepted. **Freshman Admission Statistics:** 1,162 applied, 62% admitted, 30% enrolled.

Transfer Admission Requirements: college transcript(s), minimum college GPA of 2.0 required. Lowest grade transferable C–. **General Admission Information:** Notification on a rolling basis, beginning on or about 10/15. Nonfall registration accepted. Admission may be deferred for a maximum of 1 year. Credit and/or placement offered for CEEB Advanced Placement tests.

COSTS AND FINANCIAL AID

Annual tuition $22,250. Room and board $7,600. Required fees $300. Average book expense $1,000. **Required Forms and Deadlines:** FAFSA. **Notification of Awards:** Applicants will be notified of awards on a rolling basis beginning 2/15. **Types of Aid:** *Need-based scholarships/grants:* Federal Pell, SEOG, state scholarships/grants, private scholarships, the school's own gift aid. *Loans:* Direct Subsidized Stafford, Direct Unsubsidized Stafford, Direct PLUS, PLUS, Federal Perkins, state loans, college/university loans from institutional funds. **Student Employment:** Federal Work-Study Program available. Institutional employment available. Highest amount earned per year from on-campus jobs $4,954. Off-campus job opportunities are fair. **Financial Aid Statistics:** 100% freshmen, 100% undergrads receive need-based scholarship or grant aid. 15% freshmen, 12% undergrads receive non-need-based scholarship or grant aid. 87% freshmen, 89% undergrads receive need-based self-help aid. 13% freshmen, 11% undergrads receive athletic scholarships. 99% freshmen, 99% undergrads receive any aid. 85% undergrads borrow to pay for school. Average cumulative indebtedness $24,859. **Criteria for awarding institutional aid:** *Non-need-based:* academics, alumni affiliation, art, athletics, job skills, leadership, music/drama, religious affiliation, state/district residency.

CUMBERLAND UNIVERSITY

Cumberland University, Lebanon, TN 37087-3408
Phone: 615-444-2562
E-mail: admissions@cumberland.edu • **CEEB Code:** 1146
Fax: 615-444-2569 • **Website:** www.cumberland.edu • **ACT Code:** 3954

This private school was founded in 1842. It has a 40-acre campus.

RATINGS
Admissions Selectivity Rating: 71   **Fire Safety Rating:** 64   **Green Rating:** 60*

STUDENTS AND FACULTY
Enrollment: 921. **Student Body:** 57% female, 43% male, 15% out-of-state, 3% international (27 countries represented). Asian 2%, African American 14%, Caucasian 77%, Hispanic 1%, Native American 0%.
Retention and Graduation: 69% freshmen return for sophomore year. 23% freshmen graduate within 4 years. 37% freshmen graduate within 6 years. 15% grads go on to further study within 1 year. 5% grads pursue arts and sciences degrees. 3% grads pursue law degrees. 5% grads pursue business degrees. 1% grads pursue medical degrees. **Faculty:** Student/faculty ratio 13:1. 79 full-time faculty, 57% hold PhDs, 5% are members of minority groups, 38% are women. 0% of classes are taught by teaching assistants.

ACADEMICS
Degrees: associate, bachelor's, master's. **Classes:** Most classes have fewer than 10 students. Most lab/discussion sessions have fewer than 10 students. **Majors with Highest Enrollment:** elementary education and teaching; nursing/registered nurse (rn, asn, bsn, msn). **Special Study Options:** Accelerated program, distance learning, double major, dual enrollment, honors program, independent study, internships, teacher certification program. **Disability Services:** Special programs offered to physically disabled students include tutors. **Career Services:** career/job search classes, career assessment

FACILITIES
Housing: special housing for disabled students, men's dorms, women's dorms. 100% of campus accessible to physically disabled. **Special Academic Facilities/Equipment:** Cavett Wild Game Collection.

CAMPUS LIFE
Environment: Town. **Activities:** Choral groups, dance, drama/theater, jazz band, marching band, music ensembles, musical theater, radio station, student government, student newspaper, yearbook 15 registered organizations, 13 honor societies, 2 religious organizations. 3 fraternities, 2 sororities. **Athletics (Intercollegiate):** *Men:* baseball, basketball, cheerleading, cross-country, football, golf, soccer, tennis, wrestling. *Women:* basketball, cheerleading, cross-country, golf, soccer, softball, tennis, volleyball. **On-Campus Highlights:** Labry Hall Atrium, Memorial Hall Student Lounge, Mitchell Student Center, Phillips Dining Hall Patio.

ADMISSIONS
Freshman Academic Profile: Average high school GPA 3.0. 12% in top 10% of high school class, 32% in top 25% of high school class, 70% in top 50% of high school class. 89% from public high schools. SAT Math middle 50% range

380-510. SAT Critical Reading middle 50% range 410-530. ACT middle 50% range 17-22. Minimum paper TOEFL 500. **Basis for Candidate Selection:** *Very important factors considered include:* Class rank, rigor of secondary school record, standardized test scores. *Other factors considered include:* application essay, recommendation(s), alumni/ae relation. **Freshman Admission Requirements:** High school diploma is required and GED is accepted. **Freshman Admission Statistics:** 532 applied, 66% admitted, 59% enrolled. **Transfer Admission Requirements:** college transcript(s), minimum college GPA of 2.0 required. Lowest grade transferable C. **General Admission Information:** Application Fee $25. Nonfall registration accepted. Admission may be deferred for a maximum of one year. Credit offered for CEEB Advanced Placement tests.

COSTS AND FINANCIAL AID

Annual tuition $12,130. Room and board $4,680. Required fees $100. Average book expense $1,040. **Required Forms and Deadlines:** FAFSA, institution's own financial aid form. **Notification of Awards:** Applicants will be notified of awards on or about 5/1. **Types of Aid:** *Need-based scholarships/grants:* Federal Pell, SEOG, state scholarships/grants, private scholarships, the school's own gift aid. *Loans:* Subsidized Stafford, Unsubsidized Stafford, PLUS, Federal Perkins, state loans. **Student Employment:** Federal Work-Study Program available. Off-campus job opportunities are excellent. **Financial Aid Statistics:** 56% freshmen, 59% undergrads receive need-based scholarship or grant aid. 78% freshmen, 96% undergrads receive non-need-based scholarship or grant aid. 49% freshmen, 65% undergrads receive need-based self-help aid. 85% freshmen, 96% undergrads receive athletic scholarships. 85% freshmen, 85% undergrads receive any aid. 70% undergrads borrow to pay for school. Average cumulative indebtedness $7,596.

CURRY COLLEGE

1071 Blue Hill Avenue, Milton, MA 2186
Phone: 617-333-2210
E-mail: curryadm@curry.edu • **CEEB Code:** 3285
Fax: 617-333-2114 • **Website:** www.curry.edu • **ACT Code:** 1814

This private school was founded in 1879. It has a 137-acre campus.

RATINGS
Admissions Selectivity Rating: 63   **Fire Safety Rating:** 60*   **Green Rating:** 60*

STUDENTS AND FACULTY
Enrollment: 1,709. **Student Body:** 53% female, 47% male, 40% out-of-state, 1% international (20 countries represented). Asian 1%, African American 4%, Caucasian 48%, Hispanic 2%, Native American 0%.
Retention and Graduation: 68% freshmen return for sophomore year. 44% freshmen graduate within 4 years. 53% freshmen graduate within 6 years. 17% grads go on to further study within 1 year. 10% grads pursue arts and sciences degrees. 1% grads pursue law degrees. 2% grads pursue business degrees. **Faculty:** Student/faculty ratio 12:1. 0% of classes are taught by teaching assistants.

ACADEMICS
Degrees: bachelor's, master's. **Special Study Options:** Accelerated program, double major, honors program, independent study, internships, liberal arts/career combination, student-designed major, study abroad, teacher certification program, weekend college. **Disability Services:** Special programs offered to physically disabled students include tape recorders, tutors.

FACILITIES
Housing: Coed dorms, special housing for international students, women's dorms. **Special Academic Facilities/Equipment:** On-campus preschool, nursing lab, psychology lab. **Computers:** Students can register for classes online.

CAMPUS LIFE
Environment: Village. **Activities:** Choral groups, dance, drama/theater, literary magazine, music ensembles, radio station, student government, student newspaper, television station, yearbook 1 honor societies, 2 religious organizations. **Athletics (Intercollegiate):** *Men:* baseball, basketball, cheerleading, football, ice hockey, lacrosse, soccer, tennis. *Women:* basketball, cheerleading, cross-country, lacrosse, soccer, softball, tennis. **On-Campus Highlights:** Drapkin Student Center, Levin Library, WMLN Campus Radio Station, The Suites- New Residence Hall, Hafer Academic Center.

ADMISSIONS
Freshman Academic Profile: Average high school GPA 2.3. 5% in top 10% of high school class, 22% in top 25% of high school class, 65% in top 50% of high school class. 76% from public high schools. Minimum paper TOEFL 500. **Basis for Candidate Selection:** *Important factors considered include:* Class rank,

academic GPA, recommendation(s), rigor of secondary school record. *Other factors considered include:* application essay, standardized test scores, alumni/ae relation, character/personal qualities, extracurricular activities, interview, volunteer work, work experience. **Freshman Admission Requirements:** High school diploma is required and GED is accepted. *Academic units required:* 4 English, 3 mathematics, 2 science, (2 science labs), 1 social studies, 1 history, 5 academic electives. 4 English, 3 mathematics, 2 science, (2 science labs), 1 social studies, 1 history, 5 academic electives. **Freshman Admission Statistics:** 3,509 applied, 66% admitted, 30% enrolled. **Transfer Admission Requirements:** college transcript(s), essay or personal statement, minimum college GPA of 2.0 required. Lowest grade transferable C–. **General Admission Information:** Application Fee $40. Early decision application deadline 12/1. Regular application deadline 4/1. Notification on a rolling basis, beginning on or about 1/15. Nonfall registration accepted. Admission may be deferred for a maximum of 12. Credit and/or placement offered for CEEB Advanced Placement tests.

COSTS AND FINANCIAL AID

Annual tuition $17,160. Room and board $6,870. Required fees $755. Average book expense $700. **Required Forms and Deadlines:** FAFSA, institution's own financial aid form. **Notification of Awards:** Applicants will be notified of awards on a rolling basis beginning 3/1. **Types of Aid:** *Need-based scholarships/grants:* Federal Pell, SEOG, state scholarships/grants, private scholarships, the school's own gift aid. *Loans:* Subsidized Stafford, Unsubsidized Stafford, PLUS, Federal Perkins, state loans. **Student Employment: Financial Aid Statistics:** 90% freshmen, 81% undergrads receive need-based scholarship or grant aid. 100% freshmen, 100% undergrads receive need-based self-help aid. 65% undergrads borrow to pay for school. Average cumulative indebtedness $19,125.

See page 1058.

DAEMEN COLLEGE

4380 Main Street, Amherst, NY 14226-3592
Phone: 716-839-8225 • **Financial Aid Phone:** 716-839-8254
E-mail: admissions@daemen.edu • **CEEB Code:** 2762
Fax: 716-839-8229 • **Website:** www.daemen.edu • **ACT Code:** 2874

This private school was founded in 1947. It has a 35-acre campus.

RATINGS

Admissions Selectivity Rating: 84   **Fire Safety Rating:** 79   **Green Rating:** 63

STUDENTS AND FACULTY

Enrollment: 1,872. **Student Body:** 72% female, 28% male, % out-of-state, 3% international (6 countries represented). Asian 2%, African American 10%, Caucasian 77%, Hispanic 4%, Native American 0%.
Retention and Graduation: 29% freshmen graduate within 4 years. 49% freshmen graduate within 6 years. **Faculty:** Student/faculty ratio 14:1. 120 full-time faculty, 73% hold PhDs, 7% are members of minority groups, 60% are women. 0% of classes are taught by teaching assistants.

ACADEMICS

Degrees: bachelor's, certificate, master's, post-master's certificate. **Classes:** Most classes have 10–19 students. Most lab/discussion sessions have 10–19 students. **Majors with Highest Enrollment:** elementary education and teaching; health/medical preparatory programs, other; nursing/registered nurse (rn, asn, bsn, msn). **Special Study Options:** Accelerated program, cross-registration, distance learning, double major, dual enrollment, English as a Second Language (ESL), exchange student program (domestic), honors program, independent study, internships, liberal arts/career combination, student-designed major, study abroad, teacher certification program, weekend college, Washington semester through the Washington Internship Institute. Dual degree (BS/MS) awarded at the completion of the program in physician assistant studies and professional accountancy. **Honors Programs:** The Honors Program provides an enriched curriculum relying upon multiple perspectives and using primary sources rather than textbooks. Honors program students enjoy special residential accommodations, priority registration by class rank, opportunities for domestic and international travel, and unique offerings such as field trips, access to campus speakers, and research and publication opportunities. **Combined Degree Programs:** BS/MS Health Sci/Phys. Asst.; BS/MS Accountancy; BS Nursing 1-2-1. **Disability Services:** Special programs offered to physically disabled students include note-taking services, tape recorders, tutors. **Career Services:** Alumni network, alumni services, career/job search classes, career assessment, internships, regional alumni.

FACILITIES

Housing: Coed dorms, Coed apartment-style residence halls for single students; some apartments are handicapped accessible. 92% of campus accessible

to physically disabled. **Special Academic Facilities/Equipment:** Teaching Resource Center; Franette Goldman/Carolyn Greenfield Art Gallery; Natural and Health Sciences Research Center; video conferencing center; Research & Information Commons (new). **Computers:** 60% of classrooms, 100% of dorms, 100% of libraries, 75% of dining areas, 50% of student union, 10% of common outdoor areas have wireless network access. Students can register for classes online. Administrative functions (other than registration) can be performed online.

CAMPUS LIFE

Environment: City. **Activities:** Choral groups, dance, drama/theater, literary magazine, student government, student newspaper, yearbook, Campus Ministries 45 registered organizations, 8 honor societies, 1 fraternities, 4 sororities. **Athletics (Intercollegiate):** *Men:* basketball, cross-country, golf, soccer. *Women:* basketball, cross-country, soccer, volleyball. **On-Campus Highlights:** Research and Information Commons, Modern Apartment-Style Residence Halls, Wick Student Center, Academic Computing Facilities, Athletic Facilities. **Environmental Initiatives:** College has hosted conferences and symposia on campus: Annual Environmental Summit; Green Jobs Workshop; World on Your Plate Symposium, Focus the Nation Teach-In. College offers sustainability-focused courses and majors On 1/27/2009 opened new building on campus and received Gold LEED certification from U.S. Green Building Council.

ADMISSIONS

Freshman Academic Profile: Average high school GPA 3.6. SAT Math middle 50% range 460-580. SAT Critical Reading middle 50% range 440-550. SAT Writing middle 50% range 440-540. ACT middle 50% range 21-26. Minimum web-based TOEFL 61. Minimum paper TOEFL 500. **Basis for Candidate Selection:** *Very important factors considered include:* academic GPA, rigor of secondary school record. *Important factors considered include:* Class rank, application essay, recommendation(s), interview. *Other factors considered include:* standardized test scores, alumni/ae relation, character/personal qualities, extracurricular activities, level of applicant's interest, talent/ability, volunteer work, work experience. **Freshman Admission Requirements:** High school diploma is required and GED is accepted. **Freshman Admission Statistics:** 2,938 applied, 50% admitted, 30% enrolled. **Transfer Admission Requirements:** college transcript(s), statement of good standing from prior institution(s). Minimum college GPA of 2.0 required. Lowest grade transferable C. **General Admission Information:** Application Fee $25. Notification on a rolling basis, beginning on or about 10/15. Nonfall registration accepted. Admission may be deferred for a maximum of 12 months. Credit offered for CEEB Advanced Placement tests.

COSTS AND FINANCIAL AID

Annual tuition $21,800. Room and board $10,840. Required fees $510. Average book expense $800. **Required Forms and Deadlines:** FAFSA, state aid form. **Notification of Awards:** Applicants will be notified of awards on a rolling basis beginning 2/15. **Types of Aid:** *Need-based scholarships/grants:* Federal Pell, SEOG, state scholarships/grants, private scholarships, the school's own gift aid. *Loans:* Subsidized Stafford, Unsubsidized Stafford, PLUS, Federal Perkins, college/university loans from institutional funds, Alternative Loans through private lenders. **Student Employment:** Federal Work-Study Program available. Institutional employment available. Highest amount earned per year from on-campus jobs $800. Off-campus job opportunities are fair. **Financial Aid Statistics:** 92% freshmen, 94% undergrads receive need-based scholarship or grant aid. 96% freshmen, 96% undergrads receive non-need-based scholarship or grant aid. 91% freshmen, 93% undergrads receive need-based self-help aid. 5% freshmen, 5% undergrads receive athletic scholarships. 99% freshmen, 84% undergrads receive any aid. 87% undergrads borrow to pay for school. Average cumulative indebtedness $27,444. **Criteria for awarding institutional aid:** *Non-need-based:* academics, art, athletics.

See page 1062.

DAKOTA STATE UNIVERSITY

820 North Washington Ave., Madison, SD 57042
Phone: 605-256-5139 • **Financial Aid Phone:** 605-256-5152
E-mail: admissions@dsu.edu • **CEEB Code:** 6247
Fax: 605-256-5020 • **Website:** www.dsu.edu • **ACT Code:** 3910

This public school was founded in 1881. It has a 20-acre campus.

RATINGS

Admissions Selectivity Rating: 66   **Fire Safety Rating:** 75   **Green Rating:** 62

STUDENTS AND FACULTY

Enrollment: 1,728. **Student Body:** 42% female, 58% male, 26% out-of-state, 3% international (13 countries represented). Asian 1%, African American 2%, Caucasian 86%, Hispanic 3%, Native American 1%.

Retention and Graduation: 60% freshmen return for sophomore year. 14% freshmen graduate within 4 years. 42% freshmen graduate within 6 years. **Faculty:** Student/faculty ratio 18:1. 92 full-time faculty, 73% hold PhDs, 5% are members of minority groups, 40% are women. 0% of classes are taught by teaching assistants.

ACADEMICS

Degrees: associate, bachelor's, certificate, master's. **Classes:** Most classes have 20–29 students. Most lab/discussion sessions have 10–19 students. **Majors with Highest Enrollment:** business administration and management; elementary education and teaching; information science/studies. **Special Study Options:** cooperative education program, cross-registration, distance learning, double major, dual enrollment, English as a Second Language (ESL), honors program, independent study, internships, teacher certification program. **Honors Programs:** Center of Excellence(CEX), Honors. **Disability Services:** Special programs offered to physically disabled students include note-taking services, reader services, tape recorders, tutors. **Career Services:** alumni services, career/job search classes, career assessment, internships Career Services highlights include on-campus interviews.

FACILITIES

Housing: Coed dorms, men's dorms, special housing for international students, women's dorms, apartments for single students. 80% of campus accessible to physically disabled. **Special Academic Facilities/Equipment:** Smith Zimmerman Museum **Computers:** 100% of classrooms, 100% of dorms, 100% of libraries, 100% of dining areas, 100% of student union, 100% of common outdoor areas have wireless network access. Students can register for classes online. Administrative functions (other than registration) can be performed online. Undergraduates are required to own a computer.

CAMPUS LIFE

Environment: Rural. **Activities:** Choral groups, dance, drama/theater, literary magazine, music ensembles, musical theater, pep band, radio station, student government, student newspaper, International Student Organization 33 registered organizations, 3 honor societies, 2 religious organizations. **Athletics (Intercollegiate):** *Men:* baseball, basketball, cheerleading, cross-country, football, track/field (outdoor), track/field (indoor). *Women:* basketball, cheerleading, cross-country, softball, track/field (outdoor), track/field (indoor), volleyball. **On-Campus Highlights:** Tunhiem Classroom Building, Community Center, Trojan Center, Myxers Coffee Shop, The Marketplace. **Environmental Initiatives:** LEED Silver project in progress No smoking on campus Lighting retrofits

ADMISSIONS

Freshman Academic Profile: Average high school GPA 3.1. 5% in top 10% of high school class, 20% in top 25% of high school class, 52% in top 50% of high school class. SAT Math middle 50% range 460-560. SAT Critical Reading middle 50% range 420-550. ACT middle 50% range 19-24. Minimum web-based TOEFL 79. Minimum paper TOEFL 550. **Basis for Candidate Selection:** *Important factors considered include:* Class rank, academic GPA, rigor of secondary school record, standardized test scores, level of applicant's interest. **Freshman Admission Requirements:** High school diploma is required and GED is accepted. **Freshman Admission Statistics:** 742 applied, 89% admitted, 47% enrolled. **Transfer Admission Requirements:** High school transcript, college transcript(s), minimum college GPA of 2.0 required. Lowest grade transferable D. **General Admission Information:** Application Fee $20. Nonfall registration accepted. Credit and/or placement offered for CEEB Advanced Placement tests.

COSTS AND FINANCIAL AID

Annual in-state tuition $3,726. Annual out-of-state tuition $5,591. Room and board $5,235. Required fees $4,224. Average book expense $1,000. **Required Forms and Deadlines:** FAFSAInstitutional Scholarship Application Form. **Notification of Awards:** Applicants will be notified of awards on a rolling basis beginning 4/1. **Types of Aid:** *Need-based scholarships/grants:* Federal Pell, SEOG, state scholarships/grants, private scholarships, the school's own gift aid, Agency Assistance (Veteran Benefits/ Department of Labor). *Loans:* Subsidized Stafford, Unsubsidized Stafford, PLUS, Federal Perkins, alternative commercial loans. **Student Employment:** Federal Work-Study Program available. Institutional employment available. Highest amount earned per year from on-campus jobs $5,637. Off-campus job opportunities are good. **Financial Aid Statistics:** 62% freshmen, 60% undergrads receive need-based scholarship or grant aid. 67% freshmen, 42% undergrads receive non-need-based scholarship or grant aid. 90% freshmen, 94% undergrads receive need-based self-help aid. 15% freshmen, 10% undergrads receive athletic scholarships. 81% freshmen, 81% undergrads receive any aid. 79% undergrads borrow to pay for school. Average cumulative indebtedness $25,926. **Criteria for awarding institutional aid:** *Non-need-based:* academics, alumni affiliation, art, athletics, leadership, minority status, music/drama, state/district residency.

DAKOTA WESLEYAN UNIVERSITY

1200 West University Avenue, Mitchell, SD 57301-4398
Phone: 605-995-2650 • **Financial Aid Phone:** 605-995-2656
E-mail: admissions@dwu.edu • **CEEB Code:** 6155
Fax: 605-995-2699 • **Website:** www.dwu.edu • **ACT Code:** 3906

This private school, affiliated with the Methodist Church, was founded in 1885. It has a 50-acre campus.

RATINGS

Admissions Selectivity Rating: 74   **Fire Safety Rating:** 65   **Green Rating:** 60*

STUDENTS AND FACULTY

Enrollment: 654. **Student Body:** 59% female, 41% male, 24% out-of-state, 1% international (5 countries represented). Asian 1%, African American 4%, Caucasian 90%, Hispanic 2%, Native American 2%.
Retention and Graduation: 58% freshmen return for sophomore year. 23% freshmen graduate within 4 years. 35% freshmen graduate within 6 years. 10% grads go on to further study within 1 year. **Faculty:** Student/faculty ratio 11:1. 45 full-time faculty, 64% hold PhDs, 2% are members of minority groups, 47% are women. 0% of classes are taught by teaching assistants.

ACADEMICS

Degrees: associate, bachelor's, master's, terminal associate. **Classes:** Most classes have 10–19 students. Most lab/discussion sessions have 10–19 students. **Majors with Highest Enrollment:** business/commerce; elementary education and teaching; human services. **Special Study Options:** distance learning, double major, dual enrollment, honors program, independent study, internships, liberal arts/career combination, student-designed major, study abroad, teacher certification program. **Honors Programs:** University Scholars Program, students take at least three USP courses, have a 3.5 GPA, and present original scholarship at the USP Symposium **Combined Degree Programs:** BA, M.Div. **Disability Services:** Special programs offered to physically disabled students include note-taking services, reader services, tape recorders, tutors.

FACILITIES

Housing: Coed dorms, men's dorms, women's dorms, apartments for married students, apartments for single students, Koka "honor housing" for upper class women; ADA rooms, apartments available. 100% of campus accessible to physically disabled. **Special Academic Facilities/Equipment:** Friends of the Middle Border Museum and Grounds. **Computers:** Administrative functions (other than registration) can be performed online. Undergraduates are required to own a computer.

CAMPUS LIFE

Environment: Village. **Activities:** Choral groups, concert band, drama/theater, literary magazine, music ensembles, student government, student newspaper, yearbook 5 registered organizations, 6 honor societies, 3 religious organizations. **Athletics (Intercollegiate):** *Men:* baseball, basketball, cheerleading, cross-country, football, golf, track/field (outdoor), track/field (indoor), wrestling. *Women:* basketball, cheerleading, cross-country, golf, softball, track/field (outdoor), track/field (indoor), volleyball. **On-Campus Highlights:** Athletic Department/gym/wellness center, cafeteria/coffee shop, student lounge, residence halls common lounge, residence hall computer labs.

ADMISSIONS

Freshman Academic Profile: Average high school GPA 3.0. 10% in top 10% of high school class, 35% in top 25% of high school class, 75% in top 50% of high school class. 98% from public high schools. ACT middle 50% range 22-28. Minimum paper TOEFL 500. **Basis for Candidate Selection:** *Very important factors considered include:* Class rank, rigor of secondary school record, standardized test scores. *Important factors considered include:* application essay. *Other factors considered include:* recommendation(s). **Freshman Admission Requirements:** High school diploma is required and GED is accepted. **Freshman Admission Statistics:** 423 applied, 79% admitted, 41% enrolled. **Transfer Admission Requirements:** college transcript(s), minimum college GPA of 2.0 required. Lowest grade transferable D-. **General Admission Information:** Application Fee $25. Regular application deadline 8/29. Notification on a rolling basis, beginning on or about 9/1. Nonfall registration accepted. Admission may be deferred for a maximum of no set date. Credit and/or placement offered for CEEB Advanced Placement tests.

COSTS AND FINANCIAL AID

Annual tuition $15,600. Room and board $4,744. Average book expense $900. **Required Forms and Deadlines:** FAFSA. **Notification of Awards:** Applicants will be notified of awards on a rolling basis beginning 3/1. **Types of Aid:** *Need-based scholarships/grants:* Federal Pell, SEOG, private scholarships, the school's own gift aid, Federal Nursing Scholarships, South Dakota Board of Nursing Scholarships / Loans. *Loans:* Subsidized Stafford, Unsubsidized

Stafford, PLUS, Federal Perkins, Methodist Loans, and Private Alternative Student Loans. **Student Employment:** Highest amount earned per year from on-campus jobs $3,300. **Financial Aid Statistics:** 100% freshmen, 100% undergrads receive need-based scholarship or grant aid. 68% freshmen, 41% undergrads receive non-need-based scholarship or grant aid. 100% freshmen, 97% undergrads receive need-based self-help aid. 65% freshmen, 41% undergrads receive athletic scholarships. 98% freshmen, 98% undergrads receive any aid. 98% undergrads borrow to pay for school. Average cumulative indebtedness $13,925. **Criteria for awarding institutional aid:** *Non-need-based:* academics, alumni affiliation, art, athletics, leadership, minority status, music/drama, religious affiliation.

DALLAS BAPTIST UNIVERSITY

3000 Mountain Creek Parkway, Dallas, TX 75211-9299
Phone: 214-333-5360 • **Financial Aid Phone:** 214-333-5363
E-mail: admiss@dbu.edu • **CEEB Code:** 6159
Fax: 214-333-5447 • **Website:** www.dbu.edu/ • **ACT Code:** 4080

This private school, affiliated with the Baptist Church, was founded in 1898. It has a 293-acre campus.

RATINGS
Admissions Selectivity Rating: 89   **Fire Safety Rating:** 77   **Green Rating:** 60*

STUDENTS AND FACULTY
Enrollment: 3,437. **Student Body:** 57% female, 43% male, 6% out-of-state, 6% international (52 countries represented). Asian 2%, African American 17%, Caucasian 63%, Hispanic 11%, Native American 1%.
Retention and Graduation: 71% freshmen return for sophomore year. **Faculty:** Student/faculty ratio 15:1. 129 full-time faculty, 80% hold PhDs, 13% are members of minority groups, 42% are women. 0% of classes are taught by teaching assistants.

ACADEMICS
Degrees: associate, bachelor's, certificate, master's, post-bachelor's certificate, post-master's certificate, transfer associate. **Classes:** Most classes have 10–19 students. Most lab/discussion sessions have 10–19 students. **Majors with Highest Enrollment:** business/commerce; general studies; psychology. **Special Study Options:** Accelerated program, distance learning, double major, dual enrollment, English as a Second Language (ESL), honors program, independent study, internships, study abroad, teacher certification program, weekend college. **Honors Programs:** www.dbu.edu/honors/. Special programs offered to physically disabled students include note-taking services, reader services, tape recorders, tutors. **Career Services:** alumni services, career/job search classes, career assessment, internships Career Services highlights include online job serach engine - CareerBridge.

FACILITIES
Housing: special housing for disabled students, men's dorms, women's dorms, apartments for married students, apartments for single students, wellness housing, townhomes. 75% of campus accessible to physically disabled. **Special Academic Facilities/Equipment:** Corrie ten Boom Collection **Computers:** Students can register for classes online.

CAMPUS LIFE
Environment: Metropolis. **Activities:** Choral groups, dance, drama/theater, music ensembles, musical theater, opera, student government, yearbook, Campus Ministries, International Student Organization 36 registered organizations, 4 honor societies, 3 religious organizations. **Athletics (Intercollegiate):** *Men:* baseball, cross-country, golf, soccer, tennis, track/field (outdoor). *Women:* cross-country, golf, soccer, tennis, track/field (outdoor), volleyball. **On-Campus Highlights:** Mahler Student Center, Burg Center, Coffee House, Collins Learning Center, Crowley Co-Ed.

ADMISSIONS
Freshman Academic Profile: Average high school GPA 3.5. 21% in top 10% of high school class, 48% in top 25% of high school class, 81% in top 50% of high school class. SAT Math middle 50% range 472-647. SAT Critical Reading middle 50% range 465-651. ACT middle 50% range 19-28. Minimum web-based TOEFL 71. Minimum paper TOEFL 525. **Basis for Candidate Selection:** *Very important factors considered include:* Class rank, application essay, academic GPA, rigor of secondary school record, standardized test scores, character/personal qualities, religious affiliation/commitment, talent/ability. *Important factors considered include:* extracurricular activities, first generation, interview. *Other factors considered include:* recommendation(s), alumni/ae relation, volunteer work, work experience. **Freshman Admission Requirements:** High school diploma is required and GED is accepted. **Freshman Admission**

Statistics: 2,692 applied, 41% admitted, 44% enrolled. **Transfer Admission Requirements:** college transcript(s), essay or personal statement, minimum college GPA of 2.5 required. Lowest grade transferable C. **General Admission Information:** Application Fee $25. Nonfall registration accepted. Credit offered for CEEB Advanced Placement tests.

COSTS AND FINANCIAL AID
Annual tuition $20,910. Room and board $6,498. Required fees $200. Average book expense $2,220. **Required Forms and Deadlines:** FAFSA, institution's own financial aid form. **Notification of Awards: Types of Aid:** *Need-based scholarships/grants:* Federal Pell, SEOG, state scholarships/grants, private scholarships, the school's own gift aid. *Loans:* Subsidized Stafford, Unsubsidized Stafford, PLUS, Federal Perkins, state loans, college/university loans from institutional funds. **Student Employment:** Federal Work-Study Program available. Institutional employment available. Highest amount earned per year from on-campus jobs $2,880. Off-campus job opportunities are good. **Financial Aid Statistics:** 62% freshmen, 64% undergrads receive need-based scholarship or grant aid. 95% freshmen, 87% undergrads receive non-need-based scholarship or grant aid. 78% freshmen, 78% undergrads receive need-based self-help aid. 6% freshmen, 5% undergrads receive athletic scholarships. 99% freshmen, 85% undergrads receive any aid. 72% undergrads borrow to pay for school. Average cumulative indebtedness $18,943. **Criteria for awarding institutional aid:** *Non-need-based:* academics, athletics, job skills, leadership, music/drama, religious affiliation.

DANA COLLEGE

2848 College Drive, Blair, NE 68008-1099
Phone: 402-426-7222 • **Financial Aid Phone:** 402-426-7226
E-mail: admissions@dana.edu
Fax: 402-426-7386 • **Website:** www.dana.edu/ • **ACT Code:** 2446

This private school, affiliated with the Lutheran Church, was founded in 1884. It has a 150-acre campus.

RATINGS
Admissions Selectivity Rating: 72   **Fire Safety Rating:** 83   **Green Rating:** 60*

STUDENTS AND FACULTY
Enrollment: 595. **Student Body:** 47% female, 53% male, 42% out-of-state, 1% international (3 countries represented). Asian 1%, African American 3%, Caucasian 91%, Hispanic 4%, Native American 1%.
Retention and Graduation: 60% freshmen return for sophomore year. 33% freshmen graduate within 4 years. 49% freshmen graduate within 6 years. 13% grads go on to further study within 1 year. 5% grads pursue arts and sciences degrees. 1% grads pursue law degrees. 1% grads pursue business degrees. 1% grads pursue medical degrees. **Faculty:** Student/faculty ratio 13:1. 31 full-time faculty, 81% hold PhDs, 3% are members of minority groups, 58% are women. 0% of classes are taught by teaching assistants.

ACADEMICS
Degrees: bachelor's. **Classes:** Most classes have fewer than 10 students. Most lab/discussion sessions have fewer than 10 students. **Majors with Highest Enrollment:** business/commerce; criminal justice/law enforcement administration; education. **Special Study Options:** Accelerated program, cross-registration, double major, dual enrollment, English as a Second Language (ESL), honors program, independent study, internships, liberal arts/career combination, student-designed major, study abroad, teacher certification program. **Disability Services:** Special programs offered to physically disabled students include note-taking services, reader services, tutors. **Career Services:** career/job search classes, career assessment, internships.

FACILITIES
Housing: Coed dorms, women's dorms, apartments for married students, apartments for single students. 80% of campus accessible to physically disabled. **Special Academic Facilities/Equipment:** Danish Archives. **Computers:** Administrative functions (other than registration) can be performed online.

CAMPUS LIFE
Environment: Rural. **Activities:** Choral groups, concert band, dance, drama/theater, jazz band, literary magazine, music ensembles, musical theater, radio station, student government, student newspaper, television station, yearbook 25 registered organizations, 3 honor societies, 3 religious organizations. **Athletics (Intercollegiate):** *Men:* baseball, basketball, cross-country, football, soccer, track/field (outdoor), wrestling. *Women:* basketball, cheerleading, cross-country, golf, soccer, softball, track/field (outdoor), volleyball. **On-Campus Highlights:** Gardner-Hawks Center, Dragon's Head.

ADMISSIONS

Freshman Academic Profile: Average high school GPA 3.2. 16% in top 10% of high school class, 37% in top 25% of high school class, 62% in top 50% of high school class. SAT Math middle 50% range 420-550. SAT Critical Reading middle 50% range 480-560. ACT middle 50% range 20-25. Minimum paper TOEFL 500. **Basis for Candidate Selection:** *Very important factors considered include:* academic GPA, rigor of secondary school record, standardized test scores. *Other factors considered include:* application essay, recommendation(s), extracurricular activities, interview, level of applicant's interest, volunteer work, work experience. **Freshman Admission Requirements:** High school diploma is required and GED is accepted. **Freshman Admission Statistics:** 830 applied, 72% admitted, 24% enrolled. **Transfer Admission Requirements:** college transcript(s), minimum college GPA of 2.0 required. Lowest grade transferable C. **General Admission Information:** Notification on a rolling basis, beginning on or about 9/1. Nonfall registration accepted. Admission may be deferred for a maximum of 2 Years. Credit offered for CEEB Advanced Placement tests.

COSTS AND FINANCIAL AID

Average book expense $900. **Required Forms and Deadlines:** FAFSA, institution's own financial aid form. **Notification of Awards:** Applicants will be notified of awards on a rolling basis beginning 3/4. **Types of Aid:** *Need-based scholarships/grants:* Federal Pell, SEOG, state scholarships/grants, private scholarships, the school's own gift aid. *Loans:* Subsidized Stafford, Unsubsidized Stafford, PLUS, Federal Perkins. **Student Employment:** Federal Work-Study Program available. Institutional employment available. Highest amount earned per year from on-campus jobs $1,500. Off-campus job opportunities are good. **Financial Aid Statistics:** 46% freshmen, 59% undergrads receive need-based scholarship or grant aid. 74% freshmen, 72% undergrads receive non-need-based scholarship or grant aid. 77% freshmen, 79% undergrads receive need-based self-help aid. 68% freshmen, 59% undergrads receive athletic scholarships. 86% undergrads borrow to pay for school. Average cumulative indebtedness $17,029. **Criteria for awarding institutional aid:** *Non-need-based:* academics, alumni affiliation, art, athletics, leadership, music/drama, religious affiliation, state/district residency.

DANIEL WEBSTER COLLEGE

20 University Drive, Nashua, NH 03063-1300
Phone: 603-577-6600
E-mail: admissions@dwc.edu • **CEEB Code:** 3648
Fax: 603-577-6001 • **Website:** www.dwc.edu/ • **ACT Code:** 2525

This private school was founded in 1965. It has a 50-acre campus.

RATINGS

Admissions Selectivity Rating: 65   **Fire Safety Rating:** 60*   **Green Rating:** 60*

STUDENTS AND FACULTY

Enrollment: 785. **Student Body:** 25% female, 75% male, 72% out-of-state, (11 countries represented). Asian 1%, African American 4%, Hispanic 3%, Native American 0%.
Retention and Graduation: 64% freshmen return for sophomore year. 40% freshmen graduate within 4 years. 53% freshmen graduate within 6 years. 8% grads go on to further study within 1 year. 8% grads pursue arts and sciences degrees. **Faculty:** Student/faculty ratio 14:1. 39 full-time faculty, 54% hold PhDs, 23% are women. 0% of classes are taught by teaching assistants.

ACADEMICS

Degrees: associate, bachelor's, master's, transfer associate. **Classes:** Most classes have 10–19 students. Most lab/discussion sessions have fewer than 10 students. **Majors with Highest Enrollment:** airline/commercial/professional pilot and flight crew; business/commerce; computer and information sciences. **Special Study Options:** Accelerated program, cooperative education program, cross-registration, distance learning, double major, dual enrollment, independent study, internships, study abroad. **Combined Degree Programs:** 2-2 aeronautical enginering and engineering scienc. **Disability Services:** Special programs offered to physically disabled students include tutors. **Career Services:** Alumni network, alumni services, career/job search classes, career assessment, internships.

FACILITIES

Housing: Coed dorms, men's dorms, women's dorms, Men's Townhouses Women's Townhouses Suites. 80% of campus accessible to physically disabled. **Special Academic Facilities/Equipment:** Campus is adjacent to municipal airport; over 35 aircraft are available for flight training. Three flight simulators, aviation center.

CAMPUS LIFE

Environment: Village. **Activities:** Choral groups, drama/theater, jazz band, musical theater, student government, student newspaper, student-run film society, yearbook 17 registered organizations, 2 honor societies, 1 religious organizations. **Athletics (Intercollegiate):** *Men:* baseball, basketball, cross-country, lacrosse, soccer. *Women:* basketball, cross-country, soccer, softball, volleyball.

ADMISSIONS

Freshman Academic Profile: Average high school GPA 3.1. 7% in top 10% of high school class, 21% in top 25% of high school class, 52% in top 50% of high school class. 83% from public high schools. SAT Math middle 50% range 480-610. SAT Critical Reading middle 50% range 470-570. ACT middle 50% range 19-24. Minimum paper TOEFL 520. **Basis for Candidate Selection:** *Very important factors considered include:* rigor of secondary school record. *Important factors considered include:* Class rank, recommendation(s), standardized test scores, extracurricular activities, interview. *Other factors considered include:* application essay, character/personal qualities, level of applicant's interest, talent/ability, volunteer work, work experience. **Freshman Admission Requirements:** High school diploma is required and GED is accepted. *Academic units required:* 4 English, 3 mathematics, 3 science, (2 science labs), 2 social studies, 2 history, 2 academic electives. *Academic units recommended:* 4 English, 3 mathematics, 3 science, (2 science labs), 2 social studies, 2 history, 2 academic electives. **Freshman Admission Statistics:** 823 applied. **Transfer Admission Requirements:** High school transcript, college transcript(s), minimum college GPA of 2.5 required. Lowest grade transferable C. **General Admission Information:** Application Fee $35. Nonfall registration accepted. Admission may be deferred for a maximum of 1 year. Credit and/or placement offered for CEEB Advanced Placement tests.

COSTS AND FINANCIAL AID

Average book expense $750. **Required Forms and Deadlines:** FAFSA, institution's own financial aid form. **Notification of Awards:** Applicants will be notified of awards on a rolling basis beginning 3/15. **Types of Aid:** *Need-based scholarships/grants:* Federal Pell, SEOG, state scholarships/grants, the school's own gift aid. *Loans:* Direct Subsidized Stafford, Direct Unsubsidized Stafford, Direct PLUS, Federal Perkins. **Student Employment:** Federal Work-Study Program available. Institutional employment available. Highest amount earned per year from on-campus jobs $2,000. Off-campus job opportunities are excellent. **Financial Aid Statistics:** 93% freshmen, 79% undergrads receive need-based scholarship or grant aid. 69% freshmen, 78% undergrads receive non-need-based scholarship or grant aid. 83% freshmen, 81% undergrads receive need-based self-help aid. 83% undergrads borrow to pay for school. Average cumulative indebtedness $48,000. **Criteria for awarding institutional aid:** *Non-need-based:* academics, leadership.

DARTMOUTH COLLEGE

6016 McNutt Hall, Hanover, NH 3755
Phone: 603-646-2875 • **Financial Aid Phone:** 800-443-3605
E-mail: admissions.reply@dartmouth.edu • **CEEB Code:** 3351
Fax: 603-646-1216 • **Website:** www.dartmouth.edu • **ACT Code:** 2508

This private school was founded in 1769. It has a 265-acre campus.

RATINGS

Admissions Selectivity Rating: 99   **Fire Safety Rating:** 85   **Green Rating:** 92

STUDENTS AND FACULTY

Enrollment: 4,095. **Student Body:** 50% female, 50% male, 96% out-of-state, 8% international (70 countries represented). Asian 14%, African American 7%, Caucasian 48%, Hispanic 8%, Native American 2%.
Retention and Graduation: 97% freshmen return for sophomore year. 88% freshmen graduate within 4 years. 96% freshmen graduate within 6 years. 21% grads go on to further study within 1 year. **Faculty:** Student/faculty ratio 8:1. 553 full-time faculty, 95% hold PhDs, 17% are members of minority groups, 38% are women. 0% of classes are taught by teaching assistants.

ACADEMICS

Degrees: bachelor's, doctoral, master's. **Classes:** Most classes have 10–19 students. **Majors with Highest Enrollment:** economics; political science and government; psychology. **Special Study Options:** double major, exchange student program (domestic), honors program, independent study, internships, student-designed major, study abroad, teacher certification program.

Honors Programs: Presidential Scholarship Research Program; Senior Honors Thesis; Senior Fellowship **Combined Degree Programs:** BA/BENG- 5 year program. **Disability Services:** Special programs offered to physically disabled students include note-taking services, tape recorders, tutors. **Career Services:** Alumni network, alumni services, career/job search classes, career assessment, internships, regional alumni. Career Services highlights include Unpaid internships are financially supported through the Rockefeller Center (public policy or political internships), the Dickey Center for International Understanding (overseas opportunities), the Tucker Foundation (religious or community service organizations), and through other sources on campus.

FACILITIES

Housing: Coed dorms, special housing for international students, fraternity/sorority housing, apartments for married students, cooperative housing, apartments for single students, theme housing, Academic Affinity Housing, Faculty-In-Residence Programs, Sustainable Living Center, Interfaith Living, Special Interest Housing. 75% of campus accessible to physically disabled. **Special Academic Facilities/Equipment:** Hood Museum of Art, Hopkins Center for Performing Arts, Tucker Foundation for volunteer services, observatory, centers for humanities, social science, and science. **Computers:** 100% of classrooms, 100% of dorms, 100% of libraries, 100% of dining areas, 100% of student union, 100% of common outdoor areas have wireless network access. Students can register for classes online. Administrative functions (other than registration) can be performed online. Undergraduates are required to own a computer.

CAMPUS LIFE

Environment: Village. **Activities:** Choral groups, concert band, dance, drama/theater, jazz band, literary magazine, marching band, music ensembles, musical theater, opera, pep band, radio station, student government, student newspaper, student-run film society, symphony orchestra, television station, yearbook, Campus Ministries, International Student Organization, Model UN 330 registered organizations, 26 religious organizations. 14 fraternities, 6 sororities. **Athletics (Intercollegiate):** *Men:* baseball, basketball, crew/rowing, cross-country, diving, equestrian sports, fencing, football, golf, ice hockey, lacrosse, sailing, skiing (downhill/alpine), skiingnordiccross-country, soccer, squash, swimming, tennis, track/field (outdoor), track/field (indoor). *Women:* basketball, crew/rowing, cross-country, diving, equestrian sports, fencing, field hockey, golf, ice hockey, lacrosse, sailing, skiing (downhill/alpine), skiingnordiccross-country, soccer, softball, squash, swimming, tennis, track/field (outdoor), track/field (indoor), volleyball. **On-Campus Highlights:** Hopkins Center for Creative and Performing Arts, Hood Museum of Art, Murals by Jose Clemente Orozco, Ten library system, all open to visitors, Ledyard Canoe Club, oldest in the country. **Environmental Initiatives:** As part of our commitment to reduce greenhouse gas emissions, Dartmouth commissioned an energy audit for the buildings that collectively use 75% of the energy on campus. Based on the results of this audit, the Trustees invested $12.5 million in 250 energy conservation and efficiency projects in existing buildings, which are now underway. Dartmouth established a Sustainable Living Center and is working with students to develop it as a model green dormitory and center. As part of this effort we are working on plans to push the building toward zero net energy and developing a sustainable food system for the students who live there. (See www.dartmouth.edu/~slc). Building energy metering equipment has been upgraded and the innovative Green Lite Dartmouth feedback displays will be used to provide occupants with real-time resource use information. (See greenlite.dartmouth.edu). In the first term of operation, the students reduced electricity use by 58% below past years through behavioral change alone. Dartmouth established a new tenured faculty position in Sustainability Sciences. The position has been filled and new courses in sustainability will be added in fall of 2009.

ADMISSIONS

Freshman Academic Profile: 90% in top 10% of high school class, 100% in top 50% of high school class. 55% from public high schools. SAT Math middle 50% range 680-780. SAT Critical Reading middle 50% range 670-780. SAT Writing middle 50% range 680-790. ACT middle 50% range 30-34. Minimum web-based TOEFL 250. Minimum paper TOEFL 600. **Basis for Candidate Selection:** *Very important factors considered include:* Class rank, application essay, academic GPA, recommendation(s), rigor of secondary school record, standardized test scores, character/personal qualities, extracurricular activities. *Important factors considered include:* talent/ability, volunteer work. *Other factors considered include:* alumni/ae relation, first generation, geographical residence, interview, racial/ethnic status. **Freshman Admission Requirements:** High school diploma or equivalent is not required. **Freshman Admission Statistics:** 23,110 applied, 10% admitted, 49% enrolled. **Transfer Admission Requirements:** High school transcript, college transcript(s), essay or personal statement, standardized test scores, statement of good standing from prior institution(s). Lowest grade transferable B. **General Admission Information:** Application Fee $70. Early decision application deadline 11/1. Regular application deadline 1/1. Regular notification 4/1. Nonfall registration not accepted. Admission may be deferred for a maximum of 2 years. Credit and/or placement offered for CEEB Advanced Placement tests.

COSTS AND FINANCIAL AID

Annual tuition $43,782. Room and board $12,954. Required fees $1,260. Average book expense $1,980. **Required Forms and Deadlines:** FAFSA, CSS/Financial Aid PROFILE, noncustodial PROFILE, business/farm supplement. Current W2 or Federal Tax Returns. **Notification of Awards:** Applicants will be notified of awards on or about 4/2. **Types of Aid:** *Need-based scholarships/grants:* Federal Pell, SEOG, state scholarships/grants, private scholarships, the school's own gift aid. *Loans:* Subsidized Stafford, Unsubsidized Stafford, PLUS, Federal Perkins, college/university loans from institutional funds. **Student Employment:** Federal Work-Study Program available. Institutional employment available. Off-campus job opportunities are excellent. **Financial Aid Statistics:** 98% freshmen, 97% undergrads receive need-based scholarship or grant aid. % freshmen, % undergrads receive non-need-based scholarship or grant aid. 90% freshmen, 93% undergrads receive need-based self-help aid. 44% freshmen, 51% undergrads receive any aid. 46% undergrads borrow to pay for school. Average cumulative indebtedness $17,825.

DAVENPORT UNIVERSITY

6191 Kraft Avenue S.E., Grand Rapids, MI 49512
Phone: 616-698-7111 • **Financial Aid Phone:** 313-581-4400
E-mail: gradmiss@davenport.edu
Fax: 616-698-0333 • **Website:** www.davenport.edu/

This private school was founded in 1866. It has a 43-acre campus.

RATINGS

Admissions Selectivity Rating: 61   **Fire Safety Rating:** 70   **Green Rating:** 60*

STUDENTS AND FACULTY

Enrollment: 11,736. **Student Body:** 76% female, 24% male, 2% out-of-state, 0% international (29 countries represented). Asian 1%, African American 24%, Caucasian 58%, Hispanic 4%, Native American 0%.
Retention and Graduation: 61% freshmen return for sophomore year. **Faculty:** Student/faculty ratio 14:1. 130 full-time faculty, 24% hold PhDs, % are members of minority groups, 54% are women. 0% of classes are taught by teaching assistants.

ACADEMICS

Degrees: associate, bachelor's, diploma, master's, post-bachelor's certificate. **Classes:** Most classes have fewer than 10 students. **Special Study Options:** Accelerated program, distance learning, dual enrollment, English as a Second Language (ESL), independent study, internships, student-designed major, study abroad. **Combined Degree Programs:** BA/MA. **Disability Services:** Special programs offered to physically disabled students include tutors.

FACILITIES

Housing: Coed dorms.

CAMPUS LIFE

Environment: City.

ADMISSIONS

Freshman Academic Profile: Minimum paper TOEFL 500. **Freshman Admission Requirements:** High school diploma is required and GED is accepted. *Academic units required:* 6 English, 6 mathematics, 9 social studies, 31 academic electives, 10 Interdisciplinary. *Academic units recommended:* 6 English, 6 mathematics, 9 social studies, 31 academic electives, 10 Interdisciplinary **Freshman Admission Statistics:** 1,231 applied, 93% admitted. **Transfer Admission Requirements:** High school transcript, college transcript(s), minimum college GPA of 2 required. Lowest grade transferable C. **General Admission Information:** Application Fee $25. Notification on a rolling basis, beginning on or about 9/1. Nonfall registration accepted. Admission may be deferred for a maximum of ongoing. Neither credit nor placement offered for CEEB Advanced Placement tests.

COSTS AND FINANCIAL AID

Annual tuition $8,760. Room and board $4,200. Required fees $120. Average book expense $1,000. **Required Forms and Deadlines:** FAFSAScholarship application, if applicable. **Notification of Awards:** Applicants will be notified of awards on a rolling basis beginning 3/1. **Types of Aid:** *Need-based scholarships/grants:* Federal Pell, SEOG, state scholarships/grants, private scholarships, the school's own gift aid, State of MI Nursing Scholarships. *Loans:* Subsidized Stafford, Unsubsidized Stafford, PLUS, state loans. **Student Employment: Financial Aid Statistics:** 88% freshmen, 88% undergrads receive need-based scholarship or grant aid. 64% freshmen, 35% undergrads receive non-need-based scholarship or grant aid. 83% freshmen, 92% undergrads receive need-based self-help aid. 2% freshmen, 2% undergrads receive athletic scholarships. 75% undergrads borrow to pay for school. Average cumulative indebtedness $8,439. **Criteria for awarding institutional aid:** *Non-need-based:* academics, alumni affiliation, athletics, leadership.

DAVIDSON COLLEGE

PO Box 7156, Davidson, NC 28035-7156
Phone: 704-894-2230
E-mail: admission@davidson.edu • **CEEB Code:** 5150
Fax: 704-894-2016 • **Website:** www.davidson.edu • **ACT Code:** 3086

This private school, affiliated with the Presbyterian Church, was founded in 1837. It has a 556-acre campus.

RATINGS

Admissions Selectivity Rating: 98   **Fire Safety Rating:** 60*   **Green Rating:** 91

STUDENTS AND FACULTY

Enrollment: 1,750. **Student Body:** 49% female, 51% male, 79% out-of-state, 4% international (42 countries represented). Asian 4%, African American 7%, Caucasian 71%, Hispanic 5%, Native American 0%.
Retention and Graduation: 96% freshmen return for sophomore year. 88% freshmen graduate within 4 years. 92% freshmen graduate within 6 years. 27% grads go on to further study within 1 year. **Faculty:** Student/faculty ratio 11:1. 162 full-time faculty, 96% hold PhDs, 15% are members of minority groups, 40% are women. 0% of classes are taught by teaching assistants.

ACADEMICS

Degrees: bachelor's. **Classes:** Most classes have 10–19 students. Most lab/discussion sessions have 10–19 students. **Majors with Highest Enrollment:** biology/biological sciences; English language and literature; history. **Special Study Options:** cross-registration, double major, exchange student program (domestic), honors program, independent study, student-designed major, study abroad, teacher certification program. **Disability Services:** Special programs offered to physically disabled students include note-taking services, reader services, tape recorders, tutors. **Career Services:** Alumni network, alumni services, career/job search classes, career assessment, internships.

FACILITIES

Housing: Coed dorms, cooperative housing, apartments for single students, wellness housing, theme housing, 90% of campus accessible to physically disabled. **Special Academic Facilities/Equipment:** Art gallery, scanning electron microscopes, UV-visible spectrometer, laser systems, Baker sports complex, Visual Arts building. **Computers:** Students can register for classes online.

CAMPUS LIFE

Environment: Village. **Activities:** Choral groups, concert band, dance, drama/theater, jazz band, literary magazine, music ensembles, musical theater, pep band, radio station, student government, student newspaper, symphony orchestra, yearbook, Campus Ministries, International Student Organization 151 registered organizations, 15 honor societies, 16 religious organizations. 8 fraternities. **Athletics (Intercollegiate):** *Men:* baseball, basketball, cross-country, diving, football, golf, soccer, swimming, tennis, track/field (outdoor), wrestling. *Women:* basketball, cross-country, diving, field hockey, lacrosse, soccer, swimming, tennis, track/field (outdoor), volleyball. **On-Campus Highlights:** Belk Visual Arts Center, Baker-Watt Science Complex, Baker Sports Complex, Campus Center, Lake Campus. **Environmental Initiatives:** Solar PV and solar thermal array on Baker Sports Complex Rigorous co-curricular programs, workshops, internships, student clubs, and leadership opportunities Ecological co-op - where ten students live comunally and practice sustainable living.

ADMISSIONS

Freshman Academic Profile: Average high school GPA 4.1. 82% in top 10% of high school class, 98% in top 25% of high school class, 100% in top 50% of high school class. 52% from public high schools. SAT Math middle 50% range 640-720. SAT Critical Reading middle 50% range 630-730. SAT Writing middle 50% range 630-730. ACT middle 50% range 29-33. Minimum web-based TOEFL 100. Minimum paper TOEFL 600. **Basis for Candidate Selection:** *Very important factors considered include:* recommendation(s), rigor of secondary school record, character/personal qualities, volunteer work. *Important factors considered include:* application essay, standardized test scores, extracurricular activities, interview, talent/ability. *Other factors considered include:* Class rank, alumni/ae relation. **Freshman Admission Requirements:** High school

diploma is required and GED is not accepted. *Academic units required:* 4 English, 3 mathematics, 2 science, 2 foreign language, 2 Social Studies or History. *Academic units recommended:* 4 English, 3 mathematics, 2 science, 2 foreign language, 2 social studies or history. **Freshman Admission Statistics:** 4,309 applied, 28% admitted, 40% enrolled. **Transfer Admission Requirements:** High school transcript, college transcript(s), essay or personal statement, standardized test scores, statement of good standing from prior institution(s). Minimum college GPA of 3.0 required. Lowest grade transferable C. **General Admission Information:** Application Fee $50. Early decision application deadline 11/15. Regular application deadline 1/2. Regular notification 4/1. Nonfall registration not accepted. Admission may be deferred for a maximum of 1 year. Credit and/or placement offered for CEEB Advanced Placement tests.

COSTS AND FINANCIAL AID

Annual tuition $40,405. Room and board $11,346. Required fees $404. Average book expense $1,000. **Required Forms and Deadlines:** FAFSA, CSS/Financial Aid PROFILE, noncustodial PROFILE, business/farm supplement. Noncustodial(Divorced/Separated)Parent's Statement; corporate tax return and/or noncustodial parent tax return(if applicable); parent and student tax returns and W-2 forms. **Notification of Awards:** Applicants will be notified of awards on or about 4/1. **Types of Aid:** *Need-based scholarships/grants:* Federal Pell, SEOG, state scholarships/grants, private scholarships, the school's own gift aid. *Loans:* Subsidized Stafford, Unsubsidized Stafford, PLUS, Federal Perkins, alternative loans. **Student Employment:** Federal Work-Study Program available. Institutional employment available. Off-campus job opportunities are excellent. **Financial Aid Statistics:** 96% freshmen, 96% undergrads receive need-based scholarship or grant aid. 17% freshmen, 24% undergrads receive non-need-based scholarship or grant aid. 69% freshmen, 70% undergrads receive need-based self-help aid. 6% freshmen, 8% undergrads receive athletic scholarships. 45% freshmen, 45% undergrads receive any aid. 22% undergrads borrow to pay for school. Average cumulative indebtedness $24,972. **Criteria for awarding institutional aid:** *Non-need-based:* academics, art, athletics, leadership, minority status, music/drama.

DAVIS & ELKINS COLLEGE

100 Campus Drive, Elkins, WV 26241
Phone: 304-637-1230 • **Financial Aid Phone:** 304-637-1373
E-mail: admiss@davisandelkins.edu • **CEEB Code:** 5151
Fax: 304-637-1800 • **Website:** www.davisandelkins.edu • **ACT Code:** 4518

This private school, affiliated with the Presbyterian Church, was founded in 1904. It has a 170-acre campus.

RATINGS

Admissions Selectivity Rating: 78   **Fire Safety Rating:** 62   **Green Rating:** 60*

STUDENTS AND FACULTY

Enrollment: 624. **Student Body:** 63% female, 37% male, 23% out-of-state, 0% international (15 countries represented). Asian 4%, African American 2%, Caucasian 98%, Hispanic 1%, Native American 0%.
Retention and Graduation: 64% freshmen return for sophomore year. 29% freshmen graduate within 4 years. 50% freshmen graduate within 6 years. 13% grads go on to further study within 1 year. 2% grads pursue law degrees. 11% grads pursue business degrees. **Faculty:** Student/faculty ratio 11:1. 44 full-time faculty, 84% hold PhDs, 11% are members of minority groups, 50% are women. 0% of classes are taught by teaching assistants.

ACADEMICS

Degrees: associate, bachelor's, terminal associate, transfer associate. **Classes:** Most classes have fewer than 10 students. Most lab/discussion sessions have 20–29 students. **Majors with Highest Enrollment:** business administration and management; marketing/marketing management; nursing/registered nurse (rn, asn, bsn, msn). **Special Study Options:** cooperative education program, cross-registration, double major, dual enrollment, external degree program, honors program, independent study, internships, student-designed major, study abroad, teacher certification program. **Disability Services:** Special programs offered to physically disabled students include note-taking services, reader services, tape recorders, tutors. **Career Services:** alumni services, career assessment, internships, regional alumni.

FACILITIES

Housing: Coed dorms, men's dorms, women's dorms. 80% of campus accessible to physically disabled. **Special Academic Facilities/Equipment:** planetarium, Graceland Inn and Conference Center(19th century Victorian mansion)-now used as training center for the Hospitality Program, Darby Collection-Civil War collection, Comstock collection, Pearl S. Buck collection **Computers:** Administrative functions (other than registration) can be performed online.

CAMPUS LIFE

Environment: Village. **Activities:** Choral groups, concert band, drama/theater, jazz band, literary magazine, music ensembles, musical theater, radio station, student government, student newspaper, yearbook 39 registered organizations, 7 honor societies, 1 religious organizations. 2 fraternities, 2 sororities. **Athletics (Intercollegiate):** *Men:* baseball, basketball, cross-country, golf, skiing (downhill/alpine), soccer. *Women:* basketball, cross-country, skiing (downhill/alpine), soccer, softball, volleyball. **On-Campus Highlights:** Mansions/ Halliehurst and Graceland, Icehouse, Chapel, Madden Student Center, Library, The 170 acre campus offers an historic district and newly renovated student center.

ADMISSIONS

Freshman Academic Profile: Average high school GPA 3.1. 12% in top 10% of high school class, 33% in top 25% of high school class, 71% in top 50% of high school class. 91% from public high schools. SAT Math middle 50% range 420-510. SAT Critical Reading middle 50% range 420-530. ACT middle 50% range 18-22. Minimum paper TOEFL 450. **Basis for Candidate Selection:** *Very important factors considered include:* rigor of secondary school record, level of applicant's interest. *Important factors considered include:* Class rank, academic GPA, recommendation(s), standardized test scores, character/personal qualities, extracurricular activities, talent/ability. *Other factors considered include:* application essay, alumni/ae relation, first generation, interview, volunteer work, work experience. **Freshman Admission Requirements:** High school diploma is required and GED is accepted. *Academic units required:* 4 English, 1 mathematics, 3 science, (1 science labs), 1 foreign language, 3 social studies, 2 mathematics units must include algebra I or II and geometry. *Academic units recommended:* 4 English, 1 mathematics, 3 science, (1 science labs), 1 foreign language. 3 social studies, 2 mathematics units must include algebra I or II and geometry. **Freshman Admission Statistics:** 563 applied, 55% admitted, 34% enrolled. **Transfer Admission Requirements:** High school transcript, college transcript(s), minimum college GPA of 2.0 required. Lowest grade transferable D. **General Admission Information:** Application Fee $35. Notification on a rolling basis, beginning on or about 9/30. Nonfall registration accepted. Admission may be deferred for a maximum of 1 yr. Credit and/or placement offered for CEEB Advanced Placement tests.

COSTS AND FINANCIAL AID

Average book expense $800. **Required Forms and Deadlines:** FAFSA. **Notification of Awards:** Applicants will be notified of awards on or about 5/1. **Types of Aid:** *Need-based scholarships/grants:* Federal Pell, SEOG, state scholarships/grants, private scholarships, the school's own gift aid. *Loans:* Subsidized Stafford, Unsubsidized Stafford, PLUS, Federal Perkins, state loans. **Student Employment:** Federal Work-Study Program available. Institutional employment available. Highest amount earned per year from on-campus jobs $1,000. Off-campus job opportunities are good. **Financial Aid Statistics:** 45% freshmen, 62% undergrads receive need-based scholarship or grant aid. 100% freshmen, 100% undergrads receive non-need-based scholarship or grant aid. 65% freshmen, 81% undergrads receive need-based self-help aid. 44% freshmen, 24% undergrads receive athletic scholarships. 98% freshmen, 98% undergrads receive any aid. 76% undergrads borrow to pay for school. Average cumulative indebtedness $13,380. **Criteria for awarding institutional aid:** *Non-need-based:* academics, alumni affiliation, art, athletics, leadership, minority status, music/drama, religious affiliation

DE SALES UNIVERSITY

Center Valley, PA 18034
Phone: 610-282-4443 • **Financial Aid Phone:** 610-282-4443
E-mail: admiss@desales.edu • **CEEB Code:** 2021
Fax: 610-282-0131 • **Website:** www.desales.edu

This private school, affiliated with the Roman Catholic Church, was founded in 1964. It has a 400-acre campus.

RATINGS

Admissions Selectivity Rating: 76 **Fire Safety Rating:** 78 **Green Rating:** 78

STUDENTS AND FACULTY

Enrollment: 2,468. **Student Body:** 61% female, 39% male, 22% out-of-state, 0% international (4 countries represented). Asian 2%, African American 4%, Caucasian 74%, Hispanic 8%, Native American 1%.
Retention and Graduation: 83% freshmen return for sophomore year. 54% freshmen graduate within 4 years. 67% freshmen graduate within 6 years.
Faculty: Student/faculty ratio 14:1. 105 full-time faculty, 79% hold PhDs, 7%

are members of minority groups, 49% are women. 0% of classes are taught by teaching assistants.

ACADEMICS

Degrees: bachelor's, certificate, master's, post-bachelor's certificate, post-master's certificate. **Classes:** Most classes have 20–29 students. Most lab/discussion sessions have fewer than 10 students. **Majors with Highest Enrollment:** drama and dramatics/theatre arts; nursing/registered nurse (rn, asn, bsn, msn); physician assistant. **Special Study Options:** Accelerated program, cross-registration, distance learning, double major, dual enrollment, English as a Second Language (ESL), exchange student program (domestic), honors program, independent study, internships, liberal arts/career combination, student-designed major, study abroad, teacher certification program, weekend college, Online degrees. **Honors Programs:** Faith and Reason Honors Program is competive and is limited to fifteen (15) students in each academic class. Studnets can find a description of the program at: www4.desales.edu/SCFC/FRseminars. **Combined Degree Programs:** BS/MSPAS; BSN/MSN; MBA/MNS. **Disability Services:** Special programs offered to physically disabled students include note-taking services, reader services, tape recorders, tutors. **Career Services:** Alumni network, alumni services, career/job search classes, career assessment, internships.

FACILITIES

Housing: men's dorms, women's dorms, cooperative housing, theme housing, 98% of campus accessible to physically disabled. **Computers:** 100% of classrooms, 5% of dorms, 100% of libraries, 100% of dining areas, 5% of student union, 20% of common outdoor areas have wireless network access. Students can register for classes online. Administrative functions (other than registration) can be performed online.

CAMPUS LIFE

Environment: Town. **Activities:** Choral groups, dance, drama/theater, musical theater, pep band, radio station, student government, student newspaper, television station, yearbook, Campus Ministries, International Student Organization, Model UN 42 registered organizations, 12 honor societies, 1 religious organizations. **Athletics (Intercollegiate):** *Men:* baseball, basketball, cross-country, golf, lacrosse, soccer, tennis, track/field (outdoor), track/field (indoor). *Women:* basketball, cross-country, field hockey, soccer, softball, tennis, track/field (outdoor), track/field (indoor), volleyball. **On-Campus Highlights:** Billera Athletics and Recreation Center, Hurd Science Center, Dog Pound in McShea Student Center, University Center, Labuda Center for the Performing Arts, Summer brings the Pennsylvania Shakespeare Festival to campus at the Labuda Center for the Performing Arts. **Environmental Initiatives:** Water reduction program - after adding one new residence hall we still reduced our water usage by 10% from 2008 to 2009. Open Space Land preservation recently obtained over 80 acres for campus open space and for land preservation. DeSales Dining Services Sustainability Program.

ADMISSIONS

Freshman Academic Profile: 3.2. 33% in top 10% of high school class, 45% in top 25% of high school class, 78% in top 50% of high school class. 60% from public high schools. SAT Math middle 50% range 480-600. SAT Critical Reading middle 50% range 480-590. ACT middle 50% range 20-27. Minimum paper TOEFL 550. **Basis for Candidate Selection:** *Very important factors considered include:* Class rank, academic GPA, recommendation(s), rigor of secondary school record. *Important factors considered include:* standardized test scores, extracurricular activities, interview, talent/ability. *Other factors considered include:* application essay, geographical residence, racial/ethnic status, state residency, volunteer work, work experience. **Freshman Admission Requirements:** High school diploma is required and GED is accepted. *Academic units required:* 4 English, 3 mathematics, 2 science, (2 science labs), 2 foreign language, 3 social studies, 9 history, 19 academic electives. *Academic units recommended:* 4 English, 3 mathematics, 2 science, (2 science labs), 2 foreign language, 3 social studies, 9 history, 19 academic electives. **Freshman Admission Statistics:** 2,353 applied, 72% admitted, 23% enrolled. **Transfer Admission Requirements:** High school transcript, college transcript(s), statement of good standing from prior institution(s). Minimum college GPA of 2.00 required. Lowest grade transferable 2. **General Admission Information:** Regular application deadline 8/1. Notification on a rolling basis, beginning on or about 11/1. Nonfall registration accepted. Credit offered for CEEB Advanced Placement tests.

COSTS AND FINANCIAL AID

Annual tuition $29,000. Room and board $10,970. Required fees $1,150. Average book expense $1,526. **Required Forms and Deadlines:** FAFSA, institution's own financial aid form, state aid form. **Notification of Awards:** Applicants will be notified of awards on a rolling basis beginning 2/15. **Types of Aid:** *Need-based scholarships/grants:* Federal Pell, SEOG, state scholarships/grants, private scholarships, the school's own gift aid, Federal Nursing Scholarships. *Loans:* Subsidized Stafford, Unsubsidized Stafford, PLUS, Federal Perkins, Federal Nursing, state loans. **Student Employment:** Federal Work-Study Program available. Institutional employment available. Off-campus job opportunities are good. **Financial Aid Statistics:** 100% freshmen, 94% undergrads receive need-based scholarship or grant aid. 85% freshmen, 87% undergrads receive non-need-based scholarship or grant aid. 87% freshmen, 87% undergrads receive need-based self-help aid. Average cumulative indebtedness $28,875. **Criteria for awarding institutional aid:** *Non-need-based:* academics, leadership, music/drama.

See page 1066.

DEAN COLLEGE

Office of Admission, Franklin, MA 02038-1994
Phone: 508-541-1508
E-mail: admission@dean.edu
Fax: 508-541-8726 • **Website:** www.dean.edu

This is a private school.

RATINGS
Admissions Selectivity Rating: 67   **Fire Safety Rating:** 60*   **Green Rating:** 60*

STUDENTS AND FACULTY
Enrollment: 1,106. **Student Body:** 48% female, 52% male, 53% out-of-state, 10% international. Asian 1%, African American 7%, Caucasian 50%, Hispanic 3%, Native American 1%.
Retention and Graduation: 62% freshmen return for sophomore year. **Faculty:** Student/faculty ratio 19:1. 33 full-time faculty, 36% hold PhDs, 9% are members of minority groups, 55% are women.

ACADEMICS
Degrees: associate, bachelor's, certificate. **Classes:** Most classes have 10–19 students. Most lab/discussion sessions have fewer than 10 students. **Special Study Options:** Accelerated program, double major, English as a Second Language (ESL), honors program, independent study, internships, liberal arts/career combination, study abroad.

FACILITIES
Housing: Coed dorms, women's dorms.

CAMPUS LIFE
Environment: Activities: dance, drama/theater, literary magazine, musical theater, radio station, student government, yearbook.

ADMISSIONS
Freshman Academic Profile: Average high school GPA 2.2. SAT Math middle 50% range 380-490. SAT Critical Reading middle 50% range 390-490. ACT middle 50% range 15-20. **Basis for Candidate Selection:** *Other factors considered include:* Class rank, application essay, academic GPA, recommendation(s), rigor of secondary school record, standardized test scores, alumni/ae relation, character/personal qualities, extracurricular activities, interview, level of applicant's interest, talent/ability, volunteer work, work experience. **Freshman Admission Requirements:** High school diploma is required and GED is accepted. *Academic units required:* 3 English, 1 mathematics, 1 science, (1 science labs), 1 social studies, 1 history. *Academic units recommended:* 3 English, 1 mathematics, 1 science, (1 science labs), 1 social studies, 1 history. **Freshman Admission Statistics:** 1,910 applied, 73% admitted, 39% enrolled. **Transfer Admission Requirements:** High school transcript, college transcript(s), essay or personal statement, Lowest grade transferable C–. **General Admission Information:** Application Fee $35. Notification on a rolling basis, beginning on or about 12/1. Nonfall registration accepted. Admission may be deferred for a maximum of 1 year.

COSTS AND FINANCIAL AID
Required Forms and Deadlines: FAFSA. **Notification of Awards:** Applicants will be notified of awards on a rolling basis beginning 3/1. **Types of Aid:** *Need-based scholarships/grants:* Federal Pell, SEOG, state scholarships/grants, private scholarships, the school's own gift aid. *Loans:* Subsidized Stafford, Unsubsidized Stafford, PLUS, Federal Perkins. **Student Employment: Financial Aid Statistics:** 100% freshmen, 99% undergrads receive need-based scholarship or grant aid. 13% freshmen, 13% undergrads receive non-need-based scholarship or grant aid. 93% freshmen, 94% undergrads receive need-based self-help aid. 2% freshmen, 3% undergrads receive athletic scholarships. 73% undergrads borrow to pay for school. Average cumulative indebtedness $14,531. **Criteria for awarding institutional aid:** *Non-need-based:* academics, athletics, leadership, music/drama.

DEEP SPRINGS COLLEGE

Best 378

Applications Committee, Dyer, NV 89010
Phone: 760-872-2000
E-mail: apcom@deepsprings.edu • **CEEB Code:** 4281
Fax: 760-872-4466 • **Website:** www.deepsprings.edu

This private school was founded in 1917. It has a 30000-acre campus.

RATINGS
Admissions Selectivity Rating: 99   **Fire Safety Rating:** 82   **Green Rating:** 60*

STUDENTS AND FACULTY
Enrollment: 25. **Student Body:** 0% female, 100% male, 80% out-of-state, 4% international (3 countries represented). Asian 0%, African American 0%, Caucasian 44%, Hispanic 0%, Native American 0%.
Retention and Graduation: 92% freshmen return for sophomore year. 96% grads go on to further study within 1 year. 26% grads pursue arts and sciences degrees. 11% grads pursue law degrees. 3% grads pursue business degrees. 10% grads pursue medical degrees. **Faculty:** Student/faculty ratio 4:1. 3 full-time faculty, 100% hold PhDs, 0% are members of minority groups, 67% are women. 0% of classes are taught by teaching assistants.

ACADEMICS
Degrees: associate. **Classes:** Most classes have fewer than 10 students. **Majors with Highest Enrollment:** liberal arts and sciences studies and humanities, other. **Special Study Options:** independent study, internships.

FACILITIES
Housing: men's dorms. 100% of campus accessible to physically disabled. **Special Academic Facilities/Equipment:** Ranch- 300 cattle, 20 horses, organic farm growing hay and produce; thousands of acres of wilderness surround the college

CAMPUS LIFE
Environment: Rural. **Activities:** student government 1 registered organizations. **On-Campus Highlights:** Boarding House, Dairy Barn, Horse Stables, The Upper Reservoir, The Druid.

ADMISSIONS
Freshman Academic Profile: 83% in top 10% of high school class, 93% in top 25% of high school class, 100% in top 50% of high school class. 50% from public high schools. SAT Math middle 50% range 700-800. SAT Critical Reading middle 50% range 750-800. **Basis for Candidate Selection:** *Very important factors considered include:* application essay, character/personal qualities, interview, level of applicant's interest. *Important factors considered include:* academic GPA, rigor of secondary school record, extracurricular activities, volunteer work, work experience. *Other factors considered include:* Class rank, recommendation(s), standardized test scores, racial/ethnic status, talent/ability. **Freshman Admission Requirements:** High school diploma or equivalent is not required. **Freshman Admission Statistics:** 170 applied, 7% admitted, 100% enrolled. **Transfer Admission Requirements:** High school transcript, college transcript(s), essay or personal statement, interview, standardized test scores. **General Admission Information:** Regular application deadline 11/15. Regular notification 4/15. Nonfall registration not accepted. Neither credit nor placement offered for CEEB Advanced Placement tests.

COSTS AND FINANCIAL AID
Average book expense $1,200. **Required Forms and Deadlines: Notification of Awards:** Applicants will be notified of awards on or about 4/15. **Financial Aid Statistics:** 100% freshmen, 100% undergrads receive any aid. 0% undergrads borrow to pay for school. Average cumulative indebtedness $0.

DEFIANCE COLLEGE

701 North Clinton Street, Defiance, OH 43512-1695
Phone: 419-783-2359 • **Financial Aid Phone:** 419-783-2458
E-mail: admissions@defiance.edu • **CEEB Code:** 1162
Fax: 419-783-2468 • **Website:** www.defiance.edu • **ACT Code:** 3264

This private school, affiliated with the United Church of Christ Church, was founded in 1850. It has a 150-acre campus.

RATINGS
Admissions Selectivity Rating: 72   **Fire Safety Rating:** 84   **Green Rating:** 62

STUDENTS AND FACULTY
Enrollment: 304. **Student Body:** 50% female, 50% male, 23% out-of-state, 3% international (2 countries represented). Asian 2%, African American 37%, Caucasian 237%, Hispanic 17%, Native American 5%. **Retention and Graduation:** 41% freshmen graduate within 4 years. 50% freshmen graduate within 6 years. 30% grads go on to further study within 1 year. 1% grads pursue law degrees. 29% grads pursue business degrees. 19% grads pursue medical degrees. **Faculty:** Student/faculty ratio 11:1. 40 full-time faculty, 70% hold PhDs, 10% are members of minority groups, 33% are women. 0% of classes are taught by teaching assistants.

ACADEMICS
Degrees: associate, bachelor's, certificate, master's. **Classes:** Most classes have 10–19 students. Most lab/discussion sessions have 10–19 students. **Majors with Highest Enrollment:** business administration, management and operations, other; education; forensic science and technology. **Special Study Options:** cooperative education program, distance learning, double major, dual enrollment, honors program, independent study, internships, student-designed major, study abroad, teacher certification program, weekend college. **Career Services:** Alumni network, alumni services, career/job search classes, career assessment, internships Career Services highlights include Cooperative Learning.

FACILITIES
Housing: Coed dorms, apartments for single students. 100% of campus accessible to physically disabled. **Special Academic Facilities/Equipment:** Art gallery, media center, Eisenhower archives room, curriculum resource center, Cultural Arts Center, Indian wars collection. **Computers:** 100% of classrooms, 30% of dorms, 100% of libraries, 100% of dining areas, 100% of student union, 100% of common outdoor areas have wireless network access.

CAMPUS LIFE
Environment: Rural. **Activities:** Choral groups, concert band, drama/theater, literary magazine, musical theater, pep band, student government, student newspaper, yearbook, Campus Ministries 30 registered organizations, 1 honor societies, 2 religious organizations. 1 fraternities, 2 sororities. **Athletics (Intercollegiate):** *Men:* baseball, basketball, cross-country, football, golf, soccer, tennis, track/field (outdoor), track/field (indoor). *Women:* basketball, cross-country, golf, soccer, softball, tennis, track/field (outdoor), track/field (indoor), volleyball. **On-Campus Highlights:** Smart Fitness Center, Tenzer Hall, Serrick Center, Hubbard Hall, Weaner/McMaster Center. **Environmental Initiatives:** Lowering Electrical, Gas, and Water Usage.

ADMISSIONS
Freshman Academic Profile: Average high school GPA 3.0. 12% in top 10% of high school class, 28% in top 25% of high school class, 57% in top 50% of high school class. 97% from public high schools. SAT Math middle 50% range 390-530. SAT Critical Reading middle 50% range 390-500. SAT Writing middle 50% range 350-520. ACT middle 50% range 18-23. Minimum web-based TOEFL 79. Minimum paper TOEFL 550. **Basis for Candidate Selection:** *Very important factors considered include:* academic GPA, rigor of secondary school record, standardized test scores. *Other factors considered include:* Class rank, character/personal qualities, extracurricular activities, interview, volunteer work. **Freshman Admission Requirements:** High school diploma is required and GED is accepted. **Freshman Admission Statistics:** 1,742 applied, 62% admitted, 24% enrolled. **Transfer Admission Requirements:** High school transcript, college transcript(s), essay or personal statement, statement of good standing from prior institution(s). Minimum college GPA of 2.0 required. Lowest grade transferable C. **General Admission Information:** Application Fee $25. Notification on a rolling basis, beginning on or about 9/1. Nonfall registration accepted. Admission may be deferred for a maximum of one year. Credit and/or placement offered for CEEB Advanced Placement tests.

COSTS AND FINANCIAL AID
Annual tuition $26,740. Room and board $8,850. Required fees $620. Average book expense $1,350. **Required Forms and Deadlines:** FAFSA **Notification of Awards: Types of Aid:** *Need-based scholarships/grants:* Federal Pell, SEOG, state scholarships/grants, private scholarships, the school's own gift aid.

Loans: Subsidized Stafford, Unsubsidized Stafford, PLUS, Federal Perkins, ALTERNATIVE LOANS. **Student Employment:** Federal Work-Study Program available. Institutional employment available. Off-campus job opportunities are good. **Financial Aid Statistics:** 86% freshmen, 83% undergrads receive need-based scholarship or grant aid. 100% freshmen, 97% undergrads receive non-need-based scholarship or grant aid. 93% freshmen, 92% undergrads receive need-based self-help aid. 100% freshmen, 99% undergrads receive any aid. 90% undergrads borrow to pay for school. Average cumulative indebtedness $31,410. **Criteria for awarding institutional aid:** *Non-need-based:* academics, leadership.

DELAWARE VALLEY COLLEGE

700 East Butler Avenue, Doylestown, PA 18901-2697
Phone: 215-489-2211 • **Financial Aid Phone:** 215-489-2272
E-mail: ADMITME@delval.edu • **CEEB Code:** 2510
Fax: 215-230-2968 • **Website:** www.delval.edu • **ACT Code:** 3551

This private school was founded in 1896. It has a 600-acre campus.

RATINGS
Admissions Selectivity Rating: 72   **Fire Safety Rating:** 75   **Green Rating:** 73

STUDENTS AND FACULTY
Enrollment: 1,877. **Student Body:** 58% female, 42% male, 39% out-of-state, 0% international (4 countries represented). Asian 1%, African American 4%, Caucasian 84%, Hispanic 2%, Native American 0%. **Retention and Graduation:** 76% freshmen return for sophomore year. 37% freshmen graduate within 4 years. 50% freshmen graduate within 6 years. 51% grads go on to further study within 1 year. 1% grads pursue law degrees. 9% grads pursue business degrees. 10% grads pursue medical degrees. **Faculty:** Student/faculty ratio 15:1. 82 full-time faculty, 57% hold PhDs, 10% are members of minority groups, 41% are women. 0% of classes are taught by teaching assistants.

ACADEMICS
Degrees: associate, bachelor's, certificate, master's, terminal associate, transfer associate. **Classes:** Most classes have 10–19 students. Most lab/discussion sessions have 10–19 students. **Majors with Highest Enrollment:** animal sciences; animal sciences, other; business administration and management. **Special Study Options:** Accelerated program, cross-registration, distance learning, double major, honors program, independent study, internships, study abroad, teacher certification program, weekend college. **Honors Programs:** The DVC Honors Program is an educational enrichment program designed to enhance the educational opportunities and experiences of students admitted to the program. The programs consists of an Honors Colloquium followed by independent study programs in the 3rd and 4th years. It features guest lecturers, field trips and both faculty and student-led discussions. **Disability Services:** Special programs offered to physically disabled students include note-taking services, reader services, tape recorders. **Career Services:** alumni services, career/job search classes, career assessment, internships Career Services highlights include Our required employment program requires students to work 500 hours in their field before they graduate. Delaware Valley College's Employment Program, an experience-based graduation requirement, fosters the integration of theory and practice throughout the educational continuum, and helps students develop linkages with professionals in their fields of study. The Employment Program empowers students by equipping them with the skills and abilities necessary for success as they transition from college to career. Because of the college's commitment to career-oriented education, students graduate with a level of skill and experience that far exceeds that of the average entry-level candidate. Delaware Valley College is one of only 3% of colleges nationwide with a mandatory experiential-learning requirement, making it one of the most important and unique aspects of the DelVal educational experience.

FACILITIES
Housing: Coed dorms, women's dorms. **Special Academic Facilities/Equipment:** Dairy processing plant, greenhouse and nursery lab complex, small animal science labs, poultry diagnostic lab, arboretum, equine facilities, 500+-acre farm, tissue culture lab. **Computers:** 25% of classrooms, 100% of dorms, 100% of libraries, 80% of student union, 20% of common outdoor areas have wireless network access. Students can register for classes online. Administrative functions (other than registration) can be performed online.

CAMPUS LIFE
Environment: Village. **Activities:** Choral groups, concert band, drama/theater, literary magazine, music ensembles, radio station, student government, student newspaper, yearbook 62 registered organizations, 2 honor societies, 2 religious

organizations. 5 fraternities, 3 sororities. **Athletics (Intercollegiate):** *Men:* baseball, basketball, cross-country, football, golf, soccer, track/field (outdoor), track/field (indoor), wrestling. *Women:* basketball, cheerleading, cross-country, field hockey, soccer, softball, track/field (outdoor), track/field (indoor), volleyball. **On-Campus Highlights:** Smart Classroom, Small Animal Facility, Athletic Complex, Student Center, Equine center, The campus has many unique areas that are of specific interest depending on a student's major field of study (i.e. dairy barn, equine center, etc.). **Environmental Initiatives:** Recycling Wind Energy Bio-Diesel Fuel.

ADMISSIONS
Freshman Academic Profile: Average high school GPA 3.5. 13% in top 10% of high school class, 73% in top 25% of high school class, 27% in top 50% of high school class. 85% from public high schools. SAT Math middle 50% range 460-560. SAT Critical Reading middle 50% range 450-550. SAT Writing middle 50% range 430-550. ACT middle 50% range 20-25. Minimum paper TOEFL 500. **Basis for Candidate Selection:** *Very important factors considered include:* academic GPA, standardized test scores. *Important factors considered include:* Class rank, rigor of secondary school record, interview. *Other factors considered include:* application essay, recommendation(s), alumni/ae relation, character/personal qualities, extracurricular activities, level of applicant's interest, talent/ability, volunteer work, work experience. **Freshman Admission Requirements:** High school diploma is required and GED is accepted. *Academic units required:* 3 English, 2 mathematics, 2 science, (1 science labs), 2 social studies, 6 academic electives. 3 English, 2 mathematics, 2 science, (1 science labs), 2 social studies, 6 academic electives. **Freshman Admission Statistics:** 1,770 applied, 72% admitted, 36% enrolled. **Transfer Admission Requirements:** High school transcript, college transcript(s), statement of good standing from prior institution(s). Minimum college GPA of 2.0 required. Lowest grade transferable C. **General Admission Information:** Application Fee $35. Notification on a rolling basis, beginning on or about 10/31. Nonfall registration accepted. Admission may be deferred for a maximum of 12 months. Credit and/or placement offered for CEEB Advanced Placement tests.

COSTS AND FINANCIAL AID
Annual tuition $28,596. Room and board $10,842. Required fees $2,050. Required **Forms and Deadlines:** FAFSA, state aid form. **Notification of Awards:** Applicants will be notified of awards on a rolling basis beginning 2/1. **Types of Aid:** *Need-based scholarships/grants:* Federal Pell, SEOG, state scholarships/grants, private scholarships, the school's own gift aid. *Loans:* Subsidized Stafford, Unsubsidized Stafford, PLUS, Federal Perkins, Alternative Loans. **Student Employment:** Federal Work-Study Program available. Institutional employment available. Highest amount earned per year from on-campus jobs $2,200. **Financial Aid Statistics:** 99% freshmen, 99% undergrads receive need-based scholarship or grant aid. 9% freshmen, 8% undergrads receive non-need-based scholarship or grant aid. 83% freshmen, 80% undergrads receive need-based self-help aid. 98% freshmen, 91% undergrads receive any aid. 73% undergrads borrow to pay for school. Average cumulative indebtedness $28,896. **Criteria for awarding institutional aid:** *Non-need-based:* academics, alumni affiliation, music/drama.

DELTA STATE UNIVERSITY

Highway 8 West, Cleveland, MS 38733
Phone: 662-846-4018
E-mail: dheslep@deltastate.edu
Fax: 662-846-4683 • **Website:** www.deltastate.edu • **ACT Code:** 2190

This public school was founded in 1924. It has a 332-acre campus.

RATINGS
Admissions Selectivity Rating: 86   **Fire Safety Rating:** 67   **Green Rating:** 60*

STUDENTS AND FACULTY
Enrollment: 3,156. **Student Body:** 62% female, 38% male, 10% out-of-state, 0% international (3 countries represented). Asian 1%, African American 33%, Caucasian 66%, Hispanic 1%, Native American 0%.
Retention and Graduation: 68% freshmen return for sophomore year. 24% freshmen graduate within 4 years. 48% freshmen graduate within 6 years.
Faculty: Student/faculty ratio 16:1. 162 full-time faculty, 60% hold PhDs, 7% are members of minority groups, 49% are women. 0% of classes are taught by teaching assistants.

ACADEMICS
Degrees: bachelor's, master's, post-master's certificate. **Classes: Majors with Highest Enrollment:** business/commerce; elementary education and teaching; management information systems. **Special Study Options:** cooperative educa-

---

tion program, distance learning, double major, dual enrollment, honors program, independent study, internships, teacher certification program, weekend college. **Disability Services:** Special programs offered to physically disabled students include note-taking services, reader services, tape recorders, tutors.

FACILITIES
Housing: men's dorms, women's dorms, apartments for married students, Apartments for students with dependent children. 65% of campus accessible to physically disabled. **Special Academic Facilities/Equipment:** Art museum, performing arts center, natural history museum, language lab, airport facility with 12 airplanes, flight simulator, planetarium, Art museum, Performing Arts Center, Natural History Museum, Language Lab, Airport facility, flight simulation, planetarium **Computers:** Students can register for classes online. Administrative functions (other than registration) can be performed online.

CAMPUS LIFE
Environment: Village. **Activities:** Choral groups, concert band, drama/theater, jazz band, literary magazine, marching band, music ensembles, musical theater, opera, student government, student newspaper, symphony orchestra, yearbook 46 registered organizations, 27 honor societies, 11 religious organizations. 8 fraternities, 6 sororities. **Athletics (Intercollegiate):** *Men:* baseball, basketball, diving, football, golf, soccer, swimming, tennis. *Women:* basketball, cross-country, diving, soccer, softball, swimming, tennis.

ADMISSIONS
Freshman Academic Profile: 4% in top 25% of high school class, 57% in top 50% of high school class. ACT middle 50% range 17-21. Minimum paper TOEFL 525. **Basis for Candidate Selection:** *Very important factors considered include:* Class rank, rigor of secondary school record, standardized test scores. *Other factors considered include:* recommendation(s), interview. **Freshman Admission Requirements:** High school diploma is required and GED is accepted. *Academic units required:* 4 English, 3 mathematics, 3 science, (2 science labs), 1 foreign language, 3 social studies, 1 academic electives. 4 English, 3 mathematics, 3 science, (2 science labs), 1 foreign language, 3 social studies, 1 academic electives. **Freshman Admission Statistics:** 1,289 applied, 32% admitted, 79% enrolled. **Transfer Admission Requirements:** college transcript(s), minimum college GPA of 2.0 required. Lowest grade transferable D. **General Admission Information:** Application Fee $15. Regular application deadline 8/1. Notification on a rolling basis, beginning on or about 5/15. Nonfall registration accepted. Admission may be deferred for a maximum of N/A. Credit and/or placement offered for CEEB Advanced Placement tests.

COSTS AND FINANCIAL AID
Average book expense $700. **Required Forms and Deadlines:** FAFSA, institution's own financial aid form. **Notification of Awards:** Applicants will be notified of awards on a rolling basis beginning 5/1. **Types of Aid:** *Need-based scholarships/grants:* Federal Pell, SEOG, private scholarships, the school's own gift aid. *Loans:* Subsidized Stafford, Unsubsidized Stafford, PLUS, Federal Perkins, college/university loans from institutional funds. **Student Employment:** Federal Work-Study Program available. Institutional employment available. Highest amount earned per year from on-campus jobs $1,200. Off-campus job opportunities are fair. **Criteria for awarding institutional aid:** *Non-need-based:* academics, alumni affiliation, art, athletics, leadership, music/drama, religious affiliation, state/district residency.

DENISON UNIVERSITY

Best 378

Box H, Granville, OH 43023
Phone: 740-587-6276 • **Financial Aid Phone:** 800-336-4766
E-mail: admissions@denison.edu • **CEEB Code:** 1164
Fax: 740-587-6306 • **Website:** www.denison.edu • **ACT Code:** 3266

This private school was founded in 1831. It has a 900-acre campus.

RATINGS
Admissions Selectivity Rating: 93   **Fire Safety Rating:** 87   **Green Rating:** 94

STUDENTS AND FACULTY
Enrollment: 2,266. **Student Body:** 57% female, 43% male, 70% out-of-state, 7% international (29 countries represented). Asian 3%, African American 7%, Caucasian 73%, Hispanic 6%, Native American 0%.

Retention and Graduation: 90% freshmen return for sophomore year. 76% freshmen graduate within 4 years. 79% freshmen graduate within 6 years. 26% grads go on to further study within 1 year. 16% grads pursue arts and sciences degrees. 3% grads pursue law degrees. 3% grads pursue business degrees. 3% grads pursue medical degrees. **Faculty:** Student/faculty ratio 10:1. 211 full-time faculty, 99% hold PhDs, 1676% are members of minority groups, 45% are women. 0% of classes are taught by teaching assistants.

ACADEMICS

Degrees: bachelor's. **Classes:** Most classes have 10–19 students. **Majors with Highest Enrollment:** economics; English language and literature; psychology. **Special Study Options:** double major, honors program, independent study, internships, student-designed major, study abroad, teacher certification program, 3-2 Duke U Environmental Management; 3-2 U. of Michigan Natural Resources, 3-4 Case Western Reserve Dental; 3-2 Rensselaer Poly., Washington U. (St. Louis), Case Western Reserve, Columbia U. Engineering; Washington U. (St. Louis) Occupational Therapy. **Disability Services:** Special programs offered to physically disabled students include note-taking services, reader services, tape recorders, tutors. **Career Services:** Alumni network, alumni services, career assessment, internships, regional alumni. Career Services highlights include We are proud of all of our programs.

FACILITIES

Housing: Coed dorms, men's dorms, women's dorms, cooperative housing, apartments for single students, wellness housing, theme housing, 66% of campus accessible to physically disabled. **Special Academic Facilities/Equipment:** Burmese art collection in the Dension Museum, language lab, research station in 350-acre biological reserve, observatory, high resolution spectrometer lab, nuclear magnetic resonance spectrometer, planetarium, Economics computer laboratories. **Computers:** 100% of classrooms, 100% of dorms, 100% of libraries, 100% of dining areas, 100% of student union, 100% of common outdoor areas have wireless network access. Administrative functions (other than registration) can be performed online.

CAMPUS LIFE

Environment: Village. **Activities:** Choral groups, dance, drama/theater, jazz band, music ensembles, musical theater, radio station, student government, student newspaper, student-run film society, television station, yearbook, Campus Ministries, International Student Organization 160 registered organizations, 15 honor societies, 7 religious organizations. 8 fraternities, 6 sororities. **Athletics (Intercollegiate):** *Men:* baseball, basketball, cross-country, diving, football, golf, lacrosse, soccer, swimming, tennis, track/field (outdoor), track/field (indoor). *Women:* basketball, cross-country, diving, field hockey, golf, lacrosse, soccer, softball, swimming, tennis, track/field (outdoor), track/field (indoor), volleyball. **On-Campus Highlights:** Samson Talbot Hall of Biological Science, Mitchell Recreation and Athletics Center, Swasey Chapel, Biological Reserve and Polly Anderson Fi, Burke Hall Art Gallery, Burton D. Morgan Center. **Environmental Initiatives:** The signing of the ACUPCC and the development of a standing Campus Sustainability Committee as part of the campus governance system. Completion of a comprehensive greenhouse gas inventory and campus sustainability assessment using the STARS program. Development of a Policy to build and renovate to LEED Silver or better standards.

ADMISSIONS

Freshman Academic Profile: 55% in top 10% of high school class, 86% in top 25% of high school class, 100% in top 50% of high school class. 73% from public high schools. SAT Math middle 50% range 590-670. SAT Critical Reading middle 50% range 600-690. ACT middle 50% range 27-30. Minimum paper TOEFL 599. **Basis for Candidate Selection:** *Very important factors considered include:* application essay, academic GPA, recommendation(s), rigor of secondary school record. *Important factors considered include:* extracurricular activities, interview, level of applicant's interest, talent/ability. *Other factors considered include:* Class rank, standardized test scores, alumni/ae relation, character/personal qualities, first generation, geographical residence, racial/ethnic status, state residency, volunteer work, work experience. **Freshman Admission Requirements:** High school diploma is required and GED is accepted. *Academic units required:* 4 English, 4 mathematics, 4 science, 3 foreign language, 2 social studies, 1 history, 1 academic electives. 4 English, 4 mathematics, 4 science, 3 foreign language, 2 social studies, 1 history, 1 academic electives. **Freshman Admission Statistics:** 4,772 applied, 48% admitted, 26% enrolled. **Transfer Admission Requirements:** High school transcript, college transcript(s), essay or personal statement, statement of good standing from prior institution(s). Minimum college GPA of 3.0 required. Lowest grade transferable C–. **General Admission Information:** Application Fee $40. Early decision application deadline 11/15. Regular application deadline 1/15. Regular notification 4/1. Nonfall registration not accepted. Admission may be deferred for a maximum of 1 year. Credit and/or placement offered for CEEB Advanced Placement tests.

COSTS AND FINANCIAL AID

Annual tuition $39,330. Room and board $9,960. Required fees $880. Average book expense $600. **Required Forms and Deadlines:** FAFSA. **Notification of Awards:** Applicants will be notified of awards on or about 3/28. **Types of Aid:** *Need-based scholarships/grants:* Federal Pell, SEOG, state scholarships/grants, private scholarships, the school's own gift aid. *Loans:* Direct Subsidized Stafford, Direct Unsubsidized Stafford, Direct PLUS, Federal Perkins, college/university loans from institutional funds. **Student Employment:** Federal Work-Study Program available. Institutional employment available. Highest amount earned per year from on-campus jobs $2,530. Off-campus job opportunities are fair. **Financial Aid Statistics:** 100% freshmen, 100% undergrads receive need-based scholarship or grant aid. 93% freshmen, 89% undergrads receive non-need-based scholarship or grant aid. 80% freshmen, 79% undergrads receive need-based self-help aid. 97% freshmen, 96% undergrads receive any aid. **Criteria for awarding institutional aid:** *Non-need-based:* academics, alumni affiliation, art, leadership, minority status, music/drama, state/district residency.

See page 1064.

DEPAUL UNIVERSITY

1 East Jackson Boulevard, Chicago, IL 60604-2287
Phone: 312-362-8300 • **Financial Aid Phone:** 312-362-8091
E-mail: admission@depaul.edu • **CEEB Code:** 001671-00
Fax: 312-362-5749 • **Website:** www.depaul.edu • **ACT Code:** 1012

This private school, affiliated with the Roman Catholic Church, was founded in 1898. It has a 36-acre campus.

RATINGS
Admissions Selectivity Rating: 85   **Fire Safety Rating:** 97   **Green Rating:** 80

STUDENTS AND FACULTY
Enrollment: 16,153. **Student Body:** 54% female, 46% male, 19% out-of-state, 2% international (76 countries represented). Asian 7%, African American 8%, Caucasian 56%, Hispanic 17%, Native American 0%.
Retention and Graduation: 85% freshmen return for sophomore year. 51% freshmen graduate within 4 years. 68% freshmen graduate within 6 years. 21% grads go on to further study within 1 year. **Faculty:** Student/faculty ratio 16:1. 979 full-time faculty, 88% hold PhDs, 18% are members of minority groups, 43% are women. 1% of classes are taught by teaching assistants.

ACADEMICS
Degrees: bachelor's, certificate, master's, post-bachelor's certificate, post-master's certificate. **Classes:** Most classes have 20–29 students. Most lab/discussion sessions have 10–19 students. **Majors with Highest Enrollment:** accounting; communication studies/speech communication and rhetoric; psychology. **Special Study Options:** Accelerated program, cooperative education program, distance learning, double major, dual enrollment, English as a Second Language (ESL), honors program, independent study, internships, student-designed major, study abroad, teacher certification program, weekend college. **Honors Programs:** DePaul's honors program offers small classes organized in a seminar format and taught by faculty committed to academic excellence and the attainment of lifelong learning strategies. Benefits of our scholarly community include academic advising, an Honors Lounge, a student government, peer mentoring, student-faculty dinners, newsletters, cultural outings, service activities, and many other experiences that enrich the Honors community while extending the Honors experience beyond the classroom. **Combined Degree Programs:** BA/MA, BS/MS. **Disability Services:** Special programs offered to physically disabled students include note-taking services, reader services, tape recorders, tutors. **Career Services:** Alumni network, alumni services, career/job search classes, career assessment, internships, regional alumni. Career Services highlights include In response to a mandated experiential learning requirement, we set up an university wide internship program that places 1,020 students a year in internships that meet the requirements.

FACILITIES
Housing: Coed dorms, special housing for disabled students, special housing for international students, apartments for single students, theme housing, 95% of campus accessible to physically disabled. **Special Academic Facilities/Equipment:** Monsignor Andrew J. McGowan Environmental Science & Chemistry building (gold LEED-certified, 2009), Digital Cinema laboratory with motion-capture system, Green-screen studio, converged newsroom, Merle Reskin Theatre, Art Museum, William G. McGowan Biological & Environmental Science Building (1998), Ray Meyer Fitness & Recreational Center (1999),

and Three-level student center (2002) **Computers:** 60% of classrooms, 100% of dorms, 100% of libraries, 100% of dining areas, 75% of student union, 25% of common outdoor areas have wireless network access. Students can register for classes online. Administrative functions (other than registration) can be performed online.

CAMPUS LIFE

Environment: Metropolis. **Activities:** Choral groups, concert band, dance, drama/theater, jazz band, literary magazine, marching band, music ensembles, musical theater, opera, pep band, radio station, student government, student newspaper, student-run film society, symphony orchestra, yearbook, Campus Ministries, International Student Organization, Model UN 311 registered organizations, 9 honor societies, 19 religious organizations. 9 fraternities, 13 sororities. **Athletics (Intercollegiate):** *Men:* basketball, cross-country, golf, soccer, tennis, track/field (outdoor), track/field (indoor). *Women:* basketball, cross-country, soccer, softball, tennis, track/field (outdoor), track/field (indoor), volleyball. **On-Campus Highlights:** Quad (outside center of campus), Ray Meyer Fitness Center, Student Center, Student Lounge in DePaul Center, The Bean Cafe in the Schmitt Acad. Cntr. **Environmental Initiatives:** The creation of SITF (The Sustainability Initiative Task Force) and working groups are collaborating to develop a Campus Sustainability Plan that will effectively address the challenges that sustainability poses to DePaul University, and will include strategic recommendations for further implanting sustainability initiatives in the future. The task force established four working groups to explore sustainability opportunities: curriculum, operations, research, and community engagement (CORE). SITF is also in the process of developing a web-source that will provide periodic updates and status reports to the DePaul community. DePaul University has pledged to secure LEED certification for all new campus buildings and is undertaking a program to retrofit existing facilities. In addition, 80 percent of the landscaping outside those buildings is managed organically. The university will be installing building automation systems in all new buildings that will help to improve efficiencies of operation and therefore save on energy expended. DePaul's Monsignor Andrew J. McGowan Science Building was awarded a Gold Leadership in Energy and Environmental Design (LEED) certificate by the U.S. Green Building Council. DePaul's students, faculty, and administration have all made contributions to make the University a more environmentally friendly campus. The administration has made its support for environmentalism clear by donating funds to the Student Government Association for sustainable initiatives. Students participate in classes and school community organizations to help promote environmental awareness and action.

ADMISSIONS

Freshman Academic Profile: Average high school GPA 3.6. 23% in top 10% of high school class, 52% in top 25% of high school class, 85% in top 50% of high school class. 89% from public high schools. SAT Math middle 50% range 510-630. SAT Critical Reading middle 50% range 530-640. ACT middle 50% range 23-28. Minimum web-based TOEFL 80. Minimum paper TOEFL 550. **Basis for Candidate Selection:** *Very important factors considered include:* application essay, academic GPA, rigor of secondary school record, standardized test scores. *Important factors considered include:* Class rank, recommendation(s), character/personal qualities, extracurricular activities, level of applicant's interest, talent/ability, volunteer work, work experience. *Other factors considered include:* alumni/ae relation, first generation, geographical residence, interview, racial/ethnic status, religious affiliation/commitment, state residency. **Freshman Admission Requirements:** High school diploma is required and GED is accepted. *Academic units required:* 4 English, 3 mathematics, 3 science, (2 science labs), 2 social science/history. *Academic units recommended:* 4 English, 3 mathematics, 3 science, (2 science labs), 2 social science/history. **Freshman Admission Statistics:** 18,160 applied, 62% admitted, 23% enrolled. **Transfer Admission Requirements:** college transcript(s), minimum college GPA of 2.0 required. Lowest grade transferable D. **General Admission Information:** Application Fee $40. Regular application deadline 2/1. Regular notification 3/15. Nonfall registration accepted. Admission may be deferred for a maximum of 1 year. Credit and/or placement offered for CEEB Advanced Placement tests.

COSTS AND FINANCIAL AID

Annual tuition $31,650. Room and board $11,717. Required fees $645. Average book expense $1,134. **Required Forms and Deadlines:** FAFSA. **Notification of Awards:** Applicants will be notified of awards on a rolling basis beginning 3/15. **Types of Aid:** *Need-based scholarships/grants:* Federal Pell, SEOG, state scholarships/grants, private scholarships, the school's own gift aid, Federal Academic Competitiveness Grant, Federal SMART Grant, and Federal TEACH Grant. *Loans:* Direct Subsidized Stafford, Direct Unsubsidized Stafford, Direct PLUS, Federal Perkins, Private Loans. **Student Employment:** Federal Work-Study Program available. Institutional employment available. Highest amount earned per year from on-campus jobs $14,000. Off-campus job opportunities are excellent. **Financial Aid Statistics:** 82% freshmen, 83% undergrads receive need-based scholarship or grant aid. 86% freshmen, 50% undergrads receive non-need-based scholarship or grant aid. 74% freshmen, 81% undergrads receive need-based self-help aid. 2% freshmen, 2% undergrads receive athletic

scholarships. 90% freshmen, 76% undergrads receive any aid. 63% undergrads borrow to pay for school. Average cumulative indebtedness $28,284. **Criteria for awarding institutional aid:** *Non-need-based:* academics, art, athletics, leadership, music/drama, state/district residency.

DEPAUW UNIVERSITY

101 E. Seminary Street, Greencastle, IN 46135
Phone: 765-658-4006 • **Financial Aid Phone:** 765-658-4030
E-mail: admission@depauw.edu • **CEEB Code:** 1166
Fax: 765-658-4007 • **Website:** www.depauw.edu • **ACT Code:** 1184

This private school, affiliated with the Methodist Church, was founded in 1837. It has a 1100-acre campus.

RATINGS

Admissions Selectivity Rating: 91   **Fire Safety Rating:** 65   **Green Rating:** 83

STUDENTS AND FACULTY

Enrollment: 2,298. **Student Body:** 54% female, 46% male, 58% out-of-state, 11% international (34 countries represented). Asian 3%, African American 6%, Caucasian 70%, Hispanic 4%, Native American 0%.
Retention and Graduation: 89% freshmen return for sophomore year. 74% freshmen graduate within 4 years. 23% grads go on to further study within 1 year. 15% grads pursue arts and sciences degrees. 5% grads pursue law degrees. 1% grads pursue business degrees. 2% grads pursue medical degrees. **Faculty:** Student/faculty ratio 10:1. 228 full-time faculty, 96% hold PhDs, 18% are members of minority groups, 44% are women. 0% of classes are taught by teaching assistants.

ACADEMICS

Degrees: bachelor's. **Classes:** Most classes have 10–19 students. Most lab/discussion sessions have 10–19 students. **Majors with Highest Enrollment:** communication studies/speech communication and rhetoric; economics; English composition. **Special Study Options:** double major, dual enrollment, exchange student program (domestic), honors program, independent study, internships, student-designed major, study abroad, teacher certification program. **Honors Programs:** Please visit the following website for information about DePauw's Honors Programs: http://www.depauw.edu/honors/index.asp. **Disability Services:** Special programs offered to physically disabled students include note-taking services, reader services, tape recorders, tutors. **Career Services:** Alumni network, alumni services, career/job search classes, career assessment, internships, regional alumni. Career Services highlights include http://www.depauw.edu/admin/acadaffairs/studentprograms/internship.asp.

FACILITIES

Housing: Coed dorms, special housing for disabled students, special housing for international students, fraternity/sorority housing, apartments for single students. 85% of campus accessible to physically disabled. **Special Academic Facilities/Equipment:** Recently opened Peeler Art Center housing gallery and studio space; Center for Contemporary Media; Performing Arts Center; Anthropology Museum; Shidzuo Iikudo Museum **Computers:** Students can register for classes online. Administrative functions (other than registration) can be performed online. Undergraduates are required to own a computer.

CAMPUS LIFE

Environment: Village. **Activities:** Choral groups, concert band, dance, drama/theater, jazz band, literary magazine, music ensembles, musical theater, opera, pep band, radio station, student government, student newspaper, student-run film society, symphony orchestra, television station, Campus Ministries, International Student Organization 119 registered organizations, 13 honor societies, 10 religious organizations. 13 fraternities, 11 sororities. **Athletics (Intercollegiate):** *Men:* baseball, basketball, cross-country, diving, football, golf, soccer, swimming, tennis, track/field (outdoor), track/field (indoor). *Women:* basketball, cross-country, diving, field hockey, golf, soccer, softball, swimming, tennis, track/field (outdoor), track/field (indoor), volleyball. **On-Campus Highlights:** DePauw University School of Music, Roy O. West Library, Music Library, and the Prevo Science Library, Cafe Roy coffee shop, Memorial Student Union, Bowman Park. **Environmental Initiatives:** LEED certified construction of the Janet Prindle Institute for Ethics. 2007-08 full year of campus programming, speakers, and colloquia on sustainability: Boswell Symposium on environmental justice, featuring Majora Carter (http://www.depauw.edu/admin/acadaffairs/Boswell/Symposium_2007.asp) Ubben Lecture by Ralph Nader Arts Fest 2007 on Art and the Environment DePauw Discourse on Sustainability and Global

Citizenship, featuring Bill McKibben and Robert Kennedy, Jr. Focus the Nation teach-in on global warming DePauw Colloquium on the Liberal Arts: Liberal Education in a Time of Climate Crisis Earth Week events currently in planning stages. Significant investment in/upgrades to campus utilities/infrastructure, including an HVAC audit, upgraded steam pipes, chiller planet water system replacement, lightbulb replacement, and a bike-share program, among other changes.

ADMISSIONS

Freshman Academic Profile: Average high school GPA 3.5. 44% in top 10% of high school class, 77% in top 25% of high school class, 98% in top 50% of high school class. 83% from public high schools. SAT Math middle 50% range 550-680. SAT Critical Reading middle 50% range 530-650. SAT Writing middle 50% range 530-640. ACT middle 50% range 24-30. Minimum paper TOEFL 560. **Basis for Candidate Selection:** *Very important factors considered include:* academic GPA, rigor of secondary school record, standardized test scores. *Important factors considered include:* Class rank, application essay, recommendation(s). *Other factors considered include:* alumni/ae relation, character/personal qualities, extracurricular activities, first generation, geographical residence, interview, level of applicant's interest, state residency, talent/ability, volunteer work, work experience. **Freshman Admission Requirements:** High school diploma is required and GED is accepted. **Freshman Admission Statistics:** 4,835 applied, 63% admitted, 19% enrolled. **Transfer Admission Requirements:** High school transcript, college transcript(s), essay or personal statement, statement of good standing from prior institution(s). Minimum college GPA of 3.0 required. Lowest grade transferable C. **General Admission Information:** Application Fee $40. Early decision application deadline 11/1. Regular application deadline 2/1. Regular notification 4/1. Nonfall registration accepted. Admission may be deferred for a maximum of 1 year. Credit and/or placement offered for CEEB Advanced Placement tests.

COSTS AND FINANCIAL AID

Annual tuition $38,280. Room and board $10,200. Required fees $470. Average book expense $750. **Required Forms and Deadlines:** FAFSA, institution's own financial aid form. **Notification of Awards:** Applicants will be notified of awards on or about 4/1. *Types of Aid: Need-based scholarships/grants:* Federal Pell, SEOG, state scholarships/grants, private scholarships, the school's own gift aid, United Negro College Fund. *Loans:* Direct Subsidized Stafford, Direct Unsubsidized Stafford, Direct PLUS, Subsidized Stafford, Unsubsidized Stafford, PLUS, Federal Perkins, state loans, college/university loans from institutional funds. **Student Employment:** Federal Work-Study Program available. Institutional employment available. Off-campus job opportunities are fair. **Financial Aid Statistics:** 100% freshmen, 100% undergrads receive need-based scholarship or grant aid. 27% freshmen, 22% undergrads receive non-need-based scholarship or grant aid. 67% freshmen, 74% undergrads receive need-based self-help aid. 55% undergrads borrow to pay for school. Average cumulative indebtedness $22,755. **Criteria for awarding institutional aid:** *Non-need-based:* academics, alumni affiliation, art, leadership, minority status, music/drama, religious affiliation, state/district residency.

DEVRY INSTITUTE OF TECHNOLOGY (LONG ISLAND CITY, NY)

3020 Thomson Avenue, Long Island City, NY 11101 3051
Phone: 718-472-2728
E-mail: nyemailleads@ny.devry.edu
Fax: 718-361-0004 • **Website:** www.devry.edu

This proprietary school was founded in 1931. It has a 4-acre campus.

RATINGS

Admissions Selectivity Rating: 60*   **Fire Safety Rating:** 60*   **Green Rating:** 60*

STUDENTS AND FACULTY

Enrollment: 1,839. **Student Body:** 24% female, 76% male, % out-of-state, 3% international (17 countries represented). Asian 8%, African American 40%, Caucasian 10%, Hispanic 23%, Native American 1%.
Retention and Graduation: 36% freshmen return for sophomore year. **Faculty:** Student/faculty ratio 16:1. 60 full-time faculty.

ACADEMICS

Degrees: associate, bachelor's, master's, post-bachelor's certificate, terminal associate. **Majors with Highest Enrollment:** electrical, electronic and communications engineering technology/technician. **Special Study Options:** Accelerated program, cooperative education program, distance learning, double major, weekend college. **Disability Services:** Special programs offered to physically disabled students include note-taking services, reader services, tape recorders, tutors. **Career Services:** alumni services, career/job search classes.

FACILITIES

Housing: Private apartments;student plan housing, private rooms. 100% of campus accessible to physically disabled. **Computers:** Administrative functions (other than registration) can be performed online.

CAMPUS LIFE

Environment: Activities: 4 registered organizations, 1 honor societies.

ADMISSIONS

Freshman Academic Profile: Minimum paper TOEFL 500. **Basis for Candidate Selection:** *Important factors considered include:* interview. *Other factors considered include:* standardized test scores. **Freshman Admission Requirements:** High school diploma is required and GED is accepted. *Academic units required:* 1 mathematics. *Academic units recommended:* 1 mathematics. **Transfer Admission Requirements:** college transcript(s), standardized test scores, minimum college GPA of 2.0 required. Lowest grade transferable C. **General Admission Information:** Application Fee $50. Notification on a rolling basis, beginning on or about 11/2. Nonfall registration accepted. Admission may be deferred for a maximum of 12 months. Credit offered for CEEB Advanced Placement tests.

COSTS AND FINANCIAL AID

Annual tuition $12,450. Required fees $250. Average book expense $1,200. **Required Forms and Deadlines:** FAFSA. **Notification of Awards: Types of Aid:** *Need-based scholarships/grants:* Federal Pell, SEOG, private scholarships, the school's own gift aid. *Loans:* Subsidized Stafford, Unsubsidized Stafford, PLUS, Federal Perkins, college/university loans from institutional funds. **Student Employment:** Federal Work-Study Program available. Institutional employment available. Highest amount earned per year from on-campus jobs $5,994. Off-campus job opportunities are good. **Financial Aid Statistics:** 92% freshmen, 87% undergrads receive need-based scholarship or grant aid. 97% freshmen, 98% undergrads receive need-based self-help aid.

DEVRY UNIVERSITY (ADDISON, IL)

1221 North Swift Road, Addision, IL 60101
Phone: 630-953-2000
E-mail: info@devry.edu
Fax: 630-953-1236 • **Website:** www.devry.edu

This proprietary school was founded in 1931. It has a 13-acre campus.

RATINGS

Admissions Selectivity Rating: 60*   **Fire Safety Rating:** 60*   **Green Rating:** 60*

STUDENTS AND FACULTY

Enrollment: 4,827. **Student Body:** 34% female, 66% male, 1% international (23 countries represented). Asian 8%, African American 13%, Caucasian 52%, Hispanic 8%, Native American 1%.
Retention and Graduation: 51% freshmen return for sophomore year. 33% freshmen graduate within 6 years. **Faculty:** Student/faculty ratio 19:1. 69 full-time faculty.

ACADEMICS

Degrees: associate, bachelor's, terminal associate. **Majors with Highest Enrollment:** electrical, electronic and communications engineering technology/technician. **Special Study Options:** Accelerated program, cooperative education program, distance learning, double major, weekend college. **Disability Services:** Special programs offered to physically disabled students include note-taking services, reader services, tape recorders, tutors. **Career Services:** alumni services, career/job search classes.

FACILITIES

Housing: Concord Residence. 100% of campus accessible to physically disabled. **Computers:** Students can register for classes online. Administrative functions (other than registration) can be performed online.

CAMPUS LIFE

Environment: Village. **Activities:** student government 11 registered organizations, 3 honor societies, 1 religious organizations.

ADMISSIONS

Freshman Academic Profile: Minimum paper TOEFL 500. **Basis for Candidate Selection:** *Important factors considered include:* interview. *Other factors considered include:* standardized test scores. **Freshman Admission Requirements:** High school diploma is required and GED is accepted. *Academic units required:* 1 mathematics. *Academic units recommended:* 1 mathematics. **Transfer Admission Requirements:** college transcript(s), standardized test scores, minimum college GPA of 2.0 required. Lowest grade transferable C. **General Admission Information:** Application Fee $50. Notification on a rolling basis, beginning on or about 11/2. Nonfall registration accepted. Admission may be deferred for a maximum of 12 months. Credit offered for CEEB Advanced Placement tests.

COSTS AND FINANCIAL AID
Annual tuition $11,330. Required fees $250. Average book expense $1,200. **Required Forms and Deadlines:** FAFSA. **Notification of Awards: Types of Aid:** *Need-based scholarships/grants:* Federal Pell, SEOG, private scholarships, the school's own gift aid. *Loans:* Subsidized Stafford, Unsubsidized Stafford, PLUS, Federal Perkins, college/university loans from institutional funds. **Student Employment:** Federal Work-Study Program available. Institutional employment available. Highest amount earned per year from on-campus jobs $6,750. Off-campus job opportunities are excellent. **Financial Aid Statistics:** 64% freshmen, 60% undergrads receive need-based scholarship or grant aid. 1% freshmen receive non-need-based scholarship or grant aid. 98% freshmen, 98% undergrads receive need-based self-help aid.

DEVRY UNIVERSITY (ALPHARETTA, GA)

2555 Northwinds Parkway, Alpharetta, GA 30004
Phone: 770-664-9520
E-mail: admissions@devry.com
Fax: 770-664-8824 • **Website:** www.devry.edu

This proprietary school was founded in 1931. It has a 21-acre campus.

RATINGS
Admissions Selectivity Rating: 60*   **Fire Safety Rating:** 60*   **Green Rating:** 60*

STUDENTS AND FACULTY
Enrollment: 1,286. **Student Body:** 34% female, 66% male, % out-of-state, 2% international (17 countries represented). Asian 3%, African American 32%, Caucasian 28%, Hispanic 3%, Native American 1%. **Retention and Graduation:** 40% freshmen return for sophomore year. **Faculty:** Student/faculty ratio 36:1. 38 full-time faculty.

ACADEMICS
Degrees: associate, bachelor's, master's, post-bachelor's certificate, terminal associate. **Special Study Options:** Accelerated program, cooperative education program, distance learning, double major, weekend college. **Disability Services:** Special programs offered to physically disabled students include note-taking services, reader services, tape recorders, tutors. **Career Services:** alumni services, career/job search classes.

FACILITIES
Housing: Private apartments. Student plan housing and private rooms. 98% of campus accessible to physically disabled. **Computers:** Students can register for classes online. Administrative functions (other than registration) can be performed online.

CAMPUS LIFE
Environment: City. **Activities:** student government 12 registered organizations, 4 honor societies.

ADMISSIONS
Freshman Academic Profile: Minimum paper TOEFL 500. **Basis for Candidate Selection:** *Important factors considered include:* interview. *Other factors considered include:* standardized test scores. **Freshman Admission Requirements:** High school diploma is required and GED is accepted. *Academic units required:* 1 mathematics. *Academic units recommended:* 1 mathematics. **Transfer Admission Requirements:** college transcript(s), standardized test scores, minimum college GPA of 2.0 required. Lowest grade transferable C. **General Admission Information:** Application Fee $50. Nonfall registration accepted. Admission may be deferred for a maximum of 12. Credit offered for CEEB Advanced Placement tests.

COSTS AND FINANCIAL AID
Annual tuition $11,240. Required fees $250. Average book expense $1,200. **Required Forms and Deadlines:** FAFSA. **Types of Aid:** *Need-based scholarships/grants:* Federal Pell, SEOG, private scholarships, the school's own gift aid. *Loans:* Subsidized Stafford, Unsubsidized Stafford, PLUS, Federal Perkins, college/university loans from institutional funds. **Student Employment:** **Financial Aid Statistics:** 95% freshmen, 93% undergrads receive need-based scholarship or grant aid. 2% undergrads receive non-need-based scholarship or grant aid. 97% freshmen, 96% undergrads receive need-based self-help aid.

DEVRY UNIVERSITY (CHICAGO, IL)

3300 North Cambell Avenue, Chicago, IL 60618
Phone: 773-697-2155
E-mail: keaster@chi.devry.edu
Fax: 773-697-2710 • **Website:** www.devry.edu

This proprietary school was founded in 1931. It has a 16-acre campus.

RATINGS
Admissions Selectivity Rating: 60*   **Fire Safety Rating:** 60*   **Green Rating:** 60*

STUDENTS AND FACULTY
Enrollment: 2,896. **Student Body:** 36% female, 64% male, 2% international (26 countries represented). Asian 11%, African American 69%, Caucasian 22%, Hispanic 31%, Native American 0%. **Retention and Graduation:** 46% freshmen return for sophomore year. **Faculty:** Student/faculty ratio 50:1. 74 full-time faculty.

ACADEMICS
Degrees: associate, bachelor's, terminal associate. **Majors with Highest Enrollment:** electrical, electronic and communications engineering technology/technician. **Special Study Options:** Accelerated program, cooperative education program, distance learning, double major, dual enrollment, English as a Second Language (ESL), weekend college. **Disability Services:** Special programs offered to physically disabled students include note-taking services, reader services, tape recorders, tutors. **Career Services:** alumni services, career/job search classes.

FACILITIES
Housing: men's dorms, women's dorms, apartments for married students, apartments for single students. 100% of campus accessible to physically disabled. **Computers:** Students can register for classes online. Administrative functions (other than registration) can be performed online.

CAMPUS LIFE
Environment: Metropolis. **Activities:** Choral groups, drama/theater, music ensembles, yearbook 16 registered organizations, 3 honor societies, 2 religious organizations.

ADMISSIONS
Freshman Academic Profile: Minimum paper TOEFL 500. **Basis for Candidate Selection:** *Important factors considered include:* interview. *Other factors considered include:* standardized test scores. **Freshman Admission Requirements:** High school diploma is required and GED is accepted. *Academic units required:* 1 mathematics. *Academic units recommended:* 1 mathematics. **Transfer Admission Requirements:** college transcript(s), standardized test scores, minimum college GPA of 2.0 required. Lowest grade transferable C. **General Admission Information:** Application Fee $50. Notification on a rolling basis, beginning on or about 11/2. Nonfall registration accepted. Admission may be deferred for a maximum of 12 months. Credit offered for CEEB Advanced Placement tests.

COSTS AND FINANCIAL AID
Annual tuition $11,330. Required fees $250. Average book expense $1,200. **Required Forms and Deadlines:** FAFSA. **Notification of Awards: Types of Aid:** *Need-based scholarships/grants:* Federal Pell, SEOG, private scholarships, the school's own gift aid. *Loans:* Subsidized Stafford, Unsubsidized Stafford, PLUS, Federal Perkins, college/university loans from institutional funds. **Student Employment:** Federal Work-Study Program available. Institutional employment available. Highest amount earned per year from on-campus jobs $9,000. Off-campus job opportunities are good. **Financial Aid Statistics:** 84% freshmen, 81% undergrads receive need-based scholarship or grant aid. 96% freshmen, 98% undergrads receive need-based self-help aid.

DEVRY UNIVERSITY (COLUMBUS, OH)

1350 Alum Creek Drive, Columbus, OH 43209-2705
Phone: 614-253-1525
E-mail: admissions@devry.edu
Fax: 614-253-0843 • **Website:** www.devry.edu

This proprietary school was founded in 1931. It has a 13-acre campus.

RATINGS
Admissions Selectivity Rating: 61   **Fire Safety Rating:** 60*   **Green Rating:** 60*

STUDENTS AND FACULTY

Enrollment: 3,145. **Student Body:** 25% female, 75% male, 12% out-of-state, 1% international (3 countries represented). Asian 3%, African American 20%, Caucasian 73%, Hispanic 1%, Native American 0%. **Retention and Graduation:** 40% freshmen return for sophomore year. **Faculty:** Student/faculty ratio 39:1. 83 full-time faculty.

ACADEMICS

Degrees: associate, bachelor's, master's, post-bachelor's certificate, terminal associate. **Classes: Majors with Highest Enrollment:** electrical, electronic and communications engineering technology/technician. **Special Study Options:** Accelerated program, cooperative education program, distance learning, double major, weekend college. **Disability Services:** Special programs offered to physically disabled students include note-taking services, reader services, tape recorders, tutors. **Career Services:** alumni services, career/job search classes.

FACILITIES

Housing: Private apartments Student plan housing and private rooms. 90% of campus accessible to physically disabled. **Computers:** Students can register for classes online. Administrative functions (other than registration) can be performed online.

CAMPUS LIFE

Environment: Metropolis. **Activities:** student government, student newspaper 13 registered organizations, 2 honor societies.

ADMISSIONS

Freshman Academic Profile: Minimum paper TOEFL 500. **Basis for Candidate Selection:** *Important factors considered include:* interview. *Other factors considered include:* standardized test scores. **Freshman Admission Requirements:** High school diploma is required and GED is accepted. *Academic units required:* 1 mathematics. *Academic units recommended:* 1 mathematics. **Transfer Admission Requirements:** college transcript(s), standardized test scores, minimum college GPA of 2.0 required. Lowest grade transferable C. **General Admission Information:** Application Fee $50. Notification on a rolling basis, beginning on or about 11/2. Nonfall registration accepted. Admission may be deferred for a maximum of 12 months. Credit offered for CEEB Advanced Placement tests.

COSTS AND FINANCIAL AID

Annual tuition $11,240. Required fees $250. Average book expense $1,200. **Required Forms and Deadlines:** FAFSA. **Notification of Awards: Types of Aid:** *Need-based scholarships/grants:* Federal Pell, SEOG, private scholarships, the school's own gift aid. *Loans:* Subsidized Stafford, Unsubsidized Stafford, PLUS, Federal Perkins, college/university loans from institutional funds. **Student Employment:** Federal Work-Study Program available. Institutional employment available. Highest amount earned per year from on-campus jobs $12,000. Off-campus job opportunities are excellent. **Financial Aid Statistics:** 88% freshmen, 74% undergrads receive need-based scholarship or grant aid. 1% freshmen, 1% undergrads receive non-need-based scholarship or grant aid. 96% freshmen, 98% undergrads receive need-based self-help aid.

DEVRY UNIVERSITY (DECATUR, GA)

250 N. Arcadia Avenue, Decatur, GA 30030
Phone: 404-292-2645
E-mail: dsilva@admin.atl.devry.edu
Fax: 404-292-7011 • **Website:** www.atl.devry.edu

This proprietary school was founded in 1931. It has a 23-acre campus.

RATINGS

Admissions Selectivity Rating: 61   **Fire Safety Rating:** 60*   **Green Rating:** 60*

STUDENTS AND FACULTY

Enrollment: 1,550. **Student Body:** 44% female, 56% male, 17% out-of-state, 3% international (8 countries represented). Asian 3%, African American 84%, Caucasian 15%, Hispanic 3%, Native American 0%. **Retention and Graduation:** 41% freshmen return for sophomore year. **Faculty:** Student/faculty ratio 36:1. 63 full-time faculty.

ACADEMICS

Degrees: associate, bachelor's, master's, post-bachelor's certificate, terminal associate. **Majors with Highest Enrollment:** business administration, management and operations, other. **Special Study Options:** Accelerated program, cooperative education program, distance learning, double major, weekend college. **Disability Services:** Special programs offered to physically disabled students include note-taking services, reader services, tape recorders, tutors. **Career Services:** alumni services, career/job search classes.

FACILITIES

Housing: Private apartments, student paln housing, private rooms. 100% of campus accessible to physically disabled. **Computers:** Students can register for classes online. Administrative functions (other than registration) can be performed online.

CAMPUS LIFE

Environment: City. **Activities:** 10 registered organizations, 4 honor societies.

ADMISSIONS

Freshman Academic Profile: Minimum paper TOEFL 500. **Basis for Candidate Selection:** *Important factors considered include:* interview. *Other factors considered include:* standardized test scores. **Freshman Admission Requirements:** High school diploma is required and GED is accepted. *Academic units required:* 1 mathematics. *Academic units recommended:* 1 mathematics. **Transfer Admission Requirements:** college transcript(s), standardized test scores, minimum college GPA of 2.0 required. Lowest grade transferable C. **General Admission Information:** Application Fee $50. Notification on a rolling basis, beginning on or about 11/2. Nonfall registration accepted. Admission may be deferred for a maximum of 12 months. Credit offered for CEEB Advanced Placement tests.

COSTS AND FINANCIAL AID

Annual tuition $17,104. Room and board $12,018. Required fees $250. Average book expense $1,346. **Required Forms and Deadlines:** FAFSA. **Notification of Awards: Types of Aid:** *Need-based scholarships/grants:* Federal Pell, SEOG, private scholarships, the school's own gift aid. *Loans:* Subsidized Stafford, Unsubsidized Stafford, PLUS, Federal Perkins, college/university loans from institutional funds. **Student Employment:** Federal Work-Study Program available. Institutional employment available. Highest amount earned per year from on-campus jobs $6,743. Off-campus job opportunities are good. **Financial Aid Statistics:** 94% freshmen, 93% undergrads receive need-based scholarship or grant aid. 1% freshmen, 1% undergrads receive non-need-based scholarship or grant aid. 97% freshmen, 97% undergrads receive need-based self-help aid.

DEVRY UNIVERSITY (DENVER, CO)

Office of Admissions, Denver, CO 80234-2010
Phone: 303-280-7400
E-mail: info@devry.edu
Fax: 303-280-7606 • **Website:** www.devry.edu/denver

This proprietary school was founded in 1931. It has a 13-acre campus.

RATINGS

Admissions Selectivity Rating: 60*   **Fire Safety Rating:** 60*   **Green Rating:** 60*

ACADEMICS

Degrees: associate, bachelor's, terminal associate. **Special Study Options:** Accelerated program, cooperative education program, distance learning, double major, dual enrollment, weekend college. **Disability Services:** Special programs offered to physically disabled students include note-taking services, reader services, tape recorders, tutors. **Career Services:** alumni services, career/job search classes.

FACILITIES

Housing: 100% of campus accessible to physically disabled. **Computers:** Students can register for classes online. Administrative functions (other than registration) can be performed online.

CAMPUS LIFE

Environment: City. **Activities:** 3 registered organizations.

ADMISSIONS

Freshman Academic Profile: Minimum paper TOEFL 500. **General Admission Information:** Credit offered for CEEB Advanced Placement tests.

COSTS AND FINANCIAL AID

Annual tuition $11,870. Required fees $250. Average book expense $1,200. **Student Employment:** Federal Work-Study Program available. Institutional employment available. Off-campus job opportunities are good.

DEVRY UNIVERSITY (FREMONT, CA)

6600 Dumbarton Circle, Fremont, CA 94555
Phone: 510-574-1200
E-mail: info@devry.edu
Fax: 510-742-0868 • **Website:** www.fre.devry.edu

This proprietary school was founded in 1931. It has a 17-acre campus.

RATINGS
Admissions Selectivity Rating: 60*   **Fire Safety Rating:** 60*   **Green Rating:** 60*

STUDENTS AND FACULTY
Enrollment: 1,477. **Student Body:** 26% female, 74% male, 1% international (9 countries represented). Asian 28%, African American 4%, Caucasian 15%, Hispanic 15%, Native American 1%.
Retention and Graduation: **Faculty:** Student/faculty ratio 29:1. 51 full-time faculty.

ACADEMICS
Degrees: associate, bachelor's, master's, post-bachelor's certificate, terminal associate. **Special Study Options:** Accelerated program, cooperative education program, distance learning, double major, weekend college. **Disability Services:** Special programs offered to physically disabled students include note-taking services, reader services, tape recorders, tutors. **Career Services:** alumni services, career/job search classes.

FACILITIES
Housing: There is no on campus housing. 90% of campus accessible to physically disabled. **Computers:** Students can register for classes online. Administrative functions (other than registration) can be performed online.

CAMPUS LIFE
Environment: City. **Activities:** student government 10 registered organizations, 2 honor societies.

ADMISSIONS
Freshman Academic Profile: Minimum paper TOEFL 500. **Basis for Candidate Selection:** *Important factors considered include:* interview. *Other factors considered include:* standardized test scores. **Freshman Admission Requirements:** High school diploma is required and GED is accepted. *Academic units required:* 1 mathematics. *Academic units recommended:* 1 mathematics. **Transfer Admission Requirements:** college transcript(s), standardized test scores, minimum college GPA of 2.0 required. Lowest grade transferable C. **General Admission Information:** Application Fee $50. Notification on a rolling basis, beginning on or about 11/2. Nonfall registration accepted. Admission may be deferred for a maximum of 12 months. Credit offered for CEEB Advanced Placement tests.

COSTS AND FINANCIAL AID
Annual tuition $12,450. Required fees $250. Average book expense $1,200. **Required Forms and Deadlines:** FAFSA. **Notification of Awards: Types of Aid:** *Need-based scholarships/grants:* Federal Pell, SEOG, state scholarships/grants, private scholarships, the school's own gift aid. *Loans:* Subsidized Stafford, Unsubsidized Stafford, PLUS, Federal Perkins, college/university loans from institutional funds. **Student Employment:** Federal Work-Study Program available. Institutional employment available. Highest amount earned per year from on-campus jobs $2,700. Off-campus job opportunities are good. **Financial Aid Statistics:** 64% freshmen, 65% undergrads receive need-based scholarship or grant aid. 1% freshmen, 1% undergrads receive non-need-based scholarship or grant aid. 94% freshmen, 97% undergrads receive need-based self-help aid. Average cumulative indebtedness $29,198. **Criteria for awarding institutional aid:** *Non-need-based:* academics.

DEVRY UNIVERSITY (IRVING, TX)

4800 Regent Boulevard, Irving, TX 75063-2439
Phone: 972-929-5777
E-mail: cwilliams@mail.dal.devry.edu
Fax: 972-929-2860 • **Website:** www.devry.edu

This proprietary school was founded in 1931. It has a 9-acre campus.

RATINGS
Admissions Selectivity Rating: 60*   **Fire Safety Rating:** 60*   **Green Rating:** 60*

STUDENTS AND FACULTY
Enrollment: 2,500. **Student Body:** 29% female, 71% male, 0% out-of-state, 1% international (5 countries represented). Asian 5%, African American 32%, Caucasian 42%, Hispanic 19%, Native American 0%.
Retention and Graduation: 36% freshmen return for sophomore year. **Faculty:** Student/faculty ratio 16:1. 77 full-time faculty.

ACADEMICS
Degrees: associate, bachelor's, master's, post-bachelor's certificate, terminal associate. **Majors with Highest Enrollment:** computer systems networking and telecommunications; electrical, electronic and communications engineering technology/technician. **Special Study Options:** Accelerated program, cooperative education program, distance learning, double major, weekend college. **Disability Services:** Special programs offered to physically disabled students include note-taking services, reader services, tape recorders, tutors. **Career Services:** alumni services, career/job search classes.

FACILITIES
Housing: Private apartments, student plan housing, private rooms. 100% of campus accessible to physically disabled. **Computers:** Students can register for classes online. Administrative functions (other than registration) can be performed online.

CAMPUS LIFE
Environment: Metropolis. **Activities:** student newspaper 15 registered organizations.

ADMISSIONS
Freshman Academic Profile: Minimum paper TOEFL 500. **Basis for Candidate Selection:** *Important factors considered include:* interview. *Other factors considered include:* standardized test scores. **Freshman Admission Requirements:** High school diploma is required and GED is accepted. *Academic units required:* 1 mathematics. *Academic units recommended:* 1 mathematics. **Transfer Admission Requirements:** college transcript(s), standardized test scores, statement of good standing from prior institution(s). Minimum college GPA of 2.0 required. Lowest grade transferable C. **General Admission Information:** Application Fee $50. Notification on a rolling basis, beginning on or about 11/2. Nonfall registration accepted. Admission may be deferred for a maximum of 12 months. Credit offered for CEEB Advanced Placement tests.

COSTS AND FINANCIAL AID
Annual tuition $11,240. Required fees $250. Average book expense $1,200. **Required Forms and Deadlines:** FAFSA. **Notification of Awards: Types of Aid:** *Need-based scholarships/grants:* Federal Pell, SEOG, private scholarships, the school's own gift aid. *Loans:* Subsidized Stafford, Unsubsidized Stafford, PLUS, Federal Perkins, college/university loans from institutional funds. **Student Employment:** Federal Work-Study Program available. Institutional employment available. Highest amount earned per year from on-campus jobs $7,500. Off-campus job opportunities are good. **Financial Aid Statistics:** 64% freshmen, 59% undergrads receive need-based scholarship or grant aid. 98% freshmen, 99% undergrads receive need-based self-help aid.

DEVRY UNIVERSITY (KANSAS CITY, MO)

11224 Holmes Street, Kansas City, MO 64131
Phone: 816-941-2810
E-mail: ssmeed@kc.devry.edu
Fax: 816-941-0896 • **Website:** www.devry.edu

This proprietary school was founded in 1931. It has a 8-acre campus.

RATINGS
Admissions Selectivity Rating: 60*   **Fire Safety Rating:** 60*   **Green Rating:** 60*

STUDENTS AND FACULTY
Enrollment: 1,927. **Student Body:** 26% female, 74% male, 1% international (8 countries represented). Asian 3%, African American 16%, Caucasian 76%, Hispanic 4%, Native American 1%.
Retention and Graduation: 51% freshmen return for sophomore year. **Faculty:** Student/faculty ratio 23:1. 69 full-time faculty.

ACADEMICS
Degrees: associate, bachelor's, master's, post-bachelor's certificate, terminal associate. **Majors with Highest Enrollment:** computer systems networking and telecommunications; electrical, electronic and communications engineering technology/technician. **Special Study Options:** Accelerated program, cooperative education program, distance learning, double major, weekend college. **Disability Services:** Special programs offered to physically disabled students include note-taking services, reader services, tape recorders, tutors. **Career Services:** alumni services, career/job search classes.

236

FACILITIES

Housing: Private apartments, student plan housing, private rooms. 100% of campus accessible to physically disabled. **Computers:** Students can register for classes online. Administrative functions (other than registration) can be performed online.

CAMPUS LIFE

Environment: Metropolis. **Activities:** student newspaper 8 registered organizations, 1 honor society.

ADMISSIONS

Freshman Academic Profile: Minimum paper TOEFL 500. **Basis for Candidate Selection:** *Important factors considered include:* interview. *Other factors considered include:* standardized test scores. **Freshman Admission Requirements:** High school diploma is required and GED is accepted. *Academic units required:* 1 mathematics. *Academic units recommended:* 1 mathematics. **Transfer Admission Requirements:** college transcript(s), standardized test scores, minimum college GPA of 2.0 required. Lowest grade transferable C. **General Admission Information:** Application Fee $50. Notification on a rolling basis, beginning on or about 11/2. Nonfall registration accepted. Admission may be deferred for a maximum of 12 months. Credit offered for CEEB Advanced Placement tests.

COSTS AND FINANCIAL AID

Annual tuition $11,240. Required fees $250. Average book expense $1,200. **Required Forms and Deadlines:** FAFSA. **Notification of Awards: Types of Aid:** *Need-based scholarships/grants:* Federal Pell, SEOG, private scholarships, the school's own gift aid. *Loans:* Subsidized Stafford, Unsubsidized Stafford, PLUS. **Student Employment:** Federal Work-Study Program available. Institutional employment available. Highest amount earned per year from on-campus jobs $5,625. Off-campus job opportunities are excellent. **Financial Aid Statistics:** 65% freshmen, 57% undergrads receive need-based scholarship or grant aid. 1% freshmen, 1% undergrads receive non-need-based scholarship or grant aid. 98% freshmen, 98% undergrads receive need-based self-help aid.

DEVRY UNIVERSITY (LONG BEACH, CA)

3880 Kilroy Airport Way, Long Beach, CA 90806-2449
Phone: 562-427-4162
E-mail: cblas@socal.devry.edu
Fax: 562-997-5371 • **Website:** www.devry.edu

This proprietary school was founded in 1931. It has a 25-acre campus.

RATINGS
Admissions Selectivity Rating: 60*   **Fire Safety Rating:** 60*   **Green Rating:** 60*

STUDENTS AND FACULTY

Enrollment: 1,928. **Student Body:** 26% female, 74% male, % out-of-state, 2% international (11 countries represented). Asian 27%, African American 13%, Caucasian 19%, Hispanic 33%, Native American 1%.
Retention and Graduation: 51% freshmen return for sophomore year. 25% freshmen graduate within 6 years. **Faculty:** Student/faculty ratio 44:1. 40 full-time faculty.

ACADEMICS

Degrees: associate, bachelor's, master's, post-bachelor's certificate, terminal associate. **Majors with Highest Enrollment:** business administration, management and operations, other. **Special Study Options:** Accelerated program, cooperative education program, distance learning, double major, weekend college. **Disability Services:** Special programs offered to physically disabled students include note-taking services, reader services, tape recorders, tutors. **Career Services:** alumni services, career/job search classes.

FACILITIES

Housing: men's dorms, women's dorms. 90% of campus accessible to physically disabled. **Computers:** Students can register for classes online. Administrative functions (other than registration) can be performed online.

CAMPUS LIFE

Environment: Metropolis. **Activities:** Choral groups, concert band, music ensembles, student government, student newspaper, symphony orchestra, yearbook 13 registered organizations, 5 honor societies.

ADMISSIONS

Freshman Academic Profile: Minimum paper TOEFL 500. **Basis for Candidate Selection:** *Important factors considered include:* interview. *Other factors considered include:* standardized test scores. **Freshman Admission Requirements:** High school diploma is required and GED is accepted. *Academic*

units required: 1 mathematics. *Academic units recommended:* 1 mathematics. **Transfer Admission Requirements:** college transcript(s), standardized test scores, minimum college GPA of 2.0 required. Lowest grade transferable C. **General Admission Information:** Application Fee $50. Notification on a rolling basis, beginning on or about 11/2. Nonfall registration accepted. Admission may be deferred for a maximum of 12 months. Credit offered for CEEB Advanced Placement tests.

COSTS AND FINANCIAL AID

Annual tuition $11,870. Required fees $250. Average book expense $1,200. **Required Forms and Deadlines:** FAFSA. **Notification of Awards: Types of Aid:** *Need-based scholarships/grants:* Federal Pell, SEOG, state scholarships/grants, private scholarships, the school's own gift aid. *Loans:* Subsidized Stafford, Unsubsidized Stafford, PLUS, Federal Perkins, college/university loans from institutional funds. **Student Employment:** Federal Work-Study Program available. Institutional employment available. Highest amount earned per year from on-campus jobs $6,500. Off-campus job opportunities are good. **Financial Aid Statistics:** 72% freshmen, 69% undergrads receive need-based scholarship or grant aid. 98% freshmen, 98% undergrads receive need-based self-help aid.

DEVRY UNIVERSITY (NORTH BRUNSWICK, NJ)

630 US Highway One, N. Brunswick, NJ 08902-3362
Phone: 732-435-4850
E-mail: admissions@devry.edu
Fax: 732-435-4850 • **Website:** www.devry.edu

This proprietary school was founded in 1931. It has a 15-acre campus.

RATINGS
Admissions Selectivity Rating: 60*   **Fire Safety Rating:** 60*   **Green Rating:** 60*

STUDENTS AND FACULTY

Enrollment: 2,517. **Student Body:** 21% female, 79% male, 1% international (23 countries represented). Asian 8%, African American 13%, Caucasian 43%, Hispanic 19%, Native American 0%.
Retention and Graduation: 45% freshmen return for sophomore year. **Faculty:** Student/faculty ratio 19:1. 78 full-time faculty.

ACADEMICS

Degrees: associate, bachelor's, diploma, terminal associate. **Special Study Options:** Accelerated program, cooperative education program, distance learning, double major, weekend college. **Disability Services:** Special programs offered to physically disabled students include note-taking services, reader services, tape recorders, tutors. **Career Services:** alumni services, career/job search classes.

FACILITIES

Housing: 90% of campus accessible to physically disabled. **Computers:** Students can register for classes online. Administrative functions (other than registration) can be performed online.

CAMPUS LIFE

Environment: Town. **Activities:** 13 registered organizations, 2 honor societies.

ADMISSIONS

Freshman Academic Profile: Minimum paper TOEFL 500. **Basis for Candidate Selection:** *Important factors considered include:* interview. *Other factors considered include:* standardized test scores. **Freshman Admission Requirements:** High school diploma is required and GED is accepted. *Academic units required:* 1 mathematics. *Academic units recommended:* 1 mathematics. **Transfer Admission Requirements:** college transcript(s), standardized test scores, minimum college GPA of 2.0 required. Lowest grade transferable C. **General Admission Information:** Application Fee $50. Notification on a rolling basis, beginning on or about 11/2. Nonfall registration accepted. Admission may be deferred for a maximum of 12. Credit offered for CEEB Advanced Placement tests.

COSTS AND FINANCIAL AID

Annual tuition $11,330. Required fees $250. Average book expense $1,200. **Required Forms and Deadlines:** FAFSA. **Notification of Awards: Types of Aid:** *Need-based scholarships/grants:* Federal Pell, SEOG, private scholarships, the school's own gift aid. *Loans:* Subsidized Stafford, Unsubsidized Stafford, PLUS, Federal Perkins, college/university loans from institutional funds. **Student Employment:** Federal Work-Study Program available. Institutional employment available. Off-campus job opportunities are good. **Financial Aid Statistics:** 66% freshmen, 62% undergrads receive need-based scholarship or grant aid. 1% undergrads receive non-need-based scholarship or grant aid. 97% freshmen, 98% undergrads receive need-based self-help aid.

DEVRY UNIVERSITY (ORLANDO, FL)

4000 Millenia Blvd., Orlando, FL 32839
Phone: 407-370-3131
E-mail: krochford@orl.devry.edu
Fax: 407-370-3198 • **Website:** www.devry.edu

This proprietary school was founded in 1931. It has a 11-acre campus.

RATINGS
Admissions Selectivity Rating: 60*   **Fire Safety Rating:** 60*   **Green Rating:** 60*

STUDENTS AND FACULTY
Enrollment: 1,346. **Student Body:** 29% female, 71% male, 3% international (13 countries represented). Asian 2%, African American 26%, Caucasian 30%, Hispanic 16%, Native American 0%.
Retention and Graduation: 46% freshmen return for sophomore year. **Faculty:** Student/faculty ratio 32:1. 43 full-time faculty.

ACADEMICS
Degrees: associate, bachelor's, master's, post-bachelor's certificate, terminal associate. **Majors with Highest Enrollment:** business, management, marketing, and related support services, other; communication, journalism, and related programs, other; computer and information sciences and support services, other. **Special Study Options:** Accelerated program, cooperative education program, distance learning, double major, weekend college. **Disability Services:** Special programs offered to physically disabled students include note-taking services, reader services, tape recorders, tutors. **Career Services:** alumni services, career/job search classes.

FACILITIES
Housing: men's dorms, women's dorms, apartments for married students 95% of campus accessible to physically disabled. **Computers:** Students can register for classes online. Administrative functions (other than registration) can be performed online.

CAMPUS LIFE
Environment: Metropolis. **Activities:** Choral groups, music ensembles, student government, yearbook 6 registered organizations, 2 honor societies.

ADMISSIONS
Freshman Academic Profile: Minimum paper TOEFL 500. **Basis for Candidate Selection:** *Important factors considered include:* interview. *Other factors considered include:* standardized test scores. **Freshman Admission Requirements:** High school diploma is required and GED is accepted. *Academic units required:* 1 mathematics. *Academic units recommended:* 1 mathematics. **Transfer Admission Requirements:** college transcript(s), standardized test scores, minimum college GPA of 2.0 required. Lowest grade transferable C. **General Admission Information:** Application Fee $50. Notification on a rolling basis, beginning on or about 11/2. Nonfall registration accepted. Admission may be deferred for a maximum of 12 months. Credit offered for CEEB Advanced Placement tests.

COSTS AND FINANCIAL AID
Annual tuition $11,870. Required fees $250. Average book expense $1,200.
Required Forms and Deadlines: FAFSA. **Notification of Awards: Types of Aid:** *Need-based scholarships/grants:* Federal Pell, SEOG, private scholarships, the school's own gift aid. *Loans:* Subsidized Stafford, Unsubsidized Stafford, PLUS, Federal Perkins, college/university loans from institutional funds. **Student Employment:** Federal Work-Study Program available. Institutional employment available. Highest amount earned per year from on-campus jobs $6,916. Off-campus job opportunities are fair. **Financial Aid Statistics:** 71% freshmen, 66% undergrads receive need-based scholarship or grant aid. 98% freshmen, 98% undergrads receive need-based self-help aid.

DEVRY UNIVERSITY (PHOENIX, AZ)

2149 West Dunlap, Phoenix, AZ 85021
Phone: 602-870-9222
E-mail: admissions@phx.devry.edu
Fax: 602-331-1494 • **Website:** www.devry.edu

This proprietary school was founded in 1931. It has a 12-acre campus.

RATINGS
Admissions Selectivity Rating: 60*   **Fire Safety Rating:** 60*   **Green Rating:** 60*

STUDENTS AND FACULTY
Enrollment: 1,496. **Student Body:** 24% female, 76% male, 0% international (4 countries represented). Asian 7%, African American 7%, Caucasian 58%, Hispanic 18%, Native American 6%.
Faculty: Student/faculty ratio 24:1. 73 full-time faculty.

ACADEMICS
Degrees: associate, bachelor's, master's, post-bachelor's certificate, terminal associate. **Majors with Highest Enrollment:** electrical, electronic and communications engineering technology/technician. **Special Study Options:** Accelerated program, cooperative education program, distance learning, double major, weekend college. **Disability Services:** Special programs offered to physically disabled students include note-taking services, reader services, tape recorders, tutors. **Career Services:** alumni services, career/job search classes.

FACILITIES
Housing: 100% of campus accessible to physically disabled. **Computers:** Students can register for classes online. Administrative functions (other than registration) can be performed online.

CAMPUS LIFE
Environment: Metropolis. **Activities:** student government 19 registered organizations, 2 honor societies.

ADMISSIONS
Freshman Academic Profile: Minimum paper TOEFL 500. **Basis for Candidate Selection:** *Important factors considered include:* interview. *Other factors considered include:* standardized test scores. **Freshman Admission Requirements:** High school diploma is required and GED is accepted. **Transfer Admission Requirements:** college transcript(s), standardized test scores, minimum college GPA of 2.0 required. Lowest grade transferable C. **General Admission Information:** Application Fee $50. Nonfall registration accepted. Admission may be deferred for a maximum of 12 months. Credit offered for CEEB Advanced Placement tests.

COSTS AND FINANCIAL AID
Annual tuition $11,240. Required fees $250. Average book expense $1,200.
Required Forms and Deadlines: FAFSA. **Notification of Awards: Types of Aid:** *Need-based scholarships/grants:* Federal Pell, SEOG, private scholarships, the school's own gift aid. *Loans:* Subsidized Stafford, Unsubsidized Stafford, PLUS, Federal Perkins, college/university loans from institutional funds. **Student Employment:** Federal Work-Study Program available. Institutional employment available. Highest amount earned per year from on-campus jobs $6,500. Off-campus job opportunities are excellent. **Financial Aid Statistics:** 75% freshmen, 69% undergrads receive need-based scholarship or grant aid. 1% freshmen, 1% undergrads receive non-need-based scholarship or grant aid. 96% freshmen, 96% undergrads receive need-based self-help aid. 94% undergrads borrow to pay for school. Average cumulative indebtedness $29,684. **Criteria for awarding institutional aid:** *Non-need-based:* academics.

DEVRY UNIVERSITY (POMONA, CA)

901 Corporate Center Drive, Pomona, CA 91768
Phone: 909-622-9800
E-mail: bchung@admin.pom.devry.edu
Fax: 909-868-4165 • **Website:** www.pom.devry.edu

This proprietary school was founded in 1931. It has a 13-acre campus.

RATINGS
Admissions Selectivity Rating: 60*   **Fire Safety Rating:** 60*   **Green Rating:** 60*

STUDENTS AND FACULTY
Enrollment: 1,491. **Student Body:** 4% international (19 countries represented). Asian 41%, African American 12%, Caucasian 33%, Hispanic 64%, Native American 1%.
Retention and Graduation: 49% freshmen return for sophomore year. **Faculty:** Student/faculty ratio 34:1. 49 full-time faculty.

ACADEMICS
Degrees: associate, bachelor's, master's, post-bachelor's certificate, terminal associate. **Majors with Highest Enrollment:** electrical, electronic and communications engineering technology/technician. **Special Study Options:** Accelerated program, cooperative education program, distance learning, double major, weekend college. **Disability Services:** Special programs offered to physically disabled students include note-taking services, reader services, tape recorders, tutors. **Career Services:** alumni services, career/job search classes.

FACILITIES

Housing: Private apartments, student plan housing, private rooms. 100% of campus accessible to physically disabled. **Computers:** Students can register for classes online. Administrative functions (other than registration) can be performed online.

CAMPUS LIFE

Environment: City. **Activities:** 15 registered organizations, 4 honor societies.

ADMISSIONS

Freshman Academic Profile: Minimum paper TOEFL 500. **Basis for Candidate Selection:** *Important factors considered include:* interview. *Other factors considered include:* standardized test scores**. Freshman Admission Requirements:** High school diploma is required and GED is accepted. *Academic units required:* 1 mathematics. *Academic units recommended:* 1 mathematics**. Transfer Admission Requirements:** High school transcript, standardized test scores, minimum college GPA of 2.0 required. Lowest grade transferable C. **General Admission Information:** Application Fee $50. Notification on a rolling basis, beginning on or about 11/2. Nonfall registration accepted. Admission may be deferred for a maximum of 12 months. Credit offered for CEEB Advanced Placement tests.

COSTS AND FINANCIAL AID

Annual tuition $11,870. Required fees $250. Average book expense $1,200. **Types of Aid:** *Need-based scholarships/grants:* Federal Pell, SEOG, state scholarships/grants, private scholarships. *Loans:* Subsidized Stafford, Unsubsidized Stafford, PLUS, Federal Perkins. **Student Employment:** Federal Work-Study Program available. Institutional employment available. Highest amount earned per year from on-campus jobs $6,500. Off-campus job opportunities are good. **Financial Aid Statistics:** 70% freshmen, 66% undergrads receive need-based scholarship or grant aid. 98% freshmen, 98% undergrads receive need-based self-help aid.

DEVRY UNIVERSITY (WEST HILLS, CA)

22801 Roscoe Boulevard, West Hills, CA 91304
Phone: 818-932-3001
E mail admissions@devry.com
Fax: 909-868-4165 • **Website:** www.devry.edu

This proprietary school was founded in 1931. It has a 20-acre campus.

RATINGS
Admissions Selectivity Rating: 60*   **Fire Safety Rating:** 60*   **Green Rating:** 60*

STUDENTS AND FACULTY
Enrollment: 1,161. **Student Body:** 26% female, 74% male, 3% international (13 countries represented). Asian 26%, African American 7%, Caucasian 32%, Hispanic 26%, Native American 1%.
Retention and Graduation: 46% freshmen return for sophomore year. **Faculty:** Student/faculty ratio 15:1. 19 full-time faculty.

ACADEMICS
Degrees: associate, bachelor's, master's, post-bachelor's certificate, terminal associate. **Majors with Highest Enrollment:** general studies; psychology; youth ministry. **Special Study Options:** Accelerated program, cooperative education program, distance learning, double major, weekend college. **Disability Services:** Special programs offered to physically disabled students include note-taking services, reader services, tape recorders, tutors. **Career Services:** alumni services, career/job search classes.

FACILITIES
Housing: special housing for disabled students, men's dorms, women's dorms. 100% of campus accessible to physically disabled. **Computers:** Students can register for classes online. Administrative functions (other than registration) can be performed online.

CAMPUS LIFE
Environment: Metropolis. **Activities:** dance, drama/theater, student government, student newspaper, yearbook 14 registered organizations, 3 honor societies.

ADMISSIONS
Freshman Academic Profile: Minimum paper TOEFL 500. **Basis for Candidate Selection:** *Important factors considered include:* interview. *Other factors considered include:* standardized test scores. **Freshman Admission Requirements:** High school diploma is required and GED is accepted. *Academic units required:* 1 mathematics. *Academic units recommended:* 1 mathematics. **Transfer Admission Requirements:** college transcript(s), standardized test

scores, minimum college GPA of 4.0 required. Lowest grade transferable C.
General Admission Information: Application Fee $50. Notification on a rolling basis, beginning on or about 11/2. Nonfall registration accepted. Admission may be deferred for a maximum of 12. Credit offered for CEEB Advanced Placement tests.

COSTS AND FINANCIAL AID
Annual tuition $11,870. Required fees $250. Average book expense $1,200. **Required Forms and Deadlines:** FAFSA. **Notification of Awards: Types of Aid:** *Need-based scholarships/grants:* Federal Pell, SEOG, private scholarships, the school's own gift aid. *Loans:* Subsidized Stafford, Unsubsidized Stafford, PLUS, Federal Perkins, college/university loans from institutional funds. **Student Employment:** Federal Work-Study Program available. Institutional employment available. Highest amount earned per year from on-campus jobs $6,075. Off-campus job opportunities are good. **Financial Aid Statistics:** 64% freshmen, 60% undergrads receive need-based scholarship or grant aid. 97% freshmen, 98% undergrads receive need-based self-help aid.

DICKINSON COLLEGE

P.O. Box 1773, Carlisle, PA 17013-2896
Phone: 717-245-1231 • **Financial Aid Phone:** 717-245-1308
E-mail: admit@dickinson.edu • **CEEB Code:** 2186
Fax: 717-245-1442 • **Website:** www.dickinson.edu/ • **ACT Code:** 3550

This private school was founded in 1783. It has a 308-acre campus.

RATINGS
Admissions Selectivity Rating: 94   **Fire Safety Rating:** 76   **Green Rating:** 99

STUDENTS AND FACULTY
Enrollment: 2,340. **Student Body:** 56% female, 44% male, 77% out-of-state, 7% international (40 countries represented). Asian 2%, African American 3%, Caucasian 78%, Hispanic 6%, Native American 0%.
Retention and Graduation: 91% freshmen return for sophomore year. 81% freshmen graduate within 4 years. 85% freshmen graduate within 6 years. 38% grads go on to further study within 1 year. 13% grads pursue arts and sciences degrees. 6% grads pursue law degrees. 5% grads pursue business degrees. 4% grads pursue medical degrees. **Faculty:** Student/faculty ratio 10:1. 210 full-time faculty, 93% hold PhDs, 11% are members of minority groups, 46% are women. 0% of classes are taught by teaching assistants.

ACADEMICS
Degrees: bachelor's. **Classes:** Most classes have 10–19 students. **Majors with Highest Enrollment:** international business/trade/commerce; political science and government; psychology. **Special Study Options:** Accelerated program, cross-registration, double major, English as a Second Language (ESL), exchange student program (domestic), independent study, internships, liberal arts/career combination, student-designed major, study abroad, teacher certification program. **Combined Degree Programs:** BA/JD, BA/MEng, 3-3 Dickinson School of Law (Penn State). **Disability Services:** Special programs offered to physically disabled students include note-taking services, reader services, tape recorders, tutors. **Career Services:** Alumni network, alumni services, career/job search classes, career assessment, internships, regional alumni. Career Services highlights include Dickinson College believes in the power of experiential education. We maintain a database of over 1,200 business, government and social service internships for students to apply their education in a work setting. Internships can be done for credit. Over half of Dickinson College students do at least one internship during their four years. Over one quarter of our students who go overseas perform internships while in other countries. We have a rotational program set-up with local healthcare facilities for students to explore the medical fields. For those interested in law and government, we have many opportunities available in the county court, with local law firms and in the Pennsylvania state legislature.

FACILITIES
Housing: Coed dorms, special housing for disabled students, fraternity/sorority housing, apartments for single students, theme housing, foreign languages, arts, environmental, multicultural, etc. 67% of campus accessible to physically disabled. **Special Academic Facilities/Equipment:** Art gallery, center for the arts, planetarium, observatory, scanning electron microscope, archeology. **Computers:** 10% of classrooms, 100% of dorms, 100% of libraries, 100% of dining areas, 100% of student union, 5% of common outdoor areas have wireless network access. Students can register for classes online. Administrative functions (other than registration) can be performed online.

CAMPUS LIFE

Environment: City. **Activities:** Choral groups, concert band, dance, drama/theater, jazz band, literary magazine, music ensembles, musical theater, radio station, student government, student newspaper, student-run film society, symphony orchestra, yearbook, International Student Organization, Model UN 112 registered organizations, 15 honor societies, 11 religious organizations. 6 fraternities, 6 sororities. **Athletics (Intercollegiate):** *Men:* baseball, basketball, cross-country, football, golf, lacrosse, soccer, swimming, tennis, track/field (outdoor), track/field (indoor). *Women:* basketball, cross-country, field hockey, golf, lacrosse, soccer, softball, swimming, tennis, track/field (outdoor), track/field (indoor), volleyball. **On-Campus Highlights:** Old West, designed by Benjamin Latrobe, Rector Science Complex, Waidner Spahr Library, Stern Center for Global Education, Kline Athletic Center, The Quarry (coffee shop and late night party/gathering space), Weiss Center for the Arts, and the Trout Gallery. **Environmental Initiatives:** Integrating sustainability throughout the curriculum, supported by the Center for Sustainability Education. All new buildings and major renovations constructed to a LEED Silver certification standard or higher; all projects completed since this policy was adopted in 2007 have been certified LEED Gold Signed the American College and University Presidents' Climate Commitment in 2007 and adopted a climate action plan in 2009 to become climate neutral by 2020.

ADMISSIONS

Freshman Academic Profile: 48% in top 10% of high school class, 78% in top 25% of high school class, 96% in top 50% of high school class. 61% from public high schools. SAT Math middle 50% range 600-690. SAT Critical Reading middle 50% range 590-690. SAT Writing middle 50% range 590-690. ACT middle 50% range 27-30. Minimum web-based TOEFL 89. **Basis for Candidate Selection:** *Very important factors considered include:* academic GPA, rigor of secondary school record, extracurricular activities, talent/ability, volunteer work. *Important factors considered include:* Class rank, recommendation(s), standardized test scores, alumni/ae relation, work experience. *Other factors considered include:* application essay, character/personal qualities, first generation, geographical residence, interview, level of applicant's interest, racial/ethnic status, state residency. **Freshman Admission Requirements:** High school diploma is required and GED is accepted. *Academic units required:* 4 English, 3 mathematics, 3 science, (2 science labs), 2 foreign language, 2 social studies, 2 academic electives. *Academic units recommended:* 4 English, 3 mathematics, 3 science, (2 science labs), 2 foreign language, 2 social studies, 2 academic electives. **Freshman Admission Statistics:** 5,818 applied, 40% admitted, 26% enrolled. **Transfer Admission Requirements:** High school transcript, college transcript(s), essay or personal statement, statement of good standing from prior institution(s). Minimum college GPA of 2 required. Lowest grade transferable C. **General Admission Information:** Application Fee $65. Early decision application deadline 11/15. Regular application deadline 2/1. Regular notification 3/31. Nonfall registration not accepted. Admission may be deferred for a maximum of 2 years. Credit and/or placement offered for CEEB Advanced Placement tests.

COSTS AND FINANCIAL AID

Annual tuition $44,101. Room and board $11,178. Required fees $450. Average book expense $1,000. **Required Forms and Deadlines:** FAFSA, CSS/Financial Aid PROFILE, state aid form, noncustodial PROFILE. **Notification of Awards:** Applicants will be notified of awards on or about 3/20. **Types of Aid:** *Need-based scholarships/grants:* Federal Pell, SEOG, state scholarships/grants, private scholarships, the school's own gift aid. *Loans:* Subsidized Stafford, Unsubsidized Stafford, PLUS, Federal Perkins, college/university loans from institutional funds. **Student Employment:** Federal Work-Study Program available. Institutional employment available. Off-campus job opportunities are good. **Financial Aid Statistics:** 94% freshmen, 96% undergrads receive need-based scholarship or grant aid. 11% freshmen, 8% undergrads receive non-need-based scholarship or grant aid. 87% freshmen, 92% undergrads receive need-based self-help aid. 76% freshmen, 72% undergrads receive any aid. 53% undergrads borrow to pay for school. Average cumulative indebtedness $25,574. **Criteria for awarding institutional aid:** *Non-need-based:* academics, leadership.

STUDENTS AND FACULTY

Enrollment: 2,669. **Student Body:** 59% female, 41% male, 34% out-of-state, 12% international (30 countries represented). Asian 0%, African American 1%, Caucasian 71%, Hispanic 1%, Native American 2%.
Retention and Graduation: 60% freshmen return for sophomore year. 9% freshmen graduate within 4 years. 31% freshmen graduate within 6 years.
Faculty: Student/faculty ratio 19:1. 86 full-time faculty, 52% hold PhDs, 6% are members of minority groups, 43% are women.

ACADEMICS

Degrees: associate, bachelor's, certificate, terminal associate, transfer associate. **Classes:** Most classes have 10–19 students. **Majors with Highest Enrollment:** business/commerce; nursing/registered nurse (rn, asn, bsn, msn); teacher education, multiple levels. **Special Study Options:** Accelerated program, distance learning, double major, dual enrollment, honors program, independent study, internships, liberal arts/career combination, student-designed major, study abroad, teacher certification program. **Career Services:** Alumni network, alumni services, career/job search classes, career assessment, internships.

FACILITIES

Housing: Coed dorms, special housing for disabled students, men's dorms, women's dorms, apartments for married students, apartments for single students, Apartments for upperclassmen; apartments for scholars. **Special Academic Facilities/Equipment:** Art gallery, smart classrooms **Computers:** Students can register for classes online.

CAMPUS LIFE

Environment: Rural. **Activities:** Choral groups, concert band, dance, drama/theater, jazz band, literary magazine, marching band, music ensembles, musical theater, pep band, student government, student newspaper, student-run film society, yearbook, International Student Organization 51 registered organizations, 7 honor societies, 6 religious organizations. **Athletics (Intercollegiate):** *Men:* baseball, basketball, cheerleading, cross-country, football, golf, rodeo, track/field (outdoor), track/field (indoor), wrestling. *Women:* basketball, cheerleading, cross-country, golf, rodeo, softball, track/field (outdoor), track/field (indoor), volleyball. **On-Campus Highlights:** Murphy Hall, Student Center, Common Grounds Coffee Shop, Whitney Stadium

ADMISSIONS

Freshman Academic Profile: Average high school GPA 3.2. 6% in top 10% of high school class, 19% in top 25% of high school class, 53% in top 50% of high school class. 98% from public high schools. SAT Math middle 50% range 470-590. SAT Critical Reading middle 50% range 430-530. ACT middle 50% range 18-23. Minimum paper TOEFL 525. **Basis for Candidate Selection:. Freshman Admission Requirements:** High school diploma is required and GED is accepted. *Academic units required:* 4 English, 3 mathematics, 3 science, 3 history and/or social studies. 4 English, 3 mathematics, 3 science, 3 history and/or social studies. **Freshman Admission Statistics:** 627 applied, 80% admitted, 75% enrolled. **Transfer Admission Requirements:** college transcript(s), minimum college GPA of 2.0 required. Lowest grade transferable D. **General Admission Information:** Application Fee $35. Nonfall registration accepted. Admission may be deferred for a maximum of none. Neither credit nor placement offered for CEEB Advanced Placement tests.

COSTS AND FINANCIAL AID

Annual in-state tuition $3,828. Annual out-of-state tuition $10,222. Room and board $4,076. Required fees $945. Average book expense $900. **Required Forms and Deadlines:** FAFSA. **Notification of Awards:** Applicants will be notified of awards on a rolling basis beginning 4/30. **Types of Aid:** *Need-based scholarships/grants:* Federal Pell, SEOG, state scholarships/grants, private scholarships, the school's own gift aid. *Loans:* Subsidized Stafford, Unsubsidized Stafford, PLUS, Federal Perkins, Federal Nursing. **Student Employment:** Federal Work-Study Program available. Institutional employment available. Highest amount earned per year from on-campus jobs $1,304. Off-campus job opportunities are excellent. **Financial Aid Statistics: Criteria for awarding institutional aid:** *Non-need-based:* academics, alumni affiliation, art, athletics, job skills, leadership, minority status, music/drama, state/district residency.

DICKINSON STATE UNIVERSITY

Office of Enrollment Services, Dickinson, ND 58601-4896
Phone: 701-483-2175 • **Financial Aid Phone:** 701-483-2371
E-mail: dsu.hawks@dsu.nodak.edu
Fax: 701-483-2409 • **Website:** www.dickinsonstate.com • **ACT Code:** 3210

This public school was founded in 1918. It has a 137-acre campus.

RATINGS

Admissions Selectivity Rating: 69 **Fire Safety Rating:** 60* **Green Rating:** 60*

DILLARD UNIVERSITY

2601 Gentilly Boulevard, New Orleans, LA 70122
Phone: 504-816-4670 • Financial Aid Phone: 504-816-4677
E-mail: admissions@dillard.edu • CEEB Code: 6164
Fax: 504-816-4895 • Website: www.dillard.edu • ACT Code: 1578

This private school, affiliated with the United Church of Christ Church, was founded in 1869. It has a 55-acre campus.

RATINGS
Admissions Selectivity Rating: 84   **Fire Safety Rating:** 62   **Green Rating:** 60*

STUDENTS AND FACULTY
Enrollment: 2,155. **Student Body:** 78% female, 22% male, 54% out-of-state, 0% international (12 countries represented). Asian 0%, African American 99%, Caucasian 0%, Hispanic 0%, Native American 0%.
Retention and Graduation: 78% freshmen return for sophomore year. 36% freshmen graduate within 4 years. 47% freshmen graduate within 6 years. 39% grads go on to further study within 1 year. 34% grads pursue arts and sciences degrees. 1% grads pursue law degrees. 1% grads pursue business degrees. 3% grads pursue medical degrees. **Faculty:** Student/faculty ratio 12:1. 145 full-time faculty, 68% hold PhDs, 91% are members of minority groups, 57% are women. 0% of classes are taught by teaching assistants.

ACADEMICS
Degrees: bachelor's, terminal associate. **Classes:** Most classes have 10–19 students. Most lab/discussion sessions have 20–29 students. **Special Study Options:** double major, dual enrollment, honors program, independent study, internships, liberal arts/career combination, study abroad, teacher certification program. **Career Services:** Alumni network, internships.

FACILITIES
Housing: Coed dorms, men's dorms, women's dorms, apartments for single students. 60% of campus accessible to physically disabled. **Special Academic Facilities/Equipment:** Art gallery, language lab, communication studies facilities, electron microscope, observatory, outdoor challenge course. **Computers:** Administrative functions (other than registration) can be performed online.

CAMPUS LIFE
Environment: Metropolis. **Activities:** Choral groups, dance, drama/theater, music ensembles, radio station, student government, student newspaper, yearbook 67 registered organizations, 6 honor societies, 3 religious organizations. 4 fraternities, 4 sororities. **Athletics (Intercollegiate):** *Men:* basketball, cross-country, tennis. *Women:* basketball, cross-country, tennis, volleyball. **On-Campus Highlights:** Avenue of the Oaks, Lawless Memorial Chapel, Samuel DuBois Cook, Dent Hall

ADMISSIONS
Freshman Academic Profile: Average high school GPA 3.2. 2% in top 10% of high school class, 44% in top 25% of high school class, 74% in top 50% of high school class. % from public high schools. SAT Math middle 50% range 440–520. SAT Critical Reading middle 50% range 450–530. ACT middle 50% range 19–22. Minimum paper TOEFL 550. **Basis for Candidate Selection:** *Very important factors considered include:* application essay, recommendation(s), rigor of secondary school record, standardized test scores. *Other factors considered include:* Class rank, alumni/ae relation, extracurricular activities, interview. **Freshman Admission Requirements:** High school diploma is required and GED is accepted. *Academic units required:* 4 English, 3 mathematics, 3 science, 3 social studies, 6 academic electives. *Academic units recommended:* 4 English, 3 mathematics, 3 science, 3 social studies, 6 academic electives. **Freshman Admission Statistics:** 3,106 applied, 47% admitted, 35% enrolled. **Transfer Admission Requirements:** college transcript(s), statement of good standing from prior institution(s). Minimum college GPA of 2.0 required. Lowest grade transferable C. **General Admission Information:** Application Fee $20. Regular application deadline 7/1. Nonfall registration accepted. Credit and/or placement offered for CEEB Advanced Placement tests.

COSTS AND FINANCIAL AID
Average book expense $1,000. **Required Forms and Deadlines:** FAFSA, institution's own financial aid form. **Notification of Awards:** Applicants will be notified of awards on a rolling basis beginning 3/1. **Types of Aid:** *Need-based scholarships/grants:* Federal Pell, SEOG, state scholarships/grants, private scholarships, the school's own gift aid, United Negro College Fund, Federal Nursing Scholarships. *Loans:* Direct Subsidized Stafford, Direct Unsubsidized Stafford, Direct PLUS, Subsidized Stafford, Unsubsidized Stafford, PLUS, Federal Perkins, Federal Nursing. **Student Employment:** Federal Work-Study Program available. Highest amount earned per year from on-campus jobs $2,000. Off-campus job opportunities are good. **Financial Aid Statistics:** 83% freshmen, 66% undergrads receive need-based scholarship or grant aid.

3% freshmen, 2% undergrads receive athletic scholarships. 98% freshmen, 98% undergrads receive any aid. 90% undergrads borrow to pay for school. Average cumulative indebtedness $23,585. **Criteria for awarding institutional aid:** *Non-need-based:* academics, alumni affiliation, art, athletics, music/drama, religious affiliation.

DIVINE WORD COLLEGE

Office of Admissions, Epworth, IA 52045
Phone: 563-876-3332
E-mail: svdvocations@dwci.edu • CEEB Code: 6174
Fax: 563-876-5515

This private school, affiliated with the Roman Catholic Church, was founded in 1964. It has a 30-acre campus.

RATINGS
Admissions Selectivity Rating: 63   **Fire Safety Rating:** 60*   **Green Rating:** 60*

STUDENTS AND FACULTY
Retention and Graduation: **Faculty:** Student/faculty ratio 3:1. 16 full-time faculty, 56% hold PhDs, 25% are members of minority groups, 56% are women. 0% of classes are taught by teaching assistants.

ACADEMICS
Degrees: associate, bachelor's. **Special Study Options:** double major, English as a Second Language (ESL), independent study, liberal arts/career combination.

FACILITIES
Housing: men's dorms.

CAMPUS LIFE
Environment: Rural. **Activities:** Choral groups, student government, yearbook, Campus Ministries, International Student Organization. **Athletics (Intercollegiate):** *Men:* soccer.

ADMISSIONS
Freshman Academic Profile: Minimum paper TOEFL 550. **Basis for Candidate Selection:** *Very important factors considered include:* character/personal qualities, interview, level of applicant's interest, religious affiliation/commitment, *Important factors considered include:* application essay, academic GPA, recommendation(s). *Other factors considered include:* Class rank, rigor of secondary school record, standardized test scores, extracurricular activities, geographical residence, talent/ability, volunteer work, work experience. **Freshman Admission Requirements:** High school diploma is required and GED is accepted. **Freshman Admission Statistics:** 3 applied, 67% admitted, 0% enrolled. **Transfer Admission Requirements:** High school transcript, college transcript(s), essay or personal statement, interview, statement of good standing from prior institution(s). **General Admission Information:** Application Fee $25. Nonfall registration accepted. Admission may be deferred for a maximum of one semester. Credit and/or placement offered for CEEB Advanced Placement tests.

COSTS AND FINANCIAL AID
Annual tuition $10,400. Room and board $2,700. Required fees $120. Average book expense $500. **Types of Aid:** *Need-based scholarships/grants:* Federal Pell, SEOG, state scholarships/grants, private scholarships, the school's own gift aid. *Loans:* Direct Subsidized Stafford, Direct Unsubsidized Stafford, Subsidized Stafford, PLUS, Federal Perkins, state loans. **Student Employment:** Federal Work-Study Program available.

DOANE COLLEGE

1014 Boswell Avenue, Crete, NE 68333
Phone: 402-826-8222 • Financial Aid Phone: 402-826-8260
E-mail: admissions@doane.edu • CEEB Code: 6165
Fax: 402-826-8600 • Website: www.doane.edu • ACT Code: 2448

This private school, affiliated with the United Church of Christ Church, was founded in 1872. It has a 300-acre campus.

RATINGS
Admissions Selectivity Rating: 72   **Fire Safety Rating:** 89   **Green Rating:** 61

STUDENTS AND FACULTY

Enrollment: 1,912. **Student Body:** 55% female, 45% male, 17% out-of-state, 1% international (11 countries represented). Asian 2%, African American 4%, Caucasian 86%, Hispanic 5%, Native American 1%.
Retention and Graduation: 76% freshmen return for sophomore year. 60% freshmen graduate within 4 years. 64% freshmen graduate within 6 years. 29% grads go on to further study within 1 year. 13% grads pursue arts and sciences degrees. 1% grads pursue law degrees. 1% grads pursue business degrees. 7% grads pursue medical degrees. **Faculty:** Student/faculty ratio 12:1. 78 full-time faculty, 81% hold PhDs, 4% are members of minority groups, 46% are women. 0% of classes are taught by teaching assistants.

ACADEMICS

Degrees: bachelor's, master's. **Classes:** Most classes have fewer than 10 students. Most lab/discussion sessions have fewer than 10 students. **Majors with Highest Enrollment:** biological and physical sciences; business administration and management; elementary education and teaching. **Special Study Options:** double major, English as a Second Language (ESL), honors program, independent study, internships, student-designed major, study abroad, teacher certification program. **Honors Programs:** The Honors Program is designed to enrich, in a variety of ways, the educational experience of selected Doane students. Specialized, interdisciplinary, one-credit honors seminars form the intellectual core of the program. Another component is the study abroad experience undertaken during the junior or senior year. The culminating experience is a collaborative research project. **Combined Degree Programs:** BA/MEng. **Disability Services:** Special programs offered to physically disabled students include tutors. **Career Services:** Alumni network, career assessment, internships Career Services highlights include The intenship program at Doane offers students quality internship that build upon their academic coursework. up to 12 credit hours can apply toward graduation, giving students an edge in the job market and on graduate school acceptance.

FACILITIES

Housing: Coed dorms, men's dorms, women's dorms, theme housing, 60% of campus accessible to physically disabled. **Special Academic Facilities/Equipment:** Art gallery, language lab, communication studies facilities, electron microscope, observatory, outdoor challenge course. **Computers:** 90% of classrooms, 100% of dorms, 100% of libraries, 100% of dining areas, 100% of student union, 10% of common outdoor areas have wireless network access. Students can register for classes online. Administrative functions (other than registration) can be performed online.

CAMPUS LIFE

Environment: Rural. **Activities:** Choral groups, concert band, dance, drama/theater, jazz band, literary magazine, marching band, music ensembles, musical theater, pep band, radio station, student government, student newspaper, television station, yearbook, Campus Ministries 50 registered organizations, 8 honor societies, 2 religious organizations. 5 fraternities, 4 sororities. **Athletics (Intercollegiate):** *Men:* baseball, basketball, cross-country, football, golf, soccer, tennis, track/field (outdoor), track/field (indoor). *Women:* basketball, cheerleading, cross-country, golf, soccer, softball, tennis, track/field (outdoor), track/field (indoor), volleyball. **On-Campus Highlights:** Tiger Inn, Perkins Library, The Quads, Fuhrer Field House, Heckman Auditorium. **Environmental Initiatives:** Recycling

ADMISSIONS

Freshman Academic Profile: Average high school GPA 3.5. 17% in top 10% of high school class, 46% in top 25% of high school class, 81% in top 50% of high school class. 89% from public high schools. ACT middle 50% range 21-26. Minimum paper TOEFL 525. **Basis for Candidate Selection:** *Very important factors considered include:* academic GPA, standardized test scores. *Important factors considered include:* rigor of secondary school record, alumni/ae relation, character/personal qualities, level of applicant's interest. *Other factors considered include:* Class rank, recommendation(s), extracurricular activities, interview, racial/ethnic status, talent/ability, volunteer work, work experience. **Freshman Admission Requirements:** High school diploma is required and GED is accepted. **Freshman Admission Statistics:** 1,733 applied, 76% admitted, 25% enrolled. **Transfer Admission Requirements:** High school transcript, college transcript(s), statement of good standing from prior institution(s). Minimum college GPA of 2.0 required. Lowest grade transferable C–. **General Admission Information:** Notification on a rolling basis, beginning on or about 10/1. Nonfall registration accepted. Admission may be deferred for a maximum of one year. Credit offered for CEEB Advanced Placement tests.

COSTS AND FINANCIAL AID

Annual tuition $24,960. Room and board $7,140. Required fees $620. Average book expense $900. **Required Forms and Deadlines:** FAFSA. **Notification of Awards:** Applicants will be notified of awards on a rolling basis beginning 3/1. **Types of Aid:** *Need-based scholarships/grants:* Federal Pell, SEOG, state scholarships/grants, private scholarships, the school's own gift aid. *Loans:* Subsidized Stafford, Unsubsidized Stafford, PLUS, Federal Perkins. **Student Employment:** Federal Work-Study Program available. Institutional employ-

ment available. Highest amount earned per year from on-campus jobs $1,100. Off-campus job opportunities are fair. **Financial Aid Statistics:** 99% freshmen, 88% undergrads receive need-based scholarship or grant aid. 20% freshmen, 13% undergrads receive non-need-based scholarship or grant aid. 86% freshmen, 76% undergrads receive need-based self-help aid. 15% freshmen, 15% undergrads receive athletic scholarships. 100% freshmen, 100% undergrads receive any aid. 80% undergrads borrow to pay for school. Average cumulative indebtedness $20,803. **Criteria for awarding institutional aid:** *Non-need-based:* academics, art, athletics, leadership, music/drama.

DOMINICAN COLLEGE

470 Western Highway, Orangeburg, NY 10962-1210
Phone: 845-848-7901 • **Financial Aid Phone:** 845-848-7818
E-mail: admissions@dc.edu • **CEEB Code:** 2190
Fax: 845-365-3150 • **Website:** www.dc.edu • **ACT Code:** 2730

This private school was founded in 1952. It has a 70-acre campus.

RATINGS

Admissions Selectivity Rating: 69   **Fire Safety Rating:** 90   **Green Rating:** 65

STUDENTS AND FACULTY

Enrollment: 1,559. **Student Body:** 67% female, 33% male, 25% out-of-state, 1% international (15 countries represented). Asian 8%, African American 16%, Caucasian 35%, Hispanic 24%, Native American 0%.
Retention and Graduation: 64% freshmen return for sophomore year. 24% freshmen graduate within 4 years. 35% freshmen graduate within 6 years. **Faculty:** Student/faculty ratio 15:1. 75 full-time faculty, 56% hold PhDs, 12% are members of minority groups, 72% are women. 0% of classes are taught by teaching assistants.

ACADEMICS

Degrees: associate, bachelor's, doctoral, master's. **Classes:** Most classes have 20–29 students. **Majors with Highest Enrollment:** business/commerce; nursing/registered nurse (rn, asn, bsn, msn); social sciences. **Special Study Options:** Accelerated program, cooperative education program, distance learning, dual enrollment, honors program, independent study, internships, liberal arts/career combination, teacher certification program, weekend college, Independent study. **Combined Degree Programs:** BS/MS Occupational Therapy. **Disability Services:** Special programs offered to physically disabled students include note-taking services, reader services, tutors. **Career Services:** career/job search classes, career assessment, internships, regional alumni.

FACILITIES

Housing: Coed dorms. 100% of campus accessible to physically disabled. **Special Academic Facilities/Equipment:** New State of the Art Prusmack Center for Health Care Programs and Science Education **Computers:** 100% of classrooms, 100% of dorms, 100% of libraries, 100% of dining areas, have wireless network access.

CAMPUS LIFE

Environment: Metropolis. **Activities:** Choral groups, dance, drama/theater, literary magazine, musical theater, student government, student newspaper, yearbook, Campus Ministries, Model UN 26 registered organizations, 8 honor societies, 1 religious organizations. **Athletics (Intercollegiate):** *Men:* baseball, basketball, golf, lacrosse, soccer. *Women:* basketball, cross-country, lacrosse, soccer, softball, track/field (outdoor), volleyball. **On-Campus Highlights:** Prusmack Center for Health and Science Education, Granito Center: Book Store, Health Services, Hennessy Athletic Center, Sullivan Library, Rosary Hall Lounge, Wild Onion Lounge/Cafeteria in Casey Hall. **Environmental Initiatives:** Geothermal HVAC system installed in most recently constructed academic building campus-wide recycling program, se of environmentally safe cleaning products throughout the campus, all new construction projects incorporate as many green elements as possible.

ADMISSIONS

Freshman Academic Profile: Average high school GPA 2.7. 69% from public high schools. SAT Math middle 50% range 390-490. SAT Critical Reading middle 50% range 400-480. SAT Writing middle 50% range 400-490. ACT middle 50% range 17-20. Minimum paper TOEFL 550. **Basis for Candidate Selection:** *Important factors considered include:* academic GPA, recommendation(s), standardized test scores. *Other factors considered include:* application essay, rigor of secondary school record, character/personal qualities, extracurricular activities, interview, level of applicant's interest, talent/ability, volunteer work, work experience. **Freshman Admission Requirements:** High school diploma is required and GED is accepted. *Academic units required:* 4 English, 3 mathematics, 3 science, (1 science labs), 1 foreign language, 3 social studies, 3 history, 2 academic electives. *Academic units recommended:* 4 English, 3 mathematics, 3 science, (1 science labs), 1 foreign language, 3 social studies, 3 history, 2 academic electives. **Freshman Admission Statistics:** 1,850 applied, 69% admitted, 23% enrolled. **Transfer Admission Requirements:** college transcript(s), minimum college GPA of 2.0 required. Lowest grade transferable C. **General Admission Information:** Application Fee $35. Nonfall registration accepted. Admission may be deferred for a maximum of 1 year. Credit offered for CEEB Advanced Placement tests.

COSTS AND FINANCIAL AID

Annual tuition $23,200. Room and board $11,420. Required fees $770. Average book expense $1,800. **Required Forms and Deadlines:** FAFSA, state aid form. **Notification of Awards:** Applicants will be notified of awards on a rolling basis beginning 2/1. **Types of Aid:** *Need-based scholarships/grants:* Federal Pell, SEOG, state scholarships/grants, private scholarships, the school's own gift aid. *Loans:* Subsidized Stafford, Unsubsidized Stafford, PLUS, Federal Perkins, Federal Nursing. **Student Employment:** Federal Work-Study Program available. Institutional employment available. Highest amount earned per year from on-campus jobs $2,000. Off-campus job opportunities are fair. **Financial Aid Statistics:** 100% freshmen, 93% undergrads receive need-based scholarship or grant aid. 8% freshmen, 7% undergrads receive non-need-based scholarship or grant aid. 83% freshmen, 85% undergrads receive need-based self-help aid. 6% freshmen, 5% undergrads receive athletic scholarships. 98% freshmen, 97% undergrads receive any aid. 95% undergrads borrow to pay for school. Average cumulative indebtedness $17,930. **Criteria for awarding institutional aid:** *Non-need-based:* academics, athletics.

DOMINICAN SCHOOL OF PHILOSOPHY AND THEOLOGY

2301 Vine Street, Berkeley, CA 94708
Phone: 510-883-2073
E-mail: admissions@dspt.edu
Fax: 510-849-1372 • **Website:** www.dspt.edu

This private school, affiliated with the Roman Catholic Church, was founded in 1932. It has a -1-acre campus.

RATINGS

Admissions Selectivity Rating: 60*   **Fire Safety Rating:** 60*   **Green Rating:** 60*

STUDENTS AND FACULTY

Enrollment: 5. **Student Body:** 0% international (6 countries represented). Asian 40%, African American 0%, Caucasian 20%, Hispanic 40%, Native American 0%.
Retention and Graduation: 100% freshmen return for sophomore year. 50% grads go on to further study within 1 year. 60% grads pursue arts and sciences degrees. 10% grads pursue law degrees. 50% grads pursue medical degrees. **Faculty:** Student/faculty ratio 4:1. 12 full-time faculty, 100% hold PhDs, 0% are members of minority groups, 17% are women. 10% of classes are taught by teaching assistants.

ACADEMICS

Degrees: bachelor's, certificate, first professional, master's. **Classes:** Most classes have 10–19 students. **Special Study Options:** cross-registration, independent study, study abroad, Select graduate level courses available to undergradute students.

FACILITIES

Housing: men's dorms, women's dorms, apartments for married students, apartments for single students. 50% of campus accessible to physically disabled. **Computers:** Administrative functions (other than registration) can be performed online.

CAMPUS LIFE

Environment: City. **Activities:** Choral groups, concert band, music ensembles, student government, yearbook.

ADMISSIONS

Freshman Academic Profile: Minimum paper TOEFL 550. **Freshman Admission Requirements:** High school diploma is required and GED is accepted. **Transfer Admission Requirements:** college transcript(s), essay or personal statement, minimum college GPA of 2.3 required. Lowest grade transferable C. **General Admission Information:** Application Fee $40. Nonfall registration not accepted. Admission may be deferred for a maximum of 1 year.

COSTS AND FINANCIAL AID

Annual tuition $11,880. Required fees $100. Average book expense $1,113. **Required Forms and Deadlines: Notification of Awards: Types of Aid:**

Need-based scholarships/grants: Loans: **Student Employment:** Highest amount earned per year from on-campus jobs $3,500.

DOMINICAN UNIVERSITY

7900 West Division, River Forest, IL 60305
Phone: 708-524-6800 • **Financial Aid Phone:** 708-524-6809
E-mail: domadmis@dom.edu • **CEEB Code:** 1667
Fax: 708-524-6864 • **Website:** www.dom.edu • **ACT Code:** 1126

This private school, affiliated with the Roman Catholic Church, was founded in 1901. It has a 37-acre campus.

RATINGS

Admissions Selectivity Rating: 84   **Fire Safety Rating:** 98   **Green Rating:** 78

STUDENTS AND FACULTY

Enrollment: 1,920. **Student Body:** 68% female, 32% male, 8% out-of-state, 2% international (23 countries represented). Asian 3%, African American 7%, Caucasian 49%, Hispanic 35%, Native American 0%.
Retention and Graduation: 80% freshmen return for sophomore year. 55% freshmen graduate within 4 years. 42% grads go on to further study within 1 year. **Faculty:** Student/faculty ratio 11:1. 153 full-time faculty, 88% hold PhDs, 17% are members of minority groups, 59% are women. 0% of classes are taught by teaching assistants.

ACADEMICS

Degrees: bachelor's, certificate, master's, post-bachelor's certificate, post-master's certificate. **Classes:** Most classes have 10–19 students. Most lab/discussion sessions have 10–19 students. **Majors with Highest Enrollment:** business/commerce; English language and literature; psychology. **Special Study Options:** Accelerated program, cross-registration, distance learning, double major, dual enrollment, English as a Second Language (ESL), honors program, independent study, internships, liberal arts/career combination, student-designed major, study abroad, teacher certification program. **Honors Programs:** Honors seminars for high ability students **Combined Degree Programs:** BA/MA, BA/MBA, BA/MSLIS; BA/MSSPED; 5 yr. pr. w/ Rush U. **Disability Services:** Special programs offered to physically disabled students include note-taking services, reader services, tape recorders, tutors. **Career Services:** career/job search classes, career assessment, internships Career Services highlights include We have an excellent Chicago internship program.

FACILITIES

Housing: Coed dorms, special housing for disabled students, co-ed by floor. 100% of campus accessible to physically disabled. **Special Academic Facilities/Equipment:** Art gallery, Technology Center, language lab, Recital Hall **Computers:** 70% of classrooms, 100% of libraries, 75% of dining areas, 100% of student union, have wireless network access. Students can register for classes online. Administrative functions (other than registration) can be performed online.

CAMPUS LIFE

Environment: Metropolis. **Activities:** Choral groups, dance, drama/theater, literary magazine, musical theater, student government, student newspaper, Campus Ministries, International Student Organization 76 registered organizations, 14 honor societies, 2 religious organizations. **Athletics (Intercollegiate):** *Men:* baseball, basketball, cross-country, soccer, tennis. *Women:* basketball, cross-country, soccer, softball, tennis, volleyball. **On-Campus Highlights:** Cybercafe, New science building (Parmer Hall), Reading Room, Centennial Hall (residence hall), New parking pavillion. **Environmental Initiatives:** Over half the surface parking lots have permeable pavers Newest building built to Silver Leed standards Have replaced most lighting with flourescent bulbs, have retrofitted most original windows with energy saving windows

ADMISSIONS

Freshman Academic Profile: Average high school GPA 3.4. 21% in top 10% of high school class, 49% in top 25% of high school class, 85% in top 50% of high school class. 78% from public high schools. SAT Math middle 50% range 490-600. SAT Critical Reading middle 50% range 500-590. SAT Writing middle 50% range 450-570. ACT middle 50% range 20-24. Minimum web-based TOEFL 79. Minimum paper TOEFL 550. **Basis for Candidate Selection:** *Very important factors considered include:* academic GPA. *Important factors considered include:* Class rank, rigor of secondary school record, standardized test scores. *Other factors considered include:* application essay, recommendation(s), alumni/ae relation, character/personal qualities, extracurricular activities, first generation, interview, talent/ability, volunteer work. **Freshman Admission Requirements:** High school diploma is required and GED is accepted. *Academic units required:* 4 English, 2 academic electives.

Academic units recommended: 4 English, 2 academic electives. **Freshman Admission Statistics:** 3,056 applied, 57% admitted, 23% enrolled. **Transfer Admission Requirements:** college transcript(s), essay or personal statement, minimum college GPA of 2.5 required. Lowest grade transferable C–. **General Admission Information:** Application Fee $25. Notification on a rolling basis, beginning on or about 10/15. Nonfall registration accepted. Admission may be deferred for a maximum of 1 semester. Credit offered for CEEB Advanced Placement tests.

COSTS AND FINANCIAL AID
Annual tuition $28,440. Room and board $8,818. Required fees $250. Average book expense $1,200. **Required Forms and Deadlines:** FAFSA, parent and student tax forms. **Notification of Awards:** Applicants will be notified of awards on a rolling basis beginning 3/15. **Types of Aid:** *Need-based scholarships/grants:* Federal Pell, SEOG, state scholarships/grants, private scholarships, the school's own gift aid. *Loans:* Subsidized Stafford, Unsubsidized Stafford, PLUS, Federal Perkins, state loans. **Student Employment:** Federal Work-Study Program available. Institutional employment available. Highest amount earned per year from on-campus jobs $7,730. Off-campus job opportunities are good. **Financial Aid Statistics:** 100% freshmen, 95% undergrads receive need-based scholarship or grant aid. 11% freshmen, 8% undergrads receive non-need-based scholarship or grant aid. 82% freshmen, 84% undergrads receive need-based self-help aid. % freshmen, % undergrads receive athletic scholarships. 100% freshmen, 84% undergrads receive any aid. 84% undergrads borrow to pay for school. Average cumulative indebtedness $28,281. **Criteria for awarding institutional aid:** *Non-need-based:* academics, alumni affiliation, leadership, music/drama, religious affiliation.

DOMINICAN UNIVERSITY OF CALIFORNIA

Admissions, San Rafael, CA 94901-2298
Phone: 415-485-3204 • **Financial Aid Phone:** 415-257-1302
E-mail: enroll@dominican.edu • **CEEB Code:** 4284
Fax: 415-485-3204 • **Website:** www.dominican.edu

This private school was founded in 1890. It has a 80-acre campus.

RATINGS
Admissions Selectivity Rating: 84   **Fire Safety Rating:** 99   **Green Rating:** 76

STUDENTS AND FACULTY
Enrollment: 1,426. **Student Body:** 75% female, 25% male, 6% out-of-state, 2% international (20 countries represented). Asian 23%, African American 6%, Caucasian 38%, Hispanic 16%, Native American 1%.
Retention and Graduation: 69% freshmen return for sophomore year. 31% freshmen graduate within 4 years. **Faculty:** Student/faculty ratio 11:1. 76 full-time faculty, 80% hold PhDs, 14% are members of minority groups, 64% are women. 0% of classes are taught by teaching assistants.

ACADEMICS
Degrees: bachelor's, master's, post-bachelor's certificate. **Classes:** Most classes have 10–19 students. Most lab/discussion sessions have fewer than 10 students. **Majors with Highest Enrollment:** business administration and management; nursing/registered nurse (rn, asn, bsn, msn); psychology. **Special Study Options:** Accelerated program, cross-registration, distance learning, double major, dual enrollment, English as a Second Language (ESL), exchange student program (domestic), honors program, independent study, internships, study abroad, teacher certification program, weekend college. **Honors Programs:** Honors Program Scholar in the World. **Disability Services:** Special programs offered to physically disabled students include note-taking services, reader services, tape recorders, tutors. **Career Services:** Alumni network, alumni services, career/job search classes, career assessment, internships, regional alumni., Career Services highlights include Internship Program: Most programs at Dominican University of California require an internship of 45-135 hours, undertaken after completing some coursework in the major. The internship helps students clarify and test their career goals, obtain hands-on work experience related to their major, gain professional contacts, and develop self-confidence. In addition to the completion of the internship hours, students must maintain a journal, submit a paper or give an oral presentation, and evaluate the internship at midterm and upon completion.

FACILITIES
Housing: Coed dorms, wellness housing, 65% of campus accessible to physically disabled. **Special Academic Facilities/Equipment:** Art Gallery, Science Lab, Computer Labs, Nursing Skills Lab **Computers:** 10% of classrooms, 5% of dorms, 100% of libraries, 100% of dining areas, 100% of student union, have wireless network access. Administrative functions (other than registration) can be performed online.

CAMPUS LIFE
Environment: Town. **Activities:** Choral groups, dance, drama/theater, jazz band, literary magazine, music ensembles, musical theater, radio station, student government, student newspaper, yearbook, Campus Ministries 19 registered organizations, 7 honor societies, 4 religious organizations. **Athletics (Intercollegiate):** *Men:* basketball, golf, lacrosse, soccer. *Women:* basketball, golf, soccer, softball, tennis, volleyball. **On-Campus Highlights:** Conlan Recreation Center, Caleruega Dining Hall, Guzman Lecture Hall, Alemany Library, Science Center. **Environmental Initiatives:** We established the Dominican Center for Sustainability. The Center serves as ground central for Dominican University's numerous green activities, including educational programs, scholarships, community outreach, and national and international partnerships. We created the Center to tap the wealth of intellectual capital in place at Dominican in order to support existing and emerging green programs. The Center identifies and promotes economically viable green business practices and serves as a think-tank for ongoing green projects on a community, regional, and global level. Dominican greatly expanded its academic programs focused on sustainability. We introduced a certificate program that enables nonprofit and corporate executives, as well as others who already hold an MBA, the Sustainable Enterprise Certificate provides individuals with the knowledge and tools to green their current workplaces while also advancing their careers. We also introduced a certificate program, offered through Dominican's Department of Professional and Continuing Education (PACE), designed for non-degree-seeking adults wanting to take positive steps to enhance their communities.The program offers three areas of concentration: Sustainable Careers and Advocacy, Sustainable Education, and Sustainable Lifestyles. Students will gain a high level of knowledge about sustainability issues as well as specific and practical skills to apply this knowledge to a particular area of specialization. The Institution formally adopted a Green Statement to signal its ongoing commitment to sustainability: Dominican University of California will model and instill the values, theories and practices of reverence, interdependence, sustainability, social justice and stewardship into the entirety of its learning environment. The Dominican learning environment encompasses the education programs as well as maintaining green working and living spaces, and adopting policies and business practices that minimize our environmental footprint. Dominican University strives to increase the awareness, knowledge, skills and sense of purpose within our students, faculty, staff and community to best meet the needs of the present, while creating a future that is just and sustainable for all.

ADMISSIONS
Freshman Academic Profile: Average high school GPA 3.4. 19% in top 10% of high school class, 50% in top 25% of high school class, 80% in top 50% of high school class. SAT Math middle 50% range 470-560. SAT Critical Reading middle 50% range 460-560. SAT Writing middle 50% range 460-560. ACT middle 50% range 20-25. Minimum paper TOEFL 550. **Basis for Candidate Selection:** *Very important factors considered include:* application essay, academic GPA, recommendation(s), rigor of secondary school record, standardized test scores, character/personal qualities, first generation. *Important factors considered include:* Class rank, extracurricular activities, interview, talent/ability, volunteer work, work experience. *Other factors considered include:* alumni/ae relation. **Freshman Admission Requirements:** High school diploma is required and GED is accepted. *Academic units required:* 4 English, 2 mathematics, 2 foreign language, 1 history. *Academic units recommended:* 4 English, 2 mathematics, 2 foreign language, 1 history. **Freshman Admission Statistics:** 2,819 applied, 53% admitted, 18% enrolled. **Transfer Admission Requirements:** college transcript(s), essay or personal statement, minimum college GPA of 2.0 required. Lowest grade transferable C. **General Admission Information:** Application Fee $40. Notification on a rolling basis, beginning on or about 10/15. Nonfall registration accepted. Admission may be deferred for a maximum of one term. Credit and/or placement offered for CEEB Advanced Placement tests.

COSTS AND FINANCIAL AID
Annual tuition $32,090. Room and board $12,560. Required fees $300. Average book expense $1,566. **Required Forms and Deadlines:** FAFSA, institution's own financial aid form. **Notification of Awards:** Applicants will be notified of awards on a rolling basis beginning 3/15. **Types of Aid:** *Need-based scholarships/grants:* Federal Pell, SEOG, state scholarships/grants, private scholarships, the school's own gift aid. *Loans:* Subsidized Stafford, Unsubsidized Stafford, PLUS, Federal Perkins, Private Loans. **Student Employment:** Federal Work-Study Program available. Institutional employment available. Highest amount earned per year from on-campus jobs $3,834. Off-campus job opportunities are good. **Financial Aid Statistics:** 100% freshmen, 99% undergrads receive need-based scholarship or grant aid. 7% freshmen, 7% undergrads receive non-need-based scholarship or grant aid. 74% freshmen, 82% undergrads receive need-based self-help aid. 3% freshmen, 2% undergrads receive athletic scholarships. 98% freshmen, 84% undergrads receive any aid. 93% undergrads borrow to pay for school. Average cumulative indebtedness $19,806. **Criteria for awarding institutional aid:** *Non-need-based:* academics, alumni affiliation, athletics, leadership, minority status, music/drama.

DORDT COLLEGE

498 4th Avenue Northeast, Sioux Center, IA 51250
Phone: 712-722-6080 • **Financial Aid Phone:** 712-722-6087
E-mail: admissions@dordt.edu • **CEEB Code:** 6171
Fax: 712-722-6035 • **Website:** www.dordt.edu • **ACT Code:** 1301

This private school was founded in 1955. It has a 150-acre campus.

RATINGS
Admissions Selectivity Rating: 73   **Fire Safety Rating:** 85   **Green Rating:** 60*

STUDENTS AND FACULTY
Enrollment: 1,322. **Student Body:** 47% female, 53% male, 63% out-of-state, 1% international (19 countries represented). Asian 1%, African American 2%, Caucasian 85%, Hispanic 1%, Native American 0%.
Retention and Graduation: 79% freshmen return for sophomore year. 63% freshmen graduate within 4 years. 65% freshmen graduate within 6 years. 15% grads go on to further study within 1 year. 9% grads pursue arts and sciences degrees. 1% grads pursue law degrees. 3% grads pursue business degrees. 2% grads pursue medical degrees. **Faculty:** Student/faculty ratio 14:1. 75 full-time faculty, 88% hold PhDs, 4% are members of minority groups, 24% are women. 0% of classes are taught by teaching assistants.

ACADEMICS
Degrees: associate, bachelor's, master's, terminal associate. **Classes:** Most classes have 10–19 students. Most lab/discussion sessions have 10–19 students. **Majors with Highest Enrollment:** engineering. **Special Study Options:** cooperative education program, double major, English as a Second Language (ESL), honors program, independent study, internships, liberal arts/career combination, student-designed major, study abroad, teacher certification program. **Disability Services:** Special programs offered to physically disabled students include note-taking services, reader services, tape recorders, tutors. **Career Services:** Alumni network, alumni services, career/job search classes, career assessment, internships, regional alumni.

FACILITIES
Housing: special housing for disabled students, men's dorms, women's dorms, apartments for married students, apartments for single students. 100% of campus accessible to physically disabled. **Special Academic Facilities/Equipment:** observatories 160 acre research farm for Ag program, modern recreation facilities which include indoor track, swimming and ice arena **Computers:** 100% of classrooms, 100% of dorms, 100% of libraries, 100% of dining areas, 100% of student union, 100% of common outdoor areas have wireless network access. Students can register for classes online. Administrative functions (other than registration) can be performed online.

CAMPUS LIFE
Environment: Village. **Activities:** Choral groups, concert band, dance, drama/theater, jazz band, literary magazine, music ensembles, musical theater, opera, pep band, radio station, student government, student newspaper, student-run film society, symphony orchestra, yearbook, Campus Ministries, International Student Organization 40 registered organizations, 4 honor societies, 6 religious organizations. **Athletics (Intercollegiate):** *Men:* baseball, basketball, cross-country, football, golf, ice hockey, soccer, tennis, track/field (outdoor), track/field (indoor). *Women:* basketball, cross-country, soccer, softball, tennis, track/field (outdoor), track/field (indoor), volleyball **On-Campus Highlights:** Campus Center, Recreation Center and De Wit Gymnasium, B J Haan Auditorium, Southview apartments, Covenant Hall.

ADMISSIONS
Freshman Academic Profile: Average high school GPA 3.5. 13% in top 10% of high school class, 21% in top 25% of high school class, 58% in top 50% of high school class. 30% from public high schools. SAT Math middle 50% range 520-640. SAT Critical Reading middle 50% range 490-600. SAT Writing middle 50% range 480-600. ACT middle 50% range 22-28. Minimum web-based TOEFL 80. Minimum paper TOEFL 550. **Basis for Candidate Selection:** *Very important factors considered include:* rigor of secondary school record, standardized test scores, religious affiliation/commitment. *Other factors considered include:* Class rank, character/personal qualities, extracurricular activities, talent/ability. **Freshman Admission Requirements:** High school diploma is required and GED is accepted. *Academic units required:* 3 English, 2 mathematics, 2 science, 2 foreign language, 2 history, 6 academic electives. *Academic units recommended:* 3 English, 2 mathematics, 2 science, 2 foreign language, 2 history, 6 academic electives. **Freshman Admission Statistics:** 1,102 applied, 79% admitted, 40% enrolled. **Transfer Admission Requirements:** High school transcript, college transcript(s), standardized test scores, minimum college GPA of 2.0 required. Lowest grade transferable C. **General Admission Information:** Application Fee $25. Regular application deadline 8/1. Notification on a rolling basis, beginning on or about 10/1. Nonfall registration accepted. Credit offered for CEEB Advanced Placement tests.

COSTS AND FINANCIAL AID
Annual tuition $25,100. Room and board $7,230. Required fees $420. Average book expense $910. **Required Forms and Deadlines:** FAFSA, institution's own financial aid form. **Notification of Awards:** Applicants will be notified of awards on a rolling basis beginning 3/15. *Types of Aid: Need-based scholarships/grants:* Federal Pell, SEOG, state scholarships/grants, private scholarships, the school's own gift aid. *Loans:* Direct Subsidized Stafford, Direct Unsubsidized Stafford, Direct PLUS, Subsidized Stafford, Unsubsidized Stafford, PLUS, Federal Perkins, college/university loans from institutional fundsAlternate Loans. **Student Employment:** Highest amount earned per year from on-campus jobs $1,500. Off-campus job opportunities are good. **Financial Aid Statistics:** 100% freshmen, 100% undergrads receive need-based scholarship or grant aid. 18% freshmen, 13% undergrads receive non-need-based scholarship or grant aid. 100% freshmen, 100% undergrads receive need-based self-help aid. 9% freshmen, 7% undergrads receive athletic scholarships. 98% freshmen, 98% undergrads receive any aid. 81% undergrads borrow to pay for school. Average cumulative indebtedness $21,859. **Criteria for awarding institutional aid:** *Non-need-based:* academics, alumni affiliation, athletics, job skills, leadership, minority status, music/drama, religious affiliation, state/district residency.

DOWLING COLLEGE

Idle Hour Boulevard, Oakdale, NY 11769-1999
Phone: 800-369-5464 • **Financial Aid Phone:** 631-244-3303
E-mail: admissions@dowling.edu • **CEEB Code:** 2011
Fax: 631-563-3827 • **Website:** www.dowling.edu • **ACT Code:** 2665

This private school was founded in 1959. It has a 157-acre campus.

RATINGS
Admissions Selectivity Rating: 66   **Fire Safety Rating:** 73   **Green Rating:** 60*

STUDENTS AND FACULTY
Enrollment: 3,627. **Student Body:** 61% female, 39% male, 10% out-of-state, 4% international (53 countries represented). Asian 2%, African American 9%, Caucasian 59%, Hispanic 9%, Native American 0%.
Retention and Graduation: 66% freshmen return for sophomore year. 17% freshmen graduate within 4 years. 34% freshmen graduate within 6 years. **Faculty:** Student/faculty ratio 17:1. 124 full-time faculty, 90% hold PhDs, 9% are members of minority groups, 34% are women. 0% of classes are taught by teaching assistants.

ACADEMICS
Degrees: bachelor's, master's, post-bachelor's certificate, post-master's certificate. **Classes:** Most classes have 10–19 students. **Majors with Highest Enrollment:** business/commerce; elementary education and teaching; special education and teaching. **Special Study Options:** Accelerated program, double major, English as a Second Language (ESL), honors program, independent study, internships, liberal arts/career combination, student-designed major, study abroad, teacher certification program, weekend college. **Honors Programs:** The honor programs are for highly motivated, academically superior, and creative students. **Disability Services:** Special programs offered to physically disabled students include note-taking services, reader services, tape recorders, tutors.

FACILITIES
Housing: Coed dorms. 100% of campus accessible to physically disabled. **Special Academic Facilities/Equipment:** Art gallery, cultural study center, media center, human factors lab, meteorology lab. **Computers:** Students can register for classes online. Administrative functions (other than registration) can be performed online.

CAMPUS LIFE
Environment: Town. **Activities:** Choral groups, drama/theater, jazz band, literary magazine, music ensembles, musical theater, student government, student newspaper, symphony orchestra, yearbook 29 registered organizations, 10 honor societies, 1 religious organizations. **Athletics (Intercollegiate):** *Men:* baseball, basketball, crew/rowing, golf, lacrosse, soccer, tennis. *Women:* basketball, crew/rowing, cross-country, equestrian sports, soccer, softball, tennis, volleyball. **On-Campus Highlights:** Riverside Cafe, Giordano Gallery, Loft Theatre, Connetuot River, Henry Building Atrium.

ADMISSIONS
Freshman Academic Profile: Average high school GPA 2.8. 6% in top 10% of high school class, 19% in top 25% of high school class, 50% in top 50% of high school class. 89% from public high schools. SAT Math middle 50% range 410-520. SAT Critical Reading middle 50% range 410-520. **Basis for Candidate**

Selection: *Very important factors considered include:* rigor of secondary school record. *Other factors considered include:* Class rank, application essay, academic GPA, recommendation(s), standardized test scores, alumni/ae relation, character/personal qualities, extracurricular activities, talent/ability. **Freshman Admission Requirements:** High school diploma is required and GED is accepted. **Freshman Admission Statistics:** 2,399 applied, 87% admitted, 22% enrolled. **Transfer Admission Requirements:** college transcript(s), minimum college GPA of 2.0 required. Lowest grade transferable C. **General Admission Information:** Application Fee $25. Nonfall registration accepted. Admission may be deferred for a maximum of 1 year. Credit and/or placement offered for CEEB Advanced Placement tests.

COSTS AND FINANCIAL AID
Average book expense $1,000. **Required Forms and Deadlines:** FAFSA, state aid form. **Notification of Awards:** Applicants will be notified of awards on a rolling basis beginning 2/1. **Types of Aid:** *Need-based scholarships/grants:* Federal Pell, SEOG, state scholarships/grants, private scholarships, the school's own gift aid. *Loans:* Direct Subsidized Stafford, Direct Unsubsidized Stafford, Direct PLUS, Federal Perkins, Alternative Loans. **Student Employment:** Federal Work-Study Program available. Off-campus job opportunities are good. **Financial Aid Statistics:** 99% freshmen, 98% undergrads receive need-based scholarship or grant aid. % freshmen, % undergrads receive non-need-based scholarship or grant aid. 92% freshmen, 87% undergrads receive need-based self-help aid. 2% freshmen, 3% undergrads receive athletic scholarships. 87% freshmen, 87% undergrads receive any aid. 81% undergrads borrow to pay for school. Average cumulative indebtedness $5,091. **Criteria for awarding institutional aid:** *Non-need-based:* academics, alumni affiliation, athletics.

DRAKE UNIVERSITY

2507 University Avenue, Des Moines, IA 50311-4505
Phone: 515-271-3181 • **Financial Aid Phone:** 515-271-2905
E-mail: admission@drake.edu • **CEEB Code:** 6168
Fax: 515-271-2831 • **Website:** www.drake.edu • **ACT Code:** 1302

This private school was founded in 1881. It has a 150-acre campus.

RATINGS
Admissions Selectivity Rating: 84   **Fire Safety Rating:** 89   **Green Rating:** 70

STUDENTS AND FACULTY
Enrollment: 3,310. **Student Body:** 57% female, 43% male, 62% out-of-state, 8% international (46 countries represented). Asian 3%, African American 3%, Caucasian 80%, Hispanic 3%, Native American 0%.
Retention and Graduation: 88% freshmen return for sophomore year. 66% freshmen graduate within 4 years. 74% freshmen graduate within 6 years. 22% grads go on to further study within 1 year. 9% grads pursue arts and sciences degrees. 4% grads pursue law degrees. 3% grads pursue business degrees. 4% grads pursue medical degrees. **Faculty:** Student/faculty ratio 12:1. 289 full-time faculty, 87% hold PhDs, 12% are members of minority groups, 46% are women. 0% of classes are taught by teaching assistants.

ACADEMICS
Degrees: bachelor's, certificate, first professional, first professional certificate, master's, post-bachelor's certificate. **Classes:** Most classes have 10–19 students. Most lab/discussion sessions have 10–19 students. **Majors with Highest Enrollment:** biology/biological sciences; journalism; marketing/marketing management. **Special Study Options:** Accelerated program, cooperative education program, distance learning, double major, dual enrollment, English as a Second Language (ESL), honors program, independent study, internships, liberal arts/career combination, student-designed major, study abroad, teacher certification program. **Honors Programs:** The Honors Program is designed for motivated students who want to participate in challenging, discussion-based courses on interdisciplinary and topical issues. The program provides a unique opportunity for intellectual enrichment both in and out of the classroom. **Combined Degree Programs:** BA/JD, PharmD/MBA; PharmD/MPA; PharmD/J.D.; AandS/J.D. **Disability Services:** Special programs offered to physically disabled students include note-taking services, reader services, tape recorders, tutors. **Career Services:** Alumni network, alumni services, career/job search classes, career assessment, internships, regional alumni. Career Services highlights include Our Professional and Career Development Services does exemplary programming that empowers students to pursue their professional objectives.

FACILITIES
Housing: Coed dorms, special housing for disabled students, fraternity/sorority housing, apartments for single students, theme housing. There are a total of

261 undergrad students and 58 Grad students residing in DWV Drake Realty houses 152 undergraduates and 46 graduate students Greek Life 324 undergraduate students Residence Life 831 EFR and 1795 undergraduate students. 93% of campus accessible to physically disabled. **Special Academic Facilities/Equipment:** Language lab, observatory, media service center, Anderson art gallery, Oreon E. Scott Chapel. **Computers:** 100% of classrooms, 100% of dorms, 100% of libraries, 100% of dining areas, 100% of student union, have wireless network access. Students can register for classes online. Administrative functions (other than registration) can be performed online.

CAMPUS LIFE
Environment: Metropolis. **Activities:** Choral groups, concert band, drama/theater, jazz band, literary magazine, marching band, music ensembles, musical theater, pep band, radio station, student government, student newspaper, symphony orchestra, Campus Ministries, International Student Organization, Model UN 160 registered organizations, 24 honor societies, 10 religious organizations. 7 fraternities, 6 sororities. **Athletics (Intercollegiate):** *Men:* basketball, cheerleading, cross-country, football, golf, soccer, tennis, track/field (outdoor), track/field (indoor). *Women:* basketball, cheerleading, crew/rowing, cross-country, golf, soccer, softball, tennis, track/field (outdoor), track/field (indoor), volleyball. **On-Campus Highlights:** Athletic Facilities, Olmsted Center, Anderson Gallery, Helmick Commons, Residence Halls / Residence Life. **Environmental Initiatives:** Sustainable building practices. Employees and students receive unlimited, free bus transportation on Des Moines public transportation (DART) buses. Several academic programs include strong emphasis on environmental issues and long-term sustainability.

ADMISSIONS
Freshman Academic Profile: Average high school GPA 3.7. 42% in top 10% of high school class, 75% in top 25% of high school class, 94% in top 50% of high school class. 82% from public high schools. SAT Math middle 50% range 550-660. SAT Critical Reading middle 50% range 510-640. ACT middle 50% range 24-29. Minimum paper TOEFL 545. **Basis for Candidate Selection:** *Very important factors considered include:* application essay, academic GPA, standardized test scores. *Important factors considered include:* recommendation(s), rigor of secondary school record, interview. *Other factors considered include:* Class rank, character/personal qualities, extracurricular activities, level of applicant's interest, talent/ability, volunteer work, work experience. **Freshman Admission Requirements:** High school diploma is required and GED is accepted. **Freshman Admission Statistics:** 6,357 applied, 66% admitted, 20% enrolled. **Transfer Admission Requirements:** college transcript(s), minimum college GPA of 2.0 required. Lowest grade transferable C. **General Admission Information:** Application Fee $25. Notification on a rolling basis, beginning on or about 10/1. Nonfall registration accepted. Admission may be deferred for a maximum of 12 months. Credit and/or placement offered for CEEB Advanced Placement tests.

COSTS AND FINANCIAL AID
Annual tuition $29,410. Room and board $8,680. Required fees $146. Average book expense $900. **Required Forms and Deadlines:** FAFSA. **Notification of Awards:** Applicants will be notified of awards on a rolling basis beginning 3/1. **Types of Aid:** *Need-based scholarships/grants:* Federal Pell, SEOG, state scholarships/grants, private scholarships, the school's own gift aid. *Loans:* Subsidized Stafford, Unsubsidized Stafford, PLUS, Federal Perkins, college/university loans from institutional funds, Federal Health Professional Loans. **Student Employment:** Federal Work-Study Program available. Institutional employment available. Off-campus job opportunities are good. **Financial Aid Statistics:** 99% freshmen, 98% undergrads receive need-based scholarship or grant aid. 18% freshmen, 16% undergrads receive non-need-based scholarship or grant aid. 84% freshmen, 9% undergrads receive need-based self-help aid. 4% freshmen, 3% undergrads receive athletic scholarships. 99% freshmen, 99% undergrads receive any aid. 65% undergrads borrow to pay for school. Average cumulative indebtedness $32,114. **Criteria for awarding institutional aid:** *Non-need-based:* academics, alumni affiliation, art, athletics, music/drama, state/district residency.

See page 1068.

DREW UNIVERSITY

Office of College Admissions, Madison, NJ 07940-1493
Phone: 973-408-3739 • **Financial Aid Phone:** 973-408-3112
E-mail: cadm@drew.edu • **CEEB Code:** 2193
Fax: 973-408-3068 • **Website:** www.drew.edu • **ACT Code:** 2550

This private school, affiliated with the Methodist Church, was founded in 1868. It has a 186-acre campus.

RATINGS
Admissions Selectivity Rating: 77   **Fire Safety Rating:** 96   **Green Rating:** 93

STUDENTS AND FACULTY
Enrollment: 1,552. **Student Body:** 60% female, 40% male, 35% out-of-state, 2% international (24 countries represented). Asian 5%, African American 10%, Caucasian 57%, Hispanic 14%, Native American 0%.
Retention and Graduation: 75% freshmen return for sophomore year. 66% freshmen graduate within 4 years. 69% freshmen graduate within 6 years. 25% grads go on to further study within 1 year. 20% grads pursue arts and sciences degrees. 2% grads pursue law degrees. 2% grads pursue medical degrees. **Faculty:** Student/faculty ratio :1. 160 full-time faculty, 17% are members of minority groups, 52% are women. 0% of classes are taught by teaching assistants.

ACADEMICS
Degrees: bachelor's, first professional, master's, post-bachelor's certificate, post-master's certificate. **Classes:** Most classes have 10–19 students. Most lab/discussion sessions have 10–19 students. **Majors with Highest Enrollment:** economics; political science and government; psychology. **Special Study Options:** Accelerated program, cross-registration, double major, exchange student program (domestic), independent study, internships, student-designed major, study abroad, teacher certification program, Seven-year dual degree BA/MD program with UMDNJ-New Jersey Medical school. Five-year dual degree (B.A./B.S. or B.Eng.) programs in engineering and technologies with Columbia University, Stevens Institute of Technology, and Washington University. Five-year dual degree (B.A./Master of Forestry or Master of Environmental Management)program with Duke University. **Honors Programs:** Phi Beta Kappa; Beta Beta Beta (biology), Delta Phi Alpha (German), Omicron Delta Epsilon (economics), Phi Alpha Theta (history), Pi Sigma Alpha (political science), Psi Chi (psychology), Dobro Slovo (Russian), Sigma Delta Pi (Spanish), Sigma Pi Sigma (physics), Pi Mu Epsilon (mathematics), Pi Delta Phi (French), Alpha Kappa Delta (sociology), Pinnacle (nontraditional continuing education students), and Epsilon Omega Psi (Educational Opportunity Scholars). Specialized Honors. **Combined Degree Programs:** BA/MD, Dual Degree Program with Columbia and Stevens Institute of Technology. **Disability Services:** Special programs offered to physically disabled students include note-taking services, tape recorders, tutors. **Career Services:** Alumni network, alumni services, career/job search classes, internships.

FACILITIES
Housing: Coed dorms, special housing for disabled students, wellness housing, theme housing. **Special Academic Facilities/Equipment:** Art gallery, photography gallery, multimedia language lab, child development center, research greenhouse, arboretum, observatory, laser holography lab, nuclear magnetic resonator, electron microscope, optical and radio telescopes, computer graphics laboratory, New Jersey Shakespeare Festival (professional acting company). **Computers:** 90% of classrooms, 20% of dorms, 100% of libraries, 100% of dining areas, 100% of student union, 25% of common outdoor areas have wireless network access. Students can register for classes online. Administrative functions (other than registration) can be performed online. Undergraduates are required to own a computer.

CAMPUS LIFE
Environment: Village. **Activities:** Choral groups, dance, drama/theater, literary magazine, music ensembles, radio station, student government, student newspaper, student-run film society, symphony orchestra, television station, yearbook, Campus Ministries 80 registered organizations, 17 honor societies, 9 religious organizations. **Athletics (Intercollegiate):** *Men:* baseball, basketball, cross-country, fencing, lacrosse, soccer, swimming, tennis. *Women:* basketball, cross-country, fencing, field hockey, lacrosse, soccer, softball, swimming, tennis. **On-Campus Highlights:** Dorothy Young Center for the Arts, Simon Forum, Rose Memorial Library, University Center, Commons. **Environmental Initiatives:** New residence hall, McLendon Hall, meets USGBC Leadership in Energy and Environmental Design (LEED) Silver certification Commitment to planting only native tree and plant species on campus grounds. Restoration

of forest floor through annual fern planting (Fern Fest) in sections of campus and removal of turf to create "no-mow zones." 100% composting/recycling of landscape waste

ADMISSIONS
Freshman Academic Profile: Average high school GPA 3.3. 31% in top 10% of high school class, 58% in top 25% of high school class, 85% in top 50% of high school class. 66% from public high schools. SAT Math middle 50% range 480-600. SAT Critical Reading middle 50% range 490-620. SAT Writing middle 50% range 490-610. ACT middle 50% range 21-28. Minimum paper TOEFL 550. **Basis for Candidate Selection:** *Very important factors considered include:* academic GPA, rigor of secondary school record, talent/ability. *Important factors considered include:* application essay, recommendation(s), extracurricular activities, interview, level of applicant's interest. *Other factors considered include:* Class rank, standardized test scores, alumni/ae relation, character/personal qualities, first generation, geographical residence, racial/ethnic status, volunteer work, work experience. **Freshman Admission Requirements:** High school diploma or equivalent is not required. **Freshman Admission Statistics:** 3,872 applied, 85% admitted, 11% enrolled. **Transfer Admission Requirements:** High school transcript, college transcript(s), essay or personal statement, statement of good standing from prior institution(s). Lowest grade transferable C. **General Admission Information:** Application Fee $50. Early decision application deadline 12/1. Regular application deadline 2/15. Regular notification 3/21. Nonfall registration accepted. Admission may be deferred for a maximum of 1 year. Credit and/or placement offered for CEEB Advanced Placement tests.

COSTS AND FINANCIAL AID
Annual tuition $41,688. Room and board $11,596. Required fees $932. Average book expense $1,228. **Required Forms and Deadlines:** FAFSA, CSS/Financial Aid PROFILE. **Notification of Awards:** Applicants will be notified of awards on or about 4/1. **Types of Aid:** *Need-based scholarships/grants:* Federal Pell, SEOG, state scholarships/grants, private scholarships, the school's own gift aid. *Loans:* Subsidized Stafford, Unsubsidized Stafford, PLUS, Federal Perkins, state loans. **Student Employment:** Federal Work-Study Program available. Institutional employment available. Highest amount earned per year from on-campus jobs $5,800. Off-campus job opportunities are fair. **Financial Aid Statistics:** 99% undergrads receive need-based scholarship or grant aid. 7% undergrads receive non-need-based scholarship or grant aid. 84% undergrads receive need-based self-help aid. 98% freshmen, 95% undergrads receive any aid. 66% undergrads borrow to pay for school. Average cumulative indebtedness $24,470. **Criteria for awarding institutional aid:** *Non-need-based:* academics, art, minority status, music/drama, state/district residency.

DREXEL UNIVERSITY

3141 Chestnut Street, Philadelphia, PA 19104
Phone: 215-895-2400 • **Financial Aid Phone:** 215-895-2537
E-mail: enroll@drexel.edu • **CEEB Code:** 2194
Fax: 215-895-5939 • **Website:** www.drexel.edu • **ACT Code:** 3556

This private school was founded in 1891. It has a 40-acre campus.

RATINGS
Admissions Selectivity Rating: 84   **Fire Safety Rating:** 89   **Green Rating:** 95

STUDENTS AND FACULTY
Enrollment: 15,593. **Student Body:** 46% female, 54% male, 50% out-of-state, 11% international (104 countries represented). Asian 12%, African American 6%, Caucasian 58%, Hispanic 6%, Native American 0%.
Retention and Graduation: 85% freshmen return for sophomore year. 25% freshmen graduate within 4 years. 68% freshmen graduate within 6 years. 13% grads go on to further study within 1 year. 3% grads pursue arts and sciences degrees. 1% grads pursue law degrees. 3% grads pursue business degrees. 1% grads pursue medical degrees. **Faculty:** Student/faculty ratio 11:1. 1011 full-time faculty, 83% hold PhDs, 15% are members of minority groups, 44% are women.

ACADEMICS
Degrees: associate, bachelor's, certificate, doctoral, master's, post-bachelor's certificate, post-master's certificate. **Classes:** Most classes have 10–19 students. **Majors with Highest Enrollment:** biology/biological sciences; information science/studies; mechanical engineering. **Special Study Options:** Acceler-

ated program, cooperative education program, distance learning, double major, dual enrollment, English as a Second Language (ESL), honors program, independent study, internships, study abroad, teacher certification program, weekend college, 3-3 programs in engineering with Lincoln University, Indiana Univ. of Penn. **Honors Programs:** The Pennoni Honors College enriches the University experience for students from all majors with demonstrated academic achievement and broad intellectual interests. Consider the benefits: ° Individual attention paid to your academic progress. ° A variety of small group courses with Drexel's best faculty. ° The experience of being in a small college while enjoying the diverse academic opportunities offered by a major medical and technological research University. ° Opportunities to meet students from a variety of fields who share many of your interests. ° Preparation assistance for admission to graduate or professional school, and for fellowships to further your education at home or abroad. ° Social and cultural events. ° The option of taking part in a true living-learning community in the residence halls, which have locations set aside specifically for Honors students. **Combined Degree Programs:** BA/MD, BA/MA, Engineering BS/PhD, BS/DPT, BSN/MSN, BS/MBA, BS/MS. **Disability Services:** Special programs offered to physically disabled students include note-taking services, reader services, tape recorders, tutors. **Career Services:** alumni services, career/job search classes, career assessment, internships Career Services highlights include A pioneer in co-operative education since 1919, Drexel operates one of the largest co-operative education programs in the nation (in students placed annually). Over 1,500 business, industrial, governmental, and other institutions located in 27 states and 12 foreign countries "cooperate" with Drexel in offering students the opportunity to acquire practical experience in employment related to college studies.

FACILITIES

Housing: Coed dorms, special housing for disabled students, special housing for international students, fraternity/sorority housing, apartments for single students, Freshmen required to live on campus unless living with parents. 80% of campus accessible to physically disabled. **Special Academic Facilities/Equipment:** Art museum, theatre, audiovisual center, TV studio, recreational center, center for automation technology, engineering center. **Computers:** 100% of classrooms, 100% of dorms, 100% of libraries, 100% of dining areas, 100% of student union, 100% of common outdoor areas have wireless network access. Students can register for classes online. Administrative functions (other than registration) can be performed online. Undergraduates are required to own a computer.

CAMPUS LIFE

Environment: Metropolis. **Activities:** Choral groups, concert band, dance, drama/theater, jazz band, literary magazine, music ensembles, musical theater, pep band, radio station, student government, student newspaper, student-run film society, television station, yearbook, Campus Ministries 136 registered organizations, 8 honor societies, 8 religious organizations. 12 fraternities, 11 sororities. **Athletics (Intercollegiate):** *Men:* basketball, cheerleading, crew/rowing, diving, golf, lacrosse, soccer, swimming, tennis, wrestling. *Women:* basketball, cheerleading, crew/rowing, diving, field hockey, lacrosse, soccer, softball, swimming, tennis, volleyball. **On-Campus Highlights:** Ross Commons, University Bookstore, Creese Caf, Crossroads at the Handschumacher Dining Hall, The Quad. **Environmental Initiatives:** Opening Fall 2011. Construction of a $69.5 million five story Integrated Sciences Building, 140,000 sq. ft. teaching facility, will be the first academic building in the U.S. to have a 30- to 40-ft., four-story biofilter wall. This feature will be part of the HVAC system " air intakes and outputs will be filtered through the living wall of vegetation that will upgrade energy efficiency and indoor air quality, along with controlled humidity in dry weather. The building will be the University's first LEED certified building. Opened January 2010. A new $41.6 million Recreation Center, 84,000 sq. ft., addition was the first building in the City of Philadelphia to have total storm water management. The design of a cistern and rain water reuse system was implemented to achieve a 20% reduction of post-development impervious cover. The storm water is collected in a cistern, treated and used for toilet flushing in the building. Opened August 2009 - a $42 million, 140,000 sq. ft. Residence Hall with 17-stories, housing 482 students, incorporating many environmentally sustainable features including a green roof.

ADMISSIONS

Freshman Academic Profile: Average high school GPA. 34% in top 10% of high school class, 65% in top 25% of high school class, 92% in top 50% of high school class. 70% from public high schools. SAT Math middle 50% range 580-680. SAT Critical Reading middle 50% range 540-640. SAT Writing middle 50% range 530-640. ACT middle 50% range 24-29. Minimum paper TOEFL 550. **Basis for Candidate Selection:** *Very important factors considered include:* Class rank, academic GPA, rigor of secondary school record, standardized test scores. *Important factors considered include:* application essay, recommendation(s), character/personal qualities. *Other factors considered include:* alumni/ae relation, extracurricular activities, first generation, interview, level of applicant's interest, talent/ability, volunteer work, work experience. **Freshman Admission Requirements:** High school diploma is required and

GED is accepted. *Academic units required:* 3 mathematics, 1 science, (1 science labs). *Academic units recommended:* 3 mathematics, 1 science, (1 science labs). **Freshman Admission Statistics:** 40,586 applied, 75% admitted, 10% enrolled. **Transfer Admission Requirements:** college transcript(s), minimum college GPA of 2.5 required. Lowest grade transferable C. **General Admission Information:** Application Fee $75. Regular application deadline 3/1. Nonfall registration accepted. Admission may be deferred for a maximum of 12 months. Credit and/or placement offered for CEEB Advanced Placement tests.

COSTS AND FINANCIAL AID

Annual tuition $33,800. Room and board $14,175. Required fees $2,290. Average book expense $2,000. **Required Forms and Deadlines:** FAFSA. **Notification of Awards:** Applicants will be notified of awards on a rolling basis beginning 3/15. **Types of Aid:** *Need-based scholarships/grants:* Federal Pell, SEOG, state scholarships/grants, private scholarships, the school's own gift aid, United Negro College Fund. *Loans:* Subsidized Stafford, Unsubsidized Stafford, PLUS, Federal Perkins, Federal Nursing, college/university loans from institutional funds. **Student Employment:** Federal Work-Study Program available. **Financial Aid Statistics:** 99% freshmen, 93% undergrads receive need-based scholarship or grant aid. 15% freshmen, 8% undergrads receive non-need-based scholarship or grant aid. 81% freshmen, 90% undergrads receive need-based self-help aid. 1% freshmen, 2% undergrads receive athletic scholarships. 94% freshmen, 89% undergrads receive any aid. 73% undergrads borrow to pay for school. Average cumulative indebtedness $35,082. **Criteria for awarding institutional aid:** *Non-need-based:* academics, alumni affiliation, art, athletics, leadership, music/drama.

DRURY UNIVERSITY

900 North Benton Avenue, Springfield, MO 65802-3712
Phone: 417-873-7205 • **Financial Aid Phone:** 417-873-7312
E-mail: druryad@drury.edu • **CEEB Code:** 6169
Fax: 417-866-3873 • **Website:** www.drury.edu • **ACT Code:** 2292

This private school was founded in 1873. It has a 84-acre campus.

RATINGS
Admissions Selectivity Rating: 72   **Fire Safety Rating:** 69   **Green Rating:** 93

STUDENTS AND FACULTY
Enrollment: 1,601. **Student Body:** 54% female, 46% male, 19% out-of-state, 8% international (38 countries represented). Asian 2%, African American 3%, Caucasian 83%, Hispanic 3%, Native American 0%.
Retention and Graduation: 83% freshmen return for sophomore year. 53% freshmen graduate within 4 years. 65% freshmen graduate within 6 years. 35% grads go on to further study within 1 year. 5% grads pursue arts and sciences degrees. 5% grads pursue law degrees. 9% grads pursue business degrees. 15% grads pursue medical degrees. **Faculty:** Student/faculty ratio 12:1. 135 full-time faculty, 96% hold PhDs, 10% are members of minority groups, 44% are women. 0% of classes are taught by teaching assistants.

ACADEMICS
Degrees: associate, bachelor's, master's. **Classes:** Most classes have 10–19 students. Most lab/discussion sessions have 20–29 students. **Majors with Highest Enrollment:** biology/biological sciences; business/commerce; communication studies/speech communication and rhetoric. **Special Study Options:** Accelerated program, cooperative education program, distance learning, double major, dual enrollment, English as a Second Language (ESL), honors program, independent study, internships, liberal arts/career combination, student-designed major, study abroad, teacher certification program, Drury Center in Volos, Greece; Living-Learning Communities; Washington Semester. **Honors Programs:** Drury Honors Program **Combined Degree Programs:** BA/MEng, 3+2 Occupational therapy with Washington Univ. **Disability Services:** Special programs offered to physically disabled students include note-taking services, reader services, tape recorders, tutors. **Career Services:** Alumni network, alumni services, career/job search classes, career assessment, internships, regional alumni. Career Services highlights include 75% of students complete at least one internship. Recent locations include National Public Radio in Washington, D.C.; state and federal legislators' offices, McSweeney's magazine, San Francisco; Fleishman-Hillard public relations, numerous not-for-profit organizations. Myriad opportunities are available thanks to Drury's widespread alumni base.

FACILITIES
Housing: Coed dorms, special housing for disabled students, fraternity/sorority housing, apartments for married students, apartments for single students, Living-learning communities; Leadership/community service. 97% of campus accessible to physically disabled. **Special Academic Facilities/Equipment:**

Science center with greenhouse and astronomical observaton station, new visual art center with two galleries, TV studio, radio station, teleconference facility, language lab, electronic music lab, laser lab. **Computers:** 100% of classrooms, 30% of dorms, 100% of libraries, 100% of dining areas, 75% of student union, 20% of common outdoor areas have wireless network access. Students can register for classes online. Administrative functions (other than registration) can be performed online.

CAMPUS LIFE

Environment: City. **Activities:** Choral groups, concert band, dance, drama/theater, jazz band, literary magazine, music ensembles, musical theater, opera, pep band, radio station, student government, student newspaper, student-run film society, symphony orchestra, television station, Campus Ministries, International Student Organization 90 registered organizations, 11 honor societies, 7 religious organizations. 4 fraternities, 4 sororities. **Athletics (Intercollegiate):** *Men:* baseball, basketball, cheerleading, cross-country, diving, golf, soccer, softball, swimming, tennis. *Women:* basketball, cheerleading, cross-country, diving, golf, soccer, softball, swimming, tennis, volleyball. **On-Campus Highlights:** Trustee Science Center, Sunderland Hall (new student housing), Olin Library, Pool Art Center, College Park student housing, The Drury campus is impeccably maintained and is a registered tree farm; its overall appearance is the greatest highlight of a tour. **Environmental Initiatives:** Energy Management strategies on buildings upgrading lighting, HVAC systems). Bicycle rentals for students to use for the semester for $25. Expanded recycling program, launching a zero waste campaign and partnership with neighbor institutions. Sustainability across the curriculum developments and development of a School of the Environment.

ADMISSIONS

Freshman Academic Profile: Average high school GPA 3.6. 34% in top 10% of high school class, 59% in top 25% of high school class, 93% in top 50% of high school class. 85% from public high schools. ACT middle 50% range 28-22. Minimum web-based TOEFL 72. **Basis for Candidate Selection:** *Very important factors considered include:* academic GPA. *Important factors considered include:* Class rank, application essay, recommendation(s), standardized test scores, character/personal qualities, interview. *Other factors considered include:* rigor of secondary school record, alumni/ae relation, extracurricular activities, geographical residence, level of applicant's interest, racial/ethnic status, talent/ability, volunteer work, work experience. **Freshman Admission Requirements:** High school diploma is required and GED is accepted. *Academic units required:* 4 English, 3 mathematics, 3 science, 2 foreign language, 3 social studies. *Academic units recommended:* 4 English, 3 mathematics, 3 science, 2 foreign language, 3 social studies. **Freshman Admission Statistics:** 1,043 applied, 82% admitted, 39% enrolled. **Transfer Admission Requirements:** High school transcript, college transcript(s), essay or personal statement, minimum college GPA of 2.0 required. Lowest grade transferable C. **General Admission Information:** Application Fee $25. Regular application deadline 8/1. Notification on a rolling basis, beginning on or about 10/1. Nonfall registration accepted. Admission may be deferred for a maximum of 1 semester. Credit and/or placement offered for CEEB Advanced Placement tests.

COSTS AND FINANCIAL AID

Annual tuition $21,000. Room and board $7,466. Required fees $575. Average book expense $1,500. **Required Forms and Deadlines:** FAFSA, institution's own financial aid form. **Notification of Awards:** Applicants will be notified of awards on a rolling basis beginning 3/15. **Types of Aid:** *Need-based scholarships/grants:* Federal Pell, SEOG, state scholarships/grants, private scholarships, the school's own gift aid. *Loans:* Subsidized Stafford, Unsubsidized Stafford, PLUS, Federal Perkins. **Student Employment:** Federal Work-Study Program available. Institutional employment available. Highest amount earned per year from on-campus jobs $5,993. Off-campus job opportunities are good. **Financial Aid Statistics:** 94% freshmen, 99% undergrads receive need-based scholarship or grant aid. 92% freshmen, 96% undergrads receive non-need-based scholarship or grant aid. 89% freshmen, 96% undergrads receive need-based self-help aid. 1% freshmen receive athletic scholarships. 84% freshmen, 93% undergrads receive any aid. 68% undergrads borrow to pay for school. Average cumulative indebtedness $21,550. **Criteria for awarding institutional aid:** *Non-need-based:* academics, alumni affiliation, art, athletics, job skills, leadership, minority status, music/drama, religious affiliation.

DUKE UNIVERSITY

2138 Campus Drive, Durham, NC 27708-0586
Phone: 919-684-3214 • **CEEB Code:** 5156
Website: www.duke.edu • **ACT Code:** 3088

This private school, affiliated with the Methodist Church, was founded in 1838. It has a 8500-acre campus.

RATINGS
Admissions Selectivity Rating: 98   **Fire Safety Rating:** 60*   **Green Rating:** 98

STUDENTS AND FACULTY
Enrollment: 6,066. **Student Body:** 48% female, 52% male, 85% out-of-state, 5% international (89 countries represented). Asian 15%, African American 11%, Caucasian 58%, Hispanic 7%, Native American 0%.
Retention and Graduation: 96% freshmen return for sophomore year. 86% freshmen graduate within 4 years. 92% freshmen graduate within 6 years. 38% grads go on to further study within 1 year. 14% grads pursue arts and sciences degrees. 11% grads pursue law degrees. 1% grads pursue business degrees. 12% grads pursue medical degrees. **Faculty:** Student/faculty ratio 11:1. 901 full-time faculty, 91% hold PhDs, 18% are members of minority groups, 27% are women. 4% of classes are taught by teaching assistants.

ACADEMICS
Degrees: associate, bachelor's. **Classes:** Most classes have 10–19 students. Most lab/discussion sessions have 10–19 students. **Majors with Highest Enrollment:** economics; psychology; public policy analysis **Special Study Options:** Accelerated program, cross-registration, distance learning, double major, exchange student program (domestic), honors program, independent study, internships, student-designed major, study abroad, teacher certification program, Undergrads may take grad level classes. Off-Campus Study: New York Arts Program. Other Special Programs: Semester and summer programs in ecology, geology, oceanography, physiology, and zoology at marine laboratory in Beaufort. **Combined Degree Programs:** BA/MA, BA/MEng, 3-2 and 4-1 med-tech programs. **Disability Services:** Special programs offered to physically disabled students include note-taking services, reader services, tape recorders, tutors. **Career Services:** alumni services, career/job search classes, career assessment, internships.

FACILITIES
Housing: Coed dorms, men's dorms, women's dorms, fraternity/sorority housing, apartments for single students, theme houses. **Special Academic Facilities/Equipment:** Art museum, language lab, university forest, primate center, phytotron, electron laser, nuclear magnetic resonance machine, nuclear lab. **Computers:** Students can register for classes online.

CAMPUS LIFE
Environment: City. **Activities:** Choral groups, concert band, dance, drama/theater, jazz band, literary magazine, marching band, music ensembles, musical theater, opera, pep band, radio station, student government, student newspaper, student-run film society, symphony orchestra, television station, yearbook 200 registered organizations, 10 honor societies, 25 religious organizations. 21 fraternities, 14 sororities. **Athletics (Intercollegiate):** *Men:* baseball, basketball, cross-country, diving, fencing, football, golf, lacrosse, soccer, swimming, tennis, track/field (outdoor), track/field (indoor), volleyball, wrestling. *Women:* basketball, crew/rowing, cross-country, diving, fencing, field hockey, golf, lacrosse, soccer, swimming, tennis, track/field (outdoor), track/field (indoor), volleyball. **On-Campus Highlights:** Duke Chapel, Primate Center, Sarah P. Duke Gardens, Duke Forest, Levine Science Research Center. **Environmental Initiatives:** Duke has signed the ACUPCC and made a commitment to make Duke a climate neutral institution. Duke signed a LEED building policy in 2003. The university now has 19 buildings that are certified or in the process of being certified. Sustainability has been a part of Duke's mission long before the word became fashionable. The Campus Master Plan, which guides all campus development, defines eight key principles including several that are related to the tenets of sustainability. Two of the most important of these principles are the commitment for Duke to be a university in the forest and a citizen of Durham and the region. Campus development is shaped by these goals of preserving our community within the forest while being a leader in environmental stewardship for our region. The current Strategic Plan highlights the university's efforts to employ knowledge in service to society and to make Duke a leader in addressing pressing, global issues. The sustainability principles of environment, economy and society are embedded in these guiding documents of the university.

ADMISSIONS

Freshman Academic Profile: 90% in top 10% of high school class, 98% in top 25% of high school class, 100% in top 50% of high school class. 65% from public high schools. SAT Math middle 50% range 690-800. SAT Critical Reading middle 50% range 690-770. ACT middle 50% range 29-34. **Basis for Candidate Selection:** *Very important factors considered include:* application essay, recommendation(s), rigor of secondary school record, standardized test scores, extracurricular activities, talent/ability. *Important factors considered include:* character/personal qualities. *Other factors considered include:* Class rank, academic GPA, alumni/ae relation, geographical residence, interview, racial/ethnic status, state residency, volunteer work, work experience. **Freshman Admission Requirements:** High school diploma is required and GED is not accepted. **Freshman Admission Statistics:** 18,090 applied, 22% admitted, 43% enrolled. **Transfer Admission Requirements:** High school transcript, college transcript(s), essay or personal statement, standardized test scores, Lowest grade transferable C. **General Admission Information:** Application Fee $65. Early decision application deadline 11/1. Regular application deadline 1/2. Regular notification 4/1. Nonfall registration not accepted. Admission may be deferred for a maximum of 1. Credit and/or placement offered for CEEB Advanced Placement tests.

COSTS AND FINANCIAL AID

Annual tuition $44,101. Room and board $11,830. Average book expense $970. **Required Forms and Deadlines:** FAFSA, CSS/Financial Aid PROFILE, noncustodial PROFILE, business/farm supplement. PARENT AND STUDENT INCOME TAX RETURNS. **Notification of Awards:** Applicants will be notified of awards on or about 4/1. **Types of Aid:** *Need-based scholarships/grants:* Federal Pell, SEOG, state scholarships/grants, private scholarships, the school's own gift aid, ROTC. *Loans:* Subsidized Stafford, Unsubsidized Stafford, PLUS, Federal Perkins, college/university loans from institutional funds, Private loans. **Student Employment:** Federal Work-Study Program available. Institutional employment available. Highest amount earned per year from on-campus jobs $1,400. Off-campus job opportunities are good. **Financial Aid Statistics:** 97% freshmen, 94% undergrads receive need-based scholarship or grant aid. 3% freshmen, 2% undergrads receive non-need-based scholarship or grant aid. 88% freshmen, 91% undergrads receive need-based self-help aid. Average cumulative indebtedness $16,502. **Criteria for awarding institutional aid:** *Non-need-based:* academics, alumni affiliation, art, athletics, leadership, minority status, religious affiliation, state/district residency.

DUQUESNE UNIVERSITY

600 Forbes Avenue, Pittsburgh, PA 15282
Phone: 412-396-6222 • **Financial Aid Phone:** 412-396-6607
E-mail: admissions@duq.edu
Fax: 412-396-6223 • **Website:** www.duq.edu

This private school, affiliated with the Roman Catholic Church, was founded in 1878. It has a 49-acre campus.

RATINGS

Admissions Selectivity Rating: 79   **Fire Safety Rating:** 99   **Green Rating:** 72

STUDENTS AND FACULTY

Enrollment: 5,805. **Student Body:** 58% female, 42% male, 25% out-of-state, 4% international (87 countries represented). Asian 2%, African American 4%, Caucasian 84%, Hispanic 3%, Native American 0%.
Retention and Graduation: 89% freshmen return for sophomore year. 63% freshmen graduate within 4 years. 74% freshmen graduate within 6 years. 36% grads go on to further study within 1 year. 22% grads pursue arts and sciences degrees. 5% grads pursue law degrees. 3% grads pursue business degrees. 3% grads pursue medical degrees. **Faculty:** Student/faculty ratio 14:1. 486 full-time faculty, 92% hold PhDs, 7% are members of minority groups, 45% are women. % of classes are taught by teaching assistants.

ACADEMICS

Degrees: bachelor's, master's, post-bachelor's certificate, post-master's certificate. **Classes:** Most classes have 10–19 students. Most lab/discussion sessions have fewer than 10 students. **Majors with Highest Enrollment:** accounting; nursing/registered nurse (rn, asn, bsn, msn); pharmacy (pharmd [usa], pharmd or bs/bpharm [canada]). **Special Study Options:** Accelerated program, cross-registration, distance learning, double major, dual enrollment, English as a Second Language (ESL), exchange student program (domestic), external degree program, honors program, independent study, internships, liberal arts/career

combination, student-designed major, study abroad, teacher certification program, weekend college, Students have the opportunity to study abroad on our Italian campus in Rome, Italy. **Honors Programs:** Duquesne University offers it's most qualified and outstanding freshmen the opportunity to participate in the Honors College. This selective and intellectually challenging program is available by invitation only after review of the applicant's academic record. The Honors College combines liberal arts, with opportunities for professional studies while providing the thinking, writing, and speaking skill necessary for continuing success. The foundation of Duquesne's Honors College is the Integrated Honors Program, an enhanced track of the University Core Curriculum. Special honors sections of the core courses feature some of the University's most distinguished faculty. Integrated Honors Program courses focus on our essential human heritage and on the major ideas and issues forming the background and direction of modern life. They are taught in small class sections allowing for close interaction between students and teachers and encouraging individual initiative as well as collaborative learning. **Combined Degree Programs:** BA/JD, BA/MA, BS/MSEd, BSBA/JD, BSN/MSN, BS/MS, BSBA/MBA, BA/MBA, BS/MBA, BA/BS, BS/MA. **Disability Services:** Special programs offered to physically disabled students include note-taking services, reader services, tape recorders, tutors. **Career Services:** Alumni network, alumni services, career/job search classes, career assessment, internships, regional alumni. Career Services highlights include Duquesne University's Internship Program is designed to provide students with a professional, entry-level work experience as a valuable element of their academic curriculum. The Internship Program is open to all current students. Available internship positions are posted through the DuqConnection website on an on-going basis. In addition, companies seeking interns may participate in the On-Campus Recruiting Program. It is the responsibility of the student to apply for these positions according to the posted deadline dates. Students may also seek internship opportunities through other means, such as networking and application process.

FACILITIES

Housing: Coed dorms, special housing for disabled students, fraternity/sorority housing, apartments for married students, apartments for single students, wellness housing, sorority and fraternity wings; club wings; international wings. 95% of campus accessible to physically disabled. **Special Academic Facilities/Equipment:** Student Art Gallery **Computers:** 10% of classrooms, 100% of libraries, 85% of dining areas, 100% of student union, 100% of common outdoor areas have wireless network access. Students can register for classes online. Administrative functions (other than registration) can be performed online.

CAMPUS LIFE

Environment: Metropolis. **Activities:** Choral groups, concert band, dance, drama/theater, jazz band, literary magazine, marching band, music ensembles, musical theater, opera, pep band, radio station, student government, student newspaper, student-run film society, symphony orchestra, television station, yearbook, Campus Ministries, International Student Organization, Model UN 160 registered organizations, 34 honor societies, 7 religious organizations. 10 fraternities, 7 sororities. **Athletics (Intercollegiate):** *Men:* basketball, cross-country, football, soccer, tennis, track/field (outdoor). *Women:* basketball, crew/rowing, cross-country, lacrosse, soccer, swimming, tennis, track/field (outdoor), track/field (indoor), volleyball. **On-Campus Highlights:** Power Recreation Center, Starbucks, The Red Ring, Academic Walk, The Night Spot, The Power Recreation Center is a newly opened recreation and fitness center. Starbucks is a popular coffeehouse located in the Duquesne Union. The Red Ring is a new, full service restaurant/bar with nightly musical entertainment. Academic Walk is the main walkway through campus where many activities are held. There is also a new quiet Study Lounge located on the second floor of the Union. **Environmental Initiatives:** Duquesne University relies 100 percent on clean energy. For over 14 years, the University has produced the bulk of its own electricity with a clean-burning natural gas turbine located at the heart of campus. This co-generation plant produces approximately 85 percent of the power used to light, heat and cool the campus with overall efficiency greater than 70 percent. It is Pennsylvania's first approved generation system for creating Alternative Energy Credits. Sustainable initiatives reached an exceptional level with the purchase of more than 14 million kilowatt hours of renewable energy credits. This combination of energy generation and renewable energy purchase led Duquesne University to rely 100 percent on clean energy. A highly efficient cooling system that relies on ice " the first of its kind in a Pittsburgh academic institution" has bolstered the University's efforts in responsible energy consumption. The University's last greenhouse gas emissions inventory showed that, while the student population and campus physical size increased, greenhouse gas emissions decreased. Duquesne University has pledged to seek LEED certication for all future construction projects and to observe LEED principles in all major renovations. In the past two years, the University has earned LEED Silver Rating for new construction and LEED Gold Rating for commercial interiors. A new residence hall is currently being constructed to earn at least a LEED Silver Rating. Duquesne University is committed to the continual assessment and betterment of its daily operations' environmental quality. Significant progress has been made in the areas of green cleaning, waste diversion, VOC-free products usage, "green" purchasing and other operational efforts.

ADMISSIONS

Freshman Academic Profile: Average high school GPA 3.7. 29% in top 10% of high school class, 60% in top 25% of high school class, 90% in top 50% of high school class. SAT Math middle 50% range 530-610. SAT Critical Reading middle 50% range 510-590. SAT Writing middle 50% range 510-600. ACT middle 50% range 22-27. Minimum web-based TOEFL 90. Minimum paper TOEFL 575. **Basis for Candidate Selection:** *Very important factors considered include:* application essay, academic GPA, recommendation(s), rigor of secondary school record, standardized test scores. *Important factors considered include:* Class rank, character/personal qualities, extracurricular activities, interview, talent/ability, volunteer work. *Other factors considered include:* alumni/ae relation, first generation, level of applicant's interest, racial/ethnic status, work experience. **Freshman Admission Requirements:** High school diploma is required and GED is accepted. **Freshman Admission Statistics:** 6,659 applied, 75% admitted, 31% enrolled. **Transfer Admission Requirements:** High school transcript, college transcript(s), essay or personal statement, statement of good standing from prior institution(s). Minimum college GPA of 2.5 required. Lowest grade transferable C. **General Admission Information:** Application Fee $50. Early decision application deadline 11/1. Regular application deadline 7/1. Notification on a rolling basis, beginning on or about 9/15. Nonfall registration accepted. Admission may be deferred for a maximum of One academic year. Credit and/or placement offered for CEEB Advanced Placement tests.

COSTS AND FINANCIAL AID

Annual tuition $27,668. Room and board $10,198. Required fees $2,366. Average book expense $1,000. **Required Forms and Deadlines:** FAFSA, institution's own financial aid form. **Notification of Awards:** Applicants will be notified of awards on a rolling basis beginning 3/1. **Types of Aid:** *Need-based scholarships/grants:* Federal Pell, SEOG, state scholarships/grants, private scholarships, the school's own gift aid, United Negro College Fund. *Loans:* Subsidized Stafford, Unsubsidized Stafford, PLUS, Federal Perkins, Federal Nursing, Private Alternative Loans. **Student Employment:** Federal Work-Study Program available. Institutional employment available. Off-campus job opportunities are good. **Financial Aid Statistics:** 99% freshmen, 98% undergrads receive need-based scholarship or grant aid. 98% freshmen, 92% undergrads receive non-need-based scholarship or grant aid. 87% freshmen, 87% undergrads receive need-based self-help aid. 7% freshmen, 5% undergrads receive athletic scholarships. 99% freshmen, 97% undergrads receive any aid. 80% undergrads borrow to pay for school. Average cumulative indebtedness $25,228. **Criteria for awarding institutional aid:** *Non-need based:* academics, athletics, music/drama.

D'YOUVILLE COLLEGE

One DYouville Square, Buffalo, NY 14201
Phone: 716-829-7600 • **Financial Aid Phone:** 716-829-7500
E-mail: admiss@dyc.edu • **CEEB Code:** 2197
Fax: 716-829-7790 • **Website:** www.dyc.edu • **ACT Code:** 2732

This private school was founded in 1908. It has a 7-acre campus.

RATINGS
Admissions Selectivity Rating: 70   **Fire Safety Rating:** 74   **Green Rating:** 60*

STUDENTS AND FACULTY
Enrollment: 1,982. **Student Body:** 73% female, 27% male, 4% out-of-state, 7% international (55 countries represented). Asian 3%, African American 10%, Caucasian 70%, Hispanic 4%, Native American 1%.
Retention and Graduation: 72% freshmen return for sophomore year. 32% freshmen graduate within 4 years. 52% freshmen graduate within 6 years. **Faculty:** Student/faculty ratio 8:1. 180 full-time faculty, 76% hold PhDs, 8% are members of minority groups, 61% are women. 0% of classes are taught by teaching assistants.

ACADEMICS
Degrees: bachelor's, first professional, master's, post-bachelor's certificate, post-master's certificate. **Classes:** Most classes have 10–19 students. Most lab/discussion sessions have 10–19 students. **Majors with Highest Enrollment:** business/commerce; education; nursing/registered nurse (rn, asn, bsn, msn). **Special Study Options:** Accelerated program, cooperative education program, cross-registration, distance learning, double major, dual enrollment, exchange student program (domestic), independent study, internships, liberal arts/career combination, study abroad, teacher certification program, weekend college. **Combined Degree Programs:** BS/MS. **Disability Services:** Special programs offered to physically disabled students include note-taking services, reader services, tape recorders, tutors.

FACILITIES

Housing: Coed dorms, special housing for disabled students, apartments for married students, apartments for single students, quiet floors for 3rd-5th year students. Separate male and female floors available. New apartment style housing opened 1/05. 100% of campus accessible to physically disabled. **Special Academic Facilities/Equipment:** Kavinoky Theatre (professional theatre) **Computers:** Students can register for classes online. Administrative functions (other than registration) can be performed online.

CAMPUS LIFE

Environment: City. **Activities:** Choral groups, drama/theater, literary magazine, student government, student newspaper, yearbook 25 registered organizations, 3 honor societies, 1 religious organizations. **Athletics (Intercollegiate):** *Men:* baseball, basketball, golf, soccer, volleyball. *Women:* basketball, crew/rowing, golf, soccer, softball, volleyball. **On-Campus Highlights:** New Academic Center, New Gym, Spot Spartian Cafe, Weight Room, Gross anatomy lab, New apartment style housing for junior level and up opening 1/05.

ADMISSIONS

Freshman Academic Profile: Average high school GPA. 18% in top 10% of high school class, 52% in top 25% of high school class, 87% in top 50% of high school class. 75% from public high schools. SAT Math middle 50% range 490-580. SAT Critical Reading middle 50% range 470-550. SAT Writing middle 50% range 450-540. ACT middle 50% range 21-25. Minimum paper TOEFL 500. **Basis for Candidate Selection:** *Very important factors considered include:* rigor of secondary school record, standardized test scores. *Important factors considered include:* Class rank. *Other factors considered include:* recommendation(s), alumni/ae relation, character/personal qualities, extracurricular activities, interview, talent/ability, volunteer work, work experience. **Freshman Admission Requirements:** High school diploma is required and GED is accepted. **Freshman Admission Statistics:** 1,023 applied, 80% admitted, 29% enrolled. **Transfer Admission Requirements:** High school transcript, college transcript(s), minimum college GPA of 2.0 required. Lowest grade transferable C. **General Admission Information:** Application Fee $25. Nonfall registration accepted. Admission may be deferred for a maximum of 12 months. Credit offered for CEEB Advanced Placement tests.

COSTS AND FINANCIAL AID

Annual tuition $21,930. Room and board $10,250. Required fees $310. Average book expense $1,200. **Required Forms and Deadlines:** FAFSA, institution's own financial aid form, state aid form. **Notification of Awards:** Applicants will be notified of awards on a rolling basis beginning 4/15. **Types of Aid:** *Need-based scholarships/grants:* Federal Pell, SEOG, state scholarships/grants, private scholarships, the school's own gift aid, Federal Nursing Scholarships. *Loans:* Subsidized Stafford, Unsubsidized Stafford, PLUS, Federal Perkins, Federal Nursing, college/university loans from institutional funds. **Student Employment:** Federal Work-Study Program available. Institutional employment available. Highest amount earned per year from on-campus jobs $2,000. Off-campus job opportunities are excellent. **Financial Aid Statistics:** 100% freshmen receive need-based scholarship or grant aid. 10% freshmen, 5% undergrads receive non-need-based scholarship or grant aid. 89% freshmen, 92% undergrads receive need-based self-help aid. 94% undergrads borrow to pay for school. Average cumulative indebtedness $41,281. **Criteria for awarding institutional aid:** *Non-need-based:* academics, alumni affiliation.

See page 1060.

EARLHAM COLLEGE

801 National Road West, Richmond, IN 47374-4095
Phone: 765-983-1600 • **Financial Aid Phone:** 765-983-1217
E-mail: admissions@earlham.edu • **CEEB Code:** 1195
Fax: 765-983-1560 • **Website:** www.earlham.edu • **ACT Code:** 1186

This private school, affiliated with the Quaker Church, was founded in 1847. It has a 800-acre campus.

RATINGS
Admissions Selectivity Rating: 81   **Fire Safety Rating:** 89   **Green Rating:** 84

STUDENTS AND FACULTY
Enrollment: 1,020. **Student Body:** 56% female, 44% male, 77% out-of-state, 18% international (76 countries represented). Asian 2%, African American 10%, Caucasian 44%, Hispanic 6%, Native American 1%.
Retention and Graduation: 64% freshmen graduate within 4 years. 73% freshmen graduate within 6 years. **Faculty:** Student/faculty ratio 10:1. 104 full-time faculty, 92% hold PhDs, 24% are members of minority groups, 52% are women. 0% of classes are taught by teaching assistants.

ACADEMICS

Degrees: bachelor's, first professional, master's. **Classes:** Most classes have 10–19 students. Most lab/discussion sessions have 20–29 students. **Majors with Highest Enrollment:** biology/biological sciences; history; psychology. **Special Study Options:** Accelerated program, cross-registration, double major, dual enrollment, English as a Second Language (ESL), independent study, internships, student-designed major, study abroad, teacher certification program, Teacher certification at Master's Degree level only. **Combined Degree Programs:** 3-2 in Architecture. **Disability Services:** Special programs offered to physically disabled students include note-taking services, reader services, tape recorders, tutors.

FACILITIES

Housing: Coed dorms, special housing for disabled students, men's dorms, special housing for international students, women's dorms, wellness housing, theme housing, Friendship houses. 80% of campus accessible to physically disabled. **Special Academic Facilities/Equipment:** Major academic building Landrum Bolling Center for Interdisciplinary and Social Studies opened in 2002, natural history museum, cultural centers, language labs, greenhouse, observatory, planetarium. **Computers:** 95% of classrooms, have wireless network access. Administrative functions (other than registration) can be performed online.

CAMPUS LIFE

Environment: Town. **Activities:** Choral groups, concert band, dance, drama/theater, jazz band, literary magazine, music ensembles, radio station, student government, student newspaper, student-run film society, symphony orchestra, yearbook, Campus Ministries, International Student Organization, Model UN 70 registered organizations, 1 honor societies, 15 religious organizations. **Athletics (Intercollegiate):** *Men:* baseball, basketball, cross-country, football, soccer, tennis, track/field (outdoor), track/field (indoor). *Women:* basketball, cross-country, field hockey, soccer, tennis, track/field (outdoor), track/field (indoor), volleyball. **On-Campus Highlights:** Landrum Bolling Center - Interdisciplinary Studies, Athletics and Wellness Center, Runyan Center, Natural History Museum, Coffee Shop. **Environmental Initiatives:** This year, Earlham faculty approved the proposal for environmental stsudies and environmental science majors. We completed a greenhouse gas emissions inventory using Clean Air, Cool Planet's Carbon Calculator that we will use to guide us in reducing our carbon footprint. We participated in the AASHE Sustainability Tracking Assessment and Rating System (STARS), devoting countless hours to providing as much information about our current sustainability status so that we will know how to improve it.

ADMISSIONS

Freshman Academic Profile: Average high school GPA 3.4. 30% in top 10% of high school class, 61% in top 25% of high school class, 93% in top 50% of high school class. 73% from public high schools. SAT Math middle 50% range 530-660. SAT Critical Reading middle 50% range 550-700. SAT Writing middle 50% range 530-650. ACT middle 50% range 23-30. Minimum web-based TOEFL 80. Minimum paper TOEFL 550. **Basis for Candidate Selection:** *Very important factors considered include:* Class rank, academic GPA, rigor of secondary school record, character/personal qualities. *Important factors considered include:* application essay, recommendation(s), standardized test scores, extracurricular activities, talent/ability, volunteer work. *Other factors considered include:* interview, work experience. **Freshman Admission Requirements:** High school diploma is required and GED is accepted. *Academic units required:* 4 English, 3 mathematics, 3 science, (2 science labs), 2 foreign language, 4 social studies, 2 history, 1 visual/performing arts. *Academic units recommended:* 4 English, 3 mathematics, 3 science, (2 science labs), 2 foreign language, 4 social studies, 2 history, 1 visual/performing arts. **Freshman Admission Statistics:** 1,408 applied, 75% admitted, 27% enrolled. **Transfer Admission Requirements:** High school transcript, college transcript(s), essay or personal statement, standardized test scores, statement of good standing from prior institution(s). Minimum college GPA of 2.7 required. Lowest grade transferable C. **General Admission Information:** Early decision application deadline 12/1. Regular application deadline 2/15. Regular notification 3/15. Nonfall registration accepted. Admission may be deferred for a maximum of 1 year. Credit offered for CEEB Advanced Placement tests.

COSTS AND FINANCIAL AID

Annual tuition $39,200. Room and board $7,910. Required fees $820. Average book expense $1,200. **Required Forms and Deadlines:** FAFSA. **Notification of Awards:** Applicants will be notified of awards on a rolling basis beginning 2/15. **Types of Aid:** *Need-based scholarships/grants:* Federal Pell, SEOG, state scholarships/grants, private scholarships, the school's own gift aid. *Loans:* Direct Subsidized Stafford, Direct Unsubsidized Stafford, Direct PLUS, Federal Perkins, college/university loans from institutional funds. **Student Employment:** Highest amount earned per year from on-campus jobs $2,259. **Financial Aid Statistics:** 94% freshmen, 94% undergrads receive need-based scholarship or grant aid. 52% freshmen, 58% undergrads receive non-need-based scholarship or grant aid. 67% freshmen, 64% undergrads receive need-based self-help aid. 96% freshmen, 96% undergrads receive any aid. 59% undergrads borrow to pay for school. Average cumulative indebtedness $25,577. **Criteria for award-**

ing institutional aid: *Non-need-based:* academics, minority status, religious affiliation.

EAST CAROLINA UNIVERSITY

Office of Undergraduate Admissions, Greenville, NC 27858-4353
Phone: 252-328-6640 • **Financial Aid Phone:** 252-328-4347
E-mail: admis@ecu.edu • **CEEB Code:** 5180
Fax: 252-328-6945 • **Website:** www.ecu.edu • **ACT Code:** 3094

This public school was founded in 1907. It has a 1379-acre campus.

RATINGS

Admissions Selectivity Rating: 78   **Fire Safety Rating:** 61   **Green Rating:** 63

STUDENTS AND FACULTY

Enrollment: 20,446. **Student Body:** 58% female, 42% male, 12% out-of-state, 1% international (40 countries represented). Asian 2%, African American 15%, Caucasian 73%, Hispanic 3%, Native American 1%.
Retention and Graduation: 78% freshmen return for sophomore year. 33% freshmen graduate within 4 years. 58% freshmen graduate within 6 years. **Faculty:** Student/faculty ratio 18:1. 1166 full-time faculty, 81% hold PhDs, 11% are members of minority groups, 48% are women. % of classes are taught by teaching assistants.

ACADEMICS

Degrees: bachelor's, first professional, master's, post-bachelor's certificate, post-master's certificate. **Classes:** Most classes have fewer than 10 students. Most lab/discussion sessions have fewer than 10 students. **Majors with Highest Enrollment:** construction engineering technology/technician; elementary education and teaching; nursing/registered nurse (rn, asn, bsn, msn). **Special Study Options:** Accelerated program, cooperative education program, distance learning, double major, dual enrollment, exchange student program (domestic), honors program, independent study, internships, student-designed major, study abroad, teacher certification program. **Combined Degree Programs:** BSA/MSA Accounting; MA/CAS in School Psychology. **Disability Services:** Special programs offered to physically disabled students include note-taking services, reader services, tape recorders, tutors. **Career Services:** alumni services, career/job search classes, career assessment, internships.

FACILITIES

Housing: Coed dorms, men's dorms, women's dorms, fraternity/sorority housing, First-year students floor, leadership hall, extended quiet study hours floor, upper division, academic year residence halls, music student communities, service community, engineering. 94% of campus accessible to physically disabled. **Special Academic Facilities/Equipment:** Wellington B. Gray Gallery, Museum Without Walls, Ledonia Wright Cultural Center, A.J. Fletcher Recital Hall, Hendrix Theatre, Jenkins Fine Arts Center, McGinnis Theatre, and Mendenhall Student Center. **Computers:** 68% of classrooms, 20% of dorms, 100% of libraries, 100% of dining areas, 100% of student union, 25% of common outdoor areas have wireless network access. Students can register for classes online. Administrative functions (other than registration) can be performed online.

CAMPUS LIFE

Environment: Town. **Activities:** Choral groups, concert band, dance, drama/theater, jazz band, literary magazine, marching band, music ensembles, musical theater, radio station, student government, student newspaper, student-run film society, symphony orchestra, television station, yearbook, Campus Ministries, International Student Organization, Model UN 297 registered organizations, 11 honor societies, 27 religious organizations. 20 fraternities, 13 sororities. **Athletics (Intercollegiate):** *Men:* baseball, basketball, cheerleading, cross-country, diving, football, golf, swimming, tennis, track/field (outdoor). *Women:* basketball, cheerleading, cross-country, diving, golf, soccer, softball, swimming, tennis, track/field (outdoor), volleyball. **On-Campus Highlights:** Student Recreation Center, Wright Plaza, Mendenhall Student Center, Blounts Sports Complex, Science and Technology Building, Athletic facilities include: Dowdy-Ficklen Stadium, Williams Arena in Minges Coliseum and Harrington Field. **Environmental Initiatives:** Water conservation Student life recycling Construction guidelines for sustainable buildings

ADMISSIONS

Freshman Academic Profile: Average high school GPA 3.6. 15% in top 10% of high school class, 44% in top 25% of high school class, 82% in top 50% of high school class. SAT Math middle 50% range 500-570. SAT Critical Reading middle 50% range 470-550. SAT Writing middle 50% range 450-540. ACT middle 50% range 20-24. Minimum web-based TOEFL 80. Minimum paper TOEFL 500. **Basis for Candidate Selection:** *Very important factors* *considered include:* Class rank, rigor of secondary school record, standardized test scores. *Other factors considered include:* recommendation(s), alumni/ ae relation, character/personal qualities, extracurricular activities, geographical residence, interview, state residency, talent/ability. **Freshman Admission Requirements:** High school diploma is required and GED is accepted. *Academic units required:* 4 English, 4 mathematics, 3 science, (1 science labs), 2 foreign language, 2 social studies. *Academic units recommended:* 4 English, 4 mathematics, 3 science, (1 science labs), 2 foreign language, 2 social studies. **Freshman Admission Statistics:** 15,535 applied, 62% admitted, 35% enrolled. **Transfer Admission Requirements:** High school transcript, college transcript(s), minimum college GPA of 2.0 required. Lowest grade transferable C. **General Admission Information:** Application Fee $60. Regular application deadline 3/15. Notification on a rolling basis, beginning on or about 10/1. Nonfall registration accepted. Admission may be deferred for a maximum of 1 semester. Credit and/or placement offered for CEEB Advanced Placement tests.

COSTS AND FINANCIAL AID
Annual in-state tuition $3,758. Annual out-of-state tuition $17,572. Room and board $8,300. Required fees $2,111. Average book expense $1,148. **Required Forms and Deadlines:** FAFSA. **Notification of Awards:** Applicants will be notified of awards on a rolling basis beginning 3/15. **Types of Aid:** *Need-based scholarships/grants:* Federal Pell, SEOG, state scholarships/grants, private scholarships, the school's own gift aid. *Loans:* Subsidized Stafford, Unsubsidized Stafford, PLUS, Federal Perkins, Federal Nursing. **Student Employment:** Federal Work-Study Program available. Institutional employment available. **Financial Aid Statistics:** 67% freshmen, 70% undergrads receive need-based scholarship or grant aid. 9% freshmen, 10% undergrads receive non-need-based scholarship or grant aid. 91% freshmen, 90% undergrads receive need-based self-help aid. 1% freshmen, 2% undergrads receive athletic scholarships. 73% freshmen, 54% undergrads receive any aid. 65% undergrads borrow to pay for school. Average cumulative indebtedness $25,983. **Criteria for awarding institutional aid:** *Non-need-based:* academics, alumni affiliation, art, athletics.

EAST STROUDSBURG UNIVERSITY OF PENNSYLVANIA

East Stroudsburg University, East Stroudsburg, PA 18301-2999
Phone: 570-422-3542 • **Financial Aid Phone:** 570-422-2800
E-mail: undergrads@po-box.esu.edu • **CEEB Code:** 2650
Fax: 570-422-3933 • **Website:** www4.esu.edu • **ACT Code:** 3700

This public school was founded in 1893. It has a 213-acre campus.

RATINGS
Admissions Selectivity Rating: 76   **Fire Safety Rating:** 94   **Green Rating:** 60*

STUDENTS AND FACULTY
Enrollment: 6,274. **Student Body:** 55% female, 45% male, 25% out-of-state, 1% international (24 countries represented). Asian 1%, African American 7%, Caucasian 76%, Hispanic 7%, Native American 0%.
Retention and Graduation: 34% freshmen graduate within 4 years. **Faculty:** Student/faculty ratio 17:1. 330 full-time faculty, 74% hold PhDs, 16% are members of minority groups, 51% are women. 0% of classes are taught by teaching assistants.

ACADEMICS
Degrees: associate, bachelor's, master's. **Classes:** Most classes have 20–29 students. Most lab/discussion sessions have 10–19 students. **Majors with Highest Enrollment:** business administration and management; elementary education and teaching; physical education teaching and coaching. **Special Study Options:** Accelerated program, cross-registration, distance learning, double major, dual enrollment, exchange student program (domestic), honors program, independent study, internships, student-designed major, study abroad, teacher certification program. **Honors Programs:** The Honors Program at ESU offers academically superior students an opportunity to challenge themselves intellectually both within and beyond the classroom setting. The focus of the Program was, and is, located in the area of the liberal arts general education curriculum. The goal of the program is to foster in the students an appreciation of the liberal arts perspective and a commitment to lifelong learning. **Disability Services:** Special programs offered to physically disabled students include note-taking services, reader services, tape recorders, tutors. **Career Services:** career assessment Career Services highlights include We have had several interns placed at Sanofi Pasteur, a major Parmaceutical company. Our individual career counseling services are rated very highly.

FACILITIES
Housing: Coed dorms. 95% of campus accessible to physically disabled.
Special Academic Facilities/Equipment: Natural history museum, human performance lab, TV production studios, 119-acre student-owned/operated recreation area and wildlife sanctuary, observatory, electron microscopes. **Computers:** 50% of classrooms, 100% of dorms, 100% of libraries, 100% of student union, 10% of common outdoor areas have wireless network access. Students can register for classes online. Administrative functions (other than registration) can be performed online.

CAMPUS LIFE
Environment: Village. **Activities:** Choral groups, concert band, dance, drama/theater, jazz band, literary magazine, marching band, music ensembles, musical theater, pep band, radio station, student government, student newspaper, symphony orchestra, Campus Ministries, International Student Organization 110 registered organizations, 28 honor societies, 3 religious organizations. 5 fraternities, 5 sororities. **Athletics (Intercollegiate):** *Men:* baseball, basketball, cross-country, football, soccer, tennis, track/field (outdoor), track/field (indoor), wrestling. *Women:* basketball, cross-country, field hockey, golf, lacrosse, soccer, softball, swimming, tennis, track/field (outdoor), track/field (indoor), volleyball. **On-Campus Highlights:** Recreation Center, Java CIty, University Center, Stoney Acres, The Quad.

ADMISSIONS
Freshman Academic Profile: 7% in top 10% of high school class, 30% in top 25% of high school class, 72% in top 50% of high school class. 90% from public high schools. SAT Math middle 50% range 460-550. SAT Critical Reading middle 50% range 440-530. SAT Writing middle 50% range 440-530. Minimum web-based TOEFL 83. Minimum paper TOEFL 560. **Basis for Candidate Selection:** *Very important factors considered include:* Class rank, academic GPA, rigor of secondary school record, standardized test scores. **Freshman Admission Requirements:** High school diploma is required and GED is accepted. **Freshman Admission Statistics:** 7,258 applied, 63% admitted, 26% enrolled. **Transfer Admission Requirements:** college transcript(s), minimum college GPA of 2.0 required. Lowest grade transferable C. **General Admission Information:** Application Fee $35. Regular application deadline 4/1. Notification on a rolling basis, beginning on or about 12/1. Nonfall registration accepted. Credit and/or placement offered for CEEB Advanced Placement tests.

COSTS AND FINANCIAL AID
Annual in-state tuition $5,804. Annual out-of-state tuition $14,510. Room and board $6,658. Required fees $1,974. Average book expense $1,200. **Required Forms and Deadlines:** FAFSA. **Notification of Awards:** Applicants will be notified of awards on or about 4/1. **Types of Aid:** *Need-based scholarships/grants:* Federal Pell, SEOG, state scholarships/grants, private scholarships, the school's own gift aid. *Loans:* Subsidized Stafford, Unsubsidized Stafford, PLUS, Federal Perkins. **Student Employment:** Federal Work-Study Program available. Institutional employment available. Highest amount earned per year from on-campus jobs $2,145. Off-campus job opportunities are fair. **Financial Aid Statistics:** 55% freshmen, 56% undergrads receive need-based scholarship or grant aid. 6% freshmen, 5% undergrads receive non-need-based scholarship or grant aid. 91% freshmen, 89% undergrads receive need-based self-help aid. 6% freshmen, 4% undergrads receive athletic scholarships. 75% freshmen, 84% undergrads receive any aid. 72% undergrads borrow to pay for school. Average cumulative indebtedness $27,970. **Criteria for awarding institutional aid:** *Non-need-based:* academics, alumni affiliation, art, athletics, leadership, minority status, music/drama, religious affiliation, state/district residency.

EAST TENNESSEE STATE UNIVERSITY

ETSU Box 70731, Johnson City, TN 37614
Phone: 423-439-4213 • **Financial Aid Phone:** 423-439-4300
E-mail: go2etsu@etsu.edu • **CEEB Code:** 1198
Fax: 423-439-4630 • **Website:** www.etsu.edu • **ACT Code:** 3958

This public school was founded in 1911. It has a 366-acre campus.

RATINGS
Admissions Selectivity Rating: 67   **Fire Safety Rating:** 65   **Green Rating:** 60*

STUDENTS AND FACULTY
Enrollment: 12,138. **Student Body:** 56% female, 44% male, 11% out-of-state, 1% international (63 countries represented). Asian 1%, African American 6%, Caucasian 85%, Hispanic 2%, Native American 0%.
Retention and Graduation: 20% freshmen graduate within 4 years. 44% freshmen graduate within 6 years. **Faculty:** Student/faculty ratio 18:1. 529 full-time faculty, 71% hold PhDs, 12% are members of minority groups, 44% are women.

ACADEMICS

Degrees: bachelor's, first professional, master's, post-bachelor's certificate, post-master's certificate. **Classes:** Most classes have 20–29 students. Most lab/discussion sessions have 20–29 students. **Majors with Highest Enrollment:** business administration and management; multi-/interdisciplinary studies, other; nursing/registered nurse (rn, asn, bsn, msn). **Special Study Options:** cooperative education program, distance learning, double major, dual enrollment, exchange student program (domestic), external degree program, honors program, independent study, internships, student-designed major, study abroad, teacher certification program. **Honors Programs:** University Honors Program Honors-in-Discipline Programs. **Disability Services:** Special programs offered to physically disabled students include note-taking services, reader services, tape recorders, tutors. **Career Services:** Alumni network, alumni services, career/job search classes, career assessment, internships, regional alumni.

FACILITIES

Housing: Coed dorms, special housing for disabled students, men's dorms, women's dorms, fraternity/sorority housing, apartments for married students, apartments for single students. 75% of campus accessible to physically disabled. **Special Academic Facilities/Equipment:** Regional history museum, art gallery, archives of Appalachia, planetarium. **Computers:** Students can register for classes online. Administrative functions (other than registration) can be performed online.

CAMPUS LIFE

Environment: Town. **Activities:** Choral groups, concert band, drama/theater, jazz band, literary magazine, music ensembles, pep band, radio station, student government, student newspaper, television station, Campus Ministries, International Student Organization 200 registered organizations, 19 honor societies, 13 religious organizations. 9 fraternities, 7 sororities. **Athletics (Intercollegiate):** *Men:* baseball, basketball, cheerleading, cross-country, golf, soccer, tennis, track/field (outdoor), track/field (indoor). *Women:* basketball, cheerleading, cross-country, golf, soccer, softball, tennis, track/field (outdoor), track/field (indoor), volleyball. **On-Campus Highlights:** Memorial Center, New Sherrod Library, New Physical Activities Center, The Cave- a unique pizza pub located in the DP Culp Center. Built around a huge rock formation, indoors; Amphitheater- Natural stone + earth outdoor theater.

ADMISSIONS

Freshman Academic Profile: Average high school GPA 3.3. 17% in top 10% of high school class, 43% in top 25% of high school class, 76% in top 50% of high school class. 90% from public high schools. SAT Math middle 50% range 430-540. SAT Critical Reading middle 50% range 430-550. ACT middle 50% range 19-24. Minimum paper TOEFL 500. **Basis for Candidate Selection:** *Very important factors considered include:* academic GPA, standardized test scores. *Important factors considered include:* rigor of secondary school record. *Other factors considered include:* Class rank, geographical residence, state residency. **Freshman Admission Requirements:** High school diploma is required and GED is accepted. *Academic units required:* 4 English, 3 mathematics, 2 science, (1 science labs), 2 foreign language, 1 social studies, 1 history, 1 visual/performing arts. *Academic units recommended:* 4 English, 3 mathematics, 2 science, (1 science labs), 2 foreign language, 1 social studies, 1 history, 1 visual/performing arts. **Freshman Admission Statistics:** 5,269 applied, 85% admitted, 48% enrolled. **Transfer Admission Requirements:** High school transcript, college transcript(s), minimum college GPA of 2.0 required. Lowest grade transferable D. **General Admission Information:** Application Fee $15. Nonfall registration accepted. Credit and/or placement offered for CEEB Advanced Placement tests.

COSTS AND FINANCIAL AID

Annual in-state tuition $5,208. Annual out-of-state tuition $18,768. Room and board $6,560. Required fees $1,063. Average book expense $1,090. **Required Forms and Deadlines:** FAFSA. **Notification of Awards:** Applicants will be notified of awards on a rolling basis beginning 4/15. **Types of Aid:** *Need-based scholarships/grants:* Federal Pell, SEOG, state scholarships/grants, private scholarships, the school's own gift aid, Federal Nursing Scholarships. *Loans:* Direct Subsidized Stafford, Direct Unsubsidized Stafford, Direct PLUS, Federal Perkins, Federal Nursing, state loans, college/university loans from institutional funds. **Student Employment:** Federal Work-Study Program available. Institutional employment available. Off-campus job opportunities are excellent. **Financial Aid Statistics:** 84% freshmen, 75% undergrads receive need-based scholarship or grant aid. 32% freshmen, 30% undergrads receive non-need-based scholarship or grant aid. 56% freshmen, 64% undergrads receive need-based self-help aid. 1% freshmen, 2% undergrads receive athletic scholarships. 84% freshmen, % undergrads receive any aid. 80% undergrads borrow to pay for school. Average cumulative indebtedness $20,984. **Criteria for awarding institutional aid:** *Non-need-based:* academics, alumni affiliation, art, athletics, leadership, minority status, music/drama, religious affiliation, state/district residency.

EAST TEXAS BAPTIST UNIVERSITY

One Tiger Drive, Marshall, TX 75670-1498
Phone: 903-923-2000 • **Financial Aid Phone:** 903-923-2137
E-mail: admissions@etbu.edu • **CEEB Code:** 6187
Fax: 903-923-2001 • **Website:** www.etbu.edu • **ACT Code:** 4086

This private school, affiliated with the Baptist Church, was founded in 1912. It has a 200-acre campus.

RATINGS

Admissions Selectivity Rating: 77   **Fire Safety Rating:** 63   **Green Rating:** 67

STUDENTS AND FACULTY

Enrollment: 1,110. **Student Body:** 52% female, 48% male, 9% out-of-state, 1% international (5 countries represented). Asian 1%, African American 19%, Caucasian 65%, Hispanic 11%, Native American 1%. **Retention and Graduation:** 52% freshmen return for sophomore year. 20% freshmen graduate within 4 years. 32% freshmen graduate within 6 years. **Faculty:** Student/faculty ratio 13:1. 70 full-time faculty, 87% hold PhDs, 6% are members of minority groups, 39% are women. 0% of classes are taught by teaching assistants.

ACADEMICS

Degrees: bachelor's, certificate. **Classes:** Most classes have 10–19 students. Most lab/discussion sessions have 10–19 students. **Majors with Highest Enrollment:** business/commerce; elementary education and teaching; nursing/registered nurse (rn, asn, bsn, msn). **Special Study Options:** Accelerated program, cross-registration, distance learning, double major, dual enrollment, exchange student program (domestic), honors program, independent study, internships, liberal arts/career combination, student-designed major, study abroad, teacher certification program. **Disability Services:** Special programs offered to physically disabled students include reader services, tutors. **Career Services:** alumni services, career assessment, internships Career Services highlights include Internships.

FACILITIES

Housing: men's dorms, women's dorms, apartments for married students, campus houses for married students. 95% of campus accessible to physically disabled. **Computers:** 100% of classrooms, 100% of dorms, 100% of libraries, 100% of dining areas, 100% of student union, 100% of common outdoor areas have wireless network access. Students can register for classes online. Administrative functions (other than registration) can be performed online.

CAMPUS LIFE

Environment: Village. **Activities:** Choral groups, concert band, drama/theater, jazz band, literary magazine, marching band, music ensembles, musical theater, pep band, radio station, student government, student newspaper, symphony orchestra, yearbook, Campus Ministries, International Student Organization, Model UN 38 registered organizations, 7 honor societies, 3 religious organizations. 2 fraternities, 2 sororities. **Athletics (Intercollegiate):** *Men:* baseball, basketball, cross-country, football, soccer. *Women:* basketball, cross-country, soccer, softball, volleyball. **On-Campus Highlights:** Scarborough Hall, The Quad, Bennett Student Center, Dean Healthplex, Tiger Grrill. **Environmental Initiatives:** Energy Management Recycling

ADMISSIONS

Freshman Academic Profile: Average high school GPA 3.3. 12% in top 10% of high school class, 42% in top 25% of high school class, 79% in top 50% of high school class. 88% from public high schools. SAT Math middle 50% range 440-530. SAT Critical Reading middle 50% range 410-530. ACT middle 50% range 18-22. Minimum web-based TOEFL 61. Minimum paper TOEFL 500. **Basis for Candidate Selection:** *Very important factors considered include:* Class rank, standardized test scores. *Important factors considered include:* academic GPA. *Other factors considered include:* character/personal qualities. **Freshman Admission Requirements:** High school diploma is required and GED is accepted. **Freshman Admission Statistics:** 1,462 applied, 58% admitted, 41% enrolled. **Transfer Admission Requirements:** college transcript(s), statement of good standing from prior institution(s). Minimum college GPA of 2.00 required. Lowest grade transferable D. **General Admission Information:** Application Fee $25. Notification on a rolling basis, beginning on or about 9/1. Nonfall registration accepted. Admission may be deferred for a maximum of 1 year. Credit and/or placement offered for CEEB Advanced Placement tests.

COSTS AND FINANCIAL AID

Required Forms and Deadlines: FAFSA, institution's own financial aid form. **Notification of Awards:** Applicants will be notified of awards on a rolling basis beginning 1/1. **Types of Aid:** *Need-based scholarships/grants:* Federal Pell, SEOG, state scholarships/grants, private scholarships, the school's own gift aid, Federal Nursing Scholarships. *Loans:* Subsidized Stafford, Unsubsidized Stafford, PLUS, Federal Perkins, state loans. **Student Employment:** Federal Work-Study Program available. Institutional employment available. Highest amount earned per year from on-campus jobs $2,096. Off-campus job opportunities are fair. **Financial Aid Statistics:** 79% freshmen, 76% undergrads receive need-based scholarship or grant aid. 99% freshmen, 96% undergrads receive non-need-based scholarship or grant aid. 84% freshmen, 82% undergrads receive need-based self-help aid. 99% freshmen, 99% undergrads receive any aid. 84% undergrads borrow to pay for school. Average cumulative indebtedness $23,458. **Criteria for awarding institutional aid:** *Non-need-based:* academics, alumni affiliation, leadership, music/drama, religious affiliation.

EASTERN CONNECTICUT STATE UNIVERSITY

83 Windham Street, Willimantic, CT 6226
Phone: 860-465-5286 • **Financial Aid Phone:** 860-365-5205
E-mail: admissions@easternct.edu • **CEEB Code:** 3966
Fax: 860-465-5286 • **Website:** www.easternct.edu

This public school was founded in 1889. It has a 182-acre campus.

RATINGS
Admissions Selectivity Rating: 78   Fire Safety Rating: 89   Green Rating: 86

STUDENTS AND FACULTY
Enrollment: 5,035. **Student Body:** 53% female, 47% male, 7% out-of-state, 1% international (44 countries represented). Asian 2%, African American 7%, Caucasian 79%, Hispanic 7%, Native American 0%.
Retention and Graduation: 77% freshmen return for sophomore year. 32% freshmen graduate within 4 years. 52% freshmen graduate within 6 years. 30% grads go on to further study within 1 year. **Faculty:** Student/faculty ratio 16:1. 198 full-time faculty, 96% hold PhDs, 22% are members of minority groups, 44% are women. 0% of classes are taught by teaching assistants.

ACADEMICS
Degrees: associate, bachelor's, master's. **Classes:** Most classes have 20–29 students. Most lab/discussion sessions have 10–19 students. **Majors with Highest Enrollment:** business/commerce; communication and media studies, other; psychology. **Special Study Options:** Accelerated program, cooperative education program, cross-registration, distance learning, double major, dual enrollment, exchange student program (domestic), honors program, independent study, internships, student-designed major, study abroad, teacher certification program, weekend college. **Honors Programs:** University Honor Scholars Program offers interdisciplinary and independent study opportunities. **Disability Services:** Special programs offered to physically disabled students include note-taking services, reader services, tape recorders, tutors. **Career Services:** Alumni network, alumni services, career/job search classes, career assessment, internships, regional alumni. Career Services highlights include Internships that lead to permanent employment.

FACILITIES
Housing: Coed dorms, apartments for single students. 95% of campus accessible to physically disabled. Art Gallery, Arboretum, Church Farm, Family/Child Development Center(2007), Green science bldg/labs(2008),electron microscope, planetarium, Media center with TV and radio station, Sports/Fitness Center and Studios, Center for Connecticut studies. **Computers:** 100% of libraries, 100% of dining areas, 100% of student union, 100% of common outdoor areas have wireless network access. Students can register for classes online. Administrative functions (other than registration) can be performed online.

CAMPUS LIFE
Environment: Village. **Activities:** Choral groups, concert band, dance, drama/theater, jazz band, literary magazine, music ensembles, musical theater, radio station, student government, student newspaper, television station, yearbook, International Student Organization 68 registered organizations, 17 honor societies, 3 religious organizations. **Athletics (Intercollegiate):** *Men:* baseball, basketball, cross-country, golf, lacrosse, soccer, track/field (outdoor), track/field (indoor). *Women:* basketball, cross-country, diving, field hockey, lacrosse, soccer, softball, swimming, track/field (outdoor), track/field (indoor), volleyball. **On-Campus Highlights:** Library, Student Center, Sports Center, Church Farm, Planetarium. **Environmental Initiatives:** Education Project Energy Solutions Green Campus Initiative.

ADMISSIONS
Freshman Academic Profile: Average high school GPA 3.0. 7% in top 10% of high school class, 25% in top 25% of high school class, 70% in top 50% of high school class. SAT Math middle 50% range 480-580. SAT Critical Reading middle 50% range 470-570. Minimum paper TOEFL 550. **Basis for Candidate**

Selection: *Very important factors considered include:* Class rank, standardized test scores, talent/ability. *Important factors considered include:* academic GPA, recommendation(s), rigor of secondary school record, level of applicant's interest. *Other factors considered include:* application essay, character/personal qualities, extracurricular activities, interview, volunteer work, work experience. **Freshman Admission Requirements:** High school diploma is required and GED is accepted. *Academic units required:* 4 English, 3 mathematics, 2 science, (1 science labs), 2 foreign language, 2 social studies, 3 history. 4 English, 3 mathematics, 2 science, (1 science labs), 2 foreign language, 2 social studies, 3 history. **Freshman Admission Statistics:** 3,493 applied, 65% admitted, 41% enrolled. **Transfer Admission Requirements:** High school transcript, college transcript(s), minimum college GPA of 2.0 required. Lowest grade transferable C–. **General Admission Information:** Application Fee $50. Notification on a rolling basis, beginning on or about 12/1. Nonfall registration accepted. Credit offered for CEEB Advanced Placement tests.

COSTS AND FINANCIAL AID
Annual in-state tuition $4,023. Annual out-of-state tuition $13,020. Room and board $10,048. Required fees $4,327. Average book expense $1,554. **Required Forms and Deadlines:** FAFSA. **Notification of Awards: Types of Aid:** *Need-based scholarships/grants:* Federal Pell, SEOG, state scholarships/grants, private scholarships, the school's own gift aid. *Loans:* Subsidized Stafford, Unsubsidized Stafford, PLUS, Federal Perkins. **Student Employment:** Federal Work-Study Program available. Institutional employment available. Highest amount earned per year from on-campus jobs $5,500. Off-campus job opportunities are excellent. **Financial Aid Statistics:** 68% freshmen, 66% undergrads receive need-based scholarship or grant aid. 4% freshmen, 1% undergrads receive non-need-based scholarship or grant aid. 92% freshmen, 93% undergrads receive need-based self-help aid. 69% freshmen, 75% undergrads receive any aid. 74% undergrads borrow to pay for school. Average cumulative indebtedness $24,428. **Criteria for awarding institutional aid:** *Non-need-based:* academics.

EASTERN ILLINOIS UNIVERSITY

600 Lincoln Avenue, Charleston, IL 61920
Phone: 217-581-2223 • **Financial Aid Phone:** 217-581-7812
E-mail: admissions@eiu.edu • **CEEB Code:** 1199
Fax: 217-581-7060 • **Website:** www.eiu.edu • **ACT Code:** 1016

This public school was founded in 1895. It has a 320-acre campus.

RATINGS
Admissions Selectivity Rating: 73   Fire Safety Rating: 85   Green Rating: 85

STUDENTS AND FACULTY
Enrollment: 8,861. **Student Body:** 59% female, 41% male, 2% out-of-state, 1% international (44 countries represented). Asian 1%, African American 17%, Caucasian 73%, Hispanic 4%, Native American 0%.
Retention and Graduation: 79% freshmen return for sophomore year. 33% freshmen graduate within 4 years. 30% grads go on to further study within 1 year. **Faculty:** Student/faculty ratio 15:1. 586 full-time faculty, 72% hold PhDs, 13% are members of minority groups, 46% are women.

ACADEMICS
Degrees: bachelor's, master's, post-bachelor's certificate, post-master's certificate. **Classes:** Most classes have 20–29 students. **Majors with Highest Enrollment:** biology/biological sciences; elementary education and teaching; physical education teaching and coaching. **Special Study Options:** distance learning, double major, dual enrollment, exchange student program (domestic), external degree program, honors program, independent study, internships, study abroad, teacher certification program. **Honors Programs:** Honors College. **Disability Services:** Special programs offered to physically disabled students include note-taking services, reader services, tape recorders, tutors. **Career Services:** Alumni network, alumni services, career/job search classes, career assessment, internships, regional alumni. Career Services highlights include The externship program provides early professional direction and networking to students who are narrowing their major and career choices for further development, academically and experientially.

FACILITIES
Housing: Coed dorms, special housing for disabled students, men's dorms, women's dorms, fraternity/sorority housing, apartments for married students, apartments for single students. 80% of campus accessible to physically disabled. **Special Academic Facilities/Equipment:** Arts center, electron microscope. **Computers:** 100% of classrooms, 50% of dorms, 100% of libraries, 100% of dining areas, 100% of student union, have wireless network access. Students can

register for classes online. Administrative functions (other than registration) can be performed online.

CAMPUS LIFE

Environment: Village. **Activities:** Choral groups, concert band, dance, drama/theater, jazz band, literary magazine, marching band, music ensembles, musical theater, opera, pep band, radio station, student government, student newspaper, symphony orchestra, television station, yearbook, Campus Ministries, International Student Organization 232 registered organizations, 19 honor societies, 16 religious organizations. 15 fraternities, 11 sororities. **Athletics (Intercollegiate):** *Men:* baseball, basketball, cross-country, football, golf, soccer, swimming, tennis, track/field (outdoor), track/field (indoor). *Women:* basketball, cross-country, golf, rugby, soccer, softball, swimming, tennis, track/field (outdoor), track/field (indoor), volleyball. **On-Campus Highlights:** Doudna Fine Arts Building, Old Main, Martin Luther King Jr. University Union, Pemberton Hall, Student Recreation Center. **Environmental Initiatives:** Reduced campus water consumption by over 50%. Reduced campus energy consumption by over 30%. Opened the Renewable Energy Center replacing coal with renewable biomass.

ADMISSIONS

Freshman Academic Profile: Average high school GPA 3.1. 11% in top 10% of high school class, 31% in top 25% of high school class, 66% in top 50% of high school class. ACT middle 50% range 19-24. Minimum web-based TOEFL 61. Minimum paper TOEFL 500. **Basis for Candidate Selection:** *Very important factors considered include:* academic GPA, rigor of secondary school record, standardized test scores, character/personal qualities. *Important factors considered include:* Class rank, extracurricular activities. *Other factors considered include:* application essay, recommendation(s). **Freshman Admission Requirements:** High school diploma is required and GED is accepted. *Academic units required:* 4 English, 3 mathematics, 3 science, (3 science labs), 3 social studies, 2 academic electives. *Academic units recommended:* 4 English, 3 mathematics, 3 science, (3 science labs), 3 social studies, 2 academic electives. **Freshman Admission Statistics:** 6,710 applied, 65% admitted, 30% enrolled. **Transfer Admission Requirements:** High school transcript, college transcript(s), standardized test scores, minimum college GPA of 2.0 required. **General Admission Information:** Application Fee $30. Nonfall registration accepted. Admission may be deferred for a maximum of 1 year. Credit offered for CEEB Advanced Placement tests.

COSTS AND FINANCIAL AID

Annual in-state tuition $8,370. Annual out-of-state tuition $25,110. Room and board $9,174. Required fees $2,560. Average book expense $300. **Required Forms and Deadlines:** FAFSA. **Notification of Awards:** Applicants will be notified of awards on a rolling basis beginning 3/1. **Types of Aid:** *Need-based scholarships/grants:* Federal Pell, SEOG, state scholarships/grants, private scholarships, the school's own gift aid. *Loans:* Direct Subsidized Stafford, Direct Unsubsidized Stafford, Direct PLUS, Federal Perkins, college/university loans from institutional funds. **Student Employment:** Federal Work-Study Program available. Institutional employment available. Off-campus job opportunities are fair. **Financial Aid Statistics:** 70% freshmen, 67% undergrads receive need-based scholarship or grant aid. 53% freshmen, 26% undergrads receive non-need-based scholarship or grant aid. 83% freshmen, 88% undergrads receive need-based self-help aid. 2% freshmen, 2% undergrads receive athletic scholarships. 86% freshmen, 83% undergrads receive any aid. 72% undergrads borrow to pay for school. Average cumulative indebtedness $28,575. **Criteria for awarding institutional aid:** *Non-need-based:* academics, art, athletics, leadership, music/drama.

EASTERN KENTUCKY UNIVERSITY

SSB CPO 54, Richmond, KY 40475
Phone: 859-622-2106 • **Financial Aid Phone:** 859-622-2361
E-mail: admissions@eku.edu • **CEEB Code:** 1200
Fax: 859-622-8024 • **Website:** www.eku.edu • **ACT Code:** 1512

This public school was founded in 1906. It has a 675-acre campus.

RATINGS

Admissions Selectivity Rating: 69　　**Fire Safety Rating:** 88　　**Green Rating:** 60*

STUDENTS AND FACULTY

Enrollment: 12,710. **Student Body:** 58% female, 42% male, 13% out-of-state, 1% international (36 countries represented). Asian 1%, African American 5%, Caucasian 99%, Hispanic 1%, Native American 0%.
Retention and Graduation: Faculty: Student/faculty ratio 17:1. 599 full-time faculty, 69% hold PhDs, 11% are members of minority groups, 48% are women. 0% of classes are taught by teaching assistants.

ACADEMICS

Degrees: associate, bachelor's, certificate, master's, post-bachelor's certificate. **Classes:** Most classes have 10–19 students. **Majors with Highest Enrollment:** criminal justice/law enforcement administration; elementary education and teaching; nursing/registered nurse (rn, asn, bsn, msn). **Special Study Options:** cooperative education program, distance learning, double major, English as a Second Language (ESL), honors program, independent study, internships, study abroad, teacher certification program. **Honors Programs:** Honors Program: www.honors.eku.edu. **Disability Services:** Special programs offered to physically disabled students include note-taking services, reader services, tape recorders, tutors. **Career Services:** Alumni network, alumni services, career/job search classes, career assessment, internships, regional alumni.

FACILITIES

Housing: Coed dorms, men's dorms, special housing for international students, women's dorms, fraternity/sorority housing, apartments for married students 90% of campus accessible to physically disabled. **Special Academic Facilities/Equipment:** Hummel Planetarium, Giles Gallery **Computers:** Students can register for classes online. Administrative functions (other than registration) can be performed online.

CAMPUS LIFE

Environment: Town. **Activities:** Choral groups, concert band, dance, drama/theater, jazz band, literary magazine, marching band, music ensembles, musical theater, pep band, radio station, student government, student newspaper, symphony orchestra 178 registered organizations, 30 honor societies, 11 religious organizations. 16 fraternities, 13 sororities. **Athletics (Intercollegiate):** *Men:* baseball, basketball, cheerleading, cross-country, football, golf, tennis, track/field (outdoor), track/field (indoor). *Women:* basketball, cheerleading, cross-country, golf, soccer, softball, tennis, track/field (outdoor), track/field (indoor), volleyball. **On-Campus Highlights:** Student Wellness Center (New), Library Cafe (New), Student Services Building (New), First Weekend Events

ADMISSIONS

Freshman Academic Profile: SAT Math middle 50% range 440-450. SAT Critical Reading middle 50% range 440-450. SAT Writing middle 50% range 420-430. ACT middle 50% range 18-24. Minimum paper TOEFL 500. **Basis for Candidate Selection:** *Very important factors considered include:* academic GPA, standardized test scores. *Other factors considered include:* talent/ability. **Freshman Admission Requirements:** High school diploma is required and GED is accepted. *Academic units required:* 4 English, 3 mathematics, 3 science, (1 science labs), 2 foreign language, 3 social studies, 7 academic electives, 3 Health, Physical ED. = 0.5 and Art = 1. 4 English, 3 mathematics, 3 science, (1 science labs), 2 foreign language, 3 social studies, 7 academic electives, 3 Health, Physical ED. = 0.5 and Art = 1 **Freshman Admission Statistics:** 6,928 applied, 69% admitted, 52% enrolled. **Transfer Admission Requirements:** college transcript(s), minimum college GPA of 2.0 required. Lowest grade transferable D. **General Admission Information:** Application Fee $30. Regular application deadline 8/1. Notification on a rolling basis, beginning on or about 9/1. Nonfall registration accepted. Admission may be deferred for a maximum of 1 semester. Credit offered for CEEB Advanced Placement tests.

COSTS AND FINANCIAL AID

Annual in-state tuition $6,080. Annual out-of-state tuition $16,612. Room and board $5,288. Required fees $460. Average book expense $800. **Required Forms and Deadlines:** FAFSA. **Notification of Awards:** Applicants will be notified of awards on a rolling basis beginning 4/1. **Types of Aid:** *Need-based scholarships/grants:* Federal Pell, SEOG, state scholarships/grants, private scholarships, the school's own gift aid. *Loans:* Subsidized Stafford, Unsubsidized Stafford, PLUS, Federal Perkins, college/university loans from institutional funds. **Student Employment:** Federal Work-Study Program available. Institutional employment available. Highest amount earned per year from on-campus jobs $1,800. Off-campus job opportunities are good. **Financial Aid Statistics:** 60% freshmen, 58% undergrads receive need-based scholarship or grant aid. 81% freshmen, 52% undergrads receive non-need-based scholarship or grant aid. 75% freshmen, 83% undergrads receive need-based self-help aid. 2% freshmen, 1% undergrads receive athletic scholarships. 94% freshmen, 86% undergrads receive any aid. 69% undergrads borrow to pay for school. Average cumulative indebtedness $14,976. **Criteria for awarding institutional aid:** *Non-need-based:* academics, alumni affiliation, art, athletics, job skills, leadership, minority status, music/drama.

EASTERN MENNONITE UNIVERSITY

1200 Park Rd., Harrisonburg, VA 22802
Phone: 540-432-4118 • **Financial Aid Phone:** 540-432-4137 • **CEEB Code:** 5181
Fax: 540-432-4444 • **Website:** www.emu.edu • **ACT Code:** 3708

This school, affiliated with the Mennonite Church, was founded in 1917. It has a 93-acre campus.

RATINGS
Admissions Selectivity Rating: 60*   **Fire Safety Rating:** 63   **Green Rating:** 60*

STUDENTS AND FACULTY
Student Body: (20 countries represented).
Retention and Graduation: 5% grads go on to further study within 1 year. 1% grads pursue arts and sciences degrees. 2% grads pursue medical degrees.
Faculty: 0% of classes are taught by teaching assistants.

ACADEMICS
Majors with Highest Enrollment: business administration and management; nursing/registered nurse (rn, asn, bsn, msn); psychology. **Honors Programs:** EMU's Honors Program accepts 10-14 academically-gifted first-year students into the selective Honors Program. Participation is renewable for up to 3 years. Honors students must maintain a 3.5 GPA and complete 9 SH of Honors Program Courses. Honors students gain access to many special educational opportunities and meet monthly for fellowship and discussion. **Disability Services:** Special programs offered to physically disabled students include note-taking services, reader services, tape recorders, tutors. **Career Services:** alumni services, career/job search classes, career assessment, internships, regional alumni.

FACILITIES
Housing: 75% of campus accessible to physically disabled. **Special Academic Facilities/Equipment:** D. Ralph Hostetter Museum of Natural History, M. T. Brackbill Planetarium, arboretum, Menno Simons Historical Library **Computers:** Administrative functions (other than registration) can be performed online.

CAMPUS LIFE
Environment: Town. **Activities:** 37 registered organizations, 2 honor societies, 4 religious organizations. **Athletics (Intercollegiate):** *Men:* baseball, basketball, cross-country, soccer, tennis, track/field (outdoor), track/field (indoor), volleyball. *Women:* basketball, cross-country, field hockey, soccer, softball, tennis, track/field (outdoor), track/field (indoor), volleyball. **On-Campus Highlights:** University Commons, Royals Den snack shop, Common Grounds coffeehouse, Campus Center Greeting Hall, Wood's Residence Halls, Park Woods.

ADMISSIONS
Freshman Academic Profile: Minimum paper TOEFL 550. **General Admission Information:** Credit and/or placement offered for CEEB Advanced Placement tests.

COSTS AND FINANCIAL AID
Student Employment: Federal Work-Study Program available. Institutional employment available. Highest amount earned per year from on-campus jobs $3,500. Off-campus job opportunities are good. **Financial Aid Statistics:** 91% freshmen, 93% undergrads receive any aid.

EASTERN MICHIGAN UNIVERSITY

Eastern Michigan University, Ypsilanti, MI 48197
Phone: 734-487-3060 • **Financial Aid Phone:** 734-487-0455
E-mail: admissions@emich.edu • **CEEB Code:** 1201
Fax: 734-487-1484 • **Website:** www.emich.edu • **ACT Code:** 1990

This public school was founded in 1849. It has a 460-acre campus.

RATINGS
Admissions Selectivity Rating: 79   **Fire Safety Rating:** 66   **Green Rating:** 78

STUDENTS AND FACULTY
Enrollment: 18,139. **Student Body:** 58% female, 42% male, 8% out-of-state, 2% international (70 countries represented). Asian 2%, African American 22%, Caucasian 63%, Hispanic 3%, Native American 1%.
Retention and Graduation: 76% freshmen return for sophomore year. 13% freshmen graduate within 4 years. 40% freshmen graduate within 6 years.
Faculty: Student/faculty ratio 18:1. 782 full-time faculty, 81% hold PhDs, 17% are members of minority groups, 48% are women. 3% of classes are taught by teaching assistants.

ACADEMICS
Degrees: bachelor's, doctoral, master's, post-bachelor's certificate, post-master's certificate. **Classes:** Most classes have 20–29 students. Most lab/discussion sessions have 20–29 students. **Majors with Highest Enrollment:** business administration and management; nursing/registered nurse (rn, asn, bsn, msn); psychology. **Special Study Options:** Accelerated program, cooperative education program, distance learning, double major, dual enrollment, English as a Second Language (ESL), external degree program, honors program, independent study, internships, student-designed major, study abroad, teacher certification program, weekend college, Dual enrollment note: high school students may enroll in college courses while still enrolled in high school, but are required to apply for admission to Eastern. **Combined Degree Programs:** BA/MA, BA/BBA, BA/MSA, BS/MA, BS/MOT. **Disability Services:** Special programs offered to physically disabled students include note-taking services, reader services, tape recorders, tutors. **Career Services:** Alumni network, alumni services, career/job search classes, career assessment, internships, Career Services highlights include We connect with area businesses to provide hands-on learning opportunities for our students. All three of the programs above work hand-in-hand toward helping students gain experience in their field of study (number one attributes employers look for in job candidates).

FACILITIES
Housing: Coed dorms, special housing for disabled students, special housing for international students, fraternity/sorority housing, apartments for married students, cooperative housing, apartments for single students, theme housing, house rental to sorority house. 80% of campus accessible to physically disabled. **Special Academic Facilities/Equipment:** Intermedia art gallery, paint research center, Sherzer observatory, Bruce T. Halle Library, Terrestial and Aquatics Ecology Research Facility, Coatings Research Institute, the John W. Porter Building housing the College of Education and the Marshall Building housing the College of Health and Human Services. **Computers:** 100% of classrooms, 25% of dorms, 100% of libraries, 100% of dining areas, 100% of student union, 15% of common outdoor areas have wireless network access. Students can register for classes online. Administrative functions (other than registration) can be performed online.

CAMPUS LIFE
Environment: City. **Activities:** Choral groups, concert band, dance, literary magazine, marching band, music ensembles, musical theater, pep band, radio station, student government, student newspaper, student-run film society, symphony orchestra, television station, Campus Ministries, International Student Organization 220 registered organizations, 14 honor societies, 24 religious organizations, 11 fraternities, 13 sororities. **Athletics (Intercollegiate):** *Men:* basketball, diving, football, golf, swimming, track/field (outdoor), track/field (indoor), wrestling. *Women:* basketball, crew/rowing, diving, golf, gymnastics, soccer, softball, swimming, tennis, track/field (outdoor), track/field (indoor), volleyball. **On-Campus Highlights:** New Student Center, Recreations and Intramurals Building, The Lakehouse, Halle Library, Athletic Campus. **Environmental Initiatives:** Energy performance contract Hiring an Energy & Sustainability Manager in March, 2008 Recycling initiative.

ADMISSIONS
Freshman Academic Profile: Average high school GPA 3.1. 13% in top 10% of high school class, 36% in top 25% of high school class, 71% in top 50% of high school class. 85% from public high schools. SAT Math middle 50% range 450-580. SAT Critical Reading middle 50% range 440-560. SAT Writing middle 50% range 430-555. ACT middle 50% range 18-24. Minimum paper TOEFL 500. **Basis for Candidate Selection:** *Very important factors considered include:* academic GPA, standardized test scores. *Important factors considered include:* rigor of secondary school record, character/personal qualities. *Other factors considered include:* application essay, recommendation(s), extracurricular activities, interview, talent/ability. **Freshman Admission Requirements:** High school diploma is required and GED is accepted. **Freshman Admission Statistics:** 12,787 applied, 60% admitted, 28% enrolled. **Transfer Admission Requirements:** college transcript(s), minimum college GPA of 2.0 required. Lowest grade transferable C. **General Admission Information:** Application Fee $30. Notification on a rolling basis, beginning on or about 10/1. Nonfall registration accepted. Admission may be deferred for a maximum of 1 year. Credit and/or placement offered for CEEB Advanced Placement tests.

COSTS AND FINANCIAL AID
Annual in-state tuition $7,409. Annual out-of-state tuition $21,821. Room and board $7,895. Required fees $1,275. Average book expense $900. **Required Forms and Deadlines:** FAFSA. **Notification of Awards:** Applicants will be notified of awards on a rolling basis beginning 3/1. **Types of Aid:** *Need-based scholarships/grants:* Federal Pell, SEOG, state scholarships/grants, private scholarships, the school's own gift aid. *Loans:* Subsidized Stafford, Unsubsidized Stafford, PLUS, Federal Perkins, state loans, college/university loans from institutional funds, Alternative (Private) Loans. **Student Employment:** Federal Work-Study Program available. Institutional employment available. Highest amount earned per year from on-campus jobs $13,375. Off-campus job opportunities are excellent. **Financial Aid Statistics:** 87% freshmen, 76%

undergrads receive need-based scholarship or grant aid. 49% freshmen, 29% undergrads receive non-need-based scholarship or grant aid. 85% freshmen, 87% undergrads receive need-based self-help aid. 4% freshmen, 3% undergrads receive athletic scholarships. 91% freshmen, 80% undergrads receive any aid. 63% undergrads borrow to pay for school. Average cumulative indebtedness $23,669. **Criteria for awarding institutional aid:** *Non-need-based:* academics, alumni affiliation, art, athletics, leadership, minority status, music/drama, state/district residency.

EASTERN NAZARENE COLLEGE

23 East Elm Avenue, Quincy, MA 02170-2999
Phone: 617-745-3711
E-mail: admissions@enc.edu • **CEEB Code:** 3365
Fax: 617-745-3992 • **Website:** www.enc.edu

This private school, affiliated with the Nazarene Church, was founded in 1918. It has a 19-acre campus.

RATINGS
Admissions Selectivity Rating: 61   **Fire Safety Rating:** 60*   **Green Rating:** 60*

STUDENTS AND FACULTY
Student Body: 58% out-of-state.
Retention and Graduation: 22% grads go on to further study within 1 year. 17% grads pursue arts and sciences degrees. 1% grads pursue law degrees. 2% grads pursue business degrees. 2% grads pursue medical degrees. **Faculty:** Student/faculty ratio 15:1.

ACADEMICS
Degrees: associate, bachelor's, diploma, first professional certificate, master's. **Majors with Highest Enrollment:** biology; business/commerce; communication studies/speech communication and rhetoric. **Special Study Options:** Accelerated program, cooperative education program, double major, honors program, independent study, internships, study abroad, teacher certification program. **Disability Services:** Special programs offered to physically disabled students include note-taking services, reader services, tape recorders, tutors. **Career Services:** career assessment, internships.

FACILITIES
Housing: special housing for disabled students, men's dorms, women's dorms, apartments for married students, suites-men's and women's.

CAMPUS LIFE
Environment: Village. **Activities:** Choral groups, drama/theater, music ensembles, musical theater, radio station, student government, student newspaper, yearbook 1 religious organizations. **Athletics (Intercollegiate):** *Men:* baseball, basketball, cross-country, soccer, tennis. *Women:* basketball, cross-country, soccer, softball, tennis, volleyball.

ADMISSIONS
Freshman Academic Profile: % in top 10% of high school class, % in top 25% of high school class, Minimum paper TOEFL 600. **Basis for Candidate Selection:** *Very important factors considered include:* application essay, recommendation(s), rigor of secondary school record, standardized test scores, interview. *Other factors considered include:* Class rank, character/personal qualities, extracurricular activities, religious affiliation/commitment, talent/ability, volunteer work, work experience. **Freshman Admission Requirements:** High school diploma is required and GED is accepted. *Academic units required:* 4 English, 2 mathematics, 1 science, 2 foreign language, 1 social studies, 1 history. *Academic units recommended:* 4 English, 2 mathematics, 1 science, 2 foreign language, 1 social studies, 1 history. **Freshman Transfer Admission Requirements:** High school transcript, college transcript(s), essay or personal statement, interview, standardized test scores, minimum college GPA of 2.0 required. Lowest grade transferable c. **General Admission Information:** Application Fee $25. Nonfall registration accepted.

COSTS AND FINANCIAL AID
Annual tuition $17,700. Room and board $6,590. Required fees $610. Average book expense $500. **Required Forms and Deadlines:** FAFSA, institution's own financial aid form. **Types of Aid:** *Need-based scholarships/grants:* Federal Pell, SEOG, state scholarships/grants, private scholarships, the school's own gift aid, Church Scholarships. *Loans:* Subsidized Stafford, Unsubsidized Stafford, PLUS, Federal Perkins, state loans. **Student Employment:** Federal Work-Study Program available. Highest amount earned per year from on-campus jobs $3,000. **Financial Aid Statistics:** 34% freshmen, 22% undergrads receive need-based scholarship or grant aid. 97% freshmen, 99% undergrads receive non-need-based scholarship or grant aid. 85% freshmen, 75% undergrads

receive need-based self-help aid. **Criteria for awarding institutional aid:** *Non-need-based:* academics, alumni affiliation, leadership, minority status, music/drama, religious affiliation, state/district residency.

EASTERN NEW MEXICO UNIVERSITY

Station #7, Portales, NM 88130
Phone: 575-562-2178 • **Financial Aid Phone:** 575-562-2194
E-mail: admissions@enmu.edu • **CEEB Code:** 4299
Fax: 575-562-2118 • **Website:** • **ACT Code:** 2636

This public school was founded in 1934. It has a 400-acre campus.

RATINGS
Admissions Selectivity Rating: 76   **Fire Safety Rating:** 82   **Green Rating:** 61

STUDENTS AND FACULTY
Enrollment: 3,618. **Student Body:** 57% female, 43% male, 23% out-of-state, 3% international (23 countries represented). Asian 1%, African American 5%, Caucasian 54%, Hispanic 33%, Native American 3%.
Retention and Graduation: 62% freshmen return for sophomore year. 11% freshmen graduate within 4 years. **Faculty:** Student/faculty ratio 17:1. 146 full-time faculty, 76% hold PhDs, 14% are members of minority groups, 47% are women. 3% of classes are taught by teaching assistants.

ACADEMICS
Degrees: associate, bachelor's, master's, terminal associate, transfer associate. **Classes:** Most classes have 10–19 students. Most lab/discussion sessions have 10–19 students. **Majors with Highest Enrollment:** business administration and management; elementary education and teaching; general studies. **Special Study Options:** Accelerated program, distance learning, double major, dual enrollment, English as a Second Language (ESL), exchange student program (domestic), independent study, internships, student-designed major, teacher certification program. **Disability Services:** Special programs offered to physically disabled students include note-taking services, reader services, tape recorders, tutors. **Career Services:** career assessment, internships.

FACILITIES
Housing: Coed dorms, special housing for disabled students, women's dorms, fraternity/sorority housing, apartments for married students, apartments for single students. 100% of campus accessible to physically disabled. **Special Academic Facilities/Equipment:** Natural history and historical museums, theatre, child development center, audiovisual center, electron microscopes, laser, KNEW Broadcast Center. **Computers:** Students can register for classes online. Administrative functions (other than registration) can be performed online.

CAMPUS LIFE
Environment: Village. **Activities:** Choral groups, concert band, dance, drama/theater, jazz band, literary magazine, marching band, music ensembles, radio station, student government, student newspaper, student-run film society, symphony orchestra, television station, Campus Ministries, International Student Organization 55 registered organizations, 2 honor societies, 4 religious organizations. 4 fraternities, 2 sororities. **Athletics (Intercollegiate):** *Men:* baseball, basketball, cross-country, football, rodeo, soccer, track/field (outdoor). *Women:* basketball, cross-country, rodeo, soccer, softball, track/field (outdoor), volleyball. **On-Campus Highlights:** New Science facilities/Natural History Museum, Campus Union Building, Communications-Broadcast Center, Library, University Theatre Center. **Environmental Initiatives:** Water savings project Energy management project Development of solar energy project.

ADMISSIONS
Freshman Academic Profile: Average high school GPA 3.2. 11% in top 10% of high school class, 34% in top 25% of high school class, 68% in top 50% of high school class. 98% from public high schools. SAT Math middle 50% range 430-530. SAT Critical Reading middle 50% range 420-525. ACT middle 50% range 17-23. Minimum paper TOEFL 500. **Basis for Candidate Selection:** *Very important factors considered include:* academic GPA, standardized test scores. **Freshman Admission Requirements:** High school diploma is required and GED is accepted. **Freshman Admission Statistics:** 2,164 applied, 60% admitted, 48% enrolled. **Transfer Admission Requirements:** college transcript(s), statement of good standing from prior institution(s). Minimum college GPA of 2.0 required. Lowest grade transferable D. **General Admission Information:** Nonfall registration accepted. Admission may be deferred for a maximum of 0. Credit and/or placement offered for CEEB Advanced Placement tests.

COSTS AND FINANCIAL AID
Annual in-state tuition $2,668. Annual out-of-state tuition $8,220. Room and board $5,612. Required fees $1,212. Average book expense $500. **Required**

Forms and Deadlines: FAFSA. Notification of Awards: Applicants will be notified of awards on a rolling basis beginning 4/15. Types of Aid: *Need-based scholarships/grants:* Federal Pell, SEOG, state scholarships/grants, the school's own gift aid. *Loans:* Subsidized Stafford, Unsubsidized Stafford, PLUS, Federal Perkins. Student Employment: Federal Work-Study Program available. Institutional employment available. Financial Aid Statistics: 97% freshmen, 97% undergrads receive need-based scholarship or grant aid. 88% freshmen, 56% undergrads receive non-need-based scholarship or grant aid. 25% freshmen, 27% undergrads receive need-based self-help aid. 10% freshmen, 8% undergrads receive athletic scholarships. 99% freshmen, 91% undergrads receive any aid. 1% undergrads borrow to pay for school. Average cumulative indebtedness $11,911. Criteria for awarding institutional aid: *Non-need-based:* academics, alumni affiliation, art, athletics, leadership, music/drama, state/district residency.

EASTERN OREGON UNIVERSITY

One University Blvd, La Grande, OR 97850
Phone: 1-541-962-3393 • **Financial Aid Phone:** 541-962-3456
E-mail: admissions@eou.edu • **CEEB Code:** 4300
Fax: 541-962-3418 • **Website:** www.eou.edu • **ACT Code:** 3460

This public school was founded in 1929. It has a 121-acre campus.

RATINGS
Admissions Selectivity Rating: 71   **Fire Safety Rating:** 83   **Green Rating:** 61

STUDENTS AND FACULTY
Enrollment: 3,596. **Student Body:** 62% female, 38% male, 29% out-of-state, 1% international (20 countries represented). Asian 3%, African American 2%, Caucasian 81%, Hispanic 6%, Native American 2%.
Retention and Graduation: **Faculty:** Student/faculty ratio 23:1. 118 full-time faculty, 81% hold PhDs, 7% are members of minority groups, 42% are women. 0% of classes are taught by teaching assistants.

ACADEMICS
Degrees: bachelor's, master's. **Classes:** Most classes have 10–19 students. Most lab/discussion sessions have 10–19 students. **Majors with Highest Enrollment:** business administration, management and operations, other; education, other; liberal arts and sciences/liberal studies. **Special Study Options:** cooperative education program, cross-registration, distance learning, double major, dual enrollment, exchange student program (domestic), external degree program, honors program, independent study, internships, liberal arts/career combination, student-designed major, study abroad, teacher certification program, weekend college. **Disability Services:** Special programs offered to physically disabled students include note-taking services, reader services, tape recorders, tutors. **Career Services:** alumni services, career/job search classes, career assessment, internships.

FACILITIES
Housing: Coed dorms, apartments for married students 95% of campus accessible to physically disabled. **Special Academic Facilities/Equipment:** Art gallery, archaeological museum **Computers:** 40% of classrooms, 80% of libraries, 90% of dining areas, 90% of student union, 50% of common outdoor areas have wireless network access. Students can register for classes online.

CAMPUS LIFE
Environment: Village. **Activities:** Choral groups, concert band, dance, drama/theater, jazz band, literary magazine, music ensembles, musical theater, radio station, student government, student newspaper, symphony orchestra 57 registered organizations, 2 honor societies, 4 religious organizations. **Athletics (Intercollegiate):** *Men:* basketball, cross-country, football, track/field (outdoor), track/field (indoor). *Women:* basketball, cross-country, soccer, softball, track/field (outdoor), track/field (indoor), volleyball. **On-Campus Highlights:** Loso Hall, Hoke Union, Community Stadium, Quinn Coliseum, Sports Practice Fields.

ADMISSIONS
Freshman Academic Profile: Average high school GPA 3.2. 14% in top 10% of high school class, 36% in top 25% of high school class, 73% in top 50% of high school class. 98% from public high schools. SAT Math middle 50% range 410-520. SAT Critical Reading middle 50% range 410-530. SAT Writing middle 50% range 410-500. ACT middle 50% range 18-24. Minimum paper TOEFL 520. **Basis for Candidate Selection:** *Very important factors considered include:* academic GPA, rigor of secondary school record. *Important factors considered include:* recommendation(s), talent/ability. *Other factors considered include:* Class rank, application essay, standardized test scores, extracurricular activities, first generation, geographical residence, level of applicant's interest,

volunteer work, work experience. **Freshman Admission Requirements:** High school diploma is required and GED is accepted. *Academic units required:* 4 English, 3 mathematics, 2 science, 2 foreign language. *Academic units recommended:* 4 English, 3 mathematics, 2 science, 2 foreign language. **Freshman Admission Statistics:** 1,503 applied, 67% admitted, 55% enrolled. **Transfer Admission Requirements:** college transcript(s), minimum college GPA of 2.2 required. Lowest grade transferable D-. **General Admission Information:** Application Fee $50. Regular application deadline 9/1. Notification on a rolling basis, beginning on or about 10/1. Nonfall registration accepted. Admission may be deferred for a maximum of 1 year. Credit offered for CEEB Advanced Placement tests.

COSTS AND FINANCIAL AID
Annual in-state tuition $5,918. Annual out-of-state tuition $14,400. Room and board $8,450. Required fees $1,443. Average book expense $1,350. **Required Forms and Deadlines:** FAFSA. **Notification of Awards:** Applicants will be notified of awards on a rolling basis beginning 4/1. **Types of Aid:** *Need-based scholarships/grants:* Federal Pell, SEOG, state scholarships/grants, private scholarships, the school's own gift aid. *Loans:* Subsidized Stafford, Unsubsidized Stafford, PLUS, Federal Perkins. **Student Employment:** Federal Work-Study Program available. Institutional employment available. Off-campus job opportunities are good. **Financial Aid Statistics:** 69% freshmen, 75% undergrads receive need-based scholarship or grant aid. 10% freshmen, 7% undergrads receive non-need-based scholarship or grant aid. 86% freshmen, 91% undergrads receive need-based self-help aid. 13% freshmen, 9% undergrads receive athletic scholarships. 72% undergrads borrow to pay for school. Average cumulative indebtedness $25,109. **Criteria for awarding institutional aid:** *Non-need-based:* academics, art, leadership, minority status, music/drama, state/district residency.

EASTERN UNIVERSITY

1300 Eagle Road, St. Davids, PA 19087-3696
Phone: 610-341-5967 • **Financial Aid Phone:** 610-341-5842
E-mail: ugadm@eastern.edu • **CEEB Code:** 2220
Fax: 610-341-1723 • **Website:** www.eastern.edu • **ACT Code:** 3562

This private school, affiliated with the American Baptist Church, was founded in 1952. It has a 107-acre campus.

RATINGS
Admissions Selectivity Rating: 74   **Fire Safety Rating:** 60*   **Green Rating:** 60*

STUDENTS AND FACULTY
Enrollment: 2,054. **Student Body:** 65% female, 35% male, 52% out-of-state, 1% international. Asian 1%, African American 12%, Caucasian 77%, Hispanic 5%, Native American 0%.
Retention and Graduation: 77% freshmen return for sophomore year. 56% freshmen graduate within 4 years. 63% freshmen graduate within 6 years. 19% grads go on to further study within 1 year. 24% grads pursue arts and sciences degrees. 4% grads pursue law degrees. 4% grads pursue business degrees. **Faculty:** Student/faculty ratio 13:1. 79 full-time faculty, 78% hold PhDs, 16% are members of minority groups, 42% are women. 0% of classes are taught by teaching assistants.

ACADEMICS
Degrees: associate, bachelor's, master's, post-bachelor's certificate, post-master's certificate, transfer associate. **Classes:** Most classes have fewer than 10 students. Most lab/discussion sessions have 10–19 students. **Majors with Highest Enrollment:** business, management, marketing, and related support services, other; elementary education and teaching; social work. **Special Study Options:** Accelerated program, cross-registration, double major, honors program, independent study, internships, student-designed major, study abroad, teacher certification program. **Disability Services:** Special programs offered to physically disabled students include note-taking services, reader services, tape recorders, tutors.

FACILITIES
Housing: Coed dorms, apartments for single students. 75% of campus accessible to physically disabled. **Special Academic Facilities/Equipment:** Planetarium. **Computers:** Students can register for classes online. Administrative functions (other than registration) can be performed online.

CAMPUS LIFE
Environment: Town. **Activities:** Choral groups, concert band, dance, drama/theater, jazz band, literary magazine, music ensembles, musical theater, pep band, student government, student newspaper, yearbook 94 registered organizations, 10 honor societies, 20 religious organizations. **Athletics (Intercolle-**

giate): *Men:* baseball, basketball, golf, soccer, tennis. *Women:* basketball, field hockey, lacrosse, soccer, softball, tennis, volleyball.

ADMISSIONS
Freshman Academic Profile: Average high school GPA 3.3. 19% in top 10% of high school class, 47% in top 25% of high school class, 79% in top 50% of high school class. 75% from public high schools. SAT Math middle 50% range 490-590. SAT Critical Reading middle 50% range 510-610. ACT middle 50% range 19-31. Minimum paper TOEFL 213. **Basis for Candidate Selection:** *Very important factors considered include:* Class rank, rigor of secondary school record, standardized test scores. *Important factors considered include:* application essay, recommendation(s), character/personal qualities, extracurricular activities, volunteer work. *Other factors considered include:* alumni/ae relation, interview, religious affiliation/commitment, talent/ability, work experience. **Freshman Admission Requirements:** High school diploma is required and GED is accepted. **Freshman Admission Statistics:** 1,174 applied, 77% admitted, 43% enrolled. **Transfer Admission Requirements:** High school transcript, college transcript(s), essay or personal statement, minimum college GPA of 2.0 required. Lowest grade transferable C. **General Admission Information:** Application Fee $25. Nonfall registration accepted. Admission may be deferred for a maximum of 12 months. Credit and/or placement offered for CEEB Advanced Placement tests.

COSTS AND FINANCIAL AID
Annual tuition $17,700. Room and board $7,600. Required fees $40. Average book expense $830. **Required Forms and Deadlines:** FAFSA. **Notification of Awards: Types of Aid:** *Need-based scholarships/grants:* Federal Pell, SEOG, state scholarships/grants, private scholarships, the school's own gift aid. *Loans:* Subsidized Stafford, Unsubsidized Stafford, PLUS, Federal Perkins, Alternative loans. **Student Employment:** Highest amount earned per year from on-campus jobs $1,200. **Financial Aid Statistics:** 100% freshmen receive need-based scholarship or grant aid. 34% freshmen receive non-need-based scholarship or grant aid. 88% freshmen receive need-based self-help aid. **Criteria for awarding institutional aid:** *Non-need-based:* academics, leadership, music/drama, religious affiliation, state/district residency.

EASTERN WASHINGTON UNIVERSITY

101 Sutton Hall, Cheney, WA 99004
Phone: 509-359-2397 • **Financial Aid Phone:** 509-359-2314
E-mail: admissions@ewu.edu • **CEEB Code:** 4301
Fax: 509-359-6692 • **Website:** www.ewu.edu • **ACT Code:** 4454

This public school was founded in 1882. It has a 335-acre campus.

RATINGS
Admissions Selectivity Rating: 68   **Fire Safety Rating:** 68   **Green Rating:** 90

STUDENTS AND FACULTY
Enrollment: 11,336. **Student Body:** 55% female, 45% male, 6% out-of-state, 3% international (39 countries represented). Asian 3%, African American 4%, Caucasian 66%, Hispanic 11%, Native American 1%.
Retention and Graduation: 20% freshmen graduate within 4 years. **Faculty:** Student/faculty ratio 23:1. 413 full-time faculty, 98% hold PhDs, 14% are members of minority groups, 44% are women. 0% of classes are taught by teaching assistants.

ACADEMICS
Degrees: bachelor's, certificate, master's, post-master's certificate. **Classes:** Most classes have 20–29 students. Most lab/discussion sessions have 20–29 students. **Special Study Options:** distance learning, double major, English as a Second Language (ESL), honors program, independent study, internships, student-designed major, study abroad, teacher certification program. **Honors Programs:** EWU Honors **Combined Degree Programs:** BA/MA. **Disability Services:** Special programs offered to physically disabled students include note-taking services, reader services, tape recorders.

FACILITIES
Housing: Coed dorms, special housing for disabled students, fraternity/sorority housing, apartments for married students, wellness housing, theme housing. 77% of campus accessible to physically disabled. **Special Academic Facilities/Equipment:** Anthropology museum, on-campus elementary school, education lab, primate research center, marine biology lab, ecological studies lab, wildlife refuge, planetarium. **Computers:** Students can register for classes online. Administrative functions (other than registration) can be performed online.

CAMPUS LIFE
Environment: Town. **Activities:** Choral groups, concert band, dance, drama/theater, jazz band, literary magazine, marching band, music ensembles, musi-

---

cal theater, pep band, radio station, student government, student newspaper, student-run film society, symphony orchestra, Campus Ministries, International Student Organization, Model UN 100 registered organizations, 14 honor societies, 10 religious organizations. 5 fraternities, 5 sororities. **Athletics (Intercollegiate):** *Men:* basketball, cross-country, football, golf, tennis, track/field (outdoor), track/field (indoor). *Women:* basketball, cross-country, golf, soccer, tennis, track/field (outdoor), track/field (indoor), volleyball. **On-Campus Highlights:** Pence Union Building, CyberCafe, Phase Athletic Facilities, Woodward Stadium, Central campus mall, EWU Gallery of Art. **Environmental Initiatives:** Facilities Maintenance Energy Management Program Extensive Physical Plant recycling program Recycle Mania Competition Human Powered paper vehicle competition Ride Share/alternative transportation program

ADMISSIONS
Freshman Academic Profile: Average high school GPA 3.2. 95% from public high schools. SAT Math middle 50% range 430-550. SAT Critical Reading middle 50% range 420-540. SAT Writing middle 50% range 410-520. ACT middle 50% range 18-23. Minimum web-based TOEFL 71. Minimum paper TOEFL 525. **Basis for Candidate Selection:** *Very important factors considered include:* academic GPA, standardized test scores. *Important factors considered include:* application essay, rigor of secondary school record. *Other factors considered include:* character/personal qualities, extracurricular activities, interview, talent/ability, volunteer work, work experience. **Freshman Admission Requirements:** High school diploma or equivalent is not required. *Academic units required:* 4 English, 3 mathematics, 2 science, (1 science labs), 2 foreign language, 3 social studies, 1 visual/performing arts. 4 English, 3 mathematics, 2 science, (1 science labs), 2 foreign language, 3 social studies, 1 visual/performing arts. **Freshman Admission Statistics:** 5,204 applied, 80% admitted, 38% enrolled. **Transfer Admission Requirements:** college transcript(s), essay or personal statement, minimum college GPA of 2.0 required. Lowest grade transferable D-. **General Admission Information:** Application Fee $50. Regular application deadline 8/15. Notification on a rolling basis, beginning on or about 11/1. Nonfall registration accepted. Admission may be deferred for a maximum of 1 year. Credit and/or placement offered for CEEB Advanced Placement tests.

COSTS AND FINANCIAL AID
Average book expense $1,035. **Required Forms and Deadlines:** FAFSA. **Notification of Awards:** Applicants will be notified of awards on a rolling basis beginning 4/1. **Types of Aid:** *Need-based scholarships/grants:* Federal Pell, SEOG, state scholarships/grants, private scholarships, the school's own gift aid. *Loans:* Subsidized Stafford, Unsubsidized Stafford, PLUS, Federal Perkins. **Student Employment:** Highest amount earned per year from on-campus jobs $2,457. **Financial Aid Statistics:** 74% freshmen, 74% undergrads receive need-based scholarship or grant aid. 30% freshmen, 15% undergrads receive non-need-based scholarship or grant aid. 74% freshmen, 81% undergrads receive need-based self-help aid. 2% freshmen, 2% undergrads receive athletic scholarships. 50% freshmen, 49% undergrads receive any aid. 56% undergrads borrow to pay for school. Average cumulative indebtedness $23,604. **Criteria for awarding institutional aid:** *Non-need-based:* academics, alumni affiliation, athletics, state/district residency.

ECKERD COLLEGE

Best 378

4200 54th Avenue South, St.Petersburg, FL 33711
Phone: 727-864-8331 • **Financial Aid Phone:** 727-864-8854
E-mail: admissions@eckerd.edu • **Fax:** 727-866-2304
Website: www.eckerd.edu • **ACT Code:** 731

This private school, affiliated with the Presbyterian Church, was founded in 1958. It has a 188-acre campus.

RATINGS
Admissions Selectivity Rating: 78   **Fire Safety Rating:** 73   **Green Rating:** 84

STUDENTS AND FACULTY
Enrollment: 1,866. **Student Body:** 59 % female, 41% male, 80% out-of-state, 4% international (34 countries represented). Asian 1%, African American 3%, Caucasian 80%, Hispanic 8%.
Retention and Graduation: 81% freshmen return for sophomore year. 57% freshmen graduate within 4 years. 60% freshmen graduate within 6 years. **Faculty:** Student/faculty ratio 13:1. 117 full-time faculty, 93% hold PhDs, 13%

are are members of minority groups, 38% are women. 0% of classes are taught by teaching assistants.

ACADEMICS

Degrees: bachelor's. **Classes:** Most classes have 20–29 students. Most lab/discussion sessions have 10–19 students. **Majors with Highest Enrollment:** business administration and management; environmental studies; marine biology and biological oceanography. **Special Study Options:** Accelerated program, double major, honors program, independent study, internships, liberal arts/career combination, student-designed major, study abroad. **Honors programs:** Ford Apprentice Scholar Program The Honors Program at Eckerd College **Combined degree programs:** BA/MEng. **Disability Services:** Special programs offered to physically disabled students include reader services, tape recorders, tutors. **Career services:** Alumni network, alumni services, career assessment, internships, regional alumni. Career services highlights include We are 90% successful with placing students in internship experiences.

FACILITIES

Housing: Coed dorms, women's dorms, suite-style dorms. wellness housing pet dorms. community service dorms. 95% of campus accessible to physically disabled. **Special Academic Facilities/Equipment:** Language lab, oral communications lab, marine science center. **Computers:** 100% of classrooms, 100% of dorms, 100% of libraries, 100% of dining areas, 100% of student union, 90% of common outdoor areas have wireless network access. Students can register for classes online. Administrative functions (other than registration) can be performed online.

CAMPUS LIFE

Environment: City. **Activities:** Choral groups, concert band, dance, drama/theater, literary magazine, music ensembles, radio station, student government, student newspaper, television station, Campus Ministries, International Student Organization, Model UN 74 registered organizations, 8 honor societies, 3 religious organizations. **Athletics (Intercollegiate):** *Men:* baseball, basketball, golf, sailing, soccer, tennis. *Women:* basketball, golf, sailing, soccer, softball, tennis, volleyball. **On-Campus Highlights:** Peter Armacost Library, Turley Athletic Complex, Gailbraith Marine Science Lab, Hough Campus Center/Campus Pub, Eckerd Waterfront/Wallace Boathouse, Awarded Phi Beta Kappa Chapter in Summer 2003. **Environmental Initiatives:** The yellow bike has in recent years become a new symbol of Eckerd College. The Yellow Bike Program started in the spring of 2004, and since then it has gained national recognition Students, faculty, staff, and even the College President can be spotted riding them. The goal of the program is to have less vehicle traffic which decreases greenhouse gas emissions and reduces our harm to the environment. The bikes on campus will help lead to a mostly walking campus, and an eco-friendly campus. The Yellow Bike Program was recognized in 2005 by the National Wildlife Federation, and it has gained local and national news attention. Eckerd College offers students the opportunity to offset carbon emissions by supporting sustainability efforts on campus. The "Eckerd College Offset Fund is a simple and effective way to reduce overall carbon emissions from school sponsored travel. This carbon offset represents a real reduction in greenhouse gas emissions to balance the emissions produced by flying overseas. Instead of paying money to a third-party company, Eckerd is going to apply the fund directly toward sustainability projects around campus. Last year's funds were used to purchase "Vending Miser" sensors to reduce energy use by vending machines on campus. Eckerd College was awarded a grant in 2007 to develop the first ever reusable to-go system in the United States. This innovative system utilizes a durable plastic container that is "checked out" by students to take food to go. Once the container is returned, it goes through the industrial strength dishwasher and then back into circulation. This is a closed loop method for taking food to go that models the convenience of the current disposable system.

ADMISSIONS

Freshman Academic Profile: Average high school GPA 3.3. SAT Math middle 50% range 500-610. SAT Critical Reading middle 50% range 510-620. ACT middle 50% range 23-28. Minimum web-based TOEFL 79. Minimum paper TOEFL 550. **Basis for Candidate Selection:** Very important factors considered include: academic GPA, rigor of secondary school record. Important factors considered include: application essay, recommendation(s), standardized test scores, character/personal qualities, extracurricular activities, interview, talent/ability. Other factors considered include: Class rank, alumni/ae relation, first generation, level of applicant's interest, volunteer work, work experience. **Freshman Admission Requirements:** High school diploma is required and GED is accepted. **Freshman Admission Statistics:** 3,910 applied, 71% admitted, 19% enrolled. **Transfer Admission Requirements:** college transcript(s), essay or personal statement, statement of good standing from prior institution(s). Minimum college GPA of 2.5 required. Lowest grade transferable C. **General Admission Information:** Application Fee $35. Notification on a rolling basis, beginning on or about 10/1. Nonfall registration accepted. Admission may be deferred for a maximum of 1 year. Credit and/or placement offered for CEEB Advanced Placement tests.

COSTS AND FINANCIAL AID

Annual tuition $35,620. Room and board $9,846. Required fees $306. Average book expense $1,200. **Required Forms and Deadlines:** FAFSA. **Notification of Awards:** Applicants will be notified of awards on a rolling basis beginning 2/15. **Types of Aid:** Need-based scholarships/grants: Federal Pell, SEOG, state scholarships/grants, private scholarships, the school's own gift aid. Loans: Direct Subsidized Stafford, Direct Unsubsidized Stafford, Direct PLUS, Federal Perkins, college/university loans from institutional funds. **Student Employment:** Federal Work-Study Program available. Institutional employment available. Highest amount earned per year from on-campus jobs $2,500. Off-campus job opportunities are excellent. **Financial Aid Statistics:** 100% freshmen, 99% undergrads receive need-based scholarship or grant aid. % freshmen, % undergrads receive non-need-based scholarship or grant aid. 83% freshmen, 84% undergrads receive need-based self-help aid. 1% freshmen, 2% undergrads receive athletic scholarships. 96% freshmen, 93% undergrads receive any aid. 66% undergrads borrow to pay for school. Average cumulative indebtedness $32,245. **Criteria for awarding institutional aid:** Non-need-based: academics, art, athletics, music/drama, religious affiliation, state/district residency.

EDGEWOOD COLLEGE

1000 Edgewood College Drive, Madison, WI 53711-1997
Phone: 608-663-2294 • **Financial Aid Phone:** 608-663-2206
E-mail: admissions@edgewood.edu • **CEEB Code:** 1202
Fax: 608-663-2214 • **Website:** www.edgewood.edu • **ACT Code:** 4582

This private school, affiliated with the Roman Catholic Church, was founded in 1927. It has a 55-acre campus.

RATINGS

Admissions Selectivity Rating: 72   **Fire Safety Rating:** 68   **Green Rating:** 70

STUDENTS AND FACULTY

Enrollment: 1,867. **Student Body:** 71% female, 29% male, 6% out-of-state, 2% international (34 countries represented). Asian 2%, African American 3%, Caucasian 82%, Hispanic 6%, Native American 0%. **Retention and Graduation:** 27% freshmen graduate within 4 years. 51% freshmen graduate within 6 years. **Faculty:** Student/faculty ratio 12:1. 111 full-time faculty, 80% hold PhDs, 13% are members of minority groups, 52% are women. 0% of classes are taught by teaching assistants.

ACADEMICS

Degrees: associate, bachelor's, master's. **Classes:** Most classes have 10–19 students. **Majors with Highest Enrollment:** business/commerce; elementary education and teaching; nursing/registered nurse (rn, asn, bsn, msn). **Special Study Options:** Accelerated program, double major, dual enrollment, honors program, independent study, internships, liberal arts/career combination, student-designed major, study abroad, teacher certification program. **Honors Programs:** We have an Honors Program for undergraduates. **Combined Degree Programs:** Undergraduate degrees from Edgewood and UW/Madison or Marquette. **Disability Services:** Special programs offered to physically disabled students include note-taking services, reader services, tape recorders, tutors. **Career Services:** Alumni network, alumni services, career/job search classes, career assessment, internships, regional alumni. Career Services highlights include Career assessment is providing to all incoming students. Career Services are available at no charge to alumni. Provide alumni mentor program.

FACILITIES

Housing: Coed dorms, special housing for disabled students, women's dorms, theme housing. **Special Academic Facilities/Equipment:** DeRicci Art Gallery, and Science Exploration Center. **Computers:** 90% of classrooms, 100% of dorms, 100% of libraries, 100% of dining areas, 100% of student union, 80% of common outdoor areas have wireless network access. Students can register for classes online. Administrative functions (other than registration) can be performed online.

CAMPUS LIFE

Environment: City. **Activities:** Choral groups, concert band, dance, drama/theater, jazz band, literary magazine, marching band, music ensembles, musical theater, pep band, student government, student newspaper, symphony orchestra, Campus Ministries, International Student Organization 45 registered organizations, 4 honor societies, 1 religious organizations. **Athletics (Intercollegiate):** *Men:* baseball, basketball, cross-country, golf, soccer, tennis, track/field (outdoor), track/field (indoor). *Women:* basketball, cross-country, golf, soccer, softball, tennis, track/field (outdoor), track/field (indoor), volleyball. **On-Campus Highlights:** Dominican Hall, Mazzuchelli Hall, Lake Wingra Boardwalk, Predolin Humanities Center, SondeRegger Science Center. **Environmental Initiatives:** Dominican Hall.

ADMISSIONS

Freshman Academic Profile: Average high school GPA 3.3. 9% in top 10% of high school class, 33% in top 25% of high school class, 78% in top 50% of high school class. 93% from public high schools. ACT middle 50% range 20-25. Minimum web-based TOEFL 71. Minimum paper TOEFL 525. **Basis for Candidate Selection:** *Very important factors considered include:* Class rank, academic GPA, standardized test scores. *Other factors considered include:* application essay, recommendation(s). **Freshman Admission Requirements:** High school diploma is required and GED is accepted. *Academic units required:* 4 English, 2 mathematics, 2 science, (1 science labs), 2 foreign language, 2 social studies, 1 history, 0 academic electives. *Academic units recommended:* 4 English, 2 mathematics, 2 science, (1 science labs), 2 foreign language, 2 social studies, 1 history, 0 academic electives, 0 **Freshman Admission Statistics:** 1,292 applied, 72% admitted, 32% enrolled. **Transfer Admission Requirements:** High school transcript, college transcript(s), minimum college GPA of 2.0 required. Lowest grade transferable C–. **General Admission Information:** Application Fee $25. Regular application deadline 8/14. Notification on a rolling basis, beginning on or about 9/15. Nonfall registration accepted. Admission may be deferred for a maximum of 12 months. Credit and/or placement offered for CEEB Advanced Placement tests.

COSTS AND FINANCIAL AID

Annual tuition $23,740. Room and board $8,476. Average book expense $850. **Required Forms and Deadlines:** FAFSA, institution's own financial aid form. **Notification of Awards:** Applicants will be notified of awards on a rolling basis beginning 3/15. **Types of Aid:** *Need-based scholarships/grants:* Federal Pell, SEOG, state scholarships/grants, private scholarships, the school's own gift aid. *Loans:* Subsidized Stafford, Unsubsidized Stafford, PLUS, Federal Perkins, state loans, college/university loans from institutional funds. **Student Employment:** Federal Work-Study Program available. Institutional employment available. Highest amount earned per year from on-campus jobs $2,000. Off-campus job opportunities are good. **Financial Aid Statistics:** 98% freshmen, 91% undergrads receive need-based scholarship or grant aid. 7% freshmen, 4% undergrads receive non-need-based scholarship or grant aid. 93% freshmen, 96% undergrads receive need-based self-help aid. 100% freshmen, 92% undergrads receive any aid. 78% undergrads borrow to pay for school. Average cumulative indebtedness $34,321. **Criteria for awarding institutional aid:** *Non-need-based:* academics, alumni affiliation, art, leadership, music/drama, religious affiliation.

EDINBORO UNIVERSITY OF PENNSYLVANIA

200 East Normal Street, Edinboro, PA 16444
Phone: 814-732-2761 • **Financial Aid Phone:** 814-732-5555
E-mail: eup_admissions@edinboro.edu • **CEEB Code:** 2651
Fax: 814-732-2420 • **Website:** www.edinboro.edu/ • **ACT Code:** 3702

This public school was founded in 1857. It has a 585-acre campus.

RATINGS

Admissions Selectivity Rating: 69   **Fire Safety Rating:** 93   **Green Rating:** 63

STUDENTS AND FACULTY

Enrollment: 6,301. **Student Body:** 56% female, 44% male, 11% out-of-state, 1% international (31 countries represented). Asian 1%, African American 9%, Caucasian 87%, Hispanic 2%, Native American 0%.
Retention and Graduation: 75% freshmen return for sophomore year. 24% freshmen graduate within 4 years. 47% freshmen graduate within 6 years. **Faculty:** Student/faculty ratio :1. 346 full-time faculty, 7% are members of minority groups, 46% are women. 0% of classes are taught by teaching assistants.

ACADEMICS

Degrees: associate, bachelor's, master's, post-bachelor's certificate, post-master's certificate. **Classes:** Most classes have 20–29 students. **Majors with Highest Enrollment:** art/art studies; elementary education and teaching; political science and government. **Special Study Options:** cooperative education program, cross-registration, distance learning, double major, dual enrollment, honors program, independent study, internships, liberal arts/career combination, student-designed major, study abroad, teacher certification program. **Honors Programs:** Admission to the Upper Division Honors Program, may be made by any full time EUP student who has completed 63 credit hours with an overall GPA of 3.4 or higher. They must also provide letters of support from two faculty members, secure approval of their academic advisor, and complete a proposal for the Senior Project in consultation with the Honors Director, Academic Advisor and and Faculty Member who will supervise the Senior Project. **Combined Degree Programs:** BA/MEng. **Disability Services:** Special programs offered to physically disabled students include note-taking services, reader services, tape recorders, tutors. **Career Services:** Alumni network, alumni services, career/job search classes, career assessment, internships, regional alumni. Career Services highlights include We offer our students extensive internship opportunities.

FACILITIES

Housing: Coed dorms, special housing for disabled students, Living-Learning and Suite Style housing. Choosing to become part of a living-learning community is a unique opportunity for any student to live on the same floor with others who share the same major, filed of study, or interest area. Participants will interact with faculty and staff outside of the classroom through programs, activities, and events. Residents are able to gain assistance and ideas from peers who share their strong commitment to the living-learning experience. 98% of campus accessible to physically disabled. **Special Academic Facilities/Equipment:** Planetarium, Solar Observatory, Governor George Leader Speech and Hearing Center, Bates Art Gallery, Bruce Gallery. **Computers:** 90% of classrooms, 30% of dorms, 100% of libraries, 100% of dining areas, 75% of student union, 40% of common outdoor areas have wireless network access. Students can register for classes online. Administrative functions (other than registration) can be performed online.

CAMPUS LIFE

Environment: Rural. **Activities:** Choral groups, dance, drama/theater, jazz band, literary magazine, marching band, music ensembles, opera, radio station, student government, student newspaper, student-run film society, television station, Campus Ministries, International Student Organization 157 registered organizations, 13 honor societies, 4 religious organizations. 10 fraternities, 7 sororities. **Athletics (Intercollegiate):** *Men:* basketball, cross-country, football, swimming, track/field (outdoor), track/field (indoor), wheel-chair basketball, wrestling. *Women:* basketball, cross-country, lacrosse, soccer, softball, swimming, track/field (outdoor), track/field (indoor), volleyball. **On-Campus Highlights:** Frank G. Pogue Student Center, Baron-Forness Library, R. Benjamin Wiley Arts & Sciences Center, Louis J. Cole Memorial Auditorium, McComb Fieldhouse, Planetarium. **Environmental Initiatives:** LEED Certification for all new building projects. Use of geothermal heat pumps in new construction and HVAC renovations. Energy conservation programs include lighting retrofits, fuel switch, use of variable speed drives.

ADMISSIONS

Freshman Academic Profile: Average high school GPA 3.2. 5% in top 10% of high school class, 20% in top 25% of high school class, 51% in top 50% of high school class. SAT Math middle 50% range 410-520. SAT Critical Reading middle 50% range 415-520. ACT middle 50% range 17-23. Minimum web-based TOEFL 61. Minimum paper TOEFL 500. **Basis for Candidate Selection:** *Very important factors considered include:* Class rank, academic GPA, rigor of secondary school record, standardized test scores. *Other factors considered include:* application essay, recommendation(s), character/personal qualities, extracurricular activities, interview, talent/ability, volunteer work, work experience. **Freshman Admission Requirements:** High school diploma is required and GED is accepted. **Freshman Admission Statistics:** 4,411 applied, 73% admitted, 44% enrolled. **Transfer Admission Requirements:** High school transcript, college transcript(s), statement of good standing from prior institution(s). Minimum college GPA of 2.0 required. Lowest grade transferable C–. **General Admission Information:** Application Fee $30. Notification on a rolling basis, beginning on or about 9/15. Nonfall registration accepted. Admission may be deferred for a maximum of 1 year. Credit and/or placement offered for CEEB Advanced Placement tests.

COSTS AND FINANCIAL AID

Annual in-state tuition $5,554. Annual out-of-state tuition $8,332. Room and board $7,130. Average book expense $900. **Required Forms and Deadlines:** FAFSA. **Notification of Awards:** Applicants will be notified of awards on a rolling basis beginning 3/22. **Types of Aid:** *Need-based scholarships/grants:* Federal Pell, SEOG, state scholarships/grants, private scholarships, the school's own gift aid. *Loans:* Direct Subsidized Stafford, Direct Unsubsidized Stafford, Subsidized Stafford, Unsubsidized Stafford, PLUS, Federal Perkins, Federal Nursing. **Student Employment:** Federal Work-Study Program available. Institutional employment available. Highest amount earned per year from on-campus jobs $7,233. Off-campus job opportunities are good. **Financial Aid Statistics:** 90% freshmen, 92% undergrads receive need-based scholarship or grant aid. 97% freshmen, 96% undergrads receive non-need-based scholarship or grant aid. 85% freshmen, 88% undergrads receive need-based self-help aid. 3% freshmen, 2% undergrads receive athletic scholarships. 91% freshmen, 88% undergrads receive any aid. 46% undergrads borrow to pay for school. Average cumulative indebtedness $21,518. **Criteria for awarding institutional aid:** *Non-need-based:* academics, alumni affiliation, art, athletics, job skills, leadership, minority status, music/drama, religious affiliation, state/district residency.

ELIZABETH CITY STATE UNIVERSITY

1704 Weeksville Road, Elizabeth City, NC 27909
Phone: 252-335-3305
E-mail: admissions@mail.ecsu.edu • **CEEB Code:** 5629
Fax: 252-335-3537 • **Website:** www.ecsu.edu • **ACT Code:** 3095

This public school was founded in 1891. It has a 114-acre campus.

RATINGS
Admissions Selectivity Rating: 65   **Fire Safety Rating:** 60*   **Green Rating:** 60*

STUDENTS AND FACULTY
Enrollment: 2,015. **Student Body:** 62% female, 38% male, 12% out-of-state, 0% international. Asian 0%, African American 77%, Caucasian 22%, Hispanic 1%, Native American 0%.
Retention and Graduation: 39% freshmen graduate within 4 years. 51% freshmen graduate within 6 years. 20% grads go on to further study within 1 year. 20% grads pursue arts and sciences degrees. **Faculty:** Student/faculty ratio 12:1. 114 full-time faculty, 70% hold PhDs, 80% are members of minority groups, 27% are women.

ACADEMICS
Degrees: bachelor's, master's. **Classes:** Most classes have fewer than 10 students. **Special Study Options:** cooperative education program, distance learning, double major, honors program, independent study, internships, liberal arts/career combination, teacher certification program, weekend college. **Career Services:** alumni services, career/job search classes, career assessment, internships.

FACILITIES
Housing: Coed dorms, men's dorms, women's dorms, apartments for single students, College-leased housing available. **Special Academic Facilities/Equipment:** Lab school, planetarium, science complex, music engineering station. **Computers:** Students can register for classes online. Administrative functions (other than registration) can be performed online.

CAMPUS LIFE
Environment: Village. **Activities:** Choral groups, concert band, dance, drama/theater, jazz band, literary magazine, marching band, music ensembles, musical theater, pep band, radio station, student government, student newspaper, symphony orchestra, television station, yearbook 46 registered organizations, 3 honor societies, 4 religious organizations. 4 fraternities, 4 sororities. **Athletics (Intercollegiate):** *Men:* baseball, basketball, cheerleading, cross-country, football, golf, softball, tennis, track/field (outdoor), volleyball. *Women:* baseball, basketball, cheerleading, cross-country, golf, softball, tennis, track/field (outdoor), volleyball.

ADMISSIONS
Freshman Academic Profile: 99% from public high schools. SAT Math middle 50% range 360-450. SAT Critical Reading middle 50% range 360-450. Minimum paper TOEFL 550. **Basis for Candidate Selection:** *Very important factors considered include:* rigor of secondary school record, standardized test scores, character/personal qualities, geographical residence, state residency. *Important factors considered include:* Class rank, racial/ethnic status, talent/ability. *Other factors considered include:* application essay, recommendation(s), alumni/ae relation, extracurricular activities, interview, religious affiliation/commitment, work experience. **Freshman Admission Requirements:** High school diploma is required and GED is accepted. *Academic units required:* 4 English, 3 mathematics, 3 science, 1 social studies, 1 history, 8 academic electives. *Academic units recommended:* 4 English, 3 mathematics, 3 science, 1 social studies, 1 history, 8 academic electives. **Freshman Admission Statistics:** 1,262 applied, 77% admitted, 48% enrolled. **Transfer Admission Requirements:** High school transcript, college transcript(s), statement of good standing from prior institution(s). Minimum college GPA of 2.0 required. Lowest grade transferable C. **General Admission Information:** Application Fee $30. Regular application deadline 8/1. Nonfall registration accepted. Admission may be deferred for a maximum of one year. Credit and/or placement offered for CEEB Advanced Placement tests.

COSTS AND FINANCIAL AID
Required Forms and Deadlines: FAFSA, institution's own financial aid form. **Notification of Awards:** Applicants will be notified of awards on or about 4/1. **Types of Aid:** *Need-based scholarships/grants:* Federal Pell, SEOG, state scholarships/grants, private scholarships, the school's own gift aid. *Loans:* Subsidized Stafford, Unsubsidized Stafford, PLUS, Federal Perkins, college/university loans from institutional funds. **Student Employment:** Federal Work-Study Program available. Highest amount earned per year from on-campus jobs $643. Off-campus job opportunities are fair.

ELIZABETHTOWN COLLEGE

Leffler House, Elizabethtown, PA 17022
Phone: 717-361-1400 • **Financial Aid Phone:** 717-361-1404
E-mail: admissions@etown.edu • **CEEB Code:** 2225
Fax: 717-361-1365 • **Website:** www.etown.edu • **ACT Code:** 3568

This private school, affiliated with the Church of Brethren Church, was founded in 1899. It has a 193-acre campus.

RATINGS
Admissions Selectivity Rating: 83   **Fire Safety Rating:** 61   **Green Rating:** 60*

STUDENTS AND FACULTY
Enrollment: 2,096. **Student Body:** 65% female, 35% male, 34% out-of-state, 2% international (17 countries represented). Asian 2%, African American 1%, Caucasian 82%, Hispanic 1%, Native American 0%.
Retention and Graduation: 84% freshmen return for sophomore year. 64% freshmen graduate within 4 years. 67% freshmen graduate within 6 years. 20% grads go on to further study within 1 year. **Faculty:** Student/faculty ratio 13:1. 125 full-time faculty, 82% hold PhDs, 9% are members of minority groups, 40% are women. 0% of classes are taught by teaching assistants.

ACADEMICS
Degrees: associate, bachelor's, certificate, diploma, master's, post-bachelor's certificate. **Classes:** Most classes have 10–19 students. Most lab/discussion sessions have 10–19 students. **Majors with Highest Enrollment:** biology; business/commerce; communication, journalism, and related programs, other. **Special Study Options:** Accelerated program, cooperative education program, distance learning, double major, dual enrollment, English as a Second Language (ESL), exchange student program (domestic), honors program, independent study, internships, liberal arts/career combination, study abroad, teacher certification program, 2+2, 3+3 and 4+2 (PT doctorate) programs with Thomas Jefferson University in nursing, physical therapy, labratory sceinces, diagnostic imaging, 3+2 in engineering with Penn State University, 3+2 with Duke University in Forestry, 3+3 in physical therapy with Widener University and University of Maryland, Baltimore County, 3+1 in Invasive Cardiovascular Technology with Lancaster Institute for Health Education, articulation agreements with Lehigh Unversity, Rutgers Univesity, Loyola College (MD) and Penn State University, Harrisburg to satisfy 150-hour requirment in Accounting. **Combined Degree Programs:** BA/MD, BA/MA, 3+3 physical therapy with Thomas Jefferson Univers. **Disability Services:** Special programs offered to physically disabled students include tape recorders, tutors.

FACILITIES
Housing: Coed dorms, special housing for disabled students, special housing for international students, women's dorms, apartments for single students, Off-campus houses for student service-learning groups. 75% of campus accessible to physically disabled. **Special Academic Facilities/Equipment:** Art gallery, Meetinghouse/center for Anabaptist and Pietist studies, chapel/performance center, Fourier transform multinuclear NMR spectrometer, blood gas analyzer, scanning densiometer, PCR machine, radiometer/data logger, automated ion analyzer, computerized language lab **Computers:** Students can register for classes online. Administrative functions (other than registration) can be performed online.

CAMPUS LIFE
Environment: Village. **Activities:** Choral groups, concert band, dance, drama/theater, jazz band, literary magazine, music ensembles, musical theater, pep band, radio station, student government, student newspaper, student-run film society, symphony orchestra, television station, yearbook 80 registered organizations, 16 honor societies, 6 religious organizations. **Athletics (Intercollegiate):** *Men:* baseball, basketball, cross-country, diving, golf, lacrosse, soccer, swimming, tennis, track/field (outdoor), track/field (indoor), wrestling. *Women:* basketball, cross-country, diving, field hockey, lacrosse, soccer, softball, swimming, tennis, track/field (outdoor), track/field (indoor), volleyball. **On-Campus Highlights:** Brossman Commons Students Center, The Jay's Nest Snack Bar, The Dell, The Blue Bean Cafe, The Ira R Herr Soccer Complex, During the academic year it is great to hang out in The Dell, located in the middle of campus, on a hot day for frisbee or just soaking up the sun. The Ira R Herr Soccer Complex is the place to be to see the Blue Jays men's or women's soccer team in action--either day or night--the stadium is one of the finest soccer venues in the East.

ADMISSIONS
Freshman Academic Profile: Average high school GPA 3.6. 30% in top 10% of high school class, 65% in top 25% of high school class, 93% in top 50% of high school class. 80% from public high schools. SAT Math middle 50% range 510-630. SAT Critical Reading middle 50% range 510-610. ACT middle 50% range 21-26. Minimum paper TOEFL 525. **Basis for Candidate Selection:** *Very important factors considered include:* rigor of secondary school

record. *Important factors considered include:* Class rank, recommendation(s), standardized test scores, interview, racial/ethnic status, volunteer work. *Other factors considered include:* application essay, alumni/ae relation, character/personal qualities, extracurricular activities, geographical residence, religious affiliation/commitment, state residency, talent/ability, work experience. **Freshman Admission Requirements:** High school diploma is required and GED is accepted. *Academic units required:* 4 English, 3 mathematics, 2 science, (2 science labs), 2 foreign language, 2 social studies, 2 history. *Academic units recommended:* 4 English, 3 mathematics, 2 science, (2 science labs), 2 foreign language, 2 social studies, 2 history. **Freshman Admission Statistics:** 2,923 applied, 64% admitted, 29% enrolled. **Transfer Admission Requirements:** High school transcript, college transcript(s), essay or personal statement, standardized test scores, statement of good standing from prior institution(s). Minimum college GPA of 2.5 required. Lowest grade transferable C. **General Admission Information:** Application Fee $30. Notification on a rolling basis, beginning on or about 11/15. Nonfall registration accepted. Admission may be deferred for a maximum of 1 year. Credit and/or placement offered for CEEB Advanced Placement tests.

COSTS AND FINANCIAL AID

Annual tuition $34,830. Room and board $8,800. Average book expense $1,000. **Required Forms and Deadlines:** FAFSA, institution's own financial aid form-Federal Tax Records. **Notification of Awards:** Applicants will be notified of awards on a rolling basis beginning 3/1. **Types of Aid:** *Need-based scholarships/grants:* Federal Pell, SEOG, state scholarships/grants, private scholarships, the school's own gift aid. *Loans:* Subsidized Stafford, Unsubsidized Stafford, PLUS, Federal Perkins, state loans. **Student Employment: Financial Aid Statistics:** 100% freshmen, 100% undergrads receive need-based scholarship or grant aid. 15% freshmen, 1% undergrads receive non-need-based scholarship or grant aid. 84% freshmen, 8% undergrads receive need-based self-help aid. 96% freshmen, 94% undergrads receive any aid. 82% undergrads borrow to pay for school. **Criteria for awarding institutional aid:** *Non-need-based:* academics, art, music/drama, religious affiliation.

ELMHURST COLLEGE

190 S Prospect Avenue, Elmhurst, IL 60126
Phone: 630-617-3400 • **Financial Aid Phone:** 630-617-3075
E-mail: admit@elmhurst.edu • **CEEB Code:** 1204
Fax: 630-617-5501 • **Website:** public.elmhurst.edu • **ACT Code:** 1020

This private school, affiliated with the United Church of Christ Church, was founded in 1871. It has a 38-acre campus.

RATINGS
Admissions Selectivity Rating: 78   **Fire Safety Rating:** 77   **Green Rating:** 75

STUDENTS AND FACULTY
Student Body: (36 countries represented).
Retention and Graduation: 78% freshmen return for sophomore year. 74% freshmen graduate within 6 years. 17% grads go on to further study within 1 year. 1% grads pursue law degrees. 8% grads pursue business degrees. 2% grads pursue medical degrees. **Faculty:** Student/faculty ratio 13:1. 151 full-time faculty. 0% of classes are taught by teaching assistants.

ACADEMICS
Degrees: bachelor's, master's. **Classes:** Most classes have 20–29 students. **Majors with Highest Enrollment:** business administration and management; elementary education and teaching; nursing/registered nurse (rn, asn, bsn, msn). **Special Study Options:** Accelerated program, double major, dual enrollment, honors program, independent study, internships, liberal arts/career combination, student-designed major, study abroad, teacher certification program. **Honors Programs:** The Elmhurst College Honors program provides a challenging set of educational experiences for the most academically students featuring small, stimulating seminar courses where class discussions are lively and engaging; opportunities to conduct and present professional-level research; private receptions with distinguished guest speakers; trips to theatre and dance performances, social events, and more. **Combined Degree Programs:** BA/MEng. **Disability Services:** Special programs offered to physically disabled students include note-taking services, reader services, tape recorders, tutors. **Career Services:** Alumni network, career/job search classes, career assessment, internships Career Services highlights include Elmhurst College's Center for Professional Excellence provides a comprehensive suite of services to link students' academic expereinces with opportunities to explore career options and to prepare for future careers.

FACILITIES
Housing: Coed dorms, apartments for single students. 95% of campus accessible to physically disabled. **Special Academic Facilities/Equipment:** Accelerator/art space, language lab, recording studio, computer science/technology center, four electron microscopes. **Computers:** Students can register for classes online. Administrative functions (other than registration) can be performed online.

CAMPUS LIFE
Environment: Town. **Activities:** Choral groups, concert band, dance, drama/theater, jazz band, literary magazine, music ensembles, musical theater, radio station, student government, student newspaper, symphony orchestra, yearbook, Campus Ministries, International Student Organization, Model UN 106 registered organizations, 15 honor societies, 6 religious organizations. 3 fraternities, 6 sororities. **Athletics (Intercollegiate):** *Men:* baseball, basketball, cross-country, football, golf, soccer, tennis, track/field (outdoor), wrestling. *Women:* basketball, bowling, cross-country, golf, soccer, softball, tennis, track/field (outdoor), volleyball. **On-Campus Highlights:** Alumni Circle, Frick Center, Library, Tyrrell Fitness Center, Circle Hall. **Environmental Initiatives:** Development and execution of our Sustainability Plan. It is a living document that continues to expand as goals are achieved. The construction of our LEED certified Residence Hall in 2008 with its surrounding native prairie garden and permeable paver parking lot. College/Community recycling events which include student leadership and have operated for the past two years. Within this framework we are expanding areas of cooperation to establishing a College/Community compostable material collection route and expanding initial electronic equipment recycling programs to include collection of bicycles, eye glasses, and other household products.

ADMISSIONS
Freshman Academic Profile: Average high school GPA 3.4. 92% from public high schools. SAT Math middle 50% range 515-610. SAT Critical Reading middle 50% range 480-590. SAT Writing middle 50% range 475-595. ACT middle 50% range 21-26. Minimum paper TOEFL 550. **Basis for Candidate Selection:** *Very important factors considered include:* Class rank, academic GPA, rigor of secondary school record, standardized test scores. *Important factors considered include:* application essay, recommendation(s), interview. *Other factors considered include:* alumni/ae relation, character/personal qualities, extracurricular activities, talent/ability. **Freshman Admission Requirements:** High school diploma is required and GED is accepted. *Academic units required:* 4 English, 2 mathematics, 2 science, (2 science labs), 2 social studies, 1 history, 4 academic electives. *Academic units recommended:* 4 English, 2 mathematics, 2 science, (2 science labs), 2 social studies, 1 history, 4 academic electives. **Freshman Admission Statistics:** 3,056 applied, 68% admitted, 27% enrolled. **Transfer Admission Requirements:** High school transcript, college transcript(s), statement of good standing from prior institution(s). Minimum college GPA of 2.6 required. Lowest grade transferable C. **General Admission Information:** Regular application deadline 7/15. Notification on a rolling basis, beginning on or about 11/1. Nonfall registration accepted. Admission may be deferred for a maximum of 2 years. Credit offered for CEEB Advanced Placement tests.

COSTS AND FINANCIAL AID
Annual tuition $31,450. Room and board $8,938. Required fees $200. Average book expense $1,500. **Required Forms and Deadlines:** FAFSA. **Notification of Awards:** Applicants will be notified of awards on a rolling basis beginning 2/21. **Types of Aid:** *Need-based scholarships/grants:* Federal Pell, SEOG, state scholarships/grants, private scholarships, the school's own gift aid. *Loans:* Direct Subsidized Stafford, Direct Unsubsidized Stafford, Direct PLUS, Federal Perkins, Private alternative student loans. **Student Employment:** Federal Work-Study Program available. Institutional employment available. Highest amount earned per year from on-campus jobs $3,000. Off-campus job opportunities are excellent. **Financial Aid Statistics:** 99% freshmen, 99% undergrads receive need-based scholarship or grant aid. 22% freshmen, 23% undergrads receive non-need-based scholarship or grant aid. 83% freshmen, 88% undergrads receive need-based self-help aid. 95% freshmen, 87% undergrads receive any aid. 77% undergrads borrow to pay for school. Average cumulative indebtedness $26,507. **Criteria for awarding institutional aid:** *Non-need-based:* academics, alumni affiliation, art, minority status, music/drama, religious affiliation, state/district residency.

See page 1070.

ELMIRA COLLEGE

One Park Place, Elmira, NY 14901
Phone: 607-735-1724 • **Financial Aid Phone:** 607-735-1728
E-mail: admissions@elmira.edu • **CEEB Code:** 2226
Fax: 607-735-1718 • **Website:** www.elmira.edu • **ACT Code:** 2736

This private school was founded in 1855. It has a 50-acre campus.

RATINGS
Admissions Selectivity Rating: 74   **Fire Safety Rating:** 78   **Green Rating:** 60*

STUDENTS AND FACULTY
Enrollment: 1,302. **Student Body:** 73% female, 27% male, 53% out-of-state, 4% international (31 countries represented). Asian 1%, African American 3%, Caucasian 78%, Hispanic 2%, Native American 1%.
Retention and Graduation: 71% freshmen return for sophomore year. 58% freshmen graduate within 6 years. 62% grads go on to further study within 1 year. 8% grads pursue law degrees. 6% grads pursue business degrees. 2% grads pursue medical degrees. **Faculty:** Student/faculty ratio 11:1. 92 full-time faculty, 5% are members of minority groups, 54% are women. 0% of classes are taught by teaching assistants.

ACADEMICS
Degrees: bachelor's, master's. **Classes:** Most classes have 10–19 students. Most lab/discussion sessions have 10–19 students. **Majors with Highest Enrollment:** business/commerce; elementary education and teaching; psychology. **Special Study Options:** Accelerated program, double major, English as a Second Language (ESL), exchange student program (domestic), independent study, internships, liberal arts/career combination, student-designed major, study abroad, teacher certification program. **Combined Degree Programs:** 3-2 Chemical Engineering with Clarkson University.

FACILITIES
Housing: Coed dorms, special housing for disabled students, women's dorms, apartments for single students. 25% of campus accessible to physically disabled. **Special Academic Facilities/Equipment:** Center for Mark Twain studies, American studies center.

CAMPUS LIFE
Environment: Town. **Activities:** Choral groups, concert band, dance, drama/theater, literary magazine, music ensembles, musical theater, pep band, radio station, student government, student newspaper, yearbook 85 registered organizations, 13 honor societies, 3 religious organizations. **Athletics (Intercollegiate):** *Men:* basketball, cheerleading, golf, ice hockey, lacrosse, soccer, tennis. *Women:* basketball, cheerleading, field hockey, golf, ice hockey, lacrosse, soccer, softball, tennis, volleyball. **On-Campus Highlights:** Emerson Hall, Mark Twain Study, Towers, Campus Center, The Puddle.

ADMISSIONS
Freshman Academic Profile: Average high school GPA 3.4. 35% in top 10% of high school class, 56% in top 25% of high school class, 89% in top 50% of high school class. 65% from public high schools. SAT Math middle 50% range 480-590. SAT Critical Reading middle 50% range 490-600. ACT middle 50% range 24-27. Minimum web-based TOEFL 64. Minimum paper TOEFL 500. **Basis for Candidate Selection:** *Very important factors considered include:* Class rank, academic GPA, rigor of secondary school record, character/personal qualities. *Important factors considered include:* application essay, recommendation(s), standardized test scores, extracurricular activities. *Other factors considered include:* alumni/ae relation, first generation, geographical residence, interview, level of applicant's interest, racial/ethnic status, talent/ability, volunteer work, work experience. **Freshman Admission Requirements:** High school diploma is required and GED is accepted. *Academic units required:* 4 English, 3 mathematics, 3 science, (2 science labs), 3 social studies, 1 history, 2 academic electives. *Academic units recommended:* 4 English, 3 mathematics, 3 science, (2 science labs), 3 social studies, 1 history, 2 academic electives. **Freshman Admission Statistics:** 2,424 applied, 75% admitted, 19% enrolled. **Transfer Admission Requirements:** college transcript(s), essay or personal statement, statement of good standing from prior institution(s). Minimum college GPA of 2.0 required. Lowest grade transferable C–. **General Admission Information:** Application Fee $50. Early decision application deadline 11/15. Regular application deadline 3/1. Notification on a rolling basis, beginning on or about 10/15. Nonfall registration accepted. Admission may be deferred for a maximum of 1 year. Credit and/or placement offered for CEEB Advanced Placement tests.

COSTS AND FINANCIAL AID
Annual tuition $35,500. Room and board $11,500. Required fees $1,400. Average book expense $600. **Required Forms and Deadlines:** FAFSA, state aid formState aid forms if applicable (NY, VT, RI). **Notification of Awards:** Applicants will be notified of awards on a rolling basis beginning 2/1. **Types of Aid:** *Need-based scholarships/grants:* Federal Pell, SEOG, state scholarships/grants, private scholarships, the school's own gift aid. *Loans:* Subsidized Stafford, Unsubsidized Stafford, PLUS, Federal Perkins, college/university loans from institutional funds, GATE Student Loan; Private Alternative Loans. **Student Employment:** Federal Work-Study Program available. Institutional employment available. Highest amount earned per year from on-campus jobs $1,000. Off-campus job opportunities are good. **Financial Aid Statistics:** 100% freshmen, 100% undergrads receive need-based scholarship or grant aid. 19% freshmen, 14% undergrads receive non-need-based scholarship or grant aid. 78% freshmen, 82% undergrads receive need-based self-help aid. 82% undergrads borrow to pay for school. Average cumulative indebtedness $26,528. **Criteria for awarding institutional aid:** *Non-need-based:* academics, leadership.

See page 1072.

ELON UNIVERSITY

100 Campus Drive, Elon, NC 27244-2010
Phone: 336-278-3566 • **Financial Aid Phone:** 336-278-7640
E-mail: admissions@elon.edu • **CEEB Code:** 5183
Fax: 336-278-7699 • **Website:** www.elon.edu • **ACT Code:** 3096

This private school, affiliated with the United Church of Christ Church, was founded in 1889. It has a 575-acre campus.

RATINGS
Admissions Selectivity Rating: 92   **Fire Safety Rating:** 82   **Green Rating:** 96

STUDENTS AND FACULTY
Enrollment: 5,357. **Student Body:** 59% female, 41% male, 75% out-of-state, 7% international (10 countries represented). Asian 2%, African American 6%, Caucasian 82%, Hispanic 4%, Native American 0%.
Retention and Graduation: 77% freshmen graduate within 4 years. 83% freshmen graduate within 6 years. 22% grads go on to further study within 1 year. 15% grads pursue arts and sciences degrees. 8% grads pursue law degrees. 4% grads pursue business degrees. 6% grads pursue medical degrees. **Faculty:** Student/faculty ratio 13:1. 385 full-time faculty, 86% hold PhDs, 16% are members of minority groups, 48% are women. 0% of classes are taught by teaching assistants.

ACADEMICS
Degrees: bachelor's, master's. **Classes:** Most classes have 10–19 students. Most lab/discussion sessions have 10–19 students. **Majors with Highest Enrollment:** business/commerce; communication studies/speech communication and rhetoric; education. **Special Study Options:** Accelerated program, cross-registration, distance learning, double major, dual enrollment, English as a Second Language (ESL), exchange student program (domestic), honors program, independent study, internships, liberal arts/career combination, student-designed major, study abroad, teacher certification program. **Honors Programs:** Forty freshmen are selected for the Honors Fellows program, which has benefits of specialized courses, $2,500-$10,000 scholarship renewable annually based on academic performance and participation in the program, $1,000 study abroad grant, development and presentation of their honors thesis, and housing options such as a living-learning community for Fellows. **Combined Degree Programs:** BS/BS (3-2) Engineering. **Disability Services:** Special programs offered to physically disabled students include note-taking services, reader services, tape recorders, tutors. **Career Services:** Alumni network, alumni services, career/job search classes, career assessment, internships, regional alumni. Career Services highlights include All students are required to particpate in an experiential learning experience and most Elon students particpate in internship/coop.

FACILITIES
Housing: Coed dorms, men's dorms, special housing for international students, women's dorms, fraternity/sorority housing, apartments for single students, wellness housing, theme housing, 80% of campus accessible to physically disabled. **Special Academic Facilities/Equipment:** Resource center, fine arts center with recital hall, theatre, television studios, music rooms, campus center, athletic center, art gallery. **Computers:** 100% of classrooms, 100% of dorms, 100% of libraries, 100% of dining areas, 100% of student union, 25% of common outdoor areas have wireless network access. Students can register for classes online. Administrative functions (other than registration) can be performed online.

CAMPUS LIFE

Environment: Town. **Activities:** Choral groups, concert band, dance, drama/theater, jazz band, literary magazine, marching band, music ensembles, musical theater, pep band, radio station, student government, student newspaper, student-run film society, symphony orchestra, television station, yearbook, Campus Ministries, International Student Organization, Model UN 150 registered organizations, 27 honor societies, 10 religious organizations. 11 fraternities, 12 sororities. **Athletics (Intercollegiate):** *Men:* baseball, basketball, cheerleading, cross-country, football, golf, soccer, tennis. *Women:* basketball, cheerleading, cross-country, golf, soccer, softball, tennis, track/field (outdoor), track/field (indoor), volleyball. **On-Campus Highlights:** Belk Library, Rhodes Football Stadium, Koury Business Center, Moseley Student Center, Koury Athletic Center, Lindner Hall, Academic Village. **Environmental Initiatives:** reducing greenhouse gas emissions conserving resources educating the community

ADMISSIONS

Freshman Academic Profile: Average high school GPA 4.0. 26% in top 10% of high school class, 65% in top 25% of high school class, 91% in top 50% of high school class. 67% from public high schools. SAT Math middle 50% range 560-660. SAT Critical Reading middle 50% range 570-660. SAT Writing middle 50% range 570-670. ACT middle 50% range 25-29. Minimum web-based TOEFL 79. Minimum paper TOEFL 550. **Basis for Candidate Selection:** *Very important factors considered include:* academic GPA, rigor of secondary school record, standardized test scores. *Important factors considered include:* application essay, recommendation(s), alumni/ae relation, extracurricular activities, talent/ability, volunteer work, work experience. *Other factors considered include:* Class rank, character/personal qualities, first generation, geographical residence, level of applicant's interest, racial/ethnic status, state residency. **Freshman Admission Requirements:** High school diploma is required and GED is accepted. *Academic units required:* 4 English, 3 mathematics, 3 science, (1 science labs), 2 foreign language, 1 social studies, 2 history. *Academic units recommended:* 4 English, 3 mathematics, 3 science, (1 science labs), 2 foreign language, 1 social studies, 2 history. **Freshman Admission Statistics:** 10,241 applied, 52% admitted, 27% enrolled. **Transfer Admission Requirements:** High school transcript, college transcript(s), standardized test scores, statement of good standing from prior institution(s). Minimum college GPA of 2.7 required. Lowest grade transferable C–. **General Admission Information:** Application Fee $50. Early decision application deadline 11/1. Regular application deadline 1/10. Regular notification 3/15. Nonfall registration not accepted. Admission may be deferred for a maximum of 1 year. Credit and/or placement offered for CEEB Advanced Placement tests.

COSTS AND FINANCIAL AID

Annual tuition $28,633. Room and board $9,480. Required fees $347. Average book expense $900. **Required Forms and Deadlines:** FAFSA, institution's own financial aid form, CSS/Financial Aid PROFILE. **Notification of Awards:** Applicants will be notified of awards on a rolling basis beginning 3/30. **Types of Aid:** *Need-based scholarships/grants:* Federal Pell, SEOG, state scholarships/grants, private scholarships, the school's own gift aid. *Loans:* Subsidized Stafford, Unsubsidized Stafford, PLUS, Federal Perkins, state loans, Privately funded alternative loans. **Student Employment:** Federal Work-Study Program available. Institutional employment available. Highest amount earned per year from on-campus jobs $2,500. Off-campus job opportunities are good. **Financial Aid Statistics:** 85% freshmen, 90% undergrads receive need-based scholarship or grant aid. 49% freshmen, 47% undergrads receive non-need-based scholarship or grant aid. 80% freshmen, 82% undergrads receive need-based self-help aid. 4% freshmen, 5% undergrads receive athletic scholarships. 67% freshmen, 63% undergrads receive any aid. 44% undergrads borrow to pay for school. Average cumulative indebtedness $28,183. **Criteria for awarding institutional aid:** *Non-need-based:* academics, art, athletics, leadership, music/drama, state/district residency.

EMBRY RIDDLE AERONAUTICAL UNIVERSITY— PRESCOTT

3700 Willow Creek, Prescott, AZ 86301
Phone: 928-777-6600 • **Financial Aid Phone:** 800-888-3728
E-mail: pradmit@erau.edu • **CEEB Code:** 4305
Fax: 928-777-6606 • **Website:** www.embryriddle.edu • **ACT Code:** 725

This private school was founded in 1926. It has a 539-acre campus.

RATINGS

Admissions Selectivity Rating: 70   **Fire Safety Rating:** 74   **Green Rating:** 60*

STUDENTS AND FACULTY

Enrollment: 1,647. **Student Body:** 17% female, 83% male, 79% out-of-state, 4% international (25 countries represented). Asian 6%, African American 2%, Caucasian 67%, Hispanic 9%, Native American 1%. **Retention and Graduation:** 78% freshmen return for sophomore year. 4% freshmen graduate within 4 years. 61% freshmen graduate within 6 years. 43% grads go on to further study within 1 year. 11% grads pursue arts and sciences degrees. 26% grads pursue business degrees. **Faculty:** Student/faculty ratio 15:1. 98 full-time faculty, 70% hold PhDs, 8% are members of minority groups, 18% are women. 0% of classes are taught by teaching assistants.

ACADEMICS

Degrees: bachelor's, master's. **Classes:** Most classes have 10–19 students. Most lab/discussion sessions have 10–19 students. **Majors with Highest Enrollment:** aeronautics/aviation/aerospace science and technology; aerospace, aeronautical and astronautical engineering; airline/commercial/professional pilot and flight crew. **Special Study Options:** Accelerated program, cooperative education program, distance learning, double major, dual enrollment, English as a Second Language (ESL), exchange student program (domestic), honors program, independent study, internships, Flight Training. **Disability Services:** Special programs offered to physically disabled students include note-taking services, reader services, tape recorders, tutors. **Career Services:** Alumni network, alumni services, career/job search classes, career assessment, internships, regional alumni.

FACILITIES

Housing: Coed dorms, apartments for single students. 50% of campus accessible to physically disabled. **Computers:** 100% of classrooms, 100% of dorms, 100% of libraries, 100% of dining areas, 100% of student union, 80% of common outdoor areas have wireless network access. Administrative functions (other than registration) can be performed online.

CAMPUS LIFE

Environment: Town. **Activities:** dance, literary magazine, music ensembles, radio station, student government, student newspaper 85 registered organizations, 5 honor societies, 2 religious organizations. 5 fraternities, 3 sororities. **Athletics (Intercollegiate):** *Men:* wrestling. **On-Campus Highlights:** Flight Line Facilities, Wind Tunnel Labs, Outdoor Pool and Racquetball, Tennis Area, The Hangar - Cafeteria, Two athletic facilities and weight room, Embry-Riddle Prescott is culturally diverse with students representing 49 states and 24 countries for a combined total of approximately 1700 students. Embry-Riddle Prescott is home to the Golden Eagles Flight Team, a nationally ranked flight team. In the last 22 years, the Golden Eagles are undefeated at the regional level, and the National Championship has been secured six times.

ADMISSIONS

Freshman Academic Profile: Average high school GPA 3.5. 25% in top 10% of high school class, 52% in top 25% of high school class, 82% in top 50% of high school class. Math middle 50% range 500-640. SAT Critical Reading middle 50% range 470-600. ACT middle 50% range 22-28. Minimum web-based TOEFL 79. Minimum paper TOEFL 550. **Basis for Candidate Selection:** *Very important factors considered include:* academic GPA, rigor of secondary school record, standardized test scores. *Other factors considered include:* Class rank, recommendation(s), extracurricular activities, first generation, talent/ability, volunteer work. **Freshman Admission Requirements: Freshman Admission Statistics:** 1,148 applied, 86% admitted, 42% enrolled. **Transfer Admission Requirements:** college transcript(s). **General Admission Information:** Application Fee $120. Regular application deadline 6/1. Notification on a rolling basis, beginning on or about 2/1. Nonfall registration not accepted. Admission may be deferred for a maximum of 1 year. Credit offered for CEEB Advanced Placement tests.

COSTS AND FINANCIAL AID

Annual tuition $29,520. Room and board $9,340. Required fees $900. Average book expense $1,400. **Required Forms and Deadlines:** FAFSA, institution's own financial aid form, state aid form. **Notification of Awards: Types of Aid:** *Need-based scholarships/grants:* state scholarships/grants, private scholarships, the school's own gift aid, Federal Bursaries and Grants. *Loans:* Federal and provincial loan programs administered by governments. **Student Employment:** Off-campus job opportunities are good. **Financial Aid Statistics:** 97% freshmen, 94% undergrads receive need-based scholarship or grant aid. 75% freshmen, 83% undergrads receive need-based self-help aid. 7% freshmen, 5% undergrads receive athletic scholarships. 94% freshmen, 88% undergrads receive any aid. 71% undergrads borrow to pay for school. Average cumulative indebtedness. **Criteria for awarding institutional aid:** *Non-need-based:* academics, alumni affiliation, art, athletics, leadership, minority status, music/drama, state/district residency.

EMBRY-RIDDLE AERONAUTICAL UNIVERSITY (FL)

600 South Clyde Morris Boulevard, Daytona Beach, FL 32114-3900
Phone: 386-226-6100 • **Financial Aid Phone:** 800-226-6307
E-mail: dbadmit@erau.edu • **CEEB Code:** 5190
Fax: 386-226-7070 • **Website:** www.embryriddle.edu • **ACT Code:** 725

This private school was founded in 1926. It has a 185-acre campus.

RATINGS
Admissions Selectivity Rating: 72   **Fire Safety Rating:** 80   **Green Rating:** 63

STUDENTS AND FACULTY
Enrollment: 4,484. **Student Body:** 15% female, 85% male, 65% out-of-state, 14% international (100 countries represented). Asian 6%, African American 7%, Caucasian 57%, Hispanic 9%, Native American 1%.
Retention and Graduation: 72% freshmen return for sophomore year. 30% freshmen graduate within 4 years. 54% freshmen graduate within 6 years. 41% grads go on to further study within 1 year. 7% grads pursue arts and sciences degrees. 23% grads pursue business degrees. **Faculty:** Student/faculty ratio 15:1. 249 full-time faculty, 67% hold PhDs, 10% are members of minority groups, 22% are women. 0% of classes are taught by teaching assistants.

ACADEMICS
Degrees: associate, bachelor's, master's. **Classes:** Most classes have 20–29 students. Most lab/discussion sessions have 10–19 students. **Majors with Highest Enrollment:** aeronautics/aviation/aerospace science and technology; aerospace, aeronautical and astronautical engineering; airline/commercial/professional pilot and flight crew. **Special Study Options:** Accelerated program, cooperative education program, distance learning, double major, dual enrollment, English as a Second Language (ESL), honors program, independent study, internships, student-designed major, study abroad. **Honors Programs:** The Embry-Riddle Honors Program is highly selective, offering its student members enriched educational experiences. Emphasizing Honors course work in General Education and in the majors, the Program involves selected faculty who develop innovative courses and establish mentoring relationships with students. The Program is designed to attract and retain top students and to develop their communicative, analytical, critical, and research skills, nurturing a love of life-long learning, leadership, and service. **Disability Services:** Special programs offered to physically disabled students include reader services, tape recorders, tutors. **Career Services:** Alumni network, alumni services, career/job search classes, career assessment, internships, regional alumni. Career Services highlights include Cooperative Education/Internship Program: The Co-op/Internship program provides students with practical experience which reinforces the theoretical concepts learned in the classroom. The Co-op/Internship program aids in bridging the gap between student life and the world of work. This program combines students' academic and career interests with work experience in business, industry, government, or service organizations. Key elements of the Co-op/Internship program experience are: Professional level work assignments in areas related to the student's academic major. Supervision and evaluation of performance by professionals in a chosen career field. Completion of learning objectives designed to relate academic studies to the work world.

FACILITIES
Housing: Coed dorms, apartments for married students, apartments for single students. 80% of campus accessible to physically disabled. **Special Academic Facilities/Equipment:** Fully equipped aircraft, training simulators, airway science simulation lab, wind tunnel. **Computers:** 100% of classrooms, 100% of dorms, 100% of libraries, 100% of dining areas, 100% of student union, 15% of common outdoor areas have wireless network access. Students can register for classes online. Administrative functions (other than registration) can be performed online.

CAMPUS LIFE
Environment: Town. **Activities:** Choral groups, dance, drama/theater, music ensembles, pep band, radio station, student government, student newspaper, yearbook, Campus Ministries, International Student Organization, Model UN 140 registered organizations, 12 honor societies, 5 religious organizations. 12 fraternities, 4 sororities. **Athletics (Intercollegiate):** *Men:* baseball, basketball, cheerleading, cross-country, golf, soccer, softball, tennis, track/field (outdoor), volleyball. *Women:* basketball, cheerleading, cross-country, golf, soccer, softball, tennis, track/field (outdoor), volleyball. **On-Campus Highlights:** Lehman Engineering and Technology Center, College of Aviation, Simulator Building, ICI Center (fieldhouse), The Green Garage - EcoCAR Challenge, The College of Aviation tour is a brief look at the Air Traffic Management Laboratory and its Pseudo-Pilots' Lab, the Aircraft Performance Lab, the Computer Flight Simulation Lab, the College of Aviation Student Success Center (Tutor Lab), and the Flight Tutor Lab. The COA building also contains a Weather Center and two Meteorology Labs, Basic and Advanced. **Environmental Initiatives:** Embry-Riddle Opens Green Garage Doors: EcoCAR Project Advances University Environmental Commitment Daytona Beach, Fla., Dec. 10, 2009 -- Embry-Riddle Aeronautical University has opened the doors of a new green garage, where engineering students are using aerospace techniques to develop the car of tomorrow. The garage includes a rotary vehicle lift, dedicated high-voltage room, and integrated hardware-in-the-loop laboratory donated by National Instruments. It also showcases an environmental focus at Embry-Riddle's College of Engineering. Every component in the lab was chosen to reduce environmental impact, including the floor covering, which is made from recycled tires. Interior design students from Daytona State College assisted in designing the new facility. http://givingto.erau.edu/givingnews/09releases/ecocar.html The Green Flight Challenge is a competition that is sponsored by NASA and run by the CAFE Foundation, and involves helping General Aviation move toward a "greener" way of travel. The main requirements state that a new or modified aircraft must travel 200 miles while averaging 100 mph and obtaining at least 200 passenger-mpg. Embry Riddle was accepted into the competition several weeks ago as one of the 18 teams which will compete for the $1.5 million prize in July of 2011.

ADMISSIONS
Freshman Academic Profile: Average high school GPA 3.3. 20% in top 10% of high school class, 45% in top 25% of high school class, 76% in top 50% of high school class. SAT Math middle 50% range 500-630. SAT Critical Reading middle 50% range 470-580. ACT middle 50% range 21-27. Minimum web-based TOEFL 79. Minimum paper TOEFL 550. **Basis for Candidate Selection:** *Very important factors considered include:* Class rank, academic GPA, recommendation(s), standardized test scores. *Other factors considered include:* application essay, rigor of secondary school record, alumni/ae relation, character/personal qualities, extracurricular activities, interview, level of applicant's interest, volunteer work, work experience. **Freshman Admission Requirements:** High school diploma is required and GED is accepted. *Academic units required:* 4 English, 3 mathematics, 2 science, (2 science labs), 2 social studies, 1 history, 3 academic electives. *Academic units recommended:* 4 English, 3 mathematics, 2 science, (2 science labs), 2 social studies, 1 history, 3 academic electives. **Freshman Admission Statistics:** 3,975 applied, 80% admitted, 30% enrolled. **Transfer Admission Requirements:** college transcript(s), minimum college GPA of 2.0 required. Lowest grade transferable C. **General Admission Information:** Application Fee $50. Notification on a rolling basis, beginning on or about 11/1. Nonfall registration accepted. Admission may be deferred for a maximum of 1 year. Credit and/or placement offered for CEEB Advanced Placement tests.

COSTS AND FINANCIAL AID
Annual tuition $28,680. Room and board $9,750. Required fees $1,172. Average book expense $1,428. **Required Forms and Deadlines:** FAFSA. **Notification of Awards: Types of Aid:** *Need-based scholarships/grants:* Federal Pell, SEOG, state scholarships/grants, private scholarships, the school's own gift aid. *Loans:* Direct Subsidized Stafford, Direct Unsubsidized Stafford, Direct PLUS, Subsidized Stafford. **Student Employment:** Federal Work-Study Program available. Institutional employment available. Off-campus job opportunities are good. **Financial Aid Statistics:** 99% freshmen, 95% undergrads receive need-based scholarship or grant aid. 81% freshmen, 83% undergrads receive need-based self-help aid. 3% freshmen, 4% undergrads receive athletic scholarships. 89% freshmen, 84% undergrads receive any aid. 71% undergrads borrow to pay for school. Average cumulative indebtedness. **Criteria for awarding institutional aid:** Non need based: academics, alumni affiliation, athletics, leadership.

EMERSON COLLEGE

120 Boylston Street, Boston, MA 02116-4624
Phone: 617-824-8600 • **Financial Aid Phone:** 617-824-8655
E-mail: admission@emerson.edu • **CEEB Code:** 3367
Fax: 617-824-8609 • **Website:** www.emerson.edu • **ACT Code:** 1820

This private school was founded in 1880. It has a 10-acre campus.

RATINGS
Admissions Selectivity Rating: 93   **Fire Safety Rating:** 82   **Green Rating:** 76

STUDENTS AND FACULTY
Enrollment: 3,454. **Student Body:** 59% female, 41% male, 75% out-of-state, 3% international (45 countries represented). Asian 5%, African American 3%, Caucasian 62%, Hispanic 8%, Native American 0%.

Retention and Graduation: 88% freshmen return for sophomore year. 74% freshmen graduate within 4 years. 78% freshmen graduate within 6 years. 10% grads go on to further study within 1 year. **Faculty:** Student/faculty ratio 13:1. 177 full-time faculty, 71% hold PhDs, 18% are members of minority groups, 44% are women. 3% of classes are taught by teaching assistants.

ACADEMICS

Degrees: bachelor's, certificate, master's. **Classes:** Most classes have 10–19 students. Most lab/discussion sessions have 10–19 students. **Majors with Highest Enrollment:** cinematography and film/video production; creative writing; theatre/theater. **Special Study Options:** cross-registration, double major, honors program, independent study, internships, liberal arts/career combination, student-designed major, study abroad, teacher certification program. **Combined Degree Programs:** BS/MSSp in Communication Disorders. **Disability Services:** Special programs offered to physically disabled students include note-taking services, reader services, tape recorders, tutors. **Career Services:** Alumni network, alumni services, career/job search classes, career assessment, internships, regional alumni.

FACILITIES

Housing: Coed dorms, Optional Learning Communities, such as the Writers' Block, Film Immersion Community, and Digital Culture Floor. 80% of campus accessible to physically disabled. **Special Academic Facilities/Equipment:** Emerson is home to the historic 1,200-seat Cutler Majestic Theatre and WERS-FM, Boston's oldest noncommercial broadcaster. The College has an 11-story performance and production center, housing rehearsal space, a costume shop, makeup lab, theatre design/tech center, and sound-treated TV studios. There are also digital and audio post-production labs, recording studios, a film equipment distribution center, seven clinics/programs to observe speech and hearing therapy, an integrated digital newsroom, and marketing research suite. A new 14-story campus center and residence hall houses a gymnasium and space for student organizations. Current campus construction projects include new student residences in the renovated Colonial Building and a sound stage, scene shop, black box, and cinema in the refurbished Paramount Theatre complex. **Computers:** 100% of classrooms, 100% of dorms, 100% of libraries, 100% of dining areas, 100% of student union, 100% of common outdoor areas have wireless network access. Students can register for classes online. Administrative functions (other than registration) can be performed online.

CAMPUS LIFE

Environment: Metropolis. **Activities:** Choral groups, dance, drama/theater, literary magazine, music ensembles, musical theater, radio station, student government, student newspaper, student-run film society, television station, yearbook, Campus Ministries, International Student Organization 60 registered organizations, 4 honor societies, 4 religious organizations. 4 fraternities, 3 sororities. **Athletics (Intercollegiate):** *Men:* baseball, basketball, cross-country, golf, lacrosse, soccer, tennis, track/field (indoor), volleyball. *Women:* basketball, cross-country, golf, lacrosse, soccer, softball, tennis, track/field (indoor), volleyball. **On-Campus Highlights:** WERS-FM (Boston's oldest public radio), Historic Cutler Majestic Theatre, Tufte Performance and Production Center, Journalism's Integrated Digital Newsroom, Piano Row Residence Hall/College Center, Emerson is currently remodeling the Colonial Building into student residences and renovating the Paramount Theater complex to house a sound stage, scene shop, rehearsal space, and a student residence. **Environmental Initiatives:** LEED Certified residence hall (one of only two in the city of Boston), campus center, and gymnasium. Alternative energy sources Major recycling programs.

ADMISSIONS

Freshman Academic Profile: Average high school GPA 3.6. 42% in top 10% of high school class, 77% in top 25% of high school class, 98% in top 50% of high school class. 70% from public high schools. SAT Math middle 50% range 540-640. SAT Critical Reading middle 50% range 570-670. SAT Writing middle 50% range 580-670. ACT middle 50% range 24-29. Minimum web-based TOEFL 80. Minimum paper TOEFL 550. **Basis for Candidate Selection:** *Very important factors considered include:* academic GPA, standardized test scores. *Important factors considered include:* Class rank, application essay, recommendation(s), rigor of secondary school record, character/personal qualities, extracurricular activities, talent/ability. *Other factors considered include:* alumni/ae relation, first generation, geographical residence, racial/ethnic status, volunteer work, work experience. **Freshman Admission Requirements:** High school diploma is required and GED is accepted. *Academic units required:* 4 English, 3 mathematics, 3 science, 3 foreign language, 3 social studies. *Academic units recommended:* 4 English, 3 mathematics, 3 science, 3 foreign language, 3 social studies. **Freshman Admission Statistics:** 6,943 applied, 42% admitted, 26% enrolled. **Transfer Admission Requirements:** High school transcript, college transcript(s), essay or personal statement, statement of good standing from prior institution(s). Minimum college GPA of 3.0 required. Lowest grade transferable C. **General Admission Information:** Application Fee $65. Regular application deadline 1/5. Regular notification 4/1. Nonfall registration accepted. Admission may be deferred for a maximum of 1 Year. Credit and/or placement offered for CEEB Advanced Placement tests.

COSTS AND FINANCIAL AID

Annual tuition $29,408. Room and board $12,280. Required fees $532. Average book expense $800. **Required Forms and Deadlines:** FAFSA, CSS/Financial Aid PROFILE, noncustodial PROFILE, business/farm supplement. Tax Returns. **Notification of Awards:** Applicants will be notified of awards on or about 4/1. **Types of Aid:** *Need-based scholarships/grants:* Federal Pell, SEOG, state scholarships/grants, private scholarships, the school's own gift aid. *Loans:* Subsidized Stafford, Unsubsidized Stafford, PLUS, Federal Perkins, state loans. **Student Employment:** Federal Work-Study Program available. Institutional employment available. Highest amount earned per year from on-campus jobs $2,400. Off-campus job opportunities are excellent. **Financial Aid Statistics:** 84% freshmen, 79% undergrads receive need-based scholarship or grant aid. 4% freshmen, 3% undergrads receive non-need-based scholarship or grant aid. 84% freshmen, 94% undergrads receive need-based self-help aid. 63% freshmen, 61% undergrads receive any aid. 59% undergrads borrow to pay for school. Average cumulative indebtedness $15,262. **Criteria for awarding institutional aid:** *Non-need-based:* academics, leadership, music/drama, state/district residency.

EMILY CARR UNIVERSITY OF ART & DESIGN

1399 Johnston Street, Vancouver, BC V6H 3R9
Phone: 604-844-3897
E-mail: admissions@ecuad.ca
Fax: 604-844-3089 • **Website:** www.ecuad.ca

This public school was founded in 1925. It has a 80-acre campus.

RATINGS

Admissions Selectivity Rating: 61   **Fire Safety Rating:** 60*   **Green Rating:** 60*

STUDENTS AND FACULTY

Student Body: 32% out-of-state, (55 countries represented). **Retention and Graduation:** 85% freshmen return for sophomore year. **Faculty:** 0% of classes are taught by teaching assistants.

ACADEMICS

Degrees: bachelor's, master's. **Special Study Options:** cooperative education program, cross-registration, distance learning, exchange student program (domestic), external degree program, independent study, internships, liberal arts/career combination, student-designed major, study abroad. **Disability Services:** Special programs offered to physically disabled students include note-taking services, reader services, tape recorders, tutors. **Career Services:** Alumni network, alumni services, career/job search classes, career assessment, internships, regional alumni.

FACILITIES

Housing: Off campus housing assistance. 85% of campus accessible to physically disabled. **Special Academic Facilities/Equipment:** Two Galleries A Centre for Art and Technology

CAMPUS LIFE

Environment: Activities: student government, student newspaper, yearbook 12 registered organizations.

ADMISSIONS

Freshman Academic Profile: Minimum web-based TOEFL 84. Minimum paper TOEFL 570. **Basis for Candidate Selection:** *Very important factors considered include:* character/personal qualities, level of applicant's interest, talent/ability. *Important factors considered include:* academic GPA, rigor of secondary school record. *Other factors considered include:* extracurricular activities, volunteer work, work experience. **Freshman Admission Requirements:** High school diploma is required and GED is not accepted. *Academic units required:* 3 English, 6 visual/performing arts, 6 academic electives. 3 English, 6 visual/performing arts, 6 academic electives. **Transfer Admission Requirements:** college transcript(s), essay or personal statement, statement of good standing from prior institution(s). Minimum college GPA of 2.0 required. Lowest grade transferable C. **General Admission Information:** Application Fee $40. Early decision application deadline 1/30. Regular application deadline 2/1. Regular notification 4/1. Nonfall registration accepted. Admission may be deferred for a maximum of one year. Credit and/or placement offered for CEEB Advanced Placement tests.

COSTS AND FINANCIAL AID

Annual in-state tuition $3,658. Average book expense $2,500. **Student Employment:** Institutional employment available. Highest amount earned per year from on-campus jobs $1,200. Off-campus job opportunities are good.

EMMANUEL COLLEGE

400 The Fenway, Boston, MA 2115
Phone: 617-735-9715 • **Financial Aid Phone:** 617-735-9938
E-mail: enroll@emmanuel.edu • **CEEB Code:** 3368
Fax: 617-735-9801 • **Website:** www.emmanuel.edu • **ACT Code:** 1822

This private school, affiliated with the Roman Catholic Church, was founded in 1919. It has a 17-acre campus.

RATINGS
Admissions Selectivity Rating: 89   **Fire Safety Rating:** 96   **Green Rating:** 68

STUDENTS AND FACULTY
Enrollment: 2,056. **Student Body:** 72% female, 28% male, 39% out-of-state, 1% international (36 countries represented). Asian 3%, African American 6%, Caucasian 70%, Hispanic 6%, Native American 0%. **Retention and Graduation:** 81% freshmen return for sophomore year. 50% freshmen graduate within 4 years. **Faculty:** Student/faculty ratio 14:1. 101 full-time faculty, 85% hold PhDs, 17% are members of minority groups, 60% are women. 0% of classes are taught by teaching assistants.

ACADEMICS
Degrees: bachelor's, master's, post-bachelor's certificate, post-master's certificate. **Classes:** Most classes have 10–19 students. Most lab/discussion sessions have 10–19 students. **Majors with Highest Enrollment:** biology/biological sciences; business administration and management; psychology. **Special Study Options:** Accelerated program, cross-registration, distance learning, double major, exchange student program (domestic), honors program, independent study, internships, liberal arts/career combination, student-designed major, study abroad, teacher certification program. **Honors Programs:** Emmanuel College's Honors Program is a four-year academic and co-curricular program that combines rigorous, discussion-based course work with special complementary opportunities such as cultural activities, faculty-directed research projects, and service in the community. The program begins with the yearlong Honors Colloquium, a forum for students to engage in an active and open dialogue with their peers and members of the College's faculty from across the disciplines. Students also participate in four interdisciplinary writing-intensive seminars over the course of their studies, as well as a research and presentation skills seminar in preparation for independent study as an upperclassman, and ultimately the opportunity to achieve Distinction in the Field. **Disability Services:** Special programs offered to physically disabled students include note-taking services, reader services, tape recorders, tutors. **Career Services:** Alumni network, alumni services, career/job search classes, career assessment, internships, regional alumni. Career Services highlights include Part-time Job Fair the first week of school in September.

FACILITIES
Housing: Coed dorms, special housing for disabled students, theme housing, 90% of campus accessible to physically disabled. **Special Academic Facilities/Equipment:** Academic Science Center, Lillian Immig Gallery, Academic Resource Center, Jean Yawkey Center **Computers:** Students can register for classes online. Administrative functions (other than registration) can be performed online.

CAMPUS LIFE
Environment: Metropolis. **Activities:** Choral groups, dance, drama/theater, jazz band, literary magazine, music ensembles, musical theater, pep band, radio station, student government, student newspaper, student-run film society, symphony orchestra, yearbook, Campus Ministries, International Student Organization, Model UN 48 registered organizations, 11 honor societies. **Athletics (Intercollegiate):** *Men:* basketball, cross-country, golf, soccer, track/field (outdoor), track/field (indoor), volleyball. *Women:* basketball, cross-country, lacrosse, soccer, softball, tennis, track/field (outdoor), track/field (indoor), volleyball. **On-Campus Highlights:** Jean Yawkey Center, Residence Halls, Academic Science Center, Chapel **Environmental Initiatives:** Signing onto the ACUPCC in September 2010 Making recycling units readily available across campus Pursuing sustainable practices that may result in benefits such as a healthier learning and work environment and financial savings.

ADMISSIONS
Freshman Academic Profile: Average high school GPA 3.6. 20% in top 10% of high school class, 46% in top 25% of high school class, 81% in top 50% of high school class. 78% from public high schools. SAT Math middle 50% range 500-600. SAT Critical Reading middle 50% range 510-600. SAT Writing middle 50% range 510-600. ACT middle 50% range 22-26. Minimum web-based TOEFL 79. Minimum paper TOEFL 550. **Basis for Candidate Selection:** *Very important factors considered include:* application essay, academic GPA, recommendation(s), rigor of secondary school record. *Important factors considered include:* standardized test scores, character/personal qualities, extracurricular activities, level of applicant's interest, volunteer work. *Other factors considered include:* Class rank, alumni/ae relation, first generation, geographical residence, interview, religious affiliation/commitment, talent/ability, work experience. **Freshman Admission Requirements:** High school diploma is required and GED is accepted. *Academic units required:* 4 English, 3 mathematics, 2 science, (2 science labs), 2 foreign language, 2 social studies. 4 English, 3 mathematics, 2 science, (2 science labs), 2 foreign language, 2 social studies. **Freshman Admission Statistics:** 7,851 applied, 50% admitted, 14% enrolled. **Transfer Admission Requirements:** High school transcript, college transcript(s), essay or personal statement, standardized test scores, statement of good standing from prior institution(s). Minimum college GPA of n/a required. Lowest grade transferable C. **General Admission Information:** Application Fee $40. Early decision application deadline 11/1. Regular application deadline 3/1. Notification on a rolling basis, beginning on or about 12/1. Nonfall registration accepted. Admission may be deferred for a maximum of 1 year. Credit and/or placement offered for CEEB Advanced Placement tests.

COSTS AND FINANCIAL AID
Annual tuition $33,450. Room and board $12,990. Required fees $200. Average book expense $880. **Required Forms and Deadlines:** FAFSA, institution's own financial aid form. **Notification of Awards:** Applicants will be notified of awards on a rolling basis beginning 3/15. **Types of Aid:** *Need-based scholarships/grants:* Federal Pell, SEOG, state scholarships/grants, private scholarships, the school's own gift aid. *Loans:* Direct Subsidized Stafford, Direct Unsubsidized Stafford, Direct PLUS, Federal Perkins, state loans. **Student Employment:** Federal Work-Study Program available. Institutional employment available. Highest amount earned per year from on-campus jobs $7,581. Off-campus job opportunities are excellent. **Financial Aid Statistics:** 100% freshmen, 99% undergrads receive need-based scholarship or grant aid. 100% freshmen, 95% undergrads receive non-need-based scholarship or grant aid. 82% freshmen, 84% undergrads receive need-based self-help aid. 99% freshmen, 94% undergrads receive any aid. 74% undergrads borrow to pay for school. Average cumulative indebtedness $33,452. **Criteria for awarding institutional aid:** *Non-need-based:* academics, alumni affiliation, leadership.

See page 1076.

EMMANUEL COLLEGE (GA)

P.O. Box 129, Franklin Springs, GA 30639-0129
Phone: 706-245-7226 • **Financial Aid Phone:** 706-245-2844
E-mail: admissions@emmanuelcollege.edu • **CEEB Code:** 5184
Fax: 706-245-2876 • **Website:** www.ec.edu/ • **ACT Code:**

This private school, affiliated with the Pentecostal Church, was founded in 1919. It has a 150-acre campus.

RATINGS
Admissions Selectivity Rating: 90   **Fire Safety Rating:** 61   **Green Rating:** 60*

STUDENTS AND FACULTY
Enrollment: 613. **Student Body:** 54% female, 46% male, 22% out-of-state, 1% international (4 countries represented). Asian 1%, African American 16%, Caucasian 80%, Hispanic 2%, Native American 0%. **Retention and Graduation:** 61% freshmen return for sophomore year. 18% freshmen graduate within 4 years. 34% freshmen graduate within 6 years. **Faculty:** Student/faculty ratio 13:1. 40 full-time faculty, 65% hold PhDs, 3% are members of minority groups, 40% are women. 0% of classes are taught by teaching assistants.

ACADEMICS
Degrees: associate, bachelor's, terminal associate, transfer associate. **Classes:** Most classes have fewer than 10 students. **Special Study Options:** dual enrollment, honors program, independent study, internships, teacher certification program. **Disability Services:** Special programs offered to physically disabled students include note-taking services, tutors. **Career Services:**

FACILITIES
Housing: men's dorms, women's dorms, apartments for married students 75% of campus accessible to physically disabled. **Computers:** Students can register for classes online.

CAMPUS LIFE
Environment: Rural. **Activities:** Choral groups, drama/theater, jazz band, literary magazine, music ensembles, musical theater, student government, student newspaper, yearbook 25 registered organizations, 3 honor societies, 15 religious organizations. **Athletics (Intercollegiate):** *Men:* baseball, basketball, soccer,

tennis. *Women:* basketball, soccer, softball, tennis. **On-Campus Highlights:** EC Cafe, Student Activities Center

ADMISSIONS

Freshman Academic Profile: 10% in top 10% of high school class, 50% in top 25% of high school class, 60% in top 50% of high school class. 85% from public high schools. SAT Math middle 50% range 400-550. SAT Critical Reading middle 50% range 430-570. Minimum paper TOEFL 550. **Basis for Candidate Selection:** *Very important factors considered include:* academic GPA, standardized test scores. *Important factors considered include:* level of applicant's interest. *Other factors considered include:* recommendation(s). **Freshman Admission Requirements:** High school diploma is required and GED is accepted. **Freshman Admission Statistics:** 1,661 applied, 35% admitted, 45% enrolled. **Transfer Admission Requirements:** college transcript(s), standardized test scores, Lowest grade transferable D. **General Admission Information:** Application Fee $25. Regular application deadline 8/1. Notification on a rolling basis, beginning on or about 9/1. Nonfall registration accepted. Admission may be deferred for a maximum of 1 year. Credit offered for CEEB Advanced Placement tests.

COSTS AND FINANCIAL AID

Average book expense $600. **Required Forms and Deadlines:** FAFSA, institution's own financial aid form, state aid form. **Notification of Awards:** Applicants will be notified of awards on a rolling basis beginning 3/1. **Types of Aid:** *Need-based scholarships/grants:* Federal Pell, SEOG, state scholarships/grants. *Loans:* Subsidized Stafford, Unsubsidized Stafford, PLUS. **Student Employment:** Federal Work-Study Program available. Institutional employment available. Off-campus job opportunities are good. **Financial Aid Statistics:** 84% freshmen, 92% undergrads receive need-based scholarship or grant aid. 51% freshmen, 50% undergrads receive non-need-based scholarship or grant aid. 74% freshmen, 56% undergrads receive need-based self-help aid. **Criteria for awarding institutional aid:** *Non-need-based:* academics, alumni affiliation, athletics, leadership, music/drama, religious affiliation.

EMORY AND HENRY COLLEGE

PO Box 10, Emory, VA 24327
Phone: 276-944-6133 • **Financial Aid Phone:** 866-794-0010
E-mail: ehadmiss@ehc.edu • **CEEB Code:** 5185
Fax: 276-944-6935 • **Website:** www.ehc.edu • **ACT Code:** 4350

This private school, affiliated with the Methodist Church, was founded in 1836. It has a 331-acre campus.

RATINGS

Admissions Selectivity Rating: 71   **Fire Safety Rating:** 60*   **Green Rating:** 75

STUDENTS AND FACULTY

Enrollment: 911. **Student Body:** 48% female, 52% male, 36% out-of-state, 0% international (5 countries represented). Asian 0%, African American 6%, Caucasian 57%, Hispanic 1%, Native American 0%. **Retention and Graduation:** 74% freshmen return for sophomore year. 35% freshmen graduate within 4 years. 48% freshmen graduate within 6 years. 37% grads go on to further study within 1 year. 24% grads pursue arts and sciences degrees. 31% grads pursue law degrees. 23% grads pursue business degrees. 12% grads pursue medical degrees. **Faculty:** Student/faculty ratio 10:1. 72 full-time faculty, 82% hold PhDs, 10% are members of minority groups, 49% are women. 0% of classes are taught by teaching assistants.

ACADEMICS

Degrees: bachelor's, diploma, master's. **Classes:** Most classes have 10–19 students. **Majors with Highest Enrollment:** business administration and management; education; pre-medicine/pre-medical studies. **Special Study Options:** cooperative education program, distance learning, double major, dual enrollment, honors program, independent study, internships, liberal arts/career combination, student-designed major, study abroad, teacher certification program. **Combined Degree Programs:** BA/MA. **Disability Services:** Special programs offered to physically disabled students include reader services, tape recorders, tutors. **Career Services:** career/job search classes, career assessment, internships.

FACILITIES

Housing: Coed dorms, special housing for disabled students, men's dorms, women's dorms, theme housing. **Special Academic Facilities/Equipment:** Language lab, capillary gas chromatograph, DNA vertical slab gel electrophoretic equipment, infrared spectrophotometer. Theatre Studio, Art gallery. **Computers:** 100% of classrooms, 100% of dorms, 100% of libraries, 100% of dining areas, 100% of student union, 100% of common outdoor areas have wireless network access.

CAMPUS LIFE

Environment: Rural. **Activities:** Choral groups, drama/theater, literary magazine, music ensembles, musical theater, opera, pep band, radio station, student government, student newspaper, television station, yearbook, Campus Ministries, International Student Organization 53 registered organizations, 7 honor societies, 4 religious organizations. 7 fraternities, 6 sororities. **Athletics (Intercollegiate):** *Men:* baseball, basketball, cross-country, football, golf, soccer, tennis. *Women:* basketball, cross-country, soccer, softball, swimming, tennis, volleyball. **On-Campus Highlights:** McGlothlin-Street Hall (new science buil, Memorial Chapel, Byars Hall (Arts, Music, and Theatre), King Athletic Center, Emory Mercantile (campus bookstore). **Environmental Initiatives:** Recycling is now in full swing, with a widespread distribution of recycling bins for paper, cardboard, aluminum, plastics and steel. There are thirty bins specially made for the college from sustainably-harvested local poplar. We have already reduced our trash volume significantly. We are a participant in the national Recyclemania competition, in the waste minimization category. All new campus construction will be LEED silver certified, including the use of local, sustainably harvested wood. The college food service has committed to buying a significant amount of local organic produce, eggs and meat from Appalachian Harvest, a cooperative of farmers in our region. This is for the fall semester of 2008. This is one of our most effective ways of reducing our college's environmental footprint.

ADMISSIONS

Freshman Academic Profile: Average high school GPA 3.5. 20% in top 10% of high school class, 45% in top 25% of high school class, 80% in top 50% of high school class. 92% from public high schools. SAT Math middle 50% range 445-560. SAT Critical Reading middle 50% range 430-555. SAT Writing middle 50% range 425-540. ACT middle 50% range 19-26. Minimum paper TOEFL 550. **Basis for Candidate Selection:** *Very important factors considered include:* academic GPA, recommendation(s), rigor of secondary school record, character/personal qualities, level of applicant's interest. *Important factors considered include:* application essay, standardized test scores, extracurricular activities, geographical residence, interview, state residency, talent/ability, volunteer work. *Other factors considered include:* Class rank, alumni/ae relation, first generation, racial/ethnic status, religious affiliation/commitment, work experience. **Freshman Admission Requirements:** High school diploma is required and GED is accepted. *Academic units required:* 4 English, 3 mathematics, 2 science, (2 science labs), 2 foreign language, 2 social studies, 0 academic electives, 0. *Academic units recommended:* 4 English, 3 mathematics, 2 science, (2 science labs), 2 foreign language, 2 social studies, 0 academic electives, 0 **Freshman Admission Statistics:** 1,217 applied, 72% admitted, 28% enrolled. **Transfer Admission Requirements:** High school transcript, college transcript(s), statement of good standing from prior institution(s). Minimum college GPA of 2.5 required. Lowest grade transferable C. **General Admission Information:** Application Fee $30. Notification on a rolling basis, beginning on or about 8/1. Nonfall registration accepted. Admission may be deferred for a maximum of 1 year. Credit and/or placement offered for CEEB Advanced Placement tests.

COSTS AND FINANCIAL AID

Annual tuition $23,860. Room and board $7,980. Average book expense $800. **Required Forms and Deadlines:** FAFSA, state aid form. **Notification of Awards:** Applicants will be notified of awards on a rolling basis beginning 3/1. **Types of Aid:** *Need-based scholarships/grants:* Federal Pell, SEOG, state scholarships/grants, private scholarships, the school's own gift aid. *Loans:* Subsidized Stafford, Unsubsidized Stafford, PLUS, Federal Perkins. **Student Employment: Financial Aid Statistics:** 80% freshmen, 87% undergrads receive need-based scholarship or grant aid. 20% freshmen, 13% undergrads receive non-need-based scholarship or grant aid. 70% freshmen receive need-based self-help aid. 79% undergrads borrow to pay for school. Average cumulative indebtedness $29,510. **Criteria for awarding institutional aid:** *Non-need-based:* academics, art, music/drama, religious affiliation, state/district residency.

See page 1078.

EMORY UNIVERSITY

Emory University, Boiseuillet Jones Ctr, Atlanta, GA 30322
Phone: 404-727-6036 • **Financial Aid Phone:** 404-727-6039
E-mail: admiss@emory.edu • **CEEB Code:** 5186
Fax: 404-727-4303 • **Website:** www.emory.edu • **ACT Code:** 851

This private school, affiliated with the Methodist Church, was founded in 1836. It has a 56-acre campus.

RATINGS
Admissions Selectivity Rating: 98   **Fire Safety Rating:** 74   **Green Rating:** 98

STUDENTS AND FACULTY
Enrollment: 7,337. **Student Body:** 55% female, 45% male, 72% out-of-state, 11% international (101 countries represented). Asian 24%, African American 10%, Caucasian 42%, Hispanic 5%, Native American 0%.
Retention and Graduation: 96% freshmen return for sophomore year. 83% freshmen graduate within 4 years. 37% grads go on to further study within 1 year. 21% grads pursue arts and sciences degrees. 21% grads pursue law degrees. 2% grads pursue business degrees. 30% grads pursue medical degrees.
Faculty: Student/faculty ratio 7:1. 1295 full-time faculty, 99% hold PhDs, 18% are members of minority groups, 42% are women. 10% of classes are taught by teaching assistants.

ACADEMICS
Degrees: associate, bachelor's, first professional, master's. **Classes:** Most classes have 10–19 students. Most lab/discussion sessions have 10–19 students. **Majors with Highest Enrollment:** business/commerce; economics; English language and literature. **Special Study Options:** cooperative education program, cross-registration, double major, dual enrollment, English as a Second Language (ESL), honors program, independent study, internships, liberal arts/career combination, study abroad, teacher certification program, Qualified undergraduates may take a semester of off-campus study in Washington D.C. **Combined Degree Programs:** BA/MA, 4 year BA/MA or BS/MS program. **Disability Services:** Special programs offered to physically disabled students include note-taking services, reader services, tape recorders, tutors. **Career Services:** Alumni network, alumni services, career/job search classes, career assessment, internships, regional alumni.

FACILITIES
Housing: Coed dorms, special housing for disabled students, special housing for international students, women's dorms, fraternity/sorority housing, apartments for married students, apartments for single students, theme housing. **Computers:** Students can register for classes online. Administrative functions (other than registration) can be performed online.

CAMPUS LIFE
Environment: Town. **Activities:** Choral groups, concert band, dance, drama/theater, jazz band, literary magazine, marching band, music ensembles, musical theater, opera, pep band, radio station, student government, student newspaper, student-run film society, symphony orchestra, television station, Campus Ministries, International Student Organization 51 registered organizations, 30 honor societies, 27 religious organizations. 14 fraternities, 12 sororities. **Athletics (Intercollegiate):** *Men:* baseball, basketball, cross-country, diving, golf, soccer, swimming, tennis, track/field (outdoor). *Women:* basketball, cross-country, diving, soccer, softball, swimming, tennis, track/field (outdoor), volleyball. **On-Campus Highlights:** Michael C. Carlos Museum, Lullwater Park, Clifton Health Sciences Corridor, Top of Woodruff Library, Dooley's Den at the Depot, 6) Candler Library Reading Room. **Environmental Initiatives:** Emory has among the highest number of square feet of LEED-certified space of any campus in America. Emory constructed the first LEED-certified building in the Southeast in the 1990's, the first Good LEED-EB in the U.S., and since 2001 all new and future construction must be LEED (with Silver currently the minimum). We also are auditing and retrofitting exisiting buildings - roughly 1 million square feet are currently underway with additional 1 million in planning phase. Emory has set the goal of serving 75% local or sustainable ingredients in our campus and hospital cafeterias by 2015. To reach this ambitious target, we have hired a local farmer as Emory's Farm Liaison who is building a network of other local farmers to expand production and a Sustainable Food Educator to expand awareness of sustainable food. We are also working closely with the non-profit Georgia Organics and our vendor, Sodexho, to overcome barriers to distribution from farm to plate. Finally, we've started an on-campus Farmers' Market and 8 educational food gardens on campus to allow students and staff the experience of growing their own local food. Emory has a robust alternative transportation program with one of the largest private bus fleets in metro Atlanta which is 100% alternatively fueled, running on a biodiesel blend made from the used cooking oil from our campus cafeterias and hospitals. Emory has also been named by global bike manufacturer, Fuji, as its first Fuji University and has a bike share program with free fleets of bikes at check-out locations around campus, discounted bikes for students and staff, and other incentives for biking (see www.bike.emory.edu). We give staff free public transit passes, and incentives for carpooling, walking, and vanpooling. We also have three park-n-ride facilities at shopping centers around Atlanta's perimeter highway so that staff can take our free shuttle into work instead of driving into the heart of the city.

ADMISSIONS
Freshman Academic Profile: Average high school GPA 3.8. 80% in top 10% of high school class, 96% in top 25% of high school class, 100% in top 50% of high school class. 62% from public high schools. SAT Math middle 50% range 660-760. SAT Critical Reading middle 50% range 620-710. SAT Writing middle 50% range 640-730. ACT middle 50% range 29-32. Minimum paper TOEFL 600. **Basis for Candidate Selection:** *Very important factors considered include:* application essay, academic GPA, recommendation(s), rigor of secondary school record, standardized test scores, character/personal qualities, extracurricular activities, first generation, talent/ability. *Important factors considered include:* alumni/ae relation, geographical residence, level of applicant's interest, racial/ethnic status, volunteer work, work experience. *Other factors considered include:* Class rank, interview. **Freshman Admission Requirements:** High school diploma is required and GED is not accepted. *Academic units required:* 4 English, 3 mathematics, 2 science, (2 science labs), 2 foreign language, 2 social studies, 2 history, 1 visual/performing arts, 2 academic electives. *Academic units recommended:* 4 English, 3 mathematics, 2 science, (2 science labs), 2 foreign language, 2 social studies, 2 history, 1 visual/performing arts, 2 academic electives. **Freshman Admission Statistics:** 17,021 applied, 27% admitted, 30% enrolled. **Transfer Admission Requirements:** High school transcript, college transcript(s), essay or personal statement, standardized test scores, statement of good standing from prior institution(s). Minimum college GPA of 3.00 required. Lowest grade transferable C. **General Admission Information:** Application Fee $50. Early decision application deadline 11/1. Regular application deadline 1/15. Regular notification 4/1. Nonfall registration not accepted. Admission may be deferred for a maximum of 1 year. Credit and/or placement offered for CEEB Advanced Placement tests.

COSTS AND FINANCIAL AID
Annual tuition $42,400. Room and board $12,000. Required fees $580. Average book expense $1,100. **Required Forms and Deadlines:** FAFSA, CSS/Financial Aid PROFILE, noncustodial PROFILE. **Notification of Awards:** Applicants will be notified of awards on or about 4/1. **Types of Aid:** *Need-based scholarships/grants:* Federal Pell, SEOG, state scholarships/grants, private scholarships, the school's own gift aid. *Loans:* Subsidized Stafford, Unsubsidized Stafford, PLUS, Federal Perkins, Federal Nursing, state loans, college/university loans from institutional funds. **Student Employment: Financial Aid Statistics:** 94% freshmen, 96% undergrads receive need-based scholarship or grant aid. 13% freshmen, 14% undergrads receive non-need-based scholarship or grant aid. 90% freshmen, 91% undergrads receive need-based self-help aid. 55% freshmen, 54% undergrads receive any aid. 42% undergrads borrow to pay for school. Average cumulative indebtedness $28,076. **Criteria for awarding institutional aid:** *Non-need-based:* academics, art, leadership, music/drama, religious affiliation, state/district residency.

EMPORIA STATE UNIVERSITY

1200 Commercial, Emporia, KS 66801-5087
Phone: 620-341-5465 • **Financial Aid Phone:** 620-341-5457
E-mail: go2esu@emporia.edu • **CEEB Code:** 6335
Fax: 620-341-5599 • **Website:** www.emporia.edu • **ACT Code:** 1430

This public school was founded in 1863. It has a 212-acre campus.

RATINGS
Admissions Selectivity Rating: 66   **Fire Safety Rating:** 71   **Green Rating:** 61

STUDENTS AND FACULTY
Enrollment: 4,148. **Student Body:** 59% female, 41% male, 10% out-of-state, 6% international (40 countries represented). Asian 1%, African American 5%, Caucasian 79%, Hispanic 5%, Native American 1%.
Retention and Graduation: 22% freshmen graduate within 4 years. 47% freshmen graduate within 6 years. 20% grads go on to further study within 1 year. **Faculty:** Student/faculty ratio 18:1. 260 full-time faculty, 81% hold PhDs, 9% are members of minority groups, 46% are women. 9% of classes are taught by teaching assistants.

ACADEMICS

Degrees: bachelor's, master's, post-bachelor's certificate, post-master's certificate. **Classes:** Most classes have 20–29 students. Most lab/discussion sessions have 20–29 students. **Majors with Highest Enrollment:** business/commerce; elementary education and teaching; nursing/registered nurse (rn, asn, bsn, msn). **Special Study Options:** distance learning, double major, dual enrollment, honors program, independent study, internships, student-designed major, study abroad, teacher certification program, Continuing education courses, Evening courses, Interdisciplinary or interdepartmental course of study, Learning assistance program, Pass-Fail grading option, Student Exchange program, Summer sessions, Tutorial programs, Trio programs, Service members Opportunity College, Undergrads may take grad level classes, except 800 level. **Honors Programs:** Honors Programs **Combined Degree Programs:** MLS Legal studies with KU. **Disability Services:** Special programs offered to physically disabled students include note-taking services, reader services, tape recorders, tutors. **Career Services:** Alumni network, alumni services, career assessment, internships Career Services highlights include Formal, for-credit internship program available to any student, any major.

FACILITIES

Housing: Coed dorms, special housing for disabled students, special housing for international students, fraternity/sorority housing, apartments for married students, apartments for single students, wellness housing, theme housing, 100% of campus accessible to physically disabled. **Special Academic Facilities/Equipment:** Art gallery, geology and natural history museums, Great Plains study center, planetarium. **Computers:** 25% of classrooms, 100% of libraries, 50% of student union, have wireless network access. Students can register for classes online. Administrative functions (other than registration) can be performed online.

CAMPUS LIFE

Environment: Town. **Activities:** Choral groups, concert band, dance, drama/theater, jazz band, literary magazine, marching band, music ensembles, musical theater, opera, pep band, student government, student newspaper, student-run film society, symphony orchestra, yearbook, Campus Ministries, International Student Organization 141 registered organizations, 15 honor societies, 11 religious organizations. 6 fraternities, 4 sororities. **Athletics (Intercollegiate):** *Men:* baseball, basketball, cheerleading, cross-country, football, tennis, track/field (outdoor), track/field (indoor). *Women:* basketball, cheerleading, cross-country, soccer, softball, tennis, track/field (outdoor), track/field (indoor), volleyball. **On-Campus Highlights:** Student Recreation Center, The Memorial Student Union, Beach Music Hall, Wooster Lake, William Allen White Library.

ADMISSIONS

Freshman Academic Profile: Average high school GPA 3.3. 10% in top 10% of high school class, 34% in top 25% of high school class, 67% in top 50% of high school class. 96% from public high schools. ACT middle 50% range 19-25. Minimum paper TOEFL 450. **Basis for Candidate Selection:** *Very important factors considered include:* Class rank, academic GPA, standardized test scores. *Important factors considered include:* talent/ability. *Other factors considered include:* application essay, extracurricular activities. **Freshman Admission Requirements:** High school diploma is required and GED is accepted. *Academic units required:* 4 English, 3 mathematics, 3 science, 3 social studies, 1 computer science. *Academic units recommended:* 4 English, 3 mathematics, 3 science, 3 social studies, 1 computer science. **Freshman Admission Statistics:** 1,229 applied, 92% admitted, 61% enrolled. **Transfer Admission Requirements:** college transcript(s), minimum college GPA of 2.0 required. Lowest grade transferable D. **General Admission Information:** Application Fee $30. Nonfall registration accepted. Admission may be deferred for a maximum of 1 year. Credit and/or placement offered for CEEB Advanced Placement tests.

COSTS AND FINANCIAL AID

Annual in-state tuition $3,426. Annual out-of-state tuition $12,630. Room and board $6,146. Required fees $948. Required **Forms and Deadlines:** FAFSA, state aid form. **Notification of Awards:** Applicants will be notified of awards on a rolling basis beginning 2/2. **Types of Aid:** *Need-based scholarships/grants:* Federal Pell, SEOG, state scholarships/grants, private scholarships, the school's own gift aid, Jones Foundation Grants. *Loans:* Subsidized Stafford, Unsubsidized Stafford, PLUS, Federal Perkins, Alaska Loans, alternative loans. **Student Employment:** Federal Work-Study Program available. Institutional employment available. Highest amount earned per year from on-campus jobs $3,500. Off-campus job opportunities are good. **Financial Aid Statistics:** 59% freshmen, 43% undergrads receive need-based scholarship or grant aid. 41% freshmen, 28% undergrads receive non-need-based scholarship or grant aid. 7% freshmen, 9% undergrads receive need-based self-help aid. 7% freshmen, 4% undergrads receive athletic scholarships. 61% freshmen, 57% undergrads receive any aid. 70% undergrads borrow to pay for school. Average cumulative indebtedness $17,520. **Criteria for awarding institutional aid:** *Non-need-based:* academics, alumni affiliation, art, athletics, job skills, leadership, minority status, music/drama, religious affiliation, state/district residency.

ENDICOTT COLLEGE

376 Hale Street, Beverly, MA 1915
Phone: 978-921-1000 • **Financial Aid Phone:** 978-232-2060
E-mail: admissio@endicott.edu • **CEEB Code:** 3369
Fax: 978-232-2520 • **Website:** www.endicott.edu • **ACT Code:** 1824

This private school was founded in 1939. It has a 231-acre campus.

RATINGS

Admissions Selectivity Rating: 79   **Fire Safety Rating:** 93   **Green Rating:** 88

STUDENTS AND FACULTY

Enrollment: 2,565. **Student Body:** 60% female, 40% male, 51% out-of-state, 2% international (26 countries represented). Asian 1%, African American 2%, Caucasian 82%, Hispanic 3%, Native American 0%. **Retention and Graduation:** 83% freshmen return for sophomore year. 68% freshmen graduate within 4 years. 72% freshmen graduate within 6 years. 16% grads go on to further study within 1 year. **Faculty:** Student/faculty ratio 14:1. 93 full-time faculty, 61% hold PhDs, 8% are members of minority groups, 57% are women. 0% of classes are taught by teaching assistants.

ACADEMICS

Degrees: associate, bachelor's, master's, post-bachelor's certificate, terminal associate. **Classes:** Most classes have 10–19 students. Most lab/discussion sessions have 10–19 students. **Majors with Highest Enrollment:** business administration and management; mass communication/media studies; sport and fitness administration/management. **Special Study Options:** Accelerated program, cross-registration, distance learning, dual enrollment, honors program, independent study, internships, liberal arts/career combination, student-designed major, study abroad, teacher certification program. **Honors Programs:** Alpha Phi Sigma, Eta Sigma Delta, Kappa Delta Pi, Lambda Pi Eta, Communications Mortar Board, Psi Chi, Sigma Beta Delta, National Honor Society for Criminal Justice Students, Endicott College Honors Program, International Hospitality Management Society, National Honor Society for students in Senior Year. **Disability Services:** Special programs offered to physically disabled students include note-taking services, reader services, tape recorders, tutors. **Career Services:** Alumni network, alumni services, career/job search classes, career assessment, internships, regional alumni., Career Services highlights include Internships are required for all traditional undergraduate students.

FACILITIES

Housing: Coed dorms, special housing for disabled students, special housing for international students, women's dorms, apartments for single students, theme housing, single parent housing, suites, healthy living, academic. 80% of campus accessible to physically disabled. **Special Academic Facilities/Equipment:** Center for the Arts (galleries, theaters) http://www.endicott.edu/centerforthearts, Endicott Archives Museum http://www.endicott.edu/archives, La Chanterelle, a student-run restaraunt http://www.endicott.edu/lachanterelle **Computers:** 100% of classrooms, 96% of dorms, 100% of libraries, 100% of dining areas, 100% of student union, have wireless network access. Students can register for classes online. Administrative functions (other than registration) can be performed online.

CAMPUS LIFE

Environment: Town. **Activities:** Choral groups, concert band, dance, drama/theater, jazz band, literary magazine, music ensembles, musical theater, student government, student newspaper, student-run film society, television station, yearbook, Campus Ministries, International Student Organization, Model UN 47 registered organizations, 7 honor societies, 1 religious organization. **Athletics (Intercollegiate):** *Men:* baseball, basketball, cross-country, equestrian sports, football, golf, lacrosse, soccer, tennis, volleyball. *Women:* basketball, cross-country, equestrian sports, field hockey, lacrosse, soccer, softball, tennis, volleyball. **On-Campus Highlights:** Center for the Arts, The Lodge, Post Center - Sports Complex, Callahan Center, Endicott Beaches. **Environmental Initiatives:** Wind turbine and solar feasibility studies. Endicott has undertaken a comprehensive, year-long, wind-monitoring and engineering study to determine the feasibility installing a large-scale turbine. In addition, Endicott is assessing the viability of large-scale photovoltaic installation(s). Comprehensive energy efficiency. Endicott has undertaken high efficiency lighting and boilers. In addition, the college has replaced a number of heating systems with less carbon intensive fuels. We are monitoring our building for efficiency and are creating metrics for comprehensive analysis. Several of our buildings are eligible for Energy Star designation. Waste reduction plan. We have comprehensive single-stream recycling. We compost 100% of our yard waste. We are increasing recycling capture rates throughout campus. Student projects to employ social marketing techniques are part of this strategy.

ADMISSIONS

Freshman Academic Profile: Average high school GPA 3.3. 15% in top 10% of high school class, 44% in top 25% of high school class, 80% in top 50% of high school class. 80% from public high schools. SAT Math middle 50% range 490-580. SAT Critical Reading middle 50% range 490-580. SAT Writing middle 50% range 490-580. ACT middle 50% range 21-25. Minimum web-based TOEFL 79. Minimum paper TOEFL 550. **Basis for Candidate Selection:** *Very important factors considered include:* academic GPA, rigor of secondary school record, character/personal qualities. *Important factors considered include:* Class rank, application essay, standardized test scores, alumni/ae relation, extracurricular activities, geographical residence, talent/ability, volunteer work, work experience. *Other factors considered include:* recommendation(s), first generation, interview, level of applicant's interest, racial/ethnic status, state residency. **Freshman Admission Requirements:** High school diploma is required and GED is accepted. **Freshman Admission Statistics:** 3,661 applied, 63% admitted, 28% enrolled. **Transfer Admission Requirements:** High school transcript, college transcript(s), essay or personal statement, standardized test scores, statement of good standing from prior institution(s). Minimum college GPA of 2.5 required. Lowest grade transferable C. **General Admission Information:** Application Fee $40. Regular application deadline 2/15. Notification on a rolling basis, beginning on or about 11/1. Nonfall registration accepted. Credit offered for CEEB Advanced Placement tests.

COSTS AND FINANCIAL AID

Annual tuition $25,848. Room and board $12,388. Required fees $400. Average book expense $1,018. **Required Forms and Deadlines:** FAFSA, institution's own financial aid form. **Notification of Awards:** Applicants will be notified of awards on a rolling basis beginning 3/15. **Types of Aid:** *Need-based scholarships/grants: Loans:* Subsidized Stafford, Unsubsidized Stafford, PLUS, Federal Perkins, college/university loans from institutional funds. **Student Employment:** Federal Work-Study Program available. Institutional employment available. Highest amount earned per year from on-campus jobs $1,500. Off-campus job opportunities are good. **Financial Aid Statistics:** 86% freshmen, 84% undergrads receive need-based scholarship or grant aid. 65% freshmen, 61% undergrads receive non-need-based scholarship or grant aid. 95% freshmen, 95% undergrads receive need-based self-help aid. 91% freshmen, 86% undergrads receive any aid. 73% undergrads borrow to pay for school. Average cumulative indebtedness $36,198. **Criteria for awarding institutional aid:** *Non-need-based:* academics, alumni affiliation, art, job skills, leadership, music/drama, religious affiliation, state/district residency.

ERSKINE COLLEGE

Erskine College, Due West, SC 29639
Phone: 864-379-8838 • **Financial Aid Phone:** 864-379-8832
E-mail: admissions@erskine.edu
Fax: 864-379-2172 • **Website:** www.erskine.edu

This private school, affiliated with the Presbyterian Church, was founded in 1839. It has a 85-acre campus.

RATINGS
Admissions Selectivity Rating: 74   **Fire Safety Rating:** 63   **Green Rating:** 60*

STUDENTS AND FACULTY

Enrollment: 548. **Student Body:** 53% female, 47% male, 24% out-of-state, 4% international (10 countries represented). Asian 1%, African American 8%, Caucasian 70%, Hispanic 1%, Native American 0%.
Retention and Graduation: 77% freshmen return for sophomore year. 55% freshmen graduate within 4 years. 63% freshmen graduate within 6 years. **Faculty:** Student/faculty ratio 11:1. 41 full-time faculty, 85% hold PhDs, 7% are members of minority groups, 39% are women. 0% of classes are taught by teaching assistants.

ACADEMICS

Degrees: bachelor's, certificate, master's. **Classes:** Most classes have 10–19 students. Most lab/discussion sessions have 20–29 students. **Majors with Highest Enrollment:** biology/biological sciences; business/commerce; elementary education and teaching. **Special Study Options:** double major, independent study, internships, study abroad, teacher certification program. **Combined Degree Programs:** Medical Technology w/Medical Univ. of S. Carolina. **Disability Services:** Special programs offered to physically disabled students include tutors. **Career Services:** career/job search classes

FACILITIES

Housing: men's dorms, women's dorms. 75% of campus accessible to physically disabled. **Special Academic Facilities/Equipment:** Bowie Arts Center

CAMPUS LIFE

Environment: Rural. **Activities:** Choral groups, concert band, dance, drama/theater, jazz band, literary magazine, music ensembles, musical theater, radio station, student government, student newspaper, yearbook, Campus Ministries 51 registered organizations, 6 honor societies. **Athletics (Intercollegiate):** *Men:* baseball, basketball, cross-country, golf, soccer, tennis. *Women:* basketball, cross-country, golf, lacrosse, soccer, softball, tennis, volleyball. **On-Campus Highlights:** Java City, The Phoenix, Watkins Student Center, Bowie Arts Center

ADMISSIONS

Freshman Academic Profile: 39% in top 10% of high school class, 65% in top 25% of high school class, 87% in top 50% of high school class. 85% from public high schools. SAT Math middle 50% range 480-605. SAT Critical Reading middle 50% range 460-590. ACT middle 50% range 21-26. Minimum paper TOEFL 550. **Basis for Candidate Selection:** *Very important factors considered include:* application essay, academic GPA, recommendation(s), rigor of secondary school record, standardized test scores, alumni/ae relation. *Important factors considered include:* character/personal qualities, extracurricular activities, talent/ability. *Other factors considered include:* Class rank, first generation, geographical residence, interview, level of applicant's interest, racial/ethnic status, religious affiliation/commitment, state residency, volunteer work, work experience. **Freshman Admission Requirements:** High school diploma is required and GED is accepted. *Academic units required:* 4 English, 2 mathematics, 2 science, (2 science labs). 4 English, 2 mathematics, 2 science, (2 science labs). **Freshman Admission Statistics:** 500 applied, 75% admitted, 39% enrolled. **Transfer Admission Requirements:** college transcript(s), essay or personal statement, statement of good standing from prior institution(s). Minimum college GPA of 2.0 required. Lowest grade transferable C. **General Admission Information:** Application Fee $25. Notification on a rolling basis, beginning on or about 11/15. Nonfall registration accepted. Credit and/or placement offered for CEEB Advanced Placement tests.

COSTS AND FINANCIAL AID

Required Forms and Deadlines: FAFSA, institution's own financial aid form, state aid form. **Notification of Awards:** Applicants will be notified of awards on a rolling basis beginning 12/15. **Types of Aid:** *Need-based scholarships/grants:* Federal Pell, SEOG, state scholarships/grants, private scholarships, the school's own gift aid Federal ACG, Smart & Teach Grants. *Loans:* Subsidized Stafford, Unsubsidized Stafford, PLUS, Federal Perkins, college/university loans from institutional funds. Alternative Loans. **Student Employment:** Federal Work-Study Program available. Institutional employment available. **Financial Aid Statistics:** 100% freshmen, 100% undergrads receive need-based scholarship or grant aid. 100% freshmen, 100% undergrads receive non need-based scholarship or grant aid. 95% freshmen, 99% undergrads receive need-based self-help aid. 49% freshmen, 42% undergrads receive athletic scholarships. 72% undergrads borrow to pay for school. Average cumulative indebtedness $24,450. **Criteria for awarding institutional aid:** *Non-need-based:* academics, alumni affiliation, athletics, leadership, minority status, music/drama, religious affiliation, state/district residency.

EUGENE BIBLE COLLEGE

2155 Bailey Hill Road, Eugene, OR 97405-1194
Phone: 800-322-2638 • **Financial Aid Phone:** 800-322-2638
E-mail: admissions@ebc.edu • **CEEB Code:** 4274
Fax: 541-343-5801 • **Website:** www.ebc.edu/ • **ACT Code:** 3468

This private school was founded in 1925. It has a 33-acre campus.

RATINGS
Admissions Selectivity Rating: 87   **Fire Safety Rating:** 75   **Green Rating:** 60*

STUDENTS AND FACULTY

Enrollment: 180. **Student Body:** 44% female, 56% male, 54% out-of-state, (5 countries represented).
Retention and Graduation: 68% freshmen return for sophomore year. 31% freshmen graduate within 4 years. 41% freshmen graduate within 6 years. 35% grads go on to further study within 1 year. **Faculty:** Student/faculty ratio 10:1. 10 full-time faculty, 30% hold PhDs, 20% are members of minority groups, 40% are women. 0% of classes are taught by teaching assistants.

ACADEMICS

Degrees: bachelor's, certificate. **Classes:** Most classes have 10–19 students. Most lab/discussion sessions have 10–19 students. **Majors with Highest Enrollment:** bible/biblical studies; pastoral studies/counseling; youth ministry. **Special Study Options:** cooperative education program, distance learning, double major, dual enrollment, independent study, internships, liberal arts/career combination, One year Bible Certificate obtainable by external studies program. **Career Services:**

FACILITIES

Housing: men's dorms, women's dorms, apartments for married students, apartments for single students. 75% of campus accessible to physically disabled. **Special Academic Facilities/Equipment:** Music lab, computer lab

CAMPUS LIFE

Environment: City. **Activities:** Choral groups, drama/theater, music ensembles, student government, yearbook. **Athletics (Intercollegiate):** *Men:* basketball, soccer. *Women:* soccer, volleyball. **On-Campus Highlights:** Student Center, Cafeteria, Dorm Lounges, Computer Lab, Workout Room.

ADMISSIONS

Freshman Academic Profile: Average high school GPA 3.1. 8% in top 10% of high school class, 29% in top 25% of high school class, 67% in top 50% of high school class. 90% from public high schools. SAT Math middle 50% range 430-610. SAT Critical Reading middle 50% range 450-580. ACT middle 50% range 19-24. Minimum paper TOEFL 500. **Basis for Candidate Selection:** *Very important factors considered include:* application essay, recommendation(s), character/personal qualities, religious affiliation/commitment. *Important factors considered include:* rigor of secondary school record. *Other factors considered include:* Class rank, standardized test scores, extracurricular activities, talent/ability, volunteer work, work experience. **Freshman Admission Requirements:** High school diploma is required and GED is accepted. **Freshman Admission Statistics:** 217 applied, 47% admitted, 63% enrolled. **Transfer Admission Requirements:** college transcript(s), essay or personal statement, minimum college GPA of 2.0 required. Lowest grade transferable C. **General Admission Information:** Application Fee $30. Regular application deadline 9/1. Notification on a rolling basis, beginning on or about 10/1. Nonfall registration accepted. Admission may be deferred for a maximum of 24 months. Credit offered for CEEB Advanced Placement tests.

COSTS AND FINANCIAL AID

Annual tuition $7,500. Room and board $4,575. Required fees $801. Average book expense $800. **Required Forms and Deadlines:** FAFSA. **Notification of Awards:** Applicants will be notified of awards on a rolling basis beginning 7/15. **Types of Aid:** *Need-based scholarships/grants:* Federal Pell, SEOG, the school's own gift aid. *Loans:* Direct Subsidized Stafford, Direct Unsubsidized Stafford, Direct PLUS, PLUS. **Student Employment: Financial Aid Statistics:** 100% freshmen, 100% undergrads receive need-based scholarship or grant aid. 16% freshmen, 13% undergrads receive non-need-based scholarship or grant aid. 100% freshmen, 100% undergrads 90% undergrads borrow to pay for school. Average cumulative indebtedness $25,000. **Criteria for awarding institutional aid:** *Non-need-based:* academics, alumni affiliation, athletics, leadership, music/drama.

EUGENE LANG COLLEGE THE NEW SCHOOL FOR LIBERAL ARTS

72 5th Avenue, New York, NY 10011
Phone: 212-229-5665 • **Financial Aid Phone:** 212-229-8930
E-mail: lang@newschool.edu • **CEEB Code:** 2521
Fax: 212-229-5355 • **Website:** www.newschool.edu/lang • **ACT Code:** 2828

This private school was founded in 1978.

RATINGS

Admissions Selectivity Rating: 77   **Fire Safety Rating:** 77   **Green Rating:** 93

STUDENTS AND FACULTY

Enrollment: 1,472. **Student Body:** 67% female, 33% male, 70% out-of-state, 6% international (38 countries represented). Asian 6%, African American 5%, Caucasian 57%, Hispanic 11%.
Retention and Graduation: 73% freshmen return for sophomore year. 37% freshmen graduate within 4 years. **Faculty:** Student/faculty ratio 15:1. 70 full-time faculty, 20% are are members of minority groups.

ACADEMICS

Degrees: bachelor's. **Classes:** Most classes have 10–19 students. Most lab/discussion sessions have 10–19 students. **Special Study Options:** Accelerated

program, cross-registration, distance learning, double major, dual enrollment, English as a Second Language (ESL), exchange student program (domestic), independent study, internships, liberal arts/career combination, student-designed major, study abroad, five year combined BA/BFA program. **Combined degree programs:** BA/BFA. **Disability Services:** Special programs offered to physically disabled students include note-taking services, reader services, tape recorders. **Career services:** Alumni network, alumni services, career/job search classes, career assessment, internships, regional alumni.

FACILITIES

Housing: Coed dorms, special housing for disabled students, apartments for single students. 99% of campus accessible to physically disabled. **Special Academic Facilities/Equipment:** Art gallery, photography gallery, extensive collections of contemporary art, concert hall, public lectures, conferences, cultural and intellectual events. **Computers:** 95% of classrooms, 100% of libraries, 100% of dining areas, na% of student union, 100% of common outdoor areas have wireless network access. Students can register for classes online. Administrative functions (other than registration) can be performed online.

CAMPUS LIFE

Environment: Metropolis. **Activities:** Choral groups, dance, drama/theater, jazz band, literary magazine, music ensembles, opera, radio station, student government, student newspaper, symphony orchestra, International Student Organization. 34 registered organizations. **On-Campus Highlights:** Harry Scherman Library, Raymond Fogelman Library, Lang Courtyard, University Welcome Center, Sheila C. Johnson Design Center. **Environmental Initiatives:** 1. In fall 2010, The New School Facilities Management hired an engineering firm to conduct energy audits and to retro-commission five of the most energy-intensive owned buildings on campus. The result will be a phased capital plan to address needed upgrades in these buildings, equating to 500,000gsf, that will reduce carbon emissions. 2. The New School Office for Sustainability hired a consultant to conduct a waste audit of the entire campus in fall 2009. A waste reduction strategy is currently being finalized. The immediate outcomes are new recycling signs and an enhanced post-consumer composting program in four buildings. Food scraps, napkins/paper towels and compostable cups and utensils will be collected in all food service locations plus a pilot location in a building with architecture and fine arts studios. The New School replaced two steam boilers, which were approximately 50 years old.

ADMISSIONS

Freshman Academic Profile: Average high school GPA 3.3. 29% in top 10% of high school class, 57% in top 25% of high school class, 90% in top 50% of high school class. SAT Math middle 50% range 490-605. SAT Critical Reading middle 50% range 540-660. SAT Writing middle 50% range 540-660. ACT middle 50% range 24-28. Minimum web-based TOEFL 100. Minimum paper TOEFL 600. **Basis for Candidate Selection:** Very important factors considered include: application essay, academic GPA, recommendation(s), rigor of secondary school record. Important factors considered include: standardized test scores, character/personal qualities, interview, level of applicant's interest, volunteer work. Other factors considered include: Class rank, alumni/ae relation, extracurricular activities, first generation, geographical residence, talent/ability, work experience. **Freshman Admission Requirements:** High school diploma is required and GED is accepted. **Academic units required:** 4 English. **Academic units recommended:** 4 English. **Freshman Admission Statistics:** 1515 applied, 77% admitted, 23% enrolled. **Transfer Admission Requirements:** High school transcript, college transcript(s), essay or personal statement, standardized test scores, Minimum college GPA of 3.0 required. Lowest grade transferable C. **General Admission Information:** Application Fee $50. Early decision application deadline 11/15. Regular application deadline 2/1. Notification on a rolling basis, beginning on or about 3/25. Nonfall registration accepted. Admission may be deferred for a maximum of 1 year. Neither credit nor placement offered for CEEB Advanced Placement tests.

COSTS AND FINANCIAL AID

Annual tuition 36970. Room and board $15,260. Required fees $840. Average book expense $920. **Required Forms and Deadlines:** FAFSA, state aid form. **Notification of Awards:** Applicants will be notified of awards on a rolling basis beginning 3/1. **Types of Aid:** Need-based scholarships/grants: Federal Pell, SEOG, state scholarships/grants, private scholarships, the school's own gift aid. Loans: Subsidized Stafford, Unsubsidized Stafford, PLUS, Federal Perkins. Student Employment: Federal Work-Study Program available. Institutional employment available. Off-campus job opportunities are excellent. **Financial Aid Statistics:** 94% freshmen, 90% undergrads receive need-based scholarship or grant aid. 14% freshmen, 6% undergrads receive non-need-based scholarship or grant aid. 83% freshmen, 77% undergrads receive need-based self-help aid. 65% undergrads borrow to pay for school. Average cumulative indebtedness $28,550. **Criteria for awarding institutional aid:** Non-need-based: academics, leadership.

EUREKA COLLEGE

300 East College Avenue, Eureka, IL 61530-1500
Phone: 309-467-6350 • **Financial Aid Phone:** 309-467-6311
E-mail: admissions@eureka.edu • **CEEB Code:** 1206
Fax: 309-467-6576 • **Website:** www.eureka.edu/index.html • **ACT Code:** 1022

This private school, affiliated with the Disciples of Christ Church, was founded in 1855. It has a 112-acre campus.

RATINGS
Admissions Selectivity Rating: 69   **Fire Safety Rating:** 75   **Green Rating:** 60*

STUDENTS AND FACULTY
Enrollment: 654. **Student Body:** 56% female, 44% male, 10% out-of-state, 0% international (5 countries represented). Asian 1%, African American 3%, Caucasian 73%, Hispanic 2%, Native American 0%.
Retention and Graduation: 74% freshmen return for sophomore year. 41% freshmen graduate within 4 years. 51% freshmen graduate within 6 years. 24% grads go on to further study within 1 year. 8% grads pursue arts and sciences degrees. 6% grads pursue law degrees. 2% grads pursue business degrees. 3% grads pursue medical degrees. **Faculty:** Student/faculty ratio 16:1. 35 full-time faculty, 80% hold PhDs, 3% are members of minority groups, 34% are women. 0% of classes are taught by teaching assistants.

ACADEMICS
Degrees: bachelor's, certificate. **Classes:** Most classes have 10–19 students. Most lab/discussion sessions have fewer than 10 students. **Majors with Highest Enrollment:** business/commerce; elementary education and teaching; psychology. **Special Study Options:** double major, dual enrollment, honors program, independent study, internships, liberal arts/career combination, student-designed major, study abroad, teacher certification program, weekend college, Weekend Degree Completion Cohort Program in Organizational Leadership Weekend Degree Certification in Special Education. **Honors Programs:** Academic Honors Program, Reagan Leadership Program, Sandifer Mentorship Program **Combined Degree Programs:** BA/MEng, 2-2 nursing prog with Mennonite Coll of Nursing. **Disability Services:** Special programs offered to physically disabled students include tutors.

FACILITIES
Housing: Coed dorms, special housing for disabled students, men's dorms, women's dorms, fraternity/sorority housing. 60% of campus accessible to physically disabled. **Special Academic Facilities/Equipment:** Ronald Reagan Museum Electron Microscope Peace Garden **Computers:** Administrative functions (other than registration) can be performed online.

CAMPUS LIFE
Environment: Village. **Activities:** Choral groups, concert band, dance, drama/theater, jazz band, literary magazine, musical theater, pep band, student government, student newspaper, student-run film society, yearbook 41 registered organizations, 15 honor societies, 4 religious organizations. 3 fraternities, 3 sororities. **Athletics (Intercollegiate):** *Men:* baseball, basketball, cross-country, football, golf, soccer, swimming, tennis, track/field (outdoor). *Women:* basketball, cross-country, golf, soccer, softball, swimming, tennis, track/field (outdoor), volleyball. **On-Campus Highlights:** Ronald Reagan Museum and Peace Garden, Cerf College Center, National Historic Site: Administration Building, National Historic Site: The Chapel, Lilac Arboretum, Founded in 1855 by abolitionists, Eureka College is located on 130 acres of trees and gardens. Ist college in Illinois to accept men and women on an equal basis. Small town setting located between two midsize cities--the best of both worlds! Personal. Faith-based. Liberal Arts. Pillow to Port internet access for all!.

ADMISSIONS
Freshman Academic Profile: Average high school GPA 3.2. 17% in top 10% of high school class, 44% in top 25% of high school class, 96% in top 50% of high school class. 87% from public high schools. ACT middle 50% range 18-24. Minimum paper TOEFL 500. **Basis for Candidate Selection:** *Very important factors considered include:* Class rank, recommendation(s), rigor of secondary school record, standardized test scores, character/personal qualities, extracurricular activities, volunteer work. *Important factors considered include:* talent/ability. *Other factors considered include:* application essay, alumni/ae relation, interview, work experience. **Freshman Admission Requirements: Freshman Admission Statistics:** 635 applied, 75% admitted, 31% enrolled. **Transfer Admission Requirements:** college transcript(s), statement of good standing from prior institution(s). Minimum college GPA of 2.0 required. Lowest grade transferable C. **General Admission Information:** Regular application deadline 8/1. Nonfall registration accepted. Admission may be deferred for a maximum of 1 year. Credit offered for CEEB Advanced Placement tests.

COSTS AND FINANCIAL AID
Annual tuition $15,673. Room and board $7,130. Required fees $580. Average book expense $1,000. **Required Forms and Deadlines:** FAFSA. **Notification of Awards:** Applicants will be notified of awards on or about 5/1. **Types of Aid:** *Need-based scholarships/grants:* Federal Pell, SEOG, state scholarships/grants, private scholarships, the school's own gift aid. *Loans:* Direct Subsidized Stafford, Direct Unsubsidized Stafford, Direct PLUS, Subsidized Stafford, Unsubsidized Stafford, PLUS, Federal Perkins, college/university loans from institutional funds, alternative loans. **Student Employment:** Federal Work-Study Program available. Institutional employment available. Highest amount earned per year from on-campus jobs $1,000. Off-campus job opportunities are excellent. **Financial Aid Statistics:** 100% freshmen, 100% undergrads receive need-based scholarship or grant aid. 91% freshmen, 89% undergrads receive need-based self-help aid. 100% freshmen, 94% undergrads receive any aid. 86% undergrads borrow to pay for school. Average cumulative indebtedness $14,727. **Criteria for awarding institutional aid:** *Non-need-based:* academics, alumni affiliation, art, leadership, music/drama, religious affiliation.

EVANGEL UNIVERSITY

111 North Glenstone, Springfield, MO 65802
Phone: 417-865-2811
E-mail: admissions@evangel.edu • **CEEB Code:** 6198
Fax: 417-520-0545 • **Website:** www.evangel.edu • **ACT Code:** 2296

This private school was founded in 1955. It has a 80-acre campus.

RATINGS
Admissions Selectivity Rating: 62   **Fire Safety Rating:** 60*   **Green Rating:** 60*

STUDENTS AND FACULTY
Enrollment: 1,616. **Student Body:** 56% female, 44% male, 60% out-of-state, 1% international (13 countries represented). Asian 0%, African American 2%, Caucasian 64%, Hispanic 0%, Native American 0%.
Retention and Graduation: 77% freshmen return for sophomore year. **Faculty:** 0% of classes are taught by teaching assistants.

ACADEMICS
Degrees: associate, bachelor's, master's. **Special Study Options:** cooperative education program, double major, dual enrollment, independent study, internships, teacher certification program. **Career Services:** career/job search classes, career assessment, internships.

FACILITIES
Housing: men's dorms, women's dorms, apartments for married students, Co-occupancy dorm with men and women in separate wings.

CAMPUS LIFE
Activities: Choral groups, concert band, drama/theater, jazz band, music ensembles, pep band, radio station, student government, student newspaper, television station, yearbook 14 registered organizations, 10 honor societies, 3 religious organizations. **Athletics (Intercollegiate):** *Men:* baseball, basketball, cheerleading, cross-country, football, golf, track/field (outdoor), track/field (indoor). *Women:* basketball, cheerleading, cross-country, golf, softball, track/field (outdoor), track/field (indoor), volleyball.

ADMISSIONS
Freshman Academic Profile: 76% from public high schools. Minimum paper TOEFL 490. **Basis for Candidate Selection:** *Very important factors considered include:* Class rank, recommendation(s), rigor of secondary school record, standardized test scores, religious affiliation/commitment. *Important factors considered include:* character/personal qualities. **Freshman Admission Requirements:** High school diploma is required and GED is accepted. **Freshman Admission Statistics:** 1,254 applied, 78% admitted. **Transfer Admission Requirements:** college transcript(s), statement of good standing from prior institution(s). Minimum college GPA of 2.0 required. Lowest grade transferable C. **General Admission Information:** Application Fee $35. Regular application deadline 8/15. Notification on a rolling basis, beginning on or about 9/1. Nonfall registration accepted. Admission may be deferred for a maximum of 1. Credit offered for CEEB Advanced Placement tests.

COSTS AND FINANCIAL AID
Annual tuition $13,530. Room and board $5,120. Required fees $660. Average book expense $800. **Required Forms and Deadlines:** FAFSA. **Notification of Awards:** Applicants will be notified of awards on a rolling basis beginning 4/1. **Types of Aid:** *Need-based scholarships/grants:* Federal Pell, SEOG, private scholarships. *Loans:* Direct Subsidized Stafford, Direct Unsubsidized Stafford, Direct PLUS, Subsidized Stafford, Unsubsidized Stafford, PLUS, Federal Perkins, college/university loans from institutional funds. **Student Em-**

ployment: Federal Work-Study Program available. Institutional employment available. Off-campus job opportunities are excellent. **Financial Aid Statistics:** 85% undergrads receive need-based scholarship or grant aid.

THE EVERGREEN STATE COLLEGE

2700 Evergreen Pkwy NW, Olympia, WA 98505
Phone: 360-867-6170 • **Financial Aid Phone:** 360-867-6205
E-mail: admissions@evergreen.edu • **CEEB Code:** 4292
Fax: 360-867-5114 • **Website:** www.evergreen.edu • **ACT Code:** 4457

This public school was founded in 1967. It has a 1000-acre campus.

RATINGS
Admissions Selectivity Rating: 66   **Fire Safety Rating:** 82   **Green Rating:** 86

STUDENTS AND FACULTY
Enrollment: 4,121. **Student Body:** 54% female, 46% male, 25% out-of-state, 1% international (27 countries represented). Asian 2%, African American 5%, Caucasian 67%, Hispanic 7%, Native American 2%.
Retention and Graduation: 72% freshmen return for sophomore year. 40% freshmen graduate within 4 years. 54% freshmen graduate within 6 years. 21% grads go on to further study within 1 year. 16% grads pursue arts and sciences degrees. 1% grads pursue business degrees. 1% grads pursue medical degrees.
Faculty: Student/faculty ratio 21:1. 176 full-time faculty, 88% hold PhDs, 23% are members of minority groups, 52% are women. 0% of classes are taught by teaching assistants.

ACADEMICS
Degrees: bachelor's, certificate, master's. **Classes:** Most classes have 20–29 students. **Majors with Highest Enrollment:** environmental studies; liberal arts and sciences/liberal studies; social sciences, other. **Special Study Options:** Accelerated program, double major, exchange student program (domestic), independent study, internships, student-designed major, study abroad, teacher certification program, weekend college, Learning disabilities services, summer session for credit, off-campus study. **Combined Degree Programs:** BA/BS Lib Arts; Master Environ Stud/Pub Admin. **Disability Services:** Special programs offered to physically disabled students include note-taking services, tape recorders, tutors. **Career Services:** Alumni network, alumni services, career/job search classes, career assessment, internships, Career Services highlights include Community Opportunities & Internship Fair (COIF) http://www.evergreen.edu/advising/coif.

FACILITIES
Housing: Coed dorms, special housing for disabled students, special housing for international students, apartments for married students, apartments for single students, wellness housing, theme housing: First-Year/Freshman residence halls, Quiet housing, Substance-free housing, Gender Neutral Housing, Community Action House, Sustainability House. 85% of campus accessible to physically disabled. **Special Academic Facilities/Equipment:** Longhouse Cultural Center, 4 computer music labs, 3 digital studio production studios, 4 analog audio recording studio/control room clusters, digital still imaging lab, multimedia lab, 3 nonlinear video editing suites, 4 linear analog video editing suites, color and BandW photography labs, animation stand, 2 digital animation suites, film mixing studio with 5 editing suites, 2 flatbed film edit rooms, 3 A/V classrooms, 5 A/V lecture halls, Media Loan equipment checkout facility, academic sailing fleet (two 40' wooden sailboats), organic farm, scanning electron microscope, gas chromatography mass spectrometer, FTNMR, FTIR, scientific computing laboratory, printmaking studio, ceramics studio, academic wood and metal shops, weaving studio, fine metal studio, two art galleries. **Computers:** 100% of classrooms, 95% of dorms, 100% of libraries, 100% of dining areas, 100% of student union, 80% of common outdoor areas have wireless network access. Students can register for classes online. Administrative functions (other than registration) can be performed online.

CAMPUS LIFE
Environment: City. **Activities:** Choral groups, dance, drama/theater, literary magazine, music ensembles, pep band, radio station, student government, student newspaper, student-run film society, television station, Campus Ministries, Model UN 61 registered organizations, 3 religious organizations. **Athletics (Intercollegiate):** *Men:* basketball, cross-country, soccer, track/field (outdoor), track/field (indoor). *Women:* basketball, cross-country, soccer, track/field (outdoor), track/field (indoor), volleyball. **On-Campus Highlights:** Longhouse Cultural and Education Center, Organic Farm, College Library, College Activities Building, New Seminar II Building, The Flaming Eggplant, a student-run cafe featuring organic, local, and vegan food. **Environmental Initiatives:** We have completed the planning and begun implementation of our Climate Action Plan - Carbon Neutrality by 2020. Integrating sustainability across the curriculum initiative. Free bus passes for all faculty/staff/students; first publicly funded LEED gold building in the state of Washington; 32% of food purchases from local/organic sources; campus waste diversion and composting programs; annual carbon inventory.

ADMISSIONS
Freshman Academic Profile: Average high school GPA 3.0. 13% in top 10% of high school class, 30% in top 25% of high school class, 58% in top 50% of high school class. SAT Math middle 50% range 460-590. SAT Critical Reading middle 50% range 510-640. SAT Writing middle 50% range 470-600. ACT middle 50% range 21-27. Minimum web-based TOEFL 79. Minimum paper TOEFL 550. **Basis for Candidate Selection:** *Very important factors considered include:* application essay, academic GPA, rigor of secondary school record. *Important factors considered include:* standardized test scores, first generation, level of applicant's interest. *Other factors considered include:* recommendation(s), extracurricular activities, interview, volunteer work, work experience. **Freshman Admission Requirements:** High school diploma is required and GED is accepted. *Academic units required:* 4 English, 3 mathematics, 2 science, (1 science labs), 2 foreign language, 3 social studies, 1 academic electives, 1 Fine, visual or performing arts elective or other college prep elective from the areas above. 4 English, 3 mathematics, 2 science, (1 science labs), 2 foreign language, 3 social studies, 1 academic electives, 1 Fine, visual or performing arts elective or other college prep elective from the areas above **Freshman Admission Statistics:** 1,650 applied, 98% admitted, 33% enrolled. **Transfer Admission Requirements:** college transcript(s), minimum college GPA of 2 required. Lowest grade transferable 2. **General Admission Information:** Application Fee $50. Notification on a rolling basis, beginning on or about 11/1. Nonfall registration accepted. Admission may be deferred for a maximum of One quarter. Credit offered for CEEB Advanced Placement tests.

COSTS AND FINANCIAL AID
Annual in-state tuition $7,812. Annual out-of-state tuition $18,978. Room and board $9,240. Required fees $583. Average book expense $999. **Required Forms and Deadlines:** FAFSA, institution's own financial aid form. **Notification of Awards:** Applicants will be notified of awards on a rolling basis beginning 4/1. **Types of Aid:** *Need-based scholarships/grants:* Federal Pell, SEOG, state scholarships/grants, private scholarships, the school's own gift aid, Federal Academic Competitiveness Grant (ACG); National Science and Mathematics Access to Retain Talent Grant(SMART Grant). *Loans:* Subsidized Stafford, Unsubsidized Stafford, PLUS, Federal Perkins, Private Alternative Loans. **Student Employment:** Federal Work-Study Program available. Institutional employment available. Highest amount earned per year from on-campus jobs $9,975. Off-campus job opportunities are good. **Financial Aid Statistics:** 63% freshmen, 78% undergrads receive need-based scholarship or grant aid. 15% freshmen, 11% undergrads receive non-need-based scholarship or grant aid. 70% freshmen, 79% undergrads receive need-based self-help aid. 59% freshmen, 63% undergrads receive any aid. 48% undergrads borrow to pay for school. Average cumulative indebtedness $15,706. **Criteria for awarding institutional aid:** *Non-need-based:* academics, art, athletics, state/district residency.

EXCELSIOR COLLEGE

7 Columbia Circle, Albany, NY 12203-5159
Phone: 518-464-8500 • **Financial Aid Phone:** 518-464-8500
E-mail: admissions@excelsior.edu • **CEEB Code:** 759
Fax: 518-464-8777 • **Website:** www.excelsior.edu/ • **ACT Code:** 20214

This private school was founded in 1970.

RATINGS
Admissions Selectivity Rating: 62   **Fire Safety Rating:** 60*   **Green Rating:** 60*

STUDENTS AND FACULTY
Enrollment: 32,133. **Student Body:** 58% female, 42% male, 90% out-of-state, 0% international (56 countries represented). Asian 4%, African American 17%, Caucasian 58%, Hispanic 5%, Native American 1%.

ACADEMICS
Degrees: associate, bachelor's, master's, post-bachelor's certificate, post-master's certificate. **Classes:** Most classes have 10–19 students. **Majors with

Highest Enrollment: business administration and management; liberal arts and sciences/liberal studies; nursing/registered nurse (rn, asn, msn). **Special Study Options:** Accelerated program, distance learning, external degree program, honors program, independent study. **Combined Degree Programs:** RN/MSN. **Career Services:** Alumni network, alumni services, career assessment.

FACILITIES
Housing: no housing available on campus. **Computers:** Students can register for classes online. Administrative functions (other than registration) can be performed online.

CAMPUS LIFE
Environment: City. **Activities:** 1 honor societies. **Environmental Initiatives:** EC has a staff created and led committee that looks for opportunites to create a more 'green' environment.

ADMISSIONS
Freshman Admission Requirements: High school diploma is required and GED is accepted. **Transfer Admission Requirements:** Lowest grade transferable C. **General Admission Information:** Application Fee $75. Nonfall registration accepted.

COSTS AND FINANCIAL AID
Required Forms and Deadlines: FAFSA, institution's own financial aid form. **Notification of Awards:** Applicants will be notified of awards on a rolling basis beginning 8/1. **Types of Aid:** *Need-based scholarships/grants:* Federal Pell, state scholarships/grants, private scholarships, the school's own gift aid. *Loans:* Direct Subsidized Stafford, Direct Unsubsidized Stafford, Direct PLUS. **Financial Aid Statistics:** 3% undergrads receive any aid.

FAIRFIELD UNIVERSITY

Best 378

1073 North Benson Road, Fairfield, CT 06824-5195
Phone: 203-254-4100 • **Financial Aid Phone:** 203-254-4125
E-mail: admis@fairfield.edu • **CEEB Code:** 3390
Fax: 203-254-4199 • **Website:** www.fairfield.edu • **ACT Code:** 560

This private school, affiliated with the Roman Catholic Jesuit Church, was founded in 1942. It has a 200-acre campus.

RATINGS
Admissions Selectivity Rating: 81   **Fire Safety Rating:** 87   **Green Rating:** 78

STUDENTS AND FACULTY
Enrollment: 3,696. **Student Body:** 59% female, 41% male, 64% out-of-state, 1% international (24 countries represented). Asian 2%, African American 3%, Caucasian 69%, Hispanic 8%, Native American 0%.
Retention and Graduation: 78% freshmen graduate within 4 years. 24% grads go on to further study within 1 year. 17% grads pursue arts and sciences degrees. 11% grads pursue law degrees. 37% grads pursue business degrees. 17% grads pursue medical degrees. **Faculty:** Student/faculty ratio 11:1. 263 full-time faculty, 92% hold PhDs, 5% are members of minority groups, 54% are women. 0% of classes are taught by teaching assistants.

ACADEMICS
Degrees: associate, bachelor's, master's, post-master's certificate. **Classes:** Most classes have 20–29 students. **Majors with Highest Enrollment:** finance; nursing/registered nurse (rn, asn, bsn, msn); psychology. **Special Study Options:** cross-registration, double major, exchange student program (domestic), honors program, independent study, internships, liberal arts/career combination, student-designed major, study abroad, teacher certification program, 3/2 Program with UCONN, Rensselaer Polytechnic Institute of Technology, Columbia and Stevens Institute of Technology. **Honors Programs:** Magis Scholars Four year Honors Program Corrigan Research Scholars **Combined Degree Programs:** BA/MEng, BS/MS Software Engineering. **Disability Services:** Special programs offered to physically disabled students include note-taking services, reader services, tape recorders, tutors. **Career Services:** Alumni network, alumni services, career/job search classes, career assessment, internships Career Services highlights include Fairfield's proximity to NYC, Stamford and Bridgeport maximizes student opportunities for internships in all majors from Finance to Psychology.

FACILITIES
Housing: Coed dorms, special housing for disabled students, apartments for single students, Wellness Floor; Sophomore College; Women in Math & Science; Freshmen Residence Halls; Diversity & Social Justice Floor (for Sophomores); Leadership House; Community Service House; The Green House; Empowering Women House; Extensive theme based living-learning options for sophomores. 70% of campus accessible to physically disabled. **Special Academic Facilities/Equipment:** Quick Center for the arts, 2 art galleries, media center, TV studio, language labs, computer center for teacher education, Business Experiential, Simulation & Trading Floor (BEST) at the School of Business. School of Nursing Learning Resouce center is a simulated hospital environment with a Human Patient Simulator (SimMan) for simulation based learning. **Computers:** 50% of classrooms, 100% of dorms, 100% of libraries, 100% of dining areas, 100% of student union, 5% of common outdoor areas have wireless network access. Students can register for classes online. Administrative functions (other than registration) can be performed online.

CAMPUS LIFE
Environment: Town. **Activities:** Choral groups, concert band, dance, drama/theater, jazz band, literary magazine, music ensembles, pep band, radio station, student government, student newspaper, student-run film society, television station, yearbook, Campus Ministries, International Student Organization, Model UN 110 registered organizations, 21 honor societies, 3 religious organizations. **Athletics (Intercollegiate):** *Men:* baseball, basketball, crew/rowing, cross-country, diving, golf, lacrosse, soccer, swimming, tennis. *Women:* basketball, crew/rowing, cross-country, diving, field hockey, golf, lacrosse, soccer, softball, swimming, tennis, volleyball. **On-Campus Highlights:** Quick Center for the Arts(includes Walsh Art Gallery, Kelley Theatre and Wien Theatre, Egan/Loyola Chapel, DiMenna-Nyselius Library, Leslie C. Quick, Jr. Recreation Complex, Barone Campus Center (Student Center), Jazzman's Coffee Bar. **Environmental Initiatives:** We have joined Campus Climate Pact. Built a Cogeneration facility providing 90% of campus electricity; 60% campus heating. Large scale recycling and composting/biofuels initiative. While there is no Full time dedicated staff person, sustainability efforts are performed by several folk and overseen by the Environmental Steering Committees that was convened in 2006-07 and meets quarterly.

ADMISSIONS
Freshman Academic Profile: Average high school GPA 3.4. 56% from public high schools. SAT Math middle 50% range 550-630. SAT Critical Reading middle 50% range 530-620. SAT Writing middle 50% range 540-640. ACT middle 50% range 24-27. Minimum web-based TOEFL 80. Minimum paper TOEFL 550. **Basis for Candidate Selection:** *Very important factors considered include:* application essay, academic GPA, recommendation(s), rigor of secondary school record. *Important factors considered include:* character/personal qualities, extracurricular activities, first generation, interview, talent/ability, volunteer work, work experience. *Other factors considered include:* Class rank, standardized test scores, alumni/ae relation, geographical residence, racial/ethnic status. **Freshman Admission Requirements:** High school diploma is required and GED is not accepted. *Academic units required:* 4 English, 3 mathematics, 2 science, (2 science labs), 2 foreign language, 2 social studies, 2 history, 1 academic electives. *Academic units recommended:* 4 English, 3 mathematics, 2 science, (2 science labs), 2 foreign language, 2 social studies, 2 history, 1 academic electives. **Freshman Admission Statistics:** 9,254 applied, 71% admitted, 15% enrolled. **Transfer Admission Requirements:** High school transcript, college transcript(s), essay or personal statement, statement of good standing from prior institution(s). Minimum college GPA of.03 required. Lowest grade transferable C. **General Admission Information:** Application Fee $60. Regular application deadline 1/15. Regular notification 4/1. Nonfall registration not accepted. Admission may be deferred for a maximum of 1 Year. Credit and/or placement offered for CEEB Advanced Placement tests.

COSTS AND FINANCIAL AID
Annual tuition $41,090. Room and board $12,550. Required fees $600. Average book expense $1,150. **Required Forms and Deadlines:** FAFSA, CSS/Financial Aid PROFILE, noncustodial PROFILE, business/farm supplement. **Notification of Awards:** Applicants will be notified of awards on or about 4/1. **Types of Aid:** *Need-based scholarships/grants:* Federal Pell, SEOG, state scholarships/grants, private scholarships, the school's own gift aid, Federal Nursing Scholarships. *Loans:* Subsidized Stafford, Unsubsidized Stafford, PLUS, Federal Perkins, Federal Nursing, Alternative Loans. **Student Employment:** Federal Work-Study Program available. Institutional employment available. Highest amount earned per year from on-campus jobs $1,500. Off-campus job opportunities are good. **Financial Aid Statistics:** 86% freshmen, 91% undergrads receive need-based scholarship or grant aid. 85% freshmen, 55% undergrads receive non-need-based scholarship or grant aid. 82% freshmen, 87% undergrads receive need-based self-help aid. 6% freshmen, 7% undergrads receive athletic scholarships. 87% freshmen, 78% undergrads receive any aid. 67% undergrads borrow to pay for school. Average cumulative indebtedness $28,507. **Criteria for awarding institutional aid:** *Non-need-based:* academics, alumni affiliation, art, athletics, leadership, music/drama.

FAIRLEIGH DICKINSON UNIVERSITY, COLLEGE AT FLORHAM

285 Madison Ave, Madison, NJ 7940
Phone: 800-338-8803
E-mail: globaleducation@fdu.edu • **CEEB Code:** 226241
Fax: 973-443-8088 • **Website:** www.fdu.edu • **ACT Code:** 2554

This private school was founded in 1942. It has a 178-acre campus.

RATINGS
Admissions Selectivity Rating: 65   **Fire Safety Rating:** 89   **Green Rating:** 67

STUDENTS AND FACULTY
Enrollment: 2,349. **Student Body:** 56% female, 44% male, 16% out-of-state, 1% international (25 countries represented). Asian 4%, African American 11%, Caucasian 64%, Hispanic 11%, Native American 1%.
Retention and Graduation: 72% freshmen return for sophomore year. 40% freshmen graduate within 4 years. 55% freshmen graduate within 6 years.
Faculty: Student/faculty ratio 12:1. 131 full-time faculty, 74% hold PhDs, 18% are members of minority groups, 42% are women. % of classes are taught by teaching assistants.

ACADEMICS
Degrees: bachelor's, master's, post-bachelor's certificate, post-master's certificate. **Classes: Majors with Highest Enrollment:** business administration and management; communication studies/speech communication and rhetoric; psychology. **Special Study Options:** Accelerated program, cooperative education program, cross-registration, distance learning, double major, external degree program, honors program, independent study, internships, liberal arts/career combination, student-designed major, teacher certification program, weekend college. **Combined Degree Programs:** BA/MD, BA/MA, BA/DDS, BA or BS/MAT, BA or BS/MBA, BA/MPA. **Disability Services:** Special programs offered to physically disabled students include note-taking services, reader services, tape recorders, tutors. **Career Services:** Alumni network, alumni services, career/job search classes, career assessment, internships Career Services highlights include Experiential learning.

FACILITIES
Housing: Coed dorms, special housing for disabled students 34% of campus accessible to physically disabled. **Computers:** 100% of classrooms, 100% of libraries, 100% of dining areas, 100% of student union, have wireless network access. Students can register for classes online. Administrative functions (other than registration) can be performed online.

CAMPUS LIFE
Environment: Village. **Activities:** Choral groups, dance, drama/theater, literary magazine, musical theater, radio station, student government, student newspaper, student-run film society, yearbook, Campus Ministries, International Student Organization 44 registered organizations, 9 honor societies, 3 religious organizations. 6 fraternities, 4 sororities. **Athletics (Intercollegiate):** *Men:* baseball, basketball, cross-country, football, golf, lacrosse, soccer, swimming, tennis. *Women:* basketball, cross-country, field hockey, lacrosse, soccer, softball, swimming, tennis, volleyball. **On-Campus Highlights:** Recreation Center, Bottle Hill Pub, Florham Perks, L'Orangerie of Library, Mansion gardens. **Environmental Initiatives:** Recyclemania, Recycling Bins New contruction LEED certification HVAC upgrades will be energy efficient.

ADMISSIONS
Freshman Academic Profile: Average high school GPA 3.1. 15% in top 10% of high school class, 40% in top 25% of high school class, 76% in top 50% of high school class. SAT Math middle 50% range 460-570. SAT Critical Reading middle 50% range 450-560. SAT Writing middle 50% range 450-560. Minimum web-based TOEFL 79. Minimum paper TOEFL 550. **Basis for Candidate Selection:** *Very important factors considered include:* academic GPA, rigor of secondary school record. *Important factors considered include:* standardized test scores. *Other factors considered include:* Class rank, recommendation(s), extracurricular activities, interview, volunteer work, work experience. **Freshman Admission Requirements:** High school diploma is required and GED is accepted. *Academic units required:* 4 English, 3 mathematics, 2 science, (2 science labs), 2 foreign language, 2 social studies, 2 history, 3 academic electives. *Academic units recommended:* 4 English, 3 mathematics, 2 science, (2 science labs), 2 foreign language, 2 social studies, 2 history, 3 academic electives. **Transfer Admission Requirements:** college transcript(s), minimum college GPA of 2.0 required. Lowest grade transferable C. **General Admission Information:** Application Fee $40. Notification on a rolling basis, beginning on or about 11/15. Nonfall registration accepted. Admission may be deferred for a maximum of 1 year. Credit offered for CEEB Advanced Placement tests.

COSTS AND FINANCIAL AID
Student Employment: Federal Work-Study Program available. Institutional employment available. Off-campus job opportunities are good.

FAIRLEIGH DICKINSON UNIVERSITY, METROPOLITAN CAMPUS

1000 River Road, Teaneck, NJ 07666-1966
Phone: 201-692-2553
E-mail: globaleducation@fdu.edu • **CEEB Code:** 226341
Fax: 201-692-7319 • **Website:** www.fdu.edu • **ACT Code:** 2552

This private school was founded in 1942. It has a 68-acre campus.

RATINGS
Admissions Selectivity Rating: 65   **Fire Safety Rating:** 89   **Green Rating:** 67

STUDENTS AND FACULTY
Enrollment: 4,045. **Student Body:** 58% female, 42% male, 14% out-of-state, 7% international (83 countries represented). Asian 6%, African American 14%, Caucasian 29%, Hispanic 33%, Native American 0%.
Retention and Graduation: 25% freshmen graduate within 4 years. 41% freshmen graduate within 6 years. **Faculty:** Student/faculty ratio 14:1. 191 full-time faculty, 76% hold PhDs, 20% are members of minority groups, 43% are women.

ACADEMICS
Degrees: associate, bachelor's, certificate, master's, post-bachelor's certificate, post-master's certificate, terminal associate. **Majors with Highest Enrollment:** business administration and management; nursing/registered nurse (rn, asn, bsn, msn); psychology. **Special Study Options:** Accelerated program, cooperative education program, cross-registration, distance learning, English as a Second Language (ESL), external degree program, honors program, independent study, internships, liberal arts/career combination, student-designed major, study abroad, teacher certification program, weekend college. **Combined Degree Programs:** BA/MD, BA/MA, BA/DDS, BA/MPA, BA/BS-MAT,BA/MBA,BS/DMD,BS/DC,BSEE/MSEE,BSEE/MSCE. **Disability Services:** Special programs offered to physically disabled students include note-taking services, reader services, tape recorders, tutors. **Career Services:** Alumni network, alumni services, career/job search classes, career assessment, internships Career Services highlights include Experiential Learning.

FACILITIES
Housing: Coed dorms, special housing for disabled students, °LIFE House - Substance Free Living °Global Scholars Hall °Honor's House °Academic Year Round Housing. 41% of campus accessible to physically disabled. **Computers:** 90% of classrooms, 100% of libraries, 100% of dining areas, 100% of student union, have wireless network access. Students can register for classes online. Administrative functions (other than registration) can be performed online.

CAMPUS LIFE
Environment: Town. **Activities:** Choral groups, dance, drama/theater, literary magazine, pep band, radio station, student government, student newspaper, student-run film society, yearbook, Campus Ministries, International Student Organization, Model UN 72 registered organizations, 10 honor societies, 4 religious organizations. 5 fraternities, 7 sororities. **Athletics (Intercollegiate):** *Men:* baseball, basketball, cross-country, golf, soccer, tennis, track/field (indoor). *Women:* basketball, bowling, cross-country, fencing, golf, soccer, softball, tennis, track/field (indoor), volleyball. **On-Campus Highlights:** Weiner Library, Fitness Center, Jeepers (Wireless Cafe), Knight Club, Hackensack River. **Environmental Initiatives:** Recyclemania, Recycling Bins New construction LEED certification HVAC upgrades will be energy efficient

ADMISSIONS
Freshman Academic Profile: Average high school GPA 3.2. 17% in top 10% of high school class, 43% in top 25% of high school class, 81% in top 50% of high school class. SAT Math middle 50% range 460-560. SAT Critical Reading middle 50% range 440-530. SAT Writing middle 50% range 440-540. Minimum web-based TOEFL 79. Minimum paper TOEFL 550. **Basis for Candidate Selection:** *Very important factors considered include:* academic GPA, rigor of secondary school record. *Important factors considered include:* standardized test scores. *Other factors considered include:* Class rank, recommendation(s), extracurricular activities, interview, volunteer work, work experience. **Freshman Admission Requirements:** High school diploma is required and GED is accepted. *Academic units required:* 4 English, 3 mathematics, 2 science, (2 science labs), 2 foreign language, 2 social studies, 2 history, 3 academic electives. *Academic units recommended:* 4 English, 3 mathematics, 2 science, (2 science labs), 2 foreign language, 2 social studies, 2 history, 3 academic elec-

tives. **Transfer Admission Requirements:** college transcript(s), minimum college GPA of 2.0 required. Lowest grade transferable C. **General Admission Information:** Application Fee $40. Notification on a rolling basis, beginning on or about 11/15. Nonfall registration accepted. Admission may be deferred for a maximum of 1 year. Credit offered for CEEB Advanced Placement tests.

COSTS AND FINANCIAL AID
Student Employment: Federal Work-Study Program available. Off-campus job opportunities are good.

FAIRMONT STATE UNIVERSITY, INCLUDING PIERPONT COMMUNITY & TECHNICAL COLLEGE

Office of Admissions, Fairmont State, Fairmont, WV 26554
Phone: 304-367-4892 • **Financial Aid Phone:** 304-367-4813
E-mail: admit@fairmontstate.edu • **CEEB Code:** 4520
Fax: • **Website:** www.fairmontstate.edu • **ACT Code:** 4520

This public school was founded in 1865.

RATINGS
Admissions Selectivity Rating: 67   **Fire Safety Rating:** 60*   **Green Rating:** 60*

STUDENTS AND FACULTY
Enrollment: 6,227. **Student Body:** 57% female, 43% male, 4% out-of-state, 1% international. Asian 0%, African American 4%, Caucasian 91%, Hispanic 1%, Native American 0%.
Retention and Graduation: 70% freshmen return for sophomore year. 11% freshmen graduate within 4 years. 35% freshmen graduate within 6 years. **Faculty:** Student/faculty ratio 18:1. 232 full-time faculty, 48% hold PhDs, 6% are members of minority groups, 45% are women. 0% of classes are taught by teaching assistants.

ACADEMICS
Degrees: associate, bachelor's, certificate, master's, terminal associate, transfer associate. Classes: Most classes have 10–19 students. Most lab/discussion sessions have fewer than 10 students. **Majors with Highest Enrollment:** business administration and management; criminal justice/safety studies; teacher education and professional development, specific levels and methods, other. **Special Study Options:** Accelerated program, cooperative education program, cross-registration, distance learning, double major, dual enrollment, English as a Second Language (ESL), honors program, independent study, internships, liberal arts/career combination, study abroad, teacher certification program, weekend college. **Disability Services:** Special programs offered to physically disabled students include note-taking services, reader services, tutors. **Career Services:** career/job search classes, career assessment

FACILITIES
Housing: Coed dorms, men's dorms, women's dorms, apartments for married students, apartments for single students. 100% of campus accessible to physically disabled. **Special Academic Facilities/Equipment:** Folk Life Center **Computers:** Students can register for classes online. Administrative functions (other than registration) can be performed online.

CAMPUS LIFE
Environment: Town. **Activities:** Choral groups, concert band, dance, drama/theater, jazz band, literary magazine, marching band, music ensembles, musical theater, student government, student newspaper, symphony orchestra, yearbook, Campus Ministries, International Student Organization 90 registered organizations, 4 religious organizations. 4 fraternities, 3 sororities. **Athletics (Intercollegiate):** *Men:* baseball, basketball, cross-country, football, golf, swimming, tennis. *Women:* basketball, cheerleading, cross-country, golf, softball, tennis, volleyball.

ADMISSIONS
Freshman Academic Profile: Average high school GPA 3.0. 7% in top 10% of high school class, 24% in top 25% of high school class, 57% in top 50% of high school class. SAT Math middle 50% range 390-500. SAT Critical Reading middle 50% range 400-508. ACT middle 50% range 17-22. Minimum paper TOEFL 500. **Basis for Candidate Selection:** *Very important factors considered include:* academic GPA, standardized test scores. **Freshman Admission Requirements:** High school diploma is required and GED is accepted. *Academic units required:* 4 English, 3 mathematics, 3 science, (2 science labs), 3 social studies, 1 history. *Academic units recommended:* 4 English, 3 mathematics, 3 science, (2 science labs) 3 social studies, 1 history. **Freshman Admission Statistics:** 3,400 applied, 79% admitted, 45% enrolled. **Transfer Admission Requirements:** college transcript(s), minimum college GPA of 2.00 required. Lowest grade transferable D. **General Admission Information:** Notification

on a rolling basis, beginning on or about 10/1. Nonfall registration accepted. Credit and/or placement offered for CEEB Advanced Placement tests.

COSTS AND FINANCIAL AID
Annual in-state tuition $4,656. Annual out-of-state tuition $9,956. Room and board $5,990. Average book expense $900. **Student Employment:** Federal Work-Study Program available. Institutional employment available. Off-campus job opportunities are good. **Financial Aid Statistics:** 85% freshmen, 80% undergrads receive any aid.

FAITH BAPTIST BIBLE COLLEGE AND THEOLOGICAL SEMINARY

1900 NW 4th Street, Ankeny, IA 50023
Phone: 1.888.faith.4.u • **Financial Aid Phone:** 515-964-0601
E-mail: admissions@faith.edu • **CEEB Code:** 6214
Fax: 515-964-1638 • **Website:** www.faith.edu/ • **ACT Code:** 1315

This private school, affiliated with the Baptist Church, was founded in 1921. It has a 52-acre campus.

RATINGS
Admissions Selectivity Rating: 75   **Fire Safety Rating:** 97   **Green Rating:** 60*

STUDENTS AND FACULTY
Enrollment: 290. **Student Body:** 53% female, 47% male, 39% out-of-state, 1% international. Asian 2%, African American 1%, Caucasian 93%, Hispanic 1%, Native American 0%.
Retention and Graduation: 80% freshmen return for sophomore year. 39% freshmen graduate within 4 years. 23% grads go on to further study within 1 year. **Faculty:** Student/faculty ratio 13:1. 19 full-time faculty, 63% hold PhDs, 5% are members of minority groups, 11% are women. 0% of classes are taught by teaching assistants.

ACADEMICS
Degrees: associate, bachelor's, certificate, master's. **Classes:** Most classes have fewer than 10 students. **Majors with Highest Enrollment:** bible/biblical studies; elementary education and teaching; religious education. **Special Study Options:** independent study, internships, teacher certification program.

FACILITIES
Housing: special housing for disabled students, men's dorms, women's dorms, apartments for married students, apartments for single students. **Computers:** 75% of classrooms, 100% of dorms, 100% of libraries, 100% of dining areas, 100% of student union, 60% of common outdoor areas have wireless network access.

CAMPUS LIFE
Environment: Town. **Activities:** Choral groups, concert band, dance, drama/theater, music ensembles, student government, symphony orchestra, yearbook, Campus Ministries, International Student Organization 1 registered organizations, 1 religious organizations. **Athletics (Intercollegiate):** *Men:* basketball, soccer. *Women:* basketball, soccer, volleyball. **On-Campus Highlights:** Convocation Building, Benson Hall, Library, Cray Hall, Residence Halls

ADMISSIONS
Freshman Academic Profile: Average high school GPA 3.5. 13% in top 10% of high school class, 45% in top 25% of high school class, 58% in top 50% of high school class. 33% from public high schools. SAT Math middle 50% range 440-510. SAT Critical Reading middle 50% range 470-730. SAT Writing middle 50% range 460-650. ACT middle 50% range 19-25. Minimum web-based TOEFL 173. Minimum paper TOEFL 500. **Basis for Candidate Selection:** *Very important factors considered include:* religious affiliation/commitment. *Important factors considered include:* application essay. *Other factors considered include:* Class rank, academic GPA, recommendation(s), standardized test scores, character/personal qualities, extracurricular activities, interview, level of applicant's interest, talent/ability, volunteer work. **Freshman Admission Requirements:** High school diploma is required and GED is accepted. **Freshman Admission Statistics:** 147 applied, 75% admitted, 78% enrolled. **Transfer Admission Requirements:** college transcript(s), essay or personal statement, statement of good standing from prior institution(s). Minimum college GPA of 2.0 required. Lowest grade transferable C. **General Admission Information:** Application Fee $25. Regular application deadline 8/1. Notification on a rolling basis, beginning on or about 9/1. Nonfall registration accepted. Admission may be deferred for a maximum of 1 year. Credit offered for CEEB Advanced Placement tests.

COSTS AND FINANCIAL AID

Required Forms and Deadlines: FAFSA. **Notification of Awards: Types of Aid:** *Need-based scholarships/grants:* Federal Pell, state scholarships/grants, private scholarships, the school's own gift aid. *Loans:* Subsidized Stafford, Unsubsidized Stafford, PLUS. **Student Employment:** Institutional employment available. Off-campus job opportunities are excellent. **Financial Aid Statistics:** 70% freshmen, 95% undergrads receive any aid. **Criteria for awarding institutional aid:** *Non-need-based:* academics, leadership, music/drama, state/district residency.

FARMINGDALE STATE COLLEGE

Admissions Office, Farmingdale, NY 11735
Phone: 631-420-2200
E-mail: admissions@farmingdale.edu
Fax: 631-420-2633 • **Website:** www.farmingdale.edu

This public school was founded in 1912. It has a 380-acre campus.

RATINGS

Admissions Selectivity Rating: 80   **Fire Safety Rating:** 60*   **Green Rating:** 60*

STUDENTS AND FACULTY

Enrollment: 7,257. **Student Body:** 41% female, 59% male, 3% international. Asian 7%, African American 11%, Caucasian 63%, Hispanic 14%, Native American 0%.
Retention and Graduation: 80% freshmen return for sophomore year. 21% freshmen graduate within 4 years. 45% freshmen graduate within 6 years. **Faculty:** Student/faculty ratio 20:1. 201 full-time faculty, 66% hold PhDs, 19% are members of minority groups, 45% are women. 0% of classes are taught by teaching assistants.

ACADEMICS

Degrees: associate, bachelor's, certificate, terminal associate, transfer associate. **Classes:** Most classes have 20–29 students. **Special Study Options:** distance learning, double major, dual enrollment, internships, study abroad. **Disability Services:** Special programs offered to physically disabled students include reader services, tutors. **Career Services:** alumni services, career/job search classes, career assessment, internships.

FACILITIES

Housing: 90% of campus accessible to physically disabled. **Computers:** Students can register for classes online. Administrative functions (other than registration) can be performed online.

CAMPUS LIFE

Environment: Village. **Activities:** literary magazine. **Athletics (Intercollegiate):** *Men:* baseball, basketball, cross-country, golf, lacrosse, soccer, track/field (outdoor), track/field (indoor). *Women:* basketball, cross-country, soccer, softball, track/field (outdoor), track/field (indoor), volleyball.

ADMISSIONS

Freshman Academic Profile: Average high school GPA 3.2. 92% from public high schools. SAT Math middle 50% range 480-570. SAT Critical Reading middle 50% range 450-530. ACT middle 50% range 20-24. **Basis for Candidate Selection:** *Very important factors considered include:* Class rank, rigor of secondary school record. *Important factors considered include:* talent/ability. *Other factors considered include:* application essay, recommendation(s), standardized test scores, alumni/ae relation, character/personal qualities, extracurricular activities, interview, volunteer work, work experience. **Freshman Admission Requirements:** High school diploma is required and GED is accepted. *Academic units required:* 4 English, 2 mathematics, 1 science, (1 science labs), 4 social studies. *Academic units recommended:* 4 English, 2 mathematics, 1 science, (1 science labs), 4 social studies. **Freshman Admission Statistics:** 5,398 applied, 58% admitted, 40% enrolled. **Transfer Admission Requirements:** High school transcript, college transcript(s), statement of good standing from prior institution(s). Minimum college GPA of 2.0 required. Lowest grade transferable C. **General Admission Information:** Application Fee $30. Notification on a rolling basis, beginning on or about 11/1. Nonfall registration accepted. Admission may be deferred for a maximum of 1 year. Credit and/or placement offered for CEEB Advanced Placement tests.

COSTS AND FINANCIAL AID

Annual in-state tuition $5,570. Annual out-of-state tuition $14,820. Room and board $11,790. Required fees $1,223. Average book expense $1,200. **Required Forms and Deadlines:** FAFSA, institution's own financial aid form. **Types of Aid:** *Need-based scholarships/grants:* Federal Pell, SEOG, state scholarships/grants. *Loans:* Direct Subsidized Stafford, Direct Unsubsidized Stafford, Direct PLUS, Subsidized Stafford, Unsubsidized Stafford, PLUS, Federal Perkins,

Federal Nursing, state loans. **Student Employment:** Federal Work-Study Program available. Institutional employment available. Off-campus job opportunities are good. **Financial Aid Statistics:** 68% freshmen, 71% undergrads receive need-based scholarship or grant aid. 4% freshmen, 3% undergrads receive non-need-based scholarship or grant aid. 51% freshmen, 57% undergrads receive need-based self-help aid. 39% undergrads borrow to pay for school. Average cumulative indebtedness $19,996.

FAULKNER UNIVERSITY

5345 Atlanta Highway, Montgomery, AL 36109-3398
Phone: 334-386-7200 • **Financial Aid Phone:** 334-386-7195
E-mail: admissions@faulkner.edu • **CEEB Code:** 1034
Fax: 334-386-7137 • **Website:** www.faulkner.edu • **ACT Code:** 3

This private school, affiliated with the Church of Christ Church, was founded in 1942. It has a 78-acre campus.

RATINGS

Admissions Selectivity Rating: 78   **Fire Safety Rating:** 66   **Green Rating:** 60*

STUDENTS AND FACULTY

Enrollment: 2,032. **Student Body:** 63% female, 37% male, 12% out-of-state, 1% international (15 countries represented). Asian 1%, African American 57%, Caucasian 63%, Hispanic 1%, Native American 1%.
Retention and Graduation: 59% freshmen return for sophomore year. 8% freshmen graduate within 4 years. 22% freshmen graduate within 6 years. 80% grads go on to further study within 1 year. 35% grads pursue arts and sciences degrees. 12% grads pursue law degrees. 32% grads pursue business degrees. 19% grads pursue medical degrees. **Faculty:** Student/faculty ratio 19:1. 105 full-time faculty, 67% hold PhDs, 10% are members of minority groups, 32% are women. 0% of classes are taught by teaching assistants.

ACADEMICS

Degrees: associate, bachelor's, first professional, master's. **Classes:** Most classes have fewer than 10 students. Most lab/discussion sessions have fewer than 10 students. **Majors with Highest Enrollment:** business/commerce; management information systems. **Special Study Options:** Accelerated program, cooperative education program, cross-registration, distance learning, double major, dual enrollment, honors program, independent study, internships, liberal arts/career combination, study abroad, teacher certification program, weekend college. **Honors Programs:** Great Books Honors College. **Disability Services:** Special programs offered to physically disabled students include note-taking services, reader services, tape recorders, tutors. **Career Services:** alumni services, career/job search classes, career assessment, internships Career Services highlights include All undergraduate programs have an internship. In Fall 2009 the University is starting a Spiritual Formation Program with a service-learning component.

FACILITIES

Housing: special housing for disabled students, men's dorms, women's dorms, apartments for single students. 75% of campus accessible to physically disabled. **Computers:** 100% of classrooms, 100% of dorms, 100% of libraries, 100% of dining areas, 100% of student union, 100% of common outdoor areas have wireless network access. Administrative functions (other than registration) can be performed online.

CAMPUS LIFE

Environment: City. **Activities:** Choral groups, drama/theater, music ensembles, musical theater, pep band, student government, student newspaper, yearbook, Campus Ministries 12 registered organizations, 5 honor societies, 3 religious organizations. 5 fraternities, 5 sororities. **Athletics (Intercollegiate):** *Men:* baseball, basketball, cheerleading, fishing, football, golf, soccer. *Women:* cheerleading, fishing, soccer, softball, volleyball. **On-Campus Highlights:** Cafe Sienna, Student Multiplex, Dorm Lobbies, Perry Cafeteria, Dinner Theatre.

ADMISSIONS

Freshman Academic Profile: Average high school GPA 3.1. 8% in top 10% of high school class, 10% in top 25% of high school class, 40% in top 50% of high school class. 75% from public high schools. SAT Math middle 50% range 430-550. SAT Critical Reading middle 50% range 440-560. ACT middle 50% range 18-22. Minimum paper TOEFL 450. **Basis for Candidate Selection:** *Very important factors considered include:* Class rank, recommendation(s), rigor of secondary school record, standardized test scores, character/personal qualities, extracurricular activities, interview. *Important factors considered include:* application essay, alumni/ae relation, religious affiliation/commitment, talent/ability. *Other factors considered include:* volunteer work, work experience. **Freshman Admission Requirements:** High school diploma is required and GED is accepted. **Freshman Admission Statistics:** 982 applied, 59% admitted, 48%

enrolled. **Transfer Admission Requirements:** High school transcript, college transcript(s), standardized test scores, statement of good standing from prior institution(s). Minimum college GPA of 2.0 required. Lowest grade transferable C. **General Admission Information:** Application Fee $10. Notification on a rolling basis, beginning on or about 8/1. Nonfall registration accepted. Admission may be deferred for a maximum of 12. Credit and/or placement offered for CEEB Advanced Placement tests.

COSTS AND FINANCIAL AID

Annual tuition $12,720. Room and board $6,320. Required fees $1,170. Average book expense $1,200. **Required Forms and Deadlines:** FAFSA, institution's own financial aid form, state aid form. **Notification of Awards:** Applicants will be notified of awards on a rolling basis beginning 6/1. **Types of Aid:** *Need-based scholarships/grants:* Federal Pell, SEOG, state scholarships/grants, private scholarships, the school's own gift aid. *Loans:* Subsidized Stafford, Unsubsidized Stafford, PLUS, Federal Perkins. **Student Employment:** Federal Work-Study Program available. Institutional employment available. Highest amount earned per year from on-campus jobs $1,250. **Financial Aid Statistics:** 74% freshmen, 74% undergrads receive need-based scholarship or grant aid. 59% freshmen, 59% undergrads receive non-need-based scholarship or grant aid. 87% freshmen, 87% undergrads receive need-based self-help aid. 12% freshmen, 11% undergrads receive athletic scholarships. 95% freshmen, 93% undergrads receive any aid. 87% undergrads borrow to pay for school. Average cumulative indebtedness $19,300. **Criteria for awarding institutional aid:** *Non-need-based:* academics, alumni affiliation, art, athletics, job skills, leadership, minority status, music/drama, religious affiliation, state/district residency.

FAYETTEVILLE STATE UNIVERSITY

Newbold Station, Fayetteville, NC 28301
Phone: 910-672-1371
E-mail: admissions@.uncfsu.edu • **CEEB Code:** 5212
Fax: 910-672-1414 • **Website:** www.uncfsu.edu • **ACT Code:** 3098

This public school was founded in 1867. It has a 136-acre campus.

RATINGS

Admissions Selectivity Rating: 65   **Fire Safety Rating:** 60*   **Green Rating:** 60*

STUDENTS AND FACULTY

Enrollment: 3,660. **Student Body:** 64% female, 36% male, 11% out-of-state, 0% international. Asian 1%, African American 80%, Caucasian 14%, Hispanic 4%, Native American 1%.
Retention and Graduation: 74% freshmen return for sophomore year. 14% freshmen graduate within 4 years. 39% freshmen graduate within 6 years. 11% grads go on to further study within 1 year. 10% grads pursue arts and sciences degrees. 1% grads pursue business degrees. **Faculty:** Student/faculty ratio 20:1. 202 full-time faculty, 70% hold PhDs, 77% are members of minority groups, 41% are women. 0% of classes are taught by teaching assistants.

ACADEMICS

Degrees: bachelor's, master's. **Classes:** Most classes have 20–29 students. Most lab/discussion sessions have 20–29 students. **Majors with Highest Enrollment:** business/commerce, criminal justice/police science, elementary education and teaching. **Special Study Options:** cooperative education program, distance learning, double major, honors program, independent study, internships, liberal arts/career combination, study abroad, teacher certification program, weekend college. **Career Services:** alumni services, career/job search classes, career assessment, internships.

FACILITIES

Housing: special housing for disabled students, men's dorms, women's dorms, apartments for married students, apartments for single students. 100% of campus accessible to physically disabled. **Special Academic Facilities/Equipment:** Planetarium; Observatory; Distance Learning Center; Science Labs; Health, Physical Education, and Recreation Complex; Art Gallery

CAMPUS LIFE

Environment: Activities: Choral groups, concert band, dance, drama/theater, jazz band, marching band, music ensembles, musical theater, opera, pep band, radio station, student government, student newspaper, student-run film society, television station, yearbook 56 registered organizations, 7 honor societies, 3 religious organizations. 4 fraternities, 4 sororities. **Athletics (Intercollegiate):** *Men:* basketball, cheerleading, cross-country, football, golf. *Women:* basketball, cheerleading, cross-country, softball, tennis, volleyball.

ADMISSIONS

Freshman Academic Profile: SAT Math middle 50% range 360-470. SAT Critical Reading middle 50% range 380-470. **Basis for Candidate Selection:**

Important factors considered include: Class rank, rigor of secondary school record, standardized test scores, character/personal qualities, extracurricular activities, talent/ability. **Freshman Admission Requirements:** High school diploma is required and GED is accepted.High school diploma is required and GED is not accepted. *Academic units required:* 4 English, 3 mathematics, 3 science, 1 social studies, 1 history, 6 academic electives. *Academic units recommended:* 4 English, 3 mathematics, 3 science, 1 social studies, 1 history, 6 academic electives. **Freshman Admission Statistics:** 1,570 applied, 85% admitted, 58% enrolled. **Transfer Admission Requirements:** college transcript(s), statement of good standing from prior institution(s). Lowest grade transferable C. **General Admission Information:** Application Fee $25. Regular application deadline 8/15. Notification on a rolling basis, beginning on or about 11/1. Nonfall registration accepted. Credit and/or placement offered for CEEB Advanced Placement tests.

COSTS AND FINANCIAL AID

Annual in-state tuition $1,258. Annual out-of-state tuition $10,173. Room and board $3,820. Required fees $437. Average book expense $160. **Required Forms and Deadlines:** FAFSA, institution's own financial aid form. **Notification of Awards:** Applicants will be notified of awards on or about 7/15. **Types of Aid:** *Need-based scholarships/grants:* Federal Pell, SEOG, state scholarships/grants, private scholarships, the school's own gift aid. *Loans:* Direct Subsidized Stafford, Direct Unsubsidized Stafford, Direct PLUS, Subsidized Stafford, Unsubsidized Stafford, PLUS, Federal Perkins, Federal Nursing, state loans. **Student Employment:** Federal Work-Study Program available. Off-campus job opportunities are excellent.

FELICIAN COLLEGE

262 South Main Street, Lodi, NJ 7644
Phone: 201-559-6131
E-mail: admissions@felician.edu • **CEEB Code:** 2321
Fax: 201-559-6138 • **Website:** www.felician.edu • **ACT Code:** 2559

This private school, affiliated with the Roman Catholic Church, was founded in 1942. It has a 27-acre campus.

RATINGS

Admissions Selectivity Rating: 63   **Fire Safety Rating:** 60*   **Green Rating:** 60*

STUDENTS AND FACULTY

Enrollment: 1,761. **Student Body:** 78% female, 22% male, 5% out-of-state. Asian 8%, African American 13%, Caucasian 43%, Hispanic 14%, Native American 0%.
Retention and Graduation: 60% freshmen return for sophomore year. 17% freshmen graduate within 4 years. 33% freshmen graduate within 6 years. 20% grads go on to further study within 1 year. 40% grads pursue arts and sciences degrees. 10% grads pursue law degrees. 12% grads pursue business degrees. 5% grads pursue medical degrees. **Faculty:** Student/faculty ratio 9:1. 81 full-time faculty, 57% are women. 0% of classes are taught by teaching assistants.

ACADEMICS

Degrees: associate, bachelor's, certificate, master's, post-bachelor's certificate. **Classes:** Most classes have greater than 100 students. **Majors with Highest Enrollment:** business/commerce; nursing/registered nurse (rn, asn, bsn, msn); psychology. **Special Study Options:** Accelerated program, cooperative education program, cross-registration, distance learning, double major, dual enrollment, English as a Second Language (ESL), honors program, independent study, internships, liberal arts/career combination, student-designed major, study abroad, teacher certification program, weekend college. **Combined Degree Programs:** 3-2 Clinical lab science prog w/ U of Medicine NJ. **Disability Services:** Special programs offered to physically disabled students include note-taking services, reader services, tape recorders, tutors. **Career Services:** alumni services, career/job search classes, internships.

FACILITIES

Housing: Coed dorms, special housing for disabled students, men's dorms, women's dorms. 90% of campus accessible to physically disabled. **Special Academic Facilities/Equipment:** On-campus elementary school for exceptional children.

CAMPUS LIFE

Environment: Activities: Choral groups, drama/theater, literary magazine, student government 25 registered organizations, 2 honor societies, 3 religious organizations. 1 fraternities, 2 sororities. **Athletics (Intercollegiate):** *Men:* baseball, basketball, cheerleading, cross-country, soccer, track/field (outdoor). *Women:* basketball, cheerleading, cross-country, soccer, softball, track/field (outdoor).

ADMISSIONS

Freshman Academic Profile: 70% from public high schools. SAT Math middle 50% range 400-500. SAT Writing middle 50% range 390-490. **Basis for Candidate Selection:** *Very important factors considered include:* academic GPA, standardized test scores. *Important factors considered include:* application essay, rigor of secondary school record. *Other factors considered include:* Class rank, recommendation(s), character/personal qualities, extracurricular activities, interview, volunteer work, work experience. **Freshman Admission Requirements:** High school diploma is required and GED is accepted. **Freshman Admission Statistics:** 1,479 applied, 64% admitted, 28% enrolled. **Transfer Admission Requirements:** college transcript(s), essay or personal statement, Lowest grade transferable C. **General Admission Information:** Application Fee $30. Notification on a rolling basis, beginning on or about 3/15. Nonfall registration accepted. Admission may be deferred for a maximum of 1 year. Credit and/or placement offered for CEEB Advanced Placement tests.

COSTS AND FINANCIAL AID

Annual tuition $18,900. Room and board $7,432. Required fees $1,050. Average book expense $2,163. **Required Forms and Deadlines:** FAFSA. **Notification of Awards:** Applicants will be notified of awards on a rolling basis beginning 4/1. **Types of Aid:** *Need-based scholarships/grants:* Federal Pell, SEOG, state scholarships/grants, private scholarships, the school's own gift aid. *Loans:* Subsidized Stafford, Unsubsidized Stafford, PLUS, state loans. **Student Employment:** Federal Work-Study Program available. Off-campus job opportunities are good. **Financial Aid Statistics:** 65% freshmen, 65% undergrads receive need-based scholarship or grant aid. 20% freshmen, 20% undergrads receive non-need-based scholarship or grant aid. 66% freshmen, 66% undergrads receive need-based self-help aid. 13% freshmen, 7% undergrads receive athletic scholarships. % freshmen, % undergrads receive any aid. 57% undergrads borrow to pay for school. Average cumulative indebtedness $19,500. **Criteria for awarding institutional aid:** *Non-need-based:* academics, alumni affiliation, athletics.

FERRIS STATE UNIVERSITY

1201 South State Street, Big Rapids, MI 49307
Phone: 231-591-2100 • **Financial Aid Phone:** 231-591-2110
E-mail: admissions@ferris.edu • **CEEB Code:** 1222
Fax: 231-591-3944 • **Website:** www.ferris.edu • **ACT Code:** 1994

This public school was founded in 1884. It has a 880-acre campus.

RATINGS

Admissions Selectivity Rating: 71   **Fire Safety Rating:** 75   **Green Rating:** 60*

STUDENTS AND FACULTY

Enrollment: 13,261. **Student Body:** 51% female, 49% male, 5% out-of-state, 1% international. Asian 1%, African American 7%, Caucasian 76%, Hispanic 3%, Native American 1%.
Retention and Graduation: 70% freshmen return for sophomore year. 30% freshmen graduate within 4 years. 56% freshmen graduate within 6 years. **Faculty:** Student/faculty ratio 16:1. 567 full-time faculty, 42% hold PhDs, 11% are members of minority groups, 42% are women. 0% of classes are taught by teaching assistants.

ACADEMICS

Degrees: associate, bachelor's, certificate, first professional, master's, terminal associate, transfer associate. **Classes:** Most classes have 20–29 students. Most lab/discussion sessions have 10–19 students. **Majors with Highest Enrollment:** elementary education and teaching; pharmacy (pharmd [usa], pharmd or bs/bpharm [canada]); pre-pharmacy studies. **Special Study Options:** Accelerated program, cooperative education program, cross-registration, distance learning, double major, dual enrollment, exchange student program (domestic), external degree program, honors program, independent study, internships, liberal arts/career combination, study abroad, teacher certification program, weekend college. **Disability Services:** Special programs offered to physically disabled students include note-taking services, reader services, tape recorders, tutors.

FACILITIES

Housing: Coed dorms, special housing for disabled students, special housing for international students, apartments for married students, apartments for single students, Honors, smoke-free, alcohol-free, quiet residence halls, living/earning communities. 98% of campus accessible to physically disabled. **Special Academic Facilities/Equipment:** Rankin Art Gallery, Student Recreation Center, Card Wildlife Museum, Jim Crowe Museum, Elastomer Center, FLITE **Computers:** Students can register for classes online. Administrative functions (other than registration) can be performed online.

CAMPUS LIFE

Environment: Village. **Activities:** Choral groups, concert band, dance, drama/theater, jazz band, literary magazine, music ensembles, pep band, radio station, student government, student newspaper, symphony orchestra, television station 180 registered organizations, 11 honor societies, 14 religious organizations. 8 fraternities, 6 sororities. **Athletics (Intercollegiate):** *Men:* basketball, cheerleading, cross-country, football, golf, ice hockey, tennis, track/field (outdoor). *Women:* basketball, cheerleading, cross-country, golf, soccer, softball, tennis, track/field (outdoor), volleyball. **On-Campus Highlights:** FLITE Library, Student Recreation Center, Card Wildlife Center, Center for Student Services, Ewigleben Ice Arena.

ADMISSIONS

Freshman Academic Profile: Average high school GPA 3.2. 90% from public high schools. ACT middle 50% range 19-24. Minimum web-based TOEFL 61. Minimum paper TOEFL 500. **Basis for Candidate Selection:** *Very important factors considered include:* academic GPA, standardized test scores. *Important factors considered include:* character/personal qualities. *Other factors considered include:* recommendation(s), rigor of secondary school record, alumni/ae relation, extracurricular activities, volunteer work. **Freshman Admission Requirements:** High school diploma is required and GED is accepted. **Freshman Admission Statistics:** 9,457 applied, 71% admitted, 38% enrolled. **Transfer Admission Requirements:** college transcript(s), statement of good standing from prior institution(s). Minimum college GPA of 2.0 required. Lowest grade transferable C. **General Admission Information:** Application Fee $30. Regular application deadline 8/4. Notification on a rolling basis, beginning on or about 7/1. Nonfall registration accepted. Credit and/or placement offered for CEEB Advanced Placement tests.

COSTS AND FINANCIAL AID

Annual in-state tuition $10,710. Annual out-of-state tuition $16,080. Room and board $8,744. Average book expense $1,050. **Required Forms and Deadlines:** FAFSA. **Notification of Awards:** Applicants will be notified of awards on a rolling basis beginning 4/1. **Types of Aid:** *Need-based scholarships/grants:* Federal Pell, SEOG, state scholarships/grants, private scholarships, the school's own gift aid. *Loans:* Direct Subsidized Stafford, Direct Unsubsidized Stafford, Direct PLUS, Federal Perkins, Federal Nursing, college/university loans from institutional funds, Key Loan, MI-Loan, Citi Assist. **Student Employment:** Highest amount earned per year from on-campus jobs $4,992. **Financial Aid Statistics:** 70% freshmen, 69% undergrads receive need-based scholarship or grant aid. 77% freshmen, 53% undergrads receive non-need-based scholarship or grant aid. 83% freshmen, 87% undergrads receive need-based self-help aid. 1% freshmen, 1% undergrads receive athletic scholarships. 86% freshmen, 81% undergrads receive any aid. 81% undergrads borrow to pay for school. Average cumulative indebtedness $36,930. **Criteria for awarding institutional aid:** *Non-need-based:* academics, alumni affiliation, art, athletics, leadership, minority status, music/drama, religious affiliation.

FISK UNIVERSITY

1000 17th Avenue N., Nashville, TN 37208
Phone: 1-800-443-3475
Website: www.fisk.edu

RATINGS

Admissions Selectivity Rating: 87   **Fire Safety Rating:** 60*   **Green Rating:** 60*

ACADEMICS

Special Study Options: cross-registration, double major, exchange student program (domestic), honors program, independent study, internships, student-designed major, study abroad, teacher certification program.

ADMISSIONS

Freshman Academic Profile: Average high school GPA 3.3. 10% in top 10% of high school class, 30% in top 25% of high school class, 75% in top 50% of high school class. 92% from public high schools. SAT Math middle 50% range 455-540. SAT Critical Reading middle 50% range 467-546. SAT Writing middle 50% range 447-547. ACT middle 50% range 18-23. Minimum paper TOEFL 550. **Basis for Candidate Selection:** *Very important factors considered include:* rigor of secondary school record. *Important factors considered include:* Class rank, application essay, academic GPA, standardized test scores, character/personal qualities, extracurricular activities, interview. *Other factors considered include:* recommendation(s), alumni/ae relation, geographical residence, level of applicant's interest, talent/ability, volunteer work. **Freshman Admission Requirements:** High school diploma is required and GED is accepted. *Academic units required:* 4 English, 3 mathematics, 3 science, (2 science labs), 1 foreign language, 0 social studies, 1 history, 0 computer science. *Academic units recommended:* 4 English, 3 mathematics, 3 science, (2 science labs), 1 foreign language, 0 social studies, 1 history, 0 computer science. **Freshman Admission Statistics:** 2,700 applied, 45% admitted, 51% enrolled. **Transfer Admission Requirements:** college transcript(s), essay or personal statement, statement of good standing from prior institution(s). Minimum college GPA of 2.5 required. Lowest grade transferable C. **General Admission Information:** Application Fee $50. Regular application deadline 3/1. Notification on a rolling basis, beginning on or about 9/1. Admission may be deferred for a maximum of 1 year. Credit and/or placement offered for CEEB Advanced Placement tests.

COSTS AND FINANCIAL AID

Annual tuition $15,140. Room and board $7,730. Required fees $1,100. Average book expense $1,500.

FITCHBURG STATE COLLEGE

160 Pearl Street, Fitchburg, MA 01420-2697
Phone: 978-665-3144 • **Financial Aid Phone:** 978-665-3156
E-mail: admissions@fitchburgstate.edu • **CEEB Code:** 3518
Fax: 978-665-4540 • **Website:** www.fitchburgstate.edu • **ACT Code:** 1902

This public school was founded in 1894. It has a 78-acre campus.

RATINGS

Admissions Selectivity Rating: 73   Fire Safety Rating: 85   Green Rating: 74

STUDENTS AND FACULTY

Enrollment: 3,958. **Student Body:** 54% female, 46% male, 8% out-of-state, 0% international (6 countries represented). Asian 2%, African American 4%, Caucasian 81%, Hispanic 6%, Native American 0%. **Retention and Graduation:** 73% freshmen return for sophomore year. 21% freshmen graduate within 4 years. 47% freshmen graduate within 6 years. 10% grads go on to further study within 1 year. **Faculty:** Student/faculty ratio 16:1. 184 full-time faculty, 91% hold PhDs, 11% are members of minority groups, 46% are women. 0% of classes are taught by teaching assistants.

ACADEMICS

Degrees: bachelor's, certificate, master's, post-bachelor's certificate, post-master's certificate. **Classes:** Most classes have 20–29 students. **Majors with Highest Enrollment:** business administration and management; communication studies/speech communication and rhetoric; liberal arts and sciences/liberal studies. **Special Study Options:** cross-registration, distance learning, double major, dual enrollment, honors program, independent study, internships, liberal arts/career combination, student-designed major, study abroad, teacher certification program. **Honors Programs:** Leadership Academy Honors Program. **Disability Services:** Special programs offered to physically disabled students include note-taking services, reader services, tape recorders, tutors. **Career Services:** Alumni network, alumni services, career/job search classes, career assessment, internships.

FACILITIES

Housing: Coed dorms, special housing for disabled students, apartments for single studentsAlcohol and Tobacco free housing. 80% of campus accessible to physically disabled. **Special Academic Facilities/Equipment:** Art gallery, on-campus teacher education school, 120-acre conservation area. **Computers:** 100% of classrooms, 10% of dorms, 100% of libraries, 40% of dining areas, 100% of student union, 90% of common outdoor areas have wireless network access. Students can register for classes online. Administrative functions (other than registration) can be performed online. Undergraduates are required to own a computer.

CAMPUS LIFE

Environment: Town. **Activities:** Choral groups, concert band, dance, drama/theater, jazz band, radio station, student government, student newspaper, student-run film society, Campus Ministries, International Student Organization, Model UN 60 registered organizations, 8 honor societies, 1 religious organizations. 2 fraternities, 3 sororities. **Athletics (Intercollegiate):** *Men:* baseball, basketball, cross-country, football, ice hockey, soccer, track/field (outdoor), track/field (indoor). *Women:* basketball, cross-country, field hockey, lacrosse, soccer, softball, track/field (outdoor), track/field (indoor). **On-Campus Highlights:** Campus Recreation Center, Student Center Lounge, Campus Dining Hall, Commuter Cafe, Computer Labs. **Environmental Initiatives:** Single stream recycling program Awarded LEED certification of newest residence hall Campus-wide building level utility metering.

ADMISSIONS

Freshman Academic Profile: Average high school GPA 3.1. 90% from public high schools. SAT Math middle 50% range 460-560. SAT Critical Reading

middle 50% range 450-560. SAT Writing middle 50% range 450-540. ACT middle 50% range 19-23. Minimum paper TOEFL 550. **Basis for Candidate Selection:** *Very important factors considered include:* rigor of secondary school record. *Important factors considered include:* application essay, academic GPA, standardized test scores. *Other factors considered include:* recommendation(s), alumni/ae relation, character/personal qualities, extracurricular activities, level of applicant's interest, talent/ability, volunteer work, work experience. **Freshman Admission Requirements:** High school diploma is required and GED is accepted. *Academic units required:* 4 English, 3 mathematics, 3 science, (2 science labs), 2 foreign language, 1 social studies, 1 history, 2 academic electives. 4 English, 3 mathematics, 3 science, (2 science labs), 2 foreign language, 1 social studies, 1 history, 2 academic electives. **Freshman Admission Statistics:** 3,104 applied, 70% admitted, 32% enrolled. **Transfer Admission Requirements:** college transcript(s), essay or personal statement, minimum college GPA of 2.0 required. Lowest grade transferable C. **General Admission Information:** Application Fee $25. Notification on a rolling basis, beginning on or about 12/1. Nonfall registration accepted. Admission may be deferred for a maximum of 1 year. Credit and/or placement offered for CEEB Advanced Placement tests.

COSTS AND FINANCIAL AID

Annual in-state tuition $970. Annual out-of-state tuition $7,050. Room and board $8,256. Required fees $7,330. Average book expense $800. **Required Forms and Deadlines:** FAFSA. **Notification of Awards:** Applicants will be notified of awards on a rolling basis beginning 3/15. **Types of Aid:** *Need-based scholarships/grants:* Federal Pell, SEOG, state scholarships/grants, private scholarships, the school's own gift aid. *Loans:* Direct Subsidized Stafford, Direct Unsubsidized Stafford, Direct PLUS, Federal Perkins, Federal Nursing, state loans. **Student Employment:** Federal Work-Study Program available. Institutional employment available. Off-campus job opportunities are good. **Criteria for awarding institutional aid:** *Non-need-based:* academics, alumni affiliation, job skills, leadership.

FIVE TOWNS COLLEGE

Five Towns College, Dix Hills, NY 11746
Phone: 631-656-2110 • **Financial Aid Phone:** 631-656-2164
E-mail: admissions@ftc.edu • **CEEB Code:** 3142
Fax: 631-656-2172 • **Website:** www.ftc.edu/

This proprietary school was founded in 1972. It has a 35-acre campus.

RATINGS

Admissions Selectivity Rating: 84   Fire Safety Rating: 99   Green Rating: 61

STUDENTS AND FACULTY

Enrollment: 867. **Student Body:** 30% female, 70% male, 12% out-of-state. **Faculty:** Student/faculty ratio 9:1. 38 full-time faculty, 53% are women. 0% of classes are taught by teaching assistants.

ACADEMICS

Degrees: associate, bachelor's, doctoral, master's. **Classes:** Most classes have 20–29 students. **Majors with Highest Enrollment:** film/cinema studies; music; recording arts technology/technician. **Special Study Options:** distance learning, dual enrollment, internships, liberal arts/career combination, teacher certification program. **Disability Services:** Special programs offered to physically disabled students include note-taking services, reader services, tape recorders, tutors. **Career Services:** career/job search classes, career assessment, internships.

FACILITIES

Housing: Coed dorms, wellness housing. **Computers:** 100% of classrooms, 100% of dorms, 100% of libraries, 100% of dining areas, 100% of common outdoor areas have wireless network access. Administrative functions (other than registration) can be performed online.

CAMPUS LIFE

Environment: Village. **Activities:** Choral groups, concert band, dance, drama/theater, jazz band, music ensembles, musical theater, radio station, student government, student newspaper, student-run film society, symphony orchestra, television station, yearbook. **On-Campus Highlights:** Student Center, Audio Studios, Film Video Studios, Radio Station, Court Yard.

ADMISSIONS

Freshman Academic Profile: 15% in top 10% of high school class, 40% in top 25% of high school class, 55% in top 50% of high school class. 80% from public high schools. SAT Math middle 50% range 330-590. SAT Critical Reading middle 50% range 350-560. SAT Writing middle 50% range 340-550. ACT middle 50% range 18-20. Minimum web-based TOEFL 80. Minimum paper TOEFL 520. **Basis for Candidate Selection:** *Very important factors considered include:* application essay, academic GPA, recommendation(s), rigor of secondary school record, standardized test scores, character/personal qualities, talent/ability. *Important factors considered include:* Class rank, interview, level of applicant's interest. *Other factors considered include:* extracurricular activities, volunteer work, work experience. **Freshman Admission Requirements:** High school diploma is required and GED is accepted. **Freshman Admission Statistics:** 745 applied, 41% admitted, 59% enrolled. **Transfer Admission Requirements:** High school transcript, college transcript(s), essay or personal statement, statement of good standing from prior institution(s). Minimum college GPA of 2.5 required. Lowest grade transferable C. **General Admission Information:** Application Fee $35. Early decision application deadline 12/1. Notification on a rolling basis, beginning on or about 11/1. Nonfall registration accepted. Admission may be deferred for a maximum of 1 year. Placement offered for CEEB Advanced Placement tests.

COSTS AND FINANCIAL AID

Annual tuition $18,400. Room and board $13,060. Required fees $350. Average book expense $1,200. **Required Forms and Deadlines:** FAFSA, institution's own financial aid form, state aid form. **Notification of Awards:** Applicants will be notified of awards on a rolling basis beginning 3/31. **Types of Aid:** *Need-based scholarships/grants:* Federal Pell, SEOG, state scholarships/grants, private scholarships, the school's own gift aid. *Loans:* Direct Subsidized Stafford, Direct Unsubsidized Stafford, Direct PLUS. **Student Employment:** Federal Work-Study Program available. Institutional employment available. **Financial Aid Statistics:** 88% freshmen, 89% undergrads receive need-based scholarship or grant aid. 54% freshmen, 55% undergrads receive non-need-based scholarship or grant aid. 100% freshmen, 100% undergrads receive need-based self-help aid78% freshmen, 75% undergrads receive any aid. 80% undergrads borrow to pay for school. Average cumulative indebtedness $19,000. **Criteria for awarding institutional aid:** *Non-need-based:* academics, music/drama.

See page 1082.

FLAGLER COLLEGE

Best 378

74 King Street, St. Augustine, FL 32085-1027
Phone: 800-304-4208 • **Financial Aid Phone:** 904-819-6225
E-mail: admiss@flagler.edu • **CEEB Code:** 5235
Fax: 904-826-0094 • **Website:** www.flagler.edu • **ACT Code:** 772

This private school was founded in 1968. It has a 42-acre campus.

RATINGS
Admissions Selectivity Rating: 92   **Fire Safety Rating:** 87   **Green Rating:** 67

STUDENTS AND FACULTY
Enrollment: 2,847. **Student Body:** 59% female, 41% male, 36% out-of-state, 3% international (34 countries represented). Asian 1%, African American 4%, Caucasian 78%, Hispanic 7%, Native American 1%.
Retention and Graduation: 69% freshmen return for sophomore year. 51% freshmen graduate within 4 years. 64% freshmen graduate within 6 years. 24% grads go on to further study within 1 year. 1% grads pursue arts and sciences degrees. 2% grads pursue law degrees. 3% grads pursue business degrees.
Faculty: Student/faculty ratio 18:1. 108 full-time faculty, 68% hold PhDs, 12% are members of minority groups, 48% are women. 0% of classes are taught by teaching assistants.

ACADEMICS
Degrees: bachelor's. **Classes:** Most classes have 20–29 students. **Majors with Highest Enrollment:** business/commerce; communication, journalism, and related programs, other; elementary education and teaching. **Special Study Options:** double major, external degree program, independent study, internships, liberal arts/career combination, study abroad, teacher certification program. **Combined Degree Programs:** none. **Disability Services:** Special programs offered to physically disabled students include note-taking services, reader services, tape recorders, tutors. **Career Services:** Alumni network, alumni services, career/job search classes, career assessment Career Services highlights include Most majors require students to gain internship experience.

FACILITIES
Housing: men's dorms, women's dorms. 95% of campus accessible to physically disabled. **Special Academic Facilities/Equipment:** Museum/theatre; learning disabilities clinic for student teachers; NorthEast Florida Archeological Association; Crisp-Ellert Art Gallery. **Computers:** 30% of classrooms, 100% of dorms, 100% of libraries, 100% of dining areas, 100% of student union, 80%

of common outdoor areas have wireless network access. Students can register for classes online. Administrative functions (other than registration) can be performed online.

CAMPUS LIFE
Environment: Town. **Activities:** Choral groups, drama/theater, literary magazine, radio station, student government, student newspaper, Campus Ministries 7 honor societies, 3 religious organizations. **Athletics (Intercollegiate):** *Men:* baseball, basketball, cross-country, golf, soccer, tennis. *Women:* basketball, cross-country, golf, soccer, softball, tennis, volleyball. **On-Campus Highlights:** The Student Center, Proctor Library, Campus Courtyard, Flagler College Tennis Complex, Flagler College Sports Complex. **Environmental Initiatives:** Chiller upgrades Compact flourescents and LED Green cleaning supplies

ADMISSIONS
Freshman Academic Profile: Average high school GPA. 14% in top 10% of high school class, 45% in top 25% of high school class, 90% in top 50% of high school class. 78% from public high schools. SAT Math middle 50% range 520-580. SAT Critical Reading middle 50% range 540-600. SAT Writing middle 50% range 520-580. ACT middle 50% range 22-25. Minimum web-based TOEFL 80. Minimum paper TOEFL 550. **Basis for Candidate Selection:** *Very important factors considered include:* rigor of secondary school record. *Important factors considered include:* application essay, academic GPA, standardized test scores, alumni/ae relation, extracurricular activities. *Other factors considered include:* Class rank, recommendation(s), character/personal qualities, first generation, interview, level of applicant's interest, talent/ability, volunteer work. **Freshman Admission Requirements:** High school diploma is required and GED is accepted. *Academic units required:* 4 English, 3 mathematics, 2 science, (1 science labs), 3 social studies, 1 history, 2 academic electives. *Academic units recommended:* 4 English, 3 mathematics, 2 science, (1 science labs), 3 social studies, 1 history, 2 academic electives. **Freshman Admission Statistics:** 5,347 applied, 41% admitted, 29% enrolled. **Transfer Admission Requirements:** college transcript(s), essay or personal statement, minimum college GPA of 2.0 required. Lowest grade transferable C. **General Admission Information:** Application Fee $40. Early decision application deadline 12/1. Regular application deadline 3/1. Regular notification 3/30. Nonfall registration accepted. Admission may be deferred for a maximum of 1 year. Credit and/or placement offered for CEEB Advanced Placement tests.

COSTS AND FINANCIAL AID
Annual tuition $15,340. Room and board $8,350. Average book expense $1,100. **Required Forms and Deadlines:** FAFSA, institution's own financial aid form, state aid form. **Notification of Awards:** Applicants will be notified of awards on a rolling basis beginning 4/1. **Types of Aid:** *Need-based scholarships/grants:* Federal Pell, SEOG, state scholarships/grants, private scholarships, the school's own gift aid. *Loans:* Direct Subsidized Stafford, Direct Unsubsidized Stafford, Direct PLUS, Federal Perkins, Private Alternative Loans. **Student Employment:** Federal Work-Study Program available. Institutional employment available. Highest amount earned per year from on-campus jobs $1,400. Off-campus job opportunities are excellent. **Financial Aid Statistics:** 99% freshmen, 95% undergrads receive need-based scholarship or grant aid. 8% freshmen, 8% undergrads receive non-need-based scholarship or grant aid. 90% undergrads receive need-based self-help aid. 2% freshmen, 3% undergrads receive athletic scholarships. 86% freshmen, 92% undergrads receive any aid. 68% undergrads borrow to pay for school. Average cumulative indebtedness $24,519. **Criteria for awarding institutional aid:** *Non-need-based:* academics, art, athletics, job skills, leadership, minority status, music/drama, state/district residency.

FLORIDA A&M UNIVERSITY

Suite G-9, Tallahassee, FL 32307
Phone: 850-599-3796 • **Financial Aid Phone:** 850-599-3730
E-mail: ugrdadmissions@famu.edu • **CEEB Code:** 5215
Fax: 850-599-3069 • **Website:** www.famu.edu • **ACT Code:** 726

This public school was founded in 1887. It has a 419-acre campus.

RATINGS
Admissions Selectivity Rating: 82   **Fire Safety Rating:** 68   **Green Rating:** 80

STUDENTS AND FACULTY
Enrollment: 11,027. **Student Body:** 60% female, 40% male, 17% out-of-state, 1% international (50 countries represented). Asian 1%, African American 95%, Caucasian 24%, Hispanic 1%, Native American 0%.
Retention and Graduation: 79% freshmen return for sophomore year. 33% grads go on to further study within 1 year. 3% grads pursue law degrees. 5% grads pursue business degrees. 2% grads pursue medical degrees. **Faculty:**

Student/faculty ratio 21:1. 537 full-time faculty, 75% hold PhDs, 82% are members of minority groups, 47% are women. 0% of classes are taught by teaching assistants.

ACADEMICS
Degrees: associate, bachelor's, first professional, master's. **Classes:** Most classes have fewer than 10 students. **Majors with Highest Enrollment:** business administration and management; nursing/registered nurse (rn, asn, bsn, msn); pharmacy (pharmd [usa], pharmd or bs/bpharm [canada]). **Special Study Options:** Accelerated program, cooperative education program, distance learning, double major, dual enrollment, honors program, independent study, internships, study abroad, teacher certification program, weekend college. **Honors Programs:** Florida Agricultural and Mechanical University Honors Program provides a series of challenging courses and academic enhancement experiences for undergraduate students who excel. Enhancement of academic performance in critical thinking skills, in essence, will lead to consummate intellectual engagement and strong research orientation as a launch to both graduate and professional schools, as well as career paths. The program stresses four major areas of concentration: academic achievement, development of leadership potential, community service and cultural enrichment. **Combined Degree Programs:** BA/JD, BA/MA, Pharmacy, Architecture, Occupational Therapy. **Disability Services:** Special programs offered to physically disabled students include note-taking services, reader services, tape recorders, tutors. **Career Services:** Alumni network, alumni services, career/job search classes, career assessment, internships

FACILITIES
Housing: Coed dorms, men's dorms, women's dorms, apartments for married students, outside housing (Apartment Complexes) agreement through the University. 100% of campus accessible to physically disabled. **Special Academic Facilities/Equipment:** Black Archives and Resource Ctr. Coleman Memorial Library Foster Tanner Music/Art Bldg. **Computers:** 90% of classrooms, 100% of dorms, 100% of libraries, 100% of dining areas, 100% of student union, 60% of common outdoor areas have wireless network access. Students can register for classes online. Administrative functions (other than registration) can be performed online.

CAMPUS LIFE
Environment: City. **Activities:** Choral groups, concert band, dance, drama/theater, jazz band, marching band, music ensembles, pep band, radio station, student government, student newspaper, symphony orchestra, television station, yearbook 145 registered organizations, 16 honor societies, 11 religious organizations. 4 fraternities, 4 sororities. **Athletics (Intercollegiate):** *Men:* baseball, basketball, cheerleading, cross-country, football, golf, swimming, tennis, track/field (outdoor), track/field (indoor). *Women:* basketball, bowling, cheerleading, cross-country, golf, softball, swimming, tennis, track/field (outdoor), track/field (indoor), volleyball. **On-Campus Highlights:** The Black Archives, FAMU/FSU College of Engineering, Athletic Department, Army/Navy ROTC, Alfred Lawson Jr. Multipurpose Center and Teaching Gymnasium. **Environmental Initiatives:** Establishment of an advisory body - the Environment & Sustainability Council to design and oversee the implementation of a sustainability strategic plan which informs and guides the various operatives on campus of the principles of sustainability as they apply specifically to the respective facets of the University - Administrative, Academic, Operations and Community Development of a comprehensive Recycling Program to facilitate the recycling needs of the faculty, staff, and students on campus. The recycling program engages collaborations with various external groups in the community including City and County Divisions with "green" student groups on campus. FAMU co-hosts the local staging of the annual National Conference of Mayors/Keep America Beautiful Cash for Cans Recycling Day. This is a major recycling event in Tallahassee, also co-hosted by both the City and County Recycling Divisions. FAMU's facilities planning and construction team has made the commitment to design and build all new renovation and construction projects to LEED standards.

ADMISSIONS
Freshman Academic Profile: Average high school GPA 3.1. 10% in top 10% of high school class, 34% in top 25% of high school class, 71% in top 50% of high school class. 85% from public high schools. SAT Math middle 50% range 430-520. SAT Critical Reading middle 50% range 430-510. SAT Writing middle 50% range 420-500. ACT middle 50% range 18-22. Minimum web-based TOEFL 61. Minimum paper TOEFL 500. **Basis for Candidate Selection:** *Very important factors considered include:* application essay, academic GPA, rigor of secondary school record, standardized test scores. *Other factors considered include:* Class rank, alumni/ae relation, character/personal qualities, extracurricular activities, racial/ethnic status, state residency, talent/ability, volunteer work, work experience. **Freshman Admission Requirements:** High school diploma is required and GED is accepted. *Academic units required:* 4 English, 3 mathematics, 3 science, (1 science labs), 2 foreign language, 3 social studies, 3 academic electives. *Academic units recommended:* 4 English, 3 mathematics, 3 science, (1 science labs), 2 foreign language, 3 social studies, 3 academic electives. **Freshman Admission Statistics:** 7,322 applied, 48% admitted, 52% enrolled. **Transfer Admission Requirements:** college transcript(s), minimum

college GPA of 2.0 required. Lowest grade transferable C. **General Admission Information:** Application Fee $20. Regular application deadline 5/9. Nonfall registration accepted. Credit offered for CEEB Advanced Placement tests.

COSTS AND FINANCIAL AID
Annual in-state tuition $4,929. Annual out-of-state tuition $16,869. Room and board $8,754. Required fees $258. Average book expense $1,138. **Required Forms and Deadlines:** FAFSA. **Notification of Awards:** Applicants will be notified of awards on a rolling basis beginning 3/1. **Types of Aid:** *Need-based scholarships/grants:* Federal Pell, SEOG, state scholarships/grants, private scholarships, the school's own gift aid, United Negro College Fund, Federal Nursing Scholarships. *Loans:* Direct Subsidized Stafford, Direct Unsubsidized Stafford, Direct PLUS, Federal Perkins. **Student Employment:** Federal Work-Study Program available. Institutional employment available. Highest amount earned per year from on-campus jobs $9,800. Off-campus job opportunities are good. **Financial Aid Statistics:** 90% freshmen, 87% undergrads receive need-based scholarship or grant aid. 43% freshmen, 29% undergrads receive non-need-based scholarship or grant aid. 83% freshmen, 84% undergrads receive need-based self-help aid. 2% freshmen, 2% undergrads receive athletic scholarships. 95% freshmen, 91% undergrads receive any aid. 84% undergrads borrow to pay for school. Average cumulative indebtedness $29,554. **Criteria for awarding institutional aid:** *Non-need-based:* academics, art, leadership.

FLORIDA ATLANTIC UNIVERSITY

777 Glades Road, Boca Raton, FL 33431-0991
Phone: 561-297-3040 • **Financial Aid Phone:** 561-297-3530
E-mail: admissions@fau.edu • **CEEB Code:** 5229
Fax: 561-297-2758 • **Website:** www.fau.edu • **ACT Code:** 729

This public school was founded in 1961. It has a 860-acre campus.

RATINGS
Admissions Selectivity Rating: 89   **Fire Safety Rating:** 86   **Green Rating:** 89

STUDENTS AND FACULTY
Enrollment: 24,057. **Student Body:** 56% female, 44% male, 5% out-of-state, 1% international. Asian 4%, African American 18%, Caucasian 48%, Hispanic 24%, Native American 0%.
Retention and Graduation: 78% freshmen return for sophomore year.
Faculty: Student/faculty ratio 20:1. 730 full-time faculty, 87% hold PhDs, 26% are members of minority groups, 42% are women. 15% of classes are taught by teaching assistants.

ACADEMICS
Degrees: associate, bachelor's, certificate, master's, post-master's certificate. **Classes:** Most classes have 20–29 students. Most lab/discussion sessions have 20–29 students. **Majors with Highest Enrollment:** accounting; education; nursing/registered nurse (rn, asn, bsn, msn). **Special Study Options:** Accelerated program, cooperative education program, cross-registration, distance learning, double major, dual enrollment, English as a Second Language (ESL), honors program, independent study, internships, liberal arts/career combination, study abroad, teacher certification program, weekend college. **Honors Programs:** The Harriet L. Wilkes Honors College of Florida Atlantic University, which opened in the Fall of 1999, is the first public honors institution to be built from the ground up in the United States. Its intellectual foundation is a belief in liberal arts education as the best preparation for a full and productive life. The University Scholars Program is the honors program located on the Boca Raton campus. It is for freshman and sophomore students. The historical mission of a liberal arts education has been to develop the qualities of a free and responsible citizen, one who can reason clearly, read analytically, argue persuasively in speech and in writing, and contribute in fundamental and innovative ways to a chosen field of study or work. **Combined Degree Programs:** BA/MEng. **Disability Services:** Special programs offered to physically disabled students include note-taking services, reader services, tape recorders, tutors. **Career Services:** Alumni network, alumni services, career/job search classes, career assessment, internships, regional alumni.

FACILITIES
Housing: Coed dorms, apartments for married students, apartments for single students. 100% of campus accessible to physically disabled. **Special Academic Facilities/Equipment:** Art gallery, on-campus elementary school, robotics lab, marine research facilities. **Computers:** Students can register for classes online. Administrative functions (other than registration) can be performed online.

CAMPUS LIFE
Environment: City. **Activities:** Choral groups, dance, drama/theater, jazz band, literary magazine, marching band, music ensembles, musical theater,

opera, radio station, student government, student newspaper, television station 150 registered organizations, 11 honor societies, 6 religious organizations. 9 fraternities, 4 sororities. **Athletics (Intercollegiate):** *Men:* baseball, basketball, cheerleading, cross-country, diving, football, golf, soccer, swimming, tennis. *Women:* basketball, cheerleading, cross-country, diving, golf, soccer, softball, swimming, tennis, track/field (outdoor), volleyball. **On-Campus Highlights:** Student Services Building, Student Union, Dining Hall, Breezeway, Residence Halls. **Environmental Initiatives:** All new construction is designed and built to a minimum LEED silver certification level. This has been surpassed on every project to date, FAU currently has 1 platinum, 5 gold, and 2 pending gold certified buildings. Replacement of the 2 main chillers that provide the majority of the HVAC to our main campus. This is a 1.9 million project that will reduce more than 632 metric tons of carbon and over 2500 MWH saved. Climate change has been recognized as one of the three main areas of research which FAU has committed to pursuing, and currently has more that 30 grant funded research projects dedicated to climate change in the Florida Region.

ADMISSIONS

Freshman Academic Profile: Average high school GPA 3.5. 11% in top 10% of high school class, 35% in top 25% of high school class, 78% in top 50% of high school class. SAT Math middle 50% range 490-580. SAT Critical Reading middle 50% range 480-570. SAT Writing middle 50% range 480-560. ACT middle 50% range 21-25. Minimum web-based TOEFL 80. Minimum paper TOEFL 550. **Basis for Candidate Selection:** *Very important factors considered include:* academic GPA, standardized test scores. *Important factors considered include:* Class rank, rigor of secondary school record. *Other factors considered include:* application essay, recommendation(s), alumni/ae relation, character/personal qualities, extracurricular activities, first generation, level of applicant's interest, talent/ability, volunteer work. **Freshman Admission Requirements:** High school diploma is required and GED is accepted. *Academic units required:* 4 English, 3 mathematics, 3 science, (2 science labs), 2 foreign language, 3 social studies, 3 academic electives. *Academic units recommended:* 4 English, 3 mathematics, 3 science, (2 science labs), 2 foreign language, 3 social studies, 3 academic electives. **Freshman Admission Statistics:** 27,888 applied, 39% admitted, 30% enrolled. **Transfer Admission Requirements:** college transcript(s), minimum college GPA of 3.0 required. Lowest grade transferable D-. **General Admission Information:** Application Fee $30. Regular application deadline 6/1. Notification on a rolling basis, beginning on or about 9/1. Nonfall registration accepted. Admission may be deferred for a maximum of 2 semesters. Credit offered for CEEB Advanced Placement tests.

COSTS AND FINANCIAL AID

Annual in-state tuition $5,986. Annual out-of-state tuition $21,543. Room and board $11,353. Average book expense $1,203. **Required Forms and Deadlines:** FAFSA. **Notification of Awards:** Applicants will be notified of awards on a rolling basis beginning 4/1. **Types of Aid:** *Need-based scholarships/ grants:* Federal Pell, SEOG, state scholarships/grants, private scholarships, the school's own gift aid, Federal Nursing Scholarships. *Loans:* Subsidized Stafford, Unsubsidized Stafford, PLUS, Federal Perkins, college/university loans from institutional funds. **Student Employment:** Federal Work-Study Program available. Institutional employment available. Highest amount earned per year from on-campus jobs $1,500. Off-campus job opportunities are excellent. **Financial Aid Statistics:** 91% freshmen, 86% undergrads receive need-based scholarship or grant aid. 7% freshmen, 5% undergrads receive non-need-based scholarship or grant aid. 71% freshmen, 75% undergrads receive need-based self-help aid. 1% freshmen, 1% undergrads receive athletic scholarships. 46% undergrads borrow to pay for school. Average cumulative indebtedness $19,281. **Criteria for awarding institutional aid:** *Non-need-based:* academics, athletics, music/ drama, state/district residency.

FLORIDA COLLEGE

Admissions Office, Temple Terrace, FL 33617-5578
Phone: 813-988-5131 • **Financial Aid Phone:** 813-899-6720
E-mail: Admissions@FloridaCollege.edu • **CEEB Code:** 1562
Fax: 813-899-6722 • **Website:** www.floridacollege.edu • **ACT Code:** 1482

This private school was founded in 1946.

RATINGS
Admissions Selectivity Rating: 73   **Fire Safety Rating:** 98   **Green Rating:** 60*

STUDENTS AND FACULTY
Enrollment: 532. **Student Body:** 52% female, 48% male, 67% out-of-state, 1% international (6 countries represented). Asian 1%, African American 5%, Caucasian 82%, Hispanic 6%, Native American 2%.

Faculty: Student/faculty ratio 11:1. 39 full-time faculty, 38% hold PhDs, 3% are members of minority groups, 21% are women. 0% of classes are taught by teaching assistants.

ACADEMICS
Degrees: associate, bachelor's, transfer associate. **Classes:** Most classes have fewer than 10 students. Most lab/discussion sessions have 10–19 students. **Special Study Options:** cross-registration, double major, independent study, teacher certification program. **Disability Services:** Special programs offered to physically disabled students include tape recorders, tutors. **Career Services:**

FACILITIES
Housing: special housing for disabled students, men's dorms, women's dorms.

CAMPUS LIFE
Environment: Town. **Activities:** Choral groups, concert band, drama/theater, jazz band, literary magazine, music ensembles, musical theater, pep band, student government, yearbook. **Athletics (Intercollegiate):** *Men:* basketball, cross-country, soccer. *Women:* cheerleading, cross-country, soccer, volleyball. **On-Campus Highlights:** Riverwalk, Student Center

ADMISSIONS
Freshman Academic Profile: SAT Math middle 50% range 440-585. SAT Critical Reading middle 50% range 460-595. SAT Writing middle 50% range 440-580. ACT middle 50% range 19-25. Minimum paper TOEFL 550. **Basis for Candidate Selection:** *Very important factors considered include:* academic GPA, recommendation(s), rigor of secondary school record, standardized test scores, character/personal qualities, religious affiliation/commitment. *Important factors considered include:* Class rank, level of applicant's interest. *Other factors considered include:* alumni/ae relation, talent/ability. **Freshman Admission Requirements:** High school diploma is required and GED is accepted. *Academic units required:* 4 English, 3 mathematics, 2 science, (2 science labs), 2 social studies. *Academic units recommended:* 4 English, 3 mathematics, 2 science, (2 science labs), 2 social studies. **Freshman Admission Statistics:** 322 applied, 73% admitted, 82% enrolled. **Transfer Admission Requirements:** High school transcript, college transcript(s), standardized test scores, statement of good standing from prior institution(s). Minimum college GPA of 2.0 required. Lowest grade transferable C. **General Admission Information:** Application Fee $30. Regular application deadline 8/1. Nonfall registration accepted. Placement offered for CEEB Advanced Placement tests.

COSTS AND FINANCIAL AID
Annual tuition $12,400. Room and board $7,550. Required fees $750. Average book expense $1,300. **Required Forms and Deadlines:** FAFSA, institution's own financial aid form, state aid form. **Notification of Awards:** Applicants will be notified of awards on a rolling basis beginning 3/1. **Types of Aid:** *Need-based scholarships/grants:* Federal Pell, SEOG, state scholarships/grants, private scholarships, the school's own gift aid. *Loans:* Subsidized Stafford, Unsubsidized Stafford, PLUS, Federal PerkinsAlternative Loans. **Student Employment: Financial Aid Statistics:** 66% freshmen, 66% undergrads receive need-based scholarship or grant aid. 93% freshmen, 90% undergrads receive non-need-based scholarship or grant aid. 77% freshmen, 75% undergrads receive need-based self-help aid. 12% freshmen, 11% undergrads receive athletic scholarships. **Criteria for awarding institutional aid:** *Non-need-based:* academics, athletics, music/drama, state/district residency.

FLORIDA GULF COAST UNIVERSITY

10501 FGCU Blvd. South, Fort Myers, FL 33965-6565
Phone: 239-590-7878 • **Financial Aid Phone:** 239-590-7920
E-mail: admissions@fgcu.edu • **CEEB Code:** 5221
Fax: 239-590-7894 • **Website:** • **ACT Code:** 733

This public school was founded in 1991. It has a 760-acre campus.

RATINGS
Admissions Selectivity Rating: 75   **Fire Safety Rating:** 93   **Green Rating:** 93

STUDENTS AND FACULTY
Enrollment: 12,057. **Student Body:** 55% female, 45% male, 7% out-of-state, 1% international (89 countries represented). Asian 2%, African American 7%, Caucasian 68%, Hispanic 18%, Native American 0%.
Retention and Graduation: 76% freshmen return for sophomore year.
Faculty: Student/faculty ratio 22:1. 398 full-time faculty, 74% hold PhDs, 18% are members of minority groups, 46% are women. 0% of classes are taught by teaching assistants.

ACADEMICS
Degrees: associate, bachelor's, certificate, master's, transfer associate. **Classes:** Most classes have 20–29 students. **Majors with Highest Enrollment:** busi-

The Princeton Review's Complete Book of Colleges

ness/commerce; elementary education and teaching; liberal arts and sciences/ liberal studies. **Special Study Options:** Accelerated program, cross-registration, distance learning, double major, dual enrollment, honors program, independent study, internships, student-designed major, study abroad, teacher certification program. **Honors Programs:** The University Honors Program at Florida Gulf Coast University offers special opportunities for superior students to pursue academic work that challenges their interests and abilities. The program is university-wide, which gives students full access to the faculty and the entire range of programs at FGCU. Since the honors program at Florida Gulf Coast University is exclusive, we have the ability to design a unique program for each individual student. Scholarship opportunities and special programs that support the honors student's educational, intellectual, and personal goals will be designed individually with the student and his or her faculty mentor. **Combined Degree Programs:** Nursing, BS/MS. **Disability Services:** Special programs offered to physically disabled students include note-taking services, reader services, tape recorders, tutors. **Career Services:** Alumni network, alumni services, career/job search classes, career assessment, internships.

FACILITIES

Housing: Coed dorms, special housing for disabled students, apartments for single students. 100% of campus accessible to physically disabled. **Special Academic Facilities/Equipment:** Art Gallery, Observatory **Computers:** Students can register for classes online. Administrative functions (other than registration) can be performed online.

CAMPUS LIFE

Environment: City. **Activities:** Choral groups, dance, drama/theater, literary magazine, radio station, student government, student newspaper 105 registered organizations, 7 honor societies, 8 religious organizations. 4 fraternities, 4 sororities. **Athletics (Intercollegiate):** *Men:* baseball, basketball, cross-country, golf, soccer, tennis. *Women:* basketball, cross-country, diving, golf, soccer, softball, swimming, tennis, volleyball. **On-Campus Highlights:** Alico Arena, Student Union, The Quad, The Library, Baseball/Softball fields.

ADMISSIONS

Freshman Academic Profile: Average high school GPA 3.4. 9% in top 10% of high school class, 35% in top 25% of high school class, 76% in top 50% of high school class. SAT Math middle 50% range 470-560. SAT Critical Reading middle 50% range 470-550. SAT Writing middle 50% range 450-540. ACT middle 50% range 20-23. Minimum web-based TOEFL 79. Minimum paper TOEFL 550. **Basis for Candidate Selection:** *Very important factors considered include:* academic GPA, standardized test scores. *Important factors considered include:* rigor of secondary school record. *Other factors considered include:* Class rank, recommendation(s). **Freshman Admission Requirements:** High school diploma is required and GED is accepted. *Academic units required:* 4 English, 3 mathematics, 3 science, (2 science labs), 2 foreign language, 3 social studies, 3 academic electives. 4 English, 3 mathematics, 3 science, (2 science labs), 2 foreign language, 3 social studies, 3 academic electives. **Freshman Admission Statistics:** 10,073 applied, 68% admitted, 41% enrolled. **Transfer Admission Requirements:** college transcript(s), minimum college GPA of 2.0 required. Lowest grade transferable D. **General Admission Information:** Application Fee $30. Regular application deadline 5/1. Nonfall registration accepted. Admission may be deferred for a maximum of 2 Semesters. Credit and/ or placement offered for CEEB Advanced Placement tests.

COSTS AND FINANCIAL AID

Average book expense $1,200. **Required Forms and Deadlines:** FAFSA. **Types of Aid:** *Need-based scholarships/grants:* Federal Pell, SEOG, state scholarships/grants, private scholarships, the school's own gift aid. *Loans:* Subsidized Stafford, Unsubsidized Stafford, PLUS. **Financial Aid Statistics:** 63% freshmen, 67% undergrads receive need-based scholarship or grant aid. 78% freshmen, 66% undergrads receive non-need-based scholarship or grant aid. 52% freshmen, 62% undergrads receive need-based self-help aid. 1% freshmen, 1% undergrads receive athletic scholarships. 88% freshmen, 35% undergrads receive any aid. 41% undergrads borrow to pay for school. Average cumulative indebtedness $22,171. **Criteria for awarding institutional aid:** *Non-need-based:* academics, alumni affiliation, athletics, leadership, minority status, music/drama, religious affiliation, state/district residency.

FLORIDA INSTITUTE OF TECHNOLOGY

150 West University Boulevard, Melbourne, FL 32901-6975
Phone: 321-674-8030 • **Financial Aid Phone:** 800-666-4348
E-mail: admission@fit.edu • **CEEB Code:** 5080
Fax: 321-674-8004 • **Website:** www.fit.edu • **ACT Code:** 716

This private school was founded in 1958. It has a 130-acre campus.

RATINGS

Admissions Selectivity Rating: 86   **Fire Safety Rating:** 72   **Green Rating:** 79

STUDENTS AND FACULTY

Enrollment: 2,887. **Student Body:** 28% female, 72% male, 47% out-of-state, 28% international (97 countries represented). Asian 2%, African American 5%, Caucasian 46%, Hispanic 6%, Native American 0%.
Retention and Graduation: 79% freshmen return for sophomore year. 37% freshmen graduate within 4 years. 55% freshmen graduate within 6 years. 42% grads go on to further study within 1 year. 9% grads pursue arts and sciences degrees. 1% grads pursue law degrees. 4% grads pursue business degrees. 2% grads pursue medical degrees. **Faculty:** Student/faculty ratio 14:1. 246 full-time faculty, 91% hold PhDs, 14% are members of minority groups, 23% are women. 5% of classes are taught by teaching assistants.

ACADEMICS

Degrees: associate, bachelor's, master's, post-master's certificate. **Classes:** Most classes have 10–19 students. Most lab/discussion sessions have 10–19 students. **Majors with Highest Enrollment:** aerospace, aeronautical and astronautical engineering; marine biology and biological oceanography; mechanical engineering. **Special Study Options:** Accelerated program, cooperative education program, cross-registration, distance learning, double major, dual enrollment, English as a Second Language (ESL), independent study, internships, study abroad, teacher certification program, Dual degrees in computer engineering/electrical engineering, chemical engineering/chemistry, molecular/marine biology. **Disability Services:** Special programs offered to physically disabled students include note-taking services, reader services, tutors. **Career Services:** alumni services, career/job search classes, internships Career Services highlights include Internships.

FACILITIES

Housing: Coed dorms, apartments for single students, wellness housing, 90% of campus accessible to physically disabled. **Special Academic Facilities/Equipment:** New facility openings have been the highlight of 2009, beginning in February with the dedication of the Emil Buehler Center for Aviation Training and Research at Melbourne International Airport. The center, valued at $5.1 million, consists of a main building and 17,600-square-foot hanger, located on eight acres at the airport. The new building houses the operations of F.I.T. Aviation. In August, the university's Department of Humanities got a boost with the opening of the 3,000-square-foot Ruth Funk Center for Textile Arts. The only textiles center in the state of Florida, the facility is dedicated to furthering the understanding of cultural and creative achievements in the textile and fine arts. October gave another boost to the College of Psychology and Liberal Arts with the opening of the Scott Center for Autism Treatment. The 18,000 square foot center provides services for individuals with autism spectrum disorder, training for parents, teachers and other professionals and research on effective treatments for autism. The College of Engineering and College of Science also gained a new building in October with the opening of the Harris Center for Science and Engineering. While computer science and marine biology laboratories fill two-thirds of the building, the rest is dedicated to the Harris Institute for Assured Information. The institute is already recognized for its work and numerous government and national foundation contracts. The College of Business received a tremendous boost in 2009 with a $5 million gift from Nathan M. Bisk, a leader in continuing education and online learning. The gift enhances business programs offerings and strengthens online education and marks the start of fund-raising for a new building, to be named the Nathan M. Bisk College of Business. **Computers:** 100% of classrooms, 30% of dorms, 100% of libraries, 100% of dining areas, 100% of student union, 5% of common outdoor areas have wireless network access. Students can register for classes online. Administrative functions (other than registration) can be performed online.

CAMPUS LIFE

Environment: Town. **Activities:** Choral groups, dance, drama/theater, literary magazine, pep band, radio station, student government, student newspaper, television station, Campus Ministries, International Student Organization 106 registered organizations, 8 honor societies, 3 religious organizations. 7 fraternities, 3 sororities. **Athletics (Intercollegiate):** *Men:* baseball, basketball, cross-country, golf, soccer, tennis. *Women:* basketball, crew/rowing, cross-country, golf, soccer, softball, tennis, volleyball. **On-Campus Highlights:** Student Union Building, Clemente Center for Sports & Recreation, Olin Engineering Complex, Harris Village, Botanical Gardens. **Environmental Initiatives:** All new construction to be LEED equivalent and multiple buildings on campus undergoing LEED Existing Buildings certification. Comprehensive campus-wide recycling program and green procurement program. Campus-wide sustainability minor program with students from all five colleges and 13 majors enrolled.

ADMISSIONS
Freshman Academic Profile: Average high school GPA 3.5. 31% in top 10% of high school class, 58% in top 25% of high school class, 85% in top 50% of high school class. 41% from public high schools. SAT Math middle 50% range 540-640. SAT Critical Reading middle 50% range 500-610. ACT middle 50% range 22-28. Minimum paper TOEFL 550. **Basis for Candidate Selection:** *Very important factors considered include:* rigor of secondary school record. *Important factors considered include:* academic GPA, standardized test scores, level of applicant's interest. *Other factors considered include:* Class rank, application essay, recommendation(s), alumni/ae relation, character/personal qualities, extracurricular activities, interview, work experience. **Freshman Admission Requirements:** High school diploma is required and GED is accepted. *Academic units required:* 4 English, 3 mathematics, 3 science, (3 science labs), 1 social studies, 2 history, 7 academic electives. *Academic units recommended:* 4 English, 3 mathematics, 3 science, (3 science labs), 1 social studies, 2 history, 7 academic electives. **Freshman Admission Statistics:** 7,428 applied, 59% admitted, 17% enrolled. **Transfer Admission Requirements:** college transcript(s), minimum college GPA of 2.5 required. Lowest grade transferable C. **General Admission Information:** Application Fee $50. Notification on a rolling basis, beginning on or about 7/1. Nonfall registration accepted. Admission may be deferred for a maximum of 12 month. Credit and/or placement offered for CEEB Advanced Placement tests.

COSTS AND FINANCIAL AID
Annual tuition $34,150. Room and board $12,270. Required fees $560. Average book expense $1,200. **Required Forms and Deadlines:** FAFSA, state aid form. **Notification of Awards:** Applicants will be notified of awards on a rolling basis beginning 2/15. **Types of Aid:** *Need-based scholarships/grants:* Federal Pell, SEOG, state scholarships/grants, private scholarships, the school's own gift aid. *Loans:* Subsidized Stafford, Unsubsidized Stafford, PLUS, Federal Perkins, state loans, college/university loans from institutional funds. **Student Employment:** Federal Work-Study Program available. Institutional employment available. Highest amount earned per year from on-campus jobs $15,715. Off-campus job opportunities are fair. **Financial Aid Statistics:** 100% freshmen, 99% undergrads receive need-based scholarship or grant aid. 100% freshmen, 97% undergrads receive non-need-based scholarship or grant aid. 72% freshmen, 78% undergrads receive need-based self-help aid. 3% freshmen, 3% undergrads receive athletic scholarships. 95% freshmen, 86% undergrads receive any aid. 61% undergrads borrow to pay for school. Average cumulative indebtedness $38,953. **Criteria for awarding institutional aid:** *Non-need-based:* academics, alumni affiliation, athletics, state/district residency.

FLORIDA INTERNATIONAL UNIVERSITY

Modesto Maidique Campus, Miami, FL 33199
Phone: 305-348-2363 • **Financial Aid Phone:** 305-348-7272
E-mail: admiss@fiu.edu • **CEEB Code:** 5206
Fax: 305-348-3648 • **Website:** www.fiu.edu • **ACT Code:** 776

This public school was founded in 1965. It has a 573-acre campus.

RATINGS
Admissions Selectivity Rating: 92   **Fire Safety Rating:** 87   **Green Rating:** 61

STUDENTS AND FACULTY
Enrollment: 35,006. **Student Body:** 55% female, 45% male, 3% out-of-state, 5% international (147 countries represented). Asian 3%, African American 12%, Caucasian 12%, Hispanic 66%, Native American 0%.
Retention and Graduation: 82% freshmen return for sophomore year. 16% freshmen graduate within 4 years. 43% freshmen graduate within 6 years.

ACADEMICS
Degrees: associate, bachelor's, certificate, master's, post-master's certificate. **Classes:** Most classes have 20–29 students. Most lab/discussion sessions have 20–29 students. **Majors with Highest Enrollment:** business administration and management; economics; psychology. **Special Study Options:** Accelerated program, cooperative education program, distance learning, double major, dual enrollment, exchange student program (domestic), honors program, independent study, internships, study abroad, teacher certification program, weekend college. **Combined Degree Programs:** BA/MA, BA/MEng, Economics, Asian Studies, International Relations, Lideral Studies. **Disability Services:** Special programs offered to physically disabled students include note-taking services,

reader services, tape recorders, tutors. **Career Services:** alumni services, career/job search classes, career assessment, internships, regional alumni., Career Services highlights include We are particularly proud of our Executive Protege Initiative that is designed for students who commit quality time to attend career readiness presentations and professional development actitivies. We are also proud of our yearly Federal Government Statewide Conference that brings together FIU students and federal agencies to help students freshman-graduate learn about internship and full-time opportunities in the federal government.

FACILITIES
Housing: Coed dorms, fraternity/sorority housing, apartments for married students, apartments for single students. 100% of campus accessible to physically disabled. **Special Academic Facilities/Equipment:** The Frost Art Museum, The Wolfsonian Art Museum, Natural Preserve, Biscayne Bay Preserve **Computers:** 100% of classrooms, 100% of dorms, 1000% of libraries, 100% of dining areas, 100% of student union, 100% of common outdoor areas have wireless network access. Students can register for classes online. Administrative functions (other than registration) can be performed online.

CAMPUS LIFE
Environment: Metropolis. **Activities:** Choral groups, drama/theater, jazz band, music ensembles, opera, radio station, student government, student newspaper, symphony orchestra, yearbook, Campus Ministries, International Student Organization, Model UN 250 registered organizations, 40 honor societies, 5 religious organizations. 21 fraternities, 17 sororities. **Athletics (Intercollegiate):** *Men:* baseball, basketball, cross-country, football, soccer, track/field (outdoor), track/field (indoor). *Women:* basketball, cross-country, diving, golf, soccer, softball, swimming, tennis, track/field (outdoor), track/field (indoor), volleyball. **On-Campus Highlights:** The Frost Museum, The Wolfsonian Museum, Steven and Dorothea Green Library, Graham University Center, Biscayne Bay Campus Library, The Recreational Center. **Environmental Initiatives:** Spring 2011, FIU has officially become a smoking-free campus. Providing clean and smoke-free air to it's community. The latest initiative in FIU's commitment to going green, the web-based carpool program features award-winning software that makes signing up hassle-free and completely safe. Open to all FIU students, faculty and staff, university leaders are hoping the program will save money for participants, reduce traffic and relieve parking congestion, and help improve air quality and conserve energy. Installed sensor monitor for office light and installed new xerox machines which are energy efficient and are set for double-sided copying

ADMISSIONS
Freshman Academic Profile: Average high school GPA 3.7. 19% in top 10% of high school class, 48% in top 25% of high school class, 81% in top 50% of high school class. SAT Math middle 50% range 530-610. SAT Critical Reading middle 50% range 530-600. SAT Writing middle 50% range 520-590. ACT middle 50% range 24-27. Minimum web-based TOEFL 63. Minimum paper TOEFL 500. **Basis for Candidate Selection:** *Very important factors considered include:* Class rank, academic GPA, rigor of secondary school record, standardized test scores, first generation. *Other factors considered include:* application essay, recommendation(s), alumni/ae relation, character/personal qualities, extracurricular activities, geographical residence, interview, level of applicant's interest, state residency, talent/ability, volunteer work, work experience. **Freshman Admission Requirements:** High school diploma is required and GED is accepted. *Academic units required:* 4 English, 3 mathematics, 3 science, (2 science labs), 2 foreign language, 3 social studies, 3 academic electives. 4 English, 3 mathematics, 3 science, (2 science labs), 2 foreign language, 3 social studies, 3 academic electives. **Freshman Admission Statistics:** 16,626 applied, 39% admitted, 40% enrolled. **Transfer Admission Requirements:** college transcript(s), statement of good standing from prior institution(s). Minimum college GPA of 2.0 required. Lowest grade transferable D. **General Admission Information:** Application Fee $30. Regular application deadline 5/1. Notification on a rolling basis, beginning on or about 12/1. Nonfall registration accepted. Credit offered for CEEB Advanced Placement tests.

COSTS AND FINANCIAL AID
Student Employment: Federal Work-Study Program available. Institutional employment available. Off-campus job opportunities are good. **Financial Aid Statistics:** 72% freshmen, 78% undergrads receive need-based scholarship or grant aid. 84% freshmen, 48% undergrads receive non-need-based scholarship or grant aid. 62% freshmen, 67% undergrads receive need-based self-help aid. 2% freshmen, 1% undergrads receive athletic scholarships. 89% freshmen, 74% undergrads receive any aid. 47% undergrads borrow to pay for school. Average cumulative indebtedness $17,256.

FLORIDA SOUTHERN COLLEGE

111 Lake Hollingworth Drive, Lakeland, FL 33801
Phone: 863-680-4131 • **Financial Aid Phone:** 863-680-4140
E-mail: fscadm@flsouthern.edu • **CEEB Code:** 5218
Fax: 863-680-4120 • **Website:** www.flsouthern.edu • **ACT Code:** 732

This private school, affiliated with the Methodist Church, was founded in 1883. It has a 100-acre campus.

RATINGS
Admissions Selectivity Rating: 84   **Fire Safety Rating:** 79   **Green Rating:** 61

STUDENTS AND FACULTY
Enrollment: 2,021. **Student Body:** 58% female, 42% male, 33% out-of-state, 5% international (42 countries represented). Asian 2%, African American 6%, Caucasian 75%, Hispanic 9%, Native American 0%.
Retention and Graduation: 76% freshmen return for sophomore year. 5% freshmen graduate within 4 years. 55% freshmen graduate within 6 years. 26% grads go on to further study within 1 year. 57% grads pursue arts and sciences degrees. 6% grads pursue law degrees. 17% grads pursue business degrees. 6% grads pursue medical degrees. **Faculty:** Student/faculty ratio 13:1. 123 full-time faculty, 80% hold PhDs, 16% are members of minority groups, 40% are women. 0% of classes are taught by teaching assistants.

ACADEMICS
Degrees: bachelor's, master's. **Classes:** Most classes have 20–29 students. Most lab/discussion sessions have 10–19 students. **Majors with Highest Enrollment:** biology/biological sciences; business administration and management; nursing/registered nurse (rn, asn, bsn, msn). **Special Study Options:** double major, dual enrollment, honors program, independent study, internships, liberal arts/career combination, student-designed major, study abroad, teacher certification program, FSC Honors Program   USF College of Medicine Medical Education Program. **Honors Programs:** The mission of the Florida Southern College Honors Program is to offer academically talented and highly motivated students opportunities to explore special topics through carefully constructed courses. Professors employ innovative teaching techniques that challenge students to explore subjects through multiple perspectives. The Honors Program fosters an interactive learning environment within a community of scholars. **Combined Degree Programs:** BA/MD, Priority admittance to USF School of Medicine. **Career Services:** Alumni network, alumni services, career/job search classes, career assessment, internships, regional alumni. Career Services highlights include Florida Southern College guarantees meaningful, real-world engaged learning experiences, including internships, to every student.

FACILITIES
Housing: Coed dorms, special housing for disabled students, men's dorms, women's dorms, fraternity/sorority housing, apartments for married students, apartments for single students, theme housing, 70% of campus accessible to physically disabled. **Special Academic Facilities/Equipment:** Campus designed by Frank Lloyd Wright; contains world's largest collection of Wright-designed structures at a single site. Also home to three buildings designed by world renowned architect Robert A.M. Stern: 2 residence halls and 1 classroom building, which includes an art gallery and film studies center. The science building features a planetarium; the communication building features a television studio. The latest two building additions are 1) a 24-hour, state-of-the-art Technology and Learning Center; and 2) a high-tech nursing building featuring virtual patient simulators. The college houses two newly renovated art galleries'—the Melvin and Burke Galleries. Also of note, FSC has a world-class performing arts venue seating 2200. Students enjoy a Wellness Center accompanied by an outdoor pool and a boathouse for water-skiing, sailing, and kayaking. At the center of campus is a spectacular, 50-foot high Water Dome, which is next to the library's Cyber CafÃ©, which serves Starbuck's products. A spectacular Archives Center, also adjacent to the library, was completed within the past year. **Computers:** 20% of classrooms, 20% of dorms, 100% of libraries, 100% of dining areas, 50% of student union, 50% of common outdoor areas have wireless network access. Students can register for classes online. Administrative functions (other than registration) can be performed online.

CAMPUS LIFE
Environment: City. **Activities:** Choral groups, concert band, dance, drama/theater, jazz band, literary magazine, music ensembles, musical theater, opera, pep band, student government, student newspaper, symphony orchestra, television station, yearbook, Campus Ministries, International Student Organization 70 registered organizations, 22 honor societies, 9 religious organizations. 7 fraternities, 7 sororities. **Athletics (Intercollegiate):** *Men:* baseball, basketball, cross-country, golf, lacrosse, soccer, swimming, tennis, track/field (outdoor). *Women:* basketball, cross-country, golf, soccer, softball, swimming, tennis, track/field (outdoor), volleyball. **On-Campus Highlights:** Tutu's Cyber Cafe, Wellness Center and Pool, Badcock Garden's "'outdoor living room'", The Terrace Cafe, Field House, Our sunny campus offers something for everyone, including more than 70 clubs and organizations that cater to every interest. On beautiful Lake Hollingsworth, students enjoy free kayaking, sailing, and canoeing. Our state-of-the-art Wellness Center offers classes in everything from yoga to Pilates to water aerobics in our Olympic-sized pool. If the arts are more your speed, visit the Melvin Art Gallery, which exhibits the works of students and internationally recognized artists. Take in an opera, play, or concert through the renowned Festival of Fine Arts series, or catch a movie on the Badcock Garden lawn. Our championship Division II NCAA sports programs mean there's always something to cheer about, and intramural sports such as flag football, tennis, and soccer give you a chance to get in the game. And if you've worked up an appetite, grab lunch from the Grillmaster in the Badcock Garden or enjoy a cup of Starbuck's coffee and a bagel on the patio overlooking the Water Dome at TÃ»TÃ»'s Cyber CafÃ©. **Environmental Initiatives:** Using a ground based water heating solution for the Education & visitors Center Trayless cafeteria initiative Cycling Initiative Explanation: In an effort to encourage members of the campus community to ride Bikes on short trips, we make bikes available for students, faculty, and staff to check out at no charge at the Wellness Center.

ADMISSIONS
Freshman Academic Profile: Average high school GPA 3.6. 21% in top 10% of high school class, 42% in top 25% of high school class, 75% in top 50% of high school class. 81% from public high schools. SAT Math middle 50% range 500-600. SAT Critical Reading middle 50% range 500-590. ACT middle 50% range 22-27. Minimum paper TOEFL 550. **Basis for Candidate Selection:** *Very important factors considered include:* academic GPA, rigor of secondary school record. *Important factors considered include:* application essay, recommendation(s), standardized test scores, character/personal qualities, extracurricular activities, level of applicant's interest, talent/ability. *Other factors considered include:* Class rank, alumni/ae relation, first generation, interview, racial/ethnic status, religious affiliation/commitment, volunteer work, work experience. **Freshman Admission Requirements:** High school diploma is required and GED is accepted. *Academic units required:* 4 English, 3 mathematics, 2 science, (2 science labs), 3 social studies, 3 history, 2 academic electives *Academic units recommended:* 4 English, 3 mathematics, 2 science, (2 science labs), 3 social studies, 3 history, 2 academic electives. **Freshman Admission Statistics:** 4,448 applied, 56% admitted, 22% enrolled. **Transfer Admission Requirements:** college transcript(s), essay or personal statement, statement of good standing from prior institution(s). Minimum college CPA of 2.0 required. Lowest grade transferable C. **General Admission Information:** Application Fee $30. Early decision application deadline 12/1. Regular application deadline 3/1. Notification on a rolling basis, beginning on or about 1/15. Nonfall registration accepted. Admission may be deferred for a maximum of 1 Year. Credit offered for CEEB Advanced Placement tests.

COSTS AND FINANCIAL AID
Required Forms and Deadlines: FAFSA, institution's own financial aid form. **Notification of Awards:** Applicants will be notified of awards on a rolling basis beginning 3/1. **Types of Aid:** *Need-based scholarships/grants:* Federal Pell, SEOG, state scholarships/grants, private scholarships, the school's own gift aid, Federal Nursing Scholarships. *Loans:* Subsidized Stafford, Unsubsidized Stafford, PLUS, Federal Perkins. **Student Employment:** Federal Work-Study Program available. Institutional employment available. Highest amount earned per year from on-campus jobs $1,500. Off-campus job opportunities are good. **Financial Aid Statistics:** 100% freshmen, 98% undergrads receive need-based scholarship or grant aid. 69% freshmen, 70% undergrads receive non-need-based scholarship or grant aid. 19% freshmen, 32% undergrads receive need-based self-help aid. 4% freshmen, 4% undergrads receive athletic scholarships. 99% freshmen, 98% undergrads receive any aid. 63% undergrads borrow to pay for school. Average cumulative indebtedness $26,509. **Criteria for awarding institutional aid:** *Non-need-based:* academics, alumni affiliation, art, athletics, job skills, leadership, minority status, music/drama, religious affiliation, state/district residency.

FLORIDA STATE UNIVERSITY

Best 378

PO Box 3062400, Tallahassee, FL 32306-2400
Phone: 850-644-6200 • **Financial Aid Phone:** 850-644-5716
E-mail: admissions@admin.fsu.edu • **CEEB Code:** 5219
Fax: 850-644-0197 • **Website:** www.fsu.edu • **ACT Code:** 734

This public school was founded in 1851. It has a 452-acre campus.

RATINGS
Admissions Selectivity Rating: 90   **Fire Safety Rating:** 80   **Green Rating:** 87

STUDENTS AND FACULTY
Enrollment: 31,594. **Student Body:** 55% female, 45% male, 9% out-of-state, 1% international (130 countries represented). Asian 4%, African American 10%, Caucasian 68%, Hispanic 14%, Native American 1%.
Retention and Graduation: 50% freshmen graduate within 4 years. 74% freshmen graduate within 6 years. 42% grads go on to further study within 1 year. **Faculty:** Student/faculty ratio 26:1. 1248 full-time faculty, 92% hold PhDs, 17% are members of minority groups, 37% are women. 28% of classes are taught by teaching assistants.

ACADEMICS
Degrees: associate, bachelor's, certificate, master's, post-bachelor's certificate, post-master's certificate, transfer associate. **Classes:** Most classes have 20–29 students. **Majors with Highest Enrollment:** English language and literature; finance; political science and government. **Special Study Options:** Accelerated program, cooperative education program, cross-registration, distance learning, double major, dual enrollment, English as a Second Language (ESL), honors program, independent study, internships, study abroad, teacher certification program. **Honors Programs:** The Florida State University Honors Program provides an enriched curriculum and special opportunities for exceptional, high-achieving students who are entering college for the first time. Each fall, freshmen who are admitted into this program attend the University Honors Colloquium, a weekly forum that features stimulating lectures by distinguished faculty as well as informative presentations from directors of academic programs. As they work to meet their liberal study requirements, University Honors students then have the chance to take small, honors-only courses and special topic seminars with some of the university's best researchers and teachers. With its emphasis on small classes taught by top faculty, this program provides the atmosphere of a small liberal arts college within a large research university. **Combined Degree Programs:** BA/MA. **Disability Services:** Special programs offered to physically disabled students include note-taking services, reader services, tape recorders, tutors. **Career Services:** Alumni network, alumni services, career/job search classes, career assessment, internships, regional alumni.

FACILITIES
Housing: Coed dorms, special housing for disabled students, women's dorms, fraternity/sorority housing, apartments for married students, apartments for single students, On-campus: Honors Residences; Living Learning Communities Off-campus: Cooperative housing through Southern Scholarship Foundation; off-campus private residence halls. 99% of campus accessible to physically disabled. **Special Academic Facilities/Equipment:** Art gallery, museum, developmental research school, marine lab, oceanographic institute, tandem Van de Graaff accelerator, national high magnetic field lab. **Computers:** 50% of classrooms, 25% of dorms, 90% of libraries, 100% of dining areas, 90% of student union, 70% of common outdoor areas have wireless network access. Students can register for classes online. Administrative functions (other than registration) can be performed online. Undergraduates are required to own a computer.

CAMPUS LIFE
Environment: City. **Activities:** Choral groups, concert band, dance, drama/theater, jazz band, literary magazine, marching band, music ensembles, musical theater, opera, pep band, radio station, student government, student newspaper, student-run film society, symphony orchestra, television station, yearbook, Campus Ministries, International Student Organization, Model UN 520 registered organizations, 23 honor societies, 30 religious organizations. 32 fraternities, 28 sororities. **Athletics (Intercollegiate):** *Men:* baseball, basketball, cheerleading, cross-country, diving, football, golf, swimming, tennis, track/field (outdoor), track/field (indoor). *Women:* basketball, cheerleading, cross-country, diving, golf, soccer, softball, swimming, tennis, track/field (outdoor), track/field (indoor), volleyball. **On-Campus Highlights:** Suwannee Dining Hall, Bobby E.

Leach Student Recreation Center, Bobby Bowden Field at Doak Campbell Stadium, National High Magnetic Field Laboratory, FSU Reservation. **Environmental Initiatives:** Creation of the FSU Office of Sustainability and the hiring of a full-time Director of Campus Sustainability to help build a comprehensive sustainable campus program. Dedicated energy conservation fund . FSU has set aside some capital to be used exclusively for projects that have relatively short pay backs (less than 7 years on average). Our intention is to strive for a 10% energy reduction on campus over the next several years. Concentrated growth and expansion of sustainability-related outreach and engagement programs, including the creation of an Eco-Reps program and an increase in the number of volunteers and amount of recyclable material collected at our football game recycling program. Student-initiated projects are receiving more support from staff and administrators.

ADMISSIONS
Freshman Academic Profile: Average high school GPA 3.8. 40% in top 10% of high school class, 78% in top 25% of high school class, 97% in top 50% of high school class. 84% from public high schools. SAT Math middle 50% range 560-640. SAT Critical Reading middle 50% range 550-650. SAT Writing middle 50% range 550-630. ACT middle 50% range 25-28. Minimum web-based TOEFL 80. Minimum paper TOEFL 550. **Basis for Candidate Selection:** *Very important factors considered include:* academic GPA, rigor of secondary school record. *Important factors considered include:* standardized test scores, state residency, talent/ability. *Other factors considered include:* Class rank, application essay, recommendation(s), alumni/ae relation, character/personal qualities, extracurricular activities, first generation, geographical residence, volunteer work, work experience. **Freshman Admission Requirements:** High school diploma is required and GED is accepted. *Academic units required:* 4 English, 4 mathematics, 3 science, (2 science labs), 2 foreign language, 1 social studies, 2 history, 3 academic electives. *Academic units recommended:* 4 English, 4 mathematics, 3 science, (2 science labs), 2 foreign language, 1 social studies, 2 history, 3 academic electives. **Freshman Admission Statistics:** 28,313 applied, 58% admitted, 37% enrolled. **Transfer Admission Requirements:** college transcript(s), minimum college GPA of 3.0 required. Lowest grade transferable D-. **General Admission Information:** Application Fee $30. Regular application deadline 1/21. Nonfall registration accepted. Credit and/or placement offered for CEEB Advanced Placement tests.

COSTS AND FINANCIAL AID
Annual in-state tuition $3,397. Annual out-of-state tuition $18,564. Room and board $9,626. Required fees $3,005. Average book expense $1,000. **Required Forms and Deadlines:** FAFSA. **Notification of Awards:** Applicants will be notified of awards on a rolling basis beginning 3/15. **Types of Aid:** *Need-based scholarships/grants:* Federal Pell, SEOG, state scholarships/grants, private scholarships, the school's own gift aid. *Loans:* Subsidized Stafford, Unsubsidized Stafford, PLUS, Federal Perkins. **Student Employment:** Federal Work-Study Program available. Institutional employment available. Highest amount earned per year from on-campus jobs $10,000. Off-campus job opportunities are good. **Financial Aid Statistics:** 61% freshmen, 59% undergrads receive need-based scholarship or grant aid. 95% freshmen, 80% undergrads receive non-need-based scholarship or grant aid. 61% freshmen, 67% undergrads receive need-based self-help aid. 1% freshmen, 1% undergrads receive athletic scholarships. 96% freshmen, 88% undergrads receive any aid. 54% undergrads borrow to pay for school. Average cumulative indebtedness $22,139. **Criteria for awarding institutional aid:** *Non-need-based:* academics, athletics, state/district residency.

FONTBONNE UNIVERSITY

6800 Wydown Boulevard, St. Louis, MO 63105
Phone: 314-889-1400 • **Financial Aid Phone:** 314-889-1414
E-mail: fcadmis@fontbonne.edu • **CEEB Code:** 6216
Fax: 314-889-1451 • **Website:** www.fontbonne.edu • **ACT Code:** 2298

This private school, affiliated with the Roman Catholic Church, was founded in 1917. It has a 13-acre campus.

RATINGS
Admissions Selectivity Rating: 75   **Fire Safety Rating:** 83   **Green Rating:** 60*

STUDENTS AND FACULTY
Enrollment: 1,993. **Student Body:** 72% female, 28% male, 12% out-of-state, 1% international (23 countries represented). Asian 1%, African American 34%, Caucasian 62%, Hispanic 1%, Native American 0%.
Retention and Graduation: 58% freshmen return for sophomore year. 33% freshmen graduate within 4 years. 49% freshmen graduate within 6 years. 25% grads go on to further study within 1 year. **Faculty:** Student/faculty ratio 16:1. 73 full-time faculty, 71% hold PhDs, 10% are members of minority groups, 68% are women. 0% of classes are taught by teaching assistants.

ACADEMICS

Degrees: bachelor's, certificate, master's, post-bachelor's certificate. **Classes:** Most classes have 10–19 students. Most lab/discussion sessions have 10–19 students. **Majors with Highest Enrollment:** business administration and management; elementary education and teaching; special education and teaching. **Special Study Options:** Accelerated program, cooperative education program, cross-registration, distance learning, double major, English as a Second Language (ESL), exchange student program (domestic), honors program, independent study, internships, liberal arts/career combination, student-designed major, study abroad, teacher certification program, weekend college. **Combined Degree Programs:** BA/MEng, BS/MS with Washington University. **Disability Services:** Special programs offered to physically disabled students include note-taking services, reader services, tape recorders, tutors. **Career Services:** alumni services, career/job search classes, career assessment, internships.

FACILITIES

Housing: Coed dorms, special housing for international students, apartments for single students, Off campus house which holds 13 females. 85% of campus accessible to physically disabled. **Special Academic Facilities/Equipment:** Art gallery. **Computers:** 75% of classrooms, 100% of dorms, 100% of libraries, 100% of dining areas, 100% of student union, 100% of common outdoor areas have wireless network access. Students can register for classes online. Administrative functions (other than registration) can be performed online.

CAMPUS LIFE

Environment: Metropolis. **Activities:** Choral groups, dance, drama/theater, literary magazine, music ensembles, radio station, student government, student newspaper, Campus Ministries 34 registered organizations, 7 honor societies, 4 religious organizations. **Athletics (Intercollegiate):** *Men:* baseball, basketball, cross-country, field hockey, golf, lacrosse, soccer, tennis. *Women:* basketball, bowling, cross-country, field hockey, golf, lacrosse, soccer, softball, tennis, volleyball. **On Campus Highlights:** Ryan Hall, Dunham Student Activity Center, Library, Medaille Hall, Fine Arts Center, Message from the President. On behalf of the entire Fontbonne University family, I am pleased to welcome you to our web site. As you navigate these electronic pages, I trust that you will find whatever information you seek about our University. When you explore the Fontbonne University campus, either in person or on a virtual visit like this, you will learn that Fontbonne has certain advantages that are evidenced in the following ways. Location Our campus is located in the heart of Clayton, Missouri, which is one of the most beautiful suburbs in the United States. There is easy access from our campus to Forest Park, the St. Louis Zoo, the Art Museum and the History Museum. In addition, you are approximately fifteen minutes from downtown St. Louis, home of the St. Louis Cardinals, NFL Rams and NHL Blues. Academics The academic programs are excellent, and they are taught in a values-based, student-centered context. Because of our student-faculty ratio, the faculty know you as an individual and will help you incorporate experiential learning in your academic program. Focus The individual student is the primary focus at Fontbonne University. You are the central focus of the administration, faculty and staff. We are dedicated to your academic, moral, emotional, spiritual, social, cultural, career and co-curricular development. Ultimate Goal At Fontbonne, we strive to achieve strength of curriculum and strength of character. Therefore, we will teach you not only how to make a living but also how to live a life so that you are prepared to face the challenges of the 21st century and to prevail. Fontbonne is a Catholic University sponsored by the Sisters of St. Joseph of Carondelet. We are co-educational with 2,800 students, and a student body comprised of both traditional-aged undergraduate students as well as adult learners. All of our students are taught to think critically, to act ethically and to assume responsibility as citizens and leaders for a world in need. If you are seeking a university education where the individual student is at the epicenter of all activity, then Fontbonne is for you. I invite you to visit our campus in person and come to know and value, as we do, the advantage that is a Fontbonne University education. Dennis C. Golden President.

ADMISSIONS

Freshman Academic Profile: Average high school GPA 3.1. 7% in top 10% of high school class, 28% in top 25% of high school class, 61% in top 50% of high school class. 56% from public high schools. SAT Math middle 50% range 470-625. SAT Critical Reading middle 50% range 500-625. ACT middle 50% range 18-24. Minimum paper TOEFL 525. **Basis for Candidate Selection:** *Very important factors considered include:* Class rank, academic GPA, rigor of secondary school record, standardized test scores, character/personal qualities. *Other factors considered include:* application essay, recommendation(s), alumni/ae relation, extracurricular activities, first generation, interview, level of applicant's interest, talent/ability, volunteer work, work experience. **Freshman Admission Requirements:** High school diploma is required and GED is accepted. *Academic units required:* 4 English, 3 mathematics, 3 science, (1 science labs), 3 social studies, 3 academic electives. 4 English, 3 mathematics, 3 science, (1 science labs), 3 social studies, 3 academic electives. **Freshman Admission Statistics:** 600 applied, 75% admitted, 42% enrolled. **Transfer Admission Requirements:** college transcript(s), essay or personal statement,

minimum college GPA of 2.0 required. Lowest grade transferable D. **General Admission Information:** Application Fee $25. Regular application deadline 8/1. Notification on a rolling basis, beginning on or about 8/15. Nonfall registration accepted. Admission may be deferred for a maximum of 1year. Credit and/or placement offered for CEEB Advanced Placement tests.

COSTS AND FINANCIAL AID

Annual tuition $20,860. Room and board $8,319. Required fees $440. Average book expense $650. **Required Forms and Deadlines:** FAFSA, institution's own financial aid form. **Notification of Awards: Types of Aid:** *Need-based scholarships/grants:* Federal Pell, SEOG, state scholarships/grants, private scholarships, the school's own gift aid. *Loans:* Subsidized Stafford, Unsubsidized Stafford, PLUS, Federal Perkins, state loans, college/university loans from institutional funds. **Student Employment:** Federal Work-Study Program available. **Financial Aid Statistics:** 96% freshmen, 98% undergrads receive need-based scholarship or grant aid. 99% freshmen, 68% undergrads receive non-need-based scholarship or grant aid. 93% freshmen, 91% undergrads receive need-based self-help aid. 81% undergrads borrow to pay for school. Average cumulative indebtedness $22,963. **Criteria for awarding institutional aid:** *Non-need-based:* academics, alumni affiliation, art, job skills, leadership, minority status, religious affiliation.

FORDHAM UNIVERSITY

441 East Fordham Road, Bronx, NY 10458
Phone: 718-817-4000 • **Financial Aid Phone:** 718-817-3800
E-mail: enroll@fordham.edu • **CEEB Code:** 2259
Fax: 718-367-9404 • **Website:** www.fordham.edu • **ACT Code:** 2748

This private school, affiliated with the Roman Catholic Church, was founded in 1841. It has a 93-acre campus.

RATINGS

Admissions Selectivity Rating: 93   Fire Safety Rating: 74   Green Rating: 60*

STUDENTS AND FACULTY

Enrollment: 7,451. **Student Body:** 58% female, 42% male, 46% out-of-state, 2% international (58 countries represented). Asian 7%, African American 6%, Caucasian 58%, Hispanic 13%, Native American 0%.
Retention and Graduation: 90% freshmen return for sophomore year. 72% freshmen graduate within 4 years. 25% grads go on to further study within 1 year. 10% grads pursue arts and sciences degrees. 5% grads pursue law degrees. 1% grads pursue business degrees. 2% grads pursue medical degrees. **Faculty:** Student/faculty ratio 12:1. 645 full-time faculty, 96% hold PhDs, 16% are members of minority groups, 38% are women.

ACADEMICS

Degrees: bachelor's, first professional, master's, post-master's certificate. **Classes:** Most classes have 10–19 students. Most lab/discussion sessions have 10–19 students. **Majors with Highest Enrollment:** business/commerce; communication and media studies, other; social sciences. **Special Study Options:** double major, English as a Second Language (ESL), exchange student program (domestic), honors program, independent study, internships, student-designed major, study abroad, teacher certification program, Globe Program in International Business. 3:2 Engineering Cooperative with Columbia University or Case Western Reserve University. **Honors Programs:** Each undergraduate college has its own Honors Program. All four programs offer enriched academic opportunity for qualified and interested students. Additionally, there are major programs of study designated as selective. Students must be invited into those programs and meet minimum GPA requirements for consideration. Many more majors offer Honors designation at graduation usually based upon completion of a thesis or senior project. **Combined Degree Programs:** BA/JD, BA/MA, BS/MSW, BS/MBA, 3:2 Engineering. **Disability Services:** Special programs offered to physically disabled students include note-taking services, reader services, tape recorders, tutors.

FACILITIES

Housing: Coed dorms, special housing for disabled students, apartments for single students, Residential Colleges. 80% of campus accessible to physically disabled. **Special Academic Facilities/Equipment:** television station, radio station, theaters, white and black box studio spaces, media and visual arts labs and design space, art gallery, University Church, seismic station, 113 biological field station The Louis Calder Center, in Armonk, NY **Computers:** 90%

of classrooms, 98% of dorms, 95% of libraries, 100% of dining areas, 80% of common outdoor areas have wireless network access. Students can register for classes online. Administrative functions (other than registration) can be performed online.

CAMPUS LIFE

Environment: Metropolis. **Activities:** Choral groups, concert band, dance, drama/theater, jazz band, literary magazine, music ensembles, musical theater, pep band, radio station, student government, student newspaper, student-run film society, symphony orchestra, television station, yearbook 133 registered organizations, 12 honor societies, 3 religious organizations. **Athletics (Intercollegiate):** *Men:* baseball, basketball, cross-country, diving, football, golf, soccer, squash, swimming, tennis, track/field (outdoor), track/field (indoor), water polo. *Women:* basketball, cheerleading, crew/rowing, cross-country, diving, soccer, softball, swimming, tennis, track/field (outdoor), track/field (indoor), volleyball. **On-Campus Highlights:** William D. Walsh Family Library (Rose Hill), O'Hare Hall (Residential College at Rose Hill), Edwards Parade/Keating Hall (Rose Hill), McMahon Hall (Lincoln Center), Pope Auditorium (Lincoln Center), With three distinct campuses, there are numerous noteworthy buildings including new and recently renovated academic and extracurricular space, residence halls and athletic centers/fields. Additional space to note includes student-run coffee houses, white and black box studio spaces and historic buildings designated as NYC landmarks.

ADMISSIONS

Freshman Academic Profile: Average high school GPA 3.7. 43% in top 10% of high school class, 73% in top 25% of high school class, 96% in top 50% of high school class. 47% from public high schools. SAT Math middle 50% range 560-660. SAT Critical Reading middle 50% range 570-670. SAT Writing middle 50% range 560-660. ACT middle 50% range 25-29. Minimum paper TOEFL 575. **Basis for Candidate Selection:** *Very important factors considered include:* Class rank, rigor of secondary school record, standardized test scores. *Important factors considered include:* application essay, recommendation(s), character/personal qualities, extracurricular activities, talent/ability. *Other factors considered include:* alumni/ae relation, first generation, geographical residence, racial/ethnic status, volunteer work, work experience. **Freshman Admission Requirements:** High school diploma is required and GED is accepted. *Academic units required:* 4 English, 3 mathematics, 3 science, 2 foreign language, 2 social studies, 2 history, 6 academic electives. *Academic units recommended:* 4 English, 3 mathematics, 3 science, 2 foreign language, 2 social studies, 2 history, 6 academic electives. **Freshman Admission Statistics:** 18,161 applied, 47% admitted, 20% enrolled. **Transfer Admission Requirements:** High school transcript, college transcript(s), essay or personal statement, statement of good standing from prior institution(s). Minimum college GPA of 3.0 required. Lowest grade transferable C. **General Admission Information:** Application Fee $50. Regular application deadline 1/15. Regular notification 4/1. Nonfall registration accepted. Admission may be deferred for a maximum of 1 year. Credit and/or placement offered for CEEB Advanced Placement tests.

COSTS AND FINANCIAL AID

Annual tuition $34,200. Room and board $12,980. Required fees $1,057. Average book expense $800. **Required Forms and Deadlines:** FAFSA, CSS/Financial Aid PROFILE, noncustodial PROFILE, business/farm supplement. **Notification of Awards:** Applicants will be notified of awards on or about 4/1. **Types of Aid:** *Need-based scholarships/grants:* Federal Pell, SEOG, state scholarships/grants, private scholarships, the school's own gift aid. *Loans:* Subsidized Stafford, Unsubsidized Stafford, PLUS, Federal Perkins. **Student Employment: Financial Aid Statistics:** 97% freshmen, 95% undergrads receive need-based scholarship or grant aid. 44% freshmen, 46% undergrads receive non-need-based scholarship or grant aid. 73% freshmen, 76% undergrads receive need-based self-help aid. 1% freshmen, 2% undergrads receive athletic scholarships. 88% freshmen, 83% undergrads receive any aid. 64% undergrads borrow to pay for school. Average cumulative indebtedness $38,150. **Criteria for awarding institutional aid:** *Non-need-based:* academics, athletics.

FORT HAYS STATE UNIVERSITY

600 Park Street, Hays, KS 67601-4099
Phone: 785-628-5666 • **Financial Aid Phone:** 785-628-4408
E-mail: tigers@fhsu.edu • **CEEB Code:** 6218
Fax: 785-628-4187 • **ACT Code:** 1408

This public school was founded in 1902. It has a 4160-acre campus.

RATINGS

Admissions Selectivity Rating: 64   **Fire Safety Rating:** 66   **Green Rating:** 66

STUDENTS AND FACULTY

Enrollment: 10,811. **Student Body:** 58% female, 42% male, 25% out-of-state, 36% international. Asian 1%, African American 3%, Caucasian 54%, Hispanic 4%, Native American 0%.
Retention and Graduation: 64% freshmen return for sophomore year. 18% freshmen graduate within 4 years. 42% freshmen graduate within 6 years. 20% grads go on to further study within 1 year. **Faculty:** Student/faculty ratio 18:1. 287 full-time faculty, 66% hold PhDs, 9% are members of minority groups, 43% are women. 1% of classes are taught by teaching assistants.

ACADEMICS

Degrees: associate, bachelor's, certificate, master's, post-master's certificate. **Classes:** Most classes have 10–19 students. Most lab/discussion sessions have fewer than 10 students. **Majors with Highest Enrollment:** business/commerce; elementary education and teaching; health and physical education. **Special Study Options:** distance learning, double major, dual enrollment, English as a Second Language (ESL), exchange student program (domestic), external degree program, independent study, internships, liberal arts/career combination, student-designed major, study abroad, teacher certification program. **Combined Degree Programs:** BA/MEng, 3-1 progs in allied health, dentistry, and eng. **Disability Services:** Special programs offered to physically disabled students include note-taking services, reader services, tutors. **Career Services:** Alumni network, alumni services, career/job search classes, career assessment, internships.

FACILITIES

Housing: Coed dorms, men's dorms, women's dorms, fraternity/sorority housing, apartments for married students, apartments for single students. 100% of campus accessible to physically disabled. **Special Academic Facilities/Equipment:** Paleontology, natural history, visual arts and media center, farm, NMR gas analyzer, telescope (HG). **Computers:** 100% of classrooms, 100% of dorms, 100% of libraries, 100% of dining areas, 100% of student union, 100% of common outdoor areas have wireless network access.

CAMPUS LIFE

Environment: Village. **Activities:** Choral groups, concert band, dance, drama/theater, jazz band, marching band, music ensembles, musical theater, pep band, radio station, student government, student newspaper, symphony orchestra, television station, yearbook 103 registered organizations, 20 honor societies, 2 religious organizations. 3 fraternities, 3 sororities. **Athletics (Intercollegiate):** *Men:* baseball, basketball, cheerleading, cross-country, football, golf, track/field (outdoor), track/field (indoor), wrestling. *Women:* basketball, cheerleading, cross-country, golf, softball, tennis, track/field (outdoor), track/field (indoor), volleyball. **On-Campus Highlights:** www.tigersportszone.com, www.fhsu.edu/sternberg/, www.fhsu.edu/int/kfhsradio/, www.fhsu.edu/int/kfhstv/, www.fhsu.edu/leader. **Environmental Initiatives:** Clean up of Big Creek Clean up of area neighborhoods Recycling of paper, newspapers and aluminum all over campus.

ADMISSIONS

Freshman Academic Profile: Average high school GPA 3.3. 12% in top 10% of high school class, 32% in top 25% of high school class, 63% in top 50% of high school class. 95% from public high schools. ACT middle 50% range 18-25. Minimum web-based TOEFL 61. Minimum paper TOEFL 500. **Basis for Candidate Selection:** *Other factors considered include:* Class rank, academic GPA, rigor of secondary school record, standardized test scores. **Freshman Admission Requirements:** High school diploma is required and GED is accepted. **Freshman Admission Statistics:** 1,536 applied. **Transfer Admission Requirements:** college transcript(s), minimum college GPA of 2.0 required. Lowest grade transferable D. **General Admission Information:** Application Fee $30. Nonfall registration accepted. Admission may be deferred for a maximum of 1 year. Credit offered for CEEB Advanced Placement tests.

COSTS AND FINANCIAL AID

Annual in-state tuition $3,314. Annual out-of-state tuition $12,003. Room and board $7,003. Required fees $926. Average book expense $920. **Required Forms and Deadlines:** FAFSA. **Notification of Awards: Types of Aid:** *Need-based scholarships/grants:* Federal Pell, SEOG, state scholarships/grants, private scholarships, the school's own gift aid. *Loans:* Subsidized Stafford, Unsubsidized Stafford, PLUS, Federal Perkins, college/university loans from institutional funds. **Student Employment:** Federal Work-Study Program available. Highest amount earned per year from on-campus jobs $2,000. Off-campus job opportunities are fair. **Financial Aid Statistics:** 94% freshmen, 86% undergrads receive need-based scholarship or grant aid. 7% freshmen, 3% undergrads receive non-need-based scholarship or grant aid. 80% freshmen, 83% undergrads receive need-based self-help aid. 5% freshmen, 3% undergrads receive athletic scholarships76% undergrads borrow to pay for school. Average cumulative indebtedness $19,965. **Criteria for awarding institutional aid:** *Non-need-based:* academics, alumni affiliation, art, athletics, job skills, leadership, minority status, music/drama, religious affiliation, state/district residency.

FORT LEWIS COLLEGE

1000 Rim Drive, Durango, CO 81301
Phone: 970-247-7184 • **Financial Aid Phone:** 970-247-7142
E-mail: admisson@fortlewis.edu • **CEEB Code:** 4310
Fax: 970-247-7179 • **Website:** www.fortlewis.edu • **ACT Code:** 510

This public school was founded in 1911. It has a 362-acre campus.

RATINGS
Admissions Selectivity Rating: 73   **Fire Safety Rating:** 76   **Green Rating:** 77

STUDENTS AND FACULTY
Enrollment: 3,748. **Student Body:** 48% female, 52% male, 38% out-of-state, 1% international (20 countries represented). Asian 0%, African American 1%, Caucasian 62%, Hispanic 8%, Native American 21%.
Retention and Graduation: 14% grads go on to further study within 1 year.
Faculty: Student/faculty ratio 19:1. 166 full-time faculty, 89% hold PhDs, 11% are members of minority groups, 48% are women. 0% of classes are taught by teaching assistants.

ACADEMICS
Degrees: bachelor's. **Classes:** Most classes have 10–19 students. Most lab/discussion sessions have 10–19 students. **Majors with Highest Enrollment:** biology/biological sciences; business administration and management; psychology. **Special Study Options:** Accelerated program, cooperative education program, distance learning, double major, dual enrollment, English as a Second Language (ESL), exchange student program (domestic), honors program, independent study, internships, liberal arts/career combination, student-designed major, study abroad, teacher certification program. **Honors Programs:** The John F. Reed honors program selects outstanding first and second-year students who demonstrate ability and interest in pursuing additional academic achievements and challenges. The program requires honors courses called forums which ask students to study innovative thinkers, intellectual foundations, and multidisciplinary perspectives. All of the student's work culminates in an honors thesis presented in a public forum. Students in the honors program also benefit from the honors lounge (computers, tv, fridge, reference materials, etc.), free tickets to events and mentoring by professional associates. Upon graduation, the students receive a minor in Honors called "'Rhetoric of Inquiry'". **Disability Services:** Special programs offered to physically disabled students include note-taking services, reader services, tape recorders, tutors. **Career Services:** Alumni network, alumni services, career/job search classes, career assessment, internships, regional alumni. Career Services highlights include The Skyhawks Job Source: Our new on-line, web-based system allows students to search for positions, post resumes and cover letters for employers to view. The system also allows students to apply for positions on-line. Students who up-load a resume to the site will be included in candidate searches by employers and by the Career Services Office. Students can keep track of and manage their job search activities as well.

FACILITIES
Housing: Coed dorms, special housing for disabled students, apartments for married students, apartments for single students, wellness housing, theme housing, 100% of campus accessible to physically disabled. **Special Academic Facilities/Equipment:** Center of Southwest Studies, Community Concert Hall **Computers:** 100% of classrooms, 100% of dorms, 100% of libraries, 100% of dining areas, 100% of student union, 10% of common outdoor areas have wireless network access. Students can register for classes online. Administrative functions (other than registration) can be performed online.

CAMPUS LIFE
Environment: Town. **Activities:** Choral groups, concert band, drama/theater, jazz band, literary magazine, musical theater, pep band, radio station, student government, student newspaper, Campus Ministries 65 registered organizations, 5 honor societies, 3 religious organizations. **Athletics (Intercollegiate):** *Men:* basketball, cross-country, football, golf, soccer. *Women:* basketball, cross-country, lacrosse, soccer, softball, volleyball. **On-Campus Highlights:** Center of Southwest Studies, Student Life Center, College Union Building, Residence Halls, Academic buildings, Highly qualified, committed faculty who are available, helpful, and engaged. Emphasis on active, experiential learning through community service, undergraduate research, study abroad, and internships. Student-faculty ratio of 17:1. Collaborative campus culture where student voices are heard and respected. Graduates who are twice as likely as those other schools to say their education was "excellent." Cultural diversity is a core value and key feature of Fort Lewis College. Approximately 28% of our students are from ethnic minority backgrounds. **Environmental Initiatives:** All new construction or renovation follow at minimum LEED Silver standards Waste minimization including a full-scale recycling program, event recycling, and composting within campus dining Promotion of alternative transportation options. All students and faculty receive a free bus pass, green cars receive a parking permit discount, and there is an extensive trail system for biking and walking to campus.

ADMISSIONS
Freshman Academic Profile: Average high school GPA 3.1. 11% in top 10% of high school class, 28% in top 25% of high school class, 61% in top 50% of high school class. 99% from public high schools. SAT Math middle 50% range 460-560. SAT Critical Reading middle 50% range 460-570. SAT Writing middle 50% range 430-550. ACT middle 50% range 20-25. Minimum web-based TOEFL 61. Minimum paper TOEFL 500. **Basis for Candidate Selection:** *Very important factors considered include:* Class rank, academic GPA, rigor of secondary school record, standardized test scores. *Other factors considered include:* application essay, recommendation(s), alumni/ae relation, character/personal qualities, extracurricular activities, first generation, interview, level of applicant's interest, talent/ability, volunteer work, work experience. **Freshman Admission Requirements:** High school diploma is required and GED is accepted. *Academic units required:* 4 English, 4 mathematics, 3 science, (2 science labs), 1 foreign language, 2 social studies, 1 history, 2 academic electives. 4 English, 4 mathematics, 3 science, (2 science labs), 1 foreign language, 2 social studies, 1 history, 2 academic electives. **Freshman Admission Statistics:** 2,792 applied, 71% admitted, 39% enrolled. **Transfer Admission Requirements:** college transcript(s), minimum college GPA of 2.40 required. Lowest grade transferable C–. **General Admission Information:** Application Fee $40. Regular application deadline 8/10. Notification on a rolling basis, beginning on or about 10/10. Nonfall registration accepted. Admission may be deferred for a maximum of 1 semester. Credit and/or placement offered for CEEB Advanced Placement tests.

COSTS AND FINANCIAL AID
Annual in-state tuition $2,532. Annual out-of-state tuition $16,072. Room and board $8,500. Required fees $1,691. Average book expense $1,680. **Required Forms and Deadlines:** FAFSA. **Notification of Awards:** Applicants will be notified of awards on a rolling basis beginning 3/15. **Types of Aid:** *Need-based scholarships/grants:* Federal Pell, SEOG, state scholarships/grants, private scholarships, the school's own gift aid. *Loans:* Subsidized Stafford, Unsubsidized Stafford, PLUS, Federal Perkins, college/university loans from institutional funds. **Student Employment:** Federal Work-Study Program available. Institutional employment available. Highest amount earned per year from on-campus jobs $6,905. Off-campus job opportunities are good. **Financial Aid Statistics:** 92% freshmen, 90% undergrads receive need-based scholarship or grant aid. 60% freshmen, 36% undergrads receive non-need based scholarship or grant aid. 90% freshmen, 62% undergrads receive need-based self-help aid. 12% freshmen, 8% undergrads receive athletic scholarships. 88% freshmen, 79% undergrads receive any aid. 67% undergrads borrow to pay for school. Average cumulative indebtedness $18,780. **Criteria for awarding institutional aid:** *Non-need-based:* academics, alumni affiliation, art, athletics, leadership, minority status, music/drama, state/district residency.

FRAMINGHAM STATE COLLEGE

100 State Street, Framingham, MA 01701-9101
Phone: 508-626-4500 • **Financial Aid Phone:** 508-626-4534
E-mail: admissions@framingham.edu • **CEEB Code:** 3519
Fax: 508-626-4017 • **Website:** www.framingham.edu • **ACT Code:** 1904

This public school was founded in 1839. It has a 73-acre campus.

RATINGS
Admissions Selectivity Rating: 85   **Fire Safety Rating:** 91   **Green Rating:** 95

STUDENTS AND FACULTY
Enrollment: 4,147. **Student Body:** 64% female, 36% male, 4% out-of-state, 0% international (12 countries represented). Asian 2%, African American 7%, Caucasian 76%, Hispanic 9%, Native American 0%.
Retention and Graduation: 74% freshmen return for sophomore year. 34% freshmen graduate within 4 years. 52% freshmen graduate within 6 years. 11% grads go on to further study within 1 year. **Faculty:** Student/faculty ratio 16:1. 176 full-time faculty, 87% hold PhDs, 10% are members of minority groups, 59% are women. 0% of classes are taught by teaching assistants.

ACADEMICS
Degrees: bachelor's, master's, post-bachelor's certificate. **Classes:** Most classes have 20–29 students. **Majors with Highest Enrollment:** business/commerce; family and consumer sciences/human sciences; sociology. **Special Study Options:** cross-registration, distance learning, double major, honors program,

independent study, internships, liberal arts/career combination, study abroad, teacher certification program, Pre-engineering program in conjunction with University of Massachusetts Amherst, University of Massachusetts Dartmouth, and University of Massachusetts Lowell. **Honors Programs:** The Honors Program offers challenging courses and projects for qualified students,and sponsors events which contribute to the intellectual life of the College community. **Disability Services:** Special programs offered to physically disabled students include note-taking services, reader services, tape recorders, tutors. **Career Services:** Alumni network, alumni services, career/job search classes, career assessment, internships Career Services highlights include Current working relationships with key employers in the MetroWest area with plans to expand in MetroWest, Boston and Worcester.

FACILITIES

Housing: Coed dorms, women's dorms, wellness housing, theme housing, 95% of campus accessible to physically disabled. **Special Academic Facilities/Equipment:** Mazmanian Art Gallery, McAuliffe Challenger Learning Center, Greenhouse, Early Childhood Development Lab, Education Curriculum Library,Planetarium **Computers:** 100% of classrooms, 100% of dorms, 100% of libraries, 100% of dining areas, 100% of student union, have wireless network access. Students can register for classes online. Administrative functions (other than registration) can be performed online. Undergraduates are required to own a computer.

CAMPUS LIFE

Environment: City. **Activities:** Choral groups, dance, drama/theater, literary magazine, musical theater, radio station, student government, student newspaper, Campus Ministries, International Student Organization 55 registered organizations, 11 honor societies, 4 religious organizations. **Athletics (Intercollegiate):** *Men:* baseball, basketball, cross-country, football, ice hockey, soccer. *Women:* basketball, cross-country, field hockey, lacrosse, soccer, softball, volleyball. **On-Campus Highlights:** Residence Halls, Athletic Facility, College Center, Academic Buildings, Library. **Environmental Initiatives:** Conversion of our power plant from #6 oil to natural gas, decreasing our carbon footprint from the plant by 30%. Increase of renewable power from less than 1% to 17.82% Added new course time blocks allowing for commuters, students and faculty, to deduce the number of commuting days.

ADMISSIONS

Freshman Academic Profile: 3.2. SAT Math middle 50% range 480-570. SAT Critical Reading middle 50% range 470-560. SAT Writing middle 50% range 470-560. ACT middle 50% range 19-25. Minimum web-based TOEFL 79. Minimum paper TOEFL 550. **Basis for Candidate Selection:** *Very important factors considered include:* academic GPA, rigor of secondary school record, standardized test scores. *Important factors considered include:* Class rank, application essay, recommendation(s). *Other factors considered include:* alumni/ae relation, character/personal qualities, extracurricular activities, first generation, level of applicant's interest, state residency, talent/ability, volunteer work, work experience. **Freshman Admission Requirements:** High school diploma is required and GED is accepted. *Academic units required:* 4 English, 3 mathematics, 3 science, (2 science labs), 2 foreign language, 1 social studies, 1 history, 2 academic electives. *Academic units recommended:* 4 English, 3 mathematics, 3 science, (2 science labs), 2 foreign language, 1 social studies, 1 history, 2 academic electives. **Freshman Admission Statistics:** 5,433 applied, 52% admitted, 40% enrolled. **Transfer Admission Requirements:** High school transcript, college transcript(s), essay or personal statement, minimum college GPA of 2.5 required. Lowest grade transferable C–. **General Admission Information:** Application Fee $50. Notification on a rolling basis, beginning on or about 1/15. Nonfall registration accepted. Admission may be deferred for a maximum of 12 months. Credit and/or placement offered for CEEB Advanced Placement tests.

COSTS AND FINANCIAL AID

Annual in-state tuition $970. Annual out-of-state tuition $7,050. Room and board $9,170. Required fees $6,610. Average book expense $1,000. **Required Forms and Deadlines:** FAFSA. **Notification of Awards:** Applicants will be notified of awards on a rolling basis beginning 3/15. **Types of Aid:** *Need-based scholarships/grants:* Federal Pell, SEOG, state scholarships/grants, private scholarships, the school's own gift aid. *Loans:* Subsidized Stafford, Unsubsidized Stafford, PLUS, Federal Perkins, state loans. **Student Employment:** Federal Work-Study Program available. Institutional employment available. Highest amount earned per year from on-campus jobs $1,000. Off-campus job opportunities are excellent. **Financial Aid Statistics:** 86% freshmen, 100% undergrads receive need-based scholarship or grant aid. 3% freshmen, 55% undergrads receive non-need-based scholarship or grant aid. 97% freshmen, 14% undergrads receive need-based self-help aid. 43% freshmen, 36% undergrads receive any aid. 70% undergrads borrow to pay for school. Average cumulative indebtedness $19,800. **Criteria for awarding institutional aid:** *Non-need-based:* academics.

Office of Admissions, Florence, SC 29502-0547
Phone: 843-661-1231 • **Financial Aid Phone:** 843-661-1190
E-mail: admissions@fmarion.edu • **CEEB Code:** 5442
Fax: 843-661-4635 • **Website:** www.fmarion.edu • **ACT Code:** 3856

This public school was founded in 1970. It has a 300-acre campus.

RATINGS
Admissions Selectivity Rating: 75   **Fire Safety Rating:** 73   **Green Rating:** 60*

STUDENTS AND FACULTY
Enrollment: 3,466. **Student Body:** 66% female, 34% male, 4% out-of-state, 1% international (17 countries represented). Asian 1%, African American 48%, Caucasian 46%, Hispanic 1%, Native American 1%. **Retention and Graduation:** 67% freshmen return for sophomore year. 20% freshmen graduate within 4 years. 41% freshmen graduate within 6 years. **Faculty:** Student/faculty ratio 16:1. 196 full-time faculty, 81% hold PhDs, 10% are members of minority groups, 46% are women. 0% of classes are taught by teaching assistants.

ACADEMICS
Degrees: bachelor's, master's. **Classes:** Most classes have 20–29 students. **Majors with Highest Enrollment:** biology; business/commerce; elementary education and teaching. **Special Study Options:** Accelerated program, cross-registration, distance learning, double major, dual enrollment, honors program, independent study, internships, study abroad, teacher certification program. **Combined Degree Programs:** 2-2 Forestry prog with Clemson U.; engineering,BSN. **Disability Services:** Special programs offered to physically disabled students include note-taking services, reader services, tape recorders, tutors.

FACILITIES
Housing: special housing for disabled students, men's dorms, women's dorms, apartments for single students. 100% of campus accessible to physically disabled. **Special Academic Facilities/Equipment:** Media center, planetarium, observatory. **Computers:** Students can register for classes online.

CAMPUS LIFE
Environment: Rural. **Activities:** Choral groups, drama/theater, jazz band, literary magazine, music ensembles, student government, student newspaper, television station 56 registered organizations, 13 honor societies, 5 religious organizations. 7 fraternities, 7 sororities. **Athletics (Intercollegiate):** *Men:* baseball, basketball, cross-country, golf, soccer, tennis, track/field (outdoor). *Women:* basketball, cross-country, soccer, softball, tennis, track/field (outdoor), volleyball. **On-Campus Highlights:** The Cottage, The Smith University Center, The Dooley Planetarium, The Hyman Fine Arts Center, The Hewn Timber Cabins.

ADMISSIONS
Freshman Academic Profile: Average high school GPA 3.5. 13% in top 10% of high school class, 42% in top 25% of high school class, 79% in top 50% of high school class. 90% from public high schools. SAT Math middle 50% range 430-530. SAT Critical Reading middle 50% range 410-530. SAT Writing middle 50% range 390-500. ACT middle 50% range 17-22. Minimum web-based TOEFL 61. Minimum paper TOEFL 500. **Basis for Candidate Selection:** *Very important factors considered include:* rigor of secondary school record, standardized test scores. *Important factors considered include:* Class rank. *Other factors considered include:* recommendation(s). **Freshman Admission Requirements:** High school diploma is required and GED is accepted. *Academic units required:* 4 English, 3 mathematics, 3 science, (3 science labs), 2 foreign language, 2 social studies, 1 history, 4 academic electives, 1 PE or ROTC. *Academic units recommended:* 4 English, 3 mathematics, 3 science, (3 science labs), 2 foreign language, 2 social studies, 1 history, 4 academic electives, 1 PE or ROTC **Freshman Admission Statistics:** 3,843 applied, 59% admitted, 33% enrolled. **Transfer Admission Requirements:** High school transcript, college transcript(s), statement of good standing from prior institution(s). Minimum college GPA of 2.0 required. Lowest grade transferable C. **General Admission Information:** Application Fee $30. Notification on a rolling basis, beginning on or about 9/1. Nonfall registration accepted. Admission may be deferred for a maximum of 1 semester. Credit offered for CEEB Advanced Placement tests.

COSTS AND FINANCIAL AID
Annual in-state tuition $8,467. Annual out-of-state tuition $16,934. Room and board $6,620. Required fees $335. Average book expense $1,900. **Required Forms and Deadlines:** FAFSA, institution's own financial aid form. **Notification of Awards:** Applicants will be notified of awards on a rolling basis beginning 4/15. **Types of Aid:** *Need-based scholarships/grants:* Federal Pell, SEOG, state scholarships/grants, private scholarships, the school's own gift aid. *Loans:* Subsidized Stafford, Unsubsidized Stafford, PLUS, Federal Perkins, state

loans, college/university loans from institutional funds. **Student Employment: Financial Aid Statistics:** 85% freshmen, 74% undergrads receive need-based scholarship or grant aid. 83% freshmen, 39% undergrads receive non-need-based scholarship or grant aid. 88% freshmen, 90% undergrads receive need-based self-help aid. 1% freshmen, 1% undergrads receive athletic scholarships. 88% freshmen, 82% undergrads receive any aid. Average cumulative indebtedness $26,453. **Criteria for awarding institutional aid:** *Non-need-based:* academics.

THE FRANCISCAN UNIVERSITY

400 North Bluff Blvd, Clinton, IA 52733-2967
Phone: 563-242-4153
E-mail: admissns@tfu.edu • **CEEB Code:** 6418
Fax: 563-243-6102 • **Website:** www.tfu.edu • **ACT Code:** 1342

This private school was founded in 1918. It has a 25-acre campus.

RATINGS
Admissions Selectivity Rating: 66   **Fire Safety Rating:** 60*   **Green Rating:** 60*

STUDENTS AND FACULTY
Enrollment: 416. **Student Body:** 56% female, 44% male, 46% out-of-state, 3% international (10 countries represented). Asian 1%, African American 6%, Caucasian 87%, Hispanic 3%, Native American 0%.
Retention and Graduation: 69% freshmen return for sophomore year. 25% freshmen graduate within 4 years. 34% freshmen graduate within 6 years. 25% grads go on to further study within 1 year. **Faculty:** Student/faculty ratio 12:1. 27 full-time faculty, 48% hold PhDs, 4% are members of minority groups, 44% are women. 0% of classes are taught by teaching assistants.

ACADEMICS
Degrees: associate, bachelor's, master's, transfer associate. **Classes:** Most classes have 10–19 students. Most lab/discussion sessions have fewer than 10 students. **Majors with Highest Enrollment:** education; liberal arts and sciences studies and humanities, other; social sciences. **Special Study Options:** distance learning, double major, dual enrollment, honors program, independent study, internships, student-designed major, study abroad, teacher certification program, Advanced Placement Program Summer School off campus study senior capstone or culminating academic experiences undergraduate research/creative projects writing in the disciplines. **Disability Services:** Special programs offered to physically disabled students include tutors.

FACILITIES
Housing: Coed dorms Durham Hall = 2 bedroom suites (one side floors are designated for men and one side designated for women. Sides of building joined by common lounge area) Regis Hall = single bedrooms (1 floor for women and 1 floor for men). 95% of campus accessible to physically disabled. **Special Academic Facilities/Equipment:** On-campus preschool. Indoor swimming pool, multipurpose educ. center, resident halls, 1 bedroom suites or 2 single rooms **Computers:** Administrative functions (other than registration) can be performed online.

CAMPUS LIFE
Environment: Town. **Activities:** Choral groups, music ensembles, student government, student newspaper 20 registered organizations, 2 honor societies. **Athletics (Intercollegiate):** *Men:* baseball, basketball, cross-country, golf, soccer, track/field (outdoor). *Women:* basketball, cross-country, soccer, softball, track/field (outdoor), volleyball.

ADMISSIONS
Freshman Academic Profile: Average high school GPA 2.8. 8% in top 10% of high school class, 16% in top 25% of high school class, 50% in top 50% of high school class. ACT middle 50% range 16-22. Minimum paper TOEFL 430. **Basis for Candidate Selection:** *Very important factors considered include:* Class rank, rigor of secondary school record, standardized test scores. *Other factors considered include:* recommendation(s). **Freshman Admission Requirements:** High school diploma is required and GED is accepted. **Freshman Admission Statistics:** 246 applied, 77% admitted, 28% enrolled. **Transfer Admission Requirements:** college transcript(s), statement of good standing from prior institution(s). Minimum college GPA of 2.0 required. Lowest grade transferable c. **General Admission Information:** Application Fee $20. Regular application deadline 8/15. Nonfall registration accepted. Admission may be deferred for a maximum of 1 academic year. Credit and/or placement offered for CEEB Advanced Placement tests.

COSTS AND FINANCIAL AID
Annual tuition $13,800. Room and board $5,250. Required fees $250. Average book expense $600. Required Forms and Deadlines: FAFSA. Notification

of Awards: Applicants will be notified of awards on a rolling basis beginning 3/15. Types of Aid: Need-based scholarships/grants: Federal Pell, SEOG, state scholarships/grants, private scholarships, the school's own gift aid. Loans: Subsidized Stafford, Unsubsidized Stafford, PLUS, Federal Perkins, Private Loan Company. Student Employment: Financial Aid Statistics: 100% freshmen, 100% undergrads receive need-based scholarship or grant aid. 13% freshmen, 13% undergrads receive non-need-based scholarship or grant aid. 78% freshmen, 80% undergrads receive need-based self-help aid. 23% freshmen, 12% undergrads receive athletic scholarships. 88% undergrads borrow to pay for school. Average cumulative indebtedness $15,868. Criteria for awarding institutional aid: Non-need-based: academics, alumni affiliation, art, athletics, job skills, leadership, minority status, music/drama, religious affiliation.

FRANCISCAN UNIVERSITY OF STEUBENVILLE

1235 University Boulevard., Steubenville, OH 43952-1763
Phone: 740-283-6226 • **Financial Aid Phone:** 740-283-6226
E-mail: admissions@franciscan.edu • **CEEB Code:** 1133
Fax: 740-284-5456 • **Website:** www.franciscan.edu • **ACT Code:** 3258

This private school, affiliated with the Roman Catholic Church, was founded in 1946. It has a 124-acre campus.

RATINGS
Admissions Selectivity Rating: 79   **Fire Safety Rating:** 65   **Green Rating:** 60*

STUDENTS AND FACULTY
Enrollment: 2,034. **Student Body:** 61% female, 39% male, 80% out-of-state, 1% international (20 countries represented). Asian 2%, African American 0%, Caucasian 80%, Hispanic 6%, Native American 0%.
Retention and Graduation: 84% freshmen return for sophomore year. 63% freshmen graduate within 4 years. 73% freshmen graduate within 6 years. 13% grads go on to further study within 1 year. 9% grads pursue arts and sciences degrees. 1% grads pursue business degrees. 1% grads pursue medical degrees. **Faculty:** Student/faculty ratio 15:1. 112 full-time faculty, 79% hold PhDs, 1% are members of minority groups, 26% are women. 0% of classes are taught by teaching assistants.

ACADEMICS
Degrees: associate, bachelor's, master's. **Classes:** Most classes have 10–19 students. Most lab/discussion sessions have 10–19 students. **Majors with Highest Enrollment:** business/commerce; elementary education and teaching; theology/theological studies. **Special Study Options:** Accelerated program, distance learning, double major, dual enrollment, honors program, independent study, internships, liberal arts/career combination, study abroad, teacher certification program. **Honors Programs:** We have a Great Books program. **Combined Degree Programs:** BA/MA, 4+1 in Business and Philosophy. **Disability Services:** Special programs offered to physically disabled students include note-taking services, reader services, tape recorders, tutors. **Career Services:** career/job search classes, career assessment, internships.

FACILITIES
Housing: men's dorms, women's dorms, apartments for single students. 75% of campus accessible to physically disabled. **Special Academic Facilities/Equipment:** Art Gallery **Computers:** Students can register for classes online. Administrative functions (other than registration) can be performed online.

CAMPUS LIFE
Environment: Village. **Activities:** Choral groups, drama/theater, literary magazine, music ensembles, radio station, student government, student newspaper, yearbook, Campus Ministries, International Student Organization 31 registered organizations, 3 honor societies, 6 religious organizations. 1 fraternities, 1 sororities. **On-Campus Highlights:** Heavenly Grounds Coffee Shop, Sts. Cosmas and Damian Hall-Science Building, Finnegan Fieldhouse, Christ The King Chapel, Portiuncula Chapel.

ADMISSIONS
Freshman Academic Profile: Average high school GPA 3.7. 31% in top 10% of high school class, 60% in top 25% of high school class, 84% in top 50% of high school class. 42% from public high schools. SAT Math middle 50% range 500-630. SAT Critical Reading middle 50% range 540-650. SAT Writing middle 50% range 510-630. ACT middle 50% range 23-28. Minimum paper TOEFL 550. **Basis for Candidate Selection:** *Very important factors considered include:* application essay, academic GPA, rigor of secondary school record, standardized test scores, character/personal qualities, interview. *Important factors considered include:* extracurricular activities, level of applicant's interest, talent/ability. *Other factors considered include:* recommendation(s). **Freshman Admission Requirements:** High school diploma is required and GED is accepted. **Freshman Admission Statistics:** 1,450 applied, 72% admitted,

43% enrolled. **Transfer Admission Requirements:** High school transcript, college transcript(s), essay or personal statement, minimum college GPA of 2.2 required. Lowest grade transferable C. **General Admission Information:** Application Fee $20. Regular application deadline 5/1. Notification on a rolling basis, beginning on or about 9/1. Nonfall registration accepted. Admission may be deferred for a maximum of one year. Credit and/or placement offered for CEEB Advanced Placement tests.

COSTS AND FINANCIAL AID
Average book expense $800. **Required Forms and Deadlines:** FAFSA. **Notification of Awards:** Applicants will be notified of awards on a rolling basis beginning 3/15. **Types of Aid:** *Need-based scholarships/grants:* Federal Pell, SEOG, state scholarships/grants, private scholarships, the school's own gift aid. *Loans:* Subsidized Stafford, Unsubsidized Stafford, PLUS, Federal Perkins, Alternative Loans. **Student Employment:** Federal Work-Study Program available. Institutional employment available. Highest amount earned per year from on-campus jobs $3,090. Off-campus job opportunities are good. **Financial Aid Statistics:** 91% freshmen, 93% undergrads receive need-based scholarship or grant aid. 8% freshmen, 5% undergrads receive non-need-based scholarship or grant aid. 93% freshmen, 94% undergrads receive need-based self-help aid. 63% freshmen, 62% undergrads receive any aid. 77% undergrads borrow to pay for school. Average cumulative indebtedness $21,616. **Criteria for awarding institutional aid:** *Non-need-based:* academics, leadership, religious affiliation.

FRANKLIN & MARSHALL COLLEGE

Best 378

P.O. Box 3003, Lancaster, PA 17604-3003
Phone: 717-291-3953 • **Financial Aid Phone:** 717-291-3991
E-mail: admission@fandm.edu • **CEEB Code:** 2261
Fax: 717-291-4389 • **Website:** www.fandm.edu • **ACT Code:** 3574

This private school was founded in 1787. It has a 180-acre campus.

RATINGS
Admissions Selectivity Rating: 95   **Fire Safety Rating:** 91   **Green Rating:** 91

STUDENTS AND FACULTY
Enrollment: 2,324. **Student Body:** 52% female, 48% male, 72% out-of-state, 9% international (41 countries represented). Asian 3%, African American 3%, Caucasian 72%, Hispanic 6%, Native American 0%.
Retention and Graduation: 93% freshmen return for sophomore year. 81% freshmen graduate within 4 years. 85% freshmen graduate within 6 years. 25% grads go on to further study within 1 year. 10% grads pursue arts and sciences degrees. 6% grads pursue law degrees. 1% grads pursue business degrees. 8% grads pursue medical degrees. **Faculty:** Student/faculty ratio 10:1. 213 full-time faculty, 95% hold PhDs, 11% are members of minority groups, 43% are women. 0% of classes are taught by teaching assistants.

ACADEMICS
Degrees: bachelor's. **Classes:** Most classes have 10–19 students. Most lab/discussion sessions have 10–19 students. **Majors with Highest Enrollment:** business/commerce; political science and government; psychology. **Special Study Options:** Accelerated program, cross-registration, double major, dual enrollment, exchange student program (domestic), honors program, independent study, internships, student-designed major, study abroad, teacher certification program. **Disability Services:** Special programs offered to physically disabled students include note-taking services, tutors. **Career Services:** Alumni network, alumni services, career/job search classes, career assessment, internships, regional alumni.

FACILITIES
Housing: Coed dorms, special housing for disabled students, men's dorms, special housing for international students, women's dorms, fraternity/sorority housing, apartments for single students, Arts House, French House, Community Outreach House, Sustainability House. 80% of campus accessible to physically disabled. **Special Academic Facilities/Equipment:** Art gallery, associated with natural history museums, bronze casting foundry, retail sales complex, psychology and language labs, TV and radio station, observatory/planetarium, Writers House **Computers:** 100% of classrooms, 100% of dorms, 100% of libraries, 100% of dining areas, 100% of student union, 100% of common outdoor areas have wireless network access. Students can register for classes online. Administrative functions (other than registration) can be performed online.

CAMPUS LIFE
Environment: Town. **Activities:** Choral groups, concert band, dance, drama/theater, jazz band, literary magazine, music ensembles, musical theater, radio station, student government, student newspaper, symphony orchestra, yearbook, Campus Ministries, International Student Organization, Model UN 90 registered organizations, 13 honor societies, 8 religious organizations. 7 fraternities, 3 sororities. **Athletics (Intercollegiate):** *Men:* baseball, basketball, crew/rowing, cross-country, football, golf, lacrosse, soccer, squash, swimming, tennis, track/field (outdoor), track/field (indoor), wrestling. *Women:* basketball, crew/rowing, cross-country, field hockey, golf, lacrosse, soccer, softball, squash, swimming, tennis, track/field (outdoor), track/field (indoor), volleyball. **On-Campus Highlights:** Alumni Sport and Fitness Center, Barshinger Center in Hensel Hall, Barnes and Noble Bookstore and Jazzman's Cafe, Roschel Performing Arts Center, Writers House. **Environmental Initiatives:** We have established the Wohlsen Center for the Sustainable Environment, including a Director, student staff member, and Artist-in-Residence, and partnership with the Millport Conservancy. We have a Student Sustainability House, are incorporating sustainability into 1st year orientation and support very active clubs: The Environmental Action Alliance, Fair Trade Cafe, and Dirt Army (organic garden). We have majors in Environmental Studies and Environmental Science and integrate interdisciplinary collaboration in sustainability across the curriculum.

ADMISSIONS
Freshman Academic Profile: Average high school GPA 3.5. 59% in top 10% of high school class, 87% in top 25% of high school class, 98% in top 50% of high school class. 61% from public high schools. SAT Math middle 50% range 630-710. SAT Critical Reading middle 50% range 610-680. ACT middle 50% range 28-31. Minimum paper TOEFL 600. **Basis for Candidate Selection:** *Very important factors considered include:* Class rank, academic GPA, rigor of secondary school record, character/personal qualities. *Important factors considered include:* application essay, recommendation(s), standardized test scores, extracurricular activities, interview, talent/ability, volunteer work. *Other factors considered include:* alumni/ae relation, geographical residence, level of applicant's interest, racial/ethnic status, work experience. **Freshman Admission Requirements:** High school diploma is required and GED is accepted. *Academic units required:* 4 English, 3 mathematics, 2 science, (2 science labs), 2 foreign language, 1 social studies, 2 history, 1 visual/performing arts. *Academic units recommended:* 4 English, 3 mathematics, 2 science, (2 science labs), 2 foreign language, 1 social studies, 2 history, 1 visual/performing arts. **Freshman Admission Statistics:** 5,105 applied, 38% admitted, 30% enrolled. **Transfer Admission Requirements:** High school transcript, college transcript(s), essay or personal statement, interview, standardized test scores, statement of good standing from prior institution(s). Lowest grade transferable C–. **General Admission Information:** Application Fee $60. Early decision application deadline 11/15. Regular application deadline 2/1. Regular notification 4/1. Nonfall registration accepted. Admission may be deferred for a maximum of one year. Credit and/or placement offered for CEEB Advanced Placement tests.

COSTS AND FINANCIAL AID
Annual tuition $44,260. Room and board $11,750. Required fees $100. Average book expense $1,200. **Required Forms and Deadlines:** FAFSA, CSS/Financial Aid PROFILE, noncustodial PROFILE, business/farm supplement. **Notification of Awards:** Applicants will be notified of awards on or about 4/1. **Types of Aid:** *Need-based scholarships/grants:* Federal Pell, SEOG, state scholarships/grants, private scholarships, the school's own gift aid. *Loans:* Subsidized Stafford, Unsubsidized Stafford, PLUS, Federal Perkins, college/university loans from institutional funds. **Student Employment:** Federal Work-Study Program available. Highest amount earned per year from on-campus jobs $2,175. **Financial Aid Statistics:** 97% freshmen, 96% undergrads receive need-based scholarship or grant aid. 5% freshmen, 6% undergrads receive non-need-based scholarship or grant aid. 97% freshmen, 96% undergrads receive need-based self-help aid. 50% freshmen, 44% undergrads receive any aid. 53% undergrads borrow to pay for school. Average cumulative indebtedness $31,617. **Criteria for awarding institutional aid:** *Non-need-based:* academics, art, leadership, minority status.

FRANKLIN COLLEGE

101 Branigin Blvd, Franklin, IN 46131-2623
Phone: 317-738-8062 • Financial Aid Phone: 317-738-8075
E-mail: admissions@franklincollege.edu • CEEB Code: 1228
Fax: 317-738-8274 • Website: www.franklincollege.edu • ACT Code: 1194

This private school, affiliated with the American Baptist Church, was founded in 1834. It has a 156-acre campus.

RATINGS
Admissions Selectivity Rating: 79   Fire Safety Rating: 73   Green Rating: 68

STUDENTS AND FACULTY
Enrollment: 1,053. **Student Body:** 51% female, 49% male, 7% out-of-state, 0% international (5 countries represented). Asian 1%, African American 5%, Caucasian 85%, Hispanic 1%, Native American 0%. **Retention and Graduation:** 77% freshmen return for sophomore year. 54% freshmen graduate within 4 years. 14% grads go on to further study within 1 year. 13% grads pursue arts and sciences degrees. 3% grads pursue law degrees. 2% grads pursue medical degrees. **Faculty:** Student/faculty ratio 11:1. 74 full-time faculty, 86% hold PhDs, 7% are members of minority groups, 43% are women. 0% of classes are taught by teaching assistants.

ACADEMICS
Degrees: bachelor's. **Classes:** Most classes have 10–19 students. **Majors with Highest Enrollment:** biology/biological sciences; elementary education and teaching; psychology. **Special Study Options:** double major, dual enrollment, exchange student program (domestic), independent study, internships, study abroad, teacher certification program. **Honors Programs:** The intercultural Honors Experience is a freshman-year program designed to attract and retain superior students and faculty to FC while internationalizing the FC community. The program is designed to help students build a solid intercultural foundation, introduce them to interdisciplinary learning, and provide them with opportunities and incentives to study abroad. Faculty development is an integral part of the project. **Disability Services:** Special programs offered to physically disabled students include note-taking services, reader services, tape recorders, tutors. **Career Services:** alumni services, career/job search classes, career assessment.

FACILITIES
Housing: Coed dorms, special housing for disabled students, men's dorms, women's dorms, fraternity/sorority housing. 100% of campus accessible to physically disabled. **Special Academic Facilities/Equipment:** Pulliam School of Journalism, Dietz Center for Professional Development, Leadership Center. **Computers:** 100% of classrooms, 100% of libraries, 100% of dining areas, 100% of student union, have wireless network access. Students can register for classes online. Administrative functions (other than registration) can be performed online.

CAMPUS LIFE
Environment: Village. **Activities:** Choral groups, dance, drama/theater, literary magazine, musical theater, pep band, radio station, student government, student newspaper, yearbook 66 registered organizations, 13 honor societies, 3 religious organizations. 5 fraternities, 4 sororities. **Athletics (Intercollegiate):** *Men:* baseball, basketball, cross-country, diving, football, golf, soccer, swimming, tennis, track/field (outdoor). *Women:* basketball, cheerleading, cross-country, diving, golf, soccer, softball, swimming, tennis, track/field (outdoor), volleyball. **On-Campus Highlights:** Student Center, Spurlock Center (athletic facility), library, residence hall, fraternity houses. **Environmental Initiatives:** Completing green house car emissions inventory Star purchase policy Recycling, composting program

ADMISSIONS
Freshman Academic Profile: Average high school GPA 3.4. 22% in top 10% of high school class, 53% in top 25% of high school class, 93% in top 50% of high school class. 93% from public high schools. SAT Math middle 50% range 480-570. SAT Critical Reading middle 50% range 460-560. SAT Writing middle 50% range 450-540. ACT middle 50% range 20-25. Minimum paper TOEFL 550. **Basis for Candidate Selection:** *Very important factors considered include:* Class rank, academic GPA, rigor of secondary school record, standardized test scores. *Important factors considered include:* application essay, alumni/ae relation, character/personal qualities, extracurricular activities. *Other factors considered include:* recommendation(s), first generation, geographical residence, interview, level of applicant's interest, racial/ethnic status, religious affiliation/commitment, state residency, talent/ability, volunteer work, work experience. **Freshman Admission Requirements:** High school diploma is required and GED is accepted. *Academic units required:* 4 English, 4 mathematics, 2 science, 3 social studies. 4 English, 4 mathematics, 2 science, 3 social

studies. **Freshman Admission Statistics:** 1,926 applied, 60% admitted, 26% enrolled. **Transfer Admission Requirements:** High school transcript, college transcript(s), essay or personal statement, statement of good standing from prior institution(s). Minimum college GPA of 2.0 required. Lowest grade transferable C–. **General Admission Information:** Application Fee $30. Regular notification 9/1. Nonfall registration accepted. Admission may be deferred for a maximum of 1 year. Credit and/or placement offered for CEEB Advanced Placement tests.

COSTS AND FINANCIAL AID
Annual tuition $24,470. Room and board $7,295. Required fees $185. Average book expense $1,200. **Required Forms and Deadlines:** FAFSA, institution's own financial aid form. **Notification of Awards:** Applicants will be notified of awards on or about 4/1. *Types of Aid: Need-based scholarships/grants:* Federal Pell, SEOG, state scholarships/grants, private scholarships, the school's own gift aid. *Loans:* Subsidized Stafford, Unsubsidized Stafford, PLUS, Federal Perkins, college/university loans from institutional funds. **Student Employment:** Federal Work-Study Program available. Institutional employment available. Highest amount earned per year from on-campus jobs $2,000. Off-campus job opportunities are good. **Financial Aid Statistics:** 100% freshmen, 99% undergrads receive need-based scholarship or grant aid. 11% freshmen, 11% undergrads receive non-need-based scholarship or grant aid. 88% freshmen, 88% undergrads receive need-based self-help aid. 100% freshmen, 97% undergrads receive any aid. 92% undergrads borrow to pay for school. Average cumulative indebtedness $34,160. **Criteria for awarding institutional aid:** *Non-need-based:* academics, alumni affiliation, leadership, minority status, religious affiliation, state/district residency.

FRANKLIN PIERCE COLLEGE

Admissions Office, Rindge, NH 3461
Phone: 603-899-4050 • Financial Aid Phone: 603-899-4180
E-mail: admissions@franklinpierce.edu • CEEB Code: 3395
Fax: 603-889-4394 • Website: www.franklinpierce.edu • ACT Code: 2509

This private school was founded in 1962. It has a 1200-acre campus.

RATINGS
Admissions Selectivity Rating: 64   Fire Safety Rating: 83   Green Rating: 74

STUDENTS AND FACULTY
Enrollment: 2,061. **Student Body:** 49% female, 51% male, 78% out-of-state. **Retention and Graduation:** 26% grads go on to further study within 1 year. 5% grads pursue arts and sciences degrees. 3% grads pursue law degrees. 7% grads pursue business degrees. 1% grads pursue medical degrees. **Faculty:** Student/faculty ratio 18:1. 100 full-time faculty, 68% hold PhDs, 1% are members of minority groups, 45% are women. 0% of classes are taught by teaching assistants.

ACADEMICS
Degrees: associate, bachelor's, certificate, first professional, master's, postmaster's certificate. **Classes:** Most classes have 10–19 students. Most lab/discussion sessions have fewer than 10 students. **Majors with Highest Enrollment:** accounting and business/management; criminal justice/safety studies; education; mass communication/media studies. **Special Study Options:** distance learning, double major, dual enrollment, English as a Second Language (ESL), exchange student program (domestic), honors program, independent study, internships, liberal arts/career combination, student-designed major, study abroad, teacher certification program, Walk Across Europe Program, Washington Semester, Arcadia Study Abroad. **Honors Programs:** Honors Program. **Disability Services:** Special programs offered to physically disabled students include note-taking services, reader services, tape recorders, tutors. **Career Services:** Alumni network, alumni services, career/job search classes, career assessment, internships, regional alumni. Career Services highlights include http://franklinpierce.edu/academics/career/ugrad_rindge_cpp.htm.

FACILITIES
Housing: Coed dorms, special housing for disabled students, apartments for single students, wellness housing, condominiums (townhouses). 67% of campus accessible to physically disabled. **Special Academic Facilities/Equipment:** Thoreau Art Gallery; Flynt Center; Fitzwater Communications Center; Dance Studio; Pottery Kiln; Glass Blowing Studio; TV Station; Radio Station; Grimshaw-Gudewicz Activities Center: Lakeside Activity Center **Computers:** 20% of classrooms, 20% of dorms, 100% of libraries, 80% of dining areas, 100% of student union, 50% of common outdoor areas have wireless network access. Administrative functions (other than registration) can be performed online.

CAMPUS LIFE

Environment: Rural. **Activities:** Choral groups, dance, drama/theater, literary magazine, music ensembles, musical theater, radio station, student government, student newspaper, television station, yearbook, Campus Ministries 35 registered organizations, 8 honor societies, 3 religious organizations. **Athletics (Intercollegiate):** *Men:* baseball, basketball, crew/rowing, golf, ice hockey, rugby, soccer, tennis. *Women:* basketball, crew/rowing, cross-country, field hockey, lacrosse, soccer, softball, volleyball. **On-Campus Highlights:** Peterson Hall, The Campus Center, The Northfields Activity Center, The Fitzwater Center for Communications, The Pub. **Environmental Initiatives:** Development of on enhanced on-campus recycling program. Conversion to online format materials, reducing paper waste (online catalogue, billing, forms, etc). Conversion of incandescent lighting to compact flourescent throughout campus.

ADMISSIONS

Freshman Academic Profile: Average high school GPA 2.8. 7% in top 10% of high school class, 20% in top 25% of high school class, 54% in top 50% of high school class. 89% from public high schools. SAT Math middle 50% range 430-540. SAT Critical Reading middle 50% range 440-550. SAT Writing middle 50% range 420-520. Minimum web-based TOEFL 61. Minimum paper TOEFL 500. **Basis for Candidate Selection:** *Very important factors considered include:* academic GPA, recommendation(s), character/personal qualities. *Important factors considered include:* application essay, rigor of secondary school record, standardized test scores. *Other factors considered include:* Class rank, extracurricular activities, interview, talent/ability, volunteer work, work experience. **Freshman Admission Requirements:** High school diploma is required and GED is accepted. *Academic units required:* 4 English, 3 mathematics, 2 science, (2 science labs), 3 social studies, 4 academic electives, 4. 4 English, 3 mathematics, 2 science, (2 science labs), 3 social studies, 4 academic electives, 4 **Transfer Admission Requirements:** college transcript(s), essay or personal statement, minimum college GPA of 2.0 required. Lowest grade transferable C–. **General Admission Information:** Application Fee $40. Notification on a rolling basis, beginning on or about 10/15. Nonfall registration accepted. Admission may be deferred for a maximum of 1 year. Credit and/or placement offered for CEEB Advanced Placement tests.

COSTS AND FINANCIAL AID

Annual tuition $27,700. Room and board $9,800. Required fees $1,300. Average book expense $1,000. **Required Forms and Deadlines:** FAFSA. **Notification of Awards:** Applicants will be notified of awards on a rolling basis beginning 2/1. **Types of Aid:** *Need-based scholarships/grants:* Federal Pell, SEOG, state scholarships/grants, private scholarships, the school's own gift aid. *Loans:* Subsidized Stafford, Unsubsidized Stafford, PLUS, Federal Perkins. **Student Employment:** Federal Work-Study Program available. Institutional employment available. Highest amount earned per year from on-campus jobs $2,200. Off-campus job opportunities are fair. **Financial Aid Statistics:** 99% freshmen, 99% undergrads receive need-based scholarship or grant aid. 10% freshmen, 9% undergrads receive non-need-based scholarship or grant aid. 90% freshmen, 90% undergrads receive need-based self-help aid. 4% freshmen, 5% undergrads receive athletic scholarships. 99% freshmen, 87% undergrads receive any aid. 67% undergrads borrow to pay for school. Average cumulative indebtedness $28,750. **Criteria for awarding institutional aid:** *Non-need-based:* academics, alumni affiliation, athletics, leadership, minority status, music/drama.

FRANKLIN UNIVERSITY

201 S Grant Ave, Columbus, OH 43215
Phone: 614-797-4700 • **Financial Aid Phone:**
E-mail: info@franklin.edu • **CEEB Code:** 1229
Fax: 614-224-8027 • **Website:** 201 S Grant Ave • **ACT Code:** 3275

This private school was founded in 1902. It has a 14-acre campus.

RATINGS
Admissions Selectivity Rating: 61   **Fire Safety Rating:** 60*   **Green Rating:** 60*

STUDENTS AND FACULTY
Enrollment: 5,682. **Student Body:** 55% female, 45% male, 26% out-of-state, 5% international. Asian 3%, African American 19%, Caucasian 66%, Hispanic 2%, Native American 0%.
Retention and Graduation: 72% freshmen return for sophomore year.
Faculty: Student/faculty ratio 19:1. 36 full-time faculty, 64% hold PhDs, 6% are members of minority groups, 44% are women.

ACADEMICS
Degrees: associate, bachelor's, master's. **Classes:** Most classes have 10–19 students. **Majors with Highest Enrollment:** accounting; business/commerce; computer and information science. **Special Study Options:** Acceler-

ated program, cooperative education program, cross-registration, distance learning, double major, dual enrollment, English as a Second Language (ESL), independent study, internships, study abroad, weekend college. **Combined Degree Programs:** BS/MBA. **Disability Services:** Special programs offered to physically disabled students include note-taking services, reader services, tape recorders, tutors. **Career Services:** Alumni network, alumni services, internships.

FACILITIES
Housing: 100% of campus accessible to physically disabled. **Computers:** Students can register for classes online.

CAMPUS LIFE
Environment: Activities: 6 registered organizations.

ADMISSIONS
Freshman Academic Profile: Minimum paper TOEFL 430. **Basis for Candidate Selection:.** **Freshman Admission Requirements:** High school diploma is required and GED is accepted. **Freshman Admission Statistics:** 262 applied, 100% admitted, 47% enrolled. **Transfer Admission Requirements:** college transcript(s), Lowest grade transferable C–. **General Admission Information:** Nonfall registration accepted. Admission may be deferred for a maximum of indefinite. Credit and/or placement offered for CEEB Advanced Placement tests.

COSTS AND FINANCIAL AID
Annual tuition $6,990. Average book expense $0. **Required Forms and Deadlines:** FAFSA. **Types of Aid:** *Need-based scholarships/grants:* Federal Pell, SEOG, state scholarships/grants, private scholarships, the school's own gift aid. *Loans:* Subsidized Stafford, Unsubsidized Stafford, PLUS, college/university loans from institutional funds. **Student Employment:** Federal Work-Study Program available. Institutional employment available. Off-campus job opportunities are good. **Financial Aid Statistics:** 72% freshmen, 64% undergrads receive need-based scholarship or grant aid. 89% freshmen, 84% undergrads receive non-need-based scholarship or grant aid. 97% freshmen, 96% undergrads receive need-based self-help aid. **Criteria for awarding institutional aid:** *Non-need-based:* academics, leadership, minority status.

FRANKLIN W. OLIN COLLEGE OF ENGINEERING

Needham, MA 02492-1245
Phone: 781-292-2222 • **Financial Aid Phone:** 781 292 2343
E-mail: info@olin.edu • **CEEB Code:** 2824
Fax: 781-292-2210 • **Website:** www.olin.edu • **ACT Code:** 1883

This private school was founded in 1997.

RATINGS
Admissions Selectivity Rating: 99   **Fire Safety Rating:** 89   **Green Rating:** 65

STUDENTS AND FACULTY
Enrollment: 326. **Student Body:** 48% female, 52% male, 87% out-of-state, 6% international (17 countries represented). Asian 16%, African American 1%, Caucasian 60%, Hispanic 2%, Native American 0%.
Retention and Graduation: 91% freshmen return for sophomore year. 96% freshmen graduate within 6 years. 28% grads go on to further study within 1 year. 2% grads pursue business degrees. 1% grads pursue medical degrees. **Faculty:** Student/faculty ratio 9:1. 35 full-time faculty, 109% hold PhDs, 26% are members of minority groups, 40% are women. 0% of classes are taught by teaching assistants.

ACADEMICS
Degrees: bachelor's. **Classes:** Most classes have 20–29 students. **Majors with Highest Enrollment:** electrical, electronics and communications engineering; engineering; mechanical engineering. **Special Study Options:** cross-registration, exchange student program (domestic), independent study, internships, liberal arts/career combination, student-designed major, study abroad, Passionate Pursuits program. **Career Services:** Alumni network, alumni services, career/job search classes, internships, regional alumni. Career Services highlights include Because we are a fairly new school, our network of alumni remains small but powerful. Many are now at prestigious companies or graduate school programs, and they often return to campus to talk about their company, career, grad school experience, or they perform mock interviews and/or provide advice to our current students. Due to our young age, our students are especially interested in hearing of our alumni's tales of continued development and success.

FACILITIES

Housing: Coed dorms, special housing for disabled students **Computers:** 100% of classrooms, 100% of dorms, 100% of libraries, 100% of dining areas, 100% of student union, 100% of common outdoor areas have wireless network access. Students can register for classes online. Administrative functions (other than registration) can be performed online. Undergraduates are required to own a computer.

CAMPUS LIFE

Environment: Town. **Activities:** Choral groups, dance, drama/theater, jazz band, music ensembles, musical theater, student government, student-run film society, symphony orchestra, yearbook 55 registered organizations. **Environmental Initiatives:** Replacing site-wide external lighting with LED's Installing site-wide lighting and heating sensors (60% of interior)

ADMISSIONS

Freshman Academic Profile: Average high school GPA 3.9. 95% in top 10% of high school class, 99% in top 25% of high school class, 100% in top 50% of high school class. SAT Math middle 50% range 700-780. SAT Critical Reading middle 50% range 660-740. SAT Writing middle 50% range 670-750. ACT middle 50% range 32-33. **Basis for Candidate Selection:** *Very important factors considered include:* academic GPA, rigor of secondary school record, interview, talent/ability. *Important factors considered include:* standardized test scores, character/personal qualities, extracurricular activities. *Other factors considered include:* Class rank, application essay, recommendation(s), alumni/ae relation, level of applicant's interest, volunteer work, work experience. **Freshman Admission Requirements:** High school diploma is required and GED is accepted. *Academic units required:* 4 English, 3 mathematics, 2 science, (1 science labs), 2 social studies, 1 history, 4 academic electives, 0 two years of algebra recommended. *Academic units recommended:* 4 English, 3 mathematics, 2 science, (1 science labs), 2 social studies, 1 history, 4 academic electives, 0 two years of algebra recommended **Freshman Admission Statistics:** 768 applied, 16% admitted, 69% enrolled. **Transfer Admission Requirements:** college transcript(s), minimum college GPA of 2.0 required. Lowest grade transferable C. **General Admission Information:** Application Fee $30. Regular application deadline 7/15. Notification on a rolling basis, beginning on or about 10/1. Nonfall registration accepted. Admission may be deferred for a maximum of 1 year. Credit and/or placement offered for CEEB Advanced Placement tests.

COSTS AND FINANCIAL AID

Annual tuition $40,000. Room and board $14,500. Required fees $175. Average book expense $300. **Required Forms and Deadlines:** FAFSA, state aid form. **Notification of Awards:** Applicants will be notified of awards on a rolling basis beginning 2/1. **Types of Aid:** *Need-based scholarships/grants:* Federal Pell, SEOG, state scholarships/grants, private scholarships, the school's own gift aid. *Loans:* Subsidized Stafford, Unsubsidized Stafford, PLUS, Federal Perkins. **Student Employment:** Federal Work-Study Program available. Institutional employment available. Highest amount earned per year from on-campus jobs $1,450. Off-campus job opportunities are good. **Financial Aid Statistics:** 78% freshmen, 67% undergrads receive need-based scholarship or grant aid. 100% freshmen, 100% undergrads receive non-need-based scholarship or grant aid. 100% freshmen, 100% undergrads receive need-based self-help aid. 100% freshmen, 100% undergrads receive any aid. 20% undergrads borrow to pay for school. Average cumulative indebtedness $11,900. **Criteria for awarding institutional aid:** *Non-need-based:* academics, alumni affiliation, leadership.

FREED-HARDEMAN UNIVERSITY

158 East Main Street, Henderson, TN 38340
Phone: 731-989-6651 • **Financial Aid Phone:** 731-989-6662
E-mail: jathoms1@yahoo.com • **CEEB Code:** 1230
Fax: 731-989-6047 • **Website:** web.fhu.edu • **ACT Code:** 3962

This private school, affiliated with the Church of Christ Church, was founded in 1869. It has a 122-acre campus.

RATINGS

Admissions Selectivity Rating: 86 **Fire Safety Rating:** 62 **Green Rating:** 61

STUDENTS AND FACULTY

Enrollment: 1,428. **Student Body:** 55% female, 45% male, 50% out-of-state, 3% international (26 countries represented). Asian 0%, African American 4%, Caucasian 91%, Hispanic 1%, Native American 0%.
Retention and Graduation: 74% freshmen return for sophomore year. 41% freshmen graduate within 4 years. 58% freshmen graduate within 6 years. 40% grads go on to further study within 1 year. **Faculty:** Student/faculty ratio 14:1. 108 full-time faculty, 69% hold PhDs, 5% are members of minority groups, 31% are women. 0% of classes are taught by teaching assistants.

ACADEMICS

Degrees: bachelor's, first professional, master's, post-bachelor's certificate, post-master's certificate, terminal associate. **Classes:** Most classes have 10–19 students. Most lab/discussion sessions have 10–19 students. **Majors with Highest Enrollment:** bible/biblical studies; biology/biological sciences; liberal arts and sciences studies and humanities, other. **Special Study Options:** Accelerated program, cooperative education program, cross-registration, distance learning, double major, dual enrollment, honors program, independent study, internships, liberal arts/career combination, student-designed major, study abroad, teacher certification program, 3-2 engineering, Honors College, study abroad in Belgium and Italy. **Honors Programs:** Exceptional students may be admitted to the Honors College, where he or she may graduate as an Honors College Scholar, or as an Honors College Scholar with University Honors. **Combined Degree Programs:** BBA/MBA. **Disability Services:** Special programs offered to physically disabled students include note-taking services, reader services, tutors. **Career Services:** Alumni network, career assessment, internships.

FACILITIES

Housing: men's dorms, women's dorms, apartments for single students, Some student teacher housing is available. 70% of campus accessible to physically disabled. **Special Academic Facilities/Equipment:** Child development lab, nursery school. **Computers:** Students can register for classes online. Administrative functions (other than registration) can be performed online.

CAMPUS LIFE

Environment: Rural. **Activities:** Choral groups, concert band, drama/theater, jazz band, music ensembles, musical theater, pep band, radio station, student government, student newspaper, television station, yearbook 52 registered organizations, 4 honor societies, 5 religious organizations. 6 fraternities, 6 sororities. **Athletics (Intercollegiate):** *Men:* baseball, basketball, cheerleading, soccer. *Women:* basketball, cheerleading, soccer, softball, volleyball. **On-Campus Highlights:** The Commons, The Student Center, The Sports Center, Brown Kopel Business Center, The Library.

ADMISSIONS

Freshman Academic Profile: Average high school GPA 3.4. 25% in top 10% of high school class, 51% in top 25% of high school class, 79% in top 50% of high school class. % from public high schools. SAT Math middle 50% range 480-600. SAT Critical Reading middle 50% range 480-640. ACT middle 50% range 20-26. **Basis for Candidate Selection:** *Very important factors considered include:* academic GPA, rigor of secondary school record, standardized test scores. *Other factors considered include:* recommendation(s), alumni/ae relation, character/personal qualities, extracurricular activities, racial/ethnic status, religious affiliation/commitment, volunteer work, work experience. **Freshman Admission Requirements:** High school diploma is required and GED is accepted. **Freshman Admission Statistics:** 1,326 applied, 55% admitted, 53% enrolled. **Transfer Admission Requirements:** college transcript(s), statement of good standing from prior institution(s). Lowest grade transferable D. **General Admission Information:** Notification on a rolling basis, beginning on or about 5/2. Nonfall registration accepted. Admission may be deferred for a maximum of 2 years. Credit and/or placement offered for CEEB Advanced Placement tests.

COSTS AND FINANCIAL AID

Annual tuition $13,192. Room and board $6,560. Average book expense $1,710. **Required Forms and Deadlines:** FAFSA. **Notification of Awards:** Applicants will be notified of awards on a rolling basis beginning 3/1. **Types of Aid:** *Need-based scholarships/grants:* Federal Pell, SEOG, state scholarships/grants, private scholarships, the school's own gift aid. *Loans:* Subsidized Stafford, Unsubsidized Stafford, PLUS, Federal Perkins, Alternative loan programs. **Student Employment:** Federal Work-Study Program available. Institutional employment available. Off-campus job opportunities are fair. **Financial Aid Statistics:** 97% freshmen, 91% undergrads receive need-based scholarship or grant aid. 19% freshmen, 17% undergrads receive non-need-based scholarship or grant aid. 74% freshmen, 78% undergrads receive need-based self-help aid. 4% freshmen, 4% undergrads receive athletic scholarships. 86% freshmen, % undergrads receive any aid. 76% undergrads borrow to pay for school. Average cumulative indebtedness $34,216. **Criteria for awarding institutional aid:** *Non-need-based:* academics, art, athletics, leadership, minority status, music/drama, state/district residency.

FRESNO PACIFIC UNIVERSITY

1717 S. Chestnut Ave, Fresno, CA 93702
Phone: 559-453-2039 • **Financial Aid Phone:** 559-453-2041
E-mail: ugadmis@fresno.edu
Fax: 559-453-2007 • **Website:** www.fresno.edu/

This private school, affiliated with the Mennonite Church, was founded in 1944. It has a 42-acre campus.

RATINGS
Admissions Selectivity Rating: 60*   **Fire Safety Rating:** 60*   **Green Rating:** 60*

STUDENTS AND FACULTY
Enrollment: 1,459. **Student Body:** 68% female, 32% male, % out-of-state, 2% international. Asian 4%, African American 4%, Caucasian 53%, Hispanic 26%, Native American 1%.
Retention and Graduation: 70% freshmen return for sophomore year. 48% freshmen graduate within 4 years. 62% freshmen graduate within 6 years.

ACADEMICS
Degrees: associate, bachelor's, certificate, master's, post-bachelor's certificate. **Classes:** Most classes have fewer than 10 students. Most lab/discussion sessions have fewer than 10 students. **Majors with Highest Enrollment:** bible/biblical studies; business/commerce; education. **Special Study Options:** Accelerated program, cooperative education program, cross-registration, distance learning, double major, English as a Second Language (ESL), independent study, internships, liberal arts/career combination, student-designed major, study abroad, teacher certification program. **Disability Services:** Special programs offered to physically disabled students include note-taking services, reader services, tutors. **Career Services:** alumni services, career/job search classes, career assessment, internships.

FACILITIES
Housing: special housing for disabled students, men's dorms, women's dorms, apartments for single students, houses. 100% of campus accessible to physically disabled. **Special Academic Facilities/Equipment:** English Language Training Institute.

CAMPUS LIFE
Environment: Metropolis. **Activities:** Choral groups, concert band, dance, drama/theater, jazz band, music ensembles, pep band, student government, student newspaper, yearbook 36 registered organizations, 1 honor societies, 11 religious organizations. **Athletics (Intercollegiate):** *Men:* baseball, basketball, cross-country, soccer, tennis, track/field (outdoor). *Women:* basketball, cross-country, soccer, tennis, track/field (outdoor), volleyball. **On-Campus Highlights:** Special Events Center (Gym), Steinert Campus Center, The Green (students hang out there), Bookshop, New AIMS Building.

ADMISSIONS
Basis for Candidate Selection: *Very important factors considered include:* rigor of secondary school record, standardized test scores. *Important factors considered include:* Class rank, application essay, academic GPA, recommendation(s), religious affiliation/commitment. *Other factors considered include:* character/personal qualities. **Freshman Admission Requirements:** High school diploma is required and GED is accepted. *Academic units required:* 4 English, 3 mathematics, 1 science, (1 science labs), 2 foreign language, 2 social studies. *Academic units recommended:* 4 English, 3 mathematics, 1 science, (1 science labs), 2 foreign language, 2 social studies. **Transfer Admission Requirements:** High school transcript, college transcript(s), essay or personal statement, minimum college GPA of 2.4 required. Lowest grade transferable C. **General Admission Information:** Application Fee $40. Regular application deadline 7/31. Notification on a rolling basis, beginning on or about 12/1. Nonfall registration accepted. Admission may be deferred for a maximum of NA. Credit offered for CEEB Advanced Placement tests.

COSTS AND FINANCIAL AID
Annual tuition $24,960. Required fees $276. Average book expense $1,665. **Required Forms and Deadlines:** FAFSA, institution's own financial aid form. **Notification of Awards:** Applicants will be notified of awards on a rolling basis beginning 3/2. **Types of Aid:** *Need-based scholarships/grants:* Federal Pell, SEOG, state scholarships/grants, private scholarships, the school's own gift aid. *Loans:* Subsidized Stafford, Unsubsidized Stafford, PLUS, Federal Perkins. **Student Employment:** Federal Work-Study Program available. Institutional employment available. Off-campus job opportunities are good. **Financial Aid Statistics:** 78% freshmen, 78% undergrads receive need-based scholarship or grant aid. 99% freshmen, 48% undergrads receive non-need-based scholarship or grant aid. 79% freshmen, 86% undergrads receive need-based self-help aid. 76% undergrads borrow to pay for school. Average cumulative indebtedness $16,898. **Criteria for awarding institutional aid:** *Non-need-based:* academ-

ics, alumni affiliation, art, athletics, leadership, minority status, music/drama, religious affiliation, state/district residency.

FRIENDS UNIVERSITY

2100 University Street., Wichita, KS 67213
Phone: 316-295-5100
E-mail: learn@friends.edu
Fax: 316-295-5101 • **Website:** www.friends.edu • **ACT Code:** 1918

This private school, affiliated with the Quaker Church, was founded in 1898. It has a 45-acre campus.

RATINGS
Admissions Selectivity Rating: 75   **Fire Safety Rating:** 79   **Green Rating:** 60*

STUDENTS AND FACULTY
Enrollment: 1,737. **Student Body:** 56% female, 44% male, 19% out-of-state, 0% international (13 countries represented). Asian 3%, African American 11%, Caucasian 71%, Hispanic 4%, Native American 2%.
Retention and Graduation: 60% freshmen return for sophomore year. 10% freshmen graduate within 4 years. 33% freshmen graduate within 6 years. **Faculty:** Student/faculty ratio 11:1. 75 full-time faculty, 71% hold PhDs, 5% are members of minority groups, 41% are women. 0% of classes are taught by teaching assistants.

ACADEMICS
Degrees: bachelor's, master's, terminal associate, transfer associate. **Special Study Options:** cooperative education program, cross-registration, double major, dual enrollment, external degree program, honors program, independent study, internships, student-designed major, study abroad, teacher certification program, Degree completion program for working adults. **Career Services:** career/job search classes, internships.

FACILITIES
Housing: men's dorms, women's dorms, apartments for married students, apartments for single students, University-owned houses.

CAMPUS LIFE
Environment: Activities: Choral groups, concert band, dance, drama/theater, jazz band, literary magazine, music ensembles, musical theater, pep band, student government, symphony orchestra, yearbook 32 registered organizations, 4 honor societies, 3 religious organizations. 2 fraternities, 1 sororities. **Athletics (Intercollegiate):** *Men:* baseball, basketball, cheerleading, cross-country, football, golf, soccer, tennis, track/field (outdoor). *Women:* basketball, cheerleading, cross-country, soccer, softball, tennis, track/field (outdoor), volleyball.

ADMISSIONS
Freshman Academic Profile: 3.4. 20% in top 10% of high school class, 36% in top 25% of high school class, 68% in top 50% of high school class. 84% from public high schools. SAT Math middle 50% range 400-510. SAT Critical Reading middle 50% range 390-515. ACT middle 50% range 18-26. Minimum web-based TOEFL 63. Minimum paper TOEFL 500. **Basis for Candidate Selection:** *Very important factors considered include:* rigor of secondary school record, standardized test scores. *Important factors considered include:* recommendation(s), interview. *Other factors considered include:* alumni/ae relation, extracurricular activities, racial/ethnic status, religious affiliation/commitment, talent/ability. **Freshman Admission Requirements:** High school diploma is required and GED is accepted. **Freshman Admission Statistics:** 786 applied, 58% admitted, 43% enrolled. **Transfer Admission Requirements:** college transcript(s), statement of good standing from prior institution(s). Minimum college GPA of 2.0 required. Lowest grade transferable C. **General Admission Information:** Application Fee $15. Nonfall registration accepted. Credit and/or placement offered for CEEB Advanced Placement tests.

COSTS AND FINANCIAL AID
Annual tuition $22,320. Room and board $6,600. Required fees $180. Average book expense $1,500. **Required Forms and Deadlines:** FAFSA, institution's own financial aid form. **Notification of Awards: Types of Aid:** *Need-based scholarships/grants:* Federal Pell, SEOG, private scholarships. *Loans:* Direct Subsidized Stafford, Direct Unsubsidized Stafford, Direct PLUS, Federal Perkins. **Student Employment:** Federal Work-Study Program available. Institutional employment available. Off-campus job opportunities are excellent. **Financial Aid Statistics:** 100% freshmen, 84% undergrads receive need-based scholarship or grant aid. 24% freshmen, 13% undergrads receive non-need-based scholarship or grant aid. 78% freshmen, 89% undergrads receive need-based self-help aid. 21% freshmen, 3% undergrads receive athletic scholarships. 87% freshmen, 77% undergrads receive any aid. 86% undergrads borrow to pay for school. Average cumulative indebtedness $18,750. **Criteria for awarding**

institutional aid: *Non-need-based:* academics, alumni affiliation, athletics, leadership, minority status, music/drama, religious affiliation.

FROSTBURG STATE UNIVERSITY

FSU, 101 Braddock Road, Frostburg, MD 21532
Phone: 301-687-4201 • **Financial Aid Phone:** 301-687-4301
E-mail: fsuadmissions@frostburg.edu • **CEEB Code:** 5402
Fax: 301-687-7074 • **Website:** www.frostburg.edu • **ACT Code:** 1714

This public school was founded in 1898. It has a 260-acre campus.

RATINGS
Admissions Selectivity Rating: 79   **Fire Safety Rating:** 75   **Green Rating:** 93

STUDENTS AND FACULTY
Enrollment: 4,617. **Student Body:** 49% female, 51% male, 8% out-of-state, 1% international (25 countries represented). Asian 1%, African American 25%, Caucasian 66%, Hispanic 4%, Native American 0%.
Retention and Graduation: 71% freshmen return for sophomore year. 21% freshmen graduate within 4 years. 46% freshmen graduate within 6 years.
Faculty: Student/faculty ratio 17:1. 247 full-time faculty, 79% hold PhDs, 13% are members of minority groups, 42% are women.

ACADEMICS
Degrees: bachelor's, certificate, master's, post-bachelor's certificate, post-master's certificate. **Classes:** Most classes have 20–29 students. Most lab/discussion sessions have 10–19 students. **Majors with Highest Enrollment:** business/commerce; elementary education and teaching; psychology. **Special Study Options:** Accelerated program, distance learning, double major, dual enrollment, honors program, independent study, internships, liberal arts/career combination, study abroad, teacher certification program, Learning Communities, Dual Degree Program. **Combined Degree Programs:** MBA/BS in Accounting. **Disability Services:** Special programs offered to physically disabled students include note-taking services, reader services, tape recorders, tutors.

FACILITIES
Housing: Coed dorms, women's dorms, Special interest housing: Leadership Hall Honors Housing Community Service. 100% of campus accessible to physically disabled. **Special Academic Facilities/Equipment:** Art gallery, planetarium, electron microscope. **Computers:** Students can register for classes online. Administrative functions (other than registration) can be performed online.

CAMPUS LIFE
Environment: Rural. **Activities:** Choral groups, concert band, dance, drama/theater, jazz band, literary magazine, marching band, music ensembles, musical theater, pep band, radio station, student government, student newspaper, symphony orchestra, television station 95 registered organizations, 18 honor societies, 6 religious organizations. 9 fraternities, 6 sororities. **Athletics (Intercollegiate):** *Men:* baseball, basketball, cross-country, diving, football, golf, soccer, swimming, tennis, track/field (outdoor), track/field (indoor). *Women:* basketball, cross-country, diving, field hockey, lacrosse, soccer, softball, swimming, tennis, track/field (outdoor), track/field (indoor), volleyball. **On-Campus Highlights:** Lane University Center, Cordts PE Center, Performing Arts Center, Stephanie Roper Art Gallery, Compton Science Center. **Environmental Initiatives:** Adopted an energy-efficient appliance purchasing policy requiring purchase of ENERGY STAR-certified products in all areas for which such ratings exist. Purchasing or producing at least 15 percent of our institution's electricity consumption from renewable resources. Participating in the Waste Minimization component of the national Recyclemania competition, and adopt three or more associated measures to reduce waste.

ADMISSIONS
Freshman Academic Profile: Average high school GPA 3.2. 11% in top 10% of high school class, 29% in top 25% of high school class, 67% in top 50% of high school class. % from public high schools. SAT Math middle 50% range 440-540. SAT Critical Reading middle 50% range 440-540. SAT Writing middle 50% range 420-520. ACT middle 50% range 17-21. Minimum paper TOEFL 550. **Basis for Candidate Selection:** *Very important factors considered include:* academic GPA, rigor of secondary school record, standardized test scores. *Important factors considered include:* recommendation(s), interview. *Other factors considered include:* alumni/ae relation, character/personal qualities, extracurricular activities, talent/ability. **Freshman Admission Requirements:** High school diploma is required and GED is accepted. *Academic units required:* 4 English, 3 mathematics, 3 science, (2 science labs), 2 foreign language, 3 social studies. 4 English, 3 mathematics, 3 science, (2 science labs), 2 foreign language, 3 social studies. **Freshman Admission Statistics:** 4,323 applied, 55% admitted, 35% enrolled. **Transfer Admission Requirements:** college

transcript(s), minimum college GPA of 2.0 required. Lowest grade transferable C. **General Admission Information:** Application Fee $30. Early decision application deadline 12/15. Notification on a rolling basis, beginning on or about 11/1. Nonfall registration accepted. Credit and/or placement offered for CEEB Advanced Placement tests.

COSTS AND FINANCIAL AID
Annual in-state tuition $5,304. Annual out-of-state tuition $15,196. Room and board $7,564. Required fees $1,824. Average book expense $1,200. **Required Forms and Deadlines:** FAFSA. **Notification of Awards:** Applicants will be notified of awards on a rolling basis beginning 3/15. **Types of Aid:** *Need-based scholarships/grants:* Federal Pell, SEOG, state scholarships/grants, private scholarships, the school's own gift aid. *Loans:* Direct Subsidized Stafford, Direct Unsubsidized Stafford, Direct PLUS, PLUS, Federal Perkins, college/university loans from institutional funds. **Student Employment:** Highest amount earned per year from on-campus jobs $1,000. **Financial Aid Statistics:** 75% freshmen, 73% undergrads receive need-based scholarship or grant aid. 30% freshmen, 28% undergrads receive non-need-based scholarship or grant aid. 78% freshmen, 80% undergrads receive need-based self-help aid. 72% freshmen, 65% undergrads receive any aid. 64% undergrads borrow to pay for school. Average cumulative indebtedness $18,225. **Criteria for awarding institutional aid:** *Non-need-based:* academics, alumni affiliation, art, leadership, music/drama, state/district residency.

See page 1086.

FULL SAIL UNIVERSITY

3300 University Blvd, Winter Park, FL 32792
Phone: 800-226-7625
E-mail: admissions@fullsail.com
Website: www.fullsail.edu/

This proprietary school was founded in 1979. It has a 91-acre campus.

RATINGS
Admissions Selectivity Rating: 60*   **Fire Safety Rating:** 60*   **Green Rating:** 60*

ACADEMICS
Degrees: associate, bachelor's, master's, terminal associate. **Classes: Majors with Highest Enrollment:** animation, interactive technology, video graphics and special effects; cinematography and film/video production; recording arts technology/technician. **Special Study Options:** Accelerated program.

FACILITIES
Housing: Full Sail does not feature on-campus living arrangements, but does employ a Housing Manager who is dedicated to providing information about affordable accommodations in one of the many apartment complexes near the school. The Housing Manager can also help with information regarding roommates (other incoming Full Sail students), power, phones, furniture, and helpful community programs in the Central Florida area.

CAMPUS LIFE
Environment: Metropolis.

ADMISSIONS
Basis for Candidate Selection: *Very important factors considered include:* application essay, level of applicant's interest, talent/ability. *Important factors considered include:* academic GPA, recommendation(s), standardized test scores, character/personal qualities. *Other factors considered include:* Class rank, rigor of secondary school record, extracurricular activities, interview, volunteer work. **Freshman Admission Requirements:** High school diploma is required and GED is accepted. **Transfer Admission Requirements:** college transcript(s), essay or personal statement, statement of good standing from prior institution(s). Minimum college GPA of 2.6 required. Lowest grade transferable C. **General Admission Information:** Application Fee $50. Regular application deadline 7/15. Notification on a rolling basis, beginning on or about 1/1. Nonfall registration accepted. Admission may be deferred for a maximum of 1 semester. Credit offered for CEEB Advanced Placement tests.

COSTS AND FINANCIAL AID
Required Forms and Deadlines: FAFSA, institution's own financial aid form. **Notification of Awards:** Applicants will be notified of awards on a rolling basis beginning 5/1. **Types of Aid:** *Need-based scholarships/grants:* Federal Pell, SEOG, state scholarships/grants, private scholarships, the school's own gift aid. *Loans:* Subsidized Stafford, Unsubsidized Stafford, PLUS. **Student Employment:** Federal Work-Study Program available. Institutional employment available. Off-campus job opportunities are good. **Criteria for awarding institutional aid:** *Non-need-based:* academics, art.

FURMAN UNIVERSITY

3300 Poinsett Highway, Greenville, SC 29613
Phone: 864-294-2034 • **Financial Aid Phone:** 864-294-2204
E-mail: admissions@furman.edu • **CEEB Code:** 5222
Fax: 864-294-2018 • **Website:** www.furman.edu • **ACT Code:** 3858

This private school was founded in 1826. It has a 800-acre campus.

RATINGS

Admissions Selectivity Rating: 85   **Fire Safety Rating:** 81   **Green Rating:** 94

STUDENTS AND FACULTY

Enrollment: 2,731. **Student Body:** 57% female, 43% male, 70% out-of-state, 3% international (53 countries represented). Asian 2%, African American 5%, Caucasian 81%, Hispanic 3%, Native American 0%.
Retention and Graduation: 79% freshmen graduate within 4 years. 42% grads go on to further study within 1 year. 32% grads pursue arts and sciences degrees. 4% grads pursue law degrees. 2% grads pursue business degrees. 4% grads pursue medical degrees. **Faculty:** Student/faculty ratio 11:1. 240 full-time faculty, 95% hold PhDs, 11% are members of minority groups, 35% are women. 0% of classes are taught by teaching assistants.

ACADEMICS

Degrees: bachelor's, master's, post-bachelor's certificate. **Classes:** Most classes have 10–19 students. **Majors with Highest Enrollment:** communication studies/speech communication and rhetoric; history; political science and government. **Special Study Options:** double major, independent study, internships, student-designed major, study abroad, teacher certification program. **Combined Degree Programs:** BA/MD, BA/MA, BA/DDS, Environmental Studies, Pharmacy, Nursing. **Disability Services:** Special programs offered to physically disabled students include note-taking services, reader services, tape recorders, tutors. **Career Services:** Alumni network, career/job search classes, career assessment, internships Career Services highlights include Furman's internships, both paid and unpaid, are available to virtually every student. They run the gamut from medical research to international business opportunities.

FACILITIES

Housing: Coed dorms, men's dorms, special housing for international students, women's dorms, apartments for single students, wellness housing, theme housing, lakeside cottages, language houses, eco-cottage. 98% of campus accessible to physically disabled. **Special Academic Facilities/Equipment:** Visual arts gallery and teaching facility, language lab. Astronomical lab; Center for Engaged Learning; and Center for Collaborative Learning and Communication. **Computers:** 100% of classrooms, 100% of libraries, 100% of dining areas, 100% of student union, have wireless network access. Students can register for classes online. Administrative functions (other than registration) can be performed online.

CAMPUS LIFE

Environment: City. **Activities:** Choral groups, concert band, dance, drama/theater, jazz band, literary magazine, marching band, music ensembles, musical theater, opera, pep band, radio station, student government, student newspaper, student-run film society, symphony orchestra, television station, yearbook, Campus Ministries, International Student Organization 143 registered organizations, 29 honor societies, 17 religious organizations. 7 fraternities, 7 sororities. **Athletics (Intercollegiate):** *Men:* baseball, basketball, cheerleading, cross-country, football, golf, soccer, tennis, track/field (outdoor), track/field (indoor). *Women:* basketball, cheerleading, cross-country, golf, soccer, softball, tennis, track/field (outdoor), track/field (indoor), volleyball. **On-Campus Highlights:** Charles Townes Science Center, Timmons Arena, Library, 18-hole Golf Course, Physical Activities Center, Place of Peace, David Shi Center for Sustainability. **Environmental Initiatives:** Sustainable Furman: The approval of Sustainable Furman, the university's comprehensive sustainability master plan. The plan covers all aspects of the university; the 8 goals of Sustainable Furman address sustainability in the curriculum, co-curricular activities, campus culture, renewable energy, efficiency in operations and maintenance, transportation, sustainability service, and continuing national leadership in the sustainability arena. In addition, the plan sets out a path for the university to reach carbon neutrality by 2026. Sustainability curriculum development: In recent years Furman has sought to infuse sustainability and environmental issues across the curriculum. The university offers a wide range of sustainability-related courses at all levels. The new university-wide curriculum, inaugurated in the fall of 2008, requires all students to take at least one course that focuses on the relationship between "Humans

and the Natural Environment." In 2009-2010, 31 courses in 11 departments were offered to fulfill the Humans and the Natural Environment credit. Nine departments in the natural sciences, social sciences, and humanities contribute faculty members to a multi-disciplinary Concentration in Environmental Studies. Students in the capstone course for the concentration are also involved in service learning projects in the community. The most recent new courses in sustainability have included several first-year seminars and an environmental policy course that focuses on campus/community connections. Finally, the faculty approved a new major in Sustainability Science in November 2010. Creation of the David E. Shi Center for Sustainability.

ADMISSIONS

Freshman Academic Profile: Average high school GPA. 40% in top 10% of high school class, 72% in top 25% of high school class, 92% in top 50% of high school class. 52% from public high schools. SAT Math middle 50% range 560-660. SAT Critical Reading middle 50% range 550-650. SAT Writing middle 50% range 540-650. ACT middle 50% range 25-29. Minimum paper TOEFL 570. **Basis for Candidate Selection:** *Very important factors considered include:* rigor of secondary school record. *Important factors considered include:* Class rank, application essay, academic GPA, standardized test scores, character/personal qualities, extracurricular activities. *Other factors considered include:* recommendation(s), alumni/ae relation, first generation, level of applicant's interest, racial/ethnic status, talent/ability, volunteer work, work experience. **Freshman Admission Requirements:** High school diploma is required and GED is accepted. *Academic units required:* 4 English, 3 mathematics, 2 science, (2 science labs), 2 foreign language, 3 social studies. *Academic units recommended:* 4 English, 3 mathematics, 2 science, (2 science labs), 2 foreign language, 3 social studies. **Freshman Admission Statistics:** 6,035 applied, 77% admitted, 15% enrolled. **Transfer Admission Requirements:** High school transcript, college transcript(s), essay or personal statement, standardized test scores, statement of good standing from prior institution(s). Minimum college GPA of 3.0 required. Lowest grade transferable C. **General Admission Information:** Application Fee $50. Early decision application deadline 11/15. Regular application deadline 1/15. Regular notification 3/15. Nonfall registration not accepted. Credit and/or placement offered for CEEB Advanced Placement tests.

COSTS AND FINANCIAL AID

Annual tuition $41,152. Room and board $10,509. Required fees $380. Average book expense $1,200. **Required Forms and Deadlines:** FAFSA, institution's own financial aid form, CSS/Financial Aid PROFILE, state aid formSouth Carolina residents must complete required state forms for South Carolina. **Notification of Awards:** Applicants will be notified of awards on or about 3/15. **Types of Aid:** *Need-based scholarships/grants:* Federal Pell, SEOG, state scholarships/grants, private scholarships, the school's own gift aid, Donor sponsored loans for study abroad. *Loans:* Subsidized Stafford, Unsubsidized Stafford, PLUS, Federal Perkins, state loans, Federal SMART and ACG grants. **Student Employment:** Federal Work-Study Program available. Institutional employment available. Highest amount earned per year from on-campus jobs $1,500. Off-campus job opportunities are excellent. **Financial Aid Statistics:** 100% freshmen, 99% undergrads receive need-based scholarship or grant aid. 100% freshmen, 99% undergrads receive non-need-based scholarship or grant aid. 65% freshmen, 68% undergrads receive need-based self-help aid. 8% freshmen, 9% undergrads receive athletic scholarships. 85% freshmen, 85% undergrads receive any aid. 43% undergrads borrow to pay for school. Average cumulative indebtedness $26,661. **Criteria for awarding institutional aid:** *Non-need-based:* academics, alumni affiliation, art, athletics, leadership, music/drama, religious affiliation, state/district residency.

GALLAUDET UNIVERSITY

800 Florida Avenue , NE, Washington DC, DC 20002
Phone: 202-651-5750 • **Financial Aid Phone:** 202-651-5290
E-mail: admissions.office@gallaudet.edu • **CEEB Code:** 5240
Fax: 202-651-5744 • **Website:** www.gallaudet.edu/ • **ACT Code:** 662

This private school was founded in 1864. It has a 99-acre campus.

RATINGS

Admissions Selectivity Rating: 72   **Fire Safety Rating:** 80   **Green Rating:** 61

STUDENTS AND FACULTY

Enrollment: 1,097. **Student Body:** 54% female, 46% male, 97% out-of-state, 7% international (27 countries represented). Asian 4%, African American 11%, Caucasian 62%, Hispanic 13%, Native American 0%.
Retention and Graduation: 77% freshmen return for sophomore year. 7% freshmen graduate within 4 years. 33% freshmen graduate within 6 years.

Faculty: Student/faculty ratio 8:1. 189 full-time faculty, 86% hold PhDs, 21% are members of minority groups, 67% are women. 0% of classes are taught by teaching assistants.

ACADEMICS

Degrees: bachelor's, master's, post-bachelor's certificate. **Classes:** Most classes have 10–19 students. Most lab/discussion sessions have fewer than 10 students. **Majors with Highest Enrollment:** business/commerce; psychology. **Special Study Options:** Accelerated program, cross-registration, distance learning, double major, English as a Second Language (ESL), exchange student program (domestic), honors program, independent study, internships, student-designed major, study abroad, teacher certification program, Experiential programs off-campus including orientation program for employers of deaf students and paraprofessional jobs on campus, programs for interpreter-assisted mainstreaming of students into area colleges such as Georgetown University, George Mason University, Catholic University, and Howard University. **Honors Programs:** The Gallaudet Honors Program is a Learning Community for the most academically capable and motivated students. The overall goal is to foster skills, work habits, and attitudes conducive to future achievement and lifelong learning. To this end, the Program focuses on linking rigorous, challenging, and innovative curricular offerings with co-curricular activities. It also serves as a leader in and test laboratory of curricular, co-curricular, and extracurricular innovations; successes may then be replicated for all students. **Combined Degree Programs:** BA/MA, BA or BS (Education) with MA in Teaching. **Disability Services:** Special programs offered to physically disabled students include tutors. **Career Services:** Alumni network, alumni services, career/job search classes, career assessment, internships Career Services highlights include Internship program.

FACILITIES

Housing: Coed dorms, special housing for disabled students, apartments for married students, theme housing, 100% of campus accessible to physically disabled. **Special Academic Facilities/Equipment:** Kendall Demonstration Elementary School and Model Secondary School for the Deaf **Computers:** 100% of classrooms, 100% of dorms, 100% of libraries, 100% of dining areas, 100% of student union, 20% of common outdoor areas have wireless network access. Students can register for classes online. Administrative functions (other than registration) can be performed online.

CAMPUS LIFE

Environment: Metropolis. **Activities:** dance, drama/theater, literary magazine, student government, student newspaper, student-run film society, yearbook, Campus Ministries, International Student Organization 25 registered organizations, 1 honor societies, 1 religious organizations. 5 fraternities, 4 sororities. **Athletics (Intercollegiate):** *Men:* baseball, basketball, cross-country, diving, football, soccer, swimming, tennis, track/field (outdoor), wrestling. *Women:* basketball, cross-country, diving, soccer, softball, swimming, tennis, track/field (outdoor), volleyball. **On-Campus Highlights:** Rathskellar, Cafeteria, Bison Shop, Starbucks, Student Academic Center.

ADMISSIONS

Freshman Academic Profile: SAT Math middle 50% range 350-530. SAT Critical Reading middle 50% range 350-530. ACT middle 50% range 15-20. **Basis for Candidate Selection:** *Very important factors considered include:* application essay, academic GPA, recommendation(s), rigor of secondary school record, standardized test scores. *Important factors considered include:* Class rank, first generation. *Other factors considered include:* alumni/ae relation, extracurricular activities, talent/ability. **Freshman Admission Requirements:** High school diploma is required and GED is accepted. **Freshman Admission Statistics:** 509 applied, 61% admitted, 68% enrolled. **Transfer Admission Requirements:** college transcript(s), essay or personal statement, Lowest grade transferable C–. **General Admission Information:** Application Fee $50. Nonfall registration accepted. Credit and/or placement offered for CEEB Advanced Placement tests.

COSTS AND FINANCIAL AID

Annual tuition $13,424. Room and board $11,580. Required fees $376. Average book expense $1,300. **Required Forms and Deadlines:** FAFSA, institution's own financial aid form. **Notification of Awards:** Applicants will be notified of awards on a rolling basis beginning 3/1. **Types of Aid:** *Need-based scholarships/grants:* Federal Pell, SEOG, state scholarships/grants, private scholarships, the school's own gift aid. *Loans:* Subsidized Stafford, Unsubsidized Stafford, PLUS, Federal Perkins. **Student Employment:** Federal Work-Study Program available. Institutional employment available. **Financial Aid Statistics:** 100% freshmen, 99% undergrads receive need-based scholarship or grant aid. 34% freshmen, 29% undergrads receive non-need-based scholarship or grant aid. 60% freshmen, 45% undergrads receive need-based self-help aid. 52% freshmen, 62% undergrads receive any aid. 58% undergrads borrow to pay for school. Average cumulative indebtedness $13,767. **Criteria for awarding institutional aid:** *Non-need-based:* academics, leadership, minority status.

GANNON UNIVERSITY

109 University Square, Erie, PA 16541
Phone: 814-871-7240 • **Financial Aid Phone:** 814-871-7337
E-mail: gannon.edu/admiss/default.asp • **CEEB Code:** 2270
Fax: 814-871-5803 • **Website:** www.gannon.edu • **ACT Code:** 3576

This private school, affiliated with the Roman Catholic Church, was founded in 1925. It has a 13-acre campus.

RATINGS
Admissions Selectivity Rating: 68 **Fire Safety Rating:** 95 **Green Rating:** 61

STUDENTS AND FACULTY
Enrollment: 2,652. **Student Body:** 59% female, 41% male, 24% out-of-state, 4% international (34 countries represented). Asian 1%, African American 7%, Caucasian 82%, Hispanic 2%, Native American 0%.
Retention and Graduation: 44% grads go on to further study within 1 year. 36% grads pursue arts and sciences degrees. 2% grads pursue law degrees. 3% grads pursue business degrees. 2% grads pursue medical degrees. **Faculty:** Student/faculty ratio 14:1. 197 full-time faculty, 74% hold PhDs, 10% are members of minority groups, 46% are women. 1% of classes are taught by teaching assistants.

ACADEMICS

Degrees: associate, bachelor's, certificate, master's, post-bachelor's certificate, post-master's certificate. **Classes:** Most classes have 10–19 students. Most lab/discussion sessions have 10–19 students. **Majors with Highest Enrollment:** kinesiology and exercise science; nursing/registered nurse (rn, asn, bsn, msn); physician assistant. **Special Study Options:** Accelerated program, distance learning, double major, dual enrollment, honors program, independent study, internships, liberal arts/career combination, study abroad, teacher certification program. **Honors Programs:** Gannon offers an honors program for the academically talented and highly motivated students. Last year, 246 students participated in honors classes that were small in size and staffed by Gannon's best teachers. **Combined Degree Programs:** BA/MD, BA/JD, BA/MA, BS/MBA. **Disability Services:** Special programs offered to physically disabled students include note-taking services, reader services, tape recorders, tutors. **Career Services:** Alumni network, alumni services, career/job search classes, career assessment, internships, regional alumni., Career Services highlights include The Career Road Show program we offer - it has the Career Development staff making over 55 in-class career and job search presentations each year. The program continues to grow and students benefit from learning valuable career information taught in classes within their major.

FACILITIES

Housing: Coed dorms, special housing for disabled students, apartments for single students. 85% of campus accessible to physically disabled. **Special Academic Facilities/Equipment:** Laser and spectrographic labs, Patient Simulation Center, metallurgy institute, computer-integrated manufacturing facilities, Schuster Art Gallery, Schuster Theatres, Erie Technology Incubator. **Computers:** 100% of classrooms, 100% of dorms, 100% of libraries, 100% of dining areas, 100% of student union, 100% of common outdoor areas have wireless network access. Students can register for classes online. Administrative functions (other than registration) can be performed online.

CAMPUS LIFE

Environment: City. **Activities:** Choral groups, concert band, dance, drama/theater, literary magazine, music ensembles, musical theater, pep band, radio station, student government, student newspaper, yearbook, Campus Ministries, International Student Organization, Model UN 71 registered organizations, 11 honor societies, 6 religious organizations. 5 fraternities, 5 sororities. **Athletics (Intercollegiate):** *Men:* baseball, basketball, cheerleading, cross-country, football, golf, soccer, swimming, water polo, wrestling. *Women:* basketball, cheerleading, cross-country, golf, lacrosse, soccer, softball, swimming, volleyball, water polo. **On-Campus Highlights:** Multi-purpose Athletic Field, Waldron Campus Center, A.J. Palumbo Academic Center, Carnaval Athletic Pavilion, Zurn Science Center, Schuster Art Gallery Morosky College of Health Professions and Science. **Environmental Initiatives:** Switching out all campus light fixtures to compact flourescent. Purchasing 15% of energy from wind power. Experimenting with and switching to green cleaning products.

ADMISSIONS

Freshman Academic Profile: Average high school GPA 3.5. 22% in top 10% of high school class, 52% in top 25% of high school class, 80% in top 50% of high school class. 80% from public high schools. SAT Math middle 50% range 460-580. SAT Critical Reading middle 50% range 450-570. ACT middle 50% range 20-25. Minimum web-based TOEFL 79. Minimum paper TOEFL 550. **Basis for Candidate Selection:** *Very important factors considered include:*

Class rank, academic GPA, rigor of secondary school record, standardized test scores. *Important factors considered include:* recommendation(s), level of applicant's interest. *Other factors considered include:* application essay, extracurricular activities, interview, talent/ability, volunteer work. **Freshman Admission Requirements:** High school diploma is required and GED is accepted. *Academic units required:* 4 English, 2 social studies, 1 history, 3 academic electives. *Academic units recommended:* 4 English, 2 social studies, 1 history, 3 academic electives. **Freshman Admission Statistics:** 3,633 applied, 85% admitted, 22% enrolled. **Transfer Admission Requirements:** college transcript(s), statement of good standing from prior institution(s). Minimum college GPA of 2.0 required. Lowest grade transferable C. **General Admission Information:** Application Fee $25. Notification on a rolling basis, beginning on or about 9/15. Nonfall registration accepted. Admission may be deferred for a maximum of 1 year. Credit and/or placement offered for CEEB Advanced Placement tests.

COSTS AND FINANCIAL AID
Required Forms and Deadlines: FAFSA, institution's own financial aid form. **Notification of Awards:** Applicants will be notified of awards on a rolling basis beginning 11/1. **Types of Aid:** *Need-based scholarships/grants:* Federal Pell, SEOG, state scholarships/grants, private scholarships, the school's own gift aid. *Loans:* Direct Subsidized Stafford, Direct Unsubsidized Stafford, Direct PLUS, Subsidized Stafford, Unsubsidized Stafford, PLUS, Federal Perkins. **Student Employment:** Federal Work-Study Program available. Institutional employment available. Highest amount earned per year from on-campus jobs $2,300. Off-campus job opportunities are good. **Financial Aid Statistics:** 98% freshmen, 98% undergrads receive need-based scholarship or grant aid. 14% freshmen, 14% undergrads receive non-need-based scholarship or grant aid. 88% freshmen, 89% undergrads receive need-based self-help aid. 1% freshmen, 3% undergrads receive athletic scholarships. 95% freshmen, 94% undergrads receive any aid. 92% undergrads borrow to pay for school. Average cumulative indebtedness $33,541. **Criteria for awarding institutional aid:** *Non-need-based:* academics, athletics, leadership, music/drama, religious affiliation.

GARDNER-WEBB UNIVERSITY

PO Box 817, Boiling Springs, NC 28017
Phone: 704-406-4498 • **Financial Aid Phone:** 704-406-4243
E-mail: admissions@gardner-webb.edu • **CEEB Code:** 5242
Fax: 704-406-4488 • **Website:** www.gardner-webb.edu • **ACT Code:** 3102

This private school, affiliated with the Baptist Church, was founded in 1905. It has a 250-acre campus.

RATINGS
Admissions Selectivity Rating: 77   **Fire Safety Rating:** 89   **Green Rating:** 61

STUDENTS AND FACULTY
Enrollment: 2,640. **Student Body:** 65% female, 35% male, 21% out-of-state, 0% international (22 countries represented). Asian 0%, African American 19%, Caucasian 73%, Hispanic 2%, Native American 1%.
Retention and Graduation: 36% freshmen graduate within 4 years. 49% freshmen graduate within 6 years. **Faculty:** Student/faculty ratio 13:1. 140 full-time faculty, 80% hold PhDs, 4% are members of minority groups, 46% are women. 0% of classes are taught by teaching assistants.

ACADEMICS
Degrees: associate, bachelor's, doctoral, master's. **Classes:** Most classes have fewer than 10 students. **Majors with Highest Enrollment:** business/commerce; religion/religious studies; social sciences, other. **Special Study Options:** Accelerated program, distance learning, double major, dual enrollment, English as a Second Language (ESL), honors program, independent study, internships, liberal arts/career combination, study abroad, teacher certification program. **Honors Programs:** Alpha Chi Honors Program Beta Beta Beta Delta Mu Delta Sigma Delta Pi Sigma Tau Delta Theta Alpha Kappa Pi Delta Phi Psi Chi Sigma Zeta Sigma Theta Tau Who's Who **Combined Degree Programs:** Music-Business - BM/MBA. **Disability Services:** Special programs offered to physically disabled students include note-taking services, reader services, tape recorders, tutors. **Career Services:** Alumni network, career/job search classes, career assessment, internships, Career Services highlights include Our Career Services office organizes a mock formal dinner interview and sponsors the Metrolina Career Fair and a Nursing Career Fair.

FACILITIES
Housing: special housing for disabled students, men's dorms, women's dorms, apartments for single students, wellness housing, Housing for Honor Students. 100% of campus accessible to physically disabled. **Special Academic Facilities/Equipment:** Williams Observatory, Millennium Playhouse, Broyhill Adventure Course, Lake Hollifield Complex and Carillon **Computers:** 100%

of classrooms, 100% of dorms, 100% of libraries, 100% of dining areas, 100% of student union, 100% of common outdoor areas have wireless network access. Students can register for classes online. Administrative functions (other than registration) can be performed online.

CAMPUS LIFE
Environment: Rural. **Activities:** Choral groups, concert band, dance, drama/theater, jazz band, literary magazine, marching band, music ensembles, musical theater, opera, pep band, radio station, student government, student newspaper, symphony orchestra, yearbook, Campus Ministries, International Student Organization 65 registered organizations, 12 honor societies, 11 religious organizations. **Athletics (Intercollegiate):** *Men:* baseball, basketball, cheerleading, cross-country, football, golf, soccer, swimming, tennis, track/field (outdoor), track/field (indoor), wrestling. *Women:* basketball, cheerleading, cross-country, golf, soccer, softball, swimming, tennis, track/field (outdoor), track/field (indoor), volleyball. **On-Campus Highlights:** Dover Campus Center, Suttle Wellness Center, Cafeteria, Lutz-Yelton Convocation Center, Kennel Snack Bar. **Environmental Initiatives:** recycling programs environmental science major with student projects.

ADMISSIONS
Freshman Academic Profile: Average high school GPA 3.5. 32% in top 10% of high school class, 49% in top 25% of high school class, 72% in top 50% of high school class. 84% from public high schools. SAT Math middle 50% range 420-550. SAT Critical Reading middle 50% range 440-560. ACT middle 50% range 18-23. Minimum web-based TOEFL 61. Minimum paper TOEFL 500. **Basis for Candidate Selection:** *Very important factors considered include:* academic GPA, rigor of secondary school record, standardized test scores, level of applicant's interest. *Important factors considered include:* Class rank, recommendation(s), character/personal qualities, extracurricular activities. *Other factors considered include:* application essay, interview, talent/ability, volunteer work. **Freshman Admission Requirements:** High school diploma is required and GED is accepted. **Freshman Admission Statistics:** 3,277 applied, 62% admitted, 22% enrolled. **Transfer Admission Requirements:** college transcript(s), statement of good standing from prior institution(s). Minimum college GPA of 2.25 required. Lowest grade transferable C. **General Admission Information:** Application Fee $40. Notification on a rolling basis, beginning on or about 9/1. Nonfall registration accepted. Admission may be deferred for a maximum of 2 Semesters. Credit and/or placement offered for CEEB Advanced Placement tests.

COSTS AND FINANCIAL AID
Annual tuition $22,050. Room and board $7,195. Required fees $390. Average book expense $1,000. **Required Forms and Deadlines:** FAFSA, state aid form. **Notification of Awards:** Applicants will be notified of awards on a rolling basis beginning 3/1. **Types of Aid:** *Need-based scholarships/grants:* Federal Pell, SEOG, state scholarships/grants, private scholarships, the school's own gift aid. *Loans:* Subsidized Stafford, Unsubsidized Stafford, PLUS, Federal Perkins, Federal Nursing, state loans. **Student Employment:** Federal Work-Study Program available. Institutional employment available. Off-campus job opportunities are good. **Financial Aid Statistics:** 96% freshmen, 34% undergrads receive need-based scholarship or grant aid. 77% freshmen, 70% undergrads receive non-need-based scholarship or grant aid. 66% freshmen, 75% undergrads receive need-based self-help aid. 100% freshmen receive any aid. **Criteria for awarding institutional aid:** *Non-need-based:* academics, athletics, leadership, music/drama, state/district residency.

GENEVA COLLEGE

3200 College Avenue, Beaver Falls, PA 15010
Phone: 724-847-6500 • **Financial Aid Phone:** 724-847-6530
E-mail: admissions@geneva.edu • **CEEB Code:** 2273
Fax: 724-847-6776 • **Website:** www.geneva.edu/ • **ACT Code:** 33578

This private school was founded in 1848. It has a 55-acre campus.

RATINGS
Admissions Selectivity Rating: 80   **Fire Safety Rating:** 70   **Green Rating:** 60*

STUDENTS AND FACULTY
Enrollment: 1,340. **Student Body:** 54% female, 46% male, 26% out-of-state, 1% international (7 countries represented). Asian 1%, African American 15%, Caucasian 105%, Hispanic 1%, Native American 0%.
Retention and Graduation: 78% freshmen return for sophomore year. 45% freshmen graduate within 4 years. 58% freshmen graduate within 6 years. 32% grads go on to further study within 1 year. **Faculty:** Student/faculty ratio 13:1. 84 full-time faculty, 76% hold PhDs, 8% are members of minority groups, 35% are women. 0% of classes are taught by teaching assistants.

ACADEMICS

Degrees: associate, bachelor's, master's. **Classes:** Most classes have 10–19 students. **Majors with Highest Enrollment:** bible/biblical studies; business/commerce; elementary education and teaching. **Special Study Options:** Accelerated program, cooperative education program, cross-registration, double major, dual enrollment, honors program, independent study, internships, student-designed major, study abroad, teacher certification program. **Honors Programs:** Freshmen Honors Program. **Combined Degree Programs:** BA/MA, Psychology and Business. **Disability Services:** Special programs offered to physically disabled students include note-taking services, reader services, tape recorders, tutors. **Career Services:** Alumni network, alumni services, career/job search classes, career assessment, internships.

FACILITIES

Housing: men's dorms, women's dorms, apartments for single students, 85% of campus accessible to physically disabled. **Special Academic Facilities/Equipment:** Center for Technology Development **Computers:** Students can register for classes online. Administrative functions (other than registration) can be performed online.

CAMPUS LIFE

Environment: Village. **Activities:** Choral groups, concert band, dance, drama/theater, jazz band, literary magazine, marching band, music ensembles, pep band, radio station, student government, student newspaper, yearbook 56 registered organizations, 5 honor societies, 11 religious organizations. **Athletics (Intercollegiate):** *Men:* baseball, basketball, cross-country, football, soccer, track/field (outdoor), track/field (indoor). *Women:* basketball, cheerleading, cross-country, soccer, softball, tennis, track/field (outdoor), track/field (indoor), volleyball. **On-Campus Highlights:** The Riverview Cafe (Coffee Shop), The Briagadoon (Cafe-Casual Dining), The Fitness Center, Track/Soccer Field, Skye Lounge - Student Center.

ADMISSIONS

Freshman Academic Profile: Average high school GPA 3.4. 16% in top 10% of high school class, 37% in top 25% of high school class, 71% in top 50% of high school class. 72% from public high schools. SAT Math middle 50% range 480-590. SAT Critical Reading middle 50% range 490-610. ACT middle 50% range 20-25. Minimum paper TOEFL 480. **Basis for Candidate Selection:** *Very important factors considered include:* application essay, academic GPA, rigor of secondary school record, standardized test scores. *Other factors considered include:* Class rank, recommendation(s), alumni/ae relation, character/personal qualities, extracurricular activities, interview. **Freshman Admission Requirements:** High school diploma is required and GED is accepted. *Academic units required:* 4 English, 2 mathematics, 1 science, 2 foreign language, 3 social studies, 4 academic electives. 4 English, 2 mathematics, 1 science, 2 foreign language, 3 social studies, 4 academic electives. **Freshman Admission Statistics:** 1,329 applied, 64% admitted, 35% enrolled. **Transfer Admission Requirements:** High school transcript, college transcript(s), essay or personal statement, minimum college GPA of 2.0 required. Lowest grade transferable C–. **General Admission Information:** Application Fee $40. Notification on a rolling basis, beginning on or about 9/1. Nonfall registration accepted. Admission may be deferred for a maximum of 3 years. Credit and/or placement offered for CEEB Advanced Placement tests.

COSTS AND FINANCIAL AID

Annual tuition $19,430. Room and board $7,200. Average book expense $800. **Required Forms and Deadlines:** FAFSA. **Notification of Awards:** Applicants will be notified of awards on a rolling basis beginning 3/15. **Types of Aid:** *Need-based scholarships/grants:* Federal Pell, SEOG, state scholarships/grants, private scholarships, the school's own gift aid, FSEOG. *Loans:* Subsidized Stafford, Unsubsidized Stafford, PLUS, Federal Perkins. **Student Employment:** Federal Work-Study Program available. Institutional employment available. Highest amount earned per year from on-campus jobs $2,000. Off-campus job opportunities are fair. **Financial Aid Statistics:** 100% freshmen, 99% undergrads receive need-based scholarship or grant aid. 12% freshmen, 11% undergrads receive non-need-based scholarship or grant aid. 85% freshmen, 85% undergrads receive need-based self-help aid. 3% undergrads receive athletic scholarships. 95% freshmen, 92% undergrads receive any aid. 96% undergrads borrow to pay for school. Average cumulative indebtedness $26,034. **Criteria for awarding institutional aid:** *Non-need-based:* academics, athletics, music/drama, religious affiliation.

GEORGE FOX UNIVERSITY

414 N. Meridian St., Newberg, OR 97132
Phone: 503-554-2240 • **Financial Aid Phone:** 503-554-2290
E-mail: admissions@georgefox.edu • **CEEB Code:** 4325
Fax: 503-554-3110 • **Website:** www.georgefox.edu • **ACT Code:** 3462

This private school was founded in 1891. It has a 85-acre campus.

RATINGS

Admissions Selectivity Rating: 75   **Fire Safety Rating:** 80   **Green Rating:** 60*

STUDENTS AND FACULTY

Enrollment: 2,165. **Student Body:** 60% female, 40% male, 35% out-of-state, 6% international (43 countries represented). Asian 4%, African American 2%, Caucasian 72%, Hispanic 7%, Native American 1%. **Retention and Graduation:** 53% freshmen graduate within 4 years. 64% freshmen graduate within 6 years. 11% grads go on to further study within 1 year. 6% grads pursue arts and sciences degrees. 2% grads pursue business degrees. 2% grads pursue medical degrees. **Faculty:** Student/faculty ratio 13:1. 163 full-time faculty, 77% hold PhDs, 9% are members of minority groups, 37% are women. 0% of classes are taught by teaching assistants.

ACADEMICS

Degrees: bachelor's, master's, post-bachelor's certificate, post-master's certificate. **Classes:** Most classes have 10–19 students. Most lab/discussion sessions have 10–19 students. **Majors with Highest Enrollment:** business administration and management; elementary education and teaching; nursing/registered nurse (rn, asn, bsn, msn) **Special Study Options:** Accelerated program, cross-registration, double major, dual enrollment, English as a Second Language (ESL), exchange student program (domestic), honors program, independent study, internships, student-designed major, study abroad, teacher certification program. **Honors Programs:** University Scholars, Richter Scholars, Honors Scholarships, Advance Leadership Development Program **Combined Degree Programs:** 3-1 coop. program in design and merchandising. **Disability Services:** Special programs offered to physically disabled students include note-taking services, reader services, tape recorders, tutors. **Career Services:** Alumni network, alumni services, career/job search classes, career assessment, internships, regional alumni. Career Services highlights include All.

FACILITIES

Housing: special housing for disabled students, men's dorms, women's dorms, apartments for single students, wellness housing, theme housing, houses. 98% of campus accessible to physically disabled. **Special Academic Facilities/Equipment:** nuclear magnetic resonance spectrometer, Providence Nursing Learning Lab, language lab, electron microscope. **Computers:** 100% of classrooms, 90% of dorms, 100% of libraries, 100% of dining areas, 100% of student union, 50% of common outdoor areas have wireless network access. Students can register for classes online. Administrative functions (other than registration) can be performed online.

CAMPUS LIFE

Environment: Village. **Activities:** Choral groups, concert band, drama/theater, jazz band, literary magazine, music ensembles, musical theater, pep band, radio station, student government, student newspaper, symphony orchestra, yearbook, Campus Ministries, International Student Organization 20 registered organizations, 3 honor societies, 3 religious organizations. **Athletics (Intercollegiate):** *Men:* baseball, basketball, cross-country, golf, soccer, tennis, track/field (outdoor). *Women:* basketball, cross-country, golf, soccer, softball, tennis, track/field (outdoor), volleyball. **On-Campus Highlights:** Bruin Den-Cafe in the Student Union Bldg, The Foxhole-Student-run coffee house, Dorm Movie Rooms-most have movie areas, Wheeler Sports Center **Environmental Initiatives:** LEED-certified residence hall Fleet vehicle hybrid purchases Progressive recycling program

ADMISSIONS

Freshman Academic Profile: Average high school GPA 3.6. 31% in top 10% of high school class, 62% in top 25% of high school class, 91% in top 50% of high school class. 73% from public high schools. SAT Math middle 50% range 500-620. SAT Critical Reading middle 50% range 490-630. SAT Writing middle 50% range 470-600. ACT middle 50% range 21-27. Minimum web-based TOEFL 80. Minimum paper TOEFL 550. **Basis for Candidate Selection:** *Very important factors considered include:* rigor of secondary school record. *Important factors considered include:* application essay, academic GPA, recommendation(s), standardized test scores. *Other factors considered include:* character/personal qualities, extracurricular activities, interview, religious affiliation/commitment, talent/ability, volunteer work, work experience. **Freshman Admission Requirements:** High school diploma is required and GED is accepted. **Freshman Admission Statistics:** 2,215 applied, 75% admitted, 25% enrolled. **Transfer Admission Requirements:** college transcript(s), essay or personal statement, statement of good standing from prior institution(s). Minimum college GPA of 2.6 required. Lowest grade transferable C–. **General Admission Information:** Application Fee $40. Notification on a rolling basis, beginning on or about 10/1. Nonfall registration accepted. Admission may be deferred for a maximum of 1 yr. Credit and/or placement offered for CEEB Advanced Placement tests.

COSTS AND FINANCIAL AID

Annual tuition $29,900. Room and board $9,360. Required fees $330. Average book expense $950. **Required Forms and Deadlines:** FAFSA, state aid form. **Notification of Awards:** Applicants will be notified of awards on a rolling basis beginning 3/1. **Types of Aid:** *Need-based scholarships/grants:* Federal Pell, SEOG, state scholarships/grants, private scholarships, the school's own gift aid, ACG & SMART, TEACH Grants. *Loans:* Direct Subsidized Stafford, Direct Unsubsidized Stafford, Direct PLUS, Federal Perkins, Alternative loans. **Student Employment:** Federal Work-Study Program available. Institutional employment available. Highest amount earned per year from on-campus jobs $3,715. Off-campus job opportunities are good. **Financial Aid Statistics:** 94% freshmen, 92% undergrads receive need-based scholarship or grant aid. 80% freshmen, 80% undergrads receive non-need-based scholarship or grant aid. 100% freshmen, 100% undergrads receive need-based self-help aid. 98% freshmen, 96% undergrads receive any aid. 79% undergrads borrow to pay for school. Average cumulative indebtedness $23,512. **Criteria for awarding institutional aid:** *Non-need-based:* academics, alumni affiliation, art, job skills, leadership, minority status, music/drama, religious affiliation.

GEORGE MASON UNIVERSITY

4400 University Drive, Fairfax, VA 22030-4444
Phone: 703-993-2400 • **Financial Aid Phone:** 703-993-2341
E-mail: admissions@gmu.edu • **CEEB Code:** 5827
Fax: 703-993-4622 • **Website:** www.gmu.edu • **ACT Code:** 4357

This public school was founded in 1972. It has a 806-acre campus.

RATINGS
Admissions Selectivity Rating: 89   **Fire Safety Rating:** 91   **Green Rating:** 93

STUDENTS AND FACULTY
Enrollment: 20,067. **Student Body:** 52% female, 48% male, 11% out-of-state, 4% international (134 countries represented). Asian 17%, African American 9%, Caucasian 46%, Hispanic 11%, Native American 0%.
Retention and Graduation: 86% freshmen return for sophomore year. 42% freshmen graduate within 4 years. 66% freshmen graduate within 6 years. 8% grads go on to further study within 1 year. 34% grads pursue arts and sciences degrees. 13% grads pursue law degrees. 8% grads pursue business degrees. 8% grads pursue medical degrees. **Faculty:** 1155 full-time faculty, 91% hold PhDs, 15% are members of minority groups, 41% are women. 5% of classes are taught by teaching assistants.

ACADEMICS
Degrees: bachelor's, first professional, master's, post-bachelor's certificate, post-master's certificate. **Classes:** Most classes have 20–29 students. Most lab/discussion sessions have 20–29 students. **Majors with Highest Enrollment:** biology/biological sciences; political science and government; psychology. **Special Study Options:** Accelerated program, cooperative education program, cross-registration, distance learning, double major, dual enrollment, English as a Second Language (ESL), exchange student program (domestic), external degree program, honors program, independent study, internships, liberal arts/career combination, student-designed major, study abroad, teacher certification program. **Honors Programs:** Honors Program in General Education provides small courses with outstanding faculty. The University Scholars program provides an elite group of students with exceptional academic and research opportunities in a dynamic community of learners. **Combined Degree Programs:** BS/MS. **Disability Services:** Special programs offered to physically disabled students include note-taking services, reader services, tape recorders. **Career Services:** Alumni network, alumni services, career/job search classes, career assessment, internships, regional alumni. Career Services highlights include Current initiative to increase student uptake of federal government internship opportunities (Federal Student Career Experience Program-SCEP). Students enroll for SCEP positions through Mason's Cooperative Education program. Cooperative Education employs students in the DC metro area and adds value

to student degree. Internships can be taken in concert with Co-op or stand alone.

FACILITIES
Housing: Coed dorms, special housing for disabled students, men's dorms, women's dorms, apartments for single students. 95% of campus accessible to physically disabled. **Special Academic Facilities/Equipment:** Center for the Arts, science/technology building, television studio, art galleries in Mason Hall and Johnson Center, astronomy observatory, Smithsonian Conservation and Research Center. **Computers:** 30% of classrooms, 100% of dorms, 100% of libraries, 100% of dining areas, 100% of student union, 5% of common outdoor areas have wireless network access. Students can register for classes online. Administrative functions (other than registration) can be performed online.

CAMPUS LIFE
Environment: City. **Activities:** Choral groups, concert band, dance, drama/theater, jazz band, literary magazine, music ensembles, musical theater, opera, pep band, radio station, student government, student newspaper, student-run film society, symphony orchestra, television station, yearbook, Campus Ministries, International Student Organization 250 registered organizations, 7 honor societies, 29 religious organizations. 22 fraternities, 13 sororities. **Athletics (Intercollegiate):** *Men:* baseball, basketball, cheerleading, cross-country, diving, golf, soccer, swimming, tennis, track/field (outdoor), track/field (indoor), volleyball, wrestling. *Women:* basketball, cheerleading, crew/rowing, cross-country, diving, lacrosse, soccer, softball, swimming, tennis, track/field (outdoor), track/field (indoor), volleyball. **On-Campus Highlights:** Johnson Center, Aquatic and Fitness Center, Center for the Arts, Patriot Center, Freedom Aquatic Center at Prince William. **Environmental Initiatives:** Climate neutrality: Have signed on to the American College and University Presidents Climate Committment. Our inaugural Climate Action Plan was published (last year) on the ACUPCC website (http://acupcc.aashe.org/cap/84/.) Work toward executing this plan began in January 2010. Built environment: Have committed all new buildings to be built to the USGBC LEED Silver standard, and have 6 registered projects in the queue for certification at this time. LEED standards are being worked into our Design Manual guidelines for all contractors. Transportation: Have put in place multiple shuttles to the metro and to off-campus lots; provide transportation credits to employees; free local bus rides to all Mason ID holders; bike committee examining ways to increase cycling accessibility on campus; Bike to Mason day on Earth Day being planned; van pool is offered to employees coming in from far away at a reduced monthly cost versus driving and parking; rideshare and carpooling is being promoted. Mason also offers Gunston's Go-Bus, a social shuttle service provided free to all Mason community members who travel to local establishments.

ADMISSIONS
Freshman Academic Profile: Average high school GPA 3.7. 23% in top 10% of high school class, 60% in top 25% of high school class, 93% in top 50% of high school class. 89% from public high schools. SAT Math middle 50% range 530-630. SAT Critical Reading middle 50% range 520-620. ACT middle 50% range 23-28. Minimum web-based TOEFL 88. Minimum paper TOEFL 570. **Basis for Candidate Selection:** *Very important factors considered include:* academic GPA, rigor of secondary school record. *Important factors considered include:* Class rank, application essay, recommendation(s), alumni/ae relation, character/personal qualities, talent/ability. *Other factors considered include:* standardized test scores, extracurricular activities, first generation, level of applicant's interest, volunteer work, work experience. **Freshman Admission Requirements:** High school diploma is required and GED is accepted. *Academic units required:* 4 English, 3 mathematics, 3 science, (3 science labs), 2 foreign language, 3 social studies, 3 academic electives. *Academic units recommended:* 4 English, 3 mathematics, 3 science, (3 science labs), 2 foreign language, 3 social studies, 3 academic electives. **Freshman Admission Statistics:** 17,621 applied, 55% admitted, 28% enrolled. **Transfer Admission Requirements:** college transcript(s), minimum college GPA of 2.0 required. Lowest grade transferable C. **General Admission Information:** Application Fee $70. Regular application deadline 1/15. Regular notification 4/1. Nonfall registration accepted. Admission may be deferred for a maximum of one semester. Credit and/or placement offered for CEEB Advanced Placement tests.

COSTS AND FINANCIAL AID
Annual in-state tuition $7,010. Annual out-of-state tuition $25,154. Room and board $9,250. Required fees $2,610. Average book expense $1,120. **Required Forms and Deadlines:** FAFSA. **Notification of Awards:** Applicants will be notified of awards on a rolling basis beginning 4/1. **Types of Aid:** *Need-based scholarships/grants:* Federal Pell, SEOG, state scholarships/grants, private scholarships, the school's own gift aid, Federal ACG and SMART Grants. *Loans:* Subsidized Stafford, Unsubsidized Stafford, PLUS, Federal Perkins, Federal Nursing. **Student Employment:** Federal Work-Study Program available. Institutional employment available. Highest amount earned per year from on-campus jobs $7,200. Off-campus job opportunities are excellent. **Financial Aid Statistics:** 73% freshmen, 74% undergrads receive need-based scholarship or grant aid. 33% freshmen, 17% undergrads receive non-need-based scholar-

ship or grant aid. 78% freshmen, 81% undergrads receive need-based self-help aid. 2% freshmen, 2% undergrads receive athletic scholarships. 68% freshmen, 58% undergrads receive any aid. 57% undergrads borrow to pay for school. Average cumulative indebtedness $25,822. **Criteria for awarding institutional aid:** *Non-need-based:* academics, athletics, minority status, music/drama, state/district residency.

THE GEORGE WASHINGTON UNIVERSITY

2121 Eye Street NW, Suite 201, Washington, DC 20052
Phone: 202-994-6040
E-mail: gwadm@gwu.edu • **CEEB Code:** 5246
Fax: 202-994-0325 • **Website:** www.gwu.edu • **ACT Code:** 664

This private school was founded in 1821. It has a 45-acre campus.

RATINGS
Admissions Selectivity Rating: 95   **Fire Safety Rating:** 60*   **Green Rating:** 94

STUDENTS AND FACULTY
Enrollment: 10,184. **Student Body:** 56% female, 44% male, 98% out-of-state, 7% international (134 countries represented). Asian 10%, African American 7%, Caucasian 57%, Hispanic 7%, Native American 0%.
Retention and Graduation: 94% freshmen return for sophomore year. 76% freshmen graduate within 4 years. 22% grads go on to further study within 1 year. 48% grads pursue arts and sciences degrees. 31% grads pursue law degrees. 2% grads pursue business degrees. 18% grads pursue medical degrees. **Faculty:** Student/faculty ratio 13:1. 942 full-time faculty, 92% hold PhDs, 21% are members of minority groups, 40% are women. 3% of classes are taught by teaching assistants.

ACADEMICS
Degrees: associate, bachelor's, certificate, master's, post-bachelor's certificate, post-master's certificate. **Classes:** Most classes have 10–19 students. Most lab/discussion sessions have 20–29 students. **Majors with Highest Enrollment:** business administration and management; international relations and affairs; liberal arts and sciences/liberal studies. **Special Study Options:** Accelerated program, cooperative education program, cross-registration, distance learning, double major, dual enrollment, honors program, independent study, internships, liberal arts/career combination, student-designed major, study abroad. **Combined Degree Programs:** BA/MD, BA/JD, BA/MA. **Disability Services:** Special programs offered to physically disabled students include note-taking services, reader services, tape recorders, tutors.

FACILITIES
Housing: Coed dorms, fraternity/sorority housing, apartments for single students, theme housing. **Special Academic Facilities/Equipment:** Art gallery, language lab, word processing center. **Computers:** Students can register for classes online. Administrative functions (other than registration) can be performed online.

CAMPUS LIFE
Environment: Metropolis. **Activities:** Choral groups, concert band, dance, drama/theater, jazz band, literary magazine, marching band, music ensembles, musical theater, pep band, radio station, student government, student newspaper, student-run film society, television station, yearbook, International Student Organization, Model UN 220 registered organizations, 3 honor societies, 5 religious organizations. 12 fraternities, 9 sororities. **Athletics (Intercollegiate):** *Men:* baseball, basketball, crew/rowing, cross-country, diving, fencing, golf, rugby, soccer, squash, swimming, tennis, water polo. *Women:* basketball, crew/rowing, cross-country, fencing, gymnastics, soccer, swimming, tennis, volleyball. **On-Campus Highlights:** The Smith Center, The Hippo, Media and Public Affairs Building, Kogan Plaza, Gelman Library. **Environmental Initiatives:** 1. GW's mission is to be the premier university on policy and governance for sustainable systems through practice, teaching, research, and outreach. The University is deploying a pan-university approach that bridges traditional disciplines. In Fall 2012 GW will offer an interdisciplinary Minor in Sustainability to all undergraduate students. The minor is a pan-university offering that provides students with inter-disciplinary teaching (with a team-taught course taught by faculty representing several schools) and experiential learning (which challenges students to apply knowledge, theory and methods learned in the classroom to analyze a real-world sustainability issue and/or practice). 2. Strategic Plan and

Targets including GWater Plan Commitment and ACUPCC/Climate Action Plan Commitment. In Spring 2011 GW released a comprehensive plan for water sustainability. The GWater Plan takes a holistic look at GW's water footprint. GW was one of the first universities to disclose its full water footprint and has set goals and targets to address its water sustainability across its potable water, rainfall capture, water quality and bottled water footprints. The full plan can be found here: http://www.gwu.edu/staticfile/GW/News%20and%20Events/6.%20Initiatives/1.%20Sustainability/Resources/GWater%20Plan.pdf The University's commitment to developing a plan towards carbon neutrality represents GW's environmental commitment. As an urban school with many older buildings, becoming carbon neutral will require a significant investment in order to develop the appropriate infrastructure. 3. Commitment to LEED. GW is committed to achieving a minimum of LEED Silver certification on all new construction and GW's two newest buildings " both residence halls - are LEED Gold certified. GW's commitment to designing buildings that are both comfortable for GW's students as well as environmentally friendly is part of GW's commitment to becoming a leader in urban sustainability.

ADMISSIONS
Freshman Academic Profile: 78% in top 10% of high school class, 95% in top 25% of high school class, 100% in top 50% of high school class. 70% from public high schools. SAT Math middle 50% range 610-690. SAT Critical Reading middle 50% range 600-690. SAT Writing middle 50% range 620-710. ACT middle 50% range 27-31. Minimum paper TOEFL 550. **Basis for Candidate Selection:** *Very important factors considered include:* academic GPA, rigor of secondary school record. *Important factors considered include:* Class rank, application essay, recommendation(s), standardized test scores, extracurricular activities, interview, talent/ability, volunteer work. *Other factors considered include:* alumni/ae relation, character/personal qualities, first generation, geographical residence, level of applicant's interest, racial/ethnic status, work experience. **Freshman Admission Requirements:** High school diploma is required and GED is not accepted. *Academic units required:* 4 English, 2 mathematics, 2 science, (1 science labs), 2 foreign language, 2 social studies. *Academic units recommended:* 4 English, 2 mathematics, 2 science, (1 science labs), 2 foreign language, 2 social studies. **Freshman Admission Statistics:** 21,591 applied, 33% admitted, 31% enrolled. **Transfer Admission Requirements:** High school transcript, college transcript(s), essay or personal statement, standardized test scores, Lowest grade transferable C. **General Admission Information:** Application Fee $65. Early decision application deadline 11/10. Regular application deadline 1/10. Regular notification 4/1. Nonfall registration accepted. Credit and/or placement offered for CEEB Advanced Placement tests.

COSTS AND FINANCIAL AID
Annual tuition $43,702. Room and board $13,050. Required fees $45. Average book expense $1,275. Required Forms and Deadlines: FAFSA, CSS/Financial Aid PROFILE. Notification of Awards: Applicants will be notified of awards on a rolling basis beginning 3/21. Types of Aid: Need-based scholarships/grants: Federal Pell, SEOG, state scholarships/grants, the school's own gift aid. Loans: Subsidized Stafford, Unsubsidized Stafford, PLUS, Federal Perkins. Student Employment: Federal Work-Study Program available. Institutional employment available. Highest amount earned per year from on-campus jobs $3,160. Off-campus job opportunities are excellent. Financial Aid Statistics: 97% freshmen, 95% undergrads receive need-based scholarship or grant aid. 48% freshmen, 28% undergrads receive non-need-based scholarship or grant aid. 80% freshmen, 82% undergrads receive need-based self-help aid. 2% freshmen, 2% undergrads receive athletic scholarships. Average cumulative indebtedness $32,714. Criteria for awarding institutional aid: Non-need-based: academics, art, athletics, music/drama.

GEORGETOWN COLLEGE

400 East College Street, Georgetown, KY 40324
Phone: 502-863-8009 • **Financial Aid Phone:** 502-863-8027
E-mail: admissions@georgetowncollege.edu • **CEEB Code:** 1249
Fax: 502-868-7733 • **Website:** www.georgetowncollege.edu • **ACT Code:** 1514

This private school was founded in 1787. It has a 104-acre campus.

RATINGS
Admissions Selectivity Rating: 69   **Fire Safety Rating:** 61   **Green Rating:** 69

STUDENTS AND FACULTY
Enrollment: 1,103. **Student Body:** 54% female, 46% male, 22% out-of-state, 2% international (12 countries represented). Asian 1%, African American 10%, Caucasian 83%, Hispanic 3%, Native American 0%.
Retention and Graduation: 75% freshmen return for sophomore year. 51% freshmen graduate within 4 years. 60% freshmen graduate within 6 years.

Faculty: Student/faculty ratio 9:1. 115 full-time faculty, 96% hold PhDs, 5% are members of minority groups, 48% are women. 0% of classes are taught by teaching assistants.

ACADEMICS

Degrees: bachelor's, master's. **Classes:** Most classes have 20–29 students. Most lab/discussion sessions have 10–19 students. **Majors with Highest Enrollment:** business/commerce; communication and media studies, other; psychology. **Special Study Options:** Accelerated program, cooperative education program, double major, dual enrollment, honors program, independent study, internships, liberal arts/career combination, student-designed major, study abroad, teacher certification program. **Honors Programs:** Georgetown College Academic Honors Program. **Disability Services:** Special programs offered to physically disabled students include note-taking services, reader services, tape recorders, tutors. **Career Services:** Alumni network, alumni services, career/job search classes, career assessment, internships, regional alumni.

FACILITIES

Housing: men's dorms, women's dorms, fraternity/sorority housing, apartments for upper classmen. **Special Academic Facilities/Equipment:** To name only some: the Anna Ashcraft Ensor Learning Resource Center, an aboretum, three antebellum buildings, the Asher Science Center, the Anne Wright Wilson Fine Arts Building, and the Wilson Laboratory Theatre. **Computers:** 10% of classrooms, 60% of dorms, 90% of libraries, 100% of dining areas, 100% of student union, have wireless network access. Students can register for classes online. Administrative functions (other than registration) can be performed online.

CAMPUS LIFE

Environment: Town. **Activities:** Choral groups, concert band, dance, drama/theater, literary magazine, music ensembles, musical theater, pep band, radio station, student government, student newspaper, yearbook, Campus Ministries 110 registered organizations, 20 honor societies, 8 religious organizations. 5 fraternities, 4 sororities. **Athletics (Intercollegiate):** *Men:* baseball, basketball, cross-country, football, golf, soccer, tennis, track/field (outdoor), track/field (indoor). *Women:* basketball, cheerleading, cross-country, golf, soccer, softball, tennis, track/field (outdoor), track/field (indoor), volleyball. **On-Campus Highlights:** The Ensor Learning Resource Center, Starbucks - in the Learning Resource Center, The Grille **Environmental Initiatives:** Student led "Green Team," Sustainability themed student activities, Community garden.

ADMISSIONS

Freshman Academic Profile: Average high school GPA 3.4. 27% in top 10% of high school class, 53% in top 25% of high school class, 80% in top 50% of high school class. 84% from public high schools. SAT Math middle 50% range 460-560. SAT Critical Reading middle 50% range 410-610. ACT middle 50% range 21-26. Minimum web-based TOEFL 68. Minimum paper TOEFL 520. **Basis for Candidate Selection:** *Very important factors considered include:* academic GPA, rigor of secondary school record. *Important factors considered include:* Class rank, recommendation(s), standardized test scores, character/personal qualities, extracurricular activities, talent/ability. *Other factors considered include:* application essay, alumni/ae relation, geographical residence, interview, level of applicant's interest, religious affiliation/commitment, state residency, volunteer work. **Freshman Admission Requirements:** High school diploma is required and GED is accepted. **Freshman Admission Statistics:** 1,735 applied, 82% admitted, 17% enrolled. **Transfer Admission Requirements:** High school transcript, college transcript(s), statement of good standing from prior institution(s). Minimum college GPA of 2.5 required. Lowest grade transferable C. **General Admission Information:** Application Fee $30. Regular application deadline 8/1. Notification on a rolling basis, beginning on or about 10/1. Nonfall registration accepted. Admission may be deferred for a maximum of 1 year. Credit and/or placement offered for CEEB Advanced Placement tests.

COSTS AND FINANCIAL AID

Annual tuition $30,770. Room and board $7,920. Average book expense $1,250. **Required Forms and Deadlines:** FAFSA, institution's own financial aid form. **Notification of Awards:** Applicants will be notified of awards on a rolling basis beginning 3/15. **Types of Aid:** *Need-based scholarships/grants:* Federal Pell, SEOG, state scholarships/grants, private scholarships, the school's own gift aid. *Loans:* Subsidized Stafford, Unsubsidized Stafford, PLUS, Federal Perkins, college/university loans from institutional funds. **Student Employment:** Federal Work-Study Program available. Institutional employment available. Highest amount earned per year from on-campus jobs $2,500. Off-campus job opportunities are good. **Financial Aid Statistics:** 99% freshmen, 100% undergrads receive need-based scholarship or grant aid. 17% freshmen, 25% undergrads receive non-need-based scholarship or grant aid. 75% freshmen, 74% undergrads receive need-based self-help aid. 5% freshmen, 5% undergrads receive athletic scholarships. 63% undergrads borrow to pay for school. **Criteria for awarding institutional aid:** *Non-need-based:* academics, alumni affiliation, art, athletics, leadership, minority status, music/drama, religious affiliation, state/district residency.

GEORGETOWN UNIVERSITY

37th and O Streets, NW, Washington, DC 20057
Phone: 202-687-3600 • **Financial Aid Phone:** 202-687-4547
CEEB Code: 5244
Fax: 202-687-5084 • **Website:** www.georgetown.edu • **ACT Code:** 668

This private school, affiliated with the Roman Catholic Church, was founded in 1789. It has a 104-acre campus.

RATINGS

Admissions Selectivity Rating: 98   **Fire Safety Rating:** 84   **Green Rating:** 83

STUDENTS AND FACULTY

Enrollment: 7,232. **Student Body:** 55% female, 45% male, 98% out-of-state, 8% international (138 countries represented). Asian 9%, African American 6%, Caucasian 63%, Hispanic 8%, Native American 0%.
Retention and Graduation: 96% freshmen return for sophomore year.
Faculty: Student/faculty ratio 12:1. 918 full-time faculty, 91% hold PhDs, 12% are members of minority groups, 42% are women. 8% of classes are taught by teaching assistants.

ACADEMICS

Degrees: bachelor's, certificate, first professional, master's. **Majors with Highest Enrollment:** English language and literature; international relations and affairs; political science and government. **Special Study Options:** cross-registration, double major, English as a Second Language (ESL), honors program, independent study, internships, student-designed major, study abroad. **Honors Programs:** The John Carroll Programs guide and support a highly selective group of academically talented and ambitious students from around the world. The Programs seek individuals who desire to make a lasting difference in the fields and communities they touch. For these young men and women, the Programs provide models and skills to help them make the most effective use of their undergraduate years, and to assists them in moving from the undergraduate experience to their post-graduate academic and professional lives. The Programs invite students to take as their own the Carroll motto, mentis vita pro vita mundi: the life of the mind for the life of the world. **Combined Degree Programs:** BA/MA. **Disability Services:** Special programs offered to physically disabled students include note-taking services, reader services, tape recorders, tutors. **Career Services:** Alumni network, alumni services, career/job search classes, career assessment, internships, regional alumni.

FACILITIES

Housing: Coed dorms, special housing for disabled students, apartments for single students, Freshmen and sophomores are required to live on campus. 92% of campus accessible to physically disabled. **Special Academic Facilities/Equipment:** Language lab, seismological observatory. **Computers:** Students can register for classes online. Administrative functions (other than registration) can be performed online.

CAMPUS LIFE

Environment: Metropolis. **Activities:** Choral groups, concert band, dance, drama/theater, jazz band, literary magazine, music ensembles, musical theater, pep band, radio station, student government, student newspaper, student-run film society, symphony orchestra, television station, yearbook 139 registered organizations, 14 honor societies, 20 religious organizations. **Athletics (Intercollegiate):** *Men:* baseball, basketball, crew/rowing, cross-country, diving, football, golf, lacrosse, sailing, soccer, swimming, tennis, track/field (outdoor), track/field (indoor). *Women:* basketball, crew/rowing, cross-country, diving, field hockey, golf, lacrosse, sailing, soccer, softball, swimming, tennis, track/field (outdoor), track/field (indoor), volleyball. **On-Campus Highlights:** Yates Field House, Uncommon Grounds, The Observatory, The Quadrangle, Healy Hall. **Environmental Initiatives:** Set LEED certification as the standard for new constructions & major renovations Implemented energy construction programs in utility operations Expanded recycling program to include construction waste.

ADMISSIONS

Freshman Academic Profile: 90% in top 10% of high school class, 97% in top 25% of high school class, 99% in top 50% of high school class. 46% from public high schools. SAT Math middle 50% range 650-750. SAT Critical Reading middle 50% range 640-740. ACT middle 50% range 29-33. Minimum paper TOEFL 200. **Basis for Candidate Selection:** *Very important factors considered include:* Class rank, application essay, academic GPA, recommendation(s), rigor of secondary school record, standardized test scores, character/personal qualities, talent/ability. *Important factors considered include:* extracurricular activities, interview, volunteer work. *Other factors considered include:* alumni/ae relation, geographical residence, racial/ethnic status, state residency, work experience. **Freshman Admission Requirements:** High school diploma is required and GED is accepted. **Freshman Admission Statistics:** 19,254 applied, 18% admitted, 46% enrolled. **Transfer Admission Requirements:** High school transcript, college transcript(s), essay or personal statement, standardized test scores, statement of good standing from prior institution(s). Minimum college GPA of 3.0 required. Lowest grade transferable C. **General Admission Information:** Application Fee $65. Regular application deadline 1/10. Regular notification 4/1. Nonfall registration not accepted. Admission may be deferred for a maximum of 1 year. Credit and/or placement offered for CEEB Advanced Placement tests.

COSTS AND FINANCIAL AID

Annual tuition $42,360. Room and board $13,125. Required fees $420. Average book expense $1,060. **Required Forms and Deadlines:** FAFSA, CSS/Financial Aid PROFILE, noncustodial PROFILE, business/farm supplement. Tax returns. **Notification of Awards:** Applicants will be notified of awards on or about 4/1. **Types of Aid:** *Need-based scholarships/grants:* Federal Pell, SEOG, state scholarships/grants, private scholarships, the school's own gift aid. *Loans:* Subsidized Stafford, Unsubsidized Stafford, PLUS, Federal Perkins, Federal Nursing, Alternative loans. **Student Employment:** Federal Work-Study Program available. Institutional employment available. Off-campus job opportunities are excellent. **Financial Aid Statistics:** 99% freshmen, 91% undergrads receive need-based scholarship or grant aid. 36% freshmen, 26% undergrads receive non-need-based scholarship or grant aid. 97% freshmen, 86% undergrads receive need-based self-help aid. 5% freshmen, 4% undergrads receive athletic scholarships. 39% undergrads borrow to pay for school. Average cumulative indebtedness $25,315. **Criteria for awarding institutional aid:** *Non-need-based:* athletics.

GEORGIA COLLEGE & STATE UNIVERSITY

Campus Box 23, Milledgeville, GA 31061
Phone: 478-445-1283 • **Financial Aid Phone:** 478-445-5149
E-mail: admissions@gcsu.edu • **CEEB Code:** 5252
Fax: 478-445-1914 • **Website:** www.gcsu.edu • **ACT Code:** 828

This public school was founded in 1889. It has a 590-acre campus.

RATINGS
Admissions Selectivity Rating: 79   **Fire Safety Rating:** 98   **Green Rating:** 72

STUDENTS AND FACULTY
Enrollment: 5,487. **Student Body:** 60% female, 40% male, 1% out-of-state, 1% international (44 countries represented). Asian 1%, African American 5%, Caucasian 85%, Hispanic 5%, Native American 0%.
Retention and Graduation: 86% freshmen return for sophomore year. 36% freshmen graduate within 4 years. 58% freshmen graduate within 6 years. **Faculty:** Student/faculty ratio 17:1. 304 full-time faculty, 80% hold PhDs, 16% are members of minority groups, 55% are women.

ACADEMICS
Degrees: bachelor's, master's, post-master's certificate. **Classes:** Most classes have 20–29 students. Most lab/discussion sessions have 20–29 students. **Majors with Highest Enrollment:** business/commerce; marketing/marketing management; psychology. **Special Study Options:** Accelerated program, distance learning, double major, English as a Second Language (ESL), honors program, independent study, internships, study abroad, teacher certification program. **Honors Programs:** Honors and/or Scholars Program. **Disability Services:** Special programs offered to physically disabled students include note-taking services, reader services, tape recorders, tutors. **Career Services:** Alumni network, career/job search classes, career assessment, internships.

FACILITIES
Housing: Coed dorms, special housing for international students, apartments for single students, theme housing, 90% of campus accessible to physically disabled. **Special Academic Facilities/Equipment:** Education archives museum, old governor's mansion, Museum of Fine Arts, Natural History Museum and Planetarium **Computers:** 98% of classrooms, 98% of dorms, 100% of libraries, 98% of dining areas, 100% of student union, 100% of common outdoor areas have wireless network access. Students can register for classes online. Administrative functions (other than registration) can be performed online.

CAMPUS LIFE
Environment: Town. **Activities:** Choral groups, concert band, dance, drama/theater, jazz band, literary magazine, music ensembles, musical theater, radio station, student government, student newspaper, television station, Campus Ministries, International Student Organization 238 registered organizations, 8 religious organizations. 8 fraternities, 6 sororities. **Athletics (Intercollegiate):** *Men:* baseball, basketball, cross-country, golf, tennis. *Women:* basketball, cross-country, softball, speed skating, tennis. **On-Campus Highlights:** The Depot (Wellness Center), The Centennial Center (Gymnasium), Cafeteria, Libary and Information Technology Center **Environmental Initiatives:** recycling program efficient HVAC landscaping

ADMISSIONS
Freshman Academic Profile: Average high school GPA 3.4. SAT Math middle 50% range 520-610. SAT Critical Reading middle 50% range 520-610. SAT Writing middle 50% range 510-600. ACT middle 50% range 22-26. Minimum web-based TOEFL 61. Minimum paper TOEFL 500. **Basis for Candidate Selection:** *Very important factors considered include:* academic GPA, rigor of secondary school record, standardized test scores. *Important factors considered include:* Class rank, application essay, recommendation(s), extracurricular activities, talent/ability. *Other factors considered include:* alumni/ae relation, character/personal qualities, first generation, geographical residence, level of applicant's interest, racial/ethnic status, state residency, volunteer work, work experience. **Freshman Admission Requirements:** High school diploma is required and GED is accepted. *Academic units required:* 4 English, 4 mathematics, 3 science, (2 science labs), 2 foreign language, 3 social studies. 4 English, 4 mathematics, 3 science, (2 science labs), 2 foreign language, 3 social studies. **Freshman Admission Statistics:** 3,779 applied, 70% admitted, 46% enrolled. **Transfer Admission Requirements:** college transcript(s), statement of good standing from prior institution(s). Minimum college GPA of 2.0 required. **General Admission Information:** Application Fee $40. Regular application deadline 4/1. Nonfall registration accepted. Admission may be deferred for a maximum of 1 year. Credit offered for CEEB Advanced Placement tests.

COSTS AND FINANCIAL AID
Annual in-state tuition $6,634. Annual out-of-state tuition $24,098. Room and board $9,268. Required fees $1,984. Average book expense $1,350. **Required Forms and Deadlines:** FAFSA. **Notification of Awards:** Applicants will be notified of awards on a rolling basis beginning 3/1. **Types of Aid:** *Need-based scholarships/grants:* Federal Pell, SEOG, state scholarships/grants, private scholarships, the school's own gift aid. *Loans:* Direct PLUS, Subsidized Stafford, Unsubsidized Stafford, PLUS, Federal Perkins, state loans. **Student Employment:** Federal Work-Study Program available. Institutional employment available. Highest amount earned per year from on-campus jobs $6,812. Off-campus job opportunities are good. **Financial Aid Statistics:** 36% freshmen, 42% undergrads receive need-based scholarship or grant aid. 90% freshmen, 73% undergrads receive non-need-based scholarship or grant aid. 56% freshmen, 38% undergrads receive need-based self-help aid. 5% freshmen, 4% undergrads receive athletic scholarships. **Criteria for awarding institutional aid:** *Non-need based:* academics, alumni affiliation, art, athletics, leadership, music/drama, state/district residency.

See page 1088.

GEORGIA INSTITUTE OF TECHNOLOGY

Office of Undergraduate Admissions, Atlanta, GA 30332-0320
Phone: 404-894-4154 • **Financial Aid Phone:** 404-894-4160
E-mail: admission@gatech.edu • **CEEB Code:** 5248
Fax: 404-894-9511 • **Website:** www.gatech.edu • **ACT Code:** 818

This public school was founded in 1885. It has a 450-acre campus.

RATINGS
Admissions Selectivity Rating: 93   **Fire Safety Rating:** 88   **Green Rating:** 99

STUDENTS AND FACULTY
Enrollment: 13,954. **Student Body:** 33% female, 67% male, 28% out-of-state, 9% international (82 countries represented). Asian 17%, African American 6%, Caucasian 57%, Hispanic 6%, Native American 0%.
Retention and Graduation: 95% freshmen return for sophomore year. 34% freshmen graduate within 4 years. 21% grads go on to further study within 1 year. 10% grads pursue arts and sciences degrees. 1% grads pursue law degrees. 1% grads pursue business degrees. 3% grads pursue medical degrees. **Faculty:** Student/faculty ratio 18:1. 1059 full-time faculty, 89% hold PhDs, 27% are members of minority groups, 25% are women. 3% of classes are taught by teaching assistants.

ACADEMICS

Degrees: bachelor's, master's. **Classes:** Most classes have 20–29 students. Most lab/discussion sessions have 20–29 students. **Majors with Highest Enrollment:** business administration and management; industrial engineering; mechanical engineering. **Special Study Options:** Accelerated program, cooperative education program, cross-registration, distance learning, double major, dual enrollment, English as a Second Language (ESL), honors program, independent study, internships, student-designed major, study abroad, Dual degree program (3-2); Regent's Engineering Transfer Program with 14 colleges in the University System of Georgia; Georgia Tech Regional Engineering Program (GTREP) offers undergraduate and graduate Engineering degrees in collaboration with Armstrong Atlantic state University, Georgia Southern University, and Savannah State University. **Honors Programs:** The Georgia Tech Honors Program combines the challenging academic standards of one of the finest technological universities in the world with the closer connections between students and faculty that one might expect to find in a smaller college. Our mission is to create a lively environment in which students and faculty members learn from each other through a common commitment to intellectual inquiry, careful analysis, and energetic exchange of ideas. To promote and sustain this close engagement between students and faculty, the Honors Program will offer unique opportunities to students in the first two years of their studies at Georgia Tech: 1) An Honors Program Residence where first-year students can find a supportive community of interesting people, continue their conversations beyond the classroom, and develop connections to Georgia Tech and the surrounding community; 2) Small sections of introductory core courses designed to emphasize not just mastery of the material, but innovative inquiry and exploration within the discipline and often beyond; 3) A selection of small special topics courses, each with an enrollment limit of twenty HP students, that encourage critical thinking and an interdisciplinary approach to some of the most significant issues facing the world today; 4) A program of well-coordinated advising that will help students build upon their first two years in the Honors Program as they move into their chosen undergraduate majors in the third and fourth years. **Combined Degree Programs:** BS/MS, BS/MCRP. **Disability Services:** Special programs offered to physically disabled students include note-taking services, reader services, tape recorders, tutors. **Career Services:** Alumni network, alumni services, career/job search classes, career assessment, internships, regional alumni. Career Services highlights include With more than 2,700 students participating, Georgia Tech's co-op program is currently the largest optional co-op program in the United States and has perennially been listed in U.S. News & World Report as one of the "Top Ten" co-op programs in America.

FACILITIES

Housing: Coed dorms, special housing for disabled students, men's dorms, special housing for international students, women's dorms, fraternity/sorority housing, apartments for married students, apartments for single students, theme housing. First year housing is guaranteed to all new freshman and transfer students who submit an application by May 1. 75% of campus accessible to physically disabled. **Special Academic Facilities/Equipment:** Nuclear Magnetic Resonance Spectroscopy Center Georgia Tech Research Institute Ovarian Cancer Institute Paper Museum Mechanical Properties Research Laboratory with scanning electron microscope Virtual Factory Laboratory Ferris-Goldsmith Trading Floor Advanced Technology Development Center Klaus Advanced Computing Building Electron Microscope Marcus Nanotechnology Research Center Solar Decathlon House at College of Architecture Wind Tunnel GT Smart House Clough Undergraduates Learning Commons (under construction) **Computers:** 100% of classrooms, 100% of dorms, 100% of libraries, 100% of dining areas, 100% of student union, 65% of common outdoor areas have wireless network access. Students can register for classes online. Administrative functions (other than registration) can be performed online. Undergraduates are required to own a computer.

CAMPUS LIFE

Environment: Metropolis. **Activities:** Choral groups, concert band, dance, drama/theater, jazz band, literary magazine, marching band, music ensembles, musical theater, pep band, radio station, student government, student newspaper, student-run film society, symphony orchestra, television station, yearbook, Campus Ministries, International Student Organization, Model UN 429 registered organizations, 24 honor societies, 39 religious organizations. 38 fraternities, 14 sororities. **Athletics (Intercollegiate):** *Men:* baseball, basketball, cheerleading, cross-country, diving, football, golf, swimming, tennis, track/field (outdoor), track/field (indoor). *Women:* basketball, cheerleading, cross-country, diving, softball, swimming, tennis, track/field (outdoor), track/field (indoor), volleyball. **On-Campus Highlights:** Tech Square - Bookstore/Hotel/College of, Olympic Aquatic Center/Campus Recreation, The Hill/Tech Tower, Student Center Commons and the Library W, Ferst Center for the Arts. **Environmental Initiatives:** Education: Over 264 courses across all colleges with a goal of having every student who graduates have at least one sustainability course (23 degree programs in the undergraduate and graduate levels, many continuing education and certificate programs also focus on sustainability and major areas

of sustainability. In the process of adding another dozen or so minors related to sustainability. Have updated Strategic Plan with our new President. Have included addressing the Grand Challenges in the Strategic Plan to go along with Improving the Human Condition and a Sustainable Global Economy. Are developing an option for a flexible cross disciplinary degree offering to address Grand Challenges). Research: With 21 endowed chairs and 30 research centers focusing on sustainability, Georgia Tech is home to the Strategic Energy Institute, which focuses on alternative energy and energy efficiency, the Institute of Sustainable Systems, the Sustainable Design and Manufacturing Center, and much more. Georgia Tech works at the intersection of technology, business, policy, and sustainability. The Institute has over 20 student sustainability groups on campus plus over 20 student professional organizations related to sustainability. Green Campus as role model: 1. Water Leadership (100% low flow fixtures, 2,225,000+gallons of cistern capacity, stormwater runoff management (including 80+ acre Eco-Commons in process) 2. Energy efficiency (over 7,300,000 sf of energy efficient building space (via energy retrofit, and recommissioned and new construction) resulting in an energy utilization on campus that is one half of the average per sf of other very high research universities. Green Building with LEED Gold as a minimum, is a subset of our Building and Construction Design Standard. 3. Early adapter of alternative fuel vehicles and integrating with city mass transit systems to demonstrate and facilities clean and efficient transportation options for our students and city. Students are engaged in activities such as the EcoCar Challenge (design and build the next generation environmentally friendly car) and Solar Jackets (solar race car building and competition).

ADMISSIONS

Freshman Academic Profile: Average high school GPA 3.9. SAT Math middle 50% range 660-760. SAT Critical Reading middle 50% range 600-700. SAT Writing middle 50% range 610-700. ACT middle 50% range 28-32. **Basis for Candidate Selection:** *Very important factors considered include:* academic GPA, rigor of secondary school record, extracurricular activities. *Important factors considered include:* application essay, standardized test scores, character/personal qualities, geographical residence, state residency, talent/ability, volunteer work, work experience. *Other factors considered include:* alumni/ae relation, racial/ethnic status. **Freshman Admission Requirements:** High school diploma is required and GED is accepted. *Academic units required:* 4 English, 4 mathematics, 3 science, (3 science labs), 2 foreign language, 3 social studies. 4 English, 4 mathematics, 3 science, (3 science labs), 2 foreign language, 3 social studies. **Freshman Admission Statistics:** 14,645 applied, 55% admitted, 38% enrolled. **Transfer Admission Requirements:** college transcript(s), statement of good standing from prior institution(s). Minimum college GPA of 2.7 required. Lowest grade transferable C. **General Admission Information:** Application Fee $65. Regular application deadline 1/15. Regular notification 3/15. Nonfall registration accepted. Credit and/or placement offered for CEEB Advanced Placement tests.

COSTS AND FINANCIAL AID

Annual in-state tuition $7,718. Annual out-of-state tuition $27,022. Room and board $11,440. Required fees $2,380. Average book expense $1,200. **Required Forms and Deadlines:** FAFSA, institution's own financial aid form. **Notification of Awards:** Applicants will be notified of awards on or about 4/1. **Types of Aid:** *Need-based scholarships/grants:* Federal Pell, SEOG, state scholarships/grants, private scholarships, the school's own gift aid. *Loans:* Direct Subsidized Stafford, Direct Unsubsidized Stafford, Direct PLUS, Federal Perkins, college/university loans from institutional funds. **Student Employment:** Federal Work-Study Program available. Institutional employment available. Off-campus job opportunities are excellent. **Financial Aid Statistics:** 91% freshmen, 84% undergrads receive need-based scholarship or grant aid. 79% freshmen, 64% undergrads receive non-need-based scholarship or grant aid. 52% freshmen, 65% undergrads receive need-based self-help aid. 3% freshmen, 3% undergrads receive athletic scholarships. 65% freshmen, 65% undergrads receive any aid. 44% undergrads borrow to pay for school. Average cumulative indebtedness $26,412. **Criteria for awarding institutional aid:** *Non-need-based:* academics, athletics, leadership, music/drama, state/district residency.

GEORGIA SOUTHERN UNIVERSITY

P.O. Box 8024, Statesboro, GA 30460
Phone: 912-478-5391 • **Financial Aid Phone:** 912-478-5413
E-mail: admissions@georgiasouthern.edu • **CEEB Code:** 5253
Fax: 912-478-7240 • **Website:** www.georgiasouthern.edu/ • **ACT Code:** 830

This public school was founded in 1906. It has a 700-acre campus.

RATINGS

Admissions Selectivity Rating: 87   **Fire Safety Rating:** 83   **Green Rating:** 85

STUDENTS AND FACULTY

Enrollment: 17,139. **Student Body:** 50% female, 50% male, 4% out-of-state, 1% international (72 countries represented). Asian 1%, African American 25%, Caucasian 65%, Hispanic 4%, Native American 1%.
Retention and Graduation: 77% freshmen return for sophomore year. 23% freshmen graduate within 4 years. 50% freshmen graduate within 6 years. 15% grads go on to further study within 1 year. 2% grads pursue law degrees. 12% grads pursue business degrees. 2% grads pursue medical degrees. **Faculty:** Student/faculty ratio 22:1. 761 full-time faculty, 82% hold PhDs, 18% are members of minority groups, 47% are women. 3% of classes are taught by teaching assistants.

ACADEMICS

Degrees: bachelor's, master's, post-master's certificate. **Classes:** Most classes have 20–29 students. Most lab/discussion sessions have 20–29 students. **Majors with Highest Enrollment:** biology/biological sciences; elementary education and teaching; nursing/registered nurse (rn, asn, bsn, msn). **Special Study Options:** Accelerated program, cooperative education program, distance learning, double major, English as a Second Language (ESL), honors program, independent study, internships, student-designed major, study abroad, teacher certification program. **Honors Programs:** Georgia Southern offers University Honors Program (UHP) and 1906 Scholars. The UHP is designed to offer exceptionally able and diligent students the opportunity to enroll in particularly stimulating classes and to integrate their classroom learning with the needs of the community in which they live. The 1906 Scholars, a selective group within the UHP, accepts 15-18 freshmen from the pool of approximately 400 UHP applicants. The program offers interdisciplinary course options. Weekly seminars and colloquia emphasize discussion and independent endeavor, and nurture curiosity and the sharing of ideas among students and faculty. Selected students receive a full tuition scholarship, including out-of-state fees. **Combined Degree Programs:** Bachelor's/Graduate in Accounting and Nursing. **Disability Services:** Special programs offered to physically disabled students include note-taking services, reader services, tape recorders, tutors. **Career Services:** Alumni network, alumni services, career/job search classes, career assessment, internships, regional alumni. Career Services highlights include Cooperative Education Program.

FACILITIES

Housing: Coed dorms, special housing for disabled students, special housing for international students, apartments for single students, theme housing, 47% of campus accessible to physically disabled. **Special Academic Facilities/Equipment:** Art galleries, teaching museum, performing arts center, wildlife education center, eagle cinema, broadcasting studios, planetarium, botanical garden, radio station, black box theatre, and Recreation Activity Center. **Computers:** 80% of classrooms, 45% of dorms, 100% of libraries, 100% of dining areas, 100% of student union, 20% of common outdoor areas have wireless network access. Students can register for classes online. Administrative functions (other than registration) can be performed online.

CAMPUS LIFE

Environment: Village. **Activities:** Choral groups, concert band, dance, drama/theater, jazz band, literary magazine, marching band, music ensembles, musical theater, pep band, radio station, student government, student newspaper, student-run film society, symphony orchestra, television station, Campus Ministries, International Student Organization 235 registered organizations, 17 honor societies, 20 religious organizations. 20 fraternities, 9 sororities. **Athletics (Intercollegiate):** *Men:* baseball, basketball, cheerleading, football, golf, soccer, tennis. *Women:* basketball, cheerleading, cross-country, diving, soccer, softball, swimming, tennis, track/field (outdoor), volleyball. **On-Campus Highlights:** Russell Union, Recreation Activity Center, Center for Wildlife Education, Georgia Southern Museum, Paulson Stadium, Performing Arts Center, Lamar Q. Ball Raptor Center, Georgia Southern Planetarium, Gallery 303, the Georgia Southern Botanical Gardens, Eagle Cinema, College of Information Technology and Eagle Village. **Environmental Initiatives:** New Global Sustainability Concentration & Sustainability Advisor Program American College & University Presidents Climate Commitment (ACUPCC) LEED certified (or equivalent) buildings.

ADMISSIONS

Freshman Academic Profile: Average high school GPA 3.2. 17% in top 10% of high school class, 42% in top 25% of high school class, 75% in top 50% of high school class. % from public high schools. SAT Math middle 50% range 510-600. SAT Critical Reading middle 50% range 520-590. SAT Writing middle 50% range 490-570. ACT middle 50% range 21-25. Minimum web-based TOEFL 69. Minimum paper TOEFL 523. **Basis for Candidate Selection:** *Very important factors considered include:* academic GPA, rigor of secondary school record, standardized test scores. *Other factors considered include:* Class rank. **Freshman Admission Requirements:** High school diploma is required and GED is not accepted. *Academic units required:* 4 English, 4 mathematics, 3 science, (2 science labs), 2 foreign language, 3 social studies. 4 English, 4 mathematics, 3 science, (2 science labs), 2 foreign language, 3 social studies. **Freshman Admission Statistics:** 10,525 applied, 52% admitted, 66% enrolled.

Transfer Admission Requirements: college transcript(s), statement of good standing from prior institution(s). Minimum college GPA of 2.0 required. Lowest grade transferable D. **General Admission Information:** Application Fee $30. Regular application deadline 5/1. Nonfall registration accepted. Admission may be deferred for a maximum of circumstantial. Placement offered for CEEB Advanced Placement tests.

COSTS AND FINANCIAL AID

Annual in-state tuition $4,852. Annual out-of-state tuition $17,128. Room and board $9,290. Required fees $1,872. Average book expense $1,200. **Required Forms and Deadlines:** FAFSA. **Notification of Awards:** Applicants will be notified of awards on a rolling basis beginning 4/20. **Types of Aid:** *Need-based scholarships/grants:* Federal Pell, SEOG, state scholarships/grants, private scholarships, the school's own gift aid, Hope Scholarships°, Federal Work Study, TEACH Grant°, ACG, SMART Grant. *Loans:* Direct Subsidized Stafford, Direct Unsubsidized Stafford, Direct PLUS, Federal Perkins, state loans, Service-Cancelable State Direct Student Loans, External Alternative Loans. **Student Employment:** Federal Work-Study Program available. Institutional employment available. Highest amount earned per year from on-campus jobs $2,142. Off-campus job opportunities are excellent. **Financial Aid Statistics:** 87% freshmen, 81% undergrads receive need-based scholarship or grant aid. 2% freshmen, 1% undergrads receive non-need-based scholarship or grant aid. 83% freshmen, 87% undergrads receive need-based self-help aid. 1% freshmen, 1% undergrads receive athletic scholarships. 92% freshmen, 88% undergrads receive any aid. 68% undergrads borrow to pay for school. Average cumulative indebtedness $21,562. **Criteria for awarding institutional aid:** *Non-need-based:* academics, alumni affiliation, art, athletics, leadership, minority status, music/drama, state/district residency.

GEORGIA SOUTHWESTERN STATE UNIVERSITY

800 Georgia Southwestern State University Dr., Americus, GA 31709-4693
Phone: 912-928-1273 • **Financial Aid Phone:** 229-928-1378
E-mail: gswapps@canes.gsw.edu • **CEEB Code:** 5250
Fax: 912-931-2983 • **Website:** www.gsw.edu • **ACT Code:** 824

This public school was founded in 1906. It has a 325-acre campus.

RATINGS

Admissions Selectivity Rating: 68   **Fire Safety Rating:** 60*   **Green Rating:** 60*

STUDENTS AND FACULTY

Enrollment: 2,200. **Student Body:** 65% female, 35% male, 4% out-of-state, 2% international (34 countries represented). Asian 1%, African American 31%, Caucasian 62%, Hispanic 1%, Native American 0%.
Retention and Graduation: 12% freshmen graduate within 4 years. 34% freshmen graduate within 6 years. **Faculty:** Student/faculty ratio 17:1. 92 full-time faculty, 73% hold PhDs, 20% are members of minority groups, 53% are women. 0% of classes are taught by teaching assistants.

ACADEMICS

Degrees: bachelor's, master's, post-bachelor's certificate, post-master's certificate. **Classes:** Most classes have 20–29 students. **Majors with Highest Enrollment:** accounting; business administration and management; elementary education and teaching. **Special Study Options:** Accelerated program, cooperative education program, distance learning, double major, dual enrollment, English as a Second Language (ESL), honors program, internships, study abroad, teacher certification program. **Disability Services:** Special programs offered to physically disabled students include note-taking services, reader services, tape recorders, tutors.

FACILITIES

Housing: Coed dorms, Apartment housing for upperclassmen. 100% of campus accessible to physically disabled. **Special Academic Facilities/Equipment:** Observatory, Glass-blowing studio **Computers:** Students can register for classes online. Administrative functions (other than registration) can be performed online.

CAMPUS LIFE

Environment: Village. **Activities:** Choral groups, concert band, drama/theater, jazz band, literary magazine, music ensembles, musical theater, student government, student newspaper, television station, International Student Organization 12 honor societies, 7 fraternities, 6 sororities. **Athletics (Intercollegiate):** *Men:* baseball, basketball, golf, soccer, tennis. *Women:* basketball, cross-country, soccer, softball, tennis.

ADMISSIONS

Freshman Academic Profile: Average high school GPA 3.1. 19% in top 10% of high school class, 46% in top 25% of high school class, 77% in top 50% of

high school class. SAT Math middle 50% range 430-530. SAT Critical Reading middle 50% range 440-530. ACT middle 50% range 18-21. Minimum paper TOEFL 523. **Basis for Candidate Selection:** *Very important factors considered include:* academic GPA, rigor of secondary school record, standardized test scores. *Important factors considered include:* Class rank. *Other factors considered include:* application essay, recommendation(s), extracurricular activities, interview, talent/ability. **Freshman Admission Requirements:** High school diploma is required and GED is accepted. *Academic units required:* 4 English, 4 mathematics, 3 science, (2 science labs), 2 foreign language, 1 social studies, 2 history, 2 academic electives. *Academic units recommended:* 4 English, 4 mathematics, 3 science, (2 science labs), 2 foreign language, 1 social studies, 2 history, 2 academic electives. **Freshman Admission Statistics:** 1,050 applied, 78% admitted, 52% enrolled. **Transfer Admission Requirements:** college transcript(s), minimum college GPA of 2.0 required. Lowest grade transferable D. **General Admission Information:** Application Fee $25. Early decision application deadline 12/15. Notification on a rolling basis, beginning on or about 8/1. Nonfall registration accepted. Admission may be deferred for a maximum of 12 months. Credit and/or placement offered for CEEB Advanced Placement tests.

COSTS AND FINANCIAL AID
Average book expense $1,000. **Required Forms and Deadlines:** FAFSA, institution's own financial aid form, state aid form. **Notification of Awards:** Applicants will be notified of awards on a rolling basis beginning 3/1. **Types of Aid:** *Need-based scholarships/grants:* Federal Pell, SEOG, state scholarships/grants, the school's own gift aid. *Loans:* Subsidized Stafford, Unsubsidized Stafford, PLUS, Federal Perkins. **Student Employment:** Federal Work-Study Program available. Institutional employment available. Off-campus job opportunities are fair. **Financial Aid Statistics:** 64% freshmen, 59% undergrads receive any aid. **Criteria for awarding institutional aid:** *Non-need-based:* academics, athletics, leadership.

GEORGIA STATE UNIVERSITY

PO Box 4009, Atlanta, GA 30302-4009
Phone: 404-413-2500 • **Financial Aid Phone:** 404-413-2600
E-mail: admissions@gsu.edu • **CEEB Code:** 5251
Fax: 404-413-2002 • **Website:** www.gsu.edu • **ACT Code:** 826

This public school was founded in 1913. It has a 33-acre campus.

RATINGS
Admissions Selectivity Rating: 84   **Fire Safety Rating:** 84   **Green Rating:** 60*

STUDENTS AND FACULTY
Enrollment: 23,964. **Student Body:** 59% female, 41% male, 5% out-of-state, 2% international (155 countries represented). Asian 11%, African American 39%, Caucasian 34%, Hispanic 8%, Native American 0%.
Retention and Graduation: 83% freshmen return for sophomore year. 21% freshmen graduate within 4 years. **Faculty:** Student/faculty ratio 21:1. 1142 full-time faculty, 87% hold PhDs, 25% are members of minority groups, 47% are women.

ACADEMICS
Degrees: bachelor's, certificate, first professional, master's, post-bachelor's certificate, post-master's certificate. **Classes:** Most classes have 20–29 students. **Majors with Highest Enrollment:** finance; journalism; marketing/marketing management. **Special Study Options:** Accelerated program, cooperative education program, cross-registration, distance learning, double major, dual enrollment, English as a Second Language (ESL), honors program, independent study, internships, student-designed major, study abroad, teacher certification program. **Freshman** Learning Communities. **Honors Programs:** Students have the advantage of small classes and close contact with faculty members. **Combined Degree Programs:** BA/MA, BA/MIB in French, German or Spanish. **Disability Services:** Special programs offered to physically disabled students include note-taking services, reader services, tape recorders, tutors.

FACILITIES
Housing: Coed dorms, special housing for disabled students, special housing for international students, apartments for married students, apartments for single students, Some arrangments for visiting faculty/scholars. 100% of campus accessible to physically disabled. **Special Academic Facilities/Equipment:** Cartography Production Laboratory,Commuter Student Services,Cooperative Learning Laboratory,Economic Forecasting Center,Ernest G. Welch School of Art and Design Gallery, Instructional Technology Center, James M. Cox, Jr. Multi-Media Instructional Lab and Satellite Downlink Facility,Kopleff Recital Hall,Lanette L. Suttles Child Development Center,Language Acquisition and Resource Center, Mathematics Assistance Complex, Mathematics Interactive Learning Environment, Music Media Center, Rialto Center for the Performing

Arts, Small Business Development Center, Visual Resource Center, Writing Studio. **Computers:** Students can register for classes online. Administrative functions (other than registration) can be performed online.

CAMPUS LIFE
Environment: Metropolis. **Activities:** Choral groups, concert band, dance, drama/theater, jazz band, literary magazine, music ensembles, pep band, radio station, student government, student newspaper, student-run film society, television station 201 registered organizations, 19 honor societies, 21 religious organizations. 9 fraternities, 15 sororities. **Athletics (Intercollegiate):** *Men:* baseball, basketball, cross-country, golf, soccer, tennis, track/field (outdoor), volleyball. *Women:* basketball, cross-country, golf, soccer, softball, tennis, track/field (outdoor), volleyball. **On-Campus Highlights:** Recreatoin Center, Student Housing, Aderhold Learning Center, The Rialto Center for the Performing Arts, The Student Center.

ADMISSIONS
Freshman Academic Profile: Average high school GPA 3.3. SAT Math middle 50% range 490-590. SAT Critical Reading middle 50% range 480-580. ACT middle 50% range 20-25. Minimum web-based TOEFL 79. Minimum paper TOEFL 550. **Basis for Candidate Selection:** *Very important factors considered include:* academic GPA, rigor of secondary school record, standardized test scores. *Other factors considered include:* application essay, recommendation(s), alumni/ae relation, character/personal qualities, extracurricular activities, first generation, geographical residence, interview, level of applicant's interest, state residency, talent/ability, volunteer work, work experience. **Freshman Admission Requirements:** High school diploma is required and GED is not accepted. *Academic units required:* 4 English, 4 mathematics, 3 science, (2 science labs), 2 foreign language, 2 social studies, 1 history. 4 English, 4 mathematics, 3 science, (2 science labs), 2 foreign language, 2 social studies, 1 history. **Freshman Admission Statistics:** 12,774 applied, 57% admitted, 44% enrolled. **Transfer Admission Requirements:** college transcript(s), minimum college GPA of 2.5 required. Lowest grade transferable D. **General Admission Information:** Application Fee $50. Regular application deadline 3/1. Notification on a rolling basis, beginning on or about 10/1. Nonfall registration accepted. Admission may be deferred for a maximum of 2 terms. Credit offered for CEEB Advanced Placement tests.

COSTS AND FINANCIAL AID
Annual in-state tuition $7,536. Annual out-of-state tuition $25,746. Room and board $11,546. Required fees $2,128. Average book expense $1,000. **Required Forms and Deadlines:** FAFSA. **Notification of Awards:** Applicants will be notified of awards on a rolling basis beginning 3/30. **Types of Aid:** *Need-based scholarships/grants:* Federal Pell, SEOG, state scholarships/grants, private scholarships, the school's own gift aid. *Loans:* Direct Subsidized Stafford, Direct Unsubsidized Stafford, Direct PLUS, PLUS, Federal Perkins, state loans. **Student Employment:** Federal Work-Study Program available. Institutional employment available. Off-campus job opportunities are good. **Financial Aid Statistics:** 71% freshmen, 73% undergrads receive need-based scholarship or grant aid. 97% freshmen, 95% undergrads receive non-need-based scholarship or grant aid. 54% freshmen, 60% undergrads receive need-based self-help aid. 2% freshmen, 1% undergrads receive athletic scholarships. 64% undergrads borrow to pay for school. Average cumulative indebtedness $20,439. **Criteria for awarding institutional aid:** *Non-need-based:* academics, alumni affiliation, art, athletics, minority status, music/drama, state/district residency.

GEORGIAN COURT UNIVERSITY

900 Lakewood Avenue, Lakewood, NJ 08701-2697
Phone: 732-987-2700 • **Financial Aid Phone:** 732-987-2258
E-mail: admissions@georgian.edu • **CEEB Code:** 2274
Fax: 732-987-2000 • **Website:** www.georgian.edu • **ACT Code:** 2562

This private school, affiliated with the Roman Catholic Church, was founded in 1908. It has a 156-acre campus.

RATINGS
Admissions Selectivity Rating: 70   **Fire Safety Rating:** 96   **Green Rating:** 76

STUDENTS AND FACULTY
Enrollment: 1,432. **Student Body:** 93% female, 7% male, 4% out-of-state, 0% international (9 countries represented). Asian 2%, African American 13%, Caucasian 59%, Hispanic 11%, Native American 0%.
Retention and Graduation: 71% freshmen return for sophomore year. 24% freshmen graduate within 4 years. 49% freshmen graduate within 6 years. **Faculty:** Student/faculty ratio 12:1. 97 full-time faculty, 90% hold PhDs, 15% are members of minority groups, 63% are women. 0% of classes are taught by teaching assistants.

ACADEMICS

Degrees: bachelor's, certificate, master's, post-bachelor's certificate, post-master's certificate. **Classes:** Most classes have 10–19 students. **Majors with Highest Enrollment:** elementary education and teaching; English language and literature; psychology. **Special Study Options:** Accelerated program, distance learning, double major, dual enrollment, English as a Second Language (ESL), honors program, independent study, internships, liberal arts/career combination, study abroad, teacher certification program, Undergrads may take grad level classes. Co-Op Programs: Arts, Business, Health Professions, Natural Science, Social/Behavioral Science. **Honors Programs:** Members of the University Honors Program receive an enriched academic curriculum featuring: ° Faculty chosen for their excellence as teaching-scholars ° Challenging interactive classroom format ° Emphasis on primary texts and sources ° Rigorous scholarly writing assignments and oral presentations ° Close faculty mentoring ° Preference in academic advisement and course registration ° A strong sense of belonging to a community of scholars ° Sponsorship in funding presentations at regional and national conferences ° Special advisement by faculty regarding graduate and professional school applications and prestigious fellowship opportunities ° Special recognition at commencement ceremonies **Combined Degree Programs:** BS/MBA. **Disability Services:** Special programs offered to physically disabled students include note-taking services, reader services, tape recorders, tutors. **Career Services:** Alumni network, alumni services, career/job search classes, career assessment, internships Career Services highlights include Career Connections, GCU's new online job board with research tools for students and alumni. Members can search for jobs, view the calendar of events and register for them, network with alumni, and upload their resumes. Employers can post jobs and internships directly online and search through resumes.

FACILITIES

Housing: women's dorms, wellness housing, 77% of campus accessible to physically disabled. **Special Academic Facilities/Equipment:** Art gallery, arboretum, Wellness Center, NASA ERC. **Computers:** 98% of classrooms, 77% of dorms, 100% of libraries, 50% of dining areas, 100% of student union, have wireless network access. Students can register for classes online. Administrative functions (other than registration) can be performed online.

CAMPUS LIFE

Environment: Town. **Activities:** Choral groups, concert band, dance, jazz band, literary magazine, music ensembles, student government, student newspaper, yearbook, Campus Ministries, International Student Organization, Model UN 48 registered organizations, 18 honor societies, 1 religious organizations. **Athletics (Intercollegiate):** Women: basketball, cross-country, lacrosse, soccer, softball, tennis, track/field (outdoor), volleyball. **On-Campus Highlights:** Arboretum, NASA Educational Resource Center, Art Gallery, Library, Wellness Center. **Environmental Initiatives:** We have included a sustainability commitment in our strategic plan. Our president was the 8th signatory of ACUPCC in New Jersey. GCU purchased Green-E certified renewable energy certificates equivalent to 100% of our projected campus electrical usage for 2009-10.

ADMISSIONS

Freshman Academic Profile: Average high school GPA 3.1. 8% in top 10% of high school class, 22% in top 25% of high school class, 57% in top 50% of high school class. 77% from public high schools. SAT Math middle 50% range 380-500. SAT Critical Reading middle 50% range 380-500. SAT Writing middle 50% range 400-510. Minimum web-based TOEFL 79. Minimum paper TOEFL 550. **Basis for Candidate Selection:** *Very important factors considered include:* academic GPA, rigor of secondary school record. *Important factors considered include:* standardized test scores. *Other factors considered include:* Class rank, application essay, recommendation(s), alumni/ae relation, character/personal qualities, extracurricular activities, first generation, interview, level of applicant's interest, talent/ability, volunteer work, work experience. **Freshman Admission Requirements:** High school diploma is required and GED is accepted. *Academic units required:* 4 English, 2 mathematics, (1 science labs), 2 foreign language, 1 history, 6 academic electives. 4 English, 2 mathematics, (1 science labs), 2 foreign language, 1 history, 6 academic electives. **Freshman Admission Statistics:** 876 applied, 65% admitted, 28% enrolled. **Transfer Admission Requirements:** college transcript(s), minimum college GPA of 2.0 required. Lowest grade transferable c. **General Admission Information:** Application Fee $40. Regular application deadline 8/1. Notification on a rolling basis, beginning on or about 10/1. Nonfall registration accepted. Credit and/or placement offered for CEEB Advanced Placement tests.

COSTS AND FINANCIAL AID

Annual tuition $26,740. Room and board $10,560. Required fees $1,300. **Required Forms and Deadlines:** FAFSA, institution's own financial aid form. **Notification of Awards:** Applicants will be notified of awards on a rolling basis beginning 2/1. **Types of Aid:** *Need-based scholarships/grants:* Federal Pell, SEOG, state scholarships/grants, private scholarships, the school's own gift aid. *Loans:* Subsidized Stafford, Unsubsidized Stafford, PLUS, Federal Perkins, state loans. **Student Employment:** Federal Work-Study Program available. Institutional employment available. Highest amount earned per year from on-campus jobs $2,000. Off-campus job opportunities are good. **Financial Aid**

Statistics: 100% freshmen, 95% undergrads receive need-based scholarship or grant aid. 7% freshmen, 4% undergrads receive non-need-based scholarship or grant aid. 83% freshmen, 88% undergrads receive need-based self-help aid. 1% undergrads receive athletic scholarships. 96% freshmen, 93% undergrads receive any aid. 90% undergrads borrow to pay for school. Average cumulative indebtedness $33,888. **Criteria for awarding institutional aid:** *Non-need-based:* academics, alumni affiliation, art, athletics, leadership, minority status, music/drama, religious affiliation.

GETTYSBURG COLLEGE

Admissions Office, Gettysburg, PA 17325-1484
Phone: 717-337-6100 • **Financial Aid Phone:** 717-337-6611
E-mail: admiss@gettysburg.edu • **CEEB Code:** 2275
Fax: 717-337-6145 • **Website:** www.gettysburg.edu • **ACT Code:** 3580

This private school, affiliated with the Lutheran Church, was founded in 1832. It has a 200-acre campus.

RATINGS

Admissions Selectivity Rating: 94   **Fire Safety Rating:** 90   **Green Rating:** 83

STUDENTS AND FACULTY

Enrollment: 2,585. **Student Body:** 53% female, 47% male, 73% out-of-state, 2% international (31 countries represented). Asian 2%, African American 3%, Caucasian 81%, Hispanic 4%, Native American 0%.
Retention and Graduation: 91% freshmen return for sophomore year. 80% freshmen graduate within 4 years. 40% grads go on to further study within 1 year. **Faculty:** Student/faculty ratio 10:1. 220 full-time faculty, 94% hold PhDs, 16% are members of minority groups, 42% are women. 0% of classes are taught by teaching assistants.

ACADEMICS

Degrees: bachelor's. **Classes:** Most classes have 10–19 students. **Majors with Highest Enrollment:** business/commerce; political science and government; psychology. **Special Study Options:** double major, independent study, internships, student-designed major, study abroad, teacher certification program. **Combined Degree Programs:** Optometry, Physical Therapy, Nursing. **Disability Services:** Special programs offered to physically disabled students include tape recorders. **Career Services:** Alumni network, alumni services, career/job search classes, career assessment, internships, regional alumni.

FACILITIES

Housing: Coed dorms, women's dorms, fraternity/sorority housing, apartments for single students, special interest and theme housing. **Special Academic Facilities/Equipment:** Art gallery, language lab, Child Study lab, Majestic Theatre, Sunderman Conservatory, planetarium, observatory, electron microscopes, NMR spectrometer, greenhouse, digital classrooms, wireless network, Plasma Physics labs, Science Center **Computers:** 100% of classrooms, 100% of dorms, 100% of libraries, 100% of dining areas, 100% of student union, 90% of common outdoor areas have wireless network access. Students can register for classes online. Administrative functions (other than registration) can be performed online.

CAMPUS LIFE

Environment: Village. **Activities:** Choral groups, concert band, dance, drama/theater, jazz band, literary magazine, marching band, music ensembles, radio station, student government, student newspaper, student-run film society, symphony orchestra, television station, yearbook, Campus Ministries, International Student Organization, Model UN 120 registered organizations, 16 honor societies, 7 religious organizations. 10 fraternities, 6 sororities. **Athletics (Intercollegiate):** Men: baseball, basketball, cheerleading, cross-country, football, golf, lacrosse, soccer, swimming, tennis, track/field (outdoor), track/field (indoor), wrestling. Women: basketball, cheerleading, cross-country, field hockey, golf, lacrosse, soccer, softball, swimming, tennis, track/field (outdoor), track/field (indoor), volleyball. **On-Campus Highlights:** Beautiful 200-acre campus, Musselman Library, Science Center, Center for Athletics, Recreation, and Fitness, College Union Building. **Environmental Initiatives:** The Center for Athletics, Recreation, and Fitness--a new building which has received LEED Gold certification Buying 50% of electric from renewable resources Installed water retention system under new parking lot for campus irrigation

ADMISSIONS

Freshman Academic Profile: 72% in top 10% of high school class, 92% in top 25% of high school class, 99% in top 50% of high school class. 70% from public high schools. SAT Math middle 50% range 610-670. SAT Critical Reading middle 50% range 600-690. **Basis for Candidate Selection:** *Very important factors considered include:* Class rank, academic GPA, recommendation(s), rigor of secondary school record. *Important factors considered include:* application essay, standardized test scores, character/personal qualities, extracurricular activities, interview, talent/ability, volunteer work. *Other factors considered include:* alumni/ae relation, first generation, geographical residence, level of applicant's interest, racial/ethnic status, work experience. **Freshman Admission Requirement:** High school diploma is required and GED is accepted. *Academic units required:* 4 English, 3 mathematics, 3 science, (3 science labs), 3 foreign language, 3 social studies, 3 history. *Academic units recommended:* 4 English, 3 mathematics, 3 science, (3 science labs), 3 foreign language, 3 social studies, 3 history. **Freshman Admission Statistics:** 5,620 applied, 40% admitted, 34% enrolled. **Transfer Admission Requirements:** High school transcript, college transcript(s), essay or personal statement, standardized test scores, statement of good standing from prior institution(s). Minimum college GPA of 2.5 required. Lowest grade transferable C. **General Admission Information:** Application Fee $55. Early decision application deadline 11/15. Regular application deadline 2/1. Regular notification 4/1. Nonfall registration accepted. Admission may be deferred for a maximum of 1 year. Credit and/or placement offered for CEEB Advanced Placement tests.

COSTS AND FINANCIAL AID

Annual tuition $44,210. Room and board $10,560. Average book expense $1,000. **Required Forms and Deadlines:** FAFSA, CSS/Financial Aid PROFILE, business/farm supplement. **Notification of Awards:** Applicants will be notified of awards on or about 3/26. **Types of Aid:** *Need-based scholarships/grants:* Federal Pell, SEOG, state scholarships/grants, private scholarships, the school's own gift aid. *Loans:* Subsidized Stafford, Unsubsidized Stafford, PLUS, Federal Perkins, college/university loans from institutional funds. **Student Employment:** Federal Work-Study Program available. Institutional employment available. Highest amount earned per year from on-campus jobs $1,500. Off-campus job opportunities are excellent. **Financial Aid Statistics:** 95% freshmen, 94% undergrads receive need-based scholarship or grant aid. 56% freshmen, 51% undergrads receive non-need-based scholarship or grant aid. 89% freshmen, 87% undergrads receive need-based self-help aid. 55% freshmen, 55% undergrads receive any aid. 58% undergrads borrow to pay for school. Average cumulative indebtedness $25,530. **Criteria for awarding institutional aid:** *Non-need-based:* academics, music/drama.

GIBBS COLLEGE

85 Garfield Ave., Cranston, RI 2920
Phone: 401-824-5300 • **Financial Aid Phone:** 401-824-5327
E-mail: psimonin@gbbsRI.edu
Fax: 401-824-5376 • **Website:** www.gibbsri.edu/

This proprietary school was founded in 1911. It has a 30-acre campus.

RATINGS
Admissions Selectivity Rating: 60*   **Fire Safety Rating:** 60*   **Green Rating:** 60*

STUDENTS AND FACULTY
Enrollment: 613. **Student Body:** 72% female, 28% male, 0% international (0 countries represented). Asian 5%, African American 6%, Caucasian 57%, Hispanic 22%, Native American 0%.
Retention and Graduation: Faculty: Student/faculty ratio 11:1. 17 full-time faculty, 47% hold PhDs, 12% are members of minority groups, 41% are women. 0% of classes are taught by teaching assistants.

ACADEMICS
Degrees: associate, certificate, terminal associate, transfer associate. **Classes: Majors with Highest Enrollment:** computer and information systems security; criminal justice/law enforcement administration; medical/clinical assistant. **Special Study Options:** internships, liberal arts/career combination. **Disability Services:** Special programs offered to physically disabled students include tape recorders, tutors. **Career Services:** Alumni network, alumni services, career/job search classes, career assessment.

FACILITIES
Housing: None. 100% of campus accessible to physically disabled.

CAMPUS LIFE
Environment: City. **Activities:** student government.

ADMISSIONS

Basis for Candidate Selection: *Very important factors considered include:* interview, level of applicant's interest. *Important factors considered include:* character/personal qualities. *Other factors considered include:* recommendation(s), talent/ability. **Freshman Admission Requirements:** High school diploma is required and GED is accepted. **Transfer Admission Requirements:** High school transcript, college transcript(s), interview, Lowest grade transferable C. **General Admission Information:** Application Fee $50. Nonfall registration accepted. Admission may be deferred for a maximum of 1 year. Credit and/or placement offered for CEEB Advanced Placement tests.

COSTS AND FINANCIAL AID
Annual tuition $11,250. Required fees $450.

GIBBS COLLEGE—NORWALK

10 Norden Place, Norwalk, CT 6855
Phone: 203-838-4173
E-mail: info@gibbsnorwalk.com
Fax: 203-899-0788 • **Website:** www.gibbscollege.com

This is a proprietary school.

RATINGS
Admissions Selectivity Rating: 60*   **Fire Safety Rating:** 60*   **Green Rating:** 60*

ACADEMICS
Degrees: associate, certificate, diploma. **Majors with Highest Enrollment:** business administration and management; computer and information science; management information systems.

ADMISSIONS
Freshman Admission Requirements: High school diploma is required and GED is accepted. **General Admission Information:** Nonfall registration not accepted.

COSTS AND FINANCIAL AID
Types of Aid: *Need-based scholarships/grants:* Federal Pell, SEOG.

GLENVILLE STATE COLLEGE

200 High Street, Glenville, WV 26351
Phone: 304-462-4128
E-mail: admissions@glenville.edu
Fax: 304-462-8619 • **Website:** www.glenville.edu • **ACT Code:** 4522

This public school was founded in 1872.

RATINGS
Admissions Selectivity Rating: 60*   **Fire Safety Rating:** 63   **Green Rating:** 60*

STUDENTS AND FACULTY
Enrollment: 1,374. **Student Body:** 54% female, 46% male.
Retention and Graduation: 49% freshmen return for sophomore year.
Faculty: Student/faculty ratio 20:1. 53 full-time faculty, 30% hold PhDs, 6% are members of minority groups, 36% are women. 0% of classes are taught by teaching assistants.

ACADEMICS
Degrees: associate, bachelor's, certificate. **Special Study Options:** cooperative education program, double major, honors program, internships, student-designed major, teacher certification program. **Disability Services:** Special programs offered to physically disabled students include reader services, tape recorders, tutors.

FACILITIES
Housing: Coed dorms, special housing for disabled students, men's dorms, women's dorms, apartments for married students, apartments for single students.

CAMPUS LIFE
Environment: Rural. **Activities:** Choral groups, concert band, drama/theater, jazz band, marching band, music ensembles, student government, student newspaper, yearbook 30 registered organizations, 2 religious organizations. 2 fraternities, 2 sororities. **Athletics (Intercollegiate):** *Men:* basketball, cross-

country, football, golf, track/field (outdoor). *Women:* basketball, cross-country, golf, softball, track/field (outdoor), volleyball. **On-Campus Highlights:** High Adventure, GSC Fitness Center, Fine Arts Building, PG's Snack Bar, Pioneer Village.

ADMISSIONS
Freshman Academic Profile: Minimum paper TOEFL 550. **Basis for Candidate Selection:** *Very important factors considered include:* rigor of secondary school record, standardized test scores. *Other factors considered include:* Class rank, academic GPA, recommendation(s), talent/ability. **Freshman Admission Requirements:** High school diploma is required and GED is accepted. *Academic units required:* 4 English, 3 mathematics, 3 science, (2 science labs), 3 social studies. 4 English, 3 mathematics, 3 science, (2 science labs), 3 social studies. **Freshman Admission Statistics:** 1,132 applied, 100% admitted, 41% enrolled. **Transfer Admission Requirements:** college transcript(s), minimum college GPA of 2.0 required. Lowest grade transferable C. **General Admission Information:** Nonfall registration accepted. Admission may be deferred for a maximum of 1 year. Credit offered for CEEB Advanced Placement tests.

COSTS AND FINANCIAL AID
Room and board $3,480. Average book expense $350. **Required Forms and Deadlines:** FAFSA. **Types of Aid:** *Need-based scholarships/grants:* Federal Pell, SEOG, state scholarships/grants, private scholarships, the school's own gift aid. *Loans:* Direct Subsidized Stafford, Direct Unsubsidized Stafford, Direct PLUS, Federal Perkins. **Student Employment:** Federal Work-Study Program available. Highest amount earned per year from on-campus jobs $900. Off-campus job opportunities are fair. **Financial Aid Statistics:** 81% freshmen, 82% undergrads receive need-based scholarship or grant aid. 22% freshmen, 19% undergrads receive non-need-based scholarship or grant aid. 64% freshmen, 72% undergrads receive need-based self help aid. 1% freshmen, 3% undergrads receive athletic scholarships. 71% undergrads borrow to pay for school. Average cumulative indebtedness $12,117. **Criteria for awarding institutional aid:** *Non-need-based:* academics, art, athletics, music/drama.

GOLDEN GATE UNIVERSITY

536 Mission Street, San Francisco, CA 94105
Phone: 415-442-7800
E-mail: info@ggu.edu • **CEEB Code:** 4329
Fax: 415-442-7807 • **Website:** www.ggu.edu • **ACT Code:** 278

This private school was founded in 1901.

RATINGS
Admissions Selectivity Rating: 62   **Fire Safety Rating:** 60*   **Green Rating:** 60*

STUDENTS AND FACULTY
Retention and Graduation: 15% grads go on to further study within 1 year. 30% grads pursue business degrees. **Faculty:** Student/faculty ratio 13:1. 81 full-time faculty. 0% of classes are taught by teaching assistants.

ACADEMICS
Degrees: bachelor's, certificate, first professional, master's, post-bachelor's certificate, post-master's certificate. **Classes:** Most classes have 10–19 students. **Special Study Options:** Accelerated program, cooperative education program, distance learning, dual enrollment, English as a Second Language (ESL), independent study, internships, weekend college. **Disability Services:** Special programs offered to physically disabled students include tape recorders. **Career Services:** Alumni network, alumni services, career/job search classes, career assessment, internships Career Services highlights include Virtual career center - ggucareer.com. 27/7 access to career maanagement tools and resources including self assessment, company contact databases, industry reports and job board.

FACILITIES
Housing: 100% of campus accessible to physically disabled. **Computers:** Students can register for classes online. Administrative functions (other than registration) can be performed online.

CAMPUS LIFE
Environment: Activities: student government, student newspaper 16 registered organizations, 5 honor societies.

ADMISSIONS
Freshman Academic Profile: Average high school GPA 2.7. Minimum paper TOEFL 525. **Basis for Candidate Selection:** *Very important factors considered include:* rigor of secondary school record. *Other factors considered include:*

Class rank, application essay, recommendation(s), standardized test scores. **Freshman Admission Requirements:** High school diploma is required and GED is accepted. **Transfer Admission Requirements:** college transcript(s), minimum college GPA of 2.0 required. Lowest grade transferable C–. **General Admission Information:** Application Fee $55. Notification on a rolling basis, beginning on or about 1/15. Nonfall registration accepted. Admission may be deferred for a maximum of 12 months. Credit offered for CEEB Advanced Placement tests.

COSTS AND FINANCIAL AID
Annual tuition $17,400. Average book expense $1,920. **Required Forms and Deadlines:** FAFSA, institution's own financial aid form. **Types of Aid:** *Need-based scholarships/grants:* Federal Pell, SEOG, the school's own gift aid. *Loans:* Direct Subsidized Stafford, Direct Unsubsidized Stafford, Federal Perkins, state loans. **Student Employment:** Federal Work-Study Program available. Institutional employment available. Highest amount earned per year from on-campus jobs $2,480. Off-campus job opportunities are good. **Financial Aid Statistics:** 20% undergrads receive need-based scholarship or grant aid. 24% undergrads receive non-need-based scholarship or grant aid. 100% undergrads receive need-based self-help aid. 73% undergrads borrow to pay for school. Average cumulative indebtedness $37,500. **Criteria for awarding institutional aid:** *Non-need-based:* academics, alumni affiliation, leadership.

GOLDEY-BEACOM COLLEGE

4701 Limestone Road, Wilmington, DE 19808
Phone: 302-998-8814
E-mail: admissions@gbc.edu • **CEEB Code:** 5255
Fax: 302-996-5408 • **Website:** www.goldey.gbc.edu

This private school was founded in 1886. It has a 27-acre campus.

RATINGS
Admissions Selectivity Rating: 69   **Fire Safety Rating:** 60*   **Green Rating:** 60*

STUDENTS AND FACULTY
Enrollment: 385. **Student Body:** 50% out-of-state, 8% international (60 countries represented). Asian 2%, African American 6%, Caucasian 64%, Hispanic 2%, Native American 0%. **Retention and Graduation:** 5% grads go on to further study within 1 year. 1% grads pursue law degrees. 4% grads pursue business degrees. **Faculty:** 0% of classes are taught by teaching assistants.

ACADEMICS
Degrees: associate, bachelor's, master's. **Special Study Options:** Accelerated program, cooperative education program, distance learning, independent study, internships.

FACILITIES
Housing: Coed dorms, fraternity/sorority housing, apartments for single students.

CAMPUS LIFE
Environment: Village. **Activities:** drama/theater, student government, student newspaper 4 religious organizations. **Athletics (Intercollegiate):** *Men:* soccer, softball. *Women:* softball.

ADMISSIONS
Freshman Academic Profile: Minimum paper TOEFL 500. **Basis for Candidate Selection:** *Very important factors considered include:* rigor of secondary school record, standardized test scores. *Important factors considered include:* Class rank, recommendation(s). *Other factors considered include:* character/personal qualities, interview. **Freshman Admission Requirements:** High school diploma is required and GED is accepted. *Academic units required:* 4 English, 3 mathematics, 3 science. *Academic units recommended:* 4 English, 3 mathematics, 3 science. **Freshman Admission Statistics:** 689 applied, 77% admitted, 56% enrolled. **Transfer Admission Requirements:** High school transcript, college transcript(s), minimum college GPA of 2.0 required. Lowest grade transferable 2. **General Admission Information:** Application Fee $30. Regular application deadline 8/15. Notification on a rolling basis, beginning on or about 10/1. Nonfall registration accepted. Admission may be deferred for a maximum of 12. Credit and/or placement offered for CEEB Advanced Placement tests.

COSTS AND FINANCIAL AID
Annual tuition $12,928. Room and board $4,240. Required fees $120. Average book expense $700. **Required Forms and Deadlines: Notification of Awards: Types of Aid:** *Need-based scholarships/grants:* Federal Pell, SEOG, state scholarships/grants, private scholarships, the school's own gift aid. *Loans:*

Subsidized Stafford, Unsubsidized Stafford, PLUS, Federal Perkins, state loans, college/university loans from institutional funds. **Student Employment:** Federal Work-Study Program available. Off-campus job opportunities are excellent.

GONZAGA UNIVERSITY

Best 378

502 E. Boone Avenue, Spokane, WA 99258
Phone: 509-313-6572 • **Financial Aid Phone:** 509-313-6582
E-mail: admissions@gonzaga.edu • **CEEB Code:** 4330
Fax: 509-313-5780 • **Website:** www.gonzaga.edu • **ACT Code:** 4458

This private school, affiliated with the Roman Catholic Church,, affiliated with the Catholic-Jesuit Church, was founded in 1887. It has a 108-acre campus.

RATINGS
Admissions Selectivity Rating: 89   **Fire Safety Rating:** 91   **Green Rating:** 80

STUDENTS AND FACULTY
Enrollment: 4,829. **Student Body:** 54% female, 46% male, 51% out-of-state, 2% international (20 countries represented). Asian 4%, African American 1%, Caucasian 74%, Hispanic 8%, Native American 1%.
Retention and Graduation: 68% freshmen graduate within 4 years. 81% freshmen graduate within 6 years. **Faculty:** Student/faculty ratio 11:1. 408 full-time faculty, 86% hold PhDs, 11% are members of minority groups, 42% are women. 0% of classes are taught by teaching assistants.

ACADEMICS
Degrees: bachelor's, master's. **Classes:** Most classes have 20–29 students. Most lab/discussion sessions have 10–19 students. **Majors with Highest Enrollment:** political science and government; psychology. **Special Study Options:** Accelerated program, double major, dual enrollment, English as a Second Language (ESL), exchange student program (domestic), honors program, independent study, internships, study abroad, teacher certification program. **Honors Programs:** Hogan Entrepreneurial Leadership Program- Immerses students in the fundamentals of creating and managing new ventures in the public and private sectors **Combined Degree Programs:** MAcc/JD, MBA/JD, BSN/MSN. **Disability Services:** Special programs offered to physically disabled students include note-taking services, reader services, tape recorders. **Career Services:** Alumni network, alumni services, career/job search classes, career assessment, internships, regional alumni.

FACILITIES
Housing: Coed dorms, special housing for disabled students, men's dorms, special housing for international students, women's dorms, apartments for married students, apartments for single students, theme housing, 90% of campus accessible to physically disabled. **Special Academic Facilities/Equipment:** Art center, museum, language lab, TV production center, educational center, two electron microscopes. **Computers:** 75% of classrooms, 90% of dorms, 100% of libraries, 100% of student union, 75% of common outdoor areas have wireless network access. Students can register for classes online. Administrative functions (other than registration) can be performed online.

CAMPUS LIFE
Environment: City. **Activities:** Choral groups, concert band, dance, drama/theater, jazz band, literary magazine, music ensembles, pep band, radio station, student government, student newspaper, symphony orchestra, television station, yearbook, Campus Ministries 86 registered organizations, 10 honor societies, 4 religious organizations. **Athletics (Intercollegiate):** *Men:* baseball, basketball, crew/rowing, cross-country, golf, soccer, tennis, track/field (outdoor). *Women:* basketball, crew/rowing, cross-country, golf, soccer, tennis, track/field (outdoor), volleyball. **On-Campus Highlights:** St Aloysius Cathedral, McCarthy Athletic Center, Jundt Art Museum, Bing Crosby Museum in the Crosby Student Center, The Gonzaga University Bookstore. **Environmental Initiatives:** Developing an emission inventory and a comprehensive Climate Action Plan. Formation of the Advisory Council on Stewardship and Sustainability, which reports directly to the President and has a dedicated budget. Participation in the Curriculum for the Bioregion initiative, which will expand the incorporation of sustainability across the curriculum

ADMISSIONS
Freshman Academic Profile: Average high school GPA 3.7. 38% in top 10% of high school class, 73% in top 25% of high school class, 93% in top 50% of

high school class. 59% from public high schools. SAT Math middle 50% range 550-650. SAT Critical Reading middle 50% range 540-640. ACT middle 50% range 25-29. Minimum paper TOEFL 550. **Basis for Candidate Selection:** *Very important factors considered include:* academic GPA, rigor of secondary school record, character/personal qualities, first generation. *Important factors considered include:* application essay, recommendation(s), standardized test scores, extracurricular activities, talent/ability. *Other factors considered include:* Class rank, alumni/ae relation, interview, level of applicant's interest, racial/ethnic status, volunteer work, work experience. **Freshman Admission Requirements:** High school diploma is required and GED is not accepted. *Academic units required:* 4 English, 3 mathematics, 3 science, (3 science labs), 3 foreign language, 2 social studies, 2 history, 2 academic electives. *Academic units recommended:* 4 English, 3 mathematics, 3 science, (3 science labs), 3 foreign language, 2 social studies, 2 history, 2 academic electives. **Freshman Admission Statistics:** 6,991 applied, 67% admitted, 24% enrolled. **Transfer Admission Requirements:** college transcript(s), essay or personal statement, statement of good standing from prior institution(s). Minimum college GPA of 2.7 required. Lowest grade transferable C. **General Admission Information:** Application Fee $50. Regular application deadline 2/1. Regular notification 3/15. Nonfall registration accepted. Admission may be deferred for a maximum of 1 year. Credit and/or placement offered for CEEB Advanced Placement tests.

COSTS AND FINANCIAL AID
Annual tuition $33,160. Room and board $8,730. Required fees $492. Average book expense $1,030. **Required Forms and Deadlines:** FAFSA. **Notification of Awards:** Applicants will be notified of awards on a rolling basis beginning 3/1. **Types of Aid:** *Need-based scholarships/grants:* Federal Pell, SEOG, state scholarships/grants, private scholarships, the school's own gift aid, United Negro College Fund, Federal Nursing Scholarships. *Loans:* Subsidized Stafford, Unsubsidized Stafford, PLUS, Federal Perkins, Federal Nursing, state loans, college/university loans from institutional funds. **Student Employment:** Federal Work-Study Program available. Institutional employment available. Off-campus job opportunities are excellent. **Financial Aid Statistics:** 100% freshmen, 99% undergrads receive need-based scholarship or grant aid. 25% freshmen, 18% undergrads receive non-need-based scholarship or grant aid. 67% freshmen, 70% undergrads receive need-based self-help aid. 4% freshmen, 3% undergrads receive athletic scholarships. 99% freshmen, 98% undergrads receive any aid. 66% undergrads borrow to pay for school. Average cumulative indebtedness $29,776. **Criteria for awarding institutional aid:** *Non-need-based:* academics, alumni affiliation, athletics, leadership, minority status, music/drama.

See page 1090.

GORDON COLLEGE

255 Grapevine Road, Wenham, MA 01984-1899
Phone: 978-867-4218 • **Financial Aid Phone:** 978-867-4246
E-mail: admissions@gordon.edu • **CEEB Code:** 3417
Fax: 978-867-4682 • **Website:** www.gordon.edu • **ACT Code:** 1838

This private school, affiliated with the Protestant Church, was founded in 1889. It has a 500-acre campus.

RATINGS
Admissions Selectivity Rating: 93   **Fire Safety Rating:** 84   **Green Rating:** 81

STUDENTS AND FACULTY
Enrollment: 1,563. **Student Body:** 62% female, 38% male, 68% out-of-state, 4% international (69 countries represented). Asian 3%, African American 3%, Caucasian 79%, Hispanic 7%, Native American 0%.
Retention and Graduation: 80% freshmen return for sophomore year. 60% freshmen graduate within 4 years. 74% freshmen graduate within 6 years. 21% grads go on to further study within 1 year. **Faculty:** Student/faculty ratio 13:1. 92 full-time faculty, 86% hold PhDs, 9% are members of minority groups, 35% are women. 0% of classes are taught by teaching assistants.

ACADEMICS
Degrees: bachelor's, master's. **Classes:** Most classes have 10–19 students. Most lab/discussion sessions have 10–19 students. **Majors with Highest Enrollment:** business/commerce; English language and literature; psychology. **Special Study Options:** cooperative education program, cross-registration, double major, honors program, independent study, internships, liberal arts/career combination, student-designed major, study abroad, teacher certification program, Gordon-in-Boston Urban Semester; Gordon-in-France; Italian Semester in Orvieto, Italy; Oregon Extension; Outdoor Education Immersion Semester; LaVida Wilderness Expedition; Co-Op Programs: Arts, Business, Computer Science, Education, Engineering, Health Professions, Humanities, Natural Science, Social/Behavioral Science. **Honors Programs:** The Jerusalem and Athens Forum is a new interdisciplinary honors program at Gordon Col-

lege, beginning in the academic year 2004-05. Through a variety of program components, but principally a great books course in the history of Christian thought and literature, the program strives to help students reflect on the relationship between faith and intellect, deepen their own sense of vocation, and awaken their capacities for intellectual and moral leadership. (Description taken from www.gordon.edu/jaf) The Kenneth L. Pike Honors Program provides exceptional students with an opportunity to meet unique academic goals not possible under existing Gordon programs by designing individualized, disciplined and chalenging interdisciplinary academic experiences. (Description taken from the Gordon College Academic Catalog) **Combined Degree Programs:** BA/MA, 2-2 allied health sciences prog with Thomas Jeffer. **Disability Services:** Special programs offered to physically disabled students include tape recorders, tutors. **Career Services:** Alumni network, career/job search classes, career assessment, internships Career Services highlights include Harmeling Physical Therapy Clinic located on campus provides Movement Science students hands-on experience.

FACILITIES

Housing: Coed dorms, special housing for disabled students, men's dorms, apartments for married students, apartments for single students, theme housing, International hall, mentoring hall. Also Gordon's dorms. are coed by floors and/or wings. Men and women do not live together or share facilities. 99% of campus accessible to physically disabled. **Special Academic Facilities/Equipment:** Barrington Center for the Arts; Phillips Music Center; Center for Balance and Mobility; an electron microscope; a gene sequencer; papers of British Statesman/Reformer, William Wilberforce; East-West Institute; Center for Student Leadership; Center for Christian Studies; international office for Christians in the Visual Arts (CIVA). **Computers:** Administrative functions (other than registration) can be performed online.

CAMPUS LIFE

Environment: Village. **Activities:** Choral groups, concert band, drama/theater, jazz band, literary magazine, music ensembles, musical theater, student government, student newspaper, student-run film society, symphony orchestra, yearbook, Campus Ministries, International Student Organization, Model UN 35 registered organizations, 17 honor societies, 15 religious organizations. **Athletics (Intercollegiate):** *Men:* baseball, basketball, cross-country, lacrosse, soccer, swimming, tennis, track/field (outdoor), track/field (indoor). *Women:* basketball, cross-country, field hockey, lacrosse, soccer, softball, swimming, tennis, track/field (outdoor), track/field (indoor), volleyball. **On-Campus Highlights:** Gillies Lounge/Claymore Cafe, Hiking/biking/cross country ski trails, Bennett Athletic and Recreation Center, Barrington Center for the Arts, Canoeing/swimming ponds, Gordon's campus had many lakes and trails for use by the student body. On campus recreational activities are regularly planned and/or available. **Environmental Initiatives:** Winner of MA College/University Recycling Award 2008 Green Chemistry practice and teaching Frost Hall Wetland Restoration Project.

ADMISSIONS

Freshman Academic Profile: Average high school GPA 3.6. 32% in top 10% of high school class, 68% in top 25% of high school class, 91% in top 50% of high school class. SAT Math middle 50% range 506-642. SAT Critical Reading middle 50% range 510-646. SAT Writing middle 50% range 509-641. ACT middle 50% range 23-29. Minimum web-based TOEFL 85. **Basis for Candidate Selection:** *Very important factors considered include:* application essay, academic GPA, recommendation(s), rigor of secondary school record, standardized test scores, character/personal qualities, extracurricular activities, interview, religious affiliation/commitment. *Important factors considered include:* Class rank, talent/ability. *Other factors considered include:* alumni/ae relation, racial/ethnic status, volunteer work, work experience. **Freshman Admission Requirements:** High school diploma is required and GED is accepted. *Academic units required:* 4 English, 2 mathematics, 2 science, (1 science labs), 2 foreign language, 2 social studies, 5 academic electives. *Academic units recommended:* 4 English, 2 mathematics, 2 science, (1 science labs), 2 foreign language, 2 social studies, 5 academic electives. **Freshman Admission Statistics:** 4,008 applied, 40% admitted, 29% enrolled. **Transfer Admission Requirements:** college transcript(s), essay or personal statement, interview, statement of good standing from prior institution(s). Minimum college GPA of 2.0 required. Lowest grade transferable C. **General Admission Information:** Application Fee $50. Early decision application deadline 11/15. Notification on a rolling basis, beginning on or about 12/15. Nonfall registration accepted. Admission may be deferred for a maximum of 12 months. Credit offered for CEEB Advanced Placement tests.

COSTS AND FINANCIAL AID

Annual tuition $30,740. Room and board $8,840. Required fees $1,360. Average book expense $800. **Required Forms and Deadlines:** FAFSA. **Notification of Awards:** Applicants will be notified of awards on a rolling basis beginning 4/15. **Types of Aid:** *Need-based scholarships/grants:* Federal Pell, SEOG, state scholarships/grants, private scholarships, the school's own gift aid. *Loans:* Subsidized Stafford, Unsubsidized Stafford, PLUS, Federal Perkins, state loans, college/university loans from institutional funds. **Student Employment:** Federal Work-Study Program available. Highest amount earned per year from on-campus jobs $1,500. Off-campus job opportunities are good. **Financial Aid Statistics:** 100% freshmen, 99% undergrads receive need-based scholarship or grant aid. 12% freshmen, 10% undergrads receive non-need-based scholarship or grant aid. 85% freshmen, 88% undergrads receive need-based self-help aid. 96% freshmen, 96% undergrads receive any aid. 82% undergrads borrow to pay for school. Average cumulative indebtedness $37,534. **Criteria for awarding institutional aid:** *Non-need-based:* academics, alumni affiliation, art, leadership, minority status, music/drama, religious affiliation.

GOSHEN COLLEGE

1700 South Main Street, Goshen, IN 46526-4794
Phone: 574-535-7535 • **Financial Aid Phone:** 574-535-7525
E-mail: admission@goshen.edu • **CEEB Code:** 1251
Fax: 574-535-7609 • **Website:** www.goshen.edu • **ACT Code:** 1196

This private school, affiliated with the Mennonite Church, was founded in 1894. It has a 135-acre campus.

RATINGS

Admissions Selectivity Rating: 83   **Fire Safety Rating:** 96   **Green Rating:** 69

STUDENTS AND FACULTY

Enrollment: 860. **Student Body:** 59% female, 41% male, 49% out-of-state, 9% international (37 countries represented). Asian 1%, African American 3%, Caucasian 74%, Hispanic 10%, Native American 0%. **Retention and Graduation:** 83% freshmen return for sophomore year. 55% freshmen graduate within 4 years. 70% freshmen graduate within 6 years. 10% grads go on to further study within 1 year, 6% grads pursue arts and sciences degrees. 1% grads pursue medical degrees. **Faculty:** Student/faculty ratio 10:1. 71 full-time faculty, 65% hold PhDs, 10% are members of minority groups, 51% are women. 0% of classes are taught by teaching assistants.

ACADEMICS

Degrees: bachelor's, certificate, master's. **Classes:** Most classes have 10–19 students. Most lab/discussion sessions have 10–19 students. **Majors with Highest Enrollment:** business/commerce; elementary education and teaching, nursing/registered nurse (rn, asn, bsn, msn). **Special Study Options:** cross-registration, double major, dual enrollment, independent study, internships, liberal arts/career combination, student-designed major, study abroad, teacher certification program, Adult degree completion program (one evening per week, concentrated study). **Combined Degree Programs:** BA/BS Eng. **Disability Services:** Special programs offered to physically disabled students include note-taking services, reader services, tape recorders, tutors. **Career Services:** Alumni network, career/job search classes, internships, regional alumni.

FACILITIES

Housing: Coed dorms, special housing for disabled students, men's dorms, women's dorms, apartments for married students, apartments for single students, wellness housing, 88% of campus accessible to physically disabled. **Special Academic Facilities/Equipment:** X-ray precision lab, lab kindergarten, Mennonite Historical Library. **Computers:** 100% of classrooms, 25% of dorms, 80% of libraries, 75% of dining areas, 100% of student union, have wireless network access. Students can register for classes online. Administrative functions (other than registration) can be performed online.

CAMPUS LIFE

Environment: Town. **Activities:** Choral groups, concert band, drama/theater, jazz band, music ensembles, musical theater, opera, radio station, student government, student newspaper, student-run film society, symphony orchestra, yearbook, Campus Ministries, International Student Organization 21 registered organizations, 4 religious organizations. **Athletics (Intercollegiate):** *Men:* baseball, basketball, cross-country, golf, soccer, tennis, track/field (outdoor), track/field (indoor). *Women:* basketball, cross-country, soccer, softball, tennis, track/field (outdoor), track/field (indoor), volleyball. **On-Campus Highlights:** Music Center, Gingerich Rec-Fitness Center, Science Building, Residential Halls Connector, Good Library. **Environmental Initiatives:** Built the first Platinum LEED Certified facility in Indiana at our Merry Lea Environmental Center. www.goshen.edu/merrylea Signing the President's Climate Commitment and the formation of the Ecological Stewardship Committee Have reduced campus wide gas use by 31% and electric use by 17% over the last six years during a time when actual square footage of buildings increased by 20%.

ADMISSIONS

Freshman Academic Profile: Average high school GPA 3.4. 27% in top 10% of high school class, 55% in top 25% of high school class, 88% in top 50% of high school class. 81% from public high schools. SAT Math middle 50% range 510-640. SAT Critical Reading middle 50% range 460-620. SAT Writing middle

50% range 470-570. ACT middle 50% range 21-28. Minimum paper TOEFL 550. **Basis for Candidate Selection:** *Very important factors considered include:* academic GPA, rigor of secondary school record, standardized test scores. *Important factors considered include:* Class rank, recommendation(s), character/personal qualities, interview. *Other factors considered include:* application essay, alumni/ae relation, extracurricular activities, level of applicant's interest, religious affiliation/commitment, talent/ability, volunteer work, work experience. **Freshman Admission Requirements:** High school diploma is required and GED is accepted. *Academic units required:* 4 English, 2 mathematics, 2 science, 2 foreign language, 2 social studies, 2 history. *Academic units recommended:* 4 English, 2 mathematics, 2 science, 2 foreign language, 2 social studies, 2 history. **Freshman Admission Statistics:** 608 applied, 60% admitted, 46% enrolled. **Transfer Admission Requirements:** college transcript(s), essay or personal statement, statement of good standing from prior institution(s). Lowest grade transferable C. **General Admission Information:** Application Fee $25. Regular application deadline 8/1. Notification on a rolling basis, beginning on or about 9/15. Nonfall registration accepted. Admission may be deferred for a maximum of 1 year. Credit and/or placement offered for CEEB Advanced Placement tests.

COSTS AND FINANCIAL AID

Annual tuition $26,900. Room and board $9,000. Average book expense $890. **Required Forms and Deadlines:** FAFSA, institution's own financial aid form. **Notification of Awards:** Applicants will be notified of awards on a rolling basis beginning 3/1. **Types of Aid:** *Need-based scholarships/grants:* Federal Pell, SEOG, state scholarships/grants, private scholarships, the school's own gift aid. *Loans:* Direct Subsidized Stafford, Direct Unsubsidized Stafford, Direct PLUS, Federal Perkins, Federal Nursing, college/university loans from institutional funds. **Student Employment:** Federal Work-Study Program available. Institutional employment available. Highest amount earned per year from on-campus jobs $1,001. Off-campus job opportunities are poor. **Financial Aid Statistics:** 100% freshmen, 97% undergrads receive need-based scholarship or grant aid. 18% freshmen, 14% undergrads receive non-need-based scholarship or grant aid. 78% freshmen, 81% undergrads receive need-based self-help aid. 14% freshmen, 11% undergrads receive athletic scholarships. 100% freshmen, 98% undergrads receive any aid. 72% undergrads borrow to pay for school. Average cumulative indebtedness $21,953. **Criteria for awarding institutional aid:** *Non-need-based:* academics, art, athletics, leadership, music/drama.

GOUCHER COLLEGE

1021 Dulaney Valley Road, Baltimore, MD 21204-2794
Phone: 410-337-6100 • **Financial Aid Phone:** 410-337-6141
E-mail: admissions@goucher.edu • **CEEB Code:** 5257
Fax: 410-337-6354 • **Website:** www.goucher.edu • **ACT Code:** 1696

This private school was founded in 1885. It has a 287-acre campus.

RATINGS

Admissions Selectivity Rating: 79   **Fire Safety Rating:** 88   **Green Rating:** 94

STUDENTS AND FACULTY

Enrollment: 1,469. **Student Body:** 67% female, 33% male, 73% out-of-state, 2% international (49 countries represented). Asian 3%, African American 9%, Caucasian 65%, Hispanic 7%.
Retention and Graduation: 84% freshmen return for sophomore year. 57% freshmen graduate within 4 years. 66% freshmen graduate within 6 years. 41% grads go on to further study within 1 year. 32% grads pursue arts and sciences degrees. 6% grads pursue law degrees. 1% grads pursue business degrees. **Faculty:** Student/faculty ratio 9:1. 135 full-time faculty, 90% hold PhDs, 17% are are members of minority groups, 56% are women. 0% of classes are taught by teaching assistants.

ACADEMICS

Degrees: bachelor's, master's, post-bachelor's certificate. **Classes:** Most classes have 10–19 students. **Majors with Highest Enrollment:** biology/biological sciences; business administration and management; elementary education and teaching. **Special Study Options:** cross-registration, distance learning, double major, dual enrollment, independent study, internships, student-designed major, study abroad, teacher certification program. **Combined degree programs:** BA/MEng. **Career services:** Alumni network, alumni services, career assessment, internships Career services highlights include Goucher has been linking

liberal arts education with internships for more than 75 years. Through our internship program, we help students explore career paths, enhance skills, and experience the world of work.

FACILITIES

Housing: Coed dorms, special housing for disabled students, women's dorms, apartments for single students, Wellness Housing, Theme Housing. **Special Academic Facilities/Equipment:** The Athenaeum is a 103,000-square-foot building which is open 24 hours a day and features a new, technologically superior library; a spacious open forum for performances, public discussions, and other events; a café, art gallery; a center for community service and multicultural affairs programming; and spaces for exercise, conversation, and quiet reflection and relaxation. Goucher, in collaboration with the architecture firm RMJM, approached every aspect of the Athenaeum project with an eye toward sustainable design strategies, and the project is in the process of applying for Silver certification from the Leadership in Energy and Environmental Design (LEED) Green-Building Rating System. The Silber Art Gallery in the Athenaeum provides a suitably secure gallery dedicated solely to the exhibition of art, both from the Goucher collection and from contemporary artists and collectors outside the campus. The 1,000-square-foot gallery is the new home to Goucher's permanent collection and its critically acclaimed program of contemporary art exhibitions. In addition to enabling us to display selections from the college's permanent collection, the gallery hosts a range of programming, from the traditional to the experimental, featuring the work of students, emerging artists, and established names alike. Additionally, Goucher has the Rosenberg Art Gallery and the Scientific Visualization Lab. **Computers:** 95% of classrooms, 40% of dorms, 100% of libraries, 100% of dining areas, 100% of student union, 80% of common outdoor areas have wireless network access. Students can register for classes online. Administrative functions (other than registration) can be performed online.

CAMPUS LIFE

Environment: City. **Activities:** Choral groups, dance, drama/theater, jazz band, literary magazine, music ensembles, musical theater, opera, radio station, student government, student newspaper, student-run film society, symphony orchestra, television station, yearbook, Campus Ministries, International Student Organization, Model UN 60 registered organizations, 1 honor societies, 8 religious organizations. **Athletics (Intercollegiate):** Men: basketball, cross-country, lacrosse, soccer, swimming, tennis, track/field (outdoor), track/field (indoor). Women: basketball, cross-country, equestrian sports, field hockey, lacrosse, soccer, swimming, tennis, track/field (outdoor), track/field (indoor), volleyball. **On-Campus Highlights:** The Library at the Athenaeum, Alice's Cafe, Sports and Recreation Center, Pearlstone Cafe, Gopher Hole. **Environmental Initiatives:** Our newest building, the Athenaeum, was awarded Gold certification from the Leadership in Energy and Environmental Design (LEED) rating system, the national recognized standard for measuring a building's environmental sustainability, and committing that future buildings and renovations will also be LEED certified. Goucher, in collaboration with the architecture firm RMJM, approached every aspect of the Athenaeum project with an eye toward sustainable design strategies. Goucher has completed its greenhouse gas emissions inventory and Climate Action Plan, as required by the American College and University Presidents Climate Commitment.

ADMISSIONS

Freshman Academic Profile: Average high school GPA 3.16. 26% in top 10% of high school class, 57% in top 25% of high school class, 87% in top 50% of high school class. 64% from public high schools. SAT Math middle 50% range 480-620. SAT Critical Reading middle 50% range 510-640. SAT Writing middle 50% range 500-630. ACT middle 50% range 22-28. Minimum paper TOEFL 550. **Basis for Candidate Selection:** Very important factors considered include: academic GPA, rigor of secondary school record. Important factors considered include: application essay, recommendation(s), talent/ability. Other factors considered include: Class rank, standardized test scores, alumni/ae relation, character/personal qualities, extracurricular activities, first generation, geographical residence, interview, level of applicant's interest, racial/ethnic status, state residency, volunteer work, work experience. **Freshman Admission Requirements:** High school diploma is required and GED is accepted. **Academic units required:** 4 English, 3 mathematics, 2 science, 2 foreign language, 3 social studies, 2 academic electives. **Academic units recommended:** 4 English, 3 mathematics, 2 science, 2 foreign language, 3 social studies, 2 academic electives. **Freshman Admission Statistics:** 3615 applied, 72% admitted, 16% enrolled. **Transfer Admission Requirements:** college transcript(s), essay or personal statement, Lowest grade transferable C. **General Admission Information:** Application Fee $55. Regular application deadline 2/1. Regular notification 4/1. Nonfall registration accepted. Admission may be deferred for a maximum of one year. Credit and/or placement offered for CEEB Advanced Placement tests.

COSTS AND FINANCIAL AID

Annual tuition $37,072. Room and board $11,322. Required fees $568. Average book expense $800. **Required Forms and Deadlines:** FAFSA, CSS/Financial

Aid PROFILE, noncustodial PROFILE, business/farm supplement. **Notification of Awards:** Applicants will be notified of awards on a rolling basis beginning 4/1. **Types of Aid:** Need-based scholarships/grants: Federal Pell, SEOG, state scholarships/grants, private scholarships, the school's own gift aid. Loans: Subsidized Stafford, Unsubsidized Stafford, PLUS, Federal Perkins, college/university loans from institutional funds. Student Employment: Federal Work-Study Program available. Institutional employment available. Highest amount earned per year from on-campus jobs $8,356. Off-campus job opportunities are excellent. **Financial Aid Statistics:** 98% freshmen, 97% undergrads receive need-based scholarship or grant aid. 11% freshmen, 8% undergrads receive non-need-based scholarship or grant aid. 88% freshmen, 88% undergrads receive need-based self-help aid. % freshmen, % undergrads receive athletic scholarships. 90% freshmen, 84% undergrads receive any aid. 43% undergrads borrow to pay for school. Average cumulative indebtedness 29135. **Criteria for awarding institutional aid:** Non-need-based: academics, art, leadership, music/drama.

GOVERNORS STATE UNIVERSITY

1 University Parkway, University Park, IL 60484
Phone: 708-534-4490 • **Financial Aid Phone:** 708-534-4480
E-mail: gsunow@govst.edu
Fax: 708-534-1640 • **Website:** www.govst.edu

This public school was founded in 1969. It has a 720-acre campus.

RATINGS
Admissions Selectivity Rating: 61   Fire Safety Rating: 60*   Green Rating: 60*

STUDENTS AND FACULTY
Retention and Graduation: 34% grads go on to further study within 1 year. 17% grads pursue arts and sciences degrees. 1% grads pursue law degrees. 16% grads pursue business degrees. **Faculty:** Student/faculty ratio 16:1. 203 full-time faculty, 80% hold PhDs, 25% are members of minority groups, 40% are women. 0% of classes are taught by teaching assistants.

ACADEMICS
Degrees: bachelor's, master's, post-master's certificate. **Majors with Highest Enrollment:** business/commerce, communication and media studies, other, elementary education and teaching. **Special Study Options:** cross-registration, distance learning, dual enrollment, external degree program, honors program, independent study, internships, student designed major, study abroad, teacher certification program. **Disability Services:** Special programs offered to physically disabled students include note-taking services, reader services, tape recorders, tutors. **Career Services:** Alumni network, alumni services, career/job search classes, career assessment, internships.

FACILITIES
Housing: 99% of campus accessible to physically disabled. **Special Academic Facilities/Equipment:** Manilow Sculpture Park **Computers:** Students can register for classes online. Administrative functions (other than registration) can be performed online.

CAMPUS LIFE
Environment: Village. **Activities:** drama/theater, literary magazine, student government, student newspaper, student-run film society 7 honor societies.

ADMISSIONS
Transfer Admission Requirements: college transcript(s), statement of good standing from prior institution(s). Minimum college GPA of 2.0 required. Lowest grade transferable C. **General Admission Information:** Nonfall registration not accepted.

COSTS AND FINANCIAL AID
Annual in-state tuition $4,470. Annual out-of-state tuition $13,410. Required fees $480. **Types of Aid:** *Need-based scholarships/grants:* Federal Pell, SEOG, state scholarships/grants, private scholarships, the school's own gift aid, Federal Nursing Scholarships. *Loans:* Direct Subsidized Stafford, Federal Perkins, Federal Nursing, state loans, college/university loans from institutional funds. **Student Employment:** Federal Work-Study Program available. Institutional employment available. **Criteria for awarding institutional aid:** *Non-need-based:* academics.

GRACE BIBLE COLLEGE

1011 Aldon Street SW, Grand Rapids, MI 49509-1921
Phone: 616-538-2330
E-mail: enrollment@gbcol.edu
Fax: 616-538-0599 • **Website:** www.gbcol.edu

This is a private school.

RATINGS
Admissions Selectivity Rating: 63   Fire Safety Rating: 60*   Green Rating: 60*

STUDENTS AND FACULTY
Enrollment: 153. **Student Body:** 52% female, 48% male.
Retention and Graduation: 45% freshmen return for sophomore year. 13% freshmen graduate within 4 years. 31% freshmen graduate within 6 years.

ACADEMICS
Degrees: associate, bachelor's.

CAMPUS LIFE
Environment: Village.

ADMISSIONS
Basis for Candidate Selection: *Very important factors considered include:* application essay, rigor of secondary school record, standardized test scores. *Important factors considered include:* Class rank, recommendation(s), character/personal qualities, religious affiliation/commitment. *Other factors considered include:* extracurricular activities, talent/ability, volunteer work, work experience. **Freshman Admission Requirements:** High school diploma is required and GED is accepted. **Freshman Admission Statistics:** 166 applied, 43% admitted, 56% enrolled. **General Admission Information:**

COSTS AND FINANCIAL AID
Annual tuition $11,120. Room and board $6,400. Required fees $520. **Types of Aid:** *Need-based scholarships/grants:* Federal Pell, SEOG, state scholarships/grants, private scholarships, the school's own gift aid. *Loans:* Subsidized Stafford, Unsubsidized Stafford, PLUS, state loans. **Criteria for awarding institutional aid:** *Non-need-based:* academics.

GRACE COLLEGE AND SEMINARY

200 Seminary Drive, Winona Lake, IN 46590
Phone: 800-544-7223 • **Financial Aid Phone:** 574-372-5100
E-mail: enroll@grace.edu • **CEEB Code:** 1252
Fax: 574-372-5120 • **Website:** www.grace.edu • **ACT Code:** 1198

This private school was founded in 1948. It has a 150-acre campus.

RATINGS
Admissions Selectivity Rating: 67   Fire Safety Rating: 75   Green Rating: 60*

STUDENTS AND FACULTY
Enrollment: 1,278. **Student Body:** 59% female, 41% male, 34% out-of-state, 1% international (9 countries represented). Asian 1%, African American 4%, Caucasian 82%, Hispanic 3%, Native American 0%.
Retention and Graduation: 85% freshmen return for sophomore year. 55% freshmen graduate within 4 years. 60% freshmen graduate within 6 years. **Faculty:** Student/faculty ratio 31:1. 44 full-time faculty, 55% hold PhDs, 2% are members of minority groups, 32% are women. 0% of classes are taught by teaching assistants.

ACADEMICS
Degrees: associate, bachelor's, certificate, diploma, master's. **Classes:** Most classes have 10–19 students. Most lab/discussion sessions have 10–19 students. **Majors with Highest Enrollment:** business/commerce; counseling psychology; elementary education and teaching. **Special Study Options:** cooperative education program, cross-registration, distance learning, double major, dual enrollment, exchange student program (domestic), honors program, independent study, internships, liberal arts/career combination, study abroad, teacher certification program, Degree completion. **Disability Services:** Special programs offered to physically disabled students include note-taking services, reader services, tape recorders, tutors. **Career Services:** career assessment.

FACILITIES
Housing: men's dorms, women's dorms, apartments for single students. 85% of campus accessible to physically disabled. **Special Academic Facilities/Equipment:** Reneker Museum of Winona History **Computers:** 100% of classrooms,

100% of dorms, 100% of libraries, 100% of dining areas, 100% of student union, 33% of common outdoor areas have wireless network access. Students can register for classes online. Administrative functions (other than registration) can be performed online.

CAMPUS LIFE

Environment: Village. **Activities:** Choral groups, concert band, drama/theater, music ensembles, musical theater, opera, pep band, student government, student newspaper, symphony orchestra, yearbook, Campus Ministries 9 registered organizations, 1 honor societies, 8 religious organizations. **Athletics (Intercollegiate):** *Men:* baseball, basketball, cheerleading, cross-country, golf, soccer, tennis, track/field (outdoor). *Women:* basketball, cheerleading, cross-country, soccer, softball, tennis, track/field (outdoor), volleyball. **On-Campus Highlights:** Gordon Recreation Center, Tree of Life Coffee shop, Westminster Grille, Orthopedic Capital Center.

ADMISSIONS

Freshman Academic Profile: Average high school GPA 3.5. 28% in top 10% of high school class, 56% in top 25% of high school class, 81% in top 50% of high school class. 71% from public high schools. SAT Math middle 50% range 460-600. SAT Critical Reading middle 50% range 470-580. ACT middle 50% range 21-27. **Basis for Candidate Selection:** *Very important factors considered include:* application essay, recommendation(s), rigor of secondary school record, standardized test scores, religious affiliation/commitment. *Important factors considered include:* academic GPA, character/personal qualities. *Other factors considered include:* Class rank, alumni/ae relation, extracurricular activities, interview, talent/ability. **Freshman Admission Requirements:** High school diploma is required and GED is accepted. **Freshman Admission Statistics:** 2,237 applied, 91% admitted, 18% enrolled. **Transfer Admission Requirements:** college transcript(s), essay or personal statement, standardized test scores, minimum college GPA of 2.0 required. Lowest grade transferable C–. **General Admission Information:** Application Fee $20. Regular application deadline 8/15. Notification on a rolling basis, beginning on or about 9/1. Nonfall registration accepted. Admission may be deferred for a maximum of 1 semester. Credit offered for CEEB Advanced Placement tests.

COSTS AND FINANCIAL AID

Annual tuition $23,290. Room and board $7,454. Average book expense $1,000. **Required Forms and Deadlines:** FAFSA. **Notification of Awards:** Applicants will be notified of awards on a rolling basis beginning 3/1. **Types of Aid:** *Need-based scholarships/grants:* Federal Pell, SEOG, state scholarships/grants, private scholarships, the school's own gift aid. *Loans:* Subsidized Stafford, Unsubsidized Stafford, PLUS, Federal Perkins, Alternative Educational Loan Program. **Student Employment:** Federal Work-Study Program available. Institutional employment available. Off-campus job opportunities are good. **Financial Aid Statistics:** 89% freshmen, 89% undergrads receive need-based scholarship or grant aid. 99% freshmen, 86% undergrads receive non-need-based scholarship or grant aid. 77% freshmen, 78% undergrads receive need-based self-help aid. **Criteria for awarding institutional aid:** *Non-need-based:* academics, art, athletics, leadership, music/drama.

GRACE UNIVERSITY

1311 S 9th St, Omaha, NE 68108
Phone: 402-449-2831
E-mail: admissions@graceu.com
Fax: 402-341-9587 • **Website:** www.graceuniversity.com • **ACT Code:** 2454

This private school, affiliated with the Christian (Nondenominational) Church, was founded in 1943. It has a 20-acre campus.

RATINGS

Admissions Selectivity Rating: 61   **Fire Safety Rating:** 67   **Green Rating:** 60*

STUDENTS AND FACULTY

Enrollment: 427. **Student Body:** 57% female, 43% male, 60% out-of-state, 1% international (7 countries represented). Asian 0%, African American 5%, Caucasian 99%, Hispanic 2%, Native American 0%.
Retention and Graduation: **Faculty:** Student/faculty ratio 18:1. 25 full-time faculty, 100% hold PhDs, 8% are members of minority groups, 28% are women. 0% of classes are taught by teaching assistants.

ACADEMICS

Degrees: associate, bachelor's, certificate, master's, terminal associate, transfer associate. **Majors with Highest Enrollment:** bible/biblical studies; education; youth ministry. **Special Study Options:** Accelerated program, cooperative education program, distance learning, double major, dual enrollment,

independent study, student-designed major, study abroad, teacher certification program. **Disability Services:** Special programs offered to physically disabled students include note-taking services, tape recorders. **Career Services:** career assessment, internships.

FACILITIES

Housing: men's dorms, women's dorms, apartments for married students, 100% of campus accessible to physically disabled. **Computers:** Administrative functions (other than registration) can be performed online.

CAMPUS LIFE

Environment: Metropolis. **Activities:** Choral groups, concert band, drama/theater, music ensembles, musical theater, pep band, radio station, student government, student newspaper, yearbook 6 registered organizations, 1 religious organizations. **Athletics (Intercollegiate):** *Men:* basketball, soccer. *Women:* basketball, volleyball. **On-Campus Highlights:** Dirk Lounge, Health and Fitness Center, Dorms, Dining Commons, Royal's Court.

ADMISSIONS

Freshman Academic Profile: Minimum paper TOEFL 550. **Basis for Candidate Selection:** *Very important factors considered include:* application essay, recommendation(s), rigor of secondary school record, religious affiliation/commitment. *Important factors considered include:* Class rank, standardized test scores, character/personal qualities. *Other factors considered include:* alumni/ae relation, extracurricular activities, interview, talent/ability, volunteer work, work experience. **Freshman Admission Requirements:** High school diploma is required and GED is accepted. **Transfer Admission Requirements:** High school transcript, college transcript(s), essay or personal statement, minimum college GPA of 2.0 required. Lowest grade transferable C. **General Admission Information:** Application Fee $35. Nonfall registration accepted. Admission may be deferred for a maximum of 1 year. Credit offered for CEEB Advanced Placement tests.

COSTS AND FINANCIAL AID

Required Forms and Deadlines: FAFSA, institution's own financial aid form. **Notification of Awards:** Applicants will be notified of awards on or about 4/1. **Types of Aid:** *Need-based scholarships/grants:* Federal Pell, SEOG, state scholarships/grants, private scholarships, the school's own gift aid, United Negro College Fund. *Loans:* Subsidized Stafford, Unsubsidized Stafford, PLUS, Alternative Loans. **Student Employment:** Federal Work-Study Program available. Institutional employment available. Highest amount earned per year from on-campus jobs $3,750. Off-campus job opportunities are excellent. **Financial Aid Statistics:** 94% freshmen, 89% undergrads receive need-based scholarship or grant aid. 9% freshmen, 9% undergrads receive non-need-based scholarship or grant aid. 82% freshmen, 80% undergrads receive need-based self-help aid. 77% freshmen, 78% undergrads receive any aid. 72% undergrads borrow to pay for school. Average cumulative indebtedness $11,282. **Criteria for awarding institutional aid:** *Non-need-based:* academics, alumni affiliation, leadership, music/drama, religious affiliation.

GRACELAND UNIVERSITY

1 University Place, Lamoni, IA 50140
Phone: 641-784-5196 • **Financial Aid Phone:** 641-784-5140
E-mail: admissions@graceland.edu • **CEEB Code:** 6249
Fax: 641-784-5480 • **Website:** www.graceland.edu • **ACT Code:** 1314

This private school was founded in 1895. It has a 170-acre campus.

RATINGS

Admissions Selectivity Rating: 81   **Fire Safety Rating:** 69   **Green Rating:** 81

STUDENTS AND FACULTY

Enrollment: 1,347. **Student Body:** 58% female, 42% male, 75% out-of-state, 8% international (34 countries represented). Asian 1%, African American 8%, Caucasian 65%, Hispanic 7%, Native American 1%.
Retention and Graduation: 34% freshmen graduate within 4 years. 27% grads go on to further study within 1 year. 3% grads pursue arts and sciences degrees. 3% grads pursue law degrees. 5% grads pursue business degrees. 5% grads pursue medical degrees. **Faculty:** Student/faculty ratio 15:1. 85 full-time faculty, 76% hold PhDs, 8% are members of minority groups, 54% are women. 0% of classes are taught by teaching assistants.

ACADEMICS

Degrees: bachelor's, master's, post-bachelor's certificate, post-master's certificate. **Classes:** Most classes have 10–19 students. Most lab/discussion sessions have 20–29 students. **Majors with Highest Enrollment:** business administration and management; elementary education and teaching; nursing/registered nurse (rn, asn, bsn, msn). **Special Study Options:** Accelerated program, distance learning, double major, dual enrollment, English as a Second Language (ESL), honors program, independent study, internships, liberal arts/career combination, student-designed major, study abroad, teacher certification program. **Honors Programs:** The Graceland University Honors Program includes courses in Honors English, Honors Humanities, Honors Advanced Composition, the combined Jr. and Sr. Honors Seminar, a Sr. Honors Thesis, and Honors Contracts to be created with instructors in any academic course the students choose. Completion of the Honors Program requires 21 hours of honors credit, completion of the Jr. and Sr. Honors Seminars, a Sr. Honors Thesis, and a minimum 3.5 gpa overall and in their honors work. Honors Students with a 3.75 gpa or higher are eligible for an Honors Scholarship. Incoming students with a 3.75 gap and an ACT of 27 or higher may apply for full tuition Prestigious Honors Scholarship, which are available on a competitive basis, and require an interview. Graceland University offers an Excellent Education in a caring community. So we believe the best reason to participate in the Honors Program is the people in it, and to participate in the Honors community. **Combined Degree Programs:** BSN/MSN. **Disability Services:** Special programs offered to physically disabled students include note-taking services, reader services, tape recorders, tutors. **Career Services:** Alumni network, alumni services, career/job search classes, career assessment, internships Career Services highlights include We have our own job posting site for students and alumni. We offer our career exploration and job search classes online each semester.

FACILITIES

Housing: men's dorms, women's dorms, apartments for married students 95% of campus accessible to physically disabled. **Computers:** 100% of classrooms, 91% of dorms, 100% of libraries, 100% of dining areas, 100% of student union, 30% of common outdoor areas have wireless network access. Students can register for classes online. Administrative functions (other than registration) can be performed online.

CAMPUS LIFE

Environment: Rural. **Activities:** Choral groups, concert band, dance, drama/theater, jazz band, music ensembles, musical theater, pep band, radio station, student government, student newspaper, symphony orchestra, yearbook, Campus Ministries, International Student Organization 54 registered organizations, 1 religious organizations. **Athletics (Intercollegiate):** *Men:* baseball, basketball, cross-country, football, golf, soccer, tennis, track/field (outdoor), track/field (indoor), volleyball. *Women:* basketball, cross-country, golf, soccer, softball, tennis, track/field (outdoor), track/field (indoor), volleyball. **On-Campus Highlights:** Resch Science & Technology Hall, The Helene Center for Visual Arts, The Closson Center, The Shaw Center for Performing Arts, The Higdon Administration Building. **Environmental Initiatives:** Construction of a rain garden First Year Experience curriculum has a sustainability focus Car Share Program

ADMISSIONS

Freshman Academic Profile: Average high school GPA 3.3. 14% in top 10% of high school class, 37% in top 25% of high school class, 65% in top 50% of high school class. 99% from public high schools. SAT Math middle 50% range 410-540. SAT Critical Reading middle 50% range 380-520. ACT middle 50% range 18-24. Minimum web-based TOEFL 79. Minimum paper TOEFL 550. **Basis for Candidate Selection:** *Very important factors considered include:* Class rank, academic GPA, rigor of secondary school record, standardized test scores, character/personal qualities, talent/ability. *Important factors considered include:* extracurricular activities, interview. *Other factors considered include:* application essay, recommendation(s), alumni/ae relation, religious affiliation/commitment. **Freshman Admission Requirements:** High school diploma is required and GED is accepted. **Freshman Admission Statistics:** 1,676 applied, 48% admitted, 29% enrolled. **Transfer Admission Requirements:** college transcript(s), minimum college GPA of 2.0 required. Lowest grade transferable D. **General Admission Information:** Application Fee $50. Non-fall registration accepted. Credit and/or placement offered for CEEB Advanced Placement tests.

COSTS AND FINANCIAL AID

Annual tuition $22,330. Room and board $7,580. Required fees $350. Average book expense $1,000. **Required Forms and Deadlines:** FAFSA. **Notification of Awards:** Applicants will be notified of awards on a rolling basis beginning 3/1. **Types of Aid:** *Need-based scholarships/grants:* Federal Pell, SEOG, state scholarships/grants, private scholarships, the school's own gift aid. *Loans:* Direct Subsidized Stafford, Direct Unsubsidized Stafford, Direct PLUS, Federal Perkins, state loans, college/university loans from institutional funds, Alternative loans. **Student Employment:** Federal Work-Study Program available. Institutional employment available. Highest amount earned per year from on-campus jobs $6,062. Off-campus job opportunities are poor. **Financial Aid Statistics:** 97% freshmen, 92% undergrads receive need-based scholarship or grant aid. 35% freshmen, 29% undergrads receive non-need-based scholarship or grant aid. 79% freshmen, 88% undergrads receive need-based self-help aid. 24% freshmen, 18% undergrads receive athletic scholarships. 98% freshmen, 92% undergrads receive any aid. 85% undergrads borrow to pay for school. Average cumulative indebtedness $39,022. **Criteria for awarding institutional aid:**

Non-need-based: academics, alumni affiliation, art, athletics, job skills, leadership, music/drama, religious affiliation.

See page 1092.

GRAMBLING STATE UNIVERSITY

P. O. Box 864, Grambling, LA 71245
Phone: 318-274-6423
E-mail: taylorn@gram.edu • **CEEB Code:** 6250
Fax: 318-274-3292 • **Website:** www.gram.edu • **ACT Code:** 1582

This public school was founded in 1901. It has a 340-acre campus.

RATINGS

Admissions Selectivity Rating: 63   **Fire Safety Rating:** 67   **Green Rating:** 60*

STUDENTS AND FACULTY

Enrollment: 4,171. **Student Body:** 57% female, 43% male, 34% out-of-state, 2% international (21 countries represented). Asian 0%, African American 105%, Caucasian 4%, Hispanic 0%, Native American 0%. **Retention and Graduation:** 68% freshmen return for sophomore year. 20% freshmen graduate within 4 years. 39% freshmen graduate within 6 years. 33% grads go on to further study within 1 year. 33% grads pursue arts and sciences degrees. **Faculty:** Student/faculty ratio 17:1. 243 full-time faculty, 57% hold PhDs, 78% are members of minority groups, 42% are women.

ACADEMICS

Degrees: associate, bachelor's, master's. **Special Study Options:** Accelerated program, cooperative education program, distance learning, double major, exchange student program (domestic), honors program, independent study, internships, study abroad, teacher certification program. **Career Services:** career assessment

FACILITIES

Housing: men's dorms, women's dorms, fraternity/sorority housing, Graduate Dorm. **Special Academic Facilities/Equipment:** Audiovisual and TV center, lab schools

CAMPUS LIFE

Environment: Village. **Activities:** Choral groups, dance, drama/theater, jazz band, marching band, music ensembles, radio station, student government, student newspaper, television station, yearbook 50 registered organizations, 11 honor societies, 3 religious organizations. 4 fraternities, 5 sororities. **Athletics (Intercollegiate):** *Men:* baseball, basketball, cross country, football, golf, tennis, track/field (outdoor), track/field (indoor). *Women:* basketball, cross-country, golf, soccer, softball, tennis, track/field (outdoor), track/field (indoor).

ADMISSIONS

Freshman Academic Profile: Average high school GPA 2.7. **Basis for Candidate Selection:** *Very important factors considered include:* standardized test scores. *Other factors considered include:* recommendation(s), alumni/ae relation, extracurricular activities, talent/ability. **Freshman Admission Requirements:** High school diploma is required and GED is accepted. *Academic units required:* 4 English, 3 mathematics, 3 science, 3 social studies, 8 academic electives, 2 Health and Physical Education. 4 English, 3 mathematics, 3 science, 3 social studies, 8 academic electives, 2 Health and Physical Education **Freshman Admission Statistics:** 2,923 applied, 62% admitted, 57% enrolled. **Transfer Admission Requirements:** college transcript(s), statement of good standing from prior institution(s). Minimum college GPA of 2.0 required. Lowest grade transferable C. **General Admission Information:** Application Fee $20. Early decision application deadline 4/15. Regular application deadline 8/1. Nonfall registration accepted. Admission may be deferred for a maximum of 6mos.

COSTS AND FINANCIAL AID

Annual in-state tuition $5,652. Annual out-of-state tuition $8,327. Room and board $2,912. Required fees $60. Average book expense $600. **Required Forms and Deadlines:** FAFSA, Institutional Scholarship Application. **Notification of Awards:** Applicants will be notified of awards on a rolling basis beginning 3/1. **Types of Aid:** *Need-based scholarships/grants:* Federal Pell, SEOG, state scholarships/grants. *Loans:* Direct Subsidized Stafford, Direct Unsubsidized Stafford, Direct PLUS, Subsidized Stafford, Unsubsidized Stafford, PLUS, Federal Perkins, college/university loans from institutional funds, Non-Federal Alternative/Private Loans. **Student Employment:** Federal Work-Study Program available. Institutional employment available. Highest amount earned per year from on-campus jobs $4,648. Off-campus job opportunities are good. **Financial Aid Statistics:** 84% freshmen, 87% undergrads receive need-based scholarship or grant aid. 28% freshmen, 25% undergrads receive non-need-based scholarship or grant aid. 92% freshmen, 91% undergrads receive need-based self-help aid. 4% freshmen, 5% undergrads receive athletic scholarships. 90% freshmen, 92% undergrads receive any aid. 90% undergrads borrow to pay for school. Average cumulative indebtedness $25,000. **Criteria for awarding institutional aid:** *Non-need-based:* academics, alumni affiliation, athletics, leadership, minority status, music/drama, state/district residency.

GRAND CANYON UNIVERSITY

Phoenix, AZ 85061-0197
Phone: 602-589-2855
E-mail: admissions@grand-canyon.edu • **CEEB Code:** 4331
Fax: 602-589-2580 • **Website:** www.grand-canyon.edu • **ACT Code:** 92

This private school was founded in 1949. It has a 90-acre campus.

RATINGS
Admissions Selectivity Rating: 62   **Fire Safety Rating:** 60*   **Green Rating:** 60*

STUDENTS AND FACULTY
Enrollment: 1,609. **Student Body:** 64% female, 36% male, 19% out-of-state, 3% international. Asian 2%, African American 3%, Caucasian 56%, Hispanic 7%, Native American 1%.
Retention and Graduation: 76% freshmen return for sophomore year. 32% freshmen graduate within 4 years. 50% freshmen graduate within 6 years.
Faculty: Student/faculty ratio 16:1. 97 full-time faculty, 58% hold PhDs, 3% are members of minority groups, 52% are women.

ACADEMICS
Degrees: bachelor's, diploma, master's. **Classes:** Most classes have fewer than 10 students. Most lab/discussion sessions have 10–19 students. **Special Study Options:** Accelerated program, cooperative education program, distance learning, double major, dual enrollment, English as a Second Language (ESL), exchange student program (domestic), honors program, independent study, internships, study abroad, teacher certification program. **Disability Services:** Special programs offered to physically disabled students include note-taking services, reader services, tape recorders, tutors. **Career Services:** alumni services, career assessment, internships.

FACILITIES
Housing: men's dorms, women's dorms, apartments for married students, apartments for single students. 99% of campus accessible to physically disabled. **Special Academic Facilities/Equipment:** Art gallery, dynamical systems laboratory.

CAMPUS LIFE
Environment: Activities: Choral groups, concert band, drama/theater, jazz band, literary magazine, music ensembles, musical theater, opera, student government, student newspaper 20 registered organizations, 3 honor societies, 4 religious organizations. **Athletics (Intercollegiate):** *Men:* baseball, basketball, golf, soccer. *Women:* basketball, soccer, tennis, volleyball. **On-Campus Highlights:** New Student Union, New Student Suites, Athletic Facilities, Ethington Theatre, Medical Cadaver Lab.

ADMISSIONS
Freshman Academic Profile: Minimum paper TOEFL 500. **Basis for Candidate Selection:** *Very important factors considered include:* rigor of secondary school record, standardized test scores. *Important factors considered include:* Class rank. *Other factors considered include:* application essay, recommendation(s), character/personal qualities, extracurricular activities, interview, talent/ability. **Freshman Admission Requirements:** High school diploma is required and GED is accepted. *Academic units required:* 4 English, 3 mathematics, 2 science, (2 science labs), 2 social studies. *Academic units recommended:* 4 English, 3 mathematics, 2 science, (2 science labs), 2 social studies. **Freshman Admission Statistics:** 823 applied, 69% admitted, 44% enrolled. **Transfer Admission Requirements:** college transcript(s), minimum college GPA of 2.0 required. Lowest grade transferable C. **General Admission Information:** Application Fee $50. Nonfall registration accepted. Credit offered for CEEB Advanced Placement tests.

COSTS AND FINANCIAL AID
Room and board $7,130. Average book expense $780. **Required Forms and Deadlines:** FAFSA. **Notification of Awards:** Applicants will be notified of awards on a rolling basis beginning 3/15. **Types of Aid:** *Need-based scholarships/grants:* Federal Pell, SEOG, state scholarships/grants, private scholarships, the school's own gift aid, Bureau of Indian Affairs Grant. *Loans:* Subsidized Stafford, Unsubsidized Stafford, PLUS, Federal Perkins, state loans, Alternative loans. **Student Employment:** Federal Work-Study Program available. Institutional employment available. Highest amount earned per year from on-campus jobs $1,500. Off-campus job opportunities are excellent. **Financial**

Aid Statistics: 35% freshmen, 46% undergrads receive need-based scholarship or grant aid. 92% freshmen, 74% undergrads receive non-need-based scholarship or grant aid. 61% freshmen, 78% undergrads receive need-based self-help aid. 4% freshmen, 5% undergrads receive athletic scholarships. 61% undergrads borrow to pay for school. Average cumulative indebtedness $46,640. **Criteria for awarding institutional aid:** *Non-need-based:* academics, alumni affiliation, art, athletics, job skills, leadership, minority status, music/drama, religious affiliation, state/district residency.

GRAND RAPIDS THEOLOGICAL SEMINARY

1001 E Beltline Ave. NE, Grand Rapids, MI 49525
Phone: 1-800-697-1133 • **Financial Aid Phone:** 616-949-5300
E-mail: grts@cornerstone.edu
Fax: 616-254-1623 • **Website:** grts.cornerstone.edu

This is a private school.

RATINGS
Admissions Selectivity Rating: 60*   **Fire Safety Rating:** 96   **Green Rating:** 68

STUDENTS AND FACULTY
Retention and Graduation: 15% grads go on to further study within 1 year. 10% grads pursue arts and sciences degrees. 1% grads pursue law degrees. 3% grads pursue business degrees. 1% grads pursue medical degrees. **Faculty:** Student/faculty ratio 17:1. 9 full-time faculty, 56% are women. 0% of classes are taught by teaching assistants.

ACADEMICS
Degrees: certificate, master's. **Majors with Highest Enrollment:** business/commerce; education; psychology. **Special Study Options:** distance learning, double major, dual enrollment, honors program, independent study, internships, study abroad. **Honors Programs:** Honors Program based on a "great books" curriculum. **Disability Services:** Special programs offered to physically disabled students include note-taking services, reader services, tape recorders, tutors. **Career Services:** career/job search classes, career assessment, internships Career Services highlights include The required internship of all students as part of the graduation requirements.

FACILITIES
Housing: special housing for disabled students, men's dorms, women's dorms, apartments for married students, apartments for single students. 100% of campus accessible to physically disabled. **Computers:** Students can register for classes online. Administrative functions (other than registration) can be performed online. Undergraduates are required to own a computer.

CAMPUS LIFE
Activities: student government, Campus Ministries, International Student Organization 11 registered organizations, 2 honor societies, 1 religious organizations. **Athletics (Intercollegiate):** *Men:* basketball, cross-country, golf, soccer, track/field (outdoor), track/field (indoor). *Women:* basketball, cross-country, golf, soccer, softball, track/field (outdoor), track/field (indoor), volleyball. **On-Campus Highlights:** Corum Student Union, Bernice Hansen Athletic Center, Campus Bookstore Atrium, Faber Hall Seating Area, Gordon Music Hall. **Environmental Initiatives:** On campus dialogue and focus on sustainability issues. Joining a community organization.

ADMISSIONS
Freshman Academic Profile: Minimum paper TOEFL 500. **Basis for Candidate Selection:** *Very important factors considered include:* application essay, academic GPA, recommendation(s), religious affiliation/commitment. *Important factors considered include:* standardized test scores, character/personal qualities, extracurricular activities, level of applicant's interest, volunteer work. *Other factors considered include:* rigor of secondary school record, talent/ability, work experience. **Freshman Admission Requirements:** High school diploma is required and GED is accepted. **Transfer Admission Requirements:** college transcript(s), essay or personal statement, minimum college GPA of 2.5 required. Lowest grade transferable C. **General Admission Information:** Credit and/or placement offered for CEEB Advanced Placement tests.

COSTS AND FINANCIAL AID
Types of Aid: *Need-based scholarships/grants:* state scholarships/grants, private scholarships, the school's own gift aid. *Loans:* Direct Subsidized Stafford, Direct Unsubsidized Stafford. **Student Employment:** Federal Work-Study Program available. Highest amount earned per year from on-campus jobs $5,500. Off-campus job opportunities are good. **Financial Aid Statistics:** 100% freshmen, 98% undergrads receive any aid. **Criteria for awarding institutional aid:** *Non-need-based:* academics, job skills, leadership, minority status, religious affiliation.

GRAND VALLEY STATE UNIVERSITY

1 Campus Drive, Allendale, MI 49401
Phone: 616-331-2025 • **Financial Aid Phone:** 616-331-3234
E-mail: admissions@gvsu.edu • **CEEB Code:** 1258
Fax: 616-331-2000 • **Website:** www.gvsu.edu • **ACT Code:** 2005

This public school was founded in 1960. It has a 1275-acre campus.

RATINGS
Admissions Selectivity Rating: 70   **Fire Safety Rating:** 78   **Green Rating:** 95

STUDENTS AND FACULTY
Enrollment: 21,227. **Student Body:** 58% female, 42% male, 5% out-of-state, 1% international (82 countries represented). Asian 2%, African American 5%, Caucasian 84%, Hispanic 4%, Native American 0%.
Retention and Graduation: Faculty: Student/faculty ratio 17:1. 1097 full-time faculty, 78% hold PhDs, 16% are members of minority groups, 48% are women. 0% of classes are taught by teaching assistants.

ACADEMICS
Degrees: bachelor's, certificate, master's, post-bachelor's certificate, post-master's certificate. **Classes:** Most classes have 20–29 students. Most lab/discussion sessions have 20–29 students. **Majors with Highest Enrollment:** business/commerce; health services/allied health/health sciences; psychology. **Special Study Options:** distance learning, double major, dual enrollment, English as a Second Language (ESL), honors program, independent study, internships, student-designed major, study abroad, teacher certification program. **Honors Programs:** Honor's College **Combined Degree Programs:** BA/JD, BA/MEng, Physical therapy program; Occupational Therapy; Ph. **Disability Services:** Special programs offered to physically disabled students include reader services, tape recorders, tutors. **Career Services:** Alumni network, alumni services, career/job search classes, career assessment, internships, regional alumni. Career Services highlights include We have a very strong cooperative education program in engineering that is mature and provides one year of full-time work for students. We also have very strong internship programs in the following departments: computer science, hospitality, communications, education, health majors, and social work.

FACILITIES
Housing: Coed dorms, fraternity/sorority housing, apartments for married students, apartments for single students, theme housing, 99% of campus accessible to physically disabled. **Special Academic Facilities/Equipment:** two Great Lakes research vessels, audio-visual center, performance/recital hall, pipe organ, physical therapy/human performance lab. **Computers:** 100% of classrooms, 63% of dorms, 100% of libraries, 100% of dining areas, 100% of student union, have wireless network access. Students can register for classes online. Administrative functions (other than registration) can be performed online.

CAMPUS LIFE
Environment: City. **Activities:** Choral groups, concert band, dance, drama/theater, jazz band, literary magazine, marching band, music ensembles, musical theater, pep band, radio station, student government, student newspaper, symphony orchestra, television station, Campus Ministries, International Student Organization 301 registered organizations, 20 honor societies, 20 religious organizations. 11 fraternities, 11 sororities. **Athletics (Intercollegiate):** *Men:* baseball, basketball, cross-country, diving, football, golf, swimming, tennis, track/field (outdoor), track/field (indoor). *Women:* basketball, cross-country, diving, golf, soccer, softball, swimming, tennis, track/field (outdoor), track/field (indoor), volleyball. **On-Campus Highlights:** Living Centers, Cook DeVos Center for Health Sciences, Recreation Center and Fieldhouse, Laker Turf Building, Kirkhof Center. **Environmental Initiatives:** Climate Mitigation: GVSU is a signatory to American College and University Presidents Climate Commitment and has recently completed its Climate Action Plan and set a goal of climate neutrality by 2037. The climate action plan is available online. Currently there are over 650 colleges and universities that have signed on to this agreement. LEED construction projects and bus transportation are both important climate mitigation strategies. GVSU has completed and certified 10 LEED projects with 2 more LEED projects under construction. These 12 LEED projects represent over 925,000 square feet and ~19% of total square footage. Annual bus ridership is over ~ 2MM bus rides per year for faculty and students and saves millions of dollars in annual fuel purchases and vehicle maintenance costs while reducing our carbon footprint. Waste Minimization: GVSU's currently diverts over 600 TPY of waste on our main campus from the landfill. Our recycling rate is over 30% and we have entered the national Recylemania competition again this year in a number of waste categories. We have also begun to divert waste from the landfill by composting our campus food waste. In a pilot project at a few locations, we have been able to compost ~50 tons of food waste per month. Local, fair trade, organic food purchases continue to track at a 25% + annualized rate with additional healthy, nutritional and local food options

being offered. A Farmers Market is available on campus during the growing season as well as the development of a campus community garden.

ADMISSIONS
Freshman Academic Profile: Average high school GPA 3.5. 19% in top 10% of high school class, 50% in top 25% of high school class, 88% in top 50% of high school class. Minimum paper TOEFL 550. **Basis for Candidate Selection:** *Very important factors considered include:* academic GPA, rigor of secondary school record. *Important factors considered include:* standardized test scores. *Other factors considered include:* Class rank, application essay, recommendation(s), alumni/ae relation, extracurricular activities, first generation, talent/ability, volunteer work, work experience. **Freshman Admission Requirements:** High school diploma is required and GED is accepted. *Academic units required:* 4 English, 3 mathematics, 3 science, (1 science labs), 2 foreign language, 3 social studies. 4 English, 3 mathematics, 3 science, (1 science labs), 2 foreign language, 3 social studies. **Freshman Admission Statistics:** 17,880 applied, 82% admitted, 27% enrolled. **Transfer Admission Requirements:** college transcript(s), statement of good standing from prior institution(s). Minimum college GPA of 2.5 required. Lowest grade transferable D. **General Admission Information:** Application Fee $30. Nonfall registration accepted. Credit and/or placement offered for CEEB Advanced Placement tests.

COSTS AND FINANCIAL AID
Required Forms and Deadlines: FAFSA. **Notification of Awards:** Applicants will be notified of awards on a rolling basis beginning 3/10. **Types of Aid:** *Need-based scholarships/grants:* Federal Pell, SEOG, state scholarships/grants, private scholarships, the school's own gift aid. *Loans:* Direct Subsidized Stafford, Direct Unsubsidized Stafford, Direct PLUS, Federal Perkins, Federal Nursing. **Student Employment:** Federal Work-Study Program available. Institutional employment available. Highest amount earned per year from on-campus jobs $5,200. Off-campus job opportunities are good. **Financial Aid Statistics:** 86% freshmen, 77% undergrads receive need-based scholarship or grant aid. 3% freshmen, 2% undergrads receive non-need-based scholarship or grant aid. 90% freshmen, 90% undergrads receive need-based self-help aid. 1% freshmen, 1% undergrads receive athletic scholarships. 87% freshmen, 79% undergrads receive any aid. 72% undergrads borrow to pay for school. Average cumulative indebtedness $28,728. **Criteria for awarding institutional aid:** *Non-need-based:* academics, alumni affiliation, art, athletics, music/drama, state/district residency.

GRAND VIEW UNIVERSITY

1200 Grandview Avenue, Des Moines, IA 50316-1599
Phone: 515-263-2810 • **Financial Aid Phone:** 515-263-2963
E-mail: admissions@grandview.edu • **CEEB Code:** 0251
Fax: 515-263-2974 • **Website:** www.admissions.grandview.edu • **ACT Code:** 1316

This private school, affiliated with the Lutheran Church, was founded in 1896. It has a 35-acre campus.

RATINGS
Admissions Selectivity Rating: 64   **Fire Safety Rating:** 60*   **Green Rating:** 60*

STUDENTS AND FACULTY
Enrollment: 2,163. **Student Body:** 60% female, 40% male, 12% out-of-state, 2% international (16 countries represented). Asian 2%, African American 7%, Caucasian 76%, Hispanic 3%, Native American 0%.
Retention and Graduation: 66% freshmen return for sophomore year. 23% freshmen graduate within 4 years. 41% freshmen graduate within 6 years. **Faculty:** Student/faculty ratio 14:1. 92 full-time faculty, 61% hold PhDs, 7% are members of minority groups, 58% are women. 0% of classes are taught by teaching assistants.

ACADEMICS
Degrees: associate, bachelor's, certificate, master's, post-bachelor's certificate, terminal associate, transfer associate. **Classes:** Most classes have 10–19 students. Most lab/discussion sessions have 10–19 students. **Majors with Highest Enrollment:** business/commerce; education; nursing/registered nurse (rn, asn, bsn, msn). **Special Study Options:** Accelerated program, cooperative education program, cross-registration, distance learning, double major, dual enrollment, honors program, independent study, internships, liberal arts/career combination, student-designed major, study abroad, teacher certification program, weekend college. **Honors Programs:** Logos Honors Program **Combined Degree Programs:** Dual Degrees.

FACILITIES
Housing: Coed dorms, apartments for single students. **Special Academic Facilities/Equipment:** Danish American Archives. **Computers:** Administrative functions (other than registration) can be performed online.

CAMPUS LIFE

Environment: Activities: Choral groups, concert band, dance, drama/theater, literary magazine, music ensembles, radio station, student government, student newspaper, television station, Campus Ministries, International Student Organization 28 registered organizations, 1 religious organizations. **Athletics (Intercollegiate):** *Men:* baseball, basketball, cross-country, golf, soccer. *Women:* basketball, cross-country, golf, soccer, softball, volleyball.

ADMISSIONS

Freshman Academic Profile: Average high school GPA 3.1. 11% in top 10% of high school class, 29% in top 25% of high school class, 63% in top 50% of high school class. SAT Math middle 50% range 420-490. SAT Critical Reading middle 50% range 380-450. SAT Writing middle 50% range 350-450. ACT middle 50% range 19-23. Minimum paper TOEFL 550. **Basis for Candidate Selection:** *Very important factors considered include:* Class rank, academic GPA, rigor of secondary school record, character/personal qualities. *Important factors considered include:* standardized test scores. *Other factors considered include:* alumni/ae relation, extracurricular activities, talent/ability, volunteer work, work experience. **Freshman Admission Requirements:** High school diploma is required and GED is accepted. **Freshman Admission Statistics:** 949 applied, 93% admitted, 41% enrolled. **Transfer Admission Requirements:** college transcript(s), minimum college GPA of 2.0 required. Lowest grade transferable D. **General Admission Information:** Application Fee $35. Regular application deadline 8/15. Notification on a rolling basis, beginning on or about 9/15. Nonfall registration accepted. Admission may be deferred for a maximum of 1 SEMESTER. Credit and/or placement offered for CEEB Advanced Placement tests.

COSTS AND FINANCIAL AID

Annual tuition $20,648. Room and board $7,316. Required fees $440. Average book expense $900. **Required Forms and Deadlines:** FAFSA. **Notification of Awards:** Applicants will be notified of awards on a rolling basis beginning 3/1. **Types of Aid:** *Need-based scholarships/grants:* Federal Pell, SEOG, state scholarships/grants, private scholarships, the school's own gift aid. *Loans:* Subsidized Stafford, Unsubsidized Stafford, PLUS, Federal Perkins, Federal Nursing. **Student Employment:** Federal Work-Study Program available. Institutional employment available. Highest amount earned per year from on-campus jobs $1,500. Off-campus job opportunities are excellent. **Financial Aid Statistics:** 93% freshmen, 92% undergrads receive need-based scholarship or grant aid. 13% freshmen, 8% undergrads receive non-need-based scholarship or grant aid. 84% freshmen, 87% undergrads receive need-based self-help aid. 51% freshmen, 7% undergrads receive athletic scholarships. 97% freshmen, 99% undergrads receive any aid. 81% undergrads borrow to pay for school. Average cumulative indebtedness $30,275. **Criteria for awarding institutional aid:** *Non-need-based:* academics, alumni affiliation, art, athletics, leadership, music/drama.

GRATZ COLLEGE

7605 Old York Road, Melrose Park, PA 19027
Phone: 215-635-7300
E-mail: admissions@gratz.edu
Fax: 215-635-7399 • **Website:** www.gratzcollege.edu

This is a private school.

RATINGS

Admissions Selectivity Rating: 62   **Fire Safety Rating:** 60*   **Green Rating:** 60*

STUDENTS AND FACULTY

Enrollment: 12. **Student Body:** 92% female, 8% male, 25% out-of-state, 0% international.
Retention and Graduation: 88% freshmen return for sophomore year.
Faculty: Student/faculty ratio 12:1. 8 full-time faculty, 100% hold PhDs, 0% are members of minority groups, 50% are women. 0% of classes are taught by teaching assistants.

ACADEMICS

Degrees: bachelor's, master's, post-bachelor's certificate. **Classes:** Most classes have fewer than 10 students. Most lab/discussion sessions have fewer than 10 students. **Special Study Options:** cross-registration, double major, dual enrollment, independent study, internships, liberal arts/career combination, study abroad, teacher certification program, Joint programs with area colleges and universities are offered only at the Master's level. **Career Services:** alumni services, career/job search classes, internships.

FACILITIES

Housing: The College does not offer housing. All students live off campus. 100% of campus accessible to physically disabled.

CAMPUS LIFE

Environment: Activities: Choral groups, music ensembles.

ADMISSIONS

Freshman Academic Profile: Minimum paper TOEFL 450. **Basis for Candidate Selection:** *Very important factors considered include:* application essay, recommendation(s), character/personal qualities, religious affiliation/commitment, talent/ability. *Important factors considered include:* rigor of secondary school record, interview, volunteer work. *Other factors considered include:* Class rank, standardized test scores, alumni/ae relation, extracurricular activities, racial/ethnic status, work experience. **Freshman Admission Requirements:** High school diploma is required and GED is accepted. *Academic units required:* 3 English, 2 mathematics, 2 science, (1 science labs), 2 foreign language, 3 social studies, 3 history, 2 academic electives, 0. *Academic units recommended:* 3 English, 2 mathematics, 2 science, (1 science labs), 2 foreign language, 3 social studies, 3 history, 2 academic electives, 0 **Freshman Admission Statistics:** 7 applied, 71% admitted, 100% enrolled. **Transfer Admission Requirements:** High school transcript, college transcript(s), essay or personal statement, minimum college GPA of 0 required. Lowest grade transferable C. **General Admission Information:** Application Fee $50. Nonfall registration accepted. Admission may be deferred for a maximum of 2 years. Neither credit nor placement offered for CEEB Advanced Placement tests.

COSTS AND FINANCIAL AID

Annual tuition $9,500. Required fees $400. Average book expense $550. **Required Forms and Deadlines:** FAFSA, institution's own financial aid form. **Types of Aid:** *Need-based scholarships/grants:* Federal Pell, private scholarships. *Loans:* Subsidized Stafford, Unsubsidized Stafford, PLUS. **Student Employment:** Institutional employment available. Off-campus job opportunities are good. **Financial Aid Statistics:** 100% undergrads receive need-based scholarship or grant aid. 100% undergrads receive need-based self-help aid.

GREEN MOUNTAIN COLLEGE

One Brennan Circle, Poultney, VT 05764-1199
Phone: 802-287-8000 • **Financial Aid Phone:** 802-287-8210
E-mail: admiss@greenmtn.edu • **CEEB Code:** 3418
Fax: 802-287-8099 • **Website:** www.greenmtn.edu • **ACT Code:** 4302

This private school, affiliated with the Methodist Church, was founded in 1834. It has a 155-acre campus.

RATINGS

Admissions Selectivity Rating: 76   **Fire Safety Rating:** 79   **Green Rating:** 99

STUDENTS AND FACULTY

Enrollment: 622. **Student Body:** 55% female, 45% male, 88% out-of-state, 4% international (19 countries represented). Asian 1%, African American 5%, Caucasian 66%, Hispanic 2%, Native American 1%.
Retention and Graduation: 70% freshmen return for sophomore year. 31% freshmen graduate within 4 years. 41% freshmen graduate within 6 years. 7% grads go on to further study within 1 year. **Faculty:** Student/faculty ratio 14:1. 45 full-time faculty, 93% hold PhDs, 7% are members of minority groups, 36% are women. 0% of classes are taught by teaching assistants.

ACADEMICS

Degrees: bachelor's, certificate, master's. **Classes:** Most classes have 10–19 students. Most lab/discussion sessions have 10–19 students. **Majors with Highest Enrollment:** environmental studies; parks, recreation and leisure studies; psychology. **Special Study Options:** cooperative education program, distance learning, double major, exchange student program (domestic), honors program, independent study, internships, liberal arts/career combination, student-designed major, study abroad, teacher certification program. **Honors Programs:** College Honors Program. **Disability Services:** Special programs offered to physically disabled students include note-taking services, tape recorders, tutors. Career Services highlights include All Resort Management students participate in two Co-Ops. Last year, 384 students completed 5,829 hours of service with 54 community partners. GMC has an active internship program and requires many students to complete an internship within their chosen field.

FACILITIES

Housing: Coed dorms, special housing for disabled students, substance free theme floors - recreation, education, community, Honors. **Special Academic Facilities/Equipment:** Welsh Heritage Collection, Rare Books Room, Feick Arts Center **Computers:** Students can register for classes online. Administrative functions (other than registration) can be performed online.

CAMPUS LIFE

Environment: Rural. **Activities:** Choral groups, concert band, drama/theater, jazz band, literary magazine, music ensembles, radio station, student government, student newspaper, student-run film society, yearbook 25 registered organizations, 2 honor societies, 2 religious organizations. **Athletics (Intercollegiate):** *Men:* basketball, cross-country, golf, lacrosse, skiing (downhill/alpine), soccer, tennis. *Women:* basketball, cross-country, lacrosse, skiing (downhill/alpine), soccer, softball, tennis, volleyball. **On-Campus Highlights:** Withey Student Center, Moses Coffeehouse, Surdam Art Building, Griswold Library, The Farm. **Environmental Initiatives:** Green Mountain College integrates sustainability thoroughly across curriculum. In addition to the comprehensive Environmental Liberal Arts core curriculum, other interdisciplinary academic degree offerings include a Renewable Energy and Ecological Design Certificate Program, a new Sustainable Agriculture and Food Production degree, Adventure Education, Environmental Studies, Natural Resources Management, Environmental Management, Biology, as well as a Master of Science in Environmental Studies and a Sustainable MBA program. As of July 2010, the campus move from 12% to 86% renewable energy use with 89% of the renewables used onsite as a result of our new combined heat and power(CHP) facility which shifts 85% of the College's past fuel oil usage to biomass (5,500 tons of locally sourced wood chips), reducing the use of fuel oil from 230,000 gallons to 40,700 gallons per year. The biomass fueled plant, which will be ignited in April 2010, produces 275 psig of steam for its 150 kW steam turbine generator. Thirty psig of waste steam resulting from the generation of the electricity is distributed to the buildings of the College via its underground steam distribution and condensate return piping infrastructure. GMC's conversion from fuel oil to a CHP biomass plant in combination with additional thermal efficiency improvements to be completed in 2011, will result in a reduction of the College's carbon footprint by more than 50% percent of 2007 levels, and enable the College to achieve climate neutrality by the end of 2011. This accomplishment will make GMC the FIRST college in the country to achieve carbon neutrality by actually reducing carbon emissions by more than 50 percent. Across its curriculum, the College utilizes project-based learning both on campus and in the local community to provide real-life problem solving experiences in its sustainability education offerings. By utilizing the campus as a living laboratory, students are able to make organizational, infrastructural and cultural changes that enhance the campus environment and teach practical skills. Examples include projects on the campus farm, community weatherization outreach, design for the local food cooperative, and research in renewable energy technology.

ADMISSIONS

Freshman Academic Profile: Average high school GPA 2.8. 93% from public high schools. SAT Math middle 50% range 460-570. SAT Critical Reading middle 50% range 478-613. SAT Writing middle 50% range 450-583. ACT middle 50% range 20-25. Minimum web-based TOEFL 61. Minimum paper TOEFL 500. **Basis for Candidate Selection:** *Very important factors considered include:* application essay, academic GPA, rigor of secondary school record, character/personal qualities. *Important factors considered include:* Class rank, recommendation(s), extracurricular activities, interview, volunteer work. *Other factors considered include:* standardized test scores, level of applicant's interest, talent/ability, work experience. **Freshman Admission Requirements:** High school diploma is required and GED is accepted. *Academic units required:* 4 English, 3 mathematics, 3 science, (2 science labs), 2 foreign language, 3 social studies, 1 history, 5 academic electives. *Academic units recommended:* 4 English, 3 mathematics, 3 science, (2 science labs), 2 foreign language, 3 social studies, 1 history, 5 academic electives. **Freshman Admission Statistics:** 991 applied, 69% admitted, 25% enrolled. **Transfer Admission Requirements:** High school transcript, college transcript(s), essay or personal statement, statement of good standing from prior institution(s). Minimum college GPA of 2.0 required. Lowest grade transferable C–. **General Admission Information:** Application Fee $30. Notification on a rolling basis, beginning on or about 9/1. Nonfall registration accepted. Admission may be deferred for a maximum of 1 year. Credit and/or placement offered for CEEB Advanced Placement tests.

COSTS AND FINANCIAL AID

Annual tuition $29,620. Room and board $10,948. Required fees $1,098. Average book expense $980. **Required Forms and Deadlines:** FAFSA, CSS/Financial Aid PROFILE, noncustodial PROFILE. **Notification of Awards:** Applicants will be notified of awards on a rolling basis beginning 1/1. **Types of Aid:** *Need-based scholarships/grants:* Federal Pell, SEOG, state scholarships/grants, private scholarships, the school's own gift aid. *Loans:* Subsidized Stafford, Unsubsidized Stafford, PLUS, state loans, Alternative Loans. **Student Employment: Financial Aid Statistics:** 99% freshmen, 99% undergrads receive need-based scholarship or grant aid. 3% freshmen, 7% undergrads receive non-need-based scholarship or grant aid. 92% freshmen, 89% undergrads

receive need-based self-help aid. 93% freshmen, 92% undergrads receive any aid. 79% undergrads borrow to pay for school. Average cumulative indebtedness $42,269. **Criteria for awarding institutional aid:** *Non-need-based:* academics, alumni affiliation, art, leadership, music/drama, religious affiliation.

GREENVILLE COLLEGE

315 East College Avenue, Greenville, IL 62246-0159
Phone: 618-664-7100 • **Financial Aid Phone:** 618-664-7110
E-mail: admissions@greenville.edu • **CEEB Code:** 1256
Fax: 618-664-9841 • **Website:** www.greenville.edu • **ACT Code:** 1032

This private school, affiliated with the Free Methodist Church, was founded in 1892. It has a 40-acre campus.

RATINGS

Admissions Selectivity Rating: 70   **Fire Safety Rating:** 93   **Green Rating:** 60*

STUDENTS AND FACULTY

Enrollment: 1,307. **Student Body:** 55% female, 45% male, 29% out-of-state, 1% international (14 countries represented). Asian 1%, African American 7%, Caucasian 83%, Hispanic 2%, Native American 1%.
Retention and Graduation: 67% freshmen return for sophomore year. 39% freshmen graduate within 4 years. 50% freshmen graduate within 6 years.
Faculty: Student/faculty ratio 16:1. 54 full-time faculty, 70% hold PhDs, 7% are members of minority groups, 31% are women. 0% of classes are taught by teaching assistants.

ACADEMICS

Degrees: bachelor's, master's. **Classes:** Most classes have 10–19 students. **Majors with Highest Enrollment:** elementary education and teaching; organizational behavior studies; visual and performing arts, other. **Special Study Options:** Accelerated program, cooperative education program, cross-registration, double major, external degree program, honors program, independent study, internships, liberal arts/career combination, student-designed major, study abroad, teacher certification program. **Honors Programs:** Greenville College's Honors Program is an academic program that was established in 1995 to provide a "value-added" dimension to the excellent, Christ-centered education students regularly receive at Greenville College. The Honors Program consists of a blend of enriched sections of several general education classes, special honors seminars, and experiential learning opportunities offered in an enhanced educational environment that strives for small class sizes to encourage total student participation, facilitate spirited discussions and promote greater student-faculty interaction. Outside the classroom, the Honors Programs offers a co-curricular program consisting of diversified cultural, social and educationally-oriented activities and events developed especially for program members. The Honors Program encourages its members to be persons with multi-dimensional interests who participate in a wide range of College sponsored events, activities, and organizations. Students admitted to The Honors Program automatically become members of The Honors Society, the student organization within the program which elects officers who assist with the planning and implementation of the aforementioned activities and other community building opportunities. The Greenville College Honors Program strives to emulate the guidelines, "Basic Characteristics of a Fully-Developed Honors Program," developed by the National Collegiate Honors Council. It, also, cooperates with member institutions of the Council of Christian Colleges and Universities by encouraging GC students to participate in one of the nearly twenty semester-long academic programs coordinated and promoted by CCCU that are offered at off-campus sites, both domestic and abroad. Locally, The Honors Program is administered by a director who is assisted by an Honors Council composed of faculty and students. To graduate with Honors Program recognition, students must fulfill the requirements of their academic major, earn a minimum of 25 credit hours of honors work, maintain a cumulative grade point average of 3.50 and complete a Departmental Honors Thesis under the supervision of a three-person faculty thesis committee. Graduates of the Honors Program are awarded a special medallion and receive special recognition at commencement. For additional information about The Honors Program, contact the director at (618) 664-6610. **Disability Services:** Special programs offered to physically disabled students include note-taking services, reader services, tutors.

FACILITIES

Housing: men's dorms, women's dorms, apartments for single students, All single students not living at home must live in college approved housing. 40% of campus accessible to physically disabled. **Special Academic Facilities/Equipment:** Sculpture museum, sports training annex. **Computers:** Administrative functions (other than registration) can be performed online.

CAMPUS LIFE

Environment: Village. **Activities:** Choral groups, concert band, drama/theater, jazz band, music ensembles, musical theater, pep band, radio station, student government, student newspaper, yearbook 25 registered organizations, 6 honor societies, 2 religious organizations. **Athletics (Intercollegiate):** *Men:* baseball, basketball, cross-country, football, soccer, tennis, track/field (outdoor), track/field (indoor). *Women:* basketball, cross-country, soccer, softball, tennis, track/field (outdoor), track/field (indoor), volleyball. **On-Campus Highlights:** Hogue Hall, Family Christian Bookstore, Jo's Java, Maves Art Center, Fitness Center.

ADMISSIONS

Freshman Academic Profile: Average high school GPA 3.4. 17% in top 10% of high school class, 48% in top 25% of high school class, 74% in top 50% of high school class. SAT Math middle 50% range 460-570. SAT Critical Reading middle 50% range 480-580. ACT middle 50% range 19-25. Minimum paper TOEFL 500. **Basis for Candidate Selection:** *Very important factors considered include:* Class rank, application essay, academic GPA, rigor of secondary school record, character/personal qualities, religious affiliation/commitment, talent/ability. *Important factors considered include:* recommendation(s), standardized test scores. *Other factors considered include:* alumni/ae relation, extracurricular activities, first generation, geographical residence, interview, level of applicant's interest, racial/ethnic status, volunteer work, work experience. **Freshman Admission Requirements:** High school diploma is required and GED is accepted. **Freshman Admission Statistics:** 879 applied, 82% admitted, 42% enrolled. **Transfer Admission Requirements:** High school transcript, college transcript(s), essay or personal statement, minimum college GPA of 2.0 required. Lowest grade transferable C. **General Admission Information:** Application Fee $25. Regular application deadline 8/1. Notification on a rolling basis, beginning on or about 10/15. Nonfall registration accepted. Admission may be deferred for a maximum of One year. Credit and/or placement offered for CEEB Advanced Placement tests.

COSTS AND FINANCIAL AID

Average book expense $900. **Required Forms and Deadlines:** FAFSA. **Notification of Awards:** Applicants will be notified of awards on a rolling basis beginning 3/15. **Types of Aid:** *Need-based scholarships/grants:* Federal Pell, SEOG, state scholarships/grants, private scholarships, the school's own gift aid. *Loans:* Direct Subsidized Stafford, Direct Unsubsidized Stafford, Direct PLUS, Subsidized Stafford, Unsubsidized Stafford, PLUS, Federal Perkins, college/university loans from institutional funds. **Student Employment:** Federal Work-Study Program available. Institutional employment available. Highest amount earned per year from on-campus jobs $2,407. Off-campus job opportunities are fair. **Financial Aid Statistics:** 100% freshmen, 100% undergrads receive need-based scholarship or grant aid. 8% freshmen, 7% undergrads receive non-need-based scholarship or grant aid. 90% freshmen, 91% undergrads receive need-based self-help aid. 94% freshmen, 92% undergrads receive any aid. 85% undergrads borrow to pay for school. Average cumulative indebtedness $19,820. **Criteria for awarding institutional aid:** *Non-need-based:* academics, alumni affiliation, art, leadership, minority status, music/drama, religious affiliation, state/district residency.

GRIGGS UNIVERSITY

PO Box 4437, Silver Spring, MD 20914-4437
Phone: 301-680-6579
E-mail: enrollmentservices@griggs.edu
Fax: 301-680-6526 • **Website:** www.griggs.edu

This private school, affiliated with the Seventh Day Adventist Church, was founded in 1909.

RATINGS

Admissions Selectivity Rating: 60*   **Fire Safety Rating:** 60*   **Green Rating:** 60*

STUDENTS AND FACULTY

Enrollment: 1,076. **Student Body:** 50% female, 50% male, 0% international. **Faculty:** Student/faculty ratio 3:1.

ACADEMICS

Degrees: associate, bachelor's. **Majors with Highest Enrollment:** accounting and business/management; business/commerce; computer and information sciences. **Special Study Options:** Accelerated program, distance learning, independent study.

CAMPUS LIFE

Environment: City.

ADMISSIONS

Basis for Candidate Selection: *Very important factors considered include:* rigor of secondary school record. *Important factors considered include:* application essay, religious affiliation/commitment, work experience. *Other factors considered include:* recommendation(s), standardized test scores, alumni/ae relation, character/personal qualities, extracurricular activities, interview, talent/ability, volunteer work. **Freshman Admission Requirements:** *Academic units required:* 4 English, 3 mathematics, 2 science, 3 social studies, 3 academic electives, 7 Bible, Health, Word Processing. 4 English, 3 mathematics, 2 science, 3 social studies, 3 academic electives, 7 Bible, Health, Word Processing **Transfer Admission Requirements:** college transcript(s), essay or personal statement, minimum college GPA of 2.0 required. Lowest grade transferable C. **General Admission Information:** Application Fee $60. Nonfall registration accepted.

COSTS AND FINANCIAL AID

Annual tuition $6,400. Required fees $120. Average book expense $1,000. **Types of Aid:** *Need-based scholarships/grants:* the school's own gift aid.

GRINNELL COLLEGE

1103 Park Street, Grinnell, IA 50112-1690
Phone: 641-269-3600 • **Financial Aid Phone:** 641-269-3250
E-mail: askgrin@grinnell.edu • **CEEB Code:** 6252
Fax: 641-269-4800 • **Website:** www.grinnell.edu • **ACT Code:** 1318

This private school was founded in 1846. It has a 120-acre campus.

RATINGS

Admissions Selectivity Rating: 96   **Fire Safety Rating:** 81   **Green Rating:** 82

STUDENTS AND FACULTY

Enrollment: 1,611. **Student Body:** 55% female, 45% male, 88% out-of-state, 12% international (54 countries represented). Asian 7%, African American 6%, Caucasian 58%, Hispanic 8%, Native American 0%.
Retention and Graduation: 86% freshmen graduate within 4 years. 31% grads go on to further study within 1 year. 29% grads pursue arts and sciences degrees. 3% grads pursue law degrees. 1% grads pursue business degrees. 3% grads pursue medical degrees. **Faculty:** Student/faculty ratio 9:1. 160 full-time faculty, 100% hold PhDs, 19% are members of minority groups, 44% are women. 0% of classes are taught by teaching assistants.

ACADEMICS

Degrees: bachelor's. **Classes:** Most classes have 10–19 students. Most lab/discussion sessions have 10–19 students. **Majors with Highest Enrollment:** economics; political science and government; psychology. **Special Study Options:** Accelerated program, double major, independent study, internships, liberal arts/career combination, student-designed major, study abroad, teacher certification program, Study abroad available in 32 countries, including Grinnell-in-London, Grinnell-in-Washington program, 3-2 programs available in engineering, architecture, and law. **Combined Degree Programs:** Architecture With Washington Univ, St.Louis Law Col. **Disability Services:** Special programs offered to physically disabled students include note-taking services, reader services, tape recorders, tutors. **Career Services:** Alumni network, alumni services, career assessment, internships, regional alumni. Career Services highlights include Support 12+ funded internships each summer.

FACILITIES

Housing: Coed dorms, special housing for disabled students, cooperative housing, wellness housing, theme housing, 67% of campus accessible to physically disabled. **Special Academic Facilities/Equipment:** Art galleries, language lab, nuclear magnetic resonance spectrometer, electron microscope, 24-inch reflecting telescope, 365-acre environmental research area. **Computers:** 100% of classrooms, 100% of dorms, 100% of libraries, 100% of dining areas, 100% of student union, 100% of common outdoor areas have wireless network access. Administrative functions (other than registration) can be performed online.

CAMPUS LIFE

Environment: Village. **Activities:** Choral groups, concert band, dance, drama/theater, jazz band, literary magazine, music ensembles, musical theater, pep band, radio station, student government, student newspaper, student-run film society, symphony orchestra, yearbook, Campus Ministries, International Student Organization, Model UN 240 registered organizations, 2 honor societies, 12 religious organizations. **Athletics (Intercollegiate):** *Men:* baseball, basketball, cross-country, diving, football, golf, soccer, swimming, tennis, track/field (outdoor), track/field (indoor). *Women:* basketball, cross-country, diving, golf, soccer, softball, swimming, tennis, track/field (outdoor), track/field (indoor), volleyball. **On-Campus Highlights:** Two building on campus are listed on the National Register of Historic Places: Mears Cottage and Goodnow Hall, Faulconer Gallery, Burling Library, Joe Rosenfield '25 Center, Bucksbaum Center for the Arts, Robert N. Noyce '49 Science Center; Athletic Center. **Environmental Initiatives:** All new buildings are LEED certified. The college has committed to building a wind farm near campus which will provide 50% of the campus' electricity. The college has dedicated one of its student houses as an Ecohouse and will use that house to demonstrate green technologies, energy conservation, water conservation, and local foods to the Grinnell community.

ADMISSIONS

Freshman Academic Profile: 68% in top 10% of high school class, 92% in top 25% of high school class, 100% in top 50% of high school class. 65% from public high schools. SAT Math middle 50% range 650-750. SAT Critical Reading middle 50% range 630-750. ACT middle 50% range 29-33. **Basis for Candidate Selection:** *Very important factors considered include:* Class rank, academic GPA, recommendation(s), rigor of secondary school record, standardized test scores, extracurricular activities, talent/ability. *Important factors considered include:* application essay, interview, racial/ethnic status. *Other factors considered include:* alumni/ae relation, character/personal qualities, first generation, geographical residence, level of applicant's interest, state residency, volunteer work, work experience. **Freshman Admission Requirements:** High school diploma is required and GED is accepted. **Freshman Admission Statistics:** 4,021 applied, 36% admitted, 30% enrolled. **Transfer Admission Requirements:** High school transcript, college transcript(s), essay or personal statement, standardized test scores, statement of good standing from prior institution(s). Lowest grade transferable C. **General Admission Information:** Application Fee $30. Early decision application deadline 11/15. Regular application deadline 1/2. Regular notification 4/1. Nonfall registration not accepted. Admission may be deferred for a maximum of 1 year. Credit offered for CEEB Advanced Placement tests.

COSTS AND FINANCIAL AID

Required Forms and Deadlines: FAFSA, institution's own financial aid form, noncustodial PROFILE. **Notification of Awards:** Applicants will be notified of awards on or about 4/1. **Types of Aid:** *Need-based scholarships/grants:* Federal Pell, SEOG, state scholarships/grants, private scholarships, the school's own gift aid *Loans:* Subsidized Stafford, Unsubsidized Stafford, PLUS, Federal Perkins, college/university loans from institutional funds. **Student Employment:** Federal Work-Study Program available. Institutional employment available. Highest amount earned per year from on-campus jobs $2,500. Off-campus job opportunities are excellent. **Financial Aid Statistics:** 99% freshmen, 99% undergrads receive need-based scholarship or grant aid. 20% freshmen, 9% undergrads receive non-need-based scholarship or grant aid. 78% freshmen, 87% undergrads receive need-based self-help aid. 87% freshmen, 86% undergrads receive any aid. 55% undergrads borrow to pay for school. Average cumulative indebtedness $16,226. **Criteria for awarding institutional aid:** *Non-need-based:* academics.

GROVE CITY COLLEGE

Best 378

100 Campus Drive, Grove City, PA 16127-2104
Phone: 724-458-2100 • **Financial Aid Phone:** 724-458-3300
E-mail: admissions@gcc.edu • **CEEB Code:** 2277
Fax: 724-458-3395 • **Website:** www.gcc.edu • **ACT Code:** 3582

This private school, affiliated with the Presbyterian Church, was founded in 1876. It has a 150-acre campus.

RATINGS

Admissions Selectivity Rating: 88   **Fire Safety Rating:** 86   **Green Rating:** 60*

STUDENTS AND FACULTY

Enrollment: 2,483. **Student Body:** 50% female, 50% male, 54% out-of-state, 1% international (8 countries represented). Asian 2%, African American 1%, Caucasian 93%, Hispanic 1%, Native American 0%.
Retention and Graduation: 91% freshmen return for sophomore year. 78% freshmen graduate within 4 years. 82% freshmen graduate within 6 years. 17% grads go on to further study within 1 year. 10% grads pursue arts and sciences degrees. 2% grads pursue law degrees. 4% grads pursue medical degrees.

Faculty: Student/faculty ratio 15:1. 133 full-time faculty, 92% hold PhDs, 3% are members of minority groups, 29% are women. 0% of classes are taught by teaching assistants.

ACADEMICS

Degrees: bachelor's. **Classes:** Most classes have 20–29 students. Most lab/discussion sessions have 20–29 students. **Majors with Highest Enrollment:** elementary education and teaching; English language and literature; mechanical engineering. **Special Study Options:** Accelerated program, double major, independent study, internships, study abroad, teacher certification program. **Disability Services:** Special programs offered to physically disabled students include tutors. **Career Services:** Alumni network, alumni services, career/job search classes, career assessment, internships, regional alumni. Career Services highlights include Entrepreneurship - Interships are required of most majors.

FACILITIES

Housing: men's dorms, women's dorms, fraternity/sorority housing, apartments for single students, theme housing, 100% of campus accessible to physically disabled. **Special Academic Facilities/Equipment:** Fine arts center, language lab, on-campus preschool, technological learning center. **Computers:** 100% of classrooms, 15% of dorms, 100% of libraries, 33% of dining areas, 100% of student union, 10% of common outdoor areas have wireless network access. Students can register for classes online. Administrative functions (other than registration) can be performed online. Undergraduates are required to own a computer.

CAMPUS LIFE

Environment: Rural. **Activities:** Choral groups, concert band, dance, drama/theater, jazz band, literary magazine, marching band, music ensembles, musical theater, opera, pep band, radio station, student government, student newspaper, symphony orchestra, television station, yearbook, Campus Ministries, International Student Organization 130 registered organizations, 19 honor societies, 22 religious organizations. 8 fraternities, 8 sororities. **Athletics (Intercollegiate):** *Men:* baseball, basketball, cross-country, diving, football, golf, soccer, swimming, tennis, track/field (outdoor). *Women:* basketball, cheerleading, cross-country, diving, golf, soccer, softball, swimming, tennis, track/field (outdoor), volleyball, water polo. **On-Campus Highlights:** Student Union, Chapel, Hall of Arts and Letters, Fitness Center, Ketler Recreation Room.

ADMISSIONS

Freshman Academic Profile: Average high school GPA 3.8. 43% in top 10% of high school class, 81% in top 25% of high school class, 95% in top 50% of high school class. 64% from public high schools. SAT Math middle 50% range 540-675. SAT Critical Reading middle 50% range 552-675. ACT middle 50% range 24-29. Minimum web-based TOEFL 79. Minimum paper TOEFL 550. **Basis for Candidate Selection:** *Very important factors considered include:* application essay, academic GPA, rigor of secondary school record, standardized test scores, character/personal qualities, interview, level of applicant's interest, religious affiliation/commitment. *Important factors considered include:* recommendation(s), extracurricular activities, geographical residence. *Other factors considered include:* Class rank, alumni/ae relation, first generation, racial/ethnic status, state residency, talent/ability, volunteer work, work experience. **Freshman Admission Requirements:** High school diploma is required and GED is accepted. **Freshman Admission Statistics:** 1,481 applied, 84% admitted, 54% enrolled. **Transfer Admission Requirements:** High school transcript, college transcript(s), essay or personal statement, standardized test scores, statement of good standing from prior institution(s). Minimum college GPA of 2.0 required. Lowest grade transferable C. **General Admission Information:** Application Fee $50. Early decision application deadline 11/15. Regular application deadline 2/1. Regular notification 3/15. Nonfall registration accepted. Admission may be deferred for a maximum of 1 year. Credit offered for CEEB Advanced Placement tests.

COSTS AND FINANCIAL AID

Average book expense $1,000. **Required Forms and Deadlines:** institution's own financial aid form. **Notification of Awards:** Applicants will be notified of awards on or about 3/26. **Types of Aid:** *Need-based scholarships/grants:* state scholarships/grants, private scholarships, the school's own gift aid. *Loans:* state loans, Private loans. **Student Employment:** Institutional employment available. Highest amount earned per year from on-campus jobs $1,500. Off-campus job opportunities are good. **Financial Aid Statistics:** 98% freshmen, 92% undergrads receive need-based scholarship or grant aid. 11% freshmen, 8% undergrads receive non-need-based scholarship or grant aid. 60% freshmen, 66% undergrads receive need-based self-help aid. 70% freshmen, 70% undergrads receive any aid. 60% undergrads borrow to pay for school. Average cumulative indebtedness $28,767. **Criteria for awarding institutional aid:** *Non-need-based:* academics, leadership, minority status.

GUILFORD COLLEGE

Best 378

5800 West Friendly Avenue, Greensboro, NC 27410
Phone: 336-316-2100 • **Financial Aid Phone:** 336-316-2354
E-mail: admission@guilford.edu • **CEEB Code:** 5261
Fax: 336-316-2954 • **Website:** www.guilford.edu • **ACT Code:** 3106

This private school, affiliated with the Quaker Church, was founded in 1837. It has a 340-acre campus.

RATINGS
Admissions Selectivity Rating: 73   **Fire Safety Rating:** 76   **Green Rating:** 84

STUDENTS AND FACULTY
Enrollment: 2,330. **Student Body:** 58% female, 42% male, 52% out-of-state, 1% international (13 countries represented). Asian 1%, African American 26%, Caucasian 62%, Hispanic 5%, Native American 0%.
Retention and Graduation: 47% freshmen graduate within 4 years. 25% grads go on to further study within 1 year. 18% grads pursue arts and sciences degrees. 1% grads pursue law degrees. 1% grads pursue business degrees. 1% grads pursue medical degrees. **Faculty:** Student/faculty ratio 15:1. 124 full-time faculty, 91% hold PhDs, 10% are members of minority groups, 47% are women. 0% of classes are taught by teaching assistants.

ACADEMICS
Degrees: bachelor's, certificate. **Classes:** Most classes have 10–19 students. Most lab/discussion sessions have 10–19 students. **Majors with Highest Enrollment:** business/commerce; criminal justice/safety studies; psychology. **Special Study Options:** Accelerated program, cooperative education program, cross-registration, double major, honors program, independent study, internships, liberal arts/career combination, student-designed major, study abroad, teacher certification program, weekend college, There are 3-2 degree programs available in forestry and environmental studies with Duke University, and in physician assistant training with Bowman Gray School of Medicine at Wake Forest University. Guilford also offers many internships, a Washington semester, work-study programs, accelerated degree programs in business management, computer information systems, psychology, and biology, dual majors, student-designed majors, study abroad in 9 countries, and cross-registration with members of the Greater Greensboro Consortium (8 colleges/universities). **Honors Programs:** Guilford College is a participating member of the National Collegiate Honors Council. Membership in the NCHC means that students in the Guilford College Honors Program can participate in the NCHC Honors Semesters. These semester programs are regularly offered in different sites around the world and enable Honors students from across the country to meet and learn in unique settings. In recent years, Guilford College students have participated in the Study Abroad programs sponsored by Honors Programs at other colleges and universities. The University of North Carolina at Wilmington offers an Honors Semester Program at the University of Wales Swansea. For more information visit the following site: www.swan.ac.uk. Eastern Illinois University offers a n Honors Summer Program at the Universite Catholique de Louvain in Belgium that features archaeological study of historic sites. For more information, one can visit: www.eiu.edu/~honprog/abroad.htm. Both these programs offer college credit courses that are transferable. **Combined Degree Programs:** 3-1 Physician's asst program, 3-2 Forestry/environ. **Disability Services:** Special programs offered to physically disabled students include note-taking services, reader services, tape recorders, tutors. **Career Services:** Alumni network, alumni services, career/job search classes, career assessment, internships Career Services highlights include Internships offer students up top 12 credit hours. Local, national, and international opportunities are available. Program is centralized and provides a coordinator to assist students with the process and reflection.

FACILITIES
Housing: Coed dorms, special housing for disabled students, men's dorms, special housing for international students, women's dorms, cooperative housing, apartments for single students, theme housing, special interest housing available. Alternative houses with themes and community service project requirements. 97% of campus accessible to physically disabled. Friends Historical Collection, Frank Family Science Center, art gallery, language lab, research-grade observatory + planetarium, **Computers:** 15% of classrooms, 10% of dorms, 100% of libraries, 100% of dining areas, 50% of student union, 10% of common outdoor areas have wireless network access. Students can register for classes online. Administrative functions (other than registration) can be performed online.

CAMPUS LIFE
Environment: City. **Activities:** Choral groups, concert band, dance, drama/theater, jazz band, literary magazine, music ensembles, musical theater, pep band, radio station, student government, student newspaper, student-run film society, yearbook, Campus Ministries 47 registered organizations, 1 honor societies, 8 religious organizations. **Athletics (Intercollegiate):** *Men:* baseball, basketball, cross-country, football, golf, lacrosse, rugby, soccer, tennis. *Women:* basketball, cross-country, lacrosse, rugby, soccer, softball, swimming, tennis, volleyball. **On-Campus Highlights:** Hege Library and Art Gallery, Community Center, Frank Family Science Center, Founders Student Center and the new Grill 155, The Greenleaf Cafe - coffee co-op, The Guilford College campus is a beautiful 340 acre campus situated in the western residential area of Greensboro, North Carolina. The college is bordered by woods on one end and easy access to stores on the other. **Environmental Initiatives:** Becoming signatories of the American College and Universities Presidents Climate Commitment Composting program for the on-campus dining service. Substantial commitment to local food procurement for the dining services.

ADMISSIONS
Freshman Academic Profile: Average high school GPA 3.2. 11% in top 10% of high school class, 38% in top 25% of high school class, 76% in top 50% of high school class. 72% from public high schools. SAT Math middle 50% range 490-660. SAT Critical Reading middle 50% range 480-620. SAT Writing middle 50% range 460-600. ACT middle 50% range 21-26. Minimum paper TOEFL 550. **Basis for Candidate Selection:** *Very important factors considered include:* application essay, academic GPA, rigor of secondary school record, character/personal qualities. *Important factors considered include:* Class rank, recommendation(s), standardized test scores, extracurricular activities, interview, level of applicant's interest, talent/ability, volunteer work, work experience. *Other factors considered include:* alumni/ae relation, first generation, geographical residence, racial/ethnic status, state residency. **Freshman Admission Requirements:** High school diploma is required and GED is accepted. **Freshman Admission Statistics:** 2,549 applied, 80% admitted, 24% enrolled. **Transfer Admission Requirements:** High school transcript, college transcript(s), essay or personal statement, standardized test scores, statement of good standing from prior institution(s). Minimum college GPA of 2.5 required. Lowest grade transferable C. **General Admission Information:** Application Fee $25. Regular application deadline 8/10. Notification on a rolling basis, beginning on or about 10/1. Nonfall registration accepted. Admission may be deferred for a maximum of 12 months. Credit and/or placement offered for CEEB Advanced Placement tests.

COSTS AND FINANCIAL AID
Annual tuition $31,000. Room and board $8,600. Required fees $380. Average book expense $1,350. **Required Forms and Deadlines:** FAFSA. **Notification of Awards:** Applicants will be notified of awards on a rolling basis beginning 2/15. **Types of Aid:** *Need-based scholarships/grants:* Federal Pell, SEOG, state scholarships/grants, private scholarships, the school's own gift aid. *Loans:* Subsidized Stafford, Unsubsidized Stafford, PLUS, Federal Perkins, college/university loans from institutional funds. **Student Employment:** Federal Work-Study Program available. Institutional employment available. Highest amount earned per year from on-campus jobs $6,911. Off-campus job opportunities are fair. **Financial Aid Statistics:** 89% freshmen, 93% undergrads receive need-based scholarship or grant aid. 49% freshmen, 69% undergrads receive non-need-based scholarship or grant aid. 85% freshmen, 98% undergrads receive need-based self-help aid. 95% freshmen, 90% undergrads receive any aid. 75% undergrads borrow to pay for school. Average cumulative indebtedness $25,025. **Criteria for awarding institutional aid:** *Non-need-based:* academics.

GUSTAVUS ADOLPHUS COLLEGE

800 College Avenue, Saint Peter, MN 56082
Phone: 507-933-7676 • **Financial Aid Phone:** 507-933-7527
E-mail: admission@gustavus.edu • **CEEB Code:** 6253
Fax: 507-933-7474 • **Website:** www.gustavus.edu • **ACT Code:** 2112

This private school, affiliated with the Lutheran Church, was founded in 1862. It has a 340-acre campus.

RATINGS
Admissions Selectivity Rating: 88   **Fire Safety Rating:** 91   **Green Rating:** 82

STUDENTS AND FACULTY
Enrollment: 2,513. **Student Body:** 56% female, 44% male, 18% out-of-state, 2% international (19 countries represented). Asian 4%, African American 3%, Caucasian 83%, Hispanic 3%, Native American 1%.

Retention and Graduation: 90% freshmen return for sophomore year. 82% freshmen graduate within 4 years. 26% grads go on to further study within 1 year. 9% grads pursue arts and sciences degrees. 2% grads pursue law degrees. 2% grads pursue business degrees. 3% grads pursue medical degrees. **Faculty:** Student/faculty ratio 12:1. 191 full-time faculty, 87% hold PhDs, 14% are members of minority groups, 49% are women. 0% of classes are taught by teaching assistants.

ACADEMICS

Degrees: bachelor's. **Classes:** Most classes have 10–19 students. Most lab/discussion sessions have 10–19 students. **Majors with Highest Enrollment:** biology/biological sciences; business/commerce; psychology. **Special Study Options:** cooperative education program, cross-registration, double major, dual enrollment, exchange student program (domestic), honors program, independent study, internships, liberal arts/career combination, student-designed major, study abroad, teacher certification program. **Honors Programs:** Curriculum II. **Disability Services:** Special programs offered to physically disabled students include note-taking services, reader services, tape recorders, tutors. **Career Services:** Alumni network, alumni services, career assessment, internships Career Services highlights include We have a well developed internship program offering month-long career explorations as well as full-semester and summer full-time and part-time internships for academic credit. Forty-eight percent of our graduates participate in an internship for academic credit and 93.4% participated in some type of experiential learning during their college experience.

FACILITIES

Housing: Coed dorms, special housing for disabled students, special housing for international students, apartments for single students, wellness housing, theme housing, 95% of campus accessible to physically disabled. **Special Academic Facilities/Equipment:** Art gallery, mineral museum, electron microscopes, arboretum, 14-inch computer-guided Celestron telescope, artificial intelligence laboratory, materials science laboratory, 300-MHz NMR spectrometer, five-section greenhouse. **Computers:** 100% of dorms, 100% of libraries, 100% of dining areas, 100% of student union, 50% of common outdoor areas have wireless network access. Students can register for classes online. Administrative functions (other than registration) can be performed online.

CAMPUS LIFE

Environment: Village. **Activities:** Choral groups, concert band, dance, drama/theater, jazz band, literary magazine, music ensembles, musical theater, pep band, radio station, student government, student newspaper, symphony orchestra, television station, yearbook 120 registered organizations, 11 honor societies, 8 religious organizations. 5 fraternities, 5 sororities. **Athletics (Intercollegiate):** *Men:* baseball, basketball, cross-country, diving, football, golf, ice hockey, skiingnordiccross-country, soccer, swimming, tennis, track/field (outdoor), track/field (indoor). *Women:* basketball, cross-country, diving, golf, gymnastics, ice hockey, skiingnordiccross-country, soccer, softball, swimming, tennis, track/field (outdoor), track/field (indoor), volleyball. **On-Campus Highlights:** Campus Center, Courtyard Cafe, Lund Athletic Center, Christ Chapel, Linnaeus Arboretum, With over 75% of students remaining on campus during a typical weekend (according to our Dining Service), our students actively use the entire campus. As there are no city streets intersecting our campus, Gusties enjoy their home on the hill. **Environmental Initiatives:** Seeking to acquire 5 MW of wind generator capacity Established the Johnson Center for Environmental Innovation Strong institutional commitment to recycling & energy conservation

ADMISSIONS

Freshman Academic Profile: Average high school GPA 3.7. 37% in top 10% of high school class, 74% in top 25% of high school class, 96% in top 50% of high school class. 93% from public high schools. SAT Math middle 50% range 570-670. SAT Writing middle 50% range 570-700. ACT middle 50% range 25-30. Minimum web-based TOEFL 80. Minimum paper TOEFL 550. **Basis for Candidate Selection:** *Very important factors considered include:* rigor of secondary school record. *Important factors considered include:* application essay, academic GPA, recommendation(s), standardized test scores. *Other factors considered include:* alumni/ae relation, extracurricular activities, first generation, geographical residence, interview, level of applicant's interest, racial/ethnic status, religious affiliation/commitment, state residency, talent/ability, volunteer work, work experience. **Freshman Admission Requirements:** High school diploma is required and GED is accepted. *Academic units required:* 4 English, 3 mathematics, 2 science, (2 science labs), 2 foreign language, 2 social studies, 2 history. *Academic units recommended:* 4 English, 3 mathematics, 2 science, (2 science labs), 2 foreign language, 2 social studies, 2 history. **Freshman Admission Statistics:** 4,881 applied, 63% admitted, 22% enrolled. **Transfer Admission Requirements:** High school transcript, college transcript(s), essay or personal statement, standardized test scores, statement of good standing from prior institution(s). Minimum college GPA of 2.4 required. Lowest grade transferable 2. **General Admission Information:** Notification on a rolling basis, beginning on or about 11/20. Nonfall registration accepted. Admission may be deferred for a maximum of 1 year. Credit and/or placement offered for CEEB Advanced Placement tests.

COSTS AND FINANCIAL AID

Annual tuition $37,210. Room and board $8,880. Required fees $396. Average book expense $900. **Required Forms and Deadlines:** FAFSA, CSS/Financial Aid PROFILECSS Profile required of all students applying for need-based assistance. **Notification of Awards:** Applicants will be notified of awards on a rolling basis beginning 1/20. **Types of Aid:** *Need-based scholarships/grants:* Federal Pell, SEOG, state scholarships/grants, private scholarships, the school's own gift aid. *Loans:* Direct Subsidized Stafford, Direct Unsubsidized Stafford, Direct PLUS, Federal Perkins, state loans, Alternative loans from private lenders. **Student Employment:** Federal Work-Study Program available. Institutional employment available. Highest amount earned per year from on-campus jobs $1,800. Off-campus job opportunities are good. **Financial Aid Statistics:** 99% freshmen, 97% undergrads receive need-based scholarship or grant aid. 15% freshmen, 10% undergrads receive non-need-based scholarship or grant aid. 100% freshmen, 100% undergrads receive need-based self-help aid. 96% freshmen, 95% undergrads receive any aid. 71% undergrads borrow to pay for school. Average cumulative indebtedness $28,124. **Criteria for awarding institutional aid:** *Non-need-based:* academics, alumni affiliation, art, music/drama, religious affiliation.

GWYNEDD-MERCY COLLEGE

1325 Sumneytown Pike, Gwynedd Valley, PA 19437-0901
Phone: 215-641-5510 • **Financial Aid Phone:** 215-646-7300
E-mail: admissions@gmc.edu • **CEEB Code:** 2278
Fax: 215-641-5556 • **Website:** www.gmc.edu

This private school, affiliated with the Roman Catholic Church, was founded in 1948. It has a 160-acre campus.

RATINGS

Admissions Selectivity Rating: 73   **Fire Safety Rating:** 74   **Green Rating:** 60*

STUDENTS AND FACULTY

Enrollment: 2,130. **Student Body:** 74% female, 26% male, 8% out-of-state, 0% international (28 countries represented). Asian 2%, African American 21%, Caucasian 69%, Hispanic 1%, Native American 0%.

Retention and Graduation: 76% freshmen return for sophomore year. 50% freshmen graduate within 4 years, 69% freshmen graduate within 6 years. 60% grads go on to further study within 1 year. **Faculty:** Student/faculty ratio 13:1. 75 full-time faculty, 63% hold PhDs, 0% are members of minority groups, 71% are women. 0% of classes are taught by teaching assistants.

ACADEMICS

Degrees: associate, bachelor's, certificate, master's, post-bachelor's certificate, post-master's certificate. **Classes:** Most classes have 10–19 students. Most lab/discussion sessions have 10–19 students. **Majors with Highest Enrollment:** business administration and management; education; nursing/registered nurse (rn, asn, bsn, msn). **Special Study Options:** Accelerated program, cross-registration, double major, English as a Second Language (ESL), honors program, independent study, internships, liberal arts/career combination, study abroad, teacher certification program, weekend college. **Honors Programs:** The Honors Program in Liberal Studies consists of six interdisciplinary, team-taught courses developing the theme of "The Quest for Community and Freedom: The Individual and Society." **Combined Degree Programs:** BSN/MSN. **Disability Services:** Special programs offered to physically disabled students include reader services, tutors. **Career Services:** alumni services, career assessment, internships.

FACILITIES

Housing: Coed dorms, special housing for international students 95% of campus accessible to physically disabled. **Special Academic Facilities/Equipment:** Keiss Hall (Health and Science Center), television production room and small theater, computer labs. **Computers:** Students can register for classes online.

CAMPUS LIFE

Environment: City. **Activities:** Choral groups, literary magazine, student government, student newspaper, yearbook, Campus Ministries 22 registered organizations, 10 honor societies, 1 religious organizations. **Athletics (Intercollegiate):** *Men:* baseball, basketball, cross-country, golf, soccer, tennis, track/field (outdoor), track/field (indoor). *Women:* basketball, cross-country, field hockey, lacrosse, soccer, softball, tennis, track/field (outdoor), track/field (indoor), volleyball. **On-Campus Highlights:** Assumption Hall, The Sister Isabelle Keiss Center for Health and Sciences, The Griffin Complex Student Union and Athletic Facility, Saint Bernard Lobby and Snack Bar, Loyola Hall and Saint Brigid's Hall- Residence Halls.

ADMISSIONS

Freshman Academic Profile: 4% in top 10% of high school class, 14% in top 25% of high school class, 40% in top 50% of high school class. 57% from public high schools. SAT Math middle 50% range 430-530. SAT Critical Reading middle 50% range 440-530. Minimum paper TOEFL 525. **Basis for Candidate Selection:** *Very important factors considered include:* rigor of secondary school record. *Important factors considered include:* Class rank, academic GPA, recommendation(s), standardized test scores, extracurricular activities. *Other factors considered include:* application essay, alumni/ae relation, character/personal qualities, interview, volunteer work, work experience. **Freshman Admission Requirements:** High school diploma is required and GED is accepted. *Academic units required:* 4 English, 3 mathematics, 3 science, 1 history, 3 academic electives. 4 English, 3 mathematics, 3 science, 1 history, 3 academic electives. **Freshman Admission Statistics:** 1,844 applied, 67% admitted, 25% enrolled. **Transfer Admission Requirements:** High school transcript, college transcript(s), minimum college GPA of 2.0 required. Lowest grade transferable c. **General Admission Information:** Application Fee $25. Regular application deadline 8/20. Notification on a rolling basis, beginning on or about 9/20. Nonfall registration accepted. Admission may be deferred for a maximum of 12 months. Credit and/or placement offered for CEEB Advanced Placement tests.

COSTS AND FINANCIAL AID

Annual tuition $25,160. Room and board $9,760. Required fees $450. Average book expense $600. **Required Forms and Deadlines:** FAFSA, institution's own financial aid form. **Notification of Awards:** Applicants will be notified of awards on a rolling basis beginning 3/1. **Types of Aid:** *Need-based scholarships/grants:* Federal Pell, SEOG, state scholarships/grants, private scholarships, the school's own gift aid. *Loans:* Direct Subsidized Stafford, Direct Unsubsidized Stafford, Direct PLUS, Subsidized Stafford, Unsubsidized Stafford, PLUS, Federal Perkins, Federal Nursing, Alternative loan through banks. **Student Employment:** Federal Work-Study Program available. Off-campus job opportunities are fair. **Financial Aid Statistics:** 97% freshmen, 98% undergrads receive need-based scholarship or grant aid. 77% freshmen, 77% undergrads receive non-need-based scholarship or grant aid. 91% freshmen, 83% undergrads receive need-based self-help aid. 97% freshmen, 92% undergrads receive any aid. 90% undergrads borrow to pay for school. Average cumulative indebtedness $36,255. **Criteria for awarding institutional aid:** *Non-need-based:* academics, leadership.

HAMILTON COLLEGE

Best 378

Office of Admission, Clinton, NY 13323
Phone: 315-859-4421 • **Financial Aid Phone:** 800-859-4413
E-mail: admission@hamilton.edu • **CEEB Code:** 2286
Fax: 315-859-4457 • **Website:** www.hamilton.edu • **ACT Code:** 2754

This private school was founded in 1812. It has a 1300-acre campus.

RATINGS

Admissions Selectivity Rating: 97   **Fire Safety Rating:** 92   **Green Rating:** 83

STUDENTS AND FACULTY

Enrollment: 1,867. **Student Body:** 51% female, 49% male, 67% out-of-state, 5% international (41 countries represented). Asian 8%, African American 4%, Caucasian 63%, Hispanic 7%, Native American 0%.
Retention and Graduation: 96% freshmen return for sophomore year. 85% freshmen graduate within 4 years. 91% freshmen graduate within 6 years. 21% grads go on to further study within 1 year. 5% grads pursue arts and sciences degrees. 3% grads pursue law degrees. 1% grads pursue medical degrees.
Faculty: Student/faculty ratio 9:1. 188 full-time faculty, 94% hold PhDs, 13% are members of minority groups, 43% are women. 0% of classes are taught by teaching assistants.

ACADEMICS

Degrees: bachelor's. **Classes:** Most classes have 10–19 students. Most lab/discussion sessions have 10–19 students. **Majors with Highest Enrollment:** economics; political science and government; psychology. **Special Study Options:** Accelerated program, cross-registration, double major, English as a Second Language (ESL), independent study, internships, student-designed major, study abroad, 3-2 program in Engineering with Columbia University, Rensselaer Polytechnic Institute, and Washington University(St. Louis); 3-3 program in Law with Columbia University. **Combined Degree Programs:**

BA/JD, BA/MEng, Cooperative Program with Columbia University. **Disability Services:** Special programs offered to physically disabled students include note-taking services, reader services, tape recorders, tutors. **Career Services:** Alumni network, alumni services, career/job search classes, career assessment, internships, regional alumni. Career Services highlights include The Summer Internship Fund, launched with a $1.6 million endowment in 2006, provides cost-of-living stipends each summer to a number of undergraduates who accept unpaid internships in any career field.

FACILITIES

Housing: Coed dorms, special housing for disabled students, apartments for married students, cooperative housing, apartments for single students, wellness housing. **Special Academic Facilities/Equipment:** Art gallery, language lab, fitness center, observatory, two electron microscopes. Arthur Levitt Public Affairs Center. **Computers:** 100% of classrooms, 100% of dorms, 100% of libraries, 100% of dining areas, 100% of student union, 100% of common outdoor areas have wireless network access. Students can register for classes online. Administrative functions (other than registration) can be performed online.

CAMPUS LIFE

Environment: Rural. **Activities:** Choral groups, concert band, dance, drama/theater, jazz band, literary magazine, music ensembles, musical theater, radio station, student government, student newspaper, student-run film society, symphony orchestra, yearbook, Campus Ministries, International Student Organization, Model UN 117 registered organizations, 8 honor societies, 4 religious organizations. 11 fraternities, 7 sororities. **Athletics (Intercollegiate):** *Men:* baseball, basketball, crew/rowing, cross-country, diving, football, golf, ice hockey, lacrosse, soccer, squash, swimming, tennis, track/field (outdoor), track/field (indoor). *Women:* basketball, crew/rowing, cross-country, diving, field hockey, ice hockey, lacrosse, soccer, softball, squash, swimming, tennis, track/field (outdoor), track/field (indoor), volleyball. **On-Campus Highlights:** Blood Fitness and Dance Center, Kirner-Johnson Commons, Outdoor Leadership Center/Root Glen, Science Center, Cafe Opus.

ADMISSIONS

Freshman Academic Profile: 79% in top 10% of high school class, 97% in top 25% of high school class, 100% in top 50% of high school class. 59% from public high schools. SAT Math middle 50% range 650-740. SAT Critical Reading middle 50% range 650-740. SAT Writing middle 50% range 650-740. ACT middle 50% range 29-33. **Basis for Candidate Selection:** *Very important factors considered include:* Class rank, academic GPA, rigor of secondary school record. *Important factors considered include:* application essay, recommendation(s), standardized test scores, character/personal qualities, extracurricular activities, interview. *Other factors considered include:* alumni/ae relation, first generation, geographical residence, level of applicant's interest, racial/ethnic status, talent/ability, volunteer work, work experience. **Freshman Admission Requirements:** High school diploma is required and GED is accepted. **Freshman Admission Statistics:** 5,107 applied, 27% admitted, 34% enrolled. **Transfer Admission Requirements:** High school transcript, college transcript(s), essay or personal statement, standardized test scores, statement of good standing from prior institution(s). Lowest grade transferable C. **General Admission Information:** Application Fee $75. Early decision application deadline 11/15. Regular application deadline 1/1. Regular notification 4/1. Nonfall registration accepted. Admission may be deferred for a maximum of 2 years. Credit and/or placement offered for CEEB Advanced Placement tests.

COSTS AND FINANCIAL AID

Annual tuition $43,910. Room and board $11,270. Required fees $440. Average book expense $1,300. **Required Forms and Deadlines:** FAFSA, institution's own financial aid form, CSS/Financial Aid PROFILE, state aid form, noncustodial PROFILE, business/farm supplement. **Notification of Awards:** Applicants will be notified of awards on or about 4/1. **Types of Aid:** *Need-based scholarships/grants:* Federal Pell, SEOG, state scholarships/grants, private scholarships, the school's own gift aid. *Loans:* Subsidized Stafford, Unsubsidized Stafford, PLUS, Federal Perkins, college/university loans from institutional funds. **Student Employment:** Federal Work-Study Program available. Institutional employment available. Highest amount earned per year from on-campus jobs $1,800. **Financial Aid Statistics:** 100% freshmen, 100% undergrads receive need-based scholarship or grant aid. 85% freshmen, 86% undergrads receive need-based self-help aid. 56% freshmen, 50% undergrads receive any aid. 39% undergrads borrow to pay for school. Average cumulative indebtedness $18,568. **Criteria for awarding institutional aid:** *Non-need-based:* state/district residency.

HAMLINE UNIVERSITY

, Saint Paul, MN 55104
Phone: 651-523-2207 • **Financial Aid Phone:** 651-523-3000
E-mail: CLA-admis@hamline.edu • **CEEB Code:** 6265
Fax: 651-523-2458 • **Website:** www.hamline.edu • **ACT Code:** 2114

This private school, affiliated with the Methodist Church, was founded in 1854. It has a 77-acre campus.

RATINGS
Admissions Selectivity Rating: 76   **Fire Safety Rating:** 81   **Green Rating:** 63

STUDENTS AND FACULTY
Enrollment: 1,986. **Student Body:** 58% female, 42% male, 15% out-of-state, 3% international (53 countries represented). Asian 6%, African American 5%, Caucasian 75%, Hispanic 2%, Native American 1%.
Retention and Graduation: 82% freshmen return for sophomore year. 61% freshmen graduate within 4 years. 68% freshmen graduate within 6 years. 27% grads go on to further study within 1 year. 17% grads pursue arts and sciences degrees. 4% grads pursue law degrees. 2% grads pursue business degrees. 1% grads pursue medical degrees. **Faculty:** Student/faculty ratio 14:1. 173 full-time faculty, 87% hold PhDs, 11% are members of minority groups, 49% are women. 0% of classes are taught by teaching assistants.

ACADEMICS
Degrees: bachelor's, first professional, master's, post-bachelor's certificate. **Classes:** Most classes have 10–19 students. Most lab/discussion sessions have 10–19 students. **Majors with Highest Enrollment:** business/commerce; criminal justice/police science; psychology. **Special Study Options:** cross-registration, double major, dual enrollment, English as a Second Language (ESL), exchange student program (domestic), honors program, independent study, internships, student-designed major, study abroad, teacher certification program. **Combined Degree Programs:** BA/JD, BA/MEng, 3-3 prog with Hamline School of Law. **Disability Services:** Special programs offered to physically disabled students include note-taking services, reader services, tape recorders, tutors. **Career Services:** Alumni network, alumni services, career/job search classes, career assessment, internships, regional alumni. Career Services highlights include All students must fulfill the Leadership, Education, and Development (LEAD) requirement which integrates the liberal arts with the world of work. Most students choose an internship to fulfill this requirement.

FACILITIES
Housing: Coed dorms, fraternity/sorority housing, apartments for married students, cooperative housing, apartments for single students, PRIDE (African-American), Spectrum (GLBT), Hmong, foreign language interest, theme housing. (floors organized around areas like Arts, Weekends on Campus, GLBT, and Social Justice). 80% of campus accessible to physically disabled. **Special Academic Facilities/Equipment:** theatre, music hall, art gallery, science center. **Computers:** 100% of classrooms, 100% of dorms, 100% of libraries, 100% of dining areas, 100% of student union, 100% of common outdoor areas have wireless network access. Students can register for classes online. Administrative functions (other than registration) can be performed online.

CAMPUS LIFE
Environment: Metropolis. **Activities:** Choral groups, concert band, dance, drama/theater, jazz band, literary magazine, music ensembles, musical theater, pep band, radio station, student government, student newspaper, symphony orchestra, television station, yearbook, Campus Ministries, International Student Organization, Model UN 77 registered organizations, 11 honor societies, 9 religious organizations. 1 fraternities, 2 sororities. **Athletics (Intercollegiate):** *Men:* baseball, basketball, cross-country, diving, football, ice hockey, soccer, swimming, tennis, track/field (outdoor), track/field (indoor). *Women:* basketball, cross-country, diving, gymnastics, ice hockey, soccer, softball, swimming, tennis, track/field (outdoor), track/field (indoor), volleyball. **On-Campus Highlights:** Klas Center (stadium and food service), Walker Field House, Sorin Dining Hall, Sundin Music Hall, Bush Student Center. **Environmental Initiatives:** Recycling program Energy saving projects such as chiller replacement, boiler burner replacement and lighting retrofits. Transportation initiatives (increases in bike parking and the use of electric vehicles in mail services and safety and security services, discounted transit pass).

ADMISSIONS
Freshman Academic Profile: Average high school GPA 3.4. 20% in top 10% of high school class, 49% in top 25% of high school class, 79% in top 50% of high school class. 90% from public high schools. SAT Math middle 50% range 540-640. SAT Critical Reading middle 50% range 513-645. SAT Writing middle 50% range 510-615. ACT middle 50% range 21-27. Minimum paper TOEFL 550. **Basis for Candidate Selection:** *Very important factors considered include:* Class rank, rigor of secondary school record. *Important factors considered include:* application essay, academic GPA, recommendation(s), standardized test scores, extracurricular activities, interview, talent/ability. *Other factors considered include:* alumni/ae relation, character/personal qualities, first generation, racial/ethnic status, volunteer work, work experience. **Freshman Admission Requirements:** High school diploma is required and GED is accepted. **Freshman Admission Statistics:** 2,018 applied, 78% admitted, 29% enrolled. **Transfer Admission Requirements:** college transcript(s), essay or personal statement, minimum college GPA of 2.0 required. Lowest grade transferable C–. **General Admission Information:** Notification on a rolling basis, beginning on or about 12/20. Nonfall registration accepted. Admission may be deferred for a maximum of 2 years. Credit and/or placement offered for CEEB Advanced Placement tests.

COSTS AND FINANCIAL AID
Required Forms and Deadlines: FAFSA. **Notification of Awards:** Applicants will be notified of awards on a rolling basis beginning 3/15. **Types of Aid:** *Need-based scholarships/grants:* Federal Pell, SEOG, state scholarships/grants, private scholarships, the school's own gift aid, Federal ACG and SMART grants. *Loans:* Subsidized Stafford, Unsubsidized Stafford, PLUS, Federal Perkins, state loans, Non-federal alternative loans. **Student Employment:** Federal Work-Study Program available. Institutional employment available. Highest amount earned per year from on-campus jobs $3,250. Off-campus job opportunities are excellent. **Financial Aid Statistics:** 100% freshmen, 99% undergrads receive need-based scholarship or grant aid. 15% freshmen, 10% undergrads receive non-need-based scholarship or grant aid. 87% freshmen, 91% undergrads receive need-based self-help aid. 98% freshmen, 95% undergrads receive any aid. 79% undergrads borrow to pay for school. Average cumulative indebtedness $34,598. **Criteria for awarding institutional aid:** *Non-need-based:* academics, alumni affiliation, art, job skills, leadership, minority status, music/drama, religious affiliation, state/district residency.

HAMPDEN-SYDNEY COLLEGE

PO Box 667, Hampden-Sydney, VA 23943-0667
Phone: 434-223-6120 • **Financial Aid Phone:** 434-223-6119
E-mail: hsapp@hsc.edu • **CEEB Code:** 5291
Fax: 434-223-6346 • **Website:** www.hsc.edu • **ACT Code:** 4356

This private school, affiliated with the Presbyterian Church, was founded in 1775. It has a 1200-acre campus.

RATINGS
Admissions Selectivity Rating: 86   **Fire Safety Rating:** 75   **Green Rating:** 65

STUDENTS AND FACULTY
Enrollment: 1,080. **Student Body:** 0% female, 100% male, 29% out-of-state, 1% international (19 countries represented). Asian 1%, African American 9%, Caucasian 80%, Hispanic 2%, Native American 1%.
Retention and Graduation: 63% freshmen graduate within 4 years. 68% freshmen graduate within 6 years. 20% grads go on to further study within 1 year. 7% grads pursue arts and sciences degrees. 7% grads pursue law degrees. 5% grads pursue business degrees. 4% grads pursue medical degrees. **Faculty:** Student/faculty ratio 11:1. 94 full-time faculty, 94% hold PhDs, 6% are members of minority groups, 29% are women. 0% of classes are taught by teaching assistants.

ACADEMICS
Degrees: bachelor's. **Classes:** Most classes have 10–19 students. **Majors with Highest Enrollment:** economics; history; political science and government. **Special Study Options:** cooperative education program, cross-registration, double major, dual enrollment, exchange student program (domestic), honors program, independent study, internships, study abroad, Appalachian semester, junior year exchange with members of Virginia consortium. Semester at sea and Washington semester also available. **Honors Programs:** Student Summer Research programs, Departmental Honors. **Disability Services:** Special programs offered to physically disabled students include note-taking services, reader services, tape recorders, tutors. **Career Services:** Alumni network, alumni services, career/job search classes, career assessment, internships, regional alumni. Career Services highlights include Internships - our goal is to assist all of our students who want internships with finding them.

FACILITIES

Housing: men's dorms, special housing for international students, fraternity/sorority housing, apartments for married students, apartments for single students, theme housing, language houses. 90% of campus accessible to physically disabled. **Special Academic Facilities/Equipment:** History museum, language lab, international communications center, observatory. **Computers:** 15% of classrooms, 100% of libraries, 100% of dining areas, 100% of student union, 20% of common outdoor areas have wireless network access. Students can register for classes online. Administrative functions (other than registration) can be performed online.

CAMPUS LIFE

Environment: Rural. **Activities:** Choral groups, drama/theater, literary magazine, music ensembles, pep band, radio station, student government, student newspaper, yearbook, Campus Ministries, International Student Organization 45 registered organizations, 14 honor societies, 6 religious organizations. 11 fraternities. **Athletics (Intercollegiate):** *Men:* baseball, basketball, cross-country, football, golf, lacrosse, soccer, tennis. **On-Campus Highlights:** Bortz Library, Kirby Fieldhouse (athletic facility), Gammon gym/Hall of Fame, Tiger Inn, Campus Museum. **Environmental Initiatives:** Electrical energy conservation. Removal of all underground fossil fuel tanks. Conversion from heating oil to propane for improved air quality.

ADMISSIONS

Freshman Academic Profile: Average high school GPA 3.4. 13% in top 10% of high school class, 28% in top 25% of high school class, 87% in top 50% of high school class. 64% from public high schools. SAT Math middle 50% range 510-615. SAT Critical Reading middle 50% range 490-620. SAT Writing middle 50% range 470-580. ACT middle 50% range 21-26. Minimum web-based TOEFL 100. Minimum paper TOEFL 600. **Basis for Candidate Selection:** *Very important factors considered include:* application essay, academic GPA, recommendation(s), rigor of secondary school record, standardized test scores, character/personal qualities. *Important factors considered include:* Class rank, extracurricular activities. *Other factors considered include:* first generation, interview, level of applicant's interest, talent/ability, volunteer work, work experience. **Freshman Admission Requirements:** High school diploma is required and GED is accepted. *Academic units required:* 4 English, 3 mathematics, 2 science, (1 science labs), 2 foreign language, 1 social studies, 1 history, 3 academic electives. *Academic units recommended:* 4 English, 3 mathematics, 2 science, (1 science labs), 2 foreign language, 1 social studies, 1 history, 3 academic electives. **Freshman Admission Statistics:** 2,629 applied, 56% admitted, 23% enrolled. **Transfer Admission Requirements:** High school transcript, college transcript(s), essay or personal statement, standardized test scores, statement of good standing from prior institution(s). Minimum college GPA of 2.5 required. Lowest grade transferable C. **General Admission Information:** Application Fee $30. Early decision application deadline 11/15. Regular application deadline 3/1. Regular notification 4/15. Nonfall registration accepted. Credit and/or placement offered for CEEB Advanced Placement tests.

COSTS AND FINANCIAL AID

Annual tuition $34,498. Room and board $11,166. Required fees $1,072. Average book expense $1,298. **Required Forms and Deadlines:** FAFSA, CSS/Financial Aid PROFILE, state aid form. **Notification of Awards:** Applicants will be notified of awards on or about 3/15. **Types of Aid:** *Need-based scholarships/grants:* Federal Pell, SEOG, state scholarships/grants, private scholarships, the school's own gift aid. *Loans:* Subsidized Stafford, Unsubsidized Stafford, PLUS, Federal Perkins, college/university loans from institutional funds. **Student Employment:** Federal Work-Study Program available. Institutional employment available. Highest amount earned per year from on-campus jobs $2,884. Off-campus job opportunities are fair. **Financial Aid Statistics:** 100% freshmen, 100% undergrads receive need-based scholarship or grant aid. 12% freshmen, 13% undergrads receive non-need-based scholarship or grant aid. 88% freshmen, 83% undergrads receive need-based self-help aid. 99% freshmen, 99% undergrads receive any aid. 55% undergrads borrow to pay for school. Average cumulative indebtedness $30,048. **Criteria for awarding institutional aid:** *Non-need-based:* academics, leadership, minority status, religious affiliation, state/district residency.

HAMPSHIRE COLLEGE

Admissions Office, Amherst, MA 1002
Phone: 413-559-5471 • **Financial Aid Phone:** 413-559-5484
E-mail: admissions@hampshire.edu • **CEEB Code:** 3447
Fax: 413-559-5631 • **Website:** www.hampshire.edu/ • **ACT Code:** 1842

This private school was founded in 1965. It has a 850-acre campus.

RATINGS

Admissions Selectivity Rating: 85   **Fire Safety Rating:** 70   **Green Rating:** 80

STUDENTS AND FACULTY

Enrollment: 1,475. **Student Body:** 58% female, 42% male, 82% out-of-state, 5% international (31 countries represented). Asian 2%, African American 3%, Caucasian 66%, Hispanic 9%, Native American 0%.
Retention and Graduation: 78% freshmen return for sophomore year. 51% freshmen graduate within 4 years. 63% freshmen graduate within 6 years. 10% grads go on to further study within 1 year. 8% grads pursue arts and sciences degrees. 1% grads pursue law degrees. 1% grads pursue medical degrees.
Faculty: Student/faculty ratio 12:1. 98 full-time faculty, 88% hold PhDs, 20% are members of minority groups, 56% are women. 0% of classes are taught by teaching assistants.

ACADEMICS

Degrees: bachelor's. **Classes:** Most classes have 10–19 students. Most lab/discussion sessions have 10–19 students. **Majors with Highest Enrollment:** creative writing; drama and dramatics/theatre arts; film/video and photographic arts, other. **Special Study Options:** exchange student program (domestic), independent study, internships, student-designed major, study abroad, teacher certification program. **Disability Services:** Special programs offered to physically disabled students include note-taking services, reader services, tape recorders. **Career Services:** Alumni network, alumni services, career/job search classes, career assessment, internships.

FACILITIES

Housing: Coed dorms, special housing for disabled students, special housing for international students, women's dorms, apartments for single students, theme housing, 50% of campus accessible to physically disabled. **Special Academic Facilities/Equipment:** Performing and visual arts center, bioshelter (integrated greenhouse/aquaculture facility), farm center, electronic music and TV production studios, extensive film and photography facilities, multimedia center. **Computers:** 100% of classrooms, 10% of dorms, 100% of libraries, 100% of dining areas, n/a% of student union, 50% of common outdoor areas have wireless network access. Students can register for classes online. Administrative functions (other than registration) can be performed online.

CAMPUS LIFE

Environment: Town. **Activities:** Choral groups, dance, drama/theater, jazz band, student newspaper, student-run film society, International Student Organization 94 registered organizations, 3 religious organizations. **On-Campus Highlights:** Bridge Cafe, Bookstore, Library, Eric Carle Museum of Picture Book Art, Liebling Center - Film/Photo. **Environmental Initiatives:** Constructing a new facility addition to LEED standards (minimum silver; hopefully gold); constructing a condominium community to be LEED certified. ACUPCC signatory, establishing an environmental committee and mandating emissions inventory. Formed a committee on sustainability that will engage all administrative areas, including Facilities and Grounds, Purchasing, Environmental Health and Safety, Dining Services, Campus Planning, and Information Technology. The campus sustainability committment has also been re-emphasized at the trustee committee level.

ADMISSIONS

Freshman Academic Profile: Average high school GPA 3.3. 19% in top 10% of high school class, 52% in top 25% of high school class, 85% in top 50% of high school class. 74% from public high schools. SAT Math middle 50% range 540-650. SAT Critical Reading middle 50% range 590-700. SAT Writing middle 50% range 580-670. ACT middle 50% range 25-29. Minimum web-based TOEFL 91. Minimum paper TOEFL 577. **Basis for Candidate Selection:** *Very important factors considered include:* application essay, character/personal qualities. *Important factors considered include:* recommendation(s), rigor of secondary school record, extracurricular activities, level of applicant's interest, talent/ability. *Other factors considered include:* Class rank, academic GPA, standardized test scores, alumni/ae relation, interview, racial/ethnic status, volunteer work, work experience. **Freshman Admission Requirements:** High school diploma is required and GED is accepted. *Academic units required:* 4 English, 3 mathematics, 3 science, (2 science labs), 3 foreign language, 3 history. *Academic units recommended:* 4 English, 3 mathematics, 3 science, (2 science labs), 3 foreign language, 3 history. **Freshman Admission Statistics:** 2,517 applied, 71% admitted, 20% enrolled. **Transfer Admission Requirements:** High school transcript, college transcript(s), essay or personal statement, Lowest grade transferable C. **General Admission Information:** Application Fee $60. Early decision application deadline 11/15. Regular application deadline 1/1. Regular notification 4/1. Nonfall registration accepted. Admission may be deferred for a maximum of 1 year. Placement offered for CEEB Advanced Placement tests.

COSTS AND FINANCIAL AID
Annual tuition $43,580. Room and board $11,620. Average book expense $700. **Required Forms and Deadlines:** FAFSA, CSS/Financial Aid PROFILE, noncustodial PROFILE. **Notification of Awards:** Applicants will be notified of awards on or about 4/1. **Types of Aid:** *Need-based scholarships/grants:* Federal Pell, SEOG, state scholarships/grants, private scholarships, the school's own gift aid. *Loans:* Direct Subsidized Stafford, Direct Unsubsidized Stafford, Direct PLUS, PLUS, Federal Perkins. **Student Employment:** Federal Work-Study Program available. Highest amount earned per year from on-campus jobs $2,600. **Financial Aid Statistics:** 100% freshmen, 100% undergrads receive need-based scholarship or grant aid. 45% freshmen, 54% undergrads receive non-need-based scholarship or grant aid. 100% freshmen, 100% undergrads receive need-based self-help aid. 70% freshmen, 76% undergrads receive any aid. 62% undergrads borrow to pay for school. Average cumulative indebtedness $20,430. **Criteria for awarding institutional aid:** *Non-need-based:* academics, leadership, minority status.

HAMPTON UNIVERSITY

Best 378

Office of Admissions, Hampton, VA 23668
Phone: 757-727-5328 • **Financial Aid Phone:** 757-727-5332
E-mail: admit@hamptonu.edu • **CEEB Code:** 5292
Fax: 757-727-5095 • **Website:** www.hamptonu.edu • **ACT Code:** 4358

This private school was founded in 1868. It has a 255-acre campus.

RATINGS
Admissions Selectivity Rating: 92   **Fire Safety Rating:** 64   **Green Rating:** 60*

STUDENTS AND FACULTY
Enrollment: 5,056. **Student Body:** 64% female, 36% male, 69% out-of-state, 0% international (33 countries represented). Asian 1%, African American 96%, Caucasian 12%, Hispanic 1%, Native American 0%.
Retention and Graduation: 85% freshmen return for sophomore year. 40% grads go on to further study within 1 year. 40% grads pursue arts and sciences degrees. 2% grads pursue law degrees. 5% grads pursue business degrees. 10% grads pursue medical degrees. **Faculty:** Student/faculty ratio 16:1. 363 full-time faculty, 75% hold PhDs, 79% are members of minority groups, 58% are women. 0% of classes are taught by teaching assistants.

ACADEMICS
Degrees: associate, bachelor's, certificate, first professional, master's, post-master's certificate. **Classes:** Most classes have 20–29 students. Most lab/discussion sessions have 10–19 students. **Majors with Highest Enrollment:** business/commerce; journalism; psychology. **Special Study Options:** Accelerated program, cooperative education program, cross-registration, distance learning, double major, dual enrollment, honors program, independent study, internships, study abroad, teacher certification program, Undergrads may take grad level programs. Co-Op Programs: Arts, Business, Education, Engineering, Social/Behavioral Science, Pre-college, Army ROTC, Navy ROTC. Member Tidewater Consortium. **Honors Programs:** Honors College-Designed to augment, enhance and extend the undergraduate academic experience through community, exposure and expectations. Leadership Institute - Offers the undergraduate student a curricular option that enhances the university experience. **Combined Degree Programs:** Bachelor of Arts/Master in Teaching. **Disability Services:** Special programs offered to physically disabled students include note-taking services, reader services, tape recorders, tutors. **Career Services:** Alumni network, alumni services, career/job search classes, career assessment, internships Career Services highlights include Students who experience jobs through

Cooperative Education have a chance to determine their life's work while earning academic credit.

FACILITIES
Housing: Coed dorms, men's dorms, special housing for international students, women's dorms. 90% of campus accessible to physically disabled. **Special Academic Facilities/Equipment:** African, Native American, and Oceanic museums, and gallery. New Student Center **Computers:** 100% of classrooms, 100% of dorms, 100% of libraries, 100% of dining areas, 100% of student union, 100% of common outdoor areas have wireless network access. Students can register for classes online. Administrative functions (other than registration) can be performed online.

CAMPUS LIFE
Environment: City. **Activities:** Choral groups, concert band, dance, drama/theater, jazz band, marching band, music ensembles, musical theater, opera, pep band, radio station, student government, student newspaper, symphony orchestra, television station, yearbook 85 registered organizations, 16 honor societies, 3 religious organizations. 6 fraternities, 3 sororities. **Athletics (Intercollegiate):** *Men:* basketball, cross-country, football, golf, sailing, tennis, track/field (outdoor), track/field (indoor). *Women:* basketball, bowling, cross-country, golf, sailing, softball, tennis, track/field (outdoor), track/field (indoor), volleyball. **On-Campus Highlights:** Emancipation Oak, Memorial Chapel, Huntington Memorial Museum, Booker T. Washington Monument, Student Center: bowling, fitness and movie.

ADMISSIONS
Freshman Academic Profile: Average high school GPA 3.2. 20% in top 10% of high school class, 45% in top 25% of high school class, 90% in top 50% of high school class. 90% from public high schools. SAT Math middle 50% range 464-606. SAT Critical Reading middle 50% range 481-552. ACT middle 50% range 17-26. Minimum paper TOEFL 550. **Basis for Candidate Selection:** *Very important factors considered include:* application essay, rigor of secondary school record, standardized test scores, character/personal qualities. *Important factors considered include:* Class rank, recommendation(s). *Other factors considered include:* alumni/ae relation, extracurricular activities, talent/ability, volunteer work. **Freshman Admission Requirements:** High school diploma is required and GED is accepted. *Academic units required:* 4 English, 3 mathematics, 2 science, (2 science labs), 2 social studies, 6 academic electives. *Academic units recommended:* 4 English, 3 mathematics, 2 science, (2 science labs), 2 social studies, 6 academic electives. **Freshman Admission Statistics:** 7,120 applied, 37% admitted, 43% enrolled. **Transfer Admission Requirements:** college transcript(s), essay or personal statement, statement of good standing from prior institution(s). Minimum college GPA of 2.3 required. Lowest grade transferable C. **General Admission Information:** Application Fee $35. Non fall registration accepted. Admission may be deferred for a maximum of one year. Credit and/or placement offered for CEEB Advanced Placement tests.

COSTS AND FINANCIAL AID
Annual tuition $13,358. Room and board $6,746. Required fees $1,460. Average book expense $750. **Required Forms and Deadlines:** FAFSA. **Notification of Awards:** Applicants will be notified of awards on a rolling basis beginning 4/15. **Types of Aid:** *Need-based scholarships/grants:* Federal Pell, SEOG, state scholarships/grants, private scholarships, the school's own gift aid, Federal Nursing Scholarships. *Loans:* Direct Subsidized Stafford, Direct Unsubsidized Stafford, Direct PLUS, Subsidized Stafford, Unsubsidized Stafford, PLUS, Federal Perkins, Alternative Loans. **Student Employment:** Federal Work-Study Program available. Off-campus job opportunities are excellent. **Financial Aid Statistics:** 100% freshmen, 100% undergrads receive need-based scholarship or grant aid. 24% freshmen, 29% undergrads receive non-need-based scholarship or grant aid. 82% freshmen, 100% undergrads receive need-based self-help aid. 44% freshmen, 100% undergrads receive any aid. 51% undergrads borrow to pay for school. Average cumulative indebtedness $17,125. **Criteria for awarding institutional aid:** *Non-need-based:* academics, athletics, leadership, music/drama.

HANNIBAL-LAGRANGE UNIVERSITY

2800 Palmyra Road, Hannibal, MO 63401
Phone: 573-221-3113 • **Financial Aid Phone:** 573-629-3280
E-mail: admissio@hlg.edu
Fax: 573-221-6594 • **Website:** www.hlg.edu/ • **ACT Code:** 2320

This private school, affiliated with the Southern Baptist Church, was founded in 1858. It has a 110-acre campus.

RATINGS
Admissions Selectivity Rating: 70   **Fire Safety Rating:** 67   **Green Rating:** 60*

STUDENTS AND FACULTY

Enrollment: 929. **Student Body:** 64% female, 36% male, 26% out-of-state, 10% international (11 countries represented). Asian 0%, African American 3%, Caucasian 81%, Hispanic 2%, Native American 0%.
Retention and Graduation: 58% freshmen return for sophomore year.
Faculty: Student/faculty ratio 11:1. 60 full-time faculty, 28% hold PhDs, 2% are members of minority groups, 52% are women. 0% of classes are taught by teaching assistants.

ACADEMICS

Degrees: associate, bachelor's, master's. **Majors with Highest Enrollment:** elementary education and teaching; non-profit/public/organizational management; secondary education and teaching. **Special Study Options:** Accelerated program, distance learning, dual enrollment, English as a Second Language (ESL), honors program, independent study, internships, liberal arts/career combination, student-designed major, study abroad, teacher certification program, weekend college, Adult Program. **Honors Programs:** Honors Program qualifies a student for a semester of study at Harlaxton College, Grantham, England. **Disability Services:** Special programs offered to physically disabled students include tape recorders, tutors. **Career Services:** career assessment, internships Career Services highlights include FOCUS online career exploration program.

FACILITIES

Housing: special housing for disabled students, men's dorms, women's dorms, apartments for single students. 98% of campus accessible to physically disabled. **Special Academic Facilities/Equipment:** L.A. Foster Library, T.M. Matthews Science Building, Mary Wiehe Science Building, Partee Tech. Center, Roland Fine Arts Center **Computers:** Students can register for classes online.

CAMPUS LIFE

Environment: Village. **Activities:** Choral groups, concert band, drama/theater, jazz band, music ensembles, musical theater, student government, student newspaper, yearbook, Campus Ministries, International Student Organization 22 registered organizations, 1 honor societies, 3 religious organizations. **Athletics (Intercollegiate):** *Men:* baseball, basketball, cross-country, golf, soccer, swimming, track/field (outdoor), volleyball, wrestling. *Women:* basketball, cheerleading, cross-country, golf, soccer, softball, swimming, track/field (outdoor), volleyball. **On-Campus Highlights:** Roland Fine Arts Center, Mabee Sports Complex, Common Grounds, Snack Shack, Carroll Mission Center.

ADMISSIONS

Freshman Academic Profile: 21% in top 10% of high school class, 37% in top 25% of high school class, 52% in top 50% of high school class. SAT Math middle 50% range 440-480. SAT Critical Reading middle 50% range 260-490. SAT Writing middle 50% range 420-480. ACT middle 50% range 19-24. Minimum paper TOEFL 520. **Basis for Candidate Selection:** *Very important factors considered include:* academic GPA, standardized test scores. *Important factors considered include:* rigor of secondary school record. *Other factors considered include:* Class rank, recommendation(s), character/personal qualities, level of applicant's interest, religious affiliation/commitment, talent/ability. **Freshman Admission Requirements:** High school diploma is required and GED is accepted. *Academic units recommended:* **Freshman Admission Statistics:** 696 applied, 64% admitted, 42% enrolled. **Transfer Admission Requirements:** college transcript(s), minimum college GPA of 2.0 required. Lowest grade transferable 1. **General Admission Information:** Application Fee $25. Nonfall registration accepted. Admission may be deferred for a maximum of 1 semester. Neither credit nor placement offered for CEEB Advanced Placement tests.

COSTS AND FINANCIAL AID

Annual tuition $16,170. Room and board $6,200. Required fees $720. Average book expense $800. **Required Forms and Deadlines:** FAFSA, institution's own financial aid form. **Notification of Awards: Types of Aid:** *Need-based scholarships/grants:* Federal Pell, SEOG, state scholarships/grants, private scholarships, the school's own gift aid. *Loans:* Subsidized Stafford, Unsubsidized Stafford, PLUS, Federal Perkins. **Student Employment:** Federal Work-Study Program available. Institutional employment available. Off-campus job opportunities are fair. **Criteria for awarding institutional aid:** *Non-need-based:* academics, art, athletics, music/drama, religious affiliation.

HANOVER COLLEGE

P.O. Box 108, Hanover, IN 47243-0108
Phone: 800-213-2178 • **Financial Aid Phone:** 812-866-7029
E-mail: admission@hanover.edu • **CEEB Code:** 1290
Fax: 812-866-7098 • **Website:** www.hanover.edu • **ACT Code:** 1200

This private school, affiliated with the Presbyterian Church, was founded in 1827. It has a 650-acre campus.

RATINGS

Admissions Selectivity Rating: 82   **Fire Safety Rating:** 77   **Green Rating:** 72

STUDENTS AND FACULTY

Enrollment: 1,121. **Student Body:** 56% female, 44% male, 31% out-of-state, 3% international (11 countries represented). Asian 1%, African American 4%, Caucasian 84%, Hispanic 2%, Native American 0%.
Retention and Graduation: 83% freshmen return for sophomore year. 63% freshmen graduate within 4 years. 65% freshmen graduate within 6 years. 30% grads go on to further study within 1 year. 18% grads pursue arts and sciences degrees. 4% grads pursue law degrees. 4% grads pursue business degrees. 1% grads pursue medical degrees. **Faculty:** Student/faculty ratio 12:1. 96 full-time faculty, 99% hold PhDs, 8% are members of minority groups, 38% are women. 0% of classes are taught by teaching assistants.

ACADEMICS

Degrees: bachelor's. **Classes:** Most classes have 10–19 students. **Majors with Highest Enrollment:** communication studies/speech communication and rhetoric; history; psychology. **Special Study Options:** double major, dual enrollment, independent study, internships, student-designed major, study abroad, teacher certification program, CBP (Center for Business Preparation) Business Scholar Program, Philadelphia Center and Washington Center Internship Programs. **Disability Services:** Special programs offered to physically disabled students include note-taking services, tutors. **Career Services:** Alumni network, alumni services, career/job search classes, career assessment, internships, regional alumni. Career Services highlights include Hanover College curriculum teaches students to communicate effectively, think critically, and solve problems creatively. Through a variety of experiential learning opportunities and networking events, the CBP builds upon the liberal arts foundation by emphasizing personal leadership development and team working skills.

FACILITIES

Housing: Coed dorms, men's dorms, women's dorms, fraternity/sorority housing, apartments for single students, wellness housing, theme housing, 50% of campus accessible to physically disabled. **Special Academic Facilities/Equipment:** cadaver lab, geological museum, electronic language lab, observatory **Computers:** 80% of classrooms, 100% of dorms, 50% of libraries, 100% of dining areas, 100% of student union, 20% of common outdoor areas have wireless network access. Students can register for classes online. Administrative functions (other than registration) can be performed online.

CAMPUS LIFE

Environment: Rural. **Activities:** Choral groups, concert band, dance, drama/theater, jazz band, literary magazine, music ensembles, musical theater, pep band, radio station, student government, student newspaper, student-run film society, symphony orchestra, television station, yearbook, Campus Ministries, International Student Organization 60 registered organizations, 8 honor societies, 4 religious organizations. 4 fraternities, 4 sororities. **Athletics (Intercollegiate):** *Men:* baseball, basketball, cross-country, football, golf, lacrosse, soccer, tennis, track/field (outdoor). *Women:* basketball, cross-country, golf, soccer, softball, tennis, track/field (outdoor), volleyball. **On-Campus Highlights:** Science Center, Horner Health and Recreation Center (Collier Arena), Campus Center, The Shoebox, The Point-River View, The Shoebox serves food and drinks, as does the new coffee house in Crowe Hall. **Environmental Initiatives:** As part of the long range Strategic Plan the College has identified Environmental Sustainability as a core value. Formed an Environmental Sustainability committee in 2010 with faculty, staff, and student representatives. Ofer an Environmental Science Major/Minor, Fall 2010, as part of the curriculum.

ADMISSIONS

Freshman Academic Profile: Average high school GPA 3.7. 28% in top 10% of high school class, 67% in top 25% of high school class, 93% in top 50% of high school class. 87% from public high schools. SAT Math middle 50% range 490-600. SAT Critical Reading middle 50% range 500-620. SAT Writing middle 50% range 470-580. ACT middle 50% range 22-28. Minimum web-based TOEFL 80. Minimum paper TOEFL 550. **Basis for Candidate**

Selection: *Very important factors considered include:* Class rank, academic GPA, rigor of secondary school record. *Important factors considered include:* recommendation(s), standardized test scores, talent/ability. *Other factors considered include:* application essay, alumni/ae relation, character/personal qualities, extracurricular activities, first generation, geographical residence, interview, level of applicant's interest, racial/ethnic status, state residency, volunteer work, work experience. **Freshman Admission Requirements:** High school diploma is required and GED is not accepted. *Academic units required:* 4 English, 3 mathematics, 3 science, (2 science labs), 2 foreign language, 2 social studies, 2 history, 2 academic electives. *Academic units recommended:* 4 English, 3 mathematics, 3 science, (2 science labs), 2 foreign language, 2 social studies, 2 history, 2 academic electives. **Freshman Admission Statistics:** 3,633 applied, 64% admitted, 16% enrolled. **Transfer Admission Requirements:** High school transcript, college transcript(s), essay or personal statement, standardized test scores, statement of good standing from prior institution(s). Minimum college GPA of 2.0 required. Lowest grade transferable C–. **General Admission Information:** Application Fee $40. Regular application deadline 3/1. Notification on a rolling basis, beginning on or about 9/1. Nonfall registration accepted. Admission may be deferred for a maximum of 1 year. Credit and/or placement offered for CEEB Advanced Placement tests.

COSTS AND FINANCIAL AID

Annual tuition $29,668. Room and board $9,230. Required fees $600. Average book expense $1,200. **Required Forms and Deadlines:** FAFSA. **Notification of Awards:** Applicants will be notified of awards on a rolling basis beginning 3/1. **Types of Aid:** *Need-based scholarships/grants:* Federal Pell, SEOG, state scholarships/grants, private scholarships, the school's own gift aid. *Loans:* Subsidized Stafford, Unsubsidized Stafford, PLUS, college/university loans from institutional funds. **Student Employment:** Institutional employment available. Highest amount earned per year from on-campus jobs $3,000. Off-campus job opportunities are fair. **Financial Aid Statistics:** 100% freshmen, 100% undergrads receive need-based scholarship or grant aid. 20% freshmen, 13% undergrads receive non-need-based scholarship or grant aid. 79% freshmen, 86% undergrads receive need-based self-help aid. 85% freshmen, 83% undergrads receive any aid. 74% undergrads borrow to pay for school. Average cumulative indebtedness $27,992. **Criteria for awarding institutional aid:** *Non-need-based:* academics, alumni affiliation, art, leadership, minority status, music/drama, religious affiliation, state/district residency.

HARDING UNIVERSITY

Box 12255, Scarcy, AR 72149
Phone: 501-279-4407 • **Financial Aid Phone:** 501-279-4257
E-mail: admissions@harding.edu • **CEEB Code:** 10311
Fax: 501-279-4129 • **Website:** www.harding.edu • **ACT Code:** 124

This private school, affiliated with the Church of Christ Church, was founded in 1924. It has a 275-acre campus.

RATINGS

| Admissions Selectivity Rating: 76 | Fire Safety Rating: 81 | Green Rating: 62 |

STUDENTS AND FACULTY

Enrollment: 4,241. **Student Body:** 54% female, 46% male, 71% out-of-state, 7% international (54 countries represented). Asian 1%, African American 4%, Caucasian 84%, Hispanic 3%, Native American 0%.
Retention and Graduation: 81% freshmen return for sophomore year. 40% freshmen graduate within 4 years. 61% freshmen graduate within 6 years. 36% grads go on to further study within 1 year. 2% grads pursue law degrees. 9% grads pursue business degrees. 2% grads pursue medical degrees. **Faculty:** Student/faculty ratio 17:1. 275 full-time faculty, 70% hold PhDs, 4% are members of minority groups, 35% are women. 0% of classes are taught by teaching assistants.

ACADEMICS

Degrees: bachelor's, master's, post-master's certificate. **Classes:** Most classes have 10–19 students. Most lab/discussion sessions have 10–19 students. **Majors with Highest Enrollment:** business/commerce; early childhood education and teaching; nursing/registered nurse (rn, asn, bsn, msn). **Special Study Options:** Accelerated program, cooperative education program, distance learning, double major, dual enrollment, English as a Second Language (ESL), honors program, independent study, internships, liberal arts/career combination, study abroad, teacher certification program. **Combined Degree Programs:** BA/PharmD. **Disability Services:** Special programs offered to physically disabled students include note-taking services, reader services, tape recorders, tutors. **Career Services:** alumni services, career/job search classes, career assessment, internships.

FACILITIES

Housing: special housing for disabled students, men's dorms, women's dorms, apartments for married students, apartments for single students, Approved Off-Campus Housing. 95% of campus accessible to physically disabled. **Special Academic Facilities/Equipment:** On-campus academy (prep school grades K-12). **Computers:** 95% of classrooms, 100% of libraries, 100% of dining areas, 100% of student union, 80% of common outdoor areas have wireless network access. Students can register for classes online. Administrative functions (other than registration) can be performed online.

CAMPUS LIFE

Environment: Village. **Activities:** Choral groups, concert band, drama/theater, jazz band, marching band, music ensembles, pep band, radio station, student government, student newspaper, symphony orchestra, television station, yearbook, Campus Ministries, International Student Organization 100 registered organizations, 12 honor societies, 10 religious organizations. 14 fraternities, 15 sororities. **Athletics (Intercollegiate):** *Men:* baseball, basketball, cross-country, football, golf, soccer, tennis, track/field (outdoor). *Women:* basketball, cheerleading, cross-country, golf, soccer, tennis, track/field (outdoor), volleyball. **On-Campus Highlights:** Cyber Cafe in Student Center, Front Lawn with Swings, Campus Dining until 9:00pm, Rhodes Memorial Field House, First Security Stadium. **Environmental Initiatives:** Recycling Composting Trayless Dining.

ADMISSIONS

Freshman Academic Profile: Average high school GPA 3.6. 29% in top 10% of high school class, 54% in top 25% of high school class, 80% in top 50% of high school class. 64% from public high schools. SAT Math middle 50% range 440-570. SAT Critical Reading middle 50% range 560-650. ACT middle 50% range 22-28. Minimum web-based TOEFL 79. Minimum paper TOEFL 550. **Basis for Candidate Selection:** *Very important factors considered include:* recommendation(s), rigor of secondary school record, standardized test scores, character/personal qualities, interview. *Important factors considered include:* Class rank, academic GPA, talent/ability. *Other factors considered include:* application essay, alumni/ae relation, extracurricular activities, first generation, geographical residence, level of applicant's interest, state residency, volunteer work, work experience. **Freshman Admission Requirements:** High school diploma is required and GED is accepted. *Academic units required:* 4 English, 3 mathematics, 2 science, 3 social studies, 3 academic electives. *Academic units recommended:* 4 English, 3 mathematics, 2 science, 3 social studies, 3 academic electives. **Freshman Admission Statistics:** 2,477 applied, 75% admitted, 60% enrolled. **Transfer Admission Requirements:** college transcript(s), essay or personal statement, statement of good standing from prior institution(s). Minimum college GPA of 2 required. Lowest grade transferable C. **General Admission Information:** Application Fee $40. Notification on a rolling basis, beginning on or about 5/1. Nonfall registration accepted. Admission may be deferred for a maximum of One Year. Credit and/or placement offered for CEEB Advanced Placement tests.

COSTS AND FINANCIAL AID

Annual tuition $14,790. Room and board $6,192. Required fees $450. Average book expense $900. **Required Forms and Deadlines:** FAFSA. **Notification of Awards:** Applicants will be notified of awards on a rolling basis beginning 2/15. **Types of Aid:** *Need-based scholarships/grants:* Federal Pell, SEOG, state scholarships/grants, private scholarships, the school's own gift aid, Stephens Scholars Program for African-American students. *Loans:* Subsidized Stafford, Unsubsidized Stafford, PLUS, Federal Perkins, Federal Nursing, college/university loans from institutional funds. **Student Employment:** Federal Work-Study Program available. Institutional employment available. **Financial Aid Statistics:** 98% freshmen, 91% undergrads receive need-based scholarship or grant aid. 21% freshmen, 18% undergrads receive non-need-based scholarship or grant aid. 71% freshmen, 77% undergrads receive need-based self-help aid. 5% freshmen, 4% undergrads receive athletic scholarships. 99% freshmen, 94% undergrads receive any aid. 63% undergrads borrow to pay for school. Average cumulative indebtedness $32,752. **Criteria for awarding institutional aid:** *Non-need-based:* academics, alumni affiliation, art, athletics, leadership, music/drama, religious affiliation, state/district residency.

HARDIN-SIMMONS UNIVERSITY

Box 16050, Abilene, TX 79698
Phone: 325-670-1206 • **Financial Aid Phone:** 325-670-1206
E-mail: enroll@hsutx.edu • **CEEB Code:** 6268
Fax: 325-671-2115 • **Website:** www.hsutx.edu • **ACT Code:** 4096

This private school was founded in 1891. It has a 209-acre campus.

RATINGS
Admissions Selectivity Rating: 83   **Fire Safety Rating:** 71   **Green Rating:** 67

STUDENTS AND FACULTY
Enrollment: 1,788. **Student Body:** 52% female, 48% male, 4% out-of-state, 2% international (17 countries represented). Asian 1%, African American 7%, Caucasian 71%, Hispanic 14%, Native American 1%.
Retention and Graduation: 66% freshmen return for sophomore year. 31% freshmen graduate within 4 years. 50% grads go on to further study within 1 year. 27% grads pursue arts and sciences degrees. 1% grads pursue law degrees. 8% grads pursue business degrees. 6% grads pursue medical degrees. **Faculty:** Student/faculty ratio 13:1. 137 full-time faculty, 91% hold PhDs, 4% are members of minority groups, 34% are women. 0% of classes are taught by teaching assistants.

ACADEMICS
Degrees: bachelor's, doctoral, master's, post-bachelor's certificate. **Classes:** Most classes have 10–19 students. Most lab/discussion sessions have 20–29 students. **Majors with Highest Enrollment:** biology/biological sciences; business, management, marketing, and related support services, other; education. **Special Study Options:** Accelerated program, cross-registration, distance learning, double major, dual enrollment, honors program, independent study, internships, study abroad, teacher certification program. **Honors Programs:** The Hardin-Simmons University Honors Program provides an enriched educational environment for undergraduate students of exceptional promise who have a wide variety of interests and seek an enhanced learning opportunity. The Honors Program promotes creative and critical thinking skills to equip individuals for success in today's world. The Program, which serves as an integral part of the academic community, includes courses taught by selected faculty members interested in working with highly motivated students. The Honors Program expects participants to strive for excellence and assume personal accountability for their intellectual growth. **Disability Services:** Special programs offered to physically disabled students include note-taking services, reader services, tape recorders, tutors. **Career Services:** Alumni network, alumni services, career/job search classes, career assessment, internships, regional alumni. Career Services highlights include Internship program - the Office of Career Services at HSU hosts internship listings through our online service, Career Connection. In addition, many academic departments have a specific faculty person designated to help students find internship opportunities within their field of study.

FACILITIES
Housing: special housing for disabled students, men's dorms, women's dorms, apartments for married students, apartments for single students, Single and Duplex housing with priority given to families. 100% of campus accessible to physically disabled. **Special Academic Facilities/Equipment:** Art center, observatory with 14-inch telescope, rare and fine book room, SIX WHITE HORSE facility, Holland Health Science Medical High School **Computers:** 90% of classrooms, 100% of dorms, 80% of libraries, 100% of dining areas, 100% of student union, 50% of common outdoor areas have wireless network access.

CAMPUS LIFE
Environment: City. **Activities:** Choral groups, concert band, drama/theater, jazz band, literary magazine, marching band, music ensembles, musical theater, opera, student government, student newspaper, symphony orchestra, yearbook, Campus Ministries, International Student Organization, Model UN 15 honor societies, 1 religious organizations. 4 fraternities, 4 sororities. **Athletics (Intercollegiate):** *Men:* baseball, basketball, cheerleading, cross-country, football, golf, soccer, tennis, track/field (outdoor). *Women:* basketball, cheerleading, cross-country, golf, soccer, softball, tennis, track/field (outdoor), volleyball. **On-Campus Highlights:** Moody Center (Student Center), Java City Coffee House, The Pond/Gazebo, Dorm Lobbies, The Pool, Gym/Fitness Center; Connally Mission Center; Skiles Social Science Building. **Environmental Initiatives:** Establishing a recycling program. Educating the student body, faculty, staff and alumni on sustainability.

ADMISSIONS
Freshman Academic Profile: Average high school GPA 3.6. 24% in top 10% of high school class, 54% in top 25% of high school class, 83% in top 50% of high school class. 88% from public high schools. SAT Math middle 50% range 470-590. SAT Critical Reading middle 50% range 450-560. SAT Writing middle 50% range 430-550. ACT middle 50% range 20-25. Minimum web-based TOEFL 75. Minimum paper TOEFL 550. **Basis for Candidate Selection:** *Very important factors considered include:* Class rank, academic GPA, standardized test scores. *Important factors considered include:* recommendation(s), rigor of secondary school record, character/personal qualities, talent/ability. *Other factors considered include:* alumni/ae relation, extracurricular activities, level of applicant's interest, religious affiliation/commitment. **Freshman Admission Requirements:** High school diploma is required and GED is accepted. *Academic units required:* 3 English, 2 mathematics, 2 science, 2 social studies, 7 academic electives. 3 English, 2 mathematics, 2 science, 2 social studies, 7 academic electives. **Freshman Admission Statistics:** 1,823 applied, 54% admitted, 40% enrolled. **Transfer Admission Requirements:** college transcript(s), minimum college GPA of 2.0 required. Lowest grade transferable C. **General Admission Information:** Application Fee $50. Notification on a rolling basis, beginning on or about 9/1. Nonfall registration accepted. Admission may be deferred for a maximum of 1 Year. Credit offered for CEEB Advanced Placement tests.

COSTS AND FINANCIAL AID
Annual tuition $22,350. Room and board $6,792. Required fees $1,110. Average book expense $800. **Required Forms and Deadlines:** FAFSA. **Notification of Awards:** Applicants will be notified of awards on a rolling basis beginning 2/1. **Types of Aid:** *Need-based scholarships/grants:* Federal Pell, SEOG, state scholarships/grants, private scholarships, the school's own gift aid, ACG/SMART (federal grants). *Loans:* Subsidized Stafford, Unsubsidized Stafford, PLUS, Federal Perkins, state loans, college/university loans from institutional funds. **Student Employment:** Federal Work-Study Program available. Institutional employment available. Highest amount earned per year from on-campus jobs $2,400. Off-campus job opportunities are excellent. **Financial Aid Statistics:** 68% freshmen, 70% undergrads receive need-based scholarship or grant aid. 92% freshmen, 90% undergrads receive non-need-based scholarship or grant aid. 88% freshmen, 90% undergrads receive need-based self-help aid. 98% freshmen, 91% undergrads receive any aid. 71% undergrads borrow to pay for school. Average cumulative indebtedness $40,972. **Criteria for awarding institutional aid:** *Non-need-based:* academics, art, job skills, music/drama, religious affiliation.

HARRINGTON COLLEGE OF DESIGN

200 West Madison, Chicago, IL 60606-3433
Phone: 877-939-4975
E-mail: hiid@interiordesign.edu
Fax: 312-697-8032 • **Website:** www.harringtoncollege.com • **ACT Code:** 6641

This proprietary school was founded in 1931.

RATINGS
Admissions Selectivity Rating: 62   **Fire Safety Rating:** 60*   **Green Rating:** 60*

ACADEMICS
Degrees: associate, bachelor's, certificate, diploma. **Special Study Options:** Accelerated program, internships, study abroad.

FACILITIES
Housing: apartments for single students, Independent referral housing Shared Apartment housing.

CAMPUS LIFE
Activities: student government.

ADMISSIONS
Freshman Academic Profile: Minimum paper TOEFL 500. **Basis for Candidate Selection:** *Very important factors considered include:* interview. *Important factors considered include:* character/personal qualities, talent/ability. *Other factors considered include:* Class rank, application essay, recommendation(s), rigor of secondary school record, standardized test scores, extracurricular activities, geographical residence, volunteer work, work experience. **Freshman Admission Requirements:** High school diploma is required and GED is accepted. **Freshman Admission Statistics:** 568 applied, 90% admitted, 7% enrolled. **Transfer Admission Requirements:** college transcript(s), interview, Lowest grade transferable C. **General Admission Information:** Application Fee $60. Nonfall registration accepted.

COSTS AND FINANCIAL AID
Annual tuition $6,300. Average book expense $900. **Required Forms and Deadlines:** FAFSA. **Types of Aid:** *Need-based scholarships/grants:* Federal Pell, SEOG. *Loans:* Subsidized Stafford, Unsubsidized Stafford, PLUS. **Student Employment:** Off-campus job opportunities are excellent.

HARRISBURG UNIVERSITY OF SCIENCE AND TECHNOLOGY

326 Market Street, Harrisburg, PA 17101
Phone: 717-901-5101 • **Financial Aid Phone:** 717-901-5115
E-mail: admissions@HarrisburgU.edu • **CEEB Code:** 4511
Fax: 717-901-3101 • **Website:** www.HarrisburgU.edu • **ACT Code:** 3637

This private school was founded in 2001. It has a 2-acre campus.

RATINGS
Admissions Selectivity Rating: 83   **Fire Safety Rating:** 60*   **Green Rating:** 60*

STUDENTS AND FACULTY
Enrollment: 272. **Student Body:** 46% female, 54% male, 17% out-of-state, 1% international (3 countries represented). Asian 4%, African American 32%, Caucasian 49%, Hispanic 8%, Native American 0%.
Retention and Graduation: 54% freshmen return for sophomore year. 12% freshmen graduate within 4 years. 20% freshmen graduate within 6 years. 10% grads go on to further study within 1 year. 10% grads pursue arts and sciences degrees. **Faculty:** Student/faculty ratio 11:1. 10 full-time faculty, 100% hold PhDs, 40% are members of minority groups, 50% are women. 0% of classes are taught by teaching assistants.

ACADEMICS
Degrees: bachelor's, master's. **Classes: Majors with Highest Enrollment:** biotechnology; computer and information sciences; physical sciences. **Special Study Options:** dual enrollment, internships, student-designed major. **Career Services:** internships.

FACILITIES
Housing: 100% of campus accessible to physically disabled. **Computers:** 100% of classrooms, 100% of libraries, 100% of dining areas, 100% of student union, 100% of common outdoor areas have wireless network access. Students can register for classes online. Administrative functions (other than registration) can be performed online. Undergraduates are required to own a computer.

CAMPUS LIFE
Environment: City. **On-Campus Highlights:** Conference Center

ADMISSIONS
Freshman Academic Profile: 90% from public high schools. SAT Math middle 50% range 420-550. SAT Critical Reading middle 50% range 440-530. SAT Writing middle 50% range 390-510. ACT middle 50% range 20-24. Minimum paper TOEFL 80. **Freshman Admission Statistics:** 1,827 applied, 47% admitted, 15% enrolled.

COSTS AND FINANCIAL AID
Annual tuition $23,800. Room and board $6,340. Average book expense $1,500. **Financial Aid Statistics:** 99% freshmen, 100% undergrads receive need-based scholarship or grant aid. 9% freshmen, 6% undergrads receive non-need-based scholarship or grant aid. 87% freshmen, 82% undergrads receive need-based self-help aid. 98% freshmen, 94% undergrads receive any aid. 80% undergrads borrow to pay for school. Average cumulative indebtedness $41,893.

HARTWICK COLLEGE

PO Box 4022, Oneonta, NY 13820-4020
Phone: 607-431-4154 • **Financial Aid Phone:** 607-431-4130
E-mail: admissions@hartwick.edu • **CEEB Code:** 2288
Fax: 607-431-4102 • **Website:** www.hartwick.edu/ • **ACT Code:** 2756

This private school was founded in 1797. It has a 425-acre campus.

RATINGS
Admissions Selectivity Rating: 71   **Fire Safety Rating:** 83   **Green Rating:** 82

STUDENTS AND FACULTY
Enrollment: 1,541. **Student Body:** 60% female, 40% male, 26% out-of-state, 3% international (35 countries represented). Asian 1%, African American 5%, Caucasian 69%, Hispanic 6%, Native American 1%.
Retention and Graduation: 73% freshmen return for sophomore year. 53% freshmen graduate within 4 years. 58% freshmen graduate within 6 years. 22% grads go on to further study within 1 year. **Faculty:** Student/faculty ratio 11:1. 110 full-time faculty, 85% hold PhDs, 4% are members of minority groups, 45% are women. 0% of classes are taught by teaching assistants.

ACADEMICS
Degrees: bachelor's. **Classes:** Most classes have 10–19 students. Most lab/discussion sessions have 30–39 students. **Majors with Highest Enrollment:** business/commerce; nursing/registered nurse (rn, asn, bsn, msn); psychology. **Special Study Options:** Accelerated program, cross-registration, double major, exchange student program (domestic), honors program, independent study, internships, student-designed major, study abroad, teacher certification program, January thematic term, study abroad/international internships.
Honors Programs: Requirements for the Honors Program are: Challenges—4 must be completed by graduation; Divisions—3 must be represented in Challenges; Honors Forum—a presentation of a project; Academic Excellence—a 3.50 Grade Point Average. Also, students in the Honors program can choose to live on the Honors floor in a campus residence hall. **Combined Degree Programs:** BA/JD, BA/MEng, JD with Albany Law School. **Disability Services:** Special programs offered to physically disabled students include reader services, tape recorders, tutors. **Career Services:** career/job search classes, internships, Career Services highlights include Learning outside the classroom is an integral part of preparing our students for careers after graduation and why we've designed our curriculum and teaching approaches to break down the barriers that separate the classroom from the world. As a Hartwick student, you'll get to learn "out there" and bring that experience back, making your time in the classroom more engaging and effective.

FACILITIES
Housing: Coed dorms, women's dorms, fraternity/sorority housing, apartments for single students, Housing at Pine Lake environmental campus (lodge and cabins) also available. 50% of campus accessible to physically disabled.
Special Academic Facilities/Equipment: Art and history museums, Indian artifact collection, environmental center, observatory, electron microscope, tissue culture lab, spectrophotometers. **Computers:** 100% of classrooms, 100% of dorms, 100% of libraries, 50% of dining areas, 50% of student union, have wireless network access. Students can register for classes online. Administrative functions (other than registration) can be performed online.

CAMPUS LIFE
Environment: Village. **Activities:** Choral groups, dance, drama/theater, literary magazine, music ensembles, pep band, radio station, student government, student newspaper, yearbook, Campus Ministries 70 registered organizations, 30 honor societies, 3 religious organizations. 3 fraternities, 3 sororities. **Athletics (Intercollegiate):** *Men:* basketball, cross-country, diving, football, lacrosse, soccer, swimming, tennis. *Women:* basketball, cheerleading, cross-country, diving, equestrian sports, field hockey, lacrosse, soccer, swimming, tennis, volleyball, water polo. **On-Campus Highlights:** Yager Museum, Stevens-German Library, Johnstone Science Center, Binder Athletic Facility, Dewar Student Union. **Environmental Initiatives:** Hartwick is a signatory of the Talloires Declaration and is a member of the Association for the Advancement of Sustainability in Higher Education. In 2005, the College received a Kresge Green Building Iniative planning grant to partially fund green design of its first LEED-certified building, Golisano Hall. In keeping with Hartwick's emphasis on hands-on learning, the project provided the basis for a course entitled "Sustainable Design", taught by Richard Rittelman, FAIA principal architect and Karl Seeley, PhD. of Hartwick's economics department. The LEED-certification process for Golisano Hall is currently underway. The process involves commissioning the building's systems, which are estimated to use 75% less energy than the average building on Hartwick's campus. As an institution, Hartwick has a long history of environmental awareness and action. The 125 acre Pine Lake Environmental Campus (which borders 3,000 acres of state park) was created in 1971, offering students a unique living laboratory for sustainability where ecological principles such as energy conservation, organic gardening, composting, waste reduction, and recycling are practiced every day. The lake, forests, trails, and mud bog have been the sites of more than 40 courses and 30 ongoing student/faculty research projects. Pine Lake is also a residence for 30-35 students. In 2002, students in the class "Architecture of the Sacred," finished construction on a 900-square foot strawbale house at the Lake. Built of compressed strawbale and finished with natural plaster, the house is economical and environmentally friendly and was the first "green" building constructed by Hartwick. Subsequently, students constructed a cob house, also at Pine Lake. Since 2002-03 Hartwick's academic year theme was focused on sustainablilty, including annual themes on sustainable living, food in our lives, health and the human experience, globalization, water works, climate change and balance. Several leaders in the sustainability movement, including Vandura Shiva, Bill McKibben, Peter Finn, David Orr, Winona LaDuke, and Oren Lyons have spent time on campus, led college activities, and made public presentations. The Pine Lake Institute (PLI) for Environmental and Sustainability Studies sets an example for the College and community as to how to live sustainably.

ADMISSIONS
Freshman Academic Profile: 20% in top 10% of high school class, 53% in top 25% of high school class, 81% in top 50% of high school class. 86% from public high schools. SAT Math middle 50% range 500-610. SAT Critical Reading middle 50% range 520-610. SAT Writing middle 50% range 500-600. ACT middle

50% range 24-27. Minimum web-based TOEFL 79. Minimum paper TOEFL 550. **Basis for Candidate Selection:** *Very important factors considered include:* rigor of secondary school record. *Important factors considered include:* Class rank, academic GPA, recommendation(s). *Other factors considered include:* application essay, standardized test scores, alumni/ae relation, character/personal qualities, extracurricular activities, first generation, geographical residence, interview, level of applicant's interest, racial/ethnic status, state residency, talent/ability, volunteer work, work experience. **Freshman Admission Requirements:** High school diploma is required and GED is accepted. **Freshman Admission Statistics:** 5,795 applied, 85% admitted, 9% enrolled. **Transfer Admission Requirements:** college transcript(s), essay or personal statement, statement of good standing from prior institution(s). Minimum college GPA of 2.0 required. Lowest grade transferable C–. **General Admission Information:** Application Fee $35. Early decision application deadline 11/15. Regular application deadline 2/15. Nonfall registration accepted. Admission may be deferred for a maximum of 12 months. Credit offered for CEEB Advanced Placement tests.

COSTS AND FINANCIAL AID
Average book expense $700. **Required Forms and Deadlines:** FAFSA. **Notification of Awards:** Applicants will be notified of awards on or about 3/15. **Types of Aid:** *Need-based scholarships/grants:* Federal Pell, SEOG, state scholarships/grants, private scholarships, the school's own gift aid. *Loans:* Subsidized Stafford, Unsubsidized Stafford, PLUS, Federal Perkins, Federal Nursing. **Student Employment:** Federal Work-Study Program available. Institutional employment available. Highest amount earned per year from on-campus jobs $2,000. Off-campus job opportunities are good. **Financial Aid Statistics:** 100% freshmen, 100% undergrads receive need-based scholarship or grant aid. 14% freshmen, 11% undergrads receive non-need-based scholarship or grant aid. 87% freshmen, 88% undergrads receive need-based self-help aid. 1% undergrads receive athletic scholarships. 100% freshmen, 95% undergrads receive any aid. 70% undergrads borrow to pay for school. Average cumulative indebtedness $32,627. **Criteria for awarding institutional aid:** *Non-need-based:* academics, alumni affiliation, art, athletics, leadership, music/drama, state/district residency.

HARVARD COLLEGE

Best 378

86 Brattle Street, Cambridge, MA 2138
Phone: 617-495-1551 • **Financial Aid Phone:** 617-495-1581
E-mail: college@fas.harvard.edu • **CEEB Code:** 3434
Fax: 617-495-8821 • **Website:** www.college.harvard.edu • **ACT Code:** 1840

This private school was founded in 1636. It has a 380-acre campus.

RATINGS
Admissions Selectivity Rating: 99   **Fire Safety Rating:** 60*   **Green Rating:** 98

STUDENTS AND FACULTY
Enrollment: 6,610. **Student Body:** 49% female, 51% male, 85% out-of-state, 11% international (109 countries represented). Asian 19%, African American 7%, Caucasian 45%, Hispanic 9%, Native American 0%.
Retention and Graduation: 97% freshmen return for sophomore year. 86% freshmen graduate within 4 years. 97% freshmen graduate within 6 years.
Faculty: Student/faculty ratio 7:1. 933 full-time faculty, 84% hold PhDs, 18% are members of minority groups, 33% are women. 0% of classes are taught by teaching assistants.

ACADEMICS
Degrees: bachelor's, master's, post-master's certificate. **Classes:** Most classes have fewer than 10 students. **Majors with Highest Enrollment:** economics; political science and government; sociology. **Special Study Options:** Accelerated program, cross-registration, double major, exchange student program (domestic), honors program, independent study, internships, student-designed major, study abroad, teacher certification program. **Combined Degree Programs:** BA/MA, BA/MEng. **Disability Services:** Special programs offered to physically disabled students include note-taking services, reader services, tape recorders, tutors. **Career Services:** Alumni network, alumni services

FACILITIES
Housing: Coed dorms, special housing for disabled students, apartments for married students, cooperative **Academic Facilities/Equipment:** Museums

(University Arts Museums, Museums of Cultural History, many others), language labs, observatory, many science and research laboratories and facilities, new state-of-the-art computer science facility. **Computers:** 98% of classrooms, 100% of dorms, 100% of libraries, have wireless network access. Students can register for classes online. Administrative functions (other than registration) can be performed online.

CAMPUS LIFE
Environment: City. **Activities:** Choral groups, concert band, dance, drama/theater, jazz band, literary magazine, marching band, music ensembles, musical theater, opera, pep band, radio station, student government, student newspaper, student-run film society, symphony orchestra, television station, yearbook, Campus Ministries, International Student Organization, Model UN 393 registered organizations, 1 honor societies, 28 religious organizations. **Athletics (Intercollegiate):** *Men:* baseball, basketball, crew/rowing, cross-country, diving, fencing, football, golf, ice hockey, lacrosse, sailing, skiing (downhill/alpine), skiing (nordic/cross-country), soccer, squash, swimming, tennis, track/field (outdoor), track/field (indoor), volleyball, water polo, wrestling. *Women:* basketball, crew/rowing, cross-country, diving, fencing, field hockey, golf, ice hockey, lacrosse, sailing, skiing (downhill/alpine), skiing (nordic/cross-country), soccer, softball, squash, swimming, tennis, track/field (outdoor), track/field (indoor), volleyball, water polo. **On-Campus Highlights:** Widener Library, Harvard Yard, Fogg Museum, Annenburg/Memorial Hall, Science Center. **Environmental Initiatives:** Campus-wide Sustainability Principles that provide a broad vision to guide University operations and planning (adopted in 2004) and an established University-wide Office for Sustainability (green.harvard.edu) that oversees implementation of Harvard's GHG reduction goal and sustainability commitments. The University has had a formal sustainability office for a decade initially created by a faculty and staff initiative with strong student involvement. Greenhouse Gas (GHG) Reduction Goal to reduce GHG emissions 30% below a 2006 baseline by 2016, including growth (adopted in 2008). University-wide GHG emissions have declined by 7% from FY06-FY09, including growth. When growth is excluded, emissions declined by 14% in the same time period. Comprehensive Green Building Standards for capital projects, renovations and building system upgrades that require a smart design process incorporating life cycle costing, integrated design, energy modeling when applicable and other elements that ensure all sustainable design and operations opportunities are vetted and that performance requirements are achieved in a cost-effective manner (Adopted 2009, building on the 2007 Green Building Guidelines).

ADMISSIONS
Freshman Academic Profile: Average high school GPA 4.1. 95% in top 10% of high school class, 99% in top 25% of high school class, 100% in top 50% of high school class. SAT Math middle 50% range 710-790. SAT Critical Reading middle 50% range 700-800. SAT Writing middle 50% range 710-800. ACT middle 50% range 32-35. **Basis for Candidate Selection:** *Other factors considered include:* application essay, academic GPA, recommendation(s), rigor of secondary school record, standardized test scores, alumni/ae relation, character/personal qualities, extracurricular activities, first generation, geographical residence, interview, racial/ethnic status, talent/ability, volunteer work, work experience. **Freshman Admission Requirements:** High school diploma or equivalent is not required. **Freshman Admission Statistics:** 34,303 applied, 6% admitted, 80% enrolled. **General Admission Information:** Application Fee $75. Regular application deadline 1/1. Regular notification 4/1. Nonfall registration not accepted. Admission may be deferred for a maximum of 12 months. Credit and/or placement offered for CEEB Advanced Placement tests.

COSTS AND FINANCIAL AID
Required Forms and Deadlines: FAFSA, CSS/Financial Aid PROFILE Tax forms through IDOC. **Notification of Awards:** Applicants will be notified of awards on or about 4/1. **Types of Aid:** *Need-based scholarships/grants:* Federal Pell, SEOG, state scholarships/grants, private scholarships, the school's own gift aid. *Loans:* Direct Subsidized Stafford, Direct Unsubsidized Stafford, Direct PLUS, Federal Perkins, college/university loans from institutional funds. **Student Employment:** Federal Work-Study Program available. Institutional employment available. Highest amount earned per year from on-campus jobs $19,967. Off-campus job opportunities are excellent. **Financial Aid Statistics:** 100% freshmen, 99% undergrads receive need-based scholarship or grant aid. 64% freshmen, 84% undergrads receive need-based self-help aid. 25% undergrads borrow to pay for school. Average cumulative indebtedness $13,098.

HARVEY MUDD COLLEGE

Best 378

301 Platt Boulevard, Claremont, CA 91711-5990
Phone: 909-621-8011 • **Financial Aid Phone:** 909-621-8055
E-mail: admission@hmc.edu • **CEEB Code:** 4341
Fax: 909-621-8360 • **Website:** www.hmc.edu

This private school was founded in 1955. It has a 33-acre campus.

RATINGS
Admissions Selectivity Rating: 99   **Fire Safety Rating:** 71   **Green Rating:** 78

STUDENTS AND FACULTY
Enrollment: 779. **Student Body:** 44% female, 56% male, 63% out-of-state, 6% international (18 countries represented). Asian 16%, African American 1%, Caucasian 43%, Hispanic 5%, Native American 0%.
Retention and Graduation: 98% freshmen return for sophomore year. 84% freshmen graduate within 4 years. 88% freshmen graduate within 6 years. **Faculty:** Student/faculty ratio 9:1. 86 full-time faculty, 100% hold PhDs, 22% are members of minority groups, 40% are women. 0% of classes are taught by teaching assistants.

ACADEMICS
Degrees: bachelor's. **Classes:** Most classes have 10–19 students. Most lab/discussion sessions have 10–19 students. **Majors with Highest Enrollment:** computer and information sciences; engineering; mathematics. **Special Study Options:** cross-registration, double major, dual enrollment, exchange student program (domestic), independent study, internships, liberal arts/career combination, student-designed major, study abroad, Innovative client-sponsored design projects. **Combined Degree Programs:** BS/MS math, BS/MBA, BS/MIS, BA/BS. **Career Services:** Alumni network, alumni services, career assessment, internships Career Services highlights include see http://www.hmc.edu/academicsclinicresearch/clinicprogram1/history.html.

FACILITIES
Housing: Coed dorms, apartments for married students, apartments for single students, Housing exchange program w/ Pomona College, Pitzer College, Scripps College, and Claremont McKenna College. 80% of campus accessible to physically disabled. **Computers:** 100% of classrooms, 100% of dorms, 100% of libraries, 100% of dining areas, 100% of student union, 75% of common outdoor areas have wireless network access. Students can register for classes online. Administrative functions (other than registration) can be performed online.

CAMPUS LIFE
Environment: Town. **Activities:** Choral groups, concert band, dance, drama/theater, jazz band, literary magazine, music ensembles, musical theater, pep band, radio station, student government, student newspaper, student-run film society, symphony orchestra, yearbook, Campus Ministries, International Student Organization, Model UN 109 registered organizations, 4 honor societies, 6 religious organizations. **Athletics (Intercollegiate):** *Men:* baseball, basketball, cross-country, diving, football, golf, soccer, swimming, tennis, track/field (outdoor), water polo. *Women:* basketball, cross-country, diving, golf, lacrosse, soccer, softball, swimming, tennis, track/field (outdoor), volleyball, water polo.
On-Campus Highlights: Dorm Lounges, Platt Campus Center Living Room, Liquidamber mall, Jay's Pizza Place, Linde Student Activities Center. **Environmental Initiatives:** In February 2008 Harvey Mudd College President Maria Klawe signed the American College & University Presidents Climate Commitment and Harvey Mudd College Board of Trustees adopted HMC Sustainability Policy Statement. Additionally, the Board of Trustees passed a resolution where the standard for new buildings will be at least U.S. Green Building Council LEED Silver standard or equivalent and premium rated or ENERGY STAR certified products are purchased for use on campus where possible. In 2007 a team of students lead by faculty advisers documented the historical usage of key resources and utilities " electricity, natural gas, and water for Harvey Mudd College and the other Claremont Colleges " in order to establish baselines against which to compare future usage, and to identify targets for conservation programs. The team also studied emissions, waste disposal, and recycling programs with the ultimate goal of assessing the feasibility of achieving carbon neutrality within the next decade or two. Finally the team developed recommendations for creating a more sustainable Claremont Colleges Community. The Center for Environmental Studies at Harvey Mudd College was created in May 1999 to create and coordinate interdepartmental programs related to environmental studies. The Center provides a framework through which students, faculty, and alumni can come together to identify critical issues in the relationship between human life and both natural and human-built environments, to investigate those issues, and to help articulate the important roles that science, mathematics, and engineering will take in addressing those issues. Through this framework, the Center seeks to perpetuate creative and responsible professional practices in an increasingly fragile world.

ADMISSIONS
Freshman Academic Profile: 96% in top 10% of high school class, 100% in top 25% of high school class, 100% in top 50% of high school class. 67% from public high schools. SAT Math middle 50% range 740-800. SAT Critical Reading middle 50% range 680-770. SAT Writing middle 50% range 680-760. ACT middle 50% range 33-35. Minimum web-based TOEFL 100. Minimum paper TOEFL 600. **Basis for Candidate Selection:** *Very important factors considered include:* application essay, academic GPA, recommendation(s), rigor of secondary school record, character/personal qualities, talent/ability. *Important factors considered include:* Class rank, standardized test scores, extracurricular activities. *Other factors considered include:* alumni/ae relation, first generation, geographical residence, interview, level of applicant's interest, racial/ethnic status, state residency, volunteer work, work experience. **Freshman Admission Requirements:** High school diploma is required and GED is accepted.High school diploma or equivalent is not required. *Academic units required:* 4 English, 3 mathematics, 3 science, 1 history. *Academic units recommended:* 4 English, 3 mathematics, 3 science, 1 history. **Freshman Admission Statistics:** 3,336 applied, 19% admitted, 31% enrolled. **Transfer Admission Requirements:** High school transcript, college transcript(s), essay or personal statement, statement of good standing from prior institution(s). Minimum college GPA of 3.0 required. Lowest grade transferable C. **General Admission Information:** Application Fee $60. Early decision application deadline 11/15. Regular application deadline 1/2. Regular notification 4/1. Nonfall registration not accepted. Admission may be deferred for a maximum of 12 months. Placement offered for CEEB Advanced Placement tests.

COSTS AND FINANCIAL AID
Annual tuition $44,159. Room and board $14,471. Required fees $283. Average book expense $800. **Required Forms and Deadlines:** FAFSA, CSS/Financial Aid PROFILE, state aid form, noncustodial PROFILE, business/farm supplement. **Notification of Awards:** Applicants will be notified of awards on or about 4/1. **Types of Aid:** *Need-based scholarships/grants:* Federal Pell, SEOG, state scholarships/grants, private scholarships, the school's own gift aid Federal ACG and SMART Grants. *Loans:* Subsidized Stafford, Unsubsidized Stafford, PLUS, Federal Perkins, college/university loans from institutional funds, Alternative Loans. **Student Employment:** Federal Work-Study Program available. Institutional employment available. Highest amount earned per year from on campus jobs $11,776. Off-campus job opportunities are excellent. **Financial Aid Statistics:** 96% freshmen, 97% undergrads receive need-based scholarship or grant aid. 41% freshmen, 42% undergrads receive non-need-based scholarship or grant aid. 67% freshmen, 77% undergrads receive need-based self-help aid. 48% undergrads borrow to pay for school. Average cumulative indebtedness $24,194. **Criteria for awarding institutional aid:** *Non-need-based:* academics.

HASTINGS COLLEGE

Hastings College, Hastings, NE 68901
Phone: 402-461-7403 • **Financial Aid Phone:** 402-461-7431
E-mail: mmolliconi@hastings.edu • **CEEB Code:** 6270
Fax: 402-461-7490 • **Website:** www.hastings.edu • **ACT Code:** 2456

This private school, affiliated with the Presbyterian Church, was founded in 1882. It has a 109-acre campus.

RATINGS
Admissions Selectivity Rating: 66   **Fire Safety Rating:** 68   **Green Rating:** 61

STUDENTS AND FACULTY
Enrollment: 1,067. **Student Body:** 46% female, 54% male, 28% out-of-state, 1% international (7 countries represented). Asian 1%, African American 2%, Caucasian 91%, Hispanic 3%, Native American 0%.
Retention and Graduation: 76% freshmen return for sophomore year. 52% freshmen graduate within 4 years. 61% freshmen graduate within 6 years. 24% grads go on to further study within 1 year. 16% grads pursue arts and sciences degrees. 2% grads pursue law degrees. 1% grads pursue business degrees. 1% grads pursue medical degrees. **Faculty:** Student/faculty ratio 11:1. 87 full-time faculty, 71% hold PhDs, 1% are members of minority groups, 34% are women. 0% of classes are taught by teaching assistants.

ACADEMICS
Degrees: bachelor's, master's. **Classes:** Most classes have 10–19 students. Most lab/discussion sessions have fewer than 10 students. **Majors with High-

est **Enrollment:** business/commerce; education; psychology. **Special Study Options:** double major, exchange student program (domestic), independent study, internships, student-designed major, study abroad, teacher certification program. **Combined Degree Programs:** BA/BM. **Disability Services:** Special programs offered to physically disabled students include note-taking services, reader services, tape recorders, tutors. **Career Services:** Alumni network, alumni services, career/job search classes, career assessment, internships, regional alumni. Career Services highlights include Service Learning program.

FACILITIES

Housing: Coed dorms, men's dorms, women's dorms, apartments for single students, Honors housing, one apartment complex is for quiet and alcohol-free living. 90% of campus accessible to physically disabled. **Special Academic Facilities/Equipment:** center for communication arts, glass-blowing studio, observatory, art gallery **Computers:** 95% of classrooms, 100% of libraries, 100% of dining areas, 100% of student union, have wireless network access. Administrative functions (other than registration) can be performed online.

CAMPUS LIFE

Environment: Village. **Activities:** Choral groups, concert band, dance, drama/theater, jazz band, literary magazine, marching band, music ensembles, musical theater, pep band, radio station, student government, student newspaper, symphony orchestra, television station, yearbook, Campus Ministries 85 registered organizations, 13 honor societies, 10 religious organizations. 4 fraternities, 4 sororities. **Athletics (Intercollegiate):** *Men:* baseball, basketball, cross-country, football, golf, soccer, tennis, track/field (outdoor), track/field (indoor), wrestling. *Women:* basketball, cheerleading, cross-country, golf, soccer, softball, tennis, track/field (outdoor), track/field (indoor), volleyball. **On-Campus Highlights:** Fleharty Educational Center and weight room, Hazelrigg Student Union, Perkins Library, Gray Center of Communication Arts, Dorm lounges.

ADMISSIONS

Freshman Academic Profile: Average high school GPA 3.2. 16% in top 10% of high school class, 40% in top 25% of high school class, 65% in top 50% of high school class. 88% from public high schools. SAT Math middle 50% range 490-605. SAT Critical Reading middle 50% range 500-600. ACT middle 50% range 20-26. Minimum paper TOEFL 600. **Basis for Candidate Selection:** *Very important factors considered include:* Class rank, academic GPA, recommendation(s), rigor of secondary school record, standardized test scores. *Important factors considered include:* character/personal qualities, extracurricular activities, talent/ability. *Other factors considered include:* application essay, alumni/ae relation, interview, level of applicant's interest, racial/ethnic status. **Freshman Admission Requirements:** High school diploma is required and GED is accepted. *Academic units required:* 3 English, 3 mathematics, 3 science, (3 science labs), 4 social studies, 3 history. *Academic units recommended:* 3 English, 3 mathematics, 3 science, (3 science labs), 4 social studies, 3 history. **Freshman Admission Statistics:** 1,210 applied, 81% accepted, 26% enrolled. **Transfer Admission Requirements:** High school transcript, college transcript(s), statement of good standing from prior institution(s). Minimum college GPA of 2.0 required. Lowest grade transferable C. **General Admission Information:** Application Fee $20. Notification on a rolling basis, beginning on or about 10/15. Nonfall registration accepted. Credit and/or placement offered for CEEB Advanced Placement tests.

COSTS AND FINANCIAL AID

Average book expense $730. **Required Forms and Deadlines:** FAFSA, institution's own financial aid form. **Notification of Awards:** Applicants will be notified of awards on a rolling basis beginning 3/1. **Types of Aid:** *Need-based scholarships/grants:* Federal Pell, SEOG, state scholarships/grants, private scholarships, the school's own gift aid. *Loans:* Subsidized Stafford, Unsubsidized Stafford, PLUS, Federal Perkins. **Student Employment:** Federal Work-Study Program available. Institutional employment available. Highest amount earned per year from on-campus jobs $1,000. Off-campus job opportunities are good. **Financial Aid Statistics:** 100% freshmen, 98% undergrads receive need-based scholarship or grant aid. 20% freshmen, 16% undergrads receive non-need-based scholarship or grant aid. 73% freshmen, 79% undergrads receive need-based self-help aid. 23% freshmen, 16% undergrads receive athletic scholarships. 97% freshmen, 98% undergrads receive any aid. **Criteria for awarding institutional aid:** *Non-need-based:* academics, art, athletics, leadership, music/drama.

HAVERFORD COLLEGE

370 Lancaster Avenue, Haverford, PA 19041
Phone: 610-896-1350 • **Financial Aid Phone:** 610-896-1350
E-mail: http://www.haverford.edu/admission/staff • **CEEB Code:** 2289
Fax: 610-896-1338 • **Website:** www.haverford.edu • **ACT Code:** 3409

This private school was founded in 1833. It has a 200-acre campus.

RATINGS
Admissions Selectivity Rating: 98   **Fire Safety Rating:** 74   **Green Rating:** 92

STUDENTS AND FACULTY

Enrollment: 1,205. **Student Body:** 53% female, 47% male, 86% out-of-state, 4% international (33 countries represented). Asian 7%, African American 6%, Caucasian 67%, Hispanic 9%, Native American 0%.
Retention and Graduation: 96% freshmen return for sophomore year. 89% freshmen graduate within 4 years. 94% freshmen graduate within 6 years. 13% grads go on to further study within 1 year. 8% grads pursue arts and sciences degrees. 3% grads pursue law degrees. 1% grads pursue medical degrees.
Faculty: Student/faculty ratio 8:1. 118 full-time faculty, 97% hold PhDs, 23% are members of minority groups, 47% are women. 0% of classes are taught by teaching assistants.

ACADEMICS

Degrees: bachelor's. **Classes:** Most classes have fewer than 10 students. Most lab/discussion sessions have fewer than 10 students. **Majors with Highest Enrollment:** biology/biological sciences; economics; English language and literature. **Special Study Options:** cross-registration, double major, exchange student program (domestic), independent study, internships, liberal arts/career combination, student-designed major, study abroad, teacher certification program. **Combined Degree Programs:** BA/MEng. **Disability Services:** Special programs offered to physically disabled students include note-taking services, tape recorders. **Career Services:** Alumni network, alumni services, career assessment, internships, regional alumni.

FACILITIES

Housing: Coed dorms, men's dorms, women's dorms, apartments for single students, theme housing. 60% of campus accessible to physically disabled. **Special Academic Facilities/Equipment:** Art gallery, center for cross-cultural study of religion, arboretum, observatory, foundry. **Computers:** 75% of classrooms, 75% of libraries, 100% of dining areas, 100% of student union, 80% of common outdoor areas have wireless network access. Students can register for classes online. Administrative functions (other than registration) can be performed online.

CAMPUS LIFE

Environment: Town. **Activities:** Choral groups, dance, drama/theater, literary magazine, music ensembles, musical theater, student government, student newspaper, yearbook, Campus Ministries, International Student Organization 144 registered organizations, 1 honor societies, 6 religious organizations. **Athletics (Intercollegiate):** *Men:* baseball, basketball, cross-country, fencing, lacrosse, soccer, squash, tennis, track/field (outdoor), track/field (indoor). *Women:* basketball, cross-country, fencing, field hockey, lacrosse, soccer, softball, squash, tennis, track/field (outdoor), track/field (indoor), volleyball. **On-Campus Highlights:** Integrated Natural Sciences Center, John Whitehead Campus Center, Cantor Fitzgerald Gallery, Arboretum, Douglas B. Gardner Athletic Center. **Environmental Initiatives:** Our athletic center is the 1st gold LEED certified recreation center in the US (opened in 2005). We have reached 98% for grounds recycling. We have completed a master plan to identify utility and powerhouse improvements, and will commence work on these improvements immediately.

ADMISSIONS

Freshman Academic Profile: 92% in top 10% of high school class, 100% in top 25% of high school class. 55% from public high schools. SAT Math middle 50% range 660-760. SAT Critical Reading middle 50% range 650-760. SAT Writing middle 50% range 670-760. ACT middle 50% range 29-33. Minimum paper TOEFL 600. **Basis for Candidate Selection:** *Very important factors considered include:* application essay, academic GPA, recommendation(s), rigor of secondary school record, character/personal qualities, extracurricular activities. *Important factors considered include:* Class rank, standardized test scores, talent/ability, volunteer work, work experience. *Other factors considered include:* alumni/ae relation, first generation, geographical residence, interview, level of applicant's interest, racial/ethnic status. **Freshman Admission Requirements:** High school diploma or equivalent is not required. **Freshman Admission Statistics:** 3,626 applied, 23% admitted, 39% enrolled. **Transfer**

Admission Requirements: college transcript(s), essay or personal statement, standardized test scores, statement of good standing from prior institution(s). Minimum college GPA of 3.0 required. Lowest grade transferable C. **General Admission Information:** Application Fee $60. Early decision application deadline 11/15. Regular application deadline 1/15. Regular notification 4/15. Nonfall registration not accepted. Admission may be deferred for a maximum of 12months.

COSTS AND FINANCIAL AID

Annual tuition $43,310. Room and board $13,290. Required fees $392. Average book expense $1,194. **Required Forms and Deadlines:** FAFSA, CSS/Financial Aid PROFILE, noncustodial PROFILE, business/farm supplement. CSS College Board Noncustodial Parents' Statement is required--not the Noncustodial supplement. **Notification of Awards:** Applicants will be notified of awards on or about 4/1. **Types of Aid:** *Need-based scholarships/grants:* Federal Pell, SEOG, state scholarships/grants, the school's own gift aid. *Loans:* Subsidized Stafford, Unsubsidized Stafford, PLUS, Federal Perkins. **Student Employment:** Federal Work-Study Program available. Institutional employment available. Highest amount earned per year from on-campus jobs $2,300. Off-campus job opportunities are good. **Financial Aid Statistics:** 98% freshmen, 96% undergrads receive need-based scholarship or grant aid. 91% freshmen, 94% undergrads receive need-based self-help aid. 51% freshmen, 50% undergrads receive any aid. 33% undergrads borrow to pay for school. Average cumulative indebtedness $14,171.

See page 1094.

HAWAII PACIFIC UNIVERSITY

1164 Bishop Street, Honolulu, HI 96813
Phone: 808-544-0238 • **Financial Aid Phone:** 808-544-0253
E-mail: admissions@hpu.edu • **CEEB Code:** 4352
Fax: 808-544-1136 • **Website:** www.hpu.edu • **ACT Code:** 4352

This private school was founded in 1965. It has a 135-acre campus.

RATINGS

Admissions Selectivity Rating: 67   **Fire Safety Rating:** 78   **Green Rating:** 60*

STUDENTS AND FACULTY

Enrollment: 6,262. **Student Body:** 61% female, 39% male, 40% out-of-state, 10% international (102 countries represented). Asian 31%, African American 7%, Caucasian 34%, Hispanic 7%, Native American 1%.
Retention and Graduation: 66% freshmen return for sophomore year. 68% grads go on to further study within 1 year. 20% grads pursue arts and sciences degrees. 5% grads pursue law degrees. 45% grads pursue business degrees. 3% grads pursue medical degrees. **Faculty:** Student/faculty ratio 16:1. 264 full-time faculty, 66% hold PhDs, 25% are members of minority groups, 46% are women. 0% of classes are taught by teaching assistants.

ACADEMICS

Degrees: associate, bachelor's, certificate, master's, post-bachelor's certificate, post-master's certificate. **Classes:** Most classes have 10–19 students. Most lab/discussion sessions have fewer than 10 students. **Majors with Highest Enrollment:** business, management, marketing, and related support services, other; management information systems; nursing/registered nurse (rn, asn, bsn, msn). **Special Study Options:** Accelerated program, cooperative education program, distance learning, double major, dual enrollment, English as a Second Language (ESL), honors program, independent study, internships, liberal arts/career combination, student-designed major, study abroad, weekend college. **Honors Programs:** University Scholars Honors Program: During the freshman and sophomore years University Scholars enroll in honors sections of many courses required in the general education curriculum. Normally, University Scholars are required to complete at least six of these courses, but exceptions can be made for students who have completed certain requirements through AP courses in high school or for majors with different general education requirements. At the upper-division level, University Scholars enroll in three honors seminars. The Certificate of Merit is awarded at the time of graduation to students who fulfill the University Scholars requirements. **Combined Degree Programs:** BA/MA.

FACILITIES

Housing: Coed dorms, women's dorms, apartments for married students, apartments for single students, Apartment search and referral service. 90% of campus accessible to physically disabled. **Special Academic Facilities/Equipment:** Hawaii Pacific University Art Gallery, Hawaii Pacific University Theatre. **Computers:** Students can register for classes online. Administrative functions (other than registration) can be performed online.

CAMPUS LIFE

Environment: Metropolis. **Activities:** Choral groups, dance, drama/theater, literary magazine, music ensembles, musical theater, pep band, student government, student newspaper, student-run film society 80 registered organizations, 18 honor societies, 3 religious organizations. **Athletics (Intercollegiate):** *Men:* baseball, basketball, cheerleading, cross-country, golf, tennis. *Women:* cheerleading, cross-country, golf, softball, tennis, volleyball. **On-Campus Highlights:** Frear Center, Sea Warrior Center, Windward Campus, Art Gallery, Fort Street Mall.

ADMISSIONS

Freshman Academic Profile: Average high school GPA 3.3. 20% in top 10% of high school class, 45% in top 25% of high school class, 80% in top 50% of high school class. 60% from public high schools. SAT Math middle 50% range 430-560. SAT Critical Reading middle 50% range 420-550. SAT Writing middle 50% range 350-540. ACT middle 50% range 17-24. Minimum paper TOEFL 550. **Basis for Candidate Selection:** *Very important factors considered include:* academic GPA, rigor of secondary school record. *Important factors considered include:* standardized test scores, extracurricular activities, interview. *Other factors considered include:* Class rank, application essay, recommendation(s), character/personal qualities, first generation, talent/ability, volunteer work, work experience. **Freshman Admission Requirements:** High school diploma is required and GED is accepted. **Freshman Admission Statistics:** 2,991 applied, 829% enrolled. **Transfer Admission Requirements:** college transcript(s), minimum college GPA of 2.0 required. Lowest grade transferable C. **General Admission Information:** Application Fee $50. Notification on a rolling basis, beginning on or about 1/1. Nonfall registration accepted. Admission may be deferred for a maximum of 24 months. Credit and/or placement offered for CEEB Advanced Placement tests.

COSTS AND FINANCIAL AID

Annual tuition $18,500. Room and board $12,230. Required fees $80. Average book expense $2,096. **Required Forms and Deadlines:** FAFSA. **Notification of Awards:** Applicants will be notified of awards on a rolling basis beginning 4/1. **Types of Aid:** *Need-based scholarships/grants:* Federal Pell, SEOG, state scholarships/grants, the school's own gift aid, Federal Nursing Scholarships. *Loans:* Subsidized Stafford, Unsubsidized Stafford, PLUS, Federal Perkins, Federal Nursing, Alternative loans. **Student Employment:** Highest amount earned per year from on-campus jobs $3,800. **Financial Aid Statistics:** 41% freshmen, 45% undergrads receive need-based scholarship or grant aid. 41% freshmen, 28% undergrads receive non-need-based scholarship or grant aid. 93% freshmen, 95% undergrads receive need-based self-help aid. 75% freshmen, 67% undergrads receive any aid. 36% undergrads borrow to pay for school. Average cumulative indebtedness $17,125. **Criteria for awarding institutional aid:** *Non-need-based:* academics, alumni affiliation, athletics, job skills, leadership, music/drama, religious affiliation.

See page 1096.

HEBREW COLLEGE

160 Herrick Road, Newton Centre, MA 2459
Phone: 617-559-8610 • **Financial Aid Phone:** 617-559-8642
E-mail: admissions@hebrewcollege.edu
Fax: 617 559-8601 • **Website:** www.hebrewcollege.edu

This private school, affiliated with the Jewish Church, was founded in 1921.

RATINGS

Admissions Selectivity Rating: 61   **Fire Safety Rating:** 60*   **Green Rating:** 60*

STUDENTS AND FACULTY

Enrollment: 4. **Student Body:** 50% female, 50% male, 1% out-of-state, 25% international.
Retention and Graduation: 40% grads go on to further study within 1 year.

ACADEMICS

Degrees: bachelor's, certificate, master's. **Majors with Highest Enrollment:** business administration and management; education; psychology. **Special Study Options:** cross-registration, distance learning, independent study, internships, student-designed major, Semester in Israel is encouraged.

CAMPUS LIFE

Environment: City. **Activities:** Choral groups. **On-Campus Highlights:** Library

ADMISSIONS

Freshman Academic Profile: Minimum paper TOEFL 400. **Basis for Candidate Selection:** *Very important factors considered include:* application essay, religious affiliation/commitment, talent/ability. *Important factors considered include:* Class rank, recommendation(s), rigor of secondary school record, standardized test scores, character/personal qualities, extracurricular activities, interview, volunteer work, work experience. *Other factors considered include:* alumni/ae relation, geographical residence, state residency. **Transfer Admission Requirements:** college transcript(s), essay or personal statement, interview, Lowest grade transferable C. **General Admission Information:** Regular application deadline 4/15. Nonfall registration accepted.

COSTS AND FINANCIAL AID

Annual tuition $7,920. **Student Employment:** Off-campus job opportunities are good.

HEC MONTREAL

3000 chemin de la Cote Ste-Catherine, Montreal, QC
Phone: 514-340-6151
E-mail: registraire.info@hec.ca
Fax: 514-340-6151 • **Website:** www.hec.ca

This public school was founded in 1907.

RATINGS
Admissions Selectivity Rating: 60*   **Fire Safety Rating:** 60*   **Green Rating:** 60*

STUDENTS AND FACULTY
Student Body: (102 countries represented).

ACADEMICS
Degrees: bachelor's, certificate, diploma, master's.

CAMPUS LIFE
Environment: Metropolis. **Activities:** radio station, student newspaper, yearbook, International Student Organization.

ADMISSIONS
General Admission Information: Application Fee $62. Regular application deadline 2/15. Nonfall registration accepted.

COSTS AND FINANCIAL AID
Annual in-state tuition $2,120. Room and board $9,600. Required fees $2,700. Average book expense $800.

HEIDELBERG COLLEGE

310 East Market Street, Tiffin, OH 44883
Phone: 419-448-2330 • **Financial Aid Phone:** 419-448-2293
E-mail: adminfo@heidelberg.edu • **CEEB Code:** 1292
Fax: 419-448-2334 • **Website:** www.heidelberg.edu • **ACT Code:** 3278

This private school, affiliated with the United Church of Christ Church, was founded in 1850. It has a 120-acre campus.

RATINGS
Admissions Selectivity Rating: 72   **Fire Safety Rating:** 61   **Green Rating:** 67

STUDENTS AND FACULTY
Enrollment: 1,089. **Student Body:** 48% female, 52% male, 15% out-of-state, 1% international. Asian 1%, African American 7%, Caucasian 78%, Hispanic 2%, Native American 0%.
Retention and Graduation: 61% freshmen return for sophomore year. 39% freshmen graduate within 4 years. 51% freshmen graduate within 6 years. 25% grads go on to further study within 1 year. 15% grads pursue arts and sciences degrees. 2% grads pursue law degrees. 5% grads pursue business degrees. 3% grads pursue medical degrees. **Faculty:** Student/faculty ratio 15:1. 50 full-time faculty, 86% hold PhDs, 6% are members of minority groups, 46% are women. 0% of classes are taught by teaching assistants.

ACADEMICS
Degrees: bachelor's, master's. **Classes:** Most classes have fewer than 10 students. Most lab/discussion sessions have 10–19 students. **Majors with Highest Enrollment:** biological and physical sciences; business/commerce; education. **Special Study Options:** cross-registration, double major, dual enrollment, English as a Second Language (ESL), exchange student program (domestic), honors program, independent study, internships, liberal arts/career combination, study abroad, teacher certification program. **Honors Programs:**

The Honors Program, entitled "The Life of the Mind," integrates learning and life experiences, stems from the mission of the University. It features extensive contact with the fundamental values that underpin self-worth and integrity, free inquiry, and intellectual rigor, an understanding of other cultures and traditions, and a lifelong habit of commitment to the community and concern for social responsibility. **Disability Services:** Special programs offered to physically disabled students include tutors. **Career Services:** Alumni network, career assessment, internships.

FACILITIES
Housing: Coed dorms, special housing for disabled students, women's dorms, cooperative housing, apartments for single students, theme housing, 65% of campus accessible to physically disabled. **Special Academic Facilities/Equipment:** Forest research lots, water quality lab, Center for Historic and Military Archaeology **Computers:** 80% of classrooms, 70% of dorms, 100% of libraries, 100% of dining areas, 100% of student union, have wireless network access. Students can register for classes online. Administrative functions (other than registration) can be performed online.

CAMPUS LIFE
Environment: Village. **Activities:** Choral groups, concert band, dance, drama/theater, jazz band, literary magazine, music ensembles, musical theater, opera, pep band, radio station, student government, student newspaper, student-run film society, symphony orchestra, television station, yearbook, Campus Ministries, International Student Organization, Model UN 75 registered organizations, 6 honor societies, 3 religious organizations. 5 fraternities, 4 sororities. **Athletics (Intercollegiate):** *Men:* baseball, basketball, cheerleading, cross-country, football, golf, soccer, tennis, track/field (outdoor), track/field (indoor), wrestling. *Women:* basketball, cheerleading, cross-country, golf, soccer, softball, tennis, track/field (outdoor), track/field (indoor), volleyball. **On-Campus Highlights:** Gillmor Science Center, Campus Center, Seiberling Gymnasium, Education Center

ADMISSIONS
Freshman Academic Profile: Average high school GPA 3.2. 14% in top 10% of high school class, 33% in top 25% of high school class, 62% in top 50% of high school class. 61% from public high schools. SAT Math middle 50% range 420-570. SAT Critical Reading middle 50% range 420-590. SAT Writing middle 50% range 400-550. ACT middle 50% range 19-25. Minimum paper TOEFL 550. **Basis for Candidate Selection:** *Very important factors considered include:* academic GPA, rigor of secondary school record, standardized test scores, character/personal qualities, talent/ability. *Important factors considered include:* Class rank, extracurricular activities, interview, level of applicant's interest. *Other factors considered include:* application essay, recommendation(s), alumni/ae relation, first generation, geographical residence, religious affiliation/commitment, state residency, volunteer work, work experience. **Freshman Admission Requirements:** High school diploma is required and GED is accepted. **Freshman Admission Statistics:** 1,726 applied, 71% admitted, 29% enrolled. **Transfer Admission Requirements:** High school transcript, college transcript(s), standardized test scores, statement of good standing from prior institution(s). Minimum college GPA of 2.0 required. Lowest grade transferable C–. **General Admission Information:** Application Fee $25. Regular application deadline 8/1. Notification on a rolling basis, beginning on or about 8/1. Nonfall registration accepted. Admission may be deferred for a maximum of 1 year. Credit and/or placement offered for CEEB Advanced Placement tests.

COSTS AND FINANCIAL AID
Average book expense $1,500. **Required Forms and Deadlines:** FAFSA. **Notification of Awards:** Applicants will be notified of awards on a rolling basis beginning 3/1. **Types of Aid:** *Need-based scholarships/grants:* Federal Pell, SEOG, state scholarships/grants, private scholarships, the school's own gift aid. *Loans:* Subsidized Stafford, Unsubsidized Stafford, PLUS, Federal Perkins. **Student Employment:** Federal Work-Study Program available. Institutional employment available. Highest amount earned per year from on-campus jobs $1,500. Off-campus job opportunities are good. **Financial Aid Statistics:** 100% freshmen, 100% undergrads receive need-based scholarship or grant aid. 89% freshmen, 70% undergrads receive non-need-based scholarship or grant aid. 89% freshmen, 89% undergrads receive need-based self-help aid. 99% freshmen, 97% undergrads receive any aid. 86% undergrads borrow to pay for school. Average cumulative indebtedness $35,470. **Criteria for awarding institutional aid:** *Non-need-based:* academics, music/drama, religious affiliation, state/district residency.

HELLENIC COLLEGE

50 Goddard Avenue, Brookline, MA 2445
Phone: 617-850-1260 • **Financial Aid Phone:** 617-850-1317
E-mail: admissions@hchc.edu
Fax: 617-850-1460 • **Website:** www.hchc.edu • **ACT Code:** 1843

This private school, affiliated with the Greek Orthodox Church, was founded in 1937. It has a 59-acre campus.

RATINGS
Admissions Selectivity Rating: 71　　**Fire Safety Rating:** 83　　**Green Rating:** 60*

STUDENTS AND FACULTY
Enrollment: 99. **Student Body:** 38% female, 62% male, 80% out-of-state, 8% international (9 countries represented). Caucasian 90%, Hispanic 2%. **Retention and Graduation:** 50% grads go on to further study within 1 year. **Faculty:** Student/faculty ratio 9:1. 18 full-time faculty.

ACADEMICS
Degrees: bachelor's, master's. **Classes:** Most classes have 20–29 students. **Majors with Highest Enrollment:** business/commerce. **Special Study Options:** honors program, liberal arts/career combination. **Combined Degree Programs:** BA/MA. **Disability Services:** Special programs offered to physically disabled students include tutors. **Career Services:** alumni services, regional alumni.

FACILITIES
Housing: Coed dorms, apartments for married students. 20% of campus accessible to physically disabled. **Computers:** 100% of dorms, have wireless network access.

CAMPUS LIFE
Environment: Village. **Activities:** Choral groups, student government, yearbook, Campus Ministries. **Athletics (Intercollegiate):** *Men:* basketball. *Women:* tennis.

ADMISSIONS
Freshman Academic Profile: Average high school GPA 3.1. 100% from public high schools. SAT Math middle 50% range 390-750. SAT Critical Reading middle 50% range 400-700. SAT Writing middle 50% range 390-640. ACT middle 50% range 20-29. Minimum web based TOEFL 61. Minimum paper TOEFL 500. **Basis for Candidate Selection:** *Very important factors considered include:* application essay, academic GPA, recommendation(s), rigor of secondary school record, standardized test scores, interview. *Important factors considered include:* Class rank. *Other factors considered include:* alumni/ae relation, character/personal qualities, extracurricular activities. **Freshman Admission Requirements:** High school diploma is required and GED is accepted. *Academic units required:* 4 English, 2 mathematics, 2 science, 2 foreign language, 2 social studies, 2 history. *Academic units recommended:* 4 English, 2 mathematics, 2 science, 2 foreign language, 2 social studies, 2 history. **Freshman Admission Statistics:** 64 applied, 81% admitted, 73% enrolled. **Transfer Admission Requirements:** college transcript(s), essay or personal statement, interview, minimum college GPA of 2.0 required. Lowest grade transferable C+. **General Admission Information:** Application Fee $50. Regular application deadline 8/15. Notification on a rolling basis, beginning on or about 9/1. Nonfall registration accepted. Admission may be deferred for a maximum of 2. Credit offered for CEEB Advanced Placement tests.

COSTS AND FINANCIAL AID
Annual tuition $19,900. Room and board $12,740. Required fees $500. Average book expense $1,000. **Required Forms and Deadlines:** FAFSA, institution's own financial aid form. **Notification of Awards:** Applicants will be notified of awards on a rolling basis beginning 4/1. **Types of Aid:** *Need-based scholarships/grants:* Federal Pell, SEOG, state scholarships/grants, private scholarships, the school's own gift aid. *Loans:* Subsidized Stafford, Unsubsidized Stafford, PLUS. **Student Employment:** Highest amount earned per year from on-campus jobs $1,600. **Financial Aid Statistics:** 100% freshmen, 100% undergrads receive need-based scholarship or grant aid. 98% freshmen, 96% undergrads receive any aid. 68% undergrads borrow to pay for school. Average cumulative indebtedness $23,000. **Criteria for awarding institutional aid:** *Non-need-based:* academics, alumni affiliation, religious affiliation.

HENDERSON STATE UNIVERSITY

1100 Henderson Street, Arkadelphia, AR 71999-0001
Phone: 870-230-5028 • **Financial Aid Phone:** 870-230-5148
E-mail: admissions@hsu.edu • **CEEB Code:** 6272
Fax: 870-230-5066 • **ACT Code:** 126

This public school was founded in 1890. It has a 151-acre campus.

RATINGS
Admissions Selectivity Rating: 78　　**Fire Safety Rating:** 76　　**Green Rating:** 60*

STUDENTS AND FACULTY
Enrollment: 3,354. **Student Body:** 55% female, 45% male, 13% out-of-state, 1% international (35 countries represented). Asian 1%, African American 23%, Caucasian 67%, Hispanic 3%, Native American 0%. **Retention and Graduation:** 59% freshmen return for sophomore year. 21% freshmen graduate within 4 years. 35% freshmen graduate within 6 years. **Faculty:** Student/faculty ratio 16:1. 173 full-time faculty, 69% hold PhDs, 18% are members of minority groups, 45% are women. 0% of classes are taught by teaching assistants.

ACADEMICS
Degrees: associate, bachelor's, master's. **Classes: Majors with Highest Enrollment:** business/commerce; early childhood education and teaching; nursing/registered nurse (rn, asn, bsn, msn). **Special Study Options:** cross-registration, distance learning, English as a Second Language (ESL), honors program, internships, liberal arts/career combination, teacher certification program. **Honors Programs:** The overarching purpose of the Honors College is summed up in the single ancient Greek word, areté (highest excellence), which the students and faculty of the College have taken as their motto. In working to achieve this purpose, the Honors College shares the university's goal to excel in undergraduate education, always striving to enrich the quality of learning and teaching. The program is directly involved in actively recruiting, challenging, and supporting those students who are among the most highly motivated toward achieving academic success. **Disability Services:** Special programs offered to physically disabled students include note-taking services, tutors. **Career Services:** alumni services, career assessment, internships.

FACILITIES
Housing: Coed dorms, men's dorms, special housing for international students, women's dorms, cooperative housing, honors dorm. 72% of campus accessible to physically disabled. **Special Academic Facilities/Equipment:** closed-circuit TV studio, Planetarium **Computers:** Students can register for classes online. Administrative functions (other than registration) can be performed online.

CAMPUS LIFE
Environment: Rural. **Activities:** Choral groups, concert band, dance, drama/theater, jazz band, literary magazine, marching band, music ensembles, radio station, student government, student newspaper, symphony orchestra, television station, yearbook, International Student Organization 80 registered organizations, 11 honor societies, 7 religious organizations. 9 fraternities, 6 sororities. **Athletics (Intercollegiate):** *Men:* baseball, basketball, cross-country, football, golf, swimming. *Women:* basketball, cross-country, golf, softball, swimming, tennis, volleyball. **On-Campus Highlights:** HSU Planetarium, New Reddie Athletic Center, Newly Renovated Arkansas Hall, Henderson House Bed and Breakfast, Java Spot Coffee House. **Environmental Initiatives:** Recycling paper, cans and bottles on campus. On-going "Green News" newsletter to faculty and staff that promotes living green and ways to do so.

ADMISSIONS
Freshman Academic Profile: Average high school GPA 3.2. 14% in top 10% of high school class, 39% in top 25% of high school class, 72% in top 50% of high school class. 92% from public high schools. SAT Math middle 50% range 483-558. SAT Critical Reading middle 50% range 440-528. ACT middle 50% range 18-24. Minimum paper TOEFL 500. **Basis for Candidate Selection:** *Very important factors considered include:* academic GPA, rigor of secondary school record, standardized test scores. *Other factors considered include:* Class rank, application essay, recommendation(s), character/personal qualities, interview. **Freshman Admission Requirements:** High school diploma is required and GED is accepted. *Academic units required:* 4 English, 2 mathematics, 2 science, 2 social studies, 1 history. *Academic units recommended:* 4 English, 2 mathematics, 2 science, 2 social studies, 1 history. **Freshman Admission Statistics:** 3,383 applied, 61% admitted, 38% enrolled. **Transfer Admission Requirements:** college transcript(s), Lowest grade transferable C. **General Admission Information:** Regular application deadline 7/15. Nonfall registration accepted. Admission may be deferred for a maximum of 1+. Neither credit nor placement offered for CEEB Advanced Placement tests.

COSTS AND FINANCIAL AID

Annual in-state tuition $5,832. Annual out-of-state tuition $11,664. Room and board $5,868. Required fees $1,104. Average book expense $1,200. **Required Forms and Deadlines:** FAFSA. **Notification of Awards:** Applicants will be notified of awards on a rolling basis beginning 3/1. **Types of Aid:** *Need-based scholarships/grants:* Federal Pell, SEOG, state scholarships/grants, private scholarships, the school's own gift aid. *Loans:* Direct Subsidized Stafford, Direct Unsubsidized Stafford, Direct PLUS, Subsidized Stafford, Unsubsidized Stafford, PLUS, Federal Perkins. **Student Employment:** Federal Work-Study Program available. Off-campus job opportunities are good. **Financial Aid Statistics:** 70% freshmen, 72% undergrads receive need-based scholarship or grant aid. 98% freshmen, 82% undergrads receive non-need-based scholarship or grant aid. 49% freshmen, 50% undergrads receive need-based self-help aid. 7% freshmen, 9% undergrads receive athletic scholarships. **Criteria for awarding institutional aid:** *Non-need-based:* academics, alumni affiliation, art, athletics, leadership, minority status, music/drama.

HENDRIX COLLEGE

1600 Washington Avenue, Conway, AR 72032
Phone: 501-450-1362 • **Financial Aid Phone:** 501-450-1368
E-mail: adm@hendrix.edu • **CEEB Code:** 6273
Fax: 501-450-3843 • **Website:** www.hendrix.edu • **ACT Code:** 128

This private school, affiliated with the Methodist Church, was founded in 1876. It has a 160-acre campus.

RATINGS

Admissions Selectivity Rating: 90   **Fire Safety Rating:** 74   **Green Rating:** 67

STUDENTS AND FACULTY

Enrollment: 1,365. **Student Body:** 57% female, 43% male, 53% out-of-state, 5% international (13 countries represented). Asian 3%, African American 3%, Caucasian 72%, Hispanic 5%, Native American 1%.
Retention and Graduation: 86% freshmen return for sophomore year. 63% freshmen graduate within 4 years. 72% freshmen graduate within 6 years. 63% grads go on to further study within 1 year. 43% grads pursue arts and sciences degrees. 10% grads pursue law degrees. 3% grads pursue business degrees. 6% grads pursue medical degrees. **Faculty:** Student/faculty ratio 11:1. 108 full-time faculty, 90% hold PhDs, 11% are members of minority groups, 45% are women. 0% of classes are taught by teaching assistants.

ACADEMICS

Degrees: bachelor's, master's. **Classes:** Most classes have 10–19 students. Most lab/discussion sessions have 20–29 students. **Majors with Highest Enrollment:** biochemistry/biophysics and molecular biology; biology/biological sciences; psychology. **Special Study Options:** cooperative education program, double major, English as a Second Language (ESL), independent study, internships, student-designed major, study abroad, teacher certification program, Hendrix-in-Brussels (Belgium), Hendrix-in-Costa Rica, Hendrix-in-Heilongjiang (China), Hendrix-in-Graz (Austria), Hendrix-in-London (UK), Hendrix-in-Madrid (Spain), Hendrix-in-Oxford (UK), Accademia dell'Arte, other programs with 140 colleges and universities on 6 continents including countries such as Australia, Finland, France, Ghana, Japan etc. **Combined Degree Programs:** BA/MEng, 4-1 BA/MPH Program in Public Health with UAMS. **Disability Services:** Special programs offered to physically disabled students include note-taking services, reader services, tape recorders, tutors. **Career Services:** Alumni network, alumni services, career/job search classes, career assessment, internships, regional alumni. Career Services highlights include ASK, The Alumni Sharing Knowledge Program, Internships, Grad Expo, Career Week/Fair.

FACILITIES

Housing: Coed dorms, special housing for disabled students, men's dorms, women's dorms, cooperative housing, apartments for single students, wellness housing, theme housing, co-educational foreign language house (Spanish, German, French alternating years)available; suite-style small houses; Ecology house; Christian House. 49% of campus accessible to physically disabled. **Special Academic Facilities/Equipment:** Herbarium, Wilbur A. Mills Library. **Computers:** 100% of classrooms, 100% of dorms, 100% of libraries, 100% of dining areas, 100% of student union, 100% of common outdoor areas have wireless network access. Students can register for classes online. Administrative functions (other than registration) can be performed online.

CAMPUS LIFE

Environment: Town. **Activities:** Choral groups, concert band, dance, drama/theater, jazz band, literary magazine, music ensembles, musical theater, pep band, radio station, student government, student newspaper, student-run film society, symphony orchestra, yearbook, Campus Ministries, International Student Organization, Model UN 80 registered organizations, 6 honor societies, 5 religious organizations. **Athletics (Intercollegiate):** *Men:* baseball, basketball, cross-country, diving, golf, lacrosse, soccer, swimming, tennis, track/field (outdoor). *Women:* basketball, cross-country, diving, field hockey, golf, soccer, softball, swimming, tennis, track/field (outdoor), volleyball. **On-Campus Highlights:** Student Life & Technology Center, Village at Hendrix Apartments, Wellness & Athletic Center, Charles D. Morgan Center for Physical Sc, D.W. Reynolds building for the life scie, Art Complex, Butler Plaza Fountain, the Burrow (campus center). **Environmental Initiatives:** Reduction in paper utilization Maintaining and building environmentally sound buildings Recycling

ADMISSIONS

Freshman Academic Profile: Average high school GPA 3.9. 51% in top 10% of high school class, 77% in top 25% of high school class, 96% in top 50% of high school class. 77% from public high schools. SAT Math middle 50% range 540-670. SAT Critical Reading middle 50% range 550-680. ACT middle 50% range 26-32. Minimum web-based TOEFL 79. Minimum paper TOEFL 550. **Basis for Candidate Selection:** *Very important factors considered include:* application essay, academic GPA, rigor of secondary school record, standardized test scores. *Important factors considered include:* Class rank, recommendation(s), extracurricular activities, interview. *Other factors considered include:* racial/ethnic status, talent/ability, volunteer work. **Freshman Admission Requirements:** High school diploma is required and GED is accepted. **Freshman Admission Statistics:** 1,656 applied, 83% admitted, 27% enrolled. **Transfer Admission Requirements:** college transcript(s), essay or personal statement, statement of good standing from prior institution(s). Minimum college GPA of 2.5 required. Lowest grade transferable C. **General Admission Information:** Application Fee $40. Regular application deadline 8/1. Notification on a rolling basis, beginning on or about 11/1. Nonfall registration accepted. Admission may be deferred for a maximum of 1 year. Credit and/or placement offered for CEEB Advanced Placement tests.

COSTS AND FINANCIAL AID

Annual tuition $35,600. Room and board $10,408. Required fees $300. Average book expense $1,100. **Required Forms and Deadlines:** FAFSAApplication for admission serves as primary merit-based scholarship application. **Notification of Awards:** Applicants will be notified of awards on a rolling basis beginning 2/15. **Types of Aid:** *Need-based scholarships/grants:* Federal Pell, SEOG, state scholarships/grants, private scholarships, the school's own gift aid. *Loans:* Direct Subsidized Stafford, Direct Unsubsidized Stafford, Direct PLUS, Subsidized Stafford, Unsubsidized Stafford, PLUS, Federal Perkins, Private alternative loans as selected by the student. **Student Employment:** Federal Work-Study Program available. Institutional employment available. Highest amount earned per year from on-campus jobs $1,500. Off-campus job opportunities are good. **Financial Aid Statistics:** 100% freshmen, 100% undergrads receive need-based scholarship or grant aid. 38% freshmen, 34% undergrads receive non-need-based scholarship or grant aid. 62% freshmen, 65% undergrads receive need-based self-help aid. % freshmen, % undergrads receive athletic scholarships. 100% freshmen, 100% undergrads receive any aid. 52% undergrads borrow to pay for school. Average cumulative indebtedness $24,492. **Criteria for awarding institutional aid:** *Non-need-based:* academics, art, leadership, music/drama, state/district residency.

HERITAGE UNIVERSITY

3240 Fort Road, Toppenish, WA 98948
Phone: 509-865-8508 • **Financial Aid Phone:** 509-865-8502
E-mail: 3w_Admissions@heritage.edu • **CEEB Code:** 3777
Fax: 509-865-8659 • **Website:** www.heritage.edu/

This private school was founded in 1982. It has a 20-acre campus.

RATINGS

Admissions Selectivity Rating: 63   **Fire Safety Rating:** 60*   **Green Rating:** 60*

STUDENTS AND FACULTY

Enrollment: 756. **Student Body:** 73% female, 27% male, 0% out-of-state, 0% international. Asian 1%, African American 1%, Caucasian 35%, Hispanic 56%, Native American 11%.
Retention and Graduation: 49% freshmen return for sophomore year. 30% freshmen graduate within 6 years. **Faculty:** Student/faculty ratio 10:1. 47 full-time faculty, 38% hold PhDs, 23% are members of minority groups, 49% are women. 0% of classes are taught by teaching assistants.

ACADEMICS

Degrees: associate, bachelor's, certificate, master's, post-bachelor's certificate, post-master's certificate, terminal associate, transfer associate. **Classes:** Most classes have fewer than 10 students. **Special Study Options:** cooperative education program, distance learning, double major, English as a Second Language (ESL), honors program, independent study, internships, liberal arts/career combination, teacher certification program. **Honors Programs:** Students take Honors seminar, Honors sections of general education requirements, and have frequent interactions with faculty, other scholars, and community leaders; develop and implement strategies for community improvement and participate in cultural events. **Combined Degree Programs:** N/A. **Disability Services:** Special programs offered to physically disabled students include note-taking services, reader services, tape recorders, tutors.

FACILITIES

Housing: 90% of campus accessible to physically disabled. CAMPUS LIFE **Environment:** Rural. **Activities:** drama/theater, literary magazine, music ensembles, student government, student newspaper. **On-Campus Highlights:** Student Services Center, Jewett Center, Library, Academic Skills Center

ADMISSIONS

Freshman Academic Profile: % in top 10% of high school class, Minimum paper TOEFL 500. **Basis for Candidate Selection:. Freshman Admission Requirements:** High school diploma is required and GED is accepted. **Freshman Admission Statistics:** 475 applied, 631% enrolled. **Transfer Admission Requirements:** college transcript(s), Lowest grade transferable C–. **General Admission Information:** Regular application deadline 9/1. Nonfall registration accepted. Admission may be deferred for a maximum of 3. Credit and/or placement offered for CEEB Advanced Placement tests.

COSTS AND FINANCIAL AID

Annual tuition $9,600. Required fees $45. Average book expense. **Required Forms and Deadlines:** FAFSA, institution's own financial aid form. **Notification of Awards: Types of Aid:** *Need-based scholarships/grants:* Federal Pell, SEOG, state scholarships/grants, private scholarships, the school's own gift aid. *Loans:* Subsidized Stafford, Unsubsidized Stafford, PLUS, Federal Perkins. **Student Employment: Financial Aid Statistics:** 90% freshmen, 86% undergrads receive need-based scholarship or grant aid. 2% freshmen, 2% undergrads receive non-need-based scholarship or grant aid. 57% freshmen, 72% undergrads receive need-based self-help aid. 92% undergrads borrow to pay for school. Average cumulative indebtedness $11,909.

HIGH POINT UNIVERSITY

University Station 3598, High Point, NC 27262-3598
Phone: 336-841-9216 • **Financial Aid Phone:** 336-841-9128
E-mail: admiss@highpoint.edu • **CEEB Code:** 5293
Fax: 336-888-6382 • **Website:** www.highpoint.edu • **ACT Code:** 3108

This private school, affiliated with the Methodist Church, was founded in 1924. It has a 135-acre campus.

RATINGS

Admissions Selectivity Rating: 84   **Fire Safety Rating:** 74   **Green Rating:** 81

STUDENTS AND FACULTY

Enrollment: 3,932. **Student Body:** 60% female, 40% male, 1% international (29 countries represented). Asian 1%, African American 6%, Caucasian 77%, Hispanic 2%, Native American 2%.
Retention and Graduation: 78% freshmen return for sophomore year. 61% freshmen graduate within 6 years. 31% grads go on to further study within 1 year. 21% grads pursue arts and sciences degrees. 1% grads pursue law degrees. 8% grads pursue business degrees. **Faculty:** Student/faculty ratio 15:1. 212 full-time faculty, 75% hold PhDs, 11% are members of minority groups, 48% are women. 0% of classes are taught by teaching assistants.

ACADEMICS

Degrees: bachelor's, master's, post-bachelor's certificate. **Classes:** Most classes have 10–19 students. **Majors with Highest Enrollment:** communication studies/speech communication and rhetoric; education; psychology. **Special Study Options:** Accelerated program, cooperative education program, cross-registration, double major, dual enrollment, English as a Second Language (ESL), honors program, independent study, internships, liberal arts/career combination, student-designed major, study abroad, teacher certification program, Joint degree programs in environmental science, forestry and medical technology. **Honors Programs:** More than 200 students are enrolled in the university's Honors Program. In addition to enrollment in honors courses, members of the Honors Program often present the results of their research at the Honors Symposium sponsored annually by the university's Odyssey Club, an organization of students enrolled in the Honors Program. In addition to activities for members of the Honors Program, the Odyssey Club sponsors a number of activities annually for the campus at large, including academic bowls and visiting lecturers. **Combined Degree Programs:** 3-2 programs: med tech; environ sci; forestry. **Disability Services:** Special programs offered to physically disabled students include tape recorders, tutors. **Career Services:** career/job search classes, career assessment, internships Career Services highlights include The mission of the civic engagement program is to increase students' understanding of their diverse responsibilities as stewards of their communities by: providing students with opportunities to participate in activities that contribute to the public good; encouraging students to reflect on their experiences as a means of making more permanent the practical lessons they learn in the field; instilling in students an awareness of the mutually beneficial relationship that exists between social institutions and centers of higher learning; teaching students to think critically, speak clearly, and write effectively as a means of becoming productive members of society.

FACILITIES

Housing: Coed dorms, special housing for disabled students, men's dorms, women's dorms, fraternity/sorority housing, apartments for married students, cooperative housing, apartments for single studentsThe number of apartments/houses are available for married students. is limited. 98% of campus accessible to physically disabled. **Special Academic Facilities/Equipment:** Hayworth Chapel; Hayworth Fine Arts Center; Sechrest Gallery; Smith Library; Campus Television Studio; Radio Studio/Station (WHPU) Beginning a $100 million new-construction and renovation program, the campus of High Point University is currently experiencing the greatest period of growth in our 81-year history. Currently under construction are: Blessing Residence Hall is a $10-million facility which is made possible by the generous lead gift of one anonymous donor who requested we call it the "Blessing" residence hall. It will be loaded with amenities that make it a prototype for 21st Century college residence halls. It will offer 240 fully furnished, private bedrooms arranged in suites with living rooms,kitchens and dining areas. Residents will enjoy spacious common areas, computer lounges, conference areas, laundry rooms and elevators. Slane Student Life & Wellness Center will be a centerpiece of campus. This $6.5 million, 45,000-square-foot building will connect to the current Slane Student Center via a two-story atrium, and will feature a high-performance aerobics room, rock-climbing wall, indoor track, fully equipped weight room, food court, dramatic inside & outside basketball courts, outdoor swimming pool, sand volleyball courts, and a grand student atrium with billiard tables and sitting areas. The Earl N. Phillips School of Business will be a new 27,000 square foot building which will become the home for the more than 1,000 undergraduate students pursuing a degree in one of High Point University's 12 undergraduate majors and Master of Business Administration graduate degree. The facility will feature a 200-seat, tiered lecture hall, four smaller lecture rooms, as well as traditional classrooms, a spacious auditorium, private study rooms, computer labs and faculty offices. The Jerry & Kitty Steele Sports Center will be a $5 million, 2-story, 27,000-square-foot facility featuring training & weight rooms, a hospitality/conference room, locker rooms, and an academic services room. In addition, another $5 million is being invested to build a new soccer stadium, baseball stadium, and eight-lane track. University Park will be an extraordinary outdoor experience. Featuring a network of trails and bridges, spectacular waterfalls, a 15-foot overhead trellis, multi-level reflecting pools, 65' covered walkway, and an amphitheatre, this will be the perfect place for an outdoor class, receptions, plays and programs. **Computers:** 100% of classrooms, 100% of dorms, 100% of libraries, 100% of dining areas, 100% of student union, 100% of common outdoor areas have wireless network access. Students can register for classes on-line. Administrative functions (other than registration) can be performed online.

CAMPUS LIFE

Environment: City. **Activities:** Choral groups, concert band, dance, drama/theater, literary magazine, music ensembles, musical theater, pep band, radio station, student government, student newspaper, symphony orchestra, television station, yearbook, Campus Ministries, Model UN 109 registered organizations, 14 honor societies, 8 religious organizations. 4 fraternities, 5 sororities. **Athletics (Intercollegiate):** *Men:* baseball, basketball, cheerleading, cross-country, golf, soccer, tennis, track/field (outdoor), track/field (indoor). *Women:* basketball, cheerleading, cross-country, golf, soccer, tennis, track/field (outdoor), track/field (indoor), volleyball. **On-Campus Highlights:** Slane University Center, Hayworth Fine Arts Center, Millis Athletic/Convocation Center, Hayworth Chapel, The International Promenade, High Point University is in the midst of a 5-year, $250 million campus development plan that will result in the construction of a new building for the School of Business, a new Student Activity Center, a new soccer stadium and track, a new residence hall, a new Sports Center, a new University Park, and dozens of renovations across campus. **Environmental Initiatives:** Arboreatum and Tree Campus USA Recycling Program Free Bike Rentals to students.

ADMISSIONS

Freshman Academic Profile: 3.2. 20% in top 10% of high school class, 47% in top 25% of high school class, 80% in top 50% of high school class. 66% from public high schools. SAT Math middle 50% range 510-600. SAT Critical Reading middle 50% range 490-590. SAT Writing middle 50% range 500-590. ACT middle 50% range 21-26. Minimum paper TOEFL 500. **Basis for Candidate Selection:** *Very important factors considered include:* rigor of secondary school record, standardized test scores. *Important factors considered include:* Class rank, academic GPA. *Other factors considered include:* application essay, recommendation(s), extracurricular activities, interview, talent/ability, volunteer work, work experience. **Freshman Admission Requirements:** High school diploma is required and GED is accepted. *Academic units required:* 4 English, 3 mathematics, 2 science, (2 science labs), 2 social studies, 2 history, 1 academic electives. *Academic units recommended:* 4 English, 3 mathematics, 2 science, (2 science labs), 2 social studies, 2 history, 1 academic electives. **Freshman Admission Statistics:** 6,866 applied, 59% admitted, 32% enrolled. **Transfer Admission Requirements:** High school transcript, college transcript(s), standardized test scores, statement of good standing from prior institution(s). Minimum college GPA of 2.0 required. Lowest grade transferable C. **General Admission Information:** Application Fee $40. Early decision application deadline 11/7. Regular application deadline 8/15. Notification on a rolling basis, beginning on or about 11/6. Nonfall registration accepted. Admission may be deferred for a maximum of 1 year. Credit and/or placement offered for CEEB Advanced Placement tests.

COSTS AND FINANCIAL AID

Average book expense $1,000. **Required Forms and Deadlines:** FAFSA, state aid form. **Notification of Awards:** Applicants will be notified of awards on a rolling basis beginning 4/1. **Types of Aid:** *Need-based scholarships/grants:* Federal Pell, SEOG, state scholarships/grants, private scholarships, the school's own gift aid. *Loans:* Direct Subsidized Stafford, Direct Unsubsidized Stafford, Direct PLUS, Subsidized Stafford, Unsubsidized Stafford, PLUS, Federal Perkins. **Student Employment:** Federal Work-Study Program available. Institutional employment available. Off-campus job opportunities are good. **Financial Aid Statistics:** 96% freshmen, 71% undergrads receive need-based scholarship or grant aid. 70% freshmen, 61% undergrads receive non-need-based scholarship or grant aid. 100% freshmen, 100% undergrads receive need-based self-help aid. 5% freshmen, 5% undergrads receive athletic scholarships. 78% freshmen, 84% undergrads receive any aid. 70% undergrads borrow to pay for school. Average cumulative indebtedness $9,567. **Criteria for awarding institutional aid:** *Non-need-based:* academics, alumni affiliation, art, athletics, leadership, music/drama, religious affiliation, state/district residency.

HILBERT COLLEGE

5200 South Park Avenue, Hamburg, NY 14075-1597
Phone: 716-649-7900 • **Financial Aid Phone:** 716-649-7900
E-mail: admissions@hilbert.edu • **CEEB Code:** 2334
Fax: 716-649-0702 • **Website:** www.hilbert.edu • **ACT Code:** 2759

This private school, affiliated with the Roman Catholic Church, was founded in 1957. It has a 40-acre campus.

RATINGS

Admissions Selectivity Rating: 66   **Fire Safety Rating:** 92   **Green Rating:** 60*

STUDENTS AND FACULTY

Enrollment: 998. **Student Body:** 60% female, 40% male, 10% out-of-state, 0% international (4 countries represented). Asian 0%, African American 6%, Caucasian 82%, Hispanic 2%, Native American 2%.
Retention and Graduation: 70% freshmen return for sophomore year. 49% freshmen graduate within 4 years. 50% freshmen graduate within 6 years. 15% grads go on to further study within 1 year. 4% grads pursue arts and sciences degrees. 4% grads pursue law degrees. 4% grads pursue business degrees. **Faculty:** Student/faculty ratio 13:1. 48 full-time faculty, 50% hold PhDs, 2% are members of minority groups, 48% are women. 0% of classes are taught by teaching assistants.

ACADEMICS

Degrees: associate, bachelor's, certificate, terminal associate. **Classes:** Most classes have 10–19 students. Most lab/discussion sessions have fewer than 10 students. **Majors with Highest Enrollment:** business/commerce; criminal justice/law enforcement administration; forensic science and technology. **Special Study Options:** cross-registration, distance learning, dual enrollment, honors program, independent study, internships, study abroad, Member of Western New York consortium of colleges. **Honors Programs:** About the Honors Program The Hilbert Honors Program will give you more from your college experience. You will enroll in regular classes and fulfill honors credit requirements by doing advanced work, or in lieu of projects. These special projects allow you to work one-on-one with Hilbert's outstanding honors faculty in your major and in other academic areas. As an honors student, you will also have a student mentor for your first semester and personal faculty advisement. **Disability Services:** Special programs offered to physically disabled students include note-taking services, reader services, tape recorders, tutors. **Career Services:** Alumni network, alumni services, career assessment, internships Career Services highlights include Internships are available with agencies in most majors.

FACILITIES

Housing: Coed dorms, apartments for single studentsCampus Apartments. 95% of campus accessible to physically disabled. Honors Lounge, Institute for Law and Justice, Center for Creative Media, **Computers:** 100% of classrooms, 100% of dorms, 100% of libraries, 100% of dining areas, 100% of student union, 100% of common outdoor areas have wireless network access. Students can register for classes online. Administrative functions (other than registration) can be performed online.

CAMPUS LIFE

Environment: Village. **Activities:** Choral groups, drama/theater, literary magazine, student government, student newspaper, Campus Ministries 20 registered organizations, 5 honor societies, 1 religious organizations. **Athletics (Intercollegiate):** *Men:* baseball, basketball, cross-country, golf, soccer, volleyball. *Women:* basketball, cross-country, golf, soccer, softball, volleyball. **On-Campus Highlights:** Hafner Recreation Center, Franciscan Hall Atrium, Campus Apartments, Swan Auditorium, Paczesny Hall.

ADMISSIONS

Freshman Academic Profile: Average high school GPA 2.8. 2% in top 10% of high school class, 13% in top 25% of high school class, 40% in top 50% of high school class. 85% from public high schools. SAT Math middle 50% range 400-510. SAT Critical Reading middle 50% range 400-510. ACT middle 50% range 17-22. Minimum paper TOEFL 500. **Basis for Candidate Selection:** *Very important factors considered include:* academic GPA, rigor of secondary school record. *Important factors considered include:* recommendation(s). *Other factors considered include:* application essay, character/personal qualities, extracurricular activities, interview, talent/ability, volunteer work, work experience. **Freshman Admission Requirements:** High school diploma is required and GED is accepted. *Academic units required:* 4 English, 2 mathematics, 2 science, (1 science labs), 2 social studies, 2 history, 4 academic electives. *Academic units recommended:* 4 English, 2 mathematics, 2 science, (1 science labs), 2 social studies, 2 history, 4 academic electives. **Freshman Admission Statistics:** 726 applied, 85% admitted, 35% enrolled. **Transfer Admission Requirements:** High school transcript, college transcript(s), minimum college GPA of 2.0 required. Lowest grade transferable C. **General Admission Information:** Application Fee $20. Regular application deadline 9/1. Nonfall registration accepted. Admission may be deferred for a maximum of 1 year. Credit offered for CEEB Advanced Placement tests.

COSTS AND FINANCIAL AID

Annual tuition $16,000. Room and board $6,600. Required fees $600. Average book expense $700. **Required Forms and Deadlines:** FAFSA, state aid form. **Notification of Awards:** Applicants will be notified of awards on a rolling basis beginning 3/1. **Types of Aid:** *Need-based scholarships/grants:* Federal Pell, SEOG, state scholarships/grants, private scholarships, the school's own gift aid. *Loans:* Subsidized Stafford, Unsubsidized Stafford, PLUS, Federal Perkins. **Student Employment:** Federal Work-Study Program available. Institutional employment available. Highest amount earned per year from on-campus jobs $1,250. Off-campus job opportunities are excellent. **Financial Aid Statistics:** 99% freshmen, 98% undergrads receive need-based scholarship or grant aid. 4% freshmen, 5% undergrads receive non-need-based scholarship or grant aid. 90% freshmen, 88% undergrads receive need-based self-help aid. 92% freshmen, 87% undergrads receive any aid. 93% undergrads borrow to pay for school. Average cumulative indebtedness $26,583. **Criteria for awarding institutional aid:** *Non-need-based:* academics, leadership, minority status.

HILLSDALE COLLEGE

33 East College Street, Hillsdale, MI 49242
Phone: 517-607-2327 • **Financial Aid Phone:** 517-607-2350
E-mail: admissions@hillsdale.edu • **CEEB Code:** 1295
Fax: 517-607-2223 • **Website:** www.hillsdale.edu • **ACT Code:** 2010

This private school was founded in 1844. It has a 200-acre campus.

RATINGS
Admissions Selectivity Rating: 95   **Fire Safety Rating:** 88   **Green Rating:** 60*

STUDENTS AND FACULTY
Enrollment: 1,387. **Student Body:** 53% female, 47% male, 60% out-of-state, 2% international (13 countries represented). Asian 0%, African American 0%, Caucasian 0%, Hispanic 0%, Native American 0%.
Retention and Graduation: 94% freshmen return for sophomore year. 66% freshmen graduate within 4 years. 75% freshmen graduate within 6 years. 46% grads go on to further study within 1 year. 12% grads pursue arts and sciences degrees. 5% grads pursue law degrees. 13% grads pursue business degrees. 4% grads pursue medical degrees. **Faculty:** Student/faculty ratio 10:1. 118 full-time faculty, 92% hold PhDs. 0% of classes are taught by teaching assistants.

ACADEMICS
Degrees: bachelor's. **Classes:** Most classes have fewer than 10 students. Most lab/discussion sessions have 20–29 students. **Majors with Highest Enrollment:** biology/biological sciences; business administration and management; education. **Special Study Options:** double major, dual enrollment, honors program, independent study, internships, student-designed major, study abroad, teacher certification program. **Honors Programs:** Honors Program available. **Career Services:** Alumni network, alumni services, career assessment, internships Career Services highlights include National Professional Sales Internship Program.

FACILITIES
Housing: men's dorms, women's dorms, fraternity/sorority housing, apartments for single students. **Special Academic Facilities/Equipment:** Early childhood education lab, media center, K-8 private academy,Slayton Arboretum,rare books library **Computers:** 100% of classrooms, 85% of dorms, 100% of libraries, 100% of dining areas, 100% of student union, 100% of common outdoor areas have wireless network access.

CAMPUS LIFE
Environment: Village. **Activities:** Choral groups, concert band, dance, drama/theater, jazz band, literary magazine, music ensembles, musical theater, pep band, student government, student newspaper, symphony orchestra, yearbook, Campus Ministries, International Student Organization 50 registered organizations, 26 honor societies, 4 religious organizations. 3 fraternities, 3 sororities. **Athletics (Intercollegiate):** *Men:* baseball, basketball, cheerleading, cross-country, football, track/field (outdoor), track/field (indoor). *Women:* basketball, cheerleading, cross-country, diving, equestrian sports, softball, swimming, track/field (outdoor), track/field (indoor), volleyball. **On-Campus Highlights:** Student Union, Quad (outdoor quadrangle), Sage Center for the Arts, Howard Music Hall, Sports Complex. **Environmental Initiatives:** Central heating and cooling efficiency plan Highh efficiency lighting in all new facilities Environmental controls in all buildings for energy management.

ADMISSIONS
Freshman Academic Profile: Average high school GPA 3.8. 54% in top 10% of high school class, 82% in top 25% of high school class, 99% in top 50% of high school class. 48% from public high schools. SAT Math middle 50% range 590-680. SAT Critical Reading middle 50% range 620-750. SAT Writing middle 50% range 590-730. ACT middle 50% range 27-32. Minimum web-based TOEFL 83. Minimum paper TOEFL 580. **Basis for Candidate Selection:** *Very important factors considered include:* academic GPA, rigor of secondary school record, standardized test scores, character/personal qualities, interview. *Important factors considered include:* Class rank, application essay, recommendation(s), extracurricular activities, level of applicant's interest, volunteer work, work experience. *Other factors considered include:* alumni/ae relation, talent/ability. **Freshman Admission Requirements:** High school diploma is required and GED is accepted. **Freshman Admission Statistics:** 2,207 applied, 42% admitted, 42% enrolled. **Transfer Admission Requirements:** High school transcript, college transcript(s), essay or personal statement, standardized test scores, statement of good standing from prior institution(s). Minimum college GPA of 3.25 required. Lowest grade transfer-

able C. **General Admission Information:** Application Fee $35. Early decision application deadline 11/15. Regular application deadline 2/15. Nonfall registration accepted. Admission may be deferred for a maximum of one year. Credit and/or placement offered for CEEB Advanced Placement tests.

COSTS AND FINANCIAL AID
Annual tuition $21,390. Room and board $8,640. Required fees $540. Average book expense $850. **Required Forms and Deadlines:** institution's own financial aid form, noncustodial PROFILE, business/farm supplement. **Notification of Awards:** Applicants will be notified of awards on a rolling basis beginning 2/15. **Types of Aid:** *Need-based scholarships/grants:* private scholarships, the school's own gift aid. *Loans:* college/university loans from institutional funds. **Student Employment:** Institutional employment available. Highest amount earned per year from on-campus jobs $1,300. Off-campus job opportunities are good. **Financial Aid Statistics:** 49% freshmen, 64% undergrads receive need-based scholarship or grant aid. 73% freshmen, 88% undergrads receive non-need-based scholarship or grant aid. 71% freshmen, 76% undergrads receive need-based self-help aid. 15% freshmen, 16% undergrads receive athletic scholarships. 80% freshmen, 82% undergrads receive any aid. 62% undergrads borrow to pay for school. Average cumulative indebtedness $17,000. **Criteria for awarding institutional aid:** *Non-need-based:* academics, alumni affiliation, art, athletics, leadership, music/drama.

See page 1098.

HIRAM COLLEGE

PO Box 96, Hiram, OH 44234
Phone: 330-569-5169 • **CEEB Code:** 1297
Fax: • **Website:** www.hiram.edu • **ACT Code:** 3280

This private school, affiliated with the Disciples of Christ Church, was founded in 1850. It has a 110-acre campus.

RATINGS
Admissions Selectivity Rating: 78   **Fire Safety Rating:** 61   **Green Rating:** 60*

STUDENTS AND FACULTY
Enrollment: 1,311. **Student Body:** 54% female, 46% male, 17% out-of-state, 6% international (17 countries represented). Asian 1%, African American 12%, Caucasian 74%, Hispanic 3%, Native American 0%.
Retention and Graduation: 75% freshmen return for sophomore year. 62% freshmen graduate within 4 years. 66% freshmen graduate within 6 years. 36% grads go on to further study within 1 year. 30% grads pursue arts and sciences degrees. 3% grads pursue law degrees. 1% grads pursue business degrees. 2% grads pursue medical degrees. **Faculty:** Student/faculty ratio 12:1. 74 full-time faculty, 93% hold PhDs, 3% are members of minority groups, 40% are women. 0% of classes are taught by teaching assistants.

ACADEMICS
Degrees: bachelor's, master's. **Classes:** Most classes have 10–19 students. Most lab/discussion sessions have 10–19 students. **Majors with Highest Enrollment:** biology; education. **Special Study Options:** Accelerated program, cross-registration, double major, English as a Second Language (ESL), exchange student program (domestic), independent study, internships, student-designed major, study abroad, teacher certification program, weekend college. **Combined Degree Programs:** BA(Hiram)/BS(Engineering) 5 years. **Disability Services:** Special programs offered to physically disabled students include note-taking services, reader services, tape recorders, tutors. **Career Services:** Alumni network, alumni services, career/job search classes, career assessment, internships Career Services highlights include Internships including participation in the regional ClevelandIntern.net, biomedical research, and virtual internships.

FACILITIES
Housing: Coed dorms, special housing for disabled students, women's dorms, theme housing, suite style housing. 55% of campus accessible to physically disabled. Special Academic Facilities/Equipment: Psychology lab, language lab, international center, center for literature and medicine, fitness center, health center, observatory, electron microscope, two field stations for study and research. CAMPUS LIFE
Environment: Rural. **Activities:** Choral groups, concert band, dance, drama/theater, jazz band, literary magazine, marching band, music ensembles, opera, pep band, radio station, student government, student newspaper, symphony orchestra, yearbook, Campus Ministries, International Student Organization,

Model UN 55 registered organizations, 7 honor societies, 6 religious organizations. 3 fraternities, 3 sororities. **Athletics (Intercollegiate):** *Men:* baseball, basketball, cheerleading, cross-country, diving, football, golf, soccer, swimming, tennis, track/field (outdoor), track/field (indoor). *Women:* basketball, cheerleading, cross-country, diving, golf, soccer, softball, swimming, tennis, track/field (outdoor), track/field (indoor), volleyball. **On-Campus Highlights:** James H. Barrow Field Station, The Hiram College Library, Kennedy Center(Food Court, Bookstore, ballroom,and other facilities), Hiram Church, Stevens Memorial Observatory.

ADMISSIONS

Freshman Academic Profile: Average high school GPA 3.3. 26% in top 10% of high school class, 46% in top 25% of high school class, 74% in top 50% of high school class. 86% from public high schools. SAT Math middle 50% range 450-600. SAT Critical Reading middle 50% range 450-600. SAT Writing middle 50% range 440-570. ACT middle 50% range 19-25. Minimum paper TOEFL 550. **Freshman Admission Statistics:** 2,273 applied, 63% admitted, 22% enrolled. **General Admission Information:** Credit and/or placement offered for CEEB Advanced Placement tests.

COSTS AND FINANCIAL AID

Annual tuition $26,960. Room and board $9,460. Required fees $950. Average book expense $700. **Required Forms and Deadlines:** FAFSA. **Notification of Awards:** Applicants will be notified of awards on a rolling basis beginning 3/1. **Types of Aid:** *Need-based scholarships/grants:* Federal Pell, SEOG, state scholarships/grants, private scholarships, the school's own gift aid, United Negro College Fund. *Loans:* Subsidized Stafford, Unsubsidized Stafford, PLUS, Federal Perkins, college/university loans from institutional funds. **Student Employment:** Highest amount earned per year from on-campus jobs $500. **Financial Aid Statistics:** 78% undergrads borrow to pay for school. Average cumulative indebtedness $21,247. **Criteria for awarding institutional aid:** *Non-need-based:* academics, alumni affiliation, music/drama, religious affiliation, state/district residency.

HOBART AND WILLIAM SMITH COLLEGES

Best 378

629 South Main Street, Geneva, NY 14456
Phone: 315-781-3622 • **Financial Aid Phone:** 315-781-3315
E-mail: admissions@hws.edu • **CEEB Code:** 2294
Fax: 315-781-3914 • **Website:** www.hws.edu • **ACT Code:** 2758

This private school was founded in 1822. It has a 170-acre campus.

RATINGS

Admissions Selectivity Rating: 87   **Fire Safety Rating:** 84   **Green Rating:** 91

STUDENTS AND FACULTY

Enrollment: 2,138. **Student Body:** 55% female, 45% male, 56% out-of-state, 4% international (18 countries represented). Asian 2%, African American 4%, Caucasian 63%, Hispanic 4%, Native American 0%.
Retention and Graduation: 89% freshmen return for sophomore year. 70% freshmen graduate within 4 years. 49% grads go on to further study within 1 year. 10% grads pursue arts and sciences degrees. 14% grads pursue law degrees. 11% grads pursue business degrees. 4% grads pursue medical degrees.
Faculty: Student/faculty ratio 11:1. 185 full-time faculty, 96% hold PhDs, 18% are members of minority groups, 39% are women. 0% of classes are taught by teaching assistants.

ACADEMICS

Degrees: bachelor's, master's. **Classes:** Most classes have 10–19 students.
Majors with Highest Enrollment: economics; English language and literature; history. **Special Study Options:** cross-registration, double major, dual enrollment, English as a Second Language (ESL), exchange student program (domestic), honors program, independent study, internships, student-designed major, study abroad, teacher certification program. **Combined Degree Programs:** BA/MA, 3-2 Engineer; 3-4 Architect; 4-1 MBA; 4-1 MAT. **Disability Services:** Special programs offered to physically disabled students include note-taking services, reader services, tape recorders, tutors. **Career Services:** Alumni network, alumni services, career/job search classes, career assessment, internships.

FACILITIES

Housing: Coed dorms, men's dorms, special housing for international students, women's dorms, fraternity/sorority housing, cooperative housing, apartments

for single students, Upperclass townhouses; Theme Houses; Honors Houses. **Special Academic Facilities/Equipment:** Houghton Gallery, HWS Explorer (research vessel), 100 Acre Nature Preserve, Melly Academic Center, Rosenberg science center. **Computers:** Students can register for classes online. Administrative functions (other than registration) can be performed online.

CAMPUS LIFE

Environment: Village. **Activities:** Choral groups, dance, drama/theater, jazz band, literary magazine, music ensembles, radio station, student government, student newspaper, student-run film society, symphony orchestra, yearbook 77 registered organizations, 12 honor societies, 4 religious organizations. 5 fraternities. **Athletics (Intercollegiate):** *Men:* basketball, crew/rowing, cross-country, football, golf, ice hockey, lacrosse, sailing, soccer, squash, tennis. *Women:* basketball, crew/rowing, cross-country, diving, field hockey, golf, lacrosse, sailing, soccer, squash, swimming, tennis. **On-Campus Highlights:** Scandling Center, South Hall, Stern Hall, North Hall, Bristol Field House, Trinity Hall, with the newly remodeled Salisbury Center, houses the Offices of Career Development, Public Service and Global Education. The building re-opened in January 2004. **Environmental Initiatives:** Integrating the Colleges' Sustainability living laboratory approach in the Climate Action Plan. The living laboratory approach is exemplified through student projects - class, independent study or volunteer that directly effect the colleges' impact on the environment and culture of environmental sustainability. For example, The Finger Lakes Institute's renovation was directed by a first year Energy class project that identified specific environmental parameters to be incorporated into the building. These students' vision and project qualified the Finger Lakes Institute for the Energy Star Small Business Award. This living laboratory, student oriented learning approach is at the core of the Colleges Sustainability Program and enhanced by the Colleges Climate Action Plan. The Climate Task Force (Colleges Sustainability Executive Committee) created an Energy and Climate Committee, an outcome of the Climate Action Plan. The Energy and Climate Committee is charged to reduce HWS greenhouse gas emissions through electricity and heat conservation initiatives. The Committee decreased emissions resulting from energy consumption by 10%, saving over $300,000 through investment in energy efficiency technologies " including, but certainly not limited to L.E.D. lighting, high efficiency boilers, variable speed drives, and refined building scheduling through building automation systems. 20. The student led overhaul of the Colleges waste management program led the Colleges to institutionalize composting, add over 1000 recycling bins and implement a year round E-Waste management program. The Colleges now compost nearly 100% of pre-consumer & post-consumer (must be a clean stream) food-waste from its dining facilities sending nearly 2 tons of foodwaste and compostable serviceware (used in our retail " CafÃ© and Pub operations as well as at all catered events) to the compost facility weekly. In addition, the Colleges raised its recycling rate by 25% through front end awareness building and a transition to a single stream recycling program.

ADMISSIONS

Freshman Academic Profile: 43% in top 10% of high school class, 78% in top 25% of high school class, 97% in top 50% of high school class. 60% from public high schools. SAT Math middle 50% range 560-640. SAT Critical Reading middle 50% range 560-650. ACT middle 50% range 25-28. Minimum web-based TOEFL 80. Minimum paper TOEFL 550. **Basis for Candidate Selection:** *Very important factors considered include:* rigor of secondary school record. *Important factors considered include:* Class rank, application essay, academic GPA, recommendation(s), standardized test scores, character/personal qualities, extracurricular activities, volunteer work, work experience. *Other factors considered include:* alumni/ae relation, first generation, geographical residence, interview, level of applicant's interest, racial/ethnic status, talent/ability. **Freshman Admission Requirements:** High school diploma is required and GED is accepted. *Academic units required:* 4 English, 3 mathematics, 3 science, (2 science labs), 2 foreign language, 2 social studies, 2 history, 2 academic electives. *Academic units recommended:* 4 English, 3 mathematics, 3 science, (2 science labs), 2 foreign language, 2 social studies, 2 history, 2 academic electives. **Freshman Admission Statistics:** 4,682 applied, 62% admitted, 21% enrolled. **Transfer Admission Requirements:** High school transcript, college transcript(s), essay or personal statement, standardized test scores, minimum college GPA of 2.5 required. Lowest grade transferable C. **General Admission Information:** Application Fee $45. Early decision application deadline 11/15. Regular application deadline 2/1. Regular notification 4/1. Nonfall registration not accepted. Admission may be deferred for a maximum of 2 Years. Credit offered for CEEB Advanced Placement tests.

COSTS AND FINANCIAL AID

Annual tuition $42,104. Room and board $10,582. Required fees $1,206. Average book expense $1,300. **Required Forms and Deadlines:** FAFSA, CSS/Financial Aid PROFILE, state aid form, noncustodial PROFILE, PARENT'S AND STUDENT'S TAX RETURN. **Notification of Awards:** Applicants will be notified of awards on or about 4/1. **Types of Aid:** *Need-based scholarships/grants:* Federal Pell, SEOG, state scholarships/grants, private scholarships, the school's own gift aid. *Loans:* Subsidized Stafford, Unsubsidized Stafford, PLUS, Federal Perkins. **Student Employment:** Federal Work-Study Program available. Institutional employment available. Highest amount earned per year from on-campus jobs $600. Off-campus job opportunities are good. **Financial Aid Statistics:** 98% freshmen, 99% undergrads receive need-based scholarship or grant aid. 14% freshmen, 12% undergrads receive non-need-based scholarship or grant aid. 82% freshmen, 85% undergrads receive need-based self-help aid. 80% freshmen, 76% undergrads receive any aid. 59% undergrads borrow to pay for school. Average cumulative indebtedness $31,113. **Criteria for awarding institutional aid:** *Non-need-based:* academics, art, leadership, music/drama.

HOFSTRA UNIVERSITY

Best 378

100 Hofstra University, Hempstead, NY 11549
Phone: 516-463-6700 • **Financial Aid Phone:** 516-463-8000
E-mail: admission@hofstra.edu • **CEEB Code:** 2295
Fax: 516-463-5100 • **Website:** www.hofstra.edu • **ACT Code:** 2760

This private school was founded in 1935. It has a 240-acre campus.

RATINGS

Admissions Selectivity Rating: 87   **Fire Safety Rating:** 91   **Green Rating:** 83

STUDENTS AND FACULTY

Enrollment: 6,747. **Student Body:** 53% female, 47% male, 35% out-of-state, 2% international (66 countries represented). Asian 7%, African American 9%, Caucasian 62%, Hispanic 11%, Native American 0%.
Retention and Graduation: 78% freshmen return for sophomore year. 45% freshmen graduate within 4 years. 61% freshmen graduate within 6 years. 27% grads go on to further study within 1 year. 4% grads pursue arts and sciences degrees. 4% grads pursue law degrees. 4% grads pursue business degrees. 2% grads pursue medical degrees. **Faculty:** Student/faculty ratio 14:1. 517 full-time faculty, 93% hold PhDs, 20% are members of minority groups, 43% are women. 0% of classes are taught by teaching assistants.

ACADEMICS

Degrees: bachelor's, certificate, doctoral, master's, post bachelor's certificate, post-master's certificate. **Classes:** Most classes have 10–19 students. Most lab/discussion sessions have 10–19 students. **Majors with Highest Enrollment:** business administration and management; marketing/marketing management; psychology. **Special Study Options:** Accelerated program, cross-registration, distance learning, double major, dual enrollment, English as a Second Language (ESL), external degree program, honors program, independent study, internships, liberal arts/career combination, student-designed major, study abroad, teacher certification program. **Honors Programs:** Hofstra University's Honors College (HUHC) is the leading edge of Hofstra University's pursuit of academic excellence. Serving the highly motivated, high achieving student, every aspect of its curriculum is designed to provide them with the resources they need to meet their academic objectives. Combining the support of a strong community with the freedom to pursue individual goals HUHC emphasizes student ownership and direction of their own education. At the same time, HUHC recognizes its responsibility to support students so that they can explore, reflect upon and achieve their educational objectives. HUHC is an intimate community of students, faculty and administrators committed to challenging and supporting one another in the pursuit of excellence at all levels. Its students are connected to every college, department, major and program on campus and engaged in every aspect of campus life. All entering HUHC students begin their Hofstra careers with Culture and Expression (C&E) a four-course, year-long sequence designed specifically for the honors college community. C&E is our primary tool for establishing a community among the students of each entering class. Together, they follow a common reading list, attend common lectures and take ownership of the materials via small group discussions with some of Hofstra's best faculty. C&E addresses life's biggest questions with rigor. Most importantly, it provides a broad foundation for a lifetime of learning in college and beyond. After the first year, Honors College students pursue honors work in those Hofstra courses that they find most exciting. Each semester HUHC offers an array of small, discussion based seminars, taught by professors from around the university, who are invited to offer their dream course. In addition, HUHC's Honors Option program allows students to enrich regular courses that align with their personal and intellectual passions. These honors experiences are all recognized on the transcript and count toward completion of an HUHC designation which is applied to both the student's transcript and diploma. Thus, HUHC students may choose from among any of Hofstra's more than 145 undergraduate majors and upon graduation receive a bachelor's degree with a special designation marking it as having been achieved with an extraordinary level of distinction.

HUHC sponsors a rich array of cultural and social experiences, including trips to New York City to visit museums, Broadway shows, concerts, and major league sporting events. Given our location, HUHC faculty mentors regularly organize outdoor adventures, such as sea kayaking, hiking and visits to ocean beaches. A significant percentage of HUHC students participate in a variety of HUHC-based social service programs, including those focused on serving the homeless, promoting early literacy and working toward environmental responsibility. HUHC students can be found in leadership roles in virtually every club and activity on the Hofstra campus. They are student government leaders, newspaper editors, and champions of social and political causes. They are committed to the arts and to sports (including Division I) and can be found in just about every form of meaningful activity imaginable. They come from across the United States, and increasingly from abroad. Most of all, they are curious about one another and the wider world. Many HUHC students opt to live in honors housing, where they enjoy an even greater sense of community and an exceptional level of support from a professional staff and specially selected student leaders. HUHC graduates have won prestigious grants and fellowships such as the Fulbright, the National Science Fellowship, and the Jack Kent Cooke fellowship. They've also been admitted to the most prestigious graduate and professional schools. Hofstra University also recognizes high-achieving students in many other ways, including Dean's List, Provost's Scholars, Phi Beta Kappa, Phi Eta Sigma, Golden Key, and the chance to earn baccalaureate degrees with distinction and departmental honors. **Combined Degree Programs:** BA/JD, BBA/MS, BBA/MBA. **Disability Services:** Special programs offered to physically disabled students include note-taking services, reader services, tape recorders, tutors. **Career Services:** Alumni network, alumni services, career/job search classes, career assessment, internships Career Services highlights include Comprehensive on-campus job fairs and recruiting program including internship opportunities for all majors with Fortune 500, media outlets, government, law, not-for-profit, and education, many of which lead to job opportunities for graduates.

FACILITIES

Housing: Coed dorms, special housing for disabled students, apartments for single students, Theme housing, Living-Learning Center, Honors Housing, Quiet Floors, and Women's Floors. 100% of campus accessible to physically disabled. **Special Academic Facilities/Equipment:** New state-of-the-art medical school, financial trading room, multi-media converged news room, comprehensive media production facility including a 24 hour radio station, linux beowolf cluster, digital language lab, technology, science and engineering labs, a rooftop observatory, 6 theaters including a black box teaching theater, assessment centers for client observation and counseling, child care institute, cultural center, museum, arboretum, and bird sanctuary. **Computers:** 57% of classrooms, 100% of dorms, 100% of libraries, 100% of dining areas, 100% of student union, 60% of common outdoor areas have wireless network access. Students can register for classes online. Administrative functions (other than registration) can be performed online.

CAMPUS LIFE

Environment: City. **Activities:** Choral groups, concert band, dance, drama/theater, jazz band, literary magazine, music ensembles, musical theater, opera, pep band, radio station, student government, student newspaper, student-run film society, symphony orchestra, television station, yearbook, Campus Ministries, International Student Organization 135 registered organizations, 32 honor societies, 9 religious organizations. 13 fraternities, 12 sororities. **Athletics (Intercollegiate):** *Men:* baseball, basketball, cross-country, golf, lacrosse, soccer, tennis, wrestling. *Women:* basketball, cross-country, field hockey, golf, lacrosse, soccer, softball, tennis, volleyball. **Environmental Initiatives:** New construction complies with LEED standards where feasible. The new School of Medicine Building has been committed to be LEED Silver Certified. In August 2011, Hofstra University installed a 9 KW solar array on the Living Green Learning Living Community residence house. The University is looking into expanding solar technology to more buildings on campus. Hofstra will soon be offering a Bachelor of Arts, a Bachelor of Science and a minor in Sustainability Studies. A cornerstone of the curriculum is a strong applied focus such that students will be involved with sustainability projects on campus and in the surrounding area.

ADMISSIONS

Freshman Academic Profile: Average high school GPA 3.5. 28% in top 10% of high school class, 61% in top 25% of high school class, 87% in top 50% of high school class. SAT Math middle 50% range 540-630. SAT Critical Reading middle 50% range 530-630. ACT middle 50% range 23-28. Minimum web-based TOEFL 80. Minimum paper TOEFL 550. **Basis for Candidate Selection:** *Very important factors considered include:* Class rank, application essay, academic GPA, recommendation(s), rigor of secondary school record, standardized test scores. *Important factors considered include:* character/personal qualities, extracurricular activities, interview, talent/ability. *Other factors considered include:* alumni/ae relation, geographical residence, level of applicant's interest, racial/ethnic status, volunteer work, work experience. **Freshman Admission Requirements:** High school diploma is required and GED is accepted.

Academic units required: 4 English, 3 mathematics, 3 science, (1 science labs), 2 foreign language, 3 social studies. *Academic units recommended:* 4 English, 3 mathematics, 3 science, (1 science labs), 2 foreign language, 3 social studies. **Freshman Admission Statistics:** 22,733 applied, 59% admitted, 11% enrolled. **Transfer Admission Requirements:** college transcript(s), statement of good standing from prior institution(s). Lowest grade transferable C–. **General Admission Information:** Application Fee $70. Notification on a rolling basis, beginning on or about 2/1. Nonfall registration accepted. Admission may be deferred for a maximum of 1 year. Credit and/or placement offered for CEEB Advanced Placement tests.

COSTS AND FINANCIAL AID

Annual tuition $34,400. Room and board $12,370. Required fees $1,050. Average book expense $1,000. **Required Forms and Deadlines:** FAFSA, state aid form. **Notification of Awards:** Applicants will be notified of awards on a rolling basis beginning 3/1. **Types of Aid:** *Need-based scholarships/grants:* Federal Pell, SEOG, state scholarships/grants, private scholarships, the school's own gift aid, ACG & SMART. *Loans:* Subsidized Stafford, Unsubsidized Stafford, PLUS, Federal Perkins, college/university loans from institutional funds. **Student Employment:** Federal Work-Study Program available. Institutional employment available. Highest amount earned per year from on-campus jobs $22,795. Off-campus job opportunities are excellent. **Financial Aid Statistics:** 96% freshmen, 90% undergrads receive need-based scholarship or grant aid. 14% freshmen, 10% undergrads receive non-need-based scholarship or grant aid. 79% freshmen, 80% undergrads receive need-based self-help aid. 1% freshmen, 1% undergrads receive athletic scholarships. 97% freshmen, 89% undergrads receive any aid. 67% undergrads borrow to pay for school. Average cumulative indebtedness. **Criteria for awarding institutional aid:** *Non-need-based:* academics, alumni affiliation, art, athletics, leadership, music/drama, state/district residency.

See page 1100.

HOLLINS UNIVERSITY

Best 378

PO Box 9707, Roanoke, VA 24020-1707
Phone: 540-362-6401 • **Financial Aid Phone:** 540-362-6332
E-mail: huadm@hollins.edu • **CEEB Code:** 5294
Fax: 540-362-6218 • **Website:** www.hollins.edu • **ACT Code:** 4360

This private school was founded in 1842. It has a 475-acre campus.

RATINGS
Admissions Selectivity Rating: 80   **Fire Safety Rating:** 80   **Green Rating:** 83

STUDENTS AND FACULTY
Enrollment: 607. **Student Body:** 100% female, 0% male, 43% out-of-state, 5% international (16 countries represented). Asian 2%, African American 11%, Caucasian 72%, Hispanic 5%, Native American 0%.
Retention and Graduation: 70% freshmen return for sophomore year. 51% freshmen graduate within 4 years. 24% grads go on to further study within 1 year. 24% grads pursue arts and sciences degrees. **Faculty:** Student/faculty ratio 9:1. 71 full-time faculty, 100% hold PhDs, 11% are members of minority groups, 56% are women. 2% of classes are taught by teaching assistants.

ACADEMICS
Degrees: bachelor's, master's, post-bachelor's certificate, post-master's certificate. **Classes:** Most classes have 10–19 students. Most lab/discussion sessions have 10–19 students. **Majors with Highest Enrollment:** business/commerce; English language and literature; psychology. **Special Study Options:** Accelerated program, cross-registration, double major, dual enrollment, exchange student program (domestic), independent study, internships, student-designed major, study abroad, teacher certification program. **Honors Programs:** A number of university departments offer Honors Programs. The specific nature of departmental honors varies from department to department. The programs, which are undertaken for at least the full senior year, may involve research, theses, oral or written examinations, seminars, reading programs, or any combination thereof. **Disability Services:** Special programs offered to physically disabled students include tape recorders. **Career Services:** Alumni network, alumni services, career/job search classes, career assessment, internships, regional alumni.

FACILITIES
Housing: special housing for disabled students, women's dorms, apartments for single students, wellness housing, theme housing. 38% of campus accessible to physically disabled. **Special Academic Facilities/Equipment:** Athletic complex, a writing center, language labs, campus-wide computer network, scientific equipment and instrumentation, art museum, and a state-of-the-art library. **Computers:** 90% of classrooms, 100% of dorms, 100% of libraries, 100% of dining areas, 100% of student union, 100% of common outdoor areas have wireless network access. Students can register for classes online. Administrative functions (other than registration) can be performed online.

CAMPUS LIFE
Environment: City. **Activities:** Choral groups, dance, drama/theater, literary magazine, music ensembles, musical theater, student government, student newspaper, student-run film society, television station, yearbook, Campus Ministries, International Student Organization, Model UN 28 registered organizations, 15 honor societies, 5 religious organizations. **Athletics (Intercollegiate):** *Women:* basketball, equestrian sports, golf, lacrosse, soccer, swimming, tennis. **On-Campus Highlights:** Front Quadrangle, Wetherill Visual Arts Center and Wilson Museum, Wyndham Robertson Library, Moody Center, Gymnasium, Northen Swim Cntr, Tayloe Fitness Cntr. **Environmental Initiatives:** Signing the President's Climate Agreement Completed a strategic plan (April 2009) with target of 3% annual reduction of green gasses for five years. Hollins University and Emory & Henry College have hired an energy manager for both institutions; a key component of a joint, three-year energy conservation project, supported by a grant from the Jesse Ball duPont Fund and intended to foster a culture of sustainability. The energy manager is conducting a comprehensive assessment of energy consumption on each campus; identifying strategies to further decrease energy use; developing and implementing energy policies for each institution; and enhancing educational activities to promote energy conservation by members of each campus community.

ADMISSIONS
Freshman Academic Profile: Average high school GPA 3.6. 18% in top 10% of high school class, 61% in top 25% of high school class, 89% in top 50% of high school class. 80% from public high schools. SAT Math middle 50% range 460-590. SAT Critical Reading middle 50% range 500-650. SAT Writing middle 50% range 480-630. ACT middle 50% range 21-27. Minimum web-based TOEFL 80. Minimum paper TOEFL 550. **Basis for Candidate Selection:** *Very important factors considered include:* academic GPA, standardized test scores. *Important factors considered include:* application essay, recommendation(s), talent/ability. *Other factors considered include:* Class rank, rigor of secondary school record, alumni/ae relation, character/personal qualities, extracurricular activities, first generation, interview, level of applicant's interest, volunteer work, work experience. **Freshman Admission Requirements:** High school diploma is required and GED is accepted. *Academic units required:* 4 English, 3 mathematics, 3 science, 3 foreign language, 3 social studies. 4 English, 3 mathematics, 3 science, 3 foreign language, 3 social studies. **Freshman Admission Statistics:** 814 applied, 66% admitted, 24% enrolled. **Transfer Admission Requirements:** High school transcript, college transcript(s), essay or personal statement, minimum college GPA of 2.5 required. Lowest grade transferable C. **General Admission Information:** Application Fee $40. Early decision application deadline 12/1. Notification on a rolling basis, beginning on or about 12/15. Nonfall registration accepted. Admission may be deferred for a maximum of usually one year. Credit and/or placement offered for CEEB Advanced Placement tests.

COSTS AND FINANCIAL AID
Average book expense. **Required Forms and Deadlines:** FAFSA, state aid form. **Notification of Awards:** Applicants will be notified of awards on a rolling basis beginning 3/1. **Types of Aid:** *Need-based scholarships/grants:* Federal Pell, SEOG, state scholarships/grants, private scholarships, the school's own gift aid. *Loans:* Direct Subsidized Stafford, Direct Unsubsidized Stafford, Direct PLUS, Federal Perkins, college/university loans from institutional funds, PLATO, CitiAssist, SallieMae, Nelnet, Campus Door. **Student Employment:** Federal Work-Study Program available. Institutional employment available. Highest amount earned per year from on-campus jobs $3,067. Off-campus job opportunities are good. **Financial Aid Statistics:** 100% freshmen, 100% undergrads receive need-based scholarship or grant aid. 100% freshmen, 98% undergrads receive non-need-based scholarship or grant aid. 75% freshmen, 82% undergrads receive need-based self-help aid. 100% freshmen, 98% undergrads receive any aid. 77% undergrads borrow to pay for school. Average cumulative indebtedness $31,104. **Criteria for awarding institutional aid:** *Non-need-based:* academics, alumni affiliation, art, leadership, music/drama, state/district residency.

HOLY FAMILY UNIVERSITY

9801 Frankford Avenue, Philadelphia, PA 19114-2009
Phone: 215-637-3050 • **Financial Aid Phone:** 215-637-5538
E-mail: admissions@holyfamily.edu gradstudy@holyfamily.edu • **CEEB Code:** 2297
Fax: 215-281-1022 • **Website:** www.holyfamily.edu • **ACT Code:** 3592

This private school, affiliated with the Roman Catholic Church, was founded in 1954. It has a 46-acre campus.

RATINGS
Admissions Selectivity Rating: 70   **Fire Safety Rating:** 91   **Green Rating:** 60*

STUDENTS AND FACULTY
Enrollment: 2,031. **Student Body:** 73% female, 27% male, 17% out-of-state, 1% international (12 countries represented). Asian 4%, African American 7%, Caucasian 65%, Hispanic 7%, Native American 0%.
Retention and Graduation: 79% freshmen return for sophomore year. 43% freshmen graduate within 4 years. 61% freshmen graduate within 6 years.
Faculty: Student/faculty ratio 12:1. 94 full-time faculty, 76% hold PhDs, 13% are members of minority groups, 66% are women. 0% of classes are taught by teaching assistants.

ACADEMICS
Degrees: associate, bachelor's, certificate, master's, post-bachelor's certificate. **Classes:** Most classes have 10–19 students. **Majors with Highest Enrollment:** business administration and management; elementary education and teaching; nursing/registered nurse (rn, asn, bsn, msn). **Special Study Options:** Accelerated program, cooperative education program, double major, dual enrollment, English as a Second Language (ESL), independent study, internships, study abroad, teacher certification program. **Disability Services:** Special programs offered to physically disabled students include note-taking services, reader services, tape recorders, tutors. **Career Services:** alumni services, career/job search classes, career assessment, internships Career Services highlights include Our Co-op Program. Refer to website for more details.

FACILITIES
Housing: Coed dorms, 100% of campus accessible to physically disabled. **Special Academic Facilities/Equipment:** On-campus nursery school, art gallery. **Computers:** 100% of classrooms, 100% of dorms, 100% of libraries, 100% of dining areas, 100% of student union, 100% of common outdoor areas have wireless network access. Students can register for classes online. Administrative functions (other than registration) can be performed online.

CAMPUS LIFE
Environment: Metropolis. **Activities:** Choral groups, drama/theater, literary magazine, radio station, student government, student newspaper, television station, yearbook, Campus Ministries, International Student Organization 15 registered organizations, 14 honor societies, 1 religious organizations. **Athletics (Intercollegiate):** *Men:* basketball, cross-country, golf, soccer, track/field (outdoor), track/field (indoor). *Women:* basketball, cross-country, lacrosse, soccer, softball, tennis, track/field (outdoor), track/field (indoor), volleyball. **On-Campus Highlights:** Campus Center, Education / Technology Center, Library, Student Residence Halls, Nurse Education Building.

ADMISSIONS
Freshman Academic Profile: Average high school GPA 3.0. 10% in top 10% of high school class, 32% in top 25% of high school class, 68% in top 50% of high school class. 57% from public high schools. SAT Math middle 50% range 420-500. SAT Critical Reading middle 50% range 430-510. SAT Writing middle 50% range 420-500. Minimum paper TOEFL 550. **Basis for Candidate Selection:** *Very important factors considered include:* Class rank, rigor of secondary school record, interview. *Important factors considered include:* academic GPA, standardized test scores, alumni/ae relation, character/personal qualities, level of applicant's interest. *Other factors considered include:* application essay, recommendation(s), extracurricular activities, talent/ability, volunteer work, work experience. **Freshman Admission Requirements:** High school diploma is required and GED is accepted. *Academic units required:* 4 English, 3 mathematics, 2 science, 2 history, 3 academic electives. *Academic units recommended:* 4 English, 3 mathematics, 2 science, 2 history, 3 academic electives. **Freshman Admission Statistics:** 1,270 applied, 71% admitted, 32% enrolled. **Transfer Admission Requirements:** High school transcript, college transcript(s), essay or personal statement, statement of good standing from prior institution(s). Minimum college GPA of 2.5 required. Lowest grade transferable C. **General Admission Information:** Application Fee $25. Nonfall registration not accepted. Admission may be deferred for a maximum of 1 year. Neither credit nor placement offered for CEEB Advanced Placement tests.

COSTS AND FINANCIAL AID
Annual tuition $24,940. Room and board $12,000. Required fees $650. Average book expense $1,040. **Required Forms and Deadlines:** FAFSA, institution's own financial aid form. **Notification of Awards:** Applicants will be notified of awards on a rolling basis beginning 4/1. **Types of Aid:** *Need-based scholarships/grants:* Federal Pell, SEOG, state scholarships/grants, private scholarships, the school's own gift aid. *Loans:* Subsidized Stafford, Unsubsidized Stafford, PLUS, Federal Perkins, Federal Nursing, college/university loans from institutional funds. **Student Employment:** Federal Work-Study Program available. Off-campus job opportunities are excellent. **Financial Aid Statistics:** 100% freshmen, 97% undergrads receive need-based scholarship or grant aid. 7% freshmen, 8% undergrads receive non-need-based scholarship or grant aid. 88% freshmen, 86% undergrads receive need-based self-help aid. 2% freshmen, 1% undergrads receive athletic scholarships. 87% undergrads borrow to pay for school. Average cumulative indebtedness $33,962. **Criteria for awarding institutional aid:** *Non-need-based:* academics, alumni affiliation, athletics.

HOLY NAMES UNIVERSITY

3500 Mountain Boulevard, Oakland, CA 94619-1699
Phone: 510-436-1351
E-mail: admissions@hnu.edu • **CEEB Code:** 4059
Fax: 510-436-1325 • **Website:** www.hnu.edu • **ACT Code:** 230

This private school, affiliated with the Roman Catholic Church, was founded in 1868. It has a 60-acre campus.

RATINGS
Admissions Selectivity Rating: 76   **Fire Safety Rating:** 62   **Green Rating:** 60*

STUDENTS AND FACULTY
Enrollment: 592. **Student Body:** 78% female, 22% male, 4% out-of-state, 3% international (25 countries represented). Asian 0%, African American 32%, Caucasian 28%, Hispanic 16%, Native American 1%.
Retention and Graduation: 62% freshmen return for sophomore year. 30% freshmen graduate within 4 years. 46% freshmen graduate within 6 years.
Faculty: Student/faculty ratio 12:1. 31 full-time faculty, 90% hold PhDs, 23% are members of minority groups, 68% are women. 0% of classes are taught by teaching assistants.

ACADEMICS
Degrees: bachelor's, master's, post-bachelor's certificate. **Classes:** Most classes have 10–19 students. Most lab/discussion sessions have 10–19 students. **Majors with Highest Enrollment:** business/commerce; nursing/registered nurse (rn, asn, bsn, msn); psychology. **Special Study Options:** Accelerated program, cross-registration, distance learning, double major, English as a Second Language (ESL), exchange student program (domestic), independent study, internships, liberal arts/career combination, student-designed major, study abroad, teacher certification program, weekend college, academic remediating, independent study, learning disabled services, off campus study. **Combined Degree Programs:** BA/MA. **Disability Services:** Special programs offered to physically disabled students include note-taking services, tape recorders, tutors. **Career Services:** Alumni network, alumni services, career/job search classes, career assessment, internships, regional alumni. Career Services highlights include Assistance is available for researching and obtaining positions in business, government, education and non- profits All students are encouraged to enhance their professional development. They can earn a maximum of 6 units for internship credit.

FACILITIES
Housing: Coed dorms, Single sex floor and wings. 30% of campus accessible to physically disabled. Special Academic Facilities/Equipment: Valley Center for the Performing Arts and The J.D. Kennedy Arts Center Gallery CAMPUS LIFE
Environment: Metropolis. **Activities:** Choral groups, drama/theater, music ensembles, student government, symphony orchestra 16 registered organizations, 11 honor societies, 1 religious organizations. **Athletics (Intercollegiate):** *Men:* basketball, cross-country, golf, soccer. *Women:* basketball, cross-country, soccer, volleyball. **On-Campus Highlights:** Green Banana Cafe, Gym, Soda Commons, Cafeteria, Valley Center for Performing Arts.

ADMISSIONS
Freshman Academic Profile: Average high school GPA 3.2. 12% in top 10% of high school class, 40% in top 25% of high school class, 79% in top 50% of high school class. 62% from public high schools. SAT Math middle 50% range 440-540. SAT Critical Reading middle 50% range 450-510. ACT middle 50% range 16-23. Minimum paper TOEFL 490. **Basis for Candidate Selection:** *Very important factors considered include:* rigor of secondary school record. *Important factors considered include:* application essay, recommendation(s), standardized test scores. *Other factors considered include:* Class rank, alumni/ae relation, character/personal qualities, extracurricular activities, interview, talent/

ability, volunteer work, work experience. **Freshman Admission Requirements:** High school diploma is required and GED is accepted. *Academic units required:* 4 English, 3 mathematics, 1 science, (1 science labs), 2 foreign language, 1 history, 4 academic electives. *Academic units recommended:* 4 English, 3 mathematics, 1 science, (1 science labs), 2 foreign language, 1 history, 4 academic electives. **Freshman Admission Statistics:** 211 applied, 62% admitted, 44% enrolled. **Transfer Admission Requirements:** college transcript(s), essay or personal statement, statement of good standing from prior institution(s). Minimum college GPA of 2.2 required. Lowest grade transferable C–. **General Admission Information:** Application Fee $35. Regular application deadline 8/1. Notification on a rolling basis, beginning on or about 10/1. Nonfall registration accepted. Admission may be deferred for a maximum of 1 year. Credit offered for CEEB Advanced Placement tests.

COSTS AND FINANCIAL AID

Annual tuition $19,970. Room and board $7,800. Required fees $210. Average book expense $946. **Required Forms and Deadlines:** FAFSA, institution's own financial aid form, state aid form. **Notification of Awards:** Applicants will be notified of awards on a rolling basis beginning 4/1. **Types of Aid:** *Need-based scholarships/grants:* Federal Pell, SEOG, state scholarships/grants, private scholarships, the school's own gift aid. *Loans:* Subsidized Stafford, Unsubsidized Stafford, PLUS, Federal Perkins, Alternative loans. **Student Employment:** Federal Work-Study Program available. Institutional employment available. Off-campus job opportunities are good. **Financial Aid Statistics:** 93% freshmen, 92% undergrads receive need-based scholarship or grant aid. 100% freshmen, 81% undergrads receive non-need-based scholarship or grant aid. 100% freshmen, 99% undergrads receive need-based self-help aid. 42% freshmen, 20% undergrads receive athletic scholarships. 79% freshmen, 57% undergrads receive any aid. 95% undergrads borrow to pay for school. Average cumulative indebtedness $21,000. **Criteria for awarding institutional aid:** *Non-need-based:* academics, alumni affiliation, athletics, leadership, music/drama, religious affiliation.

HOOD COLLEGE

401 Rosemont Avenue, Frederick, MD 21701
Phone: 301-696-3400 • **Financial Aid Phone:** 301-696-3411
E-mail: admissions@hood.edu • **CEEB Code:** 5296
Fax: 301-696-3819 • **Website:** www.hood.edu • **ACT Code:** 1702

This private school, affiliated with the United Church of Christ Church, was founded in 1893. It has a 50-acre campus.

RATINGS
Admissions Selectivity Rating: 72 | **Fire Safety Rating:** 95 | **Green Rating:** 61

STUDENTS AND FACULTY
Enrollment: 1,383. **Student Body:** 66% female, 34% male, 23% out-of-state, 2% international (36 countries represented). Asian 3%, African American 12%, Caucasian 69%, Hispanic 7%, Native American 0%.
Retention and Graduation: 49% freshmen graduate within 4 years. 45% grads go on to further study within 1 year. 33% grads pursue arts and sciences degrees. 4% grads pursue law degrees. 14% grads pursue business degrees.
Faculty: Student/faculty ratio 12:1. 88 full-time faculty, 95% hold PhDs, 17% are members of minority groups, 57% are women. 0% of classes are taught by teaching assistants.

ACADEMICS
Degrees: bachelor's, master's, post-bachelor's certificate. **Classes:** Most classes have 10–19 students. Most lab/discussion sessions have 10–19 students. **Majors with Highest Enrollment:** biology/biological sciences; business administration and management; psychology. **Special Study Options:** double major, dual enrollment, honors program, independent study, internships, liberal arts/career combination, student-designed major, study abroad, teacher certification program. **Honors Programs:** Our award-winning program offers exceptional undergraduate students four years of exciting coursework and co-curriular activities. Classes are small, discussion oriented, and enhanced by guest speakers and field trips. Interdisciplinary in approach, students are encouraged to engage in personal and intellectual development in the context of community memebership and service. **Combined Degree Programs:** BA Biology/MS Biomed Sci with Montgomery CC. **Disability Services:** Special programs offered to physically disabled students include note-taking services, reader services, tape recorders, tutors. **Career Services:** Alumni network, alumni services, career assessment, internships, regional alumni. Career Services highlights include Hood College has a very active internship program. In 2008-09, more than 100 students completed internships at a variety of sites throughout the Baltimore/Washington/Frederick area.

FACILITIES
Housing: Coed dorms, women's dorms, theme housing, 30% of campus accessible to physically disabled. **Special Academic Facilities/Equipment:** Art gallery, child development lab, language lab, observatory, science labs. **Computers:** 100% of classrooms, 100% of dorms, 100% of libraries, 100% of dining areas, 100% of student union, 100% of common outdoor areas have wireless network access. Students can register for classes online. Administrative functions (other than registration) can be performed online.

CAMPUS LIFE
Environment: Town. **Activities:** Choral groups, dance, drama/theater, jazz band, literary magazine, music ensembles, musical theater, radio station, student government, student newspaper, student-run film society, Campus Ministries, International Student Organization, Model UN 92 registered organizations, 14 honor societies, 6 religious organizations. **Athletics (Intercollegiate):** *Men:* basketball, cross-country, golf, lacrosse, soccer, swimming, tennis, track/field (outdoor). *Women:* basketball, cross-country, field hockey, golf, lacrosse, soccer, softball, swimming, tennis, track/field (outdoor), volleyball. **On-Campus Highlights:** Whitaker Campus Center, Hodson Science and Technology Building, Coblentz Dining Hall, Beneficial-Hodson Library, The Residence Halls.

ADMISSIONS
Freshman Academic Profile: Average high school GPA 3.5. 21% in top 10% of high school class, 52% in top 25% of high school class, 82% in top 50% of high school class. 79% from public high schools. SAT Math middle 50% range 470-590. SAT Critical Reading middle 50% range 470-610. SAT Writing middle 50% range 470-590. ACT middle 50% range 20-25. Minimum web-based TOEFL 79. Minimum paper TOEFL 550. **Basis for Candidate Selection:** *Very important factors considered include:* academic GPA, rigor of secondary school record. *Important factors considered include:* standardized test scores. *Other factors considered include:* Class rank, application essay, recommendation(s), alumni/ae relation, extracurricular activities, first generation, interview, level of applicant's interest. **Freshman Admission Requirements:** High school diploma is required and GED is accepted. *Academic units required:* 4 English, 3 mathematics, 3 science, (2 science labs), 2 foreign language, 2 social studies, 1 history, 4 academic electives. *Academic units recommended:* 4 English, 3 mathematics, 3 science, (2 science labs), 2 foreign language, 2 social studies, 1 history, 1 academic electives. **Freshman Admission Statistics:** 1,788 applied, 77% admitted, 20% enrolled. **Transfer Admission Requirements:** college transcript(s), minimum college GPA of 2.5 required. Lowest grade transferable C–. **General Admission Information:** Application Fee $35. Notification on a rolling basis, beginning on or about 12/1. Nonfall registration accepted. Admission may be deferred for a maximum of 1 yr. Credit and/or placement offered for CEEB Advanced Placement tests.

COSTS AND FINANCIAL AID
Average book expense. **Required Forms and Deadlines:** FAFSA. **Notification of Awards:** Applicants will be notified of awards on a rolling basis beginning 2/15. **Types of Aid:** *Need-based scholarships/grants:* Federal Pell, SEOG, state scholarships/grants, private scholarships, the school's own gift aid. *Loans:* Direct Subsidized Stafford, Direct Unsubsidized Stafford, Direct PLUS, Subsidized Stafford, Unsubsidized Stafford, PLUS, Federal Perkins. **Student Employment:** Federal Work-Study Program available. Institutional employment available. Highest amount earned per year from on-campus jobs $1,800. Off-campus job opportunities are good. **Financial Aid Statistics:** 100% freshmen, 100% undergrads receive need-based scholarship or grant aid. 17% freshmen, 12% undergrads receive non-need-based scholarship or grant aid. 78% freshmen, 83% undergrads receive need-based self-help aid. 98% freshmen, 94% undergrads receive any aid. 33% undergrads borrow to pay for school. Average cumulative indebtedness $18,250. **Criteria for awarding institutional aid:** *Non-need-based:* academics, alumni affiliation, music/drama.

HOPE COLLEGE

69 East 10th, Holland, MI 49422-9000
Phone: 616-395-7850 • **Financial Aid Phone:** 616-395-7765
E-mail: admissions@hope.edu • **CEEB Code:** 1301
Fax: 616-395-7130 • **Website:** www.hope.edu • **ACT Code:** 2012

This private school, affiliated with the Reformed Church Church, was founded in 1862. It has a 120-acre campus.

RATINGS
Admissions Selectivity Rating: 74 | **Fire Safety Rating:** 76 | **Green Rating:** 77

STUDENTS AND FACULTY
Enrollment: 3,251. **Student Body:** 60% female, 40% male, 32% out-of-state, 2% international (35 countries represented). Asian 2%, African American 2%, Caucasian 85%, Hispanic 6%, Native American 0%.

Retention and Graduation: 90% freshmen return for sophomore year. 67% freshmen graduate within 4 years. 77% freshmen graduate within 6 years. 25% grads go on to further study within 1 year. 8% grads pursue arts and sciences degrees. 1% grads pursue law degrees. 1% grads pursue business degrees. 10% grads pursue medical degrees. **Faculty:** Student/faculty ratio 12:1. 226 full-time faculty, 78% hold PhDs, 13% are members of minority groups, 47% are women. 0% of classes are taught by teaching assistants.

ACADEMICS

Degrees: bachelor's. **Classes:** Most classes have 10–19 students. Most lab/discussion sessions have 20–29 students. **Majors with Highest Enrollment:** business/commerce; communication studies/speech communication and rhetoric; English language and literature. **Special Study Options:** distance learning, double major, English as a Second Language (ESL), independent study, internships, student-designed major, study abroad, teacher certification program. **Disability Services:** Special programs offered to physically disabled students include note-taking services, reader services, tape recorders, tutors. **Career Services:** Alumni network, alumni services, career/job search classes, career assessment, internships, regional alumni. Career Services highlights include Hope has an extensive undergraduate research program engaging more than 200 students each summer.

FACILITIES

Housing: Coed dorms, special housing for disabled students, men's dorms, special housing for international students, women's dorms, fraternity/sorority housing, apartments for single students, wellness housing, theme housing, 95% of campus accessible to physically disabled. **Special Academic Facilities/Equipment:** Art gallery, particle accelerator, computational chemistry lab, electron microscopes, spectrometers, ultracentrifuge, observatory, new $38M science building. **Computers:** 70% of classrooms, 100% of libraries, 34% of dining areas, 100% of student union, 40% of common outdoor areas have wireless network access. Students can register for classes online. Administrative functions (other than registration) can be performed online.

CAMPUS LIFE

Environment: Town. **Activities:** Choral groups, concert band, dance, drama/theater, jazz band, literary magazine, music ensembles, radio station, student government, student newspaper, symphony orchestra, television station, yearbook, Campus Ministries, International Student Organization, Model UN 67 registered organizations, 22 honor societies, 6 religious organizations. 6 fraternities, 7 sororities. **Athletics (Intercollegiate).** *Men:* baseball, basketball, cheerleading, cross-country, diving, football, golf, soccer, swimming, tennis, track/field (outdoor), track/field (indoor). *Women:* basketball, cheerleading, cross-country, diving, golf, soccer, softball, swimming, tennis, track/field (outdoor), track/field (indoor), volleyball. **On-Campus Highlights:** DeWitt Student Center, Martha Miller Center for Global Communic, Library, Paul A Schaap Science Center, DeVos Fieldhouse, Kletz - student grill. **Environmental Initiatives:** electrical use reduction water use reduction expanded recycling.

ADMISSIONS

Freshman Academic Profile: Average high school GPA 3.8. 37% in top 10% of high school class, 64% in top 25% of high school class, 92% in top 50% of high school class. 88% from public high schools. SAT Math middle 50% range 520-670. SAT Critical Reading middle 50% range 510-660. ACT middle 50% range 23-29. Minimum web-based TOEFL 80. **Basis for Candidate Selection:** *Very important factors considered include:* academic GPA, rigor of secondary school record, standardized test scores. *Important factors considered include:* Class rank, application essay. *Other factors considered include:* recommendation(s), alumni/ac relation, character/personal qualities, extracurricular activities, first generation, geographical residence, interview, racial/ethnic status, religious affiliation/commitment, state residency, talent/ability, volunteer work, work experience. **Freshman Admission Requirements:** High school diploma is required and GED is accepted. **Freshman Admission Statistics:** 3,491 applied, 85% admitted, 30% enrolled. **Transfer Admission Requirements:** High school transcript, college transcript(s), essay or personal statement, standardized test scores, statement of good standing from prior institution(s). Minimum college GPA of 2.5 required. Lowest grade transferable C. **General Admission Information:** Application Fee $35. Notification on a rolling basis, beginning on or about 12/15. Nonfall registration accepted. Admission may be deferred for a maximum of 1 year. Credit offered for CEEB Advanced Placement tests.

COSTS AND FINANCIAL AID

Annual tuition $28,550. Room and board $8,810. Required fees $170. Average book expense $820. **Required Forms and Deadlines:** FAFSA, institution's own financial aid form, business/farm supplement. **Notification of Awards:** Applicants will be notified of awards on a rolling basis beginning 3/15. **Types of Aid:** *Need-based scholarships/grants:* Federal Pell, SEOG, state scholarships/grants, private scholarships, the school's own gift aid. *Loans:* Direct Subsidized Stafford, Direct Unsubsidized Stafford, Direct PLUS, Federal Perkins, college/university loans from institutional funds. **Student Employment:** Federal Work-Study Program available. Institutional employment available. Highest

amount earned per year from on-campus jobs $7,455. Off-campus job opportunities are good. **Financial Aid Statistics:** 86% freshmen, 84% undergrads receive need-based scholarship or grant aid. 74% freshmen, 68% undergrads receive non-need-based scholarship or grant aid. 83% freshmen, 82% undergrads receive need-based self-help aid. 96% freshmen, 92% undergrads receive any aid. 65% undergrads borrow to pay for school. Average cumulative indebtedness $37,010. **Criteria for awarding institutional aid:** *Non-need-based:* academics, art, minority status, music/drama, religious affiliation.

HOPE INTERNATIONAL UNIVERSITY

Undergraduate Admissions, Fullerton, CA 92831
Phone: 866-722-4673 • **Financial Aid Phone:** 714-879-3901
E-mail: pccadmissions@hiu.edu
Fax: 714-681-7423 • **Website:** www.hiu.edu • **ACT Code:** 356

This private school, affiliated with the Church of Christ Church, was founded in 1928. It has a 18-acre campus.

RATINGS

Admissions Selectivity Rating: 71 **Fire Safety Rating:** 65 **Green Rating:** 60*

STUDENTS AND FACULTY

Enrollment: 521. **Student Body:** 60% female, 40% male, 24% out-of-state, 2% international. Asian 5%, African American 5%, Caucasian 61%, Hispanic 16%, Native American 1%.
Retention and Graduation: 71% freshmen return for sophomore year. 1% freshmen graduate within 4 years. 50% freshmen graduate within 6 years. **Faculty:** Student/faculty ratio 15:1. 32 full-time faculty, 59% hold PhDs, 6% are members of minority groups, 25% are women. 0% of classes are taught by teaching assistants.

ACADEMICS

Degrees: associate, bachelor's, certificate, master's, post-bachelor's certificate. **Classes:** Most classes have fewer than 10 students. Most lab/discussion sessions have fewer than 10 students. **Majors with Highest Enrollment:** psychology; teacher education, multiple levels; youth ministry. **Special Study Options:** Accelerated program, cross-registration, distance learning, double major, dual enrollment, English as a Second Language (ESL), independent study, internships, liberal arts/career combination, student-designed major, study abroad, teacher certification program. **Disability Services:** Special programs offered to physically disabled students include note-taking services, tape recorders, tutors.

FACILITIES

Housing: men's dorms, women's dorms. 95% of campus accessible to physically disabled. CAMPUS LIFE
Environment: City. **Activities:** Choral groups, drama/theater, jazz band, music ensembles, musical theater, student government, student newspaper, yearbook. **Athletics (Intercollegiate):** *Men:* basketball, soccer, tennis, volleyball. *Women:* basketball, soccer, softball, tennis, volleyball. **On-Campus Highlights:** Lawson-Fulton Student Center, Darling Library, Lambda Lounge, Auditorium, The Commons.

ADMISSIONS

Freshman Academic Profile: Average high school GPA 3.3. 20% in top 10% of high school class, 37% in top 25% of high school class, 77% in top 50% of high school class. 95% from public high schools. SAT Math middle 50% range 420-530. SAT Critical Reading middle 50% range 440-540. SAT Writing middle 50% range 420-520. ACT middle 50% range 18-21. Minimum paper TOEFL 500. **Basis for Candidate Selection:** *Very important factors considered include:* Class rank, application essay, academic GPA, recommendation(s), rigor of secondary school record, standardized test scores. *Important factors considered include:* level of applicant's interest. *Other factors considered include:* character/personal qualities, extracurricular activities, interview, religious affiliation/commitment, talent/ability, volunteer work. **Freshman Admission Requirements:** High school diploma is required and GED is accepted. **Freshman Admission Statistics:** 413 applied, 71% admitted, 59% enrolled. **Transfer Admission Requirements:** college transcript(s), essay or personal statement, statement of good standing from prior institution(s). Minimum college GPA of 2.5 required. Lowest grade transferable C. **General Admission Information:** Application Fee $40. Notification on a rolling basis, beginning on or about 8/1. Nonfall registration accepted. Credit and/or placement offered for CEEB Advanced Placement tests.

COSTS AND FINANCIAL AID

Annual tuition $21,560. Room and board $6,940. Required fees $325. Average book expense $1,386. **Required Forms and Deadlines:** FAFSA, institution's own financial aid form. **Notification of Awards:** Applicants will be notified of awards on a rolling basis beginning 3/15. **Types of Aid:** *Need-based scholarships/grants:* Federal Pell, SEOG, state scholarships/grants, private scholarships, the school's own gift aid. *Loans:* Direct Subsidized Stafford, Direct Unsubsidized Stafford, Direct PLUS, Subsidized Stafford, Unsubsidized Stafford, PLUS, Federal Perkins, state loans, college/university loans from institutional funds. **Student Employment:** Federal Work-Study Program available. Institutional employment available. Off-campus job opportunities are good. **Financial Aid Statistics:** 98% freshmen, 96% undergrads receive need-based scholarship or grant aid. 19% freshmen, 15% undergrads receive non-need-based scholarship or grant aid. 74% freshmen, 79% undergrads receive need-based self-help aid. 67% freshmen, 73% undergrads receive any aid. 92% undergrads borrow to pay for school. Average cumulative indebtedness $18,627. **Criteria for awarding institutional aid:** *Non-need-based:* academics, alumni affiliation, athletics, leadership, music/drama, religious affiliation.

HOUGHTON COLLEGE

PO Box 128, Houghton, NY 14744
Phone: 585-567-9353 • **Financial Aid Phone:** 585-567-9328
E-mail: admission@houghton.edu • **CEEB Code:** 2299
Fax: 716-567-9522 • **Website:** www.houghton.edu • **ACT Code:** 2766

This private school, affiliated with the Wesleyan Church, was founded in 1883. It has a 1300-acre campus.

RATINGS
Admissions Selectivity Rating: 78   **Fire Safety Rating:** 71   **Green Rating:** 78

STUDENTS AND FACULTY
Enrollment: 1,113. **Student Body:** 66% female, 34% male, 39% out-of-state, 5% international (32 countries represented). Asian 1%, African American 3%, Caucasian 87%, Hispanic 2%, Native American 0%.
Retention and Graduation: 58% freshmen graduate within 4 years. 67% freshmen graduate within 6 years. 36% grads go on to further study within 1 year. 22% grads pursue arts and sciences degrees. 1% grads pursue law degrees. 4% grads pursue business degrees. 1% grads pursue medical degrees. **Faculty:** Student/faculty ratio 12:1. 71 full-time faculty, 92% hold PhDs, 1% are members of minority groups, 31% are women. 0% of classes are taught by teaching assistants.

ACADEMICS
Degrees: associate, bachelor's, master's. **Classes:** Most classes have 10–19 students. Most lab/discussion sessions have 10–19 students. **Majors with Highest Enrollment:** biology/biological sciences; business administration and management; elementary education and teaching. **Special Study Options:** cross-registration, double major, exchange student program (domestic), honors program, independent study, internships, liberal arts/career combination, study abroad, teacher certification program. **Honors Programs:** First-year honors program in London, England; first-year honors program in Eastern Europe; first-year honors program in math and science. **Disability Services:** Special programs offered to physically disabled students include note-taking services, tape recorders, tutors. **Career Services:** Alumni network, alumni services, career/job search classes, career assessment, internships.

FACILITIES
Housing: men's dorms, special housing for international students, women's dorms, apartments for married students, apartments for single students. 80% of campus accessible to physically disabled. **Special Academic Facilities/Equipment:** Electron microscope, Art Gallery, Greenhouse. **Computers:** 100% of classrooms, 100% of dorms, 100% of libraries, 100% of dining areas, 100% of student union, 50% of common outdoor areas have wireless network access. Students can register for classes online. Administrative functions (other than registration) can be performed online.

CAMPUS LIFE
Environment: Rural. **Activities:** Choral groups, concert band, dance, drama/theater, jazz band, literary magazine, music ensembles, musical theater, opera, student government, student newspaper, symphony orchestra, yearbook, Campus Ministries, International Student Organization 34 registered organizations, 2 honor societies, 9 religious organizations. **Athletics (Intercollegiate):** *Men:* basketball, cross-country, soccer, track/field (outdoor), track/field (indoor). *Women:* basketball, cross-country, field hockey, soccer, track/field (outdoor), track/field (indoor), volleyball. **On-Campus Highlights:** Center for the Arts, Nielsen Physical Education Center, Wesley Chapel, Campus Center, Library. **Environmental Initiatives:** The Creation Care Committee is spearheading the formulation of the long range Climate Action Plan to bring the campus to carbon neutrality. This document takes large strides in focusing the college on sustainability across the board. New construction upgrades on the Paine Science Center, which commenced October 2010, will seek LEED Silver certification.

Commencement and implementation of a composting program for all prep waste from the dining hall.

ADMISSIONS
Freshman Academic Profile: Average high school GPA 3.6. 30% in top 10% of high school class, 65% in top 25% of high school class, 91% in top 50% of high school class. 64% from public high schools. SAT Math middle 50% range 510-620. SAT Critical Reading middle 50% range 530-640. SAT Writing middle 50% range 500-620. ACT middle 50% range 22-27. Minimum web-based TOEFL 80. Minimum paper TOEFL 550. **Basis for Candidate Selection:** *Very important factors considered include:* academic GPA, religious affiliation/commitment. *Important factors considered include:* Class rank, application essay, recommendation(s), rigor of secondary school record, standardized test scores, character/personal qualities. *Other factors considered include:* alumni/ae relation, extracurricular activities, interview, level of applicant's interest, racial/ethnic status, talent/ability, volunteer work, work experience. **Freshman Admission Requirements:** High school diploma is required and GED is accepted. **Freshman Admission Statistics:** 830 applied, 73% admitted, 38% enrolled. **Transfer Admission Requirements:** college transcript(s), essay or personal statement, Lowest grade transferable C–. **General Admission Information:** Application Fee $40. Notification on a rolling basis, beginning on or about 1/1. Nonfall registration accepted. Admission may be deferred for a maximum of 2 years. Credit and/or placement offered for CEEB Advanced Placement tests.

COSTS AND FINANCIAL AID
Annual tuition $27,578. Room and board $8,012. Required fees $150. Average book expense $1,000. **Required Forms and Deadlines:** FAFSA. **Notification of Awards:** Applicants will be notified of awards on a rolling basis beginning 3/15. **Types of Aid:** *Need-based scholarships/grants:* Federal Pell, SEOG, state scholarships/grants, private scholarships, the school's own gift aid. *Loans:* Subsidized Stafford, Unsubsidized Stafford, PLUS, Federal Perkins. **Student Employment:** Federal Work-Study Program available. Institutional employment available. Highest amount earned per year from on-campus jobs $4,283. Off-campus job opportunities are poor. **Financial Aid Statistics:** 100% freshmen, 98% undergrads receive need-based scholarship or grant aid. 10% freshmen, 10% undergrads receive non-need-based scholarship or grant aid. 90% freshmen, 90% undergrads receive need-based self-help aid. 3% undergrads receive athletic scholarships. 100% freshmen, 97% undergrads receive any aid. 79% undergrads borrow to pay for school. Average cumulative indebtedness $22,197. **Criteria for awarding institutional aid:** *Non-need-based:* academics, alumni affiliation, art, athletics, music/drama, religious affiliation.

HOUSTON BAPTIST UNIVERSITY

7502 Fondren Road, Houston, TX 77074
Phone: 281-649-3211 • **Financial Aid Phone:** 281-649-3471
E-mail: unadm@hbu.edu • **CEEB Code:** 6282
Fax: 281-649-3217 • **Website:** www.hbu.edu • **ACT Code:** 4101

This private school, affiliated with the Southern Baptist Church, was founded in 1960. It has a 100-acre campus.

RATINGS
Admissions Selectivity Rating: 81   **Fire Safety Rating:** 86   **Green Rating:** 60*

STUDENTS AND FACULTY
Enrollment: 1,916. **Student Body:** 67% female, 33% male, 3% out-of-state, 6% international (36 countries represented). Asian 13%, African American 20%, Caucasian 46%, Hispanic 14%, Native American 0%.
Retention and Graduation: 74% freshmen return for sophomore year. 32% freshmen graduate within 4 years. 59% freshmen graduate within 6 years. **Faculty:** Student/faculty ratio 14:1. 103 full-time faculty, 81% hold PhDs, 10% are members of minority groups, 48% are women. 0% of classes are taught by teaching assistants.

ACADEMICS
Degrees: associate, bachelor's, master's. **Classes:** Most classes have 10–19 students. Most lab/discussion sessions have fewer than 10 students. **Majors with Highest Enrollment:** biology/biological sciences; business/commerce; psychology. **Special Study Options:** Accelerated program, double major, dual enrollment, English as a Second Language (ESL), independent study, internships, liberal arts/career combination, teacher certification program. **Combined Degree Programs:** Accelerated MATS degree Program (with BA or BS). **Career Services:** Alumni network, alumni services, career/job search classes, career assessment, internships, regional alumni. Career Services highlights include Our internship program provides opportunities for student to work with early stage companies at the BU incubators, as well as in the community. One

particularly unusual aspect of the program is that we provide opportunities for non-business students to "intern" with startups our business students are creating. One such program this year had Graphic Design students working with MBA student entrepreneurs to develop corporate identity programs for them.

FACILITIES

Housing: men's dorms, women's dorms, apartments for single students. 90% of campus accessible to physically disabled. **Special Academic Facilities/Equipment:** Museum of architecture/decorative arts, language lab, research center. **Computers:** Students can register for classes online.

CAMPUS LIFE

Environment: Metropolis. **Activities:** Choral groups, concert band, drama/theater, music ensembles, pep band, student government, student newspaper, yearbook 36 registered organizations, 9 honor societies, 3 religious organizations. 2 fraternities, 2 sororities. **Athletics (Intercollegiate):** *Men:* baseball, basketball, cheerleading. *Women:* basketball, cheerleading, softball, volleyball. **On-Campus Highlights:** Hinton Center, Baugh Center and the Bone Appetit Cafe, Bible Museum, Wellness Center, Admissions Office.

ADMISSIONS

Freshman Academic Profile: 24% in top 10% of high school class, 44% in top 25% of high school class, 79% in top 50% of high school class. 79% from public high schools. SAT Math middle 50% range 500-620. SAT Critical Reading middle 50% range 500-610. ACT middle 50% range 19-25. Minimum paper TOEFL 550. **Basis for Candidate Selection:** *Very important factors considered include:* application essay, recommendation(s), rigor of secondary school record, standardized test scores. *Important factors considered include:* Class rank, extracurricular activities, geographical residence, religious affiliation/commitment, talent/ability, volunteer work. *Other factors considered include:* alumni/ae relation, character/personal qualities, interview. **Freshman Admission Requirements:** High school diploma is required and GED is accepted. **Freshman Admission Statistics:** 867 applied, 65% admitted, 55% enrolled. **Transfer Admission Requirements:** college transcript(s), essay or personal statement, statement of good standing from prior institution(s). Minimum college GPA of 2.0 required. Lowest grade transferable C. **General Admission Information:** Application Fee $25. Nonfall registration accepted. Admission may be deferred for a maximum of None. Credit offered for CEEB Advanced Placement tests.

COSTS AND FINANCIAL AID

Average book expense. **Required Forms and Deadlines:** FAFSA. **Notification of Awards:** Applicants will be notified of awards on a rolling basis beginning 3/10. **Types of Aid:** *Need-based scholarships/grants.* Federal Pell, SEOG, state scholarships/grants, private scholarships, the school's own gift aid. *Loans:* Subsidized Stafford, Unsubsidized Stafford, PLUS, state loans, Private, non federal. **Student Employment:** Federal Work-Study Program available. Highest amount earned per year from on-campus jobs $1,800. **Financial Aid Statistics:** 99% freshmen, 97% undergrads receive need-based scholarship or grant aid. 14% freshmen, 7% undergrads receive non-need-based scholarship or grant aid. 73% freshmen, 82% undergrads receive need-based self-help aid. 3% freshmen, 1% undergrads receive athletic scholarships. 64% freshmen, 85% undergrads receive any aid. **Criteria for awarding institutional aid:** *Non-need-based:* academics, alumni affiliation, art, athletics, leadership, music/drama, religious affiliation.

HOWARD PAYNE UNIVERSITY

Howard Payne Station, Brownwood, TX 76801
Phone: 325-649-8027 • **Financial Aid Phone:** 325-649-8015
E-mail: enroll@hputx.edu
Fax: 325-649-8901 • **Website:** www.hputx.edu • **ACT Code:** 4102

This private school, affiliated with the Baptist Church, was founded in 1889. It has a 30-acre campus.

RATINGS

Admissions Selectivity Rating: 70   **Fire Safety Rating:** 70   **Green Rating:** 60*

STUDENTS AND FACULTY

Enrollment: 1,303. **Student Body:** 50% female, 50% male, 3% out-of-state, 1% international (6 countries represented). Asian 1%, African American 8%, Caucasian 75%, Hispanic 12%, Native American 1%.
Retention and Graduation: 61% freshmen return for sophomore year. 21% freshmen graduate within 4 years. 35% freshmen graduate within 6 years. 15% grads go on to further study within 1 year. 2% grads pursue law degrees. 2% grads pursue business degrees. 2% grads pursue medical degrees. **Faculty:** Student/faculty ratio 11:1. 75 full-time faculty, 59% hold PhDs, 5% are mem-

bers of minority groups, 36% are women. 0% of classes are taught by teaching assistants.

ACADEMICS

Degrees: associate, bachelor's, certificate. **Classes:** Most classes have fewer than 10 students. **Majors with Highest Enrollment:** bible/biblical studies; business/commerce; education. **Special Study Options:** Accelerated program, cooperative education program, distance learning, double major, dual enrollment, English as a Second Language (ESL), honors program, independent study, internships, liberal arts/career combination, study abroad, teacher certification program, Extension campuses are located in El Paso, Corpus Christi, Weatherford, and Harlingen, Texas. **Honors Programs:** The Douglas MacArthur Academy of Freedom is designed for academically gifted students who aspire to leadership roles in a variety of careers. The Academy program prepares students to read critically, think analytically, and communicate ideas effectively. Through a broad-based liberal arts education that emphasizes Judeo-Christian values, western civilization, free enterprise principles, and political awareness, the Academy explores the meaning and significance of traditional American values and seeks to understand the problems of contemporary society. Students develop critical thinking skills by analyzing current issues through the multidisciplinary Academy major, which includes courses from the School of Humanities, the School of Christian Studies, and the School of Business. **Disability Services:** Special programs offered to physically disabled students include tutors. **Career Services:** Alumni network, career assessment

FACILITIES

Housing: men's dorms, women's dorms, apartments for single students. 95% of campus accessible to physically disabled. **Special Academic Facilities/Equipment:** Douglas MacArthur Academy of Freedom and Museum **Computers:** Administrative functions (other than registration) can be performed online.

CAMPUS LIFE

Environment: Rural. **Activities:** Choral groups, concert band, drama/theater, jazz band, literary magazine, marching band, music ensembles, musical theater, opera, radio station, student government, student newspaper, yearbook 32 registered organizations, 3 honor societies, 4 religious organizations. 5 fraternities, 5 sororities. **Athletics (Intercollegiate):** *Men:* baseball, basketball, cheerleading, cross-country, football, tennis, track/field (outdoor). *Women:* basketball, cheerleading, cross-country, softball, tennis, track/field (outdoor), volleyball. **On-Campus Highlights:** Elliston-Cassle Wellness Center, Mabee University Center, Douglas MacArthur Academy of Freedom, Muse Mall and Plaza, Old Main Park.

ADMISSIONS

Freshman Academic Profile: Average high school GPA 3.3. 15% in top 10% of high school class, 39% in top 25% of high school class, 71% in top 50% of high school class. 94% from public high schools. SAT Math middle 50% range 440-550. SAT Critical Reading middle 50% range 440-570. ACT middle 50% range 17-23. Minimum paper TOEFL 550. **Basis for Candidate Selection:** *Very important factors considered include:* rigor of secondary school record, standardized test scores. *Important factors considered include:* recommendation(s), interview. *Other factors considered include:* Class rank, character/personal qualities, work experience. **Freshman Admission Requirements:** High school diploma is required and GED is accepted. **Freshman Admission Statistics:** 640 applied, 78% admitted, 62% enrolled. **Transfer Admission Requirements:** college transcript(s), minimum college GPA of 2.0 required. Lowest grade transferable D. **General Admission Information:** Application Fee $25. Regular application deadline 8/31. Nonfall registration accepted. Admission may be deferred for a maximum of 1 year. Credit and/or placement offered for CEEB Advanced Placement tests.

COSTS AND FINANCIAL AID

Annual tuition $11,500. Room and board $4,615. Required fees $1,000. Average book expense $1,000. **Required Forms and Deadlines:** FAFSA, institution's own financial aid form. **Notification of Awards:** Applicants will be notified of awards on a rolling basis beginning 3/1. **Types of Aid:** *Need-based scholarships/grants:* Federal Pell, SEOG, state scholarships/grants, private scholarships, the school's own gift aid. *Loans:* Subsidized Stafford, Unsubsidized Stafford, PLUS, Federal Perkins, state loans. **Student Employment:** Federal Work-Study Program available. Institutional employment available. Off-campus job opportunities are good. **Financial Aid Statistics:** 98% freshmen, 98% undergrads receive need-based scholarship or grant aid. 10% freshmen, 10% undergrads receive non-need-based scholarship or grant aid. 72% freshmen, 76% undergrads receive need-based self-help aid. 69% undergrads borrow to pay for school. Average cumulative indebtedness $18,960. **Criteria for awarding institutional aid:** *Non-need-based:* academics, alumni affiliation, art, leadership, music/drama, religious affiliation.

HOWARD UNIVERSITY

2400 Sixth Street, NW, Washington, DC 20059
Phone: 202-806-2700 • **Financial Aid Phone:** 202-806-2840
E-mail: admission@howard.edu • **CEEB Code:** 5297
Fax: 202-806-4467 • **Website:** www.howard.edu • **ACT Code:** 4102

This private school was founded in 1867. It has a 258-acre campus.

RATINGS
Admissions Selectivity Rating: 90   **Fire Safety Rating:** 89   **Green Rating:** 60*

STUDENTS AND FACULTY
Enrollment: 7,086. **Student Body:** 66% female, 34% male, 97% out-of-state, 4% international (86 countries represented). Asian 0%, African American 49%, Caucasian 0%, Hispanic 1%, Native American 0%.
Retention and Graduation: 85% freshmen return for sophomore year. 46% freshmen graduate within 4 years. 65% freshmen graduate within 6 years. 60% grads go on to further study within 1 year. 42% grads pursue arts and sciences degrees. 12% grads pursue law degrees. 15% grads pursue business degrees. 11% grads pursue medical degrees. **Faculty:** Student/faculty ratio 8:1. 1064 full-time faculty, 91% hold PhDs, 81% are members of minority groups, 42% are women.

ACADEMICS
Degrees: bachelor's, certificate, first professional, first professional certificate, master's, post-master's certificate. **Classes:** Most classes have fewer than 10 students. Most lab/discussion sessions have 10–19 students. **Majors with Highest Enrollment:** biology/biological sciences; journalism; radio and television. **Special Study Options:** Accelerated program, cooperative education program, distance learning, double major, English as a Second Language (ESL), exchange student program (domestic), honors program, independent study, internships, study abroad, teacher certification program, Tutorial program, advanced placement, continuing education. **Combined Degree Programs:** BA/MD, BA/DDS, MBA / JD, MD / PHD. **Disability Services:** Special programs offered to physically disabled students include note-taking services, reader services. **Career Services:** career/job search classes, career assessment, internships Career Services highlights include Rangel Scholars Program Internships offer exposure to Capital Hii and countries abroad. Students get personal experiences regarding the working of our political system and those of other countries from experienced state department professionals and elected government officials.

FACILITIES
Housing: Coed dorms, men's dorms, women's dorms, apartments for married students, apartments for single students. 100% of campus accessible to physically disabled. **Special Academic Facilities/Equipment:** Three art galleries, language labs, hospital. Research center with comprehensive collection on Africa and persons of African descent. **Computers:** 10% of classrooms, 100% of dorms, 100% of libraries, 10% of dining areas, 50% of student union, 10% of common outdoor areas have wireless network access. Students can register for classes online. Administrative functions (other than registration) can be performed online.

CAMPUS LIFE
Environment: Metropolis. **Activities:** Choral groups, concert band, dance, drama/theater, jazz band, literary magazine, marching band, music ensembles, musical theater, opera, pep band, radio station, student government, student newspaper, student-run film society, symphony orchestra, television station, yearbook, Campus Ministries, International Student Organization 150 registered organizations, 15 honor societies, 3 religious organizations. 10 fraternities, 8 sororities. **Athletics (Intercollegiate):** *Men:* basketball, cheerleading, cross-country, diving, football, soccer, swimming, tennis, track/field (outdoor). *Women:* basketball, bowling, boxing, cheerleading, cross-country, diving, lacrosse, soccer, softball, swimming, tennis, track/field (outdoor), volleyball. **On-Campus Highlights:** Founders Library, Rankin Chapel, Punchout, Ira Aldridge Theatre, Burr Gymnasium.

ADMISSIONS
Freshman Academic Profile: Average high school GPA 3.2. 26% in top 10% of high school class, 55% in top 25% of high school class, 84% in top 50% of high school class. 80% from public high schools. SAT Math middle 50% range 460-680. SAT Critical Reading middle 50% range 470-670. SAT Writing middle 50% range 430-670. ACT middle 50% range 19-29. Minimum paper TOEFL 550. **Basis for Candidate Selection:** *Very important factors considered include:* Class rank, rigor of secondary school record, standardized test scores.

Important factors considered include: recommendation(s), character/personal qualities. *Other factors considered include:* application essay, alumni/ae relation, extracurricular activities, talent/ability, volunteer work, work experience. **Freshman Admission Requirements:** High school diploma is required and GED is accepted. *Academic units required:* 4 English, 2 mathematics, 2 science, 2 foreign language, 2 social studies, 2 history. *Academic units recommended:* 4 English, 2 mathematics, 2 science, 2 foreign language, 2 social studies, 2 history. **Freshman Admission Statistics:** 9,750 applied, 49% admitted, 31% enrolled. **Transfer Admission Requirements:** college transcript(s), statement of good standing from prior institution(s). Minimum college GPA of 2.5 required. Lowest grade transferable C. **General Admission Information:** Application Fee $45. Early decision application deadline 11/1. Regular application deadline 2/15. Nonfall registration accepted. Admission may be deferred for a maximum of 1. Credit and/or placement offered for CEEB Advanced Placement tests.

COSTS AND FINANCIAL AID
Annual tuition $19,150. Room and board $15,341. Required fees $1,021. Average book expense $3,740. **Required Forms and Deadlines:** FAFSA. **Notification of Awards:** Applicants will be notified of awards on a rolling basis beginning 4/1. **Types of Aid:** *Need-based scholarships/grants:* Federal Pell, SEOG, state scholarships/grants, private scholarships, the school's own gift aid, Federal Nursing Scholarships. *Loans:* Direct Subsidized Stafford, Direct Unsubsidized Stafford, Direct PLUS, Federal Perkins, Federal Nursing. **Student Employment:** Federal Work-Study Program available. Institutional employment available. Highest amount earned per year from on-campus jobs $3,500. Off-campus job opportunities are excellent. **Financial Aid Statistics:** 41% freshmen, 54% undergrads receive need-based scholarship or grant aid. 56% freshmen, 41% undergrads receive non-need-based scholarship or grant aid. 34% freshmen, 57% undergrads receive need-based self-help aid. 5% freshmen, 3% undergrads receive athletic scholarships. 96% freshmen, 96% undergrads receive any aid. 80% undergrads borrow to pay for school. Average cumulative indebtedness $16,473. **Criteria for awarding institutional aid:** *Non-need-based:* academics, art, athletics, job skills, music/drama, state/district residency.

HUMBOLDT STATE UNIVERSITY

1 Harpst Street, Arcata, CA 95521-8299
Phone: 707-826-4402 • **Financial Aid Phone:** 707-826-4321
E-mail: hsuinfo@humboldt.edu • **CEEB Code:** 4345
Fax: 707-826-6190 • **Website:** www.humboldt.edu • **ACT Code:** 286

This public school was founded in 1913. It has a 161-acre campus.

RATINGS
Admissions Selectivity Rating: 69   **Fire Safety Rating:** 87   **Green Rating:** 81

STUDENTS AND FACULTY
Enrollment: 7,562. **Student Body:** 53% female, 47% male, 12% out-of-state, 1% international (40 countries represented). Asian 3%, African American 3%, Caucasian 46%, Hispanic 18%, Native American 1%.
Retention and Graduation: 73% freshmen return for sophomore year. 14% freshmen graduate within 4 years. 42% freshmen graduate within 6 years. **Faculty:** Student/faculty ratio 23:1. 228 full-time faculty, 100% hold PhDs, 14% are members of minority groups, 39% are women. % of classes are taught by teaching assistants.

ACADEMICS
Degrees: bachelor's, master's, post-bachelor's certificate. **Classes:** Most classes have 20–29 students. Most lab/discussion sessions have 20–29 students. **Majors with Highest Enrollment:** liberal arts and sciences/liberal studies; social sciences. **Special Study Options:** double major, English as a Second Language (ESL), exchange student program (domestic), student-designed major, study abroad, teacher certification program. **Disability Services:** Special programs offered to physically disabled students include note-taking services, reader services, tape recorders, tutors. **Career Services:** alumni services, career/job search classes, career assessment, internships, regional alumni. Career Services highlights include Internships allow students to get jobs in their fields after they graduate. The Career Center connects students with the internships that work best for them.

FACILITIES
Housing: Coed dorms. 75% of campus accessible to physically disabled. **Special Academic Facilities/Equipment:** Art and geology museums, marine research lab, fish hatchery, wildlife game pen, observatory, First Street Gallery **Computers:** 85% of classrooms, 100% of dorms, 100% of libraries, 100% of dining areas, 100% of student union, 80% of common outdoor areas have wireless network access. Students can register for classes online. Administrative functions (other than registration) can be performed online.

CAMPUS LIFE

Environment: Village. **Activities:** Choral groups, concert band, dance, drama/theater, jazz band, literary magazine, music ensembles, pep band, radio station, student government, student newspaper, symphony orchestra, International Student Organization, Model UN 160 registered organizations, 6 honor societies, 8 religious organizations. 2 fraternities, 4 sororities. **Athletics (Intercollegiate):** *Men:* basketball, cross-country, football, soccer, track/field (outdoor). *Women:* basketball, crew/rowing, cross-country, soccer, softball, track/field (outdoor), volleyball. **On-Campus Highlights:** Founders Hall, Campus Center for Appropriate Technology, University Center, Redwood Bowl, University Library. **Environmental Initiatives:** Campus Center for Appropriate Technology (CCAT): For 30 years, the Campus Center for Appropriate Technology's live-in demonstration home for sustainability annually exposes over 2,000 students, faculty, staff, and visitors through tours, student-taught courses, workshops, presentations and hands-on projects. The first of its kind, CCAT has been the inspiration for similar projects on college campuses across the nation. http://www.humboldt.edu/~ccat/ For the past 15 years, Humboldt State's Schatz Energy Research Center has been an international leader in the development of clean and renewable energy. Most recently, the Center unveiled a hydrogen fueling station that powers a hydrogen fueled Toyota Prius. http://www.schatzlab.org/ Humboldt Energy Independent Fund (HEIF): The Humboldt State Energy Independence Fund (HEIF) seeks to reduce the environmental impacts of energy use at HSU through student created, designed, and implemented projects. The funds for these projects come from a $10 per semester student fee (students approved the fee via a university-wide vote). Projects educate about energy, save energy or generate energy. So far, $100,000 has been commissioned towards two HEIF projects: a solar monitoring station on campus and a 10.5 kW solar installation along with a student-designed interpretive sign and energy-themed art project. http://www.humboldt.edu/~heif/

ADMISSIONS

Freshman Academic Profile: Average high school GPA 3.2. 11% in top 10% of high school class, 39% in top 25% of high school class, 78% in top 50% of high school class. 90% from public high schools. SAT Math middle 50% range 440-580. SAT Critical Reading middle 50% range 450-560. SAT Writing middle 50% range 440-550. ACT middle 50% range 18-24. Minimum web-based TOEFL 71. Minimum paper TOEFL 525. **Basis for Candidate Selection:** *Very important factors considered include:* academic GPA, standardized test scores. *Important factors considered include:* rigor of secondary school record. *Other factors considered include:* state residency. **Freshman Admission Requirements:** High school diploma is required and GED is accepted. *Academic units required:* 4 English, 3 mathematics, 2 science, (1 science labs), 2 foreign language, 1 social studies, 1 history, 1 visual/performing arts, 1 academic electives. *Academic units recommended:* 4 English, 3 mathematics, 2 science, (1 science labs), 2 foreign language, 1 social studies, 1 history, 1 visual/performing arts, 1 academic electives. **Freshman Admission Statistics:** 9,979 applied, 816% enrolled. **Transfer Admission Requirements:** college transcript(s), statement of good standing from prior institution(s). Minimum college GPA of 2.00 required. Lowest grade transferable D–. **General Admission Information:** Application Fee $55. Regular application deadline 11/30. Notification on a rolling basis, beginning on or about 12/1. Nonfall registration not accepted. Credit and/or placement offered for CEEB Advanced Placement tests.

COSTS AND FINANCIAL AID

Annual in-state tuition $5,472. Annual out-of-state tuition $16,632. Room and board $11,130. Required fees $1,658. Average book expense $1,582. **Required Forms and Deadlines:** FAFSA. **Notification of Awards:** Applicants will be notified of awards on a rolling basis beginning 4/1. **Types of Aid:** *Need-based scholarships/grants:* Federal Pell, SEOG, state scholarships/grants, private scholarships, the school's own gift aid. *Loans:* Direct Subsidized Stafford, Direct Unsubsidized Stafford, Direct PLUS, Federal Perkins. **Student Employment:** Federal Work-Study Program available. Institutional employment available. Off-campus job opportunities are good. **Financial Aid Statistics:** 82% freshmen, 83% undergrads receive need-based scholarship or grant aid. 1% freshmen, 1% undergrads receive non-need-based scholarship or grant aid. 71% freshmen, 72% undergrads receive need-based self-help aid. 2% freshmen, 1% undergrads receive athletic scholarships. 55% freshmen, 79% undergrads receive any aid. 82% undergrads borrow to pay for school. Average cumulative indebtedness $19,095. **Criteria for awarding institutional aid:** *Non-need-based:* academics, alumni affiliation, athletics, leadership, minority status, music/drama, religious affiliation.

HUMPHREYS COLLEGE

6650 Inglewood Avenue, Stockton, CA 95207
Phone: 209-478-0800 • **Financial Aid Phone:** 209-478-0800
E-mail: slopez@humphreys.edu
Fax: 209-478-0800 • **Website:** www.humphreys.edu/

This private school was founded in 1896. It has a 10-acre campus.

RATINGS
Admissions Selectivity Rating: 62   **Fire Safety Rating:** 60*   **Green Rating:** 60*

STUDENTS AND FACULTY
Enrollment: 692. **Student Body:** 85% female, 15% male, 0% out-of-state, 0% international. Asian 12%, African American 15%, Caucasian 25%, Hispanic 33%, Native American 1%.
Retention and Graduation: 64% freshmen return for sophomore year. 100% freshmen graduate within 4 years. 100% freshmen graduate within 6 years. 54% grads go on to further study within 1 year. 20% grads pursue arts and sciences degrees. 30% grads pursue law degrees. 40% grads pursue business degrees. 1% grads pursue medical degrees. **Faculty:** Student/faculty ratio 18:1. 18 full-time faculty, 17% hold PhDs, 6% are members of minority groups, 67% are women. 0% of classes are taught by teaching assistants.

ACADEMICS
Degrees: associate, bachelor's, certificate, first professional. **Classes:** Most classes have greater than 100 students. **Special Study Options:** distance learning, double major, dual enrollment, independent study, internships. **Career Services:** alumni services, internships, Career Services highlights include Internships.

FACILITIES
Housing: apartments for single students. 100% of campus accessible to physically disabled. CAMPUS LIFE
Environment: Village. **Activities:** literary magazine, student newspaper 3 registered organizations.

ADMISSIONS
Freshman Academic Profile: Average high school GPA 3.0. 0% in top 10% of high school class, 0% in top 25% of high school class, 15% in top 50% of high school class. 95% from public high schools. Minimum paper TOEFL 450. **Basis for Candidate Selection:** *Very important factors considered include:* interview. *Important factors considered include:* character/personal qualities. *Other factors considered include:* level of applicant's interest. **Freshman Admission Requirements:** High school diploma is required and GED is accepted. **Freshman Admission Statistics:** 143 applied, 81% admitted, 100% enrolled. **Transfer Admission Requirements:** High school transcript, college transcript(s), interview, minimum college GPA of 2.0 required. Lowest grade transferable C–. **General Admission Information:** Application Fee $35. Nonfall registration accepted. Admission may be deferred for a maximum of 5. Placement offered for CEEB Advanced Placement tests.

COSTS AND FINANCIAL AID
Average book expense. **Required Forms and Deadlines:** FAFSA. **Notification of Awards:** Types of Aid: *Need-based scholarships/grants:* Federal Pell, SEOG, state scholarships/grants, private scholarships. *Loans:* Subsidized Stafford, Unsubsidized Stafford, PLUS. **Student Employment:** Highest amount earned per year from on-campus jobs $1,603. Off-campus job opportunities are fair. **Financial Aid Statistics:** 100% freshmen, 100% undergrads receive need-based scholarship or grant aid. % freshmen, % undergrads receive non-need-based scholarship or grant aid. 23% freshmen, 7% undergrads receive need-based self-help aid. 98% freshmen, 98% undergrads receive any aid. 8% undergrads borrow to pay for school. Average cumulative indebtedness $28,000.

HUNTINGDON COLLEGE

1500 East Fairview Avenue, Montgomery, AL 36106-2148
Phone: 334-833-4497 • **Financial Aid Phone:** 334-833-4519
E-mail: admiss@huntingdon.edu • **CEEB Code:** 1303
Fax: 334-833-4347 • **Website:** www.huntingdon.edu • **ACT Code:** 18

This private school, affiliated with the Methodist Church, was founded in 1854. It has a 71-acre campus.

RATINGS
Admissions Selectivity Rating: 74   **Fire Safety Rating:** 96   **Green Rating:** 60*

STUDENTS AND FACULTY

Enrollment: 1,103. **Student Body:** 50% female, 50% male, 15% out-of-state, 0% international (5 countries represented). Asian 1%, African American 19%, Caucasian 52%, Hispanic 2%, Native American 0%.
Retention and Graduation: 55% freshmen return for sophomore year. 33% freshmen graduate within 4 years. 46% freshmen graduate within 6 years. 40% grads go on to further study within 1 year. 19% grads pursue arts and sciences degrees. 14% grads pursue law degrees. 11% grads pursue business degrees. 11% grads pursue medical degrees. **Faculty:** Student/faculty ratio 13:1. 51 full-time faculty, 90% hold PhDs, 4% are members of minority groups, 43% are women. 0% of classes are taught by teaching assistants.

ACADEMICS

Degrees: bachelor's. **Classes:** Most classes have fewer than 10 students. Most lab/discussion sessions have 10–19 students. **Majors with Highest Enrollment:** accounting; business/commerce; kinesiology and exercise science. **Special Study Options:** cross-registration, double major, honors program, independent study, internships, liberal arts/career combination, student-designed major, study abroad, teacher certification program, Adult Degree Completion Program in which students take classes only in the evening, all year long, dual engineering degree with Auburn University and exchange student program with universities Ireland; travel opportunities to all full-time junior and seniors within regular educational costs or for nominal additional fees. **Honors Programs:** Program Honors - An outstanding student in a particular major has the opportunity to create an individualized honors project within the major to meet a particular need and interest. **Disability Services:** Special programs offered to physically disabled students include note-taking services, reader services, tape recorders, tutors. **Career Services:** Alumni network, alumni services, career/job search classes, career assessment, internships Career Services highlights include The Internship program is exceptional. The Center for Career and Vocation currently has more internships and jobs than there are students and alumni needing such opportunities. Huntingdon College's partnership with the community and local business and industry is paying huge dividends for Huntingdon students, alumni and the College.

FACILITIES

Housing: Coed dorms, men's dorms, women's dorms. 85% of campus accessible to physically disabled. **Special Academic Facilities/Equipment:** 1. The Bowman Ecological Center is a protected area in Prattville, AL that provides space for students to collect and study samples of plants, trees, and aquatic life. 2. Sybil Smith Hall is a fully equipped music facility housing the Lucile Crowell Delchamps Recital Hall, the Julia Lightfoot Sellers Reception Hall, faculty offices and studios, rehersal rooms, classrooms, a modern electronic music laboratory, and one of the most extensive music collections in the South, with more than 10,000 records, CDs and tapes. 3. The Staton Center for Learning Enrichment Center oversees the Academic Success Centers, advises students who have not declared majors, provides academic counseling for students with provisional enrollment, serves as a resource for study halls as related to study skills and time management skills, and advises staff and faculty serving the First Year Experience (FYEx) program. 4. Leon and Myra Allman Ligon Chapel contains the newly expanded and installed Bellingrath Memorial Organ, which Dr. Harold Rohlig, professor of music, designed. The Bellingrath Memorial Organ is one of the largest of its kind among private colleges in the Southeast, with 141 ranks and a four-manual keyboard. The Chapel's Green Window, revered by alumni as a symbol of the Huntingdon experience, is framed by the new organ pipes, some of which are 32 feet in length. Ligon Chapel is the site of pageants, performances, lectures, convocations, concerts, and countless traditions at Huntingdon College. **Computers:** 40% of classrooms, 33% of dorms, 100% of libraries, 100% of dining areas, 100% of student union, have wireless network access. Administrative functions (other than registration) can be performed online. Undergraduates are required to own a computer.

CAMPUS LIFE

Environment: City. **Activities:** Choral groups, concert band, dance, drama/theater, literary magazine, marching band, music ensembles, pep band, student government, student newspaper, yearbook, Campus Ministries, International Student Organization, Model UN 50 registered organizations, 15 honor societies, 3 religious organizations. 4 fraternities, 4 sororities. **Athletics (Intercollegiate):** *Men:* baseball, basketball, cross-country, football, golf, soccer, tennis. *Women:* basketball, cross-country, golf, soccer, softball, tennis, volleyball. **On-Campus Highlights:** Flowers Hall, Houghton Memorial Library, Wilson Center, Carolyn & Wynton Blount (Residence) Hall, Julia Walker Russell Dining Hall.

ADMISSIONS

Freshman Academic Profile: Average high school GPA 3.3. 13% in top 10% of high school class, 32% in top 25% of high school class, 69% in top 50% of high school class. 80% from public high schools. SAT Math middle 50% range 408-513. SAT Critical Reading middle 50% range 428-500. ACT middle 50% range 19-24. Minimum web-based TOEFL 45. Minimum paper TOEFL 500. **Basis for Candidate Selection:** *Very important factors considered include:* academic GPA, standardized test scores. *Important factors considered include:*

rigor of secondary school record. *Other factors considered include:* Class rank, application essay, recommendation(s), interview. **Freshman Admission Requirements:** High school diploma is required and GED is accepted. **Freshman Admission Statistics:** 1,835 applied, 61% admitted, 25% enrolled. **Transfer Admission Requirements:** High school transcript, college transcript(s), statement of good standing from prior institution(s). Minimum college GPA of 2.25 required. Lowest grade transferable C. **General Admission Information:** Regular application deadline 8/15. Notification on a rolling basis, beginning on or about 9/7. Nonfall registration accepted. Admission may be deferred for a maximum of 2 semesters. Credit and/or placement offered for CEEB Advanced Placement tests.

COSTS AND FINANCIAL AID

Annual tuition $20,990. Room and board $8,000. Required fees $1,000. Average book expense $1,000. **Required Forms and Deadlines:** institution's own financial aid form. **Notification of Awards:** Applicants will be notified of awards on a rolling basis beginning 3/1. **Types of Aid:** *Need-based scholarships/grants:* Federal Pell, SEOG, state scholarships/grants, private scholarships, the school's own gift aid. *Loans:* Subsidized Stafford, Unsubsidized Stafford, PLUS, Federal Perkins. **Student Employment:** Federal Work-Study Program available. Institutional employment available. Off-campus job opportunities are excellent. **Financial Aid Statistics:** 100% freshmen, 98% undergrads receive need-based scholarship or grant aid. 13% freshmen, 14% undergrads receive non-need-based scholarship or grant aid. 79% freshmen, 79% undergrads receive need-based self-help aid. 100% freshmen, 99% undergrads receive any aid. 69% undergrads borrow to pay for school. Average cumulative indebtedness $21,034. **Criteria for awarding institutional aid:** *Non-need-based:* academics, alumni affiliation, leadership, music/drama, religious affiliation, state/district residency.

HUNTINGTON UNIVERSITY

2303 College Avenue, Huntington, IN 46750
Phone: 260-359-4000 • **Financial Aid Phone:** 800-642-6493
E-mail: admissions@huntington.edu • **CEEB Code:** 1304
Fax: 260-358-3699 • **Website:** www.huntington.edu • **ACT Code:** 1202

This private school, affiliated with the Protestant Church, was founded in 1897. It has a 170-acre campus.

RATINGS

Admissions Selectivity Rating: 65   **Fire Safety Rating:** 91   **Green Rating:** 61

STUDENTS AND FACULTY

Enrollment: 1,103. **Student Body:** 58% female, 42% male, 38% out-of-state, 3% international (19 countries represented). Asian 0%, African American 2%, Caucasian 91%, Hispanic 3%, Native American 0%.
Retention and Graduation: 73% freshmen return for sophomore year. 60% freshmen graduate within 4 years. 60% freshmen graduate within 6 years. 13% grads go on to further study within 1 year. 10% grads pursue arts and sciences degrees. 1% grads pursue law degrees. 1% grads pursue business degrees. 1% grads pursue medical degrees. **Faculty:** Student/faculty ratio 13:1. 58 full-time faculty, 79% hold PhDs, 5% are members of minority groups, 40% are women. 0% of classes are taught by teaching assistants.

ACADEMICS

Degrees: associate, bachelor's, diploma, master's, terminal associate, transfer associate. **Classes:** Most classes have 10–19 students. Most lab/discussion sessions have 10–19 students. **Majors with Highest Enrollment:** animation, interactive technology, video graphics and special effects; elementary education and teaching; nursing/registered nurse (rn, asn, bsn, msn). **Special Study Options:** Accelerated program, double major, independent study, internships, study abroad, teacher certification program, Bible and religion. **Disability Services:** Special programs offered to physically disabled students include note-taking services, reader services, tutors. **Career Services:** Alumni network, alumni services, career/job search classes, career assessment, internships, regional alumni. Career Services highlights include www.huntington.edu/erc/.

FACILITIES

Housing: special housing for disabled students, men's dorms, women's dorms, apartments for single students, college-owned houses. 62% of campus accessible to physically disabled. **Special Academic Facilities/Equipment:** Thornhill Nature Preserve **Computers:** 100% of classrooms, 100% of dorms, 100% of libraries, 100% of dining areas, 100% of student union, have wireless network access. Students can register for classes online. Administrative functions (other than registration) can be performed online.

CAMPUS LIFE

Environment: Town. **Activities:** Choral groups, concert band, dance, drama/theater, jazz band, literary magazine, music ensembles, musical theater, pep band, radio station, student government, student newspaper, student-run film society, television station, yearbook, Campus Ministries, International Student Organization 6 honor societies, 4 religious organizations. **Athletics (Intercollegiate):** *Men:* baseball, basketball, cheerleading, cross-country, golf, soccer, tennis, track/field (outdoor), track/field (indoor). *Women:* basketball, cheerleading, cross-country, golf, soccer, softball, tennis, track/field (outdoor), track/field (indoor), volleyball. **On-Campus Highlights:** Residence Halls-lounges, Habecker Dining Commons, Norm's Place-snack lounge, Merillat Complex for Physical EducationandRecreation, Merillat Centre for the Arts. **Environmental Initiatives:** Campus recycling program.

ADMISSIONS

Freshman Academic Profile: Average high school GPA 3.5. 22% in top 10% of high school class, 48% in top 25% of high school class, 83% in top 50% of high school class. SAT Math middle 50% range 453-568. SAT Critical Reading middle 50% range 450-568. SAT Writing middle 50% range 430-550. ACT middle 50% range 21-27. Minimum web-based TOEFL 75. Minimum paper TOEFL 525. **Basis for Candidate Selection:** *Very important factors considered include:* academic GPA, rigor of secondary school record, standardized test scores, religious affiliation/commitment. *Important factors considered include:* Class rank, application essay, character/personal qualities, extracurricular activities. *Other factors considered include:* recommendation(s), alumni/ae relation, first generation, interview, level of applicant's interest, racial/ethnic status, talent/ability, volunteer work, work experience. **Freshman Admission Requirements:** High school diploma is required and GED is accepted. *Academic units required:* 4 English, 3 mathematics, 2 science, (1 science labs), 2 social studies, 2 history. *Academic units recommended:* 4 English, 3 mathematics, 2 science, (1 science labs), 2 social studies, 2 history. **Freshman Admission Statistics:** 824 applied, 97% admitted, 30% enrolled. **Transfer Admission Requirements:** college transcript(s), essay or personal statement, minimum college GPA of 2.0 required. Lowest grade transferable C. **General Admission Information:** Application Fee $20. Regular application deadline 8/1. Notification on a rolling basis, beginning on or about 10/1. Nonfall registration accepted. Admission may be deferred for a maximum of 1 year. Credit and/or placement offered for CEEB Advanced Placement tests.

COSTS AND FINANCIAL AID

Annual tuition $23,300. Room and board $8,180. Required fees $740. Average book expense $1,000. **Required Forms and Deadlines:** FAFSA. **Notification of Awards:** Applicants will be notified of awards on a rolling basis beginning 3/1. **Types of Aid:** *Need-based scholarships/grants:* Federal Pell, SEOG, state scholarships/grants, private scholarships, the school's own gift aid. *Loans:* Subsidized Stafford, Unsubsidized Stafford, PLUS, Federal Perkins. **Student Employment:** Federal Work-Study Program available. Institutional employment available. Highest amount earned per year from on-campus jobs $3,500. Off-campus job opportunities are good. **Financial Aid Statistics:** 97% freshmen, 92% undergrads receive need-based scholarship or grant aid. 14% freshmen, 13% undergrads receive non-need-based scholarship or grant aid. 93% freshmen, 91% undergrads receive need-based self-help aid. 5% freshmen, 4% undergrads receive athletic scholarships. 90% freshmen, 90% undergrads receive any aid. 66% undergrads borrow to pay for school. Average cumulative indebtedness $31,149. **Criteria for awarding institutional aid:** *Non-need-based:* academics, alumni affiliation, art, athletics, leadership, music/drama, religious affiliation.

HUSSON UNIVERSITY

1 College Circle, Bangor, ME 4401
Phone: 207-941-7100 • **Financial Aid Phone:** 207-941-7156
E-mail: admit@husson.edu • **CEEB Code:** 3440
Fax: 207-941-7935 • **Website:** www.husson.edu • **ACT Code:** 1646

This private school was founded in 1898. It has a 170-acre campus.

RATINGS

Admissions Selectivity Rating: 68   **Fire Safety Rating:** 98   **Green Rating:** 71

STUDENTS AND FACULTY

Enrollment: 2,384. **Student Body:** 58% female, 42% male, 15% out-of-state, 2% international (15 countries represented). Asian 1%, African American 4%, Caucasian 88%, Hispanic 1%, Native American 1%.
Retention and Graduation: 72% freshmen return for sophomore year. 23% freshmen graduate within 4 years. 41% freshmen graduate within 6 years.
Faculty: Student/faculty ratio 16:1. 118 full-time faculty, 67% hold PhDs, 6% are members of minority groups, 49% are women. 0% of classes are taught by teaching assistants.

ACADEMICS

Degrees: associate, bachelor's, certificate, diploma, master's, post-master's certificate, terminal associate. **Classes:** Most classes have 20–29 students. Most lab/discussion sessions have fewer than 10 students. **Majors with Highest Enrollment:** business/commerce; nursing/registered nurse (rn, asn, bsn, msn); physical therapy/therapist. **Special Study Options:** Accelerated program, cooperative education program, distance learning, double major, dual enrollment, independent study, internships, liberal arts/career combination, student-designed major, teacher certification program, weekend college. **Combined Degree Programs:** BS/BS, BS/MS, DPT/BS. **Disability Services:** Special programs offered to physically disabled students include note-taking services, tape recorders, tutors. **Career Services:** Alumni network, career/job search classes, internships.

FACILITIES

Housing: Coed dorms, special housing for disabled students 85% of campus accessible to physically disabled. **Special Academic Facilities/Equipment:** White Art Gallery Dahl Anatomy Lab Kenduskeag Research Institute Gracie Theater **Computers:** 100% of classrooms, 100% of dorms, 100% of libraries, 100% of student union, have wireless network access. Students can register for classes online. Administrative functions (other than registration) can be performed online.

CAMPUS LIFE

Environment: City. **Activities:** drama/theater, literary magazine, pep band, radio station, student government, student newspaper, television station, yearbook, Campus Ministries, International Student Organization 30 registered organizations, 1 honor societies, 2 religious organizations. 2 fraternities, 3 sororities. **Athletics (Intercollegiate):** *Men:* baseball, basketball, football, golf, lacrosse, soccer. *Women:* basketball, field hockey, lacrosse, soccer, softball, swimming, tennis, volleyball. **On-Campus Highlights:** Swan Fitness Center, Campus Center, Student Lounge, Newman Gym, Library, The Meeting House, a new academic building, opened in the fall of 2008. The attached 500-seat balconied, performing arts center opened in the fall of 2009. **Environmental Initiatives:** Green Cleaning Supplies Recycle Paper Reduce printing, set maximum limit.

ADMISSIONS

Freshman Academic Profile: Average high school GPA 3.0. 13% in top 10% of high school class, 44% in top 25% of high school class, 81% in top 50% of high school class. 87% from public high schools. SAT Math middle 50% range 430-530. SAT Critical Reading middle 50% range 410-510. SAT Writing middle 50% range 400-510. ACT middle 50% range 19-23. Minimum paper TOEFL 500. **Basis for Candidate Selection:** *Very important factors considered include:* recommendation(s), rigor of secondary school record, interview. *Important factors considered include:* Class rank, application essay, academic GPA, standardized test scores, character/personal qualities, extracurricular activities. *Other factors considered include:* alumni/ae relation, first generation, level of applicant's interest, volunteer work, work experience. **Freshman Admission Requirements:** High school diploma is required and GED is accepted. **Freshman Admission Statistics:** 1,489 applied, 78% admitted, 32% enrolled. **Transfer Admission Requirements:** High school transcript, college transcript(s), essay or personal statement, minimum college GPA of 2.0 required. Lowest grade transferable C. **General Admission Information:** Application Fee $25. Notification on a rolling basis, beginning on or about 12/1. Nonfall registration accepted. Admission may be deferred for a maximum of 1 year. Credit and/or placement offered for CEEB Advanced Placement tests.

COSTS AND FINANCIAL AID

Annual tuition $14,190. Room and board $7,900. Required fees $350. Average book expense $1,150. **Required Forms and Deadlines:** FAFSA. **Notification of Awards:** Applicants will be notified of awards on a rolling basis beginning 3/1. **Types of Aid:** *Need-based scholarships/grants:* Federal Pell, SEOG, state scholarships/grants, private scholarships, the school's own gift aid. *Loans:* Subsidized Stafford, Unsubsidized Stafford, PLUS, Federal Perkins, state loans. **Student Employment:** Federal Work-Study Program available. Institutional employment available. Highest amount earned per year from on-campus jobs $1,600. Off-campus job opportunities are good. **Financial Aid Statistics:** 97% freshmen, 92% undergrads receive need-based scholarship or grant aid. 1% freshmen, 2% undergrads receive non-need-based scholarship or grant aid. 97% freshmen, 95% undergrads receive need-based self-help aid. 82% freshmen, 80% undergrads receive any aid. 98% undergrads borrow to pay for school. Average cumulative indebtedness $25,724. **Criteria for awarding institutional aid:** *Non-need-based:* academics, leadership.

HUSTON-TILLOTSON UNIVERSITY

900 Chicon Street, Austin, TX 78702
Phone: 512-505-3028 • **Financial Aid Phone:** 512-505-3028
E-mail: admission@htu.edu • **CEEB Code:** 6280
Fax: 512-505-3192 • **Website:** www.htu.edu./ • **ACT Code:** 4104

This private school was founded in 1875. It has a 35-acre campus.

RATINGS
Admissions Selectivity Rating: 64   **Fire Safety Rating:** 60*   **Green Rating:** 60*

STUDENTS AND FACULTY
Enrollment: 889. **Student Body:** 51% female, 49% male, 3% out-of-state, 3% international (11 countries represented). African American 72%, Caucasian 5%, Hispanic 19%.
Retention and Graduation: 50% freshmen return for sophomore year. 12% freshmen graduate within 4 years. 24% freshmen graduate within 6 years. **Faculty:** Student/faculty ratio 15:1. 47 full-time faculty, 70% hold PhDs, 57% are members of minority groups, 53% are women. 0% of classes are taught by teaching assistants.

ACADEMICS
Degrees: bachelor's, post-bachelor's certificate. **Classes:** Most classes have fewer than 10 students. Most lab/discussion sessions have fewer than 10 students. **Majors with Highest Enrollment:** computer and information science; education. **Special Study Options:** cross-registration, distance learning, double major, dual enrollment, external degree program, honors program, independent study, internships, liberal arts/career combination, study abroad, teacher certification program, 3-2 Engineering Program with Prairie View A&M University.

FACILITIES
Housing: men's dorms, women's dorms.

CAMPUS LIFE
Environment: Activities: Choral groups, dance, jazz band, literary magazine, music ensembles, student government, student-run film society, Campus Ministries, International Student Organization 17 registered organizations, 5 honor societies, 5 religious organizations. **Athletics (Intercollegiate):** *Men:* baseball, basketball, soccer, track/field (outdoor). *Women:* basketball, track/field (outdoor), volleyball.

ADMISSIONS
Freshman Academic Profile: Average high school GPA 2.8. 6% in top 10% of high school class, 12% in top 25% of high school class, 53% in top 50% of high school class. % from public high schools. SAT Math middle 50% range 360-460. SAT Critical Reading middle 50% range 350-460. ACT middle 50% range 14-19. Minimum web-based TOEFL 61. Minimum paper TOEFL 500. **Basis for Candidate Selection:** *Very important factors considered include:* rigor of secondary school record, standardized test scores. *Important factors considered include:* application essay, academic GPA, interview, religious affiliation/ commitment. *Other factors considered include:* recommendation(s), alumni/ ae relation, extracurricular activities, talent/ability. **Freshman Admission Requirements:** High school diploma is required and GED is accepted. *Academic units required:* 4 English, 3 mathematics, 2 science, 3 social studies, 1 computer science, 2 health, P.E. *Academic units recommended:* 4 English, 3 mathematics, 2 science, 3 social studies, 1 computer science, 2 health, P.E. **Freshman Admission Statistics:** 652 applied, 96% admitted, 43% enrolled. **Transfer Admission Requirements:** college transcript(s), essay or personal statement, minimum college GPA of 2.0 required. Lowest grade transferable C. **General Admission Information:** Application Fee $25. Regular application deadline 7/1. Notification on a rolling basis, beginning on or about 1/1. Nonfall registration accepted. Admission may be deferred for a maximum of 1 Year. Credit and/ or placement offered for CEEB Advanced Placement tests.

COSTS AND FINANCIAL AID
Annual tuition $10,396. Room and board $6,946. Required fees $2,034. Average book expense $600. **Required Forms and Deadlines:** FAFSA, institution's own financial aid form. **Notification of Awards:** Applicants will be notified of awards on a rolling basis beginning 4/1. **Types of Aid:** *Need-based scholarships/ grants:* Federal Pell, SEOG, state scholarships/grants, private scholarships, the school's own gift aid, United Negro College Fund. *Loans:* Direct Subsidized Stafford, Direct Unsubsidized Stafford, Direct PLUS, Subsidized Stafford, Unsubsidized Stafford, PLUS, state loans, Private Loans. **Student Employment:** Federal Work-Study Program available. Off-campus job opportunities are good. **Financial Aid Statistics:** 25% freshmen, 33% undergrads receive need-based scholarship or grant aid. 33% freshmen, 35% undergrads receive non-need-based scholarship or grant aid. 100% freshmen, 100% undergrads receive need-based self-help aid. 15% freshmen, 14% undergrads receive athletic

scholarships. 97% undergrads receive any aid. 89% undergrads borrow to pay for school. Average cumulative indebtedness $9,250. **Criteria for awarding institutional aid:** *Non-need-based:* academics, alumni affiliation, art, athletics, job skills, leadership, minority status, music/drama, religious affiliation, state/ district residency.

IDAHO STATE UNIVERSITY

Museum of National History 319, Pocatello, ID 83209-8270
Phone: 208-282-2475 • **Financial Aid Phone:** 208-282-2981
E-mail: info@isu.edu • **CEEB Code:** 4355
Fax: 208-282-4231 • **Website:** www.isu.edu • **ACT Code:** 918

This public school was founded in 1901. It has a 1100-acre campus.

RATINGS
Admissions Selectivity Rating: 69   **Fire Safety Rating:** 65   **Green Rating:** 61

STUDENTS AND FACULTY
Enrollment: 10,034. **Student Body:** 54% female, 46% male, 6% out-of-state, 1% international (63 countries represented). Asian 2%, African American 1%, Caucasian 82%, Hispanic 6%, Native American 2%.
Retention and Graduation: 60% freshmen return for sophomore year. 4% freshmen graduate within 4 years. 18% freshmen graduate within 6 years. **Faculty:** Student/faculty ratio 16:1. 602 full-time faculty, 76% hold PhDs, 7% are members of minority groups, 43% are women.

ACADEMICS
Degrees: associate, bachelor's, certificate, doctoral, master's, post-bachelor's certificate, post-master's certificate. **Classes:** Most classes have 10–19 students. Most lab/discussion sessions have 20–29 students. **Special Study Options:** Accelerated program, cooperative education program, cross-registration, distance learning, double major, dual enrollment, English as a Second Language (ESL), exchange student program (domestic), honors program, independent study, internships, liberal arts/career combination, student-designed major, study abroad, teacher certification program, weekend college. **Honors Programs:** Honors courses are offered in small classes and deal with interdisciplinary issues and confront some aspect of the human condition. Innovative teaching and assignments are encourages and interaction with faculty and class members is lively. **Combined Degree Programs:** BA/MA, BS/MS in chemistry. **Disability Services:** Special programs offered to physically disabled students include note-taking services, reader services, tape recorders, tutors.

FACILITIES
Housing: Coed dorms, special housing for disabled students, men's dorms, women's dorms, fraternity/sorority housing, apartments for married students, apartments for single students, Graduate Student Housing. 100% of campus accessible to physically disabled. **Special Academic Facilities/Equipment:** Museum of Natural History, Idaho Accelerator Center, Rendezvous Center **Computers:** Students can register for classes online. Administrative functions (other than registration) can be performed online.

CAMPUS LIFE
Environment: Town. **Activities:** Choral groups, concert band, dance, drama/ theater, jazz band, marching band, music ensembles, musical theater, opera, pep band, radio station, student government, student newspaper, symphony orchestra, television station, yearbook, Campus Ministries, International Student Organization 134 registered organizations, 8 honor societies, 7 religious organizations. 2 fraternities, 3 sororities. **Athletics (Intercollegiate):** *Men:* basketball, cheerleading, cross-country, football, golf, tennis, track/field (outdoor). *Women:* basketball, cheerleading, cross-country, golf, soccer, softball, tennis, track/field (outdoor), volleyball. **On-Campus Highlights:** Idaho Museum of Natural History, Rock Climbing Wall at Reed Gym, L.E. and Thelma E Stephens performing Ar, Rendezvous Center, Particle Accelerator.

ADMISSIONS
Freshman Academic Profile: Average high school GPA 3.2. 13% in top 10% of high school class, 31% in top 25% of high school class, 61% in top 50% of high school class. SAT Math middle 50% range 470-570. SAT Writing middle 50% range 460-600. ACT middle 50% range 18-24. Minimum web-based TOEFL 61. Minimum paper TOEFL 500. **Basis for Candidate Selection:** *Other factors considered include:* academic GPA, standardized test scores. **Freshman Admission Requirements:** High school diploma is required and GED is accepted. *Academic units required:* 4 English, 3 mathematics, 3 science, (1 science labs), 1 foreign language. *Academic units recommended:* 4 English, 3 mathematics, 3 science, (1 science labs), 1 foreign language. **Freshman Admission Statistics:** 3,889 applied, 73% admitted, 67% enrolled. **Transfer Admission Requirements:** High school transcript, college transcript(s), standardized test scores, minimum college GPA of 2.0 required. Lowest grade

transferable D. **General Admission Information:** Application Fee $40. Notification on a rolling basis, beginning on or about 3/1. Nonfall registration accepted. Admission may be deferred for a maximum of 3 years. Credit and/or placement offered for CEEB Advanced Placement tests.

COSTS AND FINANCIAL AID

Annual in-state tuition $3,318. Annual out-of-state tuition $13,120. Room and board $5,050. Required fees $1,650. Average book expense $900. **Required Forms and Deadlines:** FAFSA. **Notification of Awards:** Applicants will be notified of awards on a rolling basis beginning 4/1. **Types of Aid:** *Need-based scholarships/grants:* Federal Pell, SEOG, state scholarships/grants, private scholarships, the school's own gift aid, Federal Nursing Scholarships. *Loans:* Direct Subsidized Stafford, Direct Unsubsidized Stafford, Direct PLUS, Federal Perkins. **Student Employment:** Off-campus job opportunities are good. **Criteria for awarding institutional aid:** *Non-need-based:* academics, alumni affiliation, art, athletics, leadership, minority status, music/drama, state/district residency.

ILLINOIS COLLEGE

1101 West College, Jacksonville, IL 62650
Phone: 217-245-3030
E-mail: admissions@ic.edu • **CEEB Code:** 1315
Fax: 217-245-3034 • **Website:** www.ic.edu • **ACT Code:** 1034

This private school, affiliated with the Presbyterian Church, was founded in 1829. It has a 62-acre campus.

RATINGS
Admissions Selectivity Rating: 85   **Fire Safety Rating:** 60*   **Green Rating:** 60*

STUDENTS AND FACULTY

Enrollment: 854. **Student Body:** 50% female, 50% male, 10% out-of-state, 3% international. Asian 1%, African American 5%, Caucasian 82%, Hispanic 2%, Native American 1%.
Retention and Graduation: 83% freshmen return for sophomore year. 50% freshmen graduate within 4 years. 60% freshmen graduate within 6 years. 22% grads go on to further study within 1 year. 13% grads pursue arts and sciences degrees. 5% grads pursue law degrees. 2% grads pursue business degrees. 4% grads pursue medical degrees. **Faculty:** Student/faculty ratio 11:1. 74 full-time faculty, 84% hold PhDs, 9% are members of minority groups, 50% are women.

ACADEMICS

Degrees: bachelor's. **Classes:** Most classes have 10–19 students. Most lab/discussion sessions have 10–19 students. **Special Study Options:** cross-registration, double major, dual enrollment, independent study, internships, liberal arts/career combination, student-designed major, study abroad, teacher certification program. **Combined Degree Programs:** 3-2 nursing, 3-2 occupational ther and 3-1 med-tech. **Career Services:** career/job search classes, career assessment, internships.

FACILITIES

Housing: Coed dorms, men's dorms, women's dorms, apartments for single students. **Special Academic Facilities/Equipment:** Art gallery, language lab.

CAMPUS LIFE

Environment: Rural. **Activities:** Choral groups, concert band, drama/theater, literary magazine, music ensembles, student government, student newspaper, yearbook, Campus Ministries, International Student Organization, Model UN 72 registered organizations, 12 honor societies, 3 religious organizations. 4 fraternities, 3 sororities. **Athletics (Intercollegiate):** *Men:* baseball, basketball, cross-country, football, golf, soccer, tennis, track/field (outdoor), track/field (indoor), wrestling. *Women:* basketball, cheerleading, cross-country, golf, soccer, softball, tennis, track/field (outdoor), track/field (indoor), volleyball.

ADMISSIONS

Freshman Academic Profile: Average high school GPA 3.4. 26% in top 10% of high school class, 56% in top 25% of high school class, 85% in top 50% of high school class. 80% from public high schools. ACT middle 50% range 21-27. Minimum paper TOEFL 550. **Basis for Candidate Selection:** *Very important factors considered include:* academic GPA, rigor of secondary school record, character/personal qualities. *Important factors considered include:* Class rank, application essay, recommendation(s), extracurricular activities, interview, state residency, talent/ability. *Other factors considered include:* standardized test scores, alumni/ae relation, first generation, geographical residence, level of applicant's interest, racial/ethnic status, volunteer work, work experience. **Freshman Admission Requirements:** High school diploma is required and GED is accepted. *Academic units required:* 4 English, 3 mathematics, 2 science, (2 science labs), 1 social studies, 1 history, 3 academic electives. *Academic units*

recommended: 4 English, 3 mathematics, 2 science, (2 science labs), 1 social studies, 1 history, 3 academic electives. **Freshman Admission Statistics:** 1,313 applied, 55% admitted, 31% enrolled. **Transfer Admission Requirements:** High school transcript, college transcript(s), minimum college GPA of 2.50 required. Lowest grade transferable C. **General Admission Information:** Notification on a rolling basis, beginning on or about 11/15. Nonfall registration accepted. Admission may be deferred for a maximum of 1 year. Credit and/or placement offered for CEEB Advanced Placement tests.

COSTS AND FINANCIAL AID

Annual tuition $26,000. Room and board $8,500. Required fees $500. Average book expense $900. **Required Forms and Deadlines:** FAFSA. **Notification of Awards:** Applicants will be notified of awards on a rolling basis beginning 3/1. **Types of Aid:** *Need-based scholarships/grants:* Federal Pell, SEOG, state scholarships/grants, private scholarships, the school's own gift aid. *Loans:* Direct Subsidized Stafford, Direct Unsubsidized Stafford, Direct PLUS, Federal Perkins. **Student Employment:** Federal Work-Study Program available. Institutional employment available. Highest amount earned per year from on-campus jobs $800. Off-campus job opportunities are good. **Financial Aid Statistics:** 100% freshmen, 100% undergrads receive need-based scholarship or grant aid. 15% freshmen, 13% undergrads receive non-need-based scholarship or grant aid. 84% freshmen, 86% undergrads receive need-based self-help aid. 79% undergrads borrow to pay for school. Average cumulative indebtedness $29,762. **Criteria for awarding institutional aid:** *Non-need-based:* academics, art, minority status, music/drama.

ILLINOIS INSTITUTE OF TECHNOLOGY

Best 378

10 West 33rd Street, Chicago, IL 60616
Phone: 312-567-3025 • **Financial Aid Phone:** 312-567-7219
E-mail: admission@iit.edu • **CEEB Code:** 1318
Fax: 312-567-6939 • **Website:** www.iit.edu/ • **ACT Code:** 1040

This private school was founded in 1892. It has a 120-acre campus.

RATINGS
Admissions Selectivity Rating: 91   **Fire Safety Rating:** 73   **Green Rating:** 89

STUDENTS AND FACULTY

Enrollment: 2,731. **Student Body:** 31% female, 69% male, 23% out-of-state, 23% international (94 countries represented). Asian 10%, African American 7%, Caucasian 39%, Hispanic 13%, Native American 0%.
Retention and Graduation: 92% freshmen return for sophomore year. 38% freshmen graduate within 4 years. 68% freshmen graduate within 6 years. **Faculty:** Student/faculty ratio 12:1. 411 full-time faculty, 82% hold PhDs, 4% are members of minority groups, 26% are women. 0% of classes are taught by teaching assistants.

ACADEMICS

Degrees: bachelor's, master's. **Classes:** Most classes have 10–19 students. Most lab/discussion sessions have 20–29 students. **Majors with Highest Enrollment:** architecture (barch, ba/bs, march, ma/ms, phd); electrical, electronics and communications engineering; mechanical engineering. **Special Study Options:** cooperative education program, cross-registration, distance learning, double major, English as a Second Language (ESL), independent study, liberal arts/career combination, study abroad, teacher certification program, Joint enrollment: Enrollment at 2 institutions for 2 degrees. **Honors Programs:** Honors Pharmacy Program, and Honors Medical Program, Honors Law Program, Business Honors Law Program **Combined Degree Programs:** BS/MBA; BS/JD; BArch/MS; BArch/MBA; BS/MS; BS/MPA. **Disability Services:** Special programs offered to physically disabled students include note-taking services, reader services, tape recorders, tutors. **Career Services:** Alumni network, alumni services, career/job search classes, career assessment, internships, regional alumni. Career Services highlights include Co-operative Education.

FACILITIES

Housing: Coed dorms, fraternity/sorority housing, Men's/women's floors in residence halls, university apartments, arrangements for disabled students. 90% of campus accessible to physically disabled. **Special Academic Facilities/Equipment:** The Center for Accelerator and Particle Physics (CAPP), The Center for Complex Systems and Dynamics (CCSD), The Center for Digital Design and Manufacturing (CDDM), The Center for Electrochemical Science and Engineering, The Center for Excellence in Polymer Science and

Engineering, The Center for Integrative Neuroscience and Neuroengineering Research, The Center for the Management of Medical Technology (CMMT), The Center for Molecular Study of Soft Condensed Matter (CMS2), The Center for Strategic Competitiveness (CSC), The Center for the Study of Ethics in the Professions (CSEP), The Center for Synchrotron Radiation Research and Instrumentation, The Center for Work Zone Safety and Mobility (CWZSM), Electric Power and Power Electronics Center (EPPEC), Energy + Power Center, Energy and Sustainability Institute, The Engineering Center For Diabetes Research and Education (ECDRE), The Fluid Dynamics Research Center, The High Performance Computing Center (HPCC), IIT Research Institute (IITRI), The International Center for Sensor Science and Engineering (ICSSE), The International Center for Sustainable New Cities (ICSNC), The Medical Imaging Research Center (MIRC), The National Center for Food Safety and Technology (NCFST), The Particle Technology and Crystallization Center (PTCC), The Pritzker Institute of Biomedical Science and Engineering, The Thermal Processing Technology Center (TPTC), The Wireless Network and Communications Research Center (WiNCom), Main Campus design by Ludwig Mies van der Rohe, McCormick Tribune Campus Center (MTCC) design by Rem Koolhaas, residence hall designed by Helmut Jahn, IIT Research Institute (IITRI), University Technology Park At IIT (UTP), Kemper Room Art Gallery, Illinois Tech Model Railroad (ITMR) **Computers:** 100% of classrooms, 100% of dorms, 100% of libraries, 100% of dining areas, 100% of student union, have wireless network access. Students can register for classes online. Administrative functions (other than registration) can be performed online.

CAMPUS LIFE

Environment: Metropolis. **Activities:** Choral groups, concert band, dance, drama/theater, literary magazine, music ensembles, musical theater, radio station, student government, student newspaper, student-run film society, television station, yearbook, Campus Ministries, International Student Organization 100 registered organizations, 4 honor societies, 10 religious organizations. 7 fraternities, 3 sororities. **Athletics (Intercollegiate):** *Men:* baseball, cross-country, diving, soccer, swimming. *Women:* cross-country, diving, soccer, swimming, volleyball. **On-Campus Highlights:** S.R. Crown Hall (Architecture Building), McCormick Tribune Center, Keating Athletic Center, Hermann Hall, State Street Village. **Environmental Initiatives:** Creation of an Office of Campus Energy and Sustainability and the Wanger Institute of Sustainable Energy Research bringing students, faculty, staff, and alumni together to address complex sustainability issues. Implementation of a smart-micro grid on campus encompassing smart metering, energy efficiency, wind power, solar and on-site storage. Recycling Expansion: In 2008, IIT re-invigorated its recycling program under the banner of IIT Hawk Recycling and expanded into other areas to include other recyclables such as glass, cans, and batteries in addition to the paper and e-waste programs already in existence. In 2009, the program was expanded to include all campus academic, support and residence buildings and is anticipated to include all research buildings by May 2010. IIT projects an annual improvement between 5-10% in recycling rates due to the expanded program. The recycling effort will avoid approximately 750 cubic yards of landfill waste per year. Recycling reports are available to the campus community, as well as details on where recycled material ends up, at www.iit.edu/recycling. In addition, IIT has implemented commercial composting and on-site composting to eliminate landfilling of recyclable food waste.

ADMISSIONS

Freshman Academic Profile: Average high school GPA 3.9. 51% in top 10% of high school class, 82% in top 25% of high school class, 98% in top 50% of high school class. 74% from public high schools. SAT Math middle 50% range 610-710. SAT Critical Reading middle 50% range 513-630. SAT Writing middle 50% range 520-640. ACT middle 50% range 24-30. Minimum web-based TOEFL 80. Minimum paper TOEFL 550. **Basis for Candidate Selection:** *Very important factors considered include:* academic GPA, rigor of secondary school record. *Important factors considered include:* Class rank, application essay, recommendation(s), standardized test scores. *Other factors considered include:* alumni/ae relation, character/personal qualities, extracurricular activities, first generation, interview, level of applicant's interest, talent/ability, volunteer work, work experience. **Freshman Admission Requirements:** High school diploma is required and GED is accepted. *Academic units required:* 4 English, 4 mathematics, 3 science, (2 science labs), 2 foreign language, 2 social studies. *Academic units recommended:* 4 English, 4 mathematics, 3 science, (2 science labs), 2 foreign language, 2 social studies. **Freshman Admission Statistics:** 2,597 applied, 55% admitted, 29% enrolled. **Transfer Admission Requirements:** college transcript(s), essay or personal statement, statement of good standing from prior institution(s). Minimum college GPA of 3.0 required. Lowest grade transferable C. **General Admission Information:** Early decision application deadline 11/9. Notification on a rolling basis, beginning on or about 10/10. Nonfall registration accepted. Admission may be deferred for a maximum of 1 Year. Credit and/or placement offered for CEEB Advanced Placement tests.

COSTS AND FINANCIAL AID

Annual tuition $37,039. Average book expense. **Required Forms and Deadlines:** FAFSA. **Notification of Awards:** Applicants will be notified of awards on a rolling basis beginning 3/1. **Types of Aid:** *Need-based scholarships/grants:* Federal Pell, SEOG, state scholarships/grants, private scholarships, the school's own gift aid. *Loans:* Subsidized Stafford, Unsubsidized Stafford, PLUS, Federal Perkins, college/university loans from institutional funds. **Student Employment:** Federal Work-Study Program available. Institutional employment available. Off-campus job opportunities are good. **Financial Aid Statistics:** 100% freshmen, 79% undergrads receive need-based scholarship or grant aid. 14% freshmen, 11% undergrads receive non-need-based scholarship or grant aid. 72% freshmen, 9% undergrads receive need-based self-help aid. 3% freshmen, 2% undergrads receive athletic scholarships. 100% freshmen, 99% undergrads receive any aid. 62% undergrads borrow to pay for school. Average cumulative indebtedness $29,581. **Criteria for awarding institutional aid:** *Non-need-based:* academics, alumni affiliation, athletics, leadership, minority status.

ILLINOIS STATE UNIVERSITY

Office of Admissions, Normal, IL 61790-2200
Phone: 309-438-2181 • **Financial Aid Phone:** 309-438-2231
E-mail: admissions@illinoisstate.edu • **CEEB Code:** 1319
Fax: 309-438-3932 • **Website:** www.ilstu.edu • **ACT Code:** 1042

This public school was founded in 1857. It has a 850-acre campus.

RATINGS
Admissions Selectivity Rating: 79   **Fire Safety Rating:** 70   **Green Rating:** 83

STUDENTS AND FACULTY
Enrollment: 18,526. **Student Body:** 55% female, 45% male, 2% out-of-state, 1% international (59 countries represented). Asian 2%, African American 6%, Caucasian 82%, Hispanic 6%, Native American 0%.
Retention and Graduation: 85% freshmen return for sophomore year. 44% freshmen graduate within 4 years. **Faculty:** Student/faculty ratio 19:1. 882 full-time faculty, 84% hold PhDs, 15% are members of minority groups, 48% are women. 7% of classes are taught by teaching assistants.

ACADEMICS
Degrees: bachelor's, master's, post-bachelor's certificate, post-master's certificate. **Classes:** Most classes have 20–29 students. Most lab/discussion sessions have 20–29 students. **Majors with Highest Enrollment:** business administration and management; elementary education and teaching; special education and teaching. **Special Study Options:** Accelerated program, cooperative education program, distance learning, double major, dual enrollment, English as a Second Language (ESL), exchange student program (domestic), honors program, independent study, internships, student-designed major, study abroad, teacher certification program. **Combined Degree Programs:** BS/MPA. **Disability Services:** Special programs offered to physically disabled students include note-taking services, reader services, tape recorders, tutors. **Career Services:** alumni services, internships.

FACILITIES
Housing: Coed dorms, special housing for disabled students, special housing for international students, women's dorms, fraternity/sorority housing, apartments for married students, apartments for single students. 100% of campus accessible to physically disabled. **Special Academic Facilities/Equipment:** Art gallery, cultural museums, on-campus elementary and secondary schools, greenhouse, farm, planetarium. **Computers:** 100% of classrooms, 100% of dorms, 100% of libraries, 100% of dining areas, 100% of student union, have wireless network access. Students can register for classes online. Administrative functions (other than registration) can be performed online. Undergraduates are required to own a computer.

CAMPUS LIFE
Environment: City. **Activities:** Choral groups, concert band, dance, drama/theater, jazz band, literary magazine, marching band, music ensembles, musical theater, pep band, radio station, student government, student newspaper, student-run film society, symphony orchestra, television station 270 registered organizations, 23 honor societies, 22 religious organizations. 21 fraternities, 17 sororities. **Athletics (Intercollegiate):** *Men:* baseball, basketball, cheerleading, cross-country, football, golf, tennis, track/field (outdoor), track/field (indoor). *Women:* basketball, cheerleading, cross-country, diving, golf, gymnastics, soccer, softball, swimming, tennis, track/field (outdoor), track/field (indoor), volleyball. **On-Campus Highlights:** College of Business Building, Science Laboratory Building, Redbird Arena **Environmental Initiatives:** Establishing a formal Office of Sustainability with 2 full time staff, 1 graduate assistant and multiple interns. The development of a sustainability across the curriculum summer workshop for faculty Launch of a community wide food waste composting operation at the University Farm.

ADMISSIONS

Freshman Academic Profile: Average high school GPA 3.3. 87% from public high schools. ACT middle 50% range 22-26. Minimum paper TOEFL 550. **Basis for Candidate Selection:** *Very important factors considered include:* academic GPA, rigor of secondary school record, standardized test scores. *Important factors considered include:* application essay. *Other factors considered include:* Class rank, character/personal qualities, first generation, talent/ability. **Freshman Admission Requirements:** High school diploma is required and GED is accepted. *Academic units required:* 4 English, 3 mathematics, 2 science, (2 science labs), 2 foreign language, 2 social studies, 2 academic electives. 4 English, 3 mathematics, 2 science, (2 science labs), 2 foreign language, 2 social studies, 2 academic electives. **Freshman Admission Statistics:** 13,156 applied, 63% admitted, 40% enrolled. **Transfer Admission Requirements:** college transcript(s), essay or personal statement, minimum college GPA of 3.0 required. Lowest grade transferable D. **General Admission Information:** Application Fee $40. Regular application deadline 3/1. Notification on a rolling basis, beginning on or about 9/1. Nonfall registration accepted. Credit and/or placement offered for CEEB Advanced Placement tests.

COSTS AND FINANCIAL AID

Annual in-state tuition $9,630. Annual out-of-state tuition $16,590. Room and board $9,090. Required fees $2,600. Average book expense $1,074. **Required Forms and Deadlines:** FAFSA. **Notification of Awards:** Applicants will be notified of awards on a rolling basis beginning 4/1. **Types of Aid:** *Need-based scholarships/grants:* Federal Pell, SEOG, state scholarships/grants, private scholarships, the school's own gift aid, Federal Nursing Scholarships. *Loans:* Direct Subsidized Stafford, Direct Unsubsidized Stafford, Direct PLUS, Federal Perkins, Federal Nursing, college/university loans from institutional funds. **Student Employment:** Off-campus job opportunities are excellent. **Financial Aid Statistics:** 58% freshmen, 55% undergrads receive need-based scholarship or grant aid. 33% freshmen, 23% undergrads receive non need-based scholarship or grant aid. 92% freshmen, 89% undergrads receive need-based self-help aid. 1% freshmen, 1% undergrads receive athletic scholarships. 74% freshmen, 75% undergrads receive any aid. 65% undergrads borrow to pay for school. Average cumulative indebtedness $24,767. **Criteria for awarding institutional aid:** *Non-need-based:* academics, art, athletics, music/drama.

ILLINOIS WESLEYAN UNIVERSITY

Best 378

P.O. Box 2900, Bloomington, IL 61702-2900
Phone: 309-556-3031 • **Financial Aid Phone:** 309-556-3096
E-mail: iwuadmit@iwu.edu • **CEEB Code:** 1320
Fax: 309-556-3820 • **Website:** www.iwu.edu • **ACT Code:** 1044

This private school was founded in 1850. It has a 80-acre campus.

RATINGS

Admissions Selectivity Rating: 90   Fire Safety Rating: 77   Green Rating: 70

STUDENTS AND FACULTY

Enrollment: 2,007. **Student Body:** 58% female, 42% male, 12% out-of-state, 4% international (19 countries represented). Asian 5%, African American 5%, Caucasian 73%, Hispanic 5%, Native American 0%.
Retention and Graduation: 89% freshmen return for sophomore year. 78% freshmen graduate within 4 years. 35% grads go on to further study within 1 year. **Faculty:** Student/faculty ratio 11:1. 162 full-time faculty, 93% hold PhDs, 8% are members of minority groups, 43% are women. 0% of classes are taught by teaching assistants.

ACADEMICS

Degrees: bachelor's. **Classes:** Most classes have 10–19 students. Most lab/discussion sessions have 10–19 students. **Majors with Highest Enrollment:** biology/biological sciences; business/commerce; psychology. **Special Study Options:** double major, exchange student program (domestic), honors program, independent study, internships, student-designed major, study abroad, teacher certification program. **Honors Programs:** IWU offers a research honors designation to eligible senior students who successfully complete and defend an intensive, advanced research or creative project under the direction of an interdisciplinary faculty committee. Performance Honors designations are also available in the Art, Music, and Theatre Arts. **Combined Degree Programs:** 3-2 prgrms—Engrng, Forestry, or Environ. **Disability Services:** Special programs offered to physically disabled students include note-taking services, reader services, tape recorders, tutors. **Career Services:** Alumni network,

alumni services, career/job search classes, career assessment, internships, regional alumni. Career Services highlights include The Action Research Center links students in seminar and internships classes with community partners, such as social service and non-profit agencies. Students in these classes work with the partners on major projects intended to have a lasting, positive impact on the community. Projects have been as varied as those on environmental issues, historic preservation, pre-school education, crisis intervention, mentoring troubled youth, drug courts, living wage legislation, and ESL tutoring. See http://www2.iwu.edu/action/ for more details.

FACILITIES

Housing: Coed dorms, special housing for disabled students, special housing for international students, fraternity/sorority housing, apartments for single students, Groups of students with common curricular or cocurricular interests can propose and implement theme housing consistent with their educational goals in a limited number of residential buildings. Examples of past and current interest areas include the arts, languages, environmentalism, multi-faith issues, wellness, culinary arts, and internationalism. 80% of campus accessible to physically disabled. **Special Academic Facilities/Equipment:** observatory, computerized music lab, graphic design studio, Ames Library archives and special collections, visual anthropology lab, social science lab **Computers:** 60% of classrooms, 100% of libraries, 100% of dining areas, 100% of student union, have wireless network access. Students can register for classes online. Administrative functions (other than registration) can be performed online.

CAMPUS LIFE

Environment: City. **Activities:** Choral groups, concert band, dance, drama/theater, jazz band, literary magazine, music ensembles, musical theater, opera, pep band, radio station, student government, student newspaper, student-run film society, symphony orchestra, television station, yearbook, Campus Ministries, International Student Organization, Model UN 165 registered organizations, 29 honor societies, 15 religious organizations 6 fraternities, 5 sororities. **Athletics (Intercollegiate):** *Men:* baseball, basketball, cross-country, diving, football, golf, soccer, swimming, tennis, track/field (outdoor), track/field (indoor). *Women:* basketball, cross-country, diving, golf, soccer, softball, swimming, tennis, track/field (outdoor), track/field (indoor), volleyball. **On-Campus Highlights:** Ames Library, Hansen Student Center, Shirk Center for Athletics and Wellness, Center for Natural Science, The Dugout (snack bar and coffee shop). **Environmental Initiatives:** IWU has a commitment to environmental sustainability in its mission statement. IWU signed the Talloires Declaration. IWU signed the Illinois Sustainability Compact - July 22, 2009. Our new Welcome Center is LEED certified.

ADMISSIONS

Freshman Academic Profile: Average high school GPA 3.5. 45% in top 10% of high school class, 82% in top 25% of high school class, 98% in top 50% of high school class. 85% from public high schools. SAT Math middle 50% range 570-700. SAT Critical Reading middle 50% range 540-650. ACT middle 50% range 25-30. Minimum paper TOEFL 550. **Basis for Candidate Selection:** *Very important factors considered include:* academic GPA, rigor of secondary school record, interview. *Important factors considered include:* Class rank, application essay, standardized test scores, character/personal qualities, extracurricular activities, talent/ability. *Other factors considered include:* recommendation(s), alumni/ae relation, first generation, geographical residence, level of applicant's interest, racial/ethnic status, state residency, volunteer work, work experience. **Freshman Admission Requirements:** High school diploma is required and GED is accepted. **Freshman Admission Statistics:** 3,297 applied, 625% enrolled. **Transfer Admission Requirements:** High school transcript, college transcript(s), essay or personal statement, standardized test scores, minimum college GPA of 2.0 required. Lowest grade transferable C–. **General Admission Information:** Notification on a rolling basis, beginning on or about 12/15. Nonfall registration accepted. Admission may be deferred for a maximum of 1 year. Credit and/or placement offered for CEEB Advanced Placement tests.

COSTS AND FINANCIAL AID

Annual tuition $37,774. Room and board $8,838. Required fees $180. Average book expense $800. **Required Forms and Deadlines:** FAFSA, institution's own financial aid form, CSS/Financial Aid PROFILE. **Notification of Awards:** Applicants will be notified of awards on a rolling basis beginning 2/15. **Types of Aid:** *Need-based scholarships/grants:* Federal Pell, SEOG, state scholarships/grants, private scholarships, the school's own gift aid. *Loans:* Subsidized Stafford, Unsubsidized Stafford, PLUS, Federal Perkins, Federal Nursing, college/university loans from institutional funds. **Student Employment:** Federal Work-Study Program available. Institutional employment available. Off-campus job opportunities are good. **Financial Aid Statistics:** 98% freshmen, 99% undergrads receive need-based scholarship or grant aid. 13% freshmen, 10% undergrads receive non-need-based scholarship or grant aid. 78% freshmen, 86% undergrads receive need-based self-help aid. 99% freshmen, 96% undergrads receive any aid. 70% undergrads borrow to pay for school. Average cumulative indebtedness $32,964. **Criteria for awarding institutional aid:** *Non-need-based:* academics, art, music/drama.

IMMACULATA UNIVERSITY

1145 King Road, Immaculata, PA 19345-0642
Phone: 610-647-4400 x3060 • **Financial Aid Phone:** 877-428-6329
E-mail: admiss@immaculata.edu • **CEEB Code:** 2320
Fax: 610-640-0836 • **Website:** www.immaculata.edu • **ACT Code:** 3596

This private school, affiliated with the Roman Catholic Church, was founded in 2000. It has a 400-acre campus.

RATINGS
Admissions Selectivity Rating: 67   **Fire Safety Rating:** 84   **Green Rating:** 60*

STUDENTS AND FACULTY
Enrollment: 2,683. **Student Body:** 79% female, 21% male, 21% out-of-state, 1% international. Asian 3%, African American 16%, Caucasian 72%, Hispanic 4%, Native American 0%.
Retention and Graduation: 40% freshmen graduate within 4 years. 53% freshmen graduate within 6 years. **Faculty:** Student/faculty ratio 10:1. 102 full-time faculty, 79% hold PhDs, 6% are members of minority groups, 76% are women. 0% of classes are taught by teaching assistants.

ACADEMICS
Degrees: associate, bachelor's, certificate, post-bachelor's certificate. **Classes: Majors with Highest Enrollment:** business administration and management; human resources management and services, other; nursing/registered nurse (rn, asn, bsn, msn). **Special Study Options:** Accelerated program, cooperative education program, cross-registration, distance learning, double major, dual enrollment, external degree program, honors program, independent study, internships, liberal arts/career combination, study abroad, teacher certification program. **Disability Services:** Special programs offered to physically disabled students include note-taking services, reader services, tape recorders, tutors. **Career Services:** career assessment, internships.

FACILITIES
Housing: No housing is available for CLL students. 100% of campus accessible to physically disabled. **Special Academic Facilities/Equipment:** Annual art show on-campus. **Computers:** Administrative functions (other than registration) can be performed online.

CAMPUS LIFE
Environment: Town. **Activities:** Choral groups, dance, drama/theater, literary magazine, music ensembles, musical theater, student government, student newspaper, symphony orchestra, yearbook 28 registered organizations, 14 honor societies, 1 religious organizations. **Athletics (Intercollegiate):** *Men:* basketball, golf, soccer, tennis. *Women:* basketball, cross-country, field hockey, golf, lacrosse, soccer, softball, tennis, volleyball. **On-Campus Highlights:** Java Hut, Pool, Weight Room.

ADMISSIONS
Freshman Academic Profile: Average high school GPA 3.2. SAT Math middle 50% range 420-520. SAT Critical Reading middle 50% range 420-520. SAT Writing middle 50% range 430-520. ACT middle 50% range 18-21. Minimum paper TOEFL 500. **Basis for Candidate Selection:** *Important factors considered include:* level of applicant's interest. *Other factors considered include:* character/personal qualities, interview, work experience. **Freshman Admission Requirements:** High school diploma is required and GED is accepted. **Freshman Admission Statistics:** 1,650 applied, 819% enrolled. **Transfer Admission Requirements:** High school transcript, college transcript(s), minimum college GPA of 2.0 required. Lowest grade transferable C. **General Admission Information:** Application Fee $50. Nonfall registration accepted. Admission may be deferred for a maximum of 1 Year. Credit and/or placement offered for CEEB Advanced Placement tests.

COSTS AND FINANCIAL AID
Annual tuition $29,000. Room and board $11,740. Average book expense $1,790. **Required Forms and Deadlines:** FAFSA. **Notification of Awards:** Applicants will be notified of awards on a rolling basis beginning 2/1. **Types of Aid:** *Need-based scholarships/grants:* Federal Pell, state scholarships/grants, private scholarships, United Negro College Fund. *Loans:* Subsidized Stafford, Unsubsidized Stafford, PLUS, Federal Perkins. **Student Employment:** Federal Work-Study Program available. Institutional employment available. Highest amount earned per year from on-campus jobs $1,053. Off-campus job opportunities are good. **Financial Aid Statistics:** 35% undergrads receive need-based scholarship or grant aid. 5% undergrads receive non-need-based scholarship or grant aid. 73% undergrads receive need-based self-help aid. 34% undergrads receive any aid. 80% undergrads borrow to pay for school. Average cumulative indebtedness $12,000.

INDIANA INSTITUTE OF TECHNOLOGY

1600 East Washington Blvd, Fort Wayne, IN 46803
Phone: 260-422-5561
E-mail: admissions@indtech.edu • **CEEB Code:** 1805
Fax: 260-422-7696 • **Website:** www.indianatech.edu • **ACT Code:** 1208

This private school was founded in 1930. It has a 57-acre campus.

RATINGS
Admissions Selectivity Rating: 61   **Fire Safety Rating:** 60*   **Green Rating:** 60*

STUDENTS AND FACULTY
Enrollment: 2,985. **Student Body:** 56% female, 44% male, 13% out-of-state, 1% international (14 countries represented). Asian 1%, African American 17%, Caucasian 63%, Hispanic 2%, Native American 1%.
Retention and Graduation: 56% freshmen return for sophomore year. 11% freshmen graduate within 4 years. 16% freshmen graduate within 6 years. **Faculty:** Student/faculty ratio 17:1. 40 full-time faculty, 38% hold PhDs, 15% are members of minority groups, 30% are women. 0% of classes are taught by teaching assistants.

ACADEMICS
Degrees: associate, bachelor's, master's. **Classes:** Most classes have 10–19 students. **Majors with Highest Enrollment:** business/commerce; electrical, electronics and communications engineering; engineering, other. **Special Study Options:** Accelerated program, cooperative education program, distance learning, double major, external degree program, independent study, internships. **Career Services:** alumni services, career assessment, internships.

FACILITIES
Housing: Coed dorms, fraternity/sorority housing, apartments for single students. **Computers:** Students can register for classes online. Undergraduates are required to own a computer.

CAMPUS LIFE
Environment: Activities: Choral groups, dance, pep band, student government, student newspaper 14 registered organizations, 1 honor societies, 3 fraternities, 1 sororities. **Athletics (Intercollegiate):** *Men:* baseball, basketball, soccer. *Women:* basketball, soccer, softball.

ADMISSIONS
Freshman Academic Profile: Average high school GPA 2.9. 8% in top 10% of high school class, 27% in top 25% of high school class, 57% in top 50% of high school class. 80% from public high schools. Minimum paper TOEFL 500. **Basis for Candidate Selection:** *Very important factors considered include:* rigor of secondary school record, alumni/ae relation. *Important factors considered include:* Class rank, standardized test scores, interview, racial/ethnic status. *Other factors considered include:* application essay, recommendation(s), character/personal qualities, extracurricular activities, talent/ability, volunteer work, work experience. **Freshman Admission Requirements:** High school diploma is required and GED is accepted. *Academic units required:* 4 English, 3 mathematics, 2 science. *Academic units recommended:* 4 English, 3 mathematics, 2 science. **Freshman Admission Statistics:** 1,989 applied, 92% admitted, 13% enrolled. **Transfer Admission Requirements:** college transcript(s), minimum college GPA of 2.0 required. Lowest grade transferable C. **General Admission Information:** Application Fee $50. Regular application deadline 9/1. Notification on a rolling basis, beginning on or about 10/15. Nonfall registration accepted. Admission may be deferred for a maximum of 2 years. Credit and/or placement offered for CEEB Advanced Placement tests.

COSTS AND FINANCIAL AID
Annual tuition $16,680. Room and board $6,272. Average book expense $0. **Required Forms and Deadlines:** FAFSA, institution's own financial aid form. **Notification of Awards:** Applicants will be notified of awards on a rolling basis beginning 2/2. **Types of Aid:** *Need-based scholarships/grants:* Federal Pell, SEOG, state scholarships/grants, private scholarships, the school's own gift aid, United Negro College Fund. *Loans:* Subsidized Stafford, Unsubsidized Stafford, PLUS, Federal Perkins. **Student Employment:** Federal Work-Study Program available. Institutional employment available. Off-campus job opportunities are good. **Financial Aid Statistics:** 92% freshmen, 82% undergrads receive need-based scholarship or grant aid. 8% freshmen, 5% undergrads receive non-need-based scholarship or grant aid. 89% freshmen, 87% undergrads receive need-based self-help aid. 6% freshmen, 4% undergrads receive athletic scholarships. 73% undergrads borrow to pay for school. Average cumulative indebtedness $15,020. **Criteria for awarding institutional aid:** *Non-need-based:* academics, alumni affiliation, athletics, leadership, minority status, music/drama, state/district residency.

INDIANA STATE UNIVERSITY

Office of Admissions, 218 N 6th Street, Terre Haute, IN 47809
Phone: 812-237-2121 • **Financial Aid Phone:** 812-237-2215
E-mail: admissions@indstate.edu • **CEEB Code:** 1322
Fax: 812-237-8023 • **Website:** www.indstate.edu • **ACT Code:** 1206

This public school was founded in 1865. It has a 92-acre campus.

RATINGS
Admissions Selectivity Rating: 65   **Fire Safety Rating:** 79   **Green Rating:** 90

STUDENTS AND FACULTY
Enrollment: 9,816. **Student Body:** 54% female, 46% male, 17% out-of-state, 4% international (69 countries represented). Asian 1%, African American 17%, Caucasian 71%, Hispanic 3%, Native American 0%.
Retention and Graduation: Faculty: Student/faculty ratio 18:1. 485 full-time faculty, 69% hold PhDs, 14% are members of minority groups, 44% are women. 4% of classes are taught by teaching assistants.

ACADEMICS
Degrees: associate, bachelor's, certificate, master's, post-bachelor's certificate, post-master's certificate, terminal associate, transfer associate. **Classes:** Most classes have 20–29 students. **Majors with Highest Enrollment:** business administration and management; criminology; nursing/registered nurse (rn, asn, bsn, msn). **Special Study Options:** Accelerated program, cooperative education program, distance learning, double major, dual enrollment, English as a Second Language (ESL), honors program, independent study, internships, study abroad, teacher certification program. **Honors Programs:** University Honors Program. **Disability Services:** Special programs offered to physically disabled students include note-taking services, tape recorders, tutors. **Career Services:** alumni services, career assessment, internships Career Services highlights include At Indiana State, students from every discipline are able to apply what they are learning through hands-on inquiry and research, and life-changing field experiences. Our students program robots, conduct research alongside expert faculty, assist K-12 teachers in the classroom, analyze artifacts from a major archaeological dig, compose, dance, write and perform. They assist non-profit organizations, sample deep ocean sediments off the California coast, and care for patients at our community health education center. Experiential learning brings knowledge to life and gives student the kind of real-world understanding that sets you apart from students at other institutions.

FACILITIES
Housing: Coed dorms, special housing for disabled students, men's dorms, women's dorms, fraternity/sorority housing, apartments for married students, apartments for single students, theme housing, special housing for freshmen, and apartments for students with dependent children. 98% of campus accessible to physically disabled. **Special Academic Facilities/Equipment:** Music hall, art gallery, civic center, museum, flight simulator, audio-visual center, observatory, theaters. **Computers:** 100% of classrooms, 100% of dorms, 100% of libraries, 100% of dining areas, 100% of student union, have wireless network access. Students can register for classes online Administrative functions (other than registration) can be performed online. Undergraduates are required to own a computer.

CAMPUS LIFE
Environment: Town. **Activities:** Choral groups, concert band, dance, drama/theater, jazz band, literary magazine, marching band, music ensembles, musical theater, pep band, radio station, student government, student newspaper, student-run film society, symphony orchestra, yearbook, Campus Ministries, International Student Organization 130 registered organizations, 19 honor societies, 13 religious organizations. 11 fraternities, 10 sororities. **Athletics (Intercollegiate): Men:** baseball, basketball, cross-country, football, track/field (outdoor), track/field (indoor). *Women:* basketball, cross-country, golf, soccer, softball, track/field (outdoor), track/field (indoor), volleyball. **On-Campus Highlights:** Hulman Memorial Student Union, Student Recreation Center, John C. Hook's Memorial Observatory, Cunningham Memorial Library, Three Art Galleries, The Hulman Memorial Student Union Building contains the University Bookstore, The Commons(food court), Le Club(exercise club),etc. Various Libraries = Cunningham Memorial (main), Women Study, Arts and Science, etc. **Environmental Initiatives:** Signing of the ACUPPC Agreement. Policy development that will eventually be spelled out in the Climate Action Plan. President's development of an organizational structure that resulted in the development of a Climate Action Plan and two rounds of Carbon Footprint Analyses. Public and Campus Recycling efforts since 1989.

ADMISSIONS
Freshman Academic Profile: Average high school GPA 3.1. 9% in top 10% of high school class, 28% in top 25% of high school class, 68% in top 50% of high school class. SAT Math middle 50% range 410-520. SAT Critical Reading middle 50% range 400-510. SAT Writing middle 50% range 390-490. ACT middle 50% range 16-22. Minimum web-based TOEFL 61. Minimum paper TOEFL 500. **Basis for Candidate Selection:** *Very important factors considered include:* Class rank, academic GPA, rigor of secondary school record. *Important factors considered include:* application essay, recommendation(s), standardized test scores. *Other factors considered include:* character/personal qualities, extracurricular activities, interview, talent/ability. **Freshman Admission Requirements:** High school diploma is required and GED is accepted. **Freshman Admission Statistics:** 10,709 applied, 86% admitted, 29% enrolled. **Transfer Admission Requirements:** college transcript(s), minimum college GPA of 2.0 required. Lowest grade transferable C. **General Admission Information:** Application Fee $25. Regular application deadline 8/15. Nonfall registration accepted. Admission may be deferred for a maximum of 12 months. Credit offered for CEEB Advanced Placement tests.

COSTS AND FINANCIAL AID
Annual in-state tuition $7,898. Annual out-of-state tuition $17,444. Room and board $8,772. Required fees $200. Average book expense $1,170. **Required Forms and Deadlines:** FAFSA. **Notification of Awards:** Applicants will be notified of awards on a rolling basis beginning 4/15. **Types of Aid:** *Need-based scholarships/grants:* Federal Pell, SEOG, state scholarships/grants, private scholarships, the school's own gift aid. *Loans:* Subsidized Stafford, Unsubsidized Stafford, PLUS, Federal Perkins, Alternative Loans. **Student Employment:** Federal Work-Study Program available. Institutional employment available. Highest amount earned per year from on-campus jobs $13,370. Off-campus job opportunities are good. **Financial Aid Statistics:** 65% freshmen, 62% undergrads receive need-based scholarship or grant aid. 72% freshmen, 54% undergrads receive non-need-based scholarship or grant aid. 79% freshmen, 81% undergrads receive need-based self-help aid. 3% freshmen, 4% undergrads receive athletic scholarships. 79% freshmen, 72% undergrads receive any aid. 71% undergrads borrow to pay for school. Average cumulative indebtedness $24,484. **Criteria for awarding institutional aid:** *Non-need based:* academics, alumni affiliation, art, athletics, minority status, music/drama, state/district residency.

INDIANA UNIVERSITY—BLOOMINGTON

300 North Jordan Avenue, Bloomington, IN 47405-1106
Phone: 812-855-0661 • **Financial Aid Phone:** 812-855-0321
E-mail: iuadmit@indiana.edu • **CEEB Code:** 1324
Fax: 812-855-5102 • **Website:** www.indiana.edu • **ACT Code:** 1210

This public school was founded in 1820. It has a 1937-acre campus.

RATINGS
Admissions Selectivity Rating: 82   **Fire Safety Rating:** 80   **Green Rating:** 92

STUDENTS AND FACULTY
Enrollment: 31,927. **Student Body:** 51% female, 49% male, 28% out-of-state, 10% international (135 countries represented). Asian 4%, African American 4%, Caucasian 74%, Hispanic 4%, Native American 0%.
Retention and Graduation: 88% freshmen return for sophomore year. 55% freshmen graduate within 4 years. 75% freshmen graduate within 6 years. **Faculty:** Student/faculty ratio 18:1. 1941 full-time faculty, 79% hold PhDs, 18% are members of minority groups, 38% are women.

ACADEMICS
Degrees: bachelor's, certificate, diploma, doctoral, master's, post-bachelor's certificate, post-master's certificate. **Classes:** Most classes have 20–29 students. Most lab/discussion sessions have 20–29 students. **Majors with Highest Enrollment:** business/commerce; communication, journalism, and related programs, other; education. **Special Study Options:** Accelerated program, cooperative education program, distance learning, double major, dual enrollment, English as a Second Language (ESL), external degree program, honors program, independent study, internships, liberal arts/career combination, student-designed major, study abroad, teacher certification program. **Honors Programs:** Hutton Honors College and the Hudson/Holland Scholar Programs. **Disability Services:** Special programs offered to physically disabled students include note-taking services, reader services, tape recorders, tutors. **Career Services:** Alumni network, career/job search classes, career assessment, internships Career Services highlights include The New IU Alumni Connections Program tha we initated this year which brings back successful alumni to work with current students.

FACILITIES

Housing: Coed dorms, special housing for disabled students, men's dorms, special housing for international students, women's dorms, fraternity/sorority housing, apartments for married students, cooperative housing, apartments for single students, Apartments for students with dependent children. Residential language houses, and living/learning centers available, wellness center, African-American living/learning. Honor College floors, First-Year Academic Interest Group Housing; Suites for 2, 3 students. 95% of campus accessible to physically disabled. **Special Academic Facilities/Equipment:** Art Gallery, folklore, radio station, natural history museum, TV station, art museum, Mathers Museum of World Cultures, Kirkwood Observatory, Hilltop Garden and Nature Center, Arboretum, Student Recreational Sports and Aquatic Center, Auditorium, Beck Chapel, Golf Driving Range, Musical Arts Center, Health Physical Education and Recreation facilities (HPER), indoor swimming, outdoor swimming, Wildermuth Intramural Center (in HPER complex), cyclotron, Lilly Library, and more than 70 research centers. **Computers:** Students can register for classes online. Administrative functions (other than registration) can be performed online.

CAMPUS LIFE

Environment: City. **Activities:** Choral groups, concert band, dance, drama/theater, jazz band, literary magazine, marching band, music ensembles, musical theater, opera, radio station, student government, student newspaper, symphony orchestra, television station, yearbook, Campus Ministries, International Student Organization 9 religious organizations. **Athletics (Intercollegiate):** *Men:* baseball, basketball, cheerleading, cross-country, diving, football, golf, soccer, swimming, tennis, track/field (outdoor), wrestling. *Women:* basketball, cheerleading, cross-country, diving, field hockey, golf, soccer, softball, swimming, tennis, track/field (outdoor), volleyball, water polo. **On-Campus Highlights:** Indiana Memorial Union, Art Museum, Lilly Library, Assembly Hall, Student Recreational Sports Center. **Environmental Initiatives:** Established an office of sustainability in 2009 with two full time staff and 18 interns. Director of Sustainability reports to the Provost and the Vice President for Capital Projects and Facilities. A Campus Sustainability Advisory Board composed of 40 representatives of faculty, staff and students includes seven working groups staffed by nearly 200 volunteers. A Student Sustainability Council, with 22 member student organizations, advises the Office of Sustainability and also administers its own initiatives. Energy Challenge is an annual competition, conceived of and ran by student sustainability interns, to see which campus unit can most reduce its energy and water consumption based on a 3-year baseline for their own buildings. The 2010 competition included all 11 residence halls on the Bloomington campus, 26 Greek houses and 8 academic buildings competing in three separate divisions. Community based social marketing techniques are used to improve peer-to-peer learning. The Residence Hall Association is the student group most active in the residence hall competition, Greeks Go Green assist with influencing normative behavior in the Greek houses and Green Teams trade best practices in the academic buildings. In four weeks, these 14,000 participants saved over 2.5 million gallons of water and over 1 million kilowatt hours of electricity, or the equivalent of over 1000 households. The high profile of this competition, which has become a campus tradition leading up to Earth Day, has led to accelerated implementation of metering on campus and drawn attention to the need for and the paths to energy and water conservation. The Fall Energy challenge involved 11 residence halls, 27 Greek houses and 19 academic buildings encompassing over 6 million square feet and 18,000 occupants. In total, the four Energy Challenge competitions since 2008 have conserved 2,753,850 kWh of electricity and 6,061,365 gallons of water. This is enough electricity to power 2,753 average American homes for 12 weeks and enough water to fill more than 10 Olympic sized swimming pools! Approximately 4,392,252 pounds of CO_2 emissions have been avoided and $199,469 in utility savings have been achieved because of the Energy Challenge. E-Waste Days Sustainability Interns Kristin Hanks and Laura Knudsen wanted to create an electronic waste recycling program in a manner that would allow certification that the waste did not get shipped overseas to sweat shops or wind up in landfills. Another Sustainability Intern, Susan Coleman Morse, worked with various campus departments to strengthen campus e-waste recycling efforts. In collaboration with various IU departments, campuses and communities, Apple Inc and Sims Recycling, these dedicated students organized an effort that in two years has diverted more than a million pounds of electronic waste from the landfill at locations on this campus and other IU regional campuses. E-Waste Days were three-day events that invited corporations, institutions and the general public to participate. Apple Inc officials called this one of the best organized e-waste recycling efforts in the United States.

ADMISSIONS

Freshman Academic Profile: Average high school GPA 3.6. 34% in top 10% of high school class, 70% in top 25% of high school class, 95% in top 50% of high school class. SAT Math middle 50% range 540-660. SAT Critical Reading middle 50% range 510-620. SAT Writing middle 50% range 510-610. ACT middle 50% range 24-29. Minimum web-based TOEFL 79. Minimum paper TOEFL 550. **Basis for Candidate Selection:** *Very important factors*

considered include: Class rank, academic GPA, rigor of secondary school record. *Important factors considered include:* standardized test scores. *Other factors considered include:* application essay, recommendation(s), alumni/ae relation, character/personal qualities, extracurricular activities, first generation, geographical residence, interview, level of applicant's interest, racial/ethnic status, state residency, talent/ability, volunteer work, work experience. **Freshman Admission Requirements:** High school diploma is required and GED is accepted. *Academic units required:* 4 English, 3 mathematics, 1 science, (1 science labs), 2 social studies, 4 academic electives. *Academic units recommended:* 4 English, 3 mathematics, 1 science, (1 science labs), 2 social studies, 4 academic electives. **Freshman Admission Statistics:** 35,247 applied, 74% admitted, 29% enrolled. **Transfer Admission Requirements:** college transcript(s), minimum college GPA of 2.0 required. Lowest grade transferable C. **General Admission Information:** Application Fee $55. Nonfall registration accepted. Admission may be deferred for a maximum of 1 year. Credit and/or placement offered for CEEB Advanced Placement tests.

COSTS AND FINANCIAL AID

Annual in-state tuition $8,750. Annual out-of-state tuition $30,200. Room and board $8,854. Required fees $1,283. Average book expense $848. **Required Forms and Deadlines:** FAFSA. **Notification of Awards:** Applicants will be notified of awards on a rolling basis beginning 4/1. **Types of Aid:** *Need-based scholarships/grants:* Federal Pell, SEOG, state scholarships/grants, private scholarships, the school's own gift aid. *Loans:* Direct Subsidized Stafford, Direct Unsubsidized Stafford, Direct PLUS, Federal Perkins, college/university loans from institutional funds. **Student Employment:** Federal Work-Study Program available. Institutional employment available. Off-campus job opportunities are good. **Financial Aid Statistics:** 77% freshmen, 74% undergrads receive need-based scholarship or grant aid. 15% freshmen, 10% undergrads receive non-need-based scholarship or grant aid. 59% freshmen, 70% undergrads receive need-based self-help aid. 1% freshmen, 1% undergrads receive athletic scholarships. 52% undergrads borrow to pay for school. Average cumulative indebtedness $28,769. **Criteria for awarding institutional aid:** *Non-need-based:* academics, art, athletics, leadership, minority status, music/drama, religious affiliation.

INDIANA UNIVERSITY EAST

2325 Chester Boulevard, Richmond, IN 47374-1289
Phone: 765-973-8208 • **Financial Aid Phone:** 765-973-8206
E-mail: applynow@iue.edu • **CEEB Code:** 1194
Fax: 765-973-8209 • **Website:** www.iue.edu • **ACT Code:** 1216

This public school was founded in 1971. It has a 182-acre campus.

RATINGS

Admissions Selectivity Rating: 72   **Fire Safety Rating:** 60*   **Green Rating:** 60*

STUDENTS AND FACULTY

Enrollment: 2,813. **Student Body:** 67% female, 33% male, 18% out-of-state, >1% international (25 countries represented). Asian >1%, African American 4%, Caucasian 90%, Hispanic 2%, Native American >1%
Retention and Graduation: 66% freshmen return for sophomore year. 6% freshmen graduate within 4 years. 19% freshmen graduate within 6 years. **Faculty:** Student/faculty ratio 16:1. 103 full-time faculty, 57% hold PhDs, 16% are are members of minority groups, 62% are women.

ACADEMICS

Degrees: associate, bachelor's, master's, post-bachelor's certificate,. **Classes:** Most classes have 10-19 students. **Majors with Highest Enrollment:** business/commerce; elementary education and teaching; nursing/registered nurse (rn, asn, bsn, msn). **Special Study Options:** cooperative education program, cross-registration, distance learning, double major, dual enrollment, external degree program, honors program, independent study, internships, teacher certification program, weekend college, , State-wide technology program with Purdue University. Disability Services: Special programs offered to physically disabled students include note-taking services, reader services, tape recorders, tutors..

FACILITIES

Housing: Computers: Students can register for classes online. Administrative functions (other than registration) can be performed online.

CAMPUS LIFE

Environment: Town. **Activities:** drama/theater, literary magazine, student government, student newspaper, television station . **Athletics (Intercollegiate):** *Men:* basketball, golf. *Women:* volleyball.

ADMISSIONS

Freshman Academic Profile: Average high school GPA 3.04. 7% in top 10% of high school class, 24% in top 25% of high school class, 66% in top 50% of high school class. SAT Math middle 50% range 410-510. SAT Critical Reading middle 50% range 410-510. SAT Writing middle 50% range 390-480. ACT middle 50% range 18-23. Minimum web-based TOEFL 79. Minimum paper TOEFL 550. Basis for Candidate Selection: Very important factors considered include: rigor of secondary school record, standardized test scores,. Important factors considered include: Class rank, academic GPA,. Other factors considered include: geographical residence, state residency,. Freshman Admission Requirements: High school diploma is required and GED is accepted. Academic units required: 4 English, 3 mathematics, 1 science, (1 science labs), 2 social studies. Academic units recommended: 4 English, 3 mathematics, 1 science, (1 science labs), 2 social studies, Freshman Admission Statistics: 1,122 applied, 64% admitted, 58% enrolled. Transfer Admission Requirements: college transcript(s), Minimum college GPA of 2.0 required. Lowest grade transferable C. General Admission Information: Application Fee $35. Notification on a rolling basis, beginning on or about 9/1. Nonfall registration accepted. Admission may be deferred for a maximum of Contact campus.

COSTS AND FINANCIAL AID

Annual in-state tuition $5,9637. Annual out-of-state tuition $16,893. Required fees $531. Average book expense $1,012. Required Forms and Deadlines: FAFSA, institution's own financial aid form. Notification of Awards: Applicants will be notified of awards on a rolling basis beginning 5/1. Types of Aid: Need-based scholarships/grants: Federal Pell, SEOG, state scholarships/grants, private scholarships, the school's own gift aid. Loans: Direct Subsidized Stafford, Direct Unsubsidized Stafford, Direct PLUS, Federal Perkins, college/university loans from institutional funds. Financial Aid Statistics: 91% freshmen, 86% undergrads receive need-based scholarship or grant aid. 8% freshmen, 4% undergrads receive non-need-based scholarship or grant aid. 55% freshmen, 74% undergrads receive need-based self-help aid. 83% undergrads borrow to pay for school. Average cumulative indebtedness $26,897. Criteria for awarding institutional aid: Non-need-based: academics, alumni affiliation, leadership.

INDIANA UNIVERSITY—KOKOMO

2300 South Washington Street, Kokomo, IN 46904-9003
Phone: 765-455-9217 • **Financial Aid Phone:** 765 4559216
E-mail: iuadmis@iuk.edu • **CEEB Code:** 1337
Fax: 765-455-9537 • **Website:** www.iuk.edu • **ACT Code:** 1219

This public school was founded in 1945. It has a 51-acre campus.

RATINGS

Admissions Selectivity Rating: 70   **Fire Safety Rating:** 60*   **Green Rating:** 60*

STUDENTS AND FACULTY

Enrollment: 2,501. **Student Body:** 67% female, 33% male, 1% out-of-state, 0% international (19 countries represented). Asian 1%, African American 4%, Caucasian 86%, Hispanic 3%, Native American 0%.
Retention and Graduation: 64% freshmen return for sophomore year. 8% freshmen graduate within 4 years. 20% freshmen graduate within 6 years.
Faculty: Student/faculty ratio 17:1. 98 full-time faculty, 63% hold PhDs, 15% are members of minority groups, 58% are women.

ACADEMICS

Degrees: associate, bachelor's, certificate, master's, post-bachelor's certificate. **Classes:** Most classes have 20–29 students. Most lab/discussion sessions have 20–29 students. **Special Study Options:** Accelerated program, cross-registration, distance learning, double major, dual enrollment, external degree program, honors program, independent study, internships, liberal arts/career combination, study abroad, teacher certification program. **Disability Services:** Special programs offered to physically disabled students include note-taking services, reader services, tutors. **Career Services:** alumni services, career/job search classes, career assessment, internships.

FACILITIES

Housing: Special Academic Facilities/Equipment: Observatory, Art Gallery **Computers:** Students can register for classes online. Administrative functions (other than registration) can be performed online.

CAMPUS LIFE

Environment: Village. **Activities:** Choral groups, drama/theater, music ensembles, student government, student newspaper.

ADMISSIONS

Freshman Academic Profile: Average high school GPA 3.0. 5% in top 10% of high school class, 28% in top 25% of high school class, 65% in top 50% of

high school class. SAT Math middle 50% range 430-530. SAT Critical Reading middle 50% range 420-530. SAT Writing middle 50% range 400-510. ACT middle 50% range 18-23. Minimum paper TOEFL 560. **Basis for Candidate Selection:** *Very important factors considered include:* Class rank, rigor of secondary school record. *Important factors considered include:* standardized test scores. *Other factors considered include:* recommendation(s). **Freshman Admission Requirements:** High school diploma is required and GED is accepted. *Academic units required:* 4 English, 3 mathematics, 1 science, 2 social studies. *Academic units recommended:* 4 English, 3 mathematics, 1 science, 2 social studies. **Freshman Admission Statistics:** 932 applied, 767% enrolled. **Transfer Admission Requirements:** college transcript(s), minimum college GPA of 2.0 required. Lowest grade transferable C. **General Admission Information:** Application Fee $45. Nonfall registration accepted. Admission may be deferred for a maximum of Contact admissions. Credit and/or placement offered for CEEB Advanced Placement tests.

COSTS AND FINANCIAL AID

Annual in-state tuition $5,949. Annual out-of-state tuition $16,894. Required fees $592. Average book expense $924. **Required Forms and Deadlines:** FAFSA, institution's own financial aid form. **Notification of Awards:** Applicants will be notified of awards on a rolling basis beginning 5/1. **Types of Aid:** *Need-based scholarships/grants:* Federal Pell, SEOG, state scholarships/grants, private scholarships, the school's own gift aid. *Loans:* Direct Subsidized Stafford, Direct Unsubsidized Stafford, Direct PLUS, Federal Perkins, Federal Nursing, college/university loans from institutional funds. **Student Employment:** Federal Work-Study Program available. Institutional employment available. **Financial Aid Statistics:** 80% freshmen, 80% undergrads receive need-based scholarship or grant aid. 4% freshmen, 3% undergrads receive non-need-based scholarship or grant aid. 56% freshmen, 72% undergrads receive need-based self-help aid. 88% freshmen, 88% undergrads receive any aid. 70% undergrads borrow to pay for school. Average cumulative indebtedness $25,839. **Criteria for awarding institutional aid:** *Non-need-based:* academics.

INDIANA UNIVERSITY NORTHWEST

3400 Broadway, Gary, IN 46408-1197
Phone: 219-980-6991 • **Financial Aid Phone:** 209 9806778
E-mail: admit@iun.edu
Fax: 219-981-4219 • **Website:** www.iun.edu

This public school was founded in 1948. It has a 38-acre campus.

RATINGS

Admissions Selectivity Rating: 67   **Fire Safety Rating:** 60*   **Green Rating:** 60*

STUDENTS AND FACULTY

Enrollment: 4,960. **Student Body:** 69% female, 31% male, 1% out-of-state, 0% international (33 countries represented). Asian 2%, African American 23%, Caucasian 55%, Hispanic 15%, Native American 0%.
Retention and Graduation: 63% freshmen return for sophomore year. 8% freshmen graduate within 4 years. 23% freshmen graduate within 6 years.
Faculty: Student/faculty ratio 15:1. 187 full-time faculty, 70% hold PhDs, 25% are members of minority groups, 52% are women.

ACADEMICS

Degrees: associate, bachelor's, certificate, master's, post-bachelor's certificate. **Classes:** Most classes have 20–29 students. Most lab/discussion sessions have 20–29 students. **Majors with Highest Enrollment:** business/commerce; criminal justice/safety studies; nursing/registered nurse (rn, asn, bsn, msn). **Special Study Options:** Accelerated program, cooperative education program, distance learning, double major, dual enrollment, external degree program, independent study, internships, liberal arts/career combination, student-designed major, study abroad, teacher certification program, weekend college. **Disability Services:** Special programs offered to physically disabled students include reader services, tape recorders, tutors. **Career Services:** alumni services, career/job search classes, career assessment, internships.

FACILITIES

Housing: Computers: Students can register for classes online. Administrative functions (other than registration) can be performed online.

CAMPUS LIFE

Environment: Activities: Choral groups, dance, drama/theater, literary magazine, musical theater, radio station, student government, student newspaper, International Student Organization 60 registered organizations, 4 honor societies, 2 religious organizations. 2 fraternities, 3 sororities. **Athletics (Intercollegiate):** *Men:* baseball, basketball, cheerleading, golf. *Women:* basketball, cheerleading, volleyball.

ADMISSIONS

Freshman Academic Profile: Average high school GPA 2.7. 7% in top 10% of high school class, 25% in top 25% of high school class, 56% in top 50% of high school class. SAT Math middle 50% range 390-500. SAT Critical Reading middle 50% range 390-500. SAT Writing middle 50% range 380-480. ACT middle 50% range 16-24. Minimum web-based TOEFL 79. Minimum paper TOEFL 500. **Basis for Candidate Selection:** *Very important factors considered include:* Class rank, academic GPA, rigor of secondary school record, standardized test scores. *Other factors considered include:* recommendation(s). **Freshman Admission Requirements:** High school diploma is required and GED is accepted. *Academic units required:* 4 English, 3 mathematics, 2 science, 2 social studies, 4 academic electives. *Academic units recommended:* 4 English, 3 mathematics, 2 science, 2 social studies, 4 academic electives. **Freshman Admission Statistics:** 1,793 applied, 76% admitted, 66% enrolled. **Transfer Admission Requirements:** High school transcript, college transcript(s), minimum college GPA of 2.0 required. Lowest grade transferable C. **General Admission Information:** Application Fee $25. Nonfall registration accepted. Admission may be deferred for a maximum of 2 years. Credit offered for CEEB Advanced Placement tests.

COSTS AND FINANCIAL AID

Annual in-state tuition $6,043. Annual out-of-state tuition $16,894. Required fees $583. Average book expense $1,012. **Required Forms and Deadlines:** FAFSA, institution's own financial aid form. **Notification of Awards:** Applicants will be notified of awards on a rolling basis beginning 5/1. **Types of Aid:** *Need-based scholarships/grants:* Federal Pell, SEOG, state scholarships/grants, private scholarships, the school's own gift aid, Federal Nursing Scholarships. *Loans:* Direct Subsidized Stafford, Direct Unsubsidized Stafford, Direct PLUS, Federal Perkins, college/university loans from institutional funds. **Student Employment:** Federal Work-Study Program available. Off-campus job opportunities are good. **Financial Aid Statistics:** 77% freshmen, 80% undergrads receive need-based scholarship or grant aid. 2% freshmen, 1% undergrads receive non-need-based scholarship or grant aid. 66% freshmen, 78% undergrads receive need-based self-help aid. 1% freshmen receive athletic scholarships. 70% undergrads borrow to pay for school. Average cumulative indebtedness $31,686. **Criteria for awarding institutional aid:** *Non-need-based:* academics, athletics.

INDIANA UNIVERSITY OF PENNSYLVANIA

Best 378

1011 South Drive, Indiana, PA 15705
Phone: 724-357-2230 • **Financial Aid Phone:** 724-357-2218
E-mail: admissions-inquiry@iup.edu • **CEEB Code:** 2652
Fax: 724-357-6281 • **Website:** www.iup.edu • **ACT Code:** 3704

This public school was founded in 1875. It has a 342-acre campus.

RATINGS

Admissions Selectivity Rating: 76   **Fire Safety Rating:** 92   **Green Rating:** 61

STUDENTS AND FACULTY

Enrollment: 12,690. **Student Body:** 55% female, 45% male, 7% out-of-state, 2% international (63 countries represented). Asian 1%, African American 11%, Caucasian 80%, Hispanic 3%, Native American 0%.
Retention and Graduation: 75% freshmen return for sophomore year. **Faculty:** Student/faculty ratio 18:1. 620 full-time faculty, % hold PhDs, 13% are members of minority groups, 47% are women. 0% of classes are taught by teaching assistants.

ACADEMICS

Degrees: associate, bachelor's, certificate, master's, post-bachelor's certificate, post-master's certificate. **Classes:** Most classes have 20–29 students. Most lab/discussion sessions have 10–19 students. **Majors with Highest Enrollment:** criminology; management information systems; nursing/registered nurse (rn, asn, bsn, msn). **Special Study Options:** Accelerated program, cooperative education program, cross-registration, distance learning, double major, dual enrollment, English as a Second Language (ESL), exchange student program (domestic), external degree program, honors program, independent study, internships, liberal arts/career combination, student-designed major, study abroad, teacher certification program, weekend college. **Honors Programs:** Robert E. Cook Honors College. **Disability Services:** Special programs offered to physically disabled students include note-taking services, reader services, tape recorders. **Career Services:** Alumni network, alumni services,

internships Career Services highlights include Mock Interview Simulation Program - 800 participants each year.

FACILITIES

Housing: Coed dorms, special housing for disabled students, special housing for international students, apartments for married students, apartments for single students, wellness housing, theme housing, Living Learning Communities. 98% of campus accessible to physically disabled. **Special Academic Facilities/Equipment:** Art museum, natural history museum, on-campus elementary school, lodge, farm, co-generation plant, ski slope, sailing base. **Computers:** 90% of classrooms, 60% of dorms, 100% of libraries, 100% of dining areas, 80% of student union, 100% of common outdoor areas have wireless network access. Students can register for classes online. Administrative functions (other than registration) can be performed online.

CAMPUS LIFE

Environment: Village. **Activities:** Choral groups, concert band, dance, drama/theater, jazz band, marching band, music ensembles, musical theater, radio station, student government, student newspaper, symphony orchestra, television station, Campus Ministries, International Student Organization 210 registered organizations, 23 honor societies, 18 religious organizations, 18 fraternities, 14 sororities. **Athletics (Intercollegiate):** *Men:* baseball, basketball, cross-country, diving, football, golf, swimming, track/field (outdoor), track/field (indoor). *Women:* basketball, cross-country, diving, field hockey, lacrosse, soccer, softball, swimming, tennis, track/field (outdoor), track/field (indoor), volleyball. **On-Campus Highlights:** Suites on Grant, Oak Grove, Hadley Union Building Fitness Center/Foo, Stapleton Library, Miller Stadium.

ADMISSIONS

Freshman Academic Profile: 8% in top 10% of high school class, 27% in top 25% of high school class, 60% in top 50% of high school class. SAT Math middle 50% range 450-540. SAT Critical Reading middle 50% range 440-530. SAT Writing middle 50% range 430-520. Minimum web-based TOEFL 61. Minimum paper TOEFL 500. **Basis for Candidate Selection:** *Very important factors considered include:* academic GPA, standardized test scores. *Important factors considered include:* rigor of secondary school record. *Other factors considered include:* Class rank, application essay, recommendation(s), extracurricular activities. **Freshman Admission Requirements:** High school diploma is required and GED is accepted. **Freshman Admission Statistics:** 12,333 applied, 61% admitted, 39% enrolled. **Transfer Admission Requirements:** High school transcript, college transcript(s), statement of good standing from prior institution(s). Minimum college GPA of 2.0 required. Lowest grade transferable C–. **General Admission Information:** Application Fee $35. Notification on a rolling basis, beginning on or about 9/15. Nonfall registration accepted. Admission may be deferred for a maximum of 1 year. Credit offered for CEEB Advanced Placement tests.

COSTS AND FINANCIAL AID

Annual in-state tuition $6,428. Annual out-of-state tuition $16,070. Room and board $10,466. Required fees $2,244. Average book expense $1,100. **Required Forms and Deadlines:** FAFSA. **Notification of Awards:** Applicants will be notified of awards on a rolling basis beginning 3/15. **Types of Aid:** *Need-based scholarships/grants:* Federal Pell, SEOG, state scholarships/grants, private scholarships, the school's own gift aid, United Negro College Fund. *Loans:* Subsidized Stafford, Unsubsidized Stafford, PLUS, Federal Perkins, Private Alternative Loans. **Student Employment:** Federal Work-Study Program available. Institutional employment available. Highest amount earned per year from on-campus jobs $8,043. Off-campus job opportunities are good. **Financial Aid Statistics:** 68% freshmen, 70% undergrads receive need-based scholarship or grant aid. 30% freshmen, 19% undergrads receive non-need-based scholarship or grant aid. 94% freshmen, 93% undergrads receive need-based self-help aid. 2% freshmen, 2% undergrads receive athletic scholarships. 83% freshmen, 83% undergrads receive any aid. 83% undergrads borrow to pay for school. Average cumulative indebtedness $35,229. **Criteria for awarding institutional aid:** *Non-need-based:* academics, alumni affiliation, art, athletics, job skills, leadership, music/drama, state/district residency.

INDIANA UNIVERSITY—PURDUE UNIVERSITY FORT WAYNE

2101 East Coliseum Boulevard, Fort Wayne, IN 46805-1499
Phone: 260-481-6812
E-mail: ipfwadms@ipfw.edu • **CEEB Code:** 1336
Fax: 260-481-6880 • **Website:** www.ipfw.edu • **ACT Code:** 1217

This public school was founded in 1917. It has a 565-acre campus.

RATINGS
Admissions Selectivity Rating: 65   **Fire Safety Rating:** 60*   **Green Rating:** 60*

STUDENTS AND FACULTY
Enrollment: 10,587. **Student Body:** 58% female, 42% male, 5% out-of-state, 2% international (71 countries represented). Asian 2%, African American 5%, Caucasian 87%, Hispanic 2%, Native American 0%.
Retention and Graduation: 60% freshmen return for sophomore year. **Faculty:** Student/faculty ratio 19:1. 329 full-time faculty, 83% hold PhDs, 13% are members of minority groups, 37% are women. 1% of classes are taught by teaching assistants.

ACADEMICS
Degrees: associate, bachelor's, certificate, master's, post-bachelor's certificate, post-master's certificate, terminal associate, transfer associate. **Classes:** Most classes have 20–29 students. Most lab/discussion sessions have 20–29 students. **Majors with Highest Enrollment:** business/commerce; elementary education and teaching; nursing/registered nurse (rn, asn, bsn, msn). **Special Study Options:** cooperative education program, distance learning, double major, English as a Second Language (ESL), exchange student program (domestic), honors program, independent study, internships, liberal arts/career combination, student-designed major, study abroad, teacher certification program, weekend college. **Disability Services:** Special programs offered to physically disabled students include note-taking services, reader services, tape recorders, tutors. **Career Services:** Alumni network, alumni services, career/job search classes, career assessment, internships, regional alumni.

FACILITIES
Housing: Coed dorms. 100% of campus accessible to physically disabled. **Special Academic Facilities/Equipment:** Williams theatre. recital hall anthropology and geology exhibits art gallery **Computers:** Students can register for classes online. Administrative functions (other than registration) can be performed online.

CAMPUS LIFE
Environment: Village. **Activities:** Choral groups, concert band, dance, drama/theater, jazz band, literary magazine, music ensembles, musical theater, opera, pep band, student government, student newspaper, symphony orchestra, television station 65 registered organizations, 7 honor societies, 3 religious organizations. 2 fraternities, 3 sororities. **Athletics (Intercollegiate):** *Men:* baseball, basketball, cross-country, soccer, tennis, track/field (outdoor), volleyball. *Women:* basketball, cross-country, soccer, softball, tennis, track/field (outdoor), volleyball.

ADMISSIONS
Freshman Academic Profile: Average high school GPA 2.6. 7% in top 10% of high school class, 24% in top 25% of high school class, 57% in top 50% of high school class. SAT Math middle 50% range 430-550. SAT Critical Reading middle 50% range 420-540. ACT middle 50% range 17-23. Minimum paper TOEFL 550. **Basis for Candidate Selection:** *Very important factors considered include:* Class rank, rigor of secondary school record, standardized test scores. *Other factors considered include:* recommendation(s), state residency. **Freshman Admission Requirements:** High school diploma is required and GED is accepted. *Academic units required:* 4 English, 3 mathematics, 1 science, 1 foreign language, 1 social studies. *Academic units recommended:* 4 English, 3 mathematics, 1 science, 1 foreign language, 1 social studies. **Freshman Admission Statistics:** 2,471 applied, 97% admitted, 71% enrolled. **Transfer Admission Requirements:** High school transcript, college transcript(s), minimum college GPA of 2.0 required. Lowest grade transferable C–. **General Admission Information:** Application Fee $30. Regular application deadline 8/1. Notification on a rolling basis, beginning on or about 12/1. Nonfall registration accepted. Credit and/or placement offered for CEEB Advanced Placement tests.

COSTS AND FINANCIAL AID
Annual in-state tuition $3,100. Annual out-of-state tuition $7,728. Required fees $384. Average book expense $800. **Required Forms and Deadlines:** FAFSA. **Notification of Awards:** Applicants will be notified of awards on or about 4/30. **Types of Aid:** *Need-based scholarships/grants:* Federal Pell, SEOG, state scholarships/grants, private scholarships, Federal Nursing Scholarships. *Loans:*

Subsidized Stafford, Unsubsidized Stafford, PLUS, Federal Perkins, Federal Nursing. **Student Employment:** Federal Work-Study Program available. Institutional employment available. Highest amount earned per year from on-campus jobs $1,200. Off-campus job opportunities are excellent. **Financial Aid Statistics:** 56% freshmen, 69% undergrads receive need-based scholarship or grant aid. 28% freshmen, 23% undergrads receive non-need-based scholarship or grant aid. 46% freshmen, 50% undergrads receive need-based self-help aid. 3% freshmen, 3% undergrads receive athletic scholarships. 59% undergrads borrow to pay for school. Average cumulative indebtedness $13,764. **Criteria for awarding institutional aid:** *Non-need-based:* academics, alumni affiliation, art, athletics.

INDIANA UNIVERSITY—PURDUE UNIVERSITY INDIANAPOLIS

420 N University Boulevard, Indianapolis, IN 46202
Phone: 317-274-4591 • **Financial Aid Phone:** 317-274-4162
E-mail: apply@iupui.edu
Fax: 317-278-1862 • **Website:** www.iupui.edu • **ACT Code:** 1214

This public school was founded in 1969. It has a 509-acre campus.

RATINGS
Admissions Selectivity Rating: 72   **Fire Safety Rating:** 61   **Green Rating:** 60*

STUDENTS AND FACULTY
Enrollment: 21,235. **Student Body:** 57% female, 43% male, 2% out-of-state, 3% international (142 countries represented). Asian 3%, African American 11%, Caucasian 75%, Hispanic 4%, Native American 0%.
Retention and Graduation: 82% freshmen return for sophomore year. 11% freshmen graduate within 4 years. 33% freshmen graduate within 6 years. **Faculty:** Student/faculty ratio 17:1. 2247 full-time faculty, 83% hold PhDs, 23% are members of minority groups, 40% are women.

ACADEMICS
Degrees: associate, bachelor's, certificate, doctoral, master's, post-bachelor's certificate. **Classes:** Most classes have 20–29 students. Most lab/discussion sessions have 10–19 students. **Majors with Highest Enrollment:** business/commerce; elementary education and teaching; nursing/registered nurse (rn, asn, bsn, msn). **Special Study Options:** Accelerated program, cooperative education program, cross-registration, distance learning, double major, dual enrollment, English as a Second Language (ESL), exchange student program (domestic), external degree program, honors program, independent study, internships, student-designed major, study abroad, teacher certification program, weekend college. **Honors Programs:** The Honors Program provides a challenging campus-wide program for high achieving students from all academic disciplines. Honors Program students have the opportunity to enroll in smaller dynamic classes and to collaborate with faculty in independent study and research projects. Participants in the IUPUI Honors Program will be required to complete at least three credit hours of honors course work each semester. **Combined Degree Programs:** BA/MEng, BS /MS;MD/PhD; MA/MPA; MBA/JD. **Disability Services:** Special programs offered to physically disabled students include note-taking services, reader services, tape recorders, tutors.

FACILITIES
Housing: Coed dorms, special housing for international students, apartments for married students, apartments for single students. 90% of campus accessible to physically disabled. **Special Academic Facilities/Equipment:** Inlow Hall-Law School Eskenazi Hall-Herron School of Art and Design Cavanaugh Hall-School of Liberal Arts and IUPUI Enrollment Center University Library-Most high tech library in North America IUPUI Sport Complex-host of 11 Olympic Team Trails White River State Park-Indianapolis' version of the mall in Washington, D.C. **Computers:** 100% of classrooms, 100% of dorms, 100% of libraries, 100% of dining areas, 100% of student union, 100% of common outdoor areas have wireless network access. Students can register for classes online. Administrative functions (other than registration) can be performed online.

CAMPUS LIFE
Environment: Metropolis. **Activities:** Choral groups, concert band, dance, drama/theater, jazz band, literary magazine, music ensembles, pep band, student government, student newspaper, Campus Ministries, International Student Organization 154 registered organizations, 9 honor societies, 10 religious organizations. 2 fraternities, 1 sororities. **Athletics (Intercollegiate):** *Men:* basketball, cross-country, diving, golf, soccer, swimming, tennis. *Women:* basketball, cross-country, diving, golf, soccer, softball, swimming, tennis, volleyball. **On-Campus Highlights:** IUPUI Sport Complex, University College, Cavanaugh Hall, University Library, Eskenazi Hall, IU Medical Center.

ADMISSIONS

Freshman Academic Profile: Average high school GPA 3.3. 15% in top 10% of high school class, 44% in top 25% of high school class, 83% in top 50% of high school class. SAT Math middle 50% range 450-560. SAT Critical Reading middle 50% range 430-550. SAT Writing middle 50% range 420-530. ACT middle 50% range 19-25. Minimum web-based TOEFL 80. Minimum paper TOEFL 550. **Basis for Candidate Selection:** *Very important factors considered include:* rigor of secondary school record. *Important factors considered include:* academic GPA. *Other factors considered include:* Class rank, application essay, recommendation(s), standardized test scores, character/personal qualities, first generation, volunteer work, work experience. **Freshman Admission Requirements:** High school diploma is required and GED is accepted. *Academic units required:* 4 English, 3 mathematics, 3 science, (3 science labs), 2 social studies, 2 history, 4 academic electives. *Academic units recommended:* 4 English, 3 mathematics, 3 science, (3 science labs), 2 social studies, 2 history, 4 academic electives. **Freshman Admission Statistics:** 10,164 applied, 69% admitted, 43% enrolled. **Transfer Admission Requirements:** college transcript(s), minimum college GPA of 2.0 required. Lowest grade transferable C. **General Admission Information:** Application Fee $50. Nonfall registration accepted. Admission may be deferred for a maximum of 1 year. Credit and/or placement offered for CEEB Advanced Placement tests.

COSTS AND FINANCIAL AID

Annual in-state tuition $7,623. Annual out-of-state tuition $28,080. Room and board $7,944. Required fees $982. Average book expense $672. Required Forms and Deadlines: FAFSA. Notification of Awards: Applicants will be notified of awards on a rolling basis beginning 4/1. Types of Aid: Need-based scholarships/grants: Federal Pell, SEOG, state scholarships/grants, private scholarships, the school's own gift aid. Loans: Direct Subsidized Stafford, Direct Unsubsidized Stafford, Direct PLUS, Federal Perkins, Federal Nursing, college/university loans from institutional funds. Student Employment: Federal Work-Study Program available. Institutional employment available. Financial Aid Statistics: 79% freshmen, 80% undergrads receive need-based scholarship or grant aid. 6% freshmen, 4% undergrads receive non-need-based scholarship or grant aid. 72% freshmen, 81% undergrads receive need-based self-help aid. 1% freshmen. 88% freshmen, 87% undergrads receive any aid. 72% undergrads borrow to pay for school. Average cumulative indebtedness $29,673. Criteria for awarding institutional aid: Non-need-based: academics.

INDIANA UNIVERSITY—SOUTH BEND

1700 Mishawaka Avenue, South Bend, IN 46634-7111
Phone: 574-520-4834 • **Financial Aid Phone:** 574-520-4357
E-mail: admissions@iusb.edu • **CEEB Code:** 1339
Fax: 574-520-4834 • **Website:** www.iusb.edu

This public school was founded in 1922. It has a 80-acre campus.

RATINGS
Admissions Selectivity Rating: 70   **Fire Safety Rating:** 81   **Green Rating:** 60*

STUDENTS AND FACULTY

Enrollment: 6,189. **Student Body:** 61% female, 39% male, 4% out-of-state, 2% international (76 countries represented). Asian 1%, African American 8%, Caucasian 78%, Hispanic 6%, Native American 0%.
Retention and Graduation: 64% freshmen return for sophomore year. 5% freshmen graduate within 4 years. 22% freshmen graduate within 6 years.
Faculty: Student/faculty ratio 14:1. 286 full-time faculty, 66% hold PhDs, 20% are members of minority groups, 51% are women. % of classes are taught by teaching assistants.

ACADEMICS

Degrees: associate, bachelor's, certificate, diploma, master's, post-bachelor's certificate. **Classes:** Most classes have 20–29 students. Most lab/discussion sessions have 20–29 students. **Special Study Options:** Accelerated program, cross-registration, distance learning, double major, English as a Second Language (ESL), external degree program, honors program, internships, liberal arts/career combination, study abroad, teacher certification program, weekend college, Electrical, Mechanical Engineering, Computer Technology with Purdue University on Indiana University South Bend Campus. Northern Indiana Consortium for Education (NICE) - IUSB is one of six member institutions sharing library resources, faculty expertise, and academic strengths resulting in broadened course opportunities to students. **Disability Services:** Special programs offered to physically disabled students include note-taking services, reader services, tape recorders, tutors. **Career Services:** alumni services, career/job search classes, career assessment, internships.

FACILITIES

Housing: Coed dorms, special housing for international students, apartments for single students. **Computers:** Students can register for classes online. Administrative functions (other than registration) can be performed online.

CAMPUS LIFE

Environment: Activities: Choral groups, drama/theater, jazz band, literary magazine, music ensembles, musical theater, opera, student government, student newspaper, student-run film society, symphony orchestra 30 registered organizations, 1 religious organizations. 2 fraternities, 1 sororities. **Athletics (Intercollegiate):** *Men:* basketball. *Women:* basketball.

ADMISSIONS

Freshman Academic Profile: Average high school GPA 2.9. 7% in top 10% of high school class, 27% in top 25% of high school class, 63% in top 50% of high school class. SAT Math middle 50% range 430-530. SAT Critical Reading middle 50% range 420-530. SAT Writing middle 50% range 410-510. ACT middle 50% range 19-23. Minimum web-based TOEFL 71. Minimum paper TOEFL 530. **Basis for Candidate Selection:** *Very important factors considered include:* rigor of secondary school record. *Important factors considered include:* Class rank, academic GPA. *Other factors considered include:* recommendation(s), standardized test scores, extracurricular activities, interview, state residency. **Freshman Admission Requirements:** High school diploma is required and GED is accepted. *Academic units required:* 4 English, 3 mathematics, 1 science, (1 science labs), 2 social studies. *Academic units recommended:* 4 English, 3 mathematics, 1 science, (1 science labs), 2 social studies. **Freshman Admission Statistics:** 2,441 applied, 71% admitted, 57% enrolled. **Transfer Admission Requirements:** college transcript(s), minimum college GPA of 2.0 required. Lowest grade transferable C. **General Admission Information:** Application Fee $45. Nonfall registration accepted. Admission may be deferred for a maximum of Contact admissions. Neither credit nor placement offered for CEEB Advanced Placement tests.

COSTS AND FINANCIAL AID

Annual in-state tuition $6,138. Annual out-of-state tuition $16,894. Room and board $8,192. Required fees $590. Average book expense $1,496. **Required Forms and Deadlines:** FAFSA, institution's own financial aid form. **Notification of Awards:** Applicants will be notified of awards on a rolling basis beginning 5/1. **Types of Aid:** *Need-based scholarships/grants:* Federal Pell, SEOG, state scholarships/grants, private scholarships, the school's own gift aid. *Loans:* Direct Subsidized Stafford, Direct Unsubsidized Stafford, Direct PLUS, Federal Perkins, college/university loans from institutional funds. **Student Employment:** Federal Work-Study Program available. Off-campus job opportunities are good. **Financial Aid Statistics:** 81% freshmen, 83% undergrads receive need-based scholarship or grant aid. 1% freshmen, 2% undergrads receive non-need-based scholarship or grant aid. 68% freshmen, 76% undergrads receive need-based self-help aid. 71% undergrads borrow to pay for school. Average cumulative indebtedness $25,014. **Criteria for awarding institutional aid:** *Non-need-based:* academics, athletics.

INDIANA UNIVERSITY SOUTHEAST

4201 Grant Line Road, New Albany, IN 47150
Phone: 812-941-2212 • **Financial Aid Phone:** 812-941-2246
E-mail: admissions@ius.edu • **CEEB Code:** 1314
Fax: 812-941-2595 • **Website:** www.ius.edu • **ACT Code:** 1229

This public school was founded in 1941. It has a 177-acre campus.

RATINGS
Admissions Selectivity Rating: 68   **Fire Safety Rating:** 87   **Green Rating:** 63

STUDENTS AND FACULTY

Enrollment: 6,066. **Student Body:** 58% female, 42% male, 28% out-of-state, 0% international (36 countries represented). Asian 1%, African American 6%, Caucasian 86%, Hispanic 2%, Native American 0%.
Retention and Graduation: 64% freshmen return for sophomore year. 8% freshmen graduate within 4 years. 26% freshmen graduate within 6 years.
Faculty: Student/faculty ratio 15:1. 210 full-time faculty, 70% hold PhDs, 17% are members of minority groups, 53% are women.

ACADEMICS

Degrees: associate, bachelor's, certificate, master's, post-bachelor's certificate. **Classes:** Most classes have 20–29 students. Most lab/discussion sessions have 10–19 students. **Special Study Options:** Accelerated program, cross-registration, distance learning, double major, dual enrollment, external degree program, honors program, independent study, internships, student-designed major, study abroad, teacher certification program, weekend college. **Disability Services:** Special programs offered to physically disabled students include note-taking services, reader services, tutors. **Career Services:** alumni services, career/job search classes, career assessment, internships.

FACILITIES
Housing: Coed dorms. 95% of campus accessible to physically disabled. **Special Academic Facilities/Equipment:** Paul W. Ogle Center, Concert Hall, Theatre, Recital Hall, Japanese Cultural Center, Ronald L. Barr Art Gallery. **Computers:** Students can register for classes online. Administrative functions (other than registration) can be performed online.

CAMPUS LIFE
Environment: Village. **Activities:** Choral groups, concert band, drama/theater, literary magazine, music ensembles, student government, student newspaper, symphony orchestra 76 registered organizations, 1 religious organizations. 2 fraternities, 4 sororities. **Athletics (Intercollegiate):** *Men:* baseball, basketball, cross-country, tennis. *Women:* basketball, cross-country, softball, tennis, volleyball. **Environmental Initiatives:** Single stream waste recycling Campus Beautification Day. Volunteers assist grounds personnel in planting flowers and other plant life. Energy reduction capital project (completed in 2006).

ADMISSIONS
Freshman Academic Profile: Average high school GPA 3.1. 10% in top 10% of high school class, 31% in top 25% of high school class, 67% in top 50% of high school class. SAT Math middle 50% range 420-520. SAT Critical Reading middle 50% range 420-530. SAT Writing middle 50% range 410-510. ACT middle 50% range 18-22. Minimum web-based TOEFL 75. Minimum paper TOEFL 530. **Basis for Candidate Selection:** *Very important factors considered include:* Class rank, rigor of secondary school record. *Important factors considered include:* academic GPA, standardized test scores. *Other factors considered include:* recommendation(s), interview. **Freshman Admission Requirements:** High school diploma is required and GED is accepted. *Academic units required:* 4 English, 3 mathematics, 1 science, (1 science labs), 2 social studies, 4 academic electives. *Academic units recommended:* 4 English, 3 mathematics, 1 science, (1 science labs), 2 social studies, 4 academic electives. **Freshman Admission Statistics:** 2,102 applied, 77% admitted, 61% enrolled. **Transfer Admission Requirements:** college transcript(s), Lowest grade transferable C. **General Admission Information:** Application Fee $30. Nonfall registration accepted. Admission may be deferred for a maximum of Contact admissions. Credit offered for CEEB Advanced Placement tests.

COSTS AND FINANCIAL AID
Annual in-state tuition $5,960. Annual out-of-state tuition $16,894. Room and board $9,280. Required fees $616. Average book expense $1,100. **Required Forms and Deadlines:** FAFSA. **Notification of Awards:** Applicants will be notified of awards on a rolling basis beginning 5/1. **Types of Aid:** *Need-based scholarships/grants:* Federal Pell, SEOG, state scholarships/grants, private scholarships, the school's own gift aid. *Loans:* Direct Subsidized Stafford, Direct Unsubsidized Stafford, Direct PLUS, Federal Perkins, Federal Nursing, college/university loans from institutional funds. **Student Employment:** Federal Work-Study Program available. Institutional employment available. Off-campus job opportunities are excellent. **Financial Aid Statistics:** 80% freshmen, 82% undergrads receive need-based scholarship or grant aid. 3% freshmen, 2% undergrads receive non-need-based scholarship or grant aid. 61% freshmen, 72% undergrads receive need-based self-help aid. 1% freshmen, 1% undergrads receive athletic scholarships. 63% undergrads borrow to pay for school. Average cumulative indebtedness $23,532. **Criteria for awarding institutional aid:** *Non-need-based:* academics, art, athletics, leadership, minority status, music/drama.

INDIANA WESLEYAN UNIVERSITY

4201 South Washington Street, Marion, IN 46953-4974
Phone: 765-677-2138 • **Financial Aid Phone:** 765-677-2137
E-mail: admissions@indwes.edu • **CEEB Code:** 1446
Fax: 317-677-2333 • **Website:** www.indwes.edu • **ACT Code:** 1226

This private school, affiliated with the Wesleyan Church, was founded in 1920. It has a 220-acre campus.

RATINGS
Admissions Selectivity Rating: 78   **Fire Safety Rating:** 98   **Green Rating:** 63

STUDENTS AND FACULTY
Enrollment: 2,860. **Student Body:** 64% female, 36% male, 46% out-of-state, 0% international (21 countries represented). Asian 1%, African American 2%, Caucasian 91%, Hispanic 3%, Native American 0%.
Retention and Graduation: 74% freshmen return for sophomore year. 58% freshmen graduate within 4 years. 71% freshmen graduate within 6 years.
Faculty: Student/faculty ratio 14:1. 164 full-time faculty, 67% hold PhDs, 11%

are members of minority groups, 30% are women. 0% of classes are taught by teaching assistants.

ACADEMICS
Degrees: associate, bachelor's. **Classes:** Most classes have 10-19 students. Most lab/discussion sessions have 10-19 students. **Majors with Highest Enrollment:** business administration and management; elementary education and teaching; nursing/registered nurse (rn, asn, bsn, msn). **Special Study Options:** double major, dual enrollment, honors program, independent study, internships, study abroad, teacher certification program. **Honors Programs:** John Wesley Honors College **Combined Degree Programs:** BA/MA, MA/Ed.D. in Leadership. **Disability Services:** Special programs offered to physically disabled students include note-taking services, reader services, tape recorders, tutors. **Career Services:** Alumni network, alumni services, career/job search classes, career assessment, internships, regional alumni. Career Services highlights include The Center for Life Calling and Leadership enables individuals to find an overriding purpose for their lives, equips them to make life decisions based on this purpose, and empowers them to develop this purpose into world changing leadership.

FACILITIES
Housing: men's dorms, women's dorms, apartments for married students, apartments for single students. 99% of campus accessible to physically disabled. **Special Academic Facilities/Equipment:** Lee Howard art collection (European artists) Lewis Jackson Library (2003) Tom and Joanne Phillippe Performing Arts Center (1998) Bronze statues from Israel (1998-2002) Williams chapel--medieval replica (2001) Burns Hall of Science and Nursing (2000) Luckey Recreation and Wellness Center (2001) John Maxwell Business Center (1999) **Computers:** 100% of classrooms, 100% of dorms, 100% of libraries, 100% of dining areas, 100% of student union, 100% of common outdoor areas have wireless network access. Students can register for classes online. Administrative functions (other than registration) can be performed online.

CAMPUS LIFE
Environment: Town. **Activities:** Choral groups, concert band, drama/theater, jazz band, literary magazine, music ensembles, musical theater, pep band, radio station, student government, student newspaper, symphony orchestra, television station, yearbook, Campus Ministries, International Student Organization 35 registered organizations, 1 honor societies, 5 religious organizations. **Athletics (Intercollegiate):** *Men:* baseball, basketball, cheerleading, cross-country, golf, soccer, tennis, track/field (outdoor), track/field (indoor). *Women:* basketball, cheerleading, cross-country, soccer, softball, tennis, track/field (outdoor), track/field (indoor), volleyball. **On-Campus Highlights:** McConn Coffee Shop, Recreation and Wellness Center, Globe Theater, The 1920 Art Gallery, Williams Chapel, The McCoon Coffee Shop is one of the more striking facilities on any college campus--situated in a long indoor mall area of the student center--and includes a fireplace and numerous seating configurations. **Environmental Initiatives:** Creation of a multi-disciplinary Task Force for Campus Sustainabilty Researching grant opportunities for alternative energy projects Currently developing an RFP to calculate our carbon footprint

ADMISSIONS
Freshman Academic Profile: Average high school GPA 3.7. 30% in top 10% of high school class, 60% in top 25% of high school class, 86% in top 50% of high school class. SAT Math middle 50% range 480-590. SAT Critical Reading middle 50% range 470-590. SAT Writing middle 50% range 460-580. ACT middle 50% range 21-26. Minimum web-based TOEFL 79. Minimum paper TOEFL 550. **Basis for Candidate Selection:** *Very important factors considered include:* academic GPA, recommendation(s), standardized test scores, character/personal qualities. *Important factors considered include:* Class rank, rigor of secondary school record. *Other factors considered include:* application essay, alumni/ae relation, extracurricular activities, first generation, interview, level of applicant's interest, religious affiliation/commitment, talent/ability, volunteer work, work experience. **Freshman Admission Requirements:** High school diploma is required and GED is accepted. **Freshman Admission Statistics:** 3,429 applied, 66% admitted, 32% enrolled. **Transfer Admission Requirements:** college transcript(s), statement of good standing from prior institution(s). Minimum college GPA of 2.0 required. Lowest grade transferable C. **General Admission Information:** Application Fee $25. Regular application deadline 8/1. Notification on a rolling basis, beginning on or about 10/1. Nonfall registration accepted. Admission may be deferred for a maximum of 1 year. Credit offered for CEEB Advanced Placement tests.

COSTS AND FINANCIAL AID
Annual tuition $23,628. Room and board $7,560. Average book expense $1,392. **Required Forms and Deadlines:** FAFSA. **Notification of Awards:** Applicants will be notified of awards on or about 4/1. **Types of Aid:** *Need-based scholarships/grants:* Federal Pell, SEOG, state scholarships/grants, private scholarships, the school's own gift aid. *Loans:* Subsidized Stafford, Unsubsidized Stafford, PLUS, Federal Perkins, Federal Nursing, college/university loans from institutional funds. **Student Employment:** Federal Work-Study Program available. Institutional employment available. Off-campus job opportunities

are good. **Financial Aid Statistics:** 99% freshmen, 98% undergrads receive need-based scholarship or grant aid. 12% freshmen, 12% undergrads receive non-need-based scholarship or grant aid. 78% freshmen, 79% undergrads receive need-based self-help aid. 7% freshmen, 5% undergrads receive athletic scholarships. 99% freshmen, 93% undergrads receive any aid. 78% undergrads borrow to pay for school. Average cumulative indebtedness $22,940. **Criteria for awarding institutional aid:** *Non-need-based:* academics, alumni affiliation, art, athletics, leadership, music/drama.

INTERNATIONAL COLLEGE

2655 Northbrooke Drive, Naples, FL 34119
Phone: 239-513-1122 • **Financial Aid Phone:** 239-513-1122
E-mail: admit@internationalcollege.edu • **CEEB Code:** 7113
Fax: 239-598-6254 • **Website:** www.hodges.edu • **ACT Code:** 4775

This private school was founded in 1990.

RATINGS
Admissions Selectivity Rating: 62   **Fire Safety Rating:** 60*   **Green Rating:** 64

STUDENTS AND FACULTY
Enrollment: 1,475. **Student Body:** 68% female, 32% male, % out-of-state, 0% international (40 countries represented). Asian 2%, African American 16%, Caucasian 55%, Hispanic 24%, Native American 0%.
Retention and Graduation: **Faculty:** Student/faculty ratio 17:1. 61 full-time faculty, 66% hold PhDs, 8% are members of minority groups, 33% are women. 0% of classes are taught by teaching assistants.

ACADEMICS
Degrees: associate, bachelor's, certificate, master's. **Classes:** Most classes have 10–19 students. **Majors with Highest Enrollment:** business, management, marketing, and related support services, other; health professions and related clinical sciences, other; multi-/interdisciplinary studies, other. **Special Study Options:** Accelerated program, cooperative education program, distance learning, double major, English as a Second Language (ESL), independent study, internships, weekend college. **Career Services:** alumni services, career/job search classes, career assessment.

FACILITIES
Housing: 100% of campus accessible to physically disabled. **Computers:** 100% of classrooms, 100% of libraries, have wireless network access. Students can register for classes online. Administrative functions (other than registration) can be performed online.

CAMPUS LIFE
Environment: City. **Activities:** literary magazine 1 honor societies. **Environmental Initiatives:** Reduction in energy usage Recycling Programs

ADMISSIONS
Freshman Academic Profile: Minimum paper TOEFL 500. **Basis for Candidate Selection:** *Important factors considered include:* interview, level of applicant's interest. **Freshman Admission Requirements:** High school diploma is required and GED is accepted. **Freshman Admission Statistics:** 210 applied, 79% admitted, 94% enrolled. **Transfer Admission Requirements:** High school transcript, essay or personal statement, Lowest grade transferable C. **General Admission Information:** Application Fee $20. Nonfall registration accepted. Admission may be deferred for a maximum of 1 year. Credit offered for CEEB Advanced Placement tests.

COSTS AND FINANCIAL AID
Required Forms and Deadlines: FAFSA. **Notification of Awards: Types of Aid:** *Need-based scholarships/grants:* Federal Pell, SEOG, state scholarships/grants, private scholarships, the school's own gift aid. *Loans:* Subsidized Stafford, Unsubsidized Stafford, PLUS. **Student Employment:** Federal Work-Study Program available. Institutional employment available. Off-campus job opportunities are good. **Financial Aid Statistics:** 90% freshmen, 94% undergrads receive need-based scholarship or grant aid. 41% freshmen, 66% undergrads receive non-need-based scholarship or grant aid. 87% freshmen, 91% undergrads receive need-based self-help aid. 81% undergrads borrow to pay for school. Average cumulative indebtedness $18,100. **Criteria for awarding institutional aid:** *Non-need-based:* academics, leadership.

IONA COLLEGE

715 North Avenue, New Rochelle, NY 10801
Phone: 914-633-2502 • **Financial Aid Phone:** 914-633-2497
E-mail: icad@iona.edu • **CEEB Code:** 2324
Fax: 914-633-2642 • **Website:** www.iona.edu • **ACT Code:** 2770

This private school, affiliated with the Roman Catholic Church, was founded in 1940. It has a 35-acre campus.

RATINGS
Admissions Selectivity Rating: 67   **Fire Safety Rating:** 96   **Green Rating:** 76

STUDENTS AND FACULTY
Enrollment: 2,988. **Student Body:** 57% female, 43% male, 24% out-of-state, 2% international (32 countries represented). Asian 2%, African American 6%, Caucasian 63%, Hispanic 18%, Native American 0%.
Retention and Graduation: 81% freshmen return for sophomore year. 56% freshmen graduate within 4 years. 65% freshmen graduate within 6 years.
Faculty: Student/faculty ratio 14:1. 176 full-time faculty, 90% hold PhDs, 16% are members of minority groups, 38% are women. 0% of classes are taught by teaching assistants.

ACADEMICS
Degrees: bachelor's, master's, post-bachelor's certificate, post-master's certificate. **Classes:** Most classes have 20–29 students. Most lab/discussion sessions have 10–19 students. **Majors with Highest Enrollment:** finance; mass communication/media studies; psychology. **Special Study Options:** Accelerated program, distance learning, double major, honors program, independent study, internships, liberal arts/career combination, study abroad, teacher certification program, weekend college. **Honors Programs:** The Iona College Honors Degree Program is designed to meet the educational needs of the ablest and most highly motivated students at Iona. Grounded in a challenging curriculum, the program offers gifted students the resources and opportunities to develop their talents and to perform at the peak of their capabilities. The course of study is designed to develop intellectual curiosity, analytic abilities, and awareness of ethical and civic responsibilities. The program encourages the development of a nucleus of independent learners able to inspire each other academically and fosters a sense of self-respect in students, encouraging them to stretch their abilities in pursuit of lifelong learning, independent thinking, and personal fulfillment. The Honors Degree Program seeks to establish a core academic community that enriches and serves the wider college community. The program endeavors to create an intellectual atmosphere to attract and challenge superior students and faculty and to enhance the public image of the College by promoting the concept of excellence in education. The curriculum promotes an appreciation and understanding of the interrelatedness of knowledge and culture by providing a wide range of interdisciplinary courses and opportunities to study abroad. Students in the program take specially designed honors courses and advanced courses in other areas, and engage in independent research under the guidance of faculty mentors. Small class sizes encourage student participation and promote a close student-faculty relationship. Students are offered close individual guidance, both academically and in terms of career preparation. There is a faculty committee that works with students interested in applying for competitive grants and fellowships and advises them regarding graduate and professional studies. A career mentoring program affords students a unique chance to explore career opportunities by matching them with an appropriate alumnus/alumna or corporate liaison. **Combined Degree Programs:** BA/MA. **Disability Services:** Special programs offered to physically disabled students include note-taking services, reader services, tape recorders, tutors. **Career Services:** Alumni network, alumni services, career/job search classes, career assessment, internships, regional alumni.

FACILITIES
Housing: Coed dorms, special housing for disabled students, apartments for single students, Living learning communities in Science, Education, wellness housing to Honors Program Students. 100% of campus accessible to physically disabled. **Special Academic Facilities/Equipment:** Iona College Art Center, Br. Kenneth Chapman Public Art Gallary, Murphy Science Technology Center, Hynes Natural Science Center, Advanced Computer Laboratory, TV Production Studio, LaPenta Student Union, Hynes Athletic Center, Rowing tank, Arrigoni center **Computers:** 100% of classrooms, 100% of dorms, 100% of libraries, 100% of dining areas, 100% of student union, 100% of common outdoor areas have wireless network access. Students can register for classes online. Administrative functions (other than registration) can be performed online.

CAMPUS LIFE
Environment: City. **Activities:** Choral groups, dance, drama/theater, literary magazine, musical theater, pep band, radio station, student government, student newspaper, student-run film society, television station, yearbook, Campus Ministries, International Student Organization, Model UN 65 registered

organizations, 9 honor societies, 4 religious organizations. 4 fraternities, 6 sororities. **Athletics (Intercollegiate):** *Men:* baseball, basketball, crew/rowing, cross-country, diving, golf, soccer, swimming, track/field (outdoor), track/field (indoor), water polo. *Women:* basketball, crew/rowing, cross-country, diving, lacrosse, soccer, softball, swimming, track/field (outdoor), track/field (indoor), volleyball, water polo. **On-Campus Highlights:** Lapenta Student Union, Hynes Athletics Center, Ryan Library, North Residence Hall, Loftus Courtyard. **Environmental Initiatives:** Recycling Green Cleaning Lowering of emissions

ADMISSIONS

Freshman Academic Profile: Average high school GPA 3.1. 17% in top 10% of high school class, 44% in top 25% of high school class, 76% in top 50% of high school class. SAT Math middle 50% range 460-560. SAT Critical Reading middle 50% range 450-550. ACT middle 50% range 20-25. Minimum web-based TOEFL 80. Minimum paper TOEFL 550. **Basis for Candidate Selection:** *Very important factors considered include:* academic GPA, rigor of secondary school record. *Important factors considered include:* Class rank, application essay, standardized test scores, character/personal qualities, interview. *Other factors considered include:* recommendation(s), alumni/ae relation, extracurricular activities, first generation, geographical residence, level of applicant's interest, talent/ability, volunteer work, work experience. **Freshman Admission Requirements:** High school diploma is required and GED is accepted. *Academic units required:* 4 English, 3 mathematics, 2 science, (2 science labs), 2 foreign language, 1 social studies, 1 history, 1 academic electives. *Academic units recommended:* 4 English, 3 mathematics, 2 science, (2 science labs), 2 foreign language, 1 social studies, 1 history, 1 academic electives. **Freshman Admission Statistics:** 8,741 applied, 86% admitted, 10% enrolled. **Transfer Admission Requirements:** High school transcript, college transcript(s), essay or personal statement, minimum college GPA of 2.5 required. Lowest grade transferable C. **General Admission Information:** Application Fee $50. Regular application deadline 2/15. Regular notification 3/20. Nonfall registration accepted. Admission may be deferred for a maximum of 12 months. Credit and/or placement offered for CEEB Advanced Placement tests.

COSTS AND FINANCIAL AID

Annual tuition $30,670. Room and board $13,175. Required fees $2,100. Average book expense $1,500. **Required Forms and Deadlines:** FAFSA, institution's own financial aid form, state aid form. **Notification of Awards:** Applicants will be notified of awards on a rolling basis beginning 12/20. **Types of Aid:** *Need-based scholarships/grants:* Federal Pell, SEOG, state scholarships/grants, private scholarships, the school's own gift aid. *Loans:* Subsidized Stafford, Unsubsidized Stafford, PLUS, Federal Perkins, Alternative Loans. **Student Employment:** Federal Work-Study Program available. Institutional employment available. Highest amount earned per year from on-campus jobs $9,729. Off-campus job opportunities are good. **Financial Aid Statistics:** 77% freshmen, 70% undergrads receive need-based scholarship or grant aid. 98% freshmen, 97% undergrads receive non-need-based scholarship or grant aid. 82% freshmen, 83% undergrads receive need-based self-help aid. 7% freshmen, 7% undergrads receive athletic scholarships. 99% freshmen, 96% undergrads receive any aid. 71% undergrads borrow to pay for school. Average cumulative indebtedness $31,960. **Criteria for awarding institutional aid:** *Non-need-based:* academics, alumni affiliation, athletics.

See page 1104.

IOWA STATE UNIVERSITY

Best 378

100 Enrollment Services Center, Ames, IA 50011-2011
Phone: 515-294-5836 • **Financial Aid Phone:** 515-294-2223
E-mail: admissions@iastate.edu • **CEEB Code:** 6306
Fax: 515-294-2592 • **Website:** www.iastate.edu • **ACT Code:** 1320

This public school was founded in 1858. It has a 1794-acre campus.

RATINGS
Admissions Selectivity Rating: 75   **Fire Safety Rating:** 79   **Green Rating:** 88

STUDENTS AND FACULTY
Enrollment: 25,058. **Student Body:** 44% female, 56% male, 31% out-of-state, 7% international (101 countries represented). Asian 3%, African American 3%, Caucasian 79%, Hispanic 4%, Native American 0%.
Retention and Graduation: 39% freshmen graduate within 4 years. 19% grads go on to further study within 1 year. 8% grads pursue arts and sciences

degrees. 1% grads pursue law degrees. 3% grads pursue business degrees. 2% grads pursue medical degrees. **Faculty:** Student/faculty ratio 18:1. 1446 full-time faculty, 94% hold PhDs, 22% are members of minority groups, 35% are women. 11% of classes are taught by teaching assistants.

ACADEMICS

Degrees: bachelor's, master's. **Classes:** Most classes have 20–29 students. Most lab/discussion sessions have 20–29 students. **Majors with Highest Enrollment:** finance; marketing/marketing management; mechanical engineering. **Special Study Options:** Accelerated program, cooperative education program, cross-registration, distance learning, double major, dual enrollment, English as a Second Language (ESL), exchange student program (domestic), external degree program, honors program, independent study, internships, liberal arts/career combination, student-designed major, study abroad, teacher certification program, weekend college. **Honors Programs:** ISU offers both a University Honors Program and a Freshman Honors Program. Each program promotes an enhanced academic environment for students of high ability and emphasizes the development of an enriched, individualized program study that meets each student's particular needs, interests and abilities. Honors gives students a supportive community in which to pursue their goals and stretch their horizons. Benefits include uniques courses, small class sizes, research opportunities and funding, access to graduate-level courses, and priority registration. **Combined Degree Programs:** BA/MEng, BS/MS. **Disability Services:** Special programs offered to physically disabled students include note-taking services, reader services, tape recorders, tutors. **Career Services:** Alumni network, alumni services, career/job search classes, career assessment, internships. Career Services highlights include Our Learning Communities, in which students who have similar career goals live together and share academic courses, are ranked high nationally.

FACILITIES

Housing: Coed dorms, special housing for disabled students, men's dorms, special housing for international students, women's dorms, fraternity/sorority housing, apartments for married students, apartments for single students, theme housing, Learning Communities; family housing; quiet, non-smoking, or alcohol-free floors; graduate/adult undergraduate housing. 95% of campus accessible to physically disabled. **Special Academic Facilities/Equipment:** Brunnier art museum, Farm House museum, observatory, numerous institutes, research centers, College of Design Gallery, Virtual Reality Application Center, Pappajohn Center for Entrepreneurship **Computers:** 100% of classrooms, 75% of dorms, 100% of libraries, 100% of dining areas, 100% of student union, 40% of common outdoor areas have wireless network access. Students can register for classes online. Administrative functions (other than registration) can be performed online.

CAMPUS LIFE

Environment: Town. **Activities:** Choral groups, concert band, dance, drama/theater, jazz band, literary magazine, marching band, music ensembles, musical theater, opera, pep band, radio station, student government, student newspaper, student-run film society, symphony orchestra, television station 799 registered organizations, 43 honor societies, 34 religious organizations. 34 fraternities, 19 sororities. **Athletics (Intercollegiate):** *Men:* basketball, cross-country, football, golf, track/field (outdoor), track/field (indoor), wrestling. *Women:* basketball, cross-country, diving, golf, gymnastics, soccer, softball, swimming, tennis, track/field (outdoor), track/field (indoor), volleyball. **On-Campus Highlights:** Union Drive Community Center (dining center), Reiman Gardens, Lied Recreation Center, Memorial Union, Virtual Reality Lab (available to visitors also), 6. Campanile. **Environmental Initiatives:** Establishment of the Live Green Initiative (http://www.livegreen.iastate.edu/about/)that has included: 1. Hiring of a Director of Sustainability (http://www.iastate.edu/Inside/2008/1212/rankin.shtml) 2. Creation of a 13 member (students, staff, and faculty) President's Advisory Committee on Energy Conservation and Global Climate Change (http://www.committees.iastate.edu/comm-info.php?id=136) 3. Creation of a Live Green Loan Fund for energy conservation and sustainability projects (http://www.livegreen.iastate.edu/loan/) 4. Completion of an annual Symposium on Sustainability (http://www.livegreen.iastate.edu/symposium/archive/) Commitment to Sustainable Operations highlighted by: 1. Energy - through a joint contract with the City of Ames, allowing up to 10% of Iowa State University's energy to be derived from wind. In addition, there is ongoing evaluation and testing of renewable fuel sources. 2. Building and Construction - LEED Gold Certification Requirement for all new construction and major renovation projects. Specific Iowa State University required LEED credits have also been designated. In addition, for all other campus projects the incorporation of sustainable design standards is required. Currently ISU has one platinum, two gold, and one silver LEED buildings. 3. Dining Services - 12% of purchases are local, organic, or environmentally-preferable. Trayless dining in three dining centers has reduced food waste by 50%. Food waste is composted at the university's compost facility and utilized for on-campus projects. Prepared leftover food is donated to a free meal program in the Ames community. Waste in packaging is reduced through a reusable mug program, keeping 42,796 disposable coffee cups out of the landfill in 2011, and a "green" to go reusable takeway container program, currently serving 3,312 customers. 4. Campus Green Teams - Development of campus green teams dedicated to increasing sustainability efforts as related to a specific campus building, college, department, or operation. To date, there are 33 Iowa State University Green Teams. 5. Community partnership to bring 12 hybrid buses, Cybrids (17% of the total fleet), to the University and Ames community bus system, CyRide. Government of the Student Body is very active in supporting and expanding sustainability efforts including: the creation a cabinet postion of Director of Sustainability, formation of a Sustainability Committee, addition of a sustainability section to their website (http://www.gsb.iastate.edu/en/projects_and_issues/sustainability_efforts/), and the development and launching of an online Ride Share database to increase sustainability in travel and commuting for students, faculty, and staff.

ADMISSIONS

Freshman Academic Profile: Average high school GPA 3.6. 26% in top 10% of high school class, 56% in top 25% of high school class, 90% in top 50% of high school class. 92% from public high schools. SAT Math middle 50% range 530-680. SAT Critical Reading middle 50% range 460-620. ACT middle 50% range 22-28. Minimum web-based TOEFL 71. Minimum paper TOEFL 530. **Basis for Candidate Selection:** *Very important factors considered include:* Class rank, academic GPA, rigor of secondary school record, standardized test scores. *Other factors considered include:* application essay, recommendation(s), character/personal qualities, extracurricular activities, geographical residence, interview, state residency, talent/ability, volunteer work, work experience. **Freshman Admission Requirements:** High school diploma is required and GED is accepted. *Academic units required:* 4 English, 3 mathematics, 3 science, (2 science labs), 2 foreign language, 2 social studies. *Academic units recommended:* 4 English, 3 mathematics, 3 science, (2 science labs), 2 foreign language, 2 social studies. **Freshman Admission Statistics:** 16,539 applied, 83% admitted, 39% enrolled. **Transfer Admission Requirements:** college transcript(s), statement of good standing from prior institution(s). Minimum college GPA of 2.0 required. Lowest grade transferable D. **General Admission Information:** Application Fee $30. Regular application deadline 7/1. Notification on a rolling basis, beginning on or about 7/1. Nonfall registration accepted. Admission may be deferred for a maximum of 1 year. Credit and/or placement offered for CEEB Advanced Placement tests.

COSTS AND FINANCIAL AID

Annual in-state tuition $6,648. Annual out-of-state tuition $18,760. Room and board $7,721. Required fees $1,078. Average book expense $1,043. **Required Forms and Deadlines:** FAFSA. **Notification of Awards:** Applicants will be notified of awards on a rolling basis beginning 4/1. **Types of Aid:** *Need-based scholarships/grants:* Federal Pell, SEOG, state scholarships/grants, the school's own gift aid. *Loans:* Direct Subsidized Stafford, Direct Unsubsidized Stafford, Direct PLUS, Federal Perkins, state loans, college/university loans from institutional funds, Private alternative loans. **Student Employment:** Federal Work-Study Program available. Institutional employment available. Highest amount earned per year from on-campus jobs $1,877. Off-campus job opportunities are excellent. **Financial Aid Statistics:** 95% freshmen, 98% undergrads receive need-based scholarship or grant aid. 49% freshmen, 49% undergrads receive non-need-based scholarship or grant aid. 70% freshmen, 79% undergrads receive need-based self-help aid. 1% freshmen, 2% undergrads receive athletic scholarships. 87% freshmen, 80% undergrads receive any aid. 65% undergrads borrow to pay for school. Average cumulative indebtedness $30,374. **Criteria for awarding institutional aid:** *Non-need-based:* academics, art, athletics, leadership, minority status, music/drama, state/district residency.

ITHACA COLLEGE

Best 378

Ithaca College, Office of Admission, Ithaca, NY 14850-7002
Phone: 607-274-3124 • **Financial Aid Phone:** 607-274-3131
E-mail: admission@ithaca.edu • **CEEB Code:** 2325
Fax: 607-274-1900 • **Website:** www.ithaca.edu • **ACT Code:** 2772

This private school was founded in 1892. It has a 650-acre campus.

RATINGS
Admissions Selectivity Rating: 82   **Fire Safety Rating:** 89   **Green Rating:** 94

STUDENTS AND FACULTY
Enrollment: 6,228. **Student Body:** 57% female, 43% male, 56% out-of-state, 2% international (73 countries represented). Asian 3%, African American 4%, Caucasian 70%, Hispanic 6%, Native American 0%.

Retention and Graduation: 67% freshmen graduate within 4 years. **Faculty:** Student/faculty ratio 12:1. 478 full-time faculty, 94% hold PhDs, 10% are members of minority groups, 46% are women. 1% of classes are taught by teaching assistants.

ACADEMICS
Degrees: bachelor's, certificate, master's. **Classes:** Most classes have fewer than 10 students. Most lab/discussion sessions have 10–19 students. **Majors with Highest Enrollment:** business/commerce; music; radio and television. **Special Study Options:** Accelerated program, cross-registration, distance learning, double major, dual enrollment, honors program, independent study, internships, liberal arts/career combination, student-designed major, study abroad, teacher certification program, London Center (London, England), Los Angeles Program, Washington D.C. semester program, Walkabout Down Under Program(Australia),opportunities to study in over 50 countries around the world. **Honors Programs:** Students in the Humanities and Sciences Honors Program participate in a series of special intensive seminars complemented by an array of out-of-class activities. Starting in the fall of the first year, honors students begin a sequence of eight honors seminar courses that help them meet general requirements of the school. The sequence includes: a first-year seminar taken in the first semester, four intermediate seminars normally taken in the second, third and fourth semesters, a seminar on cultural themes taken in the junior year, and a capstone seminar on contemporary issues, taken in the senior year. **Combined Degree Programs:** BS/MS-Occup. Therapy and BS/DPT in Physical Therapy. **Disability Services:** Special programs offered to physically disabled students include note-taking services, reader services, tape recorders. **Career Services:** Alumni network, alumni services, career/job search classes, career assessment, internships, regional alumni. Career Services highlights include Park School of Communication Internships are normally taken during a students senior year. Sponsors include local, regional, national, and international TV, radio, advertising, public relations, motion picture, education and corporate media organizations and many corporations and non-profit organizations.

FACILITIES
Housing: Coed dorms, special housing for disabled students, women's dorms, fraternity/sorority housing, apartments for single students, theme housing. **Special Academic Facilities/Equipment:** Two newly-constructed Platinum LEED certified buildings(the Business School and the Peggy Williams Center, Art Gallery, Radio and TV stations, digital technology throughout Communications building, Observatory, Wellness Clinic, Fitness Center, Trading Room, Speech and Hearing Handicapped Clinic, Physical Therapy Clinic, Performing Arts Centers (Music And Theater), Music Recording Facility. **Computers:** 50% of classrooms, 100% of dorms, 100% of libraries, 100% of dining areas, 100% of student union, have wireless network access. Students can register for classes online. Administrative functions (other than registration) can be performed online.

CAMPUS LIFE
Environment: Town. **Activities:** Choral groups, concert band, dance, drama/theater, jazz band, literary magazine, music ensembles, musical theater, opera, pep band, radio station, student government, student newspaper, student-run film society, symphony orchestra, television station, yearbook, Campus Ministries, International Student Organization 180 registered organizations, 28 honor societies, 8 religious organizations. 3 fraternities, 1 sororities. **Athletics (Intercollegiate):** *Men:* baseball, basketball, crew/rowing, cross-country, diving, football, lacrosse, soccer, swimming, tennis, track/field (outdoor), wrestling. *Women:* basketball, crew/rowing, cross-country, diving, field hockey, golf, gymnastics, lacrosse, soccer, softball, swimming, tennis, track/field (outdoor), volleyball. **On-Campus Highlights:** IC Square and Food Court, Handwerker Gallery, Fitness Center, Business School Atrium, Library. **Environmental Initiatives:** Sustainability Initiative that spurs and chronicles progress in three separate but highly inter-related areas: development of curriculum to infuse considerations of sustainability and applied research opportunities to study and solve sustainability challenges; modification of campus operations to incorporate more sustainable decision-making; and campus in-reach and community outreach to share our experiences as a learning organization seeking to become more sustainable. Ithaca College participated as a charter member in the Sustainability Tracking, Assessment and Rating System (STARS) developed by the Association for the Advancement of Sustainability in Higher Education (AASHE). Using the STARS campus sustainability evaluation system, Ithaca College achieved a GOLD rating. We have collaborated with our regional Sodexo Facilities Management group to implement the recommendations of a comprehensive energy and resource audit and sustainability assessment of all of our dining services-related facilities including board dining halls and retail operations.

ADMISSIONS
Freshman Academic Profile: 31% in top 10% of high school class, 68% in top 25% of high school class, 92% in top 50% of high school class. 82% from public high schools. SAT Math middle 50% range 520-630. SAT Critical Reading middle 50% range 520-620. SAT Writing middle 50% range 530-630. Minimum web-based TOEFL 80. Minimum paper TOEFL 550. **Basis for Candidate**

Selection: *Very important factors considered include:* academic GPA, rigor of secondary school record, standardized test scores. *Important factors considered include:* Class rank, application essay, recommendation(s), character/personal qualities, extracurricular activities, talent/ability. *Other factors considered include:* alumni/ae relation, first generation, level of applicant's interest, volunteer work, work experience. **Freshman Admission Requirements:** High school diploma is required and GED is accepted. *Academic units required:* 4 English, 3 mathematics, 3 science, 2 foreign language, 4 social studies, 1 academic electives. 4 English, 3 mathematics, 3 science, 2 foreign language, 4 social studies, 1 academic electives. **Freshman Admission Statistics:** 13,436 applied, 68% admitted, 18% enrolled. **Transfer Admission Requirements:** High school transcript, college transcript(s), essay or personal statement, statement of good standing from prior institution(s). Minimum college GPA of 2.75 required. Lowest grade transferable C–. **General Admission Information:** Application Fee $60. Early decision application deadline 11/1. Regular application deadline 2/1. Regular notification 4/15. Notification on a rolling basis, beginning on or about 11/15. Nonfall registration accepted. Admission may be deferred for a maximum of 1 year. Credit and/or placement offered for CEEB Advanced Placement tests.

COSTS AND FINANCIAL AID

Annual tuition $35,278. Room and board $12,854. Average book expense $1,340. **Required Forms and Deadlines:** FAFSA, CSS/Financial Aid PROFILE. **Notification of Awards:** Applicants will be notified of awards on a rolling basis beginning 2/15. **Types of Aid:** *Need-based scholarships/grants:* Federal Pell, SEOG, state scholarships/grants, private scholarships, the school's own gift aid. *Loans:* Subsidized Stafford, Unsubsidized Stafford, PLUS, Federal Perkins, Alternative Loans. **Student Employment:** Federal Work-Study Program available. Institutional employment available. Highest amount earned per year from on-campus jobs $2,400. Off-campus job opportunities are good. **Financial Aid Statistics:** 96% freshmen, 97% undergrads receive need-based scholarship or grant aid, 25% freshmen, 21% undergrads receive non-need-based scholarship or grant aid. 94% freshmen, 94% undergrads receive need-based self-help aid. 93% freshmen, 92% undergrads receive any aid. **Criteria for awarding institutional aid:** *Non-need-based:* academics, alumni affiliation, leadership, minority status, music/drama.

JACKSON STATE UNIVERSITY

1400 J. R. Lynch Street, Jackson, MS 39217
Phone: 601-979-2100 • **Financial Aid Phone:** 601-979-2227
E-mail: admappl@jsums.edu • **CEEB Code:** 1341
Fax: 601-979-3445 • **Website:** www.jsums.edu • **ACT Code:** 2204

This public school was founded in 1877. It has a 150 acre campus.

RATINGS
Admissions Selectivity Rating: 66   **Fire Safety Rating:** 77   **Green Rating:** 60*

STUDENTS AND FACULTY
Enrollment: 6,844. **Student Body:** 62% female, 38% male, 17% out-of-state, 2% international (35 countries represented). Asian 0%, African American 93%, Caucasian 3%, Hispanic 0%, Native American 0%.
Retention and Graduation: 78% freshmen return for sophomore year. 22% freshmen graduate within 4 years. 42% freshmen graduate within 6 years.
Faculty: Student/faculty ratio 17:1. 378 full-time faculty, 81% hold PhDs, 81% are members of minority groups, 46% are women.

ACADEMICS
Degrees: bachelor's, master's, post-master's certificate. **Classes: Majors with Highest Enrollment:** education, other; elementary education and teaching; social work. **Special Study Options:** cooperative education program, distance learning, double major, dual enrollment, English as a Second Language (ESL), honors program, independent study, internships, study abroad, teacher certification program, weekend college, Undergrads may take grad level classes. Off-Campus Programs: Research semester at Lawrence Berkeley Lab. Co-Op Programs: Business, Computer Science, Natural Science. **Honors Programs:** Honors College. **Disability Services:** Special programs offered to physically disabled students include note-taking services, tape recorders, tutors. **Career Services:** career/job search classes, career assessment Career Services highlights include They both are important in assisting students for job placement after graduation.

FACILITIES
Housing: men's dorms, women's dorms. 100% of campus accessible to physically disabled. **Special Academic Facilities/Equipment:** Research center. **Computers:** Students can register for classes online. Administrative functions (other than registration) can be performed online.

CAMPUS LIFE
Environment: Metropolis. **Activities:** Choral groups, concert band, dance, drama/theater, jazz band, literary magazine, marching band, music ensembles, opera, pep band, radio station, student government, student newspaper, student-run film society, symphony orchestra, television station, yearbook 150 registered organizations, 20 honor societies, 11 religious organizations. 4 fraternities, 4 sororities. **Athletics (Intercollegiate):** *Men:* baseball, basketball, cross-country, football, golf, soccer, tennis, track/field (outdoor), track/field (indoor), volleyball. *Women:* basketball, cross-country, golf, soccer, softball, tennis, track/field (outdoor), track/field (indoor), volleyball.

ADMISSIONS
Freshman Academic Profile: Average high school GPA 2.9. ACT middle 50% range 17-20. Minimum paper TOEFL 525. **Basis for Candidate Selection:** *Very important factors considered include:* academic GPA, rigor of secondary school record, standardized test scores. *Important factors considered include:* level of applicant's interest. **Freshman Admission Requirements:** High school diploma is required and GED is accepted. *Academic units required:* 4 English, 3 mathematics, 3 science, 3 social studies, 2 academic electives. 4 English, 3 mathematics, 3 science, 3 social studies, 2 academic electives. **Freshman Admission Statistics:** 7,265 applied, 74% admitted, 19% enrolled. **Transfer Admission Requirements:** High school transcript, college transcript(s), minimum college GPA of 2.0 required. Lowest grade transferable C. **General Admission Information:** Nonfall registration accepted.

COSTS AND FINANCIAL AID
Annual in-state tuition $5,504. Annual out-of-state tuition $13,494. Room and board $6,494. Average book expense $800. **Required Forms and Deadlines:** FAFSA, institution's own financial aid form, state aid form. **Notification of Awards:** Applicants will be notified of awards on a rolling basis beginning 2/15. **Types of Aid:** *Need-based scholarships/grants:* Federal Pell, SEOG, state scholarships/grants, private scholarships, the school's own gift aid. *Loans:* Subsidized Stafford, Unsubsidized Stafford, PLUS, Federal Perkins, college/university loans from institutional funds. **Student Employment:** Federal Work-Study Program available. Institutional employment available. Highest amount earned per year from on-campus jobs $2,200. Off-campus job opportunities are good.

JACKSONVILLE STATE UNIVERSITY

700 Pelham Road North, Jacksonville, AL 36265
Phone: 256-782-5268 • **Financial Aid Phone:** 256-782-5006
E-mail: info@jsu.edu
Fax: 256-782-5953 • **Website:** www.jsu.edu • **ACT Code:** 20

This public school was founded in 1883. It has a 459-acre campus.

RATINGS
Admissions Selectivity Rating: 65   **Fire Safety Rating:** 62   **Green Rating:** 60*

STUDENTS AND FACULTY
Enrollment: 7,096. **Student Body:** 58% female, 42% male, 12% out-of-state, 1% international (73 countries represented). Asian 1%, African American 22%, Caucasian 71%, Hispanic 1%, Native American 1%.
Retention and Graduation: 63% freshmen return for sophomore year. 15% freshmen graduate within 4 years. 35% freshmen graduate within 6 years.
Faculty: Student/faculty ratio 21:1. 300 full-time faculty, 66% hold PhDs, 11% are members of minority groups, 44% are women. 0% of classes are taught by teaching assistants.

ACADEMICS
Degrees: bachelor's, master's, post-master's certificate. **Classes:** Most classes have 20–29 students. **Majors with Highest Enrollment:** criminal justice/safety studies; elementary education and teaching; nursing/registered nurse (rn, asn, bsn, msn). **Special Study Options:** Accelerated program, cooperative education program, distance learning, double major, dual enrollment, honors program, independent study, internships, teacher certification program. **Disability Services:** Special programs offered to physically disabled students include note-taking services, reader services, tape recorders, tutors.

FACILITIES
Housing: Coed dorms, men's dorms, special housing for international students, women's dorms, fraternity/sorority housing, apartments for married students, apartments for single students, apartments for students with dependent children. 90% of campus accessible to physically disabled. **Computers:** Students can register for classes online.

CAMPUS LIFE
Environment: Village. **Activities:** Choral groups, concert band, dance, drama/theater, jazz band, marching band, music ensembles, musical theater, pep band,

radio station, student government, student newspaper, symphony orchestra, yearbook 100 registered organizations, 13 honor societies, 8 religious organizations. 11 fraternities, 9 sororities. **Athletics (Intercollegiate):** *Men:* baseball, basketball, cheerleading, football, golf, riflery, tennis. *Women:* basketball, cheerleading, cross-country, golf, riflery, soccer, softball, tennis, track/field (outdoor), volleyball. **On-Campus Highlights:** Houston Cole Library, Theron Montgomery Bldg - Student Life, Stephenson Gym, Bibb Graves - Adm Bldg, Paul Snow Stadium.

ADMISSIONS

Freshman Academic Profile: Average high school GPA 3.0. 3% in top 10% of high school class, 13% in top 25% of high school class, 34% in top 50% of high school class. 99% from public high schools. SAT Math middle 50% range 400-530. SAT Critical Reading middle 50% range 420-530. ACT middle 50% range 17-23. Minimum paper TOEFL 500. **Basis for Candidate Selection:** *Very important factors considered include:* rigor of secondary school record, standardized test scores. **Freshman Admission Requirements:** High school diploma is required and GED is accepted. *Academic units required:* 3 English, 4 academic electives. 3 English, 4 academic electives. **Freshman Admission Statistics:** 2,419 applied, 88% admitted, 50% enrolled. **Transfer Admission Requirements:** college transcript(s), Lowest grade transferable D. **General Admission Information:** Application Fee $20. Nonfall registration accepted. Admission may be deferred for a maximum of 4. Credit and/or placement offered for CEEB Advanced Placement tests.

COSTS AND FINANCIAL AID

Annual in-state tuition $4,040. Annual out-of-state tuition $8,080. Room and board $3,312. Required fees $20. Average book expense $1,008. **Required Forms and Deadlines:** FAFSA, institution's own financial aid form. **Notification of Awards:** Applicants will be notified of awards on a rolling basis beginning 5/15. *Types of Aid: Need-based scholarships/grants:* Federal Pell, SEOG, state scholarships/grants, private scholarships, Federal Nursing Scholarships. *Loans:* Direct Subsidized Stafford, Direct Unsubsidized Stafford, Direct PLUS, college/university loans from institutional funds.

JACKSONVILLE UNIVERSITY

Office of Admissions, Jacksonville, FL 32211
Phone: 904-256-7000 • **Financial Aid Phone:** 800-558-3467
E-mail: admissions@ju.edu • **CEEB Code:** 5331
Fax: • **Website:** www.ju.edu/ • **ACT Code:** 740

This private school was founded in 1934. It has a 198-acre campus.

RATINGS
Admissions Selectivity Rating: 90   **Fire Safety Rating:** 71   **Green Rating:** 60*

STUDENTS AND FACULTY
Enrollment: 3,122. **Student Body:** 59% female, 41% male, 29% out-of-state, 1% international (50 countries represented). Asian 4%, African American 19%, Caucasian 60%, Hispanic 7%, Native American 1%.
Retention and Graduation: 60% freshmen return for sophomore year. 23% freshmen graduate within 4 years. 40% freshmen graduate within 6 years. 22% grads go on to further study within 1 year. **Faculty:** Student/faculty ratio 13:1. 180 full-time faculty, 79% hold PhDs, 9% are members of minority groups, 43% are women. 0% of classes are taught by teaching assistants.

ACADEMICS
Degrees: bachelor's, master's. **Classes:** Most classes have 10–19 students. **Majors with Highest Enrollment:** aviation/airway management and operations; business/commerce; nursing/registered nurse (rn, asn, bsn, msn). **Special Study Options:** Accelerated program, cooperative education program, distance learning, double major, dual enrollment, honors program, independent study, internships, liberal arts/career combination, student-designed major, study abroad, teacher certification program. **Honors Programs:** University Honors Program. **Disability Services:** Special programs offered to physically disabled students include note-taking services, reader services, tutors.

FACILITIES
Housing: Coed dorms, special housing for disabled students, men's dorms, women's dorms, fraternity/sorority housing, apartments for single students. **Special Academic Facilities/Equipment:** Art museum, dance pavilion, concert hall, on-campus pre-school. **Computers:** Students can register for classes online. Administrative functions (other than registration) can be performed online.

CAMPUS LIFE
Environment: Metropolis. **Activities:** Choral groups, concert band, dance, drama/theater, jazz band, literary magazine, music ensembles, musical theater, pep band, radio station, student government, student newspaper, symphony orchestra, television station, yearbook, Campus Ministries, International Student

Organization 60 registered organizations, 16 honor societies, 9 fraternities, 6 sororities. **Athletics (Intercollegiate):** *Men:* baseball, basketball, crew/rowing, cross-country, football, golf, soccer, tennis. *Women:* basketball, crew/rowing, cross-country, golf, soccer, softball, tennis, track/field (outdoor), track/field (indoor), volleyball. **On-Campus Highlights:** Alexander Brest Fine Arts Museum, Davis College of Business/ Jazzman's Cafe (New), JU Baseball Complex, Lazzara Health Sciences Center (New), Residential Apartment Village (New).

ADMISSIONS

Freshman Academic Profile: Average high school GPA 3.5. SAT Math middle 50% range 480-570. SAT Critical Reading middle 50% range 470-560. SAT ACT middle 50% range 20-26. Minimum paper TOEFL 540. **Basis for Candidate Selection:** *Very important factors considered include:* academic GPA, standardized test scores. *Important factors considered include:* rigor of secondary school record, talent/ability. *Other factors considered include:* application essay, recommendation(s), character/personal qualities, extracurricular activities, interview, volunteer work, work experience. **Freshman Admission Requirements:** High school diploma is required and GED is accepted. *Academic units required:* 4 English, 3 mathematics, 3 science, (2 science labs), 3 social studies. 4 English, 3 mathematics, 3 science, (2 science labs), 3 social studies. **Freshman Admission Statistics:** 8,096 applied, 42% admitted, 16% enrolled. **Transfer Admission Requirements:** college transcript(s), essay or personal statement, statement of good standing from prior institution(s). Minimum college GPA of 2.0 required. Lowest grade transferable C. **General Admission Information:** Notification on a rolling basis, beginning on or about 10/1. Nonfall registration accepted. Admission may be deferred for a maximum of NA. Credit and/or placement offered for CEEB Advanced Placement tests.

COSTS AND FINANCIAL AID

Average book expense. **Required Forms and Deadlines:** FAFSA, institution's own financial aid form, state aid form. **Notification of Awards:** Applicants will be notified of awards on a rolling basis beginning 2/15. **Types of Aid:** *Need-based scholarships/grants:* Federal Pell, SEOG, state scholarships/grants, private scholarships, the school's own gift aid, ACG/SMART. *Loans:* Subsidized Stafford, Unsubsidized Stafford, PLUS, Federal Perkins, state loans, college/university loans from institutional funds. **Student Employment:** Highest amount earned per year from on-campus jobs $4,677. **Financial Aid Statistics:** 98% freshmen, 99% undergrads receive need-based scholarship or grant aid. 1% freshmen, 1% undergrads receive non-need-based scholarship or grant aid. 62% freshmen, 69% undergrads receive need-based self-help aid. 2% freshmen, 4% undergrads receive athletic scholarships. 97% freshmen, 87% undergrads receive any aid. **Criteria for awarding institutional aid:** *Non-need-based:* academics, art, athletics, job skills, leadership, music/drama, state/district residency.

JAMES MADISON UNIVERSITY

Sonner Hall, MSC 0101, Harrisonburg, VA 22807
Phone: 540-568-5681 • **Financial Aid Phone:** 540-568-7820
E-mail: admissions@jmu.edu • **CEEB Code:** 5392
Fax: 540-568-3332 • **Website:** www.jmu.edu • **ACT Code:** 4370

This public school was founded in 1908. It has a 712-acre campus.

RATINGS
Admissions Selectivity Rating: 85   **Fire Safety Rating:** 74   **Green Rating:** 97

STUDENTS AND FACULTY
Enrollment: 17,575. **Student Body:** 59% female, 41% male, 27% out-of-state, 1% international (66 countries represented). Asian 5%, African American 4%, Caucasian 80%, Hispanic 4%, Native American 0%.
Retention and Graduation: 64% freshmen graduate within 4 years. 29% grads go on to further study within 1 year. 14% grads pursue arts and sciences degrees. 1% grads pursue law degrees. 2% grads pursue business degrees. 1% grads pursue medical degrees. **Faculty:** Student/faculty ratio 16:1. 924 full-time faculty, 79% hold PhDs, 8% are members of minority groups, 46% are women. 1% of classes are taught by teaching assistants.

ACADEMICS
Degrees: bachelor's, master's, post-master's certificate. **Classes:** Most classes have 20–29 students. Most lab/discussion sessions have 20–29 students. **Majors with Highest Enrollment:** community health services/liaison/counseling;

marketing/marketing management; psychology. **Special Study Options:** Accelerated program, distance learning, double major, English as a Second Language (ESL), honors program, independent study, internships, study abroad, teacher certification program, Continuing education programs offered on campus. **Honors Programs:** Academic honors program, honors scholars (3.25 or above),honors courses, and senior honors project (3.25) **Combined Degree Programs:** BS in Bio. JMU/Master of Forestry VA Tech 3-2. **Disability Services:** Special programs offered to physically disabled students include note-taking services, reader services, tape recorders. **Career Services:** Alumni network, alumni services, career/job search classes, career assessment, internships Career Services highlights include We offer a course designed for first and second year students who have not selected a major called Life and Career Planning. It is offered for academic credit and serves over 10% of the freshman class. Our assessment data has demonstrated the effectiveness of this course in enhancing students' understanding of career decision-makinng processes, career decisiveness and career decision-making self-efficacy.

FACILITIES

Housing: Coed dorms, special housing for disabled students, fraternity/sorority housing, apartments for single students, wellness housing, theme housing, 90% of campus accessible to physically disabled. **Special Academic Facilities/ Equipment:** language lab, music and fine arts buildings, herbarium, university farm, planetarium, arboretum,mineral museum,Science on a Sphere. **Computers:** 25% of classrooms, 100% of dorms, 100% of libraries, 50% of dining areas, 100% of student union, 25% of common outdoor areas have wireless network access. Students can register for classes online. Administrative functions (other than registration) can be performed online.

CAMPUS LIFE

Environment: Town. **Activities:** Choral groups, concert band, dance, drama/ theater, jazz band, literary magazine, marching band, music ensembles, musical theater, opera, pep band, radio station, student government, student newspaper, student-run film society, symphony orchestra, yearbook, Campus Ministries, International Student Organization 298 registered organizations, 28 honor societies, 28 religious organizations. 15 fraternities, 9 sororities. **Athletics (Intercollegiate):** *Men:* baseball, basketball, cheerleading, football, golf, soccer, tennis. *Women:* basketball, cheerleading, cross-country, diving, field hockey, golf, lacrosse, soccer, softball, swimming, tennis, track/field (outdoor), volleyball. **On-Campus Highlights:** Quad, Taylor Down Under, UREC, East Campus Library, Festival Student Center. **Environmental Initiatives:** JMU has a department, the Institute for Stewardship of the Natural World, that facilitates sustainability by coordinating environmental stewardship efforts across campus, advocating for priorities, and challenging all members of the JMU community to think critically about their role in achieving the long-term stewardship of Earth. Over 100 JMU citizens serve on the committees that support the department. Areas across the university are creating objectives to support the campus environmental stewardship action plan. The plan comprehensively outlines the priority environmental stewardship actions the university will take between 2011 and 2015. Examples of the many actions included in the plan are reduce waste sent to landfill, increase the accessibility of public transportation, and assess students' environmental literacy. JMU changed campus navigation patterns and implemented supporting tools which increased transit and non-motorized access. A 22% increase in transit use has occurred.

ADMISSIONS

Freshman Academic Profile: Average high school GPA 3.8. 26% in top 10% of high school class, 70% in top 25% of high school class, 98% in top 50% of high school class. 60% from public high schools. SAT Math middle 50% range 530-620. SAT Critical Reading middle 50% range 520-620. SAT Writing middle 50% range 520-610. ACT middle 50% range 23-27. Minimum paper TOEFL 550. **Basis for Candidate Selection:** *Very important factors considered include:* academic GPA, rigor of secondary school record. *Important factors considered include:* standardized test scores. *Other factors considered include:* Class rank, application essay, recommendation(s), alumni/ae relation, character/ personal qualities, extracurricular activities, geographical residence, state residency, talent/ability, volunteer work, work experience. **Freshman Admission Requirements:** High school diploma is required and GED is accepted. *Academic units required:* 4 English, 4 mathematics, 3 science, (3 science labs), 2 foreign language, 3 social studies. *Academic units recommended:* 4 English, 4 mathematics, 3 science, (3 science labs), 2 foreign language, 3 social studies. **Freshman Admission Statistics:** 22,864 applied, 629% enrolled. **Transfer Admission Requirements:** High school transcript, college transcript(s), minimum college GPA of 2.0 required. Lowest grade transferable C. **General Admission Information:** Application Fee $50. Regular application deadline 1/15. Regular notification 4/1. Nonfall registration not accepted. Admission may be deferred for a maximum of 1 year with. Credit offered for CEEB Advanced Placement tests.

COSTS AND FINANCIAL AID

Annual in-state tuition $4,862. Annual out-of-state tuition $18,850. Room and board $8,630. Required fees $3,946. Average book expense $876. **Required**

Forms and Deadlines: FAFSA. **Notification of Awards:** Applicants will be notified of awards on a rolling basis beginning 4/1. **Types of Aid:** *Need-based scholarships/grants:* Federal Pell, SEOG, state scholarships/grants, private scholarships, the school's own gift aid. *Loans:* Direct Subsidized Stafford, Direct Unsubsidized Stafford, Direct PLUS, Federal Perkins, Federal Nursing. **Student Employment:** Federal Work-Study Program available. Institutional employment available. Highest amount earned per year from on-campus jobs $3,640. Off-campus job opportunities are good. **Financial Aid Statistics:** 47% freshmen, 40% undergrads receive need-based scholarship or grant aid. 15% freshmen, 11% undergrads receive non-need-based scholarship or grant aid. 93% freshmen, 80% undergrads receive need-based self-help aid. 2% freshmen, 2% undergrads receive athletic scholarships. 59% freshmen, 53% undergrads receive any aid. 52% undergrads borrow to pay for school. Average cumulative indebtedness $22,128. **Criteria for awarding institutional aid:** *Non-need-based:* academics, alumni affiliation, art, athletics, leadership, minority status, music/drama, state/district residency.

JAMESTOWN COLLEGE

6081 College Lane, Jamestown, ND 58405-0001
Phone: 701-252-3467 • **Financial Aid Phone:** 701-252-3467
E-mail: admissions@jc.edu
Fax: 701-253-4318 • **Website:** www.jc.edu • **ACT Code:** 3200

This private school, affiliated with the Presbyterian Church, was founded in 1883. It has a 110-acre campus.

RATINGS

Admissions Selectivity Rating: 77   **Fire Safety Rating:** 65   **Green Rating:** 60*

STUDENTS AND FACULTY

Enrollment: 890. **Student Body:** 50% female, 50% male, 52% out-of-state, 8% international (14 countries represented). Asian 2%, African American 4%, Caucasian 80%, Hispanic 5%, Native American 1%.
Retention and Graduation: 68% freshmen return for sophomore year. 31% freshmen graduate within 4 years. 46% freshmen graduate within 6 years. 14% grads go on to further study within 1 year. 9% grads pursue arts and sciences degrees. 2% grads pursue law degrees. 2% grads pursue medical degrees. **Faculty:** Student/faculty ratio 14:1. 60 full-time faculty, 55% hold PhDs, 5% are members of minority groups, 50% are women. 0% of classes are taught by teaching assistants.

ACADEMICS

Degrees: bachelor's. **Classes:** Most classes have 10–19 students. Most lab/ discussion sessions have fewer than 10 students. **Majors with Highest Enrollment:** business/commerce; elementary education and teaching; nursing/registered nurse (rn, asn, bsn, msn). **Special Study Options:** cooperative education program, double major, dual enrollment, English as a Second Language (ESL), exchange student program (domestic), honors program, independent study, internships, liberal arts/career combination, student-designed major, study abroad, teacher certification program. **Honors Programs:** Character and Leadership Program. The heart of the Character in Leadership program is its academic core. Each student who participates will receive a minor in leadership. Jamestown College values its reputation for quality education and therefore is committed through its Character in Leadership Program to providing a broad and sound intellectual foundation that will enable its students to provide ethical leadership in an ever-changing world. **Disability Services:** Special programs offered to physically disabled students include note-taking services, reader services, tape recorders, tutors. **Career Services:** Alumni network, alumni services, career/job search classes, internships.

FACILITIES

Housing: Coed dorms, special housing for disabled students, apartments for married students, apartments for single students. 80% of campus accessible to physically disabled. **Computers:** 95% of classrooms, 100% of dorms, 100% of libraries, 100% of dining areas, 100% of student union, 50% of common outdoor areas have wireless network access. Students can register for classes online. Administrative functions (other than registration) can be performed online.

CAMPUS LIFE

Environment: Village. **Activities:** Choral groups, concert band, dance, drama/ theater, jazz band, literary magazine, music ensembles, musical theater, pep band, student government, student newspaper, television station, Campus Ministries, International Student Organization 35 registered organizations, 6 honor societies, 5 religious organizations. **Athletics (Intercollegiate):** *Men:* baseball, basketball, cross-country, football, golf, track/field (outdoor), track/ field (indoor), wrestling. *Women:* basketball, cross-country, golf, soccer, softball, track/field (outdoor), track/field (indoor), volleyball, wrestling. **On-Campus**

Highlights: Library lobby, Lounge/tv room outside of cafeteria, Larson Center (athletic center)/Foss Wellness Center, Residence Hall lounges, Level 2 (campus nightclub).

ADMISSIONS

Freshman Academic Profile: Average high school GPA 3.3. 15% in top 10% of high school class, 41% in top 25% of high school class, 70% in top 50% of high school class. SAT Math middle 50% range 420-550. SAT Critical Reading middle 50% range 390-510. ACT middle 50% range 20-24. Minimum web-based TOEFL 70. Minimum paper TOEFL 525. **Basis for Candidate Selection:** *Important factors considered include:* academic GPA, recommendation(s), standardized test scores. *Other factors considered include:* rigor of secondary school record, character/personal qualities, extracurricular activities, level of applicant's interest, talent/ability, volunteer work, work experience. **Freshman Admission Requirements:** High school diploma is required and GED is accepted. **Freshman Admission Statistics:** 1,031 applied, 56% admitted, 38% enrolled. **Transfer Admission Requirements:** High school transcript, college transcript(s), statement of good standing from prior institution(s). Minimum college GPA of 2.5 required. Lowest grade transferable c. **General Admission Information:** Application Fee $35. Notification on a rolling basis, beginning on or about 7/1. Nonfall registration accepted. Admission may be deferred for a maximum of 1. Credit offered for CEEB Advanced Placement tests.

COSTS AND FINANCIAL AID

Annual tuition $17,974. Room and board $6,244. Required fees $450. Average book expense $1,000. **Required Forms and Deadlines:** FAFSA. **Notification of Awards:** Applicants will be notified of awards on a rolling basis beginning 2/1. **Types of Aid:** *Need-based scholarships/grants:* Federal Pell, SEOG, state scholarships/grants, private scholarships, the school's own gift aid, Federal Nursing Scholarships. *Loans:* Subsidized Stafford, Unsubsidized Stafford, PLUS, Federal Perkins, college/university loans from institutional funds, Alternative Loans (Private). **Student Employment:** Federal Work-Study Program available. Institutional employment available. Highest amount earned per year from on-campus jobs $2,262. Off-campus job opportunities are good. **Financial Aid Statistics:** 100% freshmen, 100% undergrads receive need-based scholarship or grant aid. 18% freshmen, 16% undergrads receive non-need-based scholarship or grant aid. 78% freshmen, 79% undergrads receive need-based self-help aid. 28% freshmen, 24% undergrads receive athletic scholarships. 100% freshmen, 98% undergrads receive any aid. 83% undergrads borrow to pay for school. Average cumulative indebtedness $30,939. **Criteria for awarding institutional aid:** *Non-need-based:* academics, alumni affiliation, art, athletics, job skills, leadership, music/drama, religious affiliation.

JARVIS CHRISTIAN COLLEGE

P.O.BOX 1470, Hawkins, TX 75765-1470
Phone: 903-769-5730 • **Financial Aid Phone:** 903-769-5740
E-mail: felecia_tyiska@jarvis.edu
Fax: 903-769-1282 • **Website:** www.jarvis.edu/ • **ACT Code:** 4110

This private school, affiliated with the Disciples of Christ Church, was founded in 1912. It has a 243-acre campus.

RATINGS

Admissions Selectivity Rating: 61   **Fire Safety Rating:** 93   **Green Rating:** 60*

STUDENTS AND FACULTY

Enrollment: 547. **Student Body:** 60% female, 40% male, 15% out-of-state, 0% international (2 countries represented). Asian 0%, African American 107%, Caucasian 2%, Hispanic 4%, Native American 0%.
Retention and Graduation: 41% freshmen return for sophomore year. 17% freshmen graduate within 4 years. 19% freshmen graduate within 6 years. 2% grads go on to further study within 1 year. 1% grads pursue business degrees. **Faculty:** Student/faculty ratio 13:1. 35 full-time faculty, 46% hold PhDs, 63% are members of minority groups, 49% are women. 0% of classes are taught by teaching assistants.

ACADEMICS

Degrees: bachelor's. **Classes:** Most classes have fewer than 10 students. Most lab/discussion sessions have 10–19 students. **Majors with Highest Enrollment:** biology/biological sciences; criminal justice/law enforcement administration; health and physical education. **Special Study Options:** cross-registration, distance learning, double major, dual enrollment, English as a Second Language (ESL), honors program, independent study, internships, liberal arts/career combination, student-designed major, teacher certification program. **Honors Programs:** JETS Honors Program. **Disability Services:** Special programs offered to physically disabled students include reader services, tutors. **Career Services:** Alumni network, alumni services

FACILITIES

Housing: special housing for disabled students, men's dorms, women's dorms, apartments for married students, apartments for single students. 95% of campus accessible to physically disabled. **Special Academic Facilities/Equipment:** ARCHIVES **Computers:** 100% of classrooms, 100% of dorms, 100% of libraries, 100% of dining areas, 100% of student union, 20% of common outdoor areas have wireless network access. Students can register for classes online.

CAMPUS LIFE

Environment: Rural. **Activities:** Choral groups, drama/theater, music ensembles, pep band, student government, International Student Organization 33 registered organizations, 6 honor societies, 5 religious organizations. 4 fraternities, 4 sororities. **Athletics (Intercollegiate):** *Men:* baseball, basketball. *Women:* basketball, volleyball. **On-Campus Highlights:** E. W. Rand Health, Physical Education, and Recreat, J. N. Ervin Religion Center, Walk of Fame, Community and Technology Center, Meyer Science and Mathematics Center, Archives of the Texas Christian Missionary Fellowship of the Christian Church (Disciples of Christ).

ADMISSIONS

Freshman Academic Profile: Average high school GPA 2.6. 0% in top 10% of high school class, 6% in top 25% of high school class, 23% in top 50% of high school class. 99% from public high schools. Minimum paper TOEFL 500. **Basis for Candidate Selection:** *Other factors considered include:* Class rank, academic GPA, rigor of secondary school record, standardized test scores, character/personal qualities, extracurricular activities, talent/ability. **Freshman Admission Requirements:** High school diploma is required and GED is accepted. *Academic units required:* 3 English, 2 mathematics, 1 science, 3 social studies, 7 academic electives. *Academic units recommended:* 3 English, 2 mathematics, 1 science, 3 social studies, 7 academic electives. **Freshman Admission Statistics:** 525 applied, 92% admitted, 25% enrolled. **Transfer Admission Requirements:** High school transcript, college transcript(s), standardized test scores, Lowest grade transferable F. **General Admission Information:** Application Fee $50. Notification on a rolling basis, beginning on or about 8/1. Nonfall registration accepted. Admission may be deferred for a maximum of one year. Neither credit nor placement offered for CEEB Advanced Placement tests.

COSTS AND FINANCIAL AID

Annual tuition $8,528. Room and board $6,715. Required fees $1,080. Average book expense $1,000. **Required Forms and Deadlines:** FAFSA, institution's own financial aid form, state aid form. **Notification of Awards:** Applicants will be notified of awards on a rolling basis beginning 5/1. **Types of Aid:** *Need-based scholarships/grants:* Federal Pell, SEOG, state scholarships/grants, private scholarships, the school's own gift aid, United Negro College Fund. *Loans:* Direct Subsidized Stafford, Direct Unsubsidized Stafford, Direct PLUS, Subsidized Stafford, Unsubsidized Stafford, PLUS, Federal Perkins, UNCF INSTITUTIONAL. **Student Employment:** Federal Work-Study Program available. Highest amount earned per year from on-campus jobs $1,729. Off-campus job opportunities are fair. **Financial Aid Statistics:** 94% freshmen, 100% undergrads receive need-based scholarship or grant aid. 41% freshmen, 23% undergrads receive non-need-based scholarship or grant aid. 79% freshmen, 89% undergrads receive need-based self-help aid. 3% freshmen, 6% undergrads receive athletic scholarships. 98% freshmen, 98% undergrads receive any aid. 93% undergrads borrow to pay for school. Average cumulative indebtedness $20,000. **Criteria for awarding institutional aid:** *Non-need-based:* academics, athletics, religious affiliation, state/district residency.

JEWISH THEOLOGICAL SEMINARY, ALBERT A. LIST COLLEGE

3080 Broadway, New York, NY 10027
Phone: 212-678-8832 • **Financial Aid Phone:** 212-678-8007
E-mail: lcadmissions@jtsa.edu • **CEEB Code:** 2339
Fax: 212-280-6022 • **Website:** www.jtsa.edu • **ACT Code:** 2776

This private school, affiliated with the Jewish Church, was founded in 1886. It has a 1-acre campus.

RATINGS

Admissions Selectivity Rating: 90   **Fire Safety Rating:** 61   **Green Rating:** 61

STUDENTS AND FACULTY

Enrollment: 177. **Student Body:** 54% female, 46% male, 84% out-of-state, 3% international (10 countries represented). Asian 0%, African American 0%, Caucasian 94%, Hispanic 1%, Native American 0%.

Retention and Graduation: 89% freshmen return for sophomore year. 15% grads go on to further study within 1 year. 6% grads pursue arts and sciences degrees. 6% grads pursue law degrees. 3% grads pursue medical degrees. **Faculty:** Student/faculty ratio 6:1. 52 full-time faculty, 113% hold PhDs, 0% are members of minority groups, 29% are women. 0% of classes are taught by teaching assistants.

ACADEMICS

Degrees: bachelor's, master's. **Classes:** Most classes have fewer than 10 students. **Majors with Highest Enrollment:** bible/biblical studies; jewish/judaic studies; talmudic studies. **Special Study Options:** cross-registration, distance learning, double major, exchange student program (domestic), honors program, independent study, internships, liberal arts/career combination, student-designed major, study abroad, BA/MA program with JTS Graduate School or William Davidson School of Jewish Education. **Combined Degree Programs:** BA/MA, BA/BA and BA/BS programs with Columbia University and Barnard College. **Disability Services:** Special programs offered to physically disabled students include tape recorders, tutors. **Career Services:** Alumni network, alumni services, career/job search classes, internships Career Services highlights include Career/Job search classes and alumni network.

FACILITIES

Housing: Coed dorms, apartments for married students, apartments for single students. **Special Academic Facilities/Equipment:** The Jewish Museum and the Rare Book Room of the Library **Computers:** 100% of classrooms, 100% of dorms, 80% of libraries, 100% of dining areas, 50% of common outdoor areas have wireless network access. Students can register for classes online. Administrative functions (other than registration) can be performed online.

CAMPUS LIFE

Environment: Metropolis. **Activities:** Choral groups, concert band, dance, drama/theater, jazz band, literary magazine, music ensembles, musical theater, radio station, student government, student newspaper, yearbook 1 religious organizations. **Athletics (Intercollegiate):** *Men:* baseball, basketball, crew/rowing, soccer, tennis, track/field (outdoor), volleyball. *Women:* baseball, basketball, crew/rowing, soccer, tennis, track/field (outdoor), volleyball. **On-Campus Highlights:** The Library of the Jewish Theological Seminary **Environmental Initiatives:** 4-Day work week to save on electricity The cafeteria has replaced styrofoam products with paper products and promotes the use of reusable plates, bowls and utensils. Energy saving film applied to all windows

ADMISSIONS

Freshman Academic Profile: Average high school GPA 3.7. SAT Math middle 50% range 620-660. SAT Critical Reading middle 50% range 640-700. SAT Writing middle 50% range 620-720. ACT middle 50% range 30-32. Minimum paper TOEFL 600. **Basis for Candidate Selection:** *Very important factors considered include:* academic GPA, rigor of secondary school record, standardized test scores. *Important factors considered include:* Class rank, application essay, recommendation(s), interview. *Other factors considered include:* alumni/ae relation, character/personal qualities, extracurricular activities, first generation, level of applicant's interest, religious affiliation/commitment, talent/ability, volunteer work. **Freshman Admission Requirements:** High school diploma is required and GED is not accepted. **Freshman Admission Statistics:** 102 applied, 62% admitted, 65% enrolled. **Transfer Admission Requirements:** High school transcript, college transcript(s), essay or personal statement, standardized test scores, statement of good standing from prior institution(s). **General Admission Information:** Application Fee $65. Early decision application deadline 11/15. Regular application deadline 2/15. Regular notification 4/1. Nonfall registration accepted. Admission may be deferred for a maximum of 1. Credit and/or placement offered for CEEB Advanced Placement tests.

COSTS AND FINANCIAL AID

Annual tuition $14,200. Room and board $9,200. Required fees $800. Average book expense $500. **Required Forms and Deadlines:** FAFSA, institution's own financial aid form, CSS/Financial Aid PROFILE, state aid form, noncustodial PROFILE, business/farm supplement. **Notification of Awards:** Applicants will be notified of awards on a rolling basis beginning 4/1. **Types of Aid:** *Need-based scholarships/grants:* private scholarships, the school's own gift aid. *Loans:* Direct Subsidized Stafford, Direct Unsubsidized Stafford, college/university loans from institutional funds. **Student Employment:** Federal Work-Study Program available. Institutional employment available. Off-campus job opportunities are excellent. **Financial Aid Statistics:** 100% freshmen, 100% undergrads receive need-based scholarship or grant aid. 50% freshmen, 41% undergrads receive non-need-based scholarship or grant aid. 86% freshmen, 97% undergrads receive need-based self-help aid. 42% undergrads borrow to pay for school. Average cumulative indebtedness $16,892. **Criteria for awarding institutional aid:** *Non-need-based:* academics, alumni affiliation, leadership.

JOHN BROWN UNIVERSITY

2000 West University Street, Siloam Springs, AR 72761
Phone: 479-524-7157 • **Financial Aid Phone:** 479-524-7424
E-mail: jbuinfo@jbu.edu • **CEEB Code:** 6321
Fax: 479-524-4196 • **Website:** www.jbu.edu • **ACT Code:** 130

This private school was founded in 1919. It has a 200-acre campus.

RATINGS

Admissions Selectivity Rating: 80   **Fire Safety Rating:** 61   **Green Rating:** 61

STUDENTS AND FACULTY

Enrollment: 1,770. **Student Body:** 56% female, 44% male, 62% out-of-state, 6% international (39 countries represented). Asian 0%, African American 1%, Caucasian 59%, Hispanic 6%, Native American 1%.
Retention and Graduation: 58% freshmen graduate within 4 years. 68% freshmen graduate within 6 years. 18% grads go on to further study within 1 year. **Faculty:** Student/faculty ratio 13:1. 80 full-time faculty, 74% hold PhDs, 4% are members of minority groups, 25% are women. 0% of classes are taught by teaching assistants.

ACADEMICS

Degrees: bachelor's, master's. **Classes:** Most classes have 10–19 students. Most lab/discussion sessions have 10–19 students. **Majors with Highest Enrollment:** business administration and management; digital communication and media/multimedia; graphic design. **Special Study Options:** Accelerated program, distance learning, double major, dual enrollment, English as a Second Language (ESL), honors program, independent study, internships, liberal arts/career combination, student-designed major, study abroad, teacher certification program. **Honors Programs:** The Honors Scholars Program consists of enriched Core Curriculum courses developed especially for gifted and highly motivated students. Emphasizing the use of primary texts, instructors challenge students through individual research, critical reflection, incisive discussion, interactive projects, and professional presentations. **Disability Services:** Special programs offered to physically disabled students include note-taking services, reader services, tutors. **Career Services:** Alumni network, career/job search classes, career assessment.

FACILITIES

Housing: Coed dorms, men's dorms, women's dorms, apartments for married students, apartments for single students. 80% of campus accessible to physically disabled. **Special Academic Facilities/Equipment:** Art Gallery, Human Anatomy Lab, TV Studio, Radio Station, Outdoor Learning Center, Center for Relationship Enrichment, Soderquist Center for Business and Ethics **Computers:** 100% of classrooms, 100% of dorms, 100% of libraries, 100% of dining areas, 100% of student union, 30% of common outdoor areas have wireless network access. Students can register for classes online. Administrative functions (other than registration) can be performed online.

CAMPUS LIFE

Environment: Village. **Activities:** Choral groups, dance, drama/theater, jazz band, literary magazine, music ensembles, musical theater, pep band, radio station, student government, student newspaper, student-run film society, yearbook, Campus Ministries, International Student Organization 20 registered organizations, 3 honor societies. **Athletics (Intercollegiate):** *Men:* basketball, golf, soccer, tennis. *Women:* basketball, soccer, swimming, tennis, volleyball. **On-Campus Highlights:** Walker Student Center, California Cafe, Chapel, Walton Lifetime Health Complex, Intramural Sports. **Environmental Initiatives:** New major in Renewable Energy

ADMISSIONS

Freshman Academic Profile: Average high school GPA 3.6. 33% in top 10% of high school class, 60% in top 25% of high school class, 84% in top 50% of high school class. 65% from public high schools. SAT Math middle 50% range 520-620. SAT Critical Reading middle 50% range 500-630. SAT Writing middle 50% range 500-560. ACT middle 50% range 22-28. Minimum web-based TOEFL 85. Minimum paper TOEFL 560. **Basis for Candidate Selection:** *Very important factors considered include:* academic GPA, recommendation(s), standardized test scores. *Important factors considered include:* Class rank, application essay, character/personal qualities, interview, religious affiliation/commitment. *Other factors considered include:* rigor of secondary school record, alumni/ae relation, extracurricular activities, first generation, level of applicant's interest, talent/ability. **Freshman Admission Requirements:** High school diploma is required and GED is accepted. **Freshman Admission Statistics:** 1,170 applied, 66% admitted, 41% enrolled. **Transfer Admission Requirements:** High school transcript, college transcript(s), essay or personal statement, minimum college GPA of 2.5 required. Lowest grade transferable C. **General Admission Information:** Application Fee $25. Notification on a rolling basis, beginning on or about 11/1. Nonfall registration accepted. Admission may be deferred for a maximum of 1 year. Neither credit nor placement offered for CEEB Advanced Placement tests.

COSTS AND FINANCIAL AID

Annual tuition $20,796. Room and board $7,902. Required fees $978. Average book expense $800. **Required Forms and Deadlines:** FAFSA. **Notification of Awards:** Applicants will be notified of awards on or about 3/1. **Types of Aid:** *Need-based scholarships/grants:* Federal Pell, SEOG, state scholarships/grants, private scholarships, the school's own gift aid. *Loans:* Direct Subsidized Stafford, Direct Unsubsidized Stafford, Direct PLUS, Subsidized Stafford, Unsubsidized Stafford, PLUS, Federal Perkins, college/university loans from institutional funds. **Student Employment:** Federal Work-Study Program available. Institutional employment available. Highest amount earned per year from on-campus jobs $1,415. Off-campus job opportunities are fair. **Financial Aid Statistics:** 92% freshmen, 93% undergrads receive need-based scholarship or grant aid. 92% freshmen, 93% undergrads receive non-need-based scholarship or grant aid. 76% freshmen, 69% undergrads receive need-based self-help aid. 6% freshmen, 4% undergrads receive athletic scholarships. 90% freshmen, 87% undergrads receive any aid. 57% undergrads borrow to pay for school. Average cumulative indebtedness $24,160. **Criteria for awarding institutional aid:** *Non-need-based:* academics, alumni affiliation, art, athletics, leadership, music/drama.

JOHN CARROLL UNIVERSITY

20700 North Park Boulevard, University Heights, OH 44118-4581
Phone: 216-397-4294 • **Financial Aid Phone:** 216-397-4270
E-mail: admission@jcu.edu • **CEEB Code:** 1342
Fax: 216-397-4981 • **Website:** www.jcu.edu • **ACT Code:** 3282

This private school, affiliated with the Roman Catholic Church, was founded in 1886. It has a 60-acre campus.

RATINGS
Admissions Selectivity Rating: 72   **Fire Safety Rating:** 66   **Green Rating:** 74

STUDENTS AND FACULTY
Enrollment: 2,914. **Student Body:** 49% female, 51% male, 30% out-of-state, 2% international (20 countries represented). Asian 2%, African American 4%, Caucasian 83%, Hispanic 4%, Native American 0%.
Retention and Graduation: 87% freshmen return for sophomore year. 66% freshmen graduate within 4 years. 75% freshmen graduate within 6 years. 38% grads go on to further study within 1 year. 43% grads pursue arts and sciences degrees. 15% grads pursue law degrees. 19% grads pursue business degrees. 15% grads pursue medical degrees. **Faculty:** Student/faculty ratio 13:1. 195 full-time faculty, 97% hold PhDs, 15% are members of minority groups, 44% are women. 1% of classes are taught by teaching assistants.

ACADEMICS
Degrees: bachelor's, master's, post-bachelor's certificate. **Classes:** Most classes have 20–29 students. Most lab/discussion sessions have 10–19 students. **Majors with Highest Enrollment:** biology/biological sciences; communication studies/speech communication and rhetoric; marketing/marketing management. **Special Study Options:** Accelerated program, cooperative education program, cross-registration, double major, dual enrollment, exchange student program (domestic), honors program, independent study, internships, liberal arts/career combination, student-designed major, study abroad, teacher certification program, Undergrads may take grad level classes. Co-Op Programs: All majors. **Combined Degree Programs:** 3-4 Doctor of Nursing prog with Case Western Reserve U. **Disability Services:** Special programs offered to physically disabled students include note-taking services, reader services, tape recorders. **Career Services:** Alumni network, alumni services, career/job search classes, career assessment, internships, regional alumni. Career Services highlights include Internships are available to our students for 0-3 credits and they can be paid or unpaid. We have a large number of students working at non-profits who are eligible for scholarships.

FACILITIES
Housing: Coed dorms, special housing for disabled students, women's dorms, fraternity/sorority housing, apartments for single students, theme housing, 94% of campus accessible to physically disabled. **Computers:** 100% of classrooms, 100% of dorms, 100% of libraries, 100% of dining areas, 100% of student union, 100% of common outdoor areas have wireless network access. Students can register for classes online. Administrative functions (other than registration) can be performed online.

CAMPUS LIFE
Environment: Metropolis. **Activities:** Choral groups, dance, drama/theater, literary magazine, music ensembles, pep band, radio station, student government, student newspaper, television station, yearbook, Campus Ministries 95

registered organizations, 12 honor societies, 2 religious organizations. 4 fraternities, 5 sororities. **Athletics (Intercollegiate):** *Men:* baseball, basketball, cross-country, diving, football, golf, soccer, swimming, tennis, track/field (outdoor), track/field (indoor), wrestling. *Women:* basketball, cheerleading, cross-country, diving, golf, soccer, softball, swimming, tennis, track/field (outdoor), track/field (indoor), volleyball. **On-Campus Highlights:** Einstein Bagel Bros, Dolan Center for Science and Technology, Inn-Between Cafe, Grasselli Library, Student Center Atrium. **Environmental Initiatives:** Reuse building materials on campus or divert from landfills Reduce energy and water consumption LEED design principles used in all renovations or new buildings

ADMISSIONS
Freshman Academic Profile: Average high school GPA 3.5. 22% in top 10% of high school class, 50% in top 25% of high school class, 85% in top 50% of high school class. 54% from public high schools. SAT Math middle 50% range 500-610. SAT Critical Reading middle 50% range 490-600. SAT Writing middle 50% range 490-590. ACT middle 50% range 22-27. Minimum web-based TOEFL 79. Minimum paper TOEFL 550. **Basis for Candidate Selection:** *Very important factors considered include:* academic GPA, rigor of secondary school record. *Important factors considered include:* application essay, standardized test scores, character/personal qualities, extracurricular activities, talent/ability, volunteer work, work experience. *Other factors considered include:* Class rank, recommendation(s), alumni/ae relation, first generation, geographical residence, interview. **Freshman Admission Requirements:** High school diploma is required and GED is accepted. *Academic units required:* 4 English, 3 mathematics, 2 science, (2 science labs), 2 foreign language, 2 social studies, 3 academic electives, 2 2 units must be distributed between social studies and/or history; 4 recommended. *Academic units recommended:* 4 English, 3 mathematics, 2 science, (2 science labs), 2 foreign language, 2 social studies, 3 academic electives, 2 2 units must be distributed between social studies and/or history; 4 recommended **Freshman Admission Statistics:** 3,490 applied, 81% admitted, 24% enrolled. **Transfer Admission Requirements:** High school transcript, college transcript(s), essay or personal statement, standardized test scores, statement of good standing from prior institution(s). Lowest grade transferable 2. **General Admission Information:** Regular application deadline 2/1. Notification on a rolling basis, beginning on or about 12/15. Nonfall registration accepted. Admission may be deferred for a maximum of 1-2 terms. Credit and/or placement offered for CEEB Advanced Placement tests.

COSTS AND FINANCIAL AID
Annual tuition $32,130. Room and board $9,610. Required fees $1,050. Average book expense $1,000. **Required Forms and Deadlines:** FAFSA. **Notification of Awards:** Applicants will be notified of awards on a rolling basis beginning 2/15. **Types of Aid:** *Need-based scholarships/grants:* Federal Pell, SEOG, state scholarships/grants, private scholarships, the school's own gift aid. *Loans:* Subsidized Stafford, Unsubsidized Stafford, PLUS, Federal Perkins. **Student Employment:** Federal Work-Study Program available. Institutional employment available. Highest amount earned per year from on-campus jobs $2,747. Off-campus job opportunities are good. **Financial Aid Statistics:** 99% freshmen, 75% undergrads receive need-based scholarship or grant aid. 100% freshmen, 75% undergrads receive non-need-based scholarship or grant aid. 87% freshmen, 88% undergrads receive need-based self-help aid. 98% freshmen, 95% undergrads receive any aid. 77% undergrads borrow to pay for school. Average cumulative indebtedness $31,727. **Criteria for awarding institutional aid:** *Non-need-based:* academics, alumni affiliation, leadership, minority status, state/district residency.

JOHNS HOPKINS UNIVERSITY

3400 North Charles Street, Baltimore, MD 21218
Phone: 410-516-8171 • **Financial Aid Phone:** 410-516-8028
E-mail: gotojhu@jhu.edu • **CEEB Code:** 5332
Fax: 410-516-6025 • **Website:** www.jhu.edu

This private school was founded in 1876. It has a 140-acre campus.

RATINGS
Admissions Selectivity Rating: 99   **Fire Safety Rating:** 76   **Green Rating:** 95

STUDENTS AND FACULTY
Enrollment: 5,047. **Student Body:** 47% female, 53% male, 87% out-of-state, 9% international (71 countries represented). Asian 20%, African American 5%, Caucasian 52%, Hispanic 9%, Native American 0%.

Retention and Graduation: 86% freshmen graduate within 4 years. 92% freshmen graduate within 6 years. 38% grads go on to further study within 1 year. 3% grads pursue law degrees. 9% grads pursue medical degrees. **Faculty:** Student/faculty ratio 13:1. 505 full-time faculty, 94% hold PhDs, 16% are members of minority groups, 31% are women.

ACADEMICS

Degrees: bachelor's, certificate, diploma, master's, post-bachelor's certificate, post-master's certificate. **Classes:** Most classes have 10–19 students. Most lab/discussion sessions have 20–29 students. **Majors with Highest Enrollment:** international relations and affairs; neuroscience; public health, other. **Special Study Options:** cross-registration, double major, dual enrollment, independent study, internships, student-designed major, study abroad, Combined Bachelor's/Master's programs. **Combined Degree Programs:** BA/MA, BA/MEng, Accelerated Bachelor's/Masters Programs. **Disability Services:** Special programs offered to physically disabled students include note-taking services, reader services, tape recorders, tutors. **Career Services:** Alumni network, alumni services, career/job search classes, career assessment, internships, regional alumni. Career Services highlights include Second Decade Society summer internship grants; Medical tutorial program, wherein students shadow physicians.

FACILITIES

Housing: Coed dorms, men's dorms, women's dorms, fraternity/sorority housing, apartments for single students. **Special Academic Facilities/Equipment:** Baltimore Museum of Art, on-campus Digital Media Center, art gallery, electron microscope, Space Telescope Science Institute, four major research centers **Computers:** 95% of classrooms, 100% of dorms, 100% of libraries, 90% of dining areas, 100% of student union, 50% of common outdoor areas have wireless network access. Students can register for classes online. Administrative functions (other than registration) can be performed online.

CAMPUS LIFE

Environment: Metropolis. **Activities:** Choral groups, concert band, dance, drama/theater, jazz band, literary magazine, music ensembles, musical theater, pep band, radio station, student government, student newspaper, student-run film society, symphony orchestra, yearbook, Campus Ministries, Model UN 250 registered organizations, 17 honor societies, 20 religious organizations. 12 fraternities, 7 sororities. **Athletics (Intercollegiate):** *Men:* baseball, basketball, cross-country, diving, fencing, football, lacrosse, soccer, swimming, tennis, track/field (outdoor), track/field (indoor), water polo, wrestling. *Women:* basketball, cross-country, diving, fencing, field hockey, lacrosse, soccer, swimming, tennis, track/field (outdoor), track/field (indoor), volleyball. **On-Campus Highlights:** Mason Hall - new Visitor's Center, Mattin Student Arts Center, Homewood House Museum, Lacrosse Hall of Fame and Museum, Ralph S. O'Connor Recreation Center. Also, Charles Commons, a new building that houses 618 upperclassmen, as well as a new dining facility and retail spaces, opened in the Fall of 2007. **Environmental Initiatives:** Comprehensive climate commitment includes reaching a 51% reduction in GHG by 2025, investing over $73 million in GHG reduction projects, and seed grants for climate researchers. Recently created Energy, Environment, Health, and Sustainability Institute (EESHI) to advance greater collaboration among researchers on areas of opportunity. Strong commitment to the surrounding community through conducting sustainability assessments, facilitating collegetown sustainability networks, and providing workshops and training for community members.

ADMISSIONS

Freshman Academic Profile: Average high school GPA 3.7. 86% in top 10% of high school class, 98% in top 25% of high school class, 100% in top 50% of high school class. 58% from public high schools. SAT Math middle 50% range 670-770. SAT Critical Reading middle 50% range 640-740. SAT Writing middle 50% range 650-750. ACT middle 50% range 30-34. Minimum paper TOEFL 600. **Basis for Candidate Selection:** *Very important factors considered include:* academic GPA, recommendation(s), rigor of secondary school record, character/personal qualities. *Important factors considered include:* Class rank, application essay, standardized test scores, extracurricular activities, talent/ability, volunteer work, work experience. *Other factors considered include:* alumni/ae relation, first generation, geographical residence, interview, racial/ethnic status, state residency. **Freshman Admission Requirements:** High school diploma or equivalent is not required. **Freshman Admission Statistics:** 19,391 applied, 18% admitted, 36% enrolled. **Transfer Admission Requirements:** High school transcript, college transcript(s), essay or personal statement, statement of good standing from prior institution(s). Minimum college GPA of 3.0 required. Lowest grade transferable C. **General Admission Information:** Application Fee $70. Early decision application deadline 11/1. Regular application deadline 1/1. Regular notification 4/1. Nonfall registration not accepted. Admission may be deferred for a maximum of 2 Years. Credit offered for CEEB Advanced Placement tests.

COSTS AND FINANCIAL AID

Annual tuition $43,930. Room and board $13,390. Average book expense $1,200. **Required Forms and Deadlines:** FAFSA, CSS/Financial Aid PROFILE, noncustodial PROFILE, business/farm supplement. current year federal tax returns. **Notification of Awards:** Applicants will be notified of awards on or about 4/1. **Types of Aid:** *Need-based scholarships/grants:* Federal Pell, SEOG, state scholarships/grants, private scholarships, the school's own gift aid. *Loans:* Direct Subsidized Stafford, Direct Unsubsidized Stafford, Direct PLUS, Federal Perkins, college/university loans from institutional funds. **Student Employment:** Federal Work-Study Program available. Institutional employment available. Off-campus job opportunities are good. **Financial Aid Statistics:** 91% freshmen, 92% undergrads receive need-based scholarship or grant aid. 10% freshmen, 8% undergrads receive non-need-based scholarship or grant aid. 75% freshmen, 87% undergrads receive need-based self-help aid. 1% undergrads receive athletic scholarships. 60% freshmen, 55% undergrads receive any aid. 49% undergrads borrow to pay for school. Average cumulative indebtedness $25,266. **Criteria for awarding institutional aid:** *Non-need-based:* academics, athletics, leadership, state/district residency.

See page 1106.

JOHNSON BIBLE COLLEGE

7900 Johnson Drive, Knoxville, TN 37998
Phone: 800-827-2122 • **Financial Aid Phone:** 865-251-2303
E-mail: jbc@jbc.edu • **CEEB Code:** 1345
Fax: 865-251-2336 • **Website:** www.jbc.edu • **ACT Code:** 3968

This private school, affiliated with the Christian (Nondenominational) Church, was founded in 1893. It has a 350-acre campus.

RATINGS

Admissions Selectivity Rating: 66   **Fire Safety Rating:** 73   **Green Rating:** 60*

STUDENTS AND FACULTY

Student Body: 78% out-of-state, (12 countries represented).
Retention and Graduation: 73% freshmen return for sophomore year. 57% freshmen graduate within 6 years. **Faculty:** Student/faculty ratio 21:1. 30 full-time faculty, 63% hold PhDs, 0% are members of minority groups, 17% are women. 0% of classes are taught by teaching assistants.

ACADEMICS

Degrees: associate, bachelor's, certificate, master's. **Special Study Options:** Accelerated program, cooperative education program, distance learning, double major, English as a Second Language (ESL), honors program, independent study, internships, teacher certification program. **Disability Services:** Special programs offered to physically disabled students include reader services, tape recorders.

FACILITIES

Housing: men's dorms, women's dorms, apartments for married students. **Computers:** Students can register for classes online. Administrative functions (other than registration) can be performed online.

CAMPUS LIFE

Environment: Rural. **Activities:** Choral groups, music ensembles, musical theater, radio station, student government, yearbook 3 honor societies, 3 religious organizations. **Athletics (Intercollegiate):** *Men:* baseball, basketball, cheerleading, soccer. *Women:* basketball, cheerleading, volleyball. **On-Campus Highlights:** women's residence hall, men's residence hall, global-education-tech building.

ADMISSIONS

Freshman Academic Profile: Average high school GPA 3.0. 21% in top 10% of high school class, 48% in top 25% of high school class, 78% in top 50% of high school class. SAT Math middle 50% range 470-560. SAT Critical Reading middle 50% range 480-612. SAT Writing middle 50% range 487-562. ACT middle 50% range 20-26. Minimum paper TOEFL 500. **Basis for Candidate Selection:** *Very important factors considered include:* Class rank, recommendation(s), rigor of secondary school record, standardized test scores, character/personal qualities, religious affiliation/commitment. *Important factors considered include:* application essay, interview. *Other factors considered include:* alumni/ae relation, extracurricular activities, talent/ability, volunteer work. **Freshman Admission Requirements:** High school diploma is required and GED is accepted. **Freshman Admission Statistics:** 213 applied, 95% admitted, 58% enrolled. **Transfer Admission Requirements:** High school transcript, college transcript(s), essay or personal statement, statement of good standing from prior institution(s). Lowest grade transferable C. **General Admission Information:** Application Fee $35. Regular application deadline 7/1. Regular notification 9/1. Nonfall registration accepted. Admission may be deferred for a maximum of one year.

COSTS AND FINANCIAL AID

Annual tuition $7,000. Room and board $4,890. Required fees $770. Average book expense $1,300. **Required Forms and Deadlines:** FAFSA, institution's own financial aid form. **Notification of Awards:** Applicants will be notified of awards on or about 3/30. **Types of Aid:** *Need-based scholarships/grants:* Federal Pell, SEOG, state scholarships/grants, private scholarships, the school's own gift aid. *Loans:* Subsidized Stafford, Unsubsidized Stafford, PLUS. **Student Employment:** Federal Work-Study Program available. Institutional employment available. Highest amount earned per year from on-campus jobs $1,240. **Financial Aid Statistics:** 97% freshmen, 98% undergrads receive need-based scholarship or grant aid. 24% freshmen, 26% undergrads receive non-need-based scholarship or grant aid. 59% freshmen, 58% undergrads receive need-based self-help aid. 97% undergrads receive any aid. 63% undergrads borrow to pay for school. Average cumulative indebtedness $17,487. **Criteria for awarding institutional aid:** *Non-need-based:* academics, minority status, music/drama, religious affiliation, state/district residency.

JOHNSON STATE COLLEGE

337 College Hill, Johnson, VT 05656-9408
Phone: 802-635-1219 • **Financial Aid Phone:** 802-635-1380
E-mail: jscadmissions@jsc.edu • **CEEB Code:** 3766
Fax: 802-635-1230 • **Website:** www.jsc.edu • **ACT Code:** 4316

This public school was founded in 1828. It has a 350-acre campus.

RATINGS
Admissions Selectivity Rating: 64   **Fire Safety Rating:** 72   **Green Rating:** 60*

STUDENTS AND FACULTY
Enrollment: 1,640. **Student Body:** 62% female, 38% male, 28% out-of-state, 0% international (2 countries represented). Asian 1%, African American 3%, Caucasian 85%, Hispanic 1%, Native American 1%.
Retention and Graduation: 64% freshmen return for sophomore year. 15% freshmen graduate within 4 years. 35% freshmen graduate within 6 years. **Faculty:** Student/faculty ratio 16:1. 50 full-time faculty, 98% hold PhDs, 4% are members of minority groups, 36% are women. 0% of classes are taught by teaching assistants.

ACADEMICS
Degrees: associate, bachelor's, master's, post-bachelor's certificate, terminal associate. **Classes:** Most classes have 10–19 students. **Majors with Highest Enrollment:** elementary education and teaching; tourism and travel services management; visual and performing arts, other. **Special Study Options:** cross-registration, double major, dual enrollment, English as a Second Language (ESL), exchange student program (domestic), external degree program, honors program, independent study, internships, study abroad, teacher certification program. **Disability Services:** Special programs offered to physically disabled students include note-taking services, reader services, tape recorders, tutors. **Career Services:** Alumni network, alumni services, career/job search classes, career assessment, internships, regional alumni. Career Services highlights include Internships.

FACILITIES
Housing: Coed dorms, apartments for married students, apartments for single students, Apartments for students who have 60 credits and a 3.0 average GPA. 65% of campus accessible to physically disabled. **Special Academic Facilities/Equipment:** Art gallery, visual arts center, child development center, human performance lab, 1,000-acre nature preserve, snowboard terrain park, dance studio **Computers:** Students can register for classes online. Administrative functions (other than registration) can be performed online.

CAMPUS LIFE
Environment: Rural. **Activities:** Choral groups, concert band, dance, drama/theater, jazz band, literary magazine, music ensembles, musical theater, pep band, radio station, student government, student newspaper, yearbook, International Student Organization 30 registered organizations, 1 honor societies, 4 religious organizations. **Athletics (Intercollegiate):** *Men:* basketball, cross-country, golf, lacrosse, soccer, tennis. *Women:* basketball, cross-country, soccer, softball, tennis, volleyball. **On-Campus Highlights:** Dibden Center For the Arts, Snowboarding Hill, Baselodge, Disc Golf Course, SHAPE Athletic Facility, Located in the heart of the Green Mountains, 1 hour from Vermont largest city, Burlington. JSC has 14 buildings on 1,350 acres (including our nature preserve). **Environmental Initiatives:** We compose. We owned a 1000 acres preserved land. Bio-Diesel school bus for students' transportation.

ADMISSIONS
Freshman Academic Profile: 34% in top 10% of high school class, 66% in top 25% of high school class, 68% in top 50% of high school class. SAT Math

middle 50% range 430-550. SAT Critical Reading middle 50% range 430-550. ACT middle 50% range 20-28. Minimum web-based TOEFL 61. Minimum paper TOEFL 500. **Basis for Candidate Selection:** *Very important factors considered include:* rigor of secondary school record, standardized test scores. *Important factors considered include:* Class rank, application essay, academic GPA, recommendation(s), character/personal qualities, talent/ability. *Other factors considered include:* extracurricular activities, interview, volunteer work, work experience. **Freshman Admission Requirements:** High school diploma is required and GED is accepted. *Academic units required:* 4 English, 2 mathematics, 2 science, (1 science labs), 3 social studies, 2 history. *Academic units recommended:* 4 English, 2 mathematics, 2 science, (1 science labs), 3 social studies, 2 history. **Transfer Admission Requirements:** High school transcript, college transcript(s), essay or personal statement, statement of good standing from prior institution(s). Minimum college GPA of 2.0 required. Lowest grade transferable C–. **General Admission Information:** Application Fee $39. Notification on a rolling basis, beginning on or about 12/1. Nonfall registration accepted. Admission may be deferred for a maximum of 1 year. Credit and/or placement offered for CEEB Advanced Placement tests.

COSTS AND FINANCIAL AID

Annual in-state tuition $8,568. Annual out-of-state tuition $19,008. Room and board $8,446. Required fees $1,113. Average book expense $1,000. **Required Forms and Deadlines:** FAFSA, state aid form. **Notification of Awards:** Applicants will be notified of awards on a rolling basis beginning 4/1. **Types of Aid:** *Need-based scholarships/grants:* Federal Pell, SEOG, state scholarships/grants, private scholarships, the school's own gift aid. *Loans:* Subsidized Stafford, Unsubsidized Stafford, PLUS, Federal Perkins. **Student Employment:** Federal Work-Study Program available. Institutional employment available. Off-campus job opportunities are good. **Financial Aid Statistics:** 93% freshmen, 89% undergrads receive need-based scholarship or grant aid. 4% freshmen, 3% undergrads receive non-need-based scholarship or grant aid. 95% freshmen, 95% undergrads receive need-based self-help aid. 87% freshmen, 82% undergrads receive any aid. **Criteria for awarding institutional aid:** *Non-need-based:* academics, art, leadership, music/drama, state/district residency.

JOHNSON & WALES UNIVERSITY—DENVER

7150 Montview Boulevard, Denver, CO 80220
Phone: 303-256-9300
Fax: 303-256-9333 • **Website:** www.jwu.edu/

This private school was founded in 1914.

RATINGS
Admissions Selectivity Rating: 62   **Fire Safety Rating:** 60*   **Green Rating:** 60*

STUDENTS AND FACULTY
Enrollment: 1,672. **Student Body:** 59% female, 41% male, 56% out-of-state, 1% international. Asian 3%, African American 5%, Caucasian 49%, Hispanic 11%, Native American 1%.
Retention and Graduation: 39% freshmen graduate within 4 years. **Faculty:** Student/faculty ratio 22:1. 54 full-time faculty, 37% are women.

ACADEMICS
Degrees: associate, bachelor's. **Classes:** Most classes have 10–19 students. Most lab/discussion sessions have 20–29 students. **Majors with Highest Enrollment:** business/commerce; hotel/motel administration/management; restaurant/food services management. **Special Study Options:** cooperative education program, double major, honors program, independent study, internships, study abroad.

FACILITIES
Housing: Coed dorms, Living-Learning Communities (LLCs) and Theme Floors, are an exciting approach to combining residential and academic life at Johnson & Wales University, Denver. LLCs and theme floors provide students with an opportunity to interact with faculty, staff, and other students around a theme or academic discipline in an active and collaborative program that enhances the teaching and learning process by incorporating all aspects of a Student's collegiate experience.

CAMPUS LIFE
Environment: Activities: Choral groups, dance, literary magazine, student government, yearbook.

ADMISSIONS
Freshman Academic Profile: Average high school GPA 3.2. **Basis for Candidate Selection:** *Very important factors considered include:* Class rank, rigor of secondary school record, interview. *Important factors considered include:* extra-

curricular activities, work experience. *Other factors considered include:* academic GPA, recommendation(s), standardized test scores, alumni/ae relation, level of applicant's interest, volunteer work. **Freshman Admission Requirements:** High school diploma is required and GED is accepted. **Freshman Admission Statistics:** 2,520 applied, 724% enrolled. **Transfer Admission Requirements:** High school transcript, college transcript(s), minimum college GPA of 2.0 required. Lowest grade transferable C. **General Admission Information:** Notification on a rolling basis, beginning on or about 11/1. Nonfall registration accepted. Admission may be deferred for a maximum of 1 year.

COSTS AND FINANCIAL AID

Annual tuition $26,112. Room and board $9,750. Average book expense. **Required Forms and Deadlines:** FAFSA. **Notification of Awards:** Applicants will be notified of awards on a rolling basis beginning 3/1. **Types of Aid:** *Need-based scholarships/grants:* Federal Pell, SEOG, state scholarships/grants, private scholarships, the school's own gift aid. *Loans:* Subsidized Stafford, Unsubsidized Stafford, PLUS, Federal Perkins, state loans, college/university loans from institutional funds. **Student Employment: Financial Aid Statistics:** 91% freshmen, 84% undergrads receive need-based scholarship or grant aid. 85% freshmen, 75% undergrads receive non-need-based scholarship or grant aid. 90% freshmen, 94% undergrads receive need-based self-help aid. 74% undergrads borrow to pay for school. Average cumulative indebtedness $24,664. **Criteria for awarding institutional aid:** *Non-need-based:* academics, alumni affiliation, job skills, leadership, state/district residency.

JOHNSON & WALES UNIVERSITY— NORTH MIAMI

1701 NE 127th Street, North Miami, FL 33181
Phone: 305-892-7600
E-mail: admissions.mia@jwu.edu
Fax: 305-892-7020 • **Website:** www.jwu.edu

This is a private school.

RATINGS
Admissions Selectivity Rating: 63   **Fire Safety Rating:** 60*   **Green Rating:** 60*

STUDENTS AND FACULTY
Enrollment: 2,152. **Student Body:** 57% female, 43% male, 56% out-of-state, 9% international (countries represented). Asian 1%, African American 24%, Caucasian 23%, Hispanic 21%, Native American 1%.
Retention and Graduation: 67% freshmen return for sophomore year. 34% freshmen graduate within 4 years. **Faculty:** Student/faculty ratio 28:1. 64 full-time faculty, 34% are women.

ACADEMICS
Degrees: associate, bachelor's. **Classes:** Most classes have 10–19 students. Most lab/discussion sessions have 20–29 students. **Special Study Options:** Accelerated program, cooperative education program, honors program, independent study, internships, study abroad, weekend college.

FACILITIES
Housing: Coed dorms, special housing for disabled students

CAMPUS LIFE
Environment: Activities: dance, drama/theater, student government, student newspaper, yearbook.

ADMISSIONS
Freshman Academic Profile: Average high school GPA 3.1. **Basis for Candidate Selection:** *Very important factors considered include:* Class rank, rigor of secondary school record, interview. *Important factors considered include:* extracurricular activities, work experience. *Other factors considered include:* academic GPA, recommendation(s), standardized test scores, alumni/ae relation, volunteer work. **Freshman Admission Requirements:** High school diploma is required and GED is accepted. **Freshman Admission Statistics:** 5,414 applied, 63% admitted, 19% enrolled. **Transfer Admission Requirements:** High school transcript, college transcript(s), minimum college GPA of 2.0 required. Lowest grade transferable C. **General Admission Information:** Notification on a rolling basis, beginning on or about 11/1. Nonfall registration accepted. Admission may be deferred for a maximum of 1 year.

COSTS AND FINANCIAL AID
Annual tuition $26,112. Room and board $10,728. Average book expense $1,800. **Required Forms and Deadlines:** FAFSA. **Notification of Awards:** Applicants will be notified of awards on a rolling basis beginning 3/1. **Types**

of Aid: *Need-based scholarships/grants:* Federal Pell, SEOG, state scholarships/grants, private scholarships, the school's own gift aid. *Loans:* Subsidized Stafford, Unsubsidized Stafford, PLUS, Federal Perkins, state loans, college/university loans from institutional funds. **Student Employment: Financial Aid Statistics:** % freshmen, 94% undergrads receive need-based scholarship or grant aid. 72% freshmen, 63% undergrads receive non-need-based scholarship or grant aid. 98% freshmen, 97% undergrads receive need-based self-help aid. 82% undergrads borrow to pay for school. Average cumulative indebtedness $31,737. **Criteria for awarding institutional aid:** *Non-need-based:* academics, alumni affiliation, job skills, leadership, state/district residency.

JOHNSON & WALES UNIVERSITY— PROVIDENCE CAMPUS

8 Abbott Park Place, Providence, RI 02903-3703
Phone: 401-598-2310 • **Financial Aid Phone:**
E-mail: admissions.pvd@jwu.edu • **CEEB Code:**
Fax: 401-598-2948 • **Website:** www.jwu.edu • **ACT Code:** 3804

This private school was founded in 1914. It has a 50-acre campus.

RATINGS
Admissions Selectivity Rating: 62   **Fire Safety Rating:** 60*   **Green Rating:** 60*

STUDENTS AND FACULTY
Enrollment: 9,756. **Student Body:** 56% female, 44% male, 81% out-of-state, 10% international. Asian 2%, African American 8%, Caucasian 48%, Hispanic 8%, Native American 0%.
Retention and Graduation: 74% freshmen return for sophomore year. 41% freshmen graduate within 4 years. **Faculty:** Student/faculty ratio 28:1. 308 full-time faculty, 42% are women.

ACADEMICS
Degrees: associate, bachelor's, certificate, master's, post-master's certificate. **Classes:** Most classes have 10–19 students. Most lab/discussion sessions have 10–19 students. **Special Study Options:** Accelerated program, cooperative education program, English as a Second Language (ESL), exchange student program (domestic), external degree program, honors program, independent study, study abroad, weekend college.

FACILITIES
Housing: Coed dorms, special housing for disabled students, special housing for international students, Technology Living/Learning Community at Snowden Hall '—A wing for first-year technology majors (among other upperclassman technology majors) interested in living with other students in the same academic program. The floor Resident Assistant is an upperclassman Technology Major. Faculty from the School of Technology will be involved in programming and mentorship in this community, providing out of classroom contact with instructors and academic program content. **Special Academic Facilities/Equipment:** Culinary Archives and Museum. **Computers:** Students can register for classes online. Administrative functions (other than registration) can be performed online.

CAMPUS LIFE
Environment: City. **Activities:** Choral groups, dance, drama/theater, pep band, student government, student newspaper, yearbook. **Athletics (Intercollegiate): Men:** baseball, basketball, cheerleading, cross-country, equestrian sports, golf, ice hockey, soccer, tennis, volleyball, wrestling. *Women:* basketball, cheerleading, cross-country, equestrian sports, golf, ice hockey, soccer, softball, tennis, volleyball.

ADMISSIONS
Freshman Academic Profile: Average high school GPA 3.1. **Basis for Candidate Selection:** *Very important factors considered include:* Class rank, rigor of secondary school record, interview. *Important factors considered include:* extracurricular activities, work experience. *Other factors considered include:* academic GPA, recommendation(s), standardized test scores, level of applicant's interest, volunteer work. **Freshman Admission Requirements:** High school diploma is required and GED is accepted. **Freshman Admission Statistics:** 11,830 applied, 76% admitted, 26% enrolled. **Transfer Admission Requirements:** High school transcript, college transcript(s), minimum college GPA of 2.0 required. Lowest grade transferable C. **General Admission Information:** Notification on a rolling basis, beginning on or about 11/1. Nonfall registration accepted. Admission may be deferred for a maximum of 1 year.

COSTS AND FINANCIAL AID
Annual tuition $26,112. Room and board $10,728. Average book expense $1,800. **Required Forms and Deadlines:** FAFSA. **Notification of Awards:**

Applicants will be notified of awards on a rolling basis beginning 3/1. **Types of Aid:** *Need-based scholarships/grants:* Federal Pell, SEOG, state scholarships/grants, private scholarships, the school's own gift aid. *Loans:* Subsidized Stafford, Unsubsidized Stafford, PLUS, Federal Perkins, state loans, college/university loans from institutional funds. **Student Employment: Financial Aid Statistics:** 90% freshmen, 84% undergrads receive need-based scholarship or grant aid. 71% freshmen, 59% undergrads receive non-need-based scholarship or grant aid. 94% freshmen, 95% undergrads receive need-based self-help aid. 77% undergrads borrow to pay for school. Average cumulative indebtedness $26,193. **Criteria for awarding institutional aid:** *Non-need-based:* academics, alumni affiliation, job skills, leadership, state/district residency.

See page 1108.

JONES INTERNATIONAL UNIVERSITY

9697 E. Mineral Avenue, Centennial, CO 80112
Phone: 800-811-5663
E-mail: admissions@international.edu
Fax: 303-799-0966 • **Website:** www.jonesinternational.edu

This is a private school.

RATINGS
Admissions Selectivity Rating: 60*   **Fire Safety Rating:** 60*   **Green Rating:** 60*

STUDENTS AND FACULTY
Enrollment: 22.
Retention and Graduation: 97% freshmen return for sophomore year.

ACADEMICS
Degrees: bachelor's, certificate, master's. **Special Study Options:** Accelerated program, distance learning, external degree program.

ADMISSIONS
Basis for Candidate Selection: *Very important factors considered include:* rigor of secondary school record, interview. *Important factors considered include:* standardized test scores. *Other factors considered include:* Class rank, academic GPA, recommendation(s), character/personal qualities, extracurricular activities, talent/ability, volunteer work, work experience. **Freshman Admission Requirements:** High school diploma is required and GED is accepted. **Freshman Admission Statistics:** 22 applied, 1086% enrolled. **Transfer Admission Requirements:** High school transcript, college transcript(s), Lowest grade transferable C. **General Admission Information:** Application Fee $50. Nonfall registration accepted. Credit and/or placement offered for CEEB Advanced Placement tests.

COSTS AND FINANCIAL AID
Annual tuition $835. Required fees $75. Average book expense $100. **Required Forms and Deadlines:** FAFSA. **Notification of Awards:** Applicants will be notified of awards on a rolling basis beginning 3/1. **Types of Aid:** *Need-based scholarships/grants:* Federal Pell, SEOG, state scholarships/grants, private scholarships, the school's own gift aid. *Loans:* Subsidized Stafford, Unsubsidized Stafford, PLUS, state loans. **Criteria for awarding institutional aid:** *Non-need-based:* academics, alumni affiliation.

JUDSON COLLEGE (AL)

302 Bibb Street, Marion, AL 36756
Phone: 334-683-5110 • **Financial Aid Phone:** 334-683-5157
E-mail: admissions@judson.edu • **CEEB Code:** 1349
Fax: 334-683-5282 • **Website:** www.judson.edu • **ACT Code:** 22

This private school, affiliated with the Baptist Church, was founded in 1838. It has a 80-acre campus.

RATINGS
Admissions Selectivity Rating: 71   **Fire Safety Rating:** 66   **Green Rating:** 60*

STUDENTS AND FACULTY
Enrollment: 315. **Student Body:** 97% female, 3% male, 29% out-of-state, 1% international (3 countries represented). Asian 0%, African American 12%, Caucasian 83%, Hispanic 1%, Native American 1%.
Retention and Graduation: 61% freshmen return for sophomore year. 49% freshmen graduate within 4 years. 49% freshmen graduate within 6 years. 15%

grads go on to further study within 1 year. 83% grads pursue arts and sciences degrees. 17% grads pursue medical degrees. **Faculty:** Student/faculty ratio 11:1. 18 full-time faculty, 83% hold PhDs, 0% are members of minority groups, 39% are women. 0% of classes are taught by teaching assistants.

ACADEMICS
Degrees: bachelor's. **Classes:** Most classes have fewer than 10 students. Most lab/discussion sessions have fewer than 10 students. **Majors with Highest Enrollment:** biology/biological sciences; elementary education and teaching; psychology. **Special Study Options:** Accelerated program, cross-registration, distance learning, double major, dual enrollment, independent study, internships, student-designed major, study abroad, teacher certification program. **Disability Services:** Special programs offered to physically disabled students include tutors. **Career Services:** alumni services, career assessment, internships.

FACILITIES
Housing: women's dorms. 50% of campus accessible to physically disabled. **Special Academic Facilities/Equipment:** Alabama Women's Hall of Fame. **Computers:** 50% of classrooms, 100% of dorms, 100% of libraries, 100% of student union, have wireless network access.

CAMPUS LIFE
Environment: Rural. **Activities:** Choral groups, drama/theater, literary magazine, marching band, music ensembles, student government, student newspaper, yearbook, Campus Ministries 23 registered organizations, 8 honor societies, 1 religious organizations. **Athletics (Intercollegiate):** *Women:* basketball, equestrian sports, soccer, softball, volleyball. **On-Campus Highlights:** Residence Hall Lobbies, Gym, Computer Labs, Club House, Student Center.

ADMISSIONS
Freshman Academic Profile: Average high school GPA 3.4. 32% in top 10% of high school class, 22% in top 25% of high school class, 84% in top 50% of high school class. 78% from public high schools. SAT Math middle 50% range 470-590. SAT Critical Reading middle 50% range 540-590. SAT Writing middle 50% range 520-630. ACT middle 50% range 19-26. Minimum paper TOEFL 500. **Basis for Candidate Selection:** *Very important factors considered include:* Class rank, academic GPA, standardized test scores. *Other factors considered include:* recommendation(s), rigor of secondary school record, alumni/ae relation, character/personal qualities, extracurricular activities, level of applicant's interest, talent/ability. **Freshman Admission Requirements:** High school diploma is required and GED is accepted. *Academic units required:* 4 English, 2 mathematics, 2 science, 3 social studies, 5 academic electives. *Academic units recommended:* 4 English, 2 mathematics, 2 science, 3 social studies, 5 academic electives. **Freshman Admission Statistics:** 306 applied, 84% admitted, 38% enrolled. **Transfer Admission Requirements:** college transcript(s), minimum college GPA of 2.0 required. Lowest grade transferable C–. **General Admission Information:** Application Fee $35. Notification on a rolling basis, beginning on or about 8/1. Nonfall registration accepted. Admission may be deferred for a maximum of 1 Year. Credit and/or placement offered for CEEB Advanced Placement tests.

COSTS AND FINANCIAL AID
Annual tuition $12,327. Room and board $7,969. Required fees $220. Average book expense $1,200. **Required Forms and Deadlines:** FAFSA, institution's own financial aid form, state aid form. **Notification of Awards:** Applicants will be notified of awards on a rolling basis beginning 11/15. **Types of Aid:** *Need-based scholarships/grants:* Federal Pell, SEOG, state scholarships/grants, private scholarships, the school's own gift aid. *Loans:* Subsidized Stafford, Unsubsidized Stafford, PLUS, Federal Perkins, college/university loans from institutional funds. **Student Employment:** Federal Work-Study Program available. Institutional employment available. Highest amount earned per year from on-campus jobs $1,750. Off-campus job opportunities are poor. **Financial Aid Statistics:** 97% freshmen, 97% undergrads receive need-based scholarship or grant aid. 11% freshmen, 12% undergrads receive non-need-based scholarship or grant aid. 75% freshmen, 86% undergrads receive need-based self-help aid. 12% freshmen, 12% undergrads receive athletic scholarships. 99% freshmen, 96% undergrads receive any aid. 74% undergrads borrow to pay for school. Average cumulative indebtedness $17,185. **Criteria for awarding institutional aid:** *Non-need-based:* academics, alumni affiliation, art, athletics, music/drama, religious affiliation, state/district residency.

JUDSON COLLEGE (IL)

1151 North State Street, Elgin, IL 60123
Phone: 847-628-2510 • **Financial Aid Phone:** 847-628-2530
E-mail: admission@JudsonU.edu • **CEEB Code:** 1700
Fax: 847-628-2526 • **Website:** www.JudsonU.edu • **ACT Code:** 1101

This private school, affiliated with the Baptist Church, was founded in 1963. It has a 84-acre campus.

RATINGS
Admissions Selectivity Rating: 75   **Fire Safety Rating:** 73   **Green Rating:** 60*

STUDENTS AND FACULTY
Enrollment: 1,132. **Student Body:** 58% female, 42% male, 35% out-of-state, 3% international (25 countries represented). Asian 1%, African American 4%, Caucasian 69%, Hispanic 5%, Native American 0%.
Retention and Graduation: 72% freshmen return for sophomore year. **Faculty:** Student/faculty ratio 16:1. 54 full-time faculty, 74% hold PhDs, 13% are members of minority groups, 30% are women. 0% of classes are taught by teaching assistants.

ACADEMICS
Degrees: bachelor's, certificate, master's. **Classes:** Most classes have 10–19 students. Most lab/discussion sessions have fewer than 10 students. **Majors with Highest Enrollment:** architecture (barch, ba/bs, march, ma/ms, phd); business/commerce; elementary education and teaching. **Special Study Options:** Accelerated program, distance learning, double major, English as a Second Language (ESL), honors program, independent study, internships, study abroad, teacher certification program. **Honors Programs:** GEN101H Faith and Learning: The Consecrated Genius MAT 211H Functions and Calculus **Combined Degree Programs:** BA/MA, Architecture. **Disability Services:** Special programs offered to physically disabled students include tutors. **Career Services:** Alumni network, alumni services, career/job search classes, career assessment, internships Career Services highlights include Internships in the following areas: Architecture, Business, Education, Worship Arts, Youth Ministry.

FACILITIES
Housing: Coed dorms, special housing for disabled students, men's dorms, women's dorms, apartments for married students. **Computers:** Students can register for classes online. Administrative functions (other than registration) can be performed online.

CAMPUS LIFE
Environment: City. **Activities:** Choral groups, drama/theater, music ensembles, student government 23 registered organizations, 1 honor societies. **Athletics (Intercollegiate):** *Men:* baseball, basketball, cheerleading, soccer. *Women:* basketball, cheerleading, soccer, softball, volleyball. **On-Campus Highlights:** Harm A. Weber Academic Center, Lindner Fitness Center, Lindner Commons, Eyrie Coffee House.

ADMISSIONS
Freshman Academic Profile: Average high school GPA 3.3. 7% in top 10% of high school class, 35% in top 25% of high school class, 59% in top 50% of high school class. SAT Math middle 50% range 440-660. SAT Critical Reading middle 50% range 430-600. ACT middle 50% range 20-26. Minimum paper TOEFL 550. **Basis for Candidate Selection:** *Very important factors considered include:* rigor of secondary school record, standardized test scores. *Important factors considered include:* character/personal qualities. *Other factors considered include:* Class rank, recommendation(s), talent/ability. **Freshman Admission Requirements:** High school diploma is required and GED is accepted. **Freshman Admission Statistics:** 520 applied, 73% admitted, 44% enrolled. **Transfer Admission Requirements:** college transcript(s), minimum college GPA of 2.0 required. Lowest grade transferable C–. **General Admission Information:** Application Fee $30. Notification on a rolling basis, beginning on or about 7/1. Nonfall registration accepted. Admission may be deferred for a maximum of 1semester. Credit and/or placement offered for CEEB Advanced Placement tests.

COSTS AND FINANCIAL AID
Annual tuition $13,872. Room and board $5,570. Required fees $550. Average book expense $680. **Required Forms and Deadlines:** FAFSA. **Notification of Awards: Types of Aid:** *Need-based scholarships/grants:* Federal Pell, SEOG, state scholarships/grants, private scholarships, the school's own gift aid. *Loans:* Direct Subsidized Stafford, Direct Unsubsidized Stafford, Direct PLUS, Federal Perkins. **Student Employment:** Federal Work-Study Program available. Institutional employment available. Highest amount earned per year from on-campus jobs $1,200. Off-campus job opportunities are excellent. **Financial Aid Statistics:** 90% freshmen, 90% undergrads receive any aid. **Criteria for awarding institutional aid:** *Non-need-based:* academics, art, athletics, music/drama.

THE JUILLIARD SCHOOL

60 Lincoln Center Plaza, New York, NY 10023-6588
Phone: 212-799-2000 ext.223 • **Financial Aid Phone:** 212-799-5000
E-mail: admissions@juilliard.edu • **CEEB Code:** 2340
Fax: 212-769-6420 • **Website:** www.juilliard.edu

This private school was founded in 1905.

RATINGS
Admissions Selectivity Rating: 65   **Fire Safety Rating:** 63   **Green Rating:** 60*

STUDENTS AND FACULTY
Enrollment: 508. **Student Body:** 45% female, 55% male, 85% out-of-state, 23% international (40 countries represented). Asian 11%, African American 5%, Caucasian 43%, Hispanic 6%, Native American 0%.
Retention and Graduation: Faculty: Student/faculty ratio 5:1. 130 full-time faculty, 14% are members of minority groups, 36% are women.

ACADEMICS
Degrees: bachelor's, diploma, master's, post-master's certificate. **Classes:** Most classes have fewer than 10 students. **Majors with Highest Enrollment:** piano and organ; violin, viola, guitar and other stringed instruments; voice and opera.

FACILITIES
Housing: Coed dorms. **Special Academic Facilities/Equipment:** 2 recital halls, 1 theater (1000 ppl), 1 drama theater (200 ppl), 15 two-story studios, 35 private teaching studios, 106 practice rooms, organ studios, 200+ pianos, recording studio, The Peter Jay Sharp Special Collections Room. **Computers:** Students can register for classes online. Administrative functions (other than registration) can be performed online.

CAMPUS LIFE
Environment: Metropolis. **Activities:** student government 5 registered organizations, 2 religious organizations. **On-Campus Highlights:** Lila Acheson Wallace Library, Lincoln Center, Rose Building - cafeteria, Juilliard Bookstore

ADMISSIONS
Freshman Academic Profile: Minimum paper TOEFL 533. **Basis for Candidate Selection:** *Very important factors considered include:* interview talent/ability. *Other factors considered include:* application essay, academic GPA, recommendation(s). **Freshman Admission Requirements:** High school diploma is required and GED is accepted. **Freshman Admission Statistics:** 2,269 applied, 7% admitted, 64% enrolled. **Transfer Admission Requirements:** college transcript(s), essay or personal statement, interview, Lowest grade transferable C. **General Admission Information:** Application Fee $100. Regular application deadline 12/1. Regular notification 4/1. Nonfall registration not accepted. Neither credit nor placement offered for CEEB Advanced Placement tests.

COSTS AND FINANCIAL AID
Annual tuition $35,140. Room and board $13,280. Average book expense $700. **Required Forms and Deadlines:** FAFSA, institution's own financial aid form. **Notification of Awards:** Applicants will be notified of awards on or about 4/1. **Types of Aid:** *Need-based scholarships/grants:* Federal Pell, SEOG, state scholarships/grants, private scholarships, the school's own gift aid. *Loans:* Direct Subsidized Stafford, Direct Unsubsidized Stafford, Direct PLUS, PLUS, Federal Perkins. **Student Employment:** Highest amount earned per year from on-campus jobs $4,500. **Financial Aid Statistics:** 96% freshmen, 96% undergrads receive need-based scholarship or grant aid. 70% undergrads borrow to pay for school. Average cumulative indebtedness $24,117. **Criteria for awarding institutional aid:** *Non-need-based:* music/drama.

JUNIATA COLLEGE

Best 378

1700 Moore Street, Huntingdon, PA 16652
Phone: 814-641-3420 • **Financial Aid Phone:** 814-641-3141
E-mail: admissions@juniata.edu • **CEEB Code:** 2341
Fax: 814-641-3100 • **Website:** www.juniata.edu • **ACT Code:** 3600

This private school was founded in 1876. It has a 800-acre campus.

RATINGS
Admissions Selectivity Rating: 89   **Fire Safety Rating:** 76   **Green Rating:** 72

STUDENTS AND FACULTY
Enrollment: 1,455. **Student Body:** 55% female, 45% male, 33% out-of-state, 8% international (35 countries represented). Asian 1%, African American 2%, Caucasian 63%, Hispanic 2%, Native American 1%.
Retention and Graduation: 71% freshmen graduate within 4 years. 34% grads go on to further study within 1 year. 62% grads pursue arts and sciences degrees. 3% grads pursue law degrees. 5% grads pursue business degrees. 20% grads pursue medical degrees. **Faculty:** Student/faculty ratio 13:1. 104 full-time faculty, 92% hold PhDs, 9% are members of minority groups, 40% are women. 0% of classes are taught by teaching assistants.

ACADEMICS
Degrees: bachelor's. **Classes:** Most classes have 10–19 students. Most lab/discussion sessions have 10–19 students. **Majors with Highest Enrollment:** biology/biological sciences; business/commerce; education. **Special Study Options:** double major, dual enrollment, English as a Second Language (ESL), exchange student program (domestic), honors program, independent study, internships, student-designed major, study abroad, teacher certification program, Philadelphia Urban Semester, Marine Science Semester, Washington Semester, Cooperative Degree Programs (3-1, 3-2, etc.). **Honors Programs:** Entire college is considered to be an honors program. **Combined Degree Programs:** BA/MD, BA/JD, BA/MA, BA/DDS, BA/MEng, Dentistry,Optom etry,Podiatry,Allied Health,Nursing. **Disability Services:** Special programs offered to physically disabled students include reader services, tape recorders, tutors. **Career Services:** Alumni network, alumni services, career/job search classes, career assessment, internships Career Services highlights include At Juniata, countless opportunities abound to learn by doing. Whether students are participating in internships, studying abroad, volunteering for local charities, leading student organizations, starting their own business, designing a play, or working on individual research, Juniata students learn early in their education how to make things happen.

FACILITIES
Housing: Coed dorms, special housing for international students, women's dorms, apartments for single students, Substance-Free Housing. 75% of campus accessible to physically disabled. **Special Academic Facilities/Equipment:** Environmental Studies Field Station,Juniata Museum of Art, Early Childhood Education Center, Ceramics studio and Anagama Kiln, Nature preserve and Peace Chapel, Observatory, Electron microscopes, Nuclear magnetic resonance spectrometers, Human Interaction Lab. three story, free form theater. **Computers:** 100% of classrooms, 100% of dorms, 100% of libraries, 100% of dining areas, 100% of student union, 100% of common outdoor areas have wireless network access. Students can register for classes online. Administrative functions (other than registration) can be performed online. Undergraduates are required to own a computer.

CAMPUS LIFE
Environment: Village. **Activities:** Choral groups, concert band, dance, drama/theater, jazz band, literary magazine, music ensembles, musical theater, radio station, student government, student newspaper, symphony orchestra, television station, Campus Ministries, International Student Organization, Model UN 94 registered organizations, 12 honor societies, 7 religious organizations. **Athletics (Intercollegiate):** *Men:* baseball, basketball, cross-country, football, soccer, tennis, track/field (outdoor), track/field (indoor), volleyball. *Women:* basketball, cross-country, field hockey, soccer, softball, swimming, tennis, track/field (outdoor), track/field (indoor), volleyball. **On-Campus Highlights:** von Liebig Science Center, Juniata College Museum of Art, Ceramics Studio w/Anagama Kiln, Sill Business Incubator and Juniata College Center, Suzanne von Liebig Theatre. **Environmental Initiatives:** 60% today and 75% by 2012 Electric in Wind RECS 2 LEED Certified Buildings, one Gold with Geothermal Goals part of campus strategic plan

ADMISSIONS
Freshman Academic Profile: Average high school GPA 3.8. 42% in top 10% of high school class, 74% in top 25% of high school class, 99% in top 50% of high school class. 86% from public high schools. SAT Math middle 50% range 540-650. SAT Critical Reading middle 50% range 530-650. Minimum web-based TOEFL 79. Minimum paper TOEFL 550. **Basis for Candidate Selection:** *Very important factors considered include:* application essay, academic GPA, recommendation(s), rigor of secondary school record, standardized test scores, character/personal qualities. *Important factors considered include:* extracurricular activities, first generation, interview, talent/ability, volunteer work. *Other factors considered include:* alumni/ae relation, geographical residence, level of applicant's interest, racial/ethnic status, state residency. **Freshman Admission Requirements:** High school diploma is required and GED is accepted. *Academic units required:* 4 English, 3 mathematics, 3 science, (2 science labs), 2 foreign language, 1 social studies, 3 history. *Academic units recommended:* 4 English, 3 mathematics, 3 science, (2 science labs), 2 foreign language, 1 social studies, 3 history. **Freshman Admission Statistics:** 2,418 applied, 66% admitted, 25% enrolled. **Transfer Admission Requirements:** High school transcript, college transcript(s), essay or personal statement, minimum college GPA of 2.5 required. Lowest grade transferable C–. **General Admission Information:** Application Fee $30. Early decision application deadline 12/1. Regular application deadline 3/15. Notification on a rolling basis, beginning on or about 2/28. Nonfall registration accepted. Admission may be deferred for a maximum of 12 months. Credit and/or placement offered for CEEB Advanced Placement tests.

COSTS AND FINANCIAL AID
Annual tuition $36,410. Room and board $10,200. Required fees $760. Average book expense $600. **Required Forms and Deadlines:** FAFSA. **Notification of Awards:** Applicants will be notified of awards on a rolling basis beginning 2/28. **Types of Aid:** *Need-based scholarships/grants:* Federal Pell, SEOG, state scholarships/grants, private scholarships, the school's own gift aid. *Loans:* Subsidized Stafford, Unsubsidized Stafford, PLUS, Federal Perkins, college/university loans from institutional funds. **Student Employment:** Federal Work-Study Program available. Institutional employment available. Highest amount earned per year from on-campus jobs $4,596. Off-campus job opportunities are good. **Financial Aid Statistics:** 100% freshmen, 98% undergrads receive need-based scholarship or grant aid. 15% freshmen, 13% undergrads receive non-need-based scholarship or grant aid. 85% freshmen, 87% undergrads receive need-based self-help aid. 100% freshmen, 100% undergrads receive any aid. 72% undergrads borrow to pay for school. Average cumulative indebtedness $31,213. **Criteria for awarding institutional aid:** *Non-need-based:* academics, art, leadership.

KALAMAZOO COLLEGE

Best 378

1200 Academy Street, Kalamazoo, MI 49006
Phone: 269-337-7166 • **Financial Aid Phone:** 269-337-7192
E-mail: admission@kzoo.edu • **CEEB Code:** 1365
Fax: 269-337-7390 • **Website:** www.kzoo.edu • **ACT Code:** 2018

This private school was founded in 1833. It has a 60-acre campus.

RATINGS
Admissions Selectivity Rating: 91   **Fire Safety Rating:** 81   **Green Rating:** 77

STUDENTS AND FACULTY
Enrollment: 1,349. **Student Body:** 58% female, 42% male, 38% out-of-state, 7% international (32 countries represented). Asian 5%, African American 4%, Caucasian 65%, Hispanic 9%, Native American 0%.
Retention and Graduation: 94% freshmen return for sophomore year. 74% freshmen graduate within 4 years. 27% grads go on to further study within 1 year. **Faculty:** Student/faculty ratio 14:1. 96 full-time faculty, 92% hold PhDs, 22% are members of minority groups, 54% are women. 0% of classes are taught by teaching assistants.

ACADEMICS
Degrees: bachelor's. **Classes:** Most classes have 10–19 students. Most lab/discussion sessions have fewer than 10 students. **Majors with Highest Enrollment:** economics; English language and literature; psychology. **Special Study Options:** cross-registration, double major, dual enrollment, English as a Second Language (ESL), exchange student program (domestic), independent study,

internships, student-designed major, study abroad. **Disability Services:** Special programs offered to physically disabled students include note-taking services, tape recorders, tutors. **Career Services:** Alumni network, alumni services, career/job search classes, career assessment, internships, regional alumni. Career Services highlights included at http://www.kzoo.edu/careerdevelopment/.

FACILITIES

Housing: Coed dorms, wellness housing, theme housing, 25% of campus accessible to physically disabled. **Special Academic Facilities/Equipment:** Science center, Rare book room **Computers:** 100% of classrooms, 70% of dorms, 100% of libraries, 100% of dining areas, 100% of student union, have wireless network access. Students can register for classes online. Administrative functions (other than registration) can be performed online.

CAMPUS LIFE

Environment: City. **Activities:** Choral groups, concert band, dance, drama/theater, jazz band, literary magazine, music ensembles, musical theater, pep band, radio station, student government, student newspaper, symphony orchestra, yearbook, Campus Ministries, International Student Organization, Model UN 50 registered organizations, 3 honor societies, 5 religious organizations. **Athletics (Intercollegiate):** *Men:* baseball, basketball, cross-country, diving, football, golf, soccer, swimming, tennis. *Women:* basketball, cross-country, diving, golf, soccer, softball, swimming, tennis, volleyball. **On-Campus Highlights:** Upjohn Library Commons, The Quad, Biggby Coffee Shop, Hicks Student Center, Anderson Athletic Center. **Environmental Initiatives:** The College is currently involved in a LEED registered expansion and renovation of Hicks Student Center. The project is expected to receive Silver certification when completed in summer 2008. The College has had an active recycling operation since 1988 and is participating in Recyclemania 2012 for the eighth consecutive year. The College has consistently garnered top 5 finishes in multiple categories each year it has participated. A student initiative in early 2010 initiated a food waste composting program in campus dining services. The program is in its second full year of operation and diverts 1,500 punds of food waste every week.

ADMISSIONS

Freshman Academic Profile: Average high school GPA 3.6. 46% in top 10% of high school class, 87% in top 25% of high school class, 96% in top 50% of high school class, 75% from public high schools. SAT Math middle 50% range 520-660. SAT Critical Reading middle 50% range 540-670. SAT Writing middle 50% range 530-650. ACT middle 50% range 26-30. Minimum web-based TOEFL 80, Minimum paper TOEFL 550. **Basis for Candidate Selection:** *Very important factors considered include:* academic GPA, rigor of secondary school record, extracurricular activities, volunteer work, work experience. *Important factors considered include:* application essay, recommendation(s), standardized test scores. *Other factors considered include:* alumni/ae relation, character/personal qualities, first generation, geographical residence, interview, level of applicant's interest, racial/ethnic status, talent/ability. **Freshman Admission Requirements:** High school diploma is required and GED is accepted. *Academic units required:* 4 English, 3 mathematics, 3 science, 3 foreign language, 2 social studies, 2 history. *Academic units recommended:* 4 English, 3 mathematics, 3 science, 3 foreign language, 2 social studies, 2 history. **Freshman Admission Statistics:** 2,294 applied, 69% admitted, 21% enrolled. **Transfer Admission Requirements:** High school transcript, college transcript(s), essay or personal statement, standardized test scores, statement of good standing from prior institution(s). Lowest grade transferable C. **General Admission Information:** Application Fee $40. Early decision application deadline 11/10. Regular application deadline 2/1. Regular notification 4/1. Nonfall registration not accepted. Admission may be deferred for a maximum of 1 year. Credit and/or placement offered for CEEB Advanced Placement tests.

COSTS AND FINANCIAL AID

Annual tuition $37,392. Room and board $8,274. Required fees $318. Average book expense $900. **Required Forms and Deadlines:** FAFSA, CSS/Financial Aid PROFILE. **Notification of Awards:** Applicants will be notified of awards on a rolling basis beginning 3/21. **Types of Aid:** *Need-based scholarships/grants:* Federal Pell, SEOG, state scholarships/grants, private scholarships, the school's own gift aid. *Loans:* Direct Subsidized Stafford, Direct Unsubsidized Stafford, Direct PLUS, Federal Perkins. **Student Employment:** Federal Work-Study Program available. Institutional employment available. Off-campus job opportunities are good. **Financial Aid Statistics:** 100% freshmen, 98% undergrads receive need-based scholarship or grant aid. 97% freshmen, 93% undergrads receive non-need-based scholarship or grant aid. 85% freshmen, 88% undergrads receive need-based self-help aid. 98% freshmen, 97% undergrads receive any aid. 53% undergrads borrow to pay for school. Average cumulative indebtedness $27,845.

KANSAS CITY ART INSTITUTE

4415 Warwick Boulevard, Kansas City, MO 64111
Phone: 800-522-5224 • **Financial Aid Phone:** 816-802-3337
E-mail: admiss@kcai.edu • **CEEB Code:** 6330
Fax: 816-802-3309 • **Website:** www.kcai.edu • **ACT Code:** 2277

This private school was founded in 1885. It has a 15-acre campus.

RATINGS

STUDENTS AND FACULTY

Enrollment: 671. **Student Body:** 55% female, 45% male, 62% out-of-state, 1% international (6 countries represented). Asian 4%, African American 3%, Caucasian 80%, Hispanic 6%, Native American 1%.
Retention and Graduation: 78% freshmen return for sophomore year. 43% freshmen graduate within 4 years. 53% freshmen graduate within 6 years. 40% grads go on to further study within 1 year. **Faculty:** Student/faculty ratio 12:1. 51 full-time faculty, 84% hold PhDs, 2% are members of minority groups, 37% are women. 0% of classes are taught by teaching assistants.

ACADEMICS

Degrees: bachelor's. **Classes:** Most classes have 20–29 students. **Majors with Highest Enrollment:** design and visual communications; film/video and photographic arts, other; painting. **Special Study Options:** cross-registration, double major, exchange student program (domestic), independent study, internships, student-designed major, study abroad. **Disability Services:** Special programs offered to physically disabled students include tape recorders, tutors. **Career Services:** Alumni network, alumni services, career/job search classes, career assessment, internships, regional alumni. Career Services highlights include Community Arts and Service Learning program (CASL).

FACILITIES

Housing: Coed dorms, apartments for single students. **Special Academic Facilities/Equipment:** H and R Block Art Space **Computers:** Students can register for classes online. Administrative functions (other than registration) can be performed online.

CAMPUS LIFE

Environment: Metropolis. **Activities:** student government. **On-Campus Highlights:** Dodge Painting Building, Cafe Nerman, Jannes Library-Learning Center, H&R Block Artspace, Green space in center of campus.

ADMISSIONS

Freshman Academic Profile: Average high school GPA 3.2. 11% in top 10% of high school class, 39% in top 25% of high school class, 73% in top 50% of high school class. 80% from public high schools. SAT Math middle 50% range 430-590. SAT Critical Reading middle 50% range 430-580. SAT Writing middle 50% range 420-570. ACT middle 50% range 20-25. Minimum web-based TOEFL 79. Minimum paper TOEFL 550. **Basis for Candidate Selection:** *Very important factors considered include:* recommendation(s). *Important factors considered include:* application essay, academic GPA, rigor of secondary school record, standardized test scores. *Other factors considered include:* character/personal qualities, extracurricular activities, first generation, interview, level of applicant's interest, talent/ability, volunteer work, work experience. **Freshman Admission Requirements:** High school diploma is required and GED is accepted. **Freshman Admission Statistics:** 537 applied, 63% admitted, 41% enrolled. **Transfer Admission Requirements:** High school transcript, college transcript(s), essay or personal statement, statement of good standing from prior institution(s). Minimum college GPA of 2.5 required. Lowest grade transferable C. **General Admission Information:** Application Fee $35. Notification on a rolling basis, beginning on or about 9/1. Nonfall registration accepted. Admission may be deferred for a maximum of 12. Credit offered for CEEB Advanced Placement tests.

COSTS AND FINANCIAL AID

Annual tuition $27,220. Room and board $8,294. Average book expense $1,500. **Required Forms and Deadlines:** FAFSA. **Notification of Awards:** Applicants will be notified of awards on a rolling basis beginning 4/1. **Types of Aid:** *Need-based scholarships/grants:* Federal Pell, SEOG, state scholarships/grants, the school's own gift aid. *Loans:* Subsidized Stafford, Unsubsidized Stafford, PLUS, Federal Perkins, Alternative Loans. **Student Employment:** Federal Work-Study Program available. Institutional employment available. Highest amount earned per year from on-campus jobs $1,000. Off-campus job opportunities are good. **Financial Aid Statistics:** 100% freshmen, 100% undergrads receive need-based scholarship or grant aid. 15% freshmen, 9% undergrads receive non-need-based scholarship or grant aid. 78% freshmen, 87% undergrads receive need-based self-help aid. 99% freshmen, 95% undergrads receive any aid. 84% undergrads borrow to pay for school. Average cumulative indebtedness $34,559. **Criteria for awarding institutional aid:** *Non-need-based:* academics, art.

KANSAS STATE UNIVERSITY

Best 378

119 Anderson Hall, Manhattan, KS 66506
Phone: 785-532-6250 • **Financial Aid Phone:** 785-532-6420
E-mail: k-state@k-state.edu • **CEEB Code:** 6334
Fax: 785-532-6393 • **Website:** www.k-state.edu • **ACT Code:** 1428

This public school was founded in 1863. It has a 668-acre campus.

RATINGS
Admissions Selectivity Rating: 70   **Fire Safety Rating:** 65   **Green Rating:** 78

STUDENTS AND FACULTY
Enrollment: 19,376. **Student Body:** 47% female, 53% male, 16% out-of-state, 6% international (107 countries represented). Asian 1%, African American 4%, Caucasian 78%, Hispanic 6%, Native American 0%.
Retention and Graduation: 27% freshmen graduate within 4 years. 59% freshmen graduate within 6 years. 22% grads go on to further study within 1 year. **Faculty:** Student/faculty ratio 20:1. 1001 full-time faculty, 83% hold PhDs, 16% are members of minority groups, 39% are women. 17% of classes are taught by teaching assistants.

ACADEMICS
Degrees: associate, bachelor's, master's, post-bachelor's certificate. **Classes:** Most classes have fewer than 10 students. **Majors with Highest Enrollment:** animal sciences; business administration and management; elementary education and teaching. **Special Study Options:** Accelerated program, cooperative education program, distance learning, double major, English as a Second Language (ESL), exchange student program (domestic), honors program, independent study, internships, study abroad, teacher certification program, Minors. **Honors Programs:** The University Honors Program is an opportunity for undergraduate students from all colleges to enhance their education with special classes and opportunities for personal growth. **Combined Degree Programs:** BS/MS Architectural Engineering, BS/MS Industrial Engineering. **Disability Services:** Special programs offered to physically disabled students include note-taking services, reader services, tape recorders, tutors. **Career Services:** career/job search classes, career assessment Career Services highlights include alumni career services partnership with the K-Sstate Alumni Association provides lifelong career services.

FACILITIES
Housing: Coed dorms, men's dorms, women's dorms, fraternity/sorority housing, apartments for married students, cooperative housing, apartments for single students. 100% of campus accessible to physically disabled. **Special Academic Facilities/Equipment:** South Asian area study center, education communications center, center for cancer research, planetarium, nuclear reactor/accelerator, Beach Art museum. **Computers:** 85% of classrooms, 100% of dorms, 100% of libraries, 100% of dining areas, 100% of student union, 10% of common outdoor areas have wireless network access. Students can register for classes online. Administrative functions (other than registration) can be performed online.

CAMPUS LIFE
Environment: Town. **Activities:** Choral groups, concert band, dance, drama/theater, jazz band, marching band, music ensembles, musical theater, pep band, radio station, student government, student newspaper, symphony orchestra, television station, yearbook, Campus Ministries, International Student Organization, Model UN 594 registered organizations, 36 honor societies, 37 religious organizations. 28 fraternities, 16 sororities. **Athletics (Intercollegiate):** *Men:* baseball, basketball, cheerleading, cross-country, football, golf, track/field (outdoor), track/field (indoor). *Women:* basketball, cheerleading, crew/rowing, cross-country, equestrian sports, golf, tennis, track/field (outdoor), track/field (indoor), volleyball. **On-Campus Highlights:** Peters Recreation Complex, Sports Complexes: Wagner Field, Bramlage Coliseum, K-State Student Union, Ahearn Fieldhouse, Beach Museum of Art. **Environmental Initiatives:** A university-wide task force for long-term visioning and planning in all areas of the university, including campus operations, curriculum, research, and external relations/outreach. Development of a new 10,000 square foot recycling facility on campus. Planning to install a used functional 750kW wind turbine donated by our local utility for research and education as well as feeding renewable energy into our campus grid.

ADMISSIONS
Freshman Academic Profile: Average high school GPA 3.5. 20% in top 10% of high school class, 45% in top 25% of high school class, 74% in top 50% of high school class. 81% from public high schools. ACT middle 50% range 21-27.

Basis for Candidate Selection: *Very important factors considered include:* Class rank, academic GPA, rigor of secondary school record, standardized test scores. *Other factors considered include:* recommendation(s). **Freshman Admission Requirements:** High school diploma is required and GED is accepted. **Freshman Admission Statistics:** 9,273 applied, 99% admitted, 42% enrolled. **Transfer Admission Requirements:** college transcript(s), minimum college GPA of 2.0 required. Lowest grade transferable C. **General Admission Information:** Application Fee $30. Nonfall registration accepted. Credit and/or placement offered for CEEB Advanced Placement tests.

COSTS AND FINANCIAL AID
Annual in-state tuition $7,317. Annual out-of-state tuition $19,416. Room and board $7,450. Required fees $730. Average book expense $1,100. **Required Forms and Deadlines:** FAFSA. **Notification of Awards:** Applicants will be notified of awards on a rolling basis beginning 4/1. **Types of Aid:** *Need-based scholarships/grants:* Federal Pell, SEOG, state scholarships/grants, private scholarships, the school's own gift aid. *Loans:* Direct Subsidized Stafford, Direct Unsubsidized Stafford, Direct PLUS, Subsidized Stafford, Unsubsidized Stafford, PLUS, Federal Perkins, college/university loans from institutional funds, Alternative Student Loans. **Student Employment:** Federal Work-Study Program available. Institutional employment available. Off-campus job opportunities are good. **Financial Aid Statistics:** 63% freshmen, 61% undergrads receive need-based scholarship or grant aid. 68% freshmen, 44% undergrads receive non-need-based scholarship or grant aid. 78% freshmen, 83% undergrads receive need-based self-help aid. 66% undergrads borrow to pay for school. Average cumulative indebtedness $23,857. **Criteria for awarding institutional aid:** *Non-need-based:* academics, alumni affiliation, art, athletics, leadership, music/drama, state/district residency.

KANSAS WESLEYAN UNIVERSITY

100 E. Claflin, Salina, KS 67401
Phone: ext 1285 • **Financial Aid Phone:** 785-827-5541
Fax: 785-827-0927 • **Website:** www.kwu.edu • **ACT Code:** 1434

This private school, affiliated with the Methodist Church, was founded in 1886. It has a 28-acre campus.

RATINGS
Admissions Selectivity Rating: 79   **Fire Safety Rating:** 69   **Green Rating:** 60*

STUDENTS AND FACULTY
Enrollment: 742. **Student Body:** 57% female, 43% male, 29% out-of-state, 2% international (8 countries represented). Asian 1%, African American 7%, Caucasian 58%, Hispanic 7%, Native American 1%.
Retention and Graduation: 30% grads go on to further study within 1 year. 24% grads pursue arts and sciences degrees. **Faculty:** Student/faculty ratio 15:1. 42 full-time faculty, 67% hold PhDs, % are members of minority groups, 38% are women. 0% of classes are taught by teaching assistants.

ACADEMICS
Degrees: associate, bachelor's, master's. **Classes:** Most classes have 10–19 students. **Special Study Options:** cross-registration, double major, honors program, independent study, internships, student-designed major, study abroad, teacher certification program. **Honors Programs:** Alpha Chi Beta Beta Beta Sigma Pi Sigma Alpha Psi Omega Phi Alpha Theta. **Career Services:** alumni services, career assessment, internships, regional alumni.

FACILITIES
Housing: Coed dorms, special housing for disabled students, men's dorms, women's dorms, apartments for married students, apartments for single students. 95% of campus accessible to physically disabled.

CAMPUS LIFE
Environment: Town. **Activities:** Choral groups, concert band, dance, drama/theater, jazz band, literary magazine, music ensembles, musical theater, pep band, student government, student newspaper, symphony orchestra, yearbook, Campus Ministries, International Student Organization, Model UN 20 registered organizations, 5 honor societies, 3 religious organizations. **Athletics (Intercollegiate):** *Men:* baseball, basketball, cheerleading, cross-country, football, golf, racquetball, soccer, tennis, track/field (outdoor). *Women:* basketball, cheerleading, cross-country, golf, racquetball, soccer, softball, tennis, track/field (outdoor), volleyball. **On-Campus Highlights:** NEW Student Center & Gym, Sam's Chapel, dorms, library, Science Hall.

ADMISSIONS
Freshman Academic Profile: Average high school GPA 3.2. 9% in top 10% of high school class, 32% in top 25% of high school class, 62% in top 50% of high school class. SAT Math middle 50% range 500-590. SAT Critical Reading middle 50% range 420-520. **Basis for Candidate Selection:** *Very important*

factors considered include: academic GPA, standardized test scores. **Freshman Admission Requirements:** High school diploma is required and GED is accepted. **Freshman Admission Statistics:** 442 applied, 61% admitted, 43% enrolled. **Transfer Admission Requirements:** college transcript(s), minimum college GPA of 2.0 required. Lowest grade transferable D. **General Admission Information:** Application Fee $20. Nonfall registration accepted.

COSTS AND FINANCIAL AID
Annual tuition $18,200. Room and board $6,400. Average book expense $800. **Required Forms and Deadlines:** FAFSA. **Notification of Awards: Types of Aid:** *Need-based scholarships/grants:* Federal Pell, SEOG, state scholarships/grants, private scholarships, the school's own gift aid. *Loans:* Direct Subsidized Stafford, Direct Unsubsidized Stafford, Direct PLUS, Federal Perkins. **Student Employment:** Federal Work-Study Program available. Off-campus job opportunities are excellent. **Financial Aid Statistics:** 75% undergrads receive any aid. 75% undergrads borrow to pay for school. Average cumulative indebtedness $16,769. **Criteria for awarding institutional aid:** *Non-need-based:* academics, alumni affiliation, art, athletics, music/drama.

KEAN UNIVERSITY

PO Box 411, Union, NJ 07083-0411
Phone: 908-737-7100 • **Financial Aid Phone:** 908-737-3220
E-mail: admitme@kean.edu • **CEEB Code:** 2517
Fax: 908-737-7105 • **Website:** www.kean.edu • **ACT Code:** 2582

This public school was founded in 1855. It has a 186-acre campus.

RATINGS
Admissions Selectivity Rating: 71   **Fire Safety Rating:** 96   **Green Rating:** 70

STUDENTS AND FACULTY
Enrollment: 12,543. **Student Body:** 61% female, 39% male, 2% out-of-state, 1% international (55 countries represented). Asian 5%, African American 18%, Caucasian 37%, Hispanic 22%, Native American 0%.
Retention and Graduation: 72% freshmen return for sophomore year. 19% freshmen graduate within 4 years. 50% freshmen graduate within 6 years.
Faculty: Student/faculty ratio 17:1. 344 full-time faculty, 87% hold PhDs, 30% are members of minority groups, 51% are women. 0% of classes are taught by teaching assistants.

ACADEMICS
Degrees: bachelor's, master's, post-master's certificate. **Classes:** Most classes have 20–29 students. **Majors with Highest Enrollment:** accounting; business administration and management; psychology. **Special Study Options:** Accelerated program, cooperative education program, distance learning, double major, dual enrollment, English as a Second Language (ESL), honors program, independent study, internships, liberal arts/career combination, study abroad, teacher certification program, weekend college, 2-year bachelor's degree program for RNs, Foreign Transfer Programs, Travelearn. **Honors Programs:** NJCSTME -THE NEW JERSEY CENTER FOR SCIENCE, TECHNOLOGY and MATHEMATICS EDUCATION: 5 year B.S. / M.S. --B.S. / M.A. Scholars programs- There is a critical and immediate need for highly qualified Science and Mathematics teachers in New Jersey, especially in urban school districts. There is also a need for highly trained research technicians to work in the pharmaceutical and biotechnology industries in New Jersey. Kean University created The New Jersey Center for Science, Technology and Mathematics Education (NJCSTME) to respond to both these needs. Through NJCSTME, Kean University offers an innovative and rigorous five year combined bachelor/master degree program to qualified students who are interested either in teaching science or mathematics (teacher track) or in a career in biotechnology or computational mathematics (research track). This program prepares graduates for immediate, well paid employment, and helps future generations of New Jersey students by putting highly qualified science and math teachers in the classroom and researchers in industry laboratories. These are some of the programs important features: -It is the only program in New Jersey that offers a core curriculum that links science and math laboratory courses with a team teaching approach. This program is a great opportunity for any student interested in both mathematics and science. -Each student has both an academic advisor and a career mentor. The progress of every student in the program is closely tracked by dedicated faculty who offer personal attention and support. It is a rigorous but highly structured and very supportive program that is designed for ensuring student success. -Students participate in research seminars and presentations, team research projects under faculty leadership, and educational outreach enrichment programs at area schools to help them appreciate the career choice between teaching and research. 4 + 4 B.S. / M.D. Scholars Program-Kean University's NJ Center for Science, Technology and Mathemat-

ics Education (NJCSTME), Drexel University College of Medicine and St. Peter's University Hospital have partnered to offer a four-plus '¬four Bachelor of Science / Medical Degree (4 + 4 B.S./M.D.) Scholars Program to highly qualified incoming freshmen. Students who meet all the requirements of this joint program while in college are awarded the B.S. in science and technology degree from NJCSTME at the end of their fourth year, then proceed to enter the first year medical school class at DCOM. **Combined Degree Programs:** BA/MA, BA/MPA ,BA/MS,BS/MS,BS/MA, BS/DPT,BS/MD, BA/DPM,MSN/MPA. **Disability Services:** Special programs offered to physically disabled students include note-taking services, reader services, tape recorders, tutors. **Career Services:** alumni services, career/job search classes, career assessment, internships Career Services highlights include Interviewing Workshop.

FACILITIES
Housing: Coed dorms, special housing for disabled students, apartments for single students, Freshmen Housing, Floor for women-only housing. 100% of campus accessible to physically disabled. **Special Academic Facilities/Equipment:** Liberty Hall Museum, Holocaust Resource Center, Center for Academic Success, Harwood Arena,Human Rights Institute Wynona Moore Lipman Ethnic Studies Center **Computers:** 100% of classrooms, 100% of dorms, 100% of libraries, 100% of dining areas, 100% of student union, 100% of common outdoor areas have wireless network access. Students can register for classes online. Administrative functions (other than registration) can be performed online.

CAMPUS LIFE
Environment: City. **Activities:** Choral groups, concert band, dance, drama/theater, jazz band, literary magazine, music ensembles, musical theater, pep band, radio station, student government, student newspaper, student-run film society, symphony orchestra, television station, yearbook, Campus Ministries, International Student Organization 143 registered organizations, 23 honor societies, 6 religious organizations. 16 fraternities, 17 sororities. **Athletics (Intercollegiate):** *Men:* baseball, basketball, football, lacrosse, soccer, track/field (outdoor). *Women:* basketball, field hockey, lacrosse, soccer, softball, tennis, track/field (outdoor), volleyball. **On-Campus Highlights:** University Center, Harwood Arena and Football Field, Center for Academic Success (CAS), Kean Hall, One Stop Service Center, Liberty Hall Museum Weather Station Holocaust Resource Center Wynona Moore Lipman Ethnic Studies Center Planetarium CAS and Vaughn Eames - Art Galleries. **Environmental Initiatives:** Creation of a bachelor of science degree in sustainability. Composting all of our food waste, plates, and compostable utensils on campus. LEED Certified renovation of our Center for Academic Success building

ADMISSIONS
Freshman Academic Profile: Average high school GPA 3.1. 8% in top 10% of high school class, 31% in top 25% of high school class, 70% in top 50% of high school class. 80% from public high schools. SAT Math middle 50% range 430-520. SAT Critical Reading middle 50% range 410-500. Minimum paper TOEFL 550. **Basis for Candidate Selection:** *Very important factors considered include:* academic GPA, rigor of secondary school record. *Important factors considered include:* standardized test scores. *Other factors considered include:* Class rank, application essay, recommendation(s), alumni/ae relation, character/personal qualities, extracurricular activities, interview, talent/ability, volunteer work, work experience. **Freshman Admission Requirements:** High school diploma is required and GED is accepted. *Academic units required:* 4 English, 3 mathematics, 2 science, (2 science labs), 2 history, 5 academic electives. *Academic units recommended:* 4 English, 3 mathematics, 2 science, (2 science labs), 2 history, 5 academic electives. **Freshman Admission Statistics:** 6,015 applied, 68% admitted, 34% enrolled. **Transfer Admission Requirements:** college transcript(s), statement of good standing from prior institution(s). Minimum college GPA of 2.0 required. Lowest grade transferable C. **General Admission Information:** Application Fee $50. Regular application deadline 5/31. Notification on a rolling basis, beginning on or about 11/1. Nonfall registration accepted. Credit and/or placement offered for CEEB Advanced Placement tests.

COSTS AND FINANCIAL AID
Average book expense. **Required Forms and Deadlines:** FAFSA. **Notification of Awards:** Applicants will be notified of awards on a rolling basis beginning 3/15. **Types of Aid:** *Need-based scholarships/grants:* Federal Pell, SEOG, state scholarships/grants, private scholarships, the school's own gift aid. *Loans:* Direct Subsidized Stafford, Direct Unsubsidized Stafford, Direct PLUS, Federal Perkins. **Student Employment:** Federal Work-Study Program available. Institutional employment available. Highest amount earned per year from on-campus jobs $6,290. Off-campus job opportunities are excellent. **Financial Aid Statistics:** 66% freshmen, 67% undergrads receive need-based scholarship or grant aid. 14% freshmen, 10% undergrads receive non-need-based scholarship or grant aid. 100% freshmen, 98% undergrads receive need-based self-help aid. 76% freshmen, 72% undergrads receive any aid. 71% undergrads borrow to pay for school. Average cumulative indebtedness $30,335. **Criteria for awarding institutional aid:** *Non-need-based:* academics, alumni affiliation, art, leadership, music/drama.

KEENE STATE COLLEGE

229 Main Street, Keene, NH 03435-2604
Phone: 603-358-2276 • **Financial Aid Phone:** 603-358-2280
E-mail: admissions@keene.edu • **CEEB Code:** 3472
Fax: 603-358-2767 • **Website:** www.keene.edu • **ACT Code:** 2510

This public school was founded in 1909. It has a 150-acre campus.

RATINGS
Admissions Selectivity Rating: 69   **Fire Safety Rating:** 94   **Green Rating:** 83

STUDENTS AND FACULTY
Enrollment: 4,787. **Student Body:** 57% female, 43% male, 50% out-of-state, 0% international (6 countries represented). Asian 1%, African American 1%, Caucasian 84%, Hispanic 3%, Native American 0%.
Retention and Graduation: 76% freshmen return for sophomore year. 49% freshmen graduate within 4 years. 62% freshmen graduate within 6 years. **Faculty:** Student/faculty ratio 17:1. 206 full-time faculty, 88% hold PhDs, 8% are members of minority groups, 48% are women. 0% of classes are taught by teaching assistants.

ACADEMICS
Degrees: associate, bachelor's, certificate, master's, post-bachelor's certificate, post-master's certificate. **Classes:** Most classes have 10–19 students. **Majors with Highest Enrollment:** business administration and management; elementary education and teaching; occupational safety and health technology/technician. **Special Study Options:** cooperative education program, double major, English as a Second Language (ESL), exchange student program (domestic), honors program, independent study, internships, liberal arts/career combination, student-designed major, study abroad, teacher certification program. **Honors Programs:** The Keene State College Honors Program; National Society of Collegiate Scholars in addition to Honors Programs in: Psychology, Safety Studies. **Disability Services:** Special programs offered to physically disabled students include note-taking services, reader services, tape recorders, tutors. **Career Services:** alumni services, career/job search classes, career assessment, internships Career Services highlights include Experiential learning/service learning and commitment to the community. Students apply what they learn from their course work by working in the local community. These real-life working situations enhance student learning and help students meet their course goals.

FACILITIES
Housing: Coed dorms, women's dorms, fraternity/sorority housing, apartments for married students, apartments for single students, wellness housing, theme housing, Honors, Language/Culture, Leadership, Quiet Study, Substance Free. 98% of campus accessible to physically disabled. **Special Academic Facilities/ Equipment:** Thorne-Sagendorph Art gallery, Redfern Arts Center, Recreational Center, Science Center, Mason Library, Media Arts Center, Cohen Center for Holocaust Studies, Center for Writing, Child Development Center **Computers:** 10% of classrooms, 100% of libraries, 50% of dining areas, 80% of student union, have wireless network access. Students can register for classes online. Administrative functions (other than registration) can be performed online.

CAMPUS LIFE
Environment: Village. **Activities:** Choral groups, concert band, dance, drama/theater, jazz band, literary magazine, music ensembles, musical theater, radio station, student government, student newspaper, student-run film society, television station, yearbook, Campus Ministries, International Student Organization 100 registered organizations, 21 honor societies, 4 religious organizations. 4 fraternities, 5 sororities. **Athletics (Intercollegiate):** *Men:* baseball, basketball, cheerleading, cross-country, diving, lacrosse, soccer, swimming, track/field (outdoor), track/field (indoor). *Women:* basketball, cheerleading, cross-country, diving, field hockey, lacrosse, soccer, softball, swimming, track/field (outdoor), track/field (indoor), volleyball. **On-Campus Highlights:** Science Building, Mason Library, Young Student Center, Night Owl Cafe, Arts Center on Brickyard Pond, Spaulding Gymnasium, Zorn Dining Commons new facility, New Pondside residence hall, Bodyworks Fitness Center, New Alumni Center in progress. **Environmental Initiatives:** LEED Silver residence hall (awarded 2008) Development of cogeneration capability in steam heat plant (combined heat and power) President's Council for a Sustainable Future

ADMISSIONS
Freshman Academic Profile: Average high school GPA 3.0. 5% in top 10% of high school class, 21% in top 25% of high school class, 60% in top 50% of high school class. SAT Math middle 50% range 440-540. SAT Critical Reading middle 50% range 440-540. SAT Writing middle 50% range 440-530. ACT middle 50% range 18-23. Minimum web-based TOEFL 61. Minimum paper TOEFL 550. **Basis for Candidate Selection:** *Very important factors considered include:* rigor of secondary school record. *Important factors considered include:*

application essay, academic GPA, recommendation(s), standardized test scores. *Other factors considered include:* Class rank, alumni/ae relation, character/personal qualities, extracurricular activities, first generation, level of applicant's interest, racial/ethnic status, talent/ability, volunteer work, work experience. **Freshman Admission Requirements:** High school diploma is required and GED is accepted. *Academic units required:* 4 English, 3 mathematics, 3 science, 2 social studies, 2 academic electives. 4 English, 3 mathematics, 3 science, 2 social studies, 2 academic electives. **Freshman Admission Statistics:** 6,315 applied, 78% admitted, 24% enrolled. **Transfer Admission Requirements:** High school transcript, college transcript(s), essay or personal statement, statement of good standing from prior institution(s). Minimum college GPA of 2.0 required. Lowest grade transferable C. **General Admission Information:** Application Fee $40. Regular application deadline 4/1. Nonfall registration accepted. Admission may be deferred for a maximum of 1 year. Credit and/or placement offered for CEEB Advanced Placement tests.

COSTS AND FINANCIAL AID
Average book expense $900. **Required Forms and Deadlines:** FAFSA. **Types of Aid:** *Need-based scholarships/grants:* Federal Pell, SEOG, state scholarships/grants, private scholarships, the school's own gift aid. *Loans:* Subsidized Stafford, Unsubsidized Stafford, PLUS, Federal Perkins, college/university loans from institutional funds. **Student Employment:** Federal Work-Study Program available. Institutional employment available. Off-campus job opportunities are excellent. **Financial Aid Statistics:** 72% freshmen, 70% undergrads receive need-based scholarship or grant aid. 29% freshmen, 24% undergrads receive non-need-based scholarship or grant aid. 94% freshmen, 93% undergrads receive need-based self-help aid. 80% undergrads borrow to pay for school. Average cumulative indebtedness $33,248. **Criteria for awarding institutional aid:** *Non-need-based:* academics, alumni affiliation, art, music/drama.

KENDALL COLLEGE

900 N. North Branch Street, Chicago, IL 60622
Phone: 877-588-8860 • **Financial Aid Phone:** 866-803-9988
E-mail: admissions@kendall.edu
Fax: 312-752-2021 • **Website:** www.kendall.edu • **ACT Code:** 1703

This private school, affiliated with the Methodist Church, was founded in 1934.

RATINGS
Admissions Selectivity Rating: 62   **Fire Safety Rating:** 70   **Green Rating:** 60*

STUDENTS AND FACULTY
Enrollment: Student Body: 12% out-of-state, (19 countries represented). **Faculty:** Student/faculty ratio 19:1. 37 full-time faculty, 14% are members of minority groups, 38% are women. 0% of classes are taught by teaching assistants.

ACADEMICS
Degrees: associate, bachelor's, certificate. **Majors with Highest Enrollment:** culinary arts and related services, other; hospitality administration/management; hospitality administration/management, other. **Special Study Options:** Accelerated program, cooperative education program, distance learning, double major, internships, student-designed major, study abroad, teacher certification program. **Disability Services:** Special programs offered to physically disabled students include tutors. **Career Services:** Alumni network, alumni services, career/job search classes, career assessment, internships, regional alumni.

FACILITIES
Housing: Coed dorms, special housing for disabled students

CAMPUS LIFE
Environment: Metropolis. **Activities:** student government, student newspaper. **On-Campus Highlights:** Kitchens, Hyatt Suite, Formal Dining Room, Student-Run Cafeteria

ADMISSIONS
Freshman Academic Profile: Average high school GPA 3.2. Minimum paper TOEFL 525. **Basis for Candidate Selection:** *Very important factors considered include:* Class rank, academic GPA, recommendation(s), rigor of secondary school record, standardized test scores. *Important factors considered include:* character/personal qualities. *Other factors considered include:* application essay, extracurricular activities, geographical residence, interview, talent/ability, work experience. **Freshman Admission Requirements:** High school diploma is required and GED is accepted. *Academic units required:* 4 English, 2 mathematics, 2 science, 2 foreign language, 2 social studies. 4 English, 2 mathematics, 2 science, 2 foreign language, 2 social studies. **Transfer Admission Requirements:** college transcript(s), statement of good standing from prior

institution(s). Minimum college GPA of 2.0 required. Lowest grade transferable C. **General Admission Information:** Application Fee $50. Nonfall registration accepted. Admission may be deferred for a maximum of 2 years. Credit and/or placement offered for CEEB Advanced Placement tests.

COSTS AND FINANCIAL AID

Annual tuition $21,510. Room and board $10,200. Required fees $440. **Required Forms and Deadlines:** FAFSA, institution's own financial aid form-Verification form Federal Tax Return. **Notification of Awards:** Applicants will be notified of awards on or about 4/1. **Types of Aid:** *Need-based scholarships/grants:* Federal Pell, SEOG, state scholarships/grants, private scholarships, the school's own gift aid. *Loans:* Direct Subsidized Stafford, Direct Unsubsidized Stafford, Direct PLUS, Subsidized Stafford, Unsubsidized Stafford, PLUS, Federal Perkins, college/university loans from institutional funds. **Student Employment:** Federal Work-Study Program available. Institutional employment available. Off-campus job opportunities are excellent. **Financial Aid Statistics:** 87% undergrads receive any aid. **Criteria for awarding institutional aid:** *Non-need-based:* academics, athletics, leadership, religious affiliation.

KENDALL COLLEGE OF ART AND DESIGN OF FERRIS STATE UNIVERSITY

17 Fountain Street NW, Grand Rapids, MI 49503-3002
Phone: 616-451-2787 • **Financial Aid Phone:** 616-451-2787
E-mail: brittons@ferris.edu • **CEEB Code:** 1983
Fax: 616-831-9689 • **Website:** www.kcad.edu • **ACT Code:** 1983

This public school was founded in 1928. It has a 2-acre campus.

RATINGS
Admissions Selectivity Rating: 60*   **Fire Safety Rating:** 60*   **Green Rating:** 60*

STUDENTS AND FACULTY
Student Body: 13% out-of-state, (15 countries represented). **Retention and Graduation:** 12% grads go on to further study within 1 year. 12% grads pursue arts and sciences degrees. **Faculty:** Student/faculty ratio 15:1. 50 full-time faculty, 6% hold PhDs, 4% are members of minority groups. 0% of classes are taught by teaching assistants.

ACADEMICS
Degrees: bachelor's, master's. **Classes: Majors with Highest Enrollment:** graphic design; illustration; interior design. **Special Study Options:** cooperative education program, double major, dual enrollment, independent study, internships, liberal arts/career combination, study abroad, teacher certification program. **Disability Services:** Special programs offered to physically disabled students include note-taking services, reader services, tape recorders, tutors. **Career Services:** Alumni network, alumni services, career/job search classes, internships, regional alumni.

FACILITIES
Housing: apartments for married students, apartments for single students, Fabulous historic district with rental apartments nearby. 100% of campus accessible to physically disabled. **Computers:** 100% of classrooms, 100% of libraries, 100% of student union, have wireless network access. Students can register for classes online. Administrative functions (other than registration) can be performed online. Undergraduates are required to own a computer.

CAMPUS LIFE
Environment: Metropolis. **Activities:** 12 registered organizations, 1 religious organizations. **On-Campus Highlights:** Studio Spaces, Studio Class Rooms, Library, Student Commons, Labs.

ADMISSIONS
Freshman Academic Profile: Average high school GPA 3.1. 10% in top 10% of high school class, 20% in top 25% of high school class, 75% in top 50% of high school class. Minimum web-based TOEFL 61. Minimum paper TOEFL 500. **Basis for Candidate Selection:** *Very important factors considered include:* application essay, academic GPA, rigor of secondary school record, standardized test scores, talent/ability. *Important factors considered include:* character/personal qualities, interview. *Other factors considered include:* Class rank, recommendation(s), extracurricular activities. **Freshman Admission Requirements:** High school diploma is required and GED is accepted. **Transfer Admission Requirements:** High school transcript, college transcript(s), essay or personal statement, Lowest grade transferable C. **General Admission Information:** Application Fee $30. Nonfall registration accepted. Admission may be deferred for a maximum of one semester. Credit offered for CEEB Advanced Placement tests.

COSTS AND FINANCIAL AID

Annual in-state tuition $12,674. Annual out-of-state tuition $19,220. Required fees $420. Average book expense $3,604. **Required Forms and Deadlines:** FAFSA. **Notification of Awards:** Applicants will be notified of awards on a rolling basis beginning 4/1. **Types of Aid:** *Need-based scholarships/grants:* Federal Pell, SEOG, state scholarships/grants, private scholarships, the school's own gift aid. *Loans:* Direct Subsidized Stafford, Direct Unsubsidized Stafford, Direct PLUS, Federal PerkinsKey Alternative Loan CitiAssist Student Loan Michigan Alternative Loan. **Student Employment:** Federal Work-Study Program available. Institutional employment available. Highest amount earned per year from on-campus jobs $2,000. **Criteria for awarding institutional aid:** *Non-need-based:* academics, alumni affiliation, art.

KENNESAW STATE UNIVERSITY

1000 Chastain Road, Kennesaw, GA 30144-5591
Phone: 770-423-6300 • **Financial Aid Phone:** 770-423-6074
E-mail: ksuadmit@kennesaw.edu • **CEEB Code:** 5359
Fax: 770-420-4435 • **Website:** www.kennesaw.edu • **ACT Code:** 833

This public school was founded in 1963. It has a 384-acre campus.

RATINGS
Admissions Selectivity Rating: 84   **Fire Safety Rating:** 99   **Green Rating:** 94

STUDENTS AND FACULTY
Enrollment: 22,574. **Student Body:** 58% female, 42% male, 6% out-of-state, 2% international (129 countries represented). Asian 3%, African American 16%, Caucasian 65%, Hispanic 7%, Native American 0%. **Retention and Graduation:** 76% freshmen return for sophomore year. 14% freshmen graduate within 4 years. 41% freshmen graduate within 6 years. **Faculty:** Student/faculty ratio 21:1. 747 full-time faculty, 79% hold PhDs, 21% are members of minority groups, 54% are women. 0% of classes are taught by teaching assistants.

ACADEMICS
Degrees: bachelor's, doctoral, master's. **Classes:** Most classes have 20–29 students. Most lab/discussion sessions have 20–29 students. **Majors with Highest Enrollment:** business administration and management; elementary education and teaching; nursing/registered nurse (rn, asn, bsn, msn). **Special Study Options:** cooperative education program, cross-registration, distance learning, double major, English as a Second Language (ESL), honors program, internships, study abroad, teacher certification program, weekend college. **Honors Programs:** The Honors Program at KSU provides a unique opportunity for exceptional students to customize their college experience. Through colloquia, seminars and directed studies, honor students can tailor their experience to meet their needs and interest. Instead of being restricted to the guidelines of a course catalog, students are encouraged to think outside the box and stretch themselves in academic directions that appeal to them. To guide them in their journey, a faculty mentor is assigned to each student. Most students only know faculty in a classroom setting, but honor students develop a one-on-one relationship designed to enhance their collegiate experience. **Disability Services:** Special programs offered to physically disabled students include note-taking services, reader services, tape recorders, tutors. **Career Services:** Alumni network, alumni services, internships Career Services highlights include Internships at KSU are on the rise and fully supported by campus administration. The president of KSU has expressed he wants to see a 10% annual increase in the number of students participating in this program from now on.

FACILITIES
Housing: apartments for single students. 100% of campus accessible to physically disabled. **Computers:** 100% of classrooms, 100% of libraries, 100% of dining areas, 100% of student union, 5% of common outdoor areas have wireless network access. Students can register for classes online. Administrative functions (other than registration) can be performed online.

CAMPUS LIFE
Environment: Town. **Activities:** Choral groups, concert band, dance, drama/theater, jazz band, music ensembles, musical theater, radio station, student government, student newspaper, symphony orchestra, Campus Ministries, International Student Organization, Model UN 151 registered organizations, 20 honor societies, 18 religious organizations. 10 fraternities, 8 sororities. **Athletics (Intercollegiate):** *Men:* baseball, basketball, cross-country, golf, tennis, track/field (outdoor), track/field (indoor). *Women:* basketball, cheerleading, cross-country, golf, soccer, softball, tennis, track/field (outdoor), track/field (indoor), volleyball. **On-Campus Highlights:** Student Dining Hall, Lounge in Student Center, Game Room in Student Center, Student Recreation Center, Campus Green. **Environmental Initiatives:** Commitment by KSU President Daniel S.

Papp to reduce the university's carbon footprint, in line with a national coalition of college and university presidents. Naming of a campus Director of Sustainability who will oversee the university's "green" initiatives and teach students as a member of the faculty. Launching an undergraduate degree program with emphases in environmental science or environmental polity within KSU's existing Interdisciplinary Studies program.

ADMISSIONS

Freshman Academic Profile: Average high school GPA 3.2. 21% in top 10% of high school class, 53% in top 25% of high school class, 81% in top 50% of high school class. 90% from public high schools. SAT Math middle 50% range 490-580. SAT Critical Reading middle 50% range 500-590. SAT Writing middle 50% range 470-570. ACT middle 50% range 21-24. Minimum web-based TOEFL 75. Minimum paper TOEFL 527. **Basis for Candidate Selection:** *Very important factors considered include:* academic GPA, standardized test scores. **Freshman Admission Requirements:** High school diploma is required and GED is not accepted. *Academic units required:* 4 English, 4 mathematics, 3 science, (3 science labs), 2 foreign language, 3 social studies. 4 English, 4 mathematics, 3 science, (3 science labs), 2 foreign language, 3 social studies. **Freshman Admission Statistics:** 9,471 applied, 57% admitted, 60% enrolled. **Transfer Admission Requirements:** college transcript(s), minimum college GPA of 2.0 required. Lowest grade transferable D. **General Admission Information:** Application Fee $40. Regular application deadline 5/14. Notification on a rolling basis, beginning on or about 1/1. Nonfall registration accepted. Admission may be deferred for a maximum of 12 months. Credit offered for CEEB Advanced Placement tests.

COSTS AND FINANCIAL AID

Average book expense. **Required Forms and Deadlines:** FAFSA. **Notification of Awards:** Applicants will be notified of awards on a rolling basis beginning 4/1. **Types of Aid:** *Need-based scholarships/grants:* Federal Pell, SEOG, state scholarships/grants, private scholarships. *Loans:* Subsidized Stafford, Unsubsidized Stafford, PLUS, Federal Perkins, Federal Nursing, state loans. **Student Employment:** Federal Work-Study Program available. Institutional employment available. Highest amount earned per year from on-campus jobs $15,732. Off-campus job opportunities are good. **Financial Aid Statistics:** 80% freshmen, 87% undergrads receive need-based scholarship or grant aid. 71% freshmen, 43% undergrads receive non-need-based scholarship or grant aid. 1% freshmen, 2% undergrads receive need-based self-help aid. 2% freshmen, 1% undergrads receive athletic scholarships. 68% freshmen, 64% undergrads receive any aid. 57% undergrads borrow to pay for school. Average cumulative indebtedness $20,666. **Criteria for awarding institutional aid:** *Non-need-based:* academics, alumni affiliation, art, athletics, job skills, leadership, minority status, music/drama, state/district residency.

KENT STATE UNIVERSITY—KENT CAMPUS

161 Michael Schwartz Center, Kent, OH 44242-0001
Phone: 330-672-2444 • **Financial Aid Phone:** 330-672-2972
E-mail: admissions@kent.edu • **CEEB Code:** 1367
Fax: 330-672-2499 • **Website:** www.kent.edu • **ACT Code:** 3284

This public school was founded in 1910. It has a 1200-acre campus.

RATINGS

Admissions Selectivity Rating: 67   **Fire Safety Rating:** 79   **Green Rating:** 72

STUDENTS AND FACULTY

Enrollment: 21,588. **Student Body:** 58% female, 42% male, 11% out-of-state, 5% international (87 countries represented). Asian 1%, African American 9%, Caucasian 77%, Hispanic 3%, Native American 0%. **Retention and Graduation:** 28% freshmen graduate within 4 years. **Faculty:** Student/faculty ratio 21:1. 908 full-time faculty, 6% are members of minority groups, 51% are women. 5% of classes are taught by teaching assistants.

ACADEMICS

Degrees: associate, bachelor's, certificate, doctoral, master's, post-bachelor's certificate, post-master's certificate, terminal associate, transfer associate. **Classes:** Most classes have 20-29 students. **Majors with Highest Enrollment:** business administration and management; nursing/registered nurse (rn, asn, bsn, msn); psychology. **Special Study Options:** Accelerated program, cooperative education program, cross-registration, distance learning, double major, dual enrollment, English as a Second Language (ESL), exchange student program (domestic), external degree program, honors program, independent study, internships, liberal arts/career combination, student-designed major, study abroad, teacher certification program, weekend college. **Honors Programs:** Honors College membership at Kent State University is open to

all majors and hosts approximately 1,350 students at the Kent Campus and five Regional Campuses. Honors College classes emphasize the intellectual value in the pursuit of knowledge. Every effort is made to show students the connections between disciplines. Honors College classes are small, taught by carefully chosen faculty, and emphasize students' active involvement in their learning. Plentiful opportunities for individual study, including the Senior Honors Thesis/Project give students exciting experiences in following their intellectual curiosity. An Honors College residence complex, state-of-the-art facilities, experiences including study abroad/away opportunities and cultural programming all support bright and motivated students seeking an intellectual home within the larger university. **Combined Degree Programs:** BA/MD, BA/MA. **Disability Services:** Special programs offered to physically disabled students include note-taking services, reader services, tape recorders, tutors. **Career Services:** Alumni network, alumni services, career/job search classes, career assessment, internships, regional alumni. Career Services highlights include Kent State University is home to the first academic trading floor with live derivatives exchange data. The Olga A. Mural Financial Engineering Trading Floor cost $2.2M to build and has an annual operating budget of $450,000. The Kent State Financial Engineering students are provided experience through Industry-based Projects (Internships). Internships are ten weeks in length and begin in May.

FACILITIES

Housing: Coed dorms, special housing for disabled students, men's dorms, special housing for international students, women's dorms, fraternity/sorority housing, apartments for married students, apartments for single students. 95% of campus accessible to physically disabled. **Special Academic Facilities/Equipment:** Fashion museum, herbarium, liquid crystal institute, planetarium, airport. **Computers:** 90% of classrooms, 20% of dorms, 40% of libraries, 70% of dining areas, 100% of student union, 10% of common outdoor areas have wireless network access. Students can register for classes online. Administrative functions (other than registration) can be performed online.

CAMPUS LIFE

Environment: Town. **Activities:** Choral groups, concert band, dance, drama/theater, jazz band, literary magazine, marching band, music ensembles, pep band, radio station, student government, student newspaper, television station, Campus Ministries, International Student Organization 214 registered organizations, 10 honor societies, 15 religious organizations. 17 fraternities, 6 sororities. **Athletics (Intercollegiate):** *Men:* baseball, basketball, cheerleading, cross-country, football, golf, track/field (outdoor), track/field (indoor), wrestling. *Women:* basketball, cheerleading, cross-country, field hockey, football, golf, gymnastics, soccer, softball, track/field (outdoor), track/field (indoor), volleyball. **On-Campus Highlights:** Student Recreation and Wellness Center, Kent State University Museum, Kent Student Center Plaza, Pan African Center Gallery, May 4 Memorial. **Environmental Initiatives:** Energy production on campus including a combined heat and power plant and a solar array to be installed this spring as part of our renewable energy master plan. Ongoing energy efficiency improvement at all campuses, including performance contracting. Supporting alternative transportation by providing a free bike sharing program, supporting walk-ability on campus, and providing free public transit for students.

ADMISSIONS

Freshman Academic Profile: Average high school GPA 3.3. 13% in top 10% of high school class, 37% in top 25% of high school class, 74% in top 50% of high school class. % from public high schools. SAT Math middle 50% range 470-570. SAT Critical Reading middle 50% range 470-570. SAT Writing middle 50% range 450-560. ACT middle 50% range 20-25. Minimum paper TOEFL 525. **Basis for Candidate Selection:** *Very important factors considered include:* academic GPA, rigor of secondary school record, standardized test scores. *Other factors considered include:* Class rank, recommendation(s). **Freshman Admission Requirements:** High school diploma is required and GED is accepted. **Freshman Admission Statistics:** 14,970 applied, 89% admitted, 31% enrolled. **Transfer Admission Requirements:** college transcript(s), minimum college GPA of 2.0 required. Lowest grade transferable C. **General Admission Information:** Application Fee $40. Regular application deadline 8/1. Notification on a rolling basis, beginning on or about 10/1. Nonfall registration accepted. Admission may be deferred for a maximum of 1 year. Credit and/or placement offered for CEEB Advanced Placement tests.

COSTS AND FINANCIAL AID

Average book expense. **Required Forms and Deadlines:** FAFSA. **Notification of Awards:** Applicants will be notified of awards on or about 3/15. **Types of Aid:** *Need-based scholarships/grants:* Federal Pell, SEOG, state scholarships/grants, private scholarships, the school's own gift aid. *Loans:* Direct Subsidized Stafford, Direct Unsubsidized Stafford, Direct PLUS, Federal Perkins, Federal Nursing, state loans, college/university loans from institutional funds, Alternative Loans. **Student Employment:** Federal Work-Study Program available. Institutional employment available. Highest amount earned per year from on-campus jobs $14,000. Off-campus job opportunities are excellent. **Financial Aid Statistics:** 87% freshmen, 78% undergrads receive need-based scholarship or grant aid. 26% freshmen, 16% undergrads receive non-need-based scholarship or grant aid. 85% freshmen, 87% undergrads receive need-based self-help aid. 1% freshmen, 1% undergrads receive athletic scholarships. 92% freshmen, 85% undergrads receive any aid. 76% undergrads borrow to pay for school. Average cumulative indebtedness $31,954. **Criteria for awarding institutional aid:** *Non-need-based:* academics, alumni affiliation, art, athletics, leadership, minority status, music/drama, state/district residency.

KENTUCKY STATE UNIVERSITY

400 East Main Street, Frankfort, KY 40601
Phone: 502-597-6813 • **Financial Aid Phone:** 502-597-6033
E-mail: admissions@kysu.edu • **CEEB Code:** 1368
Fax: 502-597-5814 • **Website:** www.kysu.edu • **ACT Code:** 1516

This public school was founded in 1886. It has a 915-acre campus.

RATINGS
Admissions Selectivity Rating: 77   **Fire Safety Rating:** 78   **Green Rating:** 61

STUDENTS AND FACULTY
Enrollment: 2,084. **Student Body:** 58% female, 42% male, 43% out-of-state, 1% international (18 countries represented). Asian 0%, African American 57%, Caucasian 18%, Hispanic 1%, Native American 0%.
Retention and Graduation: 46% freshmen return for sophomore year. 4% freshmen graduate within 4 years. 14% freshmen graduate within 6 years. 34% grads go on to further study within 1 year. 5% grads pursue law degrees. 10% grads pursue business degrees. 2% grads pursue medical degrees. **Faculty:** Student/faculty ratio 14:1. 134 full-time faculty, 63% hold PhDs, 35% are members of minority groups, 42% are women. % of classes are taught by teaching assistants.

ACADEMICS
Degrees: associate, bachelor's, master's. **Classes:** Most classes have 20–29 students. Most lab/discussion sessions have fewer than 10 students. **Majors with Highest Enrollment:** business/commerce; criminal justice/safety studies; elementary education and teaching. **Special Study Options:** cooperative education program, distance learning, double major, dual enrollment, English as a Second Language (ESL), honors program, independent study, internships, liberal arts/career combination, student-designed major, study abroad, teacher certification program. **Honors Programs:** The Whitney Young School of Honors and Liberal Studies. The Honors Program is an integrated liberal arts program that emphasizes student discussion of excellent books. **Disability Services:** Special programs offered to physically disabled students include note-taking services, reader services, tape recorders, tutors. **Career Services:** Alumni network, alumni services, career assessment, internships, regional alumni. Career Services highlights include KSU Intern and Cooperative Education program. The students gain hands on experience and 85% are offered positions after graduation.

FACILITIES
Housing: Coed dorms, men's dorms, women's dorms. 100% of campus accessible to physically disabled. **Special Academic Facilities/Equipment:** Art gallery, nutrition lab, agriculture research building, research farm, fish hatchery, electron microscope. **Computers:** 100% of classrooms, 100% of dorms, 100% of libraries, 100% of dining areas, 100% of student union, 60% of common outdoor areas have wireless network access. Students can register for classes online. Administrative functions (other than registration) can be performed online.

CAMPUS LIFE
Environment: Town. **Activities:** Choral groups, concert band, dance, drama/theater, jazz band, marching band, music ensembles, musical theater, opera, pep band, student government, student newspaper, Campus Ministries, International Student Organization 30 registered organizations, 5 honor societies, 4 religious organizations. 6 fraternities, 5 sororities. **Athletics (Intercollegiate):** *Men:* baseball, basketball, cross-country, football, golf, track/field (outdoor), track/field (indoor). *Women:* basketball, cross-country, softball, track/field (outdoor), track/field (indoor), volleyball. **On-Campus Highlights:** Jackson Hall, Carl Hill Student Center, William Exum Building, Whitney Young Residence Hall, Hume Hall. **Environmental Initiatives:** Construction of a LEED Silver Building Paper Recycle Program Upgrade mechanical systems to be more efficient

ADMISSIONS
Freshman Academic Profile: Average high school GPA 2.4. SAT Math middle 50% range 350-440. SAT Critical Reading middle 50% range 378-463. SAT Writing middle 50% range 340-440. ACT middle 50% range 15-19. Minimum web-based TOEFL 70. Minimum paper TOEFL 525. **Basis for Candidate Selection:** *Very important factors considered:* academic GPA, standardized test scores. *Important factors considered:* rigor of secondary school record, first generation, level of applicant's interest, state residency. *Other*

factors considered include: application essay, recommendation(s), alumni/ae relation, character/personal qualities, extracurricular activities, geographical residence, interview. **Freshman Admission Requirements:** High school diploma is required and GED is accepted. *Academic units required:* 4 English, 3 mathematics, 3 science, 2 foreign language, 3 social studies, 1 visual/performing arts, 1 0.5 Physical Education and 0.5 Health Education. 4 English, 3 mathematics, 3 science, 2 foreign language, 3 social studies, 1 visual/performing arts, 1 0.5 Physical Education and 0.5 Health Education **Freshman Admission Statistics:** 4,193 applied, 45% admitted, 25% enrolled. **Transfer Admission Requirements:** college transcript(s), minimum college GPA of 2.0 required. Lowest grade transferable C. **General Admission Information:** Application Fee $30. Nonfall registration accepted. Credit and/or placement offered for CEEB Advanced Placement tests.

COSTS AND FINANCIAL AID
Annual in-state tuition $6,108. Annual out-of-state tuition $15,708. Room and board $6,580. Required fees $750. Average book expense $1,300. **Required Forms and Deadlines:** FAFSA. **Notification of Awards:** Applicants will be notified of awards on or about 4/1. **Types of Aid:** *Need-based scholarships/grants:* Federal Pell, SEOG, state scholarships/grants, private scholarships, the school's own gift aid, United Negro College Fund, Federal Nursing Scholarships. *Loans:* Direct Subsidized Stafford, Direct Unsubsidized Stafford, Direct PLUS. **Student Employment:** Federal Work-Study Program available. Institutional employment available. Highest amount earned per year from on-campus jobs $2,500. Off-campus job opportunities are good. **Financial Aid Statistics:** 85% freshmen, 85% undergrads receive need-based scholarship or grant aid. 84% freshmen, 82% undergrads receive need-based self-help aid. 84% freshmen, 77% undergrads receive any aid. 26% undergrads borrow to pay for school. Average cumulative indebtedness $39,623. **Criteria for awarding institutional aid:** *Non-need-based:* academics, alumni affiliation, art, athletics, minority status, music/drama.

KENTUCKY WESLEYAN COLLEGE

3000 Frederica Street, Owensboro, KY 42301
Phone: 270-852-3120 • **Financial Aid Phone:** 270-852-3130
CEEB Code: 1369
Fax: 270-852-3133 • **Website:** www.kwc.edu • **ACT Code:** 1518

This private school, affiliated with the Methodist Church, was founded in 1858. It has a 52-acre campus.

RATINGS
Admissions Selectivity Rating: 77   **Fire Safety Rating:** 75   **Green Rating:** 60*

STUDENTS AND FACULTY
Enrollment: 665. **Student Body:** 49% female, 51% male, 28% out-of-state, 2% international (8 countries represented). Asian 0%, African American 10%, Caucasian 74%, Hispanic 2%, Native American 1%.
Retention and Graduation: 54% freshmen return for sophomore year. 25% freshmen graduate within 4 years. 21% grads go on to further study within 1 year. **Faculty:** Student/faculty ratio 12:1. 48 full-time faculty, 71% hold PhDs, 6% are members of minority groups, 48% are women. 0% of classes are taught by teaching assistants.

ACADEMICS
Degrees: bachelor's. **Classes:** Most classes have 10–19 students. Most lab/discussion sessions have 10–19 students. **Majors with Highest Enrollment:** biology/biological sciences; business/commerce; criminal justice/safety studies. **Special Study Options:** double major, independent study, internships, liberal arts/career combination, student-designed major, study abroad, teacher certification program, Online Program. **Combined Degree Programs:** University of Louisville and Auburn University. **Disability Services:** Special programs offered to physically disabled students include note-taking services, tutors. **Career Services:** Alumni network, career/job search classes, career assessment, internships.

FACILITIES
Housing: Coed dorms, special housing for disabled students, men's dorms, women's dorms, fraternity/sorority housing, apartments for married students, apartments for single students. 100% of campus accessible to physically disabled. **Special Academic Facilities/Equipment:** President's Hall/Library Learning Center Ralph Center for Fine Arts. Woodward Health and Recreation Center. Yu Hak Hahn Center for the Sciences. **Computers:** 100% of classrooms, 100% of dorms, 100% of libraries, 100% of dining areas, 100% of student union, have wireless network access. Students can register for classes online. Administrative functions (other than registration) can be performed online.

CAMPUS LIFE

Environment: Town. **Activities:** Choral groups, dance, drama/theater, literary magazine, music ensembles, pep band, radio station, student government, student newspaper, yearbook, Campus Ministries 42 registered organizations, 6 honor societies, 6 religious organizations. 3 fraternities, 2 sororities. **Athletics (Intercollegiate):** *Men:* baseball, basketball, cheerleading, cross-country, football, golf, soccer. *Women:* basketball, cheerleading, cross-country, golf, soccer, softball, tennis, volleyball. **On-Campus Highlights:** Winchester Center-New Campus Center, Ralph Fine Arts Center, Yu Hak Hahn Center for the Sciences, Woodward Health and Recreation Center, The Quad, For virtual tours, visit www.kwc.edu.

ADMISSIONS

Freshman Academic Profile: Average high school GPA 3.2. 20% in top 10% of high school class, 44% in top 25% of high school class, 68% in top 50% of high school class. 90% from public high schools. SAT Math middle 50% range 435-578. SAT Critical Reading middle 50% range 388-548. SAT Writing middle 50% range 395-503. ACT middle 50% range 19-24. Minimum paper TOEFL 500. **Basis for Candidate Selection:** *Very important factors considered include:* academic GPA, standardized test scores. *Important factors considered include:* rigor of secondary school record, extracurricular activities, interview. *Other factors considered include:* Class rank, recommendation(s), alumni/ae relation, character/personal qualities, level of applicant's interest, talent/ability, volunteer work, work experience. **Freshman Admission Requirements:** High school diploma is required and GED is accepted. *Academic units required:* 4 English, 3 mathematics, 3 science, 3 social studies. *Academic units recommended:* 4 English, 3 mathematics, 3 science, 3 social studies. **Freshman Admission Statistics:** 1,187 applied, 58% admitted, 23% enrolled. **Transfer Admission Requirements:** college transcript(s), minimum college GPA of 2.0 required. Lowest grade transferable C. **General Admission Information:** Notification on a rolling basis, beginning on or about 9/1. Nonfall registration accepted. Admission may be deferred for a maximum of 12 mo. Credit and/or placement offered for CEEB Advanced Placement tests.

COSTS AND FINANCIAL AID

Annual tuition $19,640. Room and board $7,200. Required fees $600. Average book expense $1,400. **Required Forms and Deadlines:** FAFSA. **Notification of Awards:** Applicants will be notified of awards on a rolling basis beginning 2/15. **Types of Aid:** *Need-based scholarships/grants:* Federal Pell, SEOG, state scholarships/grants, private scholarships, the school's own gift aid. *Loans:* Subsidized Stafford, Unsubsidized Stafford, PLUS, Federal Perkins, college/university loans from institutional funds, Alternative Education Loans. **Student Employment:** Federal Work-Study Program available. Institutional employment available. Off-campus job opportunities are good. **Financial Aid Statistics:** 99% freshmen, 98% undergrads receive need-based scholarship or grant aid. 8% freshmen, 11% undergrads receive non-need-based scholarship or grant aid. 81% freshmen, 77% undergrads receive need-based self-help aid. 99% freshmen, 85% undergrads receive any aid. 0% undergrads borrow to pay for school. Average cumulative indebtedness $0. **Criteria for awarding institutional aid:** *Non-need-based:* academics, alumni affiliation, art, athletics, leadership, music/drama, religious affiliation, state/district residency.

KENYON COLLEGE

Kenyon College Admissions Office, Gambier, OH 43022-9623
Phone: 740-427-5776 • **Financial Aid Phone:** 740-427-5240
E-mail: admissions@kenyon.edu • **CEEB Code:** 1370
Fax: 740-427-5770 • **Website:** www.kenyon.edu • **ACT Code:** 3286

This private school was founded in 1824. It has a 1200-acre campus.

RATINGS
Admissions Selectivity Rating: 97   **Fire Safety Rating:** 67   **Green Rating:** 83

STUDENTS AND FACULTY
Enrollment: 1,647. **Student Body:** 54% female, 46% male, 84% out-of-state, 3% international (41 countries represented). Asian 6%, African American 3%, Caucasian 79%, Hispanic 5%, Native American 1%.
Retention and Graduation: 94% freshmen return for sophomore year. 83% freshmen graduate within 4 years. 25% grads go on to further study within 1 year. **Faculty:** Student/faculty ratio 10:1. 156 full-time faculty, 100% hold PhDs, 22% are members of minority groups, 42% are women. 0% of classes are taught by teaching assistants.

ACADEMICS

Degrees: bachelor's. **Classes:** Most classes have 10–19 students. **Majors with Highest Enrollment:** economics; English language and literature; political science and government. **Special Study Options:** Accelerated program, double major, exchange student program (domestic), honors program, independent study, internships, liberal arts/career combination, student-designed major, study abroad. **Honors Programs:** Honors Programs are offered by all departmental and interdepartmental majors. **Combined Degree Programs:** Education, Environmental Studies. **Disability Services:** Special programs offered to physically disabled students include note-taking services, reader services, tape recorders, tutors. **Career Services:** Alumni network, alumni services, career/job search classes, career assessment, internships, regional alumni. Career Services highlights include Our Extern program enables students to explore career options through an experiential week of job-showing during winter or spring breaks. This often helps students decide what internships and/or career paths they'd like to pursue while building a network of contacts.

FACILITIES

Housing: Coed dorms, special housing for disabled students, women's dorms, fraternity/sorority housing, apartments for single students, wellness housing, theme housing, housing options for community service, substance-free, wellness, international wing, Kosher, twp. fire dept. groups. 41% of campus accessible to physically disabled. **Special Academic Facilities/Equipment:** Horn and Olin art galleries; Bolton and Hill theaters; Black Box Theater; Rosse and Storer halls for music; new sciences quadrangle; greenhouse and observatory; environmental center; $70-million fitness, recreation, and athletics facility. new art history building under construction **Computers:** 100% of classrooms, 100% of dorms, 100% of libraries, 100% of dining areas, 33% of common outdoor areas have wireless network access. Administrative functions (other than registration) can be performed online.

CAMPUS LIFE

Environment: Rural. **Activities:** Choral groups, concert band, dance, drama/theater, jazz band, literary magazine, music ensembles, musical theater, opera, pep band, radio station, student government, student newspaper, student-run film society, symphony orchestra, yearbook, Campus Ministries, International Student Organization, Model UN 140 registered organizations, 5 honor societies, 6 religious organizations. 8 fraternities, 4 sororities. **Athletics (Intercollegiate):** *Men:* baseball, basketball, cross-country, diving, football, golf, lacrosse, soccer, swimming, tennis, track/field (outdoor), track/field (indoor). *Women:* basketball, cross-country, diving, field hockey, lacrosse, soccer, softball, swimming, tennis, track/field (outdoor), track/field (indoor), volleyball. **On-Campus Highlights:** Kenyon College Bookstore, Fitness,/Recreation, Athletic Facility, Middle Ground Coffee Shop, Brown Family Environmental Center, Horn Gallery. **Environmental Initiatives:** 1 Food for Thought (purchase of local foods for dining hall and building a county-wide sustainable food system) http://rurallife.kenyon.edu/FFT/index.html 2 Brown Family Environmental Center (academic and public sustainability programs) 3 Kenyon Environmental Sustainability Council 4 Paper/can/bottle recycling program campus wide

ADMISSIONS

Freshman Academic Profile: Average high school GPA 3.9. 59% in top 10% of high school class, 86% in top 25% of high school class, 98% in top 50% of high school class. 50% from public high schools. SAT Math middle 50% range 610-690. SAT Critical Reading middle 50% range 640-740. SAT Writing middle 50% range 640-730. ACT middle 50% range 28-32. Minimum web-based TOEFL 100. Minimum paper TOEFL 600. **Basis for Candidate Selection:** *Very important factors considered include:* application essay, academic GPA, recommendation(s), rigor of secondary school record, character/personal qualities. *Important factors considered include:* Class rank, standardized test scores, extracurricular activities, interview, level of applicant's interest, talent/ability. *Other factors considered include:* alumni/ae relation, first generation, geographical residence, racial/ethnic status, state residency, volunteer work, work experience. **Freshman Admission Requirements:** High school diploma is required and GED is accepted. *Academic units required:* 4 English, 3 mathematics, 3 science, (3 science labs), 3 foreign language, 1 social studies, 2 history, 3 academic electives. *Academic units recommended:* 4 English, 3 mathematics, 3 science, (3 science labs), 3 foreign language, 1 social studies, 2 history, 3 academic electives. **Freshman Admission Statistics:** 4,272 applied, 33% admitted, 33% enrolled. **Transfer Admission Requirements:** High school transcript, college transcript(s), essay or personal statement, standardized test scores, statement of good standing from prior institution(s). Minimum college GPA of 3.0 required. Lowest grade transferable C. **General Admission Information:** Application Fee $45. Early decision application deadline 11/15. Regular application deadline 1/15. Regular notification 4/1. Nonfall registration not accepted. Admission may be deferred for a maximum of 1 year. Credit and/or placement offered for CEEB Advanced Placement tests.

COSTS AND FINANCIAL AID

Annual tuition $42,780. Room and board $10,340. Required fees $1,640. Average book expense $1,800. **Required Forms and Deadlines:** FAFSA, CSS/Financial Aid PROFILE, noncustodial PROFILE. **Notification of Awards:**

Applicants will be notified of awards on or about 4/1. **Types of Aid:** *Need-based scholarships/grants:* Federal Pell, SEOG, state scholarships/grants, private scholarships, the school's own gift aid. *Loans:* Subsidized Stafford, Unsubsidized Stafford, PLUS, Federal Perkins, college/university loans from institutional funds. **Student Employment:** Federal Work-Study Program available. Institutional employment available. Highest amount earned per year from on-campus jobs $1,255. Off-campus job opportunities are poor. **Financial Aid Statistics:** 99% freshmen, 98% undergrads receive need-based scholarship or grant aid. 22% freshmen, 17% undergrads receive non-need-based scholarship or grant aid. 73% freshmen, 82% undergrads receive need-based self-help aid. 54% freshmen, 58% undergrads receive any aid. 55% undergrads borrow to pay for school. Average cumulative indebtedness $19,840. **Criteria for awarding institutional aid:** *Non-need-based:* academics, minority status.

KETTERING UNIVERSITY

1700 University Ave. Flint, MI 48504-6214
Phone: 810-762-7865 • **Financial Aid Phone:** 810-762-7859
E-mail: admissions@kettering.edu • **CEEB Code:** 1246
Fax: 810-762-9837 • **Website:** www.kettering.edu • **ACT Code:** 1998

This private school was founded in 1919. It has a 85-acre campus.

RATINGS
Admissions Selectivity Rating: 86   **Fire Safety Rating:** 67   **Green Rating:** 60*

STUDENTS AND FACULTY
Enrollment: 1,658. **Student Body:** 18% female, 82% male, 26% out-of-state, 3% international (20 countries represented). Asian 3%, African American 3%, Caucasian 79%, Hispanic 3%, Native American 0%.
Retention and Graduation: 92% freshmen return for sophomore year. 10% freshmen graduate within 4 years. 55% freshmen graduate within 6 years. 24% grads go on to further study within 1 year. 17% grads pursue business degrees. **Faculty:** Student/faculty ratio 14:1. 119 full-time faculty, 87% hold PhDs, 23% are members of minority groups, 24% are women. 1% of classes are taught by teaching assistants.

ACADEMICS
Degrees: bachelor's, master's. **Classes:** Most classes have 20–29 students. Most lab/discussion sessions have 10–19 students. **Majors with Highest Enrollment:** computer engineering; electrical, electronics and communications engineering; mechanical engineering. **Special Study Options:** Accelerated program, cooperative education program, distance learning, double major, dual enrollment, independent study, study abroad, Co-op is required of all undergraduate students and typically begins in the first year. Each 24 week semester is divided into 11-weeks of classes and 12-13 weeks of paid professional co-op experience in industry. Students co-op with employers in 43 states and several countries. Income from co-op is a major resource for Kettering students whose total co-op income over their 4 and 1/2-year program typically ranges between $40,000 and $65,000. In addition to study abroad some Kettering students also gain experience in foreign locations for their co-op employer. Accelerated Program, Cooperative (work-study)program, distance learning, double major, independent study. Distance learing is for graduate students only. **Combined Degree Programs:** BS/MS Engineering. **Disability Services:** Special programs offered to physically disabled students include note-taking services, reader services, tape recorders, tutors. Career Services highlights include Kettering University is a premiere cooperative education program. All students are required to complete a specified number of co-op terms to graduate. Students may start their co-op experience as early as their freshmen year.

FACILITIES
Housing: Coed dorms, fraternity/sorority housing, apartments for single students. 100% of campus accessible to physically disabled. **Special Academic Facilities/Equipment:** Art museum, Scharschburg Archieves and Industrial History Museum (principal repository for SAE Patents and Technical Papers). Kettering is renown for the variety and quality of its laboratories for student use and teaching. Labs are required in nearly all science and engineering courses. Of special note are the Bosch Automotive Electronics Systems Lab, Ford Design Simulation Studio, the GM/PACE e-Design and e-Manufacturing Studio, Center for Fuel Cell Systems and Powertrain Integration, the Crash Test Safety, Computer Intergrated Manufacturing (CIM), Polymer Processing, and Mechatronics Labs, the Lubrizol Engine Test Center, SAE Project Vehicle facilities, Biomedical, and the Environmental Scanning Electron Microscopy Lab. The Connie and Jim John Recreation Center and Kettering Park (outdoor recreation). **Computers:** 100% of classrooms, 100% of libraries, 100% of dining areas, have wireless network access. Students can register for classes online. Administrative functions (other than registration) can be performed online.

CAMPUS LIFE
Environment: City. **Activities:** drama/theater, music ensembles, radio station, student government, student newspaper, yearbook 43 registered organizations, 13 honor societies, 1 religious organizations. 13 fraternities, 6 sororities.
On-Campus Highlights: CS Mott Engineering and Science Center, Connie and Jim John Recreation Center, Frances Willson Thompson Residence Hall, Cemistry and Physics Laboratories, Engineering Laboratories, Kettering University takes great pride in our TOP ranked programs and one-of-a-kind co-op program. Kettering students earn on average $40,000-$65,000 and up to 2 1/2 years of relevant work experience while working for one of our 600+ co-op employers. Prospective students are encouraged to visit campus to learn more about our academic programs, one-of-a-kind co-op program and to meet our faculty, students and staff.

ADMISSIONS
Freshman Academic Profile: Average high school GPA 3.6. 27% in top 10% of high school class, 64% in top 25% of high school class, 63% in top 50% of high school class. SAT Math middle 50% range 540-660. SAT Critical Reading middle 50% range 490-630. ACT middle 50% range 24-33. Minimum web-based TOEFL 79. Minimum paper TOEFL 550. **Basis for Candidate Selection:** *Very important factors considered include:* academic GPA, rigor of secondary school record, standardized test scores. *Important factors considered include:* Class rank, extracurricular activities. *Other factors considered include:* application essay, recommendation(s), interview, racial/ethnic status, volunteer work, work experience. **Freshman Admission Requirements:** High school diploma is required and GED is not accepted. *Academic units required:* 3 English, 4 mathematics, 2 science, (2 science labs). *Academic units recommended:* 3 English, 4 mathematics, 2 science, (2 science labs). **Freshman Admission Statistics:** 2,140 applied, 62% admitted, 28% enrolled. **Transfer Admission Requirements:** college transcript(s), minimum college GPA of 3.0 required. Lowest grade transferable C. **General Admission Information:** Application Fee $35. Notification on a rolling basis, beginning on or about 10/15. Nonfall registration accepted. Admission may be deferred for a maximum of 1 year. Credit offered for CEEB Advanced Placement tests.

COSTS AND FINANCIAL AID
Average book expense. **Required Forms and Deadlines:** FAFSA. **Notification of Awards:** Applicants will be notified of awards on a rolling basis beginning 1/15. **Types of Aid:** *Need-based scholarships/grants:* Federal Pell, SEOG, state scholarships/grants, private scholarships, the school's own gift aid. *Loans:* Direct Subsidized Stafford, Direct Unsubsidized Stafford, Direct PLUS, Subsidized Stafford, Unsubsidized Stafford, PLUS. **Student Employment:** Federal Work Study Program available. Institutional employment available. Highest amount earned per year from on campus jobs $1,200. Off-campus job opportunities are fair. **Financial Aid Statistics:** 100% freshmen, 99% undergrads receive need-based scholarship or grant aid. 34% freshmen, 28% undergrads receive non-need-based scholarship or grant aid. 93% freshmen, 93% undergrads receive need-based self help aid. 98% freshmen, 88% undergrads receive any aid. **Criteria for awarding institutional aid:** *Non-need-based:* academics, alumni affiliation, leadership, state/district residency.

See page 1110.

KEUKA COLLEGE

Office of Admissions, Keuka Park, NY 14478-0098
Phone: 315-279-5254 • **Financial Aid Phone:** 315-279-5646
E-mail: admissions@mail.keuka.edu • **CEEB Code:** 2744
Fax: 315-536-5386 • **Website:** www.keuka.edu • **ACT Code:** 2782

This private school, affiliated with the American Baptist Church, was founded in 1890. It has a 203-acre campus.

RATINGS
Admissions Selectivity Rating: 68   **Fire Safety Rating:** 66   **Green Rating:** 60*

STUDENTS AND FACULTY
Enrollment: 1,874. **Student Body:** 75% female, 25% male, 6% out-of-state, 0% international (3 countries represented). Asian 2%, African American 7%, Caucasian 74%, Hispanic 1%, Native American 1%.
Retention and Graduation: 43% freshmen graduate within 4 years. 52% freshmen graduate within 6 years. 28% grads go on to further study within 1 year. **Faculty:** Student/faculty ratio 14:1. 79 full-time faculty, 82% hold PhDs, 1% are members of minority groups, 57% are women. 0% of classes are taught by teaching assistants.

ACADEMICS

Degrees: bachelor's, master's. **Classes:** Most classes have 20–29 students. Most lab/discussion sessions have 10–19 students. **Majors with Highest Enrollment:** business administration and management; occupational therapy/therapist; special education and teaching. **Special Study Options:** Accelerated program, cooperative education program, cross-registration, double major, dual enrollment, independent study, internships, student-designed major, study abroad, teacher certification program. **Combined Degree Programs:** Clinical Science to Chiropractic with NY Chiroprac. **Disability Services:** Special programs offered to physically disabled students include note-taking services, reader services, tape recorders, tutors. **Career Services:** Alumni network, alumni services, career/job search classes, career assessment, internships, regional alumni. Career Services highlights include Experiential learning - National Leader in Experiential, Hands-on Learning.

FACILITIES

Housing: Coed dorms, special housing for disabled students, men's dorms, women's dorms, cooperative housing, theme housing. 61% of campus accessible to physically disabled. Special Academic Facilities/Equipment: Bird Museum, Lightner Gallery

CAMPUS LIFE

Environment: Rural. **Activities:** Choral groups, concert band, dance, drama/theater, literary magazine, musical theater, radio station, student government, student newspaper, student-run film society, yearbook 32 registered organizations, 7 honor societies, 2 religious organizations. **Athletics (Intercollegiate):** *Men:* baseball, basketball, cross-country, golf, lacrosse, soccer, tennis. *Women:* basketball, cross-country, golf, lacrosse, soccer, softball, synchronized swimming, tennis, volleyball. **On-Campus Highlights:** The Weed Physical Arts Center (Gym, pool, fitness rooms, coaches offices), Dahstrom Student Center (bookstore, club offices, student affairs), Ostrander Field (soccer, lacrosse games), Hegeman Hall (classes, faculty offices), Jephson Hall (sciences, greenhouse, labs, electronic classroom).

ADMISSIONS

Freshman Academic Profile: Average high school GPA 3.1. 13% in top 10% of high school class, 34% in top 25% of high school class, 73% in top 50% of high school class. 96% from public high schools. SAT Math middle 50% range 410-530. SAT Critical Reading middle 50% range 420-510. SAT Writing middle 50% range 400-490. ACT middle 50% range 18-23. Minimum paper TOEFL 500. **Basis for Candidate Selection:** *Very important factors considered include:* rigor of secondary school record. *Important factors considered include:* Class rank, application essay, academic GPA, recommendation(s), character/personal qualities, extracurricular activities, interview. *Other factors considered include:* standardized test scores, alumni/ae relation, level of applicant's interest, talent/ability, volunteer work, work experience. **Freshman Admission Requirements:** High school diploma is required and GED is accepted. **Freshman Admission Statistics:** 840 applied, 76% admitted, 39% enrolled. **Transfer Admission Requirements:** college transcript(s), essay or personal statement, minimum college GPA of 2.0 required. Lowest grade transferable C. **General Admission Information:** Application Fee $30. Notification on a rolling basis, beginning on or about 9/1. Nonfall registration accepted. Admission may be deferred for a maximum of 12. Credit and/or placement offered for CEEB Advanced Placement tests.

COSTS AND FINANCIAL AID

Annual tuition $24,310. Room and board $9,880. Required fees $790. Average book expense $1,000. **Required Forms and Deadlines:** FAFSA. **Notification of Awards:** Applicants will be notified of awards on a rolling basis beginning 3/1. **Types of Aid:** *Need-based scholarships/grants:* Federal Pell, SEOG, state scholarships/grants, the school's own gift aid. *Loans:* Subsidized Stafford, Unsubsidized Stafford, PLUS, Federal Perkins. **Student Employment:** Highest amount earned per year from on-campus jobs $1,800. Off-campus job opportunities are good. **Financial Aid Statistics:** 90% freshmen, 78% undergrads receive need-based scholarship or grant aid. 88% freshmen, 67% undergrads receive non-need-based scholarship or grant aid. 98% freshmen, 99% undergrads receive need-based self-help aid. 92% freshmen, 93% undergrads receive any aid. 95% undergrads borrow to pay for school. Average cumulative indebtedness $19,507. **Criteria for awarding institutional aid:** *Non-need-based:* academics, alumni affiliation, leadership, minority status, religious affiliation.

One College Green, La Plume, PA 18440
Phone: 570-945-8111 • **Financial Aid Phone:** 570-945-8132
E-mail: admissions@keystone.edu • **CEEB Code:** 2351
Fax: 570-945-7916 • **Website:** www.keystone.edu • **ACT Code:** 2602

This private school was founded in 1868. It has a 270-acre campus.

RATINGS
Admissions Selectivity Rating: 69   **Fire Safety Rating:** 97   **Green Rating:** 84

STUDENTS AND FACULTY

Enrollment: 1,651. **Student Body:** 59% female, 41% male, 13% out-of-state, 0% international (9 countries represented). Asian 0%, African American 2%, Caucasian 23%, Hispanic 2%, Native American 0%. **Retention and Graduation:** 65% freshmen return for sophomore year. 25% grads go on to further study within 1 year. 1% grads pursue arts and sciences degrees. 1% grads pursue law degrees. 1% grads pursue business degrees. 1% grads pursue medical degrees. **Faculty:** Student/faculty ratio 11:1. 68 full-time faculty, 49% hold PhDs, 1% are members of minority groups, 63% are women. 0% of classes are taught by teaching assistants.

ACADEMICS

Degrees: associate, bachelor's, certificate, post-bachelor's certificate, terminal associate, transfer associate. **Classes:** Most classes have 10–19 students. Most lab/discussion sessions have fewer than 10 students. **Majors with Highest Enrollment:** business administration and management; education; security and protective services, other. **Special Study Options:** cooperative education program, cross-registration, distance learning, double major, dual enrollment, English as a Second Language (ESL), honors program, independent study, internships, study abroad, teacher certification program, weekend college. **Honors Programs:** Freshmen Honor's Program. **Disability Services:** Special programs offered to physically disabled students include note-taking services, reader services, tutors. **Career Services:** Alumni network, alumni services, career/job search classes, career assessment, internships, regional alumni. Career Services highlights include Student internship placements have included NBC Dateline, Late Night with Conan O'Brien, US Olympic Training Committee, US Secret Service, ESPN Radio, Atlantic Records, and placements abroad in several countries.

FACILITIES

Housing: Coed dorms, special housing for disabled students, women's dorms. 80% of campus accessible to physically disabled. **Special Academic Facilities/Equipment:** Linder Art Gallery; Cupillari Astronomical Observatory; Willary Water Resource Center **Computers:** 100% of classrooms, 50% of dorms, 100% of libraries, 100% of dining areas, 100% of student union, 50% of common outdoor areas have wireless network access. Students can register for classes online. Administrative functions (other than registration) can be performed online.

CAMPUS LIFE

Environment: Rural. **Activities:** Choral groups, drama/theater, literary magazine, musical theater, radio station, student government, student newspaper, yearbook, Campus Ministries, International Student Organization 22 registered organizations, 1 religious organizations. **Athletics (Intercollegiate):** *Men:* baseball, basketball, cross-country, golf, soccer, tennis, track/field (outdoor), track/field (indoor). *Women:* basketball, cross-country, field hockey, soccer, softball, tennis, track/field (outdoor), track/field (indoor), volleyball. **On-Campus Highlights:** Linder Art Gallery, 270 acre woodlands campus (trail system), Astronomical Observatory, Giants' Den, Keystone Commons. **Environmental Initiatives:** A recycling program Water reduction Energy Star Appliance policy

ADMISSIONS

Freshman Academic Profile: SAT Math middle 50% range 400-500. SAT Critical Reading middle 50% range 400-500. SAT Writing middle 50% range 380-480. ACT middle 50% range 17-22. Minimum web-based TOEFL 80. Minimum paper TOEFL 550. **Basis for Candidate Selection:** *Very important factors considered include:* academic GPA, standardized test scores. *Important factors considered include:* recommendation(s), extracurricular activities, state residency, talent/ability. *Other factors considered include:* application essay, alumni/ae relation, character/personal qualities, geographical residence, interview, work experience. **Freshman Admission Requirements:** High school diploma is required and GED is accepted. **Freshman Admission Statistics:** 1,192 applied, 743% enrolled. **Transfer Admission Requirements:** college transcript(s), essay or personal statement, standardized test scores, statement of good standing from prior institution(s). Minimum college GPA of 2 required. Lowest grade transferable 2. **General Admission Information:** Application Fee $45. Regular application deadline 5/15. Notification on a rolling basis, beginning on or about 7/20. Nonfall registration accepted.

COSTS AND FINANCIAL AID

Annual tuition $20,300. Room and board $9,800. Required fees $900. Average book expense $1,900. **Required Forms and Deadlines:** institution's own financial aid form. **Notification of Awards:** Applicants will be notified of awards on or about 8/15. **Types of Aid:** *Need-based scholarships/grants:* private scholarships, the school's own gift aid. **Loans: Student Employment: Financial Aid Statistics:** 100% freshmen, 99% undergrads receive need-based scholarship or grant aid. 76% freshmen, 72% undergrads receive non-need-based scholarship or grant aid. 90% freshmen, 91% undergrads receive need-based self-help aid. 88% freshmen, 91% undergrads receive any aid. 92% undergrads borrow to pay for school. Average cumulative indebtedness $8,675. **Criteria for awarding institutional aid:** *Non-need-based:* academics, art, athletics, leadership, music/drama, state/district residency.

KING COLLEGE

1350 King College Road, Bristol, TN 37620-2699
Phone: 423-652-4861 • **Financial Aid Phone:** 423-652-4728
E-mail: admissions@king.edu • **CEEB Code:** 1371
Fax: 423-652-4727 • **Website:** www.king.edu • **ACT Code:** 3970

This private school, affiliated with the Presbyterian Church, was founded in 1867. It has a 135-acre campus.

RATINGS

Admissions Selectivity Rating: 71   **Fire Safety Rating:** 61   **Green Rating:** 60*

STUDENTS AND FACULTY

Enrollment: 1,866. **Student Body:** 64% female, 36% male, 37% out-of-state, 3% international (29 countries represented). Asian 0%, African American 5%, Caucasian 80%, Hispanic 2%, Native American 0%.
Retention and Graduation: 36% freshmen graduate within 4 years. 50% freshmen graduate within 6 years. 32% grads go on to further study within 1 year. 39% grads pursue arts and sciences degrees. 3% grads pursue law degrees. 42% grads pursue business degrees. 5% grads pursue medical degrees. **Faculty:** Student/faculty ratio 16:1. 86 full-time faculty, 60% hold PhDs, 0% are members of minority groups, 53% are women. 0% of classes are taught by teaching assistants.

ACADEMICS

Degrees: bachelor's, master's. **Classes:** Most classes have 10–19 students. Most lab/discussion sessions have fewer than 10 students. **Majors with Highest Enrollment:** business/commerce; nursing/registered nurse (rn, asn, bsn, msn); religion/religious studies. **Special Study Options:** Accelerated program, cross-registration, double major, dual enrollment, exchange student program (domestic), honors program, independent study, internships, student-designed major, study abroad, teacher certification program. **Honors Programs:** The Jack E. Snider Honors Center allows students to interact with other students and faculty of diverse interests. Participants take selected courses that stimulate thinking and allow for creative response while engaging in special opportunities such as meeting with faculty members and outside guests. Other courses may allow honors students, for extra credit, to develop more extensive research projects. The honors seminars also examine ideas from a variety of academic disciplines. Participants serve both the campus and the larger community by tutoring and mentoring and are encouraged to explore other perspectives through study abroad experiences. **Combined Degree Programs:** BA/MEng, 3-1 Pharmacy program 3-1 Medical Technology program. **Disability Services:** Special programs offered to physically disabled students include tutors. **Career Services:** Alumni network, alumni services, career assessment, internships.

FACILITIES

Housing: special housing for disabled students, men's dorms, women's dorms. 80% of campus accessible to physically disabled. Special Academic Facilities/Equipment: Electron microscope, observatory with two reflecting telescopes, solar telescope.

CAMPUS LIFE

Environment: Town. **Activities:** Choral groups, concert band, dance, drama/theater, literary magazine, music ensembles, musical theater, pep band, student government, student newspaper, yearbook, Campus Ministries, International Student Organization 35 registered organizations, 5 honor societies, 9 religious organizations. **Athletics (Intercollegiate):** *Men:* baseball, basketball, bowling, cheerleading, cross-country, cycling, diving, golf, soccer, swimming, tennis, track/field (outdoor), track/field (indoor), wrestling. *Women:* basketball, bowling, cheerleading, cross-country, cycling, diving, golf, soccer, softball, swimming, tennis, track/field (outdoor), track/field (indoor), volleyball, wrestling. **On-Campus Highlights:** New Student Center/Athletic Complex, Campus oval, Library, Residence hall lobbies, Entrance way and sporting fields.

ADMISSIONS

Freshman Academic Profile: Average high school GPA 3.4. 17% in top 10% of high school class, 42% in top 25% of high school class, 74% in top 50% of high school class. 89% from public high schools. SAT Math middle 50% range 450-560. SAT Critical Reading middle 50% range 440-540. SAT Writing middle 50% range 415-520. ACT middle 50% range 19-24. Minimum web-based TOEFL 84. Minimum paper TOEFL 563. **Basis for Candidate Selection:** *Very important factors considered include:* academic GPA, standardized test scores. *Other factors considered include:* Class rank, application essay, recommendation(s), rigor of secondary school record, character/personal qualities, extracurricular activities, interview, level of applicant's interest. **Freshman Admission Requirements:** High school diploma is required and GED is accepted. *Academic units required:* 4 English, 3 mathematics, 1 science, (1 science labs), 2 foreign language, 2 history, 4 academic electives. 4 English, 3 mathematics, 1 science, (1 science labs), 2 foreign language, 2 history, 4 academic electives. **Freshman Admission Statistics:** 1,090 applied, 72% admitted, 27% enrolled. **Transfer Admission Requirements:** college transcript(s), minimum college GPA of 2.0 required. Lowest grade transferable C–. **General Admission Information:** Application Fee $20. Nonfall registration accepted. Admission may be deferred for a maximum of 1 semester. Credit and/or placement offered for CEEB Advanced Placement tests.

COSTS AND FINANCIAL AID

Annual tuition $23,608. Room and board $8,180. Required fees $1,352. Average book expense $600. **Required Forms and Deadlines:** FAFSA. **Notification of Awards:** Applicants will be notified of awards on a rolling basis beginning 3/1. **Types of Aid:** *Need-based scholarships/grants:* Federal Pell, SEOG, state scholarships/grants, the school's own gift aid. *Loans:* Subsidized Stafford, Unsubsidized Stafford, PLUS, Federal Perkins, state loans, college/university loans from institutional funds. **Student Employment:** Federal Work-Study Program available. Institutional employment available. Highest amount earned per year from on-campus jobs $1,236. Off-campus job opportunities are good. **Financial Aid Statistics:** 95% freshmen, 85% undergrads receive need-based scholarship or grant aid. 12% freshmen, 8% undergrads receive non-need-based scholarship or grant aid. 87% freshmen, 92% undergrads receive need-based self-help aid. 12% freshmen, 6% undergrads receive athletic scholarships. 98% freshmen, 94% undergrads receive any aid. 95% undergrads borrow to pay for school. Average cumulative indebtedness $28,946. **Criteria for awarding institutional aid:** *Non-need-based:* academics, athletics, music/drama.

See page 1112.

KING'S COLLEGE (PA)

133 North River Street, Wilkes-Barre, PA 18711
Phone: 570-208-5858 • **Financial Aid Phone:** 570-208-5868
E-mail: admissions@kings.edu • **CEEB Code:** 2353
Fax: 570-208-5971 • **Website:** www.kings.edu • **ACT Code:** 3604

This private school, affiliated with the Roman Catholic Church, was founded in 1946. It has a 48-acre campus.

RATINGS

Admissions Selectivity Rating: 75   **Fire Safety Rating:** 93   **Green Rating:** 66

STUDENTS AND FACULTY

Enrollment: 2,048. **Student Body:** 49% female, 51% male, 72% out-of-state, 0% international (5 countries represented). Asian 2%, African American 3%, Caucasian 80%, Hispanic 6%, Native American 0%.
Retention and Graduation: 62% freshmen graduate within 4 years. 68% freshmen graduate within 6 years. 24% grads go on to further study within 1 year. 19% grads pursue arts and sciences degrees. 1% grads pursue law degrees. 1% grads pursue business degrees. 3% grads pursue medical degrees. **Faculty:** Student/faculty ratio 13:1. 136 full-time faculty, 85% hold PhDs, 4% are members of minority groups, 43% are women. 0% of classes are taught by teaching assistants.

ACADEMICS

Degrees: associate, bachelor's, certificate, master's, post-bachelor's certificate. **Classes:** Most classes have 10–19 students. Most lab/discussion sessions have 10–19 students. **Majors with Highest Enrollment:** accounting; business administration and management; elementary education and teaching. **Special Study Options:** Accelerated program, cross-registration, distance learning, double major, dual enrollment, English as a Second Language (ESL), honors program, independent study, internships, student-designed major, study abroad, teacher certification program, weekend college. **Combined Degree Programs:** BS Med Studies/MS Phys Asst. **Disability Services:** Special programs offered to physically disabled students include note-taking services, reader services, tape recorders, tutors. **Career Services:** Alumni network, alumni services, career/job search classes, career assessment, internships, regional alumni.

FACILITIES

Housing: Coed dorms, special housing for disabled students, men's dorms, women's dorms, apartments for single students, wellness housing, theme housing, 99% of campus accessible to physically disabled. **Special Academic Facilities/Equipment:** Electron microscope, rooftop greenhouse, molecular biology lab, computer graphics lab **Computers:** 50% of classrooms, 25% of dorms, 100% of libraries, 100% of dining areas, 100% of student union, 100% of common outdoor areas have wireless network access. Students can register for classes online. Administrative functions (other than registration) can be performed online.

CAMPUS LIFE

Environment: City. **Activities:** Choral groups, dance, drama/theater, literary magazine, music ensembles, pep band, radio station, student government, student newspaper, yearbook, Campus Ministries 50 registered organizations, 15 honor societies, 2 religious organizations. **Athletics (Intercollegiate):** *Men:* baseball, basketball, cheerleading, cross-country, football, golf, lacrosse, soccer, swimming, tennis, wrestling. *Women:* basketball, cheerleading, cross-country, field hockey, lacrosse, soccer, softball, swimming, tennis, volleyball. **On-Campus Highlights:** Sheehy-Farmer Campus Center, McGowan School of Business, Scandlon Physical Education Center, Betzler Fields (Athletic Complex), Gateway Corners.

ADMISSIONS

Freshman Academic Profile: Average high school GPA 3.3. 14% in top 10% of high school class, 34% in top 25% of high school class, 70% in top 50% of high school class. 75% from public high schools. SAT Math middle 50% range 470-580. SAT Critical Reading middle 50% range 470-570. SAT Writing middle 50% range 460-560. Minimum web-based TOEFL 71. Minimum paper TOEFL 530. **Basis for Candidate Selection:** *Very important factors considered include:* Class rank, academic GPA, rigor of secondary school record. *Important factors considered include:* application essay, standardized test scores, character/personal qualities. *Other factors considered include:* recommendation(s), alumni/ae relation, extracurricular activities, interview, volunteer work, work experience. **Freshman Admission Requirements:** High school diploma is required and GED is accepted. *Academic units required:* 4 English, 3 mathematics, 3 science, (2 science labs), 2 foreign language, 3 social studies, 1 history. *Academic units recommended:* 4 English, 3 mathematics, 3 science, (2 science labs), 2 foreign language, 3 social studies, 1 history. **Freshman Admission Statistics:** 2,967 applied, 725% enrolled. **Transfer Admission Requirements:** High school transcript, college transcript(s), essay or personal statement, minimum college GPA of 2.0 required. Lowest grade transferable C. **General Admission Information:** Application Fee $30. Notification on a rolling basis, beginning on or about 10/1. Nonfall registration accepted. Admission may be deferred for a maximum of 1 year. Neither credit nor placement offered for CEEB Advanced Placement tests.

COSTS AND FINANCIAL AID

Average book expense. **Required Forms and Deadlines:** FAFSA, institution's own financial aid form. **Notification of Awards:** Applicants will be notified of awards on a rolling basis beginning 3/1. **Types of Aid:** *Need-based scholarships/grants:* Federal Pell, SEOG, state scholarships/grants, private scholarships, the school's own gift aid. *Loans:* Subsidized Stafford, Unsubsidized Stafford, PLUS, Federal Perkins, Private Loans. **Student Employment:** Federal Work-Study Program available. Institutional employment available. Highest amount earned per year from on-campus jobs $2,000. Off-campus job opportunities are fair. **Financial Aid Statistics:** 100% freshmen, 99% undergrads receive need-based scholarship or grant aid. 12% freshmen, 12% undergrads receive non-need-based scholarship or grant aid. 84% freshmen, 85% undergrads receive need-based self-help aid. 99% freshmen, 96% undergrads receive any aid. 82% undergrads borrow to pay for school. Average cumulative indebtedness $36,538. **Criteria for awarding institutional aid:** *Non-need-based:* academics, leadership.

KNOX COLLEGE

Best 378

2 East South Street, Campus Box 148, Galesburg, IL 61401
Phone: 309-341-7100 • **Financial Aid Phone:** 309-341-7149
E-mail: admission@knox.edu • **CEEB Code:** 1372
Fax: 309-341-7070 • **Website:** www.knox.edu • **ACT Code:** 1052

This private school was founded in 1837. It has a 82-acre campus.

RATINGS

Admissions Selectivity Rating: 83   **Fire Safety Rating:** 84   **Green Rating:** 80

STUDENTS AND FACULTY

Enrollment: 1,394. **Student Body:** 57% female, 43% male, 55% out-of-state, 11% international (37 countries represented). Asian 5%, African American 7%, Caucasian 63%, Hispanic 9%, Native American 0%.
Retention and Graduation: 88% freshmen return for sophomore year. 69% freshmen graduate within 4 years. 79% freshmen graduate within 6 years. 22% grads go on to further study within 1 year. 13% grads pursue arts and sciences degrees. 1% grads pursue law degrees. 3% grads pursue medical degrees.
Faculty: Student/faculty ratio 12:1. 110 full-time faculty, 95% hold PhDs, 15% are members of minority groups, 38% are women. 0% of classes are taught by teaching assistants.

ACADEMICS

Degrees: bachelor's. **Classes:** Most classes have 10–19 students. Most lab/discussion sessions have 10–19 students. **Majors with Highest Enrollment:** economics; education; political science and government. **Special Study Options:** double major, dual enrollment, honors program, independent study, internships, student-designed major, study abroad, teacher certification program. **Honors Programs:** Knox College is an "honors college". If you compare Knox's academic requirements, student profile, educational opportunities, and student experiences with those of an honors program at a university, Knox provides comparable and often much richer opportunities for its students. **Combined Degree Programs:** BA/JD, BA/MEng, Architecture, Environment Management, Medical Tec. **Disability Services:** Special programs offered to physically disabled students include note-taking services, tape recorders, tutors. **Career Services:** career assessment, internships Career Services highlights include Kemper Scholars Program.

FACILITIES

Housing: Coed dorms, special housing for disabled students, men's dorms, special housing for international students, women's dorms, fraternity/sorority housing, apartments for single students, wellness housing, theme housing, 60% of campus accessible to physically disabled. **Special Academic Facilities/Equipment:** Anthropology, art, and field museums, theatre with revolving stage and computerized lighting, ceramics, sculpture, painting, and printmaking studios, 760-acre biological field station, environmental climate chambers, electron microscope. **Computers:** 100% of classrooms, 100% of dorms, 100% of libraries, 100% of dining areas, 100% of student union, 90% of common outdoor areas have wireless network access. Students can register for classes online. Administrative functions (other than registration) can be performed online.

CAMPUS LIFE

Environment: Town. **Activities:** Choral groups, dance, drama/theater, jazz band, literary magazine, music ensembles, radio station, student government, student newspaper, symphony orchestra, Campus Ministries, International Student Organization, Model UN 102 registered organizations, 8 honor societies, 6 religious organizations. 5 fraternities, 3 sororities. **Athletics (Intercollegiate):** *Men:* baseball, basketball, cross-country, football, golf, soccer, swimming, tennis, track/field (outdoor), track/field (indoor), wrestling. *Women:* basketball, cross-country, golf, soccer, softball, swimming, tennis, track/field (outdoor), track/field (indoor), volleyball. **On-Campus Highlights:** Gizmo Snack Bar, Andrew Fitness Center, Hard Knox Cafe, Gizmo Patio, Seymour Library. **Environmental Initiatives:** In dining services, Knox has eliminated trays from the cafeteria, reducing water consumption and food waste. Knox students contribute to a "Green Fund" and allocate those dollars for sustainability initiatives. In the past, monies have been allocated by students to support a bike-sharing program, to reduce water consumption in the residences, and to purchase eco-friendly supplies for campus events. Knox installed a composing system for disposing of food waste in dining services. The system creates compost for the campus garden and for purchase.

ADMISSIONS

Freshman Academic Profile: Average high school GPA 3.3. 30% in top 10% of high school class, 66% in top 25% of high school class, 90% in top 50% of high school class. 75% from public high schools. SAT Math middle 50% range 580-690. SAT Critical Reading middle 50% range 570-720. SAT Writing middle 50% range 570-660. ACT middle 50% range 26-31. Minimum web-based TOEFL 80. Minimum paper TOEFL 550. **Basis for Candidate Selection:** *Very important factors considered include:* academic GPA, rigor of secondary school record. *Important factors considered include:* Class rank, application essay, recommendation(s), character/personal qualities. *Other factors considered include:* standardized test scores, alumni/ae relation, extracurricular activities, first generation, geographical residence, interview, level of applicant's interest, racial/ethnic status, state residency, talent/ability, volunteer work. **Freshman Admission Requirements:** High school diploma is required and GED is accepted. **Freshman Admission Statistics:** 2,208 applied, 78% admitted, 22% enrolled. **Transfer Admission Requirements:** High school transcript, college transcript(s), essay or personal statement, statement of good standing from prior institution(s). Minimum college GPA of 3.0 required. Lowest grade transferable C. **General Admission Information:** Application Fee $40. Regular application deadline 2/1. Regular notification 3/31. Admission may be deferred for a maximum of 1 year. Credit and/or placement offered for CEEB Advanced Placement tests.

COSTS AND FINANCIAL AID

Annual tuition $38,286. Room and board $8,400. Required fees $366. Average book expense $900. **Required Forms and Deadlines:** FAFSA, institution's own financial aid form. **Notification of Awards:** Applicants will be notified of awards on a rolling basis beginning 3/15. **Types of Aid:** *Need-based scholarships/grants:* Federal Pell, SEOG, state scholarships/grants, private scholarships, the school's own gift aid. *Loans:* Direct Subsidized Stafford, Direct Unsubsidized Stafford, Direct PLUS, Federal Perkins, college/university loans from institutional funds. **Student Employment:** Federal Work-Study Program available. Institutional employment available. Highest amount earned per year from on-campus jobs $5,479. Off-campus job opportunities are fair. **Financial Aid Statistics:** 97% freshmen, 97% undergrads receive need-based scholarship or grant aid. 23% freshmen, 16% undergrads receive non-need-based scholarship or grant aid. 95% freshmen, 94% undergrads receive need-based self-help aid. 100% freshmen, 99% undergrads receive any aid. 64% undergrads borrow to pay for school. Average cumulative indebtedness $27,542. **Criteria for awarding institutional aid:** *Non-need-based:* academics, art, music/drama.

See page 1114.

KUTZTOWN UNIVERSITY OF PENNSYLVANIA

Admissions Office, Kutztown, PA 19530-0730
Phone: 610-683-4060 • **Financial Aid Phone:** 610-683-4032
E-mail: admission@kutztown.edu • **CEEB Code:** 2653
Fax: 610-683-1375 • **Website:** www.kutztown.edu • **ACT Code:** 3706

This public school was founded in 1866. It has a 325-acre campus.

RATINGS

Admissions Selectivity Rating: 72   Fire Safety Rating: 90   Green Rating: 66

STUDENTS AND FACULTY

Enrollment: 8,916. **Student Body:** 57% female, 43% male, 11% out-of-state, 1% international (28 countries represented). Asian 1%, African American 7%, Caucasian 81%, Hispanic 6%, Native American 0%.
Retention and Graduation: 71% freshmen return for sophomore year. 32% freshmen graduate within 4 years. 54% freshmen graduate within 6 years. 29% grads go on to further study within 1 year. 26% grads pursue arts and sciences degrees. 4% grads pursue law degrees. 4% grads pursue business degrees. 16% grads pursue medical degrees. **Faculty:** Student/faculty ratio 20:1. 423 full-time faculty, 80% hold PhDs, 15% are members of minority groups, 46% are women. 0% of classes are taught by teaching assistants.

ACADEMICS

Degrees: bachelor's, master's, post-bachelor's certificate. **Classes:** Most classes have 20–29 students. Most lab/discussion sessions have 20–29 students. **Majors with Highest Enrollment:** business administration and management; criminal justice/safety studies; psychology. **Special Study Options:** cross-registration, distance learning, double major, dual enrollment, honors program, independent study, internships, liberal arts/career combination, student-designed major, study abroad, teacher certification program. **Honors Programs:** 1)University Honors Program 2)Various Honor Societies **Combined Degree Programs:** BS/MS Computer Information Science. **Disability Services:** Special programs offered to physically disabled students include note-taking services, reader

services, tape recorders, tutors. **Career Services:** Alumni network, alumni services, career/job search classes, career assessment, internships, regional alumni. Career Services highlights include Proudest of the wide array of services and events for Kutztown University students.

FACILITIES

Housing: Coed dorms, women's dorms, cooperative housing, apartments for single students, Apartment Units. 90% of campus accessible to physically disabled. **Special Academic Facilities/Equipment:** Art Gallery, German Cultural Heritage Center, Early Childhood Learning Center, Cartography Lab, Observatory, Planetarium, Daycare Center **Computers:** 25% of classrooms, 95% of dorms, 100% of libraries, 75% of dining areas, 100% of student union, 65% of common outdoor areas have wireless network access. Students can register for classes online. Administrative functions (other than registration) can be performed online.

CAMPUS LIFE

Environment: Rural. **Activities:** Choral groups, concert band, dance, drama/theater, jazz band, literary magazine, marching band, music ensembles, musical theater, radio station, student government, student newspaper, student-run film society, symphony orchestra, television station, yearbook, Campus Ministries, International Student Organization, Model UN 218 registered organizations, 15 honor societies, 11 religious organizations. 9 fraternities, 8 sororities. **Athletics (Intercollegiate):** *Men:* baseball, basketball, cross-country, football, tennis, track/field (outdoor), track/field (indoor), wrestling. *Women:* basketball, bowling, cross-country, field hockey, golf, lacrosse, soccer, softball, swimming, tennis, track/field (outdoor), track/field (indoor), volleyball. **On-Campus Highlights:** Taylor and Burnes Gourmet Coffee, Student Rec Center, Alumni Plaza-new walkway with outdoor amphitheater, Pennsylvania German Cultural Heritage Center, Academic Forum. **Environmental Initiatives:** Recycling program Guaranteed energy savings agreement

ADMISSIONS

Freshman Academic Profile: Average high school GPA 3.1. 5% in top 10% of high school class, 22% in top 25% of high school class, 60% in top 50% of high school class. 99% from public high schools. SAT Math middle 50% range 430-530. SAT Critical Reading middle 50% range 430-530. SAT Writing middle 50% range 420-510. ACT middle 50% range 17-22. Minimum web-based TOEFL 79. Minimum paper TOEFL 550. **Basis for Candidate Selection:** *Very important factors considered include:* Class rank, rigor of secondary school record, standardized test scores. *Other factors considered include:* academic GPA, recommendation(s), character/personal qualities, extracurricular activities, geographical residence, interview, racial/ethnic status, state residency, talent/ability, volunteer work, work experience. **Freshman Admission Requirements:** High school diploma is required and GED is accepted. **Freshman Admission Statistics:** 9,730 applied, 68% admitted, 30% enrolled. **Transfer Admission Requirements:** college transcript(s), statement of good standing from prior institution(s). Minimum college GPA of 2.0 required. Lowest grade transferable C-. **General Admission Information:** Application Fee $35. Notification on a rolling basis, beginning on or about 10/1. Nonfall registration accepted. Admission may be deferred for a maximum of 1 year. Credit and/or placement offered for CEEB Advanced Placement tests.

COSTS AND FINANCIAL AID

Annual in-state tuition $6,428. Annual out-of-state tuition $16,070. Room and board $8,490. Required fees $2,168. Average book expense $1,476. **Required Forms and Deadlines:** FAFSA. **Notification of Awards:** Applicants will be notified of awards on a rolling basis beginning 3/30. **Types of Aid:** *Need-based scholarships/grants:* Federal Pell, SEOG, state scholarships/grants, private scholarships, the school's own gift aid. *Loans:* Subsidized Stafford, Unsubsidized Stafford, PLUS, Federal Perkins. **Student Employment:** Federal Work-Study Program available. Institutional employment available. Highest amount earned per year from on-campus jobs $9,999. Off-campus job opportunities are fair. **Financial Aid Statistics:** 67% freshmen, 66% undergrads receive need-based scholarship or grant aid. 2% freshmen, 8% undergrads receive non-need-based scholarship or grant aid. 92% freshmen, 90% undergrads receive need-based self-help aid. 2% freshmen, 1% undergrads receive athletic scholarships. 88% freshmen, 82% undergrads receive any aid. 87% undergrads borrow to pay for school. Average cumulative indebtedness $25,250. **Criteria for awarding institutional aid:** *Non-need-based:* academics, art, athletics, leadership, minority status, music/drama.

LA ROCHE COLLEGE

9000 Babcock Boulevard, Pittsburgh, PA 15237
Phone: 412-536-1271 • **Financial Aid Phone:** 412-536-1120
E-mail: admissions@laroche.edu • **CEEB Code:** 2379
Fax: 412-847-1820 • **Website:** www.laroche.edu • **ACT Code:** 3607

This private school, affiliated with the Roman Catholic Church, was founded in 1963. It has a 43-acre campus.

RATINGS
Admissions Selectivity Rating: 79   **Fire Safety Rating:** 84   **Green Rating:** 61

STUDENTS AND FACULTY
Enrollment: 1,323. **Student Body:** 58% female, 42% male, 8% out-of-state, 11% international (39 countries represented). Asian 1%, African American 6%, Caucasian 66%, Hispanic 2%, Native American 0%.
Retention and Graduation: 66% freshmen return for sophomore year. 38% freshmen graduate within 4 years. 47% freshmen graduate within 6 years.
Faculty: Student/faculty ratio 12:1. 59 full-time faculty, 85% hold PhDs, 8% are members of minority groups, 59% are women. 0% of classes are taught by teaching assistants.

ACADEMICS
Degrees: associate, bachelor's, certificate, master's, post-bachelor's certificate, terminal associate. **Classes:** Most classes have 10–19 students. Most lab/discussion sessions have 10–19 students. **Majors with Highest Enrollment:** design and visual communications; elementary education and teaching; interior architecture. **Special Study Options:** Accelerated program, cross-registration, distance learning, double major, English as a Second Language (ESL), honors program, independent study, internships, student-designed major, study abroad, teacher certification program. **Combined Degree Programs:** BA/MA. **Disability Services:** Special programs offered to physically disabled students include note-taking services, reader services, tutors. **Career Services:** career/job search classes, career assessment, internships, regional alumni.

FACILITIES
Housing: Coed dorms. 100% of campus accessible to physically disabled.
Special Academic Facilities/Equipment: Cantellopes Art Gallery; College Center extension has state of the art smart classrooms **Computers:** 100% of classrooms, 10% of dorms, 100% of libraries, 100% of dining areas, 100% of student union, 25% of common outdoor areas have wireless network access. Students can register for classes online. Administrative functions (other than registration) can be performed online.

CAMPUS LIFE
Environment: City. **Activities:** Choral groups, dance, drama/theater, literary magazine, musical theater, radio station, student government, student newspaper, Campus Ministries, International Student Organization 40 registered organizations, 4 honor societies, 2 religious organizations. **Athletics (Intercollegiate):** *Men:* baseball, basketball, cross-country, golf, lacrosse, soccer. *Women:* basketball, cheerleading, cross-country, soccer, softball, tennis, volleyball. **On-Campus Highlights:** Sports and Fitness Center, College bookstore, Magdalen Chapel, College Center Annex

ADMISSIONS
Freshman Academic Profile: Average high school GPA 3.2. 8% in top 10% of high school class, 11% in top 25% of high school class, 56% in top 50% of high school class. 87% from public high schools. SAT Math middle 50% range 420-520. SAT Critical Reading middle 50% range 420-520. SAT Writing middle 50% range 410-510. ACT middle 50% range 18-23. **Basis for Candidate Selection:** *Very important factors considered include:* academic GPA, standardized test scores. *Important factors considered include:* level of applicant's interest. *Other factors considered include:* application essay, recommendation(s), rigor of secondary school record, character/personal qualities, interview, talent/ability, volunteer work. **Freshman Admission Requirements:** High school diploma is required and GED is accepted. *Academic units required:* 4 English, 3 mathematics, 3 science, (2 science labs), 3 social studies, 3 history. *Academic units recommended:* 4 English, 3 mathematics, 3 science, (2 science labs), 3 social studies, 3 history. **Freshman Admission Statistics:** 1,587 applied, 52% admitted, 30% enrolled. **Transfer Admission Requirements:** college transcript(s), essay or personal statement, minimum college GPA of 2.0 required. Lowest grade transferable C. **General Admission Information:** Application Fee $50. Notification on a rolling basis, beginning on or about 9/15. Nonfall registration accepted. Admission may be deferred for a maximum of 1 year. Credit offered for CEEB Advanced Placement tests.

COSTS AND FINANCIAL AID
Annual tuition $23,108. Room and board $9,732. Required fees $730. Average book expense $1,200. **Required Forms and Deadlines:** FAFSA. **Notification**

of Awards: Applicants will be notified of awards on a rolling basis beginning 3/1. **Types of Aid:** *Need-based scholarships/grants:* Federal Pell, SEOG, state scholarships/grants, private scholarships, the school's own gift aid. *Loans:* Subsidized Stafford, Unsubsidized Stafford, PLUS, Federal Perkins, Private loans. **Student Employment:** Federal Work-Study Program available. Institutional employment available. Off-campus job opportunities are excellent. **Financial Aid Statistics:** 66% freshmen, 73% undergrads receive need-based scholarship or grant aid. 99% freshmen, 100% undergrads receive non-need-based scholarship or grant aid. 90% freshmen, 100% undergrads receive need-based self-help aid. 92% freshmen, 90% undergrads receive any aid. 78% undergrads borrow to pay for school. Average cumulative indebtedness $26,296. **Criteria for awarding institutional aid:** *Non-need-based:* academics.

See page 1116.

LAFAYETTE COLLEGE

118 Markle Hall, Easton, PA 18042
Phone: 610-330-5100 • **Financial Aid Phone:** 610 330-5055
E-mail: admissions@lafayette.edu • **CEEB Code:** 2361
Fax: 610-330-5355 • **Website:** www.lafayette.edu/

This private school, affiliated with the Presbyterian Church, was founded in 1826. It has a 340-acre campus.

RATINGS
Admissions Selectivity Rating: 95   **Fire Safety Rating:** 88   **Green Rating:** 90

STUDENTS AND FACULTY
Enrollment: 2,454. **Student Body:** 47% female, 53% male, 78% out-of-state, 5% international (37 countries represented). Asian 3%, African American 5%, Caucasian 66%, Hispanic 6%, Native American 0%.
Retention and Graduation: 95% freshmen return for sophomore year. 89% freshmen graduate within 4 years. 29% grads go on to further study within 1 year. 6% grads pursue law degrees. 4% grads pursue medical degrees. **Faculty:** Student/faculty ratio 11:1. 217 full-time faculty, 98% hold PhDs, 13% are members of minority groups, 33% are women. 0% of classes are taught by teaching assistants.

ACADEMICS
Degrees: bachelor's. **Classes:** Most classes have 10–19 students. Most lab/discussion sessions have 10–19 students. **Special Study Options:** cross-registration, double major, dual enrollment, exchange student program (domestic), honors program, independent study, internships, student-designed major, study abroad, interim sessions here and abroad. **Disability Services:** Special programs offered to physically disabled students include tutors. **Career Services:** alumni services, career/job search classes, career assessment, internships.

FACILITIES
Housing: Coed dorms, special housing for disabled students, men's dorms, women's dorms, fraternity/sorority housing, apartments for single students, wellness housing, theme housing, scholars houses, Hillel House, arts houses. 100% of campus accessible to physically disabled. **Special Academic Facilities/Equipment:** Art and geological museums, center for the arts, engineering labs, INSTRON materials testing machine, electron microscopes, transform nuclear magnetic resonance spectrometer, computerized gas chromatograph/mass spectrometer. **Computers:** Students can register for classes online. Administrative functions (other than registration) can be performed online.

CAMPUS LIFE
Environment: Village. **Activities:** Choral groups, concert band, dance, drama/theater, jazz band, literary magazine, music ensembles, musical theater, pep band, radio station, student government, student newspaper, student-run film society, symphony orchestra, yearbook, Campus Ministries, International Student Organization 250 registered organizations, 14 honor societies, 7 religious organizations. 7 fraternities, 6 sororities. **Athletics (Intercollegiate):** *Men:* baseball, basketball, cheerleading, crew/rowing, cross-country, diving, equestrian sports, fencing, football, golf, gymnastics, ice hockey, lacrosse, soccer, softball, swimming, tennis, track/field (outdoor), track/field (indoor), volleyball, wrestling. *Women:* basketball, cheerleading, crew/rowing, cross-country, diving, equestrian sports, fencing, field hockey, golf, gymnastics, softball, swimming, tennis, track/field (outdoor), track/field (indoor), volleyball. **On-Campus Highlights:** Skillman and Kirby Libraries, Farinon College Center, Wil-

liams Center for the Arts **Environmental Initiatives:** In addition to signing American College and University Presidents Climate Commitment, three undertakings summarize the College's efforts towards responsible stewardship of the environment: 1. Waste Reduction - Recycling, including composting. - Purchases of materials/goods made from recycled materials and/or virgin material that is recyclable and produced from renewable sources. Resource Conservation - Seeking to enhance our energy use portfolio's renewable energy sources (i.e. electric power suppliers with more sustainable product offerings). - Installation of conservation/efficiency technology to reduce consumption of water, electric power, and natural gas. - Purchases of materials/goods made from recycled materials and/or virgin material that is recyclable and produced from renewable sources. Commitment to education and information dissemination of sustainable practices. - Information dissemination through College website, public discussions, and campus publications. - Inclusion of sustainability in our curriculum offerings (i.e. Environmental Engineering's composting initiative) and as a cornerstone of orientation week for new students (beginning in the Fall of 2008). New curriculum initiative at Metzgar property involving the growing of vegetables through sustainable and organic methods.

ADMISSIONS

Freshman Academic Profile: Average high school GPA 3.5. 62% in top 10% of high school class, 88% in top 25% of high school class, 97% in top 50% of high school class. 65% from public high schools. SAT Math middle 50% range 610-710. SAT Critical Reading middle 50% range 580-680. SAT Writing middle 50% range 580-680. ACT middle 50% range 27-30. Minimum web-based TOEFL 80. Minimum paper TOEFL 550. **Basis for Candidate Selection:** *Very important factors considered include:* academic GPA, rigor of secondary school record. *Important factors considered include:* Class rank, application essay, recommendation(s), standardized test scores, character/personal qualities, extracurricular activities, talent/ability. *Other factors considered include:* alumni/ae relation, first generation, geographical residence, interview, level of applicant's interest, racial/ethnic status, volunteer work, work experience. **Freshman Admission Requirements:** High school diploma or equivalent is not required. **Freshman Admission Statistics:** 6,660 applied, 34% admitted, 27% enrolled. **Transfer Admission Requirements:** High school transcript, college transcript(s), essay or personal statement, statement of good standing from prior institution(s). Lowest grade transferable C. **General Admission Information:** Application Fee $60. Early decision application deadline 2/15. Regular application deadline 1/1. Regular notification 4/1. Nonfall registration accepted. Admission may be deferred for a maximum of 1 year. Credit and/or placement offered for CEEB Advanced Placement tests.

COSTS AND FINANCIAL AID

Annual tuition $41,920. Room and board $12,708. Required fees $360. Average book expense $1,000. **Required Forms and Deadlines:** FAFSA, CSS/Financial Aid PROFILE, noncustodial PROFILE, business/farm supplement. **Notification of Awards:** Applicants will be notified of awards on or about 4/1. **Types of Aid:** *Need-based scholarships/grants:* Federal Pell, SEOG, state scholarships/grants, private scholarships, the school's own gift aid. *Loans:* Subsidized Stafford, Unsubsidized Stafford, PLUS, Federal Perkins, college/university loans from institutional funds, HELP loan to parents (Lafayette Loan Program). **Student Employment:** Federal Work-Study Program available. Institutional employment available. Highest amount earned per year from on-campus jobs $1,000. Off-campus job opportunities are good. **Financial Aid Statistics:** 96% freshmen, 96% undergrads receive need-based scholarship or grant aid. 28% freshmen, 23% undergrads receive non-need-based scholarship or grant aid. 90% freshmen, 93% undergrads receive need-based self-help aid. 3% freshmen, 2% undergrads receive athletic scholarships. 56% undergrads borrow to pay for school. Average cumulative indebtedness $26,717. **Criteria for awarding institutional aid:** *Non-need-based:* academics, athletics, leadership.

LAGRANGE COLLEGE

Office of Admission, LaGrange, GA 30240
Phone: 706-880-8005 • **Financial Aid Phone:** 888-253-9918
E-mail: lgcadmis@lagrange.edu • **CEEB Code:** 5362
Fax: 706-880-8010 • **Website:** www.lagrange.edu • **ACT Code:** 834

This private school, affiliated with the Methodist Church, was founded in 1831. It has a 120-acre campus.

RATINGS

Admissions Selectivity Rating: 77   **Fire Safety Rating:** 60*   **Green Rating:** 76

STUDENTS AND FACULTY

Enrollment: 860. **Student Body:** 55% female, 45% male, 11% out-of-state, 2% international (10 countries represented). Asian 1%, African American 22%, Caucasian 72%, Hispanic 2%, Native American 0%.

Retention and Graduation: 71% freshmen return for sophomore year. 39% freshmen graduate within 4 years. 55% freshmen graduate within 6 years. **Faculty:** Student/faculty ratio 10:1. 65 full-time faculty, 83% hold PhDs, 48% are women. 0% of classes are taught by teaching assistants.

ACADEMICS

Degrees: associate, bachelor's, master's. **Classes:** Most classes have 10–19 students. Most lab/discussion sessions have 10–19 students. **Majors with Highest Enrollment:** business administration and management; organizational behavior studies; teacher education, multiple levels. **Special Study Options:** double major, dual enrollment, independent study, internships, liberal arts/career combination, study abroad, teacher certification program. **Career Services:** Alumni network, alumni services, career/job search classes, career assessment, internships.

FACILITIES

Housing: Coed dorms, men's dorms, women's dorms, fraternity/sorority housing, apartments for single students, theme housing, 75% of campus accessible to physically disabled. **Special Academic Facilities/Equipment:** Lamar Dodd Art Center, Price Theater, Callaway Auditorium **Computers:** Students can register for classes online. Administrative functions (other than registration) can be performed online.

CAMPUS LIFE

Environment: Village. **Activities:** Choral groups, drama/theater, literary magazine, music ensembles, musical theater, pep band, student government, student newspaper, symphony orchestra, yearbook, Campus Ministries, International Student Organization 49 registered organizations, 11 honor societies, 8 religious organizations. 3 fraternities, 6 sororities. **Athletics (Intercollegiate):** *Men:* baseball, basketball, cross-country, football, golf, soccer, swimming, tennis. *Women:* basketball, cheerleading, cross-country, soccer, softball, swimming, tennis, volleyball. **On-Campus Highlights:** Turner Student Center, Smith Hall, Academic Quadrangle, Smith Patio, Callaway Sports Facilities. **Environmental Initiatives:** Building a LEED library Conserving water Revamped buildings along with HVAC retrofitting.

ADMISSIONS

Freshman Academic Profile: Average high school GPA 3.5. 25% in top 10% of high school class, 54% in top 25% of high school class, 92% in top 50% of high school class. SAT Math middle 50% range 460-570. SAT Critical Reading middle 50% range 460-570. ACT middle 50% range 20-25. Minimum paper TOEFL 500. **Basis for Candidate Selection:** *Very important factors considered include:* academic GPA, standardized test scores, character/personal qualities. *Important factors considered include:* Class rank, recommendation(s), extracurricular activities, level of applicant's interest. *Other factors considered include:* application essay, rigor of secondary school record, alumni/ae relation, geographical residence, interview, talent/ability, volunteer work. **Freshman Admission Requirements:** High school diploma is required and GED is accepted. *Academic units required:* 4 English, 4 mathematics, 3 science, 3 social studies. *Academic units recommended:* 4 English, 4 mathematics, 3 science, 3 social studies. **Freshman Admission Statistics:** 1,342 applied, 65% admitted, 27% enrolled. **Transfer Admission Requirements:** college transcript(s), statement of good standing from prior institution(s). Minimum college GPA 2.0 required. Lowest grade transferable 1. **General Admission Information:** Application Fee $30. Notification on a rolling basis, beginning on or about 9/15. Nonfall registration accepted. Admission may be deferred for a maximum of one term. Credit and/or placement offered for CEEB Advanced Placement tests.

COSTS AND FINANCIAL AID

Annual tuition $19,900. Room and board $8,168. **Required Forms and Deadlines:** FAFSA, state aid form. **Notification of Awards:** Applicants will be notified of awards on a rolling basis beginning 3/15. **Types of Aid:** *Need-based scholarships/grants:* Federal Pell, SEOG, state scholarships/grants, private scholarships, the school's own gift aid. *Loans:* Subsidized Stafford, Unsubsidized Stafford, PLUS, Federal Perkins, state loans. **Student Employment:** Federal Work-Study Program available. Institutional employment available. Off-campus job opportunities are excellent. **Financial Aid Statistics:** 100% freshmen, 100% undergrads receive need-based scholarship or grant aid. 24% freshmen, 17% undergrads receive non-need-based scholarship or grant aid. 69% freshmen, 77% undergrads receive need-based self-help aid. 75% undergrads borrow to pay for school. Average cumulative indebtedness $23,106. **Criteria for awarding institutional aid:** *Non-need-based:* academics, art, leadership, music/drama, religious affiliation, state/district residency.

LAKE ERIE COLLEGE

391 West Washington Street, Painesville, OH 44077-3389
Phone: 440-375-7050 • **Financial Aid Phone:** 440-375-7100
E-mail: admissions@lec.edu • **CEEB Code:** 1391
Fax: 440-375-7005 • **Website:** www.lec.edu • **ACT Code:**

This is a private school.

RATINGS
Admissions Selectivity Rating: 76   **Fire Safety Rating:** 89   **Green Rating:** 60*

STUDENTS AND FACULTY
Enrollment: 934. **Student Body:** 48% female, 52% male, 24% out-of-state, 4% international. Asian 1%, African American 8%, Caucasian 82%, Hispanic 2%, Native American 0%.
Retention and Graduation: 64% freshmen return for sophomore year. 48% freshmen graduate within 6 years. 24% grads go on to further study within 1 year. **Faculty:** Student/faculty ratio 16:1. 41 full-time faculty, 71% hold PhDs, 56% are women. 0% of classes are taught by teaching assistants.

ACADEMICS
Degrees: bachelor's, certificate, master's, post-bachelor's certificate. **Classes:** Most classes have fewer than 10 students. **Special Study Options:** Accelerated program, cross-registration, double major, dual enrollment, honors program, independent study, internships, liberal arts/career combination, student-designed major, study abroad, teacher certification program, weekend college. **Honors Programs:** LEC Scholars Program. **Disability Services:** Special programs offered to physically disabled students include note-taking services, reader services, tape recorders, tutors. **Career Services:** Alumni network, alumni services, career/job search classes, career assessment, internships.

FACILITIES
Housing: Coed dorms, women's dorms, apartments for single students, theme Housing. 90% of campus accessible to physically disabled. **Computers:** Students can register for classes online. Administrative functions (other than registration) can be performed online.

CAMPUS LIFE
Environment: Activities: Choral groups, dance, drama/theater, pep band, student government, student newspaper, yearbook, International Student Organization 15 registered organizations, 3 honor societies, 1 sororities. **Athletics (Intercollegiate):** *Men:* baseball, basketball, cross-country, equestrian sports, football, golf, soccer. *Women:* basketball, cross-country, equestrian sports, soccer, softball, volleyball.

ADMISSIONS
Freshman Academic Profile: Average high school GPA 3.2. 9% in top 10% of high school class, 38% in top 25% of high school class, 70% in top 50% of high school class. 84% from public high schools. SAT Math middle 50% range 453-540. SAT Critical Reading middle 50% range 450-550. SAT Writing middle 50% range 423-540. ACT middle 50% range 19-23. Minimum web-based TOEFL 79. Minimum paper TOEFL 550. **Basis for Candidate Selection:** *Very important factors considered include:* application essay, academic GPA, recommendation(s), rigor of secondary school record, standardized test scores, character/personal qualities, level of applicant's interest. *Important factors considered include:* Class rank, interview, talent/ability. *Other factors considered include:* alumni/ae relation, extracurricular activities, first generation, geographical residence, religious affiliation/commitment, state residency, volunteer work, work experience. **Freshman Admission Requirements:** High school diploma is required and GED is accepted. *Academic units required:* 4 English, 3 mathematics, 3 science, (2 science labs), 2 foreign language, 3 social studies. *Academic units recommended:* 4 English, 3 mathematics, 3 science, (2 science labs), 2 foreign language, 3 social studies. **Freshman Admission Statistics:** 1,509 applied, 63% admitted, 29% enrolled. **Transfer Admission Requirements:** High school transcript, college transcript(s), statement of good standing from prior institution(s). Minimum college GPA of 2.0 required. Lowest grade transferable C. **General Admission Information:** Application Fee $30. Notification on a rolling basis, beginning on or about 7/1. Nonfall registration accepted. Admission may be deferred for a maximum of 12 months. Credit and/or placement offered for CEEB Advanced Placement tests.

COSTS AND FINANCIAL AID
Annual tuition $25,976. Room and board $8,336. Required fees $1,392. Average book expense $1,100. **Required Forms and Deadlines:** FAFSA. **Notification of Awards:** Applicants will be notified of awards on a rolling basis beginning 1/20. **Types of Aid:** *Need-based scholarships/grants:* Federal Pell, SEOG, state scholarships/grants, private scholarships, the school's own gift aid. *Loans:* Subsidized Stafford, Unsubsidized Stafford, PLUS, Federal Perkins, Payment plans. **Student Employment:** Federal Work-Study Program available. Institutional employment available. Highest amount earned per year from on-campus jobs $1,200. Off-campus job opportunities are good. **Financial Aid Statistics:** 100% freshmen, 99% undergrads receive need-based scholarship or grant aid. 12% freshmen, 13% undergrads receive non-need-based scholarship or grant aid. 87% freshmen, 87% undergrads receive need-based self-help aid. 100% freshmen, 91% undergrads receive any aid. 90% undergrads borrow to pay for school. Average cumulative indebtedness $34,837. **Criteria for awarding institutional aid:** *Non-need-based:* academics, art, leadership, music/drama, state/district residency.

LAKE FOREST COLLEGE

555 North Sheridan Road, Lake Forest, IL 60045
Phone: 847-735-5000 • **Financial Aid Phone:** 847-725-5103
E-mail: admissions@lakeforest.edu • **CEEB Code:** 1392
Fax: 847-735-6291 • **Website:** www.lakeforest.edu • **ACT Code:** 1054

This private school was founded in 1857. It has a 107-acre campus.

RATINGS
Admissions Selectivity Rating: 88   **Fire Safety Rating:** 66   **Green Rating:** 68

STUDENTS AND FACULTY
Enrollment: 1,534. **Student Body:** 58% female, 42% male, 40% out-of-state, 11% international (79 countries represented). Asian 5%, African American 6%, Caucasian 60%, Hispanic 13%, Native American 0%.
Retention and Graduation: 83% freshmen return for sophomore year. 62% freshmen graduate within 4 years. 70% freshmen graduate within 6 years. 21% grads go on to further study within 1 year. 55% grads pursue arts and sciences degrees. 15% grads pursue law degrees. 3% grads pursue business degrees. 21% grads pursue medical degrees. **Faculty:** Student/faculty ratio 12:1. 100 full-time faculty, 98% hold PhDs, 17% are members of minority groups, 44% are women. 0% of classes are taught by teaching assistants.

ACADEMICS
Degrees: bachelor's, master's. **Classes:** Most classes have 10–19 students. Most lab/discussion sessions have 10–19 students. **Majors with Highest Enrollment:** business/commerce; communication studies/speech communication and rhetoric; English language and literature. **Special Study Options:** Accelerated program, double major, honors program, independent study, internships, liberal arts/career combination, student-designed major, study abroad, teacher certification program. **Honors Programs:** The Honors Fellows program recognizes those students admitted to Lake Forest College with exemplary high school careers and high promise for independent study and research at the College. Fellows are expected to think deeply and broadly, and to join their teachers and fellow students in serious intellectual inquiry and debate. They will produce independent work, research, Student Symposium presentations, Independent Scholar majors, distinguished senior theses, and provide intellectual leadership. The Richter Apprentice Scholars Program provides students, early in their academic careers, with the opportunity to conduct independent, individual research with Lake Forest College faculty. In the summer between their first and second year, each student in the Richter Program is employed for a ten week period and works one-on-one with a faculty member, doing independent research in a particular field. As the Richter Apprentice Scholars live and work together and participate in a weekly colloquium, they become a community of peers providing encouragement and support for each other's present and future intellectual and research endeavors. **Combined Degree Programs:** BA/JD, BA/MA, Accelerated BA/JD with select law schools - Acc. BA/MA with Monterey Inst. **Disability Services:** Special programs offered to physically disabled students include note-taking services, reader services, tape recorders, tutors. **Career Services:** Alumni network, alumni services, career/job search classes, career assessment, internships, regional alumni. Career Services highlights include Internships- Due to our location near Chicago and the many partnerships Lake Forest College has developed with Chicago institutions over the years, there are a myriad of internship opportunities available to our students. Experiential learning- Again, due to our location near Chicago and the relationships with area insitutions we offer dozens of courses that have been developed to utilize the rich resources of Chicago to enhance the curriculum. Beginning with our innovative First-Year Studies program students travel downtown to Chicago with professors and take advantage of the many resources.

FACILITIES

Housing: Coed dorms, special housing for disabled students, women's dorms, apartments for single students, wellness housing, 80% of campus accessible to physically disabled. **Special Academic Facilities/Equipment:** Center for Chicago Programs, art galleries, language labs, technology resource center, speech and video production room, "smart" classrooms, music/recording studio with synthesizers, public access computer labs, electron microscope, computer molecular modeling equipment, high-resolution FT-IR, NMR spectrometer, neutron howitzer, digital storage oscilloscopes, flourescence microscope **Computers:** 90% of classrooms, 100% of dorms, 100% of libraries, 75% of dining areas, 100% of student union, 10% of common outdoor areas have wireless network access. Administrative functions (other than registration) can be performed online.

CAMPUS LIFE

Environment: Village. **Activities:** Choral groups, concert band, dance, drama/theater, jazz band, literary magazine, music ensembles, musical theater, radio station, student government, student newspaper, symphony orchestra, Campus Ministries, International Student Organization, Model UN 80 registered organizations, 12 honor societies, 6 religious organizations. 2 fraternities, 4 sororities. **Athletics (Intercollegiate):** *Men:* basketball, cross-country, diving, football, handball, ice hockey, soccer, swimming, tennis. *Women:* basketball, cross-country, diving, handball, ice hockey, soccer, softball, swimming, tennis, volleyball. **On-Campus Highlights:** Donnelley and Lee Library, Mohr Student Center, Sports Center, Center for Chicago Programs, Career Advancement Center. **Environmental Initiatives:** The organic campus garden provides internship opportunities for students and it supplies the campus cafeteria with food during the summer and fall. Restoration initiatives for ravine and savannah ecosystems. The expansion of offerings of environmental studies courses.

ADMISSIONS

Freshman Academic Profile: Average high school GPA 3.6. 35% in top 10% of high school class, 63% in top 25% of high school class, 88% in top 50% of high school class. 70% from public high schools. SAT Math middle 50% range 530-670. SAT Critical Reading middle 50% range 530-620. SAT Writing middle 50% range 500-610. ACT middle 50% range 23-28. Minimum paper TOEFL 550. **Basis for Candidate Selection:** *Very important factors considered include:* academic GPA, recommendation(s), rigor of secondary school record, interview. *Important factors considered include:* application essay, character/personal qualities, extracurricular activities, level of applicant's interest, talent/ability. *Other factors considered include:* Class rank, standardized test scores, alumni/ae relation, first generation, geographical residence, volunteer work, work experience. **Freshman Admission Requirements:** High school diploma is required and GED is accepted. *Academic units required:* 4 English, 3 mathematics, 3 science, (3 science labs), 2 foreign language, 2 social studies, 2 history, 3 academic electives. *Academic units recommended:* 4 English, 3 mathematics, 3 science, (3 science labs), 2 foreign language, 2 social studies, 2 history, 3 academic electives. **Freshman Admission Statistics:** 3,479 applied, 57% admitted, 21% enrolled. **Transfer Admission Requirements:** High school transcript, college transcript(s), essay or personal statement, minimum college GPA of 2.5 required. Lowest grade transferable C–. **General Admission Information:** Application Fee $40. Early decision application deadline 12/1. Regular notification 3/20. Nonfall registration accepted. Admission may be deferred for a maximum of 12 months. Credit and/or placement offered for CEEB Advanced Placement tests.

COSTS AND FINANCIAL AID

Annual tuition $37,660. Room and board $9,050. Required fees $640. Average book expense $1,000. **Required Forms and Deadlines:** FAFSA, institution's own financial aid formFederal Income Tax return. **Notification of Awards:** Applicants will be notified of awards on a rolling basis beginning 2/1. **Types of Aid:** *Need-based scholarships/grants:* Federal Pell, SEOG, state scholarships/grants, private scholarships, the school's own gift aid. *Loans:* Subsidized Stafford, Unsubsidized Stafford, PLUS, Federal Perkins, Private loans. **Student Employment:** Federal Work-Study Program available. Institutional employment available. Off-campus job opportunities are good. **Financial Aid Statistics:** 100% freshmen, 100% undergrads receive need-based scholarship or grant aid. 78% freshmen, 82% undergrads receive need-based self-help aid. 94% freshmen, 95% undergrads receive any aid. 66% undergrads borrow to pay for school. Average cumulative indebtedness $30,801. **Criteria for awarding institutional aid:** *Non-need-based:* academics, alumni affiliation, art, leadership, music/drama, state/district residency.

See page 1118.

LAKE REGION STATE COLLEGE

1801 College Drive N, Devils Lake, ND 58301-1598
Phone: 701-662-1514 • **Financial Aid Phone:** 701-662-1516
E-mail: lrsc.admissions@lrsc.edu
Fax: 701-662-1581 • **Website:** www.lrsc.edu • **ACT Code:** 3198

This public school was founded in 1941. It has a 120-acre campus.

RATINGS

Admissions Selectivity Rating: 64   **Fire Safety Rating:** 97   **Green Rating:** 60*

STUDENTS AND FACULTY

Enrollment: 696. **Student Body:** 53% female, 47% male, 12% out-of-state, 3% international (14 countries represented). Asian 2%, African American 4%, Caucasian 82%, Hispanic 2%, Native American 5%. **Faculty:** Student/faculty ratio 13:1. 35 full-time faculty, 14% hold PhDs, 3% are members of minority groups, 51% are women. 0% of classes are taught by teaching assistants.

ACADEMICS

Degrees: associate, certificate, diploma, terminal associate, transfer associate. **Classes:** Most classes have fewer than 10 students. **Majors with Highest Enrollment:** business administration and management; criminal justice/police science; liberal arts and sciences/liberal studies. **Special Study Options:** cooperative education program, cross-registration, distance learning, dual enrollment, English as a Second Language (ESL), internships, liberal arts/career combination. **Disability Services:** Special programs offered to physically disabled students include note-taking services, reader services, tape recorders, tutors. **Career Services:** career/job search classes, internships.

FACILITIES

Housing: special housing for disabled students, men's dorms, women's dorms, apartments for married students, apartments for single students, Coed dorms. for adult students. 100% of campus accessible to physically disabled. **Special Academic Facilities/Equipment:** Paul Hoghaug Library and Law Library **Computers:** 100% of classrooms, 100% of dorms, 100% of libraries, 100% of dining areas, 100% of student union, have wireless network access. Students can register for classes online. Administrative functions (other than registration) can be performed online.

CAMPUS LIFE

Environment: Village. **Activities:** drama/theater, literary magazine, musical theater, student government, symphony orchestra 12 registered organizations, 1 religious organizations. **Athletics (Intercollegiate):** *Men:* basketball. *Women:* basketball. **On-Campus Highlights:** Student Union, Computer Lab, Recreational Area, Library, Gymnasium.

ADMISSIONS

Freshman Academic Profile: 98% from public high schools. ACT middle 50% range 18-25. Minimum web-based TOEFL 65. Minimum paper TOEFL 510. **Freshman Admission Requirements:** High school diploma is required and GED is accepted. **Freshman Admission Statistics:** 233 applied, 99% admitted, 95% enrolled. **Transfer Admission Requirements:** High school transcript, college transcript(s), statement of good standing from prior institution(s). Minimum college GPA of 2.0 required. Lowest grade transferable D. **General Admission Information:** Application Fee $35. Nonfall registration accepted. Admission may be deferred for a maximum of one semester. Credit offered for CEEB Advanced Placement tests.

COSTS AND FINANCIAL AID

Annual in-state tuition $3,065. Annual out-of-state tuition $3,065. Room and board $5,230. Required fees $843. Average book expense $900. **Required Forms and Deadlines:** FAFSA. **Notification of Awards:** Applicants will be notified of awards on a rolling basis beginning 5/15. **Types of Aid:** *Need-based scholarships/grants:* Federal Pell, SEOG, state scholarships/grants, private scholarships, the school's own gift aid, Academic Competitiveness Grant. *Loans:* Subsidized Stafford, Unsubsidized Stafford, PLUS, Federal Perkins, state loans. **Student Employment:** Federal Work-Study Program available. Institutional employment available. Off-campus job opportunities are good. **Financial Aid Statistics:** 93% freshmen, 87% undergrads receive need-based scholarship or grant aid. 1% freshmen receive non-need-based scholarship or grant aid. 86% freshmen, 90% undergrads receive need-based self-help aid. 6% freshmen, 6% undergrads receive athletic scholarships. 80% undergrads receive any aid. 71% undergrads borrow to pay for school. Average cumulative indebtedness $9,392. **Criteria for awarding institutional aid:** *Non-need-based:* academics, athletics, leadership, minority status, music/drama.

LAKE SUPERIOR STATE UNIVERSITY

650 W. Easterday Avenue, Sault Ste. Marie, MI 49783-1699
Phone: 906-635-2231 • **Financial Aid Phone:** 906-635-2678
E-mail: admissions@lssu.edu • **CEEB Code:** 1421
Fax: 906-635-6669 • **ACT Code:** 2031

This public school was founded in 1946. It has a 115-acre campus.

RATINGS
Admissions Selectivity Rating: 66   **Fire Safety Rating:** 60*   **Green Rating:** 69

STUDENTS AND FACULTY
Enrollment: 2,440. **Student Body:** 50% female, 50% male, 5% out-of-state, 7% international. Asian 1%, African American 1%, Caucasian 79%, Hispanic 2%, Native American 8%.
Retention and Graduation: 70% freshmen return for sophomore year. 13% freshmen graduate within 4 years. 33% freshmen graduate within 6 years. **Faculty:** Student/faculty ratio 17:1. 114 full-time faculty, 53% hold PhDs, 5% are members of minority groups, 46% are women. 0% of classes are taught by teaching assistants.

ACADEMICS
Degrees: associate, bachelor's, certificate, master's. **Classes:** Most classes have 20–29 students. Most lab/discussion sessions have 10–19 students. **Special Study Options:** cooperative education program, cross-registration, distance learning, double major, dual enrollment, honors program, independent study, internships, student-designed major, teacher certification program, weekend college. **Disability Services:** Special programs offered to physically disabled students include note-taking services, reader services, tape recorders, tutors.

FACILITIES
Housing: Coed dorms, men's dorms, women's dorms, fraternity/sorority housing, apartments for married students, apartments for single students. 90% of campus accessible to physically disabled. **Special Academic Facilities/Equipment:** Natural science, Michigan history, and Great Lakes shipping museums, planetarium, industrial robots, atomic absorption/flame emission spectrophotometer. **Computers:** Students can register for classes online.

CAMPUS LIFE
Environment: City. **Activities:** Choral groups, concert band, dance, drama/theater, jazz band, literary magazine, music ensembles, pep band, radio station, student government, student newspaper, symphony orchestra 60 registered organizations, 4 fraternities, 4 sororities. **Athletics (Intercollegiate):** *Men:* basketball, cross-country, ice hockey, tennis, track/field (outdoor), track/field (indoor). *Women:* basketball, cross-country, softball, tennis, track/field (outdoor), track/field (indoor), volleyball.

ADMISSIONS
Freshman Academic Profile: Average high school GPA 3.3. 14% in top 10% of high school class, 40% in top 25% of high school class, 75% in top 50% of high school class. ACT middle 50% range 20-25. Minimum paper TOEFL 550. **Basis for Candidate Selection:** *Very important factors considered include:* academic GPA, rigor of secondary school record, standardized test scores. *Other factors considered include:* Class rank, recommendation(s), geographical residence, interview. **Freshman Admission Requirements:** High school diploma is required and GED is accepted. **Freshman Admission Statistics:** 1,425 applied, 934% enrolled. **Transfer Admission Requirements:** college transcript(s), minimum college GPA of 2.0 required. Lowest grade transferable C–. **General Admission Information:** Application Fee $20. Regular application deadline 8/15. Notification on a rolling basis, beginning on or about 9/15. Nonfall registration accepted. Admission may be deferred for a maximum of 1 Year. Credit offered for CEEB Advanced Placement tests.

COSTS AND FINANCIAL AID
Annual in-state tuition $9,540. Annual out-of-state tuition $14,410. Room and board $8,481. Required fees $100. Average book expense $1,200. **Required Forms and Deadlines:** FAFSA. **Notification of Awards:** Applicants will be notified of awards on a rolling basis beginning 11/1. **Types of Aid:** *Need-based scholarships/grants:* Federal Pell, SEOG, state scholarships/grants, private scholarships, the school's own gift aid, Federal Nursing Scholarships. , third party payments. *Loans:* Direct Subsidized Stafford, Direct Unsubsidized Stafford, Direct PLUS, Federal Perkins, Federal Nursing, state loans. **Student Employment:** Highest amount earned per year from on-campus jobs $2,400. Off-campus job opportunities are good. **Financial Aid Statistics:** 75% freshmen, 75% undergrads receive need-based scholarship or grant aid. 61% freshmen, 40% undergrads receive non-need-based scholarship or grant aid. 82% freshmen, 90% undergrads receive need-based self-help aid. 10% freshmen, 9% undergrads receive athletic scholarships. 83% undergrads receive any aid. 71% undergrads borrow to pay for school. Average cumulative indebtedness $29,108.

LAKEHEAD UNIVERSITY

955 Oliver Road, Thunder Bay, ON P7B 5E1
Phone: 807-343-8500 • **Financial Aid Phone:** 807-343-8206
E-mail: admissions@lakeheadu.ca
Fax: 807-766-7209 • **Website:** www.lakeheadu.ca

This public school was founded in 1965. It has a 288-acre campus.

RATINGS
Admissions Selectivity Rating: 60*   **Fire Safety Rating:** 60*   **Green Rating:** 60*

STUDENTS AND FACULTY
Retention and Graduation: 85% freshmen return for sophomore year. **Faculty:** Student/faculty ratio 24:1.

ACADEMICS
Degrees: bachelor's, certificate, diploma, first professional, master's. **Classes:** Most classes have 30–39 students. **Majors with Highest Enrollment:** business administration and management; engineering; forestry.

FACILITIES
Housing: Coed dorms, special housing for disabled students, apartments for single students, wellness housing. **Computers:** Students can register for classes online.

CAMPUS LIFE
Environment: City. **Activities:** Choral groups, concert band, dance, drama/theater, jazz band, literary magazine, music ensembles, musical theater, radio station, student government, student newspaper, Campus Ministries, International Student Organization, Model UN. **Athletics (Intercollegiate):** *Men:* basketball, cross-country, ice hockey, skiingnordiccross-country, track/field (outdoor), track/field (indoor), wrestling. *Women:* basketball, cross-country, skiingnordiccross-country, track/field (outdoor), track/field (indoor), volleyball, wrestling.

ADMISSIONS
Freshman Admission Requirements: High school diploma is required and GED is accepted. **General Admission Information:** Application Fee $105. Regular application deadline 9/24. Nonfall registration accepted. Admission may be deferred for a maximum of one year.

COSTS AND FINANCIAL AID
Annual in-state tuition $4,670. Annual out-of-state tuition $4,670. Room and board $3,098. Required fees $825.

LAMAR UNIVERSITY

P.O. Box 10009, Beaumont, TX 77710
Phone: 409-880-8888
E-mail: admissions@hal.lamar.edu • **CEEB Code:** 6360
Fax: 409-880-8463 • **Website:** www.lamar.edu • **ACT Code:** 4114

This public school was founded in 1923. It has a 200-acre campus.

RATINGS
Admissions Selectivity Rating: 62   **Fire Safety Rating:** 60*   **Green Rating:** 60*

STUDENTS AND FACULTY
Enrollment: 9,057. **Student Body:** 55% female, 45% male, 1% out-of-state, 1% international. Asian 3%, African American 22%, Caucasian 74%, Hispanic 5%, Native American 1%.

ACADEMICS
Degrees: bachelor's, master's. **Special Study Options:** cooperative education program, distance learning, double major, dual enrollment, English as a Second Language (ESL), honors program, internships, study abroad, teacher certification program, Texas Academy for Leadership in the Humanities, a two-year residential, early admission program for gifted high school students. Students are selected during the sophomore year of high school and enter the University at the end of their junior year. **Combined Degree Programs:** 3-1 program Medicine/Dentistry 3-2 Pharmacy prog. **Disability Services:** Special programs offered to physically disabled students include note-taking services, reader services, tape recorders, tutors. **Career Services:** alumni services, career/job search classes, career assessment.

FACILITIES

Housing: Coed dorms, men's dorms, women's dorms, fraternity/sorority housing, apartments for single students. **Special Academic Facilities/Equipment:** Museum.

CAMPUS LIFE

Environment: Village. **Activities:** student government, student newspaper 145 registered organizations, 11 fraternities, 8 sororities. **Athletics (Intercollegiate):** *Men:* baseball, basketball, cross-country, golf, tennis, track/field (outdoor). *Women:* basketball, cross-country, golf, tennis, track/field (outdoor), volleyball.

ADMISSIONS

Freshman Academic Profile: 10% in top 10% of high school class, 27% in top 25% of high school class, 90% in top 50% of high school class. 96% from public high schools. Minimum paper TOEFL 500. **Freshman Admission Requirements:** High school diploma is required and GED is accepted.High school diploma is required and GED is not accepted. Minimum college GPA of 2.0 required. Lowest grade transferable D. **General Admission Information:** Regular application deadline 8/1. Nonfall registration accepted. Credit and/or placement offered for CEEB Advanced Placement tests.

COSTS AND FINANCIAL AID

Annual in-state tuition $864. Annual out-of-state tuition $5,976. Room and board $3,040. Required fees $840. **Required Forms and Deadlines:** FAFSA, institution's own financial aid form, state aid form. **Notification of Awards: Types of Aid:** *Need-based scholarships/grants: Loans:* Subsidized Stafford, PLUS. **Student Employment:** Federal Work-Study Program available. Institutional employment available. Highest amount earned per year from on-campus jobs $1,200. Off-campus job opportunities are good.

LAMBUTH UNIVERSITY

705 Lambuth Boulevard, Jackson, TN 38301-5296
Phone: 731-425-3223 • **Financial Aid Phone:** 731-425-3332
E-mail: admit@lambuth.edu • **CEEB Code:** 1394
Fax: 731-425-3406 • **Website:** www.lambuth.edu • **ACT Code:** 3974

This private school, affiliated with the Methodist Church, was founded in 1843. It has a 50-acre campus.

RATINGS

Admissions Selectivity Rating: 78   **Fire Safety Rating:** 77   **Green Rating:** 61

STUDENTS AND FACULTY

Enrollment: 765. **Student Body:** 47% female, 53% male, 21% out-of-state, (9 countries represented).
Retention and Graduation: 60% freshmen return for sophomore year. 29% freshmen graduate within 4 years. 39% freshmen graduate within 6 years. 20% grads go on to further study within 1 year. 5% grads pursue arts and sciences degrees. 5% grads pursue law degrees. 5% grads pursue business degrees. 5% grads pursue medical degrees. **Faculty:** Student/faculty ratio 12:1. 51 full-time faculty, 78% hold PhDs, 2% are members of minority groups, 41% are women. 0% of classes are taught by teaching assistants.

ACADEMICS

Degrees: bachelor's. **Classes:** Most classes have fewer than 10 students. Most lab/discussion sessions have 20–29 students. **Majors with Highest Enrollment:** business/commerce; health and physical education; psychology. **Special Study Options:** cross-registration, double major, honors program, independent study, internships, student-designed major, study abroad, teacher certification program, Washington Semester. Tennessee Legislative Internship. Interdisciplinary courses. Lambuth in London. **Honors Programs:** University Honors is a 3 semester sequence of courses designed to offer more in-depth study of classic literature and themes. Various topics are considered including art, psychology, ecology, history, ethics, politics, science, sociology, business, religion, and literature. Honors study is available in most disciplines and consists of an 8 hour sequence of research over the last 3 semesters of study in a particular discipline. **Disability Services:** Special programs offered to physically disabled students include tape recorders, tutors. **Career Services:** Alumni network, alumni services, career/job search classes, career assessment, internships, regional alumni. Career Services highlights include Excellent internships for business, communications, psychology, education and social science majors.

FACILITIES

Housing: Coed dorms, special housing for disabled students, men's dorms, women's dorms, fraternity/sorority housing, apartments for single students. 80% of campus accessible to physically disabled. **Special Academic Facilities/Equipment:** Academic Support Center, Interior Design lab, M.D. Anderson Planetarium, Oxley Biological Field Station **Computers:** 40% of classrooms,

10% of dorms, 100% of libraries, 100% of dining areas, 100% of student union, 50% of common outdoor areas have wireless network access.

CAMPUS LIFE

Environment: City. **Activities:** Choral groups, concert band, dance, drama/theater, jazz band, literary magazine, music ensembles, musical theater, student government, student newspaper, yearbook, Campus Ministries, International Student Organization, Model UN 41 registered organizations, 6 honor societies, 3 religious organizations. 3 fraternities, 3 sororities. **Athletics (Intercollegiate):** *Men:* baseball, basketball, football, golf, soccer, tennis. *Women:* basketball, golf, soccer, softball, tennis. **On-Campus Highlights:** Eagle's Nest Bistro, E/MI Studio, The Quadrangle, Eickoff Plaza, M.D. Anderson Planetarium, Oxley Square (apartment-style dorms), Computer Center, Hamilton Performing Arts Center, R. E. Womack Memorial Chapel, Greek houses, Wellness Center, Athletic Center/Olympic Pool.

ADMISSIONS

Freshman Academic Profile: Average high school GPA 3.3. 21% in top 10% of high school class, 42% in top 25% of high school class, 71% in top 50% of high school class. 85% from public high schools. SAT Math middle 50% range 460-570. SAT Critical Reading middle 50% range 440-570. ACT middle 50% range 20-25. Minimum paper TOEFL 425. **Basis for Candidate Selection:** *Very important factors considered include:* academic GPA, rigor of secondary school record, standardized test scores. *Important factors considered include:* application essay, recommendation(s), extracurricular activities, interview, level of applicant's interest. *Other factors considered include:* Class rank, alumni/ae relation, first generation, geographical residence, religious affiliation/commitment, state residency, talent/ability, volunteer work, work experience. **Freshman Admission Requirements:** High school diploma is required and GED is accepted. **Freshman Admission Statistics:** 679 applied, 62% admitted, 49% enrolled. **Transfer Admission Requirements:** college transcript(s), essay or personal statement, statement of good standing from prior institution(s). Minimum college GPA of 2.0 required. Lowest grade transferable D. **General Admission Information:** Application Fee $25. Notification on a rolling basis, beginning on or about 10/1. Nonfall registration accepted. Admission may be deferred for a maximum of one year. Credit and/or placement offered for CEEB Advanced Placement tests.

COSTS AND FINANCIAL AID

Annual tuition $17,000. Room and board $7,160. Required fees $400. Average book expense $1,200. **Required Forms and Deadlines:** FAFSA, institution's own financial aid form Admission Application. **Notification of Awards:** Applicants will be notified of awards on a rolling basis beginning 2/15. **Types of Aid:** *Need-based scholarships/grants:* Federal Pell, SEOG, state scholarships/grants, private scholarships, the school's own gift aid, Tennessee Hope Lottery Programs. *Loans:* Subsidized Stafford, Unsubsidized Stafford, PLUS, Federal Perkins. **Student Employment:** Federal Work-Study Program available. Institutional employment available. Highest amount earned per year from on-campus jobs $1,404. Off-campus job opportunities are excellent. **Financial Aid Statistics:** 98% freshmen, 97% undergrads receive need-based scholarship or grant aid. 24% freshmen, 22% undergrads receive non-need-based scholarship or grant aid. 66% freshmen, 69% undergrads receive need-based self-help aid. 9% freshmen, 9% undergrads receive athletic scholarships. 99% freshmen, 99% undergrads receive any aid. 64% undergrads borrow to pay for school. Average cumulative indebtedness $19,950. **Criteria for awarding institutional aid:** *Non-need-based:* academics, alumni affiliation, art, athletics, job skills, leadership, music/drama, religious affiliation.

LANCASTER BIBLE COLLEGE

901 Eden Rd, Lancaster, PA 17601-5036
Phone: 717-560-8271 • **Financial Aid Phone:** 717-560-8254
E-mail: admissions@lbc.edu • **CEEB Code:** 2388
Fax: 717-560-8213 • **Website:** www.lbc.edu • **ACT Code:** 3707

This private school was founded in 1933. It has a 100-acre campus.

RATINGS

Admissions Selectivity Rating: 61   **Fire Safety Rating:** 68   **Green Rating:** 60*

STUDENTS AND FACULTY

Enrollment: 702. **Student Body:** 47% female, 53% male, 26% out-of-state, 1% international. Asian 1%, African American 3%, Caucasian 71%, Hispanic 1%, Native American 0%.
Retention and Graduation: **Faculty:** Student/faculty ratio 10:1. 48 full-time faculty, 52% hold PhDs, 2% are members of minority groups, 25% are women. 0% of classes are taught by teaching assistants.

ACADEMICS

Degrees: associate, bachelor's, certificate, master's, post-bachelor's certificate. **Classes:** Most classes have fewer than 10 students. Most lab/discussion sessions have 10–19 students. **Majors with Highest Enrollment:** bible/biblical studies; elementary education and teaching; theology and religious vocations, other. **Special Study Options:** Accelerated program, double major, independent study, internships, study abroad, teacher certification program. **Disability Services:** Special programs offered to physically disabled students include note-taking services, reader services, tape recorders, tutors. **Career Services:** Alumni network, internships.

FACILITIES

Housing: men's dorms, women's dorms. 80% of campus accessible to physically disabled.

CAMPUS LIFE

Environment: Village. **Activities:** Choral groups, concert band, drama/theater, music ensembles, musical theater, student government, student newspaper, yearbook 20 registered organizations. **Athletics (Intercollegiate):** *Men:* baseball, basketball, cheerleading, soccer, volleyball. *Women:* basketball, cheerleading, lacrosse, soccer, volleyball.

ADMISSIONS

Freshman Academic Profile: 60% from public high schools. Minimum paper TOEFL 550. **Basis for Candidate Selection:** *Very important factors considered include:* application essay, recommendation(s), rigor of secondary school record, standardized test scores, character/personal qualities, religious affiliation/commitment. *Important factors considered include:* extracurricular activities. *Other factors considered include:* interview, talent/ability, volunteer work. **Freshman Admission Requirements:** High school diploma is required and GED is accepted. **Freshman Admission Statistics:** 314 applied, 97% admitted, 44% enrolled. **Transfer Admission Requirements:** High school transcript, college transcript(s), essay or personal statement, standardized test scores, statement of good standing from prior institution(s). Minimum college GPA of 2.0 required. Lowest grade transferable C. **General Admission Information:** Application Fee $25. Notification on a rolling basis, beginning on or about 9/1. Nonfall registration accepted. Admission may be deferred for a maximum of 1 year.

COSTS AND FINANCIAL AID

Annual tuition $15,930. Room and board $7,110. Required fees $630. Average book expense $1,000. **Required Forms and Deadlines:** FAFSA, state aid form. **Notification of Awards:** Applicants will be notified of awards on a rolling basis beginning 3/1. **Types of Aid:** *Need-based scholarships/grants:* Federal Pell, SEOG, state scholarships/grants, private scholarships, the school's own gift aid, Office of Vocational Rehabilitation Blindness and Visual Services Awards. *Loans:* Subsidized Stafford, Unsubsidized Stafford, PLUS, Federal Perkins, Alternative Loans. **Student Employment:** Federal Work-Study Program available. Institutional employment available. Highest amount earned per year from on-campus jobs $1,400. Off-campus job opportunities are good. **Financial Aid Statistics:** 98% freshmen, 94% undergrads receive need-based scholarship or grant aid. 97% freshmen, 79% undergrads receive non-need-based scholarship or grant aid. 83% freshmen, 88% undergrads receive need-based self-help aid. 27% undergrads borrow to pay for school. Average cumulative indebtedness $19,579. **Criteria for awarding institutional aid:** *Non-need-based:* academics, alumni affiliation, leadership, music/drama.

LANDER UNIVERSITY

320 Stanley Avenue, Greenwood, SC 29649
Phone: 864-388-8307 • **Financial Aid Phone:** 864-388-8340
E-mail: admissions@lander.edu • **CEEB Code:** 5363
Fax: 864-388-8125 • **Website:** www.lander.edu • **ACT Code:** 3860

This public school was founded in 1872. It has a 100-acre campus.

RATINGS

Admissions Selectivity Rating: 67   **Fire Safety Rating:** 61   **Green Rating:** 60*

STUDENTS AND FACULTY

Enrollment: 2,655. **Student Body:** 67% female, 33% male, 3% out-of-state, 2% international (21 countries represented). Asian 1%, African American 22%, Caucasian 74%, Hispanic 1%, Native American 0%.
Retention and Graduation: 65% freshmen return for sophomore year. 28% freshmen graduate within 4 years. 43% freshmen graduate within 6 years.
Faculty: Student/faculty ratio 20:1. 117 full-time faculty, 72% hold PhDs, 8% are members of minority groups, 44% are women. 0% of classes are taught by teaching assistants.

ACADEMICS

Degrees: bachelor's, certificate, master's. **Classes:** Most classes have 20–29 students. **Majors with Highest Enrollment:** business/commerce; elementary education and teaching; nursing/registered nurse (rn, asn, bsn, msn). **Special Study Options:** cooperative education program, distance learning, double major, dual enrollment, honors program, independent study, internships, liberal arts/career combination, student-designed major, study abroad, teacher certification program, Nursing (R.N. to B.S.N. completion) program courses now offered on the web. M.B.A. from Clemson U. offered on campus. M.Ed. Counseling/School Administration from Clemson U. offered on campus. M.Ed. Elementary Education. M.A.T. Master of Art in Teaching. Dual degree in Engineering offered in conjunction with Clemson University. **Combined Degree Programs:** BA/MEng. **Disability Services:** Special programs offered to physically disabled students include note-taking services, reader services, tape recorders, tutors. **Career Services:** internships.

FACILITIES

Housing: Coed dorms, women's dorms, apartments for single students. 100% of campus accessible to physically disabled. **Special Academic Facilities/Equipment:** Art gallery, continuing education center, media center, electronic piano instruction facility, amphitheatre. **Computers:** Students can register for classes online. Administrative functions (other than registration) can be performed online.

CAMPUS LIFE

Environment: Village. **Activities:** Choral groups, concert band, dance, drama/theater, jazz band, literary magazine, music ensembles, student government, student newspaper 65 registered organizations, 6 honor societies, 7 religious organizations. 6 fraternities, 6 sororities. **Athletics (Intercollegiate):** *Men:* baseball, basketball, golf, soccer, tennis. *Women:* basketball, cross-country, soccer, softball, tennis, volleyball. **On-Campus Highlights:** Student Center, Grill Works, Cafeteria, Student Atrium, Library.

ADMISSIONS

Freshman Academic Profile: Average high school GPA 3.4. 8% in top 10% of high school class, 30% in top 25% of high school class, 68% in top 50% of high school class. % from public high schools. SAT Math middle 50% range 440-540. SAT Critical Reading middle 50% range 430-530. ACT middle 50% range 17-22. Minimum paper TOEFL 550. **Basis for Candidate Selection:** *Very important factors considered include:* Class rank, rigor of secondary school record, standardized test scores. *Other factors considered include:* application essay, recommendation(s), alumni/ae relation, character/personal qualities, extracurricular activities, interview, talent/ability, volunteer work, work experience. **Freshman Admission Requirements:** High school diploma is required and GED is accepted. *Academic units required:* 4 English, 3 mathematics, 3 science, (3 science labs), 2 foreign language, 2 social studies, 1 history, 4 academic electives, 1 Phys. Educ./Rotc. *Academic units recommended:* 4 English, 3 mathematics, 3 science, (3 science labs), 2 foreign language, 2 social studies, 1 history, 4 academic electives, 1 Phys. Educ./Rotc **Freshman Admission Statistics:** 1,750 applied, 85% admitted, 45% enrolled. **Transfer Admission Requirements:** college transcript(s), statement of good standing from prior institution(s). Minimum college GPA of 2.0 required. Lowest grade transferable C. **General Admission Information:** Application Fee $35. Regular application deadline 8/5. Nonfall registration accepted. Admission may be deferred for a maximum of Individual. Credit and/or placement offered for CEEB Advanced Placement tests.

COSTS AND FINANCIAL AID

Annual in-state tuition $7,152. Annual out-of-state tuition $12,024. Room and board $5,176. Required fees $150. Average book expense $840. **Required Forms and Deadlines:** FAFSA. **Notification of Awards:** Applicants will be notified of awards on or about 6/1. **Types of Aid:** *Need-based scholarships/grants:* Federal Pell, SEOG, state scholarships/grants, private scholarships, the school's own gift aid, Federal Nursing Scholarships. *Loans:* Subsidized Stafford, Unsubsidized Stafford, PLUS, Federal Perkins, state loans. **Student Employment:** Federal Work-Study Program available. Highest amount earned per year from on-campus jobs $4,500. Off-campus job opportunities are good. **Financial Aid Statistics:** 57% freshmen, 58% undergrads receive need-based scholarship or grant aid. 50% freshmen, 50% undergrads receive non-need-based scholarship or grant aid. 76% freshmen, 75% undergrads receive need-based self-help aid. 80% freshmen, 80% undergrads receive any aid. 49% undergrads borrow to pay for school. Average cumulative indebtedness $13,500. **Criteria for awarding institutional aid:** *Non-need-based:* academics, art, athletics, leadership, music/drama, state/district residency.

LANDMARK COLLEGE

P.O. Box 820, Putney, VT 05346-0820
Phone: 802-387-6718 • **Financial Aid Phone:** 802-387-6736
E-mail: admissions@landmark.edu
Fax: 802-387-6868 • **Website:** www.landmark.edu/ • **ACT Code:** 4317

This private school was founded in 1984. It has a 128-acre campus.

RATINGS

Admissions Selectivity Rating: 63   **Fire Safety Rating:** 69   **Green Rating:** 60*

STUDENTS AND FACULTY

Enrollment: 487. **Student Body:** 95% out-of-state, 3% international (14 countries represented). Asian 1%, African American 5%, Caucasian 70%, Hispanic 3%, Native American 0%.
Retention and Graduation: 95% grads go on to further study within 1 year.
Faculty: Student/faculty ratio 6:1. 86 full-time faculty, 1% are members of minority groups, 64% are women. 0% of classes are taught by teaching assistants.

ACADEMICS

Degrees: associate, terminal associate, transfer associate. **Classes:** Most classes have 10–19 students. **Special Study Options:** internships, study abroad.

FACILITIES

Housing: Coed dorms, special housing for disabled students, wellness housing, 65% of campus accessible to physically disabled.

CAMPUS LIFE

Environment: Rural. **Activities:** Choral groups, dance, drama/theater, jazz band, literary magazine, music ensembles, radio station, student government.

ADMISSIONS

Freshman Academic Profile: Minimum paper TOEFL 200. **Basis for Candidate Selection:** *Very important factors considered include:* recommendation(s), interview. *Important factors considered include:* character/personal qualities, level of applicant's interest. *Other factors considered include:* Class rank, application essay, academic GPA, rigor of secondary school record, standardized test scores, extracurricular activities, talent/ability. **Freshman Admission Requirements:** High school diploma is required and GED is accepted. **Freshman Admission Statistics:** 395 applied, 54% admitted, 54% enrolled. **Transfer Admission Requirements:** High school transcript, college transcript(s), essay or personal statement, interview, Lowest grade transferable C–. **General Admission Information:** Application Fee $75. Notification on a rolling basis, beginning on or about 12/1. Nonfall registration accepted. Admission may be deferred for a maximum of 1 calendar year.

COSTS AND FINANCIAL AID

Annual tuition $48,210. Room and board $8,620. Required fees $500. Average book expense $1,200. **Required Forms and Deadlines:** FAFSA federal Tax return - parent and student. **Notification of Awards:** Applicants will be notified of awards on a rolling basis beginning 4/15. **Types of Aid:** *Need-based scholarships/grants:* Federal Pell, SEOG, state scholarships/grants, private scholarships, the school's own gift aid, Vocational Rehabilitation Grants. *Loans:* Subsidized Stafford, Unsubsidized Stafford, PLUS. **Student Employment:** Federal Work-Study Program available. Institutional employment available. Highest amount earned per year from on-campus jobs $1,500. Off-campus job opportunities are good. **Financial Aid Statistics:** 100% undergrads receive need-based scholarship or grant aid. 4% undergrads receive non-need-based scholarship or grant aid. 100% undergrads receive need-based self-help aid. 35% freshmen, 42% undergrads receive any aid. 51% undergrads borrow to pay for school. Average cumulative indebtedness $6,510. **Criteria for awarding institutional aid:** *Non-need-based:* academics, art, athletics, leadership, minority status, music/drama.

See page 1120.

LANE COLLEGE

545 Lane Avenue, Jackson, TN 38301
Phone: 731-426-7532 • **Financial Aid Phone:** 731-426-7536
E-mail: admissions@lanecollege.edu
Fax: 731-426-7559 • **Website:** www.lanecollege.edu • **ACT Code:** 3976

This private school, affiliated with the Methodist Church, was founded in 1882. It has a 25-acre campus.

RATINGS

Admissions Selectivity Rating: 77   **Fire Safety Rating:** 92   **Green Rating:** 60*

STUDENTS AND FACULTY

Enrollment: 1,512. **Student Body:** 51% female, 49% male, 37% out-of-state, 0% international (1 countries represented). Asian %, African American 100%, Caucasian 0%, Hispanic 0%, Native American 0%.
Retention and Graduation: 50% freshmen return for sophomore year. 22% freshmen graduate within 4 years. 38% freshmen graduate within 6 years. 35% grads go on to further study within 1 year. 37% grads pursue arts and sciences degrees. 6% grads pursue law degrees. 10% grads pursue business degrees. 7% grads pursue medical degrees. **Faculty:** Student/faculty ratio 17:1. 90 full-time faculty. 0% of classes are taught by teaching assistants.

ACADEMICS

Degrees: bachelor's. **Classes:** Most classes have 20–29 students. **Majors with Highest Enrollment:** business/commerce; criminal justice/law enforcement administration; multi-/interdisciplinary studies, other. **Special Study Options:** Accelerated program, independent study, internships, study abroad, teacher certification program. **Disability Services:** Special programs offered to physically disabled students include tutors. **Career Services:** alumni services, career/job search classes, career assessment, internships.

FACILITIES

Housing: men's dorms, women's dorms. 98% of campus accessible to physically disabled. **Special Academic Facilities/Equipment:** The Grand Student Center The Cyber Cafe **Computers:** 50% of classrooms, 100% of libraries, 100% of student union, 25% of common outdoor areas have wireless network access.

CAMPUS LIFE

Environment: Town. **Activities:** Choral groups, concert band, dance, drama/theater, marching band, music ensembles, student government, student newspaper, yearbook, Campus Ministries 21 registered organizations, 6 honor societies, 4 religious organizations. 4 fraternities, 4 sororities. **Athletics (Intercollegiate):** *Men:* baseball, basketball, cross-country, football, tennis, track/field (outdoor). *Women:* basketball, cheerleading, cross-country, softball, tennis, track/field (outdoor), volleyball. **On-Campus Highlights:** Pond at the Plain, Williams/Boyd Campus Center, The Cyber Cafe, Phillips Dining Hall, The Grand. **Environmental Initiatives:** See comment on previous page re: LEEDS TP3-Pollution Tennessee Pollution Prevention Partnership EPA Environmental Self-audit Program

ADMISSIONS

Freshman Academic Profile: Average high school GPA 2.8. 3% in top 10% of high school class, 12% in top 25% of high school class, 39% in top 50% of high school class. 96% from public high schools. ACT middle 50% range 14–17. Minimum paper TOEFL 339. **Basis for Candidate Selection:** *Very important factors considered include:* recommendation(s), rigor of secondary school record, character/personal qualities. *Important factors considered include:* standardized test scores. *Other factors considered include:* academic GPA, interview, level of applicant's interest, talent/ability. **Freshman Admission Requirements:** High school diploma is required and GED is accepted. **Freshman Admission Statistics:** 5,324 applied, 33% admitted, 18% enrolled. **Transfer Admission Requirements:** college transcript(s), standardized test scores, statement of good standing from prior institution(s). Lowest grade transferable C. **General Admission Information:** Regular application deadline 8/1. Notification on a rolling basis, beginning on or about 2/1. Nonfall registration accepted. Admission may be deferred for a maximum of one semester. Credit offered for CEEB Advanced Placement tests.

COSTS AND FINANCIAL AID

Annual tuition $7,860. Room and board $6,040. Required fees $700. Average book expense $1,100. **Required Forms and Deadlines:** FAFSA. **Notification of Awards:** Applicants will be notified of awards on a rolling basis beginning 3/31. **Types of Aid:** *Need-based scholarships/grants:* Federal Pell, SEOG, state scholarships/grants, private scholarships, the school's own gift aid, United Negro College Fund. *Loans:* Direct Subsidized Stafford, Direct Unsubsidized Stafford, Direct PLUS. **Student Employment:** Federal Work-Study Program available. Institutional employment available. Off-campus job opportunities are excellent. **Financial Aid Statistics:** 21% freshmen, 11% undergrads receive need-based scholarship or grant aid. 1% freshmen, 2% undergrads receive need-based self-help aid. 5% freshmen, 3% undergrads receive athletic scholarships. 96% freshmen, 98% undergrads receive any aid. 1% undergrads borrow to pay for school. Average cumulative indebtedness $370. **Criteria for awarding institutional aid:** *Non-need-based:* academics, athletics, religious affiliation.

LASALLE UNIVERSITY

1900 West Olney Avenue, Philadelphia, PA 19141-1199
Phone: 215-951-1500 • **Financial Aid Phone:** 215-951-1070
E-mail: admiss@lasalle.edu • **CEEB Code:** 2363
Fax: 215-951-1656 • **Website:** www.lasalle.edu/ • **ACT Code:** 3608

This private school, affiliated with the Roman Catholic Church, was founded in 1863. It has a 120-acre campus.

RATINGS
Admissions Selectivity Rating: 71   **Fire Safety Rating:** 72   **Green Rating:** 60*

STUDENTS AND FACULTY
Enrollment: 4,302. **Student Body:** 64% female, 36% male, 38% out-of-state, 1% international (13 countries represented). Asian 5%, African American 18%, Caucasian 55%, Hispanic 11%, Native American 0%.
Retention and Graduation: 80% freshmen return for sophomore year. 58% freshmen graduate within 4 years. 68% freshmen graduate within 6 years. **Faculty:** Student/faculty ratio 12:1. 245 full-time faculty, 80% hold PhDs, 9% are members of minority groups, 54% are women. 0% of classes are taught by teaching assistants.

ACADEMICS
Degrees: associate, bachelor's, certificate, master's, post-bachelor's certificate, post-master's certificate. **Classes:** Most classes have 20–29 students. Most lab/discussion sessions have fewer than 10 students. **Majors with Highest Enrollment:** communication, journalism, and related programs, other; education; public health/community nurse/nursing. **Special Study Options:** Accelerated program, cooperative education program, cross-registration, double major, dual enrollment, English as a Second Language (ESL), exchange student program (domestic), honors program, independent study, internships, student-designed major, study abroad, teacher certification program, 2+2 with Thomas Jefferson University. **Combined Degree Programs:** BS/MS (5 year)Speech/Language Path. and Audiology. **Disability Services:** Special programs offered to physically disabled students include note-taking services, reader services, tape recorders, tutors.

FACILITIES
Housing: Coed dorms, special housing for disabled students, fraternity/sorority housing, apartments for single students. 95% of campus accessible to physically disabled. **Special Academic Facilities/Equipment:** Art museum, Japanese tea house, language lab, child development center. **Computers:** Students can register for classes online. Administrative functions (other than registration) can be performed online.

CAMPUS LIFE
Environment: Metropolis. **Activities:** Choral groups, concert band, drama/theater, jazz band, literary magazine, music ensembles, musical theater, pep band, radio station, student government, student newspaper, student-run film society, television station, yearbook 100 registered organizations, 10 honor societies, 4 religious organizations. 7 fraternities, 5 sororities. **Athletics (Intercollegiate):** *Men:* baseball, basketball, cheerleading, crew/rowing, cross-country, diving, football, golf, soccer, swimming, tennis, track/field (outdoor), wrestling. *Women:* basketball, cheerleading, crew/rowing, cross-country, diving, field hockey, golf, lacrosse, soccer, softball, swimming, tennis, track/field (outdoor), volleyball. **On-Campus Highlights:** Hayman Center (sports facility), Connelly Library, Student Union Building-food court, coffee house, restaurant, La Salle University Art Museum, Japanese Tea Ceremony House.

ADMISSIONS
Freshman Academic Profile: Average high school GPA 3.4. 17% in top 10% of high school class, 40% in top 25% of high school class, 74% in top 50% of high school class. 35% from public high schools. SAT Math middle 50% range 440-550. SAT Critical Reading middle 50% range 440-540. ACT middle 50% range 19-23. Minimum web-based TOEFL 76. Minimum paper TOEFL 540. **Basis for Candidate Selection:** *Very important factors considered include:* rigor of secondary school record. *Important factors considered include:* Class rank, application essay, standardized test scores. *Other factors considered include:* recommendation(s), alumni/ae relation, character/personal qualities, extracurricular activities, interview, talent/ability, volunteer work, work experience. **Freshman Admission Requirements:** High school diploma is required and GED is accepted. *Academic units required:* 4 English, 3 mathematics, 1

science, (1 science labs), 2 foreign language, 1 history, 5 academic electives. 4 English, 3 mathematics, 1 science, (1 science labs), 2 foreign language, 1 history, 5 academic electives. **Freshman Admission Statistics:** 6,101 applied, 73% admitted, 21% enrolled. **Transfer Admission Requirements:** High school transcript, college transcript(s), essay or personal statement, standardized test scores, statement of good standing from prior institution(s). Minimum college GPA of 2.5 required. Lowest grade transferable C. **General Admission Information:** Application Fee $35. Notification on a rolling basis, beginning on or about 11/15. Nonfall registration accepted. Admission may be deferred for a maximum of info. not available.

COSTS AND FINANCIAL AID
Annual tuition $36,250. Room and board $12,210. Required fees $400. Average book expense $500. **Required Forms and Deadlines:** FAFSA. **Notification of Awards:** Applicants will be notified of awards on a rolling basis beginning 3/15. **Types of Aid:** *Need-based scholarships/grants:* Federal Pell, SEOG, state scholarships/grants, private scholarships, the school's own gift aid. *Loans:* Subsidized Stafford, Unsubsidized Stafford, PLUS, Federal Perkins. **Student Employment: Financial Aid Statistics:** 99% freshmen, 98% undergrads receive need-based scholarship or grant aid. 9% freshmen, 9% undergrads receive non-need-based scholarship or grant aid. 81% freshmen, 81% undergrads receive need-based self-help aid. 5% freshmen, 5% undergrads receive athletic scholarships. 94% freshmen, 76% undergrads receive any aid. 77% undergrads borrow to pay for school. Average cumulative indebtedness $37,225. **Criteria for awarding institutional aid:** *Non-need-based:* academics, athletics.

LASELL COLLEGE

Office of Undergraduate Admissions, Newton, MA 2466
Phone: 617-243-2225 • **Financial Aid Phone:** 617-243-2227
E-mail: info@lasell.edu • **CEEB Code:** 3481
Fax: 617-243-2380 • **Website:** www.lasell.edu • **ACT Code:** 1848

This private school was founded in 1851. It has a 55-acre campus.

RATINGS
Admissions Selectivity Rating: 73   **Fire Safety Rating:** 69   **Green Rating:** 60*

STUDENTS AND FACULTY
Enrollment: 1,154. **Student Body:** 71% female, 29% male, 4% international (15 countries represented). Asian 4%, African American 6%, Caucasian 75%, Hispanic 6%, Native American 0%.
Retention and Graduation: 18% grads go on to further study within 1 year. 13% grads pursue arts and sciences degrees. 5% grads pursue business degrees. **Faculty:** Student/faculty ratio 13:1. 55 full-time faculty, 45% hold PhDs, 64% are women. 0% of classes are taught by teaching assistants.

ACADEMICS
Degrees: bachelor's, master's, post-bachelor's certificate. **Classes:** Most classes have 10–19 students. Most lab/discussion sessions have 10–19 students. **Majors with Highest Enrollment:** criminology; fashion/apparel design; psychology. **Special Study Options:** double major, honors program, internships, liberal arts/career combination, study abroad. **Honors Programs:** Lasell College Honor's Program. **Career Services:** alumni services, career/job search classes, career assessment, internships.

FACILITIES
Housing: Coed dorms, women's dorms, Special interst (human services). Some houses Alcohol free. All houses Smoke free. 30% of campus accessible to physically disabled. **Special Academic Facilities/Equipment:** Center for Public Service - Yamawaki Art/Cultural Center

CAMPUS LIFE
Environment: City. **Activities:** Choral groups, dance, drama/theater, literary magazine, music ensembles, musical theater, radio station, student government, student newspaper, television station, yearbook 30 registered organizations, 1 honor societies. **Athletics (Intercollegiate):** *Men:* basketball, cross-country, lacrosse, soccer, volleyball. *Women:* basketball, cross-country, field hockey, lacrosse, soccer, softball, volleyball. **On-Campus Highlights:** Yamawaki Art and Cultural Center, Campus Center, Athletic Center, Winslow Academic Center, Edwards Student Center.

ADMISSIONS
Freshman Academic Profile: Average high school GPA 2.7. 6% in top 10% of high school class, 32% in top 25% of high school class, 79% in top 50% of high school class. 85% from public high schools. SAT Math middle 50% range 510-420. SAT Critical Reading middle 50% range 520-430. ACT middle 50% range 21-20. Minimum paper TOEFL 500. **Basis for Candidate Selection:** *Very*

important factors considered include: recommendation(s), rigor of secondary school record. *Important factors considered include:* standardized test scores, extracurricular activities, interview. *Other factors considered include:* Class rank, application essay, alumni/ae relation, character/personal qualities, talent/ability, volunteer work, work experience. **Freshman Admission Requirements:** High school diploma is required and GED is accepted. *Academic units required:* 4 English, 3 mathematics, 2 science, (2 science labs), 2 social studies, 2 history. *Academic units recommended:* 4 English, 3 mathematics, 2 science, (2 science labs), 2 social studies, 2 history. **Freshman Admission Statistics:** 2,498 applied, 65% admitted, 24% enrolled. **Transfer Admission Requirements:** college transcript(s), standardized test scores, statement of good standing from prior institution(s). Minimum college GPA of 2.3 required. Lowest grade transferable C. **General Admission Information:** Application Fee $40. Notification on a rolling basis, beginning on or about 12/15. Nonfall registration accepted. Admission may be deferred for a maximum of 1 year. Credit offered for CEEB Advanced Placement tests.

COSTS AND FINANCIAL AID

Annual tuition $18,700. Room and board $8,800. Required fees $1,000. Average book expense $1,000. **Required Forms and Deadlines:** FAFSA, institution's own financial aid form. **Notification of Awards:** Applicants will be notified of awards on a rolling basis beginning 2/15. **Types of Aid:** *Need-based scholarships/grants:* Federal Pell, SEOG, state scholarships/grants, private scholarships, the school's own gift aid. *Loans:* Subsidized Stafford, Unsubsidized Stafford, PLUS, Federal Perkins, state loans. **Student Employment:** Federal Work-Study Program available. Institutional employment available. Off-campus job opportunities are excellent. **Financial Aid Statistics:** 95% freshmen, 97% undergrads receive need-based scholarship or grant aid. 7% freshmen, 12% undergrads receive non-need-based scholarship or grant aid. 88% freshmen, 90% undergrads receive need-based self-help aid. 87% freshmen, 85% undergrads receive any aid. 87% undergrads borrow to pay for school. Average cumulative indebtedness $20,500. **Criteria for awarding institutional aid:** *Non-need-based:* academics, alumni affiliation.

LAURA AND ALVIN SIEGAL COLLEGE OF JUDAIC STUDIES

26500 Shaker Boulevard, Beachwood, OH 44122-7116
Phone: 216-464-4050 • **Financial Aid Phone:** 216-464-4050
E-mail: admissions@siegalcollege.edu
Fax: 216-464-5827

This private school, affiliated with the Jewish Church, was founded in 1963.

RATINGS

Admissions Selectivity Rating: 62   **Fire Safety Rating:** 60*   **Green Rating:** 60*

STUDENTS AND FACULTY

Enrollment: 12. **Student Body:** 67% female, 33% male, 90% out-of-state, 0% international (1 countries represented). Asian 0%, African American 0%, Caucasian 100%, Hispanic 0%, Native American 0%.
Retention and Graduation: 100% freshmen return for sophomore year.
Faculty: Student/faculty ratio 2:1. 11 full-time faculty, 82% hold PhDs, 0% are members of minority groups, 36% are women. 0% of classes are taught by teaching assistants.

ACADEMICS

Degrees: bachelor's, certificate, master's. **Majors with Highest Enrollment:** bible/biblical studies. **Special Study Options:** distance learning, double major, independent study, internships.

FACILITIES

Housing: no housing available on campus. 100% of campus accessible to physically disabled. **Computers:** Students can register for classes online.

CAMPUS LIFE

Environment: Village. **Activities:** 1 registered organizations. **On-Campus Highlights:** library, video conferencing rooms, student lounge, language media center, professors offices.

ADMISSIONS

Basis for Candidate Selection: *Very important factors considered include:* application essay, recommendation(s), interview, level of applicant's interest. *Important factors considered include:* academic GPA, rigor of secondary school record. *Other factors considered include:* Class rank, standardized test scores, character/personal qualities, extracurricular activities, talent/ability, work experience. **Freshman Admission Requirements:** High school diploma is required

and GED is accepted. **Freshman Admission Statistics:** 3 applied, 10100% enrolled. **Transfer Admission Requirements:** college transcript(s), essay or personal statement, interview, minimum college GPA of 2.7 required. Lowest grade transferable C. **General Admission Information:** Application Fee $50. Nonfall registration accepted. Admission may be deferred for a maximum of 1 year.

COSTS AND FINANCIAL AID

Annual tuition $12,600. Required fees $25. Average book expense. **Required Forms and Deadlines:** institution's own financial aid form. **Notification of Awards:** Applicants will be notified of awards on a rolling basis beginning 9/5. **Types of Aid:** *Need-based scholarships/grants:* Federal Pell, the school's own gift aid. *Loans:* Subsidized Stafford, Unsubsidized Stafford, PLUS. **Student Employment:** Off-campus job opportunities are good. **Financial Aid Statistics:** 100% freshmen receive need-based scholarship or grant aid. 0% undergrads borrow to pay for school.

LAWRENCE TECHNICAL UNIVERSITY

21000 West Ten Mile Rd. Southfield, MI 48075-1058
Phone: 248-204-3160 • **Financial Aid Phone:** 248-204-2120
E-mail: admissions@ltu.edu • **CEEB Code:** 1399
Fax: 248-204-3188 • **Website:** www.ltu.edu • **ACT Code:** 2020

This private school was founded in 1932. It has a 102-acre campus.

RATINGS

Admissions Selectivity Rating: 91   **Fire Safety Rating:** 87   **Green Rating:** 83

STUDENTS AND FACULTY

Enrollment: 1,909. **Student Body:** 27% female, 73% male, 3% out-of-state, 8% international (47 countries represented). Asian 5%, African American 9%, Caucasian 70%, Hispanic 3%, Native American 1%.
Retention and Graduation: 74% freshmen return for sophomore year.
Faculty: Student/faculty ratio 11:1. 114 full-time faculty, 67% hold PhDs, 25% are members of minority groups, 31% are women. 0% of classes are taught by teaching assistants.

ACADEMICS

Degrees: associate, bachelor's, certificate, doctoral, master's, post-bachelor's certificate. **Classes:** Most classes have 10–19 students. Most lab/discussion sessions have fewer than 10 students. **Majors with Highest Enrollment:** architecture (barch, ba/bs, march, ma/ms, phd); computer science; mechanical engineering. **Special Study Options:** cooperative education program, cross-registration, distance learning, double major, dual enrollment, English as a Second Language (ESL), honors program, independent study, internships, liberal arts/career combination, study abroad, weekend college. **Honors Programs:** The LTU Honors Program is designed for highly qualified students who want an educational experience that will take full advantage of the challenging curricula offered at Lawrence Tech. **Combined Degree Programs:** Many dual degree combinations. **Disability Services:** Special programs offered to physically disabled students include note-taking services, reader services, tape recorders, tutors. **Career Services:** Alumni network, alumni services, career/job search classes, career assessment, internships, regional alumni. Career Services highlights include "Find Your First Professional Job". A 10 week program to develop student skills to locate and secure their career goals. Classes are taught by leading employers, and each student is assigned a career counselor to help develop an individualized approach to their quest.

FACILITIES

Housing: special housing for disabled students, fraternity/sorority housing, apartments for married students, apartments for single students. 97% of campus accessible to physically disabled. **Special Academic Facilities/Equipment:** Albert Kahn Library Center for Innovative Materials Research **Computers:** 100% of classrooms, 100% of dorms, 100% of libraries, 100% of dining areas, 100% of student union, 75% of common outdoor areas have wireless network access. Students can register for classes online. Administrative functions (other than registration) can be performed online. Undergraduates are required to own a computer.

CAMPUS LIFE

Environment: City. **Activities:** drama/theater, literary magazine, music ensembles, student government, student newspaper 54 registered organizations, 7 honor societies, 1 religious organizations. 6 fraternities, 3 sororities. **On-Campus Highlights:** Atrium, Field House, Engineering Lounge, Larry Joe Coffee Bar, Housing. **Environmental Initiatives:** A. Alfred Taubman Student Services Center is a green building including geothermal wells and a vegetated roof. It serves as a living laboratory for sustainability education of architects and engineers. Establishment of the Center for Sustainability including campus standards for sustainability, a speaker series, and recycling. Academic programming including participation in the Solar Decathlon and Formula Zero international competitions.

ADMISSIONS

Freshman Academic Profile: 3.4. 26% in top 10% of high school class, 57% in top 25% of high school class, 88% in top 50% of high school class. SAT Math middle 50% range 550-630. SAT Critical Reading middle 50% range 480-610. SAT Writing middle 50% range 490-580. ACT middle 50% range 22-28. Minimum web-based TOEFL 79. Minimum paper TOEFL 550. **Basis for Candidate Selection:** *Very important factors considered include:* academic GPA, rigor of secondary school record, standardized test scores. *Other factors considered include:* application essay, recommendation(s), interview. **Freshman Admission Requirements:** High school diploma is required and GED is accepted. *Academic units required:* 4 English, 3 mathematics, 2 science, 3 social studies. *Academic units recommended:* 4 English, 3 mathematics, 2 science, 3 social studies. **Freshman Admission Statistics:** 1,819 applied, 44% admitted, 37% enrolled. **Transfer Admission Requirements:** High school transcript, college transcript(s), minimum college GPA of 2.2 required. Lowest grade transferable C. **General Admission Information:** Application Fee $30. Non-fall registration accepted. Credit and/or placement offered for CEEB Advanced Placement tests.

COSTS AND FINANCIAL AID

Average book expense. **Required Forms and Deadlines:** FAFSA. **Notification of Awards:** Applicants will be notified of awards on a rolling basis beginning 3/1. **Types of Aid:** *Need-based scholarships/grants:* Federal Pell, SEOG, state scholarships/grants, private scholarships, the school's own gift aid. *Loans:* Direct Subsidized Stafford, Direct Unsubsidized Stafford, Direct PLUS, Federal Perkins, state loans, college/university loans from institutional funds, Private Alternative Loans. **Student Employment:** Federal Work-Study Program available. Institutional employment available. Highest amount earned per year from on-campus jobs $13,110. Off-campus job opportunities are excellent. **Financial Aid Statistics:** 98% freshmen, 94% undergrads receive need-based scholarship or grant aid. 81% freshmen, 70% undergrads receive non-need-based scholarship or grant aid. 82% freshmen, 89% undergrads receive need-based self-help aid. 5% freshmen, 1% undergrads receive athletic scholarships. 86% freshmen, 48% undergrads receive any aid. 75% undergrads borrow to pay for school. Average cumulative indebtedness $41,529. **Criteria for awarding institutional aid:** *Non-need-based:* academics, alumni affiliation, art, job skills, leadership, minority status, state/district residency.

See page 1122.

LAWRENCE UNIVERSITY

Best 378

711 East Boldt Way SPC 29, Appleton, WI 54911-5699
Phone: 920-832-6500 • **Financial Aid Phone:** 920-832-6583
E-mail: excel@lawrence.edu • **CEEB Code:** 1398
Fax: 920-832-6782 • **Website:** www.lawrence.edu • **ACT Code:** 4596

This private school was founded in 1847. It has a 84-acre campus.

RATINGS

Admissions Selectivity Rating: 90   **Fire Safety Rating:** 70   **Green Rating:** 77

STUDENTS AND FACULTY

Enrollment: 1,471. **Student Body:** 53% female, 47% male, 63% out-of-state, 8% international (50 countries represented). Asian 3%, African American 3%, Caucasian 77%, Hispanic 4%, Native American 1%.
Retention and Graduation: 90% freshmen return for sophomore year. 54% freshmen graduate within 4 years. 23% grads go on to further study within 1 year. 11% grads pursue arts and sciences degrees. 2% grads pursue law degrees. 3% grads pursue medical degrees. **Faculty:** Student/faculty ratio 9:1. 161 full-time faculty, 95% hold PhDs, 12% are members of minority groups, 37% are women. 0% of classes are taught by teaching assistants.

ACADEMICS

Degrees: bachelor's. **Classes:** Most classes have 10–19 students. **Majors with Highest Enrollment:** biology/biological sciences; psychology; visual and performing arts. **Special Study Options:** double major, independent study, internships, student-designed major, study abroad, teacher certification program. **Combined Degree Programs:** BA/B-MUS. **Disability Services:** Special programs offered to physically disabled students include note-taking services,

reader services, tape recorders, tutors. **Career Services:** Alumni network, alumni services, career assessment, internships, regional alumni.

FACILITIES

Housing: Coed dorms, special housing for disabled students, men's dorms, women's dorms, apartments for married students, theme housing, theme/group houses available. 70% of campus accessible to physically disabled. **Special Academic Facilities/Equipment:** Art galleries, anthropology collection, 425-acre estate on Lake Michigan hosting retreats and seminars for students, new student center (Warch Center) electron microscope, laser physics lab, physics/computational graphics lab, nuclear magnetic resonance spectrometer **Computers:** 100% of classrooms, 20% of dorms, 100% of libraries, 100% of dining areas, 100% of student union, have wireless network access. Students can register for classes online. Administrative functions (other than registration) can be performed online.

CAMPUS LIFE

Environment: City. **Activities:** Choral groups, concert band, dance, drama/theater, jazz band, literary magazine, music ensembles, musical theater, opera, pep band, radio station, student government, student newspaper, student-run film society, symphony orchestra, yearbook, Campus Ministries, International Student Organization, Model UN 90 registered organizations, 5 honor societies, 3 religious organizations. 5 fraternities, 3 sororities. **Athletics (Intercollegiate):** *Men:* baseball, basketball, cross-country, diving, fencing, football, golf, ice hockey, soccer, swimming, tennis, track/field (outdoor), track/field (indoor), wrestling. *Women:* basketball, cross-country, diving, fencing, soccer, softball, swimming, tennis, track/field (outdoor), track/field (indoor), volleyball. **On-Campus Highlights:** Wriston Art Gallery, Music Conservatory, New Warch Campus Center -opening '09, New $18 million Science Building, Hiett Hall (new $8 million residence hall). **Environmental Initiatives:** Construction of LEED certified Student Center - Gold! Campus Garden (SLUG) http://blogs.lawrence.edu/SLUG/which provides produce to the dining hall and composts all food prep waste. Also serves an educational garden for the Community Garden Partnership of the Fox Cities. Lawrence has a long standing Environmental Studies Program and offers Majors and Minors. http:www.lawrence.edu/academics/enst/

ADMISSIONS

Freshman Academic Profile: Average high school GPA 3.6. 46% in top 10% of high school class, 71% in top 25% of high school class, 92% in top 50% of high school class. 70% from public high schools. SAT Math middle 50% range 580-710. SAT Critical Reading middle 50% range 580-720. SAT Writing middle 50% range 580-690. ACT middle 50% range 25-31. Minimum web-based TOEFL 90. Minimum paper TOEFL 577. **Basis for Candidate Selection:** *Very important factors considered include:* Class rank, academic GPA, rigor of secondary school record. *Important factors considered include:* application essay, recommendation(s), character/personal qualities, extracurricular activities, talent/ability. *Other factors considered include:* standardized test scores, alumni/ae relation, first generation, interview, racial/ethnic status, volunteer work, work experience. **Freshman Admission Requirements:** High school diploma is required and GED is not accepted. *Academic units required:* 4 English. *Academic units recommended:* 4 English. **Freshman Admission Statistics:** 2,599 applied, 76% admitted, 21% enrolled. **Transfer Admission Requirements:** High school transcript, college transcript(s), essay or personal statement, minimum college GPA of 2.75 required. Lowest grade transferable C–. **General Admission Information:** Application Fee $40. Early decision application deadline 11/15. Regular application deadline 1/15. Regular notification 4/1. Nonfall registration not accepted. Admission may be deferred for a maximum of 12 mo. Credit and/or placement offered for CEEB Advanced Placement tests.

COSTS AND FINANCIAL AID

Annual tuition $40,926. Room and board $8,496. Required fees $300. Average book expense $900. **Required Forms and Deadlines:** FAFSA, institution's own financial aid formCopies of Federal Tax Returns & W-2 forms for parent and student; Non-custodial parent form. **Notification of Awards:** Applicants will be notified of awards on a rolling basis beginning 3/1. **Types of Aid:** *Need-based scholarships/grants:* Federal Pell, SEOG, state scholarships/grants, private scholarships, the school's own gift aid. *Loans:* Direct Subsidized Stafford, Direct Unsubsidized Stafford, Direct PLUS, Federal Perkins. **Student Employment:** Federal Work-Study Program available. Institutional employment available. Highest amount earned per year from on-campus jobs $4,189. Off-campus job opportunities are good. **Financial Aid Statistics:** 100% freshmen, 98% undergrads receive need-based scholarship or grant aid. 3% freshmen, 3% undergrads receive non-need-based scholarship or grant aid. 79% freshmen, 82% undergrads receive need-based self-help aid. 95% freshmen, 94% undergrads receive any aid. 65% undergrads borrow to pay for school. Average cumulative indebtedness $30,724. **Criteria for awarding institutional aid:** *Non-need-based:* academics, alumni affiliation, leadership, minority status, music/drama.

LE MOYNE COLLEGE

Best 378

1419 Salt Springs Rd. Syracuse, NY 13214-1301
Phone: 315-445-4300 • **Financial Aid Phone:** 315-445-4400
E-mail: admission@lemoyne.edu • **CEEB Code:** 2366
Fax: 315-445-4711 • **Website:** www.lemoyne.edu • **ACT Code:** 2790

This private school, affiliated with the Roman Catholic Church, was founded in 1946. It has a 161-acre campus.

RATINGS
Admissions Selectivity Rating: 77   **Fire Safety Rating:** 91   **Green Rating:** 69

STUDENTS AND FACULTY
Enrollment: 2,549. **Student Body:** 59% female, 41% male, 6% out-of-state, 1% international (35 countries represented). Asian 2%, African American 5%, Caucasian 80%, Hispanic 5%, Native American 1%.
Retention and Graduation: 85% freshmen return for sophomore year. 58% freshmen graduate within 4 years. 69% freshmen graduate within 6 years. 35% grads go on to further study within 1 year. 15% grads pursue arts and sciences degrees. 4% grads pursue law degrees. 2% grads pursue business degrees. 10% grads pursue medical degrees. **Faculty:** Student/faculty ratio 13:1. 150 full-time faculty, 96% hold PhDs, 15% are members of minority groups, 41% are women. 0% of classes are taught by teaching assistants.

ACADEMICS
Degrees: bachelor's, master's, post-master's certificate. **Classes:** Most classes have 20–29 students. Most lab/discussion sessions have 10–19 students. **Majors with Highest Enrollment:** accounting; biology/biological sciences; psychology. **Special Study Options:** Accelerated program, double major, dual enrollment, honors program, independent study, internships, study abroad, teacher certification program, Certificate of Advanced Studies in Educational Leadership and Certificate of Advanced Studies in Nursing. **Honors Programs:** Students in the program complete a 21-hour sequence of interdisciplinary humanities courses that replaces the standard core requirements in English, history, philosophy, and religious studies. Seniors complete an honors project working in close collaboration with a faculty advisor. **Combined Degree Programs:** BA/MA, BA/DDS, BA/MEng, 3-4:Pre Optmtry (PA Coll) Pre-Podiatry (NY Coll),3-3:Dr of Physcl Thrpy. **Disability Services:** Special programs offered to physically disabled students include note-taking services, reader services, tape recorders, tutors. **Career Services:** Alumni network, alumni services, career/job search classes, career assessment, internships, regional alumni. Career Services highlights include Business and Science Internship Programs and Mock Interview week.

FACILITIES
Housing: Coed dorms, special housing for disabled students, men's dorms, women's dorms, apartments for single students, Living/Learning Communities. 96% of campus accessible to physically disabled. **Special Academic Facilities/Equipment:** Art gallery, audiovisual center, electron microscopes and Academic Support Center. **Computers:** 100% of classrooms, 75% of dorms, 100% of libraries, 100% of dining areas, 100% of student union, 100% of common outdoor areas have wireless network access. Students can register for classes online. Administrative functions (other than registration) can be performed online.

CAMPUS LIFE
Environment: City. **Activities:** Choral groups, concert band, dance, drama/theater, jazz band, literary magazine, music ensembles, musical theater, pep band, radio station, student government, student newspaper, student-run film society, television station, yearbook, Campus Ministries, International Student Organization, Model UN 70 registered organizations, 14 honor societies, 11 religious organizations. **Athletics (Intercollegiate):** *Men:* baseball, basketball, cross-country, diving, golf, lacrosse, soccer, swimming, tennis. *Women:* basketball, cross-country, diving, golf, lacrosse, soccer, softball, swimming, tennis, volleyball. **On-Campus Highlights:** The Thomas J. Niland Athletic Complex, Campus Center, The W.Carroll Coyne Center for the Performing Arts, Panasci Family Chapel, Noreen Reale Falcone Library. **Environmental Initiatives:** LEED certification on new science building. Project for LED lighting. Dining Services Food Composting.

ADMISSIONS
Freshman Academic Profile: Average high school GPA 3.4. 21% in top 10% of high school class, 55% in top 25% of high school class, 90% in top 50% of high school class. 80% from public high schools. SAT Math middle 50% range 490-610. SAT Critical Reading middle 50% range 480-580. ACT middle 50%

range 21-26. Minimum web-based TOEFL 79. Minimum paper TOEFL 550. **Basis for Candidate Selection:** *Very important factors considered include:* academic GPA, rigor of secondary school record. *Important factors considered include:* Class rank, application essay, recommendation(s), standardized test scores, extracurricular activities, interview, talent/ability, work experience. *Other factors considered include:* alumni/ae relation, character/personal qualities, geographical residence, level of applicant's interest, state residency, volunteer work. **Freshman Admission Requirements:** High school diploma is required and GED is accepted. *Academic units required:* 4 English, 3 mathematics, 3 science, 3 foreign language, 4 social studies. *Academic units recommended:* 4 English, 3 mathematics, 3 science, 3 foreign language, 4 social studies. **Freshman Admission Statistics:** 4,304 applied, 71?% enrolled. **Transfer Admission Requirements:** college transcript(s), essay or personal statement, minimum college GPA of 2.6 required. Lowest grade transferable C–. **General Admission Information:** Application Fee $35. Early decision application deadline 12/1. Notification on a rolling basis, beginning on or about 1/1. Nonfall registration accepted. Admission may be deferred for a maximum of 12 months. Credit and/or placement offered for CEEB Advanced Placement tests.

COSTS AND FINANCIAL AID
Annual tuition $28,470. Room and board $11,320. Required fees $990. Average book expense $1,300. **Required Forms and Deadlines:** FAFSA, institution's own financial aid form, state aid form. **Notification of Awards:** Applicants will be notified of awards on or about 3/15. **Types of Aid:** *Need-based scholarships/grants:* Federal Pell, SEOG, state scholarships/grants, private scholarships, the school's own gift aid. *Loans:* Subsidized Stafford, Unsubsidized Stafford, PLUS, Federal Perkins. **Student Employment:** Federal Work-Study Program available. Institutional employment available. Highest amount earned per year from on-campus jobs $2,000. Off-campus job opportunities are excellent. **Financial Aid Statistics:** 100% freshmen, 100% undergrads receive need-based scholarship or grant aid. 16% freshmen, 13% undergrads receive non-need-based scholarship or grant aid. 81% freshmen, 84% undergrads receive need-based self-help aid. 8% freshmen, 7% undergrads receive athletic scholarships. 92% freshmen, 93% undergrads receive any aid. 85% undergrads borrow to pay for school. Average cumulative indebtedness $34,532. **Criteria for awarding institutional aid:** *Non-need-based:* academics, alumni affiliation, athletics, leadership, minority status.

See page 1124.

LEBANON VALLEY COLLEGE

101 North College Avenue, Annville, PA 17003-1400
Phone: 717-867-6181 • **Financial Aid Phone:** 717-867-6126
E-mail: admission@lvc.edu • **CEEB Code:** 2364
Fax: 717-867-6026 • **Website:** www.lvc.edu • **ACT Code:** 3610

This private school, affiliated with the Methodist Church, was founded in 1866. It has a 340-acre campus.

RATINGS
Admissions Selectivity Rating: 79   **Fire Safety Rating:** 87   **Green Rating:** 65

STUDENTS AND FACULTY
Enrollment: 1,678. **Student Body:** 55% female, 45% male, 21% out-of-state, 0% international (3 countries represented). Asian 1%, African American 2%, Caucasian 87%, Hispanic 4%, Native American 0%.
Retention and Graduation: 86% freshmen return for sophomore year. 67% freshmen graduate within 4 years. 72% freshmen graduate within 6 years. 29% grads go on to further study within 1 year. 24% grads pursue arts and sciences degrees. 1% grads pursue law degrees. 2% grads pursue medical degrees. **Faculty:** Student/faculty ratio 12:1. 103 full-time faculty, 89% hold PhDs, 9% are members of minority groups, 41% are women. 0% of classes are taught by teaching assistants.

ACADEMICS
Degrees: associate, bachelor's, certificate, master's, post-bachelor's certificate, terminal associate. **Classes:** Most classes have 10–19 students. Most lab/discussion sessions have 10–19 students. **Majors with Highest Enrollment:** business/commerce; elementary education and teaching; health services/allied health/health sciences. **Special Study Options:** double major, dual enrollment, independent study, internships, liberal arts/career combination, student-designed major, study abroad, teacher certification program. **Combined Degree Programs:** Forestry/Environmental Studies - 3+2 w/ Duke. **Disability Services:** Special programs offered to physically disabled students include note-taking services, reader services, tape recorders, tutors. **Career Services:** Alumni network, alumni services, career assessment, internships Ca-

reer Services highlights include Career Connections is our on-line mentoring/networking system for connecting students with almuni who can assist in career planning and the job search.

FACILITIES

Housing: Coed dorms, special housing for disabled students, women's dorms, apartments for single students, theme housing suites. 80% of campus accessible to physically disabled. **Special Academic Facilities/Equipment:** Electric pianos, sound recording studio, transmission electron microscope, scanning electron microscope, Fourier transform infrared spectrometer, atomic absorption spectrometer, nuclear magnetic resonance spectrometer, molecular modeling lab, campus Arboretum, art gallery, therapy pool **Computers:** 100% of classrooms, 100% of dorms, 100% of libraries, 100% of dining areas, 100% of student union, 90% of common outdoor areas have wireless network access. Students can register for classes online. Administrative functions (other than registration) can be performed online.

CAMPUS LIFE

Environment: Rural. **Activities:** Choral groups, drama/theater, jazz band, literary magazine, marching band, music ensembles, musical theater, radio station, student government, student newspaper, symphony orchestra, yearbook, Campus Ministries 79 registered organizations, 6 honor societies, 14 religious organizations. 4 fraternities, 4 sororities. **Athletics (Intercollegiate):** *Men:* baseball, basketball, cross-country, football, golf, ice hockey, lacrosse, soccer, swimming, tennis, track/field (outdoor), track/field (indoor). *Women:* basketball, cross-country, field hockey, lacrosse, soccer, softball, swimming, tennis, track/field (outdoor), track/field (indoor), volleyball. **On-Campus Highlights:** Neidig Garber Science Center, Lynch Memorial - Synodinos Commons, The Peace Garden, Bishop Library, Suzanne Arnold Art Gallery and Zimmerman Recital Hall, Athletic fields are outstanding. Stanson Residence Hall, with 148 beds, was opened in Fall 2009. **Environmental Initiatives:** energy conservation recycling green products used in cleaning and grounds care

ADMISSIONS

Freshman Academic Profile: 38% in top 10% of high school class, 69% in top 25% of high school class, 93% in top 50% of high school class. 95% from public high schools. SAT Math middle 50% range 500-630. SAT Critical Reading middle 50% range 490-580. SAT Writing middle 50% range 470-580. ACT middle 50% range 20-26. Minimum web-based TOEFL 80. Minimum paper TOEFL 550. **Basis for Candidate Selection:** *Very important factors considered include:* Class rank, rigor of secondary school record. *Important factors considered include:* academic GPA, character/personal qualities, extracurricular activities, interview, level of applicant's interest, talent/ability. *Other factors considered include:* application essay, recommendation(s), standardized test scores, alumni/ae relation, first generation, geographical residence, racial/ethnic status, state residency, volunteer work, work experience. **Freshman Admission Requirements:** High school diploma is required and GED is accepted. *Academic units required:* 4 English, 3 mathematics, 2 science, 2 foreign language, 1 social studies. *Academic units recommended:* 4 English, 3 mathematics, 2 science, 2 foreign language, 1 social studies. **Freshman Admission Statistics:** 3,012 applied, 66% admitted, 20% enrolled. **Transfer Admission Requirements:** High school transcript, college transcript(s), essay or personal statement, statement of good standing from prior institution(s). Minimum college GPA of 2.0 required. Lowest grade transferable C–. **General Admission Information:** Application Fee $30. Notification on a rolling basis, beginning on or about 10/15. Nonfall registration accepted. Credit offered for CEEB Advanced Placement tests.

COSTS AND FINANCIAL AID

Annual tuition $33,670. Room and board $9,180. Required fees $800. Average book expense $1,100. **Required Forms and Deadlines:** FAFSA, institution's own financial aid form. **Notification of Awards:** Applicants will be notified of awards on a rolling basis beginning 3/1. **Types of Aid:** *Need-based scholarships/grants:* Federal Pell, SEOG, state scholarships/grants, private scholarships, the school's own gift aid. *Loans:* Subsidized Stafford, Unsubsidized Stafford, PLUS, Federal Perkins. **Student Employment:** Federal Work-Study Program available. Institutional employment available. Highest amount earned per year from on-campus jobs $901. Off-campus job opportunities are good. **Financial Aid Statistics:** 100% freshmen, 92% undergrads receive need-based scholarship or grant aid. 8% freshmen, 15% undergrads receive non-need-based scholarship or grant aid. 92% freshmen, 81% undergrads receive need-based self-help aid. 99% freshmen, 99% undergrads receive any aid. 84% undergrads borrow to pay for school. Average cumulative indebtedness $34,561. **Criteria for awarding institutional aid:** *Non-need-based:* academics, alumni affiliation, music/drama.

LEE UNIVERSITY

P.O. Box 3450, Cleveland, TN 37320-3450
Phone: 423-614-8500 • **Financial Aid Phone:** 423-614-8300
E-mail: admissions@leeuniversity.edu • **CEEB Code:** 1401
Fax: 423-614-8533 • **Website:** www.leeuniversity.edu • **ACT Code:** 3978

This private school, affiliated with the Church of God Church, was founded in 1918. It has a 115-acre campus.

RATINGS

Admissions Selectivity Rating: 72   **Fire Safety Rating:** 68   **Green Rating:** 60*

STUDENTS AND FACULTY

Enrollment: 4,217. **Student Body:** 56% female, 44% male, 56% out-of-state, 5% international (57 countries represented). Asian 1%, African American 7%, Caucasian 77%, Hispanic 4%, Native American 0%.
Retention and Graduation: 73% freshmen return for sophomore year. 33% freshmen graduate within 4 years. 49% freshmen graduate within 6 years. 20% grads go on to further study within 1 year. **Faculty:** Student/faculty ratio 18:1. 157 full-time faculty, 80% hold PhDs, 13% are members of minority groups, 31% are women. 0% of classes are taught by teaching assistants.

ACADEMICS

Degrees: bachelor's, master's, post-master's certificate. **Classes:** Most classes have 20–29 students. Most lab/discussion sessions have fewer than 10 students. **Majors with Highest Enrollment:** business administration and management; education, other; psychology. **Special Study Options:** distance learning, double major, dual enrollment, English as a Second Language (ESL), exchange student program (domestic), external degree program, honors program, independent study, internships, liberal arts/career combination, study abroad, teacher certification program. **Honors Programs:** The Kairos Scholars Honors Program. Also, several academic subject honors societies like Psychology, Business, Music and Pre-Med. **Disability Services:** Special programs offered to physically disabled students include reader services, tape recorders, tutors. **Career Services:** alumni services, career assessment, internships.

FACILITIES

Housing: men's dorms, women's dorms, apartments for married students, apartments for single students, wellness housing, Lee University leases apartments and houses for students. 71% of campus accessible to physically disabled. **Special Academic Facilities/Equipment:** Curriculum Library in the College of Education. **Computers:** 80% of classrooms, 50% of dorms, 100% of libraries, 100% of dining areas, 100% of student union, 50% of common outdoor areas have wireless network access. Students can register for classes online. Administrative functions (other than registration) can be performed online.

CAMPUS LIFE

Environment: Town. **Activities:** Choral groups, concert band, drama/theater, jazz band, literary magazine, music ensembles, musical theater, opera, pep band, student government, student newspaper, symphony orchestra, yearbook, Campus Ministries, International Student Organization, Model UN 72 registered organizations, 16 honor societies, 10 religious organizations. 5 fraternities, 4 sororities. **Athletics (Intercollegiate):** *Men:* baseball, basketball, cheerleading, cross-country, golf, soccer, tennis. *Women:* basketball, cheerleading, cross-country, soccer, softball, tennis, volleyball. **On-Campus Highlights:** Paul Conn Student Union-Bookstore, Pizza Hut, Chickfil, Conn Center-Home of Chapels, Concerts, etc. Dixon Center plays, recitals, community eents, De Vos Recreation Center, The House-Coffee House, and Jazzman's Cafe.

ADMISSIONS

Freshman Academic Profile: Average high school GPA 3.5. 26% in top 10% of high school class, 52% in top 25% of high school class, 79% in top 50% of high school class. 75% from public high schools. SAT Math middle 50% range 440-600. SAT Critical Reading middle 50% range 460-610. ACT middle 50% range 21-28. Minimum paper TOEFL 450. **Basis for Candidate Selection:** *Very important factors considered include:* academic GPA, rigor of secondary school record, standardized test scores. *Important factors considered include:* Class rank, character/personal qualities, level of applicant's interest. *Other factors considered include:* recommendation(s), alumni/ae relation, extracurricular activities, first generation, interview, talent/ability. **Freshman Admission Requirements:** High school diploma is required and GED is accepted. *Academic units required:* 4 English, 3 mathematics, 2 science, 1 foreign language, 2 social studies, 1 history. *Academic units recommended:* 4 English, 3 mathematics, 2 science, 1 foreign language, 2 social studies, 1 history. **Freshman Admission Statistics:** 1,782 applied, 89% admitted, 54% enrolled. **Transfer Admission Requirements:** college transcript(s), minimum college GPA of 2.0 required. Lowest grade transferable D. **General Admission Information:** Application Fee $25. Regular application deadline 9/1. Notification on a rolling basis, beginning on or about 9/1. Nonfall registration accepted. Admission may be deferred for a maximum of 1 semester. Credit and/or placement offered for CEEB Advanced Placement tests.

COSTS AND FINANCIAL AID

Annual tuition $12,720. Room and board $6,234. Required fees $650. Average book expense $1,100. **Required Forms and Deadlines:** FAFSA. **Notification of Awards:** Applicants will be notified of awards on a rolling basis beginning 2/1. **Types of Aid:** *Need-based scholarships/grants:* Federal Pell, SEOG, state scholarships/grants, private scholarships, the school's own gift aid. *Loans:* Subsidized Stafford, Unsubsidized Stafford, PLUS, Federal Perkins, college/university loans from institutional funds. **Student Employment:** Federal Work-Study Program available. Institutional employment available. Off-campus job opportunities are good. **Financial Aid Statistics:** 95% freshmen, 89% undergrads receive need-based scholarship or grant aid. 23% freshmen, 10% undergrads receive non-need-based scholarship or grant aid. 59% freshmen, 73% undergrads receive need-based self-help aid. 4% freshmen, 3% undergrads receive athletic scholarships. 64% undergrads borrow to pay for school. Average cumulative indebtedness $27,882. **Criteria for awarding institutional aid:** *Non-need-based:* academics, alumni affiliation, athletics, leadership, minority status, music/drama, religious affiliation, state/district residency.

LEHIGH UNIVERSITY

Best 378

27 Memorial Drive West, Bethlehem, PA 18015
Phone: 610-758-3100 • **Financial Aid Phone:** 610-758-3181
E-mail: admissions@lehigh.edu • **CEEB Code:** 2365
Fax: 610-758-4361 • **Website:** www.lehigh.edu • **ACT Code:** 3612

This private school was founded in 1865. It has a 1600-acre campus.

RATINGS

Admissions Selectivity Rating: 95   **Fire Safety Rating:** 87   **Green Rating:** 80

STUDENTS AND FACULTY

Enrollment: 4,857. **Student Body:** 43% female, 57% male, 74% out-of-state, 6% international (50 countries represented). Asian 6%, African American 4%, Caucasian 70%, Hispanic 8%, Native American 0%.
Retention and Graduation: 78% freshmen graduate within 4 years. 88% freshmen graduate within 6 years. 33% grads go on to further study within 1 year. 33% grads pursue arts and sciences degrees. 7% grads pursue law degrees. 9% grads pursue business degrees. 15% grads pursue medical degrees. **Faculty:** Student/faculty ratio 10:1. 493 full-time faculty, 97% hold PhDs, 18% are members of minority groups, 29% are women.

ACADEMICS

Degrees: bachelor's, doctoral, master's, post-bachelor's certificate, post-master's certificate. **Classes:** Most classes have 10–19 students. Most lab/discussion sessions have 10–19 students. **Majors with Highest Enrollment:** accounting; finance; mechanical engineering. **Special Study Options:** Accelerated program, cooperative education program, cross-registration, distance learning, double major, English as a Second Language (ESL), exchange student program (domestic), external degree program, honors program, independent study, internships, liberal arts/career combination, study abroad. **Honors Programs:** Integrated Business and Engineering (IBE) Honors Program, program description available http://www.lehigh.edu/~inibep/ **Combined Degree Programs:** BA/MD, BA/DDS, 7-year BA/OD Program with SUNY Optometry. **Disability Services:** Special programs offered to physically disabled students include note-taking services, reader services, tape recorders, tutors. **Career Services:** Alumni network, alumni services, career/job search classes, career assessment, internships, regional alumni. Career Services highlights include Lehigh University's Integrated Business and Engineering Honors Program infuses engineering thinking into the world of entrepreneurship and business. The interdisciplinary four-year program ends with a year-long experiential capstone project usually involving a high-tech startup. This senior project incorporates marketing, strategic planning and competitive analysis, along with product, process and system design issues.

FACILITIES

Housing: Coed dorms, special housing for disabled students, special housing for international students, fraternity/sorority housing, apartments for married students, apartments for single students, wellness housing, theme housing.

Special Academic Facilities/Equipment: Art Museum, Zoellner Arts Center Electron optical labs civil engineering lab particle accelerator electron optical labs **Computers:** 70% of classrooms, 100% of dorms, 100% of libraries, 100% of dining areas, 75% of student union, 80% of common outdoor areas have wireless network access. Students can register for classes online. Administrative functions (other than registration) can be performed online.

CAMPUS LIFE

Environment: City. **Activities:** Choral groups, concert band, dance, drama/theater, jazz band, literary magazine, marching band, music ensembles, musical theater, pep band, radio station, student government, student newspaper, student-run film society, symphony orchestra, yearbook, Campus Ministries, International Student Organization, Model UN 18 honor societies, 10 religious organizations. 21 fraternities, 9 sororities. **Athletics (Intercollegiate):** *Men:* baseball, basketball, cross-country, diving, football, golf, lacrosse, soccer, swimming, tennis, track/field (outdoor), track/field (indoor), wrestling. *Women:* basketball, crew/rowing, cross-country, diving, field hockey, golf, lacrosse, soccer, softball, swimming, tennis, track/field (outdoor), track/field (indoor), volleyball.
On-Campus Highlights: Zoellner Arts Center LU Art Galleries, Campus Square, Taylor Gymnasium, Ulrich Student Center, Goodman Campus. **Environmental Initiatives:** Lehigh's Eco-Rep program, a peer-to-peer education program focused on educating students in residential halls about sustainable lifestyles, has grown from 12 students and 2 residential halls in 2010 to 27 Eco-Reps in 14 Residential Halls and 11 Greek Houses in the 2011-2012 academic year. Sustainability Plan draft created in 2011 with a finalized and public version available in Spring 2012. A new sustainability-focused excursion, SustainabLEHIGH, was added to Lehigh's pre-orientation program. http://www.lehigh.edu/sustainability/sustainablehigh.html

ADMISSIONS

Freshman Academic Profile: 64% in top 10% of high school class, 92% in top 25% of high school class, 100% in top 50% of high school class. % from public high schools, SAT Math middle 50% range 630-730. SAT Critical Reading middle 50% range 570-670. ACT middle 50% range 28-31. Minimum web based TOEFL 90. Minimum paper TOEFL 570. **Basis for Candidate Selection:** *Very important factors considered include:* recommendation(s), rigor of secondary school record. *Important factors considered include:* application essay, standardized test scores, character/personal qualities, extracurricular activities, level of applicant's interest, talent/ability, volunteer work. *Other factors considered include:* Class rank, academic GPA, alumni/ae relation, first generation, geographical residence, racial/ethnic status, work experience. **Freshman Admission Requirements:** High school diploma or equivalent is not required. *Academic units required:* 4 English, 3 mathematics, 2 science, (2 science labs), 2 foreign language, 2 social studies, 3 academic electives. 4 English, 3 mathematics, 2 science, (2 science labs), 2 foreign language, 2 social studies, 3 academic electives. **Freshman Admission Statistics:** 11,529 applied, 33% admitted, 32% enrolled. **Transfer Admission Requirements:** High school transcript, college transcript(s), essay or personal statement, statement of good standing from prior institution(s). Minimum college GPA of 3.25 required. **General Admission Information:** Application Fee $70. Early decision application deadline 11/15. Regular application deadline 1/1. Regular notification 4/1. Nonfall registration accepted. Admission may be deferred for a maximum of 1 year. Credit and/or placement offered for CEEB Advanced Placement tests.

COSTS AND FINANCIAL AID

Annual tuition $41,920. Room and board $11,230. Required fees $300. Average book expense $1,000. **Required Forms and Deadlines:** FAFSA, CSS/Financial Aid PROFILE, noncustodial PROFILE, business/farm supplement. **Notification of Awards:** Applicants will be notified of awards on or about 3/30. **Types of Aid:** *Need-based scholarships/grants:* Federal Pell, SEOG, state scholarships/grants, private scholarships, the school's own gift aid, United Negro College Fund. *Loans:* Subsidized Stafford, Unsubsidized Stafford, PLUS, Federal Perkins, college/university loans from institutional funds. **Student Employment:** Federal Work-Study Program available. Institutional employment available. Off-campus job opportunities are good. **Financial Aid Statistics:** 96% freshmen, 97% undergrads receive need-based scholarship or grant aid. 9% freshmen, 10% undergrads receive non-need-based scholarship or grant aid. 96% freshmen, 96% undergrads receive need-based self-help aid. 3% freshmen, 2% undergrads receive athletic scholarships. 61% freshmen, 59% undergrads receive any aid. 54% undergrads borrow to pay for school. Average cumulative indebtedness $31,122. **Criteria for awarding institutional aid:** *Non-need-based:* academics, art, athletics, leadership, music/drama.

LEMOYNE-OWEN COLLEGE

807 Walker Avenue, Memphis, TN 38126
Phone: 901-942-7302 • **Financial Aid Phone:** 901-942-7313
E-mail: admission@loc.edu • **CEEB Code:** 1403
Fax: 901-942-6233 • **Website:** www.loc.edu • **ACT Code:** 3980

This private school was founded in 1862. It has a 15-acre campus.

RATINGS

Admissions Selectivity Rating: 64   **Fire Safety Rating:** 70   **Green Rating:** 60*

STUDENTS AND FACULTY

Enrollment: 720. **Student Body:** 0% female, 100% male, 3% out-of-state, 2% international. Asian 0%, African American 98%, Caucasian 0%, Hispanic 0%, Native American 0%.
Retention and Graduation: 38% freshmen graduate within 4 years. 49% freshmen graduate within 6 years. **Faculty:** Student/faculty ratio 12:1. 54 full-time faculty, 80% hold PhDs, 89% are members of minority groups, 50% are women. 85% of classes are taught by teaching assistants.

ACADEMICS

Degrees: bachelor's, post-bachelor's certificate. **Classes:** Most classes have 20–29 students. **Majors with Highest Enrollment:** business/commerce; education. **Special Study Options:** cross-registration, double major, honors program, independent study, internships, student-designed major, study abroad, teacher certification program, Undergrads may take Grad level courses. **Combined Degree Programs:** BA/MEng, Dual Degree Program in English. **Career Services:** Alumni network, alumni services, career/job search classes, career assessment, internships, regional alumni.

FACILITIES

Housing: Coed dorms, men's dorms, women's dorms. 85% of campus accessible to physically disabled. Special Academic Facilities/Equipment: Museum/gallery, language lab. CAMPUS LIFE
Environment: Metropolis. **Activities:** Choral groups, drama/theater, jazz band, music ensembles, student government, student newspaper, yearbook 5 honor societies, 6 religious organizations. 4 fraternities, 3 sororities. **Athletics (Intercollegiate):** *Men:* baseball, basketball, cross-country, tennis. *Women:* basketball, cross-country, softball, tennis, volleyball.

ADMISSIONS

Freshman Academic Profile: 95% from public high schools. Minimum paper TOEFL 475. **Basis for Candidate Selection:** *Very important factors considered include:* standardized test scores. **Freshman Admission Requirements:** High school diploma is required and GED is accepted. **Freshman Admission Statistics:** 1,118 applied, 17% admitted, 63% enrolled. **Transfer Admission Requirements:** college transcript(s), standardized test scores, minimum college GPA of 2.0 required. Lowest grade transferable C. **General Admission Information:** Application Fee $25. Regular application deadline 6/15. Nonfall registration accepted. Credit and/or placement offered for CEEB Advanced Placement tests.

COSTS AND FINANCIAL AID

Annual tuition $8,250. Room and board $4,620. Required fees $200. Average book expense $700. **Required Forms and Deadlines:** FAFSA. **Notification of Awards: Types of Aid:** *Need-based scholarships/grants:* United Negro College Fund. *Loans:* Subsidized Stafford, PLUS. **Student Employment:** Federal Work-Study Program available. Institutional employment available.

LENOIR-RHYNE COLLEGE

Admissions Office, Hickory, NC 28603
Phone: 828-328-7300
E-mail: admission@lrc.edu • **CEEB Code:** 5365
Fax: 828-328-7378 • **Website:** www.lrc.edu • **ACT Code:** 2941

This private school, affiliated with the Lutheran Church, was founded in 1891. It has a 100-acre campus.

RATINGS

Admissions Selectivity Rating: 68   **Fire Safety Rating:** 60*   **Green Rating:** 60*

STUDENTS AND FACULTY

Enrollment: 1,358. **Student Body:** 64% female, 36% male, 29% out-of-state, 0% international. Asian 1%, African American 7%, Caucasian 91%, Hispanic 1%, Native American 0%.

Retention and Graduation: 80% freshmen return for sophomore year. 40% grads go on to further study within 1 year. 1% grads pursue arts and sciences degrees. 4% grads pursue law degrees. 5% grads pursue business degrees. 4% grads pursue medical degrees. **Faculty:** Student/faculty ratio 12:1. 107 full-time faculty, 108% hold PhDs, 45% are women. 0% of classes are taught by teaching assistants.

ACADEMICS

Degrees: bachelor's, certificate, master's. **Special Study Options:** Accelerated program, double major, dual enrollment, English as a Second Language (ESL), honors program, independent study, internships, student-designed major, study abroad, teacher certification program. **Combined Degree Programs:** BA/MEng. **Disability Services:** Special programs offered to physically disabled students include note-taking services, tutors. **Career Services:** alumni services, career/job search classes, career assessment, internships.

FACILITIES

Housing: Coed dorms, special housing for disabled students, men's dorms, women's dorms, fraternity/sorority housing, Honors, Hearing Impaired. 90% of campus accessible to physically disabled. Special Academic Facilities/Equipment: Language lab. CAMPUS LIFE
Environment: Village. **Activities:** Choral groups, concert band, dance, drama/theater, jazz band, music ensembles, musical theater, pep band, radio station, student government, student newspaper, television station, yearbook 54 registered organizations, 10 honor societies, 6 religious organizations. 4 fraternities, 4 sororities. **Athletics (Intercollegiate):** *Men:* baseball, basketball, cheerleading, cross-country, football, golf, soccer. *Women:* basketball, cheerleading, cross-country, golf, soccer, softball, volleyball. **On-Campus Highlights:** McCrorie Center, Cromer College Center, Shuford Fitness Center, Living and Learning Center, Quad.

ADMISSIONS

Freshman Academic Profile: 90% from public high schools. SAT Math middle 50% range 470-580. SAT Critical Reading middle 50% range 460-570. ACT middle 50% range 17-24. Minimum paper TOEFL 500. **Basis for Candidate Selection:** *Very important factors considered include:* rigor of secondary school record, standardized test scores. *Important factors considered include:* Class rank, interview. *Other factors considered include:* application essay, recommendation(s), character/personal qualities, extracurricular activities, volunteer work, work experience. **Freshman Admission Requirements:** High school diploma is required and GED is accepted. *Academic units required:* 4 English, 3 mathematics, 1 science, (1 science labs), 2 foreign language, 1 social studies, 1 history. 4 English, 3 mathematics, 1 science, (1 science labs), 2 foreign language, 1 social studies, 1 history. **Freshman Admission Statistics:** 915 applied, 85% admitted, 35% enrolled. **Transfer Admission Requirements:** college transcript(s), statement of good standing from prior institution(s). Minimum college GPA of 2.5 required. Lowest grade transferable C. **General Admission Information:** Application Fee $25. Notification on a rolling basis, beginning on or about 9/1. Nonfall registration accepted. Admission may be deferred for a maximum of 1 year. Credit offered for CEEB Advanced Placement tests.

COSTS AND FINANCIAL AID

Annual tuition $12,870. Room and board $4,920. Required fees $486. Average book expense $700. **Required Forms and Deadlines:** FAFSA, institution's own financial aid form, state aid form. **Notification of Awards: Types of Aid:** *Need-based scholarships/grants:* Federal Pell, SEOG, state scholarships/grants, the school's own gift aid. *Loans:* Direct Subsidized Stafford, Direct Unsubsidized Stafford, Direct PLUS, Federal Perkins. **Student Employment:** Federal Work-Study Program available. Institutional employment available. Highest amount earned per year from on-campus jobs $1,000. Off-campus job opportunities are excellent. **Criteria for awarding institutional aid:** *Non-need-based:* academics, alumni affiliation, athletics, leadership, minority status, music/drama, religious affiliation, state/district residency.

LESLEY COLLEGE AT LESLEY UNIVERSITY

Office of Admissions, Cambridge, MA 2138
Phone: 617-349-8800 • **Financial Aid Phone:** 617-349-8710
E-mail: lcadmissions@lesley.edu • **CEEB Code:** 3483
Fax: 617-349-8810 • **Website:** www.lesley.edu • **ACT Code:** 1850

This private school was founded in 1909. It has a 1-acre campus.

RATINGS

Admissions Selectivity Rating: 77   **Fire Safety Rating:** 87   **Green Rating:** 67

STUDENTS AND FACULTY

Enrollment: 1,451. **Student Body:** 75% female, 25% male, 44% out-of-state, 2% international (30 countries represented). Asian 3%, African American 3%, Caucasian 60%, Hispanic 5%, Native American 1%.

Retention and Graduation: 74% freshmen return for sophomore year. 38% freshmen graduate within 4 years. **Faculty:** Student/faculty ratio 11:1. 65 full-time faculty, 83% hold PhDs, 15% are members of minority groups, 54% are women. 0% of classes are taught by teaching assistants.

ACADEMICS

Degrees: associate, bachelor's, certificate, diploma, master's, post-bachelor's certificate, post-master's certificate. **Classes:** Most classes have 10–19 students. **Majors with Highest Enrollment:** counseling psychology; elementary education and teaching; marketing/marketing management. **Special Study Options:** Accelerated program, cross-registration, distance learning, double major, dual enrollment, exchange student program (domestic), honors program, independent study, internships, liberal arts/career combination, student-designed major, study abroad, teacher certification program, Studio courses. **Combined Degree Programs:** BA/MA, BS/M.Ed. **Disability Services:** Special programs offered to physically disabled students include note-taking services, reader services, tape recorders, tutors. **Career Services:** Alumni network, alumni services, career/job search classes, career assessment, internships, regional alumni. Career Services highlights include Wellesley College funded at least one internship for more than half the class of 2009. This included grants of up $3,500 for what otherwise would have been unpaid internships over the summer.

FACILITIES

Housing: Coed dorms, women's dorms, Special Interest and themed housing. 85% of campus accessible to physically disabled. **Special Academic Facilities/Equipment:** Kresge Center for Teaching Resources and Educational Software Collection, Marran Art Gallery, Porter Exchange Gallery, AIB Main Gallery **Computers:** 100% of classrooms, 100% of libraries, 100% of dining areas, 100% of student union, 20% of common outdoor areas have wireless network access. Students can register for classes online. Administrative functions (other than registration) can be performed online.

CAMPUS LIFE

Environment: Metropolis. **Activities:** Choral groups, dance, drama/theater, literary magazine, musical theater, student government, student newspaper, Campus Ministries, International Student Organization 25 registered organizations, 2 honor societies, 2 religious organizations. **Athletics (Intercollegiate):** *Men:* basketball, cross-country, soccer, tennis, volleyball. *Women:* basketball, crew/rowing, cross-country, soccer, softball, tennis, volleyball. **On Campus Highlights:** Student Center, Ludke Library, Porter Exchange Building, Stebbins Fitness Room, Kresge Center for Teaching Resources. **Environmental Initiatives:** The continual enhancement of recycling, waste management and composting programs on campus. The formation of sustainability recommendations for faculty, staff and students. Student groups on campus are involved with and sponsor sustainability events.

ADMISSIONS

Freshman Academic Profile: Average high school GPA 2.9. 14% in top 10% of high school class, 43% in top 25% of high school class, 77% in top 50% of high school class. 83% from public high schools. SAT Math middle 50% range 470–570. SAT Critical Reading middle 50% range 490–600. SAT Writing middle 50% range 480–590. ACT middle 50% range 21–27. Minimum web-based TOEFL 61. Minimum paper TOEFL 500. **Basis for Candidate Selection:** *Very important factors considered include:* academic GPA, rigor of secondary school record. *Important factors considered include:* Class rank, application essay, recommendation(s), standardized test scores, character/personal qualities, extracurricular activities, interview, talent/ability, volunteer work. *Other factors considered include:* alumni/ae relation, first generation, geographical residence, level of applicant's interest, racial/ethnic status, work experience. **Freshman Admission Requirements:** High school diploma is required and GED is accepted. *Academic units required:* 4 English, 3 mathematics, 3 science, (2 science labs), 1 social studies, 1 history, 4 academic electives. *Academic units recommended:* 4 English, 3 mathematics, 3 science, (2 science labs), 1 social studies, 1 history, 4 academic electives. **Freshman Admission Statistics:** 2,588 applied, 68% admitted, 23% enrolled. **Transfer Admission Requirements:** High school transcript, college transcript(s), essay or personal statement, statement of good standing from prior institution(s). Minimum college GPA of 2.5 required. Lowest grade transferable C. **General Admission Information:** Application Fee $50. Notification on a rolling basis, beginning on or about 1/15. Nonfall registration accepted. Admission may be deferred for a maximum of 1 year. Credit and/or placement offered for CEEB Advanced Placement tests.

COSTS AND FINANCIAL AID

Annual tuition $30,170. Room and board $13,250. Required fees $250. Average book expense $700. **Required Forms and Deadlines:** FAFSA. **Notification of Awards:** Applicants will be notified of awards on a rolling basis beginning 2/15. **Types of Aid:** *Need-based scholarships/grants:* Federal Pell, SEOG, state scholarships/grants, private scholarships, the school's own gift aid. *Loans:* Direct Subsidized Stafford, Direct Unsubsidized Stafford, Direct PLUS, Federal Perkins, state loans. **Student Employment:** Federal Work-Study Program available. Institutional employment available. Highest amount earned per year from on-campus jobs $1,200. Off-campus job opportunities are excellent. **Financial Aid Statistics:** 73% freshmen, 75% undergrads receive need-based scholarship or grant aid. 60% freshmen, 25% undergrads receive non-need-based scholarship or grant aid. 85% freshmen, 94% undergrads receive need-based self-help aid. 70% freshmen, 70% undergrads receive any aid. 90% undergrads borrow to pay for school. Average cumulative indebtedness $18,000. **Criteria for awarding institutional aid:** *Non-need-based:* academics, art, leadership, minority status, state/district residency.

LETOURNEAU UNIVERSITY

PO Box 7001, Longview, TX 75607-7001
Phone: 903-233-4300
E-mail: admissions@letu.edu • **CEEB Code:** 6365
Fax: 903-233-4301 • **Website:** www.letu.edu • **ACT Code:** 4120

This private school was founded in 1946. It has a 162-acre campus.

RATINGS

Admissions Selectivity Rating: 77   **Fire Safety Rating:** 60*   **Green Rating:** 60*

STUDENTS AND FACULTY

Enrollment: 2,343. **Student Body:** 49% female, 51% male, 44% out-of-state, 3% international (24 countries represented). Asian 1%, African American 12%, Caucasian 65%, Hispanic 9%, Native American 1%.

Retention and Graduation: 78% freshmen return for sophomore year. 19% grads go on to further study within 1 year. **Faculty:** Student/faculty ratio 15:1, 96 full-time faculty, 15% are members of minority groups, 24% are women.

ACADEMICS

Degrees: associate, bachelor's, master's. **Classes:** Most classes have fewer than 10 students. Most lab/discussion sessions have 10–19 students. **Majors with Highest Enrollment:** aviation/airway management and operations; business/commerce; engineering. **Special Study Options:** Accelerated program, cooperative education program, distance learning, double major, dual enrollment, honors program, independent study, internships, study abroad, teacher certification program, weekend college. **Career Services:** alumni services, career/job search classes, career assessment, internships.

FACILITIES

Housing: special housing for disabled students, men's dorms, special housing for international students, women's dorms, apartments for married students, apartments for single students, theme housing, residential societies available. **Special Academic Facilities/Equipment:** Longview Citizens Resource Center; R.G. LeTourneau Memorial Museum **Computers:** Students can register for classes online. Administrative functions (other than registration) can be performed online.

CAMPUS LIFE

Environment: Town. **Activities:** Choral groups, drama/theater, jazz band, literary magazine, music ensembles, musical theater, student government, student newspaper, student-run film society, yearbook, Campus Ministries, International Student Organization 44 registered organizations, 4 honor societies, 10 religious organizations. **Athletics (Intercollegiate):** *Men:* baseball, basketball, cross-country, golf, soccer, tennis. *Women:* basketball, cross-country, golf, soccer, softball, tennis, volleyball.

ADMISSIONS

Freshman Academic Profile: Average high school GPA 3.6. 50% in top 10% of high school class, 70% in top 25% of high school class, 93% in top 50% of high school class. 56% from public high schools. SAT Math middle 50% range 550–660. SAT Critical Reading middle 50% range 510–660. SAT Writing middle 50% range 480–610. ACT middle 50% range 22–29. Minimum paper TOEFL 500. **Basis for Candidate Selection:** *Very important factors considered include:* academic GPA, rigor of secondary school record, standardized test scores. *Important factors considered include:* Class rank, application essay, character/personal qualities, religious affiliation/commitment. *Other factors considered include:* recommendation(s), alumni/ae relation, extracurricular activities, first generation, interview, racial/ethnic status, talent/ability, volunteer work. **Freshman Admission Requirements:** High school diploma is required and GED is accepted. *Academic units required:* 4 English, 3 mathematics, 3 science, (3 science labs), 2 social studies, 1 history. *Academic units recommended:* 4 English, 3 mathematics, 3 science, (3 science labs), 2 social studies, 1 history. **Freshman Admission Statistics:** 1,684 applied, 43% admitted, 50% enrolled. **Transfer Admission Requirements:** college transcript(s), essay or personal statement, minimum college GPA of 2.0 required. Lowest grade transferable C. **General Admission Information:** Application Fee $25. Regular notification 8/26. Notification on a rolling basis, beginning on or about 9/15. Nonfall registration accepted. Credit and/or placement offered for CEEB Advanced Placement tests.

COSTS AND FINANCIAL AID
Annual tuition $24,050. Room and board $8,940. Required fees $490. Average book expense $1,470. **Required Forms and Deadlines:** FAFSA. **Notification of Awards:** Applicants will be notified of awards on a rolling basis beginning 3/1. **Types of Aid:** *Need-based scholarships/grants:* Federal Pell, SEOG, state scholarships/grants, private scholarships, the school's own gift aid. *Loans:* Subsidized Stafford, Unsubsidized Stafford, PLUS, Federal Perkins, state loans. **Student Employment:** Federal Work-Study Program available. Institutional employment available. Off-campus job opportunities are excellent. **Financial Aid Statistics:** 100% freshmen, 96% undergrads receive need-based scholarship or grant aid. 8% freshmen, 6% undergrads receive non-need-based scholarship or grant aid. 71% freshmen, 53% undergrads receive need-based self-help aid. 96% undergrads receive any aid. 82% undergrads borrow to pay for school. Average cumulative indebtedness $30,295. **Criteria for awarding institutional aid:** *Non-need-based:* academics, leadership.

LEWIS & CLARK COLLEGE

0615 SW Palatine Hill Road, Portland, OR 97219-7899
Phone: 503-768-7040 • **Financial Aid Phone:** 503-768-7090
E-mail: admissions@lclark.edu • **CEEB Code:** 4384
Fax: 503-768-7055 • **Website:** www.lclark.edu • **ACT Code:** 3464

This private school was founded in 1867. It has a 137-acre campus.

RATINGS
Admissions Selectivity Rating: 92   **Fire Safety Rating:** 96   **Green Rating:** 99

STUDENTS AND FACULTY
Enrollment: 2,031. **Student Body:** 59% female, 41% male, 81% out-of-state, 5% international (69 countries represented). Asian 4%, African American 2%, Caucasian 61%, Hispanic 7%, Native American 1%.
Retention and Graduation: 88% freshmen return for sophomore year. 66% freshmen graduate within 4 years. 75% freshmen graduate within 6 years. 17% grads go on to further study within 1 year. 14% grads pursue arts and sciences degrees. 1% grads pursue law degrees. 1% grads pursue business degrees. 2% grads pursue medical degrees. **Faculty:** Student/faculty ratio 12:1. 229 full-time faculty, 95% hold PhDs, 14% are members of minority groups, 47% are women. 0% of classes are taught by teaching assistants.

ACADEMICS
Degrees: bachelor's, first professional, master's, post-master's certificate. **Classes:** Most classes have 20–29 students. Most lab/discussion sessions have 20–29 students. **Majors with Highest Enrollment:** biology/biological sciences; international relations and affairs; psychology. **Special Study Options:** Accelerated program, cross-registration, double major, dual enrollment, English as a Second Language (ESL), honors program, independent study, internships, student-designed major, study abroad, teacher certification program, Teacher certification is graduate level only. **Honors Programs:** Honors are designated by each department **Combined Degree Programs:** BA/MA, BA/MAT, 4+1 yr Masters Degree and credential. **Disability Services:** Special programs offered to physically disabled students include note-taking services, reader services, tape recorders, tutors. **Career Services:** Alumni network, alumni services, career assessment, internships, regional alumni.

FACILITIES
Housing: Coed dorms, women's dorms, Theme Floors, Apartment-style residence halls for upper-class students. 85% of campus accessible to physically disabled. **Special Academic Facilities/Equipment:** Art gallery, observatory, world music room, 85 Rank Casavant organ, renovated greenhouse. **Computers:** 50% of classrooms, 20% of dorms, 100% of libraries, 25% of common outdoor areas have wireless network access. Students can register for classes online. Administrative functions (other than registration) can be performed online.

CAMPUS LIFE
Environment: City. **Activities:** Choral groups, concert band, dance, drama/theater, jazz band, literary magazine, music ensembles, musical theater, radio station, student government, student newspaper, symphony orchestra, television

station, yearbook, Campus Ministries, International Student Organization, Model UN 70 registered organizations, 5 honor societies, 9 religious organizations. **Athletics (Intercollegiate):** *Men:* baseball, basketball, crew/rowing, cross-country, football, golf, swimming, tennis, track/field (outdoor). *Women:* basketball, crew/rowing, cross-country, golf, soccer, softball, swimming, tennis, track/field (outdoor), volleyball. **On-Campus Highlights:** Gallery of Contemporary Art, New residence halls/Maggie's Cafe, Library, Templeton Student Center, Pamplin Sports Center, Howard Hall, newest academic building. **Environmental Initiatives:** Lewis & Clark provides students, faculty, and staff with a fare-free shuttle bus system that allows access to downtown Portland, local neighborhoods, and retail stores. We installed a 100KW photovoltaic system. Students funds are used to purchase green power. Lewis & Clark established an Environmental Council in the late 1990's that has since been renamed as the Sustainability Council. The trustee investment committee has made a $3 million committment to fund sustainable energy development. Since 1991 Lewis & Clark has invested in energy conservation projects that have resulted in a current annual reduction in use of 4,000,000 kWh of electricity and 230,000 Therms of natural gas with a corresponding decrease in carbon footprint.

ADMISSIONS
Freshman Academic Profile: Average high school GPA 3.7. 40% in top 10% of high school class, 77% in top 25% of high school class, 99% in top 50% of high school class. 73% from public high schools. SAT Math middle 50% range 580-670. SAT Critical Reading middle 50% range 610-710. SAT Writing middle 50% range 590-680. ACT middle 50% range 27-30. Minimum paper TOEFL 550. **Basis for Candidate Selection:** *Very important factors considered include:* academic GPA, rigor of secondary school record, racial/ethnic status. *Important factors considered include:* Class rank, application essay, recommendation(s), standardized test scores, alumni/ae relation, character/personal qualities, extracurricular activities, first generation, talent/ability, volunteer work. *Other factors considered include:* geographical residence, interview, level of applicant's interest, state residency, work experience. **Freshman Admission Requirements:** High school diploma is required and GED is accepted. **Freshman Admission Statistics:** 5,950 applied, 66% admitted, 15% enrolled. **Transfer Admission Requirements:** High school transcript, college transcript(s), essay or personal statement, statement of good standing from prior institution(s). Minimum college GPA of 2.0 required. Lowest grade transferable C. **General Admission Information:** Application Fee $50. Regular application deadline 2/1. Regular notification 4/1. Nonfall registration accepted. Admission may be deferred for a maximum of One year. Credit and/or placement offered for CEEB Advanced Placement tests.

COSTS AND FINANCIAL AID
Annual tuition $39,970. Room and board $10,014. Required fees $360. Average book expense $1,050. **Required Forms and Deadlines:** FAFSA, CSS/Financial Aid PROFILE. **Notification of Awards:** Applicants will be notified of awards on a rolling basis beginning 3/1. **Types of Aid:** *Need-based scholarships/grants:* Federal Pell, SEOG, state scholarships/grants, private scholarships, the school's own gift aid. *Loans:* Direct Subsidized Stafford, Direct Unsubsidized Stafford, Direct PLUS, Subsidized Stafford, Unsubsidized Stafford, PLUS, Federal Perkins. **Student Employment:** Federal Work-Study Program available. Institutional employment available. Highest amount earned per year from on-campus jobs $1,800. Off-campus job opportunities are fair. **Financial Aid Statistics:** 100% freshmen, 100% undergrads receive need-based scholarship or grant aid. 8% freshmen, 7% undergrads receive non-need-based scholarship or grant aid. 92% freshmen, 90% undergrads receive need-based self-help aid. 69% freshmen, 62% undergrads receive any aid. 47% undergrads borrow to pay for school. Average cumulative indebtedness $22,956. **Criteria for awarding institutional aid:** *Non-need-based:* academics, leadership, music/drama.

See page 1126.

LEWIS UNIVERSITY

One University Parkway, Romeoville, IL 60446
Phone: 815-836-5250 • **Financial Aid Phone:** 815-836-5263
E-mail: admissions@lewisu.edu • **CEEB Code:** 1404
Fax: 815-836-5002 • **Website:** www.lewisu.edu • **ACT Code:** 1058

This private school, affiliated with the Roman Catholic Church, was founded in 1932. It has a 375-acre campus.

RATINGS
Admissions Selectivity Rating: 86   **Fire Safety Rating:** 87   **Green Rating:** 68

STUDENTS AND FACULTY
Enrollment: 4,452. **Student Body:** 57% female, 43% male, 6% out-of-state, 1% international (36 countries represented). Asian 3%, African American 8%, Caucasian 64%, Hispanic 16%, Native American 0%.

Retention and Graduation: 82% freshmen return for sophomore year. 40% freshmen graduate within 4 years. 59% freshmen graduate within 6 years. **Faculty:** Student/faculty ratio 13:1. 212 full-time faculty, 68% hold PhDs, 14% are members of minority groups, 51% are women. 0% of classes are taught by teaching assistants.

ACADEMICS

Degrees: associate, bachelor's, certificate, master's, post-master's certificate. **Classes:** Most classes have 10–19 students. Most lab/discussion sessions have 10–19 students. **Majors with Highest Enrollment:** business/commerce; criminal justice/police science; nursing/registered nurse (rn, asn, bsn, msn). **Special Study Options:** Accelerated program, distance learning, double major, dual enrollment, English as a Second Language (ESL), exchange student program (domestic), honors program, independent study, internships, liberal arts/career combination, student-designed major, study abroad, teacher certification program. **Honors Programs:** Honors Program offers academically motivated students opportunities for active and collaborative learning. Students have the opporuntiy to fulfill many of their general education requirements in a "paired course" arrangement that allows for greater integration of material and content. **Combined Degree Programs:** BA/MA, MSN-MBA / BS - MBA. **Disability Services:** Special programs offered to physically disabled students include note-taking services, tape recorders, tutors. **Career Services:** Alumni network, alumni services, career/job search classes, career assessment, internships, regional alumni. Career Services highlights include Our Alumni Volunteer Network pairs current stduents with professionals active in their field of interest for mentoring and career search guidance.

FACILITIES

Housing: Coed dorms, special housing for disabled students, theme housing, 95% of campus accessible to physically disabled. **Special Academic Facilities/Equipment:** Lewis University is located immediately adjacent to the Lewis University airport, and contains an aviation complex, which includes a Boeing 737 located on campus for use by students studying aviation maintenance. Special collections on campus include: Curriculum Collection, Eva White Memorial Aviation Collection, Library of American Civilization (ultrafiche), Library of English Literature (ultrafiche), ERIC fiche, Government Documents (Lewis University has housed a selective Federal Depository since 1952, and possesses a strong collection of the public documents generated during each decennial census), and Canal and Regional History Collection/I and M Canal Archives (one of the largest collections of documents, photographs, and artifacts pertaining to the canal era in the U.S.). **Computers:** 100% of classrooms, 100% of dorms, 100% of libraries, 100% of dining areas, 100% of student union, 100% of common outdoor areas have wireless network access. Students can register for classes online. Administrative functions (other than registration) can be performed online.

CAMPUS LIFE

Environment: Metropolis. **Activities:** Choral groups, dance, drama/theater, jazz band, literary magazine, music ensembles, musical theater, radio station, student government, student newspaper, television station, Campus Ministries, International Student Organization 45 registered organizations, 10 honor societies, 7 religious organizations. 7 fraternities, 6 sororities. **Athletics (Intercollegiate):** *Men:* baseball, basketball, cheerleading, cross-country, golf, soccer, swimming, tennis, track/field (outdoor), track/field (indoor), volleyball. *Women:* basketball, cheerleading, cross-country, golf, soccer, softball, swimming, tennis, track/field (outdoor), track/field (indoor), volleyball. **On-Campus Highlights:** Harold E. White Aviation Center, Student Recreation and Fitness Center, Philip Lynch Theatre, Student Union/Bookstore, Flyer's Den. **Environmental Initiatives:** The Lewis University Environment and Energy Conservation Council sponsors annual events such as an Earth Day event in spring where we clear out Buckthorn (an invasive plant species) from the nature trail here on campus and the Arbor Day Initiative in which we plant an assortment of native trees back into the University nature trail. Lewis sponsors an annual Come Clean, Go Green Sustainability Contest. One-half of the prize money goes toward the creation and implementation of the winning projects, which are then publicized. The other half of the prize money goes directly to the winner(s). There is an awards ceremony to honor the winning proposals and to distribute prizes. On September 24, 2010, Lewis in yet another step to show the college commitment to sustainability, joined 10 other Illiinois colleges and universities in signing the renewed Illinois Campus Sustainability Compact during a Sustainability Workshop. By signing this compact together, these institutions made themselves accountable to completing certain tasks that will work toward measured improvements and integrate sustainability in campus operations, academic and research programs, student activities, and community outreach.

ADMISSIONS

Freshman Academic Profile: Average high school GPA 3.3. 13% in top 10% of high school class, 40% in top 25% of high school class, 77% in top 50% of high school class. 80% from public high schools. SAT Math middle 50% range 500-640. SAT Critical Reading middle 50% range 480-610. SAT Writing middle 50% range 540-570. ACT middle 50% range 20-25. Minimum web-based TOEFL 79. Minimum paper TOEFL 550. **Basis for Candidate Selection:** *Very important factors considered include:* academic GPA, rigor of secondary school record, standardized test scores. *Important factors considered include:* application essay. *Other factors considered include:* Class rank, recommendation(s), alumni/ae relation, character/personal qualities, extracurricular activities, first generation, geographical residence, interview, level of applicant's interest, racial/ethnic status, talent/ability, volunteer work, work experience. **Freshman Admission Requirements:** High school diploma is required and GED is accepted. *Academic units required:* 3 English. *Academic units recommended:* 3 English. **Freshman Admission Statistics:** 5,568 applied, 56% admitted, 22% enrolled. **Transfer Admission Requirements:** college transcript(s), minimum college GPA of 2.0 required. Lowest grade transferable D. **General Admission Information:** Application Fee $40. Notification on a rolling basis, beginning on or about 10/1. Nonfall registration accepted. Admission may be deferred for a maximum of 12 months. Credit and/or placement offered for CEEB Advanced Placement tests.

COSTS AND FINANCIAL AID

Annual tuition $25,770. Room and board $9,200. Average book expense $1,000. **Required Forms and Deadlines:** FAFSA. **Notification of Awards:** Applicants will be notified of awards on a rolling basis beginning 2/1. **Types of Aid:** *Need-based scholarships/grants:* Federal Pell, SEOG, state scholarships/grants, private scholarships, the school's own gift aid, Federal Nursing Scholarships. *Loans:* Subsidized Stafford, Unsubsidized Stafford, PLUS, Federal Perkins. **Student Employment:** Federal Work-Study Program available. Institutional employment available. Highest amount earned per year from on-campus jobs $3,000. Off-campus job opportunities are good. **Financial Aid Statistics:** 100% freshmen, 94% undergrads receive need-based scholarship or grant aid. 12% freshmen, 10% undergrads receive non-need-based scholarship or grant aid. 83% freshmen, 87% undergrads receive need-based self-help aid. 2% freshmen, 2% undergrads receive athletic scholarships. 99% freshmen, 86% undergrads receive any aid. 82% undergrads borrow to pay for school. Average cumulative indebtedness $31,100. **Criteria for awarding institutional aid:** *Non-need-based:* academics, alumni affiliation, art, athletics, leadership, music/drama, religious affiliation.

LEWIS-CLARK STATE COLLEGE

500 Eighth Avenue, Lewiston, ID 83501
Phone: 208-792-2210 • **Financial Aid Phone:** 208-792-2224
E-mail: admissions@lcsc.edu • **CEEB Code:** 4385
Fax: 208-792-2876 • **Website:** www.lcsc.edu • **ACT Code:** 920

This public school was founded in 1893. It has a 44-acre campus.

RATINGS

Admissions Selectivity Rating: 77   **Fire Safety Rating:** 69   **Green Rating:** 60*

STUDENTS AND FACULTY

Enrollment: 3,027. **Student Body:** 61% female, 39% male, 14% out-of-state, 5% international (32 countries represented). Asian 2%, African American 1%, Caucasian 81%, Hispanic 4%, Native American 4%.
Retention and Graduation: 52% freshmen return for sophomore year. 7% grads go on to further study within 1 year. **Faculty:** Student/faculty ratio 18:1. 159 full-time faculty, 47% hold PhDs, 4% are members of minority groups, 53% are women. 0% of classes are taught by teaching assistants.

ACADEMICS

Degrees: associate, bachelor's, certificate, diploma, terminal associate, transfer associate. **Classes:** Most classes have fewer than 10 students. **Majors with Highest Enrollment:** business/commerce; elementary education and teaching; nursing/registered nurse (rn, asn, bsn, msn). **Special Study Options:** Accelerated program, cooperative education program, distance learning, double major, dual enrollment, English as a Second Language (ESL), independent study, internships, study abroad, teacher certification program. **Disability Services:** Special programs offered to physically disabled students include note-taking services, reader services, tape recorders, tutors.

FACILITIES

Housing: Coed dorms, apartments for married students, apartments for single students. 95% of campus accessible to physically disabled. **Special Academic Facilities/Equipment:** Museum/art gallery, Media Services **Computers:** Students can register for classes online. Administrative functions (other than registration) can be performed online.

CAMPUS LIFE

Environment: Town. **Activities:** drama/theater, jazz band, literary magazine, radio station, student government, student newspaper, Campus Ministries,

International Student Organization 52 registered organizations, 1 honor societies, 3 religious organizations. **Athletics (Intercollegiate):** *Men:* baseball, basketball, cross-country, golf, tennis. *Women:* basketball, cross-country, golf, tennis, volleyball. **On-Campus Highlights:** Information Commons in the Library, Student Union Building, Athletic Center which is under construction, Centennial Mall, Yo Espresso or Jitterz.

ADMISSIONS

Freshman Academic Profile: Average high school GPA 3.0. 7% in top 10% of high school class, 23% in top 25% of high school class, 52% in top 50% of high school class. 99% from public high schools. SAT Math middle 50% range 440-550. SAT Critical Reading middle 50% range 420-520. ACT middle 50% range 17-23. Minimum paper TOEFL 500. **Basis for Candidate Selection:** *Very important factors considered include:* academic GPA, rigor of secondary school record, standardized test scores. **Freshman Admission Requirements:** High school diploma is required and GED is accepted. *Academic units required:* 4 English, 3 mathematics, 3 science, (2 science labs). 4 English, 3 mathematics, 3 science, (2 science labs). **Freshman Admission Statistics:** 1,434 applied, 59% admitted, 74% enrolled. **Transfer Admission Requirements:** college transcript(s), minimum college GPA of 2.0 required. Lowest grade transferable D. **General Admission Information:** Application Fee $35. Nonfall registration accepted. Admission may be deferred for a maximum of 1 year. Credit and/or placement offered for CEEB Advanced Placement tests.

COSTS AND FINANCIAL AID

Annual in-state tuition $4,296. Annual out-of-state tuition $11,950. Room and board $5,400. Average book expense $1,500. **Required Forms and Deadlines:** FAFSA. **Notification of Awards:** Applicants will be notified of awards on a rolling basis beginning 4/15. **Types of Aid:** *Need-based scholarships/grants:* Federal Pell, SEOG, state scholarships/grants, private scholarships, the school's own gift aid. *Loans:* Subsidized Stafford, Unsubsidized Stafford, PLUS, Federal Perkins, Federal Nursing. **Student Employment:** Federal Work-Study Program available. Institutional employment available. **Financial Aid Statistics:** 58% freshmen, 66% undergrads receive need-based scholarship or grant aid. 55% freshmen, 24% undergrads receive non-need-based scholarship or grant aid. 77% freshmen, 82% undergrads receive need-based self-help aid. 5% freshmen, 8% undergrads receive athletic scholarships. 85% freshmen, 76% undergrads receive any aid. 61% undergrads borrow to pay for school. **Criteria for awarding institutional aid:** *Non-need-based:* academics, alumni affiliation, art, athletics, leadership, minority status, music/drama.

LIBERTY UNIVERSITY

1971 University Blvd, Lynchburg, VA 24502
Phone: 434-582-2000 • **Financial Aid Phone:** 434-582-2270
E-mail: admissions@liberty.edu • **CEEB Code:** 5385
Fax: 800-628-7977 • **Website:** www.liberty.edu/ • **ACT Code:** 4364

This private school, affiliated with the Baptist Church, was founded in 1971. It has a 4400-acre campus.

RATINGS

Admissions Selectivity Rating: 87   **Fire Safety Rating:** 72   **Green Rating:** 60*

STUDENTS AND FACULTY

Enrollment: 11,507. **Student Body:** 52% female, 48% male, 58% out-of-state, 6% international (125 countries represented). Asian 1%, African American 7%, Caucasian 69%, Hispanic 3%, Native American 0%.
Retention and Graduation: 81% freshmen return for sophomore year. 28% freshmen graduate within 4 years. 52% freshmen graduate within 6 years. **Faculty:** Student/faculty ratio 25:1. 532 full-time faculty. 0% of classes are taught by teaching assistants.

ACADEMICS

Degrees: associate, bachelor's, certificate, doctoral, master's, post-master's certificate, terminal associate. **Classes:** Most classes have 20–29 students. **Majors with Highest Enrollment:** business/commerce; psychology; religion/religious studies. **Special Study Options:** Accelerated program, cooperative education program, distance learning, double major, dual enrollment, English as a Second Language (ESL), external degree program, honors program, independent study, internships, student-designed major, teacher certification program, weekend college. **Honors Programs:** An early class registration period, smaller class size (15:1) for general education Honors seminars, and a generous scholarship based on grade point average are just a few of the benefits enjoyed by our Honors students. Once Honors students reach junior status, they petition one Honors course per semester in their desired major field of study. **Disability Services:** Special programs offered to physically disabled students include tutors. **Career**

Services: career assessment, internships, Career Services highlights include https://www.liberty.edu/academics/general/career/index.cfm?PID=6149.

FACILITIES

Housing: special housing for disabled students, men's dorms, women's dorms, apartments for single students. 94% of campus accessible to physically disabled. **Special Academic Facilities/Equipment:** Displays from the Museum of Life and Earth History are located in the Library. The Jerry Falwell Museum located in the main lobby of DeMoss Hall. **Computers:** 90% of classrooms, have wireless network access. Students can register for classes online. Administrative functions (other than registration) can be performed online.

CAMPUS LIFE

Environment: Town. **Activities:** Choral groups, concert band, drama/theater, literary magazine, marching band, music ensembles, musical theater, pep band, radio station, student government, student newspaper, symphony orchestra, television station, yearbook, Campus Ministries 25 registered organizations, 8 honor societies, 10 religious organizations. **Athletics (Intercollegiate):** *Men:* baseball, basketball, cheerleading, cross-country, football, golf, soccer, tennis, track/field (outdoor), track/field (indoor), wrestling. *Women:* basketball, cheerleading, cross-country, soccer, softball, tennis, track/field (outdoor), track/field (indoor), volleyball. **On-Campus Highlights:** LaHaye Student Center, Bookstore, Hangar (Food Court), ILRC Computer Lab, LaHaye Ice Center (Ice Arena).

ADMISSIONS

Freshman Academic Profile: Average high school GPA 3.4. 22% in top 10% of high school class, 50% in top 25% of high school class, 78% in top 50% of high school class. % from public high schools. SAT Math middle 50% range 460-570. SAT Critical Reading middle 50% range 470-580. SAT Writing middle 50% range 450-570. ACT middle 50% range 20-26. Minimum web-based TOEFL 60. Minimum paper TOEFL 500. **Basis for Candidate Selection:** *Very important factors considered include:* rigor of secondary school record, standardized test scores. *Important factors considered include:* application essay, academic GPA. *Other factors considered include:* Class rank, recommendation(s), character/personal qualities, extracurricular activities, level of applicant's interest, talent/ability. **Freshman Admission Requirements:** High school diploma is required and GED is accepted. **Freshman Admission Statistics:** 25,976 applied, 23% admitted, 45% enrolled. **Transfer Admission Requirements:** High school transcript, college transcript(s), essay or personal statement, statement of good standing from prior institution(s). Minimum college GPA of 2.0 required. Lowest grade transferable C. **General Admission Information:** Application Fee $40. Nonfall registration accepted. Admission may be deferred for a maximum of 12 months. Credit and/or placement offered for CEEB Advanced Placement tests.

COSTS AND FINANCIAL AID

Annual tuition $18,562. Room and board $7,050. Required fees $1,406. Average book expense $1,400. **Required Forms and Deadlines:** FAFSA, state aid form. **Notification of Awards:** Applicants will be notified of awards on a rolling basis beginning 3/15. **Types of Aid:** *Need-based scholarships/grants:* Federal Pell, SEOG, state scholarships/grants, private scholarships, the school's own gift aid. *Loans:* Subsidized Stafford, Unsubsidized Stafford, PLUS. **Student Employment:** Off-campus job opportunities are good. **Financial Aid Statistics:** 95% freshmen, 87% undergrads receive any aid. **Criteria for awarding institutional aid:** *Non-need-based:* academics, alumni affiliation, athletics, leadership, music/drama, religious affiliation, state/district residency.

LIFE PACIFIC COLLEGE

1100 Covina Blvd. San Dimas, CA 91773
Phone: 909-599-5433 • **Financial Aid Phone:** 909-599-5433
E-mail: adm@lifepacific.edu
Fax: 909-599-6690 • **Website:** www.lifepacific.edu/ • **ACT Code:** 489

This private school, affiliated with the Protestant Church, was founded in 1923. It has a 9-acre campus.

RATINGS

Admissions Selectivity Rating: 66   **Fire Safety Rating:** 69   **Green Rating:** 60*

STUDENTS AND FACULTY

Enrollment: 528. **Student Body:** 46% female, 54% male, 48% out-of-state, 0% international (2 countries represented).
Retention and Graduation: 69% freshmen return for sophomore year. 18% freshmen graduate within 4 years. 32% freshmen graduate within 6 years. 48% grads go on to further study within 1 year. **Faculty:** Student/faculty ratio 17:1. 12 full-time faculty, 17% hold PhDs, 8% are members of minority groups, 17% are women. 0% of classes are taught by teaching assistants.

ACADEMICS

Degrees: associate, bachelor's. **Classes:** Most classes have 10–19 students. Most lab/discussion sessions have 20–29 students. **Special Study Options:** Accelerated program, distance learning, dual enrollment, external degree program, independent study, internships. **Disability Services:** Special programs offered to physically disabled students include note-taking services, tape recorders, tutors. **Career Services:** alumni services, career/job search classes, internships Career Services highlights include Our service learning program is required for all students.

FACILITIES

Housing: men's dorms, women's dorms. 100% of campus accessible to physically disabled. **Special Academic Facilities/Equipment:** New gymnasium and Work out facilities New computer lab New Student Center New Music Facilities **Computers:** Students can register for classes online.

CAMPUS LIFE

Environment: Town. **Activities:** Choral groups, dance, drama/theater, music ensembles, student government, yearbook. **Athletics (Intercollegiate):** *Men:* basketball. *Women:* volleyball. **On-Campus Highlights:** The Cove Student Center, New Gymnasium, New Work-out room, Music Wing (new)

ADMISSIONS

Freshman Academic Profile: Average high school GPA 2.9. 5% in top 10% of high school class, 21% in top 25% of high school class, 38% in top 50% of high school class. SAT Math middle 50% range 410-510. SAT Critical Reading middle 50% range 430-540. ACT middle 50% range 14-23. Minimum paper TOEFL 550. **Basis for Candidate Selection:** *Very important factors considered include:* application essay, academic GPA, recommendation(s), standardized test scores, character/personal qualities, level of applicant's interest, religious affiliation/commitment. *Other factors considered include:* alumni/ae relation, extracurricular activities, talent/ability. **Freshman Admission Requirements:** High school diploma is required and GED is accepted. **Freshman Admission Statistics:** 102 applied, 87% admitted, 70% enrolled. **Transfer Admission Requirements:** college transcript(s), essay or personal statement, statement of good standing from prior institution(s). Minimum college GPA of 2.0 required. Lowest grade transferable C. **General Admission Information:** Application Fee $35. Regular application deadline 6/1. Nonfall registration accepted. Admission may be deferred for a maximum of 1 yr. Credit and/or placement offered for CEEB Advanced Placement tests.

COSTS AND FINANCIAL AID

Annual tuition $9,750. Room and board $5,000. Required fees $350. Average book expense $1,242. **Required Forms and Deadlines:** FAFSA. **Notification of Awards:** Applicants will be notified of awards on a rolling basis beginning 6/1. **Types of Aid:** *Need-based scholarships/grants:* Federal Pell, SEOG, state scholarships/grants, private scholarships, the school's own gift aid. *Loans:* Subsidized Stafford, Unsubsidized Stafford, PLUS. **Student Employment:** Federal Work-Study Program available. Institutional employment available. Off-campus job opportunities are excellent. **Financial Aid Statistics:** 68% freshmen, 78% undergrads receive need-based scholarship or grant aid. 18% freshmen, 4% undergrads receive non-need-based scholarship or grant aid. 78% freshmen, 80% undergrads receive need-based self-help aid. 70% undergrads borrow to pay for school. Average cumulative indebtedness $17,125. **Criteria for awarding institutional aid:** *Non-need-based:* academics, alumni affiliation, leadership, religious affiliation.

LIM COLLEGE

12 East 53rd Street, New York, NY 10022
Phone: 212-752-1530 • **Financial Aid Phone:** 212-752-1530
E-mail: admissions@limcollege.edu • **CEEB Code:** 2380
Fax: 212-750-3432 • **Website:** www.limcollege.edu • **ACT Code:** 4807

This proprietary school was founded in 1939.

RATINGS

Admissions Selectivity Rating: 79   **Fire Safety Rating:** 73   **Green Rating:** 60*

STUDENTS AND FACULTY

Enrollment: 1,308. **Student Body:** 94% female, 6% male, 57% out-of-state, 1% international (13 countries represented). Asian 6%, African American 11%, Caucasian 68%, Hispanic 14%, Native American 0%. **Retention and Graduation:** 64% freshmen return for sophomore year. 53% freshmen graduate within 4 years. **Faculty:** Student/faculty ratio 17:1. 26 full-time faculty, 38% hold PhDs, 31% are members of minority groups, 46% are women. 0% of classes are taught by teaching assistants.

ACADEMICS

Degrees: associate, bachelor's, master's. **Classes:** Most classes have 10–19 students. **Majors with Highest Enrollment:** fashion merchandising; marketing/marketing management. **Special Study Options:** cooperative education program, internships, study abroad, 3 credit trip in winter/summer to Europe. **Disability Services:** Special programs offered to physically disabled students include tape recorders, tutors. **Career Services:** Alumni network; alumni services, career/job search classes, career assessment, internships Career Services highlights include All first and second year students must participate in a 5 week internship between Thanksgiving and Christmas. All seniors must participate in a full-semester co-op.

FACILITIES

Housing: Coed dorms. 100% of campus accessible to physically disabled. **Computers:** 100% of classrooms, 100% of dorms, 100% of libraries, 100% of dining areas, 100% of student union, have wireless network access. Students can register for classes online. Administrative functions (other than registration) can be performed online.

CAMPUS LIFE

Environment: Metropolis. **Activities:** student government, yearbook 12 registered organizations, 1 honor societies. **On-Campus Highlights:** Library, Cafe 45, Cyber Lounge, 1760 Third Ave.

ADMISSIONS

Freshman Academic Profile: 84.5. 3% in top 10% of high school class, 17% in top 25% of high school class, 55% in top 50% of high school class. 73% from public high schools. SAT Math middle 50% range 420-510. SAT Critical Reading middle 50% range 440-520. SAT Writing middle 50% range 500-520. ACT middle 50% range 19-23. Minimum paper TOEFL 550. **Basis for Candidate Selection:** *Very important factors considered include:* academic GPA, interview, level of applicant's interest. *Important factors considered include:* Class rank, application essay, recommendation(s), rigor of secondary school record, standardized test scores, alumni/ae relation, character/personal qualities, extracurricular activities, talent/ability, volunteer work, work experience. *Other factors considered include:* geographical residence, racial/ethnic status, state residency. **Freshman Admission Requirements:** High school diploma is required and GED is accepted. **Freshman Admission Statistics:** 1,069 applied, 56% admitted, 51% enrolled. **Transfer Admission Requirements:** High school transcript, college transcript(s), essay or personal statement, minimum college GPA of 2.0 required. Lowest grade transferable D-. **General Admission Information:** Application Fee $40. Notification on a rolling basis, beginning on or about 12/15. Nonfall registration accepted. Admission may be deferred for a maximum of 1 semester. Credit offered for CEEB Advanced Placement tests.

COSTS AND FINANCIAL AID

Annual tuition $22,420. Room and board $19,850. Required fees $575. Average book expense $1,100. **Required Forms and Deadlines:** FAFSA, institution's own financial aid form. **Notification of Awards:** Applicants will be notified of awards on a rolling basis beginning 2/15. **Types of Aid:** *Need-based scholarships/grants:* Federal Pell, SEOG, state scholarships/grants, private scholarships, the school's own gift aid. *Loans:* Direct Subsidized Stafford, Direct Unsubsidized Stafford, Direct PLUS. **Student Employment:** Federal Work Study Program available. Institutional employment available. Off-campus job opportunities are excellent. **Financial Aid Statistics:** 72% freshmen, 75% undergrads receive need-based scholarship or grant aid. 29% freshmen, 17% undergrads receive non-need-based scholarship or grant aid. 85% freshmen, 90% undergrads receive need-based self-help aid. 85% freshmen, 85% undergrads receive any aid. 68% undergrads borrow to pay for school. Average cumulative indebtedness $27,505. **Criteria for awarding institutional aid:** *Non-need-based:* academics.

See page 1128.

LIMESTONE COLLEGE

1115 College Drive, Gaffney, SC 29340-3799
Phone: 864-488-4549 • **Financial Aid Phone:** 864-488-8700
E-mail: admiss@limestone.edu • **CEEB Code:** 5366
Fax: 864-487-8706 • **Website:** www.limestone.edu • **ACT Code:** 3862

This private school was founded in 1845. It has a 115-acre campus.

RATINGS

Admissions Selectivity Rating: 82   **Fire Safety Rating:** 76   **Green Rating:** 60*

STUDENTS AND FACULTY

Enrollment: 899. **Student Body:** 41% female, 59% male, 51% out-of-state, 9% international. Asian 0%, African American 22%, Caucasian 60%, Hispanic 4%, Native American 1%.

Retention and Graduation: 21% freshmen graduate within 4 years. 39% freshmen graduate within 6 years. **Faculty:** Student/faculty ratio 12:1. 68 full-time faculty, 87% hold PhDs, 4% are members of minority groups, 50% are women. 0% of classes are taught by teaching assistants.

ACADEMICS

Degrees: bachelor's, transfer associate. **Classes:** Most classes have 20–29 students. Most lab/discussion sessions have fewer than 10 students. **Majors with Highest Enrollment:** business/managerial economics; elementary education and teaching; health and physical education/fitness, other. **Special Study Options:** Accelerated program, distance learning, double major, honors program, independent study, internships, liberal arts/career combination, student-designed major, teacher certification program. **Honors Programs:** The Honors Program was established at Limestone College in 1983 to create a challenging academic environment for gifted and special ability students. **Disability Services:** Special programs offered to physically disabled students include tape recorders, tutors. **Career Services:** alumni services, career assessment, Career Services highlights include The student is placed in a local private or public enterprise to gain work-related experience consistent with their field of study.

FACILITIES

Housing: men's dorms, women's dorms, apartments for single students. 90% of campus accessible to physically disabled. **Special Academic Facilities/Equipment:** Computer graphic arts lab; museum of Southern history in Winnie Davis Hall **Computers:** 20% of classrooms, 20% of dorms, 100% of libraries, 100% of student union, 5% of common outdoor areas have wireless network access. Students can register for classes online. Administrative functions (other than registration) can be performed online.

CAMPUS LIFE

Environment: Town. **Activities:** Choral groups, concert band, drama/theater, jazz band, literary magazine, music ensembles, musical theater, pep band, student government, yearbook, Campus Ministries 2 religious organizations. **Athletics (Intercollegiate):** *Men:* baseball, basketball, cross-country, golf, lacrosse, soccer, swimming, tennis, track/field (outdoor), volleyball, wrestling. *Women:* basketball, cross-country, field hockey, golf, lacrosse, soccer, softball, swimming, tennis, track/field (outdoor), volleyball. **On-Campus Highlights:** Dixie Lodge, Stephenson Dining Hall, Timken Gym and Pool, Eastwood Library, Curtis Administration Building, The Walt Griffin Physical Education Center Limestone Learning Center Winnie Davis Hall of History. **Environmental Initiatives:** Community Garden

ADMISSIONS

Freshman Academic Profile: Average high school GPA 3.1. 6% in top 10% of high school class, 21% in top 25% of high school class, 53% in top 50% of high school class. 90% from public high schools. SAT Math middle 50% range 480-560. SAT Critical Reading middle 50% range 450-540. ACT middle 50% range 20-24. Minimum web-based TOEFL 75. Minimum paper TOEFL 500. **Basis for Candidate Selection:** *Very important factors considered include:* academic GPA, rigor of secondary school record, standardized test scores. *Important factors considered include:* Class rank. *Other factors considered include:* recommendation(s), interview. **Freshman Admission Requirements:** High school diploma is required and GED is accepted. *Academic units required:* 4 English, 3 mathematics, 2 science, (2 science labs), 3 social studies. 4 English, 3 mathematics, 2 science, (2 science labs), 3 social studies. **Freshman Admission Statistics:** 1,389 applied, 55% admitted, 32% enrolled. **Transfer Admission Requirements:** college transcript(s), statement of good standing from prior institution(s). Minimum college GPA of 2.0 required. Lowest grade transferable C. **General Admission Information:** Application Fee $25. Regular application deadline 8/26. Notification on a rolling basis, beginning on or about 6/1. Nonfall registration accepted. Admission may be deferred for a maximum of 18 months. Credit offered for CEEB Advanced Placement tests.

COSTS AND FINANCIAL AID

Annual tuition $22,080. Room and board $7,800. Average book expense $2,304. **Required Forms and Deadlines:** FAFSA. **Notification of Awards:** Applicants will be notified of awards on a rolling basis beginning 1/15. **Types of Aid:** *Need-based scholarships/grants:* Federal Pell, SEOG, state scholarships/grants, private scholarships, the school's own gift aid. *Loans:* Subsidized Stafford, Unsubsidized Stafford, PLUS, Federal Perkins. **Student Employment:** Federal Work-Study Program available. Institutional employment available. Highest amount earned per year from on-campus jobs $8,300. Off-campus job opportunities are good. **Financial Aid Statistics:** 100% freshmen, 100% undergrads receive need-based scholarship or grant aid. 14% freshmen, 12% undergrads receive non-need-based scholarship or grant aid. 80% freshmen, 83% undergrads receive need-based self-help aid. 11% freshmen, 9% undergrads receive athletic scholarships. 98% freshmen, 98% undergrads receive any aid. 91% undergrads borrow to pay for school. Average cumulative indebtedness $32,175. **Criteria**

for awarding institutional aid: *Non-need-based:* academics, art, athletics, job skills, leadership, music/drama, state/district residency.

See page 1130.

LINCOLN CHRISTIAN COLLEGE AND SEMINARY

100 Campus View Dr, Lincoln, IL 62656-2167
Phone: 2177323168 x:2251 • **Financial Aid Phone:** 2177323168
E-mail: coladmis@lccs.edu • **CEEB Code:**
Fax: 2177324199 • **Website:** www.lccs.edu • **ACT Code:** 1060

This private school, affiliated with the Church of Christ Church, was founded in 1944. It has a 100-acre campus.

RATINGS

Admissions Selectivity Rating: 67   **Fire Safety Rating:** 77   **Green Rating:** 60*

STUDENTS AND FACULTY

Enrollment: 601. **Student Body:** 51% female, 49% male, 40% out-of-state, 0% international (19 countries represented). Asian 0%, African American 5%, Caucasian 91%, Hispanic 2%, Native American 0%.

Retention and Graduation: 17% grads go on to further study within 1 year. **Faculty:** Student/faculty ratio 15:1. 44 full-time faculty, 45% hold PhDs, 5% are members of minority groups, 18% are women. 0% of classes are taught by teaching assistants.

ACADEMICS

Degrees: associate, bachelor's, certificate, first professional, master's. **Special Study Options:** distance learning, double major, honors program, independent study, internships, study abroad, teacher certification program, weekend college, Teacher preparatory program through University of Illinois at Springfield, Illinois State University, and Greenville College. **Honors Programs:** Students with at least sophomore standing and a cumulative grade average of 3.5 or higher may apply for acceptance into an honors degree program. The honors degree requires 5 additional semester hours of study under a mentoring professor and the completion of a capstone project. The additional work may be completed in the area of the student's ministry specialization or in an area of interest outside the specialization. Since the program is funded by memorial gifts, honors degree students do not pay tuition for the additional 5 hours. For students who complete the honors degree requirements, special recognition will be given at the Commencement service, and an honors designation will be included on the academic transcript. **Disability Services:** Special programs offered to physically disabled students include reader services, tape recorders, tutors. Career Services highlights include https://secure.lccs.edu/internship/.

FACILITIES

Housing: men's dorms, women's dorms, apartments for married students. 80% of campus accessible to physically disabled. **Computers:** 90% of classrooms, 100% of dorms, 80% of libraries, have wireless network access. Students can register for classes online. Administrative functions (other than registration) can be performed online.

CAMPUS LIFE

Environment: Village. **Activities:** Choral groups, drama/theater, music ensembles, musical theater, student government, student newspaper, Campus Ministries, International Student Organization 7 registered organizations. **Athletics (Intercollegiate):** *Men:* baseball, basketball, soccer. *Women:* basketball, softball, volleyball. **On-Campus Highlights:** The Warehouse, The CoffeeShop

ADMISSIONS

Freshman Academic Profile: 19% in top 10% of high school class, 45% in top 25% of high school class, 76% in top 50% of high school class. ACT middle 50% range 19-25. Minimum web-based TOEFL 75. Minimum paper TOEFL 550. **Basis for Candidate Selection:** *Very important factors considered include:* application essay, rigor of secondary school record, standardized test scores, level of applicant's interest, religious affiliation/commitment, state residency. *Important factors considered include:* Class rank, academic GPA, alumni/ae relation, character/personal qualities, extracurricular activities, geographical residence, racial/ethnic status, volunteer work. *Other factors considered include:* recommendation(s), interview, talent/ability, work experience. **Freshman Admission Requirements:** High school diploma is required and GED is accepted. **Freshman Admission Statistics:** 195 applied, 84% admitted, 65% enrolled. **Transfer Admission Requirements:** High school transcript, college transcript(s), essay or personal statement, minimum college GPA of 2.0 required. Lowest grade transferable 2. **General Admission Information:** Application Fee $25. Nonfall registration accepted. Admission may be deferred for a maximum of 1 semester. Credit offered for CEEB Advanced Placement tests.

COSTS AND FINANCIAL AID

Annual tuition $11,790. Room and board $5,355. Average book expense. **Required Forms and Deadlines:** FAFSA. **Notification of Awards:** Applicants will be notified of awards on a rolling basis beginning 3/1. **Types of Aid:** *Need-based scholarships/grants:* Federal Pell, SEOG, state scholarships/grants. *Loans:* Subsidized Stafford, Unsubsidized Stafford, PLUS, Federal Perkins, college/university loans from institutional funds. **Student Employment:** Federal Work-Study Program available. Institutional employment available. Off-campus job opportunities are good. **Financial Aid Statistics:** 55% freshmen, 64% undergrads receive need-based scholarship or grant aid. 84% freshmen, 79% undergrads receive non-need-based scholarship or grant aid. 67% freshmen, 72% undergrads receive need-based self-help aid. 80% freshmen, 80% undergrads receive any aid. 71% undergrads borrow to pay for school. Average cumulative indebtedness $17,625. **Criteria for awarding institutional aid:** *Non-need-based:* academics.

LINCOLN COLLEGE

300 Keokuk St, Lincoln, IL 62656
Phone: 800-569-0556
E-mail: admission@lincolncollege.com
Fax: 217-732-7715 • **Website:** www.lincolncollege.edu • **ACT Code:** 1062

This private school was founded in 1865. It has a 60-acre campus.

RATINGS
Admissions Selectivity Rating: 60*   **Fire Safety Rating:** 65   **Green Rating:** 60*

STUDENTS AND FACULTY
Faculty: 0% of classes are taught by teaching assistants.

ACADEMICS
Degrees: associate, transfer associate. **Disability Services:** Special programs offered to physically disabled students include tape recorders, tutors.

FACILITIES
Housing: 90% of campus accessible to physically disabled. **Computers.** Students can register for classes online. Administrative functions (other than registration) can be performed online.

CAMPUS LIFE
Environment: Village. **Activities:** 10 registered organizations, 1 honor societies. **Athletics (Intercollegiate):** *Men:* baseball, basketball, cheerleading, cross-country, diving, golf, soccer, swimming, wrestling. *Women:* basketball, cheerleading, cross-country, diving, golf, soccer, softball, swimming, volleyball. **On-Campus Highlights:** Meyer-Evans Student Center, Library-Museum, Heritage Resident Halls, Dooley Hall, University Hall, Johnston Center for Performing Arts.

ADMISSIONS
General Admission Information: Placement offered for CEEB Advanced Placement tests.

COSTS AND FINANCIAL AID
Student Employment: Federal Work-Study Program available. Institutional employment available. Highest amount earned per year from on-campus jobs $1,500. Off-campus job opportunities are fair. **Financial Aid Statistics:** 92% freshmen, 92% undergrads receive any aid.

LINCOLN MEMORIAL UNIVERSITY

6965 Cumberland Gap Parkway, Harrogate, TN 37752
Phone: 423-869-6280 • **Financial Aid Phone:** 423-869-6465
E-mail: admissions@lmunet.edu • **CEEB Code:** 1408
Fax: 423-869-6250 • **Website:** www.lmunet.edu • **ACT Code:** 3982

This private school was founded in 1897. It has a 1000-acre campus.

RATINGS
Admissions Selectivity Rating: 74   **Fire Safety Rating:** 60*   **Green Rating:** 60*

STUDENTS AND FACULTY
Enrollment: 1,749. **Student Body:** 73% female, 27% male, 36% out-of-state, 2% international (27 countries represented). Asian 1%, African American 4%, Caucasian 80%, Hispanic 2%, Native American 0%.

Retention and Graduation: 66% freshmen return for sophomore year. **Faculty:** Student/faculty ratio 13:1. 191 full-time faculty, 65% hold PhDs, 5% are members of minority groups, 50% are women. 0% of classes are taught by teaching assistants.

ACADEMICS
Degrees: associate, bachelor's, master's, post-bachelor's certificate, post-master's certificate. **Classes:** Most classes have fewer than 10 students. Most lab/discussion sessions have 10–19 students. **Special Study Options:** Accelerated program, distance learning, double major, dual enrollment, English as a Second Language (ESL), internships, teacher certification program. **Career Services:** alumni services

FACILITIES
Housing: Coed dorms, special housing for disabled students, men's dorms, women's dorms, apartments for married students, apartments for single students. 60% of campus accessible to physically disabled. Special Academic Facilities/Equipment: Civil War museum, including Abraham Lincoln memorabilia collection of over 6,000 books, paintings, and manuscripts. CAMPUS LIFE **Environment:** Rural. **Activities:** Choral groups, dance, drama/theater, literary magazine, music ensembles, pep band, radio station, student government, television station, yearbook, Campus Ministries, International Student Organization 26 registered organizations, 5 honor societies, 3 religious organizations. 3 fraternities, 3 sororities. **Athletics (Intercollegiate):** *Men:* baseball, basketball, cross-country, golf, soccer, tennis. *Women:* basketball, cross-country, golf, soccer, softball, tennis, volleyball.

ADMISSIONS
Freshman Academic Profile: Average high school GPA 3.4. 90% from public high schools. SAT Math middle 50% range 430-560. SAT Critical Reading middle 50% range 420-550. ACT middle 50% range 20-25. Minimum paper TOEFL 500. **Basis for Candidate Selection:** *Very important factors considered include:* academic GPA, rigor of secondary school record, standardized test scores. *Important factors considered include:* Class rank, alumni/ae relation, character/personal qualities. *Other factors considered include:* extracurricular activities, first generation, racial/ethnic status, religious affiliation/commitment, volunteer work. **Freshman Admission Requirements:** High school diploma is required and GED is accepted. *Academic units required:* 4 English, 3 mathematics, 2 science, 2 foreign language, 1 social studies, 1 history, 1 visual/performing arts. *Academic units recommended:* 4 English, 3 mathematics, 2 science, 2 foreign language, 1 social studies, 1 history, 1 visual/performing arts. **Freshman Admission Statistics:** 984 applied, 65% admitted, 39% enrolled. **Transfer Admission Requirements:** High school transcript, college transcript(s), standardized test scores, minimum college GPA of 2.0 required. Lowest grade transferable C. **General Admission Information:** Application Fee $25. Notification on a rolling basis, beginning on or about 9/1. Nonfall registration accepted. Credit offered for CEEB Advanced Placement tests.

COSTS AND FINANCIAL AID
Average book expense $1,250. **Required Forms and Deadlines:** FAFSA. **Notification of Awards:** Applicants will be notified of awards on a rolling basis beginning 4/15. **Types of Aid:** *Need-based scholarships/grants:* Federal Pell, SEOG, state scholarships/grants, private scholarships, the school's own gift aid. *Loans:* Subsidized Stafford, Unsubsidized Stafford, PLUS, Federal Perkins. **Student Employment:** Federal Work-Study Program available. Highest amount earned per year from on-campus jobs $1,500. Off-campus job opportunities are fair. **Financial Aid Statistics:** 100% freshmen, 97% undergrads receive need-based scholarship or grant aid. 17% freshmen, 9% undergrads receive non-need-based scholarship or grant aid. 42% freshmen, 59% undergrads receive need-based self-help aid. 2% freshmen, 1% undergrads receive athletic scholarships. 60% undergrads borrow to pay for school. Average cumulative indebtedness $22,439. **Criteria for awarding institutional aid:** *Non-need-based:* academics, alumni affiliation, art, athletics, leadership, music/drama.

LINCOLN UNIVERSITY (CA)

401 15th Street, Oakland, CA 94612
Phone: 510-628-8010 • **Financial Aid Phone:** 510-628-8023
E-mail: admissions@lincolnuca.edu
Fax: 510-628-8012 • **Website:** www.lincolnuca.edu

This private school was founded in 1919.

RATINGS
Admissions Selectivity Rating: 60*   **Fire Safety Rating:** 60*   **Green Rating:** 60*

STUDENTS AND FACULTY
Enrollment: 114.
Faculty: 6 full-time faculty, 100% hold PhDs, 50% are women.

ACADEMICS

Degrees: associate, bachelor's, certificate, master's. **Majors with Highest Enrollment:** bible/biblical studies; education; youth ministry. **Special Study Options:** cross-registration, double major, English as a Second Language (ESL), internships, student-designed major. **Career Services:** Alumni network, internships.

FACILITIES

Housing: Universal Student Housing Placement.

CAMPUS LIFE

Environment: Metropolis. **Activities:** student government.

ADMISSIONS

Freshman Academic Profile: Minimum paper TOEFL 500. **Basis for Candidate Selection:** *Very important factors considered include:* rigor of secondary school record. *Important factors considered include:* academic GPA. *Other factors considered include:* Class rank, standardized test scores. **Freshman Admission Requirements:** High school diploma is required and GED is accepted. **Freshman Admission Statistics:** 33 applied, 1052% enrolled. **Transfer Admission Requirements:** college transcript(s), minimum college GPA of 2.0 required. Lowest grade transferable C. **General Admission Information:** Application Fee $75. Regular application deadline 8/15. Nonfall registration accepted. Admission may be deferred for a maximum of 3 semester.

COSTS AND FINANCIAL AID

Annual tuition $7,080. Required fees $400. Average book expense $400.

LINCOLN UNIVERSITY (MO)

820 Chestnut Street, Jefferson City, MO 65102-0029
Phone: 573-681-5599 • **Financial Aid Phone:** 573-681-6156
E-mail: enroll@lincolnu.edu • **CEEB Code:** 177940
Fax: 573-681-5889 • **Website:** www.lincolnu.edu • **ACT Code:** 2322

This public school was founded in 1866. It has a 165-acre campus.

RATINGS

Admissions Selectivity Rating: 83   Fire Safety Rating: 99   Green Rating: 85

STUDENTS AND FACULTY

Enrollment: 2,394. **Student Body:** 59% female, 41% male, 16% out-of-state, 2% international (23 countries represented). Asian 0%, African American 44%, Caucasian 49%, Hispanic 2%, Native American 0%.
Retention and Graduation: 36% freshmen return for sophomore year. 9% freshmen graduate within 4 years. 24% freshmen graduate within 6 years.
Faculty: Student/faculty ratio 15:1. 132 full-time faculty, 27% are members of minority groups, 52% are women.

ACADEMICS

Degrees: associate, bachelor's, master's, post-master's certificate, terminal associate, transfer associate. **Classes:** Most classes have 20–29 students. **Majors with Highest Enrollment:** business administration and management; computer and information sciences; criminal justice/law enforcement administration. **Special Study Options:** Accelerated program, distance learning, double major, dual enrollment, exchange student program (domestic), honors program, independent study, internships, study abroad, teacher certification program, Senior Citizen Program; Learning in Retirement, Inc.; Intersession courses. **Honors Programs:** Lincoln University offers a 24-credit-hour Honors Program which features small classes, unique academic challenges, individual attention from Honors faculty, and association with other like-minded students. An Honors student has opportunities to compete for summer mentorships, work closely with a faculty member on a research or creative project; to do sustained research or creative work leading to a thesis in the student's major; and to present his/her work at regional, national, and international conferences. These students also qualify for Honors housing, certain restricted courses, and other activities. **Disability Services:** Special programs offered to physically disabled students include note-taking services, reader services, tape recorders, tutors. **Career Services:** alumni services, career assessment, internships Career Services highlights include All of the above.

FACILITIES

Housing: Coed dorms, men's dorms, women's dorms, wellness housing, Honors Student Housing. 100% of campus accessible to physically disabled. **Special Academic Facilities/Equipment:** University Archives/Ethnic Studies Center Media Center Student Support Services Center for Academic Enrichment Agriculture and Extension Information Center Education Curriculum Library **Computers:** 100% of classrooms, 100% of dorms, 100% of libraries, 100% of dining areas, 100% of student union, have wireless network access. Students can register for classes online. Administrative functions (other than registration) can be performed online.

CAMPUS LIFE

Environment: Town. **Activities:** Choral groups, concert band, dance, drama/theater, jazz band, literary magazine, marching band, music ensembles, pep band, radio station, student government, student newspaper, television station, yearbook, Campus Ministries, International Student Organization 24 registered organizations, 6 honor societies, 2 religious organizations. 4 fraternities, 2 sororities. **Athletics (Intercollegiate):** *Men:* baseball, basketball, football, golf, track/field (outdoor). *Women:* basketball, cheerleading, cross-country, golf, softball, tennis, track/field (outdoor). **On-Campus Highlights:** Clifford G. Scruggs University Center (SUC), Inman E. Page Library, Stamper Hall (Business and Economics), Richardson Fine Arts Center, Dwight T. Reed Stadium, University Farms used for agricultural research include: Busby Research Farm (273 acres); Carver Research Farm (173 acres); and Freeman Research Farm (199 acres). **Environmental Initiatives:** Composting cafeteria food waste Built and are using a cardboard collection bin for recycling from the cafeteria In the planning stages for developing an integrated and sustainable small farm operation (a microcommunity project)

ADMISSIONS

Freshman Academic Profile: Average high school GPA 2.7. 4% in top 10% of high school class, 15% in top 25% of high school class, 46% in top 50% of high school class. SAT Math middle 50% range 405-470. SAT Critical Reading middle 50% range 395-528. ACT middle 50% range 15-20. Minimum web-based TOEFL 61. Minimum paper TOEFL 500. **Basis for Candidate Selection:** *Other factors considered include:* academic GPA, state residency. **Freshman Admission Requirements:** High school diploma is required and GED is accepted. **Freshman Admission Statistics:** 2,487 applied, 43% admitted, 42% enrolled. **Transfer Admission Requirements:** college transcript(s), minimum college GPA of 2.0 required. Lowest grade transferable C. **General Admission Information:** Application Fee $20. Regular application deadline 7/15. Nonfall registration accepted. Credit and/or placement offered for CEEB Advanced Placement tests.

COSTS AND FINANCIAL AID

Annual in-state tuition $6,150. Annual out-of-state tuition $12,150. Room and board $5,271. Required fees $575. Average book expense $1,000. **Required Forms and Deadlines:** FAFSA, institution's own financial aid form. **Notification of Awards:** Applicants will be notified of awards on a rolling basis beginning 3/15. **Types of Aid:** *Need-based scholarships/grants:* Federal Pell, SEOG, state scholarships/grants, private scholarships, the school's own gift aid. *Loans:* Subsidized Stafford, Unsubsidized Stafford, PLUS. **Student Employment:** Federal Work-Study Program available. Institutional employment available. Off-campus job opportunities are fair. **Financial Aid Statistics:** 92% freshmen, 88% undergrads receive need-based scholarship or grant aid. 2% freshmen, 2% undergrads receive non-need-based scholarship or grant aid. 89% freshmen, 85% undergrads receive need-based self-help aid. 11% freshmen, 11% undergrads receive athletic scholarships. 90% freshmen, 82% undergrads receive any aid. 70% undergrads borrow to pay for school. Average cumulative indebtedness $27,910. **Criteria for awarding institutional aid:** *Non-need-based:* academics, art, athletics, job skills, leadership, minority status, music/drama, state/district residency.

LINCOLN UNIVERSITY (PA)

1570 Balitmore Pike, Lincoln University, PA 19352
Phone: 484-365-7206 • **Financial Aid Phone:** 800-561-2606
E-mail: admiss@lincoln.edu • **CEEB Code:** 2367
Fax: 484-365-8109 • **Website:** www.lincoln.edu • **ACT Code:** 3614

This public school was founded in 1854. It has a 422-acre campus.

RATINGS

Admissions Selectivity Rating: 81   Fire Safety Rating: 66   Green Rating: 64

STUDENTS AND FACULTY

Enrollment: 1,674. **Student Body:** 60% female, 40% male, 57% out-of-state, 3% international (23 countries represented). Asian 0%, African American 31%, Caucasian 1%, Hispanic 0%, Native American 0%.
Retention and Graduation: 67% freshmen return for sophomore year. 21% freshmen graduate within 4 years. 38% freshmen graduate within 6 years.
Faculty: Student/faculty ratio 17:1. 99 full-time faculty, 71% hold PhDs, 71% are members of minority groups, 64% are women. 0% of classes are taught by teaching assistants.

ACADEMICS

Degrees: bachelor's, master's. **Classes:** Most classes have 20–29 students. Most lab/discussion sessions have 10–19 students. **Majors with Highest Enrollment:** criminal justice/safety studies; elementary education and teaching. **Special Study Options:** double major, exchange student program (domestic), honors program, independent study, internships, study abroad, teacher certification program, 3-2 in advanced science/egineering with Drexel University, Pennsylvania State University, Howard University, University of Delaware, Temple University, Widener University, and New Jersey Institute of Technology. **Combined Degree Programs:** 2-2 nursing prog with West Chester U. **Disability Services:** Special programs offered to physically disabled students include reader services, tutors. **Career Services:** alumni services, internships.

FACILITIES

Housing: Coed dorms, men's dorms, women's dorms, apartments for single students. 90% of campus accessible to physically disabled. Special Academic Facilities/Equipment: African museum, fine arts center, hall for life sciences, learning resource center.

CAMPUS LIFE

Environment: Rural. **Activities:** Choral groups, dance, drama/theater, jazz band, music ensembles, radio station, student government, student newspaper, television station, yearbook 30 registered organizations, 9 honor societies, 4 fraternities, 3 sororities. **Athletics (Intercollegiate):** Men: baseball, basketball, cross-country, soccer, tennis, track/field (outdoor), track/field (indoor). Women: basketball, cross-country, soccer, tennis, track/field (outdoor), track/field (indoor), volleyball. **On-Campus Highlights:** Langston Hughes Memorial Library, Thurgood Marshall Living and Learning Ce, John Miller Dickey Hall, Student Union Building, Fredrick Douglass Memorial statue area.

ADMISSIONS

Freshman Academic Profile: Average high school GPA 2.7. 5% in top 10% of high school class, 17% in top 25% of high school class, 45% in top 50% of high school class. SAT Math middle 50% range 360-450. SAT Critical Reading middle 50% range 370-450. ACT middle 50% range 14-18. Minimum paper TOEFL 500. **Basis for Candidate Selection:** Very important factors considered include: Class rank, rigor of secondary school record. Important factors considered include: academic GPA, recommendation(s), standardized test scores, talent/ability. Other factors considered include: application essay, alumni/ae relation, character/personal qualities, extracurricular activities, first generation, geographical residence, interview, level of applicant's interest, religious affiliation/commitment, state residency, volunteer work, work experience. **Freshman Admission Requirements:** High school diploma is required and GED is accepted. Academic units required: 4 English, 3 mathematics, 3 science, 3 social studies, 5 academic electives, 3 2 arts or humanities, and 1 health and physical education is required. 4 English, 3 mathematics, 3 science, 3 social studies, 5 academic electives, 3 2 arts or humanities, and 1 health and physical education is required **Freshman Admission Statistics:** 5,488 applied, 38% admitted, 31% enrolled. **Transfer Admission Requirements:** college transcript(s), essay or personal statement, statement of good standing from prior institution(s). Minimum college GPA of 2.0 required. Lowest grade transferable C. **General Admission Information:** Application Fee $20. Notification on a rolling basis, beginning on or about 2/15. Nonfall registration accepted. Admission may be deferred for a maximum of 1 year. Credit offered for CEEB Advanced Placement tests.

COSTS AND FINANCIAL AID

Annual in-state tuition $5,472. Annual out-of-state tuition $9,312. Room and board $7,278. Required fees $2,290. Average book expense $1,330. **Required Forms and Deadlines:** FAFSA. **Notification of Awards:** Applicants will be notified of awards on a rolling basis beginning 4/1. **Types of Aid:** Need-based scholarships/grants: Federal Pell, SEOG, state scholarships/grants, private scholarships, the school's own gift aid, United Negro College Fund. Loans: Subsidized Stafford, Unsubsidized Stafford, PLUS, Federal Perkins. **Student Employment:** Federal Work-Study Program available. Institutional employment available. Highest amount earned per year from on-campus jobs $3,500. Off-campus job opportunities are fair. **Financial Aid Statistics:** 76% freshmen, 75% undergrads receive need-based scholarship or grant aid. 41% freshmen, 42% undergrads receive non-need-based scholarship or grant aid. 93% freshmen, 95% undergrads receive need-based self-help aid. 94% freshmen, 93% undergrads receive any aid. 84% undergrads borrow to pay for school. Average cumulative indebtedness $28,582. **Criteria for awarding institutional aid:** Non-need-based: academics, alumni affiliation, leadership, music/drama.

LINDENWOOD UNIVERSITY

209 South Kingshighway, Saint Charles, MO 63301-1695
Phone: 314-949-4949
E-mail: admissions@lindenwood.edu • **CEEB Code:** 6367
Fax: 314-949-4989 • **Website:** www.lindenwood.edu • **ACT Code:** 2324

This private school, affiliated with the Presbyterian Church, was founded in 1827. It has a 172-acre campus.

RATINGS

Admissions Selectivity Rating: 88   **Fire Safety Rating:** 60*   **Green Rating:** 60*

STUDENTS AND FACULTY

Enrollment: 6,330. **Student Body:** 56% female, 44% male, 20% out-of-state, 10% international. Asian 1%, African American 11%, Caucasian 62%, Hispanic 2%, Native American 0%.
Retention and Graduation: 66% freshmen return for sophomore year. 26% freshmen graduate within 4 years. 43% freshmen graduate within 6 years. 20% grads go on to further study within 1 year. 8% grads pursue arts and sciences degrees. 1% grads pursue law degrees. 10% grads pursue business degrees. 1% grads pursue medical degrees. **Faculty:** Student/faculty ratio 13:1. 190 full-time faculty, 65% hold PhDs, 8% are members of minority groups, 40% are women. 0% of classes are taught by teaching assistants.

ACADEMICS

Degrees: bachelor's, certificate, master's, post-bachelor's certificate, post-master's certificate. **Classes:** Most classes have 10–19 students. Most lab/discussion sessions have 20–29 students. **Special Study Options:** Accelerated program, cross-registration, double major, dual enrollment, English as a Second Language (ESL), honors program, independent study, internships, student-designed major, study abroad, teacher certification program. **Disability Services:** Special programs offered to physically disabled students include reader services, tutors. **Career Services:** alumni services, career assessment, internships.

FACILITIES

Housing: men's dorms, women's dorms, apartments for married students, apartments for single students. Special Academic Facilities/Equipment: University archives. Daniel Boone Campus

CAMPUS LIFE

Environment: Activities: Choral groups, concert band, dance, drama/theater, jazz band, literary magazine, marching band, music ensembles, musical theater, pep band, radio station, student government, student newspaper, symphony orchestra, television station, Campus Ministries, International Student Organization 72 registered organizations, 8 honor societies, 13 religious organizations. 1 fraternities, 1 sororities. **Athletics (Intercollegiate):** Men: baseball, basketball, cheerleading, cross-country, diving, football, golf, ice hockey, lacrosse, riflery, soccer, swimming, tennis, track/field (outdoor), track/field (indoor), volleyball, water polo, wrestling. Women: basketball, cheerleading, cross-country, diving, field hockey, golf, ice hockey, lacrosse, riflery, soccer, softball, swimming, tennis, track/field (outdoor), track/field (indoor), volleyball, water polo. **Environmental Initiatives:** Paper recycling Lighting

ADMISSIONS

Freshman Academic Profile: Average high school GPA 3.1. 10% in top 10% of high school class, 30% in top 25% of high school class, 62% in top 50% of high school class. 75% from public high schools. SAT Math middle 50% range 480-560. SAT Critical Reading middle 50% range 410-490. ACT middle 50% range 20-24. Minimum paper TOEFL 500. **Basis for Candidate Selection:** Very important factors considered include: academic GPA, standardized test scores. Important factors considered include: Class rank, rigor of secondary school record, character/personal qualities, extracurricular activities, interview, talent/ability. Other factors considered include: application essay, recommendation(s), alumni/ae relation, first generation, level of applicant's interest, volunteer work. **Freshman Admission Requirements:** High school diploma is required and GED is accepted. **Freshman Admission Statistics:** 4,020 applied, 469% enrolled. **Transfer Admission Requirements:** college transcript(s), minimum college GPA of 2.0 required. Lowest grade transferable D. **General Admission Information:** Application Fee $30. Nonfall registration accepted. Admission may be deferred for a maximum of Eval Individually. Credit and/or placement offered for CEEB Advanced Placement tests.

COSTS AND FINANCIAL AID

Annual tuition $12,960. Room and board $6,700. Required fees $300. **Required Forms and Deadlines:** FAFSA. **Notification of Awards: Types of Aid:** Need-based scholarships/grants: Federal Pell, SEOG, state scholarships/grants, private scholarships, the school's own gift aid. Loans: Subsidized Stafford, Unsubsidized Stafford, PLUS, Federal Perkins. **Student Employment:** Federal Work-Study Program available. Institutional employment available. Off-campus job opportunities are good. **Financial Aid Statistics:** 67%

freshmen, 67% undergrads receive need-based scholarship or grant aid. 26% freshmen, 30% undergrads receive non-need-based scholarship or grant aid. 91% freshmen, 93% undergrads receive need-based self-help aid. **Criteria for awarding institutional aid:** *Non-need-based:* academics, alumni affiliation, art, job skills, leadership, music/drama.

LINDSEY WILSON COLLEGE

210 Lindsey Wilson Street, Columbia, KY 42728
Phone: 800-264-0138
E-mail: admissions@lindsey.edu • **CEEB Code:** 1409
Fax: 270-384-8591 • **Website:** www.lindsey.edu • **ACT Code:** 1522

This private school, affiliated with the Methodist Church, was founded in 1903. It has a 43-acre campus.

RATINGS
Admissions Selectivity Rating: 63   **Fire Safety Rating:** 60*   **Green Rating:** 60*

STUDENTS AND FACULTY
Student Body: 6% out-of-state.
Retention and Graduation: 49% freshmen return for sophomore year. **Faculty:** Student/faculty ratio 21:1.

ACADEMICS
Degrees: associate, bachelor's, master's. **Majors with Highest Enrollment:** biology; elementary education and teaching; social sciences. **Special Study Options:** cooperative education program, English as a Second Language (ESL), internships, study abroad. **Disability Services:** Special programs offered to physically disabled students include reader services, tutors. **Career Services:** alumni services, career assessment, internships.

FACILITIES
Housing: men's dorms, women's dorms, apartments for single students. **Computers:** Students can register for classes online. Administrative functions (other than registration) can be performed online.

CAMPUS LIFE
Environment: Rural. **Activities:** Choral groups, literary magazine, student government, student newspaper, yearbook 28 registered organizations. **Athletics (Intercollegiate):** *Men:* baseball, basketball, cross-country, golf, soccer, tennis, track/field (outdoor). *Women:* basketball, cross-country, golf, soccer, softball, tennis, track/field (outdoor), volleyball.

ADMISSIONS
Freshman Academic Profile: Minimum paper TOEFL 490. **Freshman Admission Requirements:** High school diploma is required and GED is accepted. **Freshman Admission Statistics:** 1,335 applied, 57% admitted, 55% enrolled. **Transfer Admission Requirements:** college transcript(s), standardized test scores, statement of good standing from prior institution(s). Lowest grade transferable D. **General Admission Information:** Nonfall registration accepted. Placement offered for CEEB Advanced Placement tests.

COSTS AND FINANCIAL AID
Annual tuition $12,456. Room and board $5,484. Required fees $146. Average book expense $350. **Required Forms and Deadlines:** FAFSA, institution's own financial aid form, state aid form. **Notification of Awards: Types of Aid:** *Need-based scholarships/grants:* Federal Pell, SEOG, state scholarships/grants, private scholarships, the school's own gift aid. *Loans:* Subsidized Stafford, PLUS, Federal Perkins, college/university loans from institutional funds. **Student Employment:** Federal Work-Study Program available. Institutional employment available. Off-campus job opportunities are good.

LINFIELD COLLEGE

900 South East Baker Street, McMinnville, OR 97128-6894
Phone: 503-883-2213 • **Financial Aid Phone:** 503-883-2269
E-mail: admission@linfield.edu • **CEEB Code:** 4387
Fax: 503-883-2472 • **Website:** www.linfield.edu • **ACT Code:** 3466

This private school, affiliated with the American Baptist Church, was founded in 1858. It has a 193-acre campus.

RATINGS
Admissions Selectivity Rating: 70   **Fire Safety Rating:** 98   **Green Rating:** 92

STUDENTS AND FACULTY
Enrollment: 1,608. **Student Body:** 60% female, 40% male, 46% out-of-state, 3% international (24 countries represented). Asian 6%, African American 2%, Caucasian 65%, Hispanic 9%, Native American 1%.
Retention and Graduation: 88% freshmen return for sophomore year. 59% freshmen graduate within 4 years. 68% freshmen graduate within 6 years. 20% grads go on to further study within 1 year. 10% grads pursue arts and sciences degrees. 2% grads pursue law degrees. 2% grads pursue business degrees. 2% grads pursue medical degrees. **Faculty:** Student/faculty ratio 11:1. 119 full-time faculty, 95% hold PhDs, 9% are members of minority groups, 45% are women. 0% of classes are taught by teaching assistants.

ACADEMICS
Degrees: bachelor's. **Classes:** Most classes have 10–19 students. **Majors with Highest Enrollment:** business/commerce; elementary education and teaching; kinesiology and exercise science. **Special Study Options:** cross-registration, distance learning, double major, English as a Second Language (ESL), external degree program, independent study, internships, liberal arts/career combination, student-designed major, study abroad, teacher certification program, Unique January Term courses, widespread participation in off-campus international study. **Disability Services:** Special programs offered to physically disabled students include note-taking services, reader services, tape recorders, tutors. **Career Services:** Alumni network, alumni services, career/job search classes, internships, regional alumni.

FACILITIES
Housing: Coed dorms, special housing for disabled students, men's dorms, women's dorms, fraternity/sorority housing, apartments for single students, wellness housing, 80% of campus accessible to physically disabled. **Special Academic Facilities/Equipment:** New library, art gallery, anthropology museum, language classroom with murals, environmental field station, undergraduate research institute, electron microscope. **Computers:** 90% of classrooms, 90% of dorms, 100% of libraries, have wireless network access. Students can register for classes online. Administrative functions (other than registration) can be performed online.

CAMPUS LIFE
Environment: Town. **Activities:** Choral groups, concert band, dance, drama/theater, jazz band, literary magazine, music ensembles, musical theater, opera, pep band, radio station, student government, student newspaper, symphony orchestra, Campus Ministries, International Student Organization, Model UN 41 registered organizations, 18 honor societies, 5 religious organizations. 4 fraternities, 4 sororities. **Athletics (Intercollegiate):** *Men:* baseball, basketball, cross-country, football, golf, soccer, swimming, tennis, track/field (outdoor). *Women:* basketball, cross-country, golf, lacrosse, soccer, softball, swimming, tennis, track/field (outdoor), volleyball. **On-Campus Highlights:** Nicholson Library, Modern language rooms (Walker Hall, 3rd floor), Elkington and Terrell Halls, Food services and coffee shop, Athletic complex. **Environmental Initiatives:** Signatory on ACUPCC Established sustainability committee Completed part I of carbon footprint survey, Climate Action Plan 2010 & GHG Reports 2007 & 2010.

ADMISSIONS
Freshman Academic Profile: Average high school GPA 3.5. 27% in top 10% of high school class, 38% in top 25% of high school class, 92% in top 50% of high school class. 90% from public high schools. SAT Math middle 50% range 490-600. SAT Critical Reading middle 50% range 480-590. SAT Writing middle 50% range 460-575. ACT middle 50% range 21-27. Minimum web-based TOEFL 80. Minimum paper TOEFL 550. **Basis for Candidate Selection:** *Very important factors considered include:* academic GPA, rigor of secondary school record, standardized test scores. *Important factors considered include:* Class rank, application essay, recommendation(s). *Other factors considered include:* alumni/ae relation, character/personal qualities, extracurricular activities, first generation, geographical residence, level of applicant's interest, racial/ethnic status, talent/ability, volunteer work, work experience. **Freshman Admission Requirements:** High school diploma is required and GED is accepted. **Freshman Admission Statistics:** 2,338 applied, 83% admitted, 23% enrolled.

Transfer Admission Requirements: college transcript(s), essay or personal statement, Lowest grade transferable C. **General Admission Information:** Application Fee $40. Regular notification 4/1. Nonfall registration accepted. Admission may be deferred for a maximum of 1 YEAR. Credit offered for CEEB Advanced Placement tests.

COSTS AND FINANCIAL AID
Annual tuition $34,000. Room and board $9,500. Required fees $328. Average book expense $750. **Required Forms and Deadlines:** FAFSA. **Notification of Awards:** Applicants will be notified of awards on or about 4/1. **Types of Aid:** *Need-based scholarships/grants:* Federal Pell, SEOG, state scholarships/grants, private scholarships, the school's own gift aid. *Loans:* Direct Subsidized Stafford, Direct Unsubsidized Stafford, Direct PLUS, Federal Perkins, private loans from multiple lenders. **Student Employment:** Federal Work-Study Program available. Institutional employment available. Highest amount earned per year from on-campus jobs $2,250. Off-campus job opportunities are fair. **Financial Aid Statistics:** 98% freshmen, 98% undergrads receive need-based scholarship or grant aid. 100% freshmen, 98% undergrads receive non-need-based scholarship or grant aid. 80% freshmen, 85% undergrads receive need-based self-help aid. 94% freshmen, 90% undergrads receive any aid. 72% undergrads borrow to pay for school. Average cumulative indebtedness $29,793. **Criteria for awarding institutional aid:** *Non-need-based:* academics, minority status, music/drama.

LIPSCOMB UNIVERSITY

One University Park Dr. Nashville, TN 37204-3951
Phone: 615-966-1776 • **Financial Aid Phone:** 615-966-1791
E-mail: admissions@lipscomb.edu • **CEEB Code:** 1161
Fax: 615-966-1804 • **Website:** www.lipscomb.edu • **ACT Code:** 3956

This private school, affiliated with the Church of Christ Church, was founded in 1891. It has a 65-acre campus.

RATINGS
Admissions Selectivity Rating: 88   **Fire Safety Rating:** 99   **Green Rating:** 84

STUDENTS AND FACULTY
Enrollment: 2,622. **Student Body:** 58% female, 42% male, 32% out-of-state, 2% international (35 countries represented). Asian 3%, African American 9%, Caucasian 78%, Hispanic 4%, Native American 0%.
Retention and Graduation: 71% freshmen return for sophomore year. 40% freshmen graduate within 4 years. 80% grads go on to further study within 1 year. **Faculty:** Student/faculty ratio 14:1. 169 full-time faculty, 85% hold PhDs, 5% are members of minority groups, 36% are women. 0% of classes are taught by teaching assistants.

ACADEMICS
Degrees: bachelor's, first professional, master's, post-bachelor's certificate. **Classes:** Most classes have 10–19 students. Most lab/discussion sessions have 20–29 students. **Majors with Highest Enrollment:** business administration and management; elementary education and teaching; pre-nursing studies. **Special Study Options:** cross-registration, distance learning, double major, dual enrollment, honors program, independent study, internships, study abroad, teacher certification program, weekend college. **Disability Services:** Special programs offered to physically disabled students include note-taking services, reader services, tape recorders, tutors. **Career Services:** Alumni network, alumni services, career/job search classes, career assessment, internships.

FACILITIES
Housing: men's dorms, women's dorms. Out-of-town undergraduates required to live on campus except for seniors, students over 21, and married students. 100% of campus accessible to physically disabled. **Special Academic Facilities/Equipment:** On-campus elementary, middle, and secondary schools. **Computers:** 100% of classrooms, 100% of dorms, 100% of libraries, 100% of dining areas, 100% of student union, 100% of common outdoor areas have wireless network access. Students can register for classes online. Administrative functions (other than registration) can be performed online.

CAMPUS LIFE
Environment: Metropolis. **Activities:** Choral groups, concert band, drama/theater, jazz band, literary magazine, marching band, music ensembles, musical theater, pep band, radio station, student government, student newspaper, yearbook, Campus Ministries, International Student Organization 65 registered organizations. **Athletics (Intercollegiate):** *Men:* baseball, basketball, cross-country, golf, soccer, tennis, track/field (outdoor). *Women:* basketball, cheerleading, cross-country, soccer, softball, tennis, track/field (outdoor), track/field (indoor), volleyball. **On-Campus Highlights:** Student Center, SAC - Student Activity Center, Allen Arena, Willard Collins Alumni Auditorium, Bison Square.

Environmental Initiatives: - Internal Sustainability Practices: Geothermal heating and cooling in all new building and rennovation since 2005 (currently three buildings), hybrid cars for VP's, a green housekeeping program, internal sustainability audit and near completion of the state's first LEED certified academic building. - Established SE region's first SE Sustainability Academic Program: New Institute for Sustainable Practice, TN's first green MBA, TN's first sustainability undergrad degree and TN's first sustainability minor. Since 2007, Leader in State and Local Dialogue and Awareness on Sustainabilty: Hosted Tennessee's first two state wide conferences on sustainability policy and sponsored TN's first four green business summits and expos with international sustainability speakers (Dr. Brian Nattrass of Natural Step; Gary Hirshberg, CEO Stonyfield Farms; Joel Makower of Greenbiz.com; L. Hunter Lovins formerly of Rocky Mtn Institute; Don Mosely, Walmart Sustainable Facilities; Tom Szaky of Terracyle. The Fifth annual sustainable business summit planned for 2012 with Biomimicry's Janine Benyus.

ADMISSIONS
Freshman Academic Profile: Average high school GPA 3.5. 27% in top 10% of high school class, 52% in top 25% of high school class, 81% in top 50% of high school class. 72% from public high schools. SAT Math middle 50% range 490-610. SAT Critical Reading middle 50% range 480-603. ACT middle 50% range 22-28. Minimum paper TOEFL 550. **Basis for Candidate Selection:** *Very important factors considered include:* Class rank, standardized test scores, interview. *Important factors considered include:* academic GPA, recommendation(s), rigor of secondary school record, character/personal qualities. *Other factors considered include:* extracurricular activities, first generation, talent/ability, volunteer work, work experience. **Freshman Admission Requirements:** High school diploma is required and GED is accepted. *Academic units required:* 4 English, 2 mathematics, 2 science, 2 foreign language, 2 social studies, 2 academic electives. 4 English, 2 mathematics, 2 science, 2 foreign language, 2 social studies, 2 academic electives. **Freshman Admission Statistics:** 3,430 applied, 51% admitted, 36% enrolled. **Transfer Admission Requirements:** college transcript(s), interview, statement of good standing from prior institution(s). Minimum college GPA of 2.0 required. Lowest grade transferable C. **General Admission Information:** Application Fee $25. Nonfall registration accepted. Credit and/or placement offered for CEEB Advanced Placement tests.

COSTS AND FINANCIAL AID
Annual tuition $22,978. Room and board $9,224. Required fees $1,676. Average book expense $1,500. **Required Forms and Deadlines:** FAFSA. **Notification of Awards:** Applicants will be notified of awards on a rolling basis beginning 2/15. **Types of Aid:** *Need based scholarships/grants:* Federal Pell, SEOG, state scholarships/grants, private scholarships, the school's own gift aid. *Loans:* Subsidized Stafford, Unsubsidized Stafford, PLUS, Federal Perkins, Federal Nursing, alternative. **Student Employment: Financial Aid Statistics:** 63% freshmen, 64% undergrads receive need-based scholarship or grant aid. 98% freshmen, 79% undergrads receive non-need-based scholarship or grant aid. 83% freshmen, 85% undergrads receive need-based self-help aid. 2% freshmen, 2% undergrads receive athletic scholarships. 67% freshmen, 68% undergrads receive any aid. 58% undergrads borrow to pay for school. Average cumulative indebtedness $15,355. **Criteria for awarding institutional aid:** *Non-need-based:* academics, alumni affiliation, art, athletics, leadership, minority status, music/drama, religious affiliation, state/district residency.

LIVINGSTONE COLLEGE

701 West Monroe Street, Salisbury, NC 28144-5213
Phone: 704-216-6001 • **Financial Aid Phone:** 707-216-6273
E-mail: admissions@livingstone.edu
Fax: 704-216-6215 • **Website:** www.livingstone.edu

This private school, affiliated with the African Methodist Episcopal Church, was founded in 1879. It has a 272-acre campus.

RATINGS
Admissions Selectivity Rating: 68   **Fire Safety Rating:** 63   **Green Rating:** 60*

STUDENTS AND FACULTY
Enrollment: 907. **Student Body:** 43% female, 57% male, 1% international (5 countries represented). Asian 0%, African American 67%, Caucasian 1%, Hispanic 0%, Native American 0%.
Retention and Graduation: 61% freshmen return for sophomore year. 50% grads go on to further study within 1 year. 25% grads pursue arts and sciences degrees. 5% grads pursue law degrees. 15% grads pursue business degrees. 5% grads pursue medical degrees. **Faculty:** Student/faculty ratio 15:1. 54 full-time faculty, 50% hold PhDs, 33% are members of minority groups, 44% are women. 0% of classes are taught by teaching assistants.

ACADEMICS

Degrees: bachelor's. **Classes:** Most classes have fewer than 10 students. Most lab/discussion sessions have 10–19 students. **Majors with Highest Enrollment:** business administration and management; computer and information sciences; criminal justice/safety studies. **Special Study Options:** Accelerated program, cross-registration, double major, independent study, internships, teacher certification program, Community Service.

FACILITIES

Housing: special housing for disabled students, men's dorms, special housing for international students, women's dorms, apartments for married students, apartments for single students. 90% of campus accessible to physically disabled. **Special Academic Facilities/Equipment:** Heritage Hall; Poets and Dreamers Garden; NASA SEMAA Lab; and the Elizabeth Koontz Center **Computers:** Students can register for classes online. Administrative functions (other than registration) can be performed online.

CAMPUS LIFE

Environment: Town. **Activities:** Choral groups, concert band, dance, drama/theater, jazz band, marching band, music ensembles, musical theater, pep band, radio station, student government, student-run film society, yearbook 16 registered organizations, 4 honor societies, 2 religious organizations. 4 fraternities, 4 sororities. **Athletics (Intercollegiate):** *Men:* basketball, cross-country, football, track/field (outdoor). *Women:* basketball, bowling, cheerleading, cross-country, softball, tennis, track/field (outdoor), volleyball.

ADMISSIONS

Freshman Academic Profile: SAT Math middle 50% range 320-430. SAT Critical Reading middle 50% range 323-420. SAT Writing middle 50% range 320-400. ACT middle 50% range 12-16. Minimum paper TOEFL 500. **Basis for Candidate Selection:** *Important factors considered include:* academic GPA, recommendation(s). *Other factors considered include:* Class rank, application essay, rigor of secondary school record, alumni/ae relation, character/personal qualities, extracurricular activities, first generation, geographical residence, interview, level of applicant's interest, state residency, talent/ability, volunteer work, work experience. **Freshman Admission Requirements:** High school diploma is required and GED is accepted. *Academic units required:* 4 English, 3 mathematics, 2 science, 2 foreign language, 2 social studies, 1 history. 4 English, 3 mathematics, 2 science, 2 foreign language, 2 social studies, 1 history. **Freshman Admission Statistics:** 1,587 applied, 58% admitted, 28% enrolled. **Transfer Admission Requirements:** college transcript(s), statement of good standing from prior institution(s). Minimum college GPA of 2.0 required. Lowest grade transferable C. **General Admission Information:** Application Fee $25. Nonfall registration accepted. Credit and/or placement offered for CEEB Advanced Placement tests.

COSTS AND FINANCIAL AID

Average book expense. **Required Forms and Deadlines:** FAFSA, institution's own financial aid form, state aid form. **Notification of Awards: Types of Aid:** *Need-based scholarships/grants: Loans:* Subsidized Stafford, PLUS. **Student Employment:** Highest amount earned per year from on-campus jobs $1,200. **Financial Aid Statistics:** 94% freshmen, 96% undergrads receive need-based scholarship or grant aid. 8% freshmen, 6% undergrads receive non-need-based scholarship or grant aid. 76% freshmen, 86% undergrads receive need-based self-help aid. 97% undergrads borrow to pay for school. Average cumulative indebtedness $15,306.

LOCK HAVEN UNIVERSITY OF PENNSYLVANIA

LHU Office of Admissions, Lock Haven, PA 17745
Phone: 570-484-2027
E-mail: admissions@lhup.edu • **CEEB Code:** 2654
Fax: 570-484-2201 • **Website:** www.lhup.edu • **ACT Code:** 3708

This public school was founded in 1870. It has a 175-acre campus.

RATINGS

Admissions Selectivity Rating: 75   **Fire Safety Rating:** 61   **Green Rating:** 60*

STUDENTS AND FACULTY

Enrollment: 4,917. **Student Body:** 57% female, 43% male, 7% out-of-state, 1% international (39 countries represented). Asian 1%, African American 6%, Caucasian 89%, Hispanic 2%, Native American 0%.
Retention and Graduation: 28% freshmen graduate within 4 years. **Faculty:** Student/faculty ratio 21:1. 230 full-time faculty, 77% hold PhDs, 13% are members of minority groups, 47% are women. 0% of classes are taught by teaching assistants.

ACADEMICS

Degrees: associate, bachelor's, master's. **Classes:** Most classes have 20–29 students. Most lab/discussion sessions have 20–29 students. **Majors with Highest Enrollment:** elementary education and teaching; health and physical education/fitness, other; health professions and related clinical sciences, other. **Special Study Options:** cross-registration, distance learning, double major, dual enrollment, honors program, independent study, internships, student-designed major, study abroad, teacher certification program. **Honors Programs:** The University Honors Program provides students and faculty opportunities for creative intellectual engagement through a mix of special curricular and co-curricular opportunities. Students may apply for entry as a first-year freshman or after completing 1-4 semesters of college-level work. Entry as a first-year freshman may be either directly into the University Honors or through the First Year Excellence Program. Students successfully completing the First Year Excellence Program receive certificate recognition. Students completing the University Honors Program receive recognition on their transcript, on their diploma and at commencement. Students in both the First Year Excellence and University Honors Programs must participate in co-curricular activities and community service in addition to their curriculum. Engaging activity groups and Speaker Series allow students in the Honors Program to bond together and learn from each other, creating a community of both friends and scholars. **Disability Services:** Special programs offered to physically disabled students include note-taking services, reader services, tape recorders, tutors. **Career Services:** Alumni network, alumni services, career/job search classes, career assessment, internships, regional alumni.

FACILITIES

Housing: Coed dorms, apartments for single students. 98% of campus accessible to physically disabled. **Special Academic Facilities/Equipment:** Planetarium, Sloan Art Gallery, Library Archives **Computers:** Students can register for classes online. Administrative functions (other than registration) can be performed online. Undergraduates are required to own a computer.

CAMPUS LIFE

Environment: Village. **Activities:** Choral groups, concert band, dance, drama/theater, jazz band, literary magazine, marching band, music ensembles, musical theater, pep band, radio station, student government, student newspaper, symphony orchestra, television station, yearbook, Campus Ministries, International Student Organization 96 registered organizations, 10 honor societies, 7 religious organizations. 6 fraternities, 4 sororities. **Athletics (Intercollegiate):** *Men:* baseball, basketball, football, soccer, track/field (outdoor), track/field (indoor), wrestling. *Women:* basketball, field hockey, lacrosse, soccer, softball, swimming, track/field (outdoor), track/field (indoor), volleyball. **On-Campus Highlights:** Student Recreation Center, Parsons Union Building, Library, Residence Halls, Bentley Dining Hall.

ADMISSIONS

Freshman Academic Profile: Average high school GPA 3.3. 8% in top 10% of high school class, 28% in top 25% of high school class, 69% in top 50% of high school class. SAT Math middle 50% range 430-530. SAT Critical Reading middle 50% range 420-510. ACT middle 50% range 17-23. Minimum paper TOEFL 550. **Basis for Candidate Selection:** *Very important factors considered include:* Class rank, academic GPA, rigor of secondary school record, character/personal qualities, talent/ability. *Important factors considered include:* standardized test scores, racial/ethnic status. *Other factors considered include:* application essay, recommendation(s), extracurricular activities, first generation, interview, level of applicant's interest, volunteer work, work experience. **Freshman Admission Requirements:** High school diploma is required and GED is accepted. *Academic units required:* 4 English, 3 mathematics, 3 science, (2 science labs), 2 social studies, 2 history. *Academic units recommended:* 4 English, 3 mathematics, 3 science, (2 science labs), 2 social studies, 2 history. **Freshman Admission Statistics:** 5,072 applied, 61% admitted, 40% enrolled. **Transfer Admission Requirements:** college transcript(s), statement of good standing from prior institution(s). Minimum college GPA of 2.0 required. Lowest grade transferable C. **General Admission Information:** Application Fee $25. Notification on a rolling basis, beginning on or about 10/1. Nonfall registration accepted. Admission may be deferred for a maximum of 1 year. Credit and/or placement offered for CEEB Advanced Placement tests.

COSTS AND FINANCIAL AID

Annual in-state tuition $6,240. Annual out-of-state tuition $13,600. Room and board $7,056. Required fees $1,999. Average book expense $1,260. **Required Forms and Deadlines:** FAFSA. **Notification of Awards:** Applicants will be notified of awards on a rolling basis beginning 4/1. **Types of Aid:** *Need-based scholarships/grants:* Federal Pell, SEOG, state scholarships/grants, private scholarships, United Negro College Fund. *Loans:* Subsidized Stafford, Unsubsidized Stafford, PLUS, Federal Perkins, college/university loans from institutional funds. **Student Employment:** Federal Work-Study Program available. Institutional employment available. Off-campus job opportunities are good. **Financial Aid Statistics:** 66% freshmen, 66% undergrads receive need-based scholarship or grant aid. 5% freshmen, 6% undergrads receive non-need-based scholarship or grant aid. 77% freshmen, 77% undergrads receive need-based self-help aid. 4% freshmen, 5% undergrads receive athletic scholarships. 85% undergrads borrow to pay for school. Average cumulative indebtedness $23,707. **Criteria for awarding institutional aid:** *Non-need-based:* academics, art, athletics, leadership, minority status, music/drama, state/district residency.

LOMA LINDA UNIVERSITY

Office of Admissions, Loma Linda, CA 92350
Phone: 909-824-4599
Fax: 909-824-4291 • **Website:** www.llu.edu/

This private school, affiliated with the Seventh Day Adventist Church, was founded in 1905.

RATINGS
Admissions Selectivity Rating: 60*   Fire Safety Rating: 60*   Green Rating: 60*

ACADEMICS
Degrees: associate, bachelor's, certificate, master's, post-bachelor's certificate.
Special Study Options: distance learning, double major.

FACILITIES
Housing: Coed dorms, men's dorms, women's dorms, apartments for single students.

CAMPUS LIFE
Environment: Village. **Activities:** student government, student newspaper, yearbook 1 honor societies, 1 religious organizations.

ADMISSIONS
Basis for Candidate Selection: *Very important factors considered include:* application essay, recommendation(s), character/personal qualities, interview, religious affiliation/commitment. *Important factors considered include:* talent/ability, volunteer work, work experience. *Other factors considered include:* alumni/ae relation, extracurricular activities. **Freshman Admission Requirements:** High school diploma is required and GED is accepted. **Transfer Admission Requirements:** High school transcript, college transcript(s), essay or personal statement, interview, minimum college GPA of 2.0 required. Lowest grade transferable c. **General Admission Information:** Application Fee $50. Nonfall registration not accepted. Admission may be deferred for a maximum of 1.

COSTS AND FINANCIAL AID
Average book expense. **Required Forms and Deadlines: Notification of Awards: Types of Aid:** *Need-based scholarships/grants: Loans:* Subsidized Stafford, PLUS.

LONGWOOD UNIVERSITY

Admissions Office, Farmville, VA 23909
Phone: 434-395-2060 • **Financial Aid Phone:** 800-281-4677
E-mail: admissions@longwood.edu • **CEEB Code:** 5368
Fax: 434-395-2332 • **Website:** www.whylongwood.com • **ACT Code:** 4366

This public school was founded in 1839. It has a 160-acre campus.

RATINGS
Admissions Selectivity Rating: 72   Fire Safety Rating: 85   Green Rating: 78

STUDENTS AND FACULTY
Enrollment: 4,160. **Student Body:** 66% female, 34% male, 3% out-of-state, 0% international (46 countries represented). Asian 1%, African American 6%, Caucasian 82%, Hispanic 3%, Native American 0%. **Retention and Graduation:** 78% freshmen return for sophomore year. 40% freshmen graduate within 4 years. **Faculty:** Student/faculty ratio 18:1. 222 full-time faculty, 85% hold PhDs, 8% are members of minority groups, 48% are women. 0% of classes are taught by teaching assistants.

ACADEMICS
Degrees: bachelor's, master's. **Classes:** Most classes have 20–29 students. Most lab/discussion sessions have 20–29 students. **Majors with Highest Enrollment:** business/commerce; elementary education and teaching; psychology. **Special Study Options:** Accelerated program, cross-registration, distance learning, double major, dual enrollment, English as a Second Language (ESL), honors program, independent study, internships, study abroad, teacher certifica-

tion program. **Honors Programs:** The Longwood University Honors Program is designed to meet the needs of academically gifted and talented undergraduate students. Challenging courses with high academic standards enable students to expand their intellectual and creative horizons. The Honors Program focuses on the exchange of ideas and the enrichment of students' educational and cultural experiences. Learning takes place not only in the classroom, but also through cultural events, conferences, field trips, and study abroad. In keeping with the University's mission, the Longwood Honors Program strives to develop citizens who are committed to using their learning to provide service to their local communities as well as to the larger national and global communities. The concept of linking learning with the practice of citizenship is the distinctive feature of our Program. **Combined Degree Programs:** BA/MA, Special Education BA/MS and BS/MS. **Disability Services:** Special programs offered to physically disabled students include note-taking services, reader services, tape recorders, tutors. **Career Services:** career/job search classes, career assessment, internships Career Services highlights include Students must complete either am internship, study abroad program or work on a research project to graduate.

FACILITIES
Housing: Coed dorms, special housing for disabled students, women's dorms, fraternity/sorority housing, apartments for single students, Honor Student Housing. 100% of campus accessible to physically disabled. **Special Academic Facilities/Equipment:** Longwood Center for the Visual Arts **Computers:** 100% of classrooms, 100% of libraries, 100% of dining areas, 100% of student union, have wireless network access. Students can register for classes online. Administrative functions (other than registration) can be performed online. Undergraduates are required to own a computer.

CAMPUS LIFE
Environment: Village. **Activities:** Choral groups, concert band, dance, drama/theater, jazz band, literary magazine, music ensembles, pep band, radio station, student government, student newspaper, yearbook, Campus Ministries, International Student Organization 129 registered organizations, 17 honor societies, 11 religious organizations. 9 fraternities, 12 sororities. **Athletics (Intercollegiate):** *Men:* baseball, basketball, cheerleading, cross-country, golf, soccer, tennis. *Women:* basketball, cheerleading, cross-country, field hockey, golf, lacrosse, soccer, softball, tennis. **On-Campus Highlights:** Brock Commons, Lankford Student Union, Health and Fitness Center, Greenwood Library, Dorrill Dining Hall, Science Building.

ADMISSIONS
Freshman Academic Profile: Average high school GPA 3.4. 12% in top 10% of high school class, 38% in top 25% of high school class, 81% in top 50% of high school class. 92% from public high schools. SAT Math middle 50% range 470-550. SAT Critical Reading middle 50% range 470-560. ACT middle 50% range 20-24. Minimum web based TOEFL 79. Minimum paper TOEFL 550. **Basis for Candidate Selection:** *Very important factors considered include:* application essay, academic GPA, rigor of secondary school record, standardized test scores. *Important factors considered include:* Class rank, alumni/ae relation, character/personal qualities, extracurricular activities, first generation, geographical residence, racial/ethnic status, talent/ability, volunteer work. *Other factors considered include:* recommendation(s), state residency. **Freshman Admission Requirements:** High school diploma is required and GED is accepted. *Academic units required:* 4 English, 3 mathematics, 3 science, (2 science labs), 2 foreign language, 2 social studies, 2 history, 1 visual/performing arts. *Academic units recommended:* 4 English, 3 mathematics, 3 science, (2 science labs), 2 foreign language, 2 social studies, 2 history, 1 visual/performing arts. **Freshman Admission Statistics:** 4,080 applied, 75% admitted, 35% enrolled. **Transfer Admission Requirements:** High school transcript, college transcript(s), essay or personal statement, minimum college GPA of 2.50 required. Lowest grade transferable C–. **General Admission Information:** Application Fee $40. Notification on a rolling basis, beginning on or about 1/15. Nonfall registration accepted. Admission may be deferred for a maximum of 1 year. Credit offered for CEEB Advanced Placement tests.

COSTS AND FINANCIAL AID
Annual in-state tuition $6,120. Annual out-of-state tuition $17,760. Room and board $8,448. Required fees $4,770. Average book expense $1,000. **Required Forms and Deadlines:** FAFSA. **Notification of Awards:** Applicants will be notified of awards on or about 4/1. **Types of Aid:** *Need-based scholarships/grants:* Federal Pell, SEOG, state scholarships/grants, private scholarships, the school's own gift aid. *Loans:* Direct Subsidized Stafford, Direct Unsubsidized Stafford, Direct PLUS, Federal Perkins. **Student Employment:** Federal Work-Study Program available. Institutional employment available. Off-campus job opportunities are good. **Financial Aid Statistics:** 89% freshmen, 85% undergrads receive need-based scholarship or grant aid. 3% freshmen, 3% undergrads receive non-need-based scholarship or grant aid. 83% freshmen, 85% undergrads receive need-based self-help aid. 3% freshmen, 3% undergrads receive athletic scholarships. 60% freshmen, % undergrads receive any aid. 60% undergrads borrow to pay for school. Average cumulative indebtedness $23,672. **Criteria for awarding institutional aid:** *Non-need-based:* academics, alumni affiliation, art, athletics, leadership, music/drama, state/district residency.

LORAS COLLEGE

1450 Alta Vista, Dubuque, IA 52004-0178
Phone: 800-245-6727 • **Financial Aid Phone:** 563-588-7136
E-mail: admissions@loras.edu • **CEEB Code:** 6370
Fax: 563-588-7119 • **Website:** www.loras.edu • **ACT Code:** 1328

This private school, affiliated with the Roman Catholic Church, was founded in 1839. It has a 60-acre campus.

RATINGS
Admissions Selectivity Rating: 71   **Fire Safety Rating:** 90   **Green Rating:** 60*

STUDENTS AND FACULTY
Enrollment: 1,565. **Student Body:** 50% female, 50% male, 45% out-of-state, 3% international (7 countries represented). Asian 1%, African American 1%, Caucasian 93%, Hispanic 1%, Native American 0%.
Retention and Graduation: 78% freshmen return for sophomore year. 55% freshmen graduate within 4 years. 65% freshmen graduate within 6 years. 20% grads go on to further study within 1 year. 4% grads pursue arts and sciences degrees. 1% grads pursue law degrees. 2% grads pursue business degrees. 8% grads pursue medical degrees. **Faculty:** Student/faculty ratio 13:1. 111 full-time faculty, 95% hold PhDs, 5% are members of minority groups, 31% are women. 0% of classes are taught by teaching assistants.

ACADEMICS
Degrees: associate, bachelor's, master's. **Classes:** Most classes have 20–29 students. Most lab/discussion sessions have fewer than 10 students. **Majors with Highest Enrollment:** business/commerce; elementary education and teaching; secondary education and teaching. **Special Study Options:** cooperative education program, cross-registration, double major, dual enrollment, English as a Second Language (ESL), honors program, independent study, internships, liberal arts/career combination, student-designed major, study abroad, teacher certification program, Undergrads may take graduate level classes if certain qualifications are met. **Combined Degree Programs:** BA/MA, 2-2 nursing prog with U of Iowa. **Disability Services:** Special programs offered to physically disabled students include note-taking services, reader services, tape recorders. **Career Services:** internships.

FACILITIES
Housing: Coed dorms, men's dorms, women's dorms, apartments for single students. 95% of campus accessible to physically disabled. **Special Academic Facilities/Equipment:** Language lab, television studio, observatory and planetarium. **Computers:** Students can register for classes online. Administrative functions (other than registration) can be performed online. Undergraduates are required to own a computer.

CAMPUS LIFE
Environment: Town. **Activities:** Choral groups, concert band, dance, drama/theater, jazz band, music ensembles, musical theater, radio station, student government, student newspaper, television station, yearbook 71 registered organizations, 710 honor societies, 5 religious organizations. 2 fraternities, 2 sororities. **Athletics (Intercollegiate):** *Men:* baseball, basketball, cross-country, diving, football, golf, soccer, swimming, tennis, track/field (outdoor), track/field (indoor), wrestling. *Women:* basketball, cross-country, diving, golf, soccer, softball, swimming, tennis, track/field (outdoor), track/field (indoor), volleyball. **On-Campus Highlights:** Academic Resource Center, Alumni Campus Center, The Pub and Cafeteria, The Grotto

ADMISSIONS
Freshman Academic Profile: Average high school GPA 3.2. 13% in top 10% of high school class, 34% in top 25% of high school class, 65% in top 50% of high school class. 57% from public high schools. SAT Math middle 50% range 503-625. SAT Critical Reading middle 50% range 453-575. ACT middle 50% range 20-25. Minimum paper TOEFL 550. **Basis for Candidate Selection:** *Very important factors considered include:* academic GPA, rigor of secondary school record, standardized test scores. *Important factors considered include:* Class rank. *Other factors considered include:* application essay, recommendation(s), character/personal qualities, extracurricular activities, racial/ethnic status, volunteer work. **Freshman Admission Requirements:** High school diploma is required and GED is accepted. **Freshman Admission Statistics:** 1,402 applied, 82% admitted, 32% enrolled. **Transfer Admission Requirements:** High school transcript, college transcript(s), standardized test scores, minimum college GPA of 2.0 required. Lowest grade transferable C. **General Admission Information:** Application Fee $25. Nonfall registration accepted. Admission may be deferred for a maximum of Two Terms. Credit offered for CEEB Advanced Placement tests.

COSTS AND FINANCIAL AID
Annual tuition $19,990. Room and board $6,095. Required fees $1,108. Average book expense $800. **Required Forms and Deadlines:** FAFSA. **Notification**

of Awards: Applicants will be notified of awards on a rolling basis beginning 3/1. **Types of Aid:** *Need-based scholarships/grants:* Federal Pell, SEOG, state scholarships/grants, private scholarships, the school's own gift aid. *Loans:* Subsidized Stafford, Unsubsidized Stafford, PLUS, Federal Perkins, college/university loans from institutional funds. **Student Employment:** Highest amount earned per year from on-campus jobs $1,500. **Financial Aid Statistics:** 84% freshmen, 89% undergrads receive need-based scholarship or grant aid. 98% freshmen, 87% undergrads receive non-need-based scholarship or grant aid. 84% freshmen, 89% undergrads receive need-based self-help aid. 99% freshmen, 86% undergrads receive any aid. 94% undergrads borrow to pay for school. Average cumulative indebtedness $24,320. **Criteria for awarding institutional aid:** *Non-need-based:* academics, alumni affiliation, music/drama.

LOUISIANA COLLEGE

1140 College Drive, Pineville, LA 71359-0560
Phone: 318-487-7259
E-mail: admissions@lacollege.edu • **CEEB Code:** 6371
Fax: 318-487-7550 • **Website:** www.lacollege.edu • **ACT Code:** 1586

This private school, affiliated with the Baptist Church, was founded in 1906. It has a 81-acre campus.

RATINGS
Admissions Selectivity Rating: 68   **Fire Safety Rating:** 65   **Green Rating:** 60*

STUDENTS AND FACULTY
Enrollment: 1,014. **Student Body:** 56% female, 44% male, 9% out-of-state, 1% international. Asian 1%, African American 7%, Caucasian 89%, Hispanic 2%, Native American 0%.
Retention and Graduation: 59% freshmen return for sophomore year. 25% freshmen graduate within 4 years. 46% freshmen graduate within 6 years. **Faculty:** Student/faculty ratio 13:1. 68 full-time faculty, 60% hold PhDs, 0% are members of minority groups, 46% are women. 0% of classes are taught by teaching assistants.

ACADEMICS
Degrees: bachelor's. **Classes:** Most classes have fewer than 10 students. Most lab/discussion sessions have 10–19 students. **Majors with Highest Enrollment:** biology; elementary education and teaching; psychology. **Special Study Options:** double major, honors program, independent study, internships, liberal arts/career combination, student-designed major, study abroad, teacher certification program. **Honors Programs:** London Semester. **Disability Services:** Special programs offered to physically disabled students include note-taking services, reader services, tutors. **Career Services:** career/job search classes, career assessment, internships, Career Services highlights include Several majors require internships to fulfill graduation requirements. Academic credit may be available to students who wish to pursue internship opportunities outside major requirements.

FACILITIES
Housing: men's dorms, women's dorms, apartments for married students, apartments for single students. 95% of campus accessible to physically disabled. Special Academic Facilities/Equipment: Art gallery, radio station, performing arts center, theater

CAMPUS LIFE
Environment: Village. **Activities:** Choral groups, concert band, drama/theater, jazz band, literary magazine, music ensembles, musical theater, opera, pep band, radio station, student government, student newspaper, symphony orchestra, yearbook 60 registered organizations, 13 honor societies, 8 religious organizations. 4 fraternities, 3 sororities. **Athletics (Intercollegiate):** *Men:* baseball, basketball, cheerleading, football, golf, soccer. *Women:* basketball, cheerleading, cross-country, soccer, softball, tennis. **On-Campus Highlights:** Healthplex/Wellness Center, Student Center, Martin Performing Arts Center, Weathersby Fine Arts Building, Alexandria Hall.

ADMISSIONS
Freshman Academic Profile: Average high school GPA 3.5. 29% in top 10% of high school class, 54% in top 25% of high school class, 87% in top 50% of high school class. 82% from public high schools. SAT Math middle 50% range 440-600. SAT Critical Reading middle 50% range 440-570. ACT middle 50% range 21-26. Minimum paper TOEFL 550. **Basis for Candidate Selection:** *Very important factors considered include:* Class rank, rigor of secondary school record, standardized test scores. *Other factors considered include:* recommendation(s), alumni/ae relation, character/personal qualities, extracurricular activities, geographical residence, interview, racial/ethnic status, religious affiliation/commitment, state residency, talent/ability, volunteer work, work

experience. **Freshman Admission Requirements:** High school diploma is required and GED is accepted. *Academic units required:* 4 English, 3 mathematics, 3 science, (2 science labs), 2 social studies, 1 history, 4 academic electives. *Academic units recommended:* 4 English, 3 mathematics, 3 science, (2 science labs), 2 social studies, 1 history, 4 academic electives. **Freshman Admission Statistics:** 727 applied, 85% admitted, 43% enrolled. **Transfer Admission Requirements:** college transcript(s), minimum college GPA of 2.0 required. Lowest grade transferable D. **General Admission Information:** Application Fee $25. Regular application deadline 8/15. Notification on a rolling basis, beginning on or about 1/1. Nonfall registration accepted. Admission may be deferred for a maximum of 1 year. Credit and/or placement offered for CEEB Advanced Placement tests.

COSTS AND FINANCIAL AID
Annual tuition $8,850. Room and board $3,740. Required fees $800. Average book expense $750. **Required Forms and Deadlines:** FAFSA, institution's own financial aid form. **Notification of Awards:** Applicants will be notified of awards on a rolling basis beginning 3/1. **Types of Aid:** *Need-based scholarships/grants:* Federal Pell, SEOG, state scholarships/grants, private scholarships, the school's own gift aid, LEAP. *Loans:* Direct Subsidized Stafford, Direct Unsubsidized Stafford, Direct PLUS, Subsidized Stafford, Unsubsidized Stafford, PLUS, college/university loans from institutional funds. **Student Employment:** Federal Work-Study Program available. Institutional employment available. Highest amount earned per year from on-campus jobs $400. Off-campus job opportunities are excellent. **Financial Aid Statistics:** 44% freshmen, 45% undergrads receive need-based scholarship or grant aid. 100% freshmen, 98% undergrads receive non-need-based scholarship or grant aid. 57% freshmen, 57% undergrads receive need-based self-help aid. 98% freshmen, 82% undergrads receive any aid. 54% undergrads borrow to pay for school. Average cumulative indebtedness $5,742. **Criteria for awarding institutional aid:** *Non-need based:* academics, art, leadership, music/drama.

LOUISIANA STATE UNIVERSITY IN SHREVEPORT

One University Place, Shreveport, LA 71115-2399
Phone: 318-797-5061
E-mail: admissions@pilot.lsus.edu • **CEEB Code:** 6355
Fax: 318-797-5204 • **Website:** www.lsus.edu • **ACT Code:** 1593

This public school was founded in 1965. It has a 200-acre campus.

RATINGS
Admissions Selectivity Rating: 72   **Fire Safety Rating:** 60*   **Green Rating:** 60*

STUDENTS AND FACULTY
Enrollment: 3,594. **Student Body:** 62% female, 38% male, 2% out-of-state, 1% international. Asian 2%, African American 22%, Caucasian 65%, Hispanic 2%, Native American 1%.
Retention and Graduation: 53% freshmen return for sophomore year. **Faculty:** Student/faculty ratio 16:1. 155 full-time faculty, 72% hold PhDs, 12% are members of minority groups, 39% are women.

ACADEMICS
Degrees: bachelor's, master's, post-master's certificate. **Classes:** Most classes have 20–29 students. **Majors with Highest Enrollment:** business/commerce; elementary education and teaching; general studies. **Special Study Options:** cooperative education program, study abroad, teacher certification program, Undergrads may take grad level courses and evening Courses. **Combined Degree Programs:** Combined social work program w/ Grambling State U. **Disability Services:** Special programs offered to physically disabled students include note-taking services, reader services, tape recorders, tutors. **Career Services:** alumni services, career/job search classes, career assessment, internships.

FACILITIES
Housing: apartments for married students, apartments for single students. 100% of campus accessible to physically disabled. **Special Academic Facilities/Equipment:** Art center, life science museum, pioneer heritage center. **Computers:** Students can register for classes online. Administrative functions (other than registration) can be performed online.

CAMPUS LIFE
Environment: **Activities:** student government, student newspaper 52 registered organizations, 4 honor societies, 3 religious organizations. 5 fraternities, 3 sororities. **Athletics (Intercollegiate):** *Men:* baseball.

ADMISSIONS
Freshman Academic Profile: Average high school GPA 3.1. 90% from public high schools. ACT middle 50% range 18-23. Minimum paper TOEFL 500.

Basis for Candidate Selection: *Other factors considered include:* rigor of secondary school record, standardized test scores. **Freshman Admission Requirements:** High school diploma is required and GED is accepted. **Freshman Admission Statistics:** 848 applied, 65% admitted. **Transfer Admission Requirements:** college transcript(s), minimum college GPA of 2.0 required. Lowest grade transferable D. **General Admission Information:** Application Fee $10. Regular application deadline 8/1. Nonfall registration accepted. Credit offered for CEEB Advanced Placement tests.

COSTS AND FINANCIAL AID
Required Forms and Deadlines: FAFSA, institution's own financial aid form. **Types of Aid:** *Need-based scholarships/grants:* state scholarships/grants. *Loans:* Subsidized Stafford, PLUS. **Student Employment:** Federal Work-Study Program available. Institutional employment available. Highest amount earned per year from on-campus jobs $2,000. Off-campus job opportunities are good.

LOUISIANA STATE UNIVERSITY—BATON ROUGE

1146 Pleasant Hall, Baton Rouge, LA 70803
Phone: 225-578-1175 • **Financial Aid Phone:** 225-578-3103
E-mail: admissions@lsu.edu • **CEEB Code:** 6373
Fax: 225-578-4433 • **Website:** www.lsu.edu • **ACT Code:** 1590

This public school was founded in 1860. It has a 2000-acre campus.

RATINGS
Admissions Selectivity Rating: 75   **Fire Safety Rating:** 94   **Green Rating:** 89

STUDENTS AND FACULTY
Enrollment: 23,372. **Student Body:** 51% female, 49% male, 20% out-of-state, 2% international (80 countries represented). Asian 3%, African American 10%, Caucasian 78%, Hispanic 4%, Native American 0%.
Retention and Graduation: 84% freshmen return for sophomore year. 31% freshmen graduate within 4 years. **Faculty:** Student/faculty ratio 23:1. 1187 full-time faculty, 89% hold PhDs, 16% are members of minority groups, 34% are women. 9% of classes are taught by teaching assistants.

ACADEMICS
Degrees: bachelor's, doctoral, master's, post-master's certificate. **Classes:** Most classes have 20–29 students. Most lab/discussion sessions have 20–29 students. **Majors with Highest Enrollment:** biology/biological sciences; mass communication/media studies; physical education teaching and coaching. **Special Study Options:** Accelerated program, cooperative education program, cross-registration, distance learning, double major, dual enrollment, English as a Second Language (ESL), exchange student program (domestic), honors program, independent study, internships, liberal arts/career combination, student-designed major, study abroad, teacher certification program. **Honors Programs:** Admissions to the Honors College **Combined Degree Programs:** BS/MED Elementary Education/Holmes. **Disability Services:** Special programs offered to physically disabled students include note-taking services, reader services, tape recorders. **Career Services:** Alumni network, alumni services, career/job search classes, career assessment, internships Career Services highlights include We feel that the newly initiated Fellows Program will bring our Institute the creme of the crop in both students from around campus and in internships for those students. We are committed to teaching entrepreneurship to students in order that they are prepared to start new, innovative ventures sometime in their lives.

FACILITIES
Housing: Coed dorms, special housing for disabled students, men's dorms, women's dorms, fraternity/sorority housing, apartments for married students, apartments for single students, theme housing, 75% of campus accessible to physically disabled. **Special Academic Facilities/Equipment:** Art Museum, NAtural Science Museum, Rural Life Museum, Lichen/Bryophyte Mycological and Vascular Plant herbariums, on campus K-12 schools, geoscience and mycological museums, electron microscope, nuclear science center and civil war center. **Computers:** 100% of classrooms, 100% of dorms, 100% of libraries, 90% of dining areas, 100% of student union, 90% of common outdoor areas have wireless network access. Students can register for classes online. Administrative functions (other than registration) can be performed online.

CAMPUS LIFE
Environment: Metropolis. **Activities:** Choral groups, concert band, dance, drama/theater, jazz band, literary magazine, marching band, music ensembles,

musical theater, opera, pep band, radio station, student government, student newspaper, student-run film society, symphony orchestra, television station, yearbook, Campus Ministries, International Student Organization 300 registered organizations, 32 honor societies, 25 religious organizations. 23 fraternities, 15 sororities. **Athletics (Intercollegiate):** *Men:* baseball, basketball, cheerleading, cross-country, diving, football, golf, swimming, tennis, track/field (outdoor), track/field (indoor). *Women:* basketball, cheerleading, cross-country, diving, golf, gymnastics, soccer, softball, swimming, tennis, track/field (outdoor), track/field (indoor), volleyball. **On-Campus Highlights:** LSU Student Union, Mike VI Tiger Habitat, Indian Mounds, Tiger Stadium, Alex Box Stadium, FACES Laboratory. **Environmental Initiatives:** Energy efficiency programs including Recommissioning, Utility insulation, LED lighting, Class Utilization Study and IT power management enforcement Programs reducing vehicles on campus by 60%, new bus service using low-sulphur diesel and increasing ridership, new bike facility master plan Advanced Recycling Program, athletics in-stadium recycling increased by 77%, composting during fall festival events, sustainable Christmas tree

ADMISSIONS

Freshman Academic Profile: Average high school GPA 3.5. 24% in top 10% of high school class, 51% in top 25% of high school class, 81% in top 50% of high school class. 59% from public high schools. SAT Math middle 50% range 530-630. SAT Critical Reading middle 50% range 500-610. ACT middle 50% range 23-28. Minimum web-based TOEFL 79. Minimum paper TOEFL 550. **Basis for Candidate Selection:** *Very important factors considered include:* academic GPA, rigor of secondary school record, standardized test scores. *Important factors considered include:* Class rank, talent/ability. *Other factors considered include:* application essay, recommendation(s), extracurricular activities, first generation. **Freshman Admission Requirements:** High school diploma is required and GED is accepted. *Academic units required:* 4 English, 3 mathematics, 3 science, 2 foreign language, 1 social studies, 2 history. *Academic units recommended:* 4 English, 3 mathematics, 3 science, 2 foreign language, 1 social studies, 2 history. **Freshman Admission Statistics:** 14,818 applied, 845% enrolled. **Transfer Admission Requirements:** college transcript(s), minimum college GPA of 2.5 required. Lowest grade transferable D. **General Admission Information:** Application Fee $40. Regular application deadline 4/15. Nonfall registration accepted. Admission may be deferred for a maximum of 1 year. Credit offered for CEEB Advanced Placement tests.

COSTS AND FINANCIAL AID

Annual in-state tuition $5,193. Annual out-of-state tuition $20,469. Room and board $10,218. Required fees $1,796. Average book expense $1,500. **Required Forms and Deadlines:** FAFSA, institution's own financial aid form. **Notification of Awards:** Applicants will be notified of awards on a rolling basis beginning 3/1. **Types of Aid:** *Need-based scholarships/grants:* Federal Pell, SEOG, state scholarships/grants, private scholarships, the school's own gift aid, ACG/SMART. *Loans:* Subsidized Stafford, Unsubsidized Stafford, PLUS, Federal Perkins, Alternative/Grad Plus. **Student Employment:** Federal Work-Study Program available. Institutional employment available. Off-campus job opportunities are excellent. **Financial Aid Statistics:** 96% freshmen, 89% undergrads receive need-based scholarship or grant aid. 6% freshmen, 3% undergrads receive non-need-based scholarship or grant aid. 62% freshmen, 71% undergrads receive need-based self-help aid. 2% freshmen, 3% undergrads receive athletic scholarships. 92% freshmen, 83% undergrads receive any aid. 37% undergrads borrow to pay for school. Average cumulative indebtedness $20,337. **Criteria for awarding institutional aid:** *Non-need-based:* academics, alumni affiliation, art, athletics, leadership, music/drama, state/district residency.

LOUISIANA TECH UNIVERSITY

P. O. Box 3178, Ruston, LA 71272
Phone: 318-257-3036
E-mail: bulldog@latech.edu
Fax: 318-257-2499 • **Website:** www.latech.edu

This is a public school.

RATINGS
Admissions Selectivity Rating: 78   **Fire Safety Rating:** 60*   **Green Rating:** 60*

STUDENTS AND FACULTY
Enrollment: 7,101. **Student Body:** 45% female, 55% male, 9% out-of-state, 4% international. Asian 1%, African American 14%, Caucasian 66%, Hispanic 2%, Native American 0%.
Retention and Graduation: 26% freshmen graduate within 4 years. **Faculty:** Student/faculty ratio 21:1. 378 full-time faculty, 78% hold PhDs, 38% are women.

ACADEMICS
Degrees: associate, bachelor's, master's, post-bachelor's certificate. **Career Services:** Alumni network, alumni services, career/job search classes, career assessment, internships, regional alumni. Career Services highlights include The mission of the Career Center is to educate and to serve the students and graduates of Louisiana Tech University in the career education, planning, and development processes. In support of the mission of the University, the Career Center functions as a vital component in the total educational experience of students, primarily in the development, evaluation, initiation, and implementation of career plans and opportunities. Career Center services and resources provide assistance to students in the cultivation and enhancement of skills to explore career options, master job search techniques and strategies, and research employment opportunities. The Career Center provides effective and efficient service to employers in recruitment programs and activities.

ADMISSIONS
Freshman Academic Profile: Average high school GPA 3.3. 19% in top 10% of high school class, 48% in top 25% of high school class, 77% in top 50% of high school class. 85% from public high schools. SAT Math middle 50% range 460-590. SAT Critical Reading middle 50% range 440-550. ACT middle 50% range 20-26. Minimum web-based TOEFL 88. Minimum paper TOEFL 570. **Freshman Admission Statistics:** 4,734 applied, 63% admitted, 51% enrolled. **General Admission Information:** Credit offered for CEEB Advanced Placement tests.

LOURDES COLLEGE

6832 Convent Road, Sylvania, OH 43560-2898
Phone: 419-885-5291 • **Financial Aid Phone:** 419-824-3732
E-mail: AdmissionsLCAdmits@lourdes.edu • **CEEB Code:** 1427
Fax: 419-824-3916 • **Website:** www.lourdes.edu • **ACT Code:** 3598

This private school, affiliated with the Roman Catholic Church, was founded in 1958. It has a 94-acre campus.

RATINGS
Admissions Selectivity Rating: 67   **Fire Safety Rating:** 74   **Green Rating:** 61

STUDENTS AND FACULTY
Enrollment: 1,962. **Student Body:** 75% female, 25% male, 12% out-of-state, 0% international. Asian 0%, African American 14%, Caucasian 54%, Hispanic 6%, Native American 0%.
Retention and Graduation: 62% freshmen return for sophomore year. **Faculty:** Student/faculty ratio 11:1. 99 full-time faculty, 55% hold PhDs, 9% are members of minority groups, 67% are women. 2% of classes are taught by teaching assistants.

ACADEMICS
Degrees: associate, bachelor's, certificate, master's, post-bachelor's certificate. **Classes:** Most classes have 10–19 students. Most lab/discussion sessions have fewer than 10 students. **Majors with Highest Enrollment:** early childhood education and teaching; nursing/registered nurse (rn, asn, bsn, msn); social work. **Special Study Options:** distance learning, double major, dual enrollment, independent study, internships, liberal arts/career combination, student-designed major, study abroad, teacher certification program. **Disability Services:** Special programs offered to physically disabled students include note-taking services, reader services, tape recorders, tutors. **Career Services:** career/job search classes, career assessment.

FACILITIES
Special Academic Facilities/Equipment: Planetarium, Life Lab **Computers:** 100% of classrooms, 100% of libraries, 100% of dining areas, 100% of student union, have wireless network access. Students can register for classes online. Administrative functions (other than registration) can be performed online.

CAMPUS LIFE
Environment: Village. **Activities:** Choral groups, drama/theater, literary magazine, student government, Campus Ministries 25 registered organizations, 2 honor societies. **Athletics (Intercollegiate):** *Men:* basketball, golf. *Women:* golf, volleyball. **On-Campus Highlights:** McAlear Hall, Ebied Center.

ADMISSIONS
Freshman Academic Profile: Average high school GPA 3.1. 10% in top 10% of high school class, 31% in top 25% of high school class, 62% in top 50% of high school class. % from public high schools. SAT Math middle 50% range 360-490. SAT Critical Reading middle 50% range 370-480. ACT middle 50% range 17-22. Minimum web-based TOEFL 79. Minimum paper TOEFL 500.

Basis for Candidate Selection: *Very important factors considered include:* academic GPA. *Other factors considered include:* interview. **Freshman Admission Requirements:** High school diploma is required and GED is accepted. **Freshman Admission Statistics:** 1,231 applied, 71% admitted, 30% enrolled. **Transfer Admission Requirements:** college transcript(s), minimum college GPA of 2.0 required. Lowest grade transferable C. **General Admission Information:** Application Fee $25. Nonfall registration accepted. Admission may be deferred for a maximum of 4 years. Credit and/or placement offered for CEEB Advanced Placement tests.

COSTS AND FINANCIAL AID

Annual tuition $16,950. Room and board $8,000. Average book expense $1,250. **Required Forms and Deadlines:** FAFSA. **Notification of Awards:** Applicants will be notified of awards on a rolling basis beginning 3/1. **Types of Aid:** *Need-based scholarships/grants:* Federal Pell, SEOG, state scholarships/grants, private scholarships, the school's own gift aid. *Loans:* Direct Subsidized Stafford, Direct Unsubsidized Stafford, Direct PLUS, Federal Perkins, state loans, college/university loans from institutional funds. **Student Employment:** Federal Work-Study Program available. Institutional employment available. Off-campus job opportunities are excellent. **Financial Aid Statistics:** 82% freshmen, 78% undergrads receive need-based scholarship or grant aid. 93% freshmen, 65% undergrads receive non-need-based scholarship or grant aid. 87% freshmen, 91% undergrads receive need-based self-help aid. 17% freshmen, 11% undergrads receive athletic scholarships. 97% freshmen, 85% undergrads receive any aid. 80% undergrads borrow to pay for school. Average cumulative indebtedness. **Criteria for awarding institutional aid:** *Non-need-based:* academics, art, minority status, state/district residency.

LOYOLA UNIVERSITY MARYLAND

Best 378

4501 North Charles Street, Baltimore, MD 21210
Phone: 410-617-5012 • **Financial Aid Phone:** 410-617-2576 • **CEEB Code:** 5370
Fax: 410-617-2176 • **Website:** www.loyola.edu

This private school, affiliated with the Roman Catholic Church, was founded in 1852. It has a 89-acre campus.

RATINGS

Admissions Selectivity Rating: 85   **Fire Safety Rating:** 87   **Green Rating:** 82

STUDENTS AND FACULTY

Enrollment: 3,898. **Student Body:** 61% female, 39% male, 82% out-of-state, 0% international (61 countries represented). Asian 3%, African American 5%, Caucasian 81%, Hispanic 8%, Native American 0%.
Retention and Graduation: 88% freshmen return for sophomore year. 79% freshmen graduate within 4 years. 84% freshmen graduate within 6 years. 25% grads go on to further study within 1 year. 35% grads pursue arts and sciences degrees. 13% grads pursue law degrees. 11% grads pursue business degrees. 2% grads pursue medical degrees. **Faculty:** Student/faculty ratio 12:1. 350 full-time faculty, 84% hold PhDs, 15% are members of minority groups, 47% are women. 0% of classes are taught by teaching assistants.

ACADEMICS

Degrees: bachelor's, master's, post-master's certificate. **Classes:** Most classes have 20–29 students. Most lab/discussion sessions have 10–19 students. **Majors with Highest Enrollment:** business/commerce; communications technology/technician; psychology. **Special Study Options:** cross-registration, double major, dual enrollment, exchange student program (domestic), honors program, independent study, internships, liberal arts/career combination, study abroad, teacher certification program. **Honors Programs:** http://www.loyola.edu/undergraduate/academics/honors.aspx. **Disability Services:** Special programs offered to physically disabled students include note-taking services, reader services, tape recorders, tutors. **Career Services:** Alumni network, alumni services, career/job search classes, career assessment, internships.

FACILITIES

Housing: Coed dorms, cooperative housing, apartments for single students, wellness housing, theme housing, 100% of campus accessible to physically disabled. **Special Academic Facilities/Equipment:** Art gallery, advanced biology lab, humanities building, speech pathology lab and audiology center, black box theater **Computers:** 75% of classrooms, 80% of dorms, 100% of libraries, 100% of dining areas, 50% of student union, 50% of common outdoor areas have wireless network access. Students can register for classes online. Administrative functions (other than registration) can be performed online.

CAMPUS LIFE

Environment: Village. **Activities:** Choral groups, dance, drama/theater, literary magazine, music ensembles, musical theater, radio station, student government, student newspaper, television station, yearbook, Campus Ministries, International Student Organization 185 registered organizations, 25 honor societies, 4 religious organizations. **Athletics (Intercollegiate):** *Men:* basketball, crew/rowing, cross-country, diving, golf, lacrosse, soccer, swimming, tennis. *Women:* basketball, crew/rowing, cross-country, diving, lacrosse, soccer, swimming, tennis, track/field (outdoor), track/field (indoor), volleyball.
On-Campus Highlights: Loyola/Notre Dame Library, The Loyola University Art Gallery, Fitness and Aquatic Center, Boulder Garden Cafe, Primo's: The New Marketplace. **Environmental Initiatives:** Our commitment responsible building can be seen in our 100,000 sq. ft. green residential hall that was built in 2007. In 2010 we completed construction of an athletic facility that was built on a landfill and is considered an example of smart growth. Our waste management & diversion program currently diverts about 65% of our waste from a landfill. 55% of that is recycling and the other 10% is compost. We passed an energy management plan that has successfully reduced energy by 12% in the last 4 years. We are currently looking at making the plan more robust to include retrofits and possibly a greater commitment to renewable energy.

ADMISSIONS

Freshman Academic Profile: Average high school GPA 3.4. 25% in top 10% of high school class, 59% in top 25% of high school class, 85% in top 50% of high school class. 51% from public high schools. SAT Math middle 50% range 545-630. SAT Critical Reading middle 50% range 540-630. ACT middle 50% range 24-29. Minimum web-based TOEFL 79. Minimum paper TOEFL 550.
Basis for Candidate Selection: *Very important factors considered include:* application essay, recommendation(s), rigor of secondary school record, character/personal qualities. *Important factors considered include:* Class rank, alumni/ae relation, extracurricular activities, first generation, talent/ability, volunteer work. *Other factors considered include:* academic GPA, standardized test scores, geographical residence, interview, level of applicant's interest, racial/ethnic status, work experience. **Freshman Admission Requirements:** High school diploma is required and GED is accepted. *Academic units required:* 4 English, 3 mathematics, 3 science, 3 foreign language, 2 social studies, 2 history. *Academic units recommended:* 4 English, 3 mathematics, 3 science, 3 foreign language, 2 social studies, 2 history. **Freshman Admission Statistics:** 12,664 applied, 65% admitted, 13% enrolled. **Transfer Admission Requirements:** High school transcript, college transcript(s), essay or personal statement, statement of good standing from prior institution(s). Minimum college GPA of 2.7 required. Lowest grade transferable C. **General Admission Information:** Application Fee $50. Regular application deadline 6/1. Nonfall registration accepted. Admission may be deferred for a maximum of 1. Credit and/or placement offered for CEEB Advanced Placement tests.

COSTS AND FINANCIAL AID

Average book expense. **Required Forms and Deadlines:** FAFSA, CSS/Financial Aid PROFILE, noncustodial PROFILE, business/farm supplement. **Notification of Awards:** Applicants will be notified of awards on or about 4/1. **Types of Aid:** *Need-based scholarships/grants:* Federal Pell, SEOG, state scholarships/grants, private scholarships, the school's own gift aid. *Loans:* Direct Subsidized Stafford, Direct Unsubsidized Stafford, Direct PLUS, Federal Perkins, college/university loans from institutional funds. **Student Employment:** Federal Work-Study Program available. Institutional employment available. Highest amount earned per year from on-campus jobs $2,420. Off-campus job opportunities are good. **Financial Aid Statistics:** 87% freshmen, 87% undergrads receive need-based scholarship or grant aid. 10% freshmen, 8% undergrads receive non-need-based scholarship or grant aid. 90% freshmen, 87% undergrads receive need-based self-help aid. 2% freshmen, 3% undergrads receive athletic scholarships. 71% freshmen, 69% undergrads receive any aid. 63% undergrads borrow to pay for school. Average cumulative indebtedness $32,392. **Criteria for awarding institutional aid:** *Non-need-based:* academics, athletics, minority status.

LOYOLA MARYMOUNT UNIVERSITY

1 LMU Drive, Los Angeles, CA 90045-8350
Phone: 310-338-2750 • **Financial Aid Phone:** 310-338-2753
E-mail: admissions@lmu.edu • **CEEB Code:** 4403
Fax: 310-338-2797 • **Website:** www.lmu.edu • **ACT Code:** 326

This private school, affiliated with the Roman Catholic Church, was founded in 1911. It has a 128-acre campus.

RATINGS
Admissions Selectivity Rating: 92   **Fire Safety Rating:** 74   **Green Rating:** 91

STUDENTS AND FACULTY
Enrollment: 5,962. **Student Body:** 57% female, 43% male, 24% out-of-state, 4% international (80 countries represented). Asian 10%, African American 6%, Caucasian 51%, Hispanic 22%, Native American 0%.
Retention and Graduation: 66% freshmen graduate within 4 years. 75% freshmen graduate within 6 years. 29% grads go on to further study within 1 year. 18% grads pursue arts and sciences degrees. 4% grads pursue law degrees. 1% grads pursue business degrees. 1% grads pursue medical degrees. **Faculty:** Student/faculty ratio 11:1. 534 full-time faculty, 96% hold PhDs, 27% are members of minority groups, 44% are women. 1% of classes are taught by teaching assistants.

ACADEMICS
Degrees: bachelor's, first professional, first professional certificate, master's, post-bachelor's certificate, post-master's certificate. **Classes:** Most classes have 20–29 students. Most lab/discussion sessions have 10–19 students. **Majors with Highest Enrollment:** business administration and management; communication studies/speech communication and rhetoric; psychology. **Special Study Options:** cross-registration, double major, dual enrollment, honors program, independent study, internships, liberal arts/career combination, student-designed major, study abroad, teacher certification program, Encore program for adult students. **Disability Services:** Special programs offered to physically disabled students include note-taking services, reader services, tape recorders, tutors. **Career Services:** alumni services, career assessment, internships.

FACILITIES
Housing: Coed dorms, special housing for disabled students, men's dorms, women's dorms, apartments for single students. 99% of campus accessible to physically disabled. **Special Academic Facilities/Equipment:** Art gallery, theater, TV production labs, computer graphics lab. **Computers:** Students can register for classes online. Administrative functions (other than registration) can be performed online.

CAMPUS LIFE
Environment: Metropolis. **Activities:** Choral groups, dance, drama/theater, literary magazine, music ensembles, musical theater, pep band, radio station, student government, student newspaper, student-run film society, television station, yearbook 120 registered organizations, 12 honor societies, 2 religious organizations. 6 fraternities, 8 sororities. **Athletics (Intercollegiate): Men:** baseball, basketball, crew/rowing, cross-country, golf, soccer, tennis, water polo. **Women:** basketball, crew/rowing, cross-country, soccer, softball, swimming, tennis, volleyball, water polo. **Environmental Initiatives:** LEED Building Program: LMU's new $64 million library incorporates state-of-the-art technologies and energy efficiency features, complementing other LEED-certified campus buildings and signifying LMU's commitment to continued leadership in environmental stewardship. The library will also act as a 'living lab' for students studying Information Systems and IT in the context of building automation systems applications. LMU's solar energy program was the first, and is still one of the largest of its kind in the entire City of Los Angeles. Integrating on-site renewable energy generation together with extensive retro-fitting and efficiency features is a natural extension of our commitment to reducing our carbon footprint. The creation of the Environmental Stewardship and Sustainability Committee represents a tremendous step in establishing comprehensive, campus-wide policies and governance over every aspect of campus operations by instituting sustainability considerations and decision variables to be used across the university, from purchasing and procurement to academics and student life. The committee seeks to emphasize the inextricable link between ecological justice and social justice within our mission as a Jesuit university.

ADMISSIONS
Freshman Academic Profile: Average high school GPA 3.8. 36% in top 10% of high school class, 70% in top 25% of high school class, 96% in top 50% of high school class. 49% from public high schools. SAT Math middle 50% range 560-660. SAT Critical Reading middle 50% range 550-640. SAT Writing middle 50% range 560-660. ACT middle 50% range 24-29. Minimum web-based TOEFL 80. Minimum paper TOEFL 550. **Basis for Candidate Selection:** *Very important factors considered include:* academic GPA, rigor of secondary school record. *Important factors considered include:* Class rank, application essay, standardized test scores, character/personal qualities, talent/ability. *Other factors considered include:* recommendation(s), alumni/ae relation, extracurricular activities, first generation, geographical residence, interview, volunteer work, work experience. **Freshman Admission Requirements:** High school diploma is required and GED is accepted. **Freshman Admission Statistics:** 11,913 applied, 521% enrolled. **Transfer Admission Requirements:** college transcript(s), essay or personal statement, statement of good standing from prior institution(s). Minimum college GPA of 2.8 required. Lowest grade transferable C. **General Admission Information:** Application Fee $50. Notification on a rolling basis, beginning on or about 1/1. Nonfall registration accepted. Admission may be deferred for a maximum of 12. Credit and/or placement offered for CEEB Advanced Placement tests.

COSTS AND FINANCIAL AID
Annual tuition $38,212. Room and board $14,395. Required fees $688. Average book expense $1,665. **Required Forms and Deadlines:** FAFSA, CSS/Financial Aid PROFILE, business/farm supplement. **Notification of Awards:** Applicants will be notified of awards on a rolling basis beginning 3/15. **Types of Aid:** *Need-based scholarships/grants:* Federal Pell, SEOG, state scholarships/grants, private scholarships, the school's own gift aid. *Loans:* Subsidized Stafford, Unsubsidized Stafford, PLUS, Federal Perkins, college/university loans from institutional funds. **Student Employment:** Federal Work-Study Program available. Institutional employment available. Off-campus job opportunities are excellent. **Financial Aid Statistics:** 90% freshmen, 91% undergrads receive need-based scholarship or grant aid. 12% freshmen, 11% undergrads receive non-need-based scholarship or grant aid. 81% freshmen, 84% undergrads receive need-based self-help aid. 2% freshmen, 3% undergrads receive athletic scholarships. 87% freshmen, 84% undergrads receive any aid. 57% undergrads borrow to pay for school. Average cumulative indebtedness $34,629.

LOYOLA UNIVERSITY CHICAGO

820 North Michigan Avenue, Chicago, IL 60611
Phone: 312-915-6500 • **Financial Aid Phone:** 773-508-7704
E-mail: admission@luc.edu • **CEEB Code:** 1412
Fax: 312-915-7216 • **Website:** www.luc.edu/

This private school, affiliated with the Roman Catholic-Jesuit Church, was founded in 1870. It has a 105-acre campus.

RATINGS
Admissions Selectivity Rating: 90   **Fire Safety Rating:** 75   **Green Rating:** 87

STUDENTS AND FACULTY
Enrollment: 9,483. **Student Body:** 63% female, 37% male, 35% out-of-state, 1% international (105 countries represented). Asian 11%, African American 4%, Caucasian 65%, Hispanic 11%, Native American 0%.
Retention and Graduation: 51% freshmen graduate within 4 years. 70% freshmen graduate within 6 years. **Faculty:** Student/faculty ratio 15:1. 683 full-time faculty, 93% hold PhDs, 12% are members of minority groups, 46% are women. 0% of classes are taught by teaching assistants.

ACADEMICS
Degrees: bachelor's, certificate, master's, post-bachelor's certificate, post-master's certificate. **Classes:** Most classes have 10–19 students. Most lab/discussion sessions have 10–19 students. **Majors with Highest Enrollment:** biology/biological sciences; nursing/registered nurse (rn, asn, bsn, msn); psychology. **Special Study Options:** Accelerated program, distance learning, double major, dual enrollment, English as a Second Language (ESL), exchange student program (domestic), honors program, independent study, internships, study abroad, teacher certification program. **Honors Programs:** Loyola University Chicago offers an Interdisciplinary Honors Program that integrates a challenging academic program with service-learning opportunities. Taking a series of team-taught, interdisciplinary courses, students learn to perceive unexpected convergences among discrete facts, to synthesize information from many sources, and to use their knowledge to benefit society. **Combined Degree Programs:** BA/JD, BA/MA, BA/MEng, B.B.A./M.B.A. Business Administration;

B.S. Biology/M.B.A.; B.B.A./M.S.A. Ac. **Disability Services:** Special programs offered to physically disabled students include note-taking services, reader services, tape recorders, tutors. **Career Services:** Alumni network, alumni services, career/job search classes, career assessment, internships, regional alumni. Career Services highlights include The Career Development Center counselors teach 4 sections each semester of the "Career and Life Planning" course. This unique course takes students through a thorough self assessment, exploration of their passions and calling, and provides detailed information on job search skills. This self-reflective course encourages students to research and explore a variety of industries and employment options so they are more focused and confident in their internship choices and their future career goals.

FACILITIES

Housing: Coed dorms, special housing for disabled students, apartments for single students, Honors floors;Living Learning Community floors. 90% of campus accessible to physically disabled. **Special Academic Facilities/Equipment:** Renaissance art gallery, Loyola University Museum of Art (LUMA), Madonna Della Strada Chapel, The Quinlin Life Sciences Building' Bio Deisel Labs, Mock Trial Room, Mundelein Auditorium **Computers:** 75% of classrooms, 60% of dorms, 95% of libraries, 50% of dining areas, 100% of student union, 40% of common outdoor areas have wireless network access. Students can register for classes online. Administrative functions (other than registration) can be performed online.

CAMPUS LIFE

Environment: Metropolis. **Activities:** concert band, dance, drama/theater, jazz band, literary magazine, music ensembles, musical theater, pep band, radio station, student government, student newspaper, student-run film society, television station, Campus Ministries, International Student Organization, Model UN 185 registered organizations, 11 honor societies, 9 religious organizations. 6 fraternities, 9 sororities. **Athletics (Intercollegiate):** *Men:* basketball, cheer leading, cross-country, golf, soccer, track/field (outdoor), track/field (indoor), volleyball. *Women:* basketball, cheerleading, cross-country, golf, soccer, softball, track/field (outdoor), track/field (indoor), volleyball. **On-Campus Highlights:** Information Commons, Lake front Residence Halls, Joseph J. Gentile Center, Halas Athletic Center/Alumni Gym, Quinlan Life Sciences Center, LAKE SHORE CAMPUS Loyola's main residential campus is located on Chicago's North Side, minutes from downtown Chicago and the Water Tower Campus, and is set along the shore of Lake Michigan. It's home to the College of Arts and Sciences, Graduate School and Marcella Niehoff School of Nursing. The School of Education offers academic courses, programs and student advising. More than 3,000 students live in residence halls. The Lake Shore Campus includes Cudahy Library, Madonna della Strada Chapel, Joseph J. Gentile Center and the Halas Sports Center. WATER TOWER CAMPUS Loyola's downtown campus is located along Pearson Street, just off North Michigan Avenue, Chicago's "Magnificent Mile." Here, both residential and commuter students can complete one of many undergraduate degree programs, as well as take advantage of internships at many of Chicago's business and cultural institutions. The Water Tower Campus is home to the Schools of Business Administration, Education, Law and Social Work, and to selected programs in the College of Arts and Sciences. **Environmental Initiatives:** Energy reduction and conservation, transportation: Adopt green building design standards for all new construction. Lighting, heating/cooling retrofits. Biodiesel production from dining hall's waste vegetable oil used in campus shuttles. (www.luc.edu/biodiesel) Transportation: walk-to-work program, bicycle program, electric vehicles, public transit passes for students, car sharing program. 2. Education and Research: -Launching an Institute for Environmental Sustainability and a new center, Center for Urban Sustainable Living in 2013. -Courses and programs with multidisciplinary, problem solving,research-based, and experiential focus to include co-curricular activities -Undergraduate interdisciplinary environmental research fellowships -Urban food demonstration program -Sustainable agriculture courses -Green Living Learning Community -Environmental Science Department -Biodiesel production courses -Professional non-credit sustainability education courses/ workshops -Environmental topics and themes across the disciplines -Design projects that directly involve students with community organizations on environmental sustainable projects and outreach. 3. Waste Reduction, Reuse and Recycle programs: BioSoap production made from the glycerin, a by-product of biodiesel production (http://www.luc.edu/biodiesel/BioSoap.shtml) - small farm to supply food in dining hall at the Retreat and Ecology Campus - Rainwater cistern, permeable walkways, semi-permeable artificial turf and track walkway, expanded recycling to include batteries, inkjet/printer cartridges, and small personal electronics. Trayfree dining halls, nondisposable water bottle campaign and water bottle refill stations, recyclable collection during fall move-in and a spring move-out collection for students to donate reusable items (clothing, toiletries, nonperishable foods)to charities which divert items from landfills. 2011 began investigating off-site composting of dining hall plate waste.

ADMISSIONS

Freshman Academic Profile: Average high school GPA 3.7. 32% in top 10% of high school class, 65% in top 25% of high school class, 93% in top 50% of high school class. 68% from public high schools. SAT Math middle 50% range 540-650. SAT Critical Reading middle 50% range 540-660. SAT Writing middle 50% range 530-640. ACT middle 50% range 25-29. Minimum web-based TOEFL 79. Minimum paper TOEFL 550. **Basis for Candidate Selection:** *Very important factors considered include:* academic GPA, rigor of secondary school record, standardized test scores. *Important factors considered include:* application essay, recommendation(s), character/personal qualities, extracurricular activities, level of applicant's interest, volunteer work. *Other factors considered include:* Class rank, alumni/ae relation, first generation, geographical residence, interview, state residency, talent/ability, work experience. **Freshman Admission Requirements:** High school diploma is required and GED is accepted. *Academic units required:* 4 English, 3 mathematics, 3 science, 2 foreign language, 2 social studies, 1 history. *Academic units recommended:* 4 English, 3 mathematics, 3 science, 2 foreign language, 2 social studies, 1 history. **Freshman Admission Statistics:** 17,828 applied, 55% admitted, 20% enrolled. **Transfer Admission Requirements:** college transcript(s), minimum college GPA of 2.0 required. Lowest grade transferable C. **General Admission Information:** Application Fee $25. Notification on a rolling basis, beginning on or about 10/1. Nonfall registration accepted. Credit and/or placement offered for CEEB Advanced Placement tests.

COSTS AND FINANCIAL AID

Annual tuition $33,090. Room and board $12,010. Required fees $1,128. Average book expense $1,200. **Required Forms and Deadlines:** FAFSA. **Notification of Awards:** Applicants will be notified of awards on a rolling basis beginning 2/15. **Types of Aid:** *Need-based scholarships/grants:* Federal Pell, SEOG, state scholarships/grants, private scholarships, the school's own gift aid. *Loans:* Subsidized Stafford, Unsubsidized Stafford, PLUS, Federal Perkins, Federal Nursing. **Student Employment:** Federal Work-Study Program available. Institutional employment available. Highest amount earned per year from on-campus jobs $9,803. Off-campus job opportunities are good. **Financial Aid Statistics:** 98% freshmen, 96% undergrads receive need-based scholarship or grant aid. 8% freshmen, 6% undergrads receive non-need-based scholarship or grant aid. 91% freshmen, 92% undergrads receive need-based self-help aid. 1% freshmen, 1% undergrads receive athletic scholarships. 96% freshmen, 92% undergrads receive any aid. 75% undergrads borrow to pay for school. **Criteria for awarding institutional aid:** *Non-need-based:* academics, athletics, leadership, music/drama, religious affiliation.

See page 1132.

LOYOLA UNIVERSITY NEW ORLEANS

6363 St. Charles Avenue, New Orleans, LA 70118-6195
Phone: 504-865-3240 • **Financial Aid Phone:** 504-865-3231
E-mail: admit@loyno.edu • **CEEB Code:** 6374
Fax: 504-865-3383 • **Website:** www.loyno.edu • **ACT Code:** 1592

This private school, affiliated with the Roman Catholic Church,, affiliated with the Jesuit Church, was founded in 1912. It has a 26-acre campus.

RATINGS
Admissions Selectivity Rating: 60*   **Fire Safety Rating:** 60*   **Green Rating:** 60*

STUDENTS AND FACULTY
Enrollment: 3,135. **Student Body:** 59% female, 41% male, 58% out-of-state, 3% international (57 countries represented). Asian 4%, African American 15%, Caucasian 53%, Hispanic 15%, Native American 1%.
Retention and Graduation: 74% freshmen return for sophomore year. 47% freshmen graduate within 4 years. 64% grads go on to further study within 1 year. **Faculty:** Student/faculty ratio 10:1. 316 full-time faculty, 89% hold PhDs, 16% are members of minority groups, 44% are women. 0% of classes are taught by teaching assistants.

ACADEMICS
Degrees: bachelor's, master's, post-bachelor's certificate, post-master's certificate. **Classes:** Most classes have 10–19 students. Most lab/discussion sessions have fewer than 10 students. **Majors with Highest Enrollment:** marketing/ marketing management; mass communication/media studies; psychology. **Special Study Options:** Accelerated program, cross-registration, distance learning, double major, dual enrollment, English as a Second Language (ESL), exchange student program (domestic), honors program, independent study, internships, liberal arts/career combination, student-designed major, study abroad, teacher certification program, Advance placement credit. Limited weekend courses available. Evening Courses available. Also teacher certification program is available in music only. **Honors Programs:** The Loyola University Honors Program

offers the opportunity for academically superior, highly motivated students to take challenging Honors courses and to participate in special cultural and intellectual enrichment activities. The University Honors Program is open to qualified students of all undergraduate colleges and majors. The Honors courses replace other required courses, and therefore do not add to the number of requirements for graduation. **Combined Degree Programs:** RN/MSN/DNP, JD/MBA, MPS/MS, Early Law Admission. **Disability Services:** Special programs offered to physically disabled students include note-taking services, reader services, tape recorders, tutors. **Career Services:** Alumni network, alumni services, career/job search classes, career assessment, internships, regional alumni.

FACILITIES

Housing: Coed dorms, special housing for disabled students, apartments for single students, wellness housing, theme housing, honors floor available. 95% of campus accessible to physically disabled. **Special Academic Facilities/Equipment:** Collins C. Diboll Art Gallery, Humanities Lab with Perseus Project and TLG TV, Multimedia Classrooms, 24-hour Microcomputer Labs, Computer Science Lab, Graphics Lab, Visual Arts Lab, Ad Club/Communications Lab, RATHE Business Computer Lab, Multi-Media Training Center, Donnelley Center for Non-Profit Communications, Chemistry Wing, Television Broadcast Studio, Multimedia Studio, Audio Recording Studio, Editing Studio, Library Learning Commons, Multimedia Exhibit Room, Satchmo's Deli and Performance Area, Center for International Education, University Sports Complex with Suspended Pool, Career Development Center, Jesuit Social Research Institute, Learning Communities. **Computers:** 50% of classrooms, 100% of dorms, 100% of libraries, 100% of dining areas, 100% of student union, 100% of common outdoor areas have wireless network access. Students can register for classes online. Administrative functions (other than registration) can be performed online.

CAMPUS LIFE

Environment: City. **Activities:** Choral groups, concert band, dance, drama/theater, jazz band, literary magazine, music ensembles, musical theater, opera, pep band, radio station, student government, student newspaper, student-run film society, symphony orchestra, yearbook, Campus Ministries, International Student Organization 90 registered organizations, 13 honor societies, 4 religious organizations. 7 fraternities, 7 sororities. **Athletics (Intercollegiate):** *Men:* baseball, basketball, cross-country, track/field (outdoor), track/field (indoor). *Women:* basketball, cross-country, track/field (outdoor), track/field (indoor), volleyball. **On-Campus Highlights:** J. Edgar and Louise S. Monroe Library, Danna Student Center, Recreational Sports Complex, Peace Quad, Residential Quad, Collins C. Diboll Art Gallery, Humanities Lab with Perseus Project and TLG TV, Multimedia Classrooms, 24-hour Microcomputer Labs, Computer Science Lab, Graphics Lab, Visual Arts Lab, Ad Club/Communications Lab, RATHE Business Computer Lab, Multi-Media Training Center, Donnelley Center for Non-Profit Communications, Chemistry Wing, Television Broadcast Studio, Multimedia Studio, Audio Recording Studio, Editing Studio, Library Learning Commons, Multimedia Exhibit Room, Satchmo's Deli and Performance Area, Center for International Education, University Sports Complex with Suspended Pool, Career Development Center, Jesuit Social Research Institute, Learning Communities. **Environmental Initiatives:** Formation of a committee that has representatives from important units on campus, including SGA and other student organizations. Full support of the Administration, starting with the President and Provost. Have signed on to the leading sustainable action groups (Talloires Sustainability Declaration, EPA WasteWise Team, President's Climate Change,NWF Campus Ecology Program, etc.) Implemented major inventories of sustainable operations across campus.

ADMISSIONS

Freshman Academic Profile: Average high school GPA 3.7. 27% in top 10% of high school class, 47% in top 25% of high school class, 77% in top 50% of high school class. 47% from public high schools. SAT Math middle 50% range 510-620. SAT Critical Reading middle 50% range 530-650. ACT middle 50% range 22-27. Minimum paper TOEFL 550. **Basis for Candidate Selection:** *Very important factors considered include:* academic GPA, rigor of secondary school record, standardized test scores. *Important factors considered include:* application essay, recommendation(s), extracurricular activities, talent/ability. *Other factors considered include:* Class rank, alumni/ae relation, character/personal qualities, geographical residence, interview, level of applicant's interest, state residency, volunteer work, work experience. **Freshman Admission Requirements:** High school diploma is required and GED is accepted. *Academic units required:* 4 English, 2 mathematics, 2 science, 2 social studies. *Academic units recommended:* 4 English, 2 mathematics, 2 science, 2 social studies. **Freshman Admission Statistics:** 6,486 applied, 66% admitted, 21% enrolled. **Transfer Admission Requirements:** college transcript(s), essay or personal statement, statement of good standing from prior institution(s). Minimum college GPA of 2.25 required. Lowest grade transferable C. **General Admission Information:** Application Fee $20. Notification on a rolling basis, beginning on or about 10/20. Nonfall registration accepted. Credit and/or placement offered for CEEB Advanced Placement tests.

COSTS AND FINANCIAL AID

Annual tuition $35,504. Room and board $8,250. Required fees $1,106. Average book expense $1,200. **Required Forms and Deadlines:** FAFSA. **Notification of Awards:** Applicants will be notified of awards on a rolling basis beginning 3/1. **Types of Aid:** *Need-based scholarships/grants:* Federal Pell, SEOG, private scholarships, the school's own gift aid. *Loans:* Subsidized Stafford, Unsubsidized Stafford, PLUS, Federal Perkins. **Student Employment:** Federal Work-Study Program available. Institutional employment available. Highest amount earned per year from on-campus jobs $1,920. Off-campus job opportunities are excellent. **Financial Aid Statistics:** 100% freshmen, 99% undergrads receive need-based scholarship or grant aid. 10% freshmen, 12% undergrads receive non-need-based scholarship or grant aid. 84% freshmen, 81% undergrads receive need-based self-help aid. 2% freshmen, 1% undergrads receive athletic scholarships. 92% freshmen, 92% undergrads receive any aid. 66% undergrads borrow to pay for school. Average cumulative indebtedness $23,178. **Criteria for awarding institutional aid:** *Non-need-based:* academics, alumni affiliation, art, leadership.

LUBBOCK CHRISTIAN UNIVERSITY

5601 19th Street, Lubbock, TX 79407
Phone: 800-720-7151 • **Financial Aid Phone:** 806-720-7176
E-mail: admissions@lcu.edu • **CEEB Code:** 6378
Fax: 806-720-7162 • **Website:** www.lcu.edu • **ACT Code:** 4123

This private school, affiliated with the Church of Christ Church, was founded in 1957. It has a 120-acre campus.

RATINGS
Admissions Selectivity Rating: 71   **Fire Safety Rating:** 64   **Green Rating:** 60*

STUDENTS AND FACULTY
Enrollment: 1,728. **Student Body:** 56% female, 44% male, 9% out-of-state, 0% international. Asian 1%, African American 6%, Caucasian 79%, Hispanic 14%, Native American 1%.
Retention and Graduation: 67% freshmen return for sophomore year. 27% freshmen graduate within 4 years. 43% freshmen graduate within 6 years. **Faculty:** Student/faculty ratio 15:1. 79 full-time faculty, 59% hold PhDs, 0% are members of minority groups, 39% are women. 0% of classes are taught by teaching assistants.

ACADEMICS
Degrees: bachelor's, master's. **Classes:** Most classes have 10–19 students. Most lab/discussion sessions have fewer than 10 students. **Majors with Highest Enrollment:** elementary education and teaching; humanities/humanistic studies; small business administration/management. **Special Study Options:** distance learning, double major, dual enrollment, honors program, internships, liberal arts/career combination, student-designed major, study abroad, teacher certification program, weekend college. **Honors Programs:** Honors program available to all majors. **Disability Services:** Special programs offered to physically disabled students include tape recorders, tutors. **Career Services:** alumni services, career/job search classes, career assessment, internships Career Services highlights include Education - experietial learning opportunities in local schools are required with each education course.

FACILITIES
Housing: special housing for disabled students, men's dorms, women's dorms, apartments for married students, apartments for single students. 78% of campus accessible to physically disabled. **Computers:** Students can register for classes online.

CAMPUS LIFE
Environment: City. **Activities:** Choral groups, drama/theater, music ensembles, student government, student newspaper, yearbook 24 registered organizations, 3 honor societies, 4 fraternities, 4 sororities. **Athletics (Intercollegiate):** *Men:* baseball, basketball, cheerleading, golf. *Women:* basketball, cheerleading, golf, volleyball. **On-Campus Highlights:** Student Union Building, Ramona Perrin Fitness Center, Rip Griffin Athletic Center, Library, Snackbar.

ADMISSIONS
Freshman Academic Profile: Average high school GPA 3.5. 18% in top 10% of high school class, 44% in top 25% of high school class, 76% in top 50% of high school class. 76% from public high schools. SAT Math middle 50% range 440-572. SAT Critical Reading middle 50% range 450-582. ACT middle 50% range 18-24. Minimum paper TOEFL 500. **Basis for Candidate Selection:** *Very important factors considered include:* standardized test scores. *Important factors considered include:* rigor of secondary school record, character/personal

qualities. *Other factors considered include:* Class rank, recommendation(s), alumni/ae relation, racial/ethnic status, religious affiliation/commitment, talent/ability, volunteer work. **Freshman Admission Requirements:** High school diploma is required and GED is accepted. **Freshman Admission Statistics:** 771 applied, 77% admitted, 45% enrolled. **Transfer Admission Requirements:** college transcript(s), statement of good standing from prior institution(s). Lowest grade transferable C. **General Admission Information:** Application Fee $20. Regular application deadline 8/15. Notification on a rolling basis, beginning on or about 9/1. Nonfall registration accepted. Credit and/or placement offered for CEEB Advanced Placement tests.

COSTS AND FINANCIAL AID

Annual tuition $11,644. Room and board $2,125. Required fees $916. Average book expense $832. **Required Forms and Deadlines:** FAFSA, institution's own financial aid form. **Notification of Awards:** Applicants will be notified of awards on a rolling basis beginning 3/1. **Types of Aid:** *Need-based scholarships/grants:* Federal Pell, SEOG, state scholarships/grants. *Loans:* Subsidized Stafford, Unsubsidized Stafford, PLUS, Federal Perkins. **Student Employment:** Federal Work-Study Program available. Off-campus job opportunities are excellent. **Financial Aid Statistics:** 100% freshmen, 97% undergrads receive need-based scholarship or grant aid. 13% freshmen, 6% undergrads receive non-need-based scholarship or grant aid. 85% freshmen, 92% undergrads receive need-based self-help aid. 5% freshmen, 36% undergrads receive athletic scholarships. 78% freshmen, 72% undergrads receive any aid. 76% undergrads borrow to pay for school. Average cumulative indebtedness $20,244. **Criteria for awarding institutional aid:** *Non-need-based:* academics, athletics, leadership, music/drama.

LUTHER COLLEGE

700 College Drive, Decorah, IA 52101-1042
Phone: 563-387-1287 • **Financial Aid Phone:** 563-387-1018
E-mail: admissions@luther.edu • **CEEB Code:** 6375
Fax: 563-387-2159 • **Website:** www.luther.edu • **ACT Code:** 1330

This private school, affiliated with the Lutheran Church, was founded in 1861. It has a 175-acre campus.

RATINGS
Admissions Selectivity Rating: 76   **Fire Safety Rating:** 71   **Green Rating:** 89

STUDENTS AND FACULTY
Enrollment: 2,402. **Student Body:** 56% female, 44% male, 68% out-of-state, 5% international (46 countries represented). Asian 2%, African American 1%, Caucasian 86%, Hispanic 3%, Native American 0%.
Retention and Graduation: 68% freshmen graduate within 4 years. 77% freshmen graduate within 6 years. 21% grads go on to further study within 1 year. 15% grads pursue arts and sciences degrees. 2% grads pursue law degrees. 4% grads pursue medical degrees. **Faculty:** Student/faculty ratio 12:1. 178 full-time faculty, 93% hold PhDs, 6% are members of minority groups, 45% are women. 0% of classes are taught by teaching assistants.

ACADEMICS
Degrees: bachelor's. **Classes:** Most classes have 10–19 students. Most lab/discussion sessions have 10–19 students. **Majors with Highest Enrollment:** biology/biological sciences; business administration and management; music. **Special Study Options:** double major, dual enrollment, honors program, independent study, internships, student-designed major, study abroad, teacher certification program. **Disability Services:** Special programs offered to physically disabled students include note-taking services, reader services, tutors. **Career Services:** Alumni network, career/job search classes, internships.

FACILITIES
Housing: Coed dorms, special housing for disabled students, apartments for married students, apartments for single students, wellness housing, 95% of campus accessible to physically disabled. **Special Academic Facilities/Equipment:** Natural history museum, Norwegian-American museum, five art galleries, planetarium, live animal center, archaeological research center, computer music lab, two electron microscopes. **Computers:** 90% of classrooms, 75% of dorms, 90% of libraries, 90% of dining areas, 90% of student union, 25% of common outdoor areas have wireless network access. Students can register for classes online. Administrative functions (other than registration) can be performed online.

CAMPUS LIFE
Environment: Village. **Activities:** Choral groups, concert band, dance, drama/theater, jazz band, literary magazine, music ensembles, musical theater, pep band, radio station, student government, student newspaper, symphony

orchestra, yearbook, Campus Ministries, International Student Organization, Model UN 83 registered organizations, 13 honor societies, 8 religious organizations. 1 fraternities, 3 sororities. **Athletics (Intercollegiate):** *Men:* baseball, basketball, cross-country, diving, football, golf, soccer, swimming, tennis, track/field (outdoor), track/field (indoor), wrestling. *Women:* basketball, cross-country, diving, golf, soccer, softball, swimming, tennis, track/field (outdoor), track/field (indoor), volleyball. **On-Campus Highlights:** Marty's Cyber Cafe, Legends Fitness Center, The Cafeteria, Residence Hall Lounges, Sunnyside Cafe in the Center for the Arts. **Environmental Initiatives:** Energy audit and efficiency upgrades totaling $1.5 million and has reduced campus carbon footprint by 15% Built new science facility to LEED gold certification Wind turbine is expected to generate 1/3 of our electricity consumption. Geothermal energy heats and cools two of the facilities on campus reducing our need for fossil fuel heating and cooling

ADMISSIONS
Freshman Academic Profile: Average high school GPA 3.6. 32% in top 10% of high school class, 59% in top 25% of high school class, 90% in top 50% of high school class. 91% from public high schools. SAT Math middle 50% range 500-620. SAT Critical Reading middle 50% range 450-605. SAT Writing middle 50% range 450-595. ACT middle 50% range 23-28. Minimum web-based TOEFL 80. Minimum paper TOEFL 550. **Basis for Candidate Selection:** *Very important factors considered include:* Class rank, academic GPA, recommendation(s), rigor of secondary school record, standardized test scores. *Important factors considered include:* character/personal qualities, extracurricular activities, talent/ability. *Other factors considered include:* application essay, alumni/ae relation, first generation, interview, level of applicant's interest, racial/ethnic status, volunteer work. **Freshman Admission Requirements:** High school diploma is required and GED is accepted. **Freshman Admission Statistics:** 3,556 applied, 726% enrolled. **Transfer Admission Requirements:** High school transcript, college transcript(s), essay or personal statement, standardized test scores, minimum college GPA of 2.50 required. Lowest grade transferable C. **General Admission Information:** Application Fee $25. Non fall registration accepted. Admission may be deferred for a maximum of 1 year. Credit and/or placement offered for CEEB Advanced Placement tests.

COSTS AND FINANCIAL AID
Annual tuition $37,330. Room and board $6,850. Required fees $150. Average book expense $1,040. **Required Forms and Deadlines:** FAFSA, institution's own financial aid form. **Notification of Awards:** Applicants will be notified of awards on a rolling basis beginning 3/15. **Types of Aid:** *Need-based scholarships/grants:* Federal Pell, SEOG, state scholarships/grants, private scholarships, the school's own gift aid. *Loans:* Direct Subsidized Stafford, Direct Unsubsidized Stafford, Direct PLUS, Federal Perkins, college/university loans from institutional funds. **Student Employment:** Federal Work-Study Program available. Institutional employment available. Highest amount earned per year from on-campus jobs $3,190. Off-campus job opportunities are good. **Financial Aid Statistics:** 100% freshmen, 100% undergrads receive need-based scholarship or grant aid. 21% freshmen, 17% undergrads receive non-need-based scholarship or grant aid. 77% freshmen, 82% undergrads receive need-based self-help aid. 98% freshmen, 97% undergrads receive any aid. 78% undergrads borrow to pay for school. Average cumulative indebtedness $35,619. **Criteria for awarding institutional aid:** *Non-need-based:* academics, alumni affiliation, art, minority status, music/drama.

LYCOMING COLLEGE

700 College Place, Williamsport, PA 17701
Phone: 570-321-4026 • **Financial Aid Phone:** 570-321-4040
E-mail: admissions@lycoming.edu • **CEEB Code:** 2372
Fax: 570-321-4317 • **Website:** www.lycoming.edu • **ACT Code:** 3622

This private school, affiliated with the Methodist Church, was founded in 1812. It has a 39-acre campus.

RATINGS
Admissions Selectivity Rating: 73   **Fire Safety Rating:** 73   **Green Rating:** 72

STUDENTS AND FACULTY
Enrollment: 1,343. **Student Body:** 56% female, 44% male, 32% out-of-state, 3% international (7 countries represented). Asian 1%, African American 5%, Caucasian 78%, Hispanic 3%, Native American 0%.
Retention and Graduation: 81% freshmen return for sophomore year. 57% freshmen graduate within 4 years. 65% freshmen graduate within 6 years. 20% grads go on to further study within 1 year. 10% grads pursue arts and sciences degrees. 1% grads pursue law degrees. 1% grads pursue business degrees. 6% grads pursue medical degrees. **Faculty:** Student/faculty ratio 14:1. 81 full-time

faculty, 90% hold PhDs, 6% are members of minority groups, 41% are women. 0% of classes are taught by teaching assistants.

ACADEMICS

Degrees: bachelor's. **Classes:** Most classes have 10–19 students. Most lab/discussion sessions have 10–19 students. **Majors with Highest Enrollment:** biology/biological sciences; business administration and management; psychology. **Special Study Options:** Accelerated program, cross-registration, double major, honors program, independent study, internships, student-designed major, study abroad, teacher certification program. **Honors Programs:** Scholars Program offered to students through admissions process; each major also provides an Honors major option for students who wish to graduate with honors within their field of study. **Disability Services:** Special programs offered to physically disabled students include note-taking services, reader services, tape recorders, tutors. **Career Services:** Alumni network, career/job search classes, career assessment, internships Career Services highlights include Lycoming College has a successful internship program with local businesses. Williamsport, PA serves as the County Seat and offers a rich array of business and government opportunities for students. In addition, Lycoming has successfully placed students in nationally competitive internship programs with the FBI, top 5 accounting firms, Datatel, and the National Science Foundation.

FACILITIES

Housing: Coed dorms, special housing for disabled students, women's dorms, fraternity/sorority housing, apartments for single students, theme housing, Substance-free housing, Study-intensive housing, Creative Arts Society housing. 85% of campus accessible to physically disabled. **Special Academic Facilities/Equipment:** Language lab, tissue culture lab, TV studio, planetarium, video conferencing. **Computers:** 100% of classrooms, 100% of dorms, 100% of libraries, 100% of dining areas, 100% of student union, 100% of common outdoor areas have wireless network access. Students can register for classes online. Administrative functions (other than registration) can be performed online.

CAMPUS LIFE

Environment: Town. **Activities:** Choral groups, concert band, dance, drama/theater, jazz band, literary magazine, music ensembles, musical theater, pep band, radio station, student government, student newspaper, student-run film society, symphony orchestra, television station, yearbook, Campus Ministries, International Student Organization 78 registered organizations, 20 honor societies, 3 religious organizations. 5 fraternities, 5 sororities. **Athletics (Intercollegiate):** *Men:* basketball, cross-country, football, golf, lacrosse, soccer, swimming, tennis, wrestling. *Women:* basketball, cross-country, golf, lacrosse, soccer, softball, swimming, tennis, volleyball. **On-Campus Highlights:** Quad, Dining Hall, Jack's Place, Lamade Gymnasium, Recreation Center. **Environmental Initiatives:** The College has a Sustainability Committee that is comprised of faculty, administrators and students. Several initiatives have emerged from this group including using the grease waste from campus dining and converting it into biodiesel. The College has replaced older less efficient lighting systems on campus to more energy efficient systems. All residence halls and many of the other campus buildings have been retrofitted to include high EER rated lighting equipment. This has cut our energy costs in half for many buildings. New and renovated buildings are updated to include the latest technology in energy efficiency.

ADMISSIONS

Freshman Academic Profile: Average high school GPA 3.4. 20% in top 10% of high school class, 46% in top 25% of high school class, 78% in top 50% of high school class. 90% from public high schools. SAT Math middle 50% range 470-590. SAT Critical Reading middle 50% range 450-570. SAT Writing middle 50% range 440-560. ACT middle 50% range 20-26. Minimum web-based TOEFL 66. Minimum paper TOEFL 517. **Basis for Candidate Selection:** *Very important factors considered include:* rigor of secondary school record. *Important factors considered include:* Class rank, application essay, academic GPA, recommendation(s), standardized test scores, interview, racial/ethnic status. *Other factors considered include:* alumni/ae relation, character/personal qualities, extracurricular activities, first generation, geographical residence, level of applicant's interest, talent/ability, volunteer work, work experience. **Freshman Admission Requirements:** High school diploma is required and GED is accepted. *Academic units required:* 4 English, 3 mathematics, 3 science, (2 science labs), 2 foreign language, 4 social studies, 3 history, 2 academic electives. *Academic units recommended:* 4 English, 3 mathematics, 3 science, (2 science labs), 2 foreign language, 4 social studies, 3 history, 2 academic electives. **Freshman Admission Statistics:** 1,723 applied, 72% admitted, 26% enrolled. **Transfer Admission Requirements:** college transcript(s), statement of good standing from prior institution(s). Minimum college GPA of 2.0 required. Lowest grade transferable C–. **General Admission Information:** Application Fee $35. Regular application deadline 7/1. Notification on a rolling basis, beginning on or about 12/15. Nonfall registration accepted. Admission may be deferred for a maximum of 1 year. Credit offered for CEEB Advanced Placement tests.

COSTS AND FINANCIAL AID

Annual tuition $31,168. Room and board $8,970. Required fees $650. Average book expense $1,000. **Required Forms and Deadlines:** FAFSA, institution's

own financial aid form. **Notification of Awards:** Applicants will be notified of awards on a rolling basis beginning 3/1. **Types of Aid:** *Need-based scholarships/grants:* Federal Pell, SEOG, state scholarships/grants, private scholarships, the school's own gift aid. *Loans:* Subsidized Stafford, Unsubsidized Stafford, PLUS, Federal Perkins, college/university loans from institutional funds. **Student Employment:** Federal Work-Study Program available. Institutional employment available. Highest amount earned per year from on-campus jobs $4,004. Off-campus job opportunities are good. **Financial Aid Statistics:** 100% freshmen, 100% undergrads receive need-based scholarship or grant aid. 16% freshmen, 11% undergrads receive non-need-based scholarship or grant aid. 73% freshmen, 83% undergrads receive need-based self-help aid. 100% freshmen, 99% undergrads receive any aid. 85% undergrads borrow to pay for school. Average cumulative indebtedness $35,990. **Criteria for awarding institutional aid:** *Non-need-based:* academics, art, leadership, minority status, music/drama.

LYME ACADEMY COLLEGE OF FINE ARTS

84 Lyme St, Old Lyme, CT 6371
Phone: 860-434-3571 x118 • **Financial Aid Phone:** 860-434-5232
E-mail: admissions@lymeacademy.edu • **CEEB Code:** 1971
Fax: 860-434-8725 • **Website:** www.lymeacademy.edu/ • **ACT Code:**

This private school was founded in 1976. It has a 47-acre campus.

RATINGS

Admissions Selectivity Rating: 75   **Fire Safety Rating:** 60*   **Green Rating:** 60*

STUDENTS AND FACULTY

Enrollment: 92. **Student Body:** 63% female, 37% male, 47% out-of-state, 0% international (0 countries represented). Asian 1%, African American 3%, Caucasian 74%, Hispanic 1%, Native American 2%.
Retention and Graduation: 89% freshmen return for sophomore year. 53% freshmen graduate within 4 years. 10% grads go on to further study within 1 year. **Faculty:** Student/faculty ratio 14:1. 8 full-time faculty, 75% hold PhDs, 0% are members of minority groups, 38% are women. 0% of classes are taught by teaching assistants.

ACADEMICS

Degrees: bachelor's, certificate, post-bachelor's certificate. **Classes:** Most classes have 10–19 students. **Majors with Highest Enrollment:** illustration; painting; sculpture. **Special Study Options:** independent study.

FACILITIES

Housing: Currently, all housing is Off-campus. Students live in local homes as well as apartments. Contact Patti Broedlin in Student Services for assistance, lists and referrals. 95% of campus accessible to physically disabled. **Special Academic Facilities/Equipment:** Sill House Gallery, Chauncey Stillman Gallery, Academy Wood Shop, Sculpture Casting rooms **Computers:** 20% of classrooms, 100% of libraries, 100% of dining areas, 100% of student union, 40% of common outdoor areas have wireless network access.

CAMPUS LIFE

Environment: Village. **Activities:** literary magazine, student government, student-run film society. **On-Campus Highlights:** Chauncey Stillman Art Gallery, Cafe, Student Commons, Library, Sill House Art Gallery.

ADMISSIONS

Freshman Academic Profile: Average high school GPA 3.2. 85% from public high schools. SAT Math middle 50% range 395-555. SAT Critical Reading middle 50% range 440-650. SAT Writing middle 50% range 450-595. Minimum paper TOEFL 550. **Basis for Candidate Selection:** *Very important factors considered include:* academic GPA, character/personal qualities, interview, level of applicant's interest, talent/ability. *Important factors considered include:* application essay, recommendation(s), rigor of secondary school record. *Other factors considered include:* standardized test scores, racial/ethnic status. **Freshman Admission Requirements:** High school diploma is required and GED is accepted. **Freshman Admission Statistics:** 82 applied, 68% admitted, 41% enrolled. **Transfer Admission Requirements:** college transcript(s), essay or personal statement, interview, minimum college GPA of 2.0 required. Lowest grade transferable C. **General Admission Information:** Application Fee $55. Notification on a rolling basis, beginning on or about 12/1. Nonfall registration accepted. Admission may be deferred for a maximum of 1 year. Credit and/or placement offered for CEEB Advanced Placement tests.

COSTS AND FINANCIAL AID

Annual tuition $25,248. Required fees $1,536. Average book expense $1,500. **Required Forms and Deadlines:** FAFSA, CSS/Financial Aid PROFILE, business/farm supplement. Copies of previous year's Tax forms and W2's. **Notification of Awards:** Applicants will be notified of awards on a rolling basis beginning 3/1. **Types of Aid:** *Need-based scholarships/grants:* Federal Pell, SEOG, state scholarships/grants, private scholarships, the school's own gift aid. *Loans:* Subsidized Stafford, Unsubsidized Stafford, PLUS. **Student Employment:** Federal Work-Study Program available. Institutional employment available. Off-campus job opportunities are good. **Financial Aid Statistics:** 88% freshmen, 84% undergrads receive any aid. **Criteria for awarding institutional aid:** *Non-need-based:* academics, art, leadership.

LYNCHBURG COLLEGE

1501 Lakeside Drive, Lynchburg, VA 24501
Phone: 434-544-8300 • **Financial Aid Phone:** 434-544-8229
E-mail: admissions@lynchburg.edu • **CEEB Code:** 5372
Fax: 434-544-8653 • **Website:** www.lynchburg.edu • **ACT Code:** 4368

This private school, affiliated with the Disciples of Christ Church, was founded in 1903. It has a 214-acre campus.

RATINGS
Admissions Selectivity Rating: 74   **Fire Safety Rating:** 72   **Green Rating:** 70

STUDENTS AND FACULTY
Enrollment: 2,150. **Student Body:** 59% female, 41% male, 33% out-of-state, 1% international (26 countries represented). Asian 1%, African American 10%, Caucasian 79%, Hispanic 3%, Native American 0%. **Retention and Graduation:** 73% freshmen return for sophomore year. 47% freshmen graduate within 4 years. **Faculty:** Student/faculty ratio 11:1. 186 full-time faculty, 78% hold PhDs, 5% are members of minority groups, 52% are women. 0% of classes are taught by teaching assistants.

ACADEMICS
Degrees: bachelor's, master's, post-bachelor's certificate. **Classes:** Most classes have 10–19 students. Most lab/discussion sessions have 10–19 students. **Majors with Highest Enrollment:** business administration and management; communication studies/speech communication and rhetoric; teacher education and professional development, specific levels and methods, other. **Special Study Options:** Accelerated program, cross-registration, double major, dual enrollment, honors program, independent study, internships, study abroad, teacher certification program. **Honors Programs:** Westover Honors Program. **Disability Services:** Special programs offered to physically disabled students include note-taking services, reader services, tape recorders, tutors. **Career Services:** Alumni network, alumni services, career/job search classes, career assessment, internships, regional alumni. Career Services highlights include Experiential learning and internship programs are so numerous and diverse that it is impossible to select one that is most outstanding.

FACILITIES
Housing: Coed dorms, special housing for disabled students, men's dorms, special housing for international students, women's dorms, fraternity/sorority housing, apartments for single students, wellness housing, theme housing, 83% of campus accessible to physically disabled. **Special Academic Facilities/Equipment:** Daura Art Gallery, Claytor Nature Study Center, Ramsey-Freer Herbarium, Forensics cadaver lab; Centennial Hall audio-visual and television studios, Dillard Fine Arts Center **Computers:** 20% of dorms, 100% of libraries, 100% of dining areas, 100% of student union, have wireless network access. Students can register for classes online. Administrative functions (other than registration) can be performed online.

CAMPUS LIFE
Environment: City. **Activities:** Choral groups, concert band, dance, drama/theater, jazz band, literary magazine, music ensembles, musical theater, pep band, student government, student newspaper, student-run film society, symphony orchestra, yearbook, Campus Ministries, International Student Organization, Model UN 90 registered organizations, 14 honor societies, 10 religious organizations. 4 fraternities, 6 sororities. **Athletics (Intercollegiate):** *Men:* baseball, basketball, cheerleading, cross-country, golf, lacrosse, soccer, tennis, track/field (outdoor), track/field (indoor). *Women:* basketball, cheerleading, cross-country, equestrian sports, field hockey, lacrosse, soccer, softball, tennis, track/field (outdoor), track/field (indoor), volleyball. **On-Campus Highlights:** Shellenberger Field, Burton Student Center, Claytor Nature Study Center, Stingers Coffee House, Schewel Hall. **Environmental Initiatives:** Recovery

of College Lake. Working with the Army Corp of Engineers, and the state of Virginia, Lynchburg College is attempting to restore College Lake. Dr. Garren (LC President) has signed the American College & University Presidents Climate Commitment, a pledge to reverse the actions that lead to global warming. Signatories agree to develop a plan to reduce their use of greenhouse gases. Dr. Nancy Cowden, associate professor of biology, is leading the task force on LC's climate commitment. Development of Claytor Nature Study Center.

ADMISSIONS
Freshman Academic Profile: Average high school GPA 3.3. 10% in top 10% of high school class, 37% in top 25% of high school class, 75% in top 50% of high school class. 85% from public high schools. SAT Math middle 50% range 450-550. SAT Critical Reading middle 50% range 450-553. SAT Writing middle 50% range 440-550. ACT middle 50% range 18-24. Minimum paper TOEFL 525. **Basis for Candidate Selection:** *Very important factors considered include:* academic GPA, rigor of secondary school record, standardized test scores. *Important factors considered include:* Class rank, interview. *Other factors considered include:* application essay, recommendation(s), extracurricular activities, level of applicant's interest, talent/ability, volunteer work. **Freshman Admission Requirements:** High school diploma is required and GED is accepted. *Academic units required:* 4 English, 3 mathematics, 3 science, (2 science labs), 2 foreign language, 2 social studies, 2 history. *Academic units recommended:* 4 English, 3 mathematics, 3 science, (2 science labs), 2 foreign language, 2 social studies, 2 history. **Freshman Admission Statistics:** 4,474 applied, 67% admitted, 17% enrolled. **Transfer Admission Requirements:** college transcript(s), minimum college GPA of 2.0 required. Lowest grade transferable C. **General Admission Information:** Application Fee $30. Early decision application deadline 11/15. Notification on a rolling basis, beginning on or about 9/1. Non-fall registration accepted. Admission may be deferred for a maximum of 1 year. Credit offered for CEEB Advanced Placement tests.

COSTS AND FINANCIAL AID
Annual tuition $31,060. Room and board $8,680. Required fees $945. Average book expense $1,000. **Required Forms and Deadlines:** FAFSA, state aid form. **Notification of Awards:** Applicants will be notified of awards on a rolling basis beginning 3/5. **Types of Aid:** *Need-based scholarships/grants:* Federal Pell, SEOG, state scholarships/grants, private scholarships, the school's own gift aid. *Loans:* Subsidized Stafford, Unsubsidized Stafford, PLUS, Federal Perkins. **Student Employment:** Federal Work-Study Program available. Institutional employment available. Off-campus job opportunities are good. **Financial Aid Statistics:** 100% freshmen, 100% undergrads receive need-based scholarship or grant aid. 12% freshmen, 12% undergrads receive non-need-based scholarship or grant aid. 85% freshmen, 85% undergrads receive need based self-help aid. 98% freshmen, 96% undergrads receive any aid. 74% undergrads borrow to pay for school. Average cumulative indebtedness $33,353. **Criteria for awarding institutional aid:** *Non-need-based:* academics, leadership, music/drama, religious affiliation.

LYNDON STATE COLLEGE

P O Box 919, Lyndonville, VT 5851
Phone: 802-626-6413
E-mail: admissions@lyndonstate.edu • **CEEB Code:** 3767
Fax: 802-626-6335 • **Website:** www.lyndonstate.edu • **ACT Code:** 4318

This public school was founded in 1911. It has a 175-acre campus.

RATINGS
Admissions Selectivity Rating: 65   **Fire Safety Rating:** 60*   **Green Rating:** 60*

STUDENTS AND FACULTY
Enrollment: 1,273. **Student Body:** 49% female, 51% male, 40% out-of-state, 0% international. Asian 0%, African American 1%, Caucasian 52%, Hispanic 1%, Native American 0%. **Retention and Graduation:** 67% freshmen return for sophomore year. 24% freshmen graduate within 4 years. 43% freshmen graduate within 6 years. 10% grads go on to further study within 1 year. **Faculty:** Student/faculty ratio 20:1. 59 full-time faculty, 90% hold PhDs, 0% are members of minority groups, 34% are women. 0% of classes are taught by teaching assistants.

ACADEMICS
Degrees: associate, bachelor's, certificate, master's. **Classes:** Most classes have 10–19 students. Most lab/discussion sessions have 10–19 students. **Special Study Options:** Accelerated program, cooperative education program, double major, dual enrollment, exchange student program (domestic), independent study, internships, liberal arts/career combination, student-designed major, study abroad, teacher certification program. **Disability Services:** Special programs offered to physically disabled students include note-taking services, tape

recorders, tutors. **Career Services:** Alumni network, alumni services, career/job search classes, career assessment, internships, regional alumni.

FACILITIES
Housing: Coed dorms, special housing for disabled students, women's dorms, Substance free dorms. 100% of campus accessible to physically disabled. Special Academic Facilities/Equipment: Museum of college history, weather satellite lab, television studio, radio station, science labs: geology, chemistry, physics; ?GIS/GPS lab

CAMPUS LIFE
Environment: Rural. **Activities:** Choral groups, dance, drama/theater, literary magazine, musical theater, radio station, student government, student newspaper, television station 26 registered organizations, 1 honor societies, 1 religious organizations. **Athletics (Intercollegiate):** *Men:* baseball, basketball, cross-country, soccer, tennis. *Women:* basketball, cross-country, soccer, softball, tennis.

ADMISSIONS
Freshman Academic Profile: Average high school GPA 2.5. 12% in top 10% of high school class, 22% in top 25% of high school class, 69% in top 50% of high school class. SAT Math middle 50% range 410-530. SAT Critical Reading middle 50% range 418-520. Minimum paper TOEFL 500. **Basis for Candidate Selection:** *Very important factors considered include:* rigor of secondary school record. *Important factors considered include:* Class rank, recommendation(s), character/personal qualities, interview, talent/ability. *Other factors considered include:* application essay, standardized test scores, alumni/ae relation, extracurricular activities, volunteer work, work experience. **Freshman Admission Requirements:** High school diploma is required and GED is accepted. *Academic units required:* 4 English, 3 mathematics, 2 science, (2 science labs), 2 social studies, 2 history. *Academic units recommended:* 4 English, 3 mathematics, 2 science, (2 science labs), 2 social studies, 2 history. **Freshman Admission Statistics:** 994 applied, 94% admitted, 36% enrolled. **Transfer Admission Requirements:** college transcript(s), essay or personal statement, statement of good standing from prior institution(s). Minimum college GPA of 2.2 required. Lowest grade transferable C–. **General Admission Information:** Application Fee $35. Notification on a rolling basis, beginning on or about 12/1. Nonfall registration accepted. Admission may be deferred for a maximum of 1 year. Credit and/or placement offered for CEEB Advanced Placement tests.

COSTS AND FINANCIAL AID
Average book expense $600. **Required Forms and Deadlines:** FAFSA. **Notification of Awards:** Applicants will be notified of awards on a rolling basis beginning 4/1. **Types of Aid:** *Need-based scholarships/grants:* Federal Pell, SEOG, state scholarships/grants, private scholarships, the school's own gift aid. *Loans:* Direct Subsidized Stafford, Direct Unsubsidized Stafford, Direct PLUS, Federal Perkins, state loans. **Student Employment:** Federal Work-Study Program available. Institutional employment available. Highest amount earned per year from on-campus jobs $700. Off-campus job opportunities are good. **Financial Aid Statistics:** 53% freshmen, 53% undergrads receive need-based scholarship or grant aid. 21% freshmen, 8% undergrads receive non-need-based scholarship or grant aid. 99% freshmen, 100% undergrads receive need-based self-help aid. **Criteria for awarding institutional aid:** *Non-need-based:* academics, leadership.

LYNN UNIVERSITY

3601 North Military Trail, Boca Raton, FL 33431-5598
Phone: 561-237-7900 • **Financial Aid Phone:** 561-237-7186
E-mail: admission@lynn.edu • **CEEB Code:** 5437
Fax: 561-237-7100 • **Website:** www.lynn.edu • **ACT Code:** 706

This private school was founded in 1962. It has a 123-acre campus.

RATINGS
Admissions Selectivity Rating: 64   **Fire Safety Rating:** 96   **Green Rating:** 61

STUDENTS AND FACULTY
Enrollment: 1,626. **Student Body:** 48% female, 52% male, 55% out-of-state, 22% international (87 countries represented). Asian 1%, African American 8%, Caucasian 49%, Hispanic 10%, Native American 0%.
Retention and Graduation: 27% freshmen graduate within 4 years. 40% freshmen graduate within 6 years. **Faculty:** Student/faculty ratio 15:1. 93 full-time faculty, 70% hold PhDs, 9% are members of minority groups, 43% are women. 0% of classes are taught by teaching assistants.

ACADEMICS
Degrees: bachelor's, certificate, master's, post-bachelor's certificate, post-master's certificate. **Classes:** Most classes have 10–19 students. **Majors with Highest Enrollment:** business/commerce; hospitality administration/management; journalism. **Special Study Options:** Accelerated program, cooperative education program, distance learning, double major, dual enrollment, English as a Second Language (ESL), honors program, independent study, internships, liberal arts/career combination, study abroad, teacher certification program. **Honors Programs:** Honors Program. **Disability Services:** Special programs offered to physically disabled students include note-taking services, reader services, tape recorders. **Career Services:** alumni services, career/job search classes, career assessment, internships, regional alumni. Career Services highlights include Well developed internship program, with approximately 300 internship students for whom we provide services in all program areas, excluding Education and Aviation.

FACILITIES
Housing: Coed dorms, special housing for disabled students, special housing for international students, women's dorms. 100% of campus accessible to physically disabled. **Computers:** Students can register for classes online. Administrative functions (other than registration) can be performed online.

CAMPUS LIFE
Environment: City. **Activities:** Choral groups, dance, drama/theater, literary magazine, music ensembles, radio station, student government, student newspaper, student-run film society, symphony orchestra, television station, yearbook, Campus Ministries, International Student Organization 25 registered organizations, 4 honor societies, 4 religious organizations. 2 fraternities, 1 sororities. **Athletics (Intercollegiate):** *Men:* baseball, basketball, golf, soccer, tennis. *Women:* basketball, golf, soccer, softball, tennis, volleyball. **On-Campus Highlights:** The de Hoernle Sports Complex, The de Hoernle Sports and Cultural Center, The Coleman Electronic Lab, The Lynn Student Center, The Eugene M. and Christine E. Lynn Library. **Environmental Initiatives:** On campsu recycling program (paper, glass and cans) Recycling of flourescent lightbulbs Use of re-claimed water for irrigation.

ADMISSIONS
Freshman Academic Profile: Average high school GPA 2.8. 3% in top 10% of high school class, 22% in top 25% of high school class, 52% in top 50% of high school class. SAT Math middle 50% range 400-510. SAT Critical Reading middle 50% range 400-490. SAT Writing middle 50% range 390-490. ACT middle 50% range 17-22. Minimum paper TOEFL 525. **Basis for Candidate Selection:** *Very important factors considered include:* academic GPA, rigor of secondary school record, standardized test scores. *Important factors considered include:* Class rank, application essay, recommendation(s), character/personal qualities, work experience. *Other factors considered include:* alumni/ae relation, extracurricular activities, first generation, interview, state residency, talent/ability, volunteer work. **Freshman Admission Requirements:** High school diploma is required and GED is accepted. *Academic units required:* 4 English, 4 mathematics, 4 science, 2 social studies, 2 history. 4 English, 4 mathematics, 4 science, 2 social studies, 2 history. **Freshman Admission Statistics:** 2,162 applied, 95% admitted, 20% enrolled. **Transfer Admission Requirements:** college transcript(s), essay or personal statement, statement of good standing from prior institution(s). Minimum college GPA of 2.0 required. Lowest grade transferable C. **General Admission Information:** Application Fee $35. Nonfall registration accepted. Credit offered for CEEB Advanced Placement tests.

COSTS AND FINANCIAL AID
Annual tuition $31,900. Room and board $10,900. Required fees $1,500. Average book expense $1,000. **Required Forms and Deadlines:** FAFSA, institution's own financial aid form. **Notification of Awards:** Applicants will be notified of awards on a rolling basis beginning 2/1. **Types of Aid:** *Need-based scholarships/grants:* Federal Pell, SEOG, state scholarships/grants, private scholarships, the school's own gift aid. *Loans:* Direct Subsidized Stafford, Direct Unsubsidized Stafford, Direct PLUS, Subsidized Stafford, Unsubsidized Stafford, PLUS, Federal Perkins, state loans, college/university loans from institutional funds. **Student Employment:** Federal Work-Study Program available. Institutional employment available. Highest amount earned per year from on-campus jobs $16,420. Off-campus job opportunities are excellent. **Financial Aid Statistics:** 78% freshmen, 79% undergrads receive need-based scholarship or grant aid. 86% freshmen, 87% undergrads receive non-need-based scholarship or grant aid. 69% freshmen, 70% undergrads receive need-based self-help aid. 11% freshmen, 10% undergrads receive athletic scholarships. 54% freshmen, 55% undergrads receive any aid. 35% undergrads borrow to pay for school. Average cumulative indebtedness $33,472. **Criteria for awarding institutional aid:** *Non-need-based:* academics, athletics, leadership, music/drama, religious affiliation, state/district residency.

See page 1134.

LYON COLLEGE

P.O. Box 2317, Batesville, AR 72503-2317
Phone: 870-307-7250 • **Financial Aid Phone:** 870-307-7257
E-mail: admissions@lyon.edu • **CEEB Code:** 1088
Fax: 870-307-7542 • **Website:** www.lyon.edu • **ACT Code:** 112

This private school, affiliated with the Presbyterian Church, was founded in 1872. It has a 136-acre campus.

RATINGS
Admissions Selectivity Rating: 79 **Fire Safety Rating:** 70 **Green Rating:** 60*

STUDENTS AND FACULTY
Enrollment: 582. **Student Body:** 53% female, 47% male, 23% out-of-state, 4% international (8 countries represented). Asian 1%, African American 4%, Caucasian 77%, Hispanic 5%, Native American 1%.
Retention and Graduation: 72% freshmen return for sophomore year. 41% freshmen graduate within 4 years. 47% freshmen graduate within 6 years. **Faculty:** Student/faculty ratio 11:1. 41 full-time faculty, 95% hold PhDs, 10% are members of minority groups, 34% are women. 0% of classes are taught by teaching assistants.

ACADEMICS
Degrees: bachelor's. **Classes:** Most classes have 10–19 students. Most lab/discussion sessions have fewer than 10 students. **Majors with Highest Enrollment:** biology/biological sciences; business/commerce; psychology. **Special Study Options:** Accelerated program, cross-registration, double major, dual enrollment, independent study, internships, liberal arts/career combination, student-designed major, study abroad, teacher certification program. **Combined Degree Programs:** BA/MEng, BS/BEng (with U. MO. Rolla). **Disability Services:** Special programs offered to physically disabled students include tape recorders. **Career Services:** Alumni network, alumni services, career/job search classes, career assessment, internships, regional alumni.

FACILITIES
Housing: Coed dorms, special housing for disabled students, men's dorms, women's dorms, apartments for single students, Limited College-owned off-campus housing. 80% of campus accessible to physically disabled. **Special Academic Facilities/Equipment:** Ozark Regional Studies Center **Computers:** 100% of classrooms, 100% of dorms, 100% of libraries, 100% of dining areas, 100% of student union, 100% of common outdoor areas have wireless network access. Students can register for classes online. Administrative functions (other than registration) can be performed online.

CAMPUS LIFE
Environment: Village. **Activities:** Choral groups, concert band, drama/theater, literary magazine, music ensembles, student government, student newspaper, yearbook, Campus Ministries, Model UN 44 registered organizations, 9 honor societies, 7 religious organizations. 3 fraternities, 2 sororities. **Athletics (Intercollegiate):** *Men:* baseball, basketball, cheerleading, cross-country, golf, soccer. *Women:* basketball, cheerleading, cross-country, golf, soccer, softball, volleyball. **On-Campus Highlights:** Derby Center for Science and Mathematics, Becknell Gymnasium, Holloway Theater, Edwards Commons / Bookstore, Mabee Simpson Library.

ADMISSIONS
Freshman Academic Profile: Average high school GPA 3.6. 36% in top 10% of high school class, 63% in top 25% of high school class, 87% in top 50% of high school class. 84% from public high schools. SAT Math middle 50% range 490-580. SAT Critical Reading middle 50% range 430-580. SAT Writing middle 50% range 440-570. ACT middle 50% range 22-27. Minimum web-based TOEFL 79. Minimum paper TOEFL 550. **Basis for Candidate Selection:** *Very important factors considered include:* academic GPA, standardized test scores. *Important factors considered include:* rigor of secondary school record. *Other factors considered include:* Class rank, application essay, recommendation(s), character/personal qualities, extracurricular activities, interview, level of applicant's interest, talent/ability, volunteer work, work experience. **Freshman Admission Requirements:** High school diploma is required and GED is accepted. *Academic units required:* 4 English, 3 mathematics, 3 science, (2 science labs), 2 foreign language, 1 social studies, 2 history, 1 academic electives. *Academic units recommended:* 4 English, 3 mathematics, 3 science, (2 science labs), 2 foreign language, 1 social studies, 2 history, 1 academic electives. **Freshman Admission Statistics:** 926 applied, 725% enrolled. **Transfer Admission Requirements:** college transcript(s), statement of good standing from prior institution(s). Minimum college GPA of 2.75 required. Lowest grade transferable C. **General Admission Information:** Application Fee $25. Non-fall registration accepted. Admission may be deferred for a maximum of 1 year. Credit and/or placement offered for CEEB Advanced Placement tests.

COSTS AND FINANCIAL AID
Annual tuition $23,270. Room and board $7,560. Required fees $224. Average book expense $1,000. **Required Forms and Deadlines:** FAFSA. **Notification of Awards:** Applicants will be notified of awards on a rolling basis beginning 3/1. **Types of Aid:** *Need-based scholarships/grants:* Federal Pell, SEOG, state scholarships/grants, private scholarships, the school's own gift aid. *Loans:* Subsidized Stafford, Unsubsidized Stafford, PLUS, Federal Perkins. **Student Employment:** Highest amount earned per year from on-campus jobs $5,600. Off-campus job opportunities are good. **Financial Aid Statistics:** 100% freshmen, 100% undergrads receive need-based scholarship or grant aid. 29% freshmen, 23% undergrads receive non-need-based scholarship or grant aid. 71% freshmen, 75% undergrads receive need-based self-help aid. 18% freshmen, 15% undergrads receive athletic scholarships. 100% freshmen, 99% undergrads receive any aid. 72% undergrads borrow to pay for school. Average cumulative indebtedness $17,179. **Criteria for awarding institutional aid:** *Non-need-based:* academics, art, athletics, job skills, leadership, music/drama, religious affiliation.

MACALESTER COLLEGE

1600 Grand Avenue, St. Paul, MN 55105
Phone: 651-696-6357 • **Financial Aid Phone:** 651-696-6214
E-mail: admissions@macalester.edu • **CEEB Code:** 6390
Fax: 651-696-6724 • **Website:** www.macalester.edu • **ACT Code:** 2122

This private school, affiliated with the Presbyterian Church, was founded in 1874. It has a 53-acre campus.

RATINGS
Admissions Selectivity Rating: 96 **Fire Safety Rating:** 98 **Green Rating:** 94

STUDENTS AND FACULTY
Enrollment: 2,047. **Student Body:** 60% female, 40% male, 81% out-of-state, 13% international (93 countries represented). Asian 7%, African American 3%, Caucasian 66%, Hispanic 6%, Native American 0%.
Retention and Graduation: 94% freshmen return for sophomore year. 86% freshmen graduate within 4 years. 90% freshmen graduate within 6 years. 17% grads go on to further study within 1 year. 11% grads pursue arts and sciences degrees. 2% grads pursue law degrees. 1% grads pursue business degrees. 2% grads pursue medical degrees. **Faculty:** Student/faculty ratio 10:1. 174 full-time faculty, 94% hold PhDs, 18% are members of minority groups, 49% are women. 0% of classes are taught by teaching assistants.

ACADEMICS
Degrees: bachelor's. **Classes:** Most classes have 10–19 students. Most lab/discussion sessions have 10–19 students. **Majors with Highest Enrollment:** economics; English language and literature; political science and government. **Special Study Options:** cross-registration, double major, honors program, independent study, internships, student-designed major, study abroad, Combined bachelors/graduate programs: BA/Master's in Architecture with Washington University, St. Louis, Missouri -BA/BS in Engineering with Washington University, St. Louis or the University of Minnesota. **Combined Degree Programs:** 3/3 Architecture Washington U. **Disability Services:** Special programs offered to physically disabled students include note-taking services, reader services, tape recorders, tutors. **Career Services:** Alumni network, alumni services, career assessment, internships, regional alumni. Career Services highlights include Students at Macalester are civically engaged through a broad range of experientially focused programs. Last year, 302 students did internships for academic credit, 22 classes were offered that included a significant civic engagement component, 42 students worked in non-profit settings through an off-campus student employment program, and students contributed almost 50,000 hours of volunteer service to the community. This is possible due to the college's vibrant urban location and the strongly held belief of faculty, staff, and administration that experiential education and civic engagement are vital elements in a quality liberal arts education.

FACILITIES
Housing: Coed dorms, cooperative housing, apartments for single students, theme housing, Language Houses, Kosher Residence, EcoHouse. 75% of campus accessible to physically disabled. **Special Academic Facilities/Equipment:** Humanities learning center, econometrics lab, cartography lab, 250-acre nature preserve, observatory and planetarium, two electron microscopes, nucle-

ar magnetic resonance spectrometer, laser spectroscopy lab, X-ray diffractometer, International Center, Center for Scholarship and Teaching, Ethnographic lab, GIS lab, State-of-the-Art science labs. **Computers:** 100% of classrooms, 98% of dorms, 100% of libraries, 100% of dining areas, 100% of student union, 90% of common outdoor areas have wireless network access. Students can register for classes online. Administrative functions (other than registration) can be performed online.

CAMPUS LIFE

Environment: Metropolis. **Activities:** Choral groups, concert band, dance, drama/theater, jazz band, literary magazine, music ensembles, radio station, student government, student newspaper, symphony orchestra, Campus Ministries, International Student Organization, Model UN 80 registered organizations, 15 honor societies, 10 religious organizations. **Athletics (Intercollegiate):** *Men:* baseball, basketball, cross-country, diving, football, golf, soccer, swimming, tennis, track/field (outdoor), track/field (indoor). *Women:* basketball, cross-country, diving, golf, soccer, softball, swimming, tennis, track/field (outdoor), track/field (indoor), volleyball, water polo. **On-Campus Highlights:** Second Floor Campus Center, Bateman Plaza (our front patio), The Quad (our front yard), Shaw Field, Smail Gallery in the Science Center. **Environmental Initiatives:** Developed a comprehensive sustainability plan. Hired a sustainability Manager Built a LEED Platinum Building

ADMISSIONS

Freshman Academic Profile: 65% in top 10% of high school class, 93% in top 25% of high school class, 99% in top 50% of high school class. 69% from public high schools. SAT Math middle 50% range 640-730. SAT Critical Reading middle 50% range 630-740. SAT Writing middle 50% range 630-720. ACT middle 50% range 28-32. Minimum web-based TOEFL 100. Minimum paper TOEFL 600. **Basis for Candidate Selection:** *Very important factors considered include:* academic GPA, rigor of secondary school record. *Important factors considered include:* application essay, recommendation(s), standardized test scores, character/personal qualities, extracurricular activities. *Other factors considered include:* Class rank, alumni/ae relation, first generation, interview, racial/ethnic status, talent/ability, volunteer work, work experience. **Freshman Admission Requirements:** High school diploma or equivalent is not required. **Freshman Admission Statistics:** 6,030 applied, 37% admitted, 24% enrolled. **Transfer Admission Requirements:** High school transcript, college transcript(s), essay or personal statement, standardized test scores, statement of good standing from prior institution(s). Lowest grade transferable C–. **General Admission Information:** Application Fee $40. Early decision application deadline 11/15. Regular application deadline 1/15. Regular notification 3/30. Nonfall registration not accepted. Admission may be deferred for a maximum of 1 year. Credit and/or placement offered for CEEB Advanced Placement tests.

COSTS AND FINANCIAL AID

Annual tuition $43,472. Room and board $9,726. Required fees $221. Average book expense $1,050. **Required Forms and Deadlines:** FAFSA, CSS/ Financial Aid PROFILE, noncustodial PROFILE. **Notification of Awards:** Applicants will be notified of awards on or about 4/1. **Types of Aid:** *Need-based scholarships/grants:* Federal Pell, SEOG, state scholarships/grants, private scholarships, the school's own gift aid. *Loans:* Direct Subsidized Stafford, Direct Unsubsidized Stafford, Direct PLUS, Federal Perkins, state loans. **Student Employment:** Federal Work-Study Program available. Institutional employment available. Highest amount earned per year from on-campus jobs $2,800. Off-campus job opportunities are excellent. **Financial Aid Statistics:** 100% freshmen, 99% undergrads receive need-based scholarship or grant aid. 9% freshmen, 6% undergrads receive non-need-based scholarship or grant aid. 88% freshmen, 92% undergrads receive need-based self-help aid. 78% freshmen, 77% undergrads receive any aid. 60% undergrads borrow to pay for school. Average cumulative indebtedness $23,285. **Criteria for awarding institutional aid:** *Non-need-based:* academics, minority status.

MACMURRAY COLLEGE

447 East College, Jacksonville, IL 62650
Phone: 217-479-7056 • **Financial Aid Phone:** 217-479-7041
E-mail: admissions@mac.edu • **CEEB Code:** 1435
Fax: 217-291-0702 • **Website:** www.mac.edu • **ACT Code:** 1068

This private school, affiliated with the Methodist Church, was founded in 1846. It has a 60-acre campus.

RATINGS

Admissions Selectivity Rating: 71   **Fire Safety Rating:** 65   **Green Rating:** 60*

STUDENTS AND FACULTY

Enrollment: 581. **Student Body:** 66% female, 34% male, 11% out-of-state, 0% international (2 countries represented). Asian 1%, African American 13%, Caucasian 73%, Hispanic 3%, Native American 0%.
Retention and Graduation: 72% freshmen return for sophomore year. 26% freshmen graduate within 4 years. 37% freshmen graduate within 6 years. 25% grads go on to further study within 1 year. 9% grads pursue arts and sciences degrees. 1% grads pursue law degrees. 12% grads pursue business degrees. 1% grads pursue medical degrees. **Faculty:** Student/faculty ratio 14:1. 35 full-time faculty, 63% hold PhDs, 3% are members of minority groups, 74% are women. 0% of classes are taught by teaching assistants.

ACADEMICS

Degrees: associate, bachelor's. **Classes:** Most classes have 10–19 students. Most lab/discussion sessions have 10–19 students. **Majors with Highest Enrollment:** nursing/registered nurse (rn, asn, bsn, msn); special education and teaching. **Special Study Options:** cooperative education program, double major, dual enrollment, independent study, internships, liberal arts/career combination, student-designed major, study abroad, teacher certification program. **Combined Degree Programs:** BA/MEng, 3-2 Occupational Therapy prog. w/Washington U. **Disability Services:** Special programs offered to physically disabled students include note-taking services, reader services, tape recorders, tutors. **Career Services:** Alumni network, alumni services, career/job search classes, career assessment, internships, regional alumni.

FACILITIES

Housing: Coed dorms, special housing for disabled students, women's dorms. 50% of campus accessible to physically disabled. Art gallery, language lab., music hall, nursing labs,

CAMPUS LIFE

Environment: Village. **Activities:** Choral groups, dance, drama/theater, literary magazine, student government, yearbook, Campus Ministries 37 registered organizations, 2 honor societies, 2 religious organizations. 2 fraternities, 1 sororities. **Athletics (Intercollegiate):** *Men:* baseball, basketball, football, golf, soccer, wrestling. *Women:* basketball, golf, soccer, softball, volleyball. **On-Campus Highlights:** Gamble Campus, Education Complex, Jane Hall, Putnam Center for the Arts, McClelland Dining Hall.

ADMISSIONS

Freshman Academic Profile: Average high school GPA 2.8. 4% in top 10% of high school class, 28% in top 25% of high school class, 55% in top 50% of high school class. 75% from public high schools. SAT Math middle 50% range 430-500. SAT Critical Reading middle 50% range 370-470. SAT Writing middle 50% range 340-430. ACT middle 50% range 17-23. Minimum paper TOEFL 550. **Basis for Candidate Selection:** *Very important factors considered include:* academic GPA, rigor of secondary school record, standardized test scores. *Important factors considered include:* Class rank, character/personal qualities, extracurricular activities. *Other factors considered include:* application essay, recommendation(s), interview, volunteer work, work experience. **Freshman Admission Requirements:** High school diploma is required and GED is accepted. **Freshman Admission Statistics:** 800 applied, 61% admitted, 19% enrolled. **Transfer Admission Requirements:** college transcript(s), minimum college GPA of 2.0 required. Lowest grade transferable C. **General Admission Information:** Application Fee $25. Notification on a rolling basis, beginning on or about 9/1. Nonfall registration accepted. Admission may be deferred for a maximum of 12. Credit and/or placement offered for CEEB Advanced Placement tests.

COSTS AND FINANCIAL AID

Annual tuition $15,500. Room and board $5,998. Required fees $250. Average book expense $775. **Required Forms and Deadlines:** FAFSA. **Notification of Awards:** Applicants will be notified of awards on a rolling basis beginning 2/1. **Types of Aid:** *Need-based scholarships/grants:* Federal Pell, SEOG, state scholarships/grants, private scholarships, the school's own gift aid, Federal Nursing Scholarships. *Loans:* Subsidized Stafford, Unsubsidized Stafford, PLUS, Federal Perkins. **Student Employment:** Federal Work-Study Program available. Institutional employment available. Highest amount earned per year from on-campus jobs $945. **Financial Aid Statistics:** 100% freshmen, 100% undergrads receive need-based scholarship or grant aid. 9% freshmen, 7% undergrads receive non-need-based scholarship or grant aid. 79% freshmen, 86% undergrads receive need-based self-help aid. 95% freshmen, 97% undergrads receive any aid. 95% undergrads borrow to pay for school. Average cumulative indebtedness $22,469. **Criteria for awarding institutional aid:** *Non-need-based:* academics, alumni affiliation, art, leadership, music/drama, religious affiliation.

MAHARISHI UNIVERSITY OF MANAGEMENT

1000 North Fourth Street, Fairfield, IA 52557
Phone: 641-472-1110 • **Financial Aid Phone:** 641-472-1156
E-mail: admissions@mum.edu
Fax: 641-472-1179 • **Website:** www.mum.edu • **ACT Code:** 1317

This private school was founded in 1971. It has a 242-acre campus.

RATINGS
Admissions Selectivity Rating: 63   **Fire Safety Rating:** 60*   **Green Rating:** 85

STUDENTS AND FACULTY
Enrollment: 199. **Student Body:** 43% female, 57% male, 65% out-of-state, 17% international. Asian 4%, African American 2%, Caucasian 71%, Hispanic 7%, Native American 0%.
Retention and Graduation: 84% grads go on to further study within 1 year.
Faculty: Student/faculty ratio 16:1. 52 full-time faculty, 98% hold PhDs, 13% are members of minority groups, 21% are women. 0% of classes are taught by teaching assistants.

ACADEMICS
Degrees: associate, bachelor's, certificate, doctoral, master's. **Classes: Majors with Highest Enrollment:** business/commerce; environmental studies; fine/studio arts. **Special Study Options:** double major, independent study, internships, study abroad, teacher certification program, Rotating University: several one-month blocks out of each academic year, a course is offered abroad-e.g. students spend a month with professor studying Art in Italy, Literature in Switzerland, or Business in Japan.

FACILITIES
Housing: special housing for disabled students, men's dorms, women's dorms, apartments for married students, apartments for single students, Apartments for students with dependent children; "quiet" dorms. 80% of campus accessible to physically disabled. **Special Academic Facilities/Equipment:** art gallery; scanning electron microscope; real-time cell-imaging computer system; DNA synthesizer; rock-climbing wall

CAMPUS LIFE
Environment: Village. **Activities:** Choral groups, dance, drama/theater, music ensembles, musical theater, radio station, student government, student newspaper, yearbook 25 registered organizations, 3 honor societies, 1 religious organizations. **Athletics (Intercollegiate):** *Men:* golf. *Women:* golf. **On-Campus Highlights:** Golden Domes, Vedic Architecture, 60,000 sq. ft. Recreation Center, Student Cafe, Vedic Organic Greenhouses. **Environmental Initiatives:** Four-year bachelors of Science degree offered in Sustainable Living. (Include links) Construction of new Sustainable Living Center Implementation of Climate Action Plan.

ADMISSIONS
Freshman Academic Profile: Average high school GPA 3.6. 0% in top 10% of high school class, 0% in top 25% of high school class, 80% in top 50% of high school class. Minimum paper TOEFL 550. **Basis for Candidate Selection:** *Very important factors considered include:* character/personal qualities, interview. *Important factors considered include:* application essay, academic GPA, recommendation(s), rigor of secondary school record, extracurricular activities, level of applicant's interest, talent/ability. *Other factors considered include:* standardized test scores, alumni/ae relation, volunteer work, work experience. **Freshman Admission Requirements:** High school diploma is required and GED is accepted. **Freshman Admission Statistics:** 126 applied, 41% admitted, 87% enrolled. **Transfer Admission Requirements:** High school transcript, college transcript(s), essay or personal statement, interview, minimum college GPA of 2.5 required. Lowest grade transferable 2. **General Admission Information:** Application Fee $30. Notification on a rolling basis, beginning on or about 12/1. Nonfall registration accepted. Admission may be deferred for a maximum of one semester. Credit offered for CEEB Advanced Placement tests.

COSTS AND FINANCIAL AID
Annual tuition $24,000. Room and board $6,000. Required fees $430. Average book expense $800. **Required Forms and Deadlines:** FAFSA. **Notification of Awards:** Applicants will be notified of awards on a rolling basis beginning 3/1. **Types of Aid:** *Need-based scholarships/grants:* Federal Pell, SEOG, state scholarships/grants, private scholarships, the school's own gift aid, Federal Work Study, Veterans, Benefits. *Loans:* Subsidized Stafford, Unsubsidized Stafford, PLUS, Federal Perkins, college/university loans from institutional funds. **Student Employment:** Federal Work-Study Program available. Off-campus job opportunities are fair. **Financial Aid Statistics:** 100% freshmen, 100% undergrads receive need-based scholarship or grant aid. 7% undergrads receive non-need-based scholarship or grant aid. 100% freshmen, 100% undergrads receive need-based self-help aid. 93% freshmen, 98% undergrads receive any aid. 83% undergrads borrow to pay for school. Average cumulative indebtedness $22,691.

• **Criteria for awarding institutional aid:** *Non-need-based:* academics, alumni affiliation, music/drama, state/district residency.

MAINE COLLEGE OF ART

97 Spring Street, Portland, ME 4101
Phone: 207-775-3052 • **Financial Aid Phone:** 207-775-5157
E-mail: admissions@meca.edu • **CEEB Code:** 3701
Fax: 207-772-5069 • **Website:** www.meca.edu • **ACT Code:** 6908

This private school was founded in 1882.

RATINGS
Admissions Selectivity Rating: 79   **Fire Safety Rating:** 65   **Green Rating:** 60*

STUDENTS AND FACULTY
Enrollment: 425. **Student Body:** 62% female, 38% male, 2% international (7 countries represented). Asian 0%, African American 0%, Caucasian 49%, Hispanic 2%, Native American 0%.
Retention and Graduation: 73% freshmen return for sophomore year. 32% freshmen graduate within 4 years. 34% freshmen graduate within 6 years.
Faculty: Student/faculty ratio 10:1. 30 full-time faculty, 93% hold PhDs, 3% are members of minority groups, 63% are women.

ACADEMICS
Degrees: bachelor's, master's. **Classes:** Most classes have 10–19 students.
Special Study Options: cross-registration, double major, exchange student program (domestic), independent study, internships, student-designed major, study abroad, teacher certification program, Mobility program with 36 AICAD (Associated Independent Colleges of Art and Design) institutions in USA and Canada; cross-registration program with 4 other colleges and universites in the greater Portland area; BFA credit available through Provincetown, MA Fine Arts Work Center. **Disability Services:** Special programs offered to physically disabled students include note-taking services, reader services, tape recorders, tutors. **Career Services:** Alumni network, alumni services, career/job search classes, career assessment, internships, regional alumni.

FACILITIES
Housing: Coed dorms, cooperative housing. 80% of campus accessible to physically disabled. **Special Academic Facilities/Equipment:** Institute of Contemporary Art at Maine College of Art June Fitzpatrick Gallery ArtMart (art supply store)

CAMPUS LIFE
Environment: City. **Activities:** student government, student-run film society. **On-Campus Highlights:** The Gorman Student Center ("Living Room"), The Student Gallery, Individual Major Spaces, Institute of Contemporary Art at MECA, Computer Labs.

ADMISSIONS
Freshman Academic Profile: Average high school GPA 3.2. 8% in top 10% of high school class, 19% in top 25% of high school class, 48% in top 50% of high school class. SAT Math middle 50% range 440-560. SAT Critical Reading middle 50% range 480-610. ACT middle 50% range 17-23. Minimum paper TOEFL 500. **Basis for Candidate Selection:** *Very important factors considered include:* rigor of secondary school record, talent/ability. *Important factors considered include:* application essay, recommendation(s), character/personal qualities. *Other factors considered include:* Class rank, standardized test scores, alumni/ae relation, extracurricular activities, geographical residence, interview, racial/ethnic status, state residency, volunteer work, work experience. **Freshman Admission Requirements:** High school diploma is required and GED is accepted. **Freshman Admission Statistics:** 440 applied, 64% admitted, 35% enrolled. **Transfer Admission Requirements:** college transcript(s), essay or personal statement, statement of good standing from prior institution(s). Lowest grade transferable C. **General Admission Information:** Application Fee $40. Nonfall registration accepted. Admission may be deferred for a maximum of 12 months. Credit and/or placement offered for CEEB Advanced Placement tests.

COSTS AND FINANCIAL AID
Annual tuition $20,600. Room and board $8,550. Required fees $520. **Required Forms and Deadlines:** FAFSA. **Notification of Awards:** Applicants will be notified of awards on a rolling basis beginning 2/15. **Types of Aid:** *Need-based scholarships/grants:* Federal Pell, SEOG, state scholarships/grants, the school's own gift aid. *Loans:* Subsidized Stafford, Unsubsidized Stafford, PLUS, Federal Perkins. **Student Employment: Financial Aid Statistics:** 100% freshmen, 99% undergrads receive need-based scholarship or grant aid. 5% freshmen, 4% undergrads receive non-need-based scholarship or grant aid. 93% freshmen, 91% undergrads receive need-based self-help aid. 79% undergrads

borrow to pay for school. Average cumulative indebtedness $25,743. **Criteria for awarding institutional aid:** *Non-need-based:* academics, art.

MAINE MARITIME ACADEMY

Pleasant Street, Castine, ME 4420
Phone: 207-326-2206
E-mail: admissions@mma.edu • **CEEB Code:** 3505
Fax: 207-326-2515 • **Website:** www.mainemaritime.edu • **ACT Code:** 1648

This public school was founded in 1941. It has a 35-acre campus.

RATINGS
Admissions Selectivity Rating: 62   **Fire Safety Rating:** 60*   **Green Rating:** 60*

STUDENTS AND FACULTY
Enrollment: 814. **Student Body:** 15% female, 85% male, 39% out-of-state, 0% international (10 countries represented). Asian 1%, African American 0%, Caucasian 95%, Hispanic 1%, Native American 1%.
Retention and Graduation: 75% freshmen return for sophomore year. 2% grads go on to further study within 1 year. 1% grads pursue arts and sciences degrees. 1% grads pursue law degrees. **Faculty:** Student/faculty ratio 12:1. 55 full-time faculty. 0% of classes are taught by teaching assistants.

ACADEMICS
Degrees: associate, bachelor's, master's. **Classes:** Most classes have 10–19 students. Most lab/discussion sessions have 10–19 students. **Special Study Options:** cooperative education program, internships, Annual Training Cruises. **Career Services:** alumni services, career/job search classes, internships.

FACILITIES
Housing: Coed dorms, apartments for single students. 90% of campus accessible to physically disabled. **Computers:** Administrative functions (other than registration) can be performed online. Undergraduates are required to own a computer.

CAMPUS LIFE
Environment: Rural. **Activities:** concert band, drama/theater, jazz band, marching band, student government, yearbook 28 registered organizations. **Athletics (Intercollegiate):** *Men:* basketball, cross-country, football, golf, lacrosse, sailing, soccer. *Women:* basketball, cross-country, golf, sailing, soccer, softball.

ADMISSIONS
Freshman Academic Profile: 28% in top 10% of high school class, 48% in top 25% of high school class, 74% in top 50% of high school class. Minimum paper TOEFL 550. **Basis for Candidate Selection:** *Very important factors considered include:* rigor of secondary school record, character/personal qualities. *Important factors considered include:* interview. *Other factors considered include:* Class rank, recommendation(s), alumni/ae relation, extracurricular activities, talent/ability, volunteer work, work experience. **Freshman Admission Requirements:** High school diploma is required and GED is accepted. *Academic units required:* 4 English, 3 mathematics, 2 science, (2 science labs). *Academic units recommended:* 4 English, 3 mathematics, 2 science, (2 science labs). **Freshman Admission Statistics:** 613 applied, 76% admitted, 49% enrolled. **Transfer Admission Requirements:** High school transcript, college transcript(s), standardized test scores, statement of good standing from prior institution(s). Minimum college GPA of 2.0 required. Lowest grade transferable C. **General Admission Information:** Application Fee $15. Early decision application deadline 12/20. Regular application deadline 7/1. Notification on a rolling basis, beginning on or about 10/1. Nonfall registration accepted. Admission may be deferred for a maximum of 1 year. Credit offered for CEEB Advanced Placement tests.

COSTS AND FINANCIAL AID
Annual in-state tuition $4,739. Annual out-of-state tuition $8,774. Room and board $5,227. Required fees $715. Average book expense $700. **Required Forms and Deadlines: Types of Aid:** *Loans:* Subsidized Stafford, PLUS. **Student Employment:** Federal Work-Study Program available. Institutional employment available. Highest amount earned per year from on-campus jobs $1,200. Off-campus job opportunities are fair.

MALONE UNIVERSITY

2600 Cleveland Avenue NW, Canton, OH 44709
Phone: 330-471-8145 • **Financial Aid Phone:** 330-471-8161
E-mail: admissions@malone.edu • **CEEB Code:** 1439
Fax: 330-471-8149 • **Website:** www.malone.edu • **ACT Code:** 3289

This private school was founded in 1892. It has a 87-acre campus.

RATINGS
Admissions Selectivity Rating: 74   **Fire Safety Rating:** 89   **Green Rating:** 61

STUDENTS AND FACULTY
Enrollment: 1,816. **Student Body:** 58% female, 42% male, 13% out-of-state, 1% international (16 countries represented). Asian 1%, African American 8%, Caucasian 86%, Hispanic 2%, Native American 0%.
Retention and Graduation: 47% freshmen graduate within 4 years. 63% freshmen graduate within 6 years. 15% grads go on to further study within 1 year. 6% grads pursue arts and sciences degrees. 2% grads pursue business degrees. **Faculty:** Student/faculty ratio 13:1. 106 full-time faculty, 74% hold PhDs, 6% are members of minority groups, 50% are women. 0% of classes are taught by teaching assistants.

ACADEMICS
Degrees: bachelor's, master's, post-bachelor's certificate. **Classes:** Most classes have 10–19 students. Most lab/discussion sessions have 10–19 students. **Majors with Highest Enrollment:** business/commerce; early childhood education and teaching; nursing/registered nurse (rn, asn, bsn, msn). **Special Study Options:** Accelerated program, cross-registration, distance learning, double major, dual enrollment, exchange student program (domestic), honors program, independent study, internships, student-designed major, study abroad, teacher certification program, weekend college, 2 degree-completion programs for adults; management, nursing. NOTE: Weekend college is only for degree-completion programs and graduate programs. NOTE: Cooperative education credits are available; but, not entire program. **Honors Programs:** The purpose of the Malone University Honors Program is to support the university's intellectually gifted and highly motivated students, to create a community of students and faculty engaged in serious, substantive, and sustained critical inquiry, and to underscore the university's commitment to academic excellence. The Honors Program fulfills this purpose through pursuit of the following goals: 1. Challenging students to fulfill their intellectual and personal potential through enriching and stimulating experiences in and out of the classroom. 2. Cultivating an esprit de corps, committed to an earnest, cooperative, free, and open pursuit of truth. 3. Developing students' understanding of the unity of knowledge and the interrelationship of the academic disciplines. 4. Providing students the occasion for mentoring relationships with faculty. 5. Preparing students for the pursuit of original and advanced research, scholarship, and performance. 6. Equipping students for outstanding leadership in service to God, their communities, and the world. **Combined Degree Programs:** 3-1 Medical Technology program. **Disability Services:** Special programs offered to physically disabled students include note-taking services, reader services, tape recorders, tutors. **Career Services:** alumni services, career/job search classes, career assessment, internships Career Services highlights include The highest number of graduates who are hired by the employer providing experiential learning is in Nursing.

FACILITIES
Housing: special housing for disabled students, men's dorms, women's dorms, theme housing. **Special Academic Facilities/Equipment:** Child development center. **Computers:** 100% of classrooms, 85% of dorms, 100% of libraries, 100% of dining areas, 100% of student union, 40% of common outdoor areas have wireless network access. Students can register for classes online. Administrative functions (other than registration) can be performed online.

CAMPUS LIFE
Environment: City. **Activities:** Choral groups, concert band, dance, drama/theater, jazz band, literary magazine, marching band, music ensembles, musical theater, radio station, student government, student newspaper, student-run film society, television station, yearbook, Campus Ministries, International Student Organization 53 registered organizations, 11 honor societies, 9 religious organizations. **Athletics (Intercollegiate):** *Men:* baseball, basketball, cheerleading, cross-country, diving, football, golf, soccer, swimming, tennis, track/field (outdoor), track/field (indoor). *Women:* basketball, cheerleading, cross-country, diving, golf, soccer, softball, swimming, tennis, track/field (outdoor), track/field (indoor), volleyball. **On-Campus Highlights:** Hoover Dining Commons - Brehme Centennial Center, Randall Campus Center, Wellness Center, Froggy's & Regula Cafe, Classsrooms, Randall Campus Center houses the Office of Student Development; a game room, among other features. The Wellness Center houses equipment and laboratories to support the programs of the majors in the Health and Human Performance Department. Also, its aerobic exercise and weight room are available for all Malone University, students, faculty, and

staff. It was just opened in Fall 2004. **Environmental Initiatives:** Recycling Reducing Conservation

ADMISSIONS

Freshman Academic Profile: Average high school GPA 3.3. 18% in top 10% of high school class, 45% in top 25% of high school class, 76% in top 50% of high school class. 80% from public high schools. SAT Math middle 50% range 460-580. SAT Critical Reading middle 50% range 440-560. ACT middle 50% range 20-26. Minimum web-based TOEFL 79. Minimum paper TOEFL 550. **Basis for Candidate Selection:** *Very important factors considered include:* academic GPA, rigor of secondary school record, standardized test scores, character/personal qualities. *Important factors considered include:* Class rank, level of applicant's interest, religious affiliation/commitment, talent/ability. *Other factors considered include:* application essay, recommendation(s), alumni/ae relation, extracurricular activities, interview, racial/ethnic status, volunteer work. **Freshman Admission Requirements:** High school diploma is required and GED is accepted. *Academic units required:* 4 English, 3 mathematics, 3 science, (1 science labs), 2 foreign language, 2 social studies, 1 history, 1 visual/performing arts, 2 academic electives. 4 English, 3 mathematics, 3 science, (1 science labs), 2 foreign language, 2 social studies, 1 history, 1 visual/performing arts, 2 academic electives. **Freshman Admission Statistics:** 1,546 applied, 70% admitted, 33% enrolled. **Transfer Admission Requirements:** High school transcript, college transcript(s), statement of good standing from prior institution(s). Minimum college GPA of 2.0 required. **General Admission Information:** Application Fee $20. Regular application deadline 7/1. Notification on a rolling basis, beginning on or about 9/1. Nonfall registration accepted. Admission may be deferred for a maximum of 2 years. Credit and/or placement offered for CEEB Advanced Placement tests.

COSTS AND FINANCIAL AID

Annual tuition $23,860. Room and board $8,454. Required fees $676. Average book expense $930. **Required Forms and Deadlines:** FAFSA Verification worksheet and tax forms if chosen for verification. **Notification of Awards:** Applicants will be notified of awards on a rolling basis beginning 3/1. **Types of Aid:** *Need-based scholarships/grants:* Federal Pell, SEOG, state scholarships/grants, private scholarships, the school's own gift aid, Academic Competetiveness and Smart Grant. *Loans:* Subsidized Stafford, Unsubsidized Stafford, PLUS, Federal Perkins, state loans, college/university loans from institutional funds, Private Loans. **Student Employment:** Federal Work-Study Program available. Institutional employment available. Highest amount earned per year from on-campus jobs $2,500. Off-campus job opportunities are good. **Financial Aid Statistics:** 100% freshmen, 98% undergrads receive need-based scholarship or grant aid. 13% freshmen, 9% undergrads receive non-need-based scholarship or grant aid. 81% freshmen, 84% undergrads receive need-based self-help aid. 8% freshmen, 7% undergrads receive athletic scholarships. 100% freshmen, 80% undergrads receive any aid. 79% undergrads borrow to pay for school. Average cumulative indebtedness $33,263. **Criteria for awarding institutional aid:** *Non-need-based:* academics, alumni affiliation, athletics, leadership, music/drama, religious affiliation.

MANCHESTER COLLEGE

604 E. College Avenue, N. Manchester, IN 46962
Phone: 260-982-5055 • **Financial Aid Phone:** 260-982-5066
E-mail: admitinfo@manchester.edu • **CEEB Code:** 1440
Fax: 260-982-5239 • **Website:** www.manchester.edu • **ACT Code:** 1222

This private school was founded in 1889. It has a 124-acre campus.

RATINGS

Admissions Selectivity Rating: 76   **Fire Safety Rating:** 71   **Green Rating:** 72

STUDENTS AND FACULTY

Enrollment: 1,241. **Student Body:** 51% female, 49% male, 8% out-of-state, 2% international (22 countries represented). Asian 1%, African American 3%, Caucasian 87%, Hispanic 4%, Native American 0%. **Retention and Graduation:** 68% freshmen return for sophomore year. 18% grads go on to further study within 1 year. 7% grads pursue arts and sciences degrees. 2% grads pursue law degrees. 1% grads pursue business degrees. 4% grads pursue medical degrees. **Faculty:** Student/faculty ratio 15:1. 74 full-time faculty, 86% hold PhDs, 7% are members of minority groups. 0% of classes are taught by teaching assistants.

ACADEMICS

Degrees: associate, bachelor's, master's. **Classes:** Most classes have 20–29 students. **Majors with Highest Enrollment:** accounting and business/management; biochemistry; education. **Special Study Options:** Accelerated program, cross-registration, double major, dual enrollment, exchange student

program (domestic), honors program, independent study, internships, liberal arts/career combination, student-designed major, study abroad, teacher certification program. **Honors Programs:** An Honors Program for top students. **Disability Services:** Special programs offered to physically disabled students include reader services, tape recorders, tutors. **Career Services:** Alumni network, alumni services, career/job search classes, career assessment, internships, regional alumni. Career Services highlights include College-paid internships in regional businesses.

FACILITIES

Housing: Coed dorms, special housing for disabled students, apartments for married students, apartments for single students. **Special Academic Facilities/Equipment:** Language lab, observatory, environmental center and labs. **Computers:** 50% of classrooms, 100% of libraries, 100% of dining areas, 100% of student union, 5% of common outdoor areas have wireless network access. Students can register for classes online. Administrative functions (other than registration) can be performed online.

CAMPUS LIFE

Environment: Rural. **Activities:** Choral groups, concert band, dance, drama/theater, jazz band, literary magazine, music ensembles, musical theater, opera, pep band, radio station, student government, student newspaper, symphony orchestra, yearbook, Campus Ministries, International Student Organization, Model UN 47 registered organizations, 3 honor societies, 5 religious organizations. **Athletics (Intercollegiate):** *Men:* baseball, basketball, cheerleading, cross-country, football, golf, soccer, tennis, track/field (outdoor), wrestling. *Women:* basketball, cheerleading, cross-country, golf, soccer, softball, tennis, track/field (outdoor), volleyball. **On-Campus Highlights:** Athletic Facilities, Residence Halls, College Union, Petersime Chapel, Science Center, The campus is located on a well maintained wooded 125 acres. **Environmental Initiatives:** Over 25 years of active recyling on campus One of the oldest enverinmental studies majors in the country. Manchester College environmental studies program director Jerry Sweeten is 2009 Indiana Professor of the Year; see http://www.manchester.edu/OCA/PR/Files/News/SweetenPoY.htm over 25 years of dedication to reduction in energy consumption

ADMISSIONS

Freshman Academic Profile: Average high school GPA 3.4. 23% in top 10% of high school class, 52% in top 25% of high school class, 87% in top 50% of high school class. SAT Math middle 50% range 470-580. SAT Critical Reading middle 50% range 450-560. SAT Writing middle 50% range 420-540. ACT middle 50% range 20-25. Minimum web-based TOEFL 79. Minimum paper TOEFL 550. **Basis for Candidate Selection:** *Very important factors considered include:* rigor of secondary school record. *Important factors considered include:* academic GPA, recommendation(s), standardized test scores. *Other factors considered include:* Class rank, alumni/ae relation, character/personal qualities, interview, religious affiliation/commitment, talent/ability. **Freshman Admission Requirements:** High school diploma is required and GED is accepted. *Academic units required:* 4 English, 2 mathematics, 2 science, (2 science labs), 2 foreign language, 2 social studies, 1 history, 1 academic electives. *Academic units recommended:* 4 English, 2 mathematics, 2 science, (2 science labs), 2 foreign language, 2 social studies, 1 history, 1 academic electives. **Freshman Admission Statistics:** 3,861 applied, 64% admitted, 15% enrolled. **Transfer Admission Requirements:** High school transcript, college transcript(s), statement of good standing from prior institution(s). Minimum college GPA of 2.0 required. **General Admission Information:** Application Fee $25. Notification on a rolling basis, beginning on or about 9/1. Nonfall registration accepted. Admission may be deferred for a maximum of 1 year. Credit and/or placement offered for CEEB Advanced Placement tests.

COSTS AND FINANCIAL AID

Annual tuition $27,000. Room and board $9,250. Required fees $920. Average book expense $1,000. **Required Forms and Deadlines:** FAFSA. **Notification of Awards:** Applicants will be notified of awards on a rolling basis beginning 3/30. **Types of Aid:** *Need-based scholarships/grants:* Federal Pell, SEOG, state scholarships/grants, private scholarships, the school's own gift aid. *Loans:* Subsidized Stafford, Unsubsidized Stafford, PLUS, Federal Perkins. **Student Employment:** Highest amount earned per year from on-campus jobs $2,000. Off-campus job opportunities are fair. **Financial Aid Statistics:** 100% freshmen, 100% undergrads receive need-based scholarship or grant aid. 7% freshmen, 5% undergrads receive non-need-based scholarship or grant aid. 91% freshmen, 90% undergrads receive need-based self-help aid. 100% freshmen, 91% undergrads receive any aid. 85% undergrads borrow to pay for school. Average cumulative indebtedness $29,039. **Criteria for awarding institutional aid:** *Non-need-based:* academics, alumni affiliation, minority status, religious affiliation.

MANHATTAN CHRISTIAN COLLEGE

1415 Anderson, Manhattan, KS 66502-4081
Phone: 877-246-4622 • **Financial Aid Phone:** 785-539-3571
E-mail: admit@mccks.edu
Fax: 785-776-9251 • **Website:** www.mccks.edu • **ACT Code:** 1436

This private school, affiliated with the Christian (Nondenominational) Church, was founded in 1927. It has a 1-acre campus.

RATINGS
Admissions Selectivity Rating: 69   **Fire Safety Rating:** 68   **Green Rating:** 60*

STUDENTS AND FACULTY
Enrollment: 310. **Student Body:** 51% female, 49% male, 35% out-of-state, 0% international. Asian 0%, African American 4%, Caucasian 99%, Hispanic 2%, Native American 0%.
Retention and Graduation: 51% freshmen return for sophomore year. 36% freshmen graduate within 6 years. 3% grads go on to further study within 1 year. **Faculty:** Student/faculty ratio 15:1. 10 full-time faculty, 40% hold PhDs, 10% are members of minority groups, 20% are women. 0% of classes are taught by teaching assistants.

ACADEMICS
Degrees: associate, bachelor's, certificate, post-bachelor's certificate, transfer associate. **Classes:** Most classes have 10–19 students. **Majors with Highest Enrollment:** bible/biblical studies; management science; pastoral counseling and specialized ministries, other. **Special Study Options:** double major, dual enrollment, internships. **Combined Degree Programs:** Dual-degee program with Kansas State University. **Disability Services:** Special programs offered to physically disabled students include tutors. **Career Services:** career assessment, internships Career Services highlights include Internships are required as a Directed Field Experience that must be at least 10-weeks long.

FACILITIES
Housing: men's dorms, women's dorms, apartments for married students, apartments for single students. 100% of campus accessible to physically disabled.

CAMPUS LIFE
Environment: Town. **Activities:** dance, music ensembles, student government, yearbook 2 honor societies, 10 religious organizations. **Athletics (Intercollegiate):** *Men:* baseball, basketball, soccer. *Women:* basketball, soccer, volleyball. **On-Campus Highlights:** Coffin Memorial Hall, Campus Center, Residence Halls

ADMISSIONS
Freshman Academic Profile: Average high school GPA 3.4. 30% in top 10% of high school class, 40% in top 25% of high school class, 70% in top 50% of high school class. 95% from public high schools. ACT middle 50% range 19-25. Minimum paper TOEFL 550. **Basis for Candidate Selection:** *Very important factors considered include:* recommendation(s), character/personal qualities, religious affiliation/commitment. *Important factors considered include:* application essay, rigor of secondary school record, standardized test scores, talent/ability. *Other factors considered include:* extracurricular activities, interview, volunteer work. **Freshman Admission Requirements:** High school diploma is required and GED is accepted. **Freshman Admission Statistics:** 155 applied, 79% admitted, 66% enrolled. **Transfer Admission Requirements:** college transcript(s), essay or personal statement, minimum college GPA of 2.0 required. Lowest grade transferable C. **General Admission Information:** Application Fee $25. Regular application deadline 8/1. Notification on a rolling basis, beginning on or about 10/1. Nonfall registration accepted. Admission may be deferred for a maximum of 1 year. Credit and/or placement offered for CEEB Advanced Placement tests.

COSTS AND FINANCIAL AID
Annual tuition $8,826. Room and board $5,224. Required fees $110. Average book expense $1,150. **Required Forms and Deadlines:** FAFSA. **Notification of Awards:** Applicants will be notified of awards on a rolling basis beginning 5/1. **Types of Aid:** *Need-based scholarships/grants:* Federal Pell, SEOG, state scholarships/grants, private scholarships, the school's own gift aid. *Loans:* Direct Subsidized Stafford, Direct Unsubsidized Stafford, Direct PLUS, Federal Perkins. **Student Employment:** Federal Work-Study Program available. Off-campus job opportunities are good. **Financial Aid Statistics:** 53% freshmen, 89% undergrads receive need-based scholarship or grant aid. 96% freshmen, 84% undergrads receive non-need-based scholarship or grant aid. 78% freshmen, 97% undergrads receive need-based self-help aid. 55% undergrads borrow to pay for school. Average cumulative indebtedness $8,639. **Criteria for awarding institutional aid:** *Non-need-based:* academics, alumni affiliation, leadership, music/drama, religious affiliation.

MANHATTAN COLLEGE

Manhattan College Parkway, Riverdale, NY 10471
Phone: 718-862-7200 • **Financial Aid Phone:** 718-862-7100
E-mail: admit@manhattan.edu • **CEEB Code:** 2395
Fax: 718-862-8019 • **Website:** www.manhattan.edu

This private school, affiliated with the Roman Catholic Church, was founded in 1853. It has a 22-acre campus.

RATINGS
Admissions Selectivity Rating: 76   **Fire Safety Rating:** 69   **Green Rating:** 61

STUDENTS AND FACULTY
Enrollment: 3,351. **Student Body:** 44% female, 56% male, 28% out-of-state, 2% international (46 countries represented). Asian 3%, African American 4%, Caucasian 60%, Hispanic 17%, Native American 0%.
Retention and Graduation: 88% freshmen return for sophomore year. 66% freshmen graduate within 4 years. 75% freshmen graduate within 6 years. 20% grads go on to further study within 1 year. 19% grads pursue arts and sciences degrees. **Faculty:** Student/faculty ratio 12:1. 210 full-time faculty, 95% hold PhDs, 15% are members of minority groups, 39% are women. 0% of classes are taught by teaching assistants.

ACADEMICS
Degrees: bachelor's, master's. **Classes:** Most classes have 20–29 students. Most lab/discussion sessions have 10–19 students. **Majors with Highest Enrollment:** civil engineering; marketing/marketing management; special education and teaching, other. **Special Study Options:** Accelerated program, cooperative education program, cross-registration, distance learning, double major, English as a Second Language (ESL), exchange student program (domestic), honors program, independent study, internships, liberal arts/career combination, student-designed major, study abroad, teacher certification program. **Honors Programs:** Honors Enrichment Program **Combined Degree Programs:** BA/MA, BA/MEng, Education. **Disability Services:** Special programs offered to physically disabled students include note-taking services, reader services, tape recorders, tutors. **Career Services:** alumni services, career/job search classes, career assessment, internships.

FACILITIES
Housing: Coed dorms. 100% of campus accessible to physically disabled. **Special Academic Facilities/Equipment:** Research and learning center, 24-hour Internet cafe. **Computers:** 100% of classrooms, 50% of dorms, 100% of libraries, 100% of dining areas, 100% of student union, 100% of common outdoor areas have wireless network access. Students can register for classes online. Administrative functions (other than registration) can be performed online.

CAMPUS LIFE
Environment: Metropolis. **Activities:** Choral groups, concert band, dance, drama/theater, jazz band, literary magazine, music ensembles, musical theater, radio station, student government, student newspaper, symphony orchestra, television station, yearbook, Campus Ministries, International Student Organization, Model UN 64 registered organizations, 30 honor societies, 2 religious organizations. 2 fraternities, 2 sororities. **Athletics (Intercollegiate):** *Men:* baseball, basketball, cross-country, golf, lacrosse, soccer, tennis, track/field (outdoor), track/field (indoor). *Women:* basketball, cross-country, lacrosse, soccer, softball, swimming, tennis, track/field (outdoor), track/field (indoor), volleyball. **On-Campus Highlights:** Quadrangle, O'Malley Library, Internet Cafe, Galligan Exercise Center, Thomas Hall.

ADMISSIONS
Freshman Academic Profile: 88.8. 25% in top 10% of high school class, 54% in top 25% of high school class, 84% in top 50% of high school class. 57% from public high schools. SAT Math middle 50% range 480-610. SAT Critical Reading middle 50% range 470-570. SAT Writing middle 50% range 470-580. ACT middle 50% range 22-27. Minimum web-based TOEFL 80. Minimum paper TOEFL 550. **Basis for Candidate Selection:** *Very important factors considered include:* academic GPA, rigor of secondary school record, standardized test scores. *Important factors considered include:* Class rank, application essay, recommendation(s), extracurricular activities, interview. *Other factors considered include:* alumni/ae relation, character/personal qualities, talent/ability, volunteer work, work experience. **Freshman Admission Requirements:** High school diploma is required and GED is accepted. *Academic units required:* 4 English, 3 mathematics, 2 science, 2 foreign language, 3 social studies, 2 academic electives. *Academic units recommended:* 4 English, 3 mathematics, 2 science, 2 foreign language, 3 social studies, 2 academic electives. **Freshman Admission Statistics:** 6,545 applied, 70% admitted, 18% enrolled. **Transfer Admission Requirements:** High school transcript, college transcript(s), standardized test scores, statement of good standing from prior institution(s). Minimum college GPA of 2.5 required. Lowest grade transferable C. **General**

Admission Information: Application Fee $60. Early decision application deadline 11/15. Notification on a rolling basis, beginning on or about 12/15. Nonfall registration accepted. Admission may be deferred for a maximum of 1 year. Credit and/or placement offered for CEEB Advanced Placement tests.

COSTS AND FINANCIAL AID

Annual tuition $27,933. Room and board $12,220. Required fees $2,285. Average book expense $1,200. **Required Forms and Deadlines:** FAFSA. **Notification of Awards:** Applicants will be notified of awards on a rolling basis beginning 2/15. **Types of Aid:** *Need-based scholarships/grants:* Federal Pell, SEOG, state scholarships/grants, private scholarships, the school's own gift aid. *Loans:* Direct Subsidized Stafford, Direct Unsubsidized Stafford, Direct PLUS, Subsidized Stafford, Unsubsidized Stafford, PLUS, Federal Perkins. **Student Employment:** Highest amount earned per year from on-campus jobs $1,500. **Financial Aid Statistics:** 98% freshmen, 97% undergrads receive need-based scholarship or grant aid. 6% freshmen, 5% undergrads receive non-need-based scholarship or grant aid. 87% freshmen, 86% undergrads receive need-based self-help aid. 2% freshmen, 3% undergrads receive athletic scholarships. 88% freshmen, 86% undergrads receive any aid. 73% undergrads borrow to pay for school. Average cumulative indebtedness $34,189. **Criteria for awarding institutional aid:** *Non-need-based:* academics, athletics.

See page 1136.

MANHATTAN SCHOOL OF MUSIC

120 Claremont Ave, New York, NY 10027
Phone: 212-749-2802 • **Financial Aid Phone:** 917-493-4463
E-mail: admission@msmnyc.edu • **CEEB Code:** 2396
Fax: 212-749-3025 • **Website:** www.msmnyc.edu • **ACT Code:** 2809

This private school was founded in 1917. It has a 1-acre campus.

RATINGS

Admissions Selectivity Rating: 63   **Fire Safety Rating:** 74   **Green Rating:** 60*

STUDENTS AND FACULTY

Enrollment: 408. **Student Body:** 48% female, 52% male, 69% out-of-state, 20% international (27 countries represented). Asian 9%, African American 3%, Caucasian 44%, Hispanic 4%, Native American 0%.
Retention and Graduation: 82% freshmen return for sophomore year. 90% grads go on to further study within 1 year. 75% grads pursue arts and sciences degrees. 1% grads pursue law degrees. 1% grads pursue business degrees. 1% grads pursue medical degrees. **Faculty:** 1% of classes are taught by teaching assistants.

ACADEMICS

Degrees: bachelor's, diploma, master's, post-master's certificate. **Special Study Options:** cross-registration, English as a Second Language (ESL), study abroad. **Disability Services:** Special programs offered to physically disabled students include note-taking services, reader services, tape recorders, tutors. **Career Services:** Alumni network, alumni services, career/job search classes, Career Services highlights include Training in educational and community outreach.

FACILITIES

Housing: apartments for married students, apartments for single students. 75% of campus accessible to physically disabled. **Special Academic Facilities/Equipment:** Electronic music studios, electronic piano lab, recording studio, practice rooms, 1,000-seat auditorium, 3 recital halls.

CAMPUS LIFE

Environment: Metropolis. **Activities:** Choral groups, dance, drama/theater, jazz band, literary magazine, music ensembles, student government, symphony orchestra 8 registered organizations. **On-Campus Highlights:** Library, Residence Hall, Practice Rooms, Concert Halls, Cafeteria.

ADMISSIONS

Freshman Academic Profile: Minimum paper TOEFL 550. **Basis for Candidate Selection:** *Very important factors considered include:* rigor of secondary school record, interview, talent/ability. *Important factors considered include:* application essay, recommendation(s), character/personal qualities, extracurricular activities, volunteer work. *Other factors considered include:* Class rank, standardized test scores, alumni/ae relation, racial/ethnic status, work experience. **Freshman Admission Requirements:** High school diploma is required and GED is accepted. *Academic units required:* 2 English, 2 mathematics, 2 science, 3 social studies, 3 history. *Academic units recommended:* 2 English, 2 mathematics, 2 science, 3 social studies, 3 history. **Freshman Admission Statistics:** 794 applied, 40% admitted, 32% enrolled. **Transfer Admission Requirements:** college transcript(s), essay or personal statement, interview,

---

minimum college GPA of 3 required. Lowest grade transferable C. **General Admission Information:** Application Fee $100. Regular application deadline 12/1. Regular notification 4/1. Nonfall registration not accepted. Admission may be deferred for a maximum of 2 semesters. Credit offered for CEEB Advanced Placement tests.

COSTS AND FINANCIAL AID

Annual tuition $26,000. Room and board $14,250. Required fees $460. Average book expense $850. **Required Forms and Deadlines:** FAFSA, institution's own financial aid form, CSS/Financial Aid PROFILE. **Notification of Awards:** Applicants will be notified of awards on or about 4/1. **Types of Aid:** *Need-based scholarships/grants:* Federal Pell, SEOG, state scholarships/grants, the school's own gift aid. *Loans:* Subsidized Stafford, Unsubsidized Stafford, PLUS, Federal Perkins. **Student Employment:** Federal Work-Study Program available. Institutional employment available. Highest amount earned per year from on-campus jobs $4,000. Off-campus job opportunities are excellent. **Financial Aid Statistics:** 89% freshmen, 75% undergrads receive need-based scholarship or grant aid. 6% freshmen, 8% undergrads receive non-need-based scholarship or grant aid. 82% freshmen, 73% undergrads receive need-based self-help aid. 66% freshmen, 75% undergrads receive any aid. 58% undergrads borrow to pay for school. Average cumulative indebtedness $14,100. **Criteria for awarding institutional aid:** *Non-need-based:* academics, alumni affiliation, art, music/drama.

MANHATTANVILLE COLLEGE

2900 Purchase Street, Purchase, NY 10577
Phone: 914-323-5124 • **Financial Aid Phone:** 914-323-5357
E-mail: admissions@mville.edu • **CEEB Code:** 2397
Fax: 914-694-1732 • **Website:** www.mville.edu • **ACT Code:** 2800

This private school was founded in 1841. It has a 100-acre campus.

RATINGS

Admissions Selectivity Rating: 79   **Fire Safety Rating:** 95   **Green Rating:** 80

STUDENTS AND FACULTY

Enrollment: 1,733. **Student Body:** 64% female, 36% male, 40% out-of-state, 11% international (53 countries represented). Asian 3%, African American 9%, Caucasian 40%, Hispanic 16%, Native American 0%.
Retention and Graduation: 69% freshmen return for sophomore year. 51% freshmen graduate within 4 years. 56% freshmen graduate within 6 years. **Faculty:** Student/faculty ratio 11:1. 102 full-time faculty, 96% hold PhDs, 12% are members of minority groups, 49% are women. 0% of classes are taught by teaching assistants.

ACADEMICS

Degrees: bachelor's, master's, post-bachelor's certificate, post-master's certificate. **Classes:** Most classes have 10–19 students. **Majors with Highest Enrollment:** business/commerce; psychology; visual and performing arts, other. **Special Study Options:** Accelerated program, cross-registration, double major, dual enrollment, English as a Second Language (ESL), exchange student program (domestic), honors program, independent study, internships, student-designed major, study abroad, teacher certification program, weekend college. **Honors Programs:** The Castle Scholars Program offers students of exceptional ability a broader and more intensive program of study than the usual college curriculum. It provides motivated students in any major field with challenging, cross-disciplinary courses that encourage their academic and personal growth. Participation in the Castle Scholars Program encourages intellectual exchange among students and faculty and fosters independent initiative in academic and creative realms. Advised and mentored by the Program Director, Castle Scholars are well prepared for success in graduate and professional schools, as well as in the professional world. Castle Scholars build relationships with each other and with the college's faculty in specially-designed Honors Seminars and other unique academic opportunities, as well as in a host of social events throughout the year. Through their studies, research, and service, the Scholars contribute to the intellectual and social life of the college. Studies are augmented by participation in the wider New York City community. The Castle Scholars Program complements a student's chosen major and minor and is distinct from honors options within the major. Castle Scholars are recognized annually at college-wide awards receptions, and honors courses are noted on student academic transcripts. Successful completion of the program will be noted on the final transcript as well as on printed graduation materials. **Combined Degree Programs:** BA/MA, Dual BS programs. **Disability Services:** Special programs offered to physically disabled students include note-taking services, reader services, tape recorders, tutors. **Career Services:** Alumni network, alumni services, career/job search classes, career assessment, internships, regional alumni. Career Services highlights include Internships involved career-related work that enhances a student's academic program.

FACILITIES
Housing: Coed dorms. 95% of campus accessible to physically disabled. **Special Academic Facilities/Equipment:** Art gallery, art and music studios, Environmental Park, English language institute, two electron microscopes, library. **Computers:** Students can register for classes online. Administrative functions (other than registration) can be performed online.

CAMPUS LIFE
Environment: Town. **Activities:** Choral groups, concert band, dance, drama/theater, jazz band, literary magazine, music ensembles, musical theater, opera, radio station, student government, student newspaper, student-run film society, symphony orchestra, television station, yearbook, Campus Ministries, International Student Organization 46 registered organizations, 2 honor societies, 5 religious organizations. **Athletics (Intercollegiate):** *Men:* baseball, basketball, golf, ice hockey, lacrosse, soccer, tennis. *Women:* basketball, cheerleading, field hockey, ice hockey, lacrosse, soccer, softball, tennis, volleyball. **On-Campus Highlights:** The Castle, Library Cafe, Richard Berman Student Center, Kennedy Gymnasium, Quad, New Student Center. **Environmental Initiatives:** Environmental Classroom Building's Platinum Rating (LEED) New Student Center's Gold Rating (LEED) Green Cleaning

ADMISSIONS
Freshman Academic Profile: Minimum paper TOEFL 550. **Basis for Candidate Selection:** *Very important factors considered include:* rigor of secondary school record. *Important factors considered include:* application essay, recommendation(s), extracurricular activities, interview. *Other factors considered include:* alumni/ae relation, character/personal qualities, geographical residence, talent/ability, volunteer work, work experience. **Freshman Admission Requirements:** High school diploma is required and GED is accepted. *Academic units required:* 4 English, 3 mathematics, 2 science, 2 social studies, 5 academic electives. 4 English, 3 mathematics, 2 science, 2 social studies, 5 academic electives. **Freshman Admission Statistics:** 4,772 applied, 60% admitted, 19% enrolled. **Transfer Admission Requirements:** college transcript(s), statement of good standing from prior institution(s). Minimum college GPA of 2.5 required. Lowest grade transferable C. **General Admission Information:** Application Fee $70. Early decision application deadline 12/1. Regular application deadline 3/1. Notification on a rolling basis, beginning on or about 1/5. Nonfall registration accepted. Admission may be deferred for a maximum of 1 year. Credit and/or placement offered for CEEB Advanced Placement tests.

COSTS AND FINANCIAL AID
Annual tuition $34,020. Room and board $14,340. Required fees $1,350. Average book expense $800. **Required Forms and Deadlines:** FAFSA, state aid form. **Notification of Awards:** Applicants will be notified of awards on a rolling basis beginning 3/1. **Types of Aid:** *Need-based scholarships/grants:* Federal Pell, SEOG, state scholarships/grants, private scholarships, the school's own gift aid. *Loans:* Direct Subsidized Stafford, Direct Unsubsidized Stafford, Direct PLUS. **Student Employment:** Federal Work-Study Program available. Institutional employment available. Off-campus job opportunities are excellent. **Financial Aid Statistics:** 89% freshmen, 92% undergrads receive need-based scholarship or grant aid. 97% freshmen, 84% undergrads receive non-need-based scholarship or grant aid. 87% freshmen, 88% undergrads receive need-based self-help aid. 75% freshmen, 70% undergrads receive any aid. 53% undergrads borrow to pay for school. Average cumulative indebtedness $23,138. **Criteria for awarding institutional aid:** *Non-need-based:* academics, alumni affiliation, art, leadership, music/drama.

MANNES COLLEGE—
THE NEW SCHOOL FOR MUSIC

150 West 85th Street, New York, NY 10024
Phone: 212-580-0210 ext4862 • **Financial Aid Phone:** 212-229-8930
E-mail: mannesadmission@newschool.edu
Fax: 212 580 1738 • **Website:** www.mannes.edu

This private school was founded in 1916.

RATINGS
Admissions Selectivity Rating: 63   **Fire Safety Rating:** 77   **Green Rating:** 93

STUDENTS AND FACULTY
Enrollment: 200. **Student Body:** 51% female, 49% male, 35% out-of-state, 39% international (21 countries represented). Asian 11%, African American 3%, Caucasian 36%, Hispanic 4%.
Retention and Graduation: 84% freshmen return for sophomore year. 48% freshmen graduate within 4 years. **Faculty:** Student/faculty ratio 5:1. 15 full-time faculty, 40% hold PhDs, 13% are members of minority groups, 53% are women. 0% of classes are taught by teaching assistants.

ACADEMICS
Degrees: bachelor's, diploma, master's, post-bachelor's certificate, post-master's certificate. **Classes:** Most classes have fewer than 10 students. **Special Study Options:** Accelerated program, double major, English as a Second Language (ESL), independent study, internships. **Disability Services:** Special programs offered to physically disabled students include note-taking services, reader services, tape recorders. **Career Services:** Alumni network, alumni services, career/job search classes, career assessment, internships, regional alumni.

FACILITIES
Housing: Coed dorms, special housing for disabled students, apartments for single students. 99% of campus accessible to physically disabled. **Special Academic Facilities/Equipment:** Art gallery, photography gallery, extensive collections of contemporary art, concert hall, public lectures, conferences, cultural and intellectual events. **Computers:** 95% of classrooms, 100% of libraries, 100% of dining areas, na% of student union, 100% of common outdoor areas have wireless network access. Students can register for classes online. Administrative functions (other than registration) can be performed online.

CAMPUS LIFE
Environment: Metropolis. **Activities:** Choral groups, dance, drama/theater, jazz band, literary magazine, music ensembles, opera, radio station, student government, student newspaper, symphony orchestra, International Student Organization 39 registered organizations. **On-Campus Highlights:** Mannes Concert Hall **Environmental Initiatives:** 1. In Fall 2010, The New School Facilities Management hired an engineering firm to conduct energy audits and to retro-commission five of the most energy-intensive owned buildings on campus. The result will be a phased capital plan to address needed upgrades in these buildings, equating to 500,000gsf, that will reduce carbon emissions. 2. The New School Office for Sustainability hired a consultant to conduct a waste audit of the entire campus in Fall 2009. A waste reduction strategy is currently being finalized. The immediate outcomes are new recycling signs and an enhanced post-consumer composting program in four buildings. Food scraps, napkins/paper towels and compostable cups and utensils will be collected in all food service locations plus a pilot location in a building with architecture and fine arts studios. The New School replaced two steam boilers, which were approximately 50 years old. Located in Johnson/Kaplan Hall, the university's founding building, constructed in 1930, this boiler plant burned #6 heating oil, the dirtiest and most carbon-intensive heating oil. In the summer of 2010, Design, Construction, and Facilities Management upgraded the plant to house two new steam dual-fuel boilers with a thermal efficiency of 86 percent and the option to burn #2 heating oil or, eventually, natural gas, the least carbon intensive fossil fuel. This retrofit project also marks the phasing out of #6 heating oil on campus. In the summer of 2010, Design, Construction, and Facilities Management also replaced the roof at Johnson/Kaplan Hall with a white Thermoplastic Polyolefin (TPO) thermally bonded membrane with superior durability and an ENERGY STAR rating for its high reflectance. Insulation was also added to the roof. The new roof drastically reduces heat absorption in the summer months and also better insulates the building in the winter, resulting in lower cooling and heating loads and costs. Phasing out the use of T12 and incandescent lighting has been an ongoing initiative over the past two years and focused on 45 percent of the entire building portfolio (equivalent to 563,503 gross square feet, which represents nearly 72 percent of The New School's owned buildings). In FY10, the Office for Sustainability began to install campus-wide (in all spaces where The New School has operational control) occupancy sensors in bathrooms, office kitchenettes, and conference rooms. By the end of FY12, the university will phase out T12s and incandescent lighting in all university-owned buildings and launch a LED lighting demonstration project.

ADMISSIONS
Freshman Academic Profile: Average high school GPA 3.3. **Basis for Candidate Selection:** *Very important factors considered include:* level of applicant's interest, talent/ability. *Important factors considered include:* academic GPA, recommendation(s), rigor of secondary school record. *Other factors considered include:* Class rank, application essay, character/personal qualities, extracurricular activities, interview. **Freshman Admission Requirements:** High school diploma is required and GED is accepted. *Academic units required:* 4 English, 4 mathematics, 4 science, (2 science labs), 2 social studies. *Academic units recommended:* 4 English, 4 mathematics, 4 science, (2 science labs), 2 social studies. **Freshman Admission Statistics:** 505 applied, 35% admitted, 31% enrolled. **Transfer Admission Requirements:** college transcript(s), essay or personal statement, minimum college GPA of 2.0 required. Lowest grade transferable C.

The Princeton Review's Complete Book of Colleges

General Admission Information: Application Fee $100. Regular application deadline 12/1. Notification on a rolling basis, beginning on or about 4/1. Nonfall registration not accepted. Credit and/or placement offered for CEEB Advanced Placement tests.

COSTS AND FINANCIAL AID
Required Forms and Deadlines: FAFSA, state aid form. **Notification of Awards:** Applicants will be notified of awards on a rolling basis beginning 3/1. **Types of Aid:** *Need-based scholarships/grants:* Federal Pell, SEOG, state scholarships/grants, private scholarships, the school's own gift aid. *Loans:* Subsidized Stafford, Unsubsidized Stafford, PLUS, Federal Perkins. **Student Employment:** Federal Work-Study Program available. Institutional employment available. Off-campus job opportunities are good. **Financial Aid Statistics:** 56% freshmen, 88% undergrads receive need-based scholarship or grant aid. 11% freshmen, 6% undergrads receive non-need-based scholarship or grant aid. 89% freshmen, 94% undergrads receive need-based self-help aid. 68% undergrads borrow to pay for school. Average cumulative indebtedness $33,060. **Criteria for awarding institutional aid:** *Non-need-based:* music/drama.

MANSFIELD UNIVERSITY

Academy Street, Mansfield, PA 16933
Phone: 570-662-4243 • **Financial Aid Phone:** 570-664-4129
E-mail: admissions@mansfield.edu • **CEEB Code:** 2655
Fax: 570-662-4121 • **Website:** mansfield.edu • **ACT Code:** 3710

This public school was founded in 1857. It has a 174-acre campus.

RATINGS
Admissions Selectivity Rating: 68   **Fire Safety Rating:** 70   **Green Rating:** 60*

STUDENTS AND FACULTY
Enrollment: 2,819. **Student Body:** 59% female, 41% male, 19% out-of-state, 1% international (17 countries represented). Asian 1%, African American 8%, Caucasian 80%, Hispanic 2%, Native American 1%.
Retention and Graduation: 72% freshmen return for sophomore year. 36% freshmen graduate within 4 years. 54% freshmen graduate within 6 years. 23% grads go on to further study within 1 year. **Faculty:** Student/faculty ratio 19:1. 132 full-time faculty, 89% hold PhDs, 11% are members of minority groups, 42% are women. 0% of classes are taught by teaching assistants.

ACADEMICS
Degrees: associate, bachelor's, certificate, diploma, master's. **Classes:** Most classes have 20–29 students. Most lab/discussion sessions have 20–29 students. **Majors with Highest Enrollment:** criminal justice/law enforcement administration; education; music teacher education. **Special Study Options:** cross-registration, distance learning, double major, dual enrollment, exchange student program (domestic), honors program, independent study, internships, liberal arts/career combination, student-designed major, study abroad, teacher certification program. **Disability Services:** Special programs offered to physically disabled students include note-taking services, reader services, tape recorders, tutors. **Career Services:** career/job search classes, career assessment, internships.

FACILITIES
Housing: Coed dorms, fraternity/sorority housing 90% of campus accessible to physically disabled. **Special Academic Facilities/Equipment:** Science museum, two art galleries, animal collection, planetarium, solar collector. **Computers:** Students can register for classes online.

CAMPUS LIFE
Environment: Rural. **Activities:** Choral groups, concert band, dance, drama/theater, jazz band, literary magazine, marching band, music ensembles, musical theater, pep band, radio station, student government, student newspaper, symphony orchestra, television station 108 registered organizations, 10 honor societies, 4 religious organizations. 6 fraternities, 4 sororities. **Athletics (Intercollegiate):** *Men:* baseball, basketball, cross-country, football, track/field (outdoor), track/field (indoor). *Women:* basketball, cheerleading, cross-country, diving, field hockey, soccer, softball, swimming, track/field (outdoor), track/field (indoor). **On-Campus Highlights:** North Hall Library, Fitness Center, Student Union

ADMISSIONS
Freshman Academic Profile: Average high school GPA 3.3. 9% in top 10% of high school class, 31% in top 25% of high school class, 65% in top 50% of high school class. SAT Math middle 50% range 420-540. SAT Critical Reading middle 50% range 420-530. SAT Writing middle 50% range 390-500. Minimum web-based TOEFL 61. Minimum paper TOEFL 500. **Basis for Candidate**

Selection: *Very important factors considered include:* Class rank, academic GPA, rigor of secondary school record, standardized test scores. *Other factors considered include:* application essay, recommendation(s), alumni/ae relation, character/personal qualities, extracurricular activities, first generation, geographical residence, interview, talent/ability, volunteer work, work experience. **Freshman Admission Requirements:** High school diploma is required and GED is accepted. *Academic units required:* 4 English, 3 mathematics, 2 science, (2 science labs), 2 foreign language, 4 history, 6 academic electives. 4 English, 3 mathematics, 2 science, (2 science labs), 2 foreign language, 4 history, 6 academic electives. **Freshman Admission Statistics:** 2,340 applied, 77% admitted, 35% enrolled. **Transfer Admission Requirements:** college transcript(s), minimum college GPA of 2.0 required. Lowest grade transferable D. **General Admission Information:** Application Fee $25. Notification on a rolling basis, beginning on or about 7/1. Nonfall registration accepted. Admission may be deferred for a maximum of 12. Credit offered for CEEB Advanced Placement tests.

COSTS AND FINANCIAL AID
Annual in-state tuition $6,240. Annual out-of-state tuition $15,600. Room and board $7,756. Required fees $2,214. Average book expense $1,200. **Required Forms and Deadlines:** FAFSA, institution's own financial aid form. **Notification of Awards:** Applicants will be notified of awards on a rolling basis beginning 3/15. **Types of Aid:** *Need-based scholarships/grants:* Federal Pell, SEOG, state scholarships/grants, private scholarships, the school's own gift aid, United Negro College Fund, Federal Nursing Scholarships. *Loans:* Subsidized Stafford, Unsubsidized Stafford, PLUS, Federal Perkins, Federal Nursing, state loans. **Student Employment:** Federal Work-Study Program available. Institutional employment available. Highest amount earned per year from on-campus jobs $1,236. Off-campus job opportunities are fair. **Financial Aid Statistics:** 75% freshmen, 74% undergrads receive need-based scholarship or grant aid. 28% freshmen, 23% undergrads receive non need-based scholarship or grant aid. 90% freshmen, 92% undergrads receive need-based self-help aid. 11% freshmen receive athletic scholarships. 90% freshmen, 90% undergrads receive any aid. 77% undergrads borrow to pay for school. Average cumulative indebtedness $23,216. **Criteria for awarding institutional aid:** *Non-need-based:* academics, art, athletics, leadership, music/drama, state/district residency.

MARIAN COLLEGE

3200 Cold Spring Rd., Indianapolis, IN 46222-1997
Phone: 317-955-6300 • **Financial Aid Phone:** 317-955-6040
E-mail: admissions@marian.edu
Fax: 317-955-6401 • **Website:** www.marian.edu

This private school is , affiliated with the Roman Catholic Church.

RATINGS
Admissions Selectivity Rating: 78   **Fire Safety Rating:** 60*   **Green Rating:** 60*

STUDENTS AND FACULTY
Enrollment: 1,906. **Student Body:** 68% female, 32% male, 5% out-of-state, 1% international. Asian 1%, African American 16%, Caucasian 62%, Hispanic 1%, Native American 0%.
Retention and Graduation: 76% freshmen return for sophomore year. **Faculty:** Student/faculty ratio 15:1. 82 full-time faculty, 43% hold PhDs, 6% are members of minority groups, 51% are women. 0% of classes are taught by teaching assistants.

ACADEMICS
Degrees: associate, bachelor's, certificate, master's, terminal associate, transfer associate. **Classes:** Most classes have fewer than 10 students. Most lab/discussion sessions have 10–19 students. **Majors with Highest Enrollment:** business/commerce; elementary education and teaching; nursing/registered nurse (rn, asn, bsn, msn). **Special Study Options:** Accelerated program, cooperative education program, cross-registration, double major, dual enrollment, honors program, independent study, internships, liberal arts/career combination, study abroad, teacher certification program. **Disability Services:** Special programs offered to physically disabled students include note-taking services, reader services, tape recorders, tutors. **Career Services:** Alumni network, alumni services, career/job search classes, career assessment, internships.

FACILITIES
Housing: Coed dorms, cooperative housing, On-campus seminary, housing for Peace and Justice. **Computers:** 15% of classrooms, 100% of dorms, 100% of libraries, 100% of dining areas, 100% of student union, 50% of common outdoor areas have wireless network access. Administrative functions (other than registration) can be performed online.

CAMPUS LIFE

Environment: Metropolis. **Activities:** Choral groups, concert band, dance, drama/theater, marching band, music ensembles, musical theater, pep band, student government, student newspaper, yearbook, Campus Ministries, International Student Organization. **Athletics (Intercollegiate):** *Men:* baseball, basketball, cheerleading, cross-country, cycling, football, golf, tennis, track/field (outdoor), track/field (indoor). *Women:* basketball, cheerleading, cross-country, cycling, golf, softball, tennis, track/field (outdoor), track/field (indoor), volleyball.

ADMISSIONS

Freshman Academic Profile: Average high school GPA 3.2. 13% in top 10% of high school class, 36% in top 25% of high school class, 69% in top 50% of high school class. SAT Math middle 50% range 430-610. SAT Critical Reading middle 50% range 440-550. ACT middle 50% range 19-25. Minimum paper TOEFL 550. **Basis for Candidate Selection:** *Very important factors considered include:* academic GPA, rigor of secondary school record, standardized test scores. *Important factors considered include:* Class rank, recommendation(s). *Other factors considered include:* application essay, alumni/ae relation, extracurricular activities, interview, level of applicant's interest, talent/ability. **Freshman Admission Requirements:** High school diploma is required and GED is accepted. *Academic units required:* 4 English, 2 mathematics, 2 science, (2 science labs), 1 foreign language, 2 social studies, 9 academic electives. *Academic units recommended:* 4 English, 2 mathematics, 2 science, (2 science labs), 1 foreign language, 2 social studies, 9 academic electives. **Freshman Admission Statistics:** 1,376 applied, 62% admitted, 36% enrolled. **Transfer Admission Requirements:** college transcript(s), minimum college GPA of 2 required. Lowest grade transferable C–. **General Admission Information:** Application Fee $20. Regular application deadline 8/1. Notification on a rolling basis, beginning on or about 9/15. Nonfall registration accepted. Admission may be deferred for a maximum of 1 yr. Credit and/or placement offered for CEEB Advanced Placement tests.

COSTS AND FINANCIAL AID

Average book expense $700. **Required Forms and Deadlines:** FAFSA, institution's own financial aid form. **Types of Aid:** *Need-based scholarships/grants:* Federal Pell, SEOG, state scholarships/grants, private scholarships, the school's own gift aid. *Loans:* Direct Subsidized Stafford, Direct Unsubsidized Stafford, Direct PLUS, Subsidized Stafford, Unsubsidized Stafford, PLUS, Federal Perkins, state loans. **Student Employment:** Federal Work-Study Program available. **Financial Aid Statistics:** 59% freshmen, 65% undergrads receive need-based scholarship or grant aid. 78% freshmen, 87% undergrads receive non-need-based scholarship or grant aid. 78% freshmen, 79% undergrads receive need-based self-help aid. 7% freshmen, 6% undergrads receive athletic scholarships. 81% undergrads borrow to pay for school. Average cumulative indebtedness $25,107. **Criteria for awarding institutional aid:** *Non-need-based:* academics, alumni affiliation, art, athletics, leadership, music/drama, religious affiliation.

MARIAN UNIVERSITY

45 South National Avenue, Fond du Lac, WI 54935
Phone: 920-923-7650 • **Financial Aid Phone:** 920-923-7614
E-mail: admissions@marianuniversity.edu • **CEEB Code:** 1443
Fax: 920-923-8755 • **Website:** www.marianuniversity.edu • **ACT Code:** 4606

This private school, affiliated with the Roman Catholic Church, was founded in 1936. It has a 100-acre campus.

RATINGS

Admissions Selectivity Rating: 65   **Fire Safety Rating:** 62   **Green Rating:** 60*

STUDENTS AND FACULTY

Enrollment: 1,903. **Student Body:** 75% female, 25% male, 7% out-of-state, 1% international (13 countries represented). Asian 1%, African American 5%, Caucasian 88%, Hispanic 2%, Native American 1%.
Retention and Graduation: 21% freshmen graduate within 4 years. 41% freshmen graduate within 6 years. 16% grads go on to further study within 1 year. **Faculty:** Student/faculty ratio 12:1. 83 full-time faculty, 60% hold PhDs, 6% are members of minority groups, 55% are women. 0% of classes are taught by teaching assistants.

ACADEMICS

Degrees: bachelor's, master's. **Classes:** Most classes have 10–19 students. Most lab/discussion sessions have 10–19 students. **Majors with Highest Enrollment:** business/commerce; nursing/registered nurse (rn, asn, bsn, msn); teacher education and professional development, specific levels and methods, other. **Special Study Options:** Accelerated program, cooperative education program,

distance learning, double major, dual enrollment, honors program, independent study, internships, liberal arts/career combination, student-designed major, study abroad, teacher certification program, Accelerated programs for adults in business, criminal justice, nursing, operations management, and radiologic technology. **Honors Programs:** Honors. **Disability Services:** Special programs offered to physically disabled students include note-taking services, reader services, tape recorders, tutors. **Career Services:** career/job search classes, career assessment, internships Career Services highlights include 97% of students receive field experience.

FACILITIES

Housing: Coed dorms, special housing for disabled students, fraternity/sorority housing, apartments for single students, Townhouses, Penthouses and Suites. 95% of campus accessible to physically disabled. **Special Academic Facilities/Equipment:** On-campus child-care center, electron microscope. **Computers:** Students can register for classes online. Administrative functions (other than registration) can be performed online.

CAMPUS LIFE

Environment: Town. **Activities:** Choral groups, concert band, dance, drama/theater, jazz band, literary magazine, music ensembles, pep band, student government, student newspaper, symphony orchestra, Campus Ministries, Model UN 40 registered organizations, 6 honor societies, 1 religious organizations. 1 fraternities, 2 sororities. **Athletics (Intercollegiate):** *Men:* baseball, basketball, cross-country, golf, ice hockey, soccer, tennis. *Women:* basketball, cross-country, golf, ice hockey, soccer, softball, tennis, volleyball. **On-Campus Highlights:** Housing, Coffee House, Student Center, Stayer Center, Library and Academic buildings.

ADMISSIONS

Freshman Academic Profile: Average high school GPA 3.0. 9% in top 10% of high school class, 30% in top 25% of high school class, 66% in top 50% of high school class. 87% from public high schools. ACT middle 50% range 18-22. Minimum paper TOEFL 525. **Basis for Candidate Selection:** *Very important factors considered include:* Class rank, academic GPA, rigor of secondary school record, standardized test scores. *Important factors considered include:* character/personal qualities, interview, level of applicant's interest. *Other factors considered include:* application essay, recommendation(s), alumni/ae relation, extracurricular activities, talent/ability, volunteer work, work experience. **Freshman Admission Requirements:** High school diploma is required and GED is accepted. *Academic units required:* 4 English, 2 mathematics, 1 science, (1 science labs), 1 history. *Academic units recommended:* 4 English, 2 mathematics, 1 science, (1 science labs), 1 history. **Freshman Admission Statistics:** 843 applied, 86% admitted, 40% enrolled. **Transfer Admission Requirements:** High school transcript, college transcript(s), minimum college GPA of 2.0 required. Lowest grade transferable C. **General Admission Information:** Application Fee $20. Notification on a rolling basis, beginning on or about 9/15. Nonfall registration accepted. Admission may be deferred for a maximum of case by case. Credit and/or placement offered for CEEB Advanced Placement tests.

COSTS AND FINANCIAL AID

Annual tuition $19,590. Room and board $5,380. Required fees $350. Average book expense $700. **Required Forms and Deadlines:** FAFSA, institution's own financial aid form. **Notification of Awards:** Applicants will be notified of awards on a rolling basis beginning 3/1. **Types of Aid:** *Need-based scholarships/grants:* Federal Pell, SEOG, state scholarships/grants, private scholarships, the school's own gift aid. *Loans:* Subsidized Stafford, Unsubsidized Stafford, PLUS, Federal Perkins, Federal Nursing. **Student Employment:** Federal Work-Study Program available. Institutional employment available. Highest amount earned per year from on-campus jobs $2,000. Off-campus job opportunities are fair. **Financial Aid Statistics:** 100% freshmen, 97% undergrads receive need-based scholarship or grant aid. 91% freshmen, 85% undergrads receive non-need-based scholarship or grant aid. 89% freshmen, 91% undergrads receive need-based self-help aid. 99% freshmen, 94% undergrads receive any aid. 90% undergrads borrow to pay for school. Average cumulative indebtedness $22,200. **Criteria for awarding institutional aid:** *Non-need-based:* academics, state/district residency.

MARIETTA COLLEGE

215 Fifth Street, Marietta, OH 45750
Phone: 740-376-4600 • **Financial Aid Phone:** 740-376-4712
E-mail: admit@marietta.edu • **CEEB Code:** 1444
Fax: 740-376-8888 • **Website:** www.marietta.edu • **ACT Code:** 3290

This private school was founded in 1835. It has a 90-acre campus.

RATINGS
Admissions Selectivity Rating: 78   **Fire Safety Rating:** 74   **Green Rating:** 72

STUDENTS AND FACULTY
Enrollment: 1,448. **Student Body:** 46% female, 54% male, 36% out-of-state, 12% international (17 countries represented). Asian 1%, African American 5%, Caucasian 72%, Hispanic 2%, Native American 0%.
Retention and Graduation: 43% freshmen graduate within 4 years. 51% freshmen graduate within 6 years. 20% grads go on to further study within 1 year. 9% grads pursue arts and sciences degrees. 3% grads pursue law degrees. 2% grads pursue business degrees. 2% grads pursue medical degrees. **Faculty:** Student/faculty ratio 12:1. 109 full-time faculty, 89% hold PhDs, 6% are members of minority groups, 46% are women. 0% of classes are taught by teaching assistants.

ACADEMICS
Degrees: associate, bachelor's, certificate, master's. **Classes:** Most classes have 10–19 students. **Majors with Highest Enrollment:** athletic training/trainer; education; petroleum engineering. **Special Study Options:** double major, dual enrollment, English as a Second Language (ESL), exchange student program (domestic), honors program, independent study, internships, liberal arts/career combination, student-designed major, study abroad, teacher certification program. **Honors Programs:** Four Year Program for Top Scholarship Winners **Combined Degree Programs:** BA/MA. **Disability Services:** Special programs offered to physically disabled students include note-taking services, reader services, tape recorders, tutors. **Career Services:** Alumni network, alumni services, career/job search classes, career assessment, internships, regional alumni.

FACILITIES
Housing: Coed dorms, special housing for disabled students, men's dorms, women's dorms, fraternity/sorority housing, apartments for single students, wellness housing, theme housing is available. 90% of campus accessible to physically disabled. **Special Academic Facilities/Equipment:** Mass media building, fine arts center, natural science field camp, observatory, special collections in library **Computers:** 100% of classrooms, 100% of dorms, 100% of libraries, 100% of dining areas, 100% of student union, have wireless network access. Students can register for classes online. Administrative functions (other than registration) can be performed online.

CAMPUS LIFE
Environment: Town. **Activities:** Choral groups, concert band, dance, drama/theater, jazz band, literary magazine, music ensembles, musical theater, radio station, student government, student newspaper, television station, yearbook, Campus Ministries, International Student Organization, Model UN 80 registered organizations, 23 honor societies, 2 religious organizations, 3 fraternities, 3 sororities. **Athletics (Intercollegiate):** *Men:* baseball, basketball, crew/rowing, cross-country, football, soccer, tennis, track/field (outdoor), track/field (indoor). *Women:* basketball, crew/rowing, cross-country, soccer, softball, tennis, track/field (outdoor), track/field (indoor), volleyball. **On-Campus Highlights:** Gathering Place, new Upper Class Residence Hall, Legacy Library, Hermann Fine Arts Center, Dyson Baudo Recreation Center, 6. New Rickey Science Center 7. New Soccer and Softball Fields 8. Andrews Hall - Izzy's Snack Place. **Environmental Initiatives:** Added Sustainable Energy Minor under the Petroleum Engineering Program. "Energy and the Environment" selected as this year's theme for campus and community awareness events. Offer a sustainable living life style theme house.

ADMISSIONS
Freshman Academic Profile: Average high school GPA 3.5. 30% in top 10% of high school class, 56% in top 25% of high school class, 84% in top 50% of high school class. 89% from public high schools. SAT Math middle 50% range 500-630. SAT Critical Reading middle 50% range 480-620. SAT Writing middle 50% range 470-600. ACT middle 50% range 21-27. Minimum web-based TOEFL 79. Minimum paper TOEFL 550. **Basis for Candidate Selection:** *Very important factors considered include:* Class rank, academic GPA, rigor of secondary school record, standardized test scores. *Important factors considered include:* application essay, recommendation(s), character/personal qualities, interview. *Other factors considered include:* alumni/ae relation, extracurricular activities, first generation, geographical residence, level of applicant's interest, racial/ethnic status, state residency, talent/ability, volunteer work, work experi-

ence. **Freshman Admission Requirements:** High school diploma is required and GED is accepted. *Academic units required:* 4 English, 3 mathematics, 3 science, (2 science labs), 2 foreign language, 2 social studies, 2 history. 4 English, 3 mathematics, 3 science, (2 science labs), 2 foreign language, 2 social studies, 2 history. **Freshman Admission Statistics:** 4,099 applied, 70% admitted, 13% enrolled. **Transfer Admission Requirements:** college transcript(s), essay or personal statement, statement of good standing from prior institution(s). Minimum college GPA of 2.3 required. Lowest grade transferable C. **General Admission Information:** Application Fee $25. Notification on a rolling basis, beginning on or about 9/1. Nonfall registration accepted. Admission may be deferred for a maximum of 12 months. Credit and/or placement offered for CEEB Advanced Placement tests.

COSTS AND FINANCIAL AID
Annual tuition $28,950. Room and board $9,090. Required fees $740. Average book expense $1,104. **Required Forms and Deadlines:** FAFSA. **Notification of Awards:** Applicants will be notified of awards on a rolling basis beginning 3/15. **Types of Aid:** *Need-based scholarships/grants:* Federal Pell, SEOG, state scholarships/grants, private scholarships, the school's own gift aid. *Loans:* Direct Subsidized Stafford, Direct Unsubsidized Stafford, Direct PLUS, Subsidized Stafford, Unsubsidized Stafford, PLUS, Federal Perkins, college/university loans from institutional funds. **Student Employment:** Federal Work-Study Program available. Institutional employment available. Highest amount earned per year from on-campus jobs $2,000. Off-campus job opportunities are good. **Financial Aid Statistics:** 96% freshmen, 90% undergrads receive need-based scholarship or grant aid. 98% freshmen, 97% undergrads receive non-need-based scholarship or grant aid. 89% freshmen, 88% undergrads receive need-based self-help aid. 99% freshmen, 94% undergrads receive any aid. 82% undergrads borrow to pay for school. Average cumulative indebtedness $32,127. **Criteria for awarding institutional aid:** *Non-need-based:* academics, alumni affiliation, art, leadership, minority status, music/drama, state/district residency.

MARIST COLLEGE

3399 North Road, Poughkeepsie, NY 12601-1387
Phone: 845-575-3226 • **Financial Aid Phone:** 845-575-3230
E-mail: admission@marist.edu • **CEEB Code:** 2400
Fax: 845-575-3215 • **Website:** www.marist.edu/ • **ACT Code:** 2804

This private school was founded in 1929. It has a 180-acre campus.

RATINGS
Admissions Selectivity Rating: 94   **Fire Safety Rating:** 88   **Green Rating:** 66

STUDENTS AND FACULTY
Enrollment: 5,019. **Student Body:** 59% female, 41% male, 44% out-of-state (38 countries represented).
Retention and Graduation: 92% freshmen return for sophomore year. 26% grads go on to further study within 1 year. 1% grads pursue law degrees. 1% grads pursue business degrees. 1% grads pursue medical degrees. **Faculty:** Student/faculty ratio 16:1. 223 full-time faculty, 77% hold PhDs, 13% are members of minority groups, 47% are women. 0% of classes are taught by teaching assistants.

ACADEMICS
Degrees: bachelor's, certificate, master's, post-bachelor's certificate. **Classes:** Most classes have 20–29 students. Most lab/discussion sessions have 20–29 students. **Majors with Highest Enrollment:** business administration and management; psychology; special education and teaching. **Special Study Options:** Accelerated program, cooperative education program, cross-registration, distance learning, double major, dual enrollment, English as a Second Language (ESL), honors program, independent study, internships, liberal arts/career combination, study abroad, teacher certification program, weekend college, Undergrads may take grad level classes. Cooperative ed- Arts, Business, Computer Science, Education, Humanities, Natural Science, Social/Behavioral Science, Technologies. **Honors Programs:** The Marist College Honors Program brings together talented students in honors-enriched classes that often coordinate with co-curricular activities such as field trips and lectures. The cultural enrichment exchange is a highlight of the Program. It encourages students to move beyond standard curricula and engage in a broader range of experience consonant with their interests. **Combined Degree Programs:** BA/MA, BS/MS. **Disability Services:** Special programs offered to physically disabled students include note-taking services, reader services, tape recorders, tutors. **Career Services:** Alumni network, alumni services, career/job search classes, career assessment,

internships, regional alumni. Career Services highlights include We have a very extensive internship program that provides students with practical work experience and reinforces the lessons from the classroom.

FACILITIES

Housing: Coed dorms, special housing for disabled students, apartments for single students, wellness housing, garden apartments, townhouses, suites. 88% of campus accessible to physically disabled. **Special Academic Facilities/Equipment:** Art gallery, language lab, estuarine and environmental studies lab, public opinion institute, audiovisual/TV center, communications center, high tech classroom,digital state of the art library. **Computers:** 100% of classrooms, 100% of dorms, 100% of libraries, 100% of dining areas, 100% of student union, 57% of common outdoor areas have wireless network access. Students can register for classes online. Administrative functions (other than registration) can be performed online.

CAMPUS LIFE

Environment: Town. **Activities:** Choral groups, concert band, dance, drama/theater, jazz band, literary magazine, marching band, music ensembles, musical theater, pep band, radio station, student government, student newspaper, student-run film society, television station, yearbook, Campus Ministries 86 registered organizations, 16 honor societies, 6 religious organizations. 3 fraternities, 4 sororities. **Athletics (Intercollegiate):** *Men:* baseball, basketball, crew/rowing, cross-country, diving, football, lacrosse, soccer, swimming, tennis, track/field (outdoor). *Women:* basketball, crew/rowing, cross-country, diving, lacrosse, soccer, softball, swimming, tennis, track/field (outdoor), volleyball, water polo. **On-Campus Highlights:** James A Cannavino Library, James J McCann Recreation Center, Student Center, Newly Renovated Freshman Residence Halls, Tenney Stadium at Leonidoff Field. **Environmental Initiatives:** Sustainable food purchases Energy efficiency/reduction (electricity and heat), Composting, Recycling Green information technology initiatives.

ADMISSIONS

Freshman Academic Profile: Average high school GPA 3.3. 32% in top 10% of high school class, 70% in top 25% of high school class, 95% in top 50% of high school class. 69% from public high schools. SAT Math middle 50% range 560-640. SAT Critical Reading middle 50% range 540-630. SAT Writing middle 50% range 550-640. ACT middle 50% range 24-28. Minimum web-based TOEFL 80. Minimum paper TOEFL 550. **Basis for Candidate Selection:** *Very important factors considered include:* academic GPA, rigor of secondary school record, standardized test scores. *Important factors considered include:* Class rank, application essay, recommendation(s), character/personal qualities, extracurricular activities, geographical residence, state residency, talent/ability, volunteer work, work experience. *Other factors considered include:* alumni/ae relation, level of applicant's interest, racial/ethnic status. **Freshman Admission Requirements:** High school diploma is required and GED is accepted. *Academic units required:* 4 English, 3 mathematics, 3 science, (2 science labs), 2 foreign language, 2 social studies, 1 history, 2 academic electives. *Academic units recommended:* 4 English, 3 mathematics, 3 science, (2 science labs), 2 foreign language, 2 social studies, 1 history, 2 academic electives. **Freshman Admission Statistics:** 11,399 applied, 34% admitted, 31% enrolled. **Transfer Admission Requirements:** High school transcript, college transcript(s), essay or personal statement, minimum college GPA of 2.8 required. Lowest grade transferable 2. **General Admission Information:** Application Fee $50. Early decision application deadline 11/15. Regular application deadline 2/15. Regular notification 3/30. Nonfall registration accepted. Admission may be deferred for a maximum of 12 months. Credit and/or placement offered for CEEB Advanced Placement tests.

COSTS AND FINANCIAL AID

Annual tuition $28,300. Room and board $12,800. Required fees $500. Average book expense $1,700. **Required Forms and Deadlines:** FAFSA, institution's own financial aid form. **Notification of Awards:** Applicants will be notified of awards on a rolling basis beginning 3/15. **Types of Aid:** *Need-based scholarships/grants:* Federal Pell, SEOG, state scholarships/grants, private scholarships, the school's own gift aid. *Loans:* Subsidized Stafford, Unsubsidized Stafford, PLUS, Federal Perkins, Alternative Loans. **Student Employment:** Federal Work-Study Program available. Institutional employment available. Highest amount earned per year from on-campus jobs $7,920. Off-campus job opportunities are excellent. **Financial Aid Statistics:** 72% freshmen, 67% undergrads receive need-based scholarship or grant aid. 100% freshmen, 84% undergrads receive non-need-based scholarship or grant aid. 81% freshmen, 83% undergrads receive need-based self-help aid. 7% freshmen, 6% undergrads receive athletic scholarships. 66% freshmen, 51% undergrads receive any aid. 69% undergrads borrow to pay for school. Average cumulative indebtedness $32,507. **Criteria for awarding institutional aid:** *Non-need-based:* academics, athletics, music/drama, state/district residency.

MARLBORO COLLEGE

PO Box A, Marlboro, VT 05344-0300
Phone: 802-258-9236 • **Financial Aid Phone:** 802-258-9312
E-mail: admissions@marlboro.edu • **CEEB Code:** 3509
Fax: 802-451-7555 • **Website:** www.marlboro.edu • **ACT Code:** 4304

This private school was founded in 1946. It has a 350-acre campus.

RATINGS

Admissions Selectivity Rating: 83   **Fire Safety Rating:** 72   **Green Rating:** 69

STUDENTS AND FACULTY

Enrollment: 238. **Student Body:** 48% female, 52% male, 92% out-of-state, 1% international (8 countries represented). Asian 3%, African American 1%, Caucasian 63%, Hispanic 0%, Native American 1%.
Retention and Graduation: 68% freshmen return for sophomore year. 59% freshmen graduate within 4 years. 69% grads go on to further study within 1 year. **Faculty:** Student/faculty ratio 6:1. 39 full-time faculty, 90% hold PhDs, 10% are members of minority groups, 44% are women. 0% of classes are taught by teaching assistants.

ACADEMICS

Degrees: bachelor's, master's. **Classes:** Most classes have fewer than 10 students. Most lab/discussion sessions have fewer than 10 students. **Majors with Highest Enrollment:** English language and literature; social sciences; visual and performing arts, other. **Special Study Options:** double major, dual enrollment, independent study, internships, student-designed major, study abroad, World Studies Program for students interested in international relations while also integrating an internship with study abroad opportunities. **Disability Services:** Special programs offered to physically disabled students include note-taking services, reader services, tape recorders, tutors. **Career Services:** alumni services, career/job search classes, career assessment.

FACILITIES

Housing: Coed dorms, special housing for disabled students, women's dorms, apartments for married students, cooperative housing, apartments for single students, Housing is to a human scale; the largest residence hall accommodates about 30 students. 80% of campus accessible to physically disabled. **Special Academic Facilities/Equipment:** Serkin Center for the Performing Arts, Drury art gallery, theater, dance studio, observatory, darkroom, art studios, music practice and performance spaces. **Computers:** 80% of classrooms, 85% of dorms, 100% of libraries, 100% of dining areas, 100% of student union, 80% of common outdoor areas have wireless network access. Students can register for classes online. Administrative functions (other than registration) can be performed online.

CAMPUS LIFE

Environment: Rural. **Activities:** Choral groups, dance, drama/theater, literary magazine, music ensembles, musical theater, radio station, student government, student newspaper, student-run film society 22 registered organizations. **On-Campus Highlights:** The Rice-Aron Library, Whittemore Theatre, Rod Gander World Studies Center, Serkin Center for the Performing Arts, Persons Auditorium. **Environmental Initiatives:** Energy audits of all campus buildings in preparation for efficiency upgrades. Solar-powered water heater in new Total Health Center facility. Recycling.

ADMISSIONS

Freshman Academic Profile: Average high school GPA 3.1. 70% from public high schools. SAT Math middle 50% range 520-650. SAT Critical Reading middle 50% range 560-730. SAT Writing middle 50% range 530-680. Minimum web-based TOEFL 90. Minimum paper TOEFL 577. **Basis for Candidate Selection:** *Very important factors considered include:* application essay, academic GPA, rigor of secondary school record, character/personal qualities. *Important factors considered include:* extracurricular activities, interview. *Other factors considered include:* Class rank, recommendation(s), standardized test scores, alumni/ae relation, first generation, geographical residence, level of applicant's interest, state residency, talent/ability, volunteer work, work experience. **Freshman Admission Requirements:** High school diploma is required and GED is accepted. **Freshman Admission Statistics:** 256 applied, 79% admitted, 24% enrolled. **Transfer Admission Requirements:** High school transcript, college transcript(s), essay or personal statement, interview, minimum college GPA of 2.0 required. Lowest grade transferable C–. **General Admission Information:** Application Fee $50. Early decision application deadline 12/1. Regular application deadline 3/1. Notification on a rolling basis, beginning on or about 12/1. Nonfall registration accepted. Admission may be deferred for a maximum of 1 year. Credit offered for CEEB Advanced Placement tests.

COSTS AND FINANCIAL AID
Annual tuition $36,300. Room and board $9,930. Required fees $1,340. Average book expense $1,200. **Required Forms and Deadlines:** FAFSA. **Notification of Awards:** Applicants will be notified of awards on a rolling basis beginning 3/15. **Types of Aid:** *Need-based scholarships/grants:* Federal Pell, SEOG, state scholarships/grants, private scholarships, the school's own gift aid. *Loans:* Subsidized Stafford, Unsubsidized Stafford, PLUS. **Student Employment:** Federal Work-Study Program available. Institutional employment available. Highest amount earned per year from on-campus jobs $2,050. Off-campus job opportunities are fair. **Financial Aid Statistics:** 100% freshmen, 99% undergrads receive need-based scholarship or grant aid. 85% freshmen, 90% undergrads receive non-need-based scholarship or grant aid. 100% freshmen, 98% undergrads receive need-based self-help aid. 98% freshmen, 94% undergrads receive any aid. 71% undergrads borrow to pay for school. Average cumulative indebtedness $20,051. **Criteria for awarding institutional aid:** *Non-need-based:* academics, leadership.

See page 1138.

MARQUETTE UNIVERSITY

PO Box 1881, Milwaukee, WI 53201-1881
Phone: 414-288-7302 • **Financial Aid Phone:** 414-288-7390
E-mail: admissions@Marquette.edu • **CEEB Code:** 1448
Fax: 414-288-3764 • **Website:** www.marquette.edu • **ACT Code:** 4610

This private school, affiliated with the Roman Catholic-Jesuit Church,, affiliated with the Jesuit Church, was founded in 1881. It has a 93-acre campus.

RATINGS
Admissions Selectivity Rating: 89   **Fire Safety Rating:** 91   **Green Rating:** 87

STUDENTS AND FACULTY
Enrollment: 8,118. **Student Body:** 52% female, 48% male, 64% out-of-state, 3% international (48 countries represented). Asian 5%, African American 5%, Caucasian 76%, Hispanic 9%, Native American 0%.
Retention and Graduation: 88% freshmen return for sophomore year. 60% freshmen graduate within 4 years. 80% freshmen graduate within 6 years. 27% grads go on to further study within 1 year. **Faculty:** Student/faculty ratio 14:1. 634 full-time faculty, 91% hold PhDs, 15% are members of minority groups, 40% are women.

ACADEMICS
Degrees: bachelor's, doctoral, master's, post-master's certificate. **Classes:** Most classes have 10–19 students. Most lab/discussion sessions have 20–29 students. **Majors with Highest Enrollment:** nursing/registered nurse (rn, asn, bsn, msn). **Special Study Options:** Accelerated program, cooperative education program, cross-registration, double major, dual enrollment, honors program, independent study, internships, student-designed major, study abroad, teacher certification program, weekend college. **Honors Programs:** Pre-Law Scholars Program Pre-Dental Scholars Program **Combined Degree Programs:** BA/JD, BA/MA, BA/DDS, Physical Therapy, Physician Assistant Studies. **Disability Services:** Special programs offered to physically disabled students include note-taking services, reader services, tape recorders, tutors.

FACILITIES
Housing: Coed dorms, special housing for disabled students, men's dorms, special housing for international students, women's dorms, fraternity/sorority housing, apartments for married students, apartments for single students, Specialty housing for honor students, engineering students, nursing students. 90% of campus accessible to physically disabled. **Special Academic Facilities/Equipment:** Haggerty Museum of Art, Helfaer Theatre, Al McGuire Center Broadcast Facilities, Dental School/Clinic. **Computers:** 30% of classrooms, 100% of dorms, 100% of libraries, 100% of dining areas, 100% of student union, 10% of common outdoor areas have wireless network access. Students can register for classes online. Administrative functions (other than registration) can be performed online.

CAMPUS LIFE
Environment: Metropolis. **Activities:** Choral groups, concert band, dance, drama/theater, jazz band, literary magazine, music ensembles, musical theater, pep band, radio station, student government, student newspaper, symphony orchestra, television station, yearbook, Campus Ministries, International Student Organization, Model UN 230 registered organizations, 21 honor societies, 11 religious organizations. 11 fraternities, 11 sororities. **Athletics (Intercollegiate):** *Men:* basketball, cheerleading, cross-country, golf, soccer, tennis, track/field (outdoor), track/field (indoor). *Women:* basketball, cheerleading, cross-country, soccer, tennis, track/field (outdoor), track/field (indoor), volleyball. **On-Campus Highlights:** The Raynor Memorial Library and the Law, Gesu Church, Haggerty Museum of Art, Al McGuire Center, Helfaer Recreation Center, Other places of interest Alumni Memorial Union and the Golden Eagle giftshop. (Located in the AMU). **Environmental Initiatives:** All Full Time undergraduate Students receive a UPASS (Allows unlimited use of Milwaukee County Transit System Buses) Recycling garbage and electronic equipment. Marquette uses steam from the power company (waste heat) for 90% of campus heating. Marquette participates in the State of Wisconsin's Focus on Energy Program. In collaboration with Johnson Controls, Marquette was able to reduce energy use by 1,547,000 kWh (2,320,500 lbs of CO2) and annual water consumption by 13,400,000 gallons.

ADMISSIONS
Freshman Academic Profile: 38% in top 10% of high school class, 67% in top 25% of high school class, 94% in top 50% of high school class. 57% from public high schools. SAT Math middle 50% range 550-650. SAT Critical Reading middle 50% range 520-630. SAT Writing middle 50% range 530-630. ACT middle 50% range 24-29. Minimum web-based TOEFL 78. Minimum paper TOEFL 530. **Basis for Candidate Selection:** *Very important factors considered include:* academic GPA, rigor of secondary school record. *Important factors considered include:* Class rank, application essay, recommendation(s), standardized test scores. *Other factors considered include:* alumni/ae relation, character/personal qualities, extracurricular activities, first generation, geographical residence, racial/ethnic status, state residency, talent/ability, volunteer work. **Freshman Admission Requirements:** High school diploma is required and GED is accepted. *Academic units required:* 4 English, 2 mathematics, 2 science, (2 science labs), 2 social studies, 2 academic electives. *Academic units recommended:* 4 English, 2 mathematics, 2 science, (2 science labs), 2 social studies, 2 academic electives. **Freshman Admission Statistics:** 22,900 applied, 55% admitted, 15% enrolled. **Transfer Admission Requirements:** High school transcript, college transcript(s), essay or personal statement, Lowest grade transferable C. **General Admission Information:** Application Fee $30. Regular application deadline 12/1. Regular notification 1/31. Nonfall registration accepted. Admission may be deferred for a maximum of 1 year. Credit and/or placement offered for CEEB Advanced Placement tests.

COSTS AND FINANCIAL AID
Annual tuition $34,200. Required fees $440. Average book expense. **Required Forms and Deadlines:** FAFSA, MU Admissions Application. **Notification of Awards:** Applicants will be notified of awards on a rolling basis beginning 3/20. **Types of Aid:** *Need-based scholarships/grants:* Federal Pell, SEOG, state scholarships/grants, private scholarships, the school's own gift aid, Marquette Merit Based aid is not based on need, but is used to cover need. *Loans:* Direct Subsidized Stafford, Direct Unsubsidized Stafford, Direct PLUS, Federal Perkins, Federal Nursing, state loans, college/university loans from institutional funds, Private educational/alternative loans. **Student Employment:** Highest amount earned per year from on-campus jobs $2,500. Off-campus job opportunities are excellent. **Financial Aid Statistics:** 99% freshmen, 98% undergrads receive need-based scholarship or grant aid. 13% freshmen, 11% undergrads receive non-need-based scholarship or grant aid. 82% freshmen, 83% undergrads receive need-based self-help aid. 1% freshmen, 1% undergrads receive athletic scholarships. 99% freshmen, 98% undergrads receive any aid. 65% undergrads borrow to pay for school. Average cumulative indebtedness $34,602. **Criteria for awarding institutional aid:** *Non-need-based:* academics, athletics, leadership, music/drama.

See page xx.

MARS HILL COLLEGE

PO Box 370, Mars Hill, NC 28754
Phone: 828-689-1201 • **Financial Aid Phone:** 828-689-1123
E-mail: admissions@mhc.edu • **CEEB Code:** 5395
Fax: 828-689-1473 • **ACT Code:** 3124

This private school, affiliated with the Baptist Church, was founded in 1856. It has a 180-acre campus.

RATINGS
Admissions Selectivity Rating: 63   **Fire Safety Rating:** 60*   **Green Rating:** 60*

STUDENTS AND FACULTY
Enrollment: 1,177. **Student Body:** 56% female, 44% male, 35% out-of-state, 3% international (20 countries represented). Asian 0%, African American 8%, Caucasian 99%, Hispanic 1%, Native American 1%. **Retention and Graduation:** 71% freshmen return for sophomore year. **Faculty:** Student/faculty ratio 14:1. 78 full-time faculty, 63% hold PhDs, 1% are members of minority groups, 36% are women. 0% of classes are taught by teaching assistants.

ACADEMICS
Degrees: bachelor's, diploma. **Classes: Majors with Highest Enrollment:** biology/biological sciences; business/commerce; elementary education and teaching. **Special Study Options:** Accelerated program, cooperative education program, distance learning, double major, dual enrollment, English as a Second Language (ESL), honors program, independent study, internships, liberal arts/career combination, study abroad, teacher certification program. **Honors Programs:** http://www.mhc.edu/honors.asp. **Disability Services:** Special programs offered to physically disabled students include note-taking services, reader services, tape recorders, tutors.

FACILITIES
Housing: special housing for disabled students, men's dorms, women's dorms, apartments for married students, apartments for single students. **Special Academic Facilities/Equipment:** Language lab, Appalachian artifacts museum, rural life museum. **Computers:** Students can register for classes online. Administrative functions (other than registration) can be performed online.

CAMPUS LIFE
Environment: Rural. **Activities:** Choral groups, concert band, dance, drama/theater, jazz band, literary magazine, marching band, music ensembles, musical theater, radio station, student government, student newspaper, symphony orchestra, yearbook 45 registered organizations, 9 honor societies, 5 religious organizations. 6 fraternities, 5 sororities. **Athletics (Intercollegiate): Men:** baseball, basketball, cheerleading, cross-country, football, golf, lacrosse, soccer, tennis, track/field (outdoor). *Women:* basketball, cheerleading, cross-country, golf, soccer, softball, swimming, tennis, track/field (outdoor), volleyball. **On-Campus Highlights:** Wren Student Union, The Loft, The Ice Cream Shoppe, Cafeteria, Gym.

ADMISSIONS
Freshman Academic Profile: Average high school GPA 3.4. **Basis for Candidate Selection:** *Very important factors considered include:* rigor of secondary school record, standardized test scores. *Important factors considered include:* Class rank, recommendation(s), character/personal qualities, extracurricular activities, interview, talent/ability. *Other factors considered include:* alumni/ae relation, religious affiliation/commitment, volunteer work, work experience. **Freshman Admission Requirements:** High school diploma is required and GED is accepted. *Academic units required:* 4 English, 3 mathematics, 2 science, (1 science labs), 2 social studies, 2 history. *Academic units recommended:* 4 English, 3 mathematics, 2 science, (1 science labs), 2 social studies, 2 history. **Transfer Admission Requirements:** college transcript(s), statement of good standing from prior institution(s). Minimum college GPA of 2.0 required. Lowest grade transferable C. **General Admission Information:** Application Fee $25. Nonfall registration accepted.

COSTS AND FINANCIAL AID
Annual tuition $16,854. Room and board $5,900. Required fees $800. Average book expense $600. **Required Forms and Deadlines:** FAFSA, state aid form. **Types of Aid:** *Need-based scholarships/grants:* state scholarships/grants. *Loans:* Subsidized Stafford, PLUS. **Student Employment: Financial Aid Statistics:** 99% freshmen, 90% undergrads receive any aid.

MARSHALL UNIVERSITY

One John Marshall Drive, Huntington, WV 25755
Phone: 304-696-3160 • **Financial Aid Phone:** 304-696-3162
E-mail: admissions@marshall.edu • **CEEB Code:** 5396
Fax: 304-696-3135 • **Website:** www.marshall.edu • **ACT Code:** 4526

This public school was founded in 1837. It has a 70-acre campus,

RATINGS
Admissions Selectivity Rating: 69   **Fire Safety Rating:** 62   **Green Rating:** 60*

STUDENTS AND FACULTY
Enrollment: 9,365. **Student Body:** 56% female, 44% male, 24% out-of-state, 1% international. Asian 1%, African American 6%, Caucasian 86%, Hispanic 2%, Native American 0%. **Retention and Graduation:** 71% freshmen return for sophomore year. 27% grads go on to further study within 1 year. **Faculty:** Student/faculty ratio 19:1. 519 full-time faculty, 80% hold PhDs, 16% are members of minority groups, 43% are women.

ACADEMICS
Degrees: associate, bachelor's, master's, post-bachelor's certificate, post-master's certificate. **Classes:** Most classes have 20-29 students. **Majors with Highest Enrollment:** business/commerce; elementary education and teaching; psychology. **Special Study Options:** Accelerated program, cooperative education program, cross-registration, distance learning, double major, dual enrollment, English as a Second Language (ESL), exchange student program (domestic), honors program, independent study, internships, study abroad, teacher certification program. **Honors Programs:** John Marshall Scholars, Society of Yeager Scholars **Combined Degree Programs:** BS/MF Forestry (w/ Duke), BS/MEM Env Mgmt (w/ Duke). **Disability Services:** Special programs offered to physically disabled students include note-taking services, reader services, tutors. **Career Services:** Alumni network, alumni services, career/job search classes, career assessment, internships, regional alumni.

FACILITIES
Housing: Coed dorms, special housing for disabled students, women's dorms. 100% of campus accessible to physically disabled. **Special Academic Facilities/Equipment:** Art gallery, audiovisual center, language lab, superconducting nuclear magnetic resonance spectrometer. **Computers:** Students can register for classes online. Administrative functions (other than registration) can be performed online.

CAMPUS LIFE
Environment: Town. **Activities:** Choral groups, concert band, dance, drama/theater, jazz band, literary magazine, marching band, music ensembles, musical theater, opera, pep band, radio station, student government, student newspaper, symphony orchestra, television station, Campus Ministries, International Student Organization, Model UN 100 registered organizations, 11 honor societies, 10 religious organizations. 12 fraternities, 7 sororities. **Athletics (Intercollegiate): Men:** baseball, basketball, cross-country, football, golf, soccer, track/field (outdoor). *Women:* basketball, cross-country, golf, soccer, softball, swimming, tennis, track/field (outdoor), volleyball. **On-Campus Highlights:** Memorial Student Center Plaza, Drinko Library, Marshall Stadium, Henderson Center, Buskirk Field.

ADMISSIONS
Freshman Academic Profile: Average high school GPA 3.3. SAT Math middle 50% range 440-560. SAT Critical Reading middle 50% range 450-550. SAT Writing middle 50% range 430-550. ACT middle 50% range 19-24. Minimum paper TOEFL 500. **Basis for Candidate Selection:** *Very important factors considered include:* academic GPA, standardized test scores. *Other factors considered include:* rigor of secondary school record. **Freshman Admission Requirements:** High school diploma is required and GED is accepted. *Academic units required:* 4 English, 4 mathematics, 3 science, (3 science labs), 2 foreign language, 3 social studies, 1 visual/performing arts. 4 English, 4 mathematics, 3 science, (3 science labs), 2 foreign language, 3 social studies, 1 visual/performing arts. **Freshman Admission Statistics:** 2,889 applied, 80% admitted. **Transfer Admission Requirements:** college transcript(s). **General Admission Information:** Application Fee $30. Notification on a rolling basis, beginning on or about 9/1. Nonfall registration accepted. Admission may be deferred for a maximum of 1 year. Credit offered for CEEB Advanced Placement tests.

COSTS AND FINANCIAL AID
Annual in-state tuition $4,860. Annual out-of-state tuition $12,860. Room and board $8,354. Required fees $1,070. Average book expense $1,100. **Required Forms and Deadlines:** FAFSA, state aid form. **Notification of Awards:** Applicants will be notified of awards on a rolling basis beginning 5/1. **Types of**

Aid: *Need-based scholarships/grants:* Federal Pell, SEOG, state scholarships/grants, private scholarships, the school's own gift aid. *Loans:* Direct Subsidized Stafford, Direct Unsubsidized Stafford, Direct PLUS, Federal Perkins. **Student Employment:** Off-campus job opportunities are good. **Financial Aid Statistics:** 78% freshmen, 76% undergrads receive need-based scholarship or grant aid. 54% freshmen, 35% undergrads receive non-need-based scholarship or grant aid. 71% freshmen, 76% undergrads receive need-based self-help aid. 4% freshmen, 4% undergrads receive athletic scholarships. 62% undergrads borrow to pay for school. Average cumulative indebtedness $26,727. **Criteria for awarding institutional aid:** *Non-need-based:* academics, art, athletics, minority status, music/drama, state/district residency.

MARY BALDWIN COLLEGE

PO Box 1500, Staunton, VA 24402
Phone: 540-887-7019 • **Financial Aid Phone:** 540-887-7019
E-mail: admit@mbc.edu • **CEEB Code:** 5397
Fax: 540-887-7292 • **Website:** www.mbc.edu • **ACT Code:** 4374

This private school, affiliated with the Presbyterian Church, was founded in 1842. It has a 54-acre campus.

RATINGS
Admissions Selectivity Rating: 78   **Fire Safety Rating:** 75   **Green Rating:** 62

STUDENTS AND FACULTY
Enrollment: 1,391. **Student Body:** 95% female, 5% male, 19% out-of-state, 0% international (4 countries represented). Asian 0%, African American 0%, Caucasian 0%, Hispanic 0%, Native American 0%.
Retention and Graduation: 69% freshmen return for sophomore year. 20% grads go on to further study within 1 year. 5% grads pursue law degrees. 3% grads pursue business degrees. 3% grads pursue medical degrees. **Faculty:** Student/faculty ratio 12:1. 76 full-time faculty, 97% hold PhDs, 21% are members of minority groups, 59% are women. 0% of classes are taught by teaching assistants.

ACADEMICS
Degrees: bachelor's, certificate, master's. **Classes:** Most classes have 10–19 students. Most lab/discussion sessions have 10–19 students. **Majors with Highest Enrollment:** business/commerce; psychology; sociology. **Special Study Options:** Accelerated program, cooperative education program, cross-registration, distance learning, double major, dual enrollment, English as a Second Language (ESL), exchange student program (domestic), external degree program, honors program, independent study, internships, liberal arts/career combination, student-designed major, study abroad, teacher certification program, Summer exchange program with Doshisha Women's College in Kyoto, Japan. **Disability Services:** Special programs offered to physically disabled students include tape recorders, tutors. **Career Services:** alumni services, career/job search classes, career assessment, internships.

FACILITIES
Housing: special housing for international students, women's dorms, apartments for single students, Special interest (club) housing focuses on students, honors, leadership and community services available. 75% of campus accessible to physically disabled. **Special Academic Facilities/Equipment:** Audiovisual center, TV studio, communications lab, electron microscope, gas chromatoscope, greenhouse. **Computers:** 100% of classrooms, 100% of dorms, 100% of libraries, 100% of common outdoor areas have wireless network access. Students can register for classes online. Administrative functions (other than registration) can be performed online.

CAMPUS LIFE
Environment: Village. **Activities:** Choral groups, dance, drama/theater, literary magazine, marching band, music ensembles, musical theater, radio station, student government, student newspaper, student-run film society, television station, yearbook 34 registered organizations, 9 honor societies, 4 religious organizations. **Athletics (Intercollegiate):** *Women:* basketball, field hockey, soccer, softball, swimming, tennis, volleyball. **On-Campus Highlights:** Coffee House (The Nut House), SMA (VWIL) Museum, The Library, Spencer Center for Civic & Global Engage, Computer Center Labs. tray less dining hall enhancing native landscaping

ADMISSIONS
Freshman Academic Profile: Average high school GPA 3.3. 19% in top 10% of high school class, 53% in top 25% of high school class, 84% in top 50% of high school class. 75% from public high schools. SAT Math middle 50% range 400-510. SAT Critical Reading middle 50% range 420-550. SAT Writing middle 50% range 410-530. ACT middle 50% range 19-26. Minimum paper TOEFL 500. **Basis for Candidate Selection:** *Very important factors considered*

include: rigor of secondary school record, standardized test scores. *Important factors considered include:* character/personal qualities, extracurricular activities, interview. *Other factors considered include:* Class rank, application essay, recommendation(s), alumni/ae relation, talent/ability, volunteer work, work experience. **Freshman Admission Requirements:** High school diploma is required and GED is accepted. *Academic units required:* 4 English, 3 mathematics, 2 science, (1 science labs), 2 foreign language, 3 social studies. *Academic units recommended:* 4 English, 3 mathematics, 2 science, (1 science labs), 2 foreign language, 3 social studies. **Freshman Admission Statistics:** 4,909 applied, 54% admitted, 9% enrolled. **Transfer Admission Requirements:** High school transcript, college transcript(s), statement of good standing from prior institution(s). Minimum college GPA of 2.0 required. Lowest grade transferable C–. **General Admission Information:** Application Fee $35. Early decision application deadline 11/8. Notification on a rolling basis, beginning on or about 9/8. Nonfall registration accepted. Admission may be deferred for a maximum of 1 semester. Credit offered for CEEB Advanced Placement tests.

COSTS AND FINANCIAL AID
Annual tuition $27,670. Room and board $8,180. Required fees $350. Average book expense $900. **Required Forms and Deadlines:** FAFSA, state aid form. **Notification of Awards:** Applicants will be notified of awards on a rolling basis beginning 1/1. **Types of Aid:** *Need-based scholarships/grants:* Federal Pell, SEOG, state scholarships/grants, private scholarships, the school's own gift aid. *Loans:* Subsidized Stafford, Unsubsidized Stafford, PLUS, Federal Perkins, Private alternative loans. **Student Employment:** Federal Work-Study Program available. Institutional employment available. Highest amount earned per year from on-campus jobs $1,356. Off-campus job opportunities are excellent. **Financial Aid Statistics:** 100% freshmen, 99% undergrads receive need-based scholarship or grant aid. 5% freshmen, 7% undergrads receive non-need-based scholarship or grant aid. 87% freshmen, 88% undergrads receive need-based self-help aid. 90% freshmen, 95% undergrads receive any aid. 90% undergrads borrow to pay for school. Average cumulative indebtedness $27,642. **Criteria for awarding institutional aid:** *Non-need-based:* academics, leadership, state/district residency.

MARYGROVE COLLEGE

8425 West McNichols R, Detroit, MI 48221-2599
Phone: 313-927-1240
E-mail: info@marygrove.edu • **CEEB Code:** 1452
Fax: 313-927-1345 • **Website:** www.marygrove.edu • **ACT Code:** 2024

This private school, affiliated with the Roman Catholic Church, was founded in 1927. It has a 50-acre campus.

RATINGS
Admissions Selectivity Rating: 80   **Fire Safety Rating:** 60*   **Green Rating:** 60*

STUDENTS AND FACULTY
Enrollment: 662. **Student Body:** 79% female, 21% male, 2% out-of-state, 1% international. Asian 0%, African American 70%, Caucasian 5%, Hispanic 2%, Native American 0%.
Retention and Graduation: 61% freshmen return for sophomore year. 30% grads go on to further study within 1 year. 30% grads pursue arts and sciences degrees. **Faculty:** Student/faculty ratio 16:1. 65 full-time faculty, 66% hold PhDs, 25% are members of minority groups, 65% are women. 0% of classes are taught by teaching assistants.

ACADEMICS
Degrees: associate, bachelor's, certificate, master's, post-bachelor's certificate. **Classes:** Most classes have fewer than 10 students. **Majors with Highest Enrollment:** computer and information science; social work. **Special Study Options:** cooperative education program, distance learning, double major, honors program, independent study, student-designed major, study abroad, teacher certification program. **Honors Programs:** Honors program. **Disability Services:** Special programs offered to physically disabled students include tutors. **Career Services:** Alumni network, alumni services, career/job search classes, career assessment, internships, regional alumni.

FACILITIES
Housing: Coed dorms. 95% of campus accessible to physically disabled. **Special Academic Facilities/Equipment:** conference center, chapel, theatre, art gallery **Computers:** Students can register for classes online. Administrative functions (other than registration) can be performed online.

CAMPUS LIFE
Environment: Metropolis. **Activities:** Choral groups, dance, music ensembles, student government 17 registered organizations, 6 honor societies. **On-Campus Highlights:** Theater, Chapel, Conference Center, Art Gallery.

ADMISSIONS

Freshman Academic Profile: Average high school GPA 2.9. 10% in top 10% of high school class, 75% in top 25% of high school class, 100% in top 50% of high school class. 80% from public high schools. ACT middle 50% range 16-21. Minimum paper TOEFL 520. **Basis for Candidate Selection:** *Important factors considered include:* rigor of secondary school record, standardized test scores, character/personal qualities, interview, talent/ability. *Other factors considered include:* recommendation(s), extracurricular activities, volunteer work, work experience. **Freshman Admission Requirements:** High school diploma is required and GED is accepted. **Freshman Admission Statistics:** 290 applied, 40% admitted, 36% enrolled. **Transfer Admission Requirements:** college transcript(s), statement of good standing from prior institution(s). Minimum college GPA of 2.7 required. Lowest grade transferable C. **General Admission Information:** Application Fee $25. Regular application deadline 8/15. Regular notification 8/15. Nonfall registration accepted. Admission may be deferred for a maximum of 12 Months. Credit and/or placement offered for CEEB Advanced Placement tests.

COSTS AND FINANCIAL AID

Annual tuition $12,190. Room and board $6,000. Required fees $250. Average book expense $1,180. **Required Forms and Deadlines:** FAFSA, institution's own financial aid form. **Notification of Awards:** Applicants will be notified of awards on a rolling basis beginning 5/1. **Types of Aid:** *Need-based scholarships/grants:* Federal Pell, SEOG, state scholarships/grants, private scholarships, the school's own gift aid. *Loans:* Direct Subsidized Stafford, Direct Unsubsidized Stafford, Direct PLUS, Subsidized Stafford, Unsubsidized Stafford, PLUS, Federal Perkins, state loans. **Student Employment:** Federal Work-Study Program available. Highest amount earned per year from on-campus jobs $2,700. Off-campus job opportunities are good. **Criteria for awarding institutional aid:** *Non-need-based:* academics, art, leadership, music/drama.

MARYLAND INSTITUTE COLLEGE OF ART

1300 Mount Royal Avenue, Baltimore, MD 21217
Phone: 410-225-2222 • **Financial Aid Phone:** 410-225-2285
E-mail: admissions@mica.edu • **CEEB Code:** 5399
Fax: 410-225-2337 • **Website:** www.mica.edu • **ACT Code:** 1710

This private school was founded in 1826. It has a 12-acre campus.

RATINGS

Admissions Selectivity Rating: 91   **Fire Safety Rating:** 90   **Green Rating:** 61

STUDENTS AND FACULTY

Enrollment: 1,821. **Student Body:** 71% female, 29% male, 77% out-of-state, 8% international (54 countries represented). Asian 12%, African American 5%, Caucasian 55%, Hispanic 4%, Native American 0%.
Retention and Graduation: 85% freshmen return for sophomore year. 63% freshmen graduate within 4 years. 70% freshmen graduate within 6 years. 23% grads go on to further study within 1 year. **Faculty:** Student/faculty ratio 9:1. 147 full-time faculty, 79% hold PhDs, 12% are members of minority groups, 52% are women. 0% of classes are taught by teaching assistants.

ACADEMICS

Degrees: bachelor's, master's, post-bachelor's certificate. **Classes:** Most classes have 10–19 students. **Majors with Highest Enrollment:** graphic design; intermedia/multimedia; painting. **Special Study Options:** Accelerated program, cross-registration, distance learning, double major, dual enrollment, exchange student program (domestic), independent study, internships, student-designed major, study abroad, teacher certification program, Cooperative exchange programs with Johns Hopkins University, Goucher College, The Peabody Conservatory of Music, University of Baltimore, Loyola College, Notre Dame College, University of Maryland Baltimore County, Morgan State University, and Towson University; 5-year BFA/MAT program is available. **Combined Degree Programs:** BA/MA, BFA/MAT. **Disability Services:** Special programs offered to physically disabled students include note-taking services, tape recorders, tutors. **Career Services:** Alumni network, alumni services, career/job search classes, career assessment, internships, regional alumni.

FACILITIES

Housing: Coed dorms, special housing for disabled students, special housing for international students, apartments for single students. 85% of campus accessible to physically disabled. **Special Academic Facilities/Equipment:** There are seven art galleries open to the public year-round featuring work by MICA faculty, students, and nationally/internationally known artists; a nature library; and an extensive slide library containing over 220,000 slides. **Computers:** 100% of libraries, 100% of dining areas, 80% of common outdoor areas have wireless

network access. Students can register for classes online. Administrative functions (other than registration) can be performed online.

CAMPUS LIFE

Environment: Metropolis. **Activities:** Choral groups, dance, drama/theater, literary magazine, radio station, student government, student-run film society, International Student Organization 50 registered organizations, 3 religious organizations. **On-Campus Highlights:** The Gateway, our new dormitory, The Brown Center, our Digital Arts cente, The Meyerhoff House dormitory & dining, Various on-campus galleries/exhibitiions, Cafe Doris and Java Corner, two eateries. **Environmental Initiatives:** Single-Stream recycling of recyclable waste. Using an independent auditor to track the College's energy for an energy-use audit. MICA does not use chemical drain cleaners and openers to unclog plumbing because these products are highly acidic and detrimental to the environment, persons handling the products, as well as the plumbing.

ADMISSIONS

Freshman Academic Profile: 66% from public high schools. SAT Math middle 50% range 510-620. SAT Critical Reading middle 50% range 540-680. SAT Writing middle 50% range 530-660. Minimum web-based TOEFL 80. Minimum paper TOEFL 550. **Basis for Candidate Selection:** *Very important factors considered include:* academic GPA, rigor of secondary school record, level of applicant's interest, talent/ability. *Important factors considered include:* Class rank, application essay, standardized test scores, extracurricular activities, interview. *Other factors considered include:* recommendation(s), alumni/ae relation, character/personal qualities, racial/ethnic status, volunteer work. **Freshman Admission Requirements:** High school diploma is required and GED is accepted. *Academic units required:* 4 English, 2 mathematics, 2 science, (1 science labs), 4 social studies, 3 history, 6 academic electives, 2 Studio Art 2, 4 studio art recommended, 1 Art History recommended. *Academic units recommended:* 4 English, 2 mathematics, 2 science, (1 science labs), 4 social studies, 3 history, 6 academic electives, 2 Studio Art 2, 4 studio art recommended, 1 Art History recommended **Freshman Admission Statistics:** 3,132 applied, 52% admitted, 26% enrolled. **Transfer Admission Requirements:** High school transcript, college transcript(s), essay or personal statement, minimum college GPA of 2.8 required. Lowest grade transferable C. **General Admission Information:** Application Fee $60. Early decision application deadline 11/14. Regular application deadline 2/13. Regular notification 3/13. Nonfall registration accepted. Admission may be deferred for a maximum of 1 year. Credit and/or placement offered for CEEB Advanced Placement tests.

COSTS AND FINANCIAL AID

Annual tuition $37,900. Room and board $10,880. Required fees $1,440. Average book expense $1,450. **Required Forms and Deadlines:** FAFSA, institution's own financial aid form. **Notification of Awards:** Applicants will be notified of awards on or about 4/10. **Types of Aid:** *Need-based scholarships/grants:* Federal Pell, SEOG, state scholarships/grants, private scholarships, the school's own gift aid. *Loans:* Subsidized Stafford, Unsubsidized Stafford, PLUS, Federal Perkins. **Student Employment:** Federal Work-Study Program available. Institutional employment available. Off-campus job opportunities are excellent. **Financial Aid Statistics: Criteria for awarding institutional aid:** *Non-need-based:* academics, art.

MARYLHURST UNIVERSITY

PO Box 261, Marylhurst, OR 97036
Phone: 503-699-6268 • **Financial Aid Phone:** 503-699-6253
E-mail: admissions@marylhurst.edu • **CEEB Code:** 440
Fax: 503-636-9526 • **Website:** www.marylhurst.edu • **ACT Code:** 3470

This private school, affiliated with the Roman Catholic Church, was founded in 1893. It has a 68-acre campus.

RATINGS

Admissions Selectivity Rating: 60*   **Fire Safety Rating:** 60*   **Green Rating:** 60*

STUDENTS AND FACULTY

Enrollment: 775. **Student Body:** 72% female, 28% male, % out-of-state, 2% international. Asian 1%, African American 1%, Caucasian 24%, Hispanic 1%, Native American 0%.
Retention and Graduation: Faculty: Student/faculty ratio 7:1. 0% of classes are taught by teaching assistants.

ACADEMICS

Degrees: bachelor's, certificate, first professional, master's, post-bachelor's certificate, post-master's certificate. **Classes:** Most classes have fewer than 10 students. **Majors with Highest Enrollment:** business administration and management; interior design; multi-/interdisciplinary studies, other. **Special**

Study Options: Accelerated program, cooperative education program, cross-registration, distance learning, double major, English as a Second Language (ESL), independent study, internships, student-designed major, study abroad, teacher certification program, weekend college. **Disability Services:** Special programs offered to physically disabled students include note-taking services, reader services, tape recorders, tutors.

FACILITIES

Housing: 90% of campus accessible to physically disabled. **Special Academic Facilities/Equipment:** Art Gym Art Gallery Streff Gallery **Computers:** Students can register for classes online. Administrative functions (other than registration) can be performed online.

CAMPUS LIFE

Environment: City. **Activities:** Choral groups, jazz band, literary magazine, music ensembles, symphony orchestra 6 registered organizations, 1 honor societies.

ADMISSIONS

Freshman Academic Profile: Minimum web-based TOEFL 79. Minimum paper TOEFL 550. **Basis for Candidate Selection:** *Other factors considered include:* academic GPA, recommendation(s), interview. **Freshman Admission Requirements:** High school diploma is required and GED is accepted. **Transfer Admission Requirements:** High school transcript, college transcript(s), minimum college GPA of 2.0 required. Lowest grade transferable C–. **General Admission Information:** Application Fee $20. Nonfall registration accepted. Admission may be deferred for a maximum of 1 yr. Credit and/or placement offered for CEEB Advanced Placement tests.

COSTS AND FINANCIAL AID

Annual tuition $15,120. Required fees $450. **Required Forms and Deadlines:** FAFSA, institution's own financial aid form. **Notification of Awards:** Applicants will be notified of awards on a rolling basis beginning 4/15. **Types of Aid:** *Need-based scholarships/grants:* Federal Pell, SEOG, state scholarships/grants, private scholarships, the school's own gift aid. *Loans:* Subsidized Stafford, Unsubsidized Stafford, PLUS, Federal Perkins. **Student Employment: Financial Aid Statistics:** 91% freshmen, 84% undergrads receive need-based scholarship or grant aid. 9% freshmen, 2% undergrads receive non-need-based scholarship or grant aid. 73% freshmen, 87% undergrads receive need-based self-help aid. 67% undergrads borrow to pay for school. Average cumulative indebtedness $9,055. **Criteria for awarding institutional aid:** *Non-need-based:* academics.

MARYMOUNT COLLEGE

Marymount College, 30800 Palos Verdes Drive East, CA 90275-6299
Phone: 310-377-5501 • **Financial Aid Phone:** 310-303-7282
E-mail: admissions@marymountpv.edu • **CEEB Code:** 4515
Fax: 310-265-0962 • **Website:** www.marymountpv.edu/ • **ACT Code:** 316

This private school, affiliated with the Roman Catholic Church, was founded in 1932. It has a 22-acre campus.

RATINGS

Admissions Selectivity Rating: 75   **Fire Safety Rating:** 80   **Green Rating:** 67

STUDENTS AND FACULTY

Enrollment: 1,001. **Student Body:** 54% female, 46% male, 7% out-of-state, 8% international (27 countries represented). Asian 4%, African American 9%, Caucasian 32%, Hispanic 28%, Native American 0%.
Retention and Graduation: 69% freshmen return for sophomore year. 90% grads go on to further study within 1 year. **Faculty:** Student/faculty ratio 17:1. 35 full-time faculty, 74% hold PhDs, 14% are members of minority groups, 49% are women. 0% of classes are taught by teaching assistants.

ACADEMICS

Degrees: associate, bachelor's. **Classes:** Most classes have 10–19 students. **Special Study Options:** dual enrollment, English as a Second Language (ESL), honors program, internships, study abroad, weekend college. **Honors Programs:** Marymount Honors Program Phi Theta Kappa. **Disability Services:** Special programs offered to physically disabled students include note-taking services, reader services, tape recorders, tutors.

FACILITIES

Housing: Coed dorms, special housing for disabled students 100% of campus accessible to physically disabled. **Computers:** 100% of classrooms, 100% of dorms, 100% of libraries, 100% of dining areas, 100% of student union, 75% of common outdoor areas have wireless network access. Administrative functions (other than registration) can be performed online.

CAMPUS LIFE

Environment: Town. **Activities:** Choral groups, dance, drama/theater, jazz band, literary magazine, musical theater, radio station, student government, student newspaper, student-run film society, Campus Ministries, International Student Organization 2 honor societies, 2 religious organizations. **Athletics (Intercollegiate):** *Men:* soccer. *Women:* soccer.

ADMISSIONS

Freshman Academic Profile: Average high school GPA 2.9. SAT Math middle 50% range 400-520. SAT Critical Reading middle 50% range 400-500. SAT Writing middle 50% range 410-500. ACT middle 50% range 17-22. **Basis for Candidate Selection:** *Very important factors considered include:* academic GPA, rigor of secondary school record. *Other factors considered include:* Class rank, application essay, recommendation(s), standardized test scores, alumni/ae relation, character/personal qualities, extracurricular activities, interview, level of applicant's interest, talent/ability, volunteer work. **Freshman Admission Requirements:** High school diploma is required and GED is accepted. **Freshman Admission Statistics:** 2,476 applied, 58% admitted, 29% enrolled. **Transfer Admission Requirements:** High school transcript, college transcript(s), Lowest grade transferable C–. **General Admission Information:** Application Fee $40. Notification on a rolling basis, beginning on or about 12/1. Nonfall registration accepted. Admission may be deferred for a maximum of 1 year. Credit and/or placement offered for CEEB Advanced Placement tests.

COSTS AND FINANCIAL AID

Annual tuition $28,220. Room and board $12,260. Required fees $600. Average book expense $1,664. **Required Forms and Deadlines:** FAFSA. **Notification of Awards:** Applicants will be notified of awards on or about 3/1. **Types of Aid:** *Need-based scholarships/grants:* Federal Pell, SEOG, state scholarships/grants, private scholarships, the school's own gift aid. *Loans:* Subsidized Stafford, Unsubsidized Stafford, PLUS. **Student Employment:** Federal Work-Study Program available. Institutional employment available. Highest amount earned per year from on campus jobs $3,840. Off-campus job opportunities are good. **Financial Aid Statistics:** 100% freshmen, 100% undergrads receive need-based scholarship or grant aid. 88% freshmen, 88% undergrads receive non-need-based scholarship or grant aid. 5% undergrads receive athletic scholarships. 84% freshmen, 74% undergrads receive any aid. 68% undergrads borrow to pay for school. Average cumulative indebtedness $3,663. **Criteria for awarding institutional aid:** *Non-need-based:* academics, art, athletics, leadership.

MARYMOUNT MANHATTAN COLLEGE

221 East 71 Street, New York, NY 10021
Phone: 212-517-0430 • **Financial Aid Phone:** 212-517-0500
E-mail: admissions@mmm.edu • **CEEB Code:** 2405
Fax: 212-517-0448 • **Website:** www.mmm.edu • **ACT Code:** 2810

This private school was founded in 1936. It has a 1-acre campus.

RATINGS

Admissions Selectivity Rating: 71   **Fire Safety Rating:** 87   **Green Rating:** 78

STUDENTS AND FACULTY

Enrollment: 2,030. **Student Body:** 76% female, 24% male, 45% out-of-state, 3% international (36 countries represented). Asian 4%, African American 13%, Caucasian 67%, Hispanic 14%, Native American 0%.
Retention and Graduation: 62% freshmen return for sophomore year. 39% freshmen graduate within 4 years. 49% freshmen graduate within 6 years. 33% grads go on to further study within 1 year. 9% grads pursue arts and sciences degrees. 7% grads pursue law degrees. 12% grads pursue business degrees. 5% grads pursue medical degrees. **Faculty:** Student/faculty ratio 11:1. 101 full-time faculty, 82% hold PhDs, 14% are members of minority groups, 60% are women.

ACADEMICS

Degrees: associate, bachelor's, certificate. **Classes:** Most classes have 10–19 students. **Majors with Highest Enrollment:** communication and media studies, other; dance; drama and dramatics/theatre arts. **Special Study Options:** Accelerated program, distance learning, double major, dual enrollment, exchange student program (domestic), independent study, internships, liberal arts/career combination, study abroad, teacher certification program. **Disability Services:** Special programs offered to physically disabled students include note-taking services, reader services, tape recorders, tutors. **Career Services:** Alumni network, alumni services, career assessment, internships.

FACILITIES

Housing: Coed dorms. 100% of campus accessible to physically disabled. **Special Academic Facilities/Equipment:** Gallery, communications and learning center, theatre, media center, college skills center, mathematics lab, Samuel Freeman science center, Comm Arts multimedia suite. **Computers:**

40% of classrooms, 100% of libraries, have wireless network access. Students can register for classes online. Administrative functions (other than registration) can be performed online.

CAMPUS LIFE

Environment: Metropolis. **Activities:** Choral groups, dance, drama/theater, literary magazine, musical theater, radio station, student government, student newspaper, yearbook, International Student Organization 30 registered organizations, 7 honor societies, 2 religious organizations. **On-Campus Highlights:** Theresa Lang Theatre, Hewitt Gallery of Art, Science Laboratories, 55th Street Residence Hall, Shanahan Library, Student cafeterias. **Environmental Initiatives:** purchase of renewable energy recycling of paper and bottles awareness campaigns to get students and faculty and staff moving in a green direction

ADMISSIONS

Freshman Academic Profile: Average high school GPA 3.2. 70% from public high schools. SAT Math middle 50% range 470-570. SAT Critical Reading middle 50% range 490-600. SAT Writing middle 50% range 490-603. ACT middle 50% range 21-96. Minimum web-based TOEFL 80. Minimum paper TOEFL 550. **Basis for Candidate Selection:** *Very important factors considered include:* academic GPA, rigor of secondary school record, standardized test scores. *Important factors considered include:* application essay, recommendation(s), character/personal qualities, extracurricular activities, talent/ability. *Other factors considered include:* Class rank, interview, volunteer work, work experience. **Freshman Admission Requirements:** High school diploma is required and GED is accepted. *Academic units required:* 4 English, 3 mathematics, 3 science, 3 social studies, 4 academic electives. *Academic units recommended:* 4 English, 3 mathematics, 3 science, 3 social studies, 4 academic electives. **Freshman Admission Statistics:** 3,556 applied, 81% admitted, 17% enrolled. **Transfer Admission Requirements:** High school transcript, college transcript(s), essay or personal statement, statement of good standing from prior institution(s). Minimum college GPA of 2.5 required. Lowest grade transferable C–. **General Admission Information:** Application Fee $60. Notification on a rolling basis, beginning on or about 9/1. Nonfall registration accepted. Admission may be deferred for a maximum of 1 Semester. Credit and/or placement offered for CEEB Advanced Placement tests.

COSTS AND FINANCIAL AID

Annual tuition $22,420. Room and board $13,426. Required fees $1,116. Average book expense $1,000. **Required Forms and Deadlines:** FAFSA. **Notification of Awards:** Applicants will be notified of awards on a rolling basis beginning 3/15. **Types of Aid:** *Need-based scholarships/grants:* Federal Pell, SEOG, state scholarships/grants, private scholarships, the school's own gift aid. *Loans:* Subsidized Stafford, Unsubsidized Stafford, PLUS. **Student Employment:** Federal Work-Study Program available. Institutional employment available. Highest amount earned per year from on-campus jobs $2,000. Off-campus job opportunities are excellent. **Financial Aid Statistics:** 98% freshmen, 99% undergrads receive need-based scholarship or grant aid. 3% freshmen, 4% undergrads receive non-need-based scholarship or grant aid. 95% freshmen, 96% undergrads receive need-based self-help aid. 79% freshmen, 65% undergrads receive any aid. 82% undergrads borrow to pay for school. Average cumulative indebtedness $16,201.

MARYMOUNT UNIVERSITY

2807 North Glebe Road, Arlington, VA 22207
Phone: 703-284-1500 • **Financial Aid Phone:** 703-284-1530
E-mail: admissions@marymount.edu • **CEEB Code:** 5405
Fax: 703-522-0349 • **Website:** www.marymount.edu • **ACT Code:** 4378

This private school, affiliated with the Roman Catholic Church, was founded in 1950. It has a 21-acre campus.

RATINGS

Admissions Selectivity Rating: 69   Fire Safety Rating: 80   Green Rating: 60*

STUDENTS AND FACULTY

Enrollment: 2,199. **Student Body:** 75% female, 25% male, 42% out-of-state, 6% international (70 countries represented). Asian 8%, African American 15%, Caucasian 46%, Hispanic 12%, Native American 1%.
Retention and Graduation: 71% freshmen return for sophomore year.
Faculty: Student/faculty ratio 14:1. 138 full-time faculty, 89% hold PhDs, 5% are members of minority groups, 74% are women. 0% of classes are taught by teaching assistants.

ACADEMICS

Degrees: bachelor's, certificate, master's, post-bachelor's certificate, post-master's certificate. **Classes:** Most classes have 10–19 students. **Majors with Highest Enrollment:** business administration and management; interior design; nursing/registered nurse (rn, asn, bsn, msn). **Special Study Options:** Ac-

celerated program, cross-registration, distance learning, double major, English as a Second Language (ESL), honors program, independent study, internships, student-designed major, study abroad, teacher certification program. **Honors Programs:** The Honors Program at Marymount University **Combined Degree Programs:** BBA/MBA, Health Promotion Mgt. BS/MS. **Disability Services:** Special programs offered to physically disabled students include note-taking services, reader services, tape recorders, tutors. **Career Services:** Alumni network, career/job search classes, internships.

FACILITIES

Housing: Coed dorms, men's dorms, women's dorms. 75% of campus accessible to physically disabled. **Special Academic Facilities/Equipment:** Art gallery, learning resource center, audiovisual center, studio, and computer labs **Computers:** Students can register for classes online. Administrative functions (other than registration) can be performed online.

CAMPUS LIFE

Environment: City. **Activities:** Choral groups, dance, drama/theater, literary magazine, student government, student newspaper, yearbook, Campus Ministries, International Student Organization 33 registered organizations, 11 honor societies, 2 religious organizations. **Athletics (Intercollegiate):** *Men:* basketball, cross-country, golf, lacrosse, soccer, swimming. *Women:* basketball, cross-country, lacrosse, soccer, swimming, volleyball. **On-Campus Highlights:** Student Center, Gym, Bernie's Cafe, Turf field, Ballston campus. **Environmental Initiatives:** Recycling program Public transportation available Car pool incentives

ADMISSIONS

Freshman Academic Profile: Average high school GPA 3.1. 15% in top 10% of high school class, 41% in top 25% of high school class, 81% in top 50% of high school class. 68% from public high schools. SAT Math middle 50% range 450-550. SAT Critical Reading middle 50% range 450-560. SAT Writing middle 50% range 450-550. ACT middle 50% range 18-24. Minimum web-based TOEFL 79. Minimum paper TOEFL 550. **Basis for Candidate Selection:** *Very important factors considered include:* academic GPA, rigor of secondary school record, standardized test scores. *Important factors considered include:* Class rank, recommendation(s), interview, talent/ability. *Other factors considered include:* application essay, alumni/ae relation, character/personal qualities, extracurricular activities, first generation, level of applicant's interest, volunteer work, work experience. **Freshman Admission Requirements:** High school diploma is required and GED is accepted. **Freshman Admission Statistics:** 1,904 applied, 81% admitted, 26% enrolled. **Transfer Admission Requirements:** college transcript(s), statement of good standing from prior institution(s). Minimum college GPA of 2.0 required. Lowest grade transferable C. **General Admission Information:** Application Fee $40. Nonfall registration accepted. Admission may be deferred for a maximum of 1 year. Credit offered for CEEB Advanced Placement tests.

COSTS AND FINANCIAL AID

Annual tuition $23,700. Room and board $8,705. Required fees $220. Average book expense $800. **Required Forms and Deadlines:** FAFSA. **Notification of Awards:** Applicants will be notified of awards on a rolling basis beginning 3/15. **Types of Aid:** *Need-based scholarships/grants:* Federal Pell, SEOG, state scholarships/grants, private scholarships, the school's own gift aid. *Loans:* Direct Subsidized Stafford, Direct Unsubsidized Stafford, Subsidized Stafford, Unsubsidized Stafford, PLUS, Federal Perkins. **Student Employment:** Federal Work-Study Program available. Institutional employment available. Off-campus job opportunities are good. **Financial Aid Statistics:** 83% freshmen, 74% undergrads receive need-based scholarship or grant aid. 80% freshmen, 73% undergrads receive non-need-based scholarship or grant aid. 78% freshmen, 83% undergrads receive need-based self-help aid. 92% freshmen, 84% undergrads receive any aid. 70% undergrads borrow to pay for school. Average cumulative indebtedness $20,686. **Criteria for awarding institutional aid:** *Non-need-based:* academics, alumni affiliation, leadership, state/district residency.

See page 1142.

MARYVILLE COLLEGE

502 East Lamar Alexander Parkway, Maryville, TN 37804-5907
Phone: 865-981-8092 • **Financial Aid Phone:** 865-981-8100
E-mail: admissions@maryvillecollege.edu • **CEEB Code:** 1454
Fax: 865-981-8005 • **Website:** www.maryvillecollege.edu • **ACT Code:** 3988

This private school, affiliated with the Presbyterian Church, was founded in 1819. It has a 370-acre campus.

RATINGS

Admissions Selectivity Rating: 74   Fire Safety Rating: 87   Green Rating: 71

STUDENTS AND FACULTY

Enrollment: 1,114. **Student Body:** 55% female, 45% male, 24% out-of-state, 4% international (20 countries represented). Asian 1%, African American 5%, Caucasian 86%, Hispanic 2%, Native American 0%.
Retention and Graduation: 67% freshmen return for sophomore year. 43% freshmen graduate within 4 years. 51% freshmen graduate within 6 years. 28% grads go on to further study within 1 year. **Faculty:** Student/faculty ratio 12:1. 79 full-time faculty, 76% hold PhDs, 4% are members of minority groups, 54% are women. 0% of classes are taught by teaching assistants.

ACADEMICS

Degrees: bachelor's. **Classes:** Most classes have 10–19 students. Most lab/discussion sessions have 10–19 students. **Majors with Highest Enrollment:** biology/biological sciences; business/commerce; education. **Special Study Options:** double major, English as a Second Language (ESL), honors program, independent study, internships, liberal arts/career combination, student-designed major, study abroad, teacher certification program. **Honors Programs:** Presidential and Deans scholars participate in honors courses and honors tutorial practicum. Most courses may be taken with "honors" status. **Combined Degree Programs:** BA/MSN. **Disability Services:** Special programs offered to physically disabled students include note-taking services, reader services, tape recorders, tutors. **Career Services:** Alumni network, alumni services, career/job search classes, career assessment, internships, regional alumni. Career Services highlights include Internships and practica are available in almost all major fields.

FACILITIES

Housing: Coed dorms, special housing for disabled students, men's dorms, women's dorms, apartments for single students, Special Interest groups. 90% of campus accessible to physically disabled. **Special Academic Facilities/Equipment:** Art gallery, theatre, greenhouse, College Woods **Computers:** 100% of classrooms, 100% of dorms, 100% of libraries, 100% of dining areas, 100% of student union, 50% of common outdoor areas have wireless network access. Students can register for classes online. Administrative functions (other than registration) can be performed online.

CAMPUS LIFE

Environment: Town. **Activities:** Choral groups, concert band, dance, drama/theater, jazz band, literary magazine, music ensembles, musical theater, student government, student newspaper, symphony orchestra, yearbook, Campus Ministries 63 registered organizations, 15 honor societies, 5 religious organizations. **Athletics (Intercollegiate):** *Men:* baseball, basketball, cross-country, equestrian sports, football, soccer, tennis. *Women:* basketball, cross country, equestrian sports, soccer, softball, tennis, volleyball. **On-Campus Highlights:** Isaacs Student Center, Mountain Challenge, Lloyd Beach, New Lloyd Residence Hall, Center for Calling and Career, Mountain Challenge includes a 60' Alpine Tower, rock climbing wall, ropes course, and kayak roll sessions on campus. In addition there are trips offered every Saturday to nearby attractions, i.e. rock climbing, white water rafting, camping, and caving. **Environmental Initiatives:** Steam plant boiler is fueled by recycled wood products Campus-wide recycling program Purchase of green power for selected campus buildings

ADMISSIONS

Freshman Academic Profile: Average high school GPA 3.6. 34% in top 10% of high school class, 65% in top 25% of high school class, 89% in top 50% of high school class. 91% from public high schools. SAT Math middle 50% range 480-610. SAT Critical Reading middle 50% range 470-630. SAT Writing middle 50% range 450-610. ACT middle 50% range 21-28. Minimum paper TOEFL 525. **Basis for Candidate Selection:** *Very important factors considered include:* Class rank, rigor of secondary school record, standardized test scores. *Important factors considered include:* academic GPA, recommendation(s), extracurricular activities, interview. *Other factors considered include:* application essay, alumni/ae relation, character/personal qualities, first generation, level of applicant's interest, talent/ability, volunteer work. **Freshman Admission Requirements:** High school diploma is required and GED is accepted. *Academic units required:* 4 English, 3 mathematics, 2 science, (1 science labs), 2 foreign language, 2 social studies, 1 academic electives. *Academic units recommended:* 4 English, 3 mathematics, 2 science, (1 science labs), 2 foreign language, 2 social studies, 1 academic electives. **Freshman Admission Statistics:** 1,621 applied, 75% admitted, 24% enrolled. **Transfer Admission Requirements:** college transcript(s), statement of good standing from prior institution(s). Minimum college GPA of 2.0 required. Lowest grade transferable C. **General Admission Information:** Early decision application deadline 11/15. Notification on a rolling basis, beginning on or about 12/1. Nonfall registration accepted. Admission may be deferred for a maximum of 1 year. Credit and/or placement offered for CEEB Advanced Placement tests.

COSTS AND FINANCIAL AID

Annual tuition $26,272. Room and board $8,240. Required fees $675. Average book expense $880. **Required Forms and Deadlines:** FAFSA. **Types of Aid:** *Need-based scholarships/grants:* Federal Pell, SEOG, state scholarships/grants, private scholarships, the school's own gift aid. *Loans:* Direct Subsidized Stafford, Direct Unsubsidized Stafford, Direct PLUS, Subsidized Stafford, Unsubsidized Stafford, PLUS, Federal Perkins, state loans, college/university loans from institutional funds. **Student Employment:** Federal Work-Study Program available. Highest amount earned per year from on-campus jobs $2,617. Off-campus job opportunities are good. **Financial Aid Statistics:** 75% freshmen, 98% undergrads receive need-based scholarship or grant aid. 31% freshmen, 25% undergrads receive non-need-based scholarship or grant aid. 78% freshmen, 61% undergrads receive need-based self-help aid. 100% freshmen, 98% undergrads receive any aid. 92% undergrads borrow to pay for school. Average cumulative indebtedness $13,929. **Criteria for awarding institutional aid:** *Non-need-based:* academics, art, leadership, minority status, music/drama, religious affiliation, state/district residency.

MARYVILLE UNIVERSITY OF SAINT LOUIS

650 Maryville University Drive, St. Louis, MO 63141-7299
Phone: 314-529-9350 • **Financial Aid Phone:** 314-529-9360
E-mail: admissions@maryville.edu • **CEEB Code:** 6399
Fax: 314-529-9927 • **ACT Code:** 2326

This private school was founded in 1872. It has a 130-acre campus.

RATINGS

Admissions Selectivity Rating: 78   **Fire Safety Rating:** 85   **Green Rating:** 60*

STUDENTS AND FACULTY

Enrollment: 2,911. **Student Body:** 73% female, 27% male, 17% out-of-state, 2% international (14 countries represented). Asian 1%, African American 9%, Caucasian 75%, Hispanic 2%, Native American 0%.
Retention and Graduation: 87% freshmen return for sophomore year. 53% freshmen graduate within 4 years. 70% freshmen graduate within 6 years.
Faculty: Student/faculty ratio 12:1. 114 full-time faculty, 84% hold PhDs, 15% are members of minority groups, 63% are women. 0% of classes are taught by teaching assistants.

ACADEMICS

Degrees: bachelor's, certificate, master's **Classes:** Most classes have 10–19 students. Most lab/discussion sessions have fewer than 10 students. **Majors with Highest Enrollment:** business/commerce; nursing/registered nurse (rn, asn, bsn, msn); physical therapy/therapist. **Special Study Options:** Accelerated program, cooperative education program, cross-registration, distance learning, double major, dual enrollment, honors program, independent study, internships, liberal arts/career combination, student-designed major, study abroad, teacher certification program, weekend college, Washington Center, Semester at Sea. **Honors Programs:** Bascom Honors Program **Combined Degree Programs:** MU-St. Louis Univ. M.S.W. Joint Degree Program. **Disability Services:** Special programs offered to physically disabled students include note-taking services, reader services, tape recorders, tutors. **Career Services:** career/job search classes, career assessment, internships Career Services highlights include Cooperative Education - over 80 students per year participate in a co-op experience.

FACILITIES

Housing: Coed dorms, apartments for single students, wellness housing, theme housing. 90% of campus accessible to physically disabled. **Special Academic Facilities/Equipment:** University Center, art galleries, auditorium, chapel, observatory, teaching lab, clinical labs, art and design labs, videoconferencing facility with downlinking and electronic multi-media capability for presentations. **Computers:** 100% of classrooms, 100% of dorms, 100% of libraries, 100% of dining areas, 100% of student union, 100% of common outdoor areas have wireless network access. Students can register for classes online. Administrative functions (other than registration) can be performed online.

CAMPUS LIFE

Environment: Metropolis. **Activities:** Choral groups, dance, drama/theater, jazz band, literary magazine, music ensembles, pep band, student government, student newspaper, symphony orchestra, Campus Ministries 40 registered organizations, 3 honor societies, 4 religious organizations. **Athletics (Intercollegiate):** *Men:* baseball, basketball, cheerleading, cross-country, golf, soccer, tennis. *Women:* basketball, cheerleading, cross-country, golf, soccer, softball, tennis, volleyball.

ADMISSIONS

Freshman Academic Profile: Average high school GPA 3.6. 26% in top 10% of high school class, 56% in top 25% of high school class, 86% in top 50% of high school class. 77% from public high schools. ACT middle 50% range 23-27. Minimum paper TOEFL 500. **Basis for Candidate Selection:** *Very important factors considered include:* academic GPA, standardized test scores.

Important factors considered include: rigor of secondary school record, extra-curricular activities. *Other factors considered include:* Class rank, application essay, recommendation(s), character/personal qualities, interview, talent/ability. **Freshman Admission Requirements:** High school diploma is required and GED is accepted. *Academic units required:* 4 English, 3 mathematics, 2 science, 2 social studies, 8 academic electives, 3. 4 English, 3 mathematics, 2 science, 2 social studies, 8 academic electives, 3 **Freshman Admission Statistics:** 1,281 applied, 71% admitted, 40% enrolled. **Transfer Admission Requirements:** college transcript(s), minimum college GPA of 2.0 required. Lowest grade transferable C–. **General Admission Information:** Application Fee $30. Regular application deadline 8/15. Nonfall registration accepted. Admission may be deferred for a maximum of 1 year. Credit offered for CEEB Advanced Placement tests.

COSTS AND FINANCIAL AID

Annual tuition $22,786. Room and board $9,242. Required fees $960. Average book expense $1,600. **Required Forms and Deadlines:** FAFSA. **Notification of Awards:** Applicants will be notified of awards on a rolling basis beginning 3/1. **Types of Aid:** *Need-based scholarships/grants:* Federal Pell, SEOG, state scholarships/grants, private scholarships, the school's own gift aid, TEACH Grant, Academic Competiveness Grant, Smart Grant. *Loans:* Direct Subsidized Stafford, Direct Unsubsidized Stafford, Direct PLUS, Federal Perkins, Five Month Installment Deferred Payment Program. **Student Employment:** Federal Work-Study Program available. **Financial Aid Statistics:** 94% undergrads receive need-based scholarship or grant aid. 13% freshmen, 10% undergrads receive non-need-based scholarship or grant aid. 78% freshmen, 83% undergrads receive need-based self-help aid. 3% freshmen, 3% undergrads receive athletic scholarships. 72% freshmen, 65% undergrads receive any aid. 76% undergrads borrow to pay for school. Average cumulative indebtedness $21,835. **Criteria for awarding institutional aid:** *Non-need-based:* academics, alumni affiliation, art, athletics, leadership, minority status.

MARYWOOD UNIVERSITY

Best 378

Office of University Admissions, Scranton, PA 18509
Phone: 570-348-6234 • **Financial Aid Phone:** 866-279-9663
E-mail: yourfuture@marywood.edu • **CEEB Code:** 2407
Fax: 570-961-4763 • **Website:** www.marywood.edu • **ACT Code:** 3626

This private school, affiliated with the Roman Catholic Church, was founded in 1915. It has a 115-acre campus.

RATINGS
Admissions Selectivity Rating: 75   **Fire Safety Rating:** 94   **Green Rating:** 84

STUDENTS AND FACULTY
Enrollment: 2,174. **Student Body:** 69% female, 31% male, 29% out-of-state, 0% international (20 countries represented). Asian 2%, African American 1%, Caucasian 82%, Hispanic 5%, Native American 0%. **Retention and Graduation:** 51% freshmen graduate within 4 years. 30% grads go on to further study within 1 year. 10% grads pursue arts and sciences degrees. 1% grads pursue law degrees. 2% grads pursue business degrees. 2% grads pursue medical degrees. **Faculty:** Student/faculty ratio 11:1. 157 full-time faculty, 84% hold PhDs, 13% are members of minority groups, 56% are women. 0% of classes are taught by teaching assistants.

ACADEMICS
Degrees: bachelor's, master's, post-bachelor's certificate, post-master's certificate. **Classes:** Most classes have 10–19 students. **Majors with Highest Enrollment:** elementary education and teaching; nursing/registered nurse (rn, asn, bsn, msn); psychology. **Special Study Options:** cross-registration, double major, dual enrollment, English as a Second Language (ESL), honors program, independent study, internships, student-designed major, study abroad, teacher certification program. **Honors Programs:** Open Door Honors program. **Disability Services:** Special programs offered to physically disabled students include note-taking services, reader services, tape recorders, tutors. **Career Services:** alumni services, career/job search classes, career assessment, internships, regional alumni.

FACILITIES
Housing: Coed dorms, special housing for disabled students, men's dorms, women's dorms, apartments for single students, 100% of campus accessible to physically disabled. **Special Academic Facilities/Equipment:** Mellow

Athletic and Fitness Center, Mahady Gallery, Suraci Gallery, The Maslow Study Gallery for Contemporary Art, Performing Arts Center, O'Neill Center for Healthy Families, Insalaco Studio Arts Center, Center for Architectural Studies, Marywood University Arboretum, Curriculum Lab, electronic learning labs, Broadcast Studios, instructional media lab, interactive video lab, computerized editing facility, center for natural and health sciences, psycho-physiology experimental lab, psychology/education research lab, science multi-media lab, language lab, center for justice and peace, on-campus preschool and day care, video tele-conferencing lab. **Computers:** 75% of classrooms, 75% of dorms, 100% of libraries, 100% of dining areas, 100% of student union, 75% of common outdoor areas have wireless network access. Students can register for classes online. Administrative functions (other than registration) can be performed online.

CAMPUS LIFE
Environment: City. **Activities:** Choral groups, concert band, dance, drama/theater, jazz band, literary magazine, music ensembles, musical theater, radio station, student government, student newspaper, television station, Campus Ministries, International Student Organization 43 registered organizations, 31 honor societies, 1 religious organizations. 1 sororities. **Athletics (Intercollegiate):** *Men:* baseball, basketball, cross-country, diving, lacrosse, soccer, swimming, tennis. *Women:* basketball, cross-country, diving, field hockey, lacrosse, soccer, softball, swimming, tennis, volleyball. **On-Campus Highlights:** Mellow Center for Athletics and Wellness, Insalaco Center for Studio Arts, Liberal Arts Center Rotunda, Cafe Ritazza/Main Dining Room, Nazareth Student Center. **Environmental Initiatives:** Use of geothermal technology using "mine Water", geothermal harvesting for chilled Beam cooling. Purchase of wind energy and installation of a windmill on campus. Construction of our LEED Gold certified Center for Architectural Studies and commitment to pursue LEED certification for all future new construction projects.

ADMISSIONS
Freshman Academic Profile: Average high school GPA 3.2. 17% in top 10% of high school class, 46% in top 25% of high school class, 84% in top 50% of high school class. 89% from public high schools. SAT Math middle 50% range 470-570. SAT Critical Reading middle 50% range 470-560. SAT Writing middle 50% range 460-560. ACT middle 50% range 20-26. Minimum web-based TOEFL 71. Minimum paper TOEFL 530. **Basis for Candidate Selection:** *Very important factors considered include:* Class rank, academic GPA, rigor of secondary school record, standardized test scores, character/personal qualities. *Important factors considered include:* application essay, recommendation(s), interview, talent/ability. *Other factors considered include:* extracurricular activities, level of applicant's interest, volunteer work. **Freshman Admission Requirements:** High school diploma is required and GED is accepted. *Academic units required:* 4 English, 2 mathematics, 1 science, (1 science labs), 3 social studies, 6 academic electives. 4 English, 2 mathematics, 1 science, (1 science labs), 3 social studies, 6 academic electives. **Freshman Admission Statistics:** 2,284 applied, 69% admitted, 29% enrolled. **Transfer Admission Requirements:** High school transcript, college transcript(s), minimum college GPA of 2.25 required. Lowest grade transferable C. **General Admission Information:** Application Fee $35. Notification on a rolling basis, beginning on or about 10/1. Nonfall registration accepted. Credit and/or placement offered for CEEB Advanced Placement tests.

COSTS AND FINANCIAL AID
Required Forms and Deadlines: FAFSA. **Notification of Awards:** Applicants will be notified of awards on a rolling basis beginning 2/15. **Types of Aid:** *Need-based scholarships/grants:* Federal Pell, SEOG, state scholarships/grants, private scholarships, the school's own gift aid, Federal Nursing Scholarships. *Loans:* Subsidized Stafford, Unsubsidized Stafford, PLUS, Federal Perkins, state loans, Private Alternative Loans. **Student Employment:** Federal Work-Study Program available. **Financial Aid Statistics:** 87% freshmen, 88% undergrads receive need-based scholarship or grant aid. 2% freshmen, 5% undergrads receive non-need-based scholarship or grant aid. 91% freshmen, 86% undergrads receive need-based self-help aid. 99% freshmen, 99% undergrads receive any aid. 84% undergrads borrow to pay for school. Average cumulative indebtedness $41,198. **Criteria for awarding institutional aid:** *Non-need-based:* academics, art, leadership, music/drama, state/district residency.

MASSACHUSETTS COLLEGE OF ART AND DESIGN

621 Huntington Avenue, Boston, MA 2115
Phone: 617-879-7222 • **Financial Aid Phone:** 617-879-7850
E-mail: admissions@massart.edu • **CEEB Code:** 3516
Fax: 617-879-7250 • **ACT Code:** 1846

This public school was founded in 1873. It has a 5-acre campus.

RATINGS
Admissions Selectivity Rating: 78   **Fire Safety Rating:** 74   **Green Rating:** 75

STUDENTS AND FACULTY
Enrollment: 1,824. **Student Body:** 68% female, 32% male, 29% out-of-state, 2% international. Asian 6%, African American 3%, Caucasian 72%, Hispanic 5%, Native American 1%.
Retention and Graduation: 88% freshmen return for sophomore year. **Faculty:** Student/faculty ratio 10:1. 106 full-time faculty. 0% of classes are taught by teaching assistants.

ACADEMICS
Degrees: bachelor's, certificate, master's, post-bachelor's certificate. **Classes:** Most classes have 10–19 students. **Majors with Highest Enrollment:** graphic design; illustration; painting. **Special Study Options:** cross-registration, double major, exchange student program (domestic), independent study, internships, liberal arts/career combination, student-designed major, study abroad, teacher certification program. **Disability Services:** Special programs offered to physically disabled students include note-taking services, reader services, tutors. **Career Services:** Alumni network, alumni services, career/job search classes, career assessment, internships.

FACILITIES
Housing: Coed dorms, apartments for single students, Off campus housing assistance from school. Additional housing available in Simmons College dorms. 95% of campus accessible to physically disabled. **Special Academic Facilities/Equipment:** Ten art galleries, foundry, glass furnaces, ceramic kilns, video and film studios, performance spaces, Polaroid 20x24 camera, individual studio spaces, design research unit, printmaking facilities, video and photography equipment and facilities, specialized computer labs, specialized equipment and facilities for all art and design programs and levels. **Computers:** 100% of classrooms, 100% of dorms, 100% of libraries, 100% of dining areas, 100% of student union, 100% of common outdoor areas have wireless network access. Students can register for classes online. Administrative functions (other than registration) can be performed online.

CAMPUS LIFE
Environment: Metropolis. **Activities:** dance, drama/theater, music ensembles, radio station, student government, student newspaper, student-run film society, television station, yearbook 30 registered organizations, 1 honor societies, 3 religious organizations. **Athletics (Intercollegiate):** *Men:* baseball, basketball, cross-country, golf, lacrosse, soccer, softball, tennis, volleyball. *Women:* basketball, cross-country, golf, lacrosse, soccer, softball, tennis, volleyball. **On-Campus Highlights:** 10 art galleries, student studios, courtyard, cafes, student center, see http://inside.massart.edu/x942.xml for a description of student activites. **Environmental Initiatives:** http://inside.massart.edu/Administration/Administration_and_Finance/Facilities/Sustainability.html http://inside.massart.edu/Administration/Administration_and_Finance/Facilities/Sustainability.html http://inside.massart.edu/Administration/Administration_and_Finance/Facilities/Sustainability.html

ADMISSIONS
Freshman Academic Profile: Average high school GPA 3.4. SAT Math middle 50% range 490-590. SAT Critical Reading middle 50% range 500-610. SAT Writing middle 50% range 490-600. ACT middle 50% range 21-25. Minimum web-based TOEFL 85. Minimum paper TOEFL 530. **Basis for Candidate Selection:** *Very important factors considered include:* application essay, academic GPA, rigor of secondary school record, talent/ability. *Important factors considered include:* standardized test scores, state residency. *Other factors considered include:* Class rank, recommendation(s), character/personal qualities, extracurricular activities, geographical residence, volunteer work, work experience. **Freshman Admission Requirements:** High school diploma is required and GED is accepted. *Academic units required:* 4 English, 2 mathematics, 2 science, (2 science labs), 2 foreign language, 2 social studies, 2 academic electives, 2 Art electives. *Academic units recommended:* 4 English, 2 mathematics, 2 science, (2 science labs), 2 foreign language, 2 social studies, 2 academic electives, 2 Art electives **Freshman Admission Statistics:** 1,381 applied, 70% admitted, 37% enrolled. **Transfer Admission Requirements:** college transcript(s), essay or personal statement, statement of good standing from prior institution(s). Minimum college GPA of 2.5 required. Lowest

grade transferable C. **General Admission Information:** Application Fee $65. Regular application deadline 2/1. Notification on a rolling basis, beginning on or about 2/1. Nonfall registration not accepted. Admission may be deferred for a maximum of 12 months. Credit and/or placement offered for CEEB Advanced Placement tests.

COSTS AND FINANCIAL AID
Annual in-state tuition $10,400. Annual out-of-state tuition $27,500. Room and board $12,150. Average book expense $2,100. **Required Forms and Deadlines:** FAFSA. **Notification of Awards:** Applicants will be notified of awards on or about 2/1. **Types of Aid:** *Need-based scholarships/grants:* Federal Pell, SEOG, state scholarships/grants, private scholarships, the school's own gift aid. *Loans:* Direct Subsidized Stafford, Direct Unsubsidized Stafford, Direct PLUS, Subsidized Stafford, Unsubsidized Stafford, PLUS, Federal Perkins, state loans, college/university loans from institutional funds, Alternative loans (credit Based). **Student Employment:** Federal Work-Study Program available. Institutional employment available. Highest amount earned per year from on-campus jobs $800. Off-campus job opportunities are good. **Financial Aid Statistics:** 79% freshmen, 70% undergrads receive need-based scholarship or grant aid. 16% freshmen, 8% undergrads receive non-need-based scholarship or grant aid. 95% freshmen, 93% undergrads receive need-based self-help aid. 73% undergrads borrow to pay for school. Average cumulative indebtedness $25,875. **Criteria for awarding institutional aid:** *Non-need-based:* academics, art, leadership.

MASSACHUSETTS COLLEGE OF PHARMACY AND HEALTH SCIENCE

Office of Admissions, Boston, MA 2115
Phone: 617-732-2850 • **Financial Aid Phone:** 617-732-2864
E-mail: admissions@mcphs.edu • **CEEB Code:** 3512
Fax: 617-732-2118 • **Website:** www.mcphs.edu • **ACT Code:** 1860

This private school was founded in 1823. It has a 3-acre campus.

RATINGS
Admissions Selectivity Rating: 86   **Fire Safety Rating:** 99   **Green Rating:** 60*

STUDENTS AND FACULTY
Enrollment: 2,883. **Student Body:** 68% female, 32% male, 43% out-of-state, 3% international (32 countries represented). Asian 28%, African American 5%, Caucasian 53%, Hispanic 3%, Native American 0%.
Retention and Graduation: 83% freshmen return for sophomore year. 59% freshmen graduate within 4 years. 69% freshmen graduate within 6 years. **Faculty:** Student/faculty ratio 18:1. 206 full-time faculty, 85% hold PhDs, 65% are women. 0% of classes are taught by teaching assistants.

ACADEMICS
Degrees: bachelor's, certificate, master's, post-bachelor's certificate. **Classes:** Most classes have 20–29 students. Most lab/discussion sessions have 10–19 students. **Majors with Highest Enrollment:** nursing/registered nurse (rn, asn, bsn, msn); pharmacy (pharmd [usa], pharmd or bs/bpharm [canada]); pre-medicine/pre-medical studies. **Special Study Options:** Accelerated program, cross-registration, distance learning, double major, independent study, internships, study abroad. **Combined Degree Programs:** BS/MS Pharmaceutical Chemistry. **Disability Services:** Special programs offered to physically disabled students include note-taking services, reader services, tape recorders, tutors. **Career Services:** Alumni network, alumni services, regional alumni. Career Services highlights include Students in most majors have "rotations" in hospitals, pharmacies, clinics.

FACILITIES
Housing: Coed dorms, wellness housing, separate all-women floors. 100% of campus accessible to physically disabled. **Special Academic Facilities/Equipment:** Museum of Fine Arts and Isabella Stewart Gardner museum next door. **Computers:** 100% of classrooms, 100% of dorms, 100% of libraries, 100% of dining areas, 100% of student union, 100% of common outdoor areas have wireless network access. Students can register for classes online. Administrative functions (other than registration) can be performed online.

CAMPUS LIFE
Environment: Metropolis. **Activities:** Choral groups, concert band, dance, drama/theater, literary magazine, music ensembles, musical theater, student government, student newspaper, yearbook, International Student Organization 66 registered organizations, 5 honor societies, 2 religious organizations. **On-Campus Highlights:** New Building , residence hall, labs, Pharmacy Laboratory, Dental Hygiene Clinic, Cafeteria (located in Mass. College of Art), Student Lounge, In addition to the Boston campus, there are campuses in Worcester and Manchester NH with expanding program offerings.

ADMISSIONS

Freshman Academic Profile: Average high school GPA 3.5. SAT Math middle 50% range 520-620. SAT Critical Reading middle 50% range 480-570. SAT Writing middle 50% range 490-590. ACT middle 50% range 21-26. Minimum web-based TOEFL 79. Minimum paper TOEFL 550. **Basis for Candidate Selection:** *Very important factors considered include:* academic GPA, rigor of secondary school record, standardized test scores. *Other factors considered include:* Class rank, application essay, recommendation(s), alumni/ae relation, character/personal qualities, extracurricular activities, first generation, level of applicant's interest, talent/ability, volunteer work, work experience. **Freshman Admission Requirements:** High school diploma is required and GED is accepted. *Academic units required:* 4 English, 3 mathematics, 2 science, (2 science labs), 1 social studies, 1 history, 5 academic electives. 4 English, 3 mathematics, 2 science, (2 science labs), 1 social studies, 1 history, 5 academic electives. **Freshman Admission Statistics:** 3,011 applied, 55% admitted, 42% enrolled. **Transfer Admission Requirements:** college transcript(s), essay or personal statement, minimum college GPA of 2.5 required. Lowest grade transferable C. **General Admission Information:** Application Fee $70. Regular notification 2/15. Nonfall registration not accepted. Admission may be deferred for a maximum of one year. Credit and/or placement offered for CEEB Advanced Placement tests.

COSTS AND FINANCIAL AID

Annual tuition $23,800. Room and board $11,900. Required fees $750. Average book expense $850. **Required Forms and Deadlines:** FAFSA. **Notification of Awards:** Applicants will be notified of awards on a rolling basis beginning 2/1. **Types of Aid:** *Need-based scholarships/grants:* Federal Pell, SEOG, state scholarships/grants, private scholarships, the school's own gift aid. *Loans:* Direct Subsidized Stafford, Direct Unsubsidized Stafford, Direct PLUS, Subsidized Stafford, Unsubsidized Stafford, PLUS, Federal Perkins, Health Professions Loans. **Student Employment:** Federal Work-Study Program available. Off-campus job opportunities are excellent. **Financial Aid Statistics:** 85% freshmen, 78% undergrads receive need-based scholarship or grant aid. 94% freshmen, 93% undergrads receive need-based self-help aid. 90% freshmen, 90% undergrads receive any aid. **Criteria for awarding institutional aid:** *Non-need-based:* academics.

MASSACHUSETTS INSTITUTE OF TECHNOLOGY

Best 378

77 Massachusetts Avenue, Cambridge, MA 2139
Phone: 617-253-3400 • **Financial Aid Phone:** 617-253-4971
E-mail: admissions@mit.edu • **CEEB Code:** 3514
Fax: 617-258-8304 • **Website:** web.mit.edu • **ACT Code:** 1858

This private school was founded in 1861. It has a 168-acre campus.

RATINGS

Admissions Selectivity Rating: 99   **Fire Safety Rating:** 86   **Green Rating:** 90

STUDENTS AND FACULTY

Enrollment: 4,477. **Student Body:** 45% female, 55% male, 91% out-of-state, 10% international (92 countries represented). Asian 24%, African American 6%, Caucasian 37%, Hispanic 15%, Native American 0%.
Retention and Graduation: 97% freshmen return for sophomore year. 84% freshmen graduate within 4 years. 93% freshmen graduate within 6 years. 39% grads go on to further study within 1 year. 26% grads pursue arts and sciences degrees. 1% grads pursue law degrees. 1% grads pursue business degrees. 15% grads pursue medical degrees. **Faculty:** Student/faculty ratio 8:1. 1193 full-time faculty, 91% hold PhDs, 17% are members of minority groups, 24% are women.

ACADEMICS

Degrees: bachelor's, master's. **Classes:** Most classes have fewer than 10 students. Most lab/discussion sessions have 10–19 students. **Majors with Highest Enrollment:** business/commerce; computer science; mechanical engineering. **Special Study Options:** cooperative education program, cross-registration, double major, internships, study abroad, teacher certification program, Undergraduate Research Opportunities Program (UROP); Independent Activities Period (IAP); freshman learning communities. **Combined Degree Programs:** Two Bachelor's, SB/SM, SB/MEng, SB/MCP. **Disability Services:** Special programs offered to physically disabled students include note-taking services, reader services, tape recorders. **Career Services:** Alumni network, alumni services, career/job search classes, career assessment, internships, regional alumni. Career Services highlights include We have a very strong on-campus recruiting system, with over 397 employers who came to our Careers Office to interview students.

FACILITIES

Housing: Coed dorms, special housing for disabled students, women's dorms, fraternity/sorority housing, apartments for married students, cooperative housing, apartments for single students, theme housing, independent living group housing, apartments for students with dependent children, and living learning communities available. **Special Academic Facilities/Equipment:** List Visual Arts Center; MIT Museum; Ray and Maria Stata Center for Computer, Information and Intelligence Sciences; numerous labs and centers. **Computers:** 100% of classrooms, 100% of dorms, 100% of libraries, 100% of dining areas, 100% of student union, 80-98% of common outdoor areas have wireless network access. Administrative functions (other than registration) can be performed online.

CAMPUS LIFE

Environment: City. **Activities:** Choral groups, concert band, dance, drama/theater, jazz band, literary magazine, marching band, music ensembles, musical theater, radio station, student government, student newspaper, student-run film society, symphony orchestra, television station, yearbook, Campus Ministries, International Student Organization, Model UN 400 registered organizations, 10 honor societies, 29 religious organizations. 27 fraternities, 6 sororities. **Athletics (Intercollegiate):** *Men:* baseball, basketball, crew/rowing, cross-country, diving, fencing, football, golf, gymnastics, lacrosse, pistol, riflery, sailing, skiing (downhill/alpine), skiingnordiccross-country, soccer, squash, swimming, tennis, track/field (outdoor), track/field (indoor), volleyball, water polo, wrestling. *Women:* basketball, crew/rowing, cross-country, diving, fencing, field hockey, gymnastics, ice hockey, lacrosse, pistol, riflery, sailing, skiing (downhill/alpine), skiingnordiccross-country, soccer, softball, swimming, tennis, track/field (outdoor), track/field (indoor), volleyball. **On-Campus Highlights:** Ray and Maria Stata Center, Zesiger Sports and Fitness Center, Killian Court, The Infinite Corridor, The Student Center (W20), Stata Center is a 720,000 square foot building designed by Frank Gehry. Zesiger Sports and Fitness Center is our state-of-the-art athletics facility. At 778.8 feet, the Infinite Corridor is reputed to be the longest straight hallway in the world--it connects many of the buildings on central campus and runs though two popular gathering spots: Lobbies 7 and 10. **Environmental Initiatives:** In 2010, MIT established MIT Efficiency Forward a ground breaking, multi-million dollar collaborative energy conservation and efficiency program with their electric and gas utility company NSTAR. The program is a first-ever-of-its-kind with a utility company and is the single largest energy efficiency program NSTAR has developed with a customer. The program is investing nearly $14 million over the next three years, with an innovative funding strategy that leverages funds from MIT, NSTAR incentive payments, and reinvestment of energy savings. MIT has committed to a goal of reducing annual electrical use on campus by 34 million kilowatt hours within three years " equivalent to 15% of MIT's current electrical use. The total estimated savings over the lifetime of the efficiency measures is estimated in excess of $50 million. In 2010, MIT surpassed its goal by 30%, saving over 13 million kWh; Addition of cogeneration for central power supply; 60kw installed capacity of solar power. Recycling (45% recycling rate with new composting services offered for post-consumer food waste. Over 10% increase in recycling rate; trash reductions achieved also Green building (LEED) for new and existing buildings. In 2010, MIT certified a LEED Gold dorm, completed two high level LEED Gold laboratory and admistrative buildings, that use 45% and 35% less energy than a typical building of the saem size.

ADMISSIONS

Freshman Academic Profile: 98% in top 10% of high school class, 100% in top 25% of high school class, 100% in top 50% of high school class. 65% from public high schools. SAT Math middle 50% range 740-800. SAT Critical Reading middle 50% range 670-770. SAT Writing middle 50% range 680-780. ACT middle 50% range 32-35. Minimum web-based TOEFL 90. Minimum paper TOEFL 577. **Basis for Candidate Selection:** *Very important factors considered include:* character/personal qualities. *Important factors considered include:* Class rank, academic GPA, recommendation(s), rigor of secondary school record, standardized test scores, extracurricular activities, interview, talent/ability. *Other factors considered include:* application essay, alumni/ae relation, first generation, geographical residence, racial/ethnic status, volunteer work, work experience. **Freshman Admission Requirements:** High school diploma or equivalent is not required. **Freshman Admission Statistics:** 18,109 applied, 9% admitted, 70% enrolled. **Transfer Admission Requirements:** High school transcript, college transcript(s), essay or personal statement, standardized test scores, statement of good standing from prior institution(s). Lowest grade transferable B. **General Admission Information:** Application Fee $75. Regular application deadline 1/1. Regular notification 3/20. Nonfall registration not accepted. Admission may be deferred for a maximum of 2 years. Credit and/or placement offered for CEEB Advanced Placement tests.

COSTS AND FINANCIAL AID

Annual tuition $41,770. Room and board $12,188. Required fees $280. Average book expense $1,000. **Required Forms and Deadlines:** FAFSA, CSS/Finan-

The Princeton Review's Complete Book of Colleges

cial Aid PROFILE, noncustodial PROFILE, business/farm supplement. Parent's complete federal income tax returns from prior year and W2s. **Notification of Awards:** Applicants will be notified of awards on or about 4/1. **Types of Aid:** *Need-based scholarships/grants:* Federal Pell, SEOG, state scholarships/grants, private scholarships, the school's own gift aid. *Loans:* Direct Subsidized Stafford, Direct Unsubsidized Stafford, Direct PLUS, Federal Perkins, college/university loans from institutional funds. **Student Employment:** Federal Work-Study Program available. Institutional employment available. Highest amount earned per year from on-campus jobs $25,990. Off-campus job opportunities are excellent. **Financial Aid Statistics:** 96% freshmen, 96% undergrads receive need-based scholarship or grant aid. 3% freshmen, 3% undergrads receive non-need-based scholarship or grant aid. 72% freshmen, 76% undergrads receive need-based self-help aid. 86% freshmen, 77% undergrads receive any aid. 41% undergrads borrow to pay for school. Average cumulative indebtedness $20,794.

MASSACHUSETTS MARITIME ACADEMY

101 Academy Drive, Buzzards Bay, MA 2532
Phone: 800-544-3411
E-mail: admissions@maritime.edu
Fax: 508-830-5077 • **Website:** www.maritime.edu

This public school was founded in 1891. It has a 55-acre campus.

RATINGS
Admissions Selectivity Rating: 63   **Fire Safety Rating:** 60*   **Green Rating:** 60*

STUDENTS AND FACULTY
Enrollment: 923. **Student Body:** 12% female, 88% male, 28% out-of-state, 0% international (6 countries represented).
Retention and Graduation: 30% grads go on to further study within 1 year. 10% grads pursue arts and sciences degrees. 4% grads pursue law degrees. 15% grads pursue business degrees. 1% grads pursue medical degrees. **Faculty:** Student/faculty ratio 15:1. 0% of classes are taught by teaching assistants.

ACADEMICS
Degrees: bachelor's, first professional certificate, master's. **Classes: Majors with Highest Enrollment:** environmental science; environmental/environmental health engineering; ocean engineering. **Special Study Options:** cooperative education program, double major, internships, Semester-at-Sea. **Career Services:** Alumni network, alumni services, career/job search classes, internships.

FACILITIES
Housing: Coed dorms. 80% of campus accessible to physically disabled. **Special Academic Facilities/Equipment:** Maritime Ship Model Museum Training Ship Enterprise **Computers:** Undergraduates are required to own a computer.

CAMPUS LIFE
Environment: Village. **Activities:** drama/theater, jazz band, marching band, music ensembles, student government, student newspaper, yearbook 12 registered organizations, 1 honor societies, 1 religious organizations. **Athletics (Intercollegiate):** *Men:* baseball, crew/rowing, cross-country, football, lacrosse, riflery, rugby, sailing, soccer. *Women:* crew/rowing, cross-country, riflery, rugby, sailing, softball, volleyball.

ADMISSIONS
Freshman Academic Profile: Average high school GPA 2.8. 65% from public high schools. Minimum paper TOEFL 500. **Basis for Candidate Selection:** *Very important factors considered include:* rigor of secondary school record, standardized test scores. *Important factors considered include:* application essay, character/personal qualities. *Other factors considered include:* recommendation(s), alumni/ae relation, extracurricular activities, interview, talent/ability, volunteer work, work experience. **Freshman Admission Requirements:** High school diploma is required and GED is accepted. *Academic units required:* 4 English, 3 mathematics, 3 science, (2 science labs), 2 foreign language, 2 history, 2 academic electives. 4 English, 3 mathematics, 3 science, (2 science labs), 2 foreign language, 2 history, 2 academic electives. **Freshman Admission Statistics:** 808 applied, 60% admitted, 56% enrolled. **Transfer Admission Requirements:** High school transcript, college transcript(s), essay or personal statement, minimum college GPA of 2.0 required. Lowest grade transferable C. **General Admission Information:** Application Fee $50. Notification on a rolling basis, beginning on or about 12/15. Nonfall registration not accepted. Admission may be deferred for a maximum of 1. Credit and/or placement offered for CEEB Advanced Placement tests.

COSTS AND FINANCIAL AID
Annual in-state tuition $9,165. Annual out-of-state tuition $19,500. Room and board $5,500. Required fees $2,600. Average book expense $700. **Required Forms and Deadlines:** FAFSA, institution's own financial aid form. **Notification of Awards:** Applicants will be notified of awards on a rolling basis beginning 3/1. **Types of Aid:** *Need-based scholarships/grants:* Federal Pell, SEOG, state scholarships/grants, private scholarships, the school's own gift aid. *Loans:* Direct Subsidized Stafford, Direct Unsubsidized Stafford, Direct PLUS. **Student Employment:** Federal Work-Study Program available. Highest amount earned per year from on-campus jobs $650. Off-campus job opportunities are good. **Financial Aid Statistics:** 12% freshmen, 18% undergrads receive need-based scholarship or grant aid. 8% freshmen, 37% undergrads receive non-need-based scholarship or grant aid. 53% freshmen, 60% undergrads receive need-based self-help aid. 82% undergrads borrow to pay for school. Average cumulative indebtedness $12,125. **Criteria for awarding institutional aid:** *Non-need-based:* academics, leadership.

THE MASTER'S COLLEGE

21726 Placerita Canyon Road, Santa Clarita, CA 91321
Phone: 661-259-3540 • **Financial Aid Phone:** 661-259-3540
E-mail: admissions@masters.edu • **CEEB Code:** 4411
Fax: 661-288-1037 • **Website:** www.masters.edu • **ACT Code:** 303

This private school was founded in 1927. It has a 95-acre campus.

RATINGS
Admissions Selectivity Rating: 78   **Fire Safety Rating:** 96   **Green Rating:** 61

STUDENTS AND FACULTY
Enrollment: 1,053. **Student Body:** 47% female, 53% male, 33% out-of-state, 5% international (36 countries represented). Asian 5%, African American 2%, Caucasian 65%, Hispanic 5%, Native American 1%.
Retention and Graduation: 81% freshmen return for sophomore year. 53% freshmen graduate within 4 years. 60% freshmen graduate within 6 years. **Faculty:** Student/faculty ratio 10:1. 66 full-time faculty, 71% hold PhDs, 11% are members of minority groups, 17% are women. 0% of classes are taught by teaching assistants.

ACADEMICS
Degrees: bachelor's, certificate, first professional, first professional certificate, master's. **Classes:** Most classes have fewer than 10 students. **Majors with Highest Enrollment:** bible/biblical studies, business/commerce; elementary education and teaching. **Special Study Options:** Accelerated program, cooperative education program, distance learning, double major, independent study, internships, liberal arts/career combination, study abroad, teacher certification program, Israel semester. **Disability Services:** Special programs offered to physically disabled students include note-taking services, reader services, tape recorders, tutors. **Career Services:** Alumni network, alumni services, career/job search classes, career assessment, internships.

FACILITIES
Housing: men's dorms, special housing for international students, women's dorms, wellness housing. 95% of campus accessible to physically disabled. **Computers:** 100% of classrooms, 100% of dorms, 100% of libraries, 100% of dining areas, 100% of student union, 95% of common outdoor areas have wireless network access. Students can register for classes online. Administrative functions (other than registration) can be performed online. Undergraduates are required to own a computer.

CAMPUS LIFE
Environment: City. **Activities:** Choral groups, concert band, drama/theater, jazz band, music ensembles, opera, pep band, student government, symphony orchestra 15 registered organizations, 1 honor societies, 11 religious organizations. **Athletics (Intercollegiate):** *Men:* baseball, basketball, cross-country, golf, soccer, track/field (outdoor). *Women:* basketball, cross-country, soccer, tennis, track/field (outdoor), volleyball. **On-Campus Highlights:** New All-Weather Field (2005), Dining Center Remodeled (2005), Music Center, Smith Hall Dormitory, Canyon Cafe.

ADMISSIONS
Freshman Academic Profile: Average high school GPA 3.6. 24% in top 10% of high school class, 49% in top 25% of high school class, 82% in top 50% of high school class. 52% from public high schools. SAT Math middle 50% range 470-610. SAT Critical Reading middle 50% range 500-620. ACT middle 50% range 22-29. Minimum paper TOEFL 525. **Basis for Candidate Selection:** *Very important factors considered include:* application essay, academic GPA, recommendation(s), rigor of secondary school record, standardized test scores,

character/personal qualities, interview, religious affiliation/commitment. *Other factors considered include:* alumni/ae relation, extracurricular activities, level of applicant's interest, talent/ability. **Freshman Admission Requirements:** High school diploma is required and GED is accepted. *Academic units required:* 4 English, 3 mathematics, 2 science, 2 history. *Academic units recommended:* 4 English, 3 mathematics, 2 science, 2 history. **Freshman Admission Statistics:** 632 applied, 69% admitted, 48% enrolled. **Transfer Admission Requirements:** High school transcript, college transcript(s), essay or personal statement, interview, statement of good standing from prior institution(s). Minimum college GPA of 2.5 required. Lowest grade transferable C. **General Admission Information:** Application Fee $40. Notification on a rolling basis, beginning on or about 3/15. Nonfall registration accepted. Admission may be deferred for a maximum of 2 semesters. Credit and/or placement offered for CEEB Advanced Placement tests.

COSTS AND FINANCIAL AID

Annual tuition $25,250. Room and board $8,320. Required fees $390. Average book expense $1,620. **Required Forms and Deadlines:** FAFSA, institution's own financial aid form, state aid form. **Notification of Awards:** Applicants will be notified of awards on a rolling basis beginning 2/18. **Types of Aid:** *Need-based scholarships/grants:* Federal Pell, SEOG, state scholarships/grants, private scholarships, the school's own gift aid. *Loans:* Subsidized Stafford, Unsubsidized Stafford, PLUS, Federal Perkins, Alternative private loans. **Student Employment:** Federal Work-Study Program available. Institutional employment available. Highest amount earned per year from on-campus jobs $5,000. Off-campus job opportunities are excellent. **Financial Aid Statistics:** 99% freshmen, 97% undergrads receive need-based scholarship or grant aid. 9% freshmen, 11% undergrads receive non-need-based scholarship or grant aid. 90% freshmen, 87% undergrads receive need-based self-help aid. 6% freshmen, 6% undergrads receive athletic scholarships. 70% freshmen, 69% undergrads receive any aid. 54% undergrads borrow to pay for school. Average cumulative indebtedness $13,823. **Criteria for awarding institutional aid:** *Non-need-based:* academics, alumni affiliation, art, athletics, leadership, music/drama.

MAYVILLE STATE UNIVERSITY

330 Third Street Northeast, Mayville, ND 58257-1299
Phone: 701-788-4842 • **Financial Aid Phone:** 701-788-4767
E-mail: MaSU.admissions@mayvillestate.edu • **CEEB Code:** 6478
Fax: 701-788-4748 • **Website:** www.mayvillestate.edu • **ACT Code:** 3212

This public school was founded in 1889. It has a 55-acre campus.

RATINGS
Admissions Selectivity Rating: 73   **Fire Safety Rating:** 71   **Green Rating:** 60*

STUDENTS AND FACULTY
Enrollment: 990. **Student Body:** 57% female, 43% male, 38% out-of-state, 4% international (7 countries represented). Asian 1%, African American 6%, Caucasian 82%, Hispanic 5%, Native American 2%.
Retention and Graduation: 53% freshmen return for sophomore year. 20% freshmen graduate within 4 years. 36% freshmen graduate within 6 years. 6% grads go on to further study within 1 year. 2% grads pursue arts and sciences degrees. 2% grads pursue business degrees. **Faculty:** Student/faculty ratio 14:1. 41 full-time faculty, 39% hold PhDs, 2% are members of minority groups, 41% are women. 0% of classes are taught by teaching assistants.

ACADEMICS
Degrees: bachelor's, transfer associate. **Classes:** Most classes have 10–19 students. **Majors with Highest Enrollment:** business/commerce; elementary education and teaching; physical education teaching and coaching. **Special Study Options:** Accelerated program, cooperative education program, distance learning, double major, dual enrollment, independent study, internships, student-designed major, teacher certification program. **Disability Services:** Special programs offered to physically disabled students include note-taking services, tape recorders, tutors. **Career Services:** Alumni network, alumni services, career/job search classes, career assessment, internships, regional alumni. Career Services highlights include The internship program provides opportunities for students to have related work experience with a variety of local, regional and national employers.

FACILITIES
Housing: men's dorms, women's dorms, apartments for married students, apartments for single students. 80% of campus accessible to physically disabled. **Special Academic Facilities/Equipment:** Art gallery available in the Campus Center. **Computers:** 100% of classrooms, 25% of dorms, 100% of libraries, 100% of dining areas, 100% of student union, 25% of common outdoor areas have wireless network access. Students can register for classes online. Admin-

istrative functions (other than registration) can be performed online. Undergraduates are required to own a computer.

CAMPUS LIFE
Environment: Rural. **Activities:** Choral groups, concert band, drama/theater, jazz band, music ensembles, musical theater, radio station, student government, student newspaper 118 registered organizations, 1 honor societies, 2 religious organizations. **Athletics (Intercollegiate):** *Men:* baseball, basketball, football. *Women:* basketball, softball, volleyball. **On-Campus Highlights:** Lewy Lee Fieldhouse, Campus Center, Residence Halls, Library, West Hall.

ADMISSIONS
Freshman Academic Profile: 3.1. 5% in top 10% of high school class, 15% in top 25% of high school class, 46% in top 50% of high school class. 95% from public high schools. ACT middle 50% range 18-22. Minimum web-based TOEFL 68. Minimum paper TOEFL 520. **Basis for Candidate Selection:** *Very important factors considered include:* academic GPA. *Important factors considered include:* rigor of secondary school record, standardized test scores. *Other factors considered include:* character/personal qualities, interview. **Freshman Admission Requirements:** High school diploma is required and GED is accepted. *Academic units required:* 4 English, 3 mathematics, 3 science, (3 science labs), 3 social studies. *Academic units recommended:* 4 English, 3 mathematics, 3 science, (3 science labs), 3 social studies. **Freshman Admission Statistics:** 311 applied, 60% admitted, 84% enrolled. **Transfer Admission Requirements:** college transcript(s), statement of good standing from prior institution(s). Minimum college GPA of 2.0 required. Lowest grade transferable d. **General Admission Information:** Application Fee $35. Notification on a rolling basis, beginning on or about 1/1. Nonfall registration accepted. Admission may be deferred for a maximum of NA. Credit and/or placement offered for CEEB Advanced Placement tests.

COSTS AND FINANCIAL AID
Annual in-state tuition $4,484. Annual out-of-state tuition $6,727. Room and board $4,854. Required fees $1,709. Average book expense $1,000. **Required Forms and Deadlines:** FAFSA. **Notification of Awards:** Applicants will be notified of awards on a rolling basis beginning 5/1. **Types of Aid:** *Need-based scholarships/grants:* Federal Pell, SEOG, state scholarships/grants, private scholarships, the school's own gift aid. *Loans:* Subsidized Stafford, Unsubsidized Stafford, PLUS, Federal Perkins. **Student Employment:** Federal Work-Study Program available. Institutional employment available. Highest amount earned per year from on-campus jobs $1,500. Off-campus job opportunities are fair. **Financial Aid Statistics:** 89% freshmen, 88% undergrads receive need-based scholarship or grant aid. 6% freshmen, 3% undergrads receive non-need-based scholarship or grant aid. 97% freshmen, 96% undergrads receive need-based self-help aid. 26% freshmen, 18% undergrads receive athletic scholarships. 64% freshmen, 61% undergrads receive any aid. 77% undergrads borrow to pay for school. Average cumulative indebtedness $30,351. **Criteria for awarding institutional aid:** *Non-need-based:* academics, athletics, leadership, minority status, music/drama, state/district residency.

MCDANIEL COLLEGE

Westminster, MD 21157
Phone: 410-848-7000 • **Financial Aid Phone:** 410-857-2233

RATINGS
Admissions Selectivity Rating: 81   **Fire Safety Rating:** 73   **Green Rating:** 60*

STUDENTS AND FACULTY
Enrollment: 1,614. **Student Body:** 54% female, 46% male, 36% out-of-state, 0% international (21 countries represented). Asian 4%, African American 12%, Caucasian 76%, Hispanic 5%, Native American 1%.
Retention and Graduation: 68% freshmen graduate within 4 years. 74% freshmen graduate within 6 years. 44% grads go on to further study within 1 year. 16% grads pursue arts and sciences degrees. 2% grads pursue law degrees. 3% grads pursue business degrees. 7% grads pursue medical degrees. **Faculty:** Student/faculty ratio 11:1. 103 full-time faculty, 99% hold PhDs, 13% are members of minority groups, 51% are women. 0% of classes are taught by teaching assistants.

ACADEMICS
Majors with Highest Enrollment: business/commerce; psychology; sociology. **Disability Services:** Special programs offered to physically disabled students include note-taking services, reader services, tape recorders, tutors. **Career Services:** Alumni network, career/job search classes, career assessment, internships.

FACILITIES

Housing: Coed dorms, special housing for disabled students, men's dorms, women's dorms, fraternity/sorority housing, apartments for married students, apartments for single studentsSingle family homes shared by 3-10 students. 80% of campus accessible to physically disabled. **Special Academic Facilities/Equipment:** Art gallery, computer graphics and physiology labs, electron microscope, math spectrometer. **Computers:** Students can register for classes online. Administrative functions (other than registration) can be performed online.

CAMPUS LIFE

Activities: Choral groups, concert band, dance, drama/theater, jazz band, literary magazine, music ensembles, musical theater, pep band, radio station, student government, student newspaper, symphony orchestra, television station, yearbook 136 registered organizations, 22 honor societies, 5 religious organizations. 6 fraternities, 4 sororities. **Athletics (Intercollegiate):** *Men:* baseball, basketball, cross-country, football, golf, lacrosse, soccer, swimming, tennis, track/field (outdoor), track/field (indoor), volleyball, wrestling. *Women:* basketball, cross-country, field hockey, golf, lacrosse, soccer, softball, swimming, tennis, track/field (outdoor), track/field (indoor), volleyball. **On-Campus Highlights:** The Hoover Library, Peterson Hall, Golf course, Bair stadium, Academic Hall.

ADMISSIONS

Freshman Academic Profile: 3.5. 29% in top 10% of high school class, 54% in top 25% of high school class, 87% in top 50% of high school class. SAT Math middle 50% range 500-610. SAT Critical Reading middle 50% range 490-610. ACT middle 50% range 20-27. Minimum web-based TOEFL 80. Minimum paper TOEFL 550. **Freshman Admission Statistics:** 3,560 applied, 64% admitted, 19% enrolled. **General Admission Information:** Credit and/or placement offered for CEEB Advanced Placement tests.

COSTS AND FINANCIAL AID

Financial Aid Statistics: 98% freshmen, 95% undergrads receive need-based scholarship or grant aid. 21% freshmen, 12% undergrads receive non-need-based scholarship or grant aid. 74% freshmen, 79% undergrads receive need-based self-help aid. 93% freshmen, 87% undergrads receive any aid. 64% undergrads borrow to pay for school. Average cumulative indebtedness $31,919.

MCGILL UNIVERSITY

845 Sherbrooke Street West, Montreal, QC H3A 2T5
Phone: 514-398-3910 • **Financial Aid Phone:** 514-398-6013
E-mail: admissions@mcgill.ca • **CEEB Code:** 935
Fax: 514-398-4193 • **Website:** www.mcgill.ca • **ACT Code:** 5231

This public school was founded in 1821. It has a 80-acre campus.

RATINGS

Admissions Selectivity Rating: 94   **Fire Safety Rating:** 68   **Green Rating:** 79

STUDENTS AND FACULTY

Enrollment: 20,831. **Student Body:** 59% female, 41% male, 37% out-of-state, 17% international (136 countries represented). Asian 0%, African American 0%, Caucasian 0%, Hispanic 0%, Native American 0%.
Retention and Graduation: 93% freshmen return for sophomore year. 67% freshmen graduate within 4 years. 85% freshmen graduate within 6 years.
Faculty: Student/faculty ratio 16:1. 1689 full-time faculty, 95% hold PhDs, 29% are women.

ACADEMICS

Degrees: bachelor's, certificate, diploma, first professional, master's, post-bachelor's certificate. **Classes:** Most classes have 10–19 students. Most lab/discussion sessions have 20–29 students. **Majors with Highest Enrollment:** business/commerce; political science and government; psychology. **Special Study Options:** Accelerated program, cooperative education program, cross-registration, distance learning, double major, English as a Second Language (ESL), exchange student program (domestic), honors program, independent study, internships, study abroad, teacher certification program. **Honors Programs:** McGill's Faculties of Arts, Science, and Engineering, the Desautels Faculty of Management, and the McGill School of Environment offer many outstanding honours and joint honours programs. Honours programs offer specialization and research in one academic discipline while joint honours programs offer

specialization and research in a combination of disciplines. **Combined Degree Programs:** BSc/BEd;BMus/BEd;BCL/LLB;MSW/Law;MDCM/MBA;MDCM/PhD. **Disability Services:** Special programs offered to physically disabled students include note-taking services, reader services, tape recorders, tutors. **Career Services:** career/job search classes, career assessment Career Services highlights include Bilingual Mining and Materials Co-op Program.

FACILITIES

Housing: Coed dorms, special housing for disabled students, women's dorms, apartments for single students, Shared Facilities Housing: Similar to Cooperative Housing but chores and costs are not shared amongst the students. 90% of campus accessible to physically disabled. **Special Academic Facilities/Equipment:** McCord Museum of Canadian History, Redpath Museum of Natural History, Lyman Entomological Museum and Research Laboratory, Ecomuseum, Rutherford Museum, Lawrence Lande Collection of Canadiana, Canadian Architecture Collection, Morgan Arboretum, Gault Nature Reserve, Herbarium, McGill Archives (Canadian History), Islamic Studies Library, Bellairs Research Institute, McConnell Brain Imaging Centre, McConnell Winter Arena, McGill Sports Centre Gymnasiums, Percival Molson Stadium, Memorial Pool, Richard Tomlinson Fieldhouse, Outdoor Tennis Courts, McGill Arctic Research Station, McGill Subarctic Research Station, Phytotron, Schulich School of Music (world-class sound stage, recording studio), McGill Centre for Interdisciplinary Research in Music, Media and Technology, Research Greenhouse, J. S. Marshall Weather Radar Observatory, Mountain and Glen Campuses (McGill University Health Centre Teaching Hospitals), McGill Medical Simulation Centre, McGill Reproductive Centre, McGill University and Genome Quebec Innovation Centre. **Computers:** 100% of classrooms, 100% of dorms, 100% of libraries, 100% of dining areas, 100% of student union, 100% of common outdoor areas have wireless network access. Students can register for classes online. Administrative functions (other than registration) can be performed online.

CAMPUS LIFE

Environment: Metropolis. **Activities:** Choral groups, concert band, dance, drama/theater, jazz band, literary magazine, marching band, music ensembles, musical theater, opera, pep band, radio station, student government, student newspaper, student-run film society, symphony orchestra, television station, yearbook, International Student Organization 250 registered organizations, 2 honor societies, 10 religious organizations. 8 fraternities, 4 sororities. **Athletics (Intercollegiate):** *Men:* badminton, baseball, basketball, cheerleading, crew/rowing, cross-country, curling, cycling, fencing, football, golf, ice hockey, lacrosse, rugby, sailing, skiing (downhill/alpine), skiingnordiccross-country, soccer, squash, swimming, tennis, track/field (indoor), ultimate frisbee, volleyball, wrestling. *Women:* badminton, basketball, cheerleading, crew/rowing, cross-country, curling, cycling, fencing, field hockey, golf, ice hockey, lacrosse, rugby, sailing, skiing (downhill/alpine), skiingnordiccross-country, soccer, squash, swimming, synchronized swimming, tennis, track/field (indoor), ultimate frisbee, volleyball, wrestling. **On-Campus Highlights:** Arts Building, Schulich School of Music, McGill Bookstore, MacDonald Campus, Redpath Museum, To get a big-picture view of the entire campus, take a walk up Mont-Royal. From the Chateau look-out it is possible to see the entire downtown campus. **Environmental Initiatives:** Excellence in environmental research and teaching (e.g. School of Environment, GEC3, Brace, VERT, etc.) Continual investment in energy infrastructure improvements to efficiency and reduce resource consumption Conservation efforts (including Gault Reserve, Morgan Arboretum, EcoMuseum, etc.)

ADMISSIONS

Freshman Academic Profile: Average high school GPA 3.5. SAT Math middle 50% range 650-720. SAT Critical Reading middle 50% range 640-740. SAT Writing middle 50% range 650-730. ACT middle 50% range 29-32. Minimum web-based TOEFL 90. Minimum paper TOEFL 577. **Basis for Candidate Selection:** *Very important factors considered include:* academic GPA, rigor of secondary school record, standardized test scores. *Important factors considered include:* Class rank. *Other factors considered include:* recommendation(s). **Freshman Admission Requirements:** High school diploma is required and GED is not accepted. **Freshman Admission Statistics:** 21,242 applied, 54% admitted, 44% enrolled. **Transfer Admission Requirements:** High school transcript, college transcript(s), minimum college GPA of 3.00 required. Lowest grade transferable C. **General Admission Information:** Application Fee $85. Regular application deadline 1/15. Notification on a rolling basis, beginning on or about 1/30. Nonfall registration accepted. Admission may be deferred for a maximum of 1 year. Credit and/or placement offered for CEEB Advanced Placement tests.

COSTS AND FINANCIAL AID

Annual in-state tuition $1,968. Annual out-of-state tuition $5,500. Room and board $11,000. Required fees $1,500. Average book expense $1,000. **Required Forms and Deadlines:** institution's own financial aid formProvincial Government Loan Applications. **Notification of Awards:** Applicants will be notified of awards on a rolling basis beginning 3/1. **Types of Aid:** *Need-based scholarships/*

grants: private scholarships, the school's own gift aid, Canadian (Federal & Provincial) Student Assistance. *Loans:* Subsidized Stafford, Unsubsidized Stafford, PLUS, college/university loans from institutional funds. **Student Employment:** Institutional employment available. Off-campus job opportunities are fair. **Financial Aid Statistics:** 63% undergrads receive need-based scholarship or grant aid. 31% undergrads receive non-need-based scholarship or grant aid. 89% undergrads receive need-based self-help aid. 28% undergrads receive any aid. 24% undergrads borrow to pay for school. **Criteria for awarding institutional aid:** *Non-need-based:* academics, art, athletics, leadership, music/drama, state/district residency.

MCKENDREE COLLEGE

701 College Road, Lebanon, IL 62254
Phone: 618-537-6831 • **Financial Aid Phone:** 618-537-6828
E-mail: inquiry@mckendree.edu • **CEEB Code:** 1456
Fax: 618-537-6496 • **Website:** www.mckendree.edu • **ACT Code:** 1076

This private school, affiliated with the Methodist Church, was founded in 1828. It has a 100-acre campus.

RATINGS
Admissions Selectivity Rating: 73   **Fire Safety Rating:** 64   **Green Rating:** 60*

STUDENTS AND FACULTY
Enrollment: 2,118. **Student Body:** 57% female, 43% male, 13% out-of-state, 2% international (24 countries represented). Asian 1%, African American 12%, Caucasian 81%, Hispanic 2%, Native American 0%.
Retention and Graduation: 73% freshmen return for sophomore year. 37% freshmen graduate within 4 years. 58% freshmen graduate within 6 years. 14% grads go on to further study within 1 year. 5% grads pursue arts and sciences degrees. 3% grads pursue law degrees. 6% grads pursue business degrees. 1% grads pursue medical degrees. **Faculty:** Student/faculty ratio 15:1. 70 full-time faculty, 81% hold PhDs, 4% are members of minority groups, 51% are women. 0% of classes are taught by teaching assistants.

ACADEMICS
Degrees: associate, bachelor's, master's. **Classes:** Most classes have 10–19 students. Most lab/discussion sessions have 10–19 students. **Special Study Options:** Accelerated program, cooperative education program, double major, external degree program, honors program, independent study, internships, liberal arts/career combination, student-designed major, study abroad, teacher certification program, evening programs in accounting, business administration, organizational communication, 3-2 occupational therapy program with Washington University. **Disability Services:** Special programs offered to physically disabled students include note-taking services, reader services, tutors. **Career Services:** alumni services, career/job search classes, career assessment, internships Career Services highlights include internship.

FACILITIES
Housing: Coed dorms, special housing for disabled students, women's dorms, apartments for single studentsSuite-style apartments are available for both men and women. 80% of campus accessible to physically disabled. **Computers:** Students can register for classes online. Administrative functions (other than registration) can be performed online.

CAMPUS LIFE
Environment: Rural. **Activities:** Choral groups, concert band, dance, drama/theater, jazz band, literary magazine, marching band, music ensembles, musical theater, pep band, student government, student newspaper, student-run film society, yearbook 59 registered organizations, 9 honor societies, 3 religious organizations. 4 fraternities, 3 sororities. **Athletics (Intercollegiate):** *Men:* baseball, basketball, bowling, cheerleading, cross-country, football, golf, ice hockey, soccer, tennis, track/field (outdoor), track/field (indoor), wrestling. *Women:* basketball, bowling, cheerleading, cross-country, golf, ice hockey, soccer, softball, tennis, track/field (outdoor), track/field (indoor), volleyball. **On-Campus Highlights:** Marion K. Piper Academic Center, Bothwell Chapel, Melvin Price Convocation Center, The Lair-student lounge and snack bar, McKendree West Clubhouse.

ADMISSIONS
Freshman Academic Profile: Average high school GPA 3.6. 25% in top 10% of high school class, 54% in top 25% of high school class, 91% in top 50% of high school class. SAT Math middle 50% range 430-630. SAT Critical Reading middle 50% range 420-530. ACT middle 50% range 20-27. Minimum paper TOEFL 500. **Basis for Candidate Selection:** *Very important factors considered include:* rigor of secondary school record. *Important factors considered include:* Class rank, recommendation(s), standardized test scores, character/

personal qualities. *Other factors considered include:* application essay, alumni/ae relation, extracurricular activities, interview, talent/ability, volunteer work, work experience. **Freshman Admission Requirements:** High school diploma is required and GED is accepted. **Freshman Admission Statistics:** 1,150 applied, 69% admitted, 43% enrolled. **Transfer Admission Requirements:** High school transcript, college transcript(s), statement of good standing from prior institution(s). Minimum college GPA of 2.2 required. Lowest grade transferable C. **General Admission Information:** Application Fee $40. Nonfall registration accepted. Admission may be deferred for a maximum of 6. Credit and/or placement offered for CEEB Advanced Placement tests.

COSTS AND FINANCIAL AID
Annual tuition $16,400. Room and board $6,480. Required fees $200. Average book expense $1,000. **Required Forms and Deadlines:** FAFSA, institution's own financial aid form. **Notification of Awards:** Applicants will be notified of awards on a rolling basis beginning 3/1. **Types of Aid:** *Need-based scholarships/grants:* Federal Pell, SEOG, state scholarships/grants. *Loans:* Subsidized Stafford, Unsubsidized Stafford, PLUS, Federal Perkins, college/university loans from institutional funds. **Student Employment:** Federal Work-Study Program available. Institutional employment available. Highest amount earned per year from on-campus jobs $2,326. Off-campus job opportunities are good. **Financial Aid Statistics:** 100% freshmen, 99% undergrads receive need-based scholarship or grant aid. 19% freshmen, 18% undergrads receive non-need-based scholarship or grant aid. 75% freshmen, 75% undergrads receive need-based self-help aid. 12% freshmen, 12% undergrads receive athletic scholarships. 99% freshmen, 97% undergrads receive any aid. 58% undergrads borrow to pay for school. Average cumulative indebtedness $16,240. **Criteria for awarding institutional aid:** *Non-need-based:* academics, art, athletics, leadership, minority status, music/drama, religious affiliation.

MCNEESE STATE UNIVERSITY

Box 91740 MSU, Lake Charles, LA 70609
Phone: 337-475-5356
Fax: 337-475-5151 • **Website:** www.mcneese.edu

This is a public school.

RATINGS
Admissions Selectivity Rating: 60*   **Fire Safety Rating:** 60*   **Green Rating:** 60*

STUDENTS AND FACULTY
Enrollment: 7,041. **Student Body:** 61% female, 39% male, 7% out-of-state, 3% international. Asian 1%, African American 18%, Caucasian 72%, Hispanic 1%, Native American 1%.
Retention and Graduation: 64% freshmen return for sophomore year. **Faculty:** Student/faculty ratio 20:1. 316 full-time faculty, 66% hold PhDs, 15% are members of minority groups, 45% are women.

ACADEMICS
Degrees: associate, bachelor's, master's, post-master's certificate. **Classes:** Most classes have 20–29 students. Most lab/discussion sessions have 10–19 students. **Special Study Options:** Accelerated program, cooperative education program, distance learning, double major, dual enrollment, English as a Second Language (ESL), honors program, independent study, internships, study abroad, teacher certification program.

FACILITIES
Housing: Coed dorms, apartments for married students, apartments for single students.

CAMPUS LIFE
Activities: drama/theater, marching band, student government, student newspaper, yearbook.

ADMISSIONS
Freshman Academic Profile: Average high school GPA 3.2. 15% in top 10% of high school class, 35% in top 25% of high school class, 68% in top 50% of high school class. 82% from public high schools. ACT middle 50% range 19-23. Minimum paper TOEFL 550. **Basis for Candidate Selection:** *Very important factors considered include:* rigor of secondary school record, standardized test scores. *Important factors considered include:* Class rank, academic GPA. *Other factors considered include:* character/personal qualities, extracurricular activities, talent/ability, volunteer work, work experience. **Freshman Admission Requirements:** High school diploma is required and GED is accepted. **Transfer Admission Requirements:** college transcript(s), statement of good standing from prior institution(s). Minimum college GPA of 2.00 required. Lowest grade transferable C. **General Admission Information:** Application Fee $20. Nonfall registration accepted. Credit and/or placement offered for CEEB Advanced Placement tests.

COSTS AND FINANCIAL AID

Annual in-state tuition $2,226. Annual out-of-state tuition $8,292. Room and board $3,460. Required fees $1,036. Average book expense $1,200. **Required Forms and Deadlines:** FAFSA, institution's own financial aid form. **Notification of Awards:** Applicants will be notified of awards on a rolling basis beginning 4/15. **Criteria for awarding institutional aid:** *Non-need-based:* academics, alumni affiliation, art, athletics, leadership, minority status, music/drama, state/district residency.

MCPHERSON COLLEGE

P.O. Box 1402, McPherson, KS 67460
Phone: 620-241-0731 • **Financial Aid Phone:** 800-365-7402
E-mail: admiss@mcpherson.edu • **CEEB Code:** 6404
Fax: 620-241-8443 • **ACT Code:** 1440

This private school, affiliated with the Church of Brethren Church, was founded in 1887. It has a 23-acre campus.

RATINGS
Admissions Selectivity Rating: 67   **Fire Safety Rating:** 60*   **Green Rating:** 60*

STUDENTS AND FACULTY
Enrollment: 573. **Student Body:** 43% female, 57% male, 5% out-of-state, 1% international. Asian 2%, African American 9%, Caucasian 76%, Hispanic 7%, Native American 3%.
Retention and Graduation: 67% freshmen return for sophomore year. 36% freshmen graduate within 4 years. 48% freshmen graduate within 6 years. 9% grads go on to further study within 1 year. 9% grads pursue medical degrees. **Faculty:** Student/faculty ratio 15:1. 34 full-time faculty, 82% hold PhDs, 12% are members of minority groups, 32% are women. 0% of classes are taught by teaching assistants.

ACADEMICS
Degrees: bachelor's. **Classes:** Most classes have 10–19 students. Most lab/discussion sessions have 10–19 students. **Special Study Options:** cross-registration, double major, dual enrollment, English as a Second Language (ESL), independent study, internships, student-designed major, study abroad, teacher certification program. **Combined Degree Programs.** 2-2 program with Hutchinson Com Col.

FACILITIES
Housing: Coed dorms, special housing for disabled students, men's dorms, women's dorms. **Special Academic Facilities/Equipment:** Natural history museum.

CAMPUS LIFE
Environment: Village. **Activities:** Choral groups, concert band, dance, drama/theater, jazz band, music ensembles, musical theater, pep band, student government, student newspaper, yearbook, Campus Ministries. **Athletics (Intercollegiate):** *Women:* basketball, cross-country, golf, tennis, track/field (outdoor), volleyball.

ADMISSIONS
Freshman Academic Profile: Average high school GPA 3.2. 9% in top 10% of high school class, 25% in top 25% of high school class, 60% in top 50% of high school class. 99% from public high schools. SAT Math middle 50% range 450-563. SAT Critical Reading middle 50% range 448-560. ACT middle 50% range 19-24. Minimum paper TOEFL 550. **Basis for Candidate Selection:** *Very important factors considered include:* academic GPA, rigor of secondary school record, standardized test scores.*Other factors considered include:* Class rank, recommendation(s), character/personal qualities, extracurricular activities, first generation, interview, level of applicant's interest, talent/ability, volunteer work, work experience. **Freshman Admission Requirements:** High school diploma is required and GED is accepted. **Freshman Admission Statistics:** 474 applied, 87% admitted, 54% enrolled. **Transfer Admission Requirements:** High school transcript, college transcript(s), statement of good standing from prior institution(s). Minimum college GPA of 2.0 required. Lowest grade transferable C. **General Admission Information:** Application Fee $25. Non-fall registration accepted. Admission may be deferred for a maximum of i year. Credit offered for CEEB Advanced Placement tests.

COSTS AND FINANCIAL AID
Annual tuition $17,900. Room and board $6,910. Required fees $500. Average book expense $1,170. **Required Forms and Deadlines:** FAFSA, state aid form. **Notification of Awards:** Applicants will be notified of awards on a rolling basis beginning 3/1. **Types of Aid:** *Need-based scholarships/grants:* Federal Pell, SEOG, state scholarships/grants, private scholarships, the school's own gift aid, United Negro College Fund. *Loans:* Subsidized Stafford, Unsubsidized

Stafford, PLUS, Federal Perkins. **Student Employment:** Federal Work-Study Program available. Institutional employment available. Highest amount earned per year from on-campus jobs $400. Off-campus job opportunities are good. **Financial Aid Statistics:** 85% freshmen, 85% undergrads receive need-based scholarship or grant aid. 95% freshmen, 98% undergrads receive non-need-based scholarship or grant aid. 86% freshmen, 88% undergrads receive need-based self-help aid. 66% freshmen, 38% undergrads receive athletic scholarships. 91% undergrads borrow to pay for school. Average cumulative indebtedness $24,690. **Criteria for awarding institutional aid:** *Non-need-based:* academics, alumni affiliation, art, athletics, music/drama, religious affiliation, state/district residency.

MEDAILLE COLLEGE

18 Agassiz Circle, Buffalo, NY 14214
Phone: 716-884-3281
E-mail: jmatheny@medaille.edu • **CEEB Code:** 2422
Fax: 716-884-0291 • **Website:** www.medaille.edu • **ACT Code:** 2822

This private school was founded in 1937. It has a 13-acre campus.

RATINGS
Admissions Selectivity Rating: 71   **Fire Safety Rating:** 67   **Green Rating:** 60*

STUDENTS AND FACULTY
Enrollment: 1,650. **Student Body:** 67% female, 33% male, 1% out-of-state, 3% international (2 countries represented). Asian 1%, African American 16%, Caucasian 65%, Hispanic 3%, Native American 1%.
Retention and Graduation: 70% freshmen return for sophomore year. 15% freshmen graduate within 4 years. 24% freshmen graduate within 6 years. 24% grads go on to further study within 1 year. 4% grads pursue arts and sciences degrees. 1% grads pursue law degrees. 5% grads pursue business degrees. 1% grads pursue medical degrees. **Faculty:** Student/faculty ratio 15:1. 70 full-time faculty, 56% hold PhDs, 7% are members of minority groups, 43% are women. 0% of classes are taught by teaching assistants.

ACADEMICS
Degrees: associate, bachelor's, certificate, master's. **Classes:** Most classes have 10–19 students. Most lab/discussion sessions have 10–19 students. **Special Study Options:** Accelerated program, cross-registration, double major, honors program, independent study, internships, liberal arts/career combination, student-designed major, teacher certification program, weekend college, Module system for full-time evening studies. **Honors Programs:** Theodore Roosevelt Scholars Program. **Combined Degree Programs:** B.S. / M.B.A. **Disability Services:** Special programs offered to physically disabled students include note-taking services, reader services, tape recorders, tutors. **Career Services:** alumni services, career/job search classes, career assessment, internships, Career Services highlights include Internships available in each academic program, required for most academic programs.

FACILITIES
Housing: Coed dorms, men's dorms, women's dorms, apartments for married students, apartments for single students. 100% of campus accessible to physically disabled. **Special Academic Facilities/Equipment:** Veterinary technology labs., New Media Institute, Childrens Literature Collection.

CAMPUS LIFE
Environment: City. **Activities:** drama/theater, literary magazine, musical theater, radio station, student government, student newspaper, student-run film society, television station, yearbook 18 registered organizations, 2 honor societies. **Athletics (Intercollegiate):** *Men:* baseball, basketball, cheerleading, lacrosse, soccer, volleyball. *Women:* basketball, cheerleading, cross-country, lacrosse, soccer, softball, volleyball. **On-Campus Highlights:** Kevin I. Sullivan Campus Center, Cafeteria, New Media Laboratory, Computer Lab, Radio Station.

ADMISSIONS
Freshman Academic Profile: Average high school GPA 2.8. 14% in top 10% of high school class, 45% in top 25% of high school class, 75% in top 50% of high school class. 85% from public high schools. SAT Math middle 50% range 410-500. SAT Critical Reading middle 50% range 420-520. ACT middle 50% range 17-21. Minimum paper TOEFL 550. **Basis for Candidate Selection:** *Very important factors considered include:* rigor of secondary school record, standardized test scores, interview. *Important factors considered include:* application essay, recommendation(s), extracurricular activities. *Other factors considered include:* Class rank, alumni/ae relation, character/personal qualities, talent/ability, volunteer work, work experience. **Freshman Admission Requirements:** High school diploma is required and GED is accepted. *Academic units required:* 4 English, 2 mathematics, 2 science, 4 social studies. *Academic units recommended:* 4 English, 2 mathematics, 2 science, 4 social studies. **Freshman

Admission Statistics: 763 applied, 68% admitted, 55% enrolled. **Transfer Admission Requirements:** High school transcript, college transcript(s), essay or personal statement, minimum college GPA of 2.0 required. Lowest grade transferable C. **General Admission Information:** Application Fee $25. Notification on a rolling basis, beginning on or about 10/1. Nonfall registration accepted. Admission may be deferred for a maximum of 1year. Credit and/or placement offered for CEEB Advanced Placement tests.

COSTS AND FINANCIAL AID

Annual tuition $13,350. Room and board $6,400. Required fees $310. Average book expense $930. **Required Forms and Deadlines:** FAFSA, institution's own financial aid form, state aid form. **Notification of Awards:** Applicants will be notified of awards on a rolling basis beginning 5/1. **Types of Aid:** *Need-based scholarships/grants:* Federal Pell, SEOG, state scholarships/grants, private scholarships, the school's own gift aid. *Loans:* Subsidized Stafford, Unsubsidized Stafford, PLUS. **Student Employment:** Federal Work-Study Program available. Institutional employment available. Highest amount earned per year from on-campus jobs $1,500. Off-campus job opportunities are good. **Financial Aid Statistics:** 96% freshmen, 82% undergrads receive need-based scholarship or grant aid. 37% freshmen, 13% undergrads receive non-need-based scholarship or grant aid. 100% freshmen, 90% undergrads receive need-based self-help aid. 85% freshmen, 85% undergrads receive any aid. 75% undergrads borrow to pay for school. Average cumulative indebtedness $18,000. **Criteria for awarding institutional aid:** *Non-need-based:* academics.

MEDCENTER ONE COLLEGE OF NURSING

512 North 7th Street, Bismarck, ND 58501
Phone: 701-323-6271 • **Financial Aid Phone:** 701-323-6270
E-mail: msmith@mohs.org
Fax: 701-323-6289 • **Website:** www.medcenterone.com/collegeofnursing • **ACT Code:** 3197

This private school was founded in 1988.

RATINGS
Admissions Selectivity Rating: 61 **Fire Safety Rating:** 60* **Green Rating:** 60*

STUDENTS AND FACULTY
Enrollment: 91. **Student Body:** 91% female, 9% male, 6% out-of-state, 0% international (0 countries represented). Asian 1%, African American 4%, Caucasian 90%, Hispanic 1%, Native American 0%.
Retention and Graduation: Faculty: Student/faculty ratio 8:1. 10 full-time faculty, 10% hold PhDs, % are members of minority groups, 100% are women. 0% of classes are taught by teaching assistants.

ACADEMICS
Degrees: bachelor's. **Classes:** Most classes have 40-49 students. Most lab/discussion sessions have fewer than 10 students. **Majors with Highest Enrollment:** nursing/registered nurse (rn, asn, bsn, msn). **Special Study Options:** independent study, internships.

FACILITIES
Special Academic Facilities/Equipment: Alumni Corner **Computers:** 100% of classrooms, 100% of libraries, 100% of common outdoor areas have wireless network access.

CAMPUS LIFE
Environment: Rural. **Activities:** student government 2 registered organizations, 1 honor societies.**On-Campus Highlights:** Simulation Lab

ADMISSIONS
Freshman Admission Requirements: High school diploma is required and GED is accepted. **Transfer Admission Requirements:** High school transcript, college transcript(s), essay or personal statement, interview, minimum college GPA of 2.5 required. Lowest grade transferable C. **General Admission Information:** Application Fee $40. Notification on a rolling basis, beginning on or about 11/4. Nonfall registration not accepted.

COSTS AND FINANCIAL AID
Annual tuition $9,720. Required fees $889. Average book expense $1,169. **Required Forms and Deadlines:** FAFSA, institution's own financial aid form. **Notification of Awards:** Applicants will be notified of awards on a rolling basis beginning 6/1. **Types of Aid:** *Need-based scholarships/grants:* Federal Pell, SEOG, state scholarships/grants, private scholarships, the school's own gift aid. *Loans:* Subsidized Stafford, Unsubsidized Stafford, PLUS, Federal Perkins, Federal Nursing, college/university loans from institutional funds. **Student Employment:** Federal Work-Study Program available. Off-campus job opportunities are good. **Financial Aid Statistics:** 78% undergrads receive need-based scholarship or grant aid. 29% undergrads receive non-need-based

scholarship or grant aid. 77% undergrads receive need-based self-help aid. 0% undergrads borrow to pay for school. Average cumulative indebtedness $0. **Criteria for awarding institutional aid:** *Non-need-based:* academics, alumni affiliation, leadership.

MEDICAL UNIVERSITY OF SOUTH CAROLINA

41 Bee Street, Charleston, SC 29425-0203
Phone: 843-792-3281 • **Financial Aid Phone:** 843-792-2536
E-mail: oesadmis@musc.edu
Fax: 843-792-6615 • **Website:** www.musc.edu • **ACT Code:** 6440

This public school was founded in 1824. It has a 80-acre campus.

RATINGS
Admissions Selectivity Rating: 61 **Fire Safety Rating:** 60* **Green Rating:** 77

STUDENTS AND FACULTY
Enrollment: 198. **Student Body:** 79% female, 21% male, 12% out-of-state, 0% international (26 countries represented). Asian 3%, African American 11%, Caucasian 73%, Hispanic 6%, Native American 1%.
Retention and Graduation: Faculty: Student/faculty ratio 2:1. 153 full-time faculty, 92% hold PhDs, 10% are members of minority groups, 56% are women. 0% of classes are taught by teaching assistants.

ACADEMICS
Degrees: bachelor's, doctoral, master's, post-bachelor's certificate, post-master's certificate. **Classes:** Most classes have 50-59 students. **Majors with Highest Enrollment:** cardiovascular technology/technologist; nursing/registered nurse (rn, asn, bsn, msn). **Special Study Options:** Accelerated program, distance learning, Varies with the academic program selected. **Disability Services:** Special programs offered to physically disabled students include note-taking services, reader services, tape recorders, tutors. **Career Services:** internships, Career Services highlights include We are an academic health science center and each specialty has various programs for placement of these highly specialized graduates. Internship refers to post-graduate programs and are not part of the degree curriculum.

FACILITIES
Housing: No on-campus housing available. Housing available in community and promoted to students via the Off-Campus Housing Service's website. 97% of campus accessible to physically disabled. **Special Academic Facilities/Equipment:** Dental Museum, and Medical Museum, and Pharmacy Museum. **Computers:** 100% of classrooms, n/a% of dorms, 100% of libraries, 100% of dining areas, n/a% of student union, 100% of common outdoor areas have wireless network access. Students can register for classes online. Administrative functions (other than registration) can be performed online.

CAMPUS LIFE
Environment: City. **Activities:** Choral groups, dance, literary magazine, music ensembles, student government, Campus Ministries, International Student Organization 77 registered organizations, 4 honor societies.**On-Campus Highlights:** Student Activity and Fitness Center, Library, Various Student Lounges, Classroom and Laboratories **Environmental Initiatives:** Installed ground source heat pump as first renewable energy project Recycling program since 1992 with four clealy stated recycling goals that are a part of the campus wide sustainability plan: reduce, re-use, recycle, and green packaging. Green Building Projects include: energy performance contract (in progress from January 09); Constructing first LEED building (opened in 2011)

ADMISSIONS
Freshman Academic Profile: Minimum web-based TOEFL 80. Minimum paper TOEFL 550.

COSTS AND FINANCIAL AID
Annual in-state tuition $14,018. Annual out-of-state tuition $23,824. Required fees $1,140. **Required Forms and Deadlines:** FAFSA, institution's own financial aid form. **Notification of Awards:** Applicants will be notified of awards on a rolling basis beginning 4/21. **Types of Aid:** *Need-based scholarships/grants:* Federal Pell, SEOG, state scholarships/grants, private scholarships, the school's own gift aid, Federal Nursing Scholarships. *Loans:* Subsidized Stafford, Unsubsidized Stafford, PLUS, Federal Perkins, Federal Nursing, college/university loans from institutional funds. **Student Employment:** Federal Work-Study Program available. Off-campus job opportunities are good. **Financial Aid Statistics:** 49% undergrads receive need-based scholarship or grant aid. 23% undergrads receive non-need-based scholarship or grant aid. 99% undergrads receive need-based self-help aid. 0% freshmen, 75% undergrads receive any aid. **Criteria for awarding institutional aid:** *Non-need-based:* academics, alumni affiliation, minority status, state/district residency.

MEMORIAL UNIVERSITY OF NEWFOUNDLAND

Memorial University of Newfoundland, St. Johns, NF A1B 3V6
Phone: 709-777-6615
E-mail: munmed@mun.ca
Fax: 709-777-6615 • **Website:** www.med.mun.ca/admissions

This public school was founded in 1925. It has a 220-acre campus.

RATINGS
Admissions Selectivity Rating: 62   **Fire Safety Rating:** 60*   **Green Rating:** 60*

STUDENTS AND FACULTY
Faculty: Student/faculty ratio 16:1. 1012 full-time faculty, 26% are women. 3% of classes are taught by teaching assistants.

ACADEMICS
Special Study Options: Accelerated program, cooperative education program, distance learning, double major, English as a Second Language (ESL), exchange student program (domestic), honors program, internships, liberal arts/career combination, study abroad, teacher certification program. **Combined Degree Programs:** BA/BBA, BM/BEd. **Disability Services:** Special programs offered to physically disabled students include note-taking services, reader services, tape recorders, tutors. **Career Services:** alumni services, career/job search classes, career assessment, internships.

FACILITIES
Special Academic Facilities/Equipment: Olympic sized swimming pool, complete fitness centre, student eating area, indoor aerobics, track and field, soccer field, basketball courts. **Computers:** Students can register for classes on-line. Administrative functions (other than registration) can be performed online.

CAMPUS LIFE
Activities: student government 81 registered organizations. **Athletics (Intercollegiate):** *Men:* basketball, fencing, ice hockey, riflery, rugby, skiing (downhill/alpine), soccer, softball, squash, swimming, track/field (outdoor), volleyball, wrestling. *Women:* basketball, fencing, ice hockey, riflery, rugby, skiing (downhill/alpine), soccer, softball, squash, swimming, track/field (outdoor), volleyball, wrestling.

ADMISSIONS
Freshman Academic Profile: Minimum paper TOEFL 550. **Freshman Admission Requirements:** High school diploma is required and GED is accepted. *Academic units required:* 3 English, 4 mathematics, 4 science, (4 science labs), 2 social studies, 2 academic electives. 3 English, 4 mathematics, 4 science, (4 science labs), 2 social studies, 2 academic electives. **Freshman Admission Statistics:** 3,900 applied, 86% admitted, % enrolled. **Transfer Admission Requirements:** High school transcript, college transcript(s), standardized test scores. **General Admission Information:** Application Fee $80. Regular application deadline 3/1. Notification on a rolling basis, beginning on or about 6/21. Nonfall registration accepted.

COSTS AND FINANCIAL AID
Required Forms and Deadlines: F. *Types of Aid: Need-based scholarships/grants:* Universities Scholarships awarded for academic excellence. *Loans:* Canada/Newfoundland Government Student Loans. **Student Employment:** Institutional employment available. Off-campus job opportunities are good. **Financial Aid Statistics:** 63% undergrads borrow to pay for school. Average cumulative indebtedness $15,167. **Criteria for awarding institutional aid:** *Non-need-based:* academics, athletics, leadership, minority status, music/drama, state/district residency.

MEMPHIS COLLEGE OF ART

Overton Park, 1930 Poplar Avenue, Memphis, TN 38104-2764
Phone: 901-272-5151 • **Financial Aid Phone:** 901-272-5136
E-mail: info@mca.edu • **CEEB Code:** 1511
Fax: 901-272-5158 • **Website:** www.mca.edu • **ACT Code:** 3991

This private school was founded in 1936. It has a 340-acre campus.

RATINGS
Admissions Selectivity Rating: 90   **Fire Safety Rating:** 73   **Green Rating:** 69

STUDENTS AND FACULTY
Enrollment: 376. **Student Body:** 65% female, 35% male, 45% out-of-state, 2% international (13 countries represented). Asian 2%, African American 18%, Caucasian 65%, Hispanic 6%, Native American 0%.

Retention and Graduation: 76% freshmen return for sophomore year. 20% freshmen graduate within 4 years. 32% freshmen graduate within 6 years. 10% grads go on to further study within 1 year. **Faculty:** Student/faculty ratio 10:1. 25 full-time faculty, 84% hold PhDs, 8% are members of minority groups, 52% are women. 0% of classes are taught by teaching assistants.

ACADEMICS
Degrees: bachelor's, master's. **Classes:** Most classes have 10–19 students. **Special Study Options:** cross-registration, double major, exchange student program (domestic), independent study, internships, study abroad, teacher certification program, New York Studies Program. Arts Exchange possible with othe AICAD schools. **Disability Services:** Special programs offered to physically disabled students include note-taking services, reader services, tape recorders, tutors. **Career Services:** Alumni network, alumni services, career/job search classes, internships, regional alumni.

FACILITIES
Housing: Coed dorms, apartments for single students. 100% of campus accessible to physically disabled. **Special Academic Facilities/Equipment:** Art museum, numerous galleries for student exhibition. Computer writing lab. **Computers:** 100% of classrooms, 100% of dorms, 100% of libraries, 100% of dining areas, have wireless network access.

CAMPUS LIFE
Environment: Metropolis. **Activities:** student government, student newspaper.

ADMISSIONS
Freshman Academic Profile: Average high school GPA 3.2. 80% from public high schools. ACT middle 50% range 19-25. Minimum paper TOEFL 500. **Basis for Candidate Selection:** *Very important factors considered include:* academic GPA, talent/ability. *Important factors considered include:* rigor of secondary school record, standardized test scores, interview. *Other factors considered include:* Class rank, application essay, recommendation(s), character/personal qualities, extracurricular activities, level of applicant's interest, volunteer work, work experience. **Freshman Admission Requirements:** High school diploma is required and GED is accepted. **Freshman Admission Statistics:** 706 applied, 36% admitted, 30% enrolled. **Transfer Admission Requirements:** college transcript(s), minimum college GPA of 2.0 required. Lowest grade transferable C. **General Admission Information:** Application Fee $25. Notification on a rolling basis, beginning on or about 12/1. Nonfall registration accepted. Admission may be deferred for a maximum of 1 year. Credit and/or placement offered for CEEB Advanced Placement tests.

COSTS AND FINANCIAL AID
Annual tuition $24,400. Room and board $8,500. Required fees $650. Average book expense $1,650. **Required Forms and Deadlines:** FAFSA. **Notification of Awards:** Applicants will be notified of awards on a rolling basis beginning 1/15. *Types of Aid: Need-based scholarships/grants:* Federal Pell, SEOG, state scholarships/grants, private scholarships, the school's own gift aid. *Loans:* Direct Subsidized Stafford, Direct Unsubsidized Stafford, Direct PLUS, Subsidized Stafford, Unsubsidized Stafford, PLUS, Federal Perkins, college/university loans from institutional funds. **Student Employment:** Federal Work-Study Program available. Highest amount earned per year from on-campus jobs $1,000. Off-campus job opportunities are good. **Financial Aid Statistics:** 58% freshmen, 64% undergrads receive need-based scholarship or grant aid. 97% freshmen, 97% undergrads receive non-need-based scholarship or grant aid. 71% freshmen, 71% undergrads receive need-based self-help aid. 95% freshmen, 95% undergrads receive any aid. 100% undergrads borrow to pay for school. **Criteria for awarding institutional aid:** *Non-need-based:* academics, art.

MENLO COLLEGE

1000 El Camino Real, Atherton, CA 94027
Phone: 650-543-3753 • **Financial Aid Phone:** 650-543-3880
E-mail: admissions@menlo.edu • **CEEB Code:** 1236
Fax: 650-543-4103 • **Website:** www.menlo.edu • **ACT Code:** 330

This private school was founded in 1927. It has a 45-acre campus.

RATINGS
Admissions Selectivity Rating: 65   **Fire Safety Rating:** 65   **Green Rating:** 66

STUDENTS AND FACULTY
Enrollment: 681. **Student Body:** 37% female, 63% male, 19% out-of-state, 12% international (24 countries represented). Asian 6%, African American 6%, Caucasian 36%, Hispanic 21%, Native American 0%.

Retention and Graduation: 74% freshmen return for sophomore year. 34% freshmen graduate within 4 years. 42% freshmen graduate within 6 years. **Faculty:** Student/faculty ratio 14:1. 31 full-time faculty, 90% hold PhDs, 29% are members of minority groups, 48% are women. 0% of classes are taught by teaching assistants.

ACADEMICS
Degrees: bachelor's. **Classes:** Most classes have 20–29 students. Most lab/discussion sessions have 10–19 students. **Majors with Highest Enrollment:** business/commerce; psychology; sport and fitness administration/management. **Special Study Options:** Accelerated program, double major, independent study, internships, student-designed major, study abroad, Advanced Placement credit Learning disability services. **Disability Services:** Special programs offered to physically disabled students include note-taking services, reader services, tape recorders, tutors. **Career Services:** Alumni network, alumni services, career/job search classes, career assessment, internships, regional alumni.

FACILITIES
Housing: Coed dorms, special housing for disabled students, men's dorms, women's dorms. 95% of campus accessible to physically disabled. **Computers:** 33% of classrooms, 100% of libraries, 100% of dining areas, 100% of student union, have wireless network access. Students can register for classes online. Administrative functions (other than registration) can be performed online.

CAMPUS LIFE
Environment: Town. **Activities:** radio station, student government, student newspaper, student-run film society, television station, yearbook, International Student Organization 30 registered organizations, 2 honor societies. **Athletics (Intercollegiate):** *Men:* baseball, basketball, cross-country, football, golf, soccer, wrestling. *Women:* basketball, cross-country, soccer, softball, volleyball, wrestling. **On-Campus Highlights:** Library, Student Union, Dining commons **Environmental Initiatives:** Menlo offers Principles of Environmental Resource Management and Management for Small Planets class.

ADMISSIONS
Freshman Academic Profile: Average high school GPA 3.2. SAT Math middle 50% range 445-565. SAT Critical Reading middle 50% range 435-530. SAT Writing middle 50% range 435-530. ACT middle 50% range 20-25. Minimum web-based TOEFL 61. Minimum paper TOEFL 500. **Basis for Candidate Selection:** *Very important factors considered include:* rigor of secondary school record, character/personal qualities. *Important factors considered include:* Class rank, application essay, academic GPA, recommendation(s), standardized test scores, alumni/ae relation, extracurricular activities, level of applicant's interest, volunteer work. *Other factors considered include:* interview, talent/ability, work experience. **Freshman Admission Requirements:** High school diploma is required and GED is accepted. **Freshman Admission Statistics:** 1,856 applied, 92% admitted, 10% enrolled. **Transfer Admission Requirements:** college transcript(s), essay or personal statement, statement of good standing from prior institution(s). Minimum college GPA of 2.0 required. Lowest grade transferable C–. **General Admission Information:** Application Fee $40. Notification on a rolling basis, beginning on or about 12/1. Nonfall registration accepted. Admission may be deferred for a maximum of 2 semesters. Credit and/or placement offered for CEEB Advanced Placement tests.

COSTS AND FINANCIAL AID
Annual tuition $36,500. Room and board $11,902. Required fees $600. Average book expense $1,670. **Required Forms and Deadlines:** FAFSA, state aid form. **Notification of Awards:** Applicants will be notified of awards on a rolling basis beginning 12/15. **Types of Aid:** *Need-based scholarships/grants:* Federal Pell, SEOG, state scholarships/grants, the school's own gift aid, Federal ACG Grant. *Loans:* Direct Subsidized Stafford, Direct Unsubsidized Stafford, Direct PLUS, Subsidized Stafford, Unsubsidized Stafford, PLUS. **Student Employment:** Federal Work-Study Program available. Institutional employment available. Highest amount earned per year from on-campus jobs $2,000. Off-campus job opportunities are excellent. **Financial Aid Statistics:** 100% freshmen, 100% undergrads receive need-based scholarship or grant aid. 10% freshmen, 6% undergrads receive non-need-based scholarship or grant aid. 87% freshmen, 89% undergrads receive need-based self-help aid. 12% freshmen, 10% undergrads receive athletic scholarships. 97% freshmen, 96% undergrads receive any aid. 43% undergrads borrow to pay for school. Average cumulative indebtedness $25,753. **Criteria for awarding institutional aid:** *Non-need-based:* academics.

MERCER UNIVERSITY—MACON

Admissions Office, Macon, GA 31207-0001
Phone: 478-301-2650 • **Financial Aid Phone:** 478-301-2670
E-mail: admissions@mercer.edu • **CEEB Code:** 5409
Fax: 478-301-2828 • **Website:** www.mercer.edu • **ACT Code:** 838

This private school, affiliated with the Baptist Church, was founded in 1833. It has a 150-acre campus.

RATINGS
Admissions Selectivity Rating: 85   **Fire Safety Rating:** 79   **Green Rating:** 77

STUDENTS AND FACULTY
Enrollment: 2,363. **Student Body:** 49% female, 51% male, 16% out-of-state, 4% international (39 countries represented). Asian 7%, African American 19%, Caucasian 59%, Hispanic 4%, Native American 0%.
Retention and Graduation: 82% freshmen return for sophomore year. 44% freshmen graduate within 4 years. 64% freshmen graduate within 6 years. 37% grads go on to further study within 1 year. **Faculty:** Student/faculty ratio 13:1. 371 full-time faculty, 90% hold PhDs, 18% are members of minority groups, 47% are women. 0% of classes are taught by teaching assistants.

ACADEMICS
Degrees: bachelor's, master's, post-master's certificate. **Classes:** Most classes have 10–19 students. Most lab/discussion sessions have 20–29 students. **Majors with Highest Enrollment:** biology/biological sciences; business/commerce; engineering. **Special Study Options:** Accelerated program, cooperative education program, cross-registration, double major, dual enrollment, honors program, independent study, internships, liberal arts/career combination, student-designed major, study abroad, teacher certification program, Great Books program. **Honors Programs:** Qualified students may be admitted to the Honors Program in the College of Liberal Arts, the Stetson School of Business and Economics, the School of Engineering, and the Tift College of Education. The Honors Program includes honors courses, out of classroom activities, independent study, and other opportunities. **Combined Degree Programs:** BA/MEng, Pharmacy (D. Pharm), Medicine (MD), Law (JD). **Disability Services:** Special programs offered to physically disabled students include note-taking services, reader services, tape recorders, tutors. **Career Services:** Alumni network, alumni services, career/job search classes, career assessment, internships Career Services highlights include Aproximately 65% of undergraduate students participate in some form of structured experiential education prior to graduation. These experiences serve to enhance the students' academic and leadership skills and also prepares them well for their chosen career paths.

FACILITIES
Housing: Coed dorms, special housing for disabled students, men's dorms, special housing for international students, women's dorms, fraternity/sorority housing, apartments for married students, apartments for single students. 85% of campus accessible to physically disabled. **Special Academic Facilities/Equipment:** McCorkle Music Building **Computers:** 100% of classrooms, 100% of dorms, 100% of libraries, 100% of dining areas, 100% of student union, 100% of common outdoor areas have wireless network access. Students can register for classes online. Administrative functions (other than registration) can be performed online.

CAMPUS LIFE
Environment: City. **Activities:** Choral groups, concert band, dance, drama/theater, jazz band, literary magazine, music ensembles, musical theater, opera, pep band, student government, student newspaper, television station, Campus Ministries, International Student Organization 115 registered organizations, 18 honor societies, 7 religious organizations. 9 fraternities, 7 sororities. **Athletics (Intercollegiate):** *Men:* baseball, basketball, cross-country, golf, riflery, soccer, tennis. *Women:* basketball, cross-country, golf, soccer, softball, tennis, volleyball. **On-Campus Highlights:** University Center, Connell Student Center, Greek Village, Porter Patch, Jesse Mercer Plaza. **Environmental Initiatives:** We have long-standing community partnerships to improve and rehabilitate housing and commerical stock in Macon proper, which has significant positive impact on the sustability of the community. We have an active mixed paper, aluminum can, and plastic recycling program. We provide subsidies for faculty and staff to purchase homes that are within walking distance of the university. We provide free tolley service from the Macon Campus to downtown Macon.

ADMISSIONS

Freshman Academic Profile: Average high school GPA 3.7. 42% in top 10% of high school class, 70% in top 25% of high school class, 92% in top 50% of high school class. SAT Math middle 50% range 540-640. SAT Critical Reading middle 50% range 530-630. ACT middle 50% range 23-28. Minimum paper TOEFL 550. **Basis for Candidate Selection:** *Very important factors considered include:* academic GPA, rigor of secondary school record, standardized test scores, level of applicant's interest. *Important factors considered include:* character/personal qualities, extracurricular activities, talent/ability, volunteer work. *Other factors considered include:* Class rank, recommendation(s), alumni/ae relation, interview, work experience. **Freshman Admission Requirements:** High school diploma is required and GED is accepted. *Academic units required:* 4 English, 4 mathematics, 3 science, (2 science labs), 2 foreign language, 1 social studies, 2 history. 4 English, 4 mathematics, 3 science, (2 science labs), 2 foreign language, 1 social studies, 2 history. **Freshman Admission Statistics:** 3,519 applied, 63% admitted, 29% enrolled. **Transfer Admission Requirements:** college transcript(s), statement of good standing from prior institution(s). Minimum college GPA of 2.5 required. Lowest grade transferable C. **General Admission Information:** Application Fee $50. Regular application deadline 7/1. Notification on a rolling basis, beginning on or about 11/1. Nonfall registration not accepted. Admission may be deferred for a maximum of 1 year. Credit and/or placement offered for CEEB Advanced Placement tests.

COSTS AND FINANCIAL AID

Annual tuition $32,166. Room and board $10,697. Required fees $300. Average book expense $1,200. **Required Forms and Deadlines:** FAFSA, institution's own financial aid form, state aid form. **Notification of Awards:** Applicants will be notified of awards on a rolling basis beginning 3/15. **Types of Aid:** *Need-based scholarships/grants:* Federal Pell, SEOG, state scholarships/grants, the school's own gift aid, Federal Nursing Scholarships. *Loans:* Direct Subsidized Stafford, Direct Unsubsidized Stafford, Direct PLUS, Federal Perkins, Federal Nursing, college/university loans from institutional funds. **Student Employment:** Federal Work-Study Program available. Institutional employment available. Off-campus job opportunities are good. **Financial Aid Statistics:** 99% freshmen, 99% undergrads receive need-based scholarship or grant aid. 23% freshmen, 23% undergrads receive non-need-based scholarship or grant aid. 63% freshmen, 64% undergrads receive need-based self-help aid. 3% freshmen, 4% undergrads receive athletic scholarships. 99% freshmen, 98% undergrads receive any aid. 69% undergrads borrow to pay for school. Average cumulative indebtedness $31,488. **Criteria for awarding institutional aid:** *Non-need-based:* academics, art, athletics, job skills, leadership, music/drama, state/district residency.

See page 1144.

MERCY COLLEGE

555 Broadway, Dobbs Ferry, NY 10522
Phone: 914-674-7324 • **Financial Aid Phone:** 914-674-3027
E-mail: admissions@mercy.edu • **CEEB Code:** 2409
Fax: 914-674-7608 • **Website:** www.mercy.edu • **ACT Code:** 2814

This private school was founded in 1950. It has a 90-acre campus.

RATINGS

Admissions Selectivity Rating: 63   **Fire Safety Rating:** 99   **Green Rating:** 60*

STUDENTS AND FACULTY

Enrollment: 6,970. **Student Body:** 69% female, 31% male, 7% out-of-state, 1% international (43 countries represented). Asian 3%, African American 28%, Caucasian 28%, Hispanic 34%.
Retention and Graduation: 69% freshmen return for sophomore year. 20% freshmen graduate within 4 years. **Faculty:** Student/faculty ratio 18:1. 188 full-time faculty, 83% hold PhDs, 21% are are members of minority groups, 62% are women. 0% of classes are taught by teaching assistants.

ACADEMICS

Degrees: associate, bachelor's, certificate, master's, post-bachelor's certificate, post-master's certificate, terminal associate, transfer associate. **Classes:** Most classes have 10–19 students. **Majors with Highest Enrollment:** business administration and management; psychology; social sciences. **Special Study Options:** Accelerated program, cooperative education program, distance learning, double major, dual enrollment, honors program, internships, teacher certification program, weekend college, Program for college students with learning disabilities. **Honors programs:** Admission criteria to the Honors Program is a 87 or above high school average. One hundred and thirty new and transfer students were admitted in 2009–10. Students in the Honors Program take Honors

versions of General Education courses (e.g., English, speech, and math) at the lower level and complete individualized Honors project in connection with their major for a total of 24 Honors credits. **Combined degree programs:** BA/MA, accounting, education, nursing. **Disability Services:** Special programs offered to physically disabled students include note-taking services, reader services, tape recorders, tutors. **Career services:** Alumni network, alumni services, career/job search classes, career assessment, internships. Career services highlights include Cooperative Learning.

FACILITIES

Housing: Coed dorms, 100% of campus accessible to physically disabled. **Special Academic Facilities/Equipment:** Childcare center located at the Bronx campus. **Computers:** 40% of classrooms, 100% of dorms, 60% of libraries, 60% of dining areas, 60% of student union, have wireless network access. Students can register for classes online. Administrative functions (other than registration) can be performed online.

CAMPUS LIFE

Environment: Village. **Activities:** dance, student government, student newspaper, Campus Ministries, Model UN, 20 registered organizations, 1 religious organizations. **Athletics (Intercollegiate):** Men: baseball, basketball, cross-country, lacrosse, soccer, tennis, track/field (outdoor). Women: basketball, cross-country, lacrosse, soccer, softball, track/field (outdoor), volleyball. **On-Campus Highlights:** Waterfront campus on the Hudson River, new State-of-the-Art Library, student café, music and recording studio, Roy Disney Center for Computer Animation. Over 90 undergraduate and graduate programs: business, education, health and natural sciences, liberal arts, and social and behavioral sciences. Main campus in Dobbs Ferry plus additional campus locations in Bronx, Manhattan, White Plains, and Yorktown Heights.

ADMISSIONS

Freshman Academic Profile: Average high school GPA 2.8. Minimum web-based TOEFL 79. Minimum paper TOEFL 550. **Basis for Candidate Selection:** Very important factors considered include: academic GPA, character/personal qualities, extracurricular activities, talent/ability. Important factors considered include: Class rank, application essay, recommendation(s), rigor of secondary school record, standardized test scores, interview, level of applicant's interest. Other factors considered include: alumni/ae relation, volunteer work, work experience. **Freshman Admission Requirements:** High school diploma is required and GED is accepted. **Academic units required:** 4 English, 4 mathematics, 3 science, (1 science labs), 3 foreign language, 2 social studies, 2 history, 3 academic electives. **Academic units recommend:** 4 English, 4 mathematics, 3 science, (1 science labs), 3 foreign language, 2 social studies, 2 history, 3 academic electives. **Freshman Admission Statistics:** 5,766 applied. **Transfer Admission Requirements:** college transcript(s), minimum college GPA of 2.0 required. Lowest grade transferable C. **General Admission Information:** Application Fee $40. Notification on a rolling basis, beginning on or about 12/1. Nonfall registration accepted. Credit offered for CEEB Advanced Placement tests.

COSTS AND FINANCIAL AID

Annual tuition $16,996. Room and board $12,436. Required fees $560. Average book expense $1,412. **Required Forms and Deadlines:** FAFSA, state aid form. **Notification of Awards:** Applicants will be notified of awards on a rolling basis beginning 4/1. **Types of Aid:** Need-based scholarships/grants: Federal Pell, SEOG, state scholarships/grants, private scholarships, the school's own gift aid, Federal Nursing Scholarships. Loans: Subsidized Stafford, Unsubsidized Stafford, PLUS, Federal Nursing, Private Educational Loans. Student Employment: Federal Work-Study Program available. Institutional employment available. Highest amount earned per year from on-campus jobs $5,342. Off-campus job opportunities are good. **Financial Aid Statistics:** 91% freshmen, 88% undergrads receive need-based scholarship or grant aid. 35% freshmen, 31% undergrads receive non-need-based scholarship or grant aid. 79% freshmen, 85% undergrads receive need-based self-help aid. 4% freshmen, 4% undergrads receive athletic scholarships. 58% freshmen, 53% undergrads receive any aid. 71% undergrads borrow to pay for school. Average cumulative indebtedness $24,138. **Criteria for awarding institutional aid:** Non-need-based: academics, athletics.

MERCYHURST UNIVERSITY

Admissions, Erie, PA 16546
Phone: 814-824-2202 • **Financial Aid Phone:** 814-824-2288
E-mail: admissions@mercyhurst.edu • **CEEB Code:** 2410
Fax: 814-824-2071 • **Website:** admissions.mercyhurst.edu • **ACT Code:** 3629

This private school, affiliated with the Roman Catholic Church, was founded in 1926. It has a 88-acre campus.

RATINGS
Admissions Selectivity Rating: 70   **Fire Safety Rating:** 88   **Green Rating:** 60*

STUDENTS AND FACULTY
Enrollment: 668.
Faculty: Student/faculty ratio 15:1. 192 full-time faculty, 53% hold PhDs, 5% are members of minority groups, 48% are women. 0% of classes are taught by teaching assistants.

ACADEMICS
Degrees: associate, bachelor's, certificate, master's, post-bachelor's certificate, terminal associate, transfer associate. **Classes:** Most classes have fewer than 10 students. Most lab/discussion sessions have 10–19 students. **Special Study Options:** Accelerated program, cooperative education program, cross-registration, double major, exchange student program (domestic), honors program, independent study, internships, liberal arts/career combination, student-designed major, study abroad, teacher certification program, weekend college, Arts, Business, Computer Science, Education, Health Professions, History, English Home Economics, Humanities, Natural Science, Social/Behavioral Science. Off Campus Study: Washington D.C. Undergrads may take grad level classes. **Combined Degree Programs:** 3+4 Medical school program. **Disability Services:** Special programs offered to physically disabled students include note-taking services, reader services, tape recorders, tutors. **Career Services:** Alumni network, alumni services, career/job search classes, career assessment, internships.

FACILITIES
Housing: special housing for disabled students, men's dorms, women's dorms, apartments for single students. **Special Academic Facilities/Equipment:** Art gallery, college-owned restaurant for hotel/restaurant management department, observatory, archaeology lab. **Computers:** Students can register for classes online. Administrative functions (other than registration) can be performed online.

CAMPUS LIFE
Environment: Village. **Activities:** Choral groups, concert band, dance, drama/theater, literary magazine, music ensembles, musical theater, pep band, radio station, student government, student newspaper, television station, yearbook 9 honor societies, 2 religious organizations. **Athletics (Intercollegiate):** *Men:* baseball, basketball, cheerleading, crew/rowing, cross-country, football, golf, ice hockey, lacrosse, soccer, tennis, volleyball, water polo, wrestling. *Women:* basketball, cheerleading, crew/rowing, cross-country, field hockey, golf, ice hockey, lacrosse, soccer, softball, tennis, volleyball, water polo. **On-Campus Highlights:** Performing Arts Center, Mercyhurst Athletic Center, Library, Student Union, Ice Rink.

ADMISSIONS
Freshman Academic Profile: Average high school GPA 3.3. 17% in top 10% of high school class, 41% in top 25% of high school class, 76% in top 50% of high school class. 53% from public high schools. SAT Math middle 50% range 470-570. SAT Critical Reading middle 50% range 470-580. SAT Writing middle 50% range 460-560. ACT middle 50% range 20-26. Minimum web-based TOEFL 79. Minimum paper TOEFL 550. **Basis for Candidate Selection:** *Very important factors considered include:* rigor of secondary school record. *Important factors considered include:* Class rank, standardized test scores, character/personal qualities, interview, talent/ability. *Other factors considered include:* application essay, recommendation(s), alumni/ae relation, extracurricular activities, geographical residence, racial/ethnic status, religious affiliation/commitment, state residency, volunteer work, work experience. **Freshman Admission Requirements:** High school diploma is required and GED is accepted. **Freshman Admission Statistics:** 2,618 applied, 79% admitted, 32% enrolled. **Transfer Admission Requirements:** High school transcript, college transcript(s), standardized test scores, minimum college GPA of 2.0 required. Lowest grade transferable C. **General Admission Information:** Application Fee $30. Notification on a rolling basis, beginning on or about 11/15. Nonfall registration accepted. Admission may be deferred for a maximum of 1 year. Credit and/or placement offered for CEEB Advanced Placement tests.

COSTS AND FINANCIAL AID
Annual tuition $24,648. Required fees $1,698. Average book expense $1,000. **Required Forms and Deadlines:** FAFSA, institution's own financial aid form. **Notification of Awards:** Applicants will be notified of awards on a rolling basis beginning 2/15. **Types of Aid:** *Need-based scholarships/grants:* Federal Pell,

SEOG, state scholarships/grants, private scholarships, the school's own gift aid. *Loans:* Subsidized Stafford, Unsubsidized Stafford, PLUS, Federal Perkins. **Student Employment:** Federal Work-Study Program available. Institutional employment available. Highest amount earned per year from on-campus jobs $1,200. **Financial Aid Statistics:** 99% freshmen, 97% undergrads receive need-based scholarship or grant aid. 76% freshmen, 76% undergrads receive non-need-based scholarship or grant aid. 98% freshmen, 91% undergrads receive need-based self-help aid. 5% freshmen, 5% undergrads receive athletic scholarships. 93% freshmen. 95% undergrads borrow to pay for school. Average cumulative indebtedness $22,000. **Criteria for awarding institutional aid:** *Non-need-based:* academics, alumni affiliation, art, athletics, leadership, minority status, music/drama, religious affiliation.

MEREDITH COLLEGE

3800 Hillsborough Street, Raleigh, NC 27607
Phone: 919-760-8581 • **Financial Aid Phone:** 919-760-8565
E-mail: admissions@meredith.edu • **CEEB Code:** 5410
Fax: 919-760-2348 • **Website:** www.meredith.edu • **ACT Code:** 3126

This private school was founded in 1891. It has a 225-acre campus.

RATINGS
Admissions Selectivity Rating: 79   **Fire Safety Rating:** 80   **Green Rating:** 60*

STUDENTS AND FACULTY
Enrollment: 1,666. **Student Body:** 100% female, 0% male, 9% out-of-state, 3% international (47 countries represented). Asian 2%, African American 12%, Caucasian 74%, Hispanic 3%, Native American 1%.
Retention and Graduation: 77% freshmen return for sophomore year. 43% freshmen graduate within 4 years. 59% freshmen graduate within 6 years.
Faculty: Student/faculty ratio 12:1. 121 full-time faculty, 93% hold PhDs, 10% are members of minority groups, 67% are women. 0% of classes are taught by teaching assistants.

ACADEMICS
Degrees: bachelor's, master's, post-bachelor's certificate. **Classes:** Most classes have 10–19 students. Most lab/discussion sessions have fewer than 10 students. **Majors with Highest Enrollment:** business/commerce; interior design; psychology. **Special Study Options:** Accelerated program, cooperative education program, cross-registration, double major, dual enrollment, honors program, independent study, internships, liberal arts/career combination, student-designed major, study abroad, teacher certification program, Semester Programs at American U., Drew U., Marymount Manhattan. **Honors Programs:** Meredith offers an enriched academic and co-curricular Honors Program that spans the four years and involves honors courses in general education, in the major field, and a thesis or equivalent project. Interdisciplinary honors courses and weekend trips/programs enrich the experience, and a Focus on Excellence series offers a variety of outings to cultural/intellectual/entertainment venues. Scholarships are provided for Honors Program participants. **Combined Degree Programs:** BA/MEng, BS/MBA in accounting. **Disability Services:** Special programs offered to physically disabled students include note-taking services, reader services, tape recorders, tutors. **Career Services:** Alumni network, alumni services, career/job search classes, career assessment, internships.

FACILITIES
Housing: women's dorms, apartments for married students, apartments for single students. 80% of campus accessible to physically disabled. **Special Academic Facilities/Equipment:** Art gallery, amphitheatre, child-care lab, learning center and fitness center. Experimental and clinical psychology labs including an autism lab. A new Science and Mathematics Building provides a roof top telescope platform for astronomy observations, an electron microscope suite, greenhouse, and 15 student/faculty research labs. **Computers:** Students can register for classes online. Administrative functions (other than registration) can be performed online.

CAMPUS LIFE
Environment: Metropolis. **Activities:** Choral groups, concert band, dance, drama/theater, literary magazine, music ensembles, musical theater, student government, student newspaper, symphony orchestra, yearbook, Model UN 91 registered organizations, 22 honor societies, 7 religious organizations. **Athletics (Intercollegiate):** *Women:* basketball, cross-country, soccer, softball, tennis, volleyball. **On-Campus Highlights:** Science and Math Building, McIver Ampitheatre and Meredith Lake, Weatherspoon Physical Education -Dance Building, Belk Dining Hall, Cate Student Center/Bee Hive (snack bar).

ADMISSIONS
Freshman Academic Profile: Average high school GPA 3.1. 20% in top 10% of high school class, 48% in top 25% of high school class, 82% in top

50% of high school class. SAT Math middle 50% range 460-563. SAT Critical Reading middle 50% range 450-560. ACT middle 50% range 18-24. Minimum paper TOEFL 500. **Basis for Candidate Selection:** *Very important factors considered include:* Class rank, academic GPA, rigor of secondary school record. *Important factors considered include:* recommendation(s), standardized test scores, character/personal qualities. *Other factors considered include:* application essay, alumni/ae relation, extracurricular activities, interview, talent/ability, volunteer work, work experience. **Freshman Admission Requirements:** High school diploma is required and GED is not accepted. *Academic units required:* 4 English, 3 mathematics, 3 science, 2 foreign language. *Academic units recommended:* 4 English, 3 mathematics, 3 science, 2 foreign language. **Freshman Admission Statistics:** 1,599 applied, 61% admitted, 41% enrolled. **Transfer Admission Requirements:** High school transcript, college transcript(s), statement of good standing from prior institution(s). Minimum college GPA of 2.0 required. Lowest grade transferable C. **General Admission Information:** Application Fee $40. Early decision application deadline 10/15. Notification on a rolling basis, beginning on or about 11/1. Nonfall registration accepted. Admission may be deferred for a maximum of One year. Credit offered for CEEB Advanced Placement tests.

COSTS AND FINANCIAL AID

Annual tuition $29,106. Room and board $8,348. Required fees $80. Average book expense $750. **Required Forms and Deadlines:** FAFSA. **Notification of Awards:** Applicants will be notified of awards on a rolling basis beginning 3/15. **Types of Aid:** *Need-based scholarships/grants:* Federal Pell, SEOG, state scholarships/grants, private scholarships, the school's own gift aid. *Loans:* Subsidized Stafford, Unsubsidized Stafford, PLUS, Federal Perkins, college/university loans from institutional funds. **Student Employment: Financial Aid Statistics:** 100% freshmen, 99% undergrads receive need-based scholarship or grant aid. 84% freshmen, 83% undergrads receive non-need-based scholarship or grant aid. 84% freshmen, 83% undergrads receive need-based self-help aid. 73% undergrads borrow to pay for school. Average cumulative indebtedness $34,549. **Criteria for awarding institutional aid:** *Non-need-based:* academics, art, leadership, minority status, music/drama, religious affiliation, state/district residency.

MERRIMACK COLLEGE

Office of Admission, North Andover, MA 1845
Phone: 978-837-5100 • **Financial Aid Phone:** 978-837-5186
E-mail: admission@merrimack.edu • **CEEB Code:** 3525
Fax: 978-837-5133 • **Website:** www.merrimack.edu • **ACT Code:**

This private school, affiliated with the Roman Catholic Church, was founded in 1947. It has a 220-acre campus.

RATINGS

Admissions Selectivity Rating: 71   **Fire Safety Rating:** 96   **Green Rating:** 65

STUDENTS AND FACULTY

Enrollment: 2,408. **Student Body:** 48% female, 52% male, 27% out-of-state, 6% international (19 countries represented). Asian 2%, African American 3%, Caucasian 69%, Hispanic 7%, Native American 0%. **Retention and Graduation:** 80% freshmen return for sophomore year. 54% freshmen graduate within 4 years. 64% freshmen graduate within 6 years. 27% grads go on to further study within 1 year. **Faculty:** Student/faculty ratio 12:1. 138 full-time faculty, 83% hold PhDs, 9% are members of minority groups, 46% are women. 0% of classes are taught by teaching assistants.

ACADEMICS

Degrees: associate, bachelor's, master's. **Classes:** Most classes have 10–19 students. **Majors with Highest Enrollment:** business administration and management; marketing/marketing management; psychology. **Special Study Options:** Accelerated program, cooperative education program, cross-registration, double major, dual enrollment, English as a Second Language (ESL), independent study, internships, liberal arts/career combination, student-designed major, study abroad, teacher certification program, Five-year combined BA/BS program, continuing education program, center for corporate education. ESL available through Kaplan with offices on the college campus. Cross-registration available through college's membership in 10-college consortium. **Honors Programs:** The Honors Program offers students with strong academic credentials, class standing, and leadership qualities the opportunity to study with other exceptional students in smaller classes. It is an innovative and exciting approach to fulfilling the college's general education requirements and includes a variety of social and co-curricular activities. **Disability Services:** Special programs offered to physically disabled students include note-taking services, reader services, tape recorders, tutors. **Career Services:** Alumni network, alumni services, career/job search classes, career assessment, internships, regional alumni.

Career Services highlights include At Merrimack College we offer experiential opportunities for students in each major: Traditional 5 year cooperative education program; Full-time paid summer internships; Part-time paid internship opportunities during the academic year; In conjunction with academic departments, unpaid but for-academic credit internships; Service learning volunteer opportunities with local non-profit agencies.

FACILITIES

Housing: Coed dorms, special housing for disabled students, apartments for single students, wellness housing, theme housing, 90% of campus accessible to physically disabled. **Special Academic Facilities/Equipment:** Observatory, Rogers Center for the Arts. **Computers:** 100% of classrooms, 100% of libraries, 100% of dining areas, 100% of student union, have wireless network access. Students can register for classes online. Administrative functions (other than registration) can be performed online.

CAMPUS LIFE

Environment: Town. **Activities:** Choral groups, dance, drama/theater, jazz band, music ensembles, musical theater, pep band, student government, student newspaper, student-run film society, television station, yearbook, Campus Ministries, International Student Organization, Model UN 47 registered organizations, 3 honor societies, 5 religious organizations. 2 fraternities, 3 sororities. **Athletics (Intercollegiate):** *Men:* baseball, basketball, cross-country, football, ice hockey, lacrosse, soccer, tennis. *Women:* basketball, cross-country, field hockey, lacrosse, soccer, softball, tennis, volleyball. **On-Campus Highlights:** Sakowich Student Center, Rogers Center for the Arts, Santagati Hall, McQuade Library, Volpe Athletic Complex, Campus observatory open one night a week to the public. Rogers Center and the McQuade Library have art gallerys. McQuade Gallery frequently displays student art. **Environmental Initiatives:** Creation of a new Director of Sustainable Energy position in fall 2010 and the concomitant establishment of a new Energy Efficiency and Renewable Energy Advisory Board to guide and inform Merrimack's energy planning. As part of this effort, the College is developing a new renewable energy and carbon footprint reduction policy. End of the semester "Sweeps Week" is a joint Campus Ministry/Sustainability Group sponsored program that collects items, including clothing, food, toiletries, linens, house wares and textbooks, as students move out of the residence halls at the end of each academic year in May. The mission of the program is to lighten the load of students moving out by sharing their surplus of items with the local community in need. This event is linked to the new Blue, Cold and Green Festival that highlights campus sustainability activities, recruits new volunteers and encourages and catalyzes sustainable practices across campus. Development of a new interdisciplinary Environmental Studies and Sustainability Major in fall 2010. The new major has an integrated curriculum across the College's four Schools, Science and Engineering, Liberal Arts, Business, and Education.

ADMISSIONS

Freshman Academic Profile: Average high school GPA. 74% from public high schools. SAT Math middle 50% range 470-590. SAT Critical Reading middle 50% range 460-550. SAT Writing middle 50% range 460-560. ACT middle 50% range 20-25. Minimum web-based TOEFL 75. Minimum paper TOEFL 550. **Basis for Candidate Selection:** *Very important factors considered include:* application essay, academic GPA, rigor of secondary school record. *Important factors considered include:* Class rank, recommendation(s), character/personal qualities, talent/ability. *Other factors considered include:* alumni/ae relation, extracurricular activities, interview, level of applicant's interest, volunteer work, work experience. **Freshman Admission Requirements:** High school diploma is required and GED is accepted. *Academic units required:* 4 English, 3 mathematics, 3 science, (3 science labs), 2 foreign language, 1 social studies, 1 history, 3 academic electives. *Academic units recommended:* 4 English, 3 mathematics, 3 science, (3 science labs), 2 foreign language, 1 social studies, 1 history, 3 academic electives. **Freshman Admission Statistics:** 5,661 applied, 77% admitted, 16% enrolled. **Transfer Admission Requirements:** college transcript(s), essay or personal statement, minimum college GPA of 2.5 required. Lowest grade transferable C. **General Admission Information:** Application Fee $60. Regular application deadline 2/1. Regular notification 4/1. Nonfall registration accepted. Admission may be deferred for a maximum of 12 months. Credit and/or placement offered for CEEB Advanced Placement tests.

COSTS AND FINANCIAL AID

Required Forms and Deadlines: FAFSA, noncustodial PROFILE, business/farm supplement. Sibling Verification. **Notification of Awards:** Applicants will be notified of awards on or about 3/15. **Types of Aid:** *Need-based scholarships/grants:* Federal Pell, SEOG, state scholarships/grants, private scholarships, the school's own gift aid. *Loans:* Subsidized Stafford, Unsubsidized Stafford, PLUS, Federal Perkins, state loans, college/university loans from institutional funds, Alternative Loans. **Student Employment:** Federal Work-Study Program available. Highest amount earned per year from on-campus jobs $1,500. Off-campus job opportunities are good. **Financial Aid Statistics:** 100% freshmen, 98% undergrads receive need-based scholarship or grant aid. 8% freshmen, 11% undergrads receive non-need-based scholarship or grant aid. 88% freshmen, 84% undergrads receive need-based self-help aid. 5% freshmen, 6% undergrads receive athletic scholarships. 89% freshmen, 91% undergrads receive any aid. **Criteria for awarding institutional aid:** *Non-need-based:* academics, athletics, leadership, minority status, religious affiliation.

MESSIAH COLLEGE

Box 3005, Grantham, PA 17027
Phone: 717-691-6000 • **Financial Aid Phone:** 717-766-2511 Ext 3630
E-mail: admiss@messiah.edu • **CEEB Code:** 2411
Fax: 717-691-2307 • **Website:** www.messiah.edu • **ACT Code:** 3630

This private school was founded in 1909. It has a 471-acre campus.

RATINGS
Admissions Selectivity Rating: 83   **Fire Safety Rating:** 72   **Green Rating:** 85

STUDENTS AND FACULTY
Enrollment: 2,754. **Student Body:** 60% female, 40% male, 40% out-of-state, 2% international (27 countries represented). Asian 2%. African American 2%, Caucasian 87%, Hispanic 3%, Native American 0%.
Retention and Graduation: 87% freshmen return for sophomore year. 70% freshmen graduate within 4 years. 76% freshmen graduate within 6 years. 21% grads go on to further study within 1 year. 65% grads pursue arts and sciences degrees. 5% grads pursue law degrees. 2% grads pursue business degrees. 14% grads pursue medical degrees. **Faculty:** Student/faculty ratio 13:1. 175 full-time faculty, 86% hold PhDs, 5% are members of minority groups, 43% are women. 0% of classes are taught by teaching assistants.

ACADEMICS
Degrees: bachelor's. **Classes:** Most classes have 20–29 students. Most lab/discussion sessions have 10–19 students. **Majors with Highest Enrollment:** elementary education and teaching; nursing/registered nurse (rn, asn, bsn, msn); psychology. **Special Study Options:** Accelerated program, double major, dual enrollment, English as a Second Language (ESL), exchange student program (domestic), honors program, independent study, internships, student-designed major, study abroad, teacher certification program, Pass/Fail option. **Honors Programs:** The College Honors Program is designed for students who demonstrate high scholarly ability early in their academic career. The program provides a series of interdisciplinary honors courses which satisfy selected general education requirements. In addition, various campus activities are designed each semester for participants in the College Honors Program. Participation in the program culminates in an honors research project, typically during the senior year. Admission to the program is highly competitive and students selected for the College Honors Program receive either full tuition or partial tuition scholarships. **Disability Services:** Special programs offered to physically disabled students include note-taking services, reader services, tape recorders, tutors. **Career Services:** Alumni network, alumni services, career assessment, internships Career Services highlights include Internship program supports ~150 students each year.

FACILITIES
Housing: Coed dorms, special housing for disabled students, men's dorms, special housing for international students, women's dorms, apartments for single students. 80% of campus accessible to physically disabled. **Special Academic Facilities/Equipment:** Boyer Center for Advanced Studies; Brethren in Christ Historical Society and Archives; Oakes Museum of Natural History. **Computers:** 100% of classrooms, 100% of dorms, 100% of libraries, 100% of dining areas, 100% of student union, have wireless network access. Students can register for classes online. Administrative functions (other than registration) can be performed online.

CAMPUS LIFE
Environment: Village. **Activities:** Choral groups, concert band, dance, drama/theater, jazz band, literary magazine, music ensembles, musical theater, pep band, radio station, student government, student newspaper, student-run film society, symphony orchestra, yearbook, Campus Ministries, International Student Organization 71 registered organizations, 7 honor societies, 10 religious organizations. **Athletics (Intercollegiate):** *Men:* baseball, basketball, cross-country, golf, lacrosse, soccer, swimming, tennis, track/field (outdoor), track/field (indoor), ultimate frisbee, wrestling. *Women:* basketball, cross-country, field hockey, lacrosse, soccer, softball, swimming, tennis, track/field (outdoor), track/field (indoor), volleyball. **On-Campus Highlights:** Boyer Hall (Schools of Humanities, Ed. and Soc. Sci., Eisenhower Campus Center/Sollenberger Sports Cent, Oakes Museum of Natural History, Stoner Covered Bridge, Starry Athletic Complex, The scenic Yellow Breeches Creek runs through the 471 acre campus. It is a nationally recognized trout fishing stream, complete with covered bridge and swinging foot bridge. **Environmental Initiatives:** Sunflower Power Project: A full cycle of process of growing sunflowers on campus, press-

ing and processing cooking oil on campus for dining hall, and recycling used oil on campus into biodiesel fuel for on campus use. http://www.sunflowernsa.com/magazine/details.asp?ID=771 http://www.youtube.com/watch?v=w5_4LvNZu9M&feature=player_embedded Creation Care Community Garden--Community Supported Agriculture that is student run by the EarthKeepers Delivery of educational mock energy bills to students http://www.messiah.edu/sustainability/turn_it_off/index.html Recycling and composting of wastes by Facilities Management and Conference Services & Digital energy management system across campus buildings which is yielding solid energy savings

ADMISSIONS
Freshman Academic Profile: Average high school GPA 3.7. 34% in top 10% of high school class, 66% in top 25% of high school class, 89% in top 50% of high school class. 80% from public high schools. SAT Math middle 50% range 510-630. SAT Critical Reading middle 50% range 510-620. SAT Writing middle 50% range 500-620. ACT middle 50% range 21-28. Minimum web-based TOEFL 80. Minimum paper TOEFL 550. **Basis for Candidate Selection:** *Very important factors considered include:* Class rank, academic GPA, recommendation(s), rigor of secondary school record, standardized test scores, character/personal qualities, extracurricular activities, religious affiliation/commitment, talent/ability. *Important factors considered include:* application essay, volunteer work. *Other factors considered include:* alumni/ae relation, interview, level of applicant's interest, racial/ethnic status, work experience. **Freshman Admission Requirements:** High school diploma is required and GED is accepted. *Academic units required:* 4 English, 2 mathematics, 2 science, (2 science labs), 2 foreign language, 2 social studies, 4 academic electives. *Academic units recommended:* 4 English, 2 mathematics, 2 science, (2 science labs), 2 foreign language, 2 social studies, 4 academic electives. **Freshman Admission Statistics:** 3,149 applied, 64% admitted, 35% enrolled. **Transfer Admission Requirements:** college transcript(s), essay or personal statement, statement of good standing from prior institution(s). Minimum college GPA of 2.5 required. Lowest grade transferable C. **General Admission Information:** Application Fee $30. Notification on a rolling basis, beginning on or about 7/1. Nonfall registration accepted. Admission may be deferred for a maximum of 2 years. Credit and/or placement offered for CEEB Advanced Placement tests.

COSTS AND FINANCIAL AID
Annual tuition $28,640. Room and board $8,760. Required fees $820. Average book expense $1,220. **Required Forms and Deadlines:** FAFSA. **Notification of Awards:** Applicants will be notified of awards on a rolling basis beginning 3/15. **Types of Aid:** *Need-based scholarships/grants:* Federal Pell, SEOG, state scholarships/grants, private scholarships, the school's own gift aid. *Loans:* Direct Subsidized Stafford, Direct Unsubsidized Stafford, Direct PLUS, Subsidized Stafford, Unsubsidized Stafford, PLUS, Federal Perkins, Federal Nursing. **Student Employment:** Federal Work-Study Program available. Institutional employment available. Highest amount earned per year from on-campus jobs $5,730. Off-campus job opportunities are good. **Financial Aid Statistics:** 99% freshmen, 99% undergrads receive need-based scholarship or grant aid. 10% freshmen, 9% undergrads receive non-need-based scholarship or grant aid. 83% freshmen, 83% undergrads receive need-based self-help aid. 100% freshmen, 97% undergrads receive any aid. 74% undergrads borrow to pay for school. Average cumulative indebtedness $35,306. **Criteria for awarding institutional aid:** *Non-need-based:* academics, art, leadership, music/drama, religious affiliation.

METHODIST UNIVERSITY

5400 Ramsey Street, Fayetteville, NC 28311
Phone: 910-630-7027 • **Financial Aid Phone:** 910-630-7192
E-mail: admissions@methodist.edu • **CEEB Code:** 5426
Fax: 910-630-7285 • **Website:** www.methodist.edu • **ACT Code:** 3127

This private school, affiliated with the Methodist Church, was founded in 1956. It has a 600-acre campus.

RATINGS
Admissions Selectivity Rating: 75   **Fire Safety Rating:** 70   **Green Rating:** 60*

STUDENTS AND FACULTY
Enrollment: 2,226. **Student Body:** 48% female, 52% male, 30% out-of-state, 5% international (53 countries represented). Asian 1%, African American 24%, Caucasian 48%, Hispanic 6%, Native American 1%.
Retention and Graduation: 62% freshmen return for sophomore year. 16% freshmen graduate within 4 years. 44% freshmen graduate within 6 years. 38% grads go on to further study within 1 year. 8% grads pursue arts and sciences degrees. 1% grads pursue law degrees. 12% grads pursue business degrees. 7% grads pursue medical degrees. **Faculty:** Student/faculty ratio 13:1. 142 full-time faculty, 69% hold PhDs, 13% are members of minority groups, 49% are women. 0% of classes are taught by teaching assistants.

ACADEMICS

Degrees: associate, bachelor's, master's, terminal associate. **Classes:** Most classes have fewer than 10 students. Most lab/discussion sessions have 20–29 students. **Majors with Highest Enrollment:** business/commerce; cell/cellular and molecular biology; secondary education and teaching. **Special Study Options:** cooperative education program, distance learning, double major, dual enrollment, English as a Second Language (ESL), honors program, independent study, internships, liberal arts/career combination, student-designed major, study abroad, teacher certification program, weekend college, distance learning is on-line coursework available. **Honors Programs:** The Methodist College Honors Program is based on the "Great Books" and is an outstanding opportunity for high acheiving students. **Disability Services:** Special programs offered to physically disabled students include note-taking services, reader services, tape recorders, tutors. **Career Services:** career/job search classes, career assessment, internships.

FACILITIES

Housing: Coed dorms, men's dorms, women's dorms, apartments for single students, first year experience hall. 80% of campus accessible to physically disabled. **Special Academic Facilities/Equipment:** Art gallery, Nature Trail, 18 hole golf course with practice facilities for PGM students, Academic Developement Center **Computers:** Administrative functions (other than registration) can be performed online.

CAMPUS LIFE

Environment: City. **Activities:** Choral groups, concert band, dance, drama/theater, jazz band, literary magazine, marching band, music ensembles, musical theater, opera, pep band, radio station, student government, student newspaper, symphony orchestra, yearbook, Campus Ministries, Model UN 72 registered organizations, 15 honor societies, 8 religious organizations. 3 fraternities, 2 sororities. **Athletics (Intercollegiate):** *Men:* baseball, basketball, cheerleading, cross-country, football, golf, soccer, tennis, track/field (outdoor). *Women:* basketball, cheerleading, cross-country, golf, lacrosse, soccer, softball, tennis, track/field (outdoor), volleyball.

ADMISSIONS

Freshman Academic Profile: Average high school GPA 3.3. 9% in top 10% of high school class, 34% in top 25% of high school class, 73% in top 50% of high school class. 86% from public high schools. SAT Math middle 50% range 450-550. SAT Critical Reading middle 50% range 430-520. SAT Writing middle 50% range 400-490. ACT middle 50% range 17-23. Minimum paper TOEFL 500. **Basis for Candidate Selection:** *Very important factors considered include:* academic GPA, rigor of secondary school record. *Important factors considered include:* Class rank, standardized test scores, interview. *Other factors considered include:* application essay, recommendation(s), alumni/ae relation, character/personal qualities, extracurricular activities, first generation, talent/ability. **Freshman Admission Requirements:** High school diploma is required and GED is accepted. *Academic units required:* 4 English, 3 mathematics, 3 science, (1 science labs), 1 social studies, 2 history, 4 academic electives. *Academic units recommended:* 4 English, 3 mathematics, 3 science, (1 science labs), 1 social studies, 2 history, 4 academic electives. **Freshman Admission Statistics:** 3,823 applied, 61% admitted, 21% enrolled. **Transfer Admission Requirements:** High school transcript, college transcript(s), statement of good standing from prior institution(s). Minimum college GPA of 2.0 required. Lowest grade transferable C. **General Admission Information:** Application Fee $25. Notification on a rolling basis, beginning on or about 9/1. Nonfall registration accepted. Admission may be deferred for a maximum of 1 academic year. Credit and/or placement offered for CEEB Advanced Placement tests.

COSTS AND FINANCIAL AID

Annual tuition $25,160. Room and board $9,521. Required fees $465. Average book expense $1,200. **Required Forms and Deadlines:** FAFSA. **Notification of Awards:** Applicants will be notified of awards on a rolling basis beginning 3/1. **Types of Aid:** *Need-based scholarships/grants:* Federal Pell, SEOG, state scholarships/grants, private scholarships, the school's own gift aid. *Loans:* Subsidized Stafford, Unsubsidized Stafford, PLUS, Federal Perkins. **Student Employment:** Federal Work-Study Program available. Highest amount earned per year from on-campus jobs $1,600. Off-campus job opportunities are good. **Financial Aid Statistics:** 96% freshmen, 90% undergrads receive need-based scholarship or grant aid. 71% freshmen, 79% undergrads receive non-need-based scholarship or grant aid. 92% freshmen, 87% undergrads receive need-based self-help aid. 90% freshmen, 86% undergrads receive any aid. 81% undergrads borrow to pay for school. Average cumulative indebtedness $24,716. **Criteria for awarding institutional aid:** *Non-need-based:* academics, alumni affiliation, leadership, music/drama, religious affiliation, state/district residency.

METROPOLITAN COLLEGE OF NEW YORK

75 Varick Street, New York, NY 10013
Phone: 212-343-1234
E-mail: admissions@metropolitan.edu • **CEEB Code:** 4802
Fax: 212-343-8470 • **Website:** www.metropolitan.edu

This private school was founded in 1964.

RATINGS

Admissions Selectivity Rating: 62   **Fire Safety Rating:** 60*   **Green Rating:** 60*

STUDENTS AND FACULTY

Enrollment: 1,093. **Student Body:** 80% female, 20% male, 10% out-of-state, 0% international (12 countries represented). Asian 1%, Caucasian 5%, Hispanic 18%, Native American 1%.
Retention and Graduation: 72% freshmen return for sophomore year. 60% grads go on to further study within 1 year. 15% grads pursue law degrees. 24% grads pursue business degrees. **Faculty:** Student/faculty ratio 17:1. 26 full-time faculty. 0% of classes are taught by teaching assistants.

ACADEMICS

Degrees: associate, bachelor's, certificate, master's, transfer associate. **Classes:** Most classes have 10–19 students. **Special Study Options:** Accelerated program, cooperative education program, distance learning, honors program, internships, weekend college. **Combined Degree Programs:** MS/MBA. **Disability Services:** Special programs offered to physically disabled students include tutors. **Career Services:** alumni services, internships.

FACILITIES

Housing: 4% of campus accessible to physically disabled. **Computers:** Administrative functions (other than registration) can be performed online.

CAMPUS LIFE

Activities: student government, student newspaper 10 registered organizations.

ADMISSIONS

Freshman Academic Profile: 70% from public high schools. Minimum paper TOEFL 550. **Basis for Candidate Selection:** *Very important factors considered include:* interview. *Important factors considered include:* extracurricular activities, talent/ability, volunteer work, work experience. *Other factors considered include:* recommendation(s), character/personal qualities. **Freshman Admission Requirements:** High school diploma is required and GED is accepted. **Freshman Admission Statistics:** 399 applied, 78% admitted, 62% enrolled. **Transfer Admission Requirements:** High school transcript, essay or personal statement, interview. Lowest grade transferable C. **General Admission Information:** Application Fee $30. Early decision application deadline 5/2. Nonfall registration accepted. Admission may be deferred for a maximum of 12. Neither credit nor placement offered for CEEB Advanced Placement tests.

COSTS AND FINANCIAL AID

Annual tuition $12,960. Required fees $400. Average book expense $1,500. **Required Forms and Deadlines:** FAFSA, state aid form, noncustodial PROFILE. **Types of Aid:** *Need-based scholarships/grants:* Federal Pell, SEOG, state scholarships/grants, private scholarships, the school's own gift aid. *Loans:* Subsidized Stafford, Unsubsidized Stafford, PLUS, signature loan. **Student Employment:** Federal Work-Study Program available. Off-campus job opportunities are good. **Financial Aid Statistics:** 70% freshmen, 75% undergrads receive need-based scholarship or grant aid. 19% freshmen, 18% undergrads receive non-need-based scholarship or grant aid. 95% freshmen, 95% undergrads receive need-based self-help aid. 80% undergrads borrow to pay for school. Average cumulative indebtedness $24,000. **Criteria for awarding institutional aid:** *Non-need-based:* academics, leadership.

MIAMI UNIVERSITY

301 S. Campus Ave., Oxford, OH 45056
Phone: 513-529-2531 • **Financial Aid Phone:** 513-529-8734
E-mail: admission@muohio.edu • **CEEB Code:** 1463
Fax: 513-529-1550 • **Website:** www.miami.muohio.edu • **ACT Code:** 3294

This public school was founded in 1809. It has a 2000-acre campus.

RATINGS
Admissions Selectivity Rating: 84   **Fire Safety Rating:** 77   **Green Rating:** 87

STUDENTS AND FACULTY
Enrollment: 14,984. **Student Body:** 52% female, 48% male, 30% out-of-state, 5% international (73 countries represented). Asian 2%, African American 4%, Caucasian 82%, Hispanic 3%, Native American 0%.
Retention and Graduation: 89% freshmen return for sophomore year. 68% freshmen graduate within 4 years. 80% freshmen graduate within 6 years. 26% grads go on to further study within 1 year. **Faculty:** Student/faculty ratio 18:1. 841 full-time faculty, 89% hold PhDs, 17% are members of minority groups, 44% are women. 7% of classes are taught by teaching assistants.

ACADEMICS
Degrees: associate, bachelor's, certificate, doctoral, master's, post-master's certificate, terminal associate, transfer associate. **Classes:** Most classes have 20–29 students. Most lab/discussion sessions have 20–29 students. **Majors with Highest Enrollment:** finance; marketing/marketing management; psychology. **Special Study Options:** cooperative education program, cross-registration, distance learning, double major, exchange student program (domestic), honors program, independent study, internships, liberal arts/career combination, student-designed major, study abroad, teacher certification program. **Honors Programs:** Miami has a University Honors Program. Students selected to participate receive a renewable scholarship, priority registration, and other special opportunities. **Combined Degree Programs:** 3-2 forestry/env. studies with Duke; 3-1 Arts/Prof. Degree, 3-2 engineering. **Disability Services:** Special programs offered to physically disabled students include note-taking services, reader services, tape recorders, tutors. **Career Services:** Alumni network, alumni services, career/job search classes, career assessment, internships, regional alumni.

FACILITIES
Housing: Coed dorms, special housing for disabled students, men's dorms, special housing for international students, women's dorms, fraternity/sorority housing, apartments for married students, cooperative housing, apartments for single students, wellness housing, theme housing, 100% of campus accessible to physically disabled. **Special Academic Facilities/Equipment:** Geology, art, anthropology, and zoology museums, performing arts center, herbarium, ecology research center, 400-acre nature preserve, electron microscope center. **Computers:** 100% of classrooms, 100% of dorms, 100% of libraries, 100% of dining areas, 100% of student union, 65% of common outdoor areas have wireless network access. Students can register for classes online. Administrative functions (other than registration) can be performed online.

CAMPUS LIFE
Environment: Village. **Activities:** Choral groups, concert band, dance, drama/theater, jazz band, literary magazine, marching band, music ensembles, musical theater, opera, pep band, radio station, student government, student newspaper, student-run film society, symphony orchestra, television station, yearbook, Campus Ministries, International Student Organization, Model UN 304 registered organizations, 38 honor societies, 22 religious organizations. 32 fraternities, 23 sororities. **Athletics (Intercollegiate):** *Men:* baseball, basketball, cross-country, diving, football, golf, ice hockey, swimming, track/field (outdoor). *Women:* basketball, cross-country, diving, field hockey, soccer, softball, swimming, tennis, track/field (outdoor), volleyball. **On-Campus Highlights:** Farmer School of Business, McGuffey Museum, Center for the Performing Arts, Recreational Sports Center, Peabody Hall (National Historical Landmark), Formal Gardens. **Environmental Initiatives:** Our focus currently is on making sustainability a central part of campus decision-making at Miami, including: administration, operations, academic affairs, student life, and community relations. The creation of a sustainability coordinator role and standing sustainability committee now enables Miami to systematically research sustainability-related issues, set goals, implement strategies, and track progress. Our efforts have previously been scattered and uncoordinated. Now they are an ongoing priority. The university is developing a set of public commitments to measurable sustainability progress, including but not limited to a CO2 emissions reduction target. In future months

these specific targets and actions will be announced publicly, and a process of ongoing assessment of progress developed. Miami is committed to complying with Ohio House Bill 251, which mandates a 20% reduction in energy consumption by 2014. A set of energy efficiency and waste reduction strategies are underway. Miami continues to compete in Recyclemania, which now covers all campus buildings. Housing Dining and Guest Services has created a residence hall competition Unplugged, Untapped, Game On! to reduce resource consumption. An energy point of contact is now assigned in all state buildings to coordinate efficiency strategies. Building energy consumption is now metered and available publicly on-line, and will soon be communicated to building users by updated bulletin boards. Major new construction projects have been designed to LEED certification standards.

ADMISSIONS
Freshman Academic Profile: Average high school GPA 3.6. 36% in top 10% of high school class, 68% in top 25% of high school class, 96% in top 50% of high school class. 74% from public high schools. SAT Math middle 50% range 550-660. SAT Critical Reading middle 50% range 530-630. ACT middle 50% range 24-29. Minimum web-based TOEFL 80. Minimum paper TOEFL 550. **Basis for Candidate Selection:** *Very important factors considered include:* Class rank, application essay, academic GPA, recommendation(s), rigor of secondary school record, standardized test scores, character/personal qualities, talent/ability. *Other factors considered include:* alumni/ae relation, extracurricular activities, first generation, geographical residence, state residency, volunteer work, work experience. **Freshman Admission Requirements:** High school diploma is required and GED is accepted. **Freshman Admission Statistics:** 20,314 applied, 73% admitted, 25% enrolled. **Transfer Admission Requirements:** High school transcript, college transcript(s), essay or personal statement, statement of good standing from prior institution(s). Minimum college GPA of 2.0 required. Lowest grade transferable C. **General Admission Information:** Application Fee $50. Early decision application deadline 11/1. Regular application deadline 2/1. Regular notification 3/15. Nonfall registration accepted. Admission may be deferred for a maximum of 1 year. Credit offered for CEEB Advanced Placement tests.

COSTS AND FINANCIAL AID
Annual in-state tuition $13,067. Annual out-of-state tuition $28,631. Room and board $10,596. Required fees $528. Average book expense $1,438. **Required Forms and Deadlines:** FAFSA. **Notification of Awards:** Applicants will be notified of awards on a rolling basis beginning 3/20. **Types of Aid:** *Need-based scholarships/grants:* Federal Pell, SEOG, state scholarships/grants, private scholarships, the school's own gift aid. *Loans:* Direct Subsidized Stafford, Direct Unsubsidized Stafford, Direct PLUS, Federal Perkins, Federal Nursing, college/university loans from institutional funds, Bank Education Loans. **Student Employment:** Federal Work-Study Program available. Institutional employment available. Off-campus job opportunities are good. **Financial Aid Statistics:** 69% freshmen, 71% undergrads receive need-based scholarship or grant aid. 67% freshmen, 59% undergrads receive non-need-based scholarship or grant aid. 81% freshmen, 81% undergrads receive need-based self-help aid. 3% freshmen, 3% undergrads receive athletic scholarships. 54% undergrads borrow to pay for school. Average cumulative indebtedness $27,178. **Criteria for awarding institutional aid:** *Non-need-based:* academics, art, athletics, leadership, minority status, music/drama, state/district residency.

MICHIGAN STATE UNIVERSITY

250 Administration Building, East Lansing, MI 48824-1046
Phone: 517-355-8332 • **Financial Aid Phone:** 517-353-5940
E-mail: admis@msu.edu • **CEEB Code:** 1465
Fax: 517-353-1647 • **Website:** www.msu.edu • **ACT Code:** 2032

This public school was founded in 1855. It has a 5200-acre campus.

RATINGS
Admissions Selectivity Rating: 78   **Fire Safety Rating:** 60*   **Green Rating:** 84

STUDENTS AND FACULTY
Enrollment: 36,276. **Student Body:** 51% female, 49% male, 9% out-of-state, 9% international (135 countries represented). Asian 4%, African American 7%, Caucasian 72%, Hispanic 3%, Native American 0%.
Retention and Graduation: 91% freshmen return for sophomore year. 32% grads go on to further study within 1 year. 2% grads pursue law degrees. 12% grads pursue business degrees. 4% grads pursue medical degrees. **Faculty:** Student/faculty ratio 16:1.

The Princeton Review's Complete Book of Colleges

ACADEMICS

Degrees: bachelor's, certificate, master's, post-master's certificate. **Classes:** Most classes have 20–29 students. Most lab/discussion sessions have 20–29 students. **Special Study Options:** Accelerated program, cooperative education program, distance learning, double major, dual enrollment, English as a Second Language (ESL), exchange student program (domestic), honors program, independent study, internships, liberal arts/career combination, student-designed major, study abroad, teacher certification program, weekend college. **Honors Programs:** MSU's Honors College embodies MSU's long-standing commitment to provide programs of study that attract and challenge unusually talented undergraduates utilizing carefully planned, highly individualized programs of study that will meet the needs of academically talented students. **Combined Degree Programs:** BA/MA, Computer Science. **Disability Services:** Special programs offered to physically disabled students include note-taking services, reader services, tape recorders, tutors. **Career Services:** Alumni network, alumni services, career/job search classes, career assessment, internships, regional alumni.

FACILITIES

Housing: Coed dorms, special housing for disabled students, special housing for international students, women's dorms, fraternity/sorority housing, apartments for married students, cooperative housing, apartments for single students, theme housing. **Special Academic Facilities/Equipment:** Art, natural history, Michigan history and anthropology museums, art center, on-campus preschool and elementary school, biological station, experimental farms, botanical garden, planetarium, two superconducting cyclotrons, observatory. **Computers:** Students can register for classes online. Administrative functions (other than registration) can be performed online. Undergraduates are required to own a computer.

CAMPUS LIFE

Environment: Town. **Activities:** Choral groups, concert band, dance, drama/theater, jazz band, literary magazine, marching band, music ensembles, musical theater, opera, pep band, radio station, student government, student newspaper, student-run film society, symphony orchestra, television station, yearbook, Campus Ministries, International Student Organization, Model UN 500 registered organizations, 47 honor societies, 50 religious organizations. 31 fraternities, 19 sororities. **Athletics (Intercollegiate):** *Men:* baseball, basketball, cheerleading, cross-country, diving, football, golf, ice hockey, soccer, swimming, tennis, track/field (outdoor), track/field (indoor), wrestling. *Women:* basketball, cheerleading, crew/rowing, cross-country, diving, field hockey, golf, gymnastics, soccer, softball, swimming, tennis, track/field (outdoor), track/field (indoor), volleyball. **On-Campus Highlights:** MSU Student Union, Jack Breslin Student Events Center, MSU Main Library and Cyber Caf, The International Center, Wharton Center for the Performing Arts. **Environmental Initiatives:** Chicago Climate Exchange Implementing an Office of Campus Sustainability Fair Trade Products Preference.

ADMISSIONS

Freshman Academic Profile: Average high school GPA 3.6. 28% in top 10% of high school class, 68% in top 25% of high school class, 96% in top 50% of high school class. SAT Math middle 50% range 540–670. SAT Critical Reading middle 50% range 440–600. SAT Writing middle 50% range 450–600. ACT middle 50% range 23–28. Minimum web-based TOEFL 79. Minimum paper TOEFL 550. **Basis for Candidate Selection:** *Very important factors considered include:* academic GPA, rigor of secondary school record, standardized test scores. *Important factors considered include:* application essay, extracurricular activities, first generation, geographical residence. *Other factors considered include:* Class rank, recommendation(s), alumni/ae relation, character/personal qualities, level of applicant's interest, state residency, talent/ability, volunteer work, work experience. **Freshman Admission Requirements:** High school diploma is required and GED is accepted. *Academic units required:* 4 English, 3 mathematics, 2 science, 2 foreign language, 2 social studies, 1 history. *Academic units recommended:* 4 English, 3 mathematics, 2 science, 2 foreign language, 2 social studies, 1 history. **Freshman Admission Statistics:** 28,416 applied, 73% admitted, 39% enrolled. **Transfer Admission Requirements:** college transcript(s), essay or personal statement, statement of good standing from prior institution(s). Minimum college GPA of 2.0 required. Lowest grade transferable C. **General Admission Information:** Application Fee $35. Nonfall registration accepted. Credit and/or placement offered for CEEB Advanced Placement tests.

COSTS AND FINANCIAL AID

Annual in-state tuition $13,335. Annual out-of-state tuition $32,130. Room and board $8,154. Average book expense $996. **Required Forms and Deadlines:** FAFSA. **Notification of Awards:** Applicants will be notified of awards on a rolling basis beginning 3/15. **Types of Aid:** *Need-based scholarships/grants:* Federal Pell, SEOG, state scholarships/grants, private scholarships, the school's own gift aid, United Negro College Fund. *Loans:* Direct Subsidized Stafford, Direct Unsubsidized Stafford, Direct PLUS, Federal Perkins, college/university loans from institutional funds. **Student Employment:** Federal Work-Study Program available. Institutional employment available. Off-campus job opportu-

nities are excellent. **Financial Aid Statistics:** 61% freshmen, 64% undergrads receive need-based scholarship or grant aid. 40% freshmen, 26% undergrads receive non-need-based scholarship or grant aid. 90% freshmen, 90% undergrads receive need-based self-help aid. 1% freshmen, 1% undergrads receive athletic scholarships. 47% freshmen, 49% undergrads receive any aid. 45% undergrads borrow to pay for school. Average cumulative indebtedness $23,725. **Criteria for awarding institutional aid:** *Non-need-based:* academics, alumni affiliation, art, athletics, leadership, music/drama, state/district residency.

MICHIGAN TECHNOLOGICAL UNIVERSITY

1400 Townsend Drive, Houghton, MI 49931
Phone: 906-487-2335 • **Financial Aid Phone:** 906-487-1742
E-mail: mtu4u@mtu.edu • **CEEB Code:** 1464
Fax: 906-487-2125 • **Website:** www.mtu.edu • **ACT Code:** 2030

This public school was founded in 1885. It has a 925-acre campus.

RATINGS
Admissions Selectivity Rating: 80   **Fire Safety Rating:** 92   **Green Rating:** 71

STUDENTS AND FACULTY

Enrollment: 5,532. **Student Body:** 25% female, 75% male, 23% out-of-state, 6% international (59 countries represented). Asian 1%, African American 1%, Caucasian 84%, Hispanic 2%, Native American 1%. **Retention and Graduation:** 83% freshmen return for sophomore year. 29% freshmen graduate within 4 years. 20% grads go on to further study within 1 year. 5% grads pursue arts and sciences degrees. 1% grads pursue law degrees. 5% grads pursue business degrees. 3% grads pursue medical degrees. **Faculty:** Student/faculty ratio 12:1. 405 full-time faculty, 86% hold PhDs, 18% are members of minority groups, 30% are women. 8% of classes are taught by teaching assistants.

ACADEMICS

Degrees: associate, bachelor's, certificate, master's, post-bachelor's certificate, terminal associate. **Classes:** Most classes have 10–19 students. Most lab/discussion sessions have 10–19 students. **Majors with Highest Enrollment:** business administration and management, civil engineering, mechanical engineering. **Special Study Options:** cooperative education program, distance learning, double major, dual enrollment, English as a Second Language (ESL), exchange student program (domestic), honors program, independent study, internships, study abroad, teacher certification program, Dual degrees with Northwestern MI College, Adrian College, Albion College, Augsburg College (MN), College of St. Scholastica (MN), Mount Senario College, Olivet College, Northland College, University of Wisconsin-Superior, St. Norbert College (WI), Northcentral Technical College (WI), College of Lake County (IL), and Macomb Community College (MI). **Honors Programs:** Qualifying students are invited to apply to Michigan Tech's Honors Institute. Membership focuses on activities and enrichment for top scholars, rather than separate honors courses. More details are at http://honors.mtu.edu/. **Disability Services:** Special programs offered to physically disabled students include note-taking services, reader services, tape recorders, tutors. **Career Services:** alumni services, career/job search classes, career assessment, internships Career Services highlights include The MTU Career Center is proud to be able to provide career advising. We want to have students focus on a career verses a job. Advising includes graduate school, military, and professional employment. 96% of the 2007-08 graduates were placed either in a job relevant to their degree, graduate school, or military education.

FACILITIES

Housing: Coed dorms, special housing for disabled students, special housing for international students, fraternity/sorority housing, apartments for married students, apartments for single students, wellness housing, theme housing, Alcohol Free, Research Scholar, Honors Housing, ROTC, Learning Communities - Computer Science - First-year Experience - Health Summit - Forest Resources & Environmental Science - International House - Visual & Performing Arts - Leadership. 90% of campus accessible to physically disabled. **Special Academic Facilities/Equipment:** Mineralogical Museum, 4,700 Acre Research Forest, Scanning Electron Microscope, PUMA Robots, X-ray Fluorescence Spectrometer, Process Simulation and Control Center, Rozsa Center for the Performing Arts, Cleanrooms, MEMS Fabrication Facility, Environmental Scanning Electron Microscope, Transmission Electron Microscope, Radio-frequency Plasma-Assisted Deposition Chamber, Electron Lithography Equipment. **Computers:** 93% of classrooms, 10% of dorms, 100% of libraries, 100% of dining areas, 100% of student union, 10% of common outdoor areas have wireless network access. Students can register for classes online. Administrative functions (other than registration) can be performed online.

CAMPUS LIFE

Environment: Village. **Activities:** Choral groups, concert band, dance, drama/theater, jazz band, literary magazine, music ensembles, musical theater, opera, pep band, radio station, student government, student newspaper, student-run film society, symphony orchestra, Campus Ministries, International Student Organization 210 registered organizations, 16 honor societies, 16 religious organizations. 13 fraternities, 8 sororities. **Athletics (Intercollegiate):** *Men:* basketball, cross-country, football, ice hockey, skiingnordiccross-country, tennis, track/field (outdoor). *Women:* basketball, cross-country, skiingnordiccross-country, tennis, track/field (outdoor), volleyball. **On-Campus Highlights:** Student Development Complex, Rozsa Center for the Performing Arts, Mont Ripley Ski Hill, Portage Lake Golf Course, Memorial Union Building. **Environmental Initiatives:** Emphasis on multidisciplinary Emphasis on multidisciplinary sustainability research (www.mtu.edu/sfhi/initiatives/), education (www.sfi.mtu.edu/education/Education-1.htm www.mtu.edu/sfhi/educational/), and outreach (www.mtu.edu/sfhi/outreach/), such as Sustainable Futures Institute, Center for Water and Society, Environmentally Responsible Design and Manufacturing Research Group, National Institute for Climatic Change Research (Midwestern Region), Advanced Power Systems Research Center, Materials in Sustainable Transportation Infrastructure, Power and Energy Research Center, International Sustainable Engineering Initiative, IGERT for Sustainable Futures, Graduate Certificate in Sustainability, D80 Center, Peace Corps Masters International Program, International Sustainable Development Engineering Certificate, International Senior Design Programs, Sustainability Research Experience for Undergraduates, Wood-to-Wheels Graduate Enterprise, sustainability-based undergraduate Enterprise Programs (Challenge X, Clean Snowmobile, Alternative Fuels Group, Aqua Terra Tech, Efficiency Through Engineering and Construction), Undergraduate and Graduate Colloquium in Sustainability, Sustainable Futures 1 and 2 courses Commitment of Administration to sustainability in strategic plan and NCA AQIP accreditation project to move toward a carbon-neutral campus (as referenced above). Sustainability Strategic Faculty Hiring Initiative (www.mtu.edu/sfhi/) and other development efforts that are focused on strengthening Michigan Tech's sustainability infrastructure.

ADMISSIONS

Freshman Academic Profile: Average high school GPA 3.6. 29% in top 10% of high school class, 62% in top 25% of high school class, 90% in top 50% of high school class. 90% from public high schools. SAT Math middle 50% range 520-650. SAT Critical Reading middle 50% range 580-680. SAT Writing middle 50% range 490-615. ACT middle 50% range 24-29. Minimum web-based TOEFL 79. Minimum paper TOEFL 550. **Basis for Candidate Selection:** *Very important factors considered include:* academic GPA, rigor of secondary school record, standardized test scores. *Important factors considered include:* Class rank. *Other factors considered include:* application essay, recommendation(s), alumni/ae relation, character/personal qualities, extracurricular activities, interview, talent/ability, volunteer work, work experience. **Freshman Admission Requirements:** High school diploma is required and GED is accepted. *Academic units required:* 3 English, 3 mathematics, 2 science. *Academic units recommended:* 3 English, 3 mathematics, 2 science. **Freshman Admission Statistics:** 4,520 applied, 77% admitted, 33% enrolled. **Transfer Admission Requirements:** college transcript(s), statement of good standing from prior institution(s). Minimum college GPA of 2.75 required. Lowest grade transferable C. **General Admission Information:** Notification on a rolling basis, beginning on or about 9/15. Nonfall registration accepted. Admission may be deferred for a maximum of 1 year. Credit and/or placement offered for CEEB Advanced Placement tests.

COSTS AND FINANCIAL AID

Annual in-state tuition $13,095. Annual out-of-state tuition $27,000. Room and board $8,865. Required fees $258. Average book expense $1,200. **Required Forms and Deadlines:** FAFSA. **Types of Aid:** *Need-based scholarships/grants:* Federal Pell, SEOG, state scholarships/grants, private scholarships, the school's own gift aid. *Loans:* Direct Subsidized Stafford, Direct Unsubsidized Stafford, Direct PLUS, Federal Perkins, college/university loans from institutional funds, External Private Loans. **Student Employment:** Federal Work-Study Program available. Institutional employment available. Highest amount earned per year from on-campus jobs $4,500. Off-campus job opportunities are excellent. **Financial Aid Statistics:** 83% freshmen, 79% undergrads receive need-based scholarship or grant aid. 81% freshmen, 67% undergrads receive non-need-based scholarship or grant aid. 85% freshmen, 89% undergrads receive need-based self-help aid. 6% freshmen, 5% undergrads receive athletic scholarships. 98% freshmen, 89% undergrads receive any aid. 71% undergrads borrow to pay for school. Average cumulative indebtedness $33,141. **Criteria for awarding institutional aid:** *Non-need-based:* academics, alumni affiliation, art, athletics, job skills, leadership, music/drama, state/district residency.

See page 1146.

MID-AMERICA CHRISTIAN UNIVERSITY

3500 SW 119th Street, Oklahoma City, OK 73170
Phone: 405-691-3188
E-mail: info@macu.edu • **CEEB Code:** 6942
Fax: 405-692-3165 • **Website:** www.macu.edu • **ACT Code:** 4097

This private school, affiliated with the Church of God Church, was founded in 1953.

RATINGS

Admissions Selectivity Rating: 60*   **Fire Safety Rating:** 62   **Green Rating:** 60*

STUDENTS AND FACULTY

Student Body: (3 countries represented).
Faculty: 0% of classes are taught by teaching assistants.

ACADEMICS

Degrees: associate, bachelor's. **Majors with Highest Enrollment:** business/commerce; pastoral studies/counseling; theology and religious vocations, other. **Special Study Options:** Accelerated program, distance learning, double major, external degree program, internships, liberal arts/career combination, student-designed major, teacher certification program. **Combined Degree Programs:** Multidisciplinary. **Career Services:** internships.

FACILITIES

Housing: special housing for disabled students, men's dorms, women's dorms, 100% of campus accessible to physically disabled.

CAMPUS LIFE

Environment: Metropolis. **Activities:** Choral groups, student government, student newspaper, yearbook 1 honor societies, 5 religious organizations. **Athletics (Intercollegiate):** *Men:* baseball, basketball, soccer. *Women:* basketball, softball, volleyball. **On-Campus Highlights:** Gaulke Activity Center, President's Chapel, Fowler Student Center, Charles Ewing Brown Library

ADMISSIONS

Freshman Academic Profile: Minimum paper TOEFL 500. **Transfer Admission Requirements:** college transcript(s), Lowest grade transferable D. **General Admission Information:** Credit and/or placement offered for CEEB Advanced Placement tests.

COSTS AND FINANCIAL AID

Room and board $2,896. Average book expense $500. **Types of Aid:** *Loans:* Subsidized Stafford, PLUS. **Student Employment:** Federal Work-Study Program available. Off-campus job opportunities are excellent.

MIDAMERICA NAZARENE UNIVERSITY

2030 College Way, Olathe, KS 66062
Phone: 913-791-3380 • **Financial Aid Phone:** 913-971-3298
E-mail: admissions@mnu.edu • **CEEB Code:** 6437
Fax: 913-791-3481 • **Website:** www.mnu.edu • **ACT Code:** 1445

This private school, affiliated with the Nazarene Church, was founded in 1966. It has a 105-acre campus.

RATINGS

Admissions Selectivity Rating: 74   **Fire Safety Rating:** 73   **Green Rating:** 60*

STUDENTS AND FACULTY

Enrollment: 1,347. **Student Body:** 57% female, 43% male, 31% out-of-state, 2% international (12 countries represented). Asian 1%, African American 11%, Caucasian 76%, Hispanic 4%, Native American 1%.
Retention and Graduation: 76% freshmen return for sophomore year. 33% freshmen graduate within 4 years. **Faculty:** Student/faculty ratio 10:1. 86 full-time faculty, 50% hold PhDs, 5% are members of minority groups, 41% are women. 0% of classes are taught by teaching assistants.

ACADEMICS

Degrees: associate, bachelor's, master's, post-master's certificate. **Classes:** Most classes have 10–19 students. Most lab/discussion sessions have 10–19 students. **Majors with Highest Enrollment:** business/commerce; elementary education and teaching; nursing/registered nurse (rn, asn, bsn, msn). **Special Study Options:** Accelerated program, cross-registration, distance learning, double major, dual enrollment, independent study, internships, student-designed major, study abroad, teacher certification program, weekend college. **Disability Services:**

Special programs offered to physically disabled students include note-taking services, reader services, tape recorders, tutors. **Career Services:** career assessment.

FACILITIES

Housing: special housing for disabled students, men's dorms, women's dorms, apartments for single students. 90% of campus accessible to physically disabled. **Computers:** Students can register for classes online. Administrative functions (other than registration) can be performed online.

CAMPUS LIFE

Environment: City. **Activities:** Choral groups, concert band, drama/theater, jazz band, literary magazine, music ensembles, musical theater, pep band, radio station, student government, student newspaper, television station, yearbook, Campus Ministries, International Student Organization 43 registered organizations, 6 honor societies, 4 religious organizations. **Athletics (Intercollegiate):** *Men:* baseball, basketball, cheerleading, cross-country, football, soccer, track/field (outdoor), track/field (indoor). *Women:* basketball, cheerleading, cross-country, soccer, softball, track/field (outdoor), track/field (indoor), volleyball. **On-Campus Highlights:** Cook Center, Land Memorial Gym, Fitness Center, Campus Center, Bell Cultural Events Center.

ADMISSIONS

Freshman Academic Profile: Average high school GPA 3.4. 2% in top 10% of high school class, 5% in top 25% of high school class, 27% in top 50% of high school class. 88% from public high schools. SAT Math middle 50% range 440-550. SAT Critical Reading middle 50% range 410-540. ACT middle 50% range 20-25. Minimum paper TOEFL 550. **Basis for Candidate Selection:** *Very important factors considered include:* Class rank, rigor of secondary school record, standardized test scores, character/personal qualities. *Important factors considered include:* academic GPA, recommendation(s), level of applicant's interest. *Other factors considered include:* application essay, extracurricular activities, interview, talent/ability. **Freshman Admission Requirements:** High school diploma is required and GED is accepted. **Freshman Admission Statistics:** 617 applied, 65% admitted, 58% enrolled. **Transfer Admission Requirements:** college transcript(s), minimum college GPA of 2.0 required. Lowest grade transferable D. **General Admission Information:** Application Fee $25. Regular application deadline 8/1. Nonfall registration not accepted. Admission may be deferred for a maximum of 2 years. Credit offered for CEEB Advanced Placement tests.

COSTS AND FINANCIAL AID

Annual tuition $20,500. Room and board $7,000. Required fees $1,000. Average book expense $1,180. **Required Forms and Deadlines:** FAFSA. **Notification of Awards:** Applicants will be notified of awards on a rolling basis beginning 2/1. **Types of Aid:** *Need-based scholarships/grants:* Federal Pell, SEOG, state scholarships/grants, private scholarships, the school's own gift aid. *Loans:* Subsidized Stafford, Unsubsidized Stafford, PLUS, Federal Perkins. **Student Employment:** Off-campus job opportunities are good. **Financial Aid Statistics:** 77% freshmen, 94% undergrads receive need-based scholarship or grant aid. 53% freshmen, 41% undergrads receive non-need-based scholarship or grant aid. 75% freshmen, 79% undergrads receive need-based self-help aid. 46% freshmen, 36% undergrads receive athletic scholarships. 92% freshmen, 86% undergrads receive any aid. 77% undergrads borrow to pay for school. Average cumulative indebtedness $28,678. **Criteria for awarding institutional aid:** *Non-need-based:* academics, athletics, leadership, minority status, music/drama, religious affiliation, state/district residency.

MIDDLE TENNESSEE STATE UNIVERSITY

Cope Administration Building 208, Murfreesboro, TN 37132
Phone: 615-898-2111
E-mail: admissions@mtsu.edu
Fax: 615-898-5478 • **Website:** www.mtsu.edu

This is a public school.

RATINGS
Admissions Selectivity Rating: 77   **Fire Safety Rating:** 60*   **Green Rating:** 60*

STUDENTS AND FACULTY
Enrollment: 22,121. **Student Body:** 53% female, 47% male, 4% out-of-state. Asian 3%, African American 19%, Caucasian 69%, Hispanic 4%, Native American 0%.
Retention and Graduation: Faculty: Student/faculty ratio 21:1. 938 full-time faculty, 16% are members of minority groups, 46% are women.

ACADEMICS

Degrees: bachelor's, master's, post-bachelor's certificate, post-master's certificate. **Classes:** Most classes have 20–29 students. Most lab/discussion sessions have fewer than 10 students. **Special Study Options:** distance learning, double major, dual enrollment, honors program, independent study, internships, study abroad, teacher certification program.

FACILITIES

Housing: Coed dorms, special housing for disabled students, men's dorms, special housing for international students, women's dorms, fraternity/sorority housing, apartments for married students, cooperative housing, apartments for single students, wellness housing, theme housing.

CAMPUS LIFE

Activities: Choral groups, concert band, dance, drama/theater, jazz band, literary magazine, marching band, music ensembles, musical theater, opera, pep band, radio station, student government, student newspaper, symphony orchestra, television station, Campus Ministries, International Student Organization, Model UN.

ADMISSIONS

Freshman Academic Profile: 3.3. 17% in top 10% of high school class, 42% in top 25% of high school class, 78% in top 50% of high school class. SAT Math middle 50% range 460-580. SAT Critical Reading middle 50% range 460-590. ACT middle 50% range 19-24. Minimum paper TOEFL 500. **Basis for Candidate Selection:** *Very important factors considered include:* academic GPA, rigor of secondary school record, standardized test scores. *Important factors considered include:* racial/ethnic status, talent/ability. *Other factors considered include:* Class rank, recommendation(s), character/personal qualities, extracurricular activities, first generation, level of applicant's interest, volunteer work, work experience. **Freshman Admission Requirements:** High school diploma is required and GED is accepted. *Academic units required:* 4 English, 3 mathematics, 2 science, 2 foreign language, 1 social studies, 1 history, 1 visual/performing arts. 4 English, 3 mathematics, 2 science, 2 foreign language, 1 social studies, 1 history, 1 visual/performing arts. **Freshman Admission Statistics:** 9,405 applied, 67% admitted, 50% enrolled. **Transfer Admission Requirements:** college transcript(s), minimum college GPA of 2.0 required. Lowest grade transferable D. **General Admission Information:** Application Fee $25. Nonfall registration accepted. Credit offered for CEEB Advanced Placement tests.

COSTS AND FINANCIAL AID

Required Forms and Deadlines: Types of Aid: *Need-based scholarships/grants: Loans.* **Student Employment: Financial Aid Statistics:** 65% freshmen, 66% undergrads receive need-based scholarship or grant aid. 88% freshmen, 59% undergrads receive non-need-based scholarship or grant aid. 55% freshmen, 68% undergrads receive need-based self-help aid. 1% freshmen, 1% undergrads receive athletic scholarships. 59% undergrads borrow to pay for school. Average cumulative indebtedness $22,164.

MIDDLEBURY COLLEGE

The Emma Willard House, Middlebury, VT 05753-6002
Phone: 802-443-3000
E-mail: admissions@middlebury.edu • **CEEB Code:** 3526
Fax: 802-443-2056 • **Website:** www.middlebury.edu • **ACT Code:** 4306

This private school was founded in 1800. It has a 350-acre campus.

RATINGS
Admissions Selectivity Rating: 98   **Fire Safety Rating:** 90   **Green Rating:** 99

STUDENTS AND FACULTY
Enrollment: 2,487. **Student Body:** 51% female, 49% male, 94% out-of-state, 9% international (68 countries represented). Asian 6%, African American 2%, Caucasian 68%, Hispanic 7%, Native American 0%.
Retention and Graduation: 97% freshmen return for sophomore year. 88% freshmen graduate within 4 years. 94% freshmen graduate within 6 years.
Faculty: Student/faculty ratio 9:1. 255 full-time faculty, 95% hold PhDs, 16% are members of minority groups, 44% are women. 0% of classes are taught by teaching assistants.

ACADEMICS

Degrees: bachelor's, master's. **Classes:** Most classes have 10–19 students.
Majors with Highest Enrollment: economics; English language and literature; psychology. **Special Study Options:** Accelerated program, double major,
exchange student program (domestic), honors program, independent study,
internships, student-designed major, study abroad, teacher certification program, Williams College-Mystic Seaport Program in American Maritime Studies,
Oxford University summer Program, independent scholar programs with Berea
College and Swarthmore College, 3-year international major. **Disability
Services:** Special programs offered to physically disabled students include
note-taking services, reader services, tape recorders, tutors. **Career Services:**
Alumni network, alumni services, career/job search classes, career assessment,
internships, regional alumni.

FACILITIES

Housing: Coed dorms, special housing for disabled students, apartments for
single students, Multi-cultural house, environmental house, foreign language
house, 5 co-ed social houses. Commons System organizes residence halls into
5 groups, each with its own budget, government, faculty, and staff associates.
60% of campus accessible to physically disabled. **Special Academic Facilities/
Equipment:** Art museum, theatres, language lab, observatory, electron microscope, mountain campus, downhill and cross-country ski areas, golf course,
Franklin Environmental Center, organic garden. **Computers:** Students can
register for classes online. Administrative functions (other than registration) can
be performed online.

CAMPUS LIFE

Environment: Village. **Activities:** Choral groups, dance, drama/theater,
jazz band, literary magazine, music ensembles, musical theater, radio station,
student government, student newspaper, student-run film society, symphony
orchestra, yearbook 100 registered organizations. **Athletics (Intercollegiate):**
Men: baseball, basketball, cross-country, diving, football, golf, ice hockey,
lacrosse, skiing (downhill/alpine), skiingnordiccross-country, soccer, swimming, tennis, track/field (outdoor), track/field (indoor). *Women:* basketball,
cross-country, diving, field hockey, golf, ice hockey, lacrosse, skiing (downhill/
alpine), skiingnordiccross-country, soccer, softball, squash, swimming, tennis,
track/field (outdoor), track/field (indoor), volleyball. **On-Campus Highlights:**
Science - Bicentennial Hall, The Center for the Arts, Athletic Facilities, The
Commons System, Middlebury College Snow Bowl (Ski Area). **Environmental
Initiatives:** Trustees resolution in 2007 charging the entire college community
to work together to achieve carbon neutrality by 2016. Completion of a $12
million biomass gasification system that burns renewable wood chips, reduces
carbon emissions by 40% and fuel oil consumption by 1,000,000 gallons less,
and shifts fuel dollars to the local region rather than overseas oil locales. Our
Franklin Environmental Center at Hillcrest recently received LEED Platinum
certification. The first in Vermont and only the seventh nationwide.

ADMISSIONS

Freshman Academic Profile: SAT Math middle 50% range 640-740. SAT
Critical Reading middle 50% range 630-740. SAT Writing middle 50% range
650-750. ACT middle 50% range 31-33. **Basis for Candidate Selection:**
Very important factors considered include: Class rank, academic GPA, rigor of
secondary school record, character/personal qualities, extracurricular activities, talent/ability. *Important factors considered include:* application essay,
recommendation(s), standardized test scores, racial/ethnic status. *Other factors
considered include:* alumni/ae relation, first generation, geographical residence,
interview, level of applicant's interest, volunteer work, work experience. **Freshman Admission Requirements:** High school diploma or equivalent is not
required. **Freshman Admission Statistics:** 8,847 applied, 17% admitted, 39%
enrolled. **Transfer Admission Requirements:** High school transcript, college
transcript(s), essay or personal statement, statement of good standing from prior
institution(s). Minimum college GPA of 3.0 required. Lowest grade transferable
C–. **General Admission Information:** Application Fee $65. Early decision
application deadline 11/1. Regular application deadline 1/1. Regular notification
4/1. Nonfall registration accepted. Admission may be deferred for a maximum
of 1 year. Credit and/or placement offered for CEEB Advanced Placement
tests.

COSTS AND FINANCIAL AID

Annual tuition $43,731. Room and board $11,839. Required fees $380. Aver-
age book expense $1,000. **Required Forms and Deadlines:** FAFSA, CSS/
Financial Aid PROFILE, noncustodial PROFILE. **Notification of Awards:**
Applicants will be notified of awards on or about 4/1. **Types of Aid:** *Need-based
scholarships/grants:* Federal Pell, SEOG, state scholarships/grants, private
scholarships, the school's own gift aid. *Loans:* Subsidized Stafford, Unsubsidized
Stafford, PLUS, Federal Perkins, college/university loans from institutional
funds. **Student Employment: Financial Aid Statistics:** 95% freshmen, 95%
undergrads receive need-based scholarship or grant aid. 90% freshmen, 87%
undergrads receive need-based self-help aid. 49% undergrads borrow to pay for
school. Average cumulative indebtedness $17,246.

512 East Stephen Street, Midway, KY 40347-1120
Phone: 859-846-5347 • **Financial Aid Phone:** 859-846-5410
E-mail: admissions@midway.edu • **CEEB Code:** 1975
Fax: 859-846-5787 • **Website:** www.midway.edu • **ACT Code:** 1528

*This private school, affiliated with the Disciples of Christ Church, was
founded in 1847. It has a 105-acre campus.*

RATINGS

Admissions Selectivity Rating: 71   **Fire Safety Rating:** 62   **Green Rating:** 60*

STUDENTS AND FACULTY

Enrollment: 1,395. **Student Body:** 91% female, 9% male, 9% out-of-state,
0% international (1 countries represented). Asian 0%, African American 7%,
Caucasian 68%, Hispanic 1%, Native American 1%.
Retention and Graduation: 76% freshmen return for sophomore year. 26%
freshmen graduate within 4 years. 32% freshmen graduate within 6 years.
Faculty: Student/faculty ratio 15:1. 41 full-time faculty, 46% hold PhDs, 39%
are women. 0% of classes are taught by teaching assistants.

ACADEMICS

Degrees: associate, bachelor's, master's. **Classes:** Most classes have 10–19
students. Most lab/discussion sessions have 10–19 students. **Majors with Highest Enrollment:** elementary education and teaching; nursing/registered nurse
(rn, asn, bsn, msn). **Special Study Options:** Accelerated program, distance
learning, double major, dual enrollment, honors program, study abroad, teacher
certification program, weekend college. **Honors Programs:** Ruth Slack Roach
Leadership, President's Ambassadors, Gamma Beta Phi, Tri Beta. **Disability
Services:** Special programs offered to physically disabled students include
note-taking services, reader services, tape recorders, tutors.

FACILITIES

Housing: women's dorms. 75% of campus accessible to physically disabled.

CAMPUS LIFE

Environment: Rural. **Activities:** Choral groups, music ensembles, student
government, student newspaper, yearbook. **Athletics (Intercollegiate):**
Women: basketball, cross-country, equestrian sports, soccer, softball, tennis, volleyball. **On-Campus Highlights:** Anne Hart Raymond Center, Little Memorial
Library, Equestrian Center, McManus Student Center, Piper Dining Hall.

ADMISSIONS

Freshman Academic Profile: Average high school GPA 3.2. 12% in top 10%
of high school class, 25% in top 25% of high school class, 64% in top 50% of
high school class. SAT Math middle 50% range 400-560. SAT Critical Reading
middle 50% range 420-560. ACT middle 50% range 18-22. Minimum paper
TOEFL 500. **Basis for Candidate Selection:** *Very important factors considered include:* rigor of secondary school record, standardized test scores. *Important factors considered include:* alumni/ae relation. *Other factors considered
include:* Class rank, application essay, recommendation(s), character/personal
qualities, extracurricular activities, interview, talent/ability, volunteer work, work
experience. **Freshman Admission Requirements:** High school diploma is
required and GED is accepted. *Academic units required:* 4 English. *Academic
units recommended:* 4 English. **Freshman Admission Statistics:** 456 applied,
71% admitted, 63% enrolled. **Transfer Admission Requirements:** High
school transcript, college transcript(s), minimum college GPA of 2.0 required.
Lowest grade transferable c. **General Admission Information:** Application
Fee $25. Notification on a rolling basis, beginning on or about 9/5. Nonfall
registration accepted. Admission may be deferred for a maximum of 0. Credit
and/or placement offered for CEEB Advanced Placement tests.

COSTS AND FINANCIAL AID

Annual tuition $15,750. Room and board $6,000. Required fees $150. Average
book expense $1,200. **Required Forms and Deadlines:** FAFSA, institution's
own financial aid form. **Types of Aid:** *Need-based scholarships/grants:* Federal
Pell, SEOG, state scholarships/grants, private scholarships, the school's own gift
aid. *Loans:* Subsidized Stafford, Unsubsidized Stafford, PLUS, Federal Perkins,
college/university loans from institutional funds. **Student Employment:** Federal Work-Study Program available. Institutional employment available. Off-
campus job opportunities are good. **Financial Aid Statistics:** 100% freshmen,
93% undergrads receive need-based scholarship or grant aid. 8% freshmen, 8%
undergrads receive non-need-based scholarship or grant aid. 81% freshmen,
90% undergrads receive need-based self-help aid. 1% freshmen, 1% undergrads
receive athletic scholarships. 85% freshmen, 81% undergrads receive any aid.
86% undergrads borrow to pay for school. Average cumulative indebtedness
$18,223. **Criteria for awarding institutional aid:** *Non-need-based:* academ-
ics, alumni affiliation, athletics, leadership, religious affiliation.

MIDWESTERN STATE UNIVERSITY

3410 Taft Blvd., Wichita Falls, TX 76308-2099
Phone: 940-397-4334 • **Financial Aid Phone:** 940-397-4119
E-mail: admissions@mwsu.edu • **CEEB Code:** 6408
Fax: 940-397-4672 • **Website:** www.mwsu.edu • **ACT Code:** 4132

This public school was founded in 1922. It has a 255-acre campus.

RATINGS
Admissions Selectivity Rating: 73   Fire Safety Rating: 84   Green Rating: 60*

STUDENTS AND FACULTY
Enrollment: 5,358. **Student Body:** 58% female, 42% male, 5% out-of-state, 5% international (41 countries represented). Asian 4%, African American 13%, Caucasian 67%, Hispanic 9%, Native American 1%.
Retention and Graduation: 66% freshmen return for sophomore year. 9% freshmen graduate within 4 years. 28% freshmen graduate within 6 years.
Faculty: Student/faculty ratio 19:1. 206 full-time faculty, 68% hold PhDs, 11% are members of minority groups, 47% are women. 2% of classes are taught by teaching assistants.

ACADEMICS
Degrees: associate, bachelor's, master's, post-bachelor's certificate. **Classes:** Most classes have 20–29 students. Most lab/discussion sessions have 10–19 students. **Majors with Highest Enrollment:** journalism; marketing/marketing management; social sciences. **Special Study Options:** distance learning, double major, dual enrollment, English as a Second Language (ESL), honors program, independent study, internships, liberal arts/career combination, study abroad, teacher certification program. **Honors Programs:** First established in 1964 and developed upon Midwestern State University's Tradition of Excellence, the University Honors Program offers high achieving MSU students a challenging premier undergraduate learning experience. From the Honors Introductory Seminar at the beginning, through Honors designated classes taught by outstanding faculty, to the Honors Capstone Course and Graduation with Honors at the end, the MSU Honors Program serves as a powerful program from start to finish. **Combined Degree Programs:** Accounting/MBA. **Disability Services:** Special programs offered to physically disabled students include note-taking services, reader services, tape recorders, tutors. **Career Services:** Alumni network, alumni services, career/job search classes, internships Career Services highlights include career and job search.

FACILITIES
Housing: Coed dorms, special housing for disabled students, men's dorms, women's dorms, apartments for married students, apartments for single students, Housing for Honor students Biology Cooperative Housing. 99% of campus accessible to physically disabled. **Special Academic Facilities/Equipment:** Language lab, technology lab, video lab, planetarium, art museum. **Computers:** Students can register for classes online. Administrative functions (other than registration) can be performed online.

CAMPUS LIFE
Environment: City. **Activities:** Choral groups, concert band, dance, drama/theater, jazz band, literary magazine, marching band, music ensembles, pep band, student government, student newspaper, student-run film society, television station, yearbook 145 registered organizations, 23 honor societies, 15 religious organizations. 8 fraternities, 8 sororities. **Athletics (Intercollegiate):** *Men:* basketball, football, golf, soccer, tennis. *Women:* basketball, cross-country, soccer, softball, tennis, volleyball. **On-Campus Highlights:** Clark Student Center, D.L. Ligon Coliseum, Corner Perk Coffee Shop, Wellness Center, Library, Sikes Lake, an art meuseum.

ADMISSIONS
Freshman Academic Profile: Average high school GPA 3.4. 12% in top 10% of high school class, 37% in top 25% of high school class, 73% in top 50% of high school class. 96% from public high schools. SAT Math middle 50% range 450-560. SAT Critical Reading middle 50% range 440-550. SAT Writing middle 50% range 440-540. ACT middle 50% range 18-23. Minimum paper TOEFL 550. **Basis for Candidate Selection:** *Very important factors considered include:* Class rank, academic GPA, rigor of secondary school record, standardized test scores. *Other factors considered include:* application essay, alumni/ae relation, character/personal qualities, extracurricular activities, first generation, geographical residence, interview, level of applicant's interest, racial/ethnic status, state residency, talent/ability, volunteer work, work experience. **Freshman Admission Requirements:** High school diploma is required and GED is accepted. *Academic units required:* 4 English, 3 mathematics, 2 science, 6 academic electives. 4 English, 3 mathematics, 2 science, 6 academic electives. **Freshman Admission Statistics:** 1,407 applied, 69% admitted, 70% enrolled. **Transfer Admission Requirements:** college transcript(s), statement of good standing from prior institution(s). Minimum college GPA of 2.0 required. Lowest grade transferable D. **General Admission Information:** Application Fee $25. Regular application deadline 8/7. Notification on a rolling basis, beginning on or about 9/1. Nonfall registration accepted. Credit and/or placement offered for CEEB Advanced Placement tests.

COSTS AND FINANCIAL AID
Required Forms and Deadlines: FAFSA, institution's own financial aid form. **Notification of Awards:** Applicants will be notified of awards on a rolling basis beginning 3/15. **Types of Aid:** *Need-based scholarships/grants:* Federal Pell, SEOG, state scholarships/grants, private scholarships, the school's own gift aid. *Loans:* Subsidized Stafford, Unsubsidized Stafford, PLUS, Federal Perkins, state loans, college/university loans from institutional funds, Alternative Private Loans. **Student Employment:** Federal Work-Study Program available. Institutional employment available. Highest amount earned per year from on-campus jobs $9,120. Off-campus job opportunities are good. **Financial Aid Statistics:** 84% freshmen, 83% undergrads receive need-based scholarship or grant aid. 2% freshmen, 2% undergrads receive non-need-based scholarship or grant aid. 78% freshmen, 82% undergrads receive need-based self-help aid. 5% freshmen, 3% undergrads receive athletic scholarships. 72% freshmen, 76% undergrads receive any aid. 54% undergrads borrow to pay for school. Average cumulative indebtedness $17,882. **Criteria for awarding institutional aid:** *Non-need-based:* academics, alumni affiliation, art, athletics, leadership, minority status, music/drama.

MILES COLLEGE

5500 Myron Massey Blvd., Fairfield, AL 35064
Phone: 205-929-1656
E-mail: admissions@mail.miles.edu
Fax: 205-929-1627 • **Website:** miles.edu

This private school, affiliated with the Episcopal Church, was founded in 1905. It has a 37-acre campus.

RATINGS
Admissions Selectivity Rating: 60*   Fire Safety Rating: 60*   Green Rating: 60*

STUDENTS AND FACULTY
Enrollment: 1,660. **Student Body:** 57% female, 43% male, 33% out-of-state, 0% international. Asian 0%, African American 98%, Caucasian 1%, Hispanic 0%, Native American 0%.
Retention and Graduation: 70% freshmen return for sophomore year. 26% freshmen graduate within 4 years. 71% freshmen graduate within 6 years.
Faculty: Student/faculty ratio 20:1. 94 full-time faculty, 35% hold PhDs, 51% are women.

ACADEMICS
Degrees: bachelor's. **Special Study Options:** cooperative education program, double major, honors program, internships, study abroad, teacher certification program, weekend college.

FACILITIES
Housing: Coed dorms, men's dorms, women's dorms, apartments for single students.

CAMPUS LIFE
Activities: Choral groups, concert band, drama/theater, jazz band, marching band, music ensembles, pep band, student government, student newspaper, television station 8 honor societies, 1 religious organizations. **Athletics (Intercollegiate):** *Men:* baseball, basketball, cheerleading, football, tennis, track/field (outdoor). *Women:* basketball, cheerleading, softball, tennis, track/field (outdoor), volleyball.

ADMISSIONS
Freshman Academic Profile: Average high school GPA 2.4. 15% in top 10% of high school class, 31% in top 25% of high school class, 48% in top 50% of high school class. Minimum paper TOEFL 450. **Basis for Candidate Selection:** *Other factors considered include:* standardized test scores, alumni/ae relation. **Freshman Admission Requirements:** High school diploma is required and GED is accepted. *Academic units required:* 20 English, 20 mathematics, 20 science, 222 electives. 20 English, 20 mathematics, 20 science, 222 electives **Transfer Admission Requirements:** Lowest grade transferable C. **General Admission Information:** Application Fee $25. Regular application deadline 8/23. Nonfall registration accepted. Admission may be deferred for a maximum of 1 year.

COSTS AND FINANCIAL AID
Annual tuition $5,008. Room and board $2,950. Required fees $350. Average book expense $600. **Required Forms and Deadlines:** FAFSA, state aid form.

Types of Aid: *Need-based scholarships/grants:* Federal Pell, SEOG, state scholarships/grants, private scholarships, the school's own gift aid, United Negro College Fund. *Loans:* Direct Subsidized Stafford, Direct Unsubsidized Stafford, Direct PLUS, Subsidized Stafford, Unsubsidized Stafford, PLUS, Federal Perkins, state loans, college/university loans from institutional funds. **Student Employment:** Federal Work-Study Program available. Highest amount earned per year from on-campus jobs $1,000. **Criteria for awarding institutional aid:** *Non-need-based:* academics, job skills, religious affiliation, state/district residency.

MILLERSVILLE UNIVERSITY OF PENNSYLVANIA

PO Box 1002, Millersville, PA 17551-0302
Phone: 717-872-3371 • **Financial Aid Phone:** 717-872-3026
E-mail: admissions@millersville.edu • **CEEB Code:** 2656
Fax: 717-871-2147 • **Website:** www.millersville.edu • **ACT Code:** 3712

This public school was founded in 1855. It has a 250-acre campus.

RATINGS
Admissions Selectivity Rating: 77   **Fire Safety Rating:** 98   **Green Rating:** 75

STUDENTS AND FACULTY
Enrollment: 7,325. **Student Body:** 55% female, 45% male, 4% out-of-state, 0% international (57 countries represented). Asian 2%, African American 8%, Caucasian 80%, Hispanic 7%, Native American 0%.
Retention and Graduation: 36% freshmen graduate within 4 years. 65% freshmen graduate within 6 years. **Faculty:** Student/faculty ratio 22:1. 281 full-time faculty, 99% hold PhDs, 19% are members of minority groups, 48% are women. 0% of classes are taught by teaching assistants.

ACADEMICS
Degrees: associate, bachelor's, master's, post-bachelor's certificate, post-master's certificate. **Classes:** Most classes have 30–39 students. Most lab/discussion sessions have 20–29 students. **Majors with Highest Enrollment:** business administration and management; elementary education and teaching; psychology. **Special Study Options:** Accelerated program, cooperative education program, cross-registration, distance learning, double major, dual enrollment, honors program, independent study, internships, study abroad, teacher certification program, Academic Remediation; Advanced Placement Credit; Off-Campus Study; Learning Disabilities Services; Adult and Continuing Education (ACE) Program; Internet Courses; Summer Session for credit. **Honors Programs:** Honors College **Combined Degree Programs:** AS/Pre-Pharmacy; BS/Pre-Optomotry; BS/Pre-Podiatry; BS/Pre-Athl. Training. **Disability Services:** Special programs offered to physically disabled students include note-taking services, reader services, tape recorders, tutors. **Career Services:** alumni services, career/job search classes, career assessment Career Services highlights include Internships and co-ops are a winning strategy for students, employers and the university. Students develop their professional proficiency and self-confidence and get a chance to '"test drive"' their career choice. Employers get a highly motivated employee for a specific amount of time. The university gains valuable feedback regarding its instruction, curriculum, and programs.

FACILITIES
Housing: Coed dorms, wellness housing, theme housing, Academic Interest Housing for several subject areas. 85% of campus accessible to physically disabled. **Special Academic Facilities/Equipment:** Art galleries, foreign language lab, extensive inventory of scientific & technological instrumentation, weather station, T.V. studio, radio station, teleconferencing center, Distance Learning **Computers:** 100% of classrooms, 100% of dorms, 100% of libraries, 100% of dining areas, 100% of student union, 100% of common outdoor areas have wireless network access. Students can register for classes online. Administrative functions (other than registration) can be performed online.

CAMPUS LIFE
Environment: Village. **Activities:** Choral groups, concert band, dance, drama/theater, jazz band, literary magazine, marching band, music ensembles, musical theater, pep band, radio station, student government, student newspaper, symphony orchestra, television station, yearbook, Campus Ministries 120 registered organizations, 11 honor societies, 12 religious organizations. 9 fraternities, 10 sororities. **Athletics (Intercollegiate):** *Men:* baseball, basketball, cross-country, football, golf, soccer, tennis, track/field (outdoor), track/field (indoor), wrestling. *Women:* basketball, cheerleading, cross-country, field hockey, lacrosse, soccer, softball, swimming, tennis, track/field (outdoor), track/field (indoor), volleyball. **On-Campus Highlights:** Student Memorial Center, Ganser Library, Science and Technology Building, Biemesderfer Executive Center, Gordinier Dining Hall. **Environmental Initiatives:** Constructed a LEEDS certifiable building Campus recycling program Energy Conservation Program

ADMISSIONS
Freshman Academic Profile: 10% in top 10% of high school class, 37% in top 25% of high school class, 76% in top 50% of high school class. % from public high schools. SAT Math middle 50% range 470-560. SAT Critical Reading middle 50% range 460-550. SAT Writing middle 50% range 440-550. ACT middle 50% range 19-24. Minimum web-based TOEFL 65. Minimum paper TOEFL 500. **Basis for Candidate Selection:** *Very important factors considered include:* Class rank, rigor of secondary school record, standardized test scores. *Important factors considered include:* character/personal qualities, extracurricular activities, talent/ability, volunteer work, work experience. *Other factors considered include:* application essay, recommendation(s), alumni/ae relation, geographical residence, interview, racial/ethnic status, state residency. **Freshman Admission Requirements:** High school diploma is required and GED is accepted. *Academic units required:* 4 English, 3 mathematics, 3 science, (1 science labs), 3 social studies, 2 history. *Academic units recommended:* 4 English, 3 mathematics, 3 science, (1 science labs), 3 social studies, 2 history. **Freshman Admission Statistics:** 6,665 applied, 63% admitted, 31% enrolled. **Transfer Admission Requirements:** High school transcript, college transcript(s), statement of good standing from prior institution(s). Minimum college GPA of 2.0 required. Lowest grade transferable C. **General Admission Information:** Application Fee $50. Notification on a rolling basis, beginning on or about 9/15. Nonfall registration accepted. Admission may be deferred for a maximum of 1 semester. Credit and/or placement offered for CEEB Advanced Placement tests.

COSTS AND FINANCIAL AID
Annual in-state tuition $6,428. Annual out-of-state tuition $16,070. Room and board $8,834. Required fees $2,172. Average book expense $1,000. **Required Forms and Deadlines:** FAFSA. **Notification of Awards:** Applicants will be notified of awards on a rolling basis beginning 3/19. **Types of Aid:** *Need-based scholarships/grants:* Federal Pell, SEOG, state scholarships/grants, private scholarships, the school's own gift aid, Schock Scholarship. *Loans:* Subsidized Stafford, Unsubsidized Stafford, PLUS, Federal Perkins, college/university loans from institutional funds. **Student Employment:** Federal Work-Study Program available. Institutional employment available. Highest amount earned per year from on-campus jobs $12,787. Off-campus job opportunities are excellent. **Financial Aid Statistics:** 70% freshmen, 68% undergrads receive need-based scholarship or grant aid. 19% freshmen, 11% undergrads receive non-need-based scholarship or grant aid. 92% freshmen, 92% undergrads receive need-based self-help aid. 1% freshmen, 1% undergrads receive athletic scholarships. 84% freshmen, 80% undergrads receive any aid. 67% undergrads borrow to pay for school. Average cumulative indebtedness $30,210. **Criteria for awarding institutional aid:** *Non-need-based:* academics, athletics, minority status.

MILLIGAN COLLEGE

P.O. Box 210, Milligan College, TN 37682
Phone: 423-461-8730 • **Financial Aid Phone:** 423-461-8968
E-mail: admissions@milligan.edu • **CEEB Code:** 1469
Fax: 423-461-8982 • **Website:** www.milligan.edu/ • **ACT Code:** 3996

This private school was founded in 1866. It has a 181-acre campus.

RATINGS
Admissions Selectivity Rating: 76   **Fire Safety Rating:** 93   **Green Rating:** 63

STUDENTS AND FACULTY
Enrollment: 938. **Student Body:** 60% female, 40% male, 35% out-of-state, 3% international (15 countries represented). Asian 1%, African American 6%, Caucasian 84%, Hispanic 4%, Native American 0%.
Retention and Graduation: 80% freshmen return for sophomore year. 65% freshmen graduate within 6 years. 9% grads pursue arts and sciences degrees. 2% grads pursue law degrees. 2% grads pursue business degrees. 6% grads pursue medical degrees. **Faculty:** Student/faculty ratio 13:1. 68 full-time faculty, 79% hold PhDs, 3% are members of minority groups, 50% are women. 0% of classes are taught by teaching assistants.

ACADEMICS
Degrees: bachelor's, master's. **Classes:** Most classes have fewer than 10 students. Most lab/discussion sessions have fewer than 10 students. **Majors with Highest Enrollment:** bible/biblical studies; business/commerce; nursing/registered nurse (rn, asn, bsn, msn). **Special Study Options:** cross-registration, double major, independent study, internships, study abroad, teacher certification program. **Disability Services:** Special programs offered to physically disabled students include note-taking services, tape recorders, tutors. **Career Services:** Alumni network, career/job search classes, career assessment, regional alumni.

FACILITIES

Housing: men's dorms, women's dorms, apartments for married students, apartments for single students. 80% of campus accessible to physically disabled. **Computers:** 95% of classrooms, 95% of dorms, 100% of libraries, 100% of dining areas, 100% of student union, 25% of common outdoor areas have wireless network access. Students can register for classes online. Administrative functions (other than registration) can be performed online.

CAMPUS LIFE

Environment: Town. **Activities:** Choral groups, concert band, drama/theater, jazz band, literary magazine, music ensembles, musical theater, pep band, radio station, student government, student newspaper, symphony orchestra, yearbook 36 registered organizations, 5 honor societies, 5 religious organizations. **Athletics (Intercollegiate):** *Men:* baseball, basketball, cross-country, golf, mountain biking, soccer, swimming, tennis, track/field (outdoor), track/field (indoor). *Women:* basketball, cross-country, soccer, softball, swimming, tennis, track/field (outdoor), track/field (indoor), volleyball. **On-Campus Highlights:** The Gregory Center, Student Center, Residence Halls/ Dining Hall, Seeger Chapel, Athletic Facilities. **Environmental Initiatives:** Campuswide recycling Construction of a new LEED certified Wellness Center opened in March, 2010 Campuswide energy audit.

ADMISSIONS

Freshman Academic Profile: Average high school GPA 3.7. 37% in top 10% of high school class, 65% in top 25% of high school class, 89% in top 50% of high school class. 80% from public high schools. SAT Math middle 50% range 490-610. SAT Critical Reading middle 50% range 490-600. SAT Writing middle 50% range 480-560. ACT middle 50% range 21-27. Minimum web-based TOEFL 79. Minimum paper TOEFL 550. **Basis for Candidate Selection:** *Very important factors considered include:* application essay, academic GPA, rigor of secondary school record, standardized test scores, character/personal qualities, religious affiliation/commitment. *Important factors considered include:* recommendation(s), extracurricular activities. *Other factors considered include:* Class rank, alumni/ae relation, interview, racial/ethnic status, talent/ability, volunteer work, work experience. **Freshman Admission Requirements:** High school diploma is required and GED is accepted. **Freshman Admission Statistics:** 603 applied, 70% admitted, 48% enrolled. **Transfer Admission Requirements:** college transcript(s), essay or personal statement, minimum college GPA of 2.0 required. Lowest grade transferable C–. **General Admission Information:** Application Fee $30. Regular application deadline 8/1. Notification on a rolling basis, beginning on or about 10/1. Nonfall registration accepted. Admission may be deferred for a maximum of 1 year. Credit and/or placement offered for CEEB Advanced Placement tests.

COSTS AND FINANCIAL AID

Annual tuition $24,360. Room and board $5,650. Required fees $900. Average book expense $900. **Required Forms and Deadlines:** FAFSA. **Notification of Awards:** Applicants will be notified of awards on a rolling basis beginning 3/15. **Types of Aid:** *Need-based scholarships/grants:* Federal Pell, SEOG, state scholarships/grants, private scholarships, the school's own gift aid. *Loans:* Subsidized Stafford, Unsubsidized Stafford, PLUS, Federal Perkins. **Student Employment:** Federal Work-Study Program available. Institutional employment available. Off-campus job opportunities are excellent. **Financial Aid Statistics:** 100% freshmen, 98% undergrads receive need-based scholarship or grant aid. 30% freshmen, 21% undergrads receive non-need-based scholarship or grant aid. 58% freshmen, 69% undergrads receive need-based self-help aid. 21% freshmen, 16% undergrads receive athletic scholarships. 97% freshmen, 92% undergrads receive any aid. 72% undergrads borrow to pay for school. Average cumulative indebtedness $18,394. **Criteria for awarding institutional aid:** *Non-need-based:* academics, alumni affiliation, art, athletics, job skills, minority status, music/drama, religious affiliation, state/district residency.

MILLIKIN UNIVERSITY

1184 West Main Street, Decatur, IL 62522-2084
Phone: 217-424-6210 • **Financial Aid Phone:** 217-424-6317
E-mail: admis@millikin.edu • **CEEB Code:** 1470
Fax: 217-425-4669 • **Website:** www.millikin.edu • **ACT Code:** 1080

This private school, affiliated with the Presbyterian Church, was founded in 1901. It has a 75-acre campus.

RATINGS

Admissions Selectivity Rating: 82   **Fire Safety Rating:** 97   **Green Rating:** 60*

STUDENTS AND FACULTY

Enrollment: 2,221. **Student Body:** 59% female, 41% male, 11% out-of-state, 1% international (13 countries represented). Asian 1%, African American 12%, Caucasian 79%, Hispanic 5%, Native American 0%.

Retention and Graduation: 78% freshmen return for sophomore year. 45% freshmen graduate within 4 years. 55% freshmen graduate within 6 years. 23% grads go on to further study within 1 year. 13% grads pursue arts and sciences degrees. 1% grads pursue law degrees. 1% grads pursue business degrees. 2% grads pursue medical degrees. **Faculty:** Student/faculty ratio 11:1. 154 full-time faculty, 83% hold PhDs, 8% are members of minority groups, 51% are women. 0% of classes are taught by teaching assistants.

ACADEMICS

Degrees: bachelor's, master's. **Classes:** Most classes have 10–19 students. Most lab/discussion sessions have 10–19 students. **Majors with Highest Enrollment:** elementary education and teaching; music performance; nursing/registered nurse (rn, asn, bsn, msn). **Special Study Options:** Accelerated program, double major, exchange student program (domestic), honors program, independent study, internships, student-designed major, study abroad, teacher certification program. **Honors Programs:** Presidential Scholars are Millikin's best and brightest students; selection is based upon outstanding academic performance and demonstrated leadership; they receive a full tuition scholarship, renewable for up to four years. Millikin's Honors Program introduces students to college-level scholarship, research, critical thinking, and writing during the freshman and sophomore years; classes are taught as seminars - sessions involving intense discussion and requiring active participation; Millikin's strongest juniors are invited to join the next phase of the Honors Program to become James Millikin Scholars. ; James Millikin Scholars Program; Honors Program. **Disability Services:** Special programs offered to physically disabled students include note-taking services, reader services, tape recorders, tutors. **Career Services:** Alumni network, alumni services, career/job search classes, career assessment, internships Career Services highlights include Millikin's Blue Connection, a retail art gallery, serves as the practical laboratory for Millikin's innovative Art of Entrepreneurship curriculum. This gallery sells, original art, produced by Millikin alumni, faculty, staff and students. The Blue Connection retail art store is fully operated by Millikin students, a majority of which are from Art, Business and Music programs. The talents of the various majors are integrated with the concept of business ownership. The success of the venture is in the hands of the Millikin students.

FACILITIES

Housing: Coed dorms, special housing for disabled students, men's dorms, special housing for international students, women's dorms, fraternity/sorority housing, apartments for married students, apartments for single students, wellness housing, Learning Communities. 66% of campus accessible to physically disabled. **Special Academic Facilities/Equipment:** Art galleries, art museum, fitness/wellness center, recording studio, indoor sports center, greenhouse, observatory, 2 indoor sports centers, 2000 seat performance center **Computers:** 75% of classrooms, 75% of dorms, 100% of libraries, 100% of dining areas, 100% of student union, 5% of common outdoor areas have wireless network access. Students can register for classes online. Administrative functions (other than registration) can be performed online.

CAMPUS LIFE

Environment: City. **Activities:** Choral groups, concert band, dance, drama/theater, jazz band, literary magazine, music ensembles, musical theater, opera, pep band, radio station, student government, student newspaper, student-run film society, symphony orchestra, International Student Organization, Model UN 96 registered organizations, 7 honor societies, 2 religious organizations. 5 fraternities, 4 sororities. **Athletics (Intercollegiate):** *Men:* baseball, basketball, cheerleading, cross-country, football, golf, soccer, swimming, track/field (outdoor), track/field (indoor). *Women:* basketball, cheerleading, cross country, golf, soccer, softball, swimming, tennis, track/field (outdoor), track/field (indoor), volleyball. **On-Campus Highlights:** ADM-Scovill Hall, Perkinson Music Center, Albert Taylor Theatre, Decatur Indoor Sports Center, Kirkland Fine Arts Center.

ADMISSIONS

Freshman Academic Profile: Average high school GPA 3.4. 16% in top 10% of high school class, 40% in top 25% of high school class, 77% in top 50% of high school class. 90% from public high schools. SAT Math middle 50% range 460-560. SAT Critical Reading middle 50% range 440-600. SAT Writing middle 50% range 430-580. ACT middle 50% range 20-26. Minimum web-based TOEFL 79. Minimum paper TOEFL 550. **Basis for Candidate Selection:** *Very important factors considered include:* rigor of secondary school record. *Important factors considered include:* Class rank, academic GPA, recommendation(s), standardized test scores, interview. *Other factors considered include:* alumni/ae relation, character/personal qualities, extracurricular activities, level of applicant's interest, talent/ability, volunteer work, work experience. **Freshman Admission Requirements:** High school diploma is required and GED is accepted. **Freshman Admission Statistics:** 3,998 applied, 55% admitted, 24% enrolled. **Transfer Admission Requirements:** High school transcript, college transcript(s), minimum college GPA of 2.0 required. Lowest grade transferable C–. **General Admission Information:** Notification on a rolling basis, beginning on or about 9/15. Nonfall registration accepted. Admission may be deferred for a maximum of 1 year. Credit and/or placement offered for CEEB Advanced Placement tests.

COSTS AND FINANCIAL AID

Annual tuition $27,852. Room and board $8,970. Required fees $792. Average book expense $1,000. **Required Forms and Deadlines:** FAFSA. **Notification of Awards:** Applicants will be notified of awards on a rolling basis beginning 3/15. **Types of Aid:** *Need-based scholarships/grants:* Federal Pell, SEOG, state scholarships/grants, private scholarships, the school's own gift aid. *Loans:* Subsidized Stafford, Unsubsidized Stafford, PLUS, Federal Perkins, state loans. **Student Employment:** Federal Work-Study Program available. Institutional employment available. Highest amount earned per year from on-campus jobs $4,285. Off-campus job opportunities are good. **Financial Aid Statistics:** 98% freshmen, 92% undergrads receive need-based scholarship or grant aid. 100% freshmen, 92% undergrads receive non-need-based scholarship or grant aid. 83% freshmen, 85% undergrads receive need-based self-help aid. 100% freshmen, 100% undergrads receive any aid. 78% undergrads borrow to pay for school. Average cumulative indebtedness $29,871. **Criteria for awarding institutional aid:** *Non-need-based:* academics, alumni affiliation, art, leadership, minority status, music/drama.

MILLS COLLEGE

5000 MacArthur Boulevard, Oakland, CA 94613
Phone: 510-430-2135 • **Financial Aid Phone:** 510-430-2000
E-mail: admission@mills.edu • **CEEB Code:** 4485
Fax: 510-430-3314 • **Website:** www.mills.edu • **ACT Code:** 4485

This private school was founded in 1852. It has a 135-acre campus.

RATINGS

Admissions Selectivity Rating: 85   **Fire Safety Rating:** 68   **Green Rating:** 98

STUDENTS AND FACULTY

Enrollment: 933. **Student Body:** 100% female, 0% male, 19% out-of-state, 2% international (14 countries represented). Asian 12%, African American 6%, Caucasian 47%, Hispanic 21%, Native American 0%.
Retention and Graduation: 77% freshmen return for sophomore year. 51% freshmen graduate within 4 years. 30% grads go on to further study within 1 year. 5% grads pursue arts and sciences degrees. 2% grads pursue law degrees. 17% grads pursue business degrees. 2% grads pursue medical degrees. **Faculty:** Student/faculty ratio 10:1. 102 full-time faculty, 91% hold PhDs, 30% are members of minority groups, 72% are women. 0% of classes are taught by teaching assistants.

ACADEMICS

Degrees: bachelor's, certificate, master's, post-bachelor's certificate. **Classes:** Most classes have 10–19 students. Most lab/discussion sessions have 10–19 students. **Majors with Highest Enrollment:** English language and literature; political science and government; psychology. **Special Study Options:** cooperative education program, cross-registration, double major, exchange student program (domestic), independent study, internships, liberal arts/career combination, student-designed major, study abroad, teacher certification program. **Combined Degree Programs:** BA/MA, BA/MEng, BA/MBA; BA/MPP; BA/MA/Teaching Credential. **Disability Services:** Special programs offered to physically disabled students include note-taking services, reader services, tape recorders, tutors. **Career Services:** Alumni network, alumni services, career/job search classes, career assessment, internships, regional alumni. Career Services highlights include We are very proud of our expanding internship services program within Career Services. In 2006, we hired a dedicated internship coordinator for the campus and this position has focused on increasing access to local and national internships for our student population. We have also worked to track student success related to internship completion and to make the process more user friendly.

FACILITIES

Housing: Coed dorms, special housing for disabled students, women's dorms, apartments for married students, cooperative housing, apartments for single students, wellness housing, theme housing, Resumer Student Housing. 90% of campus accessible to physically disabled. **Special Academic Facilities/Equipment:** Art Museum, Center for contemporary Music, on-campus elementary school, botanical gardens. **Computers:** 100% of classrooms, 100% of dorms, 100% of libraries, 100% of dining areas, 100% of student union, 100% of common outdoor areas have wireless network access. Students can register for classes online. Administrative functions (other than registration) can be performed online.

CAMPUS LIFE

Environment: Metropolis. **Activities:** Choral groups, dance, drama/theater, literary magazine, music ensembles, musical theater, radio station, student government, student newspaper, student-run film society, yearbook, Campus Ministries, International Student Organization, Model UN 47 registered organizations, 2 honor societies, 4 religious organizations. **Athletics (Intercollegiate):** *Women:* crew/rowing, cross-country, soccer, swimming, tennis, track/field (outdoor), volleyball. **On-Campus Highlights:** The Mills College Art Museum, Haas Pavilion & Trefethen Aquatic Center, Rothwell Student Center, Lorrie Lokey Graduate School of Business, Littlefield Concert Hall. **Environmental Initiatives:** Mills recycles, composts and reuses all consumer materials to the extent possible. www.mills.edu/green/recycling Mills students, staff and faculty participate in Recycle Mania. Mills builds to LEED standards of silver or higher. Mills has been awarded a LEED Platinum for new science building and has just broken ground on a business school designed to achieve LEED Gold. Mills encourages the use and provides access to public and shared transportation by offering a Mills Shuttle service, car share and web based carpool system. Public Transit passes available to all undergraduate students, funded through student fees.

ADMISSIONS

Freshman Academic Profile: Average high school GPA 3.6. 33% in top 10% of high school class, 65% in top 25% of high school class, 92% in top 50% of high school class. 80% from public high schools. SAT Math middle 50% range 510-620. SAT Critical Reading middle 50% range 540-660. SAT Writing middle 50% range 530-640. ACT middle 50% range 23-27. Minimum web-based TOEFL 80. Minimum paper TOEFL 550. **Basis for Candidate Selection:** *Very important factors considered include:* rigor of secondary school record. *Important factors considered include:* Class rank, application essay, academic GPA, recommendation(s), standardized test scores, character/personal qualities, extracurricular activities. *Other factors considered include:* alumni/ae relation, first generation, interview, level of applicant's interest, talent/ability, volunteer work, work experience. **Freshman Admission Requirements:** High school diploma is required and GED is accepted. *Academic units required:* 4 English, 3 mathematics, 2 science, (2 science labs), 2 foreign language, 2 social studies, 2 history. *Academic units recommended:* 4 English, 3 mathematics, 2 science, (2 science labs), 2 foreign language, 2 social studies, 2 history. **Freshman Admission Statistics:** 2,031 applied, 63% admitted, 16% enrolled. **Transfer Admission Requirements:** High school transcript, college transcript(s), essay or personal statement, Lowest grade transferable C–. **General Admission Information:** Application Fee $50. Regular application deadline 8/1. Notification on a rolling basis, beginning on or about 11/1. Nonfall registration accepted. Admission may be deferred for a maximum of 1 year. Credit and/or placement offered for CEEB Advanced Placement tests.

COSTS AND FINANCIAL AID

Annual tuition $38,850. Room and board $11,580. Required fees $1,230. Average book expense $1,430. **Required Forms and Deadlines:** FAFSA, institution's own financial aid form, Noncustodial Parent Statement, if applicable. **Notification of Awards:** Applicants will be notified of awards on a rolling basis beginning 3/1. **Types of Aid:** *Need-based scholarships/grants:* Federal Pell, SEOG, state scholarships/grants, private scholarships, the school's own gift aid. *Loans:* Subsidized Stafford, Unsubsidized Stafford, PLUS, Federal Perkins, college/university loans from institutional funds. **Student Employment:** Federal Work-Study Program available. Institutional employment available. Highest amount earned per year from on-campus jobs $2,700. Off-campus job opportunities are excellent. **Financial Aid Statistics:** 96% freshmen, 95% undergrads receive need-based scholarship or grant aid. 7% freshmen, 5% undergrads receive non-need-based scholarship or grant aid. 93% freshmen, 89% undergrads receive need-based self-help aid. 99% freshmen, 95% undergrads receive any aid. 77% undergrads borrow to pay for school. Average cumulative indebtedness $27,021. **Criteria for awarding institutional aid:** *Non-need-based:* academics, leadership, minority status, music/drama.

MILLSAPS COLLEGE

Best 378

1701 North State Street, Jackson, MS 39210
Phone: 601-974-1050 • **Financial Aid Phone:** 800-352-1050
E-mail: admissions@millsaps.edu • **CEEB Code:** 1471
Fax: 601-974-1059 • **Website:** www.millsaps.edu • **ACT Code:** 2212

This private school, affiliated with the Methodist Church, was founded in 1890. It has a 100-acre campus.

RATINGS

Admissions Selectivity Rating: 86   **Fire Safety Rating:** 84   **Green Rating:** 61

STUDENTS AND FACULTY

Enrollment: 837. **Student Body:** 49% female, 51% male, 56% out-of-state, 2% international (21 countries represented). Asian 5%, African American 11%, Caucasian 75%, Hispanic 2%, Native American 1%.
Retention and Graduation: 67% freshmen graduate within 4 years. 56% grads go on to further study within 1 year. 25% grads pursue arts and sciences degrees. 8% grads pursue law degrees. 14% grads pursue business degrees. 8% grads pursue medical degrees. **Faculty:** Student/faculty ratio 8:1. 94 full-time faculty, 95% hold PhDs, 15% are members of minority groups, 43% are women. 0% of classes are taught by teaching assistants.

ACADEMICS

Degrees: bachelor's, master's. **Classes:** Most classes have 10–19 students. Most lab/discussion sessions have 10–19 students. **Majors with Highest Enrollment:** biology/biological sciences; business administration and management; English language and literature. **Special Study Options:** Accelerated program, double major, honors program, independent study, internships, liberal arts/career combination, student-designed major, study abroad, teacher certification program, The Millsaps FAITH & WORK INITIATIVE offers an array of curricular and extracurricular programs to help students discern their vocation or call in life and to pursue that call with passion, integrity and an eye toward the needs of the world. Faith & Work options include service-learning courses and the Meaning of Work course, immersion and service experiences, discussion programs with faculty and professionals, leadership and service clubs, internships, and public lecture series. Other INTERDISCIPLINARY PROGRAMS or concentrations are available in American studies, Christian education, environmental studies, film studies, human services, international studies, women's and gender studies, and church music. UNDERGRADUATE RESEARCH is available in most academic departments, including field research opportunities in the Pacific Northwest, Yellowstone, the Mexico, and Europe. Millsaps' non-profit biocultural reserve on 4500 acres in the Yucatan Peninsula of Mexico offers multi-disciplinary options for study, including archaeology, business, ecology, education, geology, history, literature, math and socio-cultural anthropology. Students may also choose among other STUDY ABROAD programs developed by Millsaps faculty--in Albania, Belgium, China, Costa Rica, England, France, Germany, Ghana, Greece, Ireland, Israel, Italy, Japan, Mexico (Yucatan), and Tanzania. PRE-PROFESSIONAL programs include dentistry, engineering, law, medicine, ministry, and social work. Millsaps students may work towards DUAL DEGREES in engineering, applied science or nursing through agreements with Auburn University, Columbia University, Vanderbilt University, Washington University, and the University of Mississippi Medical Health Center. Other distinctive programs include the FORD TEACHING FELLOWS program (research and internships for students interested in college teaching), and the Weiner PRE-MEDICAL FELLOWS program (summer research). **Honors Programs:** The Honors Program, Ford Teaching Fellows program (research and internships for students interested in college teaching), Weiner Pre-Medical Fellows Program (summer research), Lilly Fellows Faith and Work Initiative (connecting individual passions with learning, meaning, service, and career) **Combined Degree Programs:** BA/MBA-Millsaps, 3-2 BSN nursing-Univ. ofMiss., 4-2 MSN nursing-Vanderbilt. **Disability Services:** Special programs offered to physically disabled students include note-taking services, reader services, tutors. **Career Services:** Alumni network, alumni services, career assessment, internships, regional alumni. Career Services highlights include The Millsaps Career Center sponsors an internship-for-credit program designed to assist students with career choices and relate student work experiences to their education. Initially, the Career Center offers orientation and internship search assistance. During the internships, students maintain work logs, write monthly journals of their work experiences, and receive monthly feedback from the Career Center. Interns also obtain written evaluations from their supervisors and write final reports, evaluating their work sites and relating their work experiences to their education and career objectives.

FACILITIES

Housing: Coed dorms, special housing for disabled students, women's dorms, fraternity/sorority housing, wellness housing, theme housing. Our theme housing is community service housing. 90% of campus accessible to physically disabled. **Special Academic Facilities/Equipment:** Millsaps' W.M. Keck Center for Instrumental and Biochemical Comparative Archaeology is the only undergraduate facility of its kind in the world. The new multi-disciplinary research laboratory provides undergraduate students with the opportunity to explore complex archeological questions using advanced bioanalytical and biochemical techniques. 4-6 Keck Fellows assist each year in gathering the artifacts studied in the lab from the College's archaeological field programs in Yucatán, Mexico, and northern Albania. The lab houses an inductively-coupled plasma spectrometer with laser ablation, a gas-chromatography spectrometer, a liquid-chromatography spectrometer, and a portable x-ray fluorescence spectrometer. In addition, the college's other labs include a unique array of spectrometers for measuring atomic absorption, infrared transitional modes, nuclear magnetic resonance, and other forms of energy; high performance chromatographs for separation and identification of compounds; electrophoresis instruments for analyzing biomolecules and other biological materials; and an inert atmosphere reaction chamber. Other facilities include a state-of-the-art molecular biology/functional genomics research laboratory; a fluorescence microscopy suite and imaging facility; a GIS workstation with Rockware and Arcview 9.1 GIS Software; a specially-designed automated 24-hour food monitoring system for rats; a microsurgical lab for animal surgeries; an on-campus hydrogeologic monitoring station to measure the water table and water levels in four on-campus wells; and a computational modeling lab for math, chemistry and physics students which provides numerical and graphical solutions in three dimensions. The College Sorbent and Environmental Laboratory provides undergraduates with opportunities for oil spill and stormwater remediation research. Another unique facility is the college's 4,000-acre biocultural reserve and learning center in the state of Yucatan, Mexico. Here students excavate ancient Mayan archaeological sites, conduct environmental studies of the jungle, research the biology and geology of the area, and live in a sustainable solar-powered facility constructed of materials inspired by the native Mayan architecture. Millsaps' Yucatan program also includes a newly-renovated teaching and living facility for international business studies which is located in the large city of Merida. In addition, Millsaps' newly-renovated digital Language Resource Center has been equipped with 25 network computers and satellite connections for international programming. **Computers:** 100% of classrooms, 100% of dorms, 100% of libraries, 100% of dining areas, 100% of student union, 100% of common outdoor areas have wireless network access. Students can register for classes online. Administrative functions (other than registration) can be performed online.

CAMPUS LIFE

Environment: Metropolis. **Activities:** Choral groups, dance, drama/theater, literary magazine, music ensembles, musical theater, student government, student newspaper, yearbook, Campus Ministries, International Student Organization, Model UN 85 registered organizations, 28 honor societies, 12 religious organizations. 6 fraternities, 6 sororities. **Athletics (Intercollegiate):** *Men:* baseball, basketball, cross-country, football, golf, lacrosse, soccer, tennis, track/field (outdoor). *Women:* basketball, cross-country, golf, lacrosse, soccer, softball, tennis, track/field (outdoor), volleyball. **On-Campus Highlights:** Hall Activities Center (fitness/athletic facility), Campbell College Center (student activities), The Bowl (outdoor green space/campus center), Millsaps Wilson Library (study center), Fraternity Row, The Campbell College Center includes a cafeteria, a coffeehouse, live entertainment and game areas, and a bookstore. The Bowl is a natural, outdoor space in the heart of the campus where students congregate between classes to relax and to participate in outdoor activities.

ADMISSIONS

Freshman Academic Profile: Average high school GPA 3.6. 35% in top 10% of high school class, 60% in top 25% of high school class, 85% in top 50% of high school class. 55% from public high schools. SAT Math middle 50% range 520-610. SAT Critical Reading middle 50% range 490-610. SAT Writing middle 50% range 490-565. ACT middle 50% range 23-29. Minimum web-based TOEFL 80. Minimum paper TOEFL 550. **Basis for Candidate Selection:** *Very important factors considered include:* academic GPA, rigor of secondary school record, standardized test scores, character/personal qualities. *Important factors considered include:* Class rank, application essay, recommendation(s), extracurricular activities, interview, talent/ability, volunteer work. *Other factors considered include:* work experience. **Freshman Admission Requirements:** High school diploma is required and GED is accepted. *Academic units required:* 4 English, 3 mathematics, 3 science, (1 science labs), 2 social studies, 2 history. *Academic units recommended:* 4 English, 3 mathematics, 3 science, (1 science labs), 2 social studies, 2 history. **Freshman Admission Statistics:** 2,255 applied, 55% admitted, 17% enrolled. **Transfer Admission Requirements:** college transcript(s), essay or personal statement, standardized test scores, statement of good standing from prior institution(s). Minimum college GPA of 2.75 required. Lowest grade transferable C. **General Admission Information:** Notification on a rolling basis, beginning on or about 10/1. Nonfall registration accepted. Admission may be deferred for a maximum of 1 year. Credit and/or placement offered for CEEB Advanced Placement tests.

COSTS AND FINANCIAL AID
Annual tuition $29,052. Room and board $10,826. Required fees $1,922. Average book expense $1,100. **Required Forms and Deadlines:** FAFSA. **Notification of Awards:** Applicants will be notified of awards on a rolling basis beginning 3/15. **Types of Aid:** *Need-based scholarships/grants:* Federal Pell, SEOG, state scholarships/grants, private scholarships, the school's own gift aid. *Loans:* Subsidized Stafford, Unsubsidized Stafford, PLUS, Federal Perkins, college/university loans from institutional funds. **Student Employment:** Federal Work-Study Program available. Institutional employment available. Highest amount earned per year from on-campus jobs $8,429. Off-campus job opportunities are good. **Financial Aid Statistics:** 100% freshmen, 96% undergrads receive need-based scholarship or grant aid. 22% freshmen, 20% undergrads receive non-need-based scholarship or grant aid. 71% freshmen, 74% undergrads receive need-based self-help aid. 100% freshmen, 96% undergrads receive any aid. 56% undergrads borrow to pay for school. Average cumulative indebtedness $28,965. **Criteria for awarding institutional aid:** *Non-need-based:* academics, art, leadership, music/drama, religious affiliation.

MILWAUKEE INSTITUTE OF ART AND DESIGN

273 East Erie Street, Milwaukee, WI 53202
Phone: 414-847-3200 • **Financial Aid Phone:** 414-291-8272
E-mail: admissions@miad.edu • **CEEB Code:** 1506
Fax: 414-291-8077 • **Website:** 273 E. Erie Street • **ACT Code:** 4701

This private school was founded in 1974. It has a 2-acre campus.

RATINGS
Admissions Selectivity Rating: 62   Fire Safety Rating: 67   Green Rating: 60*

STUDENTS AND FACULTY
Enrollment: 643. **Student Body:** 50% female, 50% male, 37% out-of-state, 4% international (3 countries represented). Asian 3%, African American 3%, Caucasian 80%, Hispanic 9%, Native American 1%.
Retention and Graduation: 81% freshmen return for sophomore year. 38% freshmen graduate within 4 years. 46% freshmen graduate within 6 years. 6% grads go on to further study within 1 year. 4% grads pursue arts and sciences degrees. **Faculty:** Student/faculty ratio 9:1. 33 full-time faculty, 67% hold PhDs, 6% are members of minority groups, 42% are women. 0% of classes are taught by teaching assistants.

ACADEMICS
Degrees: bachelor's. **Classes:** Most classes have 10–19 students. Most lab/discussion sessions have fewer than 10 students. **Majors with Highest Enrollment:** graphic design; illustration; industrial design. **Special Study Options:** double major, exchange student program (domestic), independent study, internships, study abroad. **Disability Services:** Special programs offered to physically disabled students include note-taking services, reader services, tape recorders, tutors. **Career Services:** Alumni network, alumni services, career assessment, internships.

FACILITIES
Housing: Coed dorms. 100% of campus accessible to physically disabled. **Special Academic Facilities/Equipment:** Eisner Museum of Advertisng and Design Brook Stevens Gallery of Industrial design Frederick Layton Gallery

CAMPUS LIFE
Environment: Metropolis. **Activities:** drama/theater, literary magazine, student government, student newspaper 12 registered organizations, 2 honor societies, 1 religious organizations.

ADMISSIONS
Freshman Academic Profile: Average high school GPA 3.0. 6% in top 10% of high school class, 25% in top 25% of high school class, 56% in top 50% of high school class. Minimum paper TOEFL 550. **Basis for Candidate Selection:** *Very important factors considered include:* application essay, academic GPA, character/personal qualities, interview, level of applicant's interest, talent/ability.*Other factors considered include:* Class rank, recommendation(s), rigor of secondary school record, standardized test scores, extracurricular activities, volunteer work, work experience. **Freshman Admission Requirements:** High school diploma is required and GED is accepted. **Freshman Admission Statistics:** 416 applied, 75% admitted, 62% enrolled. **Transfer Admission Requirements:** essay or personal statement, interview, minimum college GPA of 2.0 required. Lowest grade transferable C. **General Admission Information:** Application Fee $25. Notification on a rolling basis, beginning on or about 9/1. Nonfall registration accepted. Admission may be deferred for a maximum

of 2 years. Neither credit nor placement offered for CEEB Advanced Placement tests.

COSTS AND FINANCIAL AID
Required **Forms and Deadlines:** FAFSA. **Notification of Awards:** Applicants will be notified of awards on a rolling basis beginning 4/1. **Types of Aid:** *Need-based scholarships/grants:* Federal Pell, SEOG, state scholarships/grants, private scholarships, the school's own gift aid. *Loans:* Direct Subsidized Stafford, Direct Unsubsidized Stafford, Direct PLUS. **Student Employment:** Federal Work-Study Program available. Institutional employment available. Highest amount earned per year from on-campus jobs $1,200. Off-campus job opportunities are good. **Financial Aid Statistics:** 99% freshmen, 98% undergrads receive need-based scholarship or grant aid. 9% freshmen, 6% undergrads receive non-need-based scholarship or grant aid. 91% freshmen, 94% undergrads receive need-based self-help aid. 95% freshmen, 92% undergrads receive any aid. 100% undergrads borrow to pay for school. **Criteria for awarding institutional aid:** *Non-need-based:* academics, art.

MILWAUKEE SCHOOL OF ENGINEERING

1025 North Broadway, Milwaukee, WI 53202-3109
Phone: 414-277-6763 • **Financial Aid Phone:** 800-778-7223
E-mail: explore@msoe.edu • **CEEB Code:** 1476
Fax: 414-277-7475 • **Website:** www.msoe.edu • **ACT Code:** 4616

This private school was founded in 1903. It has a 15-acre campus.

RATINGS
Admissions Selectivity Rating: 89   Fire Safety Rating: 99   Green Rating: 72

STUDENTS AND FACULTY
Enrollment: 2,378. **Student Body:** 22% female, 78% male, 31% out-of-state, 6% international (27 countries represented). Asian 3%, African American 2%, Caucasian 77%, Hispanic 4%, Native American 0%.
Retention and Graduation: 81% freshmen return for sophomore year. 36% freshmen graduate within 4 years. 56% freshmen graduate within 6 years. 11% grads go on to further study within 1 year. 1% grads pursue law degrees. 2% grads pursue business degrees. **Faculty:** Student/faculty ratio 14:1. 132 full-time faculty, 80% hold PhDs, 11% are members of minority groups, 29% are women. 0% of classes are taught by teaching assistants.

ACADEMICS
Degrees: bachelor's, master's. **Classes:** Most classes have 20–29 students. Most lab/discussion sessions have 10–19 students. **Majors with Highest Enrollment:** architectural engineering; electrical, electronics and communications engineering; mechanical engineering. **Special Study Options:** Accelerated program, distance learning, double major, dual enrollment, English as a Second Language (ESL), independent study, internships, study abroad, BS in international business and in electrical and mechanical engineering with Fachhochschule Lubeck, Germany. All students may apply to study at Czech Technical University, Prague, Czech Republic. **Combined Degree Programs:** BA/MEng, Architectural Eng. and Construction Management. **Disability Services:** Special programs offered to physically disabled students include note-taking services, reader services, tape recorders, tutors. **Career Services:** Alumni network, alumni services, career/job search classes, career assessment, internships, regional alumni. Career Services highlights include Approximatly 85% of gradates have had internship experience.

FACILITIES
Housing: Coed dorms, special housing for disabled students 85% of campus accessible to physically disabled. **Special Academic Facilities/Equipment:** Grohmann Museum, Kern Center Health, Wellness and Recreation Facility, Rader School of Business, Johnson Controls Software Engineering Lab, Fluid Power Institute, Rapid Prototyping Center, Applied Technology Center, Center for BioMolecular Modeling, Warren P. Knowles Nursing Lab, Harley Davidson Design Lab, Johnson Controls Environmental Systems Lab **Computers:** 100% of classrooms, 10% of dorms, 100% of libraries, 100% of dining areas, 100% of student union, 100% of common outdoor areas have wireless network access. Students can register for classes online. Administrative functions (other than registration) can be performed online. Undergraduates are required to own a computer.

CAMPUS LIFE
Environment: Metropolis. **Activities:** dance, drama/theater, jazz band, literary magazine, pep band, radio station, student government, symphony orchestra, Campus Ministries, International Student Organization 61 registered organizations, 6 honor societies, 4 religious organizations. 3 fraternities, 3 sororities. **Athletics (Intercollegiate):** *Men:* baseball, basketball, cheerleading, crew/

rowing, cross-country, golf, ice hockey, lacrosse, soccer, tennis, track/field (outdoor), track/field (indoor), volleyball, wrestling. *Women:* basketball, cheer-leading, cross-country, golf, soccer, softball, tennis, track/field (outdoor), track/field (indoor), volleyball. **On-Campus Highlights:** Kern Center - Health and Wellness Center, Student Life and Campus Center (dining and game room), The Grohmann Museum, Rapid Prototyping Center, School of Nursing Simulation Lab. **Environmental Initiatives:** In the Fall of 2010, MSOE initiated a compostable service ware program in the school's cafe. It included replacing hot and cold beverage cups, plates and soup bowls. At the time, there was also a dedicated collection stream setup to help divert an estimated 150 cubic yards of waste per year from going into local landfills. Efforts have been made to increase MSOE's recycling rate from 10% in 6/09 to over 60% in 1/11. In January of 2011, MSOE implemented a chemical inventory database for all chemicals on campus. The database enables the school to bar code and track chemical containers on campus. It also provides an opportunity for chemical surplus sharing across campus. The system is expected to reduce redundant purchasing and foster waste minimization on campus. In 2011 successfully implemented a chemical inventory system for all chemicals on campus; all must be processed through a gateway and entered in a data base, enabling personnel to maintain a real time inventory.

ADMISSIONS

Freshman Academic Profile: Average high school GPA 3.6. 87% from public high schools. SAT Math middle 50% range 570-680. SAT Critical Reading middle 50% range 510-610. ACT middle 50% range 24-29. Minimum web-based TOEFL 79. Minimum paper TOEFL 550. **Basis for Candidate Selection:** *Very important factors considered include:* academic GPA, rigor of secondary school record, standardized test scores.*Other factors considered include:* recommendation(s), character/personal qualities, extracurricular activities, level of applicant's interest, volunteer work, work experience. **Freshman Admission Requirements:** High school diploma is required and GED is accepted. *Academic units required:* 4 English, 4 mathematics, 2 science. *Academic units recommended:* 4 English, 4 mathematics, 2 science. **Freshman Admission Statistics:** 2,014 applied, 57% admitted, 43% enrolled. **Transfer Admission Requirements:** college transcript(s), minimum college GPA of 2.5 required. Lowest grade transferable C. **General Admission Information:** Application Fee $25. Notification on a rolling basis, beginning on or about 10/15. Nonfall registration accepted. Admission may be deferred for a maximum of 2 year. Placement offered for CEEB Advanced Placement tests

COSTS AND FINANCIAL AID

Annual tuition $31,920. Room and board $8,028. Average book expense $1,200. **Required Forms and Deadlines:** FAFSAAdmission Application. **Notification of Awards:** Applicants will be notified of awards on a rolling basis beginning 3/1. **Types of Aid:** *Need-based scholarships/grants:* Federal Pell, SEOG, state scholarships/grants, private scholarships, the school's own gift aid. *Loans:* Subsidized Stafford, Unsubsidized Stafford, PLUS, Federal Perkins, state loans. **Student Employment:** Federal Work-Study Program available. Institutional employment available. Highest amount earned per year from on-campus jobs $14,141. Off-campus job opportunities are excellent. **Financial Aid Statistics:** 100% freshmen, 100% undergrads receive need-based scholarship or grant aid. 8% freshmen, 9% undergrads receive non-need-based scholarship or grant aid. 89% freshmen, 88% undergrads receive need-based self-help aid. 99% freshmen, 97% undergrads receive any aid. 84% undergrads borrow to pay for school. Average cumulative indebtedness $38,038. **Criteria for awarding institutional aid:** *Non-need-based:* academics.

MINNEAPOLIS COLLEGE OF ART AND DESIGN

2501 Stevens Avenue, Minneapolis, MN 55404
Phone: 612-874-3760 • **Financial Aid Phone:** 612-874-3782
E-mail: admissions@mcad.edu • **CEEB Code:** 6411
Fax: 612-874-3701 • **Website:** www.mcad.edu • **ACT Code:** 2130

This private school was founded in 1886. It has a 3-acre campus.

RATINGS
Admissions Selectivity Rating: 82   **Fire Safety Rating:** 60*   **Green Rating:** 60*

STUDENTS AND FACULTY
Enrollment: 594. **Student Body:** 61% female, 39% male, 36% out-of-state, 1% international (10 countries represented). Asian 6%, African American 2%, Caucasian 72%, Hispanic 6%, Native American 1%. **Retention and Graduation:** 70% freshmen return for sophomore year. 10% grads go on to further study within 1 year. 10% grads pursue arts and sciences degrees. **Faculty:** Student/faculty ratio 13:1. 42 full-time faculty, 100% hold PhDs, 31% are women. 0% of classes are taught by teaching assistants.

ACADEMICS
Degrees: bachelor's, master's, post-bachelor's certificate. **Classes:** Most classes have 10–19 students. **Special Study Options:** cooperative education program, cross-registration, distance learning, independent study, internships, study abroad, Off-Campus Study: Arts Program in New York. Co-Op Programs: Arts. **Disability Services:** Special programs offered to physically disabled students include note-taking services, reader services, tape recorders, tutors. **Career Services:** alumni services, career assessment, internships.

FACILITIES
Housing: Coed dorms, apartments for single students. 95% of campus accessible to physically disabled. **Special Academic Facilities/Equipment:** Art gallery.

CAMPUS LIFE
Environment: Metropolis. **Activities:** radio station, student government, student-run film society. **On-Campus Highlights:** Main gallery, Student Center

ADMISSIONS
Freshman Academic Profile: Average high school GPA 3.3. 89% from public high schools. SAT Math middle 50% range 430-604. SAT Critical Reading middle 50% range 503-680. SAT Writing middle 50% range 467-644. ACT middle 50% range 21-27. Minimum paper TOEFL 550. **Basis for Candidate Selection:** *Very important factors considered include:* application essay, academic GPA, recommendation(s), standardized test scores, talent/ability. *Important factors considered include:* character/personal qualities, interview.**Freshman Admission Requirements:** High school diploma is required and GED is accepted. **Freshman Admission Statistics:** 406 applied, 64% admitted, 33% enrolled. **Transfer Admission Requirements:** High school transcript, college transcript(s), essay or personal statement, standardized test scores, minimum college GPA of 2.5 required. Lowest grade transferable C–. **General Admission Information:** Application Fee $50. Regular application deadline 5/1. Nonfall registration accepted. Admission may be deferred for a maximum of 1 semester. Credit offered for CEEB Advanced Placement tests.

COSTS AND FINANCIAL AID
Annual tuition $31,450. Room and board $4,650. Required fees $200. Average book expense $2,724. **Required Forms and Deadlines:** FAFSA. **Notification of Awards:** Applicants will be notified of awards on a rolling basis beginning 4/1. **Types of Aid:** *Need-based scholarships/grants:* Federal Pell, SEOG, state scholarships/grants, private scholarships. The school's own gift aid. *Loans:* Subsidized Stafford, Unsubsidized Stafford, PLUS, Federal Perkins, state loans. **Student Employment:** Federal Work-Study Program available. Institutional employment available. Highest amount earned per year from on-campus jobs $1,656. Off-campus job opportunities are good. **Financial Aid Statistics:** 99% freshmen, 96% undergrads receive need-based scholarship or grant aid. 3% freshmen, 4% undergrads receive non-need-based scholarship or grant aid. 97% freshmen, 96% undergrads receive need-based self-help aid. 85% undergrads borrow to pay for school. Average cumulative indebtedness $43,035. **Criteria for awarding institutional aid:** *Non-need-based:* academics, alumni affiliation, art, leadership.

MINNESOTA STATE UNIVERSITY MOORHEAD

Owens Hall, Moorhead, MN 56563
Phone: 218-477-2161 • **Financial Aid Phone:** 218-477-2251
E-mail: dragon@mnstate.edu • **CEEB Code:** 6678
Fax: 218-477-4374 • **Website:** www.mnstate.edu • **ACT Code:** 2134

This public school was founded in 1887. It has a 140-acre campus.

RATINGS
Admissions Selectivity Rating: 74   **Fire Safety Rating:** 60*   **Green Rating:** 60*

STUDENTS AND FACULTY
Enrollment: 6,582. **Student Body:** 57% female, 43% male, 5% international (56 countries represented). Asian 1%, African American 3%, Caucasian 84%, Hispanic 1%, Native American 1%. **Retention and Graduation:** **Faculty:** 286 full-time faculty, 45% are women.

ACADEMICS
Degrees: associate, bachelor's, certificate, master's, post-bachelor's certificate, post-master's certificate, transfer associate. **Classes:** Most classes have 20–29 students. Most lab/discussion sessions have 20–29 students. **Majors with Highest Enrollment:** biology/biological sciences; elementary education and teaching; mass communication/media studies. **Special Study Options:** cross-registration, distance learning, double major, dual enrollment, exchange student program (domestic), external degree program, honors program, independent

study, internships, student-designed major, study abroad, teacher certification program. **Honors Programs:** Honors Program to reward and encourage superior academic achievement. **Combined Degree Programs:** Dual degree programs w/University of MN in depts of chemistry & physics. **Disability Services:** Special programs offered to physically disabled students include note-taking services, reader services, tape recorders, tutors. **Career Services:** career/job search classes, career assessment, internships.

FACILITIES

Housing: Coed dorms, special housing for disabled students, men's dorms, women's dorms, apartments for single students, theme housing, sorority housing. 95% of campus accessible to physically disabled. **Special Academic Facilities/Equipment:** Art and biology museums on-campus, planetarium, regional science center, Center for Business, new Science Building, Center for Business, Wellness Center **Computers:** Students can register for classes online. Administrative functions (other than registration) can be performed online.

CAMPUS LIFE

Environment: City. **Activities:** Choral groups, concert band, dance, drama/theater, jazz band, literary magazine, music ensembles, musical theater, radio station, student government, student newspaper, student-run film society, symphony orchestra, television station, Campus Ministries, International Student Organization, Model UN 109 registered organizations, 6 honor societies, 11 religious organizations. 2 sororities. **Athletics (Intercollegiate):** *Men:* basketball, cross-country, football, track/field (outdoor), track/field (indoor), wrestling. *Women:* basketball, cross-country, golf, soccer, softball, swimming, tennis, track/field (outdoor), track/field (indoor), volleyball. **On-Campus Highlights:** Underground Night Club, Comstock Memorial Student Union, Regional Science Center, Nemzek Athletic Complex, Planetarium, New Science Lab Building, New Wellness Center.

ADMISSIONS

Freshman Academic Profile: 7% in top 10% of high school class, 24% in top 25% of high school class, 57% in top 50% of high school class. SAT Math middle 50% range 500-610. SAT Critical Reading middle 50% range 440-570. ACT middle 50% range 20-24. Minimum paper TOEFL 500. **Basis for Candidate Selection:** *Very important factors considered include:* Class rank, rigor of secondary school record, standardized test scores.**Freshman Admission Requirements:** High school diploma is required and GED is accepted. *Academic units required:* 4 English, 3 mathematics, 3 science, (1 science labs), 2 foreign language, 3 social studies, 1 World culture or the arts. 4 English, 3 mathematics, 3 science, (1 science labs), 2 foreign language, 3 social studies, 1 World culture or the arts **Freshman Admission Statistics:** 3,393 applied, 73% admitted, 50% enrolled. **Transfer Admission Requirements:** college transcript(s), statement of good standing from prior institution(s). Minimum college GPA of 2.0 required. Lowest grade transferable D. **General Admission Information:** Application Fee $20. Regular application deadline 8/1. Notification on a rolling basis, beginning on or about 10/1. Nonfall registration accepted. Admission may be deferred for a maximum of case by case. Credit and/or placement offered for CEEB Advanced Placement tests.

COSTS AND FINANCIAL AID

Annual in-state tuition $6,140. Annual out-of-state tuition $6,140. Room and board $6,468. Required fees $587. Average book expense $800. **Required Forms and Deadlines:** FAFSA. **Notification of Awards:** Applicants will be notified of awards on a rolling basis beginning 6/1. **Types of Aid:** *Need-based scholarships/grants:* Federal Pell, SEOG, state scholarships/grants, private scholarships, the school's own gift aid. *Loans:* Direct Subsidized Stafford, Direct Unsubsidized Stafford, Direct PLUS, Federal Perkins, state loans. **Student Employment:** Federal Work-Study Program available. Institutional employment available. Highest amount earned per year from on-campus jobs $2,200. Off-campus job opportunities are excellent. **Financial Aid Statistics:** 75% freshmen, 58% undergrads receive any aid. **Criteria for awarding institutional aid:** *Non-need-based:* academics, art, athletics, leadership, minority status, music/drama, state/district residency.

MINNESOTA STATE UNIVERSITY, MANKATO

Room 122, Mankato, MN 56001
Phone: 507-389-1822 • **Financial Aid Phone:** 507-389-1866
E-mail: admissions@mnsu.edu • **CEEB Code:** 6677
Fax: 507-389-1511 • **Website:** www.mnsu.edu • **ACT Code:** 2126

This public school was founded in 1868. It has a 354-acre campus.

RATINGS

Admissions Selectivity Rating: 77   **Fire Safety Rating:** 65   **Green Rating:** 73

STUDENTS AND FACULTY

Enrollment: 12,513. **Student Body:** 50% female, 50% male, 12% out-of-state, 4% international (80 countries represented). Asian 3%, African American 5%, Caucasian 81%, Hispanic 3%, Native American 0%.
Retention and Graduation: 70% freshmen return for sophomore year. 22% freshmen graduate within 4 years. 21% grads go on to further study within 1 year. 21% grads pursue arts and sciences degrees. 8% grads pursue business degrees. **Faculty:** Student/faculty ratio 27:1. 470 full-time faculty, 84% hold PhDs, 12% are members of minority groups, 47% are women. 4% of classes are taught by teaching assistants.

ACADEMICS

Degrees: associate, bachelor's, certificate, master's, post-master's certificate. **Classes:** Most classes have 20–29 students. Most lab/discussion sessions have 20–29 students. **Majors with Highest Enrollment:** business administration and management; elementary education and teaching; nursing/registered nurse (rn, asn, bsn, msn). **Special Study Options:** cross-registration, distance learning, double major, dual enrollment, English as a Second Language (ESL), exchange student program (domestic), external degree program, honors program, independent study, internships, student-designed major, study abroad, teacher certification program. **Disability Services:** Special programs offered to physically disabled students include note-taking services, reader services, tape recorders. **Career Services:** Alumni network, alumni services, career/job search classes, career assessment, internships Career Services highlights include Walk-in hours for student resume review and othe services.

FACILITIES

Housing: Coed dorms, special housing for disabled students 90% of campus accessible to physically disabled. **Special Academic Facilities/Equipment:** Two art galleries, day care facility, two astronomy observ- atories, main stage and studio theatres **Computers:** 100% of classrooms, 10% of dorms, 100% of libraries, 100% of dining areas, 100% of student union, 80% of common outdoor areas have wireless network access. Students can register for classes online. Administrative functions (other than registration) can be performed online.

CAMPUS LIFE

Environment: Town. **Activities:** Choral groups, concert band, dance, drama/theater, jazz band, literary magazine, music ensembles, musical theater, pep band, radio station, student government, student newspaper, symphony orchestra, Campus Ministries, International Student Organization 178 registered organizations, 18 honor societies, 15 religious organizations. 7 fraternities, 4 sororities. **Athletics (Intercollegiate):** *Men:* baseball, basketball, cross-country, diving, football, golf, ice hockey, swimming, tennis, track/field (outdoor), track/field (indoor), wrestling. *Women:* basketball, bowling, cross-country, diving, golf, ice hockey, soccer, softball, swimming, tennis, track/field (outdoor), track/field (indoor), volleyball. **On-Campus Highlights:** Student Union, Myers Field House, Campus Recreation Center, Julia Sears Residence Hall, Memorial Library. **Environmental Initiatives:** Energy retrofit of building for lighting and motors All new buildings exceed LEED compliance Purchase of three electric cars for University Security and Environmental Health and Safety Offices.

ADMISSIONS

Freshman Academic Profile: 7% in top 10% of high school class, 25% in top 25% of high school class, 67% in top 50% of high school class. 95% from public high schools. ACT middle 50% range 20-24. Minimum web-based TOEFL 61. Minimum paper TOEFL 500. **Basis for Candidate Selection:** *Very important factors considered include:* Class rank, standardized test scores.*Other factors considered include:* academic GPA, recommendation(s). **Freshman Admission Requirements:** High school diploma is required and GED is accepted. *Academic units required:* 4 English, 3 mathematics, 3 science, (3 science labs), 2 foreign language, 2 social studies, 1 history, 1 visual/performing arts. 4 English, 3 mathematics, 3 science, (3 science labs), 2 foreign language, 2 social studies, 1 history, 1 visual/performing arts. **Freshman Admission Statistics:** 7,787 applied, 61% admitted, 49% enrolled. **Transfer Admission Requirements:** college transcript(s), statement of good standing from prior institution(s). Minimum college GPA of 2.0 required. Lowest grade transferable D. **General Admission Information:** Application Fee $20. Nonfall registration accepted. Admission may be deferred for a maximum of No set time frame. Credit offered for CEEB Advanced Placement tests.

COSTS AND FINANCIAL AID

Annual in-state tuition $7,532. Annual out-of-state tuition $15,010. Room and board $7,053. Required fees $864. Average book expense $900. **Required Forms and Deadlines:** FAFSA, SELF or Alternative Loan Application or PLUS Application. **Notification of Awards:** Applicants will be notified of awards on a rolling basis beginning 3/30. **Types of Aid:** *Need-based scholarships/grants:* Federal Pell, SEOG, state scholarships/grants, private scholarships, the school's own gift aid, Federal ACG/SMART. *Loans:* Subsidized Stafford, Unsubsidized Stafford, PLUS, Federal Perkins, state loans, Alternative Loans. **Student Employment:** Federal Work-Study Program available. Institutional employment available. Off-campus job opportunities are fair. **Financial Aid Statistics:** 81% freshmen, 74% undergrads receive need-based scholarship or grant aid. 37% freshmen, 23% undergrads receive non-need-based scholar-

The Princeton Review's Complete Book of Colleges

ship or grant aid. 99% freshmen, 99% undergrads receive need-based self-help aid. 2% freshmen, 2% undergrads receive athletic scholarships. 67% freshmen, 72% undergrads receive any aid. 75% undergrads borrow to pay for school. Average cumulative indebtedness $29,587. **Criteria for awarding institutional aid:** *Non-need-based:* academics, art, athletics, leadership, minority status, music/drama.

MISERICORDIA UNIVERSITY

301 Lake Street, Dallas, PA 18612
Phone: 570-674-6264 • **Financial Aid Phone:** 570-674-6222
E-mail: admiss@misericordia.edu • **CEEB Code:** 2087
Fax: 570-675-2441 • **Website:** www.misericordia.edu • **ACT Code:** 3539

This private school, affiliated with the Roman Catholic Church, was founded in 1924. It has a 120-acre campus.

RATINGS
Admissions Selectivity Rating: 81   **Fire Safety Rating:** 85   **Green Rating:** 60*

STUDENTS AND FACULTY
Enrollment: 2,326. **Student Body:** 67% female, 33% male, 21% out-of-state, 0% international (0 countries represented). Asian 1%, African American 1%, Caucasian 95%, Hispanic 3%, Native American 0%.
Retention and Graduation: 86% freshmen return for sophomore year. 54% freshmen graduate within 4 years. 68% freshmen graduate within 6 years. 9% grads go on to further study within 1 year. **Faculty:** Student/faculty ratio 12:1. 111 full-time faculty, 83% hold PhDs, 12% are members of minority groups, 53% are women. 0% of classes are taught by teaching assistants.

ACADEMICS
Degrees: bachelor's, certificate, master's, post-bachelor's certificate, post-master's certificate. **Classes:** Most classes have 10–19 students. Most lab/discussion sessions have 10–19 students. **Majors with Highest Enrollment:** business/commerce; elementary education and teaching; nursing/registered nurse (rn, asn, bsn, msn). **Special Study Options:** Accelerated program, cross-registration, distance learning, double major, dual enrollment, honors program, independent study, internships, student-designed major, study abroad, teacher certification program, weekend college. **Honors Programs:** The Honors Program is an interdisciplinary community of undergraduate students and faculty working together to create an intellectually stimulating and challenging environment for learning. Honors students take a common sequence of core curriculum courses in place of regular core offerings, participate each semester in our Honors Explorations Seminar, and procuce a professional quality paper or project as part of the Honors Capstone. **Combined Degree Programs:** BS/MSPT and BS/MSOT and BS/MSSLP. **Disability Services:** Special programs offered to physically disabled students include tape recorders, tutors. **Career Services:** Alumni network, alumni services, career/job search classes, career assessment, internships.

FACILITIES
Housing: Coed dorms, Leadership House, Women with Children House. 100% of campus accessible to physically disabled. **Computers:** 5% of classrooms, 100% of libraries, 100% of dining areas, 100% of student union, 10% of common outdoor areas have wireless network access. Students can register for classes online. Administrative functions (other than registration) can be performed online.

CAMPUS LIFE
Environment: Town. **Activities:** Choral groups, dance, drama/theater, jazz band, literary magazine, music ensembles, radio station, student government, student newspaper, television station, yearbook, Campus Ministries 27 registered organizations, 1 honor societies, 1 religious organizations. **Athletics (Intercollegiate):** *Men:* baseball, basketball, cross-country, golf, lacrosse, soccer, swimming, tennis, track/field (outdoor). *Women:* basketball, cheerleading, cross-country, field hockey, lacrosse, soccer, softball, swimming, tennis, track/field (outdoor), volleyball. **On-Campus Highlights:** Anderson Sports and Health Center, Banks Student Life Center, Mangelsdorf Field, Bevevino Library

ADMISSIONS
Freshman Academic Profile: Average high school GPA 3.3. 23% in top 10% of high school class, 52% in top 25% of high school class, 83% in top 50% of high school class. 89% from public high schools. SAT Math middle 50% range 470-570. SAT Critical Reading middle 50% range 460-560. ACT middle 50% range 22-26. Minimum web-based TOEFL 66. Minimum paper TOEFL 550. **Basis for Candidate Selection:** *Very important factors considered include:* academic GPA, rigor of secondary school record. *Important factors considered include:* Class rank, standardized test scores. *Other factors considered include:*

application essay, recommendation(s), character/personal qualities, extracurricular activities, interview, racial/ethnic status, volunteer work, work experience. **Freshman Admission Requirements:** High school diploma is required and GED is accepted. *Academic units required:* 4 English, 4 mathematics, 4 science, 4 social studies. 4 English, 4 mathematics, 4 science, 4 social studies. **Freshman Admission Statistics:** 2,526 applied, 58% admitted, 35% enrolled. **Transfer Admission Requirements:** college transcript(s), minimum college GPA of 2.0 required. Lowest grade transferable C. **General Admission Information:** Application Fee $25. Notification on a rolling basis, beginning on or about 10/1. Nonfall registration accepted. Admission may be deferred for a maximum of 12 months. Credit and/or placement offered for CEEB Advanced Placement tests.

COSTS AND FINANCIAL AID
Annual tuition $25,890. Room and board $11,190. Required fees $1,340. Average book expense $1,000. **Required Forms and Deadlines:** FAFSA, institution's own financial aid form. **Notification of Awards:** Applicants will be notified of awards on a rolling basis beginning 3/15. **Types of Aid:** *Need-based scholarships/grants:* Federal Pell, SEOG, state scholarships/grants, private scholarships, the school's own gift aid, Federal Nursing Scholarships. *Loans:* Subsidized Stafford, Unsubsidized Stafford, PLUS, Federal Perkins, Federal Nursing, state loans. **Student Employment:** Federal Work-Study Program available. Institutional employment available. Highest amount earned per year from on-campus jobs $1,600. Off-campus job opportunities are good. **Financial Aid Statistics:** 100% freshmen, 99% undergrads receive need-based scholarship or grant aid. 18% freshmen, 15% undergrads receive non-need-based scholarship or grant aid. 85% freshmen, 84% undergrads receive need-based self-help aid. 99% freshmen, 99% undergrads receive any aid. **Criteria for awarding institutional aid:** *Non-need-based:* academics, alumni affiliation, leadership, minority status, state/district residency.

MISSISSIPPI COLLEGE

Box 4026, Clinton, MS 39058-0001
Phone: 601-925-3800 • **Financial Aid Phone:** 601-925-3212
E-mail: enrollment-services@mc.edu • **CEEB Code:** 1477
Fax: 601-925-3950 • **Website:** www.mc.edu • **ACT Code:** 2214

This private school, affiliated with the Southern Baptist Church, was founded in 1826. It has a 320-acre campus.

RATINGS
Admissions Selectivity Rating: 90   **Fire Safety Rating:** 97   **Green Rating:** 60*

STUDENTS AND FACULTY
Enrollment: 3,180. **Student Body:** 60% female, 40% male, 22% out-of-state, 3% international (16 countries represented). Asian 1%, African American 24%, Caucasian 65%, Hispanic 1%, Native American 1%.
Retention and Graduation: 76% freshmen return for sophomore year. 34% freshmen graduate within 4 years. 51% freshmen graduate within 6 years. **Faculty:** Student/faculty ratio 13:1. 194 full-time faculty, 79% hold PhDs, 3% are members of minority groups, 47% are women. 0% of classes are taught by teaching assistants.

ACADEMICS
Degrees: bachelor's, doctoral, master's, post-bachelor's certificate, post-master's certificate. **Classes:** Most classes have 10–19 students. Most lab/discussion sessions have fewer than 10 students. **Majors with Highest Enrollment:** biology/biological sciences; business administration and management; nursing/registered nurse (rn, asn, bsn, msn). **Special Study Options:** Accelerated program, distance learning, double major, dual enrollment, English as a Second Language (ESL), honors program, independent study, internships, study abroad, teacher certification program, Academic remediation, Advance Placement credit, Work-Study program, Learning disabilities services. **Honors Programs:** Honors Programs open to freshmen, sophomores, juniors, and seniors and administered by the Honors Council. Freshmen who have a high ACT score (established each year) are invited to participate in a program of study called Freshman Honors Seminar (IDS161), it is an interdisciplinary study dealing with contemporary issues and interests. Upperclassmen who maintain a high GPA may also participate in Sophomore and Senior Honors Seminars (IDS 261, 461). Successful completion of the Junior-Senior Honors Program leads to a degree "With Honors" or "With High Honors." **Combined Degree Programs:** BA/JD. **Disability Services:** Special programs offered to physically disabled students include note-taking services, reader services, tape recorders, tutors. **Career Services:** alumni services, career/job search classes, career assessment, internships.

FACILITIES

Housing: special housing for disabled students, men's dorms, women's dorms, apartments for single students. 90% of campus accessible to physically disabled. **Computers:** 60% of classrooms, 100% of dorms, 100% of libraries, 100% of dining areas, 60% of common outdoor areas have wireless network access. Students can register for classes online. Administrative functions (other than registration) can be performed online.

CAMPUS LIFE

Environment: Metropolis. **Activities:** Choral groups, concert band, dance, drama/theater, jazz band, literary magazine, marching band, music ensembles, musical theater, opera, radio station, student government, student newspaper, yearbook, Campus Ministries, International Student Organization 66 registered organizations, 22 honor societies, 6 religious organizations. 5 fraternities, 4 sororities. **Athletics (Intercollegiate):** *Men:* baseball, basketball, cross-country, football, golf, soccer, tennis, track/field (outdoor). *Women:* basketball, cheerleading, cross-country, equestrian sports, soccer, softball, tennis, track/field (outdoor), volleyball. **On-Campus Highlights:** Gore Gallery, Healthplex, Men's Rotunda and New Women's Residence Hall, Provine Chapel, Anderson Hall in BCR Student Center, Nelson Hall-Administration Building Robinson-Wright Field House.

ADMISSIONS

Freshman Academic Profile: Average high school GPA 3.4. 31% in top 10% of high school class, 54% in top 25% of high school class, 79% in top 50% of high school class. SAT Math middle 50% range 498-590. SAT Critical Reading middle 50% range 488-630. ACT middle 50% range 21-27. Minimum paper TOEFL 500. **Basis for Candidate Selection:** *Very important factors considered include:* standardized test scores. *Important factors considered include:* rigor of secondary school record, character/personal qualities, extracurricular activities, level of applicant's interest. *Other factors considered include:* Class rank, academic GPA, recommendation(s), alumni/ae relation, interview, talent/ability, volunteer work, work experience. **Freshman Admission Requirements:** High school diploma is required and GED is accepted. **Freshman Admission Statistics:** 1,821 applied, 45% admitted, 63% enrolled. **Transfer Admission Requirements:** college transcript(s), essay or personal statement, statement of good standing from prior institution(s). Minimum college GPA of 2.0 required. Lowest grade transferable C. **General Admission Information:** Early decision application deadline 12/1. Nonfall registration accepted. Admission may be deferred for a maximum of 1 year. Credit offered for CEEB Advanced Placement tests.

COSTS AND FINANCIAL AID

Annual tuition $13,720. Room and board $6,950. Required fees $710. Average book expense $1,100. **Required Forms and Deadlines:** FAFSA, state aid form. **Notification of Awards:** Applicants will be notified of awards on a rolling basis beginning 3/1. **Types of Aid:** *Need-based scholarships/grants:* Federal Pell, SEOG, state scholarships/grants, private scholarships, the school's own gift aid, Federal Nursing Scholarships. *Loans:* Subsidized Stafford, Unsubsidized Stafford, PLUS, Federal Perkins, Federal Nursing, college/university loans from institutional funds. **Student Employment:** Federal Work-Study Program available. Highest amount earned per year from on-campus jobs $3,000. Off-campus job opportunities are good. **Financial Aid Statistics:** 89% freshmen, 87% undergrads receive need-based scholarship or grant aid. 97% freshmen, 84% undergrads receive non-need-based scholarship or grant aid. 75% freshmen, 84% undergrads receive need-based self-help aid. 98% freshmen, 95% undergrads receive any aid. 54% undergrads borrow to pay for school. Average cumulative indebtedness $24,329. **Criteria for awarding institutional aid:** *Non-need-based:* academics, alumni affiliation, art, leadership, music/drama, religious affiliation.

MISSISSIPPI STATE UNIVERSITY

P. O. Box 6334, Mississippi State, MS 39762
Phone: 662-325-2224 • **Financial Aid Phone:** 662-325-2450
E-mail: admit@msstate.edu • **CEEB Code:** 1480
Fax: 662-325-1678 • **Website:** www.msstate.edu • **ACT Code:** 2220

This public school was founded in 1878. It has a 4200-acre campus.

RATINGS

Admissions Selectivity Rating: 60*   **Fire Safety Rating:** 60*   **Green Rating:** 60*

STUDENTS AND FACULTY

Enrollment: 15,585. **Student Body:** 48% female, 52% male, 22% out-of-state, 2% international (84 countries represented). Asian 1%, African American 23%, Caucasian 74%, Hispanic 2%, Native American 1%.

Retention and Graduation: 81% freshmen return for sophomore year. **Faculty:** Student/faculty ratio 19:1. 882 full-time faculty, 80% hold PhDs, 15% are members of minority groups, 38% are women. % of classes are taught by teaching assistants.

ACADEMICS

Degrees: bachelor's, doctoral, master's. **Classes:** Most classes have 20–29 students. Most lab/discussion sessions have fewer than 10 students. **Majors with Highest Enrollment:** business administration and management; elementary education and teaching; physical education teaching and coaching. **Special Study Options:** cooperative education program, distance learning, double major, dual enrollment, English as a Second Language (ESL), exchange student program (domestic), external degree program, honors program, independent study, internships, liberal arts/career combination, student-designed major, study abroad, teacher certification program, weekend college. **Honors Programs:** University Honors Program. **Disability Services:** Special programs offered to physically disabled students include note-taking services, reader services, tape recorders, tutors. **Career Services:** Alumni network, alumni services, career/job search classes, career assessment, internships, regional alumni. Career Services highlights include MSU offers a diversified Co-op program. Students are participating from several colleges and schools at the university.

FACILITIES

Housing: special housing for disabled students, men's dorms, women's dorms, fraternity/sorority housing, apartments for married students, apartments for single students, theme housing, co-residential. 95% of campus accessible to physically disabled. **Special Academic Facilities/Equipment:** Geology, archeology, music, entomological museums; art gallery; flight research lab. **Computers:** 100% of classrooms, 100% of dorms, 100% of libraries, 100% of dining areas, 100% of student union, 100% of common outdoor areas have wireless network access. Students can register for classes online. Administrative functions (other than registration) can be performed online.

CAMPUS LIFE

Environment: Town. **Activities:** Choral groups, concert band, dance, drama/theater, jazz band, literary magazine, marching band, music ensembles, musical theater, pep band, radio station, student government, student newspaper, television station, yearbook, Campus Ministries, International Student Organization, Model UN 326 registered organizations, 42 honor societies, 30 religious organizations. 17 fraternities, 11 sororities. **Athletics (Intercollegiate):** *Men:* baseball, basketball, cheerleading, cross-country, football, golf, tennis, track/field (outdoor). *Women:* basketball, cheerleading, cross-country, golf, soccer, softball, tennis, track/field (outdoor), volleyball. **On-Campus Highlights:** Scott Field Stadium, Dudy Noble Field, Humphrey Coliseum, Barnes and Noble Campus Bookstore, Sanderson Student Recreation Center. **Environmental Initiatives:** Recycling Bicycle Program Environmental Sustainability Research Center.

ADMISSIONS

Freshman Academic Profile: Average high school GPA 3.3. 27% in top 10% of high school class, 28% in top 25% of high school class, 83% in top 50% of high school class. SAT Math middle 50% range 490-620. SAT Critical Reading middle 50% range 470-610. ACT middle 50% range 20-27. Minimum web-based TOEFL 71. Minimum paper TOEFL 525. **Basis for Candidate Selection:** *Very important factors considered include:* academic GPA, standardized test scores. *Important factors considered include:* Class rank. *Other factors considered include:* rigor of secondary school record, talent/ability. **Freshman Admission Requirements:** High school diploma is required and GED is accepted. *Academic units required:* 4 English, 3 mathematics, 3 science, (2 science labs), 1 social studies, 2 history, 2 academic electives. *Academic units recommended:* 4 English, 3 mathematics, 3 science, (2 science labs), 1 social studies, 2 history, 2 academic electives. **Freshman Admission Statistics:** 10,449 applied, 69% admitted, 40% enrolled. **Transfer Admission Requirements:** college transcript(s), statement of good standing from prior institution(s). Minimum college GPA of 2.0 required. Lowest grade transferable D. **General Admission Information:** Application Fee $35. Notification on a rolling basis, beginning on or about 9/1. Nonfall registration accepted. Credit offered for CEEB Advanced Placement tests.

COSTS AND FINANCIAL AID

Annual in-state tuition $6,264. Annual out-of-state tuition $15,828. Room and board $8,486. Average book expense $1,200. **Required Forms and Deadlines:** FAFSA, State grant/scholarship application. **Notification of Awards:** Applicants will be notified of awards on a rolling basis beginning 12/1. **Types of Aid:** *Need-based scholarships/grants:* Federal Pell, SEOG, state scholarships/grants, private scholarships, the school's own gift aid, United Negro College Fund. *Loans:* Subsidized Stafford, Unsubsidized Stafford, PLUS, Federal Perkins, college/university loans from institutional funds. **Student Employment:** Federal Work-Study Program available. Institutional employment available. Off-campus job opportunities are good. **Financial Aid Statistics:** 91% freshmen, 88% undergrads receive need-based scholarship or grant aid. 13% freshmen, 6% undergrads receive non-need-based scholarship or grant aid.

73% freshmen, 79% undergrads receive need-based self-help aid. 3% freshmen, 3% undergrads receive athletic scholarships. Average cumulative indebtedness $26,139. **Criteria for awarding institutional aid:** *Non-need-based:* academics, alumni affiliation, art, athletics, job skills, leadership, minority status, music/drama, state/district residency.

MISSISSIPPI VALLEY STATE UNIVERSITY

14000 Highway 82 West, Itta Bena, MS 38941-1400
Phone: 662-254-3344 • **Financial Aid Phone:** 662-254-3338
E-mail: nbtaylor@mvsu.edu • **CEEB Code:** 1482
Fax: 662-254-3759 • **Website:** www.mvsu.edu • **ACT Code:** 2224

This public school was founded in 1950. It has a 250-acre campus.

RATINGS
Admissions Selectivity Rating: 78   Fire Safety Rating: 89   Green Rating: 70

STUDENTS AND FACULTY
Enrollment: 2,357. **Student Body:** 62% female, 38% male, 11% out-of-state, 0% international (2 countries represented). Asian 0%, African American 93%, Caucasian 4%, Hispanic 1%, Native American 0%.
Retention and Graduation: 55% freshmen return for sophomore year. 18% freshmen graduate within 4 years. 35% freshmen graduate within 6 years.
Faculty: Student/faculty ratio 21:1. 133 full-time faculty, 58% hold PhDs, 30% are members of minority groups, 46% are women. 0% of classes are taught by teaching assistants.

ACADEMICS
Degrees: bachelor's, master's. **Classes:** Most classes have fewer than 10 students. Most lab/discussion sessions have 20–29 students. **Majors with Highest Enrollment:** business, management, marketing, and related support services, other; kindergarten/preschool education and teaching; social work. **Special Study Options:** cooperative education program, distance learning, double major, honors program, internships, teacher certification program, weekend college, Co-Op Programs: Business, Computer Science, Natural Science, Social/Behavioral Science. **Disability Services:** Special programs offered to physically disabled students include tape recorders, tutors. **Career Services:** alumni services, Career Services highlights include Many of our students have received internships with the Environmental Protection Agency in Washington, DC.

FACILITIES
Housing: men's dorms, women's dorms, apartments for married students, apartments for single students. **Computers:** Students can register for classes online.

CAMPUS LIFE
Environment: Rural. **Activities:** Choral groups, concert band, drama/theater, marching band, radio station, student government, student newspaper, yearbook 35 registered organizations, 19 honor societies, 4 religious organizations. 4 fraternities, 2 sororities. **Athletics (Intercollegiate):** *Men:* baseball, basketball, cross-country, football, golf, tennis, track/field (outdoor). *Women:* basketball, cross-country, golf, soccer, softball, tennis, track/field (outdoor), volleyball. **On-Campus Highlights:** Student Union, Student Pavillion, Administration Building, Library

ADMISSIONS
Freshman Academic Profile: Average high school GPA 2.6. 96% from public high schools. ACT middle 50% range 15-19. Minimum paper TOEFL 525. **Basis for Candidate Selection:** *Very important factors considered include:* Class rank, rigor of secondary school record, standardized test scores, state residency. *Other factors considered include:* recommendation(s), extracurricular activities, interview, talent/ability. **Freshman Admission Requirements:** High school diploma is required and GED is accepted. *Academic units required:* 4 English, 3 mathematics, 3 science, (2 science labs), 1 foreign language, 3 social studies, 2 academic electives, 1 Computer Applications. *Academic units recommended:* 4 English, 3 mathematics, 3 science, (2 science labs), 1 foreign language, 3 social studies, 2 academic electives, 1 Computer Applications **Freshman Admission Statistics:** 6,086 applied, 30% admitted, 23% enrolled. **Transfer Admission Requirements:** college transcript(s), minimum college GPA of 2.0 required. Lowest grade transferable C. **General Admission Information:** Nonfall registration accepted.

COSTS AND FINANCIAL AID
Annual in-state tuition $4,575. Annual out-of-state tuition $11,410. Room and board $5,081. Required fees $25. Average book expense $1,400. **Required Forms and Deadlines:** FAFSA, institution's own financial aid form. **Notification of Awards:** Applicants will be notified of awards on or about 7/15. **Types of Aid:** *Need-based scholarships/grants:* Federal Pell, SEOG, state scholarships/grants, private scholarships, the school's own gift aid. *Loans:* Direct Unsubsi-

dized Stafford, Direct PLUS. **Student Employment:** Federal Work-Study Program available. **Financial Aid Statistics:** 95% freshmen, 95% undergrads receive any aid.

MISSOURI SOUTHERN STATE UNIVERSITY— JOPLIN

3950 E. Newman Road, Joplin, MO 64801-1595
Phone: 417-625-9378 • **Financial Aid Phone:** 417-625-9325
E-mail: admissions@mssu.edu • **CEEB Code:** 6322
Fax: 417-659-4429 • **Website:** • **ACT Code:** 2304

This public school was founded in 1937. It has a 365-acre campus.

RATINGS
Admissions Selectivity Rating: 64   Fire Safety Rating: 63   Green Rating: 60*

STUDENTS AND FACULTY
Enrollment: 5,135. **Student Body:** 59% female, 41% male, 15% out-of-state, 1% international (31 countries represented). Asian 1%, African American 3%, Caucasian 89%, Hispanic 2%, Native American 3%.
Retention and Graduation: 63% freshmen return for sophomore year. 18% freshmen graduate within 4 years. 36% freshmen graduate within 6 years.
Faculty: Student/faculty ratio 19:1. 208 full-time faculty, 64% hold PhDs, 9% are members of minority groups, 37% are women. 0% of classes are taught by teaching assistants.

ACADEMICS
Degrees: associate, bachelor's, certificate, master's. **Classes:** Most classes have 20–29 students. Most lab/discussion sessions have fewer than 10 students. **Majors with Highest Enrollment:** business/commerce; criminal justice/law enforcement administration; education. **Special Study Options:** Accelerated program, cooperative education program, distance learning, double major, dual enrollment, English as a Second Language (ESL), exchange student program (domestic), honors program, independent study, internships, liberal arts/career combination, study abroad, teacher certification program, weekend college **Honors Programs:** MSSU Honors Program. **Disability Services:** Special programs offered to physically disabled students include note-taking services, reader services, tape recorders, tutors.

FACILITIES
Housing: Coed dorms, special housing for disabled students, men's dorms, women's dorms, apartments for single students. 100% of campus accessible to physically disabled. **Special Academic Facilities/Equipment:** spiva art gallery, biology pond, forensics laboratory, child development center, indoor "livefire" firearms range, green house, law library, cyber coffee shop, international trade and quality center, graduate center, tv station, radio station, small business development center, thomas e. taylor performing arts center, health center. **Computers:** Administrative functions (other than registration) can be performed online.

CAMPUS LIFE
Environment: Town. **Activities:** Choral groups, concert band, dance, drama/theater, jazz band, literary magazine, marching band, music ensembles, musical theater, pep band, radio station, student government, student newspaper, student-run film society, symphony orchestra, television station 82 registered organizations, 12 honor societies, 9 religious organizations. 2 fraternities, 2 sororities. **Athletics (Intercollegiate):** *Men:* baseball, basketball, cheerleading, cross-country, football, golf, soccer, track/field (outdoor). *Women:* basketball, cheerleading, cross-country, soccer, softball, tennis, track/field (outdoor), volleyball. **On-Campus Highlights:** Cyber Coffee Shop, Lion's Den, Student Life Activity Center, Leggett and Platt Athletic Center, Spiva Art Gallery, In addition to MSSU's campus facilities, Missouri Southern's low crime rate, well lit campus, 24 hour security and emergency phones located in key spots help to ensure the safety of students as they enjoy Missouri Southern's campus.

ADMISSIONS
Freshman Academic Profile: 17% in top 10% of high school class, 40% in top 25% of high school class, 72% in top 50% of high school class. 98% from public high schools. ACT middle 50% range 17-19. Minimum paper TOEFL 535. **Basis for Candidate Selection:** *Very important factors considered include:* Class rank, academic GPA, rigor of secondary school record, standardized test scores. *Other factors considered include:* recommendation(s). **Freshman Admission Requirements:** High school diploma is required and GED is accepted. **Freshman Admission Statistics:** 2,669 applied, 98% admitted, 36% enrolled. **Transfer Admission Requirements:** college transcript(s), minimum college GPA of 2.0 required. Lowest grade transferable D. **General Admission Information:** Application Fee $15. Notification on a rolling basis, beginning on or about 9/1.

Nonfall registration accepted. Admission may be deferred for a maximum of 1 year. Credit and/or placement offered for CEEB Advanced Placement tests.

COSTS AND FINANCIAL AID
Average book expense $600. **Required Forms and Deadlines:** FAFSA. **Notification of Awards:** Applicants will be notified of awards on a rolling basis beginning 2/15. **Types of Aid:** *Need-based scholarships/grants:* Federal Pell, SEOG, state scholarships/grants, private scholarships. *Loans:* Direct Subsidized Stafford, Direct Unsubsidized Stafford, Direct PLUS, Federal Perkins, state loans. **Criteria for awarding institutional aid:** *Non-need-based:* academics, alumni affiliation, art, athletics, job skills, leadership, minority status, music/drama, state/district residency.

MISSOURI STATE UNIVERSITY

901 S. National, Springfield, MO 65897
Phone: 417-836-5517 • **Financial Aid Phone:** 417-835-5262
E-mail: info@missouristate.edu • **CEEB Code:** 6665
Fax: 417-836-6334 • **Website:** www.missouristate.edu • **ACT Code:** 2370

This public school was founded in 1905. It has a 450-acre campus.

RATINGS
Admissions Selectivity Rating: 72   **Fire Safety Rating:** 78   **Green Rating:** 60*

STUDENTS AND FACULTY
Enrollment: 14,463. **Student Body:** 56% female, 44% male, 7% out-of-state, 2% international. Asian 1%, African American 2%, Caucasian 77%, Hispanic 1%, Native American 1%.
Retention and Graduation: 73% freshmen return for sophomore year. 20% grads go on to further study within 1 year. 2% grads pursue arts and sciences degrees. 2% grads pursue law degrees. 10% grads pursue business degrees. 2% grads pursue medical degrees. **Faculty:** Student/faculty ratio 18:1. 728 full-time faculty, 78% hold PhDs, 7% are members of minority groups, 40% are women. 8% of classes are taught by teaching assistants.

ACADEMICS
Degrees: bachelor's, master's, post-bachelor's certificate, post-master's certificate. **Classes:** Most classes have 20–29 students. Most lab/discussion sessions have 20–29 students. **Majors with Highest Enrollment:** elementary education and teaching; management information systems; marketing/marketing management. **Special Study Options:** Accelerated program, cooperative education program, distance learning, double major, dual enrollment, English as a Second Language (ESL), exchange student program (domestic), honors program, independent study, internships, student-designed major, study abroad, teacher certification program. **Honors Programs:** The Honors College is to provide a program of enhanced, advanced study and recognition for students of unusually strong academic achievement and motivation. The Honors College is to provide these students with intellectual opportunities beyond those generally found in the more traditional programs: smaller and enriched classes, direct contact with outstanding faculty members, and the option to pursue their own intellectual, research, and creative interests. The Honors College is to provide the means whereby individual departments may develop departmental honors opportunities. These opportunities will allow students with higher academic achievement and motivation to develop their individual interests more fully through contact with faculty and students of similar interests and abilities while maintaining involvement in the University community as a whole. **Disability Services:** Special programs offered to physically disabled students include note-taking services, reader services, tape recorders, tutors.

FACILITIES
Housing: Coed dorms, special housing for disabled students, special housing for international students, fraternity/sorority housing, apartments for married students, apartments for single students, graduate student housing, non-traditional student housing, upper-class student housing, honor student housing, transfer student housing and family housing. 95% of campus accessible to physically disabled. **Special Academic Facilities/Equipment:** On-campus laboratory school (K-12), 125-acre Darr Agricultrual Center, Baker Observatory, Bull Shoals Field Station, electron microscope, molecular beam epitaxy laboratory, Ion implantation laboratory, Art and Design Gallery, Student Exhibition Center, Coger Theatre, Ellis Recital Hall, Instructional TV Studio, Computer Animation Studio, Foundry, Wehr Band Hall, Multimedia Lab, Language Lab, Juanita K. Hammons Hall for the Performing Arts. **Computers:** Students can register for classes online. Administrative functions (other than registration) can be performed online.

CAMPUS LIFE
Environment: City. **Activities:** Choral groups, concert band, dance, drama/theater, jazz band, literary magazine, marching band, music ensembles, musi-

cal theater, pep band, radio station, student government, student newspaper, student-run film society, symphony orchestra, television station 270 registered organizations, 26 honor societies, 28 religious organizations. 15 fraternities, 9 sororities. **Athletics (Intercollegiate):** *Men:* baseball, basketball, cross-country, diving, football, golf, soccer, swimming, tennis, track/field (outdoor), track/field (indoor), volleyball. *Women:* basketball, cross-country, diving, field hockey, golf, soccer, softball, swimming, tennis, track/field (outdoor), track/field (indoor), volleyball. **On-Campus Highlights:** Plaster Student Union, Meyer Library, Baker Bookstore, Hammons Fountains, Plaster Sports Complex.

ADMISSIONS
Freshman Academic Profile: Average high school GPA 3.6. 22% in top 10% of high school class, 49% in top 25% of high school class, 81% in top 50% of high school class. ACT middle 50% range 21-26. Minimum paper TOEFL 500. **Basis for Candidate Selection:** *Very important factors considered include:* Class rank, rigor of secondary school record, standardized test scores.*Other factors considered include:* application essay, recommendation(s), alumni/ae relation, character/personal qualities, extracurricular activities, interview, racial/ethnic status, talent/ability, volunteer work, work experience. **Freshman Admission Requirements:** High school diploma is required and GED is accepted. *Academic units required:* 4 English, 3 mathematics, 2 science, (1 science labs), 3 social studies, 3 academic electives. 4 English, 3 mathematics, 2 science, (1 science labs), 3 social studies, 3 academic electives. **Freshman Admission Statistics:** 6,866 applied, 77% admitted, 50% enrolled. **Transfer Admission Requirements:** college transcript(s), minimum college GPA of 2.0 required. Lowest grade transferable D. **General Admission Information:** Application Fee $30. Regular application deadline 7/20. Nonfall registration accepted. Credit and/or placement offered for CEEB Advanced Placement tests.

COSTS AND FINANCIAL AID
Annual in-state tuition $4,920. Annual out-of-state tuition $9,840. Room and board $5,294. Required fees $534. Average book expense $800. **Required Forms and Deadlines:** FAFSA. **Notification of Awards:** Applicants will be notified of awards on a rolling basis beginning 4/1. **Types of Aid:** *Need-based scholarships/grants:* Federal Pell, SEOG, state scholarships/grants, private scholarships, the school's own gift aid. *Loans:* Subsidized Stafford, Unsubsidized Stafford, PLUS, Federal Perkins, college/university loans from institutional funds. **Student Employment: Financial Aid Statistics:** 78% freshmen, 67% undergrads receive need-based scholarship or grant aid. 14% freshmen, 7% undergrads receive non-need-based scholarship or grant aid. 74% freshmen, 80% undergrads receive need-based self-help aid. 3% freshmen, 3% undergrads receive athletic scholarships. 66% undergrads borrow to pay for school. Average cumulative indebtedness $16,003. **Criteria for awarding institutional aid:** *Non-need-based:* academics, alumni affiliation, art, athletics, job skills, leadership, minority status, music/drama, state/district residency.

MISSOURI UNIVERSITY OF SCIENCE AND TECHNOLOGY

Best 378

300 W. 13th Street; 106 Parker Hall, Rolla, MO 65409-1060
Phone: 573-341-4165 • **Financial Aid Phone:** 573-341-4282
E-mail: admissions@mst.edu • **CEEB Code:** 6876
Fax: 573-341-4082 • **Website:** www.mst.edu • **ACT Code:** 2398

This public school was founded in 1870. It has a 284-acre campus.

RATINGS
Admissions Selectivity Rating: 77   **Fire Safety Rating:** 77   **Green Rating:** 68

STUDENTS AND FACULTY
Enrollment: 5,752. **Student Body:** 23% female, 77% male, 16% out-of-state, 5% international (49 countries represented). Asian 2%, African American 4%, Caucasian 80%, Hispanic 2%, Native American 0%.
Retention and Graduation: 85% freshmen return for sophomore year. 27% freshmen graduate within 4 years. **Faculty:** Student/faculty ratio 18:1. 336 full-time faculty, 91% hold PhDs, 28% are members of minority groups, 22% are women. 12% of classes are taught by teaching assistants.

ACADEMICS
Degrees: bachelor's, certificate, master's, post-bachelor's certificate. **Classes:** Most classes have 20–29 students. Most lab/discussion sessions have 20–29 students. **Majors with Highest Enrollment:** civil engineering; electrical, electronics and communications engineering; mechanical engineering. **Special**

Study Options: distance learning, double major, dual enrollment, English as a Second Language (ESL), honors program, independent study, internships, liberal arts/career combination, study abroad, teacher certification program. **Honors Programs:** Honors Academy and Master Student Fellowship Programs- http://ugs.mst.edu/honors.html **Combined Degree Programs:** BA/MEng. **Disability Services:** Special programs offered to physically disabled students include note-taking services, reader services, tape recorders, tutors. **Career Services:** Alumni network, alumni services, career/job search classes, career assessment, internships, regional alumni.

FACILITIES

Housing: Coed dorms, special housing for disabled students, fraternity/sorority housing, apartments for married students, cooperative housing, apartments for single students, wellness housing, theme housing. 95% of campus accessible to physically disabled. **Special Academic Facilities/Equipment:** Writing Center, Student Design Center, Nuclear Reactor, Observatory, Explosives Testing Lab, Underground Mine, Museum of Rocks, Minerals, and Gemstones, Centers for Environmental Research, Water Resources, Industrial Research, and Rock Mechanics Research, Geophysical Observatory, Computerized Manufacturing System, Millenium Arch, and Stonehenge. **Computers:** 100% of classrooms, 100% of dorms, 100% of libraries, 66% of dining areas, 100% of student union, 80% of common outdoor areas have wireless network access. Students can register for classes online. Administrative functions (other than registration) can be performed online.

CAMPUS LIFE

Environment: Village. **Activities:** Choral groups, concert band, dance, drama/theater, jazz band, literary magazine, marching band, music ensembles, musical theater, pep band, radio station, student government, student newspaper, symphony orchestra, yearbook, Campus Ministries, International Student Organization 202 registered organizations, 29 honor societies, 13 religious organizations. 21 fraternities, 4 sororities **Athletics (Intercollegiate):** *Men:* baseball, basketball, cross-country, football, soccer, swimming, track/field (outdoor), track/field (indoor). *Women:* basketball, cross-country, soccer, softball, track/field (outdoor), track/field (indoor), volleyball. **On-Campus Highlights:** Havener Student Center, Residential College, Student Design Team Center, Castleman Performing Arts Center, Student Recreation Center. **Environmental Initiatives:** Reducing amount of paper being consumed. Reducing amount of energy being consumed. Reducing solid waste.

ADMISSIONS

Freshman Academic Profile: Average high school GPA. 35% in top 10% of high school class, 70% in top 25% of high school class, 92% in top 50% of high school class. 85% from public high schools. SAT Math middle 50% range 610-700, SAT Critical Reading middle 50% range 520-660. ACT middle 50% range 25-31. Minimum web-based TOEFL 79. Minimum paper TOEFL 550. **Basis for Candidate Selection:** *Very important factors considered include:* Class rank, academic GPA, rigor of secondary school record, standardized test scores. *Important factors considered include:* recommendation(s). *Other factors considered include:* application essay, character/personal qualities, extracurricular activities, interview, talent/ability, volunteer work, work experience. **Freshman Admission Requirements:** High school diploma is required and GED is accepted. *Academic units required:* 4 English, 4 mathematics, 3 science, (1 science labs), 2 foreign language, 3 social studies, 1 visual/performing arts. 4 English, 4 mathematics, 3 science, (1 science labs), 2 foreign language, 3 social studies, 1 visual/performing arts. **Freshman Admission Statistics:** 2,842 applied, 90% admitted, 44% enrolled. **Transfer Admission Requirements:** college transcript(s), minimum college GPA of 2.5 required. **General Admission Information:** Application Fee $45. Regular application deadline 7/1. Notification on a rolling basis, beginning on or about 10/1. Nonfall registration accepted. Admission may be deferred for a maximum of 2 year. Credit and/or placement offered for CEEB Advanced Placement tests.

COSTS AND FINANCIAL AID

Annual in-state tuition $8,082. Annual out-of-state tuition $22,398. Room and board $8,900. Required fees $1,268. Average book expense $952. **Required Forms and Deadlines:** FAFSA. *Types of Aid: Need-based scholarships/grants:* Federal Pell, state scholarships/grants, private scholarships, the school's own gift aid. *Loans:* Subsidized Stafford, Unsubsidized Stafford, PLUS, Federal Perkins. **Student Employment:** Federal Work-Study Program available. Institutional employment available. Off-campus job opportunities are good. **Financial Aid Statistics:** 100% freshmen, 100% undergrads receive need-based scholarship or grant aid. 86% freshmen, 87% undergrads receive non-need-based scholarship or grant aid. 57% freshmen, 88% undergrads receive need-based self-help aid. 1% freshmen receive athletic scholarships. 64% undergrads borrow to pay for school. Average cumulative indebtedness $21,700. **Criteria for awarding institutional aid:** *Non-need-based:* academics, alumni affiliation, athletics, job skills, leadership, minority status, music/drama, religious affiliation, state/district residency.

MISSOURI VALLEY COLLEGE

500 East College Street, Marshall, MO 65340
Phone: 660-831-4114
E-mail: admissions@moval.edu
Fax: 660-831-4233 • **Website:** www.moval.edu • **ACT Code:** 2330

This private school, affiliated with the Presbyterian Church, was founded in 1889. It has a 150-acre campus.

RATINGS
Admissions Selectivity Rating: 72   **Fire Safety Rating:** 60*   **Green Rating:** 60*

STUDENTS AND FACULTY
Enrollment: 1,425. **Student Body:** 43% female, 57% male, 34% out-of-state, 8% international (29 countries represented). Asian 4%, African American 13%, Caucasian 70%, Hispanic 4%, Native American 1%.
Retention and Graduation: 45% freshmen return for sophomore year. 11% freshmen graduate within 4 years. 21% freshmen graduate within 6 years. 20% grads go on to further study within 1 year. **Faculty:** Student/faculty ratio 18:1. 66 full-time faculty, 53% hold PhDs, 3% are members of minority groups, 35% are women. 0% of classes are taught by teaching assistants.

ACADEMICS
Degrees: associate, bachelor's. **Classes:** Most classes have 20–29 students. Most lab/discussion sessions have 20–29 students. **Majors with Highest Enrollment:** business/commerce; criminal justice/law enforcement administration; elementary education and teaching. **Special Study Options:** double major, dual enrollment, internships, teacher certification program. **Disability Services:** Special programs offered to physically disabled students include reader services, tutors. **Career Services:** internships Career Services highlights include Many of our majors require the completion of an internship.

FACILITIES
Housing: men's dorms, women's dorms, fraternity/sorority housing, apartments for married students, apartments for single students.

CAMPUS LIFE
Environment: Rural. **Activities:** Choral groups, dance, drama/theater, literary magazine, music ensembles, musical theater, pep band, radio station, student government, student newspaper, television station, yearbook 28 registered organizations, 8 honor societies, 7 religious organizations. 4 fraternities, 2 sororities. **Athletics (Intercollegiate):** *Men:* baseball, basketball, cheerleading, cross-country, football, golf, rodeo, soccer, tennis, track/field (outdoor), track/field (indoor), volleyball, wrestling. *Women:* basketball, cheerleading, cross country, golf, rodeo, soccer, softball, tennis, track/field (outdoor), track/field (indoor), volleyball, wrestling. **On-Campus Highlights:** Burns Gym, Eckilson-Mabee Theater, Black Box Theater, Student Lounge (basement of MacDonald Hall), Tech Center Computer Lab.

ADMISSIONS
Freshman Academic Profile: Average high school GPA 2.9. 4% in top 10% of high school class, 38% in top 25% of high school class, 54% in top 50% of high school class. SAT Math middle 50% range 412-597. SAT Critical Reading middle 50% range 372-537. ACT middle 50% range 19-27. Minimum paper TOEFL 450. **Basis for Candidate Selection:** *Very important factors considered include:* character/personal qualities, interview. *Important factors considered include:* extracurricular activities, talent/ability, volunteer work. *Other factors considered include:* Class rank, recommendation(s), rigor of secondary school record, standardized test scores, alumni/ae relation, work experience. **Freshman Admission Requirements:** High school diploma is required and GED is accepted. **Freshman Admission Statistics:** 1,345 applied, 67% admitted, 45% enrolled. **Transfer Admission Requirements:** High school transcript, college transcript(s), standardized test scores, minimum college GPA of 2.0 required. Lowest grade transferable C. **General Admission Information:** Application Fee $15. Regular application deadline 9/1. Nonfall registration accepted.

COSTS AND FINANCIAL AID
Annual tuition $13,000. Room and board $5,200. Required fees $500. Average book expense $1,300. **Required Forms and Deadlines:** FAFSA, state aid form. *Types of Aid: Need-based scholarships/grants:* Federal Pell, SEOG, state scholarships/grants, private scholarships, the school's own gift aid. *Loans:* Subsidized Stafford, Unsubsidized Stafford, PLUS, Federal Perkins. **Student Employment:** Federal Work-Study Program available. Institutional employment available. Off-campus job opportunities are excellent. **Financial Aid Statistics:** 100% freshmen, 100% undergrads receive need-based scholarship or grant aid. 100% freshmen, 100% undergrads receive non-need-based scholarship or grant aid. 87% freshmen, 87% undergrads receive need-based self-help aid. 98% freshmen, 92% undergrads receive any aid. 86% undergrads borrow to pay for school. Average cumulative indebtedness $12,000.

MISSOURI WESTERN STATE COLLEGE

4525 Downs Drive, Saint Joseph, MO 64507
Phone: 816-271-4266
E-mail: admissn@mwsc.edu
Fax: 816-271-5833 • **Website:** www.mwsc.edu • **ACT Code:** 2344

This public school was founded in 1969. It has a 740-acre campus.

RATINGS
Admissions Selectivity Rating: 64   **Fire Safety Rating:** 60*   **Green Rating:** 60*

STUDENTS AND FACULTY
Enrollment: 4,652. **Student Body:** 61% female, 39% male, 9% out-of-state, 0% international (5 countries represented). Asian 1%, African American 11%, Caucasian 85%, Hispanic 2%, Native American 1%.
Retention and Graduation: 55% freshmen return for sophomore year. 16% freshmen graduate within 4 years. 35% freshmen graduate within 6 years. 20% grads go on to further study within 1 year. 11% grads pursue arts and sciences degrees. 1% grads pursue law degrees. 6% grads pursue business degrees. 2% grads pursue medical degrees. **Faculty:** Student/faculty ratio 18:1. 180 full-time faculty, 75% hold PhDs, 6% are members of minority groups, 41% are women. 0% of classes are taught by teaching assistants.

ACADEMICS
Degrees: associate, bachelor's, certificate, terminal associate, transfer associate. **Classes:** Most classes have 20–29 students. Most lab/discussion sessions have 20–29 students. **Majors with Highest Enrollment:** business/commerce; criminal justice/law enforcement administration; nursing/registered nurse (rn, asn, bsn, msn). **Special Study Options:** distance learning, double major, dual enrollment, honors program, internships, liberal arts/career combination, teacher certification program, weekend college. **Disability Services:** Special programs offered to physically disabled students include note-taking services, reader services, tutors. **Career Services:** career/job search classes, career assessment.

FACILITIES
Housing: Coed dorms, fraternity/sorority housing, apartments for single students. 99% of campus accessible to physically disabled. **Special Academic Facilities/Equipment:** Multi-media classroom building Planetarium

CAMPUS LIFE
Environment: Village. **Activities:** Choral groups, concert band, dance, drama/theater, jazz band, marching band, music ensembles, pep band, student government, student newspaper, yearbook 64 registered organizations, 5 honor societies, 7 religious organizations. 5 fraternities, 6 sororities. **Athletics (Intercollegiate):** *Men:* baseball, basketball, football, golf. *Women:* basketball, golf, softball, tennis, volleyball.

ADMISSIONS
Freshman Academic Profile: 8% in top 10% of high school class, 25% in top 25% of high school class, 55% in top 50% of high school class. 95% from public high schools. ACT middle 50% range 16-22. Minimum paper TOEFL 500. **Freshman Admission Requirements:** High school diploma is required and GED is accepted. *Academic units required:* 4 English, 3 mathematics, 2 science, (1 science labs), 3 social studies, 3 academic electives, 1 Visual/Perf Arts. *Academic units recommended:* 4 English, 3 mathematics, 2 science, (1 science labs), 3 social studies, 3 academic electives, 1 Visual/Perf Arts **Freshman Admission Statistics:** 2,421 applied, 100% admitted, 43% enrolled. **Transfer Admission Requirements:** college transcript(s), Lowest grade transferable D. **General Admission Information:** Application Fee $15. Regular application deadline 8/15. Notification on a rolling basis, beginning on or about 10/1. Nonfall registration accepted. Credit offered for CEEB Advanced Placement tests.

COSTS AND FINANCIAL AID
Annual in-state tuition $4,098. Annual out-of-state tuition $7,674. Room and board $4,058. Required fees $366. Average book expense $700. **Required Forms and Deadlines:** FAFSA, institution's own financial aid form. **Notification of Awards:** Applicants will be notified of awards on a rolling basis beginning 3/2. **Types of Aid:** *Need-based scholarships/grants:* Federal Pell, SEOG, state scholarships/grants, private scholarships, the school's own gift aid. *Loans:* Subsidized Stafford, Unsubsidized Stafford, PLUS, Federal Perkins. **Student Employment:** Federal Work-Study Program available. Institutional employment available. Highest amount earned per year from on-campus jobs $1,400. Off-campus job opportunities are good. **Financial Aid Statistics:** 66% freshmen, 67% undergrads receive need-based scholarship or grant aid. 51% freshmen, 38% undergrads receive non-need-based scholarship or grant aid. 69% freshmen, 81% undergrads receive need-based self-help aid. 3% freshmen, 5% undergrads receive athletic scholarships. Average cumulative indebtedness $15,100. **Criteria for awarding institutional aid:** *Non-need-based:* academ-

ics, alumni affiliation, art, athletics, job skills, leadership, minority status, music/drama, state/district residency.

MITCHELL COLLEGE

437 Pequot Avenue, New London, CT 6320
Phone: 860-701-5011 • **Financial Aid Phone:** 800-443-2811
E-mail: admissions@mitchell.edu • **CEEB Code:** 3528
Fax: 860-444-1209 • **Website:** www.mitchell.edu/ • **ACT Code:** 572

This private school was founded in 1938. It has a 68-acre campus.

RATINGS
Admissions Selectivity Rating: 63   **Fire Safety Rating:** 61   **Green Rating:** 60*

STUDENTS AND FACULTY
Enrollment: 785. **Student Body:** 47% female, 53% male, 42% out-of-state, 0% international. Asian 2%, African American 11%, Caucasian 68%, Hispanic 13%, Native American 1%.
Retention and Graduation: 57% freshmen return for sophomore year. **Faculty:** Student/faculty ratio 14:1. 35 full-time faculty, 74% hold PhDs, 51% are women. 0% of classes are taught by teaching assistants.

ACADEMICS
Degrees: associate, bachelor's, certificate. **Majors with Highest Enrollment:** education, other; entrepreneurship/entrepreneurial studies; sport and fitness administration/management. **Special Study Options:** dual enrollment, English as a Second Language (ESL), internships, teacher certification program. **Disability Services:** Special programs offered to physically disabled students include note-taking services, reader services, tape recorders, tutors.

FACILITIES
Housing: Coed dorms, special housing for disabled students, Four residence halls are Victorian and Colonial houses located on the waterfront. Three other residence halls are of traditional design. 50% of campus accessible to physically disabled. **Special Academic Facilities/Equipment:** Private dock w/fleet of sailboats, 2 private beaches, 26 acres of woods

CAMPUS LIFE
Environment: Town. **Activities:** Choral groups, dance, drama/theater, literary magazine, student government, student newspaper, yearbook 30 registered organizations, 2 honor societies, 2 religious organizations. **Athletics (Intercollegiate):** *Men:* baseball, basketball, cross-country, golf, lacrosse, soccer, tennis. *Women:* basketball, cross-country, golf, soccer, softball, tennis, volleyball.

ADMISSIONS
Freshman Academic Profile: Average high school GPA 2.7. Minimum paper TOEFL 500. **Basis for Candidate Selection:** *Very important factors considered include:* recommendation(s), rigor of secondary school record, interview. *Important factors considered include:* application essay, standardized test scores, character/personal qualities, extracurricular activities, talent/ability. *Other factors considered include:* Class rank, alumni/ae relation, volunteer work, work experience. **Freshman Admission Requirements:** High school diploma is required and GED is accepted. **Freshman Admission Statistics:** 1,041 applied, 60% admitted, 24% enrolled. **Transfer Admission Requirements:** High school transcript, college transcript(s), essay or personal statement, standardized test scores, minimum college GPA of 2.0 required. Lowest grade transferable C–. **General Admission Information:** Application Fee $30. Early decision application deadline 11/15. Notification on a rolling basis, beginning on or about 12/15. Nonfall registration accepted. Admission may be deferred for a maximum of 1 year. Credit and/or placement offered for CEEB Advanced Placement tests.

COSTS AND FINANCIAL AID
Annual tuition $26,774. Room and board $12,492. Required fees $1,720. Average book expense $1,500. **Required Forms and Deadlines:** FAFSA. **Notification of Awards:** Applicants will be notified of awards on a rolling basis beginning 3/1. **Types of Aid:** *Need-based scholarships/grants:* Federal Pell, SEOG, state scholarships/grants, private scholarships, the school's own gift aid. *Loans:* Subsidized Stafford, Unsubsidized Stafford, PLUS, Federal Perkins, Plato. **Student Employment: Financial Aid Statistics:** 100% freshmen, 99% undergrads receive need-based scholarship or grant aid. 93% freshmen, 87% undergrads receive non-need-based scholarship or grant aid. 93% freshmen, 95% undergrads receive need-based self-help aid. 73% undergrads borrow to pay for school. Average cumulative indebtedness $28,182. **Criteria for awarding institutional aid:** *Non-need-based:* academics, alumni affiliation, art, leadership, state/district residency.

MOLLOY COLLEGE

1000 Hempstead Avenue, Rockville Centre, NY 11570
Phone: 516-678-5000
E-mail: admissions@molloy.edu • **CEEB Code:** 2415
Fax: 516-256-2247 • **Website:** www.molloy.edu/ • **ACT Code:** 2820

This private school, affiliated with the Roman Catholic Church, was founded in 1955. It has a 35-acre campus.

RATINGS
Admissions Selectivity Rating: 74   **Fire Safety Rating:** 60*   **Green Rating:** 61

STUDENTS AND FACULTY
Enrollment: 3,371. **Student Body:** 75% female, 25% male, 1% out-of-state, 0% international. Asian 7%, African American 13%, Caucasian 63%, Hispanic 14%, Native American 0%.
Retention and Graduation: 88% freshmen return for sophomore year. 34% freshmen graduate within 4 years. 62% freshmen graduate within 6 years.
Faculty: Student/faculty ratio 10:1. 179 full-time faculty, 71% hold PhDs, 16% are members of minority groups, 76% are women. 0% of classes are taught by teaching assistants.

ACADEMICS
Degrees: associate, bachelor's, master's, post-master's certificate. **Classes:** Most classes have 10–19 students. Most lab/discussion sessions have 10–19 students. **Majors with Highest Enrollment:** business/commerce; education; nursing/registered nurse (rn, asn, bsn, msn). **Special Study Options:** double major, English as a Second Language (ESL), honors program, independent study, internships, liberal arts/career combination, student-designed major, study abroad, teacher certification program. **Combined Degree Programs:** BSW/MSW, BS/MS, BS/MBA. **Disability Services:** Special programs offered to physically disabled students include note-taking services, reader services, tape recorders, tutors. **Career Services:** Alumni network, alumni services, internships, regional alumni.

FACILITIES
Housing: 100% of campus accessible to physically disabled. **Special Academic Facilities/Equipment:** Professional Repertory Theatre Company in residence, dance studio, institute of cross-cultural and cross-ethnic studies, institute of gerontology, cablevision studio. **Computers:** 100% of classrooms, 100% of libraries, 100% of dining areas, 100% of student union, 100% of common outdoor areas have wireless network access. Students can register for classes online. Administrative functions (other than registration) can be performed online.

CAMPUS LIFE
Environment: Village. **Activities:** Choral groups, dance, drama/theater, jazz band, literary magazine, music ensembles, student government, student newspaper, yearbook, Campus Ministries 21 registered organizations, 18 honor societies, 1 religious organizations. **Athletics (Intercollegiate):** *Men:* baseball, basketball, cross-country, lacrosse, soccer, track/field (outdoor), track/field (indoor). *Women:* basketball, cross-country, lacrosse, soccer, softball, tennis, track/field (outdoor), track/field (indoor), volleyball. **On-Campus Highlights:** The Anselma Room, The Fitness Center, Center for Social and Ethical Concerns, Media Center **Environmental Initiatives:** The Sustainability Institute at Molloy College http://www.molloy.edu/si/index.asp

ADMISSIONS
Freshman Academic Profile: 3.0. 34% in top 10% of high school class, 57% in top 25% of high school class, 89% in top 50% of high school class. 70% from public high schools. SAT Math middle 50% range 490-590. SAT Critical Reading middle 50% range 480-570. SAT Writing middle 50% range 470-570. ACT middle 50% range 23-28. Minimum paper TOEFL 500. **Basis for Candidate Selection:** *Very important factors considered include:* academic GPA, rigor of secondary school record, standardized test scores. *Other factors considered include:* Class rank, application essay, recommendation(s), extracurricular activities, interview, talent/ability, volunteer work, work experience. **Freshman Admission Requirements:** High school diploma is required and GED is accepted. *Academic units required:* 4 English, 3 mathematics, 3 science, 3 foreign language, 4 social studies. *Academic units recommended:* 4 English, 3 mathematics, 3 science, 3 foreign language, 4 social studies. **Freshman Admission Statistics:** 2,304 applied, 74% admitted, 27% enrolled. **Transfer Admission Requirements:** college transcript(s), minimum college GPA of 2.0 required. Lowest grade transferable c. **General Admission Information:** Application Fee $30. Notification on a rolling basis, beginning on or about 10/15. Nonfall registration accepted. Admission may be deferred for a maximum of One Year. Credit offered for CEEB Advanced Placement tests.

COSTS AND FINANCIAL AID
Annual tuition $23,410. Room and board $12,080. Required fees $1,010. Average book expense $1,432. **Required Forms and Deadlines:** FAFSA, state aid

form. **Notification of Awards:** Applicants will be notified of awards on a rolling basis beginning 2/1. **Types of Aid:** *Need-based scholarships/grants:* Federal Pell, SEOG, state scholarships/grants, private scholarships, the school's own gift aid, Federal Nursing Scholarships. *Loans:* Subsidized Stafford, Unsubsidized Stafford, PLUS, Federal Perkins, Federal Nursing. **Student Employment:** Federal Work-Study Program available. Off-campus job opportunities are good. **Financial Aid Statistics:** 98% freshmen, 89% undergrads receive need-based scholarship or grant aid. 11% freshmen, 6% undergrads receive non-need-based scholarship or grant aid. 77% freshmen, 85% undergrads receive need-based self-help aid. 4% freshmen, 2% undergrads receive athletic scholarships. 94% freshmen, 85% undergrads receive any aid. 77% undergrads borrow to pay for school. Average cumulative indebtedness $29,823. **Criteria for awarding institutional aid:** *Non-need-based:* academics, alumni affiliation, art, athletics, leadership, music/drama, religious affiliation.

See page 1148.

MONMOUTH COLLEGE

700 East Broadway, Monmouth, IL 61462
Phone: 800-74-SCOTS • **Financial Aid Phone:** 309-457-2129
E-mail: admit@monmouthcollege.edu • **CEEB Code:** 1484
Fax: 309-457-2141 • **Website:** www.monmouthcollege.edu • **ACT Code:** 1084

This private school, affiliated with the Presbyterian Church, was founded in 1853. It has a 80-acre campus.

RATINGS
Admissions Selectivity Rating: 75   **Fire Safety Rating:** 87   **Green Rating:** 74

STUDENTS AND FACULTY
Enrollment: 1,236. **Student Body:** 54% female, 46% male, 7% out-of-state, 0% international (11 countries represented). Asian 1%, African American 13%, Caucasian 70%, Hispanic 9%, Native American 1%.
Retention and Graduation: 74% freshmen return for sophomore year. 45% freshmen graduate within 4 years. 24% grads go on to further study within 1 year. 12% grads pursue arts and sciences degrees. 1% grads pursue law degrees. 1% grads pursue medical degrees. **Faculty:** Student/faculty ratio 14:1. 84 full-time faculty, 85% hold PhDs, 5% are members of minority groups, 42% are women. 0% of classes are taught by teaching assistants.

ACADEMICS
Degrees: bachelor's. **Classes:** Most classes have 20–29 students. Most lab/discussion sessions have 10–19 students. **Majors with Highest Enrollment:** business administration and management; education; psychology. **Special Study Options:** double major, English as a Second Language (ESL), exchange student program (domestic), honors program, independent study, internships, student-designed major, study abroad, teacher certification program. **Honors Programs:** The Monmouth College Honors Program is intended for a select group of academically well-prepared and intellectually ambitious students. Acceptance into the program is determined competitively, normally occurring at the end of the first semester of the freshman year. The program consists of three levels: exploration of the history of the liberal arts as a field of inquiry, in depth seminars upon historically significant persons, events, movements and ideas, and a senior capstone course. **Combined Degree Programs:** 3/3 and 3/4 agreements in architecture, nursing, phys. therapy, med. tech. **Disability Services:** Special programs offered to physically disabled students include note-taking services, reader services, tape recorders, tutors. **Career Services:** Alumni network, alumni services, career/job search classes, career assessment, internships, regional alumni. Career Services highlights include All Monmouth students are encouraged to seek out rigorous, academically-grounded internship opportunities. The Career Center provides pre-internship orientation to professional office conduct, placement advising, maintenance of contacts with internship sponsors, and quality-control oversight of internship experiences. The Career Center coordinates closely with academic departments in selecting internship opportunities and in assisting students with placements.

FACILITIES
Housing: Coed dorms, special housing for disabled students, men's dorms, special housing for international students, women's dorms, fraternity/sorority housing, apartments for single students, wellness housing, theme housing. 70% of campus accessible to physically disabled. **Special Academic Facilities/Equipment:** Shields Art & Antiquities Collection, Wackerle Career & Leadership Center, Mellinger Teaching & Learning Center, MC-TV (student-run television station), WMCR (student-run radio station) **Computers:** 100% of classrooms, 100% of dorms, 100% of libraries, 100% of dining areas, 100% of student union, 80% of common outdoor areas have wireless network access. Students can register for classes online. Administrative functions (other than registration) can be performed online.

CAMPUS LIFE

Environment: Village. **Activities:** Choral groups, concert band, dance, drama/ theater, jazz band, literary magazine, marching band, music ensembles, musical theater, radio station, student government, student newspaper, symphony orchestra, television station, Campus Ministries, International Student Organization 67 registered organizations, 16 honor societies, 6 religious organizations. 4 fraternities, 3 sororities. **Athletics (Intercollegiate):** *Men:* baseball, basketball, cross-country, diving, football, golf, soccer, swimming, tennis, track/field (outdoor), track/field (indoor). *Women:* basketball, cross-country, diving, golf, soccer, softball, swimming, tennis, track/field (outdoor), track/field (indoor), volleyball. **On-Campus Highlights:** Stockdale Student Center, Hewes Library (including coffee shop!), Huff Athletic Center, Mellinger Teaching and Learning Center, Wallace Hall - main floor coffee/study, The nature trail at LeSuer Nature Preserve offers many opportunities for recreation and scientific study. The new Monmouth College athletic fields are available for team practice, of course, but also open to ad hoc student groups and individuals. **Environmental Initiatives:** The College has a comprehensive recycling and waste diversion program. We provide recycling receptacles for paper, glass, plastic and aluminum in every office and every bedroom in all academic buildings and residence halls, with a recycling center for electronics, flourescent lights and cell phones in the Stockdale Center (the student center). We recycle all cardboard generated at the dining service. We have a fleet of 5 hybrid cars for use by Monmouth faculty and staff for college purposes. In 2007 we retrofitted light fixtures in all of our academic buildings, and, in 2008, placed energy-efficient boilers in five buildings. Our new academic building will meet LEEDS Silver certification standards. We offer a popular organic-foods meal plan. We provide 'trayless' dining in the main cafeteria.

ADMISSIONS

Freshman Academic Profile: Average high school GPA 3.2. 12% in top 10% of high school class, 36% in top 25% of high school class, 71% in top 50% of high school class. ACT middle 50% range 19-25. Minimum web-based TOEFL 79. Minimum paper TOEFL 550. **Basis for Candidate Selection:** *Very important factors considered include:* rigor of secondary school record. *Important factors considered include:* Class rank, academic GPA, standardized test scores, character/personal qualities, extracurricular activities, interview, talent/ability. *Other factors considered include:* application essay, recommendation(s), alumni/ ae relation, first generation, geographical residence, state residency, volunteer work, work experience. **Freshman Admission Requirements:** High school diploma is required and GED is accepted. *Academic units required:* 4 English, 3 mathematics, 2 science, (1 science labs), 2 foreign language, 2 social studies, 1 history. *Academic units recommended:* 4 English, 3 mathematics, 2 science, (1 science labs), 2 foreign language, 2 social studies, 1 history. **Freshman Admission Statistics:** 2,170 applied, 65% admitted, 24% enrolled. **Transfer Admission Requirements:** college transcript(s), minimum college GPA of 2.5 required. Lowest grade transferable C–. **General Admission Information:** Notification on a rolling basis, beginning on or about 9/15. Nonfall registration accepted. Admission may be deferred for a maximum of 1 year. Placement offered for CEEB Advanced Placement tests.

COSTS AND FINANCIAL AID

Annual tuition $30,450. Room and board $7,300. Average book expense $1,000. **Required Forms and Deadlines:** FAFSA. **Notification of Awards:** Applicants will be notified of awards on a rolling basis beginning 3/1. **Types of Aid:** *Need-based scholarships/grants:* Federal Pell, SEOG, state scholarships/ grants, private scholarships, the school's own gift aid. *Loans:* Direct Subsidized Stafford, Direct Unsubsidized Stafford, Direct PLUS, Subsidized Stafford, Unsubsidized Stafford, PLUS, Federal Perkins, college/university loans from institutional funds. **Student Employment:** Federal Work-Study Program available. Institutional employment available. Highest amount earned per year from on-campus jobs $2,325. Off-campus job opportunities are fair. **Financial Aid Statistics:** 100% freshmen, 100% undergrads receive need-based scholarship or grant aid. 12% freshmen, 10% undergrads receive non-need-based scholarship or grant aid. 86% freshmen, 88% undergrads receive need-based self-help aid. 100% freshmen, 99% undergrads receive any aid. 87% undergrads borrow to pay for school. Average cumulative indebtedness $28,934. **Criteria for awarding institutional aid:** *Non-need-based:* academics, art, leadership, music/drama.

MONMOUTH UNIVERSITY (NJ)

Admission, Monmouth University, West Long Branch, NJ 07764-1898
Phone: 732-571-3456 • **Financial Aid Phone:** 732-571-3463
E-mail: admission@monmouth.edu • **CEEB Code:** 2416
Fax: 732-263-5166 • **Website:** www.monmouth.edu • **ACT Code:** 2571

This private school was founded in 1933. It has a 156-acre campus.

RATINGS

Admissions Selectivity Rating: 74   **Fire Safety Rating:** 97   **Green Rating:** 82

STUDENTS AND FACULTY

Enrollment: 4,697. **Student Body:** 59% female, 41% male, 12% out-of-state, 1% international (28 countries represented). Asian 2%, African American 4%, Caucasian 79%, Hispanic 9%, Native American 0%.
Retention and Graduation: 44% freshmen graduate within 4 years. 64% freshmen graduate within 6 years. **Faculty:** Student/faculty ratio 15:1. 266 full-time faculty, 83% hold PhDs, 15% are members of minority groups, 53% are women. 0% of classes are taught by teaching assistants.

ACADEMICS

Degrees: associate, bachelor's, certificate, master's, post-bachelor's certificate, post-master's certificate. **Classes:** Most classes have 10–19 students. **Majors with Highest Enrollment:** business administration and management; communication studies/speech communication and rhetoric; education. **Special Study Options:** Accelerated program, cooperative education program, cross-registration, distance learning, double major, dual enrollment, honors program, independent study, internships, liberal arts/career combination, student-designed major, study abroad, teacher certification program, Clinical Lab Science Program in collaboration with UMDNJ. Air Force ROTC at Rutgers University. Affiliated with Washington Center providing semester and summer internships and shorter symposia. Monmouth Medical Scholars Program allows five incoming freshmen to complete undergraduate degree at Monmouth, including nine credit clinical requirement at Monmouth Medical Center, and commence medical studies at Drexel University School of Medicine. Study Abroad in London at Regent's College and Sydney, Australia at Macquarie University. **Honors Programs:** The Honors School is committed to providing motivated students with a unique learning environment in a community of scholars. By supporting both disciplinary and interdisciplinary approaches to education, the Honors School seeks to help students develop not only depth within their intended field of study, but also an appreciation for how that knowledge is embedded within a broader context of intellectual inquiry. The Honors School also is dedicated to raising students' level of cultural, ethical, and societal awareness as its participants develop into well-rounded scholars and citizens within a global community. **Combined Degree Programs:** BA/MD, BA/MA, 5 yr programs BS/MBA, BS//MS, BA/MA, BSW/MSW , BA/MEd, BA/MSEd. **Disability Services:** Special programs offered to physically disabled students include note-taking services, reader services, tape recorders, tutors. **Career Services:** Alumni network, alumni services, career/job search classes, career assessment, internships, regional alumni. Career Services highlights include Experiential Education graduation requirement.

FACILITIES

Housing: Coed dorms, apartments for single students, wellness housing, theme housing, Honor Program Housing, Health & Wellness housing, Community Service housing. 95% of campus accessible to physically disabled. **Special Academic Facilities/Equipment:** Art gallery, instructional media center with TV and Radio stations, theatre **Computers:** 100% of classrooms, 100% of dorms, 100% of libraries, 100% of dining areas, 100% of student union, 90% of common outdoor areas have wireless network access. Students can register for classes online. Administrative functions (other than registration) can be performed online.

CAMPUS LIFE

Environment: Village. **Activities:** Choral groups, concert band, dance, drama/ theater, jazz band, literary magazine, music ensembles, musical theater, pep band, radio station, student government, student newspaper, television station, yearbook, Campus Ministries, International Student Organization, Model UN 67 registered organizations, 19 honor societies, 3 religious organizations. 7 fraternities, 6 sororities. **Athletics (Intercollegiate):** *Men:* baseball, basketball, cross-country, football, golf, soccer, tennis, track/field (outdoor), track/field (indoor). *Women:* basketball, cross-country, field hockey, golf, lacrosse, soccer, softball, tennis, track/field (outdoor), track/field (indoor). **On-Campus Highlights:** Woodrow Wilson Hall, Plangere Center for Communication, Rebecca Stafford Student Center, Multipurpose Activity Center **Environmental**

Initiatives: EPA MOU discussed above Solar power 454.5 KW solar installation on four university buildings, additional 700 KW installation on 7 buildings in 2012 Establishment of the Sustainability Advisory Council. The Monmouth University Sustainability Advisory Council (SAC) is an interdisciplinary work group comprised of students, faculty, staff & administrators that promotes environmental awareness & encourages the development of an environmentally responsible & sustainable campus community in its operations, education, research, outreach & services.

ADMISSIONS

Freshman Academic Profile: Average high school GPA 3.4. 24% in top 10% of high school class, 49% in top 25% of high school class, 85% in top 50% of high school class. 84% from public high schools. SAT Math middle 50% range 490–580. SAT Critical Reading middle 50% range 470–560. SAT Writing middle 50% range 490–580. ACT middle 50% range 22-26. Minimum web-based TOEFL 79. Minimum paper TOEFL 550. **Basis for Candidate Selection:** *Very important factors considered include:* academic GPA, rigor of secondary school record, standardized test scores. *Important factors considered include:* extracurricular activities, volunteer work, work experience. *Other factors considered include:* application essay, recommendation(s), alumni/ae relation, character/personal qualities. **Freshman Admission Requirements:** High school diploma is required and GED is accepted. *Academic units required:* 4 English, 3 mathematics, 2 science, (1 science labs), 2 history, 5 academic electives. *Academic units recommended:* 4 English, 3 mathematics, 2 science, (1 science labs), 2 history, 5 academic electives. **Freshman Admission Statistics:** 5,127 applied, 85% admitted, 23% enrolled. **Transfer Admission Requirements:** college transcript(s), statement of good standing from prior institution(s). Minimum college GPA of 2.25 required. Lowest grade transferable C. **General Admission Information:** Application Fee $50. Regular application deadline 3/1. Nonfall registration accepted. Admission may be deferred for a maximum of 2 semesters. Credit and/or placement offered for CEEB Advanced Placement tests.

COSTS AND FINANCIAL AID

Annual tuition $29,082. Room and board $10,802. Required fees $628. Average book expense $1,200. **Required Forms and Deadlines:** FAFSA. **Notification of Awards:** Applicants will be notified of awards on a rolling basis beginning 2/15. **Types of Aid:** *Need-based scholarships/grants:* Federal Pell, SEOG, state scholarships/grants, private scholarships, the school's own gift aid, Federal Nursing Scholarships. *Loans:* Direct Subsidized Stafford, Direct Unsubsidized Stafford, Direct PLUS, PLUS, Federal Perkins, state loans, college/university loans from institutional funds, Alternative Loans. **Student Employment:** Federal Work-Study Program available. Institutional employment available. Highest amount earned per year from on-campus jobs $5,000. Off-campus job opportunities are good. **Financial Aid Statistics:** 42% freshmen, 40% undergrads receive need-based scholarship or grant aid. 100% freshmen, 92% undergrads receive non-need-based scholarship or grant aid. 83% freshmen, 85% undergrads receive need-based self-help aid. 9% freshmen, 7% undergrads receive athletic scholarships. 99% freshmen, 97% undergrads receive any aid. 73% undergrads borrow to pay for school. Average cumulative indebtedness $34,361. **Criteria for awarding institutional aid:** *Non-need-based:* academics, alumni affiliation, art, athletics, leadership, religious affiliation, state/district residency.

MONROE COLLEGE

Bronx, NY 10468
Phone: 718-933-6700
E-mail: cpatrick@monroecollege.edu
Fax: 718-364-3552 • **Website:** www.monroecollege.edu/

This is a proprietary school.

RATINGS
Admissions Selectivity Rating: 63   **Fire Safety Rating:** 60*   **Green Rating:** 60*

STUDENTS AND FACULTY
Enrollment: 6,674. **Student Body:** 71% female, 29% male, 2% out-of-state, 5% international. Asian 1%, African American 46%, Caucasian 2%, Hispanic 42%, Native American 0%.
Retention and Graduation: 75% freshmen return for sophomore year. **Faculty:** Student/faculty ratio 21:1. 70 full-time faculty, 40% hold PhDs, 57% are members of minority groups, 44% are women.

ACADEMICS
Degrees: associate, bachelor's, master's. **Classes:** Most classes have 20–29 students. **Special Study Options:** distance learning, honors program, independent study, internships, weekend college.

FACILITIES
Housing: Coed dorms.

CAMPUS LIFE
Activities: literary magazine.

ADMISSIONS
Basis for Candidate Selection: *Very important factors considered include:* application essay, academic GPA, recommendation(s), rigor of secondary school record, character/personal qualities, extracurricular activities, level of applicant's interest, talent/ability. *Important factors considered include:* Class rank, standardized test scores, racial/ethnic status, volunteer work. *Other factors considered include:* first generation, geographical residence, interview, state residency, work experience. **Freshman Admission Requirements:** High school diploma or equivalent is not required. **Freshman Admission Statistics:** 2,108 applied, 67% admitted, 95% enrolled. **General Admission Information:** Application Fee $80. Regular application deadline 1/1. Regular notification 3/22. Nonfall registration not accepted. Admission may be deferred for a maximum of 1 year.

COSTS AND FINANCIAL AID
Annual tuition $11,744. Room and board $11,660. Required fees $800. Average book expense $900. **Required Forms and Deadlines:** FAFSA. **Notification of Awards:** Applicants will be notified of awards on a rolling basis beginning 4/1. **Types of Aid:** *Need-based scholarships/grants:* Federal Pell, SEOG, private scholarships, the school's own gift aid. *Loans:* Subsidized Stafford, Unsubsidized Stafford, PLUS. **Student Employment:** Institutional employment available. **Financial Aid Statistics:** 97% freshmen, 100% undergrads receive need-based scholarship or grant aid. 1% freshmen, 1% undergrads receive non-need-based scholarship or grant aid. 41% freshmen, 43% undergrads receive need-based self-help aid. 1% freshmen receive athletic scholarships. 27% undergrads borrow to pay for school. Average cumulative indebtedness $4,700. **Criteria for awarding institutional aid:** *Non-need-based:* academics, leadership.

MONTANA STATE UNIVERSITY

PO Box 172190, Bozeman, MT 59717-2190
Phone: 406-994-2452 • **Financial Aid Phone:** 406-994-2845
E-mail: admissions@montana.edu • **CEEB Code:** 4488
Fax: 406-994-1923 • **Website:** www.montana.edu • **ACT Code:** 2420

This public school was founded in 1893. It has a 1780-acre campus.

RATINGS
Admissions Selectivity Rating: 85   **Fire Safety Rating:** 86   **Green Rating:** 71

STUDENTS AND FACULTY
Enrollment: 12,614. **Student Body:** 46% female, 54% male, 34% out-of-state, 3% international (64 countries represented). Asian 0%, African American 2%, Caucasian 1%, Hispanic 3%, Native American 1%.
Retention and Graduation: 74% freshmen return for sophomore year. 20% freshmen graduate within 4 years. 31% grads go on to further study within 1 year. **Faculty:** Student/faculty ratio 17:1. 580 full-time faculty, 76% hold PhDs, 5% are members of minority groups, 39% are women. 6% of classes are taught by teaching assistants.

ACADEMICS
Degrees: bachelor's, certificate, doctoral, master's, post-master's certificate. **Classes:** Most classes have 10–19 students. Most lab/discussion sessions have 10–19 students. **Majors with Highest Enrollment:** business/commerce; family and consumer sciences/human sciences; nursing/registered nurse (rn, asn, bsn, msn). **Special Study Options:** cooperative education program, cross-registration, distance learning, double major, English as a Second Language (ESL), exchange student program (domestic), honors program, independent study, internships, student-designed major, study abroad, teacher certification program. **Honors Programs:** http://www.montana.edu/wwwuhp/ **Combined Degree Programs:** BA/MEng, BA in Environmental Design/Master of Architecture. **Disability Services:** Special programs offered to physically disabled students include note-taking services, reader services, tape recorders, tutors. **Career Services:** Alumni network, career/job search classes, career assessment, internships.

FACILITIES
Housing: Coed dorms, men's dorms, women's dorms, fraternity/sorority housing, apartments for married students, apartments for single students, wellness housing, theme housing, wellness floors, non-smoking, older student floors. 90% of campus accessible to physically disabled. **Special Academic Facilities/Equipment:** • Museum of the Rockies (History & Paleontology Museum)

• Planetarium • Studio 1080 (multi-media, interactive learning center) • Subzero Lab • Wind Tunnel • Clean Laboratory • Nano Laboratory • Ion Beam Laboratory • Electron Microscopes • Center for Biofilm Engineering • Plant Growth Center (29 green houses) • Fitness Center ($11.7 million student funded renovation completed in 2008) • Chemistry & Biochemistry Research Facility • Copeland Art Gallery (Art Gallery) • Exit Art Gallery (Student Art Gallery) • Wild Trout Research Laboratory • Burns Telecommunications Center • Plant and Animal Bioscience Research Facilities **Computers:** Students can register for classes online. Administrative functions (other than registration) can be performed online.

CAMPUS LIFE

Environment: Town. **Activities:** Choral groups, concert band, dance, drama/theater, jazz band, literary magazine, marching band, music ensembles, musical theater, pep band, radio station, student newspaper, student-run film society, television station, Campus Ministries, International Student Organization 140 registered organizations, 18 honor societies, 12 religious organizations. 9 fraternities, 4 sororities. **Athletics (Intercollegiate):** *Men:* basketball, cheerleading, cross-country, football, rodeo, skiing (downhill/alpine), skiingnordiccross-country, tennis, track/field (outdoor), track/field (indoor). *Women:* basketball, cheerleading, cross-country, golf, rodeo, skiing (downhill/alpine), skiingnordiccross-country, tennis, track/field (outdoor), track/field (indoor), volleyball. **On-Campus Highlights:** Museum of the Rockies, Planetarium, Fitness Center ($11.7 million student funded renovation completed in 2008, Burns Telecommunications Center, Chemistry & Biochemistry Research Facility, Blackbox Theatre Student Union Building Exit Art Gallery (Student Art Gallery) Copeland Art Gallery (Art Gallery). **Environmental Initiatives:** 1) Building Lighting Retrofit projects; 2)Recycling to reduce waste stream; 3)Steam Go-Generation Turbine (generates ~1/7th of campus electrical power need)

ADMISSIONS

Freshman Academic Profile: Average high school GPA 3.3. 18% in top 10% of high school class, 43% in top 25% of high school class, 73% in top 50% of high school class. SAT Math middle 50% range 500-640. SAT Critical Reading middle 50% range 500-630. SAT Writing middle 50% range 470-600. ACT middle 50% range 21-27. Minimum web-based TOEFL 71. Minimum paper TOEFL 525. **Basis for Candidate Selection:** *Very important factors considered include:* Class rank, rigor of secondary school record, standardized test scores. **Freshman Admission Requirements:** High school diploma is required and GED is accepted. *Academic units required:* 4 English, 3 mathematics, 2 science, (2 science labs), 3 social studies, 2 Two years chosen from the following: foreign language, computer science, visual/performing arts, or. 4 English, 3 mathematics, 2 science, (2 science labs), 3 social studies, 2 Two years chosen from the following: foreign language, computer science, visual/performing arts. **Freshman Admission Statistics:** 12,081 applied, 58% admitted, 39% enrolled. **Transfer Admission Requirements:** college transcript(s), standardized test scores, statement of good standing from prior institution(s). Minimum college GPA of 2.0 required. Lowest grade transferable D-. **General Admission Information:** Application Fee $30. Nonfall registration accepted. Admission may be deferred for a maximum of one year. Credit and/or placement offered for CEEB Advanced Placement tests.

COSTS AND FINANCIAL AID

Annual in-state tuition $5,330. Annual out-of-state tuition $18,599. Room and board $8,070. Required fees $1,419. Average book expense $1,190. **Required Forms and Deadlines:** FAFSA. **Notification of Awards:** Applicants will be notified of awards on a rolling basis beginning 4/1. **Types of Aid:** *Need-based scholarships/grants:* Federal Pell, SEOG, state scholarships/grants, private scholarships, the school's own gift aid, Federal Nursing Scholarships. *Loans:* Subsidized Stafford, Unsubsidized Stafford, PLUS, Federal Perkins, Federal Nursing, college/university loans from institutional funds. **Student Employment:** Institutional employment available. Highest amount earned per year from on-campus jobs $11,700. Off-campus job opportunities are good. **Financial Aid Statistics:** 76% freshmen, 74% undergrads receive need-based scholarship or grant aid. 4% freshmen, 3% undergrads receive non-need-based scholarship or grant aid. 77% freshmen, 83% undergrads receive need-based self-help aid. 1% freshmen, 1% undergrads receive athletic scholarships. 57% freshmen, 54% undergrads receive any aid. 66% undergrads borrow to pay for school. Average cumulative indebtedness $25,682. **Criteria for awarding institutional aid:** *Non-need-based:* academics, alumni affiliation, art, athletics, job skills, leadership, minority status, music/drama, state/district residency.

MONTANA STATE UNIVERSITY—BILLINGS

1500 University Drive, Billings, MT 59101
Phone: 406-657-2158 • **Financial Aid Phone:** 406-657-2288
E-mail: cjohannes@msubillings.edu • **CEEB Code:** 4298
Fax: 406-657-2051 • **Website:** www.msubillings.edu • **ACT Code:** 2416

This public school was founded in 1927. It has a 92-acre campus.

RATINGS

Admissions Selectivity Rating: 65   Fire Safety Rating: 74   Green Rating: 60*

STUDENTS AND FACULTY

Enrollment: 4,354. **Student Body:** 61% female, 39% male, 9% out-of-state, 3% international (20 countries represented). Asian 1%, African American 1%, Caucasian 84%, Hispanic 4%, Native American 4%.
Retention and Graduation: 56% freshmen return for sophomore year. 10% grads go on to further study within 1 year. 70% grads pursue arts and sciences degrees. 14% grads pursue business degrees. 1% grads pursue medical degrees. **Faculty:** Student/faculty ratio 18:1. 154 full-time faculty, 60% hold PhDs, 5% are members of minority groups, 40% are women. 0% of classes are taught by teaching assistants.

ACADEMICS

Degrees: associate, bachelor's, certificate, master's, post-bachelor's certificate, terminal associate, transfer associate. **Classes:** Most classes have 20–29 students. Most lab/discussion sessions have 10–19 students. **Majors with Highest Enrollment:** business/commerce; elementary education and teaching; liberal arts and sciences/liberal studies. **Special Study Options:** Accelerated program, cooperative education program, cross-registration, distance learning, double major, dual enrollment, English as a Second Language (ESL), external degree program, honors program, independent study, internships, student-designed major, study abroad, teacher certification program, weekend college, On-line degrees and extensive on-line course offerings. Evening College. **Honors Programs:** The MSU-Billings University Honors Program is designed for curious students who are eager to participate actively in their education. Classes in the University Honors Program tend to be smaller than other classes and emphasize class discussion. Often these classes are interdisciplinary in nature; this helps students study issues from several perspectives. Some classes are team-taught, which also enriches the discussion. **Disability Services:** Special programs offered to physically disabled students include note-taking services, reader services, tape recorders, tutors. **Career Services:** career/job search classes, career assessment, internships.

FACILITIES

Housing: Coed dorms, special housing for disabled students, men's dorms, women's dorms, apartments for married students, Apartments for students with dependent children. 99% of campus accessible to physically disabled. **Special Academic Facilities/Equipment:** Montana Center for Disabilities, Business Enterprise, Small Business Institute, Urban Institute, Public Radio, Applied Economic Research, Biological Station, Northern Plains Studies Center, Montana Business Connections, Information Commons, Academic Support Center, Advising Center, TRIO Programs, SOS Programs, Northcutt Steele Gallery, Cisel Recital Hall, Petro Theatre, MSU-Billings Downtown **Computers:** 30% of classrooms, 100% of dorms, 100% of libraries, 100% of dining areas, 100% of student union, have wireless network access. Students can register for classes online. Administrative functions (other than registration) can be performed online.

CAMPUS LIFE

Environment: City. **Activities:** Choral groups, concert band, drama/theater, jazz band, literary magazine, music ensembles, musical theater, pep band, radio station, student government, student newspaper, symphony orchestra, Campus Ministries, International Student Organization 53 registered organizations, 10 honor societies, 8 religious organizations. **Athletics (Intercollegiate):** *Men:* baseball, basketball, cross-country, golf, soccer, tennis, track/field (outdoor), track/field (indoor). *Women:* basketball, cross-country, golf, soccer, softball, tennis, track/field (outdoor), track/field (indoor), volleyball. **On-Campus Highlights:** Alterowitz Gym, MSU Billings Downtown, SUB Coffee Shop, Liberal Arts Coffee Shop, Library.

ADMISSIONS

Freshman Academic Profile: Average high school GPA 3.1. 8% in top 10% of high school class, 26% in top 25% of high school class, 66% in top 50% of high school class. 96% from public high schools. SAT Math middle 50% range 450-570. SAT Critical Reading middle 50% range 440-570. ACT middle 50% range 19-24. Minimum web-based TOEFL 68. Minimum paper TOEFL 515. **Basis for Candidate Selection:** *Very important factors considered include:* Class rank, academic GPA, rigor of secondary school record, standardized test scores, level of applicant's interest. *Other factors considered include:* character/personal qualities. **Freshman Admission Requirements:** High school diploma is required and GED is accepted. *Academic units required:* 4 English, 3 mathematics, 2 science, (2 science labs), 3 social studies, 2 For Lang, Vis Arts, Comp Sci. 4 English, 3 mathematics, 2 science, (2 science labs), 3 social studies, 2 For Lang, Vis Arts, Comp Sci **Freshman Admission Statistics:** 1,565 applied, 97% admitted, 52% enrolled. **Transfer Admission Requirements:** college transcript(s), statement of good standing from prior institution(s). Minimum college GPA of 2.0 required. Lowest grade transferable C–. **General Admission Information:** Application Fee $30. Regular application deadline 7/1. Notification on a rolling basis, beginning on or about 7/1. Nonfall registration accepted. Credit and/or placement offered for CEEB Advanced Placement tests.

COSTS AND FINANCIAL AID

Annual in-state tuition $4,397. Annual out-of-state tuition $16,726. Room and board $6,320. Required fees $1,314. Average book expense $1,230. **Required Forms and Deadlines:** FAFSA, institution's own financial aid form. **Notification of Awards:** Applicants will be notified of awards on or about 5/1. **Types of Aid:** *Need-based scholarships/grants:* Federal Pell, SEOG, state scholarships/grants, private scholarships, the school's own gift aid, Montana State University-Billings Foundation. *Loans:* Subsidized Stafford, Unsubsidized Stafford, PLUS, Federal Perkins, college/university loans from institutional funds. **Student Employment:** Federal Work-Study Program available. Institutional employment available. Highest amount earned per year from on-campus jobs $2,000. Off-campus job opportunities are excellent. **Financial Aid Statistics:** 82% freshmen, 80% undergrads receive need-based scholarship or grant aid. 3% freshmen, 3% undergrads receive non-need-based scholarship or grant aid. 77% freshmen, 83% undergrads receive need-based self-help aid. 3% freshmen, 3% undergrads receive athletic scholarships. 65% freshmen, 71% undergrads receive any aid. 73% undergrads borrow to pay for school. Average cumulative indebtedness $27,178. **Criteria for awarding institutional aid:** *Non-need-based:* academics, alumni affiliation, art, athletics, job skills, leadership, minority status, music/drama, state/district residency.

MONTANA TECH OF THE UNIVERSITY OF MONTANA

Best 378

1300 West Park Street, Butte, MT 59701
Phone: 406-496-4256 • **Financial Aid Phone:** 406-496 4213
E-mail: enrollment@mtech.edu • **CEEB Code:** 4487
Fax: 406-496-4710 • **Website:** www.mtech.edu • **ACT Code:** 24180

This public school was founded in 1893. It has a 113-acre campus.

RATINGS
Admissions Selectivity Rating: 69   **Fire Safety Rating:** 98   **Green Rating:** 60*

STUDENTS AND FACULTY
Enrollment: 2,427. **Student Body:** 39% female, 61% male, 13% out-of-state, 7% international (14 countries represented). Asian 1%, African American 0%, Caucasian 89%, Hispanic 2%, Native American 3%.
Retention and Graduation: 66% freshmen return for sophomore year. 18% freshmen graduate within 4 years. 48% freshmen graduate within 6 years.
Faculty: Student/faculty ratio 15:1. 135 full-time faculty, 58% hold PhDs, 10% are members of minority groups, 34% are women.

ACADEMICS
Degrees: associate, bachelor's, certificate, master's, post-bachelor's certificate. **Classes:** Most classes have fewer than 10 students. Most lab/discussion sessions have 10–19 students. **Majors with Highest Enrollment:** biology/biological sciences; mass communication/media studies; resort management. **Special Study Options:** cooperative education program, distance learning, double major, dual enrollment, honors program, independent study, internships, teacher certification program. **Honors Programs:** Honors program provided for all programs. Consists of honors seminar and a few extra courses. **Combined Degree Programs:** BA/MA. **Disability Services:** Special programs offered to physically disabled students include note-taking services, reader services, tape recorders, tutors. **Career Services:** alumni services, career/job search classes, career assessment, internships, regional alumni. Career Services highlights include Internships.

FACILITIES
Housing: Coed dorms, special housing for disabled students, special housing for international students, apartments for married students, apartments for single students, Apartments for families (Don't have to be married if have children). 75% of campus accessible to physically disabled. **Special Academic Facilities/Equipment:** Mineral Museum World Museum of Mining **Computers:** 30% of classrooms, 100% of libraries, 100% of dining areas, 100% of student union, have wireless network access. Students can register for classes online. Administrative functions (other than registration) can be performed online.

CAMPUS LIFE
Environment: Town. **Activities:** concert band, pep band, radio station, student government, student newspaper, yearbook, Campus Ministries 58 registered organizations, 2 honor societies, 3 religious organizations. **Athletics (Intercollegiate):** *Men:* basketball, football, golf. *Women:* basketball, golf, volleyball. **On-Campus Highlights:** Mineral Museum, Mil Building (which houses Starbucks and, HPER (athletic facility), Student Union, Mall area (outdoor located in the center.

ADMISSIONS
Freshman Academic Profile: Average high school GPA 3.4. 22% in top 10% of high school class, 47% in top 25% of high school class, 79% in top 50% of high school class. SAT Math middle 50% range 550-610. SAT Critical Reading middle 50% range 500-620. SAT Writing middle 50% range 450-580. ACT middle 50% range 21-27. Minimum web-based TOEFL 71. Minimum paper TOEFL 525. **Basis for Candidate Selection:** *Other factors considered include:* Class rank, academic GPA, standardized test scores. **Freshman Admission Requirements:** High school diploma is required and GED is accepted. *Academic units required:* 4 English, 3 mathematics, 2 science, (2 science labs), 3 social studies, 2 Combined 2 years of foreign language, visual and performing arts, computer science, or vocational ed. *Academic units recommended:* 4 English, 3 mathematics, 2 science, (2 science labs), 3 social studies, 2 Combined 2 years of foreign language, visual and performing arts, computer science, or vocational ed **Freshman Admission Statistics:** 822 applied, 90% admitted, 58% enrolled. **Transfer Admission Requirements:** college transcript(s), minimum college GPA of 2.0 required. Lowest grade transferable C. **General Admission Information:** Application Fee $30. Notification on a rolling basis, beginning on or about 8/30. Nonfall registration accepted. Admission may be deferred for a maximum of 1 year. Credit and/or placement offered for CEEB Advanced Placement tests.

COSTS AND FINANCIAL AID
Annual in state tuition $6,693. Annual out-of-state tuition $18,948. Room and board $7,626. Average book expense $900. **Required Forms and Deadlines:** FAFSA, institution's own financial aid form. **Notification of Awards:** Applicants will be notified of awards on a rolling basis beginning 3/15. **Types of Aid:** *Need-based scholarships/grants:* Federal Pell, SEOG, state scholarships/grants, private scholarships, the school's own gift aid. *Loans:* Subsidized Stafford, Unsubsidized Stafford, PLUS, Federal Perkins, college/university loans from institutional funds. **Student Employment:** Federal Work-Study Program available. Institutional employment available. Highest amount earned per year from on-campus jobs $4,200. Off-campus job opportunities are good. **Financial Aid Statistics:** 90% freshmen, 87% undergrads receive need-based scholarship or grant aid. 10% freshmen, 5% undergrads receive non-need-based scholarship or grant aid. 74% freshmen, 81% undergrads receive need-based self-help aid. 3% freshmen, 3% undergrads receive athletic scholarships. 86% freshmen, 62% undergrads receive any aid. 55% undergrads borrow to pay for school. Average cumulative indebtedness $25,360. **Criteria for awarding institutional aid:** *Non-need-based:* academics, alumni affiliation, athletics, job skills, minority status, state/district residency.

MONTCLAIR STATE UNIVERSITY

One Normal Avenue, Montclair, NJ 07043-1624
Phone: 973-655-4444 • **Financial Aid Phone:** 973-655-4461
E-mail: undergraduate.admissions@montclair.edu • **CEEB Code:** 2520
Fax: 973-655-7700 • **Website:** www.montclair.edu/ • **ACT Code:** 2572

This public school was founded in 1908. It has a 275-acre campus.

RATINGS
Admissions Selectivity Rating: 80   **Fire Safety Rating:** 99   **Green Rating:** 89

STUDENTS AND FACULTY
Enrollment: 14,222. **Student Body:** 61% female, 39% male, 3% out-of-state, 2% international (81 countries represented). Asian 5%, African American 9%, Caucasian 49%, Hispanic 23%, Native American 0%.

Retention and Graduation: 82% freshmen return for sophomore year. 35% freshmen graduate within 4 years. 63% freshmen graduate within 6 years. 25% grads go on to further study within 1 year. 3% grads pursue arts and sciences degrees. 1% grads pursue law degrees. 5% grads pursue business degrees. 2% grads pursue medical degrees. **Faculty:** Student/faculty ratio 17:1. 579 full-time faculty, 91% hold PhDs, 26% are members of minority groups, 49% are women.

ACADEMICS
Degrees: bachelor's, certificate, master's, post-bachelor's certificate. **Classes: Majors with Highest Enrollment:** business/commerce; family and consumer sciences/human sciences; psychology. **Special Study Options:** cooperative education program, double major, English as a Second Language (ESL), honors program, independent study, internships, study abroad, teacher certification program. **Combined Degree Programs:** BA/MA, 5yr BA/MA, 5yr BA/M practical anthropol. **Disability Services:** Special programs offered to physically disabled students include note-taking services, reader services, tape recorders, tutors. **Career Services:** Alumni network, alumni services, career/job search classes, career assessment, internships, regional alumni., Career Services highlights include All of our programs are exceptional.

FACILITIES
Housing: Coed dorms, special housing for disabled students, special housing for international students, women's dorms, apartments for single students, theme housing, 90% of campus accessible to physically disabled. **Special Academic Facilities/Equipment:** The Dumont Television Center, Yogi Berra Museum and Stadium,Floyd Hall Arena **Computers:** 70% of classrooms, 20% of dorms, 100% of libraries, 75% of dining areas, 50% of student union, 10% of common outdoor areas have wireless network access. Students can register for classes online. Administrative functions (other than registration) can be performed online.

CAMPUS LIFE
Environment: Town. **Activities:** Choral groups, concert band, dance, drama/theater, jazz band, literary magazine, marching band, music ensembles, musical theater, opera, pep band, radio station, student government, student newspaper, symphony orchestra, television station, yearbook, Campus Ministries, International Student Organization 121 registered organizations, 28 honor societies, 8 religious organizations. 13 fraternities, 16 sororities. **Athletics (Intercollegiate):** *Men:* baseball, basketball, diving, football, lacrosse, soccer, swimming, track/field (outdoor). *Women:* basketball, diving, field hockey, lacrosse, soccer, softball, swimming, track/field (outdoor), volleyball. **On-Campus Highlights:** Cafe Diem, University Hall, Student Center, Recreation Center, Kasser Theater. **Environmental Initiatives:** Recycling Program - campus-wide Green products used in housekeeping (This was built into the recent contract that was awarded) Food waste composter (Transitions Dining Services food waste into compost that is used by Grounds Services in plantings around campus)

ADMISSIONS
Freshman Academic Profile: Average high school GPA 3.2. 16% in top 10% of high school class, 42% in top 25% of high school class, 82% in top 50% of high school class. SAT Math middle 50% range 460-540. SAT Critical Reading middle 50% range 440-530. SAT Writing middle 50% range 450-540. Minimum web-based TOEFL 80. Minimum paper TOEFL 550. **Basis for Candidate Selection:** *Very important factors considered include:* academic GPA, rigor of secondary school record. *Important factors considered include:* Class rank, standardized test scores. *Other factors considered include:* recommendation(s), extracurricular activities, first generation, talent/ability, volunteer work, work experience. **Freshman Admission Requirements:** High school diploma is required and GED is accepted. *Academic units required:* 4 English, 3 mathematics, 2 science, (2 science labs), 2 foreign language, 2 social studies, 3 academic electives. 4 English, 3 mathematics, 2 science, (2 science labs), 2 foreign language, 2 social studies, 3 academic electives. **Freshman Admission Statistics:** 12,319 applied, 55% admitted, 33% enrolled. **Transfer Admission Requirements:** college transcript(s), statement of good standing from prior institution(s). Minimum college GPA of 2.0 required. Lowest grade transferable C–. **General Admission Information:** Application Fee $60. Regular application deadline 3/1. Notification on a rolling basis, beginning on or about 10/1. Nonfall registration accepted. Admission may be deferred for a maximum of 1 semester. Credit offered for CEEB Advanced Placement tests.

COSTS AND FINANCIAL AID
Annual in-state tuition $7,982. Annual out-of-state tuition $17,060. Room and board $11,556. Required fees $3,076. Average book expense $1,300. **Required Forms and Deadlines:** FAFSA. **Notification of Awards:** Applicants will be notified of awards on a rolling basis beginning 4/1. **Types of Aid:** *Need-based scholarships/grants:* Federal Pell, SEOG, state scholarships/grants, private scholarships, the school's own gift aid. *Loans:* Subsidized Stafford, Unsubsidized Stafford, PLUS, Federal Perkins, state loans. **Student Employment:** Federal Work-Study Program available. Institutional employment available. Highest amount earned per year from on-campus jobs $2,297. Off-campus job opportunities are good. **Financial Aid Statistics:** 93% freshmen, 92% undergrads receive need-based scholarship or grant aid. 12% freshmen, 13% undergrads re-

ceive non-need-based scholarship or grant aid. 87% freshmen, 87% undergrads receive need-based self-help aid. 67% freshmen, 58% undergrads receive any aid. 71% undergrads borrow to pay for school. Average cumulative indebtedness $28,070. **Criteria for awarding institutional aid:** *Non-need-based:* academics, alumni affiliation, art, leadership, minority status, music/drama, religious affiliation, state/district residency.

MONTREAT COLLEGE

310 Gaither Circle, Montreat, NC 28757-1267
Phone: 828-669-8011 • **Financial Aid Phone:** 800-545-4656
E-mail: admissions@montreat.edu • **CEEB Code:** 5423
Fax: 828-669-0120 • **Website:** www.montreat.edu • **ACT Code:** 3130

This private school, affiliated with the Christian (Nondenominational) Church, was founded in 1916. It has a 162-acre campus.

RATINGS
Admissions Selectivity Rating: 64   **Fire Safety Rating:** 60*   **Green Rating:** 60*

STUDENTS AND FACULTY
Enrollment: 937. **Student Body:** 60% female, 40% male, 20% out-of-state, (12 countries represented).
Retention and Graduation: Faculty: Student/faculty ratio 22:1. 46 full-time faculty, 67% hold PhDs, 13% are members of minority groups, 35% are women. 0% of classes are taught by teaching assistants.

ACADEMICS
Degrees: associate, bachelor's, master's. **Classes:** Most classes have 10–19 students. Most lab/discussion sessions have 10–19 students. **Majors with Highest Enrollment:** bible/biblical studies; business administration and management; environmental studies. **Special Study Options:** Accelerated program, double major, dual enrollment, independent study, internships, student-designed major, study abroad, teacher certification program, American Studies Program (Washington, D.C.). L.A. Film Studies Center (Los Angeles, CA). Martha's Vineyard Semester. **Disability Services:** Special programs offered to physically disabled students include reader services, tutors.

FACILITIES
Housing: men's dorms, women's dorms. 100% of campus accessible to physically disabled. **Special Academic Facilities/Equipment:** Hamilton Art Gallery Chapel of the Prodigal **Computers:** Administrative functions (other than registration) can be performed online.

CAMPUS LIFE
Environment: Village. **Activities:** Choral groups, dance, drama/theater, music ensembles, musical theater, student government, student newspaper 11 registered organizations. **Athletics (Intercollegiate):** *Men:* baseball, basketball, cross-country, golf, soccer. *Women:* basketball, cross-country, golf, soccer, softball, volleyball. **On-Campus Highlights:** Gaither Chapel, Chapel of the Prodigal (contains original Fresco), Student Game Area with LCD Flat Panel TV, Student Lounge Area with 24 Hr. Computer Access, Cavalier Grill - relaxing cafe-style eatery.

ADMISSIONS
Freshman Academic Profile: Average high school GPA 3.0. 7% in top 10% of high school class, 20% in top 25% of high school class, 59% in top 50% of high school class. SAT Math middle 50% range 430-540. SAT Critical Reading middle 50% range 410-560. ACT middle 50% range 18-22. Minimum paper TOEFL 500. **Basis for Candidate Selection:** *Very important factors considered include:* application essay, academic GPA, rigor of secondary school record, standardized test scores. *Important factors considered include:* recommendation(s), character/personal qualities, interview. *Other factors considered include:* Class rank, alumni/ae relation, extracurricular activities, first generation, level of applicant's interest, talent/ability, volunteer work, work experience. **Freshman Admission Requirements:** High school diploma is required and GED is accepted. *Academic units required:* 4 English, 3 mathematics, 3 science, 1 foreign language, 3 history. 4 English, 3 mathematics, 3 science, 1 foreign language, 3 history. **Transfer Admission Requirements:** college transcript(s), essay or personal statement, statement of good standing from prior institution(s). Minimum college GPA of 2.5 required. Lowest grade transferable C. **General Admission Information:** Application Fee $30. Regular application deadline 8/1. Notification on a rolling basis, beginning on or about 9/1. Nonfall registration accepted. Admission may be deferred for a maximum of 1 semester. Credit and/or placement offered for CEEB Advanced Placement tests.

COSTS AND FINANCIAL AID

Annual tuition $20,196. Room and board $6,540. Average book expense $1,000. **Required Forms and Deadlines:** FAFSA. **Notification of Awards:** Applicants will be notified of awards on a rolling basis beginning 2/1. **Types of Aid:** *Need-based scholarships/grants:* Federal Pell, SEOG, state scholarships/grants, private scholarships, the school's own gift aid. *Loans:* Subsidized Stafford, Unsubsidized Stafford, PLUS, Federal Perkins. **Student Employment:** Highest amount earned per year from on-campus jobs $2,212. **Financial Aid Statistics:** 95% freshmen, 98% undergrads receive need-based scholarship or grant aid. 81% freshmen, 94% undergrads receive non-need-based scholarship or grant aid. 72% freshmen, 88% undergrads receive need-based self-help aid. 68% freshmen, 62% undergrads receive athletic scholarships. 98% freshmen, 98% undergrads receive any aid. 89% undergrads borrow to pay for school. Average cumulative indebtedness $18,005. **Criteria for awarding institutional aid:** *Non-need-based:* academics, alumni affiliation, athletics, leadership, music/drama, state/district residency.

MONTSERRAT COLLEGE OF ART

23 Essex Street, Beverly, MA 1915
Phone: 978-921-4242
E-mail: admiss@montserrat.edu • **CEEB Code:** 9101
Fax: 978-921-4241 • **Website:** www.montserrat.edu • **ACT Code:** 1847

This private school was founded in 1970. It has a 12-acre campus.

RATINGS

Admissions Selectivity Rating: 68   **Fire Safety Rating:** 67   **Green Rating:** 60*

STUDENTS AND FACULTY

Enrollment: 298. **Student Body:** 62% female, 38% male, 50% out-of-state, 0% international. Asian 2%, African American 1%, Caucasian 76%, Hispanic 2%, Native American 0%.
Retention and Graduation: 51% freshmen return for sophomore year. 45% freshmen graduate within 4 years. 55% freshmen graduate within 6 years.
Faculty: Student/faculty ratio 7:1. 26 full-time faculty, 82% hold PhDs, 1% are members of minority groups, 58% are women.

ACADEMICS

Degrees: bachelor's, certificate, diploma. **Classes:** Most classes have 10–19 students. **Majors with Highest Enrollment:** graphic design; illustration; painting. **Special Study Options:** cross-registration, dual enrollment, exchange student program (domestic), independent study, internships, student-designed major, study abroad, teacher certification program. **Disability Services:** Special programs offered to physically disabled students include reader services, tape recorders. **Career Services:** career/job search classes, internships.

FACILITIES

Housing: special housing for disabled students, apartment style: coed buildings with single sex apartments. **Special Academic Facilities/Equipment:** Montserrat Gallery, 301 Gallery, Carol Schlosberg Alumni Gallery, 292 Gallery.

CAMPUS LIFE

Environment: Town. **Activities:** literary magazine, student government 5 registered organizations. **On-Campus Highlights:** Student Lounge, Hardie Building, 292 Cabot, Montserrat Gallery, 301 Gallery.

ADMISSIONS

Freshman Academic Profile: Average high school GPA 2.8. SAT Math middle 50% range 372-589. SAT Critical Reading middle 50% range 416-642. ACT middle 50% range 18-22. Minimum paper TOEFL 550. **Basis for Candidate Selection:** *Very important factors considered include:* application essay, recommendation(s), rigor of secondary school record, character/personal qualities, interview, talent/ability. *Important factors considered include:* standardized test scores. *Other factors considered include:* Class rank, extracurricular activities, volunteer work, work experience. **Freshman Admission Requirements:** High school diploma is required and GED is accepted. **Freshman Admission Statistics:** 326 applied, 85% admitted, 27% enrolled. **Transfer Admission Requirements:** college transcript(s), essay or personal statement, minimum college GPA of 2.2 required. Lowest grade transferable C. **General Admission Information:** Application Fee $40. Notification on a rolling basis, beginning on or about 12/20. Nonfall registration accepted. Admission may be deferred for a maximum of one year. Credit offered for CEEB Advanced Placement tests.

COSTS AND FINANCIAL AID

Required Forms and Deadlines: FAFSA, institution's own financial aid form, noncustodial PROFILE. **Notification of Awards:** Applicants will be notified of awards on a rolling basis beginning 3/1. **Types of Aid:** *Need-based scholarships/grants:* Federal Pell, SEOG, state scholarships/grants, private scholarships, the

school's own gift aid. *Loans:* Subsidized Stafford, Unsubsidized Stafford, PLUS, state loans. **Student Employment:** Federal Work-Study Program available. Institutional employment available. Highest amount earned per year from on-campus jobs $1,500. Off-campus job opportunities are good. **Financial Aid Statistics:** 96% freshmen, 91% undergrads receive need-based scholarship or grant aid. 93% freshmen, 78% undergrads receive non-need-based scholarship or grant aid. 100% freshmen, 100% undergrads receive need-based self-help aid. 96% freshmen, 79% undergrads receive any aid. 84% undergrads borrow to pay for school. Average cumulative indebtedness $24,006. **Criteria for awarding institutional aid:** *Non-need-based:* academics, art.

MOORE COLLEGE OF ART & DESIGN

20th Street and The Parkway, Philadelphia, PA 19103-1179
Phone: 215-965-4014 • **Financial Aid Phone:** 215-965-4042
E-mail: enroll@moore.edu • **CEEB Code:** 2417
Fax: 215-568-3547 • **Website:** www.moore.edu • **ACT Code:** 2417

This private school was founded in 1848.

RATINGS

Admissions Selectivity Rating: 80   **Fire Safety Rating:** 87   **Green Rating:** 60*

STUDENTS AND FACULTY

Enrollment: 482. **Student Body:** 100% female, 0% male, 42% out-of-state, 3% international (15 countries represented). Asian 4%, African American 16%, Caucasian 65%, Hispanic 5%, Native American 1%.
Retention and Graduation: 73% freshmen return for sophomore year. 48% freshmen graduate within 4 years. 56% freshmen graduate within 6 years.
Faculty: Student/faculty ratio 9:1. 24 full-time faculty, 50% hold PhDs, 8% are members of minority groups, 67% are women. 0% of classes are taught by teaching assistants.

ACADEMICS

Degrees: bachelor's, post-bachelor's certificate. **Classes:** Most classes have 10–19 students. **Majors with Highest Enrollment:** fashion/apparel design; fine/studio arts; graphic design. **Special Study Options:** double major, independent study, internships, study abroad, teacher certification program, arts, education student travel courses. **Disability Services:** Special programs offered to physically disabled students include tape recorders, tutors. **Career Services:** alumni services, internships, regional alumni. Career Services highlights include All majors require an internship before senior year.

FACILITIES

Housing: women's dorms. **Special Academic Facilities/Equipment:** Paley, Graham and Levy Galleries **Computers:** 100% of classrooms, 100% of dorms, 100% of libraries, 100% of dining areas, have wireless network access. Students can register for classes online. Administrative functions (other than registration) can be performed online. Undergraduates are required to own a computer.

CAMPUS LIFE

Environment: Metropolis. **Activities:** student government, yearbook 8 registered organizations. **On-Campus Highlights:** Three art galleries, Outdoor coffee shop, Internships, Leadership Fellowships, Locks Career Center for Women.

ADMISSIONS

Freshman Academic Profile: Average high school GPA 3.2. SAT Math middle 50% range 420-520. SAT Critical Reading middle 50% range 450-560. ACT middle 50% range 17-22. Minimum paper TOEFL 527. **Basis for Candidate Selection:** *Very important factors considered include:* academic GPA, rigor of secondary school record, standardized test scores, character/personal qualities, interview, level of applicant's interest, talent/ability. *Important factors considered include:* application essay, recommendation(s), extracurricular activities. *Other factors considered include:* Class rank, volunteer work, work experience. **Freshman Admission Requirements:** High school diploma is required and GED is accepted. **Freshman Admission Statistics:** 607 applied, 54% admitted, 33% enrolled. **Transfer Admission Requirements:** High school transcript, college transcript(s), essay or personal statement, statement of good standing from prior institution(s). Minimum college GPA of 2.5 required. Lowest grade transferable C. **General Admission Information:** Application Fee $40. Early decision application deadline 11/15. Regular application deadline 8/15. Notification on a rolling basis, beginning on or about 11/15. Nonfall registration accepted. Admission may be deferred for a maximum of 1 year. Credit offered for CEEB Advanced Placement tests.

COSTS AND FINANCIAL AID

Annual tuition $31,654. Room and board $12,298. Required fees $1,084. Average book expense $2,000. **Required Forms and Deadlines:** FAFSA.

Notification of Awards: Applicants will be notified of awards on a rolling basis beginning 2/15. **Types of Aid:** *Need-based scholarships/grants:* Federal Pell, SEOG, state scholarships/grants, private scholarships, the school's own gift aid. *Loans:* Subsidized Stafford, Unsubsidized Stafford, PLUS, Federal Perkins, Alternative loans. **Student Employment:** Federal Work-Study Program available. Off-campus job opportunities are good. **Financial Aid Statistics:** 97% undergrads receive any aid. **Criteria for awarding institutional aid:** *Non-need-based:* academics, art, leadership.

MORAVIAN COLLEGE

1200 Main Street, Bethlehem, PA 18018
Phone: 610-861-1320 • **Financial Aid Phone:** 610-861-1330
E-mail: admissions@moravian.edu • **CEEB Code:** 2418
Fax: 610-625-7930 • **Website:** www.moravian.edu • **ACT Code:** 2418

This private school, affiliated with the Moravian Church, was founded in 1742. It has a 60-acre campus.

RATINGS
Admissions Selectivity Rating: 71   **Fire Safety Rating:** 88   **Green Rating:** 83

STUDENTS AND FACULTY
Enrollment: 1,476. **Student Body:** 59% female, 41% male, 32% out-of-state, 0% international (9 countries represented). Asian 2%, African American 3%, Caucasian 83%, Hispanic 7%, Native American 0%.
Retention and Graduation: 76% freshmen return for sophomore year. 71% freshmen graduate within 4 years. 74% freshmen graduate within 6 years. 26% grads go on to further study within 1 year. **Faculty:** Student/faculty ratio 12:1. 100 full-time faculty, 91% hold PhDs, 9% are members of minority groups, 51% are women. 0% of classes are taught by teaching assistants.

ACADEMICS
Degrees: bachelor's, first professional, master's, post-bachelor's certificate. **Classes:** Most classes have 20–29 students. Most lab/discussion sessions have 10–19 students. **Majors with Highest Enrollment:** business/commerce; psychology; sociology. **Special Study Options:** cross-registration, double major, honors program, independent study, internships, student-designed major, study abroad, teacher certification program. **Honors Programs:** Students can do honors projects within their selected major **Combined Degree Programs:** BA/MEng, Occ. Therapy (TJU); MBA (Moravian College). **Disability Services:** Special programs offered to physically disabled students include note-taking services, reader services, tape recorders, tutors. **Career Services:** Alumni network, alumni services, career/job search classes, career assessment, internships, regional alumni.

FACILITIES
Housing: Coed dorms, men's dorms, women's dorms, fraternity/sorority housing, apartments for single students, wellness housing, theme housing. **Special Academic Facilities/Equipment:** Payne [art] Gallery, Foy [concert] Hall, greenhouse, student art studios, observation room for psychology classes, Leadership Center **Computers:** 80% of classrooms, 100% of libraries, 100% of dining areas, 100% of student union, 25% of common outdoor areas have wireless network access. Administrative functions (other than registration) can be performed online.

CAMPUS LIFE
Environment: City. **Activities:** Choral groups, concert band, dance, drama/theater, jazz band, literary magazine, marching band, music ensembles, musical theater, radio station, student government, student newspaper, symphony orchestra, yearbook, Campus Ministries, International Student Organization 80 registered organizations, 16 honor societies, 4 religious organizations. 3 fraternities, 4 sororities. **Athletics (Intercollegiate):** *Men:* baseball, basketball, cross-country, football, golf, lacrosse, soccer, tennis, track/field (outdoor), track/field (indoor). *Women:* basketball, cross-country, field hockey, lacrosse, soccer, softball, tennis, track/field (outdoor), track/field (indoor), volleyball. **On-Campus Highlights:** Alternative (on campus club/hang out), Afterwords Cafe (Library Coffe Shop), Priscilla Payne Hurd Academic Complex, Fitness Center, The Quad. **Environmental Initiatives:** Signing of the Talloires Declaration (scheduled for Earth Day 2008) Moravian College President, Dr. Christopher Thomforde, will sign the Talloires Declaration on April 22, 2008. This document, signed by over 290 university presidents in over 40 countries, promotes positive action in environmental sustainability. It also discusses the role of education, research, policy formation and information exchange in

managing the human impact on the environment. Sustainability Taskforce: Two main initiatives that were executed by the Taskforce on Sustainability during the 2007 " 2008 academic year have included a partnership with food services as well as participating in the Focus the Nation project. The partnership with food services has enabled the College to reduce the waste of paper napkins (by using new dispensers), plastic bags (by replacing with reusable bags), and food (by instituting a no tray day). Currently the partnership is actively exploring the feasibility of composting on campus. Participation in the National Teach-In "Focus the Nation" in January 2008 has increased awareness of the unsustainable nature of our fossil fuel use and climate change. This theme was introduced by a panel comprised of key members of the College and community and used in class discussions as well. In addition, the taskforce is in the process of completing a greenhouse gas emission inventory and the College's new construction is energy efficient (although not LEED). Partnership with the City of Bethlehem's Committee for Appropriate Transportation Moravian College will introduce a free Bike Loan program that will be in place by the beginning of freshman orientation in August 2008. A discount program will be available from local bike shops for purchase of bikes and helmets, etc, for Moravian College students, staff, & faculty. In addition, shared use markings on both sides of Bethlehem's Main Street will be painted by the City of Bethlehem by early summer. There will be a sign saying Moravian College Bicycle Lane that will be posted at both ends of Main St. to promote bike usage between the College's north and south campuses.

ADMISSIONS
Freshman Academic Profile: Average high school GPA 3.3. 17% in top 10% of high school class, 47% in top 25% of high school class, 78% in top 50% of high school class. 64% from public high schools. SAT Math middle 50% range 470-550. SAT Critical Reading middle 50% range 480-590. SAT Writing middle 50% range 500-570. ACT middle 50% range 22-26. Minimum paper TOEFL 550. **Basis for Candidate Selection:** *Very important factors considered include:* Class rank, academic GPA, rigor of secondary school record, alumni/ae relation, character/personal qualities. *Important factors considered include:* application essay, recommendation(s), standardized test scores, extracurricular activities, first generation, level of applicant's interest, racial/ethnic status, talent/ability, volunteer work. *Other factors considered include:* geographical residence, interview, work experience. **Freshman Admission Requirements:** High school diploma is required and GED is accepted. *Academic units required:* 4 English, 3 mathematics, 3 science, (2 science labs), 2 foreign language, 4 social studies. *Academic units recommended:* 4 English, 3 mathematics, 3 science, (2 science labs), 2 foreign language, 4 social studies. **Freshman Admission Statistics:** 2,034 applied, 79% admitted, 24% enrolled. **Transfer Admission Requirements:** High school transcript, college transcript(s), essay or personal statement, statement of good standing from prior institution(s). Minimum college GPA of 3.0 required. Lowest grade transferable C. **General Admission Information:** Application Fee $40. Early decision application deadline 2/1. Regular application deadline 3/1. Regular notification 3/15. Non-fall registration accepted. Admission may be deferred for a maximum of 1 year. Placement offered for CEEB Advanced Placement tests.

COSTS AND FINANCIAL AID
Required Forms and Deadlines: FAFSA, CSS/Financial Aid PROFILE, non-custodial PROFILE, business/farm supplement. Copies of parent and student w-2's and 1040's. **Notification of Awards:** Applicants will be notified of awards on or about 4/1. **Types of Aid:** *Need-based scholarships/grants:* Federal Pell, SEOG, state scholarships/grants, the school's own gift aid. *Loans:* Subsidized Stafford, Unsubsidized Stafford, PLUS, Federal Perkins. **Student Employment:** Highest amount earned per year from on-campus jobs $3,000. **Financial Aid Statistics:** 100% freshmen, 100% undergrads receive need-based scholarship or grant aid. 10% freshmen, 9% undergrads receive non-need-based scholarship or grant aid. 90% freshmen, 91% undergrads receive need-based self-help aid. 96% freshmen, 97% undergrads receive any aid. 79% undergrads borrow to pay for school. Average cumulative indebtedness $39,055. **Criteria for awarding institutional aid:** *Non-need-based:* academics, alumni affiliation, leadership, minority status, music/drama, religious affiliation.

MOREHEAD STATE UNIVERSITY

Admissions Center, Morehead, KY 40351
Phone: 606-783-2000 • **Financial Aid Phone:** 606-783-2011
E-mail: admissions@moreheadstate.edu
Fax: 606-783-5038 • **ACT Code:** 1530

This public school was founded in 1922. It has a 1016-acre campus.

RATINGS
Admissions Selectivity Rating: 67   **Fire Safety Rating:** 80   **Green Rating:** 67

STUDENTS AND FACULTY

Enrollment: 6,854. **Student Body:** 61% female, 39% male, 11% out-of-state, 1% international (35 countries represented). Asian 0%, African American 4%, Caucasian 91%, Hispanic 1%, Native American 0%.
Retention and Graduation: 73% freshmen return for sophomore year.
Faculty: Student/faculty ratio 17:1. 374 full-time faculty, 12% are members of minority groups, 48% are women.

ACADEMICS

Degrees: associate, bachelor's, master's, post-bachelor's certificate, post-master's certificate. **Classes:** Most classes have 20–29 students. Most lab/discussion sessions have 10–19 students. **Majors with Highest Enrollment:** elementary education and teaching; general studies; nursing/registered nurse (rn, asn, bsn, msn). **Special Study Options:** Accelerated program, cooperative education program, cross-registration, distance learning, double major, dual enrollment, exchange student program (domestic), honors program, independent study, internships, student-designed major, study abroad, teacher certification program, weekend college. **Disability Services:** Special programs offered to physically disabled students include note-taking services, reader services, tutors. **Career Services:** Alumni network, alumni services, career/job search classes, career assessment, internships.

FACILITIES

Housing: Coed dorms, special housing for disabled students, special housing for international students, fraternity/sorority housing, apartments for married students, apartments for single students, Limited housing available at agriculture complex for agriculture science students. Housing for handicapped students and private rooms available. 90% of campus accessible to physically disabled. **Special Academic Facilities/Equipment:** Ky. Folk Art Center, 320-acre agricultural complex, Space Science Center, Ky. Center for Traditional Music **Computers:** 100% of classrooms, 20% of dorms, 100% of libraries, 100% of dining areas, 100% of student union, 100% of common outdoor areas have wireless network access. Students can register for classes online. Administrative functions (other than registration) can be performed online.

CAMPUS LIFE

Environment: Village. **Activities:** Choral groups, concert band, dance, drama/theater, jazz band, literary magazine, marching band, music ensembles, musical theater, opera, pep band, radio station, student government, student newspaper, symphony orchestra, television station, yearbook 101 registered organizations, 11 honor societies, 7 religious organizations. 10 fraternities, 9 sororities. **Athletics (Intercollegiate):** *Men:* baseball, basketball, cheerleading, cross-country, football, golf, riflery, tennis, track/field (outdoor). *Women:* basketball, cheerleading, cross-country, golf, riflery, soccer, softball, tennis, track/field (outdoor), track/field (indoor), volleyball. **On-Campus Highlights:** Adron Doran University Center, Eagle Lake, MSU Wellness Center, Laughlin Health Building **Environmental Initiatives:** Environmental Education Center: Organizes educational workshops, Earth Day Activities, and community outreach.

ADMISSIONS

Freshman Academic Profile: Average high school GPA 3.3. 21% in top 10% of high school class, 48% in top 25% of high school class, 79% in top 50% of high school class. SAT Math middle 50% range 460-570. SAT Critical Reading middle 50% range 430-550. ACT middle 50% range 19-25. Minimum paper TOEFL 500. **Basis for Candidate Selection:** *Very important factors considered include:* academic GPA, rigor of secondary school record, standardized test scores. *Other factors considered include:* recommendation(s). **Freshman Admission Requirements:** High school diploma is required and GED is accepted. *Academic units required:* 4 English, 3 mathematics, 3 science, (1 science labs), 2 foreign language, 3 social studies, 1 history, 1 visual/performing arts, 7 academic electives, 1 unit history & appreciation of fine arts required. *Academic units recommended:* 4 English, 3 mathematics, 3 science, (1 science labs), 2 foreign language, 3 social studies, 1 history, 1 visual/performing arts, 7 academic electives, 1 1 unit history & appreciation of fine arts required **Freshman Admission Statistics:** 3,461 applied, 86% admitted, 46% enrolled. **Transfer Admission Requirements:** college transcript(s), statement of good standing from prior institution(s). Minimum college GPA of 2.0 required. Lowest grade transferable C. **General Admission Information:** Application Fee $30. Nonfall registration accepted. Admission may be deferred for a maximum of one semester. Credit offered for CEEB Advanced Placement tests.

COSTS AND FINANCIAL AID

Average book expense $1,200. **Required Forms and Deadlines:** FAFSA, institution's own financial aid form. **Types of Aid:** *Need-based scholarships/grants:* Federal Pell, SEOG, state scholarships/grants, private scholarships, the school's own gift aid. *Loans:* Direct Subsidized Stafford, Direct Unsubsidized Stafford, Direct PLUS, Subsidized Stafford, Unsubsidized Stafford, PLUS, Federal Perkins, college/university loans from institutional funds. **Student Employment:** Federal Work-Study Program available. Institutional employment available. **Financial Aid Statistics:** 67% freshmen, 69% undergrads receive need-based scholarship or grant aid. 45% freshmen, 63% undergrads receive non-need-based scholarship or grant aid. 66% freshmen, 74% undergrads

receive need-based self-help aid. 6% freshmen, 5% undergrads receive athletic scholarships. 69% undergrads borrow to pay for school. Average cumulative indebtedness $29,462. **Criteria for awarding institutional aid:** *Non-need-based:* academics, alumni affiliation, art, athletics, leadership, minority status, music/drama, state/district residency.

MOREHOUSE COLLEGE

830 Westview Drive, SW, Atlanta, GA 30314
Phone: 404-215-2632
E-mail: janderso@morehouse.edu • **CEEB Code:** 5415
Fax: 404-524-5635 • **Website:** www.morehouse.edu • **ACT Code:** 792

This private school was founded in 1867. It has a 61-acre campus.

RATINGS

Admissions Selectivity Rating: 77   **Fire Safety Rating:** 60*   **Green Rating:** 60*

STUDENTS AND FACULTY

Enrollment: 2,891. **Student Body:** 0% female, 100% male, 70% out-of-state, 3% international. Asian 0%, African American 94%, Caucasian 0%, Hispanic 0%, Native American 0%.
Retention and Graduation: 84% freshmen return for sophomore year. 32% freshmen graduate within 4 years. 50% freshmen graduate within 6 years. 25% grads go on to further study within 1 year. 22% grads pursue arts and sciences degrees. 5% grads pursue law degrees. 10% grads pursue business degrees. 14% grads pursue medical degrees. **Faculty:** Student/faculty ratio 15:1. 159 full-time faculty, 81% hold PhDs, 77% are members of minority groups, 31% are women.

ACADEMICS

Degrees: bachelor's. **Classes:** Most classes have fewer than 10 students. **Majors with Highest Enrollment:** biology; business/commerce; computer and information sciences. **Special Study Options:** cooperative education program, cross-registration, double major, dual enrollment, exchange student program (domestic), honors program, internships, study abroad, dual degree program in engineering and architecture with other institutions. **Combined Degree Programs:** BA/MEng, degree architecture w/ Michigan U. **Disability Services:** Special programs offered to physically disabled students include reader services, tape recorders, tutors. **Career Services:** career/job search classes, career assessment, internships.

FACILITIES

Housing: men's dorms, apartments for single students. 100% of campus accessible to physically disabled. **Special Academic Facilities/Equipment:** Three chapels, a meditation room, and an arena that was built by and used for the Oplympic games in 1996. **Computers:** Students can register for classes online. Administrative functions (other than registration) can be performed online.

CAMPUS LIFE

Activities: Choral groups, concert band, drama/theater, jazz band, literary magazine, marching band, music ensembles, pep band, student government, student newspaper, yearbook 34 registered organizations, 7 honor societies, 4 religious organizations. 6 fraternities. **Athletics (Intercollegiate):** *Men:* basketball, cross-country, football, track/field (outdoor). **On-Campus Highlights:** Forbes Arena, Graves Hall, Martin Luther King International Chapel, Century Yard, Technology Tower.

ADMISSIONS

Freshman Academic Profile: Average high school GPA 3.2. 20% in top 10% of high school class, 47% in top 25% of high school class, 77% in top 50% of high school class. 80% from public high schools. SAT Math middle 50% range 470-590. SAT Critical Reading middle 50% range 470-580. ACT middle 50% range 19-24. Minimum paper TOEFL 500. **Basis for Candidate Selection:** *Very important factors considered include:* standardized test scores. *Important factors considered include:* Class rank, application essay, recommendation(s), rigor of secondary school record. *Other factors considered include:* alumni/ac relation, character/personal qualities, extracurricular activities, geographical residence, interview, racial/ethnic status, talent/ability, volunteer work. **Freshman Admission Requirements:** High school diploma is required and GED is accepted. *Academic units required:* 4 English, 3 mathematics, 2 science, 2 foreign language, 2 social studies. 4 English, 3 mathematics, 2 science, 2 foreign language, 2 social studies. **Freshman Admission Statistics:** 2,277 applied, 67% admitted, 46% enrolled. **Transfer Admission Requirements:** college transcript(s), essay or personal statement, standardized test scores, statement of good standing from prior institution(s). Minimum college GPA of 2.5 required. Lowest grade transferable C. **General Admission Information:** Application Fee $45. Early decision application deadline 10/15. Regular application deadline 2/15. Regular notification 4/1. Nonfall registration not accepted. Admission may be deferred for a maximum of 2.

COSTS AND FINANCIAL AID

Annual tuition $14,318. Room and board $8,748. Required fees $1,422. Average book expense $850. **Required Forms and Deadlines:** FAFSA, institution's own financial aid form, CSS/Financial Aid PROFILE. **Notification of Awards:** Applicants will be notified of awards on or about 5/1. **Types of Aid:** *Need-based scholarships/grants:* Federal Pell, SEOG, state scholarships/grants, private scholarships, the school's own gift aid, United Negro College Fund. *Loans:* Direct Subsidized Stafford, Direct Unsubsidized Stafford, Direct PLUS, Subsidized Stafford, Unsubsidized Stafford, PLUS, Federal Perkins, state loans, college/university loans from institutional funds. **Student Employment:** Federal Work-Study Program available. Institutional employment available. Highest amount earned per year from on-campus jobs $1,500. Off-campus job opportunities are good. **Financial Aid Statistics:** 41% freshmen, 41% undergrads receive need-based scholarship or grant aid. 80% freshmen, 81% undergrads receive non-need-based scholarship or grant aid. 58% freshmen, 63% undergrads receive need-based self-help aid. 3% freshmen, 4% undergrads receive athletic scholarships. 53% undergrads borrow to pay for school. **Criteria for awarding institutional aid:** *Non-need-based:* academics, alumni affiliation, art, athletics, leadership, music/drama, state/district residency.

MORGAN STATE UNIVERSITY

1700 East Cold Spring Lane, Baltimore, MD 21239
Phone: 800-332-6674
E-mail: tjenness@moac.morgan.edu • **CEEB Code:** 5416
Fax: 410-319-3684 • **Website:** www.morgan.edu • **ACT Code:** 1722

This public school was founded in 1867. It has a 122-acre campus.

RATINGS
Admissions Selectivity Rating: 63   **Fire Safety Rating:** 60*   **Green Rating:** 60*

STUDENTS AND FACULTY
Student Body: 40% out-of-state.
Retention and Graduation: 76% freshmen return for sophomore year.

ACADEMICS
Degrees: bachelor's, master's. **Special Study Options:** cooperative education program, business, education, engineering, social/behavioral science. **Combined Degree Programs:** 3-3 pharmacy, 3-4 predental/premed. **Disability Services:** Special programs offered to physically disabled students include tutors. **Career Services:** career/job search classes, career assessment, internships.

FACILITIES
Housing: Coed dorms, men's dorms, women's dorms, apartments for single students. **Special Academic Facilities/Equipment:** African-American collection, new science complex and school of engineering.

CAMPUS LIFE
Activities: radio station, student government, student newspaper, television station, yearbook 250 registered organizations, 1 religious organizations. 4 fraternities, 4 sororities. **Athletics (Intercollegiate):** *Men:* basketball, cross-country, football, tennis, track/field (outdoor), volleyball. *Women:* basketball, cross-country, tennis, track/field (outdoor), volleyball. **On-Campus Highlights:** Fine Arts Center, Hughes Stadium, Mitchell Building, Research Facility, University Museum.

ADMISSIONS
Freshman Academic Profile: 10% in top 10% of high school class, 80% in top 25% of high school class, 96% in top 50% of high school class. 85% from public high schools. Minimum web-based TOEFL 88. Minimum paper TOEFL 570. **Freshman Admission Requirements:** High school diploma is required and GED is accepted. High school diploma is required and GED is, not accepted. **Transfer Admission Requirements:** Lowest grade transferable C. **General Admission Information:** Early decision application deadline 4/15. Regular application deadline 4/15. Nonfall registration accepted. Credit offered for CEEB Advanced Placement tests.

COSTS AND FINANCIAL AID
Annual in-state tuition $1,853. Annual out-of-state tuition $4,405. Room and board $5,296. Required fees $762. Average book expense $1,500. **Required Forms and Deadlines:** FAFSA, institution's own financial aid form, state aid form. **Types of Aid:** *Need-based scholarships/grants:* state scholarships/grants, United Negro College Fund. *Loans:* Subsidized Stafford, PLUS. **Student Employment:** Federal Work-Study Program available. Institutional employment available. Off-campus job opportunities are good.

MORNINGSIDE COLLEGE

1501 Morningside Avenue, Sioux City, IA 51106-1751
Phone: 712-274-5511 • **Financial Aid Phone:** 712-274-5159
E-mail: mscadm@morningside.edu • **CEEB Code:** 6415
Fax: 712-274-5101 • **Website:** www.morningside.edu • **ACT Code:** 1338

This private school, affiliated with the Methodist Church, was founded in 1894. It has a 68-acre campus.

RATINGS
Admissions Selectivity Rating: 71   **Fire Safety Rating:** 63   **Green Rating:** 60*

STUDENTS AND FACULTY
Enrollment: 1,180. **Student Body:** 54% female, 46% male, 32% out-of-state, 1% international (4 countries represented). Asian 2%, African American 1%, Caucasian 84%, Hispanic 3%, Native American 1%.
Retention and Graduation: 70% freshmen return for sophomore year. 31% freshmen graduate within 4 years. 44% freshmen graduate within 6 years. 11% grads go on to further study within 1 year. 48% grads pursue arts and sciences degrees. 10% grads pursue law degrees. **Faculty:** Student/faculty ratio 17:1. 69 full-time faculty, 77% hold PhDs, 3% are members of minority groups, 45% are women. 0% of classes are taught by teaching assistants.

ACADEMICS
Degrees: bachelor's, master's. **Classes:** Most classes have 10–19 students. Most lab/discussion sessions have 10–19 students. **Majors with Highest Enrollment:** biology/biological sciences; business administration and management; elementary education and teaching. **Special Study Options:** distance learning, double major, dual enrollment, English as a Second Language (ESL), honors program, independent study, internships, liberal arts/career combination, student-designed major, study abroad, teacher certification program, health professions. **Combined Degree Programs:** BA/MA. **Disability Services:** Special programs offered to physically disabled students include note-taking services, reader services, tape recorders, tutors. **Career Services:** Alumni network, alumni services, career/job search classes, career assessment, internships, regional alumni.

FACILITIES
Housing: Coed dorms, fraternity/sorority housing, apartments for married students, apartments for single students. 50% of campus accessible to physically disabled. **Special Academic Facilities/Equipment:** media-enhanced "smart classroom," high-speed campus internet connection, art gallery, theatre, totally renovated science facility **Computers:** 100% of classrooms, 100% of dorms, 100% of libraries, 100% of dining areas, 100% of student union, 100% of common outdoor areas have wireless network access. Students can register for classes online. Administrative functions (other than registration) can be performed online. Undergraduates are required to own a computer.

CAMPUS LIFE
Environment: City. **Activities:** Choral groups, concert band, dance, drama/theater, jazz band, literary magazine, marching band, music ensembles, musical theater, pep band, radio station, student government, student newspaper, television station, yearbook, Campus Ministries, International Student Organization 40 registered organizations, 15 honor societies, 10 religious organizations. 2 fraternities, 1 sororities. **Athletics (Intercollegiate):** *Men:* baseball, basketball, cheerleading, cross-country, football, golf, soccer, swimming, tennis, track/field (outdoor), track/field (indoor), wrestling. *Women:* basketball, cheerleading, cross-country, golf, soccer, softball, swimming, tennis, track/field (outdoor), track/field (indoor), volleyball. **On-Campus Highlights:** New Student Apartments, Health-Fitness Center, Eppley Auditorium, Olsen Student Center, Walker Science Center.

ADMISSIONS
Freshman Academic Profile: Average high school GPA 3.4. 15% in top 10% of high school class, 42% in top 25% of high school class, 78% in top 50% of high school class. 94% from public high schools. ACT middle 50% range 20-25. Minimum paper TOEFL 450. **Basis for Candidate Selection:** *Very important factors considered include:* Class rank, academic GPA, recommendation(s), rigor of secondary school record, standardized test scores. *Important factors considered include:* extracurricular activities, interview, talent/ability. *Other factors considered include:* application essay. **Freshman Admission Requirements:** High school diploma is required and GED is accepted. **Freshman Admission Statistics:** 1,349 applied, 74% admitted, 30% enrolled. **Transfer Admission Requirements:** High school transcript, college transcript(s), statement of good standing from prior institution(s). Minimum college GPA of 2.25 required. Lowest grade transferable C–. **General Admission Information:** Application Fee $25. Nonfall registration accepted. Admission may be deferred for a maximum of no limit. Credit and/or placement offered for CEEB Advanced Placement tests.

COSTS AND FINANCIAL AID

Annual tuition $21,116. Room and board $6,729. Required fees $1,130. Average book expense $800. **Required Forms and Deadlines:** FAFSA. **Notification of Awards:** Applicants will be notified of awards on a rolling basis beginning 3/31. **Types of Aid:** *Need-based scholarships/grants:* Federal Pell, SEOG, state scholarships/grants, private scholarships, the school's own gift aid. *Loans:* Subsidized Stafford, Unsubsidized Stafford, PLUS, Federal Perkins, state loans, college/university loans from institutional funds. **Student Employment:** Federal Work-Study Program available. Institutional employment available. Highest amount earned per year from on-campus jobs $9,536. Off-campus job opportunities are excellent. **Financial Aid Statistics:** 73% freshmen, 76% undergrads receive need-based scholarship or grant aid. 83% freshmen, 86% undergrads receive need-based self-help aid. 56% freshmen, 45% undergrads receive athletic scholarships. 100% freshmen, 100% undergrads receive any aid. 88% undergrads borrow to pay for school. Average cumulative indebtedness $31,208. **Criteria for awarding institutional aid:** *Non-need-based:* academics, alumni affiliation, art, athletics, job skills, leadership, music/drama, religious affiliation, state/district residency.

MORRIS COLLEGE

100 West College Street, Sumter, SC 29150
Phone: 803-934-3225 • **Financial Aid Phone:** 803-934-3238
E-mail: gscriven@morris.edu • **CEEB Code:** 5418
Fax: 803-773-8241 • **Website:** www.morris.edu/ • **ACT Code:** 3868

This private school, affiliated with the Baptist Church, was founded in 1908. It has a 34-acre campus.

RATINGS
Admissions Selectivity Rating: 62   **Fire Safety Rating:** 69   **Green Rating:** 60*

STUDENTS AND FACULTY
Enrollment: 874. **Student Body:** 58% female, 42% male, 21% out-of-state, 0% international. Asian 0%, African American 93%, Caucasian 0%, Hispanic 0%, Native American 0%.
Retention and Graduation: 40% freshmen return for sophomore year. 16% freshmen graduate within 4 years. 31% freshmen graduate within 6 years. 22% grads go on to further study within 1 year. 9% grads pursue arts and sciences degrees. 1% grads pursue law degrees. 1% grads pursue business degrees. 1% grads pursue medical degrees. **Faculty:** Student/faculty ratio 13:1. 51 full-time faculty, 71% hold PhDs, 61% are members of minority groups, 43% are women.

ACADEMICS
Degrees: bachelor's. **Classes:** Most classes have 10–19 students. Most lab/discussion sessions have fewer than 10 students. **Majors with Highest Enrollment:** business administration and management; business administration, management and operations, other; community health services/liaison/counseling. **Special Study Options:** Accelerated program, cooperative education program, double major, honors program, internships, liberal arts/career combination, study abroad, teacher certification program, Advanced degree program available for adults aged 25 and older with 60 earned credit hours. **Combined Degree Programs:** Dual degree, math/engineering with NC A&T State U. **Career Services:** Alumni network, alumni services, career/job search classes, career assessment, internships Career Services highlights include The cooperative education internship program allows students to gain invaluable paid work experience closely related to their chosen field of study while earning their undergraduate degrees. The majority of these students are hired full-time by their co-op employers upon graduation from the college.

FACILITIES
Housing: men's dorms, women's dorms. 73% of campus accessible to physically disabled. **Special Academic Facilities/Equipment:** WMMC-640AM Student Radio Station **Computers:** 100% of classrooms, 100% of dorms, 100% of libraries, 100% of dining areas, 100% of student union, 95% of common outdoor areas have wireless network access. Administrative functions (other than registration) can be performed online.

CAMPUS LIFE
Environment: Town. **Activities:** Choral groups, dance, drama/theater, literary magazine, pep band, radio station, student government, student newspaper, yearbook 55 registered organizations, 7 honor societies, 2 religious organizations. 4 fraternities, 4 sororities. **Athletics (Intercollegiate):** *Men:* baseball, basketball, cheerleading, cross-country, golf, tennis, track/field (outdoor). *Women:* basketball, cheerleading, cross-country, softball, tennis, track/field (outdoor), volleyball. **On-Campus Highlights:** Student Center, Library, Human Development Center, Outdoor Basketball Court, Auditorium, Computer Labs.

ADMISSIONS
Freshman Academic Profile: Average high school GPA 2.5. 0% in top 10% of high school class, 10% in top 25% of high school class, 31% in top 50% of high school class. 98% from public high schools. Minimum paper TOEFL 500. **Basis for Candidate Selection:** *Very important factors considered include:* academic GPA. *Important factors considered include:* Class rank, rigor of secondary school record, standardized test scores. **Freshman Admission Requirements:** High school diploma is required and GED is accepted. *Academic units required:* 4 English, 4 mathematics, 3 science, 1 foreign language, 2 social studies, 1 history, 7 academic electives, 1 Government-1/2, Economics-1/2. *Academic units recommended:* 4 English, 4 mathematics, 3 science, 1 foreign language, 2 social studies, 1 history, 7 academic electives, 1 Government-1/2, Economics-1/2 **Freshman Admission Statistics:** 2,946 applied, 85% admitted, 11% enrolled. **Transfer Admission Requirements:** High school transcript, college transcript(s), standardized test scores, statement of good standing from prior institution(s). Minimum college GPA of 2.0 required. Lowest grade transferable C. **General Admission Information:** Application Fee $20. Notification on a rolling basis, beginning on or about 11/1. Nonfall registration accepted. Admission may be deferred for a maximum of 1 semester. Credit offered for CEEB Advanced Placement tests.

COSTS AND FINANCIAL AID
Required Forms and Deadlines: FAFSA, institution's own financial aid form. **Notification of Awards:** Applicants will be notified of awards on a rolling basis beginning 6/1. **Types of Aid:** *Need-based scholarships/grants:* Federal Pell, SEOG, state scholarships/grants, private scholarships, the school's own gift aid, United Negro College Fund. *Loans:* Direct Subsidized Stafford, Direct Unsubsidized Stafford, Direct PLUS, Federal Perkins. **Student Employment:** Federal Work-Study Program available. Off-campus job opportunities are good. **Financial Aid Statistics:** 97% freshmen, 96% undergrads receive need-based scholarship or grant aid. 20% freshmen, 22% undergrads receive non-need-based scholarship or grant aid. 94% freshmen, 92% undergrads receive need-based self-help aid. 4% freshmen, 7% undergrads receive athletic scholarships. 98% freshmen, 98% undergrads receive any aid. 98% undergrads borrow to pay for school. Average cumulative indebtedness $21,500. **Criteria for awarding institutional aid:** *Non-need-based:* academics, athletics, state/district residency.

MOUNT ALLISON UNIVERSITY

65 York Street, Sackville, NB E4L1E4
Phone: 506-364-2269 • **Financial Aid Phone:** 506-364-2258
E-mail: admissions@mta.ca
Fax: 506-364-2272 • **Website:** www.mta.ca

This public school was founded in 1839. It has a 25-acre campus.

RATINGS
Admissions Selectivity Rating: 63   **Fire Safety Rating:** 92   **Green Rating:** 77

STUDENTS AND FACULTY
Enrollment: 2,396. **Student Body:** 60% female, 40% male, 45% out-of-state, 0% international (40 countries represented).
Retention and Graduation: 45% freshmen graduate within 4 years. 58% freshmen graduate within 6 years. 30% grads go on to further study within 1 year. 10% grads pursue arts and sciences degrees. 3% grads pursue law degrees. 5% grads pursue business degrees. 12% grads pursue medical degrees. **Faculty:** Student/faculty ratio 13:1. 124 full-time faculty, 100% hold PhDs, 31% are women. 0% of classes are taught by teaching assistants.

ACADEMICS
Degrees: bachelor's, master's. **Classes:** Most classes have fewer than 10 students. **Majors with Highest Enrollment:** business/commerce; chemistry; English literature (british and commonwealth); geography; sociology. **Special Study Options:** distance learning, double major, English as a Second Language (ESL), exchange student program (domestic), honors program, independent study, internships, student-designed major, study abroad. **Disability Services:** Special programs offered to physically disabled students include reader services, tutors. **Career Services:** career/job search classes.

FACILITIES
Housing: Coed dorms, special housing for disabled students, special housing for international students, women's dorms, cooperative housing, Zero environment Footprint Housing Pet Friendly Housing. One residence fosters pets for humane society). 80% of campus accessible to physically disabled. **Special Academic Facilities/Equipment:** Art gallery **Computers:** 100% of classrooms, 100% of dorms, 100% of libraries, 100% of dining areas, 100% of student union, 85% of common outdoor areas have wireless network access. Students can

register for classes online. Administrative functions (other than registration) can be performed online.

CAMPUS LIFE
Environment: Rural. **Activities:** Choral groups, concert band, dance, drama/theater, jazz band, music ensembles, musical theater, radio station, student government, student newspaper, student-run film society, symphony orchestra, yearbook, International Student Organization 106 registered organizations. **Athletics (Intercollegiate):** *Men:* badminton, basketball, football, rugby, soccer, swimming. *Women:* badminton, basketball, rugby, soccer, swimming, volleyball. **On-Campus Highlights:** Ownes Art Gallery, Jenings Dinning Hall, Library, Student Center **Environmental Initiatives:** Residence Climate Change Challenge expanded this year to include academic and administrative buildings - buildings reduced their consumption of utilities during the month of February from 10 to 25% New campus Green Plan which studied the waste generated on campus. It identified waste reduction and waste diversion programs to increase our waste diversion from 45% to 70% Introduced a clean plate program in the dining hall - students scrape their plates just like at home. A 44% reduction in food waste is the result of this "waste in your face" project.

ADMISSIONS
Freshman Academic Profile: Minimum paper TOEFL 550. **Basis for Candidate Selection:** *Very important factors considered include:* academic GPA, rigor of secondary school record, extracurricular activities, interview, talent/ability. *Important factors considered include:* recommendation(s), character/personal qualities, volunteer work. *Other factors considered include:* Class rank, application essay, standardized test scores, work experience. **Freshman Admission Requirements:** High school diploma is required and GED is accepted. **Freshman Admission Statistics:** 1,997 applied, 46% admitted, 83% enrolled. **Transfer Admission Requirements:** High school transcript, college transcript(s), essay or personal statement, statement of good standing from prior institution(s). Lowest grade transferable C–. **General Admission Information:** Application Fee $50. Regular application deadline 5/1. Nonfall registration accepted. Admission may be deferred for a maximum of not avail.

COSTS AND FINANCIAL AID
Annual in-state tuition $6,720. Annual out-of-state tuition $6,720. Room and board $5,130. Required fees $116. Average book expense $1,200. **Required Forms and Deadlines:** FAFSA, institution's own financial aid form. **Types of Aid:** *Need-based scholarships/grants:* private scholarships, the school's own gift aid. *Loans:* Subsidized Stafford, Unsubsidized Stafford, PLUS, Canada/Provincial Loan Program. **Student Employment:** Off-campus job opportunities are good. **Financial Aid Statistics:** 100% freshmen, 100% undergrads receive need-based scholarship or grant aid. **Criteria for awarding institutional aid:** *Non-need-based:* academics, alumni affiliation, art, athletics, job skills, leadership, minority status, music/drama, state/district residency.

MOUNT ALOYSIUS COLLEGE

7373 Admiral Peary Highway, Cresson, PA 16630
Phone: 814-886-6383 • **Financial Aid Phone:** 814-886-6463
E-mail: admissions@mtaloy.edu • **CEEB Code:** 2420
Fax: 814-886-6441 • **ACT Code:** 3635

This private school, affiliated with the Roman Catholic Church, was founded in 1939. It has a 125-acre campus.

RATINGS
Admissions Selectivity Rating: 69   **Fire Safety Rating:** 60*   **Green Rating:** 60*

STUDENTS AND FACULTY
Enrollment: 1,532. **Student Body:** 72% female, 28% male, 3% out-of-state, 1% international. Asian 0%, African American 2%, Caucasian 80%, Hispanic 1%, Native American 0%.
Retention and Graduation: 66% freshmen return for sophomore year. 25% freshmen graduate within 4 years. 33% freshmen graduate within 6 years.
Faculty: Student/faculty ratio 13:1. 67 full-time faculty, 49% hold PhDs, 3% are members of minority groups, 67% are women. 0% of classes are taught by teaching assistants.

ACADEMICS
Degrees: associate, bachelor's, certificate, master's, terminal associate. **Classes:** Most classes have 10–19 students. Most lab/discussion sessions have fewer than 10 students. **Special Study Options:** Accelerated program, distance learning, honors program, independent study, internships, student-designed major, teacher certification program. **Career Services:** alumni services, career/job search classes, career assessment, internships.

FACILITIES
Housing: Coed dorms. 90% of campus accessible to physically disabled. **Computers:** 100% of classrooms, 100% of dorms, 100% of libraries, 100% of dining areas, 100% of student union, 100% of common outdoor areas have wireless network access.

CAMPUS LIFE
Environment: Rural. **Activities:** Choral groups, drama/theater, student government, student newspaper 16 registered organizations, 2 honor societies, 1 religious organizations. **Athletics (Intercollegiate):** *Men:* basketball, golf, soccer. *Women:* basketball, soccer, volleyball.

ADMISSIONS
Freshman Academic Profile: Average high school GPA 3.2. 85% from public high schools. SAT Math middle 50% range 410-510. SAT Critical Reading middle 50% range 400-490. SAT Writing middle 50% range 385-490. ACT middle 50% range 18-22. Minimum web-based TOEFL 61. Minimum paper TOEFL 500. **Basis for Candidate Selection:** *Very important factors considered include:* academic GPA, rigor of secondary school record, character/personal qualities, extracurricular activities, first generation, interview, talent/ability, volunteer work. *Important factors considered include:* Class rank, recommendation(s), standardized test scores, level of applicant's interest. *Other factors considered include:* application essay. **Freshman Admission Requirements:** High school diploma is required and GED is accepted. *Academic units required:* 4 English, 3 mathematics, 3 science, 3 social studies, 3 computer science. *Academic units recommended:* 4 English, 3 mathematics, 3 science, 3 social studies, 3 computer science. **Freshman Admission Statistics:** 1,546 applied, 69% admitted, 36% enrolled. **Transfer Admission Requirements:** High school transcript, college transcript(s), minimum college GPA of 2.0 required. Lowest grade transferable C. **General Admission Information:** Application Fee $30. Notification on a rolling basis, beginning on or about 8/1. Nonfall registration accepted. Admission may be deferred for a maximum of 1 semester. Credit and/or placement offered for CEEB Advanced Placement tests.

COSTS AND FINANCIAL AID
Average book expense $2,500. **Required Forms and Deadlines:** FAFSA. **Notification of Awards:** Applicants will be notified of awards on a rolling basis beginning 3/15. **Types of Aid:** *Need-based scholarships/grants:* Federal Pell, SEOG, state scholarships/grants, private scholarships, the school's own gift aid. *Loans:* Subsidized Stafford, Unsubsidized Stafford, PLUS, Federal Perkins, Federal Nursing, Alternative loans. **Student Employment:** Federal Work-Study Program available. Institutional employment available. Off-campus job opportunities are poor. **Financial Aid Statistics:** 100% freshmen, 100% undergrads receive need-based scholarship or grant aid. 11% freshmen, 4% undergrads receive non-need-based scholarship or grant aid. 100% freshmen, 100% undergrads receive need-based self-help aid. 30% freshmen, 35% undergrads receive any aid. 91% undergrads borrow to pay for school. **Criteria for awarding institutional aid:** *Non-need-based:* academics, art, leadership, music/drama, religious affiliation.

See page 1150.

MOUNT HOLYOKE COLLEGE

Best 378

Newhall Center, South Hadley, MA 1075
Phone: 413-538-2023 • **Financial Aid Phone:** 413-538-2291
E-mail: admission@mtholyoke.edu • **CEEB Code:** 3529
Fax: 413-538-2409 • **Website:** www.mtholyoke.edu • **ACT Code:** 1866

This private school was founded in 1837. It has a 800-acre campus.

RATINGS
Admissions Selectivity Rating: 95   **Fire Safety Rating:** 79   **Green Rating:** 86

STUDENTS AND FACULTY
Enrollment: 2,291. **Student Body:** 100% female, 0% male, 77% out-of-state, 23% international (78 countries represented). Asian 7%, African American 6%, Caucasian 48%, Hispanic 8%, Native American 0%.
Retention and Graduation: 92% freshmen return for sophomore year. 79% freshmen graduate within 4 years. 22% grads go on to further study within 1 year. 15% grads pursue arts and sciences degrees. 3% grads pursue law degrees. 1% grads pursue business degrees. 2% grads pursue medical degrees. **Faculty:**

Student/faculty ratio 9:1. 231 full-time faculty, 93% hold PhDs, 23% are members of minority groups, 55% are women. 0% of classes are taught by teaching assistants.

ACADEMICS

Degrees: bachelor's, certificate, master's, post-bachelor's certificate. **Classes:** Most classes have 10–19 students. Most lab/discussion sessions have 10–19 students. **Majors with Highest Enrollment:** biology/biological sciences; English language and literature; international relations and affairs. **Special Study Options:** cooperative education program, cross-registration, double major, exchange student program (domestic), independent study, internships, liberal arts/career combination, student-designed major, study abroad, teacher certification program, Community-based learning courses and First-Year seminars. **Disability Services:** Special programs offered to physically disabled students include note-taking services, reader services, tape recorders, tutors. **Career Services:** Alumni network, alumni services, career/job search classes, career assessment, internships, regional alumni. Career Services highlights include http://www.mtholyoke.edu/cdc/internships.html.

FACILITIES

Housing: special housing for disabled students, women's dorms, apartments for single students, Special housing arrangements are available upon request. 95% of campus accessible to physically disabled. **Special Academic Facilities/Equipment:** Art and historical museums, bronze-casting foundry, child study center, audio-visual center, language learning center, greenhouse, Japanese meditation garden, equestrian center, observatory, linear accelerator, electron microscope, refracting telescope, nuclear magnetic resonance equipment, MCulloch Center for Global Initiatives, Weissman Center for Leadership and the Liberal Arts, Center for the Environment. **Computers:** 20% of classrooms, 100% of dorms, 100% of libraries, 100% of dining areas, 100% of student union, 4% of common outdoor areas have wireless network access. Students can register for classes online. Administrative functions (other than registration) can be performed online.

CAMPUS LIFE

Environment: Town. **Activities:** Choral groups, dance, drama/theater, jazz band, literary magazine, music ensembles, musical theater, radio station, student government, student newspaper, student-run film society, symphony orchestra, yearbook, Campus Ministries, International Student Organization, Model UN 150 registered organizations, 4 honor societies, 12 religious organizations. **Athletics (Intercollegiate):** *Women:* basketball, crew/rowing, cross-country, diving, equestrian sports, field hockey, golf, horseback riding, lacrosse, soccer, squash, swimming, tennis, track/field (outdoor), track/field (indoor), volleyball. **On-Campus Highlights:** Unified Science Center, Kendall Sports and Dance Complex, The Equestrian Center, Blanchard Campus Center, Williston Memorial Library. The entire campus is an exquisitely maintained botanic garden which includes an arboretum, numerous gardens, and the Talcott Greenhouse. **Environmental Initiatives:** Green Building and Energy: The College adopted a policy that all new construction will be designed as LEED silver. The recently completed Campus Police building met the criteria for LEED silver. The College has five LEED certified buildings on campus. In addition to LEED design or certification of major construction projects, the College has adopted internal Environmentally Responsible Building Principles and Guidelines to be applied to all construction and renovation projects. Our greenhouse gas inventory indicates that our emissions, primarily associated with building operations, are significantly lower per student than many of our peer institutions. Building lighting retrofits, heat recovery systems, centralized chilled water, cogeneration, and conservation programs have resulted in a 26.9% decrease in GHG emission since 2003. Recycling and Waste Reduction--The College has had an active recycling program since the early 1990's. Over 50% of our routine waste is diverted from disposal through recycling in 2011. Food waste from dining facilities, pre and post consumer, is composted. Additionally, construction debris is recycled and equestrian center waste is composted. Student ECO-Reps and the Environmental Action Coalition routinely conduct waste audits of both residence hall and administrative/academic buildings and organize a variety of information and training activities around recycling and waste reduction as well as other environmental topics. Supporting Local Agriculture--Dining Services has worked diligently to adopt environmentally friendly practices in all aspects of their work, from locating suppliers of local and organic foods to composting waste at local farms. The College procures as much of its food as possible from local growers and purveyors and used produce this year from our own new Student Garden for its Sustainable Agriculture Dinner in September. Our produce company is committed to buying from local farms anytime there is product available. A couple of years ago, Mount Holyoke and the other members of the Five Colleges formalized the buy-local effort as a Five-College initiative. One of the first Five-College efforts was a meeting with local farmers and suppliers of produce, dairy, and meat to discuss the feasibility of buying their products.

ADMISSIONS

Freshman Academic Profile: Average high school GPA 3.7. 56% in top 10% of high school class, 82% in top 25% of high school class, 97% in top 50% of high school class. 58% from public high schools. SAT Math middle 50% range 610-700. SAT Critical Reading middle 50% range 610-720. SAT Writing middle 50% range 630-720. ACT middle 50% range 28-31. Minimum web-based TOEFL 100. Minimum paper TOEFL. **Basis for Candidate Selection:** *Very important factors considered include:* Class rank, application essay, academic GPA, recommendation(s), rigor of secondary school record. *Important factors considered include:* character/personal qualities, extracurricular activities, first generation, interview, talent/ability, volunteer work, work experience. *Other factors considered include:* standardized test scores, alumni/ae relation, geographical residence, level of applicant's interest, racial/ethnic status. **Freshman Admission Requirements:** High school diploma is required and GED is accepted. **Freshman Admission Statistics:** 3,876 applied, 42% admitted, 31% enrolled. **Transfer Admission Requirements:** High school transcript, college transcript(s), essay or personal statement, statement of good standing from prior institution(s). Minimum college GPA of 3.0 required. Lowest grade transferable C–. **General Admission Information:** Application Fee $60. Early decision application deadline 11/15. Regular application deadline 1/15. Regular notification 4/1. Nonfall registration accepted. Credit and/or placement offered for CEEB Advanced Placement tests.

COSTS AND FINANCIAL AID

Annual tuition $41,270. Room and board $12,140. Required fees $186. Average book expense $950. **Required Forms and Deadlines:** FAFSA, CSS/Financial Aid PROFILE, noncustodial PROFILE, business/farm supplement. **Notification of Awards:** Applicants will be notified of awards on or about 4/1. **Types of Aid:** *Need-based scholarships/grants:* Federal Pell, SEOG, state scholarships/grants, private scholarships, the school's own gift aid. *Loans:* Direct Subsidized Stafford, Direct Unsubsidized Stafford, Direct PLUS, Federal Perkins, state loans, college/university loans from institutional funds. **Student Employment:** Federal Work-Study Program available. Institutional employment available. Highest amount earned per year from on-campus jobs $2,100. Off-campus job opportunities are fair. **Financial Aid Statistics:** 99% freshmen, 97% undergrads receive need-based scholarship or grant aid. 85% freshmen, 94% undergrads receive need-based self-help aid. 79% freshmen, 83% undergrads receive any aid. 69% undergrads borrow to pay for school. Average cumulative indebtedness $23,254. **Criteria for awarding institutional aid:** *Non-need-based:* academics, leadership.

MOUNT IDA COLLEGE

777 Dedham Street, Newton, MA 2459
Phone: 617-928-4553 • **Financial Aid Phone:** 617-928-4785
E-mail: admissions@mountida.edu • **CEEB Code:** 3530
Fax: 617-928-4507 • **Website:** www.mountida.edu • **ACT Code:** 1868

This private school was founded in 1899. It has a 72-acre campus.

RATINGS

Admissions Selectivity Rating: 67   **Fire Safety Rating:** 60*   **Green Rating:** 60*

STUDENTS AND FACULTY

Enrollment: 1,445. **Student Body:** 67% female, 33% male, 40% out-of-state, 5% international (32 countries represented). Asian 2%, African American 10%, Caucasian 56%, Hispanic 6%, Native American 0%.
Retention and Graduation: 57% freshmen return for sophomore year.
Faculty: Student/faculty ratio 13:1. 63 full-time faculty, 57% hold PhDs, 8% are members of minority groups, 60% are women. 0% of classes are taught by teaching assistants.

ACADEMICS

Degrees: associate, bachelor's, certificate, terminal associate, transfer associate. **Classes:** Most classes have 10–19 students. **Special Study Options:** Accelerated program, distance learning, English as a Second Language (ESL), honors program, independent study, internships, student-designed major, study abroad, teacher certification program. **Disability Services:** Special programs offered to physically disabled students include tape recorders, tutors. **Career Services:** Alumni network, alumni services, career assessment, internships.

FACILITIES

Housing: Coed dorms, special housing for disabled students, men's dorms, women's dorms. **Special Academic Facilities/Equipment:** Mount Ida College Art Gallery

CAMPUS LIFE

Environment: Village. **Activities:** Choral groups, dance, drama/theater, literary magazine, radio station, student government, student newspaper, yearbook, International Student Organization 22 registered organizations, 6 honor societies. **Athletics (Intercollegiate):** *Men:* basketball, football, lacrosse, soccer, volleyball. *Women:* basketball, cheerleading, cross-country, equestrian sports, soccer, softball, volleyball.

ADMISSIONS

Freshman Academic Profile: SAT Math middle 50% range 380-490. SAT Critical Reading middle 50% range 390-490. SAT Writing middle 50% range 400-500. ACT middle 50% range 15-20. Minimum web-based TOEFL 70. Minimum paper TOEFL 525. **Basis for Candidate Selection:** *Very important factors considered include:* academic GPA. *Important factors considered include:* recommendation(s), rigor of secondary school record. *Other factors considered include:* application essay, standardized test scores, character/personal qualities, extracurricular activities, interview, talent/ability, volunteer work, work experience. **Freshman Admission Requirements:** High school diploma is required and GED is accepted. **Freshman Admission Statistics:** 2,222 applied, 74% admitted, 25% enrolled. **Transfer Admission Requirements:** High school transcript, college transcript(s), essay or personal statement, statement of good standing from prior institution(s). Minimum college GPA of 2.0 required. Lowest grade transferable C. **General Admission Information:** Application Fee $45. Nonfall registration accepted. Admission may be deferred for a maximum of 1 year. Credit offered for CEEB Advanced Placement tests.

COSTS AND FINANCIAL AID

Average book expense $1,000. **Required Forms and Deadlines:** FAFSA. **Notification of Awards:** Applicants will be notified of awards on a rolling basis beginning 3/1. **Types of Aid:** *Need-based scholarships/grants:* Federal Pell, SEOG, state scholarships/grants, private scholarships, the school's own gift aid. *Loans:* Subsidized Stafford, Unsubsidized Stafford, PLUS, state loans. **Student Employment:** Federal Work-Study Program available. Institutional employment available. Highest amount earned per year from on-campus jobs $1,500. **Financial Aid Statistics:** 99% freshmen, 97% undergrads receive need-based scholarship or grant aid. 6% freshmen, 6% undergrads receive non-need-based scholarship or grant aid. 96% freshmen, 95% undergrads receive need-based self-help aid. **Criteria for awarding institutional aid:** *Non-need-based:* academics, art, leadership.

MOUNT MARY COLLEGE

2900 North Menomonee River Parkway, Milwaukee, WI 53222-4597
Phone: 414-256-1219 • **Financial Aid Phone:** 414-256-1258
E-mail: admiss@mtmary.edu • **CEEB Code:** 1490
Fax: 414-256-0180 • **Website:** www.mtmary.edu/ • **ACT Code:** 4620

This private school, affiliated with the Roman Catholic Church, was founded in 1913. It has a 80-acre campus.

RATINGS

Admissions Selectivity Rating: 79   **Fire Safety Rating:** 73   **Green Rating:** 67

STUDENTS AND FACULTY

Enrollment: 1,026. **Student Body:** 99% female, 1% male, 4% out-of-state, 1% international (13 countries represented). Asian 5%, African American 23%, Caucasian 54%, Hispanic 11%.
Retention and Graduation: 66% freshmen return for sophomore year. 10% grads go on to further study within 1 year. **Faculty:** Student/faculty ratio 15:1. 68 full-time faculty, 76% hold PhDs, 87% are women. 0% of classes are taught by teaching assistants.

ACADEMICS

Degrees: bachelor's, master's, post-bachelor's certificate, post-master's certificate. **Classes:** Most classes have 10–19 students. Most lab/discussion sessions have 10–19 students. **Majors with Highest Enrollment:** fashion/apparel design; nursing/registered nurse (rn, asn, bsn, msn). **Special Study Options:** Accelerated program, double major, honors program, independent study, internships, liberal arts/career combination, student-designed major, study abroad, teacher certification program. **Honors programs:** The purpose of the Mount Mary College Honors Program is to reward superior scholarly achievement and to provide special challenges to serious students who wish to achieve maximum benefit from their college education. Students completing the program receive the diploma citation, "Graduation in the Honors Program. **Disability Services:** Special programs offered to physically disabled students include note-taking services, reader services, tape recorders, tutors. **Career services:** career/job search classes, career assessment, internships.

FACILITIES

Housing: women's dorms, 90% of campus accessible to physically disabled. **Special Academic Facilities/Equipment:** Hagerty Library, Marian Art Gallery, Walter and Olive Stiemke Memorial Hall and Conference Center. **Computers:** 100% of dorms, have wireless network access. Students can

register for classes online. Administrative functions (other than registration) can be performed online.

CAMPUS LIFE

Environment: Metropolis. **Activities:** Choral groups, dance, literary magazine, music ensembles, student government, student newspaper, Campus Ministries, International Student Organization, Model UN. 42 registered organizations, 14 honor societies, 1 religious organizations. **Athletics (Intercollegiate):** Women: basketball, cross-country, soccer, softball, tennis, volleyball. **On-Campus Highlights:** Cyber Cafe, Gerhardinger Science and Technology Center, Haggerty Library, Notre Dame Hall, Bloechl Recreation Center.

ADMISSIONS

Freshman Academic Profile: Average high school GPA 2.9. 16% in top 10% of high school class, 41% in top 25% of high school class, 70% in top 50% of high school class. 80% from public high schools. ACT middle 50% range 17-25. Minimum web-based TOEFL 61. Minimum paper TOEFL 500. **Basis for Candidate Selection:** Very important factors considered include: academic GPA, rigor of secondary school record. Important factors considered include: Class rank, standardized test scores, character/personal qualities, talent/ability. Other factors considered include: application essay, recommendation(s), extracurricular activities, interview, volunteer work, work experience. **Freshman Admission Requirements:** High school diploma is required and GED is accepted. **Academic units required:** 4 English, 2 mathematics, 2 science, (2 science labs), 2 social studies, 2 history, 2 academic electives. **Academic units recommended:** 4 English, 2 mathematics, 2 science, (2 science labs), 2 social studies, 2 history, 2 academic electives. **Freshman Admission Statistics:** 423 applied, 53% admitted, 51% enrolled. **Transfer Admission Requirements:** High school transcript, college transcript(s), minimum college GPA of 2.0 required. Lowest grade transferable C. **General Admission Information:** Application Fee $25. Notification on a rolling basis, beginning on or about 9/15. Nonfall registration accepted. Admission may be deferred for a maximum of 1 year. Credit and/or placement offered for CEEB Advanced Placement tests.

COSTS AND FINANCIAL AID

Room and board $7,498. Required fees $450. Average book expense $1,260. **Required Forms and Deadlines:** FAFSA. **Notification of Awards:** Applicants will be notified of awards on a rolling basis beginning 3/1. **Types of Aid:** Need-based scholarships/grants: Federal Pell, SEOG, state scholarships/grants, private scholarships, the school's own gift aid. Loans: Subsidized Stafford, Unsubsidized Stafford, PLUS, Federal Perkins, state loans. Student Employment: Federal Work-Study Program available. Institutional employment available. Highest amount earned per year from on-campus jobs $1,152. **Financial Aid Statistics:** 100% freshmen, 97% undergrads receive need-based scholarship or grant aid. 6% freshmen, 4% undergrads receive non-need-based scholarship or grant aid. 93% freshmen, 93% undergrads receive need-based self-help aid. 87% freshmen, 86% undergrads receive any aid. 83% undergrads borrow to pay for school. Average cumulative indebtedness $27,145. **Criteria for awarding institutional aid:** Non-need-based: academics, alumni affiliation, art, leadership, music/drama.

MOUNT MERCY COLLEGE

1330 Elmhurst Drive Northeast, Cedar Rapids, IA 52402-4797
Phone: 319-368-6460
E-mail: admission@mtmercy.edu
Fax: 319-363-5270 • **Website:** www.mtmercy.edu

This is a private school.

RATINGS

Admissions Selectivity Rating: 68   **Fire Safety Rating:** 60*   **Green Rating:** 60*

STUDENTS AND FACULTY

Enrollment: 1,434. **Student Body:** 70% female, 30% male, 6% out-of-state, 0% international. Asian 1%, African American 2%, Caucasian 87%, Hispanic 1%, Native American 0%.
Retention and Graduation: 77% freshmen return for sophomore year. 49% freshmen graduate within 4 years. 61% freshmen graduate within 6 years. 9% grads go on to further study within 1 year. 6% grads pursue arts and sciences degrees. 1% grads pursue law degrees. 2% grads pursue business degrees. **Faculty:** Student/faculty ratio 13:1. 72 full-time faculty, 61% hold PhDs, 6% are members of minority groups, 57% are women. 0% of classes are taught by teaching assistants.

ACADEMICS

Degrees: bachelor's. **Classes:** Most classes have 10–19 students. **Majors with Highest Enrollment:** business/commerce; education; nursing/registered nurse (rn, asn, bsn, msn). **Special Study Options:** Accelerated program, cooperative education program, cross-registration, double major, dual enrollment, honors program, independent study, internships, liberal arts/career combination, student-designed major, study abroad, teacher certification program, weekend college. **Combined Degree Programs:** 2-2 programs with Kirkwood Community College. **Disability Services:** Special programs offered to physically disabled students include note-taking services, reader services, tape recorders, tutors. **Career Services:** Alumni network, alumni services, career/job search classes, career assessment, internships, regional alumni.

FACILITIES
Housing: Coed dorms, apartments for single students. 95% of campus accessible to physically disabled.

CAMPUS LIFE
Activities: Choral groups, drama/theater, literary magazine, pep band, student government, student newspaper 35 registered organizations, 16 honor societies, 7 religious organizations. **Athletics (Intercollegiate):** *Men:* baseball, basketball, cross-country, golf, soccer, track/field (outdoor). *Women:* basketball, cross-country, golf, soccer, softball, track/field (outdoor), volleyball. **On-Campus Highlights:** Lundy Commons: Game Room, TV Room, Convenience Store, Bookstore, Lounges, Hilltop Grill and Dining Hall, Busse Library, Andrea's House-144 bed, suite style campus residence, Entire campus is connected by underground tunnels.

ADMISSIONS
Freshman Academic Profile: Average high school GPA 3.4. 18% in top 10% of high school class, 44% in top 25% of high school class, 82% in top 50% of high school class. 83% from public high schools. ACT middle 50% range 20-25. Minimum paper TOEFL 550. **Basis for Candidate Selection:** *Very important factors considered include:* Class rank, rigor of secondary school record, standardized test scores. *Important factors considered include:* application essay, recommendation(s), extracurricular activities. *Other factors considered include:* character/personal qualities, interview, talent/ability, volunteer work. **Freshman Admission Requirements:** High school diploma is required and GED is accepted. **Freshman Admission Statistics:** 488 applied, 84% admitted, 48% enrolled. **Transfer Admission Requirements:** college transcript(s), statement of good standing from prior institution(s). Minimum college GPA of 2.5 required. Lowest grade transferable D. **General Admission Information:** Application Fee $20. Regular application deadline 8/30. Nonfall registration accepted. Admission may be deferred for a maximum of 1 year. Credit and/or placement offered for CEEB Advanced Placement tests.

COSTS AND FINANCIAL AID
Required Forms and Deadlines: FAFSA. **Notification of Awards:** Applicants will be notified of awards on a rolling basis beginning 3/15. **Types of Aid:** *Need-based scholarships/grants:* Federal Pell, SEOG, state scholarships/grants, the school's own gift aid. *Loans:* Direct Subsidized Stafford, Direct Unsubsidized Stafford, Direct PLUS, Federal Perkins, state loans, college/university loans from institutional funds. **Student Employment:** Federal Work-Study Program available. Institutional employment available. Off-campus job opportunities are excellent. **Financial Aid Statistics:** 100% freshmen, 99% undergrads receive need-based scholarship or grant aid. 14% freshmen, 8% undergrads receive non-need-based scholarship or grant aid. 84% freshmen, 89% undergrads receive need-based self-help aid. 71% undergrads borrow to pay for school. Average cumulative indebtedness $19,656. **Criteria for awarding institutional aid:** *Non-need-based:* academics, art, leadership, music/drama.

ACADEMICS
Degrees: associate, bachelor's, terminal associate, transfer associate. **Special Study Options:** Accelerated program, cooperative education program, distance learning, double major, dual enrollment, external degree program, honors program, independent study, internships, liberal arts/career combination, teacher certification program. **Disability Services:** Special programs offered to physically disabled students include tutors. **Career Services:** alumni services, career/job search classes, career assessment, internships.

FACILITIES
Housing: men's dorms, women's dorms, apartments for single students. 95% of campus accessible to physically disabled.

CAMPUS LIFE
Environment: Rural. **Activities:** Choral groups, concert band, music ensembles, musical theater, student government, Campus Ministries, International Student Organization 33 registered organizations, 4 honor societies, 6 religious organizations. **Athletics (Intercollegiate):** *Men:* baseball, basketball, cross-country, golf, soccer, tennis. *Women:* basketball, cross-country, soccer, softball, tennis, volleyball.

ADMISSIONS
Freshman Academic Profile: Average high school GPA 3.1. 9% in top 10% of high school class, 26% in top 25% of high school class, 59% in top 50% of high school class. SAT Math middle 50% range 420-520. SAT Critical Reading middle 50% range 410-490. ACT middle 50% range 15-20. Minimum paper TOEFL 500. **Basis for Candidate Selection:** *Very important factors considered include:* academic GPA, rigor of secondary school record, character/personal qualities. *Important factors considered include:* Class rank, standardized test scores, extracurricular activities, interview, level of applicant's interest, talent/ability. *Other factors considered include:* recommendation(s), alumni/ae relation, geographical residence. **Freshman Admission Requirements:** High school diploma is required and GED is accepted. *Academic units required:* 4 English, 3 mathematics, 3 science, (1 science labs), 3 social studies, 3 academic electives. 4 English, 3 mathematics, 3 science, (1 science labs), 3 social studies, 3 academic electives. **Freshman Admission Statistics:** 1,838 applied, 50% admitted, 37% enrolled. **Transfer Admission Requirements:** High school transcript, college transcript(s), minimum college GPA of 2.0 required. **General Admission Information:** Nonfall registration accepted.

COSTS AND FINANCIAL AID
Annual tuition $7,223. Room and board $2,775. Average book expense $950. **Required Forms and Deadlines:** FAFSA, state aid form. **Notification of Awards:** Applicants will be notified of awards on a rolling basis beginning 2/14. **Types of Aid:** *Need-based scholarships/grants:* Federal Pell, SEOG, state scholarships/grants, private scholarships, the school's own gift aid. *Loans:* Subsidized Stafford, Unsubsidized Stafford, PLUS, Federal Perkins, Federal Nursing, state loans. **Student Employment:** Federal Work-Study Program available. Off-campus job opportunities are excellent. **Financial Aid Statistics:** 97% freshmen, 93% undergrads receive need-based scholarship or grant aid. 5% freshmen, 4% undergrads receive non-need-based scholarship or grant aid. 84% freshmen, 87% undergrads receive need-based self-help aid. 7% freshmen, 2% undergrads receive athletic scholarships. 93% undergrads borrow to pay for school. Average cumulative indebtedness $16,117. **Criteria for awarding institutional aid:** *Non-need-based:* academics, art, athletics, leadership, music/drama, religious affiliation.

MOUNT OLIVE COLLEGE

634 Henderson Street, Mount Olive, NC 28365
Phone: 919-658-2502
E-mail: admissions@moc.edu • **CEEB Code:** 5435
Fax: 919-658-9816 • **Website:** www.moc.edu • **ACT Code:** 3131

This private school, affiliated with the Baptist Church, was founded in 1951. It has a 138-acre campus.

RATINGS
Admissions Selectivity Rating: 79   **Fire Safety Rating:** 60*   **Green Rating:** 60*

STUDENTS AND FACULTY
Enrollment: 3,305. **Student Body:** 68% female, 32% male, 4% out-of-state. Asian 1%, African American 35%, Caucasian 51%, Hispanic 3%, Native American 0%.
Retention and Graduation: 68% freshmen return for sophomore year. 20% grads go on to further study within 1 year. **Faculty:** Student/faculty ratio 26:1. 80 full-time faculty, 96% hold PhDs, 15% are members of minority groups, 35% are women.

MOUNT SAINT MARY COLLEGE

330 Powell Avenue, Newburgh, NY 12550
Phone: 845-569-3488 • **Financial Aid Phone:** 845-569-3298
E-mail: admissions@msmc.edu • **CEEB Code:** 2423
Fax: 845-562-6762 • **Website:** www.msmc.edu • **ACT Code:** 2819

This private school was founded in 1959. It has a 70-acre campus.

RATINGS
Admissions Selectivity Rating: 68   **Fire Safety Rating:** 95   **Green Rating:** 60*

STUDENTS AND FACULTY
Enrollment: 2,261. **Student Body:** 72% female, 28% male, 11% out-of-state, 0% international (23 countries represented). Asian 3%, African American 6%, Caucasian 58%, Hispanic 11%, Native American 1%.
Retention and Graduation: 70% freshmen return for sophomore year. 42% freshmen graduate within 4 years. 56% freshmen graduate within 6 years. 44% grads go on to further study within 1 year. 22% grads pursue arts and sciences degrees. 3% grads pursue business degrees. **Faculty:** Student/faculty ratio 14:1. 88 full-time faculty, 92% hold PhDs, 6% are members of minority groups, 61% are women. 0% of classes are taught by teaching assistants.

ACADEMICS

Degrees: bachelor's, certificate, master's, post-master's certificate. **Classes:** Most classes have 20–29 students. Most lab/discussion sessions have fewer than 10 students. **Majors with Highest Enrollment:** nursing/registered nurse (rn, asn, bsn, msn); teacher education, multiple levels. **Special Study Options:** Accelerated program, cooperative education program, cross-registration, distance learning, double major, dual enrollment, exchange student program (domestic), honors program, independent study, internships, liberal arts/career combination, student-designed major, study abroad, teacher certification program. **Honors Programs:** The Honors Program comprises academic, cultural, and social activities, each of which complements and reinforces the others. **Combined Degree Programs:** BA/MA. **Disability Services:** Special programs offered to physically disabled students include tape recorders, tutors. **Career Services:** alumni services, career/job search classes, career assessment Career Services highlights include The Co-op program helps many students get a jump start on their career choice as well as help clarify their goals.

FACILITIES

Housing: Coed dorms, special housing for disabled students, men's dorms, women's dorms. 95% of campus accessible to physically disabled. **Special Academic Facilities/Equipment:** On-campus elementary school, television studio, and radio station. Multi-media lab. **Computers:** 100% of classrooms, 100% of dorms, 100% of libraries, 100% of dining areas, 100% of student union, 40% of common outdoor areas have wireless network access. Students can register for classes online. Administrative functions (other than registration) can be performed online.

CAMPUS LIFE

Environment: Town. **Activities:** Choral groups, concert band, dance, drama/theater, literary magazine, music ensembles, musical theater, radio station, student government, student newspaper, student-run film society, yearbook, Campus Ministries 30 registered organizations, 12 honor societies, 1 religious organizations. **Athletics (Intercollegiate):** *Men:* baseball, basketball, cross-country, lacrosse, soccer, swimming, tennis. *Women:* basketball, cross-country, lacrosse, soccer, softball, swimming, tennis, volleyball. **On-Campus Highlights:** Athletic Center with indoor pool, cardio/weight rm, Knight Court Cyber Cafe', Library with wireless internet access, Multi-media production laboratory, Theater with student productions/music events. **Environmental Initiatives:** Use of high efficiency boilers. Purchase and use of water conserving plumbing fixtures, faucets, and appliances. Natural products for flooring such as cork or marmoleum.

ADMISSIONS

Freshman Academic Profile: Average high school GPA 3.1. 8% in top 10% of high school class, 30% in top 25% of high school class, 69% in top 50% of high school class. 64% from public high schools. SAT Math middle 50% range 450-560. SAT Critical Reading middle 50% range 450-540. SAT Writing middle 50% range 450-550. ACT middle 50% range 19-25. Minimum web-based TOEFL 79. Minimum paper TOEFL 550. **Basis for Candidate Selection:** *Very important factors considered include:* academic GPA, rigor of secondary school record. *Important factors considered include:* Class rank, application essay, recommendation(s), standardized test scores, character/personal qualities, interview, talent/ability. *Other factors considered include:* alumni/ae relation, extracurricular activities, first generation, level of applicant's interest, volunteer work, work experience. **Freshman Admission Requirements:** High school diploma is required and GED is accepted. **Freshman Admission Statistics:** 3,472 applied, 81% admitted, 16% enrolled. **Transfer Admission Requirements:** High school transcript, college transcript(s), standardized test scores, statement of good standing from prior institution(s). Minimum college GPA of 2.0 required. Lowest grade transferable C. **General Admission Information:** Application Fee $45. Regular application deadline 8/15. Notification on a rolling basis, beginning on or about 9/15. Nonfall registration accepted. Admission may be deferred for a maximum of 1 year. Credit and/or placement offered for CEEB Advanced Placement tests.

COSTS AND FINANCIAL AID

Annual tuition $25,300. Room and board $13,290. Required fees $950. Average book expense $1,200. **Required Forms and Deadlines:** FAFSA. **Notification of Awards:** Applicants will be notified of awards on a rolling basis beginning 3/15. **Types of Aid:** *Need-based scholarships/grants:* Federal Pell, SEOG, state scholarships/grants, private scholarships, the school's own gift aid, Federal Nursing Scholarships. , Academic Competitiveness Grant (ACG) and National Science and Mathematics Access to Retain Talent Grant (National SMART or NSG). *Loans:* Subsidized Stafford, Unsubsidized Stafford, PLUS, Federal Perkins, Federal Nursing. **Student Employment:** Federal Work-Study Program available. Institutional employment available. Highest amount earned per year from on-campus jobs $4,204. Off-campus job opportunities are good. **Financial Aid Statistics:** 100% freshmen, 100% undergrads receive need-based scholarship or grant aid. 15% freshmen, 11% undergrads receive non-need-based scholarship or grant aid. 85% freshmen, 89% undergrads receive need-based self-help aid. 99% freshmen, 90% undergrads receive any aid. 81% undergrads

borrow to pay for school. Average cumulative indebtedness $28,716. **Criteria for awarding institutional aid:** *Non-need-based:* academics.

MOUNT ST. MARY'S COLLEGE (CA)

12001 Chalon Road, Los Angeles, CA 90049-1597
Phone: 800-999-9893 • **Financial Aid Phone:** 310-954-4190
E-mail: admissions@msmc.la.edu • **CEEB Code:** 4493
Fax: 310-954-4259 • **Website:** www.msmc.la.edu • **ACT Code:** 338

This private school, affiliated with the Roman Catholic Church, was founded in 1925. It has a 53-acre campus.

RATINGS

Admissions Selectivity Rating: 70   **Fire Safety Rating:** 86   **Green Rating:** 72

STUDENTS AND FACULTY

Enrollment: 2,445. **Student Body:** 93% female, 7% male, 2% out-of-state, 1% international (7 countries represented). Asian 17%, African American 8%, Caucasian 11%, Hispanic 55%, Native American 1%.
Retention and Graduation: 44% freshmen graduate within 4 years. 61% freshmen graduate within 6 years. 50% grads go on to further study within 1 year. **Faculty:** Student/faculty ratio 13:1. 99 full-time faculty, 65% hold PhDs, 27% are members of minority groups, 77% are women. 0% of classes are taught by teaching assistants.

ACADEMICS

Degrees: associate, bachelor's, certificate, master's, post-bachelor's certificate, post-master's certificate, terminal associate, transfer associate. **Classes:** Most classes have 10–19 students. Most lab/discussion sessions have 10–19 students. **Majors with Highest Enrollment:** liberal arts and sciences/liberal studies; nursing/registered nurse (rn, asn, bsn, msn). **Special Study Options:** Accelerated program, cross-registration, double major, exchange student program (domestic), honors program, independent study, internships, student-designed major, study abroad, teacher certification program, weekend college. **Honors Programs:** Honors program is available to qualifying incoming freshmen and college students meeting eligibility requirements. **Combined Degree Programs:** BA/MA, ADN to MSN. **Disability Services:** Special programs offered to physically disabled students include note-taking services, reader services, tape recorders, tutors. **Career Services:** alumni services, career/job search classes, career assessment, internships.

FACILITIES

Housing: men's dorms, women's dorms, limited men's housing. 100% of campus accessible to physically disabled. **Special Academic Facilities/Equipment:** Drudis-Biada Art Gallery **Computers:** 100% of classrooms, 100% of dorms, 100% of libraries, 100% of dining areas, have wireless network access. Students can register for classes online. Administrative functions (other than registration) can be performed online.

CAMPUS LIFE

Environment: Metropolis. **Activities:** Choral groups, dance, drama/theater, literary magazine, music ensembles, student government, student newspaper, yearbook, Campus Ministries 29 registered organizations, 3 honor societies, 1 religious organizations. 3 sororities. **On-Campus Highlights:** Humanities Building, Chapel, Fitness Center. **Environmental Initiatives:** Water Conservation: Bottled water deliveries virtually canceled on both campuses. Activated Carbon Water filters added to bottle-free water dispensers on both campuses. Carbon Footprint: (1) Gas-powered golf carts replaced with electric vehicles on both campuses. (2) Facilities Management offices using only "Green-Certified" vendors. Full deployment of recycling containers in offices, classrooms and throughout both campuses.

ADMISSIONS

Freshman Academic Profile: Average high school GPA 3.4. 50% from public high schools. SAT Math middle 50% range 400-510. SAT Critical Reading middle 50% range 410-510. SAT Writing middle 50% range 420-520. ACT middle 50% range 16-20. Minimum paper TOEFL 550. **Basis for Candidate Selection:** *Very important factors considered include:* application essay, academic GPA, standardized test scores. *Important factors considered include:* recommendation(s), rigor of secondary school record. *Other factors considered include:* alumni/ae relation, character/personal qualities, extracurricular activities, first generation, geographical residence, racial/ethnic status, religious affiliation/commitment, state residency, talent/ability, volunteer work, work experience. **Freshman Admission Requirements:** High school diploma is required and GED is accepted. *Academic units required:* 4 English, 3 mathematics, 2 science, (2 science labs), 2 foreign language, 2 social studies, 2 history. *Academic units recommended:* 4 English, 3 mathematics, 2 science, (2 science labs), 2 foreign language, 2 social studies, 2 history. **Freshman Admission Statistics:** 2,244 applied, 71% admitted, 34% enrolled. **Transfer Admission Requirements:** college transcript(s), essay or personal statement, statement of good standing from prior institution(s). Minimum college GPA of 2.4 required. Lowest grade transferable D. **General Admission Information:** Application Fee $40. Notification on a rolling basis, beginning on or about 11/15. Nonfall registration accepted. Admission may be deferred for a maximum of 1 year. Credit and/or placement offered for CEEB Advanced Placement tests.

COSTS AND FINANCIAL AID

Annual tuition $31,924. Room and board $10,530. Required fees $970. Average book expense $1,722. **Required Forms and Deadlines:** FAFSA. **Notification of Awards:** Applicants will be notified of awards on a rolling basis beginning 3/15. **Types of Aid:** *Need-based scholarships/grants:* Federal Pell, SEOG, state scholarships/grants, private scholarships, the school's own gift aid. *Loans:* Subsidized Stafford, Unsubsidized Stafford, PLUS, Federal Nursing, college/university loans from institutional funds. **Student Employment:** Federal Work-Study Program available. Institutional employment available. Off-campus job opportunities are good. **Financial Aid Statistics:** 100% freshmen, 94% undergrads receive need-based scholarship or grant aid. 5% freshmen, 7% undergrads receive non-need-based scholarship or grant aid. 96% freshmen, 97% undergrads receive need-based self-help aid. 83% undergrads borrow to pay for school. Average cumulative indebtedness $34,998. **Criteria for awarding institutional aid:** *Non-need-based:* academics, alumni affiliation, minority status, religious affiliation, state/district residency.

MOUNT ST. MARY'S UNIVERSITY

16300 Old Emmitsburg Road, Emmitsburg, MD 21727
Phone: 301-447-5214 • **Financial Aid Phone:** 301-447-5207
E-mail: admissions@msmary.edu • **CEEB Code:** 5421
Fax: 301-447-5860 • **Website:** www.msmary.edu • **ACT Code:** 1726

This private school, affiliated with the Roman Catholic Church, was founded in 1808. It has a 1400-acre campus.

RATINGS

Admissions Selectivity Rating: 86   **Fire Safety Rating:** 83   **Green Rating:** 72

STUDENTS AND FACULTY

Enrollment: 1,831. **Student Body:** 55% female, 45% male, 48% out-of-state, 1% international (16 countries represented), Asian 2%, African American 10%, Caucasian 73%, Hispanic 9%, Native American 0%. **Retention and Graduation:** 80% freshmen return for sophomore year. 62% freshmen graduate within 4 years. 67% freshmen graduate within 6 years. 39% grads go on to further study within 1 year. 18% grads pursue arts and sciences degrees. 13% grads pursue business degrees. **Faculty:** Student/faculty ratio 14:1. 113 full-time faculty, 93% hold PhDs, 4% are members of minority groups, 43% are women. 0% of classes are taught by teaching assistants.

ACADEMICS

Degrees: bachelor's, master's, post-bachelor's certificate, post-master's certificate. **Classes:** Most classes have 20–29 students. Most lab/discussion sessions have 10–19 students. **Majors with Highest Enrollment:** business/commerce; communication studies/speech communication and rhetoric; elementary education and teaching. **Special Study Options:** Accelerated program, cross-registration, double major, dual enrollment, honors program, independent study, internships, liberal arts/career combination, student-designed major, study abroad, teacher certification program, weekend college, 3-2 with Johns Hopkins Univ. (BS in Biology; BS in Nursing) 3-3 with Sacred Heart Univ. (BS in Biology; Ph.D in PT) 4-2 with Sacred Heart Univ. (BS in Biology; MS in OT). **Honors Programs:** The Honors Program offers talented and motivated students an educational experience that integrates curricular, co-curricular, and extra-curricular learning in both interdisciplinary and major areas of study. **Combined Degree Programs:** BS Bio, BS Nursing; BS Bio, Ph.D PT; BS Bio, MS OT. **Disability Services:** Special programs offered to physically disabled students include note-taking services, reader services, tape recorders, tutors. **Career Services:** Alumni network, alumni services, career/job search classes, career assessment, internships Career Services highlights include The Mount's Internship Program provides excellent learning and networking experiences for either credit or non-credit. Internships are tailored to students' majors. 'Mount in Washington' offers full time internships in Washington D.C. The Career Center has also introduced International Internships to London, Dublin and Florence.

FACILITIES

Housing: Coed dorms, special housing for disabled students, apartments for single students, wellness housing, theme housing. 85% of campus accessible to physically disabled. **Special Academic Facilities/Equipment:** Historical art collection reflecting Catholic history in America and Marylandia. **Computers:** 100% of classrooms, 100% of dorms, 100% of libraries, 100% of dining areas, 100% of student union, 50% of common outdoor areas have wireless network access. Students can register for classes online. Administrative functions (other than registration) can be performed online.

CAMPUS LIFE

Environment: Rural. **Activities:** Choral groups, concert band, dance, drama/theater, jazz band, literary magazine, music ensembles, musical theater, pep band, radio station, student government, student newspaper, television station, yearbook, Campus Ministries, International Student Organization 68 registered organizations, 19 honor societies, 8 religious organizations. **Athletics (Intercollegiate):** *Men:* baseball, basketball, cross-country, golf, lacrosse, soccer, tennis, track/field (outdoor), track/field (indoor). *Women:* basketball, cross-country, golf, lacrosse, soccer, softball, swimming, tennis, track/field (outdoor), track/field (indoor). **On-Campus Highlights:** McGowan Student Center - Patriot Hall, Knott Athletic Recreation Convocation Complex, Knott Academic Center, Phillips Library, National Shrine Grotto of Lourdes. **Environmental Initiatives:** We have 1.1 MW photovoltaic panels being installed that will be online in summer 2012 and provide a substantial fraction of our electricity needs. Our newest dorm is a green building that uses groundwater-source geothermal heating and cooling. We have eliminated the coal-burning furnace and replaced it with a high-efficiency gas furnace. We are also decentralizing our heating/steam systems to prevent leaks and reduce transmission losses.

ADMISSIONS

Freshman Academic Profile: Average high school GPA 3.4. 17% in top 10% of high school class, 40% in top 25% of high school class, 73% in top 50% of high school class, 54% from public high schools. SAT Math middle 50% range 500-600. SAT Critical Reading middle 50% range 510-600. SAT Writing middle 50% range 490-600. ACT middle 50% range 19-23. Minimum web-based TOEFL 83. Minimum paper TOEFL 550. **Basis for Candidate Selection:** *Important factors considered include:* academic GPA, rigor of secondary school record, standardized test scores, extracurricular activities, talent/ability, volunteer work. *Other factors considered include:* application essay, recommendation(s), character/personal qualities, interview, level of applicant's interest, racial/ethnic status, work experience. **Freshman Admission Requirements:** High school diploma is required and GED is accepted. *Academic units required:* 4 English, 3 mathematics, 3 science, (2 science labs), 2 foreign language, 3 social studies, 1 academic electives. 4 English, 3 mathematics, 3 science, (2 science labs), 2 foreign language, 3 social studies, 1 academic electives. **Freshman Admission Statistics:** 5,283 applied, 55% admitted, 15% enrolled. **Transfer Admission Requirements:** college transcript(s), statement of good standing from prior institution(s). Minimum college GPA of 2.0 required. Lowest grade transferable C. **General Admission Information:** Application Fee $35. Notification on a rolling basis, beginning on or about 12/1. Nonfall registration accepted. Admission may be deferred for a maximum of 1 yr. Credit and/or placement offered for CEEB Advanced Placement tests.

COSTS AND FINANCIAL AID

Annual tuition $33,674. Room and board $11,514. Required fees $970. Average book expense $1,300. **Required Forms and Deadlines:** FAFSA, institution's own financial aid form. **Notification of Awards:** Applicants will be notified of awards on a rolling basis beginning 2/15. **Types of Aid:** *Need-based scholarships/grants:* Federal Pell, SEOG, state scholarships/grants, private scholarships, the school's own gift aid. *Loans:* Subsidized Stafford, Unsubsidized Stafford, PLUS, Federal Perkins. **Student Employment:** Federal Work-Study Program available. Institutional employment available. Off-campus job opportunities are fair. **Financial Aid Statistics:** 100% freshmen, 100% undergrads receive need-based scholarship or grant aid. 21% freshmen, 16% undergrads receive non-need-based scholarship or grant aid. 78% freshmen, 80% undergrads receive need-based self-help aid. 5% freshmen, 7% undergrads receive athletic scholarships. 99% freshmen, 98% undergrads receive any aid. 70% undergrads borrow to pay for school. Average cumulative indebtedness $32,311. **Criteria for awarding institutional aid:** *Non-need-based:* academics, art, athletics, leadership, minority status, music/drama.

MOUNT VERNON NAZARENE UNIVERSITY

800 Martinsburg Road, Mount Vernon, OH 43050
Phone: 740-392-6868 • **Financial Aid Phone:** 866-686-8243
E-mail: admissions@mvnu.edu • **CEEB Code:** 1531
Fax: 740-393-0511 • **Website:** www.mvnu.edu • **ACT Code:** 3372

This private school, affiliated with the Nazarene Church, was founded in 1964. It has a 401-acre campus.

RATINGS
Admissions Selectivity Rating: 73   **Fire Safety Rating:** 65   **Green Rating:** 66

STUDENTS AND FACULTY
Enrollment: 1,705. **Student Body:** 65% female, 35% male, 8% out-of-state, 0% international (5 countries represented). Asian 0%, African American 2%, Caucasian 64%, Hispanic 1%, Native American 0%. **Retention and Graduation:** 76% freshmen return for sophomore year. 46% freshmen graduate within 4 years. 55% freshmen graduate within 6 years. 16% grads go on to further study within 1 year. 7% grads pursue arts and sciences degrees. 1% grads pursue law degrees. 2% grads pursue business degrees. 4% grads pursue medical degrees. **Faculty:** Student/faculty ratio 13:1. 100 full-time faculty, 62% hold PhDs, 6% are members of minority groups, 39% are women. 0% of classes are taught by teaching assistants.

ACADEMICS
Degrees: associate, bachelor's, master's. **Classes:** Most classes have 10–19 students. **Majors with Highest Enrollment:** business/commerce; early childhood education and teaching; nursing/registered nurse (rn, asn, bsn, msn). **Special Study Options:** cooperative education program, cross-registration, distance learning, double major, dual enrollment, honors program, independent study, internships, liberal arts/career combination, study abroad, teacher certification program, Cooperative pre-engineering program with Olivet Nazarene University, cooperative pre-occupational therapy/physical therapy/physician's assistant programs with Chatham University, and articulation agreements with Columbus State Community College, Marion Technical College,Zane State College, Central Ohio Technical College, and North Central State College. Several opportunities for students to participate in service learning or mission trips. During the academic year, students may participate in one of the following trips: Germany, Hungary, Venezuela, Costa Rica, Nicaragua, Belize, Benin, Romania, or several out-of-state USA trips. **Honors Programs:** Honors Program for outstandning students is designed to provide rewarding challenges for the academically gifted. Specific courses, seminars, and other out-of-the ordinary experiences, both on and off campus, are offered by the Honors Program. A $250 scholarship the first year, increases to $400 in the fourth year. The Honors Program adds depth to your academic development and allows you to have input in designing your own curiculum by proposing study topics for Honors courses and by developing independent projects. You will work closely with a faculty mentor to complete an Honors Project in your major. There are also opportunities for off-campus culural enrichment and entertainment, including travel to musuems, ballet and music performances, or dinner theater. **Disability Services:** Special programs offered to physically disabled students include note-taking services, reader services, tape recorders, tutors. **Career Services:** alumni services, career/job search classes, career assessment Career Services highlights include Missions and ministry opportunities and study aboard.

FACILITIES
Housing: special housing for disabled students, men's dorms, women's dorms, apartments for single students, wellness housing. 95% of campus accessible to physically disabled. **Special Academic Facilities/Equipment:** Art gallery, nature reserve. **Computers:** 95% of classrooms, 5% of dorms, 100% of libraries, 100% of dining areas, 100% of student union, 10% of common outdoor areas have wireless network access. Administrative functions (other than registration) can be performed online.

CAMPUS LIFE
Environment: Rural. **Activities:** Choral groups, concert band, drama/theater, jazz band, literary magazine, music ensembles, musical theater, opera, pep band, radio station, student government, student newspaper, yearbook, Campus Ministries, International Student Organization 26 registered organizations, 4 honor societies, 16 religious organizations. **Athletics (Intercollegiate):** *Men:* baseball, basketball, cross-country, golf, soccer. *Women:* basketball, cross-country, soccer, softball, volleyball. **On-Campus Highlights:** The Prince Student Union, The Chapel, The Cafeteria, The Quad, The Grove. **Environmental Initiatives:** The President has made a public commitment for the University to minimize its "mark" on the environment. Dialogue on how to best develop a University-wide environmental stewardship plan has begun. The University does have an Environmental Stewardship Committee with faculty, staff, and student representation. The University is in the process of finalizing a com-prehensive environmental stewardship plan and has recent efforts to increase campus-wide recycling, and conversion of used vegetable oil into biodisel fuel.

ADMISSIONS
Freshman Academic Profile: Average high school GPA 3.3. 27% in top 10% of high school class, 51% in top 25% of high school class, 80% in top 50% of high school class. 74% from public high schools. SAT Math middle 50% range 470-590. SAT Critical Reading middle 50% range 440-590. ACT middle 50% range 20-27. Minimum web-based TOEFL 80. Minimum paper TOEFL 550. **Basis for Candidate Selection:** *Very important factors considered include:* academic GPA, standardized test scores. *Important factors considered include:* recommendation(s), rigor of secondary school record. *Other factors considered include:* application essay. **Freshman Admission Requirements:** High school diploma is required and GED is accepted. *Academic units required:* 2 foreign language. *Academic units recommended:* 2 foreign language. **Freshman Admission Statistics:** 1,000 applied, 73% admitted, 40% enrolled. **Transfer Admission Requirements:** High school transcript, college transcript(s), essay or personal statement, statement of good standing from prior institution(s). Minimum college GPA of 2.0 required. Lowest grade transferable C–. **General Admission Information:** Application Fee $25. Regular application deadline 7/15. Notification on a rolling basis, beginning on or about 9/1. Nonfall registration accepted. Admission may be deferred for a maximum of 1 year. Credit offered for CEEB Advanced Placement tests.

COSTS AND FINANCIAL AID
Annual tuition $23,690. Room and board $6,980. Average book expense $1,400. **Required Forms and Deadlines:** FAFSA, institution's own financial aid form. **Notification of Awards:** Applicants will be notified of awards on a rolling basis beginning 3/15. **Types of Aid:** *Need-based scholarships/grants:* Federal Pell, SEOG, state scholarships/grants, private scholarships, the school's own gift aid. *Loans:* Direct Subsidized Stafford, Direct Unsubsidized Stafford, Direct PLUS. **Student Employment:** Federal Work-Study Program available. Institutional employment available. Highest amount earned per year from on-campus jobs $5,866. Off-campus job opportunities are good. **Financial Aid Statistics:** 96% freshmen, 96% undergrads receive need-based scholarship or grant aid. 16% freshmen, 19% undergrads receive non-need-based scholarship or grant aid. 88% freshmen, 93% undergrads receive need-based self-help aid. 7% freshmen, 4% undergrads receive athletic scholarships. 100% freshmen, 88% undergrads receive any aid. 85% undergrads borrow to pay for school. Average cumulative indebtedness $25,313. **Criteria for awarding institutional aid:** *Non-need-based:* academics, athletics, minority status, music/drama, religious affiliation, state/district residency.

MOUNTAIN STATE UNIVERSITY

609 South Kanawha Street, Beckley, WV 25801
Phone: 304-929-4636 • **Financial Aid Phone:** 304-929-1595
E-mail: ThinkBigger@mountainstate.edu • **CEEB Code:** 5054
Fax: 304-253-3463 • **Website:** www.mountainstate.edu/ • **ACT Code:** 4510

This private school was founded in 1933. It has a 24-acre campus.

RATINGS
Admissions Selectivity Rating: 60*   **Fire Safety Rating:** 98   **Green Rating:** 65

STUDENTS AND FACULTY
Enrollment: 4,102. **Student Body:** 64% female, 36% male, 44% out-of-state, 3% international (29 countries represented). Asian 1%, African American 20%, Caucasian 67%, Hispanic 3%, Native American 1%. **Retention and Graduation:** 50% freshmen return for sophomore year. 4% freshmen graduate within 4 years. 12% freshmen graduate within 6 years. 15% grads go on to further study within 1 year. 5% grads pursue arts and sciences degrees. 2% grads pursue law degrees. 5% grads pursue business degrees. 2% grads pursue medical degrees. **Faculty:** Student/faculty ratio 19:1. 94 full-time faculty, 22% hold PhDs, 21% are members of minority groups, 83% are women. 0% of classes are taught by teaching assistants.

ACADEMICS
Degrees: associate, bachelor's, certificate, doctoral, master's, post-bachelor's certificate, post-master's certificate, terminal associate, transfer associate. **Classes:** Most classes have 10–19 students. Most lab/discussion sessions have fewer than 10 students. **Majors with Highest Enrollment:** business, management, marketing, and related support services, other; human resources management and services, other; nursing/registered nurse (rn, asn, bsn, msn). **Special Study Options:** Accelerated program, cooperative education program, cross-registration, distance learning, double major, dual enrollment, English as a Second Language (ESL), honors program, independent study, internships,

liberal arts/career combination, student-designed major, weekend college. **Honors Programs:** President's List and Dean's List. **Disability Services:** Special programs offered to physically disabled students include note-taking services, reader services, tape recorders, tutors. **Career Services:** Alumni network, career/job search classes, career assessment, internships Career Services highlights include Internships/Practicum - Qualified bachelor's degree students have an opportunity to work directly in their field of concentration.

FACILITIES

Housing: Coed dorms, Off Campus Housing for Athletes. 80% of campus accessible to physically disabled. **Special Academic Facilities/Equipment:** Robert C. Byrd Learning Resources Center, Botanical Gardens and Greenhouse **Computers:** 90% of classrooms, 100% of libraries, 50% of dining areas, have wireless network access. Students can register for classes online. Administrative functions (other than registration) can be performed online.

CAMPUS LIFE

Environment: Village. **Activities:** Choral groups, drama/theater, literary magazine, music ensembles, pep band, student government, Campus Ministries, International Student Organization 24 registered organizations, 4 honor societies, 3 religious organizations. 1 fraternities, 1 sororities. **Athletics (Intercollegiate):** *Men:* basketball, cross-country, soccer, track/field (outdoor). *Women:* cheerleading, cross-country, soccer, softball, track/field (outdoor), volleyball. **On-Campus Highlights:** Cougar Den, Learning Resources Center (LRC), John W. Eye Conference Center (JWE), Culinary Arts building, Hogan Hall, Medicinal Botanical Greenhouse.

ADMISSIONS

Freshman Academic Profile: Average high school GPA 2.8. 3% in top 10% of high school class, 11% in top 25% of high school class, 39% in top 50% of high school class. Minimum web-based TOEFL 61. Minimum paper TOEFL 500. **Basis for Candidate Selection:** *Very important factors considered include:* Class rank, application essay, academic GPA, recommendation(s), rigor of secondary school record, standardized test scores, alumni/ae relation, character/personal qualities, extracurricular activities, first generation, geographical residence, interview, level of applicant's interest, racial/ethnic status, religious affiliation/commitment, state residency, talent/ability, volunteer work, work experience. **Freshman Admission Requirements:** High school diploma is required and GED is accepted. *Academic units required:* 4 English, 2 mathematics, 2 science, (2 science labs), 3 social studies. *Academic units recommended:* 4 English, 2 mathematics, 2 science, (2 science labs), 3 social studies. **Freshman Admission Statistics:** 1,611 applied, 100% admitted, 32% enrolled. **Transfer Admission Requirements:** college transcript(s), Lowest grade transferable C. **General Admission Information:** Application Fee $25. Nonfall registration accepted. Admission may be deferred for a maximum of One Semester. Credit offered for CEEB Advanced Placement tests.

COSTS AND FINANCIAL AID

Annual tuition $7,350. Room and board $7,526. Required fees $2,250. Average book expense $2,000. **Required Forms and Deadlines:** FAFSA. **Notification of Awards:** Applicants will be notified of awards on a rolling basis beginning 4/1. **Types of Aid:** *Need-based scholarships/grants:* Federal Pell, SEOG, state scholarships/grants, private scholarships, the school's own gift aid, Federal Nursing Scholarships. *Loans:* Subsidized Stafford, Unsubsidized Stafford, PLUS, Private Educational Loans. **Student Employment:** Federal Work-Study Program available. Institutional employment available. Highest amount earned per year from on-campus jobs $1,600. Off-campus job opportunities are good. **Financial Aid Statistics:** 88% freshmen, 65% undergrads receive need-based scholarship or grant aid. 2% freshmen, 1% undergrads receive non-need-based scholarship or grant aid. 85% freshmen, 85% undergrads receive need-based self-help aid. 3% freshmen, 2% undergrads receive athletic scholarships. 50% freshmen, 54% undergrads receive any aid. 73% undergrads borrow to pay for school. Average cumulative indebtedness $36,187. **Criteria for awarding institutional aid:** *Non-need-based:* academics, athletics, state/district residency.

MUHLENBERG COLLEGE

2400 West Chew Street, Allentown, PA 18104-5596
Phone: 484-664-3200 • **Financial Aid Phone:** 484-664-3175
E-mail: admission@muhlenberg.edu • **CEEB Code:** 2424
Fax: 484-664-3234 • **Website:** www.muhlenberg.edu • **ACT Code:** 3640

This private school, affiliated with the Lutheran Church, was founded in 1848. It has a 81-acre campus.

RATINGS
Admissions Selectivity Rating: 93   **Fire Safety Rating:** 90   **Green Rating:** 77

STUDENTS AND FACULTY

Enrollment: 2,384. **Student Body:** 58% female, 42% male, 78% out-of-state, 0% international (7 countries represented). Asian 3%, African American 3%, Caucasian 76%, Hispanic 4%, Native American 0%. **Retention and Graduation:** 90% freshmen return for sophomore year. 79% freshmen graduate within 4 years. 86% freshmen graduate within 6 years. 32% grads go on to further study within 1 year. 17% grads pursue arts and sciences degrees. 5% grads pursue law degrees. 1% grads pursue business degrees. 6% grads pursue medical degrees. **Faculty:** Student/faculty ratio 12:1. 172 full-time faculty, 89% hold PhDs, 5% are members of minority groups, 50% are women. 0% of classes are taught by teaching assistants.

ACADEMICS

Degrees: associate, bachelor's, certificate, transfer associate. **Classes:** Most classes have 10–19 students. Most lab/discussion sessions have 10–19 students. **Majors with Highest Enrollment:** business/commerce; communication studies/speech communication and rhetoric; psychology. **Special Study Options:** Accelerated program, cross-registration, double major, exchange student program (domestic), honors program, independent study, internships, student-designed major, study abroad, teacher certification program. **Honors Programs:** Muhlenberg Scholar, Dana Associate, R J Fellow (each provides a $4,000 annual stipend, dedicated freshman seminar, and mentored research) **Combined Degree Programs:** BA/MD, BA/DDS, BA/DDS University of Pennsylvania, BS/MD Drexel Un. **Disability Services:** Special programs offered to physically disabled students include note-taking services, tutors. **Career Services:** Alumni network, alumni services, career/job search classes, career assessment, internships, regional alumni. Career Services highlights include The Muhlenberg Shadow Program matches students with alumni in their field of interest to spend a day on the job over winter break. Students are able to learn first-hand about career options of interest to them, and alumni enjoy the feeling of helping a student and remembering why they enjoy their jobs.

FACILITIES

Housing: Coed dorms, special housing for disabled students, special housing for international students, women's dorms, fraternity/sorority housing, apartments for single students, College-owned houses in the neighborhood surrounding the campus. 95% of campus accessible to physically disabled. **Special Academic Facilities/Equipment:** Martin art gallery, biology museum, Graver arboretum, greenhouse, mainstage theatre, recital hall, 20-foot boat for marine studies, 40-acre Raker environmental field station, two electron microscopes, dance studios, experimental theatres, proscenium theatres. **Computers:** 10% of classrooms, 20% of dorms, 100% of libraries, 100% of dining areas, 100% of student union, 10% of common outdoor areas have wireless network access. Students can register for classes online. Administrative functions (other than registration) can be performed online.

CAMPUS LIFE

Environment: City. **Activities:** concert band, dance, drama/theater, jazz band, literary magazine, music ensembles, musical theater, pep band, radio station, student government, student newspaper, student-run film society, symphony orchestra, yearbook 100 registered organizations, 12 honor societies, 7 religious organizations. 4 fraternities, 4 sororities. **Athletics (Intercollegiate):** *Men:* baseball, basketball, cheerleading, cross-country, football, golf, lacrosse, soccer, tennis, track/field (outdoor), track/field (indoor), wrestling. *Women:* basketball, cheerleading, cross-country, field hockey, golf, lacrosse, soccer, softball, tennis, track/field (outdoor), track/field (indoor), volleyball. **On-Campus Highlights:** Seegers Union by fireplace & Java Joe's, The Life Sports Center-Athletic Facility, Parents Plaza-Outdoor Courtyard, GQ, Seegers Union, Trexler Pavilion for Threatre & Dance. **Environmental Initiatives:** Sustainability programming including creation of a community garden, bike share program and sustainability house Completion of new construction and renovations incorporating sustainable technology including energy and water conservation and significant materials recycling. Large scale 5 year plan to recalibrate all campus buildings resulting from energy audit. Energy conservation and greenhouse gas reduction plan is in progress, buildings sub-metered.

ADMISSIONS

Freshman Academic Profile: Average high school GPA 3.3. 51% in top 10% of high school class, 78% in top 25% of high school class, 96% in top 50% of high school class. 72% from public high schools. SAT Math middle 50% range 560-670. SAT Critical Reading middle 50% range 560-670. SAT Writing middle 50% range 560-670. ACT middle 50% range 25-31. Minimum paper TOEFL 550. **Basis for Candidate Selection:** *Very important factors considered include:* academic GPA, rigor of secondary school record. *Important factors considered include:* application essay, recommendation(s), standardized test scores, character/personal qualities, extracurricular activities, interview, talent/ability. *Other factors considered include:* Class rank, alumni/ae relation, first generation, level of applicant's interest, racial/ethnic status, volunteer work, work experience. **Freshman Admission Requirements:** High school diploma is required and GED is accepted. *Academic units required:* 4 English, 3 mathematics, 2 science, 2 foreign language, 2 history. *Academic units recommended:* 4 English, 3 mathematics, 2 science, 2 foreign language, 2 history. **Freshman Admission Statistics:** 4,876 applied, 43% admitted, 28% enrolled. **Transfer Admission Requirements:** High school transcript, college transcript(s), essay or personal statement, interview, standardized test scores, statement of good standing from prior institution(s). Minimum college GPA of 2.5 required. Lowest grade transferable C. **General Admission Information:** Application Fee $50. Early decision application deadline 2/1. Regular application deadline 2/15. Regular notification 4/1. Nonfall registration accepted. Admission may be deferred for a maximum of 1 year. Credit and/or placement offered for CEEB Advanced Placement tests.

COSTS AND FINANCIAL AID

Annual tuition $41,225. Room and board $9,355. Required fees $285. Average book expense $1,295. **Required Forms and Deadlines:** FAFSA, institution's own financial aid form, CSS/Financial Aid PROFILE, noncustodial PROFILE. **Notification of Awards:** Applicants will be notified of awards on or about 4/1. **Types of Aid:** *Need-based scholarships/grants:* Federal Pell, SEOG, state scholarships/grants, private scholarships, the school's own gift aid. *Loans:* Subsidized Stafford, Unsubsidized Stafford, PLUS, Federal Perkins, Private. **Student Employment:** Federal Work-Study Program available. Institutional employment available. Highest amount earned per year from on-campus jobs $1,800. Off-campus job opportunities are excellent. **Financial Aid Statistics:** 95% freshmen, 93% undergrads receive need-based scholarship or grant aid. 27% freshmen, 20% undergrads receive non-need-based scholarship or grant aid. 69% freshmen, 74% undergrads receive need-based self-help aid. 83% freshmen, 81% undergrads receive any aid. 64% undergrads borrow to pay for school. Average cumulative indebtedness $26,270. **Criteria for awarding institutional aid:** *Non-need-based:* academics, art, leadership, music/drama.

MULTNOMAH BIBLE COLLEGE AND BIBLICAL SEMINARY

8435 NE Glisan Street, Portland, OR 97220-5898
Phone: 503-251-6485 • **Financial Aid Phone:** 503-251-5335
E-mail: admiss@multnomah.edu
Fax: 503-254-1268 • **Website:** www.multnomah.edu/

This private school, affiliated with the Christian (Nondenominational) Church, was founded in 1936. It has a 25-acre campus.

RATINGS

Admissions Selectivity Rating: 79   **Fire Safety Rating:** 61   **Green Rating:** 60*

STUDENTS AND FACULTY

Enrollment: 503. **Student Body:** 40% female, 60% male, 50% out-of-state, 1% international (13 countries represented). Asian 2%, African American 3%, Caucasian 78%, Hispanic 6%, Native American 0%.
Retention and Graduation: 60% freshmen return for sophomore year. 20% freshmen graduate within 4 years. 41% freshmen graduate within 6 years.
Faculty: Student/faculty ratio 115:1. 33 full-time faculty, 82% hold PhDs, 12% are women. 0% of classes are taught by teaching assistants.

ACADEMICS

Degrees: bachelor's, master's, post-bachelor's certificate. **Classes:** Most classes have fewer than 10 students. Most lab/discussion sessions have 10–19 students. **Majors with Highest Enrollment:** bible/biblical studies. **Special Study Options:** cooperative education program, distance learning, double major, internships, liberal arts/career combination, teacher certification program. **Career Services:** career/job search classes, career assessment

FACILITIES

Housing: special housing for disabled students, men's dorms, women's dorms, apartments for married students, apartments for single students, Houses for students with spouses or dependents. **Computers:** 100% of classrooms, 100% of dorms, 100% of libraries, 100% of dining areas, 30% of common outdoor areas have wireless network access. Students can register for classes online. Administrative functions (other than registration) can be performed online.

CAMPUS LIFE

Environment: Metropolis. **Activities:** Choral groups, drama/theater, music ensembles, student government, student newspaper. **Athletics (Intercollegiate):** *Men:* basketball. *Women:* volleyball. **On-Campus Highlights:** Solid Rock Cafe, A-Frame Community Lounge, STUGO Game Room, Cafeteria, Commuter Lounge, The Solid Rock Cafe, STUGO Game Room and cafeteria are all centrally located in our JCA Student Center along with a computer lab, post-office, and health center.

ADMISSIONS

Freshman Academic Profile: Average high school GPA 3.1. 0% in top 10% of high school class, 22% in top 25% of high school class, 100% in top 50% of high school class. SAT Math middle 50% range 460-590. SAT Critical Reading middle 50% range 490-610. SAT Writing middle 50% range 450-570. ACT middle 50% range 20-24. Minimum paper TOEFL 550. **Basis for Candidate Selection:** *Very important factors considered include:* academic GPA, recommendation(s), rigor of secondary school record, standardized test scores, religious affiliation/commitment. *Important factors considered include:* application essay, character/personal qualities. *Other factors considered include:* Class rank, alumni/ae relation, extracurricular activities, talent/ability, volunteer work, work experience. **Freshman Admission Requirements:** High school diploma is required and GED is accepted. **Freshman Admission Statistics:** 118 applied, 64% admitted, 43% enrolled. **Transfer Admission Requirements:** college transcript(s), essay or personal statement, statement of good standing from prior institution(s). Minimum college GPA of 2.0 required. Lowest grade transferable C–. **General Admission Information:** Application Fee $40. Regular application deadline 7/15. Notification on a rolling basis, beginning on or about 9/1. Nonfall registration accepted. Admission may be deferred for a maximum of one semester. Credit offered for CEEB Advanced Placement tests.

COSTS AND FINANCIAL AID

Annual tuition $20,990. Room and board $7,200. Required fees $50. Average book expense $1,000. **Required Forms and Deadlines:** FAFSA, institution's own financial aid form. **Notification of Awards:** Applicants will be notified of awards on a rolling basis beginning 4/1. **Types of Aid:** *Need-based scholarships/grants:* Federal Pell, SEOG, private scholarships, the school's own gift aid. *Loans:* Direct Subsidized Stafford, Subsidized Stafford, Unsubsidized Stafford, PLUS. **Student Employment:** Federal Work-Study Program available. Institutional employment available. Off-campus job opportunities are good. **Financial Aid Statistics:** 91% freshmen, 89% undergrads receive need-based scholarship or grant aid. 2% freshmen, 1% undergrads receive non-need-based scholarship or grant aid. 88% freshmen, 91% undergrads receive need-based self-help aid. 48% freshmen, 89% undergrads receive any aid. 74% undergrads borrow to pay for school. Average cumulative indebtedness $23,000. **Criteria for awarding institutional aid:** *Non-need-based:* academics, alumni affiliation, leadership, music/drama.

MURRAY STATE UNIVERSITY

102 Curris Center, Murray, KY 42071-0009
Phone: 270-809-3741 • **Financial Aid Phone:** 270-809-2546
E-mail: Admissions@murraystate.edu • **CEEB Code:** 1494
Fax: 270-809-3780 • **Website:** www.murraystate.edu • **ACT Code:** 1532

This public school was founded in 1922. It has a 350-acre campus.

RATINGS

Admissions Selectivity Rating: 69   **Fire Safety Rating:** 83   **Green Rating:** 74

STUDENTS AND FACULTY

Enrollment: 7,849. **Student Body:** 58% female, 42% male, 29% out-of-state, 3% international (51 countries represented). Asian 1%, African American 8%, Caucasian 83%, Hispanic 2%, Native American 0%.
Retention and Graduation: 70% freshmen return for sophomore year. 26% freshmen graduate within 4 years. 52% freshmen graduate within 6 years.
Faculty: Student/faculty ratio 16:1. 423 full-time faculty, 81% hold PhDs, 9% are members of minority groups, 41% are women.

ACADEMICS

Degrees: associate, bachelor's, master's, post-master's certificate. **Classes:** Most classes have fewer than 10 students. Most lab/discussion sessions have

10–19 students. **Majors with Highest Enrollment:** business/commerce; elementary education and teaching; nursing/registered nurse (rn, asn, bsn, msn). **Special Study Options:** Accelerated program, cooperative education program, cross-registration, distance learning, double major, dual enrollment, English as a Second Language (ESL), exchange student program (domestic), external degree program, honors program, independent study, internships, study abroad, teacher certification program, weekend college, agriculture, arts, business/marketing, biological sciences, communications/communication technologies, computer and information sciences, education, engineering/engineering technologies, English, foreign languages, health professions and related sciences, history, home economics, humanities and liberal arts, library sciences, mathematics, natural resources and environmental sciences, natural sciences, parks and recreation, philosophy, physical sciences, protective sciences/public administration, psychology, social/behavioral sciences, technologies, trade and industry, visual and performing arts. **Honors Programs:** The Honors Program offers a unique educational experience designed to teach able students how to learn, how to think critically and creatively, and how to communicate effectively. **Combined Degree Programs:** engineering program w/ U of L. and U. of Ky. **Disability Services:** Special programs offered to physically disabled students include note-taking services, tape recorders, tutors. **Career Services:** Alumni network, alumni services, career/job search classes, career assessment, internships, regional alumni.

FACILITIES

Housing: Coed dorms, special housing for disabled students, men's dorms, women's dorms, fraternity/sorority housing, apartments for married students, apartments for single studentsAll housing is operated under a Residential College system. 96% of campus accessible to physically disabled. **Special Academic Facilities/Equipment:** State-of-the-art 73000 square-foot Student Recreation and Wellness Center nestled in the Residential College housing complex, West Kentucky Museum,8,500 seat Regional Special Events Center **Computers:** 95% of classrooms, 90% of dorms, 100% of libraries, 100% of dining areas, 100% of student union, have wireless network access. Students can register for classes online. Administrative functions (other than registration) can be performed online.

CAMPUS LIFE

Environment: Village. **Activities:** Choral groups, concert band, dance, drama/theater, jazz band, literary magazine, marching band, music ensembles, musical theater, pep band, radio station, student government, student newspaper, student-run film society, symphony orchestra, television station, yearbook, Campus Ministries, International Student Organization 175 registered organizations, 30 honor societies, 15 religious organizations. 15 fraternities, 7 sororities. **Athletics (Intercollegiate):** *Men:* baseball, basketball, bowling, cheerleading, cross-country, equestrian sports, football, golf, horseback riding, riflery, rodeo, tennis. *Women:* basketball, cheerleading, cross-country, equestrian sports, golf, horseback riding, riflery, rodeo, soccer, softball, tennis, track/field (outdoor), volleyball. **On-Campus Highlights:** New Student Fitness Center, Curris Student Center, Regional Special Events Center, Equine Center, Residential Colleges. **Environmental Initiatives:** Installation of Voltage Regulation System (Campus wide)conserving 2.1861 of energy annually. Renewable Fuels, BioDiesel, g-35, e-10 Recycling Program Diverting 40% of waste stream from landfill.

ADMISSIONS

Freshman Academic Profile: Average high school GPA 3.5. 17% in top 10% of high school class, 41% in top 25% of high school class, 75% in top 50% of high school class. 80% from public high schools. ACT middle 50% range 21-25. Minimum paper TOEFL 500. **Basis for Candidate Selection:** *Very important factors considered include:* Class rank, academic GPA, rigor of secondary school record, standardized test scores. *Important factors considered include:* alumni/ae relation, talent/ability. *Other factors considered include:* character/personal qualities, extracurricular activities, geographical residence, interview, racial/ethnic status, state residency, volunteer work, work experience. **Freshman Admission Requirements:** High school diploma is required and GED is accepted. *Academic units required:* 4 English, 3 mathematics, 3 science, (1 science labs), 2 foreign language, 3 social studies, 5 academic electives, 2 Art Appreciation, 1/2 PE, 1/2Health. *Academic units recommended:* 4 English, 3 mathematics, 3 science, (1 science labs), 2 foreign language, 3 social studies, 5 academic electives, 2 Art Appreciation, 1/2 PE, 1/2Health **Freshman Admission Statistics:** 4,573 applied, 82% admitted, 43% enrolled. **Transfer Admission Requirements:** college transcript(s), statement of good standing from prior institution(s). Minimum college GPA of 2.0 required. Lowest grade transferable d. **General Admission Information:** Application Fee $30. Regular application deadline 8/3. Nonfall registration accepted. Admission may be deferred for a maximum of 1 year. Credit offered for CEEB Advanced Placement tests.

COSTS AND FINANCIAL AID

Annual in-state tuition $5,880. Annual out-of-state tuition $7,942. Room and board $7,638. Required fees $960. Average book expense $990. **Required Forms and Deadlines:** FAFSA, institution's own financial aid form. **Notification of Awards:** Applicants will be notified of awards on a rolling basis beginning 4/15. **Types of Aid:** *Need-based scholarships/grants:* Federal Pell, SEOG, state scholarships/grants, private scholarships, the school's own gift aid, Federal Nursing Scholarships. A wide variety of private and Foundation scholarships available. Check out the website www.murraystate.edu. *Loans:* Direct Subsidized Stafford, Direct Unsubsidized Stafford, Direct PLUS, Subsidized Stafford, Unsubsidized Stafford, PLUS, Federal Perkins, Federal Nursing, state loans, college/university loans from institutional funds. **Student Employment:** Federal Work-Study Program available. Institutional employment available. Highest amount earned per year from on-campus jobs $3,500. Off-campus job opportunities are good. **Financial Aid Statistics:** 92% freshmen, 86% undergrads receive need-based scholarship or grant aid. 11% freshmen, 6% undergrads receive non-need-based scholarship or grant aid. 61% freshmen, 78% undergrads receive need-based self-help aid. 3% freshmen, 3% undergrads receive athletic scholarships. 88% freshmen, 82% undergrads receive any aid. 47% undergrads borrow to pay for school. Average cumulative indebtedness $20,644. **Criteria for awarding institutional aid:** *Non-need-based:* academics, alumni affiliation, art, athletics, job skills, leadership, minority status, music/drama, state/district residency.

MUSICIANS INSTITUTE

1655 McCadden Place, Hollywood, CA 90028
Phone: 323-462-1384 • **Financial Aid Phone:** 323-462-1121
E-mail: admissions@mi.edu
Fax: 323-462-6978

This private school was founded in 1977.

RATINGS

Admissions Selectivity Rating: 61   **Fire Safety Rating:** 60*   **Green Rating:** 60*

STUDENTS AND FACULTY

Enrollment: 489. **Student Body:** Asian 11%, African American 7%, Caucasian 56%, Hispanic 12%, Native American 0%.
Faculty: 69 full-time faculty, 0% hold PhDs, 14% are members of minority groups, 16% are women.

ACADEMICS

Degrees: associate, bachelor's, certificate. **Majors with Highest Enrollment:** general studies; multi-/interdisciplinary studies, other. **Career Services:** Alumni network, internships.

FACILITIES

Housing: Musicians Institute's Housing Services department assists students and their parents in locating safe, comfortable, affordable, and accessible off-campus housing. MI does not own or operate student housing, but Housing Services manages a vacancy listing service for housing in a variety of locations ad difference price levels.

CAMPUS LIFE

Environment: Metropolis.

ADMISSIONS

Basis for Candidate Selection: *Very important factors considered include:* level of applicant's interest, talent/ability. *Important factors considered include:* recommendation(s), character/personal qualities, extracurricular activities, interview, work experience. *Other factors considered include:* Class rank, application essay, academic GPA, rigor of secondary school record, standardized test scores, alumni/ae relation, first generation, volunteer work. **Freshman Admission Requirements:** High school diploma is required and GED is accepted. **Freshman Admission Statistics:** 1,057 applied, 98% admitted, 64% enrolled. **Transfer Admission Requirements:** college transcript(s), essay or personal statement, minimum college GPA of 2.0 required. Lowest grade transferable C. **General Admission Information:** Application Fee $100. Notification on a rolling basis, beginning on or about 10/1. Nonfall registration accepted. Admission may be deferred for a maximum of 1 year.

COSTS AND FINANCIAL AID

Annual tuition $15,250. Required fees $400. **Required Forms and Deadlines:** FAFSA. **Types of Aid:** *Need-based scholarships/grants:* Federal Pell, SEOG, state scholarships/grants, private scholarships. *Loans:* Subsidized Stafford, Unsubsidized Stafford, PLUS, Alternative loans. **Student Employment:** **Financial Aid Statistics:** 44% freshmen, 66% undergrads receive need-based scholarship or grant aid. 32% freshmen, 60% undergrads receive need-based self-help aid. 25% undergrads borrow to pay for school.

MUSKINGUM COLLEGE

163 Stormont Street, New Concord, OH 43762
Phone: 740-826-8137 • **Financial Aid Phone:** 740-826-8137
E-mail: jzellers@muskingum.edu • **CEEB Code:** 1496
Fax: 614-826-8100 • **ACT Code:** 3305

This private school, affiliated with the Presbyterian Church, was founded in 1837. It has a 245-acre campus.

RATINGS
Admissions Selectivity Rating: 69   **Fire Safety Rating:** 60*   **Green Rating:** 60*

STUDENTS AND FACULTY
Enrollment: 1,697. **Student Body:** 52% female, 48% male, 9% out-of-state, 3% international (10 countries represented). Asian 1%, African American 6%, Caucasian 83%, Hispanic 1%, Native American 0%.
Retention and Graduation: 71% freshmen return for sophomore year. 41% freshmen graduate within 4 years. 54% freshmen graduate within 6 years. 24% grads go on to further study within 1 year. 8% grads pursue arts and sciences degrees. 3% grads pursue law degrees. 4% grads pursue business degrees. 2% grads pursue medical degrees. **Faculty:** Student/faculty ratio 14:1. 101 full-time faculty, 89% hold PhDs, 13% are members of minority groups, 45% are women. 0% of classes are taught by teaching assistants.

ACADEMICS
Degrees: bachelor's, master's. **Classes:** Most classes have fewer than 10 students. Most lab/discussion sessions have 20–29 students. **Majors with Highest Enrollment:** business/commerce; early childhood education and teaching; psychology. **Special Study Options:** Accelerated program, distance learning, double major, dual enrollment, English as a Second Language (ESL), exchange student program (domestic), independent study, internships, liberal arts/career combination, student-designed major, study abroad, teacher certification program, weekend college. **Combined Degree Programs:** BA/MEng, BA,BS,MAE. **Disability Services:** Special programs offered to physically disabled students include note-taking services, reader services, tape recorders, tutors. **Career Services:** Alumni network, alumni services, career assessment, internships, regional alumni. Career Services highlights include Muskingum Leadership Initiative - alumni identify relevant national and regional internships and communicate those opportunities to Muskingum students and faculty.

FACILITIES
Housing: Coed dorms, men's dorms, women's dorms, fraternity/sorority housing, cooperative housing, apartments for single students, theme housing. 50% of campus accessible to physically disabled. **Special Academic Facilities/Equipment:** Art gallery, on-campus nursery school, electron microscope, 57-acre biology field station and mobile biology lab. **Computers:** 15% of classrooms, 100% of libraries, 33% of dining areas, 100% of student union, 10% of common outdoor areas have wireless network access. Students can register for classes online. Administrative functions (other than registration) can be performed online.

CAMPUS LIFE
Environment: Rural. **Activities:** Choral groups, concert band, dance, drama/theater, jazz band, literary magazine, marching band, music ensembles, musical theater, pep band, radio station, student government, student newspaper, symphony orchestra, television station, yearbook, Campus Ministries, International Student Organization, Model UN 95 registered organizations, 16 honor societies, 4 religious organizations. 5 fraternities, 5 sororities. **Athletics (Intercollegiate):** *Men:* baseball, basketball, cheerleading, cross-country, football, golf, soccer, tennis, track/field (outdoor), track/field (indoor), wrestling. *Women:* basketball, cheerleading, cross-country, golf, soccer, softball, tennis, track/field (outdoor), track/field (indoor), volleyball. **On-Campus Highlights:** Philip and Betsey Caldwell Hall, Boyd Science Center, Rec Center, Patton Dining Center/Kelly Coffee House, Walter K. Chess Student Center, New music classroom building opening Fall 2010.

ADMISSIONS
Freshman Academic Profile: Average high school GPA 3.2. 18% in top 10% of high school class, 43% in top 25% of high school class, 70% in top 50% of high school class. 92% from public high schools. SAT Math middle 50% range 430-560. SAT Critical Reading middle 50% range 420-560. SAT Writing middle 50% range 430-540. ACT middle 50% range 19-24. Minimum web-based TOEFL 79. Minimum paper TOEFL 550. **Basis for Candidate Selection:** *Very important factors considered include:* academic GPA, rigor of secondary school record. *Important factors considered include:* Class rank, recommendation(s), standardized test scores. *Other factors considered include:* application essay, alumni/ae relation, character/personal qualities, extracurricular activities, geographical residence, interview, racial/ethnic status, talent/ability, work experience. **Freshman Admission Requirements:** High school diploma is required and GED is accepted. *Academic units required:* 4 English,

2 mathematics, 2 science, (1 science labs), 2 foreign language, 1 social studies, 2 history. *Academic units recommended:* 4 English, 2 mathematics, 2 science, (1 science labs), 2 foreign language, 1 social studies, 2 history. **Freshman Admission Statistics:** 2,101 applied, 77% admitted, 26% enrolled. **Transfer Admission Requirements:** High school transcript, college transcript(s), minimum college GPA of 2.0 required. Lowest grade transferable C. **General Admission Information:** Regular application deadline 8/1. Notification on a rolling basis, beginning on or about 10/1. Nonfall registration accepted. Admission may be deferred for a maximum of 1 year. Credit and/or placement offered for CEEB Advanced Placement tests.

COSTS AND FINANCIAL AID
Annual tuition $22,000. Room and board $8,950. Required fees $766. Average book expense $1,100. **Required Forms and Deadlines:** FAFSA. **Notification of Awards:** Applicants will be notified of awards on a rolling basis beginning 3/1. **Types of Aid:** *Need-based scholarships/grants:* Federal Pell, SEOG, state scholarships/grants, private scholarships, the school's own gift aid. *Loans:* Subsidized Stafford, Unsubsidized Stafford, PLUS, Federal Perkins, college/university loans from institutional funds. **Student Employment:** Federal Work-Study Program available. Institutional employment available. Highest amount earned per year from on-campus jobs $1,500. Off-campus job opportunities are fair. **Financial Aid Statistics:** 100% freshmen, 100% undergrads receive need-based scholarship or grant aid. 93% freshmen, 92% undergrads receive non-need-based scholarship or grant aid. 90% freshmen, 89% undergrads receive need-based self-help aid. 98% freshmen, 98% undergrads receive any aid. 78% undergrads borrow to pay for school. Average cumulative indebtedness $31,513. **Criteria for awarding institutional aid:** *Non-need-based:* academics, alumni affiliation, art, leadership, minority status, music/drama, religious affiliation, state/district residency.

NAROPA UNIVERSITY

2130 Araphahoe Avenue, Boulder, CO 80302
Phone: 303-546-3572 • **Financial Aid Phone:** 303-546-3534
E-mail: admissions@naropa.edu • **CEEB Code:** 908
Fax: 303-546-3583 • **Website:** www.naropa.edu/ • **ACT Code:** 4853

This private school was founded in 1974. It has a 12-acre campus.

RATINGS
Admissions Selectivity Rating: 61   **Fire Safety Rating:** 61   **Green Rating:** 94

STUDENTS AND FACULTY
Enrollment: 464. **Student Body:** 61% female, 39% male, 74% out-of-state, 3% international (24 countries represented). Asian 3%, African American 2%, Caucasian 75%, Hispanic 4%, Native American 3%.
Retention and Graduation: 64% freshmen return for sophomore year. 19% freshmen graduate within 4 years. 42% freshmen graduate within 6 years. **Faculty:** Student/faculty ratio 9:1. 51 full-time faculty, 51% hold PhDs, 12% are members of minority groups, 57% are women. 0% of classes are taught by teaching assistants.

ACADEMICS
Degrees: bachelor's, certificate, first professional, master's. **Classes:** Most classes have 10–19 students. **Majors with Highest Enrollment:** English language and literature; psychology; visual and performing arts. **Special Study Options:** double major, independent study, internships, student-designed major, study abroad, Some courses available on-line. **Disability Services:** Special programs offered to physically disabled students include note-taking services, reader services, tape recorders, tutors.

FACILITIES
Housing: apartments for married students, apartments for single students, themed housing (living and learning concept). 85% of campus accessible to physically disabled. **Special Academic Facilities/Equipment:** Maitri Rooms, meditation halls, Allen Ginsberg library and a preschool. **Computers:** 100% of classrooms, 100% of dorms, 100% of libraries, 100% of dining areas, 100% of student union, 100% of common outdoor areas have wireless network access. Students can register for classes online. Administrative functions (other than registration) can be performed online.

CAMPUS LIFE
Environment: City. **Activities:** Choral groups, dance, drama/theater, jazz band, literary magazine, music ensembles, student government 20 registered organizations, 2 religious organizations.**On-Campus Highlights:** Lincoln Building, Nalanda Event Center, Meditation Hall, Naropa Cafe, Visual Arts Studio. **Environmental Initiatives:** We compost all of our paper towels in public restrooms diverting 25% of our landfill waste into compost. The cafÃ©

composts which will divert 20-25% of organics into compost from the landfill. CFL installed in the residential halls, and are converting burned out bulbs to green bulbs throughout the campuses.

ADMISSIONS

Freshman Academic Profile: Average high school GPA 3.0. Minimum paper TOEFL 550. **Basis for Candidate Selection:** *Very important factors considered include:* application essay, academic GPA, recommendation(s), rigor of secondary school record, interview. *Important factors considered include:* character/personal qualities, extracurricular activities, talent/ability, volunteer work. *Other factors considered include:* alumni/ae relation, first generation, racial/ethnic status, work experience. **Freshman Admission Requirements:** High school diploma is required and GED is accepted. **Freshman Admission Statistics:** 139 applied, 93% admitted, 53% enrolled. **Transfer Admission Requirements:** college transcript(s), essay or personal statement, interview, Lowest grade transferable C. **General Admission Information:** Application Fee $50. Nonfall registration accepted. Admission may be deferred for a maximum of 1 year. Credit and/or placement offered for CEEB Advanced Placement tests.

COSTS AND FINANCIAL AID

Annual tuition $23,420. Room and board $8,478. Required fees $100. Average book expense $1,200. **Required Forms and Deadlines:** FAFSA. **Notification of Awards:** Applicants will be notified of awards on a rolling basis beginning 3/1. **Types of Aid:** *Need-based scholarships/grants:* Federal Pell, SEOG, private scholarships, the school's own gift aid. *Loans:* Subsidized Stafford, Unsubsidized Stafford, PLUS, Federal Perkins. **Student Employment:** Federal Work-Study Program available. Off-campus job opportunities are good. **Financial Aid Statistics:** 87% freshmen, 88% undergrads receive need-based scholarship or grant aid. 94% freshmen, 91% undergrads receive need-based self help aid. 71% freshmen, 71% undergrads receive any aid. 7% undergrads borrow to pay for school. Average cumulative indebtedness $26,582.

NATIONAL AMERICAN UNVERSITY (NM)

Albuquerque, NM 87110
Phone: 505-348-3700
E-mail: NPointer@national.edu
Fax: 505-348-3705

This proprietary school was founded in 1941. It has a 15-acre campus.

RATINGS
Admissions Selectivity Rating: 60*   **Fire Safety Rating:** 60*   **Green Rating:** 60*

STUDENTS AND FACULTY
Enrollment: 611. **Student Body:** 42% female, 58% male, 0% out-of-state, 1% international (2 countries represented). Asian 2%, African American 5%, Caucasian 42%, Hispanic 38%, Native American 6%.
Retention and Graduation: 5% grads go on to further study within 1 year. 1% grads pursue law degrees. 5% grads pursue business degrees. **Faculty:** Student/faculty ratio 10:1. 6 full-time faculty, 33% hold PhDs, 0% are members of minority groups, 50% are women. 0% of classes are taught by teaching assistants.

ACADEMICS
Degrees: associate, bachelor's, master's. **Classes:** Most classes have fewer than 10 students. **Majors with Highest Enrollment:** accounting; business/commerce; information technology. **Special Study Options:** Accelerated program, cooperative education program, distance learning, double major, dual enrollment, independent study, weekend college. **Career Services:** Alumni network, career/job search classes, internships.

FACILITIES
Housing: 100% of campus accessible to physically disabled. **Computers:** Students can register for classes online. Administrative functions (other than registration) can be performed online.

CAMPUS LIFE
Environment: Metropolis. **Activities:** student government 1 registered organizations, 1 honor societies.

ADMISSIONS
Freshman Academic Profile: 99% from public high schools. Minimum paper TOEFL 500. **Freshman Admission Requirements:** High school diploma is required and GED is accepted. **Transfer Admission Requirements:** High school transcript, college transcript(s), Lowest grade transferable C. **General Admission Information:** Application Fee $25. Regular application deadline 9/13. Nonfall registration accepted. Admission may be deferred for a maximum of 12.

COSTS AND FINANCIAL AID

Annual tuition $8,100. Required fees $315. **Types of Aid:** *Need-based scholarships/grants:* Federal Pell, SEOG, state scholarships/grants, private scholarships, the school's own gift aid. *Loans:* Direct Subsidized Stafford, Direct Unsubsidized Stafford, Direct PLUS, Subsidized Stafford, Unsubsidized Stafford, PLUS, Federal Perkins, state loans, college/university loans from institutional funds. **Student Employment:** Federal Work-Study Program available. Institutional employment available. Off-campus job opportunities are good.

NATIONAL UNIVERSITY

11255 North Torrey Pinos Road, La Jolla, CA 92037
Phone: 858-642-8180
E-mail: advisor@nu.edu • **CEEB Code:** 4557
Fax: 858-642-8710 • **Website:** www.nu.edu • **ACT Code:** 20015

This private school was founded in 1971.

RATINGS
Admissions Selectivity Rating: 60*   **Fire Safety Rating:** 60*   **Green Rating:** 60*

STUDENTS AND FACULTY
Enrollment: 4,776. **Student Body:** 57% female, 43% male, 0% out-of-state, 1% international. Asian 9%, African American 13%, Caucasian 52%, Hispanic 18%, Native American 1%.
Retention and Graduation: 40% freshmen return for sophomore year. 70% freshmen graduate within 6 years. **Faculty:** Student/faculty ratio 16:1. 151 full-time faculty, 87% hold PhDs, 19% are members of minority groups, 42% are women. 0% of classes are taught by teaching assistants.

ACADEMICS
Degrees: associate, bachelor's, certificate, diploma, master's, post-bachelor's certificate, terminal associate, transfer associate. **Classes:** Most classes have 10–19 students. **Majors with Highest Enrollment:** criminal justice/law enforcement administration; multi-/interdisciplinary studies, other. **Special Study Options:** Accelerated program, distance learning, double major, dual enrollment, English as a Second Language (ESL), teacher certification program, extensive online offerings are available. **Disability Services:** Special programs offered to physically disabled students include note-taking services, reader services, tutors. **Career Services:** career assessment, regional alumni..

FACILITIES
Housing: 100% of campus accessible to physically disabled. **Computers:** Students can register for classes online. Administrative functions (other than registration) can be performed online.

CAMPUS LIFE
Activities: literary magazine.

ADMISSIONS
Freshman Academic Profile: Minimum paper TOEFL 525. **Basis for Candidate Selection:** *Important factors considered include:* interview, work experience. *Other factors considered include:* application essay, extracurricular activities. **Freshman Admission Requirements:** High school diploma is required and GED is accepted. **Freshman Admission Statistics:** 156 applied, 100% admitted, 36% enrolled. **General Admission Information:** Application Fee $60. Nonfall registration accepted. Admission may be deferred for a maximum of 12 months. Neither credit nor placement offered for CEEB Advanced Placement tests.

COSTS AND FINANCIAL AID
Annual tuition $7,965. Required fees $60. **Required Forms and Deadlines:** FAFSA, institution's own financial aid form, state aid form. **Types of Aid:** *Need-based scholarships/grants:* Federal Pell, SEOG, state scholarships/grants, private scholarships, the school's own gift aid. *Loans:* Direct Subsidized Stafford, Direct Unsubsidized Stafford, Subsidized Stafford, Unsubsidized Stafford, PLUS, Federal Perkins. **Student Employment:** Institutional employment available. Off-campus job opportunities are good. **Financial Aid Statistics:** 65% undergrads borrow to pay for school. Average cumulative indebtedness $20,000.

NATIONAL UNIVERSITY OF HEALTH SCIENCES

200 E. Roosevelt Road, Lombard, IL 60148
Phone: 630-889-6566 • **Financial Aid Phone:** 630-889-6700
E-mail: admissions@nuhs.edu
Fax: 630-889-6554 • **Website:** www.nuhs.edu

This private school was founded in 1906. It has a 32-acre campus.

RATINGS
Admissions Selectivity Rating: 61   **Fire Safety Rating:** 60*   **Green Rating:** 60*

STUDENTS AND FACULTY
Enrollment: 74. **Student Body:** 16% female, 84% male, 70% out-of-state, 9% international (9 countries represented). Asian 11%, African American 35%, Caucasian 141%, Hispanic 11%, Native American 0%.
Retention and Graduation: 90% freshmen return for sophomore year.
Faculty: Student/faculty ratio 6:1. 46 full-time faculty, 93% hold PhDs, 17% are women.

ACADEMICS
Degrees: bachelor's, certificate, master's. **Classes:** Most classes have 40-49 students. Most lab/discussion sessions have 20–29 students. **Majors with Highest Enrollment:** biomedical sciences; massage therapy/therapeutic massage. **Special Study Options:** internships, Accelerated science prerequisite program. **Combined Degree Programs:** BS/DC.

FACILITIES
Housing: Coed dorms, men's dorms, women's dorms, apartments for married students, apartments for single students, Studio apartments. **Special Academic Facilities/Equipment:** Museum Fitness Center Learning Resource Center Health Care Clinic **Computers:** 88% of classrooms, 100% of libraries, 100% of common outdoor areas have wireless network access. Students can register for classes online.

CAMPUS LIFE
Environment: Town. **Activities:** student government, student newspaper, yearbook 24 registered organizations, 1 religious organizations. 2 fraternities, 1 sororities. **On-Campus Highlights:** Janse Hall, Student Center, Clinic, Learning Resource Center, Dormitories.

ADMISSIONS
Freshman Academic Profile: Minimum web-based TOEFL 79. Minimum paper TOEFL 550. **Freshman Admission Requirements:** High school diploma is required and GED is accepted. **Transfer Admission Requirements:** college transcript(s), statement of good standing from prior institution(s). Minimum college GPA of 2.5 required. Lowest grade transferable C. **General Admission Information:** Application Fee $55. Nonfall registration accepted. Credit offered for CEEB Advanced Placement tests.

COSTS AND FINANCIAL AID
Types of Aid: *Need-based scholarships/grants:* Federal Pell, SEOG, state scholarships/grants, private scholarships, the school's own gift aid. *Loans:* Subsidized Stafford, Unsubsidized Stafford, PLUS, Federal Perkins. **Student Employment:** Federal Work-Study Program available. Institutional employment available. Off-campus job opportunities are excellent. **Financial Aid Statistics:** 62% undergrads receive need-based scholarship or grant aid. 10% undergrads receive non-need-based scholarship or grant aid. 62% undergrads receive need-based self-help aid.

NATIONAL UNIVERSITY OF IRELAND MAYNOOTH

International Office, Maynooth, Co Kildare
Phone: 3531-708-3868
E-mail: international.applications@nuim.ie **Fax:** 35317086113
Website: www.nuim.ie/international • **ACT Code:** 5483

RATINGS
Admissions Selectivity Rating: 63   **Fire Safety Rating:** 84   **Green Rating:** 73

STUDENTS AND FACULTY
Student Body: (90 countries represented).
Retention and Graduation: 95% freshmen return for sophomore year. **Faculty:** Student/faculty ratio 12:1. 0% of classes are taught by teaching assistants.

CAMPUS LIFE
Environmental Initiatives: To provide and co-ordinate the travel strategy at NUIM to enable a lasting and maintained shift to sustainable travel in line with the University's vision of becoming a sustainable campus by providing the best range of travel options to staff, students and visitors. Implementation and promotion of a Cycle to Work scheme for staff. Launching and promotion of the Car Share database. Implementation of recycling policy and provision of waste receptacles for general, recyclable paper and plastics, and food waste.

ADMISSIONS
Freshman Academic Profile: Average high school GPA 3.4. Minimum web-based TOEFL 80. Minimum paper TOEFL 550

NAZARETH COLLEGE

4245 East Avenue, Rochester, NY 14618-3790
Phone: 585-389-2860 • **Financial Aid Phone:** 585-389-2310
E-mail: admissions@naz.edu • **CEEB Code:** 2511
Fax: 585-389-2826 • **Website:** www.naz.edu • **ACT Code:** 2826

This private school was founded in 1924. It has a 150-acre campus.

RATINGS
Admissions Selectivity Rating: 81   **Fire Safety Rating:** 62   **Green Rating:** 60*

STUDENTS AND FACULTY
Enrollment: 2,122. **Student Body:** 76% female, 24% male, 6% out-of-state, 1% international (13 countries represented). Asian 2%, African American 4%, Caucasian 75%, Hispanic 4%, Native American 0%.
Retention and Graduation: 82% freshmen return for sophomore year. 67% freshmen graduate within 4 years. 74% freshmen graduate within 6 years.
Faculty: Student/faculty ratio 10:1. 156 full-time faculty, 85% hold PhDs, 12% are members of minority groups, 59% are women. 0% of classes are taught by teaching assistants.

ACADEMICS
Degrees: bachelor's, master's, post-master's certificate. **Classes:** Most classes have 10–19 students. Most lab/discussion sessions have 10–19 students. **Majors with Highest Enrollment:** business administration, management and operations, other; education; physical therapy/therapist. **Special Study Options:** cross-registration, distance learning, double major, exchange student program (domestic), honors program, independent study, internships, study abroad, teacher certification program. **Combined Degree Programs:** BS/DPT Physical Therapy. **Disability Services:** Special programs offered to physically disabled students include note-taking services, reader services, tape recorders, tutors. **Career Services:** Alumni network, alumni services, career/job search classes, career assessment, internships, regional alumni.

FACILITIES
Housing: Coed dorms, special housing for disabled students, apartments for single students, Substance Free Quiet Floors Language House Honors First-year Experience. 80% of campus accessible to physically disabled. **Special Academic Facilities/Equipment:** Arts center, speech/hearing/language clinic, reading clinic, psychology center, center for service learning, Center for Teaching Excellence, and Center for International Education. **Computers:** Students can register for classes online.

CAMPUS LIFE
Environment: Village. **Activities:** Choral groups, concert band, dance, drama/theater, jazz band, literary magazine, music ensembles, musical theater, opera, radio station, student government, student newspaper, symphony orchestra, yearbook, Campus Ministries, International Student Organization 50 registered organizations, 19 honor societies, 5 religious organizations. **Athletics (Intercollegiate):** *Men:* basketball, cross-country, diving, equestrian sports, golf, lacrosse, soccer, swimming, tennis, track/field (outdoor), track/field (indoor), volleyball. *Women:* basketball, cross-country, diving, equestrian sports, field hockey, golf, lacrosse, soccer, softball, swimming, tennis, track/field (outdoor), track/field (indoor), volleyball. **On-Campus Highlights:** Cabaret- informal dining/coffee house, Athletic Facilities, Shults Community Center, Colie's Cafe, Library.

ADMISSIONS

Freshman Academic Profile: Average high school GPA 89.6. 28% in top 10% of high school class, 62% in top 25% of high school class, 88% in top 50% of high school class. 90% from public high schools. SAT Math middle 50% range 540-620. SAT Critical Reading middle 50% range 520-630. ACT middle 50% range 23-27. Minimum web-based TOEFL 79. Minimum paper TOEFL 550. **Basis for Candidate Selection:** *Very important factors considered include:* Class rank, application essay, academic GPA, recommendation(s), rigor of secondary school record. *Important factors considered include:* character/personal qualities, extracurricular activities, geographical residence, interview, level of applicant's interest, racial/ethnic status, state residency, talent/ability, volunteer work, work experience. *Other factors considered include:* standardized test scores, alumni/ae relation, first generation. **Freshman Admission Requirements:** High school diploma is required and GED is accepted. *Academic units required:* 4 English, 3 mathematics, 3 science, (2 science labs), 3 foreign language, 3 social studies. *Academic units recommended:* 4 English, 3 mathematics, 3 science, (2 science labs), 3 foreign language, 3 social studies. **Freshman Admission Statistics:** 2,976 applied, 70% admitted, 21% enrolled. **Transfer Admission Requirements:** college transcript(s), essay or personal statement, minimum college GPA of 2.5 required. Lowest grade transferable C. **General Admission Information:** Application Fee $40. Early decision application deadline 11/15. Regular application deadline 2/15. Regular notification 3/1. Nonfall registration accepted. Admission may be deferred for a maximum of 1 year. Credit and/or placement offered for CEEB Advanced Placement tests.

COSTS AND FINANCIAL AID

Required Forms and Deadlines: FAFSA. **Notification of Awards:** Applicants will be notified of awards on a rolling basis beginning 2/20. **Types of Aid:** *Need-based scholarships/grants:* Federal Pell, SEOG, state scholarships/grants, private scholarships, the school's own gift aid. *Loans:* Subsidized Stafford, Unsubsidized Stafford, PLUS, Federal Perkins. **Student Employment:** Federal Work-Study Program available. Institutional employment available. Off-campus job opportunities are excellent. **Financial Aid Statistics:** 91% freshmen, 93% undergrads receive need-based scholarship or grant aid. 45% freshmen, 40% undergrads receive non-need-based scholarship or grant aid. 87% freshmen, 87% undergrads receive need-based self-help aid. 89% undergrads borrow to pay for school. Average cumulative indebtedness $32,957. **Criteria for awarding institutional aid:** *Non-need-based:* academics, alumni affiliation, art, minority status, music/drama, state/district residency.

See page 1152.

NEBRASKA CHRISTIAN COLLEGE

1800 Syracuse Avenue, Norfolk, NE 68701
Phone: 402-379-5000
E-mail: admissions@nechristian.edu
Fax: 402-379-5100 • **ACT Code:** 2473

This private school was founded in 1945. It has a 40-acre campus.

RATINGS
Admissions Selectivity Rating: 63   **Fire Safety Rating:** 60*   **Green Rating:** 60*

STUDENTS AND FACULTY
Enrollment: 146. **Student Body:** 45% female, 55% male, 10% out-of-state. **Faculty:** 0% of classes are taught by teaching assistants.

ACADEMICS
Degrees: associate, bachelor's. **Special Study Options:** distance learning, internships, study abroad.

FACILITIES
Housing: Private apartments, student plan housing, private rooms.

CAMPUS LIFE
Environment: Rural. **Activities:** student newspaper. **Athletics (Intercollegiate):** *Men:* basketball, soccer. *Women:* basketball, volleyball.

ADMISSIONS
Basis for Candidate Selection: *Very important factors considered include:* recommendation(s), standardized test scores, character/personal qualities. *Important factors considered include:* Class rank, rigor of secondary school record, extracurricular activities, interview, talent/ability, volunteer work. *Other factors considered include:* alumni/ae relation, work experience. **Freshman Admission Requirements:** High school diploma is required and GED is accepted. **Freshman Admission Statistics:** 148 applied, 60% admitted, 67% enrolled. **Transfer Admission Requirements:** High school transcript, college transcript(s). **General Admission Information:** Application Fee $25. Nonfall registration accepted. Admission may be deferred for a maximum of 1.

COSTS AND FINANCIAL AID

Annual tuition $4,500. Room and board $2,960. Required fees $450. Average book expense $400. **Required Forms and Deadlines:** FAFSA, institution's own financial aid form. **Types of Aid:** *Need-based scholarships/grants:* Federal Pell, SEOG, state scholarships/grants, private scholarships, the school's own gift aid. *Loans:* Subsidized Stafford, Unsubsidized Stafford, PLUS. **Student Employment:** Federal Work-Study Program available. Institutional employment available. Highest amount earned per year from on-campus jobs $1,625. Off-campus job opportunities are excellent. **Financial Aid Statistics:** 93% freshmen, 93% undergrads receive need-based scholarship or grant aid. 63% freshmen, 57% undergrads receive need-based self-help aid. 90% undergrads borrow to pay for school. Average cumulative indebtedness $10,178. **Criteria for awarding institutional aid:** *Non-need-based:* academics, leadership, music/drama.

NEBRASKA METHODIST COLLEGE

720 North 87th Street, Omaha, NE 68114
Phone: 402-354-7200 • **Financial Aid Phone:** 402-354-7225
E-mail: admissions@methodistcollege.edu • **CEEB Code:** 6510
Fax: 402-354-7020 • **ACT Code:** 2465

This private school, affiliated with the Methodist Church, was founded in 1891. It has a 6-acre campus.

RATINGS
Admissions Selectivity Rating: 68   **Fire Safety Rating:** 63   **Green Rating:** 60*

STUDENTS AND FACULTY
Enrollment: 504. **Student Body:** 92% female, 8% male, 35% out-of-state, 0% international (3 countries represented). Asian 3%, African American 3%, Caucasian 87%, Hispanic 1%, Native American 1%.
Retention and Graduation: 81% freshmen return for sophomore year. 10% grads go on to further study within 1 year. 10% grads pursue arts and sciences degrees. **Faculty:** Student/faculty ratio 10:1. 43 full-time faculty, 28% hold PhDs, 7% are members of minority groups, 91% are women. 0% of classes are taught by teaching assistants.

ACADEMICS
Degrees: associate, bachelor's, certificate, master's, post-master's certificate. **Classes:** Most classes have 10–19 students. Most lab/discussion sessions have 10–19 students. **Majors with Highest Enrollment:** diagnostic medical sonography/sonographer and ultrasound technician; nursing/registered nurse (rn, asn, bsn, msn); radiologic technology/science - radiographer. **Special Study Options:** Accelerated program, distance learning, independent study. **Disability Services:** Special programs offered to physically disabled students include note-taking services, reader services, tape recorders, tutors. **Career Services:** Alumni network, alumni services, career/job search classes.

FACILITIES
Housing: apartments for single students. 90% of campus accessible to physically disabled. **Computers:** 100% of classrooms, 100% of libraries, 100% of dining areas, 100% of student union, have wireless network access. Students can register for classes online. Administrative functions (other than registration) can be performed online.

CAMPUS LIFE
Environment: City. **Activities:** student government 11 registered organizations, 2 honor societies. **On-Campus Highlights:** Student Center, Library, Human Cadaver Lab, Chapel

ADMISSIONS
Freshman Academic Profile: Average high school GPA 3.3. 11% in top 10% of high school class, 11% in top 25% of high school class, 50% in top 50% of high school class. 90% from public high schools. ACT middle 50% range 19-23. Minimum web-based TOEFL 80. Minimum paper TOEFL 550. **Basis for Candidate Selection:** *Very important factors considered include:* academic GPA, rigor of secondary school record, standardized test scores. *Important factors considered include:* Class rank, application essay, recommendation(s), character/personal qualities, interview. *Other factors considered include:* alumni/ae relation, first generation, geographical residence, level of applicant's interest, racial/ethnic status, state residency, volunteer work, work experience. **Freshman Admission Requirements:** High school diploma is required and GED is accepted. *Academic units required:* 4 English, 3 mathematics, 2 science, (2 science labs), 2 social studies. 4 English, 3 mathematics, 2 science, (2 science labs), 2 social studies. **Freshman Admission Statistics:** 96 applied, 76% admitted, 70% enrolled. **Transfer Admission Requirements:** High school transcript, college transcript(s), essay or personal statement, interview,

statement of good standing from prior institution(s). Minimum college GPA of 2.5 required. Lowest grade transferable C. **General Admission Information:** Application Fee $25. Regular application deadline 3/1. Notification on a rolling basis, beginning on or about 1/15. Nonfall registration accepted. Admission may be deferred for a maximum of 12 months. Neither credit nor placement offered for CEEB Advanced Placement tests.

COSTS AND FINANCIAL AID
Annual tuition $12,840. Room and board $2,625. Required fees $600. Average book expense $1,300. **Required Forms and Deadlines:** FAFSA, institution's own financial aid form. **Notification of Awards:** Applicants will be notified of awards on a rolling basis beginning 3/1. **Types of Aid:** *Need-based scholarships/grants:* Federal Pell, SEOG, state scholarships/grants, private scholarships, the school's own gift aid. *Loans:* Subsidized Stafford, Unsubsidized Stafford, PLUS, Federal Perkins, Federal Nursing, state loans, college/university loans from institutional funds, Alternative loans. **Student Employment:** Federal Work-Study Program available. Institutional employment available. Off-campus job opportunities are good. **Financial Aid Statistics:** 38% freshmen, 51% undergrads receive need-based scholarship or grant aid. 8% freshmen, 7% undergrads receive non-need-based scholarship or grant aid. 92% freshmen, 89% undergrads receive need-based self-help aid. 85% freshmen, 69% undergrads receive any aid. 86% undergrads borrow to pay for school. Average cumulative indebtedness $29,492. **Criteria for awarding institutional aid:** *Non-need-based:* academics, minority status, religious affiliation.

NEBRASKA WESLEYAN UNIVERSITY

5000 Saint Paul Ave., Lincoln, NE 68504
Phone: 402-465-2218 • **Financial Aid Phone:** 402-465-2212
E-mail: admissions@nebrwesleyan.edu • **CEEB Code:** 6470
Fax: 402-465-2177 • **Website:** www.nebrwesleyan.edu • **ACT Code:** 2474

This private school, affiliated with the Methodist Church, was founded in 1887. It has a 50-acre campus.

RATINGS
Admissions Selectivity Rating: 75   **Fire Safety Rating:** 85   **Green Rating:** 69

STUDENTS AND FACULTY
Enrollment: 1,778. **Student Body:** 61% female, 39% male, 11% out-of-state, 0% international (13 countries represented). Asian 2%, African American 2%, Caucasian 84%, Hispanic 3%, Native American 1%.
Retention and Graduation: 76% freshmen return for sophomore year. 51% freshmen graduate within 4 years. **Faculty:** Student/faculty ratio 12:1. 98 full-time faculty, 91% hold PhDs, 2% are members of minority groups, 48% are women. 0% of classes are taught by teaching assistants.

ACADEMICS
Degrees: bachelor's, certificate, master's, post-bachelor's certificate, post-master's certificate. **Classes:** Most classes have 20–29 students. Most lab/discussion sessions have 10–19 students. **Majors with Highest Enrollment:** business administration and management; communication studies/speech communication and rhetoric; psychology. **Special Study Options:** double major, dual enrollment, independent study, internships, liberal arts/career combination, study abroad, teacher certification program, weekend college, 3-2 Engineering Program with Washington Univ., Columbia Univ., or Univ. of Nebraska-Lincoln; Capitol Hill Internship Program; Chicago Center for Urban Life & Culture. **Disability Services:** Special programs offered to physically disabled students include note-taking services, reader services, tape recorders, tutors. **Career Services:** Alumni network, alumni services, career/job search classes, career assessment, internships, regional alumni. Career Services highlights include National and international service learning trips; service learning as part of coursework.

FACILITIES
Housing: Coed dorms, women's dorms, fraternity/sorority housing, apartments for single students, Townhouses; residence hall suites. 92% of campus accessible to physically disabled. **Special Academic Facilities/Equipment:** Art galleries, psychology/sleep lab, observatory and planetarium, green house, laboratory theatre, herbarium, nuclear magnetic resonance laboratory **Computers:** Students can register for classes online. Administrative functions (other than registration) can be performed online.

CAMPUS LIFE
Environment: City. **Activities:** Choral groups, concert band, drama/theater, jazz band, literary magazine, marching band, music ensembles, musical theater, opera, pep band, radio station, student government, student newspaper, symphony orchestra, Campus Ministries, International Student Organization

80 registered organizations, 18 honor societies, 5 religious organizations. 3 fraternities, 4 sororities. **Athletics (Intercollegiate):** *Men:* baseball, basketball, cross-country, football, golf, soccer, tennis, track/field (outdoor), track/field (indoor). *Women:* basketball, cross-country, golf, soccer, softball, tennis, track/field (outdoor), track/field (indoor), volleyball. **On-Campus Highlights:** Weary Center for Health and Fitness, Wesleyan Coffee House, Old Main, Roy G Story Student Center, Great Hall, Smith-Curtis. **Environmental Initiatives:** Completed light inventory; retrofitted 80% of all lights. Recycling including cans, plastic bottles, paper Updated central heating plant.

ADMISSIONS
Freshman Academic Profile: 25% in top 10% of high school class, 56% in top 25% of high school class, 85% in top 50% of high school class. ACT middle 50% range 23-28. Minimum paper TOEFL 525. **Basis for Candidate Selection:** *Very important factors considered include:* Class rank, standardized test scores. *Important factors considered include:* academic GPA, character/personal qualities, extracurricular activities, talent/ability. *Other factors considered include:* application essay, recommendation(s), rigor of secondary school record, alumni/ae relation, first generation, geographical residence, interview, racial/ethnic status, volunteer work. **Freshman Admission Requirements:** High school diploma is required and GED is accepted. **Freshman Admission Statistics:** 2,106 applied, 79% admitted, 21% enrolled. **Transfer Admission Requirements:** college transcript(s), statement of good standing from prior institution(s). Minimum college GPA of 2.0 required. Lowest grade transferable C–. **General Admission Information:** Application Fee $20. Regular application deadline 8/15. Regular notification 1/15. Nonfall registration accepted. Admission may be deferred for a maximum of 1 year. Credit offered for CEEB Advanced Placement tests.

COSTS AND FINANCIAL AID
Annual tuition $25,468. Room and board $7,432. Required fees $450. Average book expense $1,200. **Required Forms and Deadlines:** FAFSA. **Types of Aid:** *Need-based scholarships/grants:* Federal Pell, SEOG, state scholarships/grants, private scholarships, the school's own gift aid. *Loans:* Subsidized Stafford, Unsubsidized Stafford, PLUS, Federal Perkins. **Student Employment:** Federal Work-Study Program available. Institutional employment available. Highest amount earned per year from on-campus jobs $7,664. Off-campus job opportunities are good. **Financial Aid Statistics:** 100% freshmen, 99% undergrads receive need-based scholarship or grant aid. 16% freshmen, 12% undergrads receive non-need-based scholarship or grant aid. 80% freshmen, 84% undergrads receive need-based self-help aid. 99% freshmen, 96% undergrads receive any aid. 74% undergrads borrow to pay for school. Average cumulative indebtedness $28,077. **Criteria for awarding institutional aid:** *Non-need-based:* academics, art, minority status, music/drama.

NEUMANN UNIVERSITY

One Neumann Drive, Aston, PA 19014
Phone: 610-558-5616 • **Financial Aid Phone:** 610-558-5532
E-mail: neumann@neumann.edu • **CEEB Code:** 2628
Fax: 610-558-5652 • **Website:** www.neumann.edu • **ACT Code:** 3649

This private school, affiliated with the Roman Catholic Church, was founded in 1965. It has a 55-acre campus.

RATINGS
Admissions Selectivity Rating: 68   **Fire Safety Rating:** 98   **Green Rating:** 60*

STUDENTS AND FACULTY
Enrollment: 2,578. **Student Body:** 65% female, 35% male, 33% out-of-state, 2% international (17 countries represented). Asian 1%, African American 19%, Caucasian 51%, Hispanic 3%, Native American 0%.
Retention and Graduation: 74% freshmen return for sophomore year. 29% freshmen graduate within 4 years. 51% freshmen graduate within 6 years. 20% grads go on to further study within 1 year. 7% grads pursue arts and sciences degrees. 1% grads pursue law degrees. 6% grads pursue business degrees. 1% grads pursue medical degrees. **Faculty:** Student/faculty ratio 14:1. 95 full-time faculty, 79% hold PhDs, 61% are women. 0% of classes are taught by teaching assistants.

ACADEMICS
Degrees: associate, bachelor's, certificate, master's, post-bachelor's certificate, post-master's certificate, terminal associate. **Classes:** Most classes have 20–29 students. Most lab/discussion sessions have 10–19 students. **Majors with Highest Enrollment:** criminal justice/law enforcement administration; elementary education and teaching; nursing/registered nurse (rn, asn, bsn, msn). **Special Study Options:** Accelerated program, cooperative education program, distance

learning, double major, exchange student program (domestic), honors program, independent study, internships, liberal arts/career combination, student-designed major, study abroad, teacher certification program, weekend college. **Disability Services:** Special programs offered to physically disabled students include note-taking services, reader services, tape recorders, tutors. **Career Services:** Alumni network, alumni services, career/job search classes, career assessment, internships.

FACILITIES

Housing: Coed dorms, special housing for disabled students, Off campus housing. 100% of campus accessible to physically disabled. **Special Academic Facilities/Equipment:** Child development center **Computers:** 100% of classrooms, 100% of libraries, have wireless network access. Administrative functions (other than registration) can be performed online.

CAMPUS LIFE

Environment: Town. **Activities:** Choral groups, dance, drama/theater, jazz band, literary magazine, music ensembles, musical theater, radio station, student government, student newspaper, yearbook, Campus Ministries, Model UN 14 registered organizations, 4 honor societies, 2 religious organizations. **Athletics (Intercollegiate):** *Men:* baseball, basketball, cross-country, golf, ice hockey, lacrosse, soccer, tennis. *Women:* basketball, cross-country, field hockey, ice hockey, lacrosse, soccer, softball, tennis, volleyball. **On-Campus Highlights:** Life Center, Training room, On campus Chapel, Library, Computer Labs.

ADMISSIONS

Freshman Academic Profile: Average high school GPA 2.5. 60% from public high schools. SAT Math middle 50% range 390-480. SAT Critical Reading middle 50% range 390-470. SAT Writing middle 50% range 390-473. ACT middle 50% range 830-990. Minimum web-based TOEFL 68. Minimum paper TOEFL 550. **Basis for Candidate Selection:** *Very important factors considered include:* recommendation(s), rigor of secondary school record, extra-curricular activities, talent/ability. *Important factors considered include:* Class rank, standardized test scores, alumni/ae relation, character/personal qualities, interview, level of applicant's interest. *Other factors considered include:* application essay, racial/ethnic status, religious affiliation/commitment, volunteer work. **Freshman Admission Requirements:** High school diploma is required and GED is accepted. *Academic units required:* 4 English, 2 mathematics, 2 science, 2 foreign language, 2 social studies, 4 academic electives. *Academic units recommended:* 4 English, 2 mathematics, 2 science, 2 foreign language, 2 social studies, 4 academic electives. **Freshman Admission Statistics:** 3,567 applied, 71% admitted, 23% enrolled. **Transfer Admission Requirements:** college transcript(s), minimum college GPA of 2.0 required. Lowest grade transferable C. **General Admission Information:** Application Fee $35. Nonfall registration accepted. Admission may be deferred for a maximum of one year. Credit offered for CEEB Advanced Placement tests.

COSTS AND FINANCIAL AID

Annual tuition $23,262. Room and board $11,070. Required fees $970. Average book expense $1,500. **Required Forms and Deadlines:** FAFSA. **Notification of Awards:** Applicants will be notified of awards on a rolling basis beginning 3/1. **Types of Aid:** *Need-based scholarships/grants:* Federal Pell, SEOG, state scholarships/grants, private scholarships, the school's own gift aid, Federal Nursing Scholarships. *Loans:* Direct Subsidized Stafford, Direct Unsubsidized Stafford, Direct PLUS, Subsidized Stafford, Unsubsidized Stafford, PLUS, Federal Nursing. **Student Employment:** Federal Work-Study Program available. Highest amount earned per year from on-campus jobs $5,000. Off-campus job opportunities are excellent. **Financial Aid Statistics:** 100% freshmen, 95% undergrads receive need-based scholarship or grant aid. 84% freshmen, 81% undergrads receive need-based self-help aid. 97% freshmen, 95% undergrads receive any aid. 95% undergrads borrow to pay for school. **Criteria for awarding institutional aid:** *Non-need-based:* academics.

NEUMONT UNIVERSITY

10701 S. River Front Parkway, South Jordan, UT 84095
Phone: 888-638-6668 • **Financial Aid Phone:** 801-302-2870
E-mail: admissions@neumont.edu
Fax: 801-302-2880 • **Website:** www.neumont.edu/ • **ACT Code:**

This proprietary school was founded in 2003.

RATINGS

Admissions Selectivity Rating: 60*   **Fire Safety Rating:** 60*   **Green Rating:** 60*

STUDENTS AND FACULTY

Enrollment: 346. **Student Body:** 9% female, 91% male, (40 countries represented).

Retention and Graduation: 83% freshmen return for sophomore year. **Faculty:** Student/faculty ratio 17:1. 14 full-time faculty, 21% are women.

ACADEMICS

Degrees: bachelor's, master's. **Special Study Options:** Accelerated program, internships. **Disability Services:** Special programs offered to physically disabled students include note-taking services, reader services, tape recorders, tutors. **Career Services:** career/job search classes, career assessment, internships.

FACILITIES

Housing: apartments for married students, apartments for single students. **Computers:** 100% of classrooms, 100% of libraries, 100% of dining areas, 100% of student union, have wireless network access. Students can register for classes online. Undergraduates are required to own a computer.

CAMPUS LIFE

Environment: Metropolis. **Activities:** student government 8 registered organizations.

COSTS AND FINANCIAL AID

Annual tuition $21,600. Room and board $4,230. Required fees $1,400. Average book expense $1,080.

NEW COLLEGE OF CALIFORNIA

741 Valencia street, San Francisco, CA 94110
Phone: 415-437-3460 • **CEEB Code:** 4555
Fax: 415-861-0461 • **Website:** www.newcollege.edu

This private school was founded in 1971. It has a 1-acre campus.

RATINGS

Admissions Selectivity Rating: 60*   **Fire Safety Rating:** 60*   **Green Rating:** 60*

ACADEMICS

Degrees: associate, bachelor's, certificate, diploma, first professional, master's, terminal associate. **Majors with Highest Enrollment:** music teacher education; music theory and composition; voice and opera. **Special Study Options:** Accelerated program, cooperative education program, distance learning, English as a Second Language (ESL), independent study, internships, liberal arts/career combination, student-designed major, study abroad, teacher certification program, weekend college, Summer off-campus field study opportunities. **Disability Services:** Special programs offered to physically disabled students include tape recorders, tutors. **Career Services:** alumni services.

FACILITIES

Housing: 100% of campus accessible to physically disabled. **Special Academic Facilities/Equipment:** Arts studio, video editing lab, letter press lab.

CAMPUS LIFE

Environment: Metropolis. **Activities:** Choral groups, drama/theater, jazz band, literary magazine, musical theater, radio station, student newspaper.

ADMISSIONS

Basis for Candidate Selection: *Very important factors considered include:* rigor of secondary school record. *Important factors considered include:* geographical residence, interview, racial/ethnic status, state residency, work experience. *Other factors considered include:* volunteer work. **Freshman Admission Requirements:** High school diploma is required and GED is accepted. **Transfer Admission Requirements:** High school transcript, college transcript(s), essay or personal statement, Lowest grade transferable C. **General Admission Information:** Application Fee $50. Early decision application deadline 3/1. Nonfall registration accepted. Admission may be deferred for a maximum of 1 year.

COSTS AND FINANCIAL AID

Required Forms and Deadlines: FAFSA, institution's own financial aid form, state aid form. **Notification of Awards:** Applicants will be notified of awards on a rolling basis beginning 5/15. **Types of Aid:** *Need-based scholarships/grants:* Federal Pell, SEOG, state scholarships/grants, private scholarships, the school's own gift aid. *Loans:* Direct Subsidized Stafford, Direct Unsubsidized Stafford, PLUS, Federal Perkins. **Student Employment:** Federal Work-Study Program available. Highest amount earned per year from on-campus jobs $3,000. Off-campus job opportunities are good.

NEW COLLEGE OF FLORIDA

5800 Bay Shore Rd, Sarasota, FL 34243-2109
Phone: 941-487-5000 • **Financial Aid Phone:** 941-487-5000
E-mail: admissions@ncf.edu • **CEEB Code:** 5506
Fax: 941-487-5010 • **Website:** www.ncf.edu • **ACT Code:** 750

This public school was founded in 1960. It has a 118.6-acre campus.

RATINGS
Admissions Selectivity Rating: 93   **Fire Safety Rating:** 82   **Green Rating:** 69

STUDENTS AND FACULTY
Enrollment: 845. **Student Body:** 61% female, 39% male, 21% out-of-state, 0% international (16 countries represented). Asian 3%, African American 1%, Caucasian 75%, Hispanic 13%, Native American 0%.
Retention and Graduation: 86% freshmen return for sophomore year. 50% freshmen graduate within 4 years. 68% freshmen graduate within 6 years. 29% grads go on to further study within 1 year. **Faculty:** Student/faculty ratio 10:1. 69 full-time faculty, 99% hold PhDs, 12% are members of minority groups, 48% are women. 0% of classes are taught by teaching assistants.

ACADEMICS
Degrees: bachelor's. **Classes:** Most classes have 10–19 students. Most lab/discussion sessions have 10–19 students. **Majors with Highest Enrollment:** biology/biological sciences; political science and government; psychology. **Special Study Options:** cross-registration, double major, exchange student program (domestic), honors program, independent study, internships, student-designed major, study abroad, Academic contract, January interterm (independent study), Narrative evaluation/pass-fail, Senior thesis, Tutorials, Undergraduate research. Special or unique academic programs: (1) The New College academic contract whereby each student develops her/his individual academic program of coursework, tutorials, field and lab research, study abroad, and so on, in close consultation with a faculty member. See the General Catalog on the web. http://www.ncf.edu/resources-for-students (2) Non-graded, narrative evaluation which encourages exploration and mastery. (3) Intensive "Independent Study Projects" during January which can be highly individual but can also involve group activities, such as an acting workshop or an ecological tour of Florida. (4) Competitive grants programs to support student research. **Honors Programs:** New College of Florida is the state's officially-designated "honors college for the liberal arts." **Disability Services:** Special programs offered to physically disabled students include note-taking services, reader services, tape recorders. **Career Services:** Alumni network, alumni services, career/job search classes, career assessment, internships, regional alumni. Career Services highlights include The National Student Exchange program.

FACILITIES
Housing: Coed dorms, special housing for disabled students, apartments for single students. Specialized housing options may be arranged in response to student interest. 60% of campus accessible to physically disabled. **Special Academic Facilities/Equipment:** Anthropology and psychology labs. Electronic music lab. Individual studio space for senior art students. Marine biology research center with Living Ecosystem Teaching and Research Aquarium, wet lab, and seawater on tap. NMR, scanning electron microscope, inert atmosphere glovebox, transparent fume hoods, greenhouse. **Computers:** 95% of classrooms, 100% of dorms, 100% of libraries, 100% of dining areas, 100% of student union, 20% of common outdoor areas have wireless network access. Students can register for classes online. Administrative functions (other than registration) can be performed online.

CAMPUS LIFE
Environment: Town. **Activities:** Choral groups, dance, drama/theater, literary magazine, music ensembles, musical theater, radio station, student government, student newspaper, student-run film society, Campus Ministries 90 registered organizations, 5 religious organizations. **Athletics (Intercollegiate):** *Men:* sailing. *Women:* sailing. **On-Campus Highlights:** The R.V. Heiser Natural Sciences Complex, Pritzker Marine Biology Research Center, The Caples Fine Arts Complex, Four Winds Cafe (Student owned and operated), Jane Bancroft Cook Library, Historic bayfront mansions. **Environmental Initiatives:** We've had an environmental studies program since 1972. Students have voted for a green fee and have paid a lump sum to make County buses service free. We use no nitrogen fertilizer and have just replaced about 1/50 of the campus area with native grasses and wildflowers.

ADMISSIONS
Freshman Academic Profile: Average high school GPA 4.0. 44% in top 10% of high school class, 84% in top 25% of high school class, 98% in top 50% of high school class. 80% from public high schools. SAT Math middle 50% range 570-680. SAT Critical Reading middle 50% range 630-740. SAT Writing middle 50% range 600-680. ACT middle 50% range 27-31. Minimum web-based TOEFL 83. Minimum paper TOEFL 560. **Basis for Candidate Selection:** *Very important factors considered include:* application essay, academic GPA, rigor of secondary school record. *Important factors considered include:* recommendation(s), standardized test scores, character/personal qualities. *Other factors considered include:* Class rank, alumni/ae relation, extracurricular activities, first generation, geographical residence, interview, level of applicant's interest, state residency, talent/ability, volunteer work, work experience. **Freshman Admission Requirements:** High school diploma is required and GED is accepted. *Academic units required:* 4 English, 4 mathematics, 3 science, (2 science labs), 2 foreign language, 3 social studies, 2 academic electives. *Academic units recommended:* 4 English, 4 mathematics, 3 science, (2 science labs), 2 foreign language, 3 social studies, 2 academic electives. **Freshman Admission Statistics:** 1,272 applied, 56% admitted, 33% enrolled. **Transfer Admission Requirements:** college transcript(s), essay or personal statement, minimum college GPA of 2.0 required. Lowest grade transferable C. **General Admission Information:** Application Fee $30. Regular application deadline 4/15. Nonfall registration accepted. Admission may be deferred for a maximum of 1 year. Neither credit nor placement offered for CEEB Advanced Placement tests.

COSTS AND FINANCIAL AID
Annual in-state tuition $6,763. Annual out-of-state tuition $29,792. Room and board $9,486. Average book expense $800. **Required Forms and Deadlines:** FAFSA. **Notification of Awards:** Applicants will be notified of awards on a rolling basis beginning 10/1. **Types of Aid:** *Need-based scholarships/grants:* Federal Pell, SEOG, state scholarships/grants, private scholarships, the school's own gift aid, Federal Academic Competitiveness Grant. *Loans:* Subsidized Stafford, Unsubsidized Stafford, PLUS, Alternative Loans. **Student Employment:** Federal Work-Study Program available. Institutional employment available. Highest amount earned per year from on-campus jobs $5,358. Off-campus job opportunities are good. **Financial Aid Statistics:** 100% freshmen, 98% undergrads receive need-based scholarship or grant aid. 9% freshmen, 8% undergrads receive non-need-based scholarship or grant aid. 85% freshmen, 85% undergrads receive need-based self-help aid. 100% freshmen receive any aid. 32% undergrads borrow to pay for school. Average cumulative indebtedness $14,172. **Criteria for awarding institutional aid:** *Non-need-based:* academics, state/district residency.

NEW ENGLAND COLLEGE

102 Bridge Street, Henniker, NH 3242
Phone: 603-428-2223 • **Financial Aid Phone:** 603-428-2226
E-mail: admission@nec.edu • **CEEB Code:** 3657
Fax: 603-428-3155 • **Website:** www.nec.edu • **ACT Code:** 2513

This private school was founded in 1946. It has a 225-acre campus.

RATINGS
Admissions Selectivity Rating: 68   **Fire Safety Rating:** 96   **Green Rating:** 80

STUDENTS AND FACULTY
Enrollment: 947. **Student Body:** 47% female, 53% male, 59% out-of-state, 7% international. Asian 2%, African American 5%, Caucasian 65%, Hispanic 4%, Native American 0%.
Retention and Graduation: 58% freshmen return for sophomore year. 30% freshmen graduate within 4 years. 39% freshmen graduate within 6 years. 19% grads go on to further study within 1 year. 4% grads pursue arts and sciences degrees. 1% grads pursue law degrees. 11% grads pursue business degrees. **Faculty:** Student/faculty ratio 11:1. 64 full-time faculty, 69% hold PhDs, 3% are members of minority groups, 39% are women. 0% of classes are taught by teaching assistants.

ACADEMICS
Degrees: associate, bachelor's, master's. **Classes:** Most classes have 10–19 students. Most lab/discussion sessions have 10–19 students. **Majors with Highest Enrollment:** business/commerce; elementary education and teaching; sport and fitness administration/management. **Special Study Options:** Accelerated program, cross-registration, distance learning, double major, dual enrollment, English as a Second Language (ESL), exchange student program (domestic), external degree program, honors program, independent study, internships, liberal arts/career combination, student-designed major, study abroad, teacher certification program. **Honors Programs:** Honors Program for community

college honors transfers **Combined Degree Programs:** BA/JD, NEC and New York Law 3 + 3 Program. **Disability Services:** Special programs offered to physically disabled students include note-taking services, tape recorders, tutors. **Career Services:** Alumni network, career/job search classes, career assessment, internships, regional alumni., Career Services highlights include Internships and practical experience throughout the curriculum.

FACILITIES

Housing: Coed dorms, fraternity/sorority housing, theme housing, Resident freshmen and sophomores are required to live in College housing. Quiet study options, special interest housing is available. 75% of campus accessible to physically disabled. **Special Academic Facilities/Equipment:** New England Art Gallery, Graphic Design and Imaging Lab Center for Educational Innovation (High Tech Building) **Computers:** 100% of classrooms, 100% of dorms, 100% of libraries, 100% of dining areas, 100% of student union, 75% of common outdoor areas have wireless network access. Students can register for classes on-line. Administrative functions (other than registration) can be performed online.

CAMPUS LIFE

Environment: Rural. **Activities:** Choral groups, dance, drama/theater, literary magazine, radio station, student government, student newspaper, yearbook, International Student Organization 26 registered organizations, 2 honor societies, 1 religious organizations. 2 fraternities, 2 sororities. **Athletics (Intercollegiate):** *Men:* baseball, basketball, cross-country, ice hockey, lacrosse, soccer. *Women:* basketball, cheerleading, cross-country, field hockey, ice hockey, lacrosse, soccer, softball. **On-Campus Highlights:** Simon Center (Student Center), Center of Education Innovation, Fitness Center, Gilmore Dining Hall, Coffee House. **Environmental Initiatives:** Addition of sustainability to the mission statement. A complete overhaul of lighting at the College for energy efficiency. Completion of a campus wide facilities plan. Environmental Action Committee Capital budgeting to include green projects

ADMISSIONS

Freshman Academic Profile: Average high school GPA 2.6. 3% in top 10% of high school class, 12% in top 25% of high school class, 37% in top 50% of high school class. 83% from public high schools. SAT Math middle 50% range 400-540. SAT Critical Reading middle 50% range 400-530. SAT Writing middle 50% range 400-520. ACT middle 50% range 18-23. Minimum web-based TOEFL 13. Minimum paper TOEFL 550. **Basis for Candidate Selection:** *Very important factors considered include:* application essay, recommendation(s), rigor of secondary school record, extracurricular activities, interview, level of applicant's interest, talent/ability. *Important factors considered include:* character/personal qualities, volunteer work. *Other factors considered include:* Class rank, academic GPA, standardized test scores, alumni/ae relation, work experience. **Freshman Admission Requirements:** High school diploma is required and GED is accepted. *Academic units required:* 4 English, 2 mathematics, 2 science, (1 science labs), 2 social studies. *Academic units recommended:* 4 English, 2 mathematics, 2 science, (1 science labs), 2 social studies. **Freshman Admission Statistics:** 1,985 applied, 77% admitted, 17% enrolled. **Transfer Admission Requirements:** High school transcript, college transcript(s), essay or personal statement, statement of good standing from prior institution(s). Lowest grade transferable C–. **General Admission Information:** Application Fee $30. Regular application deadline 9/1. Notification on a rolling basis, beginning on or about 11/1. Nonfall registration accepted. Admission may be deferred for a maximum of 1 year. Credit and/or placement offered for CEEB Advanced Placement tests.

COSTS AND FINANCIAL AID

Annual tuition $30,100. Room and board $11,959. Required fees $300. Average book expense $1,000. **Required Forms and Deadlines:** FAFSA, institution's own financial aid form. **Notification of Awards:** Applicants will be notified of awards on a rolling basis beginning 1/12. **Types of Aid:** *Need-based scholarships/grants:* Federal Pell, SEOG, state scholarships/grants, private scholarships, the school's own gift aid. *Loans:* Direct Subsidized Stafford, Direct Unsubsidized Stafford, Direct PLUS, Subsidized Stafford, Unsubsidized Stafford, PLUS, Federal Perkins, state loans. **Student Employment:** Federal Work-Study Program available. Institutional employment available. Highest amount earned per year from on-campus jobs $2,500. Off-campus job opportunities are good. **Financial Aid Statistics:** 97% freshmen, 97% undergrads receive need-based scholarship or grant aid. 7% freshmen, 6% undergrads receive non-need-based scholarship or grant aid. 89% freshmen, 88% undergrads receive need-based self-help aid. 99% freshmen, 97% undergrads receive any aid. 85% undergrads borrow to pay for school. Average cumulative indebtedness $43,808. **Criteria for awarding institutional aid:** *Non-need-based:* academics, alumni affiliation, art, job skills, leadership, music/drama.

NEW ENGLAND CONSERVATORY OF MUSIC

290 Huntington Avenue, Boston, MA 2115
Phone: 617-585-1101
E-mail: admissions@newenglandconservatory.edu • **CEEB Code:** 3659
Fax: 617-585-1115 • **Website:** www.newenglandconservatory.edu • **ACT Code:** 1872

This private school was founded in 1867.

RATINGS

Admissions Selectivity Rating: 63   **Fire Safety Rating:** 60*   **Green Rating:** 60*

STUDENTS AND FACULTY

Enrollment: 378. **Student Body:** 45% female, 55% male, 85% out-of-state, 6% international. Asian 3%, African American 1%, Caucasian 13%, Hispanic 1%, Native American 0%.
Retention and Graduation: 98% freshmen return for sophomore year. 56% freshmen graduate within 4 years. 69% freshmen graduate within 6 years. **Faculty:** Student/faculty ratio 4:1. 88 full-time faculty, 26% hold PhDs, 6% are members of minority groups, 33% are women.

ACADEMICS

Degrees: bachelor's, diploma, master's. **Classes:** Most classes have 10–19 students. Most lab/discussion sessions have fewer than 10 students. **Majors with Highest Enrollment:** jazz/jazz studies; violin, viola, guitar and other stringed instruments; voice and opera. **Special Study Options:** cross-registration, dual enrollment, English as a Second Language (ESL), independent study, internships, study abroad. **Disability Services:** Special programs offered to physically disabled students include note-taking services, tutors. **Career Services:** Alumni network, alumni services, career/job search classes, career assessment, internships.

FACILITIES

Housing: Coed dorms. 100% of campus accessible to physically disabled. **Special Academic Facilities/Equipment:** Rare instrument collection of over 200 pieces, recording and electronic music studios. over 200 pieces, recording and electronic music studios. Jordan Hall, the Main Concert Hall, is a national Historic Landmark

CAMPUS LIFE

Activities: Choral groups, concert band, jazz band, music ensembles, musical theater, opera, student government, symphony orchestra 7 registered organizations, 1 honor societies, 1 religious organizations. 1 fraternities.

ADMISSIONS

Freshman Academic Profile: Minimum paper TOEFL 500. **Basis for Candidate Selection:** *Very important factors considered include:* talent/ability. *Important factors considered include:* rigor of secondary school record, standardized test scores. *Other factors considered include:* application essay, academic GPA, recommendation(s), character/personal qualities. **Freshman Admission Requirements:** High school diploma is required and GED is accepted. **Freshman Admission Statistics:** 1,022 applied, 28% admitted, 28% enrolled. **Transfer Admission Requirements:** college transcript(s), essay or personal statement, interview, minimum college GPA of 2.7 required. Lowest grade transferable B. **General Admission Information:** Application Fee $100. Notification on a rolling basis, beginning on or about 4/1. Nonfall registration accepted. Admission may be deferred for a maximum of 1 year. Credit offered for CEEB Advanced Placement tests.

COSTS AND FINANCIAL AID

Annual tuition $30,650. Room and board $11,300. Required fees $325. Average book expense $700. **Required Forms and Deadlines:** FAFSA, institution's own financial aid form. **Notification of Awards:** Applicants will be notified of awards on a rolling basis beginning 4/1. **Types of Aid:** *Need-based scholarships/grants:* Federal Pell, SEOG, state scholarships/grants, private scholarships, the school's own gift aid. *Loans:* Subsidized Stafford, Unsubsidized Stafford, PLUS, Federal Perkins, state loans. **Student Employment:** Federal Work-Study Program available. Institutional employment available. Off-campus job opportunities are good. **Financial Aid Statistics:** 86% freshmen, 88% undergrads receive need-based scholarship or grant aid. 39% freshmen, 51% undergrads receive non-need-based scholarship or grant aid. 65% freshmen, 71% undergrads receive need-based self-help aid. 61% undergrads borrow to pay for school. Average cumulative indebtedness $26,628. **Criteria for awarding institutional aid:** *Non-need-based:* academics, music/drama.

NEW JERSEY CITY UNIVERSITY

2039 Kennedy Boulevard, Jersey City, NJ 7305
Phone: 888-441-6528 • **Financial Aid Phone:** 201-200-3378
E-mail: admissions@njcu.edu • **CEEB Code:** 2316
Fax: 201-200-2044 • **Website:** www.njcu.edu

This public school was founded in 1927. It has a 17-acre campus.

RATINGS
Admissions Selectivity Rating: 79   **Fire Safety Rating:** 97   **Green Rating:** 61

STUDENTS AND FACULTY
Enrollment: 6,550. **Student Body:** 60% female, 40% male, % out-of-state, 1% international (6 countries represented). Asian 8%, African American 21%, Caucasian 26%, Hispanic 35%, Native American 0%.
Retention and Graduation: 64% freshmen return for sophomore year. 5% freshmen graduate within 4 years. 34% freshmen graduate within 6 years. 20% grads go on to further study within 1 year. 13% grads pursue arts and sciences degrees. 1% grads pursue law degrees. 5% grads pursue business degrees. 1% grads pursue medical degrees. **Faculty:** Student/faculty ratio 16:1. 240 full-time faculty, 91% hold PhDs, 34% are members of minority groups, 51% are women. 0% of classes are taught by teaching assistants.

ACADEMICS
Degrees: bachelor's, certificate, master's, post-bachelor's certificate, post-master's certificate. **Classes:** Most classes have 20–29 students. **Majors with Highest Enrollment:** business administration and management; corrections and criminal justice, other; psychology. **Special Study Options:** Accelerated program, cooperative education program, cross-registration, distance learning, double major, dual enrollment, English as a Second Language (ESL), honors program, independent study, internships, study abroad, teacher certification program, weekend college. **Honors Programs:** Honors program in the William Maxwell College of Arts and Sciences **Combined Degree Programs:** BA/MA. **Disability Services:** Special programs offered to physically disabled students include reader services, tape recorders, tutors. **Career Services:** career assessment, internships Career Services highlights include Cooperative education.

FACILITIES
Housing: Coed dorms. 100% of campus accessible to physically disabled. **Special Academic Facilities/Equipment:** Art galleries, lab school for special education, criminal justice institute, electron microscope, Raimondo Center for Urban Research and Public Policy. **Computers:** Students can register for classes online. Administrative functions (other than registration) can be performed online.

CAMPUS LIFE
Environment: City. **Activities:** Choral groups, concert band, dance, drama/theater, jazz band, literary magazine, music ensembles, musical theater, opera, radio station, student government, student newspaper, symphony orchestra, yearbook, Campus Ministries, International Student Organization 50 registered organizations, 2 religious organizations. 7 fraternities, 5 sororities. **Athletics (Intercollegiate):** *Men:* baseball, basketball, cross-country, soccer, track/field (outdoor), track/field (indoor), volleyball. *Women:* basketball, bowling, cross-country, soccer, softball, track/field (outdoor), track/field (indoor), volleyball. **On-Campus Highlights:** Student Union, Physical fitness center, Library, Cafeteria

ADMISSIONS
Freshman Academic Profile: 14% in top 10% of high school class, 34% in top 25% of high school class, 71% in top 50% of high school class. 75% from public high schools. SAT Math middle 50% range 390–490. SAT Critical Reading middle 50% range 370–460. Minimum paper TOEFL 500. **Basis for Candidate Selection:** *Very important factors considered include:* rigor of secondary school record, standardized test scores, level of applicant's interest, volunteer work. *Important factors considered include:* application essay, academic GPA, recommendation(s), extracurricular activities. *Other factors considered include:* character/personal qualities, interview, talent/ability. **Freshman Admission Requirements:** High school diploma is required and GED is accepted. *Academic units required:* 4 English, 4 mathematics, 4 science, (2 science labs), 4 social studies. *Academic units recommended:* 4 English, 4 mathematics, 4 science, (2 science labs), 4 social studies. **Freshman Admission Statistics:** 4,971 applied, 44% admitted, 37% enrolled. **Transfer Admission Requirements:** college transcript(s), minimum college GPA of 2.0 required. Lowest grade transferable C. **General Admission Information:** Application Fee $35. Nonfall registration accepted. Credit and/or placement offered for CEEB Advanced Placement tests.

COSTS AND FINANCIAL AID
Annual in-state tuition $10,422. Annual out-of-state tuition $18,609. Room and board $10,827. Required fees $3,062. Average book expense $2,130. **Required**

Forms and Deadlines: FAFSA. **Notification of Awards:** Applicants will be notified of awards on or about 5/15. **Types of Aid:** *Need-based scholarships/grants:* Federal Pell, SEOG, state scholarships/grants, private scholarships, the school's own gift aid, United Negro College Fund. *Loans:* Subsidized Stafford, Unsubsidized Stafford, PLUS, Federal Perkins, state loans. **Student Employment:** Federal Work-Study Program available. Institutional employment available. Off-campus job opportunities are good. **Financial Aid Statistics:** 81% freshmen, 78% undergrads receive need-based scholarship or grant aid. 11% freshmen, 8% undergrads receive non-need-based scholarship or grant aid. 55% freshmen, 68% undergrads receive need-based self-help aid. 70% freshmen, 70% undergrads receive any aid. 65% undergrads borrow to pay for school. Average cumulative indebtedness $19,233.

NEW JERSEY INSTITUTE OF TECHNOLOGY

Office of University Admissions, Newark, NJ 7102
Phone: 973-596-3300 • **Financial Aid Phone:** 973-596-3479
E-mail: admissions@njit.edu • **CEEB Code:** 2580
Fax: 973-596-3461 • **Website:** www.njit.edu • **ACT Code:** 2513

This public school was founded in 1881. It has a 48-acre campus.

RATINGS
Admissions Selectivity Rating: 82   **Fire Safety Rating:** 95   **Green Rating:** 76

STUDENTS AND FACULTY
Enrollment: 6,154. **Student Body:** 21% female, 79% male, 9% out-of-state, 5% international (83 countries represented). Asian 21%, African American 9%, Caucasian 37%, Hispanic 15%, Native American 0%.
Retention and Graduation: 82% freshmen return for sophomore year. 19% freshmen graduate within 4 years. 55% freshmen graduate within 6 years. 17% grads go on to further study within 1 year. 1% grads pursue arts and sciences degrees. 1% grads pursue business degrees. **Faculty:** Student/faculty ratio 16:1. 398 full-time faculty, 100% hold PhDs, 26% are members of minority groups, 19% are women. 0% of classes are taught by teaching assistants.

ACADEMICS
Degrees: bachelor's, doctoral, master's, post-bachelor's certificate. **Classes:** Most classes have 20–29 students. **Majors with Highest Enrollment:** architecture (barch, ba/bs, march, ma/ms, phd); civil engineering; mechanical engineering. **Special Study Options:** Accelerated program, cooperative education program, cross-registration, distance learning, double major, English as a Second Language (ESL), honors program, independent study, internships, study abroad. **Honors Programs:** The Albert Dorman Honors College at the New Jersey Institute of Technology (NJIT) enrolls over 500 exceptional students who excel in the fields of engineering, architecture, computing sciences, management, and the sciences. **Combined Degree Programs:** BA/MD, BA/MA, BS/MD, BS/DMD, BS/OD, BArch/MS Mang. **Disability Services:** Special programs offered to physically disabled students include note-taking services, reader services, tape recorders, tutors. **Career Services:** Alumni network, alumni services, career/job search classes, career assessment, internships, regional alumni. Career Services highlights include Cooperative Education at NJIT is an academically integrated program that gives students the opportunity to gain paid professional work experience before graduation. Although not mandatory, over 400 students choose to participate each year. Most co-op students work fulltime for one or two semesters. The average wage for co-op students exceeds $15.00 per hour Nearly 2600 different companies have hired NJIT students over the past decade. Employers range from large multinationals to small start-up companies. Students have completed their co-op assignments in New Jersey, ten other states, and four foreign countries.

FACILITIES
Housing: Coed dorms. 100% of campus accessible to physically disabled. **Special Academic Facilities/Equipment:** New Jersey Literary Hall of Fame and more than 50 research centers and sponsored research laboratories, including computer chip manufacturing center, manufacturing systems center, and many others **Computers:** 100% of classrooms, 100% of dorms, 100% of libraries, 100% of dining areas, 100% of student union, 100% of common outdoor areas have wireless network access. Students can register for classes online. Administrative functions (other than registration) can be performed online. Undergraduates are required to own a computer.

CAMPUS LIFE

Environment: Metropolis. **Activities:** concert band, dance, drama/theater, literary magazine, marching band, musical theater, radio station, student government, student newspaper, yearbook, International Student Organization 70 registered organizations, 10 honor societies, 5 religious organizations. 15 fraternities, 7 sororities. **Athletics (Intercollegiate):** *Men:* baseball, basketball, cheerleading, cross-country, fencing, soccer, swimming, tennis, track/field (outdoor), track/field (indoor), volleyball. *Women:* basketball, cheerleading, cross-country, fencing, soccer, swimming, tennis, track/field (outdoor), track/field (indoor), volleyball. **On-Campus Highlights:** Campus Center, Van Houten Library, Zoom Fleisher Athletic Center, East Building - Admissions, Student Mall. **Environmental Initiatives:** Recycling Energy efficiencies on equipment Water conservation devices.

ADMISSIONS

Freshman Academic Profile: 20% in top 10% of high school class, 52% in top 25% of high school class, 85% in top 50% of high school class. 85% from public high schools. SAT Math middle 50% range 550-660. SAT Critical Reading middle 50% range 470-600. SAT Writing middle 50% range 470-590. Minimum web-based TOEFL 79. Minimum paper TOEFL 550. **Basis for Candidate Selection:** *Very important factors considered include:* Class rank, rigor of secondary school record, standardized test scores. *Important factors considered include:* academic GPA. *Other factors considered include:* application essay, recommendation(s), alumni/ae relation, character/personal qualities, extracurricular activities, geographical residence, interview, level of applicant's interest, racial/ethnic status, religious affiliation/commitment, state residency, talent/ability, volunteer work, work experience. **Freshman Admission Requirements:** High school diploma is required and GED is accepted. *Academic units required:* 4 English, 4 mathematics, 2 science, (2 science labs). *Academic units recommended:* 4 English, 4 mathematics, 2 science, (2 science labs). **Freshman Admission Statistics:** 4,216 applied, 64% admitted, 38% enrolled. **Transfer Admission Requirements:** college transcript(s), minimum college GPA of 2.0 required. Lowest grade transferable C. **General Admission Information:** Application Fee $50. Regular application deadline 4/1. Notification on a rolling basis, beginning on or about 11/15. Nonfall registration accepted. Admission may be deferred for a maximum of 1 semester. Credit offered for CEEB Advanced Placement tests.

COSTS AND FINANCIAL AID

Annual in-state tuition $11,756. Annual out-of-state tuition $23,116. Room and board $11,000. Required fees $2,218. Average book expense $1,900. **Required Forms and Deadlines:** FAFSA. **Notification of Awards:** Applicants will be notified of awards on a rolling basis beginning 12/20. **Types of Aid:** *Need-based scholarships/grants:* Federal Pell, SEOG, state scholarships/grants, private scholarships, the school's own gift aid. *Loans:* Direct Subsidized Stafford, Direct Unsubsidized Stafford, Direct PLUS, Federal Perkins, state loans, college/university loans from institutional funds. **Student Employment:** Federal Work-Study Program available. Institutional employment available. Highest amount earned per year from on-campus jobs $5,500. Off-campus job opportunities are good. **Financial Aid Statistics:** 86% freshmen, 82% undergrads receive need-based scholarship or grant aid. 46% freshmen, 36% undergrads receive non-need-based scholarship or grant aid. 70% freshmen, 89% undergrads receive need-based self-help aid. 6% freshmen, 3% undergrads receive athletic scholarships. 60% freshmen, 51% undergrads receive any aid. 49% undergrads borrow to pay for school. Average cumulative indebtedness $26,045. **Criteria for awarding institutional aid:** *Non-need-based:* academics, athletics, job skills, leadership, state/district residency.

NEW MEXICO INSTITUTE OF MINING & TECHNOLOGY

Campus Station, Socorro, NM 87801
Phone: 575-835-5424 • **Financial Aid Phone:** 575-835-5333
E-mail: admission@admin.nmt.edu • **CEEB Code:** 4533
Fax: 575-835-5989 • **Website:** www.nmt.edu • **ACT Code:** 2642

This public school was founded in 1889. It has a 320-acre campus.

RATINGS

Admissions Selectivity Rating: 85   **Fire Safety Rating:** 60*   **Green Rating:** 61

STUDENTS AND FACULTY

Enrollment: 1,425. **Student Body:** 26% female, 74% male, 17% out-of-state, 3% international (33 countries represented). Asian 2%, African American 2%, Caucasian 60%, Hispanic 26%, Native American 3%. **Retention and Graduation:** 17% freshmen graduate within 4 years. 49% freshmen graduate within 6 years. **Faculty:** Student/faculty ratio 12:1. 124 full-time faculty, 96% hold PhDs, 21% are members of minority groups, 19% are women.

ACADEMICS

Degrees: bachelor's, master's, terminal associate. **Classes:** Most classes have fewer than 10 students. Most lab/discussion sessions have 10–19 students. **Majors with Highest Enrollment:** computer and information sciences; electrical, electronics and communications engineering; mechanical engineering. **Special Study Options:** Accelerated program, cooperative education program, distance learning, double major, dual major, exchange student program (domestic), independent study, internships, student-designed major, teacher certification program. **Combined Degree Programs:** BS/MS Geology, Hydrology. **Disability Services:** Special programs offered to physically disabled students include note-taking services, reader services, tape recorders, tutors. **Career Services:** career/job search classes, career assessment, internships.

FACILITIES

Housing: Coed dorms, men's dorms, women's dorms, apartments for married students, apartments for single students. **Special Academic Facilities/Equipment:** Mineral museum, observatory, radio telescope, seismic observatory and library, explosives labs. **Computers:** Students can register for classes online. Administrative functions (other than registration) can be performed online.

CAMPUS LIFE

Environment: Village. **Activities:** Choral groups, concert band, dance, drama/theater, jazz band, music ensembles, musical theater, radio station, student government, student newspaper 60 registered organizations, 7 honor societies, 3 religious organizations. **On-Campus Highlights:** Fidel Student Center, Skeen Library, Workman Center

ADMISSIONS

Freshman Academic Profile: Average high school GPA 3.7. 35% in top 10% of high school class, 63% in top 25% of high school class, 91% in top 50% of high school class. 80% from public high schools. SAT Math middle 50% range 590-700. SAT Critical Reading middle 50% range 550-670. ACT middle 50% range 23-29. Minimum paper TOEFL 540. **Basis for Candidate Selection:** *Very important factors considered include:* academic GPA, rigor of secondary school record, standardized test scores. *Other factors considered include:* Class rank, extracurricular activities, talent/ability. **Freshman Admission Requirements:** High school diploma is required and GED is accepted. *Academic units required:* 4 English, 3 mathematics, 2 science, (2 science labs), 2 social studies, 1 history, 3 academic electives. *Academic units recommended:* 4 English, 3 mathematics, 2 science, (2 science labs), 2 social studies, 1 history, 3 academic electives. **Freshman Admission Statistics:** 1,188 applied, 31% admitted, 94% enrolled. **Transfer Admission Requirements:** High school transcript, college transcript(s), statement of good standing from prior institution(s). Minimum college GPA of 2.0 required. Lowest grade transferable D. **General Admission Information:** Application Fee $15. Regular application deadline 8/1. Notification on a rolling basis, beginning on or about 3/1. Nonfall registration accepted. Admission may be deferred for a maximum of 1 year. Credit and/or placement offered for CEEB Advanced Placement tests.

COSTS AND FINANCIAL AID

Annual in-state tuition $4,828. Annual out-of-state tuition $15,699. Room and board $6,304. Required fees $668. Average book expense $1,040. **Required Forms and Deadlines:** FAFSA, institution's own financial aid form. **Notification of Awards:** Applicants will be notified of awards on a rolling basis beginning 4/1. **Types of Aid:** *Need-based scholarships/grants:* Federal Pell, SEOG, state scholarships/grants, private scholarships, the school's own gift aid. *Loans:* Subsidized Stafford, Unsubsidized Stafford, PLUS, Federal Perkins, state loans. **Student Employment:** Federal Work-Study Program available. Institutional employment available. Highest amount earned per year from on-campus jobs $3,500. Off-campus job opportunities are fair. **Financial Aid Statistics:** 56% freshmen, 62% undergrads receive need-based scholarship or grant aid. 95% freshmen, 74% undergrads receive non-need-based scholarship or grant aid. 60% freshmen, 70% undergrads receive need-based self-help aid. 34% freshmen, 39% undergrads receive any aid. 42% undergrads borrow to pay for school. Average cumulative indebtedness $18,834. **Criteria for awarding institutional aid:** *Non-need-based:* academics, alumni affiliation, minority status, state/district residency.

NEW MEXICO STATE UNIVERSITY

Box 30001, Las Cruces, NM 88003-8001
Phone: 575-646-3121
E-mail: admissions@nmsu.edu • **CEEB Code:** 4531
Fax: 575-646-6330 • **Website:** www.nmsu.edu • **ACT Code:** 2638

This public school was founded in 1888. It has a 900-acre campus.

RATINGS
Admissions Selectivity Rating: 68   **Fire Safety Rating:** 60*   **Green Rating:** 96

STUDENTS AND FACULTY
Enrollment: 13,399. **Student Body:** 53% female, 47% male, 25% out-of-state, 4% international (72 countries represented). Asian 1%, African American 3%, Caucasian 33%, Hispanic 51%, Native American 3%.
Retention and Graduation: 72% freshmen return for sophomore year. 14% freshmen graduate within 4 years. 44% freshmen graduate within 6 years.
Faculty: Student/faculty ratio 22:1. 619 full-time faculty, 89% hold PhDs, 27% are members of minority groups, 42% are women.

ACADEMICS
Degrees: associate, bachelor's, doctoral, master's, post-bachelor's certificate, post-master's certificate. **Classes:** Most classes have 20–29 students. Most lab/discussion sessions have 20–29 students. **Majors with Highest Enrollment:** business/commerce; curriculum and instruction; electrical, electronics and communications engineering. **Special Study Options:** Accelerated program, cooperative education program, cross-registration, distance learning, double major, dual enrollment, English as a Second Language (ESL), exchange student program (domestic), external degree program, honors program, independent study, internships, student-designed major, study abroad, teacher certification program, weekend college. **Disability Services:** Special programs offered to physically disabled students include note-taking services, reader services, tape recorders, tutors. **Career Services:** alumni services, career/job search classes, career assessment, internships.

FACILITIES
Housing: Coed dorms, special housing for disabled students, men's dorms, women's dorms, fraternity/sorority housing, apartments for married students, apartments for single students. 95% of campus accessible to physically disabled. **Special Academic Facilities/Equipment:** University and art department museums, theatre, horse farm, sports medicine training clinic, observatory, electron microscope, CRAY supercomputer. **Computers:** Students can register for classes online. Administrative functions (other than registration) can be performed online.

CAMPUS LIFE
Environment: City. **Activities:** Choral groups, concert band, dance, drama/theater, jazz band, literary magazine, marching band, music ensembles, musical theater, opera, pep band, radio station, student government, student newspaper, symphony orchestra, television station, Campus Ministries 263 registered organizations, 24 honor societies, 23 religious organizations. 14 fraternities, 5 sororities. **Athletics (Intercollegiate):** *Men:* baseball, basketball, cross-country, football, golf, tennis. *Women:* basketball, cross-country, golf, softball, swimming, tennis, track/field (outdoor), volleyball.

ADMISSIONS
Freshman Academic Profile: Average high school GPA 3.4. 20% in top 10% of high school class, 48% in top 25% of high school class, 81% in top 50% of high school class. SAT Math middle 50% range 430-560. SAT Critical Reading middle 50% range 420-560. SAT Writing middle 50% range 420-540. ACT middle 50% range 18-24. Minimum paper TOEFL 500. **Basis for Candidate Selection:** *Very important factors considered include:* rigor of secondary school record, standardized test scores. *Other factors considered include:* academic GPA. **Freshman Admission Requirements:** High school diploma is required and GED is accepted. *Academic units required:* 4 English, 3 mathematics, 2 science, (2 science labs), 1 foreign language. 4 English, 3 mathematics, 2 science, (2 science labs), 1 foreign language. **Freshman Admission Statistics:** 5,928 applied, 80% admitted, 43% enrolled. **Transfer Admission Requirements:** college transcript(s), minimum college GPA of 2.0 required. Lowest grade transferable C. **General Admission Information:** Application Fee $20. Nonfall registration accepted. Admission may be deferred for a maximum of 1 year. Credit offered for CEEB Advanced Placement tests.

COSTS AND FINANCIAL AID
Average book expense $1,038. **Required Forms and Deadlines:** FAFSA, institution's own financial aid form. **Notification of Awards:** Applicants will be notified of awards on or about 3/1. **Types of Aid:** *Need-based scholarships/grants:* the school's own gift aid. *Loans:* Subsidized Stafford, Unsubsidized Stafford, PLUS, Federal Perkins, college/university loans from institutional funds.

Student Employment: Federal Work-Study Program available. Institutional employment available. Off-campus job opportunities are good. **Financial Aid Statistics:** 98% freshmen, 91% undergrads receive need-based scholarship or grant aid. 13% freshmen, 9% undergrads receive non-need-based scholarship or grant aid. 53% freshmen, 66% undergrads receive need-based self-help aid. 1% freshmen, 2% undergrads receive athletic scholarships. 54% undergrads borrow to pay for school. Average cumulative indebtedness $18,922. **Criteria for awarding institutional aid:** *Non-need-based:* academics, alumni affiliation, athletics, leadership, minority status, state/district residency.

THE NEW SCHOOL FOR JAZZ & CONTEMPORARY MUSIC

New York, NY
Phone: 212-229-5896 x4589 • **Financial Aid Phone:** 212-229-8930
E-mail: jazzadm@newschool.edu
Fax: 212-229-8936 • **Website:** jazz.newschool.edu

This private school was founded in 1986.

RATINGS
Admissions Selectivity Rating: 63   **Fire Safety Rating:** 77   **Green Rating:** 89

STUDENTS AND FACULTY
Enrollment: 239. **Student Body:** 17% female, 83% male, 74% out-of-state, 30% international (27 countries represented). Asian 3%, African American 10%, Caucasian 41%, Hispanic 6%, Native American 0%.
Retention and Graduation: 73% freshmen return for sophomore year. 59% freshmen graduate within 4 years. **Faculty:** Student/faculty ratio 11:1. 3 full-time faculty, 0% hold PhDs, 33% are members of minority groups, 33% are women. 0% of classes are taught by teaching assistants.

ACADEMICS
Degrees: bachelor's. **Classes:** Most classes have fewer than 10 students. **Majors with Highest Enrollment:** jazz/jazz studies. **Special Study Options:** Accelerated program, cross-registration, dual enrollment, English as a Second Language (ESL), exchange student program (domestic), independent study, internships, study abroad, five year combined BA/BFA. **Combined Degree Programs:** BA/BFA. **Disability Services:** Special programs offered to physically disabled students include note-taking services, reader services, tape recorders. **Career Services:** Alumni network, alumni services, career/job search classes, career assessment, internships, regional alumni..

FACILITIES
Housing: Coed dorms, special housing for disabled students, apartments for single students. 99% of campus accessible to physically disabled. **Computers:** 95% of classrooms, 100% of libraries, 100% of dining areas, 100% of common outdoor areas have wireless network access. Students can register for classes online. Administrative functions (other than registration) can be performed online.

CAMPUS LIFE
Environment: Metropolis. **Activities:** Choral groups, dance, drama/theater, jazz band, literary magazine, music ensembles, opera, radio station, student government, student newspaper, symphony orchestra, International Student Organization 34 registered organizations. **On-Campus Highlights:** Jazz Center, University Welcome Center **Environmental Initiatives:** 1. In Fall 2010, The New School Facilities Management hired an engineering firm to conduct energy audits and to retro-commission five of the most energy-intensive owned buildings on campus. The result will be a phased capital plan to address needed upgrades in these buildings, equating to 500,000gsf, that will reduce carbon emissions. 2. The New School Office for Sustainability hired a consultant to conduct a waste audit of the entire campus in Fall 2009. A waste reduction strategy is currently being finalized. The immediate outcomes are new recycling signs and an enhanced post-consumer composting program in four buildings. Food scraps, napkins/paper towels and compostable cups and utensils will be collected in all food service locations plus a pilot location in a building with architecture and fine arts studios. The New School replaced two steam boilers, which were approximately 50 years old. Located in Johnson/Kaplan Hall, the university's founding building, constructed in 1930, this boiler plant burned #6 heating oil, the dirtiest and most carbon-intensive heating oil. In the summer of 2010, Design, Construction, and Facilities Management upgraded the plant to house two new steam dual-fuel boilers with a thermal efficiency of 86 percent and the option to burn #2 heating oil or, eventually, natural gas, the least carbon intensive fossil fuel. This retrofit project also marks the phasing out of #6 heating oil on campus. In the summer of 2010, Design, Construction, and Facilities Management also replaced the roof at Johnson/Kaplan Hall with a white Thermoplastic Polyolefin (TPO) thermally bonded membrane with superior

durability and an ENERGY STAR rating for its high reflectance. Insulation was also added to the roof. The new roof drastically reduces heat absorption in the summer months and also better insulates the building in the winter, resulting in lower cooling and heating loads and costs. Phasing out the use of T12 and incandescent lighting has been an ongoing initiative over the past two years and focused on 45 percent of the entire building portfolio (equivalent to 563,503 gross square feet, which represents nearly 72 percent of The New School's owned buildings). In FY10, the Office for Sustainability began to install campus-wide (in all spaces where The New School has operational control) occupancy sensors in bathrooms, office kitchenettes, and conference rooms. By the end of FY12, the university will phase out T12s and incandescent lighting in all university-owned buildings and launch a LED lighting demonstration project.

ADMISSIONS

Freshman Academic Profile: Average high school GPA 3.3. Minimum web-based TOEFL 92. Minimum paper TOEFL 550. **Basis for Candidate Selection:** *Very important factors considered include:* level of applicant's interest, talent/ability. *Important factors considered include:* rigor of secondary school record. *Other factors considered include:* application essay, academic GPA, recommendation(s), extracurricular activities. **Freshman Admission Requirements:** High school diploma is required and GED is accepted. **Freshman Admission Statistics:** 263 applied, 62% admitted, 26% enrolled. **Transfer Admission Requirements:** college transcript(s), essay or personal statement, Lowest grade transferable C. **General Admission Information:** Application Fee $100. Notification on a rolling basis, beginning on or about 4/1. Nonfall registration accepted.

COSTS AND FINANCIAL AID

Required Forms and Deadlines: FAFSA, state aid form. Notification of Awards: Applicants will be notified of awards on a rolling basis beginning 3/1. Types of Aid: Need-based scholarships/grants: Federal Pell, SEOG, state scholarships/grants, private scholarships, the school's own gift aid. Loans: Subsidized Stafford, Unsubsidized Stafford, PLUS, Federal Perkins. Student Employment: Federal Work-Study Program available. Institutional employment available. Off-campus job opportunities are excellent. Financial Aid Statistics: 91% freshmen, 81% undergrads receive need-based scholarship or grant aid. 4% freshmen, 5% undergrads receive non-need-based scholarship or grant aid. 91% freshmen, 88% undergrads receive need-based self-help aid. 69% undergrads borrow to pay for school. Average cumulative indebtedness $25,735. Criteria for awarding institutional aid: Non-need-based: academics, music/drama.

NEW WORLD SCHOOL OF THE ARTS

300 NE 2nd Avenue, Miami, FL 33132
Phone: 305-237-7007
E-mail: nwsaadm@mdc.edu
Fax: 305-237-3794 • **Website:** www.mdc.edu/nwsa

This public school was founded in 1984. It has a 2-acre campus.

RATINGS
Admissions Selectivity Rating: 61   **Fire Safety Rating:** 60*   **Green Rating:** 60*

STUDENTS AND FACULTY
Enrollment: 359. **Student Body:** 52% female, 48% male, 17% out-of-state, 0% international (17 countries represented). Asian 4%, African American 11%, Caucasian 31%, Hispanic 51%, Native American 0%.
Retention and Graduation: 50% grads pursue arts and sciences degrees. **Faculty:** Student/faculty ratio 10:1. 20 full-time faculty, 100% hold PhDs, 20% are members of minority groups, 35% are women. 0% of classes are taught by teaching assistants.

ACADEMICS
Degrees: associate, bachelor's. **Majors with Highest Enrollment:** dance; graphic design. **Special Study Options:** cooperative education program, distance learning, English as a Second Language (ESL), independent study, liberal arts/career combination.

FACILITIES
Housing: 100% of campus accessible to physically disabled. **Special Academic Facilities/Equipment:** black box theater art gallery dance recital hall **Computers:** Students can register for classes online. Administrative functions (other than registration) can be performed online.

CAMPUS LIFE
Environment: Metropolis. **Activities:** dance, drama/theater, music ensembles, musical theater, opera, student government, symphony orchestra.

ADMISSIONS
Freshman Academic Profile: Minimum paper TOEFL 550. **Basis for Candidate Selection:** *Very important factors considered include:* talent/ability. *Other factors considered include:* application essay, recommendation(s), rigor of secondary school record, character/personal qualities, interview. **Freshman Admission Requirements:** High school diploma is required and GED is accepted. **Transfer Admission Requirements:** High school transcript, college transcript(s), essay or personal statement, interview, Lowest grade transferable c. **General Admission Information:** Nonfall registration not accepted. Credit and/or placement offered for CEEB Advanced Placement tests.

COSTS AND FINANCIAL AID
Annual in-state tuition $10,000. Annual out-of-state tuition $15,000. Average book expense $600. **Required Forms and Deadlines:** FAFSA. **Types of Aid:** *Need-based scholarships/grants:* Federal Pell, SEOG, state scholarships/grants, private scholarships, the school's own gift aid. *Loans:* Direct Subsidized Stafford, Direct Unsubsidized Stafford, Direct PLUS, PLUS, Federal Perkins, state loans, college/university loans from institutional funds. **Student Employment:** Federal Work-Study Program available. Off-campus job opportunities are excellent. **Criteria for awarding institutional aid:** *Non-need-based:* art, music/drama.

NEW YORK INSTITUTE OF TECHNOLOGY

PO Box 8000, Old Westbury, NY 11568
Phone: 516-686-7520 • **Financial Aid Phone:**
E-mail: admissions@nyit.edu • **CEEB Code:** 2561
Fax: 516-686-7613 • **Website:** www.nyit.edu • **ACT Code:** 2832

This private school was founded in 1955. It has a 325-acre campus.

RATINGS
Admissions Selectivity Rating: 74   **Fire Safety Rating:** 67   **Green Rating:** 60*

STUDENTS AND FACULTY
Enrollment: 5,141. **Student Body:** 38% female, 62% male, 10% out-of-state, 7% international. Asian 10%, African American 11%, Caucasian 33%, Hispanic 10%, Native American 0%.
Retention and Graduation: 71% freshmen return for sophomore year. 14% freshmen graduate within 4 years. 32% freshmen graduate within 6 years. 29% grads go on to further study within 1 year. 21% grads pursue arts and sciences degrees. 1% grads pursue law degrees. 33% grads pursue business degrees. 2% grads pursue medical degrees. **Faculty:** Student/faculty ratio 16:1. 218 full-time faculty, 89% hold PhDs, 22% are members of minority groups, 23% are women. 0% of classes are taught by teaching assistants.

ACADEMICS
Degrees: associate, bachelor's, certificate, first professional, master's, post-bachelor's certificate, post-master's certificate, terminal associate, transfer associate. **Classes:** Most classes have 10–19 students. Most lab/discussion sessions have 10–19 students. **Majors with Highest Enrollment:** architecture (barch, ba/bs, march, ma/ms, phd); business, management, marketing, and related support services, other; communication studies/speech communication and rhetoric. **Special Study Options:** Accelerated program, cooperative education program, cross-registration, distance learning, double major, dual enrollment, English as a Second Language (ESL), honors program, independent study, internships, liberal arts/career combination, study abroad, teacher certification program, weekend college, Combined bachelor's/professional degree program in Life Sciences (BS)/Osteopathic Medicine (DO); Architectural Technology (BS)/ Energy Managment (MS); Architectural Technology (BS)/MBA; Mechanical Engineering (BS)/Energy Managment (MS); Life Sciences (BS)/Physical Therapy (MS) Life Sciences (BS)/Occupational Therapy (MS); Behavioral Sciences (BS)/Law at Touro Law Center (JD). **Combined Degree Programs:** BA/JD, BA/MA, BS/MS; BS/MBA. **Disability Services:** Special programs offered to physically disabled students include tutors. **Career Services:** Alumni network, alumni services, career/job search classes, career assessment, internships, regional alumni.

FACILITIES
Housing: Coed dorms, special housing for international students, fraternity/sorority housing, apartments for single students, Housing for graduate, life sciences, first-year experience, student leaders, student government, international, Greek Life organizations and architecture students provided. For the Manhattan Campus, housing is available off-campus. 100% of campus accessible to physically disabled. **Special Academic Facilities/Equipment:** Center for Urban/Suburban Studies; Center for Neighborhood Revitalization; Parkinson's Disease Treatment Center; Center for Energy Policy and Research; Academic Computing Labs; Center for Labor and Industrial Relations; Carleton

Group (Advertising) LI News Tonight; Education Enterprise Zone; Center for Teaching and Learning with Technology, Production House, Motion Graphics Laboratory; Academic Health Care Center; Center for Business Information Technologies; de Seversky Culinary Arts Center **Computers:** Students can register for classes online. Administrative functions (other than registration) can be performed online. Undergraduates are required to own a computer.

CAMPUS LIFE

Environment: Village. **Activities:** Choral groups, dance, drama/theater, literary magazine, musical theater, radio station, student government, student newspaper, student-run film society, television station, yearbook 100 registered organizations, 14 honor societies, 4 religious organizations. 5 fraternities, 3 sororities. **Athletics (Intercollegiate):** *Men:* baseball, basketball, cross-country, lacrosse, soccer, track/field (outdoor). *Women:* basketball, cross-country, soccer, softball, track/field (outdoor), volleyball. **On-Campus Highlights:** Libraries, Computer clusters, Radio/Television studios, CAD rooms, Motion Graphics Laboratory, Enginnering labs, Allied Health facilities, de Seversky Culinary Arts Center.

ADMISSIONS

Freshman Academic Profile: Average high school GPA 3.1. 60% from public high schools. SAT Math middle 50% range 510-630. SAT Critical Reading middle 50% range 470-580. ACT middle 50% range 20-27. Minimum paper TOEFL 550. **Basis for Candidate Selection:** *Very important factors considered include:* rigor of secondary school record. *Important factors considered include:* application essay, standardized test scores, interview. *Other factors considered include:* Class rank, recommendation(s), character/personal qualities, extracurricular activities, talent/ability, volunteer work, work experience. **Freshman Admission Requirements:** High school diploma is required and GED is accepted. *Academic units required:* 4 English, 2 mathematics, 1 science, (1 science labs), 2 social studies, 7 academic electives. *Academic units recommended:* 4 English, 2 mathematics, 1 science, (1 science labs), 2 social studies, 7 academic electives. **Freshman Admission Statistics:** 3,511 applied, 76% admitted, 33% enrolled. **Transfer Admission Requirements:** college transcript(s), essay or personal statement, minimum college GPA of 2.0 required. Lowest grade transferable C–. **General Admission Information:** Application Fee $50. Notification on a rolling basis, beginning on or about 1/1. Nonfall registration accepted. Admission may be deferred for a maximum of ONE YEAR. Credit and/or placement offered for CEEB Advanced Placement tests.

COSTS AND FINANCIAL AID

Annual tuition $16,926. Room and board $7,780. Required fees $300. Average book expense $1,200. **Required Forms and Deadlines:** FAFSA. **Notification of Awards:** Applicants will be notified of awards on a rolling basis beginning 3/15. **Types of Aid:** *Need-based scholarships/grants:* Federal Pell, SEOG, state scholarships/grants, private scholarships, the school's own gift aid. *Loans:* Subsidized Stafford, Unsubsidized Stafford, PLUS, Federal Perkins, Federal Nursing, Alternative loans. **Student Employment:** Federal Work-Study Program available. Institutional employment available. Highest amount earned per year from on-campus jobs $2,200. Off-campus job opportunities are good. **Financial Aid Statistics:** 66% freshmen, 85% undergrads receive need-based scholarship or grant aid. 73% freshmen, 68% undergrads receive non-need-based scholarship or grant aid. 88% freshmen, 89% undergrads receive need-based self-help aid. 5% freshmen, 5% undergrads receive athletic scholarships. 75% undergrads borrow to pay for school. Average cumulative indebtedness $17,125. **Criteria for awarding institutional aid:** *Non-need-based:* academics, alumni affiliation, athletics.

NEW YORK SCHOOL OF INTERIOR DESIGN

107 East 70th Street, New York, NY 10021
Phone: 212-472-1500 • **Financial Aid Phone:** 212-472-1500
E-mail: admissions@nysid.edu • **CEEB Code:** 333
Fax: 212-472-1867 • **ACT Code:** 2829

This private school was founded in 1916.

RATINGS
Admissions Selectivity Rating: 62   **Fire Safety Rating:** 60*   **Green Rating:** 60*

STUDENTS AND FACULTY
Enrollment: 614. **Student Body:** 93% female, 7% male, 36% out-of-state, 8% international. Asian 7%, African American 3%, Caucasian 74%, Hispanic 6%, Native American 0%.
Retention and Graduation: 60% freshmen return for sophomore year. 75% freshmen graduate within 6 years. **Faculty:** Student/faculty ratio 10:1. 2 full-time faculty, 50% are women. 0% of classes are taught by teaching assistants.

ACADEMICS
Degrees: associate, bachelor's, certificate, first professional, master's, transfer associate. **Classes:** Most classes have 10–19 students. **Majors with Highest Enrollment:** interior design. **Special Study Options:** independent study, internships, study abroad. **Disability Services:** Special programs offered to physically disabled students include tutors. **Career Services:** Alumni network, alumni services, internships.

FACILITIES
Housing: 100% of campus accessible to physically disabled. **Special Academic Facilities/Equipment:** Three galleries, lighting laboratory, student atelier.

CAMPUS LIFE
Environment: Metropolis. **Activities:** 1 registered organizations.

ADMISSIONS
Freshman Academic Profile: Average high school GPA 3.0. Minimum paper TOEFL 550. **Basis for Candidate Selection:** *Very important factors considered include:* application essay, rigor of secondary school record, talent/ability. *Important factors considered include:* academic GPA, recommendation(s), level of applicant's interest. *Other factors considered include:* Class rank, standardized test scores, alumni/ae relation, character/personal qualities, extracurricular activities, interview, work experience. **Freshman Admission Requirements:** High school diploma is required and GED is accepted. **Freshman Admission Statistics:** 38 applied, 76% admitted, 34% enrolled. **Transfer Admission Requirements:** High school transcript, college transcript(s), essay or personal statement, minimum college GPA of 3.0 required. Lowest grade transferable C. **General Admission Information:** Application Fee $50. Regular notification 4/1. Nonfall registration accepted. Admission may be deferred for a maximum of 1 year. Credit offered for CEEB Advanced Placement tests.

COSTS AND FINANCIAL AID
Annual tuition $18,600. Required fees $290. **Required Forms and Deadlines:** FAFSA, institution's own financial aid form, state aid form. **Notification of Awards:** Applicants will be notified of awards on a rolling basis beginning 2/1. **Types of Aid:** *Need-based scholarships/grants:* Federal Pell, SEOG, state scholarships/grants, the school's own gift aid. *Loans:* Subsidized Stafford, Unsubsidized Stafford, PLUS. **Student Employment:** Federal Work-Study Program available. Off-campus job opportunities are excellent. **Financial Aid Statistics:** 89% undergrads receive need-based scholarship or grant aid. 54% undergrads receive need-based self-help aid. 15% undergrads receive any aid. 15% undergrads borrow to pay for school. Average cumulative indebtedness $30,000.

See page 1154.

NEW YORK UNIVERSITY

665 Broadway, New York, NY 10012
Phone: 212-998-4500 • **Financial Aid Phone:** 212-998-4444
E-mail: admissions@nyu.edu • **CEEB Code:** 2562
Fax: 212-995-4902 • **Website:** www.nyu.edu • **ACT Code:** 2838

This private school was founded in 1831.

RATINGS
Admissions Selectivity Rating: 96   **Fire Safety Rating:** 88   **Green Rating:** 90

STUDENTS AND FACULTY
Enrollment: 22,080. **Student Body:** 60% female, 40% male, 65% out-of-state, 12% international (129 countries represented). Asian 19%, African American 5%, Caucasian 40%, Hispanic 10%, Native American 0%.
Retention and Graduation: 92% freshmen return for sophomore year. 79% freshmen graduate within 4 years. 85% freshmen graduate within 6 years. 22% grads go on to further study within 1 year. 2% grads pursue arts and sciences degrees. 4% grads pursue law degrees. 1% grads pursue business degrees. 3% grads pursue medical degrees. **Faculty:** Student/faculty ratio 10:1. 2525 full-time faculty, 91% hold PhDs, 42% are women.

ACADEMICS
Degrees: associate, bachelor's, certificate, diploma, doctoral, master's, post-bachelor's certificate, post-master's certificate, terminal associate, transfer associate. **Classes:** Most classes have 10–19 students. Most lab/discussion sessions have 10–19 students. **Majors with Highest Enrollment:** drama and

dramatics/theatre arts; finance; liberal arts and sciences/liberal studies. **Special Study Options:** cross-registration, distance learning, double major, English as a Second Language (ESL), exchange student program (domestic), honors program, independent study, internships, liberal arts/career combination, student-designed major, study abroad, teacher certification program, Exchange program with several historically black colleges. **Combined Degree Programs:** BA/DDS. **Disability Services:** Special programs offered to physically disabled students include note-taking services, reader services, tape recorders. **Career Services:** Alumni network, alumni services, career/job search classes, career assessment, internships, regional alumni. Career Services highlights include Students have multiple opportunites to advance their entrepreneurial learning through course work, business planning competitions, workshops, mentoring and coaching.

FACILITIES

Housing: Coed dorms, special housing for disabled students, fraternity/sorority housing, apartments for single students, wellness housing, theme housing, Choices Substance Free Communities; FYRE: First Year Residential Experience; Sophomore Year Residential Experience; Explorations Learning Communities; Mixed Sex Housing. 95% of campus accessible to physically disabled. **Special Academic Facilities/Equipment:** Bobst Library and study center; Grey Art Gallery and study center; Special academic facilities for arts, business, culture, education, international relations, language, law, media, music, public service, research, and social policy, and Skirball Center for Performing Arts. **Computers:** 70% of classrooms, 100% of libraries, 100% of dining areas, 100% of student union, 50% of common outdoor areas have wireless network access. Students can register for classes online. Administrative functions (other than registration) can be performed online.

CAMPUS LIFE

Environment: Metropolis. **Activities:** Choral groups, concert band, dance, drama/theater, jazz band, literary magazine, music ensembles, musical theater, opera, pep band, radio station, student government, student newspaper, student-run film society, symphony orchestra, television station, yearbook, Campus Ministries, International Student Organization, Model UN 407 registered organizations, 3 honor societies, 31 religious organizations. 14 fraternities, 10 sororities. **Athletics (Intercollegiate):** *Men:* basketball, cross-country, diving, fencing, golf, soccer, swimming, tennis, track/field (outdoor), track/field (indoor), volleyball, wrestling. *Women:* basketball, cross-country, diving, fencing, golf, soccer, swimming, tennis, track/field (outdoor), track/field (indoor), volleyball. **On-Campus Highlights:** Kimmel Center for Student Life, Silver Center for Arts and Science, Coles Athletic Center, Palladium Athletic Facility, Skirball Center for the Performing Arts. **Environmental Initiatives:** 1) Launched a comprehensive sustainability initiative that has learned from earlier schools' efforts, leapfrogging peer schools to achieve new levels of environmental performance -- incl. Sustainability Task Force with 75 volunteer members and 8 working groups; Green Grants program and 60 individual grants; Sustainability Advocate Program for more than 200 employees; student engagement initiatives reaching 1000s of individuals; green purchasing policy; hiring of multiple full and part-time staff sustainability staff; an annual Environmental Assessment process; released more than 130 recommendations to the university leadership; created a website that has become the networking hub of the green community on campus; launched the first bike-sharing program in New York City, its biggest clean cogeneration power plant, its largest composting program, and more! 2) Substantively reduced measured energy use 5% or more per year for five years running, with strategies ranging from efficiency upgrades to dorm competitions, and with plans to cut substantially further in each of the coming years. 3) Committed to an aggressive 10-year, 30% emissions reduction, and a long-term commitment to climate neutrality -- ambitious given that as the largest private university NYU amounts to.3% of all of NYC emissions. We achieved that 30% cut 6 years ahead of schedule, in 2011, and are continuing forward ahead of pace for climate neutrality in 2040.

ADMISSIONS

Freshman Academic Profile: Average high school GPA 3.6. SAT Math middle 50% range 630-740. SAT Critical Reading middle 50% range 620-710. SAT Writing middle 50% range 640-730. ACT middle 50% range 28-32. Minimum web-based TOEFL 100. Minimum paper TOEFL 600. **Basis for Candidate Selection:** *Very important factors considered include:* application essay, academic GPA, recommendation(s), rigor of secondary school record, standardized test scores, extracurricular activities, talent/ability. *Important factors considered include:* Class rank, alumni/ae relation, character/personal qualities, first generation, geographical residence. *Other factors considered include:* racial/ethnic status, volunteer work, work experience. **Freshman Admission Requirements:** High school diploma is required and GED is accepted. *Academic units required:* 4 English, 3 mathematics, 3 science, 2 foreign language, 4 history. 4 English, 3 mathematics, 3 science, 2 foreign language, 4 history. **Freshman Admission Statistics:** 42,807 applied, 35% admitted, 34% enrolled. **Transfer Admission Requirements:** High school transcript, college transcript(s), essay or personal statement, statement of good standing from prior institution(s).

Lowest grade transferable C. **General Admission Information:** Application Fee $65. Early decision application deadline 11/1. Regular application deadline 1/1. Regular notification 4/1. Nonfall registration not accepted. Admission may be deferred for a maximum of 12 months. Credit offered for CEEB Advanced Placement tests.

COSTS AND FINANCIAL AID

Annual tuition $40,878. Room and board $16,133. Required fees $2,326. Average book expense $1,070. **Required Forms and Deadlines:** FAFSA, state aid formEarly Decision applicants may submit an institutional form for an estimated award. **Notification of Awards:** Applicants will be notified of awards on a rolling basis beginning 4/1. **Types of Aid:** *Need-based scholarships/grants:* Federal Pell, SEOG, state scholarships/grants, private scholarships, the school's own gift aid. *Loans:* Subsidized Stafford, Unsubsidized Stafford, PLUS, Federal Perkins, Federal Nursing. **Student Employment:** Federal Work-Study Program available. Institutional employment available. Highest amount earned per year from on-campus jobs $24,026. Off-campus job opportunities are excellent. **Financial Aid Statistics:** 94% freshmen, 94% undergrads receive need-based scholarship or grant aid. 2% freshmen, 3% undergrads receive non-need-based scholarship or grant aid. 94% freshmen, 92% undergrads receive need-based self-help aid. 55% freshmen, 58% undergrads receive any aid. 54% undergrads borrow to pay for school. Average cumulative indebtedness $36,351. **Criteria for awarding institutional aid:** *Non-need-based:* academics.

See page 1156.

NEWBERRY COLLEGE

2100 College Street, Newberry, SC 29108
Phone: 803-321-5127
E-mail: admissions@newberry.edu • **CEEB Code:** 5493
Fax: 803-321-5138 • **Website:** www.newberry.edu • **ACT Code:** 3870

This private school, affiliated with the Lutheran Church, was founded in 1856. It has a 60-acre campus.

RATINGS

Admissions Selectivity Rating: 65   **Fire Safety Rating:** 62   **Green Rating:** 60*

STUDENTS AND FACULTY

Enrollment: 764. **Student Body:** 43% female, 57% male, 25% out-of-state, 2% international (8 countries represented). Asian 0%, African American 27%, Caucasian 71%, Hispanic 1%, Native American 1%.
Retention and Graduation: 58% freshmen return for sophomore year. 36% freshmen graduate within 4 years. 49% freshmen graduate within 6 years. 15% grads go on to further study within 1 year. **Faculty:** Student/faculty ratio 13:1. 46 full-time faculty, 61% hold PhDs, 9% are members of minority groups, 37% are women. 0% of classes are taught by teaching assistants.

ACADEMICS

Degrees: bachelor's. **Classes:** Most classes have fewer than 10 students. Most lab/discussion sessions have 20-29 students. **Majors with Highest Enrollment:** business/commerce; communication studies/speech communication and rhetoric; elementary education and teaching. **Special Study Options:** cooperative education program, double major, dual enrollment, honors program, independent study, internships, liberal arts/career combination, student-designed major, study abroad, teacher certification program. **Honors Programs:** Summerland Honors Program- Focus is on human identity-honors credit may substitute for cored curriculum. **Disability Services:** Special programs offered to physically disabled students include tutors. **Career Services:** alumni services, career/job search classes, internships.

FACILITIES

Housing: Coed dorms, men's dorms, women's dorms. 90% of campus accessible to physically disabled. **Special Academic Facilities/Equipment:** TV Studio

CAMPUS LIFE

Environment: Rural. **Activities:** Choral groups, concert band, drama/theater, jazz band, literary magazine, marching band, music ensembles, radio station, student government, student newspaper, television station, yearbook 50 registered organizations, 11 honor societies, 4 religious organizations. 5 fraternities, 4 sororities. **Athletics (Intercollegiate):** *Men:* baseball, basketball, cross-country, football, golf, soccer, tennis. *Women:* basketball, cheerleading, cross-country, golf, soccer, softball, tennis, volleyball. **On-Campus Highlights:** The Quad-grassy lawln area, Steele Student Center-snack bar, game room, Fitness Center in Physical Education Complex, John F. Clarkson Swimming Pool, Weber Ministries House.

ADMISSIONS

Freshman Academic Profile: Average high school GPA 3.2. 7% in top 10% of high school class, 22% in top 25% of high school class, 61% in top 50% of high school class. 88% from public high schools. SAT Math middle 50% range 460-600. SAT Critical Reading middle 50% range 490-570. ACT middle 50% range 17-22. Minimum paper TOEFL 525. **Basis for Candidate Selection:** *Very important factors considered include:* rigor of secondary school record, standardized test scores. *Important factors considered include:* Class rank. *Other factors considered include:* application essay, recommendation(s), alumni/ae relation, character/personal qualities, extracurricular activities, geographical residence, interview, racial/ethnic status, religious affiliation/commitment, state residency, talent/ability, volunteer work, work experience. **Freshman Admission Requirements:** High school diploma is required and GED is accepted. *Academic units required:* 4 English, 3 mathematics, 2 science, (2 science labs), 2 foreign language, 2 social studies, 1 history, 1 academic electives. *Academic units recommended:* 4 English, 3 mathematics, 2 science, (2 science labs), 2 foreign language, 2 social studies, 1 history, 1 academic electives. **Transfer Admission Requirements:** college transcript(s), minimum college GPA of 2.0 required. Lowest grade transferable C. **General Admission Information:** Application Fee $30. Notification on a rolling basis, beginning on or about 9/30. Nonfall registration accepted. Admission may be deferred for a maximum of 2 years. Credit and/or placement offered for CEEB Advanced Placement tests.

COSTS AND FINANCIAL AID

Annual tuition $17,470. Room and board $5,890. Required fees $631. Average book expense $1,195. **Required Forms and Deadlines:** FAFSA, institution's own financial aid form. **Types of Aid:** *Need-based scholarships/grants:* Federal Pell, SEOG, state scholarships/grants, private scholarships, the school's own gift aid. *Loans:* Subsidized Stafford, Unsubsidized Stafford, PLUS, Federal Perkins, state loans. **Student Employment:** Federal Work-Study Program available. Institutional employment available. Off-campus job opportunities are poor. **Financial Aid Statistics:** 100% freshmen, 99% undergrads receive need-based scholarship or grant aid. 24% freshmen, 22% undergrads receive non-need-based scholarship or grant aid. 68% freshmen, 69% undergrads receive need-based self-help aid. 16% freshmen, 11% undergrads receive athletic scholarships. Average cumulative indebtedness $13,477. **Criteria for awarding institutional aid:** *Non-need-based:* academics, alumni affiliation, athletics, music/drama, religious affiliation, state/district residency.

NEWMAN UNIVERSITY

3100 McCormick Avenue, Wichita, KS 67213-2097
Phone: 316-942-4291
E-mail: admissions@newmanu.edu • **CEEB Code:** 6615
Fax: 316-942-4483 • **Website:** www.newmanu.edu • **ACT Code:** 1452

This private school, affiliated with the Roman Catholic Church, was founded in 1933. It has a 53-acre campus.

RATINGS

Admissions Selectivity Rating: 60*   **Fire Safety Rating:** 60*   **Green Rating:** 60*

STUDENTS AND FACULTY

Enrollment: 1,843. **Student Body:** 62% female, 38% male, 11% out-of-state, 6% international (26 countries represented). Asian 3%, African American 5%, Caucasian 77%, Hispanic 7%, Native American 2%.
Retention and Graduation: Faculty: Student/faculty ratio 17:1. 66 full-time faculty. 0% of classes are taught by teaching assistants.

ACADEMICS

Degrees: associate, bachelor's, master's, terminal associate, transfer associate. **Classes:** Most classes have 10–19 students. Most lab/discussion sessions have 10–19 students. **Special Study Options:** cooperative education program, cross-registration, distance learning, double major, dual enrollment, independent study, internships, liberal arts/career combination, student-designed major, study abroad, teacher certification program, weekend college. **Disability Services:** Special programs offered to physically disabled students include note-taking services, reader services, tape recorders, tutors.

FACILITIES

Housing: Coed dorms, special housing for disabled students, apartments for married students, apartments for single students, Freshmen required to live in college housng first 2 years if not living with parents. 95% of campus accessible to physically disabled. **Special Academic Facilities/Equipment:** Cadaver lab; art gallery.

CAMPUS LIFE

Activities: Choral groups, drama/theater, literary magazine, radio station, student government, student newspaper 25 registered organizations, 3 honor

societies, 2 religious organizations. **Athletics (Intercollegiate):** *Men:* baseball, basketball, golf, soccer. *Women:* basketball, golf, soccer, softball, volleyball.

ADMISSIONS

Freshman Academic Profile: Average high school GPA 3.4. 12% in top 10% of high school class, 26% in top 25% of high school class, 52% in top 50% of high school class. 78% from public high schools. Minimum paper TOEFL 530. **Basis for Candidate Selection:** *Very important factors considered include:* rigor of secondary school record, standardized test scores. *Other factors considered include:* recommendation(s). **Freshman Admission Requirements:** High school diploma is required and GED is accepted. **Transfer Admission Requirements:** college transcript(s), minimum college GPA of 2.0 required. Lowest grade transferable D. **General Admission Information:** Application Fee $20. Notification on a rolling basis, beginning on or about 6/1. Nonfall registration accepted. Admission may be deferred for a maximum of 2 years. Credit offered for CEEB Advanced Placement tests.

COSTS AND FINANCIAL AID

Annual tuition $14,650. Room and board $5,060. Required fees $180. Average book expense $800. **Required Forms and Deadlines:** FAFSA, institution's own financial aid form. **Notification of Awards:** Applicants will be notified of awards on a rolling basis beginning 1/2. **Types of Aid:** *Need-based scholarships/grants:* Federal Pell, SEOG, state scholarships/grants, private scholarships, the school's own gift aid. *Loans:* Subsidized Stafford, Unsubsidized Stafford, PLUS, Federal Perkins. **Student Employment:** Highest amount earned per year from on-campus jobs $1,200. **Financial Aid Statistics:** 79% freshmen, 79% undergrads receive need-based scholarship or grant aid. 82% freshmen, 47% undergrads receive non-need-based scholarship or grant aid. 73% freshmen, 80% undergrads receive need-based self-help aid. 36% freshmen, 29% undergrads receive athletic scholarships. 69% undergrads borrow to pay for school. Average cumulative indebtedness $18,808. **Criteria for awarding institutional aid:** *Non-need-based:* academics, alumni affiliation, athletics, leadership, minority status, music/drama, religious affiliation.

NIAGARA UNIVERSITY

Bailo Hall, Niagara University, NY 14109
Phone: 716-286-8700 • **Financial Aid Phone:** 716-286-8686
E-mail: admissions@niagara.edu • **CEEB Code:** 2558
Fax: 716-286-8710 • **Website:** www.niagara.edu • **ACT Code:** 2842

This private school, affiliated with the Roman Catholic Church, was founded in 1856. It has a 160-acre campus.

RATINGS

Admissions Selectivity Rating: 75   **Fire Safety Rating:** 72   **Green Rating:** 94

STUDENTS AND FACULTY

Enrollment: 3,138. **Student Body:** 60% female, 40% male, 8% out-of-state, 16% international (12 countries represented). Asian 1%, African American 5%, Caucasian 66%, Hispanic 3%, Native American 1%.
Retention and Graduation: 81% freshmen return for sophomore year. 60% freshmen graduate within 4 years. 65% freshmen graduate within 6 years. 31% grads go on to further study within 1 year. 13% grads pursue arts and sciences degrees. 2% grads pursue law degrees. 9% grads pursue business degrees. 2% grads pursue medical degrees. **Faculty:** Student/faculty ratio 11:1. 157 full-time faculty, 94% hold PhDs, 15% are are members of minority groups, 39% are women. 0% of classes are taught by teaching assistants.

ACADEMICS

Degrees: associate, bachelor's, certificate, master's, post-bachelor's certificate, post-master's certificate. **Classes:** Most classes have 10–19 students. Most lab/discussion sessions have 10–19 students. **Majors with Highest Enrollment:** business/commerce; criminal justice/law enforcement administration; teacher education, multiple levels. **Special Study Options:** Accelerated program, cooperative education program, cross-registration, double major, dual enrollment, English as a Second Language (ESL), exchange student program (domestic), honors program, independent study, internships, liberal arts/career combination, study abroad, teacher certification program. **Combined degree programs:** BA/MA, BBA/MBA. **Disability Services:** Special programs offered to physically disabled students include note-taking services, reader services, tape recorders, tutors. **Career services:** Alumni network, career/job search classes, career assessment, internships, regional alumni. **Career services highlights include:** Students majoring in liberal arts, business, or hospitality are eligible to participate in the co-op program in their junior or senior year, enabling them to gain academic credit as well as paid work experiences in their majors.

FACILITIES

Housing: Coed dorms, apartments for single students. **Special Academic Facilities/Equipment:** Castellani Art Museum. **Computers:** Students can register for classes online.

CAMPUS LIFE

Environment: Town. **Activities:** Choral groups, dance, drama/theater, musical theater, radio station, student government, student newspaper, yearbook, Campus Ministries, International Student Organization. 70 registered organizations, 14 honor societies, 2 religious organizations. 3 fraternities, 2 sororities. **Athletics (Intercollegiate):** Men: baseball, basketball, cross-country, diving, golf, ice hockey, soccer, swimming, tennis. Women: basketball, cross-country, diving, golf, ice hockey, lacrosse, soccer, softball, swimming, tennis, volleyball. **On-Campus Highlights:** Gallagher Center, St.Vincent's Hall, Castellani Art Museum, Clet Hall, Dwyer Arena, Student Apartments.

ADMISSIONS

Freshman Academic Profile: Average high school GPA 3.3. 13% in top 10% of high school class, 41% in top 25% of high school class, 78% in top 50% of high school class. 95% from public high schools. SAT Math middle 50% range 470-580. SAT Critical Reading middle 50% range 460-570. ACT middle 50% range 20-25. Minimum paper TOEFL 500. **Basis for Candidate Selection:** Very important factors considered include: rigor of secondary school record. Important factors considered include: recommendation(s), standardized test scores, interview. Other factors considered include: Class rank, application essay, alumni/ae relation, character/personal qualities, extracurricular activities, talent/ability, volunteer work. **Freshman Admission Requirements:** High school diploma is required and GED is accepted. **Academic units required:** 4 English, 2 mathematics, 2 science, 2 foreign language, 2 social studies, 4 academic electives. **Academic units recommended:** 4 English, 2 mathematics, 2 science, 2 foreign language, 2 social studies, 4 academic electives. **Freshman Admission Statistics:** 3703 applied, 69% admitted, 25% enrolled. **Transfer Admission Requirements:** High school transcript, college transcript(s), Minimum college GPA of 2.0 required. Lowest grade transferable C. **General Admission Information:** Application Fee $30. Regular application deadline 8/1. Nonfall registration accepted. Admission may be deferred for a maximum of 12. Credit offered for CEEB Advanced Placement tests.

COSTS AND FINANCIAL AID

Annual tuition $26,100. Room and board $11,300. Required fees $1,130. Average book expense $1,050. **Required Forms and Deadlines:** FAFSA, state aid form. **Notification of Awards:** Applicants will be notified of awards on a rolling basis beginning 3/1. **Types of Aid:** Need-based scholarships/grants: Federal Pell, SEOG, state scholarships/grants, private scholarships, the school's own gift aid. Loans: Direct Subsidized Stafford, Direct Unsubsidized Stafford, Direct PLUS, Federal Perkins, Federal Nursing, state loans, college/university loans from institutional funds. Student Employment: Federal Work-Study Program available. Highest amount earned per year from on-campus jobs $1,800. Off-campus job opportunities are excellent. **Financial Aid Statistics:** 90% freshmen, 98% undergrads receive need-based scholarship or grant aid. 83% freshmen, 78% undergrads receive non-need-based scholarship or grant aid. 81% freshmen, 81% undergrads receive need-based self-help aid. 2% freshmen, 3% undergrads receive athletic scholarships. 88% freshmen, 83% undergrads receive any aid. 79% undergrads borrow to pay for school. Average cumulative indebtedness $32,114. **Criteria for awarding institutional aid:** Non-need-based: academics, athletics.

See page 1158.

NICHOLLS STATE UNIVERSITY

P.O. Box 2004, Thibodaux, LA 70310
Phone: 985-448-4507 • **Financial Aid Phone:** 985-448-4048
E-mail: nicholls@nicholls.edu • **CEEB Code:** 6221
Fax: 985-448-4929 • **Website:** www.nicholls.edu • **ACT Code:** 1580

This public school was founded in 1948. It has a 210-acre campus.

RATINGS

Admissions Selectivity Rating: 67   **Fire Safety Rating:** 76   **Green Rating:** 60*

STUDENTS AND FACULTY

Enrollment: 6,246. **Student Body:** 61% female, 39% male, 4% out-of-state, 2% international (40 countries represented). Asian 1%, African American 18%, Caucasian 73%, Hispanic 1%, Native American 2%.
Retention and Graduation: Faculty: Student/faculty ratio 20:1. 295 full-time faculty, 54% hold PhDs, 11% are members of minority groups, 51% are women. 1% of classes are taught by teaching assistants.

ACADEMICS

Degrees: associate, bachelor's, certificate, master's, post-master's certificate. **Classes:** Most classes have 20–29 students. **Majors with Highest Enrollment:** business administration and management; general studies; nursing/registered nurse (rn, asn, bsn, msn). **Special Study Options:** cooperative education program, cross-registration, distance learning, dual enrollment, honors program, independent study, internships, study abroad, teacher certification program. **Honors Programs:** You can learn advanced material in small classes taught by outstanding professors. You can enrich your college experience through intellectually stimulating courses that allow you to reach your potential. The Honors Program invites all academically talented and intellectually curious students to participate. By joining the program you can become a select member of the campus community and associate with students who share similar goals and interests. The Program is designed to meet students' needs and interests. Therefore, students in the program determine their degree of involvement. You may take as many honors courses as you choose or simply successfully complete one-three hour honors course each year. And because honors classes fit degree requirements for all majors, participants graduate on time. **Combined Degree Programs:** BA/MA. **Disability Services:** Special programs offered to physically disabled students include note-taking services, reader services, tape recorders, tutors. **Career Services:** Alumni network, alumni services, career/job search classes, career assessment, internships.

FACILITIES

Housing: special housing for disabled students, men's dorms, special housing for international students, women's dorms, apartments for married students, apartments for single students, wellness housing. **Special Academic Facilities/Equipment:** Ameen Art Gallery **Computers:** 100% of classrooms, 100% of dorms, 100% of libraries, 100% of dining areas, 100% of student union, 100% of common outdoor areas have wireless network access. Students can register for classes online. Administrative functions (other than registration) can be performed online.

CAMPUS LIFE

Environment: Village. **Activities:** Choral groups, concert band, dance, drama/theater, jazz band, literary magazine, marching band, music ensembles, musical theater, radio station, student government, student newspaper, student-run film society, television station, yearbook 121 registered organizations, 24 honor societies, 6 religious organizations. 10 fraternities, 5 sororities. **Athletics (Intercollegiate):** Men: baseball, basketball, cross-country, football, golf, tennis. Women: basketball, cross-country, golf, soccer, softball, tennis, track/field (outdoor), track/field (indoor), volleyball. **On-Campus Highlights:** Admissions Office, Student Union, Ellender Memorial Library, Guidry Stadium

ADMISSIONS

Freshman Academic Profile: Average high school GPA 3.2. 18% in top 10% of high school class, 43% in top 25% of high school class, 73% in top 50% of high school class. 68% from public high schools. ACT middle 50% range 24-20. Minimum web-based TOEFL 61. Minimum paper TOEFL 500. **Basis for Candidate Selection:** *Very important factors considered include:* rigor of secondary school record. *Important factors considered include:* standardized test scores. *Other factors considered include:* Class rank, academic GPA, talent/ability. **Freshman Admission Requirements:** High school diploma is required and GED is accepted. *Academic units required:* 4 English, 3 mathematics, 3 science, 2 foreign language, 1 social studies, 2 history, 2 academic electives. 4 English, 3 mathematics, 3 science, 2 foreign language, 1 social studies, 2 history, 2 academic electives. **Freshman Admission Statistics:** 2,420 applied, 82% admitted, 63% enrolled. **Transfer Admission Requirements:** college transcript(s), minimum college GPA of 2.0 required. Lowest grade transferable D. **General Admission Information:** Application Fee $20. Notification on a rolling basis, beginning on or about 9/1. Nonfall registration accepted. Admission may be deferred for a maximum of 1 semester. Credit and/or placement offered for CEEB Advanced Placement tests.

COSTS AND FINANCIAL AID

Annual in-state tuition $2,231. Annual out-of-state tuition $7,679. Room and board $4,556. Required fees $1,364. Average book expense $1,200. **Required Forms and Deadlines:** FAFSA, institution's own financial aid form, state aid form, noncustodial PROFILE. **Types of Aid:** *Need-based scholarships/grants:* Federal Pell, SEOG, state scholarships/grants, private scholarships, the school's own gift aid. *Loans:* Subsidized Stafford, Unsubsidized Stafford, PLUS, Federal Perkins. **Student Employment:** Federal Work-Study Program available. Institutional employment available. Highest amount earned per year from on-campus jobs $8,112. Off-campus job opportunities are fair. **Financial Aid Statistics:** 93% freshmen, 86% undergrads receive need-based scholarship or grant aid. 69% freshmen, 33% undergrads receive non-need-based scholarship or grant aid. 51% freshmen, 70% undergrads receive need-based self-help aid. 3% freshmen, 3% undergrads receive athletic scholarships. 77% freshmen, 74% undergrads receive any aid. **Criteria for awarding institutional aid:** *Non-need-based:* academics, athletics, state/district residency.

NICHOLS COLLEGE

PO Box 5000, Dudley, MA 01571-5000
Phone: 508-213-2203 • **Financial Aid Phone:** 508-213-2276
E-mail: admissions@nichols.edu • **CEEB Code:** 3666
Fax: 508-943-9885 • **Website:** www.nichols.edu • **ACT Code:** 1878

This private school was founded in 1815. It has a 200-acre campus.

RATINGS
Admissions Selectivity Rating: 67   **Fire Safety Rating:** 75   **Green Rating:** 60*

STUDENTS AND FACULTY
Enrollment: 1,214. **Student Body:** 40% female, 60% male, 35% out-of-state, 0% international (4 countries represented). Asian 1%, African American 4%, Caucasian 78%, Hispanic 3%, Native American 0%.
Retention and Graduation: 43% freshmen graduate within 4 years. 46% freshmen graduate within 6 years. 7% grads go on to further study within 1 year. 2% grads pursue business degrees. **Faculty:** Student/faculty ratio 20:1. 34 full-time faculty, 56% hold PhDs, 3% are members of minority groups, 29% are women. 0% of classes are taught by teaching assistants.

ACADEMICS
Degrees: associate, bachelor's, master's. **Classes:** Most classes have 20–29 students. Most lab/discussion sessions have 10–19 students. **Majors with Highest Enrollment:** business/commerce; criminal justice/law enforcement administration; sport and fitness administration/management. **Special Study Options:** cooperative education program, distance learning, double major, honors program, independent study, internships, liberal arts/career combination, study abroad, teacher certification program. **Combined Degree Programs:** Five year BSBA/MBA Program. **Disability Services:** Special programs offered to physically disabled students include tutors. **Career Services:** Alumni network, alumni services, career/job search classes, career assessment, internships, regional alumni.

FACILITIES
Housing: Coed dorms, men's dorms, women's dorms, apartments for single students. 80% of campus accessible to physically disabled. **Computers:** 10% of classrooms, 100% of libraries, 100% of dining areas, have wireless network access. Students can register for classes online. Administrative functions (other than registration) can be performed online.

CAMPUS LIFE
Environment: Village. **Activities:** drama/theater, literary magazine, musical theater, radio station, student government, student newspaper, yearbook 25 registered organizations, 5 honor societies, 1 religious organizations. **Athletics (Intercollegiate):** *Men:* baseball, basketball, football, golf, ice hockey, lacrosse, soccer, tennis. *Women:* basketball, field hockey, golf, ice hockey, lacrosse, soccer, softball, tennis. **On-Campus Highlights:** Athletic and Recreation Complex, The Currier Center, Snack Bar in Alumni Hall, Davis Cafe, WNRC Radio Station.

ADMISSIONS
Freshman Academic Profile: Average high school GPA 2.6. 0% in top 10% of high school class, 0% in top 25% of high school class, 0% in top 50% of high school class. 82% from public high schools. SAT Math middle 50% range 420-520. SAT Critical Reading middle 50% range 400-490. SAT Writing middle 50% range 418-473. Minimum paper TOEFL 550. **Basis for Candidate Selection:** *Very important factors considered include:* application essay, recommendation(s), rigor of secondary school record. *Important factors considered include:* academic GPA, standardized test scores, interview. *Other factors considered include:* Class rank, character/personal qualities, extracurricular activities, level of applicant's interest, talent/ability, volunteer work, work experience. **Freshman Admission Requirements:** High school diploma is required and GED is accepted. *Academic units required:* 4 English, 3 mathematics, 2 science, (2 science labs), 2 social studies, 5 academic electives. *Academic units recommended:* 4 English, 3 mathematics, 2 science, (2 science labs), 2 social studies, 5 academic electives. **Freshman Admission Statistics:** 1,894 applied, 77% admitted, 30% enrolled. **Transfer Admission Requirements:** High school transcript, college transcript(s), essay or personal statement, minimum college GPA of 2.0 required. Lowest grade transferable C. **General Admission Information:** Application Fee $25. Notification on a rolling basis, beginning on or about 10/1. Nonfall registration accepted. Admission may be deferred for a maximum of 1 year. Neither credit nor placement offered for CEEB Advanced Placement tests.

COSTS AND FINANCIAL AID
Annual tuition $25,400. Room and board $8,960. Required fees $300. Average book expense $1,050. **Required Forms and Deadlines:** FAFSA. **Notification of Awards:** Applicants will be notified of awards on a rolling basis beginning

3/15. **Types of Aid:** *Need-based scholarships/grants:* Federal Pell, SEOG, state scholarships/grants, private scholarships. *Loans:* Subsidized Stafford, Unsubsidized Stafford, PLUS, state loans. **Student Employment:** Federal Work-Study Program available. Institutional employment available. Highest amount earned per year from on-campus jobs $3,000. Off-campus job opportunities are fair. **Financial Aid Statistics:** 100% freshmen, 100% undergrads receive need-based scholarship or grant aid. 6% freshmen, 6% undergrads receive non-need-based scholarship or grant aid. 91% freshmen, 93% undergrads receive need-based self-help aid. 70% freshmen, 73% undergrads receive any aid. 84% undergrads borrow to pay for school. Average cumulative indebtedness $17,509. **Criteria for awarding institutional aid:** *Non-need-based:* academics.

See page 1160.

NORTH CAROLINA AGRICULTURAL AND TECHNICAL STATE UNIVERSITY

1601 East Market Street, Greensboro, NC 27411
Phone: 336-334-7946
E-mail: uadmit@ncat.edu
Fax: 336-334-7478 • **Website:** www.ncat.edu

This is a public school.

RATINGS
Admissions Selectivity Rating: 69   **Fire Safety Rating:** 60*   **Green Rating:** 60*

STUDENTS AND FACULTY
Enrollment: 8,921. **Student Body:** 54% female, 46% male, 16% out-of-state, 1% international. Asian 1%, African American 89%, Caucasian 4%, Hispanic 2%, Native American 0%.
Retention and Graduation: 17% freshmen graduate within 4 years. **Faculty:** 532 full-time faculty, 77% hold PhDs, 73% are members of minority groups, 44% are women.

ACADEMICS
Degrees: bachelor's, master's. **Classes:** Most classes have 20–29 students. **Special Study Options:** cooperative education program, cross-registration, distance learning, double major, external degree program, honors program, independent study, internships, study abroad, teacher certification program.

FACILITIES
Housing: Coed dorms, men's dorms, women's dorms, theme housing, graduate housing.

CAMPUS LIFE
Activities: Choral groups, concert band, dance, drama/theater, jazz band, literary magazine, marching band, music ensembles, musical theater, opera, pep band, radio station, student government, student newspaper, student-run film society, symphony orchestra, television station, yearbook, International Student Organization, Model UN.

ADMISSIONS
Freshman Academic Profile: Average high school GPA 3.1. 0% in top 10% of high school class, 6% in top 25% of high school class, 34% in top 50% of high school class. 85% from public high schools. SAT Math middle 50% range 410-500. SAT Critical Reading middle 50% range 390-480. SAT Writing middle 50% range 370-460. ACT middle 50% range 17-21. Minimum web-based TOEFL 88. Minimum paper TOEFL 570. **Basis for Candidate Selection:** *Very important factors considered include:* rigor of secondary school record, state residency. *Important factors considered include:* standardized test scores. *Other factors considered include:* Class rank, recommendation(s), alumni/ae relation, character/personal qualities, extracurricular activities, geographical residence, talent/ability, volunteer work, work experience. **Freshman Admission Requirements:** High school diploma is required and GED is accepted. *Academic units required:* 4 English, 3 mathematics, 3 science, 2 social studies, 4 academic electives. 4 English, 3 mathematics, 3 science, 2 social studies, 4 academic electives. **Freshman Admission Statistics:** 6,692 applied, 66% admitted, 42% enrolled. **Transfer Admission Requirements:** High school transcript, minimum college GPA of 2.0 required. Lowest grade transferable C. **General Admission Information:** Application Fee $35. Notification on a rolling basis, beginning on or about 9/15. Nonfall registration accepted. Admission may be deferred for a maximum of 1 semester. Credit offered for CEEB Advanced Placement tests.

COSTS AND FINANCIAL AID
Annual in-state tuition $2,791. Annual out-of-state tuition $12,425. Room and board $7,225. Required fees $1,877. Average book expense $1,400. **Required Forms and Deadlines:** FAFSA. **Notification of Awards:** Applicants will be

notified of awards on a rolling basis beginning 4/15. **Types of Aid:** *Need-based scholarships/grants:* Federal Pell, SEOG, state scholarships/grants, private scholarships, the school's own gift aid, United Negro College Fund, Federal Nursing Scholarships. *Loans:* Direct Subsidized Stafford, Direct Unsubsidized Stafford, Direct PLUS, Federal Perkins, alternative loans. **Student Employment: Financial Aid Statistics:** 78% freshmen, 75% undergrads receive need-based scholarship or grant aid. 92% freshmen, 85% undergrads receive non-need-based scholarship or grant aid. 85% freshmen, 86% undergrads receive need-based self-help aid. 3% freshmen, 2% undergrads receive athletic scholarships. 74% undergrads borrow to pay for school. Average cumulative indebtedness $20,389. **Criteria for awarding institutional aid:** *Non-need-based:* academics, alumni affiliation, athletics, minority status, music/drama, state/district residency.

NORTH CAROLINA CENTRAL UNIVERSITY

Fayetteville Street, Durham, NC 27707
Phone: 919-560-6298
E-mail: ebridges@wpo.nccu.edu • **CEEB Code:** 5495
Fax: 919-530-7625 • **Website:** www.nccu.edu • **ACT Code:** 3132

This public school was founded in 1910. It has a 130-acre campus.

RATINGS
Admissions Selectivity Rating: 65   **Fire Safety Rating:** 60*   **Green Rating:** 60*

STUDENTS AND FACULTY
Enrollment: 5,439. **Student Body:** 66% female, 34% male, 10% out-of-state, 0% international (17 countries represented). Asian 0%, African American 79%, Caucasian 3%, Hispanic 1%, Native American 0%.
Retention and Graduation: 78% freshmen return for sophomore year.
Faculty: Student/faculty ratio 18:1. 231 full-time faculty, 67% hold PhDs, 77% are members of minority groups, 47% are women. % of classes are taught by teaching assistants.

ACADEMICS
Degrees: bachelor's, first professional, master's. **Classes:** Most classes have fewer than 10 students. Most lab/discussion sessions have fewer than 10 students. **Special Study Options:** cooperative education program, double major, honors program, independent study, internships, study abroad, teacher certification program, weekend college. **Disability Services:** Special programs offered to physically disabled students include note-taking services, reader services, tape recorders, tutors. **Career Services:** alumni services, career/job search classes, internships.

FACILITIES
Housing: Coed dorms, men's dorms, women's dorms, Coed houses dormitory available. **Special Academic Facilities/Equipment:** Treasury Room collection of primary resources on black life and culture, art museum with works of Afro-American culture. **Computers:** Administrative functions (other than registration) can be performed online.

CAMPUS LIFE
Activities: Choral groups, concert band, dance, drama/theater, jazz band, literary magazine, marching band, radio station, student government, student newspaper, yearbook 4 fraternities, 4 sororities. **Athletics (Intercollegiate):** *Men:* basketball, cross-country, football, golf, tennis, track/field (outdoor). *Women:* basketball, cross-country, golf, softball, tennis, track/field (outdoor), volleyball.

ADMISSIONS
Freshman Academic Profile: Average high school GPA 2.6. 4% in top 10% of high school class, 19% in top 25% of high school class, 53% in top 50% of high school class. SAT Math middle 50% range 380-470. SAT Critical Reading middle 50% range 380-470. ACT middle 50% range 14-18. Minimum paper TOEFL 500. **Basis for Candidate Selection:** *Very important factors considered include:* rigor of secondary school record. *Important factors considered include:* Class rank, standardized test scores. *Other factors considered include:* application essay, recommendation(s), alumni/ae relation, extracurricular activities, interview, racial/ethnic status, state residency, talent/ability. **Freshman Admission Requirements:** High school diploma is required and GED is accepted. *Academic units required:* 4 English, 3 mathematics, 3 science, (1 science labs), 2 social studies, 2 history. *Academic units recommended:* 4 English, 3 mathematics, 3 science, (1 science labs), 2 social studies, 2 history. **Freshman Admission Statistics:** 2,801 applied, 83% admitted, 50% enrolled. **Transfer Admission Requirements:** High school transcript, college transcript(s), statement of good standing from prior institution(s). Minimum college GPA of 2.0 required. Lowest grade transferable C. **General Admission Information:** Application Fee $30. Regular application deadline 7/1. Nonfall registration

accepted. Admission may be deferred for a maximum of 4. Credit offered for CEEB Advanced Placement tests.

COSTS AND FINANCIAL AID
Required Forms and Deadlines: FAFSA. **Types of Aid:** *Need-based scholarships/grants:* Federal Pell, SEOG, state scholarships/grants, private scholarships, the school's own gift aid, United Negro College Fund, Federal Nursing Scholarships. *Loans:* Direct Subsidized Stafford, Direct Unsubsidized Stafford, Direct PLUS, Federal Perkins. **Student Employment:** Federal Work-Study Program available. Off-campus job opportunities are fair. **Financial Aid Statistics:** 73% freshmen, 72% undergrads receive need-based scholarship or grant aid. 87% freshmen, 47% undergrads receive non-need-based scholarship or grant aid. 83% freshmen, 87% undergrads receive need-based self-help aid. 4% freshmen, 2% undergrads receive athletic scholarships. **Criteria for awarding institutional aid:** *Non-need-based:* academics, alumni affiliation, athletics.

NORTH CAROLINA STATE UNIVERSITY

Box 7103, Raleigh, NC 27695
Phone: 919-515-2434 • **Financial Aid Phone:** 919-515-2421
E-mail: undergrad_admissions@ncsu.edu • **CEEB Code:** 5496
Fax: 919-515-5039 • **Website:** www.ncsu.edu/ • **ACT Code:** 3164

This public school was founded in 1887. It has a 2110-acre campus.

RATINGS
Admissions Selectivity Rating: 90   **Fire Safety Rating:** 93   **Green Rating:** 92

STUDENTS AND FACULTY
Enrollment: 23,514. **Student Body:** 43% female, 57% male, 8% out-of-state, 1% international (117 countries represented). Asian 5%, African American 8%, Caucasian 76%, Hispanic 4%, Native American 0%.
Retention and Graduation: 91% freshmen return for sophomore year. 31% grads go on to further study within 1 year. 46% grads pursue arts and sciences degrees. 6% grads pursue law degrees. 16% grads pursue business degrees. 1% grads pursue medical degrees. **Faculty:** Student/faculty ratio 18:1. 1733 full-time faculty, 88% hold PhDs, 17% are members of minority groups, 31% are women. 12% of classes are taught by teaching assistants.

ACADEMICS
Degrees: associate, bachelor's, certificate, master's, post-bachelor's certificate. **Classes:** Most classes have 20–29 students. Most lab/discussion sessions have 20–29 students. **Majors with Highest Enrollment:** biology/biological sciences; business administration and management; mechanical engineering. **Special Study Options:** Accelerated program, cooperative education program, cross-registration, distance learning, double major, dual enrollment, exchange student program (domestic), honors program, independent study, internships, liberal arts/career combination, student-designed major, study abroad. **Honors Programs:** The University Honors Program recruits and provides programmatic support for a diverse group of nationally outstanding students, ensuring that they benefit fully from the resources of a major land-grant, research university and the Research Triangle by emphasizing inquiry-, creativity-, and discovery-based learning. The program offers interdisciplinary seminars and a variety of credit-earning opportunites for out-of-classroom experiences. The program emphasizes participation in research by students from all disciplines. Entering students may instead choose to participate in the University Scholars program, which emphasizes enrichment activities and leadership development. There are over 30 Honors Programs located in the colleges or departments that invite students in their sophomore or junior years. These programs include honors sections of courses, honors seminars, and honors research. Some programs require a senior honor thesis. **Combined Degree Programs:** BA/BS Humanities/Engineering Humanities/Design. **Disability Services:** Special programs offered to physically disabled students include note-taking services, reader services, tape recorders. **Career Services:** career/job search classes, career assessment, internships, regional alumni.

FACILITIES
Housing: Coed dorms, special housing for disabled students, men's dorms, special housing for international students, women's dorms, fraternity/sorority housing, apartments for married students, apartments for single students, theme housing, Living/Learning Dormitories. 87% of campus accessible to physically disabled. **Special Academic Facilities/Equipment:** Art and arts/crafts galler-

ies, research farms and forest, phytophotron with controlled atmosphere growth chambers. pulp/paper and wood products labs, processing equipment for fiber, fabric, and garment manufacture, electron microscopes, nuclear reactor, stable isotope lab. **Computers:** 94% of classrooms, 100% of libraries, 92% of dining areas, 100% of student union, 52% of common outdoor areas have wireless network access. Students can register for classes online. Administrative functions (other than registration) can be performed online.

CAMPUS LIFE

Environment: Metropolis. **Activities:** Choral groups, concert band, dance, drama/theater, jazz band, literary magazine, marching band, music ensembles, musical theater, pep band, radio station, student government, student newspaper, symphony orchestra, yearbook, Campus Ministries, International Student Organization 560 registered organizations, 26 honor societies, 25 religious organizations. 33 fraternities, 17 sororities. **Athletics (Intercollegiate):** *Men:* baseball, basketball, cheerleading, cross-country, diving, football, golf, riflery, soccer, swimming, tennis, track/field (outdoor), track/field (indoor), wrestling. *Women:* basketball, cheerleading, cross-country, diving, golf, gymnastics, riflery, soccer, softball, swimming, tennis, track/field (outdoor), track/field (indoor), volleyball. **On-Campus Highlights:** RBC Center - Sports Arena, Gallery of Art and Design, Carter Finley Stadium, Talley Student Center, University Theatre. **Environmental Initiatives:** Completion and acceptance by the Chancellor of a Sustainability Strategic Plan that will help guide sustainability policies and procedures on campus. This plan is supported by a Climate Action Plan and an Energy Management Plan. Committment to a minimum of LEED Silver for all new buildings and major renovations. Currently underway is a $61 million performance contract, part of which will install an 11 Megawatt (MW) Combined Heat and Power (CHP) system on the campus.

ADMISSIONS

Freshman Academic Profile: Average high school GPA 4.3. 43% in top 10% of high school class, 83% in top 25% of high school class, 99% in top 50% of high school class. 80% from public high schools. SAT Math middle 50% range 560-660. SAT Critical Reading middle 50% range 530-620. SAT Writing middle 50% range 510-610. ACT middle 50% range 23-28. Minimum web-based TOEFL 79. Minimum paper TOEFL 550. **Basis for Candidate Selection:** *Very important factors considered include:* Class rank, academic GPA, rigor of secondary school record, standardized test scores.*Other factors considered include:* application essay, recommendation(s), alumni/ae relation, character/personal qualities, extracurricular activities, first generation, geographical residence, racial/ethnic status, state residency, talent/ability, volunteer work, work experience. **Freshman Admission Requirements:** High school diploma is required and GED is not accepted. *Academic units required:* 4 English, 4 mathematics, 3 science, (1 science labs), 2 foreign language, 1 social studies, 1 history, 1 academic electives. *Academic units recommended:* 4 English, 4 mathematics, 3 science, (1 science labs), 2 foreign language, 1 social studies, 1 history, 1 academic electives. **Freshman Admission Statistics:** 19,863 applied, 52% admitted, 44% enrolled. **Transfer Admission Requirements:** college transcript(s), minimum college GPA of 2.0 required. Lowest grade transferable C–. **General Admission Information:** Application Fee $70. Regular application deadline 2/1. Notification on a rolling basis, beginning on or about 10/15. Nonfall registration accepted. Admission may be deferred for a maximum of 1 year. Credit and/or placement offered for CEEB Advanced Placement tests.

COSTS AND FINANCIAL AID

Annual in-state tuition $5,153. Annual out-of-state tuition $17,988. Room and board $8,536. Required fees $1,865. Average book expense $1,000. **Required Forms and Deadlines:** FAFSA, institution's own financial aid form. **Notification of Awards:** Applicants will be notified of awards on a rolling basis beginning 4/1. **Types of Aid:** *Need-based scholarships/grants:* Federal Pell, SEOG, state scholarships/grants, private scholarships, the school's own gift aid, United Negro College Fund. *Loans:* Subsidized Stafford, Unsubsidized Stafford, PLUS, Federal Perkins, state loans, college/university loans from institutional funds. **Student Employment:** Federal Work-Study Program available. Institutional employment available. Highest amount earned per year from on-campus jobs $7,300. Off-campus job opportunities are excellent. **Financial Aid Statistics:** 94% freshmen, 90% undergrads receive need-based scholarship or grant aid. 23% freshmen, 14% undergrads receive non-need-based scholarship or grant aid. 79% freshmen, 81% undergrads receive need-based self-help aid. 2% freshmen, 1% undergrads receive athletic scholarships. 75% freshmen, 69% undergrads receive any aid. 55% undergrads borrow to pay for school. Average cumulative indebtedness $17,317. **Criteria for awarding institutional aid:** *Non-need-based:* academics, alumni affiliation, athletics, leadership, state/district residency.

NORTH CAROLINA WESLEYAN COLLEGE

3400 North Wesleyan Boulevard, Rocky Mount, NC 27804
Phone: 252-985-5200
E-mail: adm@ncwc.edu **Fax:** 252-985-5309 • **Website:** www.ncwc.edu

This private school, affiliated with the Methodist Church, was founded in 1956.

RATINGS

Admissions Selectivity Rating: 62   **Fire Safety Rating:** 62   **Green Rating:** 60*

STUDENTS AND FACULTY

Enrollment: 1,695. **Student Body:** 59% female, 41% male, 12% out-of-state, 0% international (1 countries represented). Asian 1%, African American 40%, Caucasian 48%, Hispanic 1%, Native American 1%.
Retention and Graduation: 57% freshmen return for sophomore year. 26% freshmen graduate within 4 years. 38% freshmen graduate within 6 years. **Faculty:** Student/faculty ratio 15:1. 45 full-time faculty, 62% hold PhDs, 0% are members of minority groups, 51% are women. 0% of classes are taught by teaching assistants.

ACADEMICS

Degrees: bachelor's, certificate. **Classes:** Most classes have 10–19 students. **Majors with Highest Enrollment:** business/commerce; computer and information science; psychology. **Special Study Options:** Accelerated program, cooperative education program, cross-registration, distance learning, double major, dual enrollment, honors program, independent study, internships, liberal arts/career combination, teacher certification program, weekend college. **Disability Services:** Special programs offered to physically disabled students include note-taking services, reader services, tape recorders, tutors. **Career Services:** career/job search classes, career assessment, internships Career Services highlights include North Carolina Wesleyan College's Internship and Career Services Center (ICSC) complements the academic program of the College. The ICSC at Wesleyan assists our students' professional development and serves as a resource to students, faculty, and the business community. By emphasizing hands-on learning as an important tool for both full time employment and in developing a career path, the ICSC helps students realize their career goals. The ICSC offers a variety of services that allows students to assess their skills and abilities, make the major declaration, and explore the world of work. Through our resource library and employer files students are able to research possible majors, minors, and careers. To prepare our students for the world of work, the ICSC offers the Career Development Workshop as a required component of the internship for traditional day students. The workshop includes resume and cover letter writing, the value of networking, interviewing skills, appropriate business attire, how to deal with racial discrimination and sexual harassment, and social etiquette. The relevance of practical experience will become evident as students begin to explore their career goals through the Extended Internship (EI) program.

FACILITIES

Housing: Coed dorms, special housing for disabled students, men's dorms, women's dorms, 70% of campus accessible to physically disabled. **Special Academic Facilities/Equipment:** Mims Gallery, Dunn Center for the Performaing Arts. **Computers:** Administrative functions (other than registration) can be performed online.

CAMPUS LIFE

Environment: Village. **Activities:** Choral groups, drama/theater, literary magazine, music ensembles, student government, student newspaper, yearbook 30 registered organizations, 2 honor societies, 2 religious organizations. 3 fraternities, 3 sororities. **Athletics (Intercollegiate):** *Men:* baseball, basketball, football, golf, soccer, tennis. *Women:* basketball, soccer, softball, tennis, volleyball. **On-Campus Highlights:** Dunn Center for the Performing Arts, Mims Gallery, Serpentine Wall, College Fountain, Bellmonte House.

ADMISSIONS

Freshman Academic Profile: Average high school GPA 2.8. 8% in top 10% of high school class, 18% in top 25% of high school class, 59% in top 50% of high school class. 85% from public high schools. SAT Math middle 50% range 5-23. SAT Critical Reading middle 50% range 4-29. Minimum paper TOEFL 500. **Basis for Candidate Selection:** *Very important factors considered include:* recommendation(s), rigor of secondary school record, standardized test scores, talent/ability. *Important factors considered include:* application essay, alumni/ae relation, character/personal qualities, extracurricular activities, interview, volunteer work, work experience. *Other factors considered include:* Class rank. **Freshman Admission Requirements:** High school diploma is required and GED is accepted. **Freshman Admission Statistics:** 651 applied, 83% admitted, 37% enrolled. **Transfer Admission Requirements:** High school transcript, college transcript(s), standardized test scores, minimum college GPA of 2.0 required. Lowest grade transferable C. **General Admission Information:** Application Fee $25. Nonfall registration accepted. Credit and/or placement offered for CEEB Advanced Placement tests.

COSTS AND FINANCIAL AID
Annual tuition $11,225. Room and board $5,555. Required fees $1,218. Average book expense $800. **Required Forms and Deadlines:** FAFSA, state aid form. **Notification of Awards:** Applicants will be notified of awards on a rolling basis beginning 2/1. **Types of Aid:** *Need-based scholarships/grants:* Federal Pell, SEOG, state scholarships/grants, private scholarships, the school's own gift aid. *Loans:* Subsidized Stafford, Unsubsidized Stafford, PLUS, Federal Perkins, Alternative Loans. **Student Employment:** Federal Work-Study Program available. Highest amount earned per year from on-campus jobs $800. **Financial Aid Statistics:** 100% undergrads borrow to pay for school. **Criteria for awarding institutional aid:** *Non-need-based:* academics, religious affiliation, state/district residency.

NORTH CENTRAL COLLEGE

Office of Admissions, Naperville, IL 60566-7063
Phone: 630-637-5800 • **Financial Aid Phone:** 630-637-5600
E-mail: admissions@noctrl.edu • **CEEB Code:** 1555
Fax: 630-637-5819 • **Website:** www.northcentralcollege.edu • **ACT Code:** 1096

This private school, affiliated with the Methodist Church, was founded in 1861. It has a 59-acre campus.

RATINGS
Admissions Selectivity Rating: 83   **Fire Safety Rating:** 92   **Green Rating:** 84

STUDENTS AND FACULTY
Enrollment: 2,662. **Student Body:** 57% female, 43% male, 7% out-of-state, 1% international (23 countries represented). Asian 2%, African American 4%, Caucasian 79%, Hispanic 8%, Native American 0%.
Retention and Graduation: 78% freshmen return for sophomore year. 57% freshmen graduate within 4 years. **Faculty:** Student/faculty ratio 16:1. 130 full-time faculty, 89% hold PhDs, 11% are members of minority groups, 47% are women. 0% of classes are taught by teaching assistants.

ACADEMICS
Degrees: bachelor's, master's, post-bachelor's certificate. **Classes:** Most classes have 20–29 students. Most lab/discussion sessions have 20–29 students. **Majors with Highest Enrollment:** business administration, management and operations, other; elementary education and teaching; finance. **Special Study Options:** Accelerated program, cross-registration, double major, dual enrollment, English as a Second Language (ESL), exchange student program (domestic), honors program, independent study, internships, student-designed major, study abroad, teacher certification program, 3-2 Engineering program with University of Illinois, University of Minnesota;Integrated 5 year Bachelor's/Master's degree programs. **Honors Programs:** The College Scholars is a comprehensive four year integrative program culminating in a senior honors thesis. The program is open to students from all academic disciplines. **Combined Degree Programs:** BA/MA, BA in Acc/MBA; Bachelor's Degree/Masters in Web and Internet Applications. **Disability Services:** Special programs offered to physically disabled students include note-taking services, reader services, tape recorders, tutors. **Career Services:** Alumni network, alumni services, career/job search classes, career assessment, internships, regional alumni. Career Services highlights include Because career-related experiences support the mission of the college, the CDC actively assists students in developing Internship opportunities. We have found that real hands on experience within the workforce increases graduates marketability following graduation, be it for seeking employment or pursuing graduate school. Today's' job market is competitive and we offer a strong resource in helping students get involved in these types of opportunities which ultimately helps them reach their goals.

FACILITIES
Housing: Coed dorms, special housing for disabled students, women's dorms, Substance-free housing. 85% of campus accessible to physically disabled. **Special Academic Facilities/Equipment:** None **Computers:** 50% of classrooms, 30% of dorms, 100% of libraries, 100% of dining areas, 100% of student union, 100% of common outdoor areas have wireless network access. Students can register for classes online. Administrative functions (other than registration) can be performed online.

CAMPUS LIFE
Environment: City. **Activities:** Choral groups, concert band, dance, drama/theater, jazz band, literary magazine, music ensembles, musical theater, opera,

pep band, radio station, student government, student newspaper, Campus Ministries, International Student Organization, Model UN 54 registered organizations, 14 honor societies, 6 religious organizations. **Athletics (Intercollegiate):** *Men:* baseball, basketball, cross-country, football, golf, soccer, swimming, tennis, track/field (outdoor), track/field (indoor), wrestling. *Women:* basketball, cheerleading, cross-country, golf, lacrosse, soccer, softball, swimming, tennis, track/field (outdoor), track/field (indoor), volleyball. **On-Campus Highlights:** Old Main - historic home of North Central College, Benedtti-Wehrli Stadium, Res/Rec Center, Fine Arts Center & Wentz Concert Hall, Oesterle Library, Rolland Boilerhouse Cafe is also a popular on-campus hangout. **Environmental Initiatives:** The College committed to building a one of a kind building with a residence hall wrapped-around a rec center and NCAA regulation sized indoor track. The building was built to LEED silver certification standards with heating and cooling from a geothermal field, occupancy sensors, precast walls made of recycled material, water efficient fixtures, bike storage, and more. The College committed to hiring a full-time sustainbility coordinator to increase program development and campus-wide involvement with sustainability issues. The College hired a sustainability consulting group in the Fall 2010 to further investigate quick-win projects, benchmarking, student involvement, and the College's sustainability mission.

ADMISSIONS
Freshman Academic Profile: Average high school GPA 3.6. 25% in top 10% of high school class, 55% in top 25% of high school class, 87% in top 50% of high school class. 89% from public high schools. ACT middle 50% range 22-27. Minimum web-based TOEFL 68. Minimum paper TOEFL 520. **Basis for Candidate Selection:** *Very important factors considered include:* academic GPA, rigor of secondary school record, standardized test scores, character/personal qualities. *Important factors considered include:* extracurricular activities, talent/ability, volunteer work. *Other factors considered include:* application essay, recommendation(s), alumni/ae relation, first generation, interview, level of applicant's interest, work experience. **Freshman Admission Requirements:** High school diploma is required and GED is accepted. *Academic units required:* 4 English, 3 mathematics, 3 science, (1 science labs), 2 social studies, 1 history, 3 academic electives. *Academic units recommended:* 4 English, 3 mathematics, 3 science, (1 science labs), 2 social studies, 1 history, 3 academic electives. **Freshman Admission Statistics:** 3,987 applied, 60% admitted, 23% enrolled. **Transfer Admission Requirements:** college transcript(s), minimum college GPA of 2.25 required. Lowest grade transferable D. **General Admission Information:** Application Fee $25. Notification on a rolling basis, beginning on or about 10/1. Nonfall registration accepted. Admission may be deferred for a maximum of 1 year. Credit and/or placement offered for CEEB Advanced Placement tests.

COSTS AND FINANCIAL AID
Annual tuition $30,891. Room and board $8,883. Required fees $180. Average book expense $1,200. **Required Forms and Deadlines:** FAFSA, institution's own financial aid formFederal income tax returns for both student and parents. **Notification of Awards:** Applicants will be notified of awards on a rolling basis beginning 3/1. **Types of Aid:** *Need-based scholarships/grants:* Federal Pell, SEOG, state scholarships/grants, private scholarships, the school's own gift aid. *Loans:* Subsidized Stafford, Unsubsidized Stafford, PLUS, Federal Perkins, state loans, college/university loans from institutional funds. **Student Employment:** Federal Work-Study Program available. Institutional employment available. Off-campus job opportunities are excellent. **Financial Aid Statistics:** 100% freshmen, 99% undergrads receive need-based scholarship or grant aid. 13% freshmen, 11% undergrads receive non-need-based scholarship or grant aid. 81% freshmen, 83% undergrads receive need-based self-help aid. 99% freshmen, 97% undergrads receive any aid. 77% undergrads borrow to pay for school. Average cumulative indebtedness $33,304. **Criteria for awarding institutional aid:** *Non-need-based:* academics, art, leadership, minority status, music/drama, religious affiliation, state/district residency.

NORTH CENTRAL UNIVERSITY

Admissions Office, Minneapolis, MN 55404
Phone: 612-343-4460
E-mail: admissions@northcentral.edu
Fax: 612-343-4146 • **Website:** www.northcentral.edu

This private school, affiliated with the Pentecostal Church, was founded in 1930. It has a 9-acre campus.

RATINGS
Admissions Selectivity Rating: 64   **Fire Safety Rating:** 67   **Green Rating:** 60*

STUDENTS AND FACULTY

Enrollment: 1,217. **Student Body:** 57% female, 43% male, 60% out-of-state, (11 countries represented).
Retention and Graduation: 75% freshmen return for sophomore year. 45% freshmen graduate within 6 years. **Faculty:** Student/faculty ratio 18:1. 40 full-time faculty, 43% hold PhDs, 13% are members of minority groups, 38% are women. 0% of classes are taught by teaching assistants.

ACADEMICS

Degrees: associate, bachelor's, certificate, diploma. **Classes:** Most classes have 10–19 students. **Majors with Highest Enrollment:** education; music; youth ministry. **Special Study Options:** distance learning, double major, exchange student program (domestic), independent study, internships. **Disability Services:** Special programs offered to physically disabled students include note-taking services, reader services, tape recorders, tutors.

FACILITIES

Housing: men's dorms, women's dorms, apartments for married students, apartments for single students.

CAMPUS LIFE

Environment: Metropolis. **Activities:** Choral groups, concert band, drama/theater, jazz band, music ensembles, radio station, student government, student newspaper, television station 30 registered organizations, 15 religious organizations. **Athletics (Intercollegiate):** *Men:* basketball, cross-country, soccer, track/field (outdoor). *Women:* basketball, cross-country, soccer, track/field (outdoor), volleyball. **On-Campus Highlights:** Chapel, Library, Cafetria, Philipps Hall, Clay Commons.

ADMISSIONS

Freshman Academic Profile: Average high school GPA 3.1. 2% in top 10% of high school class, 11% in top 25% of high school class, 32% in top 50% of high school class. SAT Math middle 50% range 440-300. SAT Critical Reading middle 50% range 480-630. ACT middle 50% range 18-24. Minimum paper TOEFL 500. **Basis for Candidate Selection:** *Very important factors considered include:* application essay, academic GPA, recommendation(s), rigor of secondary school record, standardized test scores, character/personal qualities, religious affiliation/commitment. *Important factors considered include:* extracurricular activities, talent/ability, volunteer work. *Other factors considered include:* Class rank, interview. **Freshman Admission Requirements:** High school diploma is required and GED is accepted. **Freshman Admission Statistics:** 422 applied, 98% admitted, 58% enrolled. **Transfer Admission Requirements:** High school transcript, college transcript(s), essay or personal statement, minimum college GPA of 2.0 required. Lowest grade transferable C. **General Admission Information:** Application Fee $25. Regular application deadline 6/1. Notification on a rolling basis, beginning on or about 1/1. Nonfall registration accepted. Admission may be deferred for a maximum of 1 year.

COSTS AND FINANCIAL AID

Annual tuition $12,060. Room and board $4,612. Required fees $886. Average book expense $600. **Required Forms and Deadlines:** FAFSA, state aid form. **Notification of Awards:** Applicants will be notified of awards on a rolling basis beginning 3/1. **Types of Aid:** *Need-based scholarships/grants:* Federal Pell, SEOG, state scholarships/grants, private scholarships, the school's own gift aid. *Loans:* Subsidized Stafford, Unsubsidized Stafford, PLUS, Federal Perkins, state loans.

NORTH DAKOTA STATE UNIVERSITY

Box 5454, Fargo, ND 58105
Phone: 701-231-8643 • **Financial Aid Phone:** 800-726-3188
E-mail: ndsu.admission@ndsu.edu • **CEEB Code:** 6474
Fax: 701-231-8802 • **Website:** www.ndsu.edu • **ACT Code:** 3202

This public school was founded in 1890. It has a 258-acre campus.

RATINGS

Admissions Selectivity Rating: 71   **Fire Safety Rating:** 71   **Green Rating:** 60*

STUDENTS AND FACULTY

Enrollment: 12,028. **Student Body:** 45% female, 55% male, 55% out-of-state, 4% international (79 countries represented). Asian 1%, African American 2%, Caucasian 88%, Hispanic 1%, Native American 1%.
Retention and Graduation: 24% freshmen graduate within 4 years. 52% freshmen graduate within 6 years. **Faculty:** Student/faculty ratio 18:1. 643 full-time faculty, 84% hold PhDs, 16% are members of minority groups, 37% are women.

ACADEMICS

Degrees: bachelor's, certificate, first professional, master's, post-master's certificate. **Classes:** Most classes have 20–29 students. Most lab/discussion sessions have 20–29 students. **Majors with Highest Enrollment:** business, management, marketing, and related support services, other; civil engineering; mechanical engineering. **Special Study Options:** cooperative education program, cross-registration, distance learning, double major, dual enrollment, English as a Second Language (ESL), honors program, independent study, internships, student-designed major, study abroad, teacher certification program, Tri-College Collaboration and Registration with Minnesota State University and Concordia College. Collaboration with North Dakota University System institutions. **Honors Programs:** Scholars Program. **Disability Services:** Special programs offered to physically disabled students include note-taking services, reader services, tape recorders, tutors. **Career Services:** career/job search classes, internships Career Services highlights include Cooperative Education opportunities are available for most majors. Students are paid for their work experience and earn credit.

FACILITIES

Housing: Coed dorms, men's dorms, women's dorms, apartments for married students, apartments for single students, Designated floors for engineering and architecture students. Learning communities. Wellness community. Freshmen under 19 years of age not living with a parent or guardian must live on campus. Housing is guaranteed for freshmen required to live on campus. Handicapped accessible. 100% of campus accessible to physically disabled. **Special Academic Facilities/Equipment:** Art gallery, language lab, genetics institute, regional studies institute. **Computers:** Students can register for classes online. Administrative functions (other than registration) can be performed online.

CAMPUS LIFE

Environment: City. **Activities:** Choral groups, concert band, drama/theater, jazz band, marching band, music ensembles, musical theater, pep band, radio station, student government, student newspaper 218 registered organizations, 22 honor societies, 18 religious organizations. 10 fraternities, 5 sororities. **Athletics (Intercollegiate):** *Men:* baseball, basketball, cross-country, football, golf, track/field (outdoor), track/field (indoor), wrestling. *Women:* basketball, cross-country, golf, soccer, softball, track/field (outdoor), track/field (indoor), volleyball. **On-Campus Highlights:** Wellness Center, Memorial Union, FargoDome, Alumni Center, Industrial Agricultural Communications Center, Residence Halls/Living Learning Center; Newman Outdoor Field; Technology Park.

ADMISSIONS

Freshman Academic Profile: Average high school GPA 3.4. 16% in top 10% of high school class, 40% in top 25% of high school class, 74% in top 50% of high school class. SAT Math middle 50% range 490-620. SAT Critical Reading middle 50% range 480-610. ACT middle 50% range 20-26. Minimum paper TOEFL 525. **Basis for Candidate Selection:** *Very important factors considered include:* academic GPA, rigor of secondary school record, standardized test scores. *Other factors considered include:* Class rank, recommendation(s). **Freshman Admission Requirements:** High school diploma is required and GED is accepted. *Academic units required:* 4 English, 3 mathematics, 3 science, (3 science labs), 3 social studies. *Academic units recommended:* 4 English, 3 mathematics, 3 science, (3 science labs), 3 social studies. **Freshman Admission Statistics:** 5,562 applied, 84% admitted, 53% enrolled. **Transfer Admission Requirements:** college transcript(s), minimum college GPA of 2.0 required. Lowest grade transferable D. **General Admission Information:** Application Fee $35. Regular application deadline 8/15. Notification on a rolling basis, beginning on or about 9/1. Nonfall registration accepted. Admission may be deferred for a maximum of 3 years. Credit and/or placement offered for CEEB Advanced Placement tests.

COSTS AND FINANCIAL AID

Annual in-state tuition $6,135. Annual out-of-state tuition $16,381. Room and board $6,910. Required fees $1,098. Average book expense $1,100. **Required Forms and Deadlines:** FAFSA. **Notification of Awards:** Applicants will be notified of awards on a rolling basis beginning 3/15. **Types of Aid:** *Need-based scholarships/grants:* Federal Pell, SEOG, state scholarships/grants, private scholarships, the school's own gift aid, Diversity Waivers. *Loans:* Subsidized Stafford, Unsubsidized Stafford, PLUS, Federal Perkins, Federal Nursing, Private loans from various lending institutions. **Student Employment:** Federal Work-Study Program available. Institutional employment available. Off-campus job opportunities are good. **Financial Aid Statistics:** 77% freshmen, 69% undergrads receive need-based scholarship or grant aid. 3% freshmen, 1% undergrads receive non-need-based scholarship or grant aid. 88% freshmen, 90% undergrads receive need-based self-help aid. 3% freshmen, 3% undergrads receive athletic scholarships. 85% undergrads borrow to pay for school. Average cumulative indebtedness $28,738. **Criteria for awarding institutional aid:** *Non-need-based:* academics, alumni affiliation, art, athletics, leadership, minority status, music/drama, state/district residency.

NORTH GEORGIA COLLEGE AND STATE UNIVERSITY

Office of Undergraduate Admissions, Dahlonega, GA 30597
Phone: 706-864-1800 • **Financial Aid Phone:** 706-864-1412
E-mail: admissions@northgeorgia.edu • **CEEB Code:** 5497
Fax: 706-864-1478 • **Website:** www.northgeorgia.edu • **ACT Code:** 848

This public school was founded in 1873. It has a 120-acre campus.

RATINGS
Admissions Selectivity Rating: 86   **Fire Safety Rating:** 95   **Green Rating:** 60*

STUDENTS AND FACULTY
Enrollment: 5,808. **Student Body:** 57% female, 43% male, 6% out-of-state, 1% international (48 countries represented). Asian 2%, African American 3%, Caucasian 86%, Hispanic 4%, Native American 0%.
Retention and Graduation: 78% freshmen return for sophomore year. 28% freshmen graduate within 4 years. 53% freshmen graduate within 6 years. **Faculty:** Student/faculty ratio 20:1. 247 full-time faculty, 53% are women.

ACADEMICS
Degrees: associate, bachelor's, certificate, master's, post-bachelor's certificate, post-master's certificate. **Classes:** Most classes have 20–29 students. Most lab/discussion sessions have fewer than 10 students. **Majors with Highest Enrollment:** biology/biological sciences; early childhood education and teaching; marketing/marketing management. **Special Study Options:** cooperative education program, distance learning, double major, dual enrollment, external degree program, honors program, independent study, internships, study abroad, teacher certification program, Dual degree in Engineering with GA Institute of Technology and Clemson University. **Disability Services:** Special programs offered to physically disabled students include note-taking services, reader services, tape recorders, tutors.

FACILITIES
Housing: Coed dorms, men's dorms, women's dorms, apartments for single students. 90% of campus accessible to physically disabled. **Special Academic Facilities/Equipment:** Planetarium; 2 Art galleries; Hall of fame; NGCSU museum **Computers:** Students can register for classes online. Administrative functions (other than registration) can be performed online.

CAMPUS LIFE
Environment: Rural. **Activities:** Choral groups, drama/theater, jazz band, literary magazine, marching band, music ensembles, pep band, student government, student newspaper, symphony orchestra, yearbook 60 registered organizations, 8 honor societies, 5 religious organizations. 6 fraternities, 4 sororities. **Athletics (Intercollegiate):** *Men:* baseball, basketball, cross-country, football, golf, riflery, soccer, table tennis, tennis, track/field (outdoor), volleyball, water polo. *Women:* basketball, cheerleading, cross-country, golf, riflery, soccer, softball, table tennis, tennis, track/field (outdoor), volleyball, water polo. **On-Campus Highlights:** Canteen, Commuter Lounge, Game Room, Uniform Store, Lounge Areas.

ADMISSIONS
Freshman Academic Profile: Average high school GPA 3.5. SAT Math middle 50% range 500-600. SAT Critical Reading middle 50% range 510-600. ACT middle 50% range 21-26. Minimum paper TOEFL 550. **Basis for Candidate Selection:** *Very important factors considered include:* rigor of secondary school record, standardized test scores.*Other factors considered include:* Class rank, recommendation(s), alumni/ae relation, character/personal qualities, extracurricular activities, talent/ability, volunteer work, work experience. **Freshman Admission Requirements:** High school diploma is required and GED is accepted. *Academic units required:* 4 English, 4 mathematics, 3 science, (1 science labs), 2 foreign language, 3 social studies. 4 English, 4 mathematics, 3 science, (1 science labs), 2 foreign language, 3 social studies. **Freshman Admission Statistics:** 4,226 applied, 56% admitted, 48% enrolled. **Transfer Admission Requirements:** college transcript(s), statement of good standing from prior institution(s). Minimum college GPA of 2.0 required. Lowest grade transferable C. **General Admission Information:** Application Fee $25. Regular application deadline 7/1. Nonfall registration accepted. Credit offered for CEEB Advanced Placement tests.

COSTS AND FINANCIAL AID
Annual in-state tuition $4,852. Annual out-of-state tuition $17,128. Room and board $8,430. Required fees $1,718. Average book expense $1,000. **Required Forms and Deadlines:** FAFSA, institution's own financial aid form. **Notification of Awards:** Applicants will be notified of awards on a rolling basis beginning 5/15. **Types of Aid:** *Need-based scholarships/grants:* Federal Pell, SEOG, state scholarships/grants, private scholarships, the school's own gift aid. *Loans:* Subsidized Stafford, Unsubsidized Stafford, PLUS, Federal Perkins, state loans, college/university loans from institutional funds. **Student Employment:** Financial Aid Statistics: 59% freshmen, 57% undergrads receive need-based scholarship or grant aid. 70% freshmen, 65% undergrads receive non-need-based scholarship or grant aid. 72% freshmen, 72% undergrads receive need-based self-help aid. 4% freshmen, 3% undergrads receive athletic scholarships. 57% undergrads borrow to pay for school. Average cumulative indebtedness $12,166. **Criteria for awarding institutional aid:** *Non-need-based:* academics, alumni affiliation, art, athletics, leadership, music/drama, state/district residency.

NORTH GREENVILLE COLLEGE

PO Box 1892, Tigerville, SC 29688-1892
Phone: 864-977-7001
E-mail: admissions@ngc.edu
Fax: 864-977-7177 • **Website:** www.ngc.edu

This private school, affiliated with the Southern Baptist Church, was founded in 1892.

RATINGS
Admissions Selectivity Rating: 66   **Fire Safety Rating:** 60*   **Green Rating:** 60*

STUDENTS AND FACULTY
Enrollment: 1,570. **Student Body:** 49% female, 51% male, 19% out-of-state, 2% international (19 countries represented). Asian 0%, African American 10%, Caucasian 90%, Hispanic 0%, Native American 0%.
Retention and Graduation: Faculty: Student/faculty ratio 17:1. 70 full-time faculty, 37% are women.

ACADEMICS
Degrees: associate, bachelor's, transfer associate. **Classes:** Most classes have 10–19 students. Most lab/discussion sessions have 10–19 students. **Special Study Options:** Accelerated program, cooperative education program, cross-registration, double major, English as a Second Language (ESL), external degree program, honors program, independent study, internships, student-designed major, study abroad, teacher certification program. **Disability Services:** Special programs offered to physically disabled students include tutors.

FACILITIES
Housing: men's dorms, women's dorms.

CAMPUS LIFE
Environment: Rural. **Activities:** Choral groups, concert band, drama/theater, jazz band, literary magazine, marching band, music ensembles, radio station, student government, student newspaper, television station, yearbook. **Athletics (Intercollegiate):** *Men:* baseball, basketball, cross-country, football, golf, soccer, softball, tennis. *Women:* basketball, cross-country, soccer, softball, tennis, volleyball.

ADMISSIONS
Freshman Academic Profile: Average high school GPA 3.8. 16% in top 10% of high school class, 43% in top 25% of high school class, 70% in top 50% of high school class. SAT Math middle 50% range 460-570. SAT Critical Reading middle 50% range 470-580. ACT middle 50% range 20-24. Minimum paper TOEFL 500. **Basis for Candidate Selection:** *Very important factors considered include:* Class rank, rigor of secondary school record, standardized test scores.*Other factors considered include:* application essay, recommendation(s). **Freshman Admission Requirements:** High school diploma is required and GED is accepted. **Freshman Admission Statistics:** 769 applied, 95% admitted, 56% enrolled. **Transfer Admission Requirements:** college transcript(s), minimum college GPA of 2.0 required. Lowest grade transferable C. **General Admission Information:** Application Fee $25. Regular application deadline 8/25. Nonfall registration accepted. Admission may be deferred for a maximum of 1 year.

COSTS AND FINANCIAL AID
Required Forms and Deadlines: FAFSA. **Notification of Awards:** Applicants will be notified of awards on a rolling basis beginning 2/1. **Types of Aid:** *Need-based scholarships/grants:* Federal Pell, SEOG, state scholarships/grants, private scholarships, the school's own gift aid. *Loans:* Subsidized Stafford, Unsubsidized Stafford, PLUS, Federal Perkins, state loans, college/university loans from institutional funds. **Financial Aid Statistics:** 97% freshmen, 95% undergrads receive need-based scholarship or grant aid. 25% freshmen, 24% undergrads receive need-based self-help aid. 20% freshmen, 30% undergrads receive athletic scholarships. 50% undergrads borrow to pay for school. Average cumulative indebtedness $3,500. **Criteria for awarding institutional aid:** *Non-need-based:* academics, art, athletics, music/drama, religious affiliation.

NORTH PARK UNIVERSITY

3225 West Foster Avenue, Chicago, IL 60625-4895
Phone: 773-244-5500 • **Financial Aid Phone:** 773-244-5506
E-mail: admission@northpark.edu • **CEEB Code:** 1556
Fax: 773-244-5243 • **Website:** www.northpark.edu • **ACT Code:** 1098

This private school was founded in 1891. It has a 30-acre campus.

RATINGS
Admissions Selectivity Rating: 75   **Fire Safety Rating:** 67   **Green Rating:** 60*

STUDENTS AND FACULTY
Enrollment: 2,188. **Student Body:** 63% female, 37% male, 31% out-of-state, 4% international (31 countries represented). Asian 7%, African American 9%, Caucasian 60%, Hispanic 10%, Native American 0%.
Retention and Graduation: 71% freshmen return for sophomore year. 45% freshmen graduate within 4 years. 55% freshmen graduate within 6 years. 15% grads go on to further study within 1 year. 15% grads pursue arts and sciences degrees. 2% grads pursue law degrees. 10% grads pursue business degrees. 3% grads pursue medical degrees. **Faculty:** Student/faculty ratio 14:1. 125 full-time faculty, 88% hold PhDs, 17% are members of minority groups, 50% are women. 0% of classes are taught by teaching assistants.

ACADEMICS
Degrees: bachelor's, first professional, master's, post-bachelor's certificate.
Classes: Most classes have 10–19 students. Most lab/discussion sessions have 20–29 students. **Majors with Highest Enrollment:** business administration and management; education; nursing/registered nurse (rn, asn, bsn, msn).
Special Study Options: Accelerated program, distance learning, double major, English as a Second Language (ESL), honors program, independent study, internships, liberal arts/career combination, student-designed major, study abroad, teacher certification program. **Honors Programs:** The North Park University Honors Congress brings together students of high academic ability with faculty in a learning community designed to promote academic excellence, rigorous intellectual development, community involvement, service to others, and vocational direction. As Honors Congress Scholars, students of promise are provided opportunities to excel during their first two years of undergraduate study. Honors courses during the second two years are offered in individual departments. We strive to take the words of Jesus, "To whom much is given, much is required," and give them special consideration in the Honors Congress. Our philosophy is simply this: The Honors Congress gives students of high intellectual ability an array of learning experiences from which to choose, places them sideby-side with faculty mentors who care, and offers them guidance and encouragement along the way. **Combined Degree Programs:** MDiv/MBA dual degree. **Disability Services:** Special programs offered to physically disabled students include note-taking services, reader services, tape recorders, tutors. **Career Services:** Alumni network, career/job search classes, career assessment, internships Career Services highlights include North Park has hundreds of internship opportunities available throughout the Chicago area. Students can decide between public and private, nonprofit and for profit organizations.

FACILITIES
Housing: special housing for disabled students, men's dorms, women's dorms, apartments for single students. **Special Academic Facilities/Equipment:** Art gallery, language lab, Swedish Historical Society Archives. **Computers:** 100% of libraries, 25% of dining areas, have wireless network access. Students can register for classes online. Administrative functions (other than registration) can be performed online.

CAMPUS LIFE
Environment: Metropolis. **Activities:** Choral groups, concert band, drama/theater, jazz band, literary magazine, music ensembles, musical theater, opera, pep band, student government, student newspaper, symphony orchestra, yearbook, Campus Ministries, International Student Organization 4 honor societies, 1 religious organizations. **Athletics (Intercollegiate):** *Men:* baseball, basketball, cross-country, football, golf, soccer, track/field (outdoor), track/field (indoor). *Women:* basketball, crew/rowing, cross-country, golf, soccer, softball, track/field (outdoor), track/field (indoor), volleyball. **On-Campus Highlights:** New Student Recreation Center, Brandel Library, New state of the art outdoor athletic facilities, Beautifull New Campus Quadrangle, Diverse neighborhood.

ADMISSIONS
Freshman Academic Profile: Average high school GPA 3.1. 11% in top 10% of high school class, 35% in top 25% of high school class, 66% in top 50% of high school class. 80% from public high schools. SAT Math middle 50% range 460-590. SAT Critical Reading middle 50% range 470-580. ACT middle 50% range 19-24. Minimum paper TOEFL 550. **Basis for Candidate Selection:** *Very important factors considered include:* Class rank, application essay, aca-

demic GPA, recommendation(s), rigor of secondary school record, standardized test scores, character/personal qualities, talent/ability. *Important factors considered include:* extracurricular activities, first generation, interview, racial/ethnic status, volunteer work. *Other factors considered include:* alumni/ae relation, geographical residence, level of applicant's interest, work experience. **Freshman Admission Requirements:** High school diploma is required and GED is accepted. **Freshman Admission Statistics:** 1,402 applied, 71% admitted, 42% enrolled. **Transfer Admission Requirements:** college transcript(s), essay or personal statement, statement of good standing from prior institution(s). Minimum college GPA of 2.0 required. Lowest grade transferable D. **General Admission Information:** Application Fee $40. Regular application deadline 7/1. Notification on a rolling basis, beginning on or about 9/15. Nonfall registration accepted. Admission may be deferred for a maximum of 1 year. Credit and/or placement offered for CEEB Advanced Placement tests.

COSTS AND FINANCIAL AID
Annual tuition $22,090. Room and board $8,040. Average book expense $950. **Required Forms and Deadlines:** FAFSA. **Notification of Awards:** Applicants will be notified of awards on a rolling basis beginning 3/15. **Types of Aid:** *Need-based scholarships/grants:* Federal Pell, SEOG, state scholarships/grants, private scholarships, the school's own gift aid, Federal Nursing Scholarships. *Loans:* Direct Subsidized Stafford, Direct Unsubsidized Stafford, Direct PLUS, Subsidized Stafford, Unsubsidized Stafford, PLUS, Federal Perkins, Federal Nursing. **Student Employment:** Federal Work-Study Program available. Institutional employment available. Highest amount earned per year from on-campus jobs $1,600. Off-campus job opportunities are excellent. **Financial Aid Statistics:** 70% freshmen receive need-based scholarship or grant aid. 42% freshmen receive non-need-based scholarship or grant aid. 64% freshmen receive need-based self-help aid. 90% freshmen, 90% undergrads receive any aid. 79% undergrads borrow to pay for school. Average cumulative indebtedness $21,140. **Criteria for awarding institutional aid:** *Non-need-based:* academics, art, music/drama, religious affiliation, state/district residency.

NORTHEASTERN ILLINOIS UNIVERSITY

5500 North St. Louis Avenue, Chicago, IL 60625
Phone: 773-442-4000 • **Financial Aid Phone:** 773-442-5000
E-mail: admrec@neiu.edu • **CEEB Code:** 1090
Fax: 773-442-4020 • **Website:** www.neiu.edu • **ACT Code:** 993

This public school was founded in 1961. It has a 63-acre campus.

RATINGS
Admissions Selectivity Rating: 69   **Fire Safety Rating:** 60*   **Green Rating:** 68

STUDENTS AND FACULTY
Enrollment: 9,282. **Student Body:** 56% female, 44% male, 1% out-of-state, 4% international (108 countries represented). Asian 9%, African American 10%, Caucasian 40%, Hispanic 32%, Native American 0%.
Retention and Graduation: 5% freshmen graduate within 4 years. **Faculty:** Student/faculty ratio 16:1. 414 full-time faculty, 70% hold PhDs, 26% are members of minority groups, 51% are women.

ACADEMICS
Degrees: bachelor's, master's. **Classes:** Most classes have 20–29 students. **Majors with Highest Enrollment:** accounting; elementary education and teaching; psychology. **Special Study Options:** cooperative education program, distance learning, double major, dual enrollment, exchange student program (domestic), honors program, independent study, student-designed major, study abroad, teacher certification program. **Disability Services:** Special programs offered to physically disabled students include note-taking services, reader services, tape recorders, tutors. **Career Services:** career assessment, internships.

FACILITIES
Housing: 98% of campus accessible to physically disabled. **Special Academic Facilities/Equipment:** Learning center with audiovisual, TV, multimedia, film, photography, graphic arts, and electronic instructional equipment, listening room. **Computers:** 50% of classrooms, 100% of libraries, 80% of dining areas, 100% of student union, 50% of common outdoor areas have wireless network access. Students can register for classes online. Administrative functions (other than registration) can be performed online.

CAMPUS LIFE
Environment: Metropolis. **Activities:** Choral groups, concert band, dance, drama/theater, jazz band, literary magazine, music ensembles, musical theater, radio station, student government, student newspaper 42 registered organizations, 12 honor societies, 6 religious organizations. 3 fraternities, 3 sororities. **On-Campus Highlights:** International Day, Fine Arst Building/ Art Gallery,

Ensemble Dance Company, Health and Wellness Center, Library. **Environmental Initiatives:** Recycling Environmentally Friendly Chemicals Lighting upgrades.

ADMISSIONS
Freshman Academic Profile: Average high school GPA 2.9. 10% in top 10% of high school class, 15% in top 25% of high school class, 58% in top 50% of high school class. 88% from public high schools. ACT middle 50% range 16-21. Minimum paper TOEFL 500. **Basis for Candidate Selection:** *Very important factors considered include:* Class rank, standardized test scores. **Freshman Admission Requirements:** High school diploma is required and GED is accepted. *Academic units required:* 4 English, 3 mathematics, 3 science, 3 social studies, 2 Fine Arts, Foreign Lang. or Voc. Ed (only 1 yr voc. ed. allowed). 4 English, 3 mathematics, 3 science, 3 social studies, 2 Fine Arts, Foreign Lang. or Voc. Ed (only 1 yr voc. ed. allowed) **Freshman Admission Statistics:** 5,118 applied, 64% admitted, 29% enrolled. **Transfer Admission Requirements:** college transcript(s), statement of good standing from prior institution(s). Minimum college GPA of 2.0 required. Lowest grade transferable D. **General Admission Information:** Application Fee $25. Regular application deadline 7/1. Regular notification 9/1. Nonfall registration accepted. Admission may be deferred for a maximum of 1 semester. Credit offered for CEEB Advanced Placement tests.

COSTS AND FINANCIAL AID
Required Forms and Deadlines: FAFSA, institution's own financial aid form. **Notification of Awards:** Applicants will be notified of awards on a rolling basis beginning 4/1. **Types of Aid:** *Need-based scholarships/grants:* Federal Pell, SEOG, state scholarships/grants, private scholarships, the school's own gift aid, Federal ACG, SMART. *Loans:* Subsidized Stafford, Unsubsidized Stafford, PLUS, Federal Perkins. **Student Employment:** Federal Work-Study Program available. Institutional employment available. Off-campus job opportunities are good. **Financial Aid Statistics:** 84% freshmen, 79% undergrads receive need-based scholarship or grant aid. 16% freshmen, 12% undergrads receive non-need-based scholarship or grant aid. 22% freshmen, 44% undergrads receive need-based self-help aid. 72% freshmen, 65% undergrads receive any aid. 14% undergrads borrow to pay for school. Average cumulative indebtedness $12,100. **Criteria for awarding institutional aid:** *Non-need-based:* academics, art, leadership, music/drama.

NORTHEASTERN STATE UNIVERSITY

Office of Admissions and Records, Tahlequah, OK 74464-2399
Phone: 918-444-2200 • **Financial Aid Phone:** 918-444-6402
E-mail: nsuinfo@nsuok.edu • **CEEB Code:** 6485
Fax: 918-458-2342 • **Website:** • **ACT Code:** 3408

This public school was founded in 1846. It has a 200-acre campus.

RATINGS
Admissions Selectivity Rating: 64   **Fire Safety Rating:** 60*   **Green Rating:** 60*

STUDENTS AND FACULTY
Enrollment: 8,485. **Student Body:** 61% female, 39% male, 3% out-of-state, 3% international (41 countries represented). Asian 1%, African American 6%, Caucasian 59%, Hispanic 2%, Native American 29%.
Retention and Graduation: 64% freshmen return for sophomore year. 12% freshmen graduate within 4 years. 33% freshmen graduate within 6 years. **Faculty:** Student/faculty ratio 23:1. 306 full-time faculty, 70% hold PhDs, 13% are members of minority groups, 46% are women. 2% of classes are taught by teaching assistants.

ACADEMICS
Degrees: bachelor's, first professional, master's, post-bachelor's certificate, post-master's certificate. **Classes:** Most classes have 20–29 students. Most lab/discussion sessions have 10–19 students. **Majors with Highest Enrollment:** accounting; business administration and management; elementary education and teaching. **Special Study Options:** cooperative education program, distance learning, double major, dual enrollment, honors program, independent study, internships, student-designed major, weekend college.
Honors Programs: NSU Honors Program: The Honors Program at NSU is a challenging educational option for academically talented students who enjoy learning. Honor students work with distinguished faculty members and peers in enhanced courses, pursue independent research, and participate in co-curricular cultural experiences. NSU President's Leadership Class: The President's Leadership Class is a unique scholarship/leadership program designed to identify and cultivate outstanding potential in selected freshmen entering NSU. Membership in the PLC allows students to develop close associations with

University administrators, meet scholars and dignitaries who frequently visit campus, take advantage of some of the most talented faculty members at NSU who teach special sections of selected required courses, and receive scholarship assistance which includes a tuition waiver and a stipend. The PLC Scholarship is renewable for four years if members maintain high academic standards while exercising practical leadership in University activities. **Disability Services:** Special programs offered to physically disabled students include note-taking services, reader services, tape recorders, tutors. **Career Services:** alumni services, career/job search classes, career assessment

FACILITIES
Housing: Coed dorms, special housing for disabled students, fraternity/sorority housing, apartments for married students, apartments for single students. **Computers:** Administrative functions (other than registration) can be performed online.

CAMPUS LIFE
Environment: Rural. **Activities:** Choral groups, concert band, dance, drama/theater, jazz band, literary magazine, marching band, music ensembles, musical theater, pep band, student government, student newspaper, symphony orchestra, television station 77 registered organizations, 9 honor societies, 5 religious organizations. 7 fraternities, 6 sororities. **Athletics (Intercollegiate):** *Men:* baseball, basketball, football, golf, soccer. *Women:* basketball, golf, soccer, softball, tennis. **On-Campus Highlights:** Seminary Hall, University Center, New Science Lab Building, NET Building, Seminary Suites.

ADMISSIONS
Freshman Academic Profile: Average high school GPA 3.2. ACT middle 50% range 18-23. Minimum paper TOEFL 500. **Basis for Candidate Selection:** *Very important factors considered include:* Class rank, academic GPA, rigor of secondary school record, standardized test scores. *Other factors considered include:* first generation, geographical residence, state residency. **Freshman Admission Requirements:** High school diploma is required and GED is accepted. *Academic units required:* 4 English, 3 mathematics, 2 science, (2 science labs), 2 history, 4 academic electives. *Academic units recommended:* 4 English, 3 mathematics, 2 science, (2 science labs), 2 history, 4 academic electives. **Freshman Admission Statistics:** 69% enrolled. **Transfer Admission Requirements:** college transcript(s), minimum college GPA of 2.0 required. Lowest grade transferable D. **General Admission Information:** Regular application deadline 8/1. Nonfall registration accepted. Admission may be deferred for a maximum of one semester. Credit offered for CEEB Advanced Placement tests.

COSTS AND FINANCIAL AID
Average book expense $950. **Required Forms and Deadlines:** FAFSA, institution's own financial aid form. **Notification of Awards:** Applicants will be notified of awards on a rolling basis beginning 2/15. **Types of Aid:** *Need-based scholarships/grants:* Federal Pell, SEOG, state scholarships/grants, private scholarships, the school's own gift aid. *Loans:* Subsidized Stafford, Unsubsidized Stafford, PLUS, Federal Perkins. **Student Employment:** Federal Work-Study Program available. Institutional employment available. **Financial Aid Statistics:** 68% freshmen, 70% undergrads receive need-based scholarship or grant aid. 69% freshmen, 91% undergrads receive non-need-based scholarship or grant aid. 29% freshmen, 65% undergrads receive need-based self-help aid. 4% freshmen, 13% undergrads receive athletic scholarships. 75% freshmen, 75% undergrads receive any aid. 61% undergrads borrow to pay for school. Average cumulative indebtedness $18,981. **Criteria for awarding institutional aid:** *Non need based:* academics, alumni affiliation, art, athletics, job skills, leadership, minority status, music/drama, religious affiliation, state/district residency.

NORTHEASTERN UNIVERSITY

Best 378

360 Huntington Avenue, Boston, MA 2115
Phone: 617-373-2200 • **Financial Aid Phone:** 617-373-3190
E-mail: admissions@neu.edu • **CEEB Code:** 3667
Fax: 617-373-8780 • **Website:** www.northeastern.edu • **ACT Code:** 1880

This private school was founded in 1898. It has a 73-acre campus.

RATINGS
Admissions Selectivity Rating: 97   **Fire Safety Rating:** 84   **Green Rating:** 98

STUDENTS AND FACULTY

Enrollment: 16,685. **Student Body:** 71% out-of-state, 15% international (122 countries represented). Asian 9%, African American 3%, Caucasian 52%, Hispanic 6%, Native American 0%.
Retention and Graduation: 96% freshmen return for sophomore year. 27% grads go on to further study within 1 year. **Faculty:** Student/faculty ratio 14:1. 1157 full-time faculty, 94% hold PhDs, 16% are members of minority groups, 41% are women.

ACADEMICS

Degrees: bachelor's, master's, post-master's certificate. **Classes:** Most classes have 10–19 students. **Majors with Highest Enrollment:** business/commerce; engineering; health services/allied health/health sciences. **Special Study Options:** Accelerated program, cooperative education program, cross-registration, distance learning, double major, English as a Second Language (ESL), exchange student program (domestic), honors program, independent study, internships, liberal arts/career combination, student-designed major, study abroad, teacher certification program, ROTC. **Honors Programs:** The University Honors Program offers exceptionally motivated students an undergraduate experience charted by meeting academic challenge. The program includes demanding and challenging academic opportunities, connections to an active community of thinkers committed to making a difference, and Living and Learning in the Honors Program thematic communities. The University Honors Program frames opportunities that are intellectually rigorous; promotes global awareness and civic engagement; and empowers students. **Combined Degree Programs:** BA/MA, BA/MEng. **Disability Services:** Special programs offered to physically disabled students include note-taking services, reader services, tape recorders. **Career Services:** Alumni network, alumni services, career/job search classes, career assessment, internships, regional alumni. Career Services highlights include Northeastern was in Princeton Review's Top 5 in Job Placement Career Services for 2 consecutive years; we host one of the largest Career Fairs in the region each semester '– over 500 employers participated in Fall '08 & Spring '09 Career Fairs. We have an "Employer in Residence" program where IBM, Raytheon, and Shawmut Design & Construction make available a company rep one day a week to meet with students to assist in career related topics: resumes, interviews, job openings, and career paths. We also participate in "'Call to Serve'" (Partnership for Public Service) which educates a new generation about the importance of strong civil service, helps re-establish links between federal agencies and campus, and provides students with information about federal jobs.

FACILITIES

Housing: Coed dorms, special housing for disabled students, special housing for international students, apartments for single students, wellness housing, theme housing. 95% of campus accessible to physically disabled. **Special Academic Facilities/Equipment:** John D. O'Bryant African American Institute, Egan Science/Engineering Research Center, Behrakis Health Sciences Center, Marine Science Center at Nahant, Center for Subsurfacing Sensing and Imaging Systems (CenSSIS), Center for Complex Network Research, Center for Drug Discovery, Barnett Institute of Chemical and Biological Analysis, Behrakis Health Sciences Center, Center for High Rate Nanomanufacturing, Center for Subsurface Sensing and Imaging Systems (CenSSIS), Egan Science/Engineering Research Center , Institute for Information Assurance, Institute on Urban Health Research, Dukakis Center for Urban and Regional Policy, John D. O'Bryant African-American Institute, Institute on Race and Justice, Institute for Global Innovation Management, Marine Science Center, Marino Recreation Center **Computers:** 100% of classrooms, 20% of dorms, 100% of libraries, 75% of dining areas, 100% of student union, 100% of common outdoor areas have wireless network access. Students can register for classes online. Administrative functions (other than registration) can be performed online.

CAMPUS LIFE

Environment: Metropolis. **Activities:** Choral groups, concert band, dance, drama/theater, jazz band, literary magazine, music ensembles, musical theater, pep band, radio station, student government, student newspaper, symphony orchestra, television station, yearbook, Campus Ministries, International Student Organization, Model UN 225 registered organizations, 15 honor societies, 20 religious organizations. 9 fraternities, 8 sororities. **Athletics (Intercollegiate):** *Men:* baseball, basketball, crew/rowing, cross-country, ice hockey, soccer, track/field (outdoor), track/field (indoor). *Women:* basketball, crew/rowing, cross-country, diving, field hockey, ice hockey, soccer, swimming, track/field (outdoor), track/field (indoor), volleyball. **On-Campus Highlights:** International Village, Curry Student Center, Marino Health and Fitness Center, Levine Marketplace & Stetson West Dining, Cyber Cafe. **Environmental Initiatives:** Presidents' Climate Commitment New buildings and major renovations must be LEED certifiable Aggressive energy efficiency, conservation, and use of energy management systems; recycling; composting; expanding procurement of dining services items including local produce and fair trade certified products, zero transfat, antibiotic- free poultry, pork, and locally raised beef burger, sustainable seafood, cage free eggs; corporate responsibility partnerships; active engagement with student groups, individual students, staff, and faculty; and expanding community partnerships that further demonstrate NU's sustainability commitment.

ADMISSIONS

Freshman Academic Profile: 63% in top 10% of high school class, 88% in top 25% of high school class, 99% in top 50% of high school class. % from public high schools. SAT Math middle 50% range 650-740. SAT Critical Reading middle 50% range 630-720. ACT middle 50% range 29-32. Minimum web-based TOEFL 84. **Basis for Candidate Selection:** *Very important factors considered include:* academic GPA, rigor of secondary school record. *Important factors considered include:* application essay, recommendation(s), standardized test scores, character/personal qualities, extracurricular activities, first generation, talent/ability, volunteer work. *Other factors considered include:* Class rank, alumni/ae relation, geographical residence, interview, racial/ethnic status, state residency, work experience. **Freshman Admission Requirements:** High school diploma is required and GED is accepted. *Academic units required:* 4 English, 3 mathematics, 3 science, (2 science labs), 2 foreign language, 3 social studies, 2 history. *Academic units recommended:* 4 English, 3 mathematics, 3 science, (2 science labs), 2 foreign language, 3 social studies, 2 history. **Freshman Admission Statistics:** 44,208 applied, 32% admitted, 19% enrolled. **Transfer Admission Requirements:** college transcript(s), essay or personal statement, statement of good standing from prior institution(s). Minimum college GPA of 2.0 required. Lowest grade transferable C. **General Admission Information:** Application Fee $70. Regular application deadline 1/15. Nonfall registration accepted. Admission may be deferred for a maximum of 1 year. Credit and/or placement offered for CEEB Advanced Placement tests.

COSTS AND FINANCIAL AID

Annual tuition $39,320. Room and board $13,620. Required fees $416. Average book expense $1,000. **Required Forms and Deadlines:** FAFSA, CSS/Financial Aid PROFILE. **Notification of Awards:** Applicants will be notified of awards on a rolling basis beginning 3/15. **Types of Aid:** *Need-based scholarships/grants:* Federal Pell, SEOG, state scholarships/grants, private scholarships, the school's own gift aid. *Loans:* Direct Subsidized Stafford, Direct Unsubsidized Stafford, Direct PLUS, Federal Perkins, Federal Nursing, state loans. **Student Employment:** Federal Work-Study Program available. Institutional employment available. Off-campus job opportunities are excellent. **Financial Aid Statistics:** 98% freshmen, 93% undergrads receive need-based scholarship or grant aid. 34% freshmen, 26% undergrads receive non-need-based scholarship or grant aid. 85% freshmen, 88% undergrads receive need-based self-help aid. 2% freshmen, 1% undergrads receive athletic scholarships. **Criteria for awarding institutional aid:** *Non-need-based:* academics, athletics, minority status.

See page 1162.

NORTHERN ARIZONA UNIVERSITY

PO Box 4084, Flagstaff, AZ 86011-4084
Phone: 928-523-5511 • **Financial Aid Phone:** 928-523-4951
E-mail: undergraduate.admissions@nau.edu • **CEEB Code:** 4006
Fax: 928-523-0226 • **Website:** www.nau.edu • **ACT Code:** 86

This public school was founded in 1899. It has a 740-acre campus.

RATINGS

Admissions Selectivity Rating: 72   **Fire Safety Rating:** 84   **Green Rating:** 94

STUDENTS AND FACULTY

Enrollment: 21,609. **Student Body:** 58% female, 42% male, 26% out-of-state, 4% international (61 countries represented). Asian 1%, African American 3%, Caucasian 64%, Hispanic 18%, Native American 4%.
Retention and Graduation: 76% freshmen return for sophomore year. 30% freshmen graduate within 4 years. **Faculty:** Student/faculty ratio 20:1. 900 full-time faculty, 12% are members of minority groups, 49% are women.

ACADEMICS

Degrees: bachelor's, certificate, master's, post-bachelor's certificate. **Classes:** Most classes have 20–29 students. Most lab/discussion sessions have 20–29 students. **Majors with Highest Enrollment:** biology/biological sciences; elementary education and teaching; hospitality administration/management. **Special Study Options:** Accelerated program, cooperative education program, distance learning, double major, dual enrollment, English as a Second Language (ESL), exchange student program (domestic), honors program, independent study, internships, study abroad, teacher certification program. **Honors Programs:** Honors Program. **Disability Services:** Special programs offered to physically disabled students include note-taking services, reader services, tape recorders, tutors. **Career Services:** alumni services, career/job search classes, career assessment, internships.

FACILITIES

Housing: Coed dorms, men's dorms, special housing for international students, women's dorms, fraternity/sorority housing, apartments for married students, apartments for single students. 90% of campus accessible to physically disabled. **Special Academic Facilities/Equipment:** Art gallery, art and music studios, observatory, multidisciplinary research center, 4,000-acre experimental forest. **Computers:** 100% of classrooms, 100% of dorms, 100% of libraries, 100% of dining areas, 100% of student union, 25% of common outdoor areas have wireless network access. Students can register for classes online. Administrative functions (other than registration) can be performed online.

CAMPUS LIFE

Environment: Town. **Activities:** Choral groups, concert band, dance, drama/theater, jazz band, marching band, music ensembles, musical theater, opera, radio station, student government, student newspaper, symphony orchestra, television station, yearbook, Campus Ministries, International Student Organization 193 registered organizations, 20 honor societies, 7 religious organizations. 14 fraternities, 9 sororities. **Athletics (Intercollegiate):** *Men:* basketball, cheerleading, cross-country, football, tennis, track/field (outdoor). *Women:* basketball, cheerleading, cross-country, diving, golf, soccer, swimming, tennis, track/field (outdoor), volleyball. **On-Campus Highlights:** University Union, NAU Dome, Wall Aquatic Center, Cline Library, Old Main. **Environmental Initiatives:** Green Building commitment Fifty percent of campus landscaping served by reclaimed/non-potable water ecoPass " Free city bus passes offered to all faculty and staff.

ADMISSIONS

Freshman Academic Profile: Average high school GPA 3.4. 19% in top 10% of high school class, 48% in top 25% of high school class, 81% in top 50% of high school class. SAT Math middle 50% range 470-590. SAT Critical Reading middle 50% range 470-580. SAT Writing middle 50% range 460-560. ACT middle 50% range 20-25. Minimum web-based TOEFL 70. Minimum paper TOEFL 525. **Basis for Candidate Selection:** *Important factors considered include:* Class rank, academic GPA, rigor of secondary school record, standardized test scores.**Freshman Admission Requirements:** High school diploma is required and GED is accepted. *Academic units required:* 4 English, 4 mathematics, 3 science, (1 science labs), 2 foreign language, 1 social studies, 1 history, 1 Fine Arts. 4 English, 4 mathematics, 3 science, (1 science labs), 2 foreign language, 1 social studies, 1 history, 1 Fine Arts **Freshman Admission Statistics:** 34,461 applied, 76% admitted, 16% enrolled. Minimum college GPA of 2.0 required. Lowest grade transferable C. **General Admission Information:** Application Fee $25. Nonfall registration accepted. Admission may be deferred for a maximum of 2 years. Credit and/or placement offered for CEEB Advanced Placement tests.

COSTS AND FINANCIAL AID

Average book expense $944. **Required Forms and Deadlines:** FAFSA. **Notification of Awards:** Applicants will be notified of awards on a rolling basis beginning 3/15. **Types of Aid:** *Need-based scholarships/grants:* Federal Pell, SEOG, state scholarships/grants, private scholarships, the school's own gift aid, Federal Nursing Scholarships. *Loans:* Direct Subsidized Stafford, Direct Unsubsidized Stafford, Direct PLUS, Federal Perkins, Federal Nursing, state loans, college/university loans from institutional funds. **Student Employment:** Federal Work-Study Program available. Institutional employment avail able. Off-campus job opportunities are good. **Financial Aid Statistics:** 65% freshmen, 73% undergrads receive need-based scholarship or grant aid. 56% freshmen, 42% undergrads receive non need-based scholarship or grant aid 74% freshmen, 78% undergrads receive need-based self-help aid. 2% freshmen, 2% undergrads receive athletic scholarships. 63% freshmen, 62% undergrads receive any aid. 58% undergrads borrow to pay for school. Average cumulative indebtedness $22,621. **Criteria for awarding institutional aid:** *Non-need-based:* academics, alumni affiliation, art, athletics, leadership, minority status, music/drama, state/district residency.

NORTHERN ILLINOIS UNIVERSITY

Office of Admissions, DeKalb, IL 60115-2857
Phone: 815-753-0446 • **Financial Aid Phone:** 815-753-1395
E-mail: admissions-info@niu.edu • **CEEB Code:** 1559
Fax: 815-753-1783 • **Website:** www.reg.niu.edu • **ACT Code:** 1102

This public school was founded in 1895. It has a 546-acre campus.

RATINGS

Admissions Selectivity Rating: 82   **Fire Safety Rating:** 60*   **Green Rating:** 60*

STUDENTS AND FACULTY

Enrollment: 28,551. **Student Body:** 29% female, 71% male, 2% out-of-state, 1% international. Asian 3%, African American 9%, Caucasian 35%, Hispanic 7%, Native American 0%.
Retention and Graduation: 28% freshmen graduate within 4 years. 54% freshmen graduate within 6 years. **Faculty:** Student/faculty ratio 17:1. 891 full-time faculty, 82% hold PhDs, 13% are members of minority groups, 46% are women.

ACADEMICS

Degrees: bachelor's, first professional, master's. **Classes:** Most classes have 20–29 students. Most lab/discussion sessions have 20–29 students. **Special Study Options:** cooperative education program, distance learning, double major, dual enrollment, external degree program, honors program, independent study, internships, liberal arts/career combination, student-designed major, study abroad, teacher certification program. **Combined Degree Programs:** BA/JD. **Disability Services:** Special programs offered to physically disabled students include note-taking services, tape recorders, tutors. **Career Services:** Alumni network, alumni services, career/job search classes, internships, regional alumni., Career Services highlights include Comprehensive internship and Cooperative ed. program.

FACILITIES

Housing: Coed dorms, special housing for disabled students, special housing for international students, fraternity/sorority housing, apartments for married students, quiet and alcohol-free lifestyle floors, 21 and over/graduates student floors, honors floors. Fllors with visitation policies, computer science residential program. 90% of campus accessible to physically disabled. **Special Academic Facilities/Equipment:** Art and anthropology museums, plant molecular biology center. **Computers:** Students can register for classes online.

CAMPUS LIFE

Environment: Rural. **Activities:** Choral groups, concert band, dance, drama/theater, jazz band, marching band, opera, radio station, student government, student newspaper, student-run film society, symphony orchestra, television station 200 registered organizations, 13 religious organizations. 22 fraternities, 14 sororities. **Athletics (Intercollegiate):** *Men:* baseball, basketball, diving, football, golf, soccer, swimming, tennis, wrestling. *Women:* basketball, cross-country, golf, gymnastics, soccer, softball, swimming, tennis, volleyball. **On-Campus Highlights:** Barsema Hall, Convocation Center, Holmes Student Center, Campus Life Building, Recreation Center.

ADMISSIONS

Freshman Academic Profile: 11% in top 10% of high school class, 33% in top 25% of high school class, 70% in top 50% of high school class. ACT middle 50% range 19-25. Minimum paper TOEFL 525. **Basis for Candidate Selection:** *Very important factors considered include:* Class rank, rigor of secondary school record, standardized test scores.*Other factors considered include:* application essay, recommendation(s), extracurricular activities, racial/ethnic status, talent/ability. **Freshman Admission Requirements:** High school diploma is required and GED is accepted. *Academic units required:* 4 English, 2 mathematics, 2 science, (1 science labs), 1 foreign language, 2 social studies, 1 history. *Academic units recommended:* 4 English, 2 mathematics, 2 science, (1 science labs), 1 foreign language, 2 social studies, 1 history. **Freshman Admission Statistics:** 17,842 applied, 52% admitted, 29% enrolled. **Transfer Admission Requirements:** college transcript(s), minimum college GPA of 2.0 required. Lowest grade transferable c. **General Admission Information:** Regular application deadline 8/1. Nonfall registration accepted. Credit and/or placement offered for CEEB Advanced Placement tests.

COSTS AND FINANCIAL AID

Annual in-state tuition $8,894. Annual out-of-state tuition $17,787. Room and board $10,648. Required fees $2,590. Average book expense $1,400. **Required Forms and Deadlines:** FAFSA, institution's own financial aid form, noncustodial PROFILEP. **Notification of Awards:** Applicants will be notified of awards on a rolling basis beginning 4/15. **Types of Aid:** *Need-based scholarships/grants:* Federal Pell, SEOG, state scholarships/grants, private scholarships, the school's own gift aid, Federal Nursing Scholarships. *Loans:* Subsidized Stafford, Unsubsidized Stafford, PLUS, Federal Perkins. **Student Employment:** Off-campus job opportunities are good. **Financial Aid Statistics:** 96% freshmen, 74% undergrads receive need-based scholarship or grant aid. 1% freshmen, 2% undergrads receive non-need-based scholarship or grant aid. 87% freshmen, 90% undergrads receive need-based self-help aid. 3% freshmen, 2% undergrads receive athletic scholarships. 72% undergrads borrow to pay for school. Average cumulative indebtedness $30,521. **Criteria for awarding institutional aid:** *Non-need-based:* academics, athletics.

NORTHERN KENTUCKY UNIVERSITY

Administrative Center 401, Highland Heights, KY 41099
Financial Aid Phone: 859-572-6437
E-mail: admitnku@nku.edu • **CEEB Code:** 1574
Fax: • **Website:** www.nku.edu • **ACT Code:** 1566

This public school was founded in 1968. It has a 397-acre campus.

RATINGS
Admissions Selectivity Rating: 74   **Fire Safety Rating:** 85   **Green Rating:** 79

STUDENTS AND FACULTY
Enrollment: 12,658. **Student Body:** 56% female, 44% male, 31% out-of-state, 1% international (48 countries represented). Asian 1%, African American 7%, Caucasian 84%, Hispanic 2%, Native American 0%.
Retention and Graduation: 68% freshmen return for sophomore year. 8% freshmen graduate within 4 years. **Faculty:** Student/faculty ratio 17:1. 530 full-time faculty, 68% hold PhDs, 12% are members of minority groups, 51% are women. 0% of classes are taught by teaching assistants.

ACADEMICS
Degrees: associate, bachelor's, certificate, first professional, master's, post-bachelor's certificate. **Classes:** Most classes have 20–29 students. Most lab/discussion sessions have 10–19 students. **Majors with Highest Enrollment:** elementary education and teaching; nursing/registered nurse (rn, asn, bsn, msn); psychology. **Special Study Options:** cooperative education program, cross-registration, distance learning, double major, dual enrollment, exchange student program (domestic), honors program, independent study, internships, liberal arts/career combination, study abroad, teacher certification program, weekend college, Web-based Programs. **Honors Programs:** The NKU Honors Program provides qualified students a 21-hour minor, which includes 15 semester hours of seminars, each having a maximum enrollment of 15 students, plus 6 semester hours for completing the Honors Thesis. At the core of the Honors experience, the seminars emphasize discussion and discovery of ideas. NKU's Honors Program is university-wide. The program showcases open-ended seminars not conforming to the boundaries traditionally dividing fields of experise. Honors learning affords the intellectual challenges of interdisciplinary education. **Combined Degree Programs:** MBA/JD. **Disability Services:** Special programs offered to physically disabled students include note-taking services, reader services, tape recorders, tutors. **Career Services:** alumni services, career/job search classes, career assessment, internships Career Services highlights include Cooperative Education - well organized co-op learning program out of the Career Development Center. This program has grown significantly (55%) in the last two years.

FACILITIES
Housing: Coed dorms, special housing for disabled students, men's dorms, women's dorms, cooperative housing, apartments for single students. One-Third of all college housing accessible to handicapped. 100% of campus accessible to physically disabled. **Special Academic Facilities/Equipment:** Art gallery, biology, geology, and anthropology museums, research/technical center, two electron microscopes. **Computers:** Students can register for classes online. Administrative functions (other than registration) can be performed online.

CAMPUS LIFE
Environment: Metropolis. **Activities:** Choral groups, concert band, dance, drama/theater, jazz band, literary magazine, music ensembles, musical theater, opera, pep band, radio station, student government, student newspaper, symphony orchestra, television station 125 registered organizations, 14 honor societies, 9 religious organizations. 8 fraternities, 8 sororities. **Athletics (Intercollegiate):** *Men:* baseball, basketball, cheerleading, cross-country, golf, soccer, tennis. *Women:* basketball, cheerleading, cross-country, golf, soccer, softball, tennis, volleyball. **On-Campus Highlights:** Natural Science Center, University Suites (housing), Starbucks Cafe, Albright Health Center, a full service U.S. Bank Branch. **Environmental Initiatives:** NKU has a $4.5 million ESCO (energy savings performance contract to improve lighting, HVAC and water use). Originally expected to pay for itself within 11.7 years, it has been so successful that it will pay for itself in 10 years. NKU partnered with the Transit Authority of Northern Kentucky (TANK) to provide free, unlimited bus rides to students and faculty/staff with a valid university ID. August 2007 through March 2011, this program, called U-PASS, has provided over 900,000 free rides on TANK and NKU shuttle buses for an avoidance of 2,425 metric tons of CO_2 equivalent in the Northern Kentucky atmosphere. Since 2007, the campus recycling program has expanded and now includes high-grade paper, cardboard, aluminum, steel cans, plastic/glass bottles, light bulbs, magazines, newspapers, books, and sorted office paper. Some of the more unusual things we recycle are tires and oil from the campus vehicles, plant materials for compost, wood pallets, telephone books, computer equipment, printer cartridges, plates from the print shop and

carpet. As an ACUPCC signatory, NKU has participated in RecycleMania for the past four years. Each year, students, faculty/staff and visitors to campus are encouraged to limit their waste and increase their percentage of recyclables.

ADMISSIONS
Freshman Academic Profile: Average high school GPA 3.1. 9% in top 10% of high school class, 29% in top 25% of high school class, 63% in top 50% of high school class. SAT Math middle 50% range 435-555. SAT Critical Reading middle 50% range 430-550. ACT middle 50% range 19-24. Minimum web-based TOEFL 61. Minimum paper TOEFL 500. **Basis for Candidate Selection:** *Very important factors considered include:* Class rank, academic GPA, standardized test scores. **Freshman Admission Requirements:** High school diploma is required and GED is accepted. *Academic units required:* 4 English, 3 mathematics, 3 science, (1 science labs), 2 foreign language, 3 social studies, 6 academic electives, 1 Health/Physical Education. 4 English, 3 mathematics, 3 science, (1 science labs), 2 foreign language, 3 social studies, 6 academic electives, 1 Health/Physical Education **Freshman Admission Statistics:** 7,202 applied, 66% admitted, 49% enrolled. **Transfer Admission Requirements:** college transcript(s), minimum college GPA of 2.0 required. Lowest grade transferable D. **General Admission Information:** Application Fee $30. Regular application deadline 8/1. Notification on a rolling basis, beginning on or about 10/1. Nonfall registration accepted. Credit offered for CEEB Advanced Placement tests.

COSTS AND FINANCIAL AID
Required Forms and Deadlines: FAFSA. **Notification of Awards:** Applicants will be notified of awards on a rolling basis beginning 4/1. **Types of Aid:** *Need-based scholarships/grants:* Federal Pell, SEOG, state scholarships/grants, private scholarships, the school's own gift aid. *Loans:* Subsidized Stafford, Unsubsidized Stafford, PLUS, Federal Perkins, Private Loans. **Student Employment:** Federal Work-Study Program available. Institutional employment available. Highest amount earned per year from on-campus jobs $5,625. Off-campus job opportunities are good. **Financial Aid Statistics:** 53% freshmen, 52% undergrads receive need-based scholarship or grant aid. 71% freshmen, 48% undergrads receive non-need-based scholarship or grant aid. 87% freshmen, 91% undergrads receive need-based self-help aid. 3% freshmen, 2% undergrads receive athletic scholarships. 66% freshmen, 57% undergrads receive any aid. 69% undergrads borrow to pay for school. Average cumulative indebtedness $21,535. **Criteria for awarding institutional aid:** *Non-need-based:* academics, alumni affiliation, art, athletics, job skills, leadership, minority status, music/drama, state/district residency.

NORTHERN MICHIGAN UNIVERSITY

1401 Presque Isle Avenue, Marquette, MI 49855
Phone: 906-227-2650 • **Financial Aid Phone:** 800-682-9797
E-mail: admiss@nmu.edu • **CEEB Code:** 1560
Fax: 906-227-1747 • **Website:** www.nmu.edu • **ACT Code:** 2038

This public school was founded in 1899. It has a 350-acre campus.

RATINGS
Admissions Selectivity Rating: 72   **Fire Safety Rating:** 66   **Green Rating:** 68

STUDENTS AND FACULTY
Enrollment: 7,977. **Student Body:** 53% female, 47% male, 19% out-of-state, 1% international (30 countries represented). Asian 1%, African American 2%, Caucasian 81%, Hispanic 1%, Native American 2%.
Retention and Graduation: 20% freshmen graduate within 4 years. 47% freshmen graduate within 6 years.

ACADEMICS
Degrees: associate, bachelor's, certificate, diploma, master's, post-bachelor's certificate, post-master's certificate, terminal associate, transfer associate. **Classes:** Most classes have 20–29 students. **Majors with Highest Enrollment:** art/art studies; criminal justice/safety studies; nursing/registered nurse (rn, asn, bsn, msn). **Special Study Options:** distance learning, double major, dual enrollment, English as a Second Language (ESL), honors program, independent study, internships, liberal arts/career combination, student-designed major, study abroad, teacher certification program, weekend college. **Honors Programs:** Honors Program for eligible freshmen and transfer students. **Disability Services:** Special programs offered to physically disabled students include note-taking services, reader services, tape recorders, tutors. **Career Services:** Alumni network, career/job search classes, internships Career Services highlights include The offering of internships is specific to each academic department.

FACILITIES

Housing: Coed dorms, special housing for disabled students, apartments for married students, apartments for single students, wellness housing, theme housing. 100% of campus accessible to physically disabled. **Special Academic Facilities/Equipment:** Seaborg Science Center, New Science facility, new and remodeled Music and Art and Design instructional rooms, DeVos Art Gallery. **Computers:** 100% of classrooms, 100% of dorms, 100% of libraries, 100% of dining areas, 100% of student union, 100% of common outdoor areas have wireless network access. Students can register for classes online. Administrative functions (other than registration) can be performed online.

CAMPUS LIFE

Environment: Village. **Activities:** Choral groups, concert band, dance, drama/theater, jazz band, literary magazine, marching band, music ensembles, musical theater, opera, pep band, radio station, student government, student newspaper, student-run film society, symphony orchestra, television station, Campus Ministries, International Student Organization, Model UN 308 registered organizations, 11 honor societies, 19 religious organizations. 3 fraternities, 4 sororities. **Athletics (Intercollegiate):** *Men:* basketball, football, golf, ice hockey, skiingnordiccross-country. *Women:* basketball, cross-country, diving, skiingnordiccross-country, soccer, swimming, track/field (outdoor), track/field (indoor), volleyball. **On-Campus Highlights:** Hedgcock Student Service Center, Superior Dome, New Science Facility, Market Place Dining Facility, De Vos Art Galleries, The Starbucks coffee lounge located in the library is a very popular place and doubles as a study lounge. **Environmental Initiatives:** Northern is a member of the Association for the Advancement of Sustainability in Higher Education and USGBC. Reduced energy consumption by providing computer controlled heating and cooling, thermal efficient windows for the dormitories,individual heating controls in dorm rooms, new efficient lighting and controls technology, new energy efficient architectural design components, water efficient fixtures, wells for irrigation and waterless urinals In 2007 Meyland Hall's renovation received LEED certification, a first for any building in the Upper Peninsula and the first certified residence hall in the states of MI, WI, MN, OH & IN. A total of four residence halls are now certified by LEED.

ADMISSIONS

Freshman Academic Profile: Average high school GPA 3.1. ACT middle 50% range 19-24. Minimum web-based TOEFL 61. Minimum paper TOEFL 500. **Basis for Candidate Selection:** *Very important factors considered include:* academic GPA, standardized test scores.Freshman Admission Requirements: High school diploma is required and GED is accepted. **Freshman Admission Statistics:** 6,041 applied, 68% admitted, 36% enrolled. **Transfer Admission Requirements:** college transcript(s), statement of good standing from prior institution(s). Minimum college GPA of 2.0 required. Lowest grade transferable C–. **General Admission Information:** Application Fee $30. Notification on a rolling basis, beginning on or about 9/15. Nonfall registration accepted. Admission may be deferred for a maximum of 1 year. Credit and/or placement offered for CEEB Advanced Placement tests.

COSTS AND FINANCIAL AID

Annual in-state tuition $8,646. Annual out-of-state tuition $13,542. Room and board $8,404. Required fees $64. Average book expense $900. **Required Forms and Deadlines:** FAFSA. **Notification of Awards:** Applicants will be notified of awards on a rolling basis beginning 4/1. **Types of Aid:** *Need-based scholarships/grants:* Federal Pell, SEOG, state scholarships/grants, private scholarships, the school's own gift aid, Federal Nursing Scholarships. *Loans:* Direct Subsidized Stafford, Direct Unsubsidized Stafford, Direct PLUS, Federal Perkins, state loans, Private loans. **Student Employment:** Federal Work-Study Program available. Institutional employment available. Off-campus job opportunities are fair. **Financial Aid Statistics:** 60% freshmen, 61% undergrads receive need-based scholarship or grant aid. 46% freshmen, 37% undergrads receive non-need-based scholarship or grant aid. 79% freshmen, 86% undergrads receive need-based self-help aid. 1% freshmen, 68% undergrads borrow to pay for school. Average cumulative indebtedness $29,371. **Criteria for awarding institutional aid:** *Non-need-based:* academics, art, athletics, leadership, minority status, music/drama, religious affiliation, state/district residency.

NORTHERN STATE UNIVERSITY

1200 South Jay Street, Aberdeen, SD 57401-7198
Phone: 605-626-2544 • **Financial Aid Phone:** 605-626-2640
E-mail: admission2@northern.edu • **CEEB Code:** 6487
Fax: 605-626-2587 **ACT Code:** 3916

This public school was founded in 1901. It has a 72-acre campus.

RATINGS

Admissions Selectivity Rating: 66   **Fire Safety Rating:** 70   **Green Rating:** 78

STUDENTS AND FACULTY

Enrollment: 1,769. **Student Body:** 56% female, 44% male, 21% out-of-state, 4% international (14 countries represented). Asian 1%, African American 2%, Caucasian 86%, Hispanic 3%, Native American 2%.
Retention and Graduation: 29% grads go on to further study within 1 year. **Faculty:** Student/faculty ratio 19:1. 89 full-time faculty, 79% hold PhDs, 10% are members of minority groups, 37% are women. 0% of classes are taught by teaching assistants.

ACADEMICS

Degrees: associate, bachelor's, certificate, master's. **Classes:** Most classes have 10–19 students. **Majors with Highest Enrollment:** business/commerce; elementary education and teaching; sociology. **Special Study Options:** Accelerated program, cooperative education program, cross-registration, distance learning, double major, dual enrollment, English as a Second Language (ESL), exchange student program (domestic), external degree program, honors program, independent study, internships, liberal arts/career combination, student-designed major, study abroad, teacher certification program, weekend college, International Business E Learning Certification. **Honors Programs:** Honors Program **Combined Degree Programs:** Bachelor's/MBA w/ U of South Dakota. **Disability Services:** Special programs offered to physically disabled students include note-taking services, reader services, tape recorders, tutors. **Career Services:** Alumni network, alumni services, career/job search classes, career assessment, internships, regional alumni. Career Services highlights include School of Business Programs School of Education Programs.

FACILITIES

Housing: Coed dorms, men's dorms, women's dorms, apartments for married students, apartments for single students. 90% of campus accessible to physically disabled. **Special Academic Facilities/Equipment:** State-Wide E-Learning Center; Art galleries. **Computers:** 100% of classrooms, 100% of dorms, 100% of libraries, 100% of dining areas, 100% of student union, have wireless network access. Students can register for classes online. Administrative functions (other than registration) can be performed online.

CAMPUS LIFE

Environment: Rural. **Activities:** Choral groups, concert band, dance, drama/theater, jazz band, marching band, music ensembles, musical theater, pep band, student government, student newspaper, symphony orchestra, television station, yearbook, Campus Ministries, International Student Organization 100 registered organizations, 5 honor societies, 6 religious organizations. **Athletics (Intercollegiate):** *Men:* baseball, basketball, cheerleading, cross-country, football, golf, track/field (outdoor), track/field (indoor), wrestling. *Women:* basketball, cheerleading, cross-country, golf, soccer, softball, swimming, tennis, track/field (outdoor), track/field (indoor), volleyball. **On-Campus Highlights:** NSU Student Center, NSU State-Wide E-Learning Center, NSU Barnett Athletic Center, NSU Johnson Fine Arts Center, NSU International Center of Excellence.

ADMISSIONS

Freshman Academic Profile: Average high school GPA 3.1. 9% in top 10% of high school class, 21% in top 25% of high school class, 56% in top 50% of high school class. SAT Math middle 50% range 430-560. SAT Critical Reading middle 50% range 420-550. ACT middle 50% range 19-24. Minimum web-based TOEFL 61. Minimum paper TOEFL 500. **Basis for Candidate Selection:** *Very important factors considered include:* Class rank, rigor of secondary school record, standardized test scores.*Other factors considered include:* interview, talent/ability. **Freshman Admission Requirements:** High school diploma is required and GED is accepted. *Academic units required:* 4 English, 3 mathematics, 3 science, (3 science labs), 3 social studies. 4 English, 3 mathematics, 3 science, (3 science labs), 3 social studies. **Freshman Admission Statistics:** 1,142 applied, 90% admitted, 40% enrolled. **Transfer Admission Requirements:** High school transcript, college transcript(s), statement of good standing from prior institution(s). Minimum college GPA of 2.0 required. Lowest grade transferable C. **General Admission Information:** Application Fee $20. Nonfall registration accepted. Credit and/or placement offered for CEEB Advanced Placement tests.

COSTS AND FINANCIAL AID

Annual in-state tuition $3,726. Annual out-of-state tuition $5,590. Room and board $6,174. Required fees $3,543. Average book expense $1,200. **Required Forms and Deadlines:** FAFSA. **Notification of Awards:** Applicants will be notified of awards on or about 4/15. **Types of Aid:** *Need-based scholarships/ grants:* Federal Pell, SEOG, state scholarships/grants, private scholarships, the school's own gift aid. *Loans:* Subsidized Stafford, Unsubsidized Stafford, PLUS, Federal Perkins, college/university loans from institutional funds. **Student Employment:** Federal Work-Study Program available. Institutional employment available. Off-campus job opportunities are excellent. **Criteria for awarding institutional aid:** *Non-need-based:* academics, art, athletics, leadership, minority status, music/drama, state/district residency.

NORTHLAND COLLEGE

1411 Ellis Avenue, Ashland, WI 54806-3999
Phone: 715-682-1224 • **Financial Aid Phone:** 715-682-1254
E-mail: admit@northland.edu • **CEEB Code:** 1561
Fax: 715-682-1258 • **Website:** www.northland.edu • **ACT Code:** 4624

This private school, affiliated with the United Church of Christ Church, was founded in 1892. It has a 130-acre campus.

RATINGS
Admissions Selectivity Rating: 72   Fire Safety Rating: 72   Green Rating: 97

STUDENTS AND FACULTY
Enrollment: 519. **Student Body:** 52% female, 48% male, 49% out-of-state, 4% international (6 countries represented). Asian 1%, African American 1%, Caucasian 80%, Hispanic 5%, Native American 2%.
Retention and Graduation: 63% freshmen return for sophomore year. 41% freshmen graduate within 4 years. 48% freshmen graduate within 6 years.
Faculty: Student/faculty ratio 10:1. 46 full-time faculty, 91% hold PhDs, 4% are members of minority groups, 39% are women. 0% of classes are taught by teaching assistants.

ACADEMICS
Degrees: bachelor's. **Classes:** Most classes have 10–19 students. Most lab/discussion sessions have 10–19 students. **Majors with Highest Enrollment:** biology/biological sciences; education; natural resources conservation and research, other. **Special Study Options:** distance learning, double major, dual enrollment, exchange student program (domestic), honors program, independent study, internships, student-designed major, teacher certification program, 3-2 cooperative programs in Forestry and Engineering with Michigan Technological University and Washington University Eco League consortium with 6 environmental liberal arts colleges around the country (Prescott, Green Mountain, Alaska Pacific University, Antioch College, College of the Atlantic, Northland College)engaging in student semester exchanges. **Combined Degree Programs:** 3-2 engineering. **Disability Services:** Special programs offered to physically disabled students include note-taking services, reader services, tape recorders, tutors. **Career Services:** internships.

FACILITIES
Housing: Coed dorms, women's dorms, cooperative housing, apartments for single students, theme housing. **Special Academic Facilities/Equipment:** Native American museum, language lab, field stations in nearby national forest, observatory. **Computers:** 20% of classrooms, 20% of dorms, 100% of libraries, 100% of dining areas, 100% of student union, 75% of common outdoor areas have wireless network access. Students can register for classes online. Administrative functions (other than registration) can be performed online.

CAMPUS LIFE
Environment: Village. **Activities:** Choral groups, concert band, drama/theater, jazz band, music ensembles, radio station, student government, student newspaper, symphony orchestra, yearbook, International Student Organization 30 registered organizations, 1 honor societies, 2 religious organizations. **Athletics (Intercollegiate):** *Men:* baseball, basketball, cross-country, ice hockey, skiingnordiccross-country, soccer. *Women:* basketball, cross-country, skiingnordiccross-country, soccer, softball, volleyball. **On-Campus Highlights:** Campus Center, Science Center, The Fire Ring, The Environmental Living and Learning Center, The Ravine. **Environmental Initiatives:** Signing the ACUPCC Founding member of the Billion Dollar Green Challenge Outreach through Regional Sustainability Coordinator. Inreach through student involvement in every major sustainability effort on campus.

ADMISSIONS
Freshman Academic Profile: Average high school GPA 3.3. 12% in top 10% of high school class, 41% in top 25% of high school class, 71% in top 50% of high school class. SAT Math middle 50% range 423-568. SAT Critical Reading middle 50% range 435-578. SAT Writing middle 50% range 443-575. ACT middle 50% range 20-27. Minimum paper TOEFL 525. **Basis for Candidate Selection:** *Very important factors considered include:* rigor of secondary school record. *Important factors considered include:* Class rank, application essay, academic GPA, recommendation(s), standardized test scores. *Other factors considered include:* alumni/ae relation, character/personal qualities, extracurricular activities, first generation, geographical residence, interview, level of applicant's interest, talent/ability, volunteer work, work experience. **Freshman Admission Requirements:** High school diploma is required and GED is accepted. *Academic units required:* 4 English, 3 mathematics, 3 science, (2 science labs), 3 social studies, 3 academic electives. *Academic units recommended:* 4 English, 3 mathematics, 3 science, (2 science labs), 3 social studies, 3 academic electives. **Freshman Admission Statistics:** 644 applied, 73% admitted, 31% enrolled. **Transfer Admission Requirements:** High school transcript, college transcript(s), essay or personal statement, statement of good standing from prior institution(s). Minimum college GPA of 2.0 required. Lowest grade transferable C–. **General Admission Information:** Application Fee $25. Notification on a rolling basis, beginning on or about 9/1. Nonfall registration accepted. Admission may be deferred for a maximum of 2 years. Credit and/or placement offered for CEEB Advanced Placement tests.

COSTS AND FINANCIAL AID
Annual tuition $27,622. Room and board $7,150. Required fees $946. Average book expense $800. **Required Forms and Deadlines:** FAFSA. **Notification of Awards:** Applicants will be notified of awards on a rolling basis beginning 3/1. **Types of Aid:** *Need-based scholarships/grants:* Federal Pell, SEOG, state scholarships/grants, private scholarships, the school's own gift aid, Bureau of Indian Affairs Grants. *Loans:* Direct Subsidized Stafford, Direct Unsubsidized Stafford, Direct PLUS, Subsidized Stafford, Unsubsidized Stafford, PLUS, Federal Perkins. **Student Employment:** Federal Work-Study Program available. Institutional employment available. Highest amount earned per year from on-campus jobs $1,600. Off-campus job opportunities are good. **Financial Aid Statistics:** 100% freshmen, 99% undergrads receive need-based scholarship or grant aid. 29% freshmen, 15% undergrads receive non-need-based scholarship or grant aid. 97% freshmen, 98% undergrads receive need-based self-help aid. 99% freshmen, 99% undergrads receive any aid. 80% undergrads borrow to pay for school. Average cumulative indebtedness $27,441. **Criteria for awarding institutional aid:** *Non-need-based:* academics, alumni affiliation, art, job skills, leadership, minority status, music/drama, religious affiliation, state/district residency.

NORTHWEST CHRISTIAN COLLEGE

828 East 11th Avenue, Eugene, OR 97401
Phone: 541-684-7201 • **Financial Aid Phone:** 541-684-7203
E-mail: admissions@nwcc.edu • **CEEB Code:** 4543
Fax: 541-628-7317 • **ACT Code:** 10101

This private school was founded in 1895. It has a 8-acre campus.

RATINGS
Admissions Selectivity Rating: 76   Fire Safety Rating: 64   Green Rating: 60*

STUDENTS AND FACULTY
Enrollment: 380. **Student Body:** 61% female, 39% male, 10% out-of-state, 0% international (0 countries represented). Asian 2%, African American 1%, Caucasian 64%, Hispanic 4%, Native American 2%.
Retention and Graduation: 66% freshmen return for sophomore year. 23% freshmen graduate within 4 years. 29% freshmen graduate within 6 years.
Faculty: Student/faculty ratio 10:1. 21 full-time faculty, 43% hold PhDs, 0% are members of minority groups, 52% are women. 0% of classes are taught by teaching assistants.

ACADEMICS
Degrees: associate, bachelor's, certificate, master's, post-bachelor's certificate. **Classes:** Most classes have fewer than 10 students. Most lab/discussion sessions have 10–19 students. **Majors with Highest Enrollment:** business/commerce; teacher education, multiple levels. **Special Study Options:** Accelerated program, distance learning, double major, English as a Second Language (ESL), independent study, internships, liberal arts/career combination, student-designed major, study abroad, teacher certification program. **Disability Services:** Special programs offered to physically disabled students include note-taking services, tape recorders, tutors. **Career Services:** career/job search classes, career assessment, internships, Career Services highlights include Internships required of all undergraduate students.

FACILITIES

Housing: Coed dorms, apartments for single students. 80% of campus accessible to physically disabled. **Special Academic Facilities/Equipment:** Morse Event Center with gym, athletic facilities, and weight training room plus Student Life and Athletic Offices. Library Museum and Rare Book Collections. **Computers:** Administrative functions (other than registration) can be performed online.

CAMPUS LIFE

Environment: City. **Activities:** Choral groups, concert band, drama/theater, literary magazine, music ensembles, student government, student newspaper, yearbook 10 registered organizations, 1 honor societies, 2 religious organizations. **Athletics (Intercollegiate):** *Men:* basketball, cross-country, soccer. *Women:* basketball, cross-country, soccer, softball, volleyball. **On-Campus Highlights:** Morse Event Center, Bookstore/Internet Cafe in Dormitory, Chapel, Library, Pomajevich Faculty Building.

ADMISSIONS

Freshman Academic Profile: Average high school GPA 3.3. 11% in top 10% of high school class, 42% in top 25% of high school class, 74% in top 50% of high school class. 89% from public high schools. SAT Math middle 50% range 470-560. SAT Critical Reading middle 50% range 440-540. SAT Writing middle 50% range 410-510. ACT middle 50% range 21-23. Minimum paper TOEFL 500. **Basis for Candidate Selection:** *Very important factors considered include:* academic GPA. *Important factors considered include:* Class rank, application essay, recommendation(s), standardized test scores. *Other factors considered include:* rigor of secondary school record, character/personal qualities, work experience. **Freshman Admission Requirements:** High school diploma is required and GED is accepted. *Academic units required:* 4 English, 3 mathematics, 2 science, (1 science labs), 2 foreign language, 2 social studies, 1 history. 4 English, 3 mathematics, 2 science, (1 science labs), 2 foreign language, 2 social studies, 1 history. **Freshman Admission Statistics:** 232 applied, 61% admitted, 46% enrolled. **Transfer Admission Requirements:** college transcript(s), essay or personal statement, statement of good standing from prior institution(s). Minimum college GPA of 2.2 required. Lowest grade transferable C–. **General Admission Information:** Notification on a rolling basis, beginning on or about 10/15. Nonfall registration accepted. Admission may be deferred for a maximum of 2 years. Credit and/or placement offered for CEEB Advanced Placement tests.

COSTS AND FINANCIAL AID

Average book expense $825. **Required Forms and Deadlines:** FAFSA. **Notification of Awards:** Applicants will be notified of awards on a rolling basis beginning 4/1. **Types of Aid:** *Need-based scholarships/grants:* Federal Pell, SEOG, state scholarships/grants, private scholarships, the school's own gift aid. *Loans:* Subsidized Stafford, Unsubsidized Stafford, PLUS, Federal Perkins. **Student Employment:** Federal Work-Study Program available. Institutional employment available. Off campus job opportunities are fair. **Financial Aid Statistics:** 100% freshmen, 100% undergrads receive need-based scholarship or grant aid. 13% freshmen, 6% undergrads receive non-need-based scholarship or grant aid. 75% freshmen, 85% undergrads receive need-based self-help aid. 14% freshmen, 5% undergrads receive athletic scholarships. 97% freshmen, 96% undergrads receive any aid. 79% undergrads borrow to pay for school. Average cumulative indebtedness $14,415. **Criteria for awarding institutional aid:** *Non-need-based:* academics, athletics, leadership, music/drama, religious affiliation.

NORTHWEST COLLEGE

PO Box 579, Kirkland, WA 98083-0579
Phone: 425-889-5231
E-mail: admissions@ncag.edu • **CEEB Code:** 4541
Fax: 425-889-5224 • **Website:** www.nwcollege.edu • **ACT Code:** 4466

This private school, affiliated with the Assemblies of God Church, was founded in 1934. It has a 56-acre campus.

RATINGS

Admissions Selectivity Rating: 62   **Fire Safety Rating:** 60*   **Green Rating:** 60*

STUDENTS AND FACULTY

Enrollment: 1,054. **Student Body:** 62% female, 38% male, 18% out-of-state, 2% international (9 countries represented). Asian 4%, African American 3%, Caucasian 84%, Hispanic 3%, Native American 1%. **Retention and Graduation:** 66% freshmen return for sophomore year. 35% freshmen graduate within 4 years. 43% freshmen graduate within 6 years. **Faculty:** Student/faculty ratio 15:1. 50 full-time faculty, 48% hold PhDs, 10%

are members of minority groups, 42% are women. 0% of classes are taught by teaching assistants.

ACADEMICS

Degrees: associate, bachelor's, certificate, diploma, master's, post-bachelor's certificate. **Classes:** Most classes have 20–29 students. Most lab/discussion sessions have 10–19 students. **Special Study Options:** Accelerated program, double major, English as a Second Language (ESL), independent study, internships, liberal arts/career combination, study abroad, teacher certification program. **Disability Services:** Special programs offered to physically disabled students include note-taking services, reader services, tape recorders, tutors. **Career Services:** career/job search classes, career assessment, internships.

FACILITIES

Housing: men's dorms, women's dorms, apartments for married students, apartments for single students, Apartments for students with dependent children. 80% of campus accessible to physically disabled. **Computers:** Students can register for classes online.

CAMPUS LIFE

Environment: Village. **Activities:** Choral groups, concert band, drama/theater, jazz band, music ensembles, musical theater, radio station, student government, student newspaper, symphony orchestra, yearbook 15 registered organizations, 9 religious organizations. **Athletics (Intercollegiate):** *Men:* basketball, cross-country, soccer, track/field (outdoor). *Women:* basketball, cross-country, track/field (outdoor), volleyball.

ADMISSIONS

Freshman Academic Profile: Average high school GPA 3.3. 75% from public high schools. Minimum paper TOEFL 500. **Basis for Candidate Selection:** *Very important factors considered include:* application essay, recommendation(s), rigor of secondary school record, standardized test scores, character/personal qualities. *Important factors considered include:* Class rank, extracurricular activities, religious affiliation/commitment. *Other factors considered include:* alumni/ae relation, interview, talent/ability, volunteer work. **Freshman Admission Requirements:** High school diploma is required and GED is accepted. **Freshman Admission Statistics:** 308 applied, 90% admitted, 60% enrolled. **Transfer Admission Requirements:** High school transcript, college transcript(s), essay or personal statement, statement of good standing from prior institution(s). Minimum college GPA of 2.3 required. Lowest grade transferable C. **General Admission Information:** Application Fee $30. Regular application deadline 8/1. Notification on a rolling basis, beginning on or about 10/1. Nonfall registration accepted. Admission may be deferred for a maximum of 12 months. Credit offered for CEEB Advanced Placement tests.

COSTS AND FINANCIAL AID

Annual tuition $13,200. Room and board $6,124. Required fees $324. Average book expense $850. **Required Forms and Deadlines:** FAFSA, institution's own financial aid form. **Notification of Awards:** Applicants will be notified of awards on a rolling basis beginning 4/15. **Types of Aid:** *Need-based scholarships/grants:* Federal Pell, SEOG, state scholarships/grants, private scholarships, the school's own gift aid. *Loans:* Subsidized Stafford, Unsubsidized Stafford, PLUS, Federal Perkins, state loans, alternative(private) loans. **Student Employment:** Federal Work-Study Program available. Institutional employment available. Highest amount earned per year from on-campus jobs $3,308. Off-campus job opportunities are excellent. **Financial Aid Statistics:** 99% freshmen, 94% undergrads receive need-based scholarship or grant aid. 13% freshmen, 10% undergrads receive non-need-based scholarship or grant aid. 86% freshmen, 87% undergrads receive need-based self-help aid. 4% freshmen, 4% undergrads receive athletic scholarships. 91% undergrads borrow to pay for school. Average cumulative indebtedness $20,015. **Criteria for awarding institutional aid:** *Non-need-based:* academics, art, athletics, leadership, music/drama, religious affiliation.

NORTHWEST MISSOURI STATE UNIVERSITY

800 University Drive, Maryville, MO 64468
Phone: 800-633-1175
E-mail: admissions@nwmissouri.edu • **CEEB Code:** 6488
Fax: 660-562-1121 • **ACT Code:** 2338

This public school was founded in 1905. It has a 240-acre campus.

RATINGS

Admissions Selectivity Rating: 73   **Fire Safety Rating:** 60*   **Green Rating:** 60*

STUDENTS AND FACULTY

Enrollment: 4,956. **Student Body:** 55% female, 45% male, 26% out-of-state, 2% international. Asian 1%, African American 4%, Caucasian 86%, Hispanic 2%, Native American 0%.

Retention and Graduation: 74% freshmen return for sophomore year. **Faculty:** Student/faculty ratio 21:1. 249 full-time faculty, 64% hold PhDs, 6% are members of minority groups, 45% are women. 0% of classes are taught by teaching assistants.

ACADEMICS

Degrees: bachelor's, master's, post-master's certificate. **Classes:** Most classes have 20–29 students. Most lab/discussion sessions have 20–29 students. **Special Study Options:** Accelerated program, distance learning, double major, dual enrollment, English as a Second Language (ESL), honors program, independent study, internships, study abroad, teacher certification program. **Disability Services:** Special programs offered to physically disabled students include note-taking services, reader services, tape recorders, tutors. **Career Services:** alumni services, career/job search classes, career assessment, internships.

FACILITIES

Housing: Coed dorms, special housing for disabled students, fraternity/sorority housing, apartments for single students. **Special Academic Facilities/Equipment:** State history and art collections, earth/science museum, broadcasting museum, on-campus elementary lab school, biomass energy plant. **Computers:** Students can register for classes online.

CAMPUS LIFE

Environment: Rural. **Activities:** Choral groups, concert band, dance, drama/theater, jazz band, literary magazine, marching band, music ensembles, musical theater, pep band, radio station, student government, student newspaper, student-run film society, symphony orchestra, television station, yearbook 174 registered organizations, 13 honor societies, 9 religious organizations. 10 fraternities, 6 sororities. **Athletics (Intercollegiate):** *Men:* baseball, basketball, cheerleading, cross-country, football, rodeo, tennis, track/field (outdoor), track/field (indoor). *Women:* basketball, cheerleading, cross-country, rodeo, soccer, softball, tennis, track/field (outdoor), track/field (indoor), volleyball.

ADMISSIONS

Freshman Academic Profile: Average high school GPA 3.3. 13% in top 10% of high school class, 41% in top 25% of high school class, 80% in top 50% of high school class. 90% from public high schools. SAT Math middle 50% range 480-610. SAT Critical Reading middle 50% range 450-600. ACT middle 50% range 19-24. Minimum paper TOEFL 500. **Basis for Candidate Selection:** *Very important factors considered include:* Class rank, rigor of secondary school record, standardized test scores. *Important factors considered include:* academic GPA. *Other factors considered include:* application essay, recommendation(s), character/personal qualities, extracurricular activities, interview, level of applicant's interest, state residency. **Freshman Admission Requirements:** High school diploma is required and GED is accepted. *Academic units required:* 4 English, 3 mathematics, 2 science, (1 science labs), 3 social studies, 4 academic electives. *Academic units recommended:* 4 English, 3 mathematics, 2 science, (1 science labs), 3 social studies, 4 academic electives. **Freshman Admission Statistics:** 3,759 applied, 75% admitted, 45% enrolled. **Transfer Admission Requirements:** college transcript(s), statement of good standing from prior institution(s). Minimum college GPA of 2.0 required. Lowest grade transferable D. **General Admission Information:** Application Fee $25. Nonfall registration accepted. Admission may be deferred for a maximum of info. not available.

COSTS AND FINANCIAL AID

Annual in-state tuition $5,835. Annual out-of-state tuition $10,080. Room and board $5,854. Required fees $295. Average book expense $500. **Required Forms and Deadlines:** FAFSA. **Notification of Awards:** Applicants will be notified of awards on or about 4/15. **Types of Aid:** *Need-based scholarships/grants:* Federal Pell, SEOG, state scholarships/grants, private scholarships, the school's own gift aid. *Loans:* Direct Subsidized Stafford, Direct Unsubsidized Stafford, Direct PLUS, Federal Perkins, college/university loans from institutional funds. **Student Employment:** Federal Work-Study Program available. Institutional employment available. Off-campus job opportunities are fair. **Financial Aid Statistics:** 53% freshmen, 51% undergrads receive need-based scholarship or grant aid. 75% freshmen, 50% undergrads receive non-need-based scholarship or grant aid. 89% freshmen, 88% undergrads receive need-based self-help aid. 58% undergrads borrow to pay for school. Average cumulative indebtedness $13,799. **Criteria for awarding institutional aid:** *Non-need-based:* academics, alumni affiliation, art, athletics, leadership, music/drama, state/district residency.

NORTHWEST NAZARENE UNIVERSITY

623 S. University Blvd., Nampa, ID 83686
Phone: 208-467-8000 • **Financial Aid Phone:** 208-467-8774
E-mail: admissions@nnu.edu • **CEEB Code:** 4544
Fax: 208-467-8645 • **Website:** www.nnu.edu • **ACT Code:** 924

This private school, affiliated with the Nazarene Church, was founded in 1913. It has a 85-acre campus.

RATINGS

Admissions Selectivity Rating: 77   **Fire Safety Rating:** 63   **Green Rating:** 60*

STUDENTS AND FACULTY

Enrollment: 1,263. **Student Body:** 59% female, 41% male, 51% out-of-state, 2% international (20 countries represented). Asian 2%, African American 1%, Caucasian 68%, Hispanic 6%, Native American 0%.
Retention and Graduation: Faculty: Student/faculty ratio 14:1. 103 full-time faculty, 73% hold PhDs, 6% are members of minority groups, 45% are women. 0% of classes are taught by teaching assistants.

ACADEMICS

Degrees: bachelor's, master's. **Majors with Highest Enrollment:** business/commerce; education; nursing/registered nurse (rn, asn, bsn, msn). **Special Study Options:** cooperative education program, cross-registration, distance learning, double major, English as a Second Language (ESL), exchange student program (domestic), honors program, independent study, internships, liberal arts/career combination, student-designed major, study abroad, teacher certification program, Many service and ministry programs and opportunities. **Combined Degree Programs:** 3-2 engineering program with any co-op institution. **Disability Services:** Special programs offered to physically disabled students include reader services, tape recorders, tutors. **Career Services:** Alumni network, career/job search classes, internships, regional alumni.

FACILITIES

Housing: Coed dorms, men's dorms, women's dorms, apartments for married students, apartments for single students, Off-campus housing owned the by University include rental homes and units. 70% of campus accessible to physically disabled. **Computers:** 100% of classrooms, have wireless network access. Administrative functions (other than registration) can be performed online.

CAMPUS LIFE

Environment: City. **Activities:** Choral groups, concert band, drama/theater, jazz band, literary magazine, music ensembles, musical theater, pep band, student government, student newspaper, symphony orchestra, yearbook, Campus Ministries, International Student Organization 21 registered organizations, 6 honor societies, 8 religious organizations. **Athletics (Intercollegiate):** *Men:* baseball, basketball, cross-country, golf, soccer, track/field (outdoor), track/field (indoor). *Women:* basketball, cross-country, soccer, softball, track/field (outdoor), track/field (indoor), volleyball. **On-Campus Highlights:** Helstrom Business Center, The Brandt Center, Ford Hall, Johnson Sports Center, Student Center.

ADMISSIONS

Freshman Academic Profile: 3.5. 29% in top 10% of high school class, 52% in top 25% of high school class, 81% in top 50% of high school class. SAT Math middle 50% range 470-620. SAT Critical Reading middle 50% range 470-600. SAT Writing middle 50% range 470-570. ACT middle 50% range 21-27. Minimum paper TOEFL 500. **Basis for Candidate Selection:** *Very important factors considered include:* Class rank, academic GPA, standardized test scores, character/personal qualities. *Other factors considered include:* recommendation(s), rigor of secondary school record, alumni/ae relation, extracurricular activities, religious affiliation/commitment, talent/ability. **Freshman Admission Requirements:** High school diploma is required and GED is accepted. **Freshman Admission Statistics:** 984 applied, 69% admitted, 41% enrolled. **Transfer Admission Requirements:** college transcript(s), minimum college GPA of 2.0 required. Lowest grade transferable C–. **General Admission Information:** Application Fee $25. Regular application deadline 8/15. Nonfall registration accepted. Credit and/or placement offered for CEEB Advanced Placement tests.

COSTS AND FINANCIAL AID

Annual tuition $26,150. Room and board $6,400. Required fees $400. Average book expense $1,160. **Required Forms and Deadlines:** FAFSA, institution's own financial aid form. **Notification of Awards:** Applicants will be notified of awards on a rolling basis beginning 4/1. **Types of Aid:** *Need-based scholarships/grants:* Federal Pell, SEOG, state scholarships/grants, private scholarships, the school's own gift aid. *Loans:* Subsidized Stafford, Unsubsidized Stafford, PLUS, Federal Perkins, college/university loans from institutional funds, Bank Loans. **Student Employment:** Federal Work-Study Program available. Institutional employment available. Highest amount earned per year from on-campus jobs $8,739. Off-campus job opportunities are good. **Financial Aid Statistics:** 100% freshmen, 95% undergrads receive need-based scholarship or grant aid. 14% freshmen, 8% undergrads receive non-need-based scholarship or grant aid. 72% freshmen, 79% undergrads receive need-based self-help aid. 9% freshmen, 9% undergrads receive athletic scholarships. 64% undergrads borrow to pay for school. Average cumulative indebtedness $30,499. **Criteria for awarding institutional aid:** *Non-need-based:* academics, alumni affiliation, art, athletics, leadership, minority status, music/drama, religious affiliation, state/district residency.

NORTHWESTERN COLLEGE (IA)

101 7th St SW, Orange City, IA 51041
Phone: 712-707-7130 • **Financial Aid Phone:** 712-707-7131
E-mail: admissions@nwciowa.edu • **CEEB Code:** 6490
Fax: 712-707-7164 • **Website:** www.nwciowa.edu • **ACT Code:** 1346

This private school, affiliated with the Reformed Church Church, was founded in 1882. It has a 100-acre campus.

RATINGS
Admissions Selectivity Rating: 72   **Fire Safety Rating:** 90   **Green Rating:** 61

STUDENTS AND FACULTY
Enrollment: 1,195. **Student Body:** 56% female, 44% male, 46% out-of-state, 3% international (22 countries represented). Asian 1%, African American 2%, Caucasian 87%, Hispanic 5%, Native American 1%.
Retention and Graduation: 77% freshmen return for sophomore year. 53% freshmen graduate within 4 years. 63% freshmen graduate within 6 years.
Faculty: Student/faculty ratio 12:1. 84 full-time faculty, 81% hold PhDs, 5% are members of minority groups, 37% are women. 0% of classes are taught by teaching assistants.

ACADEMICS
Degrees: bachelor's, certificate. **Classes:** Most classes have 10–19 students. **Majors with Highest Enrollment:** biology/biological sciences; business/commerce; education. **Special Study Options:** double major, English as a Second Language (ESL), honors program, independent study, internships, liberal arts/career combination, student-designed major, study abroad, teacher certification program, Off Campus Study Programs: American Studies Program (Washington, D.C.), AuSable Inst of Environmental Studies Program (Michigan), Los Angeles Film Studies Semester, Chicago Metropolitan Studies Program (Chicago), China Studies Program (Xiamen, China), Middle East Studies Program (Cairo, Egypt), Oxford Summer Program (Oxford, England), Romanian Studies Program, Russian Studies Program, Contemporary Music Center (Martha's Vineyard, MA), Latin American Studies Program (Costa Rica), Oxford Honours Programme (England), Trinity Christian College: Semester in Spain, and Creation Care Study Program. **Honors Programs:** Honors Program: Affords students an interdisciplinary approach to understanding perennial and contemporary issues, such as technology, war and peace, gender roles, work and calling, and humor. Affords students th eopportunity to delve more deeply into a topic of their choice, workinh with selected faculty members to complete a project that goes beyond the normal upper-division work at the college. Encourages graduate education by sponsoring trips to regional graduate schools and financially supporting graduate school applications. **Disability Services:** Special programs offered to physically disabled students include note-taking services, reader services, tape recorders, tutors. **Career Services:** alumni services, career/job search classes, career assessment, internships Career Services highlights include Internships.

FACILITIES
Housing: special housing for disabled students, men's dorms, women's dorms, apartments for single students, theme housing (i.e., Spanish house, etc.). 90% of campus accessible to physically disabled. **Special Academic Facilities/Equipment:** Thea G Korver Visual Arts Center-Art Gallery; DeWitt Theatre Arts Center-Proscenium Theatre, Black Box Theatre, Costume Shop. **Computers:** 75% of classrooms, 30% of dorms, 100% of libraries, 100% of dining areas, 100% of student union, 30% of common outdoor areas have wireless network access. Students can register for classes online. Administrative functions (other than registration) can be performed online.

CAMPUS LIFE
Environment: Rural. **Activities:** Choral groups, concert band, dance, drama/theater, jazz band, literary magazine, music ensembles, musical theater, pep band, student government, student newspaper, symphony orchestra, television station, yearbook 30 registered organizations, 2 honor societies, 5 religious orga-

nizations. **Athletics (Intercollegiate):** *Men:* baseball, basketball, cheerleading, cross-country, football, golf, soccer, track/field (outdoor), track/field (indoor), wrestling. *Women:* basketball, cheerleading, cross-country, golf, soccer, softball, track/field (outdoor), track/field (indoor), volleyball. **On-Campus Highlights:** Rowenhorst Student Center, Bultman Center Gym, DeWitt Theatre Arts Center, Korver Visual Arts Center.

ADMISSIONS
Freshman Academic Profile: Average high school GPA 3.5. 26% in top 10% of high school class, 54% in top 25% of high school class, 79% in top 50% of high school class. 72% from public high schools. SAT Math middle 50% range 445-630. SAT Critical Reading middle 50% range 425-605. SAT Writing middle 50% range 395-565. ACT middle 50% range 22-27. Minimum paper TOEFL 475. **Basis for Candidate Selection:** *Very important factors considered include:* Class rank, rigor of secondary school record, standardized test scores. *Important factors considered include:* application essay, academic GPA, recommendation(s), character/personal qualities, first generation, interview, level of applicant's interest, talent/ability. *Other factors considered include:* extracurricular activities, religious affiliation/commitment. **Freshman Admission Requirements:** High school diploma is required and GED is accepted. **Freshman Admission Statistics:** 1,193 applied, 74% admitted, 34% enrolled. **Transfer Admission Requirements:** college transcript(s), minimum college GPA of 2.2 required. Lowest grade transferable C. **General Admission Information:** Application Fee $25. Notification on a rolling basis, beginning on or about 10/1. Nonfall registration accepted. Admission may be deferred for a maximum of 4 years. Credit and/or placement offered for CEEB Advanced Placement tests.

COSTS AND FINANCIAL AID
Annual tuition $26,614. Room and board $8,084. Required fees $150. Average book expense $1,114. **Required Forms and Deadlines:** FAFSA. **Notification of Awards:** Applicants will be notified of awards on a rolling basis beginning 3/15. **Types of Aid:** *Need-based scholarships/grants:* Federal Pell, SEOG, state scholarships/grants, private scholarships, the school's own gift aid, United Negro College Fund. *Loans:* Subsidized Stafford, Unsubsidized Stafford, PLUS, Federal Perkins, college/university loans from institutional funds. **Student Employment:** Highest amount earned per year from on-campus jobs $2,100. Off-campus job opportunities are fair. **Financial Aid Statistics:** 96% freshmen, 95% undergrads receive need-based scholarship or grant aid. 96% freshmen, 98% undergrads receive non-need-based scholarship or grant aid. 81% freshmen, 83% undergrads receive need-based self-help aid. 7% freshmen, 8% undergrads receive athletic scholarships. 99% freshmen, 98% undergrads receive any aid. 82% undergrads borrow to pay for school. Average cumulative indebtedness $30,589. **Criteria for awarding institutional aid:** *Non-need-based:* academics, art, athletics, music/drama, religious affiliation.

NORTHWESTERN STATE UNIVERSITY

South Hall, Natchitoches, LA 71497
Phone: 318-357-4078 • **Financial Aid Phone:** 800-823-3008
E-mail: applications@nsula.edu • **CEEB Code:** 6492
Fax: 318-357-4660 • **Website:** www.nsula.edu • **ACT Code:** 1600

This public school was founded in 1884. It has a 916-acre campus.

RATINGS
Admissions Selectivity Rating: 67   **Fire Safety Rating:** 80   **Green Rating:** 66

STUDENTS AND FACULTY
Enrollment: 7,333. **Student Body:** 68% female, 32% male, 9% out-of-state, 1% international (34 countries represented). Asian 1%, African American 30%, Caucasian 57%, Hispanic 3%, Native American 1%.
Retention and Graduation: 71% freshmen return for sophomore year. 17% freshmen graduate within 4 years. 36% freshmen graduate within 6 years.
Faculty: Student/faculty ratio 19:1. 291 full-time faculty, 60% hold PhDs, 8% are members of minority groups, 55% are women. 1% of classes are taught by teaching assistants.

ACADEMICS
Degrees: associate, bachelor's, master's, post-master's certificate. **Classes:** Most classes have 10–19 students. Most lab/discussion sessions have fewer than 10 students. **Majors with Highest Enrollment:** business administration and management; general studies; nursing/registered nurse (rn, asn, bsn, msn). **Special Study Options:** cooperative education program, distance learning, double major, dual enrollment, honors program, independent study, internships, study abroad, teacher certification program. **Honors Programs:** The Louisiana Scholar's College is a special institution at Northwestern that enrolls students in a strong liberal arts program while simultaneously letting them take part in

the other great areas of NSU. **Disability Services:** Special programs offered to physically disabled students include note-taking services, reader services, tape recorders, tutors. **Career Services:** alumni services, career/job search classes, career assessment, internships.

FACILITIES

Housing: Coed dorms, special housing for disabled students, fraternity/sorority housing, apartments for married students, apartments for single students, theme housing. 96% of campus accessible to physically disabled. **Special Academic Facilities/Equipment:** Cammie G. Henry Research Center; Louisiana Creole Heritage Center; Louisiana Folklife Center; Louisiana Regional Folklife Center; The Space Science Group; Williamson Museum **Computers:** 50% of classrooms, 100% of dorms, 100% of libraries, 50% of dining areas, 100% of student union, 75% of common outdoor areas have wireless network access. Students can register for classes online. Administrative functions (other than registration) can be performed online.

CAMPUS LIFE

Environment: Village. **Activities:** Choral groups, concert band, dance, drama/theater, jazz band, literary magazine, marching band, music ensembles, musical theater, opera, pep band, radio station, student government, student newspaper, symphony orchestra, television station, yearbook, Campus Ministries, International Student Organization 109 registered organizations, 11 honor societies, 6 religious organizations. 10 fraternities, 7 sororities. **Athletics (Intercollegiate):** *Men:* baseball, basketball, cheerleading, cross-country, football, soccer, track/field (outdoor), track/field (indoor). *Women:* basketball, cheerleading, cross-country, soccer, softball, tennis, track/field (outdoor), track/field (indoor), volleyball. **On-Campus Highlights:** Wellness, Recreation, and Activity Center, Student Union, University Place Apartments, University Columns Apartments, BCM/CSO/Wellesley Foundation. **Environmental Initiatives:** NSU student groups and organizations participate in recycling, liter-abatement, campus beautification, and related "Green" service (and service-learning) activities. Professors of courses in the Arts and the Sciences have adopted "Green" topics for class assignments and projects. All Freshman are invited to attend a seminar that addresses conservation, recycling, and other sustainable practices on campus.

ADMISSIONS

Freshman Academic Profile: Average high school GPA 3.2. 16% in top 10% of high school class, 39% in top 25% of high school class, 72% in top 50% of high school class. % from public high schools. SAT Math middle 50% range 435-555. SAT Critical Reading middle 50% range 435-550. ACT middle 50% range 19-23. Minimum web-based TOEFL 61. Minimum paper TOEFL 500. **Basis for Candidate Selection:** *Very important factors considered include:* rigor of secondary school record, standardized test scores. *Important factors considered include:* Class rank, academic GPA. *Other factors considered include:* alumni/ae relation, extracurricular activities, geographical residence, state residency, talent/ability. **Freshman Admission Requirements:** High school diploma is required and GED is accepted. *Academic units required:* 4 English, 3 mathematics, 3 science, (3 science labs), 2 foreign language, 1 social studies, 2 history, 1 visual/performing arts, 1 Other: One additional math or science. 4 English, 3 mathematics, 3 science, (3 science labs), 2 foreign language, 1 social studies, 2 history, 1 visual/performing arts, 1 Other: One additional math or science **Freshman Admission Statistics:** 2,633 applied, 83% admitted, 51% enrolled. **Transfer Admission Requirements:** college transcript(s), statement of good standing from prior institution(s). Minimum college GPA of 2.0 required. Lowest grade transferable D. **General Admission Information:** Application Fee $20. Regular application deadline 7/6. Notification on a rolling basis, beginning on or about 1/1. Nonfall registration accepted. Admission may be deferred for a maximum of 3 Semesters w/o Fee. Credit and/or placement offered for CEEB Advanced Placement tests.

COSTS AND FINANCIAL AID

Required **Forms and Deadlines:** FAFSA, institution's own financial aid form. **Notification of Awards:** Applicants will be notified of awards on a rolling basis beginning 5/1. **Types of Aid:** *Need-based scholarships/grants:* Federal Pell, SEOG, state scholarships/grants, private scholarships, the school's own gift aid, United Negro College Fund, Federal Nursing Scholarships. , Third Party Scholarships. *Loans:* Subsidized Stafford, Unsubsidized Stafford, PLUS, Federal Perkins, Alternative Loans. **Student Employment:** Federal Work-Study Program available. Institutional employment available. Highest amount earned per year from on-campus jobs $9,218. Off-campus job opportunities are fair. **Financial Aid Statistics:** 64% freshmen, 65% undergrads receive need-based scholarship or grant aid. 68% freshmen, 47% undergrads receive non-need-based scholarship or grant aid. 57% freshmen, 66% undergrads receive need-based self-help aid. 6% freshmen, 5% undergrads receive athletic scholarships. 91% freshmen, 82% undergrads receive any aid. 67% undergrads borrow to pay for school. Average cumulative indebtedness $23,710. **Criteria for awarding institutional aid:** *Non-need-based:* academics, alumni affiliation, art, athletics, job skills, leadership, minority status, music/drama, religious affiliation, state/district residency.

NORTHWESTERN UNIVERSITY

PO Box 3060, Evanston, IL 60204-3060
Phone: 847-491-7271 • **Financial Aid Phone:** 847-491-7400
E-mail: ug-admission@northwestern.edu • **CEEB Code:** 1565
Fax: 555-555-5555 • **Website:** www.northwestern.edu • **ACT Code:** 1106

This private school was founded in 1851. It has a 240-acre campus.

RATINGS

Admissions Selectivity Rating: 98   **Fire Safety Rating:** 76   **Green Rating:** 83

STUDENTS AND FACULTY

Enrollment: 8,485. **Student Body:** 52% female, 48% male, 75% out-of-state, 6% international (42 countries represented). Asian 19%, African American 6%, Caucasian 56%, Hispanic 7%, Native American 0%. **Retention and Graduation:** 97% freshmen return for sophomore year. 86% freshmen graduate within 4 years. 93% freshmen graduate within 6 years. 23% grads go on to further study within 1 year. 7% grads pursue arts and sciences degrees. 3% grads pursue law degrees. 1% grads pursue business degrees. 7% grads pursue medical degrees. **Faculty:** Student/faculty ratio 7:1. 1092 full-time faculty, 100% hold PhDs, 16% are members of minority groups, 37% are women. 2% of classes are taught by teaching assistants.

ACADEMICS

Degrees: bachelor's, certificate, first professional, master's, post-master's certificate. **Classes:** Most classes have fewer than 10 students. Most lab/discussion sessions have 10–19 students. **Majors with Highest Enrollment:** economics; engineering; journalism. **Special Study Options:** Accelerated program, cooperative education program, double major, honors program, independent study, internships, liberal arts/career combination, student-designed major, study abroad, teacher certification program. **Honors Programs:** Honors Program in Medical Education, Integrated Science Program, MENU, MMSS **Combined Degree Programs:** BA/MD, BA/MA, BM/MS, BA/BS, BA/BM, BS/BM, BS/MS. **Disability Services:** Special programs offered to physically disabled students include note-taking services, reader services, tape recorders, tutors. **Career Services:** Alumni network, alumni services, career/job search classes, career assessment, internships, regional alumni. Career Services highlights include At Northwestern, all undergraduates have the opportunity to gain real-world experience through internships, field studies programs, and practicums. These programs place students in corporations, newsrooms, archaeological dig sites, and laboratories throughout Chicago, the United States, and the world.

FACILITIES

Housing: Coed dorms, men's dorms, women's dorms, fraternity/sorority housing, wellness housing, theme housing. 100% of campus accessible to physically disabled. **Special Academic Facilities/Equipment:** Art gallery, learning sciences institute, communicative disorders and materials and life sciences buildings, catalysis center, astronomical research center. Ford Motor Compay Engineering Design Center for engineering students. **Computers:** 100% of classrooms, 100% of dorms, 100% of libraries, 100% of dining areas, 100% of student union, 100% of common outdoor areas have wireless network access. Students can register for classes online.

CAMPUS LIFE

Environment: Town. **Activities:** Choral groups, concert band, dance, drama/theater, jazz band, literary magazine, marching band, music ensembles, musical theater, opera, pep band, radio station, student government, student newspaper, student-run film society, symphony orchestra, television station, yearbook, Campus Ministries, International Student Organization, Model UN 415 registered organizations, 23 honor societies, 29 religious organizations. 17 fraternities, 19 sororities. **Athletics (Intercollegiate):** *Men:* baseball, basketball, cheerleading, diving, football, golf, soccer, swimming, tennis, wrestling. *Women:* basketball, cheerleading, cross-country, diving, fencing, field hockey, golf, lacrosse, soccer, softball, swimming, tennis, volleyball. **On-Campus Highlights:** Shakespeare Garden, Dearborn Observatory, Norris Student Center, Henry Crown Sports Pavilion and Acquatic Center, The lakefill on Lake Michigan. **Environmental Initiatives:** The development of a Strategic Plan for sustainability that will detail the long-term sustainability vision and goals for Northwestern University as well as putting in place the governance and accountability for the implementation of that plan and communicating our progress to stakeholders at all levels. A comprehensive approach to Energy Efficiency and Alternative Energy consisting of several phases of energy efficiency initiatives ranging from prescriptive programs to upgrade lighting and controls to a $15M-$22M fund set-aside for the completion of campus-wide energy conservation measures identified through 3rd party audits. In addition, the University has increased its commitment to purchase of renewable energy credits to 30% of the University's usage or almost 75,000 MWh placing NU 6th nationally in green power purchases (US EPA Green Power Partnership) as well as the installation of a 17kW solar PV array on the Ford Engineering Design Center (LEED certified) A commitment to LEED certification in all new construction and major renovations; of the last six major projects, five were awarded LEED Gold and one was awarded LEED silver. The next three major projects; the Bienen school of music, the new visitors center and the new Kellogg School of Business have all targeted LEED Gold or higher.

ADMISSIONS

Freshman Academic Profile: 90% in top 10% of high school class, 99% in top 25% of high school class, 100% in top 50% of high school class. 65% from public high schools. SAT Math middle 50% range 690-780. SAT Critical Reading middle 50% range 670-750. SAT Writing middle 50% range 670-760. ACT middle 50% range 31-33. Minimum paper TOEFL 600. **Basis for Candidate Selection:** *Very important factors considered include:* Class rank, application essay, academic GPA, rigor of secondary school record, standardized test scores. *Important factors considered include:* recommendation(s), character/personal qualities, extracurricular activities, talent/ability. *Other factors considered include:* alumni/ae relation, first generation, interview, level of applicant's interest, racial/ethnic status, volunteer work, work experience. **Freshman Admission Requirements:** High school diploma or equivalent is not required. **Freshman Admission Statistics:** 25,369 applied, 27% admitted, 31% enrolled. **Transfer Admission Requirements:** High school transcript, college transcript(s), essay or personal statement, standardized test scores, statement of good standing from prior institution(s). Minimum college GPA of 3.0 required. Lowest grade transferable C. **General Admission Information:** Application Fee $65. Early decision application deadline 11/1. Regular application deadline 1/1. Regular notification 4/15. Nonfall registration accepted. Admission may be deferred for a maximum of 1 year. Credit and/or placement offered for CEEB Advanced Placement tests.

COSTS AND FINANCIAL AID

Annual tuition $43,380. Room and board $13,329. Required fees $399. Average book expense $1,737. **Required Forms and Deadlines:** FAFSA, CSS/Financial Aid PROFILE, noncustodial PROFILE, business/farm supplement. Parent and student federal tax returns. **Notification of Awards:** Applicants will be notified of awards on or about 4/15. **Types of Aid:** *Need-based scholarships/grants:* Federal Pell, SEOG, state scholarships/grants, private scholarships, the school's own gift aid, United Negro College Fund. *Loans:* Subsidized Stafford, Unsubsidized Stafford, PLUS, Federal Perkins, college/university loans from institutional funds. **Student Employment:** Federal Work-Study Program available. Institutional employment available. Off-campus job opportunities are excellent. **Financial Aid Statistics:** 94% freshmen, 94% undergrads receive need-based scholarship or grant aid. 86% freshmen, 87% undergrads receive need-based self-help aid. 4% freshmen, 5% undergrads receive athletic scholarships. 60% freshmen, 60% undergrads receive any aid. 48% undergrads borrow to pay for school. Average cumulative indebtedness $20,802. **Criteria for awarding institutional aid:** *Non-need-based:* academics, athletics, music/drama.

NORTHWOOD UNIVERSITY

4000 Whiting Drive, Midland, MI 48640
Phone: 989-837-4273 • **Financial Aid Phone:** 989-837-4320
E-mail: miadmit@northwood.edu • **CEEB Code:** 1568
Fax: 989-837-4490 • **Website:** www.northwood.edu • **ACT Code:** 2041

This private school was founded in 1959. It has a 434-acre campus.

RATINGS

Admissions Selectivity Rating: 74   **Fire Safety Rating:** 72   **Green Rating:** 60*

STUDENTS AND FACULTY

Enrollment: 1,530. **Student Body:** 38% female, 62% male, 11% out-of-state, 9% international (26 countries represented). Asian 1%, African American 8%, Caucasian 71%, Hispanic 3%, Native American 0%.
Retention and Graduation: 77% freshmen return for sophomore year. 33% freshmen graduate within 4 years. 54% freshmen graduate within 6 years.
Faculty: Student/faculty ratio 21:1. 53 full-time faculty, 38% hold PhDs, 9% are members of minority groups, 32% are women. 0% of classes are taught by teaching assistants.

ACADEMICS

Degrees: bachelor's, master's. **Classes:** Most classes have 10–19 students. **Majors with Highest Enrollment:** business administration and management; sport and fitness administration/management. **Special Study Options:** Accelerated program, distance learning, double major, dual enrollment, external degree program, honors program, independent study, internships, study abroad, weekend college. **Honors Programs:** An Honors Program began in Fall Term, 1991. In it, honors sections of six critically important courses are offered. The best instructors and the most demanding material and expectations are used. Additionally, special one credit hour seminars, which include outside speakers, are offered to sophomores and juniors. **Disability Services:** Special programs offered to physically disabled students include tutors. **Career Services:** Alumni network, alumni services, career/job search classes, career assessment, internships.

FACILITIES

Housing: men's dorms, women's dorms, apartments for single students. **Special Academic Facilities/Equipment:** Hach Student Life Center, Gerstacker Student Union. **Computers:** 100% of classrooms, 100% of dorms, 100% of libraries, 100% of dining areas, 100% of student union, have wireless network access. Students can register for classes online. Administrative functions (other than registration) can be performed online.

CAMPUS LIFE

Environment: Town. **Activities:** Choral groups, dance, drama/theater, pep band, student government, student newspaper, yearbook, International Student Organization 42 registered organizations, 2 honor societies, 2 religious organizations. 9 fraternities, 3 sororities. **Athletics (Intercollegiate):** *Men:* baseball, basketball, cheerleading, cross-country, football, golf, soccer, tennis, track/field (outdoor), track/field (indoor). *Women:* basketball, cheerleading, cross-country, golf, soccer, softball, tennis, track/field (outdoor), track/field (indoor), volleyball. **On-Campus Highlights:** Hach Student Life Center, Mid - Cat @ Northwood, Bennett Sports Center

ADMISSIONS

Freshman Academic Profile: Average high school GPA 3.3. 12% in top 10% of high school class, 40% in top 25% of high school class, 71% in top 50% of high school class. 70% from public high schools. SAT Math middle 50% range 470-580. SAT Critical Reading middle 50% range 410-540. ACT middle 50% range 20-25. Minimum paper TOEFL 500. **Basis for Candidate Selection:** *Very important factors considered include:* level of applicant's interest. *Important factors considered include:* academic GPA, standardized test scores. *Other factors considered include:* Class rank, application essay, recommendation(s), rigor of secondary school record, alumni/ae relation, character/personal qualities, extracurricular activities, interview. **Freshman Admission Requirements:** High school diploma is required and GED is accepted. **Freshman Admission Statistics:** 1,258 applied, 68% admitted, 39% enrolled. **Transfer Admission Requirements:** college transcript(s), minimum college GPA of 2.0 required. Lowest grade transferable C. **General Admission Information:** Application Fee $25. Notification on a rolling basis, beginning on or about 1/1. Nonfall registration accepted. Admission may be deferred for a maximum of 1 term. Credit and/or placement offered for CEEB Advanced Placement tests.

COSTS AND FINANCIAL AID

Required Forms and Deadlines: FAFSA. **Notification of Awards:** Applicants will be notified of awards on a rolling basis beginning 3/1. **Types of Aid:** *Need-based scholarships/grants:* Federal Pell, SEOG, state scholarships/grants, private scholarships, the school's own gift aid. *Loans:* Subsidized Stafford, Unsubsidized Stafford, PLUS, state loans. **Student Employment:** Federal Work-Study Program available. Institutional employment available. Off-campus job opportunities are fair. **Financial Aid Statistics:** 91% freshmen, 88% undergrads receive need-based scholarship or grant aid. 41% freshmen, 38% undergrads receive non-need-based scholarship or grant aid. 84% freshmen, 87% undergrads receive need-based self-help aid. 9% freshmen, 7% undergrads receive athletic scholarships. 74% undergrads borrow to pay for school. Average cumulative indebtedness $32,457. **Criteria for awarding institutional aid:** *Non-need-based:* academics, athletics, leadership, minority status.

NORTHWOOD UNIVERSITY, FLORIDA CAMPUS

2600 North Military Trail, West Palm Beach, FL 33409-2911
Phone: 561-478-5500 • **Financial Aid Phone:** 561-478-5590
E-mail: fladmit@northwood.edu • **CEEB Code:** 4072
Fax: 561-640-3328 • **Website:** • **ACT Code:** 6736

This private school was founded in 1982. It has a 90-acre campus.

RATINGS
Admissions Selectivity Rating: 78   **Fire Safety Rating:** 77   **Green Rating:** 60*

STUDENTS AND FACULTY
Enrollment: 490. **Student Body:** 36% female, 64% male, 37% out-of-state, 39% international (40 countries represented). Asian 1%, African American 10%, Caucasian 25%, Hispanic 11%, Native American 1%.
Retention and Graduation: 60% freshmen return for sophomore year. 24% freshmen graduate within 4 years. **Faculty:** Student/faculty ratio 20:1. 16 full-time faculty, 38% hold PhDs, 38% are women. 0% of classes are taught by teaching assistants.

ACADEMICS
Degrees: bachelor's. **Classes:** Most classes have 10–19 students. **Majors with Highest Enrollment:** banking and financial support services; marketing/marketing management. **Special Study Options:** Accelerated program, distance learning, double major, dual enrollment, external degree program, honors program, independent study, internships, study abroad, weekend college. **Honors Programs:** An Honors Program began in fall term 1991. In it, honors sections of a variety of critically important courses are offered. The best instructors and the most demanding material and expectations are used. Additionally, special one-credit-hour seminars, which include outside speakers, are offered to sophomores and juniors. Honor students having completed 17 credit hours in honors courses may apply for honors admission to Term in Europe, Term in Asia, or Term in Northern Europe and are eligible for a partial scholarship to support these travel abroad programs. This also provides a powerful incentive for students to successfully compete in the Honors Program. **Disability Services:** Special programs offered to physically disabled students include note-taking services. **Career Services:** Alumni network, alumni services, career/job search classes, career assessment, internships.

FACILITIES
Housing: men's dorms, women's dorms. **Special Academic Facilities/Equipment:** Art Gallery. **Computers:** 100% of classrooms, 100% of dorms, 100% of libraries, 100% of dining areas, 100% of student union, have wireless network access. Students can register for classes online. Administrative functions (other than registration) can be performed online.

CAMPUS LIFE
Environment: City. **Activities:** dance, drama/theater, student government, student newspaper, International Student Organization 23 registered organizations, 1 honor societies. **Athletics (Intercollegiate):** *Men:* baseball, basketball, golf, soccer, tennis. *Women:* basketball, golf, soccer, softball, tennis, volleyball. **On-Campus Highlights:** Countess de Hoernle Student Life Center **Environmental Initiatives:** We keep use of paper to a minimum (e-mail attachments/files, Blackboard portal). Advertising promotions in small numbers in key locations (as opposed to making up 50 flyers and posting them everywhere!) We are just starting a campus-wide paper recycling program with recycling boxes in key locations and a large bin on campus

ADMISSIONS
Freshman Academic Profile: Average high school GPA 3.2. 13% in top 10% of high school class, 27% in top 25% of high school class, 57% in top 50% of high school class. 70% from public high schools. SAT Math middle 50% range 440-550. SAT Critical Reading middle 50% range 430-510. SAT Writing middle 50% range 390-480. ACT middle 50% range 18-21. Minimum paper TOEFL 500. **Basis for Candidate Selection:** *Very important factors considered include:* academic GPA, level of applicant's interest. *Important factors considered include:* Class rank, rigor of secondary school record, standardized test scores. *Other factors considered include:* application essay, recommendation(s), alumni/ae relation, character/personal qualities, extracurricular activities, geographical residence, interview, talent/ability, volunteer work, work experience. **Freshman Admission Requirements:** High school diploma is required and GED is accepted. **Freshman Admission Statistics:** 628 applied, 54% admitted, 31% enrolled. **Transfer Admission Requirements:** High school transcript, college transcript(s), minimum college GPA of 2.0 required. Lowest grade transferable C. **General Admission Information:** Application Fee $25. Notification on a rolling basis, beginning on or about 10/1. Nonfall registration accepted. Admission may be deferred for a maximum of 1 year. Credit and/or placement offered for CEEB Advanced Placement tests.

COSTS AND FINANCIAL AID
Required **Forms and Deadlines:** FAFSA, state aid form. **Notification of Awards:** Applicants will be notified of awards on a rolling basis beginning 3/1. **Types of Aid:** *Need-based scholarships/grants:* Federal Pell, SEOG, state scholarships/grants, private scholarships, the school's own gift aid. *Loans:* Subsidized Stafford, Unsubsidized Stafford, PLUS. **Student Employment: Financial Aid Statistics:** 87% freshmen, 86% undergrads receive need-based scholarship or grant aid. 27% freshmen, 21% undergrads receive non-need-based scholarship or grant aid. 84% freshmen, 90% undergrads receive need-based self-help aid. 20% freshmen, 19% undergrads receive athletic scholarships. 61% undergrads borrow to pay for school. Average cumulative indebtedness $27,505. **Criteria for awarding institutional aid:** *Non-need-based:* academics, alumni affiliation, athletics, leadership, minority status, state/district residency.

NORTHWOOD UNIVERSITY, TEXAS CAMPUS

1114 West FM 1382, Cedar Hill, TX 75104-1204
Phone: 972-293-5400 • **Financial Aid Phone:** 972-293-5430
E-mail: txadmit@northwood.edu • **CEEB Code:** 6499
Fax: 972-291-3824 • **Website:** • **ACT Code:** 4135

This private school was founded in 1966. It has a 360-acre campus.

RATINGS
Admissions Selectivity Rating: 73   **Fire Safety Rating:** 64   **Green Rating:** 60*

STUDENTS AND FACULTY
Enrollment: 531. **Student Body:** 42% female, 58% male, 27% international (18 countries represented), Asian 2%, African American 15%, Caucasian 20%, Hispanic 26%, Native American 0%.
Retention and Graduation: 31% freshmen graduate within 4 years. **Faculty:** Student/faculty ratio 19:1. 20 full-time faculty, 25% hold PhDs, 15% are members of minority groups, 45% are women. 0% of classes are taught by teaching assistants.

ACADEMICS
Degrees: bachelor's. **Classes:** Most classes have 10–19 students. **Majors with Highest Enrollment:** entrepreneurship/entrepreneurial studies; international business/trade/commerce; marketing/marketing management. **Special Study Options:** Accelerated program, distance learning, double major, dual enrollment, external degree program, honors program, independent study, internships, study abroad, weekend college. **Honors Programs:** An Honors Program begain in Fall Term, 1991. In it, honors sections of six critically important courses are offered. The best instructors and the most demanding material and expectations are used. Additionally, special one credit hour seminars, which include outside speakers, are offered to sophomores and juniors. **Disability Services:** Special programs offered to physically disabled students include tutors. **Career Services:** Alumni network, alumni services, career assessment, internships.

FACILITIES
Housing: men's dorms, women's dorms, apartments for single students. **Special Academic Facilities/Equipment:** Butler Gallery, Hopkins Display Cases, Hach Library **Computers:** 100% of classrooms, 100% of dorms, 100% of libraries, 100% of dining areas, 100% of student union, have wireless network access. Students can register for classes online. Administrative functions (other than registration) can be performed online.

CAMPUS LIFE
Environment: Village. **Activities:** Choral groups, dance, drama/theater, student newspaper, Campus Ministries, International Student Organization 17 registered organizations, 1 honor societies, 2 religious organizations. 1 fraternities, 1 sororities. **Athletics (Intercollegiate):** *Men:* baseball, cross-country, golf, soccer, track/field (outdoor), track/field (indoor). *Women:* cross-country, golf, soccer, softball, track/field (outdoor), track/field (indoor). **Environmental Initiatives:** Paper recycling. We have two large bins in one of the parking lots. The paper is collected twice a week from offices and common areas. During the month of April and for Earth Day, we plan other activities and provide educational flyers about what everyone can do on their own.

ADMISSIONS
Freshman Academic Profile: Average high school GPA 3.3. 8% in top 10% of high school class, 27% in top 25% of high school class, 65% in top 50% of high school class. 90% from public high schools. SAT Math middle 50% range 420-520. SAT Critical Reading middle 50% range 390-500. SAT Writing middle 50% range 390-460. ACT middle 50% range 17-22. Minimum paper TOEFL 500. **Basis for Candidate Selection:** *Very important factors considered*

include: Class rank, application essay, academic GPA, recommendation(s), rigor of secondary school record, standardized test scores, character/personal qualities, extracurricular activities, interview, level of applicant's interest. *Important factors considered include:* talent/ability, volunteer work, work experience. *Other factors considered include:* alumni/ae relation, first generation. **Freshman Admission Requirements:** High school diploma is required and GED is accepted. **Freshman Admission Statistics:** 452 applied, 59% admitted, 65% enrolled. **Transfer Admission Requirements:** High school transcript, college transcript(s), essay or personal statement, minimum college GPA of 2.0 required. Lowest grade transferable C. **General Admission Information:** Application Fee $25. Notification on a rolling basis, beginning on or about 1/1. Nonfall registration accepted. Admission may be deferred for a maximum of 1 year. Credit and/or placement offered for CEEB Advanced Placement tests.

COSTS AND FINANCIAL AID

Required Forms and Deadlines: FAFSA. **Notification of Awards:** Applicants will be notified of awards on a rolling basis beginning 3/1. **Types of Aid:** *Need-based scholarships/grants:* Federal Pell, SEOG, private scholarships, the school's own gift aid. *Loans:* Subsidized Stafford, Unsubsidized Stafford, PLUS. **Student Employment: Financial Aid Statistics:** 92% freshmen, 89% undergrads receive need-based scholarship or grant aid. 24% freshmen, 22% undergrads receive non-need-based scholarship or grant aid. 90% freshmen, 91% undergrads receive need-based self-help aid. 11% freshmen, 12% undergrads receive athletic scholarships. 81% undergrads borrow to pay for school. Average cumulative indebtedness $24,254. **Criteria for awarding institutional aid:** *Non-need-based:* academics, alumni affiliation, athletics, leadership, minority status, state/district residency.

NORWICH UNIVERSITY

Admissions Office, Northfield, VT 5663
Phone: 802-485-2001
E-mail: nuadm@norwich.edu
Fax: 802-485-2032 • **Website:** www.norwich.edu

This private school was founded in 1819. It has a 1125-acre campus.

RATINGS
Admissions Selectivity Rating: 68   **Fire Safety Rating:** 60'   **Green Rating:** 60*

STUDENTS AND FACULTY
Enrollment: 2,201. **Student Body:** 26% female, 74% male, 84% out-of-state, 2% international. Asian 2%, African American 3%, Caucasian 74%, Hispanic 4%, Native American 1%.
Retention and Graduation: 85% freshmen return for sophomore year. 45% freshmen graduate within 4 years. 55% freshmen graduate within 6 years. 10% grads go on to further study within 1 year. 2% grads pursue arts and sciences degrees. 2% grads pursue law degrees. 2% grads pursue business degrees. 1% grads pursue medical degrees. **Faculty:** Student/faculty ratio 14:1. 140 full-time faculty, 9% are members of minority groups, 36% are women. 0% of classes are taught by teaching assistants.

ACADEMICS
Degrees: bachelor's, master's, post bachelor's certificate. **Classes:** Most classes have 10–19 students. **Majors with Highest Enrollment:** architecture (barch, ba/bs, march, ma/ms, phd); criminal justice/law enforcement administration; liberal arts and sciences/liberal studies. **Special Study Options:** cooperative education program, distance learning, double major, English as a Second Language (ESL), honors program, independent study, internships, study abroad. **Disability Services:** Special programs offered to physically disabled students include tutors. **Career Services:** career/job search classes.

FACILITIES
Housing: Coed dorms. 95% of campus accessible to physically disabled. **Special Academic Facilities/Equipment:** museum, architecture and art building w/galery, new library.

CAMPUS LIFE
Environment: Rural. **Activities:** Choral groups, concert band, drama/theater, jazz band, literary magazine, marching band, pep band, radio station, student government, student newspaper, yearbook 40 registered organizations, 8 honor societies, 4 religious organizations. **Athletics (Intercollegiate):** *Men:* baseball, basketball, cross-country, diving, football, ice hockey, lacrosse, riflery, rugby, soccer, swimming, track/field (outdoor), volleyball, wrestling. *Women:* basketball, cross-country, diving, riflery, rugby, soccer, softball, swimming, track/field (outdoor), volleyball.

ADMISSIONS
Freshman Academic Profile: Average high school GPA 3.1. 11% in top 10% of high school class, 37% in top 25% of high school class, 74% in top 50% of high school class. 90% from public high schools. SAT Math middle 50% range 500-640. SAT Critical Reading middle 50% range 480-580. SAT Writing middle 50% range 460-620. ACT middle 50% range 21-26. Minimum paper TOEFL 500. **Basis for Candidate Selection:** *Very important factors considered include:* rigor of secondary school record. *Important factors considered include:* extracurricular activities, talent/ability. *Other factors considered include:* Class rank, application essay, recommendation(s), standardized test scores, alumni/ae relation, character/personal qualities, interview, volunteer work, work experience. **Freshman Admission Requirements:** High school diploma is required and GED is accepted. *Academic units required:* 4 English, 3 mathematics, 2 science, (2 science labs). *Academic units recommended:* 4 English, 3 mathematics, 2 science, (2 science labs). **Freshman Admission Statistics:** 1,473 applied, 91% admitted, 37% enrolled. **Transfer Admission Requirements:** High school transcript, college transcript(s), Lowest grade transferable C–. **General Admission Information:** Application Fee $35. Early decision application deadline 11/15. Notification on a rolling basis, beginning on or about 10/1. Nonfall registration accepted. Admission may be deferred for a maximum of 1. Credit offered for CEEB Advanced Placement tests.

COSTS AND FINANCIAL AID
Annual tuition $30,048. Room and board $10,976. Required fees $1,734. Average book expense $1,000. **Required Forms and Deadlines: Types of Aid:** *Need-based scholarships/grants:* Federal Pell, SEOG. *Loans:* Direct Subsidized Stafford, Direct Unsubsidized Stafford, Subsidized Stafford, Unsubsidized Stafford, PLUS, Federal Perkins. **Student Employment:** Federal Work-Study Program available. Institutional employment available. Off-campus job opportunities are fair. **Financial Aid Statistics:** 100% freshmen, 100% undergrads receive need based scholarship or grant aid. 18% freshmen, 17% undergrads receive non-need-based scholarship or grant aid. 79% freshmen, 79% undergrads receive need-based self-help aid.

NOTRE DAME COLLEGE

4545 College Road, South Euclid, OH 44121
Phone: 216-381-1680 • **Financial Aid Phone:** 216-373-5213
E-mail: admissions@ndc.edu • **CEEB Code:** 3085
Fax: 216-373-5278 • **Website:** www.notredamecollege.edu • **ACT Code:** 3302

This private school, affiliated with the Roman Catholic Church, was founded in 1922. It has a 53-acre campus.

RATINGS
Admissions Selectivity Rating: 80   **Fire Safety Rating:** 65   **Green Rating:** 60*

STUDENTS AND FACULTY
Enrollment: 835. **Student Body:** 63% female, 37% male, 3% out-of-state, 4% international. Asian 0%, African American 24%, Caucasian 62%, Hispanic 3%, Native American 0%.
Retention and Graduation: 65% freshmen return for sophomore year. 60% grads go on to further study within 1 year. 10% grads pursue arts and sciences degrees. 5% grads pursue law degrees. 10% grads pursue business degrees. 5% grads pursue medical degrees. **Faculty:** Student/faculty ratio 19:1. 36 full-time faculty, 53% hold PhDs, 3% are members of minority groups, 58% are women. 0% of classes are taught by teaching assistants.

ACADEMICS
Degrees: associate, bachelor's, certificate, master's, post-bachelor's certificate. **Classes:** Most classes have 10–19 students. Most lab/discussion sessions have 10–19 students. **Majors with Highest Enrollment:** business/commerce; psychology; secondary education and teaching. **Special Study Options:** cooperative education program, cross-registration, distance learning, double major, independent study, internships, student-designed major, study abroad, teacher certification program, weekend college. **Disability Services:** Special programs offered to physically disabled students include tutors. **Career Services:** alumni services, career/job search classes, career assessment, internships.

FACILITIES
Housing: Coed dorms, men's dorms, women's dorms. 100% of campus accessible to physically disabled. **Special Academic Facilities/Equipment:** Tolerance Resource Center.

CAMPUS LIFE
Environment: Town. **Activities:** Choral groups, dance, drama/theater, literary magazine, pep band, student government, student newspaper, yearbook 22

registered organizations, 6 honor societies, 1 religious organizations. **Athletics (Intercollegiate):** *Men:* baseball, basketball, cross-country, golf, soccer, tennis, track/field (outdoor). *Women:* basketball, cross-country, golf, lacrosse, soccer, softball, track/field (outdoor), volleyball. **On-Campus Highlights:** Smart Classroom, Legacy Walkway, Joseph H. Keller Fitness Center, Tolerance Resource Center, Coffee Shop, Several new construction and renovations projects are underway in 2005. Check back for updates.

ADMISSIONS

Freshman Academic Profile: Average high school GPA 3.0. 4% in top 10% of high school class, 22% in top 25% of high school class, 62% in top 50% of high school class. 60% from public high schools. SAT Math middle 50% range 393-520. SAT Critical Reading middle 50% range 440-528. ACT middle 50% range 17-21. Minimum paper TOEFL 550. **Basis for Candidate Selection:** *Very important factors considered include:* academic GPA, rigor of secondary school record, standardized test scores. *Important factors considered include:* Class rank, interview, level of applicant's interest. *Other factors considered include:* application essay, recommendation(s), alumni/ae relation, character/personal qualities, extracurricular activities, talent/ability, volunteer work, work experience. **Freshman Admission Requirements:** High school diploma is required and GED is accepted. **Freshman Admission Statistics:** 1,004 applied, 51% admitted, 29% enrolled. **Transfer Admission Requirements:** High school transcript, college transcript(s), interview, minimum college GPA of 2.5 required. Lowest grade transferable C. **General Admission Information:** Application Fee $30. Notification on a rolling basis, beginning on or about 9/1. Nonfall registration accepted. Admission may be deferred for a maximum of 1 year. Credit offered for CEEB Advanced Placement tests.

COSTS AND FINANCIAL AID

Annual tuition $18,670. Room and board $6,648. Required fees $550. Average book expense $1,270. **Required Forms and Deadlines:** FAFSA. **Notification of Awards:** Applicants will be notified of awards on a rolling basis beginning 1/1. **Types of Aid:** *Need-based scholarships/grants:* Federal Pell, SEOG, state scholarships/grants, private scholarships, the school's own gift aid. *Loans:* Subsidized Stafford, Unsubsidized Stafford, PLUS, Federal Perkins, state loans, college/university loans from institutional funds. **Student Employment:** Federal Work-Study Program available. Institutional employment available. Off-campus job opportunities are good. **Financial Aid Statistics:** 100% freshmen, 100% undergrads receive need-based scholarship or grant aid. 100% freshmen, 100% undergrads receive non-need-based scholarship or grant aid. 100% freshmen, 100% undergrads receive need-based self-help aid. 6% undergrads receive athletic scholarships. 93% freshmen, 63% undergrads receive any aid. 90% undergrads borrow to pay for school. Average cumulative indebtedness $15,649. **Criteria for awarding institutional aid:** *Non-need-based:* academics, art, leadership, state/district residency.

See page 1164.

NOTRE DAME DE NAMUR UNIVERSITY

1500 Ralston Avenue, Belmont, CA 94002-1908
Phone: 650-508-3600
E-mail: admiss@ndnu.edu • **CEEB Code:** 4063
Fax: 650-508-3426 • **Website:** www.ndnu.edu • **ACT Code:** 236

This private school, affiliated with the Roman Catholic Church, was founded in 1851. It has a 80-acre campus.

RATINGS
Admissions Selectivity Rating: 70 **Fire Safety Rating:** 61 **Green Rating:** 60*

STUDENTS AND FACULTY
Enrollment: 1,180. **Student Body:** 66% female, 34% male, 7% out-of-state, 3% international. Asian 11%, African American 7%, Caucasian 27%, Hispanic 30%, Native American 1%.
Retention and Graduation: 81% freshmen return for sophomore year. 38% freshmen graduate within 4 years. 47% freshmen graduate within 6 years.
Faculty: Student/faculty ratio 12:1. 58 full-time faculty, 91% hold PhDs, 24% are members of minority groups, 55% are women. 0% of classes are taught by teaching assistants.

ACADEMICS
Degrees: bachelor's, master's, post-bachelor's certificate. **Classes:** Most classes have 10–19 students. **Special Study Options:** Accelerated program, double major, English as a Second Language (ESL), exchange student program (domestic), independent study, internships, liberal arts/career combination, student-designed major, study abroad, teacher certification program. **Disability Services:** Special programs offered to physically disabled students include

note-taking services, reader services. **Career Services:** career/job search classes, internships.

FACILITIES

Housing: Coed dorms, 2 or 3 person apartments 4-person suites. **Special Academic Facilities/Equipment:** Student art museum, professional art gallery, archives of modern Christian art, theatre, early learning center for Montessori credential training, on-campus elementary school.

CAMPUS LIFE

Environment: Village. **Activities:** Choral groups, dance, literary magazine, music ensembles, musical theater, student government, student newspaper 15 registered organizations, 3 honor societies, 1 religious organizations. **Athletics (Intercollegiate):** *Men:* basketball, cheerleading, soccer, tennis, track/field (outdoor). *Women:* basketball, cheerleading, cross-country, soccer, softball, tennis, track/field (outdoor), volleyball.

ADMISSIONS

Freshman Academic Profile: Average high school GPA 3.1. 10% in top 10% of high school class, 29% in top 25% of high school class, 62% in top 50% of high school class. 62% from public high schools. SAT Math middle 50% range 430-530. SAT Critical Reading middle 50% range 440-520. SAT Writing middle 50% range 440-530. ACT middle 50% range 18-22. Minimum web-based TOEFL 61. Minimum paper TOEFL 500. **Basis for Candidate Selection:** *Very important factors considered include:* academic GPA, rigor of secondary school record, character/personal qualities. *Important factors considered include:* Class rank, application essay, recommendation(s), standardized test scores, extracurricular activities, talent/ability, volunteer work. *Other factors considered include:* first generation, interview, work experience. **Freshman Admission Requirements:** High school diploma is required and GED is accepted. *Academic units required:* 4 English, 2 mathematics, 1 science, (1 science labs), 2 foreign language, 2 social studies, 1 history, 3 academic electives. *Academic units recommended:* 4 English, 2 mathematics, 1 science, (1 science labs), 2 foreign language, 2 social studies, 1 history, 3 academic electives. **Freshman Admission Statistics:** 2,209 applied, 75% admitted, 11% enrolled. **Transfer Admission Requirements:** college transcript(s), essay or personal statement, statement of good standing from prior institution(s). Minimum college GPA of 2.0 required. Lowest grade transferable C. **General Admission Information:** Application Fee $40. Notification on a rolling basis, beginning on or about 12/1. Nonfall registration accepted. Admission may be deferred for a maximum of 12 months. Credit offered for CEEB Advanced Placement tests.

COSTS AND FINANCIAL AID

Annual tuition $30,202. Room and board $11,970. Required fees $320. Average book expense $1,656. **Required Forms and Deadlines:** FAFSA. **Types of Aid:** *Need-based scholarships/grants:* Federal Pell, SEOG, state scholarships/grants, private scholarships. *Loans:* Subsidized Stafford, Unsubsidized Stafford, PLUS, Federal Perkins. **Student Employment:** Federal Work-Study Program available. Institutional employment available. Highest amount earned per year from on-campus jobs $1,300. Off-campus job opportunities are excellent. **Financial Aid Statistics:** 99% freshmen, 99% undergrads receive need-based scholarship or grant aid. 3% freshmen, 3% undergrads receive non-need-based scholarship or grant aid. 84% freshmen, 78% undergrads receive need-based self-help aid. 2% freshmen, 1% undergrads receive athletic scholarships. Average cumulative indebtedness $31,915. **Criteria for awarding institutional aid:** *Non-need-based:* academics, alumni affiliation, art, athletics, leadership, music/drama.

NOVA SCOTIA COLLEGE OF ART AND DESIGN

5163 Duke Street, Halifax, NS B3J3J6
Phone: 902-494-8129 • **Financial Aid Phone:** 902-494-8130
E-mail: admissions@nscad.ca
Fax: 902-425-2987 • **Website:** www.nscad.ca

This public school was founded in 1887. It has a 1-acre campus.

RATINGS
Admissions Selectivity Rating: 63 **Fire Safety Rating:** 60* **Green Rating:** 60*

STUDENTS AND FACULTY
Enrollment: 896. **Student Body:** 64% female, 36% male.
Faculty: Student/faculty ratio 11:1. 68 full-time faculty, 28% are women. 19% of classes are taught by teaching assistants.

ACADEMICS
Degrees: bachelor's, master's. **Special Study Options:** cooperative education program, distance learning, double major, exchange student program

(domestic), independent study, internships, study abroad. **Combined Degree Programs:** BFA/BD. **Disability Services:** Special programs offered to physically disabled students include note-taking services, tape recorders.

FACILITIES
Housing: men's dorms, women's dorms, apartments for married students. 25% of campus accessible to physically disabled.

CAMPUS LIFE
Environment: City. **Activities:** Choral groups, concert band, drama/theater, music ensembles, musical theater, student government, yearbook.

ADMISSIONS
Freshman Academic Profile: Minimum paper TOEFL 575. **Basis for Candidate Selection:** *Very important factors considered include:* application essay, rigor of secondary school record, talent/ability.*Other factors considered include:* recommendation(s), standardized test scores, character/personal qualities, interview, volunteer work, work experience. **Freshman Admission Requirements: Freshman Admission Statistics:** 247 applied, 43% admitted. **Transfer Admission Requirements:** college transcript(s), essay or personal statement, statement of good standing from prior institution(s). **General Admission Information:** Application Fee $50. Regular application deadline 5/15. Notification on a rolling basis, beginning on or about 3/15. Nonfall registration not accepted. Admission may be deferred for a maximum of 1 year. Placement offered for CEEB Advanced Placement tests.

NOVA SOUTHEASTERN UNIVERSITY

3301 College Avenue, Fort Lauderdale, FL 33314
Phone: 954-262-8000 • **Financial Aid Phone:** 954-262-7456
E-mail: admissions@nova.edu • **CEEB Code:** 5514
Fax: 954-262-3811 • **Website:** www.nova.edu • **ACT Code:** 6706

This private school was founded in 1964. It has a 300-acre campus.

RATINGS
Admissions Selectivity Rating: 82   **Fire Safety Rating:** 90   **Green Rating:** 61

STUDENTS AND FACULTY
Enrollment: 6,246. **Student Body:** 71% female, 29% male, 16% out-of-state, 4% international. Asian 6%, African American 24%, Caucasian 28%, Hispanic 32%, Native American 0%.
Retention and Graduation: 70% freshmen return for sophomore year. **Faculty:** Student/faculty ratio 20:1. 814 full-time faculty, 88% hold PhDs, 30% are members of minority groups, 49% are women. 0% of classes are taught by teaching assistants.

ACADEMICS
Degrees: associate, bachelor's, master's, post-bachelor's certificate, post-master's certificate. **Classes:** Most classes have 10–19 students. **Majors with Highest Enrollment:** biology/biological sciences; business administration and management; nursing/registered nurse (rn, asn, bsn, msn). **Special Study Options:** distance learning, double major, honors program, independent study, internships, study abroad, teacher certification program, Dual admission programs with NSU graduate and professional schools. **Honors Programs:** http://undergrad.nova.edu/honors/index.cfm For the academically motivated student, the NSU Honors program provides a value added experience. Students enjoy greater interaction with faculty through curricular and co-curricular activities, special invitations to events, and enhanced engagement in disciplinary inquiry. **Combined Degree Programs:** BA/MD, BA/JD, BA/MA, BA/DDS, http://www.undergrad.nova.edu/majors.cfm. **Disability Services:** Special programs offered to physically disabled students include note-taking services, reader services, tape recorders, tutors. **Career Services:** alumni services, career assessment, internships, regional alumni. Career Services highlights include Our comprehensive career development program encompassing career planning, advisement services, employment and career resources, campus relations, and employer recruitment program.

FACILITIES
Housing: Coed dorms, special housing for disabled students, special housing for international students, fraternity/sorority housing, apartments for married students, apartments for single students, wellness housing, theme housing. **Special Academic Facilities/Equipment:** Institute for Early Childhood Studies, University School for pre-kindergarten to grade 12, Oceanographic Center and Lab, Biofeedback and Learning Technology Labs, Audiology and Speech Language Pathology, and Psychology Clinics **Computers:** 100% of classrooms, 100% of dorms, 100% of libraries, 80% of dining areas, 100% of student union, 70% of common outdoor areas have wireless network access. Students can

register for classes online. Administrative functions (other than registration) can be performed online.

CAMPUS LIFE
Environment: City. **Activities:** Choral groups, dance, drama/theater, jazz band, literary magazine, music ensembles, musical theater, pep band, radio station, student government, student newspaper, International Student Organization 292 registered organizations. **Athletics (Intercollegiate):** *Men:* baseball, basketball, cross-country, golf, soccer, track/field (outdoor). *Women:* basketball, cheerleading, crew/rowing, cross-country, golf, soccer, softball, tennis, track/field (outdoor), volleyball. **On-Campus Highlights:** University Center and Performing Arts Wi, Alvin Sherman Library, Research & Inform, Health Professions Division Museum, Miniaci Performing Arts Center, Law School, University Center includes the sports arena, fitness center, flight deck, shark mural, and mall-style food court. Performing Arts Wing includes multiple theaters, costume and scenery shops, performance practice rooms for music and dance, dressing rooms, and a gallery.

ADMISSIONS
Freshman Academic Profile: SAT Math middle 50% range 470-590. SAT Critical Reading middle 50% range 460-570. ACT middle 50% range 20-25. Minimum paper TOEFL 550. **Basis for Candidate Selection:** *Very important factors considered include:* academic GPA, standardized test scores. *Important factors considered include:* rigor of secondary school record. *Other factors considered include:* application essay, recommendation(s), character/personal qualities, extracurricular activities, interview, talent/ability, volunteer work. **Freshman Admission Requirements:** High school diploma is required and GED is accepted. **Freshman Admission Statistics:** 3,780 applied, 58% admitted, 31% enrolled. **Transfer Admission Requirements:** college transcript(s), statement of good standing from prior institution(s). Minimum college GPA of 2.50 required. Lowest grade transferable D. **General Admission Information:** Application Fee $50. Regular application deadline 8/1. Nonfall registration accepted. Admission may be deferred for a maximum of 1 year. Credit and/or placement offered for CEEB Advanced Placement tests.

COSTS AND FINANCIAL AID
Annual tuition $21,600. Room and board $9,086. Required fees $550. Average book expense $1,500. **Required Forms and Deadlines:** FAFSA, state aid form. **Notification of Awards:** Applicants will be notified of awards on a rolling basis beginning 3/15. **Types of Aid:** *Need-based scholarships/grants:* Federal Pell, SEOG, state scholarships/grants, private scholarships, the school's own gift aid. *Loans:* Subsidized Stafford, Unsubsidized Stafford, PLUS, Federal Perkins. **Student Employment:** Federal Work-Study Program available. Institutional employment available. Off-campus job opportunities are good. **Financial Aid Statistics:** 97% freshmen, 96% undergrads receive need-based scholarship or grant aid. 100% freshmen, 100% undergrads receive non-need-based scholarship or grant aid. 83% freshmen, 88% undergrads receive need-based self-help aid. 12% freshmen, 7% undergrads receive athletic scholarships. 92% freshmen, 83% undergrads receive any aid. 76% undergrads borrow to pay for school. Average cumulative indebtedness $43,206. **Criteria for awarding institutional aid:** *Non-need-based:* academics, athletics, leadership, music/drama.

OAK HILLS CHRISTIAN COLLEGE

1600 Oak Hills Rd SW, Bemidji, MN 56601
Phone: 218-751-8670 • **Financial Aid Phone:** 218-751-8670
E-mail: admissions@oakhills.edu
Fax: 218-751-8825 • **Website:** www.oakhills.edu • **ACT Code:** 2167

This private school was founded in 1946. It has a 180-acre campus.

RATINGS
Admissions Selectivity Rating: 72   **Fire Safety Rating:** 63   **Green Rating:** 60*

STUDENTS AND FACULTY
Enrollment: 131. **Student Body:** 33% out-of-state, 1% international (1 countries represented). Asian 2%, African American 1%, Caucasian 79%, Native American 1%.
Retention and Graduation: 55% freshmen return for sophomore year. 38% freshmen graduate within 6 years. **Faculty:** Student/faculty ratio 13:1. 6 full-time faculty, 67% hold PhDs, 0% are members of minority groups, 33% are women. 0% of classes are taught by teaching assistants.

ACADEMICS
Degrees: associate, bachelor's, certificate, diploma. **Classes:** Most classes have fewer than 10 students. **Majors with Highest Enrollment:** bible/biblical studies; pastoral studies/counseling; youth ministry. **Special Study Options:** cooperative education program, double major, independent study, internships.

Disability Services: Special programs offered to physically disabled students include note-taking services, reader services, tape recorders, tutors. **Career Services:** Alumni network, career/job search classes, career assessment, internships.

FACILITIES

Housing: special housing for disabled students, men's dorms, women's dorms, apartments for married students, apartments for single students. 85% of campus accessible to physically disabled. **Special Academic Facilities/Equipment:** American Indian Resource Center. **Computers:** 50% of classrooms, 100% of dorms, 100% of libraries, 100% of student union, 50% of common outdoor areas have wireless network access. Students can register for classes online. Administrative functions (other than registration) can be performed online.

CAMPUS LIFE

Environment: Village. **Activities:** Choral groups, music ensembles, student government, Campus Ministries. **Athletics (Intercollegiate):** *Men:* basketball. *Women:* basketball, volleyball. **On-Campus Highlights:** The Fellowship Center Lounge, Schreiber Activity Center (SAC) Gym, Library, Chapel, Lake Front.

ADMISSIONS

Freshman Academic Profile: 5% in top 10% of high school class, 5% in top 25% of high school class, 47% in top 50% of high school class. 79% from public high schools. ACT middle 50% range 16-21. Minimum paper TOEFL 500. **Basis for Candidate Selection:** *Very important factors considered include:* Class rank, application essay, academic GPA, recommendation(s). *Other factors considered include:* rigor of secondary school record, interview. **Freshman Admission Requirements:** High school diploma is required and GED is accepted. **Freshman Admission Statistics:** 70 applied, 56% admitted, 79% enrolled. **Transfer Admission Requirements:** High school transcript, college transcript(s), essay or personal statement, minimum college GPA of 2.0 required. Lowest grade transferable C. **General Admission Information:** Application Fee $25. Notification on a rolling basis, beginning on or about 9/1. Nonfall registration accepted. Admission may be deferred for a maximum of 2 years. Credit and/or placement offered for CEEB Advanced Placement tests.

COSTS AND FINANCIAL AID

Annual tuition $14,420. Room and board $5,180. Average book expense $990. **Required Forms and Deadlines:** FAFSA, institution's own financial aid form. **Notification of Awards:** Applicants will be notified of awards on a rolling basis beginning 3/1. **Types of Aid:** *Need-based scholarships/grants:* Federal Pell, SEOG, state scholarships/grants, private scholarships, the school's own gift aid. *Loans:* Subsidized Stafford, Unsubsidized Stafford, PLUS, state loans, Alternative Loan programs. **Student Employment:** Federal Work-Study Program available. Institutional employment available. Highest amount earned per year from on-campus jobs $9. Off-campus job opportunities are excellent. **Financial Aid Statistics:** 100% freshmen, 100% undergrads receive need-based scholarship or grant aid. 75% freshmen, 86% undergrads receive need-based self-help aid. 100% freshmen, 100% undergrads receive any aid. 100% undergrads borrow to pay for school. Average cumulative indebtedness $29,440. **Criteria for awarding institutional aid:** *Non-need-based:* academics, alumni affiliation.

OAKLAND CITY UNIVERSITY

138 N. Lucretia Street, Oakland City, IN 47660
Phone: 812-749-1221
E-mail: ocuadmit@oak.edu
Fax: 812-749-1433 • **Website:** www.oak.edu

This is a private school.

RATINGS

Admissions Selectivity Rating: 76   **Fire Safety Rating:** 60*   **Green Rating:** 60*

STUDENTS AND FACULTY

Enrollment: 1,492. **Student Body:** 53% female, 47% male, 17% out-of-state, 1% international. Asian 1%, African American 13%, Caucasian 98%, Hispanic 0%, Native American 1%.
Retention and Graduation: 66% freshmen return for sophomore year. 46% freshmen graduate within 4 years. 64% freshmen graduate within 6 years. **Faculty:** Student/faculty ratio 15:1. 58 full-time faculty, 0% are members of minority groups, 47% are women.

ACADEMICS

Degrees: associate, bachelor's, certificate, doctoral, master's. **Classes:** Most classes have 10–19 students. Most lab/discussion sessions have fewer than 10 students. **Special Study Options:** distance learning, double major, dual enrollment, independent study, internships, teacher certification program.

FACILITIES

Housing: men's dorms, women's dorms, apartments for married students, apartments for single students.

CAMPUS LIFE

Activities: Choral groups, drama/theater, pep band, student government, student newspaper, yearbook, Campus Ministries.

ADMISSIONS

Freshman Academic Profile: Average high school GPA 3.2. 9% in top 10% of high school class, 16% in top 25% of high school class, 41% in top 50% of high school class. SAT Math middle 50% range 420-530. SAT Critical Reading middle 50% range 400-510. SAT Writing middle 50% range 398-500. ACT middle 50% range 17-23. **Basis for Candidate Selection:** *Very important factors considered include:* academic GPA, rigor of secondary school record, standardized test scores. *Other factors considered include:* Class rank, alumni/ae relation, character/personal qualities, interview, level of applicant's interest. **Freshman Admission Requirements:** High school diploma is required and GED is accepted. **Freshman Admission Statistics:** 620 applied, 56% admitted, 100% enrolled. **Transfer Admission Requirements:** High school transcript, college transcript(s), standardized test scores, minimum college GPA of 2.0 required. Lowest grade transferable C. **General Admission Information:** Application Fee $35. Regular application deadline 9/5. Nonfall registration accepted.

COSTS AND FINANCIAL AID

Annual tuition $15,200. Room and board $6,000. Required fees $360. Average book expense $1,500. **Required Forms and Deadlines:** FAFSA. **Notification of Awards:** Applicants will be notified of awards on a rolling basis beginning 5/1. **Types of Aid:** *Need-based scholarships/grants:* Federal Pell, SEOG, state scholarships/grants, private scholarships, the school's own gift aid. *Loans:* Subsidized Stafford, Unsubsidized Stafford, PLUS, Federal Perkins. **Criteria for awarding institutional aid:** *Non-need-based:* academics, alumni affiliation, art, athletics, minority status, music/drama, religious affiliation.

OAKLAND UNIVERSITY

Office of Admissions, Rochester, MI 48309-4401
Phone: 248-370-3360 • **Financial Aid Phone:** 248-370-2550
E-mail: ouinfo@oakland.edu • **CEEB Code:** 1497
Fax: 248-370-4462 • **Website:** www.oakland.edu • **ACT Code:** 2033

This public school was founded in 1957. It has a 1444-acre campus.

RATINGS

Admissions Selectivity Rating: 78   **Fire Safety Rating:** 80   **Green Rating:** 68

STUDENTS AND FACULTY

Enrollment: 15,727. **Student Body:** 60% female, 40% male, 1% out-of-state, 1% international (100 countries represented). Asian 4%, African American 9%, Caucasian 77%, Hispanic 2%, Native American 0%.
Retention and Graduation: 70% freshmen return for sophomore year. 15% freshmen graduate within 4 years. **Faculty:** 534 full-time faculty, 88% hold PhDs, 22% are members of minority groups, 46% are women. 1% of classes are taught by teaching assistants.

ACADEMICS

Degrees: bachelor's, doctoral, master's, post-bachelor's certificate, post-master's certificate. **Classes:** Most classes have 20–29 students. Most lab/discussion sessions have 10–19 students. **Majors with Highest Enrollment:** business/commerce; elementary education and teaching; psychology. **Special Study Options:** Accelerated program, cooperative education program, cross-registration, distance learning, double major, English as a Second Language (ESL), honors program, independent study, internships, student-designed major, study abroad, teacher certification program. **Honors Programs:** Honors College **Combined Degree Programs:** 5 year MBA program. **Disability Services:** Special programs offered to physically disabled students include note-taking services, reader services, tape recorders, tutors. **Career Services:** Alumni network, alumni services, internships.

FACILITIES

Housing: Coed dorms, special housing for disabled students, special housing for international students, fraternity/sorority housing, apartments for married students, cooperative housing, apartments for single students, wellness housing, theme housing, Living/Learning Community. 90% of campus accessible to physically disabled. **Special Academic Facilities/Equipment:** Art gallery, robotics lab, Eye Research institute, Professional theater, Meadowbrook Hall, Meadowbrook Music Festival, two golf courses, Pawley Learning center, Lowry Early Childhood Education Center, Jack's Place for Autism at OU **Computers:**

Students can register for classes online. Administrative functions (other than registration) can be performed online.

CAMPUS LIFE

Environment: Town. **Activities:** Choral groups, concert band, dance, drama/theater, jazz band, literary magazine, music ensembles, musical theater, pep band, radio station, student government, student newspaper, student-run film society, symphony orchestra, television station, Campus Ministries, International Student Organization 170 registered organizations, 9 honor societies, 12 religious organizations. 6 fraternities, 6 sororities. **Athletics (Intercollegiate):** *Men:* baseball, basketball, cross-country, diving, golf, soccer, swimming, track/field (outdoor). *Women:* basketball, cross-country, diving, golf, soccer, softball, swimming, tennis, track/field (outdoor), volleyball. **On-Campus Highlights:** Recreation Center, Pawley Hall, Oakland Center, Library, Honors College. **Environmental Initiatives:** $8 million Facility upgrade from 1998 to save on energy costs Solar electric power roof installed on the student apartments buildings Investigating Biomass energy and/ or wind power for campus heating and cooling.

ADMISSIONS

Freshman Academic Profile: Average high school GPA 3.4. 18% in top 10% of high school class, 47% in top 25% of high school class, 82% in top 50% of high school class. 90% from public high schools. ACT middle 50% range 20-26. Minimum web-based TOEFL 79. Minimum paper TOEFL 550. **Basis for Candidate Selection:** *Very important factors considered include:* Class rank, academic GPA, rigor of secondary school record. *Important factors considered include:* recommendation(s), character/personal qualities, extracurricular activities, talent/ability, volunteer work. *Other factors considered include:* application essay, standardized test scores, alumni/ae relation, first generation, interview, level of applicant's interest, work experience. **Freshman Admission Requirements:** High school diploma is required and GED is accepted. *Academic units required:* 4 English, 3 mathematics, 3 science, 3 social studies. *Academic units recommended:* 4 English, 3 mathematics, 3 science, 3 social studies. **Freshman Admission Statistics:** 12,152 applied, 62% admitted, 33% enrolled. **Transfer Admission Requirements:** college transcript(s), statement of good standing from prior institution(s). Minimum college GPA of 2.50 required. Lowest grade transferable C. **General Admission Information:** Notification on a rolling basis, beginning on or about 9/15. Nonfall registration accepted. Admission may be deferred for a maximum of 1 year. Placement offered for CEEB Advanced Placement tests.

COSTS AND FINANCIAL AID

Annual in-state tuition $11,183. Annual out-of-state tuition $25,598. Room and board $8,208. Average book expense $1,362. **Required Forms and Deadlines:** FAFSA. **Notification of Awards:** Applicants will be notified of awards on a rolling basis beginning 3/15. **Types of Aid:** *Need-based scholarships/ grants:* Federal Pell, SEOG, state scholarships/grants, private scholarships, the school's own gift aid. *Loans:* Direct Subsidized Stafford, Direct Unsubsidized Stafford, Direct PLUS, Federal Perkins, Private loans. **Student Employment:** Federal Work-Study Program available. Institutional employment available. Off-campus job opportunities are good. **Financial Aid Statistics:** 70% freshmen, 60% undergrads receive need-based scholarship or grant aid. 40% freshmen, 28% undergrads receive non-need-based scholarship or grant aid. 59% freshmen, 75% undergrads receive need-based self-help aid. 3% freshmen, 2% undergrads receive athletic scholarships. 59% freshmen, 54% undergrads receive any aid. 51% undergrads borrow to pay for school. Average cumulative indebtedness $19,967. **Criteria for awarding institutional aid:** *Non-need-based:* academics, art, athletics, leadership, music/drama, state/district residency.

OBERLIN COLLEGE

101 North Professor Street, Oberlin, OH 44074
Phone: 440-775-8411 • **Financial Aid Phone:** 440-775-8142
E-mail: college.admissions@oberlin.edu • **CEEB Code:** 1587
Fax: 440-775-6905 • **Website:** www.oberlin.edu • **ACT Code:** 3304

This private school was founded in 1833. It has a 450-acre campus.

RATINGS

Admissions Selectivity Rating: 97   **Fire Safety Rating:** 69   **Green Rating:** 89

STUDENTS AND FACULTY

Enrollment: 2,959. **Student Body:** 55% female, 45% male, 92% out-of-state, 6% international. Asian 4%, African American 6%, Caucasian 72%, Hispanic 6%, Native American 0%.
Retention and Graduation: 94% freshmen return for sophomore year. 75% freshmen graduate within 4 years. 87% freshmen graduate within 6 years. 16% grads go on to further study within 1 year. 8% grads pursue arts and sciences degrees. 3% grads pursue law degrees. 2% grads pursue business degrees. 3% grads pursue medical degrees. **Faculty:** 0% of classes are taught by teaching assistants.

ACADEMICS

Degrees: bachelor's, diploma, master's, post-master's certificate. **Classes:** Most classes have 10–19 students. Most lab/discussion sessions have fewer than 10 students. **Majors with Highest Enrollment:** biology; English language and literature; history. **Special Study Options:** cross-registration, double major, dual enrollment, English as a Second Language (ESL), exchange student program (domestic), honors program, independent study, internships, student-designed major, study abroad, teacher certification program, 5 year double degree program with Conservatory of Music and College of Arts and Sciences; 3-2 engineering. **Combined Degree Programs:** BA/B.Music. **Disability Services:** Special programs offered to physically disabled students include note-taking services, reader services, tape recorders, tutors.

FACILITIES

Housing: Coed dorms, men's dorms, women's dorms, cooperative housing, theme housing. 90% of campus accessible to physically disabled. **Special Academic Facilities/Equipment:** Allen Memorial Art museum, Theaters, music performance halls. **Computers:** Students can register for classes online. Administrative functions (other than registration) can be performed online.

CAMPUS LIFE

Environment: Rural. **Activities:** Choral groups, concert band, dance, drama/theater, jazz band, literary magazine, marching band, music ensembles, musical theater, opera, radio station, student government, student newspaper, student-run film society, symphony orchestra, yearbook, Campus Ministries, International Student Organization 125 registered organizations, 3 honor societies, 10 religious organizations. **Athletics (Intercollegiate):** *Men:* baseball, basketball, cross-country, diving, football, golf, lacrosse, soccer, swimming, tennis, track/field (outdoor), track/field (indoor). *Women:* basketball, cross-country, diving, field hockey, golf, lacrosse, soccer, softball, swimming, tennis, track/field (outdoor), track/field (indoor), volleyball. **On-Campus Highlights:** Allen Art Museum, Oberlin College Science Center, Adam Joseph Lewis Center for Environmental Studies, Mudd Library, Jesse Philips Recreational Center. **Environmental Initiatives:** Development of Campus Resource Monitoring System. oberlin.edu/dormenergy Building of social capital on campus and in the larger community. http://www.oberlin.edu/sustainability/portfolio/social_capital. html Adam Joseph Lewis Center for Environmental Studies. oberlin.edu/ajlc

ADMISSIONS

Freshman Academic Profile: Average high school GPA 3.6. 68% in top 10% of high school class, 90% in top 25% of high school class, 100% in top 50% of high school class. 60% from public high schools. Minimum paper TOEFL 600. **Basis for Candidate Selection:** *Very important factors considered include:* Class rank, academic GPA, rigor of secondary school record, standardized test scores. *Important factors considered include:* application essay, recommendation(s), character/personal qualities, extracurricular activities, first generation, talent/ability. *Other factors considered include:* alumni/ae relation, interview, level of applicant's interest, racial/ethnic status, volunteer work, work experience. **Freshman Admission Requirements:** High school diploma is required and GED is accepted. *Academic units required:* 4 English, 4 mathematics, 3 science, 3 foreign language, 3 social studies. 4 English, 4 mathematics, 3 science, 3 foreign language, 3 social studies. **Freshman Admission Statistics:** 7,395 applied, 30% admitted, 34% enrolled. **Transfer Admission Requirements:** High school transcript, college transcript(s), essay or personal statement, standardized test scores, statement of good standing from prior institution(s). Minimum college GPA of 3.0 required. Lowest grade transferable C–. **General Admission Information:** Application Fee $35. Early decision application deadline 11/15. Regular application deadline 1/15. Regular notification 4/1. Nonfall registration not accepted. Admission may be deferred for a maximum of 1 year. Credit and/or placement offered for CEEB Advanced Placement tests.

COSTS AND FINANCIAL AID

Annual tuition $44,512. Room and board $12,120. Required fees $393. Average book expense $830. **Required Forms and Deadlines:** FAFSA, institution's own financial aid form, CSS/Financial Aid PROFILE, state aid form, noncustodial PROFILE, business/farm supplement. **Notification of Awards:** Applicants will be notified of awards on or about 4/1. **Types of Aid:** *Need-based* scholarships/grants: Federal Pell, SEOG, state scholarships/grants, private scholarships, the school's own gift aid. *Loans:* Subsidized Stafford, Unsubsidized Stafford, PLUS, Federal Perkins, college/university loans from institutional funds. **Student Employment:** Highest amount earned per year from on-campus jobs $1,750. **Financial Aid Statistics:** 73% freshmen, 78% undergrads receive need-based scholarship or grant aid. 54% freshmen, 56% undergrads receive non-need-based scholarship or grant aid. 80% freshmen, 84% undergrads receive need-based self-help aid. 61% freshmen, 60% undergrads receive any aid. **Criteria for awarding institutional aid:** *Non-need-based:* academics, music/drama.

OCCIDENTAL COLLEGE

Best 378

1600 Campus Road, Los Angeles, CA 90041-3314
Phone: 323-259-2700 • **Financial Aid Phone:** 323-259-2548
E-mail: admission@oxy.edu • **CEEB Code:** 4581
Fax: 323-341-4875 • **Website:** www.oxy.edu • **ACT Code:** 350

This private school was founded in 1887. It has a 120-acre campus.

RATINGS
Admissions Selectivity Rating: 95   **Fire Safety Rating:** 67   **Green Rating:** 79

STUDENTS AND FACULTY
Enrollment: 2,172. **Student Body:** 56% female, 44% male, 54% out-of-state, 3% international (27 countries represented). Asian 13%, African American 4%, Caucasian 54%, Hispanic 16%, Native American 0%.
Retention and Graduation: 94% freshmen return for sophomore year. 80% freshmen graduate within 4 years. 84% freshmen graduate within 6 years. 10% grads go on to further study within 1 year. 17% grads pursue law degrees. 13% grads pursue medical degrees. **Faculty:** Student/faculty ratio 10:1. 184 full-time faculty, 94% hold PhDs, 28% are members of minority groups, 48% are women. 0% of classes are taught by teaching assistants.

ACADEMICS
Degrees: bachelor's, master's. **Classes:** Most classes have 10–19 students. Most lab/discussion sessions have 10–19 students. **Majors with Highest Enrollment:** economics; English language and literature; international relations and affairs. **Special Study Options:** cross-registration, double major, exchange student program (domestic), honors program, independent study, internships, student-designed major, study abroad, Richter fellowships for international research; summer undergraduate research program; endowment investment management program (Blyth Fund). **Combined Degree Programs:** BA/JD, law, Columbia; biotech with Keck Grad Institute. **Disability Services:** Special programs offered to physically disabled students include note-taking services, tape recorders. **Career Services:** Alumni network, alumni services, career/job search classes, internships, regional alumni.

FACILITIES
Housing: Coed dorms, women's dorms, fraternity/sorority housing, theme housing. 75% of campus accessible to physically disabled. **Special Academic Facilities/Equipment:** Keck Theater; Mullin Studio and Art Gallery; Moore Ornithology Collection; Smiley Geological Collection; Morse Collection of Astronomical Instruments; superconducting magnet; vivarium; greenhouses **Computers:** 100% of classrooms, 100% of dorms, 90% of libraries, 100% of dining areas, 80% of student union, 50% of common outdoor areas have wireless network access. Students can register for classes online. Administrative functions (other than registration) can be performed online.

CAMPUS LIFE
Environment: Metropolis. **Activities:** Choral groups, concert band, dance, drama/theater, jazz band, literary magazine, music ensembles, musical theater, radio station, student government, student newspaper, student-run film society, symphony orchestra, yearbook, International Student Organization 8 honor societies, 5 religious organizations. 4 fraternities, 4 sororities. **Athletics (Intercollegiate):** *Men:* baseball, basketball, cross-country, diving, football, golf, soccer, swimming, tennis, track/field (outdoor), water polo. *Women:* basketball, cross-country, diving, golf, lacrosse, soccer, softball, swimming, tennis, track/field (outdoor), volleyball, water polo. **On-Campus Highlights:** Johnson Student Center, Student Quad, Samuelson Pavilion, Clapp Library, Alumni Gymnasium. **Environmental Initiatives:** Freestanding solar array LEED silver for all new construction Student Sustainability Fund.

ADMISSIONS
Freshman Academic Profile: Average high school GPA. 60% in top 10% of high school class, 91% in top 25% of high school class, 100% in top 50% of high school class. 60% from public high schools. SAT Math middle 50% range 600-700. SAT Critical Reading middle 50% range 600-700. SAT Writing middle 50% range 610-700. ACT middle 50% range 28-32. Minimum paper TOEFL 600. **Basis for Candidate Selection:** *Very important factors considered include:* rigor of secondary school record, extracurricular activities, volunteer work, work experience. *Important factors considered include:* Class rank, application essay, recommendation(s), standardized test scores. *Other factors considered include:* academic GPA, alumni/ae relation, character/personal qualities, first generation, geographical residence, interview, level of applicant's interest, racial/ethnic status, talent/ability. **Freshman Admission Requirements:** High school diploma is required and GED is accepted. **Freshman Admission Statistics:** 6,135 applied, 39% admitted, 22% enrolled. **Transfer Admission Requirements:** High school transcript, college transcript(s), essay or personal statement, statement of good standing from prior institution(s). Minimum college GPA of 3.0 required. Lowest grade transferable D. **General Admission Information:** Application Fee $50. Early decision application deadline 11/15. Regular application deadline 1/10. Regular notification 4/1. Nonfall registration not accepted. Admission may be deferred for a maximum of 1 year. Credit and/or placement offered for CEEB Advanced Placement tests.

COSTS AND FINANCIAL AID
Annual tuition $43,490. Room and board $12,450. Required fees $1,080. Average book expense $1,213. **Required Forms and Deadlines:** FAFSA, CSS/Financial Aid PROFILE, state aid form, noncustodial PROFILE, business/farm supplement. **Notification of Awards:** Applicants will be notified of awards on a rolling basis beginning 4/1. **Types of Aid:** *Need-based scholarships/grants:* Federal Pell, SEOG, state scholarships/grants, private scholarships, the school's own gift aid. *Loans:* Subsidized Stafford, Unsubsidized Stafford, PLUS, Federal Perkins, college/university loans from institutional funds. **Student Employment:** Federal Work-Study Program available. Institutional employment available. Off-campus job opportunities are good. **Financial Aid Statistics:** 100% freshmen, 99% undergrads receive need-based scholarship or grant aid. 10% freshmen, 9% undergrads receive non-need-based scholarship or grant aid. 89% freshmen, 90% undergrads receive need-based self-help aid. 73% freshmen, 77% undergrads receive any aid. 51% undergrads borrow to pay for school. Average cumulative indebtedness $23,703. **Criteria for awarding institutional aid:** *Non-need-based:* academics, leadership, music/drama, state/district residency.

OGLETHORPE UNIVERSITY

4484 Peachtree Road N.E., Atlanta, GA 30319
Phone: 404-364-8307 • **Financial Aid Phone:** 404-364-8356
E-mail: admission@oglethorpe.edu • **CEEB Code:** 5521
Fax: 404-364-8491 • **Website:** www.oglethorpe.edu • **ACT Code:** 850

This private school was founded in 1835. It has a 102-acre campus.

RATINGS
Admissions Selectivity Rating: 72   **Fire Safety Rating:** 75   **Green Rating:** 67

STUDENTS AND FACULTY
Enrollment: 1,023. **Student Body:** 58% female, 42% male, 29% out-of-state, 5% international (24 countries represented). Asian 3%, African American 21%, Caucasian 36%, Hispanic 8%, Native American 0%.
Retention and Graduation: 80% freshmen return for sophomore year. 41% freshmen graduate within 4 years. 56% freshmen graduate within 6 years. 40% grads go on to further study within 1 year. 19% grads pursue arts and sciences degrees. 9% grads pursue law degrees. 10% grads pursue business degrees. 2% grads pursue medical degrees. **Faculty:** Student/faculty ratio 13:1. 55 full-time faculty, 93% hold PhDs, 11% are members of minority groups, 36% are women. 0% of classes are taught by teaching assistants.

ACADEMICS
Degrees: bachelor's, master's. **Classes:** Most classes have 10–19 students. **Majors with Highest Enrollment:** business/commerce; English language and literature; psychology. **Special Study Options:** Accelerated program, cooperative education program, cross-registration, double major, dual enrollment, exchange student program (domestic), honors program, independent study, internships, liberal arts/career combination, student-designed major, study abroad. **Disability Services:** Special programs offered to physically disabled students include note-taking services, tutors. **Career Services:** alumni services, career/job search classes, career assessment, internships.

FACILITIES

Housing: Coed dorms, fraternity/sorority housing 60% of campus accessible to physically disabled. **Special Academic Facilities/Equipment:** Art museum, scanning electron microscope. **Computers:** 100% of classrooms, 100% of dorms, 100% of libraries, 100% of student union, 25% of common outdoor areas have wireless network access. Administrative functions (other than registration) can be performed online.

CAMPUS LIFE

Environment: Metropolis. **Activities:** Choral groups, dance, drama/theater, jazz band, literary magazine, music ensembles, musical theater, pep band, radio station, student government, student newspaper, student-run film society, yearbook, Campus Ministries, International Student Organization 57 registered organizations, 10 honor societies, 5 religious organizations. 4 fraternities, 3 sororities. **Athletics (Intercollegiate):** *Men:* baseball, basketball, cross-country, golf, lacrosse, soccer, tennis, track/field (outdoor). *Women:* basketball, cheerleading, cross-country, golf, lacrosse, soccer, tennis, track/field (outdoor), volleyball. **On-Campus Highlights:** Oglethorpe University Museum, Phillip Weltner Library, Conant Performing Arts Center, Hermance Stadium, New Residence Halls. **Environmental Initiatives:** New buildings are built according to LEED requiesmuts use of green cleaning chemicals recycling program on campus - student organized and student run

ADMISSIONS

Freshman Academic Profile: Average high school GPA 3.4. 25% in top 10% of high school class, 54% in top 25% of high school class, 81% in top 50% of high school class. 79% from public high schools. SAT Math middle 50% range 510-610. SAT Critical Reading middle 50% range 530-620. SAT Writing middle 50% range 500-600. ACT middle 50% range 22-26. Minimum paper TOEFL 550. **Basis for Candidate Selection:** *Very important factors considered include:* academic GPA, rigor of secondary school record, standardized test scores. *Important factors considered include:* Class rank, application essay, recommendation(s), extracurricular activities, interview, level of applicant's interest, volunteer work. *Other factors considered include:* alumni/ae relation, character/personal qualities, first generation, talent/ability, work experience. **Freshman Admission Requirements:** High school diploma is required and GED is accepted. *Academic units required:* 4 English, 3 mathematics, 2 science, 3 social studies. *Academic units recommended:* 4 English, 3 mathematics, 2 science, 3 social studies. **Freshman Admission Statistics:** 2,463 applied, 83% admitted, 14% enrolled. **Transfer Admission Requirements:** college transcript(s), statement of good standing from prior institution(s). Minimum college GPA of 2.8 required. Lowest grade transferable C. **General Admission Information:** Application Fee $40. Notification on a rolling basis, beginning on or about 12/1. Nonfall registration accepted. Admission may be deferred for a maximum of 1 year. Credit and/or placement offered for CEEB Advanced Placement tests.

COSTS AND FINANCIAL AID

Annual tuition $29,900. Room and board $10,800. Required fees $250. Average book expense $1,100. **Required Forms and Deadlines:** FAFSA, institution's own financial aid form. **Notification of Awards:** Applicants will be notified of awards on a rolling basis beginning 3/1. **Types of Aid:** *Need-based scholarships/grants:* Federal Pell, SEOG, state scholarships/grants, private scholarships, the school's own gift aid. *Loans:* Direct Subsidized Stafford, Direct Unsubsidized Stafford, Direct PLUS, Federal Perkins. **Student Employment:** Federal Work-Study Program available. Institutional employment available. Off-campus job opportunities are excellent. **Financial Aid Statistics:** 97% freshmen, 99% undergrads receive need-based scholarship or grant aid. 56% freshmen, 60% undergrads receive non-need-based scholarship or grant aid. 77% freshmen, 81% undergrads receive need-based self-help aid. 95% freshmen, 95% undergrads receive any aid. 88% undergrads borrow to pay for school. Average cumulative indebtedness $22,692. **Criteria for awarding institutional aid:** *Non-need-based:* academics, music/drama.

OHIO DOMINICAN UNIVERSITY

1216 Sunbury Road, Coumbus, OH 42319-2099
Phone: 614-251-4500 • **Financial Aid Phone:** 614-251-4778
E-mail: admissions@ohiodominican.edu • **CEEB Code:** 1131
Fax: 614-251-0156 • **Website:** www.ohiodominican.edu • **ACT Code:** 3256

This private school, affiliated with the Roman Catholic Church, was founded in 1911. It has a 75-acre campus.

RATINGS

Admissions Selectivity Rating: 77   **Fire Safety Rating:** 89   **Green Rating:** 69

STUDENTS AND FACULTY

Enrollment: 1,680. **Student Body:** 59% female, 41% male, 4% out-of-state, 1% international (9 countries represented). Asian 1%, African American 28%, Caucasian 63%, Hispanic 2%, Native American 0%.
Retention and Graduation: 57% freshmen return for sophomore year. 35% freshmen graduate within 4 years. 48% freshmen graduate within 6 years. **Faculty:** Student/faculty ratio 14:1. 71 full-time faculty, 90% hold PhDs, 7% are members of minority groups, 48% are women. 0% of classes are taught by teaching assistants.

ACADEMICS

Degrees: associate, bachelor's, certificate, master's, transfer associate. **Classes:** Most classes have 10–19 students. **Majors with Highest Enrollment:** business/commerce; psychology; secondary education and teaching. **Special Study Options:** Accelerated program, cross-registration, distance learning, double major, dual enrollment, exchange student program (domestic), honors program, independent study, internships, study abroad, teacher certification program. **Honors Programs:** The Honors Program is designed for high-ability, motivated students. Honors-designed courses will be offered to specifically challenge and engage students in the program. **Career Services:** Alumni network, alumni services, career/job search classes, career assessment, internships. Career Services highlights include Students gain vital practical experience by participating in internships.

FACILITIES

Housing: Coed dorms. 90% of campus accessible to physically disabled. **Special Academic Facilities/Equipment:** Wehrle Art Gallery. **Computers:** 90% of classrooms, 100% of libraries, 100% of dining areas, na% of student union, 5% of common outdoor areas have wireless network access. Students can register for classes online. Administrative functions (other than registration) can be performed online.

CAMPUS LIFE

Environment: Metropolis. **Activities:** Choral groups, concert band, dance, drama/theater, literary magazine, marching band, music ensembles, musical theater, pep band, radio station, student government, student newspaper, Campus Ministries, Model UN 40 registered organizations, 2 honor societies, 1 religious organizations. **Athletics (Intercollegiate):** *Men:* baseball, basketball, cross-country, football, golf, soccer, tennis. *Women:* basketball, cross-country, golf, soccer, softball, tennis, volleyball. **On-Campus Highlights:** Student Center opened Fall 2009, Panther Plaza, Alumni Hall, Wehrle Hall, The Underground in Fitzpatrick Hall. **Environmental Initiatives:** New buildings are to be LEED silver certified. Recycling program is now in place. Sustainability Council with representation from faculty, staff, and students.

ADMISSIONS

Freshman Academic Profile: Average high school GPA 3.2. 14% in top 10% of high school class, 31% in top 25% of high school class, 68% in top 50% of high school class. 86% from public high schools. SAT Math middle 50% range 450-520. SAT Critical Reading middle 50% range 430-560. ACT middle 50% range 19-24. Minimum web-based TOEFL 78. Minimum paper TOEFL 550. **Basis for Candidate Selection:** *Very important factors considered include:* academic GPA, rigor of secondary school record. *Important factors considered include:* standardized test scores. *Other factors considered include:* Class rank, application essay, recommendation(s), character/personal qualities, extracurricular activities, interview, talent/ability, volunteer work, work experience. **Freshman Admission Requirements:** High school diploma is required and GED is accepted. **Freshman Admission Statistics:** 1,821 applied, 61% admitted, 28% enrolled. **Transfer Admission Requirements:** college transcript(s), Lowest grade transferable C. **General Admission Information:** Application Fee $25. Notification on a rolling basis, beginning on or about 9/4. Nonfall registration accepted. Admission may be deferred for a maximum of 1-year. Credit and/or placement offered for CEEB Advanced Placement tests.

COSTS AND FINANCIAL AID

Annual tuition $24,116. Room and board $7,900. Required fees $500. Average book expense $1,000. **Required Forms and Deadlines:** FAFSA. **Notification of Awards:** Applicants will be notified of awards on a rolling basis beginning 3/1. **Types of Aid:** *Need-based scholarships/grants:* Federal Pell, SEOG, state scholarships/grants, private scholarships, the school's own gift aid. *Loans:* Subsidized Stafford, Unsubsidized Stafford, PLUS, Federal Perkins. **Student Employment:** Federal Work-Study Program available. Off-campus job opportunities are good. **Financial Aid Statistics:** 100% freshmen, 72% undergrads receive any aid. 59% undergrads borrow to pay for school. **Criteria for awarding institutional aid:** *Non-need-based:* academics, athletics, music/drama.

OHIO NORTHERN UNIVERSITY

525 South Main Street, Ada, OH 45810
Phone: 419-772-2260 • **Financial Aid Phone:** 419-772-2272
E-mail: admissions-ug@onu.edu • **CEEB Code:** 1591
Fax: 419-772-2821 • **Website:** www.onu.edu • **ACT Code:** 3310

This private school, affiliated with the Methodist Church, was founded in 1871. It has a 300-acre campus.

RATINGS
Admissions Selectivity Rating: 84   **Fire Safety Rating:** 61   **Green Rating:** 60*

STUDENTS AND FACULTY
Enrollment: 2,313. **Student Body:** 47% female, 53% male, % out-of-state, 2% international (17 countries represented). Asian 1%, African American 3%, Caucasian 89%, Hispanic 1%, Native American 0%.
Retention and Graduation: 84% freshmen return for sophomore year. 47% freshmen graduate within 4 years. 66% freshmen graduate within 6 years.
Faculty: Student/faculty ratio 12:1. 242 full-time faculty, 75% hold PhDs, 11% are members of minority groups, 36% are women. 0% of classes are taught by teaching assistants.

ACADEMICS
Degrees: bachelor's, post-bachelor's certificate. **Classes:** Most classes have 20–29 students. **Majors with Highest Enrollment:** biological and biomedical sciences, other; business, management, marketing, and related support services, other; engineering. **Special Study Options:** cooperative education program, distance learning, double major, dual enrollment, English as a Second Language (ESL), exchange student program (domestic), honors program, independent study, internships, liberal arts/career combination, study abroad, teacher certification program, Washington semester. **Honors Programs:** Honors Program consisits of a First-Year Honors Seminar and 3 additional Honors Seminars, 2 "contract" courses and a final Honors project. **Combined Degree Programs:** BA/JD, Pharm D. **Disability Services:** Special programs offered to physically disabled students include note-taking services, reader services, tape recorders, tutors. **Career Services:** Alumni network, alumni services, career/job search classes, career assessment, internships.

FACILITIES
Housing: Coed dorms, special housing for disabled students, men's dorms, special housing for international students, women's dorms, fraternity/sorority housing, apartments for married students, cooperative housing, apartments for single students, wellness housing, theme housing, Honors Residence Halls. 95% of campus accessible to physically disabled. **Special Academic Facilities/Equipment:** Art gallery, performing arts center, language lab, sports center, pharmacy museum. **Computers:** 100% of classrooms, 100% of dorms, 100% of libraries, 100% of dining areas, 100% of student union, have wireless network access. Students can register for classes online. Administrative functions (other than registration) can be performed online.

CAMPUS LIFE
Environment: Village. **Activities:** Choral groups, concert band, dance, drama/theater, jazz band, literary magazine, marching band, music ensembles, musical theater, opera, pep band, radio station, student government, student newspaper, symphony orchestra, television station, yearbook, Campus Ministries, International Student Organization, Model UN 200 registered organizations, 40 honor societies, 27 religious organizations. 6 fraternities, 4 sororities. **Athletics (Intercollegiate):** *Men:* baseball, basketball, cross-country, diving, football, golf, soccer, swimming, tennis, track/field (outdoor), track/field (indoor), wrestling. *Women:* basketball, cross-country, diving, golf, soccer, softball, swimming, tennis, track/field (outdoor), track/field (indoor), volleyball. **On-Campus Highlights:** ONU Sports Center, Northern on Main Coffee Cafe, Performing Arts Center, New Student Apartments, James F. Dicke Hall.

ADMISSIONS
Freshman Academic Profile: Average high school GPA 3.7. 50% in top 10% of high school class, 74% in top 25% of high school class, 91% in top 50% of high school class. SAT Math middle 50% range 560-670. SAT Critical Reading middle 50% range 520-630. SAT Writing middle 50% range 510-620. ACT middle 50% range 24-29. Minimum web-based TOEFL 54. Minimum paper TOEFL 480. **Basis for Candidate Selection:** *Very important factors considered include:* academic GPA, rigor of secondary school record, standardized test scores. *Important factors considered include:* Class rank, extracurricular activities, interview. *Other factors considered include:* application essay, recommendation(s), alumni/ae relation, character/personal qualities, first generation, level of applicant's interest, talent/ability, volunteer work. **Freshman Admission Requirements:** High school diploma is required and GED is accepted. *Academic units required:* 4 English, 2 mathematics, 2 science, (2 science labs), 2 social studies, 2 history, 4 academic electives. *Academic units recommended:* 4 English, 2 mathematics, 2 science, (2 science labs), 2 social studies, 2 history, 4 academic electives. **Freshman Admission Statistics:** 3,147 applied, 81% admitted, 24% enrolled. **Transfer Admission Requirements:** High school transcript, college transcript(s), statement of good standing from prior institution(s). Minimum college GPA of 2.0 required. Lowest grade transferable C. **General Admission Information:** Application Fee $30. Regular application deadline 8/15. Notification on a rolling basis, beginning on or about 7/15. Nonfall registration accepted. Admission may be deferred for a maximum of 1 year. Credit and/or placement offered for CEEB Advanced Placement tests.

COSTS AND FINANCIAL AID
Annual tuition $35,438. Room and board $9,808. Required fees $240. Average book expense $1,800. **Required Forms and Deadlines:** FAFSA. **Notification of Awards:** Applicants will be notified of awards on a rolling basis beginning 3/1. **Types of Aid:** *Need-based scholarships/grants:* Federal Pell, SEOG, state scholarships/grants, private scholarships, the school's own gift aid, External Scholarships. *Loans:* Subsidized Stafford, Unsubsidized Stafford, PLUS, Federal Perkins, college/university loans from institutional funds, Alternative Loans, Federal Health Professions Loan. **Student Employment:** Federal Work-Study Program available. Institutional employment available. Off-campus job opportunities are good. **Financial Aid Statistics:** 100% freshmen, 100% undergrads receive need-based scholarship or grant aid. 15% freshmen, 7% undergrads receive non-need-based scholarship or grant aid. 81% freshmen, 86% undergrads receive need-based self-help aid. 85% undergrads borrow to pay for school. Average cumulative indebtedness $48,886. **Criteria for awarding institutional aid:** *Non-need-based:* academics, alumni affiliation, art, leadership, minority status, music/drama, state/district residency.

THE OHIO STATE UNIVERSITY—COLUMBUS

Undergraduate Admissions 110 Enarson Hall, Columbus, OH 43210
Phone: 614-292-3980 • **Financial Aid Phone:** 614-292-0300
E-mail: askabuckeye@osu.edu • **CEEB Code:** 1592
Fax: 614-292-4818 • **Website:** www.osu.edu • **ACT Code:** 3312

This public school was founded in 1870. It has a 3469-acre campus.

RATINGS
Admissions Selectivity Rating: 88   **Fire Safety Rating:** 76   **Green Rating:** 94

STUDENTS AND FACULTY
Enrollment: 41,877. **Student Body:** 47% female, 53% male, 12% out-of-state, 7% international (111 countries represented). Asian 5%, African American 6%, Caucasian 74%, Hispanic 3%, Native American 0%.
Retention and Graduation: 92% freshmen return for sophomore year. 53% freshmen graduate within 4 years. 82% freshmen graduate within 6 years.
Faculty: Student/faculty ratio 19:1. 3477 full-time faculty, 99% hold PhDs, 22% are members of minority groups, 35% are women. 17% of classes are taught by teaching assistants.

ACADEMICS
Degrees: associate, bachelor's, certificate, doctoral, master's, post-bachelor's certificate, post-master's certificate. **Classes:** Most classes have 20–29 students. Most lab/discussion sessions have 20–29 students. **Majors with Highest Enrollment:** biology/biological sciences; finance; political science and government. **Special Study Options:** Accelerated program, cooperative education program, cross-registration, distance learning, double major, dual enrollment, English as a Second Language (ESL), exchange student program (domestic), honors program, independent study, internships, liberal arts/career combination, student-designed major, study abroad, teacher certification program, weekend college. **Honors Programs:** The University Honors Program is dedicated to promoting the intellectual and personal development of high-performing students. It strives to promote a more active and enriching relationship between Honors students and the University by connecting them with resources and opportunities that will encourage them to maximize their potential. The University Scholars Program enables talented and motivated students to be part of smaller, selective communnities within the larger university environment. Each of the fourteen programs focuses on a common theme or academic area of interest designed to foster learning and involvement. Scholars live together, attend classes together, and experience diverse opportunities outside the classroom.

Combined Degree Programs: BA/MD, BA/DDS. **Disability Services:** Special programs offered to physically disabled students include note-taking services, reader services, tape recorders, tutors. **Career Services:** Alumni network, alumni services, career/job search classes, career assessment, internships, regional alumni.

FACILITIES

Housing: Coed dorms, special housing for disabled students, special housing for international students, women's dorms, fraternity/sorority housing, apartments for married students, cooperative housing, apartments for single students, wellness housing, theme housing. 90% of campus accessible to physically disabled. **Special Academic Facilities/Equipment:** Wexner center for the Arts, zoology museum, geology museum, art and photography galleries, nuclear research reactor, electroscience lab, biomedical engineering center, cartoon art museum **Computers:** 100% of dorms, 90% of libraries, 100% of dining areas, 100% of student union, 4% of common outdoor areas have wireless network access. Students can register for classes online. Administrative functions (other than registration) can be performed online.

CAMPUS LIFE

Environment: Metropolis. **Activities:** Choral groups, dance, drama/theater, jazz band, literary magazine, marching band, music ensembles, musical theater, opera, pep band, radio station, student government, student newspaper, student-run film society, symphony orchestra, television station, yearbook, International Student Organization 950 registered organizations, 39 honor societies, 93 religious organizations. 42 fraternities, 25 sororities. **Athletics (Intercollegiate):** *Men:* baseball, basketball, cheerleading, cross-country, diving, fencing, football, golf, gymnastics, ice hockey, lacrosse, pistol, riflery, soccer, swimming, tennis, track/field (outdoor), track/field (indoor), volleyball, wrestling. *Women:* baseball, basketball, cheerleading, crew/rowing, cross-country, diving, fencing, field hockey, golf, gymnastics, ice hockey, lacrosse, pistol, riflery, soccer, softball, swimming, synchronized swimming, tennis, track/field (outdoor), track/field (indoor), volleyball. **On-Campus Highlights:** Hale Cultural Center, Chadwick Arboretum, Jack Nicklaus Golf Museum, Schottenstein Center and Value City Arena, Wexner Center for the Arts 0. **Environmental Initiatives:** Building Energy Auditing Program http://president.osu.edu/sustainability; iee.osu.edu; http://fod.osu.edu/afp/ All-In-One Campus Recycling System http://president. osu.edu/sustainability; iee.osu.edu; http://fod.osu.edu/afp/ Ohio State boasts a holistic approach to sustainability endeavors: in depth planning, programs for the physical environment and programs for the community. The 'One Ohio State Framework Plan' is the structure for guiding the ever improving university, of which, sustainability plays a major role. The Sustainability Plan, the Climate Action Plan and the Energy and Infrastructure Plan, key elements of the Framework Plan, serve as references for the forthcoming Integrated Energy and Environment Implementation Strategy. This strategy will provide direction for all energy and environment initiatives from development of university level policies to support for individual projects and programs. Existing plans come into action on Ohio State's campus through the university's aggressive building energy auditing program and expansive 'All-In-One' recycling program. The true reach of Ohio State's planning is seen through research, curriculum and engagement programs. Several research incubators, including the Institute for Energy and the Environment, champion sustainability innovation from professors and students alike. Ohio State also demonstrates a strong commitment to developing environmentally conscious students by offering sustainability focused degrees, concentrations and courses while providing strong support for its over two dozen sustainability oriented student groups.

ADMISSIONS

Freshman Academic Profile: 54% in top 10% of high school class, 89% in top 25% of high school class, 99% in top 50% of high school class. 85% from public high schools. SAT Math middle 50% range 610-710. SAT Critical Reading middle 50% range 540-650. SAT Writing middle 50% range 550-650. ACT middle 50% range 26-30. Minimum web-based TOEFL 79. Minimum paper TOEFL 550. **Basis for Candidate Selection:** *Very important factors considered include:* Class rank, academic GPA, rigor of secondary school record, standardized test scores. *Important factors considered include:* application essay, extracurricular activities, first generation, talent/ability, volunteer work, work experience. *Other factors considered include:* recommendation(s), character/personal qualities, geographical residence, racial/ethnic status, state residency. **Freshman Admission Requirements:** High school diploma is required and GED is accepted. *Academic units required:* 4 English, 3 mathematics, 2 science, (2 science labs), 2 foreign language, 2 social studies, 1 visual/performing arts, 1 academic electives. *Academic units recommended:* 4 English, 3 mathematics, 2 science, (2 science labs), 2 foreign language, 2 social studies, 1 visual/performing arts, 1 academic electives. **Freshman Admission Statistics:** 25,816 applied, 64% admitted, 44% enrolled. **Transfer Admission Requirements:** college transcript(s), minimum college GPA of 2.0 required. Lowest grade transferable C-. **General Admission Information:** Application Fee $40. Regular application deadline 2/1. Notification on a rolling basis, beginning on or about 12/1. Nonfall registration accepted. Credit and/or placement offered for CEEB Advanced Placement tests.

COSTS AND FINANCIAL AID

Room and board $10,370. Average book expense $1,248. **Required Forms and Deadlines:** FAFSA. **Notification of Awards:** Applicants will be notified of awards on or about 4/5. **Types of Aid:** *Need-based scholarships/grants:* Federal Pell, SEOG, state scholarships/grants, private scholarships, the school's own gift aid. *Loans:* Direct Subsidized Stafford, Direct Unsubsidized Stafford, Direct PLUS, Federal Perkins, Federal Nursing, college/university loans from institutional funds. **Student Employment:** Federal Work-Study Program available. Institutional employment available. Off-campus job opportunities are good. **Financial Aid Statistics:** 85% freshmen, 76% undergrads receive need-based scholarship or grant aid. 6% freshmen, 3% undergrads receive non-need-based scholarship or grant aid. 82% freshmen, 89% undergrads receive need-based self-help aid. 1% freshmen, 1% undergrads receive athletic scholarships. 84% freshmen, 79% undergrads receive any aid. 59% undergrads borrow to pay for school. Average cumulative indebtedness $26,409. **Criteria for awarding institutional aid:** *Non-need-based:* academics, alumni affiliation, art, athletics, job skills, leadership, minority status, music/drama, state/district residency.

THE OHIO STATE UNIVERSITY AT LIMA

4240 Campus Drive, Lima, OH 45804-3596
Phone: 419-995-8434 • **Financial Aid Phone:** 614-688-5712
E-mail: admissions@lima.ohio-state.edu • **CEEB Code:** 1541
Fax: 419-995-8483 • **Website:** www.lima.ohio-state.edu • **ACT Code:** 3312

This public school was founded in 1960. It has a 565-acre campus.

RATINGS

Admissions Selectivity Rating. 05   Fire Safety Rating: 60*   Green Rating: 60*

STUDENTS AND FACULTY

Enrollment: 1,021. **Student Body:** 55% female, 45% male, 0% international (1 countries represented). Asian 2%, African American 5%, Caucasian 87%, Hispanic 3%, Native American 0%.
Retention and Graduation: 62% freshmen return for sophomore year. 19% freshmen graduate within 4 years. 38% freshmen graduate within 6 years. **Faculty:** Student/faculty ratio 20:1. 39 full-time faculty, 97% hold PhDs, 18% are members of minority groups, 41% are women. 0% of classes are taught by teaching assistants

ACADEMICS

Degrees: associate, bachelor's, master's. **Classes:** Most classes have 20-29 students. Most lab/discussion sessions have 20-29 students. **Majors with Highest Enrollment:** biology/biological sciences; elementary education and teaching; psychology. **Special Study Options:** Accelerated program, cooperative education program, cross-registration, distance learning, double major, dual enrollment, English as a Second Language (ESL), exchange student program (domestic), honors program, independent study, internships, liberal arts/career combination, student-designed major, study abroad, teacher certification program, weekend college. **Honors Programs:** The University Honors Program is dedicated to promoting the intellectual and personal development of high-performing students. It strives to promote a more active and enriching relationship between Honors students and the University by connecting them with resources and opportunities that will encourage them to maximize their potential. The University Scholars Program enables talented and motivated students to be part of smaller, selective communities within the larger university environment. Each of the fourteen programs focuses on a common theme or academic area of interest designed to foster learning and involvement. Scholars live together, attend classes together, and experience diverse opportunities outside the classroom. **Disability Services:** Special programs offered to physically disabled students include note-taking services, reader services, tape recorders, tutors. **Career Services:** Alumni network, alumni services, career/job search classes, career assessment, internships, regional alumni.

FACILITIES

Housing: 100% of campus accessible to physically disabled. **Special Academic Facilities/Equipment:** OhioSeis seismological network: http://seismic.lima. ohio-state.edu/ Geological Museum Observatory. **Computers:** 75% of classrooms, 100% of libraries, 100% of dining areas, 100% of student union, 100% of common outdoor areas have wireless network access. Students can register for classes online. Administrative functions (other than registration) can be performed online.

CAMPUS LIFE

Environment: Rural. **Activities:** Choral groups, dance, drama/theater, musical theater, pep band, student government, student-run film society, Campus Ministries, International Student Organization 32 registered organizations, 1 honor societies, 2 religious organizations.

ADMISSIONS

Freshman Academic Profile: 8% in top 10% of high school class, 30% in top 25% of high school class, 69% in top 50% of high school class. 94% from public high schools. SAT Math middle 50% range 500-593. SAT Critical Reading middle 50% range 435-583. SAT Writing middle 50% range 418-563. ACT middle 50% range 20-25. Minimum web-based TOEFL 79. Minimum paper TOEFL 550. **Basis for Candidate Selection:** *Other factors considered include:* recommendation(s), rigor of secondary school record. **Freshman Admission Requirements:** *Academic units required:* 4 English, 3 mathematics, 2 science, (2 science labs), 2 foreign language, 2 social studies, 1 visual/performing arts, 1 academic electives. *Academic units recommended:* 4 English, 3 mathematics, 2 science, (2 science labs), 2 foreign language, 2 social studies, 1 visual/performing arts, 1 academic electives. **Freshman Admission Statistics:** 1,068 applied, 99% admitted, 40% enrolled. **Transfer Admission Requirements:** college transcript(s), minimum college GPA of 2.0 required. Lowest grade transferable C–. **General Admission Information:** Application Fee $40. Regular application deadline 7/1. Notification on a rolling basis, beginning on or about 12/1. Credit and/or placement offered for CEEB Advanced Placement tests.

COSTS AND FINANCIAL AID

Average book expense $1,602. **Required Forms and Deadlines:** FAFSA. **Notification of Awards:** Applicants will be notified of awards on or about 4/5. **Types of Aid:** *Need-based scholarships/grants:* Federal Pell, SEOG, state scholarships/grants, private scholarships, the school's own gift aid. *Loans:* Direct Subsidized Stafford, Direct Unsubsidized Stafford, Direct PLUS, Federal Perkins, Federal Nursing, college/university loans from institutional funds. **Student Employment:** Federal Work-Study Program available. Institutional employment available. Off-campus job opportunities are good. **Financial Aid Statistics:** 90% freshmen, 81% undergrads receive need-based scholarship or grant aid. 1% freshmen receive non-need-based scholarship or grant aid. 93% freshmen, 94% undergrads receive need-based self-help aid. 98% freshmen, 93% undergrads receive any aid. % undergrads borrow to pay for school. Average cumulative indebtedness. **Criteria for awarding institutional aid:** *Non-need-based:* academics, alumni affiliation, art, athletics, job skills, leadership, minority status, music/drama, state/district residency.

THE OHIO STATE UNIVERSITY AT MANSFIELD

1680 University Drive, Mansfield, OH 44906
Phone: 419-755-4011 • **Financial Aid Phone:** 614-292-0300
E-mail: admissions@mansfield.ohio-state.edu • **CEEB Code:** 744
Fax: • **Website:** www.mansfield.ohio-stae.edu • **ACT Code:** 3312

This public school was founded in 1958. It has a 640-acre campus.

RATINGS

Admissions Selectivity Rating: 65 **Fire Safety Rating:** 60* **Green Rating:** 66

STUDENTS AND FACULTY

Enrollment: 1,252. **Student Body:** 54% female, 46% male, 0% out-of-state, 0% international (3 countries represented). Asian 1%, African American 7%, Caucasian 87%, Hispanic 2%, Native American 0%.
Retention and Graduation: 71% freshmen return for sophomore year. 21% freshmen graduate within 4 years. 39% freshmen graduate within 6 years. 3% grads go on to further study within 1 year. 45% grads pursue medical degrees. **Faculty:** Student/faculty ratio :1. full-time faculty. 1% of classes are taught by teaching assistants.

ACADEMICS

Degrees: associate, bachelor's, master's. **Classes:** Most classes have 10–19 students. Most lab/discussion sessions have 40-49 students. **Special Study Options:** Accelerated program, cooperative education program, cross-registration, distance learning, double major, dual enrollment, English as a Second Language (ESL), exchange student program (domestic), honors program, independent study, internships, liberal arts/career combination, student-designed major, study abroad, teacher certification program, weekend college. **Honors Programs:** The University Honors Program is dedicated to promoting the intellectual and personal development of high-performing students. It strives to promote a more active and enriching relationship between Honors students and the University by connecting them with resources and opportunities that will encourage them to maximize their potential. The University Scholars Program enables talented and motivated students to be part of smaller, selective communities within the larger university environment. Each of the fourteen programs focuses on a common theme or academic area of interest designed to foster learning and involvement. Scholars live together, attend classes together, and experience diverse opportunities outside the classroom. **Combined Degree Programs:** BA/MD, BA/DDS. **Disability Services:** Special programs offered

to physically disabled students include note-taking services, reader services, tape recorders, tutors. **Career Services:** Alumni network, alumni services.

FACILITIES

Housing: special housing for disabled students, apartments for single students, wellness housing. 90% of campus accessible to physically disabled. **Computers:** 100% of classrooms, 100% of dorms, 100% of libraries, 100% of dining areas, 100% of student union, 50% of common outdoor areas have wireless network access. Students can register for classes online. Administrative functions (other than registration) can be performed online.

CAMPUS LIFE

Environment: Town. **Activities:** Choral groups, dance, drama/theater, student newspaper, student-run film society 16 registered organizations, 2 honor societies, 2 religious organizations. **Athletics (Intercollegiate):** *Men:* baseball, basketball, soccer. *Women:* basketball, cheerleading, volleyball. **Environmental Initiatives:** Pursuing HB7 Energy Savings Performance Contract Aggressive Recycling Program Wetlands reclamation, enhancements and outdoor labaratory.

ADMISSIONS

Freshman Academic Profile: 90% from public high schools. SAT Math middle 50% range 450-570. SAT Critical Reading middle 50% range 460-570. SAT Writing middle 50% range 430-545. Minimum web-based TOEFL 79. Minimum paper TOEFL 550. **Basis for Candidate Selection:** *Other factors considered include:* recommendation(s), rigor of secondary school record. **Freshman Admission Requirements:** *Academic units required:* 4 English, 3 mathematics, 2 science, (2 science labs), 2 foreign language, 2 social studies, 1 visual/performing arts, 1 academic electives. *Academic units recommended:* 4 English, 3 mathematics, 2 science, (2 science labs), 2 foreign language, 2 social studies, 1 visual/performing arts, 1 academic electives. **Freshman Admission Statistics:** 1,500 applied, 99% admitted, 34% enrolled. **Transfer Admission Requirements:** college transcript(s), minimum college GPA of 2.0 required. Lowest grade transferable C–. **General Admission Information:** Application Fee $40. Regular application deadline 7/1. Notification on a rolling basis, beginning on or about 12/1. Nonfall registration accepted. Credit and/or placement offered for CEEB Advanced Placement tests.

COSTS AND FINANCIAL AID

Required Forms and Deadlines: FAFSA. **Notification of Awards:** Applicants will be notified of awards on or about 4/5. **Types of Aid:** *Need-based scholarships/grants:* Federal Pell, SEOG, state scholarships/grants, private scholarships, the school's own gift aid. *Loans:* Direct Subsidized Stafford, Direct Unsubsidized Stafford, Direct PLUS, Federal Perkins, Federal Nursing, college/university loans from institutional funds. **Student Employment:** Federal Work-Study Program available. Institutional employment available. Off-campus job opportunities are good. **Criteria for awarding institutional aid:** *Non-need-based:* academics, alumni affiliation, art, athletics, job skills, leadership, minority status, music/drama, state/district residency.

THE OHIO STATE UNIVERSITY AT MARION

1465 Mount Vernon Avenue, Marion, OH 43302
Phone: 740-725-6337
E-mail: moreau.1@osu.edu • **CEEB Code:** 752
Fax: • **Website:** www.marion.ohio-state.edu • **ACT Code:** 3312

This public school was founded in 1957. It has a 188-acre campus.

RATINGS

Admissions Selectivity Rating: 65 **Fire Safety Rating:** 60* **Green Rating:** 60*

STUDENTS AND FACULTY

Enrollment: 1,397. **Student Body:** 53% female, 47% male, 0% out-of-state, 0% international (1 countries represented). Asian 4%, African American 10%, Caucasian 80%, Hispanic 2%, Native American 1%.
Retention and Graduation: 13% freshmen graduate within 4 years. 37% freshmen graduate within 6 years. 13% grads go on to further study within 1 year. 49% grads pursue medical degrees. **Faculty:** Student/faculty ratio :1. full-time faculty. 11% of classes are taught by teaching assistants.

ACADEMICS

Degrees: associate, bachelor's, master's. **Classes:** Most classes have 20–29 students. Most lab/discussion sessions have 20–29 students. **Special Study Options:** Accelerated program, cooperative education program, cross-registration, distance learning, double major, dual enrollment, English as a Second Language (ESL), exchange student program (domestic), honors program, independent study, internships, liberal arts/career combination, student-designed major, study abroad, teacher certification program, weekend college. **Honors Programs:** The University Honors Program is dedicated to promoting the intellectual and personal development of high-performing students. It strives to promote a more active and enriching relationship between Honors students and the University by connecting them with resources and opportunities that will encourage them to maximize their potential. The University Scholars Program enables talented and motivated students to be part of smaller, selective communnities within the larger university environment. Each of the fourteen programs focuses on a common theme or academic area of interest designed to foster learning and involvement. Scholars live together, attend classes together, and experience diverse opportunities outside the classroom. **Combined Degree Programs:** BA/MD, BA/DDS, BA/MEng. **Disability Services:** Special programs offered to physically disabled students include note-taking services, reader services, tape recorders, tutors. **Career Services:** Alumni network, alumni services, career/job search classes, career assessment, internships, regional alumni..

FACILITIES

Housing: 100% of campus accessible to physically disabled. **Special Academic Facilities/Equipment:** Kuhn Art Gallery. **Computers:** 100% of classrooms, 100% of libraries, have wireless network access. Students can register for classes online. Administrative functions (other than registration) can be performed online.

CAMPUS LIFE

Environment: Town. **Activities:** Choral groups, literary magazine, music ensembles, student government, Campus Ministries 33 registered organizations, 1 honor societies, 3 religious organizations. **Athletics (Intercollegiate):** *Men:* basketball, gymnastics, volleyball. *Women:* gymnastics.

ADMISSIONS

Freshman Academic Profile: 93% from public high schools. SAT Math middle 50% range 490-590. SAT Critical Reading middle 50% range 470-560. SAT Writing middle 50% range 430-550. Minimum web-based TOEFL 79. Minimum paper TOEFL 550. **Basis for Candidate Selection:** *Other factors considered include:* recommendation(s), rigor of secondary school record. **Freshman Admission Requirements:** *Academic units required:* 4 English, 3 mathematics, 2 science, (2 science labs), 2 foreign language, 2 social studies, 1 visual/performing arts, 1 academic electives. *Academic units recommended:* 4 English, 3 mathematics, 2 science, (2 science labs), 2 foreign language, 2 social studies, 1 visual/performing arts, 1 academic electives. **Freshman Admission Statistics:** 964 applied, 98% admitted. **Transfer Admission Requirements:** college transcript(s), minimum college GPA of 2.0 required. Lowest grade transferable C–. **General Admission Information:** Application Fee $40. Regular application deadline 7/1. Regular notification 12/1. Nonfall registration accepted. Credit and/or placement offered for CEEB Advanced Placement tests.

COSTS AND FINANCIAL AID

Required Forms and Deadlines: FAFSA. **Notification of Awards:** Applicants will be notified of awards on or about 4/5. **Types of Aid:** *Need-based scholarships/grants:* Federal Pell, SEOG, state scholarships/grants, private scholarships, the school's own gift aid. *Loans:* Direct Subsidized Stafford, Direct Unsubsidized Stafford, Direct PLUS, Federal Perkins, Federal Nursing, college/university loans from institutional funds. **Student Employment:** Federal Work-Study Program available. Institutional employment available. Off-campus job opportunities are good. **Criteria for awarding institutional aid:** *Non-need-based:* academics, alumni affiliation, art, athletics, job skills, leadership, minority status, music/drama, state/district residency.

THE OHIO STATE UNIVERSITY—NEWARK

1179 University Drive, Newark, OH 43055
Phone: 740-366-9333 • **Financial Aid Phone:** 614-292-0300
E-mail: • **CEEB Code:** 752
Fax: 740-364-9645 • **Website:** www.newark.ohio-state.edu • **ACT Code:** 3312

This public school was founded in 1957. It has a 106-acre campus.

RATINGS
Admissions Selectivity Rating: 65   **Fire Safety Rating:** 94   **Green Rating:** 60*

STUDENTS AND FACULTY
Enrollment: 2,230. **Student Body:** 53% female, 47% male, 0% out-of-state. Asian 3%, African American 14%, Caucasian 75%, Hispanic 2%, Native American 0%.
Retention and Graduation: 61% freshmen return for sophomore year. 14% freshmen graduate within 4 years. 37% freshmen graduate within 6 years.

Faculty: Student/faculty ratio 24:1. 50 full-time faculty, 98% hold PhDs, 18% are members of minority groups, 38% are women.

ACADEMICS
Degrees: associate, bachelor's, master's. **Classes:** Most classes have 20–29 students. Most lab/discussion sessions have 20–29 students. **Majors with Highest Enrollment:** elementary education and teaching; nursing/registered nurse (rn, asn, bsn, msn); psychology. **Special Study Options:** Accelerated program, cooperative education program, cross-registration, distance learning, double major, dual enrollment, English as a Second Language (ESL), exchange student program (domestic), honors program, independent study, internships, liberal arts/career combination, student-designed major, study abroad, teacher certification program, weekend college. **Honors Programs:** The University Honors Program is dedicated to promoting the intellectual and personal development of high-performing students. It strives to promote a more active and enriching relationship between Honors students and the University by connecting them with resources and opportunities that will encourage them to maximize their potential. The University Scholars Program enables talented and motivated students to be part of smaller, selective communnities within the larger university environment. Each of the fourteen programs focuses on a common theme or academic area of interest designed to foster learning and involvement. Scholars live together, attend classes together, and experience diverse opportunities outside the classroom. **Combined Degree Programs:** BA/MD, BA/DDS, BA/MEng. **Disability Services:** Special programs offered to physically disabled students include note-taking services, reader services, tape recorders, tutors. **Career Services:** career assessment, internships.

FACILITIES
Housing: Coed dorms, apartments for single students, wellness housing. 100% of campus accessible to physically disabled. **Computers:** 100% of classrooms, 100% of dorms, 100% of libraries, 100% of dining areas, 100% of student union, have wireless network access. Students can register for classes online. Administrative functions (other than registration) can be performed online.

CAMPUS LIFE
Environment: Village. **Activities:** Choral groups, drama/theater, literary magazine, music ensembles, student government, Campus Ministries 33 registered organizations, 2 honor societies, 2 religious organizations. **Athletics (Intercollegiate):** *Men:* basketball, golf, soccer. *Women:* basketball, soccer, softball, volleyball.

ADMISSIONS
Freshman Academic Profile: 4% in top 10% of high school class, 22% in top 25% of high school class, 59% in top 50% of high school class. 92% from public high schools. SAT Math middle 50% range 450-590. SAT Critical Reading middle 50% range 440-550. SAT Writing middle 50% range 418-523. ACT middle 50% range 19-24. **Basis for Candidate Selection:** *Other factors considered include:* recommendation(s), rigor of secondary school record. **Freshman Admission Requirements:** High school diploma is required and GED is accepted. *Academic units required:* 4 English, 3 mathematics, 2 science, (2 science labs), 2 foreign language, 2 social studies, 1 academic electives, 1 visual/performing arts. *Academic units recommended:* 4 English, 3 mathematics, 2 science, (2 science labs), 2 foreign language, 2 social studies, 1 academic electives, 1 visual/performing arts **Freshman Admission Statistics:** 2,764 applied, 99% admitted, 42% enrolled. **Transfer Admission Requirements:** college transcript(s), minimum college GPA of 2.0 required. Lowest grade transferable C–. **General Admission Information:** Application Fee $40. Regular application deadline 7/1. Notification on a rolling basis, beginning on or about 12/1. Nonfall registration accepted. Credit and/or placement offered for CEEB Advanced Placement tests.

COSTS AND FINANCIAL AID
Room and board $10,370. Average book expense $1,248. **Required Forms and Deadlines:** FAFSA. **Notification of Awards:** Applicants will be notified of awards on or about 4/5. **Types of Aid:** *Need-based scholarships/grants:* Federal Pell, SEOG, state scholarships/grants, private scholarships, the school's own gift aid. *Loans:* Direct Subsidized Stafford, Direct Unsubsidized Stafford, Direct PLUS, Federal Perkins, Federal Nursing, college/university loans from institutional funds. **Student Employment:** Federal Work-Study Program available. Institutional employment available. Off-campus job opportunities are good. **Financial Aid Statistics:** 100% freshmen, 93% undergrads receive need-based scholarship or grant aid. 91% freshmen, 91% undergrads receive need-based self-help aid. 100% freshmen, 93% undergrads receive any aid. **Criteria for awarding institutional aid:** *Non-need-based:* academics, alumni affiliation, art, athletics, job skills, leadership, minority status, music/drama, state/district residency.

OHIO UNIVERSITY—ATHENS

Best 378

120 Chubb Hall, Athens, OH 45701
Phone: 740-593-4100 • **Financial Aid Phone:** 740-593-4141
E-mail: admissions@ohio.edu • **CEEB Code:** 1593
Fax: 740-593-0560 • **Website:** www.ohio.edu • **ACT Code:** 3314

This public school was founded in 1804. It has a 1762-acre campus.

RATINGS
Admissions Selectivity Rating: 72   **Fire Safety Rating:** 70   **Green Rating:** 88

STUDENTS AND FACULTY
Enrollment: 22,573. **Student Body:** 60% female, 40% male, 13% out-of-state, 4% international (107 countries represented). Asian 1%, African American 5%, Caucasian 84%, Hispanic 2%, Native American 0%.
Retention and Graduation: 79% freshmen return for sophomore year. 44% freshmen graduate within 4 years. 64% freshmen graduate within 6 years. 27% grads go on to further study within 1 year. 6% grads pursue arts and sciences degrees. 1% grads pursue law degrees. 1% grads pursue business degrees. 1% grads pursue medical degrees. **Faculty:** Student/faculty ratio 19:1. 852 full-time faculty, 81% hold PhDs, 15% are members of minority groups, 39% are women. 16% of classes are taught by teaching assistants.

ACADEMICS
Degrees: associate, bachelor's, master's. **Classes:** Most classes have 10–19 students. Most lab/discussion sessions have 10–19 students. **Majors with Highest Enrollment:** biology/biological sciences; journalism; kinesiology and exercise science. **Special Study Options:** Accelerated program, cooperative education program, cross-registration, distance learning, double major, dual enrollment, English as a Second Language (ESL), external degree program, honors program, independent study, internships, liberal arts/career combination, student-designed major, study abroad, teacher certification program.
Honors Programs: Honors Tutorial College: The most selective of Ohio University's nine undergraduate colleges the Honor's Tutorial College is the oldest, largest, and most academically diverse degree-only degree-granting college in the country. Based on Oxbridge systems of tutorial education developed in England, it offers highly motivated, talented students the opportunity to receive a substantial part of their education through tutorials (one-on-one classes or small seminars). There are generally 220 students in the Honors Tutorial College spread over 26 programs of study. To preserve the tutorial experience, HTC enrolls about 60 new students each year, and admission is highly competitive.
Disability Services: Special programs offered to physically disabled students include reader services, tape recorders, tutors. **Career Services:** Alumni network, alumni services, career/job search classes, career assessment, regional alumni. Career Services highlights include Most internships/co-ops are through college departments as our office focuses on full-time positions.

FACILITIES
Housing: Coed dorms, special housing for disabled students, special housing for international students, women's dorms, apartments for married students. 89% of campus accessible to physically disabled. **Special Academic Facilities/Equipment:** Museum of American Art, Innovation Center, Nuclear Accelerator, Electron Microscope, Biotech Center, Kennedy Museum of Art, Trisolini Gallery, Art Gallery in Multicultural Programs, Voinovich Center, & Academic & Research Center. **Computers:** 100% of classrooms, 100% of dorms, 100% of libraries, 100% of dining areas, 100% of student union, 100% of common outdoor areas have wireless network access. Students can register for classes online. Administrative functions (other than registration) can be performed online.

CAMPUS LIFE
Environment: Village. **Activities:** Choral groups, concert band, dance, drama/theater, jazz band, literary magazine, marching band, music ensembles, musical theater, opera, pep band, radio station, student government, student newspaper, student-run film society, symphony orchestra, television station, yearbook, Campus Ministries, International Student Organization 323 registered organizations, 16 honor societies, 27 religious organizations. 17 fraternities, 12 sororities. **Athletics (Intercollegiate):** *Men:* baseball, basketball, cheerleading, cross-country, football, golf, wrestling. *Women:* basketball, cheerleading, cross-country, diving, field hockey, golf, soccer, softball, swimming, track/field (outdoor), volleyball.
On-Campus Highlights: Charles J. Ping Recreation Center, Kennedy Museum of Art, Templeton-Blackburn Memorial Auditorium, Convocation Center, Alden Library, 6. Baker University Center. **Environmental Initiatives:** Ohio University is currently expanding its invessel composting system, already the

largest at any college or university in the nation, to handle all organic waste at the university. The Presidential Advisory Council for Sustainability Planning prepared a Sustainability Plan that was approved by the university last summer, allowing the group to now develop a climate action plan aimed at providing guidance toward institutional climate neutrality. The OHIO Ecohouse demonstrates affordable green technology & sustainable living to inform, engage & inspire campus & community members.

ADMISSIONS
Freshman Academic Profile: Average high school GPA 3.4. 16% in top 10% of high school class, 42% in top 25% of high school class, 81% in top 50% of high school class. 83% from public high schools. SAT Math middle 50% range 490-610. SAT Critical Reading middle 50% range 480-590. SAT Writing middle 50% range 470-580. ACT middle 50% range 21-26. **Basis for Candidate Selection:** *Very important factors considered include:* academic GPA, rigor of secondary school record. *Important factors considered include:* Class rank, standardized test scores. *Other factors considered include:* application essay, recommendation(s), alumni/ae relation, character/personal qualities, extracurricular activities, talent/ability, volunteer work, work experience. **Freshman Admission Requirements:** High school diploma is required and GED is accepted. *Academic units required:* 4 English, 3 mathematics, 3 science, 2 foreign language, 3 social studies, 1 Visual or Performing Arts. 4 English, 3 mathematics, 3 science, 2 foreign language, 3 social studies, 1 Visual or Performing Arts **Freshman Admission Statistics:** 17,466 applied, 78% admitted, 29% enrolled. **Transfer Admission Requirements:** college transcript(s), minimum college GPA of 2.0 required. Lowest grade transferable C–. **General Admission Information:** Application Fee $45. Regular application deadline 2/1. Notification on a rolling basis, beginning on or about 9/15. Nonfall registration accepted. Admission may be deferred for a maximum of 12 months. Credit and/or placement offered for CEEB Advanced Placement tests.

COSTS AND FINANCIAL AID
Annual in-state tuition $10,282. Annual out-of-state tuition $19,246. Room and board $10,010. Average book expense $886. **Required Forms and Deadlines:** FAFSA. **Notification of Awards:** Applicants will be notified of awards on or about 4/1. **Types of Aid:** *Need-based scholarships/grants:* Federal Pell, SEOG, state scholarships/grants, private scholarships, the school's own gift aid. *Loans:* Direct Subsidized Stafford, Direct Unsubsidized Stafford, Direct PLUS, Federal Perkins, Institutional short term loans are repaid in 30-60 days. **Student Employment:** Federal Work-Study Program available. Institutional employment available. Highest amount earned per year from on-campus jobs $1,784. **Financial Aid Statistics:** 44% freshmen, 43% undergrads receive need-based scholarship or grant aid. 59% freshmen, 45% undergrads receive non-need-based scholarship or grant aid. 92% freshmen, 87% undergrads receive need-based self-help aid. 2% freshmen, 2% undergrads receive athletic scholarships. 86% freshmen, 61% undergrads receive any aid. 67% undergrads borrow to pay for school. Average cumulative indebtedness $27,060. **Criteria for awarding institutional aid:** *Non-need-based:* academics, art, athletics, minority status, music/drama, religious affiliation.

OHIO UNIVERSITY—SOUTHERN

Office of Enrollment Services, Ironton, OH 45638-2214
Phone: 740-533-4600
E-mail: askousc@mail.southern.ohiou.edu
Fax: 740-533-4632 • **Website:** www.southern.ohiou.edu

This public school was founded in 1956. It has a 9-acre campus.

RATINGS
Admissions Selectivity Rating: 61   **Fire Safety Rating:** 60*   **Green Rating:** 60*

ACADEMICS
Degrees: associate, bachelor's, master's, terminal associate, transfer associate.
Special Study Options: distance learning, double major, independent study, student-designed major, teacher certification program, weekend college.

FACILITIES
Computers: Students can register for classes online. Administrative functions (other than registration) can be performed online.

CAMPUS LIFE
Environment: Village. **Activities:** Choral groups, concert band, drama/theater, literary magazine, music ensembles, radio station, student government, television station.

ADMISSIONS
Transfer Admission Requirements: college transcript(s), Lowest grade transferable C. **General Admission Information:** Application Fee $20.

COSTS AND FINANCIAL AID

Annual in-state tuition $3,087. Annual out-of-state tuition $3,219. Average book expense $700. **Required Forms and Deadlines:** FAFSA. **Types of Aid:** *Need-based scholarships/grants:* Federal Pell, SEOG, state scholarships/grants, private scholarships, the school's own gift aid. *Loans:* Direct Subsidized Stafford, Direct Unsubsidized Stafford, Direct PLUS, Federal Perkins.

OHIO VALLEY UNIVERSITY

#1 Campus View Drive, Vienna, WV 26105
Phone: 304-865-6200
E-mail: admissions@ovu.edu
Fax: 304-865-6001 • **ACT Code:** 4548

This private school was founded in 1960. It has a 267-acre campus.

RATINGS
Admissions Selectivity Rating: 82 **Fire Safety Rating:** 67 **Green Rating:** 60*

STUDENTS AND FACULTY
Enrollment: 512. **Student Body:** 53% female, 47% male, 6% out-of-state, 7% international (12 countries represented). Asian 1%, African American 4%, Caucasian 86%, Hispanic 1%, Native American 1%.
Retention and Graduation: 72% freshmen return for sophomore year. **Faculty:** Student/faculty ratio 14:1. 26 full-time faculty, 38% hold PhDs, 38% are women. 0% of classes are taught by teaching assistants.

ACADEMICS
Degrees: associate, bachelor's. **Classes:** Most classes have fewer than 10 students. Most lab/discussion sessions have fewer than 10 students. **Majors with Highest Enrollment:** business/commerce; elementary education and teaching; psychology. **Special Study Options:** double major, English as a Second Language (ESL), study abroad, teacher certification program, weekend college, Adult Education: Degree completion program in Business Administration and Saturday college available. **Disability Services:** Special programs offered to physically disabled students include tutors.

FACILITIES
Housing: men's dorms, women's dorms, apartments for married students, apartments for single students. 50% of campus accessible to physically disabled.

CAMPUS LIFE
Environment: Village. **Activities:** Choral groups, concert band, drama/theater, jazz band, literary magazine, music ensembles, musical theater, student government, student newspaper, symphony orchestra, yearbook 10 registered organizations, 2 honor societies, 3 religious organizations. 4 fraternities, 4 sororities. **Athletics (Intercollegiate):** *Men:* baseball, basketball, cross-country, golf, soccer. *Women:* basketball, cheerleading, cross-country, soccer, softball, volleyball. **On-Campus Highlights:** New men and women's dorm, Memorial Fountain

ADMISSIONS
Freshman Academic Profile: Average high school GPA 3.0. 10% in top 10% of high school class, 32% in top 25% of high school class, 57% in top 50% of high school class. 95% from public high schools. SAT Math middle 50% range 540-460. SAT Critical Reading middle 50% range 600 510. ACT middle 50% range 23-17. Minimum paper TOEFL 500. **Basis for Candidate Selection:** *Very important factors considered include:* rigor of secondary school record, standardized test scores, character/personal qualities. *Important factors considered include:* recommendation(s), alumni/ae relation, talent/ability. *Other factors considered include:* Class rank, application essay, extracurricular activities, interview, religious affiliation/commitment. **Freshman Admission Requirements:** High school diploma is required and GED is accepted. **Freshman Admission Statistics:** 326 applied, 59% admitted, 50% enrolled. **Transfer Admission Requirements:** High school transcript, college transcript(s), standardized test scores, minimum college GPA of 2.0 required. Lowest grade transferable D. **General Admission Information:** Application Fee $20. Regular application deadline 8/20. Nonfall registration accepted. Admission may be deferred for a maximum of 1 year. Credit and/or placement offered for CEEB Advanced Placement tests.

COSTS AND FINANCIAL AID
Annual tuition $12,750. Room and board $5,850. Required fees $1,512. Average book expense $1,000. **Required Forms and Deadlines:** FAFSA. **Notification of Awards:** Applicants will be notified of awards on a rolling basis beginning 3/15. **Types of Aid:** *Need-based scholarships/grants:* Federal Pell, SEOG, state scholarships/grants, private scholarships, the school's own gift aid. *Loans:* Subsidized Stafford, Unsubsidized Stafford, PLUS, Federal Perkins, Signature student loans. **Student Employment:** Federal Work-Study Program available.

Institutional employment available. Highest amount earned per year from on-campus jobs $800. Off-campus job opportunities are good. **Financial Aid Statistics:** 100% freshmen, 86% undergrads receive need-based scholarship or grant aid. 11% freshmen, 12% undergrads receive non-need-based scholarship or grant aid. 89% freshmen, 87% undergrads receive need-based self-help aid. 16% freshmen, 12% undergrads receive athletic scholarships. 81% freshmen, 89% undergrads receive any aid. 80% undergrads borrow to pay for school. Average cumulative indebtedness. **Criteria for awarding institutional aid:** *Non-need-based:* academics, athletics, job skills, leadership, music/drama, religious affiliation.

OHIO WESLEYAN UNIVERSITY

61 South Sandusky Street, Delaware, OH 43015
Phone: 740-368-3020 • **Financial Aid Phone:** 740-368-3050
E-mail: owuadmit@owu.edu • **CEEB Code:** 1594
Fax: 740-368-3314 • **Website:** www.owu.edu • **ACT Code:** 3316

This private school, affiliated with the Methodist Church, was founded in 1842. It has a 200-acre campus.

RATINGS
Admissions Selectivity Rating: 81 **Fire Safety Rating:** 72 **Green Rating:** 84

STUDENTS AND FACULTY
Enrollment: 1,812. **Student Body:** 55% female, 45% male, 47% out-of-state, 8% international (41 countries represented). Asian 2%, African American 5%, Caucasian 75%, Hispanic 3%, Native American 0%.
Retention and Graduation: 83% freshmen return for sophomore year. 61% freshmen graduate within 4 years. 68% freshmen graduate within 6 years. 32% grads go on to further study within 1 year. 14% grads pursue arts and sciences degrees. 3% grads pursue law degrees. 2% grads pursue business degrees. 14% grads pursue medical degrees. **Faculty:** Student/faculty ratio 11:1. 142 full-time faculty, 100% hold PhDs, 6% are members of minority groups, 39% are women. 0% of classes are taught by teaching assistants.

ACADEMICS
Degrees: bachelor's. **Classes:** Most classes have 10–19 students. Most lab/discussion sessions have 10–19 students. **Majors with Highest Enrollment:** economics; pre-medicine/pre-medical studies; psychology. **Special Study Options:** double major, dual enrollment, exchange student program (domestic), honors program, independent study, internships, student-designed major, study abroad, teacher certification program. **Honors Programs:** The Leland F. and Helen Schubert Honors Program recognizes the most talented students among Ohio Wesleyan's community of scholars and challenges them through Honors Tutorials, Honors Seminars, and Honors Scholarships. **Combined Degree Programs:** Pre-Medical Tech, Pre-Optometry, Pre-Physical Therap. **Disability Services:** Special programs offered to physically disabled students include note-taking services, tape recorders, tutors. **Career Services:** Alumni network, alumni services, career assessment, Career Services highlights include Alumni Networking System.

FACILITIES
Housing: Coed dorms, special housing for international students, women's dorms, fraternity/sorority housing, apartments for single students, Small Living Units (SLUs) offer unique living opportunities to groups of 10-15 OWU students. In these theme houses, students create a small community centered on promoting specific interests and concerns. 60% of campus accessible to physically disabled. **Special Academic Facilities/Equipment:** Perkins and Student Observatories Scanning electron microscope Woltemade Center for Economics, Business and Entrepreneurship Nine inch refractor telescope Ross Art Museum Newly renovated fine arts facilities Newly renovated 150,000 square foot science center with state-of-the art classrooms and equipment. Wireless Internet in some areas. Fiber optic network **Computers:** 10% of classrooms, 100% of libraries, 10% of dining areas, 10% of common outdoor areas have wireless network access. Administrative functions (other than registration) can be performed online.

CAMPUS LIFE
Environment: Town. **Activities:** Choral groups, dance, drama/theater, jazz band, literary magazine, music ensembles, musical theater, opera, pep band, radio station, student government, student newspaper, symphony orchestra, yearbook, Campus Ministries, International Student Organization, Model UN

86 registered organizations, 26 honor societies, 10 religious organizations. 11 fraternities, 7 sororities. **Athletics (Intercollegiate):** *Men:* baseball, basketball, cross-country, diving, football, golf, lacrosse, sailing, soccer, swimming, tennis, track/field (outdoor), track/field (indoor). *Women:* basketball, cross-country, diving, field hockey, lacrosse, sailing, soccer, softball, swimming, tennis, track/field (outdoor), track/field (indoor), volleyball. **On-Campus Highlights:** Science Center, Hamilton Williams Campus Center, Selby Stadium, R.W. Corns Building, Sanborn Hall (music), Beeghly Library and Ross Museum are additional popular places on campus. **Environmental Initiatives:** Waste reduction Energy efficiency and conservation Water conservation.

ADMISSIONS

Freshman Academic Profile: Average high school GPA 3.5. 32% in top 10% of high school class, 63% in top 25% of high school class, 89% in top 50% of high school class. 77% from public high schools. SAT Math middle 50% range 520-640. SAT Critical Reading middle 50% range 510-620. SAT Writing middle 50% range 500-620. ACT middle 50% range 23-28. Minimum paper TOEFL 550. **Basis for Candidate Selection:** *Very important factors considered include:* application essay, academic GPA, recommendation(s), rigor of secondary school record, character/personal qualities, interview. *Important factors considered include:* Class rank, standardized test scores, extracurricular activities, talent/ability. *Other factors considered include:* alumni/ae relation, first generation, geographical residence, level of applicant's interest, racial/ethnic status, volunteer work, work experience. **Freshman Admission Requirements:** High school diploma is required and GED is accepted. *Academic units required:* 4 English, 3 mathematics, 3 science, 2 foreign language, 3 social studies. *Academic units recommended:* 4 English, 3 mathematics, 3 science, 2 foreign language, 3 social studies. **Freshman Admission Statistics:** 3,835 applied, 74% admitted, 19% enrolled. **Transfer Admission Requirements:** High school transcript, college transcript(s), essay or personal statement, statement of good standing from prior institution(s). Minimum college GPA of 2.5 required. Lowest grade transferable C–. **General Admission Information:** Application Fee $35. Early decision application deadline 12/1. Notification on a rolling basis, beginning on or about 10/1. Nonfall registration accepted. Admission may be deferred for a maximum of 2 years. Credit and/or placement offered for CEEB Advanced Placement tests.

COSTS AND FINANCIAL AID

Annual tuition $38,890. Room and board $10,310. Required fees $260. Average book expense $1,300. **Required Forms and Deadlines:** FAFSA, institution's own financial aid form. **Notification of Awards:** Applicants will be notified of awards on a rolling basis beginning 2/15. **Types of Aid:** *Need-based scholarships/grants:* Federal Pell, SEOG, state scholarships/grants, private scholarships, the school's own gift aid. *Loans:* Subsidized Stafford, Unsubsidized Stafford, PLUS, Federal Perkins, college/university loans from institutional funds. **Student Employment:** Federal Work-Study Program available. Institutional employment available. Highest amount earned per year from on-campus jobs $2,400. Off-campus job opportunities are excellent. **Financial Aid Statistics:** 100% freshmen, 99% undergrads receive need-based scholarship or grant aid. 28% freshmen, 25% undergrads receive non-need-based scholarship or grant aid. 77% freshmen, 80% undergrads receive need-based self-help aid. 97% freshmen, 97% undergrads receive any aid. 65% undergrads borrow to pay for school. Average cumulative indebtedness $30,900. **Criteria for awarding institutional aid:** *Non-need-based:* academics, alumni affiliation, art, leadership, minority status, music/drama, religious affiliation, state/district residency.

See page 1168.

OKLAHOMA BAPTIST UNIVERSITY

500 West University, Shawnee, OK 74804
Phone: 800-654-3285 • **Financial Aid Phone:** 405-878-2016
E-mail: admissions@okbu.edu • **CEEB Code:** 6541
Fax: 405-878-2046 • **Website:** www.okbu.edu • **ACT Code:** 3414

This private school, affiliated with the Southern Baptist Church, was founded in 1910. It has a 200-acre campus.

RATINGS

Admissions Selectivity Rating: 81   **Fire Safety Rating:** 73   **Green Rating:** 60*

STUDENTS AND FACULTY

Enrollment: 1,714. **Student Body:** 59% female, 41% male, 36% out-of-state, 3% international (25 countries represented). Asian 1%, African American 5%, Caucasian 69%, Hispanic 4%, Native American 6%.
Retention and Graduation: 75% freshmen return for sophomore year. 42% freshmen graduate within 4 years. **Faculty:** Student/faculty ratio 14:1. 117 full-time faculty, 68% hold PhDs, 41% are women. 0% of classes are taught by teaching assistants.

ACADEMICS

Degrees: associate, bachelor's, master's. **Classes:** Most classes have fewer than 10 students. Most lab/discussion sessions have fewer than 10 students. **Majors with Highest Enrollment:** bible/biblical studies; elementary education and teaching; nursing/registered nurse (rn, asn, bsn, msn). **Special Study Options:** cooperative education program, double major, English as a Second Language (ESL), exchange student program (domestic), honors program, independent study, internships, student-designed major, study abroad, teacher certification program, Semester-away programs available. **Honors Programs:** The OBU Honors Program is a curricular program designed to enhance the undergraduate study experience for certain exceptionally well-qualified students. Students completing all of the requirements for gradulation in the Honors Program earn the designation "with Honors" on their OBU diplomas. **Combined Degree Programs:** BA/MA. **Disability Services:** Special programs offered to physically disabled students include note-taking services, reader services, tape recorders, tutors. **Career Services:** Alumni network, regional alumni.

FACILITIES

Housing: men's dorms, women's dorms, apartments for married students, apartments for single students. 95% of campus accessible to physically disabled. **Special Academic Facilities/Equipment:** planetarium, Baptist Historical Society Archives, Avery T. Willis Center for Global Outreach **Computers:** Students can register for classes online. Administrative functions (other than registration) can be performed online.

CAMPUS LIFE

Environment: Town. **Activities:** Choral groups, concert band, drama/theater, jazz band, literary magazine, music ensembles, musical theater, opera, pep band, student government, student newspaper, symphony orchestra, television station, yearbook, Campus Ministries 80 registered organizations, 15 honor societies, 5 religious organizations. 5 fraternities, 5 sororities. **Athletics (Intercollegiate):** *Men:* baseball, basketball, cheerleading, cross-country, golf, soccer, tennis, track/field (outdoor), track/field (indoor). *Women:* basketball, cheerleading, cross-country, golf, soccer, softball, tennis, track/field (outdoor), track/field (indoor), volleyball. **On-Campus Highlights:** Geiger Center (Student Building), Recreation and Wellness Center, Noble Complex (athletics), Mabee Learning Center (Library), Intramural Field.

ADMISSIONS

Freshman Academic Profile: Average high school GPA 3.6. 33% in top 10% of high school class, 63% in top 25% of high school class, 88% in top 50% of high school class. 90% from public high schools. SAT Math middle 50% range 470-590. SAT Critical Reading middle 50% range 480-610. ACT middle 50% range 21-26. Minimum paper TOEFL 500. **Basis for Candidate Selection:** *Very important factors considered include:* academic GPA, rigor of secondary school record. *Important factors considered include:* Class rank, recommendation(s), standardized test scores, character/personal qualities, extracurricular activities. *Other factors considered include:* application essay, alumni/ae relation, geographical residence, interview, level of applicant's interest, religious affiliation/commitment, state residency, talent/ability, volunteer work, work experience. **Freshman Admission Requirements:** High school diploma is required and GED is accepted. **Freshman Admission Statistics:** 4,909 applied, 62% admitted, 17% enrolled. **Transfer Admission Requirements:** college transcript(s), minimum college GPA of 2.5 required. Lowest grade transferable D. **General Admission Information:** Application Fee $25. Regular application deadline 8/1. Regular notification 9/1. Nonfall registration accepted. Admission may be deferred for a maximum of one year. Credit and/or placement offered for CEEB Advanced Placement tests.

COSTS AND FINANCIAL AID

Annual tuition $18,894. Room and board $6,200. Required fees $1,902. Average book expense $1,200. **Required Forms and Deadlines:** FAFSA. **Notification of Awards:** Applicants will be notified of awards on or about 3/1. **Types of Aid:** *Need-based scholarships/grants:* Federal Pell, SEOG, state scholarships/grants, private scholarships, the school's own gift aid, Federal Nursing Scholarships. , ACG SMART. *Loans:* Subsidized Stafford, Unsubsidized Stafford, PLUS, Federal Perkins, college/university loans from institutional funds. **Student Employment:** Highest amount earned per year from on-campus jobs $3,200. **Financial Aid Statistics:** 80% freshmen, 83% undergrads receive need-based scholarship or grant aid. 100% freshmen, 97% undergrads receive non-need-based scholarship or grant aid. 25% freshmen, 70% undergrads receive need-based self-help aid. 26% freshmen, 23% undergrads receive athletic scholarships. 87% freshmen, 90% undergrads receive any aid. 58% undergrads borrow to pay for school. Average cumulative indebtedness $17,008. **Criteria for awarding institutional aid:** *Non-need-based:* academics, alumni affiliation, art, athletics, job skills, leadership, music/drama, religious affiliation.

OKLAHOMA CHRISTIAN UNIVERSITY

P.O. Box 11000, Oklahoma City, OK 73136-1100
Phone: 405-425-5050 • **Financial Aid Phone:** 405-425-5190
E-mail: info@oc.edu
Fax: 405-425-5069 • **Website:** www.oc.edu • **ACT Code:** 3415

This private school, affiliated with the Church of Christ Church, was founded in 1950. It has a 240-acre campus.

RATINGS
Admissions Selectivity Rating: 90   **Fire Safety Rating:** 69   **Green Rating:** 60*

STUDENTS AND FACULTY
Enrollment: 1,910. **Student Body:** 49% female, 51% male, 63% out-of-state, 11% international (38 countries represented). Asian 1%, African American 3%, Caucasian 63%, Hispanic 3%, Native American 4%.
Retention and Graduation: 73% freshmen return for sophomore year. 31% freshmen graduate within 4 years. 48% freshmen graduate within 6 years.
Faculty: Student/faculty ratio 13:1. 116 full-time faculty, 73% hold PhDs, 30% are women. 0% of classes are taught by teaching assistants.

ACADEMICS
Degrees: bachelor's, master's. **Classes:** Most classes have 10–19 students. **Majors with Highest Enrollment:** biology/biological sciences; elementary education and teaching; nursing/registered nurse (rn, asn, bsn, msn). **Special Study Options:** cross-registration, distance learning, double major, English as a Second Language (ESL), honors program, independent study, internships, student-designed major, study abroad, teacher certification program. **Career Services:** Alumni network, alumni services, career/job search classes, career assessment, internships Career Services highlights include They are government sponsored internships with DISA, FBI, CIA, homeland security and more. Also some companies, too many to list.

FACILITIES
Housing: special housing for disabled students, men's dorms, women's dorms, apartments for married students, apartments for single students. **Special Academic Facilities/Equipment:** Art Museum Art Gallery **Computers:** 100% of classrooms, 100% of dorms, 100% of libraries, 100% of dining areas, 100% of student union, 95% of common outdoor areas have wireless network access. Students can register for classes online. Administrative functions (other than registration) can be performed online.

CAMPUS LIFE
Environment: Metropolis. **Activities:** Choral groups, concert band, drama/theater, jazz band, literary magazine, music ensembles, musical theater, opera, pep band, radio station, student government, student newspaper, symphony orchestra, television station, yearbook, Campus Ministries, International Student Organization 20 registered organizations, 5 honor societies, 2 religious organizations. 6 fraternities, 6 sororities. **Athletics (Intercollegiate):** *Men:* baseball, basketball, cross-country, golf, soccer, tennis, track/field (outdoor). *Women:* basketball, cheerleading, cross-country, soccer, softball, tennis, track/field (outdoor). **On-Campus Highlights:** Gaylord University Center, University House Commons, Lawson Commons, Payne Athletic & Fitness Center, Mabee Learning Center. **Environmental Initiatives:** Trayless Cafeteria

ADMISSIONS
Freshman Academic Profile: Average high school GPA 3.6. 30% in top 10% of high school class, 54% in top 25% of high school class, 80% in top 50% of high school class. SAT Math middle 50% range 470-640. SAT Critical Reading middle 50% range 440-620. SAT Writing middle 50% range 470-600. ACT middle 50% range 21-28. Minimum web-based TOEFL 61. Minimum paper TOEFL 500. **Basis for Candidate Selection:** *Other factors considered include:* Class rank, academic GPA, recommendation(s), rigor of secondary school record, standardized test scores, character/personal qualities, extracurricular activities, interview, talent/ability, volunteer work. **Freshman Admission Requirements:** High school diploma is required and GED is accepted. **Freshman Admission Statistics:** 2,156 applied, 45% admitted, 47% enrolled. **Transfer Admission Requirements:** High school transcript, college transcript(s), standardized test scores, statement of good standing from prior institution(s). Lowest grade transferable D. **General Admission Information:** Application Fee $25. Notification on a rolling basis, beginning on or about 9/1. Nonfall registration accepted. Admission may be deferred for a maximum of 1 year. Credit offered for CEEB Advanced Placement tests.

COSTS AND FINANCIAL AID
Annual tuition $18,800. Room and board $6,775. Average book expense $1,000. **Required Forms and Deadlines:** FAFSA. **Notification of Awards:** Applicants will be notified of awards on a rolling basis beginning 2/2. **Types of Aid:** *Need-based scholarships/grants:* Federal Pell, SEOG, state scholarships/grants, private scholarships, the school's own gift aid. *Loans:* Subsidized Stafford, Unsubsidized Stafford, PLUS, Federal Perkins. **Student Employment:** Federal Work-Study Program available. Institutional employment available. Highest amount earned per year from on-campus jobs $9,905. Off-campus job opportunities are excellent. **Financial Aid Statistics:** 58% freshmen, 58% undergrads receive need-based scholarship or grant aid. 82% freshmen, 77% undergrads receive non-need-based scholarship or grant aid. 60% freshmen, 42% undergrads receive need-based self-help aid. 9% freshmen, 9% undergrads receive athletic scholarships. 100% freshmen, 98% undergrads receive any aid. 65% undergrads borrow to pay for school. Average cumulative indebtedness $29,389. **Criteria for awarding institutional aid:** *Non-need-based:* academics, alumni affiliation, art, athletics, leadership, music/drama.

OKLAHOMA CITY UNIVERSITY

2501 North Blackwelder, Oklahoma City, OK 73106
Phone: 405-208-5050 • **Financial Aid Phone:** 405-208-5211
E-mail: uadmission@okcu.edu • **CEEB Code:** 6543
Fax: 405-208-5264 • **Website:** www.okcu.edu • **ACT Code:** 3416

This private school, affiliated with the Methodist Church, was founded in 1904. It has a 78-acre campus.

RATINGS
Admissions Selectivity Rating: 77   **Fire Safety Rating:** 88   **Green Rating:** 68

STUDENTS AND FACULTY
Enrollment: 2,227. **Student Body:** 63% female, 37% male, 42% out-of-state, 16% international (57 countries represented). Asian 2%, African American 7%, Caucasian 58%, Hispanic 6%, Native American 3%.
Retention and Graduation: 75% freshmen return for sophomore year. 42% freshmen graduate within 4 years. 60% freshmen graduate within 6 years.
Faculty: Student/faculty ratio 11:1. 198 full-time faculty, 80% hold PhDs, 17% are members of minority groups, 47% are women. 0% of classes are taught by teaching assistants.

ACADEMICS
Degrees: bachelor's, master's. **Classes:** Most classes have 10–19 students. Most lab/discussion sessions have fewer than 10 students. **Majors with Highest Enrollment:** biology/biological sciences; business/commerce; dance. **Special Study Options:** Accelerated program, cooperative education program, distance learning, double major, dual enrollment, English as a Second Language (ESL), exchange student program (domestic), external degree program, honors program, independent study, internships, student-designed major, study abroad, teacher certification program. **Honors Programs:** University Honors Program: The mission of the University Honors program is to provide an enhanced learning environment for academically gifted undergraduate students. Each new class of Honors students at OCU will be a special community of scholars. Students will have the opportunity to become acquainted with one another and the Honors program in the Honors Colloquium, a course required for all new honors students during their first semester in the program. Honors students will have the opportunities to meet with visiting scholars and participate in special events. As part of a network of Honors Programs through the National Collegiate Honors Council and the Great Plains Honors Council, students may present research at national and regional honors conferences and participate in exciting summer and semester programs. **Combined Degree Programs:** BA/JD, MBA/JD. **Disability Services:** Special programs offered to physically disabled students include reader services, tape recorders, tutors. **Career Services:** Alumni network, alumni services, career/job search classes, career assessment, internships, regional alumni. Career Services highlights include Career Fairs hosting over 200+ employers on campus.

FACILITIES
Housing: Coed dorms, special housing for disabled students, men's dorms, women's dorms, fraternity/sorority housing, apartments for married students, apartments for single students, Learning Communities. 96% of campus accessible to physically disabled. **Special Academic Facilities/Equipment:** Art museum, audiovisual center, language lab. **Computers:** 100% of classrooms, 100% of dorms, 100% of libraries, 100% of dining areas, 100% of student union, 90% of common outdoor areas have wireless network access. Students can register for classes online. Administrative functions (other than registration) can be performed online.

CAMPUS LIFE
Environment: Metropolis. **Activities:** Choral groups, concert band, dance, drama/theater, jazz band, literary magazine, music ensembles, musical theater, opera, pep band, student government, student newspaper, symphony orchestra, television station, yearbook, Campus Ministries, International Student Organi-

zation 64 registered organizations, 14 honor societies, 6 religious organizations. 2 fraternities, 4 sororities. **Athletics (Intercollegiate):** *Men:* baseball, basketball, cheerleading, crew/rowing, golf, soccer, track/field (outdoor), wrestling. *Women:* basketball, cheerleading, crew/rowing, golf, soccer, softball, track/field (outdoor), volleyball, wrestling. **On-Campus Highlights:** Tom and Brenda McDaniel Univ Center, Henry J Freede Wellness and Activity Center, Meinders' School of Business, Walker Center for Arts and Sciences, Norick Art Center. **Environmental Initiatives:** Computer recycling program, community garden Purchasing maximum % of wind power allowable by energy supplying and trading company. Install sprinkler system on well system saving city water.

ADMISSIONS

Freshman Academic Profile: Average high school GPA 3.6. 31% in top 10% of high school class, 67% in top 25% of high school class, 88% in top 50% of high school class. 87% from public high schools. SAT Math middle 50% range 510-620. SAT Critical Reading middle 50% range 510-630. SAT Writing middle 50% range 510-600. ACT middle 50% range 23-28. Minimum paper TOEFL 550. **Basis for Candidate Selection:** *Very important factors considered include:* Class rank, application essay, academic GPA, recommendation(s), standardized test scores. *Important factors considered include:* rigor of secondary school record, extracurricular activities. *Other factors considered include:* character/personal qualities, talent/ability, volunteer work, work experience. **Freshman Admission Requirements:** High school diploma is required and GED is accepted. *Academic units required:* 4 English, 3 mathematics, 3 science, (1 science labs), 2 foreign language, 3 social studies, 3 history. 4 English, 3 mathematics, 3 science, (1 science labs), 2 foreign language, 3 social studies, 3 history. **Freshman Admission Statistics:** 1,171 applied, 74% admitted, 38% enrolled. **Transfer Admission Requirements:** college transcript(s), essay or personal statement, statement of good standing from prior institution(s). Minimum college GPA of 2.0 required. Lowest grade transferable C–. **General Admission Information:** Application Fee $40. Regular application deadline 8/21. Notification on a rolling basis, beginning on or about 10/15. Nonfall registration accepted. Admission may be deferred for a maximum of 1 year. Credit and/or placement offered for CEEB Advanced Placement tests.

COSTS AND FINANCIAL AID

Annual tuition $24,740. Room and board $9,170. Required fees $3,450. Average book expense $1,500. **Required Forms and Deadlines:** FAFSA, institution's own financial aid form, tax returns if selected for verification. **Notification of Awards:** Applicants will be notified of awards on a rolling basis beginning 2/20. **Types of Aid:** *Need-based scholarships/grants:* Federal Pell, SEOG, state scholarships/grants, private scholarships, the school's own gift aid, United Negro College Fund, Native American Grants. *Loans:* Subsidized Stafford, Unsubsidized Stafford, PLUS, Federal Perkins. **Student Employment:** Federal Work-Study Program available. Institutional employment available. Highest amount earned per year from on-campus jobs $10,800. Off-campus job opportunities are good. **Financial Aid Statistics:** 95% freshmen, 98% undergrads receive need-based scholarship or grant aid. 70% freshmen, 19% undergrads receive non-need-based scholarship or grant aid. 28% freshmen, 28% undergrads receive need-based self-help aid. 10% freshmen, 8% undergrads receive athletic scholarships. 97% freshmen, 86% undergrads receive any aid. 50% undergrads borrow to pay for school. Average cumulative indebtedness $18,615. **Criteria for awarding institutional aid:** *Non-need-based:* academics, alumni affiliation, art, athletics, job skills, leadership, music/drama, religious affiliation, state/district residency.

OKLAHOMA STATE UNIVERSITY

219 Student Union, Stillwater, OK 74078
Phone: 405-744-5358 • **Financial Aid Phone:** 405-744-6604
E-mail: admissions@okstate.edu • **CEEB Code:** 6546
Fax: 405-744-7092 • **Website:** osu.okstate.edu/welcome/ • **ACT Code:** 3424

This public school was founded in 1890. It has a 840-acre campus.

RATINGS

Admissions Selectivity Rating: 74   **Fire Safety Rating:** 76   **Green Rating:** 69

STUDENTS AND FACULTY

Enrollment: 19,912. **Student Body:** 48% female, 52% male, 24% out-of-state, 2% international (108 countries represented). Asian 1%, African American 5%, Caucasian 73%, Hispanic 4%, Native American 6%. **Retention and Graduation:** 79% freshmen return for sophomore year. 35% freshmen graduate within 4 years. 62% freshmen graduate within 6 years. **Faculty:** Student/faculty ratio 20:1. 1029 full-time faculty, 91% hold PhDs, 12% are members of minority groups, 33% are women. 11% of classes are taught by teaching assistants.

ACADEMICS

Degrees: bachelor's, master's, post-bachelor's certificate, post-master's certificate. **Classes:** Most classes have 10–19 students. Most lab/discussion sessions have 10–19 students. **Special Study Options:** Accelerated program, cross-registration, distance learning, double major, dual enrollment, English as a Second Language (ESL), exchange student program (domestic), honors program, independent study, internships, student-designed major, study abroad, teacher certification program. **Combined Degree Programs:** BS/MS Accounting. **Disability Services:** Special programs offered to physically disabled students include note-taking services, reader services, tape recorders, tutors. **Career Services:** Alumni network, alumni services, career/job search classes, career assessment, internships, regional alumni. Career Services highlights include Our Entrepreneurship Empowerment in South Africa (EESA) Program involves taking 20 OSU students, pairing them with 20 South African students, and spending six weeks working with a group of historically disadvantaged, township-based entrepreneurs helping them growth their businesses. The students are taught and coached by three of our entrepreneurship faculty members. Over the years we have assisted over 120 entrepreneurs in meaningful ways.

FACILITIES

Housing: Coed dorms, special housing for disabled students, men's dorms, women's dorms, fraternity/sorority housing, apartments for married students, apartments for single students, wellness housing, theme housing, 97% of campus accessible to physically disabled. **Special Academic Facilities/Equipment:** Art, history, and natural science museums, wellness center, laser research center. **Computers:** 80% of classrooms, 80% of dorms, 100% of libraries, 80% of student union, have wireless network access. Students can register for classes online. Administrative functions (other than registration) can be performed online.

CAMPUS LIFE

Environment: Town. **Activities:** Choral groups, concert band, dance, drama/theater, jazz band, literary magazine, marching band, music ensembles, musical theater, opera, pep band, radio station, student government, student newspaper, symphony orchestra, television station, Campus Ministries, International Student Organization 300 registered organizations. **Athletics (Intercollegiate):** *Men:* baseball, basketball, cross-country, football, golf, tennis, track/field (outdoor), wrestling. *Women:* basketball, cross-country, equestrian sports, golf, soccer, softball, tennis, track/field (outdoor). **On-Campus Highlights:** Colvin Recreational Center, Gallagher/Iba Arena and Museum, Student Union Building, Library, ConocoPhillips Alumni Center. **Environmental Initiatives:** Energy conservation - turning off lights, computers, monitors, speakers, printers, etc when not in use. Reducing thermostat settings during winter and turning it up during summer.

ADMISSIONS

Freshman Academic Profile: Average high school GPA 3.5. 28% in top 10% of high school class, 58% in top 25% of high school class, 86% in top 50% of high school class. % from public high schools. SAT Math middle 50% range 510-620. SAT Critical Reading middle 50% range 490-590. ACT middle 50% range 22-28. Minimum web-based TOEFL 61. Minimum paper TOEFL 500. **Basis for Candidate Selection:** *Very important factors considered include:* Class rank, academic GPA, standardized test scores. *Other factors considered include:* application essay, recommendation(s), rigor of secondary school record, character/personal qualities, extracurricular activities, interview, talent/ability. **Freshman Admission Requirements:** High school diploma is required and GED is accepted. *Academic units required:* 4 English, 3 mathematics, 2 science, (2 science labs), 2 social studies, 1 history, 3 academic electives. *Academic units recommended:* 4 English, 3 mathematics, 2 science, (2 science labs), 2 social studies, 1 history, 3 academic electives. **Freshman Admission Statistics:** 12,056 applied, 78% admitted, 46% enrolled. **Transfer Admission Requirements:** college transcript(s), minimum college GPA of 2.25 required. Lowest grade transferable D. **General Admission Information:** Application Fee $40. Nonfall registration accepted. Admission may be deferred for a maximum of military. Credit offered for CEEB Advanced Placement tests.

COSTS AND FINANCIAL AID

Annual in-state tuition $4,425. Annual out-of-state tuition $16,440. Room and board $6,868. Required fees $3,017. Average book expense $1,080. **Required Forms and Deadlines:** FAFSACombined Admissions and Scholarship Application. **Notification of Awards:** Applicants will be notified of awards on a rolling basis beginning 10/1. **Types of Aid:** *Need-based scholarships/grants:* Federal Pell, SEOG, state scholarships/grants, private scholarships, the school's own gift aid, TEACH, ACG, SMART. *Loans:* Direct Subsidized Stafford, Direct Unsubsidized Stafford, Direct PLUS, Federal Perkins. **Student Employment:** Institutional employment available. Off-campus job opportunities are good. **Financial Aid Statistics:** 77% freshmen, 78% undergrads receive need-based scholarship or grant aid. 9% freshmen, 6% undergrads receive non-need-based scholarship or grant aid. 61% freshmen, 70% undergrads receive need-based self-help aid. 2% freshmen, 2% undergrads receive athletic scholarships. 52%

undergrads borrow to pay for school. Average cumulative indebtedness $22,736. **Criteria for awarding institutional aid:** *Non-need-based:* academics, alumni affiliation, art, athletics, leadership, minority status, music/drama, state/district residency.

OKLAHOMA WESLEYAN UNIVERSITY

2201 Silver Lake Road, Bartlesville, OK 74006
Phone: 918-335-6219
E-mail: admissions@okwu.edu • **CEEB Code:** 6135
Fax: 918-335-6229 • **Website:** www.okwu.edu • **ACT Code:** 3387

This private school was founded in 1972. It has a 127-acre campus.

RATINGS
Admissions Selectivity Rating: 77   **Fire Safety Rating:** 60*   **Green Rating:** 60*

STUDENTS AND FACULTY
Student Body: 43% out-of-state, (12 countries represented).
Retention and Graduation: 10% grads go on to further study within 1 year. 2% grads pursue arts and sciences degrees. 2% grads pursue law degrees. 5% grads pursue business degrees. 2% grads pursue medical degrees. **Faculty:** 0% of classes are taught by teaching assistants.

ACADEMICS
Degrees: associate, bachelor's, certificate, master's. **Special Study Options:** double major, English as a Second Language (ESL), independent study, internships, student-designed major, study abroad. **Disability Services:** Special programs offered to physically disabled students include tutors.

FACILITIES
Housing: men's dorms, women's dorms. 70% of campus accessible to physically disabled. **Special Academic Facilities/Equipment:** LaQuinta Mansion. **Computers:** Undergraduates are required to own a computer.

CAMPUS LIFE
Environment: Village. **Activities:** Choral groups, music ensembles, pep band, student government, student newspaper, yearbook 10 registered organizations, 2 honor societies, 3 religious organizations. **Athletics (Intercollegiate):** *Men:* baseball, basketball, cheerleading, golf, soccer. *Women:* basketball, cheerleading, soccer, softball, volleyball.

ADMISSIONS
Freshman Academic Profile: 90% from public high schools. ACT middle 50% range 19-25. Minimum paper TOEFL 500. **Basis for Candidate Selection:** *Very important factors considered include:* Class rank, recommendation(s), rigor of secondary school record, standardized test scores, character/personal qualities, religious affiliation/commitment, state residency. *Important factors considered include:* alumni/ae relation, geographical residence, interview, racial/ethnic status. *Other factors considered include:* extracurricular activities, talent/ability. **Freshman Admission Requirements:** High school diploma is required and GED is accepted. *Academic units required:* 4 English, 2 mathematics, 1 science, (1 science labs), 1 social studies, 1 history, 6 academic electives. 4 English, 2 mathematics, 1 science, (1 science labs), 1 social studies, 1 history, 6 academic electives. **Freshman Admission Statistics:** 317 applied, 60% admitted, 62% enrolled. **Transfer Admission Requirements:** High school transcript, college transcript(s), essay or personal statement, statement of good standing from prior institution(s). Minimum college GPA of 2.0 required. Lowest grade transferable D. **General Admission Information:** Application Fee $25. Nonfall registration accepted. Admission may be deferred for a maximum of 12. Credit and/or placement offered for CEEB Advanced Placement tests.

COSTS AND FINANCIAL AID
Annual tuition $8,200. Room and board $3,800. Required fees $500. **Required Forms and Deadlines: Types of Aid:** *Need-based scholarships/grants:* Federal Pell, SEOG, state scholarships/grants, private scholarships, the school's own gift aid. *Loans:* Direct Subsidized Stafford, Direct Unsubsidized Stafford, Direct PLUS, Federal Perkins. **Student Employment:** Federal Work-Study Program available. Institutional employment available. Highest amount earned per year from on-campus jobs $1,913. Off-campus job opportunities are excellent.

OLD DOMINION UNIVERSITY

108 Rollins Hall, Norfolk, VA 23529-0050
Phone: 757-683-3685 • **Financial Aid Phone:** 757-683-3683
E-mail: admissions@odu.edu • **CEEB Code:** 5126
Fax: 757-683-3255 • **Website:** www.odu.edu • **ACT Code:**

This public school was founded in 1930. It has a 188-acre campus.

RATINGS
Admissions Selectivity Rating: 73   **Fire Safety Rating:** 75   **Green Rating:** 84

STUDENTS AND FACULTY
Enrollment: 19,303. **Student Body:** 54% female, 46% male, 7% out-of-state, 1% international (131 countries represented). Asian 4%, African American 25%, Caucasian 54%, Hispanic 6%, Native American 0%.
Retention and Graduation: 80% freshmen return for sophomore year. 25% freshmen graduate within 4 years. 49% freshmen graduate within 6 years.
Faculty: Student/faculty ratio 21:1. 757 full-time faculty, 78% hold PhDs, 20% are members of minority groups, 41% are women.

ACADEMICS
Degrees: bachelor's, doctoral, master's, post-master's certificate. **Classes:** Most classes have 10–19 students. Most lab/discussion sessions have 20–29 students. **Majors with Highest Enrollment:** communication, journalism, and related programs, other; mental and social health services and allied professions, other; multi-/interdisciplinary studies, other. **Special Study Options:** Accelerated program, cooperative education program, cross-registration, distance learning, double major, dual enrollment, English as a Second Language (ESL), exchange student program (domestic), honors program, independent study, internships, liberal arts/career combination, student-designed major, study abroad, teacher certification program, weekend college, Experiential Learning. **Honors Programs:** Honors College. The Honors College was established to further the University's commitment to excellence in education. With an emphasis on teaching, innovation, and small classes, the college offers the experience of a small liberal arts college within the framework of the large university. The four-year experience offers specially designed, low-enrollment courses to honors students and selected juniors and seniors. Several out-of-class and off-campus experiences are often part of these courses '–at no extra cost to students. A one credit honors tutorial is required in the junior year, and a senior honors colloquium is taken in the final year of study. All Honors College students are awarded an annual honors stipend. **Combined Degree Programs:** BA/MD, BA/JD, BA/MA, BA/DDS, BA/MEng, 5-year Master's degree program in education. **Disability Services:** Special programs offered to physically disabled students include note-taking services, reader services, tutors. **Career Services:** Alumni network, alumni services, career/job search classes, career assessment, internships, regional alumni. Career Services highlights include The Career Advantage Program is a comprehensive series of programs, services, professional seminars, appointments, and work assignments geared toward helping you determine your future career. The cornerstone of the Career Advantage Program is the Guaranteed Practicum. All undergraduates are guaranteed a practical experience, or classroom experience working in a "real world" setting. More information is available at http://www.odu.edu/ao/cmc/cap.html.

FACILITIES
Housing: Coed dorms, special housing for disabled students, special housing for international students, apartments for single students. 95% of campus accessible to physically disabled. **Special Academic Facilities/Equipment:** Centers for urban research/service, economic education, and child study, planetarium, marine science research vessel, random wave pool. **Computers:** 100% of classrooms, 100% of dorms, 100% of libraries, 100% of dining areas, 100% of student union, 20% of common outdoor areas have wireless network access. Students can register for classes online. Administrative functions (other than registration) can be performed online.

CAMPUS LIFE
Environment: City. **Activities:** Choral groups, concert band, dance, drama/theater, jazz band, marching band, music ensembles, musical theater, pep band, radio station, student government, student newspaper, symphony orchestra, television station, Campus Ministries, International Student Organization, Model UN 155 registered organizations, 16 honor societies, 25 religious organizations. 14 fraternities, 10 sororities. **Athletics (Intercollegiate):** *Men:* baseball, basketball, diving, football, golf, sailing, soccer, tennis, wrestling. *Women:* basketball, crew/rowing, diving, field hockey, golf, lacrosse, sailing, soccer, tennis. **On-Campus Highlights:** Webb Student Center, Engineering/Computational Bldg, University Village, Constant Convocation Center, Kaufman Mall. **Environmental Initiatives:** All new contruction and major renovations are designed to LEED Silver standards at a minimum. We recycled over 1.5 million pounds of materials last year that would have otherwise gone to landfill Com-

pleted construction of a wetland restoration and breakwater installation project (in collaboration with the Army Corps of Engineers) on the west end of campus that adjoins with the Elizabeth River. The project emcompassed approximately 3/4 acres of new wetlands.

ADMISSIONS

Freshman Academic Profile: Average high school GPA 3.3. 9% in top 10% of high school class, 33% in top 25% of high school class, 78% in top 50% of high school class. 94% from public high schools. SAT Math middle 50% range 460-560. SAT Critical Reading middle 50% range 460-560. ACT middle 50% range 18-23. Minimum web-based TOEFL 79. Minimum paper TOEFL 550. **Basis for Candidate Selection:** *Very important factors considered include:* academic GPA, rigor of secondary school record, standardized test scores, extracurricular activities. *Important factors considered include:* Class rank, application essay, recommendation(s), volunteer work, work experience. *Other factors considered include:* alumni/ae relation, character/personal qualities, first generation, interview, level of applicant's interest, talent/ability. **Freshman Admission Requirements:** High school diploma is required and GED is accepted. *Academic units required:* 4 English, 3 mathematics, 3 science, 3 foreign language, 3 social studies. 4 English, 3 mathematics, 3 science, 3 foreign language, 3 social studies. **Freshman Admission Statistics:** 10,656 applied, 72% admitted, 35% enrolled. **Transfer Admission Requirements:** college transcript(s), minimum college GPA of 2.2 required. Lowest grade transferable c. **General Admission Information:** Application Fee $50. Regular application deadline 2/1. Notification on a rolling basis, beginning on or about 1/15. Nonfall registration accepted. Admission may be deferred for a maximum of 12 months. Credit and/ or placement offered for CEEB Advanced Placement tests.

COSTS AND FINANCIAL AID

Annual in-state tuition $8,190. Annual out-of-state tuition $23,070. Room and board $9,066. Required fees $260. Average book expense $1,000. **Required Forms and Deadlines:** FAFSA. **Notification of Awards:** Applicants will be notified of awards on a rolling basis beginning 2/1. **Types of Aid:** *Need-based scholarships/grants:* Federal Pell, SEOG, state scholarships/grants, private scholarships, the school's own gift aid, United Negro College Fund, Federal Nursing Scholarships. *Loans:* Direct Subsidized Stafford, Direct Unsubsidized Stafford, Direct PLUS, Federal Perkins, Federal Nursing, college/university loans from institutional funds. **Student Employment:** Federal Work-Study Program available. Institutional employment available. Highest amount earned per year from on-campus jobs $5,382. Off-campus job opportunities are excellent. **Financial Aid Statistics:** 38% freshmen, 41% undergrads receive need-based scholarship or grant aid. 46% freshmen, 29% undergrads receive non-need-based scholarship or grant aid. 63% freshmen, 68% undergrads receive need-based self-help aid. 3% freshmen, 2% undergrads receive athletic scholarships. 74% freshmen, 71% undergrads receive any aid. 75% undergrads borrow to pay for school. Average cumulative indebtedness $16,500. **Criteria for awarding institutional aid:** *Non-need-based:* academics, alumni affiliation, art, athletics, leadership, music/drama, state/district residency.

See page 1166.

OLIVET COLLEGE

320 S. Main St., Olivet, MI 49076
Phone: 269-749-7635
E-mail: admissions@olivetcollege.edu • **CEEB Code:** 1595
Fax: 269-749-6617 • **Website:** www.olivetcollege.edu • **ACT Code:** 2042

This private school, affiliated with the United Church of Christ Church, was founded in 1844. It has a 45-acre campus.

RATINGS

Admissions Selectivity Rating: 62   **Fire Safety Rating:** 60*   **Green Rating:** 60*

STUDENTS AND FACULTY

Enrollment: 1,070. **Student Body:** 42% female, 58% male, 5% out-of-state, 3% international. Asian 1%, African American 16%, Caucasian 76%, Hispanic 2%, Native American 1%.
Retention and Graduation: 65% grads go on to further study within 1 year. 72% grads pursue arts and sciences degrees. 20% grads pursue law degrees. 45% grads pursue business degrees. 10% grads pursue medical degrees.
Faculty: Student/faculty ratio 14:1. 46 full-time faculty, 46% hold PhDs, 26% are members of minority groups, 37% are women. 1% of classes are taught by teaching assistants.

ACADEMICS

Degrees: bachelor's, master's. **Special Study Options:** cooperative education program, dual enrollment, honors program, independent study, internships,

liberal arts/career combination, student-designed major, study abroad, teacher certification program, Freshman Year Experience, Portfolio Assessment, Senior Experience, and Service Learning programs. **Disability Services:** Special programs offered to physically disabled students include reader services, tape recorders, tutors. **Career Services:** career/job search classes, career assessment, internships.

FACILITIES

Housing: Coed dorms, men's dorms, special housing for international students, women's dorms, fraternity/sorority housing, apartments for married students, apartments for single students. 30% of campus accessible to physically disabled. **Computers:** Students can register for classes online. Administrative functions (other than registration) can be performed online.

CAMPUS LIFE

Environment: Rural. **Activities:** Choral groups, concert band, drama/theater, jazz band, music ensembles, musical theater, pep band, radio station, student government, student newspaper, yearbook 12 registered organizations, 1 honor societies, 1 religious organizations. 3 fraternities, 3 sororities. **Athletics (Intercollegiate):** *Men:* baseball, basketball, cross-country, diving, football, golf, soccer, swimming, track/field (outdoor), wrestling. *Women:* basketball, cheerleading, cross-country, diving, golf, soccer, softball, swimming, tennis, track/field (outdoor), volleyball.

ADMISSIONS

Freshman Academic Profile: Average high school GPA 2.9. Minimum web-based TOEFL 79. Minimum paper TOEFL 550. **Basis for Candidate Selection:** *Very important factors considered include:* rigor of secondary school record, standardized test scores, alumni/ae relation, character/personal qualities, extracurricular activities, volunteer work, work experience. *Important factors considered include:* recommendation(s), racial/ethnic status. *Other factors considered include:* Class rank, application essay, geographical residence, interview, religious affiliation/commitment, state residency, talent/ability. **Freshman Admission Requirements:** High school diploma is required and GED is accepted. **Transfer Admission Requirements:** High school transcript, college transcript(s), minimum college GPA of 2.0 required. Lowest grade transferable C–. **General Admission Information:** Application Fee $25. Notification on a rolling basis, beginning on or about 8/15. Nonfall registration accepted. Admission may be deferred for a maximum of 1 year. Credit and/or placement offered for CEEB Advanced Placement tests.

COSTS AND FINANCIAL AID

Annual tuition $17,994. Room and board $6,346. Required fees $664. Average book expense $800. **Required Forms and Deadlines:** FAFSA. **Notification of Awards:** Applicants will be notified of awards on a rolling basis beginning 2/1. **Types of Aid:** *Need-based scholarships/grants:* Federal Pell, SEOG, state scholarships/grants, private scholarships, the school's own gift aid. *Loans:* Subsidized Stafford, Unsubsidized Stafford, PLUS, Federal Perkins, state loans. **Student Employment:** Federal Work-Study Program available. Institutional employment available. Highest amount earned per year from on-campus jobs $850. Off-campus job opportunities are fair. **Financial Aid Statistics:** 100% freshmen, 100% undergrads receive need-based scholarship or grant aid. 6% freshmen, 4% undergrads receive non-need-based scholarship or grant aid. 93% freshmen, 93% undergrads receive need-based self-help aid. 80% undergrads borrow to pay for school. Average cumulative indebtedness $6,444. **Criteria for awarding institutional aid:** *Non-need-based:* academics, art, leadership, music/drama, religious affiliation.

OLIVET NAZARENE UNIVERSITY

One University Avenue, Bourbonnais, IL 60914
Phone: 815-939-5603 • **Financial Aid Phone:** 815-939-5249
E-mail: admissions@olivet.edu • **CEEB Code:** 32
Fax: 815-935-4998 • **Website:** www.olivet.edu • **ACT Code:** 1112

This private school, affiliated with the Nazarene Church, was founded in 1907. It has a 225-acre campus.

RATINGS

Admissions Selectivity Rating: 81   **Fire Safety Rating:** 63   **Green Rating:** 60*

STUDENTS AND FACULTY

Enrollment: 2,633. **Student Body:** 60% female, 40% male, 55% out-of-state, 1% international (18 countries represented). Asian 1%, African American 9%, Caucasian 86%, Hispanic 3%, Native American 0%.
Retention and Graduation: 79% freshmen return for sophomore year. 39% grads go on to further study within 1 year. 27% grads pursue arts and sciences degrees. 3% grads pursue law degrees. 13% grads pursue business degrees. 9%

grads pursue medical degrees. **Faculty:** Student/faculty ratio 20:1. 94 full-time faculty, 68% hold PhDs, 3% are members of minority groups, 34% are women. 0% of classes are taught by teaching assistants.

ACADEMICS
Degrees: associate, bachelor's, master's. **Classes:** Most classes have 20–29 students. **Majors with Highest Enrollment:** business/commerce; education; health/medical preparatory programs, other. **Special Study Options:** Accelerated program, distance learning, double major, honors program, independent study, internships, student-designed major, study abroad, teacher certification program. **Honors Programs:** Phi Delta Lambda Psi Chi (Psychology) Dappa Delta Pi (Education) Kappa Omicron Nu (FACS) Sigma Tau Delta (English) Sigma Theta Tau (Nursing) Kappa Sigma Chapter (Nursing) Phi Alpha Theta (History) Departmental Honors. **Disability Services:** Special programs offered to physically disabled students include note-taking services, reader services, tape recorders, tutors.

FACILITIES
Housing: special housing for disabled students, men's dorms, women's dorms, apartments for married students, apartments for single students. 100% of campus accessible to physically disabled. **Special Academic Facilities/Equipment:** Planetarium, "Smart" Classrooms, Radio Station **Computers:** Students can register for classes online. Administrative functions (other than registration) can be performed online.

CAMPUS LIFE
Environment: Town. **Activities:** Choral groups, concert band, dance, drama/theater, jazz band, literary magazine, marching band, music ensembles, musical theater, opera, pep band, radio station, student government, student newspaper, student-run film society, symphony orchestra, television station, yearbook 79 registered organizations, 8 honor societies, 23 religious organizations. **Athletics (Intercollegiate):** *Men:* baseball, basketball, cheerleading, cross-country, football, golf, soccer, tennis, track/field (outdoor), track/field (indoor). *Women:* basketball, cheerleading, cross-country, soccer, softball, tennis, track/field (outdoor), track/field (indoor), volleyball. **On-Campus Highlights:** Common Grounds (coffee shop), Ludwig Center (student center), McHie Arena, Fitness Center, Red Room (student lounge).

ADMISSIONS
Freshman Academic Profile: Average high school GPA 3.3. 22% in top 10% of high school class, 45% in top 25% of high school class, 75% in top 50% of high school class. 85% from public high schools. SAT Math middle 50% range 480-590. SAT Critical Reading middle 50% range 490-620. ACT middle 50% range 20-26. Minimum paper TOEFL 500. **Basis for Candidate Selection:** *Very important factors considered include:* Class rank, recommendation(s), rigor of secondary school record, standardized test scores, character/personal qualities. *Important factors considered include:* application essay, extracurricular activities, interview, talent/ability. *Other factors considered include:* religious affiliation/commitment, volunteer work, work experience. **Freshman Admission Requirements:** High school diploma is required and GED is accepted. *Academic units required:* 4 English, 3 mathematics, 3 science, 3 social studies, 2 history. *Academic units recommended:* 4 English, 3 mathematics, 3 science, 3 social studies, 2 history. **Freshman Admission Statistics:** 2,747 applied, 64% admitted, 40% enrolled. **Transfer Admission Requirements:** college transcript(s), essay or personal statement, statement of good standing from prior institution(s). Minimum college GPA of 2.0 required. Lowest grade transferable D-. **General Admission Information:** Regular application deadline 5/15. Notification on a rolling basis, beginning on or about 6/1. Nonfall registration accepted. Credit and/or placement offered for CEEB Advanced Placement tests.

COSTS AND FINANCIAL AID
Annual tuition $16,750. Room and board $6,400. Required fees $840. Average book expense $800. **Required Forms and Deadlines:** FAFSA, institution's own financial aid form. **Notification of Awards:** Applicants will be notified of awards on a rolling basis beginning 2/1. **Types of Aid:** *Need-based scholarships/grants:* Federal Pell, SEOG, state scholarships/grants, private scholarships, the school's own gift aid. *Loans:* Direct Subsidized Stafford, Direct Unsubsidized Stafford, Direct PLUS, Subsidized Stafford, Unsubsidized Stafford, PLUS, Federal Perkins. **Student Employment:** Federal Work-Study Program available. **Financial Aid Statistics:** 99% freshmen, 98% undergrads receive need-based scholarship or grant aid. 96% freshmen, 91% undergrads receive non-need-based scholarship or grant aid. 83% freshmen, 86% undergrads receive need-based self-help aid. 15% freshmen, 15% undergrads receive athletic scholarships. 96% undergrads receive any aid. 68% undergrads borrow to pay for school. Average cumulative indebtedness $20,607. **Criteria for awarding institutional aid:** *Non-need-based:* academics, art, athletics, leadership, music/drama, religious affiliation.

ONONDAGA COMMUNITY COLLEGE

4941, Syracuse, NY 13215
Phone: 315-498-2201
E-mail: occinfo@sunyocc.edu
Fax: 315-469-2107 • **Website:** www.sunyocc.edu

This public school was founded in 1961. It has a 181-acre campus.

RATINGS
Admissions Selectivity Rating: 62   **Fire Safety Rating:** 60*   **Green Rating:** 88

STUDENTS AND FACULTY
Enrollment: 5,097. **Student Body:** 54% female, 46% male, 0% out-of-state, 0% international.
Faculty: Student/faculty ratio 17:1. 179 full-time faculty, 9% are members of minority groups, 52% are women.

ACADEMICS
Degrees: associate, certificate. **Classes:** Most classes have 10–19 students. **Special Study Options:** cooperative education program, double major, dual enrollment, English as a Second Language (ESL), honors program, independent study, internships, liberal arts/career combination, study abroad. **Disability Services:** Special programs offered to physically disabled students include note-taking services, reader services, tape recorders, tutors. **Career Services:** alumni services, career/job search classes.

CAMPUS LIFE
Environment: Village. **Activities:** Choral groups, music ensembles, radio station, student government, student newspaper, television station 1 honor societies. **Athletics (Intercollegiate):** *Men:* baseball, basketball, cross-country, lacrosse, tennis. *Women:* basketball, cross-country, softball, tennis, volleyball.

ADMISSIONS
Freshman Academic Profile: 95% from public high schools. Minimum paper TOEFL 500. **Basis for Candidate Selection:** *Very important factors considered include:* rigor of secondary school record. *Other factors considered include:* recommendation(s), character/personal qualities, interview. **Freshman Admission Requirements:** High school diploma is required and GED is accepted. High school diploma or equivalent is not required. **Freshman Admission Statistics:** 2,899 applied, 79% admitted. **Transfer Admission Requirements:** High school transcript, college transcript(s), Lowest grade transferable C. **General Admission Information:** Application Fee $30. Nonfall registration accepted. Admission may be deferred for a maximum of 2 semesters.

COSTS AND FINANCIAL AID
Annual in-state tuition $3,180. Annual out-of-state tuition $9,540. Required fees $155. Average book expense. **Required Forms and Deadlines:** FAFSA, state aid form. **Notification of Awards:** Applicants will be notified of awards on or about 4/15. **Types of Aid:** *Need-based scholarships/grants:* Federal Pell, SEOG, state scholarships/grants, Federal work study. *Loans:* Subsidized Stafford, Unsubsidized Stafford, PLUS. **Student Employment:** Federal Work-Study Program available. Off-campus job opportunities are excellent. **Financial Aid Statistics:** 60% freshmen, 60% undergrads receive need-based scholarship or grant aid. 1% freshmen, 1% undergrads receive non-need-based scholarship or grant aid. 80% freshmen, 80% undergrads receive need-based self-help aid. **Criteria for awarding institutional aid:** *Non-need-based:* academics, alumni affiliation.

ORAL ROBERTS UNIVERSITY

7777 S. Lewis Avenue, Tulsa, OK 74171
Phone: 918-495-6518
E-mail: admissions@oru.edu • **CEEB Code:** 6552
Fax: 918-495-6222 • **Website:** www.oru.edu • **ACT Code:** 3427

This is a private school. It has a 500-acre campus.

RATINGS
Admissions Selectivity Rating: 73   **Fire Safety Rating:** 60*   **Green Rating:** 60*

STUDENTS AND FACULTY
Enrollment: 2,645. **Student Body:** 59% female, 41% male, 62% out-of-state, 6% international. Asian 4%, African American 15%, Caucasian 55%, Hispanic 6%, Native American 1%.

Retention and Graduation: 82% freshmen return for sophomore year. 49% freshmen graduate within 4 years. 58% freshmen graduate within 6 years. 50% grads go on to further study within 1 year. 25% grads pursue arts and sciences degrees. 1% grads pursue law degrees. 10% grads pursue business degrees. 5% grads pursue medical degrees. **Faculty:** Student/faculty ratio 14:1. 180 full-time faculty, 62% hold PhDs, 13% are members of minority groups, 37% are women. 0% of classes are taught by teaching assistants.

ACADEMICS
Degrees: bachelor's, first professional, master's. **Classes:** Most classes have 10–19 students. Most lab/discussion sessions have 20–29 students. **Majors with Highest Enrollment:** marketing/marketing management; mass communication/media studies; theology/theological studies. **Special Study Options:** Accelerated program, distance learning, double major, dual enrollment, English as a Second Language (ESL), external degree program, honors program, independent study, internships, liberal arts/career combination, student-designed major, study abroad, teacher certification program, weekend college. **Honors Programs:** ORU HOnors Program includes "Scholars" and "Fellows" -- Highly selective Includes Beta Gamma Phi and others **Combined Degree Programs:** 3-2 bachelor's/ MBA and bachelor's/MA.Ed. programs. **Disability Services:** Special programs offered to physically disabled students include note-taking services, reader services, tape recorders, tutors.

FACILITIES
Housing: men's dorms, women's dorms. 100% of campus accessible to physically disabled. **Special Academic Facilities/Equipment:** Dial Access Information Retrieval System, programmed learning facilities, early learning center, TV production studio.

CAMPUS LIFE
Activities: Choral groups, concert band, dance, drama/theater, jazz band, music ensembles, musical theater, pep band, radio station, student government, student newspaper, television station, yearbook, Campus Ministries, International Student Organization, Model UN. **Athletics (Intercollegiate):** *Men:* baseball, basketball, cheerleading, cross-country, soccer, swimming, tennis, track/field (outdoor). *Women:* basketball, cheerleading, cross-country, soccer, swimming, tennis, track/field (outdoor), volleyball. **On-Campus Highlights:** Eagle's Nest, Aerobics Center, Prayer Tower, Mabee Center (Multi-purpose Event Complex), Gabrielle Christian Salem Hall.

ADMISSIONS
Freshman Academic Profile: Average high school GPA 3.4. 23% in top 10% of high school class, 45% in top 25% of high school class, 74% in top 50% of high school class. 75% from public high schools. SAT Math middle 50% range 455-570. SAT Critical Reading middle 50% range 465-590. ACT middle 50% range 20-26. Minimum paper TOEFL 500. **Basis for Candidate Selection:** *Very important factors considered include:* application essay, academic GPA, rigor of secondary school record, standardized test scores. *Important factors considered include:* Class rank, recommendation(s). *Other factors considered include:* alumni/ae relation, character/personal qualities, religious affiliation/commitment. **Freshman Admission Requirements:** High school diploma is required and GED is accepted. **Freshman Admission Statistics:** 1,127 applied, 73% admitted, 59% enrolled. **Transfer Admission Requirements:** High school transcript, college transcript(s), essay or personal statement, minimum college GPA of 2.0 required. Lowest grade transferable 2. **General Admission Information:** Application Fee $35. Nonfall registration accepted. Credit and/or placement offered for CEEB Advanced Placement tests.

COSTS AND FINANCIAL AID
Annual tuition $20,060. Room and board $8,594. Required fees $686. Average book expense $1,500. **Required Forms and Deadlines:** FAFSA. **Types of Aid:** *Need-based scholarships/grants:* Federal Pell, SEOG, state scholarships/grants, private scholarships, the school's own gift aid. *Loans:* Subsidized Stafford, Unsubsidized Stafford, PLUS, Federal Perkins. **Student Employment:** Highest amount earned per year from on-campus jobs $1,800. **Financial Aid Statistics:** 99% freshmen, 97% undergrads receive need-based scholarship or grant aid. 29% freshmen, 36% undergrads receive non-need-based scholarship or grant aid. 64% freshmen, 93% undergrads receive need-based self-help aid. 3% freshmen, 4% undergrads receive athletic scholarships. 67% undergrads borrow to pay for school. Average cumulative indebtedness $34,555. **Criteria for awarding institutional aid:** *Non-need-based:* academics, alumni affiliation, art, athletics, job skills, leadership, music/drama.

OREGON COLLEGE OF ART AND CRAFT

8245 Southwest Barnes Road, Portland, OR 97225
Phone: 971-255-4192 • **Financial Aid Phone:** 971-255-4224
E-mail: admissions@ocac.edu • **CEEB Code:** 4236
Fax: 503-297-9651 • **Website:** www.ocac.edu • **ACT Code:** 3471

This private school was founded in 1907. It has a 9-acre campus.

RATINGS
Admissions Selectivity Rating: 61   **Fire Safety Rating:** 62   **Green Rating:** 60*

STUDENTS AND FACULTY
Enrollment: 151. **Student Body:** 73% female, 27% male, 18% out-of-state, 0% international (2 countries represented). Asian 2%, African American 0%, Caucasian 70%, Hispanic 5%, Native American 3%.
Retention and Graduation: 65% freshmen return for sophomore year. 25% freshmen graduate within 4 years. 38% freshmen graduate within 6 years. 9% grads pursue arts and sciences degrees. **Faculty:** Student/faculty ratio 7:1. 10 full-time faculty, 90% hold PhDs, 10% are members of minority groups, 50% are women. 0% of classes are taught by teaching assistants.

ACADEMICS
Degrees: bachelor's, certificate, post-bachelor's certificate. **Classes:** Most classes have fewer than 10 students. **Majors with Highest Enrollment:** drawing; fine arts and art studies, other; metal and jewelry arts. **Special Study Options:** cross-registration, exchange student program (domestic), independent study, internships, study abroad.

FACILITIES
Housing: cooperative housing, the college offers a small number of on-campus housing for new students straight from high school. In addition, the college has contract with two apartment complexes across the street from the college. 60% of campus accessible to physically disabled. **Special Academic Facilities/Equipment:** Hoffman Gallery, Centrum Gallery, and 7 specialized studios for artmaking.

CAMPUS LIFE
Environment: Metropolis. **Activities:** student government, student newspaper 1 registered organizations. **On-Campus Highlights:** Hands On Cafe, Centrum Art Gallery, Thesis Studios, Library, Computer Lab.

ADMISSIONS
Freshman Academic Profile: Average high school GPA 3.0. 20% in top 10% of high school class, 20% in top 25% of high school class, 60% in top 50% of high school class. Minimum web-based TOEFL 80. Minimum paper TOEFL 550. **Basis for Candidate Selection:** *Very important factors considered include:* application essay, academic GPA, level of applicant's interest, talent/ability. *Important factors considered include:* recommendation(s), rigor of secondary school record, character/personal qualities, interview. *Other factors considered include:* standardized test scores, alumni/ae relation, extracurricular activities, first generation, volunteer work, work experience. **Freshman Admission Requirements:** High school diploma is required and GED is accepted. **Freshman Admission Statistics:** 60 applied, 92% admitted, 47% enrolled. **Transfer Admission Requirements:** High school transcript, college transcript(s), essay or personal statement, minimum college GPA of 2.0 required. Lowest grade transferable C. **General Admission Information:** Application Fee $35. Notification on a rolling basis, beginning on or about 1/1. Nonfall registration accepted. Admission may be deferred for a maximum of 1 year. Credit and/or placement offered for CEEB Advanced Placement tests.

COSTS AND FINANCIAL AID
Annual tuition $22,614. Room and board $4,050. Required fees $1,657. Average book expense $1,000. **Required Forms and Deadlines:** FAFSA. **Notification of Awards:** Applicants will be notified of awards on a rolling basis beginning 3/15. **Types of Aid:** *Need-based scholarships/grants:* Federal Pell, SEOG, state scholarships/grants, private scholarships, the school's own gift aid. *Loans:* Subsidized Stafford, Unsubsidized Stafford, PLUS, state loans. **Student Employment:** Federal Work-Study Program available. Institutional employment available. **Financial Aid Statistics:** 100% freshmen, 84% undergrads receive need-based scholarship or grant aid. 88% freshmen, 82% undergrads receive non-need-based scholarship or grant aid. 94% freshmen, 95% undergrads receive need-based self-help aid. 90% freshmen, 93% undergrads receive any aid. 0% undergrads borrow to pay for school. Average cumulative indebtedness $0. **Criteria for awarding institutional aid:** *Non-need-based:* academics, art.

OREGON HEALTH SCIENCES UNIVERSITY

3181 SW Sam Jackson Park Rd, Portland, OR 97239
Phone: 503-494-2998 • **Financial Aid Phone:** 503-494-7800
E-mail: proginfo@ohsu.edu • **CEEB Code:** 4900
Fax: 503-494-3400 • **Website:** www.ohsu.edu

This public school was founded in 1867. It has a 120-acre campus.

RATINGS
Admissions Selectivity Rating: 61   **Fire Safety Rating:** 60*   **Green Rating:** 60*

STUDENTS AND FACULTY
Enrollment: 591. **Student Body:** 84% female, 16% male, 10% out-of-state, 1% international. Asian 5%, African American 1%, Caucasian 79%, Hispanic 5%, Native American 2%.
Faculty: 1290 full-time faculty.

ACADEMICS
Degrees: associate, bachelor's, first professional, first professional certificate, master's, post-bachelor's certificate, post-master's certificate. **Majors with Highest Enrollment:** clinical laboratory science/medical technology/technologist; emergency medical technology/technician (emt paramedic); nursing/registered nurse (rn, asn, bsn, msn). **Special Study Options:** Accelerated program, distance learning. **Combined Degree Programs:** MD/PhD, MD/MPH.

FACILITIES
Computers: Students can register for classes online.

CAMPUS LIFE
Environment: Metropolis. **Activities:** student government, student newspaper, yearbook. **On-Campus Highlights:** Portland Aerial Tram, Center for Health and Healing Cafe, Marquam Hill Hiking Trails

ADMISSIONS
Freshman Admission Requirements: High school diploma is required and GED is accepted. **Transfer Admission Requirements:** college transcript(s), essay or personal statement, standardized test scores, statement of good standing from prior institution(s). Lowest grade transferable C. **General Admission Information:** Application Fee $120. Regular application deadline 1/15.

COSTS AND FINANCIAL AID
Annual out-of-state tuition $20,176. **Types of Aid:** *Need-based scholarships/grants:* Federal Pell, SEOG, state scholarships/grants, private scholarships, the school's own gift aid, Scholarship for Disadvantaged Student. *Loans:* Direct Subsidized Stafford, Direct Unsubsidized Stafford, Direct PLUS, Federal Perkins, Federal Nursing, college/university loans from institutional funds. **Student Employment:** Federal Work-Study Program available. Institutional employment available. Off-campus job opportunities are poor. **Financial Aid Statistics:** 49% undergrads receive need-based scholarship or grant aid. 1% undergrads receive non-need-based scholarship or grant aid. 100% undergrads receive need-based self-help aid. 70% undergrads receive any aid. **Criteria for awarding institutional aid:** *Non-need-based:* academics, minority status, state/district residency.

OREGON INSTITUTE OF TECHNOLOGY

3201 Campus Drive, Klamath Falls, OR 97601
Phone: 541-885-1150 • **Financial Aid Phone:** 541-885-1280
E-mail: oit@oit.edu • **CEEB Code:** 4587
Fax: 541-885-1115 • **ACT Code:** 3484

This public school was founded in 1947. It has a 173-acre campus.

RATINGS
Admissions Selectivity Rating: 68   **Fire Safety Rating:** 61   **Green Rating:** 60*

STUDENTS AND FACULTY
Enrollment: 2,663. **Student Body:** 44% female, 56% male, 15% out-of-state, 1% international (11 countries represented). Asian 5%, African American 1%, Caucasian 81%, Hispanic 4%, Native American 2%.
Retention and Graduation: 69% freshmen return for sophomore year. **Faculty:** Student/faculty ratio 16:1. 126 full-time faculty, 33% hold PhDs, 6% are members of minority groups, 35% are women.

ACADEMICS
Degrees: associate, bachelor's, certificate, master's. **Classes:** Most classes have 10–19 students. Most lab/discussion sessions have 10–19 students. **Majors with**

Highest Enrollment: computer engineering technology/technician; computer software technology/technician; mechanical engineering/mechanical technology/technician. **Special Study Options:** cooperative education program, cross-registration, distance learning, double major, dual enrollment, external degree program, internships, study abroad. **Disability Services:** Special programs offered to physically disabled students include note-taking services, reader services, tape recorders, tutors.

FACILITIES
Housing: Coed dorms. **Special Academic Facilities/Equipment:** Shaw Historical library. **Computers:** Students can register for classes online. Administrative functions (other than registration) can be performed online.

CAMPUS LIFE
Environment: Town. **Activities:** Choral groups, pep band, radio station, student government, student newspaper, symphony orchestra, television station 30 registered organizations, 5 honor societies, 1 religious organizations. 1 fraternities, 1 sororities. **Athletics (Intercollegiate):** *Men:* baseball, basketball, cross-country, track/field (outdoor). *Women:* basketball, cross-country, soccer, softball, track/field (outdoor), volleyball. **On-Campus Highlights:** College Union Bistro, College Union Marketplace, Purvine Coffee Cart, Tech Fit, Fitness Center, Residnece Hall Lounge.

ADMISSIONS
Freshman Academic Profile: Average high school GPA 3.3. 25% in top 10% of high school class, 56% in top 25% of high school class, 92% in top 50% of high school class. SAT Math middle 50% range 480-600. SAT Critical Reading middle 50% range 460-570. ACT middle 50% range 21-26. Minimum paper TOEFL 520. **Basis for Candidate Selection:** *Very important factors considered include:* rigor of secondary school record, standardized test scores. *Other factors considered include:* Class rank, application essay, recommendation(s), character/personal qualities, interview, work experience. **Freshman Admission Requirements:** High school diploma is required and GED is accepted. *Academic units required:* 4 English, 3 mathematics, 2 science, (1 science labs), 2 foreign language, 3 social studies. 4 English, 3 mathematics, 2 science, (1 science labs), 2 foreign language, 3 social studies. **Freshman Admission Statistics:** 651 applied, 88% admitted, 46% enrolled. **Transfer Admission Requirements:** college transcript(s), minimum college GPA of 2.0 required. Lowest grade transferable D. **General Admission Information:** Application Fee $50. Regular application deadline 10/1. Notification on a rolling basis, beginning on or about 10/15. Nonfall registration accepted. Admission may be deferred for a maximum of 2 years. Credit and/or placement offered for CEEB Advanced Placement tests.

COSTS AND FINANCIAL AID
Annual in-state tuition $4,590. Annual out-of-state tuition $14,760. Room and board $6,480. Required fees $1,329. Average book expense $1,000. **Required Forms and Deadlines:** FAFSA. **Notification of Awards:** Applicants will be notified of awards on a rolling basis beginning 4/1. **Types of Aid:** *Need-based scholarships/grants:* Federal Pell, SEOG, state scholarships/grants, private scholarships, the school's own gift aid. *Loans:* Subsidized Stafford, Unsubsidized Stafford, PLUS, Federal Perkins, college/university loans from institutional funds. **Student Employment: Financial Aid Statistics:** 37% freshmen, 48% undergrads receive need-based scholarship or grant aid. 7% freshmen, 5% undergrads receive non-need-based scholarship or grant aid. 61% freshmen, 74% undergrads receive need-based self-help aid. 1% undergrads receive athletic scholarships. 89% freshmen, 86% undergrads receive any aid. 7% undergrads borrow to pay for school. Average cumulative indebtedness $22,351. **Criteria for awarding institutional aid:** *Non-need-based:* academics, athletics, leadership, minority status.

OREGON STATE UNIVERSITY

104 Kerr Administration Building, Corvallis, OR 97331-2106
Phone: 541-737-4411 • **Financial Aid Phone:** 541-737-2241
E-mail: osuadmit@oregonstate.edu • **CEEB Code:** 4586
Fax: 541-737-2482 • **Website:** oregonstate.edu • **ACT Code:**

This public school was founded in 1858. It has a 421-acre campus.

RATINGS
Admissions Selectivity Rating: 72   **Fire Safety Rating:** 72   **Green Rating:** 95

STUDENTS AND FACULTY
Enrollment: 20,464. **Student Body:** 47% female, 53% male, 21% out-of-state, 5% international (97 countries represented). Asian 7%, African American 1%, Caucasian 69%, Hispanic 7%, Native American 1%.

Retention and Graduation: 81% freshmen return for sophomore year. 29% freshmen graduate within 4 years. 60% freshmen graduate within 6 years.
Faculty: Student/faculty ratio 22:1. 856 full-time faculty, 83% hold PhDs, 14% are members of minority groups, 39% are women.

ACADEMICS

Degrees: bachelor's, certificate, doctoral, master's, post-bachelor's certificate, post-master's certificate. **Classes:** Most classes have 20–29 students. Most lab/discussion sessions have 20–29 students. **Majors with Highest Enrollment:** business administration and management; health and physical education; human development and family studies. **Special Study Options:** Accelerated program, cooperative education program, cross-registration, distance learning, double major, dual enrollment, English as a Second Language (ESL), exchange student program (domestic), external degree program, honors program, independent study, internships, liberal arts/career combination, student-designed major, study abroad, teacher certification program. **Combined Degree Programs:** 2-2 food science/technology program w/ U of Alaska. **Disability Services:** Special programs offered to physically disabled students include note-taking services, reader services, tape recorders, tutors. **Career Services:** Alumni network, alumni services, career/job search classes, career assessment, internships, regional alumni.

FACILITIES

Housing: Coed dorms, special housing for disabled students, special housing for international students, fraternity/sorority housing, apartments for married students, cooperative housing, apartments for single students, theme housing. 86% of campus accessible to physically disabled. **Special Academic Facilities/Equipment:** Museums, galleries, collections, exhibits of cultural and scientific materials, language lab. **Computers:** 100% of classrooms, 2% of dorms, 100% of libraries, 50% of dining areas, 100% of student union, 2% of common outdoor areas have wireless network access. Students can register for classes online. Administrative functions (other than registration) can be performed online.

CAMPUS LIFE

Environment: Town. **Activities:** Choral groups, concert band, dance, drama/theater, jazz band, literary magazine, marching band, music ensembles, musical theater, opera, pep band, radio station, student government, student newspaper, student-run film society, symphony orchestra, television station, yearbook, Campus Ministries, International Student Organization, Model UN 350 registered organizations, 29 honor societies, 23 religious organizations. 24 fraternities, 13 sororities. **Athletics (Intercollegiate):** *Men:* baseball, basketball, crew/rowing, football, golf, soccer, wrestling. *Women:* basketball, crew/rowing, cross-country, golf, gymnastics, soccer, softball, swimming, track/field (outdoor), volleyball. **On-Campus Highlights:** Memorial Union, Java II, Weatherford Hall, Dixon Recreation Center, Reser Stadium. **Environmental Initiatives:** Many areas of OSU research have large impacts on sustainability state- and nation-wide. Particularly the Oregon Climate Change Research Institute and our wave and wind research make global impacts. New degrees like ecological engineering offer a greener curriculum. More info at http://senergi.oregonstate.edu/home A student fee, combined with donations and administrative money, offsets about 60% of campus electrical use with a green tags purchase. We are installing a large solar hot water system on our rec center. EPA gave OSU a Green Power Leadership Award in 2008: http://oregonstate.edu/dept/ncs/newsarch/2008/Oct08/greenpowerleader.html The Student Sustainability Initiative, a student fee funded organization, is a national model for student engagement and leadership development. It funds student employees and competitive grants for student projects that make campus more sustainable and expose students to sustainable practices. http://oregonstate.edu/sustainability/ssi/

ADMISSIONS

Freshman Academic Profile: Average high school GPA 3.6. 26% in top 10% of high school class, 55% in top 25% of high school class, 90% in top 50% of high school class. SAT Math middle 50% range 490-630. SAT Critical Reading middle 50% range 480-600. SAT Writing middle 50% range 460-580. ACT middle 50% range 21-27. Minimum web-based TOEFL 80. Minimum paper TOEFL 550. **Basis for Candidate Selection:** *Very important factors considered include:* application essay, academic GPA, rigor of secondary school record. *Important factors considered include:* Class rank, character/personal qualities, level of applicant's interest, talent/ability, volunteer work. *Other factors considered include:* recommendation(s), standardized test scores, extracurricular activities, first generation, interview, work experience. **Freshman Admission Requirements:** High school diploma is required and GED is accepted. *Academic units required:* 4 English, 3 mathematics, 2 science, (1 science labs), 2 foreign language, 3 social studies. *Academic units recommended:* 4 English, 3 mathematics, 2 science, (1 science labs), 2 foreign language, 3 social studies. **Freshman Admission Statistics:** 12,330 applied, 79% admitted, 34% enrolled. **Transfer Admission Requirements:** college transcript(s), essay or personal statement, statement of good standing from prior institution(s). Minimum college GPA of 2.25 required. Lowest grade transferable D. **General Admission Information:** Application Fee $50. Regular application deadline 9/1. Notification on a rolling basis, beginning on or about 10/1. Nonfall registration

accepted. Admission may be deferred for a maximum of 1 year. Credit and/or placement offered for CEEB Advanced Placement tests.

COSTS AND FINANCIAL AID

Annual in-state tuition $6,660. Annual out-of-state tuition $20,844. Room and board $10,563. Required fees $1,478. Average book expense $1,908. **Required Forms and Deadlines:** FAFSA. **Notification of Awards:** Applicants will be notified of awards on a rolling basis beginning 4/1. **Types of Aid:** *Need-based scholarships/grants:* Federal Pell, SEOG, state scholarships/grants, private scholarships, the school's own gift aid. *Loans:* Direct Subsidized Stafford, Direct Unsubsidized Stafford, Direct PLUS, Federal Perkins, college/university loans from institutional funds. **Student Employment:** Federal Work-Study Program available. Institutional employment available. Off-campus job opportunities are good. **Financial Aid Statistics:** 84% freshmen, 78% undergrads receive need-based scholarship or grant aid. 4% freshmen, 2% undergrads receive non-need-based scholarship or grant aid. 81% freshmen, 86% undergrads receive need-based self-help aid. 2% freshmen, 3% undergrads receive athletic scholarships. 57% freshmen, 57% undergrads receive any aid. **Criteria for awarding institutional aid:** *Non-need-based:* academics, alumni affiliation, athletics, job skills, leadership, minority status, state/district residency.

OTIS COLLEGE OF ART AND DESIGN

9045 Lincoln Boulevard, Los Angeles, CA 90045
Phone: 310-665-6820 • **Financial Aid Phone:** 310-665-6880
E-mail: admissions@otis.edu • **CEEB Code:** 4394
Fax: 310-665-6821 • **Website:** www.otis.edu • **ACT Code:** 359

This private school was founded in 1918. It has a 5-acre campus.

RATINGS

Admissions Selectivity Rating: 82   **Fire Safety Rating:** 60*   **Green Rating:** 61

STUDENTS AND FACULTY

Enrollment: 1,100. **Student Body:** 66% female, 34% male, 16% international. Asian 33%, African American 4%, Caucasian 23%, Hispanic 14%, Native American 0%.
Retention and Graduation: 77% freshmen return for sophomore year. 45% freshmen graduate within 4 years. 53% freshmen graduate within 6 years. 80% grads pursue arts and sciences degrees. **Faculty:** Student/faculty ratio 5:1. 55 full-time faculty, 51% hold PhDs, 16% are members of minority groups, 53% are women. 0% of classes are taught by teaching assistants.

ACADEMICS

Degrees: bachelor's, master's. **Classes:** Most classes have 10–19 students. **Majors with Highest Enrollment:** animation, interactive technology, video graphics and special effects; fashion/apparel design; graphic design. **Special Study Options:** English as a Second Language (ESL), exchange student program (domestic), honors program, independent study, internships, study abroad. **Honors Programs:** We have an honors program for qualified enrolled students. **Disability Services:** Special programs offered to physically disabled students include tape recorders, tutors. **Career Services:** Alumni network, alumni services, career/job search classes, career assessment, internships, Career Services highlights include Strong and growing network for students to experience real world work.

FACILITIES

Housing: apartments for single students. 100% of campus accessible to physically disabled. **Special Academic Facilities/Equipment:** Art gallery, student gallery, Woodshop, Metal Shop, Photo lab, Digital Media lab, Printmaking lab, letterpress lab **Computers:** Administrative functions (other than registration) can be performed online.

CAMPUS LIFE

Environment: Metropolis. **Activities:** literary magazine, student government, student newspaper 7 registered organizations.

ADMISSIONS

Freshman Academic Profile: Average high school GPA 3.2. SAT Math middle 50% range 460-600. SAT Critical Reading middle 50% range 430-560. ACT middle 50% range 21-26. Minimum web-based TOEFL 79. Minimum paper TOEFL 550. **Basis for Candidate Selection:** *Very important factors considered include:* rigor of secondary school record, talent/ability. *Important factors considered include:* application essay, standardized test scores. *Other factors considered include:* recommendation(s), alumni/ae relation, character/personal qualities, extracurricular activities, interview, volunteer work, work experience. **Freshman Admission Requirements:** High school diploma is required and GED is accepted. *Academic units required:* 4 English, 3 mathematics,

2 science, (1 science labs), 1 social studies, 2 history. *Academic units recommended:* 4 English, 3 mathematics, 2 science, (1 science labs), 1 social studies, 2 history. **Freshman Admission Statistics:** 1,493 applied, 55% admitted, 22% enrolled. **Transfer Admission Requirements:** High school transcript, college transcript(s), essay or personal statement, statement of good standing from prior institution(s). Minimum college GPA of 2.5 required. Lowest grade transferable C. **General Admission Information:** Application Fee $50. Nonfall registration accepted. Credit offered for CEEB Advanced Placement tests.

COSTS AND FINANCIAL AID
Annual tuition $36,350. Room and board $11,800. Required fees $1,950. Average book expense $1,400. **Required Forms and Deadlines:** FAFSA, state aid form. **Notification of Awards:** Applicants will be notified of awards on a rolling basis beginning 3/1. **Types of Aid:** *Need-based scholarships/grants:* Federal Pell, SEOG, state scholarships/grants, private scholarships, the school's own gift aid. *Loans:* Subsidized Stafford, Unsubsidized Stafford, PLUS. **Student Employment:** Federal Work-Study Program available. Institutional employment available. Off-campus job opportunities are excellent. **Financial Aid Statistics:** 96% freshmen, 98% undergrads receive need-based scholarship or grant aid. 11% freshmen, 5% undergrads receive non-need-based scholarship or grant aid. 85% freshmen, 91% undergrads receive need-based self-help aid. 95% undergrads borrow to pay for school. Average cumulative indebtedness $41,482. **Criteria for awarding institutional aid:** *Non-need-based:* academics, art.

OTTERBEIN COLLEGE

Office of Admission, Westerville, OH 43081
Phone: 614-823-1500 • **Financial Aid Phone:** 614-823-1502
E-mail: uotterb@otterbein.edu • **CEEB Code:** 1597
Fax: 614-823-1200 • **Website:** www.otterbein.edu • **ACT Code:** 3318

This private school, affiliated with the Methodist Church, was founded in 1847. It has a 140-acre campus.

RATINGS
Admissions Selectivity Rating: 70   **Fire Safety Rating:** 00*   **Green Rating:** 60*

STUDENTS AND FACULTY
Student Body: 10% out-of-state, (12 countries represented).
Retention and Graduation: 92% freshmen return for sophomore year.
Faculty: Student/faculty ratio 12:1. 161 full-time faculty, 93% hold PhDs, 11% are members of minority groups, 55% are women. 0% of classes are taught by teaching assistants.

ACADEMICS
Degrees: bachelor's, master's. **Majors with Highest Enrollment:** business/commerce; education; nursing/registered nurse (rn, asn, bsn, msn). **Special Study Options:** Accelerated program, cooperative education program, cross-registration, double major, dual enrollment, exchange student program (domestic), honors program, independent study, internships, liberal arts/career combination, student-designed major, study abroad, teacher certification program, weekend college. **Honors Programs:** The Honors Program at Otterbein College is designed to provide intellectual stimulation and challenge for students with high academic ability and motivation. The four-year program provides the opportunity to participate in a community of students and faculty who have shared scholarly and creative interests. As part of that community students develop and complete their own Honors research and creative projects. Through the Honors seminars and Honors project, students develop advanced knowledge in their disciplinary fields and acquire the skills for independent work in their own areas of academic and professional interest. The Honors Program at Otterbein College is designed to provide intellectual stimulation and challenge for students with high academic ability and motivation. The four-year program provides the opportunity to participate in a community of students and faculty who have shared scholarly and creative interests. As part of that community students develop and complete their own Honors research and creative projects. Through the Honors seminars and Honors project, students develop advanced knowledge in their disciplinary fields and acquire the skills for independent work in their own areas of academic and professional interest. **Disability Services:** Special programs offered to physically disabled students include note-taking services, reader services, tape recorders, tutors. **Career Services:** Alumni network, alumni services, career/job search classes, career assessment, internships, regional alumni.

FACILITIES
Housing: Coed dorms, men's dorms, women's dorms, fraternity/sorority housing, apartments for single students, theme housing. **Special Academic Facilities/Equipment:** Language lab, horse stable, observatory and planetarium,

Celestron 8-inch and 14-inch telescopes, 3 art galleries. **Computers:** Students can register for classes online. Administrative functions (other than registration) can be performed online.

CAMPUS LIFE
Environment: Town. **Activities:** Choral groups, concert band, dance, drama/theater, jazz band, literary magazine, marching band, music ensembles, musical theater, opera, pep band, radio station, student government, student newspaper, symphony orchestra, television station, yearbook, International Student Organization 100 registered organizations, 7 fraternities, 6 sororities. **Athletics (Intercollegiate):** *Men:* baseball, basketball, cheerleading, cross-country, equestrian sports, football, golf, soccer, tennis, track/field (outdoor), track/field (indoor). *Women:* basketball, cheerleading, cross-country, equestrian sports, golf, soccer, softball, tennis, track/field (outdoor), track/field (indoor), volleyball. **On-Campus Highlights:** Clements Recreation Center, Cowen Hall- Theatre, Campus Center, Art Galleries/Art Building

ADMISSIONS
Freshman Academic Profile: Average high school GPA 3.3. 24% in top 10% of high school class, 55% in top 25% of high school class, 85% in top 50% of high school class. SAT Math middle 50% range 480-590. SAT Critical Reading middle 50% range 470-600. SAT Writing middle 50% range 460-600. ACT middle 50% range 20-25. Minimum paper TOEFL 500. **Basis for Candidate Selection:** *Important factors considered include:* Class rank, rigor of secondary school record, standardized test scores. *Other factors considered include:* application essay, recommendation(s), alumni/ae relation, character/personal qualities, extracurricular activities, interview, racial/ethnic status, talent/ability, volunteer work, work experience. **Freshman Admission Requirements:** High school diploma is required and GED is accepted. **Freshman Admission Statistics:** 3,381 applied, 82% admitted, 24% enrolled. **Transfer Admission Requirements:** college transcript(s), minimum college GPA of 2.5 required. Lowest grade transferable C–. **General Admission Information:** Application Fee $25. Notification on a rolling basis, beginning on or about 10/15. Nonfall registration accepted. Admission may be deferred for a maximum of 12. Credit and/or placement offered for CEEB Advanced Placement tests.

COSTS AND FINANCIAL AID
Annual tuition $26,319. Room and board $7,461. Average book expense $700. **Required Forms and Deadlines:** FAFSA. **Types of Aid:** *Need-based scholarships/grants:* Federal Pell, SEOG, state scholarships/grants, private scholarships, the school's own gift aid. *Loans:* Direct Subsidized Stafford, Direct Unsubsidized Stafford, Direct PLUS, Federal Perkins. **Student Employment:** Federal Work-Study Program available. Institutional employment available. Highest amount earned per year from on-campus jobs $1,800. Off-campus job opportunities are excellent. **Criteria for awarding institutional aid:** *Non-need-based:* academics, alumni affiliation, art, leadership, minority status, music/drama, religious affiliation.

OUACHITA BAPTIST UNIVERSITY

410 Ouachita St, Arkadelphia, AR 71998-0001
Phone: 870-245-5110 • **Financial Aid Phone:** 870-245-5587
E-mail: admissions@alpha.obu.edu • **CEEB Code:** 6549
Fax: 870-245-5500 • **Website:** • **ACT Code:** 134

This private school, affiliated with the Southern Baptist Church, was founded in 1886. It has a 200-acre campus.

RATINGS
Admissions Selectivity Rating: 76   **Fire Safety Rating:** 92   **Green Rating:** 60*

STUDENTS AND FACULTY
Enrollment: 1,503. **Student Body:** 54% female, 46% male, 41% out-of-state, 2% international (36 countries represented). Asian 1%, African American 7%, Caucasian 86%, Hispanic 3%, Native American 1%.
Retention and Graduation: 76% freshmen return for sophomore year. 50% freshmen graduate within 4 years. 59% freshmen graduate within 6 years. 44% grads go on to further study within 1 year. 22% grads pursue arts and sciences degrees. 2% grads pursue law degrees. 2% grads pursue business degrees. 13% grads pursue medical degrees. **Faculty:** Student/faculty ratio 12:1. 110 full-time faculty, 84% hold PhDs, 4% are members of minority groups, 36% are women. 0% of classes are taught by teaching assistants.

ACADEMICS
Degrees: bachelor's, terminal associate. **Classes:** Most classes have 10–19 students. Most lab/discussion sessions have fewer than 10 students. **Majors with Highest Enrollment:** biology/biological sciences; business administration and management; mass communication/media studies. **Special Study Options:**

cross-registration, distance learning, double major, English as a Second Language (ESL), honors program, independent study, internships, study abroad, teacher certification program. **Disability Services:** Special programs offered to physically disabled students include note-taking services, reader services, tape recorders, tutors. **Career Services:** Alumni network, alumni services, career/job search classes, career assessment, internships Career Services highlights include Tiger Career Connection (online job postings and resources).

FACILITIES

Housing: special housing for disabled students, men's dorms, women's dorms, apartments for married students, apartments for single students. 95% of campus accessible to physically disabled. **Special Academic Facilities/Equipment:** Historical archives, Senator John McClellan collection, language lab, TV studio. **Computers:** 100% of classrooms, 100% of dorms, 100% of libraries, 100% of dining areas, 100% of student union, 50% of common outdoor areas have wireless network access. Administrative functions (other than registration) can be performed online.

CAMPUS LIFE

Environment: Village. **Activities:** Choral groups, concert band, dance, drama/theater, jazz band, literary magazine, marching band, music ensembles, musical theater, opera, pep band, student government, student newspaper, television station, yearbook, Campus Ministries, International Student Organization, Model UN 60 registered organizations, 8 honor societies, 4 religious organizations. 5 fraternities, 5 sororities. **Athletics (Intercollegiate):** *Men:* baseball, basketball, diving, football, golf, soccer, swimming, tennis, wrestling. *Women:* basketball, cross-country, diving, golf, soccer, softball, swimming, tennis, volleyball. **On-Campus Highlights:** Starbuck's, Chick-fil-A, Commons (dining), Student Center, Sturgis Recreation Center. **Environmental Initiatives:** Employment of Energy Management Director Faculty and staff initiatives for reduction of utility use Re-cycling.

ADMISSIONS

Freshman Academic Profile: 38% in top 10% of high school class, 61% in top 25% of high school class, 86% in top 50% of high school class. 86% from public high schools. SAT Math middle 50% range 460-590. SAT Critical Reading middle 50% range 470-590. ACT middle 50% range 21-28. Minimum web-based TOEFL 80. Minimum paper TOEFL 550. **Basis for Candidate Selection:** *Very important factors considered include:* academic GPA, rigor of secondary school record, standardized test scores.*Other factors considered include:* character/personal qualities, talent/ability. **Freshman Admission Requirements:** High school diploma is required and GED is accepted. *Academic units required:* 4 English, 2 mathematics, 2 science, 1 social studies, 2 history, 4 academic electives. *Academic units recommended:* 4 English, 2 mathematics, 2 science, 1 social studies, 2 history, 4 academic electives. **Freshman Admission Statistics:** 1,822 applied, 69% admitted, 29% enrolled. **Transfer Admission Requirements:** college transcript(s), statement of good standing from prior institution(s). Minimum college GPA of 2.0 required. Lowest grade transferable C. **General Admission Information:** Nonfall registration accepted. Admission may be deferred for a maximum of 1 year. Credit offered for CEEB Advanced Placement tests.

COSTS AND FINANCIAL AID

Annual tuition $21,860. Room and board $6,640. Required fees $480. Average book expense $1,100. **Required Forms and Deadlines:** FAFSA. **Notification of Awards:** Applicants will be notified of awards on a rolling basis beginning 11/1. **Types of Aid:** *Need-based scholarships/grants:* Federal Pell, SEOG, state scholarships/grants, private scholarships, the school's own gift aid. *Loans:* Subsidized Stafford, Unsubsidized Stafford, PLUS, Federal Perkins, state loans, college/university loans from institutional funds, Alternative Loans. **Student Employment:** Federal Work-Study Program available. Highest amount earned per year from on-campus jobs $1,800. Off-campus job opportunities are fair. **Financial Aid Statistics:** 95% freshmen, 95% undergrads receive need-based scholarship or grant aid. 25% freshmen, 26% undergrads receive non-need-based scholarship or grant aid. 70% freshmen, 71% undergrads receive need-based self-help aid. 5% freshmen, 7% undergrads receive athletic scholarships. 98% freshmen, 96% undergrads receive any aid. 46% undergrads borrow to pay for school. Average cumulative indebtedness $24,367. **Criteria for awarding institutional aid:** *Non-need-based:* academics, alumni affiliation, art, athletics, leadership, minority status, music/drama, religious affiliation, state/district residency.

OUR LADY OF THE LAKE UNIVERSITY (OLLU)

Admissions Office, San Antonio, TX 78207-4689
Phone: 210-431-3961 • **Financial Aid Phone:** 800-324-4310
E-mail: webmaster@ollusa.edu • **CEEB Code:** 6550
Fax: 210-431-4036 • **Website:** www.ollusa.edu • **ACT Code:** 4140

This private school, affiliated with the Roman Catholic Church, was founded in 1895. It has a 75-acre campus.

RATINGS

Admissions Selectivity Rating: 79   **Fire Safety Rating:** 61   **Green Rating:** 60*

STUDENTS AND FACULTY

Enrollment: 1,554. **Student Body:** 73% female, 27% male, 2% out-of-state, 1% international. Asian 1%, African American 8%, Caucasian 17%, Hispanic 63%, Native American 1%.
Retention and Graduation: 60% freshmen return for sophomore year. 14% freshmen graduate within 4 years. 32% freshmen graduate within 6 years. 30% grads go on to further study within 1 year. **Faculty:** Student/faculty ratio 15:1. 101 full-time faculty, 80% hold PhDs, 35% are members of minority groups, 60% are women. 0% of classes are taught by teaching assistants.

ACADEMICS

Degrees: bachelor's, master's. **Classes:** Most classes have fewer than 10 students. **Special Study Options:** cooperative education program, cross-registration, distance learning, double major, dual enrollment, English as a Second Language (ESL), honors program, independent study, internships, liberal arts/career combination, study abroad, teacher certification program, weekend college, service learning. **Disability Services:** Special programs offered to physically disabled students include note-taking services, reader services, tape recorders, tutors. **Career Services:** alumni services, career assessment.

FACILITIES

Housing: Coed dorms, special housing for disabled students, men's dorms, women's dorms, wellness housing. 99% of campus accessible to physically disabled. **Special Academic Facilities/Equipment:** Lab school for children with language and learning disabilities, elementary demonstration school, intercultural institute for training and research, language lab.

CAMPUS LIFE

Activities: Choral groups, dance, drama/theater, jazz band, music ensembles, musical theater, student government, student newspaper, symphony orchestra, television station, Campus Ministries.

ADMISSIONS

Freshman Academic Profile: Average high school GPA 3.3. 22% in top 10% of high school class, 49% in top 25% of high school class, 82% in top 50% of high school class. % from public high schools. SAT Math middle 50% range 410-513. SAT Critical Reading middle 50% range 400-500. ACT middle 50% range 17-21. Minimum web-based TOEFL 79. Minimum paper TOEFL 650. **Basis for Candidate Selection:** *Very important factors considered include:* academic GPA, rigor of secondary school record, standardized test scores. *Important factors considered include:* Class rank. *Other factors considered include:* application essay, recommendation(s), alumni/ae relation, character/personal qualities, extracurricular activities, first generation, interview, talent/ability, volunteer work, work experience. **Freshman Admission Requirements:** High school diploma is required and GED is accepted. *Academic units required:* 4 English, 2 mathematics, 2 science, (2 science labs), 3 foreign language, 3 social studies, 3 academic electives. *Academic units recommended:* 4 English, 2 mathematics, 2 science, (2 science labs), 3 foreign language, 3 social studies, 3 academic electives. **Freshman Admission Statistics:** 2,109 applied, 49% admitted, 29% enrolled. **Transfer Admission Requirements:** college transcript(s), minimum college GPA of 2.0 required. Lowest grade transferable D. **General Admission Information:** Application Fee $25. Regular application deadline 7/15. Nonfall registration accepted. Admission may be deferred for a maximum of 1 year. Credit offered for CEEB Advanced Placement tests.

COSTS AND FINANCIAL AID

Annual tuition $22,256. Room and board $7,327. Required fees $456. Average book expense $1,200. **Required Forms and Deadlines:** FAFSA. **Notification of Awards:** Applicants will be notified of awards on a rolling basis beginning 4/1. **Types of Aid:** *Need-based scholarships/grants:* Federal Pell, SEOG, state scholarships/grants, private scholarships, the school's own gift aid. *Loans:* Subsidized Stafford, Unsubsidized Stafford, PLUS, Federal Perkins, state loans, Private Loans. **Student Employment:** Federal Work-Study Program available. Institutional employment available. Highest amount earned per year from on-campus jobs $1,206. Off-campus job opportunities are good. **Financial Aid Statistics:** 99% freshmen, 96% undergrads receive need-based scholarship or grant aid. 3% freshmen, 6% undergrads receive non-need-based scholarship or grant aid. 71% freshmen, 84% undergrads receive need-based self-help aid. 5% freshmen, 7% undergrads receive athletic scholarships. 91% freshmen, 89% undergrads receive any aid. 90% undergrads borrow to pay for school. Average cumulative indebtedness $32,356. **Criteria for awarding institutional aid:** *Non-need-based:* academics, alumni affiliation, art, music/drama.

PACE UNIVERSITY

1 Pace Plaza, New York, NY 10038
Phone: 212-346-1323 • **Financial Aid Phone:** 212-346-1309
E-mail: infoctr@pace.edu • **CEEB Code:** 2635
Fax: 212-346-1040 • **Website:** www.pace.edu • **ACT Code:** 2852

This private school was founded in 1906. It has a 1-acre campus.

RATINGS
Admissions Selectivity Rating: 74   **Fire Safety Rating:** 88   **Green Rating:** 65

STUDENTS AND FACULTY
Enrollment: 7,867. **Student Body:** 59% female, 41% male, 37% out-of-state, 6% international (103 countries represented). Asian 9%, African American 11%, Caucasian 47%, Hispanic 16%, Native American 0%.
Retention and Graduation: 76% freshmen return for sophomore year. 39% freshmen graduate within 4 years. 56% freshmen graduate within 6 years. 20% grads go on to further study within 1 year. **Faculty:** Student/faculty ratio 14:1. 466 full-time faculty, 88% hold PhDs, 19% are members of minority groups, 46% are women. 0% of classes are taught by teaching assistants.

ACADEMICS
Degrees: associate, bachelor's, certificate, first professional, first professional certificate, master's, post-bachelor's certificate, post-master's certificate. **Classes:** Most classes have 10–19 students. Most lab/discussion sessions have fewer than 10 students. **Majors with Highest Enrollment:** accounting; finance; nursing/registered nurse (rn, asn, bsn, msn). **Special Study Options:** Accelerated program, cooperative education program, cross-registration, distance learning, double major, dual enrollment, English as a Second Language (ESL), honors program, independent study, internships, study abroad, teacher certification program, Evening and freshman studies programs, Pre-freshman summer program, Learning Communities and Service Learning. **Honors Programs:** Pforzheimer Honors College for incoming freshmen. **Combined Degree Programs:** BA/JD, BA/MA, BBA/MBA; BA/MPA. **Disability Services:** Special programs offered to physically disabled students include note-taking services, reader services, tape recorders. **Career Services:** Alumni network, alumni services, career/job search classes, career assessment, internships, regional alumni. Career Services highlights include Cooperative Education/Internship Program.

FACILITIES
Housing: Coed dorms, apartments for single students, Apartment style for 3-4 upperclassmen. 100% of campus accessible to physically disabled. **Special Academic Facilities/Equipment:** Laboratory Theatre, Communication Center, Language Center, Center for the Arts, Art Gallery, English Language Institute. **Computers:** 20% of classrooms, 10% of dorms, 100% of libraries, 100% of dining areas, 100% of student union, have wireless network access. Students can register for classes online. Administrative functions (other than registration) can be performed online.

CAMPUS LIFE
Environment: Metropolis. **Activities:** Choral groups, dance, drama/theater, literary magazine, musical theater, radio station, student government, student newspaper, student-run film society, television station, yearbook, International Student Organization, Model UN 79 registered organizations, 25 honor societies, 4 religious organizations. 11 fraternities, 9 sororities. **Athletics (Intercollegiate):** *Men:* baseball, basketball, cross-country, football, golf, lacrosse, swimming, tennis, track/field (outdoor), track/field (indoor). *Women:* basketball, cheerleading, cross-country, equestrian sports, soccer, softball, swimming, tennis, track/field (outdoor), track/field (indoor), volleyball. **On-Campus Highlights:** Library, Fitness Center, Theater, Classrooms, Dormitories. **Environmental Initiatives:** Environmental Law Program - Pace Law School Environmental Sciences Program at Dyson College of Arts & Science New York City Mayoral Challenge and participation with the Clinton Climate Initiative

ADMISSIONS
Freshman Academic Profile: Average high school GPA 3.2. 19% in top 10% of high school class, 51% in top 25% of high school class, 86% in top 50% of high school class. 81% from public high schools. SAT Math middle 50% range 500-600. SAT Critical Reading middle 50% range 490-590. ACT middle 50% range 21-25. Minimum paper TOEFL 570. **Basis for Candidate Selection:** *Very important factors considered include:* rigor of secondary school

record, standardized test scores. *Important factors considered include:* Class rank, academic GPA. *Other factors considered include:* application essay, recommendation(s), alumni/ae relation, character/personal qualities, extracurricular activities, talent/ability, volunteer work, work experience. **Freshman Admission Requirements:** High school diploma is required and GED is accepted. *Academic units required:* 4 English, 3 mathematics, 2 science, (2 science labs), 2 foreign language, 1 social studies, 2 history, 2 academic electives. *Academic units recommended:* 4 English, 3 mathematics, 2 science, (2 science labs), 2 foreign language, 1 social studies, 2 history, 2 academic electives. **Freshman Admission Statistics:** 12,885 applied, 77% admitted, 19% enrolled. **Transfer Admission Requirements:** college transcript(s), statement of good standing from prior institution(s). Minimum college GPA of 2.5 required. Lowest grade transferable C. **General Admission Information:** Application Fee $45. Regular application deadline 3/1. Notification on a rolling basis, beginning on or about 12/15. Nonfall registration accepted. Admission may be deferred for a maximum of 12 mo. Credit offered for CEEB Advanced Placement tests.

COSTS AND FINANCIAL AID
Annual tuition $35,320. Room and board $14,720. Required fees $1,134. Average book expense $800. **Required Forms and Deadlines:** FAFSA, state aid form. **Notification of Awards:** Applicants will be notified of awards on a rolling basis beginning 2/25. **Types of Aid:** *Need-based scholarships/grants:* Federal Pell, SEOG, state scholarships/grants, private scholarships, the school's own gift aid, Federal Nursing Scholarships. , Endowed and Restricted scholarships and grants. *Loans:* Direct Subsidized Stafford, Direct Unsubsidized Stafford, Direct PLUS, Federal Perkins, Federal Nursing. **Student Employment:** Highest amount earned per year from on-campus jobs $1,564. Off-campus job opportunities are good. **Financial Aid Statistics:** 100% freshmen, 99% undergrads receive need-based scholarship or grant aid. 7% freshmen, 6% undergrads receive non-need-based scholarship or grant aid. 85% freshmen, 84% undergrads receive need-based self-help aid. 1% undergrads receive athletic scholarships. 82% freshmen, 68% undergrads receive any aid. 74% undergrads borrow to pay for school. Average cumulative indebtedness $35,895. **Criteria for awarding institutional aid:** *Non-need-based:* academics, athletics, music/drama.

PACIFIC LUTHERAN UNIVERSITY

Office of Admission, Tacoma, WA 98447
Phone: 253-535-7151 • **Financial Aid Phone:** 253-535-7134
E-mail: admissions@plu.edu • **CEEB Code:** 4597
Fax: 253-536-5136 • **Website:** www.plu.edu • **ACT Code:** 4597

This private school, affiliated with the Lutheran Church, was founded in 1890. It has a 126-acre campus.

RATINGS
Admissions Selectivity Rating: 75   **Fire Safety Rating:** 80   **Green Rating:** 92

STUDENTS AND FACULTY
Enrollment: 3,111. **Student Body:** 62% female, 38% male, 22% out-of-state, 4% international (21 countries represented). Asian 5%, African American 3%, Caucasian 72%, Hispanic 7%, Native American 1%.
Retention and Graduation: 83% freshmen return for sophomore year. 52% freshmen graduate within 4 years. 11% grads go on to further study within 1 year. **Faculty:** Student/faculty ratio 15:1. 204 full-time faculty, 88% hold PhDs, 13% are members of minority groups, 54% are women. 0% of classes are taught by teaching assistants.

ACADEMICS
Degrees: bachelor's, master's, post-bachelor's certificate, post-master's certificate. **Classes:** Most classes have 20–29 students. Most lab/discussion sessions have 10–19 students. **Majors with Highest Enrollment:** business administration and management; communication studies/speech communication and rhetoric; nursing/registered nurse (rn, asn, bsn, msn). **Special Study Options:** cooperative education program, cross-registration, double major, dual enrollment, English as a Second Language (ESL), exchange student program (domestic), honors program, independent study, internships, liberal arts/career combination, student-designed major, study abroad, teacher certification program. **Honors Programs:** International Honors Program **Combined Degree Programs:** BA/MEng. **Disability Services:** Special programs offered to physically disabled students include note-taking services, reader services, tape recorders, tutors. **Career Services:** alumni services, career/job search classes, career assessment.

FACILITIES
Housing: Coed dorms, special housing for disabled students, special housing for international students, women's dorms, apartments for married students,

apartments for single students, Foreign Languages Learning Housing. 90% of campus accessible to physically disabled. **Special Academic Facilities/Equipment:** Mary Baker Russell Music Center Wekell Art Gallery Keck Observatory Rieke Science Center Scandinavian Cultural Center Morken Center for Learning and Technology **Computers:** 25% of classrooms, 25% of dorms, 100% of libraries, 100% of dining areas, 100% of student union, 25% of common outdoor areas have wireless network access. Students can register for classes online.

CAMPUS LIFE
Environment: City. **Activities:** Choral groups, concert band, dance, drama/theater, jazz band, literary magazine, music ensembles, musical theater, opera, pep band, radio station, student government, student newspaper, student-run film society, symphony orchestra, television station, yearbook, Campus Ministries, International Student Organization 67 registered organizations, 6 honor societies, 8 religious organizations. **Athletics (Intercollegiate):** *Men:* baseball, basketball, cheerleading, crew/rowing, cross-country, football, golf, soccer, swimming, tennis, track/field (outdoor), track/field (indoor). *Women:* basketball, cheerleading, crew/rowing, cross-country, golf, soccer, softball, swimming, tennis, track/field (outdoor), track/field (indoor), volleyball. **On-Campus Highlights:** Keck Observatory, Rieke Science Center, Mary Baker Russell Music Center, Wekell Art Gallery, Names Fitness Center, Morken Center for Learning and Technology, Scandinavian Cultural Center. **Environmental Initiatives:** Successfully building a community commitment to sustainability that encompasses students, faculty and staff in part through sustainability fellowships. Including environmental goals for waste diversion, reduction of water and electricity consumption, LEED building and carbon neutrality into the campus master plan. PLU is in the leadership circle for the President's Climate Commitment and is planning to meet all goals and deadlines of that commitment.

ADMISSIONS
Freshman Academic Profile: Average high school GPA 3.6. 37% in top 10% of high school class, 67% in top 25% of high school class, 86% in top 50% of high school class. % from public high schools. SAT Math middle 50% range 490-610. SAT Critical Reading middle 50% range 480-610. SAT Writing middle 50% range 470-590. ACT middle 50% range 21-27. Minimum web-based TOEFL 79. Minimum paper TOEFL 550. **Basis for Candidate Selection:** *Very important factors considered include:* application essay, rigor of secondary school record. *Important factors considered include:* Class rank, academic GPA, recommendation(s), standardized test scores, character/personal qualities, extracurricular activities, talent/ability, volunteer work. *Other factors considered include:* interview, work experience. **Freshman Admission Requirements:** High school diploma is required and GED is accepted. *Academic units required:* 2 mathematics, 2 foreign language. *Academic units recommended:* 2 mathematics, 2 foreign language. **Freshman Admission Statistics:** 3,550 applied, 74% admitted, 24% enrolled. **Transfer Admission Requirements:** High school transcript, college transcript(s), essay or personal statement, statement of good standing from prior institution(s). Minimum college GPA of 2.5 required. Lowest grade transferable C–. **General Admission Information:** Application Fee $40. Notification on a rolling basis, beginning on or about 10/1. Nonfall registration accepted. Admission may be deferred for a maximum of 2 years. Credit and/or placement offered for CEEB Advanced Placement tests.

COSTS AND FINANCIAL AID
Annual tuition $34,440. Room and board $10,100. Required fees $300. Average book expense $1,000. **Required Forms and Deadlines:** FAFSA. **Notification of Awards:** Applicants will be notified of awards on a rolling basis beginning 3/15. **Types of Aid:** *Need-based scholarships/grants:* Federal Pell, SEOG, state scholarships/grants, private scholarships, the school's own gift aid, Federal Nursing Scholarships. *Loans:* Subsidized Stafford, Unsubsidized Stafford, PLUS, Federal Perkins, Federal Nursing, state loans. **Student Employment:** Federal Work-Study Program available. Institutional employment available. Highest amount earned per year from on-campus jobs $13,754. Off-campus job opportunities are good. **Financial Aid Statistics:** 99% freshmen, 98% undergrads receive need-based scholarship or grant aid. 80% freshmen, 80% undergrads receive non-need-based scholarship or grant aid. 89% freshmen receive need-based self-help aid. 98% freshmen, 99% undergrads receive any aid. 69% undergrads borrow to pay for school. Average cumulative indebtedness $29,649. **Criteria for awarding institutional aid:** *Non-need-based:* academics, alumni affiliation, art, leadership, music/drama, religious affiliation.

See page 1170.

PACIFIC NORTHWEST COLLEGE OF ART

1241 NW Johnson Street, Portland, OR 97209
Phone: 503-821-8972
E-mail: admissions@pnca.edu • **CEEB Code:** 4504
Fax: 503-821-8978 • **Website:** www.pnca.edu • **ACT Code:** 3477

This private school was founded in 1909. It has a 1-acre campus.

RATINGS
Admissions Selectivity Rating: 73   **Fire Safety Rating:** 64   **Green Rating:** 60*

STUDENTS AND FACULTY
Enrollment: 288. **Student Body:** 59% female, 41% male, 24% out-of-state, 0% international. Asian 3%, African American 1%, Caucasian 92%, Hispanic 3%, Native American 1%.
Retention and Graduation: 66% freshmen return for sophomore year. 18% freshmen graduate within 4 years. 33% freshmen graduate within 6 years.
Faculty: Student/faculty ratio 11:1. 13 full-time faculty, 85% hold PhDs, 0% are members of minority groups, 38% are women. 0% of classes are taught by teaching assistants.

ACADEMICS
Degrees: bachelor's. **Classes:** Most classes have 10–19 students. **Majors with Highest Enrollment:** design and visual communications; painting; photography. **Special Study Options:** cross-registration, exchange student program (domestic), independent study, internships, student-designed major, study abroad. **Combined Degree Programs:** 5-year B.A./B.F.A. program with Reed College. **Career Services:** career/job search classes, internships.

FACILITIES
Housing: apartments for single studentsHousing/student dorm available through College Housing Northwest in Portland, Oregon. 100% of campus accessible to physically disabled. **Special Academic Facilities/Equipment:** Student galleries, darkrooms, student painting studios, printmaking studio, computer labs. **Computers:** Administrative functions (other than registration) can be performed online.

CAMPUS LIFE
Environment: Metropolis. **Activities:** student government 2 registered organizations. **On-Campus Highlights:** Stevens Studios, Feldman Gallery

ADMISSIONS
Freshman Academic Profile: Average high school GPA 3.0. 89% from public high schools. SAT Math middle 50% range 370-590. SAT Critical Reading middle 50% range 440-650. ACT middle 50% range 16-26. Minimum paper TOEFL 550. **Basis for Candidate Selection:** *Very important factors considered include:* academic GPA, talent/ability. *Important factors considered include:* application essay, rigor of secondary school record, extracurricular activities, interview. *Other factors considered include:* recommendation(s), standardized test scores, character/personal qualities, level of applicant's interest. **Freshman Admission Requirements:** High school diploma is required and GED is accepted. **Freshman Admission Statistics:** 120 applied, 73% admitted, 31% enrolled. **Transfer Admission Requirements:** college transcript(s), essay or personal statement, minimum college GPA of 2.0 required. Lowest grade transferable C. **General Admission Information:** Application Fee $35. Notification on a rolling basis, beginning on or about 1/1. Nonfall registration accepted. Admission may be deferred for a maximum of 2 years. Credit and/or placement offered for CEEB Advanced Placement tests.

COSTS AND FINANCIAL AID
Annual tuition $16,490. Room and board $4,500. Required fees $806. Average book expense $98,500. **Required Forms and Deadlines:** FAFSA. **Notification of Awards:** Applicants will be notified of awards on a rolling basis beginning 4/1. **Types of Aid:** *Need-based scholarships/grants:* Federal Pell, SEOG, state scholarships/grants, private scholarships, the school's own gift aid. *Loans:* Subsidized Stafford, Unsubsidized Stafford, PLUS. **Student Employment:** Highest amount earned per year from on-campus jobs $1,000. **Financial Aid Statistics:** 77% freshmen, 97% undergrads receive need-based scholarship or grant aid. 12% undergrads receive non-need-based scholarship or grant aid. 77% freshmen, 97% undergrads receive need-based self-help aid. 79% undergrads borrow to pay for school. Average cumulative indebtedness $24,974. **Criteria for awarding institutional aid:** *Non-need-based:* academics, art.

PACIFIC STATES UNIVERSITY

3450 Wilshire blvd, 5th floor, Los Angeles, CA 90010
Phone: 323-731-2383 EXT:203
E-mail: admission@psuca.edu
Fax: 323-731-7276 • **Website:** www.psuca.edu

This private school was founded in 1928.

RATINGS
Admissions Selectivity Rating: 63 **Fire Safety Rating:** 60* **Green Rating:** 60*

STUDENTS AND FACULTY
Enrollment: 14. **Student Body:** 5% out-of-state, 57% international. Asian 14%, African American 7%, Caucasian 7%, Hispanic 0%, Native American 0%.
Retention and Graduation: 100% freshmen return for sophomore year.
Faculty: Student/faculty ratio 6:1. 7 full-time faculty, 43% hold PhDs, % are members of minority groups, 29% are women.

ACADEMICS
Degrees: bachelor's, doctoral, master's, post-bachelor's certificate. **Special Study Options:** distance learning, double major, English as a Second Language (ESL), independent study.

FACILITIES
Housing: Coed dorms.

CAMPUS LIFE
Environment: Metropolis. **Activities:** television station.

ADMISSIONS
Basis for Candidate Selection. *Important factors considered include:* standardized test scores. *Other factors considered include:* application essay, academic GPA, rigor of secondary school record, level of applicant's interest. **Freshman Admission Requirements:** High school diploma is required and GED is accepted. **Freshman Admission Statistics:** 2 applied, 50% admitted, 100% enrolled. **Transfer Admission Requirements:** college transcript(s), minimum college GPA of 2.5 required. Lowest grade transferable C. **General Admission Information:** Nonfall registration not accepted.

COSTS AND FINANCIAL AID
Annual tuition $14,055. Room and board $7,200. Required fees $540. Average book expense $1,800. **Required Forms and Deadlines:** FAFSA. **Types of Aid:** *Need-based scholarships/grants:* Federal Pell. *Loans:* Direct Subsidized Stafford, Direct Unsubsidized Stafford.

PACIFIC UNION COLLEGE

Enrollment Services, Angwin, CA 94508
Phone: 707-965-6336 • **Financial Aid Phone:** 707-965-7200
E-mail: enroll@puc.edu • **CEEB Code:** 4600
Fax: 707-965-6671 • **Website:** www.puc.edu • **ACT Code:** 362

This private school, affiliated with the Seventh Day Adventist Church, was founded in 1882. It has a 200-acre campus.

RATINGS
Admissions Selectivity Rating: 86 **Fire Safety Rating:** 81 **Green Rating:** 66

STUDENTS AND FACULTY
Enrollment: 1,524. **Student Body:** 55% female, 45% male, 18% out-of-state, 3% international (21 countries represented). Asian 19%, African American 7%, Caucasian 29%, Hispanic 24%, Native American 1%.
Retention and Graduation: 78% freshmen return for sophomore year. 23% freshmen graduate within 4 years. **Faculty:** Student/faculty ratio 13:1. 92 full-time faculty, 50% hold PhDs, 33% are members of minority groups, 49% are women. 0% of classes are taught by teaching assistants.

ACADEMICS
Degrees: associate, bachelor's, master's. **Classes:** Most classes have fewer than 10 students. Most lab/discussion sessions have fewer than 10 students. **Majors with Highest Enrollment:** business/commerce; nursing/registered nurse (rn, asn, bsn, msn); teacher education, multiple levels. **Special Study Options:** cooperative education program, double major, external degree program, honors program, independent study, internships, study abroad, teacher certification program. **Honors Programs:** The Honors Program offers an alternative general-education program for academically motivated students. There are no other general education requirements. Students fulfilling the Honors Program graduate "With Honors.". **Disability Services:** Special programs offered to physically disabled students include note-taking services, reader services, tape recorders, tutors. **Career Services:** career/job search classes, career assessment, internships Career Services highlights include Spring break externship program available to anyone that preregisters.

FACILITIES
Housing: men's dorms, women's dorms, apartments for married students. 80% of campus accessible to physically disabled. **Special Academic Facilities/Equipment:** Art gallery, natural history collection, Pitcairn Island studies center, on-campus elementary and high schools, airport, flight training facility, observatory. **Computers:** Students can register for classes online. Administrative functions (other than registration) can be performed online.

CAMPUS LIFE
Environment: Rural. **Activities:** Choral groups, concert band, drama/theater, jazz band, literary magazine, music ensembles, musical theater, radio station, student government, student newspaper, student-run film society, symphony orchestra, yearbook 24 registered organizations, 8 honor societies. **Athletics (Intercollegiate):** *Men:* basketball, cross-country, volleyball. *Women:* basketball, cross-country, volleyball. **On-Campus Highlights:** Campus Center, Clark Hall/Museum, Pacific Auditorium (Gym), Paulin Auditorium (Music), 1500 acres of hiking/biking land.

ADMISSIONS
Freshman Academic Profile: Average high school GPA 3.3. 31% from public high schools. SAT Math middle 50% range 420-580. SAT Critical Reading middle 50% range 440-590. SAT Writing middle 50% range 440-560. ACT middle 50% range 18-24. Minimum web-based TOEFL 70. Minimum paper TOEFL 525. **Basis for Candidate Selection:** *Very important factors considered include:* recommendation(s), rigor of secondary school record. *Important factors considered include:* academic GPA, character/personal qualities, level of applicant's interest. *Other factors considered include:* standardized test scores, extracurricular activities, interview, religious affiliation/commitment. **Freshman Admission Requirements:** High school diploma is required and GED is accepted. *Academic units required:* 4 English, 2 mathematics, 1 science, 1 history. *Academic units recommended:* 4 English, 2 mathematics, 1 science, 1 history. **Freshman Admission Statistics:** 2,105 applied, 47% admitted, 29% enrolled. **Transfer Admission Requirements:** High school transcript, college transcript(s), minimum college GPA of 2.0 required. Lowest grade transferable C–. **General Admission Information:** Application Fee $30. Notification on a rolling basis, beginning on or about 1/15. Nonfall registration accepted. Admission may be deferred for a maximum of 1 year. Credit offered for CEEB Advanced Placement tests.

COSTS AND FINANCIAL AID
Annual tuition $26,550. Room and board $7,485. Required fees $300. Average book expense $1,710. **Required Forms and Deadlines:** FAFSA, institution's own financial aid form, state aid form, business/farm supplement. Federal tax returns. **Types of Aid:** *Need-based scholarships/grants:* Federal Pell, SEOG, state scholarships/grants, the school's own gift aid. *Loans:* Subsidized Stafford, Unsubsidized Stafford, PLUS, Federal Perkins, college/university loans from institutional funds. **Student Employment:** Federal Work-Study Program available. Institutional employment available. Highest amount earned per year from on-campus jobs $3,000. Off-campus job opportunities are fair. **Financial Aid Statistics:** 100% freshmen, 100% undergrads receive need-based scholarship or grant aid. 23% freshmen, 36% undergrads receive non-need-based scholarship or grant aid. 96% freshmen, 97% undergrads receive need-based self-help aid. 2% freshmen receive athletic scholarships. 76% undergrads borrow to pay for school. Average cumulative indebtedness $33,662. **Criteria for awarding institutional aid:** *Non-need-based:* academics, leadership, religious affiliation.

PACIFIC UNIVERSITY

2043 College Way, Forest Grove, OR 97116
Phone: 503-352-2218 • **Financial Aid Phone:** 503-352-2222
E-mail: admissions@pacificu.edu • **CEEB Code:** 4601
Website: www.pacificu.edu

This private school was founded in 1849. It has a 60-acre campus.

RATINGS
Admissions Selectivity Rating: 75 **Fire Safety Rating:** 70 **Green Rating:** 73

STUDENTS AND FACULTY
Enrollment: 1,555. **Student Body:** 58% female, 42% male, 47% out-of-state, 2% international (32 countries represented). Asian 14%, African American 2%,

Caucasian 56%, Hispanic 8%, Native American 1%.
Retention and Graduation: 75% freshmen return for sophomore year. 51% freshmen graduate within 4 years. 61% freshmen graduate within 6 years. 24% grads go on to further study within 1 year. 11% grads pursue arts and sciences degrees. 4% grads pursue law degrees. 2% grads pursue business degrees. 2% grads pursue medical degrees. **Faculty:** Student/faculty ratio 10:1. 216 full-time faculty, 87% hold PhDs, 13% are members of minority groups, 51% are women. 0% of classes are taught by teaching assistants.

ACADEMICS

Degrees: bachelor's, master's. **Classes:** Most classes have 10–19 students. Most lab/discussion sessions have 10–19 students. **Majors with Highest Enrollment:** biology/biological sciences; business administration and management; kinesiology and exercise science. **Special Study Options:** cross-registration, double major, English as a Second Language (ESL), independent study, internships, liberal arts/career combination, study abroad, teacher certification program. **Combined Degree Programs:** 3-2 applied physics program and 4-1 computer scien. **Disability Services:** Special programs offered to physically disabled students include note-taking services, reader services, tape recorders, tutors. **Career Services:** Alumni network, alumni services, career/job search classes, career assessment, internships, regional alumni. Career Services highlights include Internships.

FACILITIES

Housing: Coed dorms, special housing for disabled students, apartments for single students, theme housing, one wing designated for women. **Special Academic Facilities/Equipment:** State history museum, performing arts center, media center, humanitarian center, Holocaust resource center, politics/law forum, Berglund Center for Internet Studies, electron microscopes. **Computers:** 100% of classrooms, 100% of dorms, 100% of libraries, 100% of dining areas, 100% of student union, 90% of common outdoor areas have wireless network access. Administrative functions (other than registration) can be performed online.

CAMPUS LIFE

Environment: Village. **Activities:** Choral groups, concert band, dance, drama/theater, jazz band, literary magazine, music ensembles, pep band, radio station, student government, student newspaper, student-run film society, Campus Ministries, International Student Organization 58 registered organizations, 2 honor societies, 4 religious organizations. 3 fraternities, 4 sororities. **Athletics (Intercollegiate):** *Men:* baseball, basketball, cross-country, golf, soccer, swimming, tennis, track/field (outdoor), wrestling. *Women:* basketball, cross-country, golf, lacrosse, soccer, softball, swimming, tennis, track/field (outdoor), volleyball, wrestling. **On-Campus Highlights:** Pacific Athletic Center, Pacific Library (New Library), Marsh Hall, Old College Hall, New Bookstore/Vera's Cafe. **Environmental Initiatives:** Sustainability Committee New LEED-certified buldings B-Street Permaculture Project.

ADMISSIONS

Freshman Academic Profile: Average high school GPA 3.6. 34% in top 10% of high school class, 66% in top 25% of high school class, 92% in top 50% of high school class. 88% from public high schools. SAT Math middle 50% range 510-610. SAT Critical Reading middle 50% range 490-600. ACT middle 50% range 21-26. Minimum paper TOEFL 550. **Basis for Candidate Selection:** *Very important factors considered include:* academic GPA, recommendation(s), rigor of secondary school record, standardized test scores, character/personal qualities, extracurricular activities, level of applicant's interest, volunteer work. *Important factors considered include:* Class rank, application essay, talent/ability. *Other factors considered include:* alumni/ae relation, first generation, work experience. **Freshman Admission Requirements:** High school diploma is required and GED is accepted. **Freshman Admission Statistics:** 2,499 applied, 75% admitted, 20% enrolled. **Transfer Admission Requirements:** college transcript(s), essay or personal statement, statement of good standing from prior institution(s). Minimum college GPA of 2.70 required. Lowest grade transferable C–. **General Admission Information:** Application Fee $40. Regular application deadline 8/15. Notification on a rolling basis, beginning on or about 10/1. Nonfall registration accepted. Admission may be deferred for a maximum of 2 years. Credit and/or placement offered for CEEB Advanced Placement tests.

COSTS AND FINANCIAL AID

Annual tuition $34,460. Room and board $9,992. Required fees $800. Average book expense $1,050. **Required Forms and Deadlines:** FAFSA. **Notification of Awards:** Applicants will be notified of awards on a rolling basis beginning 3/1. **Types of Aid:** *Need-based scholarships/grants:* Federal Pell, SEOG, state scholarships/grants, private scholarships, the school's own gift aid. *Loans:* Subsidized Stafford, Unsubsidized Stafford, PLUS, Federal Perkins, Private Alternative Loans. **Student Employment:** Federal Work-Study Program available. Institutional employment available. **Financial Aid Statistics:** 97% freshmen, 94% undergrads receive need-based scholarship or grant aid. 8% freshmen, 7% undergrads receive non-need-based scholarship or grant aid. 86% fresh-

men, 88% undergrads receive need-based self-help aid. 93% freshmen, 93% undergrads receive any aid. 74% undergrads borrow to pay for school. Average cumulative indebtedness $29,303. **Criteria for awarding institutional aid:** *Non-need-based:* academics, alumni affiliation, art, music/drama.

PALM BEACH ATLANTIC UNIVERSITY

PO Box 24708, West Palm Beach, FL 33416-4708
Phone: 561-803-2100 • **Financial Aid Phone:** 561-803-2126
E-mail: admit@pba.edu • **CEEB Code:** 5553
Fax: 561-803-2115 • **Website:** www.pba.edu • **ACT Code:** 739

This private school, affiliated with the Christian (Nondenominational) Church, was founded in 1968. It has a 25-acre campus.

RATINGS

Admissions Selectivity Rating: 66   **Fire Safety Rating:** 60*   **Green Rating:** 61

STUDENTS AND FACULTY

Enrollment: 2,334. **Student Body:** 65% female, 35% male, 27% out-of-state, 4% international (28 countries represented). Asian 2%, African American 16%, Caucasian 60%, Hispanic 13%, Native American 0%.
Retention and Graduation: 68% freshmen return for sophomore year. 39% freshmen graduate within 4 years. **Faculty:** Student/faculty ratio 31:1. 165 full-time faculty, 81% hold PhDs, 10% are members of minority groups, 48% are women. 0% of classes are taught by teaching assistants.

ACADEMICS

Degrees: associate, bachelor's, master's. **Classes:** Most classes have 10–19 students. Most lab/discussion sessions have 10–19 students. **Majors with Highest Enrollment:** accounting and business/management; education; psychology. **Special Study Options:** Accelerated program, distance learning, double major, dual enrollment, honors program, independent study, internships, student-designed major, study abroad, teacher certification program. **Honors Programs:** The Frederick M. Supper Honors Program exists to establish a community of scholars. The program encourages students to develop a thoughtful and insightful Christian worldview through enduring conversation to enable students to live the examined life and to facilitate character formation. **Combined Degree Programs:** BA/MA. **Career Services:** alumni services, career/job search classes, career assessment, internships, Career Services highlights include The Workship program is a distinctive service program at PBA which enables students to offer a Christian response to human needs by serving in nonprofit agencies, churches, and schools outside the university community.

FACILITIES

Housing: Coed dorms, men's dorms, women's dorms, apartments for married students, theme housing. **Special Academic Facilities/Equipment:** DeSantis Family Chapel; Greene Sports Complex (Cafe); Helen K.Persson Recital Hall **Computers:** Students can register for classes online. Administrative functions (other than registration) can be performed online.

CAMPUS LIFE

Environment: Metropolis. **Activities:** Choral groups, dance, drama/theater, jazz band, literary magazine, music ensembles, musical theater, pep band, radio station, student government, student newspaper, symphony orchestra, television station, yearbook, Campus Ministries, International Student Organization 56 registered organizations, 29 honor societies, 6 religious organizations. **Athletics (Intercollegiate):** *Men:* baseball, basketball, cross-country, soccer, tennis. *Women:* basketball, cross-country, soccer, softball, tennis, volleyball. **On-Campus Highlights:** DeSantis Family Chapel, Greene Complex (athletics, snack shop), Vera Lea Rinker Music Building.

ADMISSIONS

Freshman Academic Profile: SAT Math middle 50% range 445-570. SAT Critical Reading middle 50% range 470-580. ACT middle 50% range 20-25. Minimum paper TOEFL 550. **Basis for Candidate Selection:** *Very important factors considered include:* academic GPA, standardized test scores, character/personal qualities. *Important factors considered include:* application essay, recommendation(s), rigor of secondary school record, interview. *Other factors considered include:* Class rank, alumni/ae relation, extracurricular activities, religious affiliation/commitment, talent/ability, volunteer work. **Freshman Admission Requirements:** High school diploma is required and GED is accepted. *Academic units required:* 4 English, 3 mathematics, 4 science, (2 science labs). 4 English, 3 mathematics, 4 science, (2 science labs). **Freshman Admission Statistics:** 1,380 applied, 96% admitted, 34% enrolled. **Transfer Admission Requirements:** college transcript(s), essay or personal statement, minimum college GPA of 2.5 required. Lowest grade transferable C. **General Admission Information:** Notification on a rolling basis, beginning on or about

9/1. Nonfall registration accepted. Admission may be deferred for a maximum of 1 year. Credit offered for CEEB Advanced Placement tests.

COSTS AND FINANCIAL AID

Annual tuition $24,500. Room and board $8,220. Required fees $300. Average book expense $960. **Required Forms and Deadlines:** FAFSA. **Notification of Awards:** Applicants will be notified of awards on a rolling basis beginning 2/15. **Types of Aid:** *Need-based scholarships/grants:* Federal Pell, SEOG, state scholarships/grants, private scholarships, the school's own gift aid. *Loans:* Subsidized Stafford, Unsubsidized Stafford, PLUS. **Student Employment:** Federal Work-Study Program available. Institutional employment available. Off-campus job opportunities are good. **Financial Aid Statistics:** 100% freshmen, 99% undergrads receive need-based scholarship or grant aid. 11% freshmen, 9% undergrads receive non-need-based scholarship or grant aid. 73% freshmen, 79% undergrads receive need-based self-help aid. 5% freshmen, 3% undergrads receive athletic scholarships. 100% freshmen, 100% undergrads receive any aid. 67% undergrads borrow to pay for school. Average cumulative indebtedness $24,750. **Criteria for awarding institutional aid:** *Non-need-based:* academics, alumni affiliation, athletics, minority status, music/drama, state/district residency.

PALMER COLLEGE OF CHIROPRACTIC

1000 Brady Street, Davenport, IA 52803
Phone: 563-884-5656
E-mail: pcadmit@palmer.edu
Fax: 563-884-5414 • **Website:** admissons.palmer.edu

This private school was founded in 1897.

RATINGS

Admissions Selectivity Rating: 60*   **Fire Safety Rating:** 60*   **Green Rating:** 60*

STUDENTS AND FACULTY

Faculty: Student/faculty ratio 14:1.

ACADEMICS

Degrees: associate, bachelor's, first professional, master's. **Career Services:** alumni services, internships.

FACILITIES

Special Academic Facilities/Equipment: Palmer Mansion, Specific Collections, David.D.Palmer Library **Computers:** Students can register for classes online.

CAMPUS LIFE

Activities: 78 registered organizations, 1 honor societies, 3 fraternities, 1 sororities. **Athletics (Intercollegiate):** *Men:* baseball, ice hockey, rugby, soccer. *Women:* soccer, softball.

ADMISSIONS

Transfer Admission Requirements: Minimum college GPA of 2.5 required. **General Admission Information:** Application Fee $50. Nonfall registration accepted. Admission may be deferred for a maximum of 3 times.

COSTS AND FINANCIAL AID

Annual tuition $4,665. Required fees $105. Average book expense $100. **Student Employment:** Federal Work-Study Program available. Institutional employment available. Off-campus job opportunities are excellent.

PARK UNIVERSITY

8700 NW River Park Drive, Parkville, MO 64152
Phone: 816-584-6213 • **Financial Aid Phone:** 816-548-6290
E-mail: admissions@mail.park.edu • **CEEB Code:** 6574
Fax: 816-741-4462 • **ACT Code:** 2340

This private school was founded in 1875. It has a 700-acre campus.

RATINGS

Admissions Selectivity Rating: 69   **Fire Safety Rating:** 72   **Green Rating:** 60*

STUDENTS AND FACULTY

Enrollment: 1,672. **Student Body:** 56% female, 44% male, 20% out-of-state, 19% international (93 countries represented). Asian 0%, African American 10%, Caucasian 61%, Hispanic 5%, Native American 1%.

Retention and Graduation: 61% freshmen return for sophomore year. 22% freshmen graduate within 4 years. 39% freshmen graduate within 6 years. 7% grads go on to further study within 1 year. 6% grads pursue arts and sciences degrees. 1% grads pursue business degrees. **Faculty:** Student/faculty ratio 12:1. 82 full-time faculty, 66% hold PhDs, 4% are members of minority groups, 38% are women. 0% of classes are taught by teaching assistants.

ACADEMICS

Degrees: associate, bachelor's, master's, post-bachelor's certificate. **Majors with Highest Enrollment:** business/commerce; human resources management/personnel administration; management information systems. **Special Study Options:** Accelerated program, cross-registration, distance learning, double major, dual enrollment, English as a Second Language (ESL), honors program, independent study, internships, student-designed major, study abroad, teacher certification program, weekend college. **Disability Services:** Special programs offered to physically disabled students include note-taking services, reader services, tape recorders, tutors.

FACILITIES

Housing: Coed dorms, apartments for married students. 90% of campus accessible to physically disabled. **Computers:** Students can register for classes online. Administrative functions (other than registration) can be performed online.

CAMPUS LIFE

Environment: Town. **Activities:** Choral groups, drama/theater, literary magazine, radio station, student government, student newspaper, symphony orchestra, yearbook 15 registered organizations, 4 honor societies, 13 religious organizations. **Athletics (Intercollegiate):** *Men:* baseball, basketball, cross-country, soccer, track/field (outdoor), track/field (indoor), volleyball. *Women:* basketball, cross-country, golf, soccer, softball, track/field (outdoor), track/field (indoor), volleyball. **On-Campus Highlights:** Gym, Cafeteria, Classrooms (Underground), Library, Bookstore.

ADMISSIONS

Freshman Academic Profile: Average high school GPA 3.3. 14% in top 10% of high school class, 37% in top 25% of high school class, 68% in top 50% of high school class. 80% from public high schools. ACT middle 50% range 17-23. Minimum paper TOEFL 500. **Basis for Candidate Selection:** *Very important factors considered include:* Class rank, rigor of secondary school record, standardized test scores. *Other factors considered include:* application essay, recommendation(s). **Freshman Admission Requirements:** High school diploma is required and GED is accepted. **Freshman Admission Statistics:** 778 applied, 69% admitted, 39% enrolled. **Transfer Admission Requirements:** High school transcript, college transcript(s), minimum college GPA of 2.0 required. Lowest grade transferable C. **General Admission Information:** Application Fee $25. Regular application deadline 7/1. Nonfall registration accepted. Admission may be deferred for a maximum of Maximum of 1 year. Credit and/or placement offered for CEEB Advanced Placement tests.

COSTS AND FINANCIAL AID

Annual tuition $10,380. Required fees $100. Average book expense $1,800. **Required Forms and Deadlines:** FAFSA, institution's own financial aid form. **Types of Aid:** *Need-based scholarships/grants:* Federal Pell, SEOG, state scholarships/grants, private scholarships, the school's own gift aid. *Loans:* Subsidized Stafford, Unsubsidized Stafford, PLUS, Federal Perkins, college/university loans from institutional funds. **Student Employment:** Federal Work-Study Program available. **Financial Aid Statistics:** 78% freshmen, 73% undergrads receive need-based scholarship or grant aid. 75% freshmen, 53% undergrads receive non-need-based scholarship or grant aid. 56% freshmen, 71% undergrads receive need-based self-help aid. 17% freshmen, 11% undergrads receive athletic scholarships. 78% freshmen receive any aid. 41% undergrads borrow to pay for school. Average cumulative indebtedness $22,210. **Criteria for awarding institutional aid:** *Non-need-based:* academics, alumni affiliation, art, athletics, job skills, leadership, minority status, music/drama, religious affiliation.

PARSONS THE NEW SCHOOL FOR DESIGN

72 Fifth Avenue, New York, NY 10011
Phone: 212-229-8910 • **Financial Aid Phone:** 212-229-8930
E-mail: thinkparsons@newschool.edu • **CEEB Code:** 2638
Fax: 212 229 8975 • **Website:** www.parsons.edu • **ACT Code:** 2854

This private school was founded in 1896.

RATINGS

Admissions Selectivity Rating: 78   **Fire Safety Rating:** 77   **Green Rating:** 91

STUDENTS AND FACULTY

Enrollment: 4,254. **Student Body:** 79% female, 21% male, 72% out-of-state, 36% international (81 countries represented). Asian 16%, African American 4%, Caucasian 29%, Hispanic 9%.

Retention and Graduation: 86% freshmen return for sophomore year.
Faculty: Student/faculty ratio 10:1. 151 full-time faculty, 59% hold PhDs, 14% are are members of minority groups, 48% are women. 0% of classes are taught by teaching assistants.

ACADEMICS

Degrees: associate, bachelor's, certificate, master's. **Classes:** Most classes have 10–19 students. Most lab/discussion sessions have 20–29 students. **Majors with Highest Enrollment:** design and visual communications; fashion/apparel design; illustration. **Special Study Options:** Accelerated program, cross-registration, distance learning, double major, dual enrollment, English as a Second Language (ESL), exchange student program (domestic), independent study, internships, liberal arts/career combination, student-designed major, study abroad, five year combined BA/BFA. **Combined degree programs:** BA/BFA, MA/ARC. **Disability Services:** Special programs offered to physically disabled students include note-taking services, reader services, tape recorders. **Career services:** Alumni network, alumni services, career/job search classes, career assessment, internships, regional alumni.

FACILITIES

Housing: Coed dorms, special housing for disabled students, apartments for single students. 99% of campus accessible to physically disabled. **Special Academic Facilities/Equipment:** Fashion Education Center in New York's garment district with labs and studios for fashion design students. **Computers:** 95% of classrooms, 100% of libraries, 100% of dining areas, na% of student union, 100% of common outdoor areas have wireless network access. Students can register for classes online. Administrative functions (other than registration) can be performed online.

CAMPUS LIFE

Environment: Metropolis. **Activities:** Choral groups, dance, drama/theater, jazz band, literary magazine, music ensembles, radio station, student government, student newspaper, symphony orchestra, International Student Organization. 34 registered organizations. **On-Campus Highlights:** Sheila Johnson Design Center, Schwartz Fashion Center, University Welcome Center **Environmental Initiatives:** 1. In fall 2010, The New School Facilities Management hired an engineering firm to conduct energy audits and to retro-commission five of the most energy-intensive owned buildings on campus. The result will be a phased capital plan to address needed upgrades in these buildings, equating to 500,000gsf, that will reduce carbon emissions.

ADMISSIONS

Freshman Academic Profile: Average high school GPA 3.3. 25% in top 10% of high school class, 50% in top 25% of high school class, 76% in top 50% of high school class. SAT Math middle 50% range 500-640. SAT Critical Reading middle 50% range 490-600. SAT Writing middle 50% range 500-620. ACT middle 50% range 21-27. Minimum web-based TOEFL 92. Minimum paper TOEFL 580. **Basis for Candidate Selection:** Very important factors considered include: academic GPA, rigor of secondary school record, standardized test scores, level of applicant's interest, talent/ability. Important factors considered include: interview. Other factors considered include: Class rank, application essay, recommendation(s), extracurricular activities. **Freshman Admission Requirements:** High school diploma is required and GED is accepted. **Freshman Admission Statistics:** 2,590 applied, 70% admitted, 39% enrolled. **Transfer Admission Requirements:** college transcript(s), Minimum college GPA of 2.0 required. Lowest grade transferable C. **General Admission Information:** Application Fee $50. Notification on a rolling basis, beginning on or about 3/21. Nonfall registration accepted. Admission may be deferred for a maximum of 1 year. Neither credit nor placement offered for CEEB Advanced Placement tests.

COSTS AND FINANCIAL AID

Annual tuition $38,510. Room and board $15,260. Required fees 840. Average book expense $2,050. **Required Forms and Deadlines:** FAFSA, state aid form. **Notification of Awards:** Applicants will be notified of awards on a rolling basis beginning 3/1. **Types of Aid:** Need-based scholarships/grants: Federal Pell, SEOG, state scholarships/grants, private scholarships, the school's own gift aid. Loans: Subsidized Stafford, Unsubsidized Stafford, PLUS, Federal Perkins. Student Employment: Federal Work-Study Program available. Institutional employment available. Off-campus job opportunities are excellent. **Financial Aid Statistics:** 93% freshmen, 89% undergrads receive need-based scholarship or grant aid. 16% freshmen, 8% undergrads receive non-need-based scholarship or grant aid. 80% freshmen, 77% undergrads receive need-based self-help aid. 65% undergrads borrow to pay for school. Average cumulative indebtedness $32,800. **Criteria for awarding institutional aid:** Non-need-based: academics, art.

PATRICK HENRY COLLEGE

Ten Patrick Henry Circle, Purcellville, VA 20132
Financial Aid Phone: 540-441-8142
E-mail: admissions@phc.edu
Fax: 540-441-8119 • **Website:** www.phc.edu • **ACT Code:** 4383

This private school, affiliated with the Christian (Nondenominational) Church, was founded in 2000. It has a 106-acre campus.

RATINGS

Admissions Selectivity Rating: 81   **Fire Safety Rating:** 85   **Green Rating:** 61

STUDENTS AND FACULTY

Enrollment: 301. **Student Body:** 49% female, 51% male, 87% out-of-state.
Retention and Graduation: 88% freshmen return for sophomore year. 10% grads go on to further study within 1 year. 23% grads pursue law degrees.
Faculty: Student/faculty ratio 10:1. 24 full-time faculty, 96% hold PhDs. 0% of classes are taught by teaching assistants.

ACADEMICS

Degrees: bachelor's. **Classes:** Most classes have fewer than 10 students. **Majors with Highest Enrollment:** american government and politics (united states); journalism. **Special Study Options:** distance learning, liberal arts/career combination. **Disability Services:** Special programs offered to physically disabled students include tutors. **Career Services:** internships.

FACILITIES

Housing: men's dorms, women's dorms. 100% of campus accessible to physically disabled. **Computers:** 100% of classrooms, 100% of dorms, 100% of libraries, 100% of dining areas, 100% of student union, 100% of common outdoor areas have wireless network access. Students can register for classes online. Administrative functions (other than registration) can be performed online. Undergraduates are required to own a computer.

CAMPUS LIFE

Environment: Village. **Activities:** Choral groups, concert band, drama/theater, literary magazine, music ensembles, student government, student newspaper, student-run film society, yearbook, Campus Ministries, Model UN. **Athletics (Intercollegiate):** *Men:* basketball, soccer. *Women:* basketball, soccer. **On-Campus Highlights:** Student Coffee Lounge, Workout facilities, Raquetball courts **Environmental Initiatives:** water conservation energy management recycling

ADMISSIONS

Freshman Academic Profile: Average high school GPA 3.8. 15% from public high schools. SAT Math middle 50% range 540-670. SAT Critical Reading middle 50% range 640-740. SAT Writing middle 50% range 600-700. ACT middle 50% range 25-31. **Basis for Candidate Selection:** *Very important factors considered include:* application essay, academic GPA, recommendation(s), rigor of secondary school record, standardized test scores, character/personal qualities, extracurricular activities, interview, religious affiliation/commitment, talent/ability, volunteer work. *Important factors considered include:* level of applicant's interest. *Other factors considered include:* Class rank, alumni/ae relation, first generation, work experience. **Freshman Admission Requirements:** High school diploma is required and GED is accepted. *Academic units required:* 4 English, 3 mathematics, 2 science, 1 foreign language, 3 history, 5 academic electives. *Academic units recommended:* 4 English, 3 mathematics, 2 science, 1 foreign language, 3 history, 5 academic electives. **Freshman Admission Statistics:** 132 applied, 83% admitted, 41% enrolled. **Transfer Admission Requirements:** High school transcript, college transcript(s), essay or personal statement, interview, standardized test scores, statement of good standing from prior institution(s). Lowest grade transferable C. **General Admission Information:** Application Fee $40. Regular application deadline 6/15. Notification on a rolling basis, beginning on or about 10/1. Nonfall registration accepted. Admission may be deferred for a maximum of one year. Credit and/or placement offered for CEEB Advanced Placement tests.

COSTS AND FINANCIAL AID

Average book expense $500. **Required Forms and Deadlines:** institution's own financial aid form, CSS/Financial Aid PROFILE. **Types of Aid:** *Need-based scholarships/grants:* private scholarships, the school's own gift aid. *Loans:* private loans. **Student Employment:** Institutional employment available. Highest amount earned per year from on-campus jobs $2,880. Off-campus job opportunities are good. **Financial Aid Statistics:** 100% freshmen, 100% undergrads receive need-based scholarship or grant aid. 72% freshmen, 80% undergrads receive non-need-based scholarship or grant aid. 94% freshmen, 94% undergrads receive any aid. 0% undergrads borrow to pay for school. Average cumulative indebtedness $0. **Criteria for awarding institutional aid:** *Non-need-based:* academics, leadership, music/drama.

PATTEN UNIVERSITY

2433 Coolidge Avenue, Oakland, CA 94601-2699
Phone: 877-472-8836
E-mail: admissions@patten.edu
Fax: 510-534-4344 • Website: www.patten.edu

This is a private school.

RATINGS
Admissions Selectivity Rating: 61   Fire Safety Rating: 60*   Green Rating: 60*

STUDENTS AND FACULTY
Retention and Graduation: 40% freshmen return for sophomore year.

ACADEMICS
Degrees: associate, bachelor's, certificate, master's, post-bachelor's certificate, terminal associate, transfer associate.

FACILITIES
Housing: Coed dorms.

CAMPUS LIFE
Activities: 2 religious organizations.

ADMISSIONS
Freshman Academic Profile: Minimum paper TOEFL 500. General Admission Information: Regular application deadline 7/15.

COSTS AND FINANCIAL AID
Annual tuition $11,520. Room and board $6,000. Average book expense $500. Types of Aid: *Loans:* Subsidized Stafford, PLUS. Student Employment: Federal Work-Study Program available. Highest amount earned per year from on-campus jobs $550.

THE PENNSYLVANIA ACADEMY
OF THE FINE ARTS

128 North Broad Street, Philadelphia, PA 19102
Phone: 215-972-7625 • Financial Aid Phone: 215-972-2019
E-mail: admissions@pafa.edu • CEEB Code:
Fax: 215-569-0153 • Website: www.pafa.edu • ACT Code:

This private school was founded in 1804.

RATINGS
Admissions Selectivity Rating: 61   Fire Safety Rating: 60*   Green Rating: 60*

STUDENTS AND FACULTY
Student Body: 25% out-of-state, (19 countries represented).
Faculty: Student/faculty ratio 13:1. 0% of classes are taught by teaching assistants.

ACADEMICS
Degrees: bachelor's, certificate, master's, post-bachelor's certificate. Majors with Highest Enrollment: painting. Special Study Options: dual enrollment, exchange student program (domestic), independent study, internships. Combined Degree Programs: BFA in conjunction wit the University of Pennsylvania.

FACILITIES
Housing: The Pennsylvania Academy has a housing arrangement with International House, Philadelphia. We do not offer our own on-campus housing opportunities.

CAMPUS LIFE
Environment: Metropolis. Activities: student government 4 registered organizations. On-Campus Highlights: Museum of American Art, World Famous Cast Hall.

ADMISSIONS
Freshman Academic Profile: Minimum web-based TOEFL 100. Minimum paper TOEFL 600. Basis for Candidate Selection: *Very important factors considered include:* application essay, academic GPA. *Important factors considered include:* interview. *Other factors considered include:* recommendation(s), standardized test scores. Freshman Admission Requirements: High school diploma is required and GED is accepted. Transfer Admission Require-

ments: High school transcript, essay or personal statement, Lowest grade transferable C. General Admission Information: Notification on a rolling basis, beginning on or about 9/15. Neither credit nor placement offered for CEEB Advanced Placement tests.

COSTS AND FINANCIAL AID
Annual tuition $27,950. Room and board $6,800. Required fees $770. Average book expense $1,314. Required Forms and Deadlines: FAFSA. Types of Aid: *Need-based scholarships/grants:* Federal Pell, SEOG, state scholarships/grants, private scholarships, the school's own gift aid. *Loans:* Subsidized Stafford, Unsubsidized Stafford, PLUS. Student Employment: Federal Work-Study Program available. Institutional employment available. Highest amount earned per year from on-campus jobs $5,000. Off-campus job opportunities are excellent. Financial Aid Statistics: 80% freshmen, 80% undergrads receive any aid. Criteria for awarding institutional aid: *Non-need-based:* academics.

PENNSYLVANIA COLLEGE OF TECHNOLOGY

One College Avenue, Williamsport, PA 17701
Phone: 570-327-4761 • Financial Aid Phone: 570-327-4766
E-mail: admissions@pct.edu
Fax: 570-321-5551 • Website: www.pct.edu/princeton/

This public school was founded in 1989. It has a 984-acre campus.

RATINGS
Admissions Selectivity Rating: 61   Fire Safety Rating: 72   Green Rating: 60*

STUDENTS AND FACULTY
Enrollment: 6,427. Student Body: 36% female, 64% male, 9% out-of-state, 0% international. Asian 1%, African American 3%, Caucasian 93%, Hispanic 1%, Native American 1%.
Retention and Graduation: 70% freshmen return for sophomore year. Faculty: Student/faculty ratio 18:1. 297 full-time faculty, 3% are members of minority groups, 29% are women. 0% of classes are taught by teaching assistants.

ACADEMICS
Degrees: associate, bachelor's, certificate, transfer associate. Special Study Options: Accelerated program, cooperative education program, cross-registration, distance learning, dual enrollment, exchange student program (domestic), honors program, independent study, internships, student-designed major, study abroad, weekend college. Disability Services: Special programs offered to physically disabled students include note-taking services, reader services, tape recorders, tutors. Career Services: alumni services Career Services highlights include www.pct.edu/careerservices/.

FACILITIES
Housing: Coed dorms, apartments for single students, wellness housing. 100% of campus accessible to physically disabled. Computers: Students can register for classes online. Administrative functions (other than registration) can be performed online.

CAMPUS LIFE
Environment: Town. Activities: dance, radio station, student government, Campus Ministries 50 registered organizations, 3 honor societies, 4 religious organizations. 3 fraternities. Athletics (Intercollegiate): *Men:* archery, baseball, basketball, bowling, cross-country, golf, soccer, tennis, volleyball. *Women:* archery, basketball, bowling, cross-country, golf, soccer, softball, tennis, volleyball. On-Campus Highlights: Academic Facilities, Madigan Library, Campus Center, Student & Administrative Services Center, Academic Center.

ADMISSIONS
Freshman Academic Profile: Minimum paper TOEFL 500. Basis for Candidate Selection: *Very important factors considered include:* academic GPA, standardized test scores. *Important factors considered include:* application essay. *Other factors considered include:* recommendation(s), rigor of secondary school record. Freshman Admission Requirements: High school diploma is required and GED is accepted. Freshman Admission Statistics: 3,002 applied, 95% admitted, 0% enrolled. Transfer Admission Requirements: High school transcript, college transcript(s), minimum college GPA of 2.5 required. Lowest grade transferable C. General Admission Information: Application Fee $50. Regular application deadline 8/1. Nonfall registration accepted. Admission may be deferred for a maximum of One year. Credit offered for CEEB Advanced Placement tests.

COSTS AND FINANCIAL AID
Annual in-state tuition $10,020. Annual out-of-state tuition $13,050. Room and board $8,250. Required fees $1,770. Average book expense $1,000. Required

Forms and Deadlines: FAFSA, institution's own financial aid form, state aid form. Notification of Awards: Applicants will be notified of awards on a rolling basis beginning 3/1. Types of Aid: *Need-based scholarships/grants:* Federal Pell, state scholarships/grants, private scholarships, the school's own gift aid. *Loans:* Subsidized Stafford, Unsubsidized Stafford, PLUS. Student Employment: Institutional employment available. Highest amount earned per year from on-campus jobs $8,268. Off-campus job opportunities are good. Criteria for awarding institutional aid: *Non-need-based:* academics, alumni affiliation, leadership.

See page 1172.

PENNSYLVANIA STATE UNIVERSITY—ABINGTON

106 Sutherland, 1600 Woodland Rd, Abington, PA 19001
Phone: 215-881-7600
E-mail: abingtonadmissions@psu.edu
Fax: 215-881-7655 • **Website:** abington.psu.edu

This public school was founded in 1950. It has a 45-acre campus.

RATINGS
Admissions Selectivity Rating: 68   Fire Safety Rating: 60*   Green Rating: 60*

STUDENTS AND FACULTY
Enrollment: 3,033. **Student Body:** 47% female, 53% male, 6% out-of-state, 2% international. Asian 15%, African American 15%, Caucasian 55%, Hispanic 8%, Native American 0%.
Retention and Graduation: 23% freshmen graduate within 4 years. **Faculty:** Student/faculty ratio 20:1. 109 full-time faculty, 66% hold PhDs, 12% are members of minority groups, 48% are women.

ACADEMICS
Degrees: bachelor's, terminal associate, transfer associate. **Classes:** Most classes have 20–29 students. Most lab/discussion sessions have 20–29 students. **Special Study Options:** Accelerated program, cooperative education program, distance learning, double major, dual enrollment, English as a Second Language (ESL), exchange student program (domestic), external degree program, honors program, independent study, internships, liberal arts/career combination, student-designed major, study abroad.

CAMPUS LIFE
Environment: Village. **Activities:** dance, drama/theater, literary magazine, student government, student newspaper, student-run film society, Campus Ministries. **Athletics (Intercollegiate):** *Men:* basketball, soccer, softball, tennis. *Women:* basketball, field hockey, softball, tennis, volleyball.

ADMISSIONS
Freshman Academic Profile: Average high school GPA 3.0. 10% in top 10% of high school class, 28% in top 25% of high school class, 67% in top 50% of high school class. SAT Math middle 50% range 420-550. SAT Critical Reading middle 50% range 410-520. SAT Writing middle 50% range 400-510. Minimum paper TOEFL 550. **Basis for Candidate Selection:** *Very important factors considered include:* academic GPA, standardized test scores. *Important factors considered include:* rigor of secondary school record. *Other factors considered include:* Class rank, application essay, recommendation(s), alumni/ae relation, character/personal qualities, extracurricular activities, talent/ability, volunteer work, work experience. **Freshman Admission Requirements:** High school diploma is required and GED is accepted. *Academic units required:* 4 English, 3 mathematics, 3 science, 2 foreign language, 3 social studies. *Academic units recommended:* 4 English, 3 mathematics, 3 science, 2 foreign language, 3 social studies. **Freshman Admission Statistics:** 3,363 applied, 78% admitted, 31% enrolled. **Transfer Admission Requirements:** High school transcript, college transcript(s), Lowest grade transferable C. **General Admission Information:** Application Fee $50. Notification on a rolling basis, beginning on or about 11/1. Nonfall registration accepted. Admission may be deferred for a maximum of One Year.

COSTS AND FINANCIAL AID
Annual in-state tuition $12,242. Annual out-of-state tuition $18,682. Required fees $860. **Required Forms and Deadlines:** FAFSA. **Types of Aid:** *Need-based scholarships/grants:* Federal Pell, SEOG, state scholarships/grants, private scholarships, the school's own gift aid. *Loans:* Subsidized Stafford, Unsubsidized Stafford, PLUS, Federal Perkins, college/university loans from institutional funds, Private Loans. **Student Employment: Financial Aid Statistics:** 79% freshmen, 80% undergrads receive need-based scholarship or

grant aid. 47% freshmen, 25% undergrads receive non-need-based scholarship or grant aid. 84% freshmen, 85% undergrads receive need-based self-help aid. 66% undergrads borrow to pay for school. Average cumulative indebtedness $33,530. **Criteria for awarding institutional aid:** *Non-need-based:* academics, alumni affiliation, athletics, minority status.

PENNSYLVANIA STATE UNIVERSITY—ALTOONA

E108 Raymond Smith Building, Altoona, PA 16601-3760
Phone: 814-949-5466
E-mail: aaadmit@psu.edu
Fax: 814-949-5564 • **Website:** aa.psu.edu

This public school was founded in 1929.

RATINGS
Admissions Selectivity Rating: 67   Fire Safety Rating: 60*   Green Rating: 60*

STUDENTS AND FACULTY
Enrollment: 4,016. **Student Body:** 47% female, 53% male, 18% out-of-state, 1% international. Asian 2%, African American 7%, Caucasian 82%, Hispanic 4%, Native American 0%.
Retention and Graduation: 38% freshmen graduate within 4 years. 65% freshmen graduate within 6 years. **Faculty:** Student/faculty ratio 19:1. 173 full-time faculty, 72% hold PhDs, 9% are members of minority groups, 44% are women.

ACADEMICS
Degrees: bachelor's, terminal associate, transfer associate. **Classes:** Most classes have 20–29 students. Most lab/discussion sessions have 20–29 students. **Special Study Options:** cooperative education program, cross-registration, distance learning, double major, dual enrollment, English as a Second Language (ESL), exchange student program (domestic), honors program, independent study, internships, liberal arts/career combination, student-designed major, study abroad, teacher certification program.

FACILITIES
Housing: Coed dorms, special housing for disabled students, Suites, Special Interest Housing.

CAMPUS LIFE
Environment: Village. **Activities:** Choral groups, dance, drama/theater, jazz band, literary magazine, music ensembles, pep band, student government, student newspaper, student-run film society, yearbook, Campus Ministries, International Student Organization. **Athletics (Intercollegiate):** *Men:* basketball, diving, skiing (downhill/alpine), soccer, swimming, tennis, volleyball. *Women:* basketball, diving, skiing (downhill/alpine), swimming, tennis, volleyball.

ADMISSIONS
Freshman Academic Profile: Average high school GPA 3.0. 6% in top 10% of high school class, 27% in top 25% of high school class, 74% in top 50% of high school class. SAT Math middle 50% range 460-560. SAT Critical Reading middle 50% range 440-540. SAT Writing middle 50% range 440-530. **Basis for Candidate Selection:** *Very important factors considered include:* academic GPA, standardized test scores. *Important factors considered include:* rigor of secondary school record. *Other factors considered include:* Class rank, application essay, recommendation(s), alumni/ae relation, character/personal qualities, extracurricular activities, talent/ability, volunteer work, work experience. **Freshman Admission Requirements:** High school diploma is required and GED is accepted. *Academic units required:* 4 English, 3 mathematics, 3 science, 2 foreign language, 3 social studies. *Academic units recommended:* 4 English, 3 mathematics, 3 science, 2 foreign language, 3 social studies. **Freshman Admission Statistics:** 6,083 applied, 84% admitted, 31% enrolled. **Transfer Admission Requirements:** High school transcript, college transcript(s), Lowest grade transferable C. **General Admission Information:** Application Fee $50. Notification on a rolling basis, beginning on or about 11/1. Nonfall registration accepted. Admission may be deferred for a maximum of One Year.

COSTS AND FINANCIAL AID
Annual in-state tuition $12,776. Annual out-of-state tuition $19,548. Room and board $9,420. Required fees $860. Average book expense $1,536. **Required Forms and Deadlines:** FAFSA. **Types of Aid:** *Need-based scholarships/grants:* Federal Pell, SEOG, state scholarships/grants, private scholarships, the school's own gift aid. *Loans:* Subsidized Stafford, Unsubsidized Stafford, PLUS, Federal Perkins, college/university loans from institutional funds, Private Loans. **Student Employment: Financial Aid Statistics:** 62% freshmen, 65% undergrads receive need-based scholarship or grant aid. 35% freshmen, 31% undergrads receive non-need-based scholarship or grant aid. 89% freshmen,

90% undergrads receive need-based self-help aid. 66% undergrads borrow to pay for school. Average cumulative indebtedness $33,530. **Criteria for awarding institutional aid:** *Non-need-based:* academics, alumni affiliation, athletics, minority status.

PENNSYLVANIA STATE UNIVERSITY—BEAVER

100 University Drive, Monaca, PA 15061-2799 Phone: 724-773-3800 Financial Aid
Phone: 724-773-3519 • **E-mail:** br-admissions@psu.edu
Fax: 724-733-3658 • **Website:** www.br.psu.edu

This public school was founded in 1965. It has a 100-acre campus.

RATINGS
Admissions Selectivity Rating: 66   Fire Safety Rating: 60*   Green Rating: 60*

STUDENTS AND FACULTY
Enrollment: 724. **Student Body:** 45% female, 55% male, 8% out-of-state, 1% international. Asian 2%, African American 11%, Caucasian 77%, Hispanic 4%, Native American 0%.
Retention and Graduation: 29% freshmen graduate within 4 years. **Faculty:** Student/faculty ratio 18:1. 34 full-time faculty, 65% hold PhDs, 21% are members of minority groups, 53% are women.

ADMISSIONS
Freshman Academic Profile: 2.9. 7% in top 10% of high school class, 27% in top 25% of high school class, 60% in top 50% of high school class. SAT Math middle 50% range 410-550. SAT Critical Reading middle 50% range 420-520. SAT Writing middle 50% range 400-520. **Freshman Admission Statistics:** 737 applied, 86% admitted, 39% enrolled.

COSTS AND FINANCIAL AID
Annual in-state tuition $12,242. Annual out-of-state tuition $18,682. Room and board $9,420. Required fees $860. Average book expense $1,536. **Financial Aid Statistics:** 76% freshmen, 74% undergrads receive need-based scholarship or grant aid. 48% freshmen, 36% undergrads receive non-need-based scholarship or grant aid. 87% freshmen, 90% undergrads receive need-based self-help aid. 66% undergrads borrow to pay for school. Average cumulative indebtedness $33,530.

PENNSYLVANIA STATE UNIVERSITY—BERKS

Tulpehocken Road, PO Box 7009, Reading, PA 19610-6009
Phone: 610-396-6060
E-mail: admissionsbk@psu.edu
Fax: 610-396-6077 • **Website:** bk.psu.edu

This public school was founded in 1924. It has a 241-acre campus.

RATINGS
Admissions Selectivity Rating: 67   Fire Safety Rating: 60*   Green Rating: 60*

STUDENTS AND FACULTY
Enrollment: 2,666. **Student Body:** 44% female, 56% male, 9% out-of-state, 1% international. Asian 4%, African American 8%, Caucasian 75%, Hispanic 8%, Native American 0%.
Retention and Graduation: 32% freshmen graduate within 4 years. **Faculty:** Student/faculty ratio 18:1. 118 full-time faculty, 65% hold PhDs, 12% are members of minority groups, 51% are women.

ACADEMICS
Degrees: bachelor's, certificate, terminal associate, transfer associate. **Classes:** Most classes have 20–29 students. Most lab/discussion sessions have 10–19 students. **Special Study Options:** Accelerated program, cooperative education program, cross-registration, distance learning, dual enrollment, English as a Second Language (ESL), honors program, independent study, internships, study abroad, teacher certification program.

FACILITIES
Housing: Coed dorms, special housing for disabled students, Honor Students, Suites, Special Interest Houses.

CAMPUS LIFE
Environment: Village. **Activities:** Choral groups, dance, drama/theater, pep band, radio station, student government, student newspaper, student-run film

society, yearbook, Campus Ministries, International Student Organization. **Athletics (Intercollegiate):** *Men:* baseball, basketball, fencing, soccer, tennis, volleyball. *Women:* fencing, softball, tennis, volleyball.

ADMISSIONS
Freshman Academic Profile: Average high school GPA 3.0. 5% in top 10% of high school class, 25% in top 25% of high school class, 67% in top 50% of high school class. SAT Math middle 50% range 440-560. SAT Critical Reading middle 50% range 430-530. SAT Writing middle 50% range 420-520. Minimum paper TOEFL 550. **Basis for Candidate Selection:** *Very important factors considered include:* academic GPA, standardized test scores. *Important factors considered include:* rigor of secondary school record. *Other factors considered include:* Class rank, application essay, recommendation(s), alumni/ae relation, character/personal qualities, extracurricular activities, talent/ability, volunteer work, work experience. **Freshman Admission Requirements:** High school diploma is required and GED is accepted. *Academic units required:* 4 English, 3 mathematics, 3 science, 2 foreign language, 3 social studies. *Academic units recommended:* 4 English, 3 mathematics, 3 science, 2 foreign language, 3 social studies. **Freshman Admission Statistics:** 2,788 applied, 82% admitted, 38% enrolled. **Transfer Admission Requirements:** High school transcript, college transcript(s), Lowest grade transferable C. **General Admission Information:** Application Fee $50. Notification on a rolling basis, beginning on or about 11/1. Nonfall registration accepted. Admission may be deferred for a maximum of One Year.

COSTS AND FINANCIAL AID
Annual in-state tuition $12,776. Annual out-of-state tuition $19,548. Room and board $10,250. Required fees $860. Average book expense $1,536. **Required Forms and Deadlines:** FAFSA. **Types of Aid:** *Need-based scholarships/grants:* Federal Pell, SEOG, state scholarships/grants, private scholarships, the school's own gift aid. *Loans:* Direct Subsidized Stafford, Subsidized Stafford, Unsubsidized Stafford, PLUS, Federal Perkins, college/university loans from institutional funds, Private Loans. **Financial Aid Statistics:** 67% freshmen, 67% undergrads receive need-based scholarship or grant aid. 27% freshmen, 21% undergrads receive non-need-based scholarship or grant aid. 89% freshmen, 91% undergrads receive need-based self-help aid. 66% undergrads borrow to pay for school. Average cumulative indebtedness $33,530. **Criteria for awarding institutional aid:** *Non-need-based:* academics, alumni affiliation, athletics, minority status.

PENNSYLVANIA STATE UNIVERSITY— DELAWARE COUNTY

25 Yearsley Mill Road, Media, PA 19063-5596
Phone: 610-892-1200
E-mail: admissions-delco@psu.edu
Fax: 610-892-1320

This public school was founded in 1966. It has a 87-acre campus.

RATINGS
Admissions Selectivity Rating: 67   Fire Safety Rating: 60*   Green Rating: 60*

STUDENTS AND FACULTY
Enrollment: 1,455. **Student Body:** 43% female, 57% male, 4% out-of-state, 0% international. Asian 9%, African American 15%, Caucasian 74%, Hispanic 3%, Native American 0%.
Retention and Graduation: 69% freshmen return for sophomore year. **Faculty:** Student/faculty ratio 19:1. 61 full-time faculty, 57% hold PhDs, 15% are members of minority groups, 51% are women. 0% of classes are taught by teaching assistants.

ACADEMICS
Degrees: bachelor's, certificate, terminal associate, transfer associate. **Classes:** Most classes have 10–19 students. **Special Study Options:** distance learning, double major, dual enrollment, English as a Second Language (ESL), honors program, independent study, internships, study abroad, teacher certification program.

FACILITIES
Special Academic Facilities/Equipment: Culinary Archives and Museum.

CAMPUS LIFE
Environment: Village. **Activities:** Choral groups, dance, literary magazine, student government, student newspaper, student-run film society. **Athletics (Intercollegiate):** *Men:* baseball, basketball, ice hockey, riflery, soccer, tennis, volleyball. *Women:* basketball, ice hockey, riflery, soccer, tennis, volleyball.

ADMISSIONS

Freshman Academic Profile: Average high school GPA 2.9. 6% in top 10% of high school class, 23% in top 25% of high school class, 59% in top 50% of high school class. SAT Math middle 50% range 420-540. SAT Critical Reading middle 50% range 410-520. Minimum paper TOEFL 550. **Basis for Candidate Selection:** *Very important factors considered include:* academic GPA, standardized test scores. *Important factors considered include:* rigor of secondary school record. *Other factors considered include:* Class rank, application essay, recommendation(s), alumni/ae relation, character/personal qualities, extracurricular activities, talent/ability, volunteer work, work experience. **Freshman Admission Requirements:** High school diploma is required and GED is accepted. *Academic units required:* 4 English, 3 mathematics, 3 science, 2 foreign language, 3 social studies. *Academic units recommended:* 4 English, 3 mathematics, 3 science, 2 foreign language, 3 social studies. **Freshman Admission Statistics:** 1,745 applied, 80% admitted, 31% enrolled. **Transfer Admission Requirements:** High school transcript, college transcript(s), Lowest grade transferable C. **General Admission Information:** Application Fee $50. Notification on a rolling basis, beginning on or about 11/1. Nonfall registration accepted. Admission may be deferred for a maximum of One Year.

COSTS AND FINANCIAL AID

Annual in-state tuition $10,454. Annual out-of-state tuition $15,954. Room and board $3,360. Required fees $552. Average book expense $1,168. **Required Forms and Deadlines:** FAFSA. **Types of Aid:** *Need-based scholarships/ grants:* Federal Pell, SEOG, state scholarships/grants, private scholarships, the school's own gift aid. *Loans:* Subsidized Stafford, Unsubsidized Stafford, PLUS, Federal Perkins, college/university loans from institutional funds, Private Loans. **Student Employment: Financial Aid Statistics:** 76% freshmen, 77% undergrads receive need-based scholarship or grant aid. 49% freshmen, 30% undergrads receive non-need-based scholarship or grant aid. 75% freshmen, 81% undergrads receive need-based self-help aid. 67% undergrads borrow to pay for school. Average cumulative indebtedness $26,300. **Criteria for awarding institutional aid:** *Non-need-based:* academics, alumni affiliation, athletics, minority status.

PENNSYLVANIA STATE UNIVERSITY—DUBOIS

Enrollment Services House, Dubois, PA 15801-3199
Phone: 814-375-4720
E-mail: duboisinfo@psu.edu
Fax: 814-375-4784 • **Website:** www.ds.psu.edu

This public school was founded in 1935. It has a 13-acre campus.

RATINGS

Admissions Selectivity Rating: 65   **Fire Safety Rating:** 60*   **Green Rating:** 60*

STUDENTS AND FACULTY

Enrollment: 724. **Student Body:** 51% female, 49% male, 1% out-of-state, 0% international. Asian 0%, African American 1%, Caucasian 99%, Hispanic 0%, Native American 0%.
Retention and Graduation: 82% freshmen return for sophomore year.
Faculty: Student/faculty ratio 13:1. 43 full-time faculty, 65% hold PhDs, 14% are members of minority groups, 44% are women. 0% of classes are taught by teaching assistants.

ACADEMICS

Degrees: bachelor's, certificate, terminal associate, transfer associate. **Classes:** Most classes have 10–19 students. Most lab/discussion sessions have 10–19 students. **Special Study Options:** Accelerated program, cross-registration, distance learning, double major, dual enrollment, honors program, independent study, internships, student-designed major, study abroad.

FACILITIES

Housing: Indepently owned housing nearby.

CAMPUS LIFE

Environment: Village. **Activities:** Choral groups, drama/theater, literary magazine, student government, student newspaper, student-run film society. **Athletics (Intercollegiate):** *Men:* basketball. *Women:* volleyball.

ADMISSIONS

Freshman Academic Profile: Average high school GPA 2.9. 5% in top 10% of high school class, 21% in top 25% of high school class, 61% in top 50% of high school class. SAT Math middle 50% range 415-545. SAT Critical Reading middle 50% range 410-500. Minimum paper TOEFL 550. **Basis for Candidate Selection:** *Very important factors considered include:* academic GPA, standardized test scores. *Important factors considered include:* rigor of

secondary school record. *Other factors considered include:* Class rank, application essay, recommendation(s), alumni/ae relation, character/personal qualities, extracurricular activities, talent/ability, volunteer work, work experience. **Freshman Admission Requirements:** High school diploma is required and GED is accepted. *Academic units required:* 4 English, 3 mathematics, 3 science, 2 foreign language, 3 social studies. *Academic units recommended:* 4 English, 3 mathematics, 3 science, 2 foreign language, 3 social studies. **Freshman Admission Statistics:** 539 applied, 88% admitted, 48% enrolled. **Transfer Admission Requirements:** High school transcript, college transcript(s), Lowest grade transferable C. **General Admission Information:** Application Fee $50. Notification on a rolling basis, beginning on or about 11/1. Nonfall registration accepted. Admission may be deferred for a maximum of One Year.

COSTS AND FINANCIAL AID

Annual in-state tuition $10,454. Annual out-of-state tuition $15,954. Room and board $3,360. Required fees $542. Average book expense $1,168. **Required Forms and Deadlines:** FAFSA. **Notification of Awards:** Applicants will be notified of awards on a rolling basis beginning 3/1. **Types of Aid:** *Need-based scholarships/grants:* Federal Pell, SEOG, state scholarships/grants, private scholarships, the school's own gift aid. *Loans:* Subsidized Stafford, Unsubsidized Stafford, PLUS, Federal Perkins, college/university loans from institutional funds, Private Loans. **Student Employment: Financial Aid Statistics:** 84% freshmen, 88% undergrads receive need-based scholarship or grant aid. 42% freshmen, 33% undergrads receive non-need-based scholarship or grant aid. 84% freshmen, 89% undergrads receive need-based self-help aid. 67% undergrads borrow to pay for school. Average cumulative indebtedness $26,300. **Criteria for awarding institutional aid:** *Non-need-based:* academics, alumni affiliation, athletics, minority status.

PENNSYLVANIA STATE UNIVERSITY— ERIE, THE BEHREND COLLEGE

4701 College Drive, Erie, PA 16563-0105
Phone: 814-898-6100
E-mail: behrend.admissions@psu.edu
Fax: 814-898-6044 • **Website:** erie.psu.edu • **ACT Code:** 3656

This public school was founded in 1948. It has a 732-acre campus.

RATINGS

Admissions Selectivity Rating: 69   **Fire Safety Rating:** 60*   **Green Rating:** 60*

STUDENTS AND FACULTY

Enrollment: 3,940. **Student Body:** 36% female, 64% male, 9% out-of-state, 2% international. Asian 2%, African American 3%, Caucasian 86%, Hispanic 3%, Native American 0%.
Retention and Graduation: 43% freshmen graduate within 4 years. **Faculty:** Student/faculty ratio 16:1. 232 full-time faculty, 63% hold PhDs, 10% are members of minority groups, 36% are women. 0% of classes are taught by teaching assistants.

ACADEMICS

Degrees: bachelor's, certificate, master's, terminal associate, transfer associate. **Classes:** Most classes have 20–29 students. Most lab/discussion sessions have 10–19 students. **Special Study Options:** Accelerated program, cooperative education program, distance learning, double major, dual enrollment, honors program, independent study, internships, liberal arts/career combination, study abroad, teacher certification program. **Disability Services:** Special programs offered to physically disabled students include note-taking services, reader services, tape recorders, tutors. **Career Services:** alumni services, career/job search classes, career assessment, internships.

FACILITIES

Housing: Coed dorms, special housing for disabled students, men's dorms, women's dorms, apartments for single students, Suites, Special Interest Housing. **Special Academic Facilities/Equipment:** Observatory, plastics lab. **Computers:** Students can register for classes online. Administrative functions (other than registration) can be performed online.

CAMPUS LIFE

Environment: Village. **Activities:** Choral groups, concert band, dance, drama/ theater, jazz band, literary magazine, music ensembles, pep band, radio station, student government, student newspaper, student-run film society, Campus Ministries, International Student Organization 75 registered organizations, 46 honor societies, 26 religious organizations. 6 fraternities, 4 sororities. **Athletics (Intercollegiate):** *Men:* baseball, basketball, cheerleading, cross-country, golf, soccer, swimming, tennis, track/field (outdoor), water polo, wrestling. *Women:*

basketball, cheerleading, cross-country, golf, soccer, softball, swimming, tennis, track/field (outdoor), volleyball, water polo. **On-Campus Highlights:** Junker Athletic Center, Logan House, Smith Chapel and Carillon, Bruno's Caf , Reen Union Building, Historic Behrend Farmhouse.

ADMISSIONS

Freshman Academic Profile: Average high school GPA 3.2. 15% in top 10% of high school class, 43% in top 25% of high school class, 86% in top 50% of high school class. SAT Math middle 50% range 490-610. SAT Critical Reading middle 50% range 460-560. SAT Writing middle 50% range 440-550. Minimum paper TOEFL 550. **Basis for Candidate Selection:** *Very important factors considered include:* academic GPA, standardized test scores. *Important factors considered include:* rigor of secondary school record. *Other factors considered include:* Class rank, application essay, recommendation(s), alumni/ae relation, character/personal qualities, extracurricular activities, talent/ability, volunteer work, work experience. **Freshman Admission Requirements:** High school diploma is required and GED is accepted. *Academic units required:* 4 English, 3 mathematics, 3 science, 2 foreign language, 3 social studies. *Academic units recommended:* 4 English, 3 mathematics, 3 science, 2 foreign language, 3 social studies. **Freshman Admission Statistics:** 3,367 applied, 83% admitted, 39% enrolled. **Transfer Admission Requirements:** High school transcript, college transcript(s), Lowest grade transferable C. **General Admission Information:** Application Fee $50. Notification on a rolling basis, beginning on or about 11/1. Nonfall registration accepted. Admission may be deferred for a maximum of One Year. Credit offered for CEEB Advanced Placement tests.

COSTS AND FINANCIAL AID

Annual in-state tuition $12,776. Annual out-of-state tuition $19,548. Room and board $9,420. Required fees $860. Average book expense $1,536. **Required Forms and Deadlines:** FAFSA. **Notification of Awards:** Applicants will be notified of awards on a rolling basis beginning 3/1. **Types of Aid:** *Need-based scholarships/grants:* Federal Pell, SEOG, state scholarships/grants, private scholarships, the school's own gift aid. *Loans:* Subsidized Stafford, Unsubsidized Stafford, PLUS, Federal Perkins, college/university loans from institutional funds, Private Loans. **Student Employment:** Federal Work-Study Program available. Institutional employment available. Highest amount earned per year from on-campus jobs $656. Off-campus job opportunities are good. **Financial Aid Statistics:** 67% freshmen, 69% undergrads receive need-based scholarship or grant aid. 31% freshmen, 28% undergrads receive non-need-based scholarship or grant aid. 90% freshmen, 92% undergrads receive need-based self-help aid. 66% undergrads borrow to pay for school. Average cumulative indebtedness $33,530. **Criteria for awarding institutional aid:** *Non-need-based:* academics, alumni affiliation, athletics, minority status.

PENNSYLVANIA STATE UNIVERSITY— FAYETTE, THE EBERLY CAMPUS

PO Box 519, Uniontown, PA 15401-0519
Phone: 724-430-4130
E-mail: feadm@psu.edu
Fax: 724-430-4175 • **Website:** www.fe.psu.edu

This public school was founded in 1934. It has a 193-acre campus.

RATINGS

Admissions Selectivity Rating: 60*   **Fire Safety Rating:** 60*   **Green Rating:** 60*

STUDENTS AND FACULTY

Enrollment: 942. **Student Body:** 58% female, 42% male, 1% out-of-state, 0% international. Asian 0%, African American 7%, Caucasian 92%, Hispanic 1%, Native American 0%.
Retention and Graduation: Faculty: Student/faculty ratio 14:1. 55 full-time faculty, 51% hold PhDs, 7% are members of minority groups, 36% are women. 0% of classes are taught by teaching assistants.

ACADEMICS

Degrees: bachelor's, terminal associate, transfer associate. **Classes:** Most classes have 20-29 students. Most lab/discussion sessions have fewer than 10 students. **Special Study Options:** Accelerated program, cross-registration, distance learning, double major, dual enrollment, honors program, independent study, internships, student-designed major, study abroad, Weekend classes.

FACILITIES

Housing: privately owned, off-campus housing.

CAMPUS LIFE

Environment: Village. **Activities:** drama/theater, musical theater, student government.

ADMISSIONS

Freshman Academic Profile: Average high school GPA 3.0. 8% in top 10% of high school class, 37% in top 25% of high school class, 77% in top 50% of high school class. SAT Math middle 50% range 400-520. SAT Critical Reading middle 50% range 400-510. Minimum paper TOEFL 550. **Basis for Candidate Selection:** *Very important factors considered include:* academic GPA, standardized test scores. *Important factors considered include:* rigor of secondary school record. *Other factors considered include:* Class rank, application essay, recommendation(s), alumni/ae relation, character/personal qualities, extracurricular activities, talent/ability, volunteer work, work experience. **Freshman Admission Requirements:** High school diploma is required and GED is accepted. *Academic units required:* 4 English, 3 mathematics, 3 science, 2 foreign language, 3 social studies. *Academic units recommended:* 4 English, 3 mathematics, 3 science, 2 foreign language, 3 social studies. **Freshman Admission Statistics:** 605 applied, 90% admitted, 45% enrolled. **Transfer Admission Requirements:** High school transcript, college transcript(s), Lowest grade transferable C. **General Admission Information:** Application Fee $50. Notification on a rolling basis, beginning on or about 11/1. Nonfall registration accepted. Admission may be deferred for a maximum of 1 year.

COSTS AND FINANCIAL AID

Annual in-state tuition $10,454. Annual out-of-state tuition $15,954. Room and board $3,360. Required fees $542. Average book expense $1,168. **Required Forms and Deadlines:** FAFSA. **Notification of Awards:** Applicants will be notified of awards on a rolling basis beginning 3/1. **Types of Aid:** *Need-based scholarships/grants:* Federal Pell, SEOG, state scholarships/grants, private scholarships, the school's own gift aid. *Loans:* Subsidized Stafford, Unsubsidized Stafford, PLUS, Federal Perkins, college/university loans from institutional funds, Private Loans. **Financial Aid Statistics:** 87% freshmen, 89% undergrads receive need-based scholarship or grant aid. 36% freshmen, 33% undergrads receive non-need-based scholarship or grant aid. 78% freshmen, 88% undergrads receive need-based self-help aid. 67% undergrads borrow to pay for school. Average cumulative indebtedness $26,300. **Criteria for awarding institutional aid:** *Non-need-based:* academics, alumni affiliation, athletics, minority status.

PENNSYLVANIA STATE UNIVERSITY— GREATER ALLEGHENY

2809 Saucon Valley Road, Center Valley, PA 1803 8447
Phone: 610-285-5000
E-mail: admissions-lv@psu.edu
Fax: 610-285-5220 • **Website:** www.lv.psu.edu

RATINGS

Admissions Selectivity Rating: 60*   **Fire Safety Rating:** 60*   **Green Rating:** 60*

STUDENTS AND FACULTY

Enrollment: 647. **Student Body:** 47% female, 53% male, 9% out-of-state, 3% international. Asian 2%, African American 29%, Caucasian 58%, Hispanic 3%, Native American 0%.
Retention and Graduation: 70% freshmen return for sophomore year. 20% freshmen graduate within 4 years. **Faculty:** Student/faculty ratio 14:1. 36 full-time faculty, 75% hold PhDs, 22% are members of minority groups, 50% are women.

ADMISSIONS

Freshman Academic Profile: 2.8. 8% in top 10% of high school class, 30% in top 25% of high school class, 63% in top 50% of high school class. SAT Math middle 50% range 380-530. SAT Critical Reading middle 50% range 380-500. SAT Writing middle 50% range 370-490. **Freshman Admission Statistics:** 719 applied, 81% admitted, 40% enrolled.

COSTS AND FINANCIAL AID

Annual in-state tuition $12,242. Annual out-of-state tuition $18,682. Room and board $9,420. Required fees $860. Average book expense $1,536. **Financial Aid Statistics:** 84% freshmen, 79% undergrads receive need-based scholarship or grant aid. 60% freshmen, 47% undergrads receive non-need-based scholarship or grant aid. 85% freshmen, 88% undergrads receive need-based self-help aid. 66% undergrads borrow to pay for school. Average cumulative indebtedness $33,530.

PENNSYLVANIA STATE UNIVERSITY— HARRISBURG

Swatara Bldg., Middletown, PA 17057-4898
Phone: 717-948-6250
E-mail: hbgadmit@psu.edu
Fax: 717-948-6325 • **Website:** www.hbg.psu.edu

This public school was founded in 1966.

RATINGS
Admissions Selectivity Rating: 70   **Fire Safety Rating:** 60*   **Green Rating:** 60*

STUDENTS AND FACULTY
Enrollment: 3,008. **Student Body:** 44% female, 56% male, 14% out-of-state, 3% international. Asian 7%, African American 10%, Caucasian 69%, Hispanic 6%, Native American 0%.
Retention and Graduation: 84% freshmen return for sophomore year. 35% freshmen graduate within 4 years. 63% freshmen graduate within 6 years.
Faculty: Student/faculty ratio 14:1. 206 full-time faculty, 86% hold PhDs, 19% are members of minority groups, 39% are women.

ACADEMICS
Degrees: bachelor's, certificate, master's, post-bachelor's certificate, terminal associate, transfer associate. **Classes:** Most classes have 20–29 students. Most lab/discussion sessions have fewer than 10 students. **Special Study Options:** cooperative education program, cross-registration, distance learning, double major, dual enrollment, honors program, independent study, internships, student-designed major, study abroad, teacher certification program.

FACILITIES
Housing: special housing for disabled students, apartments for single students, Special Interest Housing.

CAMPUS LIFE
Environment: Village. **Activities:** Choral groups, dance, drama/theater, literary magazine, music ensembles, radio station, student government, student newspaper 2 honor societies, 1 religious organizations. **Athletics (Intercollegiate):** *Men:* basketball, skiing (downhill/alpine), soccer, tennis, track/field (outdoor), volleyball. *Women:* skiing (downhill/alpine), soccer, track/field (outdoor), volleyball.

ADMISSIONS
Freshman Academic Profile: Average high school GPA 3.1. 9% in top 10% of high school class, 37% in top 25% of high school class, 81% in top 50% of high school class. SAT Math middle 50% range 470-590. SAT Critical Reading middle 50% range 440-560. SAT Writing middle 50% range 430-540. **Basis for Candidate Selection:** *Very important factors considered include:* academic GPA, standardized test scores. *Important factors considered include:* rigor of secondary school record. *Other factors considered include:* Class rank, application essay, recommendation(s), alumni/ae relation, character/personal qualities, extracurricular activities, talent/ability, volunteer work, work experience. **Freshman Admission Requirements:** High school diploma is required and GED is accepted. *Academic units required:* 4 English, 3 mathematics, 3 science, 2 foreign language, 3 social studies. *Academic units recommended:* 4 English, 3 mathematics, 3 science, 2 foreign language, 3 social studies. **Freshman Admission Statistics:** 2,482 applied, 79% admitted, 28% enrolled. **Transfer Admission Requirements:** High school transcript, college transcript(s), Lowest grade transferable C. **General Admission Information:** Application Fee $50. Notification on a rolling basis, beginning on or about 11/1. Nonfall registration accepted. Admission may be deferred for a maximum of One Year.

COSTS AND FINANCIAL AID
Annual in-state tuition $12,776. Annual out-of-state tuition $19,548. Room and board $10,690. Required fees $852. Average book expense $1,536. **Required Forms and Deadlines:** FAFSA. **Notification of Awards:** Applicants will be notified of awards on a rolling basis beginning 3/1. **Types of Aid:** *Need-based scholarships/grants:* Federal Pell, SEOG, state scholarships/grants, private scholarships, the school's own gift aid. *Loans:* Subsidized Stafford, Unsubsidized Stafford, PLUS, Federal Perkins, college/university loans from institutional funds, Private Loans. **Student Employment: Financial Aid Statistics:** 63% freshmen, 67% undergrads receive need-based scholarship or grant aid. 35% freshmen, 27% undergrads receive non-need-based scholarship or grant aid. 84% freshmen, 86% undergrads receive need-based self-help aid. 66% undergrads borrow to pay for school. Average cumulative indebtedness $33,530. **Criteria for awarding institutional aid:** *Non-need-based:* academics, alumni affiliation, athletics, minority status.

PENNSYLVANIA STATE UNIVERSITY— HAZLETON

110 Admin. Building, Hazleton, PA 18202-1291
Phone: 570-450-3142
E-mail: admissions-hn@psu.edu
Fax: 570-450-3182 • **Website:** www.hn.psu.edu

This public school was founded in 1934. It has a 73-acre campus.

RATINGS
Admissions Selectivity Rating: 65   **Fire Safety Rating:** 60*   **Green Rating:** 60*

STUDENTS AND FACULTY
Enrollment: 1,192. **Student Body:** 40% female, 60% male, 26% out-of-state, 0% international. Asian 4%, African American 8%, Caucasian 80%, Hispanic 7%, Native American 0%.
Retention and Graduation: Faculty: Student/faculty ratio 19:1. 51 full-time faculty, 65% hold PhDs, 16% are members of minority groups, 41% are women.

ACADEMICS
Degrees: bachelor's, terminal associate, transfer associate. **Classes:** Most classes have 20–29 students. **Special Study Options:** Accelerated program, cross-registration, distance learning, double major, dual enrollment, English as a Second Language (ESL), honors program, independent study, internships, student-designed major, study abroad.

FACILITIES
Housing: Coed dorms, Townhouses, suites.

CAMPUS LIFE
Environment: Rural. **Activities:** Choral groups, dance, drama/theater, literary magazine, radio station, student government, student newspaper, Campus Ministries. **Athletics (Intercollegiate):** *Men:* baseball, basketball, soccer, tennis. *Women:* softball, tennis, volleyball.

ADMISSIONS
Freshman Academic Profile: Average high school GPA 2.9. 6% in top 10% of high school class, 24% in top 25% of high school class, 67% in top 50% of high school class. SAT Math middle 50% range 420-540. SAT Critical Reading middle 50% range 420-530. Minimum paper TOEFL 550. **Basis for Candidate Selection:** *Very important factors considered include:* academic GPA, standardized test scores. *Important factors considered include:* rigor of secondary school record. *Other factors considered include:* Class rank, application essay, recommendation(s), alumni/ae relation, character/personal qualities, extracurricular activities, talent/ability, volunteer work, work experience. **Freshman Admission Requirements:** High school diploma is required and GED is accepted. *Academic units required:* 4 English, 3 mathematics, 3 science, 2 foreign language, 3 social studies. *Academic units recommended:* 4 English, 3 mathematics, 3 science, 2 foreign language, 3 social studies. **Freshman Admission Statistics:** 1,613 applied, 89% admitted, 40% enrolled. **Transfer Admission Requirements:** High school transcript, college transcript(s), Lowest grade transferable C. **General Admission Information:** Application Fee $50. Notification on a rolling basis, beginning on or about 11/1. Nonfall registration accepted. Admission may be deferred for a maximum of One Year.

COSTS AND FINANCIAL AID
Annual in-state tuition $10,454. Annual out-of-state tuition $15,954. Room and board $7,180. Required fees $552. Average book expense $1,168. **Required Forms and Deadlines:** FAFSA. **Notification of Awards:** Applicants will be notified of awards on a rolling basis beginning 3/1. **Types of Aid:** *Need-based scholarships/grants:* Federal Pell, SEOG, state scholarships/grants, private scholarships, the school's own gift aid. *Loans:* Subsidized Stafford, Unsubsidized Stafford, PLUS, Federal Perkins, college/university loans from institutional funds, Private Loans. **Student Employment: Financial Aid Statistics:** 70% freshmen, 69% undergrads receive need-based scholarship or grant aid. 37% freshmen, 30% undergrads receive non-need-based scholarship or grant aid. 84% freshmen, 87% undergrads receive need-based self-help aid. 67% undergrads borrow to pay for school. Average cumulative indebtedness $26,300. **Criteria for awarding institutional aid:** *Non-need-based:* academics, alumni affiliation, athletics, minority status.

PENNSYLVANIA STATE UNIVERSITY— LEHIGH VALLEY

2809 Saucon Valley Road, Center Valley, PA 18034-8447
Phone: 610-285-5000
E-mail: admissions-lv@psu.edu
Fax: 610-285-5220 • **Website:** www.lv.psu.edu

This public school was founded in 1912. It has a 42-acre campus.

RATINGS
Admissions Selectivity Rating: 66   **Fire Safety Rating:** 60*   **Green Rating:** 60*

STUDENTS AND FACULTY
Enrollment: 785. **Student Body:** 44% female, 56% male, 4% out-of-state, 1% international. Asian 9%, African American 4%, Caucasian 69%, Hispanic 14%, Native American 0%.
Retention and Graduation: 24% freshmen graduate within 4 years. 47% freshmen graduate within 6 years. **Faculty:** Student/faculty ratio 16:1. 33 full-time faculty, 76% hold PhDs, 12% are members of minority groups, 55% are women.

ACADEMICS
Degrees: bachelor's, terminal associate, transfer associate. **Classes:** Most classes have 10–19 students. Most lab/discussion sessions have 10–19 students. **Special Study Options:** Accelerated program, cooperative education program, cross-registration, distance learning, dual enrollment, honors program, independent study, internships, study abroad.

CAMPUS LIFE
Activities: drama/theater, student government, student newspaper. **Athletics (Intercollegiate):** *Men:* basketball, cross-country, golf, soccer, tennis, volleyball. *Women:* basketball, golf, tennis, volleyball.

ADMISSIONS
Freshman Academic Profile: Average high school GPA 2.9. 5% in top 10% of high school class, 29% in top 25% of high school class, 66% in top 50% of high school class. SAT Math middle 50% range 440-560. SAT Critical Reading middle 50% range 420-540. SAT Writing middle 50% range 410-520. Minimum paper TOEFL 550. **Basis for Candidate Selection.** *Very important factors considered include:* academic GPA, standardized test scores. *Important factors considered include:* rigor of secondary school record. *Other factors considered include:* Class rank, application essay, recommendation(s), alumni/ae relation, character/personal qualities, extracurricular activities, talent/ability, volunteer work, work experience. **Freshman Admission Requirements:** High school diploma is required and GED is accepted. *Academic units required:* 4 English, 3 mathematics, 3 science, 2 foreign language, 3 social studies. *Academic units recommended:* 4 English, 3 mathematics, 3 science, 2 foreign language, 3 social studies. **Freshman Admission Statistics:** 951 applied, 87% admitted, 31% enrolled. **Transfer Admission Requirements:** High school transcript, college transcript(s), Lowest grade transferable C. **General Admission Information:** Application Fee $50. Notification on a rolling basis, beginning on or about 11/1. Nonfall registration accepted. Admission may be deferred for a maximum of 1 year.

COSTS AND FINANCIAL AID
Annual in-state tuition $12,242. Annual out-of-state tuition $18,682. Required fees $852. **Required Forms and Deadlines:** FAFSA. **Types of Aid:** *Need-based scholarships/grants:* Federal Pell, SEOG, state scholarships/grants, private scholarships, the school's own gift aid. *Loans:* Subsidized Stafford, Unsubsidized Stafford, PLUS, Federal Perkins, college/university loans from institutional funds, Private Loans. **Student Employment: Financial Aid Statistics:** 74% freshmen, 77% undergrads receive need-based scholarship or grant aid. 28% freshmen, 20% undergrads receive non-need-based scholarship or grant aid. 85% freshmen, 88% undergrads receive need-based self-help aid. 66% undergrads borrow to pay for school. Average cumulative indebtedness $33,530. **Criteria for awarding institutional aid:** *Non-need-based:* academics, alumni affiliation, athletics, minority status.

PENNSYLVANIA STATE UNIVERSITY— MONT ALTO

1 Campus Drive, Mont Alto, PA 17237-9703
Phone: 717-749-6130
E-mail: psuma@psu.edu
Fax: 717-749-6132 • **Website:** www.ma.psu.edu

This public school was founded in 1929. It has a 62-acre campus.

RATINGS
Admissions Selectivity Rating: 66   **Fire Safety Rating:** 60*   **Green Rating:** 60*

STUDENTS AND FACULTY
Enrollment: 1,025. **Student Body:** 59% female, 41% male, 17% out-of-state, 0% international. Asian 3%, African American 12%, Caucasian 81%, Hispanic 3%, Native American 0%.
Retention and Graduation: 74% freshmen return for sophomore year. 22% grads go on to further study within 1 year. **Faculty:** Student/faculty ratio 14:1. 52 full-time faculty, 50% hold PhDs, 8% are members of minority groups, 54% are women.

ACADEMICS
Degrees: bachelor's, terminal associate, transfer associate. **Classes:** Most classes have 10–19 students. Most lab/discussion sessions have 10–19 students. **Special Study Options:** Accelerated program, cross-registration, distance learning, double major, dual enrollment, honors program, independent study, internships, study abroad. **Honors Programs:** The Schreyer Honors College is widely recognized as one of the best and most comprehensive undergraduate Honors Programs in the United States. http://www.scholars.psu.edu/index.cfm **Combined Degree Programs:** BA/MD, BA/MEng, Science/MBA Program; JD/MBA. **Disability Services:** Special programs offered to physically disabled students include note-taking services, reader services, tape recorders, tutors.

FACILITIES
Housing: Coed dorms, special housing for disabled students, Suites, Special Interest Housing, Townhouses. 99% of campus accessible to physically disabled.

CAMPUS LIFE
Environment: Village. **Activities:** dance, drama/theater, jazz band, student government, student newspaper, Campus Ministries. **Athletics (Intercollegiate):** *Men:* basketball, soccer, tennis. *Women:* basketball, tennis.

ADMISSIONS
Freshman Academic Profile: Average high school GPA 3.0. 13% in top 10% of high school class, 31% in top 25% of high school class, 70% in top 50% of high school class. SAT Math middle 50% range 430-560. SAT Critical Reading middle 50% range 440-545. **Basis for Candidate Selection:** *Very important factors considered include:* academic GPA, standardized test scores. *Important factors considered include:* rigor of secondary school record. *Other factors considered include:* Class rank, application essay, recommendation(s), alumni/ac relation, character/personal qualities, extracurricular activities, talent/ability, volunteer work, work experience. **Freshman Admission Requirements:** High school diploma is required and GED is accepted. *Academic units required:* 4 English, 3 mathematics, 3 science, 2 foreign language, 3 social studies. *Academic units recommended:* 4 English, 3 mathematics, 3 science, 2 foreign language, 3 social studies. **Freshman Admission Statistics:** 927 applied, 89% admitted, 44% enrolled. **Transfer Admission Requirements:** High school transcript, college transcript(s), Lowest grade transferable C. **General Admission Information:** Application Fee $50. Notification on a rolling basis, beginning on or about 11/1. Nonfall registration accepted. Admission may be deferred for a maximum of One Year.

COSTS AND FINANCIAL AID
Annual in-state tuition $10,454. Annual out-of-state tuition $15,954. Room and board $7,180. Required fees $552. Average book expense $1,168. **Required Forms and Deadlines:** FAFSA. **Notification of Awards:** Applicants will be notified of awards on a rolling basis beginning 3/1. **Types of Aid:** *Need-based scholarships/grants:* Federal Pell, SEOG, state scholarships/grants, private scholarships, the school's own gift aid. *Loans:* Subsidized Stafford, Unsubsidized Stafford, PLUS, Federal Perkins, college/university loans from institutional funds, Private Loans. **Financial Aid Statistics:** 73% freshmen, 75% undergrads receive need-based scholarship or grant aid. 53% freshmen, 42% undergrads receive non-need-based scholarship or grant aid. 82% freshmen, 86% undergrads receive need-based self-help aid. 67% undergrads borrow to pay for school. Average cumulative indebtedness $26,300. **Criteria for awarding institutional aid:** *Non-need-based:* academics, alumni affiliation, athletics, minority status.

PENNSYLVANIA STATE UNIVERSITY— NEW KENSINGTON

3550 7th Street Road, Upper Barrell, PA 15068-1798
Phone: 724-334-5466
E-mail: nkadmissions@psu.edu
Fax: 724-334-6111

This public school was founded in 1958. It has a 71-acre campus.

RATINGS
Admissions Selectivity Rating: 67   **Fire Safety Rating:** 60*   **Green Rating:** 60*

STUDENTS AND FACULTY
Enrollment: 734. **Student Body:** 44% female, 56% male, 2% out-of-state, 0% international. Asian 1%, African American 3%, Caucasian 95%, Hispanic 1%, Native American 0%.
Faculty: Student/faculty ratio 14:1. 38 full-time faculty, 61% hold PhDs, 16% are members of minority groups, 45% are women.

ACADEMICS
Degrees: bachelor's, certificate, terminal associate, transfer associate. **Classes:** Most classes have fewer than 10 students. Most lab/discussion sessions have 10–19 students. **Special Study Options:** cross-registration, distance learning, double major, dual enrollment, external degree program, honors program, independent study, internships, study abroad.

CAMPUS LIFE
Activities: Choral groups, dance, drama/theater, jazz band, literary magazine, musical theater, student government, student newspaper. **Athletics (Intercollegiate):** *Men:* baseball, basketball, ice hockey, tennis, volleyball. *Women:* basketball, ice hockey, tennis, volleyball.

ADMISSIONS
Freshman Academic Profile: Average high school GPA 3.0. 9% in top 10% of high school class, 29% in top 25% of high school class, 69% in top 50% of high school class. SAT Math middle 50% range 440-570. SAT Critical Reading middle 50% range 430-540. Minimum paper TOEFL 550. **Basis for Candidate Selection:** *Very important factors considered include:* academic GPA, standardized test scores. *Important factors considered include:* rigor of secondary school record. *Other factors considered include:* Class rank, application essay, recommendation(s), alumni/ae relation, character/personal qualities, extracurricular activities, talent/ability, volunteer work, work experience. **Freshman Admission Requirements:** High school diploma is required and GED is accepted. *Academic units required:* 4 English, 3 mathematics, 3 science, 2 foreign language, 3 social studies. 4 English, 3 mathematics, 3 science, 2 foreign language, 3 social studies. **Freshman Admission Statistics:** 561 applied, 86% admitted, 44% enrolled. **Transfer Admission Requirements:** High school transcript, college transcript(s), Lowest grade transferable C. **General Admission Information:** Application Fee $50. Notification on a rolling basis, beginning on or about 11/1. Nonfall registration accepted. Admission may be deferred for a maximum of one year.

COSTS AND FINANCIAL AID
Annual in-state tuition $10,454. Annual out-of-state tuition $15,954. Room and board $3,360. Required fees $552. Average book expense $1,168. **Required Forms and Deadlines:** FAFSA. **Types of Aid:** *Need-based scholarships/grants:* Federal Pell, SEOG, state scholarships/grants, private scholarships, the school's own gift aid. *Loans:* Subsidized Stafford, Unsubsidized Stafford, PLUS, Federal Perkins, college/university loans from institutional funds, Private Loans. **Financial Aid Statistics:** 72% freshmen, 80% undergrads receive need-based scholarship or grant aid. 53% freshmen, 32% undergrads receive non-need-based scholarship or grant aid. 75% freshmen, 85% undergrads receive need-based self-help aid. 67% undergrads borrow to pay for school. Average cumulative indebtedness $26,300. **Criteria for awarding institutional aid:** *Non-need-based:* academics, alumni affiliation, athletics, minority status.

PENNSYLVANIA STATE UNIVERSITY— SCHUYLKILL

200 University Drive, Schuylkill Haven, PA 17972-2208
Phone: 570-385-6252
E-mail: sl-admissions@psu.edu
Fax: 570-385-6272 • **Website:** sl.psu.edu

This public school was founded in 1934. It has a 42-acre campus.

RATINGS
Admissions Selectivity Rating: 66   **Fire Safety Rating:** 60*   **Green Rating:** 60*

STUDENTS AND FACULTY
Enrollment: 956. **Student Body:** 54% female, 46% male, 20% out-of-state, 1% international. Asian 2%, African American 30%, Caucasian 57%, Hispanic 7%, Native American 0%.
Retention and Graduation: 30% freshmen graduate within 4 years. **Faculty:** Student/faculty ratio 17:1. 45 full-time faculty, 76% hold PhDs, 2% are members of minority groups, 42% are women.

ACADEMICS
Degrees: bachelor's, terminal associate, transfer associate. **Classes:** Most classes have 20–29 students. Most lab/discussion sessions have 10–19 students. **Special Study Options:** Accelerated program, cooperative education program, distance learning, double major, dual enrollment, honors program, independent study, internships, student-designed major, study abroad.

FACILITIES
Housing: special housing for disabled students, apartments for single students.

CAMPUS LIFE
Activities: Choral groups, dance, drama/theater, musical theater, student government, student newspaper, Campus Ministries. **Athletics (Intercollegiate):** *Men:* basketball, cross-country, softball, tennis, volleyball. *Women:* basketball, cross-country, softball, tennis, volleyball.

ADMISSIONS
Freshman Academic Profile: Average high school GPA 2.7. 4% in top 10% of high school class, 18% in top 25% of high school class, 52% in top 50% of high school class. SAT Math middle 50% range 370-490. SAT Critical Reading middle 50% range 380-500. SAT Writing middle 50% range 370-470. Minimum paper TOEFL 550. **Basis for Candidate Selection:** *Very important factors considered include:* academic GPA, standardized test scores. *Important factors considered include:* rigor of secondary school record. *Other factors considered include:* Class rank, application essay, recommendation(s), alumni/ae relation, character/personal qualities, extracurricular activities, talent/ability, volunteer work, work experience. **Freshman Admission Requirements:** High school diploma is required and GED is accepted. *Academic units required:* 4 English, 3 mathematics, 3 science, 2 foreign language, 3 social studies. *Academic units recommended:* 4 English, 3 mathematics, 3 science, 2 foreign language, 3 social studies. **Freshman Admission Statistics:** 834 applied, 79% admitted, 50% enrolled. **Transfer Admission Requirements:** High school transcript, college transcript(s), Lowest grade transferable C. **General Admission Information:** Application Fee $50. Notification on a rolling basis, beginning on or about 11/1. Nonfall registration accepted. Admission may be deferred for a maximum of 1 year.

COSTS AND FINANCIAL AID
Annual in-state tuition $12,242. Annual out-of-state tuition $18,682. Room and board $10,198. Required fees $752. Average book expense $1,536. **Required Forms and Deadlines:** FAFSA. **Types of Aid:** *Need-based scholarships/grants:* Federal Pell, SEOG, state scholarships/grants, private scholarships, the school's own gift aid. *Loans:* Subsidized Stafford, Unsubsidized Stafford, PLUS, Federal Perkins, college/university loans from institutional funds, Private Loans. **Financial Aid Statistics:** 83% freshmen, 85% undergrads receive need-based scholarship or grant aid. 47% freshmen, 35% undergrads receive non-need-based scholarship or grant aid. 91% freshmen, 92% undergrads receive need-based self-help aid. 66% undergrads borrow to pay for school. Average cumulative indebtedness $33,530. **Criteria for awarding institutional aid:** *Non-need-based:* academics, alumni affiliation, athletics, minority status.

PENNSYLVANIA STATE UNIVERSITY— SHENANGO

147 Shenango Ave, Sharon, PA 16146-1597
Phone: 724-983-2800
E-mail: psushenango@psu.edu
Fax: 724-983-2820

This public school was founded in 1965. It has a 14-acre campus.

RATINGS
Admissions Selectivity Rating: 65   **Fire Safety Rating:** 60*   **Green Rating:** 60*

STUDENTS AND FACULTY
Enrollment: 677. **Student Body:** 65% female, 35% male, 13% out-of-state, 0% international. Asian 1%, African American 8%, Caucasian 90%, Hispanic 1%, Native American 0%.
Retention and Graduation: 71% freshmen return for sophomore year. **Faculty:** Student/faculty ratio 15:1. 29 full-time faculty, 55% hold PhDs, 10% are members of minority groups, 45% ae women. 0% of classes are taught by teaching assistants.

ACADEMICS
Degrees: bachelor's, certificate, terminal associate, transfer associate. **Classes:** Most classes have 10–19 students. Most lab/discussion sessions have 10–19 students. **Special Study Options:** Accelerated program, cross-registration, distance learning, double major, dual enrollment, honors program, independent study, internships, student-designed major, study abroad.

CAMPUS LIFE
Environment: Village. **Activities:** literary magazine, student government.

ADMISSIONS
Freshman Academic Profile: Average high school GPA 2.9. 2% in top 10% of high school class, 19383% in top 25% of high school class, 61% in top 50% of high school class. SAT Math middle 50% range 400-520. SAT Critical Reading middle 50% range 400-490. Minimum paper TOEFL 550. **Basis for Candidate Selection:** *Very important factors considered include:* academic GPA, standardized test scores. *Important factors considered include:* rigor of secondary school record. *Other factors considered include:* Class rank, application essay, recommendation(s), alumni/ae relation, character/personal qualities, extracurricular activities, talent/ability, volunteer work, work experience. **Freshman Admission Requirements:** High school diploma is required and GED is accepted. *Academic units required:* 4 English, 3 mathematics, 3 science, 2 foreign language, 3 social studies. *Academic units recommended:* 4 English, 3 mathematics, 3 science, 2 foreign language, 3 social studies. **Freshman Admission Statistics:** 271 applied, 89% admitted, 61% enrolled. **Transfer Admission Requirements:** High school transcript, college transcript(s), Lowest grade transferable C. **General Admission Information:** Application Fee $50. Notification on a rolling basis, beginning on or about 11/1. Nonfall registration accepted. Admission may be deferred for a maximum of one year.

COSTS AND FINANCIAL AID
Annual in-state tuition $10,454. Annual out-of-state tuition $15,954. Room and board $3,360. Required fees $552. Average book expense $1,168. **Required Forms and Deadlines:** FAFSA. **Types of Aid:** *Need-based scholarships/grants:* Federal Pell, SEOG, state scholarships/grants, private scholarships, the school's own gift aid. *Loans:* Subsidized Stafford, Unsubsidized Stafford, PLUS, Federal Perkins, college/university loans from institutional funds, Private Loans. **Financial Aid Statistics:** 88% freshmen, 89% undergrads receive need-based scholarship or grant aid. 55% freshmen, 38% undergrads receive non-need-based scholarship or grant aid. 86% freshmen, 92% undergrads receive need-based self-help aid. 67% undergrads borrow to pay for school. Average cumulative indebtedness $26,300. **Criteria for awarding institutional aid:** *Non-need-based:* academics, alumni affiliation, athletics.

PENNSYLVANIA STATE UNIVERSITY— UNIVERSITY PARK

201 Shields Building, University Park, PA 16802-3000
Phone: 814-865-5471 • **Financial Aid Phone:** 814-865-6301
E-mail: admissions@psu.edu • **CEEB Code:** 2660
Fax: 814-863-7590 • **Website:** www.psu.edu • **ACT Code:** 3656

This public school was founded in 1855. It has a 7264-acre campus.

RATINGS
Admissions Selectivity Rating: 91   **Fire Safety Rating:** 95   **Green Rating:** 97

STUDENTS AND FACULTY
Enrollment: 38,229. **Student Body:** 46% female, 54% male, 29% out-of-state, 7% international (131 countries represented). Asian 5%, African American 4%, Caucasian 75%, Hispanic 5%, Native American 0%.
Retention and Graduation: 62% freshmen graduate within 4 years. 87% freshmen graduate within 6 years. 21% grads go on to further study within 1 year. **Faculty:** Student/faculty ratio 17:1. 2481 full-time faculty, 79% hold PhDs, 16% are members of minority groups, 38% are women.

ACADEMICS
Degrees: associate, bachelor's, certificate, doctoral, master's, post-master's certificate, terminal associate, transfer associate. **Classes:** Most classes have 20–29 students. Most lab/discussion sessions have 20–29 students. **Majors with Highest Enrollment:** business administration and management; engineering. **Special Study Options:** Accelerated program, cooperative education program, cross-registration, distance learning, double major, dual enrollment, English as a Second Language (ESL), exchange student program (domestic), external degree program, honors program, independent study, internships, liberal arts/career combination, student-designed major, study abroad, teacher certification program, weekend college. **Honors Programs:** The Schreyer Honors College is widely recognized as one of the best and most comprehensive undergraduate Honors Programs in the United States. http://www.shc.psu.edu/ **Combined Degree Programs:** BA/MD, BA/MEng, Science/MBA Program; JD/MBA. **Disability Services:** Special programs offered to physically disabled students include note-taking services, reader services, tape recorders, tutors. **Career Services:** Alumni network, alumni services, career/job search classes, career assessment, internships, regional alumni. Career Services highlights include All of our e-ship programs are based on problem-based learning for which we have gained both national and international recognition. COurse modules are transferable and scalable and have been used by students at other US schools as well as majoe overseas Universities in Germany, Slovakia, Austria, etc.

FACILITIES
Housing: Coed dorms, special housing for disabled students, men's dorms, special housing for international students, women's dorms, fraternity/sorority housing, apartments for married students, apartments for single students, Suites, Special Interest Housing. 99% of campus accessible to physically disabled. **Special Academic Facilities/Equipment:** Museums, theatres, language labs, weather station, nuclear reactor. **Computers:** 83% of classrooms, 50% of dorms, 100% of libraries, 100% of dining areas, 100% of student union, 25% of common outdoor areas have wireless network access. Students can register for classes online. Administrative functions (other than registration) can be performed online.

CAMPUS LIFE
Environment: Town. **Activities:** Choral groups, concert band, dance, drama/theater, jazz band, literary magazine, marching band, music ensembles, musical theater, opera, pep band, radio station, student government, student newspaper, student-run film society, symphony orchestra, television station, yearbook, Campus Ministries, International Student Organization, Model UN 784 registered organizations, 34 honor societies, 49 religious organizations. 58 fraternities, 32 sororities. **Athletics (Intercollegiate):** *Men:* baseball, basketball, cheerleading, cross-country, diving, fencing, football, golf, gymnastics, lacrosse, soccer, swimming, tennis, track/field (outdoor), track/field (indoor), volleyball, wrestling. *Women:* basketball, cheerleading, cross-country, diving, fencing, field hockey, golf, gymnastics, lacrosse, soccer, softball, swimming, tennis, track/field (outdoor), track/field (indoor), volleyball. **On-Campus Highlights:** Hetzel Union Building, Pattee Paterno Library, The Creamery, Old Main, The Lion Shrine. **Environmental Initiatives:** To address the issue of climate change, Penn State has established the goal of reducing greenhouse gas emissions by 17.5%, below

2005/2006 levels, by 2012. As of the FY 2009/10 inventory, we have achieved a reduction of 15.2%. More information can be found at: www.ghg.psu.edu. A team of faculty, students, administrators and staff from across the institution has been working since July 2010 ato develop a Strategic Sustainability Plan for Penn State. The mission of this strategy is to integrate sustainability into the University's teaching, research, outreach, and operational functions in a manner that creates value for the University, the Commonwealth, and society and prepares students, faculty, and staff to contribute to the world as change agents and sustainability leaders. More information can be found at http://www.green.psu.edu/about/strategic_plan.asp As one of five partners in the Greater Philadelphia Innovation Cluster (GPIC), Penn State has received a 5-year, $122 million grant to develop the Energy Innovation HUB at the Navy Yard in Philadelphia, and will use these funds to develop innovative energy efficient building technologies, designs and systems. For more information, visit: http://www.research.psu.edu/industry/theiron/fall-2010/doe-energy-innovation-hub.

ADMISSIONS

Freshman Academic Profile: Average high school GPA 3.5. 45% in top 10% of high school class, 87% in top 25% of high school class, 98% in top 50% of high school class. SAT Math middle 50% range 560-670. SAT Critical Reading middle 50% range 530-630. SAT Writing middle 50% range 540-640. Minimum web-based TOEFL 80. Minimum paper TOEFL 550. **Basis for Candidate Selection:** *Very important factors considered include:* academic GPA, standardized test scores. *Important factors considered include:* rigor of secondary school record. *Other factors considered include:* Class rank, application essay, recommendation(s), alumni/ae relation, character/personal qualities, extracurricular activities, talent/ability, volunteer work, work experience. **Freshman Admission Requirements:** High school diploma is required and GED is accepted. *Academic units required:* 4 English, 3 mathematics, 3 science, 2 foreign language, 3 social studies. *Academic units recommended:* 4 English, 3 mathematics, 3 science, 2 foreign language, 3 social studies. **Freshman Admission Statistics:** 45,502 applied, 52% admitted, 31% enrolled. **Transfer Admission Requirements:** High school transcript, college transcript(s), Lowest grade transferable C. **General Admission Information:** Application Fee $50. Notification on a rolling basis, beginning on or about 11/1. Nonfall registration accepted. Admission may be deferred for a maximum of One Year. Credit and/or placement offered for CEEB Advanced Placement tests.

COSTS AND FINANCIAL AID

Annual in-state tuition $15,562. Annual out-of-state tuition $27,864. Room and board $9,690. Required fees $882. Average book expense. **Required Forms and Deadlines:** FAFSA. **Notification of Awards:** Applicants will be notified of awards on a rolling basis beginning 3/1. **Types of Aid:** *Need-based scholarships/grants:* Federal Pell, SEOG, state scholarships/grants, private scholarships, the school's own gift aid. *Loans:* Direct Subsidized Stafford, Direct Unsubsidized Stafford, Direct PLUS, Federal Perkins, college/university loans from institutional funds, Private Loans. **Student Employment:** Federal Work-Study Program available. Institutional employment available. Off-campus job opportunities are good. **Financial Aid Statistics:** 44% freshmen, 53% undergrads receive need-based scholarship or grant aid. 45% freshmen, 34% undergrads receive non-need-based scholarship or grant aid. 84% freshmen, 88% undergrads receive need-based self-help aid. 2% freshmen, 1% undergrads receive athletic scholarships. 68% freshmen, 70% undergrads receive any aid. 66% undergrads borrow to pay for school. Average cumulative indebtedness $33,530. **Criteria for awarding institutional aid:** *Non-need-based:* academics, alumni affiliation, athletics.

PENNSYLVANIA STATE UNIVERSITY— WILKES-BARRE

PO Box PSU, Lehman, PA 18627
Phone: 570-675-9238
E-mail: wbadmissions@psu.edu
Fax: 570-675-9113 • **Website:** www.wb.psu.edu

This public school was founded in 1916. It has a 58-acre campus.

RATINGS

Admissions Selectivity Rating: 66   **Fire Safety Rating:** 60*   **Green Rating:** 60*

STUDENTS AND FACULTY

Enrollment: 563. **Student Body:** 29% female, 71% male, 4% out-of-state, 0% international. Asian 2%, African American 3%, Caucasian 93%, Hispanic 2%, Native American 0%.
Retention and Graduation: Faculty: Student/faculty ratio 13:1. 37 full-time faculty, 54% hold PhDs, 16% are members of minority groups, 16% are women.

ACADEMICS

Degrees: bachelor's, post-bachelor's certificate, terminal associate, transfer associate. **Classes:** Most classes have 10–19 students. **Special Study Options:** Accelerated program, cross-registration, distance learning, double major, dual enrollment, honors program, independent study, internships, student-designed major, study abroad.

CAMPUS LIFE

Environment: Village. **Activities:** radio station, student government, student newspaper. **Athletics (Intercollegiate):** *Men:* baseball, soccer, volleyball. *Women:* volleyball.

ADMISSIONS

Freshman Academic Profile: Average high school GPA 3.0. 9% in top 10% of high school class, 35% in top 25% of high school class, 67% in top 50% of high school class. SAT Math middle 50% range 440-560. SAT Critical Reading middle 50% range 430-530. Minimum paper TOEFL 550. **Basis for Candidate Selection:** *Very important factors considered include:* academic GPA, standardized test scores. *Important factors considered include:* rigor of secondary school record. *Other factors considered include:* Class rank, application essay, recommendation(s), alumni/ae relation, character/personal qualities, extracurricular activities, talent/ability, volunteer work, work experience. **Freshman Admission Requirements:** High school diploma is required and GED is accepted. *Academic units required:* 4 English, 3 mathematics, 3 science, 2 foreign language, 3 social studies, 0. *Academic units recommended:* 4 English, 3 mathematics, 3 science, 2 foreign language, 3 social studies, 0 **Freshman Admission Statistics:** 630 applied, 84% admitted, 33% enrolled. **Transfer Admission Requirements:** High school transcript, college transcript(s), Lowest grade transferable C. **General Admission Information:** Application Fee $50. Notification on a rolling basis, beginning on or about 11/1. Nonfall registration accepted. Admission may be deferred for a maximum of 1 year.

COSTS AND FINANCIAL AID

Annual in-state tuition $10,454. Annual out-of-state tuition $15,954. Room and board $3,360. Required fees $552. Average book expense $1,168. **Required Forms and Deadlines:** FAFSA. **Types of Aid:** *Need-based scholarships/grants:* Federal Pell, SEOG, state scholarships/grants, private scholarships, the school's own gift aid. *Loans:* Subsidized Stafford, Unsubsidized Stafford, PLUS, Federal Perkins, college/university loans from institutional funds, Private Loans. **Student Employment: Financial Aid Statistics:** 76% freshmen, 77% undergrads receive need-based scholarship or grant aid. 57% freshmen, 40% undergrads receive non-need-based scholarship or grant aid. 82% freshmen, 85% undergrads receive need-based self-help aid. 67% undergrads borrow to pay for school. Average cumulative indebtedness $26,300. **Criteria for awarding institutional aid:** *Non-need-based:* academics, alumni affiliation, athletics, minority status.

PENNSYLVANIA STATE UNIVERSITY— WORTHINGTON SCRANTON

120 Ridge View Drive, Dunmore, PA 18512-1602
Phone: 570-963-2500
E-mail: wsadmissions@psu.edu
Fax: 570-963-2524 • **Website:** www.sn.psu.edu

This public school was founded in 1923. It has a 43-acre campus.

RATINGS

Admissions Selectivity Rating: 66   **Fire Safety Rating:** 60*   **Green Rating:** 60*

STUDENTS AND FACULTY

Enrollment: 1,185. **Student Body:** 50% female, 50% male, 1% out-of-state, 0% international. Asian 1%, African American 2%, Caucasian 93%, Hispanic 3%, Native American 0%.
Faculty: Student/faculty ratio 16:1. 55 full-time faculty, 62% hold PhDs, 13% are members of minority groups, 51% are women.

ACADEMICS

Degrees: bachelor's, terminal associate, transfer associate. **Classes:** Most classes have 20–29 students. Most lab/discussion sessions have 20–29 students. **Special Study Options:** Accelerated program, cooperative education program, cross-registration, distance learning, double major, dual enrollment, honors program, independent study, internships, study abroad.

CAMPUS LIFE

Activities: Choral groups, drama/theater, jazz band, literary magazine, music ensembles, student government, student newspaper. **Athletics (Intercollegiate):** *Men:* baseball, basketball, cross-country, soccer. *Women:* volleyball.

ADMISSIONS

Freshman Academic Profile: Average high school GPA 2.8. 5% in top 10% of high school class, 19% in top 25% of high school class, 63% in top 50% of high school class. SAT Math middle 50% range 410-520. SAT Critical Reading middle 50% range 420-530. Minimum paper TOEFL 550. **Basis for Candidate Selection:** *Very important factors considered include:* academic GPA, standardized test scores. *Important factors considered include:* rigor of secondary school record. *Other factors considered include:* Class rank, application essay, recommendation(s), alumni/ae relation, character/personal qualities, extracurricular activities, talent/ability, volunteer work, work experience. **Freshman Admission Requirements:** High school diploma is required and GED is accepted. *Academic units required:* 4 English, 3 mathematics, 3 science, 2 foreign language, 3 social studies. *Academic units recommended:* 4 English, 3 mathematics, 3 science, 2 foreign language, 3 social studies. **Freshman Admission Statistics:** 903 applied, 86% admitted, 40% enrolled. **Transfer Admission Requirements:** High school transcript, college transcript(s), Lowest grade transferable C. **General Admission Information:** Application Fee $50. Notification on a rolling basis, beginning on or about 11/1. Nonfall registration accepted. Admission may be deferred for a maximum of One year.

COSTS AND FINANCIAL AID

Annual in-state tuition $10,454. Annual out-of-state tuition $15,954. Room and board $3,360. Required fees $532. Average book expense $1,168. **Required Forms and Deadlines:** FAFSA. *Types of Aid: Need-based scholarships/ grants:* Federal Pell, SEOG, state scholarships/grants, private scholarships, the school's own gift aid. *Loans:* Subsidized Stafford, Unsubsidized Stafford, PLUS, Federal Perkins, college/university loans from institutional funds, Private Loans. **Student Employment: Financial Aid Statistics:** 77% freshmen, 80% undergrads receive need-based scholarship or grant aid. 24% freshmen, 22% undergrads receive non-need-based scholarship or grant aid. 79% freshmen, 86% undergrads receive need-based self-help aid. 67% undergrads borrow to pay for school. Average cumulative indebtedness $26,300. **Criteria for awarding institutional aid:** *Non-need-based:* academics, alumni affiliation, athletics, minority status.

PENNSYLVANIA STATE UNIVERSITY—YORK

1031 Edgecomb Avenue, York, PA 17403-3398
Phone: 717-771-4040
E-mail: ykadmission@psu.edu
Fax: 717-771-4005 • **Website:** www.yk.psu.edu

This public school was founded in 1926. It has a 52-acre campus.

RATINGS
Admissions Selectivity Rating: 67   **Fire Safety Rating:** 60*   **Green Rating:** 60*

STUDENTS AND FACULTY

Enrollment: 1,070. **Student Body:** 44% female, 56% male, 5% out-of-state, 0% international. Asian 6%, African American 5%, Caucasian 83%, Hispanic 5%, Native American 0%.
Retention and Graduation: 71% freshmen return for sophomore year. **Faculty:** Student/faculty ratio 15:1. 59 full-time faculty, 61% hold PhDs, 17% are members of minority groups, 36% are women.

ACADEMICS

Degrees: bachelor's, terminal associate, transfer associate. **Classes:** Most classes have 10–19 students. Most lab/discussion sessions have fewer than 10 students. **Special Study Options:** Accelerated program, cross-registration, distance learning, double major, English as a Second Language (ESL), honors program, independent study, internships, student-designed major, study abroad.

FACILITIES

Housing: Nearby rooms, apartments, house rentals in the local community.

CAMPUS LIFE

Environment: Village. **Activities:** dance, drama/theater, literary magazine, student government, student newspaper, Campus Ministries, International Student Organization, Model UN. **Athletics (Intercollegiate):** *Men:* basketball, soccer, tennis. *Women:* tennis, volleyball.

ADMISSIONS

Freshman Academic Profile: Average high school GPA 2.8. 6% in top 10% of high school class, 24% in top 25% of high school class, 55% in top 50% of high school class. SAT Math middle 50% range 440-550. SAT Critical Reading middle 50% range 410-530. Minimum paper TOEFL 550. **Basis for Candidate Selection:** *Very important factors considered include:* academic GPA, standardized test scores. *Important factors considered include:* rigor of secondary school record. *Other factors considered include:* Class rank, applica-

tion essay, recommendation(s), alumni/ae relation, character/personal qualities, extracurricular activities, talent/ability, volunteer work, work experience. **Freshman Admission Requirements:** High school diploma is required and GED is accepted. *Academic units required:* 4 English, 3 mathematics, 3 science, 2 foreign language, 3 social studies. *Academic units recommended:* 4 English, 3 mathematics, 3 science, 2 foreign language, 3 social studies. **Freshman Admission Statistics:** 1,328 applied, 84% admitted, 30% enrolled. **Transfer Admission Requirements:** High school transcript, college transcript(s), Lowest grade transferable C. **General Admission Information:** Application Fee $50. Notification on a rolling basis, beginning on or about 11/1. Nonfall registration accepted. Admission may be deferred for a maximum of One year.

COSTS AND FINANCIAL AID

Annual in-state tuition $10,454. Annual out-of-state tuition $15,954. Room and board $3,360. Required fees $532. Average book expense $1,168. **Required Forms and Deadlines:** FAFSA. **Notification of Awards:** Applicants will be notified of awards on or about 3/1. *Types of Aid: Need-based scholarships/ grants:* Federal Pell, SEOG, state scholarships/grants, private scholarships, the school's own gift aid. *Loans:* Subsidized Stafford, Unsubsidized Stafford, PLUS, Federal Perkins, college/university loans from institutional funds, Private Loans. **Financial Aid Statistics:** 66% freshmen, 75% undergrads receive need-based scholarship or grant aid. 40% freshmen, 36% undergrads receive non-need-based scholarship or grant aid. 80% freshmen, 83% undergrads receive need-based self-help aid. 67% undergrads borrow to pay for school. Average cumulative indebtedness $26,300. **Criteria for awarding institutional aid:** *Non-need-based:* academics, alumni affiliation, athletics, minority status.

PEPPERDINE UNIVERSITY

24255 Pacific Coast Highway, Malibu, CA 90263
Phone: 310-506-4392 • **Financial Aid Phone:** 310-506-4301
E-mail: admission-seaver@pepperdine.edu • **CEEB Code:** 4630
Fax: 310-506-4861 • **Website:** www.pepperdine.edu • **ACT Code:** 373

This private school, affiliated with the Church of Christ Church, was founded in 1937. It has a 830-acre campus.

RATINGS
Admissions Selectivity Rating: 94   **Fire Safety Rating:** 64   **Green Rating:** 84

STUDENTS AND FACULTY

Enrollment: 3,480. **Student Body:** 57% female, 43% male, 38% out-of-state, 7% international (64 countries represented). Asian 9%, African American 5%, Caucasian 35%, Hispanic 12%, Native American 0%.
Retention and Graduation: 73% freshmen graduate within 4 years. **Faculty:** Student/faculty ratio 13:1. 385 full-time faculty, 90% hold PhDs, 14% are members of minority groups, 39% are women. 0% of classes are taught by teaching assistants.

ACADEMICS

Degrees: bachelor's, master's. **Classes:** Most classes have 10–19 students. Most lab/discussion sessions have 20–29 students. **Majors with Highest Enrollment:** business administration and management; communication, journalism, and related programs, other; social sciences, other. **Special Study Options:** double major, honors program, independent study, internships, student-designed major, study abroad, teacher certification program, weekend college, 3-2 programing engineering with University of Southern California, Washington University(MO), Boston University(MA). **Disability Services:** Special programs offered to physically disabled students include note-taking services, reader services, tape recorders, tutors. **Career Services:** Alumni network, alumni services, career/job search classes, career assessment, internships, regional alumni. Career Services highlights include Pepperdine has a very active internship program that reaches into the local LA areas, Washington DC, nationally through our participation in the University Career Action Network, and internationally through an internship emphasis at our international campuses. Students at Pepperdine can receive academic credit for internships. Service-learning is employed as a teaching pedagogy by a variety of faculty members. One example the senior capstone business class "Service Leadership" where class members serve on a consulting team for a nonprofit.

FACILITIES

Housing: special housing for disabled students, men's dorms, women's dorms, apartments for married students, cooperative housing, apartments for single students. Freshman and sophomores must live on campus or at home with parent or guardian if single and under age 21. **Special Academic Facilities/Equipment:** Weisman Art Museum **Computers:** 100% of classrooms, 100% of dorms, 100% of libraries, 100% of dining areas, 100% of student union, 100% of common outdoor areas have wireless network access. Students can register for classes online. Administrative functions (other than registration) can be performed online.

CAMPUS LIFE

Environment: City. **Activities:** Choral groups, concert band, dance, drama/theater, jazz band, literary magazine, music ensembles, musical theater, opera, pep band, radio station, student government, student newspaper, student-run film society, symphony orchestra, television station, yearbook, Campus Ministries, International Student Organization, Model UN 50 registered organizations, 5 honor societies, 8 religious organizations. 5 fraternities, 7 sororities. **Athletics (Intercollegiate):** *Men:* baseball, basketball, cross-country, golf, tennis, volleyball, water polo. *Women:* basketball, cheerleading, cross-country, golf, soccer, swimming, tennis, track/field (outdoor), volleyball. **On-Campus Highlights:** Theme Tower, Smother'sTheatre, The Sandbar, Payson Library, Alumni Park. **Environmental Initiatives:** Pepperdine University conserves millions of gallons of drinking water annually dating back to 1972. Pepperdine uses recycled water to irrigate over 90% of the University's managed grounds. The University carefully monitors irrigation practices and uses an automated irrigation program based upon historical trends and current climactic conditions to conserve water and reduce runoff. Pepperdine University recycles all refuse disposed of on campus since 2000. The University has an average diversion rate of 78% meaning that 78% of all refuse gets reused. Pepperdine recycles high-tech equipment. All on-campus tree trimmings and brush clearance debris are either reused for grounds maintenance or turned into compost, which is used in many areas throughout campus. Pepperdine is committed to preserving the native environment in which the campus resides. 500 acres of the campus are set aside for conservation and 20% of the actively managed area is managed completely organically. Before the 50-acre Drescher Graduate Campus construction began, soil and seeds were collected on-site and were used to replant the slopes. In an effort to blend the Graduate Campus with the surrounding environment, the surrounding slopes contain approximately 99% native vegetation.

ADMISSIONS

Freshman Academic Profile: Average high school GPA 3.6. 44% in top 10% of high school class, 81% in top 25% of high school class, 96% in top 50% of high school class. SAT Math middle 50% range 570-680. SAT Critical Reading middle 50% range 550-650. SAT Writing middle 50% range 560-670. ACT middle 50% range 25-30. Minimum web-based TOEFL 80. Minimum paper TOEFL 550. **Basis for Candidate Selection:** *Very important factors considered include:* application essay, academic GPA, recommendation(s), rigor of secondary school record, standardized test scores, character/personal qualities, extracurricular activities, talent/ability. *Important factors considered include:* religious affiliation/commitment, volunteer work. *Other factors considered include:* alumni/ae relation, first generation, racial/ethnic status, work experience. **Freshman Admission Requirements:** High school diploma is required and GED is accepted. **Freshman Admission Statistics:** 8,567 applied, 38% admitted, 24% enrolled. **Transfer Admission Requirements:** High school transcript, college transcript(s), essay or personal statement, minimum college GPA of 3.00 required. Lowest grade transferable C. **General Admission Information:** Application Fee $65. Regular application deadline 1/15. Regular notification 4/1. Nonfall registration accepted. Credit and/or placement offered for CEEB Advanced Placement tests.

COSTS AND FINANCIAL AID

Required Forms and Deadlines: FAFSA. **Notification of Awards:** Applicants will be notified of awards on or about 4/15. **Types of Aid:** *Need-based scholarships/grants:* Federal Pell, SEOG, state scholarships/grants, private scholarships, the school's own gift aid, United Negro College Fund, ACG, SMART. *Loans:* Subsidized Stafford, Unsubsidized Stafford, PLUS, Federal Perkins, college/university loans from institutional funds. **Student Employment:** Federal Work-Study Program available. Institutional employment available. Off-campus job opportunities are good. **Financial Aid Statistics:** 41% freshmen, 45% undergrads receive need-based scholarship or grant aid. 91% freshmen, 94% undergrads receive non-need-based scholarship or grant aid. 75% freshmen, 77% undergrads receive need-based self-help aid. 2% freshmen, 3% undergrads receive athletic scholarships. 56% undergrads borrow to pay for school. Average cumulative indebtedness $30,101. **Criteria for awarding institutional aid:** *Non-need-based:* academics, art, athletics, minority status, music/drama, religious affiliation.

PFEIFFER UNIVERSITY

P.O. Box 960, Misenheimer, NC 28109
Phone: 800-338-2060
E-mail: admissions@pfeiffer.edu • **CEEB Code:** 5536
Fax: 704-463-1363 • **Website:** www.pfeiffer.edu • **ACT Code:** 3140

This private school, affiliated with the Methodist Church, was founded in 1885.

RATINGS

Admissions Selectivity Rating: 72   **Fire Safety Rating:** 60*   **Green Rating:** 60*

STUDENTS AND FACULTY

Enrollment: 1,188. **Student Body:** 58% female, 42% male, 19% out-of-state, 5% international (13 countries represented). Asian 1%, African American 16%, Caucasian 59%, Hispanic 1%, Native American 0%.
Retention and Graduation: 77% freshmen return for sophomore year. 41% freshmen graduate within 4 years. 60% freshmen graduate within 6 years. 23% grads go on to further study within 1 year. 15% grads pursue arts and sciences degrees. 5% grads pursue law degrees. 20% grads pursue business degrees. 2% grads pursue medical degrees. **Faculty:** Student/faculty ratio 13:1. 65 full-time faculty, 66% hold PhDs, 11% are members of minority groups, 37% are women. 0% of classes are taught by teaching assistants.

ACADEMICS

Degrees: bachelor's, master's, post-master's certificate. **Classes:** Most classes have fewer than 10 students. **Majors with Highest Enrollment:** business/commerce; criminal justice/law enforcement administration; elementary education and teaching. **Special Study Options:** Accelerated program, cross-registration, distance learning, double major, dual enrollment, honors program, independent study, internships, study abroad, teacher certification program, Capitol Hill Internship Program. **Honors Programs:** Students who have demonstrated strong academic performance are invited to participate in the Honors Program. They enroll in honors-designated courses and are given expanded assignments or complete special projects. They live in honors housing and are invited to join the University Honors Association. Twelve students are chosen each year to serve as marshals at the graduation ceremony and the fall Academic Convocation. In addition, all Pfeiffer students are eligible to graduate cum laude, magna cum laude, and summa cum laude, depending on their grade point average. **Combined Degree Programs:** BA/MA. **Disability Services:** Special programs offered to physically disabled students include note-taking services, tutors. **Career Services:** Alumni network, alumni services, career/job search classes, career assessment, internships, regional alumni.

FACILITIES

Housing: Coed dorms, men's dorms, women's dorms. **Special Academic Facilities/Equipment:** Beth Haltiwanger Retreat Center, Francis Center for Servant Leadership, new science building **Computers:** Administrative functions (other than registration) can be performed online.

CAMPUS LIFE

Environment: Rural. **Activities:** Choral groups, concert band, drama/theater, jazz band, literary magazine, music ensembles, musical theater, pep band, student government, student newspaper, yearbook 60 registered organizations, 6 honor societies, 1 religious organizations. **Athletics (Intercollegiate):** *Men:* baseball, basketball, cheerleading, cross-country, golf, lacrosse, soccer, tennis. *Women:* basketball, cheerleading, cross-country, golf, lacrosse, soccer, softball, swimming, tennis, volleyball. **On-Campus Highlights:** Student Center, Merner Gymnasium, Chapel, Knapp Health and Fitness Center, Beth Haltiwanger Retreat Center, New science building.

ADMISSIONS

Freshman Academic Profile: Average high school GPA 3.1. 11% in top 10% of high school class, 30% in top 25% of high school class, 62% in top 50% of high school class. 90% from public high schools. SAT Math middle 50% range 450-570. SAT Critical Reading middle 50% range 430-540. ACT middle 50% range 18-24. Minimum paper TOEFL 500. **Basis for Candidate Selection:** *Very important factors considered include:* rigor of secondary school record, standardized test scores, character/personal qualities, volunteer work. *Important factors considered include:* recommendation(s), extracurricular activities, talent/ability. *Other factors considered include:* Class rank, application essay, alumni/ae relation, interview, religious affiliation/commitment, work experience. **Freshman Admission Requirements:** High school diploma is required and GED is accepted. *Academic units required:* 4 English, 3 mathematics, 2 science, (1 science labs), 2 social studies, 2 history. *Academic units recommended:* 4 English, 3 mathematics, 2 science, (1 science labs), 2 social studies, 2 history. **Freshman Admission Statistics:** 586 applied, 72% admitted, 41% enrolled. **Transfer Admission Requirements:** college transcript(s), statement of good standing from prior institution(s). Minimum college GPA of 2.0 required. Lowest grade transferable D. **General Admission Information:** Application Fee $25. Notification on a rolling basis, beginning on or about 9/1. Nonfall registration accepted. Credit offered for CEEB Advanced Placement tests.

COSTS AND FINANCIAL AID

Annual tuition $13,550. Room and board $5,430. Average book expense $500. **Required Forms and Deadlines:** FAFSA. **Notification of Awards:** Applicants will be notified of awards on a rolling basis beginning 2/15. **Types of Aid:** *Need-based scholarships/grants:* Federal Pell, SEOG, state scholarships/grants, the school's own gift aid. *Loans:* Subsidized Stafford, Unsubsidized Stafford, PLUS, Federal Perkins. **Student Employment:** Federal Work-Study Program available. Off-campus job opportunities are good. **Financial Aid Statistics:** 99% freshmen, 99% undergrads receive need-based scholarship or grant aid. 32% freshmen, 16% undergrads receive non-need-based scholarship or grant aid. 85% freshmen, 87% undergrads receive need-based self-help aid. 90% freshmen, 90% undergrads receive any aid. **Criteria for awarding institutional aid:** *Non-need-based:* academics, athletics, religious affiliation, state/district residency.

PHILADELPHIA UNIVERSITY

School House Lane and Henry Avenue, Philadelphia, PA 19144-5497
Phone: 215-951-2800 • **Financial Aid Phone:** 215-951-2940
E-mail: admissions@philau.edu • **CEEB Code:** 2666
Fax: 215-951-2907 • **Website:** www.PhilaU.edu • **ACT Code:** 3668

This private school was founded in 1884. It has a 100-acre campus.

RATINGS
Admissions Selectivity Rating: 73   **Fire Safety Rating:** 60*   **Green Rating:** 60*

STUDENTS AND FACULTY
Enrollment: 2,987. **Student Body:** 66% female, 34% male, 52% out-of-state, 2% international (30 countries represented). Asian 4%, African American 10%, Caucasian 68%, Hispanic 6%, Native American 0%.
Retention and Graduation: 79% freshmen return for sophomore year. 46% freshmen graduate within 4 years. 19% grads go on to further study within 1 year. 8% grads pursue arts and sciences degrees. 1% grads pursue law degrees. 10% grads pursue business degrees. 1% grads pursue medical degrees. **Faculty:** Student/faculty ratio 14:1. 112 full-time faculty, 71% hold PhDs, 13% are members of minority groups, 42% are women. 0% of classes are taught by teaching assistants.

ACADEMICS
Degrees: associate, bachelor's, certificate, master's, post-bachelor's certificate, post-master's certificate. **Classes:** Most classes have 10–19 students. Most lab/discussion sessions have 10–19 students. **Majors with Highest Enrollment:** architecture (barch, ba/bs, march, ma/ms, phd); fashion/apparel design; merchandising and buying operations. **Special Study Options:** distance learning, double major, honors program, independent study, internships, liberal arts/career combination, study abroad. **Honors Programs:** University Honors Program. **Combined Degree Programs:** BS/MS, BS/MBA. **Disability Services:** Special programs offered to physically disabled students include note-taking services, reader services, tape recorders, tutors. **Career Services:** alumni services, career/job search classes, career assessment, internships.

FACILITIES
Housing: Coed dorms, special housing for disabled students, women's dorms, apartments for single students, Townhouses. 63% of campus accessible to physically disabled. **Special Academic Facilities/Equipment:** The Design Center, Industrial Design Studios, Graphic Design Studios, Architecture Design Studios, CAD Labs in fashion design, interior design and architecture. **Computers:** Students can register for classes online. Administrative functions (other than registration) can be performed online.

CAMPUS LIFE
Environment: Metropolis. **Activities:** Choral groups, dance, drama/theater, student government, student newspaper, yearbook 32 registered organizations, 3 religious organizations. 1 fraternities, 1 sororities. **Athletics (Intercollegiate):** *Men:* baseball, basketball, crew/rowing, cross-country, golf, soccer, tennis. *Women:* basketball, crew/rowing, cross-country, field hockey, lacrosse, soccer, softball, tennis, volleyball. **On-Campus Highlights:** Kanbar Campus Center, Athletic and Recreation Center, Gutman Library, Architecture and Design Building, The Design Center.

ADMISSIONS
Freshman Academic Profile: Average high school GPA 3.4. 11% in top 10% of high school class, 42% in top 25% of high school class, 78% in top 50% of

high school class. 80% from public high schools. SAT Math middle 50% range 490-590. SAT Critical Reading middle 50% range 480-560. SAT Writing middle 50% range 470-560. Minimum paper TOEFL 500. **Basis for Candidate Selection:** *Very important factors considered include:* academic GPA, rigor of secondary school record, standardized test scores. *Important factors considered include:* Class rank, recommendation(s), extracurricular activities, interview. *Other factors considered include:* application essay. **Freshman Admission Requirements:** High school diploma is required and GED is accepted. *Academic units required:* 4 English, 3 mathematics, 3 science, (2 science labs), 2 social studies, 1 history, 2 academic electives. *Academic units recommended:* 4 English, 3 mathematics, 3 science, (2 science labs), 2 social studies, 1 history, 2 academic electives. **Freshman Admission Statistics:** 4,138 applied, 73% admitted, 23% enrolled. **Transfer Admission Requirements:** college transcript(s), minimum college GPA of 2.5 required. Lowest grade transferable C. **General Admission Information:** Application Fee $35. Notification on a rolling basis, beginning on or about 11/1. Nonfall registration accepted. Admission may be deferred for a maximum of 1 year. Credit and/or placement offered for CEEB Advanced Placement tests.

COSTS AND FINANCIAL AID
Required Forms and Deadlines: FAFSA. **Notification of Awards:** Applicants will be notified of awards on a rolling basis beginning 2/10. **Types of Aid:** *Need-based scholarships/grants:* Federal Pell, SEOG, state scholarships/grants, private scholarships, the school's own gift aid, Gift scholarships from outside sources (non-endowed) for which University chooses recipient which may involve a need component. *Loans:* Subsidized Stafford, Unsubsidized Stafford, PLUS, Federal Perkins, Private Loan Programs. **Student Employment:** Federal Work-Study Program available. Institutional employment available. Off-campus job opportunities are good. **Financial Aid Statistics:** 100% freshmen, 98% undergrads receive need-based scholarship or grant aid. 8% freshmen, 6% undergrads receive non-need-based scholarship or grant aid. 91% freshmen, 92% undergrads receive need-based self-help aid. 2% freshmen, 3% undergrads receive athletic scholarships. 99% freshmen, 97% undergrads receive any aid. 77% undergrads borrow to pay for school. Average cumulative indebtedness $32,337. **Criteria for awarding institutional aid:** *Non-need-based:* academics, athletics.

PIEDMONT COLLEGE

P.O. Box 10, Demorest, GA 30535
Phone: 706-776-0103 • **Financial Aid Phone:** 706-778-3000
E-mail: ugrad@piedmont.edu • **CEEB Code:** 5537
Fax: 706-776-6635 • **Website:** www.piedmont.edu • **ACT Code:** 853

This private school, affiliated with the Congregational Church, was founded in 1897. It has a 115-acre campus.

RATINGS
Admissions Selectivity Rating: 77   **Fire Safety Rating:** 63   **Green Rating:** 60*

STUDENTS AND FACULTY
Enrollment: 939. **Student Body:** 64% female, 36% male, 5% out-of-state, 0% international (23 countries represented). Asian 1%, African American 6%, Caucasian 88%, Hispanic 2%, Native American 0%.
Retention and Graduation: 69% freshmen return for sophomore year. 26% freshmen graduate within 4 years. 42% freshmen graduate within 6 years. **Faculty:** Student/faculty ratio 13:1. 98 full-time faculty, 77% hold PhDs, 5% are members of minority groups, 51% are women. 0% of classes are taught by teaching assistants.

ACADEMICS
Degrees: bachelor's, master's, post-master's certificate. **Classes:** Most classes have fewer than 10 students. Most lab/discussion sessions have 10–19 students. **Majors with Highest Enrollment:** business/commerce; elementary education and teaching; sociology. **Special Study Options:** Accelerated program, distance learning, double major, dual enrollment, honors program, independent study, internships, student-designed major, study abroad, teacher certification program. **Combined Degree Programs:** BA/MAT (Secondary Education). **Disability Services:** Special programs offered to physically disabled students include note-taking services, reader services, tape recorders, tutors. **Career Services:** Alumni network, career/job search classes, career assessment, regional alumni.

FACILITIES
Housing: Coed dorms, special housing for disabled students, men's dorms, women's dorms, apartments for single students. 98% of campus accessible to physically disabled. **Special Academic Facilities/Equipment:** Art Gallery; 4

NE Georgia Youth and Tech Center; Botanical Center; Fitness Center. **Computers:** Administrative functions (other than registration) can be performed online.

CAMPUS LIFE
Environment: Rural. **Activities:** Choral groups, concert band, drama/theater, music ensembles, opera, radio station, student government, student newspaper, student-run film society, television station, yearbook 20 registered organizations, 7 honor societies, 1 religious organizations. **Athletics (Intercollegiate):** *Men:* baseball, basketball, cross-country, golf, soccer, tennis. *Women:* basketball, cross-country, golf, soccer, softball, tennis, volleyball. **On-Campus Highlights:** Johnny Mize Athletic Center, Lane Student Center, Stewart Hall, Center for Music and Worship, Arrendale Library.

ADMISSIONS
Freshman Academic Profile: Average high school GPA 3.4. 19% in top 10% of high school class, 41% in top 25% of high school class, 79% in top 50% of high school class. SAT Math middle 50% range 460-570. SAT Critical Reading middle 50% range 480-570. ACT middle 50% range 18-23. Minimum paper TOEFL 550. **Basis for Candidate Selection:** *Very important factors considered include:* academic GPA, rigor of secondary school record, standardized test scores. *Important factors considered include:* Class rank, application essay, recommendation(s), character/personal qualities, extracurricular activities, first generation, interview, talent/ability. *Other factors considered include:* alumni/ae relation, geographical residence, level of applicant's interest, state residency, volunteer work, work experience. **Freshman Admission Requirements:** High school diploma is required and GED is accepted. **Freshman Admission Statistics:** 485 applied, 66% admitted, 52% enrolled. **Transfer Admission Requirements:** college transcript(s), statement of good standing from prior institution(s). Minimum college GPA of 2.0 required. Lowest grade transferable C. **General Admission Information:** Regular application deadline 7/11. Regular notification 7/1. Nonfall registration accepted. Admission may be deferred for a maximum of 12. Neither credit nor placement offered for CEEB Advanced Placement tests.

COSTS AND FINANCIAL AID
Annual tuition $15,500. Room and board $5,000. Average book expense $850. **Required Forms and Deadlines:** FAFSA, institution's own financial aid form, state aid form. **Types of Aid:** *Need-based scholarships/grants:* Federal Pell, SEOG, state scholarships/grants, private scholarships, the school's own gift aid. *Loans:* Direct Subsidized Stafford, Direct Unsubsidized Stafford, Direct PLUS. **Student Employment:** Federal Work-Study Program available. Institutional employment available. Highest amount earned per year from on-campus jobs $3,530. Off-campus job opportunities are good. **Financial Aid Statistics:** 67% freshmen, 71% undergrads receive need-based scholarship or grant aid. 95% freshmen, 95% undergrads receive non-need-based scholarship or grant aid. 79% freshmen, 68% undergrads receive need-based self-help aid. 96% freshmen, 87% undergrads receive any aid. 66% undergrads borrow to pay for school. Average cumulative indebtedness $14,408. **Criteria for awarding institutional aid:** *Non-need-based:* academics, art, leadership, music/drama, religious affiliation, state/district residency.

PIKEVILLE COLLEGE

Admissions Office, Pikeville, KY 41501
Phone: 606-218-5251 • **Financial Aid Phone:** 606-218-5251
E-mail: wewantyou@pc.edu • **CEEB Code:** 1980
Fax: 606-218-5255 • **Website:** www.pc.edu/default.aspx • **ACT Code:** 1540

This private school, affiliated with the Presbyterian Church, was founded in 1889. It has a 25-acre campus.

RATINGS
Admissions Selectivity Rating: 64   **Fire Safety Rating:** 73   **Green Rating:** 60*

STUDENTS AND FACULTY
Enrollment: 1,245. **Student Body:** 50% female, 50% male, 20% out-of-state, 1% international (11 countries represented). Asian 0%, African American 10%, Caucasian 86%, Hispanic 1%, Native American 0%.
Retention and Graduation: 52% freshmen return for sophomore year. 13% freshmen graduate within 4 years. 27% freshmen graduate within 6 years. 10% grads go on to further study within 1 year. 5% grads pursue arts and sciences degrees. 1% grads pursue law degrees. 2% grads pursue business degrees. 2% grads pursue medical degrees. **Faculty:** Student/faculty ratio 16:1. 68 full-time faculty, 62% hold PhDs, 3% are members of minority groups, 53% are women. 0% of classes are taught by teaching assistants.

ACADEMICS
Degrees: associate, bachelor's, post-bachelor's certificate, terminal associate, transfer associate. **Classes:** Most classes have 10-19 students. **Majors with Highest Enrollment:** business/commerce; communication studies/speech communication and rhetoric; nursing/registered nurse (rn, asn, bsn, msn). **Special Study Options:** double major, dual enrollment, independent study, internships, liberal arts/career combination, student-designed major, study abroad, teacher certification program. **Disability Services:** Special programs offered to physically disabled students include tape recorders, tutors.

FACILITIES
Housing: Coed dorms, men's dorms, women's dorms. 90% of campus accessible to physically disabled.

CAMPUS LIFE
Environment: Village. **Activities:** Choral groups, dance, literary magazine, pep band, student government, student newspaper, yearbook, Campus Ministries 40 registered organizations, 6 honor societies, 2 religious organizations. **Athletics (Intercollegiate):** *Men:* baseball, basketball, bowling, cheerleading, cross-country, football, golf, soccer, tennis. *Women:* basketball, bowling, cheerleading, cross-country, golf, soccer, softball, tennis, volleyball. **On-Campus Highlights:** Administration Building, Armington Hall, Allara Library, Record Hall, Kinzer Hall.

ADMISSIONS
Freshman Academic Profile: Average high school GPA 3.1. 14% in top 10% of high school class, 38% in top 25% of high school class, 67% in top 50% of high school class. 99% from public high schools. SAT Math middle 50% range 400-510. SAT Writing middle 50% range 390-470. ACT middle 50% range 17-22. Minimum web-based TOEFL 80. Minimum paper TOEFL 550. **Basis for Candidate Selection:** . **Freshman Admission Requirements:** High school diploma is required and GED is accepted. **Freshman Admission Statistics:** 1,858 applied, 100% admitted, 20% enrolled. **Transfer Admission Requirements:** High school transcript, college transcript(s), standardized test scores, statement of good standing from prior institution(s). Lowest grade transferable C. **General Admission Information:** Regular application deadline 8/15. Notification on a rolling basis, beginning on or about 9/15. Nonfall registration accepted. Credit and/or placement offered for CEEB Advanced Placement tests.

COSTS AND FINANCIAL AID
Annual tuition $17,050. Room and board $6,700. Average book expense $2,500. **Required Forms and Deadlines:** FAFSA, institution's own financial aid form. **Notification of Awards:** Applicants will be notified of awards on a rolling basis beginning 2/1. **Types of Aid:** *Need-based scholarships/grants:* Federal Pell, SEOG, state scholarships/grants, private scholarships, the school's own gift aid. *Loans:* Subsidized Stafford, Unsubsidized Stafford, PLUS, Federal Perkins, college/university loans from institutional funds. **Student Employment:** Federal Work-Study Program available. Off-campus job opportunities are good. **Financial Aid Statistics:** 100% freshmen, 98% undergrads receive need-based scholarship or grant aid. 57% freshmen, 46% undergrads receive non-need-based scholarship or grant aid. 86% freshmen, 84% undergrads receive need-based self-help aid. 99% freshmen, 97% undergrads receive any aid. 75% undergrads borrow to pay for school. Average cumulative indebtedness $24,954.

PINE MANOR COLLEGE

400 Heath Street, Chestnut Hill, MA 02467-2332
Phone: 617-731-7104 • **Financial Aid Phone:** 800-762-1357
E-mail: admission@pmc.edu
Fax: 617-731-7102 • **Website:** www.pmc.edu

This is a private school.

RATINGS
Admissions Selectivity Rating: 66   **Fire Safety Rating:** 61   **Green Rating:** 60*

STUDENTS AND FACULTY
Enrollment: 477. **Student Body:** 100% female, 0% male, 24% out-of-state, 8% international. Asian 4%, African American 32%, Caucasian 25%, Hispanic 21%, Native American 0%.
Retention and Graduation: 58% freshmen return for sophomore year. 31% freshmen graduate within 4 years. 39% freshmen graduate within 6 years. 27% grads go on to further study within 1 year. 11% grads pursue arts and sciences degrees. 1% grads pursue law degrees. 11% grads pursue business degrees. 4% grads pursue medical degrees. **Faculty:** Student/faculty ratio 10:1. 30 full-time faculty, 80% hold PhDs, 10% are members of minority groups, 77% are women. 0% of classes are taught by teaching assistants.

ACADEMICS

Degrees: associate, bachelor's, certificate, transfer associate. **Classes:** Most classes have 10–19 students. Most lab/discussion sessions have 10–19 students. **Majors with Highest Enrollment:** business/commerce; communication and media studies, other; psychology. **Special Study Options:** cross-registration, double major, English as a Second Language (ESL), honors program, independent study, internships, liberal arts/career combination, student-designed major, study abroad, teacher certification program. **Disability Services:** Special programs offered to physically disabled students include reader services, tape recorders, tutors. **Career Services:** alumni services, career/job search classes, career assessment, internships Career Services highlights include Recognizing a fundamental link between a liberal arts education and the professional world, Pine Manor College integrates the internship experience heavily into the curriculum. Although all students are encouraged to participate in at least one internship before senior year, each Pine Manor student must complete a senior level internship during fall semester of senior year. The PMC Internship combines student's academic knowledge with practical experience in the workplace, while providing students with the opportunity to explore career options and develop the leadership skills employers seek. Many PMC interns are offered permanent positions at their sites. After working with top professionals at Boston's best corporations, hospitals, museums, laboratories, publications and social service agencies, PMC seniors feel prepared to make informed career choices.

FACILITIES

Housing: special housing for disabled students, women's dorms. 50% of campus accessible to physically disabled. **Special Academic Facilities/Equipment:** Hess Art Gallery, Annenberg Library and Communications Center, Ann Pappajohn Child Study Center. **Computers:** Administrative functions (other than registration) can be performed online.

CAMPUS LIFE

Activities: Choral groups, dance, drama/theater, literary magazine, radio station, student government, yearbook 25 registered organizations, 1 honor societies, 1 religious organizations. **Athletics (Intercollegiate):** *Women:* basketball, cross-country, lacrosse, soccer, softball, tennis, volleyball.

ADMISSIONS

Freshman Academic Profile: Average high school GPA 2.4. 0% in top 10% of high school class, 23% in top 25% of high school class, 49% in top 50% of high school class. 89% from public high schools. SAT Math middle 50% range 340-450. SAT Critical Reading middle 50% range 360-480. ACT middle 50% range 15-19. Minimum paper TOEFL 475. **Basis for Candidate Selection:** *Very important factors considered include:* application essay, recommendation(s), rigor of secondary school record. *Important factors considered include:* standardized test scores, interview. *Other factors considered include:* Class rank, alumni/ae relation, character/personal qualities, extracurricular activities, talent/ability, volunteer work, work experience. **Freshman Admission Requirements:** High school diploma is required and GED is accepted. **Freshman Admission Statistics:** 478 applied, 75% admitted, 42% enrolled. **Transfer Admission Requirements:** college transcript(s), essay or personal statement, statement of good standing from prior institution(s). Minimum college GPA of 2.0 required. Lowest grade transferable C–. **General Admission Information:** Application Fee $25. Nonfall registration accepted. Admission may be deferred for a maximum of 1 year. Credit and/or placement offered for CEEB Advanced Placement tests.

COSTS AND FINANCIAL AID

Room and board $5,088. Required fees $826. Average book expense $900. **Required Forms and Deadlines:** FAFSA. **Notification of Awards:** Applicants will be notified of awards on a rolling basis beginning 3/1. **Types of Aid:** *Need-based scholarships/grants:* Federal Pell, SEOG, state scholarships/grants, private scholarships, the school's own gift aid. *Loans:* Subsidized Stafford, Unsubsidized Stafford, PLUS, state loans. **Student Employment:** Federal Work-Study Program available. Institutional employment available. Off-campus job opportunities are excellent. **Financial Aid Statistics:** 84% freshmen, 85% undergrads receive any aid. **Criteria for awarding institutional aid:** *Non-need-based:* academics, alumni affiliation, leadership.

PITTSBURG STATE UNIVERSITY

1701 South Broadway, Pittsburg, KS 66762
Phone: 620-235-4251 • **Financial Aid Phone:** 800-854-7488
E-mail: psuadmit@pittstate.edu • **CEEB Code:** 6336
Fax: 620-235-6003 • **Website:** www.pittstate.edu • **ACT Code:** 1449

This public school was founded in 1903. It has a 443-acre campus.

RATINGS

Admissions Selectivity Rating: 68   **Fire Safety Rating:** 81   **Green Rating:** 72

STUDENTS AND FACULTY

Enrollment: 6,166. **Student Body:** 48% female, 52% male, 26% out-of-state, 4% international (40 countries represented). Asian 0%, African American 2%, Caucasian 62%, Hispanic 3%, Native American 1%.
Retention and Graduation: 69% freshmen return for sophomore year. 24% freshmen graduate within 4 years. 48% freshmen graduate within 6 years. **Faculty:** Student/faculty ratio 19:1. 313 full-time faculty, 80% hold PhDs, 8% are members of minority groups, 41% are women. 2% of classes are taught by teaching assistants.

ACADEMICS

Degrees: associate, bachelor's, certificate, master's, post-master's certificate. **Classes:** Most classes have 20–29 students. Most lab/discussion sessions have 10–19 students. **Majors with Highest Enrollment:** biology/biological sciences; elementary education and teaching; nursing/registered nurse (rn, asn, bsn, msn). **Special Study Options:** Accelerated program, distance learning, double major, dual enrollment, English as a Second Language (ESL), honors program, independent study, internships, student-designed major, study abroad, teacher certification program. **Honors Programs:** Honors College. **Disability Services:** Special programs offered to physically disabled students include note-taking services, reader services, tape recorders. **Career Services:** Alumni network, alumni services, career/job search classes, career assessment, internships.

FACILITIES

Housing: Coed dorms, special housing for disabled students, apartments for married students, substance free and academic excellence floors are available. 90% of campus accessible to physically disabled. **Special Academic Facilities/Equipment:** planetarium, observatory, field biology reserve, nature reach, herbarium, technology center, mammal collection, greenhouse, art gallery, polymer research center, cadaver lab, Veterans Memorial Amphitheater, broadcasting lab, public radio station **Computers:** 100% of classrooms, 100% of dorms, 100% of libraries, 100% of dining areas, 100% of student union, 80% of common outdoor areas have wireless network access. Students can register for classes online. Administrative functions (other than registration) can be performed online.

CAMPUS LIFE

Environment: Village. **Activities:** Choral groups, concert band, dance, drama/theater, jazz band, literary magazine, marching band, music ensembles, pep band, radio station, student government, student newspaper, television station, yearbook, Campus Ministries, International Student Organization 150 registered organizations, 8 fraternities, 3 sororities. **Athletics (Intercollegiate):** *Men:* baseball, basketball, cheerleading, cross-country, football, golf, track/field (outdoor), track/field (indoor). *Women:* basketball, cheerleading, cross-country, softball, track/field (outdoor), track/field (indoor), volleyball. **On-Campus Highlights:** Planetarium, Veterans Memorial Amphitheater, Gorilla Village, Brandenburg Field/Carnie Smith Stadium, Timmons Chapel, Russ Hall, Kansas Technology Center, Nature Reach, Centennial Mural, Centennial Bell Tower, herbarium, art gallery, broadcasting lab, cadaver lab, polymer research lab, mammal collection, ROTC & student fitness center. **Environmental Initiatives:** Addition of Sustainability as a goal in the university strategic plan. Completing a campus sustainability plan. AASHE STARS - Bronze Rating.

ADMISSIONS

Freshman Academic Profile: Average high school GPA 3.3. 13% in top 10% of high school class, 32% in top 25% of high school class, 66% in top 50% of high school class. ACT middle 50% range 19-24. Minimum web-based TOEFL 68. Minimum paper TOEFL 520. **Basis for Candidate Selection:** *Very important factors considered include:* Class rank, academic GPA, rigor of secondary school record, standardized test scores. **Freshman Admission Requirements:** High school diploma is required and GED is accepted. **Freshman Admission Statistics:** 2,771 applied, 79% admitted, 50% enrolled. **Transfer Admission Requirements:** college transcript(s), minimum college GPA of 2.0 required. Lowest grade transferable D. **General Admission Information:** Application Fee $30. Nonfall registration accepted. Credit and/or placement offered for CEEB Advanced Placement tests.

COSTS AND FINANCIAL AID

Annual in-state tuition $4,386. Annual out-of-state tuition $13,942. Room and board $6,538. Required fees $1,108. Average book expense $1,000. **Required Forms and Deadlines:** FAFSA. **Notification of Awards:** Applicants will be notified of awards on a rolling basis beginning 3/1. **Types of Aid:** *Need-based scholarships/grants:* Federal Pell, SEOG, state scholarships/grants, private scholarships, the school's own gift aid. *Loans:* Direct Subsidized Stafford, Direct Unsubsidized Stafford, Direct PLUS, Subsidized Stafford, Unsubsidized Stafford, PLUS, Federal Perkins, Federal Nursing, college/university loans from institutional funds. **Student Employment:** Federal Work-Study Program available. Institutional employment available. Highest amount earned per year from on-campus jobs $5,100. Off-campus job opportunities are good. **Financial Aid Statistics:** 67% freshmen, 70% undergrads receive need-based scholarship or grant aid. 56% freshmen, 36% undergrads receive non-need-based scholarship or grant aid. 26% freshmen, 23% undergrads receive need-based self-help aid. 4% freshmen, 3% undergrads receive athletic scholarships. 8% undergrads borrow to pay for school. Average cumulative indebtedness $19,714. **Criteria for awarding institutional aid:** *Non-need-based:* academics, alumni affiliation, art, athletics, leadership, minority status, music/drama.

PITZER COLLEGE

Best 378

1050 North Mills Avenue, Claremont, CA 91711-6101
Phone: 909-621-8129 • **Financial Aid Phone:** 909-621-8208
E-mail: admission@pitzer.edu • **CEEB Code:** 4619
Fax: 909-621-8770 • **Website:** www.pitzer.edu • **ACT Code:** 363

This private school was founded in 1963. It has a 35-acre campus.

RATINGS

Admissions Selectivity Rating: 96   **Fire Safety Rating:** 77   **Green Rating:** 92

STUDENTS AND FACULTY

Enrollment: 1,099. **Student Body:** 62% female, 38% male, 50% out-of-state, 3% international (15 countries represented). Asian 8%, African American 6%, Caucasian 46%, Hispanic 16%, Native American 1%.
Retention and Graduation: 75% freshmen graduate within 4 years. 81% freshmen graduate within 6 years. 17% grads go on to further study within 1 year. **Faculty:** Student/faculty ratio 12:1. 74 full-time faculty, 100% hold PhDs, 36% are members of minority groups, 46% are women. 0% of classes are taught by teaching assistants.

ACADEMICS

Degrees: bachelor's. **Classes:** Most classes have 10–19 students. **Majors with Highest Enrollment:** film/cinema studies; psychology; sociology. **Special Study Options:** cooperative education program, cross-registration, double major, English as a Second Language (ESL), exchange student program (domestic), honors program, independent study, internships, liberal arts/career combination, student-designed major, study abroad. **Combined Degree Programs:** BA/MA, B.A./D.O. (Doctor of Osteopathy); BA/MBA. **Disability Services:** Special programs offered to physically disabled students include note-taking services, reader services, tape recorders, tutors. **Career Services:** Alumni network, career/job search classes, career assessment, internships Career Services highlights include Many of our courses have an internship component which provides students with practical experience as well as classroom learning.

FACILITIES

Housing: Coed dorms, special housing for disabled students, theme housing, green housing. 95% of campus accessible to physically disabled. **Special Academic Facilities/Equipment:** Theatre arts center, Black, Asian American and Chicano Study centers; film, TV, and videotape studios; arboretum; biological field station; student health services, Gold Student Center. **Computers:** 95% of classrooms, 100% of dorms, 95% of libraries, have wireless network access. Students can register for classes online. Administrative functions (other than registration) can be performed online.

CAMPUS LIFE

Environment: Town. **Activities:** Choral groups, dance, drama/theater, literary magazine, music ensembles, radio station, student government, student newspaper, symphony orchestra, Campus Ministries, International Student Organization, Model UN 120 registered organizations, 1 honor societies. **Athletics (Intercollegiate):** *Men:* baseball, basketball, cross-country, diving, football, golf,

soccer, swimming, tennis, track/field (outdoor), water polo. *Women:* basketball, cross-country, diving, soccer, softball, swimming, tennis, track/field (outdoor), volleyball, water polo. **On-Campus Highlights:** Grove House, McConnell Center, Gloria and Peter Gold Student Center, Marquis Library, The Mounds, http://www.pitzer.edu/admission/campusvisit.aspThe Claremont Colleges Consortium Pitzer students may cross-register at any of The Claremont Colleges, and may utilize all Claremont facilities, including Honnold Library, the third-largest academic library in the state, with more than 2 million volumes; Huntley Bookstore; Baxter Medical Center; McAlister Center for Religious Activities and Monsour Counseling Center. Pitzer sponsors the Joint Science Program with Claremont McKenna and Scripps colleges, and the five undergraduate colleges offer a wide range of recreational facilities, student gathering places and dining areas. Pitzer combines with Pomona College for NCAA Division III sports. **Environmental Initiatives:** New 'Green' dorms. Campus Climate challenge through Eco Center Majors in Environmental Studies and Environmental Science. Class in Environmental Justice.

ADMISSIONS

Freshman Academic Profile: Average high school GPA 3.9. 55% in top 10% of high school class, 89% in top 25% of high school class, 100% in top 50% of high school class. SAT Math middle 50% range 590-690. SAT Critical Reading middle 50% range 605-710. Minimum web-based TOEFL 70. Minimum paper TOEFL 520. **Basis for Candidate Selection:** *Very important factors considered include:* Class rank, application essay, academic GPA, recommendation(s), rigor of secondary school record, character/personal qualities, extracurricular activities, racial/ethnic status. *Important factors considered include:* first generation, geographical residence, interview, level of applicant's interest, talent/ability, volunteer work. *Other factors considered include:* standardized test scores, alumni/ae relation, work experience. **Freshman Admission Requirements:** High school diploma is required and GED is accepted. *Academic units required:* 4 English, 3 mathematics, 3 science, (3 science labs), 3 foreign language, 3 social studies, 1 history, 1 visual/performing arts. computer science. 4 English, 3 mathematics, 3 science, (3 science labs), 3 foreign language, 3 social studies, 1 history, 1 visual/performing arts. computer science. **Freshman Admission Statistics:** 3,743 applied, 24% admitted, 30% enrolled. **Transfer Admission Requirements:** college transcript(s), essay or personal statement, statement of good standing from prior institution(s). Minimum college GPA of 2.0 required. Lowest grade transferable C–. **General Admission Information:** Application Fee $60. Early decision application deadline 11/15. Regular application deadline 1/1. Regular notification 4/1. Nonfall registration not accepted. Admission may be deferred for a maximum of 1 year. Placement offered for CEEB Advanced Placement tests.

COSTS AND FINANCIAL AID

Annual tuition $38,832. Room and board $12,438. Required fees $3,718. Average book expense $1,000. **Required Forms and Deadlines:** FAFSA, CSS/Financial Aid PROFILE, state aid form, noncustodial PROFILE, business/farm supplement. **Notification of Awards:** Applicants will be notified of awards on or about 4/1. **Types of Aid:** *Need-based scholarships/grants:* Federal Pell, SEOG, state scholarships/grants, private scholarships, the school's own gift aid, Federal ACG and National SMART. *Loans:* Subsidized Stafford, Unsubsidized Stafford, PLUS, Federal Perkins, college/university loans from institutional funds. **Student Employment:** Federal Work-Study Program available. Institutional employment available. Off-campus job opportunities are good. **Financial Aid Statistics:** 95% freshmen, 98% undergrads receive need-based scholarship or grant aid. 89% freshmen, 95% undergrads receive need-based self-help aid. 34% freshmen, 40% undergrads receive any aid. 35% undergrads borrow to pay for school. Average cumulative indebtedness $22,568. **Criteria for awarding institutional aid:** *Non-need-based:* academics, leadership.

See page 1174.

PLYMOUTH STATE UNIVERSITY

17 High Street, Plymouth, NH 3264
Phone: 603-535-2237 • **Financial Aid Phone:** 877-846-5755
E-mail: plymouthadmit@plymouth.edu • **CEEB Code:** 3690
Fax: 603-535-2714 • **Website:** www.plymouth.edu • **ACT Code:** 2518

This public school was founded in 1871. It has a 170-acre campus.

RATINGS

Admissions Selectivity Rating: 70   **Fire Safety Rating:** 99   **Green Rating:** 81

STUDENTS AND FACULTY

Enrollment: 4,315. **Student Body:** 48% female, 52% male, 41% out-of-state, 1% international (34 countries represented). Asian 1%, African American 1%,

Caucasian 80%, Hispanic 2%, Native American 0%.
Retention and Graduation: 74% freshmen return for sophomore year. 40% freshmen graduate within 4 years. **Faculty:** Student/faculty ratio 16:1. 187 full-time faculty, 88% hold PhDs, 8% are members of minority groups, 45% are women. 0% of classes are taught by teaching assistants.

ACADEMICS

Degrees: bachelor's, doctoral, master's, post-bachelor's certificate, post-master's certificate. **Classes:** Most classes have 20–29 students. Most lab/discussion sessions have 10–19 students. **Majors with Highest Enrollment:** business administration and management; criminal justice/safety studies; elementary education and teaching. **Special Study Options:** cross-registration, distance learning, double major, dual enrollment, English as a Second Language (ESL), exchange student program (domestic), external degree program, honors program, independent study, internships, student-designed major, study abroad, teacher certification program. **Honors Programs:** First and Second Year Honors Program, Business Honors, Psychology Honors. **Disability Services:** Special programs offered to physically disabled students include note-taking services, reader services, tape recorders, tutors. **Career Services:** Alumni network, alumni services, career/job search classes, career assessment, internships, regional alumni.

FACILITIES

Housing: Coed dorms, special housing for disabled students, fraternity/sorority housing, apartments for married students, apartments for single students, wellness housing, theme housing, Non-traditional student apts. Quiet study/Academic. 80% of campus accessible to physically disabled. **Special Academic Facilities/Equipment:** Karl Drerup Art gallery, Silver Cultural Arts Center, Sylvestre Planetarium, Child Development and Family Center (NAEYC accredited lab school for children 2-6 years old), meteorology lab, Geographic Information System lab, psychology lab, graphic design computer lab **Computers:** 75% of classrooms, 5% of dorms, 100% of libraries, 100% of dining areas, 100% of student union, 10% of common outdoor areas have wireless network access. Students can register for classes online. Administrative functions (other than registration) can be performed online.

CAMPUS LIFE

Environment: Village. **Activities:** Choral groups, concert band, dance, drama/theater, jazz band, literary magazine, music ensembles, musical theater, radio station, student government, student newspaper, student-run film society, yearbook, Campus Ministries, International Student Organization, Model UN 80 registered organizations, 13 honor societies, 4 religious organizations. 3 sororities. **Athletics (Intercollegiate):** *Men:* baseball, basketball, football, ice hockey, lacrosse, skiing (downhill/alpine), soccer, wrestling. *Women:* basketball, cheerleading, diving, field hockey, ice hockey, lacrosse, skiing (downhill/alpine), soccer, softball, swimming, tennis, volleyball. **On-Campus Highlights:** Hartman Union Building, Silver Center for the Arts, PE Center-New-Fall '10 Ice Arena & Welcome Center, Prospect Dining Hall, Lamson Library - Information Commons. **Environmental Initiatives:** New degree program. All new campus construction must achieve LEED Silver Standard or the Equivalent Energy conservation projects.

ADMISSIONS

Freshman Academic Profile: Average high school GPA 2.9. 5% in top 10% of high school class, 18% in top 25% of high school class, 52% in top 50% of high school class. SAT Math middle 50% range 440-530. SAT Critical Reading middle 50% range 440-530. ACT middle 50% range 18-21. Minimum web-based TOEFL 68. Minimum paper TOEFL 520. **Basis for Candidate Selection:** *Very important factors considered include:* rigor of secondary school record. *Important factors considered include:* Class rank, application essay, academic GPA, recommendation(s), standardized test scores, character/personal qualities, talent/ability. *Other factors considered include:* alumni/ae relation, extracurricular activities, racial/ethnic status, volunteer work, work experience. **Freshman Admission Requirements:** High school diploma is required and GED is accepted. *Academic units required:* 4 English, 3 mathematics, 2 science, (1 science labs), 2 social studies, 1 history. *Academic units recommended:* 4 English, 3 mathematics, 2 science, (1 science labs), 2 social studies, 1 history. **Freshman Admission Statistics:** 5,279 applied, 74% admitted, 26% enrolled. **Transfer Admission Requirements:** High school transcript, college transcript(s), minimum college GPA of 2.0 required. Lowest grade transferable C. **General Admission Information:** Application Fee $45. Regular application deadline 4/1. Notification on a rolling basis, beginning on or about 11/1. Nonfall registration accepted. Admission may be deferred for a maximum of 1 year. Credit offered for CEEB Advanced Placement tests.

COSTS AND FINANCIAL AID

Required **Forms and Deadlines:** FAFSA. **Notification of Awards:** Applicants will be notified of awards on a rolling basis beginning 3/1. **Types of Aid:** *Need-based scholarships/grants:* Federal Pell, SEOG, state scholarships/grants, private scholarships, the school's own gift aid. *Loans:* Direct Subsidized Stafford, Direct Unsubsidized Stafford, Direct PLUS, Federal Perkins.

Student Employment: Federal Work-Study Program available. Institutional employment available. Highest amount earned per year from on-campus jobs $3,325. Off-campus job opportunities are good. **Financial Aid Statistics:** 64% freshmen, 59% undergrads receive need-based scholarship or grant aid. 44% freshmen, 31% undergrads receive non-need-based scholarship or grant aid. 98% freshmen, 98% undergrads receive need-based self-help aid. 91% freshmen, 86% undergrads receive any aid. 82% undergrads borrow to pay for school. Average cumulative indebtedness $31,145. **Criteria for awarding institutional aid:** *Non-need-based:* academics, music/drama.

POINT LOMA NAZARENE UNIVERSITY

3900 Lomaland Drive, San Diego, CA 92106
Phone: 619-849-2273
E-mail: admissions@pointloma.edu • **CEEB Code:** 4605
Fax: 619-849-2601 • **ACT Code:** 370

This private school, affiliated with the Nazarene Church, was founded in 1902. It has a 90-acre campus.

RATINGS

Admissions Selectivity Rating: 77   **Fire Safety Rating:** 60*   **Green Rating:** 60*

STUDENTS AND FACULTY

Enrollment: 2,337. **Student Body:** 61% female, 39% male, 21% out-of-state, 0% international (17 countries represented). Asian 6%, African American 2%, Caucasian 78%, Hispanic 11%, Native American 1%.
Retention and Graduation: 87% freshmen return for sophomore year. 60% freshmen graduate within 4 years. 70% freshmen graduate within 6 years. **Faculty:** Student/faculty ratio 16:1. 177 full-time faculty, 73% hold PhDs, 10% are members of minority groups, 40% are women. 0% of classes are taught by teaching assistants.

ACADEMICS

Degrees: bachelor's, master's. **Classes:** Most classes have 20–29 students. **Majors with Highest Enrollment:** business/commerce; liberal arts and sciences/liberal studies; psychology. **Special Study Options:** double major, honors program, independent study, internships, study abroad, teacher certification program. **Honors Programs:** Honors Scholars Program.

FACILITIES

Housing: men's dorms, women's dorms, apartments for married students, apartments for single students. 100% of campus accessible to physically disabled. **Special Academic Facilities/Equipment:** Language lab, on-campus preschool, electron microscope. **Computers:** Students can register for classes online. Administrative functions (other than registration) can be performed online.

CAMPUS LIFE

Environment: Metropolis. **Activities:** Choral groups, concert band, drama/theater, jazz band, literary magazine, music ensembles, musical theater, radio station, student government, student newspaper, television station, yearbook, Campus Ministries, International Student Organization 30 registered organizations, 2 honor societies, 7 religious organizations. 3 fraternities, 3 sororities. **Athletics (Intercollegiate):** *Men:* baseball, basketball, cross-country, golf, soccer, tennis, track/field (outdoor). *Women:* basketball, cross-country, softball, tennis, track/field (outdoor), volleyball. **On-Campus Highlights:** Point Break Cafe, Recreation Center, Ryan Library, Greek Ampitheatre, Golden Gymnasium.

ADMISSIONS

Freshman Academic Profile: Average high school GPA 3.7. 45% in top 10% of high school class, 72% in top 25% of high school class, 95% in top 50% of high school class. SAT Math middle 50% range 500-620. SAT Critical Reading middle 50% range 510-620. Minimum paper TOEFL 550. **Basis for Candidate Selection:** *Very important factors considered include:* academic GPA, rigor of secondary school record, standardized test scores, character/personal qualities, religious affiliation/commitment. *Important factors considered include:* Class rank, application essay, recommendation(s), interview. *Other factors considered include:* alumni/ae relation, extracurricular activities, first generation, level of applicant's interest, talent/ability. **Freshman Admission Requirements:** High school diploma is required and GED is accepted. **Freshman Admission Statistics:** 1,757 applied, 73% admitted, 41% enrolled. **Transfer Admission Requirements:** college transcript(s), essay or personal statement, interview, minimum college GPA of 2.0 required. Lowest grade transferable D. **General Admission Information:** Application Fee $50. Regular notification 4/1. Nonfall registration not accepted. Credit and/or placement offered for CEEB Advanced Placement tests.

COSTS AND FINANCIAL AID

Annual tuition $24,580. Room and board $8,170. Required fees $540. Average book expense $1,566. **Required Forms and Deadlines:** FAFSA, institution's own financial aid form. **Notification of Awards:** Applicants will be notified of awards on a rolling basis beginning 3/1. **Types of Aid:** *Need-based scholarships/grants:* Federal Pell, SEOG, state scholarships/grants, private scholarships, the school's own gift aid. *Loans:* Subsidized Stafford, Unsubsidized Stafford, PLUS, Federal Perkins, Federal Nursing. **Student Employment: Financial Aid Statistics:** 96% freshmen, 93% undergrads receive need-based scholarship or grant aid. 9% freshmen, 9% undergrads receive non-need-based scholarship or grant aid. 78% freshmen, 82% undergrads receive need-based self-help aid. 3% freshmen, 4% undergrads receive athletic scholarships. 86% undergrads borrow to pay for school. Average cumulative indebtedness $19,525.

POINT PARK UNIVERSITY

201 Wood Street, Pittsburgh, PA 15222
Phone: 412-392-3430 • **Financial Aid Phone:** 412-392-3930
E-mail: enroll@pointpark.edu • **CEEB Code:** 2676
Fax: 412-391-1980 • **ACT Code:** 3530

This private school was founded in 1960.

RATINGS
Admissions Selectivity Rating: 71   **Fire Safety Rating:** 94   **Green Rating:** 75

STUDENTS AND FACULTY

Enrollment: 3,316. **Student Body:** 58% female, 42% male, 20% out-of-state, 1% international (38 countries represented). Asian 1%, African American 18%, Caucasian 73%, Hispanic 3%, Native American 0%.
Retention and Graduation: 75% freshmen return for sophomore year. 41% freshmen graduate within 4 years. 50% freshmen graduate within 6 years.
Faculty: Student/faculty ratio 14:1. 129 full-time faculty, 71% hold PhDs, 15% are members of minority groups, 62% are women. 0% of classes are taught by teaching assistants.

ACADEMICS

Degrees: associate, bachelor's, certificate, master's, post-bachelor's certificate. **Classes:** Most classes have 10–19 students. **Majors with Highest Enrollment:** dance; drama and dramatics/theatre arts; teacher education and professional development, specific subject areas, other. **Special Study Options:** Accelerated program, cooperative education program, cross-registration, distance learning, double major, dual enrollment, English as a Second Language (ESL), exchange student program (domestic), honors program, independent study, internships, liberal arts/career combination, student-designed major, study abroad, teacher certification program, weekend college. **Honors Programs:** The Point Park Honors Program mission provides the foundation from which honors courses are developed. Honors courses will not be defined by more work but rather by a different kind of learning environment. Students will be introduced to the usual content and objectives of the course, but they will also develop in-depth understandings of topics. Students will be expected to use primary sources when possible and to develop appropriate research skills which should result in major documented papers or projects. Students will be encouraged to become adventurous, independent thinkers. Students should experience a variety of learning activities which may include collaborative learning, field experience, debates, documented projects, interviews, and presentations. Evaluation will be based on performance, creativity, imagination, critical thinking, and risk taking rather than on more assignments and tests. Honors students will be expected to participate in the quest for knowledge by being prepared and willing to contribute to all class activities. Honors students also may join our Honors Student Organization and participate in a variety of community service efforts and projects inside and outside the Point Park community. Students annually are offered the chance to travel for an alternative spring break, and they can present papers and research at national and regional honors conferences. Every effort is made to encourage all of them to assume leadership positions and propose their own activities and endeavors to complement their work in the classroom. Students who complete program requirements will be recognized in the program at graduation and will receive a separate certificate and notation on their transcript. **Disability Services:** Special programs offered to physically disabled students include note-taking services, reader services, tape recorders, tutors. **Career Services:** Alumni network, alumni services, career/job search classes, career assessment, internships, regional alumni..

FACILITIES

Housing: Coed dorms, special housing for disabled students, women's dorms, apartments for single students, theme housing, Living & Learning Communities; Suite Style. 95% of campus accessible to physically disabled. **Special Aca-**

demic Facilities/Equipment: Theater, day care center and elementary school, engineering technology labs, television and radio studios, digital film editing suites, dance studios. **Computers:** 100% of classrooms, 100% of libraries, 100% of dining areas, 100% of student union, 100% of common outdoor areas have wireless network access. Students can register for classes online. Administrative functions (other than registration) can be performed online.

CAMPUS LIFE

Environment: Metropolis. **Activities:** Choral groups, dance, drama/theater, literary magazine, musical theater, radio station, student government, student newspaper, student-run film society, television station, International Student Organization 25 registered organizations, 3 honor societies, 2 religious organizations. **Athletics (Intercollegiate):** *Men:* baseball, basketball, cross-country, golf, soccer. *Women:* basketball, cross-country, golf, soccer, softball, volleyball. **On-Campus Highlights:** Point Cafe, Atrium Overlook, Recreation Center, Coffee Kiosk, Outdoor Patio. **Environmental Initiatives:** Recycling LEED Building Creating a greening committee with strategic plan

ADMISSIONS

Freshman Academic Profile: Average high school GPA 3.2. 9% in top 10% of high school class, 31% in top 25% of high school class, 66% in top 50% of high school class. SAT Math middle 50% range 440-540. SAT Critical Reading middle 50% range 470-570. SAT Writing middle 50% range 450-560. ACT middle 50% range 20-25. Minimum paper TOEFL 500. **Basis for Candidate Selection:** *Other factors considered include:* Class rank, academic GPA, rigor of secondary school record, standardized test scores, talent/ability. **Freshman Admission Requirements:** High school diploma is required and GED is accepted. **Freshman Admission Statistics:** 3,357 applied, 75% admitted, 20% enrolled. **Transfer Admission Requirements:** college transcript(s), minimum college GPA of 2.0 required. Lowest grade transferable C. **General Admission Information:** Application Fee $40. Notification on a rolling basis, beginning on or about 10/1. Nonfall registration accepted. Admission may be deferred for a maximum of 1 year. Neither credit nor placement offered for CEEB Advanced Placement tests.

COSTS AND FINANCIAL AID

Required Forms and Deadlines: FAFSA. **Notification of Awards:** Applicants will be notified of awards on a rolling basis beginning 2/15. **Types of Aid:** *Need-based scholarships/grants:* Federal Pell, SEOG, state scholarships/grants, private scholarships, the school's own gift aid. *Loans:* Direct Subsidized Stafford, Direct Unsubsidized Stafford, Direct PLUS, Subsidized Stafford, Unsubsidized Stafford, PLUS, Federal Perkins. **Student Employment:** Federal Work-Study Program available. Institutional employment available. Highest amount earned per year from on-campus jobs $2,500. Off-campus job opportunities are good. **Financial Aid Statistics:** 100% freshmen, 98% undergrads receive need-based scholarship or grant aid. 9% freshmen, 8% undergrads receive non-need-based scholarship or grant aid. 87% freshmen, 88% undergrads receive need-based self-help aid. 3% freshmen, 2% undergrads receive athletic scholarships. 100% freshmen, 95% undergrads receive any aid. 80% undergrads borrow to pay for school. Average cumulative indebtedness $26,087. **Criteria for awarding institutional aid:** *Non-need-based:* academics, athletics, minority status.

POLYTECHNIC INSTITUTE OF NEW YORK UNIVERSITY—BROOKLYN

6 Metrotech Center, Brooklyn, NY 11201-2999
Phone: 718-260-5955 • **Financial Aid Phone:** 718-260-3025
E-mail: uadmit@poly.edu • **CEEB Code:** 2668
Fax: 718-260-3446 • **Website:** www.poly.edu • **ACT Code:** 2860

This private school was founded in 1854. It has a 3-acre campus.

RATINGS
Admissions Selectivity Rating: 87   **Fire Safety Rating:** 74   **Green Rating:** 78

STUDENTS AND FACULTY

Enrollment: 2,000. **Student Body:** 20% female, 80% male, 19% out-of-state, 10% international (34 countries represented). Asian 35%, African American 6%, Caucasian 30%, Hispanic 10%, Native American 0%.
Retention and Graduation: 84% freshmen return for sophomore year. 31% freshmen graduate within 4 years. 54% freshmen graduate within 6 years. 15% grads go on to further study within 1 year. **Faculty:** Student/faculty ratio 14:1. 157 full-time faculty, 91% hold PhDs, 29% are members of minority groups, 17% are women. 0% of classes are taught by teaching assistants.

ACADEMICS

Degrees: bachelor's, certificate, doctoral, master's. **Classes:** Most classes have 10–19 students. Most lab/discussion sessions have 10–19 students. **Majors with Highest Enrollment:** civil engineering; electrical, electronics and communications engineering; mechanical engineering. **Special Study Options:** Accelerated program, cooperative education program, distance learning, double major, dual enrollment, honors program, independent study, internships. **Honors Programs:** The Honors College serves as a magnet for attracting academically superior Undergraduates to the University. It accepts students of exceptional talent and promise from a variety of backgrounds. It offers outstanding Honors students the opportunity to earn a BS and possibly an MS degree in possibly as few as four years, including summers. Honors College students work one-on-one with faculty mentors, who, among other things, stress interdisciplinary research where appropriate, originality of thought, and active learning. Honors College students form a talented cadre of high-achievers who will become engineers, scientists, managers, and other professionals positioned for leadership roles in our emerging knowledge-based economy. They will also form a highly enthusiastic and supportive part of the University's alumni population and enhance the overall reputation of the University for delivering excellence in education. **Combined Degree Programs:** BA/MA, BA/MEng, 2-2 engineering program with CUNY Brooklyn Coll. **Disability Services:** Special programs offered to physically disabled students include note-taking services, tape recorders, tutors. **Career Services:** Alumni network, alumni services, career/job search classes, career assessment, internships.

FACILITIES

Housing: Coed dorms, fraternity/sorority housing. 100% of campus accessible to physically disabled. **Special Academic Facilities/Equipment:** Electron microscope, supersonic wind tunnel. Art Displays in Student Center. **Computers:** 100% of classrooms, 100% of dorms, 100% of libraries, 100% of dining areas, 100% of student union, 100% of common outdoor areas have wireless network access. Students can register for classes online. Administrative functions (other than registration) can be performed online. Undergraduates are required to own a computer.

CAMPUS LIFE

Environment: Metropolis. **Activities:** drama/theater, literary magazine, radio station, student government, student newspaper, student-run film society, yearbook 36 registered organizations, 8 honor societies, 4 religious organizations. 3 fraternities, 1 sororities. **Athletics (Intercollegiate):** *Men:* baseball, basketball, cross-country, soccer, tennis, track/field (outdoor), volleyball. *Women:* basketball, cross-country, softball, tennis, track/field (outdoor), volleyball. **On-Campus Highlights:** Recreation Center--Wunsch Student Center, Fitness Center--Jacobs Building, Bern Dibner Library for Science and Technology, Jasper H. Kane Dining Hall--Rogers Hall, Gymnasium--Jacobs Building. **Environmental Initiatives:** Enhanced/expanded recycling. Signed Presidents' Climate Committment. Accepted Mayor's Challenge--30% in 10 years.

ADMISSIONS

Freshman Academic Profile: Average high school GPA 3.5. 46% in top 10% of high school class, 81% in top 25% of high school class, 95% in top 50% of high school class. 73% from public high schools. SAT Math middle 50% range 640-720. SAT Critical Reading middle 50% range 550-650. SAT Writing middle 50% range 540-650. ACT middle 50% range 26-30. Minimum web-based TOEFL 80. Minimum paper TOEFL 550. **Basis for Candidate Selection:** *Very important factors considered include:* rigor of secondary school record, standardized test scores. *Important factors considered include:* Class rank. *Other factors considered include:* application essay, recommendation(s), interview. **Freshman Admission Requirements:** High school diploma is required and GED is accepted. *Academic units required:* 4 English, 4 mathematics, 4 science, 3 social studies, 2 academic electives. *Academic units recommended:* 4 English, 4 mathematics, 4 science, 3 social studies, 2 academic electives. **Freshman Admission Statistics:** 3,284 applied, 75% admitted, 20% enrolled. **Transfer Admission Requirements:** college transcript(s), minimum college GPA of 2.5 required. Lowest grade transferable c. **General Admission Information:** Application Fee $50. Nonfall registration accepted. Admission may be deferred for a maximum of 1. Credit and/or placement offered for CEEB Advanced Placement tests.

COSTS AND FINANCIAL AID

Annual tuition $38,334. Room and board $13,500. Required fees $1,230. Average book expense $1,500. **Required Forms and Deadlines:** FAFSA, institution's own financial aid form, CSS/Financial Aid PROFILE, state aid form. **Notification of Awards:** Applicants will be notified of awards on a rolling basis beginning 2/15. **Types of Aid:** *Need-based scholarships/grants:* Federal Pell, SEOG, state scholarships/grants, private scholarships, the school's own gift aid, United Negro College Fund. *Loans:* Subsidized Stafford, Unsubsidized Stafford, PLUS, Federal Perkins, college/university loans from institutional funds, Alternative Loans. **Student Employment:** Highest amount earned per year from on-campus jobs $10,500. Off-campus job opportunities are excellent. **Financial Aid Statistics:** 93% freshmen, 93% undergrads receive need-based

scholarship or grant aid. 89% freshmen, 60% undergrads receive non-need-based scholarship or grant aid. 86% freshmen, 88% undergrads receive need-based self-help aid. 97% freshmen, 92% undergrads receive any aid. 68% undergrads borrow to pay for school. Average cumulative indebtedness $30,560. **Criteria for awarding institutional aid:** *Non-need-based:* academics, minority status, state/district residency.

POLYTECHNIC UNIVERSITY OF PUERTO RICO

PO BOX 192017, Hato Rey, PR 00919-2017
Phone: 787-622-8000 • **Financial Aid Phone:** 787-622-8000
E-mail: • **CEEB Code:**
Fax: 787-764-8712 • **Website:** www.pupr.edu • **ACT Code:**

This private school was founded in 1966.

RATINGS

Admissions Selectivity Rating: 62   **Fire Safety Rating:** 60*   **Green Rating:** 61

STUDENTS AND FACULTY

Enrollment: 4,017. **Student Body:** 21% female, 79% male.
Retention and Graduation: 70% freshmen return for sophomore year. **Faculty:** Student/faculty ratio 19:1. 161 full-time faculty, 35% are women.

ACADEMICS

Degrees: bachelor's, master's. **Special Study Options:** cooperative education program, distance learning, honors program. **Honors Programs:** In a continuing effort to provide educational opportunities consistent with the ability of the individual student, the University invites a select group of students to enroll in and benefit from the Honor Program and corresponding Scholarship. This program consists of honors seminars, special courses, and independent study. The special courses enable students who excel to be challenged to their full intellectual capacity. The program is designed both to broaden and deepen the student's intellectual power. At the advanced level, honor students are encouraged to undertake faculty-guided independent research in their areas of special interest or competencies. These courses are conducted as seminars and involve topics at the forefront of current scientific interest. Students who excel in mathematics and physics, regardless of the major preference, are encouraged to enroll in these courses. The program also offers an opportunity for independent study for honor students whose interests lie beyond the topics ordinarily covered by the university program. **Disability Services:** Special programs offered to physically disabled students include note-taking services, tutors.

FACILITIES

Computers: 100% of classrooms, 100% of libraries, 100% of dining areas, 100% of student union, 100% of common outdoor areas have wireless network access.

CAMPUS LIFE

Environment: Metropolis. **Activities:** Choral groups, student government 20 registered organizations, 1 honor societies, 1 religious organizations. **Athletics (Intercollegiate):** *Men:* basketball, cross-country, martial arts, table tennis, tennis, track/field (outdoor), volleyball, wrestling. *Women:* cross-country, martial arts, table tennis, tennis, track/field (outdoor), volleyball.

ADMISSIONS

Freshman Admission Requirements: High school diploma is required and GED is accepted. *Academic units required:* 3 English, 3 mathematics, 3 science, 3 foreign language, 3 social studies. 3 English, 3 mathematics, 3 science, 3 foreign language, 3 social studies. **Freshman Admission Statistics:** 634 applied, 89% admitted, 73% enrolled. **Transfer Admission Requirements:** college transcript(s). **General Admission Information:** Application Fee $30. Placement offered for CEEB Advanced Placement tests.

COSTS AND FINANCIAL AID

Annual tuition $6,768. Required fees $780. Average book expense $2,312. **Required Forms and Deadlines:** FAFSA. **Student Employment:** Federal Work-Study Program available.

POMONA COLLEGE

333 N. College Way, Claremont, CA 91711-6312
Phone: 909-621-8134 • **Financial Aid Phone:** 909-621-8205
E-mail: admissions@pomona.edu • **CEEB Code:** 4607
Fax: 909-621-8952 • **Website:** www.pomona.edu • **ACT Code:** 372

This private school was founded in 1887. It has a 140-acre campus.

RATINGS
Admissions Selectivity Rating: 99   **Fire Safety Rating:** 93   **Green Rating:** 99

STUDENTS AND FACULTY
Enrollment: 1,585. **Student Body:** 52% female, 48% male, 66% out-of-state, 6% international (25 countries represented). Asian 11%, African American 6%, Caucasian 45%, Hispanic 14%, Native American 0%.
Retention and Graduation: 97% freshmen return for sophomore year. 89% freshmen graduate within 4 years. 22% grads go on to further study within 1 year. **Faculty:** Student/faculty ratio 8:1. 189 full-time faculty, 98% hold PhDs, 30% are members of minority groups, 41% are women. 0% of classes are taught by teaching assistants.

ACADEMICS
Degrees: bachelor's. **Classes:** Most classes have 10–19 students. Most lab/discussion sessions have 10–19 students. **Majors with Highest Enrollment:** biology/biological sciences; economics; English language and literature. **Special Study Options:** cross-registration, double major, exchange student program (domestic), independent study, internships, student-designed major, study abroad, The college has a 3-2 combined Bachelors (BA & BS) in Engineering with Washington University in St. Louis and the California Institute of Technology. **Combined Degree Programs:** BA/MEng. **Disability Services:** Special programs offered to physically disabled students include note-taking services, reader services, tape recorders, tutors. **Career Services:** Alumni network, alumni services, career/job search classes, career assessment, internships, regional alumni. Career Services highlights include Pomona College Internship Program (PCIP) Students receive school credit for having a part-time internship over the course of a semester, totaling at minimum 60 hours. They can choose from a list of local internship options coordinated through our Career Development Office. Students submit a written evaluation at the end of the semester.

FACILITIES
Housing: Coed dorms, theme housing, Language Residence Hall. 85% of campus accessible to physically disabled. **Special Academic Facilities/Equipment:** Oldenborg Center for Foreign Languages, Musuem of Art, Brackett Observatory **Computers:** 75% of classrooms, 50% of dorms, 100% of libraries, 100% of dining areas, 100% of student union, 100% of common outdoor areas have wireless network access. Administrative functions (other than registration) can be performed online.

CAMPUS LIFE
Environment: Town. **Activities:** Choral groups, concert band, dance, drama/theater, jazz band, literary magazine, music ensembles, musical theater, pep band, radio station, student government, student newspaper, student-run film society, symphony orchestra, television station, yearbook, Campus Ministries, International Student Organization, Model UN 280 registered organizations, 3 honor societies, 5 religious organizations. 3 fraternities. **Athletics (Intercollegiate):** *Men:* baseball, basketball, cross-country, diving, football, golf, soccer, swimming, tennis, track/field (outdoor), water polo. *Women:* basketball, cross-country, diving, golf, lacrosse, soccer, softball, swimming, tennis, track/field (outdoor), volleyball, water polo. **On-Campus Highlights:** Smith Campus Center, Sontag Greek Theater, Rains Center for Sports and Recreation, Brackett Observatory. **Environmental Initiatives:** Pomona's Environmental Analysis Program incorporates sustainability across the curriculum in a variety of disciplines. The program offers 11 tracks within its major and minor, allowing students to focus on sustainability in a variety of natural science, social science, and humanities subjects. Sustainability is well incorporated across the curriculum. Student programs and campus engagement efforts include a green office certification program, green living training for all RAs and student mentors, an annual sustainability film festival, a program where students can get free drying racks, CFL light bulbs, and compost buckets, and much more. All programming is focused on the educational experience for campus stakeholders, as well as the reduction of environmental impacts. Pomona's facilities are built with strict environmental standards dating back to 2003. All renovation, new construction, and remodel projects must develop sustainability goals and adhere to the

campus' standard specifications for fixtures, furnishings, and building systems - including high-efficiency lighting and plumbing, non-toxic materials, and energy performance analysis. Lighting, HVAC, and other systems are systematically and regularly enhanced for energy performance, making buildings more efficient. All new construction must adhere to LEED standards for a Gold certification.

ADMISSIONS
Freshman Academic Profile: 91% in top 10% of high school class, 97% in top 25% of high school class, 100% in top 50% of high school class. 68% from public high schools. SAT Math middle 50% range 680-760. SAT Critical Reading middle 50% range 680-770. SAT Writing middle 50% range 680-780. ACT middle 50% range 29-34. Minimum web-based TOEFL 100. Minimum paper TOEFL 600. **Basis for Candidate Selection:** *Very important factors considered include:* Class rank, application essay, academic GPA, recommendation(s), rigor of secondary school record, standardized test scores, character/personal qualities, extracurricular activities, talent/ability. *Important factors considered include:* interview. *Other factors considered include:* alumni/ae relation, first generation, geographical residence, racial/ethnic status, volunteer work, work experience. **Freshman Admission Requirements:** High school diploma or equivalent is not required. *Academic units required:* 4 English, 3 mathematics, 3 science, (2 science labs), 2 foreign language, 2 social studies, 3 history. *Academic units recommended:* 4 English, 3 mathematics, 3 science, (2 science labs), 2 foreign language, 2 social studies, 3 history. **Freshman Admission Statistics:** 7,456 applied, 13% admitted, 41% enrolled. **Transfer Admission Requirements:** High school transcript, college transcript(s), essay or personal statement, standardized test scores, statement of good standing from prior institution(s). Lowest grade transferable C. **General Admission Information:** Application Fee $65. Early decision application deadline 11/1. Regular application deadline 1/2. Nonfall registration not accepted. Admission may be deferred for a maximum of 1 year. Credit and/or placement offered for CEEB Advanced Placement tests.

COSTS AND FINANCIAL AID
Required Forms and Deadlines: FAFSA, CSS/Financial Aid PROFILE, noncustodial PROFILE, business/farm supplement. Tax returns for both the student and parents. **Notification of Awards:** Applicants will be notified of awards on or about 4/1. **Types of Aid:** *Need-based scholarships/grants:* Federal Pell, SEOG, state scholarships/grants, private scholarships, the school's own gift aid. *Loans:* Subsidized Stafford, Unsubsidized Stafford, PLUS, Federal Perkins, college/university loans from institutional funds. **Student Employment:** Federal Work-Study Program available. Institutional employment available. Off-campus job opportunities are good. **Financial Aid Statistics:** 100% freshmen, 100% undergrads receive need-based scholarship or grant aid. 100% freshmen, 99% undergrads receive need-based self-help aid. 55% freshmen, 54% undergrads receive any aid. 53% undergrads borrow to pay for school. Average cumulative indebtedness $10,580.

PONTIFICAL COLLEGE JOSEPHINUM

7625 North High Street, Columbus, OH 43235-1498
Phone: 614-885-5585 • **Financial Aid Phone:** 614-885-5585
E-mail: admissions@pcj.edu
Fax: 614-885-2307

This private school, affiliated with the Roman Catholic Church,, affiliated with the Seminarian Church, was founded in 1888. It has a 100-acre campus.

RATINGS
Admissions Selectivity Rating: 70   **Fire Safety Rating:** 60*   **Green Rating:** 60*

STUDENTS AND FACULTY
Enrollment: 78. **Student Body:** 0% female, 100% male, 64% out-of-state, 8% international (15 countries represented). Asian 1%, African American 0%, Caucasian 79%, Hispanic 10%, Native American 1%.
Retention and Graduation: 92% freshmen return for sophomore year. 63% freshmen graduate within 4 years. 62% freshmen graduate within 6 years. 95% grads go on to further study within 1 year. 5% grads pursue arts and sciences degrees. **Faculty:** Student/faculty ratio 4:1. 17 full-time faculty, 76% hold PhDs, 0% are members of minority groups, 35% are women. 0% of classes are taught by teaching assistants.

ACADEMICS
Degrees: bachelor's, master's. **Classes:** Most classes have 10–19 students. **Special Study Options:** cross-registration, double major, honors program, independent study.

FACILITIES
Housing: men's dorms.

CAMPUS LIFE

Environment: Metropolis. **Activities:** Choral groups 1 religious organizations.

ADMISSIONS

Freshman Academic Profile: 25% in top 10% of high school class, 35% in top 25% of high school class, 60% in top 50% of high school class. SAT Math middle 50% range 360-610. SAT Critical Reading middle 50% range 380-600. SAT Writing middle 50% range 350-610. ACT middle 50% range 17-25. Minimum paper TOEFL 550. **Basis for Candidate Selection:** *Very important factors considered include:* recommendation(s), rigor of secondary school record, standardized test scores, religious affiliation/commitment. *Important factors considered include:* application essay, academic GPA, interview. *Other factors considered include:* Class rank, character/personal qualities, extracurricular activities, talent/ability, volunteer work. **Freshman Admission Requirements:** High school diploma is required and GED is accepted. *Academic units required:* 4 English, 2 mathematics, 1 science, 1 foreign language, 2 social studies. *Academic units recommended:* 4 English, 2 mathematics, 1 science, 1 foreign language, 2 social studies. **Freshman Admission Statistics:** 8 applied, 75% admitted, 100% enrolled. **Transfer Admission Requirements:** High school transcript, college transcript(s), essay or personal statement, interview, standardized test scores, Lowest grade transferable C. **General Admission Information:** Application Fee $25. Notification on a rolling basis, beginning on or about 1/1. Nonfall registration not accepted.

COSTS AND FINANCIAL AID

Annual tuition $16,701. Room and board $7,908. Required fees $720. Average book expense $1,100. **Required Forms and Deadlines:** FAFSA, institution's own financial aid form. **Types of Aid:** *Need-based scholarships/grants:* Federal Pell, SEOG, state scholarships/grants, private scholarships, the school's own gift aid. *Loans:* Subsidized Stafford, Unsubsidized Stafford, PLUS, Federal Perkins. **Student Employment:** Federal Work-Study Program available. Highest amount earned per year from on-campus jobs $1,200. **Financial Aid Statistics:** 83% undergrads receive need-based scholarship or grant aid. 100% freshmen, 33% undergrads receive need-based self-help aid. 20% undergrads borrow to pay for school. Average cumulative indebtedness $8,575. **Criteria for awarding institutional aid:** *Non-need-based:* academics.

PORTLAND STATE UNIVERSITY

Office of Admissions and Records, Portland, OR 97207-0751
Phone: 503-725-3511 • **Financial Aid Phone:** 800-547-8887
E-mail: admissions@pdx.edu • **CEEB Code:** 4610
Fax: 503-725-5525 • **Website:** www.pdx.edu • **ACT Code:** 3492

This public school was founded in 1946. It has a 49-acre campus.

RATINGS

Admissions Selectivity Rating: 73   **Fire Safety Rating:** 65   **Green Rating:** 99

STUDENTS AND FACULTY

Enrollment: 20,119. **Student Body:** 53% female, 47% male, 11% out-of-state, 4% international (94 countries represented). Asian 8%, African American 3%, Caucasian 66%, Hispanic 8%, Native American 2%.
Retention and Graduation: 73% freshmen return for sophomore year. 8% freshmen graduate within 4 years. 35% freshmen graduate within 6 years. **Faculty:** Student/faculty ratio 16:1. 885 full-time faculty, 76% hold PhDs, 15% are members of minority groups, 46% are women. 5% of classes are taught by teaching assistants.

ACADEMICS

Degrees: bachelor's, certificate, master's, post-bachelor's certificate. **Classes:** Most classes have 20–29 students. Most lab/discussion sessions have 20–29 students. **Majors with Highest Enrollment:** business/commerce; fine/studio arts; psychology. **Special Study Options:** Accelerated program, cooperative education program, cross-registration, distance learning, double major, English as a Second Language (ESL), exchange student program (domestic), honors program, independent study, internships, study abroad, teacher certification program, Haystack Summer Program in the Arts and Sciences. **Honors Programs:** University Honors Program. **Disability Services:** Special programs offered to physically disabled students include note-taking services, reader services, tape recorders, tutors. **Career Services:** Alumni network, alumni services, career/job search classes, career assessment, internships, Career Services

highlights include The Senior Capstone's purpose is to further enhance student learning while cultivating crucial life abilities that are important both academically and professionally; establishing connections within the larger community, developing strategies for analyzing and addressing problems, and working with others trained in fields different from one's own. This 6-credit, community-based learning course is designed to provide students with the opportunity to apply, in a team context, what they have learned in the major and in their other University Studies courses to a real challenge emanating from the metropolitan community.

FACILITIES

Housing: Coed dorms, special housing for disabled students, special housing for international students, fraternity/sorority housing, apartments for married students, apartments for single students, Special housing for new students. Apartments for students with dependent children. 95% of campus accessible to physically disabled. **Special Academic Facilities/Equipment:** Art galleries, audiovisual resources, classroom multimedia computer systems, learning lab, child development center, native american center. **Computers:** 50% of dorms, 100% of libraries, 100% of dining areas, 100% of student union, have wireless network access. Students can register for classes online. Administrative functions (other than registration) can be performed online.

CAMPUS LIFE

Environment: Metropolis. **Activities:** Choral groups, concert band, dance, drama/theater, jazz band, literary magazine, music ensembles, musical theater, opera, pep band, radio station, student government, student newspaper, student-run film society, symphony orchestra, Campus Ministries, International Student Organization, Model UN 200 registered organizations, 10 honor societies, 14 religious organizations. 4 fraternities, 4 sororities. **Athletics (Intercollegiate):** *Men:* basketball, cross-country, football, tennis, track/field (outdoor), track/field (indoor). *Women:* basketball, cross-country, golf, soccer, softball, tennis, track/field (outdoor), track/field (indoor), volleyball. **On-Campus Highlights:** Park Blocks, Student Union Center **Environmental Initiatives:** Since 2002 PSU has focused on designing new buildings and retrofitting and renovating older campus buildings with sustainability in mind. Several PSU buildings serve as models of these kinds of innovative sustainable design and construction projects. These include the new Engineering Building, Broadway Housing Building, Stephen Epler Hall, and Native American Student and Community Center. In all but the latter, the US Green Building Council's LEED certification program was used as the measuring stick and standard for sustainable design and construction. The Center for Sustainable Processes and Practices collaborates with public and private partners to study eco-roof efficiency. Graduate Sustainability Certificate This graduate certificate (in process of approval) offers an integrated series of post-baccalaureate courses that comprise a multidisciplinary study of the environmental, social, and economic dimensions of sustainability.

ADMISSIONS

Freshman Academic Profile: Average high school GPA 3.4. 11% in top 10% of high school class, 41% in top 25% of high school class, 84% in top 50% of high school class. 85% from public high schools. SAT Math middle 50% range 460-580. SAT Critical Reading middle 50% range 420-580. SAT Writing middle 50% range 440-560. ACT middle 50% range 18-25. Minimum web-based TOEFL 60. Minimum paper TOEFL 527. **Basis for Candidate Selection:** *Very important factors considered include:* academic GPA, rigor of secondary school record.*Other factors considered include:* standardized test scores. **Freshman Admission Requirements:** High school diploma is required and GED is accepted. *Academic units required:* 4 English, 3 mathematics, 2 science, 2 foreign language, 2 social studies, 1 history. *Academic units recommended:* 4 English, 3 mathematics, 2 science, 2 foreign language, 2 social studies, 1 history. **Freshman Admission Statistics:** 4,954 applied, 70% admitted, 39% enrolled. **Transfer Admission Requirements:** college transcript(s), minimum college GPA of 2.25 required. Lowest grade transferable D-. **General Admission Information:** Application Fee $50. Notification on a rolling basis, beginning on or about 1/1. Nonfall registration accepted. Admission may be deferred for a maximum of One Year. Credit and/or placement offered for CEEB Advanced Placement tests.

COSTS AND FINANCIAL AID

Annual in-state tuition $6,156. Annual out-of-state tuition $21,375. Room and board $10,368. Required fees $1,608. Average book expense $1,968. **Required Forms and Deadlines:** FAFSA. **Types of Aid:** *Need-based scholarships/grants:* Federal Pell, SEOG, state scholarships/grants, private scholarships, the school's own gift aid, United Negro College Fund. *Loans:* Direct Subsidized Stafford, Direct Unsubsidized Stafford, Direct PLUS, Subsidized Stafford, Unsubsidized Stafford, PLUS, Federal Perkins, state loans. **Student Employment:** Federal Work-Study Program available. Institutional employment available. Off-campus job opportunities are excellent. **Financial Aid Statistics:** 77% freshmen, 78% undergrads receive need-based scholarship or grant aid. 2% freshmen, 1% undergrads receive non-need-based scholarship or grant aid. 80% freshmen, 90% undergrads receive need-based self-help aid. 3% freshmen,

1% undergrads receive athletic scholarships. 75% freshmen, 56% undergrads receive any aid. **Criteria for awarding institutional aid:** *Non-need-based:* academics, art, athletics, music/drama, state/district residency.

POST UNIVERSITY

PO Box 2540, Waterbury, CT 6723
Phone: 203-596-4520 • **Financial Aid Phone:** 204-596-4526
E-mail: admissions@post.edu • **CEEB Code:** 3698
Fax: 203-756-5810 • **Website:** www.post.edu • **ACT Code:** 580

This proprietary school was founded in 1890. It has a 58-acre campus.

RATINGS
Admissions Selectivity Rating: 62   **Fire Safety Rating:** 65   **Green Rating:** 61

STUDENTS AND FACULTY
Enrollment: 1,055. **Student Body:** 61% female, 39% male, 13% out-of-state, 1% international (15 countries represented). Asian 1%, African American 15%, Caucasian 33%, Hispanic 7%, Native American 0%.
Retention and Graduation: 25% grads go on to further study within 1 year. 20% grads pursue arts and sciences degrees. 5% grads pursue law degrees. 25% grads pursue business degrees. **Faculty:** 0% of classes are taught by teaching assistants.

ACADEMICS
Degrees: associate, bachelor's, certificate, master's, post-bachelor's certificate, terminal associate, transfer associate. **Classes: Majors with Highest Enrollment:** accounting; business/commerce; criminal justice/law enforcement administration. **Special Study Options:** Accelerated program, cooperative education program, cross-registration, distance learning, double major, honors program, independent study, internships, liberal arts/career combination, study abroad, weekend college. **Disability Services:** Special programs offered to physically disabled students include tape recorders, tutors. **Career Services:** alumni services, career/job search classes, career assessment, internships.

FACILITIES
Housing: Coed dorms, apartments for single students, Inquire about learning communities. 75% of campus accessible to physically disabled. **Computers:** Students can register for classes online. Administrative functions (other than registration) can be performed online.

CAMPUS LIFE
Environment: City. **Activities:** Choral groups, drama/theater, literary magazine, musical theater, student government, student newspaper 30 registered organizations. **Athletics (Intercollegiate):** *Men:* baseball, basketball, cross-country, equestrian sports, golf, soccer, tennis. *Women:* basketball, cross-country, equestrian sports, soccer, softball, tennis, volleyball. **On-Campus Highlights:** University Hall, Leever Student Center, Drubner Athletic Center.

ADMISSIONS
Freshman Academic Profile: Average high school GPA 2.7. 90% from public high schools. Minimum paper TOEFL 500. **Basis for Candidate Selection:** *Very important factors considered include:* academic GPA, interview, level of applicant's interest. *Important factors considered include:* standardized test scores, character/personal qualities, extracurricular activities, talent/ability, volunteer work. *Other factors considered include:* application essay, recommendation(s), alumni/ae relation, first generation. **Freshman Admission Requirements:** High school diploma is required and GED is accepted. *Academic units required:* 4 English, 2 mathematics, 2 science, (1 science labs), 2 foreign language, 1 social studies, 2 history, 2 academic electives. *Academic units recommended:* 4 English, 2 mathematics, 2 science, (1 science labs), 2 foreign language, 1 social studies, 2 history, 2 academic electives. **Transfer Admission Requirements:** college transcript(s), minimum college GPA of 2.0 required. Lowest grade transferable C–. **General Admission Information:** Application Fee $40. Nonfall registration accepted. Admission may be deferred for a maximum of 1 year. Credit and/or placement offered for CEEB Advanced Placement tests.

COSTS AND FINANCIAL AID
Annual tuition $22,500. Room and board $9,000. Average book expense $1,000. **Required Forms and Deadlines:** FAFSA, institution's own financial aid form. **Types of Aid:** *Need-based scholarships/grants:* Federal Pell, SEOG, state scholarships/grants, private scholarships, the school's own gift aid. *Loans:* Subsidized Stafford, Unsubsidized Stafford, PLUS, Federal Perkins, state loans, college/university loans from institutional funds. **Student Employment:** Federal Work-Study Program available. Highest amount earned per year from on-campus jobs $2,100. **Financial Aid Statistics:** 80% freshmen, 75% undergrads

receive any aid. **Criteria for awarding institutional aid:** *Non-need-based:* academics, alumni affiliation, athletics, job skills, leadership, minority status, state/district residency.

See page 1176.

PRAIRIE VIEW A&M UNIVERSITY

PO Box 519, Prairie View, TX 77446
Phone: 936-261-3500 • **Financial Aid Phone:** 1-877-782-6830
E-mail: admissions@pvamu.edu • **CEEB Code:** 6580
Fax: • **Website:** www.pvamu.edu • **ACT Code:** 4202

This public school was founded in 1876. It has a 1388-acre campus.

RATINGS
Admissions Selectivity Rating: 79   **Fire Safety Rating:** 74   **Green Rating:** 60*

STUDENTS AND FACULTY
Enrollment: 6,973. **Student Body:** 58% female, 42% male, 7% out-of-state, 1% international (40 countries represented). Asian 2%, African American 88%, Caucasian 3%, Hispanic 5%, Native American 0%.
Retention and Graduation: 71% freshmen return for sophomore year. 12% freshmen graduate within 4 years. 32% freshmen graduate within 6 years. **Faculty:** Student/faculty ratio 17:1. 394 full-time faculty, 67% hold PhDs, 80% are members of minority groups, 39% are women.

ACADEMICS
Degrees: bachelor's, doctoral, master's. **Majors with Highest Enrollment:** business administration and management; multi-/interdisciplinary studies, other; nursing/registered nurse (rn, asn, bsn, msn). **Special Study Options:** Accelerated program, cooperative education program, distance learning, double major, dual enrollment, English as a Second Language (ESL), honors program, independent study, internships, liberal arts/career combination, study abroad, teacher certification program, weekend college. **Disability Services:** Special programs offered to physically disabled students include tape recorders, tutors. **Career Services:** Alumni network, alumni services, career assessment, internships, regional alumni..

FACILITIES
Housing: Coed dorms, special housing for disabled students, apartments for single students. 90% of campus accessible to physically disabled. **Computers:** 100% of classrooms, 100% of dorms, 100% of libraries, 75% of dining areas, 75% of student union, 50% of common outdoor areas have wireless network access. Students can register for classes online.

CAMPUS LIFE
Environment: Rural. **Activities:** Choral groups, concert band, dance, drama/theater, jazz band, marching band, music ensembles, radio station, student government, student newspaper, symphony orchestra, television station, yearbook, Campus Ministries, International Student Organization 100 registered organizations, 15 honor societies, 6 religious organizations. 9 fraternities, 9 sororities. **Athletics (Intercollegiate):** *Men:* baseball, basketball, cross-country, football, golf, tennis, track/field (outdoor), track/field (indoor). *Women:* basketball, cheerleading, cross-country, golf, soccer, softball, tennis, track/field (outdoor), track/field (indoor), volleyball. **On-Campus Highlights:** Purple Zone Student Sports Bar, Memorial Student Center, Baby Dome, J.B. Coleman Library, Jazzman Coffee Cafe, University College and University Village.

ADMISSIONS
Freshman Academic Profile: Average high school GPA 2.9. 5% in top 10% of high school class, 21% in top 25% of high school class, 56% in top 50% of high school class. SAT Math middle 50% range 380-440. SAT Critical Reading middle 50% range 370-450. SAT Writing middle 50% range 360-440. ACT middle 50% range 15-19. Minimum paper TOEFL 500. **Basis for Candidate Selection:** *Very important factors considered include:* Class rank, academic GPA, rigor of secondary school record, standardized test scores. *Other factors considered include:* character/personal qualities, extracurricular activities, first generation, volunteer work, work experience. **Freshman Admission Requirements:** High school diploma is required and GED is accepted. **Freshman Admission Statistics:** 7,931 applied, 42% admitted, 52% enrolled. **Transfer Admission Requirements:** college transcript(s), statement of good standing from prior institution(s). Minimum college GPA of 2.0 required. Lowest grade transferable C. **General Admission Information:** Application Fee $25. Regular application deadline 7/1. Nonfall registration accepted. Admission may be deferred for a maximum of 1. Credit and/or placement offered for CEEB Advanced Placement tests.

COSTS AND FINANCIAL AID

Annual in-state tuition $5,076. Annual out-of-state tuition $14,376. Room and board $7,064. Required fees $1,779. Average book expense $1,000. **Required Forms and Deadlines:** FAFSA, institution's own financial aid form. **Notification of Awards:** Applicants will be notified of awards on or about 6/1. **Types of Aid:** *Need-based scholarships/grants:* Federal Pell, SEOG, state scholarships/grants, the school's own gift aid, United Negro College Fund. *Loans:* Direct Subsidized Stafford, Direct Unsubsidized Stafford, Direct PLUS, Subsidized Stafford, Unsubsidized Stafford, PLUS, Federal Perkins, college/university loans from institutional funds. **Student Employment: Financial Aid Statistics:** 69% freshmen, 63% undergrads receive need-based scholarship or grant aid. 35% freshmen, 18% undergrads receive non-need-based scholarship or grant aid. 94% freshmen, 90% undergrads receive need-based self-help aid. 1% freshmen, 4% undergrads receive athletic scholarships. 61% freshmen, 53% undergrads receive any aid. 76% undergrads borrow to pay for school. Average cumulative indebtedness $27,500. **Criteria for awarding institutional aid:** *Non-need-based:* academics, athletics.

PRATT INSTITUTE

200 Willoughby Avenue, Brooklyn, NY 11205
Phone: 718-636-3514 • **Financial Aid Phone:** 718-636-3599
E-mail: visit@pratt.edu • **CEEB Code:** 2669
Fax: 718-636-3670 • **Website:** www.pratt.edu • **ACT Code:** 2862

This private school was founded in 1887. It has a 25-acre campus.

RATINGS

Admissions Selectivity Rating: 88   **Fire Safety Rating:** 68   **Green Rating:** 83

STUDENTS AND FACULTY

Enrollment: 2,996. **Student Body:** 64% female, 36% male, 69% out-of-state, 17% international (56 countries represented). Asian 18%, African American 4%, Caucasian 48%, Hispanic 9%, Native American 0%. **Retention and Graduation:** 42% freshmen graduate within 4 years. **Faculty:** Student/faculty ratio 11:1. 130 full-time faculty, 72% hold PhDs, 15% are members of minority groups, 40% are women. 0% of classes are taught by teaching assistants.

ACADEMICS

Degrees: associate, bachelor's, master's, post-master's certificate, terminal associate, transfer associate. **Classes:** Most classes have 10-19 students. **Majors with Highest Enrollment:** design and visual communications; fashion/apparel design. **Special Study Options:** English as a Second Language (ESL), exchange student program (domestic), independent study, internships, study abroad, teacher certification program. **Combined Degree Programs:** BA/MA, art history. **Disability Services:** Special programs offered to physically disabled students include note-taking services, reader services, tutors. **Career Services:** Alumni network, alumni services, career/job search classes, career assessment, internships Career Services highlights include As part of the intership program, students can become involved with community matters, contributing their design skills to a community program.

FACILITIES

Housing: Coed dorms, special housing for disabled students, special housing for international students, apartments for single students, wellness housing, Global Learning (for international and domestic students), Healthy Choice and Quiet Floors are available. **Special Academic Facilities/Equipment:** Five art galleries, fine arts center, printmaking center, computer graphics lab. **Computers:** Undergraduates are required to own a computer.

CAMPUS LIFE

Environment: Metropolis. **Activities:** literary magazine, music ensembles, radio station, student government, student newspaper, student-run film society, television station, yearbook, Campus Ministries, International Student Organization 50 registered organizations, 4 honor societies, 3 religious organizations. 3 fraternities, 1 sororities. **Athletics (Intercollegiate):** *Men:* basketball, cross-country, soccer, tennis, track/field (outdoor), track/field (indoor). *Women:* basketball, cross-country, soccer, tennis, track/field (outdoor), volleyball. **On-Campus Highlights:** studios, galleries, three cafeterias/coffee shops, athletic center, student union, Pratt is the only East Coast art school with a traditional campus (25 acres). **Environmental Initiatives:** Our new building, breaking ground in April 2008 will be LEED gold. We received a $475K FIPSE grant "Green by Design" to embed sustainable best practices into every program, create interdisciplinary programs that center around environmental projects and create a "living laboratory" that links greening our facilities with greening our academic programs and providing educational programs to our city. We

have a new Center for Sustainable Design and Research that centers faculty and students from various programs around environmental projects and research.

ADMISSIONS

Freshman Academic Profile: Average high school GPA 3.6. 70% from public high schools. SAT Math middle 50% range 550-660. SAT Critical Reading middle 50% range 530-640. SAT Writing middle 50% range 540-650. ACT middle 50% range 25-28. Minimum paper TOEFL 550. **Basis for Candidate Selection:** *Very important factors considered include:* academic GPA, rigor of secondary school record, standardized test scores, talent/ability. *Important factors considered include:* application essay, recommendation(s), alumni/ae relation, character/personal qualities, level of applicant's interest. *Other factors considered include:* Class rank, extracurricular activities, interview, volunteer work, work experience. **Freshman Admission Requirements:** High school diploma is required and GED is accepted. **Freshman Admission Statistics:** 4,247 applied, 60% admitted, 24% enrolled. **Transfer Admission Requirements:** High school transcript, college transcript(s), essay or personal statement, statement of good standing from prior institution(s). Lowest grade transferable C. **General Admission Information:** Application Fee $50. Regular application deadline 1/5. Regular notification 4/1. Nonfall registration not accepted. Admission may be deferred for a maximum of one year. Credit and/or placement offered for CEEB Advanced Placement tests.

COSTS AND FINANCIAL AID

Annual tuition $39,282. Room and board $10,506. Required fees $1,810. **Required Forms and Deadlines:** FAFSA. **Student Employment:** Federal Work-Study Program available. Institutional employment available. Highest amount earned per year from on-campus jobs $2,500. Off-campus job opportunities are excellent. **Financial Aid Statistics:** 92% freshmen, 83% undergrads receive any aid.

PRESBYTERIAN COLLEGE

503 South Broad Street, Clinton, SC 29325
Phone: 864-833-8230 • **Financial Aid Phone:** 864-833-8287
E-mail: admissions@presby.edu • **CEEB Code:** 5540
Fax: 864-833-8195 • **Website:** www.presby.edu • **ACT Code:** 3874

This private school, affiliated with the Presbyterian Church,, affiliated with the Presbyterian USA Church, was founded in 1880. It has a 240-acre campus.

RATINGS

Admissions Selectivity Rating: 80   **Fire Safety Rating:** 91   **Green Rating:** 70

STUDENTS AND FACULTY

Enrollment: 1,153. **Student Body:** 53% female, 47% male, 34% out-of-state, 1% international (15 countries represented). Asian 1%, African American 10%, Caucasian 84%, Hispanic 2%, Native American 1%. **Retention and Graduation:** 76% freshmen return for sophomore year. 61% freshmen graduate within 4 years. 68% freshmen graduate within 6 years. 34% grads go on to further study within 1 year. 19% grads pursue arts and sciences degrees. 6% grads pursue law degrees. 2% grads pursue business degrees. 4% grads pursue medical degrees. **Faculty:** Student/faculty ratio 13:1. 98 full-time faculty, 97% hold PhDs, 9% are members of minority groups, 36% are women. 0% of classes are taught by teaching assistants.

ACADEMICS

Degrees: bachelor's. **Classes:** Most classes have 20-29 students. Most lab/discussion sessions have 20-29 students. **Majors with Highest Enrollment:** business administration and management; political science and government; psychology. **Special Study Options:** double major, dual enrollment, exchange student program (domestic), honors program, independent study, internships, study abroad, teacher certification program, Program in forestry and environmental science, 3-2 engineering program. **Honors Programs:** A variety of opportunities are available to highly motivated students with above average abilities through the normal programs of the College. These include research, internships, special projects, and directed studies. Presbyterian College also offers a special honors program for students who are chosen on the basis of their demonstrated ability. Students with a 3.20 GPA in all courses and a 3.40 GPA in all courses in the major field may, with the approval of departmental faculty, undertake an honors research program during the junior and/or senior years. Oral and written presentations of the results of the project will be required. Students who successfully complete the departmental honors research program will graduate with honors in the major field. **Disability Services:** Special programs offered to physically disabled students include tutors. **Career Services:** Alumni network, alumni services, career/job search classes, career assessment, internships, regional alumni. Career Services highlights include Internship Program: Students of all disciplines are coordinated to participate in on-campus seminar sessions at the beginning, middle, and end of the semester to reflect/review, compare/contrast their internship experience as a group.

FACILITIES

Housing: Coed dorms, men's dorms, special housing for international students, women's dorms, fraternity/sorority housing, apartments for single studentsSorority housing is not available. 95% of campus accessible to physically disabled. **Special Academic Facilities/Equipment:** Art gallery, recital hall, media center, marine/ecological center, scanning and transmission electron microscopes, visible spectrophotometer. **Computers:** 95% of classrooms, 100% of dorms, 100% of libraries, 100% of dining areas, 100% of student union, 50% of common outdoor areas have wireless network access. Students can register for classes online. Administrative functions (other than registration) can be performed online.

CAMPUS LIFE

Environment: Village. **Activities:** Choral groups, concert band, dance, drama/theater, jazz band, literary magazine, music ensembles, musical theater, opera, pep band, radio station, student government, student newspaper, symphony orchestra, yearbook, Campus Ministries 85 registered organizations, 11 honor societies, 6 religious organizations. 6 fraternities, 3 sororities. **Athletics (Intercollegiate):** *Men:* baseball, basketball, cheerleading, cross-country, football, golf, lacrosse, soccer, tennis. *Women:* basketball, cheerleading, cross-country, golf, lacrosse, soccer, softball, tennis, volleyball. **On-Campus Highlights:** Inklings Coffee House, Bailey Stadium, Springs Campus Center, Harrington Peachtree Academic Building, Thompson Library, Inklings - hot spot for open mics and up and coming bands Springs Campus Center - workout facilities, Starbucks, WPCX, ping pong Harrington Peachtree Academic Building - commonly known as H-P it is an ideal study and gathering spot in the late night hours Thompson Library - with the new expansion and renovations to the existing facilities, the library has seen a Renaissance - comfy chairs and cozy corners offer students a relaxing atmosphere for studying and researching. **Environmental Initiatives:** Energy conservation Use of alternative fuels Recycling Center

ADMISSIONS

Freshman Academic Profile: Average high school GPA 3.5. 34% in top 10% of high school class, 67% in top 25% of high school class, 91% in top 50% of high school class. SAT Math middle 50% range 510-620. SAT Critical Reading middle 50% range 498-603. ACT middle 50% range 21-27. Minimum web-based TOEFL 93. Minimum paper TOEFL 550. **Basis for Candidate Selection:** *Very important factors considered include:* Class rank, application essay, academic GPA, rigor of secondary school record, standardized test scores. *Important factors considered include:* recommendation(s), character/personal qualities, extracurricular activities. *Other factors considered include:* alumni/ae relation, first generation, interview, level of applicant's interest, talent/ability, volunteer work, work experience. **Freshman Admission Requirements:** High school diploma is required and GED is accepted. *Academic units required:* 4 English, 4 mathematics, 2 science, (2 science labs), 2 foreign language, 2 social studies, 2 history, 2 academic electives. *Academic units recommended:* 4 English, 4 mathematics, 2 science, (2 science labs), 2 foreign language, 2 social studies, 2 history, 2 academic electives. **Freshman Admission Statistics:** 1,484 applied, 67% admitted, 36% enrolled. **Transfer Admission Requirements:** High school transcript, college transcript(s), essay or personal statement, standardized test scores, statement of good standing from prior institution(s). Lowest grade transferable C. **General Admission Information:** Application Fee $40. Early decision application deadline 11/1. Regular application deadline 6/30. Regular notification 3/15. Nonfall registration accepted. Admission may be deferred for a maximum of 1 Year. Credit and/or placement offered for CEEB Advanced Placement tests.

COSTS AND FINANCIAL AID

Annual tuition $30,080. Room and board $8,750. Required fees $2,600. Average book expense $1,200. **Required Forms and Deadlines:** FAFSA. **Notification of Awards:** Applicants will be notified of awards on a rolling basis beginning 3/1. **Types of Aid:** *Need-based scholarships/grants:* Federal Pell, SEOG, state scholarships/grants, private scholarships, the school's own gift aid. *Loans:* Subsidized Stafford, Unsubsidized Stafford, PLUS, state loans, college/university loans from institutional funds, Private loans. **Student Employment:** Federal Work-Study Program available. Institutional employment available. Highest amount earned per year from on-campus jobs $1,800. Off-campus job opportunities are fair. **Financial Aid Statistics:** 100% freshmen, 100% undergrads receive need-based scholarship or grant aid. 38% freshmen, 37% undergrads receive non-need-based scholarship or grant aid. 45% freshmen, 50% undergrads receive need-based self-help aid. 8% freshmen, 11% undergrads receive athletic scholarships. 52% undergrads borrow to pay for school. Average cumulative indebtedness $23,192. **Criteria for awarding institutional aid:** *Non-need-based:* academics, alumni affiliation, art, athletics, job skills, leadership, minority status, music/drama, religious affiliation, state/district residency.

PRESCOTT COLLEGE

220 Grove Avenue, Prescott, AZ 86301
Phone: 928-350-2100 • **Financial Aid Phone:** 928-350-1112
E-mail: admissions@prescott.edu • **CEEB Code:** 9295
Fax: 928-776-5242 • **Website:** www.prescott.edu/ • **ACT Code:** 5022

This private school was founded in 1966. It has a 6-acre campus.

RATINGS
Admissions Selectivity Rating: 76   **Fire Safety Rating:** 72   **Green Rating:** 84

STUDENTS AND FACULTY

Enrollment: 671. **Student Body:** 57% female, 43% male, 75% out-of-state, 2% international (11 countries represented). Asian 1%, African American 2%, Caucasian 75%, Hispanic 6%, Native American 3%. **Retention and Graduation:** 20% freshmen graduate within 4 years. 45% freshmen graduate within 6 years. **Faculty:** Student/faculty ratio 8:1. 72 full-time faculty, 58% hold PhDs, 7% are members of minority groups, 51% are women. 0% of classes are taught by teaching assistants.

ACADEMICS

Degrees: bachelor's, master's, post-bachelor's certificate, post-master's certificate. **Classes:** Most classes have 10–19 students. **Majors with Highest Enrollment:** education, other; elementary education and teaching; environmental studies. **Special Study Options:** cross-registration, double major, exchange student program (domestic), external degree program, independent study, internships, liberal arts/career combination, student-designed major, teacher certification program, Dual Credit. **Disability Services:** Special programs offered to physically disabled students include note-taking services, tape recorders, tutors. **Career Services:** Alumni network, alumni services, career/job search classes, career assessment, regional alumni. Career Services highlights include One on one career development counseling.

FACILITIES

Housing: Coed dorms. 90% of campus accessible to physically disabled. **Special Academic Facilities/Equipment:** Wolfberry Farm: An experimental agroecology farm Kino Bay Center, MX: A field station on the Gulf of CA. Sam Hill Warehouse: Our visual arts center GIS Lab (Geographic Information Systems) Several Computer Labs Multi-Media Center **Computers:** 50% of classrooms, 100% of dorms, 100% of libraries, 100% of dining areas, 75% of common outdoor areas have wireless network access.

CAMPUS LIFE

Environment: Town. **Activities:** dance, drama/theater, literary magazine, radio station, student government, student newspaper, student-run film society, International Student Organization 18 registered organizations. **On-Campus Highlights:** Crossroads Cafe, Crossroads Library, HUB (Helping Understand Bikes), Sam Hill Visual Arts Building **Environmental Initiatives:** ACUPCC commitment and Climate Action Plan Curriculum; Environmental awareness is an integral part of our curriculum, with social and environmental literacy as college-wide learning outcomes. Local food initiatives (campus Community Supported Agriculture, college farm and gardens)

ADMISSIONS

Freshman Academic Profile: Average high school GPA 3.1. 14% in top 10% of high school class, 28% in top 25% of high school class, 86% in top 50% of high school class. 78% from public high schools. SAT Math middle 50% range 460-590. SAT Critical Reading middle 50% range 490-640. SAT Writing middle 50% range 440-650. ACT middle 50% range 22-27. Minimum web-based TOEFL 61. Minimum paper TOEFL 550. **Basis for Candidate Selection:** *Very important factors considered include:* application essay, recommendation(s), rigor of secondary school record. *Important factors considered include:* academic GPA, standardized test scores, character/personal qualities, extracurricular activities, interview, level of applicant's interest, talent/ability, volunteer work, work experience. *Other factors considered include:* first generation. **Freshman Admission Requirements:** High school diploma is required and GED is accepted. **Freshman Admission Statistics:** 551 applied, 73% admitted, 18% enrolled. **Transfer Admission Requirements:** college transcript(s), essay or personal statement, Lowest grade transferable C. **General Admission Information:** Application Fee $25. Early decision application deadline 12/1. Regular application deadline 8/15. Notification on a rolling basis, beginning on or about 1/1. Nonfall registration accepted. Admission may be deferred for a maximum of 2 terms. Credit offered for CEEB Advanced Placement tests.

COSTS AND FINANCIAL AID

Required **Forms and Deadlines:** FAFSA. **Notification of Awards:** Applicants will be notified of awards on a rolling basis beginning 3/15. **Types of Aid:** *Need-based scholarships/grants:* Federal Pell, SEOG, state scholarships/grants, private scholarships, the school's own gift aid, ACT & SMART. *Loans:* Subsidized Stafford, Unsubsidized Stafford, PLUS. **Student Employment:** Federal Work-Study Program available. Institutional employment available. Highest amount earned per year from on-campus jobs $2,744. Off-campus job opportunities are good. **Financial Aid Statistics:** 98% freshmen, 99% undergrads receive need-based scholarship or grant aid. 6% freshmen, 4% undergrads receive non-need-based scholarship or grant aid. 94% freshmen, 95% undergrads receive need-based self-help aid. 93% freshmen, 88% undergrads receive any aid. 68% undergrads borrow to pay for school. Average cumulative indebtedness $23,476. **Criteria for awarding institutional aid:** *Non-need-based:* academics, alumni affiliation, minority status, state/district residency.

PRINCETON UNIVERSITY

PO Box 430, Princeton, NJ 08544-0430
Phone: 609-258-3060 • **Financial Aid Phone:** 609-258-3330 • **CEEB Code:** 2672
Fax: 609-258-6743 • **Website:** www.princeton.edu • **ACT Code:** 2588

This private school was founded in 1746. It has a 500-acre campus.

RATINGS

Admissions Selectivity Rating: 99　　**Fire Safety Rating:** 91　　**Green Rating:** 91

STUDENTS AND FACULTY

Enrollment: 5,255. **Student Body:** 49% female, 51% male, 83% out-of-state, 11% international (107 countries represented). Asian 19%, African American 7%, Caucasian 40%, Hispanic 7%, Native American 0%.
Retention and Graduation: 98% freshmen return for sophomore year. 88% freshmen graduate within 4 years. **Faculty:** Student/faculty ratio 6:1. 859 full-time faculty, 93% hold PhDs, 19% are members of minority groups, 20% are women.

ACADEMICS

Degrees: bachelor's, master's. **Classes:** Most classes have 10-19 students. Most lab/discussion sessions have 10-19 students. **Majors with Highest Enrollment:** economics; history; political science and government. **Special Study Options:** cross-registration, exchange student program (domestic), independent study, student-designed major, study abroad, teacher certification program. **Disability Services:** Special programs offered to physically disabled students include note-taking services, reader services, tape recorders. **Career Services:** Alumni network, alumni services, career/job search classes, career assessment, internships, regional alumni.

FACILITIES

Housing: Coed dorms, special housing for disabled students, apartments for married students. **Special Academic Facilities/Equipment:** Art Museum, Natural history museum, energy and environmental studies center, plasma physics lab, Center for Jewish Life, Center for Human Values, Woodrow Wilson School of Public and International Affairs, etc. **Computers:** 100% of classrooms, 100% of dorms, 70% of libraries, 100% of dining areas, 100% of student union, 20% of common outdoor areas have wireless network access. Students can register for classes online. Administrative functions (other than registration) can be performed online.

CAMPUS LIFE

Environment: Town. **Activities:** Choral groups, concert band, dance, drama/theater, jazz band, literary magazine, marching band, music ensembles, musical theater, opera, pep band, radio station, student government, student newspaper, student-run film society, symphony orchestra, yearbook, Campus Ministries, International Student Organization, Model UN 250 registered organizations, 30 honor societies, 28 religious organizations. **Athletics (Intercollegiate):** *Men:* baseball, basketball, crew/rowing, cross-country, diving, fencing, football, golf, ice hockey, lacrosse, light weight football, soccer, squash, swimming, tennis, track/field (outdoor), track/field (indoor), volleyball, water polo, wrestling. *Women:* basketball, crew/rowing, cross-country, diving, fencing, field hockey, golf, ice hockey, lacrosse, soccer, softball, squash, swimming, tennis, track/field (outdoor), track/field (indoor), volleyball, water polo. **On-Campus Highlights:** Nassau Hall, Firestone Library, McCarter Theater, Princeton U. Art Museum,

University Chapel, Frist Campus Center. **Environmental Initiatives:** Greenhouse Gas reduction goal: 1990 levels by 2020 through local verifiable action, while adding more than 1 million gross square feet of built area, and without the purchase of offsets. 5.3 megawatt solar PV installation to be installed on campus properaty by 2012. Sustainable Building Guidelines: requiring all new buildings and major renovations to be 50% more energy efficient than code requires, 95% demolition and construction debris recycling, major building systems life cycle costing, and use of sustainable materials. Implementation of transportation demand management program to reduce by 10% the number of cars coming to campus by 2020.

ADMISSIONS

Freshman Academic Profile: Average high school GPA 3.9. 96% in top 10% of high school class, 99% in top 25% of high school class, 100% in top 50% of high school class. 58% from public high schools. SAT Math middle 50% range 710-800. SAT Critical Reading middle 50% range 700-790. SAT Writing middle 50% range 710-800. ACT middle 50% range 31-35. Minimum paper TOEFL 600. **Basis for Candidate Selection:** *Very important factors considered include:* Class rank, application essay, academic GPA, recommendation(s), rigor of secondary school record, standardized test scores, character/personal qualities, talent/ability. *Important factors considered include:* extracurricular activities. *Other factors considered include:* alumni/ae relation, first generation, geographical residence, interview, racial/ethnic status, volunteer work, work experience. **Freshman Admission Requirements:** High school diploma or equivalent is not required. **Freshman Admission Statistics:** 26,664 applied, 8% admitted, 65% enrolled. **General Admission Information:** Application Fee $65. Regular application deadline 1/1. Regular notification 3/31. Nonfall registration not accepted. Admission may be deferred for a maximum of 1 year. Credit and/or placement offered for CEEB Advanced Placement tests.

COSTS AND FINANCIAL AID

Annual tuition $38,650. Room and board $12,630. Average book expense $1,200. **Required Forms and Deadlines:** FAFSA, institution's own financial aid form. **Notification of Awards:** Applicants will be notified of awards on or about 4/1. **Types of Aid:** *Need-based scholarships/grants:* Federal Pell, SEOG, state scholarships/grants, private scholarships, the school's own gift aid. *Loans:* Subsidized Stafford, Unsubsidized Stafford, PLUS, Federal Perkins, college/university loans from institutional funds. **Student Employment:** Federal Work-Study Program available. Institutional employment available. Highest amount earned per year from on-campus jobs $3,500. Off-campus job opportunities are good. **Financial Aid Statistics:** 100% freshmen, 100% undergrads receive need-based scholarship or grant aid. 100% freshmen, 100% undergrads receive need-based self-help aid. 59% freshmen, 59% undergrads receive any aid. 24% undergrads borrow to pay for school. Average cumulative indebtedness $5,096.

See page 1178.

PRINCIPIA COLLEGE

1 Maybeck Place, Elsah, IL 62028
Phone: 618-374-5181 • **Financial Aid Phone:** 800-277-4648
E-mail: collegeadmissions@prin.edu • **CEEB Code:** 1630
Fax: 618-374-4000 • **Website:** www.principia.edu • **ACT Code:** 1118

This private school, affiliated with the Christian Science Church, was founded in 1898. It has a 2600-acre campus.

RATINGS

Admissions Selectivity Rating: 70　　**Fire Safety Rating:** 94　　**Green Rating:** 60*

STUDENTS AND FACULTY

Enrollment: 489. **Student Body:** 55% female, 45% male, 88% out-of-state, 15% international (28 countries represented). Asian 0%, African American 1%, Caucasian 68%, Hispanic 0%, Native American 0%.
Retention and Graduation: 79% freshmen return for sophomore year. **Faculty:** Student/faculty ratio 7:1. 76 full-time faculty, 45% hold PhDs, 4% are members of minority groups, 53% are women. 0% of classes are taught by teaching assistants.

ACADEMICS

Degrees: bachelor's. **Classes:** Most classes have 10-19 students. **Majors with Highest Enrollment:** business/commerce; fine/studio arts; mass communication/media studies. **Special Study Options:** double major, independent study, internships, liberal arts/career combination, student-designed major, study abroad, teacher certification program, 3-2 Engineering with Washington University (St. Louis, MO), USC (Los Angeles), and Southern Illinois University (SIU) in Edwardsville, IL. **Honors Programs:** One honors program of three courses is taught in conjunction with our First Year Experience Program (FYE). **Career Services:** Alumni network, career/job search classes, career assessment, internships, regional alumni. Career Services highlights include Internship in San Fransisco as part of a school-sponsored program for students interested in practical internships in companies and businesses in the Bay Area.

FACILITIES

Housing: men's dorms, women's dorms, apartments for married students-Houses with single-sex wings (one side for men and one side for women) and a common living room. This is not really considered "coed" because there are no shared bathrooms or men and women living together on the same floor or on alternate floors. Cottages (for 8 people) are available for non-traditionally aged students, special programs, or theme houses. 75% of campus accessible to physically disabled. **Special Academic Facilities/Equipment:** Science Center with indoor aviary, School of Nations Museum and Classrooms, Voney Art Studio, School of Government, Merrick Wing for Performing Arts

CAMPUS LIFE

Environment: Rural. **Activities:** Choral groups, dance, drama/theater, jazz band, music ensembles, musical theater, radio station, student government, student newspaper, television station, yearbook 29 registered organizations, 1 honor societies, 1 religious organizations. **Athletics (Intercollegiate):** *Men:* baseball, basketball, cross-country, diving, football, soccer, swimming, tennis, track/field (outdoor), track/field (indoor). *Women:* basketball, cross-country, diving, soccer, swimming, tennis, track/field (outdoor), track/field (indoor), volleyball. **On-Campus Highlights:** Piasa Pub, Hay Field House, Planetarium, Science Center, Chapel, By January, 2007 a new 68,000 square foot athletic training center will be built. This includes two regulation-size basketball courts and 200 meter indoor track. Also part of the facility will be a 6-lane 25-meter natatorium with four diving boards and am adjacent well-appointed fitness center.

ADMISSIONS

Freshman Academic Profile: Average high school GPA 3.3. 17% in top 10% of high school class, 39% in top 25% of high school class, 69% in top 50% of high school class. SAT Math middle 50% range 440-590. SAT Critical Reading middle 50% range 450-610. SAT Writing middle 50% range 460-590. ACT middle 50% range 20-26. Minimum web-based TOEFL 79. **Basis for Candidate Selection:** *Very important factors considered include:* application essay, rigor of secondary school record, character/personal qualities, religious affiliation/commitment. *Important factors considered include:* Class rank, recommendation(s), standardized test scores, extracurricular activities, interview, talent/ability. *Other factors considered include:* alumni/ae relation, racial/ethnic status, volunteer work, work experience. **Freshman Admission Requirements:** High school diploma is required and GED is accepted. *Academic units required:* 4 English, 4 mathematics, 2 science, (2 science labs), 2 foreign language, 2 social studies, 1 history, 1 academic electives. *Academic units recommended:* 4 English, 4 mathematics, 2 science, (2 science labs), 2 foreign language, 2 social studies, 1 history, 1 academic electives. **Freshman Admission Statistics:** 195 applied, 87% admitted, 68% enrolled. **Transfer Admission Requirements:** High school transcript, college transcript(s), essay or personal statement, minimum college GPA of 2.0 required. Lowest grade transferable C–. **General Admission Information:** Regular application deadline 3/1. Notification on a rolling basis, beginning on or about 11/1. Nonfall registration accepted. Admission may be deferred for a maximum of 1 year. Credit and/or placement offered for CEEB Advanced Placement tests.

COSTS AND FINANCIAL AID

Annual tuition $25,500. Room and board $10,000. Required fees $460. Average book expense $1,000. **Required Forms and Deadlines:** institution's own financial aid form, CSS/Financial Aid PROFILE. **Notification of Awards:** Applicants will be notified of awards on a rolling basis beginning 3/15. **Types of Aid:** *Need-based scholarships/grants:* private scholarships, the school's own gift aid. *Loans:* college/university loans from institutional funds. **Student Employment:** Highest amount earned per year from on-campus jobs $1,310. **Financial Aid Statistics:** 100% freshmen, 100% undergrads receive need-based scholarship or grant aid. 43% freshmen, 40% undergrads receive non-need-based scholarship or grant aid. 72% freshmen, 75% undergrads receive need-based self-help aid. 94% freshmen, 92% undergrads receive any aid. 64% undergrads borrow to pay for school. Average cumulative indebtedness $18,462. **Criteria for awarding institutional aid:** *Non-need-based:* academics, alumni affiliation.

PROVIDENCE COLLEGE

Harkins 222, Providence, RI 2918
Phone: 401-865-2535 • **Financial Aid Phone:** 401-865-2286
E-mail: pcadmiss@providence.edu • **CEEB Code:** 3693
Fax: 401-865-2826 • **Website:** www.providence.edu • **ACT Code:** 3806

This private school, affiliated with the Roman Catholic Church, was founded in 1917. It has a 105-acre campus.

RATINGS
Admissions Selectivity Rating: 86   **Fire Safety Rating:** 96   **Green Rating:** 69

STUDENTS AND FACULTY
Enrollment: 3,804. **Student Body:** 57% female, 43% male, 88% out-of-state, 2% international. Asian 1%, African American 4%, Caucasian 77%, Hispanic 5%, Native American 0%.
Retention and Graduation: 90% freshmen return for sophomore year. 84% freshmen graduate within 4 years. 87% freshmen graduate within 6 years.
Faculty: Student/faculty ratio 12:1. 310 full-time faculty, 95% hold PhDs, 11% are members of minority groups, 38% are women. 0% of classes are taught by teaching assistants.

ACADEMICS
Degrees: associate, bachelor's, certificate, master's, terminal associate. **Classes:** Most classes have 20–29 students. Most lab/discussion sessions have 10–19 students. **Majors with Highest Enrollment:** biology/biological sciences; business administration and management; marketing/marketing management. **Special Study Options:** cross-registration, distance learning, double major, dual enrollment, exchange student program (domestic), honors program, independent study, internships, liberal arts/career combination, student-designed major, study abroad, teacher certification program. **Honors Programs:** Liberal Arts Honors Program. **Combined Degree Programs:** Comb-plan Bio/Opt w/ NE College of Optometry. **Disability Services:** Special programs offered to physically disabled students include note-taking services, reader services, tape recorders, tutors. **Career Services:** Alumni network, alumni services, career/job search classes, career assessment, internships, regional alumni. Career Services highlights include Over 20 departments offer academic internships and field experience courses. We also have the Friar Summer Internship Partner Program in which we pair students with high quality summer internships.

FACILITIES
Housing: Coed dorms, special housing for disabled students, men's dorms, women's dorms, wellness housing. 98% of campus accessible to physically disabled. **Special Academic Facilities/Equipment:** Hunt-Cavanagh Art Gallery, Blackfriar Theatre, Science Center Complex, Computer and Language Labs, Smith Center for the Arts. **Computers:** 100% of classrooms, 50% of dorms, 100% of libraries, 100% of dining areas, 100% of student union, 20% of common outdoor areas have wireless network access. Students can register for classes online. Administrative functions (other than registration) can be performed online.

CAMPUS LIFE
Environment: City. **Activities:** Choral groups, concert band, dance, drama/theater, jazz band, literary magazine, music ensembles, musical theater, pep band, radio station, student government, student newspaper, television station, yearbook, Campus Ministries, International Student Organization 112 registered organizations, 18 honor societies, 2 religious organizations. **Athletics (Intercollegiate):** *Men:* basketball, cross-country, diving, ice hockey, lacrosse, soccer, swimming, track/field (outdoor), track/field (indoor). *Women:* basketball, cross-country, diving, field hockey, ice hockey, soccer, softball, swimming, tennis, track/field (outdoor), track/field (indoor), volleyball. **On-Campus Highlights:** McPhails- Student Activity Center, Peterson Center- Athletic Facility, Slavin Center- Student Center, Smith Center for the Arts, St. Dominic Chapel, Harkins Hall- Classrooms, Admin Offices; Blackfriars Theatre; Hunt-Cavanagh Art Gallery.

ADMISSIONS
Freshman Academic Profile: Average high school GPA 3.4. 37% in top 10% of high school class, 69% in top 25% of high school class, 95% in top 50% of high school class. 57% from public high schools. SAT Math middle 50% range 530-640. SAT Critical Reading middle 50% range 520-630. SAT Writing middle 50% range 540-640. ACT middle 50% range 23-28. Minimum web-based TOEFL 80. Minimum paper TOEFL 550. **Basis for Candidate Selection:**

Very important factors considered include: academic GPA, recommendation(s), rigor of secondary school record. *Important factors considered include:* application essay, character/personal qualities, extracurricular activities. *Other factors considered include:* Class rank, standardized test scores, alumni/ae relation, first generation, geographical residence, level of applicant's interest, racial/ethnic status, state residency, talent/ability, volunteer work, work experience. **Freshman Admission Requirements:** High school diploma is required and GED is not accepted. *Academic units required:* 4 English, 4 mathematics, 3 science, (2 science labs), 3 foreign language, 2 social studies, 2 history. *Academic units recommended:* 4 English, 4 mathematics, 3 science, (2 science labs), 3 foreign language, 2 social studies, 2 history. **Freshman Admission Statistics:** 9,652 applied, 61% admitted, 17% enrolled. **Transfer Admission Requirements:** High school transcript, college transcript(s), essay or personal statement, statement of good standing from prior institution(s). Minimum college GPA of 3.0 required. Lowest grade transferable c. **General Admission Information:** Application Fee $55. Regular application deadline 1/15. Regular notification 4/1. Nonfall registration accepted. Admission may be deferred for a maximum of 12 months. Credit and/or placement offered for CEEB Advanced Placement tests.

COSTS AND FINANCIAL AID

Annual tuition $41,350. Room and board $12,440. Required fees $856. Average book expense $900. **Required Forms and Deadlines:** FAFSA, CSS/Financial Aid PROFILE, business/farm supplement. **Notification of Awards:** Applicants will be notified of awards on or about 4/1. **Types of Aid:** *Need-based scholarships/grants:* Federal Pell, SEOG, state scholarships/grants, private scholarships, the school's own gift aid, Federal Academic Competitive Grant/Smart Grant. *Loans:* Direct Subsidized Stafford, Direct Unsubsidized Stafford, Direct PLUS, Subsidized Stafford, Unsubsidized Stafford, PLUS, Federal Perkins. **Student Employment:** Federal Work-Study Program available. Institutional employment available. Highest amount earned per year from on-campus jobs $6,500. Off-campus job opportunities are good. **Financial Aid Statistics:** 98% freshmen, 100% undergrads receive need-based scholarship or grant aid. 7% freshmen, 11% undergrads receive non-need-based scholarship or grant aid. 100% freshmen, 90% undergrads receive need-based self-help aid. 5% freshmen, 3% undergrads receive athletic scholarships. 80% freshmen, 77% undergrads receive any aid. 70% undergrads borrow to pay for school. Average cumulative indebtedness $26,832. **Criteria for awarding institutional aid:** *Non-need-based:* academics, athletics, minority status.

PURDUE UNIVERSITY—CALUMET

Office of Admissions, Hammond, IN 46323-2094
Phone: 219-989-2213 • **Financial Aid Phone:** 219-989-2301
E-mail: adms@calumet.purdue.edu • **CEEB Code:** 1638
Fax: 219-989-2775 • **Website:** www.calumet.purdue.edu/ • **ACT Code:** 1233

This public school was founded in 1946. It has a 194-acre campus.

RATINGS
Admissions Selectivity Rating: 70 **Fire Safety Rating:** 93 **Green Rating:** 60*

STUDENTS AND FACULTY
Enrollment: 8,403. **Student Body:** 55% female, 45% male, 11% out-of-state, 3% international (39 countries represented). Asian 1%, African American 19%, Caucasian 60%, Hispanic 15%, Native American 0%.
Retention and Graduation: 69% freshmen return for sophomore year. 6% freshmen graduate within 4 years. 26% freshmen graduate within 6 years. **Faculty:** Student/faculty ratio 21:1. 268 full-time faculty, 69% hold PhDs, 21% are members of minority groups, 48% are women.

ACADEMICS
Degrees: associate, bachelor's, certificate, master's, post-bachelor's certificate. **Classes:** Most classes have 20–29 students. Most lab/discussion sessions have 20–29 students. **Majors with Highest Enrollment:** elementary education and teaching; engineering; marketing/marketing management. **Special Study Options:** Accelerated program, cooperative education program, distance learning, double major, dual enrollment, English as a Second Language (ESL), honors program, independent study, internships, study abroad, teacher certification program, weekend college. **Honors Programs:** Purdue Calumet Honors Program **Combined Degree Programs:** 2-2 nursing program. **Disability Services:** Special programs offered to physically disabled students include note-taking services, reader services, tape recorders, tutors. **Career Services:** career/job search classes, career assessment, internships.

FACILITIES
Housing: apartments for single students. 100% of campus accessible to physically disabled. **Special Academic Facilities/Equipment:** Audio-visual

services, urban development institute. **Computers:** Students can register for classes online. Administrative functions (other than registration) can be performed online.

CAMPUS LIFE
Environment: City. **Activities:** Choral groups, dance, drama/theater, radio station, student government, student newspaper, Campus Ministries, International Student Organization 56 registered organizations, 25 honor societies, 3 religious organizations. 2 fraternities, 3 sororities. **Athletics (Intercollegiate):** *Men:* basketball. *Women:* basketball. **On-Campus Highlights:** Physical Education and Recreation Building, Enrollment Services Center, Challenger Learning Center of Northwest Indiana **Environmental Initiatives:** Campus-wide Recycling WEP Energy Conservation Measures Alternative Transportation including usage of electric vehicles

ADMISSIONS
Freshman Academic Profile: Average high school GPA 2.6. 10% in top 10% of high school class, 28% in top 25% of high school class, 58% in top 50% of high school class. % from public high schools. SAT Math middle 50% range 410-520. SAT Critical Reading middle 50% range 410-510. ACT middle 50% range 17-23. Minimum paper TOEFL 550. **Basis for Candidate Selection:** *Important factors considered include:* Class rank, academic GPA, rigor of secondary school record, standardized test scores. **Freshman Admission Requirements:** High school diploma is required and GED is accepted. *Academic units required:* 4 English, 2 mathematics, 1 science, (1 science labs), 2 foreign language, 1 social studies, 1 history. *Academic units recommended:* 4 English, 2 mathematics, 1 science, (1 science labs), 2 foreign language, 1 social studies, 1 history. **Freshman Admission Statistics:** 5,884 applied, 69% admitted, 33% enrolled. **Transfer Admission Requirements:** High school transcript, minimum college GPA of 2.0 required. Lowest grade transferable C. **General Admission Information:** Nonfall registration accepted. Admission may be deferred for a maximum of 1 semester. Credit offered for CEEB Advanced Placement tests.

COSTS AND FINANCIAL AID
Room and board $11. Average book expense $1,125. **Required Forms and Deadlines:** FAFSA. **Notification of Awards:** Applicants will be notified of awards on a rolling basis beginning 4/15. **Types of Aid:** *Need-based scholarships/grants:* Federal Pell, SEOG, state scholarships/grants, the school's own gift aid. *Loans:* Direct Subsidized Stafford, Direct Unsubsidized Stafford, Direct PLUS, Federal Perkins. **Student Employment:** Federal Work-Study Program available. Off-campus job opportunities are fair. **Financial Aid Statistics:** 61% freshmen, 65% undergrads receive need-based scholarship or grant aid. 27% freshmen, 16% undergrads receive non-need-based scholarship or grant aid. 67% freshmen, 77% undergrads receive need-based self-help aid. 1% freshmen, 62% undergrads borrow to pay for school. Average cumulative indebtedness $19,926. **Criteria for awarding institutional aid:** *Non-need-based:* academics, athletics, minority status, state/district residency.

PURDUE UNIVERSITY—WEST LAFAYETTE

Best 378

1080 Schleman Hall, West Lafayette, IN 47907-2050
Phone: 765-494-1776 • **Financial Aid Phone:** 765-494-0998
E-mail: admissions@purdue.edu • **CEEB Code:** 1631
Fax: 765-494-0544 • **Website:** www.purdue.edu • **ACT Code:** 1230

This public school was founded in 1869. It has a 2552-acre campus.

RATINGS
Admissions Selectivity Rating: 86 **Fire Safety Rating:** 83 **Green Rating:** 90

STUDENTS AND FACULTY
Enrollment: 29,945. **Student Body:** 43% female, 57% male, 31% out-of-state, 17% international (126 countries represented). Asian 5%, African American 3%, Caucasian 68%, Hispanic 4%, Native American 0%.
Retention and Graduation: 91% freshmen return for sophomore year. **Faculty:** Student/faculty ratio 14:1. 2041 full-time faculty, 22% are members of minority groups, 32% are women. 29% of classes are taught by teaching assistants.

ACADEMICS
Degrees: bachelor's, certificate, doctoral, master's, terminal associate. **Classes:** Most classes have 20–29 students. Most lab/discussion sessions have 20–29 students. **Majors with Highest Enrollment:** biology/biological sciences; fam-

ily and consumer sciences/human sciences; mechanical engineering. **Special Study Options:** Accelerated program, cooperative education program, cross-registration, distance learning, double major, dual enrollment, exchange student program (domestic), honors program, independent study, internships, liberal arts/career combination, study abroad, teacher certification program, weekend college. **Honors Programs:** University Honors Program. **Disability Services:** Special programs offered to physically disabled students include note-taking services, reader services, tape recorders, tutors. **Career Services:** Alumni network, alumni services, career/job search classes, career assessment, internships, regional alumni. Career Services highlights include All of the above.

FACILITIES

Housing: Coed dorms, special housing for disabled students, men's dorms, women's dorms, fraternity/sorority housing, apartments for married students, cooperative housing, apartments for single students, wellness housing, 90% of campus accessible to physically disabled. **Special Academic Facilities/Equipment:** Hall of music, child development lab, speech and hearing clinic, small animal veterinary clinic, horticulture park, linear accelerator, tornado simulator, nuclear accelerator. **Computers:** 95% of classrooms, 5% of dorms, 95% of libraries, 90% of dining areas, 95% of student union, 5% of common outdoor areas have wireless network access. Students can register for classes online. Administrative functions (other than registration) can be performed online.

CAMPUS LIFE

Environment: Town. **Activities:** Choral groups, concert band, dance, drama/theater, jazz band, literary magazine, marching band, music ensembles, musical theater, opera, pep band, radio station, student government, student newspaper, student-run film society, symphony orchestra, television station, yearbook, Campus Ministries, International Student Organization, Model UN 850 registered organizations, 25 honor societies, 66 religious organizations. 48 fraternities. 32 sororities. **Athletics (Intercollegiate):** *Men:* baseball, basketball, cross-country, diving, football, golf, swimming, tennis, track/field (outdoor), track/field (indoor), wrestling. *Women:* basketball, cross-country, diving, golf, soccer, softball, swimming, tennis, track/field (outdoor), track/field (indoor), volleyball. **On-Campus Highlights:** Pudue Memorial Union, Recreational Sports Center, Fountain areas, Libraries, Sporting events. **Environmental Initiatives:** Development and implementation of the Sustainability Strategic Plan. The Sustainability Strategic Plan also establishes eight program areas or "pillars" of sustainability focus on campus. These eight "pillars" are as follows: 1. Site Considerations 2. Water Resources 3. Energy and Built Environment 4. Materials Management 5. Food Systems 6. Academics and Research 7. Endowment / Development 8. Community Relationships Within this plan, there are 56 short-term goals (to be achieved by 2014) and 85 long-term goals (to be achieved by 2025). Development of our Comprehensive Energy Master Plan. The purpose of the CEMP is to investigate the energy production, distribution and building demand on the West Lafayette Campus. The investigation analyzed the chilled water, steam and electrical production at the utility plants, modeled the chilled water and steam distribution systems and estimated the energy savings potential in the campus buildings. The result of this analysis is a fiscally and environmentally responsible Comprehensive Energy Master Plan that provides Purdue guidance in managing the energy production and consumption on the campus as it continues to grow and evolve. Academic / research leadership in sustainability. Examples include: Purdue's Global Sustainability Initiative (GSI), led by Director Jon Harbor, focuses research and study within five major centers which include: - Energy Center - Center for the Environment - Purdue Climate Change Research Center - Purdue Water Community - Purdue Center for Global Food Security More information on GSI's programs and research activities can be found at the following: www.purdue.edu/discoverypark/sustainability/index.php. The Purdue Solar Decathlon Team " INhome (www.purdue.edu/inhome/) " recently finished second in this international competition sponsored by the Department of Energy (www.solardecathlon.gov/). This was Purdue's first foray into this competition, which was comprised of an extremely competitive group of international universities, many of which have been competing in the Solar Decathlon for years. Finishing in second place in our first attempt represents a stellar achievement for the INhome Team.

ADMISSIONS

Freshman Academic Profile: Average high school GPA 3.7. 41% in top 10% of high school class, 76% in top 25% of high school class, 97% in top 50% of high school class. SAT Math middle 50% range 550-680. SAT Critical Reading middle 50% range 510-620. SAT Writing middle 50% range 510-620. ACT middle 50% range 24-30. Minimum web-based TOEFL 79. Minimum paper TOEFL 550. **Basis for Candidate Selection:** *Very important factors considered include:* application essay, rigor of secondary school record, standardized test scores. *Important factors considered include:* Class rank, academic GPA. *Other factors considered include:* recommendation(s), alumni/ae relation, character/personal qualities, extracurricular activities, first generation, state residency, volunteer work, work experience. **Freshman Admission Requirements:** High school diploma is required and GED is accepted. *Academic units required:* 4 English, 3 mathematics, 3 science, (3 science labs), 2 foreign lan-

guage, 3 social studies. *Academic units recommended:* 4 English, 3 mathematics, 3 science, (3 science labs), 2 foreign language, 3 social studies. **Freshman Admission Statistics:** 30,903 applied, 61% admitted, 33% enrolled. **Transfer Admission Requirements:** college transcript(s), essay or personal statement, statement of good standing from prior institution(s). Minimum college GPA of 2.5 required. Lowest grade transferable C. **General Admission Information:** Application Fee $50. Regular application deadline 3/1. Notification on a rolling basis, beginning on or about 12/5. Nonfall registration accepted. Admission may be deferred for a maximum of 1 year. Credit and/or placement offered for CEEB Advanced Placement tests.

COSTS AND FINANCIAL AID

Annual in-state tuition $9,208. Annual out-of-state tuition $28,010. Room and board $10,378. Required fees $692. Average book expense $1,370. **Required Forms and Deadlines:** FAFSA. **Notification of Awards:** Applicants will be notified of awards on or about 4/15. **Types of Aid:** *Need-based scholarships/grants:* Federal Pell, SEOG, state scholarships/grants, private scholarships, the school's own gift aid, Federal Academic Competitiveness Grant (ACG) and National SMART Grant Program. *Loans:* Direct Subsidized Stafford, Direct Unsubsidized Stafford, Direct PLUS, Federal Perkins, college/university loans from institutional funds. **Student Employment:** Federal Work-Study Program available. Institutional employment available. Off-campus job opportunities are good. **Financial Aid Statistics:** 64% freshmen, 65% undergrads receive need-based scholarship or grant aid. 43% freshmen, 33% undergrads receive non-need-based scholarship or grant aid. 81% freshmen, 89% undergrads receive need-based self-help aid. 1% freshmen, 1% undergrads receive athletic scholarships. 61% freshmen, 72% undergrads receive any aid. 54% undergrads borrow to pay for school. Average cumulative indebtedness $27,798. **Criteria for awarding institutional aid:** *Non-need-based:* academics, athletics, leadership, music/drama, state/district residency.

QUEEN'S UNIVERSITY

Admission Services, Kingston, ON K7L3N6
Phone: 613-533-2218
E-mail: admission@queensu.ca • **CEEB Code:** 949
Fax: 613-533-6810 • **Website:** www.queensu.ca • **ACT Code:** 5236

This public school was founded in 1841. It has a 160-acre campus.

RATINGS

Admissions Selectivity Rating: 63   **Fire Safety Rating:** 60*   **Green Rating:** 60*

STUDENTS AND FACULTY

Enrollment: 14,130. **Student Body:** 59% female, 41% male, 18% out-of-state, (129 countries represented).
Retention and Graduation: 93% freshmen graduate within 6 years. **Faculty:** Student/faculty ratio 16:1. 1032 full-time faculty, 94% hold PhDs, 39% are women.

ACADEMICS

Degrees: bachelor's, master's. **Classes:** Most classes have 20–29 students. Most lab/discussion sessions have 20–29 students. **Majors with Highest Enrollment:** business/commerce; sport and fitness administration/management. **Special Study Options:** cooperative education program, distance learning, double major, dual enrollment, English as a Second Language (ESL), exchange student program (domestic), honors program, independent study, internships, study abroad, teacher certification program, The university owns and operates an International Study Centre (ISC) at Herstmonceux,East Sussex, England. **Disability Services:** Special programs offered to physically disabled students include note-taking services, reader services, tape recorders, tutors. **Career Services:** career/job search classes, career assessment, internships.

FACILITIES

Housing: Coed dorms, men's dorms, special housing for international students, women's dorms, apartments for married students, cooperative housing, apartments for single students. **Special Academic Facilities/Equipment:** Agnes Etherington Art Centre, Miller Museum of Geology **Computers:** Students can register for classes online. Administrative functions (other than registration) can be performed online.

CAMPUS LIFE

Environment: City. **Activities:** Choral groups, concert band, dance, drama/theater, jazz band, literary magazine, marching band, music ensembles, musical theater, opera, pep band, radio station, student government, student newspaper, student-run film society, symphony orchestra, television station, yearbook 18 religious organizations. **Athletics (Intercollegiate):** *Men:* baseball, basketball, cheerleading, crew/rowing, cross-country, curling, fencing, football, golf, ice hockey, lacrosse, mountain biking, rodeo, rugby, sailing, skiingnordiccross-country, soccer, squash, swimming, tennis, track/field (outdoor), ultimate frisbee, volleyball, water polo, wrestling. *Women:* basketball, cheerleading, crew/rowing, cross-country, curling, fencing, field hockey, ice hockey, lacrosse, mountain biking, rodeo, rugby, sailing, skiingnordiccross-country, soccer, squash, swimming, synchronized swimming, tennis, track/field (outdoor), ultimate frisbee, volleyball, water polo, wrestling. **On-Campus Highlights:** Integrated Learning Centre (ILC), Agnes Etherington Art Centre, Stauffer Library, Biosciences Complex, Chernoff Hall.

ADMISSIONS

Freshman Academic Profile: Minimum paper TOEFL 580. **Basis for Candidate Selection:** *Very important factors considered include:* academic GPA, standardized test scores. *Important factors considered include:* rigor of secondary school record, extracurricular activities, talent/ability, volunteer work. *Other factors considered include:* Class rank, recommendation(s), work experience. **Freshman Admission Requirements:** High school diploma is required and GED is accepted. **Freshman Admission Statistics:** 25,403 applied, 42% admitted, 31% enrolled. **Transfer Admission Requirements:** High school transcript, college transcript(s). **General Admission Information:** Application Fee $135. Regular application deadline 2/16. Notification on a rolling basis, beginning on or about 1/2. Nonfall registration not accepted. Admission may be deferred for a maximum of 12 months.

COSTS AND FINANCIAL AID

Required **Forms and Deadlines:** institution's own financial aid formP. **Types of Aid:** *Need-based scholarships/grants:* private scholarships, the school's own gift aid. *Loans:* college/university loans from institutional funds. **Student Employment: Financial Aid Statistics:** 30% undergrads borrow to pay for school. **Criteria for awarding institutional aid:** *Non-need-based:* academics, leadership, music/drama.

QUEENS UNIVERSITY OF CHARLOTTE

1900 Selwyn Avenue, Charlotte, NC 28274
Phone: 704-337-2212 • **Financial Aid Phone:** 704-337-2225
E-mail: admissions@queens.edu • **CEEB Code:** 5560
Fax: 704-337-2403 • **Website:** www.queens.edu • **ACT Code:** 3148

This private school, affiliated with the Presbyterian Church, was founded in 1857. It has a 30-acre campus.

RATINGS
Admissions Selectivity Rating: 72   **Fire Safety Rating:** 63   **Green Rating:** 60+

STUDENTS AND FACULTY
Enrollment: 1,911. **Student Body:** 76% female, 24% male, % out-of-state, 8% international. Asian 2%, African American 16%, Caucasian 55%, Hispanic 3%, Native American 1%.
Retention and Graduation: 70% freshmen return for sophomore year. 48% freshmen graduate within 4 years. 59% freshmen graduate within 6 years. **Faculty:** Student/faculty ratio 12:1. 123 full-time faculty, 72% hold PhDs, 7% are members of minority groups, 68% are women. 0% of classes are taught by teaching assistants.

ACADEMICS
Degrees: associate, bachelor's, master's, post-bachelor's certificate, terminal associate. **Classes:** Most classes have 10–19 students. Most lab/discussion sessions have 10–19 students. **Majors with Highest Enrollment:** business/commerce; communication and media studies, other; nursing/registered nurse (rn, asn, bsn, msn). **Special Study Options:** cross-registration, double major, dual enrollment, honors program, independent study, internships, liberal arts/career combination, student-designed major, study abroad, teacher certification program, weekend college. **Disability Services:** Special programs offered to physically disabled students include note-taking services, reader services, tape recorders, tutors. **Career Services:** Alumni network, career/job search classes, internships Career Services highlights include The Internship is a required component of the undergraduate degree here at Queens.

FACILITIES
Housing: Coed dorms, special housing for disabled studentsApartment style 2 bedroom suites for traditional-aged undergraduates 1/2 mile from campus. 60% of campus accessible to physically disabled. **Special Academic Facilities/Equipment:** Three art galleries, rare books museum.

CAMPUS LIFE
Environment: Metropolis. **Activities:** Choral groups, dance, drama/theater, literary magazine, music ensembles, musical theater, pep band, student govern-

ment, student newspaper, yearbook, Campus Ministries, International Student Organization, Model UN 38 registered organizations, 9 honor societies, 2 religious organizations. 2 fraternities, 4 sororities. **Athletics (Intercollegiate):** *Men:* basketball, cheerleading, cross-country, golf, lacrosse, soccer, tennis, track/field (outdoor). *Women:* basketball, cheerleading, cross-country, golf, lacrosse, soccer, softball, tennis, track/field (outdoor), volleyball. **On-Campus Highlights:** Fitness Center, The Lion's Den, Trexler Courtyard, Queens' Off-Campus Athletic Facility

ADMISSIONS
Freshman Academic Profile: Average high school GPA 3.5. 14% in top 10% of high school class, 39% in top 25% of high school class, 78% in top 50% of high school class. 88% from public high schools. SAT Math middle 50% range 460-570. SAT Critical Reading middle 50% range 470-580. SAT Writing middle 50% range 460-560. ACT middle 50% range 20-25. Minimum web-based TOEFL 80. Minimum paper TOEFL 550. **Basis for Candidate Selection:** *Very important factors considered include:* academic GPA, rigor of secondary school record, standardized test scores, character/personal qualities, extracurricular activities. *Important factors considered include:* Class rank, interview, volunteer work. *Other factors considered include:* application essay, recommendation(s), alumni/ae relation, first generation, talent/ability, work experience. **Freshman Admission Requirements:** High school diploma is required and GED is accepted. *Academic units required:* 4 English, 3 mathematics, 2 science, (1 science labs), 2 foreign language, 2 social studies. 4 English, 3 mathematics, 2 science, (1 science labs), 2 foreign language, 2 social studies. **Freshman Admission Statistics:** 2,199 applied, 74% admitted, 22% enrolled. **Transfer Admission Requirements:** High school transcript, college transcript(s), essay or personal statement, statement of good standing from prior institution(s). Minimum college GPA of 2.0 required. Lowest grade transferable C. **General Admission Information:** Application Fee $40. Notification on a rolling basis, beginning on or about 10/1. Nonfall registration accepted. Admission may be deferred for a maximum of 1 year. Credit and/or placement offered for CEEB Advanced Placement tests.

COSTS AND FINANCIAL AID
Required **Forms and Deadlines:** FAFSA, state aid form. **Notification of Awards:** Applicants will be notified of awards on a rolling basis beginning 3/15. **Types of Aid:** *Need-based scholarships/grants:* Federal Pell, SEOG, state scholarships/grants, private scholarships, the school's own gift aid. *Loans:* Subsidized Stafford, Unsubsidized Stafford, PLUS, Federal Perkins, state loans. **Student Employment:** Federal Work Study Program available. Highest amount earned per year from on-campus jobs $1,500. Off-campus job opportunities are excellent. **Financial Aid Statistics:** 100% freshmen, 99% undergrads receive need-based scholarship or grant aid. 18% freshmen, 15% undergrads receive non-need-based scholarship or grant aid. 79% freshmen, 83% undergrads receive need-based self-help aid. 11% freshmen, 10% undergrads receive athletic scholarships. 83% freshmen receive any aid. 86% undergrads borrow to pay for school. Average cumulative indebtedness $27,832. **Criteria for awarding institutional aid:** *Non-need-based:* academics, art, athletics, minority status, music/drama.

QUINCY UNIVERSITY

1800 College Avenue, Quincy, IL 62301-2699
Phone: 217-228-5210 • **Financial Aid Phone:** 217-228-5260
E-mail: admissions@quincy.edu • **CEEB Code:** 1645
Fax: 217-228-5479 • **Website:** www.quincy.edu • **ACT Code:** 1120

This private school, affiliated with the Roman Catholic Church, was founded in 1860. It has a 70-acre campus.

RATINGS
Admissions Selectivity Rating: 65   **Fire Safety Rating:** 70   **Green Rating:** 67

STUDENTS AND FACULTY
Enrollment: 1,186. **Student Body:** 58% female, 42% male, 25% out-of-state, 1% international (3 countries represented). Asian 1%, African American 10%, Caucasian 64%, Hispanic 1%, Native American 1%.
Retention and Graduation: 70% freshmen return for sophomore year. 42% freshmen graduate within 4 years. 56% freshmen graduate within 6 years. 22% grads go on to further study within 1 year. 11% grads pursue arts and sciences degrees. 2% grads pursue law degrees. 5% grads pursue business degrees. 2% grads pursue medical degrees. **Faculty:** Student/faculty ratio 14:1. 54 full-time faculty, 69% hold PhDs, 7% are members of minority groups, 37% are women. 0% of classes are taught by teaching assistants.

ACADEMICS

Degrees: associate, bachelor's, master's. **Classes:** Most classes have 10–19 students. Most lab/discussion sessions have fewer than 10 students. **Majors with Highest Enrollment:** elementary education and teaching; marketing/marketing management; nursing/registered nurse (rn, asn, bsn, msn). **Special Study Options:** Accelerated program, distance learning, double major, dual enrollment, honors program, independent study, internships, student-designed major, study abroad, teacher certification program, 3-2 program in engineering with Washington University; 3-1 program in medical technology with various hospitals. **Honors Programs:** The Honors Program provides a challenging course of study which adds an interdisciplinary dimension to a student's major field. The program promotes academic excellence through critical thinking, original research, exceptional writing, and public presentation of scholarship. **Combined Degree Programs:** Clinical Laboratory Science - B.S. **Disability Services:** Special programs offered to physically disabled students include note-taking services, reader services, tape recorders, tutors. **Career Services:** Alumni network, alumni services, career/job search classes, career assessment, internships, regional alumni. Career Services highlights include The University, in cooperation with the state of Illinois and local businesses and social service agencies, provides early exploratory internships to first and second year students to aid in the career development/decision-making process.

FACILITIES

Housing: Coed dorms, men's dorms, women's dorms, fraternity/sorority housing, apartments for married students, apartments for single students, theme housing, honors. 90% of campus accessible to physically disabled. **Special Academic Facilities/Equipment:** Reading center for student teachers, multimedia and graphic design labs, TV broadcast studio, temperature-controlled rare books Library archive, art gallery, 200-seat theater, environmental studies institute, hospital simulation lab, aviation facility with flight simulator, College-operated national public radio station. **Computers:** 100% of classrooms, 100% of dorms, 100% of libraries, 100% of dining areas, 100% of student union, 40% of common outdoor areas have wireless network access. Administrative functions (other than registration) can be performed online.

CAMPUS LIFE

Environment: Town. **Activities:** Choral groups, concert band, dance, drama/theater, jazz band, literary magazine, music ensembles, musical theater, opera, pep band, radio station, student government, student newspaper, symphony orchestra, television station, Campus Ministries 40 registered organizations, 8 honor societies, 2 religious organizations. 1 fraternities, 2 sororities. **Athletics (Intercollegiate):** *Men:* baseball, basketball, cross-country, football, golf, soccer, tennis, volleyball. *Women:* basketball, cross-country, golf, soccer, softball, tennis, volleyball. **On-Campus Highlights:** Health and Fitness Center, Newly renovated University Center, QU Chapel, Francis Garden, Brenner Library. **Environmental Initiatives:** Residence hall renovation: Helein Hall renovations included use of recycled furniture and the installation of an energy-efficient VRV hvac system. New 36,000 sq.ft. suite-style residence hall constructed with high energy-efficient HVAC system and outdoor green area. On-going University-wide recycling program for paper, plastic, metal, and ink cartridges.

ADMISSIONS

Freshman Academic Profile: Average high school GPA 3.3. 12% in top 10% of high school class, 36% in top 25% of high school class, 74% in top 50% of high school class. 81% from public high schools. SAT Math middle 50% range 440-520. SAT Critical Reading middle 50% range 410-510. ACT middle 50% range 19-24. Minimum web-based TOEFL 61. Minimum paper TOEFL 500. **Basis for Candidate Selection:** *Very important factors considered include:* academic GPA, rigor of secondary school record. *Important factors considered include:* Class rank, application essay, recommendation(s), standardized test scores, character/personal qualities, extracurricular activities, level of applicant's interest, volunteer work, work experience. *Other factors considered include:* interview, talent/ability. **Freshman Admission Requirements:** High school diploma is required and GED is accepted. **Freshman Admission Statistics:** 1,034 applied, 91% admitted, 28% enrolled. **Transfer Admission Requirements:** college transcript(s), statement of good standing from prior institution(s). Minimum college GPA of 2.0 required. Lowest grade transferable D. **General Admission Information:** Application Fee $25. Notification on a rolling basis, beginning on or about 9/1. Nonfall registration accepted. Credit offered for CEEB Advanced Placement tests.

COSTS AND FINANCIAL AID

Annual tuition $24,344. Room and board $11,090. Required fees $836. Average book expense $1,250. **Required Forms and Deadlines:** FAFSA. **Notification of Awards:** Applicants will be notified of awards on a rolling basis beginning 2/15. **Types of Aid:** *Need-based scholarships/grants:* Federal Pell, SEOG, state scholarships/grants, private scholarships, the school's own gift aid. *Loans:* Subsidized Stafford, Unsubsidized Stafford, PLUS, Federal Perkins. **Student Employment:** Federal Work-Study Program available. Institutional employment available. Highest amount earned per year from on-campus jobs $2,000. Off-campus job opportunities are good. **Financial Aid Statistics:** 100%

---

freshmen, 96% undergrads receive need-based scholarship or grant aid. 14% freshmen, 12% undergrads receive non-need-based scholarship or grant aid. 81% freshmen, 81% undergrads receive need-based self-help aid. 2% freshmen, 2% undergrads receive athletic scholarships. 100% freshmen, 92% undergrads receive any aid. 82% undergrads borrow to pay for school. Average cumulative indebtedness $26,080. **Criteria for awarding institutional aid:** *Non-need-based:* academics, alumni affiliation, art, athletics, music/drama.

QUINNIPIAC UNIVERSITY

275 Mount Carmel Avenue, Hamden, CT 6518
Phone: 203-582-8600 • **Financial Aid Phone:** 203-582-8750
E-mail: admissions@quinnipiac.edu • **CEEB Code:** 3712
Fax: 203-582-8906 • **Website:** www.quinnipiac.edu • **ACT Code:** 582

This private school was founded in 1929. It has a 600-acre campus.

RATINGS
Admissions Selectivity Rating: 84   **Fire Safety Rating:** 94   **Green Rating:** 76

STUDENTS AND FACULTY

Enrollment: 6,155. **Student Body:** 62% female, 38% male, 75% out-of-state, 1% international (23 countries represented). Asian 3%, African American 4%, Caucasian 79%, Hispanic 7%, Native American 0%.
Retention and Graduation: 70% freshmen graduate within 4 years. 77% freshmen graduate within 6 years. 37% grads go on to further study within 1 year. 18% grads pursue arts and sciences degrees. 2% grads pursue law degrees. 9% grads pursue business degrees. 2% grads pursue medical degrees. **Faculty:** Student/faculty ratio 12:1. 351 full-time faculty, 83% hold PhDs, 15% are members of minority groups, 51% are women. 0% of classes are taught by teaching assistants.

ACADEMICS

Degrees: bachelor's, doctoral, master's, post-bachelor's certificate, post-master's certificate. **Classes:** Most classes have 10–19 students. Most lab/discussion sessions have 10–19 students. **Majors with Highest Enrollment:** business/commerce; physical therapy/therapist; psychology. **Special Study Options:** distance learning, double major, exchange student program (domestic), honors program, independent study, internships, liberal arts/career combination, student-designed major, study abroad, teacher certification program, Online option for summer course offerings Online degrees offered at the graduate level. **Honors Programs:** The University Honors Program, limited to 60-70 freshmen who are selected following their acceptance, provides challenging coursework and opportunities for learning and service. BA/JD, BA/MA. **Career Services:** Alumni network, alumni services, career/job search classes, career assessment, internships, regional alumni. Career Services highlights include Extensive internship programs in all business and communications fields. Clinical placements in all of the health science fields.

FACILITIES

Housing: Coed dorms, apartments for single students, wellness housing, University owned houses provide housing for about 100 seniors/juniors. 100% of campus accessible to physically disabled. **Special Academic Facilities/Equipment:** Quinnipiac Polling Institute, Financial Technology Center, Motion Analysis Lab, Albert Schweitzer Institute, Critical Care Nursing Lab, Fully digital/high definition TV production studio, editing labs, news technology center. Lender family special collection room in Library on the Irish Famine, "An Gorta Mor". **Computers:** 100% of classrooms, 100% of dorms, 100% of libraries, 100% of dining areas, 100% of student union, 100% of common outdoor areas have wireless network access. Students can register for classes online. Administrative functions (other than registration) can be performed online. Undergraduates are required to own a computer.

CAMPUS LIFE

Environment: Town. **Activities:** Choral groups, dance, drama/theater, literary magazine, pep band, radio station, student government, student newspaper, television station, yearbook, Campus Ministries, International Student Organization 78 registered organizations, 8 honor societies, 3 religious organizations. 2 fraternities, 3 sororities. **Athletics (Intercollegiate):** *Men:* baseball, basketball, cross-country, ice hockey, lacrosse, soccer, tennis. *Women:* basketball, cheerleading, cross-country, field hockey, ice hockey, lacrosse, soccer, softball, tennis, track/field (outdoor), track/field (indoor), volleyball. **On-Campus Highlights:**

Arnold Bernhard Library, Recreation Center with suspended banked track, An Gorta Mor, Irish famine literature and art, Cafe Q with Zia/Starbucks, Bobcat Den/Coffee Bar, The nearby 250 acre 'York Hill' campus with the TD Bank Sports Center-twin 3500 seat arenas for ice hockey and basketball, includes residence halls with 1800 beds and a student/recreation center. About 5 miles away is the North Haven campus of 104 acres, home to the graduate programs in the School of Health Sciences. Upper division (juniors and seniors) students in Physical Therapy, Occupational Therapy, Nursing, Diagnostic Imaging and Physician Assistant programs also use this outstanding state-of-the-art facility. **Environmental Initiatives:** 100 percent of Quinnipiac electricity requirements on all three of its campuses have been purchased from renewable energy credits. 1,232 photovoltaic solar panels on the roof of the 475,000 square-foot Crescent residence hall, will convert energy from the sun to electricity and generate about 250,000kwh per year. A wind garden composed of 42 vertical-axis wind turbines will generate about 84,000 kilowatt hours per year on the York Hill campus - home to residence halls for 1800 students and the TD Bank Sports Center.

ADMISSIONS

Freshman Academic Profile: Average high school GPA 3.4. 25% in top 10% of high school class, 66% in top 25% of high school class, 92% in top 50% of high school class. 70% from public high schools. SAT Math middle 50% range 530-610. SAT Critical Reading middle 50% range 520-590. SAT Writing middle 50% range 540-610. ACT middle 50% range 23-27. Minimum web-based TOEFL 77. Minimum paper TOEFL 550. **Basis for Candidate Selection:** *Very important factors considered include:* academic GPA, rigor of secondary school record. *Important factors considered include:* Class rank, application essay, standardized test scores. *Other factors considered include:* recommendation(s), alumni/ae relation, character/personal qualities, extracurricular activities, interview, level of applicant's interest, racial/ethnic status, talent/ability, volunteer work, work experience. **Freshman Admission Requirements:** High school diploma is required and GED is accepted. *Academic units required:* 4 English, 3 mathematics, 3 science, (2 science labs), 2 foreign language, 2 social studies, 4 4 years of Science and Math req. in PT,OT, Nursing and PA. *Academic units recommended:* 4 English, 3 mathematics, 3 science, (2 science labs), 2 foreign language, 2 social studies, 4 4 years of Science and Math req. in PT,OT, Nursing and PA **Freshman Admission Statistics:** 18,642 applied, 63% admitted, 13% enrolled. **Transfer Admission Requirements:** college transcript(s), essay or personal statement, minimum college GPA of 2.5 required. Lowest grade transferable C. **General Admission Information:** Application Fee $45. Notification on a rolling basis, beginning on or about 12/15. Nonfall registration accepted. Admission may be deferred for a maximum of 12 months. Credit and/or placement offered for CEEB Advanced Placement tests.

COSTS AND FINANCIAL AID

Annual tuition $36,510. Room and board $13,610. Required fees $1,490. Average book expense $800. **Required Forms and Deadlines:** FAFSA, CSS/ Financial Aid PROFILE Students applying during 2010-2011 for the spring 2011 or fall 2011 semesters, will need to provide the CSS Profile. **Notification of Awards:** Applicants will be notified of awards on a rolling basis beginning 2/15. **Types of Aid:** *Need-based scholarships/grants:* Federal Pell, SEOG, state scholarships/grants, private scholarships, the school's own gift aid, Federal Nursing Scholarships. *Loans:* Direct Subsidized Stafford, Direct Unsubsidized Stafford, Direct PLUS, Subsidized Stafford, Unsubsidized Stafford, PLUS, Federal Perkins, Federal Nursing, state loans. **Student Employment:** Federal Work-Study Program available. Institutional employment available. Highest amount earned per year from on-campus jobs $2,100. Off-campus job opportunities are excellent. **Financial Aid Statistics:** 94% freshmen, 97% undergrads receive need-based scholarship or grant aid. 49% freshmen, 44% undergrads receive non-need-based scholarship or grant aid. 84% freshmen, 85% undergrads receive need-based self-help aid. 5% freshmen, 5% undergrads receive athletic scholarships. 72% freshmen, 70% undergrads receive any aid. 69% undergrads borrow to pay for school. Average cumulative indebtedness $39,500. **Criteria for awarding institutional aid:** *Non-need-based:* academics, athletics.

See page 1180.

RADFORD UNIVERSITY

PO Box 6903, Radford, VA 24142
Phone: 540-831-5371 • **Financial Aid Phone:** 540-831-5408
E-mail: admissions@radford.edu • **CEEB Code:** 5565
Fax: 540-831-5038 • **Website:** www.radford.edu • **ACT Code:** 4422

This public school was founded in 1910. It has a 191-acre campus.

RATINGS
Admissions Selectivity Rating: 70   **Fire Safety Rating:** 88   **Green Rating:** 81

STUDENTS AND FACULTY

Enrollment: 8,575. **Student Body:** 56% female, 44% male, 5% out-of-state, 1% international (59 countries represented). Asian 2%, African American 8%, Caucasian 81%, Hispanic 4%, Native American 0%.
Retention and Graduation: 42% freshmen graduate within 4 years. 15% grads go on to further study within 1 year. 4% grads pursue arts and sciences degrees. 1% grads pursue law degrees. 1% grads pursue business degrees. 1% grads pursue medical degrees. **Faculty:** Student/faculty ratio 19:1. 411 full-time faculty, 83% hold PhDs, 12% are members of minority groups, 48% are women. 3% of classes are taught by teaching assistants.

ACADEMICS

Degrees: bachelor's, doctoral, master's, post-bachelor's certificate, post-master's certificate. **Classes:** Most classes have 20–29 students. Most lab/discussion sessions have 20–29 students. **Majors with Highest Enrollment:** criminal justice/safety studies; multi-/interdisciplinary studies, other; physical education teaching and coaching. **Special Study Options:** Accelerated program, cross-registration, distance learning, double major, dual enrollment, honors program, independent study, internships, student-designed major, study abroad, teacher certification program. **Honors Programs:** Student members of Honors Academy work toward graduating as Highlander Scholars. To graduate as a Highlander Scholar, one must complete 27 credit hours of Honors Coursework, present their Honors Capstone Project in a public forum, and have a cumulative GPA of 3.5 at the time of graduation. The 27 hours of honors coursework are completed as follows: 6-12 credits in the Core Curriculum as honors credits (usually earned by taking Honors Classes), 12-15 in one's major as honors credits (usually by contracting the course for honors credit and a 3-6 credit hour honors capstone project in one's major (a piece of scholarship completed under the supervision of a faculty member in one's department). There is also a residential/social component to the Honors Academy. Active members in the Honors Academy enjoy early registration, and their status as a Highlander Scholar Graduate is noted on their diploma and transcript. Students are also supported financially to present the results of their work at professional and undergraduate conferences. **Combined Degree Programs:** BA/MA. **Disability Services:** Special programs offered to physically disabled students include note-taking services, reader services, tape recorders, tutors. **Career Services:** Alumni network, alumni services, career/job search classes, career assessment, internships, regional alumni. Career Services highlights include Radford University has strong job search classes and tools that now include the best software available in the field to assist students in career search training. RU makes available Optimal Resume & Optimal First Impressions software that assists with resume/ business letter development; electronic portfolio construction; and virtual interview practice utilizing video and audio tape recording. Our students also have a job board of employer posted openings, a resume posting site, and interview scheduling software powered by CSO and called Hire a Highlander. In addition, each semester the career placement office provides a series of Internship Readiness Seminars and other programs developed to enhance interviewing, business protocol and confidence in the career transition process.

FACILITIES

Housing: Coed dorms, special housing for disabled students, special housing for international students, apartments for single students, wellness housing, theme housing, 100% of campus accessible to physically disabled. **Special Academic Facilities/Equipment:** Language Lab, Art Gallery with Sculpture Garden, Planetarium, Selu Conservancy, and on-campus speech/language/hearing clinic. **Computers:** 100% of classrooms, 100% of dorms, 100% of libraries, 100% of dining areas, 100% of student union, 100% of common outdoor areas have wireless network access. Students can register for classes online. Administrative functions (other than registration) can be performed online.

CAMPUS LIFE

Environment: Village. **Activities:** Choral groups, concert band, dance, drama/ theater, jazz band, literary magazine, music ensembles, musical theater, pep band, radio station, student government, student newspaper, television station, yearbook, Campus Ministries, International Student Organization 237 registered organizations, 14 honor societies, 10 religious organizations. 15 fraternities, 10 sororities. **Athletics (Intercollegiate):** *Men:* baseball, basketball, cheerleading, cross-country, golf, soccer, tennis, track/field (outdoor), track/ field (indoor). *Women:* basketball, cheerleading, cross-country, diving, field hockey, golf, soccer, softball, swimming, tennis, track/field (outdoor), track/field (indoor), volleyball. **On-Campus Highlights:** Hurlburt Student Center-- The Bonnie, Heth Hall- Students Services, Young Hall--High Tech Classrooms, Covington Center for Arts, Muse Hall--New River Grill. **Environmental Initiatives:** Climate Action Plan (CAP)- As a signatory of the ACUPCC, Radford continues to meet the expectations by completing its first-ever greenhouse gas inventory baseline and publicly reporting the information on the ACUPCC website in January of 2011. Now, Radford is in the midst of the developing its CAP that will guide the university towards climate neutrality in the years to come. The work, to this point, has included many stakeholders across campus and beyond by volunteering their efforts to bring forth suggestions and recommendations to help Radford's campus be a more sustainable place in the short-, mid-, and long-term time frames. The CAP will be updated and revised periodically as various factors (financial, technological, etc.) change but this will be the foundational document that helps Radford reach its climate neutrality commitment. Energy Star- Since the University has already completed individual digital submetering of campus buildings for water, electricity & steam, Radford continues to expand its capabilities and earn recognition for its efforts. The digital submetering and associated information allows RU to compare various benchmarks, prioritize efforts and verify savings from energy conservation measures. Currently, Radford has 32% of its main campus buildings that have an USEPA Energy Star rating of 69 or greater With five buildings receiving actual certification (score of 75 or better), Radford has four residence halls that have received certification, which are the only ones certified in the Commonwealth of Virginia currently. Recycling Rate- For the second straight year, Radford has achieved it highest recycling rate ever topping out at over 51.68% in fiscal year 2011 even while two residence halls were closed for renovations during this time period with those students living in off-campus housing. While construction materials can have a large impact on recycling rates as well, Radford still continued to increase the amount of cardboard and mixed containers recycled, in part, through its education/awareness efforts like creating an online request a bin service, RecycleMania, YToss? move out program, & others.

ADMISSIONS

Freshman Academic Profile: Average high school GPA 3.2. 6% in top 10% of high school class, 22% in top 25% of high school class, 61% in top 50% of high school class. 92% from public high schools. SAT Math middle 50% range 460-550. SAT Critical Reading middle 50% range 460-540. SAT Writing middle 50% range 440-530. ACT middle 50% range 19-23. Minimum paper TOEFL 520. **Basis for Candidate Selection:** *Very important factors considered include:* rigor of secondary school record. *Important factors considered include:* academic GPA. *Other factors considered include:* Class rank, application essay, recommendation(s), standardized test scores, alumni/ae relation, character/personal qualities, extracurricular activities, first generation, geographical residence, level of applicant's interest, racial/ethnic status, state residency, talent/ability, volunteer work, work experience. **Freshman Admission Requirements:** High school diploma is required and GED is accepted. **Freshman Admission Statistics:** 8,192 applied, 76% admitted, 33% enrolled. **Transfer Admission Requirements:** college transcript(s), minimum college GPA of 2.0 required. Lowest grade transferable C. **General Admission Information:** Application Fee $50. Regular application deadline 2/1. Regular notification 4/1. Nonfall registration accepted. Admission may be deferred for a maximum of 1 year. Credit and/or placement offered for CEEB Advanced Placement tests.

COSTS AND FINANCIAL AID

Required Forms and Deadlines: FAFSA. **Notification of Awards:** Applicants will be notified of awards on a rolling basis beginning 4/15. **Types of Aid:** *Need-based scholarships/grants:* Federal Pell, SEOG, state scholarships/grants, private scholarships, the school's own gift aid. *Loans:* Subsidized Stafford, Unsubsidized Stafford, PLUS, Federal Perkins, Federal Nursing, state loans, college/university loans from institutional funds. **Student Employment:** Federal Work-Study Program available. Institutional employment available. Highest amount earned per year from on-campus jobs $2,610. Off-campus job opportunities are good. **Financial Aid Statistics:** 59% freshmen, 63% undergrads receive need-based scholarship or grant aid. 28% freshmen, 21% undergrads receive non-need-based scholarship or grant aid. 86% freshmen, 86% undergrads receive need-based self-help aid. 2% freshmen, 1% undergrads receive athletic scholarships. 74% freshmen, 70% undergrads receive any aid. 63% undergrads borrow to pay for school. Average cumulative indebtedness $25,241. **Criteria for awarding institutional aid:** *Non-need-based:* academics, alumni affiliation, art, athletics, leadership, music/drama, state/district residency.

RAMAPO COLLEGE OF NEW JERSEY

505 Ramapo Valley Road, Mahwah, NJ 07430-1680
Phone: 201-684-7300 • **Financial Aid Phone:** 201-684-7550
E-mail: admissions@ramapo.edu • **CEEB Code:** 2884
Fax: 201-684-7964 • **Website:** www.ramapo.edu • **ACT Code:** 2591

This public school was founded in 1971. It has a 300-acre campus.

RATINGS

Admissions Selectivity Rating: 90   **Fire Safety Rating:** 92   **Green Rating:** 73

STUDENTS AND FACULTY

Enrollment: 5,390. **Student Body:** 58% female, 42% male, 95% out-of-state, 1% international (27 countries represented). Asian 6%, African American 5%, Caucasian 69%, Hispanic 13%, Native American 0%.

Retention and Graduation: 60% freshmen graduate within 4 years. **Faculty:** Student/faculty ratio 17:1. 218 full-time faculty, % hold PhDs, 25% are members of minority groups, 49% are women. 0% of classes are taught by teaching assistants.

ACADEMICS

Degrees: bachelor's, certificate, master's. **Classes:** Most classes have 20–29 students. Most lab/discussion sessions have 10–19 students. **Majors with Highest Enrollment:** business administration and management; nursing science (ms, phd); psychology. **Special Study Options:** Accelerated program, cooperative education program, cross-registration, distance learning, double major, dual enrollment, exchange student program (domestic), external degree program, honors program, independent study, internships, liberal arts/career combination, student-designed major, study abroad, teacher certification program, The RCNJ Teacher's Education program is accredited by TEAC. Students with non-Business majors may enroll in courses to earn a Business Essentials Certificate. **Honors Programs:** http://www.ramapo.edu/honors/ The Ramapo College Honors Program is designed for students who desire a scholarly environment and an opportunity to interact with challenging faculty members and like-minded students. The Honors Program provides expanded opportunities for learning and reflection. Other benefits of the College Honors Program include residence hall options, special seminars, and exciting trips. Graduation from the College Honors Program is one indicator of a highly motivated, highly skilled, self-initiating individual. Students may participate in the College Honors Program by completing three H-option courses and receiving an Honors Certificate or by completing three H-option courses and completing a senior project, in which case the student graduates with full college honors. Full college honors is indicated on the diploma. For more information, please log onto http://www.ramapo.edu/academics/honors/ **Combined Degree Programs:** BA/MD, BA/MA, BA/DDS, BS/DR- PT, Phys.Ast., Chiro., Optom., Osteo. **Disability Services:** Special programs offered to physically disabled students include note-taking services, reader services, tape recorders, tutors. **Career Services:** Alumni network, alumni services, career/job search classes, career assessment, internships Career Services highlights include The College's Cooperative Education Program (created in the 1980-81 academic year) has placed over 8,000 students and received more than $750,000 in grant awards from Federal, State, and private sources as well as nationwide recognition through U.S. Department of Education "national demonstration model" status.

FACILITIES

Housing: Coed dorms, special housing for disabled students, special housing for international students, cooperative housing, apartments for single students, Special arrangements are made from time to time. Disabled students live in same residence halls as non-disabled students. 100% of campus accessible to physically disabled. **Special Academic Facilities/Equipment:** Art museum, media center, international telecommunications center, electron microscope, astronomical observatory, Holocaust Studies Center, new sports/fitness complex. A new Center for Science, Education and Technology is underway, as well as a Sustainability Education Center, and a Spirituality Center. **Computers:** 100% of classrooms, 100% of dorms, 100% of libraries, 100% of dining areas, 100% of student union, 60% of common outdoor areas have wireless network access. Students can register for classes online. Administrative functions (other than registration) can be performed online.

CAMPUS LIFE

Environment: Town. **Activities:** Choral groups, dance, drama/theater, literary magazine, music ensembles, musical theater, radio station, student government, student newspaper, television station, yearbook, Campus Ministries, International Student Organization, Model UN 80 registered organizations, 19 honor societies, 7 religious organizations. 10 fraternities, 11 sororities. **Athletics (Intercollegiate):** *Men:* baseball, basketball, cross-country, soccer, swimming, tennis, track/field (outdoor), track/field (indoor), volleyball. *Women:* basketball, cross-country, field hockey, lacrosse, soccer, softball, swimming, tennis, track/field (outdoor), track/field (indoor), volleyball. **On-Campus Highlights:** Berrie Center for Performing and Visual Arts, The Pavilion, The Market Place at the Birch Tree Inn, J Lee's in the Student Center, The Bill Bradley Sports and Fitness center. **Environmental Initiatives:** - Curriculum (and a new building for the Sustainability Education Center). - Recycling - Energy Conservation.

ADMISSIONS

Freshman Academic Profile: Average high school GPA 3.3. 28% in top 10% of high school class, 61% in top 25% of high school class, 90% in top 50% of high school class. SAT Math middle 50% range 510-620. SAT Critical Reading middle 50% range 490-600. SAT Writing middle 50% range 500-600. Minimum web-based TOEFL 90. Minimum paper TOEFL 550. **Basis for Candidate Selection:** *Very important factors considered include:* Class rank, academic GPA, rigor of secondary school record, standardized test scores. *Important factors considered include:* application essay, recommendation(s), extracurricular activities, talent/ability. *Other factors considered include:* alumni/ae relation, geographical residence, state residency, volunteer work, work experience. **Freshman Admission Requirements:** High school diploma is required and

GED is accepted. *Academic units required:* 4 English, 3 mathematics, 3 science, (2 science labs), 2 foreign language, 3 social studies, 3 academic electives. 4 English, 3 mathematics, 3 science, (2 science labs), 2 foreign language, 3 social studies, 3 academic electives. **Freshman Admission Statistics:** 6,299 applied, 47% admitted, 30% enrolled. **Transfer Admission Requirements:** college transcript(s), essay or personal statement, minimum college GPA of 2.5 required. Lowest grade transferable C. **General Admission Information:** Application Fee $60. Regular application deadline 3/1. Nonfall registration accepted. Admission may be deferred for a maximum of 12 months. Credit and/or placement offered for CEEB Advanced Placement tests.

COSTS AND FINANCIAL AID

Annual in-state tuition $8,480. Annual out-of-state tuition $16,960. Room and board $11,370. Required fees $4,664. Average book expense $1,200. **Required Forms and Deadlines:** FAFSA. **Notification of Awards:** Applicants will be notified of awards on a rolling basis beginning 4/1. *Types of Aid: Need-based scholarships/grants:* Federal Pell, SEOG, state scholarships/grants, private scholarships, the school's own gift aid, Federal Nursing Scholarships. , Federal TRIO Grant. *Loans:* Direct Subsidized Stafford, Direct Unsubsidized Stafford, Direct PLUS, Federal Perkins, state loans. **Student Employment:** Federal Work-Study Program available. Institutional employment available. Highest amount earned per year from on-campus jobs $9,299. Off-campus job opportunities are good. **Financial Aid Statistics:** 37% freshmen, 45% undergrads receive need-based scholarship or grant aid. 29% freshmen, 25% undergrads receive non-need-based scholarship or grant aid. 75% freshmen, 87% undergrads receive need-based self-help aid. 80% freshmen, 74% undergrads receive any aid. 67% undergrads borrow to pay for school. Average cumulative indebtedness $30,053.

See page 1182.

RANDOLPH COLLEGE

2500 Rivermont Avenue, Lynchburg, VA 24503-1555
Phone: 434-947 8100 • **Financial Aid Phone:** 434-947-8128
E-mail: admissions@randolphcollege.edu • **CEEB Code:** 5567
Fax: 434-947-8996 • **Website:** www.randolphcollege.edu • **ACT Code:** 4388

This private school, affiliated with the Methodist Church, was founded in 1891. It has a 100-acre campus.

RATINGS

Admissions Selectivity Rating: 77   **Fire Safety Rating:** 88   **Green Rating:** 94

STUDENTS AND FACULTY

Enrollment: 555. **Student Body:** 66% female, 34% male, 53% out-of-state, 12% international (33 countries represented). Asian 2%, African American 9%, Caucasian 69%, Hispanic 6%, Native American 0%.
Retention and Graduation: 75% freshmen return for sophomore year. 61% freshmen graduate within 4 years. 64% freshmen graduate within 6 years. 33% grads go on to further study within 1 year. 21% grads pursue arts and sciences degrees. 6% grads pursue law degrees. 2% grads pursue business degrees. 4% grads pursue medical degrees. **Faculty:** Student/faculty ratio 8:1. 68 full-time faculty, 94% hold PhDs, 15% are members of minority groups, 54% are women. 0% of classes are taught by teaching assistants.

ACADEMICS

Degrees: bachelor's, master's. **Classes:** Most classes have fewer than 10 students. Most lab/discussion sessions have fewer than 10 students. **Majors with Highest Enrollment:** biology/biological sciences; political science and government; psychology. **Special Study Options:** Accelerated program, cross-registration, double major, dual enrollment, exchange student program (domestic), honors program, independent study, internships, liberal arts/career combination, student-designed major, study abroad, teacher certification program, 7-college exchange with Washington and Lee University, Hollins University, Hampden-Sydney College, Mary Baldwin College, Sweet Briar College, and Randolph-Macon College. Study abroad is encouraged and facilitated. The College currently offers a program for one or two semesters in Reading,England and affiliated programs in Greece, France, Denmark, Japan, Italy, Spain, N. Ireland, Mexico, and Czech Republic. Qualified students may elect to study abroad on a Randolph College or independent program. Endowed funds provide need-based assistance for study abroad to both American and international students. American Culture Program, a 1-Semester program that includes study

on-site at key locations in and near Virginia, open to Randolph College students and students from other colleges who are accepted through a special application process. **Honors Programs:** Juniors and seniors who have a cumulative 3.45 in all academic work and a 3.7 in the major are eligible to read for Honors in the Major. The Honors Program encourages students of exceptional ability to engage in independent and intensive study in their fields of interest. **Combined Degree Programs:** BA/MA, BA/MEng, BA/MS Nursing; BS/BS Engineering. **Disability Services:** Special programs offered to physically disabled students include note-taking services, reader services, tape recorders, tutors. **Career Services:** Alumni network, alumni services, career assessment, internships, regional alumni., Career Services highlights include We are most proud of our Experiential Learning opportunities made available to our students. The Career Development Center continues to provide all aspects of Career Services and is now within the Experiential Learning Center. The Center serves as a hub for all experiential activities and is responsible for coordination of those activities including service learning, study abroad, volunteerism and internships. The Experiential Learning Center empowers Randolph College students and faculty to creatively combine learning in the classroom with experiential opportunities within our campus and beyond. Through effective communication and collaboration, we help students make meaningful connections between their academic goals and life-long pursuits.

FACILITIES

Housing: Coed dorms, women's dorms, special housing for non-traditional age students. 50% of campus accessible to physically disabled. **Special Academic Facilities/Equipment:** Maier Museum of American Art recognized as one of the most outstanding college collections in the nation, computer-equipped classrooms (including wireless computer networks and smart boards), 100-acre equestrian center, language lab, science and math resource center, learning resources center, writing lab, nursery school, nature preserves, observatory, electron microscope. **Computers:** 100% of classrooms, 100% of dorms, 100% of libraries, 100% of dining areas, 100% of student union, 100% of common outdoor areas have wireless network access. Students can register for classes online. Administrative functions (other than registration) can be performed online.

CAMPUS LIFE

Environment: City. **Activities:** Choral groups, dance, drama/theater, literary magazine, music ensembles, pep band, radio station, student government, student newspaper, student-run film society, yearbook, International Student Organization, Model UN 40 registered organizations, 7 honor societies, 6 religious organizations. **Athletics (Intercollegiate):** *Men:* basketball, cross-country, equestrian sports, horseback riding, lacrosse, soccer, tennis. *Women:* basketball, cross-country, equestrian sports, horseback riding, lacrosse, soccer, softball, swimming, tennis, volleyball. **On-Campus Highlights:** The Maier Museum of Art, Macon Bookshop (on Rivermont Avenue), The Whiteside Amphitheater, Botanical Gardens, Main Hall and Main Grounds coffee bar, Randolph College Riding Center Skeller (in Main Hall) Houston Chapel.

ADMISSIONS

Freshman Academic Profile: Average high school GPA 3.5. 27% in top 10% of high school class, 55% in top 25% of high school class, 96% in top 50% of high school class. 81% from public high schools. SAT Math middle 50% range 480-620. SAT Critical Reading middle 50% range 490-620. SAT Writing middle 50% range 470-610. ACT middle 50% range 20-25. Minimum paper TOEFL. **Basis for Candidate Selection:** *Very important factors considered include:* academic GPA, rigor of secondary school record, character/personal qualities. *Important factors considered include:* Class rank, application essay, recommendation(s), standardized test scores, extracurricular activities. *Other factors considered include:* alumni/ae relation, first generation, interview, level of applicant's interest, talent/ability, volunteer work, work experience. **Freshman Admission Requirements:** High school diploma is required and GED is accepted. *Academic units required:* 4 English, 3 mathematics, 2 science, (2 science labs), 3 foreign language, 2 history, 2 academic electives. 4 English, 3 mathematics, 2 science, (2 science labs), 3 foreign language, 2 history, 2 academic electives. **Freshman Admission Statistics:** 979 applied, 71% admitted, 25% enrolled. **Transfer Admission Requirements:** High school transcript, college transcript(s), essay or personal statement, Lowest grade transferable C–. **General Admission Information:** Application Fee $50. Regular application deadline 4/1. Regular notification 4/15. Nonfall registration accepted. Admission may be deferred for a maximum of 1 year. Credit and/or placement offered for CEEB Advanced Placement tests.

COSTS AND FINANCIAL AID

Annual tuition $31,030. Room and board $10,790. Required fees $510. Average book expense $1,000. **Required Forms and Deadlines:** FAFSA, state aid form. **Notification of Awards:** Applicants will be notified of awards on a rolling basis beginning 3/1. **Types of Aid:** *Need-based scholarships/grants:* Federal Pell, SEOG, state scholarships/grants, private scholarships, the school's own gift aid. *Loans:* Subsidized Stafford, Unsubsidized Stafford, PLUS, Federal Perkins, college/university loans from institutional funds, Private. **Student Employment:** Federal Work-Study Program available. Institutional employment available. Off-campus job opportunities are good. **Financial Aid Statistics:** 100% freshmen, 99% undergrads receive need-based scholarship or grant aid. 17% freshmen, 14% undergrads receive non-need-based scholarship or grant aid. 83% freshmen, 85% undergrads receive need-based self-help aid. 99% freshmen, 96% undergrads receive any aid. 67% undergrads borrow to pay for school. Average cumulative indebtedness $29,842. **Criteria for awarding institutional aid:** *Non-need-based:* academics, alumni affiliation, art, leadership, minority status, music/drama, religious affiliation, state/district residency.

RANDOLPH-MACON COLLEGE

P. O. Box 5005, Ashland, VA 23005
Phone: 804-752-7305 • **Financial Aid Phone:** 804-752-7259
E-mail: admissions@rmc.edu • **CEEB Code:** 5566
Fax: 804-752-4707 • **Website:** www.rmc.edu • **ACT Code:** 4386

This private school, affiliated with the Methodist Church, was founded in 1830. It has a 120-acre campus.

RATINGS
Admissions Selectivity Rating: 86   Fire Safety Rating: 83   Green Rating: 74

STUDENTS AND FACULTY
Enrollment: 1,295. **Student Body:** 52% female, 48% male, 26% out-of-state, 3% international (20 countries represented). Asian 2%, African American 12%, Caucasian 77%, Hispanic 4%, Native American 1%.
Retention and Graduation: 80% freshmen return for sophomore year. 53% freshmen graduate within 4 years. 56% freshmen graduate within 6 years. 26% grads go on to further study within 1 year. 10% grads pursue arts and sciences degrees. 3% grads pursue law degrees. 3% grads pursue business degrees. 2% grads pursue medical degrees. **Faculty:** Student/faculty ratio 12:1. 93 full-time faculty, 99% hold PhDs, 9% are members of minority groups, 44% are women. 0% of classes are taught by teaching assistants.

ACADEMICS
Degrees: bachelor's. **Classes:** Most classes have 10–19 students. **Majors with Highest Enrollment:** business/managerial economics; psychology; sociology. **Special Study Options:** Accelerated program, cross-registration, double major, dual enrollment, exchange student program (domestic), honors program, independent study, internships, liberal arts/career combination, study abroad, teacher certification program, Member of Seven College Consortium, 3-2 program in engineering with Columbia University University of Virginia, 3-2 in forestry with Duke University, 4-1 in accounting with Virginia Commonwealth University. **Honors Programs:** The Honors Program offers qualified students the opportunity to take special honors classes, participate in unique programs and events for honors students, and an Honors House for recreation and socializing. **Combined Degree Programs:** BA/MA, BA/MEng, 3:2 Forestry, 4:1 Accounting, 4:1 MBA. **Disability Services:** Special programs offered to physically disabled students include note-taking services, reader services, tape recorders, tutors. **Career Services:** Alumni network, alumni services, career/job search classes, career assessment, internships, regional alumni. Career Services highlights include Randolph-Macon offers outstanding internship opportunities to students of all class years and majors. Of greatest note is the Bassett Internship Program, open to seniors and juniors.

FACILITIES
Housing: Coed dorms, special housing for disabled students, men's dorms, special housing for international students, women's dorms, fraternity/sorority housing, apartments for single students, Honors House; Substance-free housing; Special Interest Housing. 50% of campus accessible to physically disabled. **Special Academic Facilities/Equipment:** Language lab, learning center, media center, greenhouse, observatory with telescope, electron microscopes, nuclear magnetic resonator, art gallery, fine arts center **Computers:** 20% of classrooms, 100% of dorms, 100% of libraries, 100% of dining areas, 100% of student union, 25% of common outdoor areas have wireless network access. Students can register for classes online. Administrative functions (other than registration) can be performed online.

CAMPUS LIFE
Environment: Village. **Activities:** Choral groups, concert band, dance, drama/theater, jazz band, literary magazine, music ensembles, musical theater, pep band, radio station, student government, student newspaper, student-run film society, television station, yearbook, Campus Ministries, International Student Organization 102 registered organizations, 18 honor societies, 4 religious organizations. 6 fraternities, 4 sororities. **Athletics (Intercollegiate):** *Men:* baseball, basketball, football, golf, lacrosse, soccer, tennis. *Women:* basketball, field hockey, lacrosse, soccer, softball, swimming, tennis, volleyball. **On-Cam-**

pus Highlights: Randolph-Macon Performing Arts Center, The Brock Sports and Recreation Center, Frank E. Brown Campus Center, Pace-Armistead Hall and Flippo Gallery, Washington and Franklin Hall, Campus is located on 120 acres in the suburban community of Ashland, Virginia. R-MC has six historic landmarks, including three academic buildings listed on the National Historic Register. **Environmental Initiatives:** Designing, Planning, Building and Operating a LEED-certified residence hall incorporating solar power, geothermal heat exchange, rainwater reclamation and other sustainable aspects Successfully achieving level E2 certification in the Virginia Department of Environmental Quality's Virginia Environmental Excellence Program. R-MC was the second higher-ed institution (and the first residential college) to achieve this for their entire campus. Certification of Estes Dining Hall as a Virginia Green Restaurant through the DEQ's Green Restaurant program.

ADMISSIONS
Freshman Academic Profile: Average high school GPA 3.6. 20% in top 10% of high school class, 49% in top 25% of high school class, 88% in top 50% of high school class. 80% from public high schools. SAT Math middle 50% range 490-600. SAT Critical Reading middle 50% range 500-590. SAT Writing middle 50% range 480-580. ACT middle 50% range 21-26. Minimum web-based TOEFL 80. Minimum paper TOEFL 550. **Basis for Candidate Selection:** *Very important factors considered include:* academic GPA, rigor of secondary school record. *Important factors considered include:* Class rank, application essay, recommendation(s), standardized test scores. *Other factors considered include:* alumni/ae relation, character/personal qualities, extracurricular activities, first generation, interview, racial/ethnic status, talent/ability, volunteer work, work experience. **Freshman Admission Requirements:** High school diploma is required and GED is accepted. *Academic units required:* 4 English, 3 mathematics, 3 science, (2 science labs), 2 foreign language, 1 social studies, 2 history, 1 academic electives. *Academic units recommended:* 4 English, 3 mathematics, 3 science, (2 science labs), 2 foreign language, 1 social studies, 2 history, 1 academic electives. **Freshman Admission Statistics:** 4,155 applied, 54% admitted, 18% enrolled. **Transfer Admission Requirements:** High school transcript, college transcript(s), essay or personal statement, statement of good standing from prior institution(s). Minimum college GPA of 2.0 required. Lowest grade transferable C–. **General Admission Information:** Application Fee $30. Early decision application deadline 11/15. Regular application deadline 3/1. Regular notification 4/1. Nonfall registration accepted. Admission may be deferred for a maximum of 1 year. Credit and/or placement offered for CEEB Advanced Placement tests.

COSTS AND FINANCIAL AID
Annual tuition $32,625. Room and board $10,400. Required fees $900. Average book expense $1,100. **Required Forms and Deadlines:** FAFSA, state aid formR-MC Entitlement Eligibility Form(If applicable) College Prepaid Education Program Form. **Notification of Awards:** Applicants will be notified of awards on or about 3/15. **Types of Aid:** *Need-based scholarships/grants:* Federal Pell, SEOG, state scholarships/grants, private scholarships, the school's own gift aid. *Loans:* Subsidized Stafford, Unsubsidized Stafford, PLUS, Federal Perkins, college/university loans from institutional funds. **Student Employment:** Federal Work-Study Program available. Institutional employment available. Highest amount earned per year from on-campus jobs $1,500. Off-campus job opportunities are excellent. **Financial Aid Statistics:** 100% freshmen, 100% undergrads receive need-based scholarship or grant aid. 22% freshmen, 17% undergrads receive non-need-based scholarship or grant aid. 78% freshmen, 81% undergrads receive need-based self-help aid. 99% freshmen, 99% undergrads receive any aid. 70% undergrads borrow to pay for school. Average cumulative indebtedness $31,112. **Criteria for awarding institutional aid:** *Non-need-based:* academics, alumni affiliation, leadership, minority status, religious affiliation, state/district residency.

REED COLLEGE

3203 SE Woodstock Boulevard, Portland, OR 97202-8199
Phone: 503-777-7511 • **Financial Aid Phone:** 503-777-7223
E-mail: admission@reed.edu • **CEEB Code:** 4654
Fax: 503-777-7553 • **Website:** www.reed.edu • **ACT Code:** 3494

This private school was founded in 1908. It has a 116-acre campus.

RATINGS
Admissions Selectivity Rating: 97   Fire Safety Rating: 92   Green Rating: 78

STUDENTS AND FACULTY

Enrollment: 1,418. **Student Body:** 56% female, 44% male, 87% out-of-state, 5% international (46 countries represented). Asian 6%, African American 2%, Caucasian 56%, Hispanic 4%, Native American 0%.

Retention and Graduation: 90% freshmen return for sophomore year. 59% freshmen graduate within 4 years. 79% freshmen graduate within 6 years. 65% grads go on to further study within 1 year. 48% grads pursue arts and sciences degrees. 5% grads pursue law degrees. 3% grads pursue business degrees. 4% grads pursue medical degrees. **Faculty:** Student/faculty ratio 10:1. 130 full-time faculty, 92% hold PhDs, 14% are members of minority groups, 42% are women. 0% of classes are taught by teaching assistants.

ACADEMICS

Degrees: bachelor's, master's. **Classes:** Most classes have 10–19 students. Most lab/discussion sessions have 10–19 students. **Majors with Highest Enrollment:** biology/biological sciences; English language and literature; psychology. **Special Study Options:** cross-registration, double major, dual enrollment, exchange student program (domestic), independent study, internships, liberal arts/career combination, study abroad, Computer Science By arrangement with the University of Washington, a student may obtain a bachelor of arts degree from Reed and a bachelor of science degree in computer science from the University of Washington. The program calls for three years at Reed, including completion of the general distribution requirements and major requirements in one department, the passing of the junior qualifying examination, the acquisition of a minimum of 22 Reed units (at least 20 of which, including the distribution requirements, must be earned at Reed), and two years at the University of Washington. The university will admit up to five students per year on the recommendation of Reed College. Recommended students must satisfy the university's GPA requirements for transfer students, which may differ from year to year and which are not necessarily the same for Washington residents and non-residents. Computer science degrees are also available under the engineering programs described later in this section. Course Requirements These vary, depending upon the field of the Reed major -chemistry, mathematics, or physics. Consult the Reed dual degree coordinator for specific information. In special cases, an ad hoc program with the biology or economics department, or with another department, may be approved. Engineering By arrangement with the California Institute of Technology (Caltech), the Columbia University School of Engineering and Applied Sciences, or Rensselaer Polytechnic Institute, a student may obtain a bachelor's degree in engineering (alternatively, computer science or certain earth and planetary sciences) and a bachelor of arts degree from Reed. The program calls for three years at Reed, including the completion of the general college distribution requirements, completion of major requirements in one department (excluding thesis), the passing of the junior qualifying examination, the acquisition of a minimum of 22 Reed units (at least 20 of which, including all but two units of the distribution requirement, must be earned at Reed), and two years at the engineering school. Transfer students entering these programs should expect to spend no fewer than five semesters at Reed to meet this requirement. The two degrees will be awarded concurrently; all requirements for both degrees must be met before either is awarded. Admission to the engineering school is contingent on the college's recommendation and the student's having met certain course requirements of the engineering school while at Reed. Typical course requirements are two years of physics, one or two years of chemistry, and two years of mathematics, including differential equations. Normally, students with a G.P.A. less than 3.0 should not expect to be recommended. Admission to the specific field of engineering preferred by the student is not guaranteed; the student's academic record can be relevant. Admission to Caltech is not automatic upon recommendation, but is subject to review by Caltech and may depend upon factors that cannot be anticipated. Caltech does not guarantee financial aid to otherwise eligible students. While admission to the other programs is also subject to review by the participating school, admission can usually be expected upon recommendation. Course Requirements During the freshman year: Mathematics 111/112 or 211/212; Physics 100. Consult with the Reed dual degree coordinator for information on other required courses. Forestry-Environmental Sciences By arrangement with the Nicholas School of the Environment of Duke University, a student may obtain a bachelor of arts degree at Reed and a professional master's degree from Duke (master of forestry or master of environmental management). Work at Duke emphasizes three aspects of study and research in forest and other renewable natural resources: management, science, and policy. The program calls for three years at Reed, including completion of the general college distribution and major requirements (excluding thesis), passing of the junior qualifying examination, the acquisition of a minimum of 22 Reed units (at least 20 of which, including the distribution requirements, must be earned at Reed), and two years at Duke. Students in all academic majors may qualify for the program. Course Requirements l. Biology 101,102; Mathematics 111 or 112, and Mathematics 141; and Economics 201. 2. Successful completion of the junior qualifying exam before the end of the junior year. Students should plan to take the Graduate Record Examination and make formal application for admission to Duke during the third year at Reed. In the summer following the third year, the student should begin work at Duke. Additional information may be obtained from the faculty adviser for the forestry-environmental sciences program. Pre-Medical and Pre-Veterinary Medical schools value the breadth in educational programs offered by liberal arts colleges. Work in the humanities and social sciences, as well as non-academic factors are all very important. Students should choose a major according to their academic interests and include the following laboratory and other courses to fulfill the admission requirements of most medical schools: 1. General biology: Biology 101 and 102 2. General chemistry: Chemistry 101 and 102 3. Organic chemistry: Chemistry 201 and 202 4. General physics: Physics 100, with lab 5. English or humanities: Humanities 110 6. One year of mathematics, including calculus (Mathematics 111) Course prerequisites for veterinary school usually include the courses above plus additional specific courses, such as biochemistry or upper-level biology. Since there are more than 100 domestic medical schools and 30 veterinary schools, the student may encounter variation in the number and character of admission requirements. Students should be acquainted with the specific requirements and programs of the schools to which they apply. To prepare a competitive application portfolio, students considering medical or veterinary school are strongly encouraged to consult with health professions advisers and the Career Services office early in their undergraduate careers. In addition to offering advising, the Career Services office maintains a library of resources essential to the medical school planning process, such as Medical School Admission Requirements, a publication by the American Association of Medical Colleges. The guide Preparation for Medical School at Reed is available online, and includes important timelines, health care internship information, insight into letters of evaluation, and useful web links. It is strongly recommended that students take advantage of additional resources by attending informational seminars, seeking assistance with the application process, and using mock interviews. Graduating students who plan to take time off before applying to medical or veterinary school should discuss their plans with a health-profession adviser before graduation. Visual Arts The college has made arrangements for Reed students to participate in a variety of exchange programs and summer internships at other institutions. They may choose from programs in painting and sculpture, architecture, art history, archaeology, conservation, historic preservation, and museum work. A joint five-year program is also available with the Pacific Northwest College of Art. These programs are described in more detail in the art department section of the catalog. **Combined Degree Programs:** Computing: Univ. of Washington. **Disability Services:** Special programs offered to physically disabled students include note-taking services, reader services, tape recorders, tutors. **Career Services:** Alumni network, alumni services, career/job search classes, career assessment, internships, regional alumni. Career Services highlights include http://web.reed.edu/career/students.html.

FACILITIES

Housing: Coed dorms, special housing for disabled students, women's dorms, cooperative housing, apartments for single students, wellness housing, theme housing, Reed language houses accommodate upper-division students studying Chinese, French, German, Russian, and Spanish. First-year students required to live on campus; exceptions granted for unusual situations. 85% of campus accessible to physically disabled. **Special Academic Facilities/Equipment:** Art gallery, studio art building, language labs, computerized music listening lab, nuclear research reactor, 20 music practice rooms and midi lab, 760 seat auditorium, academic support center (quantitative skills, writing, math support), educational technology center **Computers:** 100% of classrooms, 100% of dorms, 100% of libraries, 100% of dining areas, 100% of student union, 50% of common outdoor areas have wireless network access. Students can register for classes online. Administrative functions (other than registration) can be performed online.

CAMPUS LIFE

Environment: Metropolis. **Activities:** Choral groups, dance, drama/theater, literary magazine, music ensembles, radio station, student government, student newspaper, student-run film society, symphony orchestra, Campus Ministries, International Student Organization, Model UN 130 registered organizations, 1 honor societies, 5 religious organizations. **On-Campus Highlights:** Thesis Tower, Nuclear Research Reactor, Crystal Springs Canyon, Cerf Amphitheatre, The Paradox Cafe. **Environmental Initiatives:** LEED construction recycling installation for energy efficiency across campus, i.e., lighting, windows, heating.

ADMISSIONS

Freshman Academic Profile: Average high school GPA 3.9. 63% in top 10% of high school class, 90% in top 25% of high school class, 99% in top 50% of high school class. 59% from public high schools. SAT Math middle 50% range 640-710. SAT Critical Reading middle 50% range 670-750. SAT Writing middle 50% range 660-730. ACT middle 50% range 30-33. Minimum web-based TOEFL 100. Minimum paper TOEFL 600. **Basis for Candidate Selection:** *Very important factors considered include:* application essay, academic GPA, rigor of secondary school record. *Important factors considered include:* Class rank, recommendation(s), standardized test scores, interview, level of applicant's interest. *Other factors considered include:* alumni/ae relation, character/personal qualities, extracurricular activities, first generation, geographical residence, racial/ethnic status, talent/ability, volunteer work, work experience. **Freshman Admission Requirements:** High school diploma is required and GED is accepted. **Freshman Admission Statistics:** 3,075 applied, 43% admitted, 28% enrolled. **Transfer Admission Requirements:** High school transcript, college transcript(s), essay or personal statement, standardized test scores, statement of good standing from prior institution(s). Lowest grade transferable C–. **General Admission Information:** Application Fee $50. Early decision application deadline 11/15. Regular application deadline 1/15. Regular notification 4/1. Nonfall registration not accepted. Admission may be deferred for a maximum of 1 year. Credit and/or placement offered for CEEB Advanced Placement tests.

COSTS AND FINANCIAL AID

Annual tuition $44,200. Room and board $11,460. Required fees $260. Average book expense $950. **Required Forms and Deadlines:** FAFSA, institution's own financial aid form, CSS/Financial Aid PROFILE, noncustodial PROFILE. **Notification of Awards:** Applicants will be notified of awards on or about 4/1. **Types of Aid:** *Need-based scholarships/grants:* Federal Pell, SEOG, state scholarships/grants, private scholarships, the school's own gift aid. *Loans:* Subsidized Stafford, Unsubsidized Stafford, PLUS, Federal Perkins. **Student Employment:** Federal Work-Study Program available. Institutional employment available. Highest amount earned per year from on-campus jobs $12,006. **Financial Aid Statistics:** 87% freshmen, 89% undergrads receive need-based scholarship or grant aid. 92% freshmen, 93% undergrads receive need-based self-help aid. 53% freshmen, 54% undergrads receive any aid. 53% undergrads borrow to pay for school. Average cumulative indebtedness $16,910.

See page 1184.

REGENT UNIVERSITY

1000 Regent University Drive, Virginia Beach, VA 23464
Phone: 800-373-5504 • **Financial Aid Phone:** 757-352-4125
E-mail: admissions@regent.edu • **CEEB Code:**
Fax: 757-352-4381 • **Website:** www.regent.edu • **ACT Code:** 6738

This private school, affiliated with the Christian (Nondenominational) Church, was founded in 1978. It has a 70-acre campus.

RATINGS

Admissions Selectivity Rating: 68   **Fire Safety Rating:** 86   **Green Rating:** 67

STUDENTS AND FACULTY

Enrollment: 2,316. **Student Body:** 62% female, 38% male, 52% out-of-state, 2% international (66 countries represented). Asian 2%, African American 20%, Caucasian 56%, Hispanic 5%, Native American 0%.
Retention and Graduation: 78% freshmen return for sophomore year. **Faculty:** Student/faculty ratio 16:1. 171 full-time faculty, 95% hold PhDs, 22% are members of minority groups, 32% are women. 0% of classes are taught by teaching assistants.

ACADEMICS

Degrees: associate, bachelor's, doctoral, master's, post-master's certificate, terminal associate, transfer associate. **Classes:** Most classes have 20–29 students. **Majors with Highest Enrollment:** business/commerce; psychology; religion/religious studies. **Special Study Options:** distance learning, double major, dual enrollment, internships, study abroad, teacher certification program. **Disability Services:** Special programs offered to physically disabled students include note-taking services, reader services, tape recorders, tutors. **Career Services:** Alumni network, alumni services, career/job search classes, career assessment, internships, regional alumni.

FACILITIES

Housing: apartments for married students, apartments for single students. 100% of campus accessible to physically disabled. **Special Academic Facilities/Equipment:** The 31,000-square-foot Student Center on Regent's Virginia Beach Campus, opened in 2003, offers a central location for campus and student services. The building houses the University Bookstore, student organizations and meeting rooms, a cafe/coffee shop, computer lab, student lounge and offices for the Registrar, Admissions and Financial Aid. The 135,000-square-foot Communication & Performing Arts Center, opened in 2002, includes film and animation studios, a state-of-the-art main theatre, screening rooms and editing suites in one of the most technologically advanced communication buildings on the east coast. **Computers:** 80% of classrooms, 100% of dorms, 100% of libraries, 100% of student union, 50% of common outdoor areas have wireless network access. Students can register for classes online. Administrative functions (other than registration) can be performed online.

CAMPUS LIFE

Environment: City. **Activities:** Choral groups, concert band, dance, drama/theater, student government, student newspaper, Campus Ministries, International Student Organization 47 registered organizations, 4 honor societies. **On-Campus Highlights:** The Student Center, Communication & Performing Arts, The Ordinary Cafe and Coffee Shop, Robertson Hall, University Library, Robertson Hall is equipped with the latest technology in audio/video equipment and cameras for simultaneous broadcasting. The 132,000-square-foot building also boasts a 380-seat moot court/city council chamber. The 135,000-square-foot Communication & Performing Arts Center features a 750-seat theater and a 150-seat experimental theater, cinema-television production studio, film sound stage, screening theaters, technical studios and teaching labs. A back lot area offers space for sets for indoor and outdoor filming. Just opened in 2002, the 31,000-square-foot Student Center houses the University Bookstore, student organization offices, The Ordinary cafe/coffee shop, a computer lab, student lounge and meeting rooms. **Environmental Initiatives:** Our investments in "cool storage" systems since our beginning in 1978 allows us to shave peak demand when the power company desires. This helps reduce the size of the power plant needed to support this area. This results in a major decrease in greenhouse emissions for this area. This fact is recognized by VA Dominion Power --our supplier of electricity. Our campus is one of the most beautiful campuses in Virginia because we have worked diligently to acheive the proper balance between "bricks and mortar" and the natural resources we have been blessed with. Our woods have diverse species of trees and plantings and we strive to enhance the wildlife habitat. For instance den trees are highly valued and preserved. Fruit bearing tree species are highly valued and retained whenever possible. The President and facilities director intensively manages the campus grounds to retain the nature setting. Branches are chipped and composted as are tree leaves and needles. Campus aquatic ecosystems are maintained with similar intensity. We have purposely changed locations for buildings, sidewalks, storm sewer, and other underground utilities in order to preserve natural resources. Additionally we resisted City of Virginia Beach directives to build additional parking lots which would "urbanize" our campus. We hired a lawyer, contested the directive and preserved our green campus. The investments we have made in energy saving devices has been remarkable and worthwhile as evidenced by usage reduction data. ALL building light fixtures have been renovated to T8 fixtures.A state of the art monitoring system is in place. All flat roofs were replaced with white TPO roofs. Most pumps were upgraded with variable frequency drives. All chillers and boilers are high efficiency models. There is much, much more.

ADMISSIONS

Freshman Academic Profile: Average high school GPA 3.5. SAT Math middle 50% range 440-540. SAT Critical Reading middle 50% range 470-580. SAT Writing middle 50% range 450-560. ACT middle 50% range 20-26. Minimum web-based TOEFL 90. Minimum paper TOEFL 577. **Freshman Admission Requirements:** High school diploma or equivalent is not required. **Freshman Admission Statistics:** 1,497 applied, 83% admitted, 18% enrolled. **Transfer Admission Requirements:** college transcript(s), Lowest grade transferable c. **General Admission Information:** Notification on a rolling basis, beginning on or about 1/1. Nonfall registration accepted. Admission may be deferred for a maximum of aslongasneed. Credit offered for CEEB Advanced Placement tests.

COSTS AND FINANCIAL AID

Annual tuition $14,850. Room and board $8,430. Required fees $660. Average book expense $800. **Required Forms and Deadlines:** FAFSA, institution's own financial aid form. **Notification of Awards:** Applicants will be notified of awards on a rolling basis beginning 5/1. **Types of Aid:** *Need-based scholarships/grants:* Federal Pell, SEOG, state scholarships/grants, private scholarships, the school's own gift aid. *Loans:* Subsidized Stafford, Unsubsidized Stafford, PLUS, state loans. **Student Employment:** Federal Work-Study Program available. Institutional employment available. Highest amount earned per year from on-campus jobs $3,000. Off-campus job opportunities are excellent. **Financial Aid Statistics:** 98% freshmen, 94% undergrads receive need-based scholarship or grant aid. 9% freshmen, 3% undergrads receive non-need-based scholarship or grant aid. 93% freshmen, 96% undergrads receive need-based self-help aid. 91% freshmen, 90% undergrads receive any aid. 67% undergrads borrow to pay for school. Average cumulative indebtedness $49,326. **Criteria for awarding institutional aid:** *Non-need-based:* academics, alumni affiliation, art, athletics, leadership, minority status, music/drama, state/district residency.

REGIS COLLEGE

235 Wellesley Street, Weston, MA 02493-1571
Phone: 781-768-7100 • **Financial Aid Phone:** 781-768-7184
E-mail: admission@regiscollege.edu • **CEEB Code:** 3723
Fax: 781-768-7071 • **Website:** www.regiscollege.edu • **ACT Code:** 1886

This private school, affiliated with the Roman Catholic Church, was founded in 1927. It has a 131-acre campus.

RATINGS
Admissions Selectivity Rating: 69   **Fire Safety Rating:** 82   **Green Rating:** 72

STUDENTS AND FACULTY
Enrollment: 1,149. **Student Body:** 78% female, 22% male, 13% out-of-state, 1% international (12 countries represented). Asian 4%, African American 21%, Caucasian 47%, Hispanic 12%, Native American 0%. **Retention and Graduation:** 77% freshmen return for sophomore year. 41% freshmen graduate within 4 years. 28% grads go on to further study within 1 year. 16% grads pursue arts and sciences degrees. 1% grads pursue law degrees. 2% grads pursue business degrees. 2% grads pursue medical degrees. **Faculty:** Student/faculty ratio 13:1. 73 full-time faculty, 74% hold PhDs, 10% are members of minority groups, 78% are women. 0% of classes are taught by teaching assistants.

ACADEMICS
Degrees: associate, bachelor's, master's, post-master's certificate, transfer associate. **Classes:** Most classes have 10–19 students. **Majors with Highest Enrollment:** communication studies/speech communication and rhetoric; nursing/registered nurse (rn, asn, bsn, msn); political science and government. **Special Study Options:** Accelerated program, cross-registration, double major, English as a Second Language (ESL), exchange student program (domestic), honors program, independent study, internships, student-designed major, study abroad, teacher certification program. **Honors Programs:** The Honors Program at Regis College offers qualified students a stimulating and challenging learning experience, and opportunities for distinguished scholarship. It prepares students to become leaders committed to the betterment of the human condition and our society, a goal that is central to the Regis College mission. **Combined Degree Programs:** BA/MSCO; BS/MSNU. **Disability Services:** Special programs offered to physically disabled students include note-taking services, tape recorders, tutors. **Career Services:** Alumni network, alumni services, career/job search classes, career assessment, internships Career Services highlights include Internships offer students opportunities to apply classroom learning to the world of work while receiving academic credit.

FACILITIES
Housing: Coed dorms, women's dorms. 85% of campus accessible to physically disabled. **Special Academic Facilities/Equipment:** Fine arts center, philatelic museum. **Computers:** 30% of classrooms, 100% of dorms, 100% of libraries, 100% of dining areas, 100% of student union, 15% of common outdoor areas have wireless network access. Students can register for classes online. Administrative functions (other than registration) can be performed online.

CAMPUS LIFE
Environment: Village. **Activities:** Choral groups, dance, drama/theater, literary magazine, music ensembles, musical theater, radio station, student government, yearbook, Campus Ministries, Model UN 36 registered organizations, 10 honor societies, 2 religious organizations. **Athletics (Intercollegiate):** *Men:* basketball, diving, soccer, swimming. *Women:* basketball, diving, field hockey, lacrosse, soccer, softball, swimming, tennis, track/field (outdoor), track/field (indoor), volleyball. **On-Campus Highlights:** College Hall, Student Union, Tower, Athletic Complex, Fine Arts Center. **Environmental Initiatives:** Replacement of steam boilers w/high efficiency designs Replacement of mercury vapor and incandescent lighting with fluorescent Elimination of the use of salt for snow/ice control

ADMISSIONS
Freshman Academic Profile: Average high school GPA 3.0. 10% in top 10% of high school class, 32% in top 25% of high school class, 64% in top 50% of high school class. 76% from public high schools. SAT Math middle 50% range 410-520. SAT Critical Reading middle 50% range 410-520. SAT Writing middle 50% range 410-510. ACT middle 50% range 19-24. Minimum paper TOEFL 550. **Basis for Candidate Selection:** *Very important factors considered include:* application essay, academic GPA, recommendation(s), rigor of secondary school record, character/personal qualities. *Important factors considered include:* Class rank, standardized test scores, extracurricular activities, interview, talent/ability, volunteer work, work experience. *Other factors considered include:* alumni/ae relation, first generation, level of applicant's interest. **Freshman Admission Requirements:** High school diploma is required and GED is accepted. *Academic units required:* 4 English, 3 mathematics, 2 science, (1 science labs), 2 foreign language, 2 social studies, 3 academic electives. 4 English, 3 mathematics, 2 science, (1 science labs), 2 foreign language, 2 social studies, 3 academic electives. **Freshman Admission Statistics:** 2,041 applied, 73% admitted, 19% enrolled. **Transfer Admission Requirements:** High school transcript, college transcript(s), essay or personal statement, minimum college GPA of 2.0 required. Lowest grade transferable C. **General Admission Information:** Application Fee $50. Notification on a rolling basis, beginning on or about 12/1. Nonfall registration accepted. Admission may be deferred for a maximum of 1 year. Credit and/or placement offered for CEEB Advanced Placement tests.

COSTS AND FINANCIAL AID
Annual tuition $33,060. Room and board $12,800. Average book expense $1,000. **Required Forms and Deadlines:** FAFSA, institution's own financial aid form. **Notification of Awards:** Applicants will be notified of awards on a rolling basis beginning 3/15. **Types of Aid:** *Need-based scholarships/grants:* Federal Pell, SEOG, state scholarships/grants, private scholarships, the school's own gift aid, Federal Nursing Scholarships. *Loans:* Direct Subsidized Stafford, Direct Unsubsidized Stafford, Direct PLUS, Federal Perkins, Federal Nursing. **Student Employment:** Federal Work-Study Program available. Institutional employment available. Highest amount earned per year from on-campus jobs $5,355. Off-campus job opportunities are poor. **Financial Aid Statistics:** 84% freshmen, 84% undergrads receive need-based scholarship or grant aid. 73% freshmen, 73% undergrads receive non-need-based scholarship or grant aid. 96% freshmen, 97% undergrads receive need-based self-help aid. 91% freshmen, 84% undergrads receive any aid. 92% undergrads borrow to pay for school. Average cumulative indebtedness $32,643. **Criteria for awarding institutional aid:** *Non-need-based:* academics, alumni affiliation, religious affiliation.

REGIS UNIVERSITY

3333 Regis Boulevard, Denver, CO 80221-1099
Phone: 303-458-4900
E-mail: regisadm@regis.edu/college.asp • **CEEB Code:** 4656
Fax: 303-964-5534 • **Website:** www.regis.edu • **ACT Code:** 526

This private school, affiliated with the Roman Catholic Church, was founded in 1877. It has a 90-acre campus.

RATINGS
Admissions Selectivity Rating: 69   **Fire Safety Rating:** 60*   **Green Rating:** 60*

STUDENTS AND FACULTY
Enrollment: 5,345. **Student Body:** 65% female, 35% male, 24% out-of-state, 1% international. Asian 4%, African American 6%, Caucasian 66%, Hispanic 12%, Native American 1%. **Retention and Graduation:** 84% freshmen return for sophomore year. 61% freshmen graduate within 6 years. **Faculty:** Student/faculty ratio 14:1. 268 full-time faculty, 59% hold PhDs, 9% are members of minority groups, 60% are women.

ACADEMICS
Degrees: bachelor's, master's. **Classes:** Most classes have fewer than 10 students. Most lab/discussion sessions have 10–19 students. **Special Study Options:** Accelerated program, cooperative education program, cross-registration, distance learning, double major, dual enrollment, exchange student program (domestic), honors program, independent study, internships, liberal arts/career combination, student-designed major, study abroad, teacher certification program, weekend college. **Disability Services:** Special programs offered to physically disabled students include tutors. **Career Services:** alumni services, career/job search classes, internships.

FACILITIES
Housing: Coed dorms, special housing for disabled students, apartments for single students. 90% of campus accessible to physically disabled. Language lab, wellness center, **Computers:** Administrative functions (other than registration) can be performed online.

CAMPUS LIFE
Environment: Metropolis. **Activities:** Choral groups, drama/theater, literary magazine, music ensembles, musical theater, radio station, student government, student newspaper, yearbook 40 registered organizations, 1 honor societies, 1 religious organizations. **Athletics (Intercollegiate):** *Men:* baseball, basketball, cross-country, golf, soccer. *Women:* basketball, cross-country, lacrosse, soccer, softball, volleyball.

ADMISSIONS

Freshman Academic Profile: Average high school GPA. 24% in top 10% of high school class, 52% in top 25% of high school class, 82% in top 50% of high school class. SAT Math middle 50% range 470-600. SAT Critical Reading middle 50% range 490-600. ACT middle 50% range 21-26. **Basis for Candidate Selection:** *Very important factors considered include:* rigor of secondary school record, standardized test scores. *Important factors considered include:* application essay, recommendation(s). *Other factors considered include:* Class rank, character/personal qualities, extracurricular activities, interview, talent/ability, volunteer work, work experience. **Freshman Admission Requirements:** High school diploma is required and GED is accepted. **Freshman Admission Statistics:** 3,701 applied, 87% admitted, 16% enrolled. **Transfer Admission Requirements:** college transcript(s), essay or personal statement, minimum college GPA of 2.0 required. **General Admission Information:** Application Fee $40. Nonfall registration accepted. Admission may be deferred for a maximum of 0. Credit and/or placement offered for CEEB Advanced Placement tests.

COSTS AND FINANCIAL AID

Average book expense $2,000. **Required Forms and Deadlines:** FAFSA. **Notification of Awards:** Applicants will be notified of awards on a rolling basis beginning 3/15. **Types of Aid:** *Need-based scholarships/grants:* Federal Pell, SEOG, state scholarships/grants, private scholarships, the school's own gift aid, Federal Nursing Scholarships. *Loans:* Subsidized Stafford, Unsubsidized Stafford, PLUS, Federal Perkins, Federal Nursing. **Student Employment:** Federal Work-Study Program available. Highest amount earned per year from on-campus jobs $1,800. Off-campus job opportunities are good. **Financial Aid Statistics:** 96% freshmen, 75% undergrads receive need-based scholarship or grant aid. 45% freshmen, 32% undergrads receive non-need-based scholarship or grant aid. 89% freshmen, 92% undergrads receive need-based self-help aid. 5% freshmen, 4% undergrads receive athletic scholarships. **Criteria for awarding institutional aid:** *Non-need-based:* academics, athletics.

REINHARDT COLLEGE

7300 Reinhardt Circle, Waleska, GA 30183
Phone: 770-720-5526 • **Financial Aid Phone:** 770-720- 5667
E-mail: www.reinhardt.edu
Fax: 770-720-5899 • **Website:** www.reinhardt.edu • **ACT Code:** 856

This private school, affiliated with the Methodist Church, was founded in 1883. It has a 600-acre campus.

RATINGS

Admissions Selectivity Rating: 77   **Fire Safety Rating:** 93   **Green Rating:** 69

STUDENTS AND FACULTY

Enrollment: 980. **Student Body:** 55% female, 45% male, 27% out-of-state, 0% international. Asian 1%, African American 13%, Caucasian 75%, Hispanic 4%, Native American 1%.
Retention and Graduation: 23% freshmen graduate within 4 years. 35% grads go on to further study within 1 year. 20% grads pursue arts and sciences degrees. 5% grads pursue law degrees. 45% grads pursue business degrees. 5% grads pursue medical degrees. **Faculty:** Student/faculty ratio 12:1. 62 full-time faculty, 74% hold PhDs, 11% are members of minority groups, 48% are women. 0% of classes are taught by teaching assistants.

ACADEMICS

Degrees: associate, bachelor's, master's, transfer associate. **Classes:** Most classes have 10–19 students. **Majors with Highest Enrollment:** business administration and management; communication and media studies, other; elementary education and teaching. **Special Study Options:** Accelerated program, double major, dual enrollment, external degree program, honors program, independent study, internships, study abroad, teacher certification program. **Honors Programs:** The Honors Program is designed for students who are bright, curious and enjoy being challenged. Entering freshman with High Schjool GPA of at least 3.5 or a combined SAT of 1050 or higher, with verbal score of at least 580, will be invited to apply for admission to Reinhardt College's Honors Program. **Disability Services:** Special programs offered to physically disabled students include note-taking services, reader services, tape recorders, tutors. **Career Services:** alumni services, career/job search classes, career assessment, internships, regional alumni. Career Services highlights include Internships for the Price School of Education.

FACILITIES

Housing: Coed dorms, special housing for disabled students, men's dorms, women's dorms, honors house. 93% of campus accessible to physically disabled. **Special Academic Facilities/Equipment:** Funk Heritage Center, Falany Performing Arts **Computers:** 100% of classrooms, 100% of dorms, 100% of libraries, 100% of student union, 5% of common outdoor areas have wireless network access. Students can register for classes online. Administrative functions (other than registration) can be performed online.

CAMPUS LIFE

Environment: Rural. **Activities:** Choral groups, concert band, drama/theater, jazz band, music ensembles, student government, student newspaper, student-run film society, television station, yearbook, Campus Ministries, International Student Organization 40 registered organizations, 6 honor societies, 5 religious organizations. **Athletics (Intercollegiate):** *Men:* baseball, basketball, cheerleading, cross-country, golf, soccer, tennis. *Women:* basketball, cheerleading, cross-country, golf, soccer, softball, tennis, volleyball. **On-Campus Highlights:** Falany Performing Arts Center, Funk Heritage Center, Gordy Center, Library, Class room building. **Environmental Initiatives:** Recycle paper, RU Green Follow EPA guidelines concerning hazardous waste Continue to upgrade HVAC & electrical to conserve energy

ADMISSIONS

Freshman Academic Profile: Average high school GPA 3.0. 63% in top 50% of high school class. 98% from public high schools. SAT Math middle 50% range 430-530. SAT Critical Reading middle 50% range 410-540. ACT middle 50% range 17-22. Minimum paper TOEFL 500. **Basis for Candidate Selection:** *Very important factors considered include:* academic GPA, standardized test scores. *Important factors considered include:* rigor of secondary school record. *Other factors considered include:* Class rank, recommendation(s), alumni/ae relation, character/personal qualities, extracurricular activities, first generation, geographical residence, level of applicant's interest, racial/ethnic status, religious affiliation/commitment, talent/ability, volunteer work, work experience. **Freshman Admission Requirements:** High school diploma is required and GED is accepted. *Academic units required:* 4 English, 4 mathematics, 3 science, 3 social studies. *Academic units recommended:* 4 English, 4 mathematics, 3 science, 3 social studies. **Freshman Admission Statistics:** 1,310 applied, 59% admitted, 30% enrolled. **Transfer Admission Requirements:** college transcript(s), statement of good standing from prior institution(s). Minimum college GPA of 2.0 required. Lowest grade transferable C. **General Admission Information:** Application Fee $25. Nonfall registration accepted. Credit and/or placement offered for CEEB Advanced Placement tests.

COSTS AND FINANCIAL AID

Required Forms and Deadlines: FAFSA, state aid form. **Notification of Awards:** Applicants will be notified of awards on a rolling basis beginning 3/15. **Types of Aid:** *Need-based scholarships/grants:* Federal Pell, SEOG, state scholarships/grants, private scholarships, the school's own gift aid. *Loans:* Subsidized Stafford, Unsubsidized Stafford, PLUS. **Student Employment:** Federal Work-Study Program available. Highest amount earned per year from on-campus jobs $2,800. Off-campus job opportunities are good. **Financial Aid Statistics:** 99% freshmen, 98% undergrads receive need-based scholarship or grant aid. 7% freshmen, 7% undergrads receive non-need-based scholarship or grant aid. 76% freshmen, 75% undergrads receive need-based self-help aid. 9% freshmen, 7% undergrads receive athletic scholarships. 71% undergrads borrow to pay for school. Average cumulative indebtedness $21,336. **Criteria for awarding institutional aid:** *Non-need-based:* academics, art, athletics, leadership, music/drama, religious affiliation, state/district residency.

RENSSELAER POLYTECHNIC INSTITUTE

110 Eighth Street, Troy, NY 12180-3590
Phone: 518-276-6216 • **Financial Aid Phone:** 518-276-6813
E-mail: admissions@rpi.edu • **CEEB Code:** 2757
Fax: 518-276-4072 • **Website:** www.rpi.edu • **ACT Code:** 2866

This private school was founded in 1824. It has a 284-acre campus.

RATINGS

Admissions Selectivity Rating: 95   **Fire Safety Rating:** 83   **Green Rating:** 78

STUDENTS AND FACULTY

Enrollment: 5,300. **Student Body:** 29% female, 71% male, 66% out-of-state, 6% international (63 countries represented). Asian 10%, African American 2%, Caucasian 68%, Hispanic 6%, Native American 0%.
Retention and Graduation: 94% freshmen return for sophomore year. 60%

freshmen graduate within 4 years. 84% freshmen graduate within 6 years. 18% grads go on to further study within 1 year. 2% grads pursue arts and sciences degrees. 1% grads pursue business degrees. 1% grads pursue medical degrees. **Faculty:** Student/faculty ratio 15:1. 380 full-time faculty, 99% hold PhDs, 31% are members of minority groups, 21% are women. 0% of classes are taught by teaching assistants.

ACADEMICS

Degrees: bachelor's, certificate, master's. **Classes:** Most classes have 10–19 students. Most lab/discussion sessions have 10–19 students. **Majors with Highest Enrollment:** business/commerce; computer engineering; electrical, electronics and communications engineering. **Special Study Options:** Accelerated program, cooperative education program, cross-registration, double major, dual enrollment, exchange student program (domestic), honors program, independent study, internships, liberal arts/career combination, student-designed major, study abroad, The accelerated BS-Phd program in the School of Science is possible in all the science departments. Computer Science Physics Applied Physics Biology Biochemistry and Biophysics Geology Hydrogeology. **Honors Programs:** The Rensselaer Medal Program, the Presidential Scholars Program **Combined Degree Programs:** BA/MEng, BS/MBA, BS/MS, BS/M.Eng, BS/MD, BS/JD, BS/Ph.D. **Disability Services:** Special programs offered to physically disabled students include note-taking services, reader services, tape recorders, tutors. **Career Services:** Alumni network, alumni services, career/job search classes, career assessment, internships, regional alumni. Career Services highlights include Rensselaer has actively encouraged the translation of cutting edge academic research into new products and new businesses. Scientific and technological entrepreneurship is a significant part of "The Rensselaer Plan", a comprehensive strategic plan for the Institute. Historically and consistently, faculty, students, and alumni have successfully developed technologies, created innovations, and formed business ventures to bring ideas into practice to create value. Rensselaer's focus on entrepreneurship iscross-campus, interdisciplinary, and presents multiple perspectives. It involves creative thinking, and is not only ideas, but ideas to enterprise. Entrepreneurship at Rensselaer goes beyond curriculum, with a broad spectrum of technology presentations, lecture series, and mentor programs. It has a global focus, and is further focused as technology commercialization and entrepreneurship. The Lally School at Rensselaer has a strong tradition of developing entrepreneurs who create new ventures or bring their entrepreneurial management skills to established organizations. Theory and practice are combined in the classroom, and students interact with experienced entrepreneurs. The Severino Center for Technological Entrepreneurship is the focal point for both entrepreneurship scholarship and learning, and it serves as a bridge to the Rensselaer Incubator and Technology Park. Students participate in lectures and discussions, and events that include both the entire Rensselaer university community as well as professionals from successful start-ups and fast growth companies from the Tech Valley Region.

FACILITIES

Housing: Coed dorms, special housing for disabled students, fraternity/sorority housing, apartments for married students, apartments for single students, theme housing. 75% of campus accessible to physically disabled. **Special Academic Facilities/Equipment:** Shelnutt Art Gallery in the Student Union;The George M. Low Gallery (museum); Center for Terahertz Research; Nanoscale Science and Engineering Centers (NSEC); Center for Biotechnology and Interdisciplinary Studies; Gaerttner Linear Accelerator (LINAC) Laboratory; Hirsch Observatory; RPIdeaLab and Incubator Program (supports student business ventures); Rensselaer Technology Park; Darrin Fresh Water Institute at Lake George; Experimental Media and Performing Arts Center (EMPAC - under construction); Lighting Research Center; Social and Behavioral Research Laboratory; O.T. Swanson Multidisciplinary Laboratory; and other research centers and laboratories as described at www.rpi.edu/research/research_centers. html,Computational Center for Nanotechnology Innovations (CCNI); http://www.rpi.edu/dept/ess/greening/EECbooks.html **Computers:** 75% of classrooms, 75% of dorms, 100% of libraries, 75% of dining areas, 100% of student union, 75% of common outdoor areas have wireless network access. Students can register for classes online. Administrative functions (other than registration) can be performed online. Undergraduates are required to own a computer.

CAMPUS LIFE

Environment: City. **Activities:** Choral groups, concert band, dance, drama/theater, jazz band, literary magazine, music ensembles, musical theater, pep band, radio station, student government, student newspaper, student-run film society, symphony orchestra, television station, yearbook, Campus Ministries, International Student Organization 177 registered organizations, 40 honor societies, 11 religious organizations. 32 fraternities, 5 sororities. **Athletics (Intercollegiate):** *Men:* baseball, basketball, cross-country, diving, football, golf, ice hockey, lacrosse, soccer, swimming, tennis, track/field (outdoor), track/field (indoor). *Women:* basketball, cross-country, diving, field hockey, ice hockey, lacrosse, soccer, softball, swimming, tennis, track/field (outdoor), track/field (indoor). **On-Campus Highlights:** Rensselaer Union, Mueller Fitness Center, Experimental Media & Performing Arts Ctr, Houston Field House (hockey arena), ECAV, Quiet and parklike, yet full of all the conveniences of a self-con-

tained city, Rensselaer's 275-acre campus is a blend of modern style and classic charm. The Institute is in a period of tremendous growth, building new facilities that greatly enhance the lives of our students and faculty. **Environmental Initiatives:** Student Sustainability Task Force Energy Conservation Program Purchase of Wind Certificates Sustainability Initiatives in New Construction.

ADMISSIONS

Freshman Academic Profile: 66% in top 10% of high school class, 95% in top 25% of high school class, 99% in top 50% of high school class. 77% from public high schools. SAT Math middle 50% range 660-760. SAT Critical Reading middle 50% range 610-700. ACT middle 50% range 26-31. Minimum web-based TOEFL 88. Minimum paper TOEFL 570. **Basis for Candidate Selection:** *Very important factors considered include:* Class rank, academic GPA, rigor of secondary school record, standardized test scores. *Important factors considered include:* application essay, recommendation(s), character/personal qualities, extracurricular activities, level of applicant's interest. *Other factors considered include:* alumni/ae relation, geographical residence, interview, racial/ethnic status, talent/ability, volunteer work, work experience. **Freshman Admission Requirements:** High school diploma is required and GED is accepted. *Academic units required:* 4 English, 4 mathematics, 3 science, 2 social studies. *Academic units recommended:* 4 English, 4 mathematics, 3 science, 2 social studies. **Freshman Admission Statistics:** 15,222 applied, 44% admitted, 20% enrolled. **Transfer Admission Requirements:** college transcript(s), statement of good standing from prior institution(s). Minimum college GPA of 3.0 required. Lowest grade transferable C. **General Admission Information:** Application Fee $70. Early decision application deadline 11/2. Regular application deadline 1/15. Regular notification 3/13. Nonfall registration accepted. Admission may be deferred for a maximum of 1 year. Credit and/or placement offered for CEEB Advanced Placement tests.

COSTS AND FINANCIAL AID

Annual tuition $43,350. Room and board $12,450. Required fees $1,125. Average book expense $2,545. **Required Forms and Deadlines:** FAFSA, CSS/Financial Aid PROFILE. **Notification of Awards:** Applicants will be notified of awards on or about 3/25. **Types of Aid:** *Need-based scholarships/grants:* Federal Pell, SEOG, state scholarships/grants, private scholarships, the school's own gift aid, Gates Millennium Scholarship, ACG, Smart Grants. *Loans:* Subsidized Stafford, Unsubsidized Stafford, PLUS, Federal Perkins, state loans, college/university loans from institutional funds. **Student Employment:** Federal Work-Study Program available. Institutional employment available. Highest amount earned per year from on-campus jobs $2,000. Off-campus job opportunities are good. **Financial Aid Statistics:** 100% freshmen, 100% undergrads receive need-based scholarship or grant aid. 23% freshmen, 12% undergrads receive non-need-based scholarship or grant aid. 99% freshmen, 96% undergrads receive need-based self-help aid. 1% freshmen, 1% undergrads receive athletic scholarships. 95% freshmen, 95% undergrads receive any aid. 68% undergrads borrow to pay for school. Average cumulative indebtedness $31,000. **Criteria for awarding institutional aid:** *Non-need-based:* academics, alumni affiliation, art, athletics, leadership, minority status, music/drama.

RHODE ISLAND SCHOOL OF DESIGN

2 College Street, Providence, RI 2903
Phone: 401-454-6300 • **Financial Aid Phone:** 401-454-6661
E-mail: admissions@risd.edu • **CEEB Code:** 3726
Fax: 401-454-6309 • **Website:** www.risd.edu • **ACT Code:** 3812

This private school was founded in 1877. It has a 13-acre campus.

RATINGS

Admissions Selectivity Rating: 96   **Fire Safety Rating:** 60*   **Green Rating:** 60*

STUDENTS AND FACULTY

Enrollment: 1,971. **Student Body:** 70% out-of-state, 21% international (55 countries represented). Asian 18%, African American 2%, Caucasian 34%, Hispanic 7%, Native American 0%.
Faculty: Student/faculty ratio 9:1. 147 full-time faculty, 10% are members of minority groups, 44% are women.

ACADEMICS

Degrees: bachelor's, master's. **Majors with Highest Enrollment:** graphic design; illustration; industrial design. **Special Study Options:** cross-registration, exchange student program (domestic), independent study, internships, study abroad, Continuing Education program. 6-week precollege summer program for secondary school students. summer workshops for undergraduate credit. 6 week winter session study abroad courses. **Disability Services:** Special programs offered to physically disabled students include note-taking services, reader services, tape recorders.

FACILITIES

Housing: Coed dorms, apartments for single students. **Special Academic Facilities/Equipment:** Art museum with over 45 galleries, extensive facilities for glassblowing, metalsmithing, lithography, sculpture, painting, and other art disciplines, nature lab. **Computers:** Administrative functions (other than registration) can be performed online.

CAMPUS LIFE

Environment: City. **Activities:** drama/theater, literary magazine, student government, student newspaper, student-run film society, yearbook 35 registered organizations, 5 religious organizations. **On-Campus Highlights:** The RISD Museum, The Edna Lawrence Nature Lab, Metcalf 3 dimensional fine art building, 161 S. Main St. - Industrial Design Building, RISD Works.

ADMISSIONS

Freshman Academic Profile: Average high school GPA 3.5. 28% in top 10% of high school class, 54% in top 25% of high school class, 91% in top 50% of high school class. 60% from public high schools. SAT Math middle 50% range 570-690. SAT Critical Reading middle 50% range 550-670. SAT Writing middle 50% range 560-680. Minimum web-based TOEFL 93. Minimum paper TOEFL 580. **Basis for Candidate Selection:** *Very important factors considered include:* rigor of secondary school record, talent/ability. *Important factors considered include:* application essay, recommendation(s), standardized test scores, character/personal qualities. *Other factors considered include:* Class rank, alumni/ae relation, extracurricular activities, racial/ethnic status, volunteer work, work experience. **Freshman Admission Requirements:** High school diploma is required and GED is accepted. **Freshman Admission Statistics:** 3,113 applied, 25% admitted, 55% enrolled. **Transfer Admission Requirements:** college transcript(s), essay or personal statement, Lowest grade transferable C. **General Admission Information:** Application Fee $50. Regular application deadline 2/15. Regular notification 4/1. Nonfall registration accepted. Admission may be deferred for a maximum of 1 year. Credit and/or placement offered for CEEB Advanced Placement tests.

COSTS AND FINANCIAL AID

Annual tuition $41,022. Room and board $11,980. Required fees $310. Average book expense $2,781. **Required Forms and Deadlines:** FAFSA, CSS/Financial Aid PROFILE. **Notification of Awards:** Applicants will be notified of awards on or about 4/1. **Types of Aid:** *Need-based scholarships/grants:* Federal Pell, SEOG, state scholarships/grants, private scholarships, the school's own gift aid. *Loans:* Subsidized Stafford, Unsubsidized Stafford, PLUS, Federal Perkins. **Student Employment:** Federal Work-Study Program available. Institutional employment available. Highest amount earned per year from on-campus jobs $1,100. Off-campus job opportunities are good. **Financial Aid Statistics:** 66% freshmen, 95% undergrads receive need-based scholarship or grant aid. 3% freshmen, 2% undergrads receive non-need-based scholarship or grant aid. 66% freshmen, 86% undergrads receive need-based self-help aid. 32% freshmen, 41% undergrads receive any aid. 60% undergrads borrow to pay for school. Average cumulative indebtedness $32,207. **Criteria for awarding institutional aid:** *Non-need-based:* academics, art.

RHODES COLLEGE

2000 North Parkway, Memphis, TN 38112
Phone: 901-843-3700 • **Financial Aid Phone:** 901-843-3810
E-mail: adminfo@rhodes.edu • **CEEB Code:** 1730
Fax: 901-843-3631 • **Website:** www.rhodes.edu • **ACT Code:** 4008

This private school, affiliated with the Presbyterian Church, was founded in 1848. It has a 100-acre campus.

RATINGS

Admissions Selectivity Rating: 93   **Fire Safety Rating:** 76   **Green Rating:** 78

STUDENTS AND FACULTY

Enrollment: 1,887. **Student Body:** 59% female, 41% male, 73% out-of-state, 3% international (19 countries represented). Asian 6%, African American 6%, Caucasian 74%, Hispanic 3%, Native American 1%. **Retention and Graduation:** 90% freshmen return for sophomore year. 80% freshmen graduate within 4 years. 36% grads go on to further study within 1 year. **Faculty:** Student/faculty ratio 10:1. 171 full-time faculty, 98% hold PhDs, 15% are members of minority groups, 46% are women. 0% of classes are taught by teaching assistants.

ACADEMICS

Degrees: bachelor's, master's. **Classes:** Most classes have 10–19 students. Most lab/discussion sessions have 10–19 students. **Majors with Highest Enrollment:** biology/biological sciences; business/commerce; English language and literature. **Special Study Options:** cooperative education program, cross-registration, double major, dual enrollment, exchange student program (domestic), honors program, independent study, internships, liberal arts/career combination, student-designed major, study abroad, duel degree: Master of Education; Master of Science in Nursing; Master of Science in Biomedical Engineering. **Honors Programs:** The Honors program is a culminating experience in the major field, for seniors only. It is the principal means whereby a student may do more independent, intensive, and individual work than can be done in the regular degree programs. The Honors work offers an excellent introduction to graduate study as it employs the full resources of library and laboratory and encourages independent research and study. Honors is available in most majors. **Combined Degree Programs:** BA/MEd, BA/MSN, BS/MS Biomed Engineering. **Disability Services:** Special programs offered to physically disabled students include note-taking services, reader services, tape recorders, tutors. **Career Services:** Alumni network, alumni services, career/job search classes, career assessment, internships, regional alumni. Career Services highlights include The Rhodes St. Jude Summer Plus program typifies the integrated learning philosophy at Rhodes through which students take classroom skills into the community where they connect knowledge with practice and learn effective leadership through service, internships, international travel and research. The approach also assures that students return to the classroom with the discoveries, problem-solving skills, contextualization, engagement and motivation gained through their experiences. John Sexton '04 describes his experience this way: "I was able to maintain close personal relationships with Rhodes faculty--the kind of relationships a student would be unlikely to have at a larger, research-oriented school--and also access the world-class facilities and experts at St. Jude--the kinds of resources not generally available to students at small liberal arts colleges." Clearly the Summer Plus program at St. Jude Children's Research Hospital provides the best of both worlds for the Rhodes science major who is ready to commit to two summers and a good deal of the school year working at a research hospital world renowned for its development of treatments for life-threatening diseases of childhood. In this program aspiring physicians and biomedical researchers have a unique opportunity to participate in every phase of the process in which basic research is translated into therapeutic interventions from bench to bedside. The intense and sustained challenge of work in this extraordinary environment fosters both scientific curiosity and humanitarian concern.

FACILITIES

Housing: Coed dorms, men's dorms, women's dorms, apartments for single students, learning communities; Substance free; quiet study; restricted visitation; non-smoking; special interest townhouses. 90% of campus accessible to physically disabled. **Special Academic Facilities/Equipment:** 136,000 square foot library; Art gallery; archaeology lab; astronomy observation domes with 14 and 31.5 inch telescopes; machine and woodworking shops; scanning electron microscopes; cell culture lab; nuclear magnetic resonance instrument; gas chromatography systems; UV, X-ray, infrared, and atomic absorption spectrophotometers. **Computers:** 100% of classrooms, 100% of dorms, 100% of libraries, 100% of dining areas, 50% of common outdoor areas have wireless network access. Students can register for classes online. Administrative functions (other than registration) can be performed online.

CAMPUS LIFE

Environment: Metropolis. **Activities:** Choral groups, dance, drama/theater, jazz band, literary magazine, music ensembles, musical theater, pep band, radio station, student government, student newspaper, student-run film society, symphony orchestra, television station, yearbook, Campus Ministries, International Student Organization, Model UN 115 registered organizations, 14 honor societies, 8 religious organizations. 7 fraternities, 6 sororities. **Athletics (Intercollegiate):** *Men:* baseball, basketball, cross-country, football, golf, soccer, swimming, tennis, track/field (outdoor). *Women:* basketball, cross-country, field hockey, golf, soccer, softball, swimming, tennis, track/field (outdoor), volleyball. **On-Campus Highlights:** Barret Library (includes a Starbucks coffee shop), Burrow Center for Student Opportunity, Bryan Campus Life Center (home to the Ly, East Village (apartment-style dorms), McCoy Theater, The Burrow Center for Student Opportunity opened in Spring, 2008. It consolidates most student services under one roof, including a one-stop transaction center, enrolling and financing, student development and academic support, and out of class experiences. It also includes space for student organizations and is open to students 24x7. **Environmental Initiatives:** $500,000 Andrew W. Mellon Foundation grant to expand Environmental Studies initiatives through community partnerships comprehensive campus-wide recycling program centralized energy management system and Green Power Switch

ADMISSIONS

Freshman Academic Profile: Average high school GPA 3.8. 49% in top 10% of high school class, 78% in top 25% of high school class, 96% in top 50% of

high school class. 53% from public high schools. SAT Math middle 50% range 580-680. SAT Critical Reading middle 50% range 570-690. SAT Writing middle 50% range 560-680. ACT middle 50% range 26-31. Minimum paper TOEFL 550. **Basis for Candidate Selection:** *Very important factors considered include:* Class rank, academic GPA, rigor of secondary school record. *Important factors considered include:* application essay, recommendation(s), standardized test scores, alumni/ae relation, character/personal qualities, racial/ethnic status. *Other factors considered include:* extracurricular activities, first generation, geographical residence, interview, level of applicant's interest, state residency, talent/ability, volunteer work, work experience. **Freshman Admission Requirements:** High school diploma is required and GED is accepted. *Academic units required:* 4 English, 3 mathematics, 2 science, (2 science labs), 2 foreign language, 2 social studies, 3 academic electives. 4 English, 3 mathematics, 2 science, (2 science labs), 2 foreign language, 2 social studies, 3 academic electives. **Freshman Admission Statistics:** 4,138 applied, 55% admitted, 25% enrolled. **Transfer Admission Requirements:** High school transcript, college transcript(s), essay or personal statement, standardized test scores, statement of good standing from prior institution(s). Lowest grade transferable C–. **General Admission Information:** Application Fee $45. Early decision application deadline 11/1. Regular notification 4/1. Nonfall registration accepted. Admission may be deferred for a maximum of 1 year. Credit and/or placement offered for CEEB Advanced Placement tests.

COSTS AND FINANCIAL AID

Annual tuition $37,782. Room and board $9,504. Required fees $310. Average book expense $1,125. **Required Forms and Deadlines:** FAFSA, CSS/Financial Aid PROFILE, noncustodial PROFILE. **Types of Aid:** *Need-based scholarships/grants:* Federal Pell, SEOG, state scholarships/grants, private scholarships, the school's own gift aid. *Loans:* Direct Subsidized Stafford, Direct Unsubsidized Stafford, Direct PLUS, Subsidized Stafford, Unsubsidized Stafford, PLUS, Federal Perkins. **Student Employment:** Federal Work-Study Program available. Institutional employment available. Highest amount earned per year from on-campus jobs $5,140. Off-campus job opportunities are good. **Financial Aid Statistics:** 99% freshmen, 99% undergrads receive need-based scholarship or grant aid. 40% freshmen, 28% undergrads receive non-need-based scholarship or grant aid. 65% freshmen, 68% undergrads receive need-based self-help aid. 95% freshmen, 91% undergrads receive any aid. 44% undergrads borrow to pay for school. Average cumulative indebtedness $16,831. **Criteria for awarding institutional aid:** *Non-need-based:* academics, art, minority status, music/drama, religious affiliation.

RICE UNIVERSITY

Best 378

MS 17 PO Box 1892, Houston, TX 77251-1892
Phone: 713-348-7423 • **Financial Aid Phone:** 713-348-4958
E-mail: admi@rice.edu • **CEEB Code:** 6609
Fax: 713-348-5952 • **Website:** www.rice.edu • **ACT Code:** 4152

This private school was founded in 1912. It has a 300-acre campus.

RATINGS

Admissions Selectivity Rating: 98   **Fire Safety Rating:** 89   **Green Rating:** 75

STUDENTS AND FACULTY

Enrollment: 3,810. **Student Body:** 49% female, 51% male, 48% out-of-state, 10% international (51 countries represented). Asian 21%, African American 7%, Caucasian 41%, Hispanic 14%, Native American 0%.
Retention and Graduation: 84% freshmen graduate within 4 years. 92% freshmen graduate within 6 years. 48% grads go on to further study within 1 year. **Faculty:** Student/faculty ratio 6:1. 676 full-time faculty, 96% hold PhDs, 19% are members of minority groups, 30% are women. 8% of classes are taught by teaching assistants.

ACADEMICS

Degrees: bachelor's, master's. **Classes:** Most classes have 10–19 students. **Majors with Highest Enrollment:** biology/biological sciences; economics; psychology. **Special Study Options:** cross-registration, double major, dual enrollment, English as a Second Language (ESL), honors program, independent study, internships, liberal arts/career combination, student-designed major, study abroad, teacher certification program, 8 year guaranteed medical school program with The Baylor College of Medicine. **Honors Programs:** Honors Programs through individual departments. **Combined Degree Programs:** guar.med.school program with Baylor College of Med. **Disability Services:**

Special programs offered to physically disabled students include note-taking services, reader services, tape recorders. **Career Services:** Alumni network, alumni services, career/job search classes, career assessment, internships, regional alumni. Career Services highlights include We are most proud of our relationship with alumni and their support (in terms of professional advice as well as recruitment) of current undergraduate and graduate students.

FACILITIES

Housing: Coed dorms, special housing for disabled students, All undergraduate students are automatically assigned to one of nine (coed) residential colleges and keep affiliation regardless of whether they live on campus or not. 90% of campus accessible to physically disabled. **Special Academic Facilities/Equipment:** Art gallery, museum, media center, language labs, computer labs, civil engineering lab, observatory and NASA equipment for students in space physics courses. **Computers:** 100% of classrooms, 100% of dorms, 1000% of libraries, 100% of dining areas, 100% of student union, 5% of common outdoor areas have wireless network access. Students can register for classes online. Administrative functions (other than registration) can be performed online.

CAMPUS LIFE

Environment: Metropolis. **Activities:** Choral groups, concert band, dance, drama/theater, jazz band, literary magazine, marching band, music ensembles, musical theater, opera, pep band, radio station, student government, student newspaper, student-run film society, symphony orchestra, television station, yearbook, Campus Ministries, International Student Organization, Model UN 215 registered organizations, 11 honor societies, 14 religious organizations. **Athletics (Intercollegiate):** *Men:* baseball, basketball, cross-country, football, golf, tennis, track/field (outdoor), track/field (indoor). *Women:* basketball, cross-country, soccer, swimming, tennis, track/field (outdoor), track/field (indoor), volleyball. **On-Campus Highlights:** Rice Memorial Center, Baker Institute for Public Policy, Brochstein Pavilion (cafe), Shepherd School of Music, Reckling Park baseball stadium. **Environmental Initiatives:** 1. Green Building. At present, we have roughly 1,000,000 square feet of facilities on campus that are under construction that will receive some level of LEED certification, including the student dormitory Duncan College which is targeted for LEED-Gold. In addition, an off-campus child care center is pursuing LEED certification. Also, an off-campus graduate student apartment complex has been designed to LEED standards although it will not be formally submitted for certification. With this complex, we anticipate savings in energy of about 30% and water savings of 20%. Further, the complex was constructed in an area with excellent pedestrian access, and it includes extensive bicycle storage along with shuttle bus service to campus and to major nearby grocery stores. Our campus standard for on-campus LEED certification for new buildings is LEED-Silver as a minimum. The University has also enjoyed significant successes with construction waste recycling, with many of our largest projects to date logging diversion rates of 85-90% to recycling. 2. Energy Consumption and Prediction Reporting Application. Our campus energy managers have developed an application that provides in near real time a powerful building level energy consumption and predictive analysis tool that takes into account variations in weather. For a given building, we can accurately model what that building's energy consumption should be based on outdoor temperature, humidity, and past performance of the building. We then plot that versus actual consumption data from the meters. The difference between the two represents energy savings or losses. This tool allows us to see the immediate impact of energy conservation measures. To my knowledge, we are the only university with this capability to create our own weather-normalized predicted baselines. Our energy managers have partnered with Incuity Software to develop this tool into a campus energy management solution. Harvey Mudd College awarded this system with its first annual green engineering award in 2008. See http://www.incuity.com/HMC%20Award%20News%20Release.pdf 3. Green Cleaning. The custodians of our Facilities Engineering and Planning Department provide the cleaning services for all of our non-residential buildings. Almost all of the cleaning is achieved with hot water, vapor, or a single environmentally-friendly cleaning chemical called H2Orange2 by Envirox. Disposable cleaning rags have been replaced by microfiber cloths, and string mops have been replaced with microfiber flat mops. FE&P custodians can attend optional English language training classes on-campus during work hours, which earns them credit through Houston Community College. They also can enroll in optional computer training, and are offered cross-training opportunities for positions such as plumbers and administrative assistants. Most of our custodians work daytime shifts (which saves building energy and improves customer services, while also being family-friendly and safer), and they receive full employee benefits.

ADMISSIONS

Freshman Academic Profile: 90% in top 10% of high school class, 97% in top 25% of high school class, 100% in top 50% of high school class. % from public high schools. SAT Math middle 50% range 700-780. SAT Critical Reading middle 50% range 660-750. SAT Writing middle 50% range 660-760. ACT middle 50% range 30-34. Minimum web-based TOEFL 100. Minimum paper TOEFL 600. **Basis for Candidate Selection:** *Very important factors considered include:* Class rank, application essay, academic GPA, recommendation(s), rigor of secondary school record, standardized test scores, character/personal qualities, extracurricular activities, talent/ability. *Other factors considered include:* alumni/ae relation, first generation, geographical residence, interview, level of applicant's interest, racial/ethnic status, state residency, volunteer work, work experience. **Freshman Admission Requirements:** High school diploma or equivalent is not required. *Academic units required:* 4 English, 3 mathematics, 2 science, (2 science labs), 2 foreign language, 2 social studies, 3 academic electives. History = Social Studies. Nat SciandEng div require trig or adv math courses and both chem and physics. May subst. a 2nd yr of chem or bio for phys. *Academic units recommended:* 4 English, 3 mathematics, 2 science, (2 science labs), 2 foreign language, 2 social studies, 3 academic electives. History = Social Studies. Nat SciandEng div require trig or adv math courses and both chem and physics. May subst. a 2nd yr of chem or bio for phys. **Freshman Admission Statistics:** 15,133 applied, 17% admitted, 37% enrolled. **Transfer Admission Requirements:** High school transcript, college transcript(s), essay or personal statement, standardized test scores, statement of good standing from prior institution(s). Minimum college GPA of 3.2 required. Lowest grade transferable C–. **General Admission Information:** Application Fee $60. Early decision application deadline 11/1. Regular application deadline 1/2. Regular notification 4/1. Nonfall registration not accepted. Admission may be deferred for a maximum of 2 years. Credit and/or placement offered for CEEB Advanced Placement tests.

COSTS AND FINANCIAL AID

Annual tuition $36,610. Room and board $12,600. Required fees $682. Average book expense $800. **Required Forms and Deadlines:** FAFSA, CSS/Financial Aid PROFILE, noncustodial PROFILE, business/farm supplement. Tax returns and W-2s. **Notification of Awards:** Applicants will be notified of awards on a rolling basis beginning 4/1. **Types of Aid:** *Need-based scholarships/grants:* Federal Pell, SEOG, state scholarships/grants, private scholarships, the school's own gift aid. *Loans:* Subsidized Stafford, Unsubsidized Stafford, PLUS, Federal Perkins. **Student Employment:** Federal Work-Study Program available. Institutional employment available. Off-campus job opportunities are excellent. **Financial Aid Statistics:** 100% freshmen, 100% undergrads receive need-based scholarship or grant aid. 34% freshmen, 19% undergrads receive non-need-based scholarship or grant aid. 70% freshmen, 72% undergrads receive need-based self-help aid. 7% freshmen, 6% undergrads receive athletic scholarships. 66% freshmen, 64% undergrads receive any aid. 25% undergrads borrow to pay for school. Average cumulative indebtedness $18,133. **Criteria for awarding institutional aid:** *Non-need-based:* academics, art, athletics, leadership, minority status, music/drama, state/district residency.

THE RICHARD STOCKTON COLLEGE OF NEW JERSEY

101 Vera King Farris Drive, Galloway, NJ 08205-9441
Phone: 609-652-4261 • **Financial Aid Phone:** 609-652-4201
E-mail: admissions@stockton.edu • **CEEB Code:** 2889
Fax: 609-748-5541 • **Website:** www.stockton.edu • **ACT Code:**

This public school was founded in 1969. It has a 1600-acre campus.

RATINGS
Admissions Selectivity Rating: 83   **Fire Safety Rating:** 88   **Green Rating:** 84

STUDENTS AND FACULTY
Enrollment: 7,340. **Student Body:** 58% female, 42% male, 1% out-of-state, 0% international (5 countries represented). Asian 5%, African American 7%, Caucasian 75%, Hispanic 9%, Native American 0%.
Retention and Graduation: 84% freshmen return for sophomore year. 40% freshmen graduate within 4 years. 64% freshmen graduate within 6 years. 26% grads go on to further study within 1 year. 82% grads pursue arts and sciences degrees. 8% grads pursue law degrees. 5% grads pursue business degrees. **Faculty:** Student/faculty ratio 18:1. 284 full-time faculty, 96% hold PhDs, 24% are members of minority groups, 50% are women. 0% of classes are taught by teaching assistants.

ACADEMICS
Degrees: bachelor's, certificate, master's, post-bachelor's certificate, post-master's certificate. **Classes:** Most classes have 30–39 students. Most lab/discussion sessions have 10–19 students. **Majors with Highest Enrollment:** biology/biological sciences; business administration and management; psychology. **Special Study Options:** Accelerated program, distance learning, double major, English as a Second Language (ESL), honors program, independent study, internships, liberal arts/career combination, study abroad, teacher certification program, Dual degree bachelor's program in engineering with Rutger's University and New Jersey Institute of Technology, preceptorial advising, opportunities for specialized research, Washington Internship available, and Service-Learning.

Honors Programs: Stockton Honors Program **Combined Degree Programs:** BA/MD, BA/MA, BA/DDS, BA/MEng, BA/MA Criminal Justice, BS/PSM Environmental Science, BS/DPT. **Disability Services:** Special programs offered to physically disabled students include note-taking services, reader services, tape recorders, tutors. **Career Services:** Alumni network, alumni services, career/job search classes, career assessment, internships, regional alumni. We are proud of all of our programs, but we are proudest of our internship and experiential learning opportunities.

FACILITIES
Housing: Coed dorms, special housing for disabled students, apartments for single students, wellness housing, theme housing, academic units. Living/Learning Communities include themes of Diversity, Global Citizenship, Sustainability, and Wellness. 100% of campus accessible to physically disabled. **Special Academic Facilities/Equipment:** Observatory, Nacote Creek field station, Holocaust Resource Center. **Computers:** 100% of classrooms, 5% of dorms, 100% of libraries, 100% of dining areas, n/a% of student union, 10% of common outdoor areas have wireless network access. Students can register for classes online. Administrative functions (other than registration) can be performed online.

CAMPUS LIFE
Environment: Town. **Activities:** Choral groups, concert band, dance, drama/theater, literary magazine, music ensembles, musical theater, radio station, student government, student newspaper, television station, yearbook, Campus Ministries, International Student Organization 130 registered organizations, 6 honor societies, 5 religious organizations. 11 fraternities, 9 sororities. **Athletics (Intercollegiate):** *Men:* baseball, basketball, cheerleading, cross-country, lacrosse, soccer, track/field (outdoor), track/field (indoor). *Women:* basketball, cheerleading, crew/rowing, cross-country, field hockey, soccer, softball, tennis, track/field (outdoor), track/field (indoor), volleyball. **On-Campus Highlights:** Performing Arts Center, Library, Housing options, Osprey's Nest, Marine Field Station. **Environmental Initiatives:** Alternative Energy: A. Solar electrical generation: 1200 KW capacity arrays operating on campus. This includes rooftop installations and shade canopies over parking lots. An additional 700 KW is under construction, expected to be operational in June of 2012. B. The GEOTHERMAL PROJECT provides up to 1650 tons of cooling capacity and allows portions of the building to be heated and cooled using the same equipment. C. Solar hot water heating has been installed on the roof of the newest residential facility, which accommodates 390 students. THE RICHARD STOCKTON COLLEGE COASTAL RESEARCH CENTER, located on Nacote Creek in Port Republic, is housed at the College's Nacote Creek Marine and Environmental Science Field Station, which functions as a teaching and training facility for Stockton students. The CRC conducts about 20 research projects a year. The CRC is at the forefront of research groups at Richard Stockton College, and is a leader in coastal geoscience and resource studies in the Mid-Atlantic region. A Sustainability Living Learning Community supports residential students interested in and committed to sustainability. Faculty presents lectures, students engage in community service to protect the environment and staff provide additional learning opportunities and links to local, regional and national bodies of knowledge.

ADMISSIONS
Freshman Academic Profile: 23% in top 10% of high school class, 56% in top 25% of high school class, 96% in top 50% of high school class. 88% from public high schools. SAT Math middle 50% range 500-600. SAT Critical Reading middle 50% range 470-570. SAT Writing middle 50% range 470-570. ACT middle 50% range 19-21. Minimum web-based TOEFL 80. Minimum paper TOEFL 550. **Basis for Candidate Selection:** *Very important factors considered include:* Class rank, academic GPA, rigor of secondary school record. *Important factors considered include:* standardized test scores. *Other factors considered include:* application essay, recommendation(s), alumni/ae relation, character/personal qualities, extracurricular activities, level of applicant's interest, talent/ability, volunteer work, work experience. **Freshman Admission Requirements:** High school diploma is required and GED is accepted. *Academic units required:* 4 English, 3 mathematics, 2 science, (2 science labs), 2 social studies, 5 academic electives. *Academic units recommended:* 4 English, 3 mathematics, 2 science, (2 science labs), 2 social studies, 5 academic electives. **Freshman Admission Statistics:** 6,195 applied, 57% admitted, 28% enrolled. Minimum college GPA of 2.5 required. Lowest grade transferable C. **General Admission Information:** Application Fee $50. Regular application deadline 5/1. Notification on a rolling basis, beginning on or about 10/1. Nonfall registration accepted. Credit and/or placement offered for CEEB Advanced Placement tests.

COSTS AND FINANCIAL AID
Annual in-state tuition $7,717. Annual out-of-state tuition $13,923. Room and board $10,477. Required fees $4,246. Average book expense $1,486. **Required Forms and Deadlines:** FAFSA. **Notification of Awards:** Applicants will be notified of awards on a rolling basis beginning 4/1. **Types of Aid:** *Need-based scholarships/grants:* Federal Pell, SEOG, state scholarships/grants, the school's own gift aid. *Loans:* Direct Subsidized Stafford, Direct Unsubsidized Stafford,

Direct PLUS, Federal Perkins, state loans. **Student Employment:** Federal Work-Study Program available. Institutional employment available. Highest amount earned per year from on-campus jobs $1,643. Off-campus job opportunities are excellent. **Financial Aid Statistics:** 52% freshmen, 53% undergrads receive need-based scholarship or grant aid. 35% freshmen, 26% undergrads receive non-need-based scholarship or grant aid. 80% freshmen, 83% undergrads receive need-based self-help aid. 82% freshmen, 79% undergrads receive any aid. 74% undergrads borrow to pay for school. Average cumulative indebtedness $34,287. **Criteria for awarding institutional aid:** *Non-need-based:* academics, art, leadership, minority status, music/drama, state/district residency.

RICHMOND, THE AMERICAN INTERNATIONAL UNIVERSITY IN LONDON

US Office of Admissions, Boston, MA 2210
Phone: 617-450-5617 • **Financial Aid Phone:** 011-44-20-8332-8244
E-mail: us_admissions@richmond.ac.uk • **CEEB Code:** 823
Fax: 617-450-5601 • **ACT Code:** 5244

This private school was founded in 1972. It has a 6-acre campus.

RATINGS
Admissions Selectivity Rating: 88   **Fire Safety Rating:** 64   **Green Rating:** 60*

STUDENTS AND FACULTY
Enrollment: 906. **Student Body:** 51% female, 49% male, 0% international **Retention and Graduation:** 72% freshmen return for sophomore year. 35% grads go on to further study within 1 year. **Faculty:** Student/faculty ratio 12:1. 41 full-time faculty, 85% hold PhDs, % are members of minority groups, 39% are women. 0% of classes are taught by teaching assistants.

ACADEMICS
Degrees: associate, bachelor's, master's, post-bachelor's certificate, terminal associate. **Classes:** Most classes have 10–19 students. **Majors with Highest Enrollment:** business/commerce; international relations and affairs. **Special Study Options:** English as a Second Language (ESL), independent study, internships, liberal arts/career combination, study abroad, Joint Engineering program with George Washington University.

FACILITIES
Housing: Coed dorms, men's dorms, women's dorms. **Computers:** Administrative functions (other than registration) can be performed online.

CAMPUS LIFE
Environment: Metropolis. **Activities:** Choral groups, dance, drama/theater, literary magazine, music ensembles, musical theater, student government, student newspaper, yearbook 1 honor societies. **Athletics (Intercollegiate):** *Men:* rugby, soccer. *Women:* rugby. **On-Campus Highlights:** Caffe del Mondo Gourmet Coffee Shop, Wireless Computer Network, Student Common Room, Student Cafeteria.

ADMISSIONS
Freshman Academic Profile: Average high school GPA 3.3. 29% in top 10% of high school class, 40% in top 25% of high school class, 94% in top 50% of high school class. 60% from public high schools. SAT Math middle 50% range 488-610. SAT Critical Reading middle 50% range 495-625. ACT middle 50% range 24-28. Minimum paper TOEFL 550. **Basis for Candidate Selection:** *Very important factors considered include:* application essay, academic GPA, recommendation(s), rigor of secondary school record. *Important factors considered include:* extracurricular activities. *Other factors considered include:* standardized test scores, alumni/ae relation, character/personal qualities, interview, talent/ability. **Freshman Admission Requirements:** High school diploma is required and GED is accepted. *Academic units required:* 4 English, 3 mathematics, 3 science. 4 English, 3 mathematics, 3 science. **Freshman Admission Statistics:** 1,232 applied, 52% admitted, 32% enrolled. **Transfer Admission Requirements:** college transcript(s), essay or personal statement, statement of good standing from prior institution(s). Minimum college GPA of 2.5 required. Lowest grade transferable C. **General Admission Information:** Application Fee $50. Regular application deadline 8/1. Notification on a rolling basis, beginning on or about 11/1. Nonfall registration accepted. Admission may be deferred for a maximum of 1 year. Credit and/or placement offered for CEEB Advanced Placement tests.

COSTS AND FINANCIAL AID
Annual tuition $27,000. Room and board $12,900. Average book expense $1,000. **Required Forms and Deadlines:** FAFSA. **Notification of Awards:** Applicants will be notified of awards on or about 3/15. **Types of Aid:** *Need-based scholarships/grants:* private scholarships, the school's own gift aid. *Loans:*

Subsidized Stafford, Unsubsidized Stafford, PLUS, college/university loans from institutional funds. **Student Employment:** Highest amount earned per year from on-campus jobs $1,500. Off-campus job opportunities are good. **Financial Aid Statistics:** 80% freshmen, 70% undergrads receive any aid. 30% undergrads borrow to pay for school. Average cumulative indebtedness $22,000. **Criteria for awarding institutional aid:** *Non-need-based:* academics.

RIDER UNIVERSITY

2083 Lawrenceville Road, Lawrenceville, NJ 08648-3099
Phone: 609-896-5042 • **Financial Aid Phone:** 609-896-5360
E-mail: admissions@rider.edu • **CEEB Code:** 2758
Fax: 609-895-6645 • **Website:** www.rider.edu • **ACT Code:** 2590

This private school was founded in 1865. It has a 280-acre campus.

RATINGS
Admissions Selectivity Rating: 73   **Fire Safety Rating:** 75   **Green Rating:** 94

STUDENTS AND FACULTY
Enrollment: 4,409. **Student Body:** 58% female, 42% male, 22% out-of-state, 2% international (64 countries represented). Asian 4%, African American 10%, Caucasian 66%, Hispanic 9%, Native American 0%. **Retention and Graduation:** 77% freshmen return for sophomore year. 57% freshmen graduate within 4 years. 67% freshmen graduate within 6 years. 23% grads go on to further study within 1 year. 4% grads pursue arts and sciences degrees. 2% grads pursue law degrees. 4% grads pursue business degrees. 2% grads pursue medical degrees. **Faculty:** Student/faculty ratio 12:1. 257 full-time faculty, 98% hold PhDs, 16% are members of minority groups, 44% are women. 0% of classes are taught by teaching assistants.

ACADEMICS
Degrees: associate, bachelor's, master's, post-master's certificate. **Classes:** Most classes have 10–19 students. Most lab/discussion sessions have 10–19 students. **Majors with Highest Enrollment:** accounting; business/commerce, elementary education and teaching. **Special Study Options:** cooperative education program, cross-registration, distance learning, double major, honors program, independent study, internships, liberal arts/career combination, study abroad, teacher certification program, weekend college, Learning Communities. **Honors Programs:** The Baccalaureate Honors Program is designed to enrich the educational opportunities for Rider students of proven intellectual capability who choose to become Baccalaureate Scholars. Through a series of team-taught seminars, small classes, personal contact with faculty, colloquia and symposia, as well as independent study opportunities, the scholars extend their ability to think critically, coherently, and systematically about the great themes, ideals and movements of their human heritage. Students may apply, or be invited, as entering freshmen, as currently enrolled freshmen or sophomores, or as transfer freshmen or sophomores. To be considered for the program incoming freshmen must be in the top 10 percent of their high school class. **Combined Degree Programs:** BS/BA. **Disability Services:** Special programs offered to physically disabled students include reader services, tape recorders, tutors. **Career Services:** Alumni network, alumni services, internships.

FACILITIES
Housing: Coed dorms, special housing for disabled students, women's dorms, fraternity/sorority housing, apartments for single students, Suites, Special interest areas: Wellness, Quite, First Year Experience, Science, Learning Community. 73% of campus accessible to physically disabled. **Special Academic Facilities/Equipment:** Art gallery, Holocaust/Genocide Resource Center **Computers:** Students can register for classes online. Administrative functions (other than registration) can be performed online.

CAMPUS LIFE
Environment: Village. **Activities:** Choral groups, concert band, dance, drama/theater, literary magazine, music ensembles, musical theater, opera, pep band, radio station, student government, student newspaper, student-run film society, television station, yearbook, Campus Ministries, International Student Organization, Model UN 84 registered organizations, 24 honor societies, 6 religious organizations. 4 fraternities, 8 sororities. **Athletics (Intercollegiate):** *Men:* baseball, basketball, cheerleading, cross-country, diving, golf, soccer, swimming, tennis, track/field (outdoor), wrestling. *Women:* basketball, cheerleading, cross-country, diving, field hockey, soccer, softball, swimming, tennis, track/field (outdoor), volleyball. **On-Campus Highlights:** Residence Hall Quad, Alumni Gym, Student Recreation Center, Daly's Dining Hall/Cranberry Cafe, Academic

Quad. **Environmental Initiatives:** Signing the American College & University Presidents Climate Commitment and formation of the Energy and Sustainability Steering Committee in 2007 to implement strategic plan establishing sustainability initiatives for the university. Completion of a Greenhouse Gas Inventory for 2007-2008 and 2008-2009 and completion of a Carbon Neutrality Plan in 2010. Development of a student Eco-Rep program and currently employing 10 students. Building Silver LEED Certified new residence hall.

ADMISSIONS

Freshman Academic Profile: Average high school GPA 3.3. 20% in top 10% of high school class, 52% in top 25% of high school class, 86% in top 50% of high school class. SAT Math middle 50% range 470-570. SAT Critical Reading middle 50% range 460-560. SAT Writing middle 50% range 460-570. ACT middle 50% range 20-25. Minimum web-based TOEFL 80. Minimum paper TOEFL 550. **Basis for Candidate Selection:** *Very important factors considered include:* application essay, academic GPA, recommendation(s), rigor of secondary school record, standardized test scores. *Important factors considered include:* level of applicant's interest. *Other factors considered include:* Class rank, alumni/ae relation, character/personal qualities, extracurricular activities, geographical residence, interview, state residency, talent/ability, volunteer work, work experience. **Freshman Admission Requirements:** High school diploma is required and GED is accepted. *Academic units required:* 4 English, 3 mathematics. *Academic units recommended:* 4 English, 3 mathematics. **Freshman Admission Statistics:** 7,903 applied, 72% admitted, 16% enrolled. **Transfer Admission Requirements:** college transcript(s), essay or personal statement, minimum college GPA of 2.5 required. Lowest grade transferable C. **General Admission Information:** Application Fee $50. Early decision application deadline 11/15. Notification on a rolling basis, beginning on or about 12/15. Nonfall registration accepted. Admission may be deferred for a maximum of 1 year. Credit and/or placement offered for CEEB Advanced Placement tests.

COSTS AND FINANCIAL AID

Annual tuition $32,820. Room and board $12,340. Required fees $600. Average book expense $1,500. **Required Forms and Deadlines:** FAFSA. **Notification of Awards:** Applicants will be notified of awards on a rolling basis beginning 2/20. **Types of Aid:** *Need-based scholarships/grants:* Federal Pell, SEOG, state scholarships/grants, private scholarships, the school's own gift aid. *Loans:* Subsidized Stafford, Unsubsidized Stafford, PLUS, Federal Perkins, state loans, college/university loans from institutional funds. **Student Employment:** Federal Work-Study Program available. Institutional employment available. Highest amount earned per year from on-campus jobs $6,195. Off-campus job opportunities are good. **Financial Aid Statistics:** 99% freshmen, 98% undergrads receive need-based scholarship or grant aid. 15% freshmen, 14% undergrads receive non-need-based scholarship or grant aid. 84% freshmen, 85% undergrads receive need-based self-help aid. 7% freshmen, 6% undergrads receive athletic scholarships. 78% freshmen, 66% undergrads receive any aid. 75% undergrads borrow to pay for school. Average cumulative indebtedness $32,718. **Criteria for awarding institutional aid:** *Non-need-based:* academics, alumni affiliation, athletics, leadership, minority status, music/drama, state/district residency.

RINGLING SCHOOL OF ART & DESIGN

2700 N. Tamiami Trail, Sarasota, FL 34234-5895
Phone: 941-351-5100 • **Financial Aid Phone:** 941-359-7534
E-mail: admissions@ringling.edu • **CEEB Code:** 5573
Fax: 941-359-7517 • **Website:** www.ringling.edu • **ACT Code:** 6724

This private school was founded in 1931. It has a 49-acre campus.

RATINGS

Admissions Selectivity Rating: 62   **Fire Safety Rating:** 85   **Green Rating:** 68

STUDENTS AND FACULTY

Enrollment: 1,364. **Student Body:** 61% female, 39% male, 46% out-of-state, 11% international (53 countries represented). Asian 7%, African American 3%, Caucasian 61%, Hispanic 14%, Native American 0%.
Retention and Graduation: 79% freshmen return for sophomore year. 53% freshmen graduate within 4 years. 65% freshmen graduate within 6 years. 3% grads go on to further study within 1 year. 3% grads pursue arts and sciences degrees. **Faculty:** Student/faculty ratio 12:1. 92 full-time faculty, 60% hold PhDs, 5% are members of minority groups, 30% are women. 0% of classes are taught by teaching assistants.

ACADEMICS

Degrees: bachelor's, certificate. **Classes:** Most classes have 10–19 students. **Majors with Highest Enrollment:** animation, interactive technology, video graphics and special effects; graphic design; illustration. **Special Study Options:** dual enrollment, exchange student program (domestic), independent

study, internships, study abroad. **Disability Services:** Special programs offered to physically disabled students include note-taking services, reader services, tape recorders, tutors. **Career Services:** Alumni network, alumni services, career/job search classes, career assessment, internships, regional alumni. Career Services highlights include Career/job search classes '– direct approach to students on areas of interest, review of core approaches and resources Alumni services '– helping those who graduated, who, in turn, help us with recruiting, posting jobs, etc. Regional alumni '– help us with conference, workshops, visits to classes Alumni network '– same as above Internships '– growing opportunities especially in new majors and increasing success as full-time employees by those who interned at the company Career assessment '– help students (few) who need to determine best major for their goals.

FACILITIES

Housing: Coed dorms, men's dorms, women's dorms, apartments for married students, apartments for single students, wellness housing. All housing accommodations are ADA compliant. 98% of campus accessible to physically disabled. **Special Academic Facilities/Equipment:** William G. and Marie Selby Gallery, Crossley Gallery, Verman Kimbrough Memorial Library **Computers:** 60% of classrooms, 100% of dorms, 100% of libraries, 100% of dining areas, 100% of student union, 60% of common outdoor areas have wireless network access. Students can register for classes online. Administrative functions (other than registration) can be performed online.

CAMPUS LIFE

Environment: City. **Activities:** dance, drama/theater, student government, Campus Ministries, International Student Organization 22 registered organizations, 2 religious organizations. **On-Campus Highlights:** Student Center, Selby Gallery, Crossley Gallery, Verman Kimbrough Memorial Library, Hammond Commons. **Environmental Initiatives:** In 2009, the College completed the construction of two 80,000 sq.ft. LEED Gold certified buildings. A residence hall houses 228 students and the other building will increase the academic teaching space on campus. The College employs a Director of Environmental Health and Safety to develop, manage and enforce the environmental management system. An environmental audit has been completed on the academic departments and the support services. The College is currently setting up a sustainability working group to instigate a sustainability initiative for the community.

ADMISSIONS

Freshman Academic Profile: Average high school GPA 3.1. Minimum web-based TOEFL 61. Minimum paper TOEFL 500. **Basis for Candidate Selection:** *Very important factors considered include:* academic GPA, rigor of secondary school record, talent/ability. *Important factors considered include:* application essay, recommendation(s). *Other factors considered include:* alumni/ae relation, extracurricular activities, geographical residence, interview, level of applicant's interest, volunteer work, work experience. **Freshman Admission Requirements:** High school diploma is required and GED is accepted. **Freshman Admission Statistics:** 1,255 applied, 75% admitted, 33% enrolled. **Transfer Admission Requirements:** High school transcript, college transcript(s), essay or personal statement, minimum college GPA of 2.0 required. Lowest grade transferable C. **General Admission Information:** Application Fee $70. Notification on a rolling basis, beginning on or about 9/1. Nonfall registration not accepted. Admission may be deferred for a maximum of 2 years. Credit and/or placement offered for CEEB Advanced Placement tests.

COSTS AND FINANCIAL AID

Annual tuition $33,960. Room and board $11,750. Required fees $920. Average book expense $2,700. **Required Forms and Deadlines:** FAFSA. **Notification of Awards:** Applicants will be notified of awards on a rolling basis beginning 4/1. **Types of Aid:** *Need-based scholarships/grants:* Federal Pell, SEOG, state scholarships/grants, private scholarships, the school's own gift aid. *Loans:* Subsidized Stafford, Unsubsidized Stafford, PLUS. **Student Employment:** Federal Work-Study Program available. Institutional employment available. Highest amount earned per year from on-campus jobs $5,894. Off-campus job opportunities are good. **Financial Aid Statistics:** 94% freshmen, 95% undergrads receive need-based scholarship or grant aid. 2% freshmen, 5% undergrads receive non-need-based scholarship or grant aid. 96% freshmen, 3% undergrads receive need-based self-help aid. 76% freshmen, 78% undergrads receive any aid. 73% undergrads borrow to pay for school. Average cumulative indebtedness $48,515. **Criteria for awarding institutional aid:** *Non-need-based:* academics, art.

RIPON COLLEGE

PO Box 248, Ripon, WI 54971
Phone: 920-748-8337 • **Financial Aid Phone:** 920-748-8301
E-mail: adminfo@ripon.edu • **CEEB Code:** 1664
Fax: 920-748-8335 • **Website:** www.ripon.edu • **ACT Code:** 4636

This private school was founded in 1851. It has a 250-acre campus.

RATINGS
Admissions Selectivity Rating: 75   **Fire Safety Rating:** 64   **Green Rating:** 68

STUDENTS AND FACULTY
Enrollment: 904. **Student Body:** 53% female, 47% male, 25% out-of-state, 3% international (12 countries represented). Asian 1%, African American 2%, Caucasian 85%, Hispanic 5%, Native American 1%.
Retention and Graduation: 86% freshmen return for sophomore year. 72% freshmen graduate within 6 years. 33% grads go on to further study within 1 year. 17% grads pursue arts and sciences degrees. 1% grads pursue law degrees. 3% grads pursue business degrees. 9% grads pursue medical degrees. **Faculty:** Student/faculty ratio 11:1. 67 full-time faculty, 96% hold PhDs, 9% are members of minority groups, 42% are women. 0% of classes are taught by teaching assistants.

ACADEMICS
Degrees: bachelor's. **Classes:** Most classes have 10-19 students. Most lab/discussion sessions have 10-19 students. **Majors with Highest Enrollment:** business/commerce; history; psychology. **Special Study Options:** double major, exchange student program (domestic), internships, student-designed major, study abroad, teacher certification program, Argonne Science Semester (Illinois). Newberry Library Program in the Humanities (Illinois). Urban Studies Program (Chicago). Wilderness Field Station Program (Minnesota). Other semester-away programs. **Disability Services:** Special programs offered to physically disabled students include tutors. **Career Services:** Alumni network, career assessment, internships, regional alumni.

FACILITIES
Housing: Coed dorms, men's dorms, women's dorms, fraternity/sorority housing, apartments for single students. **Special Academic Facilities/Equipment:** Art gallery, language labs. **Computers:** 2% of classrooms, 30% of libraries, 100% of dining areas, 60% of student union, have wireless network access.

CAMPUS LIFE
Environment: Village. **Activities:** Choral groups, concert band, dance, drama/theater, jazz band, literary magazine, music ensembles, musical theater, radio station, student government, student newspaper, symphony orchestra, yearbook, Campus Ministries, International Student Organization 45 registered organizations, 13 honor societies, 2 religious organizations. 5 fraternities, 3 sororities. **Athletics (Intercollegiate):** *Men:* baseball, basketball, cross-country, cycling, football, golf, soccer, swimming, tennis, track/field (outdoor), track/field (indoor). *Women:* basketball, cross country, cycling, golf, soccer, softball, swimming, tennis, track/field (outdoor), track/field (indoor), volleyball. **On-Campus Highlights:** Ceresco Prairie Conservancy, Art Gallery, Storzer Athletic Center, Lane Library.

ADMISSIONS
Freshman Academic Profile: Average high school GPA 3.4. 26% in top 10% of high school class, 50% in top 25% of high school class, 82% in top 50% of high school class. 75% from public high schools. SAT Math middle 50% range 530-630. SAT Critical Reading middle 50% range 500-610. ACT middle 50% range 21-27. Minimum web-based TOEFL 79. Minimum paper TOEFL 550. **Basis for Candidate Selection:** *Very important factors considered include:* rigor of secondary school record, interview. *Important factors considered include:* Class rank, academic GPA, recommendation(s), standardized test scores, character/personal qualities, extracurricular activities. *Other factors considered include:* application essay, talent/ability, volunteer work. **Freshman Admission Requirements:** High school diploma is required and GED is accepted. *Academic units required:* 4 English, 2 mathematics, 2 science, 2 social studies. *Academic units recommended:* 4 English, 2 mathematics, 2 science, 2 social studies. **Freshman Admission Statistics:** 1,046 applied, 78% admitted, 25% enrolled. **Transfer Admission Requirements:** college transcript(s), essay or personal statement, statement of good standing from prior institution(s). Minimum college GPA of 2.0 required. Lowest grade transferable C. **General Admission Information:** Application Fee $30. Notification on a rolling basis,

beginning on or about 9/15. Nonfall registration accepted. Admission may be deferred for a maximum of 1 year. Credit and/or placement offered for CEEB Advanced Placement tests.

COSTS AND FINANCIAL AID
Annual tuition $29,835. Room and board $8,545. Required fees $275. Average book expense $750. **Required Forms and Deadlines:** FAFSA. **Notification of Awards:** Applicants will be notified of awards on a rolling basis beginning 3/1. **Types of Aid:** *Need-based scholarships/grants:* Federal Pell, SEOG, state scholarships/grants, private scholarships, the school's own gift aid. *Loans:* Subsidized Stafford, Unsubsidized Stafford, PLUS, Federal Perkins. **Student Employment:** Federal Work-Study Program available. Institutional employment available. Highest amount earned per year from on-campus jobs $1,200. Off-campus job opportunities are good. **Financial Aid Statistics:** 100% freshmen, 99% undergrads receive need-based scholarship or grant aid. 8% freshmen, 10% undergrads receive non-need-based scholarship or grant aid. 93% freshmen, 89% undergrads receive need-based self-help aid. 95% freshmen, 96% undergrads receive any aid. 82% undergrads borrow to pay for school. Average cumulative indebtedness $32,511. **Criteria for awarding institutional aid:** *Non-need-based:* academics, alumni affiliation, art, leadership, minority status, music/drama, religious affiliation, state/district residency.

See page 1186.

RIVIER COLLEGE

420 South Main Street, Nashua, NH 3060
Phone: 603-897-8219 • **Financial Aid Phone:** 603-897-8810
E-mail: rivadmit@rivier.edu • **CEEB Code:** 3728
Fax: 603-891-1799 • **Website:** www.rivier.edu • **ACT Code:** 2520

This private school, affiliated with the Roman Catholic Church, was founded in 1933. It has a 68-acre campus.

RATINGS
Admissions Selectivity Rating: 67   **Fire Safety Rating:** 82   **Green Rating:** 60*

STUDENTS AND FACULTY
Enrollment: 1,370. **Student Body:** 85% female, 15% male, 38% out-of-state, 0% international (12 countries represented). Asian 2%, African American 2%, Caucasian 75%, Hispanic 5%, Native American 1%.
Retention and Graduation: 78% freshmen return for sophomore year. 42% freshmen graduate within 4 years. 53% freshmen graduate within 6 years. **Faculty:** Student/faculty ratio 17:1. 68 full-time faculty, 75% hold PhDs, 65% are women. 0% of classes are taught by teaching assistants.

ACADEMICS
Degrees: associate, bachelor's, certificate, doctoral, master's, post-bachelor's certificate, post-master's certificate. **Classes:** Most classes have 10-19 students. Most lab/discussion sessions have fewer than 10 students. **Special Study Options:** cross-registration, double major, honors program, independent study, internships, liberal arts/career combination, student-designed major, teacher certification program. **Combined Degree Programs:** BA/MA. **Disability Services:** Special programs offered to physically disabled students include note-taking services, reader services, tape recorders, tutors.

FACILITIES
Housing: Coed dorms, Coed wellness dorm (substance free). 75% of campus accessible to physically disabled. **Special Academic Facilities/Equipment:** Art gallery, Early Childhood Center/Laboratory School, language lab, TV microscope, video/laser disk system, photospectrometer, high-performance liquid chromatograph, digital imaging lab, several art studios including a photography darkroom. **Computers:** 100% of classrooms, 100% of dorms, 100% of libraries, 100% of dining areas, 100% of student union, 100% of common outdoor areas have wireless network access. Administrative functions (other than registration) can be performed online.

CAMPUS LIFE
Environment: City. **Activities:** Choral groups, dance, drama/theater, music ensembles, student government, student newspaper, television station, yearbook 30 registered organizations, 2 honor societies, 2 religious organizations. **Athletics (Intercollegiate):** *Men:* baseball, basketball, cross-country, soccer, volleyball. *Women:* basketball, cross-country, soccer, softball, volleyball.

ADMISSIONS
Freshman Academic Profile: Average high school GPA 3.0. 6% in top 10% of high school class, 27% in top 25% of high school class, 71% in top 50% of high school class. SAT Math middle 50% range 410-510. SAT Critical Reading middle 50% range 410-510. SAT Writing middle 50% range 420-520. ACT

middle 50% range 17-21. Minimum paper TOEFL 500. **Basis for Candidate Selection:** *Very important factors considered include:* academic GPA, rigor of secondary school record. *Important factors considered include:* Class rank, application essay, standardized test scores, extracurricular activities, talent/ability, volunteer work, work experience. *Other factors considered include:* recommendation(s), character/personal qualities, interview. **Freshman Admission Requirements:** High school diploma is required and GED is accepted. **Freshman Admission Statistics:** 665 applied, 82% admitted, 36% enrolled. **Transfer Admission Requirements:** essay or personal statement, minimum college GPA of 2.0 required. Lowest grade transferable C. **General Admission Information:** Application Fee $25. Notification on a rolling basis, beginning on or about 11/1. Nonfall registration not accepted. Admission may be deferred for a maximum of 1 year. Credit and/or placement offered for CEEB Advanced Placement tests.

COSTS AND FINANCIAL AID
Annual tuition $25,410. Room and board $9,798. Required fees $600. Average book expense $1,200. **Required Forms and Deadlines:** FAFSA. **Notification of Awards:** Applicants will be notified of awards on a rolling basis beginning 3/1. **Types of Aid:** *Need-based scholarships/grants:* Federal Pell, SEOG, state scholarships/grants, private scholarships, the school's own gift aid. *Loans:* Direct Subsidized Stafford, Direct Unsubsidized Stafford, Direct PLUS, Federal Perkins, college/university loans from institutional funds. **Student Employment:** Federal Work-Study Program available. Institutional employment available. Highest amount earned per year from on-campus jobs $4,500. Off-campus job opportunities are good. **Financial Aid Statistics:** 100% freshmen, 91% undergrads receive need-based scholarship or grant aid. 4% freshmen, 4% undergrads receive non-need-based scholarship or grant aid. 91% freshmen, 93% undergrads receive need-based self-help aid. 82% freshmen, 89% undergrads receive any aid. 84% undergrads borrow to pay for school. Average cumulative indebtedness $47,649. **Criteria for awarding institutional aid:** *Non-need-based:* academics, alumni affiliation, leadership.

ROANOKE BIBLE COLLEGE

715 N. Poindexter St., Elizabeth City, NC 27909-4054
Phone: 252-334-2028 • **Financial Aid Phone:** 252-334-2020
E-mail: admissions@roanokebible.edu
Fax: 252-334-2064 • **ACT Code:** 3153

This private school was founded in 1948. It has a 20-acre campus.

RATINGS
Admissions Selectivity Rating: 80   **Fire Safety Rating:** 66   **Green Rating:** 69

STUDENTS AND FACULTY
Student Body: (1 country represented).
Retention and Graduation: 36% freshmen graduate within 4 years. 58% freshmen graduate within 6 years. **Faculty:** Student/faculty ratio 10:1. 9 full-time faculty, 56% hold PhDs, 0% are members of minority groups, 33% are women. 0% of classes are taught by teaching assistants.

ACADEMICS
Degrees: associate, bachelor's, certificate. **Classes:** Most classes have fewer than 10 students. Most lab/discussion sessions have 10–19 students. **Majors with Highest Enrollment:** bible/biblical studies. **Special Study Options:** distance learning, double major, dual enrollment, internships, Cross-cultural semester abroad. **Disability Services:** Special programs offered to physically disabled students include tape recorders, tutors.

FACILITIES
Housing: special housing for disabled students, men's dorms, women's dorms, apartments for married students, apartments for single students. 90% of campus accessible to physically disabled. **Computers:** 80% of classrooms, 100% of libraries, have wireless network access.

CAMPUS LIFE
Environment: Village. **Activities:** Choral groups, drama/theater, music ensembles, musical theater, student government, yearbook 1 honor societies. **Athletics (Intercollegiate):** *Men:* basketball. *Women:* basketball, volleyball. **On-Campus Highlights:** On the Pasquotank River, New Married Housing apartments, New student life center **Environmental Initiatives:** Geothermal heating & cooling Solar hot water Recycle program

ADMISSIONS
Freshman Academic Profile: Average high school GPA 2.8. 2% in top 10% of high school class, 14% in top 25% of high school class, 37% in top 50% of high school class. 87% from public high schools. SAT Math middle 50%

range 420-590. SAT Critical Reading middle 50% range 410-565. Minimum web-based TOEFL 80. Minimum paper TOEFL 500. **Basis for Candidate Selection:** *Very important factors considered include:* Class rank, academic GPA, recommendation(s), standardized test scores, character/personal qualities, religious affiliation/commitment. *Important factors considered include:* application essay, rigor of secondary school record. *Other factors considered include:* extracurricular activities, interview, level of applicant's interest, talent/ability, volunteer work, work experience. **Freshman Admission Requirements:** High school diploma is required and GED is accepted. *Academic units required:* 4 English, 3 mathematics, 3 science, (2 science labs), 2 social studies, 2 history, 4 academic electives. *Academic units recommended:* 4 English, 3 mathematics, 3 science, (2 science labs), 2 social studies, 2 history, 4 academic electives. **Freshman Admission Statistics:** 127 applied, 56% admitted, 58% enrolled. **Transfer Admission Requirements:** college transcript(s), essay or personal statement, statement of good standing from prior institution(s). Minimum college GPA of 2.0 required. Lowest grade transferable C. **General Admission Information:** Application Fee $50. Notification on a rolling basis, beginning on or about 9/1. Nonfall registration accepted. Admission may be deferred for a maximum of 1 semester. Credit and/or placement offered for CEEB Advanced Placement tests.

COSTS AND FINANCIAL AID
Required Forms and Deadlines: FAFSA, institution's own financial aid form. **Notification of Awards:** Applicants will be notified of awards on a rolling basis beginning 5/1. **Types of Aid:** *Need-based scholarships/grants:* Federal Pell, SEOG, state scholarships/grants, private scholarships, the school's own gift aid. *Loans:* Subsidized Stafford, Unsubsidized Stafford, PLUS, Alternative Loans. **Student Employment:** Federal Work-Study Program available. Institutional employment available. Off-campus job opportunities are good. **Financial Aid Statistics:** 100% freshmen, 100% undergrads receive need-based scholarship or grant aid. 29% freshmen, 23% undergrads receive non-need-based scholarship or grant aid. 68% freshmen, 82% undergrads receive need-based self-help aid. 88% freshmen, 90% undergrads receive any aid. 80% undergrads borrow to pay for school. Average cumulative indebtedness $21,314. **Criteria for awarding institutional aid:** *Non-need-based:* academics, alumni affiliation, art, athletics, leadership, music/drama, religious affiliation.

ROANOKE COLLEGE

Best 378

221 College Lane, Salem, VA 24153-3794
Phone: 540-375-2270 • **Financial Aid Phone:** 540-375-2235
E-mail: admissions@roanoke.edu • **CEEB Code:** 5571
Fax: 540-375-2267 • **Website:** www.roanoke.edu • **ACT Code:** 4392

This private school, affiliated with the Lutheran Church, was founded in 1842. It has a 68-acre campus.

RATINGS
Admissions Selectivity Rating: 77   **Fire Safety Rating:** 78   **Green Rating:** 84

STUDENTS AND FACULTY
Enrollment: 2,010. **Student Body:** 58% female, 42% male, 46% out-of-state, 1% international (24 countries represented). Asian 1%, African American 5%, Caucasian 85%, Hispanic 4%, Native American 0%.
Retention and Graduation: 81% freshmen return for sophomore year. 57% freshmen graduate within 4 years. 65% freshmen graduate within 6 years. 28% grads go on to further study within 1 year. **Faculty:** Student/faculty ratio 11:1. 165 full-time faculty, 84% hold PhDs, 10% are members of minority groups, 49% are women. 0% of classes are taught by teaching assistants.

ACADEMICS
Degrees: bachelor's. **Classes:** Most classes have 10–19 students. Most lab/discussion sessions have 10–19 students. **Majors with Highest Enrollment:** business/commerce; history; psychology. **Special Study Options:** Accelerated program, cross-registration, double major, dual enrollment, English as a Second Language (ESL), honors program, independent study, internships, liberal arts/career combination, study abroad, teacher certification program. **Honors Programs:** The Honors Program is designed for students with excellent academic performance, broad extracurricular interests, and leadership abilities. The Honors Program substitutes a coordinated sequence of interdisciplinary courses for a portion of the core requirements. A Plenary Enrichment Program of supplemental activities, a special scholarship, and a distinct recognition on

the diploma and transcript are provided. **Disability Services:** Special programs offered to physically disabled students include note-taking services, reader services, tape recorders, tutors. **Career Services:** Alumni network, alumni services, career/job search classes, career assessment, internships, regional alumni. Career Services highlights include Alumni Networking, which is offered to both students and alumni. Roanoke alumni are very open to helping students and fellow graduates in the career development area.

FACILITIES

Housing: Coed dorms, men's dorms, women's dorms, fraternity/sorority housing, apartments for single students, theme housing. 85% of campus accessible to physically disabled. **Special Academic Facilities/Equipment:** Fine arts center, community research center, language lab, church and society center. **Computers:** 100% of classrooms, 100% of libraries, 100% of dining areas, 100% of student union, 50% of common outdoor areas have wireless network access. Students can register for classes online. Administrative functions (other than registration) can be performed online.

CAMPUS LIFE

Environment: City. **Activities:** Choral groups, dance, drama/theater, jazz band, literary magazine, music ensembles, musical theater, pep band, radio station, student government, student newspaper, student-run film society, yearbook, Campus Ministries, International Student Organization, Model UN 85 registered organizations, 30 honor societies, 7 religious organizations. 4 fraternities, 4 sororities. **Athletics (Intercollegiate):** *Men:* baseball, basketball, cross-country, golf, lacrosse, soccer, tennis, track/field (outdoor), track/field (indoor). *Women:* basketball, cross-country, field hockey, lacrosse, soccer, softball, tennis, track/field (outdoor), track/field (indoor), volleyball. **On-Campus Highlights:** Colket Student Center, Belk Fitness Center, Fintel Library, Bast Gymnasium & Kerr Stadium, Olin Hall (performing arts). **Environmental Initiatives:** Lucas Hall was renovated for the Fall of 2010. The Lucas renovation is registered for LEED Certification. LEED stands for "Leadership in Energy and Environmental Design" and it means this construction project is environmentally sensitive in many different ways. A new residence hall being constructed for fall 2012 will also be LEED certified. Campus recycling of plastics, aluminum, cardboard, and newspaper. RCycles is an initiative of the Office of the President, RCSustain, and Fintel Library with support from East Coasters Bicycle Shop that provides the free use of bicycles to the Roanoke College campus community.

ADMISSIONS

Freshman Academic Profile: Average high school GPA 3.4. 25% in top 10% of high school class, 51% in top 25% of high school class, 87% in top 50% of high school class. 79% from public high schools. SAT Math middle 50% range 480-600. SAT Critical Reading middle 50% range 490-600. SAT Writing middle 50% range 480-590. ACT middle 50% range 20-25. Minimum web-based TOEFL 68. Minimum paper TOEFL 520. **Basis for Candidate Selection:** *Very important factors considered include:* Class rank, academic GPA, rigor of secondary school record, standardized test scores, character/personal qualities. *Important factors considered include:* recommendation(s), extracurricular activities, interview. *Other factors considered include:* application essay, alumni/ae relation, level of applicant's interest, racial/ethnic status, talent/ability, volunteer work, work experience. **Freshman Admission Requirements:** High school diploma is required and GED is accepted. *Academic units required:* 4 English, 3 mathematics, 2 science, (2 science labs), 2 social studies, 5 academic electives. *Academic units recommended:* 4 English, 3 mathematics, 2 science, (2 science labs), 2 social studies, 5 academic electives. **Freshman Admission Statistics:** 4,264 applied, 69% admitted, 18% enrolled. **Transfer Admission Requirements:** High school transcript, college transcript(s), statement of good standing from prior institution(s). Minimum college GPA of 2.2 required. Lowest grade transferable C–. **General Admission Information:** Application Fee $33. Early decision application deadline 12/1. Regular application deadline 3/15. Regular notification 4/1. Nonfall registration accepted. Admission may be deferred for a maximum of 2 years. Credit and/or placement offered for CEEB Advanced Placement tests.

COSTS AND FINANCIAL AID

Annual tuition $35,108. Room and board $11,524. Required fees $1,364. Average book expense $1,000. **Required Forms and Deadlines:** FAFSA, state aid form. **Notification of Awards:** Applicants will be notified of awards on a rolling basis beginning 11/1. *Types of Aid: Need-based scholarships/grants:* Federal Pell, SEOG, state scholarships/grants, private scholarships, the school's own gift aid. *Loans:* Subsidized Stafford, Unsubsidized Stafford, PLUS, Federal Perkins, college/university loans from institutional funds, Alternative loans. **Student Employment:** Federal Work-Study Program available. Institutional employment available. Highest amount earned per year from on-campus jobs $2,000. Off-campus job opportunities are good. **Financial Aid Statistics:** 99% freshmen, 98% undergrads receive need-based scholarship or grant aid. 99% freshmen, 97% undergrads receive non-need-based scholarship or grant aid. 78% freshmen, 80% undergrads receive need-based self-help aid. 98% freshmen, 97% undergrads receive any aid. 72% undergrads borrow to pay

for school. Average cumulative indebtedness $33,004. **Criteria for awarding institutional aid:** *Non-need-based:* academics, minority status, music/drama, religious affiliation.

ROBERT MORRIS UNIVERSITY

6001 University Boulevard, Moon Township, PA 15108-1189
Phone: 412-397-5200 • **Financial Aid Phone:** 412-397-6250
E-mail: admissionsoffice@rmu.edu • **CEEB Code:** 2769
Fax: 412-397-2425 • **Website:** www.rmu.edu • **ACT Code:** 3674

This private school was founded in 1921. It has a 230-acre campus.

RATINGS

Admissions Selectivity Rating: 68   **Fire Safety Rating:** 78   **Green Rating:** 73

STUDENTS AND FACULTY

Enrollment: 4,089. **Student Body:** 46% female, 54% male, 16% out-of-state, 4% international (47 countries represented). Asian 1%, African American 7%, Caucasian 80%, Hispanic 2%, Native American 0%.
Retention and Graduation: 76% freshmen return for sophomore year. 43% freshmen graduate within 4 years. 54% freshmen graduate within 6 years. 6% grads go on to further study within 1 year. **Faculty:** Student/faculty ratio 15:1. 196 full-time faculty, 82% hold PhDs, 12% are members of minority groups, 42% are women. 0% of classes are taught by teaching assistants.

ACADEMICS

Degrees: bachelor's, certificate, master's, post-bachelor's certificate. **Classes:** Most classes have 20-29 students. **Majors with Highest Enrollment:** accounting; business administration and management; marketing/marketing management. **Special Study Options:** cooperative education program, cross-registration, distance learning, double major, honors program, independent study, internships, study abroad, teacher certification program, weekend college, Evening, weekend and 5 week/8 week programs. **Honors Programs:** International Honors Program. **Combined Degree Programs:** BSBA/MS BS/MS. **Disability Services:** Special programs offered to physically disabled students include note-taking services, reader services, tape recorders, tutors. **Career Services:** Alumni network, alumni services, career/job search classes, career assessment, internships, regional alumni. Career Services highlights include Extensive internship and co-op placement program.

FACILITIES

Housing: Coed dorms, men's dorms, women's dorms, apartments for single students. 75% of campus accessible to physically disabled. **Computers:** 50% of classrooms, 75% of libraries, 100% of dining areas, 100% of student union, 25% of common outdoor areas have wireless network access. Students can register for classes online. Administrative functions (other than registration) can be performed online.

CAMPUS LIFE

Environment: Metropolis. **Activities:** Choral groups, drama/theater, literary magazine, marching band, musical theater, pep band, radio station, student government, student newspaper, television station, Campus Ministries, International Student Organization 97 registered organizations, 6 honor societies, 5 religious organizations. 4 fraternities, 3 sororities. **Athletics (Intercollegiate):** *Men:* basketball, football, golf, ice hockey, lacrosse, soccer, tennis, track/field (outdoor), track/field (indoor). *Women:* basketball, crew/rowing, field hockey, golf, ice hockey, lacrosse, soccer, softball, tennis, track/field (outdoor), track/field (indoor), volleyball. **On-Campus Highlights:** Student Center, RMU Island Sports Center Complex, Computer Labs, Athletic Center, Health Club. **Environmental Initiatives:** Recycling paper, cardboard, plastic, bottles and cans, and florescent bulbs.

ADMISSIONS

Freshman Academic Profile: Average high school GPA 3.4. 17% in top 10% of high school class, 44% in top 25% of high school class, 80% in top 50% of high school class. 87% from public high schools. SAT Math middle 50% range 460-580. SAT Critical Reading middle 50% range 450-570. SAT Writing middle 50% range 440-540. ACT middle 50% range 20-24. Minimum web-based TOEFL 61. Minimum paper TOEFL 500. **Basis for Candidate Selection:** *Very important factors considered include:* academic GPA, standardized test scores. *Important factors considered include:* Class rank, rigor of secondary school record, character/personal qualities, extracurricular activities, interview. *Other factors considered include:* application essay, recommendation(s), alumni/ae relation, level of applicant's interest, talent/ability, volunteer work, work experience. **Freshman Admission Requirements:** High school diploma is required and GED is accepted. *Academic units required:* 4 English, 3 mathematics, 2 science, 4 social studies, 3 academic electives. *Academic units* *recommended:* 4 English, 3 mathematics, 2 science, 4 social studies, 3 academic electives. **Freshman Admission Statistics:** 5,220 applied, 82% admitted, 20% enrolled. **Transfer Admission Requirements:** college transcript(s), statement of good standing from prior institution(s). Minimum college GPA of 2.0 required. Lowest grade transferable C. **General Admission Information:** Application Fee $30. Regular application deadline 7/1. Notification on a rolling basis, beginning on or about 8/1. Nonfall registration accepted. Admission may be deferred for a maximum of 12 months. Credit and/or placement offered for CEEB Advanced Placement tests.

COSTS AND FINANCIAL AID
Annual tuition $23,410. Room and board $11,360. Required fees $654. Average book expense $1,200. **Required Forms and Deadlines:** FAFSA. **Notification of Awards:** Applicants will be notified of awards on a rolling basis beginning 3/15. **Types of Aid:** *Need-based scholarships/grants:* Federal Pell, SEOG, state scholarships/grants, private scholarships, the school's own gift aid. *Loans:* Subsidized Stafford, Unsubsidized Stafford, PLUS, Federal Perkins, Alternative private loans. **Student Employment:** Federal Work-Study Program available. Institutional employment available. Off-campus job opportunities are good. **Financial Aid Statistics:** 100% freshmen, 95% undergrads receive need-based scholarship or grant aid. 8% freshmen, 8% undergrads receive non-need-based scholarship or grant aid. 91% freshmen, 89% undergrads receive need-based self-help aid. 3% freshmen, 3% undergrads receive athletic scholarships. 81% freshmen, 76% undergrads receive any aid. 73% undergrads borrow to pay for school. Average cumulative indebtedness $41,093. **Criteria for awarding institutional aid:** *Non-need-based:* academics, athletics.

ROBERT MORRIS UNIVERSITY (IL)

401 South State Street, Chicago, IL 60605
Phone: 800-762-5960
E-mail: enroll@robertmorris.edu
Fax: 312-935-6819

This is a private school.

RATINGS
Admissions Selectivity Rating: 85   **Fire Safety Rating:** 97   **Green Rating:** 72

STUDENTS AND FACULTY
Enrollment: 3,196. **Student Body:** 53% female, 47% male, 8% out-of-state, 1% international (27 countries represented). Asian 3%, African American 33%, Caucasian 38%, Hispanic 23%, Native American 0%.
Retention and Graduation: 49% freshmen return for sophomore year. 69% freshmen graduate within 4 years. 73% freshmen graduate within 6 years. 16% grads go on to further study within 1 year. **Faculty:** Student/faculty ratio 20:1. 125 full-time faculty, 26% hold PhDs, 23% are members of minority groups, 48% are women.

ACADEMICS
Degrees: associate, bachelor's, diploma, master's. **Classes:** Most classes have 20–29 students. **Special Study Options:** Accelerated program, cooperative education program, distance learning, dual enrollment, honors program, internships, study abroad.

FACILITIES
Housing: Coed dorms.

CAMPUS LIFE
Activities: Choral groups, dance, drama/theater, literary magazine, student newspaper.

ADMISSIONS
Freshman Academic Profile: Average high school GPA 2.7. 6% in top 10% of high school class, 19% in top 25% of high school class, 46% in top 50% of high school class. ACT middle 50% range 16-22. Minimum web-based TOEFL 80. Minimum paper TOEFL 550. **Freshman Admission Requirements:** High school diploma is required and GED is accepted. **Freshman Admission Statistics:** 2,786 applied, 34% admitted. **General Admission Information:** Application Fee $75. Nonfall registration accepted. Admission may be deferred for a maximum of 1 Year.

COSTS AND FINANCIAL AID
Annual tuition $22,800. Room and board $11,754. **Financial Aid Statistics:** 83% freshmen, 80% undergrads receive need-based scholarship or grant aid. 43% freshmen, 73% undergrads receive non-need-based scholarship or grant aid. 89% freshmen, 81% undergrads receive need-based self-help aid. 16% freshmen, 17% undergrads receive athletic scholarships. 92% freshmen, 92%

undergrads receive any aid. 96% undergrads borrow to pay for school. Average cumulative indebtedness $29,771.

ROBERTS WESLEYAN COLLEGE

2301 Westside Drive, Rochester, NY 14624-1997
Phone: 585-594-6400 • **Financial Aid Phone:** 585-594-6150
E-mail: admissions@roberts.edu • **CEEB Code:** 2805
Fax: 585-594-6371 • **Website:** www.roberts.edu • **ACT Code:** 2759

This private school was founded in 1866. It has a 75-acre campus.

RATINGS
Admissions Selectivity Rating: 83   **Fire Safety Rating:** 65   **Green Rating:** 60*

STUDENTS AND FACULTY
Enrollment: 1,332. **Student Body:** 70% female, 30% male, 8% out-of-state, 2% international (19 countries represented). Asian 1%, African American 10%, Caucasian 77%, Hispanic 4%, Native American 0%.
Retention and Graduation: 83% freshmen return for sophomore year. 54% freshmen graduate within 4 years. 57% freshmen graduate within 6 years. 26% grads go on to further study within 1 year. **Faculty:** Student/faculty ratio 11:1. 100 full-time faculty, 68% hold PhDs, 10% are members of minority groups, 48% are women. 0% of classes are taught by teaching assistants.

ACADEMICS
Degrees: bachelor's, master's. **Classes:** Most classes have 10–19 students. Most lab/discussion sessions have 10–19 students. **Majors with Highest Enrollment:** elementary education and teaching; music teacher education; nursing, other. **Special Study Options:** cross-registration, distance learning, double major, English as a Second Language (ESL), honors program, independent study, internships, study abroad, teacher certification program. **Combined Degree Programs:** BA/MEng, Pharmacy. **Disability Services:** Special programs offered to physically disabled students include note-taking services, reader services, tape recorders, tutors. **Career Services:** Alumni network, alumni services, career assessment, internships, regional alumni. Career Services highlights include Alumni Networking and shadowing programs, Alumni Career Panels, Alumni Career Services Group on Linkedin.com, Mock Interviews.

FACILITIES
Housing: Coed dorms, special housing for disabled students, men's dorms, women's dorms, apartments for married students, apartments for single students. 71% of campus accessible to physically disabled. **Special Academic Facilities/Equipment:** Davison Art Gallery **Computers:** 100% of classrooms, 100% of dorms, 100% of libraries, 100% of dining areas, 100% of student union, 70% of common outdoor areas have wireless network access. Students can register for classes online. Administrative functions (other than registration) can be performed online.

CAMPUS LIFE
Environment: City. **Activities:** Choral groups, concert band, dance, drama/theater, jazz band, music ensembles, musical theater, opera, student government, student newspaper, symphony orchestra, yearbook, Campus Ministries, International Student Organization, Model UN 28 registered organizations, 11 religious organizations. **Athletics (Intercollegiate):** *Men:* basketball, cross-country, golf, soccer, tennis, track/field (outdoor), track/field (indoor). *Women:* basketball, cross-country, soccer, tennis, track/field (outdoor), track/field (indoor), volleyball. **On-Campus Highlights:** Voller Athletic Center & Sports Complex, New B. Thomas Golisano Library, Rinker Community Service Center, BT's Cafe, Cultural Life Center.

ADMISSIONS
Freshman Academic Profile: Average high school GPA 3.4. 19% in top 10% of high school class, 49% in top 25% of high school class, 82% in top 50% of high school class. SAT Math middle 50% range 480-580. SAT Critical Reading middle 50% range 470-610. SAT Writing middle 50% range 460-590. ACT middle 50% range 21-28. Minimum web-based TOEFL 75. Minimum paper TOEFL 540. **Basis for Candidate Selection:** *Very important factors considered include:* academic GPA, rigor of secondary school record, standardized test scores, character/personal qualities, interview, religious affiliation/commitment. *Important factors considered include:* application essay, recommendation(s), extracurricular activities. *Other factors considered include:* Class rank, alumni/ae relation, level of applicant's interest, talent/ability, volunteer work. **Freshman Admission Requirements:** High school diploma is required and GED is accepted. *Academic units required:* 4 English, 3 mathematics, 3 science, (1 science labs), 3 social studies. *Academic units recommended:* 4 English, 3 mathematics, 3 science, (1 science labs), 3 social studies. **Freshman Admission Statistics:** 1,386 applied, 58% admitted, 26% enrolled. **Transfer**

Admission Requirements: college transcript(s), essay or personal statement, minimum college GPA of 2.70 required. Lowest grade transferable C. **General Admission Information:** Application Fee $35. Notification on a rolling basis, beginning on or about 10/1. Nonfall registration accepted. Admission may be deferred for a maximum of 1 year. Credit and/or placement offered for CEEB Advanced Placement tests.

COSTS AND FINANCIAL AID

Annual tuition $22,580. Room and board $8,520. Required fees $866. Average book expense $1,000. **Required Forms and Deadlines:** FAFSA, state aid form. **Notification of Awards:** Applicants will be notified of awards on a rolling basis beginning 3/30. **Types of Aid:** *Need-based scholarships/grants:* Federal Pell, SEOG, state scholarships/grants, private scholarships, the school's own gift aid. *Loans:* Direct Subsidized Stafford, Direct Unsubsidized Stafford, Direct PLUS, Federal Perkins. **Student Employment:** Federal Work-Study Program available. Institutional employment available. Highest amount earned per year from on-campus jobs $3,000. Off-campus job opportunities are fair. **Financial Aid Statistics:** 100% freshmen, 96% undergrads receive need-based scholarship or grant aid. 7% freshmen, 4% undergrads receive non-need-based scholarship or grant aid. 90% freshmen, 91% undergrads receive need-based self-help aid. 7% freshmen, 3% undergrads receive athletic scholarships. 97% freshmen, 97% undergrads receive any aid. 100% undergrads borrow to pay for school. Average cumulative indebtedness $40,349. **Criteria for awarding institutional aid:** *Non-need-based:* academics, alumni affiliation, art, athletics, music/drama, religious affiliation.

ROCHESTER COLLEGE

800 West Avon Road, Rochester Hills, MI 48307
Phone: 248-218-2031
E-mail: admissions@rc.edu • **CEEB Code:** 1516
Fax: 248-218-2035 • **Website:** www.rc.edu • **ACT Code:** 2072

This private school, affiliated with the Church of Christ Church, was founded in 1959. It has a 83-acre campus.

RATINGS
Admissions Selectivity Rating: 62   **Fire Safety Rating:** 60*   **Green Rating:** 60*

STUDENTS AND FACULTY
Student Body: 14% out-of-state, (10 countries represented). **Retention and Graduation:** 60% freshmen return for sophomore year. 8% freshmen graduate within 4 years. 12% freshmen graduate within 6 years. **Faculty:** Student/faculty ratio 15:1. 38 full time faculty, 28% hold PhDs, 34% are women. 0% of classes are taught by teaching assistants.

ACADEMICS
Degrees: associate, bachelor's, master's, transfer associate. **Special Study Options:** Accelerated program, cross-registration, double major, dual enrollment, independent study, internships, liberal arts/career combination, study abroad, teacher certification program, weekend college. **Disability Services:** Special programs offered to physically disabled students include note-taking services, reader services. **Career Services:** alumni services, career/job search classes, career assessment, internships.

FACILITIES
Housing: special housing for disabled students, men's dorms, women's dorms, apartments for married students.

CAMPUS LIFE
Environment: Village. **Activities:** Choral groups, drama/theater, jazz band, music ensembles, student government, student newspaper, yearbook 19 registered organizations, 3 honor societies, 1 religious organizations. **Athletics (Intercollegiate):** *Men:* baseball, basketball, cross-country, soccer, track/field (outdoor). *Women:* basketball, cross-country, softball, track/field (outdoor), volleyball.

ADMISSIONS
Freshman Academic Profile: Minimum paper TOEFL 500. **Basis for Candidate Selection:** *Important factors considered include:* rigor of secondary school record, standardized test scores. *Other factors considered include:* interview. **Freshman Admission Requirements:** High school diploma is required and GED is accepted. **Freshman Admission Statistics:** 277 applied, 83% admitted, 65% enrolled. **Transfer Admission Requirements:** High school transcript, college transcript(s), minimum college GPA of 2.0 required. Lowest grade transferable C. **General Admission Information:** Application Fee $25. Notification on a rolling basis, beginning on or about 9/1. Nonfall registration accepted. Admission may be deferred for a maximum of 24 months. Credit and/or placement offered for CEEB Advanced Placement tests.

COSTS AND FINANCIAL AID

Annual tuition $9,462. Room and board $5,342. Required fees $600. Average book expense $600. **Required Forms and Deadlines:** FAFSA, institution's own financial aid form. **Notification of Awards:** Applicants will be notified of awards on a rolling basis beginning 6/1. **Types of Aid:** *Need-based scholarships/grants:* Federal Pell, SEOG, state scholarships/grants, private scholarships, the school's own gift aid. *Loans:* Direct Subsidized Stafford, Direct Unsubsidized Stafford, Direct PLUS, Federal Perkins. **Student Employment:** Federal Work-Study Program available. Institutional employment available. Off-campus job opportunities are excellent. **Financial Aid Statistics:** 87% freshmen receive need-based scholarship or grant aid. 79% freshmen receive non-need-based scholarship or grant aid. 84% freshmen receive need-based self-help aid. 29% freshmen receive athletic scholarships. 45% undergrads borrow to pay for school. Average cumulative indebtedness $10,416. **Criteria for awarding institutional aid:** *Non-need-based:* academics, alumni affiliation, athletics, leadership, music/drama.

ROCHESTER INSTITUTE OF TECHNOLOGY

60 Lomb Memorial Drive, Rochester, NY 14623-5604
Phone: 585-475-5502 • **Financial Aid Phone:** 585-475-5502
E-mail: admissions@rit.edu • **CEEB Code:** 2760
Fax: 585-475-7424 • **Website:** www.rit.edu • **ACT Code:** 2870

This private school was founded in 1829. It has a 1300-acre campus.

RATINGS
Admissions Selectivity Rating: 89   **Fire Safety Rating:** 85   **Green Rating:** 96

STUDENTS AND FACULTY
Enrollment: 13,005. **Student Body:** 33% female, 67% male, 50% out-of-state, 5% international (107 countries represented). Asian 5%, African American 5%, Caucasian 62%, Hispanic 6%, Native American 0%. **Retention and Graduation:** 89% freshmen return for sophomore year. 27% freshmen graduate within 4 years. 62% freshmen graduate within 6 years. 18% grads go on to further study within 1 year. **Faculty:** Student/faculty ratio 13:1. 975 full-time faculty, 71% hold PhDs, 17% are members of minority groups, 34% are women. 0% of classes are taught by teaching assistants.

ACADEMICS
Degrees: associate, bachelor's, certificate, diploma, master's, post-bachelor's certificate, terminal associate, transfer associate. **Classes:** Most classes have 10–19 students. Most lab/discussion sessions have 10–19 students. **Majors with Highest Enrollment:** business/commerce; information technology; photography. **Special Study Options:** Accelerated program, cooperative education program, cross-registration, distance learning, double major, English as a Second Language (ESL), exchange student program (domestic), honors program, independent study, internships, liberal arts/career combination, student-designed major, study abroad, weekend college. **Honors Programs:** The RIT Honors Program provides a variety of curricular and extracurricular options, special Honors housing, and Honors scholarships. **Combined Degree Programs:** BA/MEng, BS/MS, BS/MBA. **Disability Services:** Special programs offered to physically disabled students include note-taking services, reader services, tape recorders, tutors. **Career Services:** Alumni network, alumni services, career/job search classes, career assessment, internships, regional alumni. Career Services highlights include Every academic program at RIT offers some form of experiential education opportunity. Experiential education is designed to enrich the learning experience by providing students the opportunity to apply what they are learning in the lab and classroom to real-world problems, projects, and settings. Experiential education takes many forms including cooperative education, internships, study-abroad, undergraduate research, and industry sponsored project work. Experiential education requirements and opportunities vary among academic programs. Notable among these programs at RIT is cooperative education (co-op). The College of Applied Science and Technology, the E. Philip Saunders College of Business, the B. Thomas Golisano College of Computing and Information Sciences, and the Kate Gleason College of Engineering all require co-op for undergraduate students. It is available on an optional basis in other RIT colleges. Co-op students alternate periods of full-time study with periods of full-time paid work experience in business and industry directly related to their field of study and career interests. Last year more than 3,300 students completed work assignments with nearly 1,500 employers earning collectively in excess of $30 million.

FACILITIES

Housing: Coed dorms, special housing for disabled students, special housing for international students, fraternity/sorority housing, apartments for married students, apartments for single students, Special interest floors for selected majors/ groups. Men's floors Women's floors. 95% of campus accessible to physically disabled. **Special Academic Facilities/Equipment:** Art galleries, microelectronic engineering center, RIT Inn and Conference Center, observatory, student-managed restaurant, packaging testing facility, media resource center, Sunday 2000 printing press, Center for manufacturing studies, two OC3 connections to Internet and Internet2, laser optics laboratory, an observatory, an animal care facility, more than 100 color and black-and-white photography darkrooms, electronic prepress and publishing equipment, ceramic kilns, glass furnaces, a blacksmithing area, and computer graphics and robotic labs **Computers:** 75% of classrooms, 25% of dorms, 100% of libraries, 100% of dining areas, 100% of student union, 100% of common outdoor areas have wireless network access. Students can register for classes online. Administrative functions (other than registration) can be performed online.

CAMPUS LIFE

Environment: City. **Activities:** Choral groups, concert band, dance, drama/theater, jazz band, literary magazine, music ensembles, musical theater, pep band, radio station, student government, student newspaper, student-run film society, symphony orchestra, yearbook, Campus Ministries, International Student Organization 175 registered organizations, 9 honor societies, 5 religious organizations. 19 fraternities, 10 sororities. **Athletics (Intercollegiate):** *Men:* baseball, basketball, crew/rowing, cross-country, diving, ice hockey, lacrosse, soccer, swimming, tennis, track/field (outdoor), track/field (indoor), wrestling. *Women:* basketball, cheerleading, crew/rowing, cross-country, diving, ice hockey, lacrosse, soccer, softball, swimming, tennis, track/field (outdoor), track/field (indoor), volleyball. **On-Campus Highlights:** Java Wally's (Wallace Library coffee sho, Student Life Center/Field House/Ice Aren, ESPN Zone @ RIT Student Alumni Union, Ben and Jerry's (RIT Student Alumni Uni, The Cafe and Market at Crossroads. **Environmental Initiatives:** RIT has signed of the American College & University Presidents Climate Commitment (ACUPCC) and established 2030 as the target date for neutrality. A new senior level position of Sustainability Advisor to the President has been created to coordinate campus sustainable activity and connect with the sustainability-engaged communities. In addition, there are sustainability staff within Facilities Management, Auxiliary Services and the National Technical Institute for the Deaf (NTID) The University has completed the design stage for a $38 million building project designated to house the Golisano Institute for Sustainability (GIS). When completed, the GIS will become a national center of excellence in the areas of environmental science, and will position RIT in a leadership position in sustainable research and education. The GIS building is designed to make an enduring statement through its sustainable structure, energy efficiency, innovative technology applications and positive impact on its occupants and surrounding environment. The building is targeting LEED Platinum.

ADMISSIONS

Freshman Academic Profile: Average high school GPA 3.6. 35% in top 10% of high school class, 66% in top 25% of high school class, 93% in top 50% of high school class. 85% from public high schools. SAT Math middle 50% range 570-680. SAT Critical Reading middle 50% range 540-650. SAT Writing middle 50% range 520-630. ACT middle 50% range 25-30. Minimum web-based TOEFL 79. Minimum paper TOEFL 550. **Basis for Candidate Selection:** *Very important factors considered include:* academic GPA, rigor of secondary school record. *Important factors considered include:* Class rank, standardized test scores. *Other factors considered include:* application essay, recommendation(s), alumni/ae relation, character/personal qualities, extracurricular activities, first generation, geographical residence, interview, level of applicant's interest, racial/ethnic status, talent/ability, volunteer work, work experience. **Freshman Admission Requirements:** High school diploma is required and GED is accepted. *Academic units required:* 4 English, 2 mathematics, 2 science, (1 science labs), 4 social studies, 10 academic electives. *Academic units recommended:* 4 English, 2 mathematics, 2 science, (1 science labs), 4 social studies, 10 academic electives. **Freshman Admission Statistics:** 16,353 applied, 58% admitted, 29% enrolled. **Transfer Admission Requirements:** college transcript(s), essay or personal statement, minimum college GPA of 2.7 required. Lowest grade transferable C–. **General Admission Information:** Application Fee $50. Early decision application deadline 12/1. Regular application deadline 2/1. Notification on a rolling basis, beginning on or about 3/15. Nonfall registration accepted. Admission may be deferred for a maximum of 12 months. Credit and/or placement offered for CEEB Advanced Placement tests.

COSTS AND FINANCIAL AID

Annual tuition $32,784. Room and board $10,800. Required fees $474. Average book expense $1,050. **Required Forms and Deadlines:** FAFSA, institution's own financial aid form, state aid form. **Notification of Awards:** Applicants will be notified of awards on a rolling basis beginning 3/15. **Types of Aid:** *Need-based scholarships/grants:* Federal Pell, SEOG, state scholarships/grants,

private scholarships, the school's own gift aid, NACME. *Loans:* Direct Subsidized Stafford, Direct Unsubsidized Stafford, Direct PLUS, Federal Perkins, RIT Loan program; Alternative loans. **Student Employment:** Federal Work-Study Program available. Institutional employment available. Highest amount earned per year from on-campus jobs $2,500. Off-campus job opportunities are excellent. **Financial Aid Statistics:** 100% freshmen, 93% undergrads receive need-based scholarship or grant aid. 29% freshmen, 30% undergrads receive non-need-based scholarship or grant aid. 89% freshmen, 90% undergrads receive need-based self-help aid. 87% freshmen, 77% undergrads receive any aid. Average cumulative indebtedness $26,000. **Criteria for awarding institutional aid:** *Non-need-based:* academics, art, leadership.

See page 1188.

ROCKFORD COLLEGE

Admission, Rockford, IL 61108-2393
Phone: 815-226-4050 • **Financial Aid Phone:** 815-226-4062
E-mail: RCAdmissions@rockford.edu • **CEEB Code:** 1665
Fax: 815-226-2822 • **Website:** www.rockford.edu • **ACT Code:** 1122

This private school was founded in 1847. It has a 130-acre campus.

RATINGS

Admissions Selectivity Rating: 87   **Fire Safety Rating:** 69   **Green Rating:** 60*

STUDENTS AND FACULTY

Enrollment: 857. **Student Body:** 61% female, 39% male, 10% out-of-state, 0% international. Asian 2%, African American 8%, Caucasian 69%, Hispanic 6%, Native American 0%.
Retention and Graduation: Faculty: Student/faculty ratio 9:1. 69 full-time faculty, 68% hold PhDs, 3% are members of minority groups, 42% are women. 0% of classes are taught by teaching assistants.

ACADEMICS

Degrees: bachelor's, master's. **Classes:** Most classes have 10–19 students. Most lab/discussion sessions have fewer than 10 students. **Majors with Highest Enrollment:** business/commerce; education; nursing/registered nurse (rn, asn, bsn, msn). **Special Study Options:** Accelerated program, distance learning, double major, English as a Second Language (ESL), exchange student program (domestic), honors program, independent study, internships, study abroad, teacher certification program, Community-Based Learning, Tutorial Courses, Special Studies Courses. **Honors Programs:** Honors program in Liberal Arts. **Disability Services:** Special programs offered to physically disabled students include note-taking services, reader services, tutors. **Career Services:** career assessment, internships Career Services highlights include Community-Based Learning: Founded at Rockford College in the early 1990s, our community-based learning program is based on the conviction that Rockford College is a citizen of the community and that the community has a stake in Rockford College, as well. The work that the students perform serves the dual function of providing a defined need for the community while also fulfilling a specific learning objective determined by the professor.

FACILITIES

Housing: Coed dorms, special housing for disabled students, theme housing, special housing for first-year students. We offer single rooms, double rooms, and suite style living options. **Special Academic Facilities/Equipment:** Language lab. Art Gallery. Sculpture Garden. **Computers:** Students can register for classes online. Administrative functions (other than registration) can be performed online.

CAMPUS LIFE

Environment: City. **Activities:** Choral groups, dance, drama/theater, literary magazine, music ensembles, musical theater, opera, pep band, student government, Campus Ministries, International Student Organization, Model UN 25 registered organizations, 6 honor societies, 1 religious organizations. **Athletics (Intercollegiate):** *Men:* baseball, basketball, cross-country, football, golf, soccer, tennis, track/field (outdoor), track/field (indoor). *Women:* basketball, cross-country, golf, soccer, softball, tennis, track/field (outdoor), track/field (indoor), volleyball. **On-Campus Highlights:** Residence Halls, Seaver Gym, Lion's Den-student gathering place, Football/Soccer Stadium, Clark Arts Center, Tour also highlights classroom buildings. **Environmental Initiatives:** Green Week Trayless Tuesdays in the cafeteria Recycling options readily available

ADMISSIONS

Freshman Academic Profile: Average high school GPA 3.1. 18% in top 10% of high school class, 33% in top 25% of high school class, 65% in top 50% of high school class. Minimum web-based TOEFL 79. Minimum paper TOEFL

550. **Basis for Candidate Selection:** *Very important factors considered include:* academic GPA. *Important factors considered include:* application essay, rigor of secondary school record, standardized test scores. *Other factors considered include:* Class rank, recommendation(s). **Freshman Admission Requirements:** High school diploma is required and GED is accepted. *Academic units required:* 4 English, 3 mathematics, 3 science, (3 science labs), 3 social studies, 2 academic electives. *Academic units recommended:* 4 English, 3 mathematics, 3 science, (3 science labs), 3 social studies, 2 academic electives. **Freshman Admission Statistics:** 967 applied, 41% admitted, 23% enrolled. **Transfer Admission Requirements:** college transcript(s), statement of good standing from prior institution(s). Minimum college GPA of 2.3 required. Lowest grade transferable C. **General Admission Information:** Application Fee $35. Notification on a rolling basis, beginning on or about 9/15. Nonfall registration accepted. Admission may be deferred for a maximum of 1 year. Credit and/or placement offered for CEEB Advanced Placement tests.

COSTS AND FINANCIAL AID

Annual tuition $24,750. Room and board $6,950. Average book expense $1,200. **Required Forms and Deadlines:** FAFSA. **Notification of Awards:** Applicants will be notified of awards on a rolling basis beginning 3/1. **Types of Aid:** *Need-based scholarships/grants:* Federal Pell, SEOG, state scholarships/grants, private scholarships, the school's own gift aid. *Loans:* Subsidized Stafford, Unsubsidized Stafford, PLUS, Federal Perkins. **Student Employment:** Federal Work-Study Program available. Institutional employment available. Off-campus job opportunities are excellent. **Financial Aid Statistics:** 98% freshmen, 95% undergrads receive need-based scholarship or grant aid. 12% freshmen, 16% undergrads receive non-need-based scholarship or grant aid. 95% freshmen, 98% undergrads receive need-based self-help aid. 99% freshmen, 99% undergrads receive any aid. 92% undergrads borrow to pay for school. Average cumulative indebtedness $29,987. **Criteria for awarding institutional aid:** *Non-need-based:* academics, alumni affiliation, leadership, minority status, music/drama, state/district residency.

ROCKHURST UNIVERSITY

1100 Rockhurst Road, Kansas City, MO 64110
Phone: 816-501-4100 • **Financial Aid Phone:** 816-501-4600
E-mail: admission@rockhurst.edu • **CEEB Code:** 6611
Fax: 816-501-4241 • **Website:** www.rockhurst.edu • **ACT Code:** 2342

This private school, affiliated with the Roman Catholic Church, was founded in 1910. It has a 55-acre campus.

RATINGS

Admissions Selectivity Rating: 74   **Fire Safety Rating:** 69   **Green Rating:** 60*

STUDENTS AND FACULTY

Enrollment: 1,613. **Student Body:** 60% female, 40% male, 45% out-of-state, 1% international (16 countries represented). Asian 3%, African American 6%, Caucasian 78%, Hispanic 6%, Native American 1%. **Retention and Graduation:** 86% freshmen return for sophomore year. 59% freshmen graduate within 4 years. **Faculty:** Student/faculty ratio 13:1. 123 full-time faculty, 89% hold PhDs, 11% are members of minority groups, 50% are women. 0% of classes are taught by teaching assistants.

ACADEMICS

Degrees: bachelor's, certificate, master's, post-bachelor's certificate. **Classes:** Most classes have 20–29 students. Most lab/discussion sessions have 10–19 students. **Majors with Highest Enrollment:** business/commerce; nursing/registered nurse (rn, asn, bsn, msn); psychology. **Special Study Options:** Accelerated program, cooperative education program, cross-registration, double major, dual enrollment, exchange student program (domestic), honors program, independent study, internships, study abroad, teacher certification program. **Honors Programs:** The Rockhurst University Honors Program is for motivated and talented students, regardless of major, who want to be active participants in designing their education. Students find honors courses to be more innovative, personal, and challenging than other courses. The Benefits Beginning in the first year, honors students have specially designed core courses that are usually small in enrollment and are taught by some of the University's most creative faculty. During the sophomore through senior years, honors students may earn honors credit through "honors options"--individually designed projects that allow students to explore areas of their own interest under the mentorship of a professor. An honors option is typically an offshoot of a regular course, but an option can also be arranged as an independent study course. It is through the honors option that honors students shape their curriculum. **Combined Degree Programs:** BA/MOT, BA/DPT, BS/CSD, B/MBA. **Disability Services:** Special programs offered to physically disabled students include

note-taking services, reader services, tape recorders, tutors. **Career Services:** Alumni network, alumni services, career/job search classes, career assessment, internships, regional alumni. Career Services highlights include All three add to the experiential education programs at Rockhurst.

FACILITIES

Housing: Coed dorms, special housing for disabled students, men's dorms, women's dorms, apartments for single students, RU on-campus housing. 90% of campus accessible to physically disabled. **Special Academic Facilities/Equipment:** Greenlease Art Gallery, Richardson Science Center. **Computers:** Students can register for classes online. Administrative functions (other than registration) can be performed online.

CAMPUS LIFE

Environment: Metropolis. **Activities:** Choral groups, drama/theater, literary magazine, musical theater, student government, student newspaper, yearbook 44 registered organizations, 4 honor societies, 6 religious organizations. 3 fraternities, 3 sororities. **Athletics (Intercollegiate):** *Men:* baseball, basketball, golf, soccer, tennis. *Women:* basketball, golf, soccer, softball, tennis, volleyball. **On-Campus Highlights:** New Bell Tower and Fountains, Richardson Science Center / state-of-art facility, Business School / complete computer lab and classroom renovations, Career and Learning Center, The Old Gym (historic) plus the new.

ADMISSIONS

Freshman Academic Profile: 3.6. 25% in top 10% of high school class, 56% in top 25% of high school class, 86% in top 50% of high school class. 45% from public high schools. SAT Math middle 50% range 480-600. SAT Critical Reading middle 50% range 500-640. ACT middle 50% range 23-28. Minimum paper TOEFL 550. **Basis for Candidate Selection:** *Very important factors considered include:* academic GPA, standardized test scores. *Important factors considered include:* Class rank, recommendation(s), rigor of secondary school record, character/personal qualities. *Other factors considered include:* alumni/ae relation, extracurricular activities, interview, level of applicant's interest, religious affiliation/commitment, talent/ability, volunteer work. **Freshman Admission Requirements:** High school diploma is required and GED is accepted. **Freshman Admission Statistics:** 2,184 applied, 78% admitted, 26% enrolled. **Transfer Admission Requirements:** college transcript(s), minimum college GPA of 2.5 required. Lowest grade transferable C–. **General Admission Information:** Application Fee $25. Regular notification 9/15. Nonfall registration accepted. Admission may be deferred for a maximum of 1 year. Credit and/or placement offered for CEEB Advanced Placement tests.

COSTS AND FINANCIAL AID

Annual tuition $27,700. Room and board $8,220. Required fees $740. Average book expense $1,400. **Required Forms and Deadlines:** FAFSA. **Notification of Awards:** Applicants will be notified of awards on a rolling basis beginning 1/30. **Types of Aid:** *Need-based scholarships/grants:* Federal Pell, SEOG, state scholarships/grants, private scholarships, the school's own gift aid. *Loans:* Subsidized Stafford, Unsubsidized Stafford, PLUS, Federal Perkins, Alternative Loans. **Student Employment:** Federal Work-Study Program available. Institutional employment available. Highest amount earned per year from on-campus jobs $1,650. Off-campus job opportunities are fair. **Financial Aid Statistics:** 100% freshmen, 19% undergrads receive non-need-based scholarship or grant aid. 58% freshmen, 61% undergrads receive need-based self-help aid. 8% freshmen, 11% undergrads receive athletic scholarships. 74% undergrads borrow to pay for school. Average cumulative indebtedness $20,003. **Criteria for awarding institutional aid:** *Non-need-based:* academics, alumni affiliation, athletics, leadership, music/drama, state/district residency.

ROCKY MOUNTAIN COLLEGE

1511 Poly Drive, Billings, MT 59102-1796
Phone: 406-657-1026 • **Financial Aid Phone:** 406-657-1031
E-mail: admissions@rocky.edu • **CEEB Code:** 4660
Fax: 406-657-1189 • **Website:** www.rocky.edu • **ACT Code:** 2426

This private school was founded in 1878. It has a 60-acre campus.

RATINGS

Admissions Selectivity Rating: 75   **Fire Safety Rating:** 80   **Green Rating:** 61

STUDENTS AND FACULTY

Enrollment: 984. **Student Body:** 49% female, 51% male, 44% out-of-state, 4% international (16 countries represented). Asian 1%, African American 3%, Caucasian 82%, Hispanic 4%, Native American 2%. **Retention and Graduation:** 67% freshmen return for sophomore year. 26% freshmen graduate within 4 years. 18% grads go on to further study within 1 year. 16% grads pursue arts and sciences degrees. 1% grads pursue law degrees. 1% grads pursue business degrees. **Faculty:** Student/faculty ratio 12:1. 65 full-time faculty, 77% hold PhDs, 40% are women. 0% of classes are taught by teaching assistants.

ACADEMICS

Degrees: associate, bachelor's, master's, terminal associate, transfer associate. **Classes:** Most classes have 10–19 students. Most lab/discussion sessions have fewer than 10 students. **Majors with Highest Enrollment:** biology/biological sciences; business/commerce; physician assistant. **Special Study Options:** Accelerated program, distance learning, double major, dual enrollment, English as a Second Language (ESL), honors program, independent study, internships, student-designed major, study abroad, teacher certification program. **Honors Programs:** Successful honors students find that participation in this program not only brings them closer to professionals in their chosen fields, but also grants them a substantial credential in their applications to graduate schools or employment opportunities. **Disability Services:** Special programs offered to physically disabled students include note-taking services, reader services, tape recorders, tutors. **Career Services:** Alumni network, alumni services, career/job search classes, career assessment, internships, regional alumni.

FACILITIES

Housing: Coed dorms, apartments for married students, apartments for single students, Suites. 50% of campus accessible to physically disabled. **Special Academic Facilities/Equipment:** Billings Studio Theater, museum, studio, flight simulator/flight school, equestrian facilities, geology collection. **Computers:** Students can register for classes online. Administrative functions (other than registration) can be performed online.

CAMPUS LIFE

Environment: City. **Activities:** Choral groups, concert band, drama/theater, jazz band, literary magazine, music ensembles, musical theater, pep band, student government, student newspaper, yearbook 28 registered organizations, 1 honor societies, 4 religious organizations. **Athletics (Intercollegiate):** Men: basketball, cheerleading, football, golf, skiing (downhill/alpine). Women: basketball, cheerleading, golf, skiing (downhill/alpine), soccer, volleyball. **On-Campus Highlights:** Bair Family Student Center, Educational Resource Center, Fortin Center-Gymnasium, Herb Klindt Field-Football Stadium, Losekamp Hall-Music Theatre.

ADMISSIONS

Freshman Academic Profile: Average high school GPA 3.4. 10% in top 10% of high school class, 36% in top 25% of high school class, 70% in top 50% of high school class. SAT Math middle 50% range 450-550. SAT Critical Reading middle 50% range 440-540. SAT Writing middle 50% range 420-510. ACT middle 50% range 20-25. Minimum paper TOEFL 525. **Basis for Candidate Selection:** Very important factors considered include: academic GPA, rigor of secondary school record, standardized test scores. Important factors considered include: Class rank. Other factors considered include: application essay, recommendation(s), alumni/ae relation, character/personal qualities, extracurricular activities, interview, level of applicant's interest, talent/ability, volunteer work, work experience. **Freshman Admission Requirements:** High school diploma is required and GED is accepted. Academic units required: 4 English, 2 mathematics, 2 science, (1 science labs), 1 foreign language, 2 social studies, 2 history. Academic units recommended: 4 English, 2 mathematics, 2 science, (1 science labs), 1 foreign language, 2 social studies, 2 history. **Freshman Admission Statistics:** 1,347 applied, 64% admitted, 31% enrolled. **Transfer Admission Requirements:** college transcript(s), minimum college GPA of 2.0 required. Lowest grade transferable C–. **General Admission Information:** Application Fee $25. Notification on a rolling basis, beginning on or about 9/1. Nonfall registration accepted. Admission may be deferred for a maximum of 1 year. Credit and/or placement offered for CEEB Advanced Placement tests.

COSTS AND FINANCIAL AID

Annual tuition $22,442. Room and board $7,160. Required fees $450. Average book expense $1,300. **Required Forms and Deadlines:** FAFSA, institution's own financial aid form. **Notification of Awards:** Applicants will be notified of awards on a rolling basis beginning 2/1. **Types of Aid:** Need-based scholarships/grants: Federal Pell, SEOG, state scholarships/grants, private scholarships, the school's own gift aid. Loans: Subsidized Stafford, Unsubsidized Stafford, PLUS, Federal Perkins. **Student Employment:** Federal Work-Study Program available. Institutional employment available. Highest amount earned per year from on-campus jobs $3,985. Off-campus job opportunities are good. **Financial Aid Statistics:** 98% freshmen, 97% undergrads receive need-based scholarship or grant aid. 96% freshmen, 94% undergrads receive non-need-based scholarship or grant aid. 84% freshmen, 84% undergrads receive need-based self-help aid. 26% freshmen, 27% undergrads receive athletic scholarships. 90% freshmen, 90% undergrads receive any aid. 77% undergrads borrow to pay for school. Average cumulative indebtedness $30,948. **Criteria for awarding institutional aid:** Non-need-based: academics, alumni affiliation, art, athletics, leadership, minority status, music/drama, religious affiliation, state/district residency.

ROCKY MOUNTAIN COLLEGE OF ART & DESIGN

1600 Pierce St, Denver, CO 80214
Phone: 303-753-6046
E-mail: admissions@rmcad.edu
Fax: 303-567-7281 • **Website:** www.rmcad.edu • **ACT Code:** 5359

This proprietary school was founded in 1963. It has a 23-acre campus.

RATINGS

Admissions Selectivity Rating: 61   Fire Safety Rating: 60*   Green Rating: 60*

STUDENTS AND FACULTY

Student Body: 60% out-of-state.
Faculty: Student/faculty ratio 19:1.

ACADEMICS

Degrees: bachelor's. **Special Study Options:** independent study, internships, study abroad. **Career Services:** Alumni network, alumni services, career/job search classes, career assessment, internships.

FACILITIES

Special Academic Facilities/Equipment: Philip Steele Gallery Fine Arts Exhibit Space Drive Up Gallery

CAMPUS LIFE

Environment: Metropolis. **Activities:** dance, music ensembles, student government, student newspaper, Campus Ministries.

ADMISSIONS

Freshman Academic Profile: Minimum paper TOEFL 500. **Basis for Candidate Selection:** Very important factors considered include: extracurricular activities. Important factors considered include: academic GPA. **Freshman Admission Requirements:** High school diploma is required and GED is accepted. **Transfer Admission Requirements:** college transcript(s), minimum college GPA of 2.0 required. **General Admission Information:** Nonfall registration accepted. Admission may be deferred for a maximum of one semester.

COSTS AND FINANCIAL AID

Annual tuition $19,752. Average book expense $600. **Student Employment:** Federal Work-Study Program available. Off-campus job opportunities are good.

ROGER WILLIAMS UNIVERSITY

One Old Ferry Road, Bristol, RI 02809-2921
Phone: 401-254-3500 • **Financial Aid Phone:** 401-254-3100
E-mail: admit@rwu.edu • **CEEB Code:** 3729
Fax: 401-254-3557 • **Website:** www.rwu.edu • **ACT Code:** 3814

This private school was founded in 1956. It has a 140-acre campus.

RATINGS

Admissions Selectivity Rating: 83   Fire Safety Rating: 86   Green Rating: 87

STUDENTS AND FACULTY

Enrollment: 4,297. **Student Body:** 48% female, 52% male, 82% out-of-state, 2% international (41 countries represented). Asian 1%, African American 2%, Caucasian 74%, Hispanic 2%, Native American 0%.
Retention and Graduation: 82% freshmen return for sophomore year. 40% freshmen graduate within 4 years. 56% freshmen graduate within 6 years. 13% grads go on to further study within 1 year. 2% grads pursue law degrees. **Faculty:** Student/faculty ratio 12:1. 210 full-time faculty, 84% hold PhDs, 14% are members of minority groups, 40% are women. 0% of classes are taught by teaching assistants.

ACADEMICS

Degrees: associate, bachelor's, certificate, first professional, master's, post-bachelor's certificate, terminal associate. **Classes:** Most classes have 10–19 students. Most lab/discussion sessions have 10–19 students. **Majors with Highest Enrollment:** architecture (barch, ba/bs, march, ma/ms, phd); business/commerce; psychology. **Special Study Options:** cooperative education program, distance learning, double major, dual enrollment, English as a Second Language (ESL), exchange student program (domestic), external degree program, honors program, independent study, internships, liberal arts/career combination, student-designed major, study abroad, teacher certification program, weekend college. **Honors Programs:** 1. Alpha Chi Honors Society-University-wide association for Juniors and Seniors; 2. Four-year Honors Program-For full-time students in any major which includes special sections of general education classes, a unique group service project for juniors and a required senior thesis. The program includes a variety of cultural and co-curricular activities, as well as leadership opportunities; 3. Honors Society Associations-Department-level honors associations within various disciplines **Combined Degree Programs:** BA/JD, 3-3 law program. Dual Degree Architecture program. **Disability Services:** Special programs offered to physically disabled students include note-taking services, reader services, tape recorders, tutors.

FACILITIES

Housing: Coed dorms, special housing for disabled students, apartments for single students, wellness housing, theme housing: SPECIAL INTEREST, ACADEMIC THEME HOUSING, HONORS, WELLNESS, NON-SMOKING. **Special Academic Facilities/Equipment:** Marine and Natural Sciences Building, School of Law and Law Library, Main Library, Architecture Building and Architecture Library, Performing Arts Center, Thomas J. Paolino Recreation Center, Global Heritage Hall **Computers:** 100% of classrooms, 100% of dorms, 100% of libraries, 100% of dining areas, 100% of student union, 20% of common outdoor areas have wireless network access. Students can register for classes online. Administrative functions (other than registration) can be performed online.

CAMPUS LIFE

Environment: Village. **Activities:** Choral groups, dance, drama/theater, literary magazine, musical theater, radio station, student government, student newspaper, student-run film society, yearbook, International Student Organization, Model UN 93 registered organizations, 13 honor societies, 4 religious organizations. **Athletics (Intercollegiate):** *Men:* baseball, basketball, cross-country, diving, equestrian sports, lacrosse, sailing, soccer, swimming, tennis, track/field (outdoor), track/field (indoor), wrestling. *Women:* basketball, cross-country, diving, equestrian sports, lacrosse, sailing, soccer, softball, swimming, tennis, track/field (outdoor), track/field (indoor), volleyball. **On-Campus Highlights:** Recreation Center, Library, Dining Commons, Marine Science Wet Lab, Bookstore, Students are taken to any speficic place they would also like to see. Residence Halls are available for viewing with permission from occupants at certain points in the year. **Environmental Initiatives:** All renovation and new construction on campus meets LEED Silver standards Committed to reducing power consumption, reuse resources and recycle whenever possible Incorporating the idea of sustainability in all facets of the university

ADMISSIONS

Freshman Academic Profile: Average high school GPA 3.2. 14% in top 10% of high school class, 38% in top 25% of high school class, 76% in top 50% of high school class. 85% from public high schools. SAT Math middle 50% range 520-600. SAT Critical Reading middle 50% range 500-590. SAT Writing middle 50% range 500-590. ACT middle 50% range 21-25. **Basis for Candidate Selection:** *Very important factors considered include:* application essay, academic GPA, recommendation(s), rigor of secondary school record, standardized test scores. *Important factors considered include:* Class rank, extracurricular activities. *Other factors considered include:* alumni/ae relation, first generation, level of applicant's interest, talent/ability, volunteer work, work experience. **Freshman Admission Requirements:** High school diploma is required and GED is accepted. *Academic units required:* 4 English, 3 mathematics, 2 science, (2 science labs), 2 social studies, 2 history, 2 academic electives. *Academic units recommended:* 4 English, 3 mathematics, 2 science, (2 science labs), 2 social studies, 2 history, 2 academic electives. **Freshman Admission Statistics:** 8,561 applied, 61% admitted, 18% enrolled. **Transfer Admission Requirements:** college transcript(s), essay or personal statement, minimum college GPA of 2.5 required. Lowest grade transferable C. **General Admission Information:** Application Fee $50. Regular application deadline 2/1. Regular notification 3/15. Nonfall registration accepted. Admission may be deferred for a maximum of 1 YEAR. Credit and/or placement offered for CEEB Advanced Placement tests.

COSTS AND FINANCIAL AID

Annual tuition $25,968. Room and board $12,140. Required fees $1,750. Average book expense $900. **Required Forms and Deadlines:** FAFSA, CSS/Financial Aid PROFILE. **Notification of Awards:** Applicants will be notified of awards on a rolling basis beginning 3/20. **Types of Aid:** *Need-based scholarships/grants:* Federal Pell, SEOG, state scholarships/grants, private scholarships, the school's own gift aid. *Loans:* Subsidized Stafford, Unsubsidized Stafford, PLUS, Federal Perkins. **Student Employment:** Federal Work-Study Program available. Institutional employment available. Off-campus job opportunities are excellent. **Financial Aid Statistics:** 57% freshmen, 63% undergrads receive need-based scholarship or grant aid. 76% freshmen, 57% undergrads receive non-need-based scholarship or grant aid. 89% freshmen, 92% undergrads receive need-based self-help aid. 89% freshmen, 80% undergrads receive any aid. 79% undergrads borrow to pay for school. Average cumulative indebtedness $30,874. **Criteria for awarding institutional aid:** *Non-need-based:* academics, leadership.

ROLLINS COLLEGE

1000 Holt Avenue, Winter Park, FL 32789-4499
Phone: 407-646-2161 • **Financial Aid Phone:** 407-646-2395
E-mail: admission@rollins.edu • **CEEB Code:** 5572
Fax: 407-646-1502 • **Website:** www.rollins.edu • **ACT Code:** 748

This private school was founded in 1885. It has a 70-acre campus.

RATINGS
Admissions Selectivity Rating: 89   **Fire Safety Rating:** 92   **Green Rating:** 86

STUDENTS AND FACULTY
Enrollment: 1,884. **Student Body:** 45% out-of-state, 5% international (49 countries represented). Asian 3%, African American 4%, Caucasian 69%, Hispanic 13%, Native American 0%.
Retention and Graduation: 84% freshmen return for sophomore year. 62% freshmen graduate within 4 years. 72% freshmen graduate within 6 years.
Faculty: Student/faculty ratio 10:1. 216 full-time faculty, 90% hold PhDs, 12% are members of minority groups, 43% are women. 0% of classes are taught by teaching assistants.

ACADEMICS
Degrees: bachelor's, master's. **Classes:** Most classes have 10–19 students. **Majors with Highest Enrollment:** economics; international business/trade/commerce; psychology. **Special Study Options:** Accelerated program, cross registration, double major, dual enrollment, exchange student program (domestic), honors program, independent study, internships, student-designed major, study abroad, teacher certification program. **Combined Degree Programs:** BA/MBA. **Disability Services:** Special programs offered to physically disabled students include note-taking services, reader services, tape recorders, tutors. **Career Services:** Alumni network, alumni services, career/job search classes, career assessment, internships.

FACILITIES
Housing: Coed dorms, special housing for disabled students, fraternity/sorority housing, apartments for single students, theme housing. 60% of campus accessible to physically disabled. **Special Academic Facilities/Equipment:** Art museum, theatres, fine arts center, language lab, skills development building, child development center, psychology center, "state-of-the-art" IT classroom. **Computers:** 100% of classrooms, 100% of dorms, 100% of libraries, 100% of dining areas, 100% of student union, have wireless network access. Students can register for classes online. Administrative functions (other than registration) can be performed online.

CAMPUS LIFE
Environment: Town. **Activities:** Choral groups, concert band, dance, drama/theater, jazz band, literary magazine, music ensembles, musical theater, pep band, radio station, student government, student newspaper, student-run film society, symphony orchestra, television station, yearbook, Campus Ministries, International Student Organization 125 registered organizations, 5 honor societies, 5 religious organizations. 5 fraternities, 6 sororities. **Athletics (Intercollegiate):** *Men:* baseball, basketball, crew/rowing, cross-country, golf, lacrosse, sailing, soccer, swimming, tennis, water skiing. *Women:* basketball, crew/rowing, cross-country, golf, lacrosse, sailing, soccer, softball, swimming, tennis, volleyball, water skiing. **On-Campus Highlights:** Cornell Campus Center, Alfond Sports Center, Art Gallery, Cornell Fine Arts Museum, Olin Library, Rice Family Bookstore. **Environmental Initiatives:** Reuse existing buildings, renovating and updating to conform to LEAD principles, but limited to and bound by LEAD criteria Planting of native and drought resistant foliage throughout the campus. Energy reduction initiatives including but not limited to centralized chilled water production and distribution

ADMISSIONS
Freshman Academic Profile: Average high school GPA 3.3. 38% in top 10% of high school class, 69% in top 25% of high school class, 95% in top 50% of high school class. 54% from public high schools. SAT Math middle 50% range 540-640. SAT Critical Reading middle 50% range 550-640. SAT Writing middle 50% range 540-640. ACT middle 50% range 24-29. Minimum web-based TOEFL 80. Minimum paper TOEFL 550. **Basis for Candidate Selection:** *Very important factors considered include:* academic GPA, rigor of secondary school record. *Important factors considered include:* application essay, recommendation(s), standardized test scores, extracurricular activities, talent/ability. *Other factors considered include:* Class rank, alumni/ae relation, char-

acter/personal qualities, first generation, interview, level of applicant's interest, volunteer work, work experience. **Freshman Admission Requirements:** High school diploma is required and GED is accepted. *Academic units required:* 4 English, 3 mathematics, 2 science, 2 foreign language, 2 social studies, 2 history, 2 academic electives. *Academic units recommended:* 4 English, 3 mathematics, 2 science, 2 foreign language, 2 social studies, 2 history, 2 academic electives. **Freshman Admission Statistics:** 4,542 applied, 56% admitted, 20% enrolled. **Transfer Admission Requirements:** High school transcript, college transcript(s), essay or personal statement, statement of good standing from prior institution(s). Lowest grade transferable C–. **General Admission Information:** Application Fee $40. Early decision application deadline 11/15. Regular application deadline 2/15. Regular notification 4/1. Nonfall registration accepted. Admission may be deferred for a maximum of one year. Credit and/or placement offered for CEEB Advanced Placement tests.

COSTS AND FINANCIAL AID
Annual tuition $39,900. Room and board $12,470. Average book expense $804. **Required Forms and Deadlines:** FAFSA, institution's own financial aid form. **Notification of Awards:** Applicants will be notified of awards on a rolling basis beginning 3/1. **Types of Aid:** *Need-based scholarships/grants:* Federal Pell, SEOG, state scholarships/grants, private scholarships, the school's own gift aid. *Loans:* Direct Subsidized Stafford, Direct Unsubsidized Stafford, Direct PLUS, Federal Perkins, college/university loans from institutional funds. **Student Employment:** Federal Work-Study Program available. Institutional employment available. **Financial Aid Statistics:** 100% freshmen, 99% undergrads receive need-based scholarship or grant aid. 28% freshmen, 19% undergrads receive non-need-based scholarship or grant aid. 69% freshmen, 75% undergrads receive need-based self-help aid. 8% freshmen, 6% undergrads receive athletic scholarships. 86% freshmen, 83% undergrads receive any aid. 46% undergrads borrow to pay for school. Average cumulative indebtedness $24,096. **Criteria for awarding institutional aid:** *Non-need-based:* academics, art, athletics, leadership, music/drama, state/district residency.

ROOSEVELT UNIVERSITY

430 South Michigan Avenue, Chicago, IL 60605
Phone: 312-341-3515 • **Financial Aid Phone:** 866-421-0935
E-mail: applyRU@roosevelt.edu • **CEEB Code:** 1666
Fax: 312-341-3523 • **Website:** www.roosevelt.edu/Home.aspx • **ACT Code:** 1124

This private school was founded in 1945. It has a 34-acre campus.

RATINGS
Admissions Selectivity Rating: 73   **Fire Safety Rating:** 88   **Green Rating:** 91

STUDENTS AND FACULTY
Enrollment: 3,728. **Student Body:** 64% female, 36% male, 16% out-of-state, 3% international (63 countries represented). Asian 5%, African American 21%, Caucasian 48%, Hispanic 17%, Native American 0%.
Retention and Graduation: 29% freshmen graduate within 4 years. 44% freshmen graduate within 6 years. **Faculty:** Student/faculty ratio 12:1. 243 full-time faculty, 88% hold PhDs, 23% are members of minority groups, 43% are women. 0% of classes are taught by teaching assistants.

ACADEMICS
Degrees: bachelor's, certificate, master's, post-master's certificate. **Classes:** Most classes have 10–19 students. **Majors with Highest Enrollment:** biology/biological sciences; elementary education and teaching; psychology. **Special Study Options:** Accelerated program, distance learning, double major, dual enrollment, English as a Second Language (ESL), exchange student program (domestic), honors program, independent study, internships, student-designed major, study abroad, teacher certification program. **Honors Programs:** Roosevelt Scholars program offers an enriched academic program combining the students' area of interest with an interdisciplinary approach that includes internships, and research opportunities. Scholars are eligible to receive a special merit scholarship. The Scholars website is http://www.roosevelt.edu/scholars/default.htm **Combined Degree Programs:** BA/JD, MA/JD. **Disability Services:** Special programs offered to physically disabled students include note-taking services, reader services, tape recorders, tutors.

FACILITIES
Housing: Coed dorms, apartments for single students. 100% of campus accessible to physically disabled. **Special Academic Facilities/Equipment:** The Chicago campus is approx. 1 mile from the Museum of Natural History, Aquarium, Planetarium and Contemporary Art museums; and is 2 blocks from the Art Institute of Chicago **Computers:** Students can register for classes on-line. Administrative functions (other than registration) can be performed online.

CAMPUS LIFE
Environment: Metropolis. **Activities:** dance, literary magazine, radio station, student government, student newspaper, International Student Organization 48 registered organizations, 3 honor societies, 4 religious organizations. 1 fraternities, 2 sororities. **Environmental Initiatives:** Roosevelt's new downtown Chicago Vertical campus building will be a LEED Sliver certified building for operation in staring the fall of 2012. Roosevelt's Schaumburg campus underwent a landscape development project to ensure a sustainable environment. Roosevelt's new Field House building will also be Sliver LEED certified once in operation.

ADMISSIONS
Freshman Academic Profile: Average high school GPA 3.2. 2% in top 10% of high school class, 10% in top 25% of high school class, 35% in top 50% of high school class. 80% from public high schools. SAT Math middle 50% range 470-583. SAT Critical Reading middle 50% range 490-600. SAT Writing middle 50% range 450-570. ACT middle 50% range 20-25. Minimum web-based TOEFL 40. **Basis for Candidate Selection:** *Very important factors considered include:* academic GPA, rigor of secondary school record. *Important factors considered include:* standardized test scores. *Other factors considered include:* Class rank, application essay, recommendation(s), alumni/ae relation, character/personal qualities, extracurricular activities, first generation, interview, talent/ability. **Freshman Admission Requirements:** High school diploma is required and GED is accepted. *Academic units required:* 4 English, 3 mathematics, 2 science, (2 science labs), 2 social studies. *Academic units recommended:* 4 English, 3 mathematics, 2 science, (2 science labs), 2 social studies. **Freshman Admission Statistics:** 3,862 applied, 75% admitted, 19% enrolled. **Transfer Admission Requirements:** college transcript(s), statement of good standing from prior institution(s). Minimum college GPA of 2.0 required. Lowest grade transferable D. **General Admission Information:** Application Fee $25. Notification on a rolling basis, beginning on or about 10/1. Nonfall registration accepted. Admission may be deferred for a maximum of 1 year. Credit and/or placement offered for CEEB Advanced Placement tests.

COSTS AND FINANCIAL AID
Annual tuition $26,500. Room and board $12,384. Average book expense $1,200. **Required Forms and Deadlines:** FAFSA. **Notification of Awards:** Applicants will be notified of awards on a rolling basis beginning 2/1. **Types of Aid:** *Need-based scholarships/grants:* Federal Pell, SEOG, state scholarships/grants, private scholarships, the school's own gift aid. *Loans:* Direct Subsidized Stafford, Direct Unsubsidized Stafford, Direct PLUS. **Student Employment:** **Financial Aid Statistics:** 81% freshmen, 87% undergrads receive need-based self-help aid. **Criteria for awarding institutional aid:** *Non-need-based:* academics, alumni affiliation, leadership, minority status, music/drama, state/district residency.

ROSE-HULMAN INSTITUTE OF TECHNOLOGY

Best 378

5500 Wabash Avenue-CM 1, Terre Haute, IN 47803-3999
Phone: 812-877-8213 • **Financial Aid Phone:** 812-877-8259
E-mail: admissions@rose-hulman.edu • **CEEB Code:** 1668
Fax: 812-877-8941 • **Website:** www.rose-hulman.edu • **ACT Code:** 1232

This private school was founded in 1874. It has a 200-acre campus.

RATINGS
Admissions Selectivity Rating: 93   **Fire Safety Rating:** 94   **Green Rating:** 81

STUDENTS AND FACULTY
Enrollment: 2,097. **Student Body:** 21% female, 79% male, 61% out-of-state, 7% international (14 countries represented). Asian 4%, African American 2%, Caucasian 80%, Hispanic 3%, Native American 0%.
Retention and Graduation: 70% freshmen graduate within 4 years. 82% freshmen graduate within 6 years. 22% grads go on to further study within 1 year. 19% grads pursue arts and sciences degrees. 1% grads pursue law degrees. 1% grads pursue business degrees. 2% grads pursue medical degrees. **Faculty:** Student/faculty ratio 13:1. 165 full-time faculty, 98% hold PhDs, 13% are members of minority groups, 20% are women. 0% of classes are taught by teaching assistants.

ACADEMICS
Degrees: bachelor's, master's. **Classes:** Most classes have 20–29 students. Most lab/discussion sessions have 20–29 students. **Majors with Highest**

Enrollment: chemical engineering; electrical, electronics and communications engineering; mechanical engineering. **Special Study Options:** Accelerated program, cooperative education program, cross-registration, double major, independent study, internships, study abroad. **Combined Degree Programs:** MS/MD in Biomedical Engineering. **Disability Services:** Special programs offered to physically disabled students include reader services, tutors. **Career Services:** Alumni network, alumni services, career/job search classes, career assessment, internships Career Services highlights include For the Rose-Hulman student, experiential learning continually takes place during a student's college career. Whether it is through co-curricular activities, company projects brought to the classroom, or participation in degree related internship/co-op experiences. The Rose-Hulman graduate is fully prepared to enter the workforce running.

FACILITIES

Housing: Coed dorms, men's dorms, fraternity/sorority housing, apartments for single students. 95% of campus accessible to physically disabled. **Special Academic Facilities/Equipment:** Museums-none officially. Union Bldg-collection of British Watercolors. Moench Hall Section A-Western Sculpture. All Sections-Eclectic Art. Hadley Hall-Hadley Pottery and Salty Seamon Paintings. Other art in various offices. Oakley Observatory **Computers:** 100% of classrooms, 5% of dorms, 100% of libraries, 100% of dining areas, 100% of student union, 25% of common outdoor areas have wireless network access. Students can register for classes online. Administrative functions (other than registration) can be performed online. Undergraduates are required to own a computer.

CAMPUS LIFE

Environment: Town. **Activities:** Choral groups, concert band, dance, drama/theater, jazz band, literary magazine, music ensembles, musical theater, pep band, radio station, student government, student newspaper, International Student Organization 105 registered organizations, 7 honor societies, 2 religious organizations 8 fraternities, 3 sororities. **Athletics (Intercollegiate):** *Men:* baseball, basketball, cross-country, diving, football, golf, riflery, soccer, swimming, tennis, track/field (outdoor), track/field (indoor). *Women:* basketball, cross-country, diving, golf, riflery, soccer, softball, swimming, tennis, track/field (outdoor), track/field (indoor), volleyball. **On-Campus Highlights:** Sports and Recreation Center, Hatfield Hall, White Chapel, Moench Hall, Chauncey's Place. **Environmental Initiatives:** Signing of the American College & University President's Climate Commitment Formation of a Sustainability Team responsible for instilling a culture of sustainability integrating sustainability with programs in education, operations, and communtiy service. Serving as a pilot campus for the Sustainability Tracking and Assessment Rating System (STARS) Project through the Association for the Advancement of Sustainability in Higher Education.

ADMISSIONS

Freshman Academic Profile: Average high school GPA 3.9. 60% in top 10% of high school class, 90% in top 25% of high school class, 100% in top 50% of high school class. SAT Math middle 50% range 630-730. SAT Critical Reading middle 50% range 560-670. SAT Writing middle 50% range 540-640. ACT middle 50% range 27-32. Minimum web-based TOEFL 80. Minimum paper TOEFL 550. **Basis for Candidate Selection:** *Very important factors considered include:* Class rank, rigor of secondary school record. *Important factors considered include:* academic GPA, recommendation(s), standardized test scores, character/personal qualities. *Other factors considered include:* application essay, alumni/ae relation, extracurricular activities, interview, talent/ability, volunteer work, work experience. **Freshman Admission Requirements:** High school diploma is required and GED is not accepted. *Academic units required:* 4 English, 4 mathematics, 2 science, (2 science labs), 2 social studies, 4 academic electives. *Academic units recommended:* 4 English, 4 mathematics, 2 science, (2 science labs), 2 social studies, 4 academic electives. **Freshman Admission Statistics:** 4,469 applied, 65% admitted, 21% enrolled. **Transfer Admission Requirements:** college transcript(s), essay or personal statement, statement of good standing from prior institution(s). Minimum college GPA of 3.0 required. Lowest grade transferable C. **General Admission Information:** Application Fee $40. Regular application deadline 3/1. Notification on a rolling basis, beginning on or about 10/1. Nonfall registration not accepted. Admission may be deferred for a maximum of 12 months. Credit and/or placement offered for CEEB Advanced Placement tests.

COSTS AND FINANCIAL AID

Annual tuition $38,313. Room and board $10,935. Required fees $765. Average book expense $1,500. **Required Forms and Deadlines:** FAFSA. **Notification of Awards:** Applicants will be notified of awards on or about 3/10. **Types of Aid:** *Need-based scholarships/grants:* Federal Pell, SEOG, state scholarships/grants, the school's own gift aid. *Loans:* Direct Subsidized Stafford, Direct Unsubsidized Stafford, Direct PLUS, Subsidized Stafford. **Student Employment:** Federal Work-Study Program available. Institutional employment available. Highest amount earned per year from on-campus jobs $1,500. **Financial Aid Statistics:** 100% freshmen, 100% undergrads receive need-based scholarship or grant aid. 16% freshmen, 12% undergrads receive non-need-based scholarship

or grant aid. 94% freshmen, 90% undergrads receive need-based self-help aid. 100% freshmen, 98% undergrads receive any aid. 71% undergrads borrow to pay for school. Average cumulative indebtedness $44,965. **Criteria for awarding institutional aid:** *Non-need-based:* academics, minority status.

ROSEMONT COLLEGE

1400 Montgomery Ave., Rosemont, PA 19010
Phone: 610-526-2966 • **Financial Aid Phone:** 610 527 0200
E-mail: admissions@rosemont.edu • **CEEB Code:** 2763
Fax: 610-520-4399 • **Website:** www.rosemont.edu • **ACT Code:** 3676

This private school, affiliated with the Roman Catholic Church, was founded in 1921. It has a 56-acre campus.

RATINGS

Admissions Selectivity Rating: 81   **Fire Safety Rating:** 72   **Green Rating:** 71

STUDENTS AND FACULTY

Enrollment: 519. **Student Body:** 69% female, 31% male, 25% out-of-state, 2% international (12 countries represented). Asian 4%, African American 40%, Caucasian 36%, Hispanic 6%, Native American 0%.
Retention and Graduation: 67% freshmen return for sophomore year. 56% freshmen graduate within 4 years. 58% freshmen graduate within 6 years. 36% grads go on to further study within 1 year. 35% grads pursue arts and sciences degrees. 2% grads pursue law degrees. 5% grads pursue business degrees. 9% grads pursue medical degrees. **Faculty:** Student/faculty ratio 10:1. 28 full-time faculty, 75% hold PhDs, 11% are members of minority groups, 64% are women. 0% of classes are taught by teaching assistants

ACADEMICS

Degrees: bachelor's, master's, post-bachelor's certificate. **Classes:** Most classes have 10–19 students. **Majors with Highest Enrollment:** art/art studies; biology/biological sciences; psychology. **Special Study Options:** Accelerated program, cross-registration, distance learning, double major, honors program, independent study, internships, liberal arts/career combination, student-designed major, study abroad, teacher certification program. **Combined Degree Programs:** BA/MA, BSN in conjunction with Drexel Univ. **Disability Services:** Special programs offered to physically disabled students include note-taking services, tape recorders, tutors. **Career Services:** alumni services, career/job search classes, career assessment, internships Career Services highlights include All students partake of an Internship or a form of Experiential Learning prior to graduation.

FACILITIES

Housing: women's dorms, Cornelia Connelly Hall located in the center of campus is totally redesigned. It is now a state of the art residence hall. Beginning with Fall 2009 Rosemont College welcomes men into the Undergraduate College. 45% of campus accessible to physically disabled. **Special Academic Facilities/Equipment:** McShain Performing Arts Center and Conwell Learning Center. **Computers:** 25% of classrooms, 25% of dorms, 50% of libraries, 15% of dining areas, 15% of student union, 10% of common outdoor areas have wireless network access. Students can register for classes online. Administrative functions (other than registration) can be performed online.

CAMPUS LIFE

Environment: Village. **Activities:** Choral groups, concert band, dance, drama/theater, jazz band, literary magazine, marching band, music ensembles, musical theater, opera, pep band, radio station, student government, student newspaper, yearbook, Campus Ministries 23 registered organizations, 6 honor societies, 3 religious organizations. **Athletics (Intercollegiate):** *Men:* basketball, softball, tennis. *Women:* basketball, field hockey, lacrosse, softball, tennis, volleyball. **On-Campus Highlights:** Campus Grill, The Grind Coffee Shop, Fitness Center **Environmental Initiatives:** Energy Star Procurement Policy. Waste Minimization Policy. Indoor Space Temperature Policy.

ADMISSIONS

Freshman Academic Profile: Average high school GPA 3.3. 70% from public high schools. SAT Math middle 50% range 423-540. SAT Critical Reading middle 50% range 430-550. SAT Writing middle 50% range 430-520. ACT middle 50% range 18-22. Minimum web-based TOEFL 61. Minimum paper TOEFL 500. **Basis for Candidate Selection:** *Very important factors considered include:* rigor of secondary school record, interview. *Important factors considered include:* Class rank, application essay, academic GPA, recommendation(s), standardized test scores, extracurricular activities, talent/ability, volunteer work. *Other factors considered include:* alumni/ae relation, character/personal qualities, work experience. **Freshman Admission Requirements:** High school diploma is required and GED is accepted. *Academic units required:* 4 English,

3 mathematics, 3 science, (2 science labs), 1 social studies, 1 history, 7 academic electives. *Academic units recommended:* 4 English, 3 mathematics, 3 science, (2 science labs), 1 social studies, 1 history, 7 academic electives. **Freshman Admission Statistics:** 1,090 applied, 51% admitted, 18% enrolled. **Transfer Admission Requirements:** college transcript(s), minimum college GPA of 2.5 required. Lowest grade transferable C. **General Admission Information:** Application Fee $35. Regular application deadline 8/1. Regular notification 3/15. Notification on a rolling basis, beginning on or about 3/1. Nonfall registration accepted. Admission may be deferred for a maximum of 12. Credit and/or placement offered for CEEB Advanced Placement tests.

COSTS AND FINANCIAL AID
Annual tuition $29,500. Room and board $11,900. Required fees $950. Average book expense $1,500. **Required Forms and Deadlines:** FAFSA. **Notification of Awards:** Applicants will be notified of awards on a rolling basis beginning 2/15. **Types of Aid:** *Need-based scholarships/grants:* Federal Pell, SEOG, state scholarships/grants, private scholarships, the school's own gift aid. *Loans:* Subsidized Stafford, Unsubsidized Stafford, PLUS, Federal Perkins, Alternative loans offered, payment plans offered. **Student Employment:** Federal Work-Study Program available. Institutional employment available. Highest amount earned per year from on-campus jobs $2,000. Off-campus job opportunities are good. **Financial Aid Statistics:** 100% freshmen, 100% undergrads receive need-based scholarship or grant aid. 9% freshmen, 7% undergrads receive non-need-based scholarship or grant aid. 90% freshmen, 91% undergrads receive need-based self-help aid. 92% freshmen, 92% undergrads receive any aid. 94% undergrads borrow to pay for school. Average cumulative indebtedness $24,320. **Criteria for awarding institutional aid:** *Non-need-based:* academics, art, leadership, religious affiliation.

ROWAN UNIVERSITY

Savitz Hall 201 Mullica Hill Road, Glassboro, NJ 8028
Phone: 856-256-4200 • **Financial Aid Phone:** 856-256-4250
E-mail: admissions@rowan.edu • **CEEB Code:** 2515
Fax: 856-256-4430 • **Website:** www.rowan.edu • **ACT Code:** 2560

This public school was founded in 1923. It has a 800-acre campus.

RATINGS
Admissions Selectivity Rating: 82   **Fire Safety Rating:** 89   **Green Rating:** 86

STUDENTS AND FACULTY
Enrollment: 10,499. **Student Body:** 50% female, 50% male, 4% out-of-state, (27 countries represented). Asian 4%, African American 9%, Caucasian 75%, Hispanic 9%, Native American 1%.
Retention and Graduation: 54% freshmen graduate within 4 years. **Faculty:** Student/faculty ratio 16:1. 385 full-time faculty, 81% hold PhDs, 28% are members of minority groups, 45% are women. 0% of classes are taught by teaching assistants.

ACADEMICS
Degrees: bachelor's, master's. **Classes:** Most classes have 20–29 students. **Majors with Highest Enrollment:** criminal justice/police science; elementary education and teaching; multi-/interdisciplinary studies, other. **Special Study Options:** cooperative education program, distance learning, double major, English as a Second Language (ESL), exchange student program (domestic), external degree program, honors program, independent study, internships, study abroad, teacher certification program, weekend college. **Honors Programs:** The Thomas N. Bantavoglio Honors Concentration offers qualified students access to a variety of academic, enrichment, and service experiences including honors classes, the Honors Student Organization and the 45 activities sponsored by the HSO, as well as travel for cultural and enrichment activities along the eastern seaboard. **Combined Degree Programs:** BS/MA in Mathematics; BS/MS in Computer Science. **Disability Services:** Special programs offered to physically disabled students include note-taking services, reader services, tape recorders, tutors. **Career Services:** Alumni network, alumni services, career/job search classes, career assessment, internships, regional alumni. Career Services highlights include The Rowan University undergraduate Entrepreneurship program has been nationally ranked by The Princeton Review as a Top Program for Entrepreneurship.

FACILITIES
Housing: Coed dorms, special housing for disabled students, apartments for single students, wellness housing, townhouses. 90% of campus accessible to physically disabled. **Special Academic Facilities/Equipment:** Concert hall, glass collection, student recreation center, on-campus early childhood demonstration center, greenhouse for biological studies, observatory, art gallery.

Computers: 100% of classrooms, 100% of dorms, 100% of libraries, 100% of dining areas, 100% of student union, 100% of common outdoor areas have wireless network access. Students can register for classes online. Administrative functions (other than registration) can be performed online.

CAMPUS LIFE
Environment: Town. **Activities:** Choral groups, concert band, dance, drama/theater, jazz band, literary magazine, music ensembles, musical theater, opera, pep band, radio station, student government, student newspaper, student-run film society, television station, yearbook, Campus Ministries 135 registered organizations, 10 honor societies, 6 religious organizations. 10 fraternities, 10 sororities. **Athletics (Intercollegiate):** *Men:* baseball, basketball, cross-country, diving, football, soccer, swimming, track/field (outdoor), track/field (indoor). *Women:* basketball, cross-country, diving, field hockey, lacrosse, soccer, softball, swimming, track/field (outdoor), track/field (indoor), volleyball. **On-Campus Highlights:** Recreation Center, Student Center, Campbell Library, Savitz Hall (Student Services Building), Education Hall. **Environmental Initiatives:** Rowan University purchases 35% of its electricity from wind power sources derived locally and nationally. Rowan University was the first institution of higher education in NJ to sign the American College and University Presidents Climate Commitment (ACUPCC). Rowan was among the first schools in NJ to convert to singe-stream recycling. This innovative program engages students, faculty and staff. The recycling program, coupled with other initiatives, has earned Rowan 9 major awards from federal and state agencies over the last 3 years.

ADMISSIONS
Freshman Academic Profile: Average high school GPA 3.3. 0% in top 10% of high school class, 2% in top 25% of high school class, 14% in top 50% of high school class. SAT Math middle 50% range 510-630. SAT Critical Reading middle 50% range 480-580. SAT Writing middle 50% range 480-580. Minimum web-based TOEFL 79. Minimum paper TOEFL 550. **Basis for Candidate Selection:** *Very important factors considered include:* rigor of secondary school record. *Important factors considered include:* Class rank, academic GPA, standardized test scores. *Other factors considered include:* recommendation(s), character/personal qualities, extracurricular activities, talent/ability, volunteer work, work experience. **Freshman Admission Requirements:** High school diploma is required and GED is accepted. *Academic units required:* 4 English, 3 mathematics, 2 science, (2 science labs), 2 social studies. *Academic units recommended:* 4 English, 3 mathematics, 2 science, (2 science labs), 2 social studies. **Freshman Admission Statistics:** 7,346 applied, 62% admitted, 31% enrolled. **Transfer Admission Requirements:** college transcript(s), minimum college GPA of 2.0 required. Lowest grade transferable D. **General Admission Information:** Application Fee $50. Regular application deadline 3/1. Regular notification 4/15. Notification on a rolling basis, beginning on or about 10/1. Nonfall registration accepted. Admission may be deferred for a maximum of 1 semester. Credit and/or placement offered for CEEB Advanced Placement tests.

COSTS AND FINANCIAL AID
Annual in-state tuition $8,906. Annual out-of-state tuition $16,712. Room and board $10,972. Required fees $3,474. Average book expense $1,500. **Required Forms and Deadlines:** FAFSA. **Notification of Awards:** Applicants will be notified of awards on a rolling basis beginning 3/15. **Types of Aid:** *Need-based scholarships/grants:* Federal Pell, SEOG, state scholarships/grants, private scholarships, the school's own gift aid. *Loans:* Subsidized Stafford, Unsubsidized Stafford, PLUS. **Student Employment:** Federal Work-Study Program available. Institutional employment available. Highest amount earned per year from on-campus jobs $5,800. Off-campus job opportunities are good. **Financial Aid Statistics:** 45% freshmen, 52% undergrads receive need-based scholarship or grant aid. 34% freshmen, 17% undergrads receive non-need-based scholarship or grant aid. 84% freshmen, 86% undergrads receive need-based self-help aid. 72% freshmen, 69% undergrads receive any aid. 74% undergrads borrow to pay for school. Average cumulative indebtedness $35,027. **Criteria for awarding institutional aid:** *Non-need-based:* academics, art, minority status, music/drama.

RUSH UNIVERSITY

600 South Paulina, Chicago, IL 60612-3878
Phone: 312-942-7100 • **Financial Aid Phone:** 312-942-6256
E-mail: Rush_Admissions@rush.edu
Fax: 312-942-2219 • **Website:** www.rushu.rush.edu • **ACT Code:** 1617

This private school was founded in 1972. It has a 35-acre campus.

RATINGS
Admissions Selectivity Rating: 61   **Fire Safety Rating:** 70   **Green Rating:** 60*

STUDENTS AND FACULTY

Enrollment: 258. **Student Body:** 87% female, 13% male, 15% out-of-state, 2% international. Asian 18%, African American 7%, Caucasian 69%, Hispanic 3%, Native American 0%.
Retention and Graduation: 25% grads go on to further study within 1 year. 5% grads pursue medical degrees. **Faculty:** Student/faculty ratio 8:1. 305 full-time faculty, 65% are women. 0% of classes are taught by teaching assistants.

ACADEMICS

Degrees: bachelor's, first professional, master's. **Classes:** Most classes have 10–19 students. **Majors with Highest Enrollment:** audiology/audiologist and speech-language pathology/pathologist; medicine (md); nursing/registered nurse (rn, asn, bsn, msn). **Special Study Options:** distance learning. **Combined Degree Programs:** MD/PhD. **Disability Services:** Special programs offered to physically disabled students include tape recorders, tutors. **Career Services:** Alumni network, alumni services, career/job search classes, career assessment, internships, regional alumni..

FACILITIES

Housing: apartments for married students, apartments for single students. 85% of campus accessible to physically disabled.

CAMPUS LIFE

Environment: Metropolis. **Activities:** yearbook 15 registered organizations, 2 honor societies, 1 religious organizations. **On-Campus Highlights:** Student Lounge, Computer lab (100+ stations), Library, Au Bon Pain. **Environmental Initiatives:** Launched new recycling commitment and awareness campaign on Earth Day 2008.

ADMISSIONS

Freshman Academic Profile: Minimum paper TOEFL 550. **Transfer Admission Requirements:** college transcript(s), essay or personal statement, minimum college GPA of 2.7 required. Lowest grade transferable c. **General Admission Information:** Nonfall registration not accepted. Neither credit nor placement offered for CEEB Advanced Placement tests.

COSTS AND FINANCIAL AID

Room and board $5,271. Required fees $575. Average book expense $1,000. **Required Forms and Deadlines:** FAFSA, institution's own financial aid form, business/farm supplement. **Types of Aid:** *Need-based scholarships/grants:* Federal Pell, SEOG, state scholarships/grants, private scholarships, the school's own gift aid. *Loans:* Subsidized Stafford, Unsubsidized Stafford, PLUS, Federal Perkins, Federal Nursing, college/university loans from institutional funds, credit-based loans. **Student Employment:** Federal Work-Study Program available. Institutional employment available. Off-campus job opportunities are fair. **Financial Aid Statistics:** 74% undergrads receive need-based scholarship or grant aid. 13% undergrads receive non-need-based scholarship or grant aid. 88% undergrads receive need-based self-help aid. 0% freshmen, 69% undergrads receive any aid. **Criteria for awarding institutional aid:** *Non-need-based:* academics, leadership, minority status.

RUSSELL SAGE COLLEGE

Office of Admissions, Troy, NY 12180
Phone: 518-244-2217 • **Financial Aid Phone:** 518-244-4525
E-mail: rscadm@sage.edu • **CEEB Code:** 2764
Fax: 518-244-6880 • **Website:** www.sage.edu/RSC • **ACT Code:** 2876

This private school was founded in 1916. It has a 8-acre campus.

RATINGS

Admissions Selectivity Rating: 71   **Fire Safety Rating:** 64   **Green Rating:** 60*

STUDENTS AND FACULTY

Enrollment: 801. **Student Body:** 9% out-of-state, 0% international. Asian 2%, African American 4%, Caucasian 77%, Hispanic 3%, Native American 0%.
Retention and Graduation: 79% freshmen return for sophomore year. 46% freshmen graduate within 4 years. 62% freshmen graduate within 6 years. 48% grads go on to further study within 1 year. 24% grads pursue arts and sciences degrees. 5% grads pursue business degrees. **Faculty:** Student/faculty ratio 12:1. 61 full-time faculty, 87% hold PhDs, 7% are members of minority groups, 61% are women. 0% of classes are taught by teaching assistants.

ACADEMICS

Degrees: bachelor's. **Classes:** Most classes have 10–19 students. Most lab/discussion sessions have fewer than 10 students. **Majors with Highest Enrollment:** education; nursing, other; psychology. **Special Study Options:** Accelerated program, cooperative education program, cross-registration, dis-

---

tance learning, double major, honors program, independent study, internships, liberal arts/career combination, student-designed major, study abroad, teacher certification program. **Combined Degree Programs:** BA/JD, BA/MEng. **Disability Services:** Special programs offered to physically disabled students include tutors. **Career Services:** alumni services, career/job search classes, career assessment, internships, Career Services highlights include Women in the World Curriculum.

FACILITIES

Housing: women's dorms, Honors Housing, Over 21 Senior Housing, Spanish and French Housing, Returning Adult Housing. 70% of campus accessible to physically disabled. **Special Academic Facilities/Equipment:** Schacht fine arts center (home of NYS Theatre Institute) Robison Athletic and Recreational Ctr., State of the Art lab and research facilities in biology, Historic 19th Century Brownstones. **Computers:** Students can register for classes online. Administrative functions (other than registration) can be performed online.

CAMPUS LIFE

Environment: City. **Activities:** Choral groups, dance, drama/theater, literary magazine, music ensembles, musical theater, student government, student newspaper, yearbook 40 registered organizations, 14 honor societies, 4 religious organizations. **Athletics (Intercollegiate):** *Women:* basketball, soccer, softball, tennis, volleyball. **On-Campus Highlights:** New York State Theatre Institute, Buchman Pavilion, Helen M. Upton Women's Center, Robison Athletic and Recreation Center, James L. Meader Little Theater.

ADMISSIONS

Freshman Academic Profile: Average high school GPA 3.4. 30% in top 10% of high school class, 67% in top 25% of high school class, 95% in top 50% of high school class. SAT Math middle 50% range 480-590. SAT Critical Reading middle 50% range 490-620. ACT middle 50% range 21-25. Minimum paper TOEFL 550. **Basis for Candidate Selection:** *Very important factors considered include:* rigor of secondary school record, standardized test scores. *Important factors considered include:* Class rank, recommendation(s), interview. *Other factors considered include:* application essay, academic GPA, alumni/ae relation, character/personal qualities, extracurricular activities, talent/ability, volunteer work, work experience. **Freshman Admission Requirements:** High school diploma is required and GED is accepted. *Academic units required:* 4 English, 3 mathematics, 3 science, (3 science labs), 2 foreign language, 4 social studies. *Academic units recommended:* 4 English, 3 mathematics, 3 science, (3 science labs), 2 foreign language, 4 social studies. **Freshman Admission Statistics:** 394 applied, 81% admitted, 36% enrolled. **Transfer Admission Requirements:** High school transcript, college transcript(s), statement of good standing from prior institution(s). Minimum college GPA of 2.5 required. Lowest grade transferable C–. **General Admission Information:** Application Fee $30. Early decision application deadline 12/1. Notification on a rolling basis, beginning on or about 12/15. Nonfall registration accepted. Admission may be deferred for a maximum of 1yr. Credit and/or placement offered for CEEB Advanced Placement tests.

COSTS AND FINANCIAL AID

Annual tuition $23,800. Room and board $8,370. Required fees $870. Average book expense $900. **Required Forms and Deadlines:** FAFSA, state aid form. **Notification of Awards:** Applicants will be notified of awards on a rolling basis beginning 3/12. **Types of Aid:** *Need based scholarships/grants:* Federal Pell, SEOG, state scholarships/grants, private scholarships, the school's own gift aid, Federal Nursing Scholarships. *Loans:* Subsidized Stafford, Unsubsidized Stafford, PLUS, Federal Perkins. **Student Employment:** Highest amount earned per year from on-campus jobs $3,000. Off-campus job opportunities are good. **Financial Aid Statistics:** 64% freshmen, 61% undergrads receive need-based scholarship or grant aid. 64% freshmen, 57% undergrads receive non-need-based scholarship or grant aid. 100% freshmen, 100% undergrads receive need-based self-help aid. 94% freshmen, 89% undergrads receive any aid. 91% undergrads borrow to pay for school. Average cumulative indebtedness $21,500. **Criteria for awarding institutional aid:** *Non-need-based:* academics, alumni affiliation.

RUST COLLEGE

150 Rust Avenue, Holly Springs, MS 38635
Phone: 662-252-8000 • **Financial Aid Phone:** 662-252-8000, x4062
E-mail: jb_mcdonald@rustcollege.edu
Fax: 662-252-8895 • **Website:** www.rustcollege.edu • **ACT Code:** 2240

This private school, affiliated with the Moravian Church, was founded in 1866. It has a 126-acre campus.

RATINGS

Admissions Selectivity Rating: 75   **Fire Safety Rating:** 60*   **Green Rating:** 60*

STUDENTS AND FACULTY

Enrollment: 922. **Student Body:** 63% female, 37% male, 5% international. Asian 0%, African American 93%, Caucasian 1%, Hispanic 0%, Native American 0%.
Retention and Graduation: 53% freshmen return for sophomore year. 14% freshmen graduate within 4 years. 28% freshmen graduate within 6 years. **Faculty:** Student/faculty ratio 17:1. 48 full-time faculty, 90% are members of minority groups, 40% are women. 0% of classes are taught by teaching assistants.

ACADEMICS

Degrees: associate, bachelor's. **Classes:** Most classes have 10–19 students. Most lab/discussion sessions have 10–19 students. **Majors with Highest Enrollment:** biology/biological sciences; business/commerce; computer and information sciences. **Special Study Options:** double major, honors program, independent study, internships, liberal arts/career combination, study abroad, teacher certification program, weekend college, 1)Advanced Placement Program. 2)Adult Pathway Program. Dual enrollment includes three Dual Degree Programs with other institutions and one Cooperative Program with another institution. **Disability Services:** Special programs offered to physically disabled students include tutors.

FACILITIES

Housing: men's dorms, women's dorms, Honors. 100% of campus accessible to physically disabled. **Special Academic Facilities/Equipment:** Dr. Ron Trojcak collection of African tribal art which includes fabrics, masks and statues used for religious ceremonies, weddings, ritual dance and funerals.

CAMPUS LIFE

Environment: Rural. **Activities:** Choral groups, concert band, dance, drama/theater, marching band, music ensembles, pep band, radio station, student government, student newspaper, television station, yearbook, International Student Organization 35 registered organizations, 7 honor societies, 5 religious organizations. 3 fraternities, 4 sororities. **Athletics (Intercollegiate):** *Men:* baseball, basketball, cheerleading, cross-country, soccer, tennis, track/field (outdoor). *Women:* basketball, cheerleading, cross-country, softball, tennis, track/field (outdoor), volleyball. **On-Campus Highlights:** Leontyne Price Library Exhibits, James Elam Chapel, McDonald Science Building, David Beckley Conference Center, McMillan Multi-Purpose Center.

ADMISSIONS

Freshman Academic Profile: ACT middle 50% range 14-21. Minimum paper TOEFL 540. **Basis for Candidate Selection:** *Very important factors considered include:* first generation. *Important factors considered include:* Class rank, application essay, academic GPA, recommendation(s), rigor of secondary school record, standardized test scores, alumni/ae relation, character/personal qualities, level of applicant's interest. *Other factors considered include:* talent/ability, volunteer work. **Freshman Admission Requirements:** High school diploma is required and GED is accepted. *Academic units required:* 4 English, 3 mathematics, 3 science, 3 social studies, 6 academic electives. 4 English, 3 mathematics, 3 science, 3 social studies, 6 academic electives. **Freshman Admission Statistics:** 3,983 applied, 46% admitted, 15% enrolled. **Transfer Admission Requirements:** High school transcript, college transcript(s), statement of good standing from prior institution(s). Minimum college GPA of 2.0 required. Lowest grade transferable C. **General Admission Information:** Application Fee $10. Notification on a rolling basis, beginning on or about 7/15. Nonfall registration accepted. Admission may be deferred for a maximum of one year. Credit offered for CEEB Advanced Placement tests.

COSTS AND FINANCIAL AID

Annual tuition $8,100. Room and board $3,700. Average book expense $250. **Required Forms and Deadlines:** FAFSA, institution's own financial aid form, state aid form. **Notification of Awards:** Applicants will be notified of awards on a rolling basis beginning 6/9. **Types of Aid:** *Need-based scholarships/grants:* Federal Pell, SEOG, state scholarships/grants, private scholarships, United Negro College Fund. *Loans:* Subsidized Stafford, Unsubsidized Stafford, PLUS, United Methodist. **Student Employment:** Highest amount earned per year from on-campus jobs $1,600. **Financial Aid Statistics:** 86% freshmen, 87% undergrads receive need-based scholarship or grant aid. 43% freshmen, 29% undergrads receive non-need-based scholarship or grant aid. 87% freshmen, 89% undergrads receive need-based self-help aid. 83% undergrads borrow to pay for school. Average cumulative indebtedness $18,389. **Criteria for awarding institutional aid:** *Non-need-based:* academics, leadership, music/drama, religious affiliation, state/district residency.

RUTGERS, THE STATE UNIVERSITY OF NEW JERSEY—CAMDEN

406 Penn Street, Camden, NJ 8102
Phone: 856-225-6104 • **Financial Aid Phone:** 732-932-7305
E-mail: admissions@ugadm.rutgers.edu • **CEEB Code:** 2765
Fax: 856-225-6498 • **Website:** • **ACT Code:** 2592

This public school was founded in 1927. It has a 25-acre campus.

RATINGS

Admissions Selectivity Rating: 78   **Fire Safety Rating:** 81   **Green Rating:** 60*

STUDENTS AND FACULTY

Enrollment: 3,652. **Student Body:** 57% female, 43% male, 2% out-of-state, 0% international (20 countries represented). Asian 8%, African American 15%, Caucasian 67%, Hispanic 6%, Native American 0%.
Retention and Graduation: 84% freshmen return for sophomore year. 25% freshmen graduate within 4 years. 52% freshmen graduate within 6 years. **Faculty:** Student/faculty ratio 11:1. 285 full-time faculty, 99% hold PhDs, 15% are members of minority groups, 42% are women. 4% of classes are taught by teaching assistants.

ACADEMICS

Degrees: bachelor's, master's. **Majors with Highest Enrollment:** business administration and management; nursing/registered nurse (rn, asn, bsn, msn); psychology. **Special Study Options:** Accelerated program, cooperative education program, cross-registration, distance learning, double major, dual enrollment, English as a Second Language (ESL), exchange student program (domestic), honors program, independent study, internships, liberal arts/career combination, student-designed major, study abroad, teacher certification program, weekend college, Cooperative baccalaureate program in engineering with School of Engineering (New Brunswick Campus). Interdisciplinary programs in African-American studies, general science. Cooperative baccalaureate in medical technology with approved hospital. B.A./M.A. in English, history, liberal studies or psychology; B.A./M.S. in biology, chemistry or mathematics (with the Graduate School-Camden). B.A. in economics or political science/Master of Public Administration (with the Graduate School-Camden). **Combined Degree Programs:** BA/MD, 2+4 Pharm. D. **Disability Services:** Special programs offered to physically disabled students include note-taking services, reader services, tape recorders, tutors.

FACILITIES

Housing: Coed dorms, special housing for disabled students, apartments for single students. **Computers:** Students can register for classes online. Administrative functions (other than registration) can be performed online.

CAMPUS LIFE

Environment: City. **Activities:** drama/theater, literary magazine, radio station, student government, yearbook, International Student Organization 50 registered organizations, 11 honor societies, 4 fraternities, 4 sororities. **Athletics (Intercollegiate):** *Men:* baseball, basketball, cross-country, golf, soccer, track/field (outdoor). *Women:* basketball, cross-country, soccer, softball, track/field (outdoor), volleyball.

ADMISSIONS

Freshman Academic Profile: 14% in top 10% of high school class, 40% in top 25% of high school class, 77% in top 50% of high school class. 60% from public high schools. SAT Math middle 50% range 470-570. SAT Critical Reading middle 50% range 460-560. SAT Writing middle 50% range 460-560. Minimum web-based TOEFL 79. Minimum paper TOEFL 550. **Basis for Candidate Selection:** *Very important factors considered include:* Class rank, academic GPA, rigor of secondary school record, standardized test scores. *Other factors considered include:* application essay, recommendation(s), extracurricular activities, first generation, geographical residence, racial/ethnic status, state residency, volunteer work, work experience. **Freshman Admission Requirements:** High school diploma is required and GED is accepted. *Academic units required:* 4 English, 3 mathematics, 2 science, 2 foreign language, 5 academic electives. *Academic units recommended:* 4 English, 3 mathematics, 2 science, 2 foreign language, 5 academic electives. **Freshman Admission Statistics:** 5,686 applied, 62% admitted, 14% enrolled. **Transfer Admission Requirements:** High school transcript, college transcript(s), minimum college GPA of NA required. **General Admission Information:** Application Fee $65. Regular application deadline 12/1. Nonfall registration accepted. Credit and/or placement offered for CEEB Advanced Placement tests.

COSTS AND FINANCIAL AID

Annual in-state tuition $9,926. Annual out-of-state tuition $20,985. Room and board $10,362. Required fees $2,438. Average book expense $1,474. **Required**

Forms and Deadlines: FAFSA. Types of Aid: *Need-based scholarships/ grants: Loans:* Student Employment: Federal Work-Study Program available. Institutional employment available. Financial Aid Statistics: 68% freshmen, 65% undergrads receive need-based scholarship or grant aid. 32% freshmen, 17% undergrads receive non-need-based scholarship or grant aid. 80% freshmen, 89% undergrads receive need-based self-help aid. 70% freshmen, 72% undergrads receive any aid. 76% undergrads borrow to pay for school. Average cumulative indebtedness $25,516.

RUTGERS, THE STATE UNIVERSITY OF NEW JERSEY—NEW BRUNSWICK

65 Davidson Road, Piscataway, NJ 08854-8097
Phone: 732-932-4636 • **Financial Aid Phone:** 732-932-7305
E-mail: admissions@ugadm.rutgers.edu • **CEEB Code:** 2765
Fax: 732-445-0237 • **Website:** www.rutgers.edu • **ACT Code:** 2592

This public school was founded in 1766. It has a 2695-acre campus.

RATINGS
Admissions Selectivity Rating: 86   Fire Safety Rating: 81   Green Rating: 60*

STUDENTS AND FACULTY
Enrollment: 31,226. **Student Body:** 49% female, 51% male, 6% out-of-state, 3% international (117 countries represented). Asian 25%, African American 8%, Caucasian 47%, Hispanic 12%, Native American 0%.
Retention and Graduation: 92% freshmen return for sophomore year.
Faculty: Student/faculty ratio 14:1. 1762 full-time faculty, 99% hold PhDs, 17% are members of minority groups, 40% are women. 20% of classes are taught by teaching assistants.

ACADEMICS
Degrees: bachelor's, master's, post-master's certificate. **Majors with Highest Enrollment:** biology/biological sciences; engineering. **Special Study Options:** Accelerated program, cooperative education program, cross-registration, distance learning, double major, dual enrollment, English as a Second Language (ESL), exchange student program (domestic), honors program, independent study, internships, liberal arts/career combination, student-designed major, study abroad, teacher certification program, 5-year B.A. or B.S./MBA program in Rutgers Business School; BS in business Discipline/MBA; BA or BS in Science Discipline/MBA; 8-year Bachelor/Medical Dual Degree program with UMDNJ-Robert Wood Johnson Medical School; 5-year BS/BS in Bioenvironmental Engineering with the School of Engineering; 5-year accelerated baccalaureate-M.B.A with Rutgers Business School.; Bureau of Engineering Research, supported by the university, industry, state and federal government, provides research opportunities for students and faculty; Continuing professional education; Exchange program between School of Engineering and the City University of London for qualified students majoring in civil, electrical, or mechanical engineering; 5-year (BA/BS degree) program in liberal arts and engineering; 5-year BA or BS/M.Ed. with the Graduate School of Education; Interdepartmental programs and certificate programs are available; Study Abroad in England, France, Italy, Ireland, Germany, Greece, Mexico, Israel, Australia, India, Japan, Netherlands, Scotland, South Africa, South Korea and Spain; Alumnae externship program; Language and Cultural House Program; 5-year BA/BS in cooperation with Rutgers Business School.; B.A./Master of communication and information studies (with SCILS); B.A./MLER (with School of Management and Labor Relations); Baccalaureate/M.C.R.P., M.P.H., or M.P.P with EJB School of Planning and Public Policy; Baccalaureate in Business major/Master of Human Resource Management (with School of Management and Labor Relations {SMLR}). **Combined Degree Programs:** BA/MD, 5-year BA or BS/MPP, 6-year Pharm.D., 6-year Bach. **Disability Services:** Special programs offered to physically disabled students include note-taking services, reader services, tape recorders, tutors. **Career Services:** Alumni network, alumni services, career/job search classes, career assessment, internships, regional alumni.

FACILITIES
Housing: Coed dorms, men's dorms, special housing for international students, women's dorms, fraternity/sorority housing, apartments for married students, cooperative housing, apartments for single students, theme housing, special interest housing, language and cultural houses, substance-free house, Math/Science Engineering House for women, first-year residence, transfer center,

residence for single mothers and children. **Special Academic Facilities/ Equipment:** Geology Museum, Zimmerli Museum, Mason Gross Performing Arts Center; NJ Museum of Agriculture; NJ Film Festival/RU Film Co-op; Rutgers Gardens **Computers:** Students can register for classes online. Administrative functions (other than registration) can be performed online.

CAMPUS LIFE
Environment: Town. **Activities:** Choral groups, concert band, dance, drama/ theater, jazz band, literary magazine, marching band, music ensembles, musical theater, opera, pep band, radio station, student government, student newspaper, student-run film society, symphony orchestra, television station, yearbook, Campus Ministries, International Student Organization 400 registered organizations, 24 honor societies, 29 fraternities, 15 sororities. **Athletics (Intercollegiate):** *Men:* baseball, basketball, cheerleading, cross-country, diving, football, golf, lacrosse, soccer, track/field (outdoor), track/field (indoor), wrestling. *Women:* basketball, cheerleading, crew/rowing, cross-country, diving, field hockey, golf, gymnastics, lacrosse, soccer, softball, swimming, tennis, track/field (outdoor), track/field (indoor), volleyball. **On-Campus Highlights:** Geology Museum, Jane Voorhees Zimmereli Art Museum, Rutgers Display Gardens and Heylar Woods, Hutchenson Memorial Forest.

ADMISSIONS
Freshman Academic Profile: 41% in top 10% of high school class, 77% in top 25% of high school class, 98% in top 50% of high school class. SAT Math middle 50% range 540-670. SAT Critical Reading middle 50% range 500-620. SAT Writing middle 50% range 520-640. Minimum paper TOEFL 550. **Basis for Candidate Selection:** *Very important factors considered include:* Class rank, academic GPA, rigor of secondary school record, standardized test scores.*Other factors considered include:* application essay, recommendation(s), extracurricular activities, first generation, geographical residence, interview, racial/ethnic status, state residency, talent/ability, volunteer work, work experience. **Freshman Admission Requirements:** High school diploma is required and GED is accepted. *Academic units required:* 4 English, 3 mathematics, 2 science, 2 foreign language, 5 academic electives. *Academic units recommended:* 4 English, 3 mathematics, 2 science, 2 foreign language, 5 academic electives. **Freshman Admission Statistics:** 28,635 applied, 61% admitted, 35% enrolled. **Transfer Admission Requirements:** High school transcript, college transcript(s), Lowest grade transferable C. **General Admission Information:** Application Fee $65. Regular notification 3/1. Nonfall registration accepted. Credit and/or placement offered for CEEB Advanced Placement tests.

COSTS AND FINANCIAL AID
Annual in-state tuition $10,104. Annual out-of-state tuition $22,766. Room and board $11,262. Required fees $2,651. Average book expense $1,474. **Required Forms and Deadlines:** FAFSA. **Notification of Awards:** Applicants will be notified of awards on a rolling basis beginning 2/1. **Types of Aid:** *Need-based scholarships/grants:* Federal Pell, SEOG, state scholarships/grants, private scholarships, the school's own gift aid, Outside Scholarships. *Loans:* Direct Subsidized Stafford, Direct Unsubsidized Stafford, Direct PLUS, Federal Perkins, state loans, college/university loans from institutional funds, Other Educational Loans. **Student Employment:** Highest amount earned per year from on-campus jobs $1,374. **Financial Aid Statistics:** 63% freshmen, 64% undergrads receive need-based scholarship or grant aid. 26% freshmen, 20% undergrads receive non-need-based scholarship or grant aid. 87% freshmen, 86% undergrads receive need-based self-help aid. 2% freshmen, 1% undergrads receive athletic scholarships. 67% freshmen, 69% undergrads receive any aid. 57% undergrads borrow to pay for school. Average cumulative indebtedness $23,320. **Criteria for awarding institutional aid:** *Non-need-based:* academics, alumni affiliation, art, athletics, leadership, minority status, music/drama, religious affiliation.

RUTGERS, THE STATE UNIVERSITY OF NEW JERSEY—NEWARK

249 University Avenue, Newark, NJ 07102-1896
Phone: 973-353-5205 • **Financial Aid Phone:** 732-932-7305
E-mail: admissions@ugadm.rutgers.edu • **CEEB Code:** 2765
Fax: 973-353-1440 • **Website:** • **ACT Code:** 2592

This public school was founded in 1930. It has a 36-acre campus.

RATINGS
Admissions Selectivity Rating: 82   Fire Safety Rating: 79   Green Rating: 60*

STUDENTS AND FACULTY
Enrollment: 7,241. **Student Body:** 54% female, 46% male, 16% out-of-state, 3% international (84 countries represented). Asian 23%, African American 18%, Caucasian 27%, Hispanic 23%, Native American 0%.

Retention and Graduation: 89% freshmen return for sophomore year. **Faculty:** Student/faculty ratio 11:1. 493 full-time faculty, 99% hold PhDs, 20% are members of minority groups, 38% are women. 9% of classes are taught by teaching assistants.

ACADEMICS

Degrees: bachelor's, master's. **Majors with Highest Enrollment:** biology/biological sciences; business administration and management; nursing/registered nurse (rn, asn, bsn, msn). **Special Study Options:** Accelerated program, cooperative education program, cross-registration, distance learning, double major, dual enrollment, English as a Second Language (ESL), exchange student program (domestic), honors program, independent study, internships, liberal arts/career combination, student-designed major, study abroad, teacher certification program, weekend college, 5-year baccalaureate-MBA with Rutgers Business School; Baccalaureate/M.A. in Criminal Justice with the School of Criminal Justice; Baccalaureate/MPA with the School of Public Affairs and Administration; Cooperative baccalaureate program with School of Engineering (New Brunswick campus); Cooperative baccalaureate in medical technology with affiliated hospitals; Interdisciplinary programs in archaeology, international affairs, legal studies, women's studies; continuing professional education; The College of Nursing offers a program on the New Brunswick Campus. Students are admitted in the fall semester only; Baccalaureate in Business Major/Master of Human Resource Management (with School of Management and Labor Relations in New Brunswick); Baccalaureate-master's-dual degree programs with the School of Criminal Justice and Rutgers Business School. The Honors College of Rutgers University's Newark College of Arts and Sciences is a four-year program, a college within a college, providing its by-invitation-only students with opportunities for enrichment both in and outside of the classroom. Students invited to join the Honors College benefit from small classes with first-rate faculty, co-curricular internships in major corporations and other institutions, and other special options. Reserved dormitory space, a substantial scholarship program, and research assistantships with faculty members combine to make the RU-Newark Honors College experience unique. For additional information, visit the Honors College web site at http://honorsnewark.rutgers.edu or call (973)353-5860. BA/MD, BA/MA. **Disability Services:** Special programs offered to physically disabled students include note-taking services, reader services, tape recorders, tutors.

FACILITIES

Housing: Coed dorms, fraternity/sorority housing, apartments for single students. **Special Academic Facilities/Equipment:** Institute of Jazz Studies, TV/Radio media center, Institute of Animal Behavior, Center for Crime Prevention Studies, Center for Negotiation and Conflict Resolution, Center for Molecular and Behaviorial Neuroscience, Center for Nursing Research **Computers:** Students can register for classes online. Administrative functions (other than registration) can be performed online.

CAMPUS LIFE

Activities: Choral groups, drama/theater, radio station, student government, student newspaper, yearbook, International Student Organization 80 registered organizations, 16 honor societies, 7 fraternities, 7 sororities. **Athletics (Intercollegiate):** *Men:* baseball, basketball, soccer, tennis, volleyball. *Women:* basketball, softball, tennis, volleyball. **On-Campus Highlights:** The Arts at Rutgers Newark, Robeson Campus Center, Athletic Center, Bradley Hall/Bookstore, Dana Library.

ADMISSIONS

Freshman Academic Profile: 24% in top 10% of high school class, 57% in top 25% of high school class, 88% in top 50% of high school class. SAT Math middle 50% range 490-590. SAT Critical Reading middle 50% range 460-550. SAT Writing middle 50% range 470-560. Minimum paper TOEFL 550. **Basis for Candidate Selection:** *Very important factors considered include:* Class rank, academic GPA, rigor of secondary school record, standardized test scores.*Other factors considered include:* application essay, recommendation(s), extracurricular activities, first generation, geographical residence, racial/ethnic status, state residency, volunteer work, work experience. **Freshman Admission Requirements:** High school diploma is required and GED is accepted. *Academic units required:* 4 English, 3 mathematics, 2 science, 2 foreign language, 5 academic electives. *Academic units recommended:* 4 English, 3 mathematics, 2 science, 2 foreign language, 5 academic electives. **Freshman Admission Statistics:** 11,863 applied, 58% admitted, 15% enrolled. **Transfer Admission Requirements:** High school transcript, college transcript(s), minimum college GPA of na required. **General Admission Information:** Application Fee $65. Regular notification 2/28. Nonfall registration accepted. Credit and/or placement offered for CEEB Advanced Placement tests.

COSTS AND FINANCIAL AID

Annual in-state tuition $9,926. Annual out-of-state tuition $21,388. Room and board $11,653. Required fees $2,143. Average book expense $1,474. **Required Forms and Deadlines:** FAFSA. **Notification of Awards:** Applicants will be notified of awards on a rolling basis beginning 2/1. **Types of Aid:** *Need-based*

scholarships/grants: Federal Pell, SEOG, state scholarships/grants, private scholarships, the school's own gift aid, Outside Scholarships. *Loans:* Direct Subsidized Stafford, Direct Unsubsidized Stafford, Direct PLUS, Federal Perkins, state loans, college/university loans from institutional funds, Other Educational Loans. **Student Employment: Financial Aid Statistics:** 78% freshmen, 82% undergrads receive need-based scholarship or grant aid. 16% freshmen, 11% undergrads receive non-need-based scholarship or grant aid. 77% freshmen, 78% undergrads receive need-based self-help aid. 80% freshmen, 80% undergrads receive any aid. 52% undergrads borrow to pay for school. Average cumulative indebtedness $21,863. **Criteria for awarding institutional aid:** *Non-need-based:* academics, alumni affiliation, art, athletics, job skills, minority status, music/drama, religious affiliation, state/district residency.

SACRED HEART UNIVERSITY

5151 Park Avenue, Fairfield, CT 6825
Phone: 203-371-7880 • **Financial Aid Phone:** 203-371-7980
E-mail: enroll@sacredheart.edu • **CEEB Code:** 3780
Fax: 203-365-7607 • **Website:** www.sacredheart.edu • **ACT Code:** 589

This private school, affiliated with the Roman Catholic Church, was founded in 1963. It has a 67-acre campus.

RATINGS
Admissions Selectivity Rating: 74   **Fire Safety Rating:** 79   **Green Rating:** 69

STUDENTS AND FACULTY
Enrollment: 3,996. **Student Body:** 63% female, 37% male, 59% out-of-state, 1% international (24 countries represented). Asian 2%, African American 4%, Caucasian 65%, Hispanic 6%, Native American 0%.
Retention and Graduation: 83% freshmen return for sophomore year. 50% grads go on to further study within 1 year. 18% grads pursue arts and sciences degrees. 2% grads pursue law degrees. 11% grads pursue business degrees. 1% grads pursue medical degrees. **Faculty:** Student/faculty ratio 13:1. 237 full-time faculty, 79% hold PhDs, 12% are members of minority groups, 54% are women. 0% of classes are taught by teaching assistants.

ACADEMICS
Degrees: associate, bachelor's, certificate, master's, post-bachelor's certificate, post-master's certificate. **Classes:** Most classes have 20–29 students. **Majors with Highest Enrollment:** business/commerce; nursing/registered nurse (rn, asn, bsn, msn); psychology. **Special Study Options:** Accelerated program, cooperative education program, cross-registration, distance learning, double major, English as a Second Language (ESL), exchange student program (domestic), honors program, independent study, internships, liberal arts/career combination, student-designed major, study abroad, teacher certification program, weekend college, Off-campus study: Summer program in Luxembourg, Summer, Winter Intercession, Spring Break, and Semester in Ireland. Sponsored and approved study abroad programs worldwide. Combined Degree Programs: Combined Degree Programs in physical therapy (doctoral) and occupational therapy (masters). Accelerated 5th year M.B.A. program. Accelerated MSCIS (Computer Information Systems). **Honors Programs:** The Thomas More School of Honors Studies offers a challenging curriculum of Honors-level courses. These studies will provide each student with the quest for the full meaning of our humanity exploring the following three components: (1) the cognitive, (2) the aesthetic and (3) the moral or ethical. The Program also includes advisement, cultural events, dinners with the University President and other events. **Combined Degree Programs:** BA/MA, BA/S/MBA; BA/S/DPT; BA/S/MSOT; BA/S/MAT; BS/MSCIS; BA/S/MACJ. **Disability Services:** Special programs offered to physically disabled students include note-taking services, reader services, tape recorders, tutors. **Career Services:** Alumni network, alumni services, career/job search classes, career assessment, internships, regional alumni. Career Services highlights include The Office of Career Development works diligently to facilitate professional internship opportunities for students in all academic majors and career interests.

FACILITIES
Housing: Coed dorms, special housing for disabled students, apartments for single students, wellness housing, thematic floors; living & learning communities for specific academic programs. 90% of campus accessible to physically disabled. **Special Academic Facilities/Equipment:** WHRT student radio station, WSHU National Public Radio, Edgerton Center for the Performing

Arts, Gallery of Contemporary Art **Computers:** 100% of classrooms, 100% of dorms, 100% of libraries, 100% of dining areas, 100% of student union, 100% of common outdoor areas have wireless network access. Students can register for classes online. Administrative functions (other than registration) can be performed online. Undergraduates are required to own a computer.

CAMPUS LIFE

Environment: Town. **Activities:** Choral groups, concert band, dance, drama/theater, jazz band, literary magazine, marching band, music ensembles, musical theater, pep band, radio station, student government, student newspaper, student-run film society, television station, yearbook, Campus Ministries, International Student Organization 80 registered organizations, 14 honor societies, 4 religious organizations. 4 fraternities, 6 sororities. **Athletics (Intercollegiate):** *Men:* baseball, basketball, cross-country, fencing, football, golf, ice hockey, lacrosse, soccer, tennis, track/field (outdoor), track/field (indoor), volleyball, wrestling. *Women:* basketball, bowling, crew/rowing, cross-country, diving, equestrian sports, fencing, field hockey, golf, ice hockey, lacrosse, soccer, softball, swimming, tennis, track/field (outdoor), track/field (indoor), volleyball. **On-Campus Highlights:** Pitt Health and Recreation Center, Edgerton Center for Performing Arts, Holy Grounds Cafe, Ryan-Matura Library, Hawley Lounge, New University Chapel (Chapel of the Holy Spirit) opened in Fall 2009. **Environmental Initiatives:** Lighting renewal for all new construction and renovations, as well as low energy bulbs & motion detection systems. Transfer from 28 chemicals to 6 green chemicals for custodial work. Free shuttle service for students to reduce the number of cars traveling between campuses.

ADMISSIONS

Freshman Academic Profile: Average high school GPA 3.3. 15% in top 10% of high school class, 40% in top 25% of high school class, 77% in top 50% of high school class. 67% from public high schools. SAT Math middle 50% range 510-600. SAT Critical Reading middle 50% range 500-580. SAT Writing middle 50% range 500-590. ACT middle 50% range 22-26. Minimum web-based TOEFL 92. Minimum paper TOEFL 570. **Basis for Candidate Selection:** *Very important factors considered include:* academic GPA, rigor of secondary school record. *Important factors considered include:* Class rank, application essay, recommendation(s), character/personal qualities, extracurricular activities, interview, talent/ability, volunteer work, work experience. *Other factors considered include:* standardized test scores, alumni/ae relation, first generation, geographical residence, level of applicant's interest, racial/ethnic status, religious affiliation/commitment, state residency. **Freshman Admission Requirements:** High school diploma is required and GED is accepted. *Academic units required:* 4 English, 3 mathematics, 3 science, (1 science labs), 2 foreign language, 3 social studies, 3 history, 3 academic electives. *Academic units recommended:* 4 English, 3 mathematics, 3 science, (1 science labs), 2 foreign language, 3 social studies, 3 history, 3 academic electives. **Freshman Admission Statistics:** 8,221 applied, 76% admitted, 14% enrolled. **Transfer Admission Requirements:** High school transcript, college transcript(s), essay or personal statement, minimum college GPA of 2.5 required. Lowest grade transferable C–. **General Admission Information:** Application Fee $50. Early decision application deadline 12/1. Notification on a rolling basis, beginning on or about 1/1. Nonfall registration accepted. Admission may be deferred for a maximum of 1 year. Credit and/or placement offered for CEEB Advanced Placement tests.

COSTS AND FINANCIAL AID

Annual tuition $33,780. Room and board $13,532. Required fees $250. Average book expense $1,200. **Required Forms and Deadlines:** FAFSA, CSS/Financial Aid PROFILE, noncustodial PROFILE. **Notification of Awards:** Applicants will be notified of awards on a rolling basis beginning 3/1. **Types of Aid:** *Need-based scholarships/grants:* Federal Pell, SEOG, state scholarships/grants, private scholarships, the school's own gift aid. *Loans:* Direct Subsidized Stafford, Direct Unsubsidized Stafford, Direct PLUS, Subsidized Stafford, Unsubsidized Stafford, PLUS, Federal Perkins, state loansAlternative loans. **Student Employment:** Federal Work-Study Program available. Institutional employment available. Off-campus job opportunities are excellent. **Financial Aid Statistics:** 100% freshmen, 96% undergrads receive need-based scholarship or grant aid. 9% freshmen, 9% undergrads receive non-need-based scholarship or grant aid. 85% freshmen, 84% undergrads receive need-based self-help aid. 4% freshmen, 6% undergrads receive athletic scholarships. 95% freshmen, 89% undergrads receive any aid. 74% undergrads borrow to pay for school. Average cumulative indebtedness $42,779. **Criteria for awarding institutional aid:** *Non-need-based:* academics, alumni affiliation, art, athletics, leadership, minority status, music/drama.

SAGINAW VALLEY STATE UNIVERSITY

7400 Bay Road, University Center, MI 48710
Phone: 989-964-4200 • **Financial Aid Phone:** 989-964-4103
E-mail: admissions@svsu.edu • **CEEB Code:** 1766
Fax: 989-790-0180 • **Website:** • **ACT Code:** 2057

This public school was founded in 1963. It has a 782-acre campus.

RATINGS

Admissions Selectivity Rating: 65   **Fire Safety Rating:** 86   **Green Rating:** 60*

STUDENTS AND FACULTY

Enrollment: 8,018. **Student Body:** 59% female, 41% male, 1% out-of-state, 3% international (39 countries represented). Asian 1%, African American 7%, Caucasian 82%, Hispanic 2%, Native American 1%.
Retention and Graduation: 9% freshmen graduate within 4 years. 38% freshmen graduate within 6 years. 24% grads go on to further study within 1 year. **Faculty:** Student/faculty ratio 20:1. 294 full-time faculty, 75% hold PhDs. 0% of classes are taught by teaching assistants.

ACADEMICS

Degrees: bachelor's, master's, post-master's certificate. **Classes:** Most classes have 20–29 students. Most lab/discussion sessions have 10–19 students. **Majors with Highest Enrollment:** criminal justice/safety studies; elementary education and teaching; nursing/registered nurse (rn, asn, bsn, msn). **Special Study Options:** Accelerated program, cooperative education program, distance learning, double major, dual enrollment, English as a Second Language (ESL), honors program, independent study, internships, student-designed major, study abroad, teacher certification program. **Honors Programs:** The University Honors Program allows students to pursue their major and minor degree work, while providing enriched academic experiences in Honors courses, seminars, research projects, and social activities. The Honors experience enables students to work more intensively with active teacher/scholars and to participate in interdisciplinary courses. Honors students will have ample opportunity to develop as critical thinkers, active learners, and problem solvers. **Disability Services:** Special programs offered to physically disabled students include note-taking services, reader services, tutors. **Career Services:** career assessment, internships.

FACILITIES

Housing: Coed dorms, special housing for disabled students, apartments for single students, wellness housing, theme housing. 95% of campus accessible to physically disabled. **Special Academic Facilities/Equipment:** Sculpture gallery, fine arts center, center for health and physical education, independent testing lab, center for economic and business research, applied technology research center. **Computers:** Students can register for classes online. Administrative functions (other than registration) can be performed online.

CAMPUS LIFE

Environment: City. **Activities:** Choral groups, concert band, dance, drama/theater, jazz band, literary magazine, marching band, music ensembles, musical theater, pep band, student government, student newspaper, student-run film society, Campus Ministries, International Student Organization, Model UN 110 registered organizations, 8 honor societies, 9 religious organizations. 4 fraternities, 7 sororities. **Athletics (Intercollegiate):** *Men:* baseball, basketball, bowling, cheerleading, cross-country, football, golf, soccer, track/field (outdoor), track/field (indoor). *Women:* basketball, cheerleading, cross-country, soccer, softball, tennis, track/field (outdoor), track/field (indoor), volleyball. **On-Campus Highlights:** Student Center, Student Recreation Center (Ryder), Zahnow Library, Arbury Fine Arts Center, University Village. **Environmental Initiatives:** Building buildings with energy savings in mind for many years. Spending consistently through the years for energy and utility conservation measures. Recycling upgrades, cutting down on areas mowed, etc.

ADMISSIONS

Freshman Academic Profile: Average high school GPA 3.2. 19% in top 10% of high school class, 40% in top 25% of high school class, 73% in top 50% of high school class. ACT middle 50% range 18-24. Minimum web-based TOEFL 61. Minimum paper TOEFL 500. **Basis for Candidate Selection:** *Very important factors considered include:* academic GPA, rigor of secondary school record, standardized test scores.*Other factors considered include:* recommendation(s). **Freshman Admission Requirements:** High school diploma is required and GED is accepted. *Academic units required:* 4 English, 3 mathematics, 2 science, 3 social studies. *Academic units recommended:* 4 English, 3 mathematics, 2 science, 3 social studies. **Freshman Admission Statistics:** 5,467 applied, 88% admitted, 35% enrolled. **Transfer Admission Requirements:** college transcript(s), minimum college GPA of 2.0 required. Lowest grade transferable C–. **General Admission Information:** Application

Fee $25. Nonfall registration accepted. Admission may be deferred for a maximum of 1. Credit and/or placement offered for CEEB Advanced Placement tests.

COSTS AND FINANCIAL AID
Annual in-state tuition $6,054. Annual out-of-state tuition $14,453. Room and board $6,830. Required fees $438. Average book expense $900. **Required Forms and Deadlines:** FAFSA. **Notification of Awards:** Applicants will be notified of awards on a rolling basis beginning 3/20. **Types of Aid:** *Need-based scholarships/grants:* Federal Pell, SEOG, state scholarships/grants, private scholarships, the school's own gift aid. *Loans:* Direct Subsidized Stafford, Direct Unsubsidized Stafford, Direct PLUS, state loans, CitiAssist Loans; Signature Student Loans. **Student Employment:** Federal Work-Study Program available. Institutional employment available. Off-campus job opportunities are good. **Financial Aid Statistics:** 36% freshmen, 62% undergrads receive need-based scholarship or grant aid. 77% freshmen, 47% undergrads receive non-need-based scholarship or grant aid. 73% freshmen, 82% undergrads receive need-based self-help aid. 5% freshmen, 5% undergrads receive athletic scholarships. 92% freshmen, 83% undergrads receive any aid. 68% undergrads borrow to pay for school. Average cumulative indebtedness $23,561. **Criteria for awarding institutional aid:** *Non-need-based:* academics, art, athletics, leadership, minority status, music/drama.

SAINT ANSELM COLLEGE

100 Saint Anselm Drive, Manchester, NH 03102-1310
Phone: 603-641-7500 • **Financial Aid Phone:** 603-641-7110
E-mail: admission@anselm.edu • **CEEB Code:** 3748
Fax: 603-641-7550 • **Website:** www.anselm.edu • **ACT Code:** 2522

This private school, affiliated with the Roman Catholic Church, was founded in 1889. It has a 404-acre campus.

RATINGS
Admissions Selectivity Rating: 78   **Fire Safety Rating:** 78   **Green Rating:** 60*

STUDENTS AND FACULTY
Enrollment: 1,873. **Student Body:** 58% female, 42% male, 79% out-of-state, 0% international (20 countries represented). Asian 1%, African American 2%, Caucasian 84%, Hispanic 3%, Native American 0%.
Retention and Graduation: 85% freshmen return for sophomore year. 72% freshmen graduate within 4 years. 73% freshmen graduate within 6 years. 16% grads go on to further study within 1 year. 11% grads pursue arts and sciences degrees. 3% grads pursue law degrees. 1% grads pursue business degrees. 2% grads pursue medical degrees. **Faculty:** Student/faculty ratio 11:1. 142 full-time faculty, 91% hold PhDs, 9% are members of minority groups, 51% are women. 0% of classes are taught by teaching assistants.

ACADEMICS
Degrees: bachelor's, certificate. **Classes:** Most classes have 10–19 students. Most lab/discussion sessions have 10–19 students. **Special Study Options:** cross-registration, honors program, independent study, internships, liberal arts/career combination, study abroad, teacher certification program. **Honors Programs:** Honors Program for Presidential Scholars. **Disability Services:** Special programs offered to physically disabled students include note-taking services, reader services, tape recorders, tutors. **Career Services:** Alumni network, alumni services, career/job search classes, career assessment, internships, regional alumni.

FACILITIES
Housing: Coed dorms, special housing for disabled students, men's dorms, women's dorms, apartments for single students, theme housing, Substance Free Housing. 60% of campus accessible to physically disabled. **Special Academic Facilities/Equipment:** Chapel Art Center, New Hampshire Institute of Politics, Izart Observatory, Koonz Theatre, Comisky Studio (Fine Arts), Poisson Hall **Computers:** 100% of classrooms, 100% of dorms, 100% of libraries, 100% of dining areas, 100% of student union, have wireless network access. Students can register for classes online. Administrative functions (other than registration) can be performed online.

CAMPUS LIFE
Environment: City. **Activities:** Choral groups, dance, drama/theater, jazz band, literary magazine, musical theater, radio station, student government,

student newspaper, television station, yearbook, Campus Ministries, International Student Organization, Model UN 120 registered organizations, 11 honor societies, 7 religious organizations. **Athletics (Intercollegiate):** *Men:* baseball, basketball, cross-country, football, golf, ice hockey, lacrosse, skiing (downhill/alpine), soccer, tennis. *Women:* basketball, cross-country, field hockey, golf, ice hockey, lacrosse, skiing (downhill/alpine), soccer, softball, tennis, volleyball. **On-Campus Highlights:** Joseph Hall Academic Building, Chapel Arts Center, Davidson Hall Dining Hall, Sullivan Ice Arena & Fitness Center, Abbey Church, Coffee Shop and Pub Cushing Student Center.

ADMISSIONS
Freshman Academic Profile: Average high school GPA 3.2. 65% from public high schools. SAT Math middle 50% range 510-610. SAT Critical Reading middle 50% range 500-600. SAT Writing middle 50% range 510-600. ACT middle 50% range 24-27. Minimum web-based TOEFL 80. Minimum paper TOEFL 550. **Basis for Candidate Selection:** *Very important factors considered include:* application essay, academic GPA, recommendation(s), rigor of secondary school record, standardized test scores.*Other factors considered include:* Class rank, alumni/ae relation, character/personal qualities, extracurricular activities, geographical residence, racial/ethnic status, state residency, talent/ability, volunteer work, work experience. **Freshman Admission Requirements:** High school diploma is required and GED is accepted. *Academic units required:* 4 English, 3 mathematics, 3 science, (2 science labs), 2 foreign language, 2 social studies. *Academic units recommended:* 4 English, 3 mathematics, 3 science, (2 science labs), 2 foreign language, 2 social studies. **Freshman Admission Statistics:** 4,134 applied, 71% admitted, 19% enrolled. **Transfer Admission Requirements:** High school transcript, college transcript(s), essay or personal statement, standardized test scores, statement of good standing from prior institution(s). Minimum college GPA of 2.5 required. Lowest grade transferable C. **General Admission Information:** Application Fee $55. Early decision application deadline 11/15. Regular application deadline 3/1. Notification on a rolling basis, beginning on or about 1/1. Nonfall registration accepted. Admission may be deferred for a maximum of 1 year. Credit and/or placement offered for CEEB Advanced Placement tests.

COSTS AND FINANCIAL AID
Annual tuition $32,710. Room and board $12,380. Required fees $1,100. Average book expense $1,000. **Required Forms and Deadlines:** FAFSA, CSS/Financial Aid PROFILE, noncustodial PROFILE, business/farm supplement. **Notification of Awards:** Applicants will be notified of awards on a rolling basis beginning 3/1. **Types of Aid:** *Need-based scholarships/grants:* Federal Pell, SEOG, state scholarships/grants, private scholarships, the school's own gift aid. *Loans:* Subsidized Stafford, Unsubsidized Stafford, PLUS, Federal Perkins. **Student Employment:** Federal Work-Study Program available. Institutional employment available. Off-campus job opportunities are excellent. **Financial Aid Statistics:** 100% freshmen, 99% undergrads receive need-based scholarship or grant aid. 14% freshmen, 10% undergrads receive non-need-based scholarship or grant aid. 85% freshmen, 88% undergrads receive need-based self-help aid. 5% freshmen, 3% undergrads receive athletic scholarships. 81% undergrads borrow to pay for school. Average cumulative indebtedness $38,357. **Criteria for awarding institutional aid:** *Non-need-based:* academics, alumni affiliation, athletics, state/district residency.

See page 1190.

SAINT ANTHONY COLLEGE OF NURSING

5658 East State Street, Rockford, IL 61108-2468
Phone: 815-395-5100 • **Financial Aid Phone:** 815-395-5089
E-mail: cheryldelgado@sacn.edu
Fax: 815-395-2275 • **Website:** www.sacn.edu

This private school, affiliated with the Roman Catholic Church, was founded in 1915.

RATINGS
Admissions Selectivity Rating: 60*   **Fire Safety Rating:** 64   **Green Rating:** 60*

STUDENTS AND FACULTY
Enrollment: 86. **Student Body:** 93% female, 7% male.
Retention and Graduation: 10% grads go on to further study within 1 year.

ACADEMICS
Degrees: bachelor's, master's. **Special Study Options:** distance learning, independent study.

FACILITIES
Housing: Private apartments, student plan housing, private rooms.

CAMPUS LIFE

Environment: City. **Activities:** student government, student newspaper 1 registered organizations.

ADMISSIONS

Freshman Academic Profile: Minimum paper TOEFL 550. **Basis for Candidate Selection:** *Important factors considered include:* application essay, recommendation(s), interview. *Other factors considered include:* extracurricular activities, volunteer work, work experience. **Freshman Admission Requirements:** High school diploma or equivalent is not required. **Transfer Admission Requirements:** college transcript(s), essay or personal statement, interview, minimum college GPA of 2.5 required. Lowest grade transferable C. **General Admission Information:** Application Fee $50. Regular application deadline 1/15. Credit offered for CEEB Advanced Placement tests.

COSTS AND FINANCIAL AID

Annual tuition $17,220. Required fees $192. **Types of Aid:** *Need-based scholarships/grants:* Federal Pell, state scholarships/grants, private scholarships, the school's own gift aid. *Loans:* Subsidized Stafford, Unsubsidized Stafford, PLUS. **Financial Aid Statistics:** 100% undergrads receive need-based scholarship or grant aid. 64% undergrads receive non-need-based scholarship or grant aid. 91% undergrads receive need-based self-help aid. 0% freshmen, 86% undergrads receive any aid. 90% undergrads borrow to pay for school. Average cumulative indebtedness $6,828. **Criteria for awarding institutional aid:** *Non-need-based:* academics.

SAINT CLOUD STATE UNIVERSITY

720 South 4th Avenue, Saint Cloud, MN 56301-4498
Phone: 320-308-2244 • **Financial Aid Phone:** 320-308-2047
E-mail: scsu4u@stcloudstate.edu • **CEEB Code:** 6679
Fax: 320-308-2243 • **ACT Code:** 2144

This public school was founded in 1869. It has a 920-acre campus.

RATINGS

Admissions Selectivity Rating: 68   **Fire Safety Rating:** 60*   **Green Rating:** 60*

STUDENTS AND FACULTY

Enrollment: 13,120. **Student Body:** 53% female, 47% male, 8% out-of-state, 4% international (85 countries represented). Asian 2%, African American 2%, Caucasian 72%, Hispanic 1%, Native American 1%.
Retention and Graduation: 71% freshmen return for sophomore year.
Faculty: Student/faculty ratio 17:1. 650 full-time faculty, 80% hold PhDs, 18% are members of minority groups, 41% are women. 0% of classes are taught by teaching assistants.

ACADEMICS

Degrees: associate, bachelor's, master's, post-bachelor's certificate, post-master's certificate. **Classes:** Most classes have 20–29 students. **Majors with Highest Enrollment:** elementary education and teaching; marketing/marketing management; mass communication/media studies. **Special Study Options:** Accelerated program, cooperative education program, cross-registration, distance learning, double major, dual enrollment, English as a Second Language (ESL), honors program, independent study, internships, student-designed major, study abroad, teacher certification program. **Disability Services:** Special programs offered to physically disabled students include note-taking services, reader services. **Career Services:** Alumni network, alumni services, career/job search classes, career assessment, internships.

FACILITIES

Housing: Coed dorms, special housing for international students 86% of campus accessible to physically disabled. **Special Academic Facilities/Equipment:** Art and anthropology museums, electron microscope, planetarium, G.I.S. and weather labs. **Computers:** Students can register for classes online. Administrative functions (other than registration) can be performed online.

CAMPUS LIFE

Environment: Town. **Activities:** Choral groups, concert band, dance, drama/theater, music ensembles, musical theater, opera, radio station, student government, student newspaper, symphony orchestra, television station 240 registered organizations, 6 honor societies, 12 religious organizations. 5 fraternities, 4 sororities. **Athletics (Intercollegiate):** *Men:* baseball, basketball, cheerleading, cross-country, diving, football, golf, ice hockey, rugby, swimming, tennis, track/field (outdoor), track/field (indoor), wrestling. *Women:* basketball, cheerleading, cross-country, diving, golf, ice hockey, rugby, skiing (downhill/alpine), soccer, softball, swimming, tennis, track/field (outdoor), track/field (indoor), volleyball. **On-Campus Highlights:** James W. Miller Learning Resource Center, National Hockey Center.

ADMISSIONS

Freshman Academic Profile: 7% in top 10% of high school class, 29% in top 25% of high school class, 76% in top 50% of high school class. 99% from public high schools. ACT middle 50% range 19-24. Minimum paper TOEFL 500.
Basis for Candidate Selection: *Very important factors considered include:* Class rank, rigor of secondary school record. *Other factors considered include:* application essay, academic GPA, recommendation(s), standardized test scores, extracurricular activities, talent/ability. **Freshman Admission Requirements:** High school diploma is required and GED is accepted. *Academic units required:* 4 English, 3 mathematics, 3 science, (1 science labs), 2 foreign language, 3 social studies, 1 history, 1 Fine Arts. 4 English, 3 mathematics, 3 science, (1 science labs), 2 foreign language, 3 social studies, 1 history, 1 Fine Arts **Freshman Admission Statistics:** 5,912 applied, 78% admitted, 47% enrolled. **Transfer Admission Requirements:** college transcript(s), statement of good standing from prior institution(s). Minimum college GPA of 2.0 required. Lowest grade transferable C. **General Admission Information:** Application Fee $20. Regular application deadline 6/1. Notification on a rolling basis, beginning on or about 9/15. Nonfall registration accepted. Admission may be deferred for a maximum of 24 months. Credit offered for CEEB Advanced Placement tests.

COSTS AND FINANCIAL AID

Annual in-state tuition $4,760. Annual out-of-state tuition $10,332. Room and board $4,688. Required fees $562. Average book expense $1,000. **Required Forms and Deadlines:** FAFSA, institution's own financial aid form. **Notification of Awards:** Applicants will be notified of awards on a rolling basis beginning 6/3. **Types of Aid:** *Need-based scholarships/grants:* Federal Pell, SEOG, state scholarships/grants, private scholarships, the school's own gift aid. *Loans:* Subsidized Stafford, Unsubsidized Stafford, PLUS, Federal Perkins, state loans. **Student Employment:** Federal Work-Study Program available. Institutional employment available. **Financial Aid Statistics:** 79% freshmen, 76% undergrads receive need-based scholarship or grant aid. 8% freshmen, 5% undergrads receive non-need-based scholarship or grant aid. 95% freshmen, 99% undergrads receive need-based self-help aid. 2% freshmen, 2% undergrads receive athletic scholarships. 52% undergrads borrow to pay for school. Average cumulative indebtedness $20,431. **Criteria for awarding institutional aid:** *Non-need-based:* academics, art, athletics, leadership, music/drama.

SAINT FRANCIS MEDICAL CENTER
COLLEGE OF NURSING

511 NE. Greenleaf Street, Peoria, IL 61603
Phone: 309-624-8980
E-mail: janice.e.farquharson@osfhealthcare.org
Fax: 309-624-8973 • **Website:** www.sfmccon.edu/

This is a private school.

RATINGS

Admissions Selectivity Rating: 60*   **Fire Safety Rating:** 99   **Green Rating:** 60*

STUDENTS AND FACULTY

Enrollment: 402. **Student Body:** 89% female, 11% male, % out-of-state, 0% international (2 countries represented). Asian 2%, African American 5%, Caucasian 89%, Hispanic 4%, Native American 0%.
Retention and Graduation: Faculty: Student/faculty ratio 9:1. 34 full-time faculty, 29% hold PhDs, 0% are members of minority groups, 100% are women.

ACADEMICS

Degrees: bachelor's, doctoral, master's, post-master's certificate. **Classes:** Most classes have 40-49 students. Most lab/discussion sessions have fewer than 10 students. **Special Study Options:** Accelerated program, distance learning, independent study.

FACILITIES

Housing: Coed dorms.

CAMPUS LIFE

Activities: student government.

ADMISSIONS

Freshman Admission Requirements: High school diploma is required and GED is accepted. **Transfer Admission Requirements:** High school transcript, college transcript(s), essay or personal statement, statement of good standing from prior institution(s). Minimum college GPA of 2.50 required. Lowest grade transferable C. **General Admission Information:** Application Fee $50.

COSTS AND FINANCIAL AID

Annual tuition $15,810. Room and board $3,000. Required fees $556. Average book expense $1,565. **Required Forms and Deadlines:** FAFSA, institution's own financial aid form. **Notification of Awards:** Applicants will be notified of awards on a rolling basis beginning 5/15. **Types of Aid:** *Need-based scholarships/grants:* Federal Pell, state scholarships/grants. *Loans:* Subsidized Stafford, Unsubsidized Stafford, PLUS. **Financial Aid Statistics:** 72% undergrads receive need-based scholarship or grant aid. 89% undergrads receive need-based self-help aid. **Criteria for awarding institutional aid:** *Non-need-based:* academics, alumni affiliation.

SAINT FRANCIS UNIVERSITY (PA)

PO Box 600, Loretto, PA 15940
Phone: 814-472-3000 • **Financial Aid Phone:** 814-472-3010
E-mail: admissions@francis.edu • **CEEB Code:** 2797
Fax: 814-472-3335 **ACT Code:** 3682

This private school, affiliated with the Roman Catholic Church, was founded in 1847. It has a 600-acre campus.

RATINGS

Admissions Selectivity Rating: 72   **Fire Safety Rating:** 76   **Green Rating:** 60*

STUDENTS AND FACULTY

Enrollment: 1,806. **Student Body:** 59% female, 41% male, 31% out-of-state, 3% international (25 countries represented). Asian 1%, African American 5%, Caucasian 86%, Hispanic 1%, Native American 0%.
Retention and Graduation: 83% freshmen return for sophomore year. 58% freshmen graduate within 4 years. 68% freshmen graduate within 6 years. 29% grads go on to further study within 1 year. 5% grads pursue arts and sciences degrees. 3% grads pursue law degrees. 9% grads pursue business degrees. 3% grads pursue medical degrees. **Faculty:** Student/faculty ratio 14:1. 113 full-time faculty. 0% of classes are taught by teaching assistants.

ACADEMICS

Degrees: associate, bachelor's, master's, post-bachelor's certificate. **Classes:** Most classes have 10–19 students. Most lab/discussion sessions have 10–19 students. **Majors with Highest Enrollment:** business/commerce; health professions and related clinical sciences, other; physician assistant. **Special Study Options:** cooperative education program, distance learning, double major, honors program, independent study, internships, liberal arts/career combination, student-designed major, study abroad, teacher certification program. **Honors Programs:** Honors Program **Combined Degree Programs:** BA/MD, BA/DDS, BS/MPAS, BS/MOT, BS/DPT, 3-3 BS/PharmD, 2-3 PharmD. **Disability Services:** Special programs offered to physically disabled students include note-taking services, tape recorders, tutors. **Career Services:** Alumni network, career/job search classes, career assessment, internships.

FACILITIES

Housing: Coed dorms, men's dorms, women's dorms, fraternity/sorority housing, apartments for single students, Special Housing for Honors Students, Special Housing for Campus Ministry. 30% of campus accessible to physically disabled. **Special Academic Facilities/Equipment:** Art museum, elementary-level library for education majors, physician assistant practice facilities, cadaver lab, physical therapy lab, Center of Excellence for Remote and Medically Underserved Areas. **Computers:** Administrative functions (other than registration) can be performed online. Undergraduates are required to own a computer.

CAMPUS LIFE

Environment: Rural. **Activities:** Choral groups, dance, drama/theater, literary magazine, music ensembles, pep band, radio station, student government, student newspaper, student-run film society, television station, yearbook 60 registered organizations, 9 honor societies, 10 religious organizations. 3 fraternities, 3 sororities. **Athletics (Intercollegiate):** *Men:* basketball, cross-country, football, golf, soccer, swimming, tennis, track/field (outdoor), track/field (indoor), volleyball. *Women:* basketball, cross-country, field hockey, golf, lacrosse, soccer, softball, swimming, tennis, track/field (outdoor), track/field (indoor), volleyball. **On-Campus Highlights:** Christian Hall - residence hall, JFK Student Center, Immaculate Conception Chapel, Stokes Athletics Facility, Mt. Assisi Gardens.

ADMISSIONS

Freshman Academic Profile: Average high school GPA 3.4. 20% in top 10% of high school class, 53% in top 25% of high school class, 0% in top 50% of high school class. 79% from public high schools. SAT Math middle 50% range 460-570. SAT Critical Reading middle 50% range 450-550. SAT Writing middle 50% range 440-550. ACT middle 50% range 19-24. Minimum paper TOEFL 500.

Basis for Candidate Selection: *Very important factors considered include:* Class rank, academic GPA, rigor of secondary school record, standardized test scores, extracurricular activities. *Important factors considered include:* application essay, recommendation(s), character/personal qualities, interview, level of applicant's interest, talent/ability, volunteer work. *Other factors considered include:* alumni/ae relation, work experience. **Freshman Admission Requirements:** High school diploma is required and GED is accepted. *Academic units required:* 4 English, 2 mathematics, 1 science, (1 science labs), 2 social studies, 7 academic electives. *Academic units recommended:* 4 English, 2 mathematics, 1 science, (1 science labs), 2 social studies, 7 academic electives. **Freshman Admission Statistics:** 1,575 applied, 72% admitted, 37% enrolled. **Transfer Admission Requirements:** High school transcript, college transcript(s), standardized test scores, statement of good standing from prior institution(s). Minimum college GPA of 2.0 required. Lowest grade transferable C. **General Admission Information:** Application Fee $30. Notification on a rolling basis, beginning on or about 10/1. Nonfall registration accepted. Admission may be deferred for a maximum of 12. Credit offered for CEEB Advanced Placement tests.

COSTS AND FINANCIAL AID

Annual tuition $25,484. Room and board $9,066. Required fees $1,050. Average book expense $500. **Required Forms and Deadlines:** FAFSA. **Notification of Awards:** Applicants will be notified of awards on a rolling basis beginning 10/1. **Types of Aid:** *Need-based scholarships/grants:* Federal Pell, SEOG, state scholarships/grants, private scholarships, the school's own gift aid. *Loans:* Subsidized Stafford, Unsubsidized Stafford, PLUS, Federal Perkins. **Student Employment:** Federal Work-Study Program available. Institutional employment available. Highest amount earned per year from on-campus jobs $1,000. Off-campus job opportunities are fair. **Financial Aid Statistics:** 59% freshmen, 61% undergrads receive need-based scholarship or grant aid. 100% freshmen, 99% undergrads receive non-need-based scholarship or grant aid. 57% freshmen, 70% undergrads receive need-based self-help aid. 23% freshmen, 19% undergrads receive athletic scholarships. 98% freshmen receive any aid. 95% undergrads borrow to pay for school. **Criteria for awarding institutional aid:** *Non-need-based:* academics, alumni affiliation, athletics, leadership, music/drama, religious affiliation.

See page 1192.

SAINT JOSEPH SEMINARY COLLEGE

75376 River Road, St. Benedict, LA 70457
Phone: 985-867-2248 • **Financial Aid Phone:** 985-867-2229
E-mail: georgebinderregistrar@sjasc.edu • **CEEB Code:** 6689
Fax: 985-867-2270 • **ACT Code:** 1604

This private school, affiliated with the Roman Catholic Church, was founded in 1891. It has a 1200-acre campus.

RATINGS

Admissions Selectivity Rating: 61   **Fire Safety Rating:** 60*   **Green Rating:** 60*

STUDENTS AND FACULTY

Enrollment: 100. **Student Body:** 0% female, 100% male, 34% out-of-state. Asian 5%, African American %, Caucasian 69%, Hispanic 26%, Native American 0%.
Faculty: Student/faculty ratio 7:1. 16 full-time faculty, 31% hold PhDs, 0% are members of minority groups, 44% are women. 0% of classes are taught by teaching assistants.

ACADEMICS

Degrees: bachelor's. **Classes:** Most classes have 10–19 students. **Special Study Options:** distance learning, English as a Second Language (ESL), independent study, study abroad. **Disability Services:** Special programs offered to physically disabled students include tape recorders, tutors.

FACILITIES

Housing: men's dorms. 100% of campus accessible to physically disabled.

CAMPUS LIFE

Environment: Rural. **Activities:** Choral groups, drama/theater, literary magazine, student government, student newspaper, yearbook 1 religious organizations.

ADMISSIONS

Freshman Academic Profile: Minimum paper TOEFL 520. **Basis for Candidate Selection:** *Very important factors considered include:* rigor of secondary school record, character/personal qualities, religious affiliation/commitment. *Important factors considered include:* recommendation(s), standardized test scores. *Other factors considered include:* Class rank, extracurricular activities, interview, volunteer work. **Freshman Admission Requirements:** High school diploma is required and GED is accepted. *Academic units required:* 3 English, 2 mathematics, 2 science, 2 foreign language, 1 history. *Academic units recommended:* 3 English, 2 mathematics, 2 science, 2 foreign language, 1 history. **Freshman Admission Statistics:** 11 applied, 100% admitted, 100% enrolled. **Transfer Admission Requirements:** High school transcript, college transcript(s), standardized test scores, Lowest grade transferable C. **General Admission Information:** Nonfall registration accepted. Neither credit nor placement offered for CEEB Advanced Placement tests.

COSTS AND FINANCIAL AID

Annual tuition $13,500. Room and board $13,040. Required fees $1,165. Average book expense $1,000. **Required Forms and Deadlines:** FAFSA, institution's own financial aid form, state aid form. **Notification of Awards:** Applicants will be notified of awards on a rolling basis beginning 8/3. **Types of Aid:** *Need-based scholarships/grants:* Federal Pell, SEOG, state scholarships/grants, private scholarships, the school's own gift aid. *Loans:* Subsidized Stafford, Unsubsidized Stafford, PLUS, Federal Perkins. **Financial Aid Statistics:** 100% freshmen, 100% undergrads receive need-based scholarship or grant aid. 100% freshmen, 20% undergrads receive non-need-based scholarship or grant aid. 100% freshmen, 100% undergrads receive need-based self-help aid. 18% undergrads borrow to pay for school. Average cumulative indebtedness $12,400.

SAINT JOSEPH'S COLLEGE (IN)

P.O. Box 890, Rensselaer, IN 47978
Phone: 219-866-6170 • **Financial Aid Phone:** 219-866-6163
E-mail: admissions@saintjoe.edu • **CEEB Code:** 1697
Fax: 219-866-6122 • **Website:** www.saintjoe.edu • **ACT Code:** 1240

This private school, affiliated with the Roman Catholic Church, was founded in 1889. It has a 180-acre campus.

RATINGS
Admissions Selectivity Rating: 76   **Fire Safety Rating:** 79   **Green Rating:** 60*

STUDENTS AND FACULTY
Enrollment: 1,068. **Student Body:** 61% female, 39% male, 23% out-of-state, 0% international (9 countries represented). Asian 1%, African American 10%, Caucasian 79%, Hispanic 4%, Native American 1%.
Retention and Graduation: 67% freshmen return for sophomore year. 41% freshmen graduate within 4 years. 50% freshmen graduate within 6 years. 22% grads go on to further study within 1 year. 3% grads pursue arts and sciences degrees. 3% grads pursue law degrees. 3% grads pursue business degrees. 12% grads pursue medical degrees. **Faculty:** Student/faculty ratio 13:1. 59 full-time faculty, 69% hold PhDs, 5% are members of minority groups, 39% are women. 0% of classes are taught by teaching assistants.

ACADEMICS
Degrees: associate, bachelor's, certificate, diploma, master's, terminal associate. **Classes:** Most classes have 10–19 students. Most lab/discussion sessions have 10–19 students. **Majors with Highest Enrollment:** business/commerce; elementary education and teaching; nursing/registered nurse (rn, asn, bsn, msn). **Special Study Options:** Accelerated program, cross-registration, double major, dual enrollment, honors program, independent study, internships, liberal arts/career combination, student-designed major, study abroad, teacher certification program. **Disability Services:** Special programs offered to physically disabled students include note-taking services, reader services, tape recorders, tutors. **Career Services:** Alumni network, career assessment, internships.

FACILITIES
Housing: Coed dorms, special housing for disabled students, men's dorms, women's dorms, apartments for single students. 74% of campus accessible to physically disabled. **Computers:** 100% of dorms, 100% of libraries, 100% of dining areas, have wireless network access.

CAMPUS LIFE
Environment: Village. **Activities:** Choral groups, concert band, dance, drama/theater, jazz band, literary magazine, marching band, music ensembles, musical theater, pep band, radio station, student government, student newspaper, student-run film society, television station 41 registered organizations, 4 honor societies, 7 religious organizations. **Athletics (Intercollegiate):** *Men:* baseball, basketball, cross-country, football, golf, soccer, tennis, track/field (outdoor), track/field (indoor). *Women:* basketball, cross-country, golf, soccer, softball, tennis, track/field (outdoor), track/field (indoor), volleyball. **On-Campus Highlights:** Rev. Charles Banet, C.P.P.S. Core Educati, Saint Joseph's Chapel, Lourdes Grotto, Hanson Recreation Center/Fitness Center, Lake Banet.

ADMISSIONS
Freshman Academic Profile: Average high school GPA 3.1. 14% in top 10% of high school class, 34% in top 25% of high school class, 69% in top 50% of high school class. 83% from public high schools. SAT Math middle 50% range 450-535. SAT Critical Reading middle 50% range 440-510. ACT middle 50% range 19-25. Minimum web-based TOEFL 80. Minimum paper TOEFL 550. **Basis for Candidate Selection:** *Very important factors considered include:* academic GPA, rigor of secondary school record, standardized test scores. *Important factors considered include:* Class rank, character/personal qualities, extracurricular activities, volunteer work. *Other factors considered include:* application essay, recommendation(s), alumni/ae relation, interview, talent/ability, work experience. **Freshman Admission Requirements:** High school diploma is required and GED is accepted. **Freshman Admission Statistics:** 1,718 applied, 62% admitted, 22% enrolled. **Transfer Admission Requirements:** college transcript(s), minimum college GPA of 2.0 required. Lowest grade transferable C–. **General Admission Information:** Application Fee $25. Notification on a rolling basis, beginning on or about 12/1. Nonfall registration accepted. Admission may be deferred for a maximum of 2. Credit offered for CEEB Advanced Placement tests.

COSTS AND FINANCIAL AID
Annual tuition $27,160. Room and board $8,250. Required fees $190. Average book expense $900. **Required Forms and Deadlines:** FAFSA. **Notification of Awards:** Applicants will be notified of awards on a rolling basis beginning 3/1. **Types of Aid:** *Need-based scholarships/grants:* Federal Pell, SEOG, state scholarships/grants, private scholarships, the school's own gift aid. *Loans:* Subsidized Stafford, Unsubsidized Stafford, PLUS, Federal Perkins. **Student Employment:** Federal Work-Study Program available. Institutional employment available. Highest amount earned per year from on-campus jobs $1,500. Off-campus job opportunities are poor. **Financial Aid Statistics:** 99% freshmen, 97% undergrads receive need-based scholarship or grant aid. 26% freshmen, 26% undergrads receive non-need-based scholarship or grant aid. 73% freshmen, 73% undergrads receive need-based self-help aid. 3% freshmen, 5% undergrads receive athletic scholarships. 99% freshmen, 99% undergrads receive any aid. 81% undergrads borrow to pay for school. Average cumulative indebtedness $30,963. **Criteria for awarding institutional aid:** *Non-need-based:* academics, alumni affiliation, athletics, minority status, music/drama.

SAINT JOSEPH'S COLLEGE OF MAINE

278 Whites Bridge Road, Standish, ME 04084-5263
Phone: 207-893-7746 • **Financial Aid Phone:** 207-893-6612
E-mail: admission@sjcme.edu • **CEEB Code:** 3755
Fax: 207-893-7862 • **Website:** www.sjcme.edu • **ACT Code:** 1659

This private school, affiliated with the Roman Catholic Church, was founded in 1912. It has a 350-acre campus.

RATINGS
Admissions Selectivity Rating: 67   **Fire Safety Rating:** 70   **Green Rating:** 60*

STUDENTS AND FACULTY
Enrollment: 1,034. **Student Body:** 65% female, 35% male, 44% out-of-state, 0% international (1 countries represented). Asian 0%, African American 2%, Caucasian 83%, Hispanic 1%, Native American 0%.
Retention and Graduation: 78% freshmen return for sophomore year. 56% freshmen graduate within 4 years. 62% freshmen graduate within 6 years. 15% grads go on to further study within 1 year. 1% grads pursue arts and sciences degrees. 3% grads pursue business degrees. 2% grads pursue medical degrees. **Faculty:** Student/faculty ratio 15:1. 68 full-time faculty, 82% hold PhDs, 1% are members of minority groups, 51% are women. 0% of classes are taught by teaching assistants.

ACADEMICS
Degrees: bachelor's. **Classes:** Most classes have 10–19 students. Most lab/discussion sessions have 10–19 students. **Majors with Highest Enrollment:** business/commerce; elementary education and teaching; nursing/registered nurse (rn, asn, bsn, msn). **Special Study Options:** cross-registration, distance learning, double major, dual enrollment, honors program, independent study, internships, student-designed major, study abroad, teacher certification program. **Honors Programs:** 30-40 students per year are admitted for core curriculum Honors Program. **Disability Services:** Special programs offered to physically disabled students include note-taking services, reader services, tape recorders, tutors.

FACILITIES
Housing: Coed dorms, men's dorms, women's dorms, substance-free housing. 75% of campus accessible to physically disabled. **Special Academic Facilities/**

Equipment: radio studio, telescope **Computers:** Administrative functions (other than registration) can be performed online.

CAMPUS LIFE

Environment: Rural. **Activities:** Choral groups, dance, drama/theater, literary magazine, radio station, student government, student newspaper, yearbook 25 registered organizations, 2 honor societies, 1 religious organizations. **Athletics (Intercollegiate):** *Men:* baseball, basketball, cross-country, golf, lacrosse, soccer, swimming. *Women:* basketball, cross-country, field hockey, lacrosse, soccer, softball, swimming, volleyball. **On-Campus Highlights:** Harold Alford Center, Heffernan Center, Alfond Hall, Java Joe's Cafe, Mercy Hall.

ADMISSIONS

Freshman Academic Profile: 80% from public high schools. SAT Math middle 50% range 440-540. SAT Critical Reading middle 50% range 440-520. Minimum paper TOEFL 500. **Basis for Candidate Selection:** *Very important factors considered include:* application essay, recommendation(s), rigor of secondary school record, character/personal qualities. *Important factors considered include:* Class rank, academic GPA, standardized test scores, talent/ability, volunteer work. *Other factors considered include:* extracurricular activities, interview, level of applicant's interest, work experience. **Freshman Admission Requirements:** High school diploma is required and GED is accepted. **Freshman Admission Statistics:** 1,094 applied, 82% admitted, 41% enrolled. **Transfer Admission Requirements:** college transcript(s), essay or personal statement, statement of good standing from prior institution(s). Minimum college GPA of 2.0 required. Lowest grade transferable C. **General Admission Information:** Application Fee $50. Regular application deadline 8/1. Nonfall registration accepted. Admission may be deferred for a maximum of 1 year. Credit and/or placement offered for CEEB Advanced Placement tests.

COSTS AND FINANCIAL AID

Annual tuition $21,000. Room and board $9,030. Required fees $760. Average book expense $800. **Required Forms and Deadlines:** FAFSA, institution's own financial aid form. **Notification of Awards:** Applicants will be notified of awards on a rolling basis beginning 3/1. **Types of Aid:** *Need-based scholarships/grants:* Federal Pell, SEOG, state scholarships/grants, private scholarships, the school's own gift aid, Federal Nursing Scholarships. *Loans:* Subsidized Stafford, Unsubsidized Stafford, PLUS, Federal Perkins, Federal Nursing, state loans. **Student Employment:** Federal Work-Study Program available. Institutional employment available. Highest amount earned per year from on-campus jobs $1,275. Off-campus job opportunities are good. **Financial Aid Statistics:** 100% freshmen, 100% undergrads receive need-based scholarship or grant aid. 13% freshmen, 12% undergrads receive non-need-based scholarship or grant aid. 86% freshmen, 87% undergrads receive need-based self-help aid. 98% freshmen, 95% undergrads receive any aid. 84% undergrads borrow to pay for school. Average cumulative indebtedness $35,518. **Criteria for awarding institutional aid:** *Non-need-based:* academics, leadership.

SAINT JOSEPH'S UNIVERSITY (PA)

5600 City Avenue, Philadelphia, PA 19131
Phone: 610-660-1300 • **Financial Aid Phone:** 610-660-1556
E-mail: admit@sju.edu • **CEEB Code:** 2801
Fax: 610-660-1314 • **Website:** www.sju.edu • **ACT Code:** 3684

This private school, affiliated with the Roman Catholic-Jesuit Church,, affiliated with the Jesuit Church, was founded in 1851. It has a 103-acre campus.

RATINGS

Admissions Selectivity Rating: 75   **Fire Safety Rating:** 97   **Green Rating:** 73

STUDENTS AND FACULTY

Enrollment: 5,202. **Student Body:** 53% female, 47% male, 53% out-of-state, 1% international (52 countries represented). Asian 2%, African American 7%, Caucasian 81%, Hispanic 5%, Native American 0%.
Retention and Graduation: 74% freshmen graduate within 4 years. 23% grads go on to further study within 1 year. 27% grads pursue arts and sciences degrees. 9% grads pursue law degrees. 7% grads pursue business degrees. 40% grads pursue medical degrees. **Faculty:** Student/faculty ratio 13:1. 310 full-time faculty, 89% hold PhDs, 14% are members of minority groups, 46% are women. 0% of classes are taught by teaching assistants.

ACADEMICS

Degrees: associate, bachelor's, certificate, master's, post-bachelor's certificate, post-master's certificate, transfer associate. **Classes:** Most classes have 20–29 students. Most lab/discussion sessions have 10–19 students. **Majors with Highest Enrollment:** accounting; finance; marketing/marketing management.

Special Study Options: Accelerated program, cooperative education program, distance learning, double major, dual enrollment, English as a Second Language (ESL), exchange student program (domestic), honors program, independent study, internships, student-designed major, study abroad, teacher certification program, weekend college, off campus study in Jesuit student exchange. **Honors Programs:** There are distinctive benefits attached to belonging to the SJU Honors Program: Team-taught courses allow distinguished faculty members to share their knowledge and expertise with students in a challenging academic environment. Individual honors courses stress a detailed and thorough scholarly exploration of different fields of knowledge. Honors students register ahead of other students in their year. Honors suites in the residence halls allow like-minded students to live together, even as freshmen. Honors students are provided with free tickets and transportation to concerts and performances by world-renowned institutions such as the Arden Theater Company, the Curtis Institute of Music, the Philadelphia Orchestra, the Pennsylvania Ballet, the Academy of Vocal Arts, the Philadelphia Museum of Art, and the Franklin Science Institute. Receptions, concerts and lectures are regularly sponsored by the Honors Program for Honors Students. Students have access to Claver House, a quiet retreat where honors students can study, work with personal computers and attend receptions. Students have opportunities to present research and creative work at national conferences and seminars; they are also kept informed about scholarship and funding opportunities for graduate and professional work. **Combined Degree Programs:** BS/MS in Education, Psychology; 5th yr MA in Writing Studies. **Disability Services:** Special programs offered to physically disabled students include note-taking services, reader services, tape recorders, tutors. **Career Services:** Alumni network, alumni services, career/job search classes, career assessment, internships, regional alumni. Career Services highlights include Saint Joseph's University's Erivan K. Haub School of Business Cooperative Education (Co-op) Program allows students to engage in real-world applications of their academic pursuits. Through two full-time, professionally engaging and paid experiences (creating one year of full-time work experience within the four-year degree), students discover their professional passions and bring real-world experience back to the classroom. In addition, the Co-op Program offers students substantial earning potential. Co-op students earn an average of $8,400 during their four-month work term and $17,000 during their eight-month work term. Employers asked several of these students to continue as part-time employees following their formal Co-op assignment, adding to these earnings. Employers likewise have expressed significant satisfaction with Saint Joseph's Co-op students. Rating Co-op students on dependability, attitude, quality of work and overall performance, the collective rating of all Co-op students (since the Program's inception) is a 4.4 on a scale of 5.0, and 93% of employers would hire their Co-op student(s) full-time, if a full-time job were available.

FACILITIES

Housing: Coed dorms, men's dorms, women's dorms, apartments for single students, theme housing, special accommodations upon need for disabled students. 85% of campus accessible to physically disabled. **Special Academic Facilities/Equipment:** Wall Street Trading Room Claver House - Honors Program Mandeville Hall Moot Board Room University Gallery **Computers:** 100% of classrooms, 100% of dorms, 100% of libraries, 100% of dining areas, 100% of student union, 10% of common outdoor areas have wireless network access. Students can register for classes online. Administrative functions (other than registration) can be performed online.

CAMPUS LIFE

Environment: Metropolis. **Activities:** Choral groups, concert band, dance, drama/theater, jazz band, literary magazine, music ensembles, musical theater, pep band, radio station, student government, student newspaper, student-run film society, yearbook, Campus Ministries, International Student Organization 100 registered organizations, 20 honor societies, 4 fraternities, 4 sororities. **Athletics (Intercollegiate):** *Men:* baseball, basketball, crew/rowing, cross-country, golf, lacrosse, soccer, tennis, track/field (outdoor), track/field (indoor). *Women:* basketball, crew/rowing, cross-country, field hockey, lacrosse, soccer, softball, tennis, track/field (outdoor), track/field (indoor). **On-Campus Highlights:** Campion Student Center, Hagan Arena and Athletics Center, Chapel of St. Joseph, Mandeville Hall, Maguire Sports Complex, 2008 brought the expansion of the SJU campus through the acquisition of 38 acres of property adjacent to the University as well as the construction of a new parking and retail facility. **Environmental Initiatives:** We have a full-time office of Health, Safety and Environmental compliance. We have a full-time recycling program with full-time staff. We purchase whenever possible Green products and services.

ADMISSIONS

Freshman Academic Profile: Average high school GPA 3.5. 25% in top 10% of high school class, 53% in top 25% of high school class, 84% in top 50% of high school class. 49% from public high schools. SAT Math middle 50% range 510-620. SAT Critical Reading middle 50% range 510-600. SAT Writing middle 50% range 510-610. ACT middle 50% range 22-27. Minimum web-based TOEFL 79. Minimum paper TOEFL 550. **Basis for Candidate Selection:**

Very important factors considered include: academic GPA, rigor of secondary school record. *Important factors considered include:* application essay, recommendation(s), character/personal qualities. *Other factors considered include:* Class rank, standardized test scores, alumni/ae relation, extracurricular activities, first generation, level of applicant's interest, talent/ability, volunteer work, work experience. **Freshman Admission Requirements:** High school diploma is required and GED is not accepted. *Academic units required:* 4 English, 3 mathematics, 2 science, (1 science labs), 2 foreign language, 1 history. *Academic units recommended:* 4 English, 3 mathematics, 2 science, (1 science labs), 2 foreign language, 1 history. **Freshman Admission Statistics:** 7,386 applied, 78% admitted, 21% enrolled. **Transfer Admission Requirements:** High school transcript, college transcript(s), statement of good standing from prior institution(s). Minimum college GPA of 2.5 required. Lowest grade transferable C. **General Admission Information:** Application Fee $60. Regular application deadline 2/1. Regular notification 3/15. Nonfall registration accepted. Admission may be deferred for a maximum of 1 year. Credit offered for CEEB Advanced Placement tests.

COSTS AND FINANCIAL AID
Average book expense $1,000. **Required Forms and Deadlines:** FAFSA. **Notification of Awards:** Applicants will be notified of awards on a rolling basis beginning 3/1. **Types of Aid:** *Need-based scholarships/grants:* Federal Pell, SEOG, state scholarships/grants, private scholarships, the school's own gift aid. *Loans:* Direct Subsidized Stafford, Direct Unsubsidized Stafford, Direct PLUS, Subsidized Stafford, Unsubsidized Stafford, PLUS, Federal PerkinsThe Federal Direct Student Loan Program will be in effect beginning with the Fall 2010-11 academic year. **Student Employment:** Federal Work-Study Program available. Institutional employment available. Off-campus job opportunities are excellent. **Financial Aid Statistics:** 98% freshmen, 97% undergrads receive need-based scholarship or grant aid. 96% freshmen, 92% undergrads receive non-need-based scholarship or grant aid. 74% freshmen, 72% undergrads receive need-based self-help aid. 2% freshmen, 3% undergrads receive athletic scholarships. 96% freshmen, 97% undergrads receive any aid. **Criteria for awarding institutional aid:** *Non-need-based:* academics, alumni affiliation, art, athletics, minority status, music/drama.

SAINT LEO UNIVERSITY

Office of Admission MC2008, Saint Leo, Fl 33574-6665
Phone: 352-588-8283 • **Financial Aid Phone:** 800-240-7658
E-mail: admissions@saintleo.edu • **CEEB Code:** 5638
Fax: 352-588-8257 • **Website:** www.saintleo.edu • **ACT Code:** 755

This private school, affiliated with the Roman Catholic Church, was founded in 1889. It has a 186-acre campus.

RATINGS
Admissions Selectivity Rating: 65   **Fire Safety Rating:** 97   **Green Rating:** 60*

STUDENTS AND FACULTY
Enrollment: 1,923. **Student Body:** 51% female, 49% male, 28% out-of-state, 9% international (58 countries represented). Asian 1%, African American 10%, Caucasian 55%, Hispanic 13%, Native American 0%. **Retention and Graduation:** 36% freshmen graduate within 4 years. 45% freshmen graduate within 6 years. **Faculty:** Student/faculty ratio 16:1. 101 full-time faculty, 83% hold PhDs, 11% are members of minority groups, 37% are women. 0% of classes are taught by teaching assistants.

ACADEMICS
Degrees: associate, bachelor's, certificate, master's, post-bachelor's certificate. **Classes:** Most classes have 20–29 students. Most lab/discussion sessions have 10–19 students. **Majors with Highest Enrollment:** biology/biological sciences; business administration and management; psychology. **Special Study Options:** distance learning, double major, honors program, independent study, internships, liberal arts/career combination, study abroad, teacher certification program, weekend college. **Honors Programs:** The Saint Leo University Honors Program consists of an integrated sequence of six interdisciplinary courses, spread over the first three years of college, and an extensive senior honors project carried out under the supervision of a distinguished faculty mentor. **Combined Degree Programs:** BA/DDS, BA/DO. **Disability Services:** Special programs offered to physically disabled students include note-taking services, reader services, tape recorders, tutors. **Career Services:** Alumni network, alumni services, career/job search classes, career assessment, internships.

FACILITIES
Housing: Coed dorms, special housing for disabled students, men's dorms, women's dorms, apartments for single students, wellness housing, theme hous-

ing, Freshmen only housing. 95% of campus accessible to physically disabled. **Computers:** 95% of classrooms, 85% of dorms, 100% of libraries, 100% of dining areas, 100% of student union, 90% of common outdoor areas have wireless network access. Students can register for classes online. Administrative functions (other than registration) can be performed online.

CAMPUS LIFE
Environment: Rural. **Activities:** Choral groups, concert band, dance, drama/theater, literary magazine, music ensembles, musical theater, student government, student newspaper, television station, yearbook, Campus Ministries, International Student Organization 58 registered organizations, 12 honor societies, 7 religious organizations. 6 fraternities, 4 sororities. **Athletics (Intercollegiate):** *Men:* baseball, basketball, cross-country, golf, lacrosse, soccer, swimming, tennis. *Women:* basketball, cross-country, golf, soccer, softball, swimming, tennis, volleyball. **On-Campus Highlights:** Student Community Center, Student Activities Building, Marion Bowman Activities Center, Swimming Pool, Lakefront.

ADMISSIONS
Freshman Academic Profile: Average high school GPA 3.3. 5% in top 10% of high school class, 26% in top 25% of high school class, 61% in top 50% of high school class. 78% from public high schools. SAT Math middle 50% range 440-520. SAT Critical Reading middle 50% range 440-530. SAT Writing middle 50% range 410-510. ACT middle 50% range 19-23. Minimum web-based TOEFL 80. Minimum paper TOEFL 550. **Basis for Candidate Selection:** *Very important factors considered include:* academic GPA, recommendation(s), rigor of secondary school record, standardized test scores, character/personal qualities. *Important factors considered include:* alumni/ae relation, extracurricular activities, interview, level of applicant's interest, talent/ability, volunteer work. *Other factors considered include:* Class rank, application essay, first generation, racial/ethnic status, work experience. **Freshman Admission Requirements:** High school diploma is required and GED is accepted. **Freshman Admission Statistics:** 1,981 applied, 93% admitted, 30% enrolled. **Transfer Admission Requirements:** college transcript(s), essay or personal statement, statement of good standing from prior institution(s). Minimum college GPA of 2.0 required. Lowest grade transferable D. **General Admission Information:** Application Fee $35. Regular application deadline 8/15. Notification on a rolling basis, beginning on or about 10/15. Nonfall registration accepted. Admission may be deferred for a maximum of 1 year. Credit and/or placement offered for CEEB Advanced Placement tests.

COSTS AND FINANCIAL AID
Annual tuition $18,200, Room and board $8,720. Required fees $370. Average book expense $1,200. **Required Forms and Deadlines:** FAFSA. **Notification of Awards:** Applicants will be notified of awards on a rolling basis beginning 1/31. **Types of Aid:** *Need-based scholarships/grants:* Federal Pell, SEOG, state scholarships/grants, private scholarships, the school's own gift aid, United Negro College Fund. *Loans:* Direct Subsidized Stafford, Direct Unsubsidized Stafford, Direct PLUS, Federal Perkins, Private Loans Through Lenders. **Student Employment:** Federal Work-Study Program available. Institutional employment available. Highest amount earned per year from on-campus jobs $3,500. Off-campus job opportunities are good. **Financial Aid Statistics:** 100% freshmen, 100% undergrads receive need-based scholarship or grant aid. 11% freshmen, 9% undergrads receive non-need-based scholarship or grant aid. 91% freshmen, 91% undergrads receive need-based self-help aid. 3% freshmen, 4% undergrads receive athletic scholarships. 96% freshmen, 93% undergrads receive any aid. 70% undergrads borrow to pay for school. Average cumulative indebtedness $30,015. **Criteria for awarding institutional aid:** *Non-need-based:* academics, alumni affiliation, athletics, leadership, minority status, religious affiliation, state/district residency.

SAINT LOUIS UNIVERSITY

221 N Grand Boulevard, Saint Louis, MO 63103
Phone: 314-977-2500 • **Financial Aid Phone:** 314-977-2350
E-mail: admitme@slu.edu • **CEEB Code:** 6629
Fax: 314-977-7136 • **Website:** www.slu.edu • **ACT Code:** 2352

This private school, affiliated with the Roman Catholic Church, was founded in 1818. It has a 235-acre campus.

RATINGS
Admissions Selectivity Rating: 90   **Fire Safety Rating:** 81   **Green Rating:** 83

STUDENTS AND FACULTY

Enrollment: 8,566. **Student Body:** 59% female, 41% male, 61% out-of-state, 8% international (71 countries represented). Asian 8%, African American 7%, Caucasian 65%, Hispanic 4%, Native American 0%.
Retention and Graduation: 88% freshmen return for sophomore year. 61% freshmen graduate within 4 years. 70% freshmen graduate within 6 years. 41% grads go on to further study within 1 year. 13% grads pursue arts and sciences degrees. 16% grads pursue law degrees. 18% grads pursue business degrees. 18% grads pursue medical degrees. **Faculty:** Student/faculty ratio 12:1. 740 full-time faculty, 89% hold PhDs, 15% are members of minority groups, 46% are women. 6% of classes are taught by teaching assistants.

ACADEMICS

Degrees: bachelor's, certificate, doctoral, master's, post-bachelor's certificate, post-master's certificate. **Classes:** Most classes have 10–19 students. Most lab/discussion sessions have 10–19 students. **Majors with Highest Enrollment:** biology/biological sciences; business administration and management; nursing/registered nurse (rn, asn, bsn, msn). **Special Study Options:** Accelerated program, cooperative education program, cross-registration, distance learning, double major, dual enrollment, English as a Second Language (ESL), honors program, independent study, internships, liberal arts/career combination, student-designed major, study abroad, teacher certification program. **Honors Programs:** The Honors Program at Saint Louis University offers eligible students the opportunity to develop an individual course of study that complements their undergraduate major, leading to an Honors degree in that discipline. Undergraduates from any of the schools and colleges at Saint Louis University can successfully pursue an honors degree through the University Honors Program. The Saint Louis University Honors Program offers interdisciplinary programs and opportunities with reflective and expressive elements to students in the Honors Program. The Honors Program offers seminar courses with integrated collaborative learning experiences including service learning, internships, and research. The Honors Program offers Honors students study abroad opportunities. The Honors Program offers Honors courses at the Saint Louis University Madrid Campus. The Honors Program offers teaching assistant positions to undergraduate Honors students. The Honors Program offers a residential learning community and several Freshman Interest Groups. The Honors Program provides academic, cultural, and social opportunities. The Honors Program provides peer mentorship programs. **Combined Degree Programs:** BA/MA, BA/MSW, MD/MBA, MBA/MHA. **Disability Services:** Special programs offered to physically disabled students include note-taking services, reader services, tape recorders, tutors. **Career Services:** Alumni network, alumni services, career/job search classes, career assessment, internships, regional alumni.

FACILITIES

Housing: Coed dorms, special housing for disabled students, men's dorms, women's dorms, fraternity/sorority housing, apartments for married students, apartments for single students, theme housing, Foreign Language Housing. 95% of campus accessible to physically disabled. **Special Academic Facilities/Equipment:** Saint Louis University Museum of Art (SLUMA), McNamee Gallery of Samuel Cupples House, Museum of Contemporary Religious Art (MOCRA). **Computers:** 100% of classrooms, 100% of dorms, 100% of libraries, 100% of dining areas, 100% of student union, 100% of common outdoor areas have wireless network access. Students can register for classes online. Administrative functions (other than registration) can be performed online.

CAMPUS LIFE

Environment: Metropolis. **Activities:** Choral groups, dance, drama/theater, jazz band, literary magazine, music ensembles, musical theater, pep band, radio station, student government, student newspaper, student-run film society, television station, yearbook, Campus Ministries, International Student Organization, Model UN 170 registered organizations, 25 honor societies, 36 religious organizations. 11 fraternities, 6 sororities. **Athletics (Intercollegiate):** *Men:* baseball, basketball, cross-country, diving, soccer, swimming, tennis, track/field (outdoor), track/field (indoor). *Women:* basketball, cross-country, diving, field hockey, soccer, softball, swimming, tennis, track/field (outdoor), track/field (indoor), volleyball. **On-Campus Highlights:** St. Francis Xavier Church, Busch Student Center, St. Louis University Museum of Art, Simon Recreation Center, Robert R. Hermann Soccer Stadium, Chaifetz Arena. **Environmental Initiatives:** In 2010, Saint Louis University launched the Center for Sustainability. More than just another university office, department, or team, the Center for Sustainability is a dedicated degree-granting institution and the first of its kind out of 28 Jesuit colleges and universities in the United States. The Center for Sustainability was established by a $5 million grant from the Alberici Foundation, charitable arm of the Alberici Corporation. Alberici is recognized throughout the country as a leader in green building practices. With this grant they positioned SLU to become one of the nation's leaders in the field of sustainability. Barely one-year old, the center has since received an additional $2 million in grant money from a separate source, further bolstering its mission to develop creative, collaborative solutions to the pressing environmental challenges facing society today. One way the center aims to achieve its mission is by educating the next generation of leaders in sustainability through its innovative Master of Sustainability (MOS)

program. Launched in August of 2010, the MOS program is the first of its kind in the Midwest"a unique, interdisciplinary graduate degree focused entirely on sustainability. It is a collaborative effort between SLU's college of Arts and Sciences, College of Education and Public Service, John Cook School of Business, Parks College of Engineering, Aviation, and Technology, and the School of Public Health. As a university-wide effort, the program exposes students to sustainability-related instruction across multiple disciplines, including business, public policy, engineering, social work, public health, environmental science, and government. St. Louis University co-founded the St. Louis Regional Higher Education Sustainability Consortium (STL HESC), a formal network of over 20 colleges and universities working together to advance collective sustainability initiatives throughout the region. The mission of the St. Louis Regional Higher Education Sustainability Consortium is "to connect the strengths, resources, and knowledge of St. Louis area universities and colleges, to advance collective sustainable initiatives that cultivate innovation, to eliminate non-productive competition, and to create a network that is more than the sum of its parts." St. Louis was chosen to be a pilot region in the National Climate Prosperity Project along with Denver, Portland, and the Silicon Valley. Each of these regions is developing a climate prosperity strategy based on its unique comparative advantages and implementing it through regional public‐private partnerships. In St. Louis, the pilot project is led by the St. Louis Regional Chamber and Growth Association (RCGA). The St. Louis Climate Prosperity Project engages area businesses, educational institutions, elected officials and governmental entities, and other civic organizations in the 16-county metropolitan region to broaden support around green savings, green opportunity, and green talent. Saint Louis University's Center for Sustainability has partnered with the RCGA to support and advance the goals of the Climate Prosperity Project. Saint Louis University joined the RCGA's St. Louis Green Business challenge as an inaugural member in January of 2010. The challenge was designed to encourage member institutions to adopt sustainable business practices that improve energy efficiency and indoor air quality, reduce waste and water consumption, as well as increase clean transportation options. The Center for Sustainability is also collaborating with the RCGA to help develop a regional Green Talent Strategy. The Green Talent Strategy aims to identify growth in green occupations in the St. Louis region, align job training providers with employers in green industries, and develop action plans to meet the growing talent needs of the regional green economy. In January of 2011 Saint Louis University hosted and helped organize the St. Louis Green Confluence to present the Green Talent Strategy to the St. Louis community and bring St. Louis area employers, educators, public policy makers and, citizens together to explore the future of the region's green economy. The two-day event was a collaborative effort between the Missouri Career Center, Illinois Work Net, the St. Louis Regional Chamber and Growth Association (RCGA), the St. Louis Higher Education Sustainability Consortium, St. Louis Green.com and SLU's Center for Sustainability. It featured a green economy symposium with expert speakers, a green career opportunity showcase with education workshops, and the unveiling of a new Web portal for green jobs. Climate Prosperity Project: http://www.climateprosperityproject.org/ St. Louis Green Economy Profile http://www.stlrcga.org/documents/mm/StLouis-GreenEconomy.pdf

ADMISSIONS

Freshman Academic Profile: Average high school GPA 3.8. 38% in top 10% of high school class, 68% in top 25% of high school class, 90% in top 50% of high school class. SAT Math middle 50% range 540-670. SAT Critical Reading middle 50% range 530-660. ACT middle 50% range 25-30. Minimum web-based TOEFL 80. Minimum paper TOEFL 550. **Basis for Candidate Selection:** *Very important factors considered include:* academic GPA, standardized test scores. *Important factors considered include:* application essay, rigor of secondary school record, character/personal qualities, extracurricular activities, talent/ability. *Other factors considered include:* recommendation(s), alumni/ae relation, first generation, interview, level of applicant's interest, volunteer work. **Freshman Admission Requirements:** High school diploma is required and GED is accepted. *Academic units required:* 4 English, 4 mathematics, 3 science, 3 foreign language, 3 social studies, 3 academic electives. *Academic units recommended:* 4 English, 4 mathematics, 3 science, 3 foreign language, 3 social studies, 3 academic electives. **Freshman Admission Statistics:** 13,060 applied, 64% admitted, 19% enrolled. **Transfer Admission Requirements:** college transcript(s), minimum college GPA of 2.0 required. Lowest grade transferable C. **General Admission Information:** Application Fee $25. Regular application deadline 8/1. Regular notification 8/1. Notification on a rolling basis, beginning on or about 10/1. Nonfall registration accepted. Admission may be deferred for a maximum of 1 Year. Credit and/or placement offered for CEEB Advanced Placement tests.

COSTS AND FINANCIAL AID

Annual tuition $34,740. Room and board $9,612. Required fees $516. Average book expense $1,500. **Required Forms and Deadlines:** FAFSA. **Notification of Awards:** Applicants will be notified of awards on a rolling basis beginning 3/1. **Types of Aid:** *Need-based scholarships/grants:* Federal Pell, SEOG, state scholarships/grants, private scholarships, the school's own gift aid, Federal Nursing Scholarships. *Loans:* Subsidized Stafford, Unsubsidized Stafford, PLUS, Federal Perkins, Federal Nursing, college/university loans from institutional funds. **Student Employment:** Federal Work-Study Program available. Institutional employment available. Highest amount earned per year from on-campus jobs $14,068. Off-campus job opportunities are good. **Financial Aid Statistics:** 97% freshmen, 95% undergrads receive need-based scholarship or grant aid. 11% freshmen, 8% undergrads receive non-need-based scholarship or grant aid. 76% freshmen, 79% undergrads receive need-based self-help aid. 2% freshmen, 2% undergrads receive athletic scholarships. 93% freshmen, 87% undergrads receive any aid. 63% undergrads borrow to pay for school. Average cumulative indebtedness $36,797. **Criteria for awarding institutional aid:** *Non-need-based:* academics, art, athletics, leadership, music/drama, religious affiliation.

See page 1194.

SAINT MARTIN'S UNIVERSITY

5000 Abbey Way SE, Lacey, WA 98503-7500
Phone: 360-438-4596 • **Financial Aid Phone:** 360-438-8868
E-mail: admissions@stmartin.edu • **CEEB Code:** 4674
Fax: 360-412-6189 • **Website:** www.stmartin.edu • **ACT Code:** 4474

This private school, affiliated with the Roman Catholic Church, was founded in 1895. It has a 320-acre campus.

RATINGS
Admissions Selectivity Rating: 66   **Fire Safety Rating:** 63   **Green Rating:** 60*

STUDENTS AND FACULTY
Enrollment: 1,392. **Student Body:** 52% female, 48% male, 25% out-of-state, 6% international (17 countries represented). Asian 5%, African American 8%, Caucasian 57%, Hispanic 12%, Native American 1%.
Retention and Graduation: 73% freshmen return for sophomore year. 41% freshmen graduate within 4 years. 14% grads go on to further study within 1 year. 2% grads pursue arts and sciences degrees. 2% grads pursue law degrees. 8% grads pursue business degrees. 2% grads pursue medical degrees. **Faculty:** Student/faculty ratio 12:1. 73 full-time faculty, 77% hold PhDs, 14% are members of minority groups, 36% are women, 0% of classes are taught by teaching assistants.

ACADEMICS
Degrees: bachelor's, master's, post-bachelor's certificate, post-master's certificate. **Classes:** Most classes have fewer than 10 students. Most lab/discussion sessions have fewer than 10 students. **Majors with Highest Enrollment:** biology/biological sciences; business administration and management; psychology. **Special Study Options:** distance learning, double major, English as a Second Language (ESL), exchange student program (domestic), independent study, internships, study abroad, teacher certification program. **Combined Degree Programs:** BA/MEng. **Disability Services:** Special programs offered to physically disabled students include note-taking services, reader services, tape recorders, tutors. **Career Services:** Alumni network, alumni services, career/job search classes, career assessment, regional alumni. Career Services highlights include We invite our local alumni to participate in any and all of our career-related workshops and career advising sessions and we have had a great turnout. The alumni have initiated an online mentor profile so that students may contact an alum with a question or ask advice. Many relationships can be formed by their participation in these two new activities.

FACILITIES
Housing: Coed dorms, special housing for disabled students, apartments for single students. 85% of campus accessible to physically disabled. **Special Academic Facilities/Equipment:** Cap Art Gallery, Waynick Museum **Computers:** 80% of classrooms, 10% of dorms, 100% of libraries, 100% of dining areas, 100% of student union, have wireless network access. Students can register for classes online. Administrative functions (other than registration) can be performed online.

CAMPUS LIFE
Environment: Town. **Activities:** Choral groups, concert band, dance, drama/theater, jazz band, musical theater, pep band, student government, student newspaper, Campus Ministries, International Student Organization, Model UN 23 registered organizations, 3 honor societies, 3 religious organizations. **Athletics (Intercollegiate):** *Men:* baseball, basketball, cross-country, golf, track/field (outdoor), track/field (indoor). *Women:* basketball, cross-country, golf, softball, track/field (outdoor), track/field (indoor), volleyball. **On-Campus Highlights:** O'Grady Library, Student Union Building, Recreation and Fitness Center, Baran/Burton/Spangler Halls, Abbey Church, Dining Hall renovation completed in December 2009, Spangler Residence Hall opened Fall 2005. New residence hall and new academic building opened Fall 2008. New Recreation and fitness center opened in January 2010. **Environmental Initiatives:** FoodPlus recycling-for-compost program, growing garden.

ADMISSIONS
Freshman Academic Profile: Average high school GPA 3.4. 26% in top 10% of high school class, 51% in top 25% of high school class, 82% in top 50% of high school class. 95% from public high schools. SAT Math middle 50% range 470-590. SAT Critical Reading middle 50% range 450-580. SAT Writing middle 50% range 450-560. ACT middle 50% range 19-25. Minimum web-based TOEFL 54. Minimum paper TOEFL 480. **Basis for Candidate Selection:** *Very important factors considered include:* academic GPA, rigor of secondary school record. *Important factors considered include:* application essay, recommendation(s), standardized test scores, character/personal qualities, extracurricular activities, volunteer work. *Other factors considered include:* Class rank, alumni/ae relation, interview, talent/ability, work experience. **Freshman Admission Requirements:** High school diploma is required and GED is accepted. **Freshman Admission Statistics:** 708 applied, 94% admitted, 34% enrolled. **Transfer Admission Requirements:** college transcript(s), essay or personal statement, minimum college GPA of 2.25 required. Lowest grade transferable C–. **General Admission Information:** Application Fee $35. Notification on a rolling basis, beginning on or about 10/1. Nonfall registration accepted. Credit offered for CEEB Advanced Placement tests.

COSTS AND FINANCIAL AID
Annual tuition $28,400. Room and board $9,360. Required fees $322. Average book expense $1,000. **Required Forms and Deadlines:** FAFSA. **Notification of Awards:** Applicants will be notified of awards on a rolling basis beginning 2/15. **Types of Aid:** *Need-based scholarships/grants:* Federal Pell, SEOG, state scholarships/grants, private scholarships, the school's own gift aid. *Loans:* Subsidized Stafford, Unsubsidized Stafford, PLUS, Federal Perkins, state loans, college/university loans from institutional funds, Private, alternative educational loans. **Student Employment:** Federal Work-Study Program available. Institutional employment available. Highest amount earned per year from on-campus jobs $2,100. Off-campus job opportunities are good. **Financial Aid Statistics:** 100% freshmen, 97% undergrads receive need-based scholarship or grant aid. 13% freshmen, 9% undergrads receive non-need-based scholarship or grant aid. 87% freshmen, 87% undergrads receive need-based self-help aid. 10% freshmen, 5% undergrads receive athletic scholarships. 79% undergrads borrow to pay for school. Average cumulative indebtedness $34,235. **Criteria for awarding institutional aid:** *Non-need-based:* academics, alumni affiliation, art, athletics, leadership, minority status, music/drama, religious affiliation, state/district residency.

SAINT MARY-OF-THE-WOODS COLLEGE

Office of Admission, Saint Mary-of-the-Woods, IN 47876-0068
Phone: 812-535-5106 • **Financial Aid Phone:** 812-535-5100
E-mail: smwcadms@smwc.edu • **CEEB Code:** 1704
Fax: 812-535-5010 • **Website:** www.smwc.edu • **ACT Code:** 1242

This private school, affiliated with the Roman Catholic Church, was founded in 1840. It has a 67-acre campus.

RATINGS
Admissions Selectivity Rating: 71   **Fire Safety Rating:** 99   **Green Rating:** 79

STUDENTS AND FACULTY
Enrollment: 1,176. **Student Body:** 97% female, 3% male, 30% out-of-state, (5 countries represented).
Retention and Graduation: 77% freshmen return for sophomore year. 35% freshmen graduate within 4 years. 42% freshmen graduate within 6 years. 18% grads go on to further study within 1 year. 15% grads pursue arts and sciences degrees. 1% grads pursue law degrees. 1% grads pursue business degrees. 1% grads pursue medical degrees. **Faculty:** Student/faculty ratio 8:1. 67 full-time faculty, 54% hold PhDs, 6% are members of minority groups, 66% are women. 0% of classes are taught by teaching assistants.

ACADEMICS
Degrees: associate, bachelor's, certificate, master's, post-bachelor's certificate, post-master's certificate, transfer associate. **Classes:** Most classes have fewer than 10 students. **Majors with Highest Enrollment:** biology/biological sciences; elementary education and teaching; equestrian/equine studies. **Special Study Options:** Accelerated program, cross-registration, distance learning, double major, external degree program, honors program, independent study, internships, student-designed major, study abroad, teacher certification program. **Disability Services:** Special programs offered to physically disabled students

include tutors. **Career Services:** Alumni network, alumni services, career/job search classes, career assessment, internships, regional alumni., Career Services highlights include Experiential Learning: Externship, Supplemental Learning Experience, and Internship programs.

FACILITIES

Housing: special housing for disabled students, women's dorms. 100% of campus accessible to physically disabled. **Special Academic Facilities/Equipment:** Cecilian Auditorium and Conservatory of Music SMWC Art Gallery **Computers:** 100% of classrooms, 100% of dorms, 100% of libraries, 20% of dining areas, 15% of common outdoor areas have wireless network access. Students can register for classes online. Administrative functions (other than registration) can be performed online.

CAMPUS LIFE

Environment: Town. **Activities:** Choral groups, concert band, dance, drama/theater, jazz band, literary magazine, music ensembles, musical theater, student government, student newspaper, yearbook, Campus Ministries, International Student Organization 30 registered organizations, 6 honor societies, 1 religious organizations. **Athletics (Intercollegiate):** *Women:* basketball, equestrian sports, golf, soccer, softball, track/field (outdoor). **On-Campus Highlights:** Le Fer Hall (residence hall), Mari Hulman George School of Equine Studies, Softball/Soccer Fields, Cecilian Auditorium, Church of the Immaculate Conception, Saint Mary-of-the-Woods College is a 67-acre wooded campus located five miles northwest of Terre Haute, Indiana. The peaceful and beautiful campus features a fitness trail, lake and stables amid the stately academic buildings. Besides the College, Saint Mary-of-the-Woods is common ground for the Sisters of Providence, Woods Day Care/Pre-School, Providence Center and the White Violet Center for Eco-Justice. **Environmental Initiatives:** recycling food service decreasing waste, composting, use of local/organic foods housekeeping services switched to green chemicals

ADMISSIONS

Freshman Academic Profile: Average high school GPA 3.3. 85% from public high schools. SAT Math middle 50% range 410-520. SAT Critical Reading middle 50% range 430-540. SAT Writing middle 50% range 410-550. ACT middle 50% range 18-25. Minimum web-based TOEFL 62. Minimum paper TOEFL 500. **Basis for Candidate Selection:** *Important factors considered include:* Class rank, application essay, academic GPA, recommendation(s), rigor of secondary school record, standardized test scores. *Other factors considered include:* character/personal qualities, interview, level of applicant's interest, talent/ability. **Freshman Admission Requirements:** High school diploma is required and GED is accepted. *Academic units required:* 8 English, 6 mathematics, 6 science, (2 science labs), 4 foreign language, 4 social studies, 2 history, 10 academic electives. *Academic units recommended:* 8 English, 6 mathematics, 6 science, (2 science labs), 4 foreign language, 4 social studies, 2 history, 10 academic electives. **Freshman Admission Statistics:** 417 applied, 70% admitted, 44% enrolled. **Transfer Admission Requirements:** college transcript(s), essay or personal statement, minimum college GPA of 2.0 required. Lowest grade transferable C. **General Admission Information:** Application Fee $30. Regular application deadline 8/8. Notification on a rolling basis, beginning on or about 10/1. Nonfall registration accepted. Admission may be deferred for a maximum of 1 year. Credit and/or placement offered for CEEB Advanced Placement tests.

COSTS AND FINANCIAL AID

Annual tuition $20,900. Room and board $7,890. Required fees $650. Average book expense $900. **Required Forms and Deadlines:** FAFSA. **Notification of Awards:** Applicants will be notified of awards on a rolling basis beginning 12/1. **Types of Aid:** *Need-based scholarships/grants:* Federal Pell, SEOG, state scholarships/grants, private scholarships, the school's own gift aid. *Loans:* Subsidized Stafford, Unsubsidized Stafford, PLUS, Federal Perkins. **Student Employment:** Federal Work-Study Program available. Institutional employment available. Highest amount earned per year from on-campus jobs $4,665. Off-campus job opportunities are good. **Financial Aid Statistics:** 77% freshmen, 92% undergrads receive need-based scholarship or grant aid. 76% freshmen, 12% undergrads receive non-need-based scholarship or grant aid. 49% freshmen, 83% undergrads receive need-based self-help aid. 10% freshmen, 4% undergrads receive athletic scholarships. 98% freshmen, 96% undergrads receive any aid. 89% undergrads borrow to pay for school. Average cumulative indebtedness $20,310. **Criteria for awarding institutional aid:** *Non-need-based:* academics, alumni affiliation, art, athletics, leadership, music/drama.

ST. MARY'S COLLEGE (CA)

P.O. Box 4800, Moraga, CA 94575-4800
Phone: 925-631-4224 • **Financial Aid Phone:** 925-631-4522
E-mail: smcadmit@stmarys-ca.edu • **CEEB Code:** 4675
Fax: 925-376-7193 • **Website:** www.stmarys-ca.edu • **ACT Code:** 386

This private school, affiliated with the Roman Catholic Church, was founded in 1863. It has a 420-acre campus.

RATINGS

Admissions Selectivity Rating: 77   **Fire Safety Rating:** 80   **Green Rating:** 80

STUDENTS AND FACULTY

Enrollment: 3,017. **Student Body:** 60% female, 40% male, 10% out-of-state, 2% international (22 countries represented). Asian 10%, African American 4%, Caucasian 44%, Hispanic 24%, Native American 0%.
Retention and Graduation: 88% freshmen return for sophomore year. 49% freshmen graduate within 4 years. 58% freshmen graduate within 6 years. 27% grads go on to further study within 1 year. **Faculty:** Student/faculty ratio 13:1. 194 full-time faculty, % hold PhDs, 19% are members of minority groups, 52% are women. 0% of classes are taught by teaching assistants.

ACADEMICS

Degrees: associate, bachelor's, doctoral, master's. **Classes:** Most classes have 10–19 students. **Majors with Highest Enrollment:** business administration, management and operations, other; communication and media studies, other; psychology. **Special Study Options:** double major, exchange student program (domestic), independent study, student-designed major, study abroad. **Disability Services:** Special programs offered to physically disabled students include note-taking services, reader services, tape recorders, tutors. **Career Services:** Alumni network, alumni services, career/job search classes, career assessment, internships Career Services highlights include Career Information Night Series plus our Career and Internship Fair.

FACILITIES

Housing: Coed dorms, special housing for disabled students, theme housing. 90% of campus accessible to physically disabled. **Special Academic Facilities/Equipment:** Hearst Art gallery Brousseau Hall, Science Building Geissberger Observatory. **Computers:** 100% of classrooms, 100% of libraries, 100% of dining areas, 100% of student union, 70% of common outdoor areas have wireless network access. Students can register for classes online. Administrative functions (other than registration) can be performed online.

CAMPUS LIFE

Environment: Village. **Activities:** Choral groups, dance, drama/theater, jazz band, music ensembles, musical theater, pep band, radio station, student government, student newspaper, Campus Ministries, International Student Organization 56 registered organizations, 3 religious organizations. **Athletics (Intercollegiate):** *Men:* baseball, basketball, cheerleading, cross-country, golf, soccer, tennis. *Women:* basketball, cheerleading, crew/rowing, cross-country, lacrosse, soccer, softball, tennis, volleyball. **On-Campus Highlights:** Br. Alfred Brousseau Hall, Cassin Student Union and LeFevre Quad, College Chapel, Hearst Art Gallery, Oliver Dining Hall, Power Plant (exercise facility) McKeon Pavilion, "St. Patty's Cathedral." **Environmental Initiatives:** 2007 Summer reading program for incoming students focuses on global warming. Energy conservation program (phase 2) reduces consumption by 71KW Student-run organic vegetable garden: http://stmarys-ca.edu/about-smc/sustain-smc/for-students/vegetable-garden.html

ADMISSIONS

Freshman Academic Profile: Average high school GPA 3.6. 22% in top 10% of high school class, 60% in top 25% of high school class, 90% in top 50% of high school class. 55% from public high schools. SAT Math middle 50% range 500-610. SAT Critical Reading middle 50% range 500-600. ACT middle 50% range 22-27. Minimum web-based TOEFL 71. Minimum paper TOEFL 527. **Basis for Candidate Selection:** *Very important factors considered include:* academic GPA, rigor of secondary school record, standardized test scores. *Important factors considered include:* application essay, recommendation(s), first generation. *Other factors considered include:* Class rank, alumni/ae relation, character/personal qualities, extracurricular activities, geographical residence, interview, level of applicant's interest, racial/ethnic status, religious affiliation/commitment, talent/ability, volunteer work, work experience. **Freshman Admission Requirements:** High school diploma is required and GED is accepted. *Academic units required:* 4 English, 3 mathematics, 2 science, (1 science labs), 2 foreign language, 1 social studies, 1 history, 2 academic electives. *Academic units recommended:* 4 English, 3 mathematics, 2 science, (1 science labs), 2 foreign language, 1 social studies, 1 history, 2 academic electives. **Freshman Admission Statistics:** 5,256 applied, 66% admitted, 18% enrolled. **Transfer Admission Requirements:** High school transcript, college transcript(s), essay or personal statement, minimum college GPA of 2.3 required. Lowest grade transferable C–. **General Admission Information:** Application Fee $55. Regular application deadline 2/1. Regular notification 3/15. Nonfall registration accepted. Admission may be deferred for a maximum of 12 months. Credit and/or placement offered for CEEB Advanced Placement tests.

COSTS AND FINANCIAL AID

Annual tuition $39,740. Room and board $13,660. Required fees $150. Average book expense $1,665. **Required Forms and Deadlines:** FAFSA, state aid form. **Notification of Awards:** Applicants will be notified of awards on a rolling basis beginning 3/15. **Types of Aid:** *Need-based scholarships/grants:* Federal Pell, SEOG, state scholarships/grants, private scholarships, the school's own gift aid. *Loans:* Subsidized Stafford, Unsubsidized Stafford, PLUS, Federal Perkins. **Student Employment:** Federal Work-Study Program available. Institutional employment available. Highest amount earned per year from on-campus jobs $12,744. Off-campus job opportunities are good. **Financial Aid Statistics:** 99% freshmen, 98% undergrads receive need-based scholarship or grant aid. 36% freshmen, 35% undergrads receive non-need-based scholarship or grant aid. 93% freshmen, 92% undergrads receive need-based self-help aid. 3% freshmen, 3% undergrads receive athletic scholarships. 94% freshmen, 84% undergrads receive any aid. 77% undergrads borrow to pay for school. Average cumulative indebtedness $31,828. **Criteria for awarding institutional aid:** *Non-need-based:* academics, alumni affiliation, athletics, leadership.

SAINT MARY'S COLLEGE (IN)

Admission office, Notre Dame, IN 46556
Phone: 574-284-4587 • **Financial Aid Phone:** 574-284-4557
E-mail: admission@saintmarys.edu • **CEEB Code:** 1702
Fax: 574-284-4841 • **Website:** www3.saintmarys.edu • **ACT Code:** 1244

This private school, affiliated with the Roman Catholic Church, was founded in 1844. It has a 275-acre campus.

RATINGS

Admissions Selectivity Rating: 71   **Fire Safety Rating:** 83   **Green Rating:** 61

STUDENTS AND FACULTY

Enrollment: 1,454. **Student Body:** 100% female, 0% male, 73% out-of-state, 1% international (14 countries represented). Asian 1%, African American 1%, Caucasian 80%, Hispanic 10%, Native American 0%.
Retention and Graduation: 88% freshmen return for sophomore year. 74% freshmen graduate within 4 years. 78% freshmen graduate within 6 years. 30% grads go on to further study within 1 year. 13% grads pursue arts and sciences degrees. 2% grads pursue law degrees. 2% grads pursue business degrees. 4% grads pursue medical degrees. **Faculty:** Student/faculty ratio 10:1. 123 full-time faculty, 83% hold PhDs, 11% are members of minority groups, 65% are women. 0% of classes are taught by teaching assistants.

ACADEMICS

Degrees: bachelor's. **Classes:** Most classes have 20–29 students. Most lab/discussion sessions have 10–19 students. **Majors with Highest Enrollment:** communication studies/speech communication and rhetoric; elementary education and teaching; nursing/registered nurse (rn, asn, bsn, msn). **Special Study Options:** Accelerated program, cross-registration, double major, exchange student program (domestic), independent study, internships, liberal arts/career combination, student-designed major, study abroad, teacher certification program. **Disability Services:** Special programs offered to physically disabled students include note-taking services, reader services, tape recorders, tutors. **Career Services:** Alumni network, alumni services, career/job search classes, career assessment, internships, regional alumni.

FACILITIES

Housing: special housing for disabled students, women's dorms, apartments for single students, Intercultural Living Floor. 100% of campus accessible to physically disabled. **Special Academic Facilities/Equipment:** Art gallery, early childhood development center, language lab, electron microscope. **Computers:** 80% of classrooms, 60% of dorms, 100% of libraries, 100% of dining areas, 100% of student union, have wireless network access. Students can register for classes online. Administrative functions (other than registration) can be performed online.

CAMPUS LIFE

Environment: City. **Activities:** Choral groups, dance, drama/theater, jazz band, literary magazine, marching band, music ensembles, musical theater, opera, pep band, radio station, student government, student newspaper, television station, yearbook, Campus Ministries, International Student Organization 78 registered organizations, 14 honor societies, 8 religious organizations. **Athletics (Intercollegiate):** *Women:* basketball, cross-country, diving, golf, soccer, softball, swimming, tennis, volleyball. **On-Campus Highlights:** Student Center/Noble Family Dining hall., Dalloway's Coffee House, Angela Athletic Facility, Spes Unica, Moreau Center for the Arts / O'Laughlin. **Environmental Initiatives:** Campus Recycling Program Environmental considerations in building projects - Spes Unica & Madeleva Creation of an energy management team within the Facilities Division.

ADMISSIONS

Freshman Academic Profile: Average high school GPA 3.8. 36% in top 10% of high school class, 72% in top 25% of high school class, 94% in top 50% of high school class. 53% from public high schools. SAT Math middle 50% range 500-610. SAT Critical Reading middle 50% range 510-623. SAT Writing middle 50% range 510-610. ACT middle 50% range 23-28. Minimum web-based TOEFL 80. Minimum paper TOEFL 550. **Basis for Candidate Selection:** *Important factors considered include:* academic GPA, rigor of secondary school record, standardized test scores, level of applicant's interest. *Other factors considered include:* Class rank, application essay, recommendation(s), alumni/ae relation, character/personal qualities, extracurricular activities, first generation, geographical residence, interview, racial/ethnic status, state residency, talent/ability, volunteer work, work experience. **Freshman Admission Requirements:** High school diploma is required and GED is accepted. *Academic units required:* 4 English, 3 mathematics, 2 science, (2 science labs), 2 foreign language, 2 history. *Academic units recommended:* 4 English, 3 mathematics, 2 science, (2 science labs), 2 foreign language, 2 history. **Freshman Admission Statistics:** 1,482 applied, 85% admitted, 33% enrolled. **Transfer Admission Requirements:** High school transcript, college transcript(s), essay or personal statement, standardized test scores, statement of good standing from prior institution(s). Minimum college GPA of 3.0 required. Lowest grade transferable C. **General Admission Information:** Application Fee $30. Early decision application deadline 11/15. Notification on a rolling basis, beginning on or about 1/1. Nonfall registration accepted. Credit and/or placement offered for CEEB Advanced Placement tests.

COSTS AND FINANCIAL AID

Annual tuition $32,560. Room and board $10,140. Required fees $720. Average book expense $1,100. **Required Forms and Deadlines:** FAFSA, CSS/Financial Aid PROFILE, noncustodial PROFILE. **Notification of Awards:** Applicants will be notified of awards on a rolling basis beginning 3/15. **Types of Aid:** *Need-based scholarships/grants:* Federal Pell, SEOG, state scholarships/grants, private scholarships, the school's own gift aid. *Loans:* Subsidized Stafford, Unsubsidized Stafford, PLUS, Federal Perkins. **Student Employment:** Federal Work-Study Program available. Institutional employment available. Off-campus job opportunities are good. **Financial Aid Statistics:** 98% freshmen, 99% undergrads receive need-based scholarship or grant aid. 92% freshmen, 79% undergrads receive non-need-based scholarship or grant aid. 82% freshmen, 87% undergrads receive need-based self-help aid. 99% freshmen, 96% undergrads receive any aid. 68% undergrads borrow to pay for school. Average cumulative indebtedness $31,891. **Criteria for awarding institutional aid:** *Non-need-based:* academics, art.

SAINT MARY'S UNIVERSITY OF MINNESOTA

700 Terrace Heights #2, Winona, MN 55987-1399
Phone: 507-457-1700 • **Financial Aid Phone:** 507-457-1438
E-mail: admission@smumn.edu • **CEEB Code:** 6632
Fax: 507-457-1722 • **Website:** www.smumn.edu • **ACT Code:** 2148

This private school, affiliated with the Roman Catholic Church, was founded in 1912. It has a 400-acre campus.

RATINGS

Admissions Selectivity Rating: 68   **Fire Safety Rating:** 85   **Green Rating:** 65

STUDENTS AND FACULTY

Enrollment: 1,935. **Student Body:** 53% female, 47% male, 42% out-of-state, 2% international (43 countries represented). Asian 2%, African American 5%, Caucasian 56%, Hispanic 5%, Native American 0%.
Retention and Graduation: 75% freshmen return for sophomore year. 49% freshmen graduate within 4 years. 62% freshmen graduate within 6 years. 15% grads go on to further study within 1 year. 2% grads pursue arts and sciences

degrees. 1% grads pursue law degrees. 1% grads pursue business degrees. 4% grads pursue medical degrees. **Faculty:** Student/faculty ratio 16:1. 103 full-time faculty, 85% hold PhDs, 4% are members of minority groups, 38% are women. 0% of classes are taught by teaching assistants.

ACADEMICS
Degrees: bachelor's, certificate, diploma, doctoral, master's, post-bachelor's certificate, post-master's certificate. **Classes:** Most classes have 20–29 students. Most lab/discussion sessions have 10–19 students. **Majors with Highest Enrollment:** marketing/marketing management. **Special Study Options:** cooperative education program, cross-registration, double major, dual enrollment, English as a Second Language (ESL), honors program, independent study, internships, student-designed major, study abroad, teacher certification program. **Honors Programs:** The Lasallian Honors Program at Saint Mary's University is a general education program for motivated students who wish to engage in "shared inquiry" in small seminar classes. The hallmarks of the program are study of the Great Books, service learning, and participation in a community of learners who desire to grow intellectually and spiritually, together over four years. Great Books, Shared-Inquiry Seminars The Lasallian Honors Program is an interdisciplinary program of learning in the Great Books and other notable texts of Western and Eastern traditions. All of the courses are shared-inquiry seminars: the students and the professor discuss the works together in lively, interactive, and informed conversations about the most important ideas in human history. Working Smarter Honors courses do not necessarily require more work than other general education courses. What differs is the style of learning, in student-centered seminars. You have the opportunity to participate with other motivated students in small classes taught by professors committed to engaged learning and individualized attention. Streamlined General Education A practical advantage of the Honors program is that it streamlines course requirements. Because of our interdisciplinary 4-credit program, honors students take fewer general education courses. That leaves room for a second major, extracurricular activities, an internship, and/or studying abroad. Future Benefits Participation in the Lasallian Honors Program also has rewards after graduation. When it comes time to compete for a job, internship, or acceptance to graduate school, Honors students have a clear advantage. We have an enviable record (98%) of placing our students in some of the best graduate programs in the country. Personal Growth The most important reason to join the Lasallian Honors Program is the desire to extend yourself intellectually, spiritually, and creatively. We can help you do that in a supportive and challenging academic atmosphere. You will be part of a cohort group that shares your talents and interests '– and likely will become your closest college friends. **Disability Services:** Special programs offered to physically disabled students include note-taking services, reader services, tape recorders, tutors. **Career Services:** Alumni network, alumni services, career/job search classes, career assessment, internships.

FACILITIES
Housing: Coed dorms, special housing for disabled students, men's dorms, women's dorms, apartments for single students. 93% of campus accessible to physically disabled. **Special Academic Facilities/Equipment:** Art gallery, performance center, laboratories, observatory. **Computers:** 100% of dorms, 100% of libraries, 100% of dining areas, 100% of student union, have wireless network access. Students can register for classes online. Administrative functions (other than registration) can be performed online.

CAMPUS LIFE
Environment: Town. **Activities:** Choral groups, concert band, dance, drama/theater, jazz band, literary magazine, music ensembles, musical theater, radio station, student government, student newspaper, yearbook, Campus Ministries, International Student Organization 80 registered organizations, 13 honor societies, 6 religious organizations. **Athletics (Intercollegiate):** *Men:* baseball, basketball, cross-country, diving, golf, ice hockey, skiingnordiccross-country, soccer, swimming, tennis, track/field (outdoor), track/field (indoor). *Women:* basketball, cross-country, diving, golf, ice hockey, skiingnordiccross-country, soccer, softball, swimming, tennis, track/field (outdoor), track/field (indoor), volleyball. **On-Campus Highlights:** Lillian Hogan Davis Galleries, Gostomski Fieldhouse, Page Theatre, Toner Student Center, Outdoor Track and Field Complex, Saint Mary's also offers an 18 hole disc golf course which runs through the bluffs surrounding the campus. Also, a network of trails run along the bluffs and into wooded valleys allowing for hiking, running, walking, and cross country skiing. **Environmental Initiatives:** ISO 14001 Certified Environmental Management System (EMS) Member of the Sustain Winona Collaboration Green Team - Sustainability Series

ADMISSIONS
Freshman Academic Profile: Average high school GPA 3.2. 16% in top 10% of high school class, 43% in top 25% of high school class, 69% in top 50% of high school class. 64% from public high schools. SAT Math middle 50% range 490-565. SAT Critical Reading middle 50% range 420-510. SAT Writing middle 50% range 380-540. ACT middle 50% range 19-25. Minimum web-based TOEFL 79. Minimum paper TOEFL 520. **Basis for Candidate Selection:** *Very important factors considered include:* academic GPA, rigor of secondary school record, standardized test scores. *Important factors considered include:*

Class rank, character/personal qualities, interview, talent/ability. *Other factors considered include:* application essay, recommendation(s), alumni/ae relation, extracurricular activities, level of applicant's interest, volunteer work. **Freshman Admission Requirements:** High school diploma is required and GED is accepted. *Academic units required:* 4 English, 3 mathematics, 3 science, (2 science labs), 2 social studies, 6 academic electives. *Academic units recommended:* 4 English, 3 mathematics, 3 science, (2 science labs), 2 social studies, 6 academic electives. **Freshman Admission Statistics:** 1,704 applied, 79% admitted, 24% enrolled. **Transfer Admission Requirements:** High school transcript, college transcript(s), statement of good standing from prior institution(s). Minimum college GPA of 2.0 required. Lowest grade transferable C. **General Admission Information:** Application Fee $25. Regular application deadline 5/1. Regular notification 5/1. Nonfall registration accepted. Admission may be deferred for a maximum of 1 year. Credit and/or placement offered for CEEB Advanced Placement tests.

COSTS AND FINANCIAL AID
Annual tuition $27,820. Room and board $7,440. Required fees $500. Average book expense $1,300. **Required Forms and Deadlines:** FAFSA. **Notification of Awards:** Applicants will be notified of awards on a rolling basis beginning 2/1. **Types of Aid:** *Need-based scholarships/grants:* Federal Pell, SEOG, state scholarships/grants, the school's own gift aid. *Loans:* Subsidized Stafford, Unsubsidized Stafford, PLUS, Federal Perkins, state loans. **Student Employment:** Federal Work-Study Program available. Institutional employment available. Highest amount earned per year from on-campus jobs $3,000. Off-campus job opportunities are good. **Financial Aid Statistics:** 100% freshmen, 97% undergrads receive need-based scholarship or grant aid. 88% freshmen, 80% undergrads receive need-based self-help aid. 98% freshmen, 96% undergrads receive any aid. 77% undergrads borrow to pay for school. Average cumulative indebtedness $35,134. **Criteria for awarding institutional aid:** *Non-need-based:* academics, alumni affiliation, art, leadership, minority status, music/drama.

SAINT MICHAEL'S COLLEGE

One Winooski Park, Box 7, Colchester, VT 5439
Phone: 802-654-3000 • **Financial Aid Phone:** 802-654-3244
E-mail: http://www.smcvt.edu/admissions/ • **CEEB Code:** 3757
Fax: 802-654-2906 • **Website:** www.smcvt.edu • **ACT Code:** 4312

This private school, affiliated with the Roman Catholic Church, was founded in 1904. It has a 440-acre campus.

RATINGS
Admissions Selectivity Rating: 80   **Fire Safety Rating:** 71   **Green Rating:** 93

STUDENTS AND FACULTY
Enrollment: 1,942. **Student Body:** 54% female, 46% male, 79% out-of-state, 2% international (47 countries represented). Asian 2%, African American 2%, Caucasian 87%, Hispanic 4%, Native American 0%.
Retention and Graduation: 90% freshmen return for sophomore year. 77% freshmen graduate within 4 years. 82% freshmen graduate within 6 years. 23% grads go on to further study within 1 year. 54% grads pursue arts and sciences degrees. 6% grads pursue law degrees. 7% grads pursue business degrees. 5% grads pursue medical degrees. **Faculty:** Student/faculty ratio 12:1. 155 full-time faculty, 87% hold PhDs, 8% are members of minority groups, 46% are women. 0% of classes are taught by teaching assistants.

ACADEMICS
Degrees: bachelor's, master's, post-bachelor's certificate, post-master's certificate. **Classes:** Most classes have 10–19 students. Most lab/discussion sessions have 20–29 students. **Majors with Highest Enrollment:** biology/biological sciences; business/commerce; psychology. **Special Study Options:** cross-registration, distance learning, double major, dual enrollment, English as a Second Language (ESL), honors program, independent study, internships, liberal arts/career combination, student-designed major, study abroad, teacher certification program, Research for Academic Credit: Many majors require students to complete the equivalent of a senior thesis (sometimes called a Senior Seminar) for which they receive academic credit. Students work closely with an academic advisor on these capstone projects. Independent Research with Faculty: Independent research projects with faculty members--which are not-for-credit--often lead to peer-reviewed publications and presentations at major

conferences. These projects are an exciting opportunity for students and faculty to work side-by-side, making important discoveries in their fields. For students, these opportunities not only provide excellent resume-building experience, but also the chance to work closely with a mentor. Some students may even qualify for grant-funded research stipends. **Honors Programs:** The Honors Program at Saint Michael's provides additional challenges and opportunities to outstanding students through small group discussion, research and extra-curricular activities. Saint Michael's also has chapters of several national honors societies on campus including Phi Beta Kappa, and Delta Epsilon Sigma. **Combined Degree Programs:** BA/MA, 4+1 MBA w/Clarkson, (B.S., + D.Pharm.) with Albany College of Pharmacy. **Disability Services:** Special programs offered to physically disabled students include note-taking services, reader services, tape recorders, tutors. **Career Services:** Alumni network, alumni services, career/job search classes, career assessment, internships, regional alumni. Career Services highlights include Our Internship Program gives students the opportunity to integrate their academic studies with a supervised work experience. Internships enhance classroom learning by integrating academics with the world of business. This on-the-job experience assists students in their career decision-making process. Internships provide valuable work experiences that increase job opportunities after graduation. Through this process students learn valuable job search and career defining skills.

FACILITIES

Housing: Coed dorms, special housing for disabled students, men's dorms, special housing for international students, women's dorms, apartments for single students, theme housing: 1.Honors Housing, 2. Substance Free Housing. 75% of campus accessible to physically disabled. **Special Academic Facilities/Equipment:** Holcomb Observatory,McCarthy Arts Center Gallary. **Computers:** 90% of classrooms, 100% of dorms, 100% of libraries, 100% of dining areas, 100% of student union, have wireless network access. Students can register for classes online. Administrative functions (other than registration) can be performed online.

CAMPUS LIFE

Environment: City. **Activities:** Choral groups, concert band, dance, drama/theater, jazz band, literary magazine, music ensembles, musical theater, radio station, student government, student newspaper, yearbook, Campus Ministries, International Student Organization 50 registered organizations, 11 honor societies, 1 religious organizations. **Athletics (Intercollegiate):** *Men:* baseball, basketball, cross-country, diving, golf, ice hockey, lacrosse, skiing (downhill/alpine), skiingnordiccross-country, soccer, swimming, tennis. *Women:* basketball, cross-country, diving, field hockey, ice hockey, lacrosse, skiing (downhill/alpine), skiingnordiccross-country, soccer, softball, swimming, tennis, volleyball. **On-Campus Highlights:** Alliot Student Center, McCarthy Arts Center, Chapel of Saint Michael the Archangel, Vincent C. Ross Sports Center, Tarrant Student Recreational Center. **Environmental Initiatives:** Energy Efficiency Programs: "Three Degree Challenge" to further reduce campus wide building temperatures by turning down thermostats to reduce energy consumption (in addition to reducing energy consumption, all new major appliances must be energy star certified); new building aims for LEED certification; all campus buildings on an Energy Management System to ensure efficient use of energy; Creating a culture of sustainability with each First Year class: each first year student receives a green welcome package during their orientation: 2 reusable tote bags, reusable coffee mug, bus map. A Green Office Certification program just launched (Spring 2012) to encourage faculty and staff to be more sustainable. The Academic side of the college further supports creating a culture of sustainability by having just established a new major: Environmental Studies Local Food Program: The college has a 1/4 Organic Garden to give students hands on experience with sustainable agriculture and offers 2 paid positions during the summer; the college partners with the local Intervale Food Hub to offer CSA shares for faculty, staff and students that are delivered year round right to campus; a newly establised Food Justice group was formed due to increased interests for local and fair trade food and the college has become a Fair Trade Certified university.

ADMISSIONS

Freshman Academic Profile: Average high school GPA 3.5. 27% in top 10% of high school class, 59% in top 25% of high school class, 83% in top 50% of high school class. 69% from public high schools. SAT Math middle 50% range 520-620. SAT Critical Reading middle 50% range 530-630. SAT Writing middle 50% range 520-620. ACT middle 50% range 23-28. Minimum paper TOEFL 550. **Basis for Candidate Selection:** *Very important factors considered include:* Class rank, academic GPA, rigor of secondary school record. *Important factors considered include:* application essay, recommendation(s), standardized test scores, character/personal qualities, extracurricular activities, talent/ability. *Other factors considered include:* alumni/ae relation, first generation, geographical residence, level of applicant's interest, racial/ethnic status, state residency, volunteer work, work experience. **Freshman Admission Requirements:** High school diploma is required and GED is accepted. *Academic units required:* 4 English, 3 mathematics, 3 science, (2 science labs), 3 foreign language, 3 social studies. *Academic units recommended:* 4 English, 3 mathematics, 3 science,

(2 science labs), 3 foreign language, 3 social studies. **Freshman Admission Statistics:** 4,578 applied, 78% admitted, 15% enrolled. **Transfer Admission Requirements:** High school transcript, college transcript(s), essay or personal statement, standardized test scores, minimum college GPA of 2.8 required. Lowest grade transferable C–. **General Admission Information:** Application Fee $50. Regular application deadline 2/1. Regular notification 4/1. Nonfall registration accepted. Admission may be deferred for a maximum of 1 year. Credit and/or placement offered for CEEB Advanced Placement tests.

COSTS AND FINANCIAL AID

Annual tuition $37,200. Room and board $9,350. Required fees $310. Average book expense $1,200. **Required Forms and Deadlines:** FAFSASigned copies of Parent's 2009 Federal Tax Return, Parent's Federal W-2 forms, Signed copies of Student's 2009 Federal Tax Return, Student's Federal W-2 forms, Dependent 2009-10 Verification Worksheet (Please check the Student Financial Services forms library for the latest version). **Notification of Awards:** Applicants will be notified of awards on a rolling basis beginning 1/15. **Types of Aid:** *Need-based scholarships/grants:* Federal Pell, SEOG, state scholarships/grants, private scholarships, the school's own gift aid. *Loans:* Subsidized Stafford, Unsubsidized Stafford, PLUS, Federal Perkins. **Student Employment:** Federal Work-Study Program available. Institutional employment available. Highest amount earned per year from on-campus jobs $15,649. Off-campus job opportunities are excellent. **Financial Aid Statistics:** 99% freshmen, 98% undergrads receive need-based scholarship or grant aid. 19% freshmen, 17% undergrads receive non-need-based scholarship or grant aid. 79% freshmen, 78% undergrads receive need-based self-help aid. 1% freshmen, 1% undergrads receive athletic scholarships. 97% freshmen, 96% undergrads receive any aid. 71% undergrads borrow to pay for school. Average cumulative indebtedness $33,054. **Criteria for awarding institutional aid:** *Non-need-based:* academics, alumni affiliation, art, athletics, leadership, minority status, music/drama, state/district residency.

See page 1196.

SAINT PAUL'S COLLEGE

115 College Drive, Lawrenceville, VA 23868
Phone: 434-848-1856
E-mail: admissions@saintpauls.edu
Fax: 804-848-6407 • **Website:** www.saintpauls.edu • **ACT Code:** 4394

This private school, affiliated with the Episcopal Church, was founded in 1888. It has a 185-acre campus.

RATINGS
Admissions Selectivity Rating: 65   **Fire Safety Rating:** 67   **Green Rating:** 60*

STUDENTS AND FACULTY
Enrollment: 707. **Student Body:** 52% female, 48% male, 31% out-of-state, 0% international (6 countries represented). Asian 0%, African American 99%, Caucasian 2%, Hispanic 0%, Native American 0%.
Retention and Graduation: 100% freshmen return for sophomore year. 16% freshmen graduate within 4 years. 10% grads go on to further study within 1 year. **Faculty:** Student/faculty ratio 17:1. 30 full-time faculty, 53% hold PhDs, 50% are members of minority groups, 33% are women. 0% of classes are taught by teaching assistants.

ACADEMICS
Degrees: bachelor's. **Classes:** Most classes have fewer than 10 students. Most lab/discussion sessions have fewer than 10 students. **Majors with Highest Enrollment:** business/commerce; criminal justice/police science; sociology. **Special Study Options:** Accelerated program, cooperative education program, double major, honors program, independent study, internships, liberal arts/career combination, study abroad, teacher certification program, U.S. Army ROTC. **Honors Programs:** Alpha Kappa Mu Honor Society. **Disability Services:** Special programs offered to physically disabled students include tape recorders, tutors. **Career Services:** Alumni network, alumni services, career/job search classes, career assessment, internships, regional alumni.

FACILITIES
Housing: men's dorms, women's dorms, apartments for single students. **Special Academic Facilities/Equipment:** The Saul Building (1888) (the first classroom built on SPC campus).

CAMPUS LIFE
Environment: Rural. **Activities:** Choral groups, dance, drama/theater, student government, yearbook 30 registered organizations, 2 honor societies, 2 religious organizations. 3 fraternities, 3 sororities. **Athletics (Intercollegiate):** *Men:* baseball, basketball, cross-country, golf, tennis, track/field (outdoor), track/field (indoor). *Women:* basketball, cross-country, golf, softball, tennis, track/field

(outdoor), track/field (indoor), volleyball. **On-Campus Highlights:** Student Center, Gymnasium, Library, Cafeteria, Dorms.

ADMISSIONS

Freshman Academic Profile: Average high school GPA 2.5. 3% in top 10% of high school class, 8% in top 25% of high school class, 23% in top 50% of high school class. 95% from public high schools. SAT Math middle 50% range 330-410. SAT Critical Reading middle 50% range 330-410. ACT middle 50% range 13-17. **Basis for Candidate Selection:** *Important factors considered include:* Class rank, application essay, recommendation(s), rigor of secondary school record, standardized test scores, character/personal qualities, extracurricular activities, interview, talent/ability. *Other factors considered include:* volunteer work, work experience. **Freshman Admission Requirements:** High school diploma is required and GED is accepted. *Academic units required:* 4 English, 2 mathematics, 2 science. *Academic units recommended:* 4 English, 2 mathematics, 2 science. **Freshman Admission Statistics:** 641 applied, 71% admitted, 64% enrolled. **Transfer Admission Requirements:** High school transcript, college transcript(s), essay or personal statement, statement of good standing from prior institution(s). Minimum college GPA of 2 required. Lowest grade transferable C. **General Admission Information:** Application Fee $20. Nonfall registration accepted. Neither credit nor placement offered for CEEB Advanced Placement tests.

COSTS AND FINANCIAL AID

Annual tuition $10,400. Room and board $5,890. Required fees $681. Average book expense $600. **Required Forms and Deadlines:** FAFSA, state aid form. **Notification of Awards:** Applicants will be notified of awards on a rolling basis beginning 1/7. **Types of Aid:** *Need-based scholarships/grants:* Federal Pell, SEOG, state scholarships/grants, private scholarships, the school's own gift aid, United Negro College Fund. *Loans:* Direct Subsidized Stafford, Direct Unsubsidized Stafford, Direct PLUS, Federal Perkins. **Student Employment:** Federal Work-Study Program available. Highest amount earned per year from on-campus jobs $1,300. Off-campus job opportunities are fair. **Financial Aid Statistics:** 81% freshmen, 81% undergrads receive need-based scholarship or grant aid. 85% freshmen, 86% undergrads receive non-need-based scholarship or grant aid. 89% freshmen, 88% undergrads receive need-based self-help aid. 4% freshmen, 11% undergrads receive athletic scholarships. 91% freshmen, 59% undergrads receive any aid. 80% undergrads borrow to pay for school. Average cumulative indebtedness $10,240. **Criteria for awarding institutional aid:** *Non-need-based:* academics, athletics, state/district residency.

SAINT PETER'S UNIVERSITY

2641 Kennedy Boulevard, Jersey City, NJ 7306
Phone: 201-761-7100 • **Financial Aid Phone:** 201-761-7100
E-mail: admissions@spc.edu • **CEEB Code:** 2806
Fax: 201-761-7105 • **Website:** www.spc.edu • **ACT Code:** 2604

This private school, affiliated with the Roman Catholic Church, was founded in 1872. It has a 10-acre campus.

RATINGS

Admissions Selectivity Rating: 71   **Fire Safety Rating:** 60*   **Green Rating:** 60*

STUDENTS AND FACULTY

Enrollment: 2,254. **Student Body:** 59% female, 41% male, 14% out-of-state, 3% international (43 countries represented). Asian 11%, African American 28%, Caucasian 27%, Hispanic 26%, Native American 1%. **Retention and Graduation:** 74% freshmen return for sophomore year. 33% freshmen graduate within 4 years. 51% freshmen graduate within 6 years. 27% grads go on to further study within 1 year. 9% grads pursue arts and sciences degrees. 5% grads pursue law degrees. 6% grads pursue business degrees. 7% grads pursue medical degrees. **Faculty:** Student/faculty ratio 12:1. 117 full-time faculty, 79% hold PhDs, 11% are members of minority groups, 48% are women. 0% of classes are taught by teaching assistants.

ACADEMICS

Degrees: associate, bachelor's, diploma, master's. **Classes:** Most classes have 10–19 students. **Majors with Highest Enrollment:** biology/biological sciences; criminal justice/law enforcement administration; education. **Special Study Options:** Accelerated program, cooperative education program, double major, dual enrollment, exchange student program (domestic), honors program, independent study, internships, liberal arts/career combination, student-designed major, study abroad, teacher certification program, weekend college, Joint degree in clinical and laboratory sciences with the University of Medicine and Dentistry of New Jersey (UMDNJ); Joint degree in Pharmacy with Rutgers University. **Honors Programs:** While Honors provides academic enrichment for highly motivated students, it is not a formal major or minor. Students

enrolled in the program must complete a minimum of 30 credits designated as Honors courses, which include Honors core course seminars, Honors advanced electives, and 6 credits of Honors Thesis: research and independent study. Independent study projects must be approved by the Honors Program and the respective chairs of the student's major department. Independent study projects may carry departmental as well as Honors credit. **Combined Degree Programs:** BA/MD, BA/JD, Combined-Degree programs at Seton Hall and UMDNJ. **Disability Services:** Special programs offered to physically disabled students include note-taking services, reader services, tape recorders, tutors.

FACILITIES

Housing: Coed dorms, men's dorms, women's dorms, apartments for single students. **Special Academic Facilities/Equipment:** TV production facilities, center for government affairs.

CAMPUS LIFE

Environment: City. **Activities:** Choral groups, drama/theater, literary magazine, radio station, student government, student newspaper, yearbook 45 registered organizations, 11 honor societies. **Athletics (Intercollegiate):** *Men:* baseball, basketball, cheerleading, cross-country, diving, football, golf, soccer, swimming, tennis, track/field (outdoor). *Women:* basketball, bowling, cheerleading, cross-country, diving, soccer, softball, swimming, tennis, track/field (outdoor), volleyball.

ADMISSIONS

Freshman Academic Profile: Average high school GPA 3.2. SAT Math middle 50% range 420-530. SAT Critical Reading middle 50% range 412-520. SAT Writing middle 50% range 420-510. ACT middle 50% range 17-21. Minimum web-based TOEFL 79. Minimum paper TOEFL 550. **Basis for Candidate Selection:** *Very important factors considered include:* academic GPA, rigor of secondary school record, standardized test scores. *Important factors considered include:* Class rank, application essay, recommendation(s). *Other factors considered include:* character/personal qualities, extracurricular activities, interview, talent/ability, volunteer work, work experience. **Freshman Admission Requirements:** High school diploma is required and GED is accepted. *Academic units required:* 4 English, 3 mathematics, 2 science, (1 science labs), 2 foreign language, 2 history, 3 academic electives. *Academic units recommended:* 4 English, 3 mathematics, 2 science, (1 science labs), 2 foreign language, 2 history, 3 academic electives. **Freshman Admission Statistics:** 2,779 applied, 67% admitted, 23% enrolled. **Transfer Admission Requirements:** college transcript(s), essay or personal statement, minimum college GPA of 2.0 required. Lowest grade transferable C. **General Admission Information:** Notification on a rolling basis, beginning on or about 11/1. Nonfall registration accepted. Admission may be deferred for a maximum of 24. Credit offered for CEEB Advanced Placement tests.

COSTS AND FINANCIAL AID

Annual tuition $28,900. Room and board $12,240. Required fees $900. Average book expense. **Required Forms and Deadlines:** FAFSA. **Notification of Awards:** Applicants will be notified of awards on a rolling basis beginning 2/15. **Types of Aid:** *Need-based scholarships/grants:* Federal Pell, SEOG, state scholarships/grants, the school's own gift aid. *Loans:* Subsidized Stafford, Unsubsidized Stafford, PLUS, Federal Perkins, state loans. **Student Employment:** Federal Work-Study Program available. Institutional employment available. Highest amount earned per year from on-campus jobs $1,500. Off-campus job opportunities are excellent. **Financial Aid Statistics:** 99% freshmen, 98% undergrads receive need-based scholarship or grant aid. 8% freshmen, 5% undergrads receive non-need-based scholarship or grant aid. 66% freshmen, 75% undergrads receive need-based self-help aid. 4% freshmen, 3% undergrads receive athletic scholarships. 88% freshmen, 88% undergrads receive any aid. 73% undergrads borrow to pay for school. Average cumulative indebtedness $28,638.

See page 1198.

SAINT THOMAS AQUINAS COLLEGE

125 Route 340, Sparkill, NY 10976
Phone: 845-398-4100 • **Financial Aid Phone:** 845-398-4098
E-mail: admissions@stac.edu • **CEEB Code:** 2807
Fax: 845-398-4114 • **Website:** www.stac.edu • **ACT Code:** 2897

This private school was founded in 1952. It has a 47-acre campus.

RATINGS

Admissions Selectivity Rating: 67   **Fire Safety Rating:** 87   **Green Rating:** 60*

STUDENTS AND FACULTY

Enrollment: 1,437. **Student Body:** 54% female, 46% male, 27% out-of-state, 1% international. Asian 3%, African American 6%, Caucasian 70%, Hispanic 15%, Native American 0%.

Retention and Graduation: 72% freshmen return for sophomore year. 36% grads go on to further study within 1 year. 25% grads pursue arts and sciences degrees. 5% grads pursue law degrees. 5% grads pursue business degrees. 5% grads pursue medical degrees. **Faculty:** Student/faculty ratio 16:1. 64 full-time faculty, 89% hold PhDs, 13% are members of minority groups, 50% are women. 0% of classes are taught by teaching assistants.

ACADEMICS

Degrees: associate, bachelor's, master's, post-master's certificate, terminal associate, transfer associate. **Classes:** Most classes have 20–29 students. **Majors with Highest Enrollment:** business/commerce; criminal justice/law enforcement administration; elementary education and teaching. **Special Study Options:** Accelerated program, cooperative education program, cross-registration, double major, dual enrollment, exchange student program (domestic), honors program, independent study, internships, liberal arts/career combination, study abroad, teacher certification program, Undergrads may take grad level classes--e.g. cooperative education programs: combined BS/MSW in social work in partnership with NYU; engineering Combined Degree Programs: 3-2 engineering programs with George Washington U and Manhattan Coll foreign exchange program(s): study abroad in England. **Honors Programs:** Highly selective honors program with maximum 20 student each class. Honor students receive full scholarship. **Disability Services:** Special programs offered to physically disabled students include note-taking services, tape recorders, tutors. **Career Services:** Alumni network, alumni services, career/job search classes, career assessment, internships, regional alumni.

FACILITIES

Housing: men's dorms, women's dorms, apartments for single students. 80% of campus accessible to physically disabled. **Special Academic Facilities/Equipment:** Azarian-McCullough Art Gallery, Sullivan Theatre, Spellman Technology Corridor, Costello Hall Science and Technology Center **Computers:** Students can register for classes online.

CAMPUS LIFE

Environment: Village. **Activities:** Choral groups, dance, drama/theater, literary magazine, musical theater, opera, radio station, student government, student newspaper, yearbook 35 registered organizations, 8 honor societies, 1 religious organizations. **Athletics (Intercollegiate):** *Men:* baseball, basketball, cross-country, golf, soccer, tennis, track/field (outdoor), track/field (indoor). *Women:* basketball, cross-country, lacrosse, soccer, softball, tennis, track/field (outdoor). **On-Campus Highlights:** The College Commons, The Fitness Center, The Romano Alumni Center, The Art Gallery, The Technology Corridor.

ADMISSIONS

Freshman Academic Profile: Average high school GPA 2.6. 5% in top 10% of high school class, 35% in top 25% of high school class, 50% in top 50% of high school class. 70% from public high schools. SAT Math middle 50% range 410-530. SAT Critical Reading middle 50% range 420-510. SAT Writing middle 50% range 420-520. ACT middle 50% range 17-22. Minimum paper TOEFL 530. **Basis for Candidate Selection:** *Very important factors considered include:* rigor of secondary school record. *Important factors considered include:* application essay, recommendation(s), standardized test scores, extracurricular activities, interview, talent/ability *Other factors considered include:* alumni/ae relation, volunteer work, work experience. **Freshman Admission Requirements:** High school diploma is required and GED is accepted. *Academic units required:* 4 English, 3 mathematics, 3 science, (2 science labs), 3 foreign language, 4 social studies. 4 English, 3 mathematics, 3 science, (2 science labs), 3 foreign language, 4 social studies. **Freshman Admission Statistics:** 1,331 applied, 80% admitted, 31% enrolled. **Transfer Admission Requirements:** college transcript(s), statement of good standing from prior institution(s). Minimum college GPA of 2.0 required. Lowest grade transferable C. **General Admission Information:** Application Fee $30. Early decision application deadline 12/15. Notification on a rolling basis, beginning on or about 10/1. Non-fall registration accepted. Admission may be deferred for a maximum of one year. Credit and/or placement offered for CEEB Advanced Placement tests.

COSTS AND FINANCIAL AID

Annual tuition $19,500. Room and board $9,730. Required fees $500. Average book expense $750. **Required Forms and Deadlines:** FAFSA, state aid form. **Notification of Awards:** Applicants will be notified of awards on a rolling basis beginning 3/1. **Types of Aid:** *Need-based scholarships/grants:* Federal Pell, SEOG, state scholarships/grants, private scholarships, the school's own gift aid. *Loans:* Direct Subsidized Stafford, Direct Unsubsidized Stafford, Direct PLUS, Subsidized Stafford, Unsubsidized Stafford, PLUS, Federal Perkins, Private alternative loans from lending institutions. **Student Employment:** Federal Work-Study Program available. Institutional employment available. Off-campus job opportunities are good. **Financial Aid Statistics:** 95% freshmen, 92%

undergrads receive need-based scholarship or grant aid. 12% freshmen, 11% undergrads receive non-need-based scholarship or grant aid. 76% freshmen, 76% undergrads receive need-based self-help aid. 3% freshmen, 3% undergrads receive athletic scholarships. 66% freshmen, 72% undergrads receive any aid. **Criteria for awarding institutional aid:** *Non-need-based:* academics, athletics.

SAINT VINCENT COLLEGE

Office of Admission and Financial Aid, Latrobe, PA 15650-2690
Phone: 724-537-4540 • **Financial Aid Phone:** 800-782-5549
E-mail: admission@stvincent.edu • **CEEB Code:** 2808
Fax: 724-532-5069 • **Website:** www.stvincent.edu • **ACT Code:** 3686

This private school, affiliated with the Roman Catholic Church, was founded in 1846. It has a 200-acre campus.

RATINGS

Admissions Selectivity Rating: 81   **Fire Safety Rating:** 67   **Green Rating:** 67

STUDENTS AND FACULTY

Enrollment: 1,617. **Student Body:** 50% female, 50% male, 12% out-of-state, 1% international (15 countries represented). Asian 1%, African American 3%, Caucasian 90%, Hispanic 2%, Native American 0%.

Retention and Graduation: 60% freshmen graduate within 4 years. 70% freshmen graduate within 6 years. 30% grads go on to further study within 1 year. **Faculty:** Student/faculty ratio 13:1. 91 full-time faculty, 84% hold PhDs, 2% are members of minority groups, 24% are women. 0% of classes are taught by teaching assistants.

ACADEMICS

Degrees: bachelor's, certificate, master's, post-bachelor's certificate. **Classes:** Most classes have 20–29 students. Most lab/discussion sessions have 10–19 students. **Majors with Highest Enrollment:** biology/biological sciences; history; psychology. **Special Study Options:** Accelerated program, cooperative education program, cross-registration, distance learning, double major, dual enrollment, external degree program, honors program, independent study, internships, liberal arts/career combination, study abroad, teacher certification program. **Honors Programs:** Honors Classes Professors design Honors classes to challenge and reward students who seek substantial intellectual development in college. The quality, not the quantity of work, distinguishes Honors classes from other courses. Portfolio As part of their coursework in Honors classes, all students are required to submit a short reflective essay and sample of their work at the end of each Honors class. Honors Events Dinner and evening discussions based on a reading, or attendance of a play, a film, an art exhibit, etc., on campus provide a special, congenial setting for intellectual exchange as part of a course or an extracurricular event. Off-Campus Explorations All Honors students and faculty are regularly invited to attend a play, film, art exhibit, etc. Extended trips within the U.S. or abroad may be planned during breaks or the summer. Senior Capstone Projects Honors students in majors with a senior research or capstone project will be strongly encouraged to present their work in a special colloquium at Saint Vincent and at professional meetings in their research areas. **Combined Degree Programs:** BA/JD, BA/MEng, 3-3 JD, 4-1 MBA w/ Duquesne. **Disability Services:** Special programs offered to physically disabled students include note-taking services, tutors. **Career Services:** Alumni network, alumni services, career assessment, internships, regional alumni. Career Services highlights include Students can take internship program for credit, though this is not required. Students are assisted in looking for internships in their field or industry of interest.

FACILITIES

Housing: Coed dorms, apartments for single students. 95% of campus accessible to physically disabled. **Special Academic Facilities/Equipment:** Art gallery, life sciences research center, spectrophotometer, spectrometer, physiograph work stations, data acquisition work station, planetarium, observatory, radio telescope, instructional technology resource center. **Computers:** 75% of libraries, 100% of student union, 25% of common outdoor areas have wireless network access. Students can register for classes online. Administrative functions (other than registration) can be performed online.

CAMPUS LIFE

Environment: Village. **Activities:** Choral groups, dance, drama/theater, literary magazine, music ensembles, musical theater, pep band, radio station, student government, student newspaper, television station, yearbook, Campus Ministries, International Student Organization 43 registered organizations, 12 honor societies, 2 religious organizations. **Athletics (Intercollegiate):** *Men:* baseball, basketball, cross-country, football, golf, lacrosse, soccer, swimming, tennis, track/field (outdoor). *Women:* basketball, cross-country, field hockey, golf, lacrosse, soccer, softball, swimming, tennis, volleyball. **On-Campus Highlights:** Library, Carey Student Center, St. Benedict Hall, Basilica, Chuck Noll Field. **Environmental Initiatives:** New construction on campus, including a current building project, will be green Environmental Education Center provides education opportunities to students.

ADMISSIONS

Freshman Academic Profile: Average high school GPA 3.6. 24% in top 10% of high school class, 54% in top 25% of high school class, 84% in top 50% of high school class. 67% from public high schools. SAT Math middle 50% range 490-600. SAT Critical Reading middle 50% range 480-590. SAT Writing middle 50% range 470-570. ACT middle 50% range 20-26. Minimum paper TOEFL 550. **Basis for Candidate Selection:** *Very important factors considered include:* Class rank, academic GPA, rigor of secondary school record. *Important factors considered include:* application essay, standardized test scores, character/personal qualities. *Other factors considered include:* recommendation(s), extracurricular activities, first generation, interview, talent/ability. **Freshman Admission Requirements:** High school diploma is required and GED is accepted. *Academic units required:* 4 English, 3 mathematics, 1 science, (1 science labs), 3 social studies, 5 academic electives. *Academic units recommended:* 4 English, 3 mathematics, 1 science, (1 science labs), 3 social studies, 5 academic electives. **Freshman Admission Statistics:** 1,855 applied, 62% admitted, 37% enrolled. **Transfer Admission Requirements:** High school transcript, college transcript(s), essay or personal statement, statement of good standing from prior institution(s). Minimum college GPA of 2.5 required. Lowest grade transferable C–. **General Admission Information:** Application Fee $25. Regular application deadline 5/1. Notification on a rolling basis, beginning on or about 10/1. Nonfall registration accepted. Admission may be deferred for a maximum of 1 year. Credit and/or placement offered for CEEB Advanced Placement tests.

COSTS AND FINANCIAL AID

Annual tuition $22,350. Room and board $7,242. Required fees $650. Average book expense $650. **Required Forms and Deadlines:** FAFSA, state aid form. **Notification of Awards:** Applicants will be notified of awards on a rolling basis beginning 3/1. **Types of Aid:** *Need-based scholarships/grants:* Federal Pell, SEOG, state scholarships/grants, private scholarships, the school's own gift aid, United Negro College Fund. *Loans:* Subsidized Stafford, Unsubsidized Stafford, PLUS, Federal Perkins. **Student Employment:** Federal Work-Study Program available. Institutional employment available. Highest amount earned per year from on-campus jobs $2,432. Off-campus job opportunities are good. **Financial Aid Statistics:** 10% freshmen, 100% undergrads receive need-based scholarship or grant aid. 43% freshmen, 85% undergrads receive non-need-based scholarship or grant aid. 75% freshmen, 80% undergrads receive need-based self-help aid. 10% undergrads receive athletic scholarships. 99% freshmen, 96% undergrads receive any aid. **Criteria for awarding institutional aid:** *Non-need-based:* academics, alumni affiliation, leadership, minority status, music/drama.

SAINT XAVIER UNIVERSITY

3700 West 103rd Street., Chicago, IL 60655
Phone: 773-298-3050
E-mail: admissions@sxu.edu • **CEEB Code:** 1708
Fax: 773-298-3076 • **ACT Code:** 1134

This private school, affiliated with the Roman Catholic Church, was founded in 1847. It has a 70-acre campus.

RATINGS
Admissions Selectivity Rating: 94   **Fire Safety Rating:** 60*   **Green Rating:** 60*

STUDENTS AND FACULTY
Enrollment: 3,060. **Student Body:** 70% female, 30% male, 6% out-of-state, 0% international. Asian 3%, African American 17%, Caucasian 60%, Hispanic 14%, Native American 0%.
Retention and Graduation: 29% freshmen graduate within 4 years. 53% freshmen graduate within 6 years. 10% grads go on to further study within 1 year. **Faculty:** 180 full-time faculty, 100% hold PhDs, 14% are members of minority groups, 56% are women. 0% of classes are taught by teaching assistants.

ACADEMICS
Degrees: bachelor's, certificate, master's, post-bachelor's certificate, post-master's certificate. **Classes:** Most classes have 20–29 students. Most lab/discussion sessions have 10–19 students. **Majors with Highest Enrollment:** business/commerce; elementary education and teaching; nursing/registered nurse (rn, asn, bsn, msn). **Special Study Options:** Accelerated program, cooperative edu-

cation program, distance learning, double major, dual enrollment, English as a Second Language (ESL), external degree program, honors program, independent study, internships, liberal arts/career combination, student-designed major, study abroad, teacher certification program, weekend college. **Combined Degree Programs:** BS/RN RN/MS BS/LPN. **Disability Services:** Special programs offered to physically disabled students include note-taking services, reader services, tape recorders, tutors. **Career Services:** alumni services, career/job search classes, career assessment, internships.

FACILITIES
Housing: Coed dorms, special housing for disabled students, apartments for single students. 98% of campus accessible to physically disabled. **Computers:** Students can register for classes online. Administrative functions (other than registration) can be performed online.

CAMPUS LIFE
Environment: Metropolis. **Activities:** Choral groups, concert band, jazz band, literary magazine, marching band, music ensembles, pep band, radio station, student government, student newspaper, student-run film society, symphony orchestra, yearbook, Campus Ministries, International Student Organization 41 registered organizations, 2 honor societies, 2 religious organizations. **Athletics (Intercollegiate):** *Men:* baseball, basketball, football, soccer. *Women:* basketball, cross-country, soccer, softball, volleyball. **On-Campus Highlights:** Convocation and Athletic Center, McDonough Chapel and Mercy Ministry Center, McCarthy Hall, Speech language Pathology Clinic, Art Gallery.

ADMISSIONS
Freshman Academic Profile: Average high school GPA 3.2. 17% in top 10% of high school class, 44% in top 25% of high school class, 74% in top 50% of high school class. 55% from public high schools. SAT Math middle 50% range 487-597. SAT Critical Reading middle 50% range 512-580. SAT Writing middle 50% range 455-592. ACT middle 50% range 20-25. Minimum paper TOEFL 550. **Basis for Candidate Selection:** *Very important factors considered include:* application essay, academic GPA, standardized test scores. *Important factors considered include:* rigor of secondary school record. *Other factors considered include:* recommendation(s), character/personal qualities, extracurricular activities, interview, level of applicant's interest, talent/ability, volunteer work, work experience. **Freshman Admission Requirements:** High school diploma is required and GED is accepted. **Freshman Admission Statistics:** 12,175 applied, 25% admitted, 14% enrolled. **Transfer Admission Requirements:** college transcript(s), minimum college GPA of 2.5 required. Lowest grade transferable C. **General Admission Information:** Application Fee $25. Nonfall registration accepted. Admission may be deferred for a maximum of not avail. Credit offered for CEEB Advanced Placement tests.

COSTS AND FINANCIAL AID
Annual tuition $23,610. Room and board $8,408. Required fees $855. Average book expense $1,200. **Required Forms and Deadlines:** FAFSA. **Notification of Awards:** Applicants will be notified of awards on a rolling basis beginning 2/15. **Types of Aid:** *Need-based scholarships/grants:* Federal Pell, SEOG, state scholarships/grants, private scholarships, the school's own gift aid. *Loans:* Subsidized Stafford, Unsubsidized Stafford, PLUS, Federal Perkins. **Student Employment:** Federal Work-Study Program available. Institutional employment available. Off-campus job opportunities are excellent. **Financial Aid Statistics:** 100% freshmen, 99% undergrads receive need-based scholarship or grant aid. 98% freshmen, 92% undergrads receive non-need-based scholarship or grant aid. 84% freshmen, 87% undergrads receive need-based self-help aid. 12% freshmen, 9% undergrads receive athletic scholarships. Average cumulative indebtedness $19,374. **Criteria for awarding institutional aid:** *Non-need-based:* academics, athletics, music/drama.

SALEM COLLEGE

PO Box 10548, Winston-Salem, NC 27108
Phone: 336-721-2621 • **Financial Aid Phone:** 336-721-2808
E-mail: admissions@salem.edu • **CEEB Code:** 5607
Fax: 336-917-5572 • **Website:** www.salem.edu • **ACT Code:** 3156

This private school, affiliated with the Moravian Church, was founded in 1772. It has a 57-acre campus.

RATINGS
Admissions Selectivity Rating: 84   **Fire Safety Rating:** 76   **Green Rating:** 60*

STUDENTS AND FACULTY
Enrollment: 741. **Student Body:** 98% female, 2% male, 23% out-of-state, 13% international (22 countries represented). Asian 1%, African American 19%, Caucasian 60%, Hispanic 4%, Native American 0%.

Retention and Graduation: 78% freshmen return for sophomore year. 50% freshmen graduate within 4 years. 52% freshmen graduate within 6 years. 30% grads go on to further study within 1 year. 25% grads pursue arts and sciences degrees. 3% grads pursue law degrees. 5% grads pursue business degrees. **Faculty:** Student/faculty ratio 12:1. 57 full-time faculty, 86% hold PhDs, 9% are members of minority groups, 61% are women. 0% of classes are taught by teaching assistants.

ACADEMICS

Degrees: bachelor's, master's. **Classes:** Most classes have 10–19 students. Most lab/discussion sessions have 10–19 students. **Majors with Highest Enrollment:** business/commerce; sociology. **Special Study Options:** cross-registration, double major, dual enrollment, honors program, independent study, internships, liberal arts/career combination, student-designed major, study abroad, teacher certification program. **Career Services:** Alumni network, internships.

FACILITIES

Housing: women's dorms, apartments for single students. 75% of campus accessible to physically disabled. **Special Academic Facilities/Equipment:** Art gallery, fine arts center, Center for Women Writers, videoconferencing center **Computers:** Administrative functions (other than registration) can be performed online.

CAMPUS LIFE

Environment: City. **Activities:** Choral groups, dance, drama/theater, literary magazine, marching band, music ensembles, musical theater, student government, student newspaper, yearbook 26 registered organizations, 14 honor societies, 7 religious organizations. **Athletics (Intercollegiate):** *Women:* basketball, cross-country, field hockey, swimming, tennis, volleyball. **On-Campus Highlights:** back porch of Main Hall, Salem Grille/Java City, residence hall basement lounges **Environmental Initiatives:** Recylcle committment-all residence halls and academic buildings have paper, plastic and aluminum containers Energy Conservation-1) systematically changing incandescent lights with CFL; 2)Limited installation of occupancy sensors; 3)Removal of lights in vending machines for energy conservation EPA-self audit and self disclosure program

ADMISSIONS

Freshman Academic Profile: Average high school GPA 3.7. 39% in top 10% of high school class, 67% in top 25% of high school class, 94% in top 50% of high school class. SAT Math middle 50% range 480-630. SAT Critical Reading middle 50% range 490-650. ACT middle 50% range 20-25. Minimum paper TOEFL 550. **Basis for Candidate Selection:** *Very important factors considered include:* academic GPA, rigor of secondary school record. *Important factors considered include:* Class rank, application essay, recommendation(s), standardized test scores, character/personal qualities, extracurricular activities, talent/ability. *Other factors considered include:* alumni/ae relation, first generation, interview, level of applicant's interest, volunteer work. **Freshman Admission Requirements:** High school diploma is required and GED is accepted. *Academic units required:* 4 English, 3 mathematics, 3 science, 2 foreign language, 2 history. 4 English, 3 mathematics, 3 science, 2 foreign language, 2 history. **Freshman Admission Statistics:** 420 applied, 62% admitted, 46% enrolled. **Transfer Admission Requirements:** High school transcript, college transcript(s), essay or personal statement, statement of good standing from prior institution(s). Minimum college GPA of 2.0 required. Lowest grade transferable C–. **General Admission Information:** Application Fee $30. Notification on a rolling basis, beginning on or about 10/1. Nonfall registration accepted. Admission may be deferred for a maximum of 1 year. Credit and/or placement offered for CEEB Advanced Placement tests.

COSTS AND FINANCIAL AID

Annual tuition $18,850. Room and board $10,050. Required fees $340. Average book expense $900. **Required Forms and Deadlines:** FAFSA. **Notification of Awards:** Applicants will be notified of awards on a rolling basis beginning 3/1. **Types of Aid:** *Need-based scholarships/grants:* Federal Pell, SEOG, state scholarships/grants, private scholarships, the school's own gift aid. *Loans:* Subsidized Stafford, Unsubsidized Stafford, PLUS, Federal Perkins. **Student Employment: Financial Aid Statistics:** 80% freshmen, 71% undergrads receive need-based scholarship or grant aid. 96% freshmen, 95% undergrads receive non-need-based scholarship or grant aid. 88% freshmen, 83% undergrads receive need-based self-help aid. 70% undergrads borrow to pay for school. Average cumulative indebtedness $17,125. **Criteria for awarding institutional aid:** *Non-need-based:* academics, alumni affiliation, leadership, minority status, music/drama, state/district residency.

SALEM STATE UNIVERSITY

352 Lafayette Street, Salem, MA 1970
Phone: 978-542-6210 • **Financial Aid Phone:** 978-542-6112
E-mail: admissions@salemstate.edu • **CEEB Code:** 3522
Fax: 978-542-6893 • **Website:** www.salemstate.edu

This public school was founded in 1854. It has a 108-acre campus.

RATINGS

Admissions Selectivity Rating: 79   **Fire Safety Rating:** 69   **Green Rating:** 60*

STUDENTS AND FACULTY

Enrollment: 7,296. **Student Body:** 61% female, 39% male, 3% out-of-state, 3% international. Asian 3%, African American 9%, Caucasian 76%, Hispanic 7%, Native American 0%.
Retention and Graduation: Faculty: Student/faculty ratio 14:1. 333 full-time faculty, 10% are members of minority groups, 54% are women. 0% of classes are taught by teaching assistants.

ACADEMICS

Degrees: bachelor's, master's, post-bachelor's certificate, post-master's certificate. **Classes:** Most classes have 10–19 students. Most lab/discussion sessions have 10–19 students. **Majors with Highest Enrollment:** business/commerce; criminal justice/law enforcement administration; education. **Special Study Options:** distance learning, double major, dual enrollment, English as a Second Language (ESL), honors program, independent study, internships, study abroad, teacher certification program. **Combined Degree Programs:** BS/MS Occupational Therapy. **Disability Services:** Special programs offered to physically disabled students include reader services, tape recorders.

FACILITIES

Housing: Coed dorms, Faculty in Residence. 100% of campus accessible to physically disabled. **Special Academic Facilities/Equipment:** Aquaculture center, On-campus elementary school, color TV studio, instructional media center.

CAMPUS LIFE

Environment: Village. **Activities:** Choral groups, concert band, dance, drama/theater, jazz band, literary magazine, music ensembles, musical theater, radio station, student government, student newspaper 149 registered organizations, 13 honor societies, 3 religious organizations. **Athletics (Intercollegiate):** *Men:* baseball, basketball, cross-country, diving, golf, ice hockey, lacrosse, soccer, swimming, tennis, track/field (outdoor). *Women:* basketball, cross-country, diving, field hockey, lacrosse, soccer, softball, swimming, tennis, track/field (outdoor), volleyball.

ADMISSIONS

Freshman Academic Profile: SAT Math middle 50% range 450-540. SAT Critical Reading middle 50% range 440-550. Minimum paper TOEFL 500. **Basis for Candidate Selection:** *Very important factors considered include:* academic GPA, rigor of secondary school record, standardized test scores. *Other factors considered include:* recommendation(s), character/personal qualities, extracurricular activities, interview, level of applicant's interest, talent/ability, volunteer work, work experience. **Freshman Admission Requirements:** High school diploma is required and GED is accepted. *Academic units required:* 4 English, 3 mathematics, 3 science, (2 science labs), 2 foreign language, 2 social studies, 1 history, 1 visual/performing arts, 1 computer science, 2 academic electives. *Academic units recommended:* 4 English, 3 mathematics, 3 science, (2 science labs), 2 foreign language, 2 social studies, 1 history, 1 visual/performing arts, 1 computer science, 2 academic electives. **Freshman Admission Statistics:** 5,697 applied, 57% admitted, 31% enrolled. **Transfer Admission Requirements:** college transcript(s), minimum college GPA of 2.0 required. Lowest grade transferable C–. **General Admission Information:** Application Fee $30. Notification on a rolling basis, beginning on or about 12/1. Nonfall registration accepted. Admission may be deferred for a maximum of 1 semester. Credit and/or placement offered for CEEB Advanced Placement tests.

COSTS AND FINANCIAL AID

Required Forms and Deadlines: FAFSA. **Notification of Awards:** Applicants will be notified of awards on a rolling basis beginning 6/1. **Financial Aid Statistics:** 73% freshmen, 75% undergrads receive any aid.

SALEM-TEIKYO UNIVERSITY

223 West Main Street, Salem, WV 26426-0500
Phone: 304-782-5336
E-mail: admissions@salemiu.edu • **CEEB Code:** 5608
Fax: 304-782-5592 • **Website:** www.salemiu.edu • **ACT Code:** 4530

This private school was founded in 1888. It has a 300-acre campus.

RATINGS
Admissions Selectivity Rating: 64   **Fire Safety Rating:** 60*   **Green Rating:** 60*

STUDENTS AND FACULTY
Enrollment: 439. **Student Body:** 47% female, 53% male, 56% out-of-state, 39% international (20 countries represented). Asian 1%, African American 8%, Caucasian 46%, Hispanic 2%, Native American 1%.
Retention and Graduation: 69% freshmen return for sophomore year. 3% grads go on to further study within 1 year. 2% grads pursue arts and sciences degrees. 1% grads pursue law degrees. 2% grads pursue business degrees. 1% grads pursue medical degrees. **Faculty:** Student/faculty ratio 14:1. 33 full-time faculty, 70% hold PhDs, 24% are members of minority groups, 39% are women. 0% of classes are taught by teaching assistants.

ACADEMICS
Degrees: associate, bachelor's, master's, post-master's certificate. **Classes:** Most classes have fewer than 10 students. **Special Study Options:** distance learning, double major, English as a Second Language (ESL), independent study, internships, liberal arts/career combination, study abroad, undergrads may take grad level classes foreign exchange program(s): exchange programs abroad in Japan(Teikyo U, Hachioji)and Germany(Teikyo U Berlin). Combined Bachelor's/Graduate degree in molecular biology. **Disability Services:** Special programs offered to physically disabled students include tutors. **Career Services:** career/job search classes, career assessment, internships.

FACILITIES
Housing: Coed dorms, men's dorms, women's dorms. 90% of campus accessible to physically disabled. **Special Academic Facilities/Equipment:** Living museum of culture and crafts of West Virginia settlers. Fort New Salem. Biotechnology labs,equestrian center

CAMPUS LIFE
Environment: Rural. **Activities:** Choral groups, dance, student government, student newspaper, television station, yearbook 20 registered organizations, 1 honor societies, 2 religious organizations. 4 fraternities, 4 sororities. **Athletics (Intercollegiate):** *Men:* baseball, basketball, cheerleading, equestrian sports, golf, soccer, swimming, tennis, water polo. *Women:* basketball, cheerleading, equestrian sports, soccer, softball, swimming, tennis, volleyball, water polo. **On-Campus Highlights:** Barker Center, Cafeteria, Tiger's Den, Library, Computer Labs.

ADMISSIONS
Freshman Academic Profile: SAT Math middle 50% range 420-570. SAT Critical Reading middle 50% range 380-550. ACT middle 50% range 16-22. Minimum paper TOEFL 500. **Basis for Candidate Selection:** *Very important factors considered include:* rigor of secondary school record, standardized test scores. *Important factors considered include:* recommendation(s), extracurricular activities. *Other factors considered include:* application essay, alumni/ae relation, character/personal qualities, interview, talent/ability. **Freshman Admission Requirements:** High school diploma is required and GED is accepted. **Freshman Admission Statistics:** 251 applied, 99% admitted, 24% enrolled. **Transfer Admission Requirements:** High school transcript, college transcript(s), statement of good standing from prior institution(s). Minimum college GPA of 2.5 required. Lowest grade transferable C. **General Admission Information:** Application Fee $25. Nonfall registration accepted. Admission may be deferred for a maximum of 12 months. Credit and/or placement offered for CEEB Advanced Placement tests.

COSTS AND FINANCIAL AID
Average book expense $1,000. **Required Forms and Deadlines:** FAFSA, institution's own financial aid form. **Notification of Awards:** Applicants will be notified of awards on a rolling basis beginning 2/15. **Types of Aid:** *Need-based scholarships/grants:* Federal Pell, SEOG, state scholarships/grants, private scholarships, the school's own gift aid. *Loans:* Direct Subsidized Stafford, Direct Unsubsidized Stafford, Direct PLUS, Subsidized Stafford, Unsubsidized Stafford, PLUS, Federal Perkins, college/university loans from institutional funds. **Student Employment:** Federal Work-Study Program available. Institutional employment available. Highest amount earned per year from on-campus jobs $2,000. Off-campus job opportunities are fair. **Financial Aid Statistics:** 67% freshmen, 63% undergrads receive need-based scholarship or grant aid. 9% freshmen, 38% undergrads receive non-need-based scholarship or grant aid.

94% freshmen, 89% undergrads receive need-based self-help aid. 31% freshmen, 6% undergrads receive athletic scholarships. 45% undergrads borrow to pay for school. Average cumulative indebtedness $14,449.

SALISBURY UNIVERSITY

Admissions Office, Salisbury, MD 21801
Phone: 410-543-6161 • **Financial Aid Phone:** 410-543-6165
E-mail: admissions@salisbury.edu • **CEEB Code:** 5403
Fax: 410-546-6016 • **Website:** www.salisbury.edu • **ACT Code:** 1716

This public school was founded in 1925. It has a 155-acre campus.

RATINGS
Admissions Selectivity Rating: 89   **Fire Safety Rating:** 98   **Green Rating:** 92

STUDENTS AND FACULTY
Enrollment: 7,714. **Student Body:** 57% female, 43% male, 14% out-of-state, 1% international (69 countries represented). Asian 2%, African American 11%, Caucasian 77%, Hispanic 5%, Native American 0%.
Retention and Graduation: 48% freshmen graduate within 4 years. 67% freshmen graduate within 6 years. 24% grads go on to further study within 1 year. 20% grads pursue arts and sciences degrees. 1% grads pursue law degrees. 2% grads pursue business degrees. **Faculty:** Student/faculty ratio 16:1. 404 full-time faculty, 84% hold PhDs, 14% are members of minority groups, 48% are women. 2% of classes are taught by teaching assistants.

ACADEMICS
Degrees: bachelor's, certificate, master's, post-bachelor's certificate. **Classes:** Most classes have 20–29 students. Most lab/discussion sessions have 20–29 students. **Majors with Highest Enrollment:** biology/biological sciences; business administration and management; communication studies/speech communication and rhetoric. **Special Study Options:** Accelerated program, cross-registration, distance learning, double major, dual enrollment, English as a Second Language (ESL), honors program, independent study, internships, liberal arts/career combination, student-designed major, study abroad, teacher certification program. **Honors Programs:** The Thomas E. Bellavance Honors Program **Combined Degree Programs:** BASW/BA, BS/BS Biology/Envirn., Early Chidhood Educ/Elementary Educ. **Disability Services:** Special programs offered to physically disabled students include note-taking services, reader services, tutors. **Career Services:** Alumni network, alumni services, career/job search classes, career assessment, internships, regional alumni.

FACILITIES
Housing: Coed dorms, men's dorms, women's dorms, apartments for single students, wellness housing, theme housing, affiliated off-campus apartments, quiet/study housing available. World living/learning option-community of International and American students. 47% of campus accessible to physically disabled. **Special Academic Facilities/Equipment:** Arboretum, University Galleries, Delmarva History and Culture Research Center, Small Business Development Center, Ward Museum of Wildfowl Art. **Computers:** 100% of classrooms, 100% of dorms, 100% of libraries, 100% of dining areas, 100% of student union, have wireless network access. Students can register for classes online. Administrative functions (other than registration) can be performed online.

CAMPUS LIFE
Environment: Town. **Activities:** Choral groups, concert band, dance, drama/theater, jazz band, literary magazine, music ensembles, musical theater, pep band, radio station, student government, student newspaper, student-run film society, symphony orchestra, television station, Campus Ministries, International Student Organization 126 registered organizations, 23 honor societies, 8 religious organizations. 8 fraternities, 4 sororities. **Athletics (Intercollegiate):** *Men:* baseball, basketball, cross-country, football, lacrosse, soccer, swimming, tennis, track/field (outdoor). *Women:* basketball, cross-country, field hockey, lacrosse, soccer, softball, swimming, tennis, track/field (outdoor), volleyball. **On-Campus Highlights:** Commons (housing our Dining Hall and Bookstore), Cool Beans Cyber Caf, Scarborough Leadership Center, Honors House, Maggs Physical Activities Center. **Environmental Initiatives:** Energy and water conservation partnership Minimum of LEED Silver for construction Extensive recycling and composting program

ADMISSIONS
Freshman Academic Profile: Average high school GPA 3.7. 24% in top 10% of high school class, 60% in top 25% of high school class, 92% in top

50% of high school class. 80% from public high schools. SAT Math middle 50% range 540-620. SAT Critical Reading middle 50% range 530-610. SAT Writing middle 50% range 530-600. ACT middle 50% range 22-26. Minimum paper TOEFL 550. **Basis for Candidate Selection:** *Very important factors considered include:* academic GPA, rigor of secondary school record, extracurricular activities, talent/ability. *Important factors considered include:* Class rank, standardized test scores, alumni/ae relation, geographical residence, volunteer work. *Other factors considered include:* application essay, recommendation(s), character/personal qualities, racial/ethnic status, work experience. **Freshman Admission Requirements:** High school diploma is required and GED is accepted. *Academic units required:* 4 English, 3 mathematics, 3 science, (2 science labs), 2 foreign language, 3 social studies. *Academic units recommended:* 4 English, 3 mathematics, 3 science, (2 science labs), 2 foreign language, 3 social studies. **Freshman Admission Statistics:** 8,866 applied, 53% admitted, 26% enrolled. **Transfer Admission Requirements:** college transcript(s), minimum college GPA of 2.0 required. Lowest grade transferable C. **General Admission Information:** Application Fee $45. Regular notification 3/15. Nonfall registration accepted. Credit offered for CEEB Advanced Placement tests.

COSTS AND FINANCIAL AID
Annual in-state tuition $5,576. Annual out-of-state tuition $13,922. Room and board $9,400. Required fees $2,124. Average book expense $1,300. **Required Forms and Deadlines:** FAFSA. **Notification of Awards:** Applicants will be notified of awards on a rolling basis beginning 3/15. **Types of Aid:** *Need-based scholarships/grants:* Federal Pell, SEOG, state scholarships/grants, private scholarships, the school's own gift aid. *Loans:* Direct Subsidized Stafford, Direct Unsubsidized Stafford, Federal Perkins. **Student Employment:** Federal Work-Study Program available. Institutional employment available. Off-campus job opportunities are fair. **Financial Aid Statistics:** 86% freshmen, 74% undergrads receive need-based scholarship or grant aid. 74% freshmen, 83% undergrads receive need-based self-help aid. 87% freshmen, 75% undergrads receive any aid. 59% undergrads borrow to pay for school. Average cumulative indebtedness $23,159. **Criteria for awarding institutional aid:** *Non-need-based:* academics, alumni affiliation, art, leadership, music/drama, state/district residency.

SALVE REGINA UNIVERSITY

100 Ochre Point Avenue, Newport, RI 02840-4192
Phone: 401-341-2908 • **Financial Aid Phone:** 401-341-2901
E-mail: sruadmis@salve.edu • **CEEB Code:** 3759
Fax: 401-848-2823 • **Website:** www.salve.edu • **ACT Code:** 3816

This private school, affiliated with the Roman Catholic Church, was founded in 1947. It has a 81-acre campus.

RATINGS
Admissions Selectivity Rating: 79   **Fire Safety Rating:** 88   **Green Rating:** 72

STUDENTS AND FACULTY
Enrollment: 2,020. **Student Body:** 70% female, 30% male, 80% out-of-state, 2% international (17 countries represented). Asian 1%, African American 2%, Caucasian 75%, Hispanic 6%, Native American 0%.
Retention and Graduation: 69% freshmen graduate within 4 years. 19% grads go on to further study within 1 year. **Faculty:** Student/faculty ratio 15:1. 115 full-time faculty, 78% hold PhDs, 4% are members of minority groups, 55% are women. 0% of classes are taught by teaching assistants.

ACADEMICS
Degrees: associate, bachelor's, certificate, doctoral, master's, post-bachelor's certificate, post-master's certificate. **Classes:** Most classes have 10–19 students. Most lab/discussion sessions have 20–29 students. **Majors with Highest Enrollment:** criminal justice/law enforcement administration; elementary education and teaching; nursing/registered nurse (rn, asn, bsn, msn). **Special Study Options:** Accelerated program, distance learning, double major, dual enrollment, English as a Second Language (ESL), honors program, independent study, internships, liberal arts/career combination, study abroad, teacher certification program, Washington Semester. **Honors Programs:** The Pell Honors Program is open to students from all majors who receive the Dean's, Trustee's, or Presidential Scholarships, or who are nominated by Salve Regina faculty or the Admissions Office. The goal of the Pell Honors Program is to create a learning community of students from different disciplines. The honors education is an enhancement of the core curriculum with a focus in international relations and public policy emphasizing civic responsibility and action. Students are required to take classes together, participate in either an internship or study abroad experience, and write and publicly defend a senior thesis. **Combined Degree Programs:** BA/MA, 4-1 MA, 4-1 MS, BA,BS/MBA. **Disability

Services: Special programs offered to physically disabled students include note-taking services, reader services, tape recorders, tutors. **Career Services:** Alumni network, alumni services, career/job search classes, career assessment, internships, regional alumni.

FACILITIES
Housing: Coed dorms, special housing for disabled students, men's dorms, women's dorms, apartments for single students, wellness housing. Both historic style housing and conventional style housing options are available on campus. Off-campus housing is available to upper class students. 85% of campus accessible to physically disabled. **Special Academic Facilities/Equipment:** Art gallery, theater, technology center. **Computers:** 98% of classrooms, 10% of dorms, 100% of libraries, 100% of dining areas, 100% of student union, 25% of common outdoor areas have wireless network access. Students can register for classes online. Administrative functions (other than registration) can be performed online. Undergraduates are required to own a computer.

CAMPUS LIFE
Environment: Town. **Activities:** Choral groups, concert band, dance, drama/theater, jazz band, literary magazine, music ensembles, pep band, radio station, student government, student newspaper, student-run film society, yearbook, Campus Ministries, International Student Organization, Model UN 42 registered organizations, 14 honor societies, 2 religious organizations. **Athletics (Intercollegiate):** *Men:* baseball, basketball, cross-country, football, ice hockey, lacrosse, soccer, tennis. *Women:* basketball, field hockey, ice hockey, lacrosse, soccer, softball, tennis, track/field (outdoor), volleyball. **On-Campus Highlights:** New Residence Hall, Athletic Center, O'Hare Academic & Antone Academic Cntrs, Library and Computer Labs, Historic Mansions on campus. **Environmental Initiatives:** Recycling Energy conservation Water conservation

ADMISSIONS
Freshman Academic Profile: Average high school GPA 3.2. 18% in top 10% of high school class, 40% in top 25% of high school class, 85% in top 50% of high school class. 67% from public high schools. SAT Math middle 50% range 510-600. SAT Critical Reading middle 50% range 510-600. SAT Writing middle 50% range 510-600. ACT middle 50% range 23-27. Minimum web-based TOEFL 80. Minimum paper TOEFL 500. **Basis for Candidate Selection:** *Very important factors considered include:* Class rank, academic GPA, rigor of secondary school record. *Important factors considered include:* application essay, recommendation(s), standardized test scores. *Other factors considered include:* alumni/ae relation, character/personal qualities, extracurricular activities, level of applicant's interest, racial/ethnic status, talent/ability, volunteer work, work experience. **Freshman Admission Requirements:** High school diploma is required and GED is accepted. *Academic units required:* 4 English, 3 mathematics, 2 science, (2 science labs), 2 foreign language, 1 social studies, 4 academic electives. 4 English, 3 mathematics, 2 science, (2 science labs), 2 foreign language, 1 social studies, 4 academic electives. **Freshman Admission Statistics:** 4,824 applied, 70% admitted, 16% enrolled. **Transfer Admission Requirements:** High school transcript, college transcript(s), essay or personal statement, statement of good standing from prior institution(s). Minimum college GPA of 2.7 required. Lowest grade transferable C. **General Admission Information:** Application Fee $50. Regular notification 4/1. Notification on a rolling basis, beginning on or about 12/15. Nonfall registration accepted. Admission may be deferred for a maximum of 12 months. Credit and/or placement offered for CEEB Advanced Placement tests.

COSTS AND FINANCIAL AID
Annual tuition $33,450. Room and board $11,850. Required fees $500. Average book expense $900. **Required Forms and Deadlines:** FAFSA, CSS/Financial Aid PROFILE, noncustodial PROFILE, business/farm supplement. **Notification of Awards:** Applicants will be notified of awards on or about 4/1. **Types of Aid:** *Need-based scholarships/grants:* Federal Pell, SEOG, state scholarships/grants, private scholarships, the school's own gift aid. *Loans:* Subsidized Stafford, Unsubsidized Stafford, PLUS, Federal Perkins, Federal Nursing, private loans. **Student Employment:** Federal Work-Study Program available. Institutional employment available. Highest amount earned per year from on-campus jobs $1,200. Off-campus job opportunities are good. **Financial Aid Statistics:** 99% freshmen, 95% undergrads receive need-based scholarship or grant aid. 7% freshmen, 6% undergrads receive non-need-based scholarship or grant aid. 91% freshmen, 93% undergrads receive need-based self-help aid. 82% freshmen, 77% undergrads receive any aid. 80% undergrads borrow to pay for school. Average cumulative indebtedness $40,090. **Criteria for awarding institutional aid:** *Non-need-based:* academics.

SAM HOUSTON STATE UNIVERSITY

Box 2418, Huntsville, TX 77341-2418
Phone: 936-294-1828 • **Financial Aid Phone:** 936-294-1774
E-mail: admissions@shsu.edu • **CEEB Code:** 6643
Fax: 936-294-3758 • **Website:** www.shsu.edu • **ACT Code:** 4162

This public school was founded in 1879. It has a 272-acre campus.

RATINGS
Admissions Selectivity Rating: 76   **Fire Safety Rating:** 91   **Green Rating:** 61

STUDENTS AND FACULTY
Enrollment: 15,611. **Student Body:** 58% female, 42% male, 1% out-of-state, 1% international (98 countries represented). Asian 1%, African American 17%, Caucasian 58%, Hispanic 17%, Native American 0%.
Retention and Graduation: 27% freshmen graduate within 4 years. 49% freshmen graduate within 6 years. **Faculty:** Student/faculty ratio 25:1. 620 full-time faculty, 79% hold PhDs, 16% are members of minority groups, 45% are women.

ACADEMICS
Degrees: bachelor's, doctoral, master's. **Classes:** Most classes have 20–29 students. Most lab/discussion sessions have 20–29 students. **Majors with Highest Enrollment:** business/commerce; criminal justice/safety studies; multi-/interdisciplinary studies, other. **Special Study Options:** distance learning, double major, dual enrollment, English as a Second Language (ESL), honors program, independent study, internships, teacher certification program. **Honors Programs:** The Honors student earns Honors credit in a variety of specially designated classes, and works toward the distinction of graduating 'With Honors' or 'With Highest Honors.' To qualify for graduation with honors, a student must have been a participant in the Honors Program and have completed 24 hours of Honors class credit, including participation in two interdisciplinary Honors seminars. To qualify for graduation 'With Highest Honors' a student must, in addition, complete a senior thesis in an approved discipline under the direction of a faculty member of his/her choice. The student will receive 6 credit hours of departmental course credit when completing the senior thesis. **Disability Services:** Special programs offered to physically disabled students include note-taking services, reader services, tape recorders. **Career Services:** Alumni network, alumni services, career/job search classes, career assessment, internships, regional alumni. Career Services highlights include We work closely with major public and private accounting firms as well as with a major retailer (Target) to promote their quality internship programs. We publicize, coordinate and host the interviews for these opportunities for our students and recent alumni.

FACILITIES
Housing: Coed dorms, men's dorms, women's dorms, fraternity/sorority housing, apartments for single students. 85% of campus accessible to physically disabled. **Special Academic Facilities/Equipment:** Sam Houston Memorial Museum, on-campus elementary school, communications center for photography, radio, TV, and film, agricultural complex and university farm. **Computers:** Students can register for classes online. Administrative functions (other than registration) can be performed online.

CAMPUS LIFE
Environment: Town. **Activities:** Choral groups, concert band, dance, drama/theater, jazz band, marching band, music ensembles, musical theater, pep band, radio station, student government, student newspaper, symphony orchestra, television station, yearbook, Campus Ministries, International Student Organization 185 registered organizations, 12 honor societies, 17 religious organizations. 16 fraternities, 10 sororities. **Athletics (Intercollegiate): Men:** baseball, basketball, cheerleading, cross-country, equestrian sports, football, golf, rodeo, soccer, softball, tennis, track/field (outdoor), track/field (indoor). *Women:* basketball, cheerleading, cross-country, equestrian sports, golf, rodeo, soccer, softball, tennis, track/field (outdoor), track/field (indoor), volleyball. **On-Campus Highlights:** Lowman Student Center, Health and Kinesiology Center, Computer Labs, Mall Area, Old Main Pit. **Environmental Initiatives:** Hired an Energy Manager. Adopted green approach to new building design, but short of LEED certification. Recycling of all brush and organic material picked up on campus.

ADMISSIONS
Freshman Academic Profile: 13% in top 10% of high school class, 42% in top 25% of high school class, 85% in top 50% of high school class. % from public high schools. SAT Math middle 50% range 470-550. SAT Critical Reading middle 50% range 450-540. ACT middle 50% range 19-23. Minimum paper TOEFL 550. **Basis for Candidate Selection:** *Very important factors considered include:* Class rank, standardized test scores. *Important factors considered*

include: rigor of secondary school record. *Other factors considered include:* application essay, academic GPA, recommendation(s), character/personal qualities, extracurricular activities, talent/ability, volunteer work, work experience. **Freshman Admission Requirements:** High school diploma is required and GED is accepted. *Academic units required:* 4 English, 3 mathematics, 2 science, 1 computer science, 1 academic electives. *Academic units recommended:* 4 English, 3 mathematics, 2 science, 1 computer science, 1 academic electives. **Freshman Admission Statistics:** 9,315 applied, 65% admitted, 40% enrolled. **Transfer Admission Requirements:** college transcript(s), statement of good standing from prior institution(s). Minimum college GPA of 2.0 required. Lowest grade transferable D. **General Admission Information:** Application Fee $40. Regular application deadline 8/1. Notification on a rolling basis, beginning on or about 9/1. Nonfall registration accepted. Credit and/or placement offered for CEEB Advanced Placement tests.

COSTS AND FINANCIAL AID
Annual in-state tuition $5,610. Annual out-of-state tuition $16,140. Room and board $8,092. Required fees $2,510. Average book expense $1,108. **Required Forms and Deadlines:** FAFSA, institution's own financial aid form. **Notification of Awards:** Applicants will be notified of awards on a rolling basis beginning 3/1. **Types of Aid:** *Need-based scholarships/grants:* Federal Pell, SEOG, state scholarships/grants, the school's own gift aid. *Loans:* Direct Subsidized Stafford, Direct Unsubsidized Stafford, Direct PLUS, Subsidized Stafford, Unsubsidized Stafford, PLUS, Federal Perkins, state loans, college/university loans from institutional funds. **Student Employment:** Federal Work-Study Program available. Highest amount earned per year from on-campus jobs $2,500. Off-campus job opportunities are excellent. **Financial Aid Statistics:** 79% freshmen, 71% undergrads receive any aid. **Criteria for awarding institutional aid:** *Non-need-based:* academics, alumni affiliation, art, athletics, job skills, leadership, music/drama, religious affiliation, state/district residency.

SAMFORD UNIVERSITY

800 Lakeshore Drive, Birmingham, AL 35229
Phone: 205-726-3673 • **Financial Aid Phone:** 205-726-2905
E-mail: admiss@samford.edu • **CEEB Code:** 1302
Fax: 205-726-2171 • **Website:** www.samford.edu • **ACT Code:** 16

This private school, affiliated with the Baptist Church, was founded in 1841. It has a 180-acre campus.

RATINGS
Admissions Selectivity Rating: 77   **Fire Safety Rating:** 92   **Green Rating:** 73

STUDENTS AND FACULTY
Enrollment: 2,948. **Student Body:** 65% female, 35% male, 62% out-of-state, 2% international (21 countries represented). Asian 1%, African American 7%, Caucasian 83%, Hispanic 5%, Native American 0%.
Retention and Graduation: 87% freshmen return for sophomore year. 51% freshmen graduate within 4 years. **Faculty:** Student/faculty ratio 12:1. 301 full-time faculty, 85% hold PhDs, 10% are members of minority groups, 50% are women. 0% of classes are taught by teaching assistants.

ACADEMICS
Degrees: associate, bachelor's, certificate, first professional, master's, post-master's certificate, terminal associate. **Classes:** Most classes have 10–19 students. Most lab/discussion sessions have 10–19 students. **Majors with Highest Enrollment:** biology/biological sciences; nursing/registered nurse (rn, asn, bsn, msn); teacher education, multiple levels. **Special Study Options:** Accelerated program, cooperative education program, distance learning, double major, dual enrollment, exchange student program (domestic), honors program, independent study, internships, liberal arts/career combination, study abroad, teacher certification program. **Honors Programs:** Samford University Fellows program targets academically gifted high schools students for a highly-competitive program of innovative liberal arts courses, international study and undergraduate research. **Combined Degree Programs:** The Law School sponsors seven joint-degree program. **Disability Services:** Special programs offered to physically disabled students include note-taking services, reader services, tape recorders. **Career Services:** career assessment, internships.

FACILITIES
Housing: special housing for disabled students, men's dorms, women's dorms, fraternity/sorority housing, wellness housing. 100% of campus accessible to physically disabled. **Special Academic Facilities/Equipment:** Language lab, reflective telescope, geographic information systems lab, global center, planetarium, conservatory, Pete Hanna Sports Center. **Computers:** 100% of classrooms, 100% of libraries, 100% of dining areas, 100% of student union, have

wireless network access. Students can register for classes online. Administrative functions (other than registration) can be performed online.

CAMPUS LIFE

Environment: Town. **Activities:** Choral groups, concert band, dance, drama/theater, jazz band, literary magazine, marching band, music ensembles, musical theater, radio station, student government, student newspaper, symphony orchestra, yearbook, Campus Ministries, International Student Organization, Model UN 119 registered organizations, 25 honor societies, 16 religious organizations. 6 fraternities, 6 sororities. **Athletics (Intercollegiate):** *Men:* baseball, basketball, cross-country, football, golf, tennis, track/field (outdoor). *Women:* basketball, cross-country, golf, soccer, softball, tennis, track/field (outdoor), volleyball. **On-Campus Highlights:** Sciencenter, Pete Hanna Center, University Library, Wright Center Student Center, Beeson University Center, The Quad, Hodges Chapel, Harrison Theatre, and Jane Hollock Brock Recital Hall. **Environmental Initiatives:** Bike loan program Installation of automatic towel dispensers Only "green" products used by custodial

ADMISSIONS

Freshman Academic Profile: Average high school GPA 3.7. 34% in top 10% of high school class, 61% in top 25% of high school class, 84% in top 50% of high school class. 54% from public high schools. SAT Math middle 50% range 510-630. SAT Critical Reading middle 50% range 520-630. SAT Writing middle 50% range 510-620. ACT middle 50% range 23-29. Minimum web-based TOEFL 90. Minimum paper TOEFL 575. **Basis for Candidate Selection:** *Very important factors considered include:* application essay, academic GPA, recommendation(s), rigor of secondary school record, standardized test scores, character/personal qualities, religious affiliation/commitment. *Important factors considered include:* Class rank, alumni/ae relation, extracurricular activities, interview. *Other factors considered include:* geographical residence, level of applicant's interest, racial/ethnic status, state residency, talent/ability, volunteer work, work experience. **Freshman Admission Requirements:** High school diploma is required and GED is accepted. *Academic units required:* 4 English, 3 mathematics, 3 science, 2 foreign language, 2 social studies. *Academic units recommended:* 4 English, 3 mathematics, 3 science, 2 foreign language, 2 social studies. **Freshman Admission Statistics:** 3,234 applied, 76% admitted, 29% enrolled. **Transfer Admission Requirements:** college transcript(s), essay or personal statement, statement of good standing from prior institution(s). Minimum college GPA of 2.5 required. Lowest grade transferable C–. **General Admission Information:** Application Fee $35. Notification on a rolling basis, beginning on or about 11/1. Nonfall registration accepted. Admission may be deferred for a maximum of 1 year. Credit and/or placement offered for CEEB Advanced Placement tests.

COSTS AND FINANCIAL AID

Required Forms and Deadlines: FAFSA, state aid form. **Notification of Awards:** Applicants will be notified of awards on or about 4/1. **Types of Aid:** *Need-based scholarships/grants:* Federal Pell, SEOG, state scholarships/grants, private scholarships, the school's own gift aid. *Loans:* Direct Subsidized Stafford, Direct Unsubsidized Stafford, Direct PLUS, Subsidized Stafford, Unsubsidized Stafford, PLUS, Federal Perkins. **Student Employment:** Federal Work-Study Program available. Institutional employment available. Off-campus job opportunities are excellent. **Financial Aid Statistics:** 99% freshmen, 94% undergrads receive need-based scholarship or grant aid. 23% freshmen, 17% undergrads receive non-need-based scholarship or grant aid. 73% freshmen, 80% undergrads receive need-based self-help aid. 4% freshmen, 5% undergrads receive athletic scholarships. 96% freshmen, 87% undergrads receive any aid. 52% undergrads borrow to pay for school. Average cumulative indebtedness $25,252. **Criteria for awarding institutional aid:** *Non-need-based:* academics, athletics, leadership, religious affiliation, state/district residency.

SAN DIEGO STATE UNIVERSITY

San Diego, CA 92182
Phone: 619-594-6336 • **Financial Aid Phone:** 619-594-6323 • **CEEB Code:** 4682
Website: www.sdsu.edu • **ACT Code:** 398

This public school was founded in 1897. It has a 300-acre campus.

RATINGS

Admissions Selectivity Rating: 88   **Fire Safety Rating:** 86   **Green Rating:** 91

STUDENTS AND FACULTY

Enrollment: 22,814. **Student Body:** 57% female, 43% male, 7% out-of-state, 5% international (96 countries represented). Asian 8%, African American 4%, Caucasian 43%, Hispanic 35%, Native American 0%.
Retention and Graduation: 89% freshmen return for sophomore year. 32%

freshmen graduate within 4 years. **Faculty:** Student/faculty ratio 23:1. 742 full-time faculty, 84% hold PhDs, 25% are members of minority groups, 44% are women.

ACADEMICS

Degrees: bachelor's, master's, post-bachelor's certificate. **Classes:** Most classes have 20–29 students. Most lab/discussion sessions have 20–29 students. **Majors with Highest Enrollment:** business administration and management; kinesiology and exercise science; psychology. **Special Study Options:** distance learning, double major, English as a Second Language (ESL), exchange student program (domestic), external degree program, honors program, independent study, internships, liberal arts/career combination, study abroad, teacher certification program. **Combined Degree Programs:** MBA/JD, MSW/MPH, MSW/JD, MPH/MA. **Disability Services:** Special programs offered to physically disabled students include note-taking services, reader services, tape recorders, tutors. **Career Services:** alumni services, career/job search classes, career assessment, internships.

FACILITIES

Housing: Coed dorms, special housing for international students, fraternity/sorority housing, apartments for single students, Extended Quiet Study Hours (more quiet study environment), Living/Learning Center Housing Over the Break. 99% of campus accessible to physically disabled. **Special Academic Facilities/Equipment:** Art gallery, theatre, recital hall, research bureaus for labor economics, marine studies and social science, audiovisual center, electronic boardroom, multimedia interactive fine arts technology lab, Palomar Observatory (off-campus), field studies stations (off-campus) **Computers:** Students can register for classes online. Administrative functions (other than registration) can be performed online.

CAMPUS LIFE

Environment: City. **Activities:** Choral groups, concert band, dance, drama/theater, jazz band, literary magazine, marching band, music ensembles, musical theater, opera, pep band, radio station, student government, student newspaper, student-run film society, symphony orchestra, television station, Campus Ministries, International Student Organization 264 registered organizations, 6 honor societies, 14 religious organizations. 21 fraternities, 23 sororities. **Athletics (Intercollegiate):** *Men:* baseball, basketball, football, golf, soccer, tennis. *Women:* basketball, crew/rowing, cross-country, diving, golf, soccer, softball, swimming, tennis, track/field (outdoor), track/field (indoor), volleyball, water polo. **Environmental Initiatives:** In spring 2012 SDSU opened a Student Sustainability Center in the Division of Undergraduate Studies, which is supported by a full-time staff member and is home to the Green Campus Interns program. Students can use the Center to access campus sustainability resources such as scholarships, internships, and courses; connect with faculty; work on green research projects, and utilize meeting space is available to green student organizations. The Student Center is a part of the SDSU Center for Regional Sustainability which provides faculty training and engagement opportunities on campus. SDSU has numerous green facilities upgrades, solar installations, and construction underway. The Aztec Student Union which is currently under construction and will be completed by fall 2013 is designed to LEED Platinum standards and will be the first student union in the world to seek a Platinum certification. http://as.sdsu.edu/aztec/ In fall 2011 the campus began an Energy Star building audit as a part of a campus-wide certification. Students with the SDSU Student USGBC chapter are assisting with the Energy Star certification process. Additionally the Storm and Nasatir Halls renovation and Plaza Linda Verde project, a pedestrian friendly, on-campus housing and retail complex project currently underway will be built to LEED Silver standards. http://newscenter.sdsu.edu/plazalindaverde/ SDSU is bike friendly! In 2011 the University adopted a campus area bike plan that created bike paths on major campus thoroughfares. The plan implemented a new bike policy that allows cyclists to bike on all campus streets and designated paths, giving cyclists greater access to campus and making it easy to commute by bike. New upgrades to buildings incorporate amenities for cyclists and skateboarders including facilities at the Aztec Recreation Center, transit station, and the new student union that make it easier for cyclists to get to campus and store bikes. At the weekly Farmer's Market Student can learn about bike safety and maintenance at the Enviro Business booth, pick up a bike route map, and receive free printing by peddling on the Green Campus bike generator to powers a printer with recycled paper.

ADMISSIONS

Freshman Academic Profile: Average high school GPA 3.6. 92% from public high schools. SAT Math middle 50% range 500-610. SAT Critical Reading middle 50% range 480-590. ACT middle 50% range 21-26. Minimum paper TOEFL 550. **Basis for Candidate Selection:** *Very important factors considered include:* academic GPA, rigor of secondary school record, standardized test scores. *Important factors considered include:* geographical residence, state residency. **Freshman Admission Requirements:** High school diploma is required and GED is accepted. *Academic units required:* 4 English, 3 mathematics, 2 science, (2 science labs), 2 foreign language, 1 social studies, 1 history, 1 visual/performing arts, 1 academic electives. *Academic units recommended:* 4 English,

3 mathematics, 2 science, (2 science labs), 2 foreign language, 1 social studies, 1 history, 1 visual/performing arts, 1 academic electives. **Freshman Admission Statistics:** 51,364 applied, 31% admitted, 26% enrolled. **Transfer Admission Requirements:** college transcript(s), Lowest grade transferable D-. **General Admission Information:** Application Fee $55. Regular application deadline 11/30. Regular notification 3/1. Nonfall registration not accepted. Credit offered for CEEB Advanced Placement tests.

COSTS AND FINANCIAL AID

Room and board $13,052. Required fees $7,076. Average book expense $1,717. **Required Forms and Deadlines:** FAFSA, state aid form. **Notification of Awards:** Applicants will be notified of awards on a rolling basis beginning 2/14. **Types of Aid:** *Need-based scholarships/grants:* Federal Pell, SEOG, state scholarships/grants, private scholarships, the school's own gift aid, Federal Nursing Scholarships. *Loans:* Direct Subsidized Stafford, Direct Unsubsidized Stafford, Direct PLUS, Federal Perkins, college/university loans from institutional funds. **Student Employment:** Federal Work-Study Program available. Institutional employment available. Off-campus job opportunities are good. **Financial Aid Statistics:** 65% freshmen, 72% undergrads receive need-based scholarship or grant aid. 32% freshmen, 19% undergrads receive non-need-based scholarship or grant aid. 95% freshmen, 96% undergrads receive need-based self-help aid. 3% freshmen, 2% undergrads receive athletic scholarships. 61% freshmen, 59% undergrads receive any aid. **Criteria for awarding institutional aid:** *Non-need-based:* academics, alumni affiliation, art, athletics, leadership, music/drama, state/district residency.

SAN FRANCISCO STATE UNIVERSITY

1600 Holloway Avenue, San Francisco, CA 94132
Phone: 415-338-6486 • **Financial Aid Phone:** 415-338-7000
E-mail: ugadmit@sfsu.edu • **CEEB Code:** 4684
Fax: 415-338-3880 • **Website:** www.sfsu.edu • **ACT Code:**

This public school was founded in 1899. It has a 142-acre campus.

RATINGS
Admissions Selectivity Rating: 76   **Fire Safety Rating:** 73   **Green Rating:** 98

STUDENTS AND FACULTY
Enrollment: 26,065. **Student Body:** 57% female, 43% male, 1% out-of-state, 7% international (96 countries represented). Asian 28%, African American 5%, Caucasian 26%, Hispanic 23%, Native American 0%.
Retention and Graduation: 80% freshmen return for sophomore year. **Faculty:** Student/faculty ratio 25:1. 778 full-time faculty, 79% hold PhDs, 35% are members of minority groups, 48% are women.

ACADEMICS
Degrees: bachelor's, certificate, master's, post-bachelor's certificate. **Classes:** Most classes have 20–29 students. Most lab/discussion sessions have 10–19 students. **Majors with Highest Enrollment:** biology/biological sciences; business administration and management; psychology. **Special Study Options:** cooperative education program, cross-registration, distance learning, double major, dual enrollment, English as a Second Language (ESL), honors program, independent study, internships, liberal arts/career combination, student-designed major, study abroad, teacher certification program. **Combined Degree Programs:** BA/MA. **Disability Services:** Special programs offered to physically disabled students include note-taking services, reader services, tape recorders, tutors. **Career Services:** alumni services, career/job search classes, career assessment, internships.

FACILITIES
Housing: Coed dorms, special housing for disabled students, special housing for international students, apartments for married students, apartments for single students, wellness housing, theme housing, women only floors. **Special Academic Facilities/Equipment:** Treganza Anthropology Museum, Moss Landing Marine Laboratories, Romberg Tiburon Center for Environmental Studies, Sierra Nevada Field Campus, Sutro Egyptian Collection. **Computers:** 100% of classrooms, 100% of dorms, 100% of libraries, 100% of dining areas, 100% of student union, 100% of common outdoor areas have wireless network access. Students can register for classes online. Administrative functions (other than registration) can be performed online.

CAMPUS LIFE
Environment: Metropolis. **Activities:** Choral groups, concert band, dance, drama/theater, jazz band, literary magazine, music ensembles, musical theater, opera, pep band, radio station, student government, student newspaper, student-run film society, symphony orchestra, television station, Campus Ministries, International Student Organization 213 registered organizations, 6 honor societies, 13 religious organizations. 3 fraternities, 4 sororities. **Athletics (Intercollegiate):** *Men:* baseball, basketball, cross-country, soccer, wrestling. *Women:* basketball, cross-country, soccer, softball, track/field (outdoor), track/field (indoor), volleyball. **On-Campus Highlights:** Cesar Chavez Student Center, Cox Stadium, SFSU Fine Arts Gallery, Residential Theme Communities, J. Paul Leonard Library Annex, Malcolm X Plaza, The Village at Centennial Square, and McKenna Theatre. **Environmental Initiatives:** SF State is dedicated to reducing the campus' use of resources and its impact on climate change. Some of the projects that demonstrate that are: the Buy Recycled Campaign, purchasing 15% renewable energy, implementing a green cleaning program, hiring a Sustainability Programs Manager, offering alternative transportation incentives, pursuing LEED certification for two buildings, and diverting over 72% of the waste from the landfill. SF State completed its first Greenhouse Gas Emissions Inventory in May of 2008 and its second one in January 2010. The campus' Sustainability Committee completed a Climate Action Plan in May of 2010. It outlines the campus' goal of reducing emissions below 1990 levels; 25% by 2020 and 40% by 2050. SF State passed a sustainable literacy requirement for all students. SF State already incorporates sustainability into many of its departments. Students can receive an undergraduate degree in Environmental Studies, Geography, and Urban Planning. They can receive an MBA with an emphasis in Sustainable Business and conduct research at the Romburg Tiburon Center for Environmental Studies.

ADMISSIONS
Freshman Academic Profile: Average high school GPA 3.1. 87% from public high schools. SAT Math middle 50% range 450-560. SAT Critical Reading middle 50% range 430-550. ACT middle 50% range 19-24. Minimum web-based TOEFL 61. Minimum paper TOEFL 500. **Basis for Candidate Selection:** *Very important factors considered include:* academic GPA, rigor of secondary school record, standardized test scores. *Important factors considered include:* state residency. *Other factors considered include:* recommendation(s), talent/ability. **Freshman Admission Requirements:** High school diploma is required and GED is accepted. *Academic units required:* 4 English, 3 mathematics, 2 science, (2 science labs), 2 foreign language, 1 social studies, 1 history, 1 visual/performing arts. *Academic units recommended:* 4 English, 3 mathematics, 2 science, (2 science labs), 2 foreign language, 1 social studies, 1 history, 1 visual/performing arts. **Freshman Admission Statistics:** 31,439 applied, 64% admitted, 19% enrolled. **Transfer Admission Requirements:** college transcript(s), statement of good standing from prior institution(s). Minimum college GPA of 2.0 required. Lowest grade transferable D. **General Admission Information:** Application Fee $55. Notification on a rolling basis, beginning on or about 10/1. Nonfall registration accepted. Credit offered for CEEB Advanced Placement tests.

COSTS AND FINANCIAL AID
Annual in-state tuition $5,472. Annual out-of-state tuition $11,160. Room and board $11,408. Required fees $804. Average book expense $1,754. **Required Forms and Deadlines:** FAFSA. **Notification of Awards:** Applicants will be notified of awards on a rolling basis beginning 2/1. **Types of Aid:** *Need-based scholarships/grants:* Federal Pell, SEOG, state scholarships/grants, private scholarships, the school's own gift aid. *Loans:* Direct Subsidized Stafford, Direct Unsubsidized Stafford, PLUS, Federal Perkins. **Student Employment:** Federal Work-Study Program available. Institutional employment available. **Financial Aid Statistics:** 71% freshmen, 75% undergrads receive need-based scholarship or grant aid. 10% freshmen, 6% undergrads receive non-need-based scholarship or grant aid. 99% freshmen, 99% undergrads receive need-based self-help aid. 43% undergrads borrow to pay for school. Average cumulative indebtedness $20,493. **Criteria for awarding institutional aid:** *Non-need-based:* academics, athletics.

SAN JOSE STATE UNIVERSITY

One Washington Square, San Jose, CA 95192-0016
Phone: 408-283-7500 • **Financial Aid Phone:** 408-283-7500
E-mail: admissions@sjsu.edu • **CEEB Code:** 4687
Fax: 408-924-2050 • **Website:** www.sjsu.edu • **ACT Code:**

This public school was founded in 1857. It has a 154-acre campus.

RATINGS
Admissions Selectivity Rating: 78   **Fire Safety Rating:** 60*   **Green Rating:** 65

STUDENTS AND FACULTY
Enrollment: 25,157. **Student Body:** 50% female, 50% male, 0% out-of-state, 4% international (139 countries represented). Asian 35%, African American 4%, Caucasian 24%, Hispanic 23%, Native American 0%.
Retention and Graduation: 83% freshmen return for sophomore year. 8% freshmen graduate within 4 years. 47% freshmen graduate within 6 years. **Fac-**

ulty: Student/faculty ratio 27:1. 619 full-time faculty, 30% are members of minority groups, 47% are women. 4% of classes are taught by teaching assistants.

ACADEMICS

Degrees: bachelor's, master's. **Classes:** Most classes have 20–29 students. Most lab/discussion sessions have 20–29 students. **Majors with Highest Enrollment:** art/art studies; business administration and management; electrical, electronics and communications engineering. **Special Study Options:** distance learning, double major, dual enrollment, honors program, independent study, internships, student-designed major, study abroad, teacher certification program. **Disability Services:** Special programs offered to physically disabled students include note-taking services, reader services, tutors. **Career Services:** alumni services, career/job search classes, career assessment, internships Career Services highlights include We are proud of our Neat Ideas Fair program, which was nominated for the 2008 USASBE innovative pedagogy award. The Fair is a venue for students from across the SJSU campus to display and pitch their business ideas and receive feedback from seasoned entrepreneurs, investors, lawyers, professors, and their peers.

FACILITIES

Housing: Coed dorms, special housing for disabled students, men's dorms, special housing for international students, women's dorms, fraternity/sorority housing, cooperative housing, apartments for single students. 100% of campus accessible to physically disabled. **Special Academic Facilities/Equipment:** Martin Luther King, Jr. Library (Joint with City)Child development lab, Chicano resource center, Beethoven studies center, John Steinbeck research center, art metal foundry, natural history living museum (science education), science resource center, deep-sea research ship, electro-acoustical/recording studios, nuclear science and engineering labs. **Computers:** Students can register for classes online. Administrative functions (other than registration) can be performed online.

CAMPUS LIFE

Environment: Metropolis. **Activities:** Choral groups, dance, drama/theater, literary magazine, marching band, music ensembles, musical theater, radio station, student government, student newspaper, student-run film society, symphony orchestra, Campus Ministries, International Student Organization 283 registered organizations, 13 honor societies, 20 religious organizations. 20 fraternities, 15 sororities. **Athletics (Intercollegiate):** *Men:* baseball, basketball, cheerleading, cross-country, diving, football, golf, soccer, softball, swimming, volleyball, water polo. *Women:* basketball, cheerleading, cross-country, diving, golf, gymnastics, soccer, softball, swimming, tennis, volleyball, water polo. **On-Campus Highlights:** Martin Luther King, Jr. Library, Student Union, Art Quad, Market Cafe/Burger King/Sparro, Gym.

ADMISSIONS

Freshman Academic Profile: Average high school GPA 3.3. 77% from public high schools. SAT Math middle 50% range 470-600. SAT Critical Reading middle 50% range 440-550. SAT Writing middle 50% range 450-560. ACT middle 50% range 19-25. Minimum web-based TOEFL 80. Minimum paper TOEFL 550. **Basis for Candidate Selection:** *Very important factors considered include:* academic GPA, rigor of secondary school record, standardized test scores. *Important factors considered include:* first generation.**Freshman Admission Requirements:** High school diploma is required and GED is accepted. *Academic units required:* 4 English, 3 mathematics, 2 science, (2 science labs), 2 foreign language, 1 social studies, 1 history, 1 visual/performing arts, 1 academic electives. *Academic units recommended:* 4 English, 3 mathematics, 2 science, (2 science labs), 2 foreign language, 1 social studies, 1 history, 1 visual/performing arts, 1 academic electives. **Freshman Admission Statistics:** 25,155 applied, 63% admitted, 21% enrolled. **Transfer Admission Requirements:** college transcript(s), statement of good standing from prior institution(s). Minimum college GPA of 2.0 required. Lowest grade transferable 2. **General Admission Information:** Application Fee $55. Regular application deadline 11/30. Notification on a rolling basis, beginning on or about 10/1. Nonfall registration accepted. Credit offered for CEEB Advanced Placement tests.

COSTS AND FINANCIAL AID

Annual. Annual out-of-state tuition $11,160. Room and board $10,733. Required fees $6,852. Average book expense $1,754. **Required Forms and Deadlines:** FAFSA. **Notification of Awards:** Applicants will be notified of awards on a rolling basis beginning 4/10. **Types of Aid:** *Need-based scholarships/grants:* Federal Pell, SEOG, state scholarships/grants, private scholarships, the school's own gift aid. *Loans:* Subsidized Stafford, Unsubsidized Stafford, PLUS, Federal Perkins, college/university loans from institutional funds. **Student Employment:** Federal Work-Study Program available. Institutional employment available. Off-campus job opportunities are excellent. **Financial Aid Statistics:** 68% freshmen, 71% undergrads receive need-based scholarship or grant aid. 2% freshmen, 2% undergrads receive non-need-based scholarship or grant aid. 65% freshmen, 63% undergrads receive need-based self-help aid. 40% freshmen, 39% undergrads receive any aid. 43% undergrads borrow to pay for school. Average cumulative indebtedness $17,851. **Criteria for awarding institutional aid:** *Non-need-based:* academics, athletics.

SANTA CLARA UNIVERSITY

500 El Camino Real, Santa Clara, CA 95053
Phone: 408-554-4700 • **Financial Aid Phone:** 408-554-4505
E-mail: admission@scu.edu • **CEEB Code:** 4851
Fax: 408-554-5255 • **Website:** www.scu.edu/

This private school, affiliated with the Roman Catholic Church, was founded in 1851. It has a 106-acre campus.

RATINGS

Admissions Selectivity Rating: 93   **Fire Safety Rating:** 83   **Green Rating:** 95

STUDENTS AND FACULTY

Enrollment: 5,205. **Student Body:** 50% female, 50% male, 37% out-of-state, 3% international (40 countries represented). Asian 14%, African American 3%, Caucasian 46%, Hispanic 18%, Native American 0%.
Retention and Graduation: 79% freshmen graduate within 4 years. 86% freshmen graduate within 6 years. 27% grads go on to further study within 1 year. 16% grads pursue arts and sciences degrees. 5% grads pursue law degrees. 1% grads pursue business degrees. 3% grads pursue medical degrees. **Faculty:** Student/faculty ratio 12:1. 504 full-time faculty, 92% hold PhDs, 26% are members of minority groups, 42% are women. 0% of classes are taught by teaching assistants.

ACADEMICS

Degrees: bachelor's, master's, post-bachelor's certificate, post-master's certificate. **Classes:** Most classes have 20–29 students. Most lab/discussion sessions have 10–19 students. **Majors with Highest Enrollment:** accounting; communication studies/speech communication and rhetoric; finance. **Special Study Options:** cooperative education program, double major, honors program, independent study, internships, student-designed major, study abroad, teacher certification program. **Honors Programs:** The University Honors Program provides Santa Clara's most able students with intellectual opportunities honed in small, seminar-style classes. With 14 to 17 students each, seminars emphasize analytical rigor, effective expression, and interaction among professors and students. The course of study combines broadly based, liberal learning with depth of specialization in a major field. Honors Program classes are designed to fit within the curricula of the humanities, natural and social sciences, business, and engineering. Possible majors include every undergraduate field in the University. **Combined Degree Programs:** BA/MEng. **Disability Services:** Special programs offered to physically disabled students include note-taking services, reader services, tape recorders, tutors. **Career Services:** Alumni network, alumni services, career/job search classes, career assessment, internships, regional alumni. Career Services highlights include The Career Center at Santa Clara University provides students with access to quality internships on a local, national, and international level. Employers from all sectors recruit students for internships that emphasize intentional learning, professional development, real-world experience, skill-building, and networking. Almost 4,000 internships are posted each year that target our students on NACElink. Almost one-third of these are technical internships, reflecting our location in the heart of Silicon Valley. Students also have access to thousands of internships posted on over 100 internship databases through our online resources. In addition, we provide effective and successful co-curricular internship programming through which students effectively connect with employers; educate students, faculty/staff, and parents about all aspects of internships; offer a Freshmen/Sophomore Internship Fair each February; and educate employer organizations about developing substantive internship programs that are committed to intentional learning and provide quality, engaged supervision for the student. We also provide numerous internship-related workshops for students, clubs and organizations, classes, and parents during Parent Weekend.

FACILITIES

Housing: Coed dorms, apartments for single students, theme housing. 95% of campus accessible to physically disabled. **Special Academic Facilities/Equipment:** Art and history museum (de Saisset), mission church, theatre, media lab, retail management institute, computer design center, engineering labs, Markkula Center for Applied Ethics, Center for Science, Technology, and Society, Ignatian Center for Jesuit Education **Computers:** 100% of classrooms, 100% of dorms, 100% of libraries, 100% of dining areas, 100% of student union, 90% of common outdoor areas have wireless network access. Students can register for classes online. Administrative functions (other than registration) can be performed online.

CAMPUS LIFE

Environment: City. **Activities:** Choral groups, dance, drama/theater, jazz band, literary magazine, music ensembles, musical theater, opera, pep band, radio station, student government, student newspaper, symphony orchestra, yearbook, Campus Ministries, International Student Organization, Model UN 86 registered organizations, 25 honor societies, 5 religious organizations. **Athletics (Intercollegiate):** *Men:* baseball, basketball, crew/rowing, cross-country, golf, soccer, tennis, track/field (outdoor), water polo. *Women:* basketball, crew/rowing, cross-country, golf, soccer, softball, tennis, track/field (outdoor), volleyball, water polo. **On-Campus Highlights:** Historic Mission Church; Mission gardens, Pat Malley Fitness Center, Harrington Learning Commons and Library, Benson Memorial Student Center, Leavey Activities Center, The palm tree dotted campus is gorgeous, with stunning gardens, walkways, Mission style buildings, and lots of greenery. At the heart of Santa Clara University is the historic Mission Santa Clara de Asis. Founded in 1777, it is the eighth oldest of the original 21 California missions. The current Mission Church was dedicated May 13, 1928. From then until now it has served as the University chapel, and is used by the University community for Masses, baptisms, weddings and funerals. The Mission Church is open to the public and welcomes visitors. The de Saisset Museum at Santa Clara University is the South Bay Area's free Museum of art and history. The 19,210 square foot facility was founded adjacent to the Mission Santa Clara de Asis on the Santa Clara University campus in 1955 and is currently one of only two museums in the South Bay accredited by the American Association of Museums. **Environmental Initiatives:** Santa Clara University strives to develop a culture of sustainability. Our Comprehensive Policy on Sustainability (adopted in 2004) targets our efforts toward stewardship, education, and outreach. We are a signatory of the ACUPCC in 2007, committing to transform SCU into a climate-neutral campus. The University's Sustainability Coordinator was hired in 2006. The Office of Sustainability was formally established in 2008 to support campus efforts, coordinate initiatives, serve as the "clearing-house" for campus sustainability data, and to showcase University sustainability programs to the public. The Sustainability Council was also formed at that time to guide the efforts of the Office of Sustainability. The University's Climate Neutrality Action Plan was adopted in 2010. SCU is a Charter STARS Participant, and achieved STARS Silver in 2011. EDUCATION SCU is educating its students in and outside the classroom to help them develop a deeper understanding about sustainability and its environmental, economic, and social impact on the world. In 2009, the University launched a new core curriculum that engages students in sustainability, sustainable building design, and using the campus as a living lab. SCU created the Frugal Innovation Laboratory that fosters development and application of technologies in clean energy, clean water, public health, and mobile applications, in ways that meet the needs of marginalized communities worldwide. JUSTICE AND SUSTAINABILITY SCU developed a half-acre education, demonstration, and community garden. The garden is used as a living laboratory and training facility for the Bronco Urban Gardens (BUG) Program. BUG helps communities and schools in low-income neighborhoods in San Jose build and utilize new gardens. Experiential Learning for Social Justice (ELSJ) is part of Santa Clara's new Undergraduate Core Curriculum. The ELSJ requirement, which must be completed by every undergraduate student at the University as part of their Core Curriculum, cultivates social justice, civic life, perspective, and civic engagement. ELSJ represents one of the ways that Santa Clara educates the whole person for a deeper understanding of the benefits of civic engagement and responsible citizenship.

ADMISSIONS

Freshman Academic Profile: Average high school GPA 3.6. 44% in top 10% of high school class, 81% in top 25% of high school class, 96% in top 50% of high school class. 45% from public high schools. SAT Math middle 50% range 610-700. SAT Critical Reading middle 50% range 590-680. ACT middle 50% range 27-31. Minimum web-based TOEFL 90. Minimum paper TOEFL 575. **Basis for Candidate Selection:** *Very important factors considered include:* application essay, academic GPA, recommendation(s), rigor of secondary school record. *Important factors considered include:* standardized test scores, character/personal qualities, extracurricular activities, racial/ethnic status, talent/ability, volunteer work. *Other factors considered include:* Class rank, alumni/ae relation, first generation, geographical residence, level of applicant's interest, religious affiliation/commitment, state residency, work experience. **Freshman Admission Requirements:** High school diploma is required and GED is not accepted. *Academic units required:* 4 English, 3 mathematics, 2 science, 2 foreign language, 3 social studies, 1 academic electives. *Academic units recommended:* 4 English, 3 mathematics, 2 science, 2 foreign language, 3 social studies, 1 academic electives. **Freshman Admission Statistics:** 14,339 applied, 51% admitted, 17% enrolled. **Transfer Admission Requirements:** college transcript(s), essay or personal statement, Lowest grade transferable C. **General Admission Information:** Application Fee $55. Regular application deadline 1/7. Regular notification 4/1. Nonfall registration not accepted. Admission may be deferred for a maximum of 1 year. Credit and/or placement offered for CEEB Advanced Placement tests.

COSTS AND FINANCIAL AID

Annual tuition $40,572. Room and board $12,276. **Required Forms and Deadlines:** FAFSA, CSS/Financial Aid PROFILE. **Notification of Awards:** Applicants will be notified of awards on or about 4/1. **Types of Aid:** *Need-based scholarships/grants:* Federal Pell, SEOG, state scholarships/grants, private scholarships, the school's own gift aid. *Loans:* Direct Subsidized Stafford, Direct Unsubsidized Stafford, Direct PLUS, PLUS, Federal Perkins, Private alternative loans. **Student Employment:** Federal Work-Study Program available. Institutional employment available. Off-campus job opportunities are good. **Financial Aid Statistics:** 78% freshmen, 67% undergrads receive need-based scholarship or grant aid. 51% freshmen, 43% undergrads receive non-need-based scholarship or grant aid. 64% freshmen, 66% undergrads receive need-based self-help aid. 4% freshmen, 4% undergrads receive athletic scholarships. 85% freshmen, 80% undergrads receive any aid. 46% undergrads borrow to pay for school. Average cumulative indebtedness $28,672. **Criteria for awarding institutional aid:** *Non-need-based:* academics, alumni affiliation, athletics, music/drama.

SANTA FE UNIVERSITY OF ART AND DESIGN

1600 St. Michaels Drive, Santa Fe, NM 87505-7634
Phone: 505-473-6133 • **Financial Aid Phone:** 505-473-6454
E-mail: admissions@csf.edu • **CEEB Code:** 4676
Fax: 505-473-6129 • **Website:** www.csf.edu • **ACT Code:** 2648

This private school was founded in 1874. It has a 100-acre campus.

RATINGS
Admissions Selectivity Rating: 65   **Fire Safety Rating:** 96   **Green Rating:** 60*

STUDENTS AND FACULTY
Enrollment: 544. **Student Body:** 53% female, 47% male, 70% out-of-state, 12% international. Asian 1%, African American 7%, Caucasian 45%, Hispanic 22%, Native American 3%.
Retention and Graduation: 55% freshmen return for sophomore year.
Faculty: Student/faculty ratio 13:1. 27 full-time faculty, 41% are members of minority groups, 30% are women.

ACADEMICS
Degrees: associate, bachelor's, master's, terminal associate. **Classes:** Most classes have 10–19 students. Most lab/discussion sessions have 40-49 students. **Majors with Highest Enrollment:** creative writing; drama and dramatics/theatre arts; film/cinema studies. **Special Study Options:** Accelerated program, cooperative education program, distance learning, double major, dual enrollment, exchange student program (domestic), independent study, internships, student-designed major, study abroad, teacher certification program. **Disability Services:** Special programs offered to physically disabled students include note-taking services, reader services, tape recorders, tutors. **Career Services:** career assessment, internships, regional alumni..

FACILITIES
Housing: Coed dorms, special housing for disabled students, men's dorms, women's dorms, apartments for single studentsSubstance-free floors, quiet floors, smoking floors. 95% of campus accessible to physically disabled. **Special Academic Facilities/Equipment:** Thaw Art History Library, Marion Center Photographic Library, Garson Studios, Visual Art Center, Greer Garson Theatre Centre **Computers:** Administrative functions (other than registration) can be performed online.

CAMPUS LIFE
Environment: Town. **Activities:** Choral groups, dance, drama/theater, literary magazine, music ensembles, musical theater, student government, student newspaper, television station 14 registered organizations, 1 honor societies. **Athletics (Intercollegiate):** *Men:* tennis. *Women:* tennis. **On-Campus Highlights:** Visual Arts Center, Garson Studios, Driscoll Fitness Center, Greer Garson Theatre Center, Fogelson Library.

ADMISSIONS
Freshman Academic Profile: Average high school GPA 3.1. SAT Math middle 50% range 440-583. SAT Critical Reading middle 50% range 470-590. SAT Writing middle 50% range 440-560. ACT middle 50% range 18-24. **Basis for Candidate Selection:** *Very important factors considered include:* rigor of secondary school record, character/personal qualities, interview, talent/ability. *Important factors considered include:* Class rank, application essay, academic GPA, recommendation(s), standardized test scores, extracurricular activities, volunteer work. *Other factors considered include:* alumni/ae relation, geographical residence, racial/ethnic status, state residency, work experience. **Freshman**

Admission Requirements: High school diploma is required and GED is accepted. *Academic units required:* 4 English, 2 mathematics, 2 science, (2 science labs), 2 social studies, 6 academic electives. *Academic units recommended:* 4 English, 2 mathematics, 2 science, (2 science labs), 2 social studies, 6 academic electives. **Freshman Admission Statistics:** 347 applied, 100% admitted, 45% enrolled. **Transfer Admission Requirements:** High school transcript, college transcript(s), essay or personal statement, Lowest grade transferable C–. **General Admission Information:** Application Fee $35. Notification on a rolling basis, beginning on or about 1/15. Nonfall registration accepted. Admission may be deferred for a maximum of 1 year. Credit and/or placement offered for CEEB Advanced Placement tests.

COSTS AND FINANCIAL AID

Annual tuition $28,836. Room and board $8,984. Required fees $1,300. Average book expense $1,400. **Required Forms and Deadlines:** FAFSA. **Notification of Awards:** Applicants will be notified of awards on a rolling basis beginning 3/1. **Types of Aid:** *Need-based scholarships/grants:* Federal Pell, SEOG, state scholarships/grants, private scholarships, the school's own gift aid. *Loans:* Subsidized Stafford, Unsubsidized Stafford, PLUS, Federal Perkins, state loans, college/university loans from institutional funds. **Student Employment:** Federal Work-Study Program available. Institutional employment available. Off-campus job opportunities are excellent. **Financial Aid Statistics:** 100% freshmen, 100% undergrads receive need-based scholarship or grant aid. 4% freshmen, 4% undergrads receive non-need-based scholarship or grant aid. 94% freshmen, 91% undergrads receive need-based self-help aid. 99% freshmen, **Criteria for awarding institutional aid:** *Non-need-based:* academics, alumni affiliation, art, athletics, leadership, minority status, music/drama.

SARAH LAWRENCE COLLEGE

Best 378

1 Mead Way, Bronxville, NY 10708-5999
Phone: 914-395-2510 • **Financial Aid Phone:** 914-395-2570
E-mail: slcadmit@slc.edu • **CEEB Code:** 2810
Fax: 914-395-2515 • **Website:** www.sarahlawrence.edu • **ACT Code:** 2904

This private school was founded in 1926. It has a 44-acre campus.

RATINGS

Admissions Selectivity Rating: 89   **Fire Safety Rating:** 92   **Green Rating:** 73

STUDENTS AND FACULTY

Enrollment: 1,342. **Student Body:** 73% female, 27% male, 80% out-of-state, 8% international (32 countries represented). Asian 7%, African American 6%, Caucasian 65%, Hispanic 9%, Native American 1%.
Retention and Graduation: 90% freshmen return for sophomore year. 70% freshmen graduate within 4 years. 77% freshmen graduate within 6 years. **Faculty:** Student/faculty ratio 10:1. 102 full-time faculty, % hold PhDs, 14% are members of minority groups, 44% are women. 0% of classes are taught by teaching assistants.

ACADEMICS

Degrees: bachelor's, certificate, master's, post-master's certificate. **Classes:** Most classes have 10–19 students. **Special Study Options:** double major, exchange student program (domestic), independent study, internships, student-designed major, study abroad, teacher certification program, Sarah Lawrence College has no formal majors. However students may concentrate in subject areas. All students design their own educational programs (with faculty advisement), so the equivalent of a "double major" is available. We have a 3-2 program where students can get their B.A. degree and M.S.Ed. in The Art of Teaching or M.A. in Women's History. We also have a 3-2 program in which the student receives a B.A. in the Liberal Arts from Sarah Lawrence and a B.S. in Engineering from Columbia. **Combined Degree Programs:** BA/MA, BA/MEng, B.A./M.A. Education, MSW/MA with NYU , MA/JD with Pace Law School. **Disability Services:** Special programs offered to physically disabled students include note-taking services, reader services, tape recorders, tutors. **Career Services:** Alumni network, alumni services, career/job search classes, career assessment, internships, Career Services highlights include We are proud of both our Internship program as well as our Service Learning and Community Partnership program which offers experiential learning. The Internship Program provides high quality placements in work environments closely related to our students' career, personal, and academic interests. Since Sarah Lawrence College is a 25 minute train ride away from New York City, and NYC is the hub

for so many career fields, our office has access to some of the most prestigious organizations available which consistently seek out our students. Our students' stellar performance in the workplace creates future internship opportunities for other students and full-time post-graduation employment.

FACILITIES

Housing: Coed dorms, men's dorms, women's dorms, wellness housing, theme housing. First year students required to live on campus unless living at home. 50% of campus accessible to physically disabled. **Special Academic Facilities/ Equipment:** Performing arts center including a concert hall, dance studios,and theatres; visual arts center including studios, gallery, film theatre, sound stage, visual resources library; music building including music library; science center, early childhood center, greenhouse. **Computers:** 100% of classrooms, 30% of dorms, 100% of libraries, 100% of dining areas, 100% of common outdoor areas have wireless network access. Administrative functions (other than registration) can be performed online.

CAMPUS LIFE

Environment: Metropolis. **Activities:** Choral groups, dance, drama/theater, jazz band, literary magazine, music ensembles, musical theater, radio station, student government, student newspaper, student-run film society, symphony orchestra, yearbook, Campus Ministries, International Student Organization, Model UN 30 registered organizations, 3 religious organizations. **Athletics (Intercollegiate):** *Men:* basketball, crew/rowing, cross-country, equestrian sports, soccer, tennis. *Women:* crew/rowing, cross-country, equestrian sports, softball, swimming, tennis, volleyball. **On-Campus Highlights:** Campbell Sports Center, Communitea House, Siegel Center, Library, Heimbold Visual Arts Center. **Environmental Initiatives:** A new, sustainable dorm opened in 08-09 and a green roof on another dorm. A LEED certified visual arts building A campus-wide sustainability committee

ADMISSIONS

Freshman Academic Profile: Average high school GPA 3.6. 43% in top 10% of high school class, 76% in top 25% of high school class, 97% in top 50% of high school class. Minimum web-based TOEFL 100. Minimum paper TOEFL 600. **Basis for Candidate Selection:** *Very important factors considered include:* application essay, recommendation(s), rigor of secondary school record. *Important factors considered include:* academic GPA, extracurricular activities, talent/ability. *Other factors considered include:* Class rank, alumni/ae relation, character/personal qualities, first generation, geographical residence, interview, level of applicant's interest, racial/ethnic status, volunteer work, work experience. **Freshman Admission Requirements:** High school diploma is required and GED is accepted. *Academic units required:* 4 English, 2 mathematics, 2 science, 2 foreign language, 2 history. *Academic units recommended:* 4 English, 2 mathematics, 2 science, 2 foreign language, 2 history. **Freshman Admission Statistics:** 2,165 applied, 62% admitted, 26% enrolled. **Transfer Admission Requirements:** High school transcript, college transcript(s), essay or personal statement, statement of good standing from prior institution(s). Lowest grade transferable C. **General Admission Information:** Application Fee $60. Early decision application deadline 11/1. Regular application deadline 1/1. Regular notification 4/1. Nonfall registration not accepted. Admission may be deferred for a maximum of 1 year. Credit offered for CEEB Advanced Placement tests.

COSTS AND FINANCIAL AID

Annual tuition $45,900. Room and board $14,312. Required fees $1,024. Average book expense $600. **Required Forms and Deadlines:** FAFSA, CSS/Financial Aid PROFILE, state aid form, noncustodial PROFILE. **Notification of Awards:** Applicants will be notified of awards on or about 4/1. **Types of Aid:** *Need-based scholarships/grants:* Federal Pell, SEOG, state scholarships/grants, private scholarships, the school's own gift aid. *Loans:* Subsidized Stafford, Unsubsidized Stafford, PLUS, Federal Perkins. **Student Employment:** Federal Work-Study Program available. Institutional employment available. Highest amount earned per year from on-campus jobs $1,500. Off-campus job opportunities are good. **Financial Aid Statistics:** 100% freshmen, 100% undergrads receive need-based scholarship or grant aid. 10% freshmen, 6% undergrads receive non-need-based scholarship or grant aid. 75% freshmen, 80% undergrads receive need-based self-help aid. 61% undergrads borrow to pay for school. Average cumulative indebtedness $19,922.

SAVANNAH COLLEGE OF ART AND DESIGN

PO Box 3146, Savannah, GA 31402-3146
Phone: 912-525-5100 • **Financial Aid Phone:** 800-869-7223
E-mail: admission@scad.edu • **CEEB Code:** 5631
Fax: 912-525-5986 • **Website:** www.scad.edu • **ACT Code:** 855

This private school was founded in 1978.

RATINGS
Admissions Selectivity Rating: 80   **Fire Safety Rating:** 89   **Green Rating:** 61

STUDENTS AND FACULTY
Enrollment: 9,036. **Student Body:** 64% female, 36% male, 77% out-of-state, 11% international (112 countries represented). Asian 5%, African American 9%, Caucasian 50%, Hispanic 6%, Native American 0%.
Retention and Graduation: 81% freshmen return for sophomore year. 51% freshmen graduate within 4 years. 65% freshmen graduate within 6 years.
Faculty: Student/faculty ratio 18:1. 519 full-time faculty, 76% hold PhDs, 12% are members of minority groups, 39% are women. 0% of classes are taught by teaching assistants.

ACADEMICS
Degrees: bachelor's, certificate, master's, post-bachelor's certificate. **Classes:** Most classes have 10–19 students. **Majors with Highest Enrollment:** animation, interactive technology, video graphics and special effects; fashion/apparel design; graphic design. **Special Study Options:** distance learning, double major, dual enrollment, English as a Second Language (ESL), independent study, internships, study abroad, teacher certification program, Summer quarter programs in New York City and Europe; apprenticeships with artists or designers and internships with museums, agencies, media production companies, architectural firms, and other companies in the U.S. or abroad. **Disability Services:** Special programs offered to physically disabled students include note-taking services, tape recorders, tutors. **Career Services:** Alumni network, alumni services, career/job search classes, career assessment, internships, regional alumni.

FACILITIES
Housing: Coed dorms, women's dorms, apartments for single students, Learning communities. Accommodations for disabled students are handled on an individual basis. 85% of campus accessible to physically disabled. **Special Academic Facilities/Equipment:** Art galleries; computer, video, photography, and design labs; SCAD Museum of Art **Computers:** 80% of classrooms, 100% of dorms, 100% of libraries, 100% of dining areas, 100% of student union, 50% of common outdoor areas have wireless network access. Students can register for classes online. Administrative functions (other than registration) can be performed online.

CAMPUS LIFE
Environment: City. **Activities:** Choral groups, dance, drama/theater, music ensembles, musical theater, radio station, student government, student newspaper, television station, International Student Organization 68 registered organizations, 2 honor societies, 3 religious organizations. **Athletics (Intercollegiate):** *Men:* baseball, basketball, cross-country, equestrian sports, golf, lacrosse, soccer, swimming, tennis. *Women:* basketball, cross-country, equestrian sports, golf, lacrosse, soccer, softball, swimming, tennis, volleyball. **On-Campus Highlights:** SCAD Museum of Art, Club SCAD, Jen Library, Cafe SCAD, Trustees Theatre.

ADMISSIONS
Freshman Academic Profile: Average high school GPA 3.5. 16% in top 10% of high school class, 42% in top 25% of high school class, 77% in top 50% of high school class. SAT Math middle 50% range 460-580. SAT Critical Reading middle 50% range 480-600. SAT Writing middle 50% range 460-590. ACT middle 50% range 21-27. Minimum web-based TOEFL 85. Minimum paper TOEFL 550. **Basis for Candidate Selection:** *Very important factors considered include:* academic GPA, standardized test scores. *Important factors considered include:* rigor of secondary school record, level of applicant's interest. *Other factors considered include:* Class rank, application essay, recommendation(s), character/personal qualities, extracurricular activities, interview, talent/ability, volunteer work, work experience. **Freshman Admission Requirements:** High school diploma is required and GED is accepted. **Freshman Admission Statistics:** 8,977 applied, 62% admitted, 32% enrolled. **Transfer Admission Requirements:** college transcript(s), minimum college GPA of 2.0 required. Lowest grade transferable C. **General Admission Information:** Application Fee $50. Regular application deadline 8/1. Nonfall registration accepted. Admission may be deferred for a maximum of 2 consec qtr. Credit and/or placement offered for CEEB Advanced Placement tests.

COSTS AND FINANCIAL AID
Annual tuition $31,905. Room and board $12,990. Average book expense $2,496. **Required Forms and Deadlines:** FAFSA, institution's own financial aid form, state aid form. **Notification of Awards:** Applicants will be notified of awards on a rolling basis beginning 4/1. **Types of Aid:** *Need-based scholarships/ grants:* Federal Pell, SEOG, state scholarships/grants, private scholarships, the school's own gift aid. *Loans:* Direct Subsidized Stafford, Direct Unsubsidized Stafford, Direct PLUS, state loans. **Student Employment:** Federal Work-Study Program available. Institutional employment available. Off-campus job opportunities are excellent. **Financial Aid Statistics:** 62% freshmen, 66% undergrads receive need-based scholarship or grant aid. 98% freshmen, 83% undergrads receive non-need-based scholarship or grant aid. 98% freshmen, 98% undergrads receive need-based self-help aid. 1% freshmen, 1% undergrads receive athletic scholarships. 62% undergrads borrow to pay for school. Average cumulative indebtedness $37,776. **Criteria for awarding institutional aid:** *Non-need-based:* academics, alumni affiliation, art, athletics, music/drama, state/ district residency.

SAVANNAH STATE UNIVERSITY

College Station, Savannah, GA 31404
Phone: 912-356-2181
E-mail: SSUAdmissions@savstate.edu • **CEEB Code:** 5609
Fax: 912-356-2256 • **Website:** www.savstate.edu • **ACT Code:** 858

This public school was founded in 1890. It has a 165-acre campus.

RATINGS
Admissions Selectivity Rating: 61   **Fire Safety Rating:** 60*   **Green Rating:** 60*

STUDENTS AND FACULTY
Student Body: 15% out-of-state, (18 countries represented).
Retention and Graduation: 7% grads go on to further study within 1 year. 7% grads pursue arts and sciences degrees.

ACADEMICS
Degrees: bachelor's, master's. **Special Study Options:** internships, study abroad, Undergrads may take grad level classes Off-campus study: summer quarter programs in New York City and Europe; apprenticeships with artists or designers and internships with musuems, agencies, media production companies, architectural firms, and other companies in the U.S. or abroad Foreign Exchange Program(s): study abroad in England, France, Germany, Italy, and Spain. **Career Services:** internships.

FACILITIES
Housing: Coed dorms, men's dorms, women's dorms, fraternity/sorority housing.

CAMPUS LIFE
Activities: 8 honor societies, 3 religious organizations. 5 fraternities, 4 sororities.

ADMISSIONS
Freshman Admission Requirements: High school diploma is required and GED is accepted. High school diploma is required and GED is not accepted. Minimum college GPA of 2.0 required. Lowest grade transferable D. **General Admission Information:** Early decision application deadline 3/1. Regular application deadline 9/1. Nonfall registration accepted. Credit and/or placement offered for CEEB Advanced Placement tests.

COSTS AND FINANCIAL AID
Room and board $3,495. Average book expense $750. **Required Forms and Deadlines:** FAFSA, institution's own financial aid form. **Types of Aid:** *Need-based scholarships/grants:* state scholarships/grants. *Loans:* Subsidized Stafford, PLUS. **Student Employment:** Off-campus job opportunities are good.

SCHOOL OF THE ART INSTITUTE OF CHICAGO

36 South Wabash Avenue, Chicago, IL 60603
Phone: 312-629-6100 • **Financial Aid Phone:** 312-629-6600
E-mail: admiss@saic.edu • **CEEB Code:** 1713
Fax: 312-629-6101 • **Website:** www.saic.edu • **ACT Code:** 1136

This private school was founded in 1866.

RATINGS
Admissions Selectivity Rating: 75   **Fire Safety Rating:** 85   **Green Rating:** 61

STUDENTS AND FACULTY

Enrollment: 2,549. **Student Body:** 70% female, 30% male, 62% out-of-state, 2% international (68 countries represented). Asian 0%, African American 0%, Caucasian 5%, Hispanic 0%, Native American 0%.

Retention and Graduation: Faculty: Student/faculty ratio 9:1. 160 full-time faculty, 90% hold PhDs, 18% are members of minority groups, 43% are women.

ACADEMICS

Degrees: bachelor's, master's, post-bachelor's certificate. **Classes:** Most classes have 10–19 students. **Special Study Options:** cooperative education program, cross-registration, double major, English as a Second Language (ESL), exchange student program (domestic), independent study, internships, student-designed major, study abroad, teacher certification program, credit/no credit grading option; multi-disciplinary curriculum; 6 credit off-campus requirement. **Disability Services:** Special programs offered to physically disabled students include note-taking services, reader services, tape recorders, tutors. **Career Services:** Alumni network, alumni services, career/job search classes, career assessment, internships, Career Services highlights include SAIC's Cooperative Education Program is the recipient of the National Society for Experiential Education (NSEE) Experiential Education Higher Education Program of the Year Award. The award recognizes an "outstanding educational institution that has demonstrated an exceptional commitment to experiential education in their classrooms or on their campuses."

FACILITIES

Housing: Coed dorms, special housing for disabled students 99% of campus accessible to physically disabled. **Special Academic Facilities/Equipment:** The School is directly affiliated with the Art Institute of Chicago. Other resources include: The Gene Siskel Film Center; Fashion Resource Center, John M. Flaxman Library and Screening Room Galleries (Betty Rymer, Sullivan Galleries, Student Union Galleries, project space and Gallery X), Joan Flasch Artists' Book Collection,Poetry Center, Roger Brown Resources, Video Data Bank, The Poetry Center, Visiting Artists' Program, Media Center **Computers:** Students can register for classes online. Administrative functions (other than registration) can be performed online. Undergraduates are required to own a computer.

CAMPUS LIFE

Environment: Metropolis. **Activities:** dance, drama/theater, literary magazine, radio station, student government, student newspaper, student-run film society, television station, Campus Ministries, International Student Organization 43 registered organizations, 2 religious organizations.**On-Campus Highlights:** Studio Classrooms, Residence Halls, The Art Institute of Chicago, Gene Siskel Film Center, Galleries. **Environmental Initiatives:** Incandescent light bulbs in dorm rooms have been replaced with CFLs and new low-flow restrictions have been installed in all dorm room showers and sinks. ¢ Expected results are 206 Metric Tons of CO2 not being release into the atmosphere and 1,7 Million Gallons of Water Saved annually ¢Fan drives in the MacLean Building were replaced with Variable Frequency Drives; it's like putting a dimmer switch on the fan that moves the air. ¢Annual reduction of 183 metric tons of CO2 SURPLUS is a system for material re-use at SAIC. SURPLUS is a service station where used and excess materials can be made available for other students to take and use for free. Students can bring anything they no longer need"materials, former art projects, etc., as long as they meet the material guidelines posted"and take away stuff that they can use. SURPLUS provides a constantly changing resource for materials for artmaking, and it keeps quantities of used and excess materials that the school produces out of the landfills.

ADMISSIONS

Freshman Academic Profile: SAT Math middle 50% range 500-620. SAT Critical Reading middle 50% range 510-630. ACT middle 50% range 21-27. Minimum web-based TOEFL 79. Minimum paper TOEFL 550. **Basis for Candidate Selection:** *Very important factors considered include:* application essay, recommendation(s), rigor of secondary school record, standardized test scores, character/personal qualities, level of applicant's interest, talent/ability. *Important factors considered include:* Class rank, academic GPA, extracurricular activities, first generation, racial/ethnic status, volunteer work. *Other factors considered include:* alumni/ae relation, geographical residence, interview, state residency, work experience. **Freshman Admission Requirements:** High school diploma is required and GED is accepted. **Freshman Admission Statistics:** 3,004 applied, 78% admitted, 25% enrolled. **Transfer Admission Requirements:** High school transcript, college transcript(s), essay or personal statement, Lowest grade transferable C. **General Admission Information:** Application Fee $65. Regular application deadline 6/1. Notification on a rolling basis, beginning on or about 10/1. Nonfall registration accepted. Admission may be deferred for a maximum of 1 year. Credit offered for CEEB Advanced Placement tests.

COSTS AND FINANCIAL AID

Annual tuition $38,340. Room and board $13,810. Required fees $680. Average book expense $1,710. **Required Forms and Deadlines:** FAFSA. **Notification of Awards:** Applicants will be notified of awards on a rolling basis beginning

3/1. **Types of Aid:** *Need-based scholarships/grants:* Federal Pell, SEOG, state scholarships/grants, private scholarships, the school's own gift aid. *Loans:* Subsidized Stafford, Unsubsidized Stafford, PLUS, Federal Perkins, Alternative/private. **Student Employment:** Off-campus job opportunities are fair. **Financial Aid Statistics:** 100% freshmen, 99% undergrads receive need-based scholarship or grant aid. 6% freshmen, 4% undergrads receive non-need-based scholarship or grant aid. 91% freshmen, 94% undergrads receive need-based self-help aid. 51% freshmen, 55% undergrads receive any aid. 53% undergrads borrow to pay for school. Average cumulative indebtedness $39,914. **Criteria for awarding institutional aid:** *Non-need-based:* academics, art.

See page 1200.

SCHOOL OF THE MUSEUM OF FINE ARTS

230 The Fenway, Boston, MA 2115
Phone: 617-369-3626 • **Financial Aid Phone:** 617-369-3645
E-mail: admissions@smfa.edu • **CEEB Code:** 3794
Fax: 617-369-4264 • **Website:** • **ACT Code:** 1895

This private school was founded in 1876. It has a 14-acre campus.

RATINGS

Admissions Selectivity Rating: 62   **Fire Safety Rating:** 87   **Green Rating:** 65

STUDENTS AND FACULTY

Enrollment: 426. **Student Body:** 68% female, 32% male, 65% out-of-state, 9% international (45 countries represented). Asian 4%, African American 3%, Caucasian 55%, Hispanic 10%, Native American 0%.

Retention and Graduation: 68% freshmen return for sophomore year. 31% freshmen graduate within 4 years. 50% freshmen graduate within 6 years. **Faculty:** Student/faculty ratio 9:1. 49 full-time faculty, 78% hold PhDs, 8% are members of minority groups, 51% are women. 8% of classes are taught by teaching assistants.

ACADEMICS

Degrees: bachelor's, certificate, diploma, master's, post-bachelor's certificate. **Classes:** Most classes have 10–19 students. **Majors with Highest Enrollment:** art teacher education; fine arts and art studies, other; fine/studio arts. **Special Study Options:** cross-registration, double major, English as a Second Language (ESL), exchange student program (domestic), independent study, internships, liberal arts/career combination, student-designed major, study abroad, teacher certification program, Combined Degree opportunity (BFA + BS or BA). All-studio elective program (Diploma). 5th Year study / Certificate for Diploma recipients. Joint BFA with Northeastern University. **Combined Degree Programs:** BA/BFA, BS/BFA, BFA/Diploma. **Disability Services:** Special programs offered to physically disabled students include reader services, tape recorders. **Career Services:** Alumni network, alumni services, internships, Career Services highlights include Our internship program gives students the opportunity to earn studio credit, gain valuable experience, and make contacts in the local art scene. Students in the internship program receive extensive preparation, support and guidance throughout their internship.

FACILITIES

Housing: Coed dorms, Professional off-campus housing assistance. 100% of campus accessible to physically disabled. **Special Academic Facilities/Equipment:** Museum of Fine Arts, Boston; Art galleries; welding equipment; darkrooms; digital equipment; kilns; and more! **Computers:** 100% of classrooms, 100% of dorms, 100% of libraries, 100% of dining areas, 100% of student union, have wireless network access. Students can register for classes online. Administrative functions (other than registration) can be performed online.

CAMPUS LIFE

Environment: Metropolis. **Activities:** student government, student-run film society 10 registered organizations. **On-Campus Highlights:** Classrooms and Studios, Museum of Fine Arts, Boston, Galleries and Exhibition Spaces, Museum and School Libraries, "Art in progress - everywhere you look." **Environmental Initiatives:** Migration from toxic (mostly wet photo and paint) to non-toxic art materials and solvents. Also disposal of hazardous waste. Re-use of supplies (where students swap or sell supplies to others) Recycling of ink cartridges, paper, etc.

ADMISSIONS

Freshman Academic Profile: Minimum web-based TOEFL 79. Minimum paper TOEFL 550. **Basis for Candidate Selection:** *Very important factors considered include:* rigor of secondary school record, talent/ability. *Important factors considered include:* application essay, academic GPA, interview, level of applicant's interest. *Other factors considered include:* Class rank, recommendation(s), standardized test scores, alumni/ae relation, character/personal qualities, extracurricular activities, first generation, geographical residence, volunteer work, work experience. **Freshman Admission Requirements:** High school diploma is required and GED is accepted. **Freshman Admission Statistics:** 643 applied, 89% admitted, 18% enrolled. **Transfer Admission Requirements:** college transcript(s), essay or personal statement, minimum college GPA of 1.75 required. Lowest grade transferable C–. **General Admission Information:** Application Fee $65. Notification on a rolling basis, beginning on or about 3/15. Nonfall registration accepted. Admission may be deferred for a maximum of 1 year. Neither credit nor placement offered for CEEB Advanced Placement tests.

COSTS AND FINANCIAL AID

Annual tuition $36,828. Required fees $1,200. Average book expense $1,600. **Required Forms and Deadlines:** FAFSA, institution's own financial aid form. **Notification of Awards:** Applicants will be notified of awards on a rolling basis beginning 4/15. *Types of Aid: Need-based scholarships/grants:* Federal Pell, SEOG, state scholarships/grants, private scholarships, the school's own gift aid. *Loans:* Subsidized Stafford, Unsubsidized Stafford, PLUS, state loans. **Student Employment:** Federal Work-Study Program available. Institutional employment available. Highest amount earned per year from on-campus jobs $3,500. Off-campus job opportunities are excellent. **Financial Aid Statistics:** 88% freshmen, 95% undergrads receive need-based scholarship or grant aid. 99% freshmen, 5% undergrads receive non-need-based scholarship or grant aid. 89% freshmen, 86% undergrads receive need-based self-help aid. 82% freshmen, 86% undergrads receive any aid. 61% undergrads borrow to pay for school. Average cumulative indebtedness $22,614. **Criteria for awarding institutional aid:** *Non-need-based:* art.

SCHOOL OF VISUAL ARTS

209 East 23rd Street, New York, NY 10010
Phone: 212-592-2100 • **Financial Aid Phone:** 212-592-2030
E-mail: admissions@sva.edu • **CEEB Code:** 2835
Fax: 212-592-2116 • **Website:** www.sva.edu • **ACT Code:** 2895

This proprietary school was founded in 1947.

RATINGS
Admissions Selectivity Rating: 76   **Fire Safety Rating:** 96   **Green Rating:** 60*

STUDENTS AND FACULTY
Enrollment: 3,332. **Student Body:** 55% female, 45% male, 57% out-of-state, 15% international (55 countries represented). Asian 13%, African American 3%, Caucasian 49%, Hispanic 10%, Native American 1%.
Retention and Graduation: 86% freshmen return for sophomore year. 60% freshmen graduate within 4 years. 67% freshmen graduate within 6 years.
Faculty: Student/faculty ratio 9:1. 163 full-time faculty, 24% hold PhDs, 4% are members of minority groups, 31% are women.

ACADEMICS
Degrees: bachelor's, master's. **Classes:** Most classes have 10–19 students. **Majors with Highest Enrollment:** film/video and photographic arts, other; graphic design; photography. **Special Study Options:** English as a Second Language (ESL), exchange student program (domestic), honors program, internships, liberal arts/career combination, study abroad, teacher certification program. **Honors Programs:** SVA offers an honors program for incoming freshmen; program involves a two year commitment, with an optional third year. **Disability Services:** Special programs offered to physically disabled students include note-taking services, reader services, tape recorders, tutors. **Career Services:** Alumni network, alumni services, internships.

FACILITIES
Housing: Coed dorms, women's dorms. 100% of campus accessible to physically disabled. **Special Academic Facilities/Equipment:** Visual Art Museum, Milton Glaser Design Study Center and Archives, 8 student galleries **Computers:** 100% of classrooms, 100% of libraries, 100% of student union, have wireless network access. Students can register for classes online. Administrative functions (other than registration) can be performed online.

CAMPUS LIFE
Environment: Metropolis. **Activities:** literary magazine, radio station, student government, student-run film society, yearbook 23 registered organizations, 3 religious organizations. **On-Campus Highlights:** Visual Arts Gallery, Westside Gallery, Visual Arts Museum, Visual Arts Student Association, Student Lounge. **Environmental Initiatives:** Yes, we do recycle our trash, but we do it off site. Due to space limitations we don't have an area to collect and sort out recyclables from our trash, nor do we have the space to store the recyclables prior

to shipment to an appropriate recycler. To accomplish this we rely on an outside contractor to collect our trash and sort it at their facilities. They ensure that anything that can be recycled from our trash finds its way to the recyclers. SVA recycles batteries used in electronic equipment as well as computers, monitors printers and other consumer electronics. We also recycle florescent light bulbs and electronic components. We monitor the waste water that comes from areas like the Photo Labs, Printmaking and the Sculpture Labs. The waste water is tested to make sure that it is in compliance with all city, state and federal regulations. We also do periodic air and water quality checks.

ADMISSIONS

Freshman Academic Profile: Average high school GPA 3.1. 60% from public high schools. SAT Math middle 50% range 460-590. SAT Critical Reading middle 50% range 450-580. SAT Writing middle 50% range 450-580. ACT middle 50% range 20-25. Minimum paper TOEFL 550. **Basis for Candidate Selection:** *Very important factors considered include:* application essay, academic GPA, rigor of secondary school record, interview, level of applicant's interest, talent/ability. *Other factors considered include:* recommendation(s), standardized test scores, alumni/ae relation, extracurricular activities, volunteer work, work experience. **Freshman Admission Requirements:** High school diploma is required and GED is accepted. **Freshman Admission Statistics:** 2,821 applied, 67% admitted, 35% enrolled. **Transfer Admission Requirements:** college transcript(s), essay or personal statement, statement of good standing from prior institution(s). Minimum college GPA of 2.0 required. Lowest grade transferable C. **General Admission Information:** Application Fee $50. Notification on a rolling basis, beginning on or about 2/1. Nonfall registration not accepted. Admission may be deferred for a maximum of 1 year. Credit offered for CEEB Advanced Placement tests.

COSTS AND FINANCIAL AID

Annual tuition $26,800. Room and board $12,700. Average book expense $3,150. **Required Forms and Deadlines:** FAFSA, state aid form. **Notification of Awards:** Applicants will be notified of awards on a rolling basis beginning 2/15. *Types of Aid: Need-based scholarships/grants:* Federal Pell, SEOG, state scholarships/grants, private scholarships, the school's own gift aid, Alternate loans. *Loans:* Subsidized Stafford, Unsubsidized Stafford, Federal Perkins. **Student Employment:** Federal Work-Study Program available. Off-campus job opportunities are fair. **Financial Aid Statistics:** 68% freshmen, 68% undergrads receive need-based scholarship or grant aid. 19% freshmen, 19% undergrads receive non-need-based scholarship or grant aid. 96% freshmen, 97% undergrads receive need-based self-help aid. 60% freshmen, 55% undergrads receive any aid. 55% undergrads borrow to pay for school. Average cumulative indebtedness $34,480. **Criteria for awarding institutional aid:** *Non-need-based:* art.

SCHREINER UNIVERSITY

2100 Memorial Boulevard, Kerrville, TX 78028-5697
Phone: 830-792-7217 • **Financial Aid Phone:** 830-792-7217
E-mail: admissions@schreiner.edu • **CEEB Code:** 6647
Fax: 830-896-3232 • **Website:** www.schreiner.edu • **ACT Code:** 4168

This private school, affiliated with the Presbyterian Church, was founded in 1923. It has a 175-acre campus.

RATINGS
Admissions Selectivity Rating: 75   **Fire Safety Rating:** 61   **Green Rating:** 60*

STUDENTS AND FACULTY
Enrollment: 1,059. **Student Body:** 57% female, 43% male, 3% out-of-state, 0% international. Asian 1%, African American 4%, Caucasian 64%, Hispanic 28%, Native American 0%.
Retention and Graduation: 71% freshmen return for sophomore year. 23% freshmen graduate within 4 years. 34% freshmen graduate within 6 years.
Faculty: Student/faculty ratio 14:1. 56 full-time faculty, 68% hold PhDs, 9% are members of minority groups, 46% are women. 0% of classes are taught by teaching assistants.

ACADEMICS
Degrees: associate, bachelor's, certificate, master's, post-bachelor's certificate, post-master's certificate. **Classes:** Most classes have 20–29 students. Most lab/discussion sessions have 20–29 students. **Majors with Highest Enrollment:** biology/biological sciences; design and applied arts, other; psychology. **Special Study Options:** Accelerated program, double major, dual enrollment, honors program, independent study, internships, liberal arts/career combination, student-designed major, study abroad, teacher certification program, weekend college. **Disability Services:** Special programs offered to physically disabled

students include note-taking services, reader services, tape recorders, tutors. **Career Services:** Alumni network, alumni services, career/job search classes, career assessment, internships, regional alumni.

FACILITIES

Housing: Coed dorms, special housing for disabled students, apartments for married students, apartments for single students. 95% of campus accessible to physically disabled. **Computers:** 100% of classrooms, 100% of dorms, 100% of libraries, 100% of dining areas, 100% of student union, 30% of common outdoor areas have wireless network access.

CAMPUS LIFE

Environment: Town. **Activities:** Choral groups, dance, drama/theater, literary magazine, music ensembles, musical theater, pep band, student government, student newspaper, symphony orchestra, Campus Ministries 35 registered organizations, 5 honor societies, 7 religious organizations. 2 fraternities, 2 sororities. **Athletics (Intercollegiate):** *Men:* baseball, basketball, golf, soccer, tennis. *Women:* basketball, cheerleading, golf, soccer, softball, tennis, volleyball. **On-Campus Highlights:** Caillioux Campus Activity Center, Logan Library, Griffin Welcome Center, Deitert Auditorium, Gus Schreiner Student Center.

ADMISSIONS

Freshman Academic Profile: Average high school GPA 3.5. 13% in top 10% of high school class, 40% in top 25% of high school class, 74% in top 50% of high school class. SAT Math middle 50% range 450-550. SAT Critical Reading middle 50% range 430-550. SAT Writing middle 50% range 410-510. ACT middle 50% range 19-24. Minimum web-based TOEFL 79. Minimum paper TOEFL 550. **Basis for Candidate Selection:** *Important factors considered include:* Class rank, application essay, academic GPA, rigor of secondary school record, standardized test scores, character/personal qualities, interview, level of applicant's interest, volunteer work, work experience. *Other factors considered include:* recommendation(s), extracurricular activities, talent/ability. **Freshman Admission Requirements:** High school diploma is required and GED is accepted. **Freshman Admission Statistics:** 1,153 applied, 63% admitted, 37% enrolled. **Transfer Admission Requirements:** college transcript(s), minimum college GPA of 2.0 required. Lowest grade transferable D. **General Admission Information:** Application Fee $25. Regular application deadline 8/1. Nonfall registration accepted. Admission may be deferred for a maximum of 1 semester. Credit and/or placement offered for CEEB Advanced Placement tests.

COSTS AND FINANCIAL AID

Annual tuition $20,940. Room and board $10,062. Required fees $600. Average book expense $1,200. **Required Forms and Deadlines:** FAFSATAFSA. **Notification of Awards:** Applicants will be notified of awards on a rolling basis beginning 2/15. **Types of Aid:** *Need-based scholarships/grants:* Federal Pell, SEOG, state scholarships/grants, private scholarships, the school's own gift aid. *Loans:* Direct Subsidized Stafford, Direct Unsubsidized Stafford, Direct PLUS, Subsidized Stafford, Unsubsidized Stafford, PLUS, state loans. **Student Employment:** Federal Work-Study Program available. Institutional employment available. Off-campus job opportunities are good. **Financial Aid Statistics:** 100% freshmen, 100% undergrads receive need-based scholarship or grant aid. 12% freshmen, 9% undergrads receive non-need-based scholarship or grant aid. 80% freshmen, 83% undergrads receive need-based self-help aid. 100% freshmen, 97% undergrads receive any aid. 36% undergrads borrow to pay for school. Average cumulative indebtedness $20,900. **Criteria for awarding institutional aid:** *Non-need-based:* academics, art, leadership, music/drama, religious affiliation.

SCRIPPS COLLEGE

Best 378

1030 Columbia Avenue, Claremont, CA 91711
Phone: 909-621-8149 • **Financial Aid Phone:** 909-621-8275
E-mail: admission@scrippscollege.edu • **CEEB Code:** 4693
Fax: 909-607-7508 • **Website:** www.scrippscollege.edu • **ACT Code:** 426

This private school was founded in 1926. It has a 37-acre campus.

RATINGS

Admissions Selectivity Rating: 97	Fire Safety Rating: 73	Green Rating: 79

STUDENTS AND FACULTY

Enrollment: 956. **Student Body:** 52% out-of-state, 4% international (20 countries represented). Asian 17%, African American 5%, Caucasian 48%, Hispanic 8%, Native American 1%.

Retention and Graduation: 91% freshmen return for sophomore year. 83% freshmen graduate within 4 years. 88% freshmen graduate within 6 years. **Faculty:** Student/faculty ratio 11:1. 85 full-time faculty, 100% hold PhDs, 21% are members of minority groups, 55% are women. 0% of classes are taught by teaching assistants.

ACADEMICS

Degrees: bachelor's, post-bachelor's certificate. **Classes:** Most classes have 10–19 students. Most lab/discussion sessions have 10–19 students. **Majors with Highest Enrollment:** English language and literature; international relations and affairs; psychology. **Special Study Options:** Accelerated program, cross-registration, double major, dual enrollment, exchange student program (domestic), independent study, internships, student-designed major, study abroad. **Honors Programs:** Honors Programs in all academic majors available. **Combined Degree Programs:** BA/MA, BA/MEng, BA/MBA. **Disability Services:** Special programs offered to physically disabled students include note-taking services, reader services, tape recorders, tutors. **Career Services:** Alumni network, alumni services, career/job search classes, career assessment, internships, regional alumni. Career Services highlights include Career Planning & Resources offers a variety of internship resources to assist students in their internship search. Scripps is a member of the National Internship Consortium, with 16 schools across the country sharing over 9000 internship listings. CP&R is pleased to offer a number of internship grants, which allow students to pursue opportunities without having to worry about compensation.

FACILITIES

Housing: special housing for disabled students, women's dorms, apartments for single students, Small college owned houses. 85% of campus accessible to physically disabled. **Special Academic Facilities/Equipment:** Art center, music complex, dance studio, humanities museum and institute, science center, biological field station, field house **Computers:** 100% of classrooms, 100% of dorms, 100% of libraries, 100% of dining areas, 100% of common outdoor areas have wireless network access. Administrative functions (other than registration) can be performed online.

CAMPUS LIFE

Environment: Town. **Activities:** Choral groups, dance, drama/theater, literary magazine, music ensembles, radio station, student government, student newspaper, symphony orchestra, yearbook, Campus Ministries, International Student Organization, Model UN 200 registered organizations, 5 honor societies, 7 religious organizations. **Athletics (Intercollegiate):** *Women:* basketball, cross-country, diving, golf, lacrosse, soccer, softball, swimming, tennis, track/field (outdoor), volleyball, water polo. **On-Campus Highlights:** Williamson Gallery, Rare book room, Denison Library, Margaret Fowler Garden, Malott Commons, Graffitti Wall, Sallie Tiernan Field House. **Environmental Initiatives:** Establishment of a sustainability committee to serve as an advisory counsel to president regarding campus operations - Working with students on recycling/composting programs/fallen fruit projects and student garden. - Carboard baling. Requesting information from building contractors on sustainability practices/materials.

ADMISSIONS

Freshman Academic Profile: Average high school GPA 4.1. 79% in top 10% of high school class, 93% in top 25% of high school class, 100% in top 50% of high school class. 60% from public high schools. SAT Math middle 50% range 640-710. SAT Critical Reading middle 50% range 640-740. SAT Writing middle 50% range 660-740. ACT middle 50% range 29-32. Minimum web-based TOEFL 100. Minimum paper TOEFL 600. **Basis for Candidate Selection:** *Very important factors considered include:* Class rank, application essay, academic GPA, recommendation(s), rigor of secondary school record, standardized test scores, alumni/ae relation, character/personal qualities, extracurricular activities, first generation, interview, racial/ethnic status, talent/ability, volunteer work, work experience. *Important factors considered include:* geographical residence. **Freshman Admission Requirements:** High school diploma is required and GED is accepted. *Academic units required:* 4 English, 3 mathematics, 3 science, 3 foreign language, 3 social studies. 4 English, 3 mathematics, 3 science, 3 foreign language, 3 social studies. **Freshman Admission Statistics:** 2,163 applied, 36% admitted, 33% enrolled. **Transfer Admission Requirements:** High school transcript, college transcript(s), essay or personal statement, standardized test scores, statement of good standing from prior institution(s). Minimum college GPA of 3.0 required. Lowest grade transferable C. **General Admission Information:** Application Fee $60. Early decision application deadline 11/1. Regular application deadline 1/1. Regular notification 4/1. Nonfall registration accepted. Admission may be deferred for a maximum of one year. Credit offered for CEEB Advanced Placement tests.

COSTS AND FINANCIAL AID

Annual tuition $43,406. Room and board $13,468. Required fees $214. Average book expense $800. **Required Forms and Deadlines:** FAFSA, CSS/Financial Aid PROFILE, state aid form, noncustodial PROFILE, business/farm supplement. Verification worksheet, signed copies of parent Institution Verification form, parent and student federal tax returns. **Notification of Awards:** Applicants will be notified of awards on or about 4/1. **Types of Aid:** *Need-based scholarships/grants:* Federal Pell, SEOG, state scholarships/grants, private scholarships, the school's own gift aid. *Loans:* Subsidized Stafford, Unsubsidized Stafford, PLUS, Federal Perkins, college/university loans from institutional funds. **Student Employment:** Federal Work-Study Program available. Institutional employment available. Off-campus job opportunities are good. **Financial Aid Statistics:** 99% freshmen, 98% undergrads receive need-based scholarship or grant aid. 13% freshmen, 22% undergrads receive non-need-based scholarship or grant aid. 83% freshmen, 92% undergrads receive need-based self-help aid. 54% freshmen, 58% undergrads receive any aid. 44% undergrads borrow to pay for school. Average cumulative indebtedness $21,864. **Criteria for awarding institutional aid:** *Non-need-based:* academics, leadership.

SEATTLE PACIFIC UNIVERSITY

3307 3rd Avenue West, Seattle, WA 98119-1997
Phone: 206-281-2021 • **Financial Aid Phone:** 206-281-2061
E-mail: admissions@spu.edu • **CEEB Code:** 4694
Fax: 206-281-2669 • **Website:** www.spu.edu • **ACT Code:** 4476

This private school, affiliated with the Methodist Church, was founded in 1891. It has a 35-acre campus.

RATINGS
Admissions Selectivity Rating: 73   **Fire Safety Rating:** 60*   **Green Rating:** 93

STUDENTS AND FACULTY
Enrollment: 3,231. **Student Body:** 67% female, 33% male, 39% out-of-state, 1% international (43 countries represented). Asian 10%, African American 4%, Caucasian 67%, Hispanic 8%, Native American 0%.
Retention and Graduation: 84% freshmen return for sophomore year. 55% freshmen graduate within 4 years. 72% freshmen graduate within 6 years.
Faculty: Student/faculty ratio 15:1. 202 full-time faculty, 89% hold PhDs, 9% are members of minority groups, 42% are women. 0% of classes are taught by teaching assistants.

ACADEMICS
Degrees: bachelor's, doctoral, master's, post-master's certificate. **Classes:** Most classes have 10–19 students. Most lab/discussion sessions have fewer than 10 students. **Majors with Highest Enrollment:** biology/biological sciences; business/commerce; nursing/registered nurse (rn, asn, bsn, msn). **Special Study Options:** distance learning, double major, exchange student program (domestic), external degree program, honors program, independent study, internships, liberal arts/career combination, student-designed major, study abroad, teacher certification program. **Honors Programs:** University Scholars. **Disability Services:** Special programs offered to physically disabled students include note-taking services, reader services, tape recorders. **Career Services:** Alumni network, alumni services, career/job search classes, career assessment, internships Career Services highlights include Very strong internship program. Also great 1 & 2 credit classes offered as electives.

FACILITIES
Housing: Coed dorms, apartments for married students, apartments for single students, theme housing. **Special Academic Facilities/Equipment:** Art gallery, theatre facilities **Computers:** 100% of classrooms, 90% of dorms, 100% of libraries, 100% of dining areas, 100% of student union, 50% of common outdoor areas have wireless network access. Students can register for classes online. Administrative functions (other than registration) can be performed online.

CAMPUS LIFE
Environment: Metropolis. **Activities:** Choral groups, drama/theater, jazz band, literary magazine, music ensembles, musical theater, pep band, radio station, student government, student newspaper, symphony orchestra, yearbook, Campus Ministries 63 registered organizations, 1 honor societies, 7 religious organizations. **Athletics (Intercollegiate):** *Men:* badminton, basketball, bowling, crew/rowing, cross-country, football, soccer, softball, table tennis, tennis, track/field (outdoor), track/field (indoor), volleyball, weight lifting. *Women:* badminton, basketball, bowling, crew/rowing, cross-country, football, gymnastics, soccer, softball, table tennis, tennis, track/field (outdoor), track/field (indoor), volleyball, weight lifting. **On-Campus Highlights:** Pura Vida Coffee Shop, Royal Brougham Pavilion, Weter Lounge, Student Union Building, The Science Building. **Environmental Initiatives:** 1. June 2010 completion of a solar photovoltaic installation atop our physics and engineering building. The installation was conceived as part of a senior honors project and returns to the grid the approximate amount of electricity consumed by our electric maintenance vehicles. A visible production meter in the second floor hallway allows students in the

recently created Appropriate and Sustainable Engineering major to monitor its production. 2. New buildings on campus are required to meet a minimum LEED Silver standard. Beyond that, certain LEED credits focusing on energy efficiency, renewable energy, stormwater management, and habitat restoration are designated as priority credits for Seattle Pacific to achieve. 3. Spring 2010 completion of a climate action plan adopting a 2036 target for climate neutrality. The plan covers four distinct areas: planning and development, energy infrastructure, transportation options, and education for a sustainable future. The plan was assembled with input from a 20-person sustainability committee with representation from students, faculty, staff, and the administration.

ADMISSIONS
Freshman Academic Profile: Average high school GPA 3.5. 26% in top 10% of high school class, 57% in top 25% of high school class, 87% in top 50% of high school class. SAT Math middle 50% range 500-610. SAT Critical Reading middle 50% range 500-620. SAT Writing middle 50% range 500-600. ACT middle 50% range 22-27. Minimum web-based TOEFL 79. Minimum paper TOEFL 550. **Basis for Candidate Selection:** *Very important factors considered include:* application essay, academic GPA, recommendation(s), rigor of secondary school record, standardized test scores. *Important factors considered include:* character/personal qualities, extracurricular activities, first generation, interview, level of applicant's interest, racial/ethnic status, religious affiliation/commitment, talent/ability, volunteer work, work experience. *Other factors considered include:* Class rank, alumni/ae relation, geographical residence. **Freshman Admission Requirements:** High school diploma is required and GED is accepted. **Freshman Admission Statistics:** 4,559 applied, 79% admitted, 22% enrolled. **Transfer Admission Requirements:** college transcript(s), essay or personal statement, minimum college GPA of 2.5 required. Lowest grade transferable C. **General Admission Information:** Application Fee $45. Regular application deadline 2/1. Regular notification 3/1. Nonfall registration accepted. Credit offered for CEEB Advanced Placement tests.

COSTS AND FINANCIAL AID
Annual tuition $31,701. Room and board $9,492. Required fees $366. Average book expense $999. **Required Forms and Deadlines:** FAFSA. **Notification of Awards:** Applicants will be notified of awards on a rolling basis beginning 3/11. **Types of Aid:** *Need-based scholarships/grants:* Federal Pell, SEOG, state scholarships/grants, private scholarships, the school's own gift aid. *Loans:* Subsidized Stafford, Unsubsidized Stafford, PLUS, Federal Perkins, Federal Nursing, college/university loans from institutional funds. **Student Employment:** Federal Work-Study Program available. Institutional employment available. **Financial Aid Statistics:** 100% freshmen, 99% undergrads receive need-based scholarship or grant aid. 94% freshmen, 95% undergrads receive need-based self-help aid. 1% freshmen, 1% undergrads receive athletic scholarships. 67% undergrads borrow to pay for school. Average cumulative indebtedness $28,263. **Criteria for awarding institutional aid:** *Non-need-based:* academics, alumni affiliation, art, athletics, leadership, minority status, music/drama, religious affiliation.

SEATTLE UNIVERSITY

Best 378

Admissions Office, Seattle, WA 98122-1090
Phone: 206-296-2000 • **Financial Aid Phone:** 206-296-2000
E-mail: admissions@seattleu.edu • **CEEB Code:** 4695
Fax: 206-296-5656 • **Website:** www.seattleu.edu • **ACT Code:** 4478

This private school, affiliated with the Roman Catholic-Jesuit Church, was founded in 1891. It has a 50-acre campus.

RATINGS
Admissions Selectivity Rating: 81   **Fire Safety Rating:** 79   **Green Rating:** 95

STUDENTS AND FACULTY
Enrollment: 4,559. **Student Body:** 59% female, 41% male, 44% out-of-state, 10% international (56 countries represented). Asian 16%, African American 4%, Caucasian 48%, Hispanic 9%, Native American 1%.
Retention and Graduation: 87% freshmen return for sophomore year. 62% freshmen graduate within 4 years. 77% freshmen graduate within 6 years.
Faculty: Student/faculty ratio 12:1. 504 full-time faculty, 74% hold PhDs, 15% are members of minority groups, 51% are women. 0% of classes are taught by teaching assistants.

The Princeton Review's Complete Book of Colleges

ACADEMICS

Degrees: bachelor's, master's, post-bachelor's certificate, post-master's certificate. **Classes:** Most classes have 10–19 students. Most lab/discussion sessions have 10–19 students. **Majors with Highest Enrollment:** finance; marketing/marketing management; nursing/registered nurse (rn, asn, bsn, msn). **Special Study Options:** cooperative education program, cross-registration, double major, English as a Second Language (ESL), honors program, independent study, internships, liberal arts/career combination, student-designed major, study abroad. **Honors Programs:** The University Honors program provides students of high ability and motivation the opportunity to join a small, select, two-year-long learning community. The program is taken in the freshman and sophomore years and fulfills most of the University's Core Curriculum requirements. Honors Programs are also offered within majors. **Combined Degree Programs:** BA/MBA. **Disability Services:** Special programs offered to physically disabled students include note-taking services, reader services, tape recorders, tutors. **Career Services:** Alumni network, alumni services, career/job search classes, career assessment, internships.

FACILITIES

Housing: Coed dorms, special housing for disabled students, apartments for single students, theme housing. 95% of campus accessible to physically disabled. **Special Academic Facilities/Equipment:** Observatory, electron microscope, St. Ignatius Chapel **Computers:** 100% of classrooms, 20% of dorms, 100% of libraries, 100% of dining areas, 100% of student union, 95% of common outdoor areas have wireless network access. Students can register for classes online. Administrative functions (other than registration) can be performed online.

CAMPUS LIFE

Environment: Metropolis. **Activities:** Choral groups, drama/theater, jazz band, literary magazine, music ensembles, pep band, radio station, student government, student newspaper, Campus Ministries 130 registered organizations. **Athletics (Intercollegiate):** *Men:* baseball, basketball, cross-country, golf, soccer, swimming, tennis, track/field (outdoor), track/field (indoor). *Women:* basketball, cross-country, golf, soccer, softball, swimming, tennis, track/field (outdoor), track/field (indoor), volleyball. **On-Campus Highlights:** Chapel of Saint Ignatius, Brand new Student Center, Award Winning Grounds and Open Space, Sullivan Hall, home of the School of Law **Environmental Initiatives:** Plastic bottled water is not sold anywhere on campus including: the bookstore, vending machines, athletics concession stands, restaurants, and catered events. Free, filtered water and bottle fillers are available at over 30 water fountains throughout campus. The Bookstore is selling a 27 ounce, steel water bottle at a discounted price to make owning a bottle affordable. Compost bins for collecting food waste are located in the restaurants, outside campus buildings, the library, a few staff offices, each residence hall resident's room and each residence hall floor's waste closet. All to-go ware from campus eateries is made from plant-based compostable materials. Our campus compost facility annually turns 52,000 pounds of food waste into compost - which is applied on our landscape. All new construction and major renovations must achieve LEED Gold certification. There are three completed LEED Gold buildings, a fourth is being built and one LEED Certified building. Two homes were renovated to a Built Green 3-Star rating out of three possible stars.

ADMISSIONS

Freshman Academic Profile: Average high school GPA 3.6. 26% in top 10% of high school class, 58% in top 25% of high school class, 89% in top 50% of high school class. SAT Math middle 50% range 540-640. SAT Critical Reading middle 50% range 530-640. SAT Writing middle 50% range 530-630. ACT middle 50% range 24-29. Minimum web-based TOEFL 68. Minimum paper TOEFL 520. **Basis for Candidate Selection:** *Very important factors considered include:* academic GPA, rigor of secondary school record, standardized test scores, character/personal qualities. *Important factors considered include:* application essay, recommendation(s), extracurricular activities, level of applicant's interest. *Other factors considered include:* Class rank, alumni/ae relation, first generation, geographical residence, interview, racial/ethnic status, religious affiliation/commitment, state residency, talent/ability, volunteer work, work experience. **Freshman Admission Requirements:** High school diploma is required and GED is accepted. *Academic units required:* 4 English, 3 mathematics, 2 science, (2 science labs), 2 foreign language, 2 social studies, 1 history, 2 academic electives. *Academic units recommended:* 4 English, 3 mathematics, 2 science, (2 science labs), 2 foreign language, 2 social studies, 1 history, 2 academic electives. **Freshman Admission Statistics:** 6,862 applied, 71% admitted, 18% enrolled. **Transfer Admission Requirements:** college transcript(s), essay or personal statement, statement of good standing from prior institution(s). Minimum college GPA of 2.25 required. Lowest grade transferable C–. **General Admission Information:** Application Fee $50. Notification on a rolling basis, beginning on or about 2/1. Nonfall registration accepted. Admission may be deferred for a maximum of 1 year. Credit and/or placement offered for CEEB Advanced Placement tests.

COSTS AND FINANCIAL AID

Required Forms and Deadlines: FAFSA. **Notification of Awards:** Applicants will be notified of awards on a rolling basis beginning 3/21. **Types of Aid:** *Need-based scholarships/grants:* Federal Pell, SEOG, state scholarships/grants, private scholarships, the school's own gift aid, Federal Nursing Scholarships. *Loans:* Direct Subsidized Stafford, Direct Unsubsidized Stafford, Direct PLUS, Federal Perkins, Federal Nursing. **Financial Aid Statistics:** 89% freshmen, 90% undergrads receive need-based scholarship or grant aid. 65% freshmen, 43% undergrads receive non-need-based scholarship or grant aid. 77% freshmen, 80% undergrads receive need-based self-help aid. 1% freshmen, 1% undergrads receive athletic scholarships. 96% freshmen, 87% undergrads receive any aid. 73% undergrads borrow to pay for school. Average cumulative indebtedness $29,498. **Criteria for awarding institutional aid:** *Non-need-based:* academics, alumni affiliation, athletics, leadership, minority status, music/drama, state/district residency.

See page 1202.

SETON HALL UNIVERSITY

Enrollment Services, South Orange, NJ 7079
Phone: 973-761-9332 • **Financial Aid Phone:** 973-761-9332
E-mail: thehall@shu.edu • **CEEB Code:** 2811
Fax: 973-275-2040 • **Website:** www.shu.edu • **ACT Code:** 2606

This private school, affiliated with the Roman Catholic Church, was founded in 1856. It has a 58-acre campus.

RATINGS

Admissions Selectivity Rating: 76   **Fire Safety Rating:** 81   **Green Rating:** 60*

STUDENTS AND FACULTY

Enrollment: 5,295. **Student Body:** 59% female, 41% male, 22% out-of-state, 2% international (71 countries represented). Asian 8%, African American 13%, Caucasian 51%, Hispanic 16%, Native American 0%.
Retention and Graduation: 30% grads go on to further study within 1 year. 9% grads pursue arts and sciences degrees. 7% grads pursue law degrees. 5% grads pursue business degrees. 9% grads pursue medical degrees. **Faculty:** 4% of classes are taught by teaching assistants.

ACADEMICS

Degrees: bachelor's, first professional, master's, post-master's certificate. **Classes:** Most classes have 10–19 students. Most lab/discussion sessions have 10–19 students. **Majors with Highest Enrollment:** communication studies/speech communication and rhetoric; criminal justice/safety studies; nursing/registered nurse (rn, asn, bsn, msn). **Special Study Options:** Accelerated program, cooperative education program, cross-registration, distance learning, double major, dual enrollment, English as a Second Language (ESL), honors program, independent study, internships, study abroad, teacher certification program. **Honors Programs:** University Honors Program fosters intellectual development through academic challenge. A structured sequence of colloquia and seminars helps to develop critical thinking abilities. Student study the great texts of the past and also have the opportunity to attend operas, theater, museums, concerts and other cultural events. **Combined Degree Programs:** BA/MA, BA/MEng, BS/MS Phys Asst or OT or Athl Trng, BS/D Phys Ther. **Disability Services:** Special programs offered to physically disabled students include note-taking services, reader services, tape recorders, tutors. **Career Services:** Alumni network, career/job search classes, career assessment, internships, regional alumni. Career Services highlights include Internships.

FACILITIES

Housing: Coed dorms, special housing for disabled students, apartments for single students. 94% of campus accessible to physically disabled. **Special Academic Facilities/Equipment:** Art, natural history, museums, theatre-in-the-round, archaeological research center, TV studio, radio station. **Computers:** 100% of classrooms, 100% of dorms, 100% of libraries, 100% of dining areas, 100% of student union, 100% of common outdoor areas have wireless network access. Students can register for classes online. Administrative functions (other than registration) can be performed online. Undergraduates are required to own a computer.

CAMPUS LIFE

Environment: Village. **Activities:** Choral groups, drama/theater, pep band, radio station, student government, television station 100 registered organizations,

13 honor societies, 3 religious organizations. **Athletics (Intercollegiate):** *Men:* baseball, basketball, cross-country, diving, golf, soccer, swimming, track/field (outdoor). *Women:* basketball, cross-country, diving, soccer, softball, swimming, tennis, track/field (outdoor). **On-Campus Highlights:** Jubilee Hall, University Center, Walsh Library, Recreation Center, Chapel.

ADMISSIONS
Freshman Academic Profile: Average high school GPA 3.5. 37% in top 10% of high school class, 61% in top 25% of high school class, 86% in top 50% of high school class. 70% from public high schools. SAT Math middle 50% range 510-610. SAT Critical Reading middle 50% range 490-590. SAT Writing middle 50% range 490-600. ACT middle 50% range 22-27. Minimum paper TOEFL 550. **Freshman Admission Statistics:** 10,180 applied, 84% admitted, 17% enrolled.

COSTS AND FINANCIAL AID
Financial Aid Statistics: 91% freshmen, 86% undergrads receive any aid.

See page 1204.

SETON HILL UNIVERSITY

1 Seton Hill Drive, Greensburg, PA 15601
Phone: 724-838-4255 • **Financial Aid Phone:** 724-838-4293
E-mail: admit@setonhill.edu • **CEEB Code:** 2812
Fax: 724-830-1294 • **Website:** www.setonhill.edu • **ACT Code:** 3688

This private school, affiliated with the Roman Catholic Church, was founded in 1883. It has a 200-acre campus.

RATINGS
Admissions Selectivity Rating: 75   **Fire Safety Rating:** 80   **Green Rating:** 60*

STUDENTS AND FACULTY
Enrollment: 1,583. **Student Body:** 64% female, 36% male, 22% out-of-state, (13 countries represented). **Retention and Graduation:** 42% freshmen graduate within 4 years. 26% grads go on to further study within 1 year. 56% grads pursue arts and sciences degrees. 3% grads pursue law degrees. 18% grads pursue business degrees. 5% grads pursue medical degrees. **Faculty:** Student/faculty ratio 14:1. 98 full-time faculty, 87% hold PhDs, 5% are members of minority groups, 55% are women. 0% of classes are taught by teaching assistants.

ACADEMICS
Degrees: bachelor's, certificate, master's, post-bachelor's certificate, post-master's certificate. **Classes:** Most classes have 10–19 students. **Majors with Highest Enrollment:** business/commerce; fine/studio arts; psychology. **Special Study Options:** Accelerated program, cross-registration, distance learning, double major, dual enrollment, English as a Second Language (ESL), exchange student program (domestic), honors program, independent study, internships, liberal arts/career combination, student-designed major, study abroad, teacher certification program, weekend college. **Honors Programs:** Honors Program has designated curriculum components. **Combined Degree Programs:** BA/JD, BS/DO, /DPharm with Lake Erie Coll of Osteopath Med, BA/Law with Duquesne U. **Disability Services:** Special programs offered to physically disabled students include note-taking services, reader services, tape recorders, tutors. **Career Services:** Alumni network, alumni services, career assessment, internships, regional alumni. Career Services highlights include Internships encouraged or required in every major.

FACILITIES
Housing: Coed dorms, men's dorms, women's dorms, Special housing for honors students. 95% of campus accessible to physically disabled. **Special Academic Facilities/Equipment:** Art gallery, concert hall, theatre, Child Development Center, NEW- Performing Arts Center, Studio 215, smart classrooms. **Computers:** 100% of classrooms, 100% of dorms, 100% of libraries, 100% of dining areas, 100% of common outdoor areas have wireless network access. Students can register for classes online. Administrative functions (other than registration) can be performed online.

CAMPUS LIFE
Environment: Town. **Activities:** Choral groups, concert band, dance, drama/theater, jazz band, literary magazine, marching band, music ensembles, musical theater, pep band, student government, student newspaper, symphony orchestra, Campus Ministries, International Student Organization 53 registered organizations, 4 honor societies, 7 religious organizations. **Athletics (Intercollegiate):** *Men:* baseball, basketball, cross-country, football, lacrosse, soccer, track/field (outdoor), track/field (indoor), wrestling. *Women:* basketball, cross-country, equestrian sports, field hockey, golf, lacrosse, soccer, softball, tennis,

track/field (outdoor), track/field (indoor), volleyball. **On-Campus Highlights:** Griffin's Cove, McKenna Recreation Center, Sullivan Lounge, Residence Halls, Lowe Dining Hall, New additions to Seton Hill include the Center for Performing Arts and Visual Arts Center; both of these venues are located in downtown Greensburg within walking distance of campus. **Environmental Initiatives:** Association of Independent Colleges and Universities of Pennsylvania self/peer assessment program

ADMISSIONS
Freshman Academic Profile: Average high school GPA 3.5. 20% in top 10% of high school class, 45% in top 25% of high school class, 77% in top 50% of high school class. SAT Math middle 50% range 460-560. SAT Critical Reading middle 50% range 450-560. SAT Writing middle 50% range 440-560. ACT middle 50% range 20-25. Minimum paper TOEFL 550. **Basis for Candidate Selection:** *Very important factors considered include:* academic GPA, rigor of secondary school record, interview. *Important factors considered include:* Class rank, standardized test scores, character/personal qualities, extracurricular activities, talent/ability. *Other factors considered include:* application essay, recommendation(s), alumni/ae relation, level of applicant's interest, volunteer work, work experience. **Freshman Admission Requirements:** High school diploma is required and GED is accepted. *Academic units required:* 4 English, 2 mathematics, 1 science, (1 science labs), 2 social studies, 4 academic electives. *Academic units recommended:* 4 English, 2 mathematics, 1 science, (1 science labs), 2 social studies, 4 academic electives. **Freshman Admission Statistics:** 2,150 applied, 66% admitted, 24% enrolled. **Transfer Admission Requirements:** High school transcript, college transcript(s), statement of good standing from prior institution(s). Minimum college GPA of 2.0 required. Lowest grade transferable C–. **General Admission Information:** Application Fee $35. Regular application deadline 8/15. Notification on a rolling basis, beginning on or about 9/1. Nonfall registration accepted. Admission may be deferred for a maximum of 12 months. Credit and/or placement offered for CEEB Advanced Placement tests.

COSTS AND FINANCIAL AID
Annual tuition $28,346. Room and board $9,944. Required fees $1,100. Average book expense $1,000. **Required Forms and Deadlines:** FAFSA, institution's own financial aid form, state aid form. **Notification of Awards:** Applicants will be notified of awards on a rolling basis beginning 11/15. **Types of Aid:** *Need-based scholarships/grants:* Federal Pell, SEOG, state scholarships/grants, private scholarships, the school's own gift aid. *Loans:* Subsidized Stafford, Unsubsidized Stafford, PLUS, Federal Perkins, college/university loans from institutional funds, Alternative. **Student Employment:** Federal Work-Study Program available. Institutional employment available. Highest amount earned per year from on-campus jobs $1,000. Off-campus job opportunities are good. **Financial Aid Statistics:** 100% freshmen, 99% undergrads receive need-based scholarship or grant aid. 14% freshmen, 12% undergrads receive non-need-based scholarship or grant aid. 82% freshmen, 84% undergrads receive need-based self-help aid. 9% freshmen, 9% undergrads receive athletic scholarships. 98% freshmen, 90% undergrads receive any aid. 90% undergrads borrow to pay for school. Average cumulative indebtedness $32,290. **Criteria for awarding institutional aid:** *Non-need-based:* academics, alumni affiliation, art, athletics, job skills, music/drama, religious affiliation.

SEWANEE—THE UNIVERSITY OF THE SOUTH

Best 378

735 University Avenue, Sewanee, TN 37383-1000
Phone: 931-598-1238 • **Financial Aid Phone:** 800-522-2234
E-mail: admiss@sewanee.edu • **CEEB Code:** 1842
Fax: 931-538-3248 • **Website:** www.sewanee.edu • **ACT Code:** 4924

This private school, affiliated with the Episcopal Church, was founded in 1857. It has a 13000-acre campus.

RATINGS
Admissions Selectivity Rating: 91   **Fire Safety Rating:** 89   **Green Rating:** 87

STUDENTS AND FACULTY
Enrollment: 1,450. **Student Body:** 52% female, 48% male, 74% out-of-state, 2% international (23 countries represented). Asian 2%, African American 4%, Caucasian 85%, Hispanic 4%, Native American 0%.
Retention and Graduation: 86% freshmen return for sophomore year. 74% freshmen graduate within 4 years. 24% grads go on to further study within 1

year. **Faculty:** Student/faculty ratio 10:1. 136 full-time faculty, 96% hold PhDs, 18% are members of minority groups, 40% are women. 0% of classes are taught by teaching assistants.

ACADEMICS

Degrees: bachelor's, master's, post-bachelor's certificate, post-master's certificate. **Classes:** Most classes have 10–19 students. Most lab/discussion sessions have 20–29 students. **Majors with Highest Enrollment:** economics; English language and literature; history. **Special Study Options:** double major, independent study, internships, student-designed major, study abroad. **Disability Services:** Special programs offered to physically disabled students include note-taking services, reader services, tape recorders. **Career Services:** Alumni network, alumni services, career assessment, internships, regional alumni. Career Services highlights include Sewanee's Internship Fund Program- Thanks to the help of alumni and the donors of Sewanee's 25 endowed internship funds, 150 students received a total of almost $300,000 in stipends or paid internships in 2007. Sewanee students interned in 20 states and 20 countries in 2007, and these endowed funds enabled the students to do meaningful internships that would otherwise have been unpaid.

FACILITIES

Housing: Coed dorms, special housing for disabled students, men's dorms, special housing for international students, women's dorms, fraternity/sorority housing, apartments for married students, cooperative housing, apartments for single students, wellness housing, theme housing, Substance-free housing & Living and Learning Communities. **Special Academic Facilities/Equipment:** Art gallery, observatory, keyboard collection, materials analysis lab with electron microscope. **Computers:** 80% of classrooms, 80% of dorms, 100% of libraries, 100% of dining areas, 100% of student union, 25% of common outdoor areas have wireless network access. Students can register for classes online. Administrative functions (other than registration) can be performed online.

CAMPUS LIFE

Environment: Rural. **Activities:** Choral groups, concert band, dance, drama/theater, jazz band, literary magazine, music ensembles, musical theater, radio station, student government, student newspaper, student-run film society, symphony orchestra, yearbook, Campus Ministries, International Student Organization, Model UN 110 registered organizations, 9 honor societies, 11 religious organizations. 12 fraternities, 9 sororities. **Athletics (Intercollegiate):** Men: baseball, basketball, cross-country, diving, equestrian sports, football, golf, lacrosse, soccer, swimming, tennis, track/field (outdoor), track/field (indoor). Women: basketball, cheerleading, cross-country, diving, equestrian sports, field hockey, golf, lacrosse, soccer, softball, swimming, tennis, track/field (outdoor), track/field (indoor), volleyball. **On-Campus Highlights:** Outdoor recreation on Sewanee's 10,000 a, All Saints' Chapel, Abbo's Alley Ravine Garden, Memorial Cross and University View, University Golf and Tennis Club. **Environmental Initiatives:** In pursuit of a goal from our 2008 Strategic Planning Addendum, our Sustainability Steering Committee is undertaking the development of a Sustainability Master Plan. The plan, the result of collaborative work of over 60 persons, is scheduled to be completed by May 2011. We are in serious pursuit of a variety of energy conservation and renewable energy initiatives outlined in our Climate Action Plan. Student education and involvement. The number of Environmental Studies majors has more than doubled since 2002; Sewanee Environmental Institute (summer program) began in 2009; co-curricular activites in GreenHouse, Sustain Sewanee, and research.

ADMISSIONS

Freshman Academic Profile: Average high school GPA 3.6. 35% in top 10% of high school class, 66% in top 25% of high school class, 93% in top 50% of high school class. 42% from public high schools. SAT Math middle 50% range 580-660. SAT Critical Reading middle 50% range 590-690. SAT Writing middle 50% range 570-660. ACT middle 50% range 26-30. Minimum web-based TOEFL 80. Minimum paper TOEFL 550. **Basis for Candidate Selection:** Very important factors considered include: academic GPA, recommendation(s), rigor of secondary school record. Important factors considered include: application essay, standardized test scores, character/personal qualities, extracurricular activities, volunteer work, work experience. Other factors considered include: Class rank, alumni/ae relation, first generation, geographical residence, interview, level of applicant's interest, racial/ethnic status, talent/ability. **Freshman Admission Requirements:** High school diploma is required and GED is not accepted. Academic units required: 4 English, 3 mathematics, 2 science, (2 science labs), 2 foreign language, 1 social studies, 1 history. Academic units recommended: 4 English, 3 mathematics, 2 science, (2 science labs), 2 foreign language, 1 social studies, 1 history. **Freshman Admission Statistics:** 3,369 applied, 59% admitted, 23% enrolled. **Transfer Admission Requirements:** High school transcript, college transcript(s), essay or personal statement, standardized test scores, statement of good standing from prior institution(s). Minimum college GPA of 3.00 required. Lowest grade transferable C. **General Admission Information:** Application Fee $45. Early decision application deadline 11/15. Regular application deadline 2/1. Regular notification 3/17. Nonfall registration not accepted. Admission may be deferred for a maximum

of 12 months. Credit and/or placement offered for CEEB Advanced Placement tests.

COSTS AND FINANCIAL AID

Annual tuition $34,442. Room and board $9,916. Required fees $272. Average book expense $800. **Required Forms and Deadlines:** FAFSA, institution's own financial aid form. **Notification of Awards:** Applicants will be notified of awards on or about 4/1. **Types of Aid:** Need-based scholarships/grants: Federal Pell, SEOG, state scholarships/grants, private scholarships, the school's own gift aid. Loans: Subsidized Stafford, Unsubsidized Stafford, PLUS, Federal Perkins, state loans, college/university loans from institutional funds, private alternative loans. **Student Employment:** Federal Work-Study Program available. Institutional employment available. Highest amount earned per year from on-campus jobs $1,500. Off-campus job opportunities are fair. **Financial Aid Statistics:** 98% freshmen, 96% undergrads receive need-based scholarship or grant aid. 80% freshmen, 72% undergrads receive need-based self-help aid. 71% freshmen, 73% undergrads receive any aid. 42% undergrads borrow to pay for school. Average cumulative indebtedness $32,609. **Criteria for awarding institutional aid:** Non-need-based: academics, minority status, religious affiliation.

SHASTA BIBLE COLLEGE

2951 Goodwater Ave., Redding, CA 96002
Phone: 530-221-4275
E-mail: admissions@shasta.edu
Fax: 530-221-6929 • **Website:** www.shasta.edu • **ACT Code:** 427

This private school, affiliated with the Baptist Church, was founded in 1970. It has a 63 acre campus.

RATINGS

Admissions Selectivity Rating: 61   **Fire Safety Rating:** 60*   **Green Rating:** 60*

STUDENTS AND FACULTY

Enrollment: 89. **Student Body:** 21% out-of-state, 3% international (5 countries represented). Asian 0%, African American 1%, Caucasian 73%, Hispanic 1%, Native American 0%.
Retention and Graduation: 40% freshmen return for sophomore year. 100% freshmen graduate within 4 years. 100% grads go on to further study within 1 year. 20% grads pursue arts and sciences degrees. **Faculty:** Student/faculty ratio 12:1. 7 full-time faculty, 71% hold PhDs, 14% are members of minority groups, 14% are women.

ACADEMICS

Degrees: associate, bachelor's, certificate, diploma, master's. **Classes:** Most classes have 10–19 students. **Majors with Highest Enrollment:** electrical, electronic and communications engineering technology/technician. **Special Study Options:** distance learning, double major, external degree program, independent study, teacher certification program, weekend college, Master's in School Administration. **Combined Degree Programs:** BA/MA. **Disability Services:** Special programs offered to physically disabled students include tutors.

FACILITIES

Housing: Coed dorms. 100% of campus accessible to physically disabled.

CAMPUS LIFE

Environment: Rural. **Activities:** radio station, student government, television station, yearbook.

ADMISSIONS

Freshman Academic Profile: 30% from public high schools. Minimum paper TOEFL 500. **Basis for Candidate Selection:** Very important factors considered include: application essay, recommendation(s), character/personal qualities, religious affiliation/commitment, volunteer work. Important factors considered include: extracurricular activities, work experience. Other factors considered include: Class rank, standardized test scores, alumni/ae relation, interview, talent/ability. **Freshman Admission Requirements:** High school diploma is required and GED is accepted. **Freshman Admission Statistics:** 38 applied, 100% admitted, 100% enrolled. **Transfer Admission Requirements:** High school transcript, college transcript(s), minimum college GPA of 2.0 required. Lowest grade transferable C. **General Admission Information:** Application Fee $35. Nonfall registration accepted. Admission may be deferred for a maximum of 1 Semester. Neither credit nor placement offered for CEEB Advanced Placement tests.

COSTS AND FINANCIAL AID

Annual tuition $5,300. Room and board $1,200. Required fees $135. Average book expense $250. **Notification of Awards:** Applicants will be notified of awards on a rolling basis beginning 1/2. **Types of Aid:** *Need-based scholarships/grants:* Federal Pell, state scholarships/grants. **Student Employment:** Federal Work-Study Program available. Highest amount earned per year from on-campus jobs $700. Off-campus job opportunities are excellent.

SHAW UNIVERSITY

118 East South Street, Raleigh, NC 27601
Phone: 919-546-8275 • **Financial Aid Phone:** 919-546-8240
E-mail: admissions@shawu.edu • **CEEB Code:** 5612
Fax: 919-546-8271 • **Website:** www.shawu.edu • **ACT Code:** 3158

This private school, affiliated with the Baptist Church, was founded in 1865. It has a 30-acre campus.

RATINGS
Admissions Selectivity Rating: 71   **Fire Safety Rating:** 60*   **Green Rating:** 60*

STUDENTS AND FACULTY
Enrollment: 2,649. **Student Body:** 64% female, 36% male, 36% out-of-state, 2% international (11 countries represented). Asian 0%, African American 85%, Caucasian 1%, Hispanic 0%, Native American 0%.
Retention and Graduation: 11% freshmen graduate within 4 years. 25% freshmen graduate within 6 years. **Faculty:** Student/faculty ratio 15:1. 112 full-time faculty, 63% hold PhDs, 84% are members of minority groups, 34% are women. 0% of classes are taught by teaching assistants.

ACADEMICS
Degrees: associate, bachelor's, first professional, master's. **Classes:** Most classes have fewer than 10 students. **Majors with Highest Enrollment:** business/commerce; criminal justice/safety studies; psychology. **Special Study Options:** Accelerated program, cross-registration, distance learning, double major, dual enrollment, honors program, independent study, internships, student-designed major, study abroad, teacher certification program, weekend college. **Disability Services:** Special programs offered to physically disabled students include tape recorders, tutors.

FACILITIES
Housing: men's dorms, women's dorms. **Special Academic Facilities/Equipment:** TV and film production facilities. Curriculum and Materials Center. **Computers:** Students can register for classes online. Administrative functions (other than registration) can be performed online.

CAMPUS LIFE
Environment: City. **Activities:** Choral groups, concert band, dance, drama/theater, jazz band, marching band, music ensembles, musical theater, pep band, radio station, student government, student newspaper, yearbook 4 honor societies, 4 fraternities, 4 sororities. **Athletics (Intercollegiate):** *Men:* baseball, basketball, cross-country, football, golf, tennis, track/field (outdoor), track/field (indoor). *Women:* basketball, bowling, cross-country, softball, tennis, track/field (outdoor), track/field (indoor), volleyball.

ADMISSIONS
Freshman Academic Profile: Average high school GPA 2.4. 2% in top 10% of high school class, 9% in top 25% of high school class, 33% in top 50% of high school class. 90% from public high schools. SAT Math middle 50% range 310-420. SAT Critical Reading middle 50% range 320-420. SAT Writing middle 50% range 330-420. ACT middle 50% range 12-17. **Basis for Candidate Selection:** *Very important factors considered include:* academic GPA, recommendation(s), first generation, geographical residence, level of applicant's interest. *Important factors considered include:* Class rank, application essay, rigor of secondary school record, standardized test scores, character/personal qualities, extracurricular activities, state residency, volunteer work, work experience. *Other factors considered include:* alumni/ae relation, talent/ability. **Freshman Admission Requirements:** High school diploma is required and GED is accepted. *Academic units required:* 3 English, 2 mathematics, 2 science, 2 social studies, 9 academic electives. 3 English, 2 mathematics, 2 science, 2 social studies, 9 academic electives. **Freshman Admission Statistics:** 5,361 applied, 49% admitted, 28% enrolled. **Transfer Admission Requirements:** college transcript(s), Lowest grade transferable C. **General Admission Information:** Application Fee $25. Regular application deadline 7/30. Notification on a rolling basis, beginning on or about 8/1. Nonfall registration accepted. Admission may be deferred for a maximum of indefinite. Credit and/or placement offered for CEEB Advanced Placement tests.

COSTS AND FINANCIAL AID

Required Forms and Deadlines: FAFSA, institution's own financial aid form, state aid form. **Notification of Awards:** Applicants will be notified of awards on a rolling basis beginning 2/1. **Types of Aid:** *Need-based scholarships/grants:* Federal Pell, SEOG, state scholarships/grants, private scholarships, the school's own gift aid, United Negro College Fund. *Loans:* Subsidized Stafford, Unsubsidized Stafford, PLUS, Federal Perkins. **Student Employment:** Federal Work-Study Program available. Institutional employment available. Off-campus job opportunities are excellent. **Criteria for awarding institutional aid:** *Non-need-based:* academics, alumni affiliation, art, athletics, music/drama, religious affiliation.

SHAWNEE STATE UNIVERSITY

940 Second Street, Portsmouth, OH 45662
Phone: 740-351-4778 • **Financial Aid Phone:** 740-351-4243
E-mail: to_ssu@shawnee.edu • **CEEB Code:** 1790
Fax: 740-351-3111 • **Website:** www.shawnee.edu • **ACT Code:** 3336

This public school was founded in 1986. It has a 50-acre campus.

RATINGS
Admissions Selectivity Rating: 67   **Fire Safety Rating:** 90   **Green Rating:** 61

STUDENTS AND FACULTY
Enrollment: 4,411. **Student Body:** 57% female, 43% male, 11% out-of-state, 1% international (21 countries represented). Asian 0%, African American 6%, Caucasian 85%, Hispanic 1%, Native American 1%.
Retention and Graduation: 49% freshmen return for sophomore year. 16% freshmen graduate within 4 years. 28% freshmen graduate within 6 years. 23% grads go on to further study within 1 year. 1% grads pursue law degrees. 3% grads pursue business degrees. 2% grads pursue medical degrees. **Faculty:** Student/faculty ratio 19:1. 152 full-time faculty, 59% hold PhDs, 8% are members of minority groups, 47% are women. 0% of classes are taught by teaching assistants.

ACADEMICS
Degrees: associate, bachelor's, certificate, master's. **Classes:** Most classes have 10–19 students. Most lab/discussion sessions have 20–29 students. **Majors with Highest Enrollment:** general studies; nursing/registered nurse (rn, asn, bsn, msn); psychology. **Special Study Options:** cross-registration, distance learning, double major, dual enrollment, English as a Second Language (ESL), honors program, independent study, internships, student-designed major, study abroad, teacher certification program. **Disability Services:** Special programs offered to physically disabled students include note-taking services, reader services, tape recorders, tutors. **Career Services:** alumni services, career/job search classes, career assessment, internships.

FACILITIES
Housing: Coed dorms, list of housing in community available. 100% of campus accessible to physically disabled. **Special Academic Facilities/Equipment:** Vern Riffe Center for the Arts **Computers:** Students can register for classes online.

CAMPUS LIFE
Environment: Town. **Activities:** Choral groups, drama/theater, literary magazine, music ensembles, musical theater, student government, student newspaper, Campus Ministries 36 registered organizations, 2 honor societies, 3 religious organizations. 1 fraternities, 1 sororities. **Athletics (Intercollegiate):** *Men:* baseball, basketball, cross-country, golf, soccer. *Women:* basketball, cross-country, soccer, softball, tennis, volleyball. **On-Campus Highlights:** Vern Riffe Center for the Arts, University Center **Environmental Initiatives:** geo-thermal chiller plant for new building single-stream recycle program pulper for food waste in new kitchen

ADMISSIONS
Freshman Academic Profile: 10% in top 10% of high school class, 28% in top 25% of high school class, 60% in top 50% of high school class. SAT Math middle 50% range 410-560. SAT Critical Reading middle 50% range 403-530. SAT Writing middle 50% range 383-510. ACT middle 50% range 17-23. Minimum web-based TOEFL 60. Minimum paper TOEFL 500. **Freshman Admission Requirements:** High school diploma is required and GED is accepted. **Freshman Admission Statistics:** 4,340 applied, 82% admitted, 33% enrolled. **Transfer Admission Requirements:** High school transcript, college transcript(s), minimum college GPA of 1.0 required. Lowest grade transferable D. **General Admission Information:** Nonfall registration accepted. Admission may be deferred for a maximum of one year. Credit and/or placement offered for CEEB Advanced Placement tests.

COSTS AND FINANCIAL AID

Annual in-state tuition $5,918. Annual out-of-state tuition $10,893. Room and board $9,012. Required fees $1,070. Average book expense $1,440. **Required Forms and Deadlines:** FAFSA, institution's own financial aid form. **Notification of Awards:** Applicants will be notified of awards on a rolling basis beginning 5/1. **Types of Aid:** *Need-based scholarships/grants:* Federal Pell, SEOG, state scholarships/grants, private scholarships, the school's own gift aid. *Loans:* Subsidized Stafford, Unsubsidized Stafford, PLUS, state loans. **Student Employment:** Off-campus job opportunities are fair. **Criteria for awarding institutional aid:** *Non-need-based:* academics, art, athletics, minority status, music/drama, state/district residency.

SHENANDOAH UNIVERSITY

1460 University Drive, Winchester, VA 22601-5195
Phone: 540-665-4581 • **Financial Aid Phone:** 540-665-4538
E-mail: admit@su.edu • **CEEB Code:** 5613
Fax: 540-665-4627 • **Website:** www.su.edu • **ACT Code:** 4396

This private school, affiliated with the Methodist Church, was founded in 1875. It has a 100-acre campus.

RATINGS

Admissions Selectivity Rating: 67   **Fire Safety Rating:** 97   **Green Rating:** 85

STUDENTS AND FACULTY

Enrollment: 1,902. **Student Body:** 56% female, 44% male, 36% out-of-state, 4% international (70 countries represented) Asian 4%, African American 13%, Caucasian 68%, Hispanic 3%, Native American 2%.
Retention and Graduation: Faculty: Student/faculty ratio 10:1. 229 full-time faculty, 72% hold PhDs, 9% are members of minority groups, 54% are women. 1% of classes are taught by teaching assistants.

ACADEMICS

Degrees: associate, bachelor's, certificate, first professional, master's, post-bachelor's certificate, post-master's certificate, terminal associate. **Classes:** Most classes have 10–19 students. Most lab/discussion sessions have fewer than 10 students. **Majors with Highest Enrollment:** business/commerce; drama and dramatics/theatre arts; nursing/registered nurse (rn, asn, bsn, msn). **Special Study Options:** Accelerated program, cooperative education program, distance learning, double major, English as a Second Language (ESL), independent study, internships, liberal arts/career combination, student-designed major, study abroad, teacher certification program, weekend college. **Combined Degree Programs:** Pharmacy/MBA; DPT/MBA; DPT/Athletic Training. **Disability Services:** Special programs offered to physically disabled students include note-taking services, reader services, tape recorders, tutors.

FACILITIES

Housing: Coed dorms, special housing for disabled students, special housing for international students 91% of campus accessible to physically disabled. **Special Academic Facilities/Equipment:** None **Computers:** 100% of classrooms, 100% of dorms, 100% of libraries, 100% of dining areas, 100% of student union, 25% of common outdoor areas have wireless network access. Students can register for classes online. Administrative functions (other than registration) can be performed online.

CAMPUS LIFE

Environment: Town. **Activities:** Choral groups, concert band, dance, drama/theater, jazz band, music ensembles, musical theater, opera, radio station, student government, student newspaper, symphony orchestra, television station 65 registered organizations, 2 honor societies, 2 religious organizations. 7 fraternities, 1 sororities. **Athletics (Intercollegiate):** *Men:* baseball, basketball, cross-country, football, golf, lacrosse, soccer, tennis. *Women:* basketball, cross-country, field hockey, lacrosse, soccer, softball, tennis, volleyball. **On-Campus Highlights:** Ohrstrom-Bryant Theatre, Aikens Athletic Center, Alson H. Smith, Jr. Library, Health Professions Building, Goodson Chapel/Recital Hall. **Environmental Initiatives:** Green space reclamation/campus renovation projects Relamping of all campus lighting Transportation including downsizing of campus fleet and purchase of electric and hybrid vehicles

ADMISSIONS

Freshman Academic Profile: Average high school GPA 3.4. SAT Math middle 50% range 450-570. SAT Critical Reading middle 50% range 440-550. SAT Writing middle 50% range 430-548. ACT middle 50% range 19-25. Minimum web-based TOEFL 61. Minimum paper TOEFL 500. **Basis for Candidate Selection:** *Very important factors considered include:* academic GPA, rigor of secondary school record, interview, talent/ability. *Important factors considered*

include: recommendation(s), standardized test scores, extracurricular activities, volunteer work. *Other factors considered include:* application essay, character/personal qualities, level of applicant's interest, work experience. **Freshman Admission Requirements:** High school diploma is required and GED is accepted. *Academic units required:* 4 English, 3 mathematics, 2 science, (1 science labs), 2 foreign language, 2 social studies, 2 history, 2 academic electives. *Academic units recommended:* 4 English, 3 mathematics, 2 science, (1 science labs), 2 foreign language, 2 social studies, 2 history, 2 academic electives. **Freshman Admission Statistics:** 1,833 applied, 85% admitted, 30% enrolled. **Transfer Admission Requirements:** college transcript(s), statement of good standing from prior institution(s). Minimum college GPA of 2.0 required. Lowest grade transferable C. **General Admission Information:** Application Fee $30. Regular notification 8/7. Notification on a rolling basis, beginning on or about 10/6. Nonfall registration accepted. Admission may be deferred for a maximum of 12 months. Credit and/or placement offered for CEEB Advanced Placement tests.

COSTS AND FINANCIAL AID

Average book expense $1,500. **Required Forms and Deadlines:** FAFSA, state aid form. **Notification of Awards:** Applicants will be notified of awards on a rolling basis beginning 3/15. **Types of Aid:** *Need-based scholarships/grants:* Federal Pell, SEOG, state scholarships/grants, private scholarships, the school's own gift aid, Federal Nursing Scholarships. *Loans:* Direct Subsidized Stafford, Direct Unsubsidized Stafford, Direct PLUS, Federal Perkins, Federal Nursing, college/university loans from institutional funds. **Student Employment:** Highest amount earned per year from on-campus jobs $1,500. **Financial Aid Statistics:** 100% freshmen, 100% undergrads receive need-based scholarship or grant aid. 100% freshmen, 100% undergrads receive non-need-based scholarship or grant aid. 97% freshmen, 98% undergrads receive need-based self-help aid. 85% freshmen, 85% undergrads receive any aid. 85% undergrads borrow to pay for school. Average cumulative indebtedness $3,100. **Criteria for awarding institutional aid:** *Non-need-based:* academics, job skills, music/drama, religious affiliation, state/district residency.

SHEPHERD UNIVERSITY

Office of Admissions, Shepherdstown, WV 25443-5000
Phone: 304-876-5212 • **Financial Aid Phone:** 304-876-5470
E-mail: admissions@shepherd.edu • **CEEB Code:** 5615
Fax: 304-876-5165 • **Website:** www.shepherd.edu • **ACT Code:** 4532

This public school was founded in 1871. It has a 323-acre campus.

RATINGS

Admissions Selectivity Rating: 69   **Fire Safety Rating:** 77   **Green Rating:** 61

STUDENTS AND FACULTY

Enrollment: 3,852. **Student Body:** 58% female, 42% male, 37% out-of-state, 0% international (15 countries represented). Asian 2%, African American 7%, Caucasian 82%, Hispanic 3%, Native American 1%.
Retention and Graduation: 63% freshmen return for sophomore year. 20% freshmen graduate within 4 years. 43% freshmen graduate within 6 years. 43% grads go on to further study within 1 year. 56% grads pursue arts and sciences degrees. 23% grads pursue business degrees. 7% grads pursue medical degrees. **Faculty:** Student/faculty ratio 18:1. 142 full-time faculty, 85% hold PhDs, 13% are members of minority groups, 44% are women. 0% of classes are taught by teaching assistants.

ACADEMICS

Degrees: bachelor's, master's. **Classes:** Most classes have 20–29 students. Most lab/discussion sessions have 20–29 students. **Majors with Highest Enrollment:** business/commerce; nursing/registered nurse (rn, asn, bsn, msn); teacher education, multiple levels. **Special Study Options:** cooperative education program, double major, dual enrollment, honors program, independent study, internships, study abroad, teacher certification program. **Honors Programs:** See Honors Program on Web site www.shepherd.edu **Combined Degree Programs:** MedStep with WVU School of Medicine. **Disability Services:** Special programs offered to physically disabled students include note-taking services, reader services, tape recorders, tutors. **Career Services:** Alumni network, alumni services, career/job search classes, career assessment, internships, regional alumni.

FACILITIES

Housing: Coed dorms, special housing for disabled students, apartments for single students, theme housing, suites, first-year housing. 90% of campus accessible to physically disabled. **Special Academic Facilities/Equipment:** Nursery school, elementary education lab, art gallery, theaters, Fazioli Concert

Grand Piano, George Tyler Moore Center for the Study of the Civil War, Robert C. Byrd Center for Legislative Studies **Computers:** 90% of classrooms, 100% of libraries, 100% of dining areas, 100% of student union, 1% of common outdoor areas have wireless network access. Students can register for classes on-line. Administrative functions (other than registration) can be performed online.

CAMPUS LIFE
Environment: Village. **Activities:** Choral groups, concert band, drama/theater, jazz band, literary magazine, marching band, music ensembles, musical theater, pep band, radio station, student government, student newspaper, symphony orchestra, Campus Ministries, International Student Organization 85 registered organizations, 9 honor societies, 4 religious organizations. 4 fraternities, 3 sororities. **Athletics (Intercollegiate):** *Men:* baseball, basketball, football, golf, soccer, tennis. *Women:* basketball, lacrosse, soccer, softball, tennis, volleyball. **On-Campus Highlights:** Butcher Athletic Center, Center for Contemporary Arts, Scarborough Library, Wellness Center, Student Center. **Environmental Initiatives:** Recycling Upgrading HVAC equipment Constructing new buildings to LEED standards

ADMISSIONS
Freshman Academic Profile: Average high school GPA 3.2. 97% from public high schools. SAT Math middle 50% range 450-540. SAT Critical Reading middle 50% range 460-560. ACT middle 50% range 19-24. Minimum web-based TOEFL 79. Minimum paper TOEFL 550. **Basis for Candidate Selection:** *Very important factors considered include:* academic GPA, rigor of secondary school record, standardized test scores. *Important factors considered include:* talent/ability. *Other factors considered include:* Class rank, application essay, recommendation(s), alumni/ae relation, character/personal qualities, extracurricular activities, interview, level of applicant's interest. **Freshman Admission Requirements:** High school diploma is required and GED is accepted. *Academic units required:* 4 English, 4 mathematics, 3 science, (3 science labs), 2 foreign language, 2 social studies, 1 history, 1 visual/performing arts, 5 academic electives. 4 English, 4 mathematics, 3 science, (3 science labs), 2 foreign language, 2 social studies, 1 history, 1 visual/performing arts, 5 academic electives. **Freshman Admission Statistics:** 2,023 applied, 81% admitted, 46% enrolled. **Transfer Admission Requirements:** college transcript(s), minimum college GPA of 2.0 required. Lowest grade transferable D. **General Admission Information:** Application Fee $45. Regular application deadline 8/15. Notification on a rolling basis, beginning on or about 9/15. Nonfall registration accepted. Admission may be deferred for a maximum of 12 months. Credit and/or placement offered for CEEB Advanced Placement tests.

COSTS AND FINANCIAL AID
Annual in-state tuition $5,834. Annual out-of-state tuition $15,136. Room and board $8,424. Average book expense $1,000. **Required Forms and Deadlines:** FAFSA, state aid form. **Notification of Awards:** Applicants will be notified of awards on a rolling basis beginning 3/15. **Types of Aid:** *Need-based scholarships/grants:* Federal Pell, SEOG, state scholarships/grants, private scholarships, the school's own gift aid. *Loans:* Direct Subsidized Stafford, Direct Unsubsidized Stafford, Direct PLUS, Federal Perkins. **Student Employment:** Federal Work-Study Program available. Institutional employment available. Highest amount earned per year from on-campus jobs $12,181. Off-campus job opportunities are good. **Financial Aid Statistics:** 66% freshmen, 69% undergrads receive need-based scholarship or grant aid. 45% freshmen, 28% undergrads receive non-need-based scholarship or grant aid. 68% freshmen, 78% undergrads receive need-based self-help aid. 8% freshmen, 6% undergrads receive athletic scholarships. 91% freshmen, 80% undergrads receive any aid. 69% undergrads borrow to pay for school. Average cumulative indebtedness $23,940. **Criteria for awarding institutional aid:** *Non-need-based:* academics, art, athletics, job skills, leadership, minority status, music/drama, state/district residency.

SHIMER COLLEGE

Shimer College, Chicago, IL 60616
Phone: 312-235-3506 • **Financial Aid Phone:** 312-235-3507
E-mail: admission@shimer.edu • **CEEB Code:** 1717
Fax: 312-235-3501 • **Website:** shimer.edu • **ACT Code:** 1142

This private school was founded in 1853. It has a 140-acre campus.

RATINGS
Admissions Selectivity Rating: 80   **Fire Safety Rating:** 60*   **Green Rating:** 65

STUDENTS AND FACULTY
Enrollment: 125. **Student Body:** 48% female, 52% male, 52% out-of-state, 0% international (4 countries represented). Asian 4%, African American 2%, Caucasian 78%, Hispanic 4%, Native American 0%.

Retention and Graduation: 84% freshmen return for sophomore year. **Faculty:** Student/faculty ratio 9:1. 11 full-time faculty, 100% hold PhDs, 18% are members of minority groups, 36% are women. 0% of classes are taught by teaching assistants.

ACADEMICS
Degrees: bachelor's. **Classes:** Most classes have 10-19 students. **Majors with Highest Enrollment:** humanities/humanistic studies; natural sciences; social sciences. **Special Study Options:** cross-registration, double major, independent study, internships, liberal arts/career combination, study abroad, weekend college, one-on-one tutorials with faculty member for in depth study in any area of interest to the student. **Combined Degree Programs:** BA/JD. **Career Services:** Alumni network, alumni services, career/job search classes, internships, regional alumni. Career Services highlights include Shimer students may intern off campus during their program. Funded internships are available.

FACILITIES
Housing: Coed dorms, women's dorms, apartments for married students, apartments for single students. 100% of campus accessible to physically disabled. **Special Academic Facilities/Equipment:** The Galvin Library has over one million volumes and 120 digital databases. The MTCC (student center) is an amazing place to eat, play and hang out. **Computers:** 100% of classrooms, 100% of dorms, 100% of libraries, 100% of dining areas, 100% of student union, 100% of common outdoor areas have wireless network access.

CAMPUS LIFE
Environment: Metropolis. **Activities:** Choral groups, concert band, drama/theater, jazz band, literary magazine, music ensembles, radio station, student government, student newspaper, International Student Organization 10 religious organizations. **On-Campus Highlights:** The Shimer College space on the IIT Camp, The Galvin Library/Art Galery, McCormic Tribune Campus Center, Crown Hall, Keating Sports Center, Students are strongly encouraged to visit when classes are in session. The best way to know if Shimer is a good fit for you is if you sit in on a class!.

ADMISSIONS
Freshman Academic Profile: Average high school GPA 3.1. 50% from public high schools. SAT Math middle 50% range 490-570. SAT Critical Reading middle 50% range 620-710. SAT Writing middle 50% range 500-690. ACT middle 50% range 26-29. Minimum paper TOEFL 625. **Basis for Candidate Selection:** *Very important factors considered include:* application essay, recommendation(s), interview, level of applicant's interest. *Important factors considered include:* rigor of secondary school record, character/personal qualities, talent/ability, volunteer work. *Other factors considered include:* Class rank, academic GPA, standardized test scores, alumni/ae relation, extracurricular activities, first generation, geographical residence, work experience. **Freshman Admission Requirements:** High school diploma or equivalent is not required. **Freshman Admission Statistics:** 31 applied, 74% admitted, 35% enrolled. **Transfer Admission Requirements:** college transcript(s), essay or personal statement, interview, Lowest grade transferable C. **General Admission Information:** Application Fee $25. Regular application deadline 8/1. Notification on a rolling basis, beginning on or about 9/15. Nonfall registration accepted. Admission may be deferred for a maximum of 2 years. Neither credit nor placement offered for CEEB Advanced Placement tests.

COSTS AND FINANCIAL AID
Annual tuition $26,510. Room and board $10,626. Required fees $4,720. Average book expense $800. **Required Forms and Deadlines:** FAFSA, institution's own financial aid form. **Notification of Awards:** Applicants will be notified of awards on a rolling basis beginning 2/1. **Types of Aid:** *Need-based scholarships/grants:* Federal Pell, SEOG, state scholarships/grants, private scholarships, the school's own gift aid. *Loans:* Subsidized Stafford, Unsubsidized Stafford, PLUS, Federal Perkins. **Student Employment:** Federal Work-Study Program available. Institutional employment available. Highest amount earned per year from on-campus jobs $1,500. Off-campus job opportunities are excellent. **Financial Aid Statistics:** 100% freshmen, 100% undergrads receive need-based scholarship or grant aid. 79% freshmen, 46% undergrads receive non-need-based scholarship or grant aid. 100% freshmen, 100% undergrads receive need-based self-help aid. 74% freshmen, 84% undergrads receive any aid. 100% undergrads borrow to pay for school. Average cumulative indebtedness $30,000. **Criteria for awarding institutional aid:** *Non-need-based:* academics, alumni affiliation.

SHIPPENSBURG UNIVERSITY OF PENNSYLVANIA

Old Main 105, Shippensburg, PA 17257-2299
Phone: 717-477-1231 • **Financial Aid Phone:** 717-477-1131
E-mail: admiss@ship.edu • **CEEB Code:** 2657
Fax: 717-477-4016 • **Website:** www.ship.edu • **ACT Code:** 3714

This public school was founded in 1871. It has a 200-acre campus.

RATINGS
Admissions Selectivity Rating: 68   **Fire Safety Rating:** 87   **Green Rating:** 72

STUDENTS AND FACULTY
Enrollment: 6,654. **Student Body:** 50% female, 50% male, 6% out-of-state, 0% international (26 countries represented). Asian 1%, African American 8%, Caucasian 82%, Hispanic 3%, Native American 0%.
Retention and Graduation: 70% freshmen return for sophomore year. 40% freshmen graduate within 4 years. 57% freshmen graduate within 6 years.
Faculty: Student/faculty ratio 20:1. 329 full-time faculty, 88% hold PhDs, 14% are members of minority groups, 44% are women. 0% of classes are taught by teaching assistants.

ACADEMICS
Degrees: bachelor's, certificate, master's, post-bachelor's certificate, post-master's certificate. **Classes:** Most classes have 20–29 students. Most lab/discussion sessions have 10–19 students. **Majors with Highest Enrollment:** criminal justice/safety studies; elementary education and teaching; psychology. **Special Study Options:** Accelerated program, cooperative education program, distance learning, double major, dual enrollment, honors program, independent study, internships, study abroad, teacher certification program, Raider Plan. **Honors Programs:** Program in General Education and Psychology **Combined Degree Programs:** 3-2 EngProg/PSU and U of Md; Chem and Bio/Med Tech. **Disability Services:** Special programs offered to physically disabled students include note-taking services, reader services, tape recorders, tutors. **Career Services:** Alumni network, alumni services, career/job search classes, career assessment, internships, regional alumni. Career Services highlights include Pennsylvania has been working to transform itself from a manufacturing economy to a diversified service-based economy with strength in technology intensive industries. Pennsylvania's workforce development strategy seeks to align education and training to High Priority Occupations (HPOs), which are fields with identified skill needs and job openings. Internships are a vital link between education and employment. Shippensburg University, and each of the 14 Pennsylvania State System of Higher Education (PASSHE) Universities, received a $30,000 grant to increase internships in the Commonwealth during the 2007-2008 and 2008-2009 academic years. This Economic Development-Internships grant program is designed to help meet the Commonwealth goals to develop and retain employment in the state. The grant project will enhance resources for all stakeholders by increasing university-wide coordination and institutional capacity to manage and increase internships. Student teaching, practicuums, field experiences, and internships are offered by all three colleges at both the undergraduate and graduate levels. Students gain professional experience directly related to their major by working part- or full-time during the fall or spring semesters or during the summer. Students earn credit based upon the number of hours worked; they are supervised by a faculty advisor and are expected to develop a rapport with their employer to fully understand and satisfy the duties and responsibilities of their assignment. Students are expected to complete a variety of academic assignments related to their experience and in a number of programs, also participate in a seminar course associated with their experiential learning placement. Responsibility for assessment rests within the academic departments and is incorporated into departmental five-year program reviews.

FACILITIES
Housing: Coed dorms, wellness housing, theme housing, suites, Apartment Complex Off-Campus. 91% of campus accessible to physically disabled. **Special Academic Facilities/Equipment:** art gallery, vertebrate museum, on-campus elementary school, planetarium, electron microscope, NMR spectrometer, greenhouse, herbarium,Fashion Archives, Women's Center, Closed Circuit TV **Computers:** 95% of classrooms, 10% of dorms, 100% of libraries, 100% of dining areas, 95% of student union, 75% of common outdoor areas have wireless network access. Students can register for classes online. Administrative functions (other than registration) can be performed online.

CAMPUS LIFE
Environment: Village. **Activities:** Choral groups, concert band, dance, drama/theater, jazz band, literary magazine, marching band, music ensembles, musical theater, radio station, student government, student newspaper, television station, yearbook, Campus Ministries, International Student Organization 200 registered organizations, 23 honor societies, 8 religious organizations. 12 fraternities, 15 sororities. **Athletics (Intercollegiate):** *Men:* baseball, basketball, cross-country, football, soccer, swimming, track/field (outdoor), track/field (indoor), wrestling. *Women:* basketball, cross-country, field hockey, lacrosse, soccer, softball, swimming, tennis, track/field (outdoor), track/field (indoor), volleyball. **On-Campus Highlights:** Ceddia Union Building, Heiges Field House, Student Recreation Center, Ritazza Coffee Shop, Student Fitness Center, Starbucks, Quiznos, Chick-fil-A, Dauphin Humanities Center, Lehman Library, Learning Assistant Center, Reisner Dining Hall. **Environmental Initiatives:** Energy Conservation Iniatives Go green carbon footprint analysis 1. CUB Leed Certification 2. Solar panels at Reisner Dining Hall 3. LEED Certification of new student housing.

ADMISSIONS
Freshman Academic Profile: Average high school GPA 3.2. 8% in top 10% of high school class, 26% in top 25% of high school class, 59% in top 50% of high school class. 89% from public high schools. SAT Math middle 50% range 440-550. SAT Critical Reading middle 50% range 440-530. SAT Writing middle 50% range 420-520. ACT middle 50% range 17-22. Minimum web-based TOEFL 66. Minimum paper TOEFL 550. **Basis for Candidate Selection:** *Very important factors considered include:* Class rank, academic GPA, rigor of secondary school record, standardized test scores.*Other factors considered include:* application essay, recommendation(s), character/personal qualities, extracurricular activities, interview, level of applicant's interest, talent/ability, volunteer work, work experience. **Freshman Admission Requirements:** High school diploma is required and GED is accepted. **Freshman Admission Statistics:** 6,402 applied, 81% admitted, 29% enrolled. **Transfer Admission Requirements:** college transcript(s), statement of good standing from prior institution(s). Minimum college GPA of 2.2 required. Lowest grade transferable C. **General Admission Information:** Application Fee $30. Nonfall registration accepted. Admission may be deferred for a maximum of 1 year. Credit and/or placement offered for CEEB Advanced Placement tests.

COSTS AND FINANCIAL AID
Annual in-state tuition $6,428. Annual out-of-state tuition $14,464. Room and board $7,910. Required fees $2,726. Average book expense $1,200. **Required Forms and Deadlines:** FAFSA. **Types of Aid:** *Need-based scholarships/grants:* Federal Pell, SEOG, state scholarships/grants, private scholarships, the school's own gift aid, Academic Competitiveness Grant (ACG)and Smart Grant. *Loans:* Subsidized Stafford, Unsubsidized Stafford, PLUS, Federal Perkins, Alternative loans. **Student Employment:** Federal Work-Study Program available. Off-campus job opportunities are good. **Financial Aid Statistics:** 69% freshmen, 68% undergrads receive need-based scholarship or grant aid. 3% freshmen, 3% undergrads receive non-need-based scholarship or grant aid. 95% freshmen, 95% undergrads receive need-based self-help aid. 4% freshmen, 4% undergrads receive athletic scholarships. 91% freshmen, 86% undergrads receive any aid. 78% undergrads borrow to pay for school. Average cumulative indebtedness $27,661. **Criteria for awarding institutional aid:** *Non-need-based:* academics, athletics.

SHORTER COLLEGE

315 Shorter Avenue, Rome, GA 30165
Phone: 706-233-7319 • **Financial Aid Phone:** 706-233-7227
E-mail: admissions@shorter.edu • **CEEB Code:** 5616
Fax: 706-233-7224 • **Website:** www.shorter.edu • **ACT Code:** 860

This private school, affiliated with the Southern Baptist Church, was founded in 1873. It has a 150-acre campus.

RATINGS
Admissions Selectivity Rating: 74   **Fire Safety Rating:** 76   **Green Rating:** 61

STUDENTS AND FACULTY
Enrollment: 1,581. **Student Body:** 55% female, 45% male, 12% out-of-state, 3% international (22 countries represented). Asian 1%, African American 17%, Caucasian 69%, Hispanic 4%, Native American 0%.
Retention and Graduation: 68% freshmen return for sophomore year. 33% freshmen graduate within 4 years. 43% freshmen graduate within 6 years. 30% grads go on to further study within 1 year. **Faculty:** Student/faculty ratio 13:1. 92 full-time faculty, 70% hold PhDs, 9% are members of minority groups, 50% are women. 0% of classes are taught by teaching assistants.

ACADEMICS
Degrees: bachelor's. **Classes:** Most classes have 10–19 students. Most lab/discussion sessions have 10–19 students. **Majors with Highest Enrollment:**

business administration and management; education; visual and performing arts. **Special Study Options:** cross-registration, double major, dual enrollment, honors program, independent study, internships, student-designed major, study abroad, teacher certification program, weekend college. **Honors Programs:** Academy of Aristaeus: a four-year honors program featuring seminar discussions and a research project. **Disability Services:** Special programs offered to physically disabled students include note-taking services, reader services, tape recorders, tutors. **Career Services:** career/job search classes, career assessment, Career Services highlights include Most majors include required internships.

FACILITIES

Housing: men's dorms, women's dorms, apartments for single students. 70% of campus accessible to physically disabled. **Special Academic Facilities/Equipment:** Shorter History Museum **Computers:** Students can register for classes online. Administrative functions (other than registration) can be performed online.

CAMPUS LIFE

Environment: Town. **Activities:** Choral groups, concert band, dance, drama/theater, literary magazine, marching band, music ensembles, musical theater, opera, pep band, radio station, student government, student newspaper, student-run film society, yearbook, Campus Ministries, International Student Organization, Model UN 34 registered organizations, 10 honor societies, 3 religious organizations. 3 fraternities, 3 sororities. **Athletics (Intercollegiate):** *Men:* baseball, basketball, cheerleading, cross-country, football, golf, soccer, tennis, track/field (outdoor). *Women:* basketball, cheerleading, cross-country, golf, lacrosse, soccer, softball, tennis, track/field (outdoor), volleyball. **On-Campus Highlights:** Fitton Student Union, Winthrop-King Activities Center, Brookes Chapel, Ledbetter Baseball Complex .

ADMISSIONS

Freshman Academic Profile: Average high school GPA 3.3. 21% in top 10% of high school class, 47% in top 25% of high school class, 77% in top 50% of high school class. 95% from public high schools. SAT Math middle 50% range 430-550. SAT Critical Reading middle 50% range 420-550. SAT Writing middle 50% range 410-530. ACT middle 50% range 18-24. Minimum paper TOEFL 500. **Basis for Candidate Selection:** *Very important factors considered include:* academic GPA, standardized test scores. *Important factors considered include:* Class rank, application essay, rigor of secondary school record, talent/ability. *Other factors considered include:* recommendation(s), alumni/ae relation, character/personal qualities, extracurricular activities, first generation, interview, level of applicant's interest, volunteer work, work experience. **Freshman Admission Requirements:** High school diploma is required and GED is accepted. *Academic units required:* 4 English, 4 mathematics, 3 science, 2 foreign language, 3 history. 4 English, 4 mathematics, 3 science, 2 foreign language, 3 history. **Freshman Admission Statistics:** 1,944 applied, 65% admitted, 32% enrolled. **Transfer Admission Requirements:** college transcript(s), statement of good standing from prior institution(s). Minimum college GPA of 2.0 required. Lowest grade transferable C. **General Admission Information:** Application Fee $25. Notification on a rolling basis, beginning on or about 11/1. Nonfall registration accepted. Admission may be deferred for a maximum of 2 YEARS. Credit and/or placement offered for CEEB Advanced Placement tests.

COSTS AND FINANCIAL AID

Annual tuition $17,500. Room and board $8,600. Required fees $370. Average book expense $1,200. **Required Forms and Deadlines:** FAFSA, institution's own financial aid form, state aid form. **Notification of Awards:** Applicants will be notified of awards on a rolling basis beginning 4/1. **Types of Aid:** *Need-based scholarships/grants:* Federal Pell, SEOG, state scholarships/grants, private scholarships, the school's own gift aid. *Loans:* Subsidized Stafford, Unsubsidized Stafford, PLUS, Federal Perkins, We have moved to using Direct Loans from the US Government. **Student Employment:** Federal Work-Study Program available. Institutional employment available. Highest amount earned per year from on-campus jobs $2,000. Off-campus job opportunities are good. **Financial Aid Statistics:** 99% freshmen, 99% undergrads receive need-based scholarship or grant aid. 16% freshmen, 15% undergrads receive non-need-based scholarship or grant aid. 79% freshmen, 75% undergrads receive need-based self-help aid. 15% freshmen, 11% undergrads receive athletic scholarships. 99% freshmen, 99% undergrads receive any aid. 93% undergrads borrow to pay for school. Average cumulative indebtedness $25,441. **Criteria for awarding institutional aid:** *Non-need-based:* academics, art, athletics, music/drama, religious affiliation.

SIENA COLLEGE

515 Loudon Road, Loudonville, NY 12211
Phone: 518-783-2423 • **Financial Aid Phone:** 888-287-4362
E-mail: admit@siena.edu • **CEEB Code:** 2814
Fax: 518-783-2436 • **Website:** www.siena.edu • **ACT Code:** 2878

This private school, affiliated with the Roman Catholic Church, was founded in 1937. It has a 166-acre campus.

RATINGS
Admissions Selectivity Rating: 85   **Fire Safety Rating:** 89   **Green Rating:** 61

STUDENTS AND FACULTY
Enrollment: 3,149. **Student Body:** 52% female, 48% male, 19% out-of-state, 2% international (14 countries represented). Asian 4%, African American 3%, Caucasian 82%, Hispanic 6%, Native American 0%.
Retention and Graduation: 89% freshmen return for sophomore year. 69% freshmen graduate within 4 years. 31% grads go on to further study within 1 year. 9% grads pursue arts and sciences degrees. 4% grads pursue law degrees. 5% grads pursue business degrees. 2% grads pursue medical degrees. **Faculty:** Student/faculty ratio 12:1. 210 full-time faculty, 89% hold PhDs, 8% are members of minority groups, 42% are women. 0% of classes are taught by teaching assistants.

ACADEMICS
Degrees: bachelor's, certificate. **Classes:** Most classes have 20–29 students. Most lab/discussion sessions have 10–19 students. **Majors with Highest Enrollment:** finance; marketing/marketing management; psychology. **Special Study Options:** Accelerated program, cross-registration, double major, English as a Second Language (ESL), honors program, independent study, internships, liberal arts/career combination, study abroad, teacher certification program, Semester in Washington D.C., Gettysburg Semester. **Honors Programs:** College-wide Honors program. **Combined Degree Programs:** BA/MD, BA/JD, BA/MA, BA/DDS, BA/MEng, BBA/MBA. **Disability Services:** Special programs offered to physically disabled students include note-taking services, reader services, tape recorders, tutors. **Career Services:** Alumni network, alumni services, career/job search classes, career assessment, internships, regional alumni. Career Services highlights include Students at Siena cultivate internships in almost every field.

FACILITIES
Housing: Coed dorms, special housing for disabled students, special housing for international students, apartments for single students, Quiet Living Area available; on-campus townhouses (men and women). 90% of campus accessible to physically disabled. **Special Academic Facilities/Equipment:** Hickey Financial Center **Computers:** 20% of classrooms, 40% of dorms, 100% of libraries, 100% of dining areas, 100% of student union, have wireless network access. Students can register for classes online. Administrative functions (other than registration) can be performed online.

CAMPUS LIFE
Environment: Town. **Activities:** Choral groups, dance, drama/theater, literary magazine, musical theater, opera, pep band, radio station, student government, student newspaper, symphony orchestra, television station, yearbook, Campus Ministries, Model UN 70 registered organizations, 15 honor societies, 2 religious organizations. **Athletics (Intercollegiate):** *Men:* baseball, basketball, cross-country, golf, lacrosse, soccer, tennis. *Women:* basketball, cross-country, field hockey, golf, lacrosse, soccer, softball, swimming, tennis, volleyball, water polo. **On-Campus Highlights:** Sarazen Student Union, J. Spencer and Patricia Standish Library, MAC/ARC - Athletic Facilities, Siena Hall, Academic Quad, Hickey Financial Technical Center.

ADMISSIONS
Freshman Academic Profile: 89.6. 22% in top 10% of high school class, 57% in top 25% of high school class, 89% in top 50% of high school class. % from public high schools. SAT Math middle 50% range 520-620. SAT Critical Reading middle 50% range 500-600. SAT Writing middle 50% range 500-600. ACT middle 50% range 22-27. Minimum web-based TOEFL 79. Minimum paper TOEFL 550. **Basis for Candidate Selection:** *Very important factors considered include:* academic GPA, rigor of secondary school record. *Important factors considered include:* recommendation(s), standardized test scores. *Other factors considered include:* Class rank, application essay, alumni/ae relation, character/personal qualities, extracurricular activities, first generation, interview, level of applicant's interest, racial/ethnic status, talent/ability, volunteer work, work experience. **Freshman Admission Requirements:** High school diploma is required and GED is accepted. *Academic units required:* 4 English, 3 mathematics, 3 science, (3 science labs), 1 social studies, 2 history. *Academic units recommended:* 4 English, 3 mathematics, 3 science, (3 science labs), 1 social studies, 2 history. **Freshman Admission Statistics:** 9,577 applied, 57% admit-

ted, 13% enrolled. **Transfer Admission Requirements:** college transcript(s), statement of good standing from prior institution(s). Minimum college GPA of 2.5 required. Lowest grade transferable C+. **General Admission Information:** Application Fee $50. Early decision application deadline 12/1. Regular application deadline 3/1. Regular notification 3/15. Nonfall registration accepted. Admission may be deferred for a maximum of 1 year. Credit and/or placement offered for CEEB Advanced Placement tests.

COSTS AND FINANCIAL AID

Annual tuition $28,665. Room and board $11,970. Required fees $250. Average book expense $1,250. **Required Forms and Deadlines:** FAFSA, state aid form. **Notification of Awards:** Applicants will be notified of awards on or about 4/1. **Types of Aid:** *Need-based scholarships/grants:* Federal Pell, SEOG, state scholarships/grants, private scholarships, the school's own gift aid. *Loans:* Subsidized Stafford, Unsubsidized Stafford, PLUS, Federal Perkins. **Student Employment:** Highest amount earned per year from on-campus jobs $1,000. **Financial Aid Statistics:** 99% freshmen, 98% undergrads receive need-based scholarship or grant aid. 96% freshmen, 79% undergrads receive non-need-based scholarship or grant aid. 78% freshmen, 81% undergrads receive need-based self-help aid. 8% freshmen, 8% undergrads receive athletic scholarships. 98% freshmen, 98% undergrads receive any aid. 77% undergrads borrow to pay for school. Average cumulative indebtedness $29,700. **Criteria for awarding institutional aid:** *Non-need-based:* academics, athletics, leadership, minority status, state/district residency.

SIERRA NEVADA COLLEGE

999 Tahoe Blvd., Incline Village, NV 89451
Phone: 775-831-1314 • **Financial Aid Phone:** 775 8311314 x 7404
E-mail: admissions@sierranevada.edu • **CEEB Code:** 9192
Fax: 775-831-6223 • **Website:** www.sierraneveda.edu • **ACT Code:** 2497

This private school was founded in 1969. It has a 25-acre campus.

RATINGS

Admissions Selectivity Rating: 72 **Fire Safety Rating:** 93 **Green Rating:** 73

STUDENTS AND FACULTY

Enrollment: 529. **Student Body:** 42% female, 58% male, 84% out-of-state, 8% international (14 countries represented). Asian 2%, African American 1%, Caucasian 69%, Hispanic 2%, Native American 2%.
Retention and Graduation: 79% freshmen return for sophomore year. 34% freshmen graduate within 4 years. 49% freshmen graduate within 6 years.
Faculty: Student/faculty ratio 14:1. 34 full-time faculty, 35% hold PhDs, 15% are members of minority groups, 41% are women. 0% of classes are taught by teaching assistants.

ACADEMICS

Degrees: bachelor's, post-bachelor's certificate. **Majors with Highest Enrollment:** business, management, marketing, and related support services, other; environmental science; humanities/humanistic studies. **Special Study Options:** double major, honors program, internships, study abroad, teacher certification program. **Combined Degree Programs:** BA/Dr. Pharmacy. **Disability Services:** Special programs offered to physically disabled students include note-taking services, tutors. **Career Services:** career/job search classes, career assessment, internships.

FACILITIES

Housing: Coed dorms. 50% of campus accessible to physically disabled. **Special Academic Facilities/Equipment:** McLean Observatory.

CAMPUS LIFE

Environment: Village. **Activities:** literary magazine, student government, student newspaper 10 registered organizations, 1 honor societies, 2 religious organizations. **Athletics (Intercollegiate):** *Men:* equestrian sports, skiing (downhill/alpine). *Women:* equestrian sports, skiing (downhill/alpine).

ADMISSIONS

Freshman Academic Profile: Average high school GPA 2.9. 82% from public high schools. SAT Math middle 50% range 440-550. SAT Critical Reading middle 50% range 440-550. SAT Writing middle 50% range 420-540. ACT middle 50% range 19-25. Minimum web-based TOEFL 59. Minimum paper TOEFL 500. **Basis for Candidate Selection:** *Important factors considered include:* application essay, recommendation(s), rigor of secondary school record. *Other factors considered include:* Class rank, standardized test scores, alumni/ae relation, character/personal qualities, extracurricular activities, geographical residence, interview, racial/ethnic status, talent/ability, volunteer work, work experience. **Freshman Admission Requirements:** High school diploma is required and GED is accepted. **Freshman Admission Statistics:** 709 applied,

69% admitted, 14% enrolled. **Transfer Admission Requirements:** college transcript(s), essay or personal statement, Lowest grade transferable C. **General Admission Information:** Notification on a rolling basis, beginning on or about 12/15. Nonfall registration accepted. Admission may be deferred for a maximum of 1 year. Credit and/or placement offered for CEEB Advanced Placement tests.

COSTS AND FINANCIAL AID

Annual tuition $26,945. Room and board $11,492. Required fees $709. Average book expense $727. **Required Forms and Deadlines:** FAFSA. **Notification of Awards:** Applicants will be notified of awards on a rolling basis beginning 3/1. **Types of Aid:** *Need-based scholarships/grants:* Federal Pell, SEOG, state scholarships/grants, private scholarships, the school's own gift aid. *Loans:* Direct Subsidized Stafford, Direct PLUS. **Student Employment:** Federal Work-Study Program available. Institutional employment available. Off-campus job opportunities are excellent. **Financial Aid Statistics:** 100% freshmen, 100% undergrads receive need-based scholarship or grant aid. 100% freshmen, 100% undergrads receive non-need-based scholarship or grant aid. 100% freshmen, 100% undergrads receive need-based self-help aid. 26% freshmen, 5% undergrads receive athletic scholarships. 62% freshmen, 65% undergrads receive any aid. 50% undergrads borrow to pay for school. Average cumulative indebtedness $27,000. **Criteria for awarding institutional aid:** *Non-need-based:* academics, art, athletics, state/district residency.

SIMMONS COLLEGE

300 The Fenway, Boston, MA 2115
Phone: 617-521-2051 • **Financial Aid Phone:** 617-521-2001
E-mail: ugadm@simmons.edu • **CEEB Code:** 3761
Fax: 617-521-3190 • **Website:** www.simmons.edu • **ACT Code:** 1892

This private school was founded in 1899. It has a 12-acre campus.

RATINGS

Admissions Selectivity Rating: 85 **Fire Safety Rating:** 92 **Green Rating:** 79

STUDENTS AND FACULTY

Enrollment: 1,934. **Student Body:** 100% female, 0% male, 39% out-of-state, 3% international (46 countries represented). Asian 7%, African American 6%, Caucasian 69%, Hispanic 4%, Native American 0%.
Retention and Graduation: 75% freshmen return for sophomore year. 61% freshmen graduate within 4 years. 70% freshmen graduate within 6 years. 30% grads go on to further study within 1 year. 20% grads pursue arts and sciences degrees. 1% grads pursue law degrees. 1% grads pursue business degrees. 2% grads pursue medical degrees. **Faculty:** Student/faculty ratio 13:1. 231 full-time faculty, 81% hold PhDs, 24% are members of minority groups, 69% are women. 0% of classes are taught by teaching assistants.

ACADEMICS

Degrees: bachelor's, diploma, doctoral, master's, post-bachelor's certificate, post-master's certificate. **Classes:** Most classes have 10–19 students. **Majors with Highest Enrollment:** nursing/registered nurse (rn, asn, bsn, msn); psychology. **Special Study Options:** Accelerated program, cross-registration, double major, dual enrollment, English as a Second Language (ESL), exchange student program (domestic), honors program, independent study, internships, liberal arts/career combination, student-designed major, study abroad, teacher certification program, Exhange program with Mills College (CA), Spellman College (GA), Fisk University (TN), American University (DC), Colleges of the Fenway exchange program, double-degree programs with Massachusetts College of Pharmacy and Health Sciences, and with Hebrew College. **Honors Programs:** One Honors Program **Combined Degree Programs:** BA/MA, BA/MEng, BA/MAT BS/MS BA/MBA BA/MSW. **Disability Services:** Special programs offered to physically disabled students include note-taking services, reader services, tape recorders, tutors. **Career Services:** Alumni network, alumni services, career/job search classes, career assessment, internships, regional alumni. Career Services highlights include Internships that lead to job placement.

FACILITIES

Housing: special housing for disabled students, women's dorms, wellness housing, theme housing. 99% of campus accessible to physically disabled. **Special Academic Facilities/Equipment:** Art gallery, media center, science center with dream/sleep analysis lab, physical therapy clinic areas, sports center with pool **Computers:** 100% of classrooms, 5% of dorms, 100% of libraries, 100% of dining areas, 100% of student union, have wireless network access. Students can register for classes online. Administrative functions (other than registration) can be performed online.

CAMPUS LIFE

Environment: City. **Activities:** Choral groups, dance, drama/theater, literary magazine, radio station, student government, student newspaper, student-run film society, symphony orchestra, yearbook 91 registered organizations, 4 honor societies, 4 religious organizations. **Athletics (Intercollegiate):** *Women:* basketball, crew/rowing, diving, field hockey, lacrosse, soccer, softball, swimming, tennis, volleyball. **On-Campus Highlights:** Java City, Beatley Library, Park Science Center, Palace Road Building/Pottruck Technology, School of Management. **Environmental Initiatives:** Recycling and waste management program Mechanical equipment upgrades to improve efficiency and performance LEED certified new building

ADMISSIONS

Freshman Academic Profile: Average high school GPA 3.2. 19% in top 10% of high school class, 55% in top 25% of high school class, 89% in top 50% of high school class. SAT Math middle 50% range 490-600. SAT Critical Reading middle 50% range 500-590. SAT Writing middle 50% range 510-610. ACT middle 50% range 22-26. Minimum web-based TOEFL 83. Minimum paper TOEFL 560. **Basis for Candidate Selection:** *Very important factors considered include:* academic GPA, rigor of secondary school record. *Important factors considered include:* Class rank, application essay, recommendation(s), standardized test scores. *Other factors considered include:* extracurricular activities, interview, talent/ability, volunteer work, work experience. **Freshman Admission Requirements:** High school diploma is required and GED is accepted. *Academic units required:* 4 English, 3 mathematics, 3 science, 3 foreign language, 3 social studies, 3 history. *Academic units recommended:* 4 English, 3 mathematics, 3 science, 3 foreign language, 3 social studies, 3 history. **Freshman Admission Statistics:** 3,522 applied, 57% admitted, 18% enrolled. **Transfer Admission Requirements:** High school transcript, college transcript(s), essay or personal statement, statement of good standing from prior institution(s). Minimum college GPA of 2.8 required. Lowest grade transferable C+. **General Admission Information:** Application Fee $55. Regular application deadline 2/1. Regular notification 4/15. Nonfall registration accepted. Admission may be deferred for a maximum of 1 Year. Credit and/or placement offered for CEEB Advanced Placement tests.

COSTS AND FINANCIAL AID

Annual tuition $31,280. Room and board $12,470. Required fees $950. Average book expense $1,280. **Required Forms and Deadlines:** FAFSA, institution's own financial aid form. **Notification of Awards:** Applicants will be notified of awards on a rolling basis beginning 3/15. **Types of Aid:** *Need-based scholarships/grants:* Federal Pell, SEOG, state scholarships/grants, private scholarships, the school's own gift aid. *Loans:* Direct Subsidized Stafford, Direct Unsubsidized Stafford, Direct PLUS, state loans, college/university loans from institutional funds. **Student Employment:** Federal Work-Study Program available. Institutional employment available. Highest amount earned per year from on-campus jobs $2,000. Off-campus job opportunities are excellent. **Financial Aid Statistics:** 100% freshmen, 99% undergrads receive need-based scholarship or grant aid. 5% freshmen, 4% undergrads receive non-need-based scholarship or grant aid. 93% freshmen, 94% undergrads receive need-based self-help aid. 94% freshmen, 85% undergrads receive any aid. 78% undergrads borrow to pay for school. Average cumulative indebtedness $45,237. **Criteria for awarding institutional aid:** *Non-need-based:* academics, alumni affiliation, leadership, minority status.

See page 1206.

SIMPSON COLLEGE (IA)

701 North C Street, Indianola, IA 50125
Phone: 515-961-1624
E-mail: admiss@simpson.edu • **CEEB Code:** 6650
Fax: 515-961-1870 • **Website:** www.simpson.edu • **ACT Code:** 1354

This private school, affiliated with the Methodist Church, was founded in 1860. It has a 63-acre campus.

RATINGS

Admissions Selectivity Rating: 74   **Fire Safety Rating:** 60*   **Green Rating:** 60*

STUDENTS AND FACULTY

Enrollment: 1,758. **Student Body:** 60% female, 40% male, 10% out-of-state, 2% international (13 countries represented). Asian 1%, African American 1%, Caucasian 93%, Hispanic 1%, Native American 0%.

Retention and Graduation: 78% freshmen return for sophomore year. 57% freshmen graduate within 4 years. 67% freshmen graduate within 6 years. 11% grads go on to further study within 1 year. 6% grads pursue arts and sciences degrees. 2% grads pursue law degrees. 1% grads pursue business degrees. 2% grads pursue medical degrees. **Faculty:** Student/faculty ratio 14:1. 84 full-time faculty, 87% hold PhDs, 6% are members of minority groups, 29% are women. 0% of classes are taught by teaching assistants.

ACADEMICS

Degrees: bachelor's, post-bachelor's certificate. **Classes:** Most classes have 10–19 students. Most lab/discussion sessions have 10–19 students. **Special Study Options:** Accelerated program, cooperative education program, double major, English as a Second Language (ESL), honors program, independent study, internships, liberal arts/career combination, student-designed major, study abroad, teacher certification program, weekend college, International Program. **Disability Services:** Special programs offered to physically disabled students include note-taking services, reader services, tape recorders, tutors. **Career Services:** alumni services, career/job search classes, career assessment, internships.

FACILITIES

Housing: Coed dorms, men's dorms, women's dorms, fraternity/sorority housing, apartments for single students, Simpson College owns several homes surrounding campus known as theme houses. Group of students petition for those houses on a yearly basis. **Special Academic Facilities/Equipment:** The biology department hosts a human cadaver lab while Dunn library boasts the Avery O ' Craven Room which houses an extensive antebellum collection.

CAMPUS LIFE

Environment: Village. **Activities:** Choral groups, concert band, dance, drama/theater, jazz band, literary magazine, music ensembles, opera, pep band, radio station, student government, student newspaper, yearbook 89 registered organizations, 15 honor societies, 17 religious organizations. 4 fraternities, 4 sororities. **Athletics (Intercollegiate):** *Men:* baseball, basketball, cheerleading, cross-country, football, golf, soccer, tennis, track/field (outdoor), track/field (indoor), wrestling. *Women:* basketball, cheerleading, cross-country, golf, soccer, softball, swimming, tennis, track/field (outdoor), track/field (indoor), volleyball. **On-Campus Highlights:** Carse Fitness Center, Blank Performing Arts Center, Carver Science Center and Open Atrium, Pfeiffer Dining Hall, Brenton Student Center.

ADMISSIONS

Freshman Academic Profile: 21% in top 10% of high school class, 57% in top 25% of high school class, 90% in top 50% of high school class. 96% from public high schools. ACT middle 50% range 22-27. Minimum paper TOEFL 550. **Basis for Candidate Selection:** *Very important factors considered include:* Class rank, rigor of secondary school record, standardized test scores. *Important factors considered include:* recommendation(s), character/personal qualities. *Other factors considered include:* alumni/ae relation, extracurricular activities, interview, volunteer work. **Freshman Admission Requirements:** High school diploma is required and GED is accepted. **Freshman Admission Statistics:** 1,442 applied, 76% admitted, 38% enrolled. **Transfer Admission Requirements:** High school transcript, college transcript(s), standardized test scores, minimum college GPA of 2.5 required. Lowest grade transferable C–. **General Admission Information:** Nonfall registration accepted. Admission may be deferred for a maximum of 24 months. Credit and/or placement offered for CEEB Advanced Placement tests.

COSTS AND FINANCIAL AID

Annual tuition $17,908. Room and board $6,062. Required fees $189. Average book expense $800. **Required Forms and Deadlines:** FAFSA. **Notification of Awards:** Applicants will be notified of awards on a rolling basis beginning 3/15. **Types of Aid:** *Need-based scholarships/grants:* Federal Pell, SEOG, state scholarships/grants, private scholarships, the school's own gift aid. *Loans:* Subsidized Stafford, Unsubsidized Stafford, PLUS, Federal Perkins, state loans, college/university loans from institutional funds, Private Educational Loans. **Student Employment:** Federal Work-Study Program available. Institutional employment available. Highest amount earned per year from on-campus jobs $735. Off-campus job opportunities are fair. **Financial Aid Statistics:** 100% freshmen, 99% undergrads receive need-based scholarship or grant aid. 15% freshmen, 10% undergrads receive non-need-based scholarship or grant aid. 84% freshmen, 87% undergrads receive need-based self-help aid. 91% undergrads borrow to pay for school. Average cumulative indebtedness $20,940. **Criteria for awarding institutional aid:** *Non-need-based:* academics, alumni affiliation, art, leadership, minority status, music/drama, religious affiliation, state/district residency.

SIMPSON UNIVERSITY

2211 College View Dr., Redding, CA 96003
Phone: 530-226-4606 • **Financial Aid Phone:** 530-224-5600
E-mail: admissions@simpsonuniversity.edu • **CEEB Code:**
Fax: 530-226-4861 • **Website:** www.simpsonuniversity.edu • **ACT Code:** 430

This private school, affiliated with the Christian & Missionary Allianc Church, was founded in 1921. It has a 92-acre campus.

RATINGS
Admissions Selectivity Rating: 79   **Fire Safety Rating:** 66   **Green Rating:** 60*

STUDENTS AND FACULTY
Retention and Graduation: 61% freshmen return for sophomore year. **Faculty:** Student/faculty ratio 17:1. 38 full-time faculty, 55% hold PhDs. 0% of classes are taught by teaching assistants.

ACADEMICS
Degrees: associate, bachelor's, certificate, master's. **Classes:** Most classes have 10–19 students. Most lab/discussion sessions have 10–19 students. **Majors with Highest Enrollment:** elementary education and teaching; organizational behavior studies; psychology. **Special Study Options:** Accelerated program, distance learning, double major, honors program, independent study, internships, student-designed major, study abroad, teacher certification program, weekend college. **Honors Programs:** Oxford Honours Programme through the CCCU (Coalition of Christian Colleges and Universities). **Disability Services:** Special programs offered to physically disabled students include note-taking services, reader services, tutors. **Career Services:** career/job search classes, career assessment.

FACILITIES
Housing: special housing for disabled students, men's dorms, special housing for international students, women's dorms, apartments for married students. 95% of campus accessible to physically disabled. **Computers:** Students can register for classes online. Administrative functions (other than registration) can be performed online.

CAMPUS LIFE
Environment: City. **Activities:** Choral groups, drama/theater, jazz band, music ensembles, pep band, student government, student newspaper, yearbook 17 registered organizations, 1 honor societies, 20 religious organizations. **Athletics (Intercollegiate): Men:** baseball, basketball. *Women:* basketball. **On-Campus Highlights:** Chapel (Heritage Student Life Center), Athletic Events (Heritage Student Life Center), Music Department (Heritage Student Life Center), Bible/Theology Classes (La-Baume Rudat Bldg.), AandB Coffee Shop and Bookstore (Owen Center).

ADMISSIONS
Freshman Academic Profile: Average high school GPA 3.3. 19% in top 10% of high school class, 47% in top 25% of high school class, 79% in top 50% of high school class. 63% from public high schools. SAT Math middle 50% range 430-560. SAT Critical Reading middle 50% range 450-590. ACT middle 50% range 18-23. Minimum paper TOEFL 500. **Basis for Candidate Selection:** *Very important factors considered include:* recommendation(s), rigor of secondary school record, standardized test scores, character/personal qualities, religious affiliation/commitment. *Important factors considered include:* Class rank, volunteer work. *Other factors considered include:* application essay, extracurricular activities, interview, talent/ability. **Freshman Admission Requirements:** High school diploma is required and GED is accepted. **Freshman Admission Statistics:** 938 applied, 59% admitted, 34% enrolled. **Transfer Admission Requirements:** High school transcript, college transcript(s), essay or personal statement, statement of good standing from prior institution(s). Minimum college GPA of 2.0 required. Lowest grade transferable C. **General Admission Information:** Application Fee $20. Nonfall registration accepted. Admission may be deferred for a maximum of 24 months. Credit and/or placement offered for CEEB Advanced Placement tests.

COSTS AND FINANCIAL AID
Annual tuition $17,000. Room and board $5,900. Average book expense $1,200. **Required Forms and Deadlines:** FAFSA, institution's own financial aid form. **Notification of Awards:** Applicants will be notified of awards on a rolling basis beginning 3/16. **Types of Aid:** *Need-based scholarships/grants:* Federal Pell, SEOG, state scholarships/grants, private scholarships, the school's own gift aid. *Loans:* Subsidized Stafford, Unsubsidized Stafford, PLUS, Federal Perkins, Alternative Loans. **Student Employment:** Federal Work-Study Program available. Institutional employment available. Off-campus job opportunities are good. **Financial Aid Statistics:** 100% freshmen, 95% undergrads receive need-based scholarship or grant aid. 100% freshmen, 95% undergrads receive non-need-based scholarship or grant aid. 97% freshmen, 93% undergrads receive need-based self-help aid. 96% freshmen, 96% undergrads receive any aid. 89%

undergrads borrow to pay for school. Average cumulative indebtedness $17,600. **Criteria for awarding institutional aid:** *Non-need-based:* academics, alumni affiliation, leadership, minority status, music/drama, religious affiliation, state/district residency.

SKIDMORE COLLEGE

815 North Broadway, Saratoga Springs, NY 12866-1632
Phone: 518-580-5570 • **Financial Aid Phone:** 518-580-5750
E-mail: admissions@skidmore.edu • **CEEB Code:** 2815
Fax: 518-580-5584 • **Website:** www.skidmore.edu • **ACT Code:** 2906

This private school was founded in 1903. It has a 750-acre campus.

RATINGS
Admissions Selectivity Rating: 94   **Fire Safety Rating:** 93   **Green Rating:** 60*

STUDENTS AND FACULTY
Enrollment: 2,631. **Student Body:** 61% female, 39% male, 67% out-of-state, 6% international (51 countries represented). Asian 6%, African American 4%, Caucasian 65%, Hispanic 8%, Native American 0%. **Retention and Graduation:** 84% freshmen graduate within 4 years. 88% freshmen graduate within 6 years. **Faculty:** Student/faculty ratio 9:1. 245 full-time faculty, 86% hold PhDs, 14% are members of minority groups, 59% are women. 0% of classes are taught by teaching assistants.

ACADEMICS
Degrees: bachelor's, master's. **Classes:** Most classes have 10–19 students. Most lab/discussion sessions have 10–19 students. **Majors with Highest Enrollment:** business/commerce; English language and literature; psychology. **Special Study Options:** Accelerated program, cross-registration, double major, dual enrollment, exchange student program (domestic), honors program, independent study, internships, liberal arts/career combination, student-designed major, study abroad, teacher certification program. **Honors Programs:** Honors Forum **Disability Services:** Special programs offered to physically disabled students include note-taking services, reader services, tape recorders, tutors. **Career Services:** Alumni network, alumni services, career/job search classes, career assessment, internships, regional alumni. Career Services highlights include Alumni Network.

FACILITIES
Housing: Coed dorms, special housing for disabled students, special housing for international students, women's dorms, apartments for single students, gender neutral wing. 75% of campus accessible to physically disabled. **Special Academic Facilities/Equipment:** Tang Teaching Museum and Art Gallery, center for child study, art, music, dance, and theatre facilities, electron microscope, spectrometer. **Computers:** Students can register for classes online. Administrative functions (other than registration) can be performed online.

CAMPUS LIFE
Environment: Town. **Activities:** Choral groups, concert band, dance, drama/theater, jazz band, literary magazine, music ensembles, musical theater, opera, radio station, student government, student newspaper, symphony orchestra, television station, yearbook, Campus Ministries, International Student Organization, Model UN 80 registered organizations, 10 honor societies, 3 religious organizations. **Athletics (Intercollegiate): Men:** baseball, basketball, crew/rowing, diving, golf, ice hockey, lacrosse, soccer, swimming, tennis. *Women:* basketball, crew/rowing, diving, equestrian sports, field hockey, lacrosse, soccer, softball, swimming, tennis, volleyball. **On-Campus Highlights:** Tang Teaching Museum, Lucy Scribner Library, Case Student Center, Woodlawn Village Apartments, Murray-Atkins Dining Hall.

ADMISSIONS
Freshman Academic Profile: 43% in top 10% of high school class, 78% in top 25% of high school class, 95% in top 50% of high school class. 55% from public high schools. SAT Math middle 50% range 560-670. SAT Critical Reading middle 50% range 560-670. SAT Writing middle 50% range 560-680. ACT middle 50% range 26-30. Minimum paper TOEFL 590. **Basis for Candidate Selection:** *Very important factors considered include:* rigor of secondary school record. *Important factors considered include:* Class rank, application essay, academic GPA, recommendation(s), character/personal qualities, extracurricular activities, talent/ability, volunteer work, work experience. *Other factors considered include:* standardized test scores, alumni/ae relation, first generation, geographical residence, interview, level of applicant's interest, racial/ethnic

status. **Freshman Admission Requirements:** High school diploma is required and GED is accepted. **Freshman Admission Statistics:** 5,702 applied, 42% admitted, 27% enrolled. **Transfer Admission Requirements:** High school transcript, college transcript(s), essay or personal statement, standardized test scores, statement of good standing from prior institution(s). Minimum college GPA of 2.7 required. Lowest grade transferable C. **General Admission Information:** Application Fee $60. Early decision application deadline 11/15. Regular application deadline 1/15. Regular notification 4/1. Nonfall registration not accepted. Admission may be deferred for a maximum of 2 years. Credit and/or placement offered for CEEB Advanced Placement tests.

COSTS AND FINANCIAL AID

Annual tuition $43,183. Room and board $11,744. Required fees $882. Average book expense $1,300. **Required Forms and Deadlines:** FAFSA, CSS/Financial Aid PROFILE. **Notification of Awards:** Applicants will be notified of awards on or about 4/1. **Types of Aid:** *Need-based scholarships/grants:* Federal Pell, SEOG, state scholarships/grants, the school's own gift aid. *Loans:* Subsidized Stafford, Unsubsidized Stafford, PLUS, Federal Perkins. **Student Employment:** Federal Work-Study Program available. Institutional employment available. Highest amount earned per year from on-campus jobs $2,300. Off-campus job opportunities are fair. **Financial Aid Statistics:** 96% freshmen, 97% undergrads receive need-based scholarship or grant aid. 2% freshmen, 3% undergrads receive non-need-based scholarship or grant aid. 100% freshmen, 82% undergrads receive need-based self-help aid. 55% freshmen, 51% undergrads receive any aid. 42% undergrads borrow to pay for school. Average cumulative indebtedness $22,753. **Criteria for awarding institutional aid:** *Non-need-based:* music/drama.

See page 1208.

SLIPPERY ROCK UNIVERSITY
OF PENNSYLVANIA

1 Morrow Way, Slippery Rock, PA 16057
Phone: 724-738-2015 • **Financial Aid Phone:** 724-738-2044
E-mail: asktherock@sru.edu • **CEEB Code:** 2658
Fax: 724-738-2913 • **Website:** www.sru.edu • **ACT Code:** 3716

This public school was founded in 1889. It has a 600-acre campus.

RATINGS
Admissions Selectivity Rating: 76 **Fire Safety Rating:** 95 **Green Rating:** 97

STUDENTS AND FACULTY
Enrollment: 7,769. **Student Body:** 57% female, 43% male, 11% out-of-state, 1% international (37 countries represented). Asian 0%, African American 5%, Caucasian 86%, Hispanic 2%, Native American 0%.
Retention and Graduation: 81% freshmen return for sophomore year. 38% freshmen graduate within 4 years. 62% freshmen graduate within 6 years. 18% grads go on to further study within 1 year. 36% grads pursue arts and sciences degrees. 2% grads pursue law degrees. 10% grads pursue business degrees. 1% grads pursue medical degrees. **Faculty:** Student/faculty ratio 20:1. 355 full-time faculty, 89% hold PhDs, 16% are members of minority groups, 49% are women. 0% of classes are taught by teaching assistants.

ACADEMICS
Degrees: bachelor's, certificate, master's, post-bachelor's certificate. **Classes:** Most classes have 20–29 students. Most lab/discussion sessions have fewer than 10 students. **Majors with Highest Enrollment:** business administration and management; elementary education and teaching; kinesiology and exercise science. **Special Study Options:** distance learning, double major, dual enrollment, exchange student program (domestic), honors program, independent study, internships, liberal arts/career combination, student-designed major, study abroad, teacher certification program. **Honors Programs:** Undergraduate Honors Program **Combined Degree Programs:** Pre-Osteo 3+4 and Pre-Pharm 3+3 LECOM; Pre-Chiro 3+3 Logan; Pre-PT 3+3 SRU. **Disability Services:** Special programs offered to physically disabled students include note-taking services, reader services, tape recorders, tutors. **Career Services:** alumni services, career/job search classes, career assessment, internships Career Services highlights include The Office of Career Services offers students and alumni the opportunity to meet individually with career counselors.

FACILITIES
Housing: Coed dorms, special housing for disabled students, apartments for single students, theme housing. 80% of campus accessible to physically disabled. **Special Academic Facilities/Equipment:** Special education school for student teachers, physical therapy clinic, microvideo system, planetarium, electron microscope. Residence Halls have academic interest floors with special

facilities for specific majors whereby students can interact with faculty and have academically related programs where they live. **Computers:** 80% of classrooms, 100% of dorms, 100% of libraries, 50% of dining areas, 100% of student union, 5% of common outdoor areas have wireless network access. Students can register for classes online. Administrative functions (other than registration) can be performed online.

CAMPUS LIFE
Environment: Rural. **Activities:** Choral groups, concert band, dance, drama/theater, jazz band, literary magazine, marching band, music ensembles, musical theater, radio station, student government, student newspaper, student-run film society, symphony orchestra, television station, Campus Ministries, International Student Organization, Model UN 145 registered organizations, 37 honor societies, 4 religious organizations. 9 fraternities, 8 sororities. **Athletics (Intercollegiate):** *Men:* baseball, basketball, cheerleading, cross-country, football, soccer, track/field (outdoor), track/field (indoor). *Women:* basketball, cheerleading, cross-country, field hockey, lacrosse, soccer, softball, tennis, track/field (outdoor), track/field (indoor), volleyball. **On-Campus Highlights:** Aebersold Recreation Center, New Residential Suite Living Complexes, Bailey Library, Advanced Science and Technology Building, University Union. **Environmental Initiatives:** Recycling Green building designs and renovations Green procurement practices

ADMISSIONS
Freshman Academic Profile: Average high school GPA 3.4. 12% in top 10% of high school class, 37% in top 25% of high school class, 80% in top 50% of high school class. 75% from public high schools. SAT Math middle 50% range 470-550. SAT Critical Reading middle 50% range 450-540. SAT Writing middle 50% range 440-530. ACT middle 50% range 19-23. Minimum web-based TOEFL 61. Minimum paper TOEFL 500. **Basis for Candidate Selection:** *Important factors considered include:* Class rank, academic GPA, rigor of secondary school record, standardized test scores. *Other factors considered include:* application essay, recommendation(s), talent/ability. **Freshman Admission Requirements:** High school diploma is required and GED is accepted. **Freshman Admission Statistics:** 6,276 applied, 63% admitted, 39% enrolled. **Transfer Admission Requirements:** college transcript(s), minimum college GPA of 2.0 required. Lowest grade transferable C. **General Admission Information:** Application Fee $30. Notification on a rolling basis, beginning on or about 6/15. Nonfall registration accepted. Admission may be deferred for a maximum of 1 year. Credit and/or placement offered for CEEB Advanced Placement tests.

COSTS AND FINANCIAL AID
Annual in-state tuition $6,428. Annual out-of-state tuition $9,642. Room and board $9,364. Required fees $2,319. Average book expense $1,470. **Required Forms and Deadlines:** FAFSA. **Notification of Awards:** Applicants will be notified of awards on a rolling basis beginning 3/15. **Types of Aid:** *Need-based scholarships/grants:* Federal Pell, SEOG, state scholarships/grants, private scholarships, the school's own gift aid. *Loans:* Subsidized Stafford, Unsubsidized Stafford, PLUS, Federal Perkins. **Student Employment:** Federal Work-Study Program available. Institutional employment available. Highest amount earned per year from on-campus jobs $4,000. Off-campus job opportunities are good. **Financial Aid Statistics:** 64% freshmen, 64% undergrads receive need-based scholarship or grant aid. 36% freshmen, 22% undergrads receive non-need-based scholarship or grant aid. 93% freshmen, 92% undergrads receive need-based self-help aid. 5% freshmen, 3% undergrads receive athletic scholarships. 87% freshmen, 83% undergrads receive any aid. 85% undergrads borrow to pay for school. Average cumulative indebtedness $28,959. **Criteria for awarding institutional aid:** *Non-need-based:* academics, alumni affiliation, art, athletics, job skills, leadership, minority status, music/drama, state/district residency.

SMITH COLLEGE

7 College Lane, Northampton, MA 1063
Phone: 413-585-2500 • **Financial Aid Phone:** 413-585-2530
E-mail: admission@smith.edu • **CEEB Code:** 3762
Fax: 413-585-2527 • **Website:** www.smith.edu • **ACT Code:** 1894

This private school was founded in 1871. It has a 147-acre campus.

RATINGS
Admissions Selectivity Rating: 96 **Fire Safety Rating:** 78 **Green Rating:** 92

STUDENTS AND FACULTY

Enrollment: 2,664. **Student Body:** 78% out-of-state, 12% international (59 countries represented). Asian 12%, African American 5%, Caucasian 47%, Hispanic 9%, Native American 0%.
Retention and Graduation: 93% freshmen return for sophomore year. 81% freshmen graduate within 4 years. **Faculty:** Student/faculty ratio 9:1. 275 full-time faculty, 99% hold PhDs, 17% are members of minority groups, 55% are women. 0% of classes are taught by teaching assistants.

ACADEMICS

Degrees: bachelor's, master's, post-bachelor's certificate, post-master's certificate. **Classes:** Most classes have 10–19 students. **Majors with Highest Enrollment:** economics; political science and government; psychology. **Special Study Options:** Accelerated program, cross-registration, double major, exchange student program (domestic), honors program, independent study, internships, study abroad, teacher certification program. **Disability Services:** Special programs offered to physically disabled students include note-taking services, reader services, tape recorders, tutors. **Career Services:** Alumni network, alumni services, career/job search classes, career assessment, internships, regional alumni. Career Services highlights include Praxis internship program: guaranteed $2000 stipend per student for summer internship.

FACILITIES

Housing: women's dorms, cooperative housing, Apartment complex for limited number of juniors and seniors. Also,one senior house, french speaking house, and Ada Comstock (non-traditional age) house. 85% of campus accessible to physically disabled. **Special Academic Facilities/Equipment:** Art museum, printing, darkroom, and sculpture facilities, dance, electronic music, television, and theatre studios, recital hall, rehearsal rooms, multimedia language lab, early childhood/elementary education campus school, two electronic classrooms, physiology and horticultural labs, animal care facilities, two electron microscopes, greenhouses, observatories. **Computers:** 85% of classrooms, 100% of dorms, 100% of libraries, 100% of dining areas, 100% of student union, 50% of common outdoor areas have wireless network access. Students can register for classes online. Administrative functions (other than registration) can be performed online.

CAMPUS LIFE

Environment: Town. **Activities:** Choral groups, concert band, dance, drama/theater, jazz band, literary magazine, music ensembles, musical theater, radio station, student government, student newspaper, television station, yearbook, Campus Ministries, International Student Organization, Model UN 133 registered organizations, 3 honor societies, 9 religious organizations. **Athletics (Intercollegiate):** *Women:* basketball, crew/rowing, cross-country, diving, equestrian sports, field hockey, lacrosse, skiing (downhill/alpine), soccer, softball, squash, swimming, tennis, track/field (outdoor), track/field (indoor), volleyball. **On-Campus Highlights:** Smith Art Museum, The Botanical Gardens, Campus Center, Mendenhall Center for Performing Arts, Lyman Plant House. **Environmental Initiatives:** A new natural gas fired cogeneration facility went online in October 2008, which generates most campus electric use and achieves 80% efficiency with new absorption chillers. Constructed a LEED Gold Certified Science and Engineering facility. Implemented 18 energy efficiency projects and 7 conservation programs over past 4 years; these have generated substantial economic and environmental benefits and have reduced greenhouse gas emissions associated with electricity consumption by 18% and steam production by 15%. A recurring fund is being established to fund ongoing efficiency projects.

ADMISSIONS

Freshman Academic Profile: Average high school GPA 3.9. 66% in top 10% of high school class, 90% in top 25% of high school class, 99% in top 50% of high school class. 62% from public high schools. SAT Math middle 50% range 600-710. SAT Critical Reading middle 50% range 610-720. SAT Writing middle 50% range 620-720. ACT middle 50% range 27-31. Minimum web-based TOEFL 90. Minimum paper TOEFL 600. **Basis for Candidate Selection:** *Very important factors considered include:* academic GPA, recommendation(s), rigor of secondary school record, character/personal qualities. *Important factors considered include:* Class rank, application essay, extracurricular activities, interview, talent/ability. *Other factors considered include:* standardized test scores, alumni/ae relation, first generation, racial/ethnic status, volunteer work, work experience. **Freshman Admission Requirements:** High school diploma or equivalent is not required. **Freshman Admission Statistics:** 4,341 applied, 42% admitted, 35% enrolled. **Transfer Admission Requirements:** High school transcript, college transcript(s), essay or personal statement, statement of good standing from prior institution(s). Lowest grade transferable C. **General Admission Information:** Application Fee $60. Early decision application deadline 11/15. Regular application deadline 1/15. Regular notification 4/1. Nonfall registration not accepted. Admission may be deferred for a maximum of 1 year. Credit and/or placement offered for CEEB Advanced Placement tests.

COSTS AND FINANCIAL AID

Annual tuition $41,190. Room and board $13,860. Required fees $270. Average book expense $800. **Required Forms and Deadlines:** FAFSA, CSS/Financial

Aid PROFILE, noncustodial PROFILE, business/farm supplement. **Notification of Awards:** Applicants will be notified of awards on or about 4/1. **Types of Aid:** *Need-based scholarships/grants:* Federal Pell, SEOG, state scholarships/grants, the school's own gift aid. *Loans:* Direct Subsidized Stafford, Direct Unsubsidized Stafford, PLUS, Federal Perkins, state loans, college/university loans from institutional funds. **Student Employment:** Federal Work-Study Program available. Institutional employment available. Highest amount earned per year from on-campus jobs $2,558. Off-campus job opportunities are excellent. **Financial Aid Statistics:** 96% freshmen, 95% undergrads receive need-based scholarship or grant aid. 1% freshmen, 1% undergrads receive non-need-based scholarship or grant aid. 97% freshmen, 96% undergrads receive need-based self-help aid. 70% freshmen, 71% undergrads receive any aid. 67% undergrads borrow to pay for school. Average cumulative indebtedness $23,071. **Criteria for awarding institutional aid:** *Non-need-based:* academics, state/district residency.

SOKA UNIVERSITY OF AMERICA

1 University Drive, Aliso Viejo, CA 92656-4105
Phone: 949-480-4150 • **Financial Aid Phone:** 949-480-4048
E-mail: admission@soka.edu • **CEEB Code:** 4066
Fax: 949-480-4151 • **Website:** www.soka.edu • **ACT Code:** 467

This private school was founded in 2001. It has a 103-acre campus.

RATINGS

Admissions Selectivity Rating: 93   **Fire Safety Rating:** 93   **Green Rating:** 60*

STUDENTS AND FACULTY

Enrollment: 360. **Student Body:** 62% female, 38% male, 61% out-of-state, 53% international (28 countries represented). Asian 19%, African American 3%, Caucasian 10%, Hispanic 4%, Native American 0%.
Retention and Graduation: 91% freshmen return for sophomore year. 40% grads go on to further study within 1 year. 34% grads pursue arts and sciences degrees. 2% grads pursue law degrees. 2% grads pursue business degrees. 2% grads pursue medical degrees. **Faculty:** Student/faculty ratio 8:1. 38 full-time faculty, 95% hold PhDs, 32% are members of minority groups, 45% are women. 0% of classes are taught by teaching assistants.

ACADEMICS

Degrees: bachelor's, master's. **Classes:** Most classes have 10–19 students. Most lab/discussion sessions have 10–19 students. **Special Study Options:** English as a Second Language (ESL), independent study, internships, liberal arts/career combination, study abroad. **Disability Services:** Special programs offered to physically disabled students include note-taking services, reader services, tape recorders, tutors.

FACILITIES

Housing: Coed dorms, special housing for disabled students 100% of campus accessible to physically disabled. **Special Academic Facilities/Equipment:** Art Gallery, Athenaeum (Reception Center). **Computers:** Students can register for classes online. Administrative functions (other than registration) can be performed online. Undergraduates are required to own a computer.

CAMPUS LIFE

Environment: Town. **Activities:** Choral groups, concert band, dance, drama/theater, jazz band, literary magazine, music ensembles, student government, student newspaper, student-run film society, symphony orchestra, yearbook 38 registered organizations, 1 religious organizations. **Athletics (Intercollegiate):** *Men:* cross-country, diving, soccer, swimming, track/field (outdoor). *Women:* cross-country, diving, soccer, swimming, track/field (outdoor). **On-Campus Highlights:** Founders Hall Art Gallery, Student Center Dining Hall, Student Center Bookstore, Recreation Center, Ikeda Library, Hiking trail along canyon rim surrounding campus.

ADMISSIONS

Freshman Academic Profile: Average high school GPA 3.7. 43% in top 10% of high school class, 80% in top 25% of high school class, 94% in top 50% of high school class. 60% from public high schools. SAT Math middle 50% range 570-680. SAT Critical Reading middle 50% range 460-640. SAT Writing middle 50% range 490-630. ACT middle 50% range 23-24. **Basis for Candidate Selection:** *Very important factors considered include:* Class rank, application essay, academic GPA, recommendation(s), rigor of secondary school record, character/personal qualities, extracurricular activities, level of applicant's interest. *Important factors considered include:* standardized test scores, talent/ability, volunteer work. *Other factors considered include:* geographical residence, interview, racial/ethnic status, work experience. **Freshman Admission Requirements:** High school diploma is required and GED is accepted. **Freshman Admission Statistics:** 321 applied, 40% admitted, 68% enrolled. **General Admission Information:** Application Fee $45. Regular application deadline

1/6. Regular notification 3/15. Nonfall registration not accepted. Admission may be deferred for a maximum of 1 yr. Neither credit nor placement offered for CEEB Advanced Placement tests.

COSTS AND FINANCIAL AID
Annual tuition $22,108. Room and board $8,600. Average book expense $1,000. **Required Forms and Deadlines:** FAFSA. **Notification of Awards:** Applicants will be notified of awards on a rolling basis beginning 3/15. **Types of Aid:** *Need-based scholarships/grants:* Federal Pell, SEOG, state scholarships/grants, private scholarships, the school's own gift aid, Hispanic Educational Endowment Fund (HEEF). *Loans:* Subsidized Stafford, Unsubsidized Stafford, PLUS, college/university loans from institutional funds. **Student Employment:** Highest amount earned per year from on-campus jobs $5,400. **Financial Aid Statistics:** 35% freshmen, 84% undergrads receive need-based scholarship or grant aid. 35% freshmen, 28% undergrads receive non-need-based scholarship or grant aid. 34% freshmen, 61% undergrads receive need-based self-help aid. 100% freshmen, 100% undergrads receive any aid. 85% undergrads borrow to pay for school. Average cumulative indebtedness $17,125. **Criteria for awarding institutional aid:** *Non-need-based:* academics.

SONOMA STATE UNIVERSITY

1801 East Cotati Avenue, Rohnert Park, CA 94928
Phone: 707-664-2778 • **Financial Aid Phone:** 707-664-2389
E-mail: student.outreach@sonoma.edu • **CEEB Code:** 4723
Fax: 707-664-2060 • **Website:** www.sonoma.edu • **ACT Code:** 431

This public school was founded in 1960. It has a 269-acre campus.

RATINGS
Admissions Selectivity Rating: 66   **Fire Safety Rating:** 78   **Green Rating:** 68

STUDENTS AND FACULTY
Enrollment: 8,058. **Student Body:** 60% female, 40% male, 1% out-of-state, 1% international (21 countries represented). Asian 5%, African American 2%, Caucasian 64%, Hispanic 17%, Native American 1%.
Retention and Graduation: 79% freshmen return for sophomore year. 27% freshmen graduate within 4 years. **Faculty:** Student/faculty ratio 25:1. 241 full-time faculty, 92% hold PhDs, 7% are members of minority groups, 48% are women. 1% of classes are taught by teaching assistants.

ACADEMICS
Degrees: bachelor's, master's. **Classes:** Most classes have 20–29 students. **Majors with Highest Enrollment:** business/commerce; liberal arts and sciences studies and humanities, other; psychology. **Special Study Options:** Accelerated program, cooperative education program, cross-registration, distance learning, double major, dual enrollment, English as a Second Language (ESL), exchange student program (domestic), external degree program, honors program, independent study, internships, liberal arts/career combination, student-designed major, study abroad, teacher certification program, Combined Degree Programs: bachelors/MBA; bachelors/MPA. **Combined Degree Programs:** BA/MA. **Disability Services:** Special programs offered to physically disabled students include note-taking services, reader services, tape recorders, tutors. **Career Services:** career/job search classes.

FACILITIES
Housing: Coed dorms, men's dorms, special housing for international students, women's dorms, apartments for single students, Housing for focused learning communities - freshman seminar dorms, healthy living dorms; women in math/science dorms. 99% of campus accessible to physically disabled. **Special Academic Facilities/Equipment:** Performing arts center, observatory, electron microscope, seismograph, information technology center, environmental technology center, high technology high school, nature preserve **Computers:** 95% of classrooms, 90% of dorms, 100% of libraries, 85% of dining areas, 100% of student union, 20% of common outdoor areas have wireless network access. Students can register for classes online. Administrative functions (other than registration) can be performed online. Undergraduates are required to own a computer.

CAMPUS LIFE
Environment: Town. **Activities:** Choral groups, dance, drama/theater, jazz band, literary magazine, music ensembles, musical theater, opera, pep band, radio station, student government, student newspaper, symphony orchestra 109

registered organizations, 2 honor societies, 4 religious organizations. 5 fraternities, 9 sororities. **Athletics (Intercollegiate):** *Men:* baseball, basketball, soccer, tennis. *Women:* basketball, cross-country, soccer, softball, tennis, track/field (outdoor), volleyball. **On-Campus Highlights:** Schultz Information Center, Environmental Technology Center, Charlie Brown's (coffee shop), Observatory, University Recreation Center. **Environmental Initiatives:** Energy efficiency Recycling Education

ADMISSIONS
Freshman Academic Profile: Average high school GPA 3.2. 72% from public high schools. SAT Math middle 50% range 450-560. SAT Critical Reading middle 50% range 440-550. ACT middle 50% range 18-23. Minimum web-based TOEFL 61. Minimum paper TOEFL 500. **Basis for Candidate Selection:** *Very important factors considered include:* academic GPA, rigor of secondary school record, standardized test scores. *Other factors considered include:* first generation, geographical residence, state residency. **Freshman Admission Requirements:** High school diploma is required and GED is accepted. *Academic units required:* 4 English, 3 mathematics, 2 science, (1 science labs), 2 foreign language, 2 history, 1 visual/performing arts, 1 academic electives, 1 visual/performing arts, US govt. 4 English, 3 mathematics, 2 science, (1 science labs), 2 foreign language, 2 history, 1 visual/performing arts, 1 academic electives, 1 visual/performing arts, US govt **Freshman Admission Statistics:** 13,239 applied, 92% admitted, 14% enrolled. **Transfer Admission Requirements:** college transcript(s), minimum college GPA of 2.0 required. Lowest grade transferable D. **General Admission Information:** Application Fee $55. Regular application deadline 11/30. Regular notification 3/1. Notification on a rolling basis, beginning on or about 11/1. Nonfall registration accepted. Credit and/or placement offered for CEEB Advanced Placement tests.

COSTS AND FINANCIAL AID
Annual out-of-state tuition $15,826. Room and board $11,241. Required fees $6,898. Average book expense $1,754. **Required Forms and Deadlines:** FAFSA. **Notification of Awards:** Applicants will be notified of awards on a rolling basis beginning 3/25. **Types of Aid:** *Need-based scholarships/grants:* Federal Pell, SEOG, state scholarships/grants, private scholarships, ACG, SMART. *Loans:* Direct Subsidized Stafford, Direct Unsubsidized Stafford, Direct PLUS, Federal Perkins. **Student Employment:** Federal Work-Study Program available. Institutional employment available. Highest amount earned per year from on-campus jobs $9,000. Off-campus job opportunities are good. **Financial Aid Statistics:** 55% freshmen, 76% undergrads receive need-based scholarship or grant aid. 17% freshmen, 14% undergrads receive non-need-based scholarship or grant aid. 90% freshmen, 90% undergrads receive need-based self-help aid. 1% freshmen, 2% undergrads receive athletic scholarships. 40% freshmen, 51% undergrads receive any aid. 63% undergrads borrow to pay for school. Average cumulative indebtedness $13,125. **Criteria for awarding institutional aid:** *Non-need-based:* academics, alumni affiliation, art, athletics, leadership, minority status, music/drama.

SOUTH DAKOTA SCHOOL OF MINES & TECHNOLOGY

501 East St. Joseph Street, Rapid City, SD 57701-3995
Phone: 605-394-2414 • **Financial Aid Phone:** 605-394-2274
E-mail: admissions@sdsmt.edu • **CEEB Code:** 3470
Fax: 605-394-1979 • **Website:** www.sdsmt.edu • **ACT Code:** 3922

This public school was founded in 1885. It has a 118-acre campus.

RATINGS
Admissions Selectivity Rating: 69   **Fire Safety Rating:** 97   **Green Rating:** 79

STUDENTS AND FACULTY
Enrollment: 1,939. **Student Body:** 22% female, 78% male, 46% out-of-state, 3% international (36 countries represented). Asian 1%, African American 1%, Caucasian 86%, Hispanic 3%, Native American 2%.
Retention and Graduation: 20% freshmen graduate within 4 years. 55% freshmen graduate within 6 years. 26% grads go on to further study within 1 year. 1% grads pursue law degrees. 1% grads pursue business degrees. 2% grads pursue medical degrees. **Faculty:** Student/faculty ratio 14:1. 142 full-time faculty, 88% hold PhDs, 15% are members of minority groups, 23% are women.

ACADEMICS
Degrees: associate, bachelor's, master's, terminal associate. **Classes:** Most classes have 20–29 students. **Majors with Highest Enrollment:** civil engineering; electrical, electronics and communications engineering; mechanical engineering. **Special Study Options:** cooperative education program, cross-

registration, distance learning, dual enrollment, English as a Second Language (ESL), independent study, internships, liberal arts/career combination, study abroad, Distance Education - SDSMT offfers an M.S. degree in Technology Management via the internet. Dual Degrees - We do not offer double majors but students may graduate with more than one degree by completing a minimum of thirty (30) semester hours of credit in residence beyond the credit hours used for the first B.S. degree. **Disability Services:** Special programs offered to physically disabled students include note-taking services, reader services, tape recorders, tutors. **Career Services:** Alumni network, alumni services, career/job search classes, career assessment, internships, regional alumni. Career Services highlights include Both the cooperative/internship programs are very successful and usually lead to permanent employment for the students after graduation.

FACILITIES

Housing: Coed dorms, special housing for disabled students, fraternity/sorority housing, apartments for married students, apartments for single students, wellness housing, SDSM&T recently acquired apartments which can be rented by single students. or groups of students or married students. with families. 80% of campus accessible to physically disabled. **Special Academic Facilities/ Equipment:** Museum of geology and paleontology, electron microscope, engineering/mining experiment station, supersonic wind tunnel,3-D visualization lab, polymer processing lab, friction stir welding lab, high-frequency microwave lab, tech development lab, fluid computational dynamics lab, robotics lab, clean manufacturing lab, institute atmospheric science and other research institutes. **Computers:** 100% of classrooms, 100% of dorms, 100% of libraries, 100% of dining areas, 100% of student union, 100% of common outdoor areas have wireless network access. Students can register for classes online. Administrative functions (other than registration) can be performed online.

CAMPUS LIFE

Environment: Town. **Activities:** Choral groups, concert band, dance, drama/ theater, jazz band, music ensembles, pep band, radio station, student government, student newspaper, Campus Ministries, International Student Organization 67 registered organizations - 6 honor societies, 9 religious organizations. 4 fraternities, 2 sororities. **Athletics (Intercollegiate):** *Men:* basketball, cross-country, football, golf, track/field (outdoor), track/field (indoor). *Women:* basketball, cross-country, golf, track/field (outdoor), track/field (indoor), volleyball. **On-Campus Highlights:** O'Harra Stadium (football and track), King (Sports) Center - basketball, pool, exercise, Geology and Paleontology Museum, Surbeck Student Center, Apex Gallery. **Environmental Initiatives:** A minimum of LEED Silver is required on all new construction or renovation Working on a Sustainable Engineering Minor RecycleMania

ADMISSIONS

Freshman Academic Profile: Average high school GPA 3.5. 23% in top 10% of high school class, 55% in top 25% of high school class, 87% in top 50% of high school class. SAT Math middle 50% range 520-660. SAT Critical Reading middle 50% range 470-610. SAT Writing middle 50% range 450-560. ACT middle 50% range 24-29. Minimum web-based TOEFL 83. Minimum paper TOEFL 560. **Basis for Candidate Selection:** *Very important factors considered include:* Class rank, academic GPA, rigor of secondary school record, standardized test scores.*Other factors considered include:* character/personal qualities, extracurricular activities, talent/ability, volunteer work, work experience. **Freshman Admission Requirements:** High school diploma is required and GED is accepted. *Academic units required:* 4 English, 4 mathematics, 4 science, (3 science labs), 2 foreign language, 3 social studies, 1 visual/performing arts. 4 English, 4 mathematics, 4 science, (3 science labs), 2 foreign language, 3 social studies, 1 visual/performing arts. **Freshman Admission Statistics:** 1,127 applied, 88% admitted, 46% enrolled. **Transfer Admission Requirements:** college transcript(s), statement of good standing from prior institution(s). Minimum college GPA of 2.0 required. Lowest grade transferable D. **General Admission Information:** Application Fee $20. Notification on a rolling basis, beginning on or about 11/1. Nonfall registration accepted. Admission may be deferred for a maximum of 12 months. Credit and/or placement offered for CEEB Advanced Placement tests.

COSTS AND FINANCIAL AID

Annual in-state tuition $3,897. Annual out-of-state tuition $5,843. Room and board $5,890. Required fees $4,510. Average book expense $1,780. **Required Forms and Deadlines:** FAFSA, Freshman Scholarship Application Form. **Notification of Awards:** Applicants will be notified of awards on a rolling basis beginning 5/1. **Types of Aid:** *Need-based scholarships/grants:* Federal Pell, SEOG, state scholarships/grants, private scholarships, the school's own gift aid, SMART grants, ACG grants. *Loans:* Subsidized Stafford, Unsubsidized Stafford, PLUS, Federal Perkins, Private alternative loans. **Student Employment:** Federal Work-Study Program available. Institutional employment available. Highest amount earned per year from on-campus jobs $2,000. Off-campus job opportunities are good. **Financial Aid Statistics:** 74% freshmen, 64% undergrads receive need-based scholarship or grant aid. 61% freshmen, 38% undergrads receive non-need-based scholarship or grant aid. 81% freshmen,

87% undergrads receive need-based self-help aid. 5% freshmen, 4% undergrads receive athletic scholarships. 89% freshmen, 79% undergrads receive any aid. 60% undergrads borrow to pay for school. Average cumulative indebtedness $18,331. **Criteria for awarding institutional aid:** *Non-need-based:* academics, athletics, leadership, minority status.

SOUTH DAKOTA STATE UNIVERSITY

SAD 200, Brookings, SD 57007-0649
Phone: 605-688-4121 • **Financial Aid Phone:** 605-688-4695
E-mail: sdsu.admissions@sdstate.edu • **CEEB Code:** 6653
Fax: 605-688-6891 • **Website:** www.sdstate.edu • **ACT Code:** 3924

This public school was founded in 1881. It has a 272-acre campus.

RATINGS
Admissions Selectivity Rating: 65 **Fire Safety Rating:** 74 **Green Rating:** 80

STUDENTS AND FACULTY
Enrollment: 10,060. **Student Body:** 51% female, 49% male, 33% out-of-state, 1% international (63 countries represented). Asian 1%, African American 1%, Caucasian 83%, Hispanic 1%, Native American 1%.
Retention and Graduation: Faculty: Student/faculty ratio 19:1. 467 full-time faculty, 71% hold PhDs, 14% are members of minority groups, 46% are women.

ACADEMICS
Degrees: associate, bachelor's, certificate, master's, post-bachelor's certificate, post-master's certificate, terminal associate. **Classes:** Most classes have 20–29 students. Most lab/discussion sessions have 20–29 students. **Special Study Options:** Accelerated program, cooperative education program, cross-registration, distance learning, double major, dual enrollment, exchange student program (domestic), honors program, independent study, internships, liberal arts/career combination, study abroad, teacher certification program, We offer help and courses in ESL but it is not an official program. **Honors Programs:** Have an Honors College. See website http://www3.sdstate.edu/Academics/HonorsCollege/ **Combined Degree Programs:** BS/MS in Economics. **Disability Services:** Special programs offered to physically disabled students include note-taking services, reader services, tape recorders, tutors. **Career Services:** career/job search classes, career assessment, internships.

FACILITIES
Housing: Coed dorms, special housing for disabled students, special housing for international students, fraternity/sorority housing, apartments for married students, apartments for single students, wellness housing, limited single rooms with optional meal plan for upperclassmen. Students out of high school less than 2 yrs are required to live in campus housing unless living with family. **Special Academic Facilities/Equipment:** SD Art Museum, SD Agricultural Heritage Museum, Northern Plains Bio-stress Laboratory, Animal Disease Research and Diagnostic Lab, McCrory Gardens, new Center for Infectious Disease Research and Vaccinology, EROS-SDSU GISc Center of Excellence. **Computers:** 30% of classrooms, 100% of dorms, 100% of libraries, 100% of dining areas, 100% of student union, 20% of common outdoor areas have wireless network access. Students can register for classes online. Administrative functions (other than registration) can be performed online

CAMPUS LIFE
Environment: Village. **Activities:** Choral groups, concert band, dance, drama/ theater, jazz band, literary magazine, marching band, music ensembles, musical theater, pep band, radio station, student government, student newspaper, symphony orchestra, yearbook 200 registered organizations, 32 honor societies, 14 religious organizations. 6 fraternities, 4 sororities. **Athletics (Intercollegiate):** *Men:* baseball, basketball, cross-country, diving, football, golf, swimming, tennis, track/field (outdoor), track/field (indoor), wrestling. *Women:* basketball, cross-country, diving, equestrian sports, golf, soccer, softball, swimming, tennis, track/field (outdoor), track/field (indoor), volleyball. **On-Campus Highlights:** Performing Arts Center, Dairy Bar, University Student Union, Frost Arena, South Dakota Art Museum, Northern Plains Bio-Stress Laboratory Enterprise Institute SD Ag Heritage Museum. **Environmental Initiatives:** Asbestos Abatement Recycling Energy Reduction Measures

ADMISSIONS
Freshman Academic Profile: Average high school GPA 3.3. 15% in top 10% of high school class, 39% in top 25% of high school class, 71% in top 50% of high school class. ACT middle 50% range 19-25. Minimum web-based TOEFL 61. Minimum paper TOEFL 500. **Basis for Candidate Selection:** *Very important factors considered include:* Class rank, academic GPA, standardized test scores. *Important factors considered include:* rigor of secondary school record. *Other factors considered include:* recommendation(s). **Freshman Admis-**

sion Requirements: High school diploma is required and GED is accepted. *Academic units required:* 4 English, 3 mathematics, 3 science, (3 science labs), 3 social studies, 1 Fine arts. *Academic units recommended:* 4 English, 3 mathematics, 3 science, (3 science labs), 3 social studies, 1 Fine arts **Freshman Admission Statistics:** 4,673 applied, 92% admitted, 52% enrolled. **Transfer Admission Requirements:** High school transcript, college transcript(s), statement of good standing from prior institution(s). Minimum college GPA of 2.0 required. Lowest grade transferable D. **General Admission Information:** Application Fee $20. Nonfall registration accepted. Admission may be deferred for a maximum of 12 Months. Credit and/or placement offered for CEEB Advanced Placement tests.

COSTS AND FINANCIAL AID

Average book expense $1,100. **Required Forms and Deadlines:** FAFSA. **Notification of Awards:** Applicants will be notified of awards on a rolling basis beginning 4/1. **Types of Aid:** *Need-based scholarships/grants:* Federal Pell, SEOG, state scholarships/grants, private scholarships, the school's own gift aid, United Negro College Fund, Federal Nursing Scholarships. , Federal SMART grants; Federal Academic Comp Grants, TEACH Grants, TRIO. *Loans:* Subsidized Stafford, Unsubsidized Stafford, PLUS, Federal Perkins, Federal Nursing, college/university loans from institutional funds, Health Profession loans. Private alternative loans. **Student Employment:** Federal Work-Study Program available. Institutional employment available. Highest amount earned per year from on-campus jobs $5,880. Off-campus job opportunities are good. **Financial Aid Statistics:** 62% freshmen, 62% undergrads receive need-based scholarship or grant aid. 69% freshmen, 83% undergrads receive non-need-based scholarship or grant aid. 95% freshmen, 98% undergrads receive need-based self-help aid. 7% freshmen, 3% undergrads receive athletic scholarships. 93% freshmen, 89% undergrads receive any aid. 74% undergrads borrow to pay for school. Average cumulative indebtedness $20,860. **Criteria for awarding institutional aid:** *Non-need-based:* academics, art, athletics, job skills, leadership, minority status, music/drama, state/district residency.

SOUTHAMPTON COLLEGE OF LONG ISLAND UNIVERSITY

239 Montauk Highway, Southampton, NY 11968
Phone: 631-287-8200
E-mail: admissions@southampton.liunet.edu • **CEEB Code:** 2853
Fax: 516-287-8130 • **Website:** www.southampton.liu.edu • **ACT Code:** 2853

This private school was founded in 1963. It has a 110-acre campus.

RATINGS
Admissions Selectivity Rating: 63   **Fire Safety Rating:** 60*   **Green Rating:** 60*

STUDENTS AND FACULTY
Enrollment: 1,147. **Student Body:** 67% female, 33% male, 35% out-of-state, 5% international (20 countries represented). Asian 1%, African American 5%, Caucasian 62%, Hispanic 5%, Native American 1%.
Retention and Graduation: 68% freshmen return for sophomore year. **Faculty:** Student/faculty ratio 18:1. 66 full-time faculty.

ACADEMICS
Degrees: bachelor's, master's, post-bachelor's certificate. **Classes:** Most classes have 10–19 students. Most lab/discussion sessions have 10–19 students. **Majors with Highest Enrollment:** biopsychology; business/commerce; marine biology. **Special Study Options:** Accelerated program, cooperative education program, distance learning, double major, dual enrollment, English as a Second Language (ESL), exchange student program (domestic), honors program, independent study, internships, liberal arts/career combination, student-designed major, study abroad, teacher certification program, Undergrads may take grad level classes. Co-Op Programs: Arts, Business, Education, Health Professions, Humanities, Natural Science, Social/Behaviorial Science, All majors. Off-Campus Study: United Nations, Semester at Sea. Other Special Programs: Travel abroad also available through Friends World Program. **Career Services:** Alumni network, alumni services, career/job search classes, career assessment, internships.

FACILITIES
Housing: Coed dorms, women's dormsNon-smoking and substance free; honors; quiet. **Special Academic Facilities/Equipment:** Art galleries, on-campus nursery school, psychobiology lab, marine station and fleet of research vessels, Silicon Graphics Computer Lab. **Computers:** Administrative functions (other than registration) can be performed online.

CAMPUS LIFE
Environment: Village. **Activities:** Choral groups, drama/theater, literary magazine, music ensembles, musical theater, radio station, student government, student newspaper, student-run film society, yearbook 40 registered organizations, 4 honor societies, 2 religious organizations. **Athletics (Intercollegiate):** *Men:* basketball, cross-country, lacrosse, soccer, tennis, volleyball. *Women:* basketball, cross-country, soccer, softball, tennis, volleyball.

ADMISSIONS
Freshman Academic Profile: Average high school GPA 3.2. 19% in top 10% of high school class, 40% in top 25% of high school class, 77% in top 50% of high school class. 87% from public high schools. Minimum paper TOEFL 525. **Basis for Candidate Selection:** *Very important factors considered include:* rigor of secondary school record, standardized test scores. *Important factors considered include:* application essay, recommendation(s), character/personal qualities, talent/ability. *Other factors considered include:* Class rank, extracurricular activities, interview, volunteer work, work experience. **Freshman Admission Requirements:** High school diploma is required and GED is accepted. *Academic units required:* 4 English, 2 mathematics, 2 science, (1 science labs), 2 social studies, 2 history. *Academic units recommended:* 4 English, 2 mathematics, 2 science, (1 science labs), 2 social studies, 2 history. **Freshman Admission Statistics:** 1,354 applied, 63% admitted, 24% enrolled. Minimum college GPA of 2.0 required. Lowest grade transferable C. **General Admission Information:** Application Fee $30. Notification on a rolling basis, beginning on or about 11/15. Nonfall registration accepted. Admission may be deferred for a maximum of 1 year. Credit and/or placement offered for CEEB Advanced Placement tests.

COSTS AND FINANCIAL AID
Average book expense $600. **Required Forms and Deadlines:** FAFSA, state aid form. **Notification of Awards:** Applicants will be notified of awards on a rolling basis beginning 3/1. **Types of Aid:** *Need-based scholarships/grants:* Federal Pell, SEOG, state scholarships/grants, private scholarships, the school's own gift aid. *Loans:* Direct Subsidized Stafford, Direct Unsubsidized Stafford, Direct PLUS, Federal Perkins. **Student Employment:** Federal Work-Study Program available. Institutional employment available. Highest amount earned per year from on-campus jobs $1,000. Off-campus job opportunities are good. **Financial Aid Statistics:** 91% freshmen, 87% undergrads receive need-based scholarship or grant aid. 71% freshmen, 51% undergrads receive non-need-based scholarship or grant aid. 100% freshmen, 100% undergrads receive need-based self-help aid. 1% freshmen, 6% undergrads receive athletic scholarships. 81% freshmen, 77% undergrads receive any aid. 89% undergrads borrow to pay for school. Average cumulative indebtedness $19,800. **Criteria for awarding institutional aid:** *Non-need-based:* academics, alumni affiliation, art, athletics, leadership.

SOUTHEAST MISSOURI STATE UNIVERSITY

One University Plaza, Cape Girardeau, MO 63701
Phone: 573-651-2590 • **Financial Aid Phone:** 573-651-2253
E-mail: admissions@semo.edu • **CEEB Code:** 6655
Fax: 573-651-5936 • **Website:** www.semo.edu • **ACT Code:** 2366

This public school was founded in 1873. It has a 400-acre campus.

RATINGS
Admissions Selectivity Rating: 65   **Fire Safety Rating:** 85   **Green Rating:** 70

STUDENTS AND FACULTY
Enrollment: 9,510. **Student Body:** 57% female, 43% male, 15% out-of-state, 6% international (53 countries represented). Asian 1%, African American 9%, Caucasian 80%, Hispanic 1%, Native American 0%.
Retention and Graduation: 74% freshmen return for sophomore year. 23% freshmen graduate within 4 years. 46% freshmen graduate within 6 years. **Faculty:** Student/faculty ratio 22:1. 395 full-time faculty, 75% hold PhDs, 14% are members of minority groups, 49% are women. 4% of classes are taught by teaching assistants.

ACADEMICS
Degrees: associate, bachelor's, certificate, master's, post-master's certificate. **Classes:** Most classes have 20–29 students. **Majors with Highest Enrollment:** communication studies/speech communication and rhetoric; elementary education and teaching; general studies. **Special Study Options:** Accelerated program, distance learning, double major, dual enrollment, English as a Second Language (ESL), honors program, independent study, internships, liberal arts/career combination, student-designed major, study abroad, teacher certification program. **Honors Programs:** The Honors Program encourages intellectual

perspective, addresses special needs of outstanding students and contributes to the general advancement of learning. **Disability Services:** Special programs offered to physically disabled students include note-taking services, reader services, tape recorders, tutors. **Career Services:** Alumni network, alumni services, career/job search classes, career assessment, internships, regional alumni. Career Services highlights include Career Linkages assists in locating experiential learning opportunities.

FACILITIES

Housing: Coed dorms, fraternity/sorority housing, wellness housing, apartments for students with dependents. 100% of campus accessible to physically disabled. **Special Academic Facilities/Equipment:** River Campus at Southeast; Crisp Museum;Bedell Performance Hall; Center for Faulkner Studies; Center for Scholarship in Teaching and Learning; Missouri Statewide Early Literacy Intervention Program (MSELIP); Writing Center; University Demonstration Farm; 4 corporate video studios, 2 radio stations; Southeast Explorer; SHOW (Southeast Health on Wheels); Linda Godwin Center for Science and Math Education; **Computers:** 15% of dorms, 90% of libraries, 90% of dining areas, 90% of student union, 10% of common outdoor areas have wireless network access. Students can register for classes online. Administrative functions (other than registration) can be performed online.

CAMPUS LIFE

Environment: Town. **Activities:** Choral groups, concert band, dance, drama/theater, jazz band, literary magazine, marching band, music ensembles, musical theater, opera, pep band, radio station, student government, student newspaper, symphony orchestra, Campus Ministries, International Student Organization, Model UN 136 registered organizations, 8 honor societies, 14 religious organizations. 11 fraternities, 7 sororities. **Athletics (Intercollegiate):** *Men:* baseball, basketball, cheerleading, cross-country, football, track/field (outdoor), track/field (indoor). *Women:* basketball, cheerleading, cross-country, gymnastics, soccer, softball, tennis, track/field (outdoor), track/field (indoor), volleyball. **On-Campus Highlights:** River Campus at Southeast, Recreation Center & Aquatic Center, Kent Library Information Commons, Otto and Della Seabaugh Polytechnic Bldg, Robert A. Dempster Hall, River Campus: Holland School of Visual adn Performing Arts,Bedell Performance Hall, Crisp Regional Museum, Rust Flexible Theatre, Glenn Convocation Center, Shuck Music Recital Hall. **Environmental Initiatives:** Waste Management Energy management-conduct energy savings workshops and energy audits for area companies. Green certified products.

ADMISSIONS

Freshman Academic Profile: Average high school GPA 3.3. 17% in top 10% of high school class, 42% in top 25% of high school class, 72% in top 50% of high school class. SAT Math middle 50% range 445-615. SAT Critical Reading middle 50% range 420-560. ACT middle 50% range 20-25. Minimum web-based TOEFL 61. Minimum paper TOEFL 500. **Basis for Candidate Selection:** *Very important factors considered include:* academic GPA, rigor of secondary school record, standardized test scores.*Other factors considered include:* Class rank. **Freshman Admission Requirements:** High school diploma is required and GED is accepted. *Academic units required:* 4 English, 3 mathematics, 3 science, (1 science labs), 2 social studies, 1 history, 1 visual/performing arts, 3 academic electives. 4 English, 3 mathematics, 3 science, (1 science labs), 2 social studies, 1 history, 1 visual/performing arts, 3 academic electives. **Freshman Admission Statistics:** 4,161 applied, 97% admitted, 47% enrolled. **Transfer Admission Requirements:** college transcript(s), minimum college GPA of 2.0 required. Lowest grade transferable D. **General Admission Information:** Application Fee $25. Regular application deadline 7/1. Notification on a rolling basis, beginning on or about 9/1. Nonfall registration accepted. Credit offered for CEEB Advanced Placement tests.

COSTS AND FINANCIAL AID

Annual in-state tuition $5,814. Annual out-of-state tuition $11,049. Room and board $8,110. Required fees $936. Average book expense $478. **Required Forms and Deadlines:** FAFSA. **Notification of Awards:** Applicants will be notified of awards on a rolling basis beginning 4/1. **Types of Aid:** *Need-based scholarships/grants:* Federal Pell, SEOG, state scholarships/grants, private scholarships, the school's own gift aid. *Loans:* Subsidized Stafford, Unsubsidized Stafford, PLUS, Federal Perkins, state loans. **Student Employment:** Federal Work-Study Program available. Institutional employment available. Off-campus job opportunities are fair. **Financial Aid Statistics:** 93% freshmen, 87% undergrads receive need-based scholarship or grant aid. 10% freshmen, 6% undergrads receive non-need-based scholarship or grant aid. 70% freshmen, 76% undergrads receive need-based self-help aid. 2% freshmen, 2% undergrads receive athletic scholarships. 87% freshmen, 82% undergrads receive any aid. 64% undergrads borrow to pay for school. **Criteria for awarding institutional aid:** *Non-need-based:* academics, alumni affiliation, art, athletics, job skills, leadership, minority status, music/drama, state/district residency.

SOUTHEASTERN BIBLE COLLEGE

2545 Valleydale Road, Birmingham, AL 35244
Phone: 205-970-9211
E-mail: info@sebc.edu
Fax: 205-970-9207 • **Website:** www.sebc.edu

This private school was founded in 1935. It has a 10-acre campus.

RATINGS
Admissions Selectivity Rating: 64   **Fire Safety Rating:** 60*   **Green Rating:** 60*

STUDENTS AND FACULTY
Enrollment: 174. **Student Body:** 40% female, 60% male, 9% out-of-state, 1% international. Asian 0%, African American 32%, Caucasian 57%, Hispanic 1%, Native American 1%.
Retention and Graduation: 70% freshmen return for sophomore year. 8% freshmen graduate within 4 years. 17% freshmen graduate within 6 years.
Faculty: Student/faculty ratio 14:1. 6 full-time faculty, 100% hold PhDs, 0% are members of minority groups, 17% are women. 0% of classes are taught by teaching assistants.

ACADEMICS
Degrees: associate, bachelor's, diploma, terminal associate. **Classes:** Most classes have fewer than 10 students. **Majors with Highest Enrollment:** bible/biblical studies; elementary education and teaching; youth ministry. **Special Study Options:** independent study, internships. **Disability Services:** Special programs offered to physically disabled students include note-taking services, tape recorders.

FACILITIES
Housing: men's dorms, women's dorms, apartments for married students. 100% of campus accessible to physically disabled.

CAMPUS LIFE
Environment: Metropolis. **Activities:** Choral groups, music ensembles, student government. **On-Campus Highlights:** Gannett-Estes Library.

ADMISSIONS
Freshman Academic Profile: Average high school GPA 0.1. SAT Math middle 50% range 370-680. SAT Critical Reading middle 50% range 370-470. SAT Writing middle 50% range 210-440. ACT middle 50% range 19-24.
Basis for Candidate Selection: *Very important factors considered include:* recommendation(s), rigor of secondary school record, standardized test scores, character/personal qualities, religious affiliation/commitment. *Important factors considered include:* application essay. *Other factors considered include:* alumni/ae relation, interview. **Freshman Admission Requirements:** High school diploma is required and GED is accepted. *Academic units required:* 4 English, 4 mathematics, 4 science. 4 English, 4 mathematics, 4 science. **Freshman Admission Statistics:** 24 applied, 100% admitted, 58% enrolled. **Transfer Admission Requirements:** High school transcript, college transcript(s), essay or personal statement, minimum college GPA of 2.0 required. Lowest grade transferable C. **General Admission Information:** Application Fee $20. Regular application deadline 8/1. Notification on a rolling basis, beginning on or about 9/1. Nonfall registration accepted. Admission may be deferred for a maximum of 1 year. Credit offered for CEEB Advanced Placement tests.

COSTS AND FINANCIAL AID
Required Forms and Deadlines: FAFSA, institution's own financial aid form. **Notification of Awards:** Applicants will be notified of awards on or about 6/1. **Types of Aid:** *Need-based scholarships/grants:* Federal Pell, SEOG, state scholarships/grants. *Loans:* Subsidized Stafford, Unsubsidized Stafford, PLUS. **Student Employment:** Federal Work-Study Program available. Highest amount earned per year from on-campus jobs $2,000. Off-campus job opportunities are excellent. **Financial Aid Statistics:** 100% freshmen, 70% undergrads receive need-based scholarship or grant aid. 36% freshmen, 30% undergrads receive non-need-based scholarship or grant aid. 100% freshmen, 93% undergrads receive need-based self-help aid. 63% undergrads borrow to pay for school. Average cumulative indebtedness $22,713. **Criteria for awarding institutional aid:** *Non-need-based:* academics, alumni affiliation, state/district residency.

SOUTHEASTERN LOUISIANA UNIVERSITY

SLU 10752, Hammond, LA 70402
Phone: 985-549-2066 • **Financial Aid Phone:** 985-549-2244
E-mail: admissions@selu.edu • **CEEB Code:** 6656
Fax: 985-549-5632 • **Website:** www.selu.edu • **ACT Code:** 1608

This public school was founded in 1925. It has a 365-acre campus.

RATINGS
Admissions Selectivity Rating: 66   **Fire Safety Rating:** 83   **Green Rating:** 60*

STUDENTS AND FACULTY
Enrollment: 12,295. **Student Body:** 61% female, 39% male, 4% out-of-state, 2% international (52 countries represented). Asian 1%, African American 16%, Caucasian 69%, Hispanic 5%, Native American 0%.
Faculty: Student/faculty ratio 23:1. 489 full-time faculty, 65% hold PhDs, 13% are members of minority groups, 55% are women. 0% of classes are taught by teaching assistants.

ACADEMICS
Degrees: associate, bachelor's, master's. **Classes:** Most classes have 20–29 students. Most lab/discussion sessions have 20–29 students. **Majors with Highest Enrollment:** business administration and management; general studies; nursing/registered nurse (rn, asn, bsn, msn). **Special Study Options:** Accelerated program, cross-registration, distance learning, double major, dual enrollment, English as a Second Language (ESL), honors program, independent study, internships, liberal arts/career combination, study abroad, teacher certification program. **Honors Programs:** reduced size classes, scholarships, honors residence hall, achievement awards, and honor academic credit shown on the transcript. **Disability Services:** Special programs offered to physically disabled students include note-taking services, tape recorders, tutors. **Career Services:** alumni services, career assessment, internships Career Services highlights include The University offers a wide range of courses and curricula that address emerging regional, national and international priorities. The University embraces active partnerships that benefit students, faculty and the region we serve. Programs enable students to understand themselves and the world around them in a broad intellectual perspective. Such a perspective provides students the opportunity to live full, rich, balanced lives and to assume positions of leadership in the public and private sector. Graduates are prepared to think critically, communicate effectively and become lifelong learners. Emphasis is placed on preparation for careers or graduate study through undergraduate research in collaboration with faculty, "hands-on" internships, field experiences, work-study placements, cooperative education, service-learning, and opportunities to study abroad. Many of these opportunities earn college credit. Southeastern also has honors tracks in place for all degree programs. Undergraduate research programs such as Undergraduate Research and Creative Activities Grants Programs in the College of Arts, Humanities and Social Sciences, PROFIT (Preferred Research Option for Intensive Training) in the College of Business, SOAR (Student Opportunities for Achievement and Research) in the College of Nursing and Health Sciences, SURE (Student Undergraduate Research in Education) in the College of Education and Human Development, and STAR (Science and Technology Awards for Research) in the College of Science and Technology provide opportunities for undergraduate students to conduct research and engage in creative ventures with Southeastern faculty members.

FACILITIES
Housing: Coed dorms, women's dorms, fraternity/sorority housing, apartments for single students. 95% of campus accessible to physically disabled. **Special Academic Facilities/Equipment:** Contemporary Art Gallery, Radio Station, Television Station, Columbia Theatre, Maritime Museum **Computers:** 5% of classrooms, 100% of dorms, 100% of libraries, 50% of dining areas, 25% of student union, 25% of common outdoor areas have wireless network access. Students can register for classes online. Administrative functions (other than registration) can be performed online.

CAMPUS LIFE
Environment: Village. **Activities:** Choral groups, concert band, dance, drama/theater, jazz band, literary magazine, marching band, music ensembles, musical theater, opera, pep band, radio station, student government, student newspaper, student-run film society, symphony orchestra, television station, yearbook, Campus Ministries, International Student Organization 105 registered organizations, 11 honor societies, 12 religious organizations. 7 fraternities, 8 sororities. **Athletics (Intercollegiate):** *Men:* baseball, basketball, cross-country, football, golf, track/field (outdoor), track/field (indoor). *Women:* basketball, cross-country, soccer, softball, tennis, track/field (outdoor), track/field (indoor), volleyball. **On-Campus Highlights:** Student Union, Student Recreation Center, Library, Bookstore, Campus Dining Complex. **Environmental Initiatives:** computer recycling program campus shuttle Ponchartrain wetland environmental research.

ADMISSIONS
Freshman Academic Profile: Average high school GPA 3.2. 13% in top 10% of high school class, 35% in top 25% of high school class, 66% in top 50% of high school class. ACT middle 50% range 20-24. Minimum web-based TOEFL 61. Minimum paper TOEFL 500. **Basis for Candidate Selection:** *Very important factors considered include:* Class rank, academic GPA, rigor of secondary school record, standardized test scores. **Freshman Admission Requirements:** High school diploma is required and GED is accepted. *Academic units required:* 4 English, 3 mathematics, 3 science, 2 foreign language, 3 social studies, 1 visual/performing arts, 1 Mathematics or Science. 4 English, 3 mathematics, 3 science, 2 foreign language, 3 social studies, 1 visual/performing arts, 1 Mathematics or Science **Freshman Admission Statistics:** 3,562 applied, 89% admitted, 77% enrolled. **Transfer Admission Requirements:** college transcript(s), statement of good standing from prior institution(s). Minimum college GPA of 2.0 required. Lowest grade transferable D. **General Admission Information:** Application Fee $20. Regular application deadline 8/1. Nonfall registration accepted. Admission may be deferred for a maximum of 1 year. Credit and/or placement offered for CEEB Advanced Placement tests.

COSTS AND FINANCIAL AID
Annual in-state tuition $3,853. Annual out-of-state tuition $14,712. Room and board $7,020. Required fees $1,389. Average book expense $1,200. **Required Forms and Deadlines:** FAFSAInstitutional form for college scholarships only. **Notification of Awards:** Applicants will be notified of awards on a rolling basis beginning 3/1. **Types of Aid:** *Need-based scholarships/grants:* Federal Pell, SEOG, state scholarships/grants, private scholarships, the school's own gift aid, Federal Nursing Scholarships. *Loans:* Subsidized Stafford, Unsubsidized Stafford, PLUS, Federal Perkins, college/university loans from institutional funds. **Student Employment:** Federal Work-Study Program available. Institutional employment available. Highest amount earned per year from on-campus jobs $13,009. Off-campus job opportunities are good. **Financial Aid Statistics:** 65% freshmen, 68% undergrads receive need-based scholarship or grant aid. 55% freshmen, 65% undergrads receive non-need-based scholarship or grant aid. 55% freshmen, 65% undergrads receive need-based self-help aid. 3% freshmen, 3% undergrads receive athletic scholarships. 90% freshmen, 79% undergrads receive any aid. 60% undergrads borrow to pay for school. Average cumulative indebtedness $19,661. **Criteria for awarding institutional aid:** *Non-need-based:* academics, athletics, job skills, leadership, music/drama, state/district residency.

SOUTHEASTERN OKLAHOMA STATE UNIVERSITY

1405 North 4th Avenue, Durant, OK 74701-0609
Phone: 580-745-2060 • **Financial Aid Phone:** 580-745-2186
E-mail: admissions@se.edu • **CEEB Code:** 6657
Fax: 580-745-4502 • **Website:** • **ACT Code:** 3438

This public school was founded in 1909. It has a 268-acre campus.

RATINGS
Admissions Selectivity Rating: 66   **Fire Safety Rating:** 75   **Green Rating:** 60*

STUDENTS AND FACULTY
Enrollment: 3,465. **Student Body:** 55% female, 45% male, 22% out-of-state, 1% international (28 countries represented). Asian 1%, African American 5%, Caucasian 59%, Hispanic 3%, Native American 31%.
Retention and Graduation: 19% freshmen graduate within 4 years. **Faculty:** Student/faculty ratio 18:1. 143 full-time faculty, 74% hold PhDs, 17% are members of minority groups, 41% are women. 0% of classes are taught by teaching assistants.

ACADEMICS
Degrees: bachelor's, master's, post-master's certificate. **Classes:** Most classes have 20–29 students. Most lab/discussion sessions have 20–29 students. **Majors with Highest Enrollment:** elementary education and teaching; occupational safety and health technology/technician; psychology. **Special Study Options:** distance learning, double major, honors program, independent study, internships, teacher certification program. **Honors Programs:** Our Honors program offers six different scholarships ranging in value from $6,400 to $26,400 over four years. **Disability Services:** Special programs offered to physically disabled students include note-taking services, reader services, tape recorders, tutors. **Career Services:** Alumni network, career/job search classes, career assessment, internships.

FACILITIES

Housing: Coed dorms, apartments for single students. 100% of campus accessible to physically disabled. **Special Academic Facilities/Equipment:** Visual and Performing Arts Gallery. **Computers:** 65% of classrooms, 50% of dorms, 100% of libraries, 100% of dining areas, 100% of student union, 50% of common outdoor areas have wireless network access. Students can register for classes online. Administrative functions (other than registration) can be performed online.

CAMPUS LIFE

Environment: Village. **Activities:** Choral groups, concert band, dance, drama/theater, jazz band, literary magazine, marching band, music ensembles, musical theater, opera, pep band, radio station, student government, student newspaper, yearbook, Campus Ministries, International Student Organization 70 registered organizations, 12 honor societies, 8 religious organizations. 2 fraternities, 2 sororities. **Athletics (Intercollegiate):** *Men:* baseball, basketball, football, golf, tennis. *Women:* basketball, cross-country, softball, tennis, volleyball. **On-Campus Highlights:** Shearer Hall and Suites (New Apartments), New Student Union, Newly Renovated Football Stadium, New Basketball Arena, "Campus of a Thousand Magnolias".

ADMISSIONS

Freshman Academic Profile: Average high school GPA 3.3. 16% in top 10% of high school class, 40% in top 25% of high school class, 77% in top 50% of high school class. 99% from public high schools. ACT middle 50% range 18-23. Minimum paper TOEFL 500. **Basis for Candidate Selection:** *Very important factors considered include:* Class rank, academic GPA, standardized test scores. *Other factors considered include:* recommendation(s), rigor of secondary school record, character/personal qualities, interview, level of applicant's interest, state residency, talent/ability. **Freshman Admission Requirements:** High school diploma is required and GED is accepted. *Academic units required:* 4 English, 3 mathematics, 2 science, (2 science labs), 3 history, 2 academic electives. *Academic units recommended:* 4 English, 3 mathematics, 2 science, (2 science labs), 3 history, 2 academic electives. **Freshman Admission Statistics:** 916 applied, 82% admitted, 82% enrolled. **Transfer Admission Requirements:** college transcript(s), minimum college GPA of 2.0 required. Lowest grade transferable D. **General Admission Information:** Application Fee $20. Nonfall registration accepted. Credit offered for CEEB Advanced Placement tests.

COSTS AND FINANCIAL AID

Annual in-state tuition $3,639. Annual out-of-state tuition $10,010. Room and board $2,005. Required fees $677. Average book expense $800. **Required Forms and Deadlines:** FAFSA, institution's own financial aid form. **Notification of Awards:** Applicants will be notified of awards on a rolling basis beginning 4/15. **Types of Aid:** *Need-based scholarships/grants:* Federal Pell, SEOG, state scholarships/grants, private scholarships, the school's own gift aid. *Loans:* Subsidized Stafford, Unsubsidized Stafford, PLUS, Federal Perkins. **Student Employment:** Federal Work-Study Program available. Institutional employment available. Highest amount earned per year from on-campus jobs $8,259. Off-campus job opportunities are good. **Financial Aid Statistics:** 71% freshmen, 81% undergrads receive need-based scholarship or grant aid. 45% freshmen, 33% undergrads receive non-need-based scholarship or grant aid. 37% freshmen, 59% undergrads receive need-based self-help aid. 10% freshmen, 7% undergrads receive athletic scholarships. 66% freshmen, 65% undergrads receive any aid. 37% undergrads borrow to pay for school. Average cumulative indebtedness $6,852. **Criteria for awarding institutional aid:** *Non-need-based:* academics, alumni affiliation, art, athletics, leadership, minority status, music/drama, state/district residency.

SOUTHERN ADVENTIST UNIVERSITY

P.O. Box 370, Collegedale, TN 37315
Phone: 423-236-2835 • **Financial Aid Phone:** 423-236-2894
E-mail: admissions@southern.edu • **CEEB Code:** 3518
Fax: 423-236-1835 • **ACT Code:** 4006

This private school, affiliated with the Seventh Day Adventist Church, was founded in 1892. It has a 1000-acre campus.

RATINGS

Admissions Selectivity Rating: 69   **Fire Safety Rating:** 84   **Green Rating:** 61

STUDENTS AND FACULTY

Enrollment: 2,584. **Student Body:** 55% female, 45% male, 69% out-of-state, 5% international. Asian 6%, African American 12%, Caucasian 58%, Hispanic 19%, Native American 0%.
Retention and Graduation: 72% freshmen return for sophomore year. 23% freshmen graduate within 4 years. 48% freshmen graduate within 6 years. 15%

grads go on to further study within 1 year. 10% grads pursue arts and sciences degrees. 1% grads pursue business degrees. 3% grads pursue medical degrees. **Faculty:** Student/faculty ratio 15:1. 146 full-time faculty, 64% hold PhDs, 12% are members of minority groups, 42% are women. 0% of classes are taught by teaching assistants.

ACADEMICS

Degrees: associate, bachelor's, certificate, master's, post-master's certificate. **Majors with Highest Enrollment:** biology/biological sciences; business/commerce; nursing/registered nurse (rn, asn, bsn, msn). **Special Study Options:** double major, dual enrollment, English as a Second Language (ESL), honors program, independent study, internships, study abroad, teacher certification program. **Honors Programs:** Southern Scholars program includes special projects, inter-disciplinary studies, and designated honors courses to provide a challenging and intellectually stimulating educational experience. **Combined Degree Programs:** BA/MA, Nursing. **Disability Services:** Special programs offered to physically disabled students include note-taking services, reader services, tape recorders, tutors.

FACILITIES

Housing: men's dorms, women's dorms, apartments for married students, apartments for single students. 70% of campus accessible to physically disabled. **Special Academic Facilities/Equipment:** Near-Eastern archaeology teaching collection **Computers:** 100% of classrooms, 5% of dorms, 100% of libraries, 80% of dining areas, 10% of common outdoor areas have wireless network access. Students can register for classes online. Administrative functions (other than registration) can be performed online.

CAMPUS LIFE

Environment: Rural. **Activities:** Choral groups, concert band, drama/theater, jazz band, music ensembles, radio station, student government, student newspaper, student-run film society, symphony orchestra, television station, yearbook, Campus Ministries, International Student Organization 30 registered organizations, 8 honor societies, 3 religious organizations. **On Campus Highlights:** Student Center, Wellness Center, The Village Market, KRs Place, Library. **Environmental Initiatives:** Establishing environmental sustainability committee. Campus-wide chemical cleanout Using green listed chemicals for cleaning

ADMISSIONS

Freshman Academic Profile: Average high school GPA 3.4. 18% from public high schools. SAT Math middle 50% range 430-560. SAT Critical Reading middle 50% range 460-580. ACT middle 50% range 19-25. Minimum paper TOEFL 550. **Basis for Candidate Selection:** *Very important factors considered include:* academic GPA, rigor of secondary school record, standardized test scores. **Freshman Admission Requirements:** High school diploma is required and GED is accepted. *Academic units required:* 3 English, 2 mathematics, 2 science, 1 social studies, 1 history, 9 academic electives. *Academic units recommended:* 3 English, 2 mathematics, 2 science, 1 social studies, 1 history, 9 academic electives. **Freshman Admission Statistics:** 1,452 applied, 80% admitted, 54% enrolled. **Transfer Admission Requirements:** college transcript(s), minimum college GPA of 2 required. Lowest grade transferable D. **General Admission Information:** Application Fee $25. Regular application deadline 9/8. Nonfall registration accepted. Admission may be deferred for a maximum of 1 year. Credit and/or placement offered for CEEB Advanced Placement tests.

COSTS AND FINANCIAL AID

Annual tuition $17,534. Room and board $5,786. Required fees $790. Average book expense $1,100. **Required Forms and Deadlines:** FAFSA **Notification of Awards:** Applicants will be notified of awards on a rolling basis beginning 2/15. **Types of Aid:** *Need-based scholarships/grants:* Federal Pell, SEOG, state scholarships/grants, private scholarships, the school's own gift aid. *Loans:* Subsidized Stafford, Unsubsidized Stafford, PLUS, Federal Perkins, Federal Nursing, college/university loans from institutional funds. **Student Employment:** Federal Work-Study Program available. Institutional employment available. Highest amount earned per year from on-campus jobs $2,000. Off-campus job opportunities are good. **Financial Aid Statistics:** 99% freshmen, 98% undergrads receive need-based scholarship or grant aid. 82% freshmen, 55% undergrads receive non-need-based scholarship or grant aid. 83% freshmen, 86% undergrads receive need-based self-help aid. 95% undergrads receive any aid. 65% undergrads borrow to pay for school. Average cumulative indebtedness $27,121. **Criteria for awarding institutional aid:** *Non-need-based:* academics, alumni affiliation, art, leadership, music/drama.

SOUTHERN ARKANSAS UNIVERSITY

P. O. Box 9382, Magnolia, AR 71754
Phone: 870-235-4040 • **Financial Aid Phone:** 870-235-4023
E-mail: muleriders@saumag.edu • **CEEB Code:** 142
Fax: 870-235-5072 • **ACT Code:** 142

This public school was founded in 1909. It has a 1418-acre campus.

RATINGS
Admissions Selectivity Rating: 64   **Fire Safety Rating:** 60*   **Green Rating:** 60*

STUDENTS AND FACULTY
Enrollment: 2,671. **Student Body:** 57% female, 43% male, 21% out-of-state, 6% international (29 countries represented). Asian 1%, African American 29%, Caucasian 62%, Hispanic 1%, Native American 1%.
Retention and Graduation: 62% freshmen return for sophomore year. 19% freshmen graduate within 4 years. 39% freshmen graduate within 6 years. **Faculty:** Student/faculty ratio 16:1. 148 full-time faculty, % hold PhDs, 38% are women. 0% of classes are taught by teaching assistants.

ACADEMICS
Degrees: associate, bachelor's, master's. **Classes:** Most classes have fewer than 10 students. Most lab/discussion sessions have 20–29 students. **Special Study Options:** cross-registration, distance learning, double major, dual enrollment, honors program, internships, teacher certification program. **Disability Services:** Special programs offered to physically disabled students include tape recorders, tutors.

FACILITIES
Housing: Coed dorms, men's dorms, women's dorms, apartments for married students, apartments for single students. 95% of campus accessible to physically disabled. **Computers:** Students can register for classes online. Administrative functions (other than registration) can be performed online.

CAMPUS LIFE
Environment: Rural. **Activities:** Choral groups, concert band, drama/theater, jazz band, marching band, music ensembles, musical theater, pep band, radio station, student government, student newspaper, yearbook 80 registered organizations, 10 honor societies, 7 religious organizations. 5 fraternities, 6 sororities. **Athletics (Intercollegiate):** *Men:* baseball, basketball, cheerleading, cross-country, football, golf, rodeo, track/field (outdoor). *Women:* basketball, cheerleading, cross-country, rodeo, softball, tennis, track/field (outdoor), volleyball.

ADMISSIONS
Freshman Academic Profile: Average high school GPA 3.2. 70% in top 50% of high school class. 99% from public high schools. ACT middle 50% range 17-23. Minimum paper TOEFL 500. **Basis for Candidate Selection:** *Very important factors considered include:* Class rank, rigor of secondary school record, standardized test scores.*Other factors considered include:* application essay, recommendation(s). **Freshman Admission Requirements:** High school diploma is required and GED is accepted. **Freshman Admission Statistics:** 1,417 applied, 100% admitted, 42% enrolled. **Transfer Admission Requirements:** college transcript(s), statement of good standing from prior institution(s). Lowest grade transferable C. **General Admission Information:** Regular application deadline 8/27. Nonfall registration accepted. Admission may be deferred for a maximum of N/A. Credit offered for CEEB Advanced Placement tests.

COSTS AND FINANCIAL AID
Annual in-state tuition $4,260. Annual out-of-state tuition $6,450. Room and board $3,980. Required fees $630. Average book expense $1,000. **Required Forms and Deadlines:** FAFSA. **Notification of Awards:** Applicants will be notified of awards on a rolling basis beginning 4/15. **Types of Aid:** *Need-based scholarships/grants:* Federal Pell, SEOG, state scholarships/grants, private scholarships, the school's own gift aid. *Loans:* Subsidized Stafford, Unsubsidized Stafford, PLUS, Federal Perkins. **Student Employment:** Highest amount earned per year from on-campus jobs $4,900. **Financial Aid Statistics:** 65% freshmen, 93% undergrads receive need-based scholarship or grant aid. 94% freshmen, 60% undergrads receive non-need-based scholarship or grant aid. 82% freshmen, 85% undergrads receive need-based self-help aid. 85% freshmen, 82% undergrads receive any aid. 61% undergrads borrow to pay for school. Average cumulative indebtedness $14,423. **Criteria for awarding institutional aid:** *Non-need-based:* academics, alumni affiliation, art, athletics, leadership, minority status, music/drama, state/district residency.

SOUTHERN CALIFORNIA INSTITUTE OF ARCHITECTURE

SCI-Arc Admissions Office, Los Angeles, CA 90013-1822
Phone: 213.356.5320 • **Financial Aid Phone:** 213-356-5346
E-mail: admissions@sciarc.edu
Fax: 213-613-2260 • **Website:** www.sciarc.edu

This private school was founded in 1972.

RATINGS
Admissions Selectivity Rating: 61   **Fire Safety Rating:** 60*   **Green Rating:** 60*

STUDENTS AND FACULTY
Enrollment: 245. **Student Body:** 40% out-of-state, 20% international (45 countries represented). Asian 24%, African American 1%, Caucasian 30%, Hispanic 18%.
Retention and Graduation: 93% freshmen return for sophomore year. **Faculty:** Student/faculty ratio 15:1. 36 full-time faculty, 25% are women. **Degrees:** bachelor's, master's. **Special Study Options:** internships, study abroad. **Career Services:** Alumni network, internships.

FACILITIES
Special Academic Facilities/Equipment: SCI-Arc gallery, Wood/Metal Shop, Digital Fabrication shop **Computers:** Students can register for classes online.

CAMPUS LIFE
Environment: Metropolis. **Activities:** student government. **On-Campus Highlights:** SCI-Arc Gallery, Kappe Library, Wood/Metal Shop, Studios

ADMISSIONS
Freshman Academic Profile: Minimum web-based TOEFL 83. Minimum paper TOEFL 560. **Basis for Candidate Selection:** *Very important factors considered include:* application essay, academic GPA, recommendation(s), character/personal qualities, level of applicant's interest, talent/ability. *Important factors considered include:* rigor of secondary school record. *Other factors considered include:* standardized test scores, extracurricular activities, racial/ethnic status, volunteer work, work experience. **Freshman Admission Requirements:** High school diploma is required and GED is accepted. **Freshman Admission Statistics:** 70 applied, 91% admitted, 41% enrolled. **Transfer Admission Requirements:** college transcript(s), essay or personal statement, Lowest grade transferable C. **General Admission Information:** Application Fee $75. Regular application deadline 2/1. Regular notification 4/1. Nonfall registration not accepted. Admission may be deferred for a maximum of 1 year.

COSTS AND FINANCIAL AID
Annual tuition $27,500. Required fees $350. **Required Forms and Deadlines:** FAFSA, institution's own financial aid formTax returns or parents' tax returns. **Types of Aid:** *Need-based scholarships/grants:* Federal Pell, SEOG, state scholarships/grants, the school's own gift aid. *Loans:* Subsidized Stafford, Unsubsidized Stafford, PLUS. **Student Employment:** Federal Work-Study Program available. **Criteria for awarding institutional aid:** *Non-need-based:* academics, state/district residency.

SOUTHERN CONNECTICUT STATE UNIVERSITY

SCSU-Admissions House, New Haven, CT 06515-1202
Phone: 203-392-5656
E-mail: adminfo@scsu.ctstateu.edu • **CEEB Code:** 3662
Fax: 203-392-5727 • **Website:** www.southernct.edu • **ACT Code:**

This public school was founded in 1893. It has a 168-acre campus.

RATINGS
Admissions Selectivity Rating: 69   **Fire Safety Rating:** 60*   **Green Rating:** 85

STUDENTS AND FACULTY
Enrollment: 8,525. **Student Body:** 60% female, 40% male, 4% out-of-state, 0% international (39 countries represented). Asian 3%, African American 16%, Caucasian 62%, Hispanic 10%, Native American 0%.
Retention and Graduation: 12% freshmen graduate within 4 years. 44% freshmen graduate within 6 years. 27% grads go on to further study within 1 year. **Faculty:** Student/faculty ratio 17:1. 403 full-time faculty, 90% hold PhDs, 14% are members of minority groups, 45% are women.

ACADEMICS

Degrees: bachelor's, master's, post-master's certificate. **Classes:** Most classes have 20–29 students. Most lab/discussion sessions have 10–19 students. **Special Study Options:** Accelerated program, cooperative education program, cross-registration, distance learning, double major, exchange student program (domestic), external degree program, honors program, independent study, internships, liberal arts/career combination, student-designed major, study abroad, teacher certification program, Undergrads may take grad level classes Cooperative Education Programs: Arts, Business, Computer Science, Education, Health Professions, Humanities, Natural Science, Social/Behavioral Science, Technologies. Domestic Exchange Program(s): Exchange programs with other members of state university system. Foreign Exchange Program(s): Study abroad in England, France, and Spain. Evening division. **Disability Services:** Special programs offered to physically disabled students include note-taking services, reader services, tape recorders, tutors. **Career Services:** career/job search classes, internships.

FACILITIES

Housing: Coed dorms, special housing for disabled students, apartments for single students, Freshmen have their own residence halls. Students must be 19 or older to live in upper-classman residence halls. 95% of campus accessible to physically disabled. **Special Academic Facilities/Equipment:** Art gallery, language lab, child development center, communication disorders center, planetarium and observatory, closed-circuit TV center.

CAMPUS LIFE

Environment: Village. **Activities:** Choral groups, concert band, drama/theater, literary magazine, marching band, music ensembles, pep band, radio station, student government, student newspaper, yearbook 63 registered organizations, 3 religious organizations. 2 fraternities, 4 sororities. **Athletics (Intercollegiate):** *Men:* baseball, basketball, cross-country, football, golf, gymnastics, ice hockey, rugby, soccer, softball, swimming, track/field (outdoor), track/field (indoor), volleyball, wrestling. *Women:* basketball, cheerleading, cross-country, field hockey, golf, gymnastics, rugby, soccer, softball, swimming, track/field (outdoor), track/field (indoor), volleyball.

ADMISSIONS

Freshman Academic Profile: 5% in top 10% of high school class, 21% in top 25% of high school class, 60% in top 50% of high school class. 88% from public high schools. SAT Math middle 50% range 410–530. SAT Critical Reading middle 50% range 420–520. SAT Writing middle 50% range 420–530. ACT middle 50% range 17–22. Minimum paper TOEFL 525. **Basis for Candidate Selection:** *Very important factors considered include:* rigor of secondary school record. *Important factors considered include:* application essay, academic GPA, recommendation(s), standardized test scores. *Other factors considered include:* Class rank, alumni/ae relation, character/personal qualities, extracurricular activities, first generation, racial/ethnic status, talent/ability, volunteer work, work experience. **Freshman Admission Requirements:** High school diploma is required and GED is accepted. *Academic units required:* 4 English, 3 mathematics, 2 science, (1 science labs), 2 foreign language, 2 social studies, 2 history. *Academic units recommended:* 4 English, 3 mathematics, 2 science, (1 science labs), 2 foreign language, 2 social studies, 2 history. **Freshman Admission Statistics:** 4,978 applied, 75% admitted, 37% enrolled. **Transfer Admission Requirements:** college transcript(s), essay or personal statement, statement of good standing from prior institution(s). Minimum college GPA of 2.0 required. Lowest grade transferable C–. **General Admission Information:** Application Fee $50. Regular application deadline 7/1. Notification on a rolling basis, beginning on or about 12/1. Nonfall registration accepted. Admission may be deferred for a maximum of 2 years. Credit offered for CEEB Advanced Placement tests.

COSTS AND FINANCIAL AID

Annual in-state tuition $4,285. Annual out-of-state tuition $15,137. Room and board $10,687. Required fees $4,256. Average book expense $1,400. **Required Forms and Deadlines:** FAFSA. **Types of Aid:** *Need-based scholarships/grants:* Federal Pell, SEOG, state scholarships/grants, the school's own gift aid. *Loans:* Subsidized Stafford, Unsubsidized Stafford, PLUS, Federal Perkins. **Student Employment:** Federal Work-Study Program available. Institutional employment available. Highest amount earned per year from on-campus jobs $1,400. Off-campus job opportunities are good. **Financial Aid Statistics:** 75% freshmen, 76% undergrads receive need-based scholarship or grant aid. 25% freshmen, 15% undergrads receive non-need-based scholarship or grant aid. 79% freshmen, 88% undergrads receive need-based self-help aid. 1% freshmen, 2% undergrads receive athletic scholarships. **Criteria for awarding institutional aid:** *Non-need-based:* academics, alumni affiliation, athletics.

SOUTHERN ILLINOIS UNIVERSITY— CARBONDALE

Undergraduate Admissions, 425 Clocktower, Carbondale, IL 62901-4512
Phone: 618-536-4405 • **Financial Aid Phone:** 618-453-4334
E-mail: joinsiuc@siu.edu • **CEEB Code:** 1726
Website: www.siuc.edu • **ACT Code:** 1144

This public school was founded in 1869. It has a 1136-acre campus.

RATINGS

Admissions Selectivity Rating: 84   **Fire Safety Rating:** 84   **Green Rating:** 87

STUDENTS AND FACULTY

Enrollment: 14,077. **Student Body:** 44% female, 56% male, 13% out-of-state, 3% international (95 countries represented). Asian 2%, African American 22%, Caucasian 64%, Hispanic 6%, Native American 0%.
Retention and Graduation: 61% freshmen return for sophomore year. 26% freshmen graduate within 4 years. 41% grads go on to further study within 1 year. 1% grads pursue law degrees. 1% grads pursue medical degrees. **Faculty:** Student/faculty ratio 15:1. 869 full-time faculty, 79% hold PhDs, 20% are members of minority groups, 36% are women. 30% of classes are taught by teaching assistants.

ACADEMICS

Degrees: associate, bachelor's, first professional, first professional certificate, master's, post-bachelor's certificate. **Classes:** Most classes have 10–19 students. Most lab/discussion sessions have 20–29 students. **Majors with Highest Enrollment:** business administration and management; elementary education and teaching; health/health care administration/management. **Special Study Options:** cooperative education program, distance learning, double major, English as a Second Language (ESL), honors program, independent study, internships, student-designed major, study abroad, teacher certification program, ROTC: Army; Air Force. **Honors Programs:** University Honors Program - to reward its best undergraduates for their high academic achievement, intended to give the Honors Student a taste of the private-college experience at a state-university price. Classes are small, unique in character, and specially designed for University Honors Students by outstanding SIUC faculty. **Combined Degree Programs:** JD/MD, MA/MBA, MS/MBA, MBA/JD, MBA/MS, MSW/JD. **Disability Services:** Special programs offered to physically disabled students include note-taking services, reader services, tape recorders, tutors. **Career Services:** alumni services, career/job search classes, career assessment, internships Career Services highlights include Extern Program - a job shadowing program. Business students typically comprise the largest number of participants of this campus-wide program, resulting in a 53+% job/internship offer rate.

FACILITIES

Housing: Coed dorms, special housing for disabled students, men's dorms, women's dorms, fraternity/sorority housing, apartments for married students, apartments for single students, Living Learning Communities; Residential College; General Living Learning; Freshman Interest Groups. 99% of campus accessible to physically disabled. **Special Academic Facilities/Equipment:** Art, natural history, and science museums, outdoor education center, center for crime studies, advertising and public relations agencies, child development lab, community human services center, airport training facility, archaeological research center, fisheries and wildlife research labs, coal research center, electron microscopy center. SIUC's two newest additions: Troutt-Wittmann Academic and Training Center; Student Health Center. **Computers:** 15% of classrooms, 100% of libraries, 95% of dining areas, 100% of student union, 70% of common outdoor areas have wireless network access. Students can register for classes online. Administrative functions (other than registration) can be performed online.

CAMPUS LIFE

Environment: Town. **Activities:** Choral groups, concert band, dance, drama/theater, jazz band, literary magazine, marching band, music ensembles, musical theater, opera, pep band, radio station, student government, student newspaper, student-run film society, symphony orchestra, television station, yearbook, Campus Ministries, International Student Organization 408 registered organizations, 26 honor societies, 25 religious organizations. 20 fraternities, 8 sororities. **Athletics (Intercollegiate):** *Men:* baseball, basketball, cheerleading, cross-country, diving, football, golf, swimming, tennis, track/field (outdoor), track/field (indoor). *Women:* basketball, cheerleading, cross-country, diving, golf, softball, swimming, tennis, track/field (outdoor), track/field (indoor), volleyball. **On-Campus Highlights:** Morris Library, Student Center, Recreation Center, Campus Lake, Faner Museum. **Environmental Initiatives:** $4.0M campus-wide energy efficiency and conservation project to reduce purchased utilities. Vermicomposting facility to compost food waste from campus dining halls and turn it into fertilizer for campus plantings. The facility is heated by a clean-burning oil furnace fired with used motor oil from campus vehicles and is insulated with a soy-based foam product for energy conservation. New Transportation Education Center (currently in design phase) will be Certified under U.S. Green Building Council's LEED-NC 2.2 rating system.

ADMISSIONS

Freshman Academic Profile: 2.8. 9% in top 10% of high school class, 30% in top 25% of high school class, 61% in top 50% of high school class. % from public high schools. SAT Math middle 50% range 450-570. SAT Critical Reading middle 50% range 440-550. ACT middle 50% range 18-24. Minimum paper TOEFL 520. **Basis for Candidate Selection:** *Very important factors considered include:* Class rank, standardized test scores. *Important factors considered include:* academic GPA. *Other factors considered include:* recommendation(s), rigor of secondary school record, extracurricular activities, talent/ability, volunteer work, work experience. **Freshman Admission Requirements:** High school diploma is required and GED is accepted. *Academic units required:* 4 English, 3 mathematics, 3 science, 3 social studies, 2 academic electives. 4 English, 3 mathematics, 3 science, 3 social studies, 2 academic electives. **Freshman Admission Statistics:** 14,535 applied, 51% admitted, 31% enrolled. **Transfer Admission Requirements:** college transcript(s), statement of good standing from prior institution(s). Minimum college GPA of 2.0 required. Lowest grade transferable D. **General Admission Information:** Application Fee $30. Notification on a rolling basis, beginning on or about 9/1. Nonfall registration accepted. Credit and/or placement offered for CEEB Advanced Placement tests.

COSTS AND FINANCIAL AID

Required Forms and Deadlines: FAFSA. **Notification of Awards:** Applicants will be notified of awards on a rolling basis beginning 3/21. **Types of Aid:** *Need-based scholarships/grants:* Federal Pell, SEOG, state scholarships/grants, private scholarships, the school's own gift aid. *Loans:* Direct Subsidized Stafford, Direct Unsubsidized Stafford, Direct PLUS, Federal Perkins, college/university loans from institutional funds. **Student Employment:** Federal Work-Study Program available. Institutional employment available. Highest amount earned per year from on-campus jobs $9,122. Off-campus job opportunities are good. **Financial Aid Statistics:** 43% freshmen, 30% undergrads receive need-based scholarship or grant aid. 81% freshmen, 76% undergrads receive non-need-based scholarship or grant aid. 89% freshmen, 87% undergrads receive need-based self-help aid. 2% freshmen, 2% undergrads receive athletic scholarships. 82% freshmen, 86% undergrads receive any aid. 68% undergrads borrow to pay for school. Average cumulative indebtedness $32,652. **Criteria for awarding institutional aid:** *Non-need-based:* academics, alumni affiliation, art, athletics, leadership, minority status, music/drama.

SOUTHERN ILLINOIS UNIVERSITY— EDWARDSVILLE

PO Box 1600, Edwardsville, IL 62026-1080
Phone: 618-650-3705 • **Financial Aid Phone:** 618-650-3880
E-mail: admissions@siue.edu • **CEEB Code:** 1759
Fax: 618-650-5013 • **Website:** www.siue.edu • **ACT Code:** 1147

This public school was founded in 1957. It has a 2660-acre campus.

RATINGS
Admissions Selectivity Rating: 68   **Fire Safety Rating:** 88   **Green Rating:** 71

STUDENTS AND FACULTY
Enrollment: 11,290. **Student Body:** 53% female, 47% male, 1% international (48 countries represented). Asian 1%, African American 15%, Caucasian 75%, Hispanic 4%, Native American 0%.
Retention and Graduation: 30% freshmen graduate within 4 years. 52% freshmen graduate within 6 years. **Faculty:** Student/faculty ratio 18:1. 626 full-time faculty, 79% hold PhDs, 17% are members of minority groups, 50% are women. 4% of classes are taught by teaching assistants.

ACADEMICS
Degrees: bachelor's, first professional, first professional certificate, master's, post-bachelor's certificate, post-master's certificate. **Classes:** Most classes have 10–19 students. Most lab/discussion sessions have 10–19 students. **Majors with Highest Enrollment:** business/managerial economics. **Special Study Options:** Accelerated program, cooperative education program, cross-registration, distance learning, double major, English as a Second Language (ESL), honors program, independent study, internships, student-designed major, study abroad, teacher certification program, Independent Study; elementary and secondary teacher certificate programs in art, music, social studies, English,kinesiology, biology, chemistry, foreign languages, history, math, physics, speech com-

munication. **Combined Degree Programs:** Econ and Finance; Chemistry; Biological Sciences. **Disability Services:** Special programs offered to physically disabled students include note-taking services, reader services, tape recorders, tutors. **Career Services:** Alumni network, alumni services, career/job search classes, career assessment, internships, regional alumni. Career Services highlights include Through the SIUE Co-op program, students work in professional assignments for employers throughout the U.S. and globally.

FACILITIES
Housing: Coed dorms, special housing for disabled students, fraternity/sorority housing, apartments for married students, apartments for single students, Focused Interest Communities. 100% of campus accessible to physically disabled. **Special Academic Facilities/Equipment:** Art gallery, anthropology museum, language lab, center for advanced manufacturing and production, technology commercialization center, electron microscope, psychomotorskills lab, new engineering building and lab. **Computers:** Administrative functions (other than registration) can be performed online.

CAMPUS LIFE
Environment: Village. **Activities:** Choral groups, concert band, dance, drama/theater, jazz band, literary magazine, music ensembles, musical theater, opera, pep band, radio station, student government, student newspaper, symphony orchestra, Campus Ministries 140 registered organizations, 15 honor societies, 9 religious organizations. 10 fraternities, 7 sororities. **Athletics (Intercollegiate):** *Men:* baseball, basketball, cross-country, golf, soccer, tennis, track/field (outdoor), track/field (indoor), wrestling. *Women:* basketball, cross-country, golf, soccer, softball, tennis, track/field (outdoor), track/field (indoor), volleyball. **On-Campus Highlights:** Morris University Center, Starbucks Coffee, Auntie Anne's Pretzels, New School of Engineering Building, New School of Pharmacy Building, The SIUE campus sits on 2,660 acres of beautiful woodlands and lakes just 25 minutes from St. Louis, Missouri. Also, SIUE residence halls are among the newest in the state.

ADMISSIONS
Freshman Academic Profile: 17% in top 10% of high school class, 42% in top 25% of high school class, 75% in top 50% of high school class. ACT middle 50% range 20-25. Minimum web-based TOEFL 79. Minimum paper TOEFL 550. **Basis for Candidate Selection:** *Very important factors considered include:* Class rank, rigor of secondary school record, standardized test scores. **Freshman Admission Requirements:** High school diploma is required and GED is accepted. *Academic units required:* 4 English, 3 mathematics, 3 science, (3 science labs), 3 social studies, 2 academic electives. *Academic units recommended:* 4 English, 3 mathematics, 3 science, (3 science labs), 3 social studies, 2 academic electives. **Freshman Admission Statistics:** 7,660 applied, 82% admitted, 33% enrolled. **Transfer Admission Requirements:** college transcript(s), minimum college GPA of 2 required. Lowest grade transferable D. **General Admission Information:** Application Fee $30. Regular application deadline 5/1. Notification on a rolling basis, beginning on or about 9/1. Nonfall registration accepted. Admission may be deferred for a maximum of 12. Credit and/or placement offered for CEEB Advanced Placement tests.

COSTS AND FINANCIAL AID
Annual in-state tuition $6,948. Annual out-of-state tuition $17,370. Room and board $9,421. Required fees $2,303. Average book expense $765. **Required Forms and Deadlines:** FAFSA. **Notification of Awards:** Applicants will be notified of awards on a rolling basis beginning 3/15. **Types of Aid:** *Need-based scholarships/grants:* Federal Pell, SEOG, state scholarships/grants, private scholarships, the school's own gift aid, Federal Nursing Scholarships. , Presidential Scholars Program, Chancellor's Scholars Program, Johnetta Haley Scholarship Program, Provost Scholarship. *Loans:* Direct Subsidized Stafford, Direct Unsubsidized Stafford, Direct PLUS, Subsidized Stafford, Unsubsidized Stafford, PLUS, Federal Perkins, college/university loans from institutional funds, HPL. **Student Employment:** Highest amount earned per year from on-campus jobs $1,348. **Financial Aid Statistics:** 68% freshmen, 62% undergrads receive need-based scholarship or grant aid. 28% freshmen, 18% undergrads receive non-need-based scholarship or grant aid. 87% freshmen, 87% undergrads receive need-based self-help aid. 1% freshmen, 1% undergrads receive athletic scholarships. 75% freshmen, 67% undergrads receive any aid. 46% undergrads borrow to pay for school. Average cumulative indebtedness $25,998. **Criteria for awarding institutional aid:** *Non-need-based:* academics, art, athletics, leadership, minority status, music/drama.

SOUTHERN METHODIST UNIVERSITY

PO Box 750181, Dallas, TX 75275-0181
Phone: 214-768-3417 • **Financial Aid Phone:** 214-768-3417
E-mail: ugadmission@smu.edu • **CEEB Code:** 6660
Fax: 214-768-1083 • **Website:** www.smu.edu • **ACT Code:** 4171

This private school, affiliated with the Methodist Church, was founded in 1911. It has a 210-acre campus.

RATINGS
Admissions Selectivity Rating: 92   **Fire Safety Rating:** 93   **Green Rating:** 80

STUDENTS AND FACULTY
Enrollment: 6,175. **Student Body:** 51% female, 49% male, 48% out-of-state, 7% international (92 countries represented). Asian 7%, African American 6%, Caucasian 66%, Hispanic 12%, Native American 0%.
Retention and Graduation: 91% freshmen return for sophomore year. 68% freshmen graduate within 4 years. 79% freshmen graduate within 6 years. **Faculty:** Student/faculty ratio 11:1. 723 full-time faculty, 84% hold PhDs, 18% are members of minority groups, 38% are women.

ACADEMICS
Degrees: bachelor's, certificate, doctoral, master's, post-bachelor's certificate. **Classes:** Most classes have 10–19 students. Most lab/discussion sessions have 20–29 students. **Majors with Highest Enrollment:** business administration and management; public relations/image management; social sciences. **Special Study Options:** Accelerated program, cooperative education program, distance learning, double major, English as a Second Language (ESL), exchange student program (domestic), honors program, independent study, internships, student-designed major, study abroad, teacher certification program. **Honors Programs:** The University Honors Program is designed to prepare Honors students for a new millennium to ensure that they can cope with the challenges of rapid change while taking advantage of the possibilities such a volatile and versatile world presents. The BBA Honors Program, which is separate from the University Honors Program, is composed of special sections of courses in accounting, finance, statistics, operations management, marketing, and management. Advertising Honors Program: A student may apply for the Temerlin Advertising Institute Honors program after completion of his or her first semester as a declared Advertising major. **Combined Degree Programs:** BS/BA in Comp. Sci. and Music; 3-2 Bachelor's MBA. **Disability Services:** Special programs offered to physically disabled students include note-taking services, reader services, tape recorders, tutors. **Career Services:** alumni services, career/job search classes, career assessment, internships.

FACILITIES
Housing: Coed dorms, fraternity/sorority housing, apartments for married students, apartments for single students, wellness housing, theme housing. 95% of campus accessible to physically disabled. **Special Academic Facilities/Equipment:** Art, natural history, and paleontology museums, southwest film/video archives, sculpture garden, performing arts theatres, pollen analysis and geothermal labs, electron microbe lab, microscopy lab, seismological observatory, institute of technology services, TV studio. **Computers:** 30% of classrooms, 100% of dorms, 100% of libraries, 100% of dining areas, 100% of student union, 10% of common outdoor areas have wireless network access. Students can register for classes online. Administrative functions (other than registration) can be performed online.

CAMPUS LIFE
Environment: Metropolis. **Activities:** Choral groups, concert band, dance, drama/theater, jazz band, literary magazine, marching band, music ensembles, musical theater, opera, pep band, radio station, student government, student newspaper, student-run film society, symphony orchestra, yearbook, Campus Ministries, International Student Organization 180 registered organizations, 15 honor societies, 27 religious organizations. 15 fraternities, 13 sororities. **Athletics (Intercollegiate):** *Men:* basketball, diving, football, golf, soccer, swimming, tennis, volleyball, water polo. *Women:* basketball, crew/rowing, cross-country, diving, equestrian sports, golf, soccer, swimming, tennis, track/field (outdoor), volleyball, water polo. **On-Campus Highlights:** Gerald J Ford Stadium, Meadows Museum, Hughes Trigg Student Center, Dallas Hall, Fondren Library. **Environmental Initiatives:** Broad academic commitment: research from Geothermal Energy Lab has revealed widespread availability of green energy source. Geothermal Lab's partnership with Google.org has resulted in sophisticated mapping of geothermal resources across North America. Lab hosts annual geothermal conference attended by the international community. Undergraduate and Graduate environmental degrees available through three portals: the Environmental Studies and Environmental Science programs in Dedman College of Science and Humanities, and the Environmental and Civil Engineering Department of the Lyle School of Engineering. 9 LEED Gold buildings: Embrey (engineering, first on-campus LEED building in Texas), Caruth (engineering), 7 casitas on SMU-in-Taos campus. 2 LEED-registered buildings: Simmons (education-expected to get LEED Gold) and Prothro (theology - expected to get LEED Silver). All new and major renovated buildings to be built to LEED Silver or comparable standard. Formal Sustainability Committee with wide-ranging commitment to education, outreach and campus sustainability best practices. Committee meets monthly, works with students, faculty and staff.

ADMISSIONS
Freshman Academic Profile: Average high school GPA 3.6. 47% in top 10% of high school class, 76% in top 25% of high school class, 96% in top 50% of high school class. 52% from public high schools. SAT Math middle 50% range 600-690. SAT Critical Reading middle 50% range 590-680. SAT Writing middle 50% range 570-680. ACT middle 50% range 27-31. Minimum web-based TOEFL 80. Minimum paper TOEFL 550. **Basis for Candidate Selection:** *Very important factors considered include:* Class rank, application essay, academic GPA, recommendation(s), rigor of secondary school record, standardized test scores. *Important factors considered include:* character/personal qualities, extracurricular activities, talent/ability, volunteer work, work experience. *Other factors considered include:* alumni/ae relation, first generation, interview, level of applicant's interest. **Freshman Admission Requirements:** High school diploma is required and GED is not accepted. *Academic units required:* 4 English, 3 mathematics, 3 science, (2 science labs), 2 foreign language, 1 social studies, 2 history. *Academic units recommended:* 4 English, 3 mathematics, 3 science, (2 science labs), 2 foreign language, 1 social studies, 2 history. **Freshman Admission Statistics:** 11,217 applied, 54% admitted, 24% enrolled. **Transfer Admission Requirements:** college transcript(s), essay or personal statement, minimum college GPA of 2.7 required. Lowest grade transferable C–. **General Admission Information:** Application Fee $60. Regular application deadline 3/15. Notification on a rolling basis, beginning on or about 12/31. Nonfall registration accepted. Admission may be deferred for a maximum of 1 year. Credit and/or placement offered for CEEB Advanced Placement tests.

COSTS AND FINANCIAL AID
Annual tuition $38,870. Room and board $13,955. Required fees $4,930. Average book expense $800. **Required Forms and Deadlines:** FAFSA, CSS/Financial Aid PROFILE, noncustodial PROFILE, business/farm supplement. **Notification of Awards:** Applicants will be notified of awards on a rolling basis beginning 3/15. **Types of Aid:** *Need-based scholarships/grants:* Federal Pell, SEOG, state scholarships/grants, private scholarships, the school's own gift aid. *Loans:* Subsidized Stafford, Unsubsidized Stafford, PLUS, Federal Perkins, state loans, college/university loans from institutional funds. **Student Employment:** Off campus job opportunities are good. **Financial Aid Statistics:** 70% freshmen, 76% undergrads receive need-based scholarship or grant aid. 74% freshmen, 65% undergrads receive non-need-based scholarship or grant aid. 80% freshmen, 84% undergrads receive need-based self-help aid. 5% freshmen, 5% undergrads receive athletic scholarships. 74% freshmen, 71% undergrads receive any aid. 30% undergrads borrow to pay for school. Average cumulative indebtedness $30,987. **Criteria for awarding institutional aid:** *Non-need-based:* academics, art, athletics, leadership, music/drama, religious affiliation, state/district residency.

SOUTHERN NEW HAMPSHIRE UNIVERSITY

2500 North River Road, Manchester, NH 03106-1045
Phone: 603-645-9611 • **Financial Aid Phone:** 603-645-9645
E-mail: admission@snhu.edu • **CEEB Code:** 3649
Fax: 603-645-9693 • **Website:** www.snhu.edu • **ACT Code:** 2514

This private school was founded in 1932. It has a 300-acre campus.

RATINGS
Admissions Selectivity Rating: 67   **Fire Safety Rating:** 96   **Green Rating:** 87

STUDENTS AND FACULTY
Enrollment: 1,929. **Student Body:** 52% female, 48% male, 55% out-of-state, 5% international (79 countries represented). Asian 1%, African American 1%, Caucasian 75%, Hispanic 2%, Native American 0%.
Retention and Graduation: 49% freshmen graduate within 4 years. 12% grads go on to further study within 1 year. **Faculty:** Student/faculty ratio 16:1. 120 full-time faculty, 76% hold PhDs, 12% are members of minority groups, 38% are women. 0% of classes are taught by teaching assistants.

ACADEMICS

Degrees: associate, bachelor's, certificate, master's, post-bachelor's certificate, post-master's certificate. **Classes:** Most classes have 10–19 students. **Majors with Highest Enrollment:** business administration and management; culinary arts/chef training; psychology. **Special Study Options:** Accelerated program, cooperative education program, distance learning, double major, dual enrollment, English as a Second Language (ESL), honors program, independent study, internships, student-designed major, study abroad, teacher certification program, weekend college. **Honors Programs:** Three-Year Honors Program (B.S. in Business Administration) and our traditional four-year honors program (available in conjunction with most majors) **Combined Degree Programs:** Three-Year Bachelor's Degree + 1-Year M.B.A. **Disability Services:** Special programs offered to physically disabled students include note-taking services, reader services, tape recorders, tutors. **Career Services:** Alumni network, alumni services, career/job search classes, career assessment, internships Career Services highlights include Active internship program at the undergraduate and graduate level.

FACILITIES

Housing: Coed dorms, special housing for disabled students, apartments for single students, wellness housing, theme housing. 85% of campus accessible to physically disabled. **Special Academic Facilities/Equipment:** Art Gallery **Computers:** 100% of classrooms, 40% of dorms, 100% of libraries, 100% of dining areas, 100% of student union, have wireless network access. Students can register for classes online. Undergraduates are required to own a computer.

CAMPUS LIFE

Environment: City. **Activities:** Choral groups, concert band, dance, drama/theater, jazz band, literary magazine, musical theater, radio station, student government, student newspaper, television station, yearbook, Campus Ministries, International Student Organization, Model UN 58 registered organizations, 7 honor societies, 1 religious organizations. 3 fraternities, 3 sororities. **Athletics (Intercollegiate):** *Men:* baseball, basketball, cheerleading, cross-country, golf, ice hockey, lacrosse, soccer, tennis. *Women:* basketball, cheerleading, cross-country, lacrosse, soccer, softball, tennis, volleyball. **On-Campus Highlights:** Center for Financial Studies, Fitness Center / Athletic Complex, Robert Frost Hall (Academic Building), McIninch Art Gallery, Last Chapter Pub, In addition to our five most popular places on campus, we also have a gourmet restaurant on campus run by our culinary and hospitality students, a bakery and coffee shop. **Environmental Initiatives:** Renewable Energy Hedge from 2007-2022 based on 17,500 megawatt hours of wind power output with PPM Energy Inc. By a financial swap, the hedge will flat line SNHU energy budget, and 100% offset energy green house gas use in the voluntary market with RECs, and provide the wind developer a consistent stream of income to facilitate more wind construction. This represents a new sustainable model of utility cost control based on long-term agreements between energy users and renewable developers. The establishment of the SNHU School of Liberal Arts Bachelor of Arts in Environment, Ethics and Public Policy. This new degree program represents the effort by SNHU to provide an interdisciplinary approach to training the next generation of ecological leaders with a wide range of interests, backgrounds and skills, able to respond to the challenges posed by sustainability ion the 21st century. The development of campus sustainability energy plan based on development of initiatives for interconnected campus islands of sustainability. Under development are initiatives including use of sawdust for wood gasification for cogeneration units to supply electricity and heat; the use of geothermal systems based on innovative use of ground water near the Merrimack River for heat pumps; real time price control for optimization of energy use based on 5-minte ISO-NE price signals.

ADMISSIONS

Freshman Academic Profile: Average high school GPA 3.0. 88% from public high schools. SAT Math middle 50% range 440-540. SAT Critical Reading middle 50% range 440-520. SAT Writing middle 50% range 430-520. ACT middle 50% range 18-24. Minimum web-based TOEFL 71. Minimum paper TOEFL 530. **Basis for Candidate Selection:** *Very important factors considered include:* academic GPA, rigor of secondary school record. *Important factors considered include:* application essay, recommendation(s), character/personal qualities, extracurricular activities, first generation, level of applicant's interest. *Other factors considered include:* Class rank, standardized test scores, alumni/ae relation, interview, talent/ability, volunteer work, work experience. **Freshman Admission Requirements:** High school diploma is required and GED is accepted. *Academic units required:* 4 English, (2 science labs). 4 English, (2 science labs). **Freshman Admission Statistics:** 3,124 applied, 84% admitted, 18% enrolled. **Transfer Admission Requirements:** High school transcript, college transcript(s), essay or personal statement, minimum college GPA of 2.50 required. Lowest grade transferable C–. **General Admission Information:** Application Fee $40. Nonfall registration accepted. Admission may be deferred for a maximum of 1 year. Credit and/or placement offered for CEEB Advanced Placement tests.

COSTS AND FINANCIAL AID

Required Forms and Deadlines: FAFSA. **Notification of Awards:** Applicants will be notified of awards on a rolling basis beginning 3/1. **Types of Aid:** *Need-based scholarships/grants:* Federal Pell, SEOG, state scholarships/grants, private scholarships, the school's own gift aid. *Loans:* Direct Subsidized Stafford, Direct Unsubsidized Stafford, Direct PLUS, Subsidized Stafford. **Student Employment:** Federal Work-Study Program available. Institutional employment available. Off-campus job opportunities are good. **Financial Aid Statistics:** 94% freshmen, 93% undergrads receive any aid. **Criteria for awarding institutional aid:** *Non-need-based:* academics, alumni affiliation, athletics, leadership, state/district residency.

SOUTHERN OREGON UNIVERSITY

Office of Admissions, Ashland, OR 97520-5032
Phone: 541-552-6411 • **Financial Aid Phone:** 541-552-6600
E-mail: admissions@sou.edu • **CEEB Code:** 4702
Fax: 541-552-6614 • **Website:** www.sou.edu • **ACT Code:** 3496

This public school was founded in 1926. It has a 175-acre campus.

RATINGS

Admissions Selectivity Rating: 66   **Fire Safety Rating:** 84   **Green Rating:** 97

STUDENTS AND FACULTY

Enrollment: 4,337. **Student Body:** 55% female, 45% male, 31% out-of-state, 2% international (32 countries represented). Asian 2%, African American 2%, Caucasian 70%, Hispanic 9%, Native American 2%.
Retention and Graduation: 68% freshmen return for sophomore year. 16% freshmen graduate within 4 years. **Faculty:** Student/faculty ratio 20:1. 199 full-time faculty, 82% hold PhDs, 13% are members of minority groups, 41% are women. 0% of classes are taught by teaching assistants.

ACADEMICS

Degrees: bachelor's, master's, post-bachelor's certificate. **Majors with Highest Enrollment:** business/commerce; criminology; psychology. **Special Study Options:** Accelerated program, cooperative education program, cross-registration, distance learning, double major, dual enrollment, English as a Second Language (ESL), exchange student program (domestic), external degree program, honors program, independent study, internships, liberal arts/career combination, student-designed major, study abroad, teacher certification program, Undergrads may take grad level classes. Nursing programs with Oregon Health Sciences U. Exchange programs with Coll of the Redwoods, Coll of the Siskiyous, and Shasta Coll. Member of National Student Exchange(NSE). Exchange programs abroad in Korea(Dankook U) and Mexico(U of Guanajuato). Study abroad also in Asian, European, and South American countries. Concurrent enrollment with Rogue Community College. **Disability Services:** Special programs offered to physically disabled students include note-taking services, reader services, tape recorders, tutors. **Career Services:** Alumni network, alumni services, career/job search classes, career assessment, internships, regional alumni.

FACILITIES

Housing: Coed dorms, special housing for disabled students, special housing for international students, apartments for married students, apartments for single students, Special quiet, substance free, nonsmoking, older students or freshman only residence halls. **Special Academic Facilities/Equipment:** Art and history museums, art galleries, on-campus preschool and kindergarten, National Guard armory, United States Wildlife Forensics Lab. **Computers:** Students can register for classes online. Administrative functions (other than registration) can be performed online.

CAMPUS LIFE

Environment: Village. **Activities:** Choral groups, concert band, dance, drama/theater, jazz band, literary magazine, music ensembles, musical theater, opera, pep band, radio station, student government, student newspaper, student-run film society, symphony orchestra, television station, International Student Organization 52 registered organizations, 13 honor societies, 5 religious organizations. **Athletics (Intercollegiate):** *Men:* basketball, cross-country, football, track/field (outdoor), wrestling. *Women:* basketball, cross-country, soccer, softball, tennis, track/field (outdoor), volleyball. **On-Campus Highlights:** Hannon Library, Center for the Visual Arts, Student Union, Theatre Building, Music Building. **Environmental Initiatives:** Through the student-initiated Green Energy Fee, SOU purchases Renewable Energy Certificates (RECs) to offset 100% of its electricity consumption and carbon offsets to offset 100% of its natural gas consumption. Among the 54 colleges and universities that are U.S. EPA Green Power Partners, SOU ranked #12 on the EPA's April 6, 2010 Top 20 College & University list. The Higher Education Center, jointly owned with

Rogue Community College, received LEED Platinum certification in 2010, making it the first building in the Oregon University System to achieve the highest level of LEED certification. SOU has replaced two aging boilers in its Central Heat Plant with new boilers that can utilize biomass fuel.

ADMISSIONS

Freshman Academic Profile: Average high school GPA 3.3. 90% from public high schools. SAT Math middle 50% range 460-560. SAT Critical Reading middle 50% range 450-570. SAT Writing middle 50% range 430-540. ACT middle 50% range 19-26. Minimum paper TOEFL 520. **Basis for Candidate Selection:** *Very important factors considered include:* rigor of secondary school record, standardized test scores. *Other factors considered include:* application essay, recommendation(s), character/personal qualities, extracurricular activities, talent/ability, volunteer work, work experience. **Freshman Admission Requirements:** High school diploma is required and GED is accepted. *Academic units required:* 4 English, 3 mathematics, 2 science, 2 foreign language, 3 social studies. 4 English, 3 mathematics, 2 science, 2 foreign language, 3 social studies. **Freshman Admission Statistics:** 2,063 applied, 92% admitted, 37% enrolled. **Transfer Admission Requirements:** college transcript(s), minimum college GPA of 2.2 required. Lowest grade transferable D-. **General Admission Information:** Application Fee $50. Notification on a rolling basis, beginning on or about 9/1. Nonfall registration accepted. Admission may be deferred for a maximum of 1 year. Credit and/or placement offered for CEEB Advanced Placement tests.

COSTS AND FINANCIAL AID

Annual in-state tuition $6,183. Annual out-of-state tuition $18,900. Room and board $10,332. Required fees $1,338. Average book expense $900. **Required Forms and Deadlines:** FAFSA Institutional scholarship application. **Notification of Awards:** Applicants will be notified of awards on a rolling basis beginning 4/1. **Types of Aid:** *Need-based scholarships/grants:* Federal Pell, SEOG, state scholarships/grants, private scholarships, the school's own gift aid. *Loans:* Direct Subsidized Stafford, Direct Unsubsidized Stafford, Direct PLUS, Federal Perkins, state loans, college/university loans from institutional funds. **Student Employment:** Federal Work-Study Program available. Institutional employment available. Off-campus job opportunities are excellent. **Financial Aid Statistics:** 92% freshmen, 87% undergrads receive need-based scholarship or grant aid. 6% freshmen, 3% undergrads receive non-need-based scholarship or grant aid. 85% freshmen, 89% undergrads receive need-based self-help aid. 2% freshmen, 2% undergrads receive athletic scholarships. 80% freshmen, 80% undergrads receive any aid. 80% undergrads borrow to pay for school. Average cumulative indebtedness $25,113. **Criteria for awarding institutional aid:** *Non-need-based:* academics, art, athletics, leadership, minority status, music/drama, state/district residency.

SOUTHERN POLYTECHNIC STATE UNIVERSITY

1100 South Marietta Parkway, Marietta, GA 30060-2896
Phone: 678-915-4188 • **Financial Aid Phone:** 678-915-7920
E-mail: admiss@spsu.edu • **CEEB Code:** 5626
Fax: 678-915-7292 • **Website:** www.spsu.edu/index.htm • **ACT Code:** 865

This public school was founded in 1948. It has a 198-acre campus.

RATINGS

Admissions Selectivity Rating: 73   **Fire Safety Rating:** 94   **Green Rating:** 78

STUDENTS AND FACULTY

Enrollment: 5,324. **Student Body:** 18% female, 82% male, 2% out-of-state, 4% international (51 countries represented). Asian 6%, African American 22%, Caucasian 55%, Hispanic 8%, Native American 0%.
Retention and Graduation: 7% freshmen graduate within 4 years. 37% freshmen graduate within 6 years. **Faculty:** Student/faculty ratio 19:1. 219 full-time faculty, 71% hold PhDs, 29% are members of minority groups, 32% are women. 0% of classes are taught by teaching assistants.

ACADEMICS

Degrees: associate, bachelor's, certificate, master's, post-bachelor's certificate. **Classes:** Most classes have 20-29 students. Most lab/discussion sessions have 10-19 students. **Majors with Highest Enrollment:** architecture (barch, ba/bs, march, ma/ms, phd); construction management; mechanical engineering. **Special Study Options:** cooperative education program, cross-registration, distance learning, double major, dual enrollment, honors program, independent study, internships, study abroad. **Honors Programs:** The SPSU Honors Program provides academically talented students the opportunity to develop their talents and skills in an expanded and enriched curriculum. It features seminar-size classes that demand intellectual rigor. The program provides students with a community of peers and ample opportunity for social interaction within the peer group and with Honors faculty. Students work closely with faculty and have opportunities to expand their learning through independent study, special projects, and research. **Disability Services:** Special programs offered to physically disabled students include note-taking services, reader services, tape recorders, tutors. **Career Services:** alumni services, career/job search classes, career assessment, internships Career Services highlights include We are very proud of our co-op and internship programs. Industry actually seek our students and value them greatly.

FACILITIES

Housing: Coed dorms, special housing for disabled students, men's dorms, apartments for single students. 100% of campus accessible to physically disabled. **Computers:** 100% of classrooms, 100% of libraries, 100% of dining areas, 100% of student union, 60% of common outdoor areas have wireless network access. Students can register for classes online. Administrative functions (other than registration) can be performed online.

CAMPUS LIFE

Environment: City. **Activities:** Choral groups, jazz band, pep band, radio station, student government, student newspaper, Campus Ministries, International Student Organization 87 registered organizations, 3 honor societies, 8 fraternities, 3 sororities. **Athletics (Intercollegiate):** *Men:* baseball, basketball, cheerleading, soccer. *Women:* basketball, cheerleading. **On-Campus Highlights:** Student Activities Center, Health and Wellness Center, Library, Gym, Administration Building. **Environmental Initiatives:** Transportation Master Plan to reduce SOVs. Commitment to build all new and renovated buildings to LEED silver certification. Reducing the university's carbon footprint by using EMS, green building materials, and voluntary recycling.

ADMISSIONS

Freshman Academic Profile: 3.3. 12% in top 10% of high school class, 42% in top 25% of high school class, 79% in top 50% of high school class. SAT Math middle 50% range 540-635. SAT Critical Reading middle 50% range 500-600. SAT Writing middle 50% range 470-570. ACT middle 50% range 21-26. Minimum web-based TOEFL 79. Minimum paper TOEFL 550. **Basis for Candidate Selection:** *Very important factors considered include:* academic GPA, rigor of secondary school record, standardized test scores. **Freshman Admission Requirements:** High school diploma is required and GED is not accepted. *Academic units required:* 4 English, 4 mathematics, 3 science, (2 science labs), 2 foreign language, 3 social studies, 2 academic electives. 4 English, 4 mathematics, 3 science, (2 science labs), 2 foreign language, 3 social studies, 2 academic electives. **Freshman Admission Statistics:** 1,535 applied, 79% admitted, 65% enrolled. **Transfer Admission Requirements:** college transcript(s), minimum college GPA of 2.0 required. Lowest grade transferable C. **General Admission Information:** Application Fee $20. Regular application deadline 8/1. Notification on a rolling basis, beginning on or about 9/1. Nonfall registration accepted. Admission may be deferred for a maximum of 1 term. Credit and/or placement offered for CEEB Advanced Placement tests.

COSTS AND FINANCIAL AID

Annual in-state tuition $5,256. Annual out-of-state tuition $18,704. Room and board $8,820. Required fees $1,422. Average book expense $1,700. **Required Forms and Deadlines:** FAFSA. **Notification of Awards:** Applicants will be notified of awards on a rolling basis beginning 6/1. **Types of Aid:** *Need-based scholarships/grants:* Federal Pell, SEOG, state scholarships/grants, private scholarships, the school's own gift aid. *Loans:* Subsidized Stafford, Unsubsidized Stafford, PLUS, state loans. **Student Employment:** Federal Work-Study Program available. Institutional employment available. Off-campus job opportunities are good. **Financial Aid Statistics:** 45% freshmen, 56% undergrads receive need-based scholarship or grant aid. 73% freshmen, 35% undergrads receive non-need-based scholarship or grant aid. 59% freshmen, 70% undergrads receive need-based self-help aid. 1% freshmen, 1% undergrads receive athletic scholarships. 93% freshmen, 77% undergrads receive any aid. 61% undergrads borrow to pay for school. Average cumulative indebtedness $6,850. **Criteria for awarding institutional aid:** *Non-need-based:* academics, athletics.

SOUTHERN UNIVERSITY AND A&M COLLEGE

P.O. Box 9901, Baton Rouge, LA 70813
Phone: 225-771-2430 • **Financial Aid Phone:** 225-771-2790
E-mail: admit@subr.edu • **CEEB Code:** 6663
Fax: 225-771-2500 • **Website:** subr.edu • **ACT Code:** 1610

This public school was founded in 1880. It has a 884-acre campus.

RATINGS

Admissions Selectivity Rating: 68   **Fire Safety Rating:** 69   **Green Rating:** 60*

STUDENTS AND FACULTY

Enrollment: 6,830. **Student Body:** 61% female, 39% male, 19% out-of-state, 2% international (48 countries represented). Asian 0%, African American 96%, Caucasian 3%, Hispanic 0%, Native American 0%.

Retention and Graduation: 65% freshmen return for sophomore year. 7% freshmen graduate within 4 years. 29% freshmen graduate within 6 years. 16% grads go on to further study within 1 year. 15% grads pursue arts and sciences degrees. 1% grads pursue law degrees. **Faculty:** Student/faculty ratio 16:1. 405 full-time faculty, 66% hold PhDs, 85% are members of minority groups, 47% are women. 0% of classes are taught by teaching assistants.

ACADEMICS

Degrees: associate, bachelor's, master's, post-master's certificate. **Classes:** Most classes have 20–29 students. Most lab/discussion sessions have 10–19 students. **Majors with Highest Enrollment:** biology/biological sciences; business administration and management; nursing/registered nurse (rn, asn, bsn, msn). **Special Study Options:** cooperative education program, cross-registration, distance learning, double major, dual enrollment, exchange student program (domestic), honors program, independent study, internships, study abroad, teacher certification program, weekend college, Undergrads may take grad level classes. Cooperative Education Programs: Engineering Combined Degree Programs: Dual degree programs with Jackson State U and Xavier U. **Honors Programs:** The Honors College provides an enhances educational experience for students who have a history of strong academic achievement and who have demonstrated exceptional creativity or talent. The College also provides cultural and intellectual opportunities that are designed to motivae students to perform at the highest level of excellence that they are capable of and through which they may become knowledgeable and effective leaders. **Disability Services:** Special programs offered to physically disabled students include note-taking services, tape recorders, tutors. **Career Services:** career/job search classes, internships Career Services highlights include The 3.0 credit hour co-op education course.

FACILITIES

Housing: special housing for disabled students, men's dorms, women's dorms. 100% of campus accessible to physically disabled. **Special Academic Facilities/Equipment:** Jazz institute Southern Museum of Art. **Computers:** 100% of classrooms, 20% of dorms, 100% of libraries, 50% of dining areas, 90% of student union, 25% of common outdoor areas have wireless network access. Students can register for classes online. Administrative functions (other than registration) can be performed online.

CAMPUS LIFE

Environment: Metropolis. **Activities:** Choral groups, concert band, dance, drama/theater, jazz band, literary magazine, marching band, music ensembles, musical theater, pep band, student government, student newspaper, yearbook 88 registered organizations, 11 honor societies, 6 religious organizations. 4 fraternities, 4 sororities. **Athletics (Intercollegiate):** *Men:* baseball, basketball, cross-country, football, golf, tennis, track/field (outdoor). *Women:* basketball, cross-country, golf, softball, tennis, track/field (outdoor), volleyball. **On-Campus Highlights:** SUBR Museum of Art, Smith - Brown Student Union, Site of the original Red Stick for Baton, Bluff over the Mississippi River **Environmental Initiatives:** MS4-Stormwater Permit with the Parish of East Baton Rouge Full-time Environmental, Safety and Health Director Storm Water Plan (Debris Management)

ADMISSIONS

Freshman Academic Profile: Average high school GPA 2.8. 3% in top 10% of high school class, 13% in top 25% of high school class, 40% in top 50% of high school class. SAT Math middle 50% range 380-460. ACT middle 50% range 15-18. **Basis for Candidate Selection:** *Very important factors considered include:* Class rank, academic GPA, rigor of secondary school record, standardized test scores.*Other factors considered include:* talent/ability. **Freshman Admission Requirements:** High school diploma is required and GED is accepted. *Academic units required:* 4 English, 3 mathematics, 3 science, 2 foreign language, 2 social studies, 1 history, 1 Computer Science, Arts (1.5 credits). 4 English, 3 mathematics, 3 science, 2 foreign language, 2 social studies, 1 history, 1 Computer Science, Arts (1.5 credits) **Freshman Admission Statistics:** 2,179 applied, 56% admitted, 91% enrolled. **Transfer Admission Requirements:** High school transcript, college transcript(s), standardized test scores, statement of good standing from prior institution(s). Minimum college GPA of 2.0 required. Lowest grade transferable C. **General Admission Information:** Application Fee $20. Regular application deadline 7/1. Nonfall registration accepted. Admission may be deferred for a maximum of 2 semesters. Credit offered for CEEB Advanced Placement tests.

COSTS AND FINANCIAL AID

Annual in-state tuition $3,666. Annual out-of-state tuition $9,458. Room and board $5,784. Average book expense $1,200. **Required Forms and Deadlines:** FAFSA, institution's own financial aid form. **Notification of Awards:** Applicants will be notified of awards on a rolling basis beginning 6/30. **Types of Aid:** *Need-based scholarships/grants:* Federal Pell, SEOG, state scholarships/

grants, private scholarships, the school's own gift aid. *Loans:* Direct Subsidized Stafford, Direct Unsubsidized Stafford, Direct PLUS, Subsidized Stafford, Unsubsidized Stafford, PLUS, college/university loans from institutional fundsTOPS TH Harris LEAP. **Student Employment:** Federal Work-Study Program available. Institutional employment available. Highest amount earned per year from on-campus jobs $1,000. Off-campus job opportunities are fair. **Financial Aid Statistics:** 80% freshmen, 77% undergrads receive need-based scholarship or grant aid. 21% freshmen, 18% undergrads receive non-need-based scholarship or grant aid. 79% freshmen, 89% undergrads receive need-based self-help aid. 5% freshmen, 3% undergrads receive athletic scholarships. 89% freshmen, 85% undergrads receive any aid. 85% undergrads borrow to pay for school. Average cumulative indebtedness $23,000. **Criteria for awarding institutional aid:** *Non-need-based:* academics, athletics.

SOUTHERN UTAH UNIVERSITY

S. Utah University, 351 W University Bvd, Cedar City, UT 84720
Phone: 435-586-7740
E-mail: admissioninfo@suu.edu • **CEEB Code:** 4092
Fax: 435-865-8223 • **Website:** www.suu.edu • **ACT Code:** 4271

This public school was founded in 1897. It has a 113-acre campus.

RATINGS

Admissions Selectivity Rating: 80   **Fire Safety Rating:** 60*   **Green Rating:** 60*

STUDENTS AND FACULTY

Enrollment: 5,767. **Student Body:** 54% female, 46% male, 16% out-of-state, 4% international (76 countries represented). Asian 1%, African American 1%, Caucasian 83%, Hispanic 5%, Native American 2%.

Retention and Graduation: 20% freshmen graduate within 4 years. 36% freshmen graduate within 6 years. **Faculty:** Student/faculty ratio 21:1. 254 full-time faculty, 74% hold PhDs, 9% are members of minority groups, 35% are women. 0% of classes are taught by teaching assistants.

ACADEMICS

Degrees: associate, bachelor's, certificate, diploma, master's, terminal associate, transfer associate. **Classes:** Most classes have 20–29 students. Most lab/discussion sessions have 20–29 students. **Special Study Options:** cooperative education program, distance learning, double major, English as a Second Language (ESL), honors program, independent study, internships, liberal arts/career combination, teacher certification program, weekend college. **Disability Services:** Special programs offered to physically disabled students include reader services, tape recorders, tutors. **Career Services:** alumni services, career/job search classes, career assessment, internships.

FACILITIES

Housing: Coed dorms, special housing for disabled students, men's dorms, special housing for international students, women's dorms, fraternity/sorority housing, apartments for single students.

CAMPUS LIFE

Environment: Village. **Activities:** Choral groups, concert band, dance, drama/theater, jazz band, literary magazine, marching band, music ensembles, musical theater, opera, pep band, radio station, student government, student newspaper, symphony orchestra, television station, yearbook. **Athletics (Intercollegiate):** *Men:* baseball, basketball, cross-country, football, golf, track/field (outdoor). *Women:* basketball, cross-country, gymnastics, softball, tennis, track/field (outdoor).

ADMISSIONS

Freshman Academic Profile: Average high school GPA 3.5. 17% in top 10% of high school class, 41% in top 25% of high school class, 77% in top 50% of high school class. SAT Math middle 50% range 460-570. SAT Critical Reading middle 50% range 460-560. SAT Writing middle 50% range 430-540. ACT middle 50% range 20-26. Minimum web-based TOEFL 71. Minimum paper TOEFL 525. **Basis for Candidate Selection:** *Very important factors considered include:* academic GPA, standardized test scores.*Other factors considered include:* first generation, racial/ethnic status. **Freshman Admission Requirements:** High school diploma is required and GED is accepted. **Freshman Admission Statistics:** 6,375 applied, 57% admitted, 35% enrolled. **Transfer Admission Requirements:** college transcript(s), minimum college GPA of 2.25 required. Lowest grade transferable D. **General Admission Information:** Application Fee $40. Nonfall registration accepted. Credit and/or placement offered for CEEB Advanced Placement tests.

COSTS AND FINANCIAL AID

Room and board $6,458. **Required Forms and Deadlines:** FAFSA. **Notification of Awards:** Applicants will be notified of awards on a rolling basis beginning 11/1. **Types of Aid:** *Need-based scholarships/grants:* Federal Pell, SEOG, state scholarships/grants, private scholarships, the school's own gift aid. *Loans:* Subsidized Stafford, Unsubsidized Stafford, PLUS, Federal Perkins. **Student Employment:** Federal Work-Study Program available. Institutional employment available. Highest amount earned per year from on-campus jobs $2,000. Off-campus job opportunities are good. **Financial Aid Statistics:** 99% freshmen, 92% undergrads receive need-based scholarship or grant aid. 26% freshmen, 13% undergrads receive non-need-based scholarship or grant aid. 4% freshmen, 8% undergrads receive need-based self-help aid. 5% freshmen, 6% undergrads receive athletic scholarships. Average cumulative indebtedness $13,478. **Criteria for awarding institutional aid:** *Non-need-based:* academics, alumni affiliation, art, athletics, job skills, leadership, minority status, music/drama, state/district residency.

SOUTHERN VERMONT COLLEGE

982 Mansion Drive, Bennington, VT 5201
Phone: 802-447-6304 • **Financial Aid Phone:** 800-660-3561
E-mail: admis@svc.edu • **CEEB Code:** 3796
Fax: 802-447-4695 • **Website:** www.svc.edu • **ACT Code:** 4310

This private school was founded in 1974. It has a 371-acre campus.

RATINGS
Admissions Selectivity Rating: 69   **Fire Safety Rating:** 60*   **Green Rating:** 60*

STUDENTS AND FACULTY
Enrollment: 464. **Student Body:** 64% female, 36% male, 66% out-of-state. **Retention and Graduation:** 61% freshmen return for sophomore year. **Faculty:** Student/faculty ratio 11:1. 16 full-time faculty, 25% hold PhDs, 0% are members of minority groups, 44% are women. 0% of classes are taught by teaching assistants.

ACADEMICS
Degrees: associate, bachelor's, terminal associate, transfer associate. **Special Study Options:** Accelerated program, cooperative education program, distance learning, double major, dual enrollment, honors program, independent study, internships, liberal arts/career combination, student-designed major, study abroad. **Disability Services:** Special programs offered to physically disabled students include note-taking services, tape recorders, tutors. **Career Services:** Alumni network, alumni services, career/job search classes, career assessment, internships.

FACILITIES
Housing: Coed dorms, quiet, substance-free and non-smoking, Freshmen and upper-classmen residence halls. 60% of campus accessible to physically disabled. **Special Academic Facilities/Equipment:** Mountaineers Field House and Fitness Center Apartment style Resident Halls and courtyard Dining Hall and Student Center Everett Mansion

CAMPUS LIFE
Environment: Rural. **Activities:** drama/theater, literary magazine, music ensembles, radio station, student government, student newspaper, yearbook 14 registered organizations, 1 honor societies. **Athletics (Intercollegiate):** *Men:* baseball, basketball, cross-country, rugby, soccer, volleyball. *Women:* basketball, cross-country, rugby, soccer, softball, volleyball.

ADMISSIONS
Freshman Academic Profile: Average high school GPA 2.6. 0% in top 10% of high school class, 5% in top 25% of high school class, 35% in top 50% of high school class. 85% from public high schools. SAT Math middle 50% range 390-490. SAT Critical Reading middle 50% range 420-510. Minimum paper TOEFL 500. **Basis for Candidate Selection:** *Very important factors considered include:* application essay, recommendation(s), rigor of secondary school record, interview. *Important factors considered include:* standardized test scores, character/personal qualities, extracurricular activities, volunteer work. *Other factors considered include:* Class rank, work experience. **Freshman Admission Requirements:** High school diploma is required and GED is accepted. *Academic units required:* 4 English, 2 mathematics. *Academic units recommended:* 4 English, 2 mathematics. **Freshman Admission Statistics:** 373 applied, 71% admitted, 37% enrolled. **Transfer Admission Requirements:** High school transcript, college transcript(s), essay or personal statement, minimum college GPA of 2.0 required. Lowest grade transferable C. **General Admission Information:** Application Fee $30. Notification on a rolling basis, beginning on or about 12/1. Nonfall registration accepted. Admission may be deferred for a maximum of 1 year. Credit offered for CEEB Advanced Placement tests.

COSTS AND FINANCIAL AID
Annual tuition $14,374. Room and board $6,948. Average book expense $500. **Required Forms and Deadlines:** FAFSA, institution's own financial aid form. **Notification of Awards:** Applicants will be notified of awards on or about 3/1. **Types of Aid:** *Need-based scholarships/grants:* Federal Pell, SEOG, state scholarships/grants, private scholarships, the school's own gift aid, Southern Vermont College Opportunity Grant Everett Scholarship Leadership Scholarship Vermont Resident Scholarship TRIO Scholarship. *Loans:* Direct Subsidized Stafford, Direct Unsubsidized Stafford, Direct PLUS. **Student Employment:** Federal Work-Study Program available. Off-campus job opportunities are good. **Financial Aid Statistics:** 89% freshmen, 90% undergrads receive need-based scholarship or grant aid. 94% freshmen, 94% undergrads receive need-based self-help aid. 75% freshmen, 75% undergrads receive any aid. **Criteria for awarding institutional aid:** *Non-need-based:* academics, leadership.

SOUTHERN WESLEYAN UNIVERSITY

Wesleyan Drive, Central, SC 29630-1020
Phone: 864-644-5550 • **Financial Aid Phone:** 864-644-5500
E-mail: admissions@swu.edu • **CEEB Code:** 5896
Fax: 864-644-5972 • **Website:** www.swu.edu • **ACT Code:** 3837

This private school, affiliated with the Wesleyan Church, was founded in 1906. It has a 330-acre campus.

RATINGS
Admissions Selectivity Rating: 64   **Fire Safety Rating:** 68   **Green Rating:** 60*

STUDENTS AND FACULTY
Enrollment: 1,444. **Student Body:** 60% female, 40% male, 28% out-of-state. 1% international (9 countries represented). Asian 0%, African American 27%, Caucasian 61%, Hispanic 2%, Native American 1%. **Retention and Graduation:** 70% freshmen return for sophomore year. 33% freshmen graduate within 4 years. 39% freshmen graduate within 6 years. **Faculty:** Student/faculty ratio 18:1. 58 full-time faculty, 72% hold PhDs, 12% are members of minority groups, 31% are women. 0% of classes are taught by teaching assistants.

ACADEMICS
Degrees: associate, bachelor's, master's. **Classes:** Most classes have 10–19 students. Most lab/discussion sessions have 20–29 students. **Majors with Highest Enrollment:** business/commerce; elementary education and teaching; religion/religious studies. **Special Study Options:** cross-registration, double major, dual enrollment, English as a Second Language (ESL), honors program, independent study, internships, student-designed major, study abroad, teacher certification program. **Honors Programs:** The honors program consists of specialized coursework, non-credit academic experiences, and service opportunities. Honors students must complete a research-based Honors Major Project in their Junior or Senior years. **Disability Services:** Special programs offered to physically disabled students include note-taking services, reader services, tape recorders, tutors. **Career Services:** career/job search classes, career assessment, internships Career Services highlights include Career assessment.

FACILITIES
Housing: Coed dorms, special housing for disabled students, women's dorms, apartments for single students. 90% of campus accessible to physically disabled. **Special Academic Facilities/Equipment:** Freedom's Hill Historic Site, Clayton Genealogical Research library, Electron Microscope lab **Computers:** 100% of classrooms, 50% of dorms, 100% of libraries, 100% of dining areas, 100% of student union, 25% of common outdoor areas have wireless network access. Students can register for classes online. Administrative functions (other than registration) can be performed online.

CAMPUS LIFE
Environment: Town. **Activities:** Choral groups, concert band, drama/theater, jazz band, literary magazine, music ensembles, musical theater, student government, yearbook, Campus Ministries 12 registered organizations, 2 honor societies, 3 religious organizations. **Athletics (Intercollegiate):** *Men:* baseball, basketball, cross-country, golf, soccer. *Women:* basketball, cross-country, soccer, softball, volleyball. **On-Campus Highlights:** Jennings Campus Center, Java City Coffee Shop, Historic Tysinger Gymnasium, Student Apartment Complex **Environmental Initiatives:** Voluntary recycling of paper and plastic in residence halls and academic buildings. Materials are collected by the city.

ADMISSIONS
Freshman Academic Profile: Average high school GPA 3.5. 13% in top 10% of high school class, 34% in top 25% of high school class, 75% in top 50% of

high school class. SAT Math middle 50% range 445-550. SAT Critical Reading middle 50% range 430-540. SAT Writing middle 50% range 420-520. ACT middle 50% range 18-22. Minimum paper TOEFL 500. **Basis for Candidate Selection:** *Very important factors considered include:* academic GPA, standardized test scores. *Other factors considered include:* Class rank, rigor of secondary school record, character/personal qualities, religious affiliation/commitment. **Freshman Admission Requirements:** High school diploma is required and GED is accepted. *Academic units required:* 4 English, 2 mathematics, 2 science, 2 social studies. 4 English, 2 mathematics, 2 science, 2 social studies. **Transfer Admission Requirements:** college transcript(s), minimum college GPA of 2.0 required. Lowest grade transferable C. **General Admission Information:** Application Fee $25. Regular application deadline 8/1. Nonfall registration accepted. Admission may be deferred for a maximum of 1 semester. Credit and/or placement offered for CEEB Advanced Placement tests.

COSTS AND FINANCIAL AID
Annual tuition $19,950. Room and board $8,410. Required fees $600. Average book expense $1,020. **Required Forms and Deadlines:** FAFSA, institution's own financial aid form. **Notification of Awards:** Applicants will be notified of awards on a rolling basis beginning 2/1. **Types of Aid:** *Need-based scholarships/grants:* Federal Pell, SEOG, state scholarships/grants, private scholarships, the school's own gift aid. *Loans:* Subsidized Stafford, Unsubsidized Stafford, PLUS, Federal Perkins. **Student Employment:** Federal Work-Study Program available. Institutional employment available. Off-campus job opportunities are good. **Financial Aid Statistics:** 100% freshmen, 91% undergrads receive need-based scholarship or grant aid. 16% freshmen, 8% undergrads receive non-need-based scholarship or grant aid. 73% freshmen, 80% undergrads receive need-based self-help aid. 5% freshmen, 2% undergrads receive athletic scholarships. 100% freshmen, 99% undergrads receive any aid. 81% undergrads borrow to pay for school. Average cumulative indebtedness $27,106. **Criteria for awarding institutional aid:** *Non-need-based:* academics, athletics, music/drama, religious affiliation.

SOUTHWEST BAPTIST UNIVERSITY

1600 University Avenue, Bolivar, MO 65613-2597
Phone: 417-328-1810 • **Financial Aid Phone:** 417-328-1823
E-mail: admitme@sbuniv.edu • **CEEB Code:** 6664
Fax: 417-328-1808 • **ACT Code:** 2368

This private school, affiliated with the Southern Baptist Church, was founded in 1878. It has a 180-acre campus.

RATINGS
Admissions Selectivity Rating: 66   **Fire Safety Rating:** 65   **Green Rating:** 60*

STUDENTS AND FACULTY
Enrollment: 2,646. **Student Body:** 66% female, 34% male, 29% out-of-state, 1% international (16 countries represented). Asian 1%, African American 4%, Caucasian 86%, Hispanic 1%, Native American 1%.
Retention and Graduation: 70% freshmen return for sophomore year. 38% freshmen graduate within 4 years. 48% freshmen graduate within 6 years. **Faculty:** Student/faculty ratio 13:1. 116 full-time faculty, 59% hold PhDs, 2% are members of minority groups, 41% are women. 0% of classes are taught by teaching assistants.

ACADEMICS
Degrees: associate, bachelor's, certificate, master's, post-master's certificate. **Classes:** Most classes have fewer than 10 students. Most lab/discussion sessions have 10–19 students. **Majors with Highest Enrollment:** business administration and management; elementary education and teaching; psychology. **Special Study Options:** cooperative education program, distance learning, double major, dual enrollment, exchange student program (domestic), honors program, independent study, internships, student-designed major, study abroad, teacher certification program. **Honors Programs:** Our academic honors program consists of the following components: academics, servant leadership, intercultural experiences, spiritual growth, and enrichment opportunities. **Disability Services:** Special programs offered to physically disabled students include note-taking services, reader services, tutors. **Career Services:** career/job search classes, career assessment.

FACILITIES
Housing: special housing for disabled students, men's dorms, women's dorms, apartments for single students. 95% of campus accessible to physically disabled. **Special Academic Facilities/Equipment:** The Driskell Art Gallery Jester Learning and Performance Center Meyer Wellness and Sports Center **Computers:** 100% of classrooms, 100% of dorms, 100% of libraries, 100% of

dining areas, 100% of student union, 40% of common outdoor areas have wireless network access. Administrative functions (other than registration) can be performed online.

CAMPUS LIFE
Environment: Village. **Activities:** Choral groups, concert band, drama/theater, jazz band, music ensembles, musical theater, opera, pep band, student government, student newspaper, symphony orchestra, yearbook, Campus Ministries 34 registered organizations, 8 honor societies, 10 religious organizations. **Athletics (Intercollegiate): Men:** baseball, basketball, cheerleading, cross-country, football, golf, tennis, track/field (outdoor), track/field (indoor). **Women:** basketball, cheerleading, cross-country, soccer, softball, tennis, track/field (outdoor), track/field (indoor), volleyball. **On-Campus Highlights:** Meyer Wellness and Sports Center, Jester Learning and Performance Center, Felix Goodson Student Union, Harriet K. Hutchens Library, Plaster Stadium.

ADMISSIONS
Freshman Academic Profile: Average high school GPA 3.5. 22% in top 10% of high school class, 41% in top 25% of high school class, 67% in top 50% of high school class. SAT Math middle 50% range 450-600. SAT Critical Reading middle 50% range 410-560. ACT middle 50% range 20-26. Minimum paper TOEFL 550. **Basis for Candidate Selection:** *Very important factors considered include:* Class rank, academic GPA, standardized test scores. *Important factors considered include:* application essay, recommendation(s), rigor of secondary school record. *Other factors considered include:* character/personal qualities, interview, talent/ability. **Freshman Admission Requirements:** High school diploma is required and GED is accepted. **Freshman Admission Statistics:** 1,617 applied, 92% admitted, 31% enrolled. **Transfer Admission Requirements:** High school transcript, college transcript(s), standardized test scores, minimum college GPA of 2.0 required. Lowest grade transferable D. **General Admission Information:** Application Fee $30. Notification on a rolling basis, beginning on or about 9/1. Nonfall registration accepted. Admission may be deferred for a maximum of 1 year. Credit and/or placement offered for CEEB Advanced Placement tests.

COSTS AND FINANCIAL AID
Annual tuition $16,500. Room and board $5,720. Required fees $780. Average book expense $1,000. **Required Forms and Deadlines:** FAFSA, institution's own financial aid form. **Notification of Awards:** Applicants will be notified of awards on a rolling basis beginning 3/1. **Types of Aid:** *Need-based scholarships/grants:* Federal Pell, SEOG, state scholarships/grants, private scholarships, the school's own gift aid. *Loans:* Subsidized Stafford, Unsubsidized Stafford, PLUS, Federal Perkins, Federal Nursing, Alternative loans. **Student Employment:** Federal Work-Study Program available. Institutional employment available. Off-campus job opportunities are good. **Financial Aid Statistics:** 66% freshmen, 68% undergrads receive need-based scholarship or grant aid. 93% freshmen, 80% undergrads receive non-need-based scholarship or grant aid. 80% freshmen, 84% undergrads receive need-based self-help aid. 16% freshmen, 12% undergrads receive athletic scholarships. 88% freshmen, 71% undergrads receive any aid. 69% undergrads borrow to pay for school. Average cumulative indebtedness $22,913. **Criteria for awarding institutional aid:** *Non-need-based:* academics, alumni affiliation, art, athletics, job skills, leadership, minority status, music/drama, religious affiliation, state/district residency.

SOUTHWEST MINNESOTA STATE UNIVERSITY

Admission Office, Marshall, MN 56258
Phone: 800-642-0684
E-mail: shearerr@southwest.msus.edu • **CEEB Code:** 6703
Fax: 507-537-7154 • **Website:** www.southwest.msus.edu • **ACT Code:** 2151

This public school was founded in 1963. It has a 216-acre campus.

RATINGS
Admissions Selectivity Rating: 64   **Fire Safety Rating:** 60*   **Green Rating:** 60*

STUDENTS AND FACULTY
Retention and Graduation: 66% freshmen return for sophomore year.

ACADEMICS
Degrees: associate, bachelor's, master's. **Special Study Options:** study abroad, Exchange program abroad in Japan. Study abroad also in Chile and China. **Disability Services:** Special programs offered to physically disabled students include note-taking services, reader services, tape recorders, tutors. **Career Services:** alumni services, career/job search classes, career assessment, internships.

FACILITIES

Housing: apartments for single students. **Special Academic Facilities/ Equipment:** Art gallery, natural history museum, science museum, planetarium, greenhouse, wildlife area.

CAMPUS LIFE

Environment: Rural. **Activities:** literary magazine, radio station, student government, student newspaper, television station, yearbook 65 registered organizations, 1 honor societies, 5 religious organizations. **Athletics (Intercollegiate):** *Men:* cross-country. *Women:* basketball, cross-country, softball, tennis, volleyball.

ADMISSIONS

Freshman Academic Profile: ACT middle 50% range 19-24. Minimum paper TOEFL 500. **Freshman Admission Requirements:** High school diploma is required and GED is accepted.High school diploma is required and GED is not accepted. **Transfer Admission Requirements:** Minimum college GPA of 2.0 required. Lowest grade transferable C. **General Admission Information:** Application Fee $20. Nonfall registration accepted. Credit offered for CEEB Advanced Placement tests.

COSTS AND FINANCIAL AID

Annual in-state tuition $2,648. Annual out-of-state tuition $5,965. Room and board $3,000. Required fees $484. Average book expense $800. **Required Forms and Deadlines:** FAFSA, institution's own financial aid form. **Types of Aid:** *Need-based scholarships/grants:* Federal Pell, SEOG, state scholarships/ grants, private scholarships, the school's own gift aid. *Loans:* Subsidized Stafford, Unsubsidized Stafford, PLUS, Federal Perkins, college/university loans from institutional funds. **Student Employment:** Federal Work-Study Program available. Institutional employment available. Highest amount earned per year from on campus jobs $2,602. Off-campus job opportunities are excellent.

SOUTHWESTERN COLLEGE (AZ)

2625 East Cactus Road, Phoenix, AZ 85032
Phone: 602-386-4100 • **Financial Aid Phone:** 602-386-4106
E-mail: admissions@arizonachristian.edu;
Fax: 602-404-2159 • **Website:** www.arizonachristian.edu

This private school, affiliated with the Baptist Church, was founded in 1960. It has a 17-acre campus.

RATINGS

Admissions Selectivity Rating: 65   **Fire Safety Rating:** 77   **Green Rating:** 60*

STUDENTS AND FACULTY

Enrollment: 175. **Student Body:** 57% female, 43% male, 27% out-of-state, 4% international. Asian 4%, African American 13%, Caucasian 131%, Hispanic 13%, Native American 1%.
Retention and Graduation: 56% freshmen return for sophomore year. 70% freshmen graduate within 4 years. 70% freshmen graduate within 6 years. **Faculty:** Student/faculty ratio 16:1. 13 full-time faculty, 69% hold PhDs.

ACADEMICS

Degrees: associate, bachelor's, certificate.

FACILITIES

Housing: men's dorms, women's dorms, apartments for single students.

CAMPUS LIFE

Environment: Village. **Activities:** Choral groups, drama/theater, music ensembles, student government, student newspaper, yearbook. **Athletics (Intercollegiate):** *Men:* basketball. *Women:* basketball, volleyball.

ADMISSIONS

Freshman Academic Profile: 72% from public high schools. SAT Math middle 50% range 450-560. SAT Critical Reading middle 50% range 460-570. ACT middle 50% range 19-24. Minimum web-based TOEFL 61. Minimum paper TOEFL 500. **Basis for Candidate Selection:** *Very important factors considered include:* application essay, recommendation(s), rigor of secondary school record, standardized test scores, religious affiliation/commitment. *Important factors considered include:* character/personal qualities. *Other factors considered include:* extracurricular activities, interview. **Freshman Admission Requirements:** High school diploma is required and GED is accepted. **Transfer Admission Requirements:** High school transcript, college transcript(s), essay or personal statement, statement of good standing from prior institution(s). Minimum college GPA of 2.0 required. Lowest grade transferable C. **General Admission Information:** Application Fee $25. Nonfall registration accepted. Admission may be deferred for a maximum of 1semester.

COSTS AND FINANCIAL AID

Annual tuition $17,982. Room and board $7,374. Required fees $986. Average book expense $1,600. **Required Forms and Deadlines:** FAFSA. **Notification of Awards:** Applicants will be notified of awards on a rolling basis beginning 5/1. **Types of Aid:** *Need-based scholarships/grants:* Federal Pell, SEOG, state scholarships/grants. *Loans:* Subsidized Stafford, Unsubsidized Stafford, PLUS, Federal Perkins. **Student Employment:** Federal Work-Study Program available. Institutional employment available. **Criteria for awarding institutional aid:** *Non-need-based:* academics, alumni affiliation, leadership, music/drama, religious affiliation.

SOUTHWESTERN COLLEGE (KS)

100 College Street, Winfield, KS 67156
Phone: 620-229-6236 • **Financial Aid Phone:** 620-229-6215
E-mail: scadmit@sckans.edu • **CEEB Code:** 6670
Fax: 620-229-6344 • **Website:** www.sckans.edu • **ACT Code:** 1464

This private school, affiliated with the Methodist Church, was founded in 1885. It has a 85-acre campus.

RATINGS

Admissions Selectivity Rating: 65   **Fire Safety Rating:** 75   **Green Rating:** 76

STUDENTS AND FACULTY

Enrollment: 1,471. **Student Body:** 48% female, 52% male, 34% out-of-state, 1% international (12 countries represented). Asian 2%, African American 8%, Caucasian 63%, Hispanic 6%, Native American 2%.
Retention and Graduation: 70% freshmen return for sophomore year. 29% freshmen graduate within 4 years. 45% freshmen graduate within 6 years. **Faculty:** Student/faculty ratio 12:1. 47 full-time faculty, 60% hold PhDs, 6% are members of minority groups, 38% are women. 0% of classes are taught by teaching assistants.

ACADEMICS

Degrees: bachelor's, master's, post-bachelor's certificate, post-master's certificate. **Classes:** Most classes have lower than 10 students. Most lab/discussion sessions have fewer than 10 students. **Majors with Highest Enrollment:** business administration and management; elementary education and teaching; nursing/registered nurse (rn, asn, bsn, msn). **Special Study Options:** Accelerated program, distance learning, double major, honors program, independent study, internships, student-designed major, teacher certification program. **Disability Services:** Special programs offered to physically disabled students include reader services, tape recorders, tutors.

FACILITIES

Housing: Coed dorms, men's dorms, women's dorms, apartments for married students, apartments for single students. 90% of campus accessible to physically disabled. **Special Academic Facilities/Equipment:** Ruth Warren Abbott Horticulture Lab Floyd and Ethel Moore Biological Field Station Norman E. Hege Education Center **Computers:** 100% of classrooms, 100% of dorms, 100% of libraries, 100% of dining areas, 100% of student union, 100% of common outdoor areas have wireless network access. Students can register for classes online. Administrative functions (other than registration) can be performed online.

CAMPUS LIFE

Environment: Village. **Activities:** Choral groups, concert band, dance, drama/ theater, jazz band, music ensembles, musical theater, pep band, radio station, student government, student newspaper, symphony orchestra, television station, yearbook, Campus Ministries, International Student Organization 25 registered organizations, 2 honor societies, 7 religious organizations. 2 fraternities. **Athletics (Intercollegiate):** *Men:* basketball, cheerleading, cross-country, football, golf, soccer, tennis, track/field (outdoor), track/field (indoor). *Women:* basketball, cheerleading, cross-country, golf, soccer, softball, tennis, track/field (outdoor), track/field (indoor), volleyball. **On-Campus Highlights:** Brand new Women's residence hall, Beech Science Center, Historic Stewart Field House, Christy Administration Building, Roy L. Smith Student Center (Newly re-modeled Cafeteria and bookstore). **Environmental Initiatives:** Kansas Envirothon RecycleMania Encouraging Students to Recycle Old Cell Phones.

ADMISSIONS

Freshman Academic Profile: Average high school GPA 3.3. 16% in top 10% of high school class, 44% in top 25% of high school class, 73% in top 50% of high school class. 95% from public high schools. SAT Math middle 50% range 430-550. SAT Critical Reading middle 50% range 380-540. SAT Writing middle 50% range 390-560. ACT middle 50% range 19-24. Minimum web-based TOEFL 80. Minimum paper TOEFL 550. **Basis for Candidate Selection:** *Very important factors considered include:* academic GPA, rigor of secondary school record, standardized test scores. *Important factors considered include:* application essay. *Other factors considered include:* Class rank, recommendation(s), alumni/ae relation, character/personal qualities, extracurricular activities, interview, talent/ability. **Freshman Admission Requirements:** High school diploma is required and GED is accepted. *Academic units required:* 4 English, 3 mathematics, 2 science, (1 science labs), 1 history. 4 English, 3 mathematics, 2 science, (1 science labs), 1 history. **Freshman Admission Statistics:** 293 applied, 90% admitted, 45% enrolled. **Transfer Admission Requirements:** college transcript(s), essay or personal statement, minimum college GPA of 2.25 required. Lowest grade transferable C. **General Admission Information:** Application Fee $25. Regular application deadline 8/25. Notification on a rolling basis, beginning on or about 9/15. Nonfall registration accepted. Credit offered for CEEB Advanced Placement tests.

COSTS AND FINANCIAL AID
Annual tuition $19,530. Room and board $5,750. Required fees $150. Average book expense $600. **Required Forms and Deadlines:** FAFSA. **Types of Aid:** *Need-based scholarships/grants:* Federal Pell, SEOG, state scholarships/grants, the school's own gift aid. *Loans:* Direct Subsidized Stafford, Direct Unsubsidized Stafford, Direct PLUS, Subsidized Stafford, Unsubsidized Stafford, PLUS, Federal Perkins. **Student Employment:** Federal Work-Study Program available. Institutional employment available. Off-campus job opportunities are fair. **Financial Aid Statistics:** 100% freshmen, 98% undergrads receive need-based scholarship or grant aid. 9% freshmen, 7% undergrads receive non-need-based scholarship or grant aid. 82% freshmen, 85% undergrads receive need-based self-help aid. 25% freshmen, 25% undergrads receive athletic scholarships. 100% freshmen, 99% undergrads receive any aid. 86% undergrads borrow to pay for school. Average cumulative indebtedness $27,973. **Criteria for awarding institutional aid:** *Non-need-based:* academics, athletics, leadership, minority status, music/drama.

SOUTHWESTERN OKLAHOMA STATE UNIVERSITY

100 Campus Drive, Weatherford, OK 73096
Phone: 580-774-3782
E-mail: admissions@swosu.edu • **CEEB Code:** 6673
Fax: 580-774-7131 • **Website:** www.swosu.edu • **ACT Code:** 3340

This public school was founded in 1901. It has a 73-acre campus.

RATINGS
Admissions Selectivity Rating: 65   **Fire Safety Rating:** 60*   **Green Rating:** 60*

STUDENTS AND FACULTY
Enrollment: 4,247. **Student Body:** 58% female, 42% male, 12% out-of-state, 3% international. Asian 1%, African American 5%, Caucasian 79%, Hispanic 4%, Native American 7%.
Retention and Graduation: 65% freshmen return for sophomore year.
Faculty: Student/faculty ratio 21:1. 211 full-time faculty, 59% hold PhDs, 8% are members of minority groups, 43% are women. 5% of classes are taught by teaching assistants.

ACADEMICS
Degrees: associate, bachelor's, first professional, master's. **Classes:** Most classes have 10–19 students. Most lab/discussion sessions have 20–29 students. **Special Study Options:** Accelerated program, distance learning, double major, independent study, internships, student-designed major, teacher certification program, weekend college. **Career Services:** alumni services, career/job search classes, career assessment

FACILITIES
Housing: men's dorms, women's dorms, apartments for married students, apartments for single students. **Special Academic Facilities/Equipment:** Writing lab, museum.

CAMPUS LIFE
Environment: Village. **Activities:** Choral groups, concert band, drama/theater, jazz band, literary magazine, marching band, music ensembles, musical theater, pep band, student government, student newspaper, symphony orchestra, television station, yearbook 3 religious organizations. 3 fraternities, 3 sororities.
Athletics (Intercollegiate): *Men:* baseball, basketball, football, golf, tennis, track/field (outdoor). *Women:* basketball, tennis.

ADMISSIONS
Freshman Academic Profile: Average high school GPA 3.4. 20% in top 10% of high school class, 43% in top 25% of high school class, 74% in top 50% of high school class. 98% from public high schools. ACT middle 50% range 18-24. Minimum paper TOEFL 500. **Basis for Candidate Selection:** *Very important factors considered include:* Class rank, academic GPA, standardized test scores. **Freshman Admission Requirements:** High school diploma is required and GED is accepted. *Academic units required:* 4 English, 3 mathematics, 2 science, (2 science labs), 1 social studies, 2 history, 3 Computer Science or Foreign Language. *Academic units recommended:* 4 English, 3 mathematics, 2 science, (2 science labs), 1 social studies, 2 history, 3 Computer Science or Foreign Language **Freshman Admission Statistics:** 1,301 applied, 89% admitted, 74% enrolled. **Transfer Admission Requirements:** college transcript(s), minimum college GPA of 2.0 required. Lowest grade transferable D. **General Admission Information:** Application Fee $15. Nonfall registration accepted. Admission may be deferred for a maximum of 1 year. Credit and/or placement offered for CEEB Advanced Placement tests.

COSTS AND FINANCIAL AID
Annual in-state tuition $2,700. Annual out-of-state tuition $7,200. Room and board $3,550. Required fees $750. Average book expense $1,200. **Required Forms and Deadlines:** FAFSA, institution's own financial aid form. **Notification of Awards:** Applicants will be notified of awards on or about 3/20. **Types of Aid:** *Need-based scholarships/grants:* Federal Pell, SEOG, state scholarships/grants, private scholarships, the school's own gift aid. *Loans:* Subsidized Stafford, Unsubsidized Stafford, PLUS, Alternative loans through various institutions. **Student Employment:** Federal Work-Study Program available. Institutional employment available. Off-campus job opportunities are fair. **Financial Aid Statistics:** 65% freshmen, 72% undergrads receive need-based scholarship or grant aid. 78% freshmen, 68% undergrads receive non-need-based scholarship or grant aid. 81% freshmen, 88% undergrads receive need-based self-help aid. 4% freshmen, 4% undergrads receive athletic scholarships. 58% undergrads borrow to pay for school. Average cumulative indebtedness $12,222. **Criteria for awarding institutional aid:** *Non-need-based:* academics, alumni affiliation, art, athletics, music/drama, state/district residency.

SOUTHWESTERN UNIVERSITY

Best 378

Admission Office, Georgetown, TX 78627-0770
Phone: 512-863-1200 • **Financial Aid Phone:** 512-863-1259
E-mail: admission@southwestern.edu • **CEEB Code:** 6674
Fax: 512-863-9601 • **Website:** www.southwestern.edu • **ACT Code:** 4186

This private school, affiliated with the Methodist Church, was founded in 1840. It has a 703-acre campus.

RATINGS
Admissions Selectivity Rating: 87   **Fire Safety Rating:** 92   **Green Rating:** 68

STUDENTS AND FACULTY
Enrollment: 1,341. **Student Body:** 60% female, 40% male, 9% out-of-state, 0% international (9 countries represented). Asian 4%, African American 3%, Caucasian 73%, Hispanic 17%, Native American 1%.
Retention and Graduation: 85% freshmen return for sophomore year. 57% freshmen graduate within 4 years. 72% freshmen graduate within 6 years. 25% grads go on to further study within 1 year. 18% grads pursue arts and sciences degrees. 6% grads pursue law degrees. 1% grads pursue business degrees. 3% grads pursue medical degrees. **Faculty:** Student/faculty ratio 10:1. 122 full-time faculty, 98% hold PhDs, 15% are members of minority groups, 52% are women. 0% of classes are taught by teaching assistants.

ACADEMICS
Degrees: bachelor's. **Classes:** Most classes have 10–19 students. Most lab/discussion sessions have 10–19 students. **Majors with Highest Enrollment:** business/commerce; communication studies/speech communication and rhetoric; political science and government. **Special Study Options:** double major, honors program, independent study, internships, liberal arts/career combination, student-designed major, study abroad, teacher certification program. **Disability Services:** Special programs offered to physically disabled students include note-taking services, reader services, tape recorders, tutors. **Career Services:** Alumni network, alumni services, career assessment, internships, regional alumni.

FACILITIES

Housing: Coed dorms, special housing for disabled students, men's dorms, special housing for international students, women's dorms, fraternity/sorority housing, apartments for married students, apartments for single students. 100% of campus accessible to physically disabled. **Special Academic Facilities/ Equipment:** Alma Thomas Fine Arts Center Red and Charline McCombs Campus Center Corbin J. Robertson Center for Fitness and Wellness Fountainwood Astronomical Observatory **Computers:** 100% of classrooms, 100% of dorms, 100% of libraries, 100% of dining areas, 100% of student union, 50% of common outdoor areas have wireless network access. Students can register for classes online. Administrative functions (other than registration) can be performed online.

CAMPUS LIFE

Environment: Town. **Activities:** Choral groups, concert band, dance, drama/ theater, jazz band, literary magazine, music ensembles, musical theater, radio station, student government, student newspaper, student-run film society 99 registered organizations, 14 honor societies, 10 religious organizations. 4 fraternities, 4 sororities. **Athletics (Intercollegiate):** Men: baseball, basketball, cross-country, diving, golf, lacrosse, soccer, swimming, tennis, track/field (outdoor). Women: basketball, cross-country, diving, golf, soccer, softball, swimming, tennis, track/field (outdoor), volleyball. **On-Campus Highlights:** Robertson Center-indoor olympic size pool, McCombs Center-Student Center, Fountainwood Observatory, Korovva Milkbar-student run coffee house, Academic Mall-grassy area in the middle of campus. **Environmental Initiatives:** Signed Talloires Declaration in Spring 2007. Gold Certification under the Leadership in Energy and Environmental Design (LEED'®) Green Building Rating System'„¢ for New Admission Center in 2009. Second LEED certfied buliding project slated for opening 2010.

ADMISSIONS

Freshman Academic Profile: 45% in top 10% of high school class, 82% in top 25% of high school class, 96% in top 50% of high school class. SAT Math middle 50% range 560-650. SAT Critical Reading middle 50% range 560-680. ACT middle 50% range 25-30. Minimum paper TOEFL 570. **Basis for Candidate Selection:** Very important factors considered include: Class rank, application essay, academic GPA, recommendation(s), rigor of secondary school record, standardized test scores. Important factors considered include: alumni/ ae relation, character/personal qualities, extracurricular activities, first generation, geographical residence, interview, level of applicant's interest, racial/ethnic status, talent/ability, volunteer work, work experience. **Freshman Admission Requirements:** High school diploma is required and GED is accepted. Academic units required: 4 English, 4 mathematics, 3 science, (2 science labs), 2 foreign language, 2 social studies, 1 history, 1 academic electives. Academic units recommended: 4 English, 4 mathematics, 3 science, (2 science labs), 2 foreign language, 2 social studies, 1 history, 1 academic electives. **Freshman Admission Statistics:** 2,613 applied, 65% admitted, 20% enrolled. **Transfer Admission Requirements:** High school transcript, college transcript(s), essay or personal statement, statement of good standing from prior institution(s). Minimum college GPA of 3.0 required. Lowest grade transferable C. **General Admission Information:** Application Fee $40. Early decision application deadline 11/1. Regular notification 4/1. Nonfall registration accepted. Admission may be deferred for a maximum of 1 year. Credit offered for CEEB Advanced Placement tests.

COSTS AND FINANCIAL AID

Annual tuition $33,440. Room and board $9,680. Average book expense $1,000. **Required Forms and Deadlines:** FAFSA. **Notification of Awards:** Applicants will be notified of awards on a rolling basis beginning 3/1. **Types of Aid:** Need-based scholarships/grants: Federal Pell, SEOG, state scholarships/ grants, private scholarships, the school's own gift aid. Loans: Direct Subsidized Stafford, Direct Unsubsidized Stafford, Direct PLUS, Federal Perkins, state loans, college/university loans from institutional funds. **Student Employment:** Federal Work-Study Program available. Institutional employment available. Off-campus job opportunities are good. **Financial Aid Statistics:** 100% freshmen, 99% undergrads receive need-based scholarship or grant aid. 84% freshmen, 83% undergrads receive non-need-based scholarship or grant aid. 79% freshmen, 84% undergrads receive need-based self-help aid. 61% undergrads borrow to pay for school. Average cumulative indebtedness $31,848. **Criteria for awarding institutional aid:** Non-need-based: academics, art, minority status, music/drama, religious affiliation.

SPELMAN COLLEGE

350 Spelman Lane, Atlanta, GA 30314-4399
Phone: 404-270-5193 • **Financial Aid Phone:** 404-270-5212
E-mail: admiss@spelman.edu • **CEEB Code:** 5628
Fax: 404-270-5201 • **Website:** www.spelman.edu • **ACT Code:** 794

This private school was founded in 1881. It has a 32-acre campus.

RATINGS

Admissions Selectivity Rating: 91   **Fire Safety Rating:** 95   **Green Rating:** 74

STUDENTS AND FACULTY

Enrollment: 2,145. **Student Body:** 100% female, 0% male, 73% out-of-state, 1% international (11 countries represented). Asian 0%, African American 82%, Caucasian 0%, Hispanic 0%, Native American 0%.
Retention and Graduation: 90% freshmen return for sophomore year. 64% freshmen graduate within 4 years. 72% freshmen graduate within 6 years.
Faculty: Student/faculty ratio 11:1. 174 full-time faculty, 89% hold PhDs, 85% are members of minority groups, 70% are women. 0% of classes are taught by teaching assistants.

ACADEMICS

Degrees: bachelor's. **Classes:** Most classes have 10–19 students. Most lab/ discussion sessions have 20–29 students. **Majors with Highest Enrollment:** political science and government; psychology. **Special Study Options:** cross-registration, double major, exchange student program (domestic), honors program, independent study, internships, liberal arts/career combination, student-designed major, study abroad, teacher certification program. **Honors Programs:** Ethel Waddell Githii Honors Program. **Disability Services:** Special programs offered to physically disabled students include note-taking services, reader services, tape recorders, tutors. **Career Services:** Alumni network, alumni services, career/job search classes, career assessment, internships.

FACILITIES

Housing: women's dorms, apartments for single students. **Special Academic Facilities/Equipment:** Nursery-elementary school for child development majors, language lab, electron microscope. **Computers:** Students can register for classes online. Administrative functions (other than registration) can be performed online.

CAMPUS LIFE

Environment: Metropolis. **Activities:** Choral groups, dance, drama/theater, jazz band, student government, student newspaper, yearbook, Campus Ministries, International Student Organization 17 registered organizations, 18 honor societies, 9 religious organizations. 4 sororities. **Athletics (Intercollegiate):** Women: basketball, cross-country, golf, soccer, softball, tennis, volleyball. **On-Campus Highlights:** Sister's Chapel, The Spelman College Art Museum, Camille Olivia Hanks-Cosby Academic Center, Albro, Falconer, Manley Science Center, The Oval and Alumni Arch.

ADMISSIONS

Freshman Academic Profile: Average high school GPA 3.6. 30% in top 10% of high school class, 64% in top 25% of high school class, 90% in top 50% of high school class. 84% from public high schools. SAT Math middle 50% range 460-540. SAT Critical Reading middle 50% range 470-570. ACT middle 50% range 20-24. Minimum paper TOEFL 500. **Basis for Candidate Selection:** Very important factors considered include: application essay, academic GPA, rigor of secondary school record, standardized test scores, character/personal qualities. Important factors considered include: recommendation(s), extracurricular activities. Other factors considered include: Class rank, alumni/ae relation, first generation, geographical residence, level of applicant's interest, volunteer work, work experience. **Freshman Admission Requirements:** High school diploma is required and GED is accepted. Academic units required: 4 English, 3 mathematics, 3 science, (2 science labs), 2 foreign language, 3 social studies, 2 history, 2 academic electives. Academic units recommended: 4 English, 3 mathematics, 3 science, (2 science labs), 2 foreign language, 3 social studies, 2 history, 2 academic electives. **Freshman Admission Statistics:** 6,081 applied, 38% admitted, 23% enrolled. **Transfer Admission Requirements:** High school transcript, college transcript(s), minimum college GPA of 2.0 required. Lowest grade transferable C. **General Admission Information:** Application Fee $35. Early decision application deadline 11/1. Regular application deadline 2/1. Regular notification 4/1. Nonfall registration not accepted. Admission may be deferred for a maximum of one year. Credit offered for CEEB Advanced Placement tests.

COSTS AND FINANCIAL AID

Annual tuition $20,569. Room and board $11,541. Required fees $3,225. Average book expense $2,000. **Required Forms and Deadlines:** institution's own financial aid form, CSS/Financial Aid PROFILE. **Types of Aid:** *Need-based scholarships/grants:* Federal Pell, SEOG, state scholarships/grants, private scholarships, the school's own gift aid, United Negro College Fund. *Loans:* Subsidized Stafford, Unsubsidized Stafford, PLUS. **Student Employment:** Federal Work-Study Program available. Institutional employment available. Off-campus job opportunities are good. **Financial Aid Statistics:** 97% freshmen, 94% undergrads receive need-based scholarship or grant aid. 2% undergrads receive non-need-based scholarship or grant aid. 73% freshmen, 73% undergrads receive need-based self-help aid. 94% freshmen, 93% undergrads receive any aid. 74% undergrads borrow to pay for school. Average cumulative indebtedness $33,898. **Criteria for awarding institutional aid:** *Non-need-based:* academics, alumni affiliation, leadership, music/drama, state/district residency.

SPRING ARBOR UNIVERSITY

106 East Main Street, Spring Arbor, MI 49283-9799
Phone: 517-750-6458 • **Financial Aid Phone:** 800-968-0011
E-mail: admissions@admin.arbor.edu • **CEEB Code:** 1732
Fax: 517-750-6620 • **Website:** www.arbor.edu • **ACT Code:** 2056

This private school was founded in 1873. It has a 100-acre campus.

RATINGS
Admissions Selectivity Rating: 76   **Fire Safety Rating:** 74   **Green Rating:** 61

STUDENTS AND FACULTY
Enrollment: 3,053. **Student Body:** 69% female, 31% male, 12% out-of-state, (8 countries represented).
Retention and Graduation: 77% freshmen return for sophomore year. 30% freshmen graduate within 4 years. 50% freshmen graduate within 6 years. 22% grads go on to further study within 1 year. 8% grads pursue arts and sciences degrees. 3% grads pursue business degrees. 8% grads pursue medical degrees. **Faculty:** Student/faculty ratio 15:1. 81 full-time faculty, 69% hold PhDs, 11% are members of minority groups, 31% are women. 0% of classes are taught by teaching assistants.

ACADEMICS
Degrees: associate, bachelor's, master's, post-bachelor's certificate. **Classes:** Most classes have 10–19 students. Most lab/discussion sessions have 10–19 students. **Majors with Highest Enrollment:** business administration, management and operations, other; education; theological and ministerial studies, other. **Special Study Options:** Accelerated program, cross-registration, distance learning, double major, dual enrollment, English as a Second Language (ESL), honors program, independent study, internships, student-designed major, study abroad, teacher certification program, weekend college, Off-Campus Study: Washington Journalism semester, Los Angeles Film Studies program, AuSable Inst of Environmental Studies Program (Michigan). Study abroad programs available: China, Latin America Middle East, Oxford Honors, Russian, Japan, Jerusalem Univ., Russia @ St. Petersburg, People's Republic of China @ Sichuan College. Other programs/destinations are available through petition. **Combined Degree Programs:** BA/MEng. **Disability Services:** Special programs offered to physically disabled students include note-taking services, reader services, tape recorders, tutors. **Career Services:** Alumni network, alumni services, career/job search classes, career assessment, internships, regional alumni.

FACILITIES
Housing: special housing for disabled students, men's dorms, special housing for international students, women's dorms, apartments for married students, apartments for single students. 80% of campus accessible to physically disabled. **Special Academic Facilities/Equipment:** State-of-the-art academic building (Poling Center); the Poling Center features the CP Federal Credit Union Trading Center and is equipped with some of the same technology that is used daily on Wall Street including: An electronic wrap-around ticker, large light emitting diode (LED) financial data board, Bloomberg terminal, and continuous financial news feeds. Radio and TV studios, commercial writing/computer graphics lab, science center, art gallery. **Computers:** 90% of classrooms, 100% of dorms, 100% of libraries, 100% of dining areas, 75% of common outdoor areas have wireless network access. Students can register for classes online. Administrative functions (other than registration) can be performed online.

CAMPUS LIFE
Environment: Rural. **Activities:** Choral groups, concert band, drama/theater, jazz band, literary magazine, music ensembles, musical theater, pep band, radio station, student government, student newspaper, student-run film society, symphony orchestra, television station, yearbook, Campus Ministries, International Student Organization 50 registered organizations. **Athletics (Intercollegiate):** *Men:* baseball, basketball, cross-country, golf, soccer, tennis, track/field (outdoor), track/field (indoor). *Women:* basketball, cross-country, soccer, softball, tennis, track/field (outdoor), track/field (indoor), volleyball. **On-Campus Highlights:** Sacred Grounds (Starbucks), Ganton Art Gallery, Poling Center, University Plaza, McKenna Carillon Tower, State-of-the-Art Academic Building (Poling Center) houses a trading center that is equipped with some of the same technology used on Wall Street.

ADMISSIONS
Freshman Academic Profile: Average high school GPA 3.4. 22% in top 10% of high school class, 48% in top 25% of high school class, 75% in top 50% of high school class. 82% from public high schools. SAT Math middle 50% range 540-610. SAT Critical Reading middle 50% range 425-635. SAT Writing middle 50% range 410-610. ACT middle 50% range 20-26. Minimum paper TOEFL 525. **Basis for Candidate Selection:** *Very important factors considered include:* rigor of secondary school record, standardized test scores, character/personal qualities. *Important factors considered include:* academic GPA. *Other factors considered include:* Class rank, application essay, recommendation(s), extracurricular activities, interview, religious affiliation/commitment, talent/ability. **Freshman Admission Requirements:** High school diploma is required and GED is accepted. *Academic units required:* 4 English, 3 mathematics, 3 science, (3 science labs), 3 history, 1 Physical Education or Health Related Course. *Academic units recommended:* 4 English, 3 mathematics, 3 science, (3 science labs), 3 history, 1 Physical Education or Health Related Course **Freshman Admission Statistics:** 2,674 applied, 70% admitted, 17% enrolled. **Transfer Admission Requirements:** High school transcript, college transcript(s), essay or personal statement, minimum college GPA of 2.0 required. Lowest grade transferable C. **General Admission Information:** Application Fee $30. Regular application deadline 8/1. Notification on a rolling basis, beginning on or about 9/1. Nonfall registration accepted. Admission may be deferred for a maximum of No Set Time. Credit offered for CEEB Advanced Placement tests.

COSTS AND FINANCIAL AID
Annual tuition $21,998. Room and board $7,900. Required fees $540. Average book expense $800. **Required Forms and Deadlines:** FAFSA. **Notification of Awards:** Applicants will be notified of awards on a rolling basis beginning 3/1. **Types of Aid:** *Need-based scholarships/grants:* Federal Pell, SEOG, state scholarships/grants, private scholarships, the school's own gift aid. *Loans:* Subsidized Stafford, Unsubsidized Stafford, PLUS, Federal Perkins, MI-Loan Program and Alternative Loans. **Student Employment:** Federal Work-Study Program available. Institutional employment available. Highest amount earned per year from on-campus jobs $1,550. Off-campus job opportunities are fair. **Financial Aid Statistics:** 100% freshmen, 99% undergrads receive need-based scholarship or grant aid. 13% freshmen, 10% undergrads receive non-need-based scholarship or grant aid. 82% freshmen, 86% undergrads receive need-based self-help aid. 10% freshmen, 18% undergrads receive athletic scholarships. 100% freshmen, 93% undergrads receive any aid. 87% undergrads borrow to pay for school. Average cumulative indebtedness $32,791. **Criteria for awarding institutional aid:** *Non-need-based:* academics, art, athletics, minority status, music/drama, religious affiliation.

SPRING HILL COLLEGE

4000 Dauphin Street, Mobile, AL 36608
Phone: 251-380-3030 • **Financial Aid Phone:** 251-380-3460
E-mail: admit@shc.edu • **CEEB Code:** 1733
Fax: 251-460-2186 • **Website:** www.shc.edu • **ACT Code:** 42

This private school, affiliated with the Roman Catholic Church, was founded in 1830. It has a 450-acre campus.

RATINGS
Admissions Selectivity Rating: 89   **Fire Safety Rating:** 87   **Green Rating:** 60*

STUDENTS AND FACULTY
Enrollment: 1,187. **Student Body:** 61% female, 39% male, 60% out-of-state, 1% international (9 countries represented). Asian 1%, African American 17%, Caucasian 65%, Hispanic 8%, Native American 1%.
Retention and Graduation: 74% freshmen return for sophomore year. 55% freshmen graduate within 4 years. 62% freshmen graduate within 6 years. **Faculty:** Student/faculty ratio 12:1. 78 full-time faculty, 92% hold PhDs, 13%

are members of minority groups, 49% are women. 0% of classes are taught by teaching assistants.

ACADEMICS

Degrees: bachelor's, certificate, master's, post-bachelor's certificate, post-master's certificate. **Classes:** Most classes have 10–19 students. Most lab/discussion sessions have 20–29 students. **Majors with Highest Enrollment:** biology/biological sciences; business administration and management; nursing/registered nurse (rn, asn, bsn, msn). **Special Study Options:** Accelerated program, distance learning, double major, dual enrollment, honors program, independent study, internships, student-designed major, study abroad, teacher certification program, 3-2 engineering with Auburn University, University of Alabama Birmingham, Marquette University, University of Florida, and Texas A&M University. Marine biology classes at Dauphin Island Sea Lab in conjunction with the Marine Environmental Sciences Consortium. **Honors Programs:** SHC's 4-year Honors Program offers a challenging and rewarding course of study to academically gifted and motivated students. It is comprised of academic courses; seminar experiences; and additional opportunities for service, leadership, cultural exploration, and social interaction both on and off campus. Honors courses cover material in greater depth, use primary materials when possible, stress student participation and responsibility, and encourage high individual achievement. **Disability Services:** Special programs offered to physically disabled students include tutors. **Career Services:** Alumni network, alumni services, career/job search classes, career assessment, internships, regional alumni.

FACILITIES

Housing: Coed dorms, men's dorms, women's dorms, apartments for single students. 90% of campus accessible to physically disabled. **Special Academic Facilities/Equipment:** Public radio broadcasting station, theater **Computers:** 50% of classrooms, 15% of dorms, 100% of libraries, 100% of dining areas, 100% of student union, 25% of common outdoor areas have wireless network access. Students can register for classes online. Administrative functions (other than registration) can be performed online.

CAMPUS LIFE

Environment: Metropolis. **Activities:** Choral groups, dance, drama/theater, literary magazine, student government, student newspaper, yearbook, Campus Ministries 66 registered organizations, 16 honor societies, 5 religious organizations. 3 fraternities, 5 sororities. **Athletics (Intercollegiate):** *Men:* baseball, basketball, cross-country, golf, soccer, tennis. *Women:* basketball, cross-country, golf, soccer, softball, tennis, volleyball. **On-Campus Highlights:** Arthur Outlaw Recreation Center, Golf Course, Burke Library, Java City Coffee Shop, Dorn Field. **Environmental Initiatives:** Construction of new LEED-certified Student Center Use of a college-wide energy control system Expansion of recycling program.

ADMISSIONS

Freshman Academic Profile: Average high school GPA 3.4. 20% in top 10% of high school class, 47% in top 25% of high school class, 81% in top 50% of high school class. SAT Math middle 50% range 483-600. SAT Critical Reading middle 50% range 480-620. SAT Writing middle 50% range 480-593. ACT middle 50% range 21-26. Minimum web-based TOEFL 80. Minimum paper TOEFL 550. **Basis for Candidate Selection:** *Very important factors considered include:* academic GPA, rigor of secondary school record, standardized test scores. *Important factors considered include:* Class rank, recommendation(s), interview. *Other factors considered include:* application essay, alumni/ae relation, character/personal qualities, extracurricular activities, talent/ability, volunteer work. **Freshman Admission Requirements:** High school diploma is required and GED is accepted. **Freshman Admission Statistics:** 2,817 applied, 47% admitted, 10% enrolled. **Transfer Admission Requirements:** college transcript(s), statement of good standing from prior institution(s). Minimum college GPA of 2.5 required. Lowest grade transferable C–. **General Admission Information:** Application Fee $25. Regular application deadline 7/15. Notification on a rolling basis, beginning on or about 11/1. Nonfall registration accepted. Admission may be deferred for a maximum of 1 year. Credit and/or placement offered for CEEB Advanced Placement tests.

COSTS AND FINANCIAL AID

Required Forms and Deadlines: FAFSA, state aid form. **Notification of Awards:** Applicants will be notified of awards on a rolling basis beginning 2/15. **Types of Aid:** *Need-based scholarships/grants:* Federal Pell, SEOG, state scholarships/grants, private scholarships, the school's own gift aid, ACG, SMART, and TEACH grants. *Loans:* Direct Subsidized Stafford, Direct Unsubsidized Stafford, Direct PLUS, Subsidized Stafford, Unsubsidized Stafford, PLUS, Federal Perkins, Alternative loans (Citiassist, Signature). **Student Employment:** Federal Work-Study Program available. Institutional employment available. Highest amount earned per year from on-campus jobs $1,759. Off-campus job opportunities are good. **Financial Aid Statistics:** 98% freshmen, 96% undergrads receive need-based scholarship or grant aid. 96% freshmen, 97% undergrads receive non-need-based scholarship or grant aid. 98% freshmen, 97% undergrads receive need-based self-help aid. 12% freshmen,

9% undergrads receive athletic scholarships. %71% undergrads borrow to pay for school. Average cumulative indebtedness $30,356. **Criteria for awarding institutional aid:** *Non-need-based:* academics, alumni affiliation, athletics, job skills, leadership, minority status, state/district residency.

SPRINGFIELD COLLEGE (MA)

263 Alden Street, Springfield, MA 1109
Phone: 413-748-3136
E-mail: admissions@spfldcol.edu • **CEEB Code:** 3763
Fax: 413-748-3694 • **Website:** www.spfldcol.edu

This private school was founded in 1885. It has a 80-acre campus.

RATINGS
Admissions Selectivity Rating: 78   **Fire Safety Rating:** 60*   **Green Rating:** 60*

STUDENTS AND FACULTY
Retention and Graduation: 82% freshmen return for sophomore year. 58% freshmen graduate within 4 years. 68% freshmen graduate within 6 years. 20% grads go on to further study within 1 year. **Faculty:** 5% of classes are taught by teaching assistants.

ACADEMICS
Degrees: bachelor's, master's. **Special Study Options:** cooperative education program, cross-registration, distance learning, double major, English as a Second Language (ESL), independent study, internships, liberal arts/career combination, study abroad, teacher certification program, weekend college. **Career Services:** alumni services, career/job search classes, career assessment.

FACILITIES
Housing: Coed dorms, special housing for disabled students, men's dorms, special housing for international students, women's dorms, apartments for married students, apartments for single students. **Special Academic Facilities/Equipment:** International center, college-operated summer day camp, hypermedia lab, centers for allied health sciences, emergency medical services management, occupational therapy, and physician assistant.

CAMPUS LIFE
Activities: Choral groups, concert band, dance, drama/theater, jazz band, literary magazine, marching band, music ensembles, musical theater, opera, pep band, radio station, student government, student newspaper, student-run film society, symphony orchestra, yearbook. **Athletics (Intercollegiate):** *Men:* baseball, basketball, cross-country, diving, football, golf, gymnastics, lacrosse, soccer, swimming, tennis, track/field (outdoor), volleyball, wrestling. *Women:* basketball, cross-country, diving, field hockey, golf, gymnastics, lacrosse, soccer, softball, swimming, tennis, track/field (outdoor), volleyball. **On-Campus Highlights:** Cheney Hall-dining hall, Caf -dining hall, Wellness Center.

ADMISSIONS
Freshman Academic Profile: 84% from public high schools. SAT Math middle 50% range 450-550. SAT Critical Reading middle 50% range 440-550. Minimum paper TOEFL 525. **Basis for Candidate Selection:** *Other factors considered include:* Class rank, application essay, recommendation(s), rigor of secondary school record, alumni/ae relation, character/personal qualities, extracurricular activities, geographical residence, interview, racial/ethnic status, religious affiliation/commitment, talent/ability, volunteer work, work experience. **Freshman Admission Requirements:** High school diploma is required and GED is accepted. **Freshman Admission Statistics:** 2,249 applied, 59% admitted, 38% enrolled. **Transfer Admission Requirements:** college transcript(s), essay or personal statement, interview, statement of good standing from prior institution(s). Minimum college GPA of 2.5 required. Lowest grade transferable C. **General Admission Information:** Application Fee $40. Early decision application deadline 12/1. Regular application deadline 4/11. Nonfall registration accepted. Admission may be deferred for a maximum of 12. Credit and/or placement offered for CEEB Advanced Placement tests.

COSTS AND FINANCIAL AID
Average book expense. **Student Employment:** Federal Work-Study Program available. Institutional employment available. Highest amount earned per year from on-campus jobs $1,100. Off-campus job opportunities are good.

ST JOHN FISHER COLLEGE

3690 East Avenue, Rochester, NY 14618-3597
Phone: 585-385-8064 • **Financial Aid Phone:** 585-385-8042
E-mail: admissions@sjfc.edu • **CEEB Code:** 2798
Fax: 585-385-8386 • **Website:** www.sjfc.edu/ • **ACT Code:** 2798

This private school, affiliated with the Roman Catholic Church, affiliated with the The College is guided by its Catholic heritage. Church, was founded in 1948. It has a 154-acre campus.

RATINGS
Admissions Selectivity Rating: 78   **Fire Safety Rating:** 93   **Green Rating:** 61

STUDENTS AND FACULTY
Enrollment: 2,937. **Student Body:** 59% female, 41% male, 3% out-of-state, 0% international (10 countries represented). Asian 2%, African American 4%, Caucasian 85%, Hispanic 4%, Native American 0%.
Retention and Graduation: 84% freshmen return for sophomore year. 66% freshmen graduate within 4 years. 75% freshmen graduate within 6 years.
Faculty: Student/faculty ratio 13:1. 223 full-time faculty, 88% hold PhDs, 16% are members of minority groups, 52% are women. 0% of classes are taught by teaching assistants.

ACADEMICS
Degrees: bachelor's, master's, post-bachelor's certificate, post-master's certificate. **Classes:** Most classes have 20–29 students. Most lab/discussion sessions have 10–19 students. **Majors with Highest Enrollment:** business administration and management; elementary education and teaching; nursing/registered nurse (rn, asn, bsn, msn). **Special Study Options:** Accelerated program, cross-registration, distance learning, double major, exchange student program (domestic), honors program, independent study, internships, liberal arts/career combination, student-designed major, study abroad, teacher certification program, weekend college. **Honors Programs:** St John Fisher College Honors Program; Science Scholars Program. **Disability Services:** Special programs offered to physically disabled students include note-taking services, reader services, tape recorders, tutors. **Career Services:** Alumni network, career/job search classes, career assessment, internships, regional alumni.

FACILITIES
Housing: Coed dorms, special housing for disabled students, women's dorms. 100% of campus accessible to physically disabled. **Special Academic Facilities/Equipment:** Student Campus Center, State-of-the-Art Laboratories, Two Electron Microscopes, Multimedia Computer Lab, TV Studio Childcare Center (for observation and development), Cyber Cafe, Skalny Welcome Center Art Gallery **Computers:** 25% of classrooms, 100% of libraries, 50% of dining areas, 100% of student union, 10% of common outdoor areas have wireless network access. Students can register for classes online. Administrative functions (other than registration) can be performed online.

CAMPUS LIFE
Environment: City. **Activities:** Choral groups, dance, drama/theater, literary magazine, musical theater, student government, student newspaper, television station, yearbook, Campus Ministries 70 registered organizations, 10 honor societies, 4 religious organizations. **Athletics (Intercollegiate):** *Men:* baseball, basketball, football, golf, lacrosse, soccer, tennis. *Women:* basketball, golf, lacrosse, soccer, softball, tennis, volleyball. **On-Campus Highlights:** Campus Center, Cyber Cafe, Golisano Gateway, Growney Stadium, Student Life Center.

ADMISSIONS
Freshman Academic Profile: Average high school GPA 3.5. 21% in top 10% of high school class, 52% in top 25% of high school class, 87% in top 50% of high school class. 88% from public high schools. SAT Math middle 50% range 500-600. SAT Critical Reading middle 50% range 470-560. SAT Writing middle 50% range 450-550. ACT middle 50% range 22-26. Minimum web-based TOEFL 80. Minimum paper TOEFL 550. **Basis for Candidate Selection:** *Very important factors considered include:* academic GPA, recommendation(s), rigor of secondary school record, alumni/ae relation, character/personal qualities. *Important factors considered include:* Class rank, application essay, standardized test scores, extracurricular activities, interview, level of applicant's interest, talent/ability, volunteer work, work experience. *Other factors considered include:* first generation, geographical residence, state residency. **Freshman Admission Requirements:** High school diploma is required and GED is not accepted. **Freshman Admission Statistics:** 3,769 applied, 64% admitted, 24% enrolled. **Transfer Admission Requirements:** college transcript(s), statement of good standing from prior institution(s). Minimum college GPA of 2.0 required. Lowest grade transferable C. **General Admission Information:** Application Fee $30. Early decision application deadline 12/1. Notification on a rolling basis, beginning on or about 12/1. Nonfall registration not accepted.

Admission may be deferred for a maximum of 2 semesters. Credit offered for CEEB Advanced Placement tests.

COSTS AND FINANCIAL AID
Annual tuition $26,810. Room and board $10,720. Required fees $560. Average book expense $900. **Required Forms and Deadlines:** FAFSA, state aid form. **Notification of Awards:** Applicants will be notified of awards on a rolling basis beginning 3/22. **Types of Aid:** *Need-based scholarships/grants:* Federal Pell, SEOG, state scholarships/grants, private scholarships, the school's own gift aid, Federal Nursing Scholarships. *Loans:* Direct Subsidized Stafford, Direct Unsubsidized Stafford, Direct PLUS, Federal Perkins, Bureau of Indian Affairs; Adult Vocational; Federal College Work Study. **Student Employment:** Federal Work-Study Program available. Institutional employment available. Off-campus job opportunities are good. **Financial Aid Statistics:** 100% freshmen, 100% undergrads receive need-based scholarship or grant aid. 67% freshmen, 59% undergrads receive non-need-based scholarship or grant aid. 93% freshmen, 95% undergrads receive need-based self-help aid. 82% freshmen, 82% undergrads receive any aid. 82% undergrads borrow to pay for school. Average cumulative indebtedness $32,157. **Criteria for awarding institutional aid:** *Non-need-based:* academics, leadership.

ST. AMBROSE UNIVERSITY

518 West Locust Street, Davenport, IA 52803-2898
Phone: 563-333-6300 • **Financial Aid Phone:** 563-333-6314
E-mail: admit@sau.edu • **CEEB Code:** 6617
Fax: 563-333-6297 • **Website:** www.sau.edu • **ACT Code:** 1352

This private school, affiliated with the Roman Catholic Church, was founded in 1882. It has a 118-acre campus.

RATINGS
Admissions Selectivity Rating: 68   **Fire Safety Rating:** 73   **Green Rating:** 60*

STUDENTS AND FACULTY
Enrollment: 2,686. **Student Body:** 59% female, 41% male, 58% out-of-state, 1% international (14 countries represented). Asian 1%, African American 3%, Caucasian 83%, Hispanic 6%, Native American 0%.
Retention and Graduation: 78% freshmen return for sophomore year. 49% freshmen graduate within 4 years. 62% freshmen graduate within 6 years. 23% grads go on to further study within 1 year. **Faculty:** Student/faculty ratio 11:1. 211 full-time faculty, 69% hold PhDs, 8% are members of minority groups, 49% are women. 0% of classes are taught by teaching assistants.

ACADEMICS
Degrees: bachelor's, certificate, master's, post-bachelor's certificate, post-master's certificate. **Classes:** Most classes have 10–19 students. Most lab/discussion sessions have 20–29 students. **Majors with Highest Enrollment:** business/commerce; nursing/registered nurse (rn, asn, bsn, msn); psychology. **Special Study Options:** Accelerated program, cooperative education program, distance learning, double major, independent study, internships, liberal arts/career combination, student-designed major, study abroad, teacher certification program, weekend college, We have overseas academic experiences in England, Ireland, Lithuania, and Ecuador. Our students can, also, take advantage of the overseas experiences thru Central College in Iowa. **Combined Degree Programs:** BS/D.Phys Therapy, BS/MOT, and BA/MED. **Disability Services:** Special programs offered to physically disabled students include note-taking services, reader services, tape recorders, tutors. **Career Services:** Alumni network, alumni services, career/job search classes, career assessment, internships Career Services highlights include Internships: 70% of our Business majors complete at least one internship.

FACILITIES
Housing: Coed dorms, special housing for disabled students, men's dorms, women's dorms, apartments for single students, The University owns several houses next to campus and will rent them out to graduate or married studens. 96% of campus accessible to physically disabled. **Special Academic Facilities/Equipment:** Art gallery, observatory, language lab, and distance learning classrooms (5). **Computers:** 1% of classrooms, 27% of dorms, 100% of libraries, 100% of student union, have wireless network access. Students can register for classes online. Administrative functions (other than registration) can be performed online.

CAMPUS LIFE
Environment: City. **Activities:** Choral groups, concert band, dance, drama/theater, jazz band, literary magazine, music ensembles, musical theater, opera, pep band, radio station, student government, student newspaper, symphony orchestra, television station, Campus Ministries, International Student Organi-

zation 26 registered organizations, 12 honor societies, 3 religious organizations. **Athletics (Intercollegiate):** *Men:* baseball, basketball, bowling, cheerleading, cross-country, football, golf, soccer, tennis, track/field (outdoor), track/field (indoor), volleyball. *Women:* basketball, bowling, cheerleading, cross-country, golf, soccer, softball, tennis, track/field (outdoor), track/field (indoor), volleyball. **On-Campus Highlights:** Rogalski Center (Student Union), Cafeteria, Coffee Shop and Bookstore, Chapel, Galvin Fine Arts Building. **Environmental Initiatives:** STORM WATER DETENTION In order to minimize storm water flow into underground storm sewers, the following areas have been developed to detain water during storm events and allow a slower release into the ground. - Townhouse west 2,154 gallons - University Center parking lot islands 9,694 gallons - University Center west grounds 71,808 gallons - Lombard Street at University Center 10,771 gallons - LINK east entry 1,212 gallons - Rohlman north 2,100 gallons - Cosgrove north grounds 8,617 gallons TOTAL: 106,356 gallons of detention STORM WATER RETENTION AREAS In order to minimize underground storm water flows, the following areas have been developed to capture storm water and re use the water for irrigation purposes: - Franklin Hall west retention tanks 12,000 gallons - Chapel east grounds retention tanks 12,000 gallons - New Hall retention tanks 21,000 gallons We have changed cleaning products to use those products that are Green Sealed Certified. - We use mirco fiber rags in glass and mirror cleaning and we use no glass cleaning chemical of any kind. - We use compact fluorescent light bulbs everywhere they can be used for the last 11 years and as we replace old fixtures we replace them with new ones to accomodate the compact fluorescent bulbs. - We no longer use paper or disposable rags or mops. - We no longer use mop oil for our dust mops but instead we use them dry or we use pack vacuums to cut down on the dust.

ADMISSIONS

Freshman Academic Profile: Average high school GPA 3.2. 19% in top 10% of high school class, 37% in top 25% of high school class, 65% in top 50% of high school class. 70% from public high schools. ACT middle 50% range 20-25. Minimum paper TOEFL 500. **Basis for Candidate Selection:** *Very important factors considered include:* Class rank, academic GPA, rigor of secondary school record, standardized test scores. *Other factors considered include:* application essay, recommendation(s), alumni/ae relation, character/personal qualities, extracurricular activities, first generation, geographical residence, interview, racial/ethnic status, talent/ability, volunteer work. **Freshman Admission Requirements:** High school diploma is required and GED is accepted. **Freshman Admission Statistics:** 2,257 applied, 84% admitted, 29% enrolled. **Transfer Admission Requirements:** High school transcript, college transcript(s), standardized test scores, statement of good standing from prior institution(s). Minimum college GPA of 2.0 required. Lowest grade transferable D. **General Admission Information:** Application Fee $25. Notification on a rolling basis, beginning on or about 10/1. Nonfall registration accepted. Admission may be deferred for a maximum of 1 semester. Credit and/or placement offered for CEEB Advanced Placement tests.

COSTS AND FINANCIAL AID

Annual tuition $25,730. Room and board $9,195. Required fees $240. Average book expense $1,200. **Required Forms and Deadlines:** FAFSA. **Notification of Awards:** Applicants will be notified of awards on a rolling basis beginning 2/15. **Types of Aid:** *Need-based scholarships/grants:* Federal Pell, SEOG, state scholarships/grants, private scholarships, the school's own gift aid. *Loans:* Direct Subsidized Stafford, Direct Unsubsidized Stafford, Direct PLUS, Federal Perkins. **Student Employment:** Federal Work Study Program available. Institutional employment available. Highest amount earned per year from on-campus jobs $6,128. Off-campus job opportunities are excellent. **Financial Aid Statistics:** 99% freshmen, 97% undergrads receive need-based scholarship or grant aid. 58% freshmen, 49% undergrads receive non-need-based scholarship or grant aid. 74% freshmen, 79% undergrads receive need-based self-help aid. 6% freshmen, 7% undergrads receive athletic scholarships. 99% freshmen, 88% undergrads receive any aid. 80% undergrads borrow to pay for school. Average cumulative indebtedness $37,263. **Criteria for awarding institutional aid:** *Non-need-based:* academics, art, athletics, music/drama.

ST. ANDREWS PRESBYTERIAN COLLEGE

1700 Dogwood Mile, Laurinburg, NC 28352
Phone: 910-277-5555 • **Financial Aid Phone:** 910-277-5560
E-mail: admissions@sapc.edu • **CEEB Code:** 5214
Fax: 910-277-5087 • **Website:** sapc.edu • **ACT Code:** 3146

This private school, affiliated with the Presbyterian Church, was founded in 1958. It has a 600-acre campus.

RATINGS
Admissions Selectivity Rating: 74   **Fire Safety Rating:** 60*   **Green Rating:** 60*

STUDENTS AND FACULTY

Enrollment: 422. **Student Body:** 59% female, 41% male, 54% out-of-state, 3% international (8 countries represented). Asian 2%, African American 14%, Caucasian 77%, Hispanic 2%, Native American 1%. **Retention and Graduation:** 34% freshmen graduate within 4 years. 45% freshmen graduate within 6 years. 40% grads go on to further study within 1 year. **Faculty:** Student/faculty ratio 10:1. 30 full-time faculty, 73% hold PhDs, 3% are members of minority groups, 40% are women. 0% of classes are taught by teaching assistants.

ACADEMICS

Degrees: bachelor's, certificate. **Classes:** Most classes have 10–19 students. **Majors with Highest Enrollment:** business/commerce; elementary education and teaching; English language and literature. **Special Study Options:** double major, honors program, independent study, internships, student-designed major, study abroad, teacher certification program, weekend college, online classes. **Disability Services:** Special programs offered to physically disabled students include note-taking services, reader services, tape recorders, tutors. **Career Services:** Alumni network, alumni services, career/job search classes, career assessment, internships, regional alumni.

FACILITIES

Housing: Coed dorms, men's dorms, women's dorms. 90% of campus accessible to physically disabled. **Special Academic Facilities/Equipment:** Art gallery, anthropology museum, science lab, electron microscopy center with three electron microscopes, psychology lab, artronics graphics computer, Scottish Heritage Foundation. **Computers:** 100% of libraries, 50% of dining areas, 100% of student union, have wireless network access. Administrative functions (other than registration) can be performed online.

CAMPUS LIFE

Environment: Rural. **Activities:** Choral groups, drama/theater, literary magazine, student government, student newspaper, yearbook, Campus Ministries 30 registered organizations, 3 honor societies, 1 religious organizations. **Athletics (Intercollegiate):** *Men:* baseball, basketball, cross-country, equestrian sports, golf, horseback riding, lacrosse, soccer, track/field (outdoor), wrestling. *Women:* basketball, cross-country, equestrian sports, horseback riding, lacrosse, soccer, softball, track/field (outdoor), volleyball, wrestling. **On-Campus Highlights:** Equestrian Center, Morgan Jones Science Labs, Electronic and Fine Arts Center, Athletic Facilities, Art Studios.

ADMISSIONS

Freshman Academic Profile: Average high school GPA 3.0 SAT Math middle 50% range 480-540. SAT Critical Reading middle 50% range 480-540. Minimum paper TOEFL 550. **Basis for Candidate Selection:** *Important factors considered include:* academic GPA, standardized test scores, character/personal qualities, extracurricular activities. *Other factors considered include:* Class rank, application essay, recommendation(s), rigor of secondary school record, first generation, interview, talent/ability, volunteer work, work experience. **Freshman Admission Requirements:** High school diploma is required and GED is accepted. *Academic units required:* 3 English, 3 mathematics, 3 science, 1 foreign language, 3 social studies. 3 English, 3 mathematics, 3 science, 1 foreign language, 3 social studies. **Freshman Admission Statistics:** 582 applied, 69% admitted, 24% enrolled. **Transfer Admission Requirements:** High school transcript, college transcript(s), statement of good standing from prior institution(s). Minimum college GPA of 2.5 required. Lowest grade transferable C–. **General Admission Information:** Application Fee $30. Notification on a rolling basis, beginning on or about 9/1. Nonfall registration accepted. Admission may be deferred for a maximum of one term. Credit offered for CEEB Advanced Placement tests.

COSTS AND FINANCIAL AID

Required Forms and Deadlines: FAFSA, state aid form. **Notification of Awards:** Applicants will be notified of awards on a rolling basis beginning 10/1. **Types of Aid:** *Need-based scholarships/grants:* Federal Pell, SEOG, state scholarships/grants, private scholarships, the school's own gift aid. *Loans:* Subsidized Stafford, Unsubsidized Stafford, PLUS. **Student Employment:** Federal Work-Study Program available. Institutional employment available. Highest amount earned per year from on-campus jobs $2,000. **Financial Aid Statistics:** 100% freshmen, 100% undergrads receive need-based scholarship or grant aid. 17% freshmen, 16% undergrads receive non-need-based scholarship or grant aid. 81% freshmen, 80% undergrads receive need-based self-help aid. 19% freshmen, 14% undergrads receive athletic scholarships. 99% freshmen, 98% undergrads receive any aid. 72% undergrads borrow to pay for school. Average cumulative indebtedness $22,599. **Criteria for awarding institutional aid:** *Non-need-based:* academics, alumni affiliation, art, athletics, leadership, music/drama.

ST. BONAVENTURE UNIVERSITY

Best 378

3261 West State Road, St. Bonaventure, NY 14778
Phone: 716-375-2400 • **Financial Aid Phone:** 800-462-5050
E-mail: admissions@sbu.edu • **CEEB Code:** 2793
Fax: 716-375-4005 • **Website:** www.sbu.edu • **ACT Code:** 2882

This private school, affiliated with the Roman Catholic Church, was founded in 1858. It has a 500-acre campus.

RATINGS
Admissions Selectivity Rating: 70   **Fire Safety Rating:** 62   **Green Rating:** 67

STUDENTS AND FACULTY
Enrollment: 1,848. **Student Body:** 52% female, 48% male, 76% out-of-state, 2% international (32 countries represented). Asian 3%, African American 5%, Caucasian 69%, Hispanic 5%, Native American 1%.
Retention and Graduation: 81% freshmen return for sophomore year. 49% freshmen graduate within 4 years. 64% freshmen graduate within 6 years. 51% grads go on to further study within 1 year. **Faculty:** Student/faculty ratio 12:1. 154 full-time faculty, 81% hold PhDs, 8% are members of minority groups, 35% are women.

ACADEMICS
Degrees: bachelor's, master's, post-bachelor's certificate, post-master's certificate. **Classes:** Most classes have 10–19 students. Most lab/discussion sessions have 10–19 students. **Majors with Highest Enrollment:** business/commerce; elementary education and teaching; journalism. **Special Study Options:** Accelerated program, cross-registration, distance learning, double major, dual enrollment, exchange student program (domestic), honors program, independent study, internships, liberal arts/career combination, student-designed major, study abroad, teacher certification program, weekend college. **Combined Degree Programs:** BA/MA. **Disability Services:** Special programs offered to physically disabled students include note-taking services, reader services, tutors. **Career Services:** Alumni network, career/job search classes, career assessment, internships, regional alumni.

FACILITIES
Housing: special housing for disabled students, men's dorms, women's dorms, apartments for single students. 93% of campus accessible to physically disabled. **Special Academic Facilities/Equipment:** Quick Center for the Arts, Digital Conferencing and Media Center, Franciscan Center for Social Concern, Franciscan Institute **Computers:** 100% of classrooms, have wireless network access. Students can register for classes online.

CAMPUS LIFE
Environment: Village. **Activities:** Choral groups, concert band, dance, drama/theater, jazz band, literary magazine, music ensembles, pep band, radio station, student government, student newspaper, television station, yearbook 47 registered organizations, 7 honor societies, 6 religious organizations. **Athletics (Intercollegiate):** *Men:* baseball, basketball, cross-country, diving, golf, soccer, swimming, tennis. *Women:* basketball, cross-country, diving, lacrosse, soccer, softball, swimming, tennis. **On-Campus Highlights:** Reilly Center, Richter Center, Quick Arts Center, Allegany River Trail, Golf Course and Clubhouse, Several major construction projects are taking place between 2006 and 2008, including renovation and addition to Hickey Dining Hall, renovation of Shay-Loughlen Residence Hall and addition of rare books wing to Friedsam Library. **Environmental Initiatives:** New campus construction: St. Bonaventure's William F. Walsh Science Center and the Friedsam Memorial Library Rare Books addition use underground water for cooling systems, reducing the release of carbon dioxide. Fall 2010, Townhouse 23 was dedicated as a "green building." Students living in the 8-apartment complex will work toward sustainable living by composting, recycling and monitoring and limiting their energy use. In April 2010, SBU hosted a week long campus wide event called Eco-Fest. The celebration included a tree planting, a walking tour of the Allegany River Trail and a recycled craft fair.

ADMISSIONS
Freshman Academic Profile: Average high school GPA 3.3. 18% in top 10% of high school class, 42% in top 25% of high school class, 72% in top 50% of high school class. SAT Math middle 50% range 460-600. SAT Critical Reading middle 50% range 460-570. SAT Writing middle 50% range 440-550. ACT middle 50% range 21-26. Minimum paper TOEFL 550. **Basis for Candidate Selection:** *Very important factors considered include:* academic GPA,

recommendation(s), rigor of secondary school record, character/personal qualities, interview. *Important factors considered include:* application essay, standardized test scores, extracurricular activities, level of applicant's interest, talent/ability, volunteer work. *Other factors considered include:* Class rank, alumni/ae relation, first generation, work experience. **Freshman Admission Requirements:** High school diploma is required and GED is accepted. *Academic units required:* 4 English, 3 mathematics, 3 science, 2 foreign language, 4 social studies. *Academic units recommended:* 4 English, 3 mathematics, 3 science, 2 foreign language, 4 social studies. **Freshman Admission Statistics:** 2,456 applied, 79% admitted, 25% enrolled. **Transfer Admission Requirements:** High school transcript, college transcript(s), statement of good standing from prior institution(s). Minimum college GPA of 2.0 required. Lowest grade transferable C. **General Admission Information:** Application Fee $30. Regular application deadline 4/15. Notification on a rolling basis, beginning on or about 10/1. Nonfall registration accepted. Admission may be deferred for a maximum of 1 year. Credit and/or placement offered for CEEB Advanced Placement tests.

COSTS AND FINANCIAL AID
Annual tuition $27,762. Room and board $10,704. Required fees $965. Average book expense $800. **Required Forms and Deadlines:** FAFSA, institution's own financial aid form, state aid form. **Notification of Awards:** Applicants will be notified of awards on a rolling basis beginning 4/1. **Types of Aid:** *Need-based scholarships/grants:* Federal Pell, SEOG, state scholarships/grants, private scholarships, the school's own gift aid. *Loans:* Subsidized Stafford, Unsubsidized Stafford, PLUS, Federal Perkins, college/university loans from institutional funds. **Student Employment:** Highest amount earned per year from on-campus jobs $815. **Financial Aid Statistics:** 77% freshmen, 77% undergrads receive need-based scholarship or grant aid. 94% freshmen, 94% undergrads receive non-need-based scholarship or grant aid. 80% freshmen, 84% undergrads receive need-based self-help aid. 11% freshmen, 11% undergrads receive athletic scholarships. 99% freshmen, 99% undergrads receive any aid. 80% undergrads borrow to pay for school. Average cumulative indebtedness $37,102. **Criteria for awarding institutional aid:** *Non-need-based:* academics, art, athletics, minority status, music/drama, religious affiliation, state/district residency.

ST. CHARLES BORROMENO SEMINARY

100 East Wynnewood Road, Wynnewood, PA 19096
Phone: 610-785-6271 • **Financial Aid Phone:** 610-785-6582
E-mail: dandrassy@adphila.org • **CEEB Code:** 2794
Fax: 610-617-9267 • **ACT Code:** 5923

This private school, affiliated with the Roman Catholic Church, was founded in 1832. It has a 77-acre campus.

RATINGS
Admissions Selectivity Rating: 66   **Fire Safety Rating:** 82   **Green Rating:** 60*

STUDENTS AND FACULTY
Enrollment: 53. **Student Body:** 0% female, 100% male, 42% out-of-state, 4% international (3 countries represented). Asian 4%, African American 0%, Caucasian 92%, Hispanic 0%, Native American 0%.
Retention and Graduation: 75% freshmen return for sophomore year. 33% freshmen graduate within 4 years. 33% freshmen graduate within 6 years. 90% grads go on to further study within 1 year. **Faculty:** Student/faculty ratio 7:1. 21 full-time faculty, 67% hold PhDs, 0% are members of minority groups, 14% are women. 0% of classes are taught by teaching assistants.

ACADEMICS
Degrees: bachelor's, first professional, master's. **Classes:** Most classes have 10–19 students. **Special Study Options:** Accelerated program, English as a Second Language (ESL), independent study.

FACILITIES
Housing: Men's dorms, men's and women's dorms. available during Summer sessions. 75% of campus accessible to physically disabled. **Computers:** Students can register for classes online.

CAMPUS LIFE
Environment: Town. **Activities:** Choral groups, drama/theater, music ensembles, student government, student newspaper 3 registered organizations, 1 honor societies, 2 religious organizations.

ADMISSIONS
Freshman Academic Profile: 22% in top 10% of high school class, 44% in top 25% of high school class, 67% in top 50% of high school class. 40% from public

high schools. SAT Math middle 50% range 470-590. SAT Critical Reading middle 50% range 460-710. Minimum paper TOEFL 450. **Basis for Candidate Selection:** *Very important factors considered include:* application essay, recommendation(s), rigor of secondary school record, character/personal qualities, interview, religious affiliation/commitment. *Important factors considered include:* Class rank, standardized test scores. *Other factors considered include:* extracurricular activities, talent/ability, work experience. **Freshman Admission Requirements:** High school diploma is required and GED is accepted. **Freshman Admission Statistics:** 11 applied, 100% admitted, 91% enrolled. **Transfer Admission Requirements:** High school transcript, college transcript(s), essay or personal statement, minimum college GPA of 2.0 required. Lowest grade transferable C. **General Admission Information:** Regular application deadline 7/15. Nonfall registration accepted. Credit and/or placement offered for CEEB Advanced Placement tests.

COSTS AND FINANCIAL AID
Required Forms and Deadlines: FAFSA, institution's own financial aid form. **Student Employment:** Federal Work-Study Program available. Institutional employment available. Off-campus job opportunities are poor. **Financial Aid Statistics:** 100% freshmen, 100% undergrads receive any aid. 0% undergrads borrow to pay for school. Average cumulative indebtedness $0.

ST. EDWARD'S UNIVERSITY

3001 South Congress Avenue, Austin, TX 78704
Phone: 512-448-8500 • **Financial Aid Phone:** 512-448-8523
E-mail: seu.admit@stedwards.edu • **CEEB Code:** 6619
Fax: 512-464-8877 • **Website:** www.stedwards.edu • **ACT Code:** 4156

This private school, affiliated with the Roman Catholic Church, was founded in 1885. It has a 160-acre campus.

RATINGS
Admissions Selectivity Rating: 83   **Fire Safety Rating:** 80   **Green Rating:** 78

STUDENTS AND FACULTY
Enrollment: 4,224. **Student Body:** 61% female, 39% male, 11% out of state, 7% international (44 countries represented). Asian 2%, African American 4%, Caucasian 40%, Hispanic 35%, Native American 1%
Retention and Graduation: 53% freshmen graduate within 4 years. 69% freshmen graduate within 6 years. **Faculty:** Student/faculty ratio 13:1. 214 full-time faculty, 90% hold PhDs, 13% are members of minority groups, 47% are women. 0% of classes are taught by teaching assistants.

ACADEMICS
Degrees: bachelor's, master's, post-bachelor's certificate. **Classes:** Most classes have 20–29 students. **Majors with Highest Enrollment:** biology/biological sciences; communication and media studies; other; psychology. **Special Study Options:** double major, honors program, internships, study abroad, teacher certification program. **Honors Programs:** Honors Program. **Disability Services:** Special programs offered to physically disabled students include note-taking services, reader services, tutors. **Career Services:** Alumni network, alumni services, career/job search classes, career assessment, internships, regional alumni. Career Services highlights include Service learning initiatives are an integral part of many courses. Faculty receive training on how to integrate service learning into their courses, whereby learning outcomes are achieved while serving the community.

FACILITIES
Housing: Coed dorms, special housing for disabled students, women's dorms, apartments for single students, Community-style living (casas, casitas) and two living-learning communities: Global Understanding and Social Justice. 90% of campus accessible to physically disabled. **Special Academic Facilities/Equipment:** Fine arts facility with digital photography lab; natural sciences center including state-of-the-art labs, classrooms and seminar rooms; interdisciplinary research lab at Wild Basin Wilderness Preserve. **Computers:** 100% of classrooms, 100% of dorms, 100% of libraries, 100% of dining areas, 100% of student union, 100% of common outdoor areas have wireless network access. Students can register for classes online. Administrative functions (other than registration) can be performed online.

CAMPUS LIFE
Environment: Metropolis. **Activities:** Choral groups, dance, drama/theater, literary magazine, music ensembles, musical theater, student government, student newspaper, student-run film society, symphony orchestra, television station, Campus Ministries, International Student Organization 95 registered organizations, 10 honor societies, 3 religious organizations. **Athletics (Intercollegiate):** *Men:* baseball, basketball, golf, soccer, tennis. *Women:* basketball,

golf, soccer, softball, tennis, volleyball. **On-Campus Highlights:** Historic Main Building (view of Austin), Meadows Coffee House, New 119,000 sq ft residential villa 2009, John Brooks Williams Natural Sciences Center, Meditation and Prayer Grotto/Sorin Oak, Sorin Oak is the largest oak tree in Austin at 14.6 feet in circumference. **Environmental Initiatives:** Performance contract to reduce utility consumption across campus: lighting retrofit, thermal storage tank for chilled water supply, replaced steam system with individual building hot water boilers, installed low flow plumbing fixtures (toilets, urinals, shower heads,faucet aerators). Installed variable frequency drives, replaced motors with high efficiency models, cool seal reflective roof on new construction, coordinated building site layout designs and landscaping for hot Texas environment. Eliminated all R-11 refrigerant on campus, replaced 4 older (1980s) chillers with high efficiency models.

ADMISSIONS
Freshman Academic Profile: 20% in top 10% of high school class, 55% in top 25% of high school class, 88% in top 50% of high school class. 72% from public high schools. SAT Math middle 50% range 510-610. SAT Critical Reading middle 50% range 510-620. SAT Writing middle 50% range 490-610. ACT middle 50% range 22-27. Minimum web-based TOEFL 61. Minimum paper TOEFL 500. **Basis for Candidate Selection:** *Very important factors considered include:* application essay, academic GPA, rigor of secondary school record, standardized test scores. *Important factors considered include:* Class rank, recommendation(s), extracurricular activities, volunteer work. *Other factors considered include:* alumni/ae relation, character/personal qualities, first generation, geographical residence, interview, level of applicant's interest, racial/ethnic status, religious affiliation/commitment, talent/ability, work experience. **Freshman Admission Requirements:** High school diploma is required and GED is accepted. *Academic units required:* 4 English, 3 mathematics, 2 science, (2 science labs), 2 foreign language, 1 social studies, 2 history. *Academic units recommended:* 4 English, 3 mathematics, 2 science, (2 science labs), 2 foreign language, 1 social studies, 2 history. **Freshman Admission Statistics:** 4,209 applied, 63% admitted, 29% enrolled. **Transfer Admission Requirements:** High school transcript, college transcript(s), essay or personal statement, minimum college GPA of 2.50 required. Lowest grade transferable C. **General Admission Information:** Application Fee $45. Regular application deadline 5/1. Notification on a rolling basis, beginning on or about 11/1. Nonfall registration accepted. Admission may be deferred for a maximum of One Year. Credit and/or placement offered for CEEB Advanced Placement tests.

COSTS AND FINANCIAL AID
Annual tuition $33,320. Room and board $10,954. Required fees $400. Average book expense $1,100. **Required Forms and Deadlines:** FAFSA. **Notification of Awards:** Applicants will be notified of awards on a rolling basis beginning 1/15. **Types of Aid:** *Need-based scholarships/grants:* Federal Pell, SEOG, state scholarships/grants, private scholarships, the school's own gift aid, Endowed scholarships. *Loans:* Direct PLUS, Subsidized Stafford, Unsubsidized Stafford, PLUS, Federal Perkins, state loans, Alternative educational loans. **Student Employment:** Federal Work-Study Program available. Institutional employment available. Highest amount earned per year from on-campus jobs $4,800. Off-campus job opportunities are good. **Financial Aid Statistics:** 87% freshmen, 90% undergrads receive need-based scholarship or grant aid. 68% freshmen, 67% undergrads receive non-need-based scholarship or grant aid. 77% freshmen, 79% undergrads receive need-based self-help aid. 5% freshmen, 4% undergrads receive athletic scholarships. 91% freshmen, 86% undergrads receive any aid. 70% undergrads borrow to pay for school. Average cumulative indebtedness $34,314. **Criteria for awarding institutional aid:** *Non-need-based.* academics, art, athletics, leadership, music/drama, state/district residency.

ST. FRANCIS COLLEGE (NY)

180 Remsen Street, Brooklyn Heights, NY 11201
Phone: 718-489-5200
E-mail: admissions@stfranciscollege.edu • **CEEB Code:** 2796
Fax: 718-522-1274 • **Website:** www.stfranciscollege.edu • **ACT Code:** 2884

This private school, affiliated with the Roman Catholic Church, was founded in 1884. It has a 1-acre campus.

RATINGS
Admissions Selectivity Rating: 66   **Fire Safety Rating:** 60*   **Green Rating:** 60*

STUDENTS AND FACULTY
Enrollment: 2,294. **Student Body:** 57% female, 43% male, 1% out-of-state, 13% international (52 countries represented). Asian 2%, African American 20%, Caucasian 49%, Hispanic 14%, Native American 0%.

Retention and Graduation: 76% freshmen return for sophomore year. 21% freshmen graduate within 4 years. 44% freshmen graduate within 6 years.
Faculty: Student/faculty ratio 18:1. 69 full-time faculty, 77% hold PhDs, 14% are members of minority groups, 38% are women. 0% of classes are taught by teaching assistants.

ACADEMICS

Degrees: associate, bachelor's, master's. **Classes:** Most classes have 10–19 students. Most lab/discussion sessions have 20–29 students. **Special Study Options:** Accelerated program, cooperative education program, cross-registration, double major, dual enrollment, honors program, independent study, internships, study abroad, teacher certification program, Accelerated biomedical science program with New York Colllege of Podiatric Medicine; medical technology program with St. Vincent's Catholic Medical Centers of New York and New York Methodist Hospital; joint program in radiological sciences with St. Vincent's Catholic Medical Centers of New York; 7 year cooperative program with the New York University College of Dentistry; can complete B.A. at St. Francis and Master of Science in Computer Science from Polytechnic University. **Honors Programs:** One college wide program that is not department specific. **Combined Degree Programs:** BA/DDS, MS/Computer Science. **Disability Services:** Special programs offered to physically disabled students include note-taking services, reader services, tape recorders, tutors. **Career Services:** Alumni network, alumni services, career/job search classes, career assessment, internships, regional alumni.

FACILITIES

Housing: Students may apply for housing in the recently opened dormitory at Polytechnic University, a few minutes walk from St. Francis College. 100% of campus accessible to physically disabled.

CAMPUS LIFE

Environment: Metropolis. **Activities:** Choral groups, drama/theater, literary magazine, student government, student newspaper, yearbook 25 registered organizations, 1 honor societies, 1 religious organizations. 1 fraternities, 1 sororities. **Athletics (Intercollegiate):** *Men:* basketball, cross-country, diving, golf, soccer, swimming, tennis, track/field (outdoor), track/field (indoor), water polo. *Women:* basketball, bowling, cross-country, diving, fencing, golf, swimming, tennis, track/field (outdoor), track/field (indoor), volleyball, water polo.

ADMISSIONS

Freshman Academic Profile: Average high school GPA 3.1. 44% from public high schools. SAT Math middle 50% range 400-550. SAT Critical Reading middle 50% range 410-540. Minimum paper TOEFL 500. **Basis for Candidate Selection:** *Very important factors considered include:* rigor of secondary school record, standardized test scores. *Important factors considered include:* Class rank, application essay, recommendation(s), alumni/ae relation, character/personal qualities, interview, talent/ability. *Other factors considered include:* extracurricular activities, volunteer work. **Freshman Admission Requirements:** High school diploma is required and GED is accepted. *Academic units required:* 4 English, 3 mathematics, 2 science, (1 science labs), 2 foreign language, 4 social studies, 1 academic electives, 1 Music/art. 4 English, 3 mathematics, 2 science, (1 science labs), 2 foreign language, 4 social studies, 1 academic electives, 1 Music/art **Freshman Admission Statistics:** 1,304 applied, 88% admitted, 38% enrolled. **Transfer Admission Requirements:** High school transcript, college transcript(s), essay or personal statement, statement of good standing from prior institution(s). Minimum college GPA of 2.0 required. Lowest grade transferable C. **General Admission Information:** Application Fee $35. Nonfall registration accepted. Admission may be deferred for a maximum of 12 months. Placement offered for CEEB Advanced Placement tests.

COSTS AND FINANCIAL AID

Annual tuition $13,500. **Required Forms and Deadlines:** FAFSA, institution's own financial aid form, state aid form. **Types of Aid:** *Need-based scholarships/grants:* Federal Pell, SEOG, state scholarships/grants, private scholarships, the school's own gift aid. *Loans:* Subsidized Stafford, Unsubsidized Stafford, PLUS, Federal Perkins. **Student Employment:** Federal Work-Study Program available. Institutional employment available. Off-campus job opportunities are good. **Financial Aid Statistics:** 100% undergrads receive need-based scholarship or grant aid. 34% undergrads receive non-need-based scholarship or grant aid. 56% undergrads receive need-based self-help aid. 7% undergrads receive athletic scholarships. **Criteria for awarding institutional aid:** *Non-need-based:* academics, athletics.

ST. JOHN'S COLLEGE (MD)

P.O. Box 2800, Annapolis, MD 21404
Phone: 410-626-2522 • **Financial Aid Phone:** 410-295-6932
E-mail: admissions@sjca.edu • **CEEB Code:** 5598
Website: www.sjca.edu • **ACT Code:** 1732

This private school was founded in 1696. It has a 36-acre campus.

RATINGS

Admissions Selectivity Rating: 82   **Fire Safety Rating:** 95   **Green Rating:** 69

STUDENTS AND FACULTY

Enrollment: 449. **Student Body:** 45% female, 55% male, 83% out-of-state, 9% international (14 countries represented). Asian 2%, African American 2%, Caucasian 76%, Hispanic 7%, Native American 0%.
Retention and Graduation: 81% freshmen return for sophomore year. 61% freshmen graduate within 4 years. 13% grads go on to further study within 1 year. 12% grads pursue arts and sciences degrees. 1% grads pursue law degrees.
Faculty: Student/faculty ratio 8:1. 58 full-time faculty, 76% hold PhDs, 7% are members of minority groups, 28% are women. 0% of classes are taught by teaching assistants.

ACADEMICS

Degrees: bachelor's, master's. **Classes:** Most classes have 10–19 students. **Majors with Highest Enrollment:** liberal arts and sciences studies and humanities, other. **Special Study Options:** internships, Students may spend one or more years at the college's Santa Fe, N.Mex., campus. **Disability Services:** Special programs offered to physically disabled students include reader services, tape recorders. **Career Services:** alumni services, career assessment, internships, regional alumni. Career Services highlights include Hodson Internships allowing students to receive a stipend for internships which offer them a substantial opportunity to explore a career and learn related skills.

FACILITIES

Housing: Coed dorms, special housing for disabled students 80% of campus accessible to physically disabled. **Special Academic Facilities/Equipment:** Art gallery, planetarium, pendulum, Ptolemy stone, Faraday cage, laboratories. **Computers:** 20% of dorms, 30% of common outdoor areas have wireless network access. Administrative functions (other than registration) can be performed online.

CAMPUS LIFE

Environment: Town. **Activities:** Choral groups, dance, drama/theater, literary magazine, music ensembles, student government, student newspaper, student-run film society, yearbook 64 registered organizations, 3 religious organizations. **On-Campus Highlights:** Mitchell Art Gallery, Greenfiled Library, McDowell Hall, Caroll Barrister House, French Monument, The entire campus is a registered national landmark. **Environmental Initiatives:** purchasing renewable energy credits for 100% of our electric consumption installing a new central heating plant and distribution system that will reduce fossil fuel consumption for heating by approximately 25%, as well as smokestack emissions stabilization of 800'+ of waterfront with removal of bulkhead and installation/ restoration of natural wetland

ADMISSIONS

Freshman Academic Profile: 21% in top 10% of high school class, 55% in top 25% of high school class, 82% in top 50% of high school class. 60% from public high schools. SAT Math middle 50% range 570-680. SAT Critical Reading middle 50% range 620-730. ACT middle 50% range 27-30. Minimum web-based TOEFL 100. Minimum paper TOEFL 600. **Basis for Candidate Selection:** *Very important factors considered include:* application essay. *Important factors considered include:* recommendation(s), rigor of secondary school record, character/personal qualities. *Other factors considered include:* Class rank, academic GPA, standardized test scores, alumni/ae relation, extracurricular activities, first generation, interview, racial/ethnic status, talent/ability. **Freshman Admission Requirements:** High school diploma is required and GED is accepted. *Academic units required:* 3 mathematics, 2 foreign language. *Academic units recommended:* 3 mathematics, 2 foreign language. **Freshman Admission Statistics:** 378 applied, 82% admitted, 38% enrolled. **Transfer Admission Requirements:** High school transcript, college transcript(s), essay or personal statement. **General Admission Information:** Nonfall registration accepted. Admission may be deferred for a maximum of 1 year. Neither credit nor placement offered for CEEB Advanced Placement tests.

COSTS AND FINANCIAL AID

Annual tuition $44,554. Room and board $10,644. Required fees $450. Average book expense $630. **Required Forms and Deadlines:** FAFSA, CSS/Financial Aid PROFILE, state aid form, noncustodial PROFILE, business/farm supplement. **Notification of Awards:** Applicants will be notified of awards on a rolling basis beginning 12/1. **Types of Aid:** *Need-based scholarships/grants:* Federal Pell, SEOG, state scholarships/grants, private scholarships, the school's own gift aid. *Loans:* Subsidized Stafford, Unsubsidized Stafford, PLUS, Federal Perkins, college/university loans from institutional funds. **Student Employment:** Federal Work-Study Program available. Institutional employment available. Highest amount earned per year from on-campus jobs $2,999. Off-campus job opportunities are good. **Financial Aid Statistics:** 99% freshmen, 96% undergrads receive need-based scholarship or grant aid. 4% freshmen, 5% undergrads receive non-need-based scholarship or grant aid. 96% freshmen, 96% undergrads receive need-based self-help aid. 82% freshmen, 71% undergrads receive any aid. 69% undergrads borrow to pay for school. Average cumulative indebtedness $29,265.

ST. JOHN'S COLLEGE (NM)

1160 Camino Cruz Blanca, Santa Fe, NM 87505
Phone: 505-984-6060 • **Financial Aid Phone:** 505-984-6058
E-mail: admissions@sjcsf.edu • **CEEB Code:** 4737
Fax: 505-984-6162 • **Website:** www.sjcsf.edu • **ACT Code:** 2649

This private school was founded in 1696. It has a 250-acre campus.

RATINGS
Admissions Selectivity Rating: 80   **Fire Safety Rating:** 61   **Green Rating:** 77

STUDENTS AND FACULTY
Enrollment: 349. **Student Body:** 43% female, 57% male, 79% out-of-state, 13% international (24 countries represented). Asian 3%, African American 1%, Caucasian 64%, Hispanic 11%, Native American 1%.
Retention and Graduation: 70% freshmen return for sophomore year. 49% freshmen graduate within 4 years. 13% grads go on to further study within 1 year. 9% grads pursue arts and sciences degrees. 3% grads pursue law degrees. **Faculty:** Student/faculty ratio 7:1. 58 full-time faculty, 79% hold PhDs, 3% are members of minority groups, 28% are women. 0% of classes are taught by teaching assistants.

ACADEMICS
Degrees: bachelor's, master's. **Classes:** Most classes have 10–19 students. **Special Study Options:** Accelerated program, internships. **Career Services:** Alumni network, alumni services, career/job search classes, internships, regional alumni., Career Services highlights include Ariel Internship Program provides stipends to undergraduates for a limited number of summer internship opportunities regardless of financial need. SJC recognizes that internships have become a significant component of modern academia, whether a student continues on to graduate school or enters the work force.

FACILITIES
Housing: Coed dorms, special housing for disabled students, men's dorms, women's dorms, apartments for married students, apartments for single students, wellness housing, single-sex suites are available. 70% of campus accessible to physically disabled. **Special Academic Facilities/Equipment:** Art gallery. **Computers:** 75% of classrooms, 10% of dorms, 100% of dining areas, 100% of student union, 10% of common outdoor areas have wireless network access. Administrative functions (other than registration) can be performed online.

CAMPUS LIFE
Environment: City. **Activities:** Choral groups, concert band, dance, drama/theater, jazz band, literary magazine, music ensembles, musical theater, student government, student newspaper, student-run film society 27 registered organizations. **On-Campus Highlights:** Placita/Fish Pond, Student Activities Center, Great Hall, Coffee Shop, Levan Hall (new building). **Environmental Initiatives:** Paper, glass, plastic, cardboard recycling Compost food from Cafeteria Rainwater collection from roofs

ADMISSIONS
Freshman Academic Profile: 16% in top 10% of high school class, 41% in top 25% of high school class, 70% in top 50% of high school class. 68% from public high schools. SAT Math middle 50% range 550-680. SAT Critical Reading middle 50% range 580-740. SAT Writing middle 50% range 560-670. ACT middle 50% range 25-29. Minimum paper TOEFL 550. **Basis for Candidate Selection:** *Very important factors considered include:* application essay. *Important factors considered include:* recommendation(s), rigor of secondary school record, character/personal qualities, level of applicant's interest. *Other factors considered include:* Class rank, academic GPA, standardized test scores, alumni/ae relation, extracurricular activities, first generation, interview, racial/ethnic status, talent/ability, volunteer work, work experience. **Freshman Admission Requirements:** High school diploma is required and GED is accepted. *Academic units required:* 3 mathematics, 2 foreign language. *Academic units recommended:* 3 mathematics, 2 foreign language. **Freshman Admission Statistics:** 251 applied. **Transfer Admission Requirements:** High school transcript, college transcript(s), essay or personal statement. **General Admission Information:** Nonfall registration accepted. Admission may be deferred for a maximum of 2 semesters. Neither credit nor placement offered for CEEB Advanced Placement tests.

COSTS AND FINANCIAL AID
Annual tuition $44,554. Room and board $9,994. Required fees $450. Average book expense $630. **Required Forms and Deadlines:** FAFSA, CSS/Financial Aid PROFILE, noncustodial PROFILE, business/farm supplement. **Notification of Awards:** Applicants will be notified of awards on a rolling basis beginning 12/10. **Types of Aid:** *Need-based scholarships/grants:* Federal Pell, SEOG, state scholarships/grants, private scholarships, the school's own gift aid, Academic Competitiveness Grant/SMART Grants. *Loans:* Subsidized Stafford, Unsubsidized Stafford, PLUS, Federal Perkins, college/university loans from institutional funds. **Student Employment:** Federal Work-Study Program available. Institutional employment available. Highest amount earned per year from on-campus jobs $2,800. Off-campus job opportunities are excellent. **Financial Aid Statistics:** 100% freshmen, 96% undergrads receive need-based scholarship or grant aid. 100% freshmen, 100% undergrads receive need-based self-help aid. 81% freshmen, 75% undergrads receive any aid. 77% undergrads borrow to pay for school. Average cumulative indebtedness $26,750.

ST. JOHN'S COLLEGE, DEPARTMENT OF NURSING (IL)

421 North Ninth Street, Springfield, IL 62702-5317
Phone: 217-525-5628
E-mail: College@st-johns.org
Fax: 217-757-6870 • **Website:** www.st-johns.org/collegeofnursing

This private school, affiliated with the Roman Catholic Church, was founded in 1992.

RATINGS
Admissions Selectivity Rating: 61   **Fire Safety Rating:** 60*   **Green Rating:** 60*

STUDENTS AND FACULTY
Enrollment: 83. **Student Body:** 93% female, 7% male, 10% out-of-state, 1% international (1 countries represented). Asian 0%, African American 1%, Caucasian 98%, Hispanic 0%, Native American 0%.
Retention and Graduation: Faculty: Student/faculty ratio 4:1. 12 full-time faculty, 17% hold PhDs, 0% are members of minority groups, 100% are women. 0% of classes are taught by teaching assistants.

ACADEMICS
Degrees: bachelor's. **Classes:** Most classes have 30–39 students. Most lab/discussion sessions have fewer than 10 students. **Majors with Highest Enrollment:** nursing/registered nurse (rn, asn, bsn, msn).

FACILITIES
Housing: Coed dorms, apartments for single students Campus Apartments.

CAMPUS LIFE
Activities: Choral groups, drama/theater, literary magazine, student government, student newspaper, Campus Ministries 1 registered organizations.

ADMISSIONS
Freshman Academic Profile: 100% in top 50% of high school class. Minimum paper TOEFL 500. **Basis for Candidate Selection:** *Very important factors considered include:* Class rank, application essay, academic GPA, recommendation(s), rigor of secondary school record, standardized test scores, alumni/ae relation, character/personal qualities, extracurricular activities, interview, level of applicant's interest, volunteer work. *Other factors considered include:* talent/ability, work experience. **Freshman Admission Require-**

ments: High school diploma is required and GED is accepted. *Academic units required:* 4 English, 3 mathematics, 3 science, (3 science labs), 3 social studies, 2 academic electives. 4 English, 3 mathematics, 3 science, (3 science labs), 3 social studies, 2 academic electives. **Transfer Admission Requirements:** High school transcript, college transcript(s), interview, statement of good standing from prior institution(s). Minimum college GPA of 2.5 required. Lowest grade transferable c. **General Admission Information:** Application Fee $50. Nonfall registration not accepted. Neither credit nor placement offered for CEEB Advanced Placement tests.

COSTS AND FINANCIAL AID
Annual tuition $11,708. Required fees $444. Average book expense $750.

ST. JOHN'S UNIVERSITY

8000 Utopia Parkway, Queens, NY 11439
Phone: 718-990-2000 • **Financial Aid Phone:** 718-990-2000
E-mail: admhelp@stjohns.edu • **CEEB Code:** 2799
Fax: 718-990-2096 • **Website:** www.stjohns.edu • **ACT Code:** 2888

This private school, affiliated with the Roman Catholic Church, was founded in 1870. It has a 122-acre campus.

RATINGS
Admissions Selectivity Rating: 87   **Fire Safety Rating:** 93   **Green Rating:** 96

STUDENTS AND FACULTY
Enrollment: 11,191. **Student Body:** 52% female, 48% male, 29% out-of-state, 5% international (115 countries represented). Asian 18%, African American 19%, Caucasian 35%, Hispanic 16%, Native American 0%.
Retention and Graduation: 76% freshmen return for sophomore year. 37% freshmen graduate within 4 years. 43% grads go on to further study within 1 year. 8% grads pursue arts and sciences degrees. 6% grads pursue law degrees. 12% grads pursue business degrees. 2% grads pursue medical degrees. **Faculty:** Student/faculty ratio 17:1. 643 full-time faculty, 91% hold PhDs, 25% are members of minority groups, 43% are women. 0% of classes are taught by teaching assistants.

ACADEMICS
Degrees: associate, bachelor's, certificate, diploma, doctoral, master's, post-bachelor's certificate, post-master's certificate, terminal associate, transfer associate. **Classes:** Most classes have 20–29 students. Most lab/discussion sessions have 20–29 students. **Majors with Highest Enrollment:** liberal arts and sciences/liberal studies; pharmacy (pharmd [usa], pharmd or bs/bpharm [canada]); psychology. **Special Study Options:** Accelerated program, cross-registration, distance learning, double major, dual enrollment, English as a Second Language (ESL), honors program, independent study, internships, liberal arts/career combination, study abroad, teacher certification program, weekend college.
Honors Programs: The University Honors Program is available to qualified incoming freshmen. The program primarily comprises honors versions of the courses which are part of the core curriculum. Honors students must complete 30 credits of honors-designated courses to complete the program. Additional options for obtaining honors credits are also available. The program also features a range of special activities and events. **Combined Degree Programs:** BA/JD, BA/MA, BS/MA;BS/MS;BS/MBA;BS/OD;BS/JD;MBA/JD. **Disability Services:** Special programs offered to physically disabled students include note-taking services, reader services, tape recorders, tutors. **Career Services:** alumni services, career/job search classes, career assessment, internships.

FACILITIES
Housing: Coed dorms, apartments for single students, theme housing. Some off-campus apartments are available on a limited basis. 90% of campus accessible to physically disabled. **Special Academic Facilities/Equipment:** University Gallery; Instuctional Media Center; Institute of Asian Studies; Health Education Resource Center; Center for Psychological Services; TV Center; Speech and Hearing Center and Reading and Writing Education Center. **Computers:** 100% of classrooms, 90% of dorms, 100% of libraries, 100% of dining areas, 100% of student union, 100% of common outdoor areas have wireless network access. Students can register for classes online. Administrative functions (other than registration) can be performed online. Undergraduates are required to own a computer.

CAMPUS LIFE
Environment: Metropolis. **Activities:** Choral groups, dance, drama/theater, jazz band, literary magazine, music ensembles, musical theater, pep band, radio station, student government, student newspaper, television station, yearbook, Campus Ministries 180 registered organizations. **Athletics (Intercollegiate):** *Men:* baseball, basketball, fencing, golf, lacrosse, soccer, softball, table tennis, tennis, volleyball, weight lifting. *Women:* basketball, cross-country, fencing, soccer, softball, table tennis, tennis, track/field (outdoor), track/field (indoor), volleyball, weight lifting. **On-Campus Highlights:** The Great Lawn, D'Angelo Center, The University Library **Environmental Initiatives:** Senior management signed the NYC Mayoral Challenge committing to 30% reduction in carbon emissions by the year 2017. Senior management signed a Memorandum of Understanding with the EPA committing to continuous improvement in eight EPA Voluntary Partnership Programs. St. John's is a charter participant of STARS ("Sustainability Tracking, Assessment and Rating System"). Also, establishment of a Sustainability Office within the university's central administration for the purpose of advancing the university efforts for a sustainable future and hiring 17 student workers as Sustainability Coordinators.

ADMISSIONS
Freshman Academic Profile: Average high school GPA 3.3. 17% in top 10% of high school class, 40% in top 25% of high school class, 71% in top 50% of high school class. 62% from public high schools. SAT Math middle 50% range 490-620. SAT Critical Reading middle 50% range 480-590. ACT middle 50% range 21-27. Minimum web-based TOEFL 100. Minimum paper TOEFL 600. **Basis for Candidate Selection:** *Very important factors considered include:* academic GPA, standardized test scores. *Important factors considered include:* rigor of secondary school record. *Other factors considered include:* Class rank, application essay, recommendation(s), alumni/ae relation, character/personal qualities, extracurricular activities, geographical residence, interview, level of applicant's interest, volunteer work, work experience. **Freshman Admission Requirements:** High school diploma is required and GED is accepted. *Academic units required:* 4 English. *Academic units recommended:* 4 English. **Freshman Admission Statistics:** 51,634 applied, 53% admitted, 10% enrolled. **Transfer Admission Requirements:** college transcript(s), Lowest grade transferable C. **General Admission Information:** Application Fee $50. Notification on a rolling basis, beginning on or about 12/1. Nonfall registration accepted. Admission may be deferred for a maximum of 1 year. Credit and/or placement offered for CEEB Advanced Placement tests.

COSTS AND FINANCIAL AID
Annual tuition $34,750. Room and board $15,270. Required fees $770. Average book expense $1,045. **Required Forms and Deadlines:** FAFSA. **Notification of Awards:** Applicants will be notified of awards on a rolling basis beginning 3/15. **Types of Aid:** *Need-based scholarships/grants:* Federal Pell, SEOG, state scholarships/grants, private scholarships, the school's own gift aid. *Loans:* Direct Subsidized Stafford, Direct Unsubsidized Stafford, Direct PLUS, Federal Perkins. **Student Employment:** Federal Work-Study Program available. Institutional employment available. Highest amount earned per year from on-campus jobs $5,000. Off-campus job opportunities are good. **Financial Aid Statistics:** 90% freshmen, 89% undergrads receive need-based scholarship or grant aid. 90% freshmen, 75% undergrads receive non-need-based scholarship or grant aid. 87% freshmen, 84% undergrads receive need-based self-help aid. 1% freshmen, 2% undergrads receive athletic scholarships. 97% freshmen, 96% undergrads receive any aid. 71% undergrads borrow to pay for school. Average cumulative indebtedness $29,199. **Criteria for awarding institutional aid:** *Non-need-based:* academics, alumni affiliation, art, athletics, leadership, music/drama, religious affiliation.

ST. JOSEPH'S COLLEGE

245 Clinton Avenue, Brooklyn, NY 11205
Phone: 718-636-6868 • **Financial Aid Phone:** 631-447-3214
E-mail: www.sjcny.edu
Fax: 718-636-8303 • **Website:** www.sjcny.edu

This is a private school.

RATINGS
Admissions Selectivity Rating: 73   **Fire Safety Rating:** 60*   **Green Rating:** 60*

STUDENTS AND FACULTY
Enrollment: 1,037. **Student Body:** 76% female, 24% male, 1% out-of-state, 0% international. Asian 7%, African American 36%, Caucasian 38%, Hispanic 14%, Native American 0%.
Retention and Graduation: 81% freshmen return for sophomore year. 70% freshmen graduate within 4 years. 73% freshmen graduate within 6 years. 61%

grads go on to further study within 1 year. 5% grads pursue arts and sciences degrees. 2% grads pursue law degrees. 3% grads pursue business degrees. 1% grads pursue medical degrees. **Faculty:** Student/faculty ratio 11:1. 50 full-time faculty, 66% hold PhDs, 60% are women. 0% of classes are taught by teaching assistants.

ACADEMICS

Degrees: bachelor's, certificate, master's. **Classes:** Most classes have fewer than 10 students. Most lab/discussion sessions have fewer than 10 students. **Special Study Options:** Accelerated program, honors program, independent study, internships, teacher certification program, weekend college, Biomedical Program with New York College of Podiatric medicine. **Honors Programs:** Freshman Honors Program provides enriched inter-disciplinary courses. Capstone course includes a travel or global studies component. Honors indicated on transcript. **Combined Degree Programs:** BS/MBA. **Disability Services:** Special programs offered to physically disabled students include note-taking services, reader services, tape recorders. **Career Services:** alumni services, career/job search classes, career assessment, internships.

FACILITIES

Housing: 95% of campus accessible to physically disabled. **Special Academic Facilities/Equipment:** Clare Rose Playhouse. **Computers:** Students can register for classes online.

CAMPUS LIFE

Activities: Choral groups, dance, drama/theater, literary magazine, musical theater, student government, student newspaper, yearbook, Campus Ministries 34 registered organizations, 8 honor societies, 2 religious organizations. 2 fraternities, 2 sororities. **On-Campus Highlights:** Athletic Center with pool, Eagles Nest Cafeteria, Student Lounge, Quad Area, Clare Rose Playhouse.

ADMISSIONS

Freshman Academic Profile: 50% from public high schools. SAT Math middle 50% range 430-540. SAT Critical Reading middle 50% range 410-510. SAT Writing middle 50% range 400-500. Minimum web-based TOEFL 100. Minimum paper TOEFL 600. **Basis for Candidate Selection:** *Very important factors considered include:* academic GPA, rigor of secondary school record, standardized test scores. *Important factors considered include:* Class rank, application essay, recommendation(s), extracurricular activities, interview. *Other factors considered include:* alumni/ae relation, talent/ability, volunteer work, work experience. **Freshman Admission Requirements:** High school diploma is required and GED is accepted. *Academic units required:* 4 English, 3 mathematics, 2 science, 2 foreign language, 4 social studies, 3 academic electives. *Academic units recommended:* 4 English, 3 mathematics, 2 science, 2 foreign language, 4 social studies, 3 academic electives. **Freshman Admission Statistics:** 825 applied, 62% admitted, 25% enrolled. **Transfer Admission Requirements:** college transcript(s), interview, statement of good standing from prior institution(s). Minimum college GPA of 2.0 required. **General Admission Information:** Application Fee $25. Credit and/or placement offered for CEEB Advanced Placement tests.

COSTS AND FINANCIAL AID

Annual tuition $15,400. Required fees $563. **Required Forms and Deadlines:** FAFSA, institution's own financial aid form, state aid form. **Notification of Awards:** Applicants will be notified of awards on a rolling basis beginning 3/15. **Types of Aid:** *Need-based scholarships/grants:* Federal Pell, SEOG, state scholarships/grants, private scholarships, the school's own gift aid. *Loans:* Subsidized Stafford, Unsubsidized Stafford, PLUS, Federal Perkins. **Student Employment:** Federal Work-Study Program available. Institutional employment available. Off-campus job opportunities are good. **Financial Aid Statistics:** 95% freshmen, 94% undergrads receive need-based scholarship or grant aid. 70% freshmen, 62% undergrads receive non-need-based scholarship or grant aid. 86% freshmen, 86% undergrads receive need-based self-help aid. 48% undergrads borrow to pay for school. Average cumulative indebtedness $18,582. **Criteria for awarding institutional aid:** *Non-need-based:* academics.

See page 1210.

ST. JOSEPH'S COLLEGE, NEW YORK (PATCHOGUE)

155 West Roe Blvd, Patchogue, NY 11772
Phone: 631-447-3219 • **Financial Aid Phone:** 631-447-3214
E-mail: longislandas@sjcny.edu • **CEEB Code:** 2802
Fax: 631-447-1734 • **Website:** www.sjcny.edu • **ACT Code:** 2923

This private school was founded in 1916. It has a 30-acre campus.

RATINGS

Admissions Selectivity Rating: 73   **Fire Safety Rating:** 60*   **Green Rating:** 60*

STUDENTS AND FACULTY

Enrollment: 3,727. **Student Body:** 72% female, 28% male, 0% out-of-state, 0% international. Asian 1%, African American 4%, Caucasian 73%, Hispanic 6%, Native American 0%.
Retention and Graduation: 83% freshmen return for sophomore year. 51% freshmen graduate within 4 years. 68% freshmen graduate within 6 years. 61% grads go on to further study within 1 year. 5% grads pursue arts and sciences degrees. 2% grads pursue law degrees. 3% grads pursue business degrees. 1% grads pursue medical degrees. **Faculty:** Student/faculty ratio 16:1. 111 full-time faculty, 68% hold PhDs, 59% are women. 0% of classes are taught by teaching assistants.

ACADEMICS

Degrees: bachelor's, certificate, master's. **Classes:** Most classes have 10–19 students. **Majors with Highest Enrollment:** elementary education and teaching; psychology; secondary education and teaching. **Special Study Options:** Accelerated program, cross-registration, double major, honors program, internships, liberal arts/career combination, study abroad, teacher certification program, weekend college. **Honors Programs:** Freshman Honors Program provides enriched inter-disciplinary courses. Capstone course includes a travel or global studies component. Honors indicated on transcript. **Combined Degree Programs:** BS/MBA. **Disability Services:** Special programs offered to physically disabled students include note-taking services, reader services, tape recorders. **Career Services:** alumni services, career/job search classes, career assessment, internships.

FACILITIES

Housing: 95% of campus accessible to physically disabled. **Special Academic Facilities/Equipment:** Clare Rose Playhouse. **Computers:** Students can register for classes online.

CAMPUS LIFE

Environment: Town. **Activities:** Choral groups, dance, drama/theater, jazz band, literary magazine, music ensembles, musical theater, student government, student newspaper, yearbook, Campus Ministries 34 registered organizations, 8 honor societies, 2 religious organizations. 2 fraternities, 2 sororities. **Athletics (Intercollegiate):** *Men:* baseball, basketball, cross-country, golf, soccer, tennis, track/field (outdoor). *Women:* basketball, cross-country, equestrian sports, soccer, softball, swimming, tennis, track/field (outdoor), volleyball. **On-Campus Highlights:** Athletic Center with pool, Eagles Nest Cafeteria, Student Lounge, Quad Area, Clare Rose Playhouse.

ADMISSIONS

Freshman Academic Profile: 88% from public high schools. SAT Math middle 50% range 490-590. SAT Critical Reading middle 50% range 480-560. SAT Writing middle 50% range 460-550. Minimum paper TOEFL 550. **Basis for Candidate Selection:** *Very important factors considered include:* Class rank, academic GPA, rigor of secondary school record, standardized test scores. *Important factors considered include:* application essay, recommendation(s), character/personal qualities, extracurricular activities, interview. *Other factors considered include:* alumni/ae relation, first generation, level of applicant's interest, talent/ability, volunteer work, work experience. **Freshman Admission Requirements:** High school diploma is required and GED is accepted. *Academic units required:* 4 English, 3 mathematics, 3 science, (3 science labs), 2 foreign language, 4 social studies, 2 academic electives. 4 English, 3 mathematics, 3 science, (3 science labs), 2 foreign language, 4 social studies, 2 academic electives. **Freshman Admission Statistics:** 1,375 applied, 74% admitted, 50% enrolled. **Transfer Admission Requirements:** college transcript(s), minimum college GPA of 2.0 required. **General Admission Information:** Application Fee $25. Notification on a rolling basis, beginning on or about 11/15. Nonfall registration accepted. Admission may be deferred for a maximum of 2 years. Credit offered for CEEB Advanced Placement tests.

COSTS AND FINANCIAL AID

Annual tuition $15,400. Required fees $563. **Required Forms and Deadlines:** FAFSA, institution's own financial aid form, state aid form. **Notification** of Awards: Applicants will be notified of awards on or about 3/15. **Types of Aid:** *Need-based scholarships/grants:* Federal Pell, SEOG, state scholarships/grants, private scholarships, the school's own gift aid. *Loans:* Subsidized Stafford, Unsubsidized Stafford, PLUS, Federal Perkins. **Student Employment:** Federal Work-Study Program available. Institutional employment available. Off-campus job opportunities are good. **Financial Aid Statistics:** 91% freshmen, 82% undergrads receive need-based scholarship or grant aid. 74% freshmen, 65% undergrads receive non-need-based scholarship or grant aid. 84% freshmen, 83% undergrads receive need-based self-help aid. 69% undergrads borrow to pay for school. Average cumulative indebtedness $14,028. **Criteria for awarding institutional aid:** *Non-need-based:* academics.

ST. LAWRENCE UNIVERSITY

Best 378

Payson Hall, Canton, NY 13617
Phone: 315-229-5261 • **Financial Aid Phone:** 315-229-5265
E-mail: admissions@stlawu.edu • **CEEB Code:** 2805
Fax: 315-229-5818 • **Website:** www.stlawu.edu • **ACT Code:** 2896

This private school was founded in 1856. It has a 1000-acre campus.

RATINGS
Admissions Selectivity Rating: 93   **Fire Safety Rating:** 74   **Green Rating:** 91

STUDENTS AND FACULTY
Enrollment: 2,335. **Student Body:** 54% female, 46% male, 56% out-of-state, 6% international (50 countries represented). Asian 1%, African American 3%, Caucasian 83%, Hispanic 4%, Native American 0%.
Retention and Graduation: 90% freshmen return for sophomore year. 76% freshmen graduate within 4 years. 80% freshmen graduate within 6 years. 20% grads go on to further study within 1 year. 18% grads pursue arts and sciences degrees. 3% grads pursue law degrees. 1% grads pursue business degrees. 2% grads pursue medical degrees. **Faculty:** Student/faculty ratio 12:1. 171 full-time faculty, 98% hold PhDs, 13% are members of minority groups, 47% are women. 0% of classes are taught by teaching assistants.

ACADEMICS
Degrees: bachelor's, master's, post-master's certificate. **Classes:** Most classes have 10–19 students. Most lab/discussion sessions have 10–19 students. **Majors with Highest Enrollment:** economics; political science and government; psychology. **Special Study Options:** cross-registration, double major, exchange student program (domestic), independent study, internships, student-designed major, study abroad, teacher certification program, Community-based learning. **Honors Programs:** The University Fellows program offers a $3500 stipend plus room for summer research on campus. This is a competitive program for students who wish to undertake a serious, independent academic project as their summer employment. **Combined Degree Programs:** BA/MEng, 4 + 1 Business Program; 3-2 engineering programs. **Disability Services:** Special programs offered to physically disabled students include note-taking services, reader services, tape recorders, tutors. **Career Services:** Alumni network, alumni services, career/job search classes, career assessment, internships Career Services highlights include Alumni Network.

FACILITIES
Housing: Coed dorms, special housing for disabled students, special housing for international students, women's dorms, fraternity/sorority housing, apartments for single students, theme housing. 60% of campus accessible to physically disabled. **Special Academic Facilities/Equipment:** Art gallery, arts technology center, language lab, center for international education, environmental research facility, 76-acre forest preserve, two electron microscopes, microscopy and sleep labs, Neuroscience lab, sustainability lab **Computers:** 100% of classrooms, 100% of dorms, 100% of libraries, 100% of dining areas, 100% of student union, 100% of common outdoor areas have wireless network access. Students can register for classes online. Administrative functions (other than registration) can be performed online.

CAMPUS LIFE
Environment: Village. **Activities:** Choral groups, concert band, dance, drama/theater, jazz band, literary magazine, music ensembles, radio station, student government, student newspaper, student-run film society, yearbook, Campus Ministries, International Student Organization, Model UN 117 registered organizations, 22 honor societies, 4 religious organizations. 2 fraternities, 4

sororities. **Athletics (Intercollegiate):** *Men:* baseball, basketball, crew/rowing, cross-country, equestrian sports, football, golf, ice hockey, lacrosse, skiing (downhill/alpine), skiingnordiccross-country, soccer, squash, swimming, tennis, track/field (outdoor), track/field (indoor). *Women:* basketball, crew/rowing, cross-country, equestrian sports, field hockey, golf, ice hockey, lacrosse, skiing (downhill/alpine), skiingnordiccross-country, soccer, softball, squash, swimming, tennis, track/field (outdoor), track/field (indoor), volleyball. **On-Campus Highlights:** Newell Field House, Brewer Bookstore, Johnson Hall of Science, Owen D. Young Library, Student Center, Student Center opened January 2004, Newell Center for Arts Technology opened 2007, LEED Gold Johnson Hall of Science opened fall 2007. **Environmental Initiatives:** Pledge of climate neutrality Energy audits of all on and off campus buildings and appropriate retrofits of energy and water efficiency measures. Beginning to re-source our electricity to renewable sources (15% currently) and analyzing a renewable source for our heat.

ADMISSIONS
Freshman Academic Profile: Average high school GPA 3.5. 44% in top 10% of high school class, 76% in top 25% of high school class, 95% in top 50% of high school class. 68% from public high schools. SAT Math middle 50% range 580-660. SAT Critical Reading middle 50% range 570-660. SAT Writing middle 50% range 570-660. ACT middle 50% range 25-29. Minimum web-based TOEFL 82. Minimum paper TOEFL 600. **Basis for Candidate Selection:** *Very important factors considered include:* application essay, academic GPA, recommendation(s), character/personal qualities. *Important factors considered include:* Class rank, rigor of secondary school record, extracurricular activities, interview, racial/ethnic status. *Other factors considered include:* standardized test scores, alumni/ae relation, first generation, geographical residence, level of applicant's interest, talent/ability, volunteer work, work experience. **Freshman Admission Requirements:** High school diploma is required and GED is accepted. **Freshman Admission Statistics:** 4,273 applied, 43% admitted, 35% enrolled. **Transfer Admission Requirements:** High school transcript, college transcript(s), essay or personal statement, statement of good standing from prior institution(s). Lowest grade transferable C. **General Admission Information:** Application Fee $60. Early decision application deadline 11/15. Regular application deadline 2/1. Nonfall registration accepted. Admission may be deferred for a maximum of 1 year. Credit offered for CEEB Advanced Placement tests.

COSTS AND FINANCIAL AID
Annual tuition $44,075. Room and board $11,435. Required fees $325. Average book expense $750. **Required Forms and Deadlines:** FAFSA, noncustodial PROFILE, business/farm supplement. Institution's own financial aid form OR CSS/Financial Aid PROFILE. **Notification of Awards:** Applicants will be notified of awards on or about 3/30. **Types of Aid:** *Need-based scholarships/grants:* Federal Pell, SEOG, state scholarships/grants, private scholarships, the school's own gift aid. *Loans:* Direct Subsidized Stafford, Direct Unsubsidized Stafford, Direct PLUS, Federal Perkins, college/university loans from institutional funds. **Student Employment:** Federal Work-Study Program available. Institutional employment available. Highest amount earned per year from on-campus jobs $2,000. Off-campus job opportunities are poor. **Financial Aid Statistics:** 99% freshmen, 99% undergrads receive need-based scholarship or grant aid. 22% freshmen, 14% undergrads receive non-need-based scholarship or grant aid. 68% freshmen, 76% undergrads receive need-based self-help aid. 1% freshmen, 2% undergrads receive athletic scholarships. 89% freshmen, 85% undergrads receive any aid. 61% undergrads borrow to pay for school. Average cumulative indebtedness $26,270. **Criteria for awarding institutional aid:** *Non-need-based:* academics, alumni affiliation, athletics, leadership, minority status, state/district residency.

See page 1212.

ST. LOUIS COLLEGE OF PHARMACY

4588 Parkview Place, St. Louis, MO 63110
Phone: 314-367-8700
E-mail: pkulage@stlcop.edu • **CEEB Code:** 6626
Fax: 314-446-8310 • **Website:** www.stlcop.edu • **ACT Code:** 2346

This private school was founded in 1864. It has a 7-acre campus.

RATINGS
Admissions Selectivity Rating: 78   **Fire Safety Rating:** 69   **Green Rating:** 60*

STUDENTS AND FACULTY
Faculty: Student/faculty ratio 13:1. 64 full-time faculty, 91% hold PhDs, 0% are members of minority groups, 59% are women.

ACADEMICS

Degrees: first professional, master's. **Career Services:** alumni services, internships.

FACILITIES

Housing: Coed dorms, fraternity/sorority housing, apartments for single students.

CAMPUS LIFE

Activities: Choral groups, concert band, drama/theater, literary magazine, musical theater, student government, student newspaper, Campus Ministries 2 honor societies, 6 religious organizations. 5 fraternities. **Athletics (Intercollegiate):** *Men:* basketball, cheerleading, cross-country. *Women:* cheerleading, cross-country, volleyball.

ADMISSIONS

Freshman Academic Profile: Average high school GPA 3.4. 20% in top 10% of high school class, 35% in top 25% of high school class, 98% in top 50% of high school class. SAT Math middle 50% range 628-687. SAT Critical Reading middle 50% range 536-562. ACT middle 50% range 25-26. Minimum paper TOEFL 550. **Basis for Candidate Selection:** *Very important factors considered include:* rigor of secondary school record, standardized test scores. *Important factors considered include:* Class rank. *Other factors considered include:* application essay, recommendation(s), alumni/ae relation, character/personal qualities, extracurricular activities, volunteer work, work experience. **Freshman Admission Requirements:** High school diploma is required and GED is accepted. *Academic units required:* 4 English, 3 mathematics, 2 science, (2 science labs). *Academic units recommended:* 4 English, 3 mathematics, 2 science, (2 science labs). **Freshman Admission Statistics:** 356 applied, 80% admitted, 59% enrolled. **Transfer Admission Requirements:** college transcript(s), essay or personal statement, standardized test scores, minimum college CPA of 3.0 required. Lowest grade transferable C. **General Admission Information:** Application Fee $35. Regular application deadline 4/2. Notification on a rolling basis, beginning on or about 9/2. Nonfall registration accepted. Credit offered for CEEB Advanced Placement tests.

COSTS AND FINANCIAL AID

Average book expense $1,000. **Required Forms and Deadlines:** FAFSA, institution's own financial aid form. **Notification of Awards:** Applicants will be notified of awards on a rolling basis beginning 2/10. **Types of Aid:** *Need-based scholarships/grants:* Federal Pell, SEOG, state scholarships/grants, private scholarships, the school's own gift aid. *Loans:* Subsidized Stafford, Unsubsidized Stafford, PLUS, Federal Perkins, Health Professions Loan. **Student Employment:** Federal Work-Study Program available. Institutional employment available. Highest amount earned per year from on-campus jobs $800. Off-campus job opportunities are excellent. **Criteria for awarding institutional aid:** *Non-need-based:* job skills, state/district residency.

ST. MARY'S COLLEGE OF MARYLAND

Admissions Office - 18952 E. Fisher Rd., St. Marys City, MD 20686-3001
Phone: 240-895-5000 • **Financial Aid Phone:** 240-895-3000
E-mail: admissions@smcm.edu • **CEEB Code:** 5601
Fax: 240-895-5001 • **Website:** www.smcm.edu • **ACT Code:** 1736

This public school was founded in 1840. It has a 319-acre campus.

RATINGS

Admissions Selectivity Rating: 82   **Fire Safety Rating:** 77   **Green Rating:** 93

STUDENTS AND FACULTY

Enrollment: 1,863. **Student Body:** 59% female, 41% male, 11% out-of-state, 2% international (33 countries represented). Asian 2%, African American 7%, Caucasian 77%, Hispanic 5%, Native American 0%.
Retention and Graduation: 87% freshmen return for sophomore year. 72% freshmen graduate within 4 years. 81% freshmen graduate within 6 years. 50% grads go on to further study within 1 year. 24% grads pursue arts and sciences degrees. 5% grads pursue law degrees. 4% grads pursue medical degrees. **Faculty:** 0% of classes are taught by teaching assistants.

ACADEMICS

Degrees: bachelor's, master's. **Classes:** Most classes have 10–19 students. Most lab/discussion sessions have 10–19 students. **Majors with Highest Enroll-**

ment: biology/biological sciences; English language and literature; psychology. **Special Study Options:** double major, dual enrollment, exchange student program (domestic), honors program, independent study, internships, student-designed major, study abroad, teacher certification program. **Honors Programs:** Nitze Scholars Program. **Disability Services:** Special programs offered to physically disabled students include note-taking services, reader services, tape recorders, tutors. **Career Services:** Alumni network, alumni services, career/job search classes, career assessment, internships, regional alumni. Career Services highlights include Our rigorous credit internship program supports students' academic and career goals through the availability of part- to full-time work-learning experiences in the local community and beyond.

FACILITIES

Housing: Coed dorms, special housing for disabled students, men's dorms, women's dorms, apartments for single students, wellness housing, theme housing. There are a variety of different housing options at SMCM. Townhouses for upper-class students as well as suites are offered. There is also special interest housing (ex. SAFE house which is substance and alcohol free housing) and living learning centers (ex. international house, Women in Science House (WiSH), eco-house). 95% of campus accessible to physically disabled. **Special Academic Facilities/Equipment:** Art gallery, archaeological sites, Historic St. Mary's City, historic state house of early Maryland settlers, electron microscope, freshwater and saltwater research facilities, research boat. **Computers:** 100% of classrooms, 20% of dorms, 100% of libraries, 100% of dining areas, 100% of student union, 100% of common outdoor areas have wireless network access. Students can register for classes online. Administrative functions (other than registration) can be performed online.

CAMPUS LIFE

Environment: Rural. **Activities:** Choral groups, dance, drama/theater, jazz band, literary magazine, music ensembles, musical theater, radio station, student government, student newspaper, symphony orchestra, television station, yearbook, Campus Ministries, International Student Organization 117 registered organizations, 8 honor societies, 4 religious organizations. **Athletics (Intercollegiate):** *Men:* baseball, basketball, cross-country, lacrosse, sailing, soccer, swimming, tennis. *Women:* basketball, cross-country, field hockey, lacrosse, sailing, soccer, swimming, tennis, volleyball. **On-Campus Highlights:** Student Center, Library, Athletics and Recreation Center (ARC), Waterfront, Garden of Remembrance. **Environmental Initiatives:** In 2007, students voted overwhelmingly (94%) to increase student fees $25 to purchase renewable energy credits (RECs) to offset 100% of the College's annual purchased electrical consumption. In the last year the College has been able to increase its purchase of renewable energy credits by 15% allowing the school to offset over 85% of GHG emissions from campus buildings. From 2006-2008, the College completed a $2.8 million energy performance contract (EPC) which reduced the College's electricity consumption 16.5%, oil consumption 24%, and water consumption 35%. The College is currently reviewing the possibility of second EPC. In addition to these large projects, smaller in-house renovations and energy conservation programs have yielded large dividends for the campus and the environment. St. Mary's pioneered Maryland's first major public LEED certified building, Goodpastor Hall, which uses 40% less energy than a conventional building and saves over 300,000 gallons of water each year. The College Strategic Plan now mandates that all new building be at lease LEED Silver certifiable or equivalent. To date the College has constructed 3 "green" buildings totaling over 54,000 NASF of space and has 1 additional 20,000 NASF green building currently in design.

ADMISSIONS

Freshman Academic Profile: Average high school GPA 3.3. 32% in top 10% of high school class, 67% in top 25% of high school class, 92% in top 50% of high school class. 76% from public high schools. SAT Math middle 50% range 540-650. SAT Critical Reading middle 50% range 570-670. SAT Writing middle 50% range 540-650. ACT middle 50% range 25-30. **Basis for Candidate Selection:** *Very important factors considered include:* academic GPA, rigor of secondary school record. *Important factors considered include:* application essay, recommendation(s), standardized test scores, extracurricular activities, first generation, talent/ability, volunteer work. *Other factors considered include:* alumni/ae relation, geographical residence, interview, racial/ethnic status, state residency, work experience. **Freshman Admission Requirements:** High school diploma is required and GED is accepted. *Academic units required:* 4 English, 3 mathematics, 3 science, (2 science labs), 2 foreign language, 2 social studies, 1 history, 3. *Academic units recommended:* 4 English, 3 mathematics, 3 science, (2 science labs), 2 foreign language, 2 social studies, 1 history, 3 **Freshman Admission Statistics:** 1,985 applied, 72% admitted, 29% enrolled. **Transfer Admission Requirements:** college transcript(s), essay or personal statement, minimum college GPA of 3.0 required. Lowest grade transferable C–. **General Admission Information:** Application Fee $50. Early decision application deadline 11/1. Regular application deadline 1/1. Regular notification 4/1. Nonfall registration accepted. Credit and/or placement offered for CEEB Advanced Placement tests.

COSTS AND FINANCIAL AID

Annual in-state tuition $12,485. Annual out-of-state tuition $25,045. Room and board $11,305. Required fees $2,528. Average book expense $1,000. **Required Forms and Deadlines:** FAFSA. **Notification of Awards:** Applicants will be notified of awards on or about 4/1. **Types of Aid:** *Need-based scholarships/grants:* Federal Pell, SEOG, state scholarships/grants, private scholarships, the school's own gift aid. *Loans:* Subsidized Stafford, Unsubsidized Stafford, PLUS, Federal Perkins. **Student Employment:** Federal Work-Study Program available. Institutional employment available. Highest amount earned per year from on-campus jobs $1,100. Off-campus job opportunities are good. **Financial Aid Statistics:** 75% freshmen, 74% undergrads receive need-based scholarship or grant aid. 51% freshmen, 52% undergrads receive non-need-based scholarship or grant aid. 69% freshmen, 76% undergrads receive need-based self-help aid. 79% freshmen, 77% undergrads receive any aid. 54% undergrads borrow to pay for school. Average cumulative indebtedness $23,834. **Criteria for awarding institutional aid:** *Non-need-based:* academics, alumni affiliation.

See page 1214.

ST. MARY'S UNIVERSITY

One Camino Santa Maria, San Antonio, TX 78228-8503
Phone: 210-436-3126 • **Financial Aid Phone:** 210-436-3141
E-mail: uadm@stmarytx.edu • **CEEB Code:** 6637
Fax: 210-431-6742 • **Website:** www.stmarytx.edu/ • **ACT Code:** 4158

This private school, affiliated with the Roman Catholic Church, was founded in 1852. It has a 135-acre campus.

RATINGS

Admissions Selectivity Rating: 79   **Fire Safety Rating:** 76   **Green Rating:** 62

STUDENTS AND FACULTY

Enrollment: 2,426. **Student Body:** 58% female, 42% male, 6% out-of-state, 2% international (19 countries represented). Asian 3%, African American 4%, Caucasian 18%, Hispanic 70%, Native American 0%.
Retention and Graduation: 78% freshmen return for sophomore year. 34% freshmen graduate within 4 years. 60% freshmen graduate within 6 years. **Faculty:** Student/faculty ratio 13:1. 196 full-time faculty, 92% hold PhDs, 21% are members of minority groups, 36% are women. 0% of classes are taught by teaching assistants.

ACADEMICS

Degrees: bachelor's, master's. **Classes:** Most classes have 20–29 students. Most lab/discussion sessions have 20–29 students. **Majors with Highest Enrollment:** biology/biological sciences; political science and government; psychology. **Special Study Options:** cross-registration, distance learning, double major, dual enrollment, English as a Second Language (ESL), exchange student program (domestic), honors program, independent study, internships, liberal arts/career combination, study abroad, teacher certification program, Evening Studies Program. **Honors Programs:** The Honors Program offers an academically challenging and personally enriching course of study designed to cultivate critical analysis, clear oral and written expression, aesthetic awareness and ethical judgment. In and out of the classroom we seek to prepare our future graduates for lives of leadership and service to their communities. **Combined Degree Programs:** BA/MA, B.Phil/M.Div. **Disability Services:** Special programs offered to physically disabled students include note-taking services, reader services, tape recorders, tutors. **Career Services:** Alumni network, alumni services, career/job search classes, career assessment, internships, regional alumni.

FACILITIES

Housing: Coed dorms, Science Learning, Living Community; Residence hall for students 22 yrs. old or above/non traditional. 80% of campus accessible to physically disabled. **Computers:** 100% of classrooms, 100% of dorms, 100% of libraries, 100% of dining areas, 100% of student union, 80% of common outdoor areas have wireless network access. Students can register for classes online. Administrative functions (other than registration) can be performed online. Undergraduates are required to own a computer.

CAMPUS LIFE

Environment: Metropolis. **Activities:** Choral groups, concert band, dance, drama/theater, jazz band, literary magazine, music ensembles, musical theater, pep band, student government, student newspaper, Campus Ministries, International Student Organization 91 registered organizations, 1 religious organizations. 4 fraternities, 4 sororities. **Athletics (Intercollegiate):** *Men:* baseball, basketball, cheerleading, golf, soccer, tennis. *Women:* basketball, cheerleading, cross-country, golf, soccer, softball, tennis, volleyball. **On-Campus Highlights:** Alumni Athletics and Convocation Center, University Center, Java City Coffee

Shop, The Quad, Barrett Memorial Bell Tower, Pecan Grove and the new 278-bed Founders Hall round out the list of popular campus spots. Founders Hall opened in fall 2009. Designed for freshmen, it provides spacious rooms, welcoming indoor and outdoor common spaces, and a cyber cafe. **Environmental Initiatives:** Energy efficiency electric motors, chillers, lighting Water conservation Pilot program(Recycling).

ADMISSIONS

Freshman Academic Profile: Average high school GPA 3.4. 28% in top 10% of high school class, 63% in top 25% of high school class, 87% in top 50% of high school class. 78% from public high schools. SAT Math middle 50% range 480-570. SAT Critical Reading middle 50% range 460-560. SAT Writing middle 50% range 450-540. ACT middle 50% range 20-20. Minimum web-based TOEFL 80. Minimum paper TOEFL 550. **Basis for Candidate Selection:** *Very important factors considered include:* academic GPA, rigor of secondary school record. *Important factors considered include:* Class rank, standardized test scores. *Other factors considered include:* application essay, recommendation(s), alumni/ae relation, character/personal qualities, extracurricular activities, geographical residence, interview, talent/ability, volunteer work, work experience. **Freshman Admission Requirements:** High school diploma is required and GED is accepted. *Academic units required:* 4 English, 3 mathematics, 3 science, 2 foreign language, 3 social studies, 1 academic electives. *Academic units recommended:* 4 English, 3 mathematics, 3 science, 2 foreign language, 3 social studies, 1 academic electives. **Freshman Admission Statistics:** 3,743 applied, 61% admitted, 25% enrolled. **Transfer Admission Requirements:** college transcript(s), minimum college GPA of 2.5 required. Lowest grade transferable C–. **General Admission Information:** Application Fee $30. Notification on a rolling basis, beginning on or about 10/20. Nonfall registration accepted. Admission may be deferred for a maximum of 1 year. Credit and/or placement offered for CEEB Advanced Placement tests.

COSTS AND FINANCIAL AID

Annual tuition $21,980. Room and board $7,550. Required fees $576. **Required Forms and Deadlines:** FAFSA. **Notification of Awards:** Applicants will be notified of awards on a rolling basis beginning 3/1. **Types of Aid:** *Need-based scholarships/grants:* Federal Pell, SEOG, state scholarships/grants, private scholarships, the school's own gift aid. *Loans:* Direct Subsidized Stafford, Direct Unsubsidized Stafford, Direct PLUS, Federal Perkins, state loans. **Student Employment:** Federal Work-Study Program available. Institutional employment available. Off-campus job opportunities are good. **Financial Aid Statistics:** 98% freshmen, 97% undergrads receive need-based scholarship or grant aid. 83% freshmen, 69% undergrads receive non-need-based scholarship or grant aid. 90% freshmen, 93% undergrads receive need-based self-help aid. 8% freshmen, 7% undergrads receive athletic scholarships. 96% freshmen, 91% undergrads receive any aid. 79% undergrads borrow to pay for school. Average cumulative indebtedness $27,416. **Criteria for awarding institutional aid:** *Non-need-based:* academics, alumni affiliation, athletics, leadership, minority status, music/drama, state/district residency.

ST. NORBERT COLLEGE

100 Grant Street, De Pere, WI 54115-2099
Phone: 920-403-3005 • **Financial Aid Phone:** 920-403-3071
E-mail: admit@snc.edu • **CEEB Code:** 1706
Fax: 920-403-4072 • **Website:** www.snc.edu • **ACT Code:** 4644

This private school, affiliated with the Roman Catholic Church, was founded in 1898. It has a 93-acre campus.

RATINGS

Admissions Selectivity Rating: 72   **Fire Safety Rating:** 81   **Green Rating:** 79

STUDENTS AND FACULTY

Enrollment: 2,208. **Student Body:** 59% female, 41% male, 25% out-of-state, 4% international (36 countries represented). Asian 1%, African American 1%, Caucasian 90%, Hispanic 2%, Native American 1%.
Retention and Graduation: 84% freshmen return for sophomore year. 68% freshmen graduate within 4 years. 75% freshmen graduate within 6 years. 23% grads go on to further study within 1 year. **Faculty:** Student/faculty ratio 14:1. 139 full-time faculty, 87% hold PhDs, 8% are members of minority groups, 41% are women. 0% of classes are taught by teaching assistants.

ACADEMICS

Degrees: bachelor's, master's. **Classes:** Most classes have 10–19 students. Most lab/discussion sessions have 10–19 students. **Majors with Highest Enrollment:** business/commerce; communication studies/speech communication and rhetoric; elementary education and teaching. **Special Study Options:** distance learning, double major, English as a Second Language (ESL), honors program, independent study, internships, student-designed major, study abroad, teacher certification program, Foundation for International Education (London)Internships; Washington Semester. **Honors Programs:** The Honors Program at St. Norbert College offers a sophisticated and demanding program of studies and readings to provide the most academically talented students with an enriched academic curriculum that is stimulating and challenging. **Disability Services:** Special programs offered to physically disabled students include note-taking services, reader services, tape recorders, tutors. **Career Services:** Alumni network, alumni services, career assessment, internships, regional alumni. Career Services highlights include Students can begin internships on campus or off campus after their freshmen year. Strong emphasis is placed on learning contracts.

FACILITIES
Housing: Coed dorms, special housing for disabled students, special housing for international students, women's dorms, fraternity/sorority housing, apartments for single students, Townhouses Off-campus college owned housing. 72% of campus accessible to physically disabled. **Special Academic Facilities/ Equipment:** New state-of-the-art Mulva Library, Center for leadership and service, Bush Art Center with three art galleries, scanning electron microscope, visual and performing arts center, center for international education, riverfront campus center with marina, peace and justice center, Career Services, children's center in cooperation with early childhood education, center of economic education,survey center, Kress Inn, conference services, academic support services, St. Joseph Church, chapels in residence halls, women's center and Journey-Men (men's center). **Computers:** 100% of classrooms, 60% of dorms, 100% of libraries, 100% of dining areas, 100% of student union, have wireless network access. Students can register for classes online. Administrative functions (other than registration) can be performed online.

CAMPUS LIFE
Environment: Village. **Activities:** Choral groups, concert band, drama/theater, jazz band, literary magazine, music ensembles, musical theater, pep band, radio station, student government, student newspaper, student-run film society, television station, Campus Ministries, International Student Organization 63 registered organizations, 10 honor societies, 3 religious organizations. 3 fraternities, 4 sororities. **Athletics (Intercollegiate):** *Men:* baseball, basketball, cross-country, football, golf, ice hockey, soccer, tennis, track/field (outdoor), track/field (indoor). *Women:* basketball, cross-country, golf, ice hockey, soccer, softball, tennis, track/field (outdoor), track/field (indoor), volleyball. **On-Campus Highlight:** The Ray Van Den Houvel Campus Center, The Bush Fine Arts Center, The F.K. Bemis International Center, Austin E Cofrin Hall, New Mulva Library with Coffee Shop. **Environmental Initiatives:** Designed new Mulva Library with solar water heating system. Converting all campus outdoor lighting to meet "night sky" compliance. Plan and design of future science building will meet Gold standards of LEED certification.

ADMISSIONS
Freshman Academic Profile: 25% in top 10% of high school class, 58% in top 25% of high school class, 85% in top 50% of high school class. 74% from public high schools. ACT middle 50% range 22-27. Minimum web-based TOEFL 80. Minimum paper TOEFL 550. **Basis for Candidate Selection:** *Very important factors considered include:* academic GPA, standardized test scores. *Important factors considered include:* rigor of secondary school record. *Other factors considered include:* Class rank, application essay, recommendation(s), alumni/ae relation, character/personal qualities, extracurricular activities, first generation, geographical residence, interview, level of applicant's interest, racial/ethnic status, religious affiliation/commitment, state residency, talent/ability, volunteer work, work experience. **Freshman Admission Requirements:** High school diploma is required and GED is accepted. **Freshman Admission Statistics:** 2,377 applied, 80% admitted, 31% enrolled. **Transfer Admission Requirements:** High school transcript, college transcript(s), essay or personal statement, standardized test scores, minimum college GPA of 2.5 required. Lowest grade transferable C. **General Admission Information:** Application Fee $25. Notification on a rolling basis, beginning on or about 10/1. Nonfall registration accepted. Admission may be deferred for a maximum of 2 years. Credit and/or placement offered for CEEB Advanced Placement tests.

COSTS AND FINANCIAL AID
Annual tuition $30,165. Room and board $7,813. Required fees $510. Average book expense $950. **Required Forms and Deadlines:** FAFSA. **Notification of Awards:** Applicants will be notified of awards on a rolling basis beginning 3/15. **Types of Aid:** *Need-based scholarships/grants:* Federal Pell, SEOG, state scholarships/grants, private scholarships, the school's own gift aid. *Loans:* Direct Subsidized Stafford, Direct Unsubsidized Stafford, Direct PLUS, Federal Perkins, state loans, college/university loans from institutional funds. **Student Employment:** Federal Work-Study Program available. Institutional employment available. Off-campus job opportunities are good. **Financial Aid Statistics:** 99% freshmen, 97% undergrads receive need-based scholarship or grant aid. 3% freshmen, 3% undergrads receive non-need-based scholarship

or grant aid. 79% freshmen, 79% undergrads receive need-based self-help aid. 97% freshmen, 99% undergrads receive any aid. 67% undergrads borrow to pay for school. Average cumulative indebtedness $31,331. **Criteria for awarding institutional aid:** *Non-need-based:* academics, art, leadership, minority status, music/drama, state/district residency.

See page 1216.

ST. OLAF COLLEGE

1520 St. Olaf Avenue, Northfield, MN 55057
Phone: 507-786-3025 • **Financial Aid Phone:** 507-786-3019
E-mail: admissions@stolaf.edu • **CEEB Code:** 6638
Fax: 507-786-3832 • **Website:** www.stolaf.edu • **ACT Code:** 2150

This private school, affiliated with the Lutheran Church, was founded in 1874. It has a 300-acre campus.

RATINGS
Admissions Selectivity Rating: 92   **Fire Safety Rating:** 66   **Green Rating:** 80

STUDENTS AND FACULTY
Enrollment: 3,125. **Student Body:** 56% female, 44% male, 49% out-of-state, 5% international (63 countries represented). Asian 5%, African American 2%, Caucasian 81%, Hispanic 4%, Native American 0%.
Retention and Graduation: 83% freshmen graduate within 4 years. 86% freshmen graduate within 6 years. 30% grads go on to further study within 1 year. 13% grads pursue arts and sciences degrees. 1% grads pursue law degrees. 5% grads pursue medical degrees. **Faculty:** Student/faculty ratio 12:1. 223 full-time faculty, 94% hold PhDs, 13% are members of minority groups, 44% are women. 0% of classes are taught by teaching assistants.

ACADEMICS
Degrees: bachelor's. **Classes:** Most classes have 10–19 students. Most lab/ discussion sessions have 20-29 students. **Majors with Highest Enrollment:** biology/biological sciences; economics; English language and literature. **Special Study Options:** cross-registration, double major, dual enrollment, independent study, internships, student-designed major, study abroad, teacher certification program. **Combined Degree Programs:** Law w/Columbia University. **Disability Services:** Special programs offered to physically disabled students include note-taking services, reader services, tape recorders, tutors. **Career Services:** Alumni network, alumni services, career/job search classes, career assessment, internships, regional alumni., Career Services highlights include The Center for Experiential Learning is proud of creating a comprehensive service that is linked to the academic program and offers many types of experiences to complement students' academic programs. THE CEL houses four programs: internships, service and civic leadership, entrepreneurial studies, and Career Services. The CEL has been bery successful in creating programming that meets the needs of students during their four years at St. Olaf. Some programs of which we are proud: entrepreneurial grants to start student-run businesses, service trips, civic engagement initiatives connected to specific courses, career-related seminars preseented in collaboration with academic departments, case study challenges created in conjunction with our corporate partners. Our academic internship program offers students an opportunity to receive credit for experiential learning. Since 2000, there have been over 900 Academic Internships completed by St. Olaf students at over 700 different organizations world wide.

FACILITIES
Housing: Coed dorms, special housing for disabled students, theme housing, honor houses, language houses, quiet halls, first-year only dorms. Disabled students accommodated in dorm of their choice. 80% of campus accessible to physically disabled. **Special Academic Facilities/Equipment:** Finstad Program for Entrepreneurial Studies, Kierkegaard Library, Flaten Art Museum, Norwegian American Historical Association archives. **Computers:** 100% of classrooms, 100% of dorms, 100% of libraries, 100% of dining areas, 100% of student union, 100% of common outdoor areas have wireless network access. Students can register for classes online. Administrative functions (other than registration) can be performed online.

CAMPUS LIFE
Environment: Village. **Activities:** Choral groups, concert band, dance, drama/ theater, jazz band, literary magazine, music ensembles, musical theater, opera,

pep band, radio station, student government, student newspaper, student-run film society, symphony orchestra, television station, Campus Ministries, International Student Organization, Model UN 193 registered organizations, 18 honor societies, 16 religious organizations. **Athletics (Intercollegiate):** *Men:* baseball, basketball, cross-country, diving, football, golf, ice hockey, skiing (downhill/alpine), skiingnordiccross-country, soccer, swimming, tennis, track/field (outdoor), track/field (indoor), wrestling. *Women:* basketball, cross-country, diving, golf, ice hockey, skiing (downhill/alpine), skiingnordiccross-country, soccer, softball, swimming, tennis, track/field (outdoor), track/field (indoor), volleyball. **On-Campus Highlights:** Regents Hall of Natural Science & Math, Buntrock Commons, Tostrud Recreation Center, The Lion's Pause, Dittman Art Museum, Beautiful 300 acre campus. **Environmental Initiatives:** In 2009 St. Olaf College's new 200,000 square-foot Regents Hall of Natural and Mathematical Sciences earned platinum certification -- the highest rating attainable -- from the U.S. Green Building Council's Leadership in Energy and Environmental Design(LEED)rating system. The building is the largest and most complex academic facility in the nation to earn the prestigious platinum rating. In 2005 St. Olaf became the first liberal arts college in the nation to construct a utility-grade wind turbine for the sole purpose of providing energy to the campus (Carleton College was the first to construct a turbine, but the electricity it produces is sold to an energy company and added to the general power grid). St. Olaf College's 1.65 megawatt self-generating wind turbine directly supplies up to one-third of the electricity used by the college. All food waste (100 percent) from the college's food services operation " preparation, production, line, and plate " is collected and composted in an on-campus in-vessel system, which comes to nearly 175 tons annually. One hundred percent of the compost generated is used on college-owned land, including in the landscaping and maintenance of the grounds. Compost is also supplied to the St. Olaf student-run organic farm.

ADMISSIONS

Freshman Academic Profile: Average high school GPA 3.6. 50% in top 10% of high school class, 80% in top 25% of high school class, 97% in top 50% of high school class. 78% from public high schools. SAT Math middle 50% range 580-700. SAT Critical Reading middle 50% range 580-700. SAT Writing middle 50% range 570-690. ACT middle 50% range 26-31. Minimum web-based TOEFL 90. **Basis for Candidate Selection:** *Very important factors considered include:* application essay, academic GPA, rigor of secondary school record. *Important factors considered include:* Class rank, recommendation(s), standardized test scores, character/personal qualities, extracurricular activities. *Other factors considered include:* alumni/ae relation, first generation, geographical residence, interview, level of applicant's interest, racial/ethnic status, religious affiliation/commitment, state residency, talent/ability, volunteer work, work experience. **Freshman Admission Requirements:** High school diploma is required and GED is accepted. **Freshman Admission Statistics:** 3,937 applied, 60% admitted, 36% enrolled. **Transfer Admission Requirements:** High school transcript, college transcript(s), essay or personal statement, standardized test scores, statement of good standing from prior institution(s). Minimum college GPA of 2.50 required. Lowest grade transferable C. **General Admission Information:** Application Fee $40. Early decision application deadline 11/15. Regular notification 3/20. Nonfall registration not accepted. Admission may be deferred for a maximum of 1 year. Credit and/or placement offered for CEEB Advanced Placement tests.

COSTS AND FINANCIAL AID

Annual tuition $39,560. Room and board $9,090. Average book expense $1,000. **Required Forms and Deadlines:** FAFSA, CSS/Financial Aid PROFILE, noncustodial PROFILE, business/farm supplement. **Notification of Awards:** Applicants will be notified of awards on a rolling basis beginning 3/1. **Types of Aid:** *Need-based scholarships/grants:* Federal Pell, SEOG, state scholarships/grants, private scholarships, the school's own gift aid. *Loans:* Subsidized Stafford, Unsubsidized Stafford, PLUS, Federal Perkins, Federal Nursing, state loans, college/university loans from institutional funds. **Student Employment:** Federal Work-Study Program available. Off-campus job opportunities are fair. **Financial Aid Statistics:** 100% freshmen, 100% undergrads receive need-based scholarship or grant aid. 46% freshmen, 27% undergrads receive non-need-based scholarship or grant aid. 100% freshmen, 100% undergrads receive need-based self-help aid. 92% freshmen, 90% undergrads receive any aid. 61% undergrads borrow to pay for school. Average cumulative indebtedness $27,637. **Criteria for awarding institutional aid:** *Non-need-based:* academics, leadership, music/drama.

ST. THOMAS UNIVERSITY

16401 Northwest 37th Avenue, Miami Gardens, FL 33054
Phone: 305-628-6546 • **Financial Aid Phone:** 305-628-6547
E-mail: signup@stu.edu • **CEEB Code:** 5076
Fax: 305-628-6591 • **Website:** www.stu.edu • **ACT Code:** 719

This private school, affiliated with the Roman Catholic Church, was founded in 1961. It has a 140-acre campus.

RATINGS
Admissions Selectivity Rating: 81   **Fire Safety Rating:** 68   **Green Rating:** 60*

STUDENTS AND FACULTY
Enrollment: 1,111. **Student Body:** 55% female, 45% male, 92% out-of-state, 12% international (57 countries represented). Asian 1%, African American 19%, Caucasian 10%, Hispanic 32%, Native American 0%. **Retention and Graduation:** 70% freshmen return for sophomore year. 22% freshmen graduate within 4 years. **Faculty:** Student/faculty ratio 14:1. 105 full-time faculty, 89% hold PhDs, 30% are members of minority groups, 47% are women. 0% of classes are taught by teaching assistants.

ACADEMICS
Degrees: bachelor's, certificate, master's, post-bachelor's certificate, post-master's certificate. **Classes:** Most classes have 10–19 students. Most lab/discussion sessions have 10–19 students. **Majors with Highest Enrollment:** business administration and management; organizational behavior studies; psychology. **Special Study Options:** distance learning, double major, dual enrollment, honors program, independent study, internships, liberal arts/career combination, teacher certification program. **Honors Programs:** The St. Thomas University Honors Program is designed to provide an intensive and stimulating alternative for students who wish to enhance their college academic experience. Qualified students are offered the opportunity to take Honors courses in the subjects of their choice, and, if they desire, to work for an Honors degree. **Combined Degree Programs:** BA/JD. **Disability Services:** Special programs offered to physically disabled students include note-taking services, reader services, tape recorders, tutors. **Career Services:** career/job search classes, career assessment, internships.

FACILITIES
Housing: men's dorms, women's dorms. 80% of campus accessible to physically disabled. **Special Academic Facilities/Equipment:** Multimedia computer equipment, TV studio, Art Atrium Gallery. **Computers:** 100% of libraries, 100% of dining areas, have wireless network access. Students can register for classes online. Administrative functions (other than registration) can be performed online.

CAMPUS LIFE
Environment: Metropolis. **Activities:** Choral groups, literary magazine, music ensembles, student government, television station, yearbook, Campus Ministries, International Student Organization 26 registered organizations, 4 honor societies, 2 religious organizations. **Athletics (Intercollegiate):** *Men:* baseball, basketball, cross-country, golf, soccer, tennis. *Women:* basketball, cross-country, soccer, softball, tennis, volleyball. **On-Campus Highlights:** Campus Chapel, Library, Fernandez Family Center, Kennedy Hall.

ADMISSIONS
Freshman Academic Profile: Average high school GPA 3.0. 6% in top 10% of high school class, 17% in top 25% of high school class, 53% in top 50% of high school class. SAT Math middle 50% range 408-500. SAT Critical Reading middle 50% range 410-510. SAT Writing middle 50% range 400-490. ACT middle 50% range 16-21. Minimum paper TOEFL 525. **Basis for Candidate Selection:** *Very important factors considered include:* Class rank, academic GPA, standardized test scores. *Important factors considered include:* application essay, recommendation(s), rigor of secondary school record, alumni/ae relation, level of applicant's interest. *Other factors considered include:* character/personal qualities, extracurricular activities, talent/ability, volunteer work, work experience. **Freshman Admission Requirements:** High school diploma is required and GED is accepted. *Academic units required:* 4 English, 3 mathematics, 2 science, 3 social studies, 6 academic electives. 4 English, 3 mathematics, 2 science, 3 social studies, 6 academic electives. **Freshman Admission Statistics:** 727 applied, 46% admitted, 63% enrolled. **Transfer Admission Requirements:** college transcript(s), essay or personal statement, statement of good standing from prior institution(s). Minimum college GPA of 2.0 required. Lowest grade transferable C–. **General Admission Information:** Application Fee $40. Nonfall registration accepted. Admission may be deferred for a maximum of One year. Credit and/or placement offered for CEEB Advanced Placement tests.

COSTS AND FINANCIAL AID

Required Forms and Deadlines: FAFSA, state aid form. **Notification of Awards:** Applicants will be notified of awards on a rolling basis beginning 3/1. **Types of Aid:** *Need-based scholarships/grants:* Federal Pell, SEOG, state scholarships/grants, private scholarships, the school's own gift aid. *Loans:* Subsidized Stafford, Unsubsidized Stafford, PLUS, Federal Perkins. **Student Employment:** Federal Work-Study Program available. Institutional employment available. Off-campus job opportunities are good. **Financial Aid Statistics:** 77% freshmen, 76% undergrads receive need-based scholarship or grant aid. 100% freshmen, 99% undergrads receive non-need-based scholarship or grant aid. 56% freshmen, 55% undergrads receive need-based self-help aid. 12% freshmen, 15% undergrads receive athletic scholarships. **Criteria for awarding institutional aid:** *Non-need-based:* academics, athletics, leadership.

ST. THOMAS UNIVERSITY

Admissions Office, St. Thomas University, Fredericton, NB E3B 5G3
Phone: 506-452-0532
E-mail: admissions@stu.ca
Fax: 506-452-0617 • **Website:** www.stu.ca

This private school, affiliated with the Roman Catholic Church, was founded in 1910. It has a 21-acre campus.

RATINGS
Admissions Selectivity Rating: 62   **Fire Safety Rating:** 95   **Green Rating:** 70

STUDENTS AND FACULTY
Enrollment: 2,475. **Student Body:** 66% female, 34% male, 27% out-of-state, 5% international (42 countries represented).
Retention and Graduation: 69% freshmen return for sophomore year. 41% freshmen graduate within 4 years. 54% freshmen graduate within 6 years.
Faculty: Student/faculty ratio 19:1. 109 full-time faculty, 95% hold PhDs, 39% are women. 0% of classes are taught by teaching assistants.

ACADEMICS
Degrees: bachelor's, certificate, first professional, post-bachelor's certificate. **Classes:** Most classes have 10–19 students. **Majors with Highest Enrollment:** criminology; English language and literature; psychology. **Special Study Options:** Accelerated program, cross-registration, double major, English as a Second Language (ESL), exchange student program (domestic), honors program, independent study, student-designed major, study abroad, teacher certification program, Aquinas Program: Thematically linked courses from various disciplines. **Disability Services:** Special programs offered to physically disabled students include note-taking services, reader services, tape recorders, tutors. **Career Services:** career/job search classes, career assessment, internships.

FACILITIES
Housing: Coed dorms, women's dorms. 80% of campus accessible to physically disabled. **Computers:** 100% of dorms, 100% of libraries, 100% of dining areas, have wireless network access. Students can register for classes online. Administrative functions (other than registration) can be performed online.

CAMPUS LIFE
Environment: Town. **Activities:** Choral groups, drama/theater, jazz band, music ensembles, musical theater, radio station, student government, student newspaper, student-run film society, yearbook, Campus Ministries, International Student Organization, Model UN 5 religious organizations. **Athletics (Intercollegiate):** *Men:* basketball, cross-country, golf, ice hockey, rugby, soccer, volleyball. *Women:* basketball, cross-country, golf, ice hockey, rugby, soccer, volleyball. **On-Campus Highlights:** Margaret Norrie McCain Hall, Lower courtyard, J.B. O'Keefe Fitness Centre, Sir James Dunn Hall, The Black Box Theatre. **Environmental Initiatives:** Recycle bins in all areas. Reduction of plastic and styrofoam products in cafeteria. Promotion of reduced energy usage.

ADMISSIONS
Freshman Academic Profile: Average high school GPA 3.3. Minimum web-based TOEFL 88. Minimum paper TOEFL 570. **Basis for Candidate Selection:** *Very important factors considered include:* academic GPA. *Other factors considered include:* application essay, recommendation(s), standardized test scores. **Freshman Admission Requirements:** High school diploma is required and GED is not accepted. **Freshman Admission Statistics:** 1,345 applied, 81% admitted, 58% enrolled. **Transfer Admission Requirements:** college transcript(s), statement of good standing from prior institution(s). Lowest grade transferable D. **General Admission Information:** Application Fee $35. Regular application deadline 8/31. Notification on a rolling basis, beginning

on or about 10/15. Nonfall registration accepted. Admission may be deferred for a maximum of 1 year. Credit and/or placement offered for CEEB Advanced Placement tests.

COSTS AND FINANCIAL AID
Average book expense $1,000.

STANFORD UNIVERSITY

Undergraduate Admission, Stanford, CA 94305-6106
Phone: 650-723-2091 • **Financial Aid Phone:** 650-723-3058
E-mail: admission@stanford.edu • **CEEB Code:** 4704
Fax: 650-725-2846 • **Website:** www.stanford.edu • **ACT Code:** 434

This private school was founded in 1885. It has a 8180-acre campus.

RATINGS
Admissions Selectivity Rating: 99   **Fire Safety Rating:** 77   **Green Rating:** 99

STUDENTS AND FACULTY
Enrollment: 6,999. **Student Body:** 48% female, 52% male, 54% out-of-state, 7% international (82 countries represented). Asian 19%, African American 6%, Caucasian 38%, Hispanic 17%, Native American 1%.
Retention and Graduation: 98% freshmen return for sophomore year. 80% freshmen graduate within 4 years. 95% freshmen graduate within 6 years. 25% grads go on to further study within 1 year. 62% grads pursue arts and sciences degrees. 3% grads pursue law degrees. 1% grads pursue business degrees. 9% grads pursue medical degrees. **Faculty:** Student/faculty ratio 5:1. 1486 full-time faculty, 99% hold PhDs, 22% are members of minority groups, 25% are women. 5% of classes are taught by teaching assistants.

ACADEMICS
Degrees: bachelor's, master's. **Classes:** Most classes have 10–19 students. Most lab/discussion sessions have 10–19 students. **Majors with Highest Enrollment:** biology/biological sciences; economics; international relations and affairs. **Special Study Options:** distance learning, double major, exchange student program (domestic), honors program, independent study, internships, student designed major, study abroad, Marine research center, Bing Stanford in Washington program, exchange programs with Dartmouth, Howard, Morehouse and Spelman, undergraduate research opportunities, Bing Honors College, overseas study. **Honors Programs:** About 100 student annually participate in Bing Honors College. About 25 percent of each graduating class earn departmental honors. **Combined Degree Programs:** BA/MA, Many bachelors/masters coterminal degree. **Disability Services:** Special programs offered to physically disabled students include note-taking services, reader services, tape recorders, tutors. **Career Services:** Alumni network, alumni services, career/job search classes, career assessment, internships, regional alumni. Career Services highlights include The Haas Center for Public Service at Stanford connects academic study with public service to strengthen communities and develop effective public leaders.

FACILITIES
Housing: Coed dorms, special housing for disabled students, women's dorms, fraternity/sorority housing, apartments for married students, cooperative housing, apartments for single students, theme housing: academic, cross-cultural, language theme and ethnic theme houses. 98% of campus accessible to physically disabled. **Special Academic Facilities/Equipment:** Art museum, marine station, observatory, biological preserve, linear accelerator. **Computers:** 100% of classrooms, 100% of dorms, 100% of libraries, 100% of dining areas, 100% of student union, 75% of common outdoor areas have wireless network access. Students can register for classes online. Administrative functions (other than registration) can be performed online.

CAMPUS LIFE
Environment: City. **Activities:** Choral groups, concert band, dance, drama/theater, jazz band, literary magazine, marching band, music ensembles, musical theater, opera, pep band, radio station, student government, student newspaper, student-run film society, symphony orchestra, television station, yearbook, Campus Ministries, International Student Organization, Model UN 600 registered organizations, 40 religious organizations. 17 fraternities, 11 sororities. **Athletics (Intercollegiate):** *Men:* baseball, basketball, crew/rowing, cross-country, diving, fencing, football, golf, gymnastics, sailing, soccer, swimming, tennis, track/field (outdoor), volleyball, water polo, wrestling. *Women:* basketball, crew/

rowing, cross-country, diving, fencing, field hockey, golf, gymnastics, lacrosse, sailing, soccer, softball, squash, swimming, synchronized swimming, tennis, track/field (outdoor), volleyball, water polo. **On-Campus Highlights:** Cantor Center for the Visual Arts, Rodin Sculpture Garden, Memorial Church, Observation Deck at Hoover Tower, athletic facilities, The Stanford campus is among the most beautiful anywhere and is a popular destination for tourists and other visitors. **Environmental Initiatives:** a) $438 million on the campus energy systems improvement (CESI) project for emissions reduction infrastructure;<http://news.stanford.edu/news/2011/december/trustees-december-meeting-121511.html> b) $250 million initiative on Sustainability in research (the Stanford Challenge) c) $70 million over the past ten years in energy retrofits, recommissioning and energy efficiency projects. Since 2002, energy retrofits of older buildings have resulted in an estimated savings of 176 million kilowatt‐hours of electricity, about 8 months of Stanford's current electricity use. Water consumption has been reduced from 2.7 million gallons per day to 2.15 million since 2001. New constructions and major renovations have energy and water standards comparable to LEED-NC GOLD. http://sustainable.stanford.edu/climate_action http://sustainable.stanford.edu/energy http://sustainable.stanford.edu/guidelines 2.Stanford's award-winning Transportation Demand Management program has been recognized by the EPA. It includes a free bus system powered by biodiesel and hybid buses; a commute club, free or pre-tax passes on public transportation; car rental options; commute planning assistance; charter services; and a bike program. A smaller percentage of faculty, staff and student commute by single-occupancy vehicle than the national average (46 versus 77 percent).Commute emissions are down to 1990 levels. http://transportation.stanford.edu/ 3.Stanford's recycling program, started by students in the 1970s and recognized by the EPA, diverts 64 percent of waste from landfills (including construction and demolition debris). The ultimate goal is towards zero waste.

ADMISSIONS

Freshman Academic Profile: 94% in top 10% of high school class, 99% in top 25% of high school class, 100% in top 50% of high school class. 58% from public high schools. SAT Math middle 50% range 700-790. SAT Critical Reading middle 50% range 680-780. SAT Writing middle 50% range 700-780. ACT middle 50% range 31-34. **Basis for Candidate Selection:** *Very important factors considered include:* Class rank, application essay, academic GPA, recommendation(s), rigor of secondary school record, standardized test scores, character/personal qualities, extracurricular activities, talent/ability.*Other factors considered include:* alumni/ae relation, first generation, geographical residence, racial/ethnic status, volunteer work, work experience. **Freshman Admission Requirements:** High school diploma is required and GED is accepted. **Freshman Admission Statistics:** 36,632 applied, 7% admitted, 73% enrolled. **Transfer Admission Requirements:** High school transcript, college transcript(s), essay or personal statement, standardized test scores, statement of good standing from prior institution(s). Lowest grade transferable C–. **General Admission Information:** Application Fee $90. Regular application deadline 1/1. Regular notification 4/1. Nonfall registration not accepted. Admission may be deferred for a maximum of 2 years. Credit and/or placement offered for CEEB Advanced Placement tests.

COSTS AND FINANCIAL AID

Annual tuition $41,250. Room and board $12,721. Required fees $537. Average book expense $1,500. **Required Forms and Deadlines:** FAFSA, CSS/Financial Aid PROFILE. **Notification of Awards:** Applicants will be notified of awards on a rolling basis beginning 4/3. **Types of Aid:** *Need-based scholarships/grants:* Federal Pell, SEOG, state scholarships/grants, private scholarships, the school's own gift aid. *Loans:* Subsidized Stafford, Unsubsidized Stafford, PLUS, Federal Perkins. **Student Employment:** Federal Work-Study Program available. Institutional employment available. Off-campus job opportunities are good. **Financial Aid Statistics:** 95% freshmen, 96% undergrads receive need-based scholarship or grant aid. 2% freshmen, 2% undergrads receive non-need-based scholarship or grant aid. 65% freshmen, 78% undergrads receive need-based self-help aid. 7% freshmen, 7% undergrads receive athletic scholarships. 70% undergrads receive any aid. 25% undergrads borrow to pay for school. Average cumulative indebtedness $18,833.

STATE UNIVERSITY OF NEW YORK—ALFRED STATE COLLEGE, COLLEGE OF TECHNOLOGY

Huntington Administration Bldg., Alfred, NY 14802
Phone: 607-587-4215 • **Financial Aid Phone:** 607-587-4253
E-mail: admissions@alfredstate.edu • **CEEB Code:** 2522
Fax: 607-587-4299 • **Website:** www.alfredstate.edu • **ACT Code:** 2910

This public school was founded in 1908. It has a 840-acre campus.

RATINGS
Admissions Selectivity Rating: 74   **Fire Safety Rating:** 78   **Green Rating:** 76

STUDENTS AND FACULTY
Enrollment: 3,531. **Student Body:** 37% female, 63% male, 6% out-of-state, (19 countries represented). Asian 2%, African American 9%, Caucasian 78%, Hispanic 5%, Native American 0%.
Retention and Graduation: 81% freshmen return for sophomore year. 53% freshmen graduate within 4 years. 66% freshmen graduate within 6 years. 38% grads go on to further study within 1 year. **Faculty:** Student/faculty ratio 18:1. 181 full-time faculty, 19% hold PhDs, 6% are members of minority groups, 30% are women. 0% of classes are taught by teaching assistants.

ACADEMICS
Degrees: associate, bachelor's, certificate, terminal associate, transfer associate. **Classes:** Most classes have 10–19 students. Most lab/discussion sessions have 10–19 students. **Majors with Highest Enrollment:** architectural technology/technician; automotive engineering technology/technician; engineering technology. **Special Study Options:** cooperative education program, cross-registration, distance learning, honors program, independent study, internships, student-designed major, study abroad, Internet courses. **Honors Programs:** Participants complete a series of seminars, as well as a substantial honors project and 10 hours of volunteer community service. **Disability Services:** Special programs offered to physically disabled students include note-taking services, reader services, tape recorders, tutors. **Career Services:** Alumni network, career/job search classes.

FACILITIES
Housing: Coed dorms, special housing for disabled students, Suite, corridor, singles, smoke-free, over 21 yrs, over 24 yrs, wellness living, quiet study, same curriculum housing, baccalaureate, single room options; and computer life style New upperclassmen apartment suite complex. 100% of campus accessible to physically disabled. **Computers:** 100% of classrooms, 100% of dorms, 100% of libraries, 100% of dining areas, 100% of common outdoor areas have wireless network access. Students can register for classes online. Administrative functions (other than registration) can be performed online.

CAMPUS LIFE
Environment: Rural. **Activities:** Choral groups, concert band, drama/theater, jazz band, literary magazine, music ensembles, musical theater, radio station, student government, student newspaper, symphony orchestra, yearbook 60 registered organizations, 4 honor societies, 3 fraternities, 2 sororities. **Athletics (Intercollegiate):** *Men:* baseball, basketball, cheerleading, cross-country, football, lacrosse, soccer, swimming, track/field (outdoor), wrestling. *Women:* basketball, cheerleading, cross-country, soccer, softball, swimming, track/field (outdoor), volleyball. **On-Campus Highlights:** Pioneer Center, Orvis (Athletic Center), Peach Pit, Central Dining Hall, Upperclassmen Apartment Suite Complex. **Environmental Initiatives:** Energy conservation, greenhouse gas inventory and shrinking our carbon footprint through renewable energy. Increase recycling and reduce what is going to the landfill. Composting and establishing a community garden.

ADMISSIONS
Freshman Academic Profile: Average high school GPA 2.8. SAT Math middle 50% range 430-540. SAT Critical Reading middle 50% range 410-420. SAT Writing middle 50% range 290-490. ACT middle 50% range 18-23. Minimum web-based TOEFL 61. Minimum paper TOEFL 500. **Basis for Candidate Selection:** *Very important factors considered include:* academic GPA, rigor of secondary school record. *Important factors considered include:* Class rank. *Other factors considered include:* application essay, recommendation(s), standardized test scores, alumni/ae relation, character/personal qualities, extracurricular activities, interview, talent/ability, volunteer work, work experience. **Freshman Admission Requirements:** High school diploma is required and GED is accepted. **Freshman Admission Statistics:** 3,890 applied, 55% admitted, 51% enrolled. **Transfer Admission Requirements:** High school transcript, college transcript(s), statement of good standing from prior institution(s). Minimum college GPA of 2.4 required. Lowest grade transferable C. **General Admission Information:** Application Fee $40. Notification on a rolling basis, beginning on

or about 11/1. Nonfall registration accepted. Admission may be deferred for a maximum of 1 semester. Credit and/or placement offered for CEEB Advanced Placement tests.

COSTS AND FINANCIAL AID

Annual in-state tuition $5,570. Annual out-of-state tuition $10,714. Room and board $10,450. Required fees $1,272. Average book expense $1,200. **Required Forms and Deadlines:** FAFSA, state aid form. **Notification of Awards:** Applicants will be notified of awards on a rolling basis beginning 3/3. **Types of Aid:** *Need-based scholarships/grants:* Federal Pell, SEOG, state scholarships/grants, private scholarships, the school's own gift aid. *Loans:* Subsidized Stafford, Unsubsidized Stafford, PLUS, Federal Perkins, Federal Nursing. **Student Employment:** Federal Work-Study Program available. Institutional employment available. Off-campus job opportunities are fair. **Financial Aid Statistics:** 87% freshmen, 87% undergrads receive need-based scholarship or grant aid. 27% freshmen, 25% undergrads receive non-need-based scholarship or grant aid. 89% freshmen, 87% undergrads receive need-based self-help aid. 1% freshmen, 1% undergrads receive athletic scholarships. 82% freshmen, 82% undergrads receive any aid. 87% undergrads borrow to pay for school. Average cumulative indebtedness $29,772.

STATE UNIVERSITY OF NEW YORK AT BINGHAMTON

PO Box 6001, Binghamton, NY 13902-6001
Phone: 607-777-2171 • **Financial Aid Phone:** 607-777-2428
E-mail: admit@binghamton.edu • **CEEB Code:** 2535
Fax: 607-777-4445 • **Website:** www.binghamton.edu • **ACT Code:** 2956

This public school was founded in 1946. It has a 930-acre campus.

RATINGS
Admissions Selectivity Rating: 94   **Fire Safety Rating:** 79   **Green Rating:** 94

STUDENTS AND FACULTY
Enrollment: 12,296. **Student Body:** 47% female, 53% male, 12% out-of-state, 11% international (107 countries represented). Asian 13%, African American 5%, Caucasian 53%, Hispanic 9%, Native American 0%.
Retention and Graduation: 91% freshmen return for sophomore year. 68% freshmen graduate within 4 years. 40% grads go on to further study within 1 year. 11% grads pursue arts and sciences degrees. 5% grads pursue law degrees. 7% grads pursue business degrees. 8% grads pursue medical degrees. **Faculty:** Student/faculty ratio 20:1. 604 full-time faculty, 90% hold PhDs, 25% are members of minority groups, 40% are women. 6% of classes are taught by teaching assistants.

ACADEMICS
Degrees: bachelor's, master's, post-master's certificate. **Classes:** Most classes have 20–29 students. Most lab/discussion sessions have 20–29 students. **Majors with Highest Enrollment:** biology/biological sciences; business administration and management; engineering. **Special Study Options:** Accelerated program, cross-registration, distance learning, double major, dual enrollment, English as a Second Language (ESL), exchange student program (domestic), honors program, independent study, internships, liberal arts/career combination, student-designed major, study abroad, teacher certification program, Teacher Certification Program is graduate only. **Honors Programs:** Binghamton University Scholars Program--See http://scholars.binghamton.edu Each academic department offers an honors program. Binghamton also has a PricewaterhouseCoopers Scholars program for students in the School of Management. **Combined Degree Programs:** BA/MA, >40 combined degrees for BA or BS with MBA/MPA/MAT/MA/MS. **Disability Services:** Special programs offered to physically disabled students include note-taking services, reader services, tape recorders. **Career Services:** Alumni network, alumni services, career/job search classes, career assessment, internships, regional alumni. Career Services highlights include Binghamton's Career Development Center has received numerous awards for excellence from the SUNY Career Development Organization in regard to programming, operations and recruitment.

FACILITIES
Housing: Coed dorms, special housing for disabled students, apartments for single students, wellness housing, theme housing. 90% of campus accessible to physically disabled. **Special Academic Facilities/Equipment:** Art gallery, performing arts center, indoor/outdoor theater, multi-climate and teaching greenhouse, sculpture foundry, 8,000-seat Events Center, Analytical and Diagnostics Laboratory, Electron Microscopy Facility, Public Archaeology Facility, 930-acre Nature Preserve. **Computers:** 95% of classrooms, 100% of dorms, 100% of libraries, 100% of dining areas, 100% of student union, 60% of common outdoor areas have wireless network access. Students can register for classes online. Administrative functions (other than registration) can be performed online.

CAMPUS LIFE
Environment: City. **Activities:** Choral groups, concert band, dance, drama/theater, jazz band, literary magazine, music ensembles, musical theater, opera, pep band, radio station, student government, student newspaper, student-run film society, symphony orchestra, television station, yearbook, Campus Ministries, International Student Organization, Model UN 23 honor societies, 15 religious organizations. 23 fraternities, 23 sororities. **Athletics (Intercollegiate):** *Men:* baseball, basketball, cross-country, diving, golf, lacrosse, soccer, swimming, tennis, track/field (outdoor), track/field (indoor), wrestling. *Women:* basketball, cross-country, diving, lacrosse, soccer, softball, swimming, tennis, track/field (outdoor), track/field (indoor), volleyball. **On-Campus Highlights:** University Union, Fitspace, Nature Preserve, Events Center, Anderson Center for the Arts, Rosefsky Art Gallery, Libraries. **Environmental Initiatives:** Binghamton University's goal is to design, construct, operate and maintain all new buildings following guidelines set forth by the U.S. Green Building Council's LEED rating system. Since 2004, Binghamton has obtained LEED and LEED Silver certification on three buildings. Seven other recently completed buildings are on track for LEED silver and higher certifications. Our new Engineering & Science Building completed in 2011 features state of the art energy efficient lighting and HVAC equipment as well as geothermal and photovoltaic systems. Energy Conservation and Waste Management Programs: Since 2005, Binghamton University has continually invested in energy conservation projects such as installation of efficient lighting, occupancy sensors, variable speed drives on motors, free-cooling devices to take advantage of cooler outdoor temperatures, solar hot water heater and constant improvements to our energy management system. As a result, Binghamton's overall electricity consumption was reduced by 9% from 2005 to 2010. Recent building construction activities unfortunately added to the energy usage on campus. The primary focus of the Energy Team has shifted to fine-tuning the building automation systems on these new buildings to ensure optimum energy performance of these buildings. Waste Management Program has also made tremendous progress in areas such as recycling, waste reduction, composting and community outreach. The University's waste production has been reduced by 470 tons, or 19% since 2008. Binghamton University currently offers free public transportation to students, faculty and staff for commuting within the Broome County area. Additionally, campus fleet vehicles have been rapidly replaced by plug-in electric vehicles. The University also encourages car pooling through various programs such as offering preferred parking spaces for High Occupancy Vehicles, Broome-Tioga Green-Ride, and hourly car rentals on campus for car poolers' convenience. Nearly 70% of Binghamton University's 930-acre campus is in its natural state. The core of this undeveloped land is officially designated the Nature Preserve, encompassing 187 acres of land which includes a 20 acre wetland. Binghamton uses this large, valuable resource for teaching and learning, research, ecology, arts, literature and outdoor recreation. • **Website:** http://naturepreserve.binghamton.edu

ADMISSIONS
Freshman Academic Profile: Average high school GPA 3.6. 55% in top 10% of high school class, 88% in top 25% of high school class, 99% in top 50% of high school class. 89% from public high schools. SAT Math middle 50% range 630-710. SAT Critical Reading middle 50% range 590-675. SAT Writing middle 50% range 580-670. ACT middle 50% range 27-30. Minimum web-based TOEFL 83. Minimum paper TOEFL 560. **Basis for Candidate Selection:** *Very important factors considered include:* academic GPA, rigor of secondary school record, standardized test scores. *Important factors considered include:* Class rank, application essay, recommendation(s), extracurricular activities, first generation. *Other factors considered include:* alumni/ae relation, character/personal qualities, geographical residence, level of applicant's interest, racial/ethnic status, state residency, talent/ability, volunteer work, work experience. **Freshman Admission Requirements:** High school diploma is required and GED is accepted. *Academic units required:* 4 English, 3 mathematics, 2 science, 3 foreign language, 2 social studies. *Academic units recommended:* 4 English, 3 mathematics, 2 science, 3 foreign language, 2 social studies. **Freshman Admission Statistics:** 28,232 applied, 43% admitted, 22% enrolled. **Transfer Admission Requirements:** college transcript(s), Lowest grade transferable C–. **General Admission Information:** Application Fee $40. Regular notification 4/1. Nonfall registration accepted. Admission may be deferred for a maximum of 1 year. Credit offered for CEEB Advanced Placement tests.

COSTS AND FINANCIAL AID
Annual in-state tuition $5,570. Annual out-of-state tuition $14,720. Room and board $12,446. Required fees $2,075. Average book expense $1,000. **Required**

Forms and Deadlines: FAFSA, state aid form. **Notification of Awards:** Applicants will be notified of awards on a rolling basis beginning 4/1. **Types of Aid:** *Need-based scholarships/grants:* Federal Pell, SEOG, state scholarships/grants, private scholarships, the school's own gift aid. *Loans:* Direct Subsidized Stafford, Direct Unsubsidized Stafford, Direct PLUS, Federal Perkins, Federal Nursing, college/university loans from institutional funds. **Student Employment:** Federal Work-Study Program available. Institutional employment available. Highest amount earned per year from on-campus jobs $5,700. Off-campus job opportunities are excellent. **Financial Aid Statistics:** 81% freshmen, 82% undergrads receive need-based scholarship or grant aid. 14% freshmen, 10% undergrads receive non-need-based scholarship or grant aid. 98% freshmen, 98% undergrads receive need-based self-help aid. 3% freshmen, 3% undergrads receive athletic scholarships. 79% freshmen, 70% undergrads receive any aid. 53% undergrads borrow to pay for school. Average cumulative indebtedness $23,710. **Criteria for awarding institutional aid:** *Non-need-based:* academics, art, athletics, leadership, minority status, music/drama, state/district residency.

STATE UNIVERSITY OF NEW YORK— BROCKPORT

350 New Campus Drive, Brockport, NY 14420
Phone: 585-395-2751 • **Financial Aid Phone:** 585-395-2501
E-mail: admit@brockport.edu • **CEEB Code:** 2537
Fax: 585-395-5452 • **Website:** www.brockport.edu • **ACT Code:** 2928

This public school was founded in 1835. It has a 464-acre campus.

RATINGS
Admissions Selectivity Rating: 88   **Fire Safety Rating:** 78   **Green Rating:** 79

STUDENTS AND FACULTY
Student Body: 1% out-of-state, (15 countries represented).
Retention and Graduation: 44% freshmen graduate within 4 years. 32% grads go on to further study within 1 year. 10% grads pursue arts and sciences degrees. 2% grads pursue law degrees. 4% grads pursue business degrees. **Faculty:** Student/faculty ratio 18:1. 335 full-time faculty, 89% hold PhDs, 15% are members of minority groups, 47% are women. 0% of classes are taught by teaching assistants.

ACADEMICS
Degrees: bachelor's, master's, post-master's certificate. **Classes:** Most classes have 20–29 students. Most lab/discussion sessions have 10–19 students. **Majors with Highest Enrollment:** business administration and management; health professions and related clinical sciences, other; physical education teaching and coaching. **Special Study Options:** Accelerated program, cross-registration, distance learning, double major, dual enrollment, honors program, independent study, internships, student-designed major, study abroad, teacher certification program. **Honors Programs:** 1)College Honors Program, which designs to let students complete general education requirements in small classes; 2) Delta College, which is a time-variable degree program for highly-motivated students. **Disability Services:** Special programs offered to physically disabled students include note-taking services, reader services, tape recorders, tutors. **Career Services:** Alumni network, alumni services, career/job search classes, career assessment, internships, regional alumni. Career Services highlights include Brockport has a 91% placement rate for recent graduates.

FACILITIES
Housing: Coed dorms, special housing for international students, apartments for single students, wellness housing, Extended housing (open during college breaks-excludes summer). 95% of campus accessible to physically disabled. **Special Academic Facilities/Equipment:** aquaculture ponds, weather information system, high-resolution germanium detector, research vessel on Lake Ontario, electron microscope, low- temperature physics lab, vacuum deposition lab, computational; physics lab, 2 supercomputers, Doppler Radar system, ultramodern dance facilities including green room, hydrotherapy room, student learning center, academic computing center, and two theaters. **Computers:** 100% of classrooms, 100% of dorms, 100% of libraries, 100% of dining areas, 100% of student union, 80% of common outdoor areas have wireless network access. Students can register for classes online. Administrative functions (other than registration) can be performed online.

CAMPUS LIFE
Environment: Village. **Activities:** Choral groups, dance, drama/theater, literary magazine, music ensembles, musical theater, radio station, student government, student newspaper, television station, Campus Ministries, International Student Organization, Model UN 71 registered organizations, 20 honor societies, 8 religious organizations. 6 fraternities, 3 sororities. **Athletics (Intercollegiate):** *Men:* baseball, basketball, cross-country, diving, football, ice hockey, lacrosse, soccer, swimming, track/field (outdoor), track/field (indoor), wrestling. *Women:* basketball, cross-country, diving, field hockey, gymnastics, lacrosse, soccer, softball, swimming, tennis, track/field (outdoor), track/field (indoor), volleyball. **On-Campus Highlights:** Seymour College Union, Drake Memorial Library, Hartwell Performance Center, Harrison Dining Hall, Tuttle Athletic Complex, Smith Hall Science Center Dailey Hall Computing Center Tower Fine Arts Center. **Environmental Initiatives:** We received the 2010 Pollution Prevention Award from the Rochester Business Journal for our comprehensive programs and continuing efforts to improve our sustainability performance. Developed a comprehensive environmental management system and a Facilities Master Plan in order to continuously improve our environmental performanace. Invested over $50 million in several sustainable building projects (LEED Silver) that will reduce our impact on the environment and result in long term energy savings.

ADMISSIONS
Freshman Academic Profile: Average high school GPA 3.5. 12% in top 10% of high school class, 43% in top 25% of high school class, 86% in top 50% of high school class. SAT Math middle 50% range 500-580. SAT Critical Reading middle 50% range 480-570. SAT Writing middle 50% range 460-560. ACT middle 50% range 21-25. Minimum web-based TOEFL 71. Minimum paper TOEFL 530. **Basis for Candidate Selection:** *Very important factors considered include:* academic GPA, rigor of secondary school record. *Important factors considered include:* Class rank, application essay, recommendation(s), standardized test scores, character/personal qualities, extracurricular activities, talent/ability, volunteer work, work experience. *Other factors considered include:* interview, level of applicant's interest, racial/ethnic status. **Freshman Admission Requirements:** High school diploma is required and GED is accepted. *Academic units required:* 4 English, 3 mathematics, 3 science, (1 science labs), 4 social studies, 3 academic electives. *Academic units recommended:* 4 English, 3 mathematics, 3 science, (1 science labs), 4 social studies, 3 academic electives. **Freshman Admission Statistics:** 8,575 applied, 46% admitted, 27% enrolled. **Transfer Admission Requirements:** college transcript(s), minimum college GPA of 2.5 required. Lowest grade transferable D-. **General Admission Information:** Application Fee $40. Notification on a rolling basis, beginning on or about 11/15. Nonfall registration accepted. Admission may be deferred for a maximum of 1 year. Credit and/or placement offered for CEEB Advanced Placement tests.

COSTS AND FINANCIAL AID
Annual in-state tuition $5,570. Annual out-of-state tuition $14,820. Room and board $10,940. Required fees $1,311. Average book expense $1,050. **Required Forms and Deadlines:** FAFSA, state aid form. **Notification of Awards:** Applicants will be notified of awards on a rolling basis beginning 3/15. **Types of Aid:** *Need-based scholarships/grants:* Federal Pell, SEOG, state scholarships/grants, private scholarships, the school's own gift aid. *Loans:* Direct Subsidized Stafford, Direct Unsubsidized Stafford, Direct PLUS, Federal Perkins, Federal Nursing, Private Alternative loans. **Student Employment:** Federal Work-Study Program available. Institutional employment available. Highest amount earned per year from on-campus jobs $14,059. Off-campus job opportunities are good. **Financial Aid Statistics:** 83% freshmen, 85% undergrads receive need-based scholarship or grant aid. 36% freshmen, 21% undergrads receive non-need-based scholarship or grant aid. 85% freshmen, 86% undergrads receive need-based self-help aid. 91% freshmen, 84% undergrads receive any aid. 81% undergrads borrow to pay for school. Average cumulative indebtedness $26,785. **Criteria for awarding institutional aid:** *Non-need-based:* academics, alumni affiliation, art, athletics, leadership, minority status, music/drama.

STATE UNIVERSITY OF NEW YORK— BUFFALO STATE COLLEGE

1300 Elmwood Avenue, Buffalo, NY 14222
Phone: 716-878-4017 • **Financial Aid Phone:** 716-878-4902
E-mail: admissions@buffalostate.edu • **CEEB Code:** 2533
Fax: 716-878-6100 • **ACT Code:** 2930

This public school was founded in 1871. It has a 115-acre campus.

RATINGS
Admissions Selectivity Rating: 64   **Fire Safety Rating:** 68   **Green Rating:** 69

STUDENTS AND FACULTY

Enrollment: 9,796. **Student Body:** 58% female, 42% male, 1% out-of-state, 1% international (41 countries represented). Asian 2%, African American 16%, Caucasian 65%, Hispanic 7%, Native American 1%.
Retention and Graduation: 76% freshmen return for sophomore year. 22% grads go on to further study within 1 year. 3% grads pursue arts and sciences degrees. 3% grads pursue law degrees. 7% grads pursue business degrees. **Faculty:** 402 full-time faculty, 90% hold PhDs, 17% are members of minority groups, 46% are women. 0% of classes are taught by teaching assistants.

ACADEMICS

Degrees: bachelor's, master's, post-master's certificate. **Majors with Highest Enrollment:** business/commerce; elementary education and teaching. **Special Study Options:** cooperative education program, cross-registration, distance learning, double major, dual enrollment, English as a Second Language (ESL), exchange student program (domestic), honors program, independent study, internships, liberal arts/career combination, study abroad, teacher certification program. **Disability Services:** Special programs offered to physically disabled students include note-taking services, reader services, tape recorders, tutors. **Career Services:** Alumni network, alumni services, career/job search classes, career assessment, internships.

FACILITIES

Housing: Coed dorms, special housing for international students, Apartments for students with dependent children. 100% of campus accessible to physically disabled. **Special Academic Facilities/Equipment:** Burchfield Penney Art center, anthropology museum, concert hall with pipe organ, nature preserve. **Computers:** 10% of classrooms, 30% of libraries, 100% of dining areas, 50% of student union, 10% of common outdoor areas have wireless network access. Students can register for classes online. Administrative functions (other than registration) can be performed online.

CAMPUS LIFE

Environment: City. **Activities:** Choral groups, concert band, dance, drama/theater, jazz band, literary magazine, music ensembles, radio station, student government, student newspaper, student-run film society, television station, yearbook, International Student Organization 75 registered organizations, 5 religious organizations. 10 fraternities, 10 sororities. **Athletics (Intercollegiate):** Men: basketball, cross-country, diving, football, ice hockey, soccer, swimming, track/field (outdoor), track/field (indoor). Women: basketball, cheerleading, cross-country, diving, ice hockey, lacrosse, soccer, softball, swimming, tennis, track/field (outdoor), track/field (indoor), volleyball. **On-Campus Highlights:** Burchfield Penny Art Center, Sports Arena, Houston Gymnasium/Fitness Center, Rockwell Hall/Performing Arts Center, Campus House. **Environmental Initiatives:** 1) Creation of a campus wide recycling program for plastic, glass, metal, paper, cardboard, light bulbs, electronics, electronic media (printer cartridges, dvds, cds, VHS, cassettes, etc), batteries, shrink wrap, bubble wrap, and many other misc items! This was applied to every building on campus including the residential halls. 2) "Don't Throw it Out Program" - Move out program for Residential students to bring unwanted furniture, food, clothing, shoes, appliances, etc to centrally located drop off stations. This excess waste, and these items are then donated to nonprofit organizations. 3) Environmental Information Fair- 20 - 30 organizations ranging from county depts. to coummnity organizations that congriagte on campus with the purpose of educating the campus population about environmental events and information that applies to their everyday life. It is a campus event that serves to create awareness among the campus and surrounding community. It is intended to promote and encourage a cleaner Western New York as we inform the community about going green.

ADMISSIONS

Freshman Academic Profile: Average high school GPA 3.2. 8% in top 10% of high school class, 35% in top 25% of high school class, 82% in top 50% of high school class. SAT Math middle 50% range 450-540. SAT Critical Reading middle 50% range 440-530. SAT Writing middle 50% range 430-520. Minimum paper TOEFL 500. **Basis for Candidate Selection:** Very important factors considered include: academic GPA, rigor of secondary school record, standardized test scores. Important factors considered include: Class rank. Other factors considered include: application essay, recommendation(s), character/personal qualities, extracurricular activities, first generation, interview, talent/ability, volunteer work, work experience. **Freshman Admission Requirements:** High school diploma is required and GED is accepted. Academic units required: 2 mathematics, 2 science. Academic units recommended: 2 mathematics, 2 science. **Transfer Admission Requirements:** college transcript(s), statement of good standing from prior institution(s). Minimum college GPA of 2.0 required. Lowest grade transferable C. **General Admission Information:** Application Fee $40. Early decision application deadline 11/15. Notification on a rolling basis, beginning on or about 12/15. Nonfall registration accepted. Admission may be deferred for a maximum of 1 year. Credit offered for CEEB Advanced Placement tests.

COSTS AND FINANCIAL AID

Annual in-state tuition $5,270. Annual out-of-state tuition $14,230. Room and board $10,168. Required fees $1,083. Average book expense $990. **Required Forms and Deadlines:** FAFSA. **Notification of Awards:** Applicants will be notified of awards on a rolling basis beginning 5/1. **Types of Aid:** Need-based scholarships/grants: Federal Pell, SEOG, state scholarships/grants. Loans: Subsidized Stafford, Unsubsidized Stafford, PLUS, Federal Perkins. **Student Employment:** **Financial Aid Statistics:** 84% freshmen, 81% undergrads receive need-based scholarship or grant aid. 10% freshmen, 6% undergrads receive non-need-based scholarship or grant aid. 62% freshmen, 65% undergrads receive need-based self-help aid. 71% freshmen, 68% undergrads receive any aid. 69% undergrads borrow to pay for school. Average cumulative indebtedness $17,657. **Criteria for awarding institutional aid:** Non-need-based: academics, minority status.

STATE UNIVERSITY OF NEW YORK—CANTON

French Hall, Canton, NY 13617
Phone: 315-386-7123
E-mail: admissions@canton.edu • **CEEB Code:** 2523
Fax: 315-386-7929 • **Website:** www.canton.edu • **ACT Code:** 2912

This public school was founded in 1906. It has a 555-acre campus.

RATINGS

Admissions Selectivity Rating: 61   **Fire Safety Rating:** 60*   **Green Rating:** 60*

STUDENTS AND FACULTY

Enrollment: 2,110. **Student Body:** 48% female, 52% male, 0% international (5 countries represented). Asian 0%, African American 8%, Caucasian 86%, Hispanic 3%, Native American 2%.
Retention and Graduation: 81% freshmen return for sophomore year. 45% grads go on to further study within 1 year. **Faculty:** Student/faculty ratio 23:1. 83 full-time faculty, 20% hold PhDs, 2% are members of minority groups, 66% are women. 0% of classes are taught by teaching assistants.

ACADEMICS

Degrees: associate, bachelor's, certificate, terminal associate, transfer associate. **Classes:** Most classes have 20-29 students. Most lab/discussion sessions have 10-19 students. **Special Study Options:** cooperative education program, cross-registration, distance learning, dual enrollment, internships, liberal arts/career combination, student-designed major. **Disability Services:** Special programs offered to physically disabled students include note-taking services, reader services, tape recorders, tutors. **Career Services:** career/job search classes, career assessment, internships.

FACILITIES

Housing: Coed dorms, single sex wings, Intensive Quiet Atmosphere, Relaxed Atmosphere, Suites, Private Rooms, Computer Floors, 21+ Floor, Grasse River Community (Pet floor), Umoja Ahora Community (multicultural), North Country Experience, Alcohol Free, Smoke Free. 100% of campus accessible to physically disabled. **Special Academic Facilities/Equipment:** Criminal Investigation Labs, radio station, distance learning classrooms

CAMPUS LIFE

Environment: Rural. **Activities:** Choral groups, literary magazine, radio station, student government, student newspaper, yearbook 50 registered organizations, 2 honor societies, 1 religious organizations. 3 fraternities, 3 sororities. **Athletics (Intercollegiate):** Men: basketball, football, ice hockey, lacrosse, soccer. Women: basketball, soccer, softball, volleyball.

ADMISSIONS

Freshman Academic Profile: Minimum paper TOEFL 550. **Basis for Candidate Selection:** Very important factors considered include: rigor of secondary school record. Other factors considered include: Class rank, recommendation(s), standardized test scores, character/personal qualities, extracurricular activities, interview, talent/ability, work experience. **Freshman Admission Requirements:** High school diploma is required and GED is accepted. **Freshman Admission Statistics:** 1,830 applied, 98% admitted, 45% enrolled. **Transfer Admission Requirements:** High school transcript, college transcript(s), Lowest grade transferable c. **General Admission Information:** Application Fee $40. Notification on a rolling basis, beginning on or about 12/1. Nonfall registration accepted. Admission may be deferred for a maximum of 1 year.

COSTS AND FINANCIAL AID

Required Forms and Deadlines: FAFSA, state aid form. **Notification of Awards:** Applicants will be notified of awards on a rolling basis beginning 2/3.

Types of Aid: *Need-based scholarships/grants:* Federal Pell, SEOG, private scholarships. *Loans:* Direct Subsidized Stafford, Direct Unsubsidized Stafford, Direct PLUS, Federal Perkins. **Student Employment:** Federal Work-Study Program available. Institutional employment available. Off-campus job opportunities are fair. **Financial Aid Statistics:** Average cumulative indebtedness $6,000.

STATE UNIVERSITY OF NEW YORK— COBLESKILL

Office of Admissions, Cobleskill, NY 12043
Phone: 518-255-5525 • **Financial Aid Phone:** 518-255-5623
E-mail: admissions@cobleskill.edu • **CEEB Code:** 2524
Fax: 518-255-6769 • **Website:** www.cobleskill.edu • **ACT Code:** 2914

This public school was founded in 1916. It has a 750-acre campus.

RATINGS
Admissions Selectivity Rating: 66 **Fire Safety Rating:** 73 **Green Rating:** 76

STUDENTS AND FACULTY
Enrollment: 2,559. **Student Body:** 47% female, 53% male, 10% out-of-state, 3% international (9 countries represented). Asian 1%, African American 8%, Caucasian 73%, Hispanic 5%, Native American 0%.
Retention and Graduation: 74% freshmen return for sophomore year. 48% freshmen graduate within 4 years. 52% freshmen graduate within 6 years. 63% grads go on to further study within 1 year. **Faculty:** Student/faculty ratio 18:1. 110 full-time faculty, 31% hold PhDs, 9% are members of minority groups, 36% are women. 0% of classes are taught by teaching assistants.

ACADEMICS
Degrees: associate, bachelor's, certificate, terminal associate, transfer associate. **Classes:** Most classes have 10–19 students. Most lab/discussion sessions have 10–19 students. **Special Study Options:** cross-registration, distance learning, English as a Second Language (ESL), honors program, internships, study abroad, weekend college. **Disability Services:** Special programs offered to physically disabled students include note-taking services, reader services, tape recorders, tutors. **Career Services:** alumni services, career/job search classes, career assessment, internships Career Services highlights include A 15 week internship is required for nearly all of the baccalaureate programs. It is the capstone ot our 4-year degrees.

FACILITIES
Housing: Coed dorms, special housing for disabled students, men's dorms, women's dorms, LIfestyle floors: designated quiet study lifestyle, wellness lifestyle, sustainability lifestyle, sophomore experience, upper class experience. **Special Academic Facilities/Equipment:** Art museum, 650 acre agricultural campus, distance learning classrooms, ski area, adult study center. **Computers:** Students can register for classes online. Administrative functions (other than registration) can be performed online.

CAMPUS LIFE
Environment: Rural. **Activities:** drama/theater, student government, student newspaper, Campus Ministries, International Student Organization 40 registered organizations, 1 honor societies, 1 religious organizations. **Athletics (Intercollegiate):** *Men:* baseball, basketball, cross-country, diving, equestrian sports, golf, lacrosse, soccer, swimming, tennis, track/field (outdoor), volleyball. *Women:* basketball, cross-country, diving, equestrian sports, golf, soccer, softball, swimming, tennis, track/field (outdoor), volleyball. **On-Campus Highlights:** Bouck Hall/Student Union, Brickyard Point, American Heritage, Foundation Equestrian Center, Grosvenor Art Gallery. **Environmental Initiatives:** recycling - paper, plastics, metals, galss and cardboard box waste reduction in dining halls, offices - "Taste Don't Waste" program purchase of green cleaning supplies, recycled building products such as carpet - wear washing chemicals in dining halls

ADMISSIONS
Freshman Academic Profile: 3% in top 10% of high school class, 10% in top 25% of high school class, 37% in top 50% of high school class. 98% from public high schools. SAT Math middle 50% range 400-520. SAT Critical Reading middle 50% range 390-500. ACT middle 50% range 17-22. Minimum paper TOEFL 500. **Basis for Candidate Selection:** *Important factors considered include:* academic GPA, rigor of secondary school record, standardized test scores. *Other factors considered include:* Class rank, application essay, recommendation(s), extracurricular activities, geographical residence, interview, level of applicant's interest, state residency, work experience. **Freshman Admission Requirements:** High school diploma is required and GED is ac-

cepted. *Academic units required:* 1 English, 2 mathematics, 1 science, 1 history, 1 academic electives. *Academic units recommended:* 1 English, 2 mathematics, 1 science, 1 history, 1 academic electives. **Freshman Admission Statistics:** 3,045 applied, 81% admitted, 40% enrolled. **Transfer Admission Requirements:** college transcript(s), minimum college GPA of 2.25 required. Lowest grade transferable D. **General Admission Information:** Application Fee $40. Notification on a rolling basis, beginning on or about 11/1. Nonfall registration accepted. Admission may be deferred for a maximum of 2 semesters. Credit offered for CEEB Advanced Placement tests.

COSTS AND FINANCIAL AID
Annual in-state tuition $4,350. Annual out-of-state tuition $10,610. Room and board $8,650. Required fees $1,064. Average book expense $1,200. **Required Forms and Deadlines:** FAFSA, state aid form. **Notification of Awards:** Applicants will be notified of awards on a rolling basis beginning 3/20. **Types of Aid:** *Need-based scholarships/grants:* Federal Pell, SEOG, state scholarships/grants, private scholarships, the school's own gift aid. *Loans:* Subsidized Stafford, Unsubsidized Stafford, PLUS, Federal Perkins. **Student Employment:** Federal Work-Study Program available. Institutional employment available. Highest amount earned per year from on-campus jobs $800. Off-campus job opportunities are fair. **Financial Aid Statistics:** 62% freshmen, 97% undergrads receive need-based scholarship or grant aid. 26% freshmen, 12% undergrads receive non-need-based scholarship or grant aid. 70% freshmen, 93% undergrads receive need-based self-help aid. 77% freshmen, 68% undergrads receive any aid. 80% undergrads borrow to pay for school. Average cumulative indebtedness $21,353. **Criteria for awarding institutional aid:** *Non-need-based:* academics, alumni affiliation, leadership, state/district residency.

STATE UNIVERSITY OF NEW YORK—COLLEGE OF ENVIRONMENTAL SCIENCE AND FORESTRY

Office of Undergraduate Admissions, Syracuse, NY 13210
Phone: 315-470-6600 • **Financial Aid Phone:** 315-470-6706
E-mail: esfinfo@esf.edu • **CEEB Code:** 2530
Fax: 315-470-6933 • **Website:** www.esf.edu • **ACT Code:** 2948

This public school was founded in 1911. It has a 25000-acre campus.

RATINGS
Admissions Selectivity Rating: 88 **Fire Safety Rating:** 94 **Green Rating:** 90

STUDENTS AND FACULTY
Enrollment: 1,652. **Student Body:** 44% female, 56% male, 18% out-of-state, 2% international (37 countries represented). Asian 4%, African American 2%, Caucasian 90%, Hispanic 3%, Native American 0%.
Retention and Graduation: 83% freshmen return for sophomore year. 48% freshmen graduate within 4 years. 66% freshmen graduate within 6 years. 20% grads go on to further study within 1 year. **Faculty:** Student/faculty ratio 13:1. 145 full-time faculty, 94% hold PhDs, 13% are members of minority groups, 29% are women. 0% of classes are taught by teaching assistants.

ACADEMICS
Degrees: associate, bachelor's, master's, post-bachelor's certificate. **Classes:** Most classes have 10–19 students. Most lab/discussion sessions have 10–19 students. **Majors with Highest Enrollment:** environmental biology; environmental science; landscape architecture (bs, bsla, bla, msla, mla, phd). **Special Study Options:** cooperative education program, cross-registration, distance learning, double major, English as a Second Language (ESL), honors program, independent study, internships, study abroad, teacher certification program, Associate degrees in forest technology & land surveying technology are offered at The Ranger School campus. Graduates of these degrees may then continue their studies at the Syracuse campus to complete bachelor degrees, usually in forest resources management or natural resources management. **Honors Programs:** Lower Division Honors Program: freshmen & sophomores, all academic programs, highly selective, associated scholarship, mentoring, honors seminar, honors writing course. Upper Division Thesis Honors Program: juniors and seniors, 16 of 20 academic programs eligible, intensive research or creative projects guided by faculty mentors, thesis exploration seminar, related course work, Honors Thesis/Project course. **Combined Degree Programs:** BS/Doctor of Physical Therapy. **Disability Services:** Special programs offered to physically disabled students include note-taking services, reader services, tape recorders, tutors. **Career Services:** Alumni network, alumni services, career/job search classes, career assessment, internships, regional alumni. Career Services highlights include Experiential learning is "built in to" all aspects of learning at ESF. Service Learning is an integral part of an ESF education. Required and voluntary undergraduate research, internships and field experiences

The Princeton Review's Complete Book of Colleges

are components of every degree program. Learn more at http://www.esf.edu/students/servicelearning/.

FACILITIES

Housing: Coed dorms, special housing for disabled students, special housing for international students, fraternity/sorority housing, apartments for married students, apartments for single students, theme housing. 100% of campus accessible to physically disabled. **Special Academic Facilities/Equipment:** Museums, art galleries, plant growth and animal environmental simulation chambers, wildlife collection, electron microscope, paper making facility, photogrammetric and geodetic facilities, hydrology flumes. **Computers:** 50% of classrooms, 100% of dorms, 100% of libraries, 100% of dining areas, 100% of student union, 10% of common outdoor areas have wireless network access. Students can register for classes online. Administrative functions (other than registration) can be performed online.

CAMPUS LIFE

Environment: City. **Activities:** Choral groups, concert band, dance, drama/theater, jazz band, literary magazine, marching band, music ensembles, musical theater, pep band, radio station, student government, student newspaper, student-run film society, symphony orchestra, television station, yearbook, Campus Ministries, International Student Organization 300 registered organizations, 1 honor societies, 13 religious organizations. 26 fraternities, 21 sororities. **Athletics (Intercollegiate):** *Men:* cross-country, golf, soccer. *Women:* cross-country, golf, soccer. **On-Campus Highlights:** Library, Green houses, Wildlife collection, Laboratories & Studios, Student lounge, snack bar, student store, SUNY-ESF is on the campus of Syracuse University. The most popular sites on that campus are the Carrier Dome, Crouse College (a historic building), Schine Student Center, Hendricks Chapel. **Environmental Initiatives:** (1) College uses a 250 kilowatt carbonate fuel cell to generate approximately 17% of electrical power. (2)photovoltaic arrays/green roof (3) College owns and manages 25,000 acres of forest (providing carbon offsets). Faculty at SUNY-ESF are conducting nationally recognized and government supported research in the development of ethanol and other renewable products from wood bioimass. We have partnered with the NY State government and private industry to develop the state's first "biorefinery" aimed at producing ethanol and other chemical products from wood sugars. The College has also developed a genetically engineered species of fast growth willow that is being grown as an alternative to corn use in ethanol production. Forty percent of all College vehicles (cars, maintenance vehicles, buses, GEM, etc.) are powered with renewable fuels, electric or hybrid technologies. One fifth of all vehicles are powered with biodeisel, and a significant part of our biodeisel fuel is produced on campus from waste cooking oil.

ADMISSIONS

Freshman Academic Profile: Average high school GPA 3.7. 37% in top 10% of high school class, 73% in top 25% of high school class, 97% in top 50% of high school class. 90% from public high schools. SAT Math middle 50% range 560-630. SAT Critical Reading middle 50% range 540-640. ACT middle 50% range 24-28. Minimum web-based TOEFL 79. Minimum paper TOEFL 550. **Basis for Candidate Selection:** *Very important factors considered include:* application essay, academic GPA, rigor of secondary school record, standardized test scores, level of applicant's interest. *Important factors considered include:* Class rank, recommendation(s), character/personal qualities, extracurricular activities, talent/ability, volunteer work, work experience. *Other factors considered include:* alumni/ae relation, first generation, geographical residence, interview, racial/ethnic status, state residency. **Freshman Admission Requirements:** High school diploma is required and GED is accepted. *Academic units required:* 4 English, 3 mathematics, 3 science, (3 science labs), 3 social studies. history. *Academic units recommended:* 4 English, 3 mathematics, 3 science, (3 science labs), 3 social studies. history. **Freshman Admission Statistics:** 1,866 applied, 47% admitted, 33% enrolled. **Transfer Admission Requirements:** High school transcript, college transcript(s), minimum college GPA of 2.25 required. Lowest grade transferable C. **General Admission Information:** Application Fee $40. Notification on a rolling basis, beginning on or about 2/1. Nonfall registration accepted. Admission may be deferred for a maximum of 1 year. Credit offered for CEEB Advanced Placement tests.

COSTS AND FINANCIAL AID

Annual in-state tuition $5,570. Annual out-of-state tuition $14,820. Room and board $14,400. Required fees $977. Average book expense $1,200. **Required Forms and Deadlines:** FAFSA, state aid form. **Notification of Awards:** Applicants will be notified of awards on a rolling basis beginning 3/15. **Types of Aid:** *Need-based scholarships/grants:* Federal Pell, SEOG, state scholarships/grants, private scholarships, the school's own gift aid Federal SMART Grants, Federal ACG Grants. *Loans:* Subsidized Stafford, Unsubsidized Stafford, PLUS, Federal Perkins. **Student Employment:** Federal Work-Study Program available. Institutional employment available. Highest amount earned per year from on-campus jobs $1,200. Off-campus job opportunities are excellent. **Financial Aid Statistics:** 96% freshmen, 100% undergrads receive need-based scholarship or grant aid. 50% freshmen, 48% undergrads receive non-need-

based scholarship or grant aid. 100% freshmen, 100% undergrads receive need-based self-help aid. 86% freshmen, 68% undergrads receive any aid. 80% undergrads borrow to pay for school. Average cumulative indebtedness $23,982. **Criteria for awarding institutional aid:** *Non-need-based:* academics, alumni affiliation, state/district residency.

STATE UNIVERSITY OF NEW YORK— THE COLLEGE AT OLD WESTBURY

PO Box 307, Old Westbury, NY 11568-0307
Phone: 516-876-3073 • **Financial Aid Phone:** 516-876-3247
E-mail: enroll@oldwestbury.edu • **CEEB Code:** 2866
Fax: 516-876-3307 • **Website:** www.oldwestbury.edu • **ACT Code:** 2939

This public school was founded in 1968. It has a 605-acre campus.

RATINGS
Admissions Selectivity Rating: 82   **Fire Safety Rating:** 84   **Green Rating:** 78

STUDENTS AND FACULTY
Enrollment: 4,077. **Student Body:** 59% female, 41% male, 1% out-of-state, 1% international (58 countries represented). Asian 9%, African American 30%, Caucasian 34%, Hispanic 21%, Native American 1%.
Retention and Graduation: 80% freshmen return for sophomore year. 21% freshmen graduate within 4 years. 35% freshmen graduate within 6 years.
Faculty: Student/faculty ratio 18:1. 148 full-time faculty, 84% hold PhDs, 38% are members of minority groups, 55% are women. 0% of classes are taught by teaching assistants.

ACADEMICS
Degrees: bachelor's, certificate, master's. **Classes:** Most classes have 20–29 students. Most lab/discussion sessions have 20–29 students. **Majors with Highest Enrollment:** accounting; elementary education and teaching; psychology. **Special Study Options:** cross-registration, distance learning, double major, English as a Second Language (ESL), exchange student program (domestic), honors program, independent study, internships, liberal arts/career combination, study abroad, teacher certification program, Disabled Student Services; Minority Access to Research Centers, Minority Biomedical Research **Honors Programs:** The Honors College teaches students to integrate learning methods by using in-depth primary source material and complex and intellectually challenging secondary sources. The program emphasizes critical thinking and experiential learning. **Combined Degree Programs:** BS/DO. **Disability Services:** Special programs offered to physically disabled students include note-taking services, reader services, tape recorders, tutors. **Career Services:** Alumni network, alumni services, career/job search classes, career assessment, internships, regional alumni. Career Services highlights include The Community Engagement and Partnership Center founded in 2006, and its First-Year Experience Program, Old Westbury shares its resources to support the programmatic efforts of non-profit organizations and to address issues of shared concern within various communities. The college, as a whole, is using its influential role as a regional employer and developer to contribute directly and tangibly to community revitalization efforts. Critical to this effort is the student community engagement component. Implemented by CEPC and the FYE, the College has initiated a voluntary course-embedded community-based learning and action program in which students engage in community service in areas related to their course of study.

FACILITIES
Housing: Coed dorms, Honors College residence. 90% of campus accessible to physically disabled. **Special Academic Facilities/Equipment:** Art gallery, language lab, TV studio, radio station, recital hall, physical recreation center and Maguire Theatre. **Computers:** 100% of classrooms, 60% of dorms, 100% of libraries, 100% of dining areas, 100% of student union, 30% of common outdoor areas have wireless network access. Students can register for classes online. Administrative functions (other than registration) can be performed online.

CAMPUS LIFE
Environment: Village. **Activities:** Choral groups, dance, drama/theater, radio station, student government, student newspaper, student-run film society, yearbook, Campus Ministries, International Student Organization 55 registered organizations, 5 honor societies, 2 religious organizations. 6 fraternities, 4 sororities. **Athletics (Intercollegiate):** *Men:* baseball, basketball, cross-country, golf, soccer, swimming, ultimate frisbee, volleyball. *Women:* basketball, cross-country, soccer, softball, swimming, ultimate frisbee, volleyball. **On-Campus Highlights:** Student Union, Clark Center (athletic facility), Library, Theatre, Art Gallery. **Environmental Initiatives:** SEMPRA Energy Contract; One (1)

solar installation; Gas consortium; Energy STAR purchases New building to be constructed and completed by 2011 will be Leeds Platinum.

ADMISSIONS

Freshman Academic Profile: Average high school GPA 3.1. 85% from public high schools. SAT Math middle 50% range 470-550. SAT Critical Reading middle 50% range 450-520. SAT Writing middle 50% range 430-510. ACT middle 50% range 20-22. Minimum web-based TOEFL 65. Minimum paper TOEFL 513. **Basis for Candidate Selection:** *Very important factors considered include:* application essay, academic GPA, rigor of secondary school record. *Important factors considered include:* recommendation(s), standardized test scores. *Other factors considered include:* character/personal qualities, extracurricular activities, interview, talent/ability, volunteer work, work experience. **Freshman Admission Requirements:** High school diploma is required and GED is accepted. *Academic units required:* 4 English, 3 mathematics, 3 science, (2 science labs), 2 foreign language, 4 social studies, 2 academic electives. *Academic units recommended:* 4 English, 3 mathematics, 3 science, (2 science labs), 2 foreign language, 4 social studies, 2 academic electives. **Freshman Admission Statistics:** 3,855 applied, 52% admitted, 21% enrolled. **Transfer Admission Requirements:** college transcript(s), essay or personal statement, minimum college GPA of 2.0 required. Lowest grade transferable C. **General Admission Information:** Application Fee $40. Notification on a rolling basis, beginning on or about 1/7. Nonfall registration accepted. Admission may be deferred for a maximum of one year. Credit and/or placement offered for CEEB Advanced Placement tests.

COSTS AND FINANCIAL AID

Annual in-state tuition $5,570. Annual out-of-state tuition $14,820. Room and board $9,700. Required fees $1,054. Average book expense $1,000. **Required Forms and Deadlines:** FAFSA, institution's own financial aid form, state aid form. **Notification of Awards:** Applicants will be notified of awards on or about 4/15. **Types of Aid:** *Need-based scholarships/grants:* Federal Pell, SEOG, state scholarships/grants, private scholarships, the school's own gift aid. *Loans:* Subsidized Stafford, Unsubsidized Stafford, PLUS, Federal Perkins, Federal College Work Study Grants Federal Pell Grants Federal Supplemental Education Opportunity Grants State Educational Opportunity Program Grants Supplemental State Tuition Grants Aid for Part-time Study Grants Tuition Assistance Program Federal Parent Loans Alternative Loans. **Student Employment:** Federal Work-Study Program available. Institutional employment available. Off-campus job opportunities are good. **Financial Aid Statistics:** 80% freshmen, % undergrads receive need-based scholarship or grant aid. 11% freshmen, 3% undergrads receive non-need-based scholarship or grant aid. 62% freshmen, 54% undergrads receive need-based self-help aid. 72% freshmen, 67% undergrads receive any aid. 53% undergrads borrow to pay for school. Average cumulative indebtedness $17,395. **Criteria for awarding institutional aid:** *Non-need-based:* academics, state/district residency.

STATE UNIVERSITY OF NEW YORK— COLLEGE AT ONEONTA

---

116 Alumni Hall, Oneonta, NY 13820
Phone: 607-436-2524 • **Financial Aid Phone:** 607-436-2532
E-mail: admissions@oneonta.edu • **CEEB Code:** 2542
Fax: 607-436-3074 • **Website:** www.oneonta.edu • **ACT Code:** 2940

This public school was founded in 1889. It has a 250-acre campus.

RATINGS
Admissions Selectivity Rating: 91   **Fire Safety Rating:** 83   **Green Rating:** 83

STUDENTS AND FACULTY

Enrollment: 5,808. **Student Body:** 59% female, 41% male, 14% out-of-state, 2% international (21 countries represented). Asian 2%, African American 3%, Caucasian 81%, Hispanic 4%, Native American 0%.
Retention and Graduation: 84% freshmen return for sophomore year. 53% freshmen graduate within 4 years. 67% freshmen graduate within 6 years. 27% grads go on to further study within 1 year. **Faculty:** Student/faculty ratio 18:1. 253 full-time faculty, 86% hold PhDs, 19% are members of minority groups, 42% are women. 0% of classes are taught by teaching assistants.

ACADEMICS

Degrees: bachelor's, master's, post-bachelor's certificate, post-master's certificate. **Classes:** Most classes have 10–19 students. **Majors with Highest Enrollment:** communication studies/speech communication and rhetoric; elementary education and teaching; visual and performing arts. **Special Study Options:** cross-registration, distance learning, double major, English as a Sec-

ond Language (ESL), honors program, independent study, internships, liberal arts/career combination, study abroad, teacher certification program, Variety of 3-1, 3-2, and 2-2 programs with other colleges and universities. **Honors Programs:** Oneonta Honors Program **Combined Degree Programs:** BA/MA, BA/MEng, acc't, bus. admin., mgmt., fashion, art, med. sci. **Disability Services:** Special programs offered to physically disabled students include note-taking services, reader services, tape recorders, tutors. **Career Services:** Alumni network, alumni services, career/job search classes, career assessment, internships, regional alumni. Career Services highlights include Internships available in all academic majors.

FACILITIES

Housing: Coed dorms, Special interest wings in residence halls; apartment-style suites in new hall. 90% of campus accessible to physically disabled. **Special Academic Facilities/Equipment:** Science Discovery Center, Biological Field Station, digital planetarium, observatory, College Camp, children's center **Computers:** 100% of classrooms, 100% of dorms, 100% of libraries, 100% of dining areas, 100% of student union, 100% of common outdoor areas have wireless network access. Students can register for classes online. Administrative functions (other than registration) can be performed online.

CAMPUS LIFE

Environment: Village. **Activities:** Choral groups, concert band, dance, drama/theater, jazz band, literary magazine, music ensembles, musical theater, opera, pep band, radio station, student government, student newspaper, student-run film society, symphony orchestra, television station, yearbook, Campus Ministries, International Student Organization, Model UN 70 registered organizations, 14 honor societies, 4 religious organizations. 4 fraternities, 6 sororities. **Athletics (Intercollegiate):** *Men:* baseball, basketball, cross-country, diving, lacrosse, soccer, swimming, tennis, track/field (outdoor), track/field (indoor), wrestling. *Women:* basketball, cross-country, diving, field hockey, lacrosse, soccer, softball, swimming, tennis, track/field (outdoor), track/field (indoor), volleyball. **On-Campus Highlights:** Alumni Field House, Center for Multicultural Experiences, Hunt College Union, College Camp, Center for Social Responsibility and Community, Newly remodeled Science Building with state-of-the-art Digital Planetarium. **Environmental Initiatives:** Recycling program Green construction standards Campus Sustainability Committee

ADMISSIONS

Freshman Academic Profile: Average high school GPA 3.6. 90% from public high schools. SAT Math middle 50% range 520-600. SAT Critical Reading middle 50% range 500-580. ACT middle 50% range 22-25. Minimum web-based TOEFL 61. Minimum paper TOEFL 500. **Basis for Candidate Selection:** *Very important factors considered include:* rigor of secondary school record. *Important factors considered include:* application essay, academic GPA, standardized test scores, extracurricular activities, interview, talent/ability, volunteer work. *Other factors considered include:* recommendation(s), alumni/ae relation, level of applicant's interest, racial/ethnic status, work experience. **Freshman Admission Requirements:** High school diploma is required and GED is accepted. *Academic units required:* 4 English, 2 mathematics, 2 science, (2 science labs), 2 foreign language, 3 social studies. *Academic units recommended:* 4 English, 2 mathematics, 2 science, (2 science labs), 2 foreign language, 3 social studies. **Freshman Admission Statistics:** 12,338 applied, 43% admitted, 22% enrolled. **Transfer Admission Requirements:** college transcript(s), minimum college GPA of 2.5 required. Lowest grade transferable C–. **General Admission Information:** Application Fee $40. Notification on a rolling basis, beginning on or about 11/15. Nonfall registration accepted. Admission may be deferred for a maximum of 12 months. Credit offered for CEEB Advanced Placement tests.

COSTS AND FINANCIAL AID

Annual in-state tuition $5,270. Annual out-of-state tuition $14,320. Room and board $10,164. Required fees $1,326. Average book expense $1,200. **Required Forms and Deadlines:** FAFSA, state aid form. **Notification of Awards:** Applicants will be notified of awards on a rolling basis beginning 3/1. **Types of Aid:** *Need-based scholarships/grants:* Federal Pell, SEOG, state scholarships/grants, private scholarships, the school's own gift aid. *Loans:* Subsidized Stafford, Unsubsidized Stafford, PLUS, Federal Perkins. **Student Employment:** Federal Work-Study Program available. Institutional employment available. Highest amount earned per year from on-campus jobs $1,800. Off-campus job opportunities are good. **Financial Aid Statistics:** 72% freshmen, 75% undergrads receive need-based scholarship or grant aid. 11% freshmen, 13% undergrads receive need-based self-help aid. 83% freshmen, 66% undergrads receive any aid. 75% undergrads borrow to pay for school. Average cumulative indebtedness $13,697. **Criteria for awarding institutional aid:** *Non-need-based:* academics, alumni affiliation, leadership, minority status, music/drama, state/district residency.

STATE UNIVERSITY OF NEW YORK—CORTLAND

PO Box 2000, Cortland, NY 13045-0900
Phone: 607-753-4712 • **Financial Aid Phone:** 607-753-4717
E-mail: admissions@cortland.edu • **CEEB Code:** 2538
Fax: 607-753-5998 • **Website:** www.cortland.edu • **ACT Code:** 2932

This public school was founded in 1868. It has a 191-acre campus.

RATINGS
Admissions Selectivity Rating: 91   **Fire Safety Rating:** 62   **Green Rating:** 60*

STUDENTS AND FACULTY
Enrollment: 6,344. **Student Body:** 57% female, 43% male, 3% out-of-state, 1% international (14 countries represented). Asian 1%, African American 3%, Caucasian 77%, Hispanic 8%, Native American 0%.
Retention and Graduation: 85% freshmen return for sophomore year. 46% freshmen graduate within 4 years. 67% freshmen graduate within 6 years. **Faculty:** Student/faculty ratio 17:1. 284 full-time faculty, 75% hold PhDs, 13% are members of minority groups, 53% are women. 0% of classes are taught by teaching assistants.

ACADEMICS
Degrees: bachelor's, master's, post-master's certificate. **Classes:** Most classes have 20–29 students. Most lab/discussion sessions have 20–29 students. **Special Study Options:** cooperative education program, cross-registration, distance learning, double major, dual enrollment, exchange student program (domestic), honors program, independent study, internships, liberal arts/career combination, student-designed major, study abroad, teacher certification program. **Disability Services:** Special programs offered to physically disabled students include note-taking services, reader services, tape recorders, tutors.

FACILITIES
Housing: Coed dorms, special housing for disabled students, special housing for international students, cooperative housing, apartments for single students, wellness housing, Leadership House, Transfer Floor, Quiet Atmosphere. 75% of campus accessible to physically disabled. **Special Academic Facilities/Equipment:** Natural science museum, greenhouse, center for speech and hearing disorders, classrooms with integrated technologies, specialized labs to support various program offerings. **Computers:** Students can register for classes online. Administrative functions (other than registration) can be performed online.

CAMPUS LIFE
Environment: Village. **Activities:** Choral groups, dance, drama/theater, literary magazine, music ensembles, musical theater, radio station, student government, student newspaper, student-run film society, symphony orchestra, television station, yearbook, Campus Ministries, International Student Organization, Model UN 100 registered organizations, 16 honor societies, 3 religious organizations. 2 fraternities, 5 sororities. **Athletics (Intercollegiate):** *Men:* baseball, basketball, cheerleading, cross-country, diving, football, gymnastics, ice hockey, lacrosse, soccer, swimming, track/field (outdoor), track/field (indoor), wrestling. *Women:* basketball, cheerleading, cross-country, diving, field hockey, golf, gymnastics, ice hockey, lacrosse, soccer, softball, swimming, tennis, track/field (outdoor), track/field (indoor), volleyball. **On-Campus Highlights:** Corey Union, Stadium Complex, Fitness Facilities, Dining Halls, Library.

ADMISSIONS
Freshman Academic Profile: Average high school GPA. 91% from public high schools. SAT Math middle 50% range 520-600. SAT Critical Reading middle 50% range 490-560. ACT middle 50% range 26-23. Minimum paper TOEFL 550. **Basis for Candidate Selection:** *Very important factors considered include:* rigor of secondary school record, standardized test scores. *Important factors considered include:* application essay, recommendation(s), extracurricular activities, talent/ability. *Other factors considered include:* Class rank, alumni/ae relation, geographical residence, interview, racial/ethnic status, state residency, volunteer work, work experience. **Freshman Admission Requirements:** High school diploma is required and GED is accepted. *Academic units required:* 4 English, 3 mathematics, 3 science, 3 foreign language, 4 social studies. *Academic units recommended:* 4 English, 3 mathematics, 3 science, 3 foreign language, 4 social studies. **Freshman Admission Statistics:** 12,348 applied, 41% admitted, 24% enrolled. **Transfer Admission Requirements:** High school transcript, college transcript(s), minimum college GPA of 2.5 required. Lowest grade transferable C–. **General Admission Information:** Application Fee $40. Early decision application deadline 11/15. Notification on a rolling basis, beginning on or about 1/2. Nonfall registration accepted. Admission may be deferred for a maximum of 1 year. Credit offered for CEEB Advanced Placement tests.

COSTS AND FINANCIAL AID
Annual in-state tuition $5,270. Annual out-of-state tuition $14,320. Room and board $11,060. Required fees $1,304. Average book expense $1,000. **Required**

Forms and Deadlines: FAFSA, state aid form. **Notification of Awards:** Applicants will be notified of awards on a rolling basis beginning 3/15. **Types of Aid:** *Need-based scholarships/grants:* Federal Pell, SEOG, state scholarships/grants, private scholarships, the school's own gift aid. *Loans:* Subsidized Stafford, Unsubsidized Stafford, PLUS, Federal Perkins. **Student Employment:** **Financial Aid Statistics:** 70% freshmen, 74% undergrads receive need-based scholarship or grant aid. 48% freshmen, 28% undergrads receive non-need-based scholarship or grant aid. 89% freshmen, 89% undergrads receive need-based self-help aid. 78% undergrads borrow to pay for school. Average cumulative indebtedness $26,303. **Criteria for awarding institutional aid:** *Non-need-based:* academics, art, leadership, minority status, music/drama, state/district residency.

STATE UNIVERSITY OF NEW YORK—DELHI

Bush Hall, Delhi, NY 13753
Phone: 607-746-4550
E-mail: enroll@Delhi.edu
Fax: 607-746-4104 • **Website:** www.delhi.edu

This is a public school.

RATINGS
Admissions Selectivity Rating: 61   **Fire Safety Rating:** 60*   **Green Rating:** 60*

STUDENTS AND FACULTY
Enrollment: 1,791. **Student Body:** 44% female, 56% male, 4% out-of-state, 1% international. Asian 2%, African American 11%, Caucasian 84%, Hispanic 7%, Native American 0%.

ACADEMICS
Degrees: associate, bachelor's, certificate, terminal associate, transfer associate. **Special Study Options:** distance learning, English as a Second Language (ESL), honors program, internships, student-designed major, weekend college.

FACILITIES
Housing: Coed dorms.

CAMPUS LIFE
Activities: Choral groups, dance, drama/theater, music ensembles, musical theater, radio station, student government, student newspaper, yearbook. **Athletics (Intercollegiate):** *Men:* basketball, cross-country, diving, golf, lacrosse, soccer, swimming, tennis, track/field (outdoor), track/field (indoor), wrestling. *Women:* basketball, cross-country, diving, golf, soccer, softball, swimming, tennis, track/field (outdoor), track/field (indoor), volleyball.

ADMISSIONS
Basis for Candidate Selection: *Very important factors considered include:* rigor of secondary school record. *Important factors considered include:* recommendation(s), character/personal qualities, talent/ability. *Other factors considered include:* Class rank, application essay, standardized test scores, alumni/ae relation, extracurricular activities, geographical residence, interview, state residency, volunteer work, work experience. **Freshman Admission Requirements:** High school diploma is required and GED is accepted. *Academic units required:* 4 English, 1 mathematics, 1 science, 3 social studies, 1 history. *Academic units recommended:* 4 English, 1 mathematics, 1 science, 3 social studies, 1 history. **Transfer Admission Requirements:** High school transcript, college transcript(s), Lowest grade transferable C. **General Admission Information:** Application Fee $30. Notification on a rolling basis, beginning on or about 11/1. Nonfall registration accepted. Admission may be deferred for a maximum of 12.

COSTS AND FINANCIAL AID
Financial Aid Statistics: 78% undergrads receive need-based scholarship or grant aid. 61% undergrads receive non-need-based scholarship or grant aid. 83% undergrads receive need-based self-help aid. **Criteria for awarding institutional aid:** *Non-need-based:* academics, leadership, state/district residency.

STATE UNIVERSITY OF NEW YORK— DOWNSTATE MEDICAL CENTER

450 Clarkson Avenue, Box 60, Brooklyn, NY 11203-2098
Phone: 718-270-2446
E-mail: admissions@netmail.hscbklyn.edu
Fax: 718-270-7592 • **Website:** www.sunydownstate.edu

This is a public school.

RATINGS
Admissions Selectivity Rating: 60*   **Fire Safety Rating:** 60*   **Green Rating:** 60*

ACADEMICS
Degrees: bachelor's, certificate, master's.

ADMISSIONS
Transfer Admission Requirements: college transcript(s), essay or personal statement, standardized test scores, statement of good standing from prior institution(s). Lowest grade transferable C.

STATE UNIVERSITY OF NEW YORK— EMPIRE STATE COLLEGE

Two Union Avenue, Saratoga, NY 12866
Phone: 518-587-2100 • **Financial Aid Phone:** 518-587-2100
E-mail: admissions@esc.edu • **CEEB Code:** 2214
Fax: 518-587-9759 • **Website:** esc.edu • **ACT Code:** 2737

This public school was founded in 1971.

RATINGS
Admissions Selectivity Rating: 62   **Fire Safety Rating:** 60*   **Green Rating:** 60*

STUDENTS AND FACULTY
Enrollment: 10,128. **Student Body:** 62% female, 38% male, 8% out-of-state, 0% international. Asian 2%, African American 18%, Caucasian 66%, Hispanic 5%, Native American 1%.
Faculty: Student/faculty ratio 9:1. 202 full-time faculty, 96% hold PhDs, 19% are members of minority groups, 64% are women. 0% of classes are taught by teaching assistants.

ACADEMICS
Degrees: associate, bachelor's, master's. **Majors with Highest Enrollment:** business/commerce; community organization and advocacy; physical sciences, other. **Special Study Options:** cross-registration, distance learning, double major, dual enrollment, external degree program, independent study, internships, student-designed major, Student-designed courses of study. **Combined Degree Programs:** BA/MA, BS/MA ; B.P.S./MA.

FACILITIES
Computers: Students can register for classes online. Administrative functions (other than registration) can be performed online.

CAMPUS LIFE
Environment: Village. **Activities:** literary magazine.

ADMISSIONS
Freshman Academic Profile: Minimum paper TOEFL 550. **Basis for Candidate Selection:** *Very important factors considered include:* application essay, character/personal qualities.*Other factors considered include:* recommendation(s), rigor of secondary school record, talent/ability. **Freshman Admission Requirements:** High school diploma is required and GED is accepted. **Freshman Admission Statistics:** 1,536 applied, 79% admitted, 72% enrolled. **Transfer Admission Requirements:** High school transcript, essay or personal statement, Lowest grade transferable C. **General Admission Information:** Nonfall registration accepted. Admission may be deferred for a maximum of 3 years.

COSTS AND FINANCIAL AID
Annual in-state tuition $5,570. Annual out-of-state tuition $14,820. Required fees $395. **Required Forms and Deadlines:** FAFSA, state aid form. **Types of Aid:** *Need-based scholarships/grants:* Federal Pell, SEOG, state scholarships/grants, private scholarships, the school's own gift aid. *Loans:* Subsidized Stafford, Unsubsidized Stafford, PLUS, Federal Perkins. **Student Employ-**

ment: Federal Work-Study Program available. **Financial Aid Statistics:** 63% undergrads receive any aid.

STATE UNIVERSITY OF NEW YORK—FASHION INSTITUTE OF TECHNOLOGY

Seventh Avenue at 27th Street, New York, NY 10001
Phone: 212-217-7675
E-mail: fitinfo@fitsuny.edu
Website: www.fitnyc.suny.edu

This public school was founded in 1944.

RATINGS
Admissions Selectivity Rating: 61   **Fire Safety Rating:** 60*   **Green Rating:** 60*

STUDENTS AND FACULTY
Student Body: 17% out-of-state.

FACILITIES
Housing: Coed dorms, men's dorms, women's dorms, apartments for single students.

CAMPUS LIFE
Activities: literary magazine, radio station, student government, student newspaper, yearbook 70 registered organizations, 7 honor societies, 1 religious organizations.

ADMISSIONS
General Admission Information: Regular application deadline 1/15.

COSTS AND FINANCIAL AID
Annual in-state tuition $2,500. Annual out-of-state tuition $5,950. Room and board $5,600. Required fees $210. Average book expense $1,200. **Required Forms and Deadlines:** FAFSA, institution's own financial aid form, state aid form. **Types of Aid:** *Loans:* Subsidized Stafford, PLUS. **Student Employment:** Federal Work-Study Program available. Highest amount earned per year from on-campus jobs $1,400.

See page 1080.

STATE UNIVERSITY OF NEW YORK—FREDONIA

178 Central Avenue, Fredonia, NY 14063
Phone: 716-673-3251 • **Financial Aid Phone:** 716-673-3253
E-mail: admissions@fredonia.edu • **CEEB Code:** 2539
Fax: 716-673-3249 • **Website:** www.fredonia.edu • **ACT Code:** 2934

This public school was founded in 1826. It has a 249-acre campus.

RATINGS
Admissions Selectivity Rating: 85   **Fire Safety Rating:** 76   **Green Rating:** 93

STUDENTS AND FACULTY
Enrollment: 5,347. **Student Body:** 56% female, 44% male, 2% out-of-state, 1% international (8 countries represented). Asian 1%, African American 3%, Caucasian 84%, Hispanic 4%, Native American 0%.
Retention and Graduation: 44% freshmen graduate within 4 years. 63% freshmen graduate within 6 years. 44% grads go on to further study within 1 year. **Faculty:** Student/faculty ratio 17:1. 253 full-time faculty, 90% hold PhDs, 14% are members of minority groups, 46% are women. 2% of classes are taught by teaching assistants.

ACADEMICS
Degrees: bachelor's, master's, post-master's certificate. **Classes:** Most classes have 10–19 students. Most lab/discussion sessions have 20–29 students. **Majors with Highest Enrollment:** business/commerce; elementary education and teaching; music, other. **Special Study Options:** Accelerated program, distance learning, double major, honors program, independent study, internships, student-designed major, study abroad, teacher certification program. **Combined Degree Programs:** BA/DDS, 3+4 Optometry with SUNY State College of Optometry. **Disability Services:** Special programs offered to physically disabled students include note-taking services, reader services, tape recorders, tutors. **Career Services:** Alumni network, alumni services, career/job search classes, career assessment, internships.

FACILITIES
Housing: Coed dorms, special housing for disabled students, men's dorms, women's dorms, apartments for single students. 85% of campus accessible to physically disabled. **Special Academic Facilities/Equipment:** Art center, education and local history museums, teacher education research center, developmental reading center, Sheldon Communications Lab, SMART classrooms, greenhouse. **Computers:** 100% of classrooms, 100% of libraries, 100% of dining areas, 100% of student union, 85% of common outdoor areas have wireless network access. Students can register for classes online. Administrative functions (other than registration) can be performed online.

CAMPUS LIFE
Environment: Village. **Activities:** Choral groups, concert band, dance, drama/theater, jazz band, literary magazine, music ensembles, musical theater, opera, pep band, radio station, student government, student newspaper, symphony orchestra, television station, Campus Ministries, International Student Organization 152 registered organizations, 22 honor societies, 5 religious organizations. 3 fraternities, 3 sororities. **Athletics (Intercollegiate):** *Men:* baseball, basketball, cross-country, diving, ice hockey, soccer, swimming, track/field (outdoor), track/field (indoor). *Women:* basketball, cheerleading, cross-country, diving, lacrosse, soccer, softball, swimming, tennis, track/field (outdoor), track/field (indoor), volleyball. **On-Campus Highlights:** University Commons, Michael C. Rockefeller Arts Center, Library, Natatorium-Swimming pool and diving area, Rosch Recital Hall. **Environmental Initiatives:** Campus owned gas well Recycle Mania Sustainability Committee.

ADMISSIONS
Freshman Academic Profile: Average high school GPA 3.3. 13% in top 10% of high school class, 41% in top 25% of high school class, 81% in top 50% of high school class. 95% from public high schools. SAT Math middle 50% range 490-570. SAT Critical Reading middle 50% range 480-590. ACT middle 50% range 21-25. Minimum web-based TOEFL 62. Minimum paper TOEFL 500. **Basis for Candidate Selection:** *Very important factors considered include:* academic GPA, rigor of secondary school record. *Important factors considered include:* Class rank, recommendation(s), standardized test scores, extracurricular activities. *Other factors considered include:* application essay, alumni/ae relation, character/personal qualities, first generation, level of applicant's interest, racial/ethnic status, talent/ability, volunteer work, work experience. **Freshman Admission Requirements:** High school diploma is required and GED is accepted. *Academic units required:* 4 English, 3 mathematics, 3 science, 3 foreign language, 4 social studies. *Academic units recommended:* 4 English, 3 mathematics, 3 science, 3 foreign language, 4 social studies. **Freshman Admission Statistics:** 5,918 applied, 53% admitted, 35% enrolled. **Transfer Admission Requirements:** college transcript(s), minimum college GPA of 2.0 required. Lowest grade transferable D. **General Admission Information:** Application Fee $40. Early decision application deadline 11/1. Notification on a rolling basis, beginning on or about 12/1. Nonfall registration accepted. Admission may be deferred for a maximum of 1 year. Credit and/or placement offered for CEEB Advanced Placement tests.

COSTS AND FINANCIAL AID
Annual in-state tuition $5,570. Annual out-of-state tuition $14,820. Room and board $10,790. Required fees $1,488. Average book expense $1,000. **Required Forms and Deadlines:** FAFSA, state aid form. **Notification of Awards:** Applicants will be notified of awards on a rolling basis beginning 3/10. **Types of Aid:** *Need-based scholarships/grants:* Federal Pell, SEOG, state scholarships/grants, private scholarships, the school's own gift aid. *Loans:* Subsidized Stafford, Unsubsidized Stafford, PLUS, Federal Perkins. **Student Employment:** Federal Work-Study Program available. Highest amount earned per year from on-campus jobs $1,000. Off-campus job opportunities are good. **Financial Aid Statistics:** 82% freshmen, 83% undergrads receive need-based scholarship or grant aid. 31% freshmen, 23% undergrads receive non-need-based scholarship or grant aid. 91% freshmen, 90% undergrads receive need-based self-help aid. 81% freshmen, 85% undergrads receive any aid. 86% undergrads borrow to pay for school. Average cumulative indebtedness $23,725. **Criteria for awarding institutional aid:** *Non-need-based:* academics, alumni affiliation, art, athletics, leadership, minority status, music/drama.

STATE UNIVERSITY OF NEW YORK AT GENESEO

1 College Circle, Geneseo, NY 14454-1401
Phone: 585-245-5571 • **Financial Aid Phone:** 585-245-5731
E-mail: admissions@geneseo.edu • **CEEB Code:** 2540
Fax: 585-245-5550 • **Website:** www.geneseo.edu • **ACT Code:** 2936

This public school was founded in 1871. It has a 220-acre campus.

RATINGS
Admissions Selectivity Rating: 94   **Fire Safety Rating:** 90   **Green Rating:** 87

STUDENTS AND FACULTY
Enrollment: 5,454. **Student Body:** 57% female, 43% male, 2% out-of-state, 4% international (42 countries represented). Asian 6%, African American 2%, Caucasian 75%, Hispanic 5%, Native American 0%.
Retention and Graduation: 91% freshmen return for sophomore year. 69% freshmen graduate within 4 years. 81% freshmen graduate within 6 years. 42% grads go on to further study within 1 year. 16% grads pursue arts and sciences degrees. 7% grads pursue law degrees. 13% grads pursue business degrees. 12% grads pursue medical degrees. **Faculty:** Student/faculty ratio 20:1. 241 full-time faculty, 88% hold PhDs, 11% are members of minority groups, 41% are women. 0% of classes are taught by teaching assistants.

ACADEMICS
Degrees: bachelor's, master's. **Classes:** Most classes have 20–29 students. Most lab/discussion sessions have 10–19 students. **Majors with Highest Enrollment:** biology/biological sciences; business administration and management; psychology. **Special Study Options:** cross-registration, double major, dual enrollment, English as a Second Language (ESL), honors program, independent study, internships, study abroad, teacher certification program, Albany semester, Washington semester, 3/2 Engineering, 3-3 Engineering, 4/1 MBA, 3/4 Dentistry, 3/4 Optometry, 3/4 Osteopathic Medicine, 3/2 or 3/1 nursing, 3/3 physical therapy, pre-med and pre-law advisory program. **Combined Degree Programs:** BA/MA, BA/DDS, BA/DO; BA/OD. **Disability Services:** Special programs offered to physically disabled students include note-taking services, reader services, tape recorders. **Career Services:** Alumni network, alumni services, career/job search classes, career assessment, internships Career Services highlights include Career Partners Network.

FACILITIES
Housing: Coed dorms, special housing for disabled students, special housing for international students, Town houses and special interest housing is available. Some fraternities and sororities have housing independent of college. 95% of campus accessible to physically disabled. **Special Academic Facilities/Equipment:** Four theatres, electron microscopes. Integrated Science Center **Computers:** 100% of classrooms, 60% of dorms, 100% of libraries, 100% of dining areas, 100% of student union, 10% of common outdoor areas have wireless network access. Students can register for classes online. Administrative functions (other than registration) can be performed online. Undergraduates are required to own a computer.

CAMPUS LIFE
Environment: Village. **Activities:** Choral groups, dance, drama/theater, jazz band, literary magazine, music ensembles, musical theater, pep band, radio station, student government, student newspaper, symphony orchestra, television station, Campus Ministries, International Student Organization, Model UN 175 registered organizations, 12 honor societies, 7 religious organizations. 8 fraternities, 11 sororities. **Athletics (Intercollegiate):** *Men:* basketball, cross-country, diving, ice hockey, lacrosse, soccer, swimming, track/field (outdoor), track/field (indoor). *Women:* basketball, cross-country, diving, equestrian sports, field hockey, lacrosse, soccer, softball, swimming, tennis, track/field (outdoor), track/field (indoor), volleyball. **On-Campus Highlights:** MacVittie College Union, The Gazebo, Milne Library, Alumni Fieldhouse (Workout Center), College Green. **Environmental Initiatives:** Signing of the Presidents Climate Commitment. Currently developing our Climate Action Plan. Establishment of Geneseo's Environmental Impact and Sustainability Task Force. Gold Lecture Series - Live Green Task Force Work/Initiatives.

ADMISSIONS
Freshman Academic Profile: Average high school GPA 3.7. 47% in top 10% of high school class, 85% in top 25% of high school class, 99% in top 50% of high school class. 82% from public high schools. SAT Math middle 50% range 600-90. SAT Critical Reading middle 50% range 590-690. ACT middle 50%

range 27-30. Minimum web-based TOEFL 71. Minimum paper TOEFL 525. **Basis for Candidate Selection:** *Very important factors considered include:* rigor of secondary school record, standardized test scores. *Important factors considered include:* Class rank, application essay, academic GPA, recommendation(s), extracurricular activities, racial/ethnic status, talent/ability. *Other factors considered include:* alumni/ae relation, character/personal qualities, first generation, level of applicant's interest, volunteer work, work experience. **Freshman Admission Requirements:** High school diploma is required and GED is accepted. **Freshman Admission Statistics:** 9,569 applied, 43% admitted, 24% enrolled. **Transfer Admission Requirements:** High school transcript, college transcript(s), minimum college GPA of 3.0 required. Lowest grade transferable D. **General Admission Information:** Application Fee $40. Early decision application deadline 11/15. Regular application deadline 1/1. Regular notification 3/1. Nonfall registration accepted. Admission may be deferred for a maximum of 1 year. Credit offered for CEEB Advanced Placement tests.

COSTS AND FINANCIAL AID

Annual in-state tuition $5,570. Annual out-of-state tuition $14,820. Room and board $10,476. Required fees $1,523. Average book expense $950. **Required Forms and Deadlines:** FAFSA, state aid form. **Notification of Awards:** Applicants will be notified of awards on a rolling basis beginning 3/15. **Types of Aid:** *Need-based scholarships/grants:* Federal Pell, SEOG, state scholarships/grants. *Loans:* Subsidized Stafford, Unsubsidized Stafford, PLUS, Federal Perkins. **Student Employment:** Federal Work-Study Program available. Institutional employment available. Highest amount earned per year from on-campus jobs $3,500. Off-campus job opportunities are poor. **Financial Aid Statistics:** 86% freshmen, 96% undergrads receive need-based scholarship or grant aid. 19% freshmen, 41% undergrads receive non-need-based scholarship or grant aid. 82% freshmen, 95% undergrads receive need-based self-help aid. 53% freshmen, 70% undergrads receive any aid. 67% undergrads borrow to pay for school. Average cumulative indebtedness $21,000. **Criteria for awarding institutional aid:** *Non-need-based:* academics, art, leadership, minority status, music/drama, religious affiliation, state/district residency.

STATE UNIVERSITY OF NEW YORK—INSTITUTE OF TECHNOLOGY AT UTICA/ROME

PO Box 3050, Utica, NY 13504
Phone: 315-792-7500
E-mail: admissions@sunyit.edu • **CEEB Code:** 2896
Fax: 315-792-7837 • **Website:** www.sunyit.edu • **ACT Code:** 2953

This public school was founded in 1966. It has a 850-acre campus.

RATINGS
Admissions Selectivity Rating: 81   **Fire Safety Rating:** 60*   **Green Rating:** 60*

STUDENTS AND FACULTY
Enrollment: 1,993. **Student Body:** 43% female, 57% male, 2% out-of-state, 1% international. Asian 2%, African American 7%, Caucasian 89%, Hispanic 3%, Native American 1%.
Retention and Graduation: 50% freshmen graduate within 6 years. **Faculty:** Student/faculty ratio 19:1. 97 full-time faculty, 78% hold PhDs, 24% are members of minority groups, 38% are women.

ACADEMICS
Degrees: bachelor's, master's, post-master's certificate. **Classes:** Most classes have 10–19 students. Most lab/discussion sessions have 10–19 students. **Special Study Options:** Accelerated program, cross-registration, distance learning, double major, dual enrollment, English as a Second Language (ESL), independent study, internships, study abroad. **Combined Degree Programs:** Computer/Info Science - BS/MS, Nursing - BS/MS. **Disability Services:** Special programs offered to physically disabled students include note-taking services, reader services, tape recorders, tutors. **Career Services:** alumni services, career/job search classes, career assessment, internships, regional alumni.

FACILITIES
Housing: Coed dorms, special housing for disabled students 98% of campus accessible to physically disabled. **Special Academic Facilities/Equipment:** Gannett Gallery, New York State Telecommunications Museum. **Computers:** Students can register for classes online. Administrative functions (other than registration) can be performed online.

CAMPUS LIFE
Environment: Village. **Activities:** drama/theater, jazz band, music ensembles, radio station, student government, student newspaper, television station, year-

book, International Student Organization 30 registered organizations, 4 honor societies, 1 religious organizations. **Athletics (Intercollegiate):** Men: baseball, basketball, golf, lacrosse, soccer. Women: basketball, cross-country, golf, soccer, softball, volleyball.

ADMISSIONS
Freshman Academic Profile: 10% in top 10% of high school class, 33% in top 25% of high school class, 79% in top 50% of high school classSAT Math middle 50% range 490-600. SAT Critical Reading middle 50% range 450-560. ACT middle 50% range 22-25. Minimum paper TOEFL 550. **Basis for Candidate Selection:** *Very important factors considered include:* academic GPA, standardized test scores. *Important factors considered include:* rigor of secondary school record, extracurricular activities. *Other factors considered include:* application essay, recommendation(s), interview, talent/ability, volunteer work, work experience. **Freshman Admission Requirements:** High school diploma is required and GED is accepted. *Academic units required:* 4 English, 3 mathematics, 3 science, (3 science labs), 2 social studies, 2 history. *Academic units recommended:* 4 English, 3 mathematics, 3 science, (3 science labs), 2 social studies, 2 history. **Freshman Admission Statistics:** 1,770 applied, 38% admitted, 30% enrolled. **Transfer Admission Requirements:** college transcript(s), statement of good standing from prior institution(s). Minimum college GPA of 2.5 required. Lowest grade transferable D. **General Admission Information:** Application Fee $40. Regular application deadline 8/1. Notification on a rolling basis, beginning on or about 1/15. Nonfall registration accepted. Admission may be deferred for a maximum of 1 year. Neither credit nor placement offered for CEEB Advanced Placement tests.

COSTS AND FINANCIAL AID
Annual in-state tuition $4,970. Annual out-of-state tuition $12,870. Room and board $8,750. Required fees $1,120. Average book expense $1,000. **Required Forms and Deadlines:** FAFSA, state aid form. **Notification of Awards:** Applicants will be notified of awards on a rolling basis beginning 3/17. **Types of Aid:** *Need-based scholarships/grants:* Federal Pell, SEOG, state scholarships/grants, private scholarships. *Loans:* Direct Subsidized Stafford, Direct Unsubsidized Stafford, Direct PLUS, Federal Perkins, Federal Nursing. **Student Employment:** Federal Work-Study Program available. Institutional employment available. Off-campus job opportunities are good. **Financial Aid Statistics:** 94% freshmen, 89% undergrads receive need-based scholarship or grant aid. 86% freshmen, 82% undergrads receive need-based self-help aid. **Criteria for awarding institutional aid:** *Non-need-based:* academics.

STATE UNIVERSITY OF NEW YORK— MARITIME COLLEGE

6 Pennyfield Ave, Throggs Neck, NY 10465
Phone: 718-409-7200 • **Financial Aid Phone:** 718-409-7254
E-mail: admissions@sunymaritime.edu
Fax: 718-409-7465 • **Website:** www.sunymaritime.edu • **ACT Code:** 2954

This public school was founded in 1874. It has a 56-acre campus.

RATINGS
Admissions Selectivity Rating: 83   **Fire Safety Rating:** 77   **Green Rating:** 70

STUDENTS AND FACULTY
Enrollment: 1,578. **Student Body:** 10% female, 90% male, 27% out-of-state, 3% international. Asian 3%, African American 3%, Caucasian 55%, Hispanic 8%, Native American 0%.
Retention and Graduation: 81% freshmen return for sophomore year. 5% grads go on to further study within 1 year. **Faculty:** Student/faculty ratio 14:1. 97 full-time faculty, 41% hold PhDs, 8% are members of minority groups, 21% are women. 0% of classes are taught by teaching assistants.

ACADEMICS
Degrees: associate, bachelor's, master's. **Classes:** Most classes have 20–29 students. Most lab/discussion sessions have 20–29 students. **Majors with Highest Enrollment:** engineering; transportation/transportation management. **Special Study Options:** cooperative education program, distance learning, double major, dual enrollment, English as a Second Language (ESL), honors program, independent study, internships, United States Coast Guard-issued deck and engine license program. **Honors Programs:** Honors Program **Combined Degree Programs:** BS/MS. **Disability Services:** Special programs offered to physically disabled students include note-taking services, reader services, tape recorders, tutors. **Career Services:** Alumni network, alumni services, career/job search classes, career assessment, internships, regional alumni. Career Services highlights include SUNY Maritime Colleges undergraduate students

achieve 99% career placement and earn the top average starting salaries in America. The average starting salary for the Class of 2008 was $61,000. Students who choose to participate in the Regiment of Cadets experience the benefits of a structured learning environment, along with opportunities to develop leadership ability and excel in leadership roles. Each summer, the Regiment of Cadets embarks on a Summer Sea Term onboard the Training Ship Empire State. The training ship is 565 feet long and 17,000 tons. While students reside and operate the Training Ship Empire State, they see the world, stopping in four our more international ports (i.e. Greece, Italy, Ireland, Turkey, etc).

FACILITIES

Housing: Coed dorms, special housing for disabled studentsMost undergraduates required to live in on-campus housing. 81% of campus accessible to physically disabled. **Special Academic Facilities/Equipment:** Maritime Industry Museum, Fort Schuyler(National Historic Landmark), Bridge Simulator, Liquid Cargo Simulator, 565 ft. Training Ship Empire State VI, Diesel Simulator, 2 Research Ships, State-of-the-Art Electrical Engineering Lab, NY State Strategic Center for Port and Maritime Security (224 ft USS Stalwart), Computerized Weather Station, Maritime College Waterfront Sailboat Fleet:20 Vanguard 420's, 6 Vanguard FJ's, 1 Laser, J-105, J-35, J-24, Colgate 26 **Computers:** 75% of classrooms, 30% of dorms, 100% of libraries, 50% of student union, have wireless network access. Students can register for classes online.

CAMPUS LIFE

Environment: Metropolis. **Activities:** Choral groups, jazz band, marching band, music ensembles, pep band, student government, yearbook, Campus Ministries, International Student Organization 30 registered organizations, 4 religious organizations. **Athletics (Intercollegiate):** *Men:* baseball, basketball, cross-country, football, ice hockey, lacrosse, riflery, soccer, swimming. *Women:* basketball, crew/rowing, cross-country, lacrosse, riflery, soccer, softball, swimming, volleyball. **On-Campus Highlights:** Fort Schuyler, Empire State VI **Environmental Initiatives:** Energy Reduction Programs with NYPA Building a green building with DASNY Partnering with energy management companies

ADMISSIONS

Freshman Academic Profile: SAT Math middle 50% range 520-600. SAT Critical Reading middle 50% range 490-570. SAT Writing middle 50% range 450-550. ACT middle 50% range 22-25. Minimum web-based TOEFL 79. Minimum paper TOEFL 550. **Basis for Candidate Selection:** *Very important factors considered include:* academic GPA, rigor of secondary school record, standardized test scores. *Important factors considered include:* recommendation(s), talent/ability, volunteer work, work experience. *Other factors considered include:* Class rank, application essay, alumni/ae relation, extracurricular activities, first generation, interview, level of applicant's interest. **Freshman Admission Requirements:** High school diploma is required and GED is accepted. *Academic units required:* 3 English, 3 mathematics, 3 science, (1 science labs), 1 foreign language, 3 social studies, 3 history. *Academic units recommended:* 3 English, 3 mathematics, 3 science, (1 science labs) 1 foreign language, 3 social studies, 3 history. **Freshman Admission Statistics:** 1,317 applied, 58% admitted, 44% enrolled. **Transfer Admission Requirements:** High school transcript, college transcript(s), minimum college GPA of 2.5 required. Lowest grade transferable 2. **General Admission Information:** Application Fee $40. Notification on a rolling basis, beginning on or about 9/15. Nonfall registration accepted. Credit offered for CEEB Advanced Placement tests.

COSTS AND FINANCIAL AID

Annual in-state tuition $5,570. Annual out-of-state tuition $14,820. Room and board $10,444. Required fees $1,212. Average book expense $1,380. **Required Forms and Deadlines:** FAFSA, institution's own financial aid form. **Notification of Awards:** Applicants will be notified of awards on a rolling basis beginning 3/15. **Types of Aid:** *Need-based scholarships/grants:* Federal Pell, SEOG, state scholarships/grants, private scholarships, the school's own gift aid. *Loans:* Subsidized Stafford, Unsubsidized Stafford, PLUS, Federal Perkins, state loans. **Student Employment:** Federal Work-Study Program available. Institutional employment available. Highest amount earned per year from on-campus jobs $9,896. Off-campus job opportunities are fair. **Financial Aid Statistics:** 64% undergrads receive need-based scholarship or grant aid. 82% undergrads receive need-based self-help aid. 7% undergrads receive athletic scholarships. **Criteria for awarding institutional aid:** *Non-need-based:* academics, leadership, state/district residency.

STATE UNIVERSITY OF NEW YORK—NEW PALTZ

100 Hawk Drive, New Paltz, NY 12561-2499
Phone: 845-257-3200 • **Financial Aid Phone:** 845-257-3250
E-mail: admissions@newpaltz.edu • **CEEB Code:** 2541
Fax: 845-257-3209 • **Website:** www.newpaltz.edu • **ACT Code:** 2938

This public school was founded in 1828. It has a 216-acre campus.

RATINGS

Admissions Selectivity Rating: 91 **Fire Safety Rating:** 82 **Green Rating:** 84

STUDENTS AND FACULTY

Enrollment: 6,439. **Student Body:** 62% female, 38% male, 4% out-of-state, 2% international (60 countries represented). Asian 4%, African American 5%, Caucasian 67%, Hispanic 13%, Native American 0%.
Retention and Graduation: 88% freshmen return for sophomore year. 52% freshmen graduate within 4 years. **Faculty:** Student/faculty ratio 16:1. 337 full-time faculty, 81% hold PhDs, 16% are members of minority groups, 51% are women. 2% of classes are taught by teaching assistants.

ACADEMICS

Degrees: bachelor's, master's, post-master's certificate. **Classes:** Most classes have 20–29 students. **Majors with Highest Enrollment:** business administration and management; education; fine/studio arts. **Special Study Options:** cooperative education program, cross-registration, distance learning, double major, dual enrollment, English as a Second Language (ESL), exchange student program (domestic), honors program, independent study, internships, liberal arts/career combination, student-designed major, study abroad, teacher certification program. **Honors Programs:** The Honors Program exists to challenge New Paltz Students beyond what is usually expected of them. It was designed around the philosophy that intense and rigorous courses, taught by outstanding instructors and filled with motivated, focused students would create the optimal learning environment. The Honors Program is small, consisting of around 100 students. Once admitted to the Program, students take special Honors seminars, which are interdisciplinary and small in size (usually around 10 students). Unlike traditional lecture courses, Honors seminars emphasize dialogue and non-lecture based learning: students are expected to come to class with something to say and to actively participate in debate and discussion. **Combined Degree Programs:** BS/DO BS/OD BS/MS. **Disability Services:** Special programs offered to physically disabled students include note taking services, reader services, tape recorders, tutors. **Career Services:** alumni services, career/job search classes, career assessment, internships Career Services highlights include Internship stipend program provides SUNY New Paltz students with scholarship stipends. These funds allow students to participate in career related experiences regardless of financial constraints.

FACILITIES

Housing: Coed dorms, special housing for disabled students, men's dorms, special housing for international students, women's dorms, The First-Year Initiative, Honors Housing, Art Program Housing. 90% of campus accessible to physically disabled. **Special Academic Facilities/Equipment:** Samuel Dorsky Museum of Art, Resnick Engineering Hall, Coykendall Media Center, Communication Disorders Training Center and Clinic; Music Therapy Training Center and Clinic; Shepherd Recital Hall, Honors Center; Martin Luther King, Jr. Study Center; Fournier Mass Spectrometer;Raymond Kurdt Theatre Collection; more **Computers:** 70% of classrooms, 45% of dorms, 100% of libraries, 90% of dining areas, 90% of student union, 10% of common outdoor areas have wireless network access. Students can register for classes online. Administrative functions (other than registration) can be performed online.

CAMPUS LIFE

Environment: Village. **Activities:** Choral groups, concert band, dance, drama/theater, jazz band, literary magazine, music ensembles, musical theater, radio station, student government, student newspaper, symphony orchestra, television station, Campus Ministries, International Student Organization, Model UN 196 registered organizations, 12 honor societies, 10 religious organizations. 11 fraternities, 17 sororities. **Athletics (Intercollegiate):** *Men:* baseball, basketball, cross-country, diving, soccer, swimming, tennis, volleyball. *Women:* basketball, cross-country, diving, field hockey, lacrosse, soccer, softball, swimming, tennis, volleyball. **On-Campus Highlights:** Samuel Dorsky Museum of Art, Lenape and Esopus Residence Halls, Athletic and Wellness Center, Student Union, Hasbrouck Dining Hall. **Environmental Initiatives:** Investment of large amounts of $ to energy management, for example all new construction of 5000sq.or larger ft will be LEED certified with a target of silver or higher all renovation will be be have a target of LEED certification using LEED criteria guidelines. Upgrade of recycling efforts including coninued participation in recylomania, and, increased capture of recylcing materials in construction projects tripling the recycling capture to well over 300 tons, and joining the EPA Waste Wise Program. Participation in the President's climate commitment

ADMISSIONS

Freshman Academic Profile: 90.2. 29% in top 10% of high school class, 62% in top 25% of high school class, 88% in top 50% of high school class. SAT Math middle 50% range 520-610. SAT Critical Reading middle 50% range 510-610. SAT Writing middle 50% range 510-600. ACT middle 50% range 23-27. Minimum paper TOEFL 550. **Basis for Candidate Selection:** *Very important factors considered include:* academic GPA, rigor of secondary school record, standardized test scores. *Important factors considered include:* application essay, recommendation(s). *Other factors considered include:* Class rank, extracurricular activities, talent/ability, volunteer work, work experience. **Freshman Admission Requirements:** High school diploma is required and GED is accepted. *Academic units required:* 4 English, 3 mathematics, 3 science, (2 science labs), 2 foreign language, 4 social studies, 1 history. *Academic units recommended:* 4 English, 3 mathematics, 3 science, (2 science labs), 2 foreign language, 4 social studies, 1 history. **Freshman Admission Statistics:** 12,892 applied, 44% admitted, 20% enrolled. **Transfer Admission Requirements:** college transcript(s), statement of good standing from prior institution(s). Minimum college GPA of 2.75 required. Lowest grade transferable C–. **General Admission Information:** Application Fee $40. Regular application deadline 4/1. Notification on a rolling basis, beginning on or about 1/1. Nonfall registration not accepted. Credit and/or placement offered for CEEB Advanced Placement tests.

COSTS AND FINANCIAL AID

Required Forms and Deadlines: FAFSA, state aid form. **Notification of Awards:** Applicants will be notified of awards on a rolling basis beginning 4/1. **Types of Aid:** *Need-based scholarships/grants:* Federal Pell, SEOG, state scholarships/grants, private scholarships, the school's own gift aid. *Loans:* Subsidized Stafford, Unsubsidized Stafford, PLUS, Federal Perkins. **Student Employment:** Federal Work-Study Program available. Institutional employment available. Highest amount earned per year from on-campus jobs $8,569. Off-campus job opportunities are good. **Financial Aid Statistics:** 50% freshmen, 54% undergrads receive need-based scholarship or grant aid. 4% freshmen, 5% undergrads receive non-need-based scholarship or grant aid. 91% freshmen, 89% undergrads receive need-based self-help aid. 63% undergrads borrow to pay for school. Average cumulative indebtedness $24,445. **Criteria for awarding institutional aid:** *Non-need-based:* academics, alumni affiliation, art, music/drama.

See page 1218.

STATE UNIVERSITY OF NEW YORK—OSWEGO

229 Sheldon Hall, Oswego, NY 13126-3599
Phone: 315-312-2250 • **Financial Aid Phone:** 315-312-2248
E-mail: admiss@oswego.edu • **CEEB Code:** 2543
Fax: 315-312-3260 • **Website:** www.oswego.edu • **ACT Code:** 2942

This public school was founded in 1861. It has a 696-acre campus.

RATINGS

Admissions Selectivity Rating: 91 **Fire Safety Rating:** 74 **Green Rating:** 91

STUDENTS AND FACULTY

Enrollment: 7,113. **Student Body:** 52% female, 48% male, 2% out-of-state, 1% international (20 countries represented). Asian 2%, African American 5%, Caucasian 82%, Hispanic 8%, Native American 0%.
Retention and Graduation: 80% freshmen return for sophomore year. 38% freshmen graduate within 4 years. 58% freshmen graduate within 6 years. 19% grads go on to further study within 1 year. 22% grads pursue arts and sciences degrees. 4% grads pursue law degrees. 6% grads pursue business degrees. 5% grads pursue medical degrees. **Faculty:** Student/faculty ratio 18:1. 338 full-time faculty, 88% hold PhDs, 16% are members of minority groups, 43% are women. 0% of classes are taught by teaching assistants.

ACADEMICS

Degrees: bachelor's, master's, post-master's certificate. **Classes:** Most classes have 10–19 students. Most lab/discussion sessions have 20–29 students. **Majors with Highest Enrollment:** business/commerce; elementary education and teaching. **Special Study Options:** Accelerated program, cross-registration, distance learning, double major, dual enrollment, English as a Second Language (ESL), exchange student program (domestic), external degree program, honors program, independent study, internships, liberal arts/career combination, study abroad, teacher certification program. **Honors Programs:** Over 275 students participate in our campus wide Honors Program. Students will take smaller courses based on the program's core multidisciplinary courses in the social sciences, the natural sciences, the humanities, and philosophy, as well as several

other courses in math, English, and a foreign language. The courses emphasize the interrelatedness of the disciplines, their historical and intellectual origins, their roles in modern society, and their impact on life in the future. **Combined Degree Programs:** BA/MA, BS/MBA - 5 year accounting BS/MBA program. **Disability Services:** Special programs offered to physically disabled students include note-taking services, reader services, tape recorders, tutors. **Career Services:** Alumni network, alumni services, career/job search classes, career assessment, internships, regional alumni. Career Services highlights include We currently have 133 student in Internship Program 43 male student and 90 female students, involving 78 organizations.

FACILITIES

Housing: Coed dorms, wellness housing, theme housing, Global living and learning center, suites for upperclassmen, nontraditional student housing, first-year experience residence hall for incoming freshmen only, housing for 21 and over single suites, several rooms equipped with special equipment to meet needs of disabled students available. 85% of campus accessible to physically disabled. **Special Academic Facilities/Equipment:** Tyler Hall Art Galleries, Rice Creek Biological Field Station, curriculum materials center, electron microscopy lab, planetarium. **Computers:** 80% of classrooms, 10% of dorms, 100% of libraries, 100% of dining areas, 100% of student union, have wireless network access. Students can register for classes online. Administrative functions (other than registration) can be performed online.

CAMPUS LIFE

Environment: Village. **Activities:** Choral groups, concert band, dance, drama/theater, jazz band, literary magazine, music ensembles, musical theater, radio station, student government, student newspaper, student-run film society, symphony orchestra, television station, yearbook, International Student Organization 148 registered organizations, 21 honor societies, 6 religious organizations. 13 fraternities, 10 sororities. **Athletics (Intercollegiate): Men:** baseball, basketball, cross-country, diving, golf, ice hockey, lacrosse, soccer, swimming, tennis, track/field (outdoor), track/field (indoor), wrestling. *Women:* basketball, cross-country, diving, field hockey, ice hockey, lacrosse, soccer, softball, swimming, tennis, track/field (outdoor), track/field (indoor), volleyball. **On-Campus Highlights:** Romney Fieldhouse/ Campus Ctr(Hockey and Conference), Hewitt Union; The Student Union, Rich Hall; The School of Business, Tyler Hall; The Fine Arts Building, Penfield Library and Cafe, Rice Creek Biological field station; The Sweete Shoppe in the Hewitt Union!; Laker Hall (Field House); Johnson Hall (1st Year Residence Hall). **Environmental Initiatives:** Commitment to LEED Gold for construction projects President's Climate Commitment (ACUPCC) Actively pursuing on-site generation and geothermal sources.

ADMISSIONS

Freshman Academic Profile: Average high school GPA 3.5. 16% in top 10% of high school class, 55% in top 25% of high school class, 87% in top 50% of high school class. SAT Math middle 50% range 530-600. SAT Critical Reading middle 50% range 530-600. ACT middle 50% range 22-26. Minimum web-based TOEFL 80. Minimum paper TOEFL 550. **Basis for Candidate Selection:** *Very important factors considered include:* academic GPA, rigor of secondary school record. *Important factors considered include:* Class rank, standardized test scores. *Other factors considered include:* application essay, recommendation(s), character/personal qualities, extracurricular activities, first generation, interview, level of applicant's interest, racial/ethnic status, talent/ability, volunteer work, work experience. **Freshman Admission Requirements:** High school diploma is required and GED is accepted. *Academic units required:* 4 English, 3 mathematics, 3 science, (2 science labs), 2 foreign language, 4 social studies. *Academic units recommended:* 4 English, 3 mathematics, 3 science, (2 science labs), 2 foreign language, 4 social studies. **Freshman Admission Statistics:** 9,746 applied, 48% admitted, 27% enrolled. **Transfer Admission Requirements:** college transcript(s), minimum college GPA of 2.5 required. Lowest grade transferable D. **General Admission Information:** Application Fee $40. Early decision application deadline 11/15. Notification on a rolling basis, beginning on or about 1/15. Nonfall registration accepted. Admission may be deferred for a maximum of 12 months. Credit offered for CEEB Advanced Placement tests.

COSTS AND FINANCIAL AID

Annual in-state tuition $5,570. Annual out-of-state tuition $14,820. Room and board $12,310. Required fees $1,271. Average book expense $800. **Required Forms and Deadlines:** FAFSA, state aid form. **Notification of Awards:** Applicants will be notified of awards on a rolling basis beginning 3/1. **Types of Aid:** *Need-based scholarships/grants:* Federal Pell, SEOG, state scholarships/grants, private scholarships, the school's own gift aid. *Loans:* Subsidized Stafford, Unsubsidized Stafford, PLUS, Federal Perkins. **Student Employment:** Federal Work-Study Program available. Institutional employment available. Highest amount earned per year from on-campus jobs $2,000. **Financial Aid Statistics:** 87% freshmen, 85% undergrads receive need-based scholarship or grant aid. 40% freshmen, 2% undergrads receive non-need-based scholarship or grant aid. 92% freshmen, 93% undergrads receive need-based self-help aid.

85% freshmen, 83% undergrads receive any aid. 80% undergrads borrow to pay for school. Average cumulative indebtedness $26,611. **Criteria for awarding institutional aid:** *Non-need-based:* academics, state/district residency.

STATE UNIVERSITY OF NEW YORK— PLATTSBURGH

1001 Kehoe Bldg., Plattsburgh, NY 12901
Phone: 518-564-2040
E-mail: admissions@plattsburgh.edu • **CEEB Code:** 2544
Fax: 518-564-2045 • **Website:** www.plattsburgh.edu • **ACT Code:** 2944

This public school was founded in 1889. It has a 300-acre campus.

RATINGS
Admissions Selectivity Rating: 79   **Fire Safety Rating:** 60*   **Green Rating:** 60*

STUDENTS AND FACULTY
Enrollment: 5,328. **Student Body:** 58% female, 42% male, 4% out-of-state, 7% international (56 countries represented). Asian 2%, African American 5%, Caucasian 76%, Hispanic 3%, Native American 0%.
Retention and Graduation: 75% freshmen return for sophomore year. 37% freshmen graduate within 4 years. 59% freshmen graduate within 6 years. 34% grads go on to further study within 1 year. 31% grads pursue arts and sciences degrees. 1% grads pursue law degrees. 2% grads pursue business degrees. 1% grads pursue medical degrees. **Faculty:** Student/faculty ratio 18:1. 250 full-time faculty, 90% hold PhDs, 12% are members of minority groups, 36% are women. 0% of classes are taught by teaching assistants.

ACADEMICS
Degrees: bachelor's, master's, post-bachelor's certificate, post-master's certificate. **Classes:** Most classes have 10–19 students. Most lab/discussion sessions have 20–29 students. **Majors with Highest Enrollment:** business/commerce; early childhood education; special education and teaching. **Special Study Options:** cooperative education program, cross-registration, distance learning, double major, dual enrollment, English as a Second Language (ESL), exchange student program (domestic), honors program, independent study, internships, liberal arts/career combination, student-designed major, study abroad, teacher certification program. **Honors Programs:** The honors program is offered in two levels, General Honors and Advance Honors. Each seminar in General Honors program is limited to about 15 students and is taught by faculty who have a reputation of excellence in teaching. Occasionally distance-learning experiences are available which allow students to work with faculty at other colleges and universities in the US; Advance Honors' work continues the goals and ideals of General Honors, except the work is focused in student's major and requires that students design and carry out a project in research, in performance, in fieldwork, or whatever else would be appropriate to a particular major. **Combined Degree Programs:** 3-2 French, Spanish; 3-1 Medical Tech. and Cytote. **Disability Services:** Special programs offered to physically disabled students include note-taking services, reader services, tape recorders, tutors. **Career Services:** Alumni network, alumni services, career/job search classes, career assessment, internships.

FACILITIES
Housing: Coed dorms, special housing for disabled students, special housing for international students, Wellness floor, Substance free building and floors, Quiet floors, Men's floor, Women's floors, Extended logding. 95% of campus accessible to physically disabled. **Special Academic Facilities/Equipment:** Art galleries, sculpture courtyard, theatre and concert halls, communications/lecture hall, interactive video for telecourses, radio and TV broadcasting facilities, planetarium, on-site research center for biotechnology and environmental science, enzymology lab, electron microscope, remote sensing lab, NMR spectrophotometer, computer-operated infrared spectrophotometer, gas chromatograph, mass spectrometer, computerized liquid scintillation counter, facility for analysis of environmental pollutants in lake water, sediments and biota, lake research/sampling vesel with differential GPS navigation equipment, ubductively coupled plasma/mass spectrometer, ion chromatograph/high performance liquid chromatograph, mercury detector. **Computers:** Students can register for classes online. Administrative functions (other than registration) can be performed online.

CAMPUS LIFE
Environment: Village. **Activities:** Choral groups, concert band, drama/theater, jazz band, literary magazine, music ensembles, radio station, student government, student newspaper, student-run film society, symphony orchestra, television station, yearbook 97 registered organizations, 26 honor societies, 3

religious organizations. 6 fraternities, 7 sororities. **Athletics (Intercollegiate):** *Men:* basketball, cross-country, golf, ice hockey, lacrosse, rugby, soccer, track/field (outdoor), track/field (indoor). *Women:* basketball, cross-country, golf, ice hockey, rugby, soccer, softball, tennis, track/field (outdoor), track/field (indoor), volleyball. **On-Campus Highlights:** Fitness Center, Art Museums, College Field House, Computer Labs, College Center.

ADMISSIONS
Freshman Academic Profile: Average high school GPA 3.0. 11% in top 10% of high school class, 33% in top 25% of high school class, 75% in top 50% of high school class. 98% from public high schools. SAT Math middle 50% range 480-560. SAT Critical Reading middle 50% range 480-560. ACT middle 50% range 19-24. Minimum paper TOEFL 450. **Basis for Candidate Selection:** *Very important factors considered include:* rigor of secondary school record, standardized test scores, interview. *Important factors considered include:* Class rank, application essay, recommendation(s), alumni/ae relation, character/personal qualities, extracurricular activities, racial/ethnic status, talent/ability. *Other factors considered include:* volunteer work, work experience. **Freshman Admission Requirements:** High school diploma is required and GED is accepted. *Academic units required:* 4 English, 3 mathematics, 3 science, 3 foreign language, 3 social studies, 1 history. *Academic units recommended:* 4 English, 3 mathematics, 3 science, 3 foreign language, 3 social studies, 1 history. **Freshman Admission Statistics:** 6,798 applied, 62% admitted, 23% enrolled. **Transfer Admission Requirements:** college transcript(s), minimum college GPA of 2.3 required. Lowest grade transferable D. **General Admission Information:** Application Fee $40. Early decision application deadline 11/15. Regular application deadline 8/1. Notification on a rolling basis, beginning on or about 1/15. Nonfall registration accepted. Admission may be deferred for a maximum of 1 year. Credit and/or placement offered for CEEB Advanced Placement tests.

COSTS AND FINANCIAL AID
Annual in-state tuition $4,350. Annual out-of-state tuition $10,300. Room and board $6,500. Required fees $850. Average book expense $850. **Required Forms and Deadlines:** FAFSA, state aid form. **Notification of Awards:** Applicants will be notified of awards on a rolling basis beginning 3/15. **Types of Aid:** *Need-based scholarships/grants:* Federal Pell, SEOG, state scholarships/grants, private scholarships, the school's own gift aid, Scholarships for disavantaged students, State Educational Opportunity Program. *Loans:* Direct Subsidized Stafford, Direct Unsubsidized Stafford, Direct PLUS, Federal Perkins, Federal Nursing, Grace Appleton Loan, privately endowed administered by a Trust Company; Awarded by the College. **Student Employment:** Federal Work-Study Program available. Institutional employment available. Highest amount earned per year from on-campus jobs $1,510. Off campus job opportunities are good. **Financial Aid Statistics:** 91% freshmen, 90% undergrads receive need-based scholarship or grant aid. 33% freshmen, 30% undergrads receive non-need based scholarship or grant aid. 87% freshmen, 87% undergrads receive need-based self-help aid. 73% undergrads borrow to pay for school. Average cumulative indebtedness $16,158. **Criteria for awarding institutional aid:** *Non-need-based:* academics, alumni affiliation, art, leadership, music/drama, state/district residency.

STATE UNIVERSITY OF NEW YORK— PURCHASE COLLEGE

Best 378

735 Anderson Hill Road, Purchase, NY 10577
Phone: 914-251-6300
E-mail: admissions@purchase.edu • **CEEB Code:** 2878
Fax: 914-251-6314 • **Website:** www.purchase.edu • **ACT Code:** 2931

This public school was founded in 1967. It has a 550-acre campus.

RATINGS
Admissions Selectivity Rating: 93   **Fire Safety Rating:** 60*   **Green Rating:** 89

STUDENTS AND FACULTY
Enrollment: 3,900. **Student Body:** 56% female, 44% male, 17% out-of-state, 2% international (39 countries represented). Asian 2%, African American 7%, Caucasian 52%, Hispanic 16%, Native American 0%.
Retention and Graduation: 83% freshmen return for sophomore year. 52% freshmen graduate within 4 years. **Faculty:** Student/faculty ratio 16:1. 159 full-time faculty, 49% hold PhDs, 11% are members of minority groups, 57% are women. 1% of classes are taught by teaching assistants.

ACADEMICS

Degrees: bachelor's, master's, post-master's certificate. **Classes:** Most classes have 10–19 students. Most lab/discussion sessions have fewer than 10 students. **Majors with Highest Enrollment:** liberal arts and sciences/liberal studies; visual and performing arts. **Special Study Options:** cross-registration, distance learning, double major, English as a Second Language (ESL), independent study, internships, liberal arts/career combination, student-designed major, study abroad. **Disability Services:** Special programs offered to physically disabled students include note-taking services, reader services, tape recorders, tutors. **Career Services:** alumni services, career/job search classes, career assessment, internships.

FACILITIES

Housing: Coed dorms, special housing for disabled students, special housing for international students, apartments for married students, apartments for single students, wellness housing, theme housing. 100% of campus accessible to physically disabled. **Special Academic Facilities/Equipment:** Museum, four-theatre performing arts center, visual arts facility, children's center, recording studio, electron microscopes. **Computers:** Students can register for classes online. Administrative functions (other than registration) can be performed online.

CAMPUS LIFE

Environment: Town. **Activities:** Choral groups, dance, drama/theater, jazz band, literary magazine, music ensembles, musical theater, radio station, student government, student newspaper, student-run film society, television station 30 registered organizations. **Athletics (Intercollegiate):** *Men:* baseball, basketball, cross-country, golf, soccer, tennis, volleyball. *Women:* basketball, cross-country, soccer, softball, tennis, volleyball. **On-Campus Highlights:** The Performing Arts Center, The Neuberger Museum, State-of-the-Art Athletic Complex, Starbucks, Fort Awesome, New Student Services building. **Environmental Initiatives:** Commited to reduce GHG emissions by 80% by 2050 (Presidents Climate Commitment) Have campus policy that all new buildings constructed be LEED Silver Certified or better Purchase biodegradable and recycled paper products for dining halls and 100% recycled copy paper.

ADMISSIONS

Freshman Academic Profile: Average high school GPA 3.2. 10% in top 10% of high school class, 39% in top 25% of high school class, 71% in top 50% of high school class. SAT Math middle 50% range 480-570. SAT Critical Reading middle 50% range 500-610. SAT Writing middle 50% range 480-600. ACT middle 50% range 21-27. Minimum paper TOEFL 550. **Basis for Candidate Selection:** *Very important factors considered include:* application essay, academic GPA, talent/ability. *Important factors considered include:* standardized test scores. *Other factors considered include:* Class rank, recommendation(s), rigor of secondary school record, character/personal qualities, extracurricular activities, interview. **Freshman Admission Requirements:** High school diploma is required and GED is accepted. **Freshman Admission Statistics:** 8,907 applied, 33% admitted, 23% enrolled. **Transfer Admission Requirements:** college transcript(s), minimum college GPA of 3.0 required. Lowest grade transferable D. **General Admission Information:** Application Fee $40. Early decision application deadline 11/1. Regular application deadline 7/15. Regular notification 5/1. Nonfall registration accepted. Admission may be deferred for a maximum of 1 year. Credit and/or placement offered for CEEB Advanced Placement tests.

COSTS AND FINANCIAL AID

Annual in-state tuition $5,570. Annual out-of-state tuition $14,820. Room and board $11,566. Required fees $1,660. Average book expense $1,168. **Required Forms and Deadlines:** FAFSA, state aid form. **Notification of Awards:** Applicants will be notified of awards on a rolling basis beginning 3/1. **Types of Aid:** *Need-based scholarships/grants:* Federal Pell, SEOG, state scholarships/grants, private scholarships, the school's own gift aid. *Loans:* Direct Subsidized Stafford, Direct Unsubsidized Stafford, Direct PLUS, Federal Perkins. **Student Employment:** Federal Work-Study Program available. Institutional employment available. Off-campus job opportunities are excellent. **Financial Aid Statistics:** 83% freshmen, 83% undergrads receive need-based scholarship or grant aid. 1% freshmen, 1% undergrads receive non-need-based scholarship or grant aid. 98% freshmen, 97% undergrads receive need-based self-help aid. 60% undergrads borrow to pay for school. Average cumulative indebtedness $26,684. **Criteria for awarding institutional aid:** *Non-need-based:* academics, art, minority status, music/drama.

STATE UNIVERSITY OF NEW YORK—POTSDAM

44 Pierrepont Avenue, Potsdam, NY 13676
Phone: 315-267-2180 • **Financial Aid Phone:** 315-267-2162
E-mail: admissions@potsdam.edu • **CEEB Code:** 2545
Fax: 315-267-2163 • **Website:** www.potsdam.edu • **ACT Code:** 2946

This public school was founded in 1816. It has a 240-acre campus.

RATINGS

Admissions Selectivity Rating: 63   **Fire Safety Rating:** 76   **Green Rating:** 80

STUDENTS AND FACULTY

Enrollment: 3,850. **Student Body:** 58% female, 42% male, 3% out-of-state, 1% international (30 countries represented). Asian 1%, African American 5%, Caucasian 76%, Hispanic 7%, Native American 1%.
Retention and Graduation: 32% freshmen graduate within 4 years. 51% freshmen graduate within 6 years. 41% grads go on to further study within 1 year. 14% grads pursue arts and sciences degrees. 1% grads pursue law degrees. 2% grads pursue business degrees. 2% grads pursue medical degrees. **Faculty:** Student/faculty ratio 14:1. 261 full-time faculty, 87% hold PhDs, 12% are members of minority groups, 46% are women.

ACADEMICS

Degrees: bachelor's, master's. **Classes:** Most classes have 10–19 students. Most lab/discussion sessions have 10–19 students. **Majors with Highest Enrollment:** business administration and management; education; other; music teacher education. **Special Study Options:** cross-registration, distance learning, double major, dual enrollment, exchange student program (domestic), honors program, independent study, internships, liberal arts/career combination, student-designed major, study abroad, teacher certification program, First-year students may enroll in interdisciplinary program to study art, literature, science, and sociology of the Adirondacks. Extension offers undergraduate and graduate courses with emphasis on teacher education. Combined degree options in engineering with Clarkson University and SUNY Binghamton; accounting, engineering or management with SUNY Institute of Technology. **Honors Programs:** The Honors Program is designed to offer special curricular, co-curricular, and extra curricular opportunities for our college's most academically talented students. Benefits include priority registration, honors courses, field trips, mentoring, housing, and select study abroad options. **Combined Degree Programs:** BA/MA, BA/MST. **Disability Services:** Special programs offered to physically disabled students include note-taking services, reader services, tape recorders, tutors. **Career Services:** Alumni network, alumni services, career/job search classes, career assessment

FACILITIES

Housing: Coed dorms, special housing for disabled students, special housing for international students, apartments for single students, wellness housing, theme housing. First year experience, Quiet study , International House, Transfer student housing, Sustainability. 95% of campus accessible to physically disabled. **Special Academic Facilities/Equipment:** Art gallery, anthropology museum, ecology museum, three performance halls, theatre, synthesizer music studios, planetarium, electron microscope, nuclear magnetic resonator, seismograph. **Computers:** 20% of classrooms, 100% of dorms, 100% of libraries, 100% of dining areas, 100% of student union, 40% of common outdoor areas have wireless network access. Students can register for classes online. Administrative functions (other than registration) can be performed online.

CAMPUS LIFE

Environment: Village. **Activities:** Choral groups, concert band, dance, drama/theater, jazz band, literary magazine, music ensembles, musical theater, opera, radio station, student government, student newspaper, symphony orchestra, yearbook, Campus Ministries, International Student Organization 100 registered organizations, 17 honor societies, 3 religious organizations. 4 fraternities, 7 sororities. **Athletics (Intercollegiate):** *Men:* basketball, cross-country, diving, equestrian sports, golf, ice hockey, lacrosse, soccer, swimming. *Women:* basketball, cross-country, diving, equestrian sports, ice hockey, lacrosse, soccer, softball, swimming, tennis, volleyball. **On-Campus Highlights:** Hosmer Concert Hall, Maxcy Athletic Complex, Townhouses, Gibson Art Gallery, Barrrington Student Union, Becky's Place (new dining facility) Minerva's Cafe. **Environmental Initiatives:** Increase recycle efforts Increase purchase of green products and energy star equipment Increase purchase of renewable energy

ADMISSIONS

Freshman Academic Profile: 9% in top 10% of high school class, 31% in top 25% of high school class, 74% in top 50% of high school class. 94% from public high schools. Minimum web-based TOEFL 79. Minimum paper TOEFL 550. **Basis for Candidate Selection:** *Very important factors considered include:* academic GPA, rigor of secondary school record. *Important factors considered* *include:* Class rank, application essay, recommendation(s), character/personal qualities, extracurricular activities, interview, talent/ability. *Other factors considered include:* standardized test scores, alumni/ae relation, level of applicant's interest, volunteer work, work experience. **Freshman Admission Requirements:** High school diploma is required and GED is accepted. *Academic units required:* 4 English, 2 mathematics, 2 science, (1 science labs), 4 social studies, 1 visual/performing arts. *Academic units recommended:* 4 English, 2 mathematics, 2 science, (1 science labs), 4 social studies, 1 visual/performing arts. **Freshman Admission Statistics:** 5,022 applied, 65% admitted, 27% enrolled. **Transfer Admission Requirements:** college transcript(s), minimum college GPA of 2.0 required. Lowest grade transferable D. **General Admission Information:** Application Fee $40. Notification on a rolling basis, beginning on or about 10/1. Nonfall registration accepted. Admission may be deferred for a maximum of 1 year. Credit and/or placement offered for CEEB Advanced Placement tests.

COSTS AND FINANCIAL AID

Annual in-state tuition $5,570. Annual out-of-state tuition $14,820. Room and board $10,180. Required fees $1,272. Average book expense $1,200. **Required Forms and Deadlines:** FAFSA, state aid form. **Notification of Awards:** Applicants will be notified of awards on a rolling basis beginning 2/1. **Types of Aid:** *Need-based scholarships/grants:* Federal Pell, SEOG, state scholarships/grants, private scholarships, the school's own gift aid, VESID, Veteran Benefits, BIA, Native American, Academic Achievement (ACG), SMART (National Math & Science Grant). *Loans:* Direct Subsidized Stafford, Direct Unsubsidized Stafford, Direct PLUS, Federal Perkins, college/university loans from institutional funds, Alternative Loans. **Student Employment:** Federal Work-Study Program available. Institutional employment available. Off-campus job opportunities are good. **Financial Aid Statistics:** 93% freshmen, 89% undergrads receive need-based scholarship or grant aid. 42% freshmen, 31% undergrads receive non-need-based scholarship or grant aid. 88% freshmen, 87% undergrads receive need-based self-help aid. 91% freshmen, 95% undergrads receive any aid. 78% undergrads borrow to pay for school. Average cumulative indebtedness $20,734. **Criteria for awarding institutional aid:** *Non-need-based:* academics, art, leadership, minority status, music/drama.

STATE UNIVERSITY OF NEW YORK— STONY BROOK UNIVERSITY

Office of Admissions, Stony Brook, NY 11794-1901
Phone: 631-632-6868 • **Financial Aid Phone:** 631-632-6840
E-mail: enroll@stonybrook.edu • **CEEB Code:** 2548
Fax: 631-632-9898 • **Website:** www.stonybrook.edu/ • **ACT Code:** 2952

This public school was founded in 1957. It has a 1450-acre campus.

RATINGS
Admissions Selectivity Rating: 94   **Fire Safety Rating:** 77   **Green Rating:** 98

STUDENTS AND FACULTY
Enrollment: 15,618. **Student Body:** 47% female, 53% male, 8% out-of-state, 9% international (110 countries represented). Asian 25%, African American 6%, Caucasian 38%, Hispanic 10%, Native American 0%.
Retention and Graduation: 90% freshmen return for sophomore year. 47% freshmen graduate within 4 years. 69% freshmen graduate within 6 years. 35% grads go on to further study within 1 year. **Faculty:** Student/faculty ratio 18:1. 957 full-time faculty, 97% hold PhDs, 18% are members of minority groups, 34% are women. % of classes are taught by teaching assistants.

ACADEMICS
Degrees: bachelor's, doctoral, master's, post-bachelor's certificate, post-master's certificate. **Classes:** Most classes have 20–29 students. Most lab/discussion sessions have 20–29 students. **Majors with Highest Enrollment:** biology/biological sciences; business/commerce; psychology. **Special Study Options:** cross-registration, distance learning, double major, English as a Second Language (ESL), exchange student program (domestic), honors program, independent study, internships, student-designed major, study abroad, teacher certification program, Albany Semester, Undergrads may take grad level courses BS/MS programs, BE/MS, BS/MA Living Learning Centers in residence halls, Honors College, undergraduate research and creative activities program where undergraduates work with faculty on research projects, university learning communities and (WISE) Women in Science and Engineering. **Honors Programs:** BA/

MD **Combined Degree Programs:** BA/MA, MD/PhD. **Disability Services:** Special programs offered to physically disabled students include note-taking services, reader services, tape recorders, tutors. **Career Services:** Alumni network, alumni services, career/job search classes, career assessment, internships, regional alumni. Career Services highlights include Career Services internship program modeled after successful corporate internship programs. Includes career counseling, marketing, graphics, human resources, and technology.

FACILITIES
Housing: Coed dorms, special housing for disabled students, apartments for married students, apartments for single students, -Single sex floors in coed dorms. -Living Learning Centers -First year resident members of each College are housed together in the same residential Quadrangle. 75% of campus accessible to physically disabled. **Special Academic Facilities/Equipment:** SAC Gallery, Staller Gallery, Wang Center, Tabler Center for the Arts **Computers:** 50% of classrooms, 50% of dorms, 50% of libraries, 50% of dining areas, 50% of student union, 50% of common outdoor areas have wireless network access. Students can register for classes online. Administrative functions (other than registration) can be performed online.

CAMPUS LIFE
Environment: Town. **Activities:** Choral groups, concert band, dance, drama/theater, jazz band, literary magazine, marching band, music ensembles, musical theater, opera, pep band, radio station, student government, student newspaper, student-run film society, symphony orchestra, yearbook, Campus Ministries 292 registered organizations, 6 honor societies, 25 religious organizations. 17 fraternities, 16 sororities. **Athletics (Intercollegiate):** *Men:* baseball, basketball, cross-country, diving, football, lacrosse, soccer, swimming, tennis, track/field (outdoor), track/field (indoor). *Women:* basketball, cross-country, diving, lacrosse, soccer, softball, swimming, tennis, track/field (outdoor), track/field (indoor), volleyball. **On-Campus Highlights:** Staller Center for the Arts, Sports Complex and Stadium, Student Activities Center, University Hospital, The Charles B. Wang Center, Building and Grounds: Main campus, 1,100 acres. Research and Development Campus, 246 acres adjacent to the main campus. Stony Brook Southampton, 82 acres. Stony Brook Manhattan. New buildings: Humanities Building, undergraduate apartments; Center for Excellence in Wireless and Information Technology under construction. **Environmental Initiatives:** Signing of ACUPCC. Commitment to obtain carbon nuetrality by 2050. Creation of Environmental Stewardship Department which focuses on energy reduction, waste reduction and all areas of sustainability for the campus. We have a Sustainability Task Force which meets routinely and works on projects each academic year.

ADMISSIONS
Freshman Academic Profile: Average high school GPA 3.7. 42% in top 10% of high school class, 75% in top 25% of high school class, 95% in top 50% of high school class. 90% from public high schools. SAT Math middle 50% range 600-700. SAT Critical Reading middle 50% range 530-640. SAT Writing middle 50% range 530-640. ACT middle 50% range 25-29. Minimum web-based TOEFL 80. Minimum paper TOEFL 550. **Basis for Candidate Selection:** *Very important factors considered include:* academic GPA, rigor of secondary school record, standardized test scores. *Important factors considered include:* Class rank. *Other factors considered include:* application essay, recommendation(s), alumni/ae relation, character/personal qualities, extracurricular activities, first generation, interview, level of applicant's interest, state residency, talent/ability, volunteer work, work experience. **Freshman Admission Requirements:** High school diploma is required and GED is accepted. *Academic units required:* 4 English, 3 mathematics, 3 science, 2 foreign language, 4 social studies. *Academic units recommended:* 4 English, 3 mathematics, 3 science, 2 foreign language, 4 social studies. **Freshman Admission Statistics:** 27,513 applied, 40% admitted, 24% enrolled. **Transfer Admission Requirements:** college transcript(s), minimum college GPA of 3.0 required. Lowest grade transferable C. **General Admission Information:** Application Fee $40. Notification on a rolling basis, beginning on or about 2/1. Nonfall registration accepted. Admission may be deferred for a maximum of 2 semesters. Credit and/or placement offered for CEEB Advanced Placement tests.

COSTS AND FINANCIAL AID
Annual in-state tuition $5,570. Annual out-of-state tuition $16,190. Room and board $10,934. Required fees $1,990. Average book expense $900. **Required Forms and Deadlines:** FAFSA Program Specific Forms. **Notification of Awards:** Applicants will be notified of awards on a rolling basis beginning 3/1. **Types of Aid:** *Need-based scholarships/grants:* Federal Pell, SEOG, state scholarships/grants, the school's own gift aid. *Loans:* Direct Subsidized Stafford, Direct Unsubsidized Stafford, Direct PLUS, Federal Perkins. **Student Employment:** Federal Work-Study Program available. Institutional employment available. Highest amount earned per year from on-campus jobs $12,638. Off-campus job opportunities are excellent. **Financial Aid Statistics:** 90% freshmen, 86% undergrads receive need-based scholarship or grant aid. 8% freshmen, 4% undergrads receive non-need-based scholarship or grant aid. 96% freshmen, 97% undergrads receive need-based self-help aid. 1% freshmen,

1% undergrads receive athletic scholarships. 78% freshmen, 71% undergrads receive any aid. 59% undergrads borrow to pay for school. Average cumulative indebtedness $20,933. **Criteria for awarding institutional aid:** *Non-need-based:* academics, alumni affiliation, athletics, leadership, music/drama.

STATE UNIVERSITY OF NEW YORK—UNIVERSITY AT ALBANY

Office of Undergraduate Admissions, Albany, NY 12222
Phone: 518-442-5435 • **Financial Aid Phone:** 518-442-3202
E-mail: ugadmissions@albany.edu • **CEEB Code:** 2532
Fax: 518-442-5383 • **Website:** www.albany.edu • **ACT Code:** 2926

This public school was founded in 1844. It has a 795-acre campus.

RATINGS
Admissions Selectivity Rating: 88   **Fire Safety Rating:** 76   **Green Rating:** 94

STUDENTS AND FACULTY
Enrollment: 12,425. **Student Body:** 48% female, 52% male, 5% out-of-state, 3% international (84 countries represented). Asian 7%, African American 12%, Caucasian 59%, Hispanic 11%, Native American 0%.
Retention and Graduation: 84% freshmen return for sophomore year. 53% freshmen graduate within 4 years. 65% freshmen graduate within 6 years. 51% grads go on to further study within 1 year. 13% grads pursue arts and sciences degrees. 6% grads pursue law degrees. 3% grads pursue business degrees. 4% grads pursue medical degrees. **Faculty:** Student/faculty ratio 19:1. 590 full-time faculty, 96% hold PhDs, 20% are members of minority groups, 38% are women. 11% of classes are taught by teaching assistants.

ACADEMICS
Degrees: bachelor's, master's, post-bachelor's certificate, post-master's certificate. **Classes:** Most classes have 20–29 students. Most lab/discussion sessions have 20–29 students. **Majors with Highest Enrollment:** business administration and management; English language and literature; psychology. **Special Study Options:** Accelerated program, cross-registration, distance learning, double major, dual enrollment, English as a Second Language (ESL), honors program, independent study, internships, liberal arts/career combination, student-designed major, study abroad, Accelerated 5 year Bachelors/Masters programs in 40 fields; Internships with New York State Legislature; Combined Bachelors/Law degree with Albany Law school; 3+2 Engineering Program with RPI, Clarkson, and others; Biology/Dental Program with Boston University Goldman School of Dental Medicine, Bachelors/Doctor of Optometry with SUNY State College; Early Assurance Program with Albany Medical College and SUNY Upstate Medical College. **Honors Programs:** Our Presidential Scholars program combines merit scholarships, honors courses, priority registration, special housing, and faculty mentor opportunities. **Combined Degree Programs:** BA/JD, BA/MA, BA/MEng, Accelerated 5 yr Bachelors/Masters in 40 fields. **Disability Services:** Special programs offered to physically disabled students include note-taking services, reader services, tape recorders, tutors. **Career Services:** Alumni network, alumni services, career/job search classes, career assessment, internships, regional alumni. Career Services highlights include Internships with New York State Legislature; On-Campus Recruiting for graduates and those seeking internships.

FACILITIES
Housing: Coed dorms, special housing for international students, apartments for married students, apartments for single students, wellness housing, theme housingDisabled Student Services provides individualized services including information on accessible housing. 99% of campus accessible to physically disabled. **Special Academic Facilities/Equipment:** Performing Arts Center, Art Museum, art and dance studios, sculpture foundry, nuclear accelerator and advanced materials facilities, a peptide synthesis facility, recombinatnt DNA sequencing laboratories, and atmospheric science's Whiteface Mountain observational facility. **Computers:** 75% of classrooms, 100% of dorms, 100% of libraries, 75% of dining areas, 100% of student union, 75% of common outdoor areas have wireless network access. Students can register for classes online. Administrative functions (other than registration) can be performed online.

CAMPUS LIFE
Environment: City. **Activities:** Choral groups, concert band, dance, drama/theater, jazz band, literary magazine, music ensembles, musical theater, pep

band, radio station, student government, student newspaper, student-run film society, symphony orchestra, television station, yearbook, Campus Ministries, International Student Organization 200 registered organizations, 20 honor societies, 17 religious organizations. 11 fraternities, 18 sororities. **Athletics (Intercollegiate):** *Men:* baseball, basketball, cross-country, football, lacrosse, soccer, track/field (outdoor), track/field (indoor). *Women:* basketball, cross-country, field hockey, golf, lacrosse, soccer, softball, tennis, track/field (outdoor), track/field (indoor), volleyball. **On-Campus Highlights:** Campus Center with bookstore, cafes, and lounges, SEFCU Arena, Science Library /Main Library, Performing Arts Center, University Art Museum, Students often find that a visit to the University at Albany helps them decide whether this is the university for them. Visitors can attend an information session and join a student-led tour during the academic year or the summer. The tour visits classrooms, academic and other facilities, a residence hall and a dining area. Information Sessions begin at 10:00 a.m. and 12:00 p.m. Your visit includes a QandA session and campus tour. Please allow two hours for your visit. **Environmental Initiatives:** energy conservation waste reduction alternative transport.

ADMISSIONS
Freshman Academic Profile: Average high school GPA 3.3. 16% in top 10% of high school class, 51% in top 25% of high school class, 88% in top 50% of high school class. SAT Math middle 50% range 520-610. SAT Critical Reading middle 50% range 500-580. ACT middle 50% range 22-26. Minimum web-based TOEFL 79. Minimum paper TOEFL 550. **Basis for Candidate Selection:** *Very important factors considered include:* Class rank, academic GPA, recommendation(s), rigor of secondary school record, standardized test scores, character/personal qualities. *Important factors considered include:* application essay. *Other factors considered include:* alumni/ae relation, extracurricular activities, first generation, geographical residence, talent/ability, volunteer work, work experience. **Freshman Admission Requirements:** High school diploma is required and GED is accepted. *Academic units required:* 4 English, 2 mathematics, 2 science, (2 science labs), 1 foreign language, 3 social studies, 2 history, 4 academic electives. *Academic units recommended:* 4 English, 2 mathematics, 2 science, (2 science labs), 1 foreign language, 3 social studies, 2 history, 4 academic electives. **Freshman Admission Statistics:** 21,054 applied, 51% admitted, 22% enrolled. **Transfer Admission Requirements:** college transcript(s), essay or personal statement, statement of good standing from prior institution(s). Minimum college GPA of 2.5 required. Lowest grade transferable C. **General Admission Information:** Application Fee $50. Regular application deadline 3/1. Notification on a rolling basis, beginning on or about 1/1. Nonfall registration accepted. Admission may be deferred for a maximum of 1 year. Credit and/or placement offered for CEEB Advanced Placement tests.

COSTS AND FINANCIAL AID
Annual in-state tuition $5,570. Annual out-of-state tuition $16,190. Room and board $11,276. Required fees $1,902. Average book expense $1,200. **Required Forms and Deadlines:** FAFSANY State residents should apply for TAP on-line at www.tapweb.org. **Notification of Awards:** Applicants will be notified of awards on a rolling basis beginning 3/20. **Types of Aid:** *Need-based scholarships/grants:* Federal Pell, SEOG, state scholarships/grants, private scholarships, the school's own gift aid, NY State residents should apply for TAP on-line at <http://www.tapweb.org>. *Loans:* Subsidized Stafford, Unsubsidized Stafford, PLUS, Federal Perkins. **Student Employment:** Federal Work-Study Program available. Institutional employment available. Highest amount earned per year from on-campus jobs $5,532. Off-campus job opportunities are good. **Financial Aid Statistics:** 82% freshmen, 84% undergrads receive need-based scholarship or grant aid. 3% freshmen, 2% undergrads receive non-need-based scholarship or grant aid. 84% freshmen, 83% undergrads receive need-based self-help aid. 2% freshmen, 2% undergrads receive athletic scholarships. 64% freshmen, 62% undergrads receive any aid. 70% undergrads borrow to pay for school. Average cumulative indebtedness $23,039. **Criteria for awarding institutional aid:** *Non-need-based:* academics, athletics, state/district residency.

STATE UNIVERSITY OF NEW YORK—
UNIVERSITY AT BUFFALO

12 Capen Hall, Buffalo, NY 14260-1660
Phone: 716-645-6900 • **Financial Aid Phone:** 716-645-2450
E-mail: ub-admissions@buffalo.edu • **CEEB Code:** 2925
Fax: 716-645-6411 • **Website:** www.buffalo.edu • **ACT Code:** 2978

This public school was founded in 1846. It has a 1346-acre campus.

RATINGS
Admissions Selectivity Rating: 87   **Fire Safety Rating:** 61   **Green Rating:** 61

STUDENTS AND FACULTY
Enrollment: 19,101. **Student Body:** 46% female, 54% male, 4% out-of-state, 16% international (110 countries represented). Asian 12%, African American 7%, Caucasian 52%, Hispanic 7%, Native American 0%. **Retention and Graduation:** 87% freshmen return for sophomore year. 40% grads go on to further study within 1 year. **Faculty:** Student/faculty ratio :1. 1170 full-time faculty, 95% hold PhDs, 25% are members of minority groups, 36% are women. 11% of classes are taught by teaching assistants.

ACADEMICS
Degrees: bachelor's, doctoral, master's, post-master's certificate. **Classes:** Most classes have 20–29 students. Most lab/discussion sessions have 20–29 students. **Majors with Highest Enrollment:** business/commerce; engineering; social sciences. **Special Study Options:** Accelerated program, cooperative education program, cross-registration, distance learning, double major, dual enrollment, English as a Second Language (ESL), exchange student program (domestic), honors program, independent study, internships, liberal arts/career combination, student-designed major, study abroad, teacher certification program, Certificate programs, Combined Degree Programs, Early Assurance Program with School of Medicine & Dentistry, Honors College & Learning Communities. **Honors Programs:** There is a University Honors College as well as Honors Programs within the majors. Undergraduate research is an option in a variety of disciplines and often affords the student an opportunity to participate in cutting-edge research activities. See http://honors.buffalo.edu **Combined Degree Programs:** BA/MA, BA/MS, BS/MS, BA/MBA, BS/MBA, BA/MA, BA/MSW, BS/DDS, BA/EDM, BA/MFA. **Disability Services:** Special programs offered to physically disabled students include note-taking services, reader services, tape recorders, tutors. **Career Services:** Alumni network, alumni services, career/job search classes, internships.

FACILITIES
Housing: Coed dorms, special housing for disabled students, special housing for international students, apartments for married students, apartments for single students, theme housing, Honors Housing, Academic Interest Housing. **Freshman Housing.** See http://www.ub-housing.buffalo.edu/special. 90% of campus accessible to physically disabled. **Special Academic Facilities/Equipment:** UB Center for the Arts, Slee Concert Hall, Anthropology Research Museum, Multidisciplinary Center for Earthquake Engineering Research (MCEER), New York State Center of Excellence in Bioinformatics and Life Sciences, Center for Computational Research (CCR), Poetry and Rare Books Collection, Center of Excellence for Document Analysis and Recognition Center, New York State Center for Engineering Design and Industrial Innovation, Pharmacy Museum, The Virtual Site Museum, Electronic Poetry Center, Archeological Survey Center, Anderson Gallery, Alfiero Center and numerous research centers **Computers:** Students can register for classes online. Administrative functions (other than registration) can be performed online.

CAMPUS LIFE
Environment: City. **Activities:** Choral groups, concert band, dance, drama/theater, jazz band, literary magazine, marching band, music ensembles, musical theater, pep band, radio station, student government, student newspaper, student-run film society, symphony orchestra, television station, Campus Ministries, International Student Organization 215 registered organizations, 29 honor societies, 35 religious organizations. 22 fraternities, 17 sororities. **Athletics (Intercollegiate):** *Men:* baseball, basketball, cross-country, football, soccer, swimming, tennis, track/field (outdoor), wrestling. *Women:* basketball, crew/rowing, cross-country, soccer, softball, swimming, tennis, track/field (outdoor), volleyball. **On-Campus Highlights:** Center for the Arts, Alumni Arena and Athletic Stadium, Center for Computational Research, Apartment style student housing, The Commons (on-campus shopping).

ADMISSIONS
Freshman Academic Profile: Average high school GPA 3.3. 28% in top 10% of high school class, 62% in top 25% of high school class, 94% in top 50% of high school class. SAT Math middle 50% range 550-650. SAT Critical Reading middle 50% range 500-600. ACT middle 50% range 23-28. Minimum web-based TOEFL 79. Minimum paper TOEFL 550. **Basis for Candidate Selection:** *Very important factors considered include:* academic GPA, rigor of secondary school record, standardized test scores. *Important factors considered include:* Class rank, recommendation(s), interview. *Other factors considered include:* application essay, character/personal qualities, extracurricular activities, first generation, geographical residence, racial/ethnic status, talent/ability, volunteer work, work experience. **Freshman Admission Requirements:** High school diploma is required and GED is accepted. **Freshman Admission Statistics:** 22,009 applied, 57% admitted, 29% enrolled. **Transfer Admission Requirements:** High school transcript, college transcript(s), essay or personal statement, minimum college GPA of 2.5 required. Lowest grade transferable D. **General Admission Information:** Application Fee $40. Early decision application deadline 11/1. Notification on a rolling basis, beginning on or about 2/1. Nonfall registration accepted. Credit and/or placement offered for CEEB Advanced Placement tests.

COSTS AND FINANCIAL AID
Annual in-state tuition $5,570. Annual out-of-state tuition $16,190. Room and board $11,310. Required fees $2,419. Average book expense $1,034. **Required Forms and Deadlines:** FAFSA. **Notification of Awards:** Applicants will be notified of awards on a rolling basis beginning 2/1. **Types of Aid:** *Need-based scholarships/grants:* Federal Pell, SEOG, state scholarships/grants, private scholarships, the school's own gift aid, Federal Nursing Scholarships. *Loans:* Direct Subsidized Stafford, Direct Unsubsidized Stafford, Direct PLUS, Federal Perkins, Federal Nursing, college/university loans from institutional funds. **Student Employment:** Federal Work-Study Program available. Institutional employment available. Off-campus job opportunities are good. **Financial Aid Statistics:** 98% freshmen, 64% undergrads receive need based scholarship or grant aid. 23% freshmen, 31% undergrads receive non-need-based scholarship or grant aid. 97% freshmen, 82% undergrads receive need-based self-help aid. 1% freshmen, 1% undergrads receive athletic scholarships. 45% undergrads borrow to pay for school. Average cumulative indebtedness $16,025. **Criteria for awarding institutional aid:** *Non-need-based:* academics, athletics, minority status, music/drama, state/district residency.

STATE UNIVERSITY OF NEW YORK—
UPSTATE MEDICAL UNIVERSITY

766 Irving Avenue, Syracuse, NY 13210
Phone: 315-464-4570 • **Financial Aid Phone:** 315-464-4329
E-mail: admiss@upstate.edu • **CEEB Code:** 2547
Fax: 315-464-8867 • **Website:** • **ACT Code:** 2981

This public school was founded in 1850. It has a 25-acre campus.

RATINGS
Admissions Selectivity Rating: 61   **Fire Safety Rating:** 72   **Green Rating:** 61

STUDENTS AND FACULTY
Enrollment: 328. **Student Body:** 75% female, 25% male, 9% out-of-state. **Faculty:** 43 full-time faculty, 60% hold PhDs, 2% are members of minority groups, 70% are women. 0% of classes are taught by teaching assistants.

ACADEMICS
Degrees: bachelor's, first professional, master's, post-master's certificate. **Classes:** Most classes have fewer than 10 students. **Majors with Highest Enrollment:** medicine (md). **Disability Services:** Special programs offered to physically disabled students include note-taking services, reader services, tape recorders, tutors. **Career Services:** Alumni network, regional alumni..

FACILITIES
Housing: Coed dorms, apartments for married students, apartments for single students. 100% of campus accessible to physically disabled. **Special Academic Facilities/Equipment:** 350 bed Tertiary Care Hospital **Computers:** Administrative functions (other than registration) can be performed online.

CAMPUS LIFE
Environment: City. **Activities:** student government, International Student Organization 51 registered organizations, 3 religious organizations. **On-Campus Highlights:** Weiskotten Hall, Silverman Hall, University Hospital, Institute for Human Performance, Campus Activities Building.

ADMISSIONS

Freshman Academic Profile: Minimum paper TOEFL 550. **Freshman Admission Requirements:** High school diploma is required and GED is accepted. **Transfer Admission Requirements:** High school transcript, college transcript(s), essay or personal statement, interview, minimum college GPA of 2.0 required. Lowest grade transferable C–. **General Admission Information:** Application Fee $40. Nonfall registration not accepted. Admission may be deferred for a maximum of 1 Year.

COSTS AND FINANCIAL AID

Annual in-state tuition $4,970. Annual out-of-state tuition $13,380. Room and board $10,422. Required fees $575. Average book expense $1,070. **Required Forms and Deadlines:** FAFSA. **Notification of Awards:** Applicants will be notified of awards on a rolling basis beginning 6/1. **Types of Aid:** *Need-based scholarships/grants:* Federal Pell, SEOG, state scholarships/grants, the school's own gift aid. *Loans:* Subsidized Stafford, Unsubsidized Stafford, PLUS, Federal Perkins. **Student Employment:** Federal Work-Study Program available. Institutional employment available. Off-campus job opportunities are excellent. **Financial Aid Statistics:** 18% undergrads receive need-based scholarship or grant aid. 27% undergrads receive non-need-based scholarship or grant aid. 13% undergrads receive need-based self-help aid. 78% freshmen receive any aid.

STEPHEN F. AUSTIN STATE UNIVERSITY

P. O. Box 13051, Nacogdoches, TX 75962
Phone: 936-468-2504 • **Financial Aid Phone:** 936-468-2403
E-mail: admissions@sfasu.edu • **CEEB Code:** 6682
Fax: 936-468-3849 • **Website:** www.sfasu.edu • **ACT Code:** 4188

This public school was founded in 1923. It has a 401-acre campus.

RATINGS

Admissions Selectivity Rating: 71   **Fire Safety Rating:** 65   **Green Rating:** 60*

STUDENTS AND FACULTY

Enrollment: 9,568. **Student Body:** 59% female, 41% male, 2% out-of-state, 1% international (42 countries represented). Asian 1%, African American 16%, Caucasian 74%, Hispanic 7%, Native American 1%.
Retention and Graduation: 66% freshmen return for sophomore year. 17% freshmen graduate within 4 years. 35% freshmen graduate within 6 years. **Faculty:** Student/faculty ratio 18:1. 434 full-time faculty, 76% hold PhDs, 7% are members of minority groups, 41% are women. % of classes are taught by teaching assistants.

ACADEMICS

Degrees: bachelor's, master's. **Classes:** Most classes have 20–29 students. Most lab/discussion sessions have 10–19 students. **Majors with Highest Enrollment:** health and physical education; multi-/interdisciplinary studies, other; nursing/registered nurse (rn, asn, bsn, msn). **Special Study Options:** Accelerated program, distance learning, double major, dual enrollment, honors program, independent study, internships, liberal arts/career combination, student-designed major, study abroad, teacher certification program. **Honors Programs:** www.sfasu.edu/honors/ **Combined Degree Programs:** BBA(Accounting)/MPAC(Professional Accountancy). **Disability Services:** Special programs offered to physically disabled students include note-taking services, reader services, tape recorders, tutors.

FACILITIES

Housing: Coed dorms, special housing for disabled students, men's dorms, women's dorms, fraternity/sorority housing, apartments for married students, apartments for single students, Apartments for students with dependent children. 99% of campus accessible to physically disabled. **Special Academic Facilities/Equipment:** Stone Fort Museum, Planetarium, Arboretum, Observatory, GIS Lab, Forest Resources Institute, Soils Analysis Lab, East Texas Historical Assoc., East Texas Research Center, Science Research Center, Research Feed Mill. **Computers:** Students can register for classes online. Administrative functions (other than registration) can be performed online.

CAMPUS LIFE

Environment: Town. **Activities:** Choral groups, concert band, dance, drama/theater, jazz band, literary magazine, marching band, music ensembles, musical theater, opera, pep band, radio station, student government, student newspaper, student-run film society, symphony orchestra, television station, yearbook 21 registered organizations, 15 honor societies, 25 religious organizations. 25 fraternities, 14 sororities. **Athletics (Intercollegiate):** *Men:* basketball, cross-country, football, golf, track/field (outdoor), track/field (indoor). *Women:* bas-

ketball, cross-country, soccer, softball, tennis, track/field (outdoor), track/field (indoor), volleyball. **On-Campus Highlights:** Stone Fort Museum, University Center, Art Galleries - Art Center, Griffith Gallery, Library, Arboretum.

ADMISSIONS

Freshman Academic Profile: 16% in top 10% of high school class, 44% in top 25% of high school class, 83% in top 50% of high school class. 90% from public high schools. SAT Math middle 50% range 450-550. SAT Critical Reading middle 50% range 450-560. ACT middle 50% range 18-23. Minimum paper TOEFL 550. **Basis for Candidate Selection:** *Very important factors considered include:* Class rank, rigor of secondary school record, standardized test scores.*Other factors considered include:* extracurricular activities, geographical residence, talent/ability, volunteer work, work experience. **Freshman Admission Requirements:** High school diploma is required and GED is accepted. *Academic units required:* 4 English, 3 mathematics, 3 science, 2 foreign language. *Academic units recommended:* 4 English, 3 mathematics, 3 science, 2 foreign language. **Freshman Admission Statistics:** 5,873 applied, 75% admitted, 38% enrolled. **Transfer Admission Requirements:** college transcript(s), minimum college GPA of 2.0 required. Lowest grade transferable D. **General Admission Information:** Application Fee $25. Notification on a rolling basis, beginning on or about 9/1. Nonfall registration accepted. Credit and/or placement offered for CEEB Advanced Placement tests.

COSTS AND FINANCIAL AID

Annual in-state tuition $3,360. Annual out-of-state tuition $11,100. Room and board $5,012. Required fees $938. Average book expense $905. **Required Forms and Deadlines:** FAFSA. **Notification of Awards:** Applicants will be notified of awards on a rolling basis beginning 5/1. **Types of Aid:** *Need-based scholarships/grants:* Federal Pell, SEOG, state scholarships/grants, private scholarships, the school's own gift aid. *Loans:* Subsidized Stafford, Unsubsidized Stafford, PLUS, Federal Perkins, state loans, college/university loans from institutional funds, Alternative loans. **Student Employment:** Highest amount earned per year from on-campus jobs $4,100. **Financial Aid Statistics:** 76% freshmen, 79% undergrads receive need-based scholarship or grant aid. 54% freshmen, 44% undergrads receive non-need-based scholarship or grant aid. 73% freshmen, 82% undergrads receive need-based self-help aid. 3% freshmen, 3% undergrads receive athletic scholarships. 46% freshmen, 47% undergrads receive any aid. 62% undergrads borrow to pay for school. Average cumulative indebtedness $16,624. **Criteria for awarding institutional aid:** *Non-need-based:* academics, alumni affiliation, art, athletics, leadership, music/drama, state/district residency.

STEPHENS COLLEGE

Best 378

1200 East Broadway, Columbia, MO 65215
Phone: 573-876-7207 • **Financial Aid Phone:** 573-876-7106
E-mail: apply@stephens.edu • **CEEB Code:** 6683
Fax: 573-876-7237 • **Website:** www.stephens.edu/ • **ACT Code:** 2374

This private school was founded in 1833. It has a 86-acre campus.

RATINGS

Admissions Selectivity Rating: 74   **Fire Safety Rating:** 75   **Green Rating:** 61

STUDENTS AND FACULTY

Enrollment: 672. **Student Body:** 98% female, 2% male, 47% out-of-state, 0% international (3 countries represented). Asian 1%, African American 15%, Caucasian 73%, Hispanic 2%, Native American 1%.
Retention and Graduation: 74% freshmen return for sophomore year. 52% freshmen graduate within 4 years. 57% freshmen graduate within 6 years. 19% grads go on to further study within 1 year. 14% grads pursue arts and sciences degrees. 57% grads pursue business degrees. **Faculty:** Student/faculty ratio 8:1. 52 full-time faculty, 42% hold PhDs, 2% are members of minority groups, 71% are women. 0% of classes are taught by teaching assistants.

ACADEMICS

Degrees: associate, bachelor's, master's, post-bachelor's certificate. **Classes:** Most classes have 10–19 students. Most lab/discussion sessions have 10–19 students. **Majors with Highest Enrollment:** drama and dramatics/theatre arts; fashion/apparel design; health information/medical records administration/administrator. **Special Study Options:** cross-registration, distance learning, double major, dual enrollment, external degree program, independent study, internships, liberal arts/career combination, student-designed major, study abroad, teacher certification program. **Combined Degree Programs:** BA/JD, BA/MA, Occupational Therapy with Washington University. **Disability Services:** Special programs offered to physically disabled students include note-taking services, tutors. **Career Services:** Alumni network, alumni services, career/job search classes, career assessment, internships, regional alumni. Career Services highlights include Internships.

FACILITIES

Housing: special housing for disabled students, women's dorms, fraternity/sorority housing, apartments for single students, Pet Friendly Residence. 80% of campus accessible to physically disabled. **Special Academic Facilities/Equipment:** Art gallery and historical costume collections, on-campus pre-school, kindergarten, and elementary school, language lab. **Computers:** 100% of classrooms, 100% of dorms, 100% of libraries, 100% of dining areas, 100% of student union, have wireless network access. Students can register for classes online. Administrative functions (other than registration) can be performed online.

CAMPUS LIFE

Environment: City. **Activities:** Choral groups, dance, drama/theater, literary magazine, music ensembles, musical theater, radio station, student government, student newspaper, student-run film society, television station 28 registered organizations, 11 honor societies, 3 religious organizations. 2 sororities. **Athletics (Intercollegiate):** *Women:* basketball, cross-country, softball, swimming, tennis, volleyball. **On-Campus Highlights:** Equestrian Stables, The Commons, Senior Hall, The Quad, Residence Halls. **Environmental Initiatives:** Recycling Decreased energy usage Meeting LEED criteria on building projects and operations.

ADMISSIONS

Freshman Academic Profile: Average high school GPA 3.3. 0% in top 10% of high school class, 8% in top 25% of high school class, 34% in top 50% of high school class. 86% from public high schools. SAT Math middle 50% range 440-540. SAT Critical Reading middle 50% range 480-590. SAT Writing middle 50% range 450-560. ACT middle 50% range 19-26. Minimum paper TOEFL 550. **Basis for Candidate Selection:** *Very important factors considered include:* application essay, rigor of secondary school record, standardized test scores. *Important factors considered include:* academic GPA, recommendation(s), extracurricular activities. *Other factors considered include:* Class rank, character/personal qualities, interview, level of applicant's interest, talent/ability, volunteer work, work experience. **Freshman Admission Requirements:** High school diploma is required and GED is accepted. *Academic units required:* 4 English, 3 mathematics, 2 science, 2 foreign language, 1 social studies. *Academic units recommended:* 4 English, 3 mathematics, 2 science, 2 foreign language, 1 social studies. **Freshman Admission Statistics:** 613 applied, 70% admitted, 33% enrolled. **Transfer Admission Requirements:** High school transcript, college transcript(s), essay or personal statement, minimum college GPA of 2.0 required. Lowest grade transferable C–. **General Admission Information:** Application Fee $25. Notification on a rolling basis, beginning on or about 9/15. Nonfall registration accepted. Admission may be deferred for a maximum of 1 year. Credit offered for CEEB Advanced Placement tests.

COSTS AND FINANCIAL AID

Annual tuition $27,210. Room and board $9,694. Required fees $100. Average book expense $1,750. **Required Forms and Deadlines:** FAFSA. **Notification of Awards:** Applicants will be notified of awards on a rolling basis beginning 3/1. **Types of Aid:** *Need-based scholarships/grants:* Federal Pell, SEOG, state scholarships/grants, private scholarships, the school's own gift aid, Federal ACG Federal SMART Grant. *Loans:* Subsidized Stafford, Unsubsidized Stafford, PLUS, Federal Perkins. **Student Employment:** Federal Work-Study Program available. Institutional employment available. Highest amount earned per year from on-campus jobs $1,600. Off-campus job opportunities are good. **Financial Aid Statistics:** 100% freshmen, 97% undergrads receive need-based scholarship or grant aid. 94% freshmen, 90% undergrads receive non-need-based scholarship or grant aid. 100% freshmen, 100% undergrads receive need-based self-help aid. 11% freshmen, 10% undergrads receive athletic scholarships. 99% freshmen, 95% undergrads receive any aid. 83% undergrads borrow to pay for school. Average cumulative indebtedness $22,293. **Criteria for awarding institutional aid:** *Non-need-based:* academics, alumni affiliation, athletics, leadership, music/drama, state/district residency.

STERLING COLLEGE

125 W. Cooper, Sterling, KS 67579
Phone: 620-278-4275 • **Financial Aid Phone:** 620-278-4207
E-mail: admissions@sterling.edu • **CEEB Code:** 6684
Fax: 620-278-4416 • **Website:** www.sterlingcollege.edu • **ACT Code:** 1466

This private school, affiliated with the Presbyterian Church, was founded in 1887. It has a 42-acre campus.

RATINGS

Admissions Selectivity Rating: 79　　　**Fire Safety Rating:** 64　　　**Green Rating:** 60*

STUDENTS AND FACULTY

Enrollment: 693. **Student Body:** 50% female, 50% male, 49% out-of-state, 1% international (6 countries represented). Asian 2%, African American 8%, Caucasian 79%, Hispanic 7%, Native American 2%.
Retention and Graduation: 62% freshmen return for sophomore year. 35% freshmen graduate within 4 years. 41% freshmen graduate within 6 years. **Faculty:** Student/faculty ratio 13:1. 41 full-time faculty, 46% hold PhDs, 10% are members of minority groups, 27% are women. 0% of classes are taught by teaching assistants.

ACADEMICS

Degrees: bachelor's. **Classes:** Most classes have fewer than 10 students. Most lab/discussion sessions have 20–29 students. **Majors with Highest Enrollment:** business/commerce; elementary education and teaching; health and physical education. **Special Study Options:** distance learning, double major, dual enrollment, external degree program, honors program, independent study, internships, student-designed major, study abroad, teacher certification program. **Honors Programs:** The honors program is still being developed. At this point honors level general education classes are offered in interdisciplinary history and literature. **Disability Services:** Special programs offered to physically disabled students include tutors. **Career Services:** Alumni network, alumni services, career assessment, internships.

FACILITIES

Housing: men's dorms, women's dorms. 80% of campus accessible to physically disabled. **Special Academic Facilities/Equipment:** History/cultural museum. **Computers:** Administrative functions (other than registration) can be performed online.

CAMPUS LIFE

Environment: Rural. **Activities:** Choral groups, concert band, drama/theater, jazz band, literary magazine, music ensembles, musical theater, radio station, student government, student newspaper, television station, yearbook, Campus Ministries 16 registered organizations, 4 honor societies, 2 religious organizations. **Athletics (Intercollegiate):** *Men:* baseball, basketball, cross-country, football, golf, soccer, track/field (outdoor). *Women:* basketball, cheerleading, cross-country, golf, soccer, softball, track/field (outdoor), volleyball. **On-Campus Highlights:** Gleason Phy. Educ. Center, Student Union, Cooper Hall, Evan's Hall, Campbell Hall.

ADMISSIONS

Freshman Academic Profile: Average high school GPA 3.2. 7% in top 10% of high school class, 14% in top 25% of high school class, 54% in top 50% of high school class. 80% from public high schools. SAT Math middle 50% range 420-530. SAT Critical Reading middle 50% range 410-500. SAT Writing middle 50% range 410-490. ACT middle 50% range 19-24. Minimum web-based TOEFL 70. Minimum paper TOEFL 525. **Basis for Candidate Selection:** *Very important factors considered include:* rigor of secondary school record, standardized test scores, character/personal qualities. *Important factors considered include:* application essay, academic GPA, recommendation(s), extracurricular activities, interview, level of applicant's interest, religious affiliation/commitment, volunteer work. *Other factors considered include:* Class rank, alumni/ae relation, first generation, talent/ability, work experience. **Freshman Admission Requirements:** High school diploma is required and GED is accepted. **Freshman Admission Statistics:** 821 applied, 50% admitted, 36% enrolled. **Transfer Admission Requirements:** college transcript(s), essay or personal statement, minimum college GPA of 2.2 required. Lowest grade transferable C–. **General Admission Information:** Application Fee $25. Notification on a rolling basis, beginning on or about 9/15. Nonfall registration accepted. Admission may be deferred for a maximum of 1 semester. Credit offered for CEEB Advanced Placement tests.

COSTS AND FINANCIAL AID

Annual tuition $19,950. Room and board $7,166. Average book expense $700. **Required Forms and Deadlines:** FAFSA. **Notification of Awards:** Applicants will be notified of awards on a rolling basis beginning 1/1. **Types of Aid:** *Need-based scholarships/grants:* Federal Pell, SEOG, state scholarships/grants, private scholarships, the school's own gift aid. *Loans:* Subsidized Stafford, Unsubsidized Stafford, PLUS, Federal Perkins. **Student Employment:** Federal Work-Study Program available. Institutional employment available. Highest amount earned per year from on-campus jobs $1,100. Off-campus job opportunities are fair. **Financial Aid Statistics:** 100% freshmen, 96% undergrads receive any aid. **Criteria for awarding institutional aid:** *Non-need-based:* academics, art, athletics, leadership, music/drama.

See page 1220.

STERLING COLLEGE (VT)

PO Box 72, Craftsbury Common, VT 5827
Phone: 802-586-7711 • **Financial Aid Phone:** 802-586-7711
E-mail: admissions@sterlingcollege.edu • **CEEB Code:** 3752
Fax: 802-586-2596 • **Website:** www.sterlingcollege.edu • **ACT Code:** 6946

This private school was founded in 1958. It has a 430-acre campus.

RATINGS
Admissions Selectivity Rating: 62   **Fire Safety Rating:** 60*   **Green Rating:** 74

STUDENTS AND FACULTY
Enrollment: 98. **Student Body:** 43% female, 57% male, 77% out-of-state, 0% international (1 countries represented). Asian 1%, African American 0%, Caucasian 76%, Hispanic 1%, Native American 0%.
Retention and Graduation: 47% freshmen return for sophomore year. 27% freshmen graduate within 4 years. 38% freshmen graduate within 6 years. 25% grads go on to further study within 1 year. **Faculty:** Student/faculty ratio 5:1. 16 full-time faculty, 25% hold PhDs, 0% are members of minority groups, 50% are women. 0% of classes are taught by teaching assistants.

ACADEMICS
Degrees: bachelor's. **Classes:** Most classes have 10–19 students. **Majors with Highest Enrollment:** agriculture, agriculture operations, and related sciences, other; natural resources conservation and research, other; parks, recreation and leisure studies. **Special Study Options:** double major, dual enrollment, exchange student program (domestic), independent study, internships, student-designed major, study abroad, Global Field Studies to Japan, Scandinavia, Belize, Alaska, Sierra Nevada, Newfoundland, Iceland, James Bay, and more. **Disability Services:** Special programs offered to physically disabled students include tutors. **Career Services:** Alumni network, alumni services, career/job search classes, career assessment, internships Career Services highlights include The Internship is a ten-week experience (working full time) and two courses prior and post to the experience. It is a total of 8 credits and a requirement of all second year students. Past Internship sites have included: 58 federal agencies, including National Forests, National Parks, and National Wildlife Refuges, 18 state agencies, 94 educational organizations including environmental, outdoor adventure, classroom, and interpretative centers,112 agricultural producers, 24 environmental advocacy organizations, 21 wildlife rehabilitation, veterinary medicine, and animal shelter organizations, 30 for-profit green businesses, 36 research institutions, and several national organizations including The Sierra Club, National Audubon Society, PETA, Heifer Project International, The Nature Conservancy, Outward Bound, and NOLS.

FACILITIES
Housing: Coed dorms, wellness housing. **Special Academic Facilities/ Equipment:** Library serves as art gallery. There is a 6 - 8 week rotation of Vermont artist displays. Campus also includes wind and solar-powered barns that serves as an instructional facility and lab, a greenhouse provides a working lab for plant and soil studies. Other facilities include: a woodshop, logging shop, sugarhouse, root cellar, darkroom, certified organic gardens, and a 32' tall climbing wall provides students with the ability to develop leadership and technical rock-climbing skills. The Center for Northern Studies at Sterling College includes a 300 acre boreal forest. **Computers:** 100% of classrooms, 100% of dorms, 100% of libraries, 100% of dining areas, 100% of student union, 100% of common outdoor areas have wireless network access. Administrative functions (other than registration) can be performed online.

CAMPUS LIFE
Environment: Rural. **Activities:** Choral groups, dance, drama/theater, music ensembles, student government, student-run film society, yearbook. **On-Campus Highlights:** Challenge Course and Climbing Wall, Organic Gardens and Livestock Farm, Dining Hall serves local, organic food, 300-acre Boreal Forest, Wind and Solar Powered Barns, Student Lounge, Dancing Goat Cafe, Recreation Room, Lean-tos, XC ski trails, nature trails, Computer labs, common areas in dorms, front porch.

ADMISSIONS
Freshman Academic Profile: Average high school GPA 3.0. 11% in top 10% of high school class, 21% in top 25% of high school class, 79% in top 50% of high school class. 70% from public high schools. Minimum web-based TOEFL 61. Minimum paper TOEFL 500. **Basis for Candidate Selection:** *Very important factors considered include:* academic GPA, recommendation(s), rigor of secondary school record, level of applicant's interest. *Important factors considered include:* Class rank, application essay, character/personal qualities, extracurricular activities, interview, talent/ability, volunteer work. *Other factors considered include:* standardized test scores, alumni/ae relation, geographical residence, work experience. **Freshman Admission Requirements:** High school diploma is required and GED is accepted. *Academic units required:* 4 English, 3 mathematics, 2 science, (2 science labs), 2 social studies, 2 history. *Academic units recommended:* 4 English, 3 mathematics, 2 science, (2 science labs), 2 social studies, 2 history. **Freshman Admission Statistics:** 104 applied, 78% admitted, 33% enrolled. **Transfer Admission Requirements:** High school transcript, college transcript(s), essay or personal statement, minimum college GPA of 2.0 required. Lowest grade transferable C. **General Admission Information:** Application Fee $35. Regular application deadline 2/15. Regular notification 4/1. Nonfall registration accepted. Admission may be deferred for a maximum of One year. Credit and/or placement offered for CEEB Advanced Placement tests.

COSTS AND FINANCIAL AID
Annual tuition $23,196. Room and board $7,554. Required fees $400. Average book expense $900. **Required Forms and Deadlines:** FAFSA, institution's own financial aid form, state aid form. **Notification of Awards:** Applicants will be notified of awards on a rolling basis beginning 2/1. **Types of Aid:** *Need-based scholarships/grants:* Federal Pell, SEOG, state scholarships/grants, private scholarships, the school's own gift aid. *Loans:* Subsidized Stafford, Unsubsidized Stafford, PLUS. **Student Employment:** Federal Work-Study Program available. Institutional employment available. Highest amount earned per year from on-campus jobs $1,500. Off-campus job opportunities are fair. **Financial Aid Statistics:** 100% freshmen, 100% undergrads receive need-based scholarship or grant aid. 22% undergrads receive non-need-based scholarship or grant aid. 100% freshmen, 100% undergrads receive need-based self-help aid. 71% freshmen, 74% undergrads receive any aid. 40% undergrads borrow to pay for school. Average cumulative indebtedness $15,880. **Criteria for awarding institutional aid:** *Non-need-based:* academics, leadership, state/district residency.

STETSON UNIVERSITY

421 N. Woodland Blvd, DeLand, FL 32723
Phone: 386-822-7100 • **Financial Aid Phone:** 800-688-7120
E-mail: admissions@stetson.edu • **CEEB Code:** 5630
Fax: 386-822-7112 • **ACT Code:** 756

This private school was founded in 1883. It has a 175-acre campus.

RATINGS
Admissions Selectivity Rating: 86   **Fire Safety Rating:** 71   **Green Rating:** 87

STUDENTS AND FACULTY
Enrollment: 2,508. **Student Body:** 56% female, 44% male, 22% out-of-state, 4% international (40 countries represented). Asian 2%, African American 7%, Caucasian 67%, Hispanic 15%, Native American 0%.
Retention and Graduation: 79% freshmen return for sophomore year. 56% freshmen graduate within 4 years. 64% freshmen graduate within 6 years. 33% grads go on to further study within 1 year. 14% grads pursue arts and sciences degrees. 5% grads pursue law degrees. 7% grads pursue business degrees. 6% grads pursue medical degrees. **Faculty:** Student/faculty ratio 12:1. 243 full-time faculty, 95% hold PhDs, 10% are members of minority groups, 41% are women. 0% of classes are taught by teaching assistants.

ACADEMICS
Degrees: bachelor's, master's. **Classes:** Most classes have 10–19 students. Most lab/discussion sessions have 10–19 students. **Majors with Highest Enrollment:** business administration and management; elementary education and teaching; psychology. **Special Study Options:** Accelerated program, double major, honors program, independent study, internships, liberal arts/career combination, student-designed major, study abroad, teacher certification program, weekend college. **Combined Degree Programs:** BA/JD, Cooperative Program in Forestry and Environ. Studies. **Disability Services:** Special programs offered to physically disabled students include note-taking services, reader services, tape recorders, tutors. **Career Services:** Alumni network, alumni services, career/job search classes, career assessment, internships, regional alumni.

FACILITIES

Housing: Coed dorms, men's dorms, women's dorms, fraternity/sorority housing, apartments for single students, wellness housing, theme housing, "Pet" Dorm (pets allowed), Foreign Language House, French House, The Service Station (community service house). **Special Academic Facilities/Equipment:** Language lab, art gallery, greenhouse with growth chambers, mineral museum, electron microscopes. **Computers:** 90% of classrooms, 100% of dorms, 100% of libraries, 95% of dining areas, 100% of student union, 30% of common outdoor areas have wireless network access. Students can register for classes online. Administrative functions (other than registration) can be performed online.

CAMPUS LIFE

Environment: Town. **Activities:** Choral groups, concert band, dance, drama/theater, jazz band, literary magazine, music ensembles, musical theater, opera, pep band, radio station, student government, student newspaper, student-run film society, symphony orchestra, Campus Ministries, International Student Organization, Model UN 125 registered organizations, 24 honor societies, 8 religious organizations. 6 fraternities, 5 sororities. **Athletics (Intercollegiate):** *Men:* baseball, basketball, crew/rowing, cross-country, golf, soccer, tennis. *Women:* basketball, crew/rowing, cross-country, golf, soccer, softball, tennis, volleyball. **On-Campus Highlights:** Lynn Business Center, DuPont-Ball Library, Homer and Dolly Hand Art Center, Hollis Center, Sage Hall. **Environmental Initiatives:** The Stetson College of Law is home to the Institute for Biodiversity Law and Policy. The Institute serves as an interdisciplinary focal point for education, research and service activities related to biodiversity issues, and is committed to environmental education and service from the local to the global scale. Each semester, the Institute sponsors several biodiversity lectures. Stetson has recycled more than 1 million lbs. of paper and 42,000 lbs. of plastic. In the 2008-2009 year alone, 106 tons of paper, 7,790 pounds of plastic and 1,060 pounds of aluminum were recycled at the DeLand campus. Other items that are recycled include metals when possible, concrete and construction materials. Stetson University uses LEED system as design criteria for all new projects. Stetson's Eugene M. and Christine Lynn Business Center was the first LEED-certified building in the state of Florida (2003).

ADMISSIONS

Freshman Academic Profile: Average high school GPA 3.8. 51% in top 10% of high school class, 18% in top 25% of high school class, 89% in top 50% of high school class. 76% from public high schools. SAT Math middle 50% range 525-630. SAT Critical Reading middle 50% range 530-630. SAT Writing middle 50% range 510-610. ACT middle 50% range 23-28. Minimum web-based TOEFL 79. Minimum paper TOEFL 550. **Basis for Candidate Selection:** *Very important factors considered include:* academic GPA, rigor of secondary school record. *Important factors considered include:* Class rank, application essay, recommendation(s), standardized test scores, character/personal qualities, extracurricular activities, interview, talent/ability, volunteer work, work experience. *Other factors considered include:* alumni/ae relation, geographical residence, racial/ethnic status, state residency. **Freshman Admission Requirements:** High school diploma is required and GED is accepted. *Academic units required:* 4 English, 3 mathematics, 3 science, 2 foreign language, 2 social studies. 4 English, 3 mathematics, 3 science, 2 foreign language, 2 social studies. **Freshman Admission Statistics:** 4,862 applied, 60% admitted, 28% enrolled. **Transfer Admission Requirements:** High school transcript, college transcript(s), essay or personal statement, standardized test scores, statement of good standing from prior institution(s). Minimum college GPA of 2.0 required. Lowest grade transferable C. **General Admission Information:** Application Fee $40. Early decision application deadline 11/1. Notification on a rolling basis, beginning on or about 12/1. Nonfall registration accepted. Admission may be deferred for a maximum of 1. Credit and/or placement offered for CEEB Advanced Placement tests.

COSTS AND FINANCIAL AID

Annual tuition $36,344. Room and board $10,688. Required fees $300. Average book expense $1,200. **Required Forms and Deadlines:** FAFSA, institution's own financial aid form. **Notification of Awards:** Applicants will be notified of awards on a rolling basis beginning 2/15. **Types of Aid:** *Need-based scholarships/grants:* Federal Pell, SEOG, state scholarships/grants, private scholarships, the school's own gift aid. *Loans:* Subsidized Stafford, Unsubsidized Stafford, PLUS, Federal Perkins. **Student Employment:** Federal Work-Study Program available. Institutional employment available. Highest amount earned per year from on-campus jobs $4,000. Off-campus job opportunities are good. **Financial Aid Statistics:** 100% freshmen, 100% undergrads receive need-based scholarship or grant aid. 23% freshmen, 18% undergrads receive non-need-based scholarship or grant aid. 74% freshmen, 79% undergrads receive need-based self-help aid. 4% freshmen, 3% undergrads receive athletic scholarships. 99% freshmen, 97% undergrads receive any aid. 77% undergrads borrow to pay for school. Average cumulative indebtedness $32,750. **Criteria for awarding institutional aid:** *Non-need-based:* academics, alumni affiliation, art, athletics, leadership, minority status, music/drama, religious affiliation, state/district residency.

STEVENS INSTITUTE OF TECHNOLOGY

Castle Point on Hudson, Hoboken, NJ 7030
Phone: 201-216-5194 • **Financial Aid Phone:** 201-216-5555
E-mail: admissions@stevens.edu • **CEEB Code:** 2819
Fax: 201-216-8348 • **Website:** www.stevens.edu • **ACT Code:** 2610

This private school was founded in 1870. It has a 55-acre campus.

RATINGS

Admissions Selectivity Rating: 94   **Fire Safety Rating:** 96   **Green Rating:** 63

STUDENTS AND FACULTY

Enrollment: 2,369. **Student Body:** 27% female, 73% male, 40% out-of-state, 4% international (40 countries represented). Asian 9%, African American 2%, Caucasian 42%, Hispanic 7%, Native American 0%.
Retention and Graduation: 90% freshmen return for sophomore year. 30% freshmen graduate within 4 years. 75% freshmen graduate within 6 years. 24% grads go on to further study within 1 year. 5% grads pursue arts and sciences degrees. 2% grads pursue law degrees. 1% grads pursue business degrees. 4% grads pursue medical degrees. **Faculty:** Student/faculty ratio 7:1. 226 full-time faculty, 25% are members of minority groups, 20% are women. 0% of classes are taught by teaching assistants.

ACADEMICS

Degrees: bachelor's, doctoral, master's, post-bachelor's certificate. **Majors with Highest Enrollment:** business administration and management; computer/information technology services administration and management, other; mechanical engineering. **Special Study Options:** Accelerated program, cooperative education program, cross-registration, distance learning, double major, dual enrollment, honors program, independent study, internships, study abroad, Dual enrollment program with NYU. **Honors Programs:** The Scholars Program allows high-achieving students to participate in research over the summer or take up to four tuition-free courses each summer. Scholars students may also complete their Bachelor's in three years or a combined bachelor's and Master's in four years at no extra cost. **Combined Degree Programs:** BA/MD, BA/JD, BA/DDS, BS/MS; BS/DMD; BS/JD; BS/MD. **Disability Services:** Special programs offered to physically disabled students include note-taking services, tutors. **Career Services:** Alumni network, alumni services, career/job search classes, career assessment, internships, regional alumni. Career Services highlights include Our educational philosophy encourages experience with real-world practitioners in business, science and engineering, therefore, 100% of Stevens students participate in coop, research or internships; 40% of students participate in coop.

FACILITIES

Housing: Coed dorms, women's dorms, fraternity/sorority housing, apartments for married students, apartments for single students. Freshmen not living at home must live on campus. 100% of campus accessible to physically disabled. **Special Academic Facilities/Equipment:** Art museum, electron microscope, ocean engineering lab, HDTV research facility, advanced telecommunications institute, environmental lab, design/manufacturing institute, wind tunnel, robotics lab, product management center, polymer processing institute. DeBaun Theater, a multi-media facility, wireless campus network **Computers:** 95% of classrooms, 100% of dorms, 100% of libraries, 100% of dining areas, 100% of student union, 99% of common outdoor areas have wireless network access. Students can register for classes online. Administrative functions (other than registration) can be performed online. Undergraduates are required to own a computer.

CAMPUS LIFE

Environment: Town. **Activities:** Choral groups, concert band, dance, drama/theater, jazz band, literary magazine, music ensembles, musical theater, pep band, radio station, student government, student newspaper, student-run film society, symphony orchestra, television station, yearbook, Campus Ministries, International Student Organization 120 registered organizations, 12 honor societies, 6 religious organizations. 10 fraternities, 3 sororities. **Athletics (Intercollegiate):** *Men:* baseball, basketball, cross-country, fencing, lacrosse, soccer, swimming, tennis, track/field (outdoor), track/field (indoor), volleyball, wrestling. *Women:* basketball, cross-country, equestrian sports, fencing, field hockey, lacrosse, soccer, swimming, tennis, track/field (outdoor), track/field (indoor), volleyball. **On-Campus Highlights:** Schaefer Athletic Center, DeBaun Auditorium, Castle Point, overlooking Manhattan, Babbio Center, Wesley J. Howe Center. **Environmental Initiatives:** Green minor Green Book Award.

ADMISSIONS

Freshman Academic Profile: Average high school GPA 3.8. 58% in top 10% of high school class, 88% in top 25% of high school class, 98% in top 50% of high school class. 72% from public high schools. SAT Math middle 50% range 620-700. SAT Critical Reading middle 50% range 560-640. SAT Writing middle 50% range 550-650. ACT middle 50% range 25-30. Minimum web-based TOEFL 82. Minimum paper TOEFL 550. **Basis for Candidate Selection:** *Very important factors considered include:* application essay, academic GPA, recommendation(s), rigor of secondary school record, standardized test scores, character/personal qualities, extracurricular activities, interview, volunteer work, work experience. *Important factors considered include:* Class rank, talent/ability. *Other factors considered include:* alumni/ae relation. **Freshman Admission Requirements:** High school diploma is required and GED is not accepted. *Academic units required:* 4 English, 4 mathematics, 3 science, (3 science labs). *Academic units recommended:* 4 English, 4 mathematics, 3 science, (3 science labs). **Freshman Admission Statistics:** 3,239 applied, 47% admitted, 36% enrolled. **Transfer Admission Requirements:** High school transcript, college transcript(s), essay or personal statement, interview, minimum college GPA of 3.0 required. Lowest grade transferable C. **General Admission Information:** Application Fee $55. Early decision application deadline 11/15. Regular application deadline 2/1. Regular notification 3/15. Nonfall registration accepted. Admission may be deferred for a maximum of 1 year. Credit and/or placement offered for CEEB Advanced Placement tests.

COSTS AND FINANCIAL AID

Required Forms and Deadlines: FAFSA. **Notification of Awards:** Applicants will be notified of awards on a rolling basis beginning 3/30. **Types of Aid:** *Need-based scholarships/grants:* Federal Pell, SEOG, state scholarships/grants, private scholarships, the school's own gift aid. *Loans:* Direct Subsidized Stafford, Direct Unsubsidized Stafford, Direct PLUS, Subsidized Stafford, Federal Perkins, state loans, Signature Loans, TERI Loans, NJ CLASS, CitiAssist. **Student Employment:** Federal Work-Study Program available. Institutional employment available. Highest amount earned per year from on-campus jobs $1,300. Off-campus job opportunities are excellent. **Financial Aid Statistics:** 83% freshmen, 67% undergrads receive need-based scholarship or grant aid. 79% freshmen, 79% undergrads receive non-need-based scholarship or grant aid. 83% freshmen, 81% undergrads receive need-based self-help aid. 82% freshmen, 75% undergrads receive any aid. 66% undergrads borrow to pay for school. Average cumulative indebtedness $35,319. **Criteria for awarding institutional aid:** *Non-need-based:* academics, leadership, minority status, music/drama.

See page 1222.

STEVENSON UNIVERSITY

1525 Greenspring Valley Road, Stevenson, MD 21153-0641
Phone: 410-486-7001 • **Financial Aid Phone:** 443-352-4369
E-mail: admissions@stevenson.edu
Fax: 443-352-4440 • **Website:** www.stevenson.edu

This private school was founded in 1947. It has a 150-acre campus.

RATINGS

Admissions Selectivity Rating: 78 ·   **Fire Safety Rating:** 70   **Green Rating:** 60*

STUDENTS AND FACULTY

Enrollment: 3,855. **Student Body:** 65% female, 35% male, 15% out-of-state, 0% international (7 countries represented). Asian 3%, African American 27%, Caucasian 59%, Hispanic 4%, Native American 0%. **Retention and Graduation:** 49% freshmen graduate within 4 years. 64% freshmen graduate within 6 years. 17% grads go on to further study within 1 year. **Faculty:** Student/faculty ratio 15:1. 121 full-time faculty, 71% hold PhDs, 14% are members of minority groups, 55% are women. 0% of classes are taught by teaching assistants.

ACADEMICS

Degrees: bachelor's, master's. **Classes:** Most classes have 10–19 students. **Majors with Highest Enrollment:** business administration and management; legal assistant/paralegal; nursing/registered nurse (rn, asn, bsn, msn). **Special Study Options:** Accelerated program, cooperative education program, cross-registration, distance learning, double major, dual enrollment, honors program, independent study, internships, liberal arts/career combination, student-designed major, study abroad, teacher certification program. **Honors Programs:** Consistent with its mission, the Stevenson University Honors Program seeks to admit academically outstanding students who are interested in challenging themselves through a unique and stimulating curriculum that extends beyond traditional academic boundaries. **Disability Services:** Special programs offered to physically disabled students include note-taking services, reader services, tape recorders, tutors. **Career Services:** Alumni network, alumni services, career assessment, internships.

FACILITIES

Housing: apartments for single students, suite style (2 bedrooms share 1 bath); accommodations made for students with disabilities. 100% of campus accessible to physically disabled. **Special Academic Facilities/Equipment:** Art gallery and theatre. **Computers:** Students can register for classes online. Administrative functions (other than registration) can be performed online.

CAMPUS LIFE

Environment: Village. **Activities:** Choral groups, dance, drama/theater, jazz band, literary magazine, music ensembles, pep band, student government, student newspaper, symphony orchestra, Campus Ministries, International Student Organization 40 registered organizations, 10 honor societies, 4 religious organizations. 2 sororities. **Athletics (Intercollegiate):** *Men:* baseball, basketball, cheerleading, cross-country, golf, lacrosse, soccer, tennis, track/field (indoor), volleyball. *Women:* basketball, cheerleading, cross-country, field hockey, lacrosse, soccer, softball, tennis, track/field (indoor), volleyball. **On-Campus Highlights:** Rockland Center (Dining Hall/Student Ce), Avalon Community Center, The Wellness Center/Caves, Garrison Hall, Theater.

ADMISSIONS

Freshman Academic Profile: Average high school GPA 3.4. 22% in top 10% of high school class, 47% in top 25% of high school class, 82% in top 50% of high school class. 70% from public high schools. SAT Math middle 50% range 440-550. SAT Critical Reading middle 50% range 440-540. SAT Writing middle 50% range 440-540. ACT middle 50% range 18-24. Minimum paper TOEFL 550. **Basis for Candidate Selection:** *Very important factors considered include:* academic GPA, rigor of secondary school record. *Important factors considered include:* application essay, standardized test scores, extracurricular activities, talent/ability. *Other factors considered include:* Class rank, recommendation(s), alumni/ae relation, character/personal qualities, geographical residence, interview, level of applicant's interest, volunteer work, work experience. **Freshman Admission Requirements:** High school diploma is required and GED is accepted. *Academic units required:* 4 English, 3 mathematics, 3 science, (2 science labs), 2 social studies, 1 history, 4 academic electives. *Academic units recommended:* 4 English, 3 mathematics, 3 science, (2 science labs), 2 social studies, 1 history, 4 academic electives. **Freshman Admission Statistics:** 5,735 applied, 59% admitted, 26% enrolled. **Transfer Admission Requirements:** college transcript(s), statement of good standing from prior institution(s). Minimum college GPA of 2.5 required. Lowest grade transferable C. **General Admission Information:** Application Fee $40. Notification on a rolling basis, beginning on or about 12/1. Nonfall registration accepted. Admission may be deferred for a maximum of 1 year. Credit and/or placement offered for CEEB Advanced Placement tests.

COSTS AND FINANCIAL AID

Annual tuition $23,562. Room and board $11,894. Required fees $1,748. Average book expense $1,250. **Required Forms and Deadlines:** FAFSA. **Notification of Awards:** Applicants will be notified of awards on a rolling basis beginning 3/15. **Types of Aid:** *Need-based scholarships/grants:* Federal Pell, SEOG, state scholarships/grants, private scholarships, the school's own gift aid. *Loans:* Direct Subsidized Stafford, Direct Unsubsidized Stafford, Direct PLUS, Federal Perkins. **Student Employment:** Federal Work-Study Program available. Institutional employment available. Off-campus job opportunities are excellent. **Financial Aid Statistics:** 99% freshmen, 96% undergrads receive need-based scholarship or grant aid. 9% freshmen, 8% undergrads receive non-need-based scholarship or grant aid. 79% freshmen, 79% undergrads receive need-based self-help aid. % freshmen, % undergrads receive athletic scholarships. 69% undergrads borrow to pay for school. Average cumulative indebtedness $28,032. **Criteria for awarding institutional aid:** *Non-need-based:* academics, art, leadership, music/drama.

STONEHILL COLLEGE

Best 378

320 Washington Street, Easton, MA 02357-5610
Phone: 508-565-1373 • **Financial Aid Phone:** 508-565-1088
E-mail: admissions@stonehill.edu • **CEEB Code:** 3770
Fax: 508-565-1545 • **Website:** www.stonehill.edu • **ACT Code:** 1918

This private school, affiliated with the Roman Catholic Church, was founded in 1948. It has a 375-acre campus.

RATINGS
Admissions Selectivity Rating: 80   **Fire Safety Rating:** 90   **Green Rating:** 84

STUDENTS AND FACULTY
Enrollment: 2,599. **Student Body:** 61% female, 39% male, 55% out-of-state, 1% international. Asian 2%, African American 3%, Caucasian 86%, Hispanic 4%, Native American 0%. **Retention and Graduation:** 86% freshmen return for sophomore year. 79% freshmen graduate within 4 years. 18% grads go on to further study within 1 year. 6% grads pursue arts and sciences degrees. 1% grads pursue law degrees. 1% grads pursue business degrees. 1% grads pursue medical degrees. **Faculty:** Student/faculty ratio 13:1. 168 full-time faculty, 86% hold PhDs, 10% are members of minority groups, 42% are women. 0% of classes are taught by teaching assistants.

ACADEMICS
Degrees: bachelor's. **Classes:** Most classes have 20–29 students. Most lab/discussion sessions have 10–19 students. **Majors with Highest Enrollment:** biology/biological sciences; English language and literature; psychology. **Special Study Options:** cross-registration, double major, dual enrollment, honors program, independent study, internships, liberal arts/career combination, student-designed major, study abroad, teacher certification program. **Honors Programs:** The Honors Program, which requires 5 honors courses and a Senior Honors Experience. **Disability Services:** Special programs offered to physically disabled students include note-taking services, reader services, tape recorders, tutors. **Career Services:** Alumni network, alumni services, career/job search classes, career assessment, internships Career Services highlights include We are very proud of the fact that 79% of our senior class has completed some type of internship-related experience.

FACILITIES
Housing: Coed dorms, special housing for disabled students, women's dorms, wellness housing, Special interest housing. 80% of campus accessible to physically disabled. **Special Academic Facilities/Equipment:** Institute for law and society, observatory, Stonehill Industrial History Center, shovel museum **Computers:** 30% of classrooms, 80% of dorms, 100% of libraries, 100% of dining areas, 50% of student union, 20% of common outdoor areas have wireless network access. Students can register for classes online. Administrative functions (other than registration) can be performed online.

CAMPUS LIFE
Environment: Village. **Activities:** Choral groups, dance, drama/theater, literary magazine, music ensembles, musical theater, pep band, radio station, student government, student newspaper, student-run film society, yearbook, Campus Ministries 76 registered organizations, 19 honor societies, 3 religious organizations. **Athletics (Intercollegiate):** *Men:* baseball, basketball, cross-country, football, ice hockey, soccer, tennis, track/field (outdoor), track/field (indoor). *Women:* basketball, cross-country, equestrian sports, field hockey, lacrosse, soccer, softball, tennis, track/field (outdoor), track/field (indoor), volleyball. **On-Campus Highlights:** The Hill (entertainment/dining social space), The MacPhaidin Library, The Roche Dining Commons, The Residence Courts (housing/social space), The Sally Blair Ames Sports Complex. **Environmental Initiatives:** Joined AASHE (Association for the Advancement of Sustainability in HIgher Education) and will participated in the STARS survey. Zip Cars - the College has two zip cars to provide a community car sharing program. "Thinking Outside the Bottle" proposal was implemented. The College has eliminated the majority of bottled water.

ADMISSIONS
Freshman Academic Profile: Average high school GPA 3.3. 35% in top 10% of high school class, 65% in top 25% of high school class, 90% in top 50% of high school class. 65% from public high schools. SAT Math middle 50% range 530-630. SAT Critical Reading middle 50% range 520-620. SAT Writing middle 50% range 530-630. ACT middle 50% range 24-27. Minimum web-based TOEFL 79. Minimum paper TOEFL 550. **Basis for Candidate Selection:**

Very important factors considered include: Class rank, academic GPA, rigor of secondary school record, character/personal qualities, talent/ability. *Important factors considered include:* application essay, recommendation(s), extracurricular activities, level of applicant's interest, volunteer work, work experience. *Other factors considered include:* standardized test scores, alumni/ae relation, first generation, geographical residence, interview, racial/ethnic status, religious affiliation/commitment. **Freshman Admission Requirements:** High school diploma is required and GED is accepted. *Academic units required:* 4 English, 3 mathematics, 1 science, (1 science labs), 2 foreign language, 3 history, 3 academic electives. *Academic units recommended:* 4 English, 3 mathematics, 1 science, (1 science labs), 2 foreign language, 3 history, 3 academic electives. **Freshman Admission Statistics:** 6,117 applied, 80% admitted, 17% enrolled. **Transfer Admission Requirements:** High school transcript, college transcript(s), essay or personal statement, statement of good standing from prior institution(s). Minimum college GPA of 2.0 required. Lowest grade transferable C. **General Admission Information:** Application Fee $60. Early decision application deadline 11/1. Regular application deadline 1/15. Regular notification 3/15. Nonfall registration accepted. Admission may be deferred for a maximum of 1 year. Credit and/or placement offered for CEEB Advanced Placement tests.

COSTS AND FINANCIAL AID
Annual tuition $35,110. Room and board $13,310. Average book expense $893. **Required Forms and Deadlines:** FAFSA, CSS/Financial Aid PROFILE, noncustodial PROFILE, business/farm supplement. **Notification of Awards:** Applicants will be notified of awards on or about 4/1. **Types of Aid:** *Need-based scholarships/grants:* Federal Pell, SEOG, state scholarships/grants, private scholarships, the school's own gift aid. *Loans:* Direct Subsidized Stafford, Direct Unsubsidized Stafford, Direct PLUS, Federal Perkins, state loans. **Student Employment:** Federal Work-Study Program available. Institutional employment available. Highest amount earned per year from on-campus jobs $2,505. Off-campus job opportunities are good. **Financial Aid Statistics:** 82% freshmen, 82% undergrads receive need based scholarship or grant aid. 18% freshmen, 17% undergrads receive non-need-based scholarship or grant aid. 62% freshmen, 64% undergrads receive need-based self-help aid. 3% freshmen, 3% undergrads receive athletic scholarships. 93% freshmen, 93% undergrads receive any aid. 73% undergrads borrow to pay for school. Average cumulative indebtedness $27,794. **Criteria for awarding institutional aid:** *Non-need-based:* academics, athletics, job skills, leadership, minority status, music/drama.

SUFFOLK UNIVERSITY

Best 378

8 Ashburton Place, Boston, MA 2108
Phone: 617-573-8460 • **Financial Aid Phone:** 617-573-8470
E-mail: admission@suffolk.edu • **CEEB Code:** 3771
Fax: 617-573-1574 • **Website:** www.suffolk.edu • **ACT Code:** 1920

This private school was founded in 1906.

RATINGS
Admissions Selectivity Rating: 70   **Fire Safety Rating:** 97   **Green Rating:** 89

STUDENTS AND FACULTY
Enrollment: 5,646. **Student Body:** 56% female, 44% male, 33% out-of-state, 17% international (107 countries represented). Asian 7%, African American 5%, Caucasian 43%, Hispanic 10%, Native American 0%. **Retention and Graduation:** 76% freshmen return for sophomore year. 40% freshmen graduate within 4 years. 56% freshmen graduate within 6 years. 26% grads go on to further study within 1 year. 9% grads pursue arts and sciences degrees. 3% grads pursue law degrees. 7% grads pursue business degrees. 1% grads pursue medical degrees. **Faculty:** Student/faculty ratio 12:1. 392 full-time faculty, 86% hold PhDs, 15% are members of minority groups, 43% are women.

ACADEMICS
Degrees: associate, bachelor's, certificate, diploma, master's, post-bachelor's certificate, post-master's certificate. **Classes:** Most classes have 10–19 students. Most lab/discussion sessions have 10–19 students. **Majors with Highest Enrollment:** business/corporate communications; interior design; sociology. **Special Study Options:** Accelerated program, cooperative education program, cross-registration, distance learning, double major, English as a Second Language (ESL), honors program, independent study, internships, liberal arts/career combination, study abroad, weekend college. **Honors Programs:** A Community of Scholars Suffolk University honors students work in collabo-

ration with their school's program director and advisory committee to plan events that bring the honors community together on a regular basis outside of the classroom. Lectures by Suffolk University scholars or by noted intellectuals outside of the University, a variety of social events, visits to cultural and historical sites, and public service projects offer intellectual challenge, promote leadership, and develop networking skills with faculty, alumni, community, business, and government leaders. The program provides honors scholars with a broader context for their academic pursuits, while strengthening their sense of community. Special Benefits and Recognition for Honors Scholars: Honors scholars are eligible for a full tuition scholarship. In addition, honors scholars enjoy the following benefits and recognition: Guaranteed housing in University residence halls through the sophomore year; Priority course registration; Special honors program advisors; Application assistance, when applicable, for Fulbright, Marshall, Rhodes, and other post-graduate academic and scholarship programs; Honors Program designation on official academic transcript; and Special listing in commencement program. http://www.suffolk.edu/admission/gchonors. htm **Combined Degree Programs:** BA/JD, BA/MA. **Disability Services:** Special programs offered to physically disabled students include note-taking services, reader services, tape recorders, tutors. **Career Services:** Alumni network, alumni services, career/job search classes, career assessment, internships, regional alumni. Career Services highlights include The Co-op Program offers both part-time and full-time work options and is available to full-time undergraduate and graduate students. By combining relevant work experience with academic studies, students have the best opportunity for personal, professional and career development. Additionally, students are able to subsidize their education costs while building their resumes in preparation for their professional lives. Students can work either part-time (the most popular option) or full-time. Part-time co-ops usually involve working 15-25 hours per week while continuing to take a full load of courses. Students working full-time must have completed a full load of courses the previous semester and then must return to school for the semester after their co-op placement. Co-ops are available for all majors. Most positions are located in businesses and organizations within easy commuting distance of campus, so that students can balance their work and academic schedules. Some of the employers who have participated in the Suffolk Co-op Program include: 96.9 FM Biogen Boston Globe Cape Cod Potato Chips Commonwealth of Massachusetts EF Education Ernst and Young, LLP Fidelity Investments Greater Boston Convention and Visitors Bureau Investors Bank and Trust Mass General Hospital Massport North Suffolk Mental Health Association PricewaterhouseCoopers Eligibility for participation in Co-op Program: Undergraduates must have a minimum 2.5 GPA Undergraduates have completed their freshman year Transfer students must have completed one semester at Suffolk University Full-time graduate students are eligible upon enrollment in their degree program. Student interested in Co-op must call the office at 617-573-8480 to schedule an appointment with a counselor.

FACILITIES

Housing: Coed dorms, apartments for single students. **Special Academic Facilities/Equipment:** Marine biology field station in Maine, NESAD art gallery, Adams art gallery, C. Walsh Theatre and 10 West Street Theatre **Computers:** 100% of classrooms, 100% of dorms, 100% of libraries, 100% of dining areas, 100% of student union, 20% of common outdoor areas have wireless network access. Students can register for classes online. Administrative functions (other than registration) can be performed online.

CAMPUS LIFE

Environment: Metropolis. **Activities:** Choral groups, dance, drama/theater, literary magazine, music ensembles, musical theater, radio station, student government, student newspaper, television station, yearbook, Campus Ministries, International Student Organization 75 registered organizations, 11 honor societies, 3 religious organizations. 1 fraternities, 1 sororities. **Athletics (Intercollegiate):** *Men:* baseball, basketball, cross-country, golf, ice hockey, soccer, tennis. *Women:* basketball, cross-country, softball, tennis, volleyball. **On-Campus Highlights:** Donahue Student Lounge, Donahue Cafe, Sawyer Library, NESAD Gallery, Alumni Park, Sawyer Computer Lab, Donahue Computer Lab, Sawyer Lounge, 150 Tremont St Dining Room. **Environmental Initiatives:** Energy efficiency and conservation Green Building Practices Waste Reduction and Recycling.

ADMISSIONS

Freshman Academic Profile: Average high school GPA 3.2. 14% in top 10% of high school class, 41% in top 25% of high school class, 78% in top 50% of high school class. 66% from public high schools. SAT Math middle 50% range 460-570. SAT Critical Reading middle 50% range 440-560. SAT Writing middle 50% range 450-570. ACT middle 50% range 19-24. Minimum web-based TOEFL 71. Minimum paper TOEFL 525. **Basis for Candidate Selection:** *Very important factors considered include:* rigor of secondary school record. *Important factors considered include:* Class rank, application essay, academic GPA, standardized test scores, character/personal qualities. *Other factors*

considered include: recommendation(s), alumni/ae relation, extracurricular activities, first generation, geographical residence, interview, level of applicant's interest, talent/ability, volunteer work, work experience. **Freshman Admission Requirements:** High school diploma is required and GED is accepted. *Academic units required:* 4 English, 3 mathematics, 2 science, (1 science labs), 2 foreign language, 1 history, 4 academic electives. *Academic units recommended:* 4 English, 3 mathematics, 2 science, (1 science labs), 2 foreign language, 1 history, 4 academic electives. **Freshman Admission Statistics:** 9,418 applied, 78% admitted, 17% enrolled. **Transfer Admission Requirements:** High school transcript, college transcript(s), essay or personal statement, minimum college GPA of 2.5 required. Lowest grade transferable C. **General Admission Information:** Application Fee $50. Regular application deadline 3/1. Notification on a rolling basis, beginning on or about 2/5. Nonfall registration accepted. Admission may be deferred for a maximum of 1 year. Credit and/or placement offered for CEEB Advanced Placement tests.

COSTS AND FINANCIAL AID

Required Forms and Deadlines: FAFSA, institution's own financial aid form. **Notification of Awards:** Applicants will be notified of awards on a rolling basis beginning 2/5. **Types of Aid:** *Need-based scholarships/grants:* Federal Pell, SEOG, state scholarships/grants, private scholarships, the school's own gift aid. *Loans:* Direct Subsidized Stafford, Direct Unsubsidized Stafford, Direct PLUS, Federal Perkins, state loans, college/university loans from institutional funds. **Student Employment:** Federal Work-Study Program available. Institutional employment available. Highest amount earned per year from on-campus jobs $8,217. Off-campus job opportunities are excellent. **Financial Aid Statistics:** 95% freshmen, 92% undergrads receive need-based scholarship or grant aid. 36% freshmen, 36% undergrads receive non-need-based scholarship or grant aid. 93% freshmen, 91% undergrads receive need-based self-help aid. 80% freshmen, 84% undergrads receive any aid. 77% undergrads borrow to pay for school. Average cumulative indebtedness $33,823. **Criteria for awarding institutional aid:** *Non-need-based:* academics, alumni affiliation.

SUSQUEHANNA UNIVERSITY

514 University Avenue, Selinsgrove, PA 17870
Phone: 570-372-4260 • **Financial Aid Phone:** 570-372-4450
E-mail: suadmiss@susqu.edu • **CEEB Code:** 2820
Fax: 570-372-2722 • **Website:** www.susqu.edu • **ACT Code:** 3720

This private school, affiliated with the Lutheran Church, was founded in 1858. It has a 306-acre campus.

RATINGS
Admissions Selectivity Rating: 85   **Fire Safety Rating:** 97   **Green Rating:** 66

STUDENTS AND FACULTY
Enrollment: 2,151. **Student Body:** 54% female, 46% male, 49% out-of-state, 1% international (17 countries represented). Asian 1%, African American 5%, Caucasian 86%, Hispanic 5%, Native American 0%.
Retention and Graduation: 70% freshmen graduate within 4 years. 23% grads go on to further study within 1 year. **Faculty:** Student/faculty ratio 12:1. 141 full-time faculty, 93% hold PhDs, 17% are members of minority groups, 45% are women. 0% of classes are taught by teaching assistants.

ACADEMICS
Degrees: bachelor's. **Classes:** Most classes have 10–19 students. Most lab/discussion sessions have 10–19 students. **Majors with Highest Enrollment:** business administration and management; communication studies/speech communication and rhetoric; creative writing. **Special Study Options:** Accelerated program, cross-registration, distance learning, double major, dual enrollment, exchange student program (domestic), honors program, independent study, internships, student-designed major, study abroad, teacher certification program. **Honors Programs:** Recognized as a model for similar programs throughout the country, the Honors Program at Susquehanna offers a challenging curriculum to students interested in a more self-directed and interdisciplinary approach at the undergraduate level. The program is well suited to the aggressively curious, active learner who values breadth of study and multiple perspectives. Discussion groups, lectures, off-campus visits and residential programs complement Honors Program courses. **Combined Degree Programs:** BA/DDS, BA/M.E.M. or BA/M.F. with Duke Universit. **Disability Services:** Special programs offered to physically disabled students include

note-taking services, reader services, tape recorders, tutors. **Career Services:** Alumni network, alumni services, career/job search classes, career assessment, internships, regional alumni. Career Services highlights include Susquehanna University and the Center for Career Services support and encourage student participation in credit internships. Gundaker Enrichment Fund Grants provide qualifying students with supplemental support for internships or volunteer activities. Awards from the funds are intended to provide a range of experiential learning opportunities for students. In addition, Susquehanna University has partnerships with several programs offering students opportunities to combine internships and academic coursework for university credit.

FACILITIES

Housing: Coed dorms, special housing for disabled students, special housing for international students, fraternity/sorority housing, apartments for single students, theme housing. 90% of campus accessible to physically disabled. **Special Academic Facilities/Equipment:** Art gallery, electronic music lab, child development center, foreign language broadcast system, teaching theatre, greenhouse, rare book room, ecological field station, electron microscope, reflecting telescope, fluorescent microscopes, video conference center, and the new Business and Communications Building featuring three multimedia classrooms, three computer laboratories/classrooms, conference and seminar rooms, student team study rooms and alcoves, two video studios, seminar/observation rooms and a room for faculty instructional development. The building facilitates use of laptop computers by offering informational technology dataports for every seat in the classrooms, team study areas and student lounges and faculty offices. **Computers:** 90% of classrooms, 10% of dorms, 100% of libraries, 100% of dining areas, 100% of student union, 30% of common outdoor areas have wireless network access. Students can register for classes online. Administrative functions (other than registration) can be performed online.

CAMPUS LIFE

Environment: Town. **Activities:** Choral groups, concert band, dance, drama/theater, jazz band, literary magazine, music ensembles, musical theater, opera, pep band, radio station, student government, student newspaper, student-run film society, symphony orchestra, television station, yearbook, Campus Ministries, International Student Organization 120 registered organizations, 24 honor societies, 12 religious organizations. 4 fraternities, 5 sororities. **Athletics (Intercollegiate):** *Men:* baseball, basketball, crew/rowing, cross-country, football, golf, lacrosse, soccer, swimming, tennis, track/field (outdoor), track/field (indoor). *Women:* basketball, crew/rowing, cross-country, field hockey, golf, lacrosse, soccer, softball, swimming, tennis, track/field (outdoor), track/field (indoor), volleyball. **On-Campus Highlights:** Sports and Fitness Complex, Business and Communications Center, Blough-Weis Library, Trax (campus nightclub), Java City in the Campus Center. **Environmental Initiatives:** New science facility and new student housing are LEED certified. This housing and two units built in 2010 utilize geo-thermal energy for heating and cooling. Actively pursuing alternative sources of fuel to replace coal-fired power plant. Cut fuel usage 25% last year by installing highly-efficient insulated steam lines. Susquehanna University is a flagship member of the Graduation Pledge Alliance, a national student organization whose mission is to promote socially and environmentally responsible actions by graduating seniors. Commitments include participation in a recycling cooperative with the borough.

ADMISSIONS

Freshman Academic Profile: Average high school GPA 3.3. 22% in top 10% of high school class, 55% in top 25% of high school class, 84% in top 50% of high school class. 76% from public high schools. SAT Math middle 50% range 510–600. SAT Critical Reading middle 50% range 510–610. SAT Writing middle 50% range 490–590. ACT middle 50% range 23–28. Minimum web-based TOEFL 81. Minimum paper TOEFL 550. **Basis for Candidate Selection:** *Very important factors considered include:* academic GPA, rigor of secondary school record. *Important factors considered include:* Class rank, application essay, recommendation(s), standardized test scores, alumni/ae relation, character/personal qualities, extracurricular activities, interview, level of applicant's interest, racial/ethnic status, talent/ability, volunteer work, work experience. *Other factors considered include:* first generation, geographical residence, religious affiliation/commitment, state residency. **Freshman Admission Requirements:** High school diploma is required and GED is accepted. *Academic units required:* 4 English, 3 mathematics, 3 science, (2 science labs), 2 foreign language, 2 social studies, 2 history, 2 academic electives. *Academic units recommended:* 4 English, 3 mathematics, 3 science, (2 science labs), 2 foreign language, 2 social studies, 2 history, 2 academic electives. **Freshman Admission Statistics:** 3,458 applied, 49% admitted, 37% enrolled. **Transfer Admission Requirements:** High school transcript, college transcript(s), essay or personal statement, statement of good standing from prior institution(s). Minimum college GPA of 2.0 required. Lowest grade transferable C–. **General Admission Information:** Application Fee $35. Early decision application deadline 11/15. Regular application deadline 3/1. Notification on a rolling basis, beginning on or about 12/15. Nonfall registration accepted. Admission may be deferred for a maximum of one year. Credit and/or placement offered for CEEB Advanced Placement tests.

COSTS AND FINANCIAL AID

Annual tuition $36,800. Room and board $10,000. Required fees $480. Average book expense $850. **Required Forms and Deadlines:** FAFSA, CSS/Financial Aid PROFILE, business/farm supplement. Prior year Federal tax return. **Notification of Awards:** Applicants will be notified of awards on or about 3/1. **Types of Aid:** *Need-based scholarships/grants:* Federal Pell, SEOG, state scholarships/grants, private scholarships, the school's own gift aid. *Loans:* Subsidized Stafford, Unsubsidized Stafford, PLUS, Federal Perkins, college/university loans from institutional funds. **Student Employment:** Federal Work-Study Program available. Institutional employment available. Highest amount earned per year from on-campus jobs $8,337. Off-campus job opportunities are good. **Financial Aid Statistics:** 100% freshmen, 99% undergrads receive need-based scholarship or grant aid. 13% freshmen, 13% undergrads receive non-need-based scholarship or grant aid. 86% freshmen, 85% undergrads receive need-based self-help aid. 97% freshmen, 96% undergrads receive any aid. 76% undergrads borrow to pay for school. Average cumulative indebtedness $32,952. **Criteria for awarding institutional aid:** *Non-need-based:* academics, alumni affiliation, leadership, minority status, music/drama.

SWARTHMORE COLLEGE

500 College Avenue, Swarthmore, PA 19081
Phone: 610-328-8300 • **Financial Aid Phone:** 610-328-8358
E-mail: admissions@swarthmore.edu • **CEEB Code:** 2821
Fax: 610-328-8580 • **Website:** www.swarthmore.edu • **ACT Code:** 3722

This private school was founded in 1864. It has a 399-acre campus.

RATINGS

Admissions Selectivity Rating: 99   **Fire Safety Rating:** 86   **Green Rating:** 85

STUDENTS AND FACULTY

Enrollment: 1,532. **Student Body:** 51% female, 49% male, 88% out-of-state, 8% international (58 countries represented). Asian 14%, African American 6%, Caucasian 43%, Hispanic 13%, Native American 0%. **Retention and Graduation:** 86% freshmen graduate within 4 years. 92% freshmen graduate within 6 years. 21% grads go on to further study within 1 year. 11% grads pursue arts and sciences degrees. 3% grads pursue law degrees. 1% grads pursue business degrees. 2% grads pursue medical degrees. **Faculty:** Student/faculty ratio 8:1. 171 full-time faculty, 99% hold PhDs, 16% are members of minority groups, 42% are women. 0% of classes are taught by teaching assistants.

ACADEMICS

Degrees: bachelor's. **Classes:** Most classes have 10–19 students. Most lab/discussion sessions have fewer than 10 students. **Majors with Highest Enrollment:** biology/biological sciences; economics; political science and government. **Special Study Options:** Accelerated program, cross-registration, double major, exchange student program (domestic), honors program, independent study, internships, student-designed major, study abroad, teacher certification program, Swarthmore offers cooperative exchange programs with Rice and Tufts universities and Harvey Mudd, Pomona, Mills and Middlebury colleges. **Honors Programs:** Swarthmore's Honors Program features faculty working with small groups of dedicated and accomplished students; an emphasis on independent learning; students entering into a dialogue with peers, teachers, and examiners; a demanding program of study in major and minor fields; and an examination at the end of two years' study by outside scholars. **Combined Degree Programs:** BA/BS in engineering and another major. **Disability Services:** Special programs offered to physically disabled students include note-taking services, reader services, tape recorders, tutors. **Career Services:** Alumni network, alumni services, career/job search classes, career assessment, internships, regional alumni. Career services highlights include Swarthmore's externship program matches 200 students annually with over 300 alumni sponsors in diverse career fields and locations nationwide.

FACILITIES

Housing: Coed dorms, men's dorms, women's dorms, Gender Neutral housing (students of any gender may share rooms and/or share bathrooms). 85% of campus accessible to physically disabled. **Special Academic Facilities/Equipment:** The Campus is a 399-acre, nationally registered arboretum. The Lang Performing Arts Center's resources include an art gallery, dance studios, cinema, and theater performance space. Highlights of Swarthmore's library facilities include the Friends Historical Library and the Peace Collection. The athletics facilities include a lighted stadium complex, a 400-meter dual durometer track, and synthetic grass playing field, state-of-the-art fitness center and three indoor tennis courts with Rebound Ace surface. The Science Center has been recognized by the U.S. Green Building Council for "leadership in energy and environmental design." The College's two newest residence halls feature loft-style rooms and environmentally friendly green roofs. **Computers:** 100% of classrooms, 100% of dorms, 100% of libraries, 100% of dining areas, 100% of student union, 100% of common outdoor areas have wireless network access. Students can register for classes online. Administrative functions (other than registration) can be performed online.

CAMPUS LIFE

Environment: Village. **Activities:** Choral groups, dance, drama/theater, jazz band, literary magazine, music ensembles, opera, student government, student newspaper, student-run film society, symphony orchestra, yearbook, Campus Ministries, International Student Organization 138 registered organizations, 3 honor societies, 12 religious organizations. 2 fraternities. **Athletics (Intercollegiate):** *Men:* baseball, basketball, cross-country, golf, lacrosse, soccer, swimming, tennis, track/field (outdoor), track/field (indoor). *Women:* badminton, basketball, cross-country, field hockey, lacrosse, soccer, softball, swimming, tennis, track/field (outdoor), track/field (indoor), volleyball. **On-Campus Highlights:** Kohlberg & Eldridge Commons Coffee Bars, Parrish Beach (the central campus lawn), Scott Outdoor Amphitheater, Mullan Tennis & Fitness Center, Paces (student-run cafe), Recent years have seen an exciting array of student projects and student spaces develop at Swarthmore. Among them: The acclaimed War News Radio (www.warnewsradio.org), the nation's only student-run national radio program focusing on the wars in Iraq and Afghanistan, now carried by more than 60 stations worldwide; the Genocide Intervention Network (www.genocideintervention.net), a student-founded group that is raising hundreds of thousands of dollars to support peace-keeping in Darfur; two new dormitories, whose student-influenced integrative design features loft-style doubles, wide halls, generous lounge and community kitchens'—all aimed at promoting robust hall social life; and the Lang Center for Civic and Social Responsibility (www.swarthmore.edu/langcenter) which prepares students for leadership in civic engagement, public service, advocacy, and social action. **Environmental Initiatives:** 100% of the College's electrical demands are met by renewable energy credits The College has approximately 14,300 sq. feet of green roof The College's Sustainability Committee is comprised of faculty, staff, and students and is charged with making recommendations to improve environmental sustainability on campus. A newly formed Climate Action Plan Committee will focus on establishing requirements to meet the ACUPCC climate commitment.

ADMISSIONS

Freshman Academic Profile: 92% in top 10% of high school class, 99% in top 25% of high school class, 100% in top 50% of high school class. 58% from public high schools. SAT Math middle 50% range 670-770. SAT Critical Reading middle 50% range 680-780. SAT Writing middle 50% range 680-770. ACT middle 50% range 30-33. Basis **for Candidate Selection:** *Very important factors considered include:* Class rank, application essay, academic GPA, recommendation(s), rigor of secondary school record, character/personal qualities. *Important factors considered include:* standardized test scores, extracurricular activities. *Other factors considered include:* alumni/ae relation, first generation, geographical residence, interview, level of applicant's interest, racial/ethnic status, talent/ability, volunteer work, work experience. **Freshman Admission Requirements:** High school diploma or equivalent is not required. **Freshman Admission Statistics:** 6,589 applied, 14% admitted, 40% enrolled. **Transfer Admission Requirements:** High school transcript, college transcript(s), essay or personal statement, standardized test scores, statement of good standing from prior institution(s). Lowest grade transferable C. **General Admission Information:** Application Fee $60. Early decision application deadline 11/15. Regular application deadline 1/2. Regular notification 4/1. Nonfall registration not accepted. Admission may be deferred for a maximum of 1 Year. Credit and/or placement offered for CEEB Advanced Placement tests.

COSTS AND FINANCIAL AID

Annual tuition $42,744. Room and board $12,670. Required fees $336. Average book expense $1,180. **Required Forms and Deadlines:** FAFSA, institution's own financial aid form, CSS/Financial Aid PROFILE, state aid form, noncustodial PROFILE, business/farm supplement. Federal Tax Return, W2 Statements, Year-end paycheck stub. **Notification of Awards:** Applicants will be notified of awards on or about 4/1. **Types of Aid:** *Need-based scholarships/grants:* Federal Pell, SEOG, state scholarships/grants, private scholarships, the school's own gift aid. *Loans:* Subsidized Stafford, Unsubsidized Stafford, PLUS, Federal Perkins, state loans, college/university loans from institutional funds. **Student Employment:** Federal Work-Study Program available. Institutional employment available. Highest amount earned per year from on-campus jobs $1,760. Off-campus job opportunities are good. **Financial Aid Statistics:** 100% freshmen, 100% undergrads receive need-based scholarship or grant aid. 99% freshmen, 98% undergrads receive need-based self-help aid. 49% freshmen, 53% undergrads receive any aid. 34% undergrads borrow to pay for school. Av-

erage cumulative indebtedness $20,020. **Criteria for awarding institutional aid:** *Non-need-based:* academics, leadership, state/district residency.

See page 1224.

SWEET BRIAR COLLEGE

P. O. Box 1052, Sweet Briar, VA 24595
Phone: 434-381-6142 • **Financial Aid Phone:** 434-381-6156
E-mail: admissions@sbc.edu • **CEEB Code:** 5634
Fax: 434-381-6152 • **Website:** www.sbc.edu • **ACT Code:** 4406

This private school was founded in 1901. It has a 3250-acre campus.

RATINGS
Admissions Selectivity Rating: 72   **Fire Safety Rating:** 98   **Green Rating:** 78

STUDENTS AND FACULTY
Enrollment: 566. **Student Body:** 100% female, 0% male, 0% out-of-state, 1% international (16 countries represented). Asian 3%, African American 9%, Caucasian 77%, Hispanic 6%, Native American 2%.
Retention and Graduation: 74% freshmen return for sophomore year. 61% freshmen graduate within 4 years. 26% grads go on to further study within 1 year. 12% grads pursue arts and sciences degrees. 5% grads pursue medical degrees. **Faculty:** Student/faculty ratio 8:1. 78 full-time faculty, 85% hold PhDs, 10% are members of minority groups, 46% are women. 0% of classes are taught by teaching assistants.

ACADEMICS
Degrees: bachelor's, master's. **Classes:** Most classes have 10–19 students. Most lab/discussion sessions have fewer than 10 students. **Majors with Highest Enrollment:** biology/biological sciences; business/commerce; psychology. **Special Study Options:** Accelerated program, cross-registration, double major, dual enrollment, exchange student program (domestic), honors program, independent study, internships, liberal arts/career combination, student-designed major, study abroad, teacher certification program. **Honors Programs:** The Honors Program was established and continues to evolve in response to the needs of students who demonstrate exceptional initiative, ability, and creativity. The program consists of challenging courses, Summer Research Fellowships, opportunities for independent work, and a series of extracurricular activities. The program also brings advanced graduate degree candidates to campus, providing role models for students considering graduate studies. **Combined Degree Programs:** BA/MEng, BA/BS Eng. with Columbia, VaTech, Wash. Univ. **Disability Services:** Special programs offered to physically disabled students include tutors. **Career Services:** Alumni network, alumni services, career/job search classes, career assessment, internships, regional alumni. Career Services highlights include The Internship Program has developed into a strong, professionalized program, with resources for providing students with internship and other experiential opportunities for all College majors and fields of interest. The Career Services team has been on the road recently presenting at state and regional conferences on the collaborative relationships forged between college and community. These relationships have greatly augmented the internship program.

FACILITIES
Housing: women's dorms, Substance-free, Eco Floor, Academic House, International Corridor. 75% of campus accessible to physically disabled. **Special Academic Facilities/Equipment:** Art museum and galleries, college and local history museums, environmental education/nature center, kindergarten/nursery school, riding center, electron microscope, DNA sequencing equipment, 400MHz nuclear magnetic resonance spectrometer. **Computers:** 60% of classrooms, 50% of dorms, 100% of libraries, 100% of dining areas, 100% of student union, 30% of common outdoor areas have wireless network access. Students can register for classes online. Administrative functions (other than registration) can be performed online.

CAMPUS LIFE
Environment: Rural. **Activities:** Choral groups, dance, drama/theater, literary magazine, music ensembles, musical theater, radio station, student government, student newspaper, student-run film society, symphony orchestra, television station, yearbook, Campus Ministries 61 registered organizations, 11 honor societies, 3 religious organizations. **Athletics (Intercollegiate):** *Women:* field hockey, horseback riding, lacrosse, soccer, softball, swimming, tennis, volleyball. **On-Campus Highlights:** Bistro, Riding Center, Boathouse, Book Shop,

Art Barn. **Environmental Initiatives:** Recycling Geothermal Performance Contracting

ADMISSIONS

Freshman Academic Profile: Average high school GPA 3.5. 24% in top 10% of high school class, 53% in top 25% of high school class, 87% in top 50% of high school class. 75% from public high schools. SAT Math middle 50% range 450-570. SAT Critical Reading middle 50% range 490-610. SAT Writing middle 50% range 460-590. ACT middle 50% range 22-27. Minimum web-based TOEFL 79. Minimum paper TOEFL 550. **Basis for Candidate Selection:** *Very important factors considered include:* academic GPA, rigor of secondary school record. *Important factors considered include:* application essay, recommendation(s), standardized test scores, interview. *Other factors considered include:* Class rank, alumni/ae relation, character/personal qualities, extracurricular activities, first generation, racial/ethnic status, talent/ability, volunteer work, work experience. **Freshman Admission Requirements:** High school diploma is required and GED is accepted. *Academic units required:* 4 English, 3 mathematics, 3 science, (2 science labs), 2 foreign language, 3 social studies. *Academic units recommended:* 4 English, 3 mathematics, 3 science, (2 science labs), 2 foreign language, 3 social studies. **Freshman Admission Statistics:** 763 applied, 79% admitted, 29% enrolled. **Transfer Admission Requirements:** High school transcript, college transcript(s), essay or personal statement, standardized test scores, statement of good standing from prior institution(s). Minimum college GPA of 2.5 required. Lowest grade transferable C–. **General Admission Information:** Application Fee $40. Early decision application deadline 12/1. Regular application deadline 2/1. Regular notification 3/15. Nonfall registration accepted. Admission may be deferred for a maximum of one year. Credit and/or placement offered for CEEB Advanced Placement tests.

COSTS AND FINANCIAL AID

Annual tuition $31,850. Room and board $11,440. Required fees $475. Average book expense $1,168. **Required Forms and Deadlines:** FAFSA, noncustodial PROFILE. **Notification of Awards:** Applicants will be notified of awards on or about 3/1. **Types of Aid:** *Need-based scholarships/grants:* Federal Pell, SEOG, state scholarships/grants, private scholarships, the school's own gift aid. *Loans:* Direct Subsidized Stafford, Direct Unsubsidized Stafford, Direct PLUS, Federal Perkins, college/university loans from institutional funds. **Student Employment:** Federal Work-Study Program available. Institutional employment available. Highest amount earned per year from on-campus jobs $1,000. Off-campus job opportunities are fair. **Financial Aid Statistics:** 100% freshmen, 100% undergrads receive need-based scholarship or grant aid. 18% freshmen, 15% undergrads receive non-need-based scholarship or grant aid. 79% freshmen, 81% undergrads receive need-based self-help aid. 100% freshmen, 98% undergrads receive any aid. 63% undergrads borrow to pay for school. Average cumulative indebtedness $23,596. **Criteria for awarding institutional aid:** *Non-need-based:* academics, art, leadership, music/drama, state/district residency.

See page 1226.

SYRACUSE UNIVERSITY

100 Crouse-Hinds Hall, Syracuse, NY 13244-2130
Phone: 315-443-3611 • **Financial Aid Phone:** 315-443-1513
E-mail: orange@syr.edu • **CEEB Code:** 2823
Fax: 315-443-4226 • **Website:** www.syr.edu • **ACT Code:** 2968

This private school was founded in 1870. It has a 200-acre campus.

RATINGS

Admissions Selectivity Rating: 90   **Fire Safety Rating:** 86   **Green Rating:** 90

STUDENTS AND FACULTY

Enrollment: 14,429. **Student Body:** 56% female, 44% male, 55% out-of-state, 8% international (82 countries represented). Asian 8%, African American 9%, Caucasian 56%, Hispanic 10%, Native American 1%.
Retention and Graduation: 23% grads go on to further study within 1 year. 3% grads pursue arts and sciences degrees. 1% grads pursue law degrees. 3% grads pursue business degrees. 2% grads pursue medical degrees. **Faculty:** Student/faculty ratio 16:1. 1019 full-time faculty, 86% hold PhDs, 19% are members of minority groups, 37% are women.

ACADEMICS

Degrees: associate, bachelor's, certificate, master's, post-bachelor's certificate, post-master's certificate. **Classes:** Most classes have 10–19 students. Most lab/discussion sessions have 20–29 students. **Majors with Highest Enrollment:** commercial and advertising art; psychology; radio and television. **Special Study Options:** Accelerated program, cooperative education program, distance learning, double major, dual enrollment, English as a Second Language (ESL), honors program, independent study, internships, liberal arts/career combination, student-designed major, study abroad, teacher certification program, SU offers many undergraduate research opportunities, pre-professional programs, and minors. **Honors Programs:** The University Honors program combines the benefits of a small intimate community with the advantages of diversity and opportunity found only at larger institutions. Students enjoy provocative coursework in small classes taught by some of the University's most able and experienced faculty, as well as some of the nation's leading research scholars. In the Honors Thesis Project upper class students are closely guided by faculty to pursue intensive research on a topic of their choice. **Combined Degree Programs:** BA/JD, BA/MEng. **Disability Services:** Special programs offered to physically disabled students include note-taking services, reader services, tape recorders, tutors. **Career Services:** Alumni network, alumni services, career/job search classes, career assessment, internships, regional alumni. Career Services highlights include Syracuse University's South Side Entrepreneurial Connect Project (SSECP), launched in June of 2004, works with the challenged inner city neighborhoods on the south side of Syracuse to create sustainable small business ventures. The goal of the SSECP is to foster the development of an entrepreneurial community within the south side through increasing the number of new start ups and developing a supportive infrastructure that ensures the long-term sustainability of existing small businesses within the community. In this comprehensive initiative, students are intimately involved in all facets of SSECP management and implementation, including: consultation teams with faculty and students from other disciplines that work closely with entrepreneurs in creating and growing ventures; management of a microcredit fund for inner city entrepreneurs; organizing community functions; legal counseling for entrepreneurs from Law School students; youth mentoring and empowerment programs; assistance in coordinating our South Side Entrepreneurs Association; resource mapping and connecting; involvement in the cross-marketing program; and research projects that provide insights that enable the sustainability of the inner city entrepreneurial development model that guides our efforts. Our students intern and work in the SSIC, and it has become the nerve center for a wide range of entrepreneurial initiatives and activities involving the inner city of Syracuse.

FACILITIES

Housing: Coed dorms, special housing for disabled students, special housing for international students, fraternity/sorority housing, apartments for married students, apartments for single students, wellness housing, theme housing, International living center, single-sex floors and wings of residence halls, numerous learning communities, and interest housing available. 92% of campus accessible to physically disabled. **Special Academic Facilities/Equipment:** SUArt Galleries; The Warehouse Gallery; digital media convergence center; Syracuse Center of Excellence in Environmental and Energy Systems; Fidelity MOTUS 622i flight simulator for aerospace engineering; Ballentine Investment Institute; community darkrooms; Syracuse Stage professional equity theater; Bernice M. Wright Child Development Laboratory School; Belfer Audio Laboratory and Archive; Gebbie Speech, Language, and Hearing Clinic; Life Sciences Complex; SU Library Special Collections Research Center; UPSTATE: A Center for Design, Research and Real Estate at the SU School of Architecture; Center on Human Policy; Center for Emerging Network Technologies; JPMorgan Chase Technology Center **Computers:** 75% of classrooms, 100% of dorms, 100% of libraries, 100% of dining areas, 100% of student union, 75% of common outdoor areas have wireless network access. Students can register for classes online. Administrative functions (other than registration) can be performed online.

CAMPUS LIFE

Environment: Metropolis. **Activities:** Choral groups, concert band, dance, drama/theater, jazz band, literary magazine, marching band, music ensembles, musical theater, pep band, radio station, student government, student newspaper, student-run film society, symphony orchestra, television station, yearbook, Campus Ministries, International Student Organization 347 registered organizations, 43 honor societies, 30 religious organizations. 29 fraternities, 19 sororities. **Athletics (Intercollegiate):** *Men:* basketball, cheerleading, crew/rowing, cross-country, diving, football, lacrosse, soccer, swimming, track/field (outdoor). *Women:* basketball, cheerleading, crew/rowing, cross-country, diving, field hockey, ice hockey, lacrosse, soccer, softball, swimming, tennis, track/field (outdoor), volleyball. **On-Campus Highlights:** Schine Student Center, Bird Library Cafe, Hendricks Chapel, Whitman School, Archbold Athletic Complex. **Environmental Initiatives:** First research university east of California to achieve "Climate Registered" status from The Climate Registry. One of the requirements is that our GHG inventory is third-party verified. Established two sustainability-related endowed professorships within the L.C. Smith College of Engineering. Hired a University Professor of Sustainability Policy within the Maxwell School. Established a co-major in Energy and Its Impacts within the College of Arts and Sciences. Hired a VP for Sustainability Initiatives. Integrated sustainable concepts throughout the first-year curriculum of the College of Visual and Performing Arts. Have developed a financially responsible approach to carbon neutrality which can be used as a model by businesses and other organizations. The plan is managerially conservative, fully self-funding in the long term, and meets the university's standards for internal investment of endowment funds.

ADMISSIONS

Freshman Academic Profile: Average high school GPA 3.6. 38% in top 10% of high school class, 72% in top 25% of high school class, 95% in top 50% of high school class. 68% from public high schools. SAT Math middle 50% range 540-650. SAT Critical Reading middle 50% range 510-620. SAT Writing middle 50% range 520-630. ACT middle 50% range 23-28. Minimum web-based TOEFL 85. Minimum paper TOEFL 550. **Basis for Candidate Selection:** *Very important factors considered include:* Class rank, application essay, academic GPA, recommendation(s), rigor of secondary school record, standardized test scores, character/personal qualities, extracurricular activities, interview, level of applicant's interest, talent/ability. *Important factors considered include:* alumni/ae relation, first generation, geographical residence, state residency, volunteer work, work experience. *Other factors considered include:* racial/ethnic status. **Freshman Admission Requirements:** High school diploma is required and GED is accepted. *Academic units required:* 4 English, 4 mathematics, 4 science, (4 science labs), 3 foreign language, 4 social studies. 4 English, 4 mathematics, 4 science, (4 science labs), 3 foreign language, 4 social studies. **Freshman Admission Statistics:** 25,790 applied, 51% admitted, 26% enrolled. **Transfer Admission Requirements:** college transcript(s), essay or personal statement, statement of good standing from prior institution(s). Lowest grade transferable C. **General Admission Information:** Application Fee $70. Early decision application deadline 11/1. Regular application deadline 1/1. Notification on a rolling basis, beginning on or about 3/15. Nonfall registration accepted. Admission may be deferred for a maximum of 1 year. Credit and/or placement offered for CEEB Advanced Placement tests.

COSTS AND FINANCIAL AID

Annual tuition $37,610. Room and board $13,692. Required fees $1,394. Average book expense $1,342. **Required Forms and Deadlines:** FAFSA, CSS/Financial Aid PROFILE, noncustodial PROFILE. **Notification of Awards:** Applicants will be notified of awards on or about 3/21. **Types of Aid:** *Need-based scholarships/grants:* Federal Pell, SEOG, state scholarships/grants, private scholarships, the school's own gift aid. *Loans:* Direct Subsidized Stafford, Direct Unsubsidized Stafford, Direct PLUS, Federal Perkins. **Student Employment:** Federal Work-Study Program available. Institutional employment available. Off-campus job opportunities are good. **Financial Aid Statistics:** 91% freshmen, 91% undergrads receive need-based scholarship or grant aid. 7% freshmen, 6% undergrads receive non-need-based scholarship or grant aid. 95% freshmen, 96% undergrads receive need-based self-help aid. 2% freshmen, 2% undergrads receive athletic scholarships. 75% freshmen, 75% undergrads receive any aid. 61% undergrads borrow to pay for school. Average cumulative indebtedness $33,504. **Criteria for awarding institutional aid:** *Non-need-based:* academics, art, athletics, music/drama, state/district residency.

TALLADEGA COLLEGE

627 West Battle Street, Talladega, AL 35160
Phone: 205-761-6235 • **Financial Aid Phone:** 256-761-6341
E-mail: admissions@talladega.edu
Fax: 205-362-0274 • **Website:** www.talladega.edu • **ACT Code:** 26

This private school, affiliated with the United Church of Christ Church, was founded in 1867. It has a 50-acre campus.

RATINGS

Admissions Selectivity Rating: 77	Fire Safety Rating: 82	Green Rating: 60*

STUDENTS AND FACULTY

Enrollment: 601. **Student Body:** 58% female, 42% male, 48% out-of-state, 0% international. Asian 0%, African American 95%, Caucasian 0%, Hispanic 4%, Native American 0%.
Retention and Graduation: 43% freshmen return for sophomore year. 27% freshmen graduate within 4 years. 41% freshmen graduate within 6 years. 25% grads go on to further study within 1 year. 25% grads pursue arts and sciences degrees. 25% grads pursue law degrees. 25% grads pursue business degrees. 25% grads pursue medical degrees. **Faculty:** Student/faculty ratio 16:1. 29 full-time faculty, 62% hold PhDs, 66% are members of minority groups, 45% are women. 0% of classes are taught by teaching assistants.

ACADEMICS

Degrees: bachelor's. **Classes:** Most classes have fewer than 10 students. Most lab/discussion sessions have fewer than 10 students. **Majors with Highest Enrollment:** biology/biological sciences; business/commerce; psychology. **Special Study Options:** double major, dual enrollment, independent study, internships, teacher certification program. **Disability Services:** Special programs offered to physically disabled students include note-taking services, tape recorders, tutors. **Career Services:** Alumni network, alumni services, career assessment, internships.

FACILITIES

Housing: men's dorms, women's dorms. 100% of campus accessible to physically disabled. **Special Academic Facilities/Equipment:** Savery Library, Home of the famous Amistad Murals, historic Swayne Hall, which is listed on the National Register; DeForest Chapel, which has the stained glass windows by famous artist, David Driskell; Goodnow Art Building **Computers:** 100% of libraries, 50% of common outdoor areas have wireless network access. Administrative functions (other than registration) can be performed online.

CAMPUS LIFE

Environment: Rural. **Activities:** Choral groups, concert band, dance, drama/theater, jazz band, student government, student newspaper, yearbook 40 registered organizations, 8 honor societies, 1 religious organizations. 4 fraternities, 4 sororities. **Athletics (Intercollegiate):** *Men:* baseball, basketball, golf. *Women:* basketball, cheerleading, volleyball. **On-Campus Highlights:** Savery Library, DeForest Chapel, Swayne Hall, Callanan Hall, Fanning Hall.

ADMISSIONS

Freshman Academic Profile: Average high school GPA 2.7. 90% from public high schools. SAT Math middle 50% range 340-410. SAT Critical Reading middle 50% range 320-460. ACT middle 50% range 16-19. Minimum paper TOEFL 500. **Basis for Candidate Selection:** *Very important factors considered include:* application essay, recommendation(s), rigor of secondary school record, standardized test scores, character/personal qualities, extracurricular activities, talent/ability, volunteer work, work experience. *Important factors considered include:* Class rank. *Other factors considered include:* interview. **Freshman Admission Requirements:** High school diploma is required and GED is accepted. *Academic units required:* 4 English, 2 mathematics, 2 science, 3 social studies, 2 physical education or health. *Academic units recommended:* 4 English, 2 mathematics, 2 science, 3 social studies, 2 physical education or health. **Freshman Admission Statistics:** 2,000 applied, 40% admitted, 38% enrolled. **Transfer Admission Requirements:** High school transcript, college transcript(s), essay or personal statement, standardized test scores, statement of good standing from prior institution(s). Minimum college GPA of 2.0 required. Lowest grade transferable C. **General Admission Information:** Application Fee $25. Nonfall registration accepted. Admission may be deferred for a maximum of 2 years. Credit and/or placement offered for CEEB Advanced Placement tests.

COSTS AND FINANCIAL AID

Annual tuition $6,720. Room and board $4,290. Required fees $408. Average book expense $1,000. **Required Forms and Deadlines:** FAFSA, institution's own financial aid form, CSS/Financial Aid PROFILE, state aid form. **Notification of Awards:** Applicants will be notified of awards on or about 4/1. **Types of Aid:** *Need-based scholarships/grants:* Federal Pell, SEOG, state scholarships/grants, private scholarships, the school's own gift aid, United Negro College Fund. *Loans:* Subsidized Stafford, Unsubsidized Stafford, PLUS, Federal Perkins. **Student Employment:** Highest amount earned per year from on-campus jobs $1,200. Off-campus job opportunities are good. **Financial Aid Statistics:** 45% freshmen, 26% undergrads receive need-based scholarship or grant aid. 45% freshmen, 26% undergrads receive non-need-based scholarship or grant aid. 90% freshmen, 90% undergrads receive any aid. 80% undergrads borrow to pay for school. Average cumulative indebtedness $5,000. **Criteria for awarding institutional aid:** *Non-need-based:* academics, alumni affiliation, art, athletics, music/drama.

TARLETON STATE UNIVERSITY

PO Box T-0030, Stephenville, TX 76402
Phone: 254-968-9125 • **Financial Aid Phone:** 254-968-9070
E-mail: uadm@tarleton.edu • **CEEB Code:** 6817
Fax: 254-968-9951 • **Website:** • **ACT Code:** 4204

This public school was founded in 1899. It has a 125-acre campus.

RATINGS

Admissions Selectivity Rating: 69	Fire Safety Rating: 87	Green Rating: 62

STUDENTS AND FACULTY

Enrollment: 8,856. **Student Body:** 59% female, 41% male, 2% out-of-state, 1% international (22 countries represented). Asian 1%, African American 6%, Caucasian 76%, Hispanic 14%, Native American 1%.
Retention and Graduation: 67% freshmen return for sophomore year. 18% freshmen graduate within 4 years. 40% freshmen graduate within 6 years.
Faculty: Student/faculty ratio 18:1. 318 full-time faculty, 66% hold PhDs, 10% are members of minority groups, 41% are women. 2% of classes are taught by teaching assistants.

ACADEMICS

Degrees: associate, bachelor's, master's. **Classes:** Most classes have 20–29 students. Most lab/discussion sessions have 10–19 students. **Majors with Highest Enrollment:** business/commerce; education. **Special Study Options:** Accelerated program, distance learning, double major, dual enrollment, honors program, internships, study abroad, teacher certification program, Undergrads may take grad level classes. **Honors Programs:** Offer honors classes in core curriculum subjects, including English, history, political science, chemistry, biology, geology, and speech. Courses offer intellectually challenging material, innovative approaches to the subject, increased opportunities for honing critical thinking and writing skills, and the opportunity to interact closely with similarly motivated students and with outstanding faculty. **Disability Services:** Special programs offered to physically disabled students include note-taking services, reader services, tutors. **Career Services:** career/job search classes, career assessment, internships Career Services highlights include Education Department and Student Teaching opportunities.

FACILITIES

Housing: Coed dorms, special housing for disabled students, men's dorms, special housing for international students, women's dorms, fraternity/sorority housing, apartments for married students, cooperative housing, apartments for single students. **Special Academic Facilities/Equipment:** Planetarium in Science Bldg. W.K. Gordon Center for Industrial History of Texas **Computers:** 100% of classrooms, 100% of dorms, 100% of libraries, 100% of student union, have wireless network access. Students can register for classes online. Administrative functions (other than registration) can be performed online.

CAMPUS LIFE

Environment. Village. **Activities:** Choral groups, concert band, dance, drama/theater, jazz band, literary magazine, marching band, music ensembles, musical theater, opera, pep band, radio station, student government, student newspaper, student-run film society, symphony orchestra, television station, yearbook, Campus Ministries, International Student Organization 117 registered organizations, 13 honor societies, 13 religious organizations. 7 fraternities, 8 sororities. **Athletics (Intercollegiate):** *Men:* baseball, basketball, cheerleading, cross-country, football, rodeo, track/field (outdoor) *Women:* basketball, cheerleading, cross-country, golf, rodeo, softball, tennis, track/field (outdoor), volleyball. **On-Campus Highlights:** Barry B. Thompson Student Center, New Recreational Sports Facility, Dick Smith Library, Wisdom Gym, Science Bldg with Planetarium. **Environmental Initiatives:** 15% Electric from wind In compliance with SB12

ADMISSIONS

Freshman Academic Profile: 9% in top 10% of high school class, 23% in top 25% of high school class, 76% in top 50% of high school class. 97% from public high schools. SAT Math middle 50% range 450-550. SAT Critical Reading middle 50% range 430-530. SAT Writing middle 50% range 410-500. ACT middle 50% range 19-23. Minimum web-based TOEFL 190. Minimum paper TOEFL 520. **Basis for Candidate Selection:** *Very important factors considered include:* Class rank, rigor of secondary school record, standardized test scores. *Important factors considered include:* academic GPA. **Freshman Admission Requirements:** High school diploma is required and GED is accepted. *Academic units required:* 4 English, 3 mathematics, 2 science, (2 science labs), 2 social studies, 1 history, 2 academic electives. *Academic units recommended:* 4 English, 3 mathematics, 2 science, (2 science labs), 2 social studies, 1 history, 2 academic electives. **Freshman Admission Statistics:** 4,643 applied, 76% admitted, 49% enrolled. **Transfer Admission Requirements:** college transcript(s), minimum college GPA of 2.0 required. Lowest grade transferable D. **General Admission Information:** Application Fee $25. Regular application deadline 8/1. Nonfall registration accepted. Credit offered for CEEB Advanced Placement tests.

COSTS AND FINANCIAL AID

Annual in-state tuition $3,696. Annual out-of-state tuition $12,120. Room and board $7,633. Required fees $1,826. Average book expense $1,174. **Required Forms and Deadlines:** FAFSA. **Notification of Awards:** Applicants will be notified of awards on a rolling basis beginning 2/1. **Types of Aid:** *Need-based scholarships/grants:* Federal Pell, SEOG, state scholarships/grants, private scholarships, the school's own gift aid. *Loans:* Subsidized Stafford, Unsubsidized Stafford, PLUS, state loans, college/university loans from institutional funds. **Student Employment: Financial Aid Statistics:** 64% freshmen, 64% undergrads receive need-based scholarship or grant aid. 31% freshmen, 23% un-

dergrads receive non-need-based scholarship or grant aid. 66% freshmen, 60% undergrads receive need-based self-help aid. 57% freshmen, 37% undergrads receive any aid. 56% undergrads borrow to pay for school. Average cumulative indebtedness $15,548. **Criteria for awarding institutional aid:** *Non-need-based:* academics, alumni affiliation, art, athletics, leadership, music/drama.

TAYLOR UNIVERSITY

236 West Reade Avenue, Upland, IN 46989-1001
Phone: 765-998-5134 • **Financial Aid Phone:** 765-998-5358
E-mail: admissions@tayloru.edu • **CEEB Code:** 1802
Fax: 765-998-4925 • **Website:** www.taylor.edu • **ACT Code:** 1248

This private school was founded in 1846. It has a 952-acre campus.

RATINGS

Admissions Selectivity Rating: 73 **Fire Safety Rating:** 89 **Green Rating:** 78

STUDENTS AND FACULTY

Enrollment: 1,887. **Student Body:** 54% female, 46% male, 62% out-of-state, 4% international (27 countries represented). Asian 2%, African American 2%, Caucasian 89%, Hispanic 2%, Native American 0%.
Retention and Graduation: 88% freshmen return for sophomore year. 69% freshmen graduate within 4 years. 77% freshmen graduate within 6 years. 18% grads go on to further study within 1 year. 3% grads pursue arts and sciences degrees. 1% grads pursue law degrees. 2% grads pursue business degrees. 1% grads pursue medical degrees. **Faculty:** Student/faculty ratio 12:1. 134 full-time faculty, 81% hold PhDs, 7% are members of minority groups, 28% are women. 0% of classes are taught by teaching assistants.

ACADEMICS

Degrees: associate, bachelor's, certificate, diploma, master's. **Classes:** Most classes have 10–19 students. Most lab/discussion sessions have 10–19 students. **Majors with Highest Enrollment:** biology/biological sciences; elementary education and teaching; psychology. **Special Study Options:** cooperative education program, distance learning, double major, dual enrollment, exchange student program (domestic), honors program, independent study, internships, student-designed major, study abroad, teacher certification program. **Honors Programs:** Honors Program emphasizes to a greater extent than the general curriculum, integration of faith and learning, ideas and values in content and discussion and student initiative in format. Also offer Freshmen Irish Studies Program in Ireland. **Combined Degree Programs:** BA/MA, BA and MA in Environmental Science. **Disability Services:** Special programs offered to physically disabled students include note-taking services, reader services, tape recorders, tutors. **Career Services:** Alumni network, alumni services, career assessment, internships, regional alumni.

FACILITIES

Housing: men's dorms, women's dorms, apartments for married students, apartments for single students, Some off-campus apartments available to upperclassmen with special permission. 85% of campus accessible to physically disabled. **Special Academic Facilities/Equipment:** Compton Art Gallery, Edwin W. Brown Collection/CS Lewis and Friends. **Computers:** 100% of classrooms, 100% of dorms, 100% of libraries, 100% of dining areas, 100% of student union, 50% of common outdoor areas have wireless network access Students can register for classes online. Administrative functions (other than registration) can be performed online.

CAMPUS LIFE

Environment: Rural. **Activities:** Choral groups, concert band, drama/theater, jazz band, literary magazine, music ensembles, musical theater, opera, pep band, radio station, student government, student newspaper, student-run film society, symphony orchestra, television station, yearbook, Campus Ministries, International Student Organization, Model UN 87 registered organizations, 7 honor societies, 23 religious organizations. **Athletics (Intercollegiate):** *Men:* baseball, basketball, cross-country, football, golf, soccer, tennis, track/field (outdoor), track/field (indoor). *Women:* basketball, cross-country, soccer, softball, tennis, track/field (outdoor), track/field (indoor), volleyball. **On-Campus Highlights:** The Jumping Bean (Student coffee shop), Kesler Student Activities Center, Modelle Metcalf Visual Arts Center, Rediger Chapel and Auditorium, Mitchell Theater. **Environmental Initiatives:** The 127,000 sq. ft. Euler Science Complex, scheduled to be completed in the summer of 2012, is designed to LEED specifications and includes innovative sustainability features. This includes two 50kW wind turbines and a 10kW photovoltaic system. Students are engaged in sustainability through various initiatives including the national RecycleMania competition and Campus Conservation Nationals (residence hall electricity and water conservation competition). Taylor hired its first Coordinator of Sustainability and Stewardship in 2010 to help lead the campus on the path to environmental, social, and economic sustainability.

ADMISSIONS

Freshman Academic Profile: Average high school GPA 3.7. 44% in top 10% of high school class, 72% in top 25% of high school class, 91% in top 50% of high school class. 80% from public high schools. SAT Math middle 50% range 510-650. SAT Critical Reading middle 50% range 510-660. SAT Writing middle 50% range 490-640. ACT middle 50% range 25-30. Minimum paper TOEFL 550. **Basis for Candidate Selection:** *Very important factors considered include:* application essay, academic GPA, recommendation(s), rigor of secondary school record, standardized test scores, character/personal qualities, religious affiliation/commitment. *Important factors considered include:* Class rank, extracurricular activities, interview, volunteer work. *Other factors considered include:* alumni/ae relation, first generation, geographical residence, racial/ethnic status, state residency, talent/ability, work experience. **Freshman Admission Requirements:** High school diploma is required and GED is accepted. *Academic units required:* 4 English, 3 mathematics, 3 science, (3 science labs), 2 social studies, 3 academic electives. *Academic units recommended:* 4 English, 3 mathematics, 3 science, (3 science labs), 2 social studies, 3 academic electives. **Freshman Admission Statistics:** 1,787 applied, 84% admitted, 34% enrolled. **Transfer Admission Requirements:** High school transcript, college transcript(s), essay or personal statement, standardized test scores, statement of good standing from prior institution(s). Minimum college GPA of 2.5 required. Lowest grade transferable C+. **General Admission Information:** Application Fee $25. Regular application deadline 8/1. Notification on a rolling basis, beginning on or about 10/1. Nonfall registration accepted. Admission may be deferred for a maximum of 2 years. Credit and/or placement offered for CEEB Advanced Placement tests.

COSTS AND FINANCIAL AID

Annual tuition $27,850. Room and board $7,757. Required fees $238. Average book expense $3,000. **Required Forms and Deadlines:** FAFSA. **Notification of Awards:** Applicants will be notified of awards on a rolling basis beginning 3/1. **Types of Aid:** *Need-based scholarships/grants:* Federal Pell, SEOG, state scholarships/grants, private scholarships, the school's own gift aid. *Loans:* Direct Subsidized Stafford, Direct Unsubsidized Stafford, Direct PLUS, Federal Perkins, college/university loans from institutional funds. **Student Employment:** Federal Work-Study Program available. Institutional employment available. Highest amount earned per year from on-campus jobs $3,500. Off-campus job opportunities are poor. **Financial Aid Statistics:** 100% freshmen, 98% undergrads receive need-based scholarship or grant aid. 17% freshmen, 14% undergrads receive non-need-based scholarship or grant aid. 83% freshmen, 86% undergrads receive need-based self-help aid. 4% freshmen, 5% undergrads receive athletic scholarships. 98% freshmen, 91% undergrads receive any aid. 60% undergrads borrow to pay for school. Average cumulative indebtedness $26,003. **Criteria for awarding institutional aid:** *Non-need-based:* academics, alumni affiliation, art, athletics, leadership, minority status, music/drama, religious affiliation, state/district residency.

TEMPLE UNIVERSITY

Best 378

1801 North Broad Street 041-09-, Philadelphia, PA 19122-6096
Phone: 215-204-7200 • **Financial Aid Phone:** 215-204-8760
E-mail: TUADM@TEMPLE.EDU • **CEEB Code:** 2906
Fax: 215-204-5694 • **Website:** www.temple.edu • **ACT Code:** 3724

This public school was founded in 1888. It has a 330-acre campus.

RATINGS

Admissions Selectivity Rating: 79   **Fire Safety Rating:** 91   **Green Rating:** 93

STUDENTS AND FACULTY

Enrollment: 26,981. **Student Body:** 51% female, 49% male, 18% out-of-state, 3% international (82 countries represented). Asian 10%, African American 14%, Caucasian 61%, Hispanic 5%, Native American 0%.
Retention and Graduation: 87% freshmen return for sophomore year. 37% freshmen graduate within 4 years. 68% freshmen graduate within 6 years.
Faculty: Student/faculty ratio 15:1. 1451 full-time faculty, 85% hold PhDs, 18% are members of minority groups, 40% are women.

ACADEMICS

Degrees: associate, bachelor's, certificate, diploma, doctoral, master's, post-bachelor's certificate, post-master's certificate, terminal associate, transfer as-

sociate. **Classes:** Most classes have 20–29 students. Most lab/discussion sessions have 20–29 students. **Majors with Highest Enrollment:** elementary education and teaching; marketing/marketing management; psychology. **Special Study Options:** cooperative education program, cross-registration, distance learning, double major, dual enrollment, English as a Second Language (ESL), exchange student program (domestic), honors program, independent study, internships, liberal arts/career combination, study abroad, teacher certification program, Programs are offered in a number of foreign countries: Japan, Italy, Costa Rica, France, Germany, Ghana, India, Spain, Turkey, United Kingdom and Brazil. **Honors Programs:** 1) Honors Certificate Program 2) Honors Scholars Program **Combined Degree Programs:** BA/MA, M.B.A./M.A and M.B.A./M.S. and B.F.A with Teaching Certification. **Disability Services:** Special programs offered to physically disabled students include note-taking services, reader services, tape recorders, tutors. **Career Services:** Alumni network, alumni services, career/job search classes, career assessment, internships, regional alumni.

FACILITIES

Housing: Coed dorms, special housing for disabled students, apartments for single students, Living/Learning Centers are available. 100% of campus accessible to physically disabled. **Special Academic Facilities/Equipment:** Blockson Collection, Urban Archieves, observatory **Computers:** 40% of classrooms, 30% of dorms, 80% of libraries, 90% of dining areas, 100% of student union, 40% of common outdoor areas have wireless network access. Students can register for classes online. Administrative functions (other than registration) can be performed online.

CAMPUS LIFE

Environment: Metropolis. **Activities:** Choral groups, concert band, dance, drama/theater, jazz band, literary magazine, marching band, music ensembles, musical theater, opera, pep band, radio station, student government, student newspaper, student-run film society, symphony orchestra, television station, yearbook, Campus Ministries, International Student Organization 232 registered organizations, 12 honor societies, 24 religious organizations. 11 fraternities, 9 sororities. **Athletics (Intercollegiate):** *Men:* baseball, basketball, cheerleading, crew/rowing, cross-country, football, golf, gymnastics, soccer, table tennis, tennis, track/field (outdoor), track/field (indoor). *Women:* basketball, cheerleading, crew/rowing, cross-country, fencing, field hockey, gymnastics, lacrosse, soccer, softball, table tennis, tennis, track/field (outdoor), track/field (indoor), volleyball. **On-Campus Highlights:** The Tech Center, Howard Gittis Student Center, Liacouras Center (athletic/convocation center), The Shops at Liacouras Walk, Bell Tower, 6. Independence Blue Cross Student Recreation Center 7. Alumni Circle 8. Rock Hall 9. Student Pavilion 10. Campus mall. **Environmental Initiatives:** 1. President Hart signed the American College and University Presidents Climate Commitment in April 2008 The Office of Sustainability was established July 2008. 3. Completion of Climate Action Plan in May 2010.

ADMISSIONS

Freshman Academic Profile: Average high school GPA 3.4. 18% in top 10% of high school class, 51% in top 25% of high school class, 89% in top 50% of high school class. 76% from public high schools. SAT Math middle 50% range 510-610. SAT Critical Reading middle 50% range 500-600. SAT Writing middle 50% range 490-590. ACT middle 50% range 21-26. Minimum web-based TOEFL 79. Minimum paper TOEFL 550. **Basis for Candidate Selection:** *Very important factors considered include:* academic GPA, rigor of secondary school record. *Important factors considered include:* Class rank, standardized test scores. *Other factors considered include:* application essay, recommendation(s), alumni/ae relation, character/personal qualities, extracurricular activities, talent/ability, volunteer work, work experience. **Freshman Admission Requirements:** High school diploma is required and GED is accepted. *Academic units required:* 4 English, 3 mathematics, 2 science, (1 science labs), 2 foreign language, 2 social studies, 1 history, 1 academic electives. *Academic units recommended:* 4 English, 3 mathematics, 2 science, (1 science labs), 2 foreign language, 2 social studies, 1 history, 1 academic electives. **Freshman Admission Statistics:** 18,731 applied, 67% admitted, 33% enrolled. **Transfer Admission Requirements:** High school transcript, college transcript(s), essay or personal statement, minimum college GPA of 2.50 required. Lowest grade transferable C. **General Admission Information:** Application Fee $50. Regular application deadline 3/1. Notification on a rolling basis, beginning on or about 10/15. Nonfall registration accepted. Admission may be deferred for a maximum of 1 year. Credit and/or placement offered for CEEB Advanced Placement tests.

COSTS AND FINANCIAL AID

Annual in-state tuition $13,006. Annual out-of-state tuition $22,832. Room and board $10,276. Required fees $590. Average book expense $1,000. **Required Forms and Deadlines:** FAFSA. **Notification of Awards:** Applicants will be notified of awards on a rolling basis beginning 2/15. **Types of Aid:** *Need-based scholarships/grants:* Federal Pell, SEOG, state scholarships/grants, private scholarships, the school's own gift aid, Federal Nursing Scholarships. *Loans:*

Subsidized Stafford, Unsubsidized Stafford, PLUS, Federal Perkins, Federal Nursing, state loans, college/university loans from institutional funds. **Student Employment:** Federal Work-Study Program available. Institutional employment available. Off-campus job opportunities are excellent. **Financial Aid Statistics:** 83% freshmen, 81% undergrads receive need-based scholarship or grant aid. 54% freshmen, 34% undergrads receive non-need-based scholarship or grant aid. 84% freshmen, 88% undergrads receive need-based self-help aid. 2% freshmen, 2% undergrads receive athletic scholarships. 88% freshmen, 81% undergrads receive any aid. 76% undergrads borrow to pay for school. Average cumulative indebtedness $33,500. **Criteria for awarding institutional aid:** *Non-need-based:* academics, art, athletics, music/drama.

See page 1228.

TENNESSEE STATE UNIVERSITY

3500 John Merritt Boulevard, Nashville, TN 37209-1561
Phone: 615-963-3101
E-mail: jcade@tnstate.edu
Fax: 615-963-5108 • **Website:** www.tnstate.edu

This is a public school.

RATINGS
Admissions Selectivity Rating: 89   **Fire Safety Rating:** 60*   **Green Rating:** 60*

STUDENTS AND FACULTY
Enrollment: 7,000. **Student Body:** 63% female, 37% male, 40% out of state, 1% international. Asian 1%, African American 83%, Caucasian 15%, Hispanic 1%, Native American 0%.
Retention and Graduation: 77% freshmen return for sophomore year. **Faculty:** Student/faculty ratio 22:1. 383 full-time faculty, 74% hold PhDs, 37% are members of minority groups, 42% are women.

ACADEMICS
Degrees: associate, bachelor's, master's. **Classes:** Most classes have fewer than 10 students. Most lab/discussion sessions have 10-10 students. **Special Study Options:** cooperative education program, cross-registration, double major, exchange student program (domestic), honors program, independent study, internships, liberal arts/career combination, teacher certification program, On-line Degree (courses offered via computer approved by Tennessee Board of Regents).

FACILITIES
Housing: Coed dorms, men's dorms, women's dorms, apartments for single students.

CAMPUS LIFE
Environment: Activities: Choral groups, drama/theater, jazz band, marching band, music ensembles, radio station, student government, student newspaper, yearbook.

ADMISSIONS
Freshman Academic Profile: Average high school GPA 3.0. 90% from public high schools. SAT Math middle 50% range 430-510. SAT Critical Reading middle 50% range 430-510. ACT middle 50% range 18-21. Minimum paper TOEFL 500. **Basis for Candidate Selection:** *Very important factors considered include:* standardized test scores, state residency. *Important factors considered include:* Class rank, recommendation(s), rigor of secondary school record, geographical residence. *Other factors considered include:* alumni/ae relation, character/personal qualities, extracurricular activities, talent/ability. **Freshman Admission Requirements:** High school diploma is required and GED is accepted. *Academic units required:* 4 English, 3 mathematics, 2 science, (1 science labs), 2 foreign language, 1 social studies, 1 academic electives. 4 English, 3 mathematics, 2 science, (1 science labs), 2 foreign language, 1 social studies, 1 history, 1 academic electives. **Freshman Admission Statistics:** 6,344 applied, 35% admitted, 59% enrolled. **Transfer Admission Requirements:** college transcript(s), minimum college GPA of 2.9 required. Lowest grade transferable C. **General Admission Information:** Application Fee $15. Regular application deadline 8/1. Credit and/or placement offered for CEEB Advanced Placement tests.

COSTS AND FINANCIAL AID
Annual in-state tuition $3,272. Annual out-of-state tuition $10,230. Room and board $3,060. Required fees $150. Average book expense $850. **Required Forms and Deadlines:** FAFSA, CSS/Financial Aid PROFILE, noncustodial PROFILE. **Types of Aid:** *Need-based scholarships/grants:* Federal Pell, SEOG. *Loans:* Direct Subsidized Stafford, Direct Unsubsidized Stafford, Direct PLUS, Subsidized Stafford, Unsubsidized Stafford, PLUS, Federal Perkins.

Financial Aid Statistics: 66% freshmen, 64% undergrads receive need-based scholarship or grant aid. 25% freshmen, 24% undergrads receive non-need-based scholarship or grant aid. 77% freshmen, 76% undergrads receive need-based self-help aid. 1% freshmen.

TENNESSEE TECHNOLOGICAL UNIVERSITY

PO Box 5006, Cookeville, TN 38505
Phone: 931-372-3888 • **Financial Aid Phone:** 931-372-3073
E-mail: admissions@tntech.edu • **CEEB Code:** 1804
Fax: 931-372-6250 • **Website:** www.tntech.edu • **ACT Code:** 4012

This public school was founded in 1915. It has a 235-acre campus.

RATINGS
Admissions Selectivity Rating: 68   **Fire Safety Rating:** 71   **Green Rating:** 60*

STUDENTS AND FACULTY
Enrollment: 9,647. **Student Body:** 45% female, 55% male, 3% out-of-state, 6% international. Asian 1%, African American 4%, Caucasian 84%, Hispanic 2%, Native American 0%.
Retention and Graduation: 70% freshmen return for sophomore year. 20% freshmen graduate within 4 years. **Faculty:** Student/faculty ratio 21:1. 389 full-time faculty, 72% hold PhDs, 13% are members of minority groups, 40% are women. 1% of classes are taught by teaching assistants.

ACADEMICS
Degrees: bachelor's, master's, post-master's certificate. **Classes:** Most classes have 20-29 students. Most lab/discussion sessions have 20-29 students. **Majors with Highest Enrollment:** business/commerce; elementary education and teaching; mechanical engineering. **Special Study Options:** cooperative education program, distance learning, double major, dual enrollment, honors program, internships, study abroad, teacher certification program. **Disability Services:** Special programs offered to physically disabled students include note-taking services, reader services, tape recorders, tutors. **Career Services:** Alumni network, alumni services, career/job search classes, internships, regional alumni.

FACILITIES
Housing: Good dorms, special housing for disabled students, men's dorms, special housing for international students, women's dorms, apartments for married students, apartments for single students. 99% of campus accessible to physically disabled. **Special Academic Facilities/Equipment:** 300-acre farm lab, electric power center, water resources center, manufacturing center. **Computers:** Students can register for classes online. Administrative functions (other than registration) can be performed online.

CAMPUS LIFE
Environment: Rural. **Activities:** Choral groups, concert band, dance, drama/theater, jazz band, literary magazine, marching band, music ensembles, musical theater, opera, pep band, radio station, student government, student newspaper, symphony orchestra, television station, yearbook 182 registered organizations, 26 honor societies, 16 religious organizations, 12 fraternities, 8 sororities. **Athletics (Intercollegiate):** *Men:* baseball, basketball, cheerleading, cross-country, football, golf, riflery, tennis. *Women:* basketball, cheerleading, cross-country, golf, riflery, soccer, softball, tennis, track/field (outdoor), track/field (indoor), volleyball. **On-Campus Highlights:** Recreation/ Fitness Center, Barnes and Noble Bookstore, Joan Derryberry Art Gallery, New Residence Halls, Bryan Fine Arts Music Auditorium.

ADMISSIONS
Freshman Academic Profile: Average high school GPA 3.4. 24% in top 10% of high school class, 50% in top 25% of high school class, 82% in top 50% of high school class. 80% from public high schools. SAT Math middle 50% range 490-640. SAT Critical Reading middle 50% range 480-600. ACT middle 50% range 20-26. Minimum paper TOEFL 500. **Basis for Candidate Selection:** *Very important factors considered include:* academic GPA, rigor of secondary school record, standardized test scores. *Other factors considered include:* application essay, recommendation(s), alumni/ae relation, character/personal qualities, extracurricular activities, interview. **Freshman Admission Requirements:** High school diploma is required and GED is accepted. *Academic units required:* 4 English, 3 mathematics, 2 science, (1 science labs), 2 foreign language, 1 social studies, 1 history, 1 visual / performing art. 4 English, 3 mathematics, 2 science, (1 science labs), 2 foreign language, 1 social studies, 1 history, 1 visual / performing art **Freshman Admission Statistics:** 4,553 applied, 94% admitted, 45% enrolled. **Transfer Admission Requirements:** college transcript(s), minimum college GPA of 2.0 required. Lowest grade transferable D. **General Admission Information:** Application Fee $15. Regular application deadline 8/1. Nonfall registration accepted. Admission may

be deferred for a maximum of 1 semester. Credit and/or placement offered for CEEB Advanced Placement tests.

COSTS AND FINANCIAL AID
Annual in-state tuition $5,004. Annual out-of-state tuition $18,000. Room and board $7,382. Required fees $1,034. Average book expense $1,500. **Required Forms and Deadlines:** FAFSA. **Notification of Awards:** Applicants will be notified of awards on a rolling basis beginning 3/15. **Types of Aid:** *Need-based scholarships/grants:* Federal Pell, SEOG, state scholarships/grants, private scholarships, the school's own gift aid, United Negro College Fund. *Loans:* Direct Subsidized Stafford, Direct Unsubsidized Stafford, PLUS, Federal Perkins, state loans, college/university loans from institutional funds. **Student Employment: Financial Aid Statistics:** 61% freshmen, 63% undergrads receive need-based scholarship or grant aid. 91% freshmen, 68% undergrads receive non-need-based scholarship or grant aid. 50% freshmen, 59% undergrads receive need-based self-help aid. 2% freshmen, 2% undergrads receive athletic scholarships. 91% freshmen, 89% undergrads receive any aid. 44% undergrads borrow to pay for school. Average cumulative indebtedness $9,510. **Criteria for awarding institutional aid:** *Non-need-based:* academics, alumni affiliation, art, athletics, leadership, minority status, music/drama.

TENNESSEE WESLEYAN COLLEGE

P.O. Box 40, Athens, TN 37371-0040
Phone: 423-745-7504 • **Financial Aid Phone:** 423-746-5209
E-mail: twilliams@twcnet.edu
Fax: 423-745-9335 • **Website:** www.twcnet.edu • **ACT Code:** 4014

This private school was founded in 1857. It has a 40-acre campus.

RATINGS
Admissions Selectivity Rating: 68   **Fire Safety Rating:** 73   **Green Rating:** 60*

STUDENTS AND FACULTY
Enrollment: 847. **Student Body:** 68% female, 32% male, 6% out-of-state, 3% international (13 countries represented). Asian 1%, African American 3%, Caucasian 75%, Hispanic 2%, Native American 0%.
Retention and Graduation: 65% freshmen return for sophomore year. 16% freshmen graduate within 4 years. 32% freshmen graduate within 6 years. **Faculty:** Student/faculty ratio 13:1. 46 full-time faculty, 59% hold PhDs, 2% are members of minority groups, 50% are women. 0% of classes are taught by teaching assistants.

ACADEMICS
Degrees: bachelor's. **Classes:** Most classes have 10–19 students. Most lab/discussion sessions have 10–19 students. **Majors with Highest Enrollment:** business/commerce; education; nursing/registered nurse (rn, asn, bsn, msn). **Special Study Options:** Accelerated program, double major, honors program, independent study, internships, student-designed major, study abroad, teacher certification program. **Disability Services:** Special programs offered to physically disabled students include note-taking services, tape recorders, tutors. **Career Services:** alumni services, internships Career Services highlights include Cyber and Sounds Cafe.

FACILITIES
Housing: men's dorms, women's dorms, apartments for single studentsResidency Exemption Policy: All students are required to live on campus unless they: are married; have custody of a child; is a military veteran eligible for benefits under Public Law 358, GI Bill effective 6/66; is a resident in the home of parents or legal guardian who live within the commuting area; is an independent student as defined by financial aid criteria; established residency in the commuting area for 6 months immediately prior to making application to Tennessee Wesleyan College; or enrolled as a senior. 56% of campus accessible to physically disabled. Special Academic Facilities/Equipment: Old College - building is on historical register

CAMPUS LIFE
Environment: Town. **Activities:** Choral groups, drama/theater, literary magazine, musical theater, student government, student newspaper, yearbook 19 registered organizations, 5 honor societies, 3 religious organizations. 2 sororities. **Athletics (Intercollegiate):** *Men:* baseball, basketball, cheerleading, cross-country, golf, soccer, tennis. *Women:* basketball, cheerleading, cross-country, golf, soccer, softball, tennis, volleyball. **On-Campus Highlights:** Student Activity Center, Student Theatre, Athletic Events (intramural sports), J. Wesley Grill and Starbucks Coffee House, Merner-Pfeiffer Library (book signings, special ev, College Quad.

ADMISSIONS
Freshman Academic Profile: Average high school GPA 3.2. 96% from public high schools. ACT middle 50% range 18-24. Minimum paper TOEFL 500. **Basis for Candidate Selection:** *Very important factors considered include:* academic GPA, rigor of secondary school record, standardized test scores. *Important factors considered include:* application essay, recommendation(s), level of applicant's interest. *Other factors considered include:* Class rank, alumni/ae relation, extracurricular activities, first generation, interview. **Freshman Admission Requirements:** High school diploma is required and GED is accepted. **Freshman Admission Statistics:** 515 applied, 77% admitted, 42% enrolled. **Transfer Admission Requirements:** college transcript(s), minimum college GPA of 2.0 required. Lowest grade transferable D. **General Admission Information:** Application Fee $25. Regular application deadline 8/20. Nonfall registration accepted. Admission may be deferred for a maximum of 1 semester. Credit and/or placement offered for CEEB Advanced Placement tests.

COSTS AND FINANCIAL AID
Annual tuition $14,000. Room and board $5,500. Required fees $550. Average book expense $1,000. **Required Forms and Deadlines:** FAFSA, institution's own financial aid form. **Notification of Awards:** Applicants will be notified of awards on a rolling basis beginning 2/1. **Types of Aid:** *Need-based scholarships/grants:* Federal Pell, SEOG, state scholarships/grants, private scholarships, the school's own gift aid. *Loans:* Subsidized Stafford, Unsubsidized Stafford, PLUS, Federal Perkins, United Methodist. **Student Employment:** Highest amount earned per year from on-campus jobs $2,800. **Financial Aid Statistics:** 100% freshmen, 99% undergrads receive need-based scholarship or grant aid. 17% freshmen, 12% undergrads receive non-need-based scholarship or grant aid. 66% freshmen, 75% undergrads receive need-based self-help aid. 20% freshmen, 13% undergrads receive athletic scholarships. 99% freshmen, 99% undergrads receive any aid. 81% undergrads borrow to pay for school. Average cumulative indebtedness $15,042. **Criteria for awarding institutional aid:** *Non-need-based:* academics, alumni affiliation, art, athletics, job skills, leadership, minority status, music/drama, religious affiliation, state/district residency.

TEXAS A&M UNIVERSITY—COLLEGE STATION

Best 378

P.O. Box 30014, College Station, TX 77843-3014
Phone: 979-845-3741 • **Financial Aid Phone:** 979-845-3236
E-mail: admissions@tamu.edu • **CEEB Code:** 6003
Fax: 979-847-8737 • **Website:** www.tamu.edu • **ACT Code:** 4198

This public school was founded in 1876. It has a 5200-acre campus.

RATINGS
Admissions Selectivity Rating: 83   **Fire Safety Rating:** 84   **Green Rating:** 91

STUDENTS AND FACULTY
Enrollment: 40,094. **Student Body:** 48% female, 52% male, 3% out-of-state, 1% international (127 countries represented). Asian 5%, African American 3%, Caucasian 69%, Hispanic 18%, Native American 0%.
Retention and Graduation: 92% freshmen return for sophomore year. 49% freshmen graduate within 4 years. 80% freshmen graduate within 6 years. **Faculty:** Student/faculty ratio 22:1. 2034 full-time faculty, 92% hold PhDs, 25% are members of minority groups, 32% are women. 25% of classes are taught by teaching assistants.

ACADEMICS
Degrees: bachelor's, master's, post-bachelor's certificate. **Classes:** Most classes have 20–29 students. Most lab/discussion sessions have 20–29 students. **Majors with Highest Enrollment:** biological and physical sciences; multi-/interdisciplinary studies, other; operations management and supervision. **Special Study Options:** Accelerated program, cooperative education program, cross-registration, distance learning, double major, dual enrollment, English as a Second Language (ESL), exchange student program (domestic), honors program, independent study, internships, study abroad, teacher certification program. **Disability Services:** Special programs offered to physically disabled students include note-taking services, reader services, tape recorders, tutors. **Career Services:** Alumni network, alumni services, career/job search classes, internships.

FACILITIES

Housing: Coed dorms, special housing for disabled students, men's dorms, women's dorms, fraternity/sorority housing, apartments for married students, cooperative housing, apartments for single students, theme housing, Honors Dorm. 65% of campus accessible to physically disabled. **Special Academic Facilities/Equipment:** Bush Library/Museum; Jordan International Collection; Corps of Cadets Center/Museum; Forsyth Center Gallary; MSC Visual Arts Gallary; J.Wayne Stark University Center Gallaries Oran W. Nicks Low Speed Wind Tunnel Astronomical Observatory Ocean Drilling Program Building **Computers:** 100% of classrooms, 10% of dorms, 100% of libraries, 100% of dining areas, 100% of student union, have wireless network access. Students can register for classes online. Administrative functions (other than registration) can be performed online.

CAMPUS LIFE

Environment: City. **Activities:** Choral groups, concert band, dance, drama/theater, jazz band, literary magazine, marching band, music ensembles, musical theater, radio station, student government, student newspaper, student-run film society, symphony orchestra, television station, yearbook, Campus Ministries, International Student Organization 725 registered organizations, 34 honor societies, 77 religious organizations. 33 fraternities, 23 sororities. **Athletics (Intercollegiate):** *Men:* baseball, basketball, cross-country, diving, football, golf, riflery, swimming, tennis, track/field (outdoor), track/field (indoor). *Women:* basketball, cross-country, diving, equestrian sports, golf, riflery, soccer, softball, swimming, tennis, track/field (outdoor), track/field (indoor), volleyball. **On-Campus Highlights:** Student Recreation Center, Kyle Field, Corps of Cadets, George Bush Presidential Library/Museum, Research Park. **Environmental Initiatives:** Energy Stewardship Program Paper Recycling Transportation Fuel.

ADMISSIONS

Freshman Academic Profile: 60% in top 10% of high school class, 91% in top 25% of high school class, 99% in top 50% of high school class. SAT Math middle 50% range 560-670. SAT Critical Reading middle 50% range 520-640. SAT Writing middle 50% range 499-620. ACT middle 50% range 24-30. Minimum paper TOEFL 550. **Basis for Candidate Selection:** *Very important factors considered include:* Class rank, academic GPA, rigor of secondary school record, standardized test scores, extracurricular activities, talent/ability. *Important factors considered include:* application essay, first generation, geographical residence, state residency, volunteer work, work experience. *Other factors considered include:* recommendation(s), character/personal qualities. **Freshman Admission Requirements:** High school diploma is required and GED is accepted. *Academic units required:* 4 English, 3 mathematics, 3 science, (2 science labs), 2 foreign language, 2 social studies, 1 history. *Academic units recommended:* 4 English, 3 mathematics, 3 science, (2 science labs), 2 foreign language, 2 social studies, 1 history. **Freshman Admission Statistics:** 27,798 applied, 67% admitted, 44% enrolled. **Transfer Admission Requirements:** High school transcript, college transcript(s), minimum college GPA of 2.5 required. Lowest grade transferable D. **General Admission Information:** Application Fee $60. Regular application deadline 1/15. Notification on a rolling basis, beginning on or about 4/1. Nonfall registration accepted. Credit offered for CEEB Advanced Placement tests.

COSTS AND FINANCIAL AID

Annual in-state tuition $5,297. Annual out-of-state tuition $21,826. Room and board $8,400. Required fees $3,209. Average book expense $1,272. **Required Forms and Deadlines:** FAFSA, institution's own financial aid formFinancial Aid Transcripts (for transfer students). **Notification of Awards:** Applicants will be notified of awards on a rolling basis beginning 4/1. **Types of Aid:** *Need-based scholarships/grants:* Federal Pell, SEOG, state scholarships/grants, private scholarships, the school's own gift aid. *Loans:* Subsidized Stafford, Unsubsidized Stafford, PLUS, Federal Perkins, state loans, college/university loans from institutional funds. **Student Employment:** Federal Work-Study Program available. Institutional employment available. Highest amount earned per year from on-campus jobs $2,639. Off-campus job opportunities are excellent. **Financial Aid Statistics:** 95% freshmen, 86% undergrads receive need-based scholarship or grant aid. 16% freshmen, 9% undergrads receive non-need-based scholarship or grant aid. 54% freshmen, 67% undergrads receive need-based self-help aid. 75% freshmen, 65% undergrads receive any aid. 46% undergrads borrow to pay for school. Average cumulative indebtedness $22,716. **Criteria for awarding institutional aid:** *Non-need-based:* academics, alumni affiliation, art, athletics, job skills, leadership, music/drama, state/district residency.

TEXAS A&M UNIVERSITY—COMMERCE

P.O. Box 3011, Commerce, TX 75429
Phone: 903-886-5106
E-mail: admissions@tamu-commerce.edu
Fax: 903-886-5888 • **ACT Code:** 6188

This public school was founded in 1889. It has a 140-acre campus.

RATINGS

Admissions Selectivity Rating: 84   Fire Safety Rating: 60*   Green Rating: 60*

STUDENTS AND FACULTY

Retention and Graduation: 35% freshmen graduate within 6 years. **Faculty:** Student/faculty ratio 16:1. 294 full-time faculty, 64% hold PhDs, 14% are members of minority groups, 37% are women. 10% of classes are taught by teaching assistants.

ACADEMICS

Degrees: bachelor's, master's. **Classes:** Most classes have 10–19 students. **Majors with Highest Enrollment:** business/commerce; computer and information science; criminal justice/safety studies. **Special Study Options:** cooperative education program, distance learning, double major, dual enrollment, honors program, independent study, internships, study abroad, teacher certification program, weekend college, Week-end classes for graduate students only. Selected courses available online. **Combined Degree Programs:** BA/MD. **Disability Services:** Special programs offered to physically disabled students include reader services, tape recorders, tutors. **Career Services:** career/job search classes, internships.

FACILITIES

Housing: Coed dorms, special housing for disabled students, men's dorms, special housing for international students, women's dorms, fraternity/sorority housing, apartments for married students, apartments for single students. 35% of campus accessible to physically disabled. **Computers:** Students can register for classes online. Administrative functions (other than registration) can be performed online.

CAMPUS LIFE

Environment: Rural. **Activities:** Choral groups, concert band, dance, drama/theater, jazz band, literary magazine, marching band, music ensembles, musical theater, pep band, radio station, student government, student newspaper, student-run film society, television station, yearbook 110 registered organizations, 12 honor societies, 10 religious organizations. 9 fraternities, 9 sororities. **Athletics (Intercollegiate):** *Men:* basketball, cheerleading, cross-country, football, golf, track/field (outdoor). *Women:* basketball, cheerleading, cross-country, golf, soccer, track/field (outdoor), volleyball.

ADMISSIONS

Freshman Academic Profile: Average high school GPA 3.4. 13% in top 10% of high school class, 26% in top 25% of high school class, 33% in top 50% of high school class. 98% from public high schools. SAT Math middle 50% range 460-560. SAT Critical Reading middle 50% range 440-540. ACT middle 50% range 17-23. Minimum paper TOEFL 500. **Basis for Candidate Selection:** *Very important factors considered include:* Class rank, rigor of secondary school record, standardized test scores. *Other factors considered include:* work experience. **Freshman Admission Requirements:** High school diploma is required and GED is accepted. *Academic units required:* 4 English, 3 mathematics, 2 science, 2 History and Social Studies. *Academic units recommended:* 4 English, 3 mathematics, 2 science, 2 History and Social Studies **Freshman Admission Statistics:** 1,899 applied, 51% admitted, 58% enrolled. **Transfer Admission Requirements:** college transcript(s), standardized test scores, statement of good standing from prior institution(s). Minimum college GPA of 2.0 required. Lowest grade transferable D. **General Admission Information:** Application Fee $25. Regular application deadline 8/1. Notification on a rolling basis, beginning on or about 10/1. Nonfall registration accepted. Admission may be deferred for a maximum of 1 year. Credit and/or placement offered for CEEB Advanced Placement tests.

COSTS AND FINANCIAL AID

Annual in-state tuition $9,232. Annual out-of-state tuition $25,732. Room and board $6,220. Required fees $1,106. Average book expense $1,010. **Required Forms and Deadlines:** FAFSA. **Notification of Awards:** Applicants will be notified of awards on a rolling basis beginning 6/1. **Types of Aid:** *Need-based scholarships/grants:* Federal Pell, SEOG, state scholarships/grants, private scholarships, the school's own gift aid. *Loans:* Direct Subsidized Stafford, Direct Unsubsidized Stafford, Subsidized Stafford, Unsubsidized Stafford, PLUS, Federal Perkins. **Student Employment:** Federal Work-Study Program available. Institutional employment available. Highest amount earned per year from on-campus jobs $2,500. Off-campus job opportunities are good. **Financial Aid Statistics:** 98% freshmen, 95% undergrads receive need-based scholarship or grant aid. 77% freshmen, 84% undergrads receive need-based self-help aid. 3% freshmen, 2% undergrads receive athletic scholarships. 63% undergrads borrow to pay for school. Average cumulative indebtedness $20,688. **Criteria for awarding institutional aid:** *Non-need-based:* academics, art, athletics, minority status.

TEXAS A&M UNIVERSITY AT GALVESTON

Admissions Office, Galveston, TX 77553
Phone: 409-740-4414 • **Financial Aid Phone:** 409-740-4500
E-mail: seaaggie@tamug.edu • **CEEB Code:** 6835
Fax: 409-740-4731 • **Website:** www.tamug.edu • **ACT Code:** 6592

This public school was founded in 1963. It has a 150-acre campus.

RATINGS
Admissions Selectivity Rating: 72   **Fire Safety Rating:** 80   **Green Rating:** 60*

STUDENTS AND FACULTY
Enrollment: 1,566. **Student Body:** 40% female, 60% male, 20% out-of-state, 0% international (13 countries represented). Asian 1%, African American 2%, Caucasian 55%, Hispanic 7%, Native American 1%.
Retention and Graduation: 66% freshmen return for sophomore year. 16% freshmen graduate within 4 years. 33% freshmen graduate within 6 years. 60% grads go on to further study within 1 year. 35% grads pursue arts and sciences degrees. 3% grads pursue law degrees. 5% grads pursue business degrees. 2% grads pursue medical degrees. **Faculty:** Student/faculty ratio 14:1. 92 full-time faculty, 65% hold PhDs, 13% are members of minority groups, 20% are women. 1% of classes are taught by teaching assistants.

ACADEMICS
Degrees: bachelor's, master's. **Classes:** Most classes have 10–19 students. **Majors with Highest Enrollment:** marine biology and biological oceanography; naval architecture and marine engineering. **Special Study Options:** Accelerated program, cooperative education program, double major, dual enrollment, independent study, internships, study abroad, teacher certification program, Merchant Marine Certification NROTC Naval Sciences. **Combined Degree Programs:** BS/License Option and BA/License Option. **Disability Services:** Special programs offered to physically disabled students include note-taking services, reader services, tutors. **Career Services:** Alumni network, career assessment, internships, regional alumni. Career Services highlights include http://www.tamug.edu/career/.

FACILITIES
Housing: Coed dorms, special housing for disabled students, women's dorms, Privatized apartment housing available next to campus. 90% of campus accessible to physically disabled. **Special Academic Facilities/Equipment:** USTS Texas Clipper II, Radar School/Ship Bridge Simulator, Engineering Laboratory Building, Sea Camp, Center for Bioacoustics, Center for Marine Training and Safety/TEEX, Laboratory for Oceanographic and Environmental Research, Galveston Bay Information Center, Center for Ports and Waterways, Coastal Zone Laboratory, GulfCet, Marine Mammal Research Program, Naval Science, Texas State Maritime Academy, Texas Institute of Oceanography, Texas Marine Mammal Stranding Network, Sea Turtle/Fisheries Ecology Lab. **Computers:** Students can register for classes online. Administrative functions (other than registration) can be performed online.

CAMPUS LIFE
Environment: Town. **Activities:** Choral groups, dance, drama/theater, literary magazine, student government, student newspaper, television station, yearbook 45 registered organizations, 16 honor societies, 4 religious organizations. **Athletics (Intercollegiate):** *Men:* crew/rowing, sailing. *Women:* crew/rowing, sailing. **On-Campus Highlights:** Mary Moody Northen Student Center, P.E. Facility, Small Boat Basin, Training Ship - Sirius, Jack K. Williams Library.

ADMISSIONS
Freshman Academic Profile: 11% in top 10% of high school class, 40% in top 25% of high school class, 73% in top 50% of high school class. 82% from public high schools. SAT Math middle 50% range 490-600. SAT Critical Reading middle 50% range 460-590. ACT middle 50% range 20-25. Minimum paper TOEFL 550. **Basis for Candidate Selection:** *Very important factors considered include:* Class rank, rigor of secondary school record, standardized test scores. *Important factors considered include:* application essay, academic GPA, recommendation(s), character/personal qualities, extracurricular activities, talent/ability, volunteer work, work experience. *Other factors considered include:* alumni/ae relation, first generation, interview, level of applicant's interest. **Freshman Admission Requirements:** High school diploma is required

and GED is accepted. *Academic units required:* 4 English, 3 mathematics, 3 science, (2 science labs), 3 social studies, 1 computer. *Academic units recommended:* 4 English, 3 mathematics, 3 science, (2 science labs), 3 social studies, 1 computer **Freshman Admission Statistics:** 1,181 applied, 78% admitted, 50% enrolled. **Transfer Admission Requirements:** High school transcript, college transcript(s), essay or personal statement, minimum college GPA of 2.5 required. Lowest grade transferable C. **General Admission Information:** Application Fee $45. Nonfall registration accepted. Admission may be deferred for a maximum of 1 Semester. Credit offered for CEEB Advanced Placement tests.

COSTS AND FINANCIAL AID
Annual in-state tuition $4,680. Annual out-of-state tuition $13,020. Room and board $5,203. Required fees $1,375. Average book expense $1,381. **Required Forms and Deadlines:** FAFSA. **Notification of Awards:** Applicants will be notified of awards on or about 3/15. **Types of Aid:** *Need-based scholarships/ grants:* Federal Pell, SEOG, state scholarships/grants, private scholarships, the school's own gift aid. *Loans:* Direct Subsidized Stafford, Direct Unsubsidized Stafford, Direct PLUS, Subsidized Stafford, Unsubsidized Stafford, PLUS, Federal Perkins, college/university loans from institutional funds. **Student Employment:** Federal Work-Study Program available. Institutional employment available. Highest amount earned per year from on-campus jobs $2,100. Off-campus job opportunities are good. **Financial Aid Statistics:** 51% freshmen, 56% undergrads receive need-based scholarship or grant aid. 5% freshmen, 9% undergrads receive non-need-based scholarship or grant aid. 1% freshmen, 3% undergrads receive need-based self-help aid. 46% freshmen, 48% undergrads receive any aid. 70% undergrads borrow to pay for school. Average cumulative indebtedness $16,000. **Criteria for awarding institutional aid:** *Non-need-based:* academics, leadership, state/district residency.

TEXAS A&M UNIVERSITY—KINGSVILLE

MSC 105, Kingsville, TX 78363
Phone: 361-593-2315
E-mail: ksossrx@tamuk.edu
Fax: 361-593-2195 • **Website:** www.tamuk.edu

This is a public school.

RATINGS
Admissions Selectivity Rating: 61   **Fire Safety Rating:** 60*   **Green Rating:** 60*

STUDENTS AND FACULTY
Enrollment: 5,087. **Student Body:** 47% female, 53% male, 2% out-of-state, 1% international. Asian 1%, African American 4%, Caucasian 23%, Hispanic 57%, Native American 0%.
Retention and Graduation: 59% freshmen return for sophomore year. **Faculty:** Student/faculty ratio 15:1. 276 full-time faculty, 70% hold PhDs, 24% are members of minority groups, 35% are women.

ACADEMICS
Degrees: bachelor's, master's, post-bachelor's certificate, post-master's certificate. **Classes:** Most classes have 10–19 students. Most lab/discussion sessions have 20–29 students. **Special Study Options:** Accelerated program, cooperative education program, distance learning, double major, English as a Second Language (ESL), honors program, internships, study abroad, teacher certification program.

FACILITIES
Housing: Coed dorms, men's dorms, women's dorms, apartments for married students.

CAMPUS LIFE
Environment: Activities: Choral groups, concert band, dance, drama/theater, jazz band, marching band, music ensembles, musical theater, pep band, radio station, student government, student newspaper, television station.

ADMISSIONS
Basis for Candidate Selection: *Important factors considered include:* Class rank, rigor of secondary school record, standardized test scores. **Freshman Admission Statistics:** 2,105 applied, 99% admitted, 43% enrolled. Minimum college GPA of 2.0 required. **General Admission Information:** Application Fee $15. Nonfall registration not accepted. Admission may be deferred for a maximum of varies.

COSTS AND FINANCIAL AID
Annual in-state tuition $1,380. Annual out-of-state tuition $7,590. Room and board $3,966. Required fees $1,602. Average book expense $614. **Required Forms and Deadlines:** FAFSA. **Financial Aid Statistics:** 92% freshmen, 100% undergrads receive need-based scholarship or grant aid. 31% freshmen, 71% undergrads receive non-need-based scholarship or grant aid. 87%

freshmen, 82% undergrads receive need-based self-help aid. 46% undergrads borrow to pay for school. Average cumulative indebtedness $2,867.

TEXAS A&M UNIVERSITY—TEXARKANA

P.O. Box 5518, Texarkana, TX 75505
Phone: 903-223-3069 • **E-mail:** admissions@tamut.edu
Fax: 903-223-3140

This public school was founded in 1971. It has a 1-acre campus.

RATINGS
Admissions Selectivity Rating: 60* **Fire Safety Rating:** 60* **Green Rating:** 60*

STUDENTS AND FACULTY
Enrollment: 1,030. **Student Body:** 71% female, 29% male, 0% international. Asian 1%, African American 16%, Caucasian 78%, Hispanic 6%, Native American 1%.
Retention and Graduation: Faculty: Student/faculty ratio 13:1. 59 full-time faculty, 15% are members of minority groups, 41% are women.

ACADEMICS
Degrees: bachelor's, master's. **Majors with Highest Enrollment:** accounting; general studies; multi-/interdisciplinary studies, other. **Special Study Options:** cross-registration, distance learning, independent study, internships, liberal arts/career combination, study abroad, teacher certification program. **Disability Services:** Special programs offered to physically disabled students include note-taking services, tape recorders. **Career Services:** career/job search classes.

FACILITIES
Housing: 100% of campus accessible to physically disabled. **Computers:** Students can register for classes online. Administrative functions (other than registration) can be performed online.

CAMPUS LIFE
Environment: Village. **Activities:** student government, student newspaper 20 registered organizations, 5 honor societies, 1 religious organizations.

ADMISSIONS
Freshman Academic Profile: Minimum paper TOEFL 550. **Transfer Admission Requirements:** college transcript(s), minimum college GPA of 2.0 required. Lowest grade transferable D. **General Admission Information:** Nonfall registration not accepted. Credit offered for CEEB Advanced Placement tests.

COSTS AND FINANCIAL AID
Required Forms and Deadlines: FAFSA, institution's own financial aid formOther documents may be required upon review of student aid reports. **Notification of Awards:** Applicants will be notified of awards on or about 6/1. **Types of Aid:** *Need-based scholarships/grants:* Federal Pell, SEOG, state scholarships/grants, private scholarships, the school's own gift aid. *Loans:* Subsidized Stafford, Unsubsidized Stafford, PLUS, college/university loans from institutional funds. **Student Employment:** Federal Work-Study Program available. Off-campus job opportunities are good. **Criteria for awarding institutional aid:** *Non-need-based:* academics, alumni affiliation, leadership, state/district residency.

TEXAS CHRISTIAN UNIVERSITY

Best 378

Office of Admissions, Fort Worth, TX 76129
Phone: 817-257-7490 • **Financial Aid Phone:** 817-257-7858
E-mail: frogmail@tcu.edu • **CEEB Code:** 6820
Fax: 817-257-7268 • **Website:** www.tcu.edu • **ACT Code:** 4206

This private school, affiliated with the Disciples of Christ Church, was founded in 1873. It has a 300-acre campus.

RATINGS
Admissions Selectivity Rating: 93 **Fire Safety Rating:** 79 **Green Rating:** 69

STUDENTS AND FACULTY
Enrollment: 8,171. **Student Body:** 59% female, 41% male, 29% out-of-state, 5% international (76 countries represented). Asian 3%, African American 5%, Caucasian 74%, Hispanic 10%, Native American 1%.
Retention and Graduation: 87% freshmen return for sophomore year. 55% freshmen graduate within 4 years. 74% freshmen graduate within 6 years. 31% grads go on to further study within 1 year. **Faculty:** Student/faculty ratio 14:1. 544 full-time faculty, 84% hold PhDs, 12% are members of minority groups, 43% are women. 2% of classes are taught by teaching assistants.

ACADEMICS
Degrees: bachelor's, certificate, first professional, first professional certificate, master's, post-bachelor's certificate. **Classes:** Most classes have 10–19 students. Most lab/discussion sessions have 20–29 students. **Majors with Highest Enrollment:** business administration and management; nursing/registered nurse (rn, asn, bsn, msn); public relations, advertising, and applied communication, other any instructional program in organizational communication, public relations, and advertising not listed above. **Special Study Options:** Accelerated program, cross-registration, distance learning, double major, dual enrollment, English as a Second Language (ESL), honors program, independent study, internships, liberal arts/career combination, study abroad, teacher certification program. **Honors Programs:** John V. Roach Honors College The Honors College offers programs for students of all majors and complements all areas of study on campus. Entering freshmen who complete the Honors College requirements will graduate with a John V. Roach Honors College Diploma, as well as a specialized degree from the college of their chosen major(s). **Combined Degree Programs:** BSE/MED. **Disability Services:** Special programs offered to physically disabled students include note-taking services. **Career Services:** Alumni network, alumni services, career/job search classes, career assessment, internships, regional alumni. Career Services highlights include Career Services and entrepreneurship.

FACILITIES
Housing: Coed dorms, men's dorms, women's dorms, fraternity/sorority housing, apartments for married students, apartments for single students, wellness housing, theme housing, designated rooms available for ADA needs. 97% of campus accessible to physically disabled. **Special Academic Facilities/Equipment:** Art exhibition hall, Tandy film library, speech/hearing clinic, TV studios, computer labs, observatory, Moncrief Meteorite, special collections, alumni and visitors center, cable TV, radio station, performance hall, variety of athletic facilities. **Computers:** 100% of classrooms, 100% of dorms, 100% of libraries, 100% of dining areas, 100% of student union, 100% of common outdoor areas have wireless network access. Students can register for classes online. Administrative functions (other than registration) can be performed online.

CAMPUS LIFE
Environment: Metropolis. **Activities:** Choral groups, concert band, dance, drama/theater, jazz band, literary magazine, marching band, music ensembles, musical theater, opera, pep band, radio station, student government, student newspaper, television station, yearbook, Campus Ministries, International Student Organization, Model UN 200 registered organizations, 29 honor societies, 17 religious organizations. 15 fraternities, 18 sororities. **Athletics (Intercollegiate):** *Men:* baseball, basketball, cross-country, diving, football, golf, swimming, tennis, track/field (outdoor), track/field (indoor). *Women:* basketball, cross-country, diving, equestrian sports, golf, riflery, soccer, swimming, tennis, track/field (outdoor), track/field (indoor), volleyball. **On-Campus Highlights:** Amon Carter Stadium, University Recreation Center, Monnig Meteorite Collection, Brown Lupton University Union, Campus Commons/Frog Fountain. **Environmental Initiatives:** American Colleges and Universities President's Climate Commitment Climate Commitment Curriculum Committee - planning how to integrate concepts of climate neutrality and sustainability into the curriculum of all TCU students. Academic research initiatives in areas such as green roofs, wind energy, and alternative fuels.

ADMISSIONS
Freshman Academic Profile: 38% in top 10% of high school class, 73% in top 25% of high school class, 95% in top 50% of high school class. 62% from public high schools. SAT Math middle 50% range 540-650. SAT Critical Reading middle 50% range 520-630. SAT Writing middle 50% range 540-640. ACT middle 50% range 24-29. Minimum web-based TOEFL 80. Minimum paper TOEFL 550. **Basis for Candidate Selection:** *Very important factors considered include:* Class rank, application essay, academic GPA, recommendation(s), rigor of secondary school record, standardized test scores, character/personal qualities. *Important factors considered include:* extracurricular activities, first generation, geographical residence, level of applicant's interest, racial/ethnic status, religious affiliation/commitment, talent/ability, volunteer work, work experience. *Other factors considered include:* alumni/ae relation, interview. **Freshman Admission Requirements:** High school diploma is required and GED is not accepted. *Academic units required:* 4 English, 3 mathematics, 3 science, 2 foreign language, 3 social studies, 2 academic electives. *Academic units recommended:* 4 English, 3 mathematics, 3 science, 2 foreign language, 3

social studies, 2 academic electives. **Freshman Admission Statistics:** 19,168 applied, 38% admitted, 26% enrolled. **Transfer Admission Requirements:** college transcript(s), essay or personal statement, minimum college GPA of 2.0 required. Lowest grade transferable C. **General Admission Information:** Application Fee $40. Regular application deadline 2/15. Regular notification 4/1. Nonfall registration accepted. Admission may be deferred for a maximum of 1 year. Credit offered for CEEB Advanced Placement tests.

COSTS AND FINANCIAL AID

Annual tuition $34,500. Room and board $10,650. Required fees $90. Average book expense $1,200. **Required Forms and Deadlines:** FAFSA. **Notification of Awards:** Applicants will be notified of awards on a rolling basis beginning 3/15. **Types of Aid:** *Need-based scholarships/grants:* Federal Pell, SEOG, state scholarships/grants, private scholarships, the school's own gift aid. *Loans:* Subsidized Stafford, Unsubsidized Stafford, PLUS, Federal Perkins, Federal Nursing, state loans. **Student Employment:** Federal Work-Study Program available. Institutional employment available. Highest amount earned per year from on-campus jobs $12,750. Off-campus job opportunities are excellent. **Financial Aid Statistics:** 97% freshmen, 91% undergrads receive need-based scholarship or grant aid. 64% freshmen, 58% undergrads receive non-need-based scholarship or grant aid. 73% freshmen, 75% undergrads receive need-based self-help aid. 3% freshmen, 3% undergrads receive athletic scholarships. 76% freshmen, 72% undergrads receive any aid. 41% undergrads borrow to pay for school. Average cumulative indebtedness $38,516. **Criteria for awarding institutional aid:** *Non-need-based:* academics, alumni affiliation, art, minority status, music/drama, religious affiliation, state/district residency.

TEXAS COLLEGE

2404 North Grand Ave., Tyler, TX 75702
Phone: 903-593-8311
E-mail: afrancis@texascollege.edu
Fax: 903-593-0588 • **Website:** www.texascollege.edu • **ACT Code:** 4210

This private school, affiliated with the Methodist Church, was founded in 1894. It has a 25-acre campus.

RATINGS
Admissions Selectivity Rating: 61   **Fire Safety Rating:** 62   **Green Rating:** 60*

STUDENTS AND FACULTY
Enrollment: 1,035. **Student Body:** 49% female, 51% male, 15% out-of-state, 0% international (2 countries represented). Asian 0%, African American 95%, Caucasian 2%, Hispanic 2%, Native American 0%.
Retention and Graduation: 5% grads go on to further study within 1 year. 5% grads pursue arts and sciences degrees. 2% grads pursue business degrees. 1% grads pursue medical degrees. **Faculty:** Student/faculty ratio 10:1. 28 full-time faculty, 46% hold PhDs, 79% are members of minority groups, 46% are women. 0% of classes are taught by teaching assistants.

ACADEMICS
Degrees: associate, bachelor's. **Classes:** Most classes have 30–39 students. **Majors with Highest Enrollment:** business/commerce; social work; sociology. **Special Study Options:** Accelerated program, distance learning, dual enrollment, independent study, internships, teacher certification program. **Honors Programs:** None **Combined Degree Programs:** NA. **Career Services:** alumni services, career assessment, internships.

FACILITIES
Housing: men's dorms, women's dorms, apartments for single students. 80% of campus accessible to physically disabled. Special Academic Facilities/Equipment: Moody Science-Business Center; D. R. Glass Library; Willie Lee Glass Community Development Services Center

CAMPUS LIFE
Environment: City. **Activities:** Choral groups, jazz band, marching band, student government, yearbook 31 registered organizations, 3 religious organizations. 3 fraternities, 3 sororities. **Athletics (Intercollegiate):** *Men:* baseball, basketball, cheerleading, football, track/field (outdoor). *Women:* basketball, cheerleading, softball, track/field (outdoor), volleyball. **On-Campus Highlights:** Gus F. Taylor Gymnasium, Student Union, D. R. Glass Library, Moody Science-Business Center, Mattie Fair Hall (women's residence hall).

ADMISSIONS
Freshman Academic Profile: 98% from public high schools. Minimum paper TOEFL 500. **Basis for Candidate Selection:** *Very important factors considered include:* rigor of secondary school record. **Freshman Admission Requirements:** High school diploma is required and GED is accepted.

Academic units required: 4 English, 2 mathematics, 2 science, 2 social studies, 2 history, 4 academic electives. 4 English, 2 mathematics, 2 science, 2 social studies, 2 history, 4 academic electives. **Freshman Admission Statistics:** 1,066 applied, 98% admitted, 32% enrolled. **Transfer Admission Requirements:** college transcript(s), statement of good standing from prior institution(s). Lowest grade transferable C. **General Admission Information:** Application Fee $20. Regular notification 8/15. Notification on a rolling basis, beginning on or about 4/1. Nonfall registration accepted. Admission may be deferred for a maximum of 1 year.

COSTS AND FINANCIAL AID
Annual tuition $6,305. Room and board $4,730. Required fees $20. Average book expense $800. **Required Forms and Deadlines:** FAFSA, institution's own financial aid form. **Notification of Awards:** Applicants will be notified of awards on a rolling basis beginning 4/15. **Types of Aid:** *Need-based scholarships/grants:* Federal Pell, SEOG, state scholarships/grants, private scholarships, the school's own gift aid, United Negro College Fund. *Loans:* state loans. **Student Employment:** Federal Work-Study Program available. Off-campus job opportunities are good. **Financial Aid Statistics:** 100% freshmen, 100% undergrads receive need-based scholarship or grant aid. 100% freshmen, 15% freshmen, 14% undergrads receive athletic scholarships. 100% freshmen, 90% undergrads receive any aid. 90% undergrads borrow to pay for school. Average cumulative indebtedness $2,500.

TEXAS LUTHERAN UNIVERSITY

1000 West Court Street, Seguin, TX 78155
Phone: 830-372-8050 • **Financial Aid Phone:** 830-372-8078
E-mail: admissions@tlu.edu
Fax: 830-372-8096 • **Website:** www.tlu.edu

This private school, affiliated with the Lutheran Church, was founded in 1891. It has a 184-acre campus.

RATINGS
Admissions Selectivity Rating: 82   **Fire Safety Rating:** 78   **Green Rating:** 67

STUDENTS AND FACULTY
Enrollment: 1,269. **Student Body:** 53% female, 47% male, 3% out-of-state, 0% international (7 countries represented). Asian 1%, African American 9%, Caucasian 56%, Hispanic 29%, Native American 0%.
Retention and Graduation: 67% freshmen return for sophomore year. 27% freshmen graduate within 4 years. 46% freshmen graduate within 6 years. **Faculty:** Student/faculty ratio 14:1. 74 full-time faculty, 76% hold PhDs, 15% are members of minority groups, 45% are women. 0% of classes are taught by teaching assistants.

ACADEMICS
Degrees: bachelor's. **Classes:** Most classes have 10–19 students. **Majors with Highest Enrollment:** accounting; business/commerce; education. **Special Study Options:** double major, dual enrollment, exchange student program (domestic), honors program, independent study, internships, study abroad, teacher certification program, senior seminars. **Disability Services:** Special programs offered to physically disabled students include note-taking services, reader services, tutors. **Career Services:** Alumni network, alumni services, career/job search classes, internships.

FACILITIES
Housing: Coed dorms, men's dorms, women's dorms, apartments for married students, apartments for single students. 95% of campus accessible to physically disabled. **Special Academic Facilities/Equipment:** Mexican-American studies center, geological museum. **Computers:** 100% of classrooms, 100% of dorms, 100% of libraries, 100% of dining areas, 100% of student union, 100% of common outdoor areas have wireless network access. Students can register for classes online. Administrative functions (other than registration) can be performed online.

CAMPUS LIFE
Environment: Town. **Activities:** Choral groups, concert band, dance, drama/theater, jazz band, literary magazine, music ensembles, musical theater, pep band, student government, student newspaper, symphony orchestra, Campus Ministries, International Student Organization 53 registered organizations, 10 honor societies, 3 religious organizations. 5 fraternities, 4 sororities. **Athletics (Intercollegiate):** *Men:* baseball, basketball, football, golf, soccer, tennis. *Women:* basketball, cross-country, golf, soccer, softball, tennis, track/field (outdoor), track/field (indoor), volleyball. **On-Campus Highlights:** Lucky's Snack Shack, Fitness Center, Alumni Student Center, Residence Halls, Hein Dining Hall. **Environmental Initiatives:** Installation of more efficient HVAC system

campus wide. Installation of rainwater collection system creation of a sustainability committee and recycling Program

ADMISSIONS

Freshman Academic Profile: Average high school GPA 3.6. 19% in top 10% of high school class, 49% in top 25% of high school class, 87% in top 50% of high school class. 95% from public high schools. SAT Math middle 50% range 470-570. SAT Critical Reading middle 50% range 430-550. SAT Writing middle 50% range 410-520. ACT middle 50% range 18-24. Minimum web-based TOEFL 80. Minimum paper TOEFL 550. **Basis for Candidate Selection:** *Very important factors considered include:* Class rank, application essay, academic GPA, recommendation(s), rigor of secondary school record, standardized test scores. *Important factors considered include:* character/personal qualities, interview, talent/ability, volunteer work. *Other factors considered include:* extracurricular activities, level of applicant's interest, work experience. **Freshman Admission Requirements:** High school diploma is required and GED is accepted. *Academic units required:* 4 English, 3 mathematics, 3 science, (2 science labs), 2 foreign language, 3 social studies. *Academic units recommended:* 4 English, 3 mathematics, 3 science, (2 science labs), 2 foreign language, 3 social studies. **Freshman Admission Statistics:** 1,852 applied, 53% admitted, 36% enrolled. **Transfer Admission Requirements:** High school transcript, college transcript(s), essay or personal statement, statement of good standing from prior institution(s). Minimum college GPA of 2.25 required. Lowest grade transferable C. **General Admission Information:** Application Fee $25. Regular application deadline 8/1. Notification on a rolling basis, beginning on or about 10/1. Nonfall registration accepted. Admission may be deferred for a maximum of 1 year. Credit and/or placement offered for CEEB Advanced Placement tests.

COSTS AND FINANCIAL AID

Annual tuition $24,860. Room and board $7,940. Required fees $130. Average book expense $950. **Required Forms and Deadlines:** FAFSA. **Notification of Awards:** Applicants will be notified of awards on a rolling basis beginning 3/1. **Types of Aid:** *Need-based scholarships/grants:* Federal Pell, SEOG, state scholarships/grants, the school's own gift aid. *Loans:* Subsidized Stafford, Unsubsidized Stafford, PLUS, Federal Perkins, state loans. **Student Employment:** Federal Work-Study Program available. Institutional employment available. Off-campus job opportunities are good. **Financial Aid Statistics:** 100% freshmen, 99% undergrads receive need-based scholarship or grant aid. 17% freshmen, 12% undergrads receive non-need-based scholarship or grant aid. 91% freshmen, 86% undergrads receive need-based self-help aid. 99% freshmen, 99% undergrads receive any aid. 73/75% undergrads borrow to pay for school. Average cumulative indebtedness $37,145. **Criteria for awarding institutional aid:** *Non-need-based:* academics, alumni affiliation, leadership, music/drama, religious affiliation.

TEXAS STATE UNIVERSITY—SAN MARCOS

429 North Guadalupe St., San Marcos, TX 78666
Phone: 512-245-2364 • **Financial Aid Phone:** 512-245 2315
E-mail: admissions@txstate.edu • **CEEB Code:** 6667
Fax: 512-245-8044 • **Website:** www.txstate.edu • **ACT Code:** 4178

This public school was founded in 1899. It has a 455-acre campus.

RATINGS
Admissions Selectivity Rating: 75   **Fire Safety Rating:** 92   **Green Rating:** 76

STUDENTS AND FACULTY
Enrollment: 29,458. **Student Body:** 55% female, 45% male, 1% out-of-state, 1% international (66 countries represented). Asian 2%, African American 6%, Hispanic 29%, Native American 0%.
Retention and Graduation: 77% freshmen return for sophomore year. 27% freshmen graduate within 4 years. 54% freshmen graduate within 6 years. 22% grads go on to further study within 1 year. 12% grads pursue arts and sciences degrees. 2% grads pursue law degrees. 4% grads pursue business degrees. 1% grads pursue medical degrees. **Faculty:** Student/faculty ratio 20:1. 1196 full-time faculty, 72% hold PhDs, 24% are members of minority groups, 49% are women. 5% of classes are taught by teaching assistants.

ACADEMICS
Degrees: bachelor's, doctoral, master's, post-bachelor's certificate. **Classes:** Most classes have 20-29 students. Most lab/discussion sessions have 20-29 students. **Majors with Highest Enrollment:** business administration and management; multi-/interdisciplinary studies, other; psychology. **Special Study Options:** Accelerated program, distance learning, double major, dual enrollment, English as a Second Language (ESL), exchange student program (domestic), honors program, independent study, internships, study abroad, teacher certification program, weekend college. English as a Second Language is offered to international students or any students for that matter, who wish to improve their

command of the English language. But it is not offered as a degree program. **Honors Programs:** To graduate in the University Honors Program, a student must complete at least five Honors Classes (which includes the Honors Thesis course) and maintain a minimum GPA of 3.25. Honors courses substitute for certain general education core curriculum and inidividual departmental requirements and thus become integral parts of the degree program. **Combined Degree Programs:** BA/MD, BA/DDS, See 2008-2010 undgrad catalog page 63 and 64. **Disability Services:** Special programs offered to physically disabled students include note-taking services, reader services, tape recorders, tutors. **Career Services:** Alumni network, alumni services, career/job search classes, career assessment Career Services highlights include Experiential learning through the College of Education. All teacher education majors participate on practice teaching with a supervising teacher mentoring.

FACILITIES
Housing: Coed dorms, special housing for disabled students, men's dorms, women's dorms, fraternity/sorority housing, apartments for married students, apartments for single students, Non-smoking, honors, access for the disabled, but not separate housing. 88% of campus accessible to physically disabled. **Special Academic Facilities/Equipment:** Child development center, aquifer research center, two demonstration farms, physical anthropology and archaeology laboratories. Southwestern Writer's Collection. Observatory with a 17 inch telescope. **Computers:** 100% of classrooms, 100% of dorms, 100% of libraries, 100% of dining areas, 100% of student union, 100% of common outdoor areas have wireless network access. Students can register for classes online. Administrative functions (other than registration) can be performed online.

CAMPUS LIFE
Environment: Town. **Activities:** Choral groups, concert band, dance, drama/theater, jazz band, literary magazine, marching band, music ensembles, musical theater, opera, pep band, radio station, student government, student newspaper, student-run film society, symphony orchestra, yearbook, Campus Ministries, International Student Organization, Model UN 254 registered organizations, 16 honor societies, 27 religious organizations. 18 fraternities, 14 sororities. **Athletics (Intercollegiate):** *Men:* baseball, basketball, cheerleading, cross-country, football, golf, track/field (outdoor). *Women:* basketball, cheerleading, cross-country, golf, soccer, softball, tennis, track/field (outdoor), volleyball. **On-Campus Highlights:** LBJ Student Center, Alkek Library, Student Recreation Center, The Quad, Sewell Park, The Quad is a walk way that runs the length of the campus which most academic buildings open on to. Student gather here to socialize between classes. Sewell Park is a general recreational park where students gather to swim, sun bathe, throw frisbees, and play ball. The San Marcos river runs through the park. **Environmental Initiatives:** Established the Texas Rivers Systems Institute. Our programs and projects demonstrate our deep commitment to the careful stewardship of the world's freshwater resources. Through collaborative research, public advocacy, and education on river systems, the Institute affirms the unique role of water in our lives. As one of the earth's most remarkable resources, we are dedicated to preserving and protecting this irreplaceable gift - water. The James and Marilyn Lovell Center for Environmental Geography and Hazards Research located within Texas State University-San Marcos' Department of Geography (one of the largest such departments in the United States), the JMLC provides a focal point around which its scholars can gather to share ideas and mentor students. Faculty Scholars seek to better understand Earth's environment, to analyze and reduce the impacts of natural and technological hazards, and through their work to improve policies directed toward Earth's environment and its hazards. Full-time position of coordinator of recycling and waste management for a campus wide recycling program.

ADMISSIONS
Freshman Academic Profile: 11% in top 10% of high school class, 47% in top 25% of high school class, 90% in top 50% of high school class. 98% from public high schools. SAT Math middle 50% range 490-580. SAT Critical Reading middle 50% range 460-560. SAT Writing middle 50% range 450-540. ACT middle 50% range 21-25. Minimum web-based TOEFL 78. Minimum paper TOEFL 550. **Basis for Candidate Selection:** *Very important factors considered include:* Class rank, standardized test scores. *Other factors considered include:* application essay, rigor of secondary school record, talent/ability. **Freshman Admission Requirements:** High school diploma is required and GED is accepted. *Academic units required:* 4 English, 3 mathematics, 3 science, (2 science labs), 2 foreign language, 1 visual/performing arts, 1 computer science, 3 PE 1.5, Eco.0.5, Health Ed. 0.5, Speech 0.5. *Academic units recommended:* 4 English, 3 mathematics, 3 science, (2 science labs), 2 foreign language, 1 visual/performing arts, 1 computer science, 3 PE 1.5, Eco.0.5, Health Ed. 0.5, Speech 0.5 **Freshman Admission Statistics:** 10,418 applied, 69% admitted, 59% enrolled. **Transfer Admission Requirements:** college transcript(s), statement of good standing from prior institution(s). Minimum college GPA of 2.2 required. Lowest grade transferable D. **General Admission Information:** Application Fee $60. Regular application deadline 5/1. Notification on a rolling basis, beginning on or about 9/1. Nonfall registration accepted. Admission may be deferred for a maximum of indefinite, fee req. Credit offered for CEEB Advanced Placement tests.

COSTS AND FINANCIAL AID

Annual in-state tuition $6,510. Annual out-of-state tuition $17,040. Room and board $7,070. Required fees $2,262. Average book expense $1,090. **Required Forms and Deadlines:** FAFSA. **Notification of Awards:** Applicants will be notified of awards on a rolling basis beginning 5/1. **Types of Aid:** *Need-based scholarships/grants:* Federal Pell, SEOG, state scholarships/grants, private scholarships, the school's own gift aid. *Loans:* Direct Subsidized Stafford, Direct Unsubsidized Stafford, Direct PLUS, Subsidized Stafford, Unsubsidized Stafford, PLUS, Federal Perkins, state loans, college/university loans from institutional funds, Alternative Loans, Emergency tuition loans. **Student Employment:** Federal Work-Study Program available. Institutional employment available. Highest amount earned per year from on-campus jobs $9,264. Off-campus job opportunities are good. **Financial Aid Statistics:** 84% freshmen, 82% undergrads receive need-based scholarship or grant aid. 3% freshmen, 1% undergrads receive non-need-based scholarship or grant aid. 80% freshmen, 83% undergrads receive need-based self-help aid. 1% freshmen, 1% undergrads receive athletic scholarships. 75% freshmen, 65% undergrads receive any aid. 62% undergrads borrow to pay for school. Average cumulative indebtedness $23,575. **Criteria for awarding institutional aid:** *Non-need-based:* academics, art, athletics, leadership, music/drama, state/district residency.

TEXAS TECH UNIVERSITY

Box 45005, Lubbock, TX 79409-5005
Phone: 806-742-1480 • **Financial Aid Phone:** 806-742-3681
E-mail: admissions@ttu.edu • **CEEB Code:** 6827
Fax: 806-742-0062 • **Website:** www.ttu.edu • **ACT Code:** 4220

This public school was founded in 1923. It has a 1839-acre campus.

RATINGS

Admissions Selectivity Rating: 80   **Fire Safety Rating:** 92   **Green Rating:** 87

STUDENTS AND FACULTY

Enrollment: 26,276. **Student Body:** 45% female, 55% male, 6% out-of-state, 3% international (76 countries represented). Asian 3%, African American 6%, Caucasian 66%, Hispanic 19%, Native American 0%.
Retention and Graduation: 81% freshmen return for sophomore year. 37% freshmen graduate within 4 years. **Faculty:** Student/faculty ratio 24:1. 1156 full-time faculty, 89% hold PhDs, 12% are members of minority groups, 37% are women. 17% of classes are taught by teaching assistants.

ACADEMICS

Degrees: bachelor's, first professional, master's, post-bachelor's certificate. **Classes:** Most classes have 10–19 students. Most lab/discussion sessions have 20–29 students. **Majors with Highest Enrollment:** health and physical education; mechanical engineering; psychology. **Special Study Options:** Accelerated program, cooperative education program, distance learning, double major, dual enrollment, English as a Second Language (ESL), external degree program, honors program, independent study, internships, liberal arts/career combination, student-designed major, study abroad, teacher certification program. **Honors Programs:** Honors Studies is a special program under our Honors College for highly motivated and academically talented students who want to maximize their college education. It is designed to provide such students with a unique and broadly integrated intellectual experience that is complementary to virtually every major and career path. **Combined Degree Programs:** BA/MA, MBA/JD; MBA/MD; MPA/JD; MBA/M.Arch; MBA/MS;MS/MS;MBA/MA;JD/MSA;JD/MS;MPA/MA. **Disability Services:** Special programs offered to physically disabled students include note-taking services, reader services, tape recorders, tutors. **Career Services:** alumni services, career/job search classes, internships, regional alumni.

FACILITIES

Housing: Coed dorms, special housing for disabled students, men's dorms, women's dorms, apartments for single students. 100% of campus accessible to physically disabled. **Special Academic Facilities/Equipment:** Museum, child development center, textile research center, agricultural research center, planetarium, ranching heritage center, semi-arid land studies center, ranching heritage center, seismological observatory. **Computers:** Students can register for classes online. Administrative functions (other than registration) can be performed online.

CAMPUS LIFE

Environment: City. **Activities:** Choral groups, concert band, dance, drama/theater, jazz band, marching band, music ensembles, musical theater, pep band, radio station, student government, student newspaper, symphony orchestra, television station, yearbook, Campus Ministries, International Student Organi-

zation 399 registered organizations, 33 honor societies, 35 religious organizations. 25 fraternities, 18 sororities. **Athletics (Intercollegiate):** *Men:* baseball, basketball, cross-country, football, golf, tennis, track/field (outdoor), track/field (indoor). *Women:* basketball, cross-country, golf, soccer, softball, tennis, track/field (outdoor), track/field (indoor), volleyball. **On-Campus Highlights:** Student Union Building, Student Recreation Center, Library, Classrooms, United Spirit Arena, Jones AT&T Stadium, Museums, National Ranching and Heritage Center. **Environmental Initiatives:** Reduction of energy consumption per gross square foot. Reduction of waste hauled to landfill. Courses that stress design of sustainable buildings.

ADMISSIONS

Freshman Academic Profile: 20% in top 10% of high school class, 52% in top 25% of high school class, 86% in top 50% of high school class. % from public high schools. SAT Math middle 50% range 520-620. SAT Critical Reading middle 50% range 500-590. SAT Writing middle 50% range 470-570. ACT middle 50% range 22-27. Minimum web-based TOEFL 79. Minimum paper TOEFL 550. **Basis for Candidate Selection:** *Very important factors considered include:* Class rank, academic GPA, rigor of secondary school record, standardized test scores. *Important factors considered include:* application essay, alumni/ae relation, character/personal qualities, extracurricular activities, talent/ability, volunteer work, work experience. *Other factors considered include:* recommendation(s), first generation, level of applicant's interest, racial/ethnic status. **Freshman Admission Requirements:** High school diploma is required and GED is accepted. *Academic units required:* 4 English, 3 mathematics, 2 science, (2 science labs), 2 foreign language. 4 English, 3 mathematics, 2 science, (2 science labs), 2 foreign language. **Freshman Admission Statistics:** 18,027 applied, 64% admitted, 39% enrolled. **Transfer Admission Requirements:** college transcript(s), statement of good standing from prior institution(s). Minimum college GPA of 2.25 required. Lowest grade transferable D-. **General Admission Information:** Application Fee $50. Regular application deadline 5/1. Nonfall registration accepted. Credit offered for CEEB Advanced Placement tests.

COSTS AND FINANCIAL AID

Annual in-state tuition $6,077. Annual out-of-state tuition $16,607. Room and board $8,275. Required fees $2,865. Average book expense $1,200. **Required Forms and Deadlines:** FAFSA. **Types of Aid:** *Need-based scholarships/grants:* Federal Pell, SEOG, state scholarships/grants, private scholarships, the school's own gift aid. *Loans:* Subsidized Stafford, Unsubsidized Stafford, PLUS, Federal Perkins, state loans, college/university loans from institutional funds. **Student Employment:** Federal Work-Study Program available. Institutional employment available. Highest amount earned per year from on-campus jobs $5,017. Off-campus job opportunities are excellent. **Financial Aid Statistics:** 62% freshmen, 72% undergrads receive need-based scholarship or grant aid. 45% freshmen, 27% undergrads receive non-need-based scholarship or grant aid. 73% freshmen, 81% undergrads receive need-based self-help aid. 2% freshmen, 2% undergrads receive athletic scholarships. 60% undergrads borrow to pay for school. Average cumulative indebtedness $20,424. **Criteria for awarding institutional aid:** *Non-need-based:* academics, art, athletics, job skills, leadership, music/drama.

TEXAS WOMAN'S UNIVERSITY

P.O. Box 425589, Denton, TX 76204-5589
Phone: 940-898-3188 • **Financial Aid Phone:** 940-898-3050
E-mail: admissions@twu.edu • **CEEB Code:** 6826
Fax: 940-898-3081 • **Website:** www.twu.edu • **ACT Code:** 4224

This public school was founded in 1901. It has a 270-acre campus.

RATINGS

Admissions Selectivity Rating: 78   **Fire Safety Rating:** 98   **Green Rating:** 60*

STUDENTS AND FACULTY

Enrollment: 7,389. **Student Body:** 93% female, 7% male, 1% out-of-state, 2% international (62 countries represented). Asian 8%, African American 21%, Caucasian 51%, Hispanic 18%, Native American 1%.
Retention and Graduation: 71% freshmen return for sophomore year. 22% freshmen graduate within 4 years. 44% freshmen graduate within 6 years. 4% grads go on to further study within 1 year. **Faculty:** Student/faculty ratio 17:1. 306 full-time faculty, 17% are members of minority groups, 71% are women.

ACADEMICS

Degrees: bachelor's, master's, post-bachelor's certificate, post-master's certificate. **Classes:** Most classes have 10–19 students. **Special Study Options:** cross-registration, distance learning, double major, dual enrollment, honors program, independent study, internships, study abroad, teacher certification program. **Honors Programs:** Honors Scholars Program www.twu.edu/honors/index.html **Combined Degree Programs:** BA/MEng, 3-2 program with UNT. **Disability Services:** Special programs offered to physically disabled students include note-taking services, reader services, tape recorders, tutors. **Career Services:** internships.

FACILITIES

Housing: Coed dorms, special housing for disabled students, special housing for international students, women's dorms, apartments for married students, apartments for single students, wellness housing, theme housing. 100% of campus accessible to physically disabled. **Special Academic Facilities/Equipment:** Museum, radiation lab, language lab, Texas First Ladies Gown Collection Texas Women's Hall of Fame **Computers:** Students can register for classes online. Administrative functions (other than registration) can be performed online.

CAMPUS LIFE

Environment: City. **Activities:** Choral groups, dance, drama/theater, jazz band, music ensembles, musical theater, opera, student government, student newspaper, television station, International Student Organization 94 registered organizations, 16 honor societies, 10 religious organizations. 9 sororities. **Athletics (Intercollegiate):** *Women:* basketball, gymnastics, soccer, softball, volleyball. **On-Campus Highlights:** Student Union, Pioneer Hall, Mega Computer Lab, Guinn/Stark High Rise Resident Halls, Little Chapel-in-the-Woods, TWU has four campuses - two in Dallas, one in Houston and the 270 acre main campus in Denton. The Denton Campus houses the Texas Women's Hall of Fame and the Gowns of Texas First Ladies Collection; The Houston Campus is located in the Houston Medical Center and recently opened the new facility; The Dallas campuses have begun construction on a new multi-million dollar facility.

ADMISSIONS

Freshman Academic Profile: Average high school GPA 3.2. 18% in top 10% of high school class, 29% in top 25% of high school class, 77% in top 50% of high school class. 93% from public high schools. SAT Math middle 50% range 420-530. SAT Critical Reading middle 50% range 420-520. ACT middle 50% range 18-22. Minimum paper TOEFL 550. **Basis for Candidate Selection:** *Very important factors considered include:* Class rank, rigor of secondary school record, standardized test scores. *Important factors considered include:* academic GPA. **Freshman Admission Requirements:** High school diploma is required and GED is accepted. *Academic units required:* 4 English, 3 mathematics, 2 science, 2 social studies, 2 academic electives. *Academic units recommended:* 4 English, 3 mathematics, 2 science, 2 social studies, 3 academic electives. **Freshman Admission Statistics:** 3,649 applied, 56% admitted, 41% enrolled. **Transfer Admission Requirements:** college transcript(s), minimum college GPA of 2.0 required. Lowest grade transferable D. **General Admission Information:** Application Fee $30. Notification on a rolling basis, beginning on or about 10/1. Nonfall registration accepted. Admission may be deferred for a maximum of 2 years. Credit and/or placement offered for CEEB Advanced Placement tests.

COSTS AND FINANCIAL AID

Annual in-state tuition $4,740. Annual out-of-state tuition $13,080. Room and board $6,074. Required fees $1,320. Average book expense $930. **Required Forms and Deadlines:** FAFSAFinancial Aid Certification and Information Form must be completed prior to disbursement of financial aid. **Notification of Awards:** Applicants will be notified of awards on a rolling basis beginning 3/1. **Types of Aid:** *Need-based scholarships/grants:* Federal Pell, SEOG, state scholarships/grants, private scholarships, the school's own gift aid, Federal Nursing Scholarships. , Leaveraging Educational Assistance Partnership Grant. *Loans:* Subsidized Stafford, Unsubsidized Stafford, PLUS, Federal Perkins, Federal Nursing, state loans, college/university loans from institutional funds, Alternative non-federal loans. **Student Employment:** Highest amount earned per year from on-campus jobs $5,120. **Financial Aid Statistics:** 66% freshmen, 72% undergrads receive need-based scholarship or grant aid. 67% freshmen, 34% undergrads receive non-need-based scholarship or grant aid. 92% freshmen, 95% undergrads receive need-based self-help aid. 1% undergrads receive athletic scholarships. 77% freshmen, 85% undergrads receive any aid. 58% undergrads borrow to pay for school. Average cumulative indebtedness $19,409. **Criteria for awarding institutional aid:** *Non-need-based:* academics, art, athletics, music/drama.

THIEL COLLEGE

75 College Avenue, Greenville, PA 16125
Phone: 724-589-2345 • **Financial Aid Phone:** 724-589-2178
E-mail: admissions@thiel.edu • **CEEB Code:** 2910
Fax: 724-589-2013 • **Website:** www.thiel.edu • **ACT Code:** 3730

This private school, affiliated with the Lutheran Church, was founded in 1866. It has a 135-acre campus.

RATINGS

Admissions Selectivity Rating: 71   **Fire Safety Rating:** 84   **Green Rating:** 67

STUDENTS AND FACULTY

Enrollment: 1,019. **Student Body:** 43% female, 57% male, 37% out-of-state, 3% international (14 countries represented). Asian 0%, African American 6%, Caucasian 69%, Hispanic 2%, Native American 0%. **Retention and Graduation:** 67% freshmen return for sophomore year. 30% freshmen graduate within 4 years. 13% grads go on to further study within 1 year. 86% grads pursue arts and sciences degrees. 1% grads pursue law degrees. 12% grads pursue business degrees. 1% grads pursue medical degrees. **Faculty:** Student/faculty ratio 13:1. 64 full-time faculty, 73% hold PhDs, 8% are members of minority groups, 41% are women. 0% of classes are taught by teaching assistants.

ACADEMICS

Degrees: associate, bachelor's. **Classes:** Most classes have 10–19 students. Most lab/discussion sessions have 20–29 students. **Majors with Highest Enrollment:** biology/biological sciences; business/commerce; elementary education and teaching. **Special Study Options:** cooperative education program, distance learning, double major, dual enrollment, English as a Second Language (ESL), honors program, independent study, internships, liberal arts/career combination, study abroad, teacher certification program. **Honors Programs:** Four year Honors Program with special courses for honors students. **Disability Services:** Special programs offered to physically disabled students include note-taking services, reader services, tape recorders, tutors. **Career Services:** Alumni network, career/job search classes, career assessment, internships.

FACILITIES

Housing: Coed dorms, fraternity/sorority housing, apartments for single students. 90% of campus accessible to physically disabled. **Special Academic Facilities/Equipment:** Art Gallery, Blackbox Theater, Star Bucks Bistro **Computers:** Students can register for classes online. Undergraduates are required to own a computer.

CAMPUS LIFE

Environment: Rural. **Activities:** Choral groups, concert band, dance, drama/theater, literary magazine, musical theater, pep band, radio station, student government, student newspaper, symphony orchestra, television station, yearbook, Campus Ministries 40 registered organizations, 8 honor societies, 4 religious organizations. 3 fraternities, 4 sororities. **Athletics (Intercollegiate):** *Men:* baseball, basketball, cheerleading, cross-country, football, golf, soccer, track/field (outdoor), track/field (indoor), wrestling. *Women:* basketball, cheerleading, cross-country, soccer, softball, track/field (outdoor), track/field (indoor), volleyball. **On-Campus Highlights:** Howard Miller Student Center, Robinson Black Box Theater, new student apartments, Alumni Stadium, Paul Bush Memorial Fitness Center.

ADMISSIONS

Freshman Academic Profile: Average high school GPA 3.0. 12% in top 10% of high school class, 25% in top 25% of high school class, 46% in top 50% of high school class. 88% from public high schools. SAT Math middle 50% range 420-520. SAT Critical Reading middle 50% range 410-510. ACT middle 50% range 18-23. Minimum paper TOEFL 450. **Basis for Candidate Selection:** *Very important factors considered include:* application essay, academic GPA, recommendation(s), rigor of secondary school record, standardized test scores, interview, level of applicant's interest. *Important factors considered include:* Class rank, character/personal qualities. *Other factors considered include:* extracurricular activities, talent/ability, volunteer work, work experience. **Freshman Admission Requirements:** High school diploma is required and GED is accepted. **Freshman Admission Statistics:** 1,856 applied, 68% admitted, 28% enrolled. **Transfer Admission Requirements:** High school transcript, college transcript(s), essay or personal statement, interview, standardized test scores, statement of good standing from prior institution(s). Minimum college GPA of 2.0 required. Lowest grade transferable C. **General Admission Information:** Application Fee $35. Regular application deadline 6/30. Notification on a rolling basis, beginning on or about 9/15. Nonfall registration accepted. Admission may be deferred for a maximum of 1 year. Credit and/or placement offered for CEEB Advanced Placement tests.

COSTS AND FINANCIAL AID

Required Forms and Deadlines: FAFSA, state aid form. **Notification of Awards:** Applicants will be notified of awards on a rolling basis beginning 2/15. **Types of Aid:** *Need-based scholarships/grants:* Federal Pell, SEOG, state scholarships/grants, private scholarships, the school's own gift aid. *Loans:* Subsidized Stafford, Unsubsidized Stafford, PLUS, Federal Perkins, college/university loans from institutional funds. **Student Employment:** Federal Work-Study Program available. Institutional employment available. Off-campus job opportunities are fair. **Financial Aid Statistics:** 100% undergrads receive need-based scholarship or grant aid. 100% undergrads receive need-based self-help aid. **Criteria for awarding institutional aid:** *Non-need-based:* academics, alumni affiliation, leadership, religious affiliation, state/district residency.

THOMAS AQUINAS COLLEGE

Best 378

10000 Ojai Road, Santa Paula, CA 93060
Phone: 805-525-4417 • **Financial Aid Phone:** 800-634-9797
E-mail: admissions@thomasaquinas.edu • **CEEB Code:** 4828
Fax: 805-421-5905 • **Website:** www.thomasaquinas.edu • **ACT Code:** 425

This private school, affiliated with the Roman Catholic Church, was founded in 1971. It has a 131-acre campus.

RATINGS

Admissions Selectivity Rating: 87   **Fire Safety Rating:** 91   **Green Rating:** 60*

STUDENTS AND FACULTY

Enrollment: 370. **Student Body:** 51% female, 49% male, 60% out-of-state, 4% international (6 countries represented). Asian 1%, African American 0%, Caucasian 75%, Hispanic 12%, Native American 0%. **Retention and Graduation:** 85% freshmen return for sophomore year. 72% freshmen graduate within 4 years. 76% freshmen graduate within 6 years. 24% grads go on to further study within 1 year. 8% grads pursue arts and sciences degrees. 1% grads pursue law degrees. 1% grads pursue medical degrees. **Faculty:** Student/faculty ratio 12:1. 30 full-time faculty, 77% hold PhDs, 10% are women. 0% of classes are taught by teaching assistants.

ACADEMICS

Degrees: bachelor's. **Classes:** Most classes have 10–19 students. **Special Study Options:** The sole academic program offered: a "cross-disciplinary" curriculum of liberal education through reading and analyzing the "Great Books," with special emphasis on philosophy, theology, mathematics, science, and literature. **Career Services:** Alumni network, alumni services, career/job search classes, career assessment, internships, regional alumni., Career Services highlights include Career Assessment: We work directly with our students, one on one, in order to help them determine their strengths. We then talk with them about their various interests, and advise them on possible options, given their strengths and interests. We encourage them to talk to people within those fields, including networking with our alumni. We also have guest speakers and discernment classes that help as well.

FACILITIES

Housing: men's dorms, women's dorms, Students living with their families may live off campus. 100% of campus accessible to physically disabled. Special Academic Facilities/Equipment: St. Bernardine Library CAMPUS LIFE **Environment:** Rural. **Activities:** Choral groups, dance, drama/theater, music ensembles, musical theater 2 registered organizations, 4 religious organizations. **On-Campus Highlights:** St. Joseph Commons, The Dumb Ox Coffee Shop, Dorm Commons, St. Bernardine Library, Student Lounge. **Environmental Initiatives:** The College recycles recyclable material. 100% of the campus landscape waste is made into either mulch or wood chips for further use. Green products are used for some cleaning applications.

ADMISSIONS

Freshman Academic Profile: Average high school GPA 3.8. 44% in top 10% of high school class, 67% in top 25% of high school class, 100% in top 50% of high school class. 8% from public high schools. SAT Math middle 50% range 560-660. SAT Critical Reading middle 50% range 620-700. SAT Writing middle 50% range 580-690. ACT middle 50% range 25-29. Minimum paper TOEFL 570. **Basis for Candidate Selection:** *Very important factors considered include:* application essay, recommendation(s), rigor of secondary school record, standardized test scores, character/personal qualities, level of applicant's interest. *Important factors considered include:* academic GPA. *Other factors considered include:* Class rank, extracurricular activities, interview, religious affiliation/

commitment, talent/ability, volunteer work, work experience. **Freshman Admission Requirements:** High school diploma is required and GED is accepted. *Academic units required:* 4 English, 3 mathematics, 2 science, 2 foreign language, 2 history. *Academic units recommended:* 4 English, 3 mathematics, 2 science, 2 foreign language, 2 history. **Freshman Admission Statistics:** 165 applied, 81% admitted, 63% enrolled. **General Admission Information:** Notification on a rolling basis, beginning on or about 10/1. Nonfall registration not accepted. Admission may be deferred for a maximum of 1 year. Neither credit nor placement offered for CEEB Advanced Placement tests.

COSTS AND FINANCIAL AID

Annual tuition $24,500. Room and board $7,950. Average book expense $50. **Required Forms and Deadlines:** FAFSA, institution's own financial aid form, state aid form, business/farm supplement. Tax return, Noncustodial Parent Statement. **Notification of Awards:** Applicants will be notified of awards on a rolling basis beginning 1/1. **Types of Aid:** *Need-based scholarships/grants:* Federal Pell, state scholarships/grants, private scholarships, the school's own gift aid. *Loans:* Subsidized Stafford, Unsubsidized Stafford, PLUS, college/university loans from institutional funds, Canadian student Loans. **Student Employment:** Off-campus job opportunities are fair. **Financial Aid Statistics:** 99% freshmen, 94% undergrads receive need-based scholarship or grant aid. 97% freshmen, 99% undergrads receive need-based self-help aid. 81% freshmen, 79% undergrads receive any aid. 63% undergrads borrow to pay for school. Average cumulative indebtedness $17,820.

THOMAS COLLEGE

180 West River Road, Waterville, ME 4901
Phone: 207-859-1101 • **Financial Aid Phone:** 207-859-1105
E-mail: admiss@thomas.edu • **CEEB Code:** 2052
Fax: 207-859-1114 • **Website:** www.thomas.edu • **ACT Code:** 1663

This private school was founded in 1894. It has a 120-acre campus.

RATINGS

Admissions Selectivity Rating: 66   **Fire Safety Rating:** 89   **Green Rating:** 60*

STUDENTS AND FACULTY

Enrollment: 739. **Student Body:** 49% female, 51% male, 20% out-of-state, 0% international. Asian 1%, African American 2%, Caucasian 88%, Hispanic 1%, Native American 0%. **Retention and Graduation:** 51% freshmen graduate within 6 years. 7% grads go on to further study within 1 year. 7% grads pursue business degrees. **Faculty:** Student/faculty ratio 18:1. 21 full-time faculty, 48% hold PhDs, 0% are members of minority groups, 38% are women. 0% of classes are taught by teaching assistants.

ACADEMICS

Degrees: associate, bachelor's, master's, terminal associate, transfer associate. **Classes:** Most classes have 20–29 students. **Majors with Highest Enrollment:** accounting; accounting and business/management; sport and fitness administration/management. **Special Study Options:** cross-registration, distance learning, double major, internships, study abroad, teacher certification program. **Combined Degree Programs:** BS/MBA. **Career Services:** career assessment, internships.

FACILITIES

Housing: Coed dorms. Residence halls are designated coed--male or female by floor or suite, not by building. 71% of campus accessible to physically disabled. **Computers:** Students can register for classes online. Administrative functions (other than registration) can be performed online.

CAMPUS LIFE

Environment: Rural. **Activities:** Choral groups, dance, drama/theater, student government, student newspaper, yearbook 26 registered organizations, 3 honor societies, 1 fraternities, 1 sororities. **Athletics (Intercollegiate):** *Men:* baseball, basketball, golf, lacrosse, soccer, tennis. *Women:* basketball, field hockey, lacrosse, soccer, softball, volleyball.

ADMISSIONS

Freshman Academic Profile: Average high school GPA 2.7. 7% in top 10% of high school class, 19% in top 25% of high school class, 54% in top 50% of high school class. SAT Math middle 50% range 390-510. SAT Critical Reading middle 50% range 400-500. SAT Writing middle 50% range 380-500. ACT middle 50% range 13-22. Minimum paper TOEFL 530. **Basis for Candidate Selection:** *Very important factors considered include:* Class rank, application essay, academic GPA, recommendation(s), rigor of secondary school record, standardized test scores. *Important factors considered include:* character/personal qualities, extracurricular activities, interview. *Other factors considered* *include:* alumni/ae relation, first generation, level of applicant's interest, talent/ability, volunteer work, work experience. **Freshman Admission Requirements:** High school diploma is required and GED is accepted. **Freshman Admission Statistics:** 668 applied, 81% admitted, 45% enrolled. **Transfer Admission Requirements:** High school transcript, college transcript(s), essay or personal statement, minimum college GPA of 2.0 required. Lowest grade transferable C. **General Admission Information:** Application Fee $50. Notification on a rolling basis, beginning on or about 12/1. Nonfall registration accepted. Admission may be deferred for a maximum of 2 years. Credit and/or placement offered for CEEB Advanced Placement tests.

COSTS AND FINANCIAL AID

Annual tuition $17,280. Room and board $7,430. Required fees $450. Average book expense $800. **Required Forms and Deadlines:** FAFSA. **Notification of Awards:** Applicants will be notified of awards on a rolling basis beginning 3/15. **Types of Aid:** *Need-based scholarships/grants:* Federal Pell, SEOG, state scholarships/grants, private scholarships, the school's own gift aid. *Loans:* Direct Subsidized Stafford, Direct Unsubsidized Stafford, Direct PLUS, Federal Perkins. **Student Employment:** Federal Work-Study Program available. Institutional employment available. Off-campus job opportunities are excellent. **Financial Aid Statistics:** 100% freshmen, 98% undergrads receive need-based scholarship or grant aid. 31% freshmen, 19% undergrads receive non-need-based scholarship or grant aid. 90% freshmen, 90% undergrads receive need-based self-help aid. 95% freshmen, 90% undergrads receive any aid. 75% undergrads borrow to pay for school. Average cumulative indebtedness $38,734. **Criteria for awarding institutional aid:** *Non-need-based:* academics.

THOMAS EDISON STATE COLLEGE

101 West State Street, Trenton, NJ 08608-1176
Phone: 888-442-8372 • **Financial Aid Phone:** 609-633-9658
E-mail: admissions@tesc.edu • **CEEB Code:** 2612
Fax: 609-984-8447 • **Website:** www.tesc.edu • **ACT Code:** 274872

This public school was founded in 1972. It has a 2-acre campus.

RATINGS
Admissions Selectivity Rating: 61   Fire Safety Rating: 60*   Green Rating: 61

STUDENTS AND FACULTY
Enrollment: 19,404. **Student Body:** 59% out-of-state, 1% international (68 countries represented). Asian 4%, African American 16%, Caucasian 60%, Hispanic 8%, Native American 1%.

ACADEMICS
Degrees: associate, bachelor's, certificate, master's, post-bachelor's certificate, post-master's certificate. **Majors with Highest Enrollment:** business administration and management; liberal arts and sciences/liberal studies; nuclear engineering technology/technician. **Special Study Options:** distance learning, dual enrollment, external degree program, independent study, Joint degree program with the University of Medicine and Dentistry of New Jersey for Bachelor of Science in Health Sciences. Graduates of associate degree and diploma programs of nursing may enroll for a BSN degree only (RN-BSN program), or both a BSN and a MSN degree (RN BSN/MSN program) with preparation as a Nurse Educator at the Master's level. **Combined Degree Programs:** BSN/MSN. **Career Services:** Alumni network

FACILITIES
Housing: Thomas Edison State College serves adult students at a distance. The College doesn't own/operate any housing units and/or dorms. 97% of campus accessible to physically disabled. **Computers:** Students can register for classes online. Administrative functions (other than registration) can be performed online.

CAMPUS LIFE
Environment: City. **Activities:** 3 honor societies. **On-Campus Highlights:** Prudence Townsend Kelsey Memorial Roo **Environmental Initiatives:** Solar panels installed on 2 facilities. Purchased hybrid vehicle for Vice Presidents to use. Adopted recycling programs.

ADMISSIONS
Freshman Academic Profile: Minimum web-based TOEFL 79. Minimum paper TOEFL 550. **Freshman Admission Requirements:** High school diploma is required and GED is accepted. **Transfer Admission Requirements:** college transcript(s), Lowest grade transferable D. **General Admission Information:** Application Fee $75. Credit offered for CEEB Advanced Placement tests.

COSTS AND FINANCIAL AID

Annual in-state tuition $5,508. Annual out-of-state tuition $8,111. **Required Forms and Deadlines:** FAFSA, institution's own financial aid form. **Types of Aid:** *Need-based scholarships/grants:* Federal Pell, state scholarships/grants, private scholarships. *Loans:* Subsidized Stafford, Unsubsidized Stafford, PLUS, state loans, Private Educational Loans. **Financial Aid Statistics** 17% undergrads receive any aid.

THOMAS JEFFERSON UNIVERSITY

130 South 9th Street, Philadelphia, PA 19107
Phone: 215-503-8890 • **Financial Aid Phone:** 215-955-2867
E-mail: jchp@jefferson.edu • **CEEB Code:** 2903
Fax: 215-503-7241 • **Website:** www.jefferson.edu/jchp

This private school was founded in 1967.

RATINGS
Admissions Selectivity Rating: 61   Fire Safety Rating: 70   Green Rating: 60*

STUDENTS AND FACULTY
Enrollment: 827. **Student Body:** 83% female, 17% male, 27% out-of-state, 1% international. Asian 8%, African American 9%, Caucasian 71%, Hispanic 3%, Native American 0%.
Retention and Graduation: Faculty: Student/faculty ratio 14:1. 82 full-time faculty, 43% hold PhDs, 12% are members of minority groups, 85% are women.

ACADEMICS
Degrees: associate, bachelor's, master's, post-bachelor's certificate, post-master's certificate, transfer associate. **Classes: Majors with Highest Enrollment:** clinical laboratory science/medical technology/technologist; health services/allied health/health sciences; nursing/registered nurse (rn, asn, bsn, msn). **Special Study Options:** Accelerated program, distance learning, double major, independent study, internships, study abroad. **Disability Services:** Special programs offered to physically disabled students include note-taking services, reader services, tutors. **Career Services:** Alumni network, alumni services, career/job search classes, career assessment, regional alumni.

FACILITIES
Housing: Coed dorms, special housing for disabled students, apartments for married students, apartments for single students. 80% of campus accessible to physically disabled. **Special Academic Facilities/Equipment:** Copy of the famous Gross Clinic, New building with simulation labs. Located in the heart of Center City close to all historical sights as well as cultural events and museums. **Computers:** 100% of classrooms, 100% of dorms, 100% of libraries, have wireless network access. Students can register for classes online. Administrative functions (other than registration) can be performed online.

CAMPUS LIFE
Environment: Metropolis. **Activities:** Choral groups, student government, yearbook, International Student Organization. **On-Campus Highlights:** New Education and Research Building, Famous painting called the Gross Clinic, Close to Historic Sites, Close to famous museums, Many fine restaurants and theaters, Jefferson is located in Center City Philadelphia, near the Convention Center with many fine restaurants, shops and other cultural sights.

ADMISSIONS
Freshman Admission Requirements: High school diploma is required and GED is accepted. **Transfer Admission Requirements:** college transcript(s), essay or personal statement, statement of good standing from prior institution(s). Minimum college GPA of 2.5 required. Lowest grade transferable C. **General Admission Information:** Application Fee $50. Notification on a rolling basis, beginning on or about 11/1. Nonfall registration accepted.

COSTS AND FINANCIAL AID
Annual tuition $23,685. Room and board $8,280. Required fees $400. Average book expense $1,495. **Required Forms and Deadlines:** FAFSA, institution's own financial aid form. **Types of Aid:** *Need-based scholarships/grants:* Federal Pell, SEOG, state scholarships/grants, private scholarships, the school's own gift aid, Federal Nursing Scholarships. *Loans:* Direct Subsidized Stafford, Direct Unsubsidized Stafford, Subsidized Stafford, Unsubsidized Stafford, PLUS, Federal Perkins, Federal Nursing, state loans, college/university loans from institutional funds. **Student Employment:** Federal Work-Study Program available. Institutional employment available. Off-campus job opportunities are excellent. **Criteria for awarding institutional aid:** *Non-need-based:* academics, leadership, state/district residency.

THOMAS MORE COLLEGE

333 Thomas More Pkwy., Crestview Hill, KY 41017-3495
Phone: 859-344-3332 • **Financial Aid Phone:** 859-344-3319
E-mail: admissions@thomasmore.edu • **CEEB Code:** 3892
Fax: 859-344-3444 • **Website:** www.thomasmore.edu • **ACT Code:** 1560

This private school, affiliated with the Roman Catholic Church, was founded in 1921. It has a 100-acre campus.

RATINGS
Admissions Selectivity Rating: 80   **Fire Safety Rating:** 61   **Green Rating:** 60*

STUDENTS AND FACULTY
Enrollment: 1,371. **Student Body:** 51% female, 49% male, 66% out-of-state, 1% international. Asian 1%, African American 5%, Caucasian 79%, Hispanic 0%, Native American 0%.
Retention and Graduation: 62% freshmen return for sophomore year. 39% freshmen graduate within 4 years. 55% freshmen graduate within 6 years. 25% grads go on to further study within 1 year. 44% grads pursue arts and sciences degrees. 6% grads pursue law degrees. 5% grads pursue business degrees. 5% grads pursue medical degrees. **Faculty:** Student/faculty ratio 15:1. 71 full-time faculty, 66% hold PhDs, 7% are members of minority groups, 39% are women. 0% of classes are taught by teaching assistants.

ACADEMICS
Degrees: associate, bachelor's, certificate, master's, terminal associate. **Classes:** Most classes have 10–19 students. Most lab/discussion sessions have 10–19 students. **Majors with Highest Enrollment:** business/commerce; teacher education and professional development, specific subject areas, other. **Special Study Options:** Accelerated program, cooperative education program, cross-registration, double major, dual enrollment, English as a Second Language (ESL), honors program, independent study, internships, liberal arts/career combination, student-designed major, study abroad, teacher certification program, weekend college. **Honors Programs:** Thomas More Honors Program . **Disability Services:** Special programs offered to physically disabled students include note-taking services, reader services, tape recorders, tutors.

FACILITIES
Housing: Coed dorms, men's dorms, women's dorms. 99% of campus accessible to physically disabled. **Special Academic Facilities/Equipment:** www2. thomasmore.edu/undergrad_admissions/resources.cfm?group=Resources **Computers:** Students can register for classes online. Administrative functions (other than registration) can be performed online.

CAMPUS LIFE
Environment: Village. **Activities:** Choral groups, drama/theater, literary magazine, student government, yearbook 29 registered organizations, 5 honor societies, 1 religious organizations. 1 fraternities. **Athletics (Intercollegiate):** *Men:* baseball, basketball, cross-country, football, golf, soccer, tennis. *Women:* basketball, cross-country, golf, soccer, softball, tennis, volleyball. **On-Campus Highlights:** Steigerwald Student Center, Connor Convocation Center (Athletic Center), Bank of KY Observatory at Thomas More College, Biology Field Station on the Ohio River, Murphy Hall.

ADMISSIONS
Freshman Academic Profile: Average high school GPA 2.9. 7% in top 10% of high school class, 31% in top 25% of high school class, 85% in top 50% of high school class. 69% from public high schools. SAT Math middle 50% range 460-600. SAT Critical Reading middle 50% range 460-580. ACT middle 50% range 19-24. Minimum paper TOEFL 515. **Basis for Candidate Selection:** *Very important factors considered include:* rigor of secondary school record, standardized test scores. *Important factors considered include:* Class rank. *Other factors considered include:* application essay, recommendation(s), character/personal qualities, extracurricular activities, interview, talent/ability, volunteer work. **Freshman Admission Requirements:** High school diploma is required and GED is accepted. *Academic units required:* 4 English, 3 mathematics, 3 science, (1 science labs), 2 foreign language, 3 social studies. *Academic units recommended:* 4 English, 3 mathematics, 3 science, (1 science labs), 2 foreign language, 3 social studies. **Freshman Admission Statistics:** 1,363 applied, 61% admitted, 31% enrolled. **Transfer Admission Requirements:** college transcript(s), statement of good standing from prior institution(s). Minimum college GPA of 2.0 required. Lowest grade transferable C. **General Admission Information:** Application Fee $25. Notification on a rolling basis, beginning on or about 3/15. Nonfall registration accepted. Admission may be deferred for a maximum of 1 year. Credit and/or placement offered for CEEB Advanced Placement tests.

COSTS AND FINANCIAL AID
Annual tuition $19,500. Room and board $5,400. Required fees $450. Average book expense $800. **Required Forms and Deadlines:** FAFSA, institution's own financial aid form. **Notification of Awards:** Applicants will be notified of awards on a rolling basis beginning 3/1. **Types of Aid:** *Need-based scholarships/grants:* Federal Pell, SEOG, private scholarships, the school's own gift aid, United Negro College Fund. *Loans:* Subsidized Stafford, Unsubsidized Stafford, PLUS, Federal Perkins, Federal Nursing, college/university loans from institutional funds. **Student Employment:** Highest amount earned per year from on-campus jobs $1,400. **Financial Aid Statistics:** 96% freshmen, 90% undergrads receive need-based scholarship or grant aid. 66% freshmen, 61% undergrads receive need-based self-help aid. 90% freshmen, 74% undergrads receive any aid. 62% undergrads borrow to pay for school. Average cumulative indebtedness $21,980. **Criteria for awarding institutional aid:** *Non-need-based:* academics, alumni affiliation, art, job skills, leadership, minority status, music/drama, religious affiliation.

See page 1230.

THOMAS MORE COLLEGE OF LIBERAL ARTS

6 Manchester Street, Merrimack, NH 03054-4818
Phone: 603-880-8308
E-mail: admissions@thomasmorecollege.edu
Fax: 603-880-9280 • **Website:** www.thomasmorecollege.edu • **ACT Code:** 3892

This private school, affiliated with the Roman Catholic Church, was founded in 1978. It has a 13-acre campus.

RATINGS
Admissions Selectivity Rating: 63   **Fire Safety Rating:** 60*   **Green Rating:** 60*

STUDENTS AND FACULTY
Enrollment: 92. **Student Body:** 84% out-of-state, 4% international. Asian 0%, African American 0%, Caucasian 52%, Hispanic 1%, Native American 0%.
Retention and Graduation: 60% freshmen return for sophomore year. 52% grads go on to further study within 1 year. 48% grads pursue arts and sciences degrees. 8% grads pursue law degrees. 2% grads pursue business degrees. 2% grads pursue medical degrees. **Faculty:** Student/faculty ratio 12:1. 5 full-time faculty, 100% hold PhDs, 20% are women. 0% of classes are taught by teaching assistants.

ACADEMICS
Degrees: bachelor's. **Classes:** Most classes have 10–19 students. **Majors with Highest Enrollment:** biology; business/commerce; computer and information sciences. **Special Study Options:** internships, study abroad, Spring semester in Rome for all sophomores.

FACILITIES
Housing: men's dorms, women's dorms. 70% of campus accessible to physically disabled.

CAMPUS LIFE
Environment: Village. **Activities:** Choral groups, drama/theater.

ADMISSIONS
Basis for Candidate Selection: *Very important factors considered include:* application essay, recommendation(s), character/personal qualities, interview. *Important factors considered include:* talent/ability. *Other factors considered include:* Class rank, academic GPA, rigor of secondary school record, standardized test scores, extracurricular activities, level of applicant's interest, religious affiliation/commitment. **Freshman Admission Requirements:** High school diploma is required and GED is accepted. *Academic units required:* 4 English, 3 mathematics, 2 science, (2 science labs), 2 foreign language, 2 social studies, 2 history. *Academic units recommended:* 4 English, 3 mathematics, 2 science, (2 science labs), 2 foreign language, 2 social studies, 2 history. **Freshman Admission Statistics:** 75 applied, 55% admitted, 63% enrolled. **Transfer Admission Requirements:** college transcript(s), essay or personal statement, Lowest grade transferable C. **General Admission Information:** Notification on a rolling basis, beginning on or about 1/6. Nonfall registration accepted. Admission may be deferred for a maximum of n/a. Neither credit nor placement offered for CEEB Advanced Placement tests.

COSTS AND FINANCIAL AID
Annual tuition $11,100. Room and board $8,000. Average book expense $525. **Required Forms and Deadlines:** FAFSA. **Notification of Awards:** Applicants will be notified of awards on a rolling basis beginning 3/15. **Types of Aid:** *Need-based scholarships/grants:* Federal Pell, SEOG, state scholarships/grants, private scholarships, the school's own gift aid. *Loans:* Subsidized Stafford, Unsubsidized Stafford, PLUS. **Student Employment:** Off-campus job opportunities are good. **Financial Aid Statistics:** 100% freshmen, 100% undergrads receive need-based scholarship or grant aid. 70% freshmen, 62%

undergrads receive need-based self-help aid. 79% undergrads borrow to pay for school. Average cumulative indebtedness $22,555. **Criteria for awarding institutional aid:** *Non-need-based:* academics.

THOMPSON RIVERS UNIVERSITY

TRU Admissions, Kamloops, BC V2C 5N3
Phone: 250-828-5071
E-mail: admissions@tru.ca
Fax: 250-371-5513 • **Website:** www.tru.ca

This public school was founded in 1970. It has a 200-acre campus.

RATINGS
Admissions Selectivity Rating: 61   **Fire Safety Rating:** 60*   **Green Rating:** 60*

STUDENTS AND FACULTY
Enrollment: 4,497. **Student Body:** 61% female, 39% male, 15% out-of-state, (43 countries represented).
Retention and Graduation: Faculty: Student/faculty ratio 20:1. 375 full-time faculty, 28% hold PhDs. 0% of classes are taught by teaching assistants.

ACADEMICS
Degrees: associate, bachelor's, certificate, diploma, master's, post-bachelor's certificate, terminal associate, transfer associate. **Classes:** Most classes have 20–29 students. Most lab/discussion sessions have 10–19 students. **Special Study Options:** Accelerated program, cooperative education program, distance learning, double major, English as a Second Language (ESL), external degree program, honors program, independent study, internships, liberal arts/career combination, study abroad, teacher certification program. **Disability Services:** Special programs offered to physically disabled students include note-taking services, reader services, tape recorders, tutors. **Career Services:** Alumni network, career/job search classes, career assessment

FACILITIES
Housing: 95% of campus accessible to physically disabled. **Computers:** Students can register for classes online. Administrative functions (other than registration) can be performed online.

CAMPUS LIFE
Environment: Activities: literary magazine, student government 5 religious organizations. **Athletics (Intercollegiate):** *Men:* baseball, basketball, soccer, volleyball. *Women:* basketball, soccer, volleyball.

ADMISSIONS
Freshman Academic Profile: 95% from public high schools. **Basis for Candidate Selection:** *Very important factors considered include:* rigor of secondary school record. *Important factors considered include:* standardized test scores. *Other factors considered include:* recommendation(s), character/personal qualities, interview, racial/ethnic status, talent/ability, volunteer work, work experience. **Transfer Admission Requirements:** High school transcript, college transcript(s). **General Admission Information:** Application Fee $60. Regular application deadline 3/1. Notification on a rolling basis, beginning on or about 10/1. Nonfall registration accepted. Admission may be deferred for a maximum of 1 Year. Neither credit nor placement offered for CEEB Advanced Placement tests.

COSTS AND FINANCIAL AID
Room and board $2,100. Required fees $200. Average book expense $1,000. **Student Employment:** Off-campus job opportunities are good.

TIFFIN UNIVERSITY

155 Miami Street, Tiffin, OH 44883
Phone: 419-448-3423 • **Financial Aid Phone:** 419-448-3415
E-mail: admiss@tiffin.edu • **CEEB Code:** 1817
Website: www.tiffin.edu/ • **ACT Code:** 3334

This private school was founded in 1888. It has a 110-acre campus.

RATINGS
Admissions Selectivity Rating: 88   **Fire Safety Rating:** 76   **Green Rating:** 61

STUDENTS AND FACULTY
Enrollment: 5,016. **Student Body:** 64% female, 36% male, 51% out-of-state, 2% international (34 countries represented). Asian 0%, African American 30%, Caucasian 25%, Hispanic 1%, Native American 1%.

Retention and Graduation: 66% freshmen return for sophomore year. 29% freshmen graduate within 4 years. 25% grads go on to further study within 1 year. **Faculty:** Student/faculty ratio 19:1. 85 full-time faculty, 56% hold PhDs, 7% are members of minority groups, 47% are women. 0% of classes are taught by teaching assistants.

ACADEMICS
Degrees: associate, bachelor's, certificate, master's, post-bachelor's certificate. **Classes:** Most classes have fewer than 10 students. Most lab/discussion sessions have fewer than 10 students. **Majors with Highest Enrollment:** business administration and management; forensic science and technology; marketing/marketing management. **Special Study Options:** Accelerated program, cross-registration, distance learning, double major, dual enrollment, English as a Second Language (ESL), honors program, independent study, internships, study abroad, teacher certification program. **Honors Programs:** We offer a Freshman Honors Program . **Career Services:** Alumni network, alumni services, career/job search classes, career assessment, internships, regional alumni.

FACILITIES
Housing: Coed dorms, special housing for disabled students, men's dorms, special housing for international students, women's dorms, fraternity/sorority housing, apartments for married students, theme housing. 85% of campus accessible to physically disabled. **Special Academic Facilities/Equipment:** University Art Gallery Multi-Media Lab **Computers:** 100% of classrooms, 25% of dorms, 100% of libraries, 100% of dining areas, 100% of student union, have wireless network access. Students can register for classes online. Administrative functions (other than registration) can be performed online.

CAMPUS LIFE
Environment: Village. **Activities:** Choral groups, concert band, dance, drama/theater, jazz band, literary magazine, marching band, music ensembles, musical theater, pep band, student government, student newspaper, Campus Ministries, International Student Organization 32 registered organizations, 1 honor societies, 2 religious organizations. 3 fraternities, 3 sororities. **Athletics (Intercollegiate):** *Men:* baseball, basketball, cheerleading, cross-country, equestrian sports, football, golf, soccer, tennis, track/field (outdoor), track/field (indoor). *Women:* basketball, cheerleading, cross-country, equestrian sports, golf, lacrosse, soccer, softball, tennis, track/field (outdoor), track/field (indoor), volleyball. **On-Campus Highlights:** Gillmor Student Center, Hayes Center for the Arts, Hertzer Technology Center, Main Classroom Building, Franks Hall. **Environmental Initiatives:** Establishment of a Green Committee and formation of a Green Technologies Minor and Concentration All future buildings will be considered for LEED certification (silver level) Paper recycling program has been implemented at the University along with a trayless program in the dining hall.

ADMISSIONS
Freshman Academic Profile: Average high school GPA 3.0. 75% from public high schools. SAT Math middle 50% range 420-540. SAT Critical Reading middle 50% range 440-523. ACT middle 50% range 18-23. Minimum web-based TOEFL 61. Minimum paper TOEFL 500. **Basis for Candidate Selection:** *Very important factors considered include:* academic GPA, rigor of secondary school record, standardized test scores. *Important factors considered include:* Class rank, application essay, recommendation(s), extracurricular activities, geographical residence, state residency. *Other factors considered include:* alumni/ae relation, character/personal qualities, first generation, interview, level of applicant's interest, racial/ethnic status, talent/ability, volunteer work. **Freshman Admission Requirements:** High school diploma is required and GED is accepted. *Academic units required:* 4 English, 3 mathematics, 3 science, 3 social studies. *Academic units recommended:* 4 English, 3 mathematics, 3 science, 3 social studies. **Freshman Admission Statistics:** 5,228 applied, 39% admitted, 65% enrolled. **Transfer Admission Requirements:** High school transcript, college transcript(s), minimum college GPA of 2.0 required. Lowest grade transferable C. **General Admission Information:** Application Fee $20. Notification on a rolling basis, beginning on or about 9/15. Nonfall registration accepted. Credit offered for CEEB Advanced Placement tests.

COSTS AND FINANCIAL AID
Annual tuition $20,700. Room and board $9,573. Average book expense $2,000. **Required Forms and Deadlines:** FAFSA. **Notification of Awards:** Applicants will be notified of awards on a rolling basis beginning 1/15. **Types of Aid:** *Need-based scholarships/grants:* Federal Pell, SEOG, state scholarships/grants, private scholarships, the school's own gift aid. *Loans:* Direct Subsidized Stafford, Direct Unsubsidized Stafford, Direct PLUS, Subsidized Stafford, Unsubsidized Stafford, PLUS, Federal Perkins, college/university loans from institutional funds. **Student Employment:** Federal Work-Study Program available. Institutional employment available. Highest amount earned per year from on-campus jobs $1,600. Off-campus job opportunities are good. **Financial Aid Statistics:** 99% freshmen, 99% undergrads receive need-based scholarship or grant aid. 7% freshmen, 4% undergrads receive non-need-based scholarship or grant aid. 93% freshmen, 96% undergrads receive need-based self-help aid. 4% freshmen, 3% undergrads receive athletic scholarships. 95% freshmen, 95% undergrads receive any aid. 73% undergrads borrow to pay for school. Average

cumulative indebtedness $30,119. **Criteria for awarding institutional aid:** *Non-need-based:* academics, alumni affiliation, athletics, music/drama, state/district residency.

TOCCOA FALLS COLLEGE

Toccoa Falls College, Toccoa Falls, GA 30598
Phone: 888-785-5624 • **Financial Aid Phone:** 706-886-6831
E-mail: admissions@tfc.edu
Fax: 706-282-6012 • **Website:** www.tfc.edu • **ACT Code:** 868

This private school, affiliated with the Christian & Missionary Allianc Church, was founded in 1907. It has a 1100-acre campus.

RATINGS
Admissions Selectivity Rating: 87   **Fire Safety Rating:** 62   **Green Rating:** 60*

STUDENTS AND FACULTY
Enrollment: 858. **Student Body:** 54% female, 46% male, 46% out-of-state, 1% international. Asian 8%, African American 3%, Caucasian 86%, Hispanic 2%, Native American 0%.
Retention and Graduation: 60% freshmen return for sophomore year. 46% freshmen graduate within 4 years. 55% freshmen graduate within 6 years.
Faculty: Student/faculty ratio 17:1. 47 full-time faculty, 57% hold PhDs, 4% are members of minority groups, 21% are women. 0% of classes are taught by teaching assistants.

ACADEMICS
Degrees: associate, bachelor's, certificate. **Classes:** Most classes have fewer than 10 students. **Majors with Highest Enrollment:** counseling psychology; elementary education and teaching; missions/missionary studies and missiology. **Special Study Options:** distance learning, double major, dual enrollment, independent study, internships, teacher certification program. **Disability Services:** Special programs offered to physically disabled students include notetaking services, reader services, tutors. **Career Services:** career assessment.

FACILITIES
Housing: men's dorms, special housing for international students, women's dorms, apartments for married students, Mobile home court living available for married students. 70% of campus accessible to physically disabled. **Computers:** 40% of classrooms, 50% of dorms, 100% of libraries, 100% of dining areas, 50% of student union, 1% of common outdoor areas have wireless network access. Students can register for classes online. Administrative functions (other than registration) can be performed online.

CAMPUS LIFE
Environment: Rural. **Activities:** Choral groups, concert band, drama/theater, jazz band, music ensembles, radio station, student government, student newspaper, yearbook, Campus Ministries. **Athletics (Intercollegiate):** *Men:* baseball, basketball, cross-country, golf, soccer, tennis. *Women:* basketball, cheerleading, cross-country, golf, soccer, tennis, volleyball. **On-Campus Highlights:** The Waterfall, Student Center, Gymnatorium, Eagle's Nest, Grace Chapel & Performing Arts Center.

ADMISSIONS
Freshman Academic Profile: Average high school GPA 3.4. 12% in top 10% of high school class, 38% in top 25% of high school class, 70% in top 50% of high school class. 57% from public high schools. SAT Math middle 50% range 430-550. SAT Critical Reading middle 50% range 460-570. ACT middle 50% range 18-25. Minimum paper TOEFL 500. **Basis for Candidate Selection:** *Very important factors considered include:* application essay, academic GPA, recommendation(s), rigor of secondary school record, standardized test scores, character/personal qualities, religious affiliation/commitment. *Other factors considered include:* extracurricular activities, interview, level of applicant's interest, talent/ability, volunteer work, work experience. **Freshman Admission Requirements:** High school diploma is required and GED is accepted. **Freshman Admission Statistics:** 1,188 applied, 45% admitted, 31% enrolled. **Transfer Admission Requirements:** college transcript(s), essay or personal statement, minimum college GPA of 2.0 required. Lowest grade transferable C–. **General Admission Information:** Application Fee $20. Regular application deadline 8/1. Regular notification 3/1. Nonfall registration accepted. Admission may be deferred for a maximum of 2 years. Credit and/or placement offered for CEEB Advanced Placement tests.

COSTS AND FINANCIAL AID
Annual tuition $15,450. Room and board $5,650. Required fees $125. Average book expense $1,000. **Required Forms and Deadlines:** FAFSA, institution's own financial aid form, state aid form. **Notification of Awards:** Applicants will be notified of awards on a rolling basis beginning 3/1. **Types of Aid:**

Need-based scholarships/grants: Federal Pell, SEOG, state scholarships/grants, private scholarships, the school's own gift aid. *Loans:* Subsidized Stafford, Unsubsidized Stafford, PLUS, Federal Perkins, state loans, college/university loans from institutional funds. **Student Employment:** Highest amount earned per year from on-campus jobs $6,000. **Financial Aid Statistics:** 44% freshmen, 52% undergrads receive need-based scholarship or grant aid. 95% freshmen, 100% undergrads receive non-need-based scholarship or grant aid. 20% freshmen, 16% undergrads receive need-based self-help aid. 100% freshmen, 98% undergrads receive any aid. 78% undergrads borrow to pay for school. Average cumulative indebtedness $6,284. **Criteria for awarding institutional aid:** *Non-need-based:* academics, alumni affiliation, leadership, music/drama, religious affiliation, state/district residency.

TOUGALOO COLLEGE

500 West Country Line Road, Tougaloo, MS 39174
Phone: 888-424-2566 • **Financial Aid Phone:** 601-977-7769
E-mail: jjacobs@mail.tougaloo.edu
Fax: 601-977-6185 • **Website:** tougaloo.edu

This private school, affiliated with the Church of Christ Church, was founded in 1869. It has a 500-acre campus.

RATINGS
Admissions Selectivity Rating: 64   **Fire Safety Rating:** 98   **Green Rating:** 60*

STUDENTS AND FACULTY
Enrollment: 967. **Student Body:** 72% female, 28% male, 18% out-of-state, 0% international (3 countries represented). Asian 0%, African American 99%, Caucasian 0%, Hispanic 0%, Native American 0%.
Retention and Graduation: 70% freshmen return for sophomore year. 63% freshmen graduate within 4 years. 100% freshmen graduate within 6 years. 69% grads go on to further study within 1 year. 50% grads pursue arts and sciences degrees. 20% grads pursue law degrees. 10% grads pursue business degrees. 20% grads pursue medical degrees. **Faculty:** Student/faculty ratio 15:1. 78 full-time faculty, 60% hold PhDs, 55% are members of minority groups, 51% are women. 0% of classes are taught by teaching assistants.

ACADEMICS
Degrees: associate, bachelor's, certificate, terminal associate, transfer associate. **Classes:** Most classes have 20–29 students. Most lab/discussion sessions have 10–19 students. **Special Study Options:** cooperative education program, cross-registration, double major, dual enrollment, exchange student program (domestic), honors program, independent study, internships, liberal arts/career combination, study abroad, teacher certification program. **Honors Programs:** There is a general Honors Program. **Combined Degree Programs:** Nursing with Univ. of MS Medical School. **Disability Services:** Special programs offered to physically disabled students include tape recorders, tutors. **Career Services:** Alumni network, alumni services, career/job search classes, career assessment, internships.

FACILITIES
Housing: men's dorms, women's dorms. 70% of campus accessible to physically disabled. **Special Academic Facilities/Equipment:** Tougaloo Art Collections Bailey-Ward Black Collection **Computers:** Students can register for classes online. Administrative functions (other than registration) can be performed online.

CAMPUS LIFE
Environment: City. **Activities:** Choral groups, dance, drama/theater, jazz band, literary magazine, music ensembles, student government, student newspaper, television station, yearbook 50 registered organizations, 2 honor societies, 7 religious organizations. 4 fraternities, 4 sororities. **Athletics (Intercollegiate):** *Men:* baseball, basketball, cross-country, golf, tennis, track/field (outdoor). *Women:* basketball, cross-country, golf, softball, tennis, track/field (outdoor). **On-Campus Highlights:** Woodworth Chapel, L. Zenobia Coleman Library and Archives, Warren Hall Student Center, Owens Health and Wellness Center, Blackmon Administration Center.

ADMISSIONS
Freshman Academic Profile: Average high school GPA 3.2. 95% from public high schools. ACT middle 50% range 16-21. Minimum paper TOEFL 500. **Basis for Candidate Selection:** *Important factors considered include:* recommendation(s), rigor of secondary school record, standardized test scores, character/personal qualities, talent/ability. *Other factors considered include:* Class rank, application essay, alumni/ae relation, extracurricular activities, interview. **Freshman Admission Requirements:** High school diploma is required and GED is accepted. *Academic units required:* 3 English, 2 mathematics, 2 science, 1 social studies, 1 history, 7 academic electives. *Academic units recommended:* 3 English, 2 mathematics, 2 science, 1 social studies, 1 history, 7

academic electives. **Transfer Admission Requirements:** college transcript(s), standardized test scores, statement of good standing from prior institution(s). Minimum college GPA of 2.0 required. Lowest grade transferable C. **General Admission Information:** Application Fee $25. Notification on a rolling basis, beginning on or about 10/15. Nonfall registration accepted. Admission may be deferred for a maximum of 1 semester. Credit and/or placement offered for CEEB Advanced Placement tests.

COSTS AND FINANCIAL AID

Annual tuition $9,240. Room and board $6,330. Required fees $470. Average book expense $1,200. **Required Forms and Deadlines:** FAFSA, institution's own financial aid form, CSS/Financial Aid PROFILE. **Notification of Awards:** Applicants will be notified of awards on a rolling basis beginning 10/15. **Types of Aid:** *Need-based scholarships/grants:* Federal Pell, SEOG, state scholarships/grants, private scholarships, the school's own gift aid, United Negro College Fund. *Loans:* Direct Subsidized Stafford, Direct PLUS, Unsubsidized Stafford, Federal Perkins, Federal Nursing. **Student Employment:** Federal Work-Study Program available. Highest amount earned per year from on-campus jobs $2,800. Off-campus job opportunities are excellent. **Financial Aid Statistics:** 96% freshmen, 96% undergrads receive need-based scholarship or grant aid. 18% undergrads receive non-need-based scholarship or grant aid. 23% undergrads receive need-based self-help aid. 1% undergrads receive athletic scholarships. 95% freshmen, 95% undergrads receive any aid. 85% undergrads borrow to pay for school. Average cumulative indebtedness $8,000. **Criteria for awarding institutional aid:** *Non-need-based:* academics, art, athletics, leadership, music/drama.

TOWSON UNIVERSITY

8000 York Road, Towson, MD 21252-0001
Phone: 410-704-2113 • **Financial Aid Phone:** 410-704-4236
E-mail: admissions@towson.edu • **CEEB Code:** 5404
Fax: 410-704-3030 • **Website:** www.towson.edu • **ACT Code:** 1718

This public school was founded in 1866. It has a 328-acre campus.

RATINGS

Admissions Selectivity Rating: 87   **Fire Safety Rating:** 81   **Green Rating:** 83

STUDENTS AND FACULTY

Enrollment: 17,503. **Student Body:** 61% female, 39% male, 16% out-of-state, 2% international (74 countries represented). Asian 4%, African American 14%, Caucasian 67%, Hispanic 5%, Native American 0%.
Retention and Graduation: 39% freshmen graduate within 4 years. 66% freshmen graduate within 6 years. **Faculty:** Student/faculty ratio 17:1. 848 full-time faculty, 74% hold PhDs, 17% are members of minority groups, 55% are women. 0% of classes are taught by teaching assistants.

ACADEMICS

Degrees: bachelor's, master's, post-bachelor's certificate, post-master's certificate. **Classes:** Most classes have 20–29 students. Most lab/discussion sessions have 10–19 students. **Majors with Highest Enrollment:** business administration, management and operations, other; elementary education and teaching; social sciences. **Special Study Options:** cooperative education program, cross-registration, distance learning, double major, dual enrollment, English as a Second Language (ESL), exchange student program (domestic), honors program, independent study, internships, liberal arts/career combination, student-designed major, study abroad, teacher certification program. **Honors Programs:** Honors College . **Disability Services:** Special programs offered to physically disabled students include note-taking services, reader services. **Career Services:** Alumni network, alumni services, career/job search classes, career assessment, internships, regional alumni. Career Services highlights include internships.

FACILITIES

Housing: Coed dorms, special housing for disabled students, special housing for international students, apartments for single students, 80% of campus accessible to physically disabled. **Special Academic Facilities/Equipment:** Art galleries, animal museum, Asian art collection, elementary school, media center, speech/language clinic, planetarium/observatory, herbarium, electron microscope, argon laser. **Computers:** 100% of classrooms, 100% of dorms, 100% of libraries, 100% of dining areas, 100% of student union, 100% of common outdoor areas have wireless network access. Students can register for classes online. Administrative functions (other than registration) can be performed online.

CAMPUS LIFE

Environment: Metropolis. **Activities:** Choral groups, concert band, dance, drama/theater, jazz band, literary magazine, marching band, music ensembles, musical theater, pep band, radio station, student government, student news-

paper, symphony orchestra, television station, yearbook, Campus Ministries, International Student Organization 198 registered organizations, 15 honor societies, 12 religious organizations. 12 fraternities, 10 sororities. **Athletics (Intercollegiate):** *Men:* baseball, basketball, cheerleading, cross-country, diving, football, golf, lacrosse, soccer, swimming, tennis. *Women:* basketball, cheerleading, cross-country, diving, field hockey, gymnastics, lacrosse, soccer, softball, swimming, tennis, track/field (outdoor), volleyball. **On-Campus Highlights:** Johnny Unitas Stadium, University Union, Burdick Hall-athletic facilities, The Den, Towson Center-events. **Environmental Initiatives:** Sign the American College and University President's Climate Committment (ACUPCC) in 2007 pledging to become/achieve climate neutrality RecycleMania Partcipate in B-CaUSE which is comprised of 12 institutions of higher education from the Baltimore region

ADMISSIONS

Freshman Academic Profile: Average high school GPA 3.6. 19% in top 10% of high school class, 50% in top 25% of high school class, 89% in top 50% of high school class. SAT Math middle 50% range 500-600. SAT Critical Reading middle 50% range 490-580. SAT Writing middle 50% range 500-590. ACT middle 50% range 21-25. Minimum web-based TOEFL 61. Minimum paper TOEFL 500. **Basis for Candidate Selection:** *Very important factors considered include:* academic GPA. *Important factors considered include:* rigor of secondary school record, standardized test scores. *Other factors considered include:* Class rank, application essay, recommendation(s), first generation, talent/ability. **Freshman Admission Requirements:** High school diploma is required and GED is accepted. *Academic units required:* 4 English, 3 mathematics, 3 science, (2 science labs), 2 foreign language, 3 social studies, 6 academic electives. 4 English, 3 mathematics, 3 science, (2 science labs), 2 foreign language, 3 social studies, 6 academic electives. **Freshman Admission Statistics:** 18,128 applied, 52% admitted, 26% enrolled. **Transfer Admission Requirements:** college transcript(s), minimum college GPA of 2.0 required. Lowest grade transferable D. **General Admission Information:** Application Fee $45. Regular application deadline 2/15. Notification on a rolling basis, beginning on or about 10/15. Nonfall registration accepted. Admission may be deferred for a maximum of Up to 1 year. Credit and/or placement offered for CEEB Advanced Placement tests.

COSTS AND FINANCIAL AID

Annual in-state tuition $5,660. Annual out-of-state tuition $17,282. Room and board $10,644. Required fees $2,472. Average book expense $1,080. **Required Forms and Deadlines:** FAFSA. **Notification of Awards:** Applicants will be notified of awards on a rolling basis beginning 3/21. **Types of Aid:** *Need-based scholarships/grants:* Federal Pell, SEOG, state scholarships/grants, private scholarships, the school's own gift aid. *Loans:* Direct Subsidized Stafford, Direct Unsubsidized Stafford, Direct PLUS, Federal Perkins. **Student Employment:** Federal Work-Study Program available. Institutional employment available. Off-campus job opportunities are excellent. **Financial Aid Statistics:** 51% freshmen, 50% undergrads receive need-based scholarship or grant aid. 41% freshmen, 27% undergrads receive non-need-based scholarship or grant aid. 74% freshmen, 76% undergrads receive need-based self-help aid. 3% freshmen, 2% undergrads receive athletic scholarships. 75% freshmen, 73% undergrads receive any aid. 60% undergrads borrow to pay for school. Average cumulative indebtedness $23,812. **Criteria for awarding institutional aid:** *Non-need-based:* academics, art, athletics, music/drama.

TRANSYLVANIA UNIVERSITY

300 North Broadway, Lexington, KY 40508-1797
Phone: 859-233-8242 • **Financial Aid Phone:** 859-233-8239
E-mail: admissions@transy.edu • **CEEB Code:** 1808
Fax: 859-281-3649 • **Website:** www.transy.edu • **ACT Code:** 1550

This private school, affiliated with the Christian (Nondenominational) Church, was founded in 1780. It has a 36-acre campus.

RATINGS

Admissions Selectivity Rating: 81   **Fire Safety Rating:** 83   **Green Rating:** 73

STUDENTS AND FACULTY

Enrollment: 1,070. **Student Body:** 58% female, 42% male, 18% out-of-state, 1% international (7 countries represented). Asian 2%, African American 3%, Caucasian 86%, Hispanic 2%, Native American 0%.
Retention and Graduation: 68% freshmen graduate within 4 years. 74% freshmen graduate within 6 years. 39% grads go on to further study within 1

year. 8% grads pursue arts and sciences degrees. 4% grads pursue law degrees. 3% grads pursue business degrees. 3% grads pursue medical degrees. **Faculty:** Student/faculty ratio 11:1. 90 full-time faculty, 93% hold PhDs, 7% are members of minority groups, 40% are women. 0% of classes are taught by teaching assistants.

ACADEMICS

Degrees: bachelor's. **Classes:** Most classes have 10–19 students. Most lab/discussion sessions have 10–19 students. **Majors with Highest Enrollment:** biology/biological sciences; business/commerce; psychology. **Special Study Options:** double major, independent study, internships, liberal arts/career combination, student-designed major, study abroad, teacher certification program. **Disability Services:** Special programs offered to physically disabled students include note-taking services, reader services, tape recorders, tutors. **Career Services:** Alumni network, alumni services, career/job search classes, career assessment, internships, regional alumni. Career Services highlights include Internship Programs.

FACILITIES

Housing: Coed dorms, special housing for disabled students, men's dorms, women's dorms, apartments for single students, theme housing, efficiency apartment option for upperclassmen. Units with facilities for disabled students. 90% of campus accessible to physically disabled. **Special Academic Facilities/Equipment:** Art gallery, museum of early scientific apparatus, medical museum, language lab, transmission electron microscope. **Computers:** 20% of classrooms, 20% of dorms, 75% of libraries, 20% of dining areas, 100% of student union, 10% of common outdoor areas have wireless network access. Administrative functions (other than registration) can be performed online.

CAMPUS LIFE

Environment: City. **Activities:** Choral groups, concert band, dance, drama/theater, jazz band, literary magazine, music ensembles, musical theater, opera, pep band, radio station, student government, student newspaper, yearbook 55 registered organizations, 10 honor societies, 7 religious organizations. 4 fraternities, 4 sororities. **Athletics (Intercollegiate):** *Men:* baseball, basketball, cheerleading, cross-country, diving, golf, soccer, swimming, tennis, track/field (outdoor). *Women:* basketball, cheerleading, cross-country, diving, field hockey, golf, soccer, softball, swimming, tennis, track/field (outdoor), volleyball. **On-Campus Highlights:** Beck Athletic and Recreation Center, William T. Young Campus Center, Mitchell Fine Arts Center, Little Theater, 1780 Cafe. **Environmental Initiatives:** Developing a comprehensive sustainability master plan. Comprehensive environmental policy including commitment to build to LEED silver. Ongoing outreach to faculty, staff, and students on a variety of sustainability issues.

ADMISSIONS

Freshman Academic Profile: Average high school GPA 3.7. 40% in top 10% of high school class, 72% in top 25% of high school class, 93% in top 50% of high school class. 78% from public high schools. SAT Math middle 50% range 520-640. SAT Critical Reading middle 50% range 510-630. ACT middle 50% range 24-30. Minimum web-based TOEFL 80. Minimum paper TOEFL 550. **Basis for Candidate Selection:** *Very important factors considered include:* academic GPA, rigor of secondary school record, standardized test scores. *Important factors considered include:* application essay, recommendation(s), extracurricular activities. *Other factors considered include:* Class rank, alumni/ae relation, character/personal qualities, first generation, geographical residence, interview, talent/ability, volunteer work, work experience. **Freshman Admission Requirements:** High school diploma is required and GED is accepted. *Academic units required:* 4 English, 3 mathematics, 3 science, 2 social studies. academic electives. *Academic units recommended:* 4 English, 3 mathematics, 3 science, 2 social studies. academic electives. **Freshman Admission Statistics:** 1,569 applied, 85% admitted, 25% enrolled. **Transfer Admission Requirements:** High school transcript, college transcript(s), essay or personal statement, minimum college GPA of 2.75 required. Lowest grade transferable C–. **General Admission Information:** Application Fee $30. Regular application deadline 2/1. Regular notification 3/1. Nonfall registration accepted. Admission may be deferred for a maximum of 12 months. Credit and/or placement offered for CEEB Advanced Placement tests.

COSTS AND FINANCIAL AID

Annual tuition $28,645. Room and board $8,750. Required fees $1,220. Average book expense $1,000. **Required Forms and Deadlines:** FAFSA. **Notification of Awards:** Applicants will be notified of awards on a rolling basis beginning 3/15. **Types of Aid:** *Need-based scholarships/grants:* Federal Pell, SEOG, state scholarships/grants, private scholarships, the school's own gift aid. *Loans:* Subsidized Stafford, Unsubsidized Stafford, PLUS, Federal Perkins, college/university loans from institutional funds. **Student Employment:** Federal Work-Study Program available. Institutional employment available. Off-campus job opportunities are excellent. **Financial Aid Statistics:** 100% freshmen, 100% undergrads receive need-based scholarship or grant aid. 17% freshmen, 14% undergrads receive non-need-based scholarship or grant aid. 81% fresh-

men, 79% undergrads receive need-based self-help aid. 99% freshmen, 98% undergrads receive any aid. 66% undergrads borrow to pay for school. Average cumulative indebtedness $26,604. **Criteria for awarding institutional aid:** *Non-need-based:* academics, art, leadership, minority status, music/drama, religious affiliation, state/district residency.

See page 1232.

TRENT UNIVERSITY

Registrar's Office, 1600 West Bank Dr., Peterborough, ON K9J 7B8
Phone: 705-748-1011 x 7140
E-mail: amaxie@trentu.ca
Fax: 705-748-1629 • **Website:** www.trentu.ca

This is a public school.

RATINGS
Admissions Selectivity Rating: 60* **Fire Safety Rating:** 60* **Green Rating:** 60*

ACADEMICS
Degrees: bachelor's, diploma, doctoral, master's, transfer associate. **Special Study Options:** Accelerated program, double major, English as a Second Language (ESL), exchange student program (domestic), honors program, liberal arts/career combination, student-designed major, study abroad, teacher certification program.

FACILITIES
Housing: Coed dorms, special housing for disabled students, women's dorms, apartments for married students, apartments for single students, theme housing

CAMPUS LIFE
Activities: Choral groups, dance, drama/theater, jazz band, literary magazine, radio station, student government, student newspaper, student-run film society, yearbook, International Student Organization, Model UN.

ADMISSIONS
Transfer Admission Requirements: High school transcript, college transcript(s), minimum college GPA of 2.65 required. Lowest grade transferable C.

COSTS AND FINANCIAL AID
Annual in-state tuition $6,200. Average book expense $1,000. **Required Forms and Deadlines:** institution's own financial aid formOSAP. **Types of Aid:** *Need-based scholarships/grants:* state scholarships/grants, private scholarships, the school's own gift aid. *Loans:* college/university loans from institutional funds. **Criteria for awarding institutional aid:** *Non-need-based:* academics.

TREVECCA NAZARENE UNIVERSITY

333 Murfreesboro Road, Nashville, TN 37210
Phone: 615-248-1320 • **Financial Aid Phone:** 615-248-1242
E-mail: admissions_und@trevecca.edu
Fax: 615-248-7406 • **Website:** www.trevecca.edu • **ACT Code:** 4016

This private school, affiliated with the Nazarene Church, was founded in 1901. It has a 65-acre campus.

RATINGS
Admissions Selectivity Rating: 65 **Fire Safety Rating:** 60* **Green Rating:** 60*

STUDENTS AND FACULTY
Enrollment: 1,409. **Student Body:** 55% female, 45% male, 34% out-of-state, 2% international (13 countries represented). Asian 1%, African American 8%, Caucasian 73%, Hispanic 2%, Native American 1%.
Retention and Graduation: 74% freshmen return for sophomore year. 40% freshmen graduate within 4 years. 54% freshmen graduate within 6 years. **Faculty:** Student/faculty ratio 15:1. 89 full-time faculty, 88% hold PhDs, 6% are members of minority groups, 31% are women.

ACADEMICS
Degrees: associate, bachelor's, master's. **Classes:** Most classes have 10–19 students. **Majors with Highest Enrollment:** business administration and management; elementary education and teaching; religion/religious studies. **Special Study Options:** double major, internships, study abroad, teacher certification program, Four adult degree-completion programs offer non-traditional

class schedules (night/on-line). **Disability Services:** Special programs offered to physically disabled students include note-taking services, reader services, tutors. **Career Services:** career/job search classes, internships.

FACILITIES

Housing: men's dorms, women's dorms, apartments for married students, apartments for single students.. **Computers:** 100% of classrooms, 100% of dorms, 100% of libraries, 100% of dining areas, 100% of student union, 100% of common outdoor areas have wireless network access. Administrative functions (other than registration) can be performed online.

CAMPUS LIFE

Environment: Metropolis. **Activities:** Choral groups, concert band, drama/theater, jazz band, literary magazine, marching band, music ensembles, musical theater, pep band, radio station, student government, student newspaper, symphony orchestra, television station, yearbook, Campus Ministries, International Student Organization. **Athletics (Intercollegiate):** *Men:* baseball, basketball, golf, soccer. *Women:* basketball, golf, soccer, softball, volleyball. **On-Campus Highlights:** Library, Student Center

ADMISSIONS

Freshman Academic Profile: Average high school GPA 3.3. SAT Math middle 50% range 450-570. SAT Critical Reading middle 50% range 480-590. ACT middle 50% range 19-26. Minimum paper TOEFL 500. **Basis for Candidate Selection:** *Very important factors considered include:* academic GPA, standardized test scores, character/personal qualities. *Important factors considered include:* level of applicant's interest. *Other factors considered include:* Class rank, application essay, recommendation(s), extracurricular activities, interview, talent/ability. **Freshman Admission Requirements:** High school diploma is required and GED is accepted. **Transfer Admission Requirements:** college transcript(s), Lowest grade transferable D. **General Admission Information:** Application Fee $25. Regular application deadline 8/1. Nonfall registration accepted. Admission may be deferred for a maximum of n/a. Credit offered for CEEB Advanced Placement tests.

COSTS AND FINANCIAL AID

Required Forms and Deadlines: FAFSA. **Notification of Awards:** Applicants will be notified of awards on a rolling basis beginning 3/1. **Types of Aid:** *Need-based scholarships/grants:* Federal Pell, SEOG, state scholarships/grants, private scholarships, the school's own gift aid. *Loans:* Subsidized Stafford, Unsubsidized Stafford, PLUS, Federal Perkins. **Student Employment:** Federal Work-Study Program available. Institutional employment available. Off-campus job opportunities are good. **Financial Aid Statistics:** 94% undergrads receive any aid. 74% undergrads borrow to pay for school. **Criteria for awarding institutional aid:** *Non-need-based.* academics, alumni affiliation, art, athletics, leadership, minority status, music/drama, religious affiliation.

TRINE UNIVERSITY

1 University Avenue, Angola, IN 46703
Phone: 260-665-4100 • **Financial Aid Phone:** 260-664-4158
E-mail: admit@trine.edu • **CEEB Code:** 1811
Fax: 260-665-4578 • **Website:** www.trine.edu • **ACT Code:** 1250

This private school was founded in 1881. It has a 400-acre campus.

RATINGS

Admissions Selectivity Rating: 85   **Fire Safety Rating:** 86   **Green Rating:** 76

STUDENTS AND FACULTY

Enrollment: 1,384. **Student Body:** 31% female, 69% male, 43% out-of-state, 2% international (10 countries represented). Asian 1%, African American 3%, Caucasian 69%, Hispanic 1%, Native American 0%.
Retention and Graduation: 25% grads go on to further study within 1 year. 10% grads pursue arts and sciences degrees. 5% grads pursue law degrees. 10% grads pursue business degrees. **Faculty:** Student/faculty ratio 15:1. 69 full-time faculty, 65% hold PhDs, 4% are members of minority groups, 25% are women. 0% of classes are taught by teaching assistants.

ACADEMICS

Degrees: associate, bachelor's, master's. **Classes:** Most classes have 20–29 students. Most lab/discussion sessions have 10–19 students. **Majors with Highest Enrollment:** civil engineering; criminal justice/safety studies; mechanical engineering. **Special Study Options:** cooperative education program, distance learning, double major, dual enrollment, English as a Second Language (ESL), honors program, internships, liberal arts/career combination, study abroad, teacher certification program. **Honors Programs:** Honors program began with Fall 2006 entering class of freshmen. **Combined Degree Programs:** BA/MEng. **Disability Services:** Special programs offered to physically disabled

students include tutors. **Career Services:** Alumni network, alumni services, career/job search classes, career assessment, internships, regional alumni. Career Services highlights include Students may elect to incorporate cooperative education (Co-op) as a part of their academic curriculum. Co-op students alternate semesters of employment with semesters of full-time study, that provides both academic knowledge,relevant work experience, and a salary or stipend. A Co-op background is highly regarded by prospective employers; seniors seeking full-time employment with the cooperative education credential are consistently selected over candidates without this major-related experience.

FACILITIES

Housing: Coed dorms, men's dorms, women's dorms, apartments for single students, Honors housing. 95% of campus accessible to physically disabled. **Special Academic Facilities/Equipment:** Lewis Hershey Museum; Wells Gallery of Engravings; Zollner Golf Course **Computers:** 100% of classrooms, 100% of dorms, 100% of libraries, 100% of dining areas, 100% of student union, have wireless network access. Students can register for classes online. Administrative functions (other than registration) can be performed online.

CAMPUS LIFE

Environment: Village. **Activities:** Choral groups, dance, drama/theater, music ensembles, pep band, radio station, student government, student newspaper, yearbook 35 registered organizations, 13 honor societies, 3 religious organizations. 8 fraternities, 6 sororities. **Athletics (Intercollegiate):** *Men:* baseball, basketball, cross-country, football, golf, lacrosse, soccer, tennis, track/field (outdoor), track/field (indoor), wrestling. *Women:* basketball, cross-country, golf, lacrosse, soccer, softball, tennis, track/field (outdoor), track/field (indoor), volleyball. **On-Campus Highlights:** University Center/Ctr for online Technol, Fawick Hall of Engineering, Taylor Hall of Humanities, Zollner Golf Course (on campus), Hershey Hall (Recreational Facilities). **Environmental Initiatives:** IDEM - MS4 Storm Water Program-- Erosion control best management practices, public outreach, World Wide Water Sampling Day, Water retention projects, water gardens, storm water inlet identification Audubon Certification - green chemicals on golf course, campus, and athletic fields, water-based paints Green Cleaning chemicals and floor scrubbing equipment that reduces water consumption

ADMISSIONS

Freshman Academic Profile: Average high school GPA 3.4. 22% in top 10% of high school class, 48% in top 25% of high school class, 85% in top 50% of high school class. 80% from public high schools. SAT Math middle 50% range 490-600. SAT Critical Reading middle 50% range 440-570. ACT middle 50% range 20-25. Minimum web-based TOEFL 80. Minimum paper TOEFL 550. **Basis for Candidate Selection:** *Very important factors considered include:* Class rank, academic GPA, rigor of secondary school record, standardized test scores. *Important factors considered include:* application essay, recommendation(s), extracurricular activities, interview. *Other factors considered include:* alumni/ae relation, character/personal qualities, talent/ability, volunteer work, work experience. **Freshman Admission Requirements:** High school diploma is required and GED is accepted. *Academic units required:* 4 English, 3 mathematics, 3 science, (2 science labs), 3 social studies, 2 history, 3 academic electives. 4 English, 3 mathematics, 3 science, (2 science labs), 3 social studies, 2 history, 3 academic electives. **Freshman Admission Statistics:** 2,277 applied, 53% admitted, 36% enrolled. **Transfer Admission Requirements:** High school transcript, college transcript(s), statement of good standing from prior institution(s). Minimum college GPA of 2.0 required. Lowest grade transferable C. **General Admission Information:** Regular application deadline 8/1. Nonfall registration accepted. Admission may be deferred for a maximum of 12 months. Credit and/or placement offered for CEEB Advanced Placement tests.

COSTS AND FINANCIAL AID

Annual tuition $27,660. Room and board $8,800. Required fees $130. Average book expense $1,600. **Required Forms and Deadlines:** FAFSA. **Notification of Awards:** Applicants will be notified of awards on a rolling basis beginning 2/15. **Types of Aid:** *Need-based scholarships/grants:* Federal Pell, SEOG, state scholarships/grants, private scholarships, the school's own gift aid. *Loans:* Subsidized Stafford, Unsubsidized Stafford, PLUS. **Student Employment:** Federal Work-Study Program available. Highest amount earned per year from on-campus jobs $2,420. Off-campus job opportunities are good. **Financial Aid Statistics:** 65% freshmen, 53% undergrads receive need-based scholarship or grant aid. 100% freshmen, 100% undergrads receive non-need-based scholarship or grant aid. 100% freshmen, 100% undergrads receive need-based self-help aid. 99% freshmen, 98% undergrads receive any aid. 79% undergrads borrow to pay for school. Average cumulative indebtedness $17,380. **Criteria for awarding institutional aid:** *Non-need-based:* academics, music/drama.

TRINITY BIBLE COLLEGE

50 South 6th Avenue, Ellendale, ND 58436-7150
Phone: 701-349-5403
E-mail: admissions@trinitybiblecollege.edu
Fax: 701-349-5443 • **Website:** www.trinitybiblecollege.edu

This is a private school.

RATINGS
Admissions Selectivity Rating: 61   **Fire Safety Rating:** 60*   **Green Rating:** 60*

STUDENTS AND FACULTY
Enrollment: 305. **Student Body:** 54% female, 46% male, 60% out-of-state, 0% international. Asian 1%, African American 3%, Caucasian 91%, Hispanic 2%, Native American 4%.
Retention and Graduation: 77% freshmen return for sophomore year. 44% freshmen graduate within 6 years.

ACADEMICS
Degrees: associate, bachelor's, certificate. **Special Study Options:** distance learning, double major, dual enrollment, independent study, teacher certification program.

FACILITIES
Housing: apartments for married students, apartments for single students.

CAMPUS LIFE
Activities: student government.

ADMISSIONS
Basis for Candidate Selection: *Very important factors considered include:* recommendation(s), standardized test scores, character/personal qualities. *Important factors considered include:* application essay. *Other factors considered include:* rigor of secondary school record, religious affiliation/commitment. **Freshman Admission Requirements:** High school diploma is required and GED is accepted. **Transfer Admission Requirements:** High school transcript, college transcript(s), essay or personal statement, statement of good standing from prior institution(s). Lowest grade transferable C. **General Admission Information:** Application Fee $25. Notification on a rolling basis, beginning on or about 9/2. Nonfall registration accepted. Admission may be deferred for a maximum of Indefinitely.

COSTS AND FINANCIAL AID
Annual tuition $9,680. Room and board $4,370. Required fees $1,478. Average book expense $700. **Required Forms and Deadlines:** FAFSAInformation provided on student application for admission. **Notification of Awards:** Applicants will be notified of awards on a rolling basis beginning 3/1. **Types of Aid:** *Need-based scholarships/grants:* Federal Pell, SEOG, state scholarships/grants, private scholarships, the school's own gift aid. *Loans:* Subsidized Stafford, Unsubsidized Stafford, PLUS, Federal Perkins. **Student Employment: Financial Aid Statistics:** 100% freshmen, 100% undergrads receive need-based scholarship or grant aid. 99% freshmen, 98% undergrads receive need-based self-help aid. **Criteria for awarding institutional aid:** *Non-need-based:* academics, alumni affiliation, art, leadership, music/drama, religious affiliation.

TRINITY CHRISTIAN COLLEGE

6601 West College Drive, Palos Heights, IL 60463
Phone: 708-239-4708 • **Financial Aid Phone:** 708-239-4706
E-mail: admissions@trnty.edu • **CEEB Code:** 1820
Fax: 708-239-4826 • **Website:** www.trnty.edu • **ACT Code:** 1165

This private school was founded in 1959. It has a 60-acre campus.

RATINGS
Admissions Selectivity Rating: 70   **Fire Safety Rating:** 77   **Green Rating:** 67

STUDENTS AND FACULTY
Enrollment: 1,215. **Student Body:** 66% female, 34% male, 28% out-of-state, 3% international (8 countries represented). Asian 2%, African American 10%, Caucasian 73%, Hispanic 9%, Native American 1%.
Retention and Graduation: 80% freshmen return for sophomore year. 46% freshmen graduate within 4 years. 56% freshmen graduate within 6 years. 12% grads go on to further study within 1 year. 4% grads pursue arts and sciences degrees. 1% grads pursue law degrees. 1% grads pursue business degrees. 2%

grads pursue medical degrees. **Faculty:** Student/faculty ratio 11:1. 83 full-time faculty, 69% hold PhDs, 11% are members of minority groups, 47% are women. 0% of classes are taught by teaching assistants.

ACADEMICS
Degrees: bachelor's. **Classes:** Most classes have 10–19 students. Most lab/discussion sessions have 10–19 students. **Majors with Highest Enrollment:** business/commerce; elementary education and teaching; nursing/registered nurse (rn, asn, bsn, msn). **Special Study Options:** cooperative education program, double major, English as a Second Language (ESL), honors program, independent study, internships, liberal arts/career combination, study abroad, teacher certification program. **Honors Programs:** The Trinity Honors Program challenges and academically supports gifted students through seminars, unique opportunities within the major program, and participation in co-curricular activities. **Disability Services:** Special programs offered to physically disabled students include reader services, tape recorders, tutors. **Career Services:** Alumni network, alumni services, career assessment, internships, regional alumni. Career Services highlights include Chicago Semester Internships.

FACILITIES
Housing: Coed dorms, apartments for married students, apartments for single students. 98% of campus accessible to physically disabled. **Special Academic Facilities/Equipment:** Dutch Heritage Center. **Computers:** 100% of classrooms, 100% of dorms, 100% of libraries, 100% of dining areas, 100% of student union, 15% of common outdoor areas have wireless network access. Students can register for classes online. Administrative functions (other than registration) can be performed online.

CAMPUS LIFE
Environment: Metropolis. **Activities:** Choral groups, concert band, dance, drama/theater, jazz band, music ensembles, musical theater, student government, student newspaper, yearbook, Campus Ministries 15 registered organizations, 2 honor societies, 1 religious organizations. **Athletics (Intercollegiate):** *Men:* baseball, basketball, cross-country, soccer, track/field (outdoor), track/field (indoor). *Women:* basketball, cross-country, soccer, softball, track/field (outdoor), track/field (indoor), volleyball. **On-Campus Highlights:** Bootsma Bookstore/Cafe, West Hall Rec, Chapel, South Hall Lobby **Environmental Initiatives:** Recycling of paper, aluminum, and glass Maintenance of a nature trail on campus Recycling of all electronics

ADMISSIONS
Freshman Academic Profile: Average high school GPA 3.3. 15% in top 10% of high school class, 34% in top 25% of high school class, 62% in top 50% of high school class. 54% from public high schools. SAT Math middle 50% range 460-540. SAT Critical Reading middle 50% range 480-620. ACT middle 50% range 18-26. Minimum paper TOEFL 550. **Basis for Candidate Selection:** *Very important factors considered include:* academic GPA, rigor of secondary school record, standardized test scores. *Important factors considered include:* Class rank, application essay, recommendation(s), character/personal qualities, extracurricular activities, interview, level of applicant's interest, religious affiliation/commitment, talent/ability. *Other factors considered include:* alumni/ae relation, first generation, geographical residence, racial/ethnic status, state residency, volunteer work, work experience. **Freshman Admission Requirements:** High school diploma is required and GED is accepted. *Academic units required:* 3 English, 3 mathematics, 2 science, 2 social studies. *Academic units recommended:* 3 English, 3 mathematics, 2 science, 2 social studies. **Freshman Admission Statistics:** 691 applied, 82% admitted, 33% enrolled. **Transfer Admission Requirements:** college transcript(s), essay or personal statement, interview, statement of good standing from prior institution(s). Minimum college GPA of 2.0 required. Lowest grade transferable C. **General Admission Information:** Application Fee $20. Notification on a rolling basis, beginning on or about 9/1. Nonfall registration accepted. Admission may be deferred for a maximum of 2 semesters. Credit and/or placement offered for CEEB Advanced Placement tests.

COSTS AND FINANCIAL AID
Annual tuition $17,920. Room and board $7,010. Average book expense $925. **Required Forms and Deadlines:** FAFSA, institution's own financial aid form. **Notification of Awards:** Applicants will be notified of awards on or about 3/15. **Types of Aid:** *Need-based scholarships/grants:* Federal Pell, SEOG, state scholarships/grants, private scholarships, the school's own gift aid. *Loans:* Subsidized Stafford, Unsubsidized Stafford, PLUS, Federal Perkins, Federal Nursing. **Student Employment:** Federal Work-Study Program available. Institutional employment available. Highest amount earned per year from on-campus jobs $10,905. Off-campus job opportunities are good. **Financial Aid Statistics:** 100% freshmen, 97% undergrads receive need-based scholarship or grant aid. 14% freshmen, 10% undergrads receive non-need-based scholarship or grant aid. 81% freshmen, 85% undergrads receive need-based self-help aid. 5% freshmen, 5% undergrads receive athletic scholarships. 99% freshmen, 98% undergrads receive any aid. 79% undergrads borrow to pay for school. Average cumulative indebtedness $28,124. **Criteria for awarding institutional aid:**

Non-need-based: academics, alumni affiliation, art, athletics, leadership, minority status, music/drama, religious affiliation, state/district residency.

TRINITY COLLEGE (CT)

300 Summit Street, Hartford, CT 6016
Phone: 860-297-2180 • **Financial Aid Phone:** 860-297-2047
E-mail: admissions.office@trincoll.edu • **CEEB Code:** 3899
Fax: 860-297-2287 • **Website:** www.trincoll.edu • **ACT Code:** 598

This private school was founded in 1823. It has a 100-acre campus.

RATINGS
Admissions Selectivity Rating: 95   **Fire Safety Rating:** 91   **Green Rating:** 80

STUDENTS AND FACULTY
Enrollment: 2,223. **Student Body:** 48% female, 52% male, 82% out-of-state, 8% international (48 countries represented). Asian 5%, African American 6%, Caucasian 66%, Hispanic 7%, Native American 0%. **Retention and Graduation:** 88% freshmen return for sophomore year. 77% freshmen graduate within 4 years. 83% freshmen graduate within 6 years. 19% grads go on to further study within 1 year. 10% grads pursue arts and sciences degrees. 4% grads pursue law degrees. 1% grads pursue business degrees. 1% grads pursue medical degrees. **Faculty:** Student/faculty ratio 10:1. 175 full time faculty, 93% hold PhDs, 21% are members of minority groups, 41% are women. 0% of classes are taught by teaching assistants.

ACADEMICS
Degrees: bachelor's, master's. **Classes:** Most classes have 10–19 students. Most lab/discussion sessions have 10–19 students. **Majors with Highest Enrollment:** economics, English language and literature; political science and government. **Special Study Options:** Accelerated program, cross-registration, double major, exchange student program (domestic), honors program, independent study, internships, liberal arts/career combination, student-designed major, study abroad, teacher certification program, 5-year BS/MS in Electrical Engineering or Mechanical Engineering with Rensselaer Polytechnic Institute, Community Learning Initiative. **Combined Degree Programs:** BA/MEng, BA/MS in Elect, Engg,or Mech Engg. with RPI. **Disability Services:** Special programs offered to physically disabled students include note-taking services, reader services, tape recorders, tutors. **Career Services:** Alumni network, alumni services, career/job search classes, career assessment, internships, regional alumni. Career Services highlights include Our academic internships provide real-life experiences within the framework of an academic analysis. They range from internships in for-profit governmental to non-profit organizations. Over half of our students take courses with a community-based experiential component also linking community engagement with an academic course.

FACILITIES
Housing: Coed dorms, special housing for disabled students, fraternity/sorority housing, Community service dorm, quiet dorm, wellness and substance-free, 21+ only, cooking. All dorms are non-smoking. 60% of campus accessible to physically disabled. **Special Academic Facilities/Equipment:** Watkinson Library; Austin Arts Center. **Computers:** 95% of classrooms, 85% of dorms, 100% of libraries, 100% of dining areas, 100% of student union, 90% of common outdoor areas have wireless network access. Students can register for classes online. Administrative functions (other than registration) can be performed online.

CAMPUS LIFE
Environment: Metropolis. **Activities:** Choral groups, dance, drama/theater, jazz band, literary magazine, music ensembles, musical theater, radio station, student government, student newspaper, student-run film society, yearbook, Campus Ministries, International Student Organization, Model UN 105 registered organizations, 5 honor societies, 5 religious organizations. 7 fraternities, 3 sororities. **Athletics (Intercollegiate):** *Men:* baseball, basketball, crew/rowing, cross-country, diving, football, golf, ice hockey, lacrosse, soccer, squash, swimming, tennis, track/field (outdoor), track/field (indoor), wrestling. *Women:* basketball, crew/rowing, cross-country, diving, field hockey, ice hockey, lacrosse, soccer, softball, squash, swimming, tennis, track/field (outdoor), track/field (indoor), volleyball. **On-Campus Highlights:** The Learning Corridor, Library, The Science/Engineering Labs, Summit Suites (newest residence hall), The Chapel. **Environmental Initiatives:** Energy conservation measures to help reduce and eliminate greenhouse gas emissions in accordance with the Presidents'

Climate Commitment. Development of The Treehouse (Trinity Recreational and Environmental Education House) as a social house where students can come together and share their common interests of nature appreciation and conservation. Participation in RecycleMania.

ADMISSIONS
Freshman Academic Profile: 69% in top 10% of high school class, 90% in top 25% of high school class, 100% in top 50% of high school class. 40% from public high schools. SAT Math middle 50% range 600-700. SAT Critical Reading middle 50% range 590-690. SAT Writing middle 50% range 600-700. ACT middle 50% range 26-30. **Basis for Candidate Selection:** *Very important factors considered include:* rigor of secondary school record. *Important factors considered include:* Class rank, application essay, academic GPA, recommendation(s), standardized test scores, character/personal qualities, extracurricular activities, interview, racial/ethnic status, talent/ability. *Other factors considered include:* alumni/ae relation, first generation, geographical residence, level of applicant's interest, volunteer work, work experience. **Freshman Admission Requirements:** High school diploma is required and GED is accepted. *Academic units required:* 4 English, 3 mathematics, 2 science, (2 science labs), 3 foreign language, 2 history. 4 English, 3 mathematics, 2 science, (2 science labs), 3 foreign language, 2 history. **Freshman Admission Statistics:** 7,720 applied, 34% admitted, 23% enrolled. **Transfer Admission Requirements:** High school transcript, college transcript(s), essay or personal statement, standardized test scores, statement of good standing from prior institution(s). Minimum college GPA of 3.0 required. Lowest grade transferable C–. **General Admission Information:** Application Fee $60. Early decision application deadline 11/15. Regular application deadline 1/1. Regular notification 4/1. Nonfall registration not accepted. Admission may be deferred for a maximum of 12 months. Credit and/or placement offered for CEEB Advanced Placement tests.

COSTS AND FINANCIAL AID
Annual tuition $43,570. Room and board $11,800. Required fees $2,160. Average book expense $1,000. **Required Forms and Deadlines:** FAFSA, CSS/Financial Aid PROFILE, noncustodial PROFILE, business/farm supplement. Federal Income tax returns. **Notification of Awards:** Applicants will be notified of awards on or about 4/1. **Types of Aid:** *Need-based scholarships/grants:* Federal Pell, SEOG, state scholarships/grants, private scholarships, the school's own gift aid. *Loans:* Direct Subsidized Stafford, Direct Unsubsidized Stafford, Direct PLUS, Subsidized Stafford, Unsubsidized Stafford, PLUS, Federal Perkins, college/university loans from institutional funds. **Student Employment:** Federal Work-Study Program available. Institutional employment available. Highest amount earned per year from on-campus jobs $6,000. Off-campus job opportunities are good. **Financial Aid Statistics:** 97% freshmen, 95% undergrads receive need-based scholarship or grant aid. 4% freshmen, 3% undergrads receive non-need-based scholarship or grant aid. 70% freshmen, 78% undergrads receive need-based self-help aid. 38% freshmen, 41% undergrads receive any aid. 41% undergrads borrow to pay for school. Average cumulative indebtedness $18,868. **Criteria for awarding institutional aid:** *Non-need-based:* academics, leadership.

See page 1234.

TRINITY COLLEGE OF FLORIDA

2430 Welbilt Boulevard, Trinity, FL 34655
Phone: 727-569-1411 • **Financial Aid Phone:** 727-569-1413
E-mail: admissions@trinitycollege.edu • **CEEB Code:**
Fax: 727-569-1410 • **Website:** www.trinitycollege.edu • **ACT Code:** 4876

This private school was founded in 1932. It has a 40-acre campus.

RATINGS
Admissions Selectivity Rating: 66   **Fire Safety Rating:** 76   **Green Rating:** 60*

STUDENTS AND FACULTY
Enrollment: 210. **Student Body:** 39% female, 61% male, 28% out-of-state, 1% international (2 countries represented). Asian 0%, African American 18%, Caucasian 64%, Hispanic 16%, Native American 0%. **Retention and Graduation:** 67% freshmen return for sophomore year. 30% freshmen graduate within 4 years. 14% grads go on to further study within 1 year. **Faculty:** Student/faculty ratio 14:1. 6 full-time faculty, 83% hold PhDs, 0% are members of minority groups, 17% are women. 0% of classes are taught by teaching assistants.

ACADEMICS
Degrees: associate, bachelor's, certificate, terminal associate. **Classes:** Most classes have fewer than 10 students. **Majors with Highest Enrollment:** pastoral studies/counseling; pre-theology/pre-ministerial studies; youth ministry. **Special Study Options:** Accelerated program, double major, dual enrollment,

honors program, independent study, internships, weekend college. **Honors Programs:** Our honors program consists of 4 Great Books Seminars . **Disability Services:** Special programs offered to physically disabled students include tutors. **Career Services:** career assessment, internships.

FACILITIES

Housing: special housing for disabled students, men's dorms, women's dorms, Apartments available for double occupancy or more. 100% of campus accessible to physically disabled. **Computers:** 100% of classrooms, 100% of dorms, 100% of libraries, 100% of dining areas, 100% of student union, have wireless network access.

CAMPUS LIFE

Environment: City. **Activities:** Choral groups, drama/theater, student government, yearbook, Campus Ministries 4 religious organizations. **Athletics (Intercollegiate):** *Men:* basketball. *Women:* volleyball. **On-Campus Highlights:** Epiphanies Coffee Shop, Library, Lounge Areas, Outdoor Gazebo, Horseshoe Pits.

ADMISSIONS

Freshman Academic Profile: Average high school GPA 2.8. SAT Math middle 50% range 370-480. SAT Critical Reading middle 50% range 460-550. ACT middle 50% range 19-23. Minimum paper TOEFL 500. **Basis for Candidate Selection:** *Very important factors considered include:* application essay, academic GPA, recommendation(s), standardized test scores, religious affiliation/commitment. *Important factors considered include:* character/personal qualities. *Other factors considered include:* extracurricular activities. **Freshman Admission Requirements:** High school diploma is required and GED is accepted. *Academic units required:* 4 English, 4 mathematics, 4 science, 2 foreign language, 2 social studies, 2 history. 0. *Academic units recommended:* 4 English, 4 mathematics, 4 science, 2 foreign language, 2 social studies, 2 history. academic electives. **Freshman Admission Statistics:** 79 applied, 85% admitted, 49% enrolled. **Transfer Admission Requirements:** High school transcript, college transcript(s), essay or personal statement, minimum college GPA of 2.0 required. Lowest grade transferable C. **General Admission Information:** Application Fee $25. Regular application deadline 8/2. Nonfall registration accepted. Admission may be deferred for a maximum of 1 year. Credit and/or placement offered for CEEB Advanced Placement tests.

COSTS AND FINANCIAL AID

Annual tuition $11,024. Room and board $6,656. Required fees $800. Average book expense $1,185. **Required Forms and Deadlines:** FAFSA, institution's own financial aid form. **Types of Aid:** *Need-based scholarships/grants:* Federal Pell, SEOG, state scholarships/grants, private scholarships, the school's own gift aid. *Loans:* Subsidized Stafford, Unsubsidized Stafford, PLUS, Private Loans. **Student Employment:** Federal Work-Study Program available. Institutional employment available. Highest amount earned per year from on-campus jobs $4,350. Off-campus job opportunities are excellent. **Financial Aid Statistics:** 100% freshmen, 86% undergrads receive need-based scholarship or grant aid. 100% freshmen, 74% undergrads receive non-need-based scholarship or grant aid. 75% freshmen, 79% undergrads receive need-based self-help aid. 99% freshmen, 99% undergrads receive any aid. 80% undergrads borrow to pay for school. Average cumulative indebtedness $20,523. **Criteria for awarding institutional aid:** *Non-need-based:* academics, music/drama.

TRINITY INTERNATIONAL UNIVERSITY

2065 Half Day Road, Deerfield, IL 60015
Phone: 847-317-7000 • **Financial Aid Phone:** 847-317-7033
E-mail: tcadmissions@tiu.edu • **CEEB Code:** 1810
Fax: 847-317-8097 • **Website:** www.tiu.edu • **ACT Code:** 1150

This private school was founded in 1897. It has a 111-acre campus.

RATINGS

Admissions Selectivity Rating: 79   **Fire Safety Rating:** 70   **Green Rating:** 60*

STUDENTS AND FACULTY

Enrollment: 950. **Student Body:** 57% female, 43% male, 41% out-of-state, 1% international (38 countries represented). Asian 5%, African American 17%, Caucasian 63%, Hispanic 4%, Native American 0%.
Retention and Graduation: 66% freshmen return for sophomore year. 40% freshmen graduate within 4 years. 52% freshmen graduate within 6 years. 32% grads go on to further study within 1 year. **Faculty:** Student/faculty ratio 12:1. 43 full-time faculty, 84% hold PhDs, 14% are members of minority groups, 42% are women. 0% of classes are taught by teaching assistants.

ACADEMICS

Degrees: bachelor's, certificate, first professional, master's, post-bachelor's certificate. **Classes:** Most classes have 20–29 students. Most lab/discussion sessions have 10–19 students. **Majors with Highest Enrollment:** business/commerce; elementary education and teaching; theology and religious vocations, other. **Special Study Options:** cross-registration, double major, dual enrollment, honors program, independent study, internships, study abroad, teacher certification program, REACH (for nontraditional students with previous college credit), Graduate courses. **Honors Programs:** Trinity has adopted a model for an Honors Program that is intended to enhance the breadth and depth of your liberal-arts learning, but without the burden of many additional requirements. Hence, you will do honors work in the areas of your disciplinary major, general education, and special interdisciplinary classes, but virtually all of your honors work will also fulfill regular Trinity requirements. **Combined Degree Programs:** BA/MA. **Disability Services:** Special programs offered to physically disabled students include note-taking services, reader services, tape recorders, tutors. **Career Services:** alumni services, career/job search classes, career assessment, internships, Career Services highlights include Students in Trinity International University's Athletic Training Education Program have benefited through Trinity's partnership with Condell Health Network in Libertyville, Illinois. Condell's internship opportunities provide our students with necessary clinical experience while they work under the supervision of certified athletic trainers.

FACILITIES

Housing: special housing for disabled students, men's dorms, women's dorms, apartments for married students, apartments for single students. 75% of campus accessible to physically disabled. **Special Academic Facilities/Equipment:** None **Computers:** 100% of classrooms, 50% of dorms, 100% of libraries, 100% of student union, have wireless network access. Students can register for classes online. Administrative functions (other than registration) can be performed online.

CAMPUS LIFE

Environment: Village. **Activities:** Choral groups, concert band, drama/theater, jazz band, music ensembles, musical theater, pep band, student government, student newspaper, symphony orchestra, yearbook, Campus Ministries 33 registered organizations, 2 honor societies. **Athletics (Intercollegiate):** *Men:* baseball, basketball, football, soccer. *Women:* basketball, soccer, softball, volleyball. **On-Campus Highlights:** Lew Student Center, Trinity Hall, McLennan Academic Building, Rodine Global Ministry Building, Melton Dining Hall.

ADMISSIONS

Freshman Academic Profile: Average high school GPA 3.3. 37% in top 10% of high school class, 43% in top 25% of high school class, 68% in top 50% of high school class. 69% from public high schools. SAT Math middle 50% range 440-600. SAT Critical Reading middle 50% range 445-610. ACT middle 50% range 19-26. Minimum paper TOEFL 530. **Basis for Candidate Selection:** *Very important factors considered include:* Class rank, application essay, academic GPA, recommendation(s), standardized test scores, character/personal qualities, religious affiliation/commitment. *Other factors considered include:* rigor of secondary school record, extracurricular activities, first generation, talent/ability. **Freshman Admission Requirements:** High school diploma is required and GED is accepted. *Academic units required:* 4 English, 2 mathematics, 2 science, (1 science labs), 2 foreign language, 2 social studies, 2 history, 2 visual/performing arts. 4 English, 2 mathematics, 2 science, (1 science labs), 2 foreign language, 2 social studies, 2 history, 2 visual/performing arts. **Freshman Admission Statistics:** 548 applied, 63% admitted, 39% enrolled. **Transfer Admission Requirements:** High school transcript, college transcript(s), essay or personal statement, statement of good standing from prior institution(s). Minimum college GPA of 2.0 required. Lowest grade transferable C–. **General Admission Information:** Application Fee $25. Notification on a rolling basis, beginning on or about 9/1. Nonfall registration accepted. Admission may be deferred for a maximum of 12 months. Credit and/or placement offered for CEEB Advanced Placement tests.

COSTS AND FINANCIAL AID

Annual tuition $21,980. Room and board $7,430. Required fees $390. **Required Forms and Deadlines:** FAFSA. **Notification of Awards:** Applicants will be notified of awards on a rolling basis beginning 2/15. **Types of Aid:** *Need-based scholarships/grants:* Federal Pell, SEOG, state scholarships/grants, private scholarships, the school's own gift aid. *Loans:* Subsidized Stafford, Unsubsidized Stafford, PLUS, Federal Perkins. **Student Employment:** Federal Work-Study Program available. Institutional employment available. Off-campus job opportunities are excellent. **Financial Aid Statistics:** 95% freshmen, 95% undergrads receive need-based scholarship or grant aid. 95% freshmen, 95% undergrads receive non-need-based scholarship or grant aid. 82% freshmen, 78% undergrads receive need-based self-help aid. 90% freshmen, 86% undergrads receive any aid. 79% undergrads borrow to pay for school. Average cumulative indebtedness $22,155. **Criteria for awarding institutional aid:** *Non-need-based:* academics, alumni affiliation, athletics, minority status, music/drama, religious affiliation.

TRINITY LUTHERAN COLLEGE

4221 228th Avenue SE, Issaquah, WA 98029
Phone: 425-961-5510 • **Financial Aid Phone:** 425-961-5514
E-mail: admission@tlc.edu
Fax: 425-392-0404 • **Website:** www.tlc.edu

This private school, affiliated with the Lutheran Church, was founded in 1944.

RATINGS
Admissions Selectivity Rating: 62   **Fire Safety Rating:** 74   **Green Rating:** 60*

STUDENTS AND FACULTY
Enrollment: 91. **Student Body:** 53% female, 47% male, 35% out-of-state, 0% international. Asian 4%, African American 1%, Caucasian 112%, Hispanic 4%, Native American 1%.
Retention and Graduation: 78% freshmen return for sophomore year. **Faculty:** Student/faculty ratio :1. 13 full-time faculty.

ACADEMICS
Degrees: associate, bachelor's, diploma, post-bachelor's certificate, terminal associate, transfer associate. **Classes: Majors with Highest Enrollment:** bible/biblical studies; music, other; youth ministry. **Special Study Options:** double major, independent study, internships, liberal arts/career combination, student-designed major, study abroad, teacher certification program. **Disability Services:** Special programs offered to physically disabled students include note-taking services, reader services, tape recorders, tutors. **Career Services:** Alumni network, alumni services, career assessment, internships, regional alumni., Career Services highlights include 10 week internships are a graduation requirement for all students.

FACILITIES
Housing: Coed dorms, special housing for disabled students, men's dorms, women's dorms, apartments for married students, apartments for single students, Special housing for married students. and non-traditional age students. **Computers:** Administrative functions (other than registration) can be performed online.

CAMPUS LIFE
Environment: Village. **Activities:** Choral groups, drama/theater, music ensembles, musical theater, student government, student newspaper, yearbook. **Athletics (Intercollegiate): Men:** basketball, softball. **Women:** softball. **On-Campus Highlights:** Student Center, The Running Cup, Chapel, YMCA, Bookstore.

ADMISSIONS
Freshman Academic Profile: 0% in top 10% of high school class, 33% in top 25% of high school class, 60% in top 50% of high school class. Minimum paper TOEFL 525. **Basis for Candidate Selection:** *Very important factors considered include:* recommendation(s), character/personal qualities. *Important factors considered include:* academic GPA, rigor of secondary school record, standardized test scores, religious affiliation/commitment, volunteer work. *Other factors considered include:* alumni/ae relation, extracurricular activities, first generation, level of applicant's interest, talent/ability, work experience. **Freshman Admission Requirements:** High school diploma is required and GED is accepted. **Transfer Admission Requirements:** college transcript(s), minimum college GPA of 2.0 required. Lowest grade transferable C–. **General Admission Information:** Application Fee $30. Regular application deadline 8/15. Nonfall registration accepted. Admission may be deferred for a maximum of 2 years. Credit and/or placement offered for CEEB Advanced Placement tests.

COSTS AND FINANCIAL AID
Annual tuition $13,714. Room and board $6,078. Required fees $450. Average book expense $500. **Required Forms and Deadlines:** FAFSA, institution's own financial aid form. **Notification of Awards:** Applicants will be notified of awards on a rolling basis beginning 1/1. **Types of Aid:** *Need-based scholarships/grants:* Federal Pell, SEOG, private scholarships, the school's own gift aid. *Loans:* Direct Subsidized Stafford, Direct Unsubsidized Stafford, Direct PLUS, Subsidized Stafford, PLUS. **Student Employment:** Federal Work-Study Program available. Institutional employment available. Off-campus job opportunities are excellent. **Criteria for awarding institutional aid:** *Non-need-based:* academics, alumni affiliation, art, leadership, music/drama, religious affiliation.

TRINITY UNIVERSITY

One Trinity Place, San Antonio, TX 78212-7200
Phone: 210-999-7207
E-mail: admissions@trinity.edu • **CEEB Code:** 6831
Fax: 210-999-8164 • **Website:** www.trinity.edu • **ACT Code:** 4226

This private school was founded in 1869. It has a 117-acre campus.

RATINGS
Admissions Selectivity Rating: 91   **Fire Safety Rating:** 87   **Green Rating:** 73

STUDENTS AND FACULTY
Enrollment: 2,330. **Student Body:** 54% female, 46% male, 29% out-of-state, 7% international (69 countries represented). Asian 8%, African American 4%, Caucasian 60%, Hispanic 15%, Native American 0%.
Retention and Graduation: 89% freshmen return for sophomore year. 71% freshmen graduate within 4 years. 40% grads go on to further study within 1 year. 5% grads pursue law degrees. 4% grads pursue medical degrees. **Faculty:** Student/faculty ratio 9:1. 240 full-time faculty, 98% hold PhDs, 20% are members of minority groups, 41% are women. 0% of classes are taught by teaching assistants.

ACADEMICS
Degrees: bachelor's, master's. **Classes:** Most classes have 10–19 students. Most lab/discussion sessions have 10–19 students. **Majors with Highest Enrollment:** business administration, management and operations, other; English language and literature. **Special Study Options:** Accelerated program, double major, honors program, independent study, internships, liberal arts/career combination, student-designed major, study abroad, teacher certification program. **Honors Programs:** Honors Program **Combined Degree Programs:** BA/MA, BA/MA-education; BS/MS-accounting. **Disability Services:** Special programs offered to physically disabled students include note-taking services, reader services, tutors. **Career Services:** Alumni network, career assessment, internships Career Services highlights include The Alumni Network is an amazing program. With over 500 alumni in our Career Network making themselves available for networking with students and fellow graduates.

FACILITIES
Housing: Coed dorms, wellness housing, theme housing. **Special Academic Facilities/Equipment:** Steiren Theatre, Richardson Communication Center, Ruth Taylor Arts Complex including art gallery, Laurie Auditorium **Computers:** 100% of classrooms, 100% of dorms, 100% of libraries, 100% of dining areas, 100% of student union, 100% of common outdoor areas have wireless network access. Students can register for classes online. Administrative functions (other than registration) can be performed online.

CAMPUS LIFE
Environment: Metropolis. **Activities:** Choral groups, concert band, dance, drama/theater, jazz band, literary magazine, music ensembles, musical theater, opera, pep band, radio station, student government, student newspaper, student-run film society, symphony orchestra, television station, yearbook, Campus Ministries, International Student Organization, Model UN 130 registered organizations, 24 honor societies, 4 religious organizations. 7 fraternities, 6 sororities. **Athletics (Intercollegiate): Men:** baseball, basketball, cross-country, diving, football, golf, soccer, swimming, tennis, track/field (outdoor). **Women:** basketball, cross-country, diving, golf, soccer, softball, swimming, tennis, track/field (outdoor), volleyball. **On-Campus Highlights:** Stieren Theatre, Laurie Auditorium, Coates Library, Bell Athletic Center, Coates University Center, Northrup Hall.

ADMISSIONS
Freshman Academic Profile: Average high school GPA 3.7. 47% in top 10% of high school class, 81% in top 25% of high school class, 98% in top 50% of high school class. 64% from public high schools. SAT Math middle 50% range 580-670. SAT Critical Reading middle 50% range 570-680. SAT Writing middle 50% range 550-660. ACT middle 50% range 26-31. Minimum paper TOEFL 600. **Basis for Candidate Selection:** *Very important factors considered include:* Class rank, academic GPA, rigor of secondary school record. *Important factors considered include:* application essay, recommendation(s), standardized test scores, character/personal qualities, extracurricular activities, interview, talent/ability. *Other factors considered include:* alumni/ae relation, first generation, geographical residence, level of applicant's interest, racial/ethnic status, volunteer work, work experience. **Freshman Admission Requirements:** High

school diploma is required and GED is accepted. *Academic units required:* 4 English, 3 mathematics, 3 science, (2 science labs), 2 foreign language, 3 social studies. *Academic units recommended:* 4 English, 3 mathematics, 3 science, (2 science labs), 2 foreign language, 3 social studies. **Freshman Admission Statistics:** 4,402 applied, 64% admitted, 21% enrolled. **Transfer Admission Requirements:** High school transcript, college transcript(s), essay or personal statement, statement of good standing from prior institution(s). Minimum college GPA of 3.0 required. Lowest grade transferable C–. **General Admission Information:** Application Fee $50. Early decision application deadline 11/1. Regular application deadline 2/1. Regular notification 4/1. Nonfall registration not accepted. Admission may be deferred for a maximum of 1 year. Credit and/or placement offered for CEEB Advanced Placement tests.

COSTS AND FINANCIAL AID

Annual tuition $32,568. Room and board $10,496. Required fees $1,110. Average book expense $1,000. **Required Forms and Deadlines:** FAFSA. **Notification of Awards:** Applicants will be notified of awards on or about 4/1. **Types of Aid:** *Need-based scholarships/grants:* Federal Pell, SEOG, state scholarships/grants, private scholarships, the school's own gift aid. *Loans:* Subsidized Stafford, Unsubsidized Stafford, PLUS, Federal Perkins, state loans, college/university loans from institutional funds. **Student Employment:** Federal Work-Study Program available. Institutional employment available. Off-campus job opportunities are good. **Financial Aid Statistics:** 100% freshmen, 99% undergrads receive need-based scholarship or grant aid. 15% freshmen, 12% undergrads receive non-need-based scholarship or grant aid. 79% freshmen, 80% undergrads receive need-based self-help aid. 94% freshmen, 86% undergrads receive any aid. 46% undergrads borrow to pay for school. Average cumulative indebtedness $42,987. **Criteria for awarding institutional aid:** *Non-need-based:* academics, leadership, music/drama.

TRINITY (WASHINGTON) UNIVERSITY

125 Michigan Avenue, NE, Washington, DC 20017
Phone: 202-884-9400 • **Financial Aid Phone:** 202-884-9530
E-mail: admissions@trinitydc.edu • **CEEB Code:** 5796
Fax: 202-884-9403 • **Website:** www.trinitydc.edu • **ACT Code:** 696

This private school was founded in 1897. It has a 26-acre campus.

RATINGS

Admissions Selectivity Rating: 64   **Fire Safety Rating:** 61   **Green Rating:** 60*

STUDENTS AND FACULTY

Enrollment: 962. **Student Body:** 98% female, 2% male, 48% out-of-state, 1% international (42 countries represented). Asian 2%, African American 68%, Caucasian 7%, Hispanic 11%, Native American 1%.
Retention and Graduation: 66% freshmen return for sophomore year. 29% freshmen graduate within 4 years. 44% freshmen graduate within 6 years.
Faculty: Student/faculty ratio 11:1. 61 full-time faculty, 100% hold PhDs, 30% are members of minority groups, 72% are women. 0% of classes are taught by teaching assistants.

ACADEMICS

Degrees: bachelor's, master's, post-bachelor's certificate. **Classes:** Most classes have 10–19 students. **Majors with Highest Enrollment:** business administration and management; communication studies/speech communication and rhetoric; social psychology. **Special Study Options:** Accelerated program, cross-registration, distance learning, double major, dual enrollment, honors program, independent study, internships, student-designed major, study abroad, teacher certification program, weekend college. **Honors Programs:** The Honors Program at Trinity encourages students to take advantage of small, seminar-style classes with the rich cultural benefits of our location in the nation's capital. It provides academically motivated students with the intellectual stimulation that comes not only from courses designed specifically for them by faculty members but also from intensive debate and discussion with their peers. **Combined Degree Programs:** BA/BS - with GWU or Univ. Maryland. **Disability Services:** Special programs offered to physically disabled students include note-taking services, reader services, tape recorders, tutors. **Career Services:** Alumni network, alumni services, career/job search classes, career assessment, internships, regional alumni. Career Services highlights include Service learning component of required first year seminar.

FACILITIES

Housing: women's dorms. **Special Academic Facilities/Equipment:** Art Gallery, Media Technology Center, Writing Center, Marilley Computer Classroom **Computers:** Students can register for classes online.

CAMPUS LIFE

Activities: Choral groups, dance, drama/theater, literary magazine, student government, student newspaper, student-run film society, yearbook 34 registered organizations, 5 honor societies, 2 religious organizations. **Athletics (Intercollegiate):** *Women:* basketball, field hockey, lacrosse, soccer, softball, swimming, tennis, volleyball. **On-Campus Highlights:** Trinity Center for Women and Girls in Sports, University Chapel, Main Hall.

ADMISSIONS

Freshman Academic Profile: Average high school GPA 2.8. SAT Math middle 50% range 330-480. SAT Critical Reading middle 50% range 360-482. ACT middle 50% range 13-18. Minimum paper TOEFL 550. **Basis for Candidate Selection:** *Very important factors considered include:* rigor of secondary school record, character/personal qualities. *Important factors considered include:* application essay, recommendation(s), alumni/ae relation, extracurricular activities, talent/ability, volunteer work. *Other factors considered include:* Class rank, standardized test scores, geographical residence, interview, work experience. **Freshman Admission Requirements:** High school diploma is required and GED is accepted. *Academic units required:* 4 English, 3 mathematics, 2 science, (1 science labs), 2 foreign language, 3 social studies, 2 history. 4 English, 3 mathematics, 2 science, (1 science labs), 2 foreign language, 3 social studies, 2 history. **Freshman Admission Statistics:** 441 applied, 86% admitted, 39% enrolled. **Transfer Admission Requirements:** college transcript(s), essay or personal statement, minimum college GPA of 2.5 required. Lowest grade transferable C. **General Admission Information:** Application Fee $40. Nonfall registration accepted. Admission may be deferred for a maximum of 1 year. Credit and/or placement offered for CEEB Advanced Placement tests.

COSTS AND FINANCIAL AID

Annual tuition $17,200. Room and board $7,574. Required fees $160. Average book expense $1,000. **Required Forms and Deadlines:** FAFSA. **Notification of Awards:** Applicants will be notified of awards on a rolling basis beginning 2/1. **Types of Aid:** *Need-based scholarships/grants:* Federal Pell, SEOG, state scholarships/grants, private scholarships, the school's own gift aid. *Loans:* Subsidized Stafford, Unsubsidized Stafford, PLUS, Federal Perkins. **Student Employment:** Federal Work-Study Program available. Institutional employment available. Highest amount earned per year from on-campus jobs $2,000. Off-campus job opportunities are excellent. **Financial Aid Statistics:** 100% freshmen, 97% undergrads receive need-based scholarship or grant aid. 8% freshmen, 4% undergrads receive non-need-based scholarship or grant aid. 81% freshmen, 85% undergrads receive need-based self-help aid. 97% freshmen, 94% undergrads receive any aid. 78% undergrads borrow to pay for school. Average cumulative indebtedness $29,875. **Criteria for awarding institutional aid:** *Non-need-based:* academics, alumni affiliation, leadership.

TRINITY WESTERN UNIVERSITY

P.O Box 1409, Blaine, WA 98231
Phone: 604-513-2019
E-mail: admissions@twu.ca • **CEEB Code:** 876
Fax: 604-513-2064 • **Website:** www.twu.ca • **ACT Code:** 5242

This private school was founded in 1962. It has a 100-acre campus.

RATINGS

Admissions Selectivity Rating: 62   **Fire Safety Rating:** 60*   **Green Rating:** 60*

STUDENTS AND FACULTY

Enrollment: 1,968. **Student Body:** 57% female, 43% male, 3% out-of-state. **Retention and Graduation:** 80% freshmen return for sophomore year. 15% grads go on to further study within 1 year. 3% grads pursue law degrees. 3% grads pursue medical degrees. **Faculty:** Student/faculty ratio 18:1. 77 full-time faculty, 90% hold PhDs, 4% are members of minority groups, 18% are women. 0% of classes are taught by teaching assistants.

ACADEMICS

Degrees: bachelor's, certificate, diploma, first professional, master's. **Majors with Highest Enrollment:** electrical, electronic and communications engineering technology/technician. **Special Study Options:** cooperative education program, double major, English as a Second Language (ESL), honors program, internships, study abroad. **Career Services:** alumni services, career/job search classes, career assessment, internships.

FACILITIES

Housing: 95% of campus accessible to physically disabled. **Special Academic Facilities/Equipment:** Museum of Biblical History **Computers:** Administrative functions (other than registration) can be performed online.

CAMPUS LIFE

Environment: Town. **Activities:** drama/theater, literary magazine, student government, student newspaper, student-run film society 33 registered organizations. **Athletics (Intercollegiate):** *Men:* basketball, cross-country, ice hockey, rugby, soccer, track/field (outdoor), volleyball. *Women:* basketball, cross-country, rugby, soccer, track/field (outdoor), volleyball.

ADMISSIONS

Freshman Academic Profile: Minimum paper TOEFL 570. **Basis for Candidate Selection:** *Very important factors considered include:* recommendation(s), rigor of secondary school record, standardized test scores. *Important factors considered include:* application essay. *Other factors considered include:* Class rank, character/personal qualities, extracurricular activities, religious affiliation/commitment, talent/ability. **Freshman Admission Requirements:** High school diploma is required and GED is accepted. *Academic units required:* 4 English, 3 mathematics, 2 science, (1 science labs), 2 social studies, 2 academic electives. 4 English, 3 mathematics, 2 science, (1 science labs), 2 social studies, 2 academic electives. **Freshman Admission Statistics:** 1,371 applied, 78% admitted, 39% enrolled. **Transfer Admission Requirements:** High school transcript, college transcript(s), essay or personal statement, minimum college GPA of 2.0 required. Lowest grade transferable D. **General Admission Information:** Application Fee $35. Regular application deadline 6/15. Notification on a rolling basis, beginning on or about 10/15. Nonfall registration accepted. Admission may be deferred for a maximum of 3 semesters. Credit and/or placement offered for CEEB Advanced Placement tests.

COSTS AND FINANCIAL AID

Annual tuition $10,350. Room and board $5,990. Required fees $120. Average book expense $800. **Required Forms and Deadlines:** institution's own financial aid form. **Notification of Awards:** Applicants will be notified of awards on a rolling basis beginning 4/1. **Types of Aid:** *Need-based scholarships/grants:* state scholarships/grants, private scholarships, the school's own gift aid. *Loans:* Direct Subsidized Stafford, Direct Unsubsidized Stafford, Direct PLUS. **Student Employment:** Institutional employment available. Highest amount earned per year from on-campus jobs $1,000. Off-campus job opportunities are good. **Financial Aid Statistics:** 2% freshmen, 18% undergrads receive need-based scholarship or grant aid. 2% freshmen, 3% undergrads receive non-need-based scholarship or grant aid. 34% freshmen, 35% undergrads receive need-based self-help aid. 65% undergrads borrow to pay for school. Average cumulative indebtedness $17,000. **Criteria for awarding institutional aid:** *Non-need based:* academics, athletics, leadership, music/drama.

TROY UNIVERSITY—TROY (FORMERLY TROY STATE UNIVERSITY)

111 Adams Administration, Troy, AL 36082
Phone: 334-670-3179 • **Financial Aid Phone:** 334-670-3186
E-mail: admit@troy.edu • **CEEB Code:** 1738
Fax: 334-670-3733 • **Website:** www.troy.edu • **ACT Code:** 48

This public school was founded in 1887. It has a 512-acre campus.

RATINGS

Admissions Selectivity Rating: 70   **Fire Safety Rating:** 80   **Green Rating:** 65

STUDENTS AND FACULTY

Enrollment: 17,768. **Student Body:** 63% female, 37% male, 40% out-of-state, 2% international. Asian 1%, African American 39%, Caucasian 48%, Hispanic 3%, Native American 1%.
Retention and Graduation: 71% freshmen return for sophomore year. 15% freshmen graduate within 4 years. 35% freshmen graduate within 6 years. **Faculty:** Student/faculty ratio 19:1. 552 full-time faculty, 75% hold PhDs, 16% are members of minority groups, 44% are women. 1% of classes are taught by teaching assistants.

ACADEMICS

Degrees: associate, bachelor's, doctoral, master's, post-master's certificate. **Classes:** Most classes have 10–19 students. Most lab/discussion sessions have 20–29 students. **Majors with Highest Enrollment:** business administration and management; criminal justice/safety studies; liberal arts and sciences studies and humanities, other. **Special Study Options:** Accelerated program, cross-registration, distance learning, double major, dual enrollment, English as a Second Language (ESL), external degree program, honors program, independent study, internships, study abroad, teacher certification program, weekend college. **Honors Programs:** The University Honors Program, open to students

in all undergraduate divisions of the university, is administered by the Honors Council and the director of university honors. The purpose of the University Honors Program is to offer the academically superior student a specially designed program, within a supportive community, that fosters critical thinking, intellectual development and social responsibility. This enhanced program is designed to provide a balance of common experience and flexibility addressed to individual achievement as well as a comprehensive framework on which to build disciplinary studies. The Honors Program also has an honors house on campus which houses both male and female students. Students should consult with the director of the University Honors Program and the director of University Housing for availabilities and stipulations. The house serves as a residence and a focal point for meetings and activities with the Honors Alliance, faculty and staff in the Honors Program. The official student voice within the program is the University Honors Alliance. Membership to the University Honors Alliance is offered to any student with a 3.3 grade point average or higher. There is an annual membership fee of $5. **Disability Services:** Special programs offered to physically disabled students include note-taking services, reader services, tape recorders, tutors.

FACILITIES

Housing: Coed dorms, men's dorms, special housing for international students, women's dorms, fraternity/sorority housing, apartments for married students, apartments for single students, Substance Free Housing Honor Student Housing. 95% of campus accessible to physically disabled. **Special Academic Facilities/Equipment:** Art museum, recording studio. **Computers:** Students can register for classes online.

CAMPUS LIFE

Environment: Town. **Activities:** Choral groups, concert band, dance, drama/theater, jazz band, marching band, music ensembles, musical theater, opera, pep band, radio station, student government, student newspaper, symphony orchestra, television station, yearbook 125 registered organizations, 22 honor societies, 7 religious organizations. 12 fraternities, 9 sororities. **Athletics (Intercollegiate):** *Men:* baseball, basketball, cheerleading, cross-country, football, golf, rodeo, tennis, track/field (outdoor). *Women:* basketball, cheerleading, cross-country, golf, rodeo, soccer, softball, tennis, track/field (outdoor), volleyball. **On-Campus Highlights:** Movie Gallery Veterans Stadium, Malone Art Gallery, Hall of Honor/National Band Hall of Fame, Trojan Center, Rosa Parks Museum - Montgomery Campus. **Environmental Initiatives:** recycling alternative fuel sources landscaping

ADMISSIONS

Freshman Academic Profile: 54% in top 25% of high school class, 84% in top 50% of high school class. ACT middle 50% range 18–24. Minimum paper TOEFL 500. **Basis for Candidate Selection:** *Very important factors considered include:* academic GPA, rigor of secondary school record, standardized test scores. *Other factors considered include:* application essay, recommendation(s), alumni/ae relation, character/personal qualities, extracurricular activities, interview, talent/ability. **Freshman Admission Requirements:** High school diploma is required and GED is accepted. *Academic units required:* 4 English, 4 mathematics, 4 science, 4 social studies. *Academic units recommended:* 4 English, 4 mathematics, 4 science, 4 social studies. **Freshman Admission Statistics:** 5,646 applied, 72% admitted, 51% enrolled. **Transfer Admission Requirements:** college transcript(s), minimum college GPA of 2.0 required. Lowest grade transferable D. **General Admission Information:** Application Fee $30. Nonfall registration accepted. Admission may be deferred for a maximum of 2 years. Credit and/or placement offered for CEEB Advanced Placement tests.

COSTS AND FINANCIAL AID

Annual in-state tuition $7,470. Annual out-of-state tuition $14,940. Room and board $7,071. Required fees $1,600. Average book expense $1,090. **Required Forms and Deadlines:** FAFSA, institution's own financial aid form. **Notification of Awards:** Applicants will be notified of awards on a rolling basis beginning 5/1. **Types of Aid:** *Need-based scholarships/grants:* Federal Pell, SEOG, state scholarships/grants, private scholarships, the school's own gift aid. *Loans:* Subsidized Stafford, Unsubsidized Stafford, PLUS, Federal Perkins. **Student Employment: Financial Aid Statistics:** 62% freshmen, 71% undergrads receive need-based scholarship or grant aid. 52% freshmen, 29% undergrads receive non-need-based scholarship or grant aid. 99% freshmen receive need-based self-help aid. 4% freshmen, 3% undergrads receive athletic scholarships. **Criteria for awarding institutional aid:** *Non-need-based:* academics, athletics, leadership, music/drama.

TRUMAN STATE UNIVERSITY

100 E. Normal Ave., Kirksville, MO 63501
Phone: 660-785-4114 • **Financial Aid Phone:** 660-785-4130
E-mail: admissions@truman.edu • **CEEB Code:** 6483
Fax: 660-785-7456 • **Website:** www.truman.edu • **ACT Code:** 2336

This public school was founded in 1867. It has a 140-acre campus.

RATINGS
Admissions Selectivity Rating: 88   **Fire Safety Rating:** 86   **Green Rating:** 66

STUDENTS AND FACULTY
Enrollment: 5,452. **Student Body:** 59% female, 41% male, 17% out-of-state, 6% international (54 countries represented). Asian 2%, African American 4%, Caucasian 81%, Hispanic 3%, Native American 0%.
Retention and Graduation: 89% freshmen return for sophomore year. 57% freshmen graduate within 4 years. 74% freshmen graduate within 6 years. 57% grads go on to further study within 1 year. **Faculty:** Student/faculty ratio 17:1. 316 full-time faculty, 84% hold PhDs, 10% are members of minority groups, 40% are women. 1% of classes are taught by teaching assistants.

ACADEMICS
Degrees: bachelor's, master's. **Classes:** Most classes have 20–29 students. Most lab/discussion sessions have 20–29 students. **Majors with Highest Enrollment:** biology/biological sciences; business administration and management; English language and literature. **Special Study Options:** double major, dual enrollment, honors program, independent study, internships, student-designed major, study abroad, teacher certification program. **Honors Programs:** General Honors Program: Students must complete five upper-level courses in math, social science, science and humanities with a 3.5 GPA in these 5 courses. Departmental honors are also available in some disciplines. **Disability Services:** Special programs offered to physically disabled students include note-taking services, reader services, tape recorders, tutors. **Career Services:** Alumni network, alumni services, career assessment, internships, regional alumni. Career Services highlights include Truman offers a wide variety of experiential internships through the "Truman in Washington" program in Washington, D.C. Included are work-experience opportunities in such areas as foreign affairs/diplomacy, government affairs, criminal justice, international relations, health and human services, and communications as well as other areas.

FACILITIES
Housing: Coed dorms, special housing for disabled students, special housing for international students, apartments for married students, apartments for single students, theme housing, sorority housing, French language housing, and Spanish language housing. 98% of campus accessible to physically disabled. **Special Academic Facilities/Equipment:** Art gallery, local history and artifacts museum, human performance lab, greenhouse, observatory, IR and NMR instrumentation, and convergent media center (TV studio, newspaper, and radio station). **Computers:** 100% of classrooms, 100% of dorms, 100% of libraries, 75% of dining areas, 100% of student union, 90% of common outdoor areas have wireless network access. Students can register for classes online. Administrative functions (other than registration) can be performed online.

CAMPUS LIFE
Environment: Village. **Activities:** Choral groups, concert band, dance, drama/theater, jazz band, literary magazine, marching band, music ensembles, musical theater, opera, pep band, radio station, student government, student newspaper, student-run film society, symphony orchestra, television station, Campus Ministries, International Student Organization, Model UN 282 registered organizations, 18 honor societies, 16 religious organizations. 16 fraternities, 11 sororities. **Athletics (Intercollegiate):** *Men:* baseball, basketball, cross-country, football, golf, soccer, swimming, tennis, track/field (outdoor), track/field (indoor), wrestling. *Women:* basketball, cross-country, golf, soccer, softball, swimming, tennis, track/field (outdoor), track/field (indoor), volleyball. **On-Campus Highlights:** Student Recreation Center, Pickler Memorial Library, Student Union Building, The Quadrangle, Jazzman's Coffee Shop. **Environmental Initiatives:** Energy Plan: committed to achieve at least a 5% reduction in total energy used on campus by the year 2015. Compost Program: all waste from the residence halls and cafeterias is composted and used in landscaping and farm projects (including the community garden) on campus. Local foods coordination: grant received that pays for a local food coordinator to work on initiatives begun by Truman students, faculty and Sodexo food staff members.

ADMISSIONS
Freshman Academic Profile: Average high school GPA 3.8. 46% in top 10% of high school class, 79% in top 25% of high school class, 97% in top 50% of high school class. SAT Math middle 50% range 550-650. SAT Critical Reading middle 50% range 550-710. ACT middle 50% range 24-29. Minimum web-based TOEFL 79. Minimum paper TOEFL 550. **Basis for Candidate Selection:** *Very important factors considered include:* Class rank, academic GPA, rigor of secondary school record, standardized test scores. *Important factors considered include:* application essay. *Other factors considered include:* recommendation(s), alumni/ae relation, character/personal qualities, extracurricular activities, first generation, geographical residence, racial/ethnic status, state residency, talent/ability, volunteer work, work experience. **Freshman Admission Requirements:** High school diploma is required and GED is accepted. *Academic units required:* 4 English, 3 mathematics, 3 science, (1 science labs), 2 foreign language, 2 social studies, 1 history, 1 visual/performing arts. *Academic units recommended:* 4 English, 3 mathematics, 3 science, (1 science labs), 2 foreign language, 2 social studies, 1 history, 1 visual/performing arts. **Freshman Admission Statistics:** 4,445 applied, 74% admitted, 39% enrolled. **Transfer Admission Requirements:** college transcript(s), essay or personal statement. **General Admission Information:** Nonfall registration accepted. Admission may be deferred for a maximum of 12 months. Credit and/or placement offered for CEEB Advanced Placement tests.

COSTS AND FINANCIAL AID
Annual in-state tuition $6,978. Annual out-of-state tuition $12,714. Room and board $7,504. Required fees $238. Average book expense $1,000. **Required Forms and Deadlines:** FAFSA, institution's own financial aid form. **Notification of Awards:** Applicants will be notified of awards on a rolling basis beginning 3/1. **Types of Aid:** *Need-based scholarships/grants:* Federal Pell, SEOG, state scholarships/grants, private scholarships, the school's own gift aid, Federal ACG, SMART and TEACH Grants. *Loans:* Subsidized Stafford, Unsubsidized Stafford, PLUS, Federal Perkins, Federal Nursing, college/university loans from institutional funds, Alternative loans. **Student Employment:** Federal Work-Study Program available. Institutional employment available. Highest amount earned per year from on-campus jobs $4,208. Off-campus job opportunities are good. **Financial Aid Statistics:** 99% freshmen, 92% undergrads receive need-based scholarship or grant aid. 96% freshmen, 78% undergrads receive non-need-based scholarship or grant aid. 76% freshmen, 81% undergrads receive need-based self-help aid. 5% freshmen, 5% undergrads receive athletic scholarships. 99% freshmen, 91% undergrads receive any aid. 52% undergrads borrow to pay for school. Average cumulative indebtedness $22,922. **Criteria for awarding institutional aid:** *Non-need-based:* academics, alumni affiliation, art, athletics, leadership, minority status, music/drama, state/district residency.

See page 1236.

TUFTS UNIVERSITY

Bendetson Hall, Medford, MA 2155
Phone: 617-627-3170 • **Financial Aid Phone:** 617-627-2000
E-mail: admissions.inquiry@ase.tufts.edu • **CEEB Code:** 3901
Fax: 617-627-3860 • **Website:** www.tufts.edu • **ACT Code:** 1922

This private school was founded in 1852. It has a 150-acre campus.

RATINGS
Admissions Selectivity Rating: 98   **Fire Safety Rating:** 89   **Green Rating:** 83

STUDENTS AND FACULTY
Enrollment: 5,186. **Student Body:** 51% female, 49% male, 77% out-of-state, 7% international (93 countries represented). Asian 10%, African American 4%, Caucasian 57%, Hispanic 7%, Native American 0%.
Retention and Graduation: 97% freshmen return for sophomore year. 87% freshmen graduate within 4 years. 92% freshmen graduate within 6 years. **Faculty:** Student/faculty ratio 9:1. 699 full-time faculty, 93% hold PhDs, 17% are members of minority groups, 40% are women. 1% of classes are taught by teaching assistants.

ACADEMICS
Degrees: bachelor's, master's, post-bachelor's certificate, post-master's certificate. **Classes:** Most classes have 10–19 students. Most lab/discussion sessions have 10–19 students. **Majors with Highest Enrollment:** economics; English language and literature; international relations and affairs. **Special Study Options:** cross-registration, double major, exchange student program (domestic),

honors program, independent study, internships, liberal arts/career combination, student-designed major, study abroad, teacher certification program. **Combined Degree Programs:** BA/MD, BA/MA, BA/DDS, 5-yr BA/BFA with museum school of Fine Arts; 5-yr. **Disability Services:** Special programs offered to physically disabled students include note-taking services, reader services, tape recorders, tutors. **Career Services:** Alumni network, alumni services, career/job search classes, career assessment, internships, regional alumni. Career Services highlights include Thanks to our proximity to Boston, most of our students are able to pursue an internship during their 4 years, many for academic credit. Tufts also has a program geared at providing a stipend to students who pursue an internship with non-profit or public sector organizations.

FACILITIES

Housing: Coed dorms, special housing for disabled students, women's dorms, fraternity/sorority housing, cooperative housing, Special Interest Housing. **Special Academic Facilities/Equipment:** Language lab, nutrition institute, research lab for physical electronics, bioelectrical and biochemical labs, computer-aided design (CAD) facility, electro-optics technology and environmental management centers. **Computers:** 50% of classrooms, 20% of dorms, 100% of libraries, 75% of dining areas, 100% of student union, 75% of common outdoor areas have wireless network access. Students can register for classes online. Administrative functions (other than registration) can be performed online.

CAMPUS LIFE

Environment: Town. **Activities:** Choral groups, concert band, dance, drama/theater, jazz band, literary magazine, marching band, music ensembles, musical theater, opera, pep band, radio station, student government, student newspaper, student-run film society, symphony orchestra, television station, yearbook, Campus Ministries, International Student Organization, Model UN 160 registered organizations, 4 honor societies, 6 religious organizations. 11 fraternities, 3 sororities. **Athletics (Intercollegiate):** *Men:* baseball, basketball, crew/rowing, cross-country, diving, football, golf, ice hockey, lacrosse, sailing, soccer, squash, swimming, tennis, track/field (outdoor), track/field (indoor). *Women:* basketball, cheerleading, crew/rowing, cross-country, diving, fencing, field hockey, golf, lacrosse, sailing, soccer, softball, squash, swimming, tennis, track/field (outdoor), track/field (indoor), volleyball. **On-Campus Highlights:** The Aidekman Arts Center, Tisch Library, Edwin Ginn Library, Cousens Gymnasium, Ellis Oval, Meyer Campus Center. **Environmental Initiatives:** Reduced green house gas emissions to below 1990 levels; LEED Gold building and comprehensive energy efficiency efforts Comprehensive recycling and green purchasing and green dining initiatives

ADMISSIONS

Freshman Academic Profile: 90% in top 10% of high school class, 99% in top 25% of high school class, 100% in top 50% of high school class. 57% from public high schools. SAT Math middle 50% range 680-760. SAT Critical Reading middle 50% range 670-760. SAT Writing middle 50% range 680-760. ACT middle 50% range 30-33. Minimum web-based TOEFL 100. Minimum paper TOEFL 600. **Basis for Candidate Selection:** *Very important factors considered include:* application essay, academic GPA, rigor of secondary school record, character/personal qualities. *Important factors considered include:* Class rank, recommendation(s), standardized test scores, extracurricular activities, talent/ability, volunteer work, work experience. *Other factors considered include:* alumni/ae relation, first generation, geographical residence, interview, racial/ethnic status. **Freshman Admission Requirements:** High school diploma is required and GED is accepted. **Freshman Admission Statistics:** 16,369 applied, 21% admitted, 37% enrolled. **Transfer Admission Requirements:** High school transcript, college transcript(s), essay or personal statement, standardized test scores, statement of good standing from prior institution(s). Lowest grade transferable C. **General Admission Information:** Application Fee $70. Early decision application deadline 11/1. Regular application deadline 1/1. Regular notification 4/1. Nonfall registration not accepted. Admission may be deferred for a maximum of 12 Months. Credit and/or placement offered for CEEB Advanced Placement tests.

COSTS AND FINANCIAL AID

Annual tuition $43,688. Room and board $11,880. Required fees $978. Average book expense $800. **Required Forms and Deadlines:** FAFSA, CSS/Financial Aid PROFILE, noncustodial PROFILE, Parent and Student Federal Income Tax Returns. **Notification of Awards:** Applicants will be notified of awards on or about 4/1. **Types of Aid:** *Need-based scholarships/grants:* Federal Pell, SEOG, state scholarships/grants, the school's own gift aid. *Loans:* Direct Subsidized Stafford, Direct Unsubsidized Stafford, Federal Perkins, college/university loans from institutional funds. **Student Employment:** Federal Work-Study Program available. Institutional employment available. Off-campus job opportunities are good. **Financial Aid Statistics:** 94% freshmen, 92% undergrads receive need-based scholarship or grant aid. 4% freshmen, 4% undergrads receive non-need-based scholarship or grant aid. 85% freshmen, 93% undergrads receive need-based self-help aid. 45% freshmen, 45% undergrads receive any aid. 37% undergrads borrow to pay for school. Average cumulative indebtedness $32,068. **Criteria for awarding institutional aid:** *Non-need-based:* academics.

TULANE UNIVERSITY

6823 St. Charles Avenue, New Orleans, LA 70118
Phone: 504-865-5260 • **Financial Aid Phone:** 504-865-5723
E-mail: undergrad.admission@tulane.edu • **CEEB Code:** 6832
Fax: 504-862-8715 • **Website:** www.tulane.edu • **ACT Code:** 1614

This private school was founded in 1834. It has a 110-acre campus.

RATINGS
Admissions Selectivity Rating: 96   **Fire Safety Rating:** 84   **Green Rating:** 87

STUDENTS AND FACULTY
Enrollment: 8,357. **Student Body:** 58% female, 42% male, 71% out-of-state, 3% international (37 countries represented). Asian 4%, African American 10%, Caucasian 71%, Hispanic 6%, Native American 0%.
Retention and Graduation: 89% freshmen return for sophomore year. **Faculty:** Student/faculty ratio 9:1. 652 full-time faculty, 93% hold PhDs, 22% are members of minority groups, 37% are women.

ACADEMICS
Degrees: associate, bachelor's, certificate, doctoral, master's, post-bachelor's certificate. **Classes:** Most classes have 10–19 students. **Majors with Highest Enrollment:** business/commerce; health services/allied health/health sciences; psychology. **Special Study Options:** Accelerated program, cross-registration, distance learning, double major, English as a Second Language (ESL), exchange student program (domestic), honors program, independent study, internships, liberal arts/career combination, student-designed major, study abroad, teacher certification program. **Honors Programs:** Tulane Honors Program **Combined Degree Programs:** BA/MD, BA/JD, BA/MA, Integrated Graduate Studies 4+1 programs. **Disability Services:** Special programs offered to physically disabled students include note-taking services, reader services, tape recorders, tutors. **Career Services:** Alumni network, alumni services, career/job search classes, career assessment, internships, regional alumni.

FACILITIES
Housing: Coed dorms, special housing for disabled students, special housing for international students, women's dorms, apartments for married students, apartments for single students, wellness housing. 60% of campus accessible to physically disabled. **Special Academic Facilities/Equipment:** Newcomb Art Gallery, Amistad Research Center, Latin American Library, Maxwell Music Library, Hogan Jazz Archives, Louisiana Special Collection, Manuscripts Department, Koch Herbarium, Tulane Museum of Natural History, Government Documents. **Computers:** 100% of classrooms, 100% of dorms, 100% of libraries, 100% of dining areas, 100% of student union, 100% of common outdoor areas have wireless network access. Students can register for classes online. Administrative functions (other than registration) can be performed online.

CAMPUS LIFE
Environment: City. **Activities:** Choral groups, concert band, dance, drama/theater, jazz band, literary magazine, marching band, music ensembles, musical theater, pep band, radio station, student government, student newspaper, student-run film society, television station, yearbook 250 registered organizations, 43 honor societies, 16 religious organizations. 15 fraternities, 11 sororities. **Athletics (Intercollegiate):** *Men:* baseball, basketball, cross-country, football, tennis, track/field (outdoor). *Women:* basketball, cross-country, diving, golf, swimming, tennis, track/field (outdoor), track/field (indoor), volleyball. **On-Campus Highlights:** Amistad Research Center, Newcomb Art Gallery, Reily Recreation Center, Howard Tilton Memorial Library, PJ's Coffee Shop. **Environmental Initiatives:** Almost every school within the university offers undergraduates or graduates an environmental major or focus. These include a top-ranked Environmental Law program, Environmental Health Sciences degrees at the graduate and undergraduate levels, an Environmental Science degree, an interdisciplinary Environmental Studies degree and studios that focus on sustainable design in the School of Architecture. In addition, the Ecology and Evolutionary Biology and Earth and Environmental Sciences departments have strong programs that address coastal sustainability and global environmental change. Tulane's Center for Public Service and the public service requirement ensures that academic inquiry is integrated with active civic engagement, largely within the context of helping New Orleans rebuild as a more sustainable community. Tulane has a number of green building projects on campus, and since Hurricane Katrina many Tulane students, staff and faculty have been engaged in sustainable building, design, and neighborhood planning projects in the larger community. Most recently on campus, the renovation of the Lavin-Bernick Center for University Life included the installation of natural ventilation and daylighting features, including solar chimneys, extensive fans,

exterior sunshades, and lighting systems that adjust to daylight. Off-campus, projects such as a Tulane-facilitated energy efficient neighborhood plan and green, affordable homes designed and constructed by Tulane architecture students have advanced sustainable rebuilding efforts in New Orleans. Tulane is currently implementing numerous energy efficiency and water conservation measures that will reduce annual uptown campus greenhouse gas emissions by a projected 10%. In addition to heating, cooling, lighting and water conversation improvements, the university has student-led energy savings education programs, such as the country's first Energy Star Showcase Dorm Room. To further this effort to reduce energy use and carbon emissions, Tulane has joined the Presidents Climate Commitment.

ADMISSIONS

Freshman Academic Profile: Average high school GPA 3.5. 52% in top 10% of high school class, 83% in top 25% of high school class, 97% in top 50% of high school class. SAT Math middle 50% range 620-710. SAT Critical Reading middle 50% range 630-720. SAT Writing middle 50% range 640-720. ACT middle 50% range 29-32. Minimum paper TOEFL 550. **Basis for Candidate Selection:** *Very important factors considered include:* Class rank, academic GPA, rigor of secondary school record, standardized test scores. *Important factors considered include:* application essay, recommendation(s), character/personal qualities. *Other factors considered include:* alumni/ae relation, extracurricular activities, first generation, interview, talent/ability, volunteer work, work experience. **Freshman Admission Requirements:** High school diploma is required and GED is accepted. **Freshman Admission Statistics:** 30,080 applied, 27% admitted, 20% enrolled. **Transfer Admission Requirements:** High school transcript, college transcript(s), essay or personal statement, minimum college GPA of 2.5 required. Lowest grade transferable C. **General Admission Information:** Regular application deadline 1/15. Regular notification 4/1. Nonfall registration accepted. Admission may be deferred for a maximum of 1 year. Credit and/or placement offered for CEEB Advanced Placement tests.

COSTS AND FINANCIAL AID

Annual tuition $41,500. Room and board $11,547. Required fees $3,740. Average book expense $1,200. **Required Forms and Deadlines:** FAFSA, CSS/Financial Aid PROFILE, noncustodial PROFILE, business/farm supplement. **Notification of Awards:** Applicants will be notified of awards on a rolling basis beginning 3/15. **Types of Aid:** *Need-based scholarships/grants:* Federal Pell, SEOG, state scholarships/grants, private scholarships, the school's own gift aid, Academic Competitiveness Grant, SMART Grant. *Loans:* Subsidized Stafford, Unsubsidized Stafford, PLUS, Federal Perkins. **Student Employment:** Federal Work-Study Program available. Institutional employment available. Highest amount earned per year from on-campus jobs $2,500. Off-campus job opportunities are good. **Financial Aid Statistics:** 98% freshmen, 96% undergrads receive need-based scholarship or grant aid. 31% freshmen, 26% undergrads receive non-need-based scholarship or grant aid. 64% freshmen, 66% undergrads receive need-based self-help aid. 3% freshmen, 3% undergrads receive athletic scholarships. 41% undergrads borrow to pay for school. Average cumulative indebtedness $35,100. **Criteria for awarding institutional aid:** *Non-need-based:* academics, athletics, leadership, music/drama, state/district residency.

TUSCULUM COLLEGE

PO Box 5051, Greenville, TN 37743
Phone: 423-636-7300 • **Financial Aid Phone:** 800-729-0256
E-mail: admissions@tusculum.edu • **CEEB Code:** 1812
Fax: 423-638-7166 • **ACT Code:** 4018

This private school, affiliated with the Presbyterian Church, was founded in 1794. It has a 142-acre campus.

RATINGS
Admissions Selectivity Rating: 67   **Fire Safety Rating:** 69   **Green Rating:** 60*

STUDENTS AND FACULTY
Enrollment: 2,600. **Student Body:** 60% female, 40% male, 18% out-of-state, 2% international (8 countries represented). Asian 0%, African American 11%, Caucasian 83%, Hispanic 2%, Native American 0%.
Retention and Graduation: 62% freshmen return for sophomore year. 26% freshmen graduate within 4 years. 42% freshmen graduate within 6 years. 10% grads go on to further study within 1 year. 12% grads pursue arts and sciences degrees. 1% grads pursue law degrees. 5% grads pursue business degrees. 2% grads pursue medical degrees. **Faculty:** Student/faculty ratio 16:1. 75 full-time faculty, 63% hold PhDs, 3% are members of minority groups, 44% are women. 0% of classes are taught by teaching assistants.

ACADEMICS
Degrees: bachelor's, master's. **Classes:** Most classes have 10–19 students.
Majors with Highest Enrollment: biology/biological sciences; business

administration and management; elementary education and teaching. **Special Study Options:** double major, honors program, independent study, internships, student-designed major, study abroad, teacher certification program, 16 month accelerated evening program for non-traditional students. **Honors Programs:** Honors program for those students meeting gpa and act standards - available after the first semester. **Disability Services:** Special programs offered to physically disabled students include tutors. **Career Services:** Alumni network, alumni services, career assessment, internships, regional alumni. Career Services highlights include Service-Learning.

FACILITIES
Housing: Coed dorms, men's dorms, women's dorms, apartments for single students. 80% of campus accessible to physically disabled. **Special Academic Facilities/Equipment:** The Andrew Johnson Presidential Museum and Library. The College Archives. The Charles Coffin Collection. **Computers:** Administrative functions (other than registration) can be performed online.

CAMPUS LIFE
Environment: Village. **Activities:** dance, drama/theater, radio station, student government, student newspaper, yearbook 12 registered organizations, 1 honor societies, 2 religious organizations. 1 fraternities, 1 sororities. **Athletics (Intercollegiate):** *Men:* baseball, basketball, cheerleading, cross-country, football, golf, soccer, tennis. *Women:* basketball, cheerleading, cross-country, golf, soccer, softball, tennis, volleyball. **On-Campus Highlights:** Niswonger Commons Center, Perk Coffee House, Indoor Athletic Facility.

ADMISSIONS
Freshman Academic Profile: Average high school GPA 2.9. 16% in top 10% of high school class, 42% in top 25% of high school class, 78% in top 50% of high school class. SAT Math middle 50% range 410-540. SAT Critical Reading middle 50% range 410-540. ACT middle 50% range 18-23. Minimum paper TOEFL 550. **Basis for Candidate Selection:** *Very important factors considered include:* rigor of secondary school record, standardized test scores. *Important factors considered include:* application essay. *Other factors considered include:* Class rank, recommendation(s), character/personal qualities, extracurricular activities, interview, talent/ability, volunteer work. **Freshman Admission Requirements:** High school diploma is required and GED is accepted. *Academic units required:* 4 English, 3 mathematics, 2 science, 3 social studies. 4 English, 3 mathematics, 2 science, 3 social studies. **Freshman Admission Statistics:** 1,456 applied, 81% admitted, 24% enrolled. **Transfer Admission Requirements:** college transcript(s), statement of good standing from prior institution(s). Minimum college GPA of 2.0 required. Lowest grade transferable D. **General Admission Information:** Notification on a rolling basis, beginning on or about 1/3. Nonfall registration accepted. Admission may be deferred for a maximum of 12 months. Credit offered for CEEB Advanced Placement tests.

COSTS AND FINANCIAL AID
Required Forms and Deadlines: FAFSA. **Notification of Awards:** Applicants will be notified of awards on a rolling basis beginning 3/15. **Types of Aid:** *Need-based scholarships/grants:* Federal Pell, SEOG, state scholarships/grants, private scholarships, the school's own gift aid. *Loans:* Subsidized Stafford, Unsubsidized Stafford, PLUS, Federal Perkins. **Student Employment:** Federal Work-Study Program available. Institutional employment available. Off-campus job opportunities are good. **Financial Aid Statistics:** 75% freshmen, 62% undergrads receive need-based scholarship or grant aid. 91% freshmen, 58% undergrads receive non-need-based scholarship or grant aid. 77% freshmen, 80% undergrads receive need-based self-help aid. 15% freshmen, 14% undergrads receive athletic scholarships. 90% freshmen, 85% undergrads receive any aid. Average cumulative indebtedness $14,633. **Criteria for awarding institutional aid:** *Non-need-based:* academics, athletics, leadership, music/drama, state/district residency.

TUSKEGEE UNIVERSITY

Old Administration Building, Tuskegee, AL 36088
Phone: 334-727-8500 • **Financial Aid Phone:** 334-727-8500
E-mail: admissions@tuskegee.edu • **CEEB Code:** 1813
Fax: 334-727-5750 • **Website:** www.tuskegee.edu • **ACT Code:** 50

This private school was founded in 1881. It has a 5200-acre campus.

RATINGS
Admissions Selectivity Rating: 83   **Fire Safety Rating:** 78   **Green Rating:** 76

STUDENTS AND FACULTY

Enrollment: 2,598. **Student Body:** 57% female, 43% male, 69% out-of-state, 2% international (19 countries represented). Asian 0%, African American 82%, Caucasian 0%, Hispanic 0%, Native American 0%.

Retention and Graduation: 73% freshmen return for sophomore year. 17% freshmen graduate within 4 years. 23% grads go on to further study within 1 year. 11% grads pursue arts and sciences degrees. 2% grads pursue law degrees. 4% grads pursue business degrees. 3% grads pursue medical degrees. **Faculty:** Student/faculty ratio 14:1. 271 full-time faculty, 77% hold PhDs, 66% are members of minority groups, 35% are women. 0% of classes are taught by teaching assistants.

ACADEMICS

Degrees: bachelor's, doctoral, master's. **Classes:** Most classes have 10–19 students. **Majors with Highest Enrollment:** electrical, electronics and communications engineering; veterinary medicine (dvm). **Special Study Options:** cooperative education program, double major, dual enrollment, honors program, independent study, internships, teacher certification program. **Career Services:** Alumni network, career/job search classes, career assessment, internships, regional alumni.

FACILITIES

Housing: Coed dorms, men's dorms, women's dorms, apartments for married students, apartments for single students. **Special Academic Facilities/Equipment:** Agricultural and natural history museum, electron microscopes, two nursery schools. **Computers:** 100% of classrooms, 100% of dorms, 100% of libraries, 100% of dining areas, 100% of student union, 100% of common outdoor areas have wireless network access. Students can register for classes online.

CAMPUS LIFE

Environment: Rural. **Activities:** Choral groups, drama/theater, marching band, student government, student newspaper, yearbook, Campus Ministries, International Student Organization 36 registered organizations, 22 honor societies, 6 religious organizations. 5 fraternities, 6 sororities. **Athletics (Intercollegiate):** *Men:* baseball, basketball, cheerleading, cross-country, diving, fencing, football, golf, gymnastics, riflery, soccer, swimming, tennis, track/field (outdoor), track/field (indoor), volleyball. *Women:* basketball, cheerleading, cross-country, diving, fencing, golf, gymnastics, riflery, soccer, swimming, tennis, track/field (outdoor), track/field (indoor), volleyball **On-Campus Highlights:** George Washington Carver Museum, Kellogg Conference Center, Tuskegee Chapel, The Tuskegee Cemetery, General Daniel.

ADMISSIONS

Freshman Academic Profile: Average high school GPA 3.2. 20% in top 10% of high school class, 60% in top 25% of high school class, 100% in top 50% of high school class. SAT Math middle 50% range 400-520. SAT Critical Reading middle 50% range 400-510. ACT middle 50% range 18-22. Minimum paper TOEFL 500. **Basis for Candidate Selection:** *Very important factors considered include:* Class rank, academic GPA, recommendation(s), rigor of secondary school record, standardized test scores, talent/ability. *Important factors considered include:* alumni/ae relation, character/personal qualities. *Other factors considered include:* application essay, extracurricular activities, first generation, geographical residence, interview, state residency, volunteer work, work experience. **Freshman Admission Requirements:** High school diploma is required and GED is accepted. *Academic units required:* 4 English, 3 mathematics, 2 science, 3 social studies, 4 academic electives. 4 English, 3 mathematics, 2 science, 3 social studies, 4 academic electives. **Freshman Admission Statistics:** 10,022 applied, 35% admitted, 18% enrolled. **Transfer Admission Requirements:** college transcript(s), minimum college GPA of 2.0 required. Lowest grade transferable C. **General Admission Information:** Application Fee $25. Regular application deadline 7/15. Regular notification 3/15. Notification on a rolling basis, beginning on or about 3/1. Nonfall registration accepted. Credit and/or placement offered for CEEB Advanced Placement tests.

COSTS AND FINANCIAL AID

Annual tuition $18,100. Room and board $8,510. Required fees $1,425. Average book expense $1,282. **Required Forms and Deadlines:** FAFSA, institution's own financial aid form, CSS/Financial Aid PROFILE. **Types of Aid:** *Need-based scholarships/grants:* Federal Pell, SEOG, state scholarships/grants, private scholarships, the school's own gift aid, United Negro College Fund, Federal Nursing Scholarships. *Loans:* Direct Subsidized Stafford, Direct Unsubsidized Stafford, Direct PLUS, Subsidized Stafford, Unsubsidized Stafford, PLUS, Federal Perkins, Federal Nursing, state loans, college/university loans from institutional funds. **Student Employment:** Federal Work-Study Program available. Institutional employment available. Highest amount earned per year from on-campus jobs $1,540. Off-campus job opportunities are good. **Financial Aid Statistics:** 84% freshmen, 86% undergrads receive need-based scholarship or grant aid. 56% freshmen, 48% undergrads receive non-need-based scholarship or grant aid. 59% freshmen, 62% undergrads receive need-based self-help aid. 8% freshmen, 5% undergrads receive athletic scholarships. 80% freshmen, 92% undergrads receive any aid. 91% undergrads borrow to pay for school. Average cumulative indebtedness $23,000. **Criteria for awarding institutional aid:** *Non-need-based:* academics, athletics, state/district residency.

UNION COLLEGE (NE)

3800 South 48th Street, Lincoln, NE 68506-4300
Phone: 402-486-2504 • **Financial Aid Phone:** 402-426-2505
E-mail: ucenroll@ucollege.edu
Fax: 402-486-2566 • **Website:** www.ucollege.edu • **ACT Code:** 2480

This private school, affiliated with the Seventh Day Adventist Church, was founded in 1891.

RATINGS

Admissions Selectivity Rating: 87   **Fire Safety Rating:** 61   **Green Rating:** 60*

STUDENTS AND FACULTY

Enrollment: 845. **Student Body:** 56% female, 44% male, 79% out-of-state, 11% international (34 countries represented). Asian 2%, African American 2%, Caucasian 75%, Hispanic 6%, Native American 1%.

Retention and Graduation: 69% freshmen return for sophomore year. 21% grads go on to further study within 1 year. 8% grads pursue arts and sciences degrees. 2% grads pursue law degrees. 5% grads pursue business degrees. 6% grads pursue medical degrees. **Faculty:** Student/faculty ratio 13:1. 54 full-time faculty, 54% hold PhDs, 13% are members of minority groups, 35% are women. 0% of classes are taught by teaching assistants.

ACADEMICS

Degrees: associate, bachelor's, master's. **Classes:** Most classes have fewer than 10 students. **Majors with Highest Enrollment:** business/commerce; nursing/registered nurse (rn, asn, bsn, msn); physician assistant. **Special Study Options:** cross-registration, distance learning, double major, dual enrollment, English as a Second Language (ESL), honors program, independent study, internships, student-designed major, study abroad, teacher certification program. **Honors Programs:** The honors program is available for students who have demonstrated superior scholastic ability. **Disability Services:** Special programs offered to physically disabled students include note-taking services, reader services, tape recorders, tutors. **Career Services:** career assessment, internships.

FACILITIES

Housing: men's dorms, women's dorms, apartments for married students, apartments for single students. 75% of campus accessible to physically disabled. **Computers:** Administrative functions (other than registration) can be performed online.

CAMPUS LIFE

Environment: Village. **Activities:** Choral groups, concert band, drama/theater, literary magazine, music ensembles, student government, student newspaper, yearbook 1 honor societies, 3 religious organizations. **Athletics (Intercollegiate):** *Men:* basketball, volleyball. *Women:* basketball, volleyball. **On-Campus Highlights:** Cafeteria, The Ortner Center, The Arboretum, Dick Administration Bldg., Larson Life Style Center.

ADMISSIONS

Freshman Academic Profile: 17% in top 10% of high school class, 14% in top 25% of high school class, 57% in top 50% of high school class. 10% from public high schools. ACT middle 50% range 19-25. Minimum paper TOEFL 550. **Basis for Candidate Selection:** *Very important factors considered include:* recommendation(s), rigor of secondary school record, standardized test scores, character/personal qualities. *Important factors considered include:* Class rank, extracurricular activities, interview, religious affiliation/commitment. *Other factors considered include:* application essay, alumni/ae relation, geographical residence, state residency, talent/ability. **Freshman Admission Requirements:** High school diploma is required and GED is accepted. *Academic units required:* 3 English, 2 mathematics, 2 science, (1 science labs), 1 social studies, 1 history, 3 academic electives. *Academic units recommended:* 3 English, 2 mathematics, 2 science, (1 science labs), 1 social studies, 1 history, 3 academic electives. **Freshman Admission Statistics:** 635 applied, 43% admitted, 66% enrolled. **Transfer Admission Requirements:** High school transcript, college transcript(s), minimum college GPA of 2.0 required. Lowest grade transferable C–. **General Admission Information:** Nonfall registration accepted. Credit and/or placement offered for CEEB Advanced Placement tests.

COSTS AND FINANCIAL AID

Annual tuition $13,990. Room and board $4,720. Required fees $420. Average book expense $950. **Required Forms and Deadlines:** FAFSA. **Notification of Awards:** Applicants will be notified of awards on a rolling basis beginning 5/1. **Types of Aid:** *Need-based scholarships/grants:* Federal Pell, SEOG, state scholarships/grants, private scholarships, the school's own gift aid. *Loans:* Subsidized Stafford, Unsubsidized Stafford, PLUS, Federal Perkins, Federal Nursing, college/university loans from institutional funds. **Student Employment:** Highest amount earned per year from on-campus jobs $1,300. **Financial Aid Statistics:** 100% freshmen, 100% undergrads receive need-based scholarship or grant aid. 14% freshmen, 11% undergrads receive non-need-based scholarship or grant aid. 85% freshmen, 88% undergrads receive need-based self-help aid. 100% freshmen, 58% undergrads receive any aid. **Criteria for awarding institutional aid:** *Non-need-based:* academics, leadership, religious affiliation.

UNION COLLEGE (NY)

Grant Hall, Schenectady, NY 12308
Phone: 518-388-6112 • **Financial Aid Phone:** 518-388-6123
E-mail: admissions@union.edu • **CEEB Code:** 2920
Fax: 518-388-6986 • **Website:** www.union.edu • **ACT Code:** 2970

This private school was founded in 1795. It has a 100-acre campus.

RATINGS
Admissions Selectivity Rating: 95   **Fire Safety Rating:** 88   **Green Rating:** 87

STUDENTS AND FACULTY
Enrollment: 2,192. **Student Body:** 46% female, 54% male, 60% out-of-state, 5% international (39 countries represented). Asian 6%, African American 4%, Caucasian 75%, Hispanic 7%, Native American 0%.
Retention and Graduation: 94% freshmen return for sophomore year. 76% freshmen graduate within 4 years. 83% freshmen graduate within 6 years. 30% grads go on to further study within 1 year. 10% grads pursue arts and sciences degrees. 3% grads pursue law degrees. 3% grads pursue business degrees. 3% grads pursue medical degrees. **Faculty:** Student/faculty ratio 10:1. 202 full-time faculty, 98% hold PhDs, 13% are members of minority groups, 42% are women. 0% of classes are taught by teaching assistants.

ACADEMICS
Degrees: bachelor's. **Classes:** Most classes have 10–19 students. Most lab/discussion sessions have 10–19 students. **Majors with Highest Enrollment:** economics; English language and literature; political science and government. **Special Study Options:** Accelerated program, cross-registration, double major, dual enrollment, honors program, independent study, internships, liberal arts/career combination, student-designed major, study abroad, teacher certification program. **Honors Programs:** The Union Scholars program offers selected students the opportunity to take full advantage of the diverse intellectual experiences at Union. Specific features of the program are an enriched two-term version of First-Year Preceptorial; a sophomore independent study project with a professor of the student's choosing; the option to participate as a junior in a program in which students take a leadership role in the College's intellectual and social life; and a Scholars Colloquium run by students for presenting faculty and student research, in the senior year. Union Scholars use their extra courses to create an enriched program that meets their specific needs and interests. **Combined Degree Programs:** BA/JD, BS/MS or MBA/MD; BS/MS;BA or BS/MBA(joint pgms). **Disability Services:** Special programs offered to physically disabled students include note-taking services, reader services, tape recorders. **Career Services:** Alumni network, alumni services, career/job search classes, career assessment, internships, regional alumni. Career Services highlights include Faculty,alumni, and athletics involvement in student career planning.

FACILITIES
Housing: Coed dorms, fraternity/sorority housing, apartments for single students, theme housing, Minerva Houses. Up to 45 students live in each. All students and faculty members have (Minerva) house affiliations. Each house contributes intellectual, cultural, and social events to the campus. **Special Academic Facilities/Equipment:** The Nott Memorial and its Mandeville Gallery; Yulman Theater; Burns Arts Atrium; Taylor Music Center and its Emerson Auditorium; Special Collections at Schaffer Library; Memorial Chapel; Jackson's Garden, an eight-acre formal garden and woodland. Academic facilities include the F.W. Olin Center, with high technology classrooms and laboratories, a multi-media auditorium, collaborative computer classrooms, and a 20-inch remote-controlled telescope. Science and engineering facilities include superconducting nuclear magnetic resonance spectrometer, two electron microscopes, tandem pelletron positive ion accelerator, a fully accessible machine lab, and Aerogel fabrication and analysis lab. **Computers:** 100% of classrooms, 75% of dorms, 100% of libraries, 100% of dining areas, 100% of student union, 100% of common outdoor areas have wireless network access. Students can register for classes online. Administrative functions (other than registration) can be performed online.

CAMPUS LIFE
Environment: Town. **Activities:** Choral groups, concert band, dance, drama/theater, jazz band, literary magazine, music ensembles, radio station, student government, student newspaper, student-run film society, symphony orchestra, television station, yearbook, Campus Ministries, International Student Organization, Model UN 100 registered organizations, 13 honor societies, 7 religious organizations. 12 fraternities, 5 sororities. **Athletics (Intercollegiate):** *Men:* baseball, basketball, crew/rowing, cross-country, diving, football, ice hockey, lacrosse, soccer, swimming, tennis, track/field (outdoor), track/field (indoor). *Women:* basketball, crew/rowing, cross-country, diving, field hockey, ice hockey, lacrosse, soccer, softball, swimming, tennis, track/field (outdoor), track/field (indoor), volleyball. **On-Campus Highlights:** The Nott Memorial, Schaffer Library, Reamer Campus Center, Jackson's Garden, Memorial Chapel. **Environmental Initiatives:** Presidential Green Grants. Performance of extensive Energy Audit resulting in $1.5M in energy projects. Conversion to electric vehicles.

ADMISSIONS
Freshman Academic Profile: Average high school GPA 3.5. 58% in top 10% of high school class, 79% in top 25% of high school class, 97% in top 50% of high school class. 63% from public high schools. SAT Math middle 50% range 620-700. SAT Critical Reading middle 50% range 590-680. SAT Writing middle 50% range 590-680. ACT middle 50% range 28-32. Minimum web-based TOEFL 90. Minimum paper TOEFL 600. **Basis for Candidate Selection:** *Very important factors considered include:* Class rank, academic GPA, rigor of secondary school record. *Important factors considered include:* recommendation(s), standardized test scores, character/personal qualities, extracurricular activities, talent/ability. *Other factors considered include:* application essay, alumni/ae relation, first generation, geographical residence, interview, level of applicant's interest, racial/ethnic status, state residency, volunteer work, work experience. **Freshman Admission Requirements:** High school diploma is required and GED is not accepted. *Academic units required:* 4 English, 3 mathematics, 2 science, (2 science labs), 2 foreign language, 1 social studies, 1 history. *Academic units recommended:* 4 English, 3 mathematics, 2 science, (2 science labs), 2 foreign language, 1 social studies, 1 history. **Freshman Admission Statistics:** 5,565 applied, 38% admitted, 28% enrolled. **Transfer Admission Requirements:** High school transcript, college transcript(s), essay or personal statement, statement of good standing from prior institution(s). Minimum college GPA of 3.0 required. Lowest grade transferable C. **General Admission Information:** Application Fee $50. Early decision application deadline 11/15. Regular application deadline 1/15. Regular notification 4/1. Nonfall registration not accepted. Admission may be deferred for a maximum of one year. Credit and/or placement offered for CEEB Advanced Placement tests.

COSTS AND FINANCIAL AID
Annual tuition $44,748. Room and board $11,070. Required fees $471. Average book expense $542. **Required Forms and Deadlines:** FAFSA, CSS/Financial Aid PROFILE, state aid form, noncustodial PROFILE, business/farm supplement. **Types of Aid:** *Need-based scholarships/grants:* Federal Pell, SEOG, state scholarships/grants, private scholarships, the school's own gift aid. *Loans:* Direct Subsidized Stafford, Direct Unsubsidized Stafford, Direct PLUS, Federal Perkins, college/university loans from institutional funds. **Student Employment:** Federal Work-Study Program available. Institutional employment available. Highest amount earned per year from on-campus jobs $3,800. Off-campus job opportunities are good. **Financial Aid Statistics:** 95% freshmen, 94% undergrads receive need-based scholarship or grant aid. 25% freshmen, 20% undergrads receive non-need-based scholarship or grant aid. 86% freshmen, 94% undergrads receive need-based self-help aid. 76% freshmen, 71% undergrads receive any aid. 58% undergrads borrow to pay for school. Average cumulative indebtedness $27,336. **Criteria for awarding institutional aid:** *Non-need-based:* academics.

See page 1238.

UNION COLLEGE (KY)

310 College Street, Barbourville, KY 40906
Phone: 606-546-1229 • **Financial Aid Phone:** 606-546-1224
E-mail: enrollme@unionky.edu • **CEEB Code:**
Fax: 606-546-1667 • **Website:** www.unionky.edu • **ACT Code:** 15520

This private school, affiliated with the Methodist Church, was founded in 1879.

RATINGS
Admissions Selectivity Rating: 90   **Fire Safety Rating:** 63   **Green Rating:** 60*

STUDENTS AND FACULTY

Enrollment: 811. **Student Body:** 46% female, 54% male, 25% out-of-state, 3% international (9 countries represented). Asian 0%, African American 12%, Caucasian 79%, Hispanic 1%, Native American 0%.
Retention and Graduation: 14% freshmen graduate within 4 years. 28% freshmen graduate within 6 years. **Faculty:** Student/faculty ratio 16:1. 61 full-time faculty, 72% hold PhDs, 10% are members of minority groups, 44% are women. 0% of classes are taught by teaching assistants.

ACADEMICS

Degrees: bachelor's, master's, post-bachelor's certificate, post-master's certificate. **Classes:** Most classes have 10–19 students. Most lab/discussion sessions have 10–19 students. **Majors with Highest Enrollment:** business administration and management; psychology; special education and teaching. **Special Study Options:** distance learning, double major, honors program, independent study, internships, liberal arts/career combination, student-designed major, study abroad, teacher certification program. **Disability Services:** Special programs offered to physically disabled students include reader services, tape recorders, tutors. **Career Services:** Alumni network, career/job search classes, career assessment, internships, regional alumni.

FACILITIES

Housing: men's dorms, women's dorms, apartments for married students, apartments for single students. 50% of campus accessible to physically disabled. **Computers:** 100% of classrooms, 100% of dorms, 100% of libraries, 100% of dining areas, 100% of student union, 100% of common outdoor areas have wireless network access. Students can register for classes online. Administrative functions (other than registration) can be performed online.

CAMPUS LIFE

Environment: Rural. **Activities:** Choral groups, drama/theater, literary magazine, pep band, student government, television station, yearbook 23 registered organizations, 2 honor societies, 2 religious organizations. **Athletics (Intercollegiate):** *Men:* baseball, basketball, bowling, cheerleading, cross-country, cycling, football, golf, soccer, swimming, tennis, track/field (outdoor). *Women:* basketball, bowling, cheerleading, cross-country, cycling, golf, soccer, softball, swimming, tennis, track/field (outdoor), volleyball. **On-Campus Highlights:** Student Center, Sharp Center Coffee Shop, Fitness Center

ADMISSIONS

Freshman Academic Profile: Average high school GPA 2.9. SAT Math middle 50% range 438-508. SAT Critical Reading middle 50% range 415-455. ACT middle 50% range 17-21. Minimum paper TOEFL 550. **Basis for Candidate Selection:** *Important factors considered include:* Class rank, academic GPA, rigor of secondary school record, standardized test scores, level of applicant's interest. *Other factors considered include:* recommendation(s), alumni/ae relation, character/personal qualities, extracurricular activities, first generation, geographical residence, talent/ability, volunteer work. **Freshman Admission Requirements:** High school diploma is required and GED is accepted. **Freshman Admission Statistics:** 1,226 applied, 28% admitted, 55% enrolled. **Transfer Admission Requirements:** college transcript(s), minimum college GPA of 2.0 required. Lowest grade transferable 2. **General Admission Information:** Application Fee $10. Nonfall registration accepted.

COSTS AND FINANCIAL AID

Annual tuition $18,244. Room and board $5,950. Required fees $605. Average book expense $1,400. **Required Forms and Deadlines:** FAFSA. **Notification of Awards:** Applicants will be notified of awards on a rolling basis beginning 3/1. **Types of Aid:** *Need-based scholarships/grants:* Federal Pell, SEOG, state scholarships/grants, private scholarships, the school's own gift aid. *Loans:* Subsidized Stafford, Unsubsidized Stafford, PLUS, college/university loans from institutional funds. **Student Employment:** Federal Work-Study Program available. Institutional employment available. Off-campus job opportunities are fair. **Financial Aid Statistics:** 93% freshmen, 96% undergrads receive need-based scholarship or grant aid. 11% freshmen, 12% undergrads receive non-need-based scholarship or grant aid. 93% freshmen, 90% undergrads receive need-based self-help aid. 73% undergrads borrow to pay for school. Average cumulative indebtedness $22,388. **Criteria for awarding institutional aid:** *Non-need-based:* academics, athletics, job skills, religious affiliation, state/district residency.

UNION INSTITUTE & UNIVERSITY

440 East McMillan Street, Cincinnati, OH 45206
Phone: 513-861-6400 • **Financial Aid Phone:** 800-486-3116
E-mail: admissions@myunion.edu
Fax: 513-861-3238 • **Website:** www.myunion.edu

This private school was founded in 1964.

RATINGS

Admissions Selectivity Rating: 61   **Fire Safety Rating:** 60*   **Green Rating:** 61

STUDENTS AND FACULTY

Enrollment: 1,101. **Student Body:** 53% female, 47% male, 16% out-of-state, 0% international (24 countries represented). Asian 1%, African American 27%, Caucasian 35%, Hispanic 14%, Native American 1%.
Retention and Graduation: 90% freshmen return for sophomore year. 9% freshmen graduate within 4 years. 9% freshmen graduate within 6 years. **Faculty:** Student/faculty ratio 9:1. 31 full-time faculty, 84% hold PhDs, 19% are members of minority groups, 52% are women. 0% of classes are taught by teaching assistants.

ACADEMICS

Degrees: bachelor's, doctoral, master's, post-bachelor's certificate, post-master's certificate. **Majors with Highest Enrollment:** child development; criminal justice/law enforcement administration; liberal arts and sciences studies and humanities, other. **Special Study Options:** cross-registration, distance learning, external degree program, independent study, internships, teacher certification program. **Career Services:** alumni services, career assessment.

FACILITIES

Housing: Housing (not university-owned) available for learners participating in brief on-campus residencies at Montpelier, Vermont center (applicable to BA and MEd programs only). 100% of campus accessible to physically disabled. **Computers:** Students can register for classes online. Administrative functions (other than registration) can be performed online.

CAMPUS LIFE

Environment: Metropolis.

ADMISSIONS

Basis for Candidate Selection: *Very important factors considered include:* application essay, recommendation(s), interview. *Important factors considered include:* level of applicant's interest. *Other factors considered include:* character/personal qualities, extracurricular activities, talent/ability, volunteer work, work experience. **Freshman Admission Requirements:** High school diploma is required and GED is accepted. **Transfer Admission Requirements:** college transcript(s), essay or personal statement, interview. Lowest grade transferable D. **General Admission Information:** Application Fee $35. Nonfall registration accepted. Admission may be deferred for a maximum of 12 months. Credit offered for CEEB Advanced Placement tests.

COSTS AND FINANCIAL AID

Required Forms and Deadlines: FAFSA, institution's own financial aid form F. **Notification of Awards:** Applicants will be notified of awards on a rolling basis beginning 5/1. **Types of Aid:** *Need-based scholarships/grants:* Federal Pell, SEOG, state scholarships/grants, private scholarships, the school's own gift aid. *Loans:* Subsidized Stafford, Unsubsidized Stafford, PLUS, Federal Perkins. **Student Employment:** Federal Work-Study Program available. Off-campus job opportunities are good. **Criteria for awarding institutional aid:** *Non-need-based:* academics, state/district residency.

UNION UNIVERSITY

1050 Union University Drive, Jackson, TN 38305-3697
Phone: 731-661-5000 • **Financial Aid Phone:** 731-661-5015
E-mail: rgrimm@uu.edu • **CEEB Code:** 1826
Fax: 731-661-5017 • **Website:** • **ACT Code:** 4020

This private school, affiliated with the Southern Baptist Church, was founded in 1823. It has a 360-acre campus.

RATINGS

Admissions Selectivity Rating: 79   **Fire Safety Rating:** 76   **Green Rating:** 71

STUDENTS AND FACULTY

Enrollment: 2,520. **Student Body:** 61% female, 39% male, 32% out-of-state, 2% international (36 countries represented). Asian 1%, African American 16%, Caucasian 84%, Hispanic 2%, Native American 0%.
Retention and Graduation: 92% freshmen return for sophomore year. 50% freshmen graduate within 4 years. 40% grads go on to further study within 1 year. **Faculty:** Student/faculty ratio 11:1. 242 full-time faculty, 79% hold PhDs, 9% are members of minority groups, 48% are women. 0% of classes are taught by teaching assistants.

ACADEMICS

Degrees: associate, bachelor's, diploma, doctoral, master's, post-master's certificate, transfer associate. **Classes:** Most classes have 10–19 students. Most lab/discussion sessions have 10–19 students. **Majors with Highest Enrollment:** christian studies; elementary education and teaching; nursing/registered nurse (rn, asn, bsn, msn). **Special Study Options:** Accelerated program, cross-registration, distance learning, double major, dual enrollment, English as a Second Language (ESL), exchange student program (domestic), honors program, independent study, internships, study abroad, teacher certification program. **Disability Services:** Special programs offered to physically disabled students include note-taking services, reader services, tape recorders, tutors. **Career Services:** Alumni network, alumni services, career/job search classes, career assessment, internships, regional alumni. Career Services highlights include Our department is proudest of the career development and recruitment opportunities that are discpline-specific (What Can I Do With a Major In.? workshops) and recruitment-specific (College to Career, professional development and prep; Career "U"niversity, internship opportunities; the Job Market, career recruitment, and Teacher Expo, education recruitment).

FACILITIES

Housing: special housing for disabled students, men's dorms, women's dorms, apartments for married students. 98% of campus accessible to physically disabled. **Special Academic Facilities/Equipment:** Elementary education lab, 21st-century classroom, TV communications truck, nursing/health assessment labs, health and wellness center, art gallery. **Computers:** 75% of classrooms, 100% of dorms, 100% of libraries, 50% of dining areas, 100% of student union, have wireless network access. Administrative functions (other than registration) can be performed online.

CAMPUS LIFE

Environment: City. **Activities:** Choral groups, concert band, drama/theater, jazz band, literary magazine, music ensembles, pep band, student government, student newspaper, student-run film society, yearbook, Campus Ministries, International Student Organization 67 registered organizations, 12 honor societies, 4 religious organizations. 3 fraternities, 3 sororities. **Athletics (Intercollegiate):** *Men:* baseball, basketball, cheerleading, cross-country, golf, soccer. *Women:* basketball, cheerleading, cross-country, soccer, softball, volleyball. **On-Campus Highlights:** Bowld Commons, New Residence Life Complexes, Pharmacy Building, White Hall, Jennings Hall, Athletic Facility, Penick Academic Complex, Barefoot's Joe Coffee Shop. **Environmental Initiatives:** Campus-wide recycling campaign for aluminum, plastics (#1 and #2) and paper. This includes pick up from all student residential areas as well as all buildings/offices. Particpation in recyclemania.org; organizing new student sustainability organization to help with consistent and active marketing of the program. Working towards energy efficiency in all new buildings/appliances; implemented new composting initiative.

ADMISSIONS

Freshman Academic Profile: Average high school GPA 3.7. 41% in top 10% of high school class, 67% in top 25% of high school class, 87% in top 50% of high school class. 59% from public high schools. SAT Math middle 50% range 520-670. SAT Critical Reading middle 50% range 510-690. ACT middle 50% range 22-29. Minimum web-based TOEFL 80. Minimum paper TOEFL 550. **Basis for Candidate Selection:** *Very important factors considered include:* academic GPA, rigor of secondary school record, character/personal qualities, level of applicant's interest. *Important factors considered include:* Class rank, standardized test scores, extracurricular activities, interview, religious affiliation/commitment, talent/ability. *Other factors considered include:* application essay, recommendation(s), alumni/ae relation, first generation, volunteer work, work experience. **Freshman Admission Requirements:** High school diploma is required and GED is accepted. *Academic units required:* 4 English, 3 mathematics, 3 science, (2 science labs), 1 foreign language, 2 social studies, 1 history, 1 academic electives. *Academic units recommended:* 4 English, 3 mathematics, 3 science, (2 science labs), 1 foreign language, 2 social studies, 1 history, 1 academic electives. **Freshman Admission Statistics:** 2,051 applied, 75% admitted, 31% enrolled. **Transfer Admission Requirements:** college transcript(s), statement of good standing from prior institution(s). Minimum college GPA of 2.3 required. Lowest grade transferable C. **General Admission Information:** Application Fee $35. Regular application deadline 8/1. Notification on a rolling basis, beginning on or about 10/1. Nonfall registration accepted. Admission may be deferred for a maximum of 1 year. Credit offered for CEEB Advanced Placement tests.

COSTS AND FINANCIAL AID

Annual tuition $24,940. Room and board $8,430. Required fees $710. Average book expense $1,200. **Required Forms and Deadlines:** FAFSA, institution's own financial aid form. **Notification of Awards:** Applicants will be notified of awards on a rolling basis beginning 12/1. **Types of Aid:** *Need-based scholarships/grants:* Federal Pell, SEOG, state scholarships/grants, private scholarships, the school's own gift aid. *Loans:* Direct Subsidized Stafford, Direct Unsubsidized Stafford, Direct PLUS, Federal Perkins, Alternative Loans. **Student Employment:** Federal Work-Study Program available. Institutional employment available. Highest amount earned per year from on-campus jobs $1,500. Off-campus job opportunities are excellent. **Financial Aid Statistics:** 71% freshmen, 69% undergrads receive need-based scholarship or grant aid. 100% freshmen, 77% undergrads receive non-need-based scholarship or grant aid. 54% freshmen, 68% undergrads receive need-based self-help aid. 11% freshmen, 8% undergrads receive athletic scholarships. 94% freshmen, 84% undergrads receive any aid. 61% undergrads borrow to pay for school. Average cumulative indebtedness $26,936. **Criteria for awarding institutional aid:** *Non-need-based:* academics, alumni affiliation, art, athletics, leadership, minority status, music/drama, religious affiliation.

UNITED STATES AIR FORCE ACADEMY

Best 378

HQ USAFA/ RRS, USAF Academy, CO 80840-5025
Phone: 719-333-2520
E-mail: rr_webmail@usafa.edu
Fax: 719-333-3012 • **Website:** www.academyadmissions.com • **ACT Code:** 530

This public school was founded in 1954. It has a 18000-acre campus.

RATINGS

Admissions Selectivity Rating: 98   **Fire Safety Rating:** 89   **Green Rating:** 66

STUDENTS AND FACULTY

Enrollment: 4,120. **Student Body:** 22% female, 78% male, 92% out-of-state, 1% international (38 countries represented). Asian 7%, African American 7%, Caucasian 65%, Hispanic 9%, Native American 1%.
Retention and Graduation: 93% freshmen return for sophomore year. 78% freshmen graduate within 4 years. 80% freshmen graduate within 6 years. 9% grads go on to further study within 1 year. 7% grads pursue arts and sciences degrees. 1% grads pursue medical degrees. **Faculty:** Student/faculty ratio 8:1. 516 full-time faculty, 55% hold PhDs, 14% are members of minority groups, 20% are women. 0% of classes are taught by teaching assistants.

ACADEMICS

Degrees: bachelor's. **Classes:** Most classes have 10–19 students. Most lab/discussion sessions have 10–19 students. **Majors with Highest Enrollment:** aerospace, aeronautical and astronautical engineering; business/commerce; social sciences. **Special Study Options:** double major, English as a Second Language (ESL), exchange student program (domestic), honors program, independent study, internships, student-designed major, study abroad, Academically At-Risk Program Hospital Instruction Program Extra Instruction Program Summer Programs.

FACILITIES

Housing: Coed dormsAll students are required to live on campus all four years. **Special Academic Facilities/Equipment:** Language learning center, laser and optics research center, USAFA observatory, Dept. of Engineering Mechanics Lab, US Air Force Academy visitor's center, consolidated educational training facility, Air Force Academy cadet chapel, American Legion Memorial Tower, Clune area athletic and speaking events (seats 6,000), air garden, Falcon Stadium, Aeronautics Lab, Meterology Lab, Arnold Hall Broadway Theater, ballroom and conference rooms, and historical displays. **Computers:** 100% of classrooms, 100% of libraries, 100% of student union, have wireless network access. Students can register for classes online. Administrative functions (other than registration) can be performed online. Undergraduates are required to own a computer.

CAMPUS LIFE

Environment: Metropolis. **Activities:** Choral groups, dance, drama/theater, marching band, musical theater, pep band, radio station, yearbook, Campus Ministries, Model UN 77 registered organizations, 2 honor societies, 14 religious organizations. **Athletics (Intercollegiate):** *Men:* baseball, basketball, boxing, cheerleading, cross-country, diving, fencing, football, golf, gymnastics, ice hockey, lacrosse, riflery, soccer, swimming, tennis, track/field (outdoor), track/field (indoor), water polo, wrestling. *Women:* basketball, cheerleading, cross-country, diving, fencing, gymnastics, riflery, soccer, swimming, tennis, track/field (outdoor), track/field (indoor), volleyball. **On-Campus Highlights:** USAF Academy Chapel, Thunderbird Lookout and Air Field, Falcon Stadium, Cadet Sports Complex, Visitor Center. **Environmental Initiatives:** Solar Hydro Geo Thermal (Ground-Source Heat Pumps)

ADMISSIONS

Freshman Academic Profile: 62% in top 10% of high school class, 88% in top 25% of high school class, 97% in top 50% of high school class. SAT Math middle 50% range 630-720. SAT Critical Reading middle 50% range 600-690. ACT middle 50% range 29-32. **Basis for Candidate Selection:** *Very important factors considered include:* Class rank, application essay, academic GPA, recommendation(s), rigor of secondary school record, standardized test scores, character/personal qualities, interview. *Important factors considered include:* extracurricular activities, talent/ability, volunteer work, work experience. *Other factors considered include:* alumni/ae relation, first generation, geographical residence, racial/ethnic status, state residency. **Freshman Admission Requirements:** High school diploma is required and GED is accepted. **Freshman Admission Statistics:** 12,274 applied, 10% admitted, 84% enrolled. **Transfer Admission Requirements:** High school transcript, college transcript(s), essay or personal statement, interview, standardized test scores, minimum college GPA of 2.0 required. **General Admission Information:** Regular application deadline 2/15. Notification on a rolling basis, beginning on or about 11/15. Nonfall registration not accepted. Credit and/or placement offered for CEEB Advanced Placement tests.

COSTS AND FINANCIAL AID

Room and board $0. Average book expense $0. **Financial Aid Statistics:** 0% undergrads borrow to pay for school. Average cumulative indebtedness $0.

See page 1240.

UNITED STATES COAST GUARD ACADEMY

31 Mohegan Avenue, New London, CT 06320-8103
Phone: 860-444-8503 • **Financial Aid Phone:** 860-444-8309
E-mail: USCGA.Admissions@uscga.edu • **CEEB Code:** 5807
Fax: 860-701-6700 • **Website:** www.uscga.edu • **ACT Code:** 600

This public school was founded in 1876. It has a 120-acre campus.

RATINGS
Admissions Selectivity Rating: 96   **Fire Safety Rating:** 85   **Green Rating:** 77

STUDENTS AND FACULTY
Enrollment: 967. **Student Body:** 32% female, 68% male, 95% out-of-state, 2% international (15 countries represented). Asian 4%, African American 3%, Caucasian 71%, Hispanic 12%, Native American 1%. **Retention and Graduation:** 94% freshmen return for sophomore year. 83% freshmen graduate within 4 years. **Faculty:** Student/faculty ratio 8:1. 122 full-time faculty, 52% hold PhDs, 16% are members of minority groups, 34% are women. 0% of classes are taught by teaching assistants.

ACADEMICS
Degrees: bachelor's. **Classes:** Most classes have 10–19 students. Most lab/discussion sessions have fewer than 10 students. **Majors with Highest Enrollment:** business administration and management; civil engineering; political science and government. **Special Study Options:** double major, exchange student program (domestic), honors program, independent study, internships. **Career Services:** Alumni network, career assessment, regional alumni., Career Services highlights include All graduates are "employed" and assigned to operational field units upon graduation.

FACILITIES
Housing: Coed dorms 95% of campus accessible to physically disabled. **Special Academic Facilities/Equipment:** CG Museum; Library; Visitors Center; Alumni Center **Computers:** 100% of classrooms, 65% of dorms, 100% of libraries, 50% of dining areas, 100% of student union, 50% of common outdoor areas have wireless network access. Students can register for classes online.

Administrative functions (other than registration) can be performed online. Undergraduates are required to own a computer.

CAMPUS LIFE
Environment: City. **Activities:** Choral groups, concert band, dance, drama/theater, jazz band, marching band, pep band, yearbook, Campus Ministries 2 honor societies, 7 religious organizations. **Athletics (Intercollegiate):** *Men:* baseball, basketball, crew/rowing, cross-country, diving, football, pistol, riflery, sailing, soccer, swimming, tennis, track/field (outdoor), track/field (indoor), wrestling. *Women:* basketball, cheerleading, crew/rowing, cross-country, diving, pistol, riflery, sailing, soccer, softball, swimming, track/field (outdoor), track/field (indoor), volleyball. **On-Campus Highlights:** Coast Guard Barque EAGLE, Coast Guard Museum, Sailing Center and Waterfront, Souvenier Shop (Military Exchange), Coast Guard Academy Chapel and Crown Park. **Environmental Initiatives:** Federal Electronic Recycling Challenge Participant and winner 2008 and 2009. Recyclemania http://www.campusdish.com/en-US/csne/uscga/ Sustainability Federal electronics challenge facility partner 2009 and 2010.

ADMISSIONS
Freshman Academic Profile: Average high school GPA 3.8. 45% in top 10% of high school class, 83% in top 25% of high school class, 98% in top 50% of high school class. 81% from public high schools. SAT Math middle 50% range 610-680. SAT Critical Reading middle 50% range 550-640. SAT Writing middle 50% range 530-640. ACT middle 50% range 25-29. Minimum paper TOEFL 560. **Basis for Candidate Selection:** *Very important factors considered include:* Class rank, academic GPA, rigor of secondary school record, standardized test scores, character/personal qualities, extracurricular activities. *Important factors considered include:* application essay, recommendation(s), talent/ability. *Other factors considered include:* alumni/ae relation, interview, level of applicant's interest, volunteer work, work experience. **Freshman Admission Requirements:** High school diploma is required and GED is accepted. *Academic units required:* 4 English, 4 mathematics, 3 science, (3 science labs). 4 English, 4 mathematics, 3 science, (3 science labs). **Freshman Admission Statistics:** 1,982 applied, 16% admitted, 71% enrolled. **Transfer Admission Requirements:** High school transcript, essay or personal statement, standardized test scores, statement of good standing from prior institution(s). **General Admission Information:** Regular application deadline 2/1. Notification on a rolling basis, beginning on or about 12/15. Nonfall registration not accepted. Placement offered for CEEB Advanced Placement tests.

COSTS AND FINANCIAL AID
Room and board $0. Average book expense $0. **Financial Aid Statistics:** 0% freshmen, 0% undergrads receive any aid.

UNITED STATES MERCHANT MARINE ACADEMY

Office of Admissions, Kings Point, NY 11024-1699
Phone: 516-773-5391 • **Financial Aid Phone:** 516-773-5295
E-mail: admissions@usmma.edu • **CEEB Code:** 2923
Fax: 516-773-5390 • **Website:** www.usmma.edu • **ACT Code:** 2974

This public school was founded in 1943. It has a 82-acre campus.

RATINGS
Admissions Selectivity Rating: 97   **Fire Safety Rating:** 60*   **Green Rating:** 60*

STUDENTS AND FACULTY
Enrollment: 1,058. **Student Body:** (4 countries represented). **Retention and Graduation:** 92% freshmen return for sophomore year. **Faculty:** 88 full-time faculty.

ACADEMICS
Degrees: bachelor's, master's. **Classes:** Most classes have 10–19 students. Most lab/discussion sessions have 10–19 students. **Majors with Highest Enrollment:** engineering; naval architecture and marine engineering; transportation and materials moving, other. **Special Study Options:** honors program, independent study, internships. **Career Services:** Alumni network, alumni services, career/job search classes, career assessment, internships.

FACILITIES
Housing: Coed dorms. All students required to live on campus in dormitories provided. **Special Academic Facilities/Equipment:** American Merchant Ma-

rine Museum **Computers:** Students can register for classes online. Administrative functions (other than registration) can be performed online. Undergraduates are required to own a computer.

CAMPUS LIFE
Environment: Village. **Activities:** Choral groups, concert band, drama/theater, marching band, student government, student newspaper, yearbook, Campus Ministries 3 religious organizations. **Athletics (Intercollegiate):** *Men:* baseball, basketball, crew/rowing, cross-country, diving, football, golf, lacrosse, riflery, sailing, soccer, swimming, tennis, track/field (outdoor), volleyball, water polo, wrestling. *Women:* basketball, crew/rowing, cross-country, diving, golf, riflery, sailing, softball, swimming, tennis, track/field (outdoor), volleyball.

ADMISSIONS
Freshman Academic Profile: Average high school GPA 3.6. 24% in top 10% of high school class, 62% in top 25% of high school class, 92% in top 50% of high school class. 75% from public high schools. SAT Math middle 50% range 600-680. SAT Critical Reading middle 50% range 555-635. ACT middle 50% range 25-29. Minimum web-based TOEFL 73. Minimum paper TOEFL 533. **Basis for Candidate Selection:** *Very important factors considered include:* rigor of secondary school record, standardized test scores, character/personal qualities. *Important factors considered include:* Class rank, application essay, academic GPA, recommendation(s), extracurricular activities, level of applicant's interest, talent/ability. *Other factors considered include:* geographical residence, interview, racial/ethnic status, state residency, volunteer work, work experience. **Freshman Admission Requirements:** High school diploma is required and GED is accepted. *Academic units required:* 4 English, 3 mathematics, 3 science, (1 science labs), 8 academic electives. *Academic units recommended:* 4 English, 3 mathematics, 3 science, (1 science labs), 8 academic electives. **Freshman Admission Statistics:** 2,076 applied, 20% admitted, 69% enrolled. **Transfer Admission Requirements:** High school transcript, college transcript(s), essay or personal statement, standardized test scores, statement of good standing from prior institution(s). Minimum college GPA of 2.5 required. **General Admission Information:** Regular application deadline 3/1. Notification on a rolling basis, beginning on or about 11/1. Nonfall registration not accepted. Credit offered for CEEB Advanced Placement tests.

COSTS AND FINANCIAL AID
Required fees $882. Average book expense $767. **Required Forms and Deadlines:** FAFSA, institution's own financial aid form. **Notification of Awards:** Applicants will be notified of awards on a rolling basis beginning 1/31. **Types of Aid:** *Need-based scholarships/grants:* Federal Pell, private scholarships, Federal SMART Grants & Federal Academic Competitiveness Grants. *Loans:* Direct PLUS, Subsidized Stafford, Unsubsidized Stafford, PLUS. **Student Employment:** Off-campus job opportunities are poor.

UNITED STATES MILITARY ACADEMY (WEST POINT)

Best 378

646 Swift Road, West Point, NY 10996-1905
Phone: 845-938-4041
E-mail: admissions@usma.edu • **CEEB Code:** 2924
Fax: 845-938-3021 • **Website:** www.westpoint.edu • **ACT Code:** 2976

This public school was founded in 1802. It has a 16080-acre campus.

RATINGS
Admissions Selectivity Rating: 98   **Fire Safety Rating:** 81   **Green Rating:** 73

STUDENTS AND FACULTY
Enrollment: 4,592. **Student Body:** 93% out-of-state, 1% international (35 countries represented). Asian 5%, African American 7%, Caucasian 71%, Hispanic 9%, Native American 1%.
Retention and Graduation: 96% freshmen return for sophomore year. 78% freshmen graduate within 4 years. 36% grads go on to further study within 1 year. 1% grads pursue arts and sciences degrees. 2% grads pursue medical degrees. **Faculty:** Student/faculty ratio 7:1. 617 full-time faculty, 45% hold PhDs, 10% are members of minority groups, 18% are women. 0% of classes are taught by teaching assistants.

ACADEMICS
Degrees: bachelor's. **Classes:** Most classes have 10–19 students. Most lab/discussion sessions have 10–19 students. **Majors with Highest Enrollment:**

business administration and management; economics; engineering/industrial management. **Special Study Options:** double major, exchange student program (domestic), honors program, independent study, internships, study abroad, Opportunities to attend Army Schools (Airborne, Air Assault, etc.) to learn special skills.

FACILITIES
Housing: Coed dorms, Coed dorms are called barracks. **Special Academic Facilities/Equipment:** West Point Museum.(oldest of U.S. army museums. The athletic facilities rate as highly as the academic plant. Arvin gymnasium, featuring swimming pools, wrestling, squash, racquetball, handball, and volleyball courts has undergone a major renovation to modernize and improve its contribution to the physical development of the corps of cadets. Michie Stadium, home of the Army football team, is considered one of America's most picturesque stadiums to watch a college football game. Holleder Center houses Tate Rink for the Army hockey team and Christl Arena is the home of the Army men and women's basketball teams. Additionally, the Shea Stadium outdoor track facility and Gillis Field House indoor practice facility are newly renovated to include an all-weather track, an astroturf football field and new lighting. There is also a redesigned 18-hole golf course and a new indoor tennis facility. Eisenhower Hall, the modern "student union," contains a 4,500- seat auditorium, a 1,000-seat snack bar and cafeteria, a large ballroom, and other social and recreational rooms. About 60 major productions, to include Broadway shows, musicals, popular rock, jazz, country/western, and alternative music concerts are staged annually in the theater. The new cadet library, Jefferson Hall opened this year. **Computers:** 100% of classrooms, 100% of libraries, 100% of student union, have wireless network access. Students can register for classes online. Administrative functions (other than registration) can be performed online. Undergraduates are required to own a computer.

CAMPUS LIFE
Environment: Village. **Activities:** Choral groups, drama/theater, jazz band, music ensembles, pep band, radio station, student government, student newspaper, television station, yearbook, Campus Ministries, International Student Organization, Model UN 105 registered organizations, 7 honor societies, 13 religious organizations. **Athletics (Intercollegiate):** *Men:* baseball, basketball, cross-country, football, golf, gymnastics, ice hockey, lacrosse, riflery, soccer, swimming, tennis, track/field (outdoor), track/field (indoor), wrestling. *Women:* basketball, cross-country, riflery, soccer, softball, swimming, tennis, track/field (outdoor), track/field (indoor), volleyball. **On-Campus Highlights:** Cadet Chapel, West Point Museum, Eisenhower Hall, Michie Stadium, Trophy Point, Fort Putnam, West Point Cemetery. **Environmental Initiatives:** West Point was selected as an Army Garrison net zero energy pilot program with a target date of 2020. Achieve net zero energy consumption for buildings within the U.S. Military Academy by 2020. The West Point Forest provides opportunities for sequestering large amounts of carbon. West Point is exploring projects to maximize long term carbon storage in the forest soils. West Point is investigating novel approaches to minimizing the carbon foot print of its wastewater treatment system. One approach focuses on extracting energy from wastewater solids. Another approach focuses on extracting energy from separated urine.

ADMISSIONS
Freshman Academic Profile: 50% in top 10% of high school class, 76% in top 25% of high school class, 95% in top 50% of high school class. 73% from public high schools. SAT Math middle 50% range 600-690. SAT Critical Reading middle 50% range 570-680. SAT Writing middle 50% range 550-660. ACT middle 50% range 26-31. Minimum web-based TOEFL 75. Minimum paper TOEFL 500. **Basis for Candidate Selection:** *Very important factors considered include:* Class rank, application essay, academic GPA, recommendation(s), rigor of secondary school record, standardized test scores, character/personal qualities, extracurricular activities, talent/ability. *Important factors considered include:* geographical residence, interview, level of applicant's interest, racial/ethnic status, volunteer work. *Other factors considered include:* alumni/ae relation, state residency, work experience. **Freshman Admission Requirements:** High school diploma is required and GED is accepted. **Freshman Admission Statistics:** 15,171 applied, 9% admitted, 86% enrolled. **General Admission Information:** Regular application deadline 2/28. Notification on a rolling basis, beginning on or about 11/15. Nonfall registration not accepted. Placement offered for CEEB Advanced Placement tests.

COSTS AND FINANCIAL AID
Average book expense $0. **Types of Aid:** *Need-based scholarships/grants:* All students receive an annual salary of approximately $10,148. Room and board, medical and dental care is provided by the institution. A one-time deposit of $2,900 is required upon admission to pay for the initial issue of uniforms, books, supplies, equipment and fees. If needed, loans for the deposit are available for $100 to $2,400. *Loans:* All students receive an annual salary of approximately $10,148. Room and board, medical and dental care is provided by the institution. A one-time deposit of $2,900 is required upon admission to pay for the initial issue of uniforms, books, supplies, equipment and fees. If needed, loans for the deposit are available for $100 to $2,400.

UNITED STATES NAVAL ACADEMY

117 Decatur Road, Annapolis, MD 21402
Phone: 410-293-4361
E-mail: webmail@usna.edu • **CEEB Code:** 5809
Fax: 410-293-1815 • **Website:** www.usna.edu • **ACT Code:** 1742

This public school was founded in 1845. It has a 330-acre campus.

RATINGS
Admissions Selectivity Rating: 98   **Fire Safety Rating:** 68   **Green Rating:** 60*

STUDENTS AND FACULTY
Enrollment: 4,536. **Student Body:** 21% female, 79% male, 93% out-of-state, 1% international (31 countries represented). Asian 5%, African American 7%, Caucasian 65%, Hispanic 12%, Native American 0%.
Retention and Graduation: 89% freshmen graduate within 4 years. 90% freshmen graduate within 6 years. 6% grads go on to further study within 1 year. 1% grads pursue medical degrees. **Faculty:** Student/faculty ratio 9:1. 478 full-time faculty, 70% hold PhDs, 11% are members of minority groups, 26% are women. 0% of classes are taught by teaching assistants.

ACADEMICS
Degrees: bachelor's. **Classes:** Most classes have 10–19 students. **Majors with Highest Enrollment:** economics; political science and government; systems engineering. **Special Study Options:** double major, exchange student program (domestic), honors program, independent study, Voluntary Graduate Education Program. **Honors Programs:** Voluntary Graduate Education Program - second semester seniors may enroll in graduate school at a nearby college or university. Career Services highlights include The United States Navy and the United States Marine Corps hire all our graduates.

FACILITIES
Housing: Coed dormsNo options. All midshipmen live in same dormitory. **Special Academic Facilities/Equipment:** Naval history museum, Naval Institute Proceedings, propulsion lab, wind tunnels, flight simulator, ship tow tanks, satellite dish, coastal chamber facilities, fleet of small training craft (power and sail), oceanographic research vessel. **Computers:** Students can register for classes online. Administrative functions (other than registration) can be performed online. Undergraduates are required to own a computer.

CAMPUS LIFE
Environment: Town. **Activities:** Choral groups, concert band, drama/theater, jazz band, literary magazine, marching band, musical theater, pep band, radio station, student government, yearbook, Campus Ministries, International Student Organization 70 registered organizations, 10 honor societies, 8 religious organizations. **Athletics (Intercollegiate):** *Men:* baseball, basketball, crew/rowing, cross-country, diving, football, golf, gymnastics, lacrosse, light weight football, riflery, sailing, soccer, squash, swimming, tennis, track/field (outdoor), track/field (indoor), water polo, wrestling. *Women:* basketball, crew/rowing, cross-country, diving, lacrosse, riflery, sailing, soccer, swimming, tennis, track/field (outdoor), track/field (indoor), volleyball. **On-Campus Highlights:** Bancroft Hall, U.S. Naval Academy Museum, Armel-Leftwich Visitor Center, U.S. Naval Academy Chapel, Lejeune Hall.

ADMISSIONS
Freshman Academic Profile: 53% in top 10% of high school class, 80% in top 25% of high school class, 94% in top 50% of high school class. 60% from public high schools. SAT Math middle 50% range 600-700. SAT Critical Reading middle 50% range 560-670. **Basis for Candidate Selection:** *Very important factors considered include:* Class rank, application essay, academic GPA, recommendation(s), rigor of secondary school record, character/personal qualities, extracurricular activities, interview, level of applicant's interest. *Important factors considered include:* standardized test scores, talent/ability. *Other factors considered include:* alumni/ae relation, first generation, geographical residence, racial/ethnic status, state residency, volunteer work, work experience. **Freshman Admission Requirements:** High school diploma or equivalent is not required. **Freshman Admission Statistics:** 20,601 applied, 7% admitted, 87% enrolled. **General Admission Information:** Regular application deadline 1/31. Regular notification 4/15. Notification on a rolling basis, beginning on or about 9/1. Nonfall registration not accepted. Credit and/or placement offered for CEEB Advanced Placement tests.

COSTS AND FINANCIAL AID
Average book expense $0. **Financial Aid Statistics:** 0% freshmen, 0% undergrads receive any aid. 0% undergrads borrow to pay for school. Average cumulative indebtedness $0.

UNITY COLLEGE

PO Box 532, Unity, ME 4988
Phone: 800-624-1024 • **Financial Aid Phone:** 207-948-3131 ext 235
E-mail: admissions@unity.edu • **CEEB Code:** 6858
Fax: 207-948-9776 • **Website:** www.unity.edu • **ACT Code:** 3925

This is a private school.

RATINGS
Admissions Selectivity Rating: 78   **Fire Safety Rating:** 89   **Green Rating:** 93

STUDENTS AND FACULTY
Enrollment: 574. **Student Body:** 55% female, 45% male, 75% out-of-state, 0% international. Asian 1%, African American 1%, Caucasian 93%, Hispanic 2%, Native American 2%.
Retention and Graduation: 83% freshmen return for sophomore year. 37% freshmen graduate within 4 years. 46% freshmen graduate within 6 years. 24% grads go on to further study within 1 year. 22% grads pursue arts and sciences degrees. 1% grads pursue law degrees. **Faculty:** Student/faculty ratio 12:1. 37 full-time faculty, 89% hold PhDs, 0% are members of minority groups, 54% are women.

ACADEMICS
Degrees: associate, bachelor's.

CAMPUS LIFE
Environmental Initiatives: We only offer environmental degree programs and every student studies sustainability through our Environmental Stewardship Core curriculum. Campus sustainability efforts are an outgrowth of our academic focus. Charter signatory to the ACUPCC and active leaders in the higher education sustainability community. Unity's TerraHaus is the nation's first student residence built to strict Passive House energy performance standards. Our campus also boasts the net-zero energy, LEED Platinum president's home, Unity House.

ADMISSIONS
Freshman Academic Profile: Average high school GPA 3.3. 14% in top 10% of high school class, 33% in top 25% of high school class, 55% in top 50% of high school class. SAT Math middle 50% range 490-560. SAT Critical Reading middle 50% range 480-560. SAT Writing middle 50% range 450-520. ACT middle 50% range 22-25. Minimum paper TOEFL 550. **Freshman Admission Statistics:** 737 applied, 61% admitted, 38% enrolled. **General Admission Information:** Credit and/or placement offered for CEEB Advanced Placement tests.

COSTS AND FINANCIAL AID
Annual tuition $22,440. Room and board $8,380. Required fees $800. Average book expense $500. **Required Forms and Deadlines: Types of Aid:** *Need-based scholarships/grants: Loans:* **Student Employment: Financial Aid Statistics:** 100% freshmen, 100% undergrads receive need-based scholarship or grant aid. 8% freshmen, 3% undergrads receive non-need-based scholarship or grant aid. 91% freshmen, 95% undergrads receive need-based self-help aid. 98% freshmen, 98% undergrads receive any aid.

UNIVERSITÉ LAVAL—FACULTÉ DES SCIENCES DE L'ADMINISTRATION

2345 Allée des bibliothÃ¨ques, local 2440, Québec, Qc G1V 0A6
Phone: 418-656-3080 • **Financial Aid Phone:** 418-656-3332
E-mail: reg@reg.ulaval.ca
Fax: 1 418 656-5216 • **Website:** www.fsa.ulaval.ca

This public school was founded in 1924.

RATINGS
Admissions Selectivity Rating: 62   **Fire Safety Rating:** 60*   **Green Rating:** 73

STUDENTS AND FACULTY
Enrollment: 2,009. **Student Body:** 43% female, 57% male, 3% international. **Retention and Graduation:** 75% freshmen return for sophomore year. 65% freshmen graduate within 4 years. 68% freshmen graduate within 6 years.

ACADEMICS
Degrees: bachelor's, certificate, diploma, master's, post-bachelor's certificate. **Special Study Options:** cooperative education program, exchange student program (domestic), internships, student-designed major, study abroad. **Disability Services:** Special programs offered to physically disabled students include note-taking services, reader services, tape recorders. **Career Services:** Alumni network, alumni services, career/job search classes, internships.

FACILITIES
Housing: Coed dorms, men's dorms, women's dorms. 100% of campus accessible to physically disabled. **Computers:** 100% of classrooms, 100% of dorms, 100% of libraries, 100% of dining areas, 100% of student union, 100% of common outdoor areas have wireless network access. Students can register for classes online. Administrative functions (other than registration) can be performed online. Undergraduates are required to own a computer.

CAMPUS LIFE
Environment: Metropolis. **Activities:** Choral groups, concert band, dance, drama/theater, jazz band, literary magazine, music ensembles, radio station, student government, student newspaper, International Student Organization, Model UN 200 registered organizations. **Athletics (Intercollegiate):** *Men:* badminton, basketball, diving, golf, rugby, skiing (downhill/alpine), skiingnordiccross-country, soccer, swimming, track/field (outdoor), track/field (indoor), volleyball. *Women:* badminton, basketball, diving, golf, rugby, skiing (downhill/alpine), skiingnordiccross-country, soccer, swimming, track/field (outdoor), track/field (indoor), volleyball. **Environmental Initiatives:** Table de concertation sur le développement durabla See http://www.developpementdurable. ulaval.ca/agir/la_table_de_concertation_sur_le_developpement_durable/ Fonds de développement durable/Sustainable Developement: 2M$ in 5 years to support on-campus sustainable development projects. All other initiatives: http://www.developpementdurable.ulaval.ca/agir/

ADMISSIONS
Basis for Candidate Selection: *Very important factors considered include:* academic GPA, rigor of secondary school record. *Other factors considered include:* standardized test scores, extracurricular activities, work experience. **Freshman Admission Requirements:** High school diploma is required and GED is not accepted. **Freshman Admission Statistics:** 1,377 applied, 71% admitted, 57% enrolled. **General Admission Information:** Application Fee $30. Nonfall registration accepted.

COSTS AND FINANCIAL AID
Annual in-state tuition $2,500. Annual out-of-state tuition $5,956. Room and board $2,232. Average book expense $2,000. **Student Employment:** Off-campus job opportunities are good.

UNIVERSITY OF ADVANCING TECHNOLOGY (UAT)

2625 W. Baseline Rd., Tempe, AZ 85283-1056
Phone: 602-383-8228 • **Financial Aid Phone:** 602-383-8228
E-mail: admissions@uat.edu
Fax: 602-383-8222 • **Website:** www.uat.edu

This proprietary school was founded in 1983.

RATINGS
Admissions Selectivity Rating: 61   **Fire Safety Rating:** 60*   **Green Rating:** 60*

STUDENTS AND FACULTY
Enrollment: 1,090. **Student Body:** 6% out-of-state, 0% international. Asian 4%, African American 7%, Caucasian 61%, Hispanic 6%, Native American 1%. **Faculty:** Student/faculty ratio 12:1. 31 full-time faculty, 16% hold PhDs, 35% are women. 0% of classes are taught by teaching assistants.

ACADEMICS
Degrees: associate, bachelor's, diploma, master's. **Classes:** Most classes have 20–29 students. **Special Study Options:** Accelerated program, cooperative education program, distance learning, double major, independent study, internships, student-designed major. **Career Services:** Alumni network, alumni services, career/job search classes, career assessment, internships, regional alumni. Career Services highlights include UAT expends its resources on seeking out internship opportunities for all of our majors. For example, many of our game

design students are currently interns at Rainbow Studios, Buena Vista Games and many other prominent game development companies. Internships are also a graduation requirements for all UAT students.

FACILITIES
Housing: 100% of campus accessible to physically disabled. **Computers:** Administrative functions (other than registration) can be performed online.

CAMPUS LIFE
Environment: Metropolis. **Activities:** student government 1 religious organizations. **On-Campus Highlights:** Cuban Pete's Cafe, UAT Library, Computer Commons, Campus Game Stations

ADMISSIONS
Freshman Academic Profile: Minimum paper TOEFL 550. **Basis for Candidate Selection:** *Very important factors considered include:* character/personal qualities, interview, level of applicant's interest, talent/ability. *Important factors considered include:* rigor of secondary school record. *Other factors considered include:* academic GPA, standardized test scores, volunteer work. **Freshman Admission Requirements:** High school diploma is required and GED is accepted. **Transfer Admission Requirements:** High school transcript, college transcript(s), minimum college GPA of 2.0 required. Lowest grade transferable C. **General Admission Information:** Nonfall registration accepted. Admission may be deferred for a maximum of 1 year.

COSTS AND FINANCIAL AID
Annual tuition $19,400. Average book expense $1,000. **Required Forms and Deadlines:** FAFSA. **Types of Aid:** *Need-based scholarships/grants:* Federal Pell, SEOG, private scholarships, the school's own gift aid. *Loans:* Subsidized Stafford, Unsubsidized Stafford, PLUS. **Financial Aid Statistics:** 72% undergrads borrow to pay for school. Average cumulative indebtedness.

THE UNIVERSITY OF AKRON

The University of Akron, Akron, OH 44325-2001
Phone: 330-972-7100 • **Financial Aid Phone:** 800-621-3847
E-mail: admissions@uakron.edu • **CEEB Code:** 1829
Fax: 330-972-7022 • **Website:** www.uakron.edu • **ACT Code:** 3338

This public school was founded in 1870. It has a 223-acre campus.

RATINGS
Admissions Selectivity Rating: 60*   **Fire Safety Rating:** 60*   **Green Rating:** 60*

STUDENTS AND FACULTY
Enrollment: 21,445. **Student Body:** 48% female, 52% male, 3% out-of-state, 1% international (57 countries represented). Asian 2%, African American 17%, Caucasian 73%, Hispanic 2%, Native American 0%. **Retention and Graduation:** 71% freshmen return for sophomore year. **Faculty:** Student/faculty ratio 21:1. 781 full-time faculty, 80% hold PhDs, 18% are members of minority groups, 42% are women. 4% of classes are taught by teaching assistants.

ACADEMICS
Degrees: associate, bachelor's, certificate, doctoral, master's, post-bachelor's certificate, post-master's certificate. **Classes:** Most classes have 20–29 students. Most lab/discussion sessions have 10–19 students. **Majors with Highest Enrollment:** biology/biological sciences; mechanical engineering; nursing/registered nurse (rn, asn, bsn, msn). **Special Study Options:** Accelerated program, cooperative education program, distance learning, double major, English as a Second Language (ESL), external degree program, honors program, independent study, internships, student-designed major, study abroad, teacher certification program, weekend college, Undergraduates may take graduate level courses. Co-Op Programs: Arts, Business, Computer Science, Engineering, Family and Consumer Sciences, Humanities, Natural Science, Technologies. Dual Enrollment offered for select graduate level programs. **Honors Programs:** Honors Delegates, Engineering Program, Emerging Leaders Program **Combined Degree Programs:** BA/MD, RN/MSN in Nursing, BS/MS in Accounting and Math. **Disability Services:** Special programs offered to physically disabled students include note-taking services, reader services, tape recorders, tutors. **Career Services:** alumni services, career/job search classes, career assessment, internships Career Services highlights include One of two finalists for the "Most innovative Pedagogy for Entrepreneurship Education Award" at the United States Assocatiation for Small Business and Entrepreneurship (USASBE) annual conference, 2009.

FACILITIES
Housing: Coed dorms, special housing for disabled students, men's dorms, special housing for international students, women's dorms, fraternity/sorority hous-

ing, Honors student dormitory. 90% of campus accessible to physically disabled. Performing arts hall, nursery center, language lab, speech and hearing center, nursing learning resource labs, institute of polymer science and engineering, chemical lab, institute for health and social policy, Bliss Institute of Applied Politics. **Computers:** 100% of classrooms, 100% of dorms, 100% of libraries, 100% of dining areas, 100% of student union, 100% of common outdoor areas have wireless network access. Students can register for classes online. Administrative functions (other than registration) can be performed online.

CAMPUS LIFE

Environment: City. **Activities:** Choral groups, concert band, dance, drama/theater, jazz band, marching band, music ensembles, musical theater, pep band, radio station, student government, student newspaper, symphony orchestra, television station, yearbook, Campus Ministries, International Student Organization 216 registered organizations, 30 honor societies, 12 religious organizations. 15 fraternities, 8 sororities. **Athletics (Intercollegiate):** *Men:* baseball, basketball, cheerleading, cross-country, football, golf, riflery, soccer, track/field (outdoor), track/field (indoor). *Women:* basketball, cheerleading, cross-country, diving, riflery, soccer, softball, swimming, tennis, track/field (outdoor), track/field (indoor), volleyball. **On-Campus Highlights:** Recreation Center, Student Union (includes food court, Starbucks), E.J. Thomas Performing Arts Hall, James A. Rhodes Arena, Robertson Cafe, Student Recreation and Wellness Center, which features a 56-foot rock-climbing wall, recreation pool, "lazy river", spa, ball courts and fitness facilities; Student Union with a movie theatre, bowling and billiards, a food court and a Starbucks Cafe.

ADMISSIONS

Freshman Academic Profile: Average high school GPA 3.0. 12% in top 10% of high school class, 30% in top 25% of high school class, 58% in top 50% of high school class. SAT Math middle 50% range 435-590. SAT Critical Reading middle 50% range 440-570. ACT middle 50% range 18-24. Minimum web-based TOEFL 61. Minimum paper TOEFL 500. **Basis for Candidate Selection:** *Very important factors considered include:* Class rank, academic GPA, rigor of secondary school record, standardized test scores. **Freshman Admission Requirements:** High school diploma is required and GED is accepted. **Freshman Admission Statistics:** 14,413 applied, 74% admitted, 42% enrolled. **Transfer Admission Requirements:** college transcript(s), statement of good standing from prior institution(s). Lowest grade transferable D-. **General Admission Information:** Application Fee $30. Regular application deadline 8/10. Notification on a rolling basis, beginning on or about 9/15. Nonfall registration accepted. Admission may be deferred for a maximum of 2 Semesters. Credit offered for CEEB Advanced Placement tests.

COSTS AND FINANCIAL AID

Annual in-state tuition $8,004. Annual out-of-state tuition $15,927. Room and board $9,586. Required fees $1,541. Average book expense $900. **Required Forms and Deadlines:** FAFSA, institution's own financial aid form. **Notification of Awards:** Applicants will be notified of awards on a rolling basis beginning 4/1. **Types of Aid:** *Need-based scholarships/grants:* Federal Pell, SEOG. *Loans:* Subsidized Stafford, Unsubsidized Stafford, PLUS, Federal Perkins, Federal Nursing. **Student Employment:** Federal Work-Study Program available. Institutional employment available. Highest amount earned per year from on-campus jobs $5,800. Off-campus job opportunities are excellent. **Financial Aid Statistics:** 63% freshmen, 58% undergrads receive need-based scholarship or grant aid. 47% freshmen, 41% undergrads receive non-need-based scholarship or grant aid. 79% freshmen, 77% undergrads receive need-based self-help aid. 78% freshmen, 81% undergrads receive any aid. 69% undergrads borrow to pay for school. Average cumulative indebtedness $28,421. **Criteria for awarding institutional aid:** *Non-need-based:* academics, art, athletics, leadership, music/drama, state/district residency.

UNIVERSITY OF ALABAMA AT BIRMINGHAM

Office of Undergraduate Admissions, Birmingham, AL 35294-1150
Phone: 205-934-8221 • **Financial Aid Phone:** 205-934-8223
E-mail: undergradadmit@uab.edu • **CEEB Code:** 1856
Fax: 205-975-7114 • **Website:** www.uab.edu/home • **ACT Code:** 56

This public school was founded in 1969. It has a 183-acre campus.

RATINGS
Admissions Selectivity Rating: 75   **Fire Safety Rating:** 91   **Green Rating:** 62

STUDENTS AND FACULTY
Enrollment: 11,014. **Student Body:** 58% female, 42% male, 7% out-of-state, 2% international (87 countries represented). Asian 5%, African American 27%, Caucasian 59%, Hispanic 2%, Native American 0%.
Retention and Graduation: Faculty: Student/faculty ratio 18:1. 858 full-time faculty, 86% hold PhDs, 22% are members of minority groups, 45% are women.

ACADEMICS
Degrees: bachelor's, certificate, doctoral, master's, post-bachelor's certificate, post-master's certificate. **Classes:** Most classes have 10–19 students. Most lab/discussion sessions have 20–29 students. **Majors with Highest Enrollment:** accounting; biology/biological sciences; psychology. **Special Study Options:** Accelerated program, cooperative education program, cross-registration, distance learning, double major, dual enrollment, English as a Second Language (ESL), honors program, independent study, internships, student-designed major, study abroad, teacher certification program. **Honors Programs:** The University Honors Program is designed for students who want to satisfy their intellectual curiosity both inside and outside the classroom. The program is limited in size to 200 students who represent a wide variety of disciplines, backgrounds and interests. Without delaying progress toward a degree, the Honors Program provides students an opportunity to participate in a community of committed scholars, to form close relationships with faculty, to explore new ideas, and to share their ideas, interests, and lives on a daily basis in the Honors House. Students have opportunities to work on independent projects, to travel, and to participate in special extracurricular activities. Those who complete the program are recognized with the designation "With University Honors" on their transcripts and in the graduation program. Please visit our Univeristy Honors website for more information: http://main.uab.edu/show.asp?durki=80738 **Combined Degree Programs:** BA/MD, BA/MA, Fifth Year BS/MS in Biology Program; EMSAP. **Disability Services:** Special programs offered to physically disabled students include note-taking services, reader services, tape recorders. **Career Services:** alumni services, career/job search classes, career assessment, regional alumni.

FACILITIES
Housing: Coed dorms, special housing for disabled students, special housing for international students, apartments for married students, apartments for single students, theme housing. 100% of campus accessible to physically disabled. **Special Academic Facilities/Equipment:** Museum of health sciences. **Computers:** Students can register for classes online. Administrative functions (other than registration) can be performed online.

CAMPUS LIFE
Environment: Metropolis. **Activities:** Choral groups, concert band, dance, drama/theater, jazz band, literary magazine, marching band, music ensembles, musical theater, opera, pep band, radio station, student government, student newspaper, Campus Ministries, International Student Organization 150 registered organizations, 45 honor societies, 9 religious organizations. 9 fraternities, 8 sororities. **Athletics (Intercollegiate):** *Men:* baseball, basketball, football, golf, soccer, tennis. *Women:* basketball, cross-country, golf, riflery, soccer, softball, synchronized swimming, tennis, track/field (outdoor), track/field (indoor), volleyball. **On-Campus Highlights:** Student Rec Center, Commons Dining Hall, Hill University Center, Blazer Hall, Heritage Hall. **Environmental Initiatives:** Recycling Air Handler Condensate Recovery System Building Energy Set-backs

ADMISSIONS
Freshman Academic Profile: Average high school GPA 3.5. 26% in top 10% of high school class, 56% in top 25% of high school class, 80% in top 50% of high school class. ACT middle 50% range 21-27. Minimum web-based TOEFL 61. Minimum paper TOEFL 500. **Basis for Candidate Selection:** *Very important factors considered include:* academic GPA, rigor of secondary school record, standardized test scores. **Freshman Admission Requirements:** High school diploma is required and GED is accepted. *Academic units required:* 4 English, 3 mathematics, 3 science, (2 science labs), 1 foreign language, 3 social studies, 3 academic electives. 4 English, 3 mathematics, 3 science, (2 science labs), 1 foreign language, 3 social studies, 3 academic electives. **Freshman Admission Statistics:** 6,046 applied, 73% admitted, 38% enrolled. **Transfer Admission Requirements:** college transcript(s), minimum college GPA of 2.0 required. **General Admission Information:** Application Fee $35. Regular application deadline 3/1. Nonfall registration accepted. Admission may be deferred for a maximum of 1 year. Credit offered for CEEB Advanced Placement tests.

COSTS AND FINANCIAL AID
Annual in-state tuition $8,400. Annual out-of-state tuition $19,230. Room and board $9,294. Average book expense $1,000. **Required Forms and Deadlines:** FAFSA. **Notification of Awards:** Applicants will be notified of awards on a rolling basis beginning 4/1. **Types of Aid:** *Need-based scholarships/grants:* Federal Pell, SEOC, state scholarships/grants, private scholarships, the school's own gift aid, United Negro College Fund. *Loans:* Direct Subsidized Stafford, Direct Unsubsidized Stafford, Direct PLUS, Federal Perkins, state loans, college/university loans from institutional funds. **Student Employment:** Federal

Work-Study Program available. Institutional employment available. Off-campus job opportunities are excellent. **Financial Aid Statistics:** 63% freshmen, 67% undergrads receive need-based scholarship or grant aid. 58% freshmen, 31% undergrads receive non-need-based scholarship or grant aid. 76% freshmen, 81% undergrads receive need-based self-help aid. 4% freshmen, 4% undergrads receive athletic scholarships. Average cumulative indebtedness $21,503. **Criteria for awarding institutional aid:** *Non-need-based:* academics, alumni affiliation, art, athletics, leadership, minority status, music/drama.

THE UNIVERSITY OF ALABAMA IN HUNTSVILLE

UAH Office of Admissions, Huntsville, AL 35899
Phone: 256-824-6070 • **Financial Aid Phone:** 256-824-2761
E-mail: admitme@uah.edu • **CEEB Code:** 1854
Fax: 256-824-6073 • **Website:** www.uah.edu • **ACT Code:** 53

This public school was founded in 1950. It has a 400-acre campus.

RATINGS

Admissions Selectivity Rating: 76   **Fire Safety Rating:** 87   **Green Rating:** 74

STUDENTS AND FACULTY

Enrollment: 5,703. **Student Body:** 46% female, 54% male, 10% out-of-state, 3% international (82 countries represented). Asian 3%, African American 14%, Caucasian 70%, Hispanic 3%, Native American 1%.
Retention and Graduation: 79% freshmen return for sophomore year. 16% freshmen graduate within 4 years. 47% freshmen graduate within 6 years. **Faculty:** Student/faculty ratio 16:1. 309 full-time faculty, 86% hold PhDs, 22% are members of minority groups, 39% are women. 2% of classes are taught by teaching assistants.

ACADEMICS

Degrees: bachelor's, doctoral, master's, post-bachelor's certificate, post-master's certificate. **Classes:** Most classes have 20–29 students. Most lab/discussion sessions have fewer than 10 students. **Majors with Highest Enrollment:** biology/biological sciences; mechanical engineering; nursing/registered nurse (rn, asn, bsn, msn). **Special Study Options:** cooperative education program, cross-registration, distance learning, double major, dual enrollment, English as a Second Language (ESL), honors program, independent study, internships, study abroad, teacher certification program, Intensive English Program. **Honors Programs:** The Honors Program at UAH provides academically talented undergraduate students with opportunities to develop their special talents and skills within an expanded and enriched version of the curriculum leading to an Honors Diploma. Honors coursework parallels regular offerings in all majors and programs. The courses include special interdisciplinary seminars, and opportunities for independent study and research/creative work, including the opportunity to work closely with faculty on special student projects. Students may participate in an Honors internship that offers active involvement in a business enterprise, professional organization, or government agency that has particular interest and relevance to the student's course of study. Participating students also benefit from the interaction the Honors Program affords with other talented and highly motivated students. See honors.uah.edu for more information. **Combined Degree Programs:** BA/MA, Biological Sciences, Physics, Computer Science. **Disability Services:** Special programs offered to physically disabled students include note-taking services, reader services, tape recorders, tutors. **Career Services:** alumni services, career/job search classes, career assessment, internships Career Services highlights include Coop program is one of the largest in the state of Alabama and is accredited by the Accreditation Council for Cooperative Education.

FACILITIES

Housing: Coed dorms, special housing for disabled students, fraternity/sorority housing, apartments for married students, cooperative housing, apartments for single students, theme housing, Athletic Teammates. 98% of campus accessible to physically disabled. **Special Academic Facilities/Equipment:** Art museum and galleries, observatory with a Solar Magnetometer, optics building, centers for applied optics, micro-gravity research, robotics, solar research, space plasma, and aeronomic research. **Computers:** 25% of classrooms, 30% of dorms, 100% of libraries, 100% of dining areas, 100% of student union, 90% of common outdoor areas have wireless network access. Students can register for classes online. Administrative functions (other than registration) can be performed online.

CAMPUS LIFE

Environment: City. **Activities:** Choral groups, concert band, dance, drama/theater, jazz band, literary magazine, music ensembles, pep band, student government, student newspaper, Campus Ministries, International Student Organization 52 registered organizations, 24 honor societies, 5 religious organi-

zations. 7 fraternities, 4 sororities. **Athletics (Intercollegiate):** *Men:* baseball, basketball, cheerleading, cross-country, ice hockey, soccer, tennis, track/field (outdoor), track/field (indoor). *Women:* basketball, cheerleading, cross-country, soccer, softball, tennis, track/field (outdoor), track/field (indoor), volleyball. **On-Campus Highlights:** University Fitness Center, Shelby Center, Salmon Library, University Center, Central Campus Residence Hall. **Environmental Initiatives:** A hazard chemical waste and waste minimization program has been in effect for over 15 years. Improved environmental awareness communications and training/learning opportunities will soon be available on the OEHS web site. The energy conservation program included the upgrade of the Central Plant boilers which are now among the most energy efficient and environmentally friendly in the state of Alabama. A recycling program that has been in place for over 20 years.

ADMISSIONS

Freshman Academic Profile: Average high school GPA 3.9. 26% in top 10% of high school class, 51% in top 25% of high school class, 83% in top 50% of high school class. 92% from public high schools. SAT Math middle 50% range 510-640. SAT Critical Reading middle 50% range 500-640. ACT middle 50% range 22-29. Minimum web-based TOEFL 62. Minimum paper TOEFL 500. **Basis for Candidate Selection:** *Very important factors considered include:* academic GPA, rigor of secondary school record, standardized test scores. *Other factors considered include:* Class rank, application essay, recommendation(s), level of applicant's interest. **Freshman Admission Requirements:** High school diploma is required and GED is accepted. *Academic units required:* 4 English, 3 mathematics, 3 science, 4 social studies, 6 academic electives. *Academic units recommended:* 4 English, 3 mathematics, 3 science, 4 social studies, 6 academic electives. **Freshman Admission Statistics:** 1,938 applied, 78% admitted, 41% enrolled. **Transfer Admission Requirements:** college transcript(s), statement of good standing from prior institution(s). Minimum college GPA of 2.0 required. Lowest grade transferable D. **General Admission Information:** Application Fee $30. Regular application deadline 8/19. Nonfall registration accepted. Admission may be deferred for a maximum of 1 year. Credit and/or placement offered for CEEB Advanced Placement tests.

COSTS AND FINANCIAL AID

Annual in-state tuition $8,784. Annual out-of-state tuition $21,108. Room and board $7,910. Average book expense $1,592. **Required Forms and Deadlines:** FAFSA. **Notification of Awards:** Applicants will be notified of awards on a rolling basis beginning 4/1. **Types of Aid:** *Need-based scholarships/grants:* Federal Pell, SEOG, state scholarships/grants, private scholarships, the school's own gift aid, Federal Nursing Scholarships. *Loans:* Direct Subsidized Stafford, Direct Unsubsidized Stafford, Direct PLUS. **Student Employment:** Federal Work-Study Program available. Institutional employment available. Off-campus job opportunities are fair. **Financial Aid Statistics:** 88% freshmen, 78% undergrads receive need-based scholarship or grant aid. 11% freshmen, 5% undergrads receive non-need-based scholarship or grant aid. 77% freshmen, 90% undergrads receive need-based self-help aid. 5% freshmen, 4% undergrads receive athletic scholarships. 89% freshmen, 78% undergrads receive any aid. 53% undergrads borrow to pay for school. Average cumulative indebtedness $25,437. **Criteria for awarding institutional aid:** *Non-need-based:* academics, art, athletics, leadership, minority status, music/drama.

THE UNIVERSITY OF ALABAMA AT TUSCALOOSA

Best 378

Box 870132, Tuscaloosa, AL 35487-0132
Phone: 205-348-5666 • **Financial Aid Phone:** 205-348-6756
E-mail: admissions@ua.edu • **CEEB Code:** 1830
Fax: 205-348-9046 • **Website:** www.ua.edu • **ACT Code:** 52

This public school was founded in 1831. It has a 1000-acre campus.

RATINGS

Admissions Selectivity Rating: 88   **Fire Safety Rating:** 66   **Green Rating:** 78

STUDENTS AND FACULTY

Enrollment: 27,364. **Student Body:** 54% female, 46% male, 40% out-of-state, 2% international (68 countries represented). Asian 1%, African American 12%, Caucasian 79%, Hispanic 3%, Native American 0%.

Retention and Graduation: 41% freshmen graduate within 4 years. 67% freshmen graduate within 6 years. 27% grads go on to further study within 1 year. 4% grads pursue law degrees. 2% grads pursue medical degrees. **Faculty:** Student/faculty ratio 20:1. 1202 full-time faculty, 85% hold PhDs, 17% are members of minority groups, 44% are women. 15% of classes are taught by teaching assistants.

ACADEMICS

Degrees: bachelor's, doctoral, master's, post-master's certificate. **Classes:** Most classes have 10–19 students. Most lab/discussion sessions have 20–29 students. **Majors with Highest Enrollment:** elementary education and teaching; finance; nursing/registered nurse (rn, asn, bsn, msn). **Special Study Options:** Accelerated program, cooperative education program, cross-registration, distance learning, double major, dual enrollment, English as a Second Language (ESL), exchange student program (domestic), external degree program, honors program, independent study, internships, liberal arts/career combination, student-designed major, study abroad, teacher certification program, weekend college. **Honors Programs:** University Honors College is composed of the University Honors Program, Computer-Based Honors Program and the International Honors Program. There is also a program called the University Fellows Experience. **Combined Degree Programs:** BS-MBA. **Disability Services:** Special programs offered to physically disabled students include note-taking services, reader services, tape recorders, tutors. **Career Services:** Alumni network, alumni services, career/job search classes, career assessment, internships, regional alumni. Career Services highlights include Cooperative Education is a special academic program at The University of Alabama. In order to promote, encourage, and improve the education of students and to provide maximum service to industry, business, and government agencies, The University of Alabama offers qualified students and approved employers the opportunity to participate in Cooperative Education (Co-op) where students alternate periods of full-time study with periods of full-time employment.

FACILITIES

Housing: Coed dorms, special housing for disabled students, men's dorms, special housing for international students, women's dorms, fraternity/sorority housing, apartments for married students, apartments for single students, theme housing, apartments for visiting scholars. 98% of campus accessible to physically disabled. **Special Academic Facilities/Equipment:** Art gallery, natural history museum, concert hall, archaeologic site and museum, arboretum, observatory, simulated coal mine, robotics lab, wind tunnel, artificial intelligence lab, jet propulsion engine mini-lab, special collections building. **Computers:** 55% of classrooms, 100% of dorms, 100% of libraries, 75% of dining areas, 100% of student union, 22% of common outdoor areas have wireless network access. Students can register for classes online. Administrative functions (other than registration) can be performed online.

CAMPUS LIFE

Environment: City. **Activities:** Choral groups, concert band, dance, drama/theater, jazz band, literary magazine, marching band, music ensembles, musical theater, opera, pep band, radio station, student government, student newspaper, student-run film society, symphony orchestra, television station, yearbook, Campus Ministries, International Student Organization, Model UN 294 registered organizations, 66 honor societies, 30 religious organizations. 31 fraternities, 23 sororities. **Athletics (Intercollegiate):** *Men:* baseball, basketball, cross-country, diving, football, golf, swimming, tennis, track/field (outdoor), track/field (indoor). *Women:* basketball, crew/rowing, cross-country, diving, golf, gymnastics, soccer, softball, swimming, tennis, track/field (outdoor), track/field (indoor), volleyball. **On-Campus Highlights:** University of Alabama Museum of Natural History, Amelia Gayle Gorgas Library, Bryant-Denny Stadium, The Gorgas House Museum (built in 1829), Paul W. Bryant Museum, Located right on campus is a wonderful blend of cultures and ethnic foods. Interesting shops, a new shopping center, great coffee shops, local and visiting musical talent--all located on University Blvd. **Environmental Initiatives:** Recycling has increased by 181% over fiscal year 2008. Currently we are recycling over 1,300 tons of recyclable material. Community Recycling after the tornados of April 2011. As a result of an aggressive energy reduction program, The Univeristy of Alabama uses 27% less energy per square foot than the national average for universities.

ADMISSIONS

Freshman Academic Profile: Average high school GPA 3.6. 43% in top 10% of high school class, 60% in top 25% of high school class, 82% in top 50% of high school class. SAT Math middle 50% range 500-640. SAT Critical Reading middle 50% range 500-620. SAT Writing middle 50% range 490-610. ACT middle 50% range 22-30. Minimum web-based TOEFL 71. Minimum paper TOEFL 525. **Basis for Candidate Selection:** *Very important factors considered include:* academic GPA, rigor of secondary school record, standardized test scores. *Important factors considered include:* Class rank. *Other factors considered include:* application essay, recommendation(s), alumni/ae relation, character/personal qualities, extracurricular activities, first generation, interview, talent/ability, volunteer work, work experience. **Freshman Admission Requirements:** High school diploma is required and GED is accepted.

Academic units required: 4 English, 3 mathematics, 3 science, (2 science labs), 1 foreign language, 4 social studies, 1 history, 5 academic electives. *Academic units recommended:* 4 English, 3 mathematics, 3 science, (2 science labs), 1 foreign language, 4 social studies, 1 history, 5 academic electives. **Freshman Admission Statistics:** 26,409 applied, 53% admitted, 45% enrolled. **Transfer Admission Requirements:** college transcript(s), minimum college GPA of 2.0 required. Lowest grade transferable D. **General Admission Information:** Application Fee $40. Notification on a rolling basis, beginning on or about 8/1. Nonfall registration accepted. Credit and/or placement offered for CEEB Advanced Placement tests.

COSTS AND FINANCIAL AID

Annual in-state tuition $9,200. Annual out-of-state tuition $22,950. Room and board $8,650. Average book expense $1,100. **Required Forms and Deadlines:** FAFSA. **Notification of Awards:** Applicants will be notified of awards on a rolling basis beginning 4/1. *Types of Aid: Need-based scholarships/grants:* Federal Pell, SEOG, state scholarships/grants, private scholarships, the school's own gift aid, Federal Nursing Scholarships. *Loans:* Direct Subsidized Stafford, Direct Unsubsidized Stafford, Direct PLUS, Federal Perkins, college/university loans from institutional funds. **Student Employment:** Federal Work-Study Program available. Institutional employment available. Highest amount earned per year from on-campus jobs $2,466. Off-campus job opportunities are good. **Financial Aid Statistics:** 78% freshmen, 74% undergrads receive need-based scholarship or grant aid. 55% freshmen, 40% undergrads receive non-need-based scholarship or grant aid. 78% freshmen, 85% undergrads receive need-based self-help aid. 2% freshmen, 2% undergrads receive athletic scholarships. 65% freshmen, 62% undergrads receive any aid. 42% undergrads borrow to pay for school. Average cumulative indebtedness $26,714. **Criteria for awarding institutional aid:** *Non-need-based:* academics, alumni affiliation, art, athletics, leadership, minority status, music/drama, state/district residency.

UNIVERSITY OF ALASKA ANCHORAGE

3211 Providence Drive, Anchorage, AK 99508-8046
Phone: 907-786-1480
E-mail: enroll@uaa.alaska.edu • **CEEB Code:** 4896
Fax: 907-780-4800 • **Website:** www.uaa.alaska.edu/ • **ACT Code:** 137

This public school was founded in 1954. It has a 384-acre campus.

RATINGS

Admissions Selectivity Rating: 71   **Fire Safety Rating:** 67   **Green Rating:** 60*

STUDENTS AND FACULTY

Enrollment: 13,390. **Student Body:** 58% female, 42% male, 10% out-of-state, 0% international (35 countries represented). Asian 7%, African American 4%, Caucasian 58%, Hispanic 7%, Native American 12%.
Retention and Graduation: 73% freshmen return for sophomore year. **Faculty:** Student/faculty ratio 12:1. 680 full-time faculty, 53% hold PhDs, 12% are members of minority groups, 52% are women. 0% of classes are taught by teaching assistants.

ACADEMICS

Degrees: associate, bachelor's, certificate, master's, post-bachelor's certificate, post-master's certificate. **Classes:** Most classes have fewer than 10 students. Most lab/discussion sessions have 10–19 students. **Special Study Options:** cooperative education program, cross-registration, distance learning, double major, dual enrollment, English as a Second Language (ESL), exchange student program (domestic), honors program, independent study, internships, liberal arts/career combination, student-designed major, study abroad, teacher certification program. **Honors Programs:** University Honors Program . **Disability Services:** Special programs offered to physically disabled students include note-taking services, reader services, tape recorders. **Career Services:** alumni services, career/job search classes, career assessment, internships.

FACILITIES

Housing: Coed dorms, special housing for disabled students, special housing for international students, apartments for single students, wellness housing, separate floors for: Alaska natives studying engineering, nursing students, honor students, language and cultures, first-year students under age 20, healthy lifestyle, quiet lifestyle, WWAMI program, Far East exchange program. 95% of campus accessible to physically disabled. **Special Academic Facilities/Equipment:** Kimura and student Center Galleries. **Computers:** Students can register for classes online. Administrative functions (other than registration) can be performed online.

CAMPUS LIFE

Environment: City. **Activities:** Choral groups, dance, drama/theater, jazz band, literary magazine, music ensembles, musical theater, opera, radio station, student government, student newspaper, student-run film society, Campus Ministries, International Student Organization, Model UN 70 registered organizations, 5 honor societies, 5 religious organizations. 1 fraternities, 2 sororities. **Athletics (Intercollegiate):** *Men:* basketball, cross-country, ice hockey, skiing (downhill/alpine), skiingnordiccross-country. *Women:* basketball, cross-country, gymnastics, skiing (downhill/alpine), skiingnordiccross-country, volleyball. **On-Campus Highlights:** Campus Center, Wells Fargo Sports Center, Creakside Eatery, Cuddy Center, Student Health Center, The University of Alaska Anchorage campus has covered walkways across much of the campus as well as bike trails that connect the camus to the town's bike trail system. Student Housing is adjacent to the campus with shuttle buses running every 15 minutes throughout the main campus and University Center area of campus.

ADMISSIONS

Freshman Academic Profile: 13% in top 10% of high school class, 32% in top 25% of high school class, 62% in top 50% of high school class. 95% from public high schools. SAT Math middle 50% range 440-570. SAT Critical Reading middle 50% range 430-580. Minimum paper TOEFL 450. **Basis for Candidate Selection:** *Very important factors considered include:* rigor of secondary school record. *Other factors considered include:* Class rank, standardized test scores, talent/ability. **Freshman Admission Requirements:** High school diploma is required and GED is accepted. **Freshman Admission Statistics:** 3,924 applied, 76% admitted, 43% enrolled. **Transfer Admission Requirements:** college transcript(s), statement of good standing from prior institution(s). Minimum college GPA of 2.0 required. Lowest grade transferable C. **General Admission Information:** Application Fee $50. Regular application deadline 7/1. Nonfall registration accepted. Admission may be deferred for a maximum of 1 years. Credit offered for CEEB Advanced Placement tests.

COSTS AND FINANCIAL AID

Annual in-state tuition $4,950. Annual out-of-state tuition $17,400. Room and board $9,827. Required fees $832. Average book expense $1,575. **Required Forms and Deadlines:** FAFSA, institution's own financial aid form. **Notification of Awards:** Applicants will be notified of awards on a rolling basis beginning 3/15. **Types of Aid:** *Need-based scholarships/grants:* Federal Pell, SEOG, state scholarships/grants, private scholarships, the school's own gift aid, Federal Work Study. *Loans:* Subsidized Stafford, Unsubsidized Stafford, PLUS, state loans. **Student Employment:** Federal Work-Study Program available. Institutional employment available. Off-campus job opportunities are good. **Financial Aid Statistics:** 84% freshmen, 74% undergrads receive need-based scholarship or grant aid. 11% freshmen, 3% undergrads receive non-need-based scholarship or grant aid. 66% freshmen, 75% undergrads receive need-based self-help aid. 2% freshmen, 1% undergrads receive athletic scholarships. 49% undergrads borrow to pay for school. Average cumulative indebtedness $30,363. **Criteria for awarding institutional aid:** *Non-need-based:* academics, athletics.

UNIVERSITY OF ALASKA FAIRBANKS

PO Box 757480, Fairbanks, AK 99775-7480
Phone: 907-474-7500 • **Financial Aid Phone:** 888-474-7256
E-mail: admissions@uaf.edu • **CEEB Code:** 4866
Fax: 907-474-5379 • **Website:** www.uaf.edu • **ACT Code:** 64

This public school was founded in 1917. It has a 2250-acre campus.

RATINGS
Admissions Selectivity Rating: 72   **Fire Safety Rating:** 87   **Green Rating:** 83

STUDENTS AND FACULTY
Enrollment: 5,769. **Student Body:** 56% female, 44% male, 12% out-of-state, 1% international (55 countries represented). Asian 1%, African American 3%, Caucasian 48%, Hispanic 5%, Native American 14%.
Retention and Graduation: 74% freshmen return for sophomore year. 12% freshmen graduate within 4 years. 33% freshmen graduate within 6 years.
Faculty: Student/faculty ratio 12:1. 344 full-time faculty, 58% hold PhDs, 20% are members of minority groups, 43% are women.

ACADEMICS
Degrees: associate, bachelor's, certificate, master's, post-bachelor's certificate, terminal associate, transfer associate. **Classes: Majors with Highest Enrollment:** biology/biological sciences; business administration and management; elementary education and teaching. **Special Study Options:** Accelerated program, cooperative education program, distance learning, double major, dual enrollment, exchange student program (domestic), external degree program, honors program, independent study, internships, student-designed major, study abroad, teacher certification program, Legislative Aide Intern Program; Undergraduate Research Opportunities. **Honors Programs:** The Honors Program at UAF provides superior undergraduate students with intellectual opportunities

greater than those generally found in university lecture halls. Honors students experience small classes, direct contact with top faculty members, a flexible curriculum and great encouragement to pursue their own intellectual interests. **Combined Degree Programs:** BS/MS Computer Science, BS/MS Mechanical Engineering. **Disability Services:** Special programs offered to physically disabled students include note-taking services, reader services, tape recorders, tutors. **Career Services:** Alumni network, alumni services, career/job search classes, career assessment, internships.

FACILITIES
Housing: Coed dorms, special housing for disabled students, apartments for married students, apartments for single students, wellness housing, Alaska Native cultural housing. 90% of campus accessible to physically disabled. **Special Academic Facilities/Equipment:** Museum of natural/cultural history of Alaska and the North, Cray Super Computer, extensive telecommunication network, Geophysical Institute, NASA earth station, Poker Flat Research Range, electron microscope, microprobe, International Arctic Research Center, Institute of Arctic Biology, Institute of Northern Engineering, Arctic Region Supercomputing Center, Institute of Marine Biology, Agriculture and Forestry Experiment Station, Office of Electronic Miniaturization, Alaska Native Language Center, Georgeson Botanical Gardens, Cold Climate Housing Research Center,Large Animal Research Station **Computers:** 100% of classrooms, 100% of dorms, 100% of libraries, 100% of dining areas, 100% of student union, 50% of common outdoor areas have wireless network access. Students can register for classes online. Administrative functions (other than registration) can be performed online.

CAMPUS LIFE
Environment: City. **Activities:** Choral groups, concert band, dance, drama/theater, jazz band, literary magazine, music ensembles, pep band, radio station, student government, student newspaper, symphony orchestra, television station, Campus Ministries, International Student Organization, Model UN 122 registered organizations, 11 honor societies, 10 religious organizations. 1 fraternities, 1 sororities. **Athletics (Intercollegiate):** *Men:* basketball, cross-country, ice hockey, riflery, skiingnordiccross-country. *Women:* basketball, cross-country, riflery, skiingnordiccross-country, volleyball. **On-Campus Highlights:** Wood Center (includes food court), Student Recreation Center (SRC), Rasmuson Library, Groomed cross-country ski trails on campus, Hess Recreation Center, Wood Center (includes food court, coffee shop, bowling alley and pool tables, Outdoor Adventures, the Pub and various spaces for groups to gather or hold meetings) The 2,250 acre Fairbanks campus includes two lakes and 17 miles of ski and hiking trails as well as a major student recreation complex. We often refer to UAF as having a 360-million-acre campus because research and field work might take you anywhere in Alaska.

ADMISSIONS
Freshman Academic Profile: Average high school GPA 3.2. 14% in top 10% of high school class, 34% in top 25% of high school class, 61% in top 50% of high school class. SAT Math middle 50% range 450-590. SAT Critical Reading middle 50% range 470-590. SAT Writing middle 50% range 440-560. ACT middle 50% range 18-25. Minimum web-based TOEFL 79. Minimum paper TOEFL 550. **Basis for Candidate Selection:** *Very important factors considered include:* academic GPA, standardized test scores. **Freshman Admission Requirements:** High school diploma is required and GED is not accepted. *Academic units required:* 4 English, 3 mathematics, 3 science, (1 science labs), 3 social studies. *Academic units recommended:* 4 English, 3 mathematics, 3 science, (1 science labs), 3 social studies. **Freshman Admission Statistics:** 1,541 applied, 75% admitted, 76% enrolled. **Transfer Admission Requirements:** college transcript(s), minimum college GPA of 2.0 required. Lowest grade transferable C. **General Admission Information:** Application Fee $50. Regular application deadline 7/1. Regular notification 9/1. Notification on a rolling basis, beginning on or about 1/1. Nonfall registration accepted. Admission may be deferred for a maximum of 1 calendar year. Credit and/or placement offered for CEEB Advanced Placement tests.

COSTS AND FINANCIAL AID
Annual in-state tuition $5,580. Annual out-of-state tuition $18,270. Room and board $7,200. Required fees $970. Average book expense $1,400. **Required Forms and Deadlines:** FAFSA. **Notification of Awards:** Applicants will be notified of awards on a rolling basis beginning 3/1. **Types of Aid:** *Need-based scholarships/grants:* Federal Pell, SEOG, state scholarships/grants, private scholarships, the school's own gift aid. *Loans:* Subsidized Stafford, Unsubsidized Stafford, PLUS, state loans. **Student Employment:** Federal Work-Study Program available. Institutional employment available. Highest amount earned per year from on-campus jobs $5,320. Off-campus job opportunities are good. **Financial Aid Statistics:** 85% freshmen, 79% undergrads receive need-based scholarship or grant aid. 20% freshmen, 11% undergrads receive non-need-based scholarship or grant aid. 51% freshmen, 68% undergrads receive need-based self-help aid. 3% freshmen, 2% undergrads receive athletic scholarships. 84% freshmen, 74% undergrads receive any aid. 44% undergrads borrow to pay for school. Average cumulative indebtedness $29,762. **Criteria for awarding institutional aid:** *Non-need-based:* academics, art, athletics, leadership, minority status, music/drama, state/district residency.

UNIVERSITY OF ARIZONA

PO Box 210040, Tucson, AZ 85721-0040
Phone: 520-621-3237 • **Financial Aid Phone:** 520-621-1858
E-mail: admissions@arizona.edu • **CEEB Code:** 4832
Fax: 520-621-9799 • **Website:** www.arizona.edu • **ACT Code:** 96

This public school was founded in 1885. It has a 378-acre campus.

RATINGS
Admissions Selectivity Rating: 78   **Fire Safety Rating:** 85   **Green Rating:** 96

STUDENTS AND FACULTY
Enrollment: 31,217. **Student Body:** 52% female, 48% male, 29% out-of-state, 5% international (116 countries represented). Asian 6%, African American 3%, Caucasian 57%, Hispanic 23%, Native American 1%.
Retention and Graduation: 80% freshmen return for sophomore year. 35% freshmen graduate within 4 years. **Faculty:** Student/faculty ratio 22:1. full-time faculty.

ACADEMICS
Degrees: bachelor's, master's, post-bachelor's certificate, post-master's certificate. **Classes:** Most classes have 20–29 students. Most lab/discussion sessions have 20–29 students. **Majors with Highest Enrollment:** cell/cellular and molecular biology; political science and government; psychology. **Special Study Options:** Accelerated program, cooperative education program, cross-registration, distance learning, double major, dual enrollment, English as a Second Language (ESL), exchange student program (domestic), external degree program, independent study, internships, liberal arts/career combination, study abroad, teacher certification program, weekend college. **Honors Programs:** For information on our Honors College, visit: http://www.honors.arizona.edu/ . **Disability Services:** Special programs offered to physically disabled students include note-taking services, reader services, tape recorders, tutors. **Career Services:** alumni services, career/job search classes, career assessment, internships.

FACILITIES
Housing: Coed dorms, special housing for disabled students, special housing for international students, women's dorms, fraternity/sorority housing, apartments for single students. 85% of campus accessible to physically disabled. **Special Academic Facilities/Equipment:** Art, photography, and natural history museums, tree-ring lab, planetarium, optical sciences center, nuclear reactor. **Computers:** 100% of classrooms, 100% of dorms, 100% of libraries, 100% of dining areas, 100% of student union, 75% of common outdoor areas have wireless network access. Students can register for classes online. Administrative functions (other than registration) can be performed online.

CAMPUS LIFE
Environment: Metropolis. **Activities:** Choral groups, concert band, dance, drama/theater, jazz band, literary magazine, marching band, music ensembles, musical theater, opera, pep band, radio station, student government, student newspaper, symphony orchestra, television station, yearbook, Campus Ministries, International Student Organization, Model UN 504 registered organizations, 13 honor societies, 13 religious organizations. 25 fraternities, 20 sororities. **Athletics (Intercollegiate):** *Men:* baseball, basketball, cross-country, diving, football, golf, swimming, tennis, track/field (outdoor). *Women:* basketball, cross-country, diving, golf, gymnastics, soccer, softball, swimming, tennis, track/field (outdoor), track/field (indoor), volleyball. **On-Campus Highlights:** Flandrau Science Center, Center for Creative Photography, UA Museum of Art, Athletics Events, Arizona State Museum. **Environmental Initiatives:** The University of Arizona's top environmental commitments are conducting comprehensive research on environmental issues ranging from biodiversity, management, and global change. Research and advocacy for the development and adoption of solar energy sources. By the pursuing operating procedures that promote energy efficiency and lower environmental impact while providing world class service.

ADMISSIONS
Freshman Academic Profile: Average high school GPA 3.4. 32% in top 10% of high school class, 63% in top 25% of high school class, 90% in top 50% of high school class. 94% from public high schools. SAT Math middle 50% range 500-630. SAT Critical Reading middle 50% range 483-600. SAT Writing middle 50% range 480-590. ACT middle 50% range 21-27. Minimum web-based TOEFL 61. **Basis for Candidate Selection:** *Very important factors considered include:* academic GPA, rigor of secondary school record. *Other factors considered include:* Class rank, application essay, recommendation(s), standardized test scores, character/personal qualities, extracurricular activities, first gen-eration, geographical residence, interview, racial/ethnic status, state residency, talent/ability, volunteer work, work experience. **Freshman Admission Requirements:** High school diploma is required and GED is accepted. *Academic units required:* 4 English, 3 mathematics, 3 science, (3 science labs), 2 foreign language, 1 social studies, 1 history, 1 Fine Art. *Academic units recommended:* 4 English, 3 mathematics, 3 science, (3 science labs), 2 foreign language, 1 social studies, 1 history, 1 Fine Art **Freshman Admission Statistics:** 26,329 applied, 77% admitted, 37% enrolled. **Transfer Admission Requirements:** college transcript(s), Lowest grade transferable C. **General Admission Information:** Application Fee $50. Regular application deadline 5/1. Notification on a rolling basis, beginning on or about 11/1. Nonfall registration accepted. Credit offered for CEEB Advanced Placement tests.

COSTS AND FINANCIAL AID
Annual in-state tuition $9,114. Annual out-of-state tuition $25,310. Room and board $9,714. Required fees $921. Average book expense $1,000. **Required Forms and Deadlines:** FAFSA. **Types of Aid:** *Need-based scholarships/grants:* Federal Pell, SEOG, state scholarships/grants, private scholarships, the school's own gift aid, Federal Nursing Scholarships. *Loans:* Subsidized Stafford, Unsubsidized Stafford, PLUS, Federal Perkins, Federal Nursing, college/university loans from institutional funds. **Student Employment:** Federal Work-Study Program available. Institutional employment available. Off-campus job opportunities are good. **Financial Aid Statistics:** 92% freshmen, 89% undergrads receive need-based scholarship or grant aid. 12% freshmen, 8% undergrads receive non-need-based scholarship or grant aid. 59% freshmen, 67% undergrads receive need-based self-help aid. 1% freshmen, 1% undergrads receive athletic scholarships. 49% undergrads borrow to pay for school. Average cumulative indebtedness $22,269. **Criteria for awarding institutional aid:** *Non-need-based:* academics, art, music/drama.

UNIVERSITY OF ARKANSAS—FAYETTEVILLE

232 Silas Hunt Hall, Fayetteville, AR 72701
Phone: 479-575-5346 • **Financial Aid Phone:** 479-575-3806
E-mail: uofa@uark.edu • **CEEB Code:** 6866
Fax: 479-575-7515 • **Website:** www.uark.edu • **ACT Code:** 144

This public school was founded in 1871. It has a 410-acre campus.

RATINGS
Admissions Selectivity Rating: 85   **Fire Safety Rating:** 82   **Green Rating:** 90

STUDENTS AND FACULTY
Enrollment: 18,617. **Student Body:** 49% female, 51% male, 33% out-of-state, 3% international (106 countries represented). Asian 3%, African American 5%, Caucasian 80%, Hispanic 5%, Native American 1%.
Retention and Graduation: 83% freshmen return for sophomore year. 34% freshmen graduate within 4 years. 59% freshmen graduate within 6 years.
Faculty: Student/faculty ratio 18:1. 900 full-time faculty, 86% hold PhDs, 14% are members of minority groups, 35% are women. % of classes are taught by teaching assistants.

ACADEMICS
Degrees: bachelor's, master's, post-bachelor's certificate, post-master's certificate. **Classes:** Most classes have 20–29 students. Most lab/discussion sessions have 20–29 students. **Majors with Highest Enrollment:** finance; journalism; marketing/marketing management. **Special Study Options:** Accelerated program, cooperative education program, distance learning, double major, dual enrollment, English as a Second Language (ESL), honors program, independent study, internships, liberal arts/career combination, student-designed major, study abroad, teacher certification program. **Honors Programs:** The Honors College provides exceptional opportunities for outstanding undergraduates. The College incorporates 4 areas of responsiblity: recruitment, administration of honors fellowships, coordination of honors program and curricula, and coordination of related services. **Combined Degree Programs:** BA/MD, BA/JD, BA/DDS, MBA/JD. **Disability Services:** Special programs offered to physically disabled students include note-taking services, reader services, tape recorders, tutors. **Career Services:** Alumni network, alumni services, career assessment, internships.

FACILITIES

Housing: Coed dorms, women's dorms, fraternity/sorority housing, apartments for single students, Suites with private bedrooms. Special interest floors. Enhanced learning centers. First year experience program area. Adaptable housing for disabled students. Several residences remain open over holiday and winter breaks. Honors housing. Sophmore and beyond program area. 100% of campus accessible to physically disabled. **Special Academic Facilities/Equipment:** Public Radio-KUAF, High Density Electronics Center, Reynolds Center for Enterprise Development, Center for Excellence in Poultry Science, Genesis Small Business Incubation Center, Chemical Hazards Research Center (NEW) Honors College **Computers:** Students can register for classes online. Administrative functions (other than registration) can be performed online.

CAMPUS LIFE

Environment: Town. **Activities:** Choral groups, concert band, dance, drama/theater, jazz band, literary magazine, marching band, music ensembles, musical theater, opera, pep band, radio station, student government, student newspaper, student-run film society, symphony orchestra, television station, yearbook, Campus Ministries, International Student Organization 340 registered organizations, 39 honor societies, 32 religious organizations. 16 fraternities, 11 sororities. **Athletics (Intercollegiate):** *Men:* baseball, basketball, cross-country, football, golf, tennis, track/field (outdoor), track/field (indoor). *Women:* basketball, cross-country, diving, golf, gymnastics, soccer, softball, swimming, tennis, track/field (outdoor), track/field (indoor), volleyball. **On-Campus Highlights:** Bud Walton Arena, Old Main, Reynolds Razorback Stadium, Greek AmphiTheater, Senior Walk (every graduate's name engraved). **Environmental Initiatives:** ACUPCC Signatory, GHG inventory, climate action plan $52 million investment in conservation on campus Razorback Recycling

ADMISSIONS

Freshman Academic Profile: Average high school GPA 3.6. 31% in top 10% of high school class, 58% in top 25% of high school class, 87% in top 50% of high school class. 84% from public high schools. SAT Math middle 50% range 520-630. SAT Critical Reading middle 50% range 500-610. ACT middle 50% range 23-28. Minimum web-based TOEFL 79. Minimum paper TOEFL 550. **Basis for Candidate Selection:** *Very important factors considered include:* Class rank, academic GPA, rigor of secondary school record, standardized test scores. *Other factors considered include:* application essay, recommendation(s), alumni/ae relation, character/personal qualities, extracurricular activities, first generation, geographical residence, racial/ethnic status, state residency, talent/ability, volunteer work, work experience. **Freshman Admission Requirements:** High school diploma is required and GED is accepted. *Academic units required:* 4 English, 4 mathematics, 3 science, (2 science labs), 3 social studies, 2 academic electives. *Academic units recommended:* 4 English, 4 mathematics, 3 science, (2 science labs), 3 social studies, 2 academic electives. **Freshman Admission Statistics:** 16,633 applied, 61% admitted, 44% enrolled. **Transfer Admission Requirements:** college transcript(s), minimum college GPA of 2.0 required. Lowest grade transferable C–. **General Admission Information:** Application Fee $40. Regular application deadline 8/1. Notification on a rolling basis, beginning on or about 9/15. Nonfall registration accepted. Credit and/or placement offered for CEEB Advanced Placement tests.

COSTS AND FINANCIAL AID

Annual in-state tuition $6,140. Annual out-of-state tuition $17,022. Room and board $8,672. Required fees $1,412. Average book expense $1,214. **Required Forms and Deadlines:** FAFSA. **Notification of Awards:** Applicants will be notified of awards on a rolling basis beginning 4/1. **Types of Aid:** *Need-based scholarships/grants:* Federal Pell, SEOG, state scholarships/grants, private scholarships, the school's own gift aid. *Loans:* Subsidized Stafford, Unsubsidized Stafford, PLUS, Federal Perkins, state loans, college/university loans from institutional funds, Alternative Loans. **Student Employment:** Federal Work-Study Program available. Institutional employment available. Highest amount earned per year from on-campus jobs $3,000. **Financial Aid Statistics:** 87% freshmen, 81% undergrads receive need-based scholarship or grant aid. 21% freshmen, 14% undergrads receive non-need-based scholarship or grant aid. 57% freshmen, 69% undergrads receive need-based self-help aid. 2% freshmen, 2% undergrads receive athletic scholarships. 45% undergrads borrow to pay for school. Average cumulative indebtedness $21,562. **Criteria for awarding institutional aid:** *Non-need-based:* academics, alumni affiliation, art, athletics, leadership, minority status, music/drama, state/district residency.

See page 1242.

2801 South University Avenue, Little Rock, AR 72204
Phone: 501-569-3127
E-mail: admissions@ualr.edu
Fax: 501-569-8915 • **Website:** www.ualr.edu

This is a public school.

RATINGS

Admissions Selectivity Rating: 62   **Fire Safety Rating:** 60*   **Green Rating:** 60*

STUDENTS AND FACULTY

Retention and Graduation: 59% freshmen return for sophomore year.

ACADEMICS

Degrees: associate, bachelor's, certificate, master's, post-bachelor's certificate.

FACILITIES

Housing: Coed dorms, men's dorms, women's dorms, fraternity/sorority housing

CAMPUS LIFE

Activities: radio station, student government, student newspaper, television station, yearbook.

ADMISSIONS

Freshman Academic Profile: 93% from public high schools. Minimum paper TOEFL 500. **Freshman Admission Requirements:** High school diploma is required and GED is accepted. **Transfer Admission Requirements:** college transcript(s), minimum college GPA of 2.0 required. Lowest grade transferable C. **General Admission Information:** Nonfall registration accepted. Credit offered for CEEB Advanced Placement tests.

COSTS AND FINANCIAL AID

Annual in-state tuition $1,131. Annual out-of-state tuition $2,916. Room and board $2,435. Required fees $138. Average book expense $1,000. **Required Forms and Deadlines:** FAFSA, state aid form. **Types of Aid:** *Need-based scholarships/grants:* state scholarships/grants. *Loans:* Subsidized Stafford, PLUS.

UNIVERSITY OF ARKANSAS AT PINE BLUFF

1200 N. University Drive, Pine Bluff, AR 71601
Phone: 870-575-8492
E-mail: fultone@uapb.edu
Fax: 870-575-4608 • **Website:** www.uapb.edu

This is a public school.

RATINGS

Admissions Selectivity Rating: 60*   **Fire Safety Rating:** 60*   **Green Rating:** 60*

STUDENTS AND FACULTY

Enrollment: 3,048. **Student Body:** 58% female, 42% male, 33% out-of-state, 0% international. Asian 0%, African American 96%, Caucasian 3%, Hispanic 0%, Native American 0%.
Retention and Graduation: 57% freshmen return for sophomore year. 14% freshmen graduate within 4 years. 32% freshmen graduate within 6 years.
Faculty: Student/faculty ratio 18:1. 164 full-time faculty, 46% are members of minority groups, 54% are women.

ACADEMICS

Degrees: associate, bachelor's, certificate, master's. **Classes:** Most classes have fewer than 10 students. **Special Study Options:** cooperative education program, distance learning, double major, dual enrollment, honors program, internships, study abroad, teacher certification program.

FACILITIES

Housing: men's dorms, women's dorms.

CAMPUS LIFE

Activities: Choral groups, concert band, drama/theater, jazz band, marching band, radio station, student government, student newspaper, television station, yearbook.

ADMISSIONS

Freshman Academic Profile: 93% from public high schools. SAT Math middle 50% range 350-450. SAT Critical Reading middle 50% range 350-440. ACT middle 50% range 14-18. Minimum paper TOEFL 500. **Basis for Candidate Selection:** *Very important factors considered include:* rigor of secondary school record, standardized test scores. *Important factors considered include:* academic GPA. **Freshman Admission Requirements:** High school diploma is required and GED is accepted. *Academic units required:* 4 English, 3 mathematics, 3 science, (2 science labs), 2 foreign language, 1 social studies, 2 history, 4 academic electives. 4 English, 3 mathematics, 3 science, (2 science labs), 2 foreign language, 1 social studies, 2 history, 4 academic electives. **Freshman Admission Statistics:** 2,169 applied, 64% admitted, 59% enrolled. **Transfer Admission Requirements:** High school transcript, college transcript(s). **General Admission Information:** Nonfall registration accepted. Credit offered for CEEB Advanced Placement tests.

COSTS AND FINANCIAL AID

Annual in-state tuition $3,300. Annual out-of-state tuition $7,710. Room and board $6,070. Required fees $1,199. Average book expense $1,000. **Required Forms and Deadlines:** FAFSA. **Types of Aid:** *Need-based scholarships/grants:* Federal Pell, SEOG, state scholarships/grants, private scholarships, the school's own gift aid. *Loans:* Subsidized Stafford, Unsubsidized Stafford, Federal Perkins.

THE UNIVERSITY OF THE ARTS

320 South Broad Street, Philadelphia, PA 19102
Phone: 215-717-6049
E-mail: admissions@uarts.edu • **CEEB Code:** 2664
Fax: 215-717-6045 • **Website:** www.uarts.edu • **ACT Code:** 3664

This private school was founded in 1876. It has a 18-acre campus.

RATINGS

Admissions Selectivity Rating: 88   **Fire Safety Rating:** 60*   **Green Rating:** 60*

STUDENTS AND FACULTY

Enrollment: 2,100. **Student Body:** 54% female, 46% male, 62% out-of-state, 3% international (40 countries represented). Asian 3%, African American 11%, Caucasian 65%, Hispanic 4%, Native American 0%. **Retention and Graduation:** 76% freshmen return for sophomore year. 55% freshmen graduate within 4 years. 62% freshmen graduate within 6 years. 68% grads go on to further study within 1 year. **Faculty:** Student/faculty ratio 9:1. 114 full-time faculty, 49% hold PhDs, 8% are members of minority groups, 38% are women. 0% of classes are taught by teaching assistants.

ACADEMICS

Degrees: bachelor's, certificate, diploma, master's, post-bachelor's certificate. **Classes:** Most classes have 10–19 students. **Majors with Highest Enrollment:** drama and dramatics/theatre arts; graphic design; photography. **Special Study Options:** Accelerated program, cross-registration, double major, dual enrollment, English as a Second Language (ESL), exchange student program (domestic), independent study, internships, study abroad, teacher certification program. **Combined Degree Programs:** BFA/MAT Teaching Visual Arts, BM/MAT Music Ed. **Disability Services:** Special programs offered to physically disabled students include note-taking services, reader services, tape recorders, tutors. **Career Services:** alumni services, career/job search classes, career assessment, internships.

FACILITIES

Housing: Coed dorms, apartments for single students. 85% of campus accessible to physically disabled. Special Academic Facilities/Equipment: Rosenwald-Wolf Gallery, Merriam Theater, Arts Bank, Borowsky Center for Publication arts, Gershman Y

CAMPUS LIFE

Environment: Metropolis. **Activities:** Choral groups, concert band, dance, drama/theater, jazz band, music ensembles, musical theater, radio station, student government 5 registered organizations, 1 religious organizations.

ADMISSIONS

Freshman Academic Profile: Average high school GPA 2.9. 10% in top 10% of high school class, 32% in top 25% of high school class, 66% in top 50% of high school class. 85% from public high schools. SAT Math middle 50% range 450-570. SAT Critical Reading middle 50% range 470-580. SAT Writing middle 50% range 460-580. ACT middle 50% range 19-26. Minimum paper TOEFL 500. **Basis for Candidate Selection:** *Very important factors considered include:* rigor of secondary school record, interview, talent/ability. *Important fac-*

tors considered include: Class rank, application essay, standardized test scores, character/personal qualities, extracurricular activities. *Other factors considered include:* recommendation(s), alumni/ae relation, racial/ethnic status, volunteer work, work experience. **Freshman Admission Requirements:** High school diploma is required and GED is accepted. *Academic units required:* 4 English. *Academic units recommended:* 4 English. **Freshman Admission Statistics:** 2,349 applied, 49% admitted, 49% enrolled. **Transfer Admission Requirements:** High school transcript, college transcript(s), essay or personal statement, standardized test scores, minimum college GPA of 2.0 required. Lowest grade transferable C. **General Admission Information:** Application Fee $60. Notification on a rolling basis, beginning on or about 11/1. Nonfall registration accepted. Admission may be deferred for a maximum of 12 months. Credit and/or placement offered for CEEB Advanced Placement tests.

COSTS AND FINANCIAL AID

Annual tuition $23,380. Room and board $7,800. Required fees $950. Average book expense $2,000. **Required Forms and Deadlines:** FAFSA. **Notification of Awards:** Applicants will be notified of awards on a rolling basis beginning 3/15. **Types of Aid:** *Need-based scholarships/grants:* Federal Pell, SEOG, state scholarships/grants, private scholarships, the school's own gift aid, merit scholarships. *Loans:* Subsidized Stafford, Unsubsidized Stafford, PLUS, Federal Perkinsalternative loans. **Student Employment:** Federal Work-Study Program available. Institutional employment available. Highest amount earned per year from on-campus jobs $1,200. Off-campus job opportunities are excellent. **Financial Aid Statistics:** 67% freshmen, 45% undergrads receive need-based scholarship or grant aid. 100% freshmen, 100% undergrads receive non-need-based scholarship or grant aid. 100% freshmen, 100% undergrads receive need-based self-help aid. 87% freshmen, 90% undergrads receive any aid. 85% undergrads borrow to pay for school. Average cumulative indebtedness $17,500. **Criteria for awarding institutional aid:** *Non-need-based:* academics, art, music/drama.

See page 1244.

UNIVERSITY OF BALTIMORE

1420 North Charles Street, Baltimore, MD 21201
Phone: 410-837-4777 • **Financial Aid Phone:** 410-837-4763
E-mail: admissions@ubmail.ubalt.edu • **CEEB Code:** 5810
Fax: 410-837-4793 • **Website:** www.ubalt.edu/admissionsad/01FF09.cfm?ad_source=princetonreview

This public school was founded in 1925. It has a 47-acre campus.

RATINGS

Admissions Selectivity Rating: 74   **Fire Safety Rating:** 60*   **Green Rating:** 79

STUDENTS AND FACULTY

Enrollment: 3,399. **Student Body:** 57% female, 43% male, 4% out-of-state, 2% international. Asian 4%, African American 46%, Caucasian 37%, Hispanic 4%, Native American 0%. **Retention and Graduation:** 18% grads go on to further study within 1 year. 10% grads pursue arts and sciences degrees. 2% grads pursue law degrees. 9% grads pursue business degrees. **Faculty:** Student/faculty ratio 19:1. 182 full-time faculty, 85% hold PhDs, 23% are members of minority groups, 45% are women. 0% of classes are taught by teaching assistants.

ACADEMICS

Degrees: bachelor's, master's, post-bachelor's certificate. **Classes:** Most classes have 20–29 students. **Majors with Highest Enrollment:** business/commerce; criminal justice/police science; health/health care administration/management. **Special Study Options:** Accelerated program, cooperative education program, distance learning, honors program, independent study, internships, student-designed major, study abroad. **Combined Degree Programs:** BA/JD, BA/MA, MBA/JD. **Disability Services:** Special programs offered to physically disabled students include note-taking services, reader services, tape recorders, tutors. **Career Services:** Alumni network, alumni services, career/job search classes, career assessment, internships, regional alumni. Career Services highlights include The internship program serves students who do not have experimental learning built into their academic units.

FACILITIES

Housing: The University works with several apartment complexes in the area to provide direct leases to students. 100% of campus accessible to physically disabled. **Computers:** Students can register for classes online. Administrative functions (other than registration) can be performed online.

CAMPUS LIFE

Environment: Metropolis. **Activities:** drama/theater, literary magazine, student government, student newspaper, International Student Organization 26 registered organizations, 11 honor societies, 2 religious organizations. **On-Campus Highlights:** Student Union **Environmental Initiatives:** 30% energy reduction contract with Energy Systems Group Single steam recycling Certificate of Sustainabilty (MBA Program) Creation of Human Ecology and Sustainabilty Minor in 2010 and major in 2011.

ADMISSIONS

Freshman Academic Profile: Average high school GPA 2.9. SAT Math middle 50% range 410-540. SAT Critical Reading middle 50% range 420-560. SAT Writing middle 50% range 420-530. ACT middle 50% range 17-21. Minimum paper TOEFL 550. **Basis for Candidate Selection:** *Important factors considered include:* Class rank, academic GPA, rigor of secondary school record, standardized test scores. *Other factors considered include:* application essay, recommendation(s), alumni/ae relation, character/personal qualities, extracurricular activities, first generation, talent/ability, volunteer work, work experience. **Freshman Admission Requirements:** High school diploma is required and GED is accepted. *Academic units required:* 4 English, 3 mathematics, 3 science, (2 science labs), 3 social studies, 4 academic electives. 4 English, 3 mathematics, 3 science, (2 science labs), 3 social studies, 4 academic electives. **Freshman Admission Statistics:** 730 applied, 64% admitted, 47% enrolled. **Transfer Admission Requirements:** college transcript(s), minimum college GPA of 2.0 required. Lowest grade transferable D. **General Admission Information:** Application Fee $30. Regular notification 4/1. Nonfall registration accepted. Admission may be deferred for a maximum of 1 year. Credit and/or placement offered for CEEB Advanced Placement tests.

COSTS AND FINANCIAL AID

Annual in-state tuition $5,818. Annual out-of-state tuition $16,068. Required fees $1,846. **Required Forms and Deadlines:** FAFSA. **Types of Aid:** *Need-based scholarships/grants:* Federal Pell, SEOG, state scholarships/grants, private scholarships, the school's own gift aid. *Loans:* Direct Subsidized Stafford, Direct Unsubsidized Stafford, Direct PLUS. **Student Employment:** Federal Work-Study Program available. Institutional employment available. **Financial Aid Statistics:** 90% freshmen, 91% undergrads receive need-based scholarship or grant aid. 65% freshmen, 72% undergrads receive need-based self-help aid. 97% freshmen, 66% undergrads receive any aid. 55% undergrads borrow to pay for school. Average cumulative indebtedness $0. **Criteria for awarding institutional aid:** *Non-need-based:* academics, state/district residency.

UNIVERSITY OF BRIDGEPORT

126 Park Avenue, Bridgeport, CT 6604
Phone: 203-576-4552 • **Financial Aid Phone:** 203-576-4568
E-mail: admit@.bridgeport.edu • **CEEB Code:** 3914
Fax: 203-576-4941 • **ACT Code:** 602

This private school was founded in 1927. It has a 86-acre campus.

RATINGS

Admissions Selectivity Rating: 75 **Fire Safety Rating:** 89 **Green Rating:** 60*

STUDENTS AND FACULTY

Enrollment: 2,248. **Student Body:** 68% female, 32% male, 35% out-of-state, 11% international (80 countries represented). Asian 3%, African American 37%, Caucasian 27%, Hispanic 15%, Native American 0%.
Retention and Graduation: 52% freshmen return for sophomore year. 15% grads go on to further study within 1 year. 10% grads pursue arts and sciences degrees. 10% grads pursue law degrees. 10% grads pursue business degrees. 5% grads pursue medical degrees. **Faculty:** Student/faculty ratio 12:1. 125 full-time faculty, 82% hold PhDs, 19% are members of minority groups, 37% are women. 0% of classes are taught by teaching assistants.

ACADEMICS

Degrees: associate, bachelor's, certificate, master's, post-master's certificate. **Classes:** Most classes have 10–19 students. **Majors with Highest Enrollment:** business/commerce; dental hygiene/hygienist; psychology. **Special Study Options:** Accelerated program, cooperative education program, cross-registration, distance learning, double major, English as a Second Language (ESL), honors program, independent study, internships, liberal arts/career combination, student-designed major, study abroad, teacher certification program, weekend college. **Combined Degree Programs:** BS/DC, BS/MBA. **Disability Services:** Special programs offered to physically disabled students include note-taking services, reader services, tape recorders, tutors. **Career Services:** Alumni network, alumni services, career/job search classes, career assessment, internships, regional alumni.

FACILITIES

Housing: Coed dorms, Mens, Womens floors. 80% of campus accessible to physically disabled. **Computers:** 80% of classrooms, 100% of dorms, 100% of libraries, 30% of dining areas, 50% of student union, have wireless network access. Students can register for classes online. Administrative functions (other than registration) can be performed online.

CAMPUS LIFE

Environment: City. **Activities:** Choral groups, dance, literary magazine, music ensembles, student government, student newspaper, yearbook, International Student Organization 30 registered organizations, 11 honor societies, 6 religious organizations. 2 fraternities, 4 sororities. **Athletics (Intercollegiate):** *Men:* baseball, basketball, cross-country, soccer, swimming. *Women:* basketball, cross-country, gymnastics, lacrosse, soccer, softball, swimming, volleyball. **On-Campus Highlights:** Arnold Bernhard Center, Wheeler Recreation Center, John J. Cox Student Center, The University Gallery, Hubbell Gymnasium.

ADMISSIONS

Freshman Academic Profile: Average high school GPA 2.8. 7% in top 10% of high school class, 29% in top 25% of high school class, 64% in top 50% of high school class. 89% from public high schools. SAT Math middle 50% range 410-500. SAT Critical Reading middle 50% range 400-490. SAT Writing middle 50% range 400-480. ACT middle 50% range 15-20. Minimum web-based TOEFL 61. Minimum paper TOEFL 500. **Basis for Candidate Selection:** *Very important factors considered include:* rigor of secondary school record, standardized test scores. *Important factors considered include:* Class rank, application essay, academic GPA, recommendation(s), talent/ability. *Other factors considered include:* alumni/ae relation, character/personal qualities, extracurricular activities, interview, level of applicant's interest, volunteer work, work experience. **Freshman Admission Requirements:** High school diploma is required and GED is accepted. *Academic units required:* 4 English, 3 mathematics, 2 science, (2 science labs), 2 social studies, 5 academic electives. *Academic units recommended:* 4 English, 3 mathematics, 2 science, (2 science labs), 2 social studies, 5 academic electives. **Freshman Admission Statistics:** 8,165 applied, 55% admitted, 10% enrolled. **Transfer Admission Requirements:** college transcript(s), essay or personal statement, minimum college GPA of 2.0 required. Lowest grade transferable C–. **General Admission Information:** Application Fee $25. Notification on a rolling basis, beginning on or about 10/1. Nonfall registration accepted. Admission may be deferred for a maximum of 1 year. Credit and/or placement offered for CEEB Advanced Placement tests.

COSTS AND FINANCIAL AID

Annual tuition $23,400. Room and board $11,080. Required fees $2,065. Average book expense $1,500. **Required Forms and Deadlines:** FAFSA, institution's own financial aid form. **Notification of Awards:** Applicants will be notified of awards on a rolling basis beginning 3/1. **Types of Aid:** *Need-based scholarships/grants:* Federal Pell, SEOG, state scholarships/grants, private scholarships, the school's own gift aid. *Loans:* Direct Subsidized Stafford, Direct Unsubsidized Stafford, Direct PLUS, Subsidized Stafford, Unsubsidized Stafford, PLUS, Federal Perkins. **Student Employment:** Federal Work-Study Program available. Institutional employment available. Highest amount earned per year from on-campus jobs $2,000. Off-campus job opportunities are good. **Financial Aid Statistics:** 94% freshmen, 91% undergrads receive need-based scholarship or grant aid. 97% freshmen, 94% undergrads receive non-need-based scholarship or grant aid. 97% freshmen, 96% undergrads receive need-based self-help aid. 5% freshmen, 9% undergrads receive athletic scholarships. 98% freshmen, 98% undergrads receive any aid. **Criteria for awarding institutional aid:** *Non-need-based:* academics, athletics, leadership, music/drama, state/district residency.

THE UNIVERSITY OF BRITISH COLUMBIA

Room 2016, Vancouver, BC V6T 1Z1
Phone: 1-604-822-3014 • **Financial Aid Phone:** 604-822-5111
E-mail: askme@interchange.ubc.ca • **CEEB Code:**
Fax: 604-822-3599 • **Website:** www.ubc.ca • **ACT Code:**

This public school was founded in 1908. It has a 1000-acre campus.

RATINGS

Admissions Selectivity Rating: 60* **Fire Safety Rating:** 70 **Green Rating:** 96

STUDENTS AND FACULTY

Enrollment: 29,717. **Student Body:** 54% female, 46% male, (144 countries represented).
Retention and Graduation: 31% freshmen graduate within 4 years. 50% grads go on to further study within 1 year. **Faculty:** Student/faculty ratio 15:1.

Degrees: bachelor's, certificate, diploma, doctoral, master's. **Classes:** Most classes have 50-59 students. Most lab/discussion sessions have 20-29 students. **Majors with Highest Enrollment:** biological and physical sciences; computer and information sciences; psychology. **Special Study Options:** cooperative education program, distance learning, double major, dual enrollment, English as a Second Language (ESL), exchange student program (domestic), honors program, internships, liberal arts/career combination, student-designed major, study abroad, teacher certification program, Cross-disciplinary first year options. **Honors Programs:** UBC offers many honours programs for academically strong undergraduates **Combined Degree Programs:** BA/BSc. **Disability Services:** Special programs offered to physically disabled students include note-taking services, reader services, tape recorders, tutors. **Career Services:** Alumni network, alumni services, career/job search classes, career assessment, internships, regional alumni. Career Services highlights include Outstanding Coop (Work Learn) programs in six major Faculties.

FACILITIES

Housing: Coed dorms, special housing for disabled students, men's dorms, special housing for international students, women's dorms, fraternity/sorority housing, apartments for married students, apartments for single students, theme housing: national theme housing in association with partner universities in Japan, Mexico, Korea, and Hong Kong SAR. 90% of campus accessible to physically disabled. **Special Academic Facilities/Equipment:** Museum of Anthropology Barber Learning Centre Beaty Biodiversity Museum Geological Museum TRIUMF, sub-atomic particle research Botanical Gardens Nitobe Garden Belkin Art Gallery Chan Centre for Performing Arts Liu International Studies Centre St.John's College (Graduate College) Pulp and Paper Centre Centre for Intergrated Systems Research Wall Centre for Interdisciplinary Studies **Computers:** 100% of classrooms, 100% of dorms, 100% of libraries, 100% of dining areas, 100% of student union, 100% of common outdoor areas have wireless network access. Students can register for classes online. Administrative functions (other than registration) can be performed online.

CAMPUS LIFE

Environment: Metropolis. **Activities:** Choral groups, concert band, dance, drama/theater, literary magazine, music ensembles, musical theater, opera, radio station, student government, student newspaper, student-run film society, symphony orchestra, International Student Organization 250 registered organizations, 1 honor societies, 7 religious organizations. 9 fraternities, 8 sororities. **Athletics (Intercollegiate):** *Men:* baseball, basketball, crew/rowing, cross-country, field hockey, football, golf, ice hockey, rugby, soccer, swimming, track/field (outdoor), volleyball. *Women:* basketball, crew/rowing, cross-country, field hockey, golf, ice hockey, rugby, soccer, swimming, track/field (outdoor), volleyball. **On-Campus Highlights:** Koerner Library, Museum of Anthropology, Chan Centre, Student Union Building, Barber Learning Centre. **Environmental Initiatives:** UBC is a signatory to the Talloires Declaration. It has integrated sustainability into its vision statement and strategic plan and formed a President's Advisory Council on Sustainability. The UBC Sustainability Office opened in 1998 " the first of its kind in a Canadian university. UBC has created an advisory committee of faculty, staff, students and alumni on socially responsible investing. The committee advises the Board of Governors on issues of transparency, proxy votes, and socially responsible investment practices. UBC met 2012 Kyoto Protocol targets in 2006, having reduced over the past 16 years greenhouse gas emissions by 25 per cent. UBC currently reduces carbon emissions by 14,000 tonnes annually. UBC recently finished a capital upgrade campaign that rebuilt or retrofitted nearly 300 buildings on campus to increase energy and water efficiency and reduce emissions. In addition to the numerous green building on campus, all new construction is required to achieve LEED Gold certification and all new residential constructions follows equivalent residential construction guidelines set forth in UBC's Residential Environmental Assessment Program. Numerous other initiatives: Initiatives such as the Student Ambassadors Initiative, Sustainability Pledge Program and Student Environment Centre fully engage students in sustainable living. UBC's dining services exclusively serves local eggs, poultry and milk. UBC currently offers more than 300 sustainability-related courses. UBC Okanagan heating energy is projected to come from fully sustainable resources (ground source) within the next two to three years. For other commitments see: http://www.sustain.ubc.ca/

ADMISSIONS

Basis for Candidate Selection: *Very important factors considered include:* academic GPA, rigor of secondary school record. *Other factors considered include:* application essay, recommendation(s), standardized test scores, character/personal qualities, extracurricular activities, level of applicant's interest, talent/ability, volunteer work, work experience. **Freshman Admission Requirements:** High school diploma is required and GED is not accepted. *Academic units required:* 4 English, 3 mathematics, 12 academic electives. 4 English, 3 mathematics, 12 academic electives. **Transfer Admission Requirements:** college transcript(s), statement of good standing from prior institution(s). **General Admission Information:** Application Fee $100. Regular application deadline 2/28. Notification on a rolling basis, beginning on or about 2/15. Nonfall registration accepted. Admission may be deferred for a maximum of up to one year. Credit and/or placement offered for CEEB Advanced Placement tests.

COSTS AND FINANCIAL AID

Required Forms and Deadlines: institution's own financial aid form. **Types of Aid:** *Need-based scholarships/grants:* Provincial scholarships and grants are available for Canadian citizens permanent residents of Canada. International students are eligible for modest merit awards. No application is necessary for merit-based awards. International students of outstanding academic merit and personal accomplishment who would otherwise not have the means to attend university may be nominated for awards, of which a limited number are awarded annually of between $15,000 -$35,000, depending on means. These awards are by nomination only (deadline for nominations February 1). Athletic scholarships are available for outstanding athletes, at head coach discretion in accordance with CIS rules. *Loans:* Direct Subsidized Stafford, Direct Unsubsidized Stafford, Direct PLUS, Subsidized Stafford, Unsubsidized Stafford, PLUS. **Student Employment:** Institutional employment available. Off-campus job opportunities are good. **Criteria for awarding institutional aid:** *Non-need-based:* academics, athletics, leadership.

UNIVERSITY OF CALIFORNIA—BERKELEY

110 Sproul Hall, Berkeley, CA 94720-5800
CEEB Code: 4833
Website: www.berkeley.edu • **ACT Code:** 444

This public school was founded in 1868. It has a 1232-acre campus.

RATINGS
Admissions Selectivity Rating: 98 **Fire Safety Rating:** 83 **Green Rating:** 96

STUDENTS AND FACULTY
Student Body: 11% out-of-state.
Retention and Graduation: 71% freshmen graduate within 4 years. 91% freshmen graduate within 6 years. **Faculty:** 0% of classes are taught by teaching assistants.

ACADEMICS
Degrees: bachelor's, master's, post-bachelor's certificate. **Majors with Highest Enrollment:** computer engineering; English language and literature; political science and government. **Special Study Options:** Accelerated program, cross-registration, double major, dual enrollment, English as a Second Language (ESL), exchange student program (domestic), honors program, independent study, internships, student-designed major, study abroad, teacher certification program. **Combined Degree Programs:** 10 Engineering Double Majors BS Degree. **Disability Services:** Special programs offered to physically disabled students include note-taking services, reader services, tape recorders, tutors. **Career Services:** alumni services, career/job search classes, career assessment, internships.

FACILITIES
Housing: Coed dorms, special housing for disabled students, men's dorms, special housing for international students, women's dorms, fraternity/sorority housing, apartments for married students, cooperative housing, apartments for single students, theme housing. 95% of campus accessible to physically disabled. **Special Academic Facilities/Equipment:** Lawrence Berkeley National Lab, Pacific Film Archive, Earthquake Data Center, Museums of art, anthropology, natural history, paleontology,Botanical Garden **Computers:** Students can register for classes online. Administrative functions (other than registration) can be performed online.

CAMPUS LIFE
Environment: Activities: Choral groups, concert band, dance, drama/theater, jazz band, literary magazine, marching band, music ensembles, musical theater, pep band, radio station, student government, student newspaper, student-run film society, symphony orchestra, television station, yearbook, International Student Organization, Model UN 300 registered organizations, 6 honor societies, 28 religious organizations. 38 fraternities, 19 sororities. **Athletics (Intercollegiate):** *Men:* baseball, basketball, crew/rowing, cross-country, diving, football, golf, gymnastics, rugby, sailing, soccer, swimming, tennis, track/field (outdoor), water polo. *Women:* basketball, crew/rowing, cross-country, diving, field hockey, golf, gymnastics, lacrosse, sailing, soccer, softball, swimming, tennis, track/field (outdoor), volleyball, water polo. **On-Campus Highlights:** Botanical Gardens, Lawrence Hall of Science, Museum of Anthropology, Museum of Art **Environmental Initiatives:** Planning and Reporting: Completion of 2008 Campus

Sustainability Assessment, 2009, 2010, and 2011 Campus Sustainability Reports, 2009 Campus Sustainability Plan; Establishment of campus Sustainability Metrics; Completion of 2009 Climate Action Plan; System-wide sustainability metrics included in UCOP Accountability Framework Implementation: We aggressively pursue measures to reduce greenhouse gas emissions on campus in order to achieve our goal of achieving 1990 levels by 2014. The results of the UC Berkeley 2010 Greenhouse Gas Inventory reveal an increase in greenhouse gas (GHG) emissions of 0.8% or about 1,400 metric tons CO2e (carbon dioxide equivalent) relative to the 2009 inventory. Even with this small increase in 2010, emissions are still almost 5% below 2008 levels. Electricity use in 2010 is down 1.1% on the main campus and 1.5% overall relative to 2009. The campus goal of achieving a 25% reduction in fuel from fleet and commute was met and exceeded (down over 30% since 1990). The drive-alone rate for faculty and staff dropped by four percentage points (to 43%). In addition, green fleet vehicles are over over 21% of the total fleet. Our planned strategies for further reducing our emissions include increasing the efficiency of our energy usage (especially in existing buildings), providing incentives for occupant-controlled electricity consumption, and promoting sustainable transportation. We will be commissioning all large buildings in the next 3-4 years, having recently completed energy efficiency projects that will reduce emissions by 6,800 tons each year. The promotion of tap water as part of the I Heart Tap Water campaign has reduced bottled water sales by at least 25%. Our new Green Department and Event certifications have been successful -- at least 26,000 faculty, staff, students, and guests have been participants in a certified event or department. Communication and Coordination: We continue to expand our outreach to and coordination with students, faculty, and staff. Across campus, UC Berkeley works to be more sustainable in the nine areas covered by this report, complemented by numerous campus-wide and administrative measures. These measures " campus committees and organizations, grants, communication tools, reports, and other similar initiatives " are a vital part of any sustainable institution and help define the culture of sustainability at UC Berkeley. The work over the years can be seen in the extent to which sustainability has been institutionalized on campus. One example is the nearly $1 million of student fees awards by The Green Initiative Fund. In addition to our newsletter, we have updated our websites, guest lectured at numerous classes, and launched a Facebook page. We also host Student Sustainability Forums two times a year, intended to be a space for members of the campus community to become more informed about how various campus entities are working towards sustainability and to provide networking opportunities.

ADMISSIONS

Freshman Academic Profile: Average high school GPA 3.8. 98% in top 10% of high school class, 100% in top 25% of high school class, 100% in top 50% of high school class. SAT Math middle 50% range 630-770. SAT Critical Reading middle 50% range 590-720. SAT Writing middle 50% range 620-750. ACT middle 50% range 27-33. Minimum web-based TOEFL 80. Minimum paper TOEFL 550. **Basis for Candidate Selection:** *Very important factors considered include:* application essay, academic GPA, rigor of secondary school record, state residency. *Important factors considered include:* standardized test scores, character/personal qualities, extracurricular activities, talent/ability, volunteer work, work experience. *Other factors considered include:* first generation, geographical residence. **Freshman Admission Requirements:** High school diploma is required and GED is accepted. *Academic units required:* 4 English, 3 mathematics, 2 science, (2 science labs), 2 foreign language, 2 history, 1 visual/performing arts, 1 academic electives. *Academic units recommended:* 4 English, 3 mathematics, 2 science, (2 science labs), 2 foreign language, 2 history, 1 visual/performing arts, 1 academic electives. **Freshman Admission Statistics:** 61,731 applied, 18% admitted, 36% enrolled. **Transfer Admission Requirements:** essay or personal statement, minimum college GPA of 2.4 required. Lowest grade transferable D. **General Admission Information:** Application Fee $60. Regular application deadline 11/30. Nonfall registration accepted. Neither credit nor placement offered for CEEB Advanced Placement tests.

COSTS AND FINANCIAL AID

Annual in-state tuition $11,220. Annual out-of-state tuition $34,098. Room and board $15,000. Required fees $1,654. Average book expense $1,214. **Required Forms and Deadlines:** FAFSA, state aid form. **Notification of Awards:** Applicants will be notified of awards on or about 4/15. **Types of Aid:** *Need-based scholarships/grants:* Federal Pell, SEOG, state scholarships/grants, private scholarships, the school's own gift aid. *Loans:* Direct Subsidized Stafford, Direct Unsubsidized Stafford, Direct PLUS, Federal Perkins. **Student Employment:** Federal Work-Study Program available. Institutional employment available. Off-campus job opportunities are excellent. **Criteria for awarding institutional aid:** *Non-need-based:* academics.

UNIVERSITY OF CALIFORNIA—DAVIS

178 Mrak Hall, One Shields Ave, Davis, CA 95616
Phone: 530-752-2971 • **Financial Aid Phone:** 530-752-2396
E-mail: undergraduateadmissions@ucdavis.edu • **CEEB Code:** 4834
Fax: 530-752-1280 • **Website:** www.ucdavis.edu • **ACT Code:** 454

This public school was founded in 1908. It has a 5200-acre campus.

RATINGS

Admissions Selectivity Rating: 93   **Fire Safety Rating:** 76   **Green Rating:** 94

STUDENTS AND FACULTY

Enrollment: 25,588. **Student Body:** 55% female, 45% male, 3% out-of-state, 4% international (121 countries represented). Asian 37%, African American 2%, Caucasian 32%, Hispanic 16%, Native American 0%.
Retention and Graduation: 93% freshmen return for sophomore year. 51% freshmen graduate within 4 years. 82% freshmen graduate within 6 years. 40% grads go on to further study within 1 year. 23% grads pursue arts and sciences degrees. 4% grads pursue law degrees. 1% grads pursue business degrees. 12% grads pursue medical degrees. **Faculty:** Student/faculty ratio 16:1. 1422 full-time faculty, 98% hold PhDs, 24% are members of minority groups, 36% are women.

ACADEMICS

Degrees: bachelor's, doctoral, master's, post-bachelor's certificate, post-master's certificate. **Classes:** Most classes have 20–29 students. Most lab/discussion sessions have 20–29 students. **Majors with Highest Enrollment:** biology/biological sciences; economics; psychology. **Special Study Options:** Accelerated program, cross-registration, double major, dual enrollment, English as a Second Language (ESL), honors program, independent study, internships, student-designed major, study abroad, teacher certification program, Washington DC Center. **Honors Programs:** The Davis Honors Challenge (DHC) is an innovative, open-application, campuswide honors program for highly motivated students. In addition to a mentor program and a residential living-learning option for first-year students, DHC offers students the opportunity to participate in an honors program for four years. Integrated Studies Honors Program (ISHP), the oldest continuous residential learning community in the UC system, is an invitational, residential honors program for first-year students. ISHP provides an academic residential community similar to those of the best small colleges and helps students integrate knowledge from the arts and humanities, natural sciences and engineering, and social sciences. **Disability Services:** Special programs offered to physically disabled students include note-taking services, reader services, tape recorders, tutors.

FACILITIES

Housing: Coed dorms, special housing for disabled students, women's dorms, apartments for married students, cooperative housing, apartments for single students, wellness housing, theme housing, Special Interest Communities: Davis Honors Challenge; Hammarskjöld International Relations; Integrated Studies; Multiethnic Program; Music, Arts & Performance; Quiet; Program Rainbow House; Women's Community. **Special Academic Facilities/Equipment:** Art galleries, 150-acre university arboretum, equestrian center, craft center, student experimental farm, nuclear lab, human performance lab, natural reserves, early childhood lab, raptor center, primate research center. **Computers:** Students can register for classes online. Administrative functions (other than registration) can be performed online.

CAMPUS LIFE

Environment: Town. **Activities:** Choral groups, concert band, dance, drama/theater, jazz band, literary magazine, marching band, music ensembles, musical theater, pep band, radio station, student government, student newspaper, student-run film society, symphony orchestra, television station, yearbook, Campus Ministries, International Student Organization, Model UN 364 registered organizations, 1 honor societies, 50 religious organizations. 28 fraternities, 21 sororities. **Athletics (Intercollegiate):** *Men:* baseball, basketball, cross-country, diving, football, golf, soccer, swimming, tennis, track/field (outdoor), track/field (indoor), water polo, wrestling. *Women:* basketball, crew/rowing, cross-country, diving, field hockey, golf, gymnastics, lacrosse, soccer, softball, swimming, tennis, track/field (outdoor), track/field (indoor), volleyball, water polo. **On-Campus Highlights:** Mondavi Center for the Performing Arts, Memorial Union/Coffee House, Activities and Recreation Center (The ARC), Sciences Laboratory Building, The UC Davis Arboretum, http://daviswiki.org/. **Environmental Initiatives:** UC Davis is taking action to reduce greenhouse gas emissions and energy use on campus through programs like the Strategic Energy Partnership Program, which is improving energy conservation and energy efficiency on campus and has identified retrofit and recommissioning projects that will save more than 28 million kilowatt-hours and 2 million therms over the next three years. The campus installed a 756kW solar photovoltaic system, which is expected to generate 10,879,388 kWh during 2012. UC Davis has also embarked on an ambitious initiative to reduce lighting energy use by 60% in five years, which will reduce energy use and greenhouse gas emissions (read more at www.sustainability.ucdavis.edu/news/2010/november/smart_lighting.html). Work on climate issues at UC Davis includes everything from the campus Climate Action Plan (CAP) and energy use reduction to studying pollution in the Arctic atmosphere and building global climate models. UC Davis faculty and student research on climate change spans a wide range of investigation from basic inquiry to solution-based engineering work (learn more at climatechange.ucdavis.edu/). The CAP analyzes campus issues around greenhouse gas emissions reductions, energy use and energy sourcing (find out more at www.sustainability.ucdavis.edu/progress/climate/index.html). UC Davis, a leader in bicycling, is one of two campuses to achieve the Gold level designation for a Bicycle Friendly University from the League of American Bicyclists. On any given day, up to 20,000 bikes are on campus. The Bike Barn helps on-campus cyclists with over 10,000 repairs per year. Unitrans, the community bus system (www.unitrans.ucdavis.edu), is operated by UC Davis students, has a fleet of clean busses that runs on compressed natural gas, and provides more than 3,000,000 rides per year. UC Davis undergraduate students make remarkable use of buses with more than 92 percent of local trips on these environmentally friendly alternative transportation systems. UC Davis conducted a Bikeway and Transit Network Study, which outlines plans for additional bicycling infrastructure. UC Davis is a leader in green building design. For the Davis campus, new buildings must be at least 25% more efficient than required by California's strict energy code. New buildings must also be designed to meet LEED Silver as a minimum and they typically achieve LEED Gold or Platinum. Five completed projects at UC Davis have been awarded LEED ratings, three at Platinum level and two at Gold level. The Winery, Brewery and Food Science Laboratory is the first such facility in the world to be awarded LEED Platinum, the highest rating given by the US Green Building Council and features on-site solar power generation, extensive daylighting, a large capacity rainwater capture system and is designed as a test bed for innovative production processes to capture carbon dioxide, re-use process water and dramatically reduce energy use. The Gallagher Hall Graduate School of Management and Conference Center also earned LEED Platinum certification and employs a radiant heating and cooling system coupled with a ground source heat pump and on-site photovoltaic panels. The UC Davis Tahoe Environmental Research Center was one of the very first laboratory buildings in the world to be awarded LEED Platinum. Of 16 major projects in progress,1 is expected to achieve LEED Platinum, 7 are expected to achieve Gold, 7 are expected to achieve Silver, and 1 (started before policy adoption of Silver certification) is expected to achieve Certified; in addition, one project is pursuing a Living Building Challenge rating. The campus also has the first two dormitory buildings in the state with Energy Star certifications: Webster Hall has an advanced thermostat control system and score of 76 and Emerson Hall has a score of 82.

ADMISSIONS

Freshman Academic Profile: Average high school GPA 4.0. 84% from public high schools. SAT Math middle 50% range 570-690. SAT Critical Reading middle 50% range 520-640. SAT Writing middle 50% range 540-660. ACT middle 50% range 24-30. Minimum web-based TOEFL 60. Minimum paper TOEFL 550. **Basis for Candidate Selection:** *Very important factors considered include:* academic GPA, rigor of secondary school record, standardized test scores. *Important factors considered include:* application essay, character/personal qualities, extracurricular activities, first generation, talent/ability. *Other factors considered include:* state residency, volunteer work, work experience. **Freshman Admission Requirements:** High school diploma is required and GED is accepted. *Academic units required:* 4 English, 3 mathematics, 2 science, (2 science labs), 2 foreign language, 2 social studies, 1 visual/performing arts, 1 academic electives. *Academic units recommended:* 4 English, 3 mathematics, 2 science, (2 science labs), 2 foreign language, 2 social studies, 1 visual/performing arts, 1 academic electives. **Freshman Admission Statistics:** 49,333 applied, 46% admitted, 23% enrolled. **Transfer Admission Requirements:** High school transcript, college transcript(s), essay or personal statement, statement of good standing from prior institution(s). Lowest grade transferable D-. **General Admission Information:** Application Fee $60. Regular application deadline 11/30. Regular notification 3/15. Nonfall registration not accepted. Credit and/or placement offered for CEEB Advanced Placement tests.

COSTS AND FINANCIAL AID

Annual in-state tuition $11,220. Annual out-of-state tuition $34,098. Room and board $13,503. Required fees $2,657. Average book expense $1,602. **Required Forms and Deadlines:** FAFSA. **Notification of Awards:** Applicants will be notified of awards on a rolling basis beginning 3/12. **Types of Aid:** *Need-based scholarships/grants:* Federal Pell, SEOG, state scholarships/grants, private

scholarships, the school's own gift aid, specify):Academic Competitiveness Grant (ACG) and National Science and Mathematics Access to Retain Talent Grant (SMART). *Loans:* Direct Subsidized Stafford, Direct Unsubsidized Stafford, Direct PLUS, Federal Perkins, college/university loans from institutional funds. **Student Employment:** Highest amount earned per year from on-campus jobs $7,280. **Financial Aid Statistics:** 97% freshmen, 97% undergrads receive need-based scholarship or grant aid. 1% freshmen, 1% undergrads receive non-need-based scholarship or grant aid. 71% freshmen, 68% undergrads receive need-based self-help aid. 1% freshmen, 1% undergrads receive athletic scholarships. 54% undergrads receive any aid. 52% undergrads borrow to pay for school. Average cumulative indebtedness $18,386. **Criteria for awarding institutional aid:** *Non-need-based:* academics, athletics.

UNIVERSITY OF CALIFORNIA—IRVINE

Office of Admissions and Relations with Schools, Irvine, CA 92697-1075
Phone: 949-824-6703 • **Financial Aid Phone:** 949-824-8262
E-mail: admissions@uci.edu • **CEEB Code:** 4859
Fax: 949-824-2951

This public school was founded in 1965. It has a 1500-acre campus.

RATINGS

Admissions Selectivity Rating: 96	Fire Safety Rating: 72	Green Rating: 99

STUDENTS AND FACULTY

Enrollment: 22,216. **Student Body:** 54% female, 46% male, 1% out-of-state, 6% international (88 countries represented). Asian 47%, African American 2%, Caucasian 18%, Hispanic 20%, Native American 0%.
Retention and Graduation: 93% freshmen return for sophomore year. 66% freshmen graduate within 4 years. 86% freshmen graduate within 6 years. **Faculty:** Student/faculty ratio 19:1. 1467 full-time faculty, 98% hold PhDs, 30% are members of minority groups, 35% are women. % of classes are taught by teaching assistants.

ACADEMICS

Degrees: bachelor's, master's, post-bachelor's certificate. **Classes.** Most classes have 20–29 students. Most lab/discussion sessions have fewer than 10 students. **Majors with Highest Enrollment:** biology/biological sciences; psychology; social psychology. **Special Study Options:** Accelerated program, distance learning, double major, dual enrollment, English as a Second Language (ESL), honors program, independent study, internships, liberal arts/career combination, study abroad, teacher certification program. **Honors Programs:** Campuswide Honors Program (CHP) **Combined Degree Programs:** 3-2 MBA. **Disability Services:** Special programs offered to physically disabled students include note-taking services, reader services, tape recorders. **Career Services:** Alumni network, alumni services, career/job search classes, career assessment, internships.

FACILITIES

Housing: Coed dorms, special housing for disabled students, men's dorms, special housing for international students, women's dorms, fraternity/sorority housing, apartments for married students, cooperative housing, apartments for single students, theme housing. 95% of campus accessible to physically disabled. **Special Academic Facilities/Equipment:** Museum of systemic biology, freshwater marsh reserve, electron microscope, nuclear reactor, laser institute, research facilities. **Computers:** 90% of classrooms, 100% of libraries, 100% of dining areas, 100% of student union, have wireless network access. Students can register for classes online. Administrative functions (other than registration) can be performed online.

CAMPUS LIFE

Environment: City. **Activities:** Choral groups, concert band, dance, drama/theater, jazz band, literary magazine, music ensembles, musical theater, opera, pep band, radio station, student government, student newspaper, student-run film society, symphony orchestra, yearbook, International Student Organization, Model UN 484 registered organizations, 18 honor societies, 51 religious organizations. 21 fraternities, 23 sororities. **Athletics (Intercollegiate):** *Men:* baseball, basketball, cross-country, golf, sailing, soccer, tennis, track/field (outdoor), volleyball, water polo. *Women:* basketball, cross-country, golf, sailing, soccer, tennis, track/field (outdoor), volleyball, water polo. **On-Campus Highlights:** Anteater Recreation Center, Bren Events Center, Cross-Cultural Center, Beall Center for Art and Technology, Arts Plaza. **Environmental Initiatives:** UCI worked closely with the U.S. Green Building Council to be the first university to develop campus-wide prototype LEED credits. This effort was followed by the USGBC adopting the Application Guide to Multiple Building and On-Campus Building Projects which effectively streamlines and economizes the

LEED certification process for all universities nationwide. In 2008, UCI signed an agreement with SunEdison to finance, build, and operate a solar photovoltaic energy system on campus. In March 2009, UCI began purchasing energy generated by the system which is expected to produce more than 24 million kWh and offset 25.6 million pounds of CO_2e over 20 years. In 2009, the system produced over 1.2 million kWh. 3. UCI operates the largest and most successful Sustainable Transportation Program (measured in terms of reduced single-occupant automobile ridership) in Orange County. UCI's alternative transportation initiatives reduce more than 23 million vehicle miles and 20,000 metric tons of greenhouse gas emissions annually. In 2008, this program was awarded the Governor's Environmental and Economic Leadership Award, California's highest environmental honor.

ADMISSIONS

Freshman Academic Profile: Average high school GPA 3.9. 96% in top 10% of high school class, 100% in top 25% of high school class, 100% in top 50% of high school class. 79% from public high schools. SAT Math middle 50% range 540-670. SAT Critical Reading middle 50% range 470-610. SAT Writing middle 50% range 490-620. Minimum web-based TOEFL 80. Minimum paper TOEFL 550. **Basis for Candidate Selection:** *Very important factors considered include:* application essay, academic GPA, rigor of secondary school record, standardized test scores, extracurricular activities, level of applicant's interest, talent/ability, volunteer work, work experience. *Important factors considered include:* character/personal qualities. *Other factors considered include:* first generation, state residency. **Freshman Admission Requirements:** High school diploma is required and GED is accepted. *Academic units required:* 4 English, 3 mathematics, 2 science, (2 science labs), 2 foreign language. social studies, 2 history, 1 visual/performing arts, 1 academic electives. *Academic units recommended:* 4 English, 3 mathematics, 2 science, (2 science labs), 2 foreign language. social studies, 2 history, 1 visual/performing arts, 1 academic electives. **Freshman Admission Statistics:** 56,508 applied, 42% admitted, 21% enrolled. **Transfer Admission Requirements:** High school transcript, college transcript(s), essay or personal statement, minimum college GPA of 2.0 required. Lowest grade transferable C. **General Admission Information:** Application Fee $60. Regular application deadline 11/30. Regular notification 3/31. Nonfall registration not accepted. Credit offered for CEEB Advanced Placement tests.

COSTS AND FINANCIAL AID

Annual in-state tuition $11,220. Annual out-of-state tuition $34,098. Room and board $11,735. Required fees $3,006. Average book expense $1,567. **Required Forms and Deadlines:** FAFSA, state aid formGPA verification form to state agency. **Notification of Awards:** Applicants will be notified of awards on a rolling basis beginning 4/1. **Types of Aid:** *Need-based scholarships/grants:* Federal Pell, SEOG, state scholarships/grants, private scholarships, the school's own gift aid. *Loans:* Direct Subsidized Stafford, Direct Unsubsidized Stafford, Direct PLUS, Subsidized Stafford, Unsubsidized Stafford, PLUS, Federal Perkins, college/university loans from institutional funds, Private Loans. **Student Employment:** Federal Work-Study Program available. Institutional employment available. **Financial Aid Statistics:** 93% freshmen, 92% undergrads receive need-based scholarship or grant aid. 1% freshmen, 1% undergrads receive non-need-based scholarship or grant aid. 81% freshmen, 71% undergrads receive need-based self-help aid. 1% freshmen, 1% undergrads receive athletic scholarships. 49% undergrads borrow to pay for school. Average cumulative indebtedness $18,719. **Criteria for awarding institutional aid:** *Non-need-based:* academics, art, athletics, job skills, leadership, music/drama, state/district residency.

UNIVERSITY OF CALIFORNIA—LOS ANGELES

Best 378

1147 Murphy Hall, Los Angeles, CA 90095-1436
Phone: 310-825-3101 • **Financial Aid Phone:** 310-206-0400
E-mail: ugadm@saonet.ucla.edu • **CEEB Code:** 4837
Fax: 310-206-1206 • **Website:** www.ucla.edu • **ACT Code:** 448

This public school was founded in 1919. It has a 419-acre campus.

RATINGS

Admissions Selectivity Rating: 98   **Fire Safety Rating:** 95   **Green Rating:** 99

STUDENTS AND FACULTY

Enrollment: 27,933. **Student Body:** 55% female, 45% male, 7% out-of-state, 10% international (138 countries represented). Asian 32%, African American 3%, Caucasian 30%, Hispanic 18%, Native American 0%.

Retention and Graduation: 71% freshmen graduate within 4 years. 91% freshmen graduate within 6 years. **Faculty:** Student/faculty ratio 17:1. 1989 full-time faculty, 98% hold PhDs, 25% are members of minority groups, 36% are women. 0% of classes are taught by teaching assistants.

ACADEMICS

Degrees: bachelor's, first professional, master's. **Classes:** Most classes have 10–19 students. Most lab/discussion sessions have 20–29 students. **Majors with Highest Enrollment:** business/managerial economics; political science and government; psychology. **Special Study Options:** Accelerated program, double major, English as a Second Language (ESL), honors program, independent study, internships, liberal arts/career combination, student-designed major, study abroad. **Honors Programs:** The College Honors Program. **Disability Services:** Special programs offered to physically disabled students include note-taking services, reader services, tape recorders, tutors. **Career Services:** Alumni network, alumni services, career/job search classes, career assessment, internships, regional alumni. Career Services highlights include Based at the UC Washington Center, CAPPP students carry out a research project on a topic of their own choosing, and complete a challenging, substantive internship at one of DC's hundreds of government agencies, think tanks, NGOs, non-profits, media outlets, advocacy, trade, and business organizations. Program participants earn up to 16 upper division units while remaining full-time UCLA students.

FACILITIES

Housing: Coed dorms, special housing for disabled students, fraternity/sorority housing, apartments for married students, apartments for single students, wellness housing, theme housing. 100% of campus accessible to physically disabled. **Special Academic Facilities/Equipment:** Art gallery, cultural history museum, sculpture garden, graphic arts center, numerous study centers, research institutes, UCLA Armand Hammer Museum of Art and Cultural Center, Murphy Sculpture Garden, Fowler Museum of Cultural History **Computers:** Students can register for classes online. Administrative functions (other than registration) can be performed online.

CAMPUS LIFE

Environment: Metropolis. **Activities:** Choral groups, concert band, dance, drama/theater, jazz band, literary magazine, marching band, music ensembles, musical theater, opera, pep band, radio station, student government, student newspaper, student-run film society, symphony orchestra, television station, yearbook, Campus Ministries, International Student Organization, Model UN 870 registered organizations, 21 honor societies, 38 religious organizations. 36 fraternities, 28 sororities. **Athletics (Intercollegiate):** *Men:* baseball, basketball, cross-country, football, golf, soccer, tennis, track/field (outdoor), track/field (indoor), volleyball, water polo. *Women:* basketball, crew/rowing, cross-country, diving, golf, gymnastics, soccer, softball, swimming, tennis, track/field (outdoor), track/field (indoor), volleyball, water polo. **On-Campus Highlights:** The UCLA Library, UCLA Fowler Museum of Cultural History, UCLA Book Store, DeNeve Plaza, Kerckhoff Coffee House. **Environmental Initiatives:** The University of California and state legislation set a target of reducing greenhouse gas emissions to 1990 levels by 2020. UCLA's comprehensive Climate Action Plan lays out a plan for the university to achieve that goal by 2012, eight years ahead. The plan catalogues the steps the university has taken in the past and contains a detailed financial feasibility analysis for the initiatives that the university will undertake in energy and transportation to reduce greenhouse gas emissions. The initiatives outlined in the Climate Action Plan, in addition to addressing a critical environmental issue, will also conserve university resources and result in significant cost reductions. The energy initiatives have an average payback period of less than 5 years, with some lighting initiatives paying back through cost savings in less than a year. By demonstrating that it is possible to address climate change through concrete verifiable emissions reductions even in the toughest budget situation, UCLA is setting an example for the rest of California and the nation. The plan also catalogues academic and research initiatives at UCLA focused on climate change and sustainability. UCLA is a living laboratory for climate and sustainability research. Undergraduate and graduate students engage with staff and faculty to pilot new technologies and policies on the university campus. With over 25 research centers focused on climate and sustainability, UCLA is creating the technology and training the leaders of tomorrow, while leading by example in our own operations. UCLA's greenhouse gas emissions come from mobile sources like the campus fleet and commutes, as well as buildings and energy. Sustainable transportation efforts at UCLA began before the term was coined. UCLA's been greening its transportation since 1984, when the campus had to address transportation issues in preparation for the olympics. Due to its location within the Los Angeles Basin and the South Coast Air Quality Management District, the campus has long endured traffic congestion and focused on reducing emissions. In the 1990s UCLA began a well developed transportation program that included vanpools, carpools and a campus shuttle. Now that suite of programs has expanded to include car-sharing through Zipcar, department bicycles and bicycle loaner programs, subsidized transit passes with five different transit agencies. 2010 the new UCLA Police Station won a green building award from the Los Angeles Business Council during their 40th Annual Architectural Awards. The Police Station was the third building on campus to achieve LEED Certification from the US Green Building Council. Green buildings use less energy and water and generate less waste than standard buildings. The Leadership in Energy and Environmental Design (LEED) Green Building Rating System recognizes buildings that meet strict environmental criteria and addresses a variety of building features including energy use, water efficiency, GHG emissions, building materials, site and landscaping, and transportation infrastructure. UCLA, along with the other campuses in the UC System, requires all new construction and major renovations to achieve LEED Silver or higher certification. This policy is part of a comprehensive Sustainable Practices Policy, developed by the 10 campuses of the UC system, which covers clean energy, climate, waste, purchasing, and food, in addition to green buildings.

ADMISSIONS

Freshman Academic Profile: Average high school GPA 4.2. 97% in top 10% of high school class, 100% in top 25% of high school class, 100% in top 50% of high school class. 68% from public high schools. SAT Math middle 50% range 600-760. SAT Critical Reading middle 50% range 560-680. SAT Writing middle 50% range 590-710. ACT middle 50% range 25-31. Minimum web-based TOEFL 83. Minimum paper TOEFL 550. **Basis for Candidate Selection:** *Very important factors considered include:* application essay, academic GPA, rigor of secondary school record, standardized test scores. *Important factors considered include:* character/personal qualities, extracurricular activities, talent/ability, volunteer work, work experience. *Other factors considered include:* first generation, geographical residence. **Freshman Admission Requirements:** High school diploma is required and GED is accepted. *Academic units required:* 4 English, 3 mathematics, 2 science, (2 science labs), 2 foreign language, 2 history, 1 academic electives, 1 Visual and Performing Arts. *Academic units recommended:* 4 English, 3 mathematics, 2 science, (2 science labs), 2 foreign language, 2 history, 1 academic electives, 1 Visual and Performing Arts **Freshman Admission Statistics:** 72,697 applied, 22% admitted, 35% enrolled. **Transfer Admission Requirements:** college transcript(s), essay or personal statement, statement of good standing from prior institution(s). Minimum college GPA of 2.4 required. Lowest grade transferable D. **General Admission Information:** Application Fee $60. Regular application deadline 11/30. Notification on a rolling basis, beginning on or about 3/31. Nonfall registration not accepted. Credit and/or placement offered for CEEB Advanced Placement tests.

COSTS AND FINANCIAL AID

Annual in-state tuition $11,120. Annual out-of-state tuition $34,098. Room and board $12,675. Required fees $1,472. Average book expense $1,521. **Required Forms and Deadlines:** FAFSA. **Notification of Awards:** Applicants will be notified of awards on a rolling basis beginning 3/15. **Types of Aid:** *Need-based scholarships/grants:* Federal Pell, SEOG, state scholarships/grants, private scholarships, the school's own gift aid, United Negro College Fund, Federal Nursing Scholarships. *Loans:* Subsidized Stafford, Unsubsidized Stafford, PLUS, Federal Perkins, Federal Nursing, state loans, college/university loans from institutional funds. **Student Employment:** Federal Work-Study Program available. Institutional employment available. Off-campus job opportunities are good. **Financial Aid Statistics:** 96% freshmen, 95% undergrads receive need-based scholarship or grant aid. 2% freshmen, 1% undergrads receive non-need-based scholarship or grant aid. 66% freshmen, 69% undergrads receive need-based self-help aid. 1% freshmen, 1% undergrads receive athletic scholarships. 56% freshmen, 54% undergrads receive any aid. 45% undergrads borrow to pay for school. Average cumulative indebtedness $18,203. **Criteria for awarding institutional aid:** *Non-need-based:* academics, alumni affiliation, athletics.

UNIVERSITY OF CALIFORNIA—RIVERSIDE

Best 378

3106 Student Services Building, Riverside, CA 92521
Phone: 951-827-3411 • **Financial Aid Phone:** 951-827-3878
E-mail: admit@ucr.edu • **CEEB Code:** 4839
Fax: 951-827-6344 • **Website:** www.ucr.edu

This public school was founded in 1954. It has a 1200-acre campus.

RATINGS

Admissions Selectivity Rating: 93   **Fire Safety Rating:** 86   **Green Rating:** 93

STUDENTS AND FACULTY

Enrollment: 18,537. **Student Body:** 52% female, 48% male, 0% out-of-state, 2% international (100 countries represented). Asian 36%, African American 6%, Caucasian 15%, Hispanic 35%, Native American 0%.

Retention and Graduation: 42% freshmen graduate within 4 years. 69% freshmen graduate within 6 years. **Faculty:** Student/faculty ratio 19:1. 751 full-time faculty, 98% hold PhDs, 33% are members of minority groups, 33% are women. 0% of classes are taught by teaching assistants.

ACADEMICS

Degrees: bachelor's, master's, post-bachelor's certificate. **Classes:** Most classes have 20–29 students. Most lab/discussion sessions have 20–29 students. **Majors with Highest Enrollment:** biology/biological sciences; business administration and management; psychology. **Special Study Options:** Accelerated program, cross-registration, double major, English as a Second Language (ESL), honors program, independent study, internships, student-designed major, study abroad, teacher certification program. **Disability Services:** Special programs offered to physically disabled students include note-taking services, reader services, tape recorders, tutors. **Career Services:** Alumni network, alumni services, career/job search classes, career assessment, internships Career Services highlights include Today's students do not always have the time to come to the brinks and mortar home of the traditional Career Center. The UCR Career Center has responded by developing state-of-the-art best practices to deliver services whether this is job search, internships, or career counseling. These new alternatives and virtual services range from a highly interactive website using podcast and YouTube features to providing workshops either in the classroom or in a virtual environment.

FACILITIES

Housing: Coed dorms, special housing for disabled students, special housing for international students, apartments for married students, apartments for single students, theme housing. **Special Academic Facilities/Equipment:** Art gallery, photography museum, botanical gardens, audio-visual resource center/studios, media resource center, statistical consulting center, citrus research center and agricultural experiment station, air pollution research center, center for environmental research and technology, water resources center, geophysics and planetary physics institute, center for bibliographical studies, center for family studies, center for crime and justice studies, natural reserve system, water resources center, salinity lab. **Computers:** 100% of classrooms, 15% of dorms, 100% of libraries, 100% of dining areas, 100% of student union, 100% of common outdoor areas have wireless network access. Students can register for classes online. Administrative functions (other than registration) can be performed online.

CAMPUS LIFE

Environment: City. **Activities:** Choral groups, concert band, dance, drama/theater, jazz band, literary magazine, music ensembles, musical theater, pep band, radio station, student government, student newspaper, student run film society, International Student Organization 264 registered organizations, 9 honor societies, 27 religious organizations. 20 fraternities, 20 sororities. **Athletics (Intercollegiate):** *Men:* baseball, basketball, cross-country, golf, soccer, tennis, track/field (outdoor), track/field (indoor). *Women:* basketball, cross-country, golf, soccer, softball, tennis, track/field (outdoor), track/field (indoor), volleyball. **On-Campus Highlights:** Basketball Games, Student Recreation Center and intramural sports, The Barn (music and comedy acts), Coffee Bean and Tea Leaf, The Highlander Union Building (HUB). **Environmental Initiatives:** UCR has a funded non-restrictive Office of Sustainability charged with coordinating sustainability initiatives throughout the campus supported by the Chancellor's Committee on Sustainability with the Chancellor serving as chair. UCR has an active engagement with the community including continuing education training courses on sustainability, a year long themed seminar on sustainability, and the development of a sustainability focused community garden. UCR takes a systems thinking approach to developing the built environment of the campus; integrating transportation, research, academics, design, energy, water and waste conservation into all projects.

ADMISSIONS

Freshman Academic Profile: Average high school GPA 3.6. 94% in top 10% of high school class, 100% in top 25% of high school class, 100% in top 50% of high school class. 90% from public high schools. SAT Math middle 50% range 500-630. SAT Critical Reading middle 50% range 470-580. SAT Writing middle 50% range 480-590. ACT middle 50% range 20-25. Minimum web-based TOEFL 80. Minimum paper TOEFL 550. **Basis for Candidate Selection:** *Very important factors considered include:* academic GPA, rigor of secondary school record, standardized test scores, state residency. *Important factors considered include:* application essay. *Other factors considered include:* first generation. **Freshman Admission Requirements:** High school diploma is required and GED is accepted. *Academic units required:* 4 English, 3 mathematics, 2 science, (2 science labs), 2 foreign language, 2 history, 1 visual/performing arts, 1 academic electives. *Academic units recommended:* 4 English, 3 mathematics, 2 science, (2 science labs), 2 foreign language, 2 history, 1 visual/performing arts, 1 academic electives. **Freshman Admission Statistics:** 30,395 applied, 63% admitted, 21% enrolled. **Transfer Admission Requirements:** college transcript(s), essay or personal statement, statement of good standing from prior institution(s). Minimum college GPA of 2.4 required. Lowest grade transferable D-. **General Admission Information:** Application Fee $60. Regular application deadline 11/30. Notification on a rolling basis, beginning on or about 2/1. Nonfall registration not accepted. Credit and/or placement offered for CEEB Advanced Placement tests.

COSTS AND FINANCIAL AID
Annual in-state tuition $11,220. Annual out-of-state tuition $34,098. Room and board $13,200. Required fees $1,740. Average book expense $1,800. **Required Forms and Deadlines:** FAFSA, state aid form. **Notification of Awards:** Applicants will be notified of awards on a rolling basis beginning 3/1. **Types of Aid:** *Need-based scholarships/grants:* Federal Pell, SEOG, state scholarships/ grants, private scholarships, the school's own gift aid. *Loans:* Direct Subsidized Stafford, Direct Unsubsidized Stafford, Direct PLUS, Federal Perkins, college/ university loans from institutional funds. **Student Employment:** Federal Work-Study Program available. Institutional employment available. Off-campus job opportunities are excellent. **Financial Aid Statistics:** 95% freshmen, 94% undergrads receive need-based scholarship or grant aid. 2% freshmen, 1% undergrads receive non-need-based scholarship or grant aid. 79% freshmen, 75% undergrads receive need-based self-help aid. 78% freshmen, 76% undergrads receive any aid. 73% undergrads borrow to pay for school. Average cumulative indebtedness $21,373. **Criteria for awarding institutional aid:** *Non-needbased:* academics, art, athletics, job skills, leadership, music/drama, state/district residency.

UNIVERSITY OF CALIFORNIA—SAN DIEGO

9500 Gilman Drive, La Jolla, CA 92093-0021
Phone: 858-534-4831 • **Financial Aid Phone:** 858-534-4480
E-mail: admissionsinfo@ucsd.edu • **CEEB Code:** 4836
Fax: 858-534-5723 • **Website:** www.ucsd.edu

This public school was founded in 1960. It has a 1,976-acre campus.

RATINGS
Admissions Selectivity Rating: 97   **Fire Safety Rating:** 81   **Green Rating:** 93

STUDENTS AND FACULTY
Enrollment: 22,676. **Student Body:** 49% female, 51% male, 4% out-of-state, 13% international (87 countries represented). Asian 39%, African American 2%, Caucasian 22%, Hispanic 15%.
Retention and Graduation: 94% freshmen return for sophomore year. 57% freshmen graduate within 4 years. 86% freshmen graduate within 6 years. 40% grads go on to further study within 1 year. 34% grads pursue arts and sciences degrees. 15% grads pursue law degrees. 8% grads pursue business degrees. 16% grads pursue medical degrees. **Faculty:** Student/faculty ratio 19:1. 982 full-time faculty, 98% hold PhDs, 24% are members of minority groups, 28% are women. 0% of classes are taught by teaching assistants.

ACADEMICS
Degrees: bachelor's, master's. **Classes:** Most classes have 10–19 students. Most lab/discussion sessions have 20–29 students. **Majors with Highest Enrollment:** biology/biological sciences; economics; psychology. **Special Study Options:** Accelerated program, cooperative education program, cross-registration, double major, English as a Second Language (ESL), exchange student program (domestic), honors program, independent study, internships, liberal arts/career combination, student-designed major, study abroad, teacher certification program, Summer sessions for credit; special services for students with learning disabilities; Research programs, freshman honors program, in-depth academic assignments working in small groups or one-to-one with faculty. **Honors programs:** Each of UCSD's six colleges offers an honors program. Honors programs differ from college to college and year to year. **Combined degree programs:** BA/MD, BA/MA, Psychology, Experimental Psychology, Chemistry, Biochemistry, Cognitive Sci. **Disability Services:** Special programs offered to physically disabled students include note-taking services, reader services, tape recorders, tutors. **Career services:** Alumni network, alumni services, career/ job search classes, career assessment, internships, regional alumni.

FACILITIES
Housing: Coed dorms, special housing for disabled students, men's dorms, special housing for international students, women's dorms, fraternity/sorority housing, apartments for married students, cooperative housing, apartments for single students, International House for international students and others interested in international living. 100% of campus accessible to physically disabled. **Special Academic Facilities/Equipment:** Art galleries, center for

U.S.-Mexican studies, music recording studio, audiovisual center, center for music experimentation, aquarium, structural lab, San Diego supercomputer center,electron microscopes lab, the UC San Diego Medical Center, Scripps Institution of Oceanography, California Institute for Telecommunications and Information Technology (Calit2), Institute on Global Conflict and Cooperation; Institute of the Americas. **Computers:** 100% of classrooms, 100% of dorms, 100% of libraries, 100% of dining areas, 100% of student union, 30% of common outdoor areas have wireless network access. Students can register for classes online. Administrative functions (other than registration) can be performed online.

CAMPUS LIFE
Environment: Metropolis. **Activities:** Choral groups, concert band, dance, drama/theater, jazz band, literary magazine, marching band, music ensembles, musical theater, opera, pep band, radio station, student government, student newspaper, student-run film society, symphony orchestra, television station, yearbook, Campus Ministries, International Student Organization, Model UN. 406 registered organizations, 5 honor societies, 46 religious organizations. 19 fraternities, 14 sororities. **Athletics (Intercollegiate):** *Men:* baseball, basketball, crew/rowing, cross-country, diving, fencing, golf, soccer, swimming, tennis, track/field (outdoor), volleyball, water polo. *Women:* basketball, crew/ rowing, cross-country, diving, fencing, soccer, softball, swimming, tennis, track/ field (outdoor), volleyball, water polo. **On-Campus Highlights:** Geisel Library, Stuart Art (sculpture) Gallery, Sun God Statue, Ocean Cliffs, Stephen Birch Aquarium and Museum, Price Center Expansion. **Environmental Initiatives:** The LEED Gold Certified Sustainability Resource Center (SRC) provides a centralized, collaborative space in which to realize the common goals of maximizing campus environmental, social, and economic stewardship and sustainability; reducing the campus impact on the environment; maximizing campus and local outreach and participation; and, establishing a model for contributing to local, national, and global sustainability.

ADMISSIONS
Freshman Academic Profile: Average high school GPA 4.0. 100% in top 10% of high school class, 100% in top 25% of high school class, 100% in top 50% of high school class. SAT Math middle 50% range 620-730. SAT Critical Reading middle 50% range 550-660. SAT Writing middle 50% range 580-683. ACT middle 50% range 26-31. Minimum paper TOEFL 550. **Basis for Candidate Selection:** *Very important factors considered include:* application essay, academic GPA, rigor of secondary school record, standardized test scores, character/personal qualities, state residency, talent/ability. *Important factors considered include:* extracurricular activities, volunteer work. *Other factors considered include:* first generation, work experience. **Freshman Admission Requirements:** High school diploma is required and GED is accepted. *Academic units required:* 4 English, 3 mathematics, 2 science, (2 science labs), 2 foreign language, 2 history, 1 visual/performing arts, 1 academic electives. *Academic units recommended:* 4 English, 3 mathematics, 2 science, (2 science labs), 2 foreign language, 2 history, 1 visual/performing arts, 1 academic electives. **Freshman Admission Statistics:** 60,805 applied, 38% admitted, 20% enrolled. **Transfer Admission Requirements:** college transcript(s), essay or personal statement, statement of good standing from prior institution(s). Minimum college GPA of 2.4 required. Lowest grade transferable D. **General Admission Information:** Application Fee $60. Regular application deadline 11/30. Regular notification 3/31. Notification on a rolling basis, beginning on or about 3/15. Nonfall registration accepted. Credit and/or placement offered for CEEB Advanced Placement tests.

COSTS AND FINANCIAL AID
Annual in-state tuition $10,152. Annual out-of-state tuition $33,030. Room and board $11,684. Required fees $1,976. Average book expense $1,456. **Required Forms and Deadlines:** FAFSA, state aid form. **Notification of Awards:** Applicants will be notified of awards on a rolling basis beginning 3/15. **Types of Aid:** *Need-based scholarships/grants:* Federal Pell, SEOG, state scholarships/ grants, private scholarships, the school's own gift aid, Federal Academic Competitive Grant Federal National SMART Grant. *Loans:* Subsidized Stafford, Unsubsidized Stafford, PLUS, Federal Perkins, college/university loans from institutional funds, Alternative Loans. **Student Employment:** Federal Work-Study Program available. Institutional employment available. Highest amount earned per year from on-campus jobs $15,840. Off-campus job opportunities are good. **Financial Aid Statistics:** 97% freshmen, 96% undergrads receive need-based scholarship or grant aid. 1% freshmen, 85% freshmen, 84% undergrads receive need-based self-help aid. 2% freshmen, 1% undergrads receive athletic scholarships. 77% freshmen, 63% undergrads receive any aid. 52% undergrads borrow to pay for school. Average cumulative indebtedness $19,936. **Criteria for awarding institutional aid:** Non-need-based: academics, art, athletics, leadership, minority status, music/drama.

UNIVERSITY OF CALIFORNIA—SANTA BARBARA

Office of Admissions, Santa Barbara, CA 93106-2014
Phone: 805-893-2881 • **Financial Aid Phone:** 805-893-2118
E-mail: admissions@sa.ucsb.edu • **CEEB Code:** 4835
Fax: 805-893-2676 • **Website:** www.ucsb.edu

This public school was founded in 1909. It has a 989-acre campus.

RATINGS
Admissions Selectivity Rating: 93   **Fire Safety Rating:** 90   **Green Rating:** 99

STUDENTS AND FACULTY
Enrollment: 18,617. **Student Body:** 52% female, 48% male, 4% out-of-state, 2% international (72 countries represented). Asian 20%, African American 4%, Caucasian 45%, Hispanic 24%, Native American 1%.
Retention and Graduation: 92% freshmen return for sophomore year. 66% freshmen graduate within 4 years. 80% freshmen graduate within 6 years.
Faculty: Student/faculty ratio 17:1. 886 full-time faculty, 100% hold PhDs, 18% are members of minority groups, 34% are women.

ACADEMICS
Degrees: bachelor's, master's, post-bachelor's certificate, post-master's certificate. **Classes:** Most classes have fewer than 10 students. Most lab/discussion sessions have 20–29 students. **Majors with Highest Enrollment:** biology/biological sciences; economics; psychology. **Special Study Options:** Accelerated program, cross-registration, double major, dual enrollment, English as a Second Language (ESL), exchange student program (domestic), honors program, independent study, internships, student-designed major, study abroad, teacher certification program, Undergrads may take grad level classes. Off-Campus Study: Washington, DC. Freshman Seminars, pre professional programs and advising, academic minors, and undergraduate research. **Honors programs:** The College Honors Program is designed to give students in the College of Letters and Science the opportunity to pursue their interests as part of a small community of scholars. The program connects such students to the resources of a large university, while providing an intimate collegiate atmosphere where students work closely with peers and professors in small classes, research laboratories, and special program and activities. **Combined degree programs:** BA/MA, BS/MS. **Disability Services:** Special programs offered to physically disabled students include note-taking services, reader services, tape recorders, tutors. **Career services:** career/job search classes, career assessment, internships.

FACILITIES
Housing: Coed dorms, fraternity/sorority housing, apartments for married students, cooperative housing, apartments for single students, Wellness Housing, Theme Housing. **Special Academic Facilities/Equipment:** Art museum, centers for black studies, Chicano studies, and study of developing nations, institutes for applied behavioral sciences, community/organizational research, marine science, and theoretical physics, Channel Islands field station. **Computers:** 100% of dorms, 100% of dining areas, 100% of student union, have wireless network access. Students can register for classes online. Administrative functions (other than registration) can be performed online.

CAMPUS LIFE
Environment: City. **Activities:** Choral groups, concert band, dance, drama/theater, jazz band, literary magazine, music ensembles, musical theater, opera, pep band, radio station, student government, student newspaper, student-run film society, symphony orchestra, television station, yearbook, Campus Ministries, International Student Organization, Model UN. 508 registered organizations, 5 honor societies, 19 religious organizations. 17 fraternities, 18 sororities. **Athletics (Intercollegiate): Men:** baseball, basketball, cross-country, diving, golf, gymnastics, soccer, swimming, tennis, track/field (outdoor), volleyball, water polo. **Women:** basketball, cross-country, diving, gymnastics, soccer, softball, swimming, tennis, track/field (outdoor), volleyball, water polo. **On-Campus Highlights:** Storke Tower Plaza/University Center, University Art Museum, UCSB Davidson Library, Recreation Center, Career and Counseling Services Center. **Environmental Initiatives:** 1) Green buildings: minimum silver and strive for gold LEED certification. UCSB has the most LEED EB buildings in the UC System. All cleaning products and soaps used by the custodial staff are Green Seal certified. Plus toilet tissue, seat covers, and brown paper towels have 100% recycled content. 2) Energy: through HVAC and lighting retrofits, delamping, Flex Your Power campaigns, etc., the campus has decreased its per-square-footage electrical consumption by 31% and its natural gas consumption

by 23% since 1998. 3) Creation of a high-level Chancellor's Sustainability Committee that includes administration, deans, Nobel laureates, senior faculty, staff and students in charge of making recommendations for sustainability projects to the Chancellor.

ADMISSIONS
Freshman Academic Profile: Average high school GPA 3.9. 96% in top 10% of high school class, 98% in top 25% of high school class, 100% in top 50% of high school class. 87% from public high schools. SAT Math middle 50% range 570-690. SAT Critical Reading middle 50% range 550-670. SAT Writing middle 50% range 550-670. ACT middle 50% range 24-60. Minimum web-based TOEFL 79. Minimum paper TOEFL 550. **Basis for Candidate Selection:** *Very important factors considered include:* application essay, academic GPA, rigor of secondary school record, standardized test scores. *Other factors considered include:* Class rank, character/personal qualities, extracurricular activities, first generation, state residency, talent/ability, volunteer work, work experience. **Freshman Admission Requirements:** High school diploma is required and GED is accepted. *Academic units required:* 4 English, 3 mathematics, (2 science labs), 2 foreign language, 2 history, 1 visual/performing arts, 1 academic electives. *Academic units recommended:* 4 English, 3 mathematics, (2 science labs), 2 foreign language, 2 history, 1 visual/performing arts, 1 academic electives. **Freshman Admission Statistics:** 49,008 applied, 46% admitted, 18% enrolled. **Transfer Admission Requirements:** High school transcript, college transcript(s), essay or personal statement, minimum college GPA of 2.4 required. Lowest grade transferable D. **General Admission Information:** Application Fee $60. Regular application deadline 11/30. Regular notification 3/1. Nonfall registration not accepted. Credit and/or placement offered for CEEB Advanced Placement tests.

COSTS AND FINANCIAL AID
Annual in-state tuition $11,220. Annual out-of-state tuition $33,030. Room and board $13,110. Required fees $2,356. Average book expense $1,414. **Required Forms and Deadlines:** FAFSA. **Notification of Awards:** Applicants will be notified of awards on a rolling basis beginning 3/15. **Types of Aid.** *Need-based scholarships/grants:* Federal Pell, SEOG, state scholarships/grants, private scholarships, the school's own gift aid, Work Study is also available as need-based aid. *Loans:* Direct Subsidized Stafford, Direct Unsubsidized Stafford, Direct PLUS, Federal Perkins. **Student Employment:** Federal Work-Study Program available. Institutional employment available. Off-campus job opportunities are good. **Criteria for awarding institutional aid:** Non-need-based: academics, athletics.

UNIVERSITY OF CALIFORNIA—SANTA CRUZ

Office of Admissions, Cook House, Santa Cruz, CA 95064
Phone: 831-459-4008 • **Financial Aid Phone:** 831-459-2963
E-mail: admissions@ucsc.edu • **CEEB Code:** 4860
Fax: 831-459-4452 • **Website:** www.ucsc.edu

This public school was founded in 1965. It has a 2000-acre campus.

RATINGS
Admissions Selectivity Rating: 93   **Fire Safety Rating:** 73   **Green Rating:** 99

STUDENTS AND FACULTY
Enrollment: 15,978. **Student Body:** 53% female, 47% male, 3% out-of-state, 0% international (89 countries represented). Asian 15%, African American 1%, Caucasian 32%, Hispanic 19%.
Retention and Graduation: 50% freshmen graduate within 4 years. 73% freshmen graduate within 6 years. **Faculty:** Student/faculty ratio 19:1. 557 full-time faculty, 25% are members of minority groups, 37% are women. 0% of classes are taught by teaching assistants.

ACADEMICS
Degrees: bachelor's, doctoral, master's, post-bachelor's certificate. **Classes:** Most classes have 10–19 students. Most lab/discussion sessions have 10–19 students. **Majors with Highest Enrollment:** art/art studies; business/commerce; psychology. **Special Study Options:** cooperative education program, cross-registration, double major, exchange student program (domestic), independent study, internships, student-designed major, study abroad, teacher certification program. **Combined degree programs:** BA/MA, Economics/Applied Economics, Business Management Economics, Global Economic. **Disability Services:** Special programs offered to physically disabled students include

note-taking services, reader services, tape recorders, tutors. **Career services:** Alumni network, alumni services, career/job search classes, career assessment, internships Career services highlights include Chancellor's Undergraduate Internship Program (CUIP)—CUIP provides professional level on-campus internships in administrative departments throughout campus. Interns work with a mentor to develop personal and professional skills and take a lead role in producing a product or result in thir one-year internship. Interns receive a scholarship equivalent to their registration fees for a year in exchange for 450 hours of work. Students attend a 2-unit leadership seminar led by the Dean of Undergraduate Education during both Fall and Spring quarters. This program places an average of 35 students per year. Professions Training Program and Bonner Leaders (PTP/BL)- The PTP/BL service-learning program provides internships in local non-profit organizations along with an academic component focused on leadership development. Students receive a $1000 scholarship for 300 hours of work. This program is a partnership with the Bonner Foundation and AmeriCorps and places 15-20 students each year.

FACILITIES

Housing: Coed dorms, men's dorms, special housing for international students, women's dorms, apartments for married students, apartments for single students, Theme Housing, university-sponsored off-campus housing, RV Park, University Inn and Conference Center. **Special Academic Facilities/Equipment:** Eloise Pickard Smith Gallery, Mary Porter Sesnon Gallery, Center for Agroecology, Wellness Center, Long Marine Laboratory **Computers:** 100% of classrooms, 100% of dorms, 100% of libraries, 100% of dining areas, 100% of student union, have wireless network access. Students can register for classes online. Administrative functions (other than registration) can be performed online.

CAMPUS LIFE

Environment: City. **Activities:** Choral groups, dance, drama/theater, jazz band, literary magazine, music ensembles, musical theater, opera, radio station, student government, student newspaper, student-run film society, symphony orchestra, television station, Campus Ministries, International Student Organization, Model UN. 138 registered organizations, 3 honor societies, 19 religious organizations. 9 fraternities, 11 sororities. **Athletics (Intercollegiate):** *Men:* basketball, diving, soccer, swimming, tennis, volleyball. *Women:* basketball, cross-country, diving, golf, soccer, swimming, tennis, volleyball. **On-Campus Highlights:** Arboretum, Farm and Garden, East Field House, Bay Tree Bookstore/Grad Student Commons, Pogonip Open Area Reserve. **Environmental Initiatives:** Climate Action Plan; 2014 Achieve Zero Waste by 2020 (and 75% diversion by 2012); Campus Sustainability Plan (with specific environmental targets in 8 topic areas including increasing water conservation, already at 40% lower per capita than 20 years ago).

ADMISSIONS

Freshman Academic Profile: Average high school GPA 3.6. 96% in top 10% of high school class, 100% in top 25% of high school class, 100% in top 50% of high school class. 87% from public high schools. SAT Math middle 50% range 490-630. SAT Critical Reading middle 50% range 470-610. SAT Writing middle 50% range 480-620. ACT middle 50% range 20-27. Minimum web-based TOEFL 83. Minimum paper TOEFL 550. **Basis for Candidate Selection:** *Very important factors considered include:* application essay, academic GPA, rigor of secondary school record, standardized test scores, state residency. *Important factors considered include:* Class rank, character/personal qualities, extracurricular activities, first generation, geographical residence, talent/ability. *Other factors considered include:* volunteer work, work experience. **Freshman Admission Requirements:** High school diploma is required and GED is accepted. *Academic units required:* 4 English, 3 mathematics, 2 science, (2 science labs), 2 foreign language, 1 social studies, 1 history, 1 visual/performing arts, 1 academic electives, 1. *Academic units recommended:* 4 English, 3 mathematics, 2 science, (2 science labs), 2 foreign language, 1 social studies, 1 history, 1 visual/performing arts, 1 academic electives. **Freshman Admission Statistics:** 33,142 applied, 61% admitted, 19% enrolled. **Transfer Admission Requirements:** college transcript(s), essay or personal statement, statement of good standing from prior institution(s). Minimum college GPA of 2.4 required. Lowest grade transferable D. **General Admission Information:** Application Fee $60. Regular application deadline 11/30. Regular notification 3/31. Notification on a rolling basis, beginning on or about 3/15. Nonfall registration accepted. Neither credit nor placement offered for CEEB Advanced Placement tests.

COSTS AND FINANCIAL AID

Annual in-state tuition $12,192. Annual out-of-state tuition $35,070. Room and board $14,856. Required fees $1,224. Average book expense $1,407. **Required Forms and Deadlines:** FAFSA, state aid formCA Student Adi Commission GPA verification form for CA residents. **Notification of Awards:** Applicants will be notified of awards on a rolling basis beginning 4/1. **Types of Aid:** *Need-based scholarships/grants:* Federal Pell, SEOG, state scholarships/grants, private scholarships, the school's own gift aid. *Loans:* Direct Subsidized Stafford, Direct Unsubsidized Stafford, Direct PLUS, Federal Perkins.

Student Employment: Federal Work-Study Program available. Institutional employment available. Off-campus job opportunities are excellent. **Financial Aid Statistics:** 87% freshmen, 88% undergrads receive need-based scholarship or grant aid. 1% freshmen, 1% undergrads receive non-need-based scholarship or grant aid. 91% freshmen, 90% undergrads receive need-based self-help aid. 59% freshmen, 56% undergrads receive any aid. 53% undergrads borrow to pay for school. Average cumulative indebtedness $16,024. **Criteria for awarding institutional aid:** Non-need-based: academics, alumni affiliation, art, leadership, music/drama.

UNIVERSITY OF CENTRAL ARKANSAS

201 Donaghey Avenue, Conway, AR 72035
Phone: 501-450-3128 • **Financial Aid Phone:** 501-450-3140
E-mail: admissions@uca.edu • **CEEB Code:** 6012
Fax: 501-450-5228 • **Website:** www.uca.edu/ • **ACT Code:** 118

This public school was founded in 1907. It has a 262-acre campus.

RATINGS

Admissions Selectivity Rating: 63   **Fire Safety Rating:** 61   **Green Rating:** 60*

STUDENTS AND FACULTY

Enrollment: 9,028. **Student Body:** 58% female, 42% male, 8% out-of-state, 3% international (61 countries represented). Asian 2%, African American 18%, Caucasian 67%, Hispanic 3%, Native American 1%. **Retention and Graduation:** 70% freshmen return for sophomore year.

ACADEMICS

Degrees: associate, bachelor's, certificate, master's, post-bachelor's certificate, post-master's certificate. **Classes:** Most classes have 20–29 students. **Special Study Options:** Accelerated program, cooperative education program, distance learning, double major, dual enrollment, English as a Second Language (ESL), honors program, independent study, internships, liberal arts/career combination, study abroad, teacher certification program, 5 year professional program in Physical and Occupational Therapy. **Disability Services:** Special programs offered to physically disabled students include note-taking services, reader services, tape recorders. **Career services:** internships.

FACILITIES

Housing: Coed dorms, special housing for disabled students, men's dorms, special housing for international students, women's dorms, fraternity/sorority housing, apartments for married students, apartments for single students, Residential colleges are offered, as well as Honors housing. **Special Academic Facilities/Equipment:** Greenhouse, Baum Gellery, HPER Center, Planetarium, Technology Plaza, Smartboards, H.L. Minton Center for Geospatial Analysis and Research **Computers:** 100% of classrooms, 100% of dorms, 100% of libraries, 100% of dining areas, 100% of student union, 100% of common outdoor areas have wireless network access. Students can register for classes online. Administrative functions (other than registration) can be performed online.

CAMPUS LIFE

Environment: Town. **Activities:** Choral groups, concert band, dance, drama/theater, jazz band, literary magazine, marching band, music ensembles, pep band, radio station, student government, student newspaper, student-run film society, symphony orchestra, television station, yearbook, Campus Ministries, International Student Organization, Model UN. 158 registered organizations, 11 honor societies, 16 religious organizations. 12 fraternities, 8 sororities. **Athletics (Intercollegiate):** *Men:* baseball, basketball, cheerleading, cross-country, football, golf, soccer, tennis, track/field (outdoor), track/field (indoor). *Women:* basketball, cheerleading, cross-country, golf, soccer, softball, tennis, track/field (outdoor), track/field (indoor), volleyball. **On-Campus Highlights:** Student Center, HPER Center, Baum Gallery, Estes Stadium, Farris Center.

ADMISSIONS

Freshman Academic Profile: Average high school GPA 3.3. Minimum web-based TOEFL 61. Minimum paper TOEFL 500. **Basis for Candidate Selection:** *Very important factors considered include:* academic GPA, standardized test scores. *Important factors considered include:* Class rank. **Freshman Admission Requirements:** High school diploma is required and GED is accepted. **Freshman Admission Statistics:** 3,659 applied, 90% admitted, 66% enrolled. **Transfer Admission Requirements:** college transcript(s), statement of good standing from prior institution(s). Minimum college GPA of 2.0 required. Lowest grade transferable C. **General Admission Information:** Notification on a rolling basis, beginning on or about 10/1. Nonfall registration accepted. Credit and/or placement offered for CEEB Advanced Placement tests.

COSTS AND FINANCIAL AID
Required Forms and Deadlines: FAFSA. **Notification of Awards:** Applicants will be notified of awards on a rolling basis beginning 5/4. **Types of Aid:** *Need-based scholarships/grants:* Federal Pell, SEOG, state scholarships/grants, private scholarships, the school's own gift aid, Federal Nursing Scholarships. *Loans:* Subsidized Stafford, Unsubsidized Stafford, PLUS, Federal Perkins, Federal Nursing, state loans, External Loans. **Student Employment:** Federal Work-Study Program available. Institutional employment available. **Criteria for awarding institutional aid:** Non-need-based: academics, art, athletics, leadership, minority status, music/drama, state/district residency.

UNIVERSITY OF CENTRAL FLORIDA

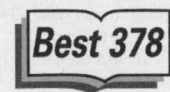

P.O. Box 160111, Orlando, FL 32816-0111
Phone: 407-823-3000 • **Financial Aid Phone:** 407-823-2827
E-mail: admission@ucf.edu • **CEEB Code:** 5233
Fax: 407-823-5625 • **Website:** www.ucf.edu • **ACT Code:** 735

This public school was founded in 1963. It has a 1415-acre campus.

RATINGS
Admissions Selectivity Rating: 92   **Fire Safety Rating:** 84   **Green Rating:** 89

STUDENTS AND FACULTY
Enrollment: 50,722. **Student Body:** 55% female, 45% male, 5% out-of-state, 1% international (148 countries represented). Asian 5%, African American 10%, Caucasian 59%, Hispanic 20%.
Retention and Graduation: 35% freshmen graduate within 4 years. 65% freshmen graduate within 6 years. **Faculty:** Student/faculty ratio 32:1. 1318 full-time faculty, 78% hold PhDs, 24% are members of minority groups, 40% are women. 5% of classes are taught by teaching assistants.

ACADEMICS
Degrees: associate, bachelor's, certificate, master's, post-bachelor's certificate. **Classes:** Most classes have 20–29 students. Most lab/discussion sessions have 30–39 students. **Majors with Highest Enrollment:** health services/allied health/health sciences; marketing/marketing management; psychology. **Special Study Options:** cooperative education program, distance learning, double major, dual enrollment, English as a Second Language (ESL), honors program, internships, study abroad, teacher certification program. **Honors programs:** The Burnett Honors College offers two main tracks, University Honors and Honors in the Major, and a special accelerated Medical School program in partnership with University of South Florida. **Combined degree programs:** BA/MD, BA/MA, BA/MEng, BS/MS. **Disability Services:** Special programs offered to physically disabled students include note-taking services, reader services, tape recorders, tutors. **Career services:** career/job search classes, career assessment.

FACILITIES
Housing: Coed dorms, men's dorms, women's dorms, fraternity/sorority housing, apartments for single students, Wellness Housing, Theme Housing, affiliated student residences available across street from campus with university resident assistants. On-campus: Honors Center; Living Learning Communities, Lead Scholars Center. 97% of campus accessible to physically disabled. **Special Academic Facilities/Equipment:** Center for research and education in optics and lasers, arboretum, observatory, New student union, student recreation center. **Computers:** 100% of classrooms, 100% of dorms, 100% of libraries, 90% of dining areas, 100% of student union, 90% of common outdoor areas have wireless network access. Students can register for classes online. Administrative functions (other than registration) can be performed online.

CAMPUS LIFE
Environment: City. **Activities:** Choral groups, concert band, drama/theater, jazz band, literary magazine, marching band, music ensembles, musical theater, pep band, radio station, student government, student newspaper, student-run film society, symphony orchestra, Campus Ministries, International Student Organization, Model UN. 361 registered organizations, 36 honor societies, 29 religious organizations. 21 fraternities, 18 sororities. **Athletics (Intercollegiate):** *Men:* baseball, basketball, cheerleading, cross-country, football, golf, soccer, tennis. *Women:* basketball, cheerleading, crew/rowing, cross-country, golf, soccer, softball, tennis, track/field (outdoor), track/field (indoor), volleyball. **On-Campus Highlights:** Student Union, Recreation and Wellness Center,

Bookstore (Barnes and Noble caf), Reflecting Pond, New Arena and Football Stadium. **Environmental Initiatives:** In House Building Commissioning Team, Full Time Sustainability Marketing and Outreach, Goal to get all major educational buildings Energy Star and LEED certified.

ADMISSIONS
Freshman Academic Profile: Average high school GPA 3.8. 32% in top 10% of high school class, 75% in top 25% of high school class, 97% in top 50% of high school class. SAT Math middle 50% range 550-650. SAT Critical Reading middle 50% range 530-630. SAT Writing middle 50% range 510-610. ACT middle 50% range 24-28. Minimum web-based TOEFL 80. Minimum paper TOEFL 550. **Basis for Candidate Selection:** *Very important factors considered include:* academic GPA, rigor of secondary school record, standardized test scores. *Important factors considered include:* application essay, recommendation(s). *Other factors considered include:* Class rank, alumni/ae relation, character/personal qualities, extracurricular activities, first generation, geographical residence, interview, level of applicant's interest, state residency, talent/ability, volunteer work, work experience. **Freshman Admission Requirements:** High school diploma is required and GED is accepted. *Academic units required:* 4 English, 4 mathematics, 3 science, (2 science labs), 2 foreign language, 3 social studies, 2 academic electives. *Academic units recommended:* 4 English, 4 mathematics, 3 science, (2 science labs), 2 foreign language, 3 social studies, 2 academic electives. **Freshman Admission Statistics:** 33,281 applied, 46% admitted, 40% enrolled. **Transfer Admission Requirements:** college transcript(s), minimum college GPA of 2.0 required. Lowest grade transferable D. **General Admission Information:** Application Fee $30. Regular application deadline 5/1. Notification on a rolling basis, beginning on or about 10/1. Nonfall registration accepted. Credit offered for CEEB Advanced Placement tests.

COSTS AND FINANCIAL AID
Annual in-state tuition $6,247. Annual out-of-state tuition $22,345. Room and board $9,357. Required fees Average book expense $1,146. **Required Forms and Deadlines:** FAFSA. **Notification of Awards:** Applicants will be notified of awards on a rolling basis beginning 3/15. **Types of Aid:** *Need-based scholarships/grants:* Federal Pell, SEOG, state scholarships/grants, private scholarships, the school's own gift aid, University scholarships and grants. *Loans:* Subsidized Stafford, Unsubsidized Stafford, PLUS, Federal Perkins. **Student Employment:** Federal Work-Study Program available. Institutional employment available. **Financial Aid Statistics:** 49% freshmen, 56% undergrads receive need-based scholarship or grant aid. 66% freshmen, 67% undergrads receive non-need-based scholarship or grant aid. 38% freshmen, 50% undergrads receive need-based self help aid. 1% freshmen, 1% undergrads receive athletic scholarships. 90% freshmen, 80% undergrads receive any aid. 46% undergrads borrow to pay for school. Average cumulative indebtedness $20,086. **Criteria for awarding institutional aid:** Non-need-based: academics, alumni affiliation, athletics, leadership, state/district residency.

See page 1246.

UNIVERSITY OF CENTRAL MISSOURI

Office of Admissions, Warrensburg, MO 64093
Phone: 660-543-4290 • **Financial Aid Phone:** 660-543-4040
E-mail: admit@ucmovmb.edu • **CEEB Code:** 6090
Fax: 660-543-8517 • **Website:** www.cmsu.edu • **ACT Code:** 2272

This public school was founded in 1871. It has a 1561-acre campus.

RATINGS
Admissions Selectivity Rating: 67   **Fire Safety Rating:** 67   **Green Rating:** 60*

STUDENTS AND FACULTY
Enrollment: 8,441. **Student Body:** 56% female, 44% male, 7% out-of-state, 2% international (53 countries represented). Asian 1%, African American 5%, Caucasian 76%, Hispanic 2%.
Retention and Graduation: 68% freshmen return for sophomore year. 23% freshmen graduate within 4 years. 50% freshmen graduate within 6 years. **Faculty:** Student/faculty ratio 19:1. 449 full-time faculty, 73% hold PhDs, 7% are members of minority groups, 40% are women. 4% of classes are taught by teaching assistants.

ACADEMICS
Degrees: associate, bachelor's, master's, post-bachelor's certificate, post-master's certificate. **Classes:** Most classes have 20–29 students. **Majors with Highest Enrollment:** criminal justice/law enforcement administration; education; marketing/marketing management. **Special Study Options:** Accelerated program, cooperative education program, cross-registration, distance learning,

double major, dual enrollment, English as a Second Language (ESL), honors program, internships, student-designed major, study abroad, teacher certification program, weekend college. **Disability Services:** Special programs offered to physically disabled students include note-taking services, reader services, tape recorders, tutors.

FACILITIES

Housing: Coed dorms, special housing for disabled students, special housing for international students, women's dorms, fraternity/sorority housing, apartments for married students, apartments for single students, Economy Suites and Townhouses. 95% of campus accessible to physically disabled. **Special Academic Facilities/Equipment:** Art gallery,Nance Museum and Library of Antiquities, natural history museum, English language center, child development lab, speech and hearing lab, 260-acre farm, Missouri Safety center, National Police Institute, driving/safety range, center for technology and business research,airport for aviation program.Extended campus,Lee's Summit,MO. KCMW-FM,KMOS-TV, Public Broadcasting Stations **Computers:** Students can register for classes online. Administrative functions (other than registration) can be performed online.

CAMPUS LIFE

Environment: Rural. **Activities:** Choral groups, concert band, dance, drama/theater, jazz band, literary magazine, marching band, music ensembles, musical theater, opera, pep band, radio station, student government, student newspaper, student-run film society, symphony orchestra, television station, yearbook 150 registered organizations, 24 honor societies, 14 religious organizations. 9 fraternities, 10 sororities. **Athletics (Intercollegiate):** *Men:* baseball, basketball, bowling, cross-country, football, golf, soccer, track/field (outdoor), wrestling. *Women:* basketball, bowling, cross-country, soccer, softball, track/field (outdoor), volleyball. **On-Campus Highlights:** Union Commons, Library, Pertle Springs, Multi-purpose building.

ADMISSIONS

Freshman Academic Profile: Average high school GPA 3.3. 12% in top 10% of high school class, 36% in top 25% of high school class, 71% in top 50% of high school class. 90% from public high schools. ACT middle 50% range 20-24. Minimum paper TOEFL 500. **Basis for Candidate Selection:** *Very important factors considered include:* Class rank, rigor of secondary school record, standardized test scores. *Other factors considered include:* recommendation(s), alumni/ae relation, character/personal qualities, extracurricular activities, talent/ability. **Freshman Admission Requirements:** High school diploma is required and GED is accepted. *Academic units required:* 4 English, 3 mathematics, 2 science, (1 science labs), 3 social studies, 3 academic electives, 1 arts. *Academic units recommended:* 4 English, 3 mathematics, 2 science, (1 science labs), 3 social studies, 3 academic electives, 1 arts. **Freshman Admission Statistics:** 3,631 applied, 84% admitted, 52% enrolled. **Transfer Admission Requirements:** college transcript(s), minimum college GPA of 2.0 required. Lowest grade transferable C. **General Admission Information:** Application Fee $30. Regular application deadline 8/18. Notification on a rolling basis, beginning on or about 9/3. Nonfall registration accepted. Admission may be deferred for a maximum of 3 semesters. Credit offered for CEEB Advanced Placement tests.

COSTS AND FINANCIAL AID

Required Forms and Deadlines: FAFSA. **Notification of Awards:** Applicants will be notified of awards on or about 3/1. **Types of Aid:** *Need-based scholarships/grants:* Federal Pell, SEOG, state scholarships/grants, private scholarships, the school's own gift aid. *Loans:* Direct Subsidized Stafford, Direct Unsubsidized Stafford, Direct PLUS, Federal Perkins, state loans. **Student Employment:** Highest amount earned per year from on-campus jobs $2,000. **Financial Aid Statistics:** 50% freshmen, 58% undergrads receive need-based scholarship or grant aid. 70% freshmen, 53% undergrads receive non-need-based scholarship or grant aid. 83% freshmen, 90% undergrads receive need-based self-help aid. 5% freshmen, 5% undergrads receive athletic scholarships. 51% freshmen, 61% undergrads receive any aid. 68% undergrads borrow to pay for school. Average cumulative indebtedness $13,184. **Criteria for awarding institutional aid:** Non-need-based: academics, alumni affiliation, art, athletics, leadership, minority status, music/drama, state/district residency.

UNIVERSITY OF CENTRAL OKLAHOMA

100 North University Drive, Edmond, OK 73034
Phone: 405-974-2338 • **Financial Aid Phone:** 405-974-3334
E-mail: admituco@uco.edu • **CEEB Code:** 6091
Fax: 405-341-4964 • **ACT Code:** 3390

This public school was founded in 1890. It has a 200-acre campus.

RATINGS

Admissions Selectivity Rating: 70   **Fire Safety Rating:** 82   **Green Rating:** 76

STUDENTS AND FACULTY

Enrollment: 14,019. **Student Body:** 58% female, 42% male, 3% out-of-state, 6% international (75 countries represented). Asian 3%, African American 9%, Caucasian 60%, Hispanic 4%, Native American 5%.
Retention and Graduation: 61% freshmen return for sophomore year. **Faculty:** Student/faculty ratio 21:1. 441 full-time faculty, 68% hold PhDs, 13% are members of minority groups, 48% are women.

ACADEMICS

Degrees: bachelor's, certificate, master's. **Classes:** Most classes have 20–29 students. Most lab/discussion sessions have 10–19 students. **Majors with Highest Enrollment:** business administration and management; elementary education and teaching; nursing/registered nurse (rn, asn, bsn, msn). **Special Study Options:** Accelerated program, distance learning, double major, dual enrollment, English as a Second Language (ESL), honors program, independent study, internships, teacher certification program. **Disability Services:** Special programs offered to physically disabled students include note-taking services, reader services, tape recorders, tutors. **Career services:** alumni services, career/job search classes, career assessment, internships.

FACILITIES

Housing: Coed dorms, men's dorms, women's dorms, fraternity/sorority housing, apartments for married students, apartments for single students. 95% of campus accessible to physically disabled. **Special Academic Facilities/Equipment:** Art and history museums, archives. **Computers:** 100% of classrooms, 100% of dorms, 100% of libraries, 100% of dining areas, 100% of student union, 50% of common outdoor areas have wireless network access. Students can register for classes online. Administrative functions (other than registration) can be performed online.

CAMPUS LIFE

Environment: Metropolis. **Activities:** Choral groups, concert band, dance, drama/theater, jazz band, marching band, music ensembles, musical theater, pep band, radio station, student government, student newspaper, symphony orchestra, television station, yearbook 150 registered organizations, 27 honor societies, 16 religious organizations. 9 fraternities, 10 sororities. **Athletics (Intercollegiate):** *Men:* baseball, basketball, football, golf, wrestling. *Women:* basketball, cross-country, golf, soccer, softball, tennis, volleyball. **On-Campus Highlights:** Starbucks, Wellness Center, University Center **Environmental Initiatives:** Use 100% wind power Waterless Urinals Motion sensor lighting

ADMISSIONS

Freshman Academic Profile: Average high school GPA 3.3. 12% in top 10% of high school class, 35% in top 25% of high school class, 72% in top 50% of high school class. ACT middle 50% range 19-23. Minimum web-based TOEFL 83. Minimum paper TOEFL 560. **Basis for Candidate Selection:** *Very important factors considered include:* Class rank, academic GPA, rigor of secondary school record, standardized test scores. *Other factors considered include:* extracurricular activities, talent/ability. **Freshman Admission Requirements:** High school diploma is required and GED is accepted. *Academic units required:* 4 English, 3 mathematics, 2 science, (2 science labs), 1 social studies, 2 history. *Academic units recommended:* 4 English, 3 mathematics, 2 science, (2 science labs), 1 social studies, 2 history. **Freshman Admission Statistics:** 4,614 applied, 69% admitted, 67% enrolled. **Transfer Admission Requirements:** college transcript(s), statement of good standing from prior institution(s). Minimum college GPA of 2.0 required. Lowest grade transferable D. **General Admission Information:** Application Fee $25. Notification on a rolling basis, beginning on or about 4/1. Nonfall registration accepted. Admission may be deferred for a maximum of 1 semester. Credit and/or placement offered for CEEB Advanced Placement tests.

COSTS AND FINANCIAL AID

Annual in-state tuition $3,681. Annual out-of-state tuition $10,110. Room and board $7,468. Required fees $542. Average book expense $1,000. **Required Forms and Deadlines:** FAFSA, institution's own financial aid form. **Notification of Awards:** Applicants will be notified of awards on a rolling basis beginning 5/1. **Types of Aid:** *Need-based scholarships/grants:* Federal Pell, SEOG, state scholarships/grants, private scholarships, the school's own gift aid.

Loans: Subsidized Stafford, Unsubsidized Stafford, PLUS, Federal Perkins. **Student Employment:** Federal Work-Study Program available. Institutional employment available. Highest amount earned per year from on-campus jobs $7,200. Off-campus job opportunities are excellent. **Financial Aid Statistics:** 88% freshmen, 89% undergrads receive need-based scholarship or grant aid. 2% freshmen, 4% undergrads receive non-need-based scholarship or grant aid. 100% freshmen, 100% undergrads receive need-based self-help aid. 2% freshmen, 2% undergrads receive athletic scholarships. 66% freshmen, 75% undergrads receive any aid. 48% undergrads borrow to pay for school. Average cumulative indebtedness $17,385. **Criteria for awarding institutional aid:** Non-need-based: academics, alumni affiliation, art, athletics, leadership, minority status, music/drama, state/district residency.

UNIVERSITY OF CHARLESTON

2300 MacCorkle Ave SE, Charleston, WV 25304
Phone: 304-357-4750 • **Financial Aid Phone:** 304-357-4950
E-mail: admissions@ucwv.edu • **CEEB Code:** 5419
Fax: 304-357-4781 • **Website:** www.ucwv.edu/ • **ACT Code:** 4528

This private school was founded in 1888. It has a 24-acre campus.

RATINGS
Admissions Selectivity Rating: 79   **Fire Safety Rating:** 78   **Green Rating:** 61

STUDENTS AND FACULTY
Enrollment: 1,016. **Student Body:** 59% female, 41% male, 37% out-of-state, 0% international (34 countries represented). Asian 1%, African American 12%, Caucasian 66%, Hispanic 3%.
Retention and Graduation: 70% freshmen return for sophomore year. 28% freshmen graduate within 4 years. **Faculty:** Student/faculty ratio 15:1. 83 full-time faculty, 61% are women.

ACADEMICS
Degrees: associate, bachelor's, master's. **Classes:** Most classes have 10–19 students. Most lab/discussion sessions have fewer than 10 students. **Majors with Highest Enrollment:** biology/biological sciences; business administration and management; health services/allied health/health sciences. **Special Study Options:** double major, English as a Second Language (ESL), independent study, internships, liberal arts/career combination, study abroad. **Disability Services:** Special programs offered to physically disabled students include note-taking services, reader services, tape recorders, tutors.

FACILITIES
Housing: Coed dorms, special housing for disabled students, apartments for single students. **Special Academic Facilities/Equipment:** Erma Byrd Art Gallery **Computers:** 75% of classrooms, 100% of dorms, 100% of libraries, 100% of dining areas, 100% of student union, 50% of common outdoor areas have wireless network access. Students can register for classes online. Administrative functions (other than registration) can be performed online.

CAMPUS LIFE
Environment: City. **Activities:** Choral groups, dance, drama/theater, music ensembles, pep band, student government, student newspaper, yearbook, Campus Ministries, International Student Organization, Model UN. 39 registered organizations, 7 honor societies, 2 religious organizations, 2 fraternities, 3 sororities. **Athletics (Intercollegiate):** *Men:* baseball, basketball, football, golf, soccer, tennis. *Women:* basketball, crew/rowing, cross-country, golf, soccer, softball, tennis, track/field (outdoor), volleyball. **On-Campus Highlights:** New Fitness Center, School of Pharmacy, Coffee Tavern, University of Charleston Stadium, Graduate School of Business. **Environmental Initiatives:** Recycling on campus Planting trees Energy conservation specifically electricity

ADMISSIONS
Freshman Academic Profile: Average high school GPA 3.3. SAT Math middle 50% range 440-540. SAT Critical Reading middle 50% range 430-530. ACT middle 50% range 20-26. Minimum web-based TOEFL 79. Minimum paper TOEFL 550. **Basis for Candidate Selection:** *Very important factors considered include:* academic GPA, standardized test scores. *Important factors considered include:* Class rank, rigor of secondary school record, alumni/ae relation, extracurricular activities. *Other factors considered include:* application essay, recommendation(s), character/personal qualities, first generation, interview, level of applicant's interest, talent/ability, volunteer work, work experience. **Freshman Admission Requirements:** High school diploma is required and GED is accepted. *Academic units required:* 1 Algebra for BS Nursing. *Academic units recommended:* 1 Algebra for BS Nursing **Freshman Admission Statistics:** 1,641 applied, 56% admitted, 26% enrolled. **Transfer Admission Requirements:** college transcript(s), minimum college GPA of 2.25 required.

Lowest grade transferable C. **General Admission Information:** Application Fee $25. Notification on a rolling basis, beginning on or about 10/1. Nonfall registration accepted. Credit and/or placement offered for CEEB Advanced Placement tests.

COSTS AND FINANCIAL AID
Average book expense $1,500. **Required Forms and Deadlines:** FAFSA. **Notification of Awards:** Applicants will be notified of awards on a rolling basis beginning 3/1. **Types of Aid:** *Need-based scholarships/grants:* Federal Pell, SEOG, state scholarships/grants, private scholarships, the school's own gift aid, TEACH/Academic Competitiveness/SMART. *Loans:* Subsidized Stafford, Unsubsidized Stafford, PLUS, Federal Perkins, Federal Nursing. **Student Employment:** Federal Work-Study Program available. Off-campus job opportunities are good. **Financial Aid Statistics:** 59% freshmen, 57% undergrads receive need-based scholarship or grant aid. 93% freshmen, 88% undergrads receive non-need-based scholarship or grant aid. 53% freshmen, 55% undergrads receive need-based self-help aid. 30% freshmen, 28% undergrads receive athletic scholarships. 93% undergrads borrow to pay for school. Average cumulative indebtedness $24,000. **Criteria for awarding institutional aid:** Non-need-based: academics, alumni affiliation, athletics, leadership, music/drama.

THE UNIVERSITY OF CHICAGO

Best 378

1101 E 58th Street, Chicago, IL 60637
Phone: 773-702-8650 • **Financial Aid Phone:** 773-702-8655
E-mail: collegeadmissions@uchicago.edu • **CEEB Code:** 1832
Fax: 773-702-4199 • **Website:** collegeadmissions@uchicago.edu • **ACT Code:** 1152

This private school was founded in 1890. It has a 211-acre campus.

RATINGS
Admissions Selectivity Rating: 99   **Fire Safety Rating:** 93   **Green Rating:** 90

STUDENTS AND FACULTY
Enrollment: 5,587. **Student Body:** 47% female, 53% male, 81% out-of-state, 9% international (103 countries represented). Asian 18%, African American 5%, Caucasian 46%, Hispanic 8%.
Retention and Graduation: 99% freshmen return for sophomore year. 86% freshmen graduate within 4 years. 92% freshmen graduate within 6 years. **Faculty:** Student/faculty ratio 6:1. 1,961 full-time faculty, 99% hold PhDs, 20% are members of minority groups, 30% are women.

ACADEMICS
Degrees: bachelor's, doctoral, master's. **Classes:** Most classes have fewer than 10 students. Most lab/discussion sessions have 10–19 students. **Majors with Highest Enrollment:** biology/biological sciences; economics; political science and government. **Special Study Options:** Accelerated program, cross-registration, double major, dual enrollment, English as a Second Language (ESL), exchange student program (domestic), honors program, independent study, internships, student-designed major, study abroad, teacher certification program. **Combined degree programs:** BA/MA. **Career services:** Alumni network, alumni services, career/job search classes, career assessment, internships, regional alumni. Career services highlights include Internship program: Jeff Metcalf Fellows Program provides outstanding opportunities for both students and hosting organizations.

FACILITIES
Housing: Coed dorms, special housing for disabled students, special housing for international students, fraternity/sorority housing, apartments for married students, cooperative housing. **Special Academic Facilities/Equipment:** Smart Museum, Renaissance Society, Oriental Institute, Business and Economics Resource Center, D'Angelo Law Library, Echhart Library, John Crerar Library, Joseph Regenstein Library, Special Collections Research Center, Social Services Administration Library, Yerkes Obsevatory Library, On Campus Lab School(PreK-12),Argonne National Laboratory, Enrico Fermi Institute, Court Theater, Observatory, Two Telescopes, Fermi National Accelerator Laboratory. **Computers:** 100% of classrooms, 100% of dorms, 100% of libraries, 100% of dining areas, 100% of student union, 100% of common outdoor areas have wireless network access. Students can register for classes online.

CAMPUS LIFE
Environment: Metropolis. **Activities:** Choral groups, concert band, dance, drama/theater, jazz band, literary magazine, music ensembles, musical theater,

pep band, radio station, student government, student newspaper, student-run film society, symphony orchestra, yearbook, Campus Ministries, International Student Organization, Model UN. 400 registered organizations, 5 honor societies, 36 religious organizations. 10 fraternities, 3 sororities. **Athletics (Intercollegiate):** *Men:* baseball, basketball, cross-country, diving, football, soccer, swimming, tennis, track/field (outdoor), track/field (indoor), volleyball, wrestling. *Women:* basketball, cross-country, diving, soccer, softball, swimming, tennis, track/field (outdoor), track/field (indoor), volleyball. **On-Campus Highlights:** Gerald Ratner Athletics Center, Joseph Regenstein Library, Robie House, Court Theatre, Rockefeller Memorial Chapel. **Environmental Initiatives:** Formation of the Program on the Global Environment Facilities Services has increased university attention in this area by leading the construction of energy efficient central utilities plants to provide steam and chilled water, aggressive program promoting alternative transportation, green roof initiatives, and LEED Silver certification pursuit on renovation project. Support of the Sustainability Council to engage students, faculty and staff in sustainability issues and hiring of a full-time sustainability officer.

ADMISSIONS

Freshman Academic Profile: Average high school GPA 97% in top 10% of high school class, 99% in top 25% of high school class, 100% in top 50% of high school class. 62% from public high schools. SAT Math middle 50% range 710-790. SAT Critical Reading middle 50% range 710-780. SAT Writing middle 50% range 700-780. ACT middle 50% range 31-34. Minimum web-based TOEFL 104. Minimum paper TOEFL 600. **Basis for Candidate Selection:** *Very important factors considered include:* application essay, recommendation(s), rigor of secondary school record, character/personal qualities, talent/ability. *Important factors considered include:* Class rank, academic GPA, extracurricular activities, volunteer work. *Other factors considered include:* standardized test scores, alumni/ae relation, first generation, interview, level of applicant's interest, racial/ethnic status, work experience. **Freshman Admission Requirements:** High school diploma or equivalent is not required. *Academic units recommended:* **Freshman Admission Statistics:** 25,268 applied, 13% admitted, 46% enrolled. **Transfer Admission Requirements:** High school transcript, college transcript(s), essay or personal statement, standardized test scores, statement of good standing from prior institution(s). Minimum college GPA of 3.0 required. **General Admission Information:** Application Fee $65. Regular application deadline 1/2. Regular notification 4/1. Nonfall registration not accepted. Admission may be deferred for a maximum of 1 year. Credit and/or placement offered for CEEB Advanced Placement tests.

COSTS AND FINANCIAL AID

Annual tuition $43,581. Room and board $13,137. Required fees $993. Average book expense $3,679. **Required Forms and Deadlines:** FAFSA, institution's own financial aid form, CSS/Financial Aid PROFILE, noncustodial PROFILE. **Notification of Awards:** Applicants will be notified of awards on or about 4/15. **Types of Aid:** *Need-based scholarships/grants:* Federal Pell, SEOG, state scholarships/grants, private scholarships, the school's own gift aid. *Loans:* Subsidized Stafford, Unsubsidized Stafford, PLUS, Federal Perkins. **Student Employment: Financial Aid Statistics:** 100% freshmen, 99% undergrads receive need-based scholarship or grant aid. 64% freshmen, 79% undergrads receive need-based self-help aid. 64% freshmen, 58% undergrads receive any aid. 43% undergrads borrow to pay for school. Average cumulative indebtedness $23,930. **Criteria for awarding institutional aid:** Non-need-based: academics, leadership.

See page 1248.

UNIVERSITY OF CINCINNATI

Best 378

P.O. Box 210091, Cincinnati, OH 45221-0091
Phone: 513-556-1100 • **Financial Aid Phone:** 513-556-6982
E-mail: admissions@uc.edu • **CEEB Code:** 1833
Fax: 513-556-1105 • **Website:** www.uc.edu • **ACT Code:** 3340

This public school was founded in 1819. It has a 392-acre campus.

RATINGS
Admissions Selectivity Rating: 82   **Fire Safety Rating:** 91   **Green Rating:** 91

STUDENTS AND FACULTY
Enrollment: 22,543. **Student Body:** 51% female, 49% male, 14% out-of-state, 3% international (111 countries represented). Asian 3%, African American 8%, Caucasian 78%, Hispanic 2%.

Retention and Graduation: 85% freshmen return for sophomore year. 22% freshmen graduate within 4 years. 59% freshmen graduate within 6 years. **Faculty:** Student/faculty ratio 18:1. 1,160 full-time faculty, 80% hold PhDs, 17% are members of minority groups, 42% are women.

ACADEMICS
Degrees: associate, bachelor's, certificate, first professional, master's, post-bachelor's certificate, terminal associate, transfer associate. **Classes:** Most classes have 20–29 students. **Majors with Highest Enrollment:** communication studies/speech communication and rhetoric; marketing/marketing management; psychology. **Special Study Options:** Accelerated program, cooperative education program, distance learning, double major, English as a Second Language (ESL), honors program, independent study, internships, liberal arts/career combination, study abroad, teacher certification program, weekend college. **Honors programs:** www.uc.edu/honors **Disability Services:** Special programs offered to physically disabled students include note-taking services, reader services, tape recorders, tutors. **Career services:** Alumni network, alumni services, career/job search classes, career assessment, internships, regional alumni. Career services highlights include Cooperative Learning: UC Professional Practice Program—over 100 years of service.

FACILITIES
Housing: Coed dorms, men's dorms, women's dorms, fraternity/sorority housing, apartments for married students, apartments for single students. **Special Academic Facilities/Equipment:** Art museum, language lab, observatory. **Computers:** 50% of classrooms, 75% of libraries, 75% of dining areas, 55% of student union, 75% of common outdoor areas have wireless network access. Students can register for classes online. Administrative functions (other than registration) can be performed online.

CAMPUS LIFE
Environment: Metropolis. **Activities:** Choral groups, concert band, dance, drama/theater, jazz band, marching band, music ensembles, musical theater, opera, pep band, radio station, student government, student newspaper, student-run film society, symphony orchestra, yearbook 250 registered organizations, 16 honor societies, 23 religious organizations. 23 fraternities, 10 sororities. **Athletics (Intercollegiate):** *Men:* baseball, basketball, cheerleading, cross-country, diving, football, golf, soccer, swimming, track/field (outdoor). *Women:* basketball, cheerleading, cross-country, diving, golf, lacrosse, soccer, swimming, tennis, track/field (outdoor), track/field (indoor), volleyball. **Environmental Initiatives:** Completed greenhouse gas inventory and Climate Action Plan implementation. Energy initiatives in new and existing buildings, including minimum LEED Silver standard for all new buildings and major renovations, compliance with Ohio House Bill 251 to reduce energy use by 20% by 2014 using 2004 as the baseline and commissioning standards.

ADMISSIONS
Freshman Academic Profile: Average high school GPA 3.4. 22% in top 10% of high school class, 50% in top 25% of high school class, 83% in top 50% of high school class. SAT Math middle 50% range 520-640. SAT Critical Reading middle 50% range 500-620. SAT Writing middle 50% range 480-590. ACT middle 50% range 22-27. Minimum paper TOEFL 515. **Basis for Candidate Selection:** *Very important factors considered include:* Class rank, academic GPA, rigor of secondary school record, standardized test scores. *Other factors considered include:* application essay, extracurricular activities. **Freshman Admission Requirements:** High school diploma is required and GED is accepted. *Academic units required:* 4 English, 3 mathematics, 2 science, 2 foreign language, 2 social studies, 2 academic electives. *Academic units recommended:* 4 English, 3 mathematics, 2 science, 2 foreign language, 2 social studies, 2 academic electives. **Freshman Admission Statistics:** 17,020 applied, 65% admitted, 39% enrolled. **General Admission Information:** Application Fee $40. Regular application deadline 9/1. Nonfall registration accepted. Admission may be deferred for a maximum of one year. Credit and/or placement offered for CEEB Advanced Placement tests.

COSTS AND FINANCIAL AID
Annual in-state tuition $9,124. Annual out-of-state tuition $24,156. Room and board $10,170. Required fees $1,660. Average book expense $1,540. **Required Forms and Deadlines:** FAFSA. **Notification of Awards:** Applicants will be notified of awards on a rolling basis beginning 3/10. **Types of Aid:** *Need-based scholarships/grants:* Federal Pell, SEOG, state scholarships/grants, private scholarships, the school's own gift aid, United Negro College Fund, Federal Nursing Scholarships. ACG, SMART, TEACH. *Loans:* Subsidized Stafford, Unsubsidized Stafford, PLUS, Federal Perkins, Federal Nursing, state loans, college/university loans from institutional funds. **Student Employment:** Federal Work-Study Program available. Institutional employment available. Off-campus job opportunities are excellent. **Financial Aid Statistics:** 43% freshmen, 47% undergrads receive need-based scholarship or grant aid. 47% freshmen, 35% undergrads receive non-need-based scholarship or grant aid. 19% freshmen, 16% undergrads receive need-based self-help aid. 1% freshmen, 1% undergrads receive athletic scholarships. 76% freshmen, 83% undergrads receive any aid.

67% undergrads borrow to pay for school. Average cumulative indebtedness $27,593. **Criteria for awarding institutional aid:** Non-need-based: academics, alumni affiliation, art, athletics, leadership, minority status, music/drama, state/district residency.

UNIVERSITY OF COLORADO—
COLORADO SPRINGS

Admissions Office, Colorado Springs, CO 80933-7150
Phone: 719-262-3383 • **Financial Aid Phone:** 719-262-3460
E-mail: admrec@uccs.edu • **CEEB Code:** 4874
Fax: 719-262-3116 • **Website:** www.uccs.edu • **ACT Code:** 535

This public school was founded in 1965. It has a 504-acre campus.

RATINGS
Admissions Selectivity Rating: 79   **Fire Safety Rating:** 74   **Green Rating:** 60*

STUDENTS AND FACULTY
Enrollment: 6,098. **Student Body:** 60% female, 40% male, 7% out-of-state, 0% international (35 countries represented). Asian 5%, African American 4%, Caucasian 76%, Hispanic 9%, Native American 1%.
Retention and Graduation: 64% freshmen return for sophomore year. 19% freshmen graduate within 4 years. 40% freshmen graduate within 6 years.
Faculty: Student/faculty ratio 18:1. 200 full-time faculty, 100% hold PhDs, 14% are members of minority groups, 36% are women. 1% of classes are taught by teaching assistants.

ACADEMICS
Degrees: bachelor's, certificate, master's, post-bachelor's certificate, post-master's certificate. **Classes:** Most classes have 10–19 students. Most lab/discussion sessions have 20–29 students. **Special Study Options:** Accelerated program, cooperative education program, cross-registration, distance learning, double major, dual enrollment, English as a Second Language (ESL), exchange student program (domestic), independent study, internships, liberal arts/career combination, student-designed major, study abroad, teacher certification program **Disability Services:** Special programs offered to physically disabled students include note-taking services, reader services, tape recorders, tutors.

FACILITIES
Housing: Coed dorms, special housing for disabled students, men's dorms, women's dorms, apartments for single students. 100% of campus accessible to physically disabled. **Special Academic Facilities/Equipment:** Gallery of contemporary art. **Computers:** Students can register for classes online.

CAMPUS LIFE
Environment: Metropolis. **Activities:** Choral groups, dance, drama/theater, jazz band, literary magazine, music ensembles, musical theater, radio station, student government, student newspaper, student-run film society 55 registered organizations, 7 religious organizations. 1 sororities. **Athletics (Intercollegiate):** *Men:* basketball, cross-country, golf, soccer, tennis, track/field (outdoor). *Women:* basketball, cross-country, softball, tennis, track/field (outdoor), volleyball. **On-Campus Highlights:** El Pomar Center (Kramer family Library), University Center, The Lodge, Gallery of Contemporary Art

ADMISSIONS
Freshman Academic Profile: Average high school GPA 3.4. 16% in top 10% of high school class, 42% in top 25% of high school class, 78% in top 50% of high school class. SAT Math middle 50% range 470-610. SAT Critical Reading middle 50% range 470-590. SAT Writing middle 50% range 450-560. ACT middle 50% range 20-25. Minimum paper TOEFL 550. **Basis for Candidate Selection:** *Very important factors considered include:* Class rank, academic GPA, rigor of secondary school record, standardized test scores. *Important factors considered include:* recommendation(s), level of applicant's interest. *Other factors considered include:* application essay, alumni/ae relation, character/personal qualities, extracurricular activities, geographical residence, state residency, talent/ability, volunteer work. **Freshman Admission Requirements:** High school diploma is required and GED is accepted. *Academic units required:* 4 English, 3 mathematics, 3 science, (2 science labs), 2 foreign language, 2 social studies, 1 academic electives. *Academic units recommended:* 4 English, 3 mathematics, 3 science, (2 science labs), 2 foreign language, 2 social studies, 1 academic electives. **Freshman Admission Statistics:** 3,243 applied, 63% admitted, 37% enrolled. **Transfer Admission Requirements:** High school transcript, college transcript(s), minimum college GPA of 2.0 required. Lowest grade transferable C. **General Admission Information:** Application Fee $50. Regular application deadline 7/1. Notification on a rolling basis, beginning on or about 10/1. Nonfall registration accepted. Admission may be deferred for

a maximum of 12 months. Neither credit nor placement offered for CEEB Advanced Placement tests.

COSTS AND FINANCIAL AID
Annual in-state tuition $5,490. Annual out-of-state tuition $22,950. Room and board $7,662. Required fees $1,047. Average book expense $1,296. **Required Forms and Deadlines:** FAFSA. **Notification of Awards:** Applicants will be notified of awards on a rolling basis beginning 4/15. **Types of Aid:** *Need-based scholarships/grants:* Federal Pell, SEOG, state scholarships/grants, private scholarships, the school's own gift aid, Federal Nursing Scholarships. *Loans:* Subsidized Stafford, Unsubsidized Stafford, PLUS, Federal Perkins, college/university loans from institutional funds. **Student Employment: Financial Aid Statistics:** 60% freshmen, 56% undergrads receive need-based scholarship or grant aid. 69% freshmen, 80% undergrads receive need-based self-help aid. 2% freshmen, 1% undergrads receive athletic scholarships. 45% undergrads borrow to pay for school. Average cumulative indebtedness $12,694. **Criteria for awarding institutional aid:** Non-need-based: academics, athletics, leadership, state/district residency.

UNIVERSITY OF COLORADO—DENVER

P.O. Box 173364, Denver, CO 80217
Phone: 303-556-2704 • **Financial Aid Phone:** 303-556-2886
E-mail: admissions@cudenver.edu • **CEEB Code:** 4875
Fax: 303-556-4838 • **Website:** www.cudenver.edu • **ACT Code:** 533

This public school was founded in 1912. It has a 127-acre campus.

RATINGS
Admissions Selectivity Rating: 78   **Fire Safety Rating:** 60*   **Green Rating:** 63

STUDENTS AND FACULTY
Enrollment: 8,327. **Student Body:** 55% female, 45% male, 4% out-of-state, 1% international (57 countries represented). Asian 10%, African American 5%, Caucasian 63%, Hispanic 12%, Native American 1%.
Retention and Graduation: 71% freshmen return for sophomore year. 7% grads go on to further study within 1 year. 19% grads pursue arts and sciences degrees. 8% grads pursue business degrees. **Faculty:** Student/faculty ratio 15:1. 2,186 full-time faculty, 81% hold PhDs, 11% are members of minority groups, 47% are women.

ACADEMICS
Degrees: bachelor's, first professional, master's, post-master's certificate. **Classes:** Most classes have 20–29 students. Most lab/discussion sessions have 20–29 students. **Majors with Highest Enrollment:** biology/biological sciences; business/commerce; psychology. **Special Study Options:** Accelerated program, cooperative education program, cross-registration, distance learning, double major, English as a Second Language (ESL), honors program, independent study, internships, student-designed major, study abroad, teacher certification program, weekend college. **Combined degree programs:** , BS/MBA. **Disability Services:** Special programs offered to physically disabled students include note-taking services, reader services, tape recorders, tutors. **Career services:** alumni services, career assessment, internships.

FACILITIES
Housing: Coed dorms. 100% of campus accessible to physically disabled. **Special Academic Facilities/Equipment:** Emmanual Gallery **Computers:** Students can register for classes online. Administrative functions (other than registration) can be performed online.

CAMPUS LIFE
Environment: Metropolis. **Activities:** Choral groups, dance, drama/theater, jazz band, music ensembles, musical theater, student government, student newspaper 77 registered organizations, 5 honor societies, 4 religious organizations. **On-Campus Highlights:** PE/Events Center and Emmanuel Gallery, The Auraria Library, Tivoli Student Union, St. Elizabeth's Church, King Academic and Performing Arts Center.

ADMISSIONS
Freshman Academic Profile: Average high school GPA 3.3. 17% in top 10% of high school class, 43% in top 25% of high school class, 78% in top 50% of high school class. SAT Math middle 50% range 490-590. SAT Critical Reading middle 50% range 490-600. ACT middle 50% range 19-25. Minimum web-based TOEFL 71. Minimum paper TOEFL 525. **Basis for Candidate Selection:** *Very important factors considered include:* Class rank, academic GPA, rigor of secondary school record, standardized test scores. *Important factors considered include:* application essay, recommendation(s), level of applicant's interest. *Other factors considered include:* character/personal qualities,

extracurricular activities, talent/ability. **Freshman Admission Requirements:** High school diploma is required and GED is accepted. *Academic units required:* 4 English, 3 mathematics, 3 science, 2 foreign language, 2 social studies, 1 academic electives. *Academic units recommended:* 4 English, 3 mathematics, 3 science, 2 foreign language, 2 social studies, 1 academic electives. **Freshman Admission Statistics:** 3,521 applied, 68% admitted, 45% enrolled. **Transfer Admission Requirements:** college transcript(s), statement of good standing from prior institution(s). Minimum college GPA of 2.4 required. Lowest grade transferable C–. **General Admission Information:** Application Fee $50. Non-fall registration accepted. Admission may be deferred for a maximum of 12 mos. Credit and/or placement offered for CEEB Advanced Placement tests.

COSTS AND FINANCIAL AID

Annual in-state tuition $5,054. Annual out-of-state tuition $17,010. Room and board $9,990. Required fees $878. Average book expense $1,700. **Required Forms and Deadlines:** FAFSA, institution's own financial aid form. **Notification of Awards:** Applicants will be notified of awards on a rolling basis beginning 5/1. **Types of Aid:** *Need-based scholarships/grants:* Federal Pell, SEOG, state scholarships/grants, private scholarships, the school's own gift aid, Federal Nursing Scholarships. *Loans:* Direct Subsidized Stafford, Direct Unsubsidized Stafford, Direct PLUS, Subsidized Stafford, Unsubsidized Stafford, PLUS, Federal Perkins, Federal Nursing. **Student Employment:** Federal Work-Study Program available. Off-campus job opportunities are good. **Financial Aid Statistics:** 97% freshmen, 86% undergrads receive need-based scholarship or grant aid. 12% freshmen, 5% undergrads receive non-need-based scholarship or grant aid. 73% freshmen, 87% undergrads receive need-based self-help aid. 44% undergrads borrow to pay for school. Average cumulative indebtedness $16,321. **Criteria for awarding institutional aid:** Non-need-based: academics, art, leadership, music/drama.

UNIVERSITY OF COLORADO DENVER AND HEALTH SCIENCES CENTER

4200 E. 9th Ave, Denver, CO 80262
Phone: 303-315-7676 • **Financial Aid Phone:** 303-315-8364
E-mail: student.services@uchsc.edu
Fax: 303-315-3358 • **Website:** www.uchsc.edu

This public school was founded in 1883.

RATINGS
Admissions Selectivity Rating: 60*   **Fire Safety Rating:** 60*   **Green Rating:** 60*

STUDENTS AND FACULTY
Enrollment: 359. **Student Body:** 90% female, 10% male, 1% international. Asian 5%, African American 2%, Caucasian 79%, Hispanic 6%, Native American 1%.
Retention and Graduation: Faculty: Student/faculty ratio 2:1. 1342 full-time faculty, 97% hold PhDs.

ACADEMICS
Degrees: bachelor's, first professional, master's, post-master's certificate. **Special Study Options:** cross-registration, distance learning, independent study, internships.

FACILITIES
Housing: 90% of campus accessible to physically disabled. **Computers:** Students can register for classes online. Administrative functions (other than registration) can be performed online.

CAMPUS LIFE
Environment: Metropolis. **Activities:** dance, drama/theater, musical theater, student government, student newspaper, yearbook.

ADMISSIONS
Freshman Academic Profile: Minimum paper TOEFL 550. **Transfer Admission Requirements:** college transcript(s), essay or personal statement, minimum college GPA of 2.0 required. Lowest grade transferable C. **General Admission Information:** Nonfall registration not accepted.

COSTS AND FINANCIAL AID
Types of Aid: *Need-based scholarships/grants:* Federal Pell, SEOG, state scholarships/grants, private scholarships, the school's own gift aid. *Loans:* Direct Subsidized Stafford, Direct Unsubsidized Stafford, Direct PLUS, Federal Perkins, Federal Nursing, college/university loans from institutional funds. **Financial Aid Statistics:** 26% undergrads receive need-based scholarship or grant aid. 16% undergrads receive non-need-based scholarship or grant aid. 100% undergrads receive need-based self-help aid. 93% undergrads borrow to pay for school. Average cumulative indebtedness $21,592.

UNIVERSITY OF COLORADO—BOULDER

552 UCB, Boulder, CO 80309-0552
Phone: 303-492-6301 • **Financial Aid Phone:** 303-492-5091
CEEB Code: 4841
Fax: 303-492-7115 • **Website:** www.colorado.edu/ • **ACT Code:** 532

This public school was founded in 1876. It has a 600-acre campus.

RATINGS
Admissions Selectivity Rating: 76   **Fire Safety Rating:** 84   **Green Rating:** 96

STUDENTS AND FACULTY
Enrollment: 25,239. **Student Body:** 46% female, 54% male, 37% out-of-state, 3% international (107 countries represented). Asian 5%, African American 2%, Caucasian 75%, Hispanic 9%.
Retention and Graduation: 84% freshmen return for sophomore year. 41% freshmen graduate within 4 years. 65% freshmen graduate within 6 years. 20% grads go on to further study within 1 year. 5% grads pursue arts and sciences degrees. 2% grads pursue law degrees. 2% grads pursue business degrees. 1% grads pursue medical degrees. **Faculty:** Student/faculty ratio 18:1. 1384 full-time faculty, 89% hold PhDs, 17% are members of minority groups, 36% are women. 11% of classes are taught by teaching assistants.

ACADEMICS
Degrees: bachelor's, master's, post-master's certificate. **Classes:** Most classes have 10–19 students. Most lab/discussion sessions have 20–29 students. **Majors with Highest Enrollment:** international/global studies; physiology; psychology. **Special Study Options:** Accelerated program, cooperative education program, cross-registration, distance learning, double major, dual enrollment, English as a Second Language (ESL), exchange student program (domestic), honors program, independent study, internships, liberal arts/career combination, student-designed major, study abroad, teacher certification program, °Research and combined BA/MA include Undergraduate Research Opportunities and Concurrent Bachelor's/Master's Programs. °°Small Group Academic Programs include Residence Hall Academic Programs, FallFEST, and Presidents Leadership Class. **Honors programs:** The CU Honors Program provides special educational opportunities for academically prepared, highly motivated undergraduate students. The Honors Program offers a wide-ranging curriculum supported by thoughtful advising and close contact with faculty. The program aspires to provide the best education possible for the leaders of the future. The Honors Residential Academic Program (HRAP) is a residential academic program within the general Honors Program. Qualified first-year students who are invited to participate in the Honors Program may elect to live in an honors part of the Kittredge residence hall complex. **Combined degree programs:** BA/MA, BS/MS. **Disability Services:** Special programs offered to physically disabled students include note-taking services, reader services, tape recorders, tutors. **Career services:** Alumni network, alumni services, career/job search classes, career assessment, internships, regional alumni. Career services highlights include International and National Voluntary Service Training (INVST) Based on service learning principles, INVST is a two-year leadership-training program in community service. It offers a unique educational experience to all majors in the College of Arts and Sciences. Aspects of the program include small innovative classes, a community-building experience in the mountains, two summer programs of service in the US and abroad, and supervised community service positions during the fall and spring semesters. Issues of global development, nonviolent social change, interpersonal conflict and conflict resolution, community development, and solving community problems are all addressed, with focus on poverty, racism, and other manifestations of social inequality and injustice.

FACILITIES
Housing: Coed dorms, special housing for disabled students, fraternity/sorority housing, apartments for married students, apartments for single students, Wellness Housing, Theme Housing. Residential academic programs within specific dorms. 80% of campus accessible to physically disabled. **Special Academic Facilities/Equipment:** Art galleries, natural history museum, heritage center, observatory, planetarium and science center, electron microscopes, outdoor theater, video interactive foreign language laboratory, mountain research station, centrifuge, hands-on teaching and learning laboratory for engineering, multipurpose cultural/athletics/educational events and conference center, a premier concert hall, and an innovative multi-disciplinary Information Technology center. **Computers:** 100% of classrooms, 65% of dorms, 100% of libraries, 100% of dining areas, 100% of student union, 50% of common outdoor areas

have wireless network access. Students can register for classes online. Administrative functions (other than registration) can be performed online.

CAMPUS LIFE

Environment: City. **Activities:** Choral groups, concert band, dance, drama/theater, jazz band, literary magazine, marching band, music ensembles, musical theater, opera, pep band, radio station, student government, student newspaper, student-run film society, symphony orchestra, television station, Campus Ministries, International Student Organization, Model UN. 300 registered organizations, 26 honor societies, 35 religious organizations. 20 fraternities, 19 sororities. **Athletics (Intercollegiate):** *Men:* basketball, cross-country, football, golf, skiing (downhill/alpine), skiing nordic cross-country, track/field (outdoor), track/field (indoor). *Women:* basketball, cross-country, golf, skiing (downhill/alpine), skiing nordic cross-country, soccer, tennis, track/field (outdoor), track/field (indoor), volleyball. **On-Campus Highlights:** University Memorial Center (UMC), Student Recreation Center, Norlin Library, ATLAS Building, Farrand Field, CU-Boulder's Outdoor Program, at the Recreation Center, offers many opportunities to explore the wonderful backcountry regions of Colorado and other unique locations. The program provides recreational experiences emphasizing adventure, skill acquisition, environmental awareness, safety, challenge, a sense of community, and fun. **Environmental Initiatives:** EDUCATION AND RESEARCH: Campus commitment to environmental education and research has helped CU-Boulder become one of the nation's top environmental research universities. CU-Boulder's reputation and performance as a national leader in environmental issues and sustainability helps recruit and retain faculty with the recognized expertise to win leading-edge research awards, to contribute to the global sustainability knowledge base, and to enhance an already respected environmental studies department—one with integrated environmental content across the campus. Environmental Studies is an interdisciplinary program that draws from curricula in the earth and natural sciences as well as the social sciences. Undergraduate students have the opportunity to participate in three residential academic programs (RAPs) that emphasize environmental studies and sustainability. All offer smaller courses in the residences halls. The Baker RAP consists of a cohort of students with interest in the environment and in future careers in working on environmental problems, such as sustainable use of our resources. The Sustainable by Design RAP includes students with an interest in resource-efficient design, renewable energy, and environmental and social impacts of community development. The Social Entrepreneurship for Equitable Development & Sustainability RAP guides students in developing innovative, self-sustaining solutions for addressing critical social and environmental issues around the globe.

ADMISSIONS

Freshman Academic Profile: Average high school GPA 3.6. 25% in top 10% of high school class, 56% in top 25% of high school class, 88% in top 50% of high school class. SAT Math middle 50% range 510-650. SAT Critical Reading middle 50% range 530-630. ACT middle 50% range 23-28. Minimum web-based TOEFL 75. Minimum paper TOEFL 537. **Basis for Candidate Selection:** *Very important factors considered include:* Class rank, application essay, academic GPA, recommendation(s), rigor of secondary school record. *Important factors considered include:* standardized test scores, character/personal qualities, first generation, state residency. *Other factors considered include:* alumni/ae relation, extracurricular activities, geographical residence, level of applicant's interest, talent/ability, volunteer work, work experience. **Freshman Admission Requirements:** High school diploma is required and GED is accepted. *Academic units required:* 4 English, 4 mathematics, 3 science, (2 science labs), 3 foreign language, 3 social studies, 1 history, 1 geography. *Academic units recommended:* 4 English, 4 mathematics, 3 science, (2 science labs), 3 foreign language, 3 social studies, 1 history, 1 geography. **Freshman Admission Statistics:** 21,744 applied, 84% admitted, 36% enrolled. **Transfer Admission Requirements:** High school transcript, college transcript(s), essay or personal statement, Lowest grade transferable C–. **General Admission Information:** Application Fee $50. Regular application deadline 1/15. Regular notification 4/1. Nonfall registration accepted. Admission may be deferred for a maximum of 12 months. Credit and/or placement offered for CEEB Advanced Placement tests.

COSTS AND FINANCIAL AID

Annual in-state tuition $8,056. Annual out-of-state tuition $28,850. Room and board $11,730. Required fees $1,426. Average book expense $1,800. **Required Forms and Deadlines:** FAFSA Tax return required. **Notification of Awards:** Applicants will be notified of awards on a rolling basis beginning 3/1. **Types of Aid:** *Need-based scholarships/grants:* Federal Pell, SEOG, state scholarships/grants, private scholarships, the school's own gift aid. *Loans:* Direct Subsidized Stafford, Direct Unsubsidized Stafford, Direct PLUS, Federal Perkins, college/university loans from institutional funds, Private lenders. **Student Employment:** Federal Work-Study Program available. Institutional employment available. Highest amount earned per year from on-campus jobs $12,050. Off-campus job opportunities are excellent. **Financial Aid Statistics:** 68% freshmen, 70% undergrads receive need-based scholarship or grant aid. 2% freshmen, 2% undergrads receive non-need-based scholarship or grant aid. 91%

freshmen, 93% undergrads receive need-based self-help aid. 1% freshmen, 1% undergrads receive athletic scholarships. 72% freshmen, 62% undergrads receive any aid. 45% undergrads borrow to pay for school. Average cumulative indebtedness $23,413. **Criteria for awarding institutional aid:** Non-need-based: academics, alumni affiliation, art, athletics, leadership, music/drama, state/district residency.

UNIVERSITY OF CONNECTICUT

2131 Hillside Road, Storrs, CT 06268-3088
Phone: 860-486-3137 • **Financial Aid Phone:** 860-486-2819
E-mail: beahusky@uconn.edu • **CEEB Code:** 3915
Fax: 860-486-1476 • **Website:** www.uconn.edu • **ACT Code:** 604

This public school was founded in 1881. It has a 4104-acre campus.

RATINGS

Admissions Selectivity Rating: 92   **Fire Safety Rating:** 81   **Green Rating:** 91

STUDENTS AND FACULTY

Enrollment: 17,450. **Student Body:** 49% female, 51% male, 23% out-of-state, 2% international (104 countries represented). Asian 8%, African American 6%, Caucasian 64%, Hispanic 7%.
Retention and Graduation: 92% freshmen return for sophomore year. 68% freshmen graduate within 4 years. 83% freshmen graduate within 6 years. 32% grads go on to further study within 1 year. 19% grads pursue arts and sciences degrees. 2% grads pursue law degrees. 3% grads pursue business degrees. 1% grads pursue medical degrees. **Faculty:** Student/faculty ratio 18:1. 1036 full-time faculty, 94% hold PhDs, 21% are members of minority groups, 66% are women. 20% of classes are taught by teaching assistants.

ACADEMICS

Degrees: associate, bachelor's, doctoral, master's, post-bachelor's certificate, post-master's certificate, terminal associate, transfer associate. **Classes:** Most classes have 10-19 students. Most lab/discussion sessions have 10-19 students. **Majors with Highest Enrollment:** business/commerce; political science and government; psychology. **Special Study Options:** Accelerated program, cooperative education program, distance learning, double major, dual enrollment, English as a Second Language (ESL), exchange student program (domestic), honors program, independent study, internships, liberal arts/career combination, student-designed major, study abroad, teacher certification program, Winter inter-session, summer session, and urban semester. **Honors programs:** Honors Scholar Program for all Undergraduates **Combined degree programs:** BA/MD, BA/MA, BA/DDS, Pharm.D. **Disability Services:** Special programs offered to physically disabled students include note-taking services, reader services, tape recorders, tutors.

FACILITIES

Housing: Coed dorms, special housing for disabled students, men's dorms, special housing for international students, women's dorms, fraternity/sorority housing, apartments for married students, apartments for single students, Wellness Housing, Theme Housing, Special Interests, Honors, Foreign Languages, Older-Student Housing, Freshman Year Experience Housing, "Global House," Women in Math, Science, and Engineering, Other learning communities. 90% of campus accessible to physically disabled. **Special Academic Facilities/Equipment:** Art and natural history museums, child development labs, national undersea research center, arboretum, institute for social inquiry, institute of materials science, electron microscope labs. **Computers:** 90% of libraries, 5% of dining areas, 25% of student union, have wireless network access. Students can register for classes online. Administrative functions (other than registration) can be performed online.

CAMPUS LIFE

Environment: Town. **Activities:** Choral groups, concert band, dance, drama/theater, jazz band, literary magazine, marching band, music ensembles, musical theater, opera, pep band, radio station, student government, student newspaper, student-run film society, symphony orchestra, television station, yearbook, Campus Ministries, International Student Organization, Model UN. 303 registered organizations, 29 honor societies, 17 religious organizations. 14 fraternities, 12 sororities. **Athletics (Intercollegiate):** *Men:* baseball, basketball, cross-country, diving, football, golf, ice hockey, soccer, swimming, tennis, track/field (outdoor), track/field (indoor). *Women:* basketball, crew/rowing, cross-country, diving, field hockey, ice hockey, lacrosse, soccer, softball, swimming, tennis, track/field (outdoor), track/field (indoor), volleyball. **On-Campus Highlights:** William Benton Museum of Art, Dairy Product Salesroom, Puppetry Museum, Green Houses, Jorgensen Auditorium and Connecticut Repertory Theater. **Environmental Initiatives:** Signed ACUPCC and began developing Climate Action Plan and began implementing several of its more than 200 strategies related to energy, transportation, sustainable development and environmental literacy. Adopted Sustainable Design & Construction Policy setting LEED Silver rating as minimum performance standard for all new construction and major renovation projects " especially significant because UConn has 8 years and $1 billion remaining on a 20-year, $2.3 billion, state bond-funded capital improvement program.

ADMISSIONS

Freshman Academic Profile: 43% in top 10% of high school class, 82% in top 25% of high school class, 98% in top 50% of high school class. 86% from public high schools. SAT Math middle 50% range 580-670. SAT Critical Reading middle 50% range 550-640. SAT Writing middle 50% range 550-650. ACT middle 50% range 25-29. Minimum web-based TOEFL 79. Minimum paper TOEFL 550. **Basis for Candidate Selection:** *Very important factors considered include:* Class rank, academic GPA, rigor of secondary school record, standardized test scores. *Important factors considered include:* application essay, recommendation(s), character/personal qualities, extracurricular activities, first generation, racial/ethnic status, talent/ability, volunteer work. *Other factors considered include:* alumni/ae relation, geographical residence, level of applicant's interest, state residency, work experience. **Freshman Admission Requirements:** High school diploma is required and GED is accepted. *Academic units required:* 4 English, 3 mathematics, 2 science, (2 science labs), 2 foreign language, 2 social studies, 3 academic electives. *Academic units recommended:* 4 English, 3 mathematics, 2 science, (2 science labs), 2 foreign language, 2 social studies, 3 academic electives. **Freshman Admission Statistics:** 27,247 applied, 47% admitted, 26% enrolled. **Transfer Admission Requirements:** High school transcript, college transcript(s), essay or personal statement, minimum college GPA of 2.7 required. Lowest grade transferable C. **General Admission Information:** Application Fee $70. Regular application deadline 2/1. Notification on a rolling basis, beginning on or about 1/1. Nonfall registration accepted. Admission may be deferred for a maximum of 1 year. Credit and/or placement offered for CEEB Advanced Placement tests.

COSTS AND FINANCIAL AID

Annual in-state tuition $8,712. Annual out-of-state tuition $26,544. Room and board $11,380. Required fees $2,530. Average book expense $850. **Required Forms and Deadlines:** FAFSA. **Notification of Awards:** Applicants will be notified of awards on a rolling basis beginning 3/1. **Types of Aid:** *Need-based scholarships/grants:* Federal Pell, SEOG, state scholarships/grants, private scholarships, the school's own gift aid. *Loans:* Subsidized Stafford, Unsubsidized Stafford, PLUS, Federal Perkins. **Student Employment:** Federal Work-Study Program available. Institutional employment available. Highest amount earned per year from on-campus jobs $3,500. Off-campus job opportunities are good. **Financial Aid Statistics:** 79% freshmen, 76% undergrads receive need-based scholarship or grant aid. 70% freshmen, 51% undergrads receive non-need-based scholarship or grant aid. 73% freshmen, 77% undergrads receive need-based self-help aid. 2% freshmen, 2% undergrads receive athletic scholarships. 49% freshmen, 48% undergrads receive any aid. 63% undergrads borrow to pay for school. Average cumulative indebtedness $23,822. **Criteria for awarding institutional aid:** Non-need-based: academics, art, athletics, leadership, minority status, music/drama.

UNIVERSITY OF THE CUMBERLANDS

6178 College Station Drive, Williamsburg, KY 40769
Phone: 606-539-4241 • **Financial Aid Phone:** 606-539-4220
E-mail: admiss@ucumberlands.edu • **CEEB Code:** 1145
Fax: 606-539-4303 • **Website:** ACT Code: 1510

This private school was founded in 1888. It has a 50-acre campus.

RATINGS

Admissions Selectivity Rating: 60*   **Fire Safety Rating:** 60*   **Green Rating:** 60*

STUDENTS AND FACULTY

Enrollment: 1,389. Student Body: 53% female, 47% male, 38% out-of-state, 2% international (22 countries represented). Asian 1%, African American 5%, Caucasian 65%, Hispanic 1%, Native American 0%.
Retention and Graduation: 62% freshmen return for sophomore year. 22% freshmen graduate within 4 years. 42% freshmen graduate within 6 years. 7% grads go on to further study within 1 year. 3% grads pursue arts and sciences degrees. 1% grads pursue law degrees. 2% grads pursue business degrees. 3% grads pursue medical degrees. Faculty: Student/faculty ratio 14:1. 85 full-time

faculty, 74% hold PhDs, 6% are are members of minority groups, 36% are women. 0% of classes are taught by teaching assistants.

ACADEMICS

Degrees: bachelor's, master's. Classes: Most classes have 10–19 students. Most lab/discussion sessions have fewer than 10 students. Majors with Highest Enrollment: biology/biological sciences; business/commerce; elementary education and teaching. Special Study Options: Accelerated program, cooperative education program, distance learning, double major, dual enrollment, English as a Second Language (ESL), honors program, independent study, internships, liberal arts/career combination, student-designed major, study abroad, teacher certification program. Disability Services: Special programs offered to physically disabled students include tutors. Career services: Alumni network, alumni services, career/job search classes, career assessment, internships, regional alumni. Career services highlights include Internships with Rollins Corporation.

FACILITIES

Housing: men's dorms, women's dorms. 55% of campus accessible to physically diasbled. Special Academic Facilities/Equipment: Natural Science History, distance learning lab, and student art museums. Computers: Students can register for classes online. Administrative functions (other than registration) can be performed online.

CAMPUS LIFE

Environment: Rural. Activities: Choral groups, concert band, dance, drama/theater, jazz band, marching band, music ensembles, musical theater, pep band, radio station, student government, student newspaper, television station 45 registered organizations, 11 honor societies, 18 religious organizations. Athletics (Intercollegiate): Men: baseball, basketball, cheerleading; cross-country, football, golf, soccer, swimming, tennis, track/field (outdoor), wrestling. Women: basketball, cheerleading, cross-country, golf, soccer, softball, swimming, tennis, track/field (outdoor), volleyball, wrestling. On-Campus Highlights: Cumberland Inn and Museum, Wayne Rollins Center, Rollins Fine Arts Center, Taylor Stadium, Boswelll Campus Center.

ADMISSIONS

Freshman Academic Profile: Average high school GPA 3.4. 20% in top 10% of high school class, 44% in top 25% of high school class, 79% in top 50% of high school class. 90% from public high schools. SAT Math middle 50% range 410-570. SAT Critical Reading middle 50% range 410-560. ACT middle 50% range 19-24. Minimum paper TOEFL 550. Basis for Candidate Selection: Very important factors considered include: rigor of secondary school record. Other factors considered include: Class rank, application essay, academic GPA, recommendation(s), standardized test scores, character/personal qualities, extracurricular activities, first generation, interview, level of applicant's interest, talent/ability, volunteer work. Freshman Admission Requirements: High school diploma is required and GED is accepted. Academic units required: 4 English, 3 mathematics, 2 science, 1 social studies. Academic units recommended: 4 English, 3 mathematics, 2 science, 1 social studies. Freshman Admission Statistics: 849 applied, 83% admitted, 50% enrolled. Transfer Admission Requirements: college transcript(s), essay or personal statement, statement of good standing from prior institution(s). Minimum college GPA of 2.0 required. Lowest grade transferable C. General Admission Information: Application Fee $30. Regular notification 8/15. Notification on a rolling basis, beginning on or about 9/1. Nonfall registration accepted. Admission may be deferred for a maximum of 1 semester. Credit offered for CEEB Advanced Placement tests.

COSTS AND FINANCIAL AID

Annual tuition $13,298. Room and board $6,626. Required fees $360. Average book expense $1,000. Required Forms and Deadlines: FAFSA. Notification of Awards: Applicants will be notified of awards on a rolling basis beginning 2/1. Types of Aid: Need-based scholarships/grants: Federal Pell, SEOG, state scholarships/grants, private scholarships, the school's own gift aid. Loans: Subsidized Stafford, Unsubsidized Stafford, PLUS, Federal Perkins, college/university loans from institutional funds. Student Employment: Federal Work-Study Program available. Institutional employment available. Highest amount earned per year from on-campus jobs $2,400. Off-campus job opportunities are fair. Financial Aid Statistics: 100% freshmen, 100% undergrads receive need-based scholarship or grant aid. 100% freshmen, 100% undergrads receive non-need-based scholarship or grant aid. 77% freshmen, 69% undergrads receive need-based self-help aid. 4% freshmen, 3% undergrads receive athletic scholarships. 94% freshmen, 92% undergrads receive any aid. 72% undergrads borrow to pay for school. Average cumulative indebtedness $19,118. Criteria for awarding institutional aid: Non-need-based: academics, alumni affiliation, art, athletics, leadership, music/drama, religious affiliation, state/district residency.

See page 1250.

UNIVERSITY OF DALLAS

1845 East Northgate Drive, Irving, TX 75062
Phone: 972-721-5266 • **Financial Aid Phone:** 972-721-5266
E-mail: ugadmis@udallas.edu • **CEEB Code:** 6868
Fax: 972-721-5017 • **Website:** www.udallas.edu • **ACT Code:** 4234

This private school, affiliated with the Roman Catholic Church, was founded in 1956. It has a 450-acre campus.

RATINGS
Admissions Selectivity Rating: 87   **Fire Safety Rating:** 82   **Green Rating:** 61

STUDENTS AND FACULTY
Enrollment: 1,353. **Student Body:** 52% female, 48% male, 52% out-of-state, 3% international (53 countries represented). Asian 4%, African American 1%, Caucasian 69%, Hispanic 17%.
Retention and Graduation: 80% freshmen return for sophomore year. 60% freshmen graduate within 4 years. 69% freshmen graduate within 6 years. 40% grads go on to further study within 1 year. 14% grads pursue arts and sciences degrees. 3% grads pursue law degrees. 4% grads pursue business degrees. 3% grads pursue medical degrees. **Faculty:** Student/faculty ratio 10:1. 139 full-time faculty, 88% hold PhDs, 8% are members of minority groups, 34% are women. 0% of classes are taught by teaching assistants.

ACADEMICS
Degrees: bachelor's, master's, post-bachelor's certificate, post-master's certificate. **Classes:** Most classes have 20–29 students. Most lab/discussion sessions have 10–19 students. **Majors with Highest Enrollment:** biology/biological sciences; business administration and management; English language and literature. **Special Study Options:** double major, dual enrollment, independent study, internships, liberal arts/career combination, student-designed major, study abroad, teacher certification program. **Combined degree programs:** BA/MA, BA/MBA, BA/M-Psy, BA/MA Philosophy. **Disability Services:** Special programs offered to physically disabled students include note-taking services, reader services, tape recorders, tutors. **Career services:** Alumni network, alumni services, career/job search classes, career assessment, internships Career services highlights include Recruiting program for graduating students.

FACILITIES
Housing: Coed dorms, men's dorms, women's dorms, apartments for single students. 50% of campus accessible to physically disabled. **Special Academic Facilities/Equipment:** Art gallery, theater, language science, and computer labs, observatory. **Computers:** 50% of classrooms, 100% of dorms, 100% of libraries, 20% of dining areas, 100% of student union, 50% of common outdoor areas have wireless network access. Students can register for classes online. Administrative functions (other than registration) can be performed online.

CAMPUS LIFE
Environment: City. **Activities:** Choral groups, dance, drama/theater, literary magazine, music ensembles, musical theater, radio station, student government, student newspaper, student-run film society, yearbook, Campus Ministries, International Student Organization 35 registered organizations, 4 honor societies, 5 religious organizations. **Athletics (Intercollegiate):** *Men:* baseball, basketball, cross-country, golf, lacrosse, soccer, track/field (outdoor). *Women:* basketball, cross-country, lacrosse, soccer, softball, track/field (outdoor), volleyball. **On-Campus Highlights:** Church of the Incarnation, Capp Bar, The Mall, The Rathskeller, Art Village. **Environmental Initiatives:** Student Government recycling committee and Environmental Alliance Club. SG provides recycling receptacles for cans and papers. Replacing all water faucets with reduction flow fixtures (low flow). Energy survey of all buildings to determine current efficiency and needed improvements. Upgraded HVAC systems in many buildings.

ADMISSIONS
Freshman Academic Profile: Average high school GPA 3.7. 53% in top 10% of high school class, 72% in top 25% of high school class, 85% in top 50% of high school class. 43% from public high schools. SAT Math middle 50% range 530-640. SAT Critical Reading middle 50% range 550-670. SAT Writing middle 50% range 530-660. ACT middle 50% range 23-29. Minimum web-based TOEFL 79. Minimum paper TOEFL 550. **Basis for Candidate Selection:** *Very important factors considered include:* application essay, academic GPA, recommendation(s), rigor of secondary school record, standardized test scores, character/personal qualities. *Important factors considered include:* Class rank, talent/ability. *Other factors considered include:* alumni/ae relation, extracurricu-

lar activities, first generation, interview, level of applicant's interest, volunteer work, work experience. **Freshman Admission Requirements:** High school diploma is required and GED is accepted. *Academic units required:* 4 English, 3 mathematics, 3 science, 2 foreign language, 3 social studies, 3 history, 2 visual/performing arts, 4 academic electives. *Academic units recommended:* 4 English, 3 mathematics, 3 science, 2 foreign language, 3 social studies, 3 history, 2 visual/performing arts, 4 academic electives. **Freshman Admission Statistics:** 1,178 applied, 88% admitted, 34% enrolled. **Transfer Admission Requirements:** college transcript(s), essay or personal statement, statement of good standing from prior institution(s). Minimum college GPA of 2.5 required. Lowest grade transferable C–. **General Admission Information:** Application Fee $40. Regular application deadline 8/1. Notification on a rolling basis, beginning on or about 3/1. Nonfall registration accepted. Admission may be deferred for a maximum of 1 year. Credit and/or placement offered for CEEB Advanced Placement tests.

COSTS AND FINANCIAL AID
Annual tuition $30,850. Room and board $10,500. Required fees $2,160. Average book expense $1,200. **Required Forms and Deadlines:** FAFSA. **Notification of Awards:** Applicants will be notified of awards on a rolling basis beginning 3/30. *Types of Aid: Need-based scholarships/grants:* Federal Pell, SEOG, state scholarships/grants, the school's own gift aid. *Loans:* Subsidized Stafford, Unsubsidized Stafford, PLUS, state loans. **Student Employment:** Federal Work-Study Program available. Institutional employment available. Highest amount earned per year from on-campus jobs $1,500. Off-campus job opportunities are fair. **Financial Aid Statistics:** 99% freshmen, 98% undergrads receive need-based scholarship or grant aid. 55% freshmen, 50% undergrads receive non-need-based scholarship or grant aid. 76% freshmen, 78% undergrads receive need-based self-help aid. 96% freshmen, 93% undergrads receive any aid. 58% undergrads borrow to pay for school. Average cumulative indebtedness $31,466. **Criteria for awarding institutional aid:** Non-need-based: academics, art, leadership, music/drama.

UNIVERSITY OF DAYTON

300 College Park, Dayton, OH 45469-1300
Phone: 937-229-4411 • **Financial Aid Phone:** 800-427-5029
E-mail: admission@udayton.edu • **CEEB Code:** 1834
Fax: 937-229-4729 • **Website:** www.udayton.edu • **ACT Code:** 3342

This private school, affiliated with the Roman Catholic Church, was founded in 1850. It has a 259-acre campus.

RATINGS
Admissions Selectivity Rating: 86   **Fire Safety Rating:** 72   **Green Rating:** 85

STUDENTS AND FACULTY
Enrollment: 7,793. **Student Body:** 48% female, 52% male, 43% out-of-state, 6% international (70 countries represented). Asian 1%, African American 3%, Caucasian 84%, Hispanic 2%.
Retention and Graduation: 88% freshmen return for sophomore year. 60% freshmen graduate within 4 years. 78% freshmen graduate within 6 years. 26% grads go on to further study within 1 year. **Faculty:** Student/faculty ratio 16:1. 508 full-time faculty, 89% hold PhDs, 16% are members of minority groups, 37% are women. 3% of classes are taught by teaching assistants.

ACADEMICS
Degrees: bachelor's, master's, post-master's certificate. **Classes:** Most classes have 20–29 students. Most lab/discussion sessions have 10–19 students. **Majors with Highest Enrollment:** business, management, marketing, and related support services, other; mechanical engineering; psychology. **Special Study Options:** Accelerated program, cooperative education program, cross-registration, distance learning, double major, dual enrollment, English as a Second Language (ESL), exchange student program (domestic), honors program, independent study, internships, liberal arts/career combination, student-designed major, study abroad, teacher certification program, Distance learning courses are offered, but not programs; domestic exchange only among other Marianist institutions; student-designed major is general studies. **Honors programs:** The University Honors Program offers courses, programming, fellowship advising, funding, guidance and benefits to undergraduates who have superior academic records, culminating in an Honors-designated diploma. Through the Honors Program, students can develop their academic talents, explore the world, under-

take extensive, self-directed research, and apply their knowledge for the benefit of others. **Combined degree programs:** BA/MA, ACC/MBA. **Disability Services:** Special programs offered to physically disabled students include note-taking services, reader services, tape recorders, tutors. **Career services:** Alumni network, alumni services, career/job search classes, career assessment, internships, regional alumni.

FACILITIES

Housing: Coed dorms, special housing for disabled students, men's dorms, special housing for international students, women's dorms, fraternity/sorority housing, apartments for single students, Wellness Housing, Theme Housing-University-owned houses. 95% of campus accessible to physically disabled. **Special Academic Facilities/Equipment:** UD Research Institute, Bombeck Family Learning Center, Learning Teaching Center, Davis Center for Portfolio Management, Marian Library, ArtStreet living-learning complex, RecPlex. **Computers:** 100% of classrooms, 100% of dorms, 100% of libraries, 100% of dining areas, 100% of student union, 100% of common outdoor areas have wireless network access. Students can register for classes online. Administrative functions (other than registration) can be performed online. Undergraduates are required to own a computer.

CAMPUS LIFE

Environment: City. **Activities:** Choral groups, concert band, dance, drama/theater, jazz band, literary magazine, marching band, music ensembles, musical theater, opera, pep band, radio station, student government, student newspaper, symphony orchestra, television station, yearbook, Campus Ministries, International Student Organization, Model UN. 200 registered organizations, 14 honor societies, 30 religious organizations. 13 fraternities, 9 sororities. **Athletics (Intercollegiate):** *Men:* baseball, basketball, cheerleading, cross-country, football, golf, soccer, tennis. *Women:* basketball, cheerleading, crew/rowing, cross-country, golf, soccer, softball, tennis, track/field (outdoor), track/field (indoor), volleyball. **On-Campus Highlights:** John F. Kennedy Memorial Union, Ryan C. Harris Learning-Teaching Center, University of Dayton Arena, University of Dayton Science Center, Kettering Laboratories; UDRI, ArtStreet, an innovative living-learning complex, combines student residential quarters with performance and visual arts spaces, a recording studio, radio station and cafe. Mariant Hall, a multifunctional facility consisting of student housing, a book store, post office, credit union, food emporium, worship space and learning center, was completed in fall 2004. A $22 million addition to and renovation of Sherman and Wohlleben Halls, home to UD science programs, connects them and provides close to 55,000 square feet for new laboratories, classrooms, offices and gathering spaces. A fitness and recreation complex, or RecPlex, opened in January 2006. It consists of three levels and totals 129,540 square feet. **Environmental Initiatives:** Composting program that has eliminated ~90% of waste from all campus dining halls complete with a total conversion to compostable disposable products for takeout and washable service ware for dine-in customers. A commingle single-stream recycling program for plastic, steel and aluminum cans, cardboard and paper, with additional recycling of ink and toner, electronics, scrap metal, batteries, and construction and renovation debris.

Freshman Academic Profile: Average high school GPA 3.6. 26% in top 10% of high school class, 57% in top 25% of high school class, 88% in top 50% of high school class. 52% from public high schools. SAT Math middle 50% range 503-640. SAT Critical Reading middle 50% range 510-620. ACT middle 50% range 24-29. Minimum web-based TOEFL 70. Minimum paper TOEFL 523. **Basis for Candidate Selection:** *Very important factors considered include:* academic GPA. *Important factors considered include:* Class rank, rigor of secondary school record, standardized test scores, talent/ability. *Other factors considered include:* application essay, recommendation(s), alumni/ae relation, character/personal qualities, extracurricular activities, first generation, interview, racial/ethnic status, volunteer work, work experience. **Freshman Admission Requirements:** High school diploma is required and GED is accepted. *Academic units required:* 2 units of foreign language are required for admission to the College of Arts and Sciences. *Academic units recommended:* 2 units of foreign language are required for admission to the College of Arts and Sciences **Freshman Admission Statistics:** 15,101 applied, 55% admitted, 25% enrolled. **Transfer Admission Requirements:** High school transcript, college transcript(s), essay or personal statement, minimum college GPA of 2.0 required. Lowest grade transferable C–. **General Admission Information:** Regular application deadline 3/1. Nonfall registration accepted. Admission may be deferred for a maximum of 2 years. Credit and/or placement offered for CEEB Advanced Placement tests.

COSTS AND FINANCIAL AID

Annual tuition $32,000. Room and board $10,350. Required fees $1,400. Average book expense $1,000. **Required Forms and Deadlines:** FAFSA. **Notification of Awards:** Applicants will be notified of awards on a rolling basis beginning 3/15. **Types of Aid:** *Need-based scholarships/grants:* Federal Pell, SEOG, state scholarships/grants, private scholarships, the school's own gift aid, ACG, SMART. *Loans:* Subsidized Stafford, Unsubsidized Stafford, PLUS, Fed-

eral Perkins. **Student Employment:** Federal Work-Study Program available. Institutional employment available. Off-campus job opportunities are good. **Financial Aid Statistics:** 100% freshmen, 100% undergrads receive need-based scholarship or grant aid. 23% freshmen, 22% undergrads receive non-need-based scholarship or grant aid. 80% freshmen, 83% undergrads receive need-based self-help aid. 2% freshmen, 2% undergrads receive athletic scholarships. 94% freshmen, 89% undergrads receive any aid. 62% undergrads borrow to pay for school. Average cumulative indebtedness $40,628. **Criteria for awarding institutional aid:** Non-need-based: academics, alumni affiliation, art, athletics, leadership, music/drama, state/district residency.

UNIVERSITY OF DELAWARE

210 South College Ave., Newark, DE 19716-6210
Phone: 302-831-8123 • **Financial Aid Phone:** 302-831-8761
E-mail: admissions@udel.edu • **CEEB Code:** 5811
Fax: 302-831-6905 • **Website:** www.udel.edu • **ACT Code:** 634

This public school was founded in 1743. It has a 1000-acre campus.

RATINGS

Admissions Selectivity Rating: 91   **Fire Safety Rating:** 95   **Green Rating:** 85

STUDENTS AND FACULTY

Enrollment: 16,340. **Student Body:** 57% female, 43% male, 59% out-of-state, 4% international (60 countries represented). Asian 4%, African American 4%, Caucasian 78%, Hispanic 6%.

Retention and Graduation: 65% freshmen graduate within 4 years. 78% freshmen graduate within 6 years. 26% grads go on to further study within 1 year. 10% grads pursue arts and sciences degrees. 8% grads pursue law degrees. 4% grads pursue business degrees. 6% grads pursue medical degrees. **Faculty:** Student/faculty ratio 15:1. 1190 full-time faculty, 86% hold PhDs, 18% are members of minority groups, 39% are women. 5% of classes are taught by teaching assistants.

ACADEMICS

Degrees: associate, bachelor's, master's. **Classes:** Most classes have 20–29 students. Most lab/discussion sessions have 10–19 students. **Majors with Highest Enrollment:** biology/biological sciences; nursing/registered nurse (rn, asn, bsn, msn); psychology. **Special Study Options:** Accelerated program, cooperative education program, distance learning, double major, dual enrollment, English as a Second Language (ESL), honors program, independent study, internships, liberal arts/career combination, student-designed major, study abroad, teacher certification program. **Honors programs:** University Honors Program, http://honors.udel.edu/ **Combined degree programs:** , 4+1 BS Hotel Restaurant and Inst. Mgmt./MBA. **Disability Services:** Special programs offered to physically disabled students include note-taking services, reader services, tape recorders, tutors. **Career services:** Alumni network, alumni services, career/job search classes, career assessment, internships Career services highlights include Extensive web-based career workshop series. Strong relationships with academic departments and colleges to deliver services to students. Discovery Learning: internships, study abroad, undergraduate research, and service learning.

FACILITIES

Housing: Coed dorms, special housing for disabled students, women's dorms, fraternity/sorority housing, apartments for married students, apartments for single students, Theme Housing, Special-interest housing. 95% of campus accessible to physically disabled. **Special Academic Facilities/Equipment:** $20 million Lammont du Pont Laboratory, $11 million Biotechnology Center, $1,8 million Fischer Greenhouse Laboratory, 23,000-seat Delaware Football Stadium, 350-acre Agricultural Teachning and Research Complex, 35-acre Woodlot harboring numerous wild species of animals and birds, 28 micro-computing sites, 6-acre Morris Library containing pver 2.8 million books and over 270 networked databases, 2 student/University centers, art coservation laboratories at Winterthur Museum and Gardens, Bob Carpenter Sports/Convocation Center, livestock arena and working farm, composites manufacturing science laboratory, Delaware Field House, Fred P. Rullo Stadium, Gerald Culley foreign language media center, historic costume and textile collection, laboratory for the analysis of cultural materials, medical technology laboratories, the mineralogical museum, nursing practice practice laboratories, orthopedic and biomechanical engineering center, Rust and Gold ice skating arenas, textiles, botanical gardens, the University gallery, University honors center, University laboratory preschool, Vita Nova, 40+ research centers and institutes, Center for the Arts **Computers:** 100% of classrooms, 100% of dorms, 100% of libraries, 100% of dining areas, 100% of student union, 50% of common outdoor areas have wireless network access. Students can register for classes online. Administrative functions (other than registration) can be performed online.

CAMPUS LIFE
Environment: Town. **Activities:** Choral groups, concert band, dance, drama/theater, jazz band, literary magazine, marching band, music ensembles, musical theater, opera, pep band, radio station, student government, student newspaper, student-run film society, symphony orchestra, television station, Campus Ministries, International Student Organization, Model UN. 250 registered organizations, 23 honor societies, 24 religious organizations. 22 fraternities, 15 sororities. **Athletics (Intercollegiate):** *Men:* baseball, basketball, cross-country, diving, football, golf, lacrosse, soccer, swimming, tennis, track/field (outdoor). *Women:* basketball, crew/rowing, cross-country, diving, field hockey, lacrosse, soccer, softball, swimming, tennis, track/field (outdoor), track/field (indoor), volleyball. **On-Campus Highlights:** Trabant University Center, Gore Hall, Memorial Hall, Morris Library, Delaware Stadium/Bob Carpenter Center. **Environmental Initiatives:** Carbon Footprint Initiative In April of last year the University of Delaware launched the Carbon Footprint Initiative, a comprehensive effort to produce a greenhouse gas inventory and a climate action plan. This effort has been led by Dr. John Byrne, Distinguished Professor of Public Policy and member of the International Panel on Climate Change. The Carbon Footprint Initiative included a comprehensive inventory of all emissions as well as energy audits of 21 representative buildings across campus. A University Climate Action Plan was produced detailing specific implementation steps and produced a goal of reducing University emissions by 20% by 2020. Expanding Renewable Energy Use Over the last six months, the University has initiated two separate projects to expand the amount of renewable energy used by the University. In October, the University signed an agreement to install a 2MW wind turbine on its Lewes Campus in 2010. See: http://www.udel.edu/udaily/2010/oct/gamesa101909.html In addition to pursuing the use of wind power, the University also issued a request for proposals for up to six megawatts of solar power to be installed at its Newark campus. The University is currently in the process of evaluating proposals. Implementation of Green Liasions Program and Single Stream Recycling In the fall of 2009, the University launched a Green Liaison Program (GLP)with the goal of raising environemental awareness and encouraging environmental action in the University community. Members of the campus community are encouraged to identify and implement environmentally-friendly initiatives. The program is open to all students, staff and faculty. See: http://www.udel.edu/udaily/2010/sep/green091609.html See: http://www.udel.edu/sustainability/green/ In the fall of 2009, the University redesigned its campus recycling program. Every campus building, including all dorm rooms and offices, now have a single stream recycling container next to all trash receptacles. The expansion of the University recycling program raised the University's diversion rate to it's highest point in history: 31% in the month of October. See: http://www.udel.edu/udaily/2010/nov/recycle113009.html See: http://www.udel.edu/udaily/2010/aug/recycle082709.html

ADMISSIONS
Freshman Academic Profile: Average high school GPA 3.6. 38% in top 10% of high school class, 79% in top 25% of high school class, 98% in top 50% of high school class. 80% from public high schools. SAT Math middle 50% range 560-660. SAT Critical Reading middle 50% range 540-640. SAT Writing middle 50% range 550-650. ACT middle 50% range 25-29. Minimum web-based TOEFL 90. Minimum paper TOEFL 570. **Basis for Candidate Selection:** *Very important factors considered include:* academic GPA, rigor of secondary school record, state residency. *Important factors considered include:* application essay, recommendation(s), standardized test scores, character/personal qualities, extracurricular activities, talent/ability, volunteer work, work experience. *Other factors considered include:* Class rank, alumni/ae relation, first generation, geographical residence, interview, level of applicant's interest, racial/ethnic status. **Freshman Admission Requirements:** High school diploma is required and GED is accepted. *Academic units required:* 4 English, 3 mathematics, 3 science, (2 science labs), 2 foreign language, 2 social studies, 2 history, 2 academic electives. *Academic units recommended:* 4 English, 3 mathematics, 3 science, (2 science labs), 2 foreign language, 2 social studies, 2 history, 2 academic electives. **Freshman Admission Statistics:** 23,647 applied, 58% admitted, 28% enrolled. **Transfer Admission Requirements:** High school transcript, college transcript(s), essay or personal statement, statement of good standing from prior institution(s). Minimum college GPA of 2.5 required. Lowest grade transferable C. **General Admission Information:** Application Fee $75. Regular application deadline 1/15. Regular notification 3/15. Nonfall registration accepted. Admission may be deferred for a maximum of 1 year. Credit offered for CEEB Advanced Placement tests.

COSTS AND FINANCIAL AID
Annual in-state tuition $10,150. Annual out-of-state tuition $27,240. Room and board $10,758. Required fees $1,532. Average book expense $800. **Required**

Forms and Deadlines: FAFSA. **Notification of Awards:** Applicants will be notified of awards on a rolling basis beginning 3/15. **Types of Aid:** *Need-based scholarships/grants:* Federal Pell, SEOG, state scholarships/grants, private scholarships, the school's own gift aid. *Loans:* Direct Subsidized Stafford, Direct Unsubsidized Stafford, Direct PLUS, Federal Perkins, Federal Nursing, college/university loans from institutional funds. **Student Employment:** Federal Work-Study Program available. Institutional employment available. Highest amount earned per year from on-campus jobs $2,000. Off-campus job opportunities are excellent. **Financial Aid Statistics:** 83% freshmen, 69% undergrads receive need-based scholarship or grant aid. 53% freshmen, 28% undergrads receive non-need-based scholarship or grant aid. 77% freshmen, 85% undergrads receive need-based self-help aid. 3% freshmen, 3% undergrads receive athletic scholarships. 57% freshmen, 55% undergrads receive any aid. 58% undergrads borrow to pay for school. Average cumulative indebtedness $31,002. **Criteria for awarding institutional aid:** Non-need-based: academics, alumni affiliation, art, athletics, leadership, minority status, music/drama, state/district residency.

See page 1252.

UNIVERSITY OF DENVER

Office of Admission, Denver, CO 80208
Phone: 303-871-2036 • **Financial Aid Phone:** 303-871-4020
E-mail: admission@du.edu • **CEEB Code:** 4842
Fax: 303-871-3301 • **Website:** www.du.edu • **ACT Code:** 534

This private school was founded in 1864. It has a 125-acre campus.

RATINGS
Admissions Selectivity Rating: 90 **Fire Safety Rating:** 77 **Green Rating:** 93

STUDENTS AND FACULTY
Enrollment: 5,379. **Student Body:** 56% female, 44% male, 50% out-of-state, 9% international (83 countries represented), Asian 4%, African American 3%, Caucasian 68%, Hispanic 8%, Native American 1%. **Retention and Graduation:** 86% freshmen return for sophomore year. 61% freshmen graduate within 4 years. **Faculty:** Student/faculty ratio 11:1. 671 full-time faculty, 90% hold PhDs, 14% are members of minority groups, 43% are women. 1% of classes are taught by teaching assistants.

ACADEMICS
Degrees: bachelor's, certificate, doctoral, master's, post-bachelor's certificate, post-master's certificate. **Classes:** Most classes have 10–19 students. Most lab/discussion sessions have 20–29 students. **Majors with Highest Enrollment:** biology/biological sciences; business, management, marketing, and related support services, other; business/commerce. **Special Study Options:** Accelerated program, cooperative education program, distance learning, double major, dual enrollment, English as a Second Language (ESL), honors program, independent study, internships, student-designed major, study abroad, teacher certification program, weekend college, Learning disabilities services. **Honors programs:** The University of Denver offers a challenging Honors Program for talented students who seek an advanced liberal education, lively dialogue with their peers and faculty on important issues, study abroad in first-rate universities, and inspiring in-depth work in their majors. The aim of the program is to challenge students to cultivate strong habits of critical thinking, creativity, and scholarship and to offer close support for advanced work. Students in the Honors Program have the best of both worlds: the small classes and close community of a liberal arts college and the opportunities and resources of a research university. **Combined degree programs:** BA/MA, BA/MPP, BSBA/MBA, BA or BS and MSW, BS/MS in Engineering, others. **Disability Services:** Special programs offered to physically disabled students include note-taking services, reader services, tape recorders, tutors. **Career services:** Alumni network, alumni services, career/job search classes, career assessment, internships, regional alumni. Career services highlights include The Backpacks to Briefcases program guides and supports students from their first year at Daniels through their transition to the working world. To symbolize this important time of growth, Daniels students receive a complimentary backpack when they enroll and briefcases embossed with the Daniels logo when they graduate. The mission of Backpacks to Briefcases is two-fold: —Help students get the most of out of their college experience. —Prepare students to realize their full potential when transitioning to the business world. This mission is accomplished through fun and informative workshops, professional development programs,

networking opportunities and other memorable experiences. Past events have included a "Fashion your Future" fashion show and seminar of business attire and etiquette, a Career Conference on "Negotiating your Career Path in a Difficult Economy" with specialized breakout sessions for everyone from first-year students to graduating seniors, and a workshop on "The Art of Small Talk" to help you make a great first impression at networking receptions, job fairs and other events.

FACILITIES

Housing: Coed dorms, fraternity/sorority housing, apartments for married students, apartments for single students, Wellness Housing, Theme Housing. 85% of campus accessible to physically disabled. **Special Academic Facilities/Equipment:** Art gallery, performing arts center, centers for Judaic and Latin American studies, Anthropology Museum, center for child study, center for gifted and talented children, regional conservation center, high altitude research lab, law enforcement technology center, observatory. **Computers:** 75% of classrooms, 10% of dorms, 100% of libraries, 100% of dining areas, 100% of student union, 50% of common outdoor areas have wireless network access. Students can register for classes online. Administrative functions (other than registration) can be performed online. Undergraduates are required to own a computer.

CAMPUS LIFE

Environment: Metropolis. **Activities:** Choral groups, concert band, dance, drama/theater, jazz band, literary magazine, music ensembles, musical theater, opera, pep band, radio station, student government, student newspaper, student-run film society, symphony orchestra, Campus Ministries, International Student Organization, Model UN. 160 registered organizations, 19 honor societies, 14 religious organizations. 9 fraternities, 6 sororities. **Athletics (Intercollegiate):** *Men:* basketball, diving, golf, ice hockey, lacrosse, skiing (downhill/alpine), skiingnordiccross-country, soccer, swimming, tennis. *Women:* basketball, diving, golf, gymnastics, lacrosse, skiing (downhill/alpine), skiingnordiccross-country, soccer, swimming, tennis, volleyball. **On-Campus Highlights:** Campus Green (Driscoll Lawn), Ritchie Center (athletic facility), Newman Center (performing arts), Daniels College of Business building, Jazzman's Cafe (located inside Driscoll Center). **Environmental Initiatives:** The University of Denver expanded from single stream recycling to outdoor bins and composting in two campus dining halls. The University of Denver established the Reserve Energy Fund in 2009, a regenerate funding mechanism in which current savings from energy conservation projects fund future conservation initiatives. The University of Denver hosted the Rocky Mountain Sustainability Summit February 17-18, 2011. Summit sessions and keynote speakers will focus on sustainability issues in higher education, making the business case for sustainability, educating on environmental justice issues, moving from talk to action in the area of sustainability on campus, and focusing on regional sustainability issues.

ADMISSIONS

Freshman Academic Profile: Average high school GPA 3.7. 44% in top 10% of high school class, 78% in top 25% of high school class, 97% in top 50% of high school class. SAT Math middle 50% range 560-660. SAT Critical Reading middle 50% range 550-640. SAT Writing middle 50% range 530-640. ACT middle 50% range 25-30. Minimum web-based TOEFL 80. Minimum paper TOEFL 550. **Basis for Candidate Selection:** *Very important factors considered include:* academic GPA, rigor of secondary school record, standardized test scores, character/personal qualities. *Important factors considered include:* application essay, recommendation(s), extracurricular activities, interview, level of applicant's interest, talent/ability, volunteer work, work experience. **Freshman Admission Requirements:** High school diploma is required and GED is accepted. *Academic units recommended:* **Freshman Admission Statistics:** 11,448 applied, 68% admitted, 16% enrolled. **Transfer Admission Requirements:** college transcript(s), essay or personal statement, statement of good standing from prior institution(s). Lowest grade transferable C. **General Admission Information:** Application Fee $50. Regular application deadline 1/15. Regular notification 3/15. Nonfall registration accepted. Admission may be deferred for a maximum of 12 months. Credit and/or placement offered for CEEB Advanced Placement tests.

COSTS AND FINANCIAL AID

Required Forms and Deadlines: FAFSA, CSS/Financial Aid PROFILE, noncustodial PROFILE. **Notification of Awards:** Applicants will be notified of awards on or about 4/1. **Types of Aid:** *Need-based scholarships/grants:* Federal Pell, SEOG, state scholarships/grants, private scholarships, the school's own gift aid. *Loans:* Direct Subsidized Stafford, Direct Unsubsidized Stafford, Direct PLUS, Subsidized Stafford, Unsubsidized Stafford, PLUS, Federal Perkins, college/university loans from institutional funds. **Student Employment:** Off-campus job opportunities are excellent. **Financial Aid Statistics:** 97% freshmen, 97% undergrads receive need-based scholarship or grant aid. 23% freshmen, 19% undergrads receive non-need-based scholarship or grant aid. 74% freshmen, 79% undergrads receive need-based self-help aid. 3% freshmen, 4% undergrads receive athletic scholarships. 84% freshmen, 85% undergrads receive any aid. 43% undergrads borrow to pay for school. Average cumulative indebtedness $30,268. **Criteria for awarding institutional aid:**

Non-need-based: academics, art, athletics, leadership, music/drama, state/district residency.

UNIVERSITY OF DETROIT MERCY

4001 W McNichols Rd, Detroit, MI 48221-3038
Phone: 313-993-1245
E-mail: admissions@udmercy.edu • **CEEB Code:** 1835
Fax: 313-993-3326 • **Website:** www.udmercy.edu • **ACT Code:** 2060

This private school, affiliated with the Roman CatholiC–Jesuit Church, was founded in 1877. It has a 70-acre campus.

RATINGS

Admissions Selectivity Rating: 68   **Fire Safety Rating:** 60*   **Green Rating:** 60*

STUDENTS AND FACULTY

Enrollment: 2,986. **Student Body:** 68% female, 32% male, 4% out-of-state, 3% international (countries represented). Asian 2%, African American 32%, Caucasian 52%, Hispanic 2%, Native American 1%.
Retention and Graduation: 76% freshmen return for sophomore year. 33% freshmen graduate within 4 years. 54% freshmen graduate within 6 years. 20% grads go on to further study within 1 year. 5% grads pursue arts and sciences degrees. 4% grads pursue law degrees. 8% grads pursue business degrees. 3% grads pursue medical degrees. **Faculty:** Student/faculty ratio 15:1. 270 full-time faculty, 85% hold PhDs, 14% are members of minority groups, 44% are women. 0% of classes are taught by teaching assistants.

ACADEMICS

Degrees: associate, bachelor's, certificate, first professional, first professional certificate, master's, post-bachelor's certificate, post-master's certificate, terminal associate, transfer associate. **Classes: Special Study Options:** Accelerated program, cooperative education program, double major, dual enrollment, English as a Second Language (ESL), honors program, independent study, internships, liberal arts/career combination, study abroad, teacher certification program, weekend college. **Combined degree programs:** BA/DDS. **Disability Services:** Special programs offered to physically disabled students include note-taking services. **Career services:** alumni services, career/job search classes, career assessment, internships.

FACILITIES

Housing: Coed dorms, fraternity/sorority housing, apartments for married students, Peace and Justice Floor Honors Floors WISE (Women in Science and Engineering) floor.

CAMPUS LIFE

Environment: Activities: dance, drama/theater, literary magazine, pep band, radio station, student government, student newspaper 55 registered organizations, 1 honor societies, 7 fraternities, 3 sororities. **Athletics (Intercollegiate):** *Men:* baseball, basketball, cheerleading, cross-country, fencing, golf, soccer, track/field (outdoor), track/field (indoor). *Women:* basketball, cheerleading, cross-country, fencing, soccer, softball, tennis, track/field (outdoor), track/field (indoor).

ADMISSIONS

Freshman Academic Profile: Average high school GPA 3.3. 22% in top 10% of high school class, 50% in top 25% of high school class, 83% in top 50% of high school class. ACT middle 50% range 19-25. **Basis for Candidate Selection:** *Very important factors considered include:* rigor of secondary school record, standardized test scores. *Other factors considered include:* Class rank, application essay, recommendation(s), alumni/ae relation, extracurricular activities, interview, volunteer work. **Freshman Admission Requirements:** High school diploma is required and GED is accepted. *Academic units required:* 4 English, 3 mathematics, 2 science, (1 science labs), 1 social studies, 1 history. *Academic units recommended:* 4 English, 3 mathematics, 2 science, (1 science labs), 1 social studies, 1 history. **Freshman Admission Statistics:** 2,181 applied, 81% admitted, 27% enrolled. **Transfer Admission Requirements:** college transcript(s), minimum college GPA of 2.0 required. Lowest grade transferable C. **General Admission Information:** Application Fee $25. Regular application deadline 7/1. Notification on a rolling basis, beginning on or about 9/1. Nonfall registration accepted. Admission may be deferred for a maximum of 12. Credit and/or placement offered for CEEB Advanced Placement tests.

COSTS AND FINANCIAL AID

Annual tuition $20,400. Room and board $7,040. Required fees $570. Average book expense $1,300. **Required Forms and Deadlines:** FAFSA. **Notification of Awards:** Applicants will be notified of awards on or about 3/1. **Types of Aid:** *Need-based scholarships/grants:* Federal Pell, SEOG, state scholarships/grants, private scholarships, the school's own gift aid, Federal Nursing Scholarships.

Loans: Subsidized Stafford, Unsubsidized Stafford, PLUS, Federal Perkins, Federal Nursing, college/university loans from institutional funds. **Student Employment:** Federal Work-Study Program available. Institutional employment available. Off-campus job opportunities are good. **Financial Aid Statistics:** 83% freshmen, 92% undergrads receive need-based scholarship or grant aid. 83% undergrads receive non-need-based scholarship or grant aid. 74% freshmen, 89% undergrads receive need-based self-help aid. 2% freshmen, 1% undergrads receive athletic scholarships. **Criteria for awarding institutional aid:** Non-need-based: academics, athletics, leadership, minority status, music/drama, religious affiliation.

UNIVERSITY OF DUBUQUE

2000 University Avenue, Dubuque, IA 52001-5050
Phone: 319-589-3200 • **Financial Aid Phone:** 563-589-3396
E-mail: admssns@dbq.edu • **CEEB Code:** 6869
Fax: 319-589-3690 • **Website:** www.dbq.edu • **ACT Code:** 1358

This private school, affiliated with the Presbyterian Church, was founded in 1852. It has a 56-acre campus.

RATINGS
Admissions Selectivity Rating: 70   **Fire Safety Rating:** 97   **Green Rating:** 78

STUDENTS AND FACULTY
Enrollment: 1,542. **Student Body:** 44% female, 56% male, 53% out-of-state, 1% international (countries represented). Asian 2%, African American 12%, Caucasian 73%, Hispanic 3%, Native American 1%.
Retention and Graduation: 68% freshmen return for sophomore year. 21% freshmen graduate within 4 years. 38% freshmen graduate within 6 years. 20% grads go on to further study within 1 year. 10% grads pursue arts and sciences degrees. 2% grads pursue law degrees. 3% grads pursue business degrees. 2% grads pursue medical degrees. **Faculty:** Student/faculty ratio 14:1. 87 full-time faculty, 56% hold PhDs, 6% are members of minority groups, 39% are women. 0% of classes are taught by teaching assistants.

ACADEMICS
Degrees: associate, bachelor's, master's. **Classes:** Most classes have 10–19 students. Most lab/discussion sessions have fewer than 10 students. **Majors with Highest Enrollment:** airline/commercial/professional pilot and flight crew; animation, interactive technology, video graphics and special effects; business/commerce. **Special Study Options:** cooperative education program, cross-registration, distance learning, double major, dual enrollment, independent study, internships, liberal arts/career combination, student-designed major, study abroad, teacher certification program. Undergrads may take grad level classes. Off-Campus Study: Semester-away programs. **Combined degree programs:** BA/MA, 3-3. M.Div. program, BBA/MBA (4+1). **Disability Services:** Special programs offered to physically disabled students include note-taking services, reader services, tape recorders, tutors. **Career services:** Alumni network, alumni services, career/job search classes, career assessment, internships, regional alumni.

FACILITIES
Housing: Coed dorms, special housing for disabled students, apartments for married students, apartments for single students, Houses and Townhouses and Suites. 50% of campus accessible to physically disabled. **Special Academic Facilities/Equipment:** Art gallery, language labs, electron microscope, gas chromatograph/mass spectrometer, floating science lab on the Mississippi River, computer graphics/interactive media stduios, multimedia project production studio in the new Charles C. Myers Library **Computers:** 20% of classrooms, 100% of libraries, 100% of student union, have wireless network access. Students can register for classes online. Administrative functions (other than registration) can be performed online.

CAMPUS LIFE
Environment: Town. **Activities:** Choral groups, dance, drama/theater, jazz band, literary magazine, music ensembles, musical theater, pep band, student government, student newspaper, student-run film society, yearbook, Campus Ministries, International Student Organization 50 registered organizations, 2 honor societies, 3 religious organizations. 7 fraternities, 4 sororities. **Athletics (Intercollegiate):** *Men:* baseball, basketball, cross-country, football, golf, soccer, tennis, track/field (outdoor), track/field (indoor), wrestling. *Women:* basketball, cross-country, golf, soccer, softball, tennis, track/field (outdoor), track/field (indoor), volleyball. **On-Campus Highlights:** Coffee Shop, Stoltz Sports Center, Library, Student Union, Chlapaty Recreation & Wellness Center. **Environmental Initiatives:** Campus-wide recycling Heating, cooling, recycling, etc. standards

ADMISSIONS
Freshman Academic Profile: Average high school GPA 3.0. 7% in top 10% of high school class, 24% in top 25% of high school class, 54% in top 50% of high school class. 85% from public high schools. SAT Math middle 50% range 420-550. SAT Critical Reading middle 50% range 440-550. ACT middle 50% range 18-23. Minimum paper TOEFL 500. **Basis for Candidate Selection:** *Very important factors considered include:* Class rank, application essay, recommendation(s), rigor of secondary school record, standardized test scores, character/personal qualities. *Other factors considered include:* alumni/ae relation, extracurricular activities, interview, talent/ability, volunteer work, work experience. **Freshman Admission Requirements:** High school diploma is required and GED is accepted. *Academic units required:* 4 English, 3 mathematics, 3 science, (0 science labs), 3 social studies, 3 academic electives. *Academic units recommended:* 4 English, 3 mathematics, 3 science, (0 science labs), 3 social studies, 3 academic electives. **Freshman Admission Statistics:** 1,288 applied, 76% admitted, 42% enrolled. **Transfer Admission Requirements:** college transcript(s), minimum college GPA of 2.0 required. Lowest grade transferable C. **General Admission Information:** Application Fee $25. Notification on a rolling basis, beginning on or about 9/1. Nonfall registration accepted. Admission may be deferred for a maximum of 1 year. Credit offered for CEEB Advanced Placement tests.

COSTS AND FINANCIAL AID
Annual tuition $21,000. Room and board $7,370. Required fees $590. Average book expense $950. **Required Forms and Deadlines:** FAFSA. **Notification of Awards:** Applicants will be notified of awards on a rolling basis beginning 3/1. **Types of Aid:** *Need-based scholarships/grants:* Federal Pell, SEOG, state scholarships/grants, private scholarships, the school's own gift aid. *Loans:* Direct Subsidized Stafford, Direct Unsubsidized Stafford, Direct PLUS, Subsidized Stafford, Unsubsidized Stafford, PLUS, Federal Perkins, state loans, college/university loans from institutional funds. **Student Employment:** Federal Work-Study Program available. Institutional employment available. Highest amount earned per year from on campus jobs $1,500. Off-campus job opportunities are excellent. **Financial Aid Statistics:** 99% freshmen, 98% undergrads receive need-based scholarship or grant aid. 16% freshmen, 12% undergrads receive non-need-based scholarship or grant aid. 80% freshmen, 83% undergrads receive need-based self-help aid. 85% freshmen, 85% undergrads receive any aid. 95% undergrads borrow to pay for school. Average cumulative indebtedness $39,365. **Criteria for awarding institutional aid:** Non-need-based: academics, alumni affiliation, leadership, music/drama, state/district residency.

UNIVERSITY OF EVANSVILLE

1800 Lincoln Avenue, Evansville, IN 47722
Phone: 812-488-2468 • **Financial Aid Phone:** 812-488-2364
E-mail: admission@evansville.edu • **CEEB Code:** 1208
Fax: 812-488-4076 • **Website:** www.evansville.edu • **ACT Code:** 1188

This private school, affiliated with the Methodist Church, was founded in 1854. It has a 75-acre campus.

RATINGS
Admissions Selectivity Rating: 73   **Fire Safety Rating:** 73   **Green Rating:** 70

STUDENTS AND FACULTY
Enrollment: 2,498. **Student Body:** 59% female, 41% male, 43% out-of-state, 7% international (45 countries represented). Asian 1%, African American 3%, Caucasian 80%, Hispanic 3%.
Retention and Graduation: 56% freshmen graduate within 4 years. 68% freshmen graduate within 6 years. 19% grads go on to further study within 1 year. **Faculty:** Student/faculty ratio 13:1. 179 full-time faculty, 86% hold PhDs, 10% are members of minority groups, 40% are women. 0% of classes are taught by teaching assistants.

ACADEMICS
Degrees: associate, bachelor's, master's. **Classes:** Most classes have 10–19 students. Most lab/discussion sessions have 20–29 students. **Majors with Highest Enrollment:** drama and dramatics/theatre arts; kinesiology and exercise science; nursing/registered nurse (rn, asn, bsn, msn). **Special Study Options:** Accelerated program, cooperative education program, double major, dual enrollment, English as a Second Language (ESL), external degree program, honors program, independent study, internships, student-designed major, study abroad, teacher certification program. **Honors programs:** The Honors Program incorporates unique courses with distinct learning environments to provide enhanced educational learning experiences for exceptional students. Students openly discuss different viewpoints in small, seminar-style classes offered in various academic disciplines. Intellectually curious students who desire academic challenges will enjoy the collaborative learning atmosphere of the

Honors Program, as well as the opportunity to engage in advanced independent study, a senior project, and special social programs. **Combined degree programs:** , BS/MS in health services administration. **Disability Services:** Special programs offered to physically disabled students include note-taking services, tutors. **Career services:** Alumni network, alumni services, career/job search classes, career assessment, internships, regional alumni.

FACILITIES

Housing: Coed dorms, men's dorms, women's dorms, fraternity/sorority housing, apartments for single students, Theme Housing. 87% of campus accessible to physically disabled. **Computers:** 100% of classrooms, 100% of dorms, 100% of libraries, 100% of dining areas, 100% of student union, 100% of common outdoor areas have wireless network access. Students can register for classes online. Administrative functions (other than registration) can be performed online.

CAMPUS LIFE

Environment: City. **Activities:** Choral groups, concert band, dance, drama/theater, jazz band, literary magazine, music ensembles, musical theater, opera, pep band, radio station, student government, student newspaper, student-run film society, symphony orchestra, yearbook, Campus Ministries, International Student Organization, Model UN. 154 registered organizations, 11 honor societies, 10 religious organizations. 6 fraternities, 5 sororities. **Athletics (Intercollegiate):** *Men:* baseball, basketball, cross-country, diving, golf, soccer, swimming. *Women:* basketball, cross-country, diving, golf, soccer, softball, swimming, tennis, volleyball. **On-Campus Highlights:** Koch Center, Fitness Center, School of Business Administration, Ridgway Student Center, Jazzman's Cafe, The library and Memorial Plaza are also popular places on campus. **Environmental Initiatives:** Placed first in Indiana and 20th nationwide during 2011 Recyclemania tournament. Recycling of paper, plastic, aluminum, cardboard, newspaper, magazines, books, electronic equipment, batteries and ink cartridges. LEED certification of new buildings.

ADMISSIONS

Freshman Academic Profile: Average high school GPA 3.8. 40% in top 10% of high school class, 70% in top 25% of high school class, 95% in top 50% of high school class. SAT Math middle 50% range 510-620. SAT Critical Reading middle 50% range 500-630. SAT Writing middle 50% range 490-610. ACT middle 50% range 23-29. Minimum web-based TOEFL 61. Minimum paper TOEFL 500. **Basis for Candidate Selection:** *Very important factors considered include:* academic GPA, rigor of secondary school record. *Important factors considered include:* standardized test scores, extracurricular activities. *Other factors considered include:* Class rank, recommendation(s), alumni/ae relation, character/personal qualities, level of applicant's interest, racial/ethnic status, talent/ability, volunteer work, work experience. **Freshman Admission Requirements:** High school diploma is required and GED is accepted. *Academic units required:* 4 English, 3 mathematics, 2 science, (2 science labs), 1 social studies, 1 history. *Academic units recommended:* 4 English, 3 mathematics, 2 science, (2 science labs) 1 social studies, 1 history. **Freshman Admission Statistics:** 2,879 applied, 80% admitted, 22% enrolled. **Transfer Admission Requirements:** High school transcript, college transcript(s), statement of good standing from prior institution(s). Minimum college GPA of 2.0 required. Lowest grade transferable C. **General Admission Information:** Application Fee $35. Regular application deadline 2/1. Regular notification 2/15. Nonfall registration accepted. Admission may be deferred for a maximum of 1 year. Credit and/or placement offered for CEEB Advanced Placement tests.

COSTS AND FINANCIAL AID

Annual tuition $29,740. Room and board $10,010. Required fees $816. Average book expense $1,000. **Required Forms and Deadlines:** FAFSA. **Notification of Awards:** Applicants will be notified of awards on a rolling basis beginning 3/25. **Types of Aid:** *Need-based scholarships/grants:* Federal Pell, SEOG, state scholarships/grants, the school's own gift aid. *Loans:* Direct Subsidized Stafford, Direct Unsubsidized Stafford, Direct PLUS, Federal Perkins, Federal Nursing, college/university loans from institutional funds. **Student Employment:** Federal Work-Study Program available. Institutional employment available. Highest amount earned per year from on-campus jobs $1,300. Off-campus job opportunities are good. **Financial Aid Statistics:** 99% freshmen, 99% undergrads receive need-based scholarship or grant aid. 100% freshmen, 92% undergrads receive non-need-based scholarship or grant aid. 60% freshmen, 67% undergrads receive need-based self-help aid. 3% freshmen, 3% undergrads receive athletic scholarships. 99% freshmen, 94% undergrads receive any aid. 73% undergrads borrow to pay for school. Average cumulative indebtedness $27,679. **Criteria for awarding institutional aid:** Non-need-based: academics, alumni affiliation, art, athletics, leadership, minority status, music/drama, religious affiliation, state/district residency.

THE UNIVERSITY OF FINDLAY

1000 North Main Street, Findlay, OH 45840
Phone: 419-434-4732 • **E-mail:** admissions@findlay.edu • **CEEB Code:** 1223
Fax: 419-434-4898 • **ACT Code:** 3272

This private school was founded in 1882. It has a 175-acre campus.

RATINGS

Admissions Selectivity Rating: 60*   **Fire Safety Rating:** 60*   **Green Rating:** 60*

STUDENTS AND FACULTY

Enrollment: 3,381. Student Body: 57% female, 43% male, 20% out-of-state, 1% international (countries represented). Asian 4%, African American 4%, Caucasian 72%, Hispanic 2%, Native American 0%.
Retention and Graduation: 72% freshmen return for sophomore year. 32% freshmen graduate within 4 years. 53% freshmen graduate within 6 years. 18% grads go on to further study within 1 year. 3% grads pursue arts and sciences degrees. 4% grads pursue law degrees. 3% grads pursue business degrees. 1% grads pursue medical degrees. Faculty: Student/faculty ratio 16:1. 160 full-time faculty, 51% hold PhDs, 41% are are members of minority groups, 40% are women. 0% of classes are taught by teaching assistants.

ACADEMICS

Degrees: associate, bachelor's, master's. Classes: Most classes have 10–19 students. Special Study Options: Accelerated program, cooperative education program, distance learning, double major, dual enrollment, English as a Second Language (ESL), external degree program, honors program, independent study, internships, liberal arts/career combination, student-designed major, study abroad, teacher certification program, weekend college, BS in nursing with Mount Carmel College of Nursing, 3-1 arrangement with Art Institute Consortium. Combined degree programs: 3-1 medical technology and nuclear medicine tech. Disability Services: Special programs offered to physically disabled students include note-taking services, tutors. Career services: alumni services, career/job search classes, career assessment, internships.

FACILITIES

Housing: special housing for disabled students, men's dorms, special housing for international students, women's dorms, fraternity/sorority housing, apartments for single students, Honors house, Special Interest houses. 90% of campus accessible to physically diasbled. Special Academic Facilities/Equipment: Fine arts pavilion, planetarium. Mazza Gallery (Children's Book Illustrations.)

CAMPUS LIFE

Environment: Village. Activities: Choral groups, concert band, drama/theater, jazz band, literary magazine, marching band, music ensembles, musical theater, pep band, radio station, student government, student newspaper, student-run film society, television station, yearbook 40 registered organizations, 1 honor societies, 1 religious organizations. 3 fraternities, 2 sororities. Athletics (Intercollegiate): Men: baseball, basketball, cross-country, diving, equestrian sports, football, golf, ice hockey, soccer, swimming, tennis, track/field (outdoor), track/field (indoor), volleyball, wrestling. Women: basketball, cross-country, diving, equestrian sports, golf, ice hockey, soccer, softball, swimming, tennis, track/field (outdoor), track/field (indoor), volleyball.

ADMISSIONS

Freshman Academic Profile: Average high school GPA 3.4. 26% in top 10% of high school class, 54% in top 25% of high school class, 80% in top 50% of high school class. 92% from public high schools. SAT Math middle 50% range 470-580. SAT Critical Reading middle 50% range 470-580. SAT Writing middle 50% range 460-590. ACT middle 50% range 20-25. Minimum paper TOEFL 500. Basis for Candidate Selection: Very important factors considered include: application essay, academic GPA, recommendation(s), rigor of secondary school record, standardized test scores. Important factors considered include: interview. Other factors considered include: Class rank, alumni/ae relation, character/personal qualities, extracurricular activities, religious affiliation/commitment, talent/ability, volunteer work. Freshman Admission Requirements: High school diploma is required and GED is accepted. Freshman Admission Statistics: 2,708 applied, 72% admitted, 37% enrolled. Transfer Admission Requirements: college transcript(s), Minimum college GPA of 2.0 required. Lowest grade transferable C. General Admission Information: Regular application deadline 7/1. Notification on a rolling basis, beginning on or about 9/1. Nonfall registration accepted. Admission may be deferred for a maximum of 1 year. Credit and/or placement offered for CEEB Advanced Placement tests.

COSTS AND FINANCIAL AID

Required Forms and Deadlines: FAFSA. Notification of Awards: Applicants will be notified of awards on a rolling basis beginning 3/1. Types of Aid: Need-based scholarships/grants: Federal Pell, SEOG, state scholarships/grants, private scholarships, the school's own gift aid. Loans: Direct Subsidized Stafford, Direct Unsubsidized Stafford, Direct PLUS, Federal Perkins, college/university loans from institutional funds. Student Employment: Federal Work-Study Program available. Institutional employment available. Highest amount earned per year from on-campus jobs $600. Off-campus job opportunities are excellent. Financial Aid Statistics: 94% freshmen, 86% undergrads receive need-based scholarship or grant aid. 24% freshmen, 23% undergrads receive non-need-based scholarship or grant aid. 99% freshmen, 86% undergrads receive need-based self-help aid. 15% freshmen, 10% undergrads receive athletic scholarships. 85% undergrads borrow to pay for school. Average cumulative indebtedness $17,000. Criteria for awarding institutional aid: Non-need-based: academics, alumni affiliation, athletics, music/drama, religious affiliation, state/district residency.

See page 1254.

UNIVERSITY OF FLORIDA

201 Criser Hall, Gainesville, FL 32611-4000
Phone: 352-392-1365 • **Financial Aid Phone:** 352-392-6684
CEEB Code: 5812
Fax: 904-392-3987 • **Website:** www.ufl.edu

This public school was founded in 1853. It has a 2000-acre campus.

RATINGS

Admissions Selectivity Rating: 95   **Fire Safety Rating:** 60*   **Green Rating:** 87

STUDENTS AND FACULTY

Enrollment: 31,988. **Student Body:** 55% female, 45% male, 3% out-of-state, 1% international (152 countries represented). Asian 8%, African American 9%, Caucasian 59%, Hispanic 18%.
Retention and Graduation: Faculty: Student/faculty ratio 21:1. 3416 full-time faculty, 76% hold PhDs, 25% are members of minority groups, 33% are women. 33% of classes are taught by teaching assistants.

ACADEMICS

Degrees: bachelor's, first professional, master's. **Classes:** Most classes have 10–19 students. Most lab/discussion sessions have 10–19 students. **Majors with Highest Enrollment:** finance; political science and government; psychology. **Special Study Options:** Accelerated program, cooperative education program, cross-registration, distance learning, double major, dual enrollment, English as a Second Language (ESL), exchange student program (domestic), external degree program, honors program, independent study, internships, liberal arts/career combination, student-designed major, study abroad, teacher certification program, weekend college, Adult/Continuing Education, TV-delivered credit-bearing courses, Honors Program, and distance learning courses. **Honors programs:** The University of Florida Honors Program blends the vast resources of a research university with the individualized attention often available only at small liberal arts colleges. With small classes taught by the top faculty at the university, the program offers students the opportunity to make the most of their educational experience. Close interaction with faculty often leads to undergraduate research projects, and students are encouraged to pursue such activities. Students in the Honors Program have the opportunity to live in the Honors Residential College at Hume Hall, the university's newest and most modern dormitory, where they will be surrounded by like-minded individuals and engage in a unique living-learning community. **Combined degree programs:** , http://www.registrar.ufl.edu/catalog/programs/combined.html. **Disability Services:** Special programs offered to physically disabled students include note-taking services, reader services, tape recorders. **Career services:** alumni services, career/job search classes, career assessment, internships Career services highlights include Major Career Showcase conducted each semester - one of the largest fairs of its type nationally. Number one Career Center in U.S. for 2010.

FACILITIES

Housing: Coed dorms, special housing for disabled students, special housing for international students, fraternity/sorority housing, apartments for married students, apartments for single students, Honors Residential College at Hume Hall, International House at Weaver Hall, Career Exploration Community at Graham Hall, Wellness Communities at Springs and Beaty Towers, Faculty-In-Residence Program, First-Year Experience Program, No-Visitation by Opposite Sex Floor available by request, East Hall Engineering Community, Community Service Floor in Fletcher, Fine Arts Living Learning Community in Reid hall, Global Learning Community in Yulee. 98% of campus accessible to physically disabled. **Special Academic Facilities/Equipment:** Natural history museum, art museum, art gallery, center for the performing arts, Aeolian Skin-

ner organ, cast-bell carillon, citrus research center, coastal engineering wave tank, 100-kilowatt training and research reactor, academic computing center, microkelvin lab, self-contained intensive care hyperbaric chamber. **Computers:** 80% of classrooms, 100% of dorms, 100% of libraries, 100% of dining areas, 100% of student union, 100% of common outdoor areas have wireless network access. Students can register for classes online. Administrative functions (other than registration) can be performed online.

CAMPUS LIFE

Environment: City. **Activities:** Choral groups, concert band, dance, drama/theater, jazz band, literary magazine, marching band, music ensembles, musical theater, pep band, radio station, student government, student newspaper, student-run film society, symphony orchestra, television station, yearbook 853 registered organizations. **Athletics (Intercollegiate):** *Men:* baseball, basketball, cross-country, diving, football, golf, swimming, tennis, track/field (outdoor), track/field (indoor). *Women:* basketball, cross-country, diving, golf, gymnastics, lacrosse, soccer, softball, swimming, tennis, track/field (outdoor), track/field (indoor), volleyball. **On-Campus Highlights:** Center for Performing Arts, Florida Museum of Natural History, Cancer & Genetic Research Complex, Brain Institute, Lake Alice Wildlife Reserve. **Environmental Initiatives:** Zero Waste by 2015: As a result of Dr. Machen's goal for Zero Waste by 2015, UF now recycles over 6,500 tons of material annually, approximately 43% of the waste stream. Additionally, UF strives to recycle at least 75% of its deconstruction debris and has instituted an Electronics Reuse/Recycling Policy and accompanying step-by-step guide for disposal and recycling. Indoor collection of paper, cans & bottles is institution-wide. UF initiated a Tail-gator recycling program for home game days in 2006. This volunteer-based program collected over 17,000 lbs of recyclables from 6 home games in the first year and over 26,000 lbs during the 2007 season. With expansion into the stadium in 2009, the program diverted more than 55,000 lbs of recyclables. This program continues to grow through self-service stations and other outreach on campus and within the stadium. UF researchers recycle Helium on campus and the Veterinary Medical Center repurposes animal waste through a composting partnership with the Forestry Service. Carbon Neutrality by 2025: UF completed its first greenhouse gas inventory and assessment in 2004. In October 2006, UF President J. Bernard Machen, was the first to sign the American College and University Presidents Climate Commitment, which committed UF to creating an action plan for becoming carbon neutral and to adding the impacts of air travel and commuting to its original greenhouse gas inventory. In 2009, UF completed a carbon inventory and developed a carbon action plan in accordance with the ACUPCC. UF hosted the first-ever carbon neutral college football game against FSU in 2007. The game inspired a Gator alumnus and his family to start a non-profit that generated all of the carbon offsets required for a fully carbon neutral 2008 home football season " the first of its kind in the NCAA, and in 2009, this partnership continued to work on carbon emissions in athletics, taking the entire athletic program carbon neutral. This commitment continued through the 2012 season. LEED Gold certification is required for all new construction: In 2001, UF adopted the Leadership in Energy and Environmental Design (LEED) standards for all major new construction and renovation projects. In 2006, this commitment was re-confirmed and strengthened by requiring LEED-Silver criteria for design and construction of all major new construction and renovation projects to deliver high performance and sustainable building design. To date, the campus boasts one Platinum certified building, 7 Gold certified buildings, 3 Silver certified buildings, and 10 certified buildings. The first Platinum and Gold certified buildings in the state were on the UF campus. The Facilities, Planning, and Construction Department, which administers this program, has undertaken a LEED portfolio program for existing buildings; UF was selected by the US Green Building Council as one of 12 entities to pursue this portfolio approach. The Campus Historic District is listed on the National Register of Historic Places; the university is committed to preservation of the campus in a manner that meets its goals for energy efficiency. UF built its first green roof atop the Charles R. Perry Construction Yard building this year. The roof, which contains soil and live plants, helps reduce storm water runoff and insulates the building against heat and sound. In support of the indoor health of the built environment, Green Seal-certified cleaning products are used by custodial staff whenever possible.

ADMISSIONS

Freshman Academic Profile: Average high school GPA 4.2. 74% in top 10% of high school class, 93% in top 25% of high school class, 99% in top 50% of high school class. 62% from public high schools. SAT Math middle 50% range 590-690. SAT Critical Reading middle 50% range 570-670. ACT middle 50% range 24-30. **Basis for Candidate Selection:** *Very important factors considered include:* academic GPA, rigor of secondary school record. *Important factors considered include:* application essay, character/personal qualities, extracurricular activities, first generation, talent/ability. *Other factors considered include:* Class rank, standardized test scores, alumni/ae relation, geographical residence, level of applicant's interest, state residency, volunteer work, work experience. **Freshman Admission Requirements:** High school diploma is required and GED is accepted. *Academic units required:* 4 English, 3 mathematics, 3 science, (2 science labs), 2 foreign language, 3 social studies,

3 academic electives. *Academic units recommended:* 4 English, 3 mathematics, 3 science, (2 science labs), 2 foreign language, 3 social studies, 3 academic electives. **Freshman Admission Statistics:** 27,295 applied, 43% admitted, 55% enrolled. **Transfer Admission Requirements:** High school transcript, college transcript(s), standardized test scores, minimum college GPA of 2.0 required. **General Admission Information:** Application Fee $30. Regular application deadline 11/1. Nonfall registration accepted. Credit and/or placement offered for CEEB Advanced Placement tests.

COSTS AND FINANCIAL AID

Annual in-state tuition $6,143. Annual out-of-state tuition $28,420. Room and board $9,370. Average book expense $1,080. **Required Forms and Deadlines:** FAFSA. **Notification of Awards:** Applicants will be notified of awards on a rolling basis beginning 4/1. **Types of Aid:** *Need-based scholarships/grants:* Federal Pell, SEOG, state scholarships/grants, private scholarships, the school's own gift aid State, Academic, Creative arts/performance, Special achievements/activities, Special characteristics, Athletic and ROTC. *Loans:* Direct Subsidized Stafford, Direct Unsubsidized Stafford, Direct PLUS, Federal Perkins, college/university loans from institutional funds. **Student Employment:** Federal Work-Study Program available. Institutional employment available. Highest amount earned per year from on-campus jobs $19,744. Off-campus job opportunities are fair. **Financial Aid Statistics:** 66% freshmen, 68% undergrads receive need-based scholarship or grant aid. 98% freshmen, 83% undergrads receive non-need-based scholarship or grant aid. 36% freshmen, 49% undergrads receive need-based self-help aid. 1% freshmen, 1% undergrads receive athletic scholarships. 98% freshmen, 90% undergrads receive any aid. 39% undergrads borrow to pay for school. Average cumulative indebtedness $16,841. **Criteria for awarding institutional aid:** Non-need-based: academics, art, athletics, leadership, minority status, music/drama, state/district residency.

UNIVERSITY OF GEORGIA

Terrell Hall, Athens, GA 30602
Phone: 706-542-8776 • **Financial Aid Phone:** 706-542-6147
E-mail: admproc@uga.edu • **CEEB Code:** 5813
Fax: 706-542-1466 • **Website:** www.uga.edu • **ACT Code:** 872

This public school was founded in 1785. It has a 324-acre campus.

RATINGS

Admissions Selectivity Rating: 90 **Fire Safety Rating:** 77 **Green Rating:** 98

STUDENTS AND FACULTY

Enrollment: 26,060. **Student Body:** 57% female, 43% male, 9% out-of-state, 1% international (121 countries represented). Asian 8%, African American 7%, Caucasian 74%, Hispanic 5%.
Retention and Graduation: 94% freshmen return for sophomore year. 55% freshmen graduate within 4 years. 83% freshmen graduate within 6 years. 22% grads go on to further study within 1 year. **Faculty:** Student/faculty ratio 18:1. 1841 full-time faculty, 94% hold PhDs, 20% are members of minority groups, 37% are women. 19% of classes are taught by teaching assistants.

ACADEMICS

Degrees: bachelor's, certificate, doctoral, master's, post-bachelor's certificate, post-master's certificate. **Classes:** Most classes have 20–29 students. **Majors with Highest Enrollment:** biology/biological sciences; English language and literature; psychology. **Special Study Options:** Accelerated program, cooperative education program, cross-registration, distance learning, double major, dual enrollment, exchange student program (domestic), external degree program, honors program, independent study, internships, liberal arts/career combination, student-designed major, study abroad, teacher certification program.
Honors programs: General Honors Program (university-wide), Foundation Fellows, Center for Undergraduate Research Summer Research Fellows, CURO Apprentice Program **Disability Services:** Special programs offered to physically disabled students include note-taking services, reader services, tape recorders, tutors. **Career services:** Alumni network, alumni services, career/job search classes, career assessment, internships, regional alumni. Career services highlights include Career Academy: Approximately 200 students participated. This event is scheduled the day '"before"' classes start at UGA and is dedicated to help students begin their job search. The University of Georgia Career Academy is a one-day, intensive career conference that jump starts the career skills of participating students so that they can immediately launch a successful job search campaign. During the event, students heard from employers

representing McKesson, Eli Lilly, Altria, Target, FBI, Sherwin Williams, Liberty Mutual, State Department, Unum, E & J Gallo, and PWC.

FACILITIES

Housing: Coed dorms, special housing for disabled students, special housing for international students, women's dorms, fraternity/sorority housing, apartments for married students, apartments for single students, Theme Housing-Honors and Language focused dorms. are available. 90% of campus accessible to physically disabled. **Special Academic Facilities/Equipment:** Miller Learning Center, Georgia Museum of Art, Georgia Museum of Natural History, Ramsey Student Center for Physical Activities, Performing Arts Center, Tate Student Center **Computers:** 90% of classrooms, 15% of dorms, 100% of libraries, 100% of dining areas, 100% of student union, 100% of common outdoor areas have wireless network access. Students can register for classes online. Administrative functions (other than registration) can be performed online.

CAMPUS LIFE

Environment: City. **Activities:** Choral groups, concert band, dance, drama/theater, jazz band, literary magazine, marching band, music ensembles, musical theater, opera, pep band, radio station, student government, student newspaper, student-run film society, symphony orchestra, television station, yearbook, Campus Ministries, International Student Organization, Model UN. 597 registered organizations, 22 honor societies, 35 religious organizations. 34 fraternities, 25 sororities. **Athletics (Intercollegiate):** *Men:* baseball, basketball, cross-country, diving, football, golf, swimming, tennis, track/field (outdoor), track/field (indoor). *Women:* basketball, cross-country, diving, equestrian sports, golf, gymnastics, soccer, softball, swimming, tennis, track/field (outdoor), track/field (indoor), volleyball. **On-Campus Highlights:** Zell B. Miller Learning Center, Sanford Stadium, Ramsey Student Center for Physical Activ, Performing and Visual Arts Complex, Tate Student Center. **Environmental Initiatives:** Sustainability is a primary directive in the University's 2020 Strategic Plan (http://www.oap.uga.edu/sp/UGA2020-final.pdf). Administratively in 2010, UGA established an Office of Sustainability to coordinate, communicate and advance sustainability initiatives. UGA's commitment to advancing sustainability is evident in its academic and research programs (http://www.sustainability.uga.edu/site/academics). UGA recently expanded its already long list of cross-disciplinary research programs to include the Bioenergy Systems Research Institute, the Georgia Initiative for Climate & Society and the Center for Integrative Conservation Research. In 2007, UGA created the Eugene Odom School of Ecology, the world's first stand-alone school devoted to teaching, research and public service in the areas of ecology and environmental studies. More than 600 members of the UGA faculty are involved in sustainability research and education - in clean energy, integrative conservation, water resources, infectious diseases, invasive species, sustainable design, organic agriculture, and more " and over 15% of all courses offered incorporate sustainability into the curriculum. UGA offers 137 service-learning courses where academic learning is applied through service to the campus and local community. The Go Green Alliance Student Organization, which represents nearly 30 student groups focused on sustainability issues, works closely with the Office of Sustainability to engage in direct and meaningful sustainability action on campus and in the community. UGA's commitment to sustainability is evident in its physical campus development. While increasing campus density, UGA has created over 50 acres of new green space since adoption of the Physical Master Plan in 1998. UGA certified its first LEED building, the Tate Student Center Expansion, at the Gold Level in 2010. Since then, Residence Hall Building 1516 and the Georgia Museum of Art received LEED-Gold certification and three other buildings are currently tracking certification at the gold level. In total, UGA will have over 600,000 s.f. of LEED certified building space. In response to recent historic drought conditions, UGA has taken aggressive steps to improve water quality and decrease potable water use by over 20% including installing 60 rain gardens throughout campus; planting native species; installing low-flow fixtures in all campus buildings; reducing water use in research labs; installing 18 cisterns totaling 550,000 gallons of storage capacity for harvesting rain and condensate water to be reused in campus buildings and landscapes; and incorporating an experimental gray-water reuse system in LEED-Gold Certified Residence Hall Building 1516. UGA has reduced electrical energy consumption per square foot of building space by 8% since 2007 through campus-wide infrastructure, lighting and mechanical system improvements. The UGA campus offers over 19 miles of bike ways and the largest campus transit system in the country with over 9 million riders annually. UGA was the first college in the US to receive campus-wide CIMS Green Building Certification with Honors, verifying its commitment to practicing social, environmental, and economic sustainability in its Green Cleaning Program.

ADMISSIONS

Freshman Academic Profile: Average high school GPA 3.8. 48% in top 10% of high school class, 90% in top 25% of high school class, 99% in top 50% of high school class. 81% from public high schools. SAT Math middle 50% range 580-570. SAT Critical Reading middle 50% range 560-660. SAT Writing middle 50% range 570-670. ACT middle 50% range 26-30. Minimum web-based

TOEFL 80. Minimum paper TOEFL 550. **Basis for Candidate Selection:** *Very important factors considered include:* academic GPA, rigor of secondary school record. *Important factors considered include:* standardized test scores. *Other factors considered include:* application essay, recommendation(s), character/personal qualities, extracurricular activities, first generation, talent/ability, volunteer work, work experience. **Freshman Admission Requirements:** High school diploma is required and GED is accepted. *Academic units required:* 4 English, 4 mathematics, 3 science, (2 science labs), 2 foreign language, 3 social studies. *Academic units recommended:* 4 English, 4 mathematics, 3 science, (2 science labs), 2 foreign language, 3 social studies. **Freshman Admission Statistics:** 18,458 applied, 56% admitted, 48% enrolled. **Transfer Admission Requirements:** college transcript(s), Lowest grade transferable D. **General Admission Information:** Application Fee $60. Regular application deadline 1/15. Nonfall registration accepted. Admission may be deferred for a maximum of one year. Credit and/or placement offered for CEEB Advanced Placement tests.

COSTS AND FINANCIAL AID
Required Forms and Deadlines: FAFSA. **Notification of Awards:** Applicants will be notified of awards on a rolling basis beginning 5/15. **Types of Aid:** *Need-based scholarships/grants:* Federal Pell, SEOG, state scholarships/grants, private scholarships, the school's own gift aid. *Loans:* Direct Subsidized Stafford, Direct Unsubsidized Stafford, Direct PLUS, Federal Perkins, state loans, college/university loans from institutional funds. **Student Employment: Financial Aid Statistics:** 97% freshmen, 90% undergrads receive need-based scholarship or grant aid. 16% freshmen, 11% undergrads receive non-need-based scholarship or grant aid. 67% freshmen, 73% undergrads receive need-based self-help aid. 2% freshmen, 2% undergrads receive athletic scholarships. 45% freshmen, 45% undergrads receive any aid. 44% undergrads borrow to pay for school. Average cumulative indebtedness $19,621. **Criteria for awarding institutional aid:** Non-need-based: academics, athletics, state/district residency.

UNIVERSITY OF GREAT FALLS

1301 20th Street South, Great Falls, MT 59405
Phone: 406-791-5200 • **Financial Aid Phone:** 406-791-5235
E-mail: enroll@ugf.edu • **CEEB Code:** 4058
Fax: 406-791-5209 • **Website:** www.ugf.edu • **ACT Code:** 2410

This private school, affiliated with the Roman Catholic Church, was founded in 1932. It has a 44-acre campus.

RATINGS
Admissions Selectivity Rating: 70   **Fire Safety Rating:** 60*   **Green Rating:** 60*

STUDENTS AND FACULTY
Enrollment: 612. **Student Body:** 63% female, 37% male, 20% out-of-state, (countries represented).
Retention and Graduation: 59% freshmen return for sophomore year. 20% grads pursue arts and sciences degrees. 100% grads pursue medical degrees.
Faculty: Student/faculty ratio 12:1. 33 full-time faculty, 61% hold PhDs, 6% are members of minority groups, 33% are women. 0% of classes are taught by teaching assistants.

ACADEMICS
Degrees: associate, bachelor's, master's, terminal associate, transfer associate. **Classes:** Most classes have fewer than 10 students. **Majors with Highest Enrollment:** criminal justice/safety studies; elementary education and teaching; psychology. **Special Study Options:** cooperative education program, distance learning, double major, independent study, internships, liberal arts/career combination, teacher certification program. **Disability Services:** Special programs offered to physically disabled students include note-taking services, reader services, tape recorders, tutors. **Career services:** Alumni network, alumni services, career/job search classes, internships.

FACILITIES
Housing: Coed dorms, apartments for married students, apartments for single students. 85% of campus accessible to physically disabled. **Special Academic Facilities/Equipment:** Art museum; Dr. Hong Herbarium. **Computers:** 70% of classrooms, 100% of dorms, 100% of libraries, 100% of student union, have wireless network access. Students can register for classes online.

CAMPUS LIFE
Environment: Town. **Activities:** Choral groups, concert band, dance, drama/theater, jazz band, music ensembles, musical theater, pep band, radio station, student government, student newspaper, symphony orchestra, Campus Ministries 10 registered organizations, 2 honor societies, 1 religious organizations.

Athletics (Intercollegiate): *Men:* basketball, cheerleading, cross-country, golf, track/field (outdoor), wrestling. *Women:* basketball, cheerleading, cross-country, golf, soccer, softball, track/field (outdoor), volleyball. **On-Campus Highlights:** Student Center, Wellness Center, Athletic Facility, Art Gallery.

ADMISSIONS
Freshman Academic Profile: Average high school GPA 3.4. 87% from public high schools. SAT Math middle 50% range 360-490. SAT Critical Reading middle 50% range 330-430. ACT middle 50% range 18-24. Minimum paper TOEFL 500. **Basis for Candidate Selection:** *Important factors considered include:* application essay, academic GPA, rigor of secondary school record, standardized test scores, character/personal qualities, interview, level of applicant's interest, religious affiliation/commitment. *Other factors considered include:* Class rank, recommendation(s), extracurricular activities, first generation, racial/ethnic status, talent/ability, volunteer work, work experience. **Freshman Admission Requirements:** High school diploma is required and GED is accepted. *Academic units required:* 4 English, 3 mathematics, 3 science, (1 science labs), 1 social studies, 3 history, 5 academic electives. *Academic units recommended:* 4 English, 3 mathematics, 3 science, (1 science labs), 1 social studies, 3 history, 5 academic electives. **Freshman Admission Statistics:** 351 applied, 57% admitted, 74% enrolled. **Transfer Admission Requirements:** college transcript(s), essay or personal statement, minimum college GPA of 2.0 required. Lowest grade transferable C. **General Admission Information:** Application Fee $35. Regular application deadline 8/30. Notification on a rolling basis, beginning on or about 10/1. Nonfall registration accepted. Admission may be deferred for a maximum of 2 Semesters. Credit and/or placement offered for CEEB Advanced Placement tests.

COSTS AND FINANCIAL AID
Annual tuition $15,500. Room and board $6,490. Required fees $900. Average book expense $500. **Required Forms and Deadlines:** FAFSA. **Notification of Awards:** Applicants will be notified of awards on a rolling basis beginning 3/1. **Types of Aid:** *Need-based scholarships/grants:* Federal Pell, SEOG, state scholarships/grants, private scholarships, the school's own gift aid. *Loans:* Subsidized Stafford, Unsubsidized Stafford, PLUS, Federal Perkins. **Student Employment:** Federal Work-Study Program available. Institutional employment available. Highest amount earned per year from on-campus jobs $2,000. Off-campus job opportunities are fair. **Financial Aid Statistics:** 69% freshmen, 73% undergrads receive need-based scholarship or grant aid. 92% freshmen, 92% undergrads receive non-need-based scholarship or grant aid. 90% freshmen, 93% undergrads receive need-based self-help aid. 47% freshmen, 38% undergrads receive athletic scholarships. 46% freshmen, 50% undergrads receive any aid. 83% undergrads borrow to pay for school. **Criteria for awarding institutional aid:** Non-need-based: academics, alumni affiliation, art, athletics, job skills, leadership, minority status, music/drama, religious affiliation, state/district residency.

UNIVERSITY OF HARTFORD

200 Bloomfield Avenue, West Hartford, CT 6117
Phone: 860-768-4296 • **Financial Aid Phone:** 800-947-4303
E-mail: admissions@mail.hartford.edu • **CEEB Code:** 3436
Fax: 860-768-4961 • **Website:** www.hartford.edu • **ACT Code:** 606

This private school was founded in 1877. It has a 320-acre campus.

RATINGS
Admissions Selectivity Rating: 78   **Fire Safety Rating:** 69   **Green Rating:** 60*

STUDENTS AND FACULTY
Enrollment: 5,318. **Student Body:** 51% female, 49% male, 61% out-of-state, 3% international (65 countries represented). Asian 3%, African American 10%, Caucasian 67%, Hispanic 5%.
Retention and Graduation: 78% freshmen return for sophomore year. 45% freshmen graduate within 4 years. 54% freshmen graduate within 6 years. 22% grads go on to further study within 1 year. 39% grads pursue arts and sciences degrees. 2% grads pursue law degrees. 14% grads pursue business degrees. 2% grads pursue medical degrees. **Faculty:** Student/faculty ratio 13:1. 325 full-time faculty, 72% hold PhDs, 11% are members of minority groups, 36% are women. 0% of classes are taught by teaching assistants.

ACADEMICS
Degrees: associate, bachelor's, certificate, diploma, master's, post-bachelor's certificate, post-master's certificate. **Classes:** Most classes have 10–19 students. Most lab/discussion sessions have fewer than 10 students. **Majors with Highest Enrollment:** architectural engineering technology/technician; communication studies/speech communication and rhetoric; psychology. **Special Study**

Options: cooperative education program, cross-registration, distance learning, double major, dual enrollment, English as a Second Language (ESL), exchange student program (domestic), honors program, independent study, internships, liberal arts/career combination, student-designed major, study abroad, teacher certification program. **Combined degree programs:** , BS Health Science/MS Physical Therapy. **Disability Services:** Special programs offered to physically disabled students include note-taking services, reader services, tutors.

FACILITIES

Housing: Coed dorms, special housing for disabled students, women's dorms, apartments for single students, Honors Housing. **Special Academic Facilities/ Equipment:** Museum of presidential memorabilia, Art Gallery, off-campus child care center for student teaching, learning skills and language lab, audio-visual aids center, 8,000-acre environmental center. **Computers:** Students can register for classes online. Administrative functions (other than registration) can be performed online.

CAMPUS LIFE

Environment: Metropolis. **Activities:** Choral groups, concert band, dance, drama/theater, jazz band, literary magazine, music ensembles, musical theater, opera, pep band, radio station, student government, student newspaper, symphony orchestra, television station, yearbook 93 registered organizations, 22 honor societies, 7 religious organizations. 16 fraternities, 14 sororities. **Athletics (Intercollegiate):** *Men:* baseball, basketball, cross-country, golf, lacrosse, soccer, tennis, track/field (outdoor), track/field (indoor). *Women:* basketball, cross-country, golf, soccer, softball, tennis, track/field (outdoor), track/field (indoor), volleyball. **On-Campus Highlights:** Museum of American Political Life, Art Gallery, Sports Center, Java City Coffee House, Hawk's Nest.

ADMISSIONS

Freshman Academic Profile: 76% from public high schools. SAT Math middle 50% range 490-590. SAT Critical Reading middle 50% range 480-580. ACT middle 50% range 21-25. Minimum paper TOEFL 550. **Basis for Candidate Selection:** *Very important factors considered include:* rigor of secondary school record. *Important factors considered include:* Class rank, standardized test scores. *Other factors considered include:* application essay, recommendation(s), character/personal qualities, extracurricular activities, interview, talent/ability. **Freshman Admission Requirements:** High school diploma is required and GED is accepted. *Academic units required:* 4 English, 2 mathematics, 2 science, 2 social studies, 2 history, 4 academic electives. *Academic units recommended:* 4 English, 2 mathematics, 2 science, 2 social studies, 2 history, 4 academic electives. **Freshman Admission Statistics:** 12,065 applied, 66% admitted, 19% enrolled. **Transfer Admission Requirements:** college transcript(s), minimum college GPA of 2.2 required. Lowest grade transferable C–. **General Admission Information:** Application Fee $35. Notification on a rolling basis, beginning on or about 10/1. Nonfall registration accepted. Admission may be deferred for a maximum of 1 year. Credit and/or placement offered for CEEB Advanced Placement tests.

COSTS AND FINANCIAL AID

Annual tuition $24,576. Room and board $9,922. Required fees $1,190. Average book expense $860. **Required Forms and Deadlines:** FAFSA, institution's own financial aid form. **Notification of Awards:** Applicants will be notified of awards on a rolling basis beginning 3/1. **Types of Aid:** *Need-based scholarships/ grants:* Federal Pell, SEOG, state scholarships/grants, private scholarships, the school's own gift aid. *Loans:* Subsidized Stafford, Unsubsidized Stafford, PLUS, Federal Perkins. **Student Employment: Financial Aid Statistics:** 97% freshmen, 95% undergrads receive need-based scholarship or grant aid. 96% freshmen, 94% undergrads receive non-need-based scholarship or grant aid. 90% freshmen, 92% undergrads receive need-based self-help aid. 2% freshmen, 3% undergrads receive athletic scholarships. 97% freshmen, 95% undergrads receive any aid. 66% undergrads borrow to pay for school. Average cumulative indebtedness $25,553. **Criteria for awarding institutional aid:** Non-need-based: academics, art, athletics, music/drama.

See page 1256.

UNIVERSITY OF HAWAII AT HILO

200 West Kawili Street, Hilo, HI 96720-4091
Phone: 808-974-7414 • **Financial Aid Phone:** 808-974-7323
E-mail: uhhadm@hawaii.edu • **CEEB Code:**
Fax: 808-933-0861 • **Website:** • **ACT Code:** 904

This public school was founded in 1970. It has a 225-acre campus.

RATINGS

Admissions Selectivity Rating: 72   **Fire Safety Rating:** 60*   **Green Rating:** 60*

STUDENTS AND FACULTY

Enrollment: 3,385. **Student Body:** 59% female, 41% male, 35% out-of-state, 5% international (countries represented). Asian 19%, African American 1%, Caucasian 24%, Hispanic 10%, Native American 1%.
Retention and Graduation: 12% freshmen graduate within 4 years. 36% freshmen graduate within 6 years. **Faculty:** Student/faculty ratio 14:1. 227 full-time faculty, 44% are women. 0% of classes are taught by teaching assistants.

ACADEMICS

Degrees: bachelor's, certificate, first professional, master's, post-bachelor's certificate. **Classes:** Most classes have 10–19 students. **Majors with Highest Enrollment:** business, management, marketing, and related support services, other; psychology. **Special Study Options:** cross-registration, distance learning, double major, dual enrollment, English as a Second Language (ESL), exchange student program (domestic), honors program, independent study, internships, student-designed major, study abroad, teacher certification program. **Disability Services:** Special programs offered to physically disabled students include note-taking services, reader services, tape recorders, tutors. **Career services:** Alumni network, alumni services, career assessment, internships Career services highlights include Service Learning opportunities.

FACILITIES

Housing: Coed dorms, special housing for disabled students, apartments for married students, apartments for single students. 90% of campus accessible to physically disabled. **Computers:** Students can register for classes online. Administrative functions (other than registration) can be performed online.

CAMPUS LIFE

Environment: Town. **Activities:** Choral groups, dance, drama/theater, jazz band, literary magazine, music ensembles, radio station, student government, student newspaper 43 registered organizations, 4 religious organizations. **Athletics (Intercollegiate):** *Men:* baseball, basketball, cross-country, golf, tennis. *Women:* cross-country, softball, tennis, volleyball. **On-Campus Highlights:** University Classroom Building (opened Fall '02), University Campus Center Plaza (opened Sp '04), University Lava Landing (Student Cyber Lounge), University Mo`okini Library, University Theatre, Student Life Center Facilities (opened Spr '08).

ADMISSIONS

Freshman Academic Profile: Average high school GPA 3.3. 17% in top 10% of high school class, 47% in top 25% of high school class, 82% in top 50% of high school class. SAT Math middle 50% range 440-600. SAT Critical Reading middle 50% range 440-560. ACT middle 50% range 17-24. Minimum paper TOEFL 500. **Basis for Candidate Selection:** *Very important factors considered include:* rigor of secondary school record. *Important factors considered include:* Class rank, standardized test scores. *Other factors considered include:* application essay, recommendation(s), extracurricular activities, talent/ability. **Freshman Admission Requirements:** High school diploma is required and GED is accepted. *Academic units required:* 4 English, 3 mathematics, 3 science, (3 science labs), 7 academic electives. *Academic units recommended:* 4 English, 3 mathematics, 3 science, (3 science labs), 7 academic electives. **Freshman Admission Statistics:** 1,500 applied, 72% admitted, 44% enrolled. **Transfer Admission Requirements:** college transcript(s), minimum college GPA of 2.0 required. Lowest grade transferable C. **General Admission Information:** Application Fee $50. Regular application deadline 7/1. Notification on a rolling basis, beginning on or about 10/1. Nonfall registration accepted. Admission may be deferred for a maximum of 1 semester. Credit offered for CEEB Advanced Placement tests.

COSTS AND FINANCIAL AID

Annual in-state tuition $5,640. Room and board $7,134. Required fees $304. Average book expense $1,017. **Required Forms and Deadlines:** FAFSA. **Notification of Awards:** Applicants will be notified of awards on a rolling basis beginning 4/12. **Types of Aid:** *Need-based scholarships/grants:* Federal Pell, SEOG, state scholarships/grants, private scholarships, the school's own gift aid. *Loans:* Subsidized Stafford, Unsubsidized Stafford, PLUS, Federal Perkins, state loans. **Student Employment:** Federal Work-Study Program available. Institutional employment available. Highest amount earned per year from on-campus jobs $1,832. **Financial Aid Statistics:** 78% freshmen, 79% undergrads receive need-based scholarship or grant aid. 15% freshmen, 17% undergrads receive non-need-based scholarship or grant aid. 56% freshmen, 65% undergrads receive need-based self-help aid. 3% freshmen, 3% undergrads receive athletic scholarships. 53% undergrads borrow to pay for school. Average cumulative indebtedness $11,944. **Criteria for awarding institutional aid:** Non-need-based: academics, art, athletics, leadership, minority status, music/drama.

UNIVERSITY OF HAWAII AT MANOA

Best 378

2600 Campus Road, Honolulu, HI 96822
Phone: 808-956-8975 • **Financial Aid Phone:** 808-956-7251
E-mail: uhmanoa.admissions@hawaii.edu • **CEEB Code:** 4867
Fax: 808-956-4148 • **Website:** manoa.hawaii.edu • **ACT Code:** 902

This public school was founded in 1907. It has a 320-acre campus.

RATINGS
Admissions Selectivity Rating: 78   **Fire Safety Rating:** 87   **Green Rating:** 87

STUDENTS AND FACULTY
Enrollment: 13,583. **Student Body:** 54% female, 46% male, 23% out-of-state, 4% international (98 countries represented). Asian 67%, African American 1%, Caucasian 24%, Hispanic 3%, Native American 1%.
Retention and Graduation: Faculty: Student/faculty ratio 15:1. 1200 full-time faculty, 87% hold PhDs, 34% are members of minority groups, 41% are women.

ACADEMICS
Degrees: bachelor's, master's, post-bachelor's certificate. **Classes:** Most classes have 10–19 students. Most lab/discussion sessions have 20–29 students. **Majors with Highest Enrollment:** art/art studies; biology/biological sciences; hospitality administration/management, other. **Special Study Options:** cooperative education program, distance learning, double major, English as a Second Language (ESL), exchange student program (domestic), honors program, independent study, internships, student-designed major, study abroad, teacher certification program. **Honors programs:** Selected Studies Program **Combined degree programs:** , Architecture. **Disability Services:** Special programs offered to physically disabled students include note-taking services, reader services, tape recorders. **Career services:** alumni services, career/job search classes, career assessment, internships. Career services highlights include Research has shown that out of classroom experiences are positively linked to academic persistence and educational attainment. Work-based experiences can contribute to students finding meaning in their academic pursuits, and vice versa. As a result, a partnership with the Colleges of Arts and Sciences was implemented The Arts & Sciences Internship Program (ASIP) supports the mission of the Center for Career Development and Student Employment (CCDSE) at UH, to empower students to engage in career life planning through awareness, exploration, experience, and reflection.

FACILITIES
Housing: Coed dorms, special housing for disabled students, apartments for married students, apartments for single students. 40% of campus accessible to physically disabled. **Special Academic Facilities/Equipment:** UH Art and Commons Galleries, John Young Museum, John F. Kennedy Theatre, Lyon Arboretum, Waikiki Aquarium, Sunset (travel industry) Library, Chuck Gee Technology Learning Center, Advanced Computing Research Laboratory, Environmental Engineering Lab, Hawaii Center for Advanced Communications, Coral Reef Science Laboratory, traditionally designed Korean Studies Building, Coconut Island marine biology labs, Wong Audio-Visual Center, language lab, speech and hearing and dental hygiene clinics, law library, Hawaiian loʻi(garden), electron microscope and laser laboratories, ship and submersible research fleet, and Maui Super Computer,Jakuan Tea House. **Computers:** Students can register for classes online. Administrative functions (other than registration) can be performed online.

CAMPUS LIFE
Environment: Metropolis. **Activities:** Choral groups, concert band, dance, drama/theater, jazz band, literary magazine, marching band, music ensembles, musical theater, pep band, radio station, student government, student newspaper, student-run film society, symphony orchestra, Campus Ministries, International Student Organization 161 registered organizations, 7 honor societies, 24 religious organizations. 3 fraternities, 2 sororities. **Athletics (Intercollegiate):** *Men:* baseball, basketball, cheerleading, diving, football, golf, sailing, swimming, tennis, volleyball. *Women:* basketball, cheerleading, cross-country, diving, golf, sailing, soccer, softball, swimming, tennis, track/field (outdoor), track/field (indoor), volleyball, water polo. **On-Campus Highlights:** Campus Center, Queen Liliʻuokalani Ctr for Student Svcs, Quad Courtyard, Sinclair Library, Hamilton Library. **Environmental Initiatives:** Creation & convening of Manoa Sustainability Corps Manoa Green Days-our energy reduction program to consolidate building uses & completely shut down buildings Sustainable UH- a student run sustainability organization

ADMISSIONS
Freshman Academic Profile: Average high school GPA 3.4. 28% in top 10% of high school class, 60% in top 25% of high school class,. 66% from public high schools. SAT Math middle 50% range 510-620. SAT Critical Reading middle 50% range 480-580. SAT Writing middle 50% range 480-570. ACT middle 50% range 21-25. Minimum web-based TOEFL 61. Minimum paper TOEFL 500. **Basis for Candidate Selection:** *Very important factors considered include:* academic GPA, rigor of secondary school record, standardized test scores. *Important factors considered include:* Class rank, state residency. *Other factors considered include:* application essay, recommendation(s), extracurricular activities, geographical residence, interview, talent/ability. **Freshman Admission Requirements:** High school diploma is required and GED is accepted. *Academic units required:* 4 English, 3 mathematics, 3 science, 3 social studies, 5 academic electives, 4 College Prep Courses. *Academic units recommended:* 4 English, 3 mathematics, 3 science, 3 social studies, 5 academic electives, 4 College Prep Courses **Freshman Admission Statistics:** 7,196 applied, 67% admitted, 40% enrolled. **Transfer Admission Requirements:** college transcript(s), minimum college GPA of 2.5 required. Lowest grade transferable D. **General Admission Information:** Application Fee $50. Regular application deadline 5/1. Notification on a rolling basis, beginning on or about 12/1. Nonfall registration accepted. Credit and/or placement offered for CEEB Advanced Placement tests.

COSTS AND FINANCIAL AID
Annual in-state tuition $8,664. Annual out-of-state tuition $24,912. Room and board $10,029. Required fees $740. Average book expense $1,212. **Required Forms and Deadlines:** FAFSA. **Notification of Awards:** Applicants will be notified of awards on a rolling basis beginning 4/1. **Types of Aid:** *Need-based scholarships/grants:* Federal Pell, SEOG, state scholarships/grants, private scholarships, the school's own gift aid. *Loans:* Subsidized Stafford, Unsubsidized Stafford, PLUS, Federal Perkins, Federal Nursing, state loans. **Student Employment:** Federal Work-Study Program available. Institutional employment available. Highest amount earned per year from on-campus jobs $5,897. Off-campus job opportunities are good. **Financial Aid Statistics:** 97% freshmen, 92% undergrads receive need-based scholarship or grant aid. 25% freshmen, 17% undergrads receive non-need-based scholarship or grant aid. 56% freshmen, 65% undergrads receive need-based self-help aid. 3% freshmen, 2% undergrads receive athletic scholarships. 62% freshmen, 59% undergrads receive any aid. 41% undergrads borrow to pay for school. Average cumulative indebtedness $20,653. **Criteria for awarding institutional aid:** Non-need-based: academics, alumni affiliation, art, athletics, leadership, music/drama.

UNIVERSITY OF HAWAII—WEST OAHU

96-129 Ala Ike, Pearl City, HI 96782
Phone: 808-454-4700 • **Financial Aid Phone:** 808-454-4700
E-mail: admissions@uhwo.hawaii.edu • **CEEB Code:** 1042
Fax: 808-453-6075 • **Website:** www.uhwo.hawaii.edu • **ACT Code:** 6465

This public school was founded in 1976.

RATINGS
Admissions Selectivity Rating: 63   **Fire Safety Rating:** 60*   **Green Rating:** 74

STUDENTS AND FACULTY
Enrollment: 1,950. **Student Body:** 67% female, 33% male, 2% out-of-state, 0% international (16 countries represented). Asian 41%, African American 1%, Caucasian 14%, Hispanic 1%.
Retention and Graduation: Faculty: Student/faculty ratio 18:1. 51 full-time faculty, 92% hold PhDs, 51% are members of minority groups, 41% are women. 0% of classes are taught by teaching assistants.

ACADEMICS
Degrees: bachelor's, certificate. **Classes:** Most classes have 10–19 students. Most lab/discussion sessions have 20–29 students. **Majors with Highest Enrollment:** business/commerce; psychology; public administration. **Special Study Options:** distance learning, double major, teacher certification program. **Disability Services:** Special programs offered to physically disabled students include note-taking services, reader services.

FACILITIES
Housing: 100% of campus accessible to physically disabled. **Computers:** 10% of classrooms, 30% of common outdoor areas have wireless network access. Students can register for classes online.

CAMPUS LIFE
Environment: Town. **Activities:** student government 12 registered organizations, 1 honor societies. **Environmental Initiatives:** All buildings being con-

structed at new campus are LEED Silver Certified or above. Engagement with community farming programs to develop sustainable food sources and uses. Engagement with community programs, partners, and organizations to develop sustainable approaches and practices in education.

ADMISSIONS

Freshman Academic Profile: Average high school GPA 74% from public high schools. Minimum web-based TOEFL 79. Minimum paper TOEFL 550. **Basis for Candidate Selection:** *Very important factors considered include:* academic GPA. *Important factors considered include:* rigor of secondary school record. *Other factors considered include:* application essay, recommendation(s), standardized test scores, extracurricular activities, first generation, geographical residence, state residency. **Freshman Admission Requirements:** High school diploma is required and GED is accepted. *Academic units required:* 4 English, 3 mathematics, 3 science, 3 social studies, 5 academic electives, 4 College prepatory courses. *Academic units recommended:* 4 English, 3 mathematics, 3 science, 3 social studies, 5 academic electives, 4 College prepatory courses **Freshman Admission Statistics:** 908 applied, 51% admitted, 64% enrolled. Minimum college GPA of 2.0 required. Lowest grade transferable D. **General Admission Information:** Application Fee $50. Regular application deadline 8/1. Notification on a rolling basis, beginning on or about 2/1. Nonfall registration accepted. Admission may be deferred for a maximum of 1 semester. Credit and/or placement offered for CEEB Advanced Placement tests.

COSTS AND FINANCIAL AID

Annual in-state tuition $5,592. Annual out-of-state tuition $16,656. **Required Forms and Deadlines:** FAFSA. **Notification of Awards:** Applicants will be notified of awards on a rolling basis beginning 4/1. **Types of Aid:** *Need-based scholarships/grants:* Federal Pell, SEOG, state scholarships/grants, private scholarships, the school's own gift aid. *Loans:* Subsidized Stafford, Unsubsidized Stafford, PLUS. **Student Employment:** Federal Work-Study Program available. Institutional employment available. Highest amount earned per year from on-campus jobs $8,000. Off-campus job opportunities are good. **Financial Aid Statistics:** 40% freshmen, 69% undergrads receive need-based scholarship or grant aid. 70% freshmen, 10% undergrads receive non-need-based scholarship or grant aid. 20% freshmen, 62% undergrads receive need-based self-help aid.

UNIVERSITY OF HOUSTON

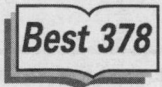

Office of Admissions, Houston, TX 77204-2023
Phone: 713-743-1010 • **Financial Aid Phone:** 713-743-9051
E-mail: admissions@uh.edu • **CEEB Code:** 6870
Fax: 713-743-7542 • **Website:** www.uh.edu • **ACT Code:** 4236

This public school was founded in 1927. It has a 551-acre campus.

RATINGS

Admissions Selectivity Rating: 86 **Fire Safety Rating:** 93 **Green Rating:** 83

STUDENTS AND FACULTY

Enrollment: 31,367. **Student Body:** 49% female, 51% male, 2% out-of-state, 4% international (119 countries represented). Asian 21%, African American 12%, Caucasian 30%, Hispanic 29%. **Retention and Graduation:** 83% freshmen return for sophomore year. 16% freshmen graduate within 4 years. 46% freshmen graduate within 6 years. **Faculty:** Student/faculty ratio 22:1. 1383 full-time faculty, 85% hold PhDs, 25% are members of minority groups, 38% are women. 1% of classes are taught by teaching assistants.

ACADEMICS

Degrees: bachelor's, first professional, master's. **Classes:** Most classes have 20–29 students. Most lab/discussion sessions have 20–29 students. **Majors with Highest Enrollment:** business administration and management; engineering; psychology. **Special Study Options:** Accelerated program, cooperative education program, cross-registration, distance learning, double major, dual enrollment, English as a Second Language (ESL), exchange student program (domestic), honors program, independent study, internships, study abroad, teacher certification program, weekend college, Academic Enrichment programs, certification programs, affiliated studies, and continuing education. **Honors programs:** The Honors College at the University of Houston is a nationally recognized, intellectually stimulating learning community. As a vibrant, leading presence within the university, The Honors College attracts highly talented and motivated students and educators to a collegial environment where tradition is honored and possibilities are both realized and created. **Combined**

degree programs: , JD/MBA, MBA/MA, MBA/MIE, MBA/MSW. **Disability Services:** Special programs offered to physically disabled students include note-taking services, reader services, tape recorders, tutors. **Career services:** Alumni network, alumni services, career/job search classes, career assessment, internships Career services highlights include The Campus Recruitment program is the one we are most proud of.

FACILITIES

Housing: Coed dorms, special housing for disabled students, fraternity/sorority housing, apartments for married students, apartments for single students, Special housing for honors students, upper level and graduate students. Cambridge Oaks and Cullen Oaks Apartments. 98% of campus accessible to physically disabled. **Special Academic Facilities/Equipment:** Art gallery, language lab, human development lab school, University Hilton (staffed in part by students in Coll. of Hotel and Restaurant Management), opera studio. **Computers:** 100% of classrooms, 25% of dorms, 100% of libraries, 25% of dining areas, 100% of student union, 25% of common outdoor areas have wireless network access. Students can register for classes online. Administrative functions (other than registration) can be performed online.

CAMPUS LIFE

Environment: Metropolis. **Activities:** Choral groups, concert band, dance, drama/theater, jazz band, literary magazine, marching band, music ensembles, musical theater, opera, pep band, radio station, student government, student newspaper, student-run film society, symphony orchestra, television station, yearbook, Campus Ministries, International Student Organization 350 registered organizations, 25 honor societies, 39 religious organizations. 21 fraternities, 19 sororities. **Athletics (Intercollegiate):** *Men:* baseball, basketball, cross-country, football, golf, track/field (outdoor), track/field (indoor). *Women:* basketball, cross-country, diving, soccer, softball, swimming, tennis, track/field (outdoor), track/field (indoor), volleyball. **On-Campus Highlights:** University Center, Campus Recreation and Wellness Center, UNIVERSITY CENTER SATELLITE, Blaffer Gallery, Campus Activities. **Environmental Initiatives:** Energy conservation/retro commissioning of existing buildings; clean energy Sustainable Transportation Recycling/waste minimization

ADMISSIONS

Freshman Academic Profile: 32% in top 10% of high school class, 68% in top 25% of high school class, 92% in top 50% of high school class. 92% from public high schools. SAT Math middle 50% range 530-640. SAT Critical Reading middle 50% range 490-600. ACT middle 50% range 22-27. Minimum web-based TOEFL 79. Minimum paper TOEFL 550. **Basis for Candidate Selection:** *Very important factors considered include:* Class rank, rigor of secondary school record. *Important factors considered include:* academic GPA, standardized test scores. *Other factors considered include:* recommendation(s), character/personal qualities, extracurricular activities, first generation, talent/ability, volunteer work, work experience. **Freshman Admission Requirements:** High school diploma is required and GED is accepted. *Academic units recommended:* **Freshman Admission Statistics:** 17,020 applied, 56% admitted, 37% enrolled. **Transfer Admission Requirements:** college transcript(s), minimum college GPA of 2.0 required. Lowest grade transferable C–. **General Admission Information:** Application Fee $50. Regular application deadline 4/1. Nonfall registration accepted. Admission may be deferred for a maximum of 12 months. Credit and/or placement offered for CEEB Advanced Placement tests.

COSTS AND FINANCIAL AID

Annual in-state tuition $8,970. Annual out-of-state tuition $19,500. Room and board $8,753. Required fees $918. Average book expense $1,200. **Required Forms and Deadlines:** FAFSA. **Notification of Awards:** Applicants will be notified of awards on a rolling basis beginning 5/1. **Types of Aid:** *Need-based scholarships/grants:* Federal Pell, SEOG, state scholarships/grants, private scholarships, the school's own gift aid. *Loans:* Subsidized Stafford, Unsubsidized Stafford, PLUS, Federal Perkins, state loans. **Student Employment:** Federal Work-Study Program available. Institutional employment available. Off-campus job opportunities are good. **Financial Aid Statistics:** 91% freshmen, 85% undergrads receive need-based scholarship or grant aid. 9% freshmen, 3% undergrads receive non-need-based scholarship or grant aid. 68% freshmen, 84% undergrads receive need-based self-help aid. 1% freshmen, 1% undergrads receive athletic scholarships. 80% freshmen, 74% undergrads receive any aid. 47% undergrads borrow to pay for school. Average cumulative indebtedness $16,582. **Criteria for awarding institutional aid:** Non-need-based: academics, alumni affiliation, art, athletics, job skills, leadership, music/drama, state/ district residency.

UNIVERSITY OF HOUSTON—CLEAR LAKE

2700 Bay Area Boulevard, Houston, TX 77058-1098
Phone: 281-283-2521 • **Financial Aid Phone:** 281-283-2480
E-mail: admissions@uhcl.edu • **CEEB Code:** 6916
Fax: 281-283-2530

This public school was founded in 1974. It has a 524-acre campus.

RATINGS
Admissions Selectivity Rating: 60*   **Fire Safety Rating:** 60*   **Green Rating:** 60*

STUDENTS AND FACULTY
Enrollment: 4,689. **Student Body:** 68% female, 32% male, 0% out-of-state, 2% international (45 countries represented). Asian 6%, African American 9%, Caucasian 49%, Hispanic 32%.
Retention and Graduation: Faculty: Student/faculty ratio 17:1. 247 full-time faculty, 86% hold PhDs, 27% are members of minority groups, 46% are women.

ACADEMICS
Degrees: bachelor's, certificate, doctoral, master's, post-bachelor's certificate, post-master's certificate. **Classes:** Most classes have 10–19 students. **Majors with Highest Enrollment:** accounting; education; psychology. **Special Study Options:** cooperative education program, distance learning, double major, dual enrollment, independent study, internships, student-designed major, study abroad, teacher certification program, weekend college. **Combined degree programs:** BS/MS, BS/MHBA. **Disability Services:** Special programs offered to physically disabled students include note-taking services, reader services, tape recorders, tutors. **Career services:** Alumni network, alumni services, career/job search classes, career assessment, internships.

FACILITIES
Housing: Privatized Housing Apartments. 100% of campus accessible to physically disabled. **Special Academic Facilities/Equipment:** Student Art Gallery Fitness Center/Fitness Zone **Computers:** 100% of classrooms, 100% of libraries, 100% of dining areas, 100% of student union, 100% of common outdoor areas have wireless network access. Students can register for classes online. Administrative functions (other than registration) can be performed online

CAMPUS LIFE
Environment: Metropolis. **Activities:** literary magazine, student government, student newspaper, student-run film society, International Student Organization 70 registered organizations, 16 honor societies, 5 religious organizations. **On-Campus Highlights:** Student Serivce Building, Bayou Building, Library, Delta Building, Computer Labs.

ADMISSIONS
Freshman Academic Profile: Minimum web-based TOEFL 79. Minimum paper TOEFL 550. **Transfer Admission Requirements:** college transcript(s), standardized test scores, statement of good standing from prior institution(s). Minimum college GPA of 2.0 required. Lowest grade transferable D-. **General Admission Information:** Application Fee $35. Regular application deadline 8/1. Nonfall registration accepted. Admission may be deferred for a maximum of 1 year.

COSTS AND FINANCIAL AID
Annual in-state tuition $5,142. Annual out-of-state tuition $16,992. Room and board Required fees $1,372. Average book expense **Required Forms and Deadlines: Notification of Awards: Types of Aid:** *Need-based scholarships/grants:* Federal Pell, SEOG, state scholarships/grants, private scholarships, the school's own gift aid. *Loans:* Direct Subsidized Stafford, Direct Unsubsidized Stafford, Direct PLUS, Federal Perkins, state loans. **Student Employment:** Federal Work-Study Program available. Institutional employment available. Off-campus job opportunities are good. **Financial Aid Statistics:** 41% undergrads receive any aid.

UNIVERSITY OF HOUSTON—DOWNTOWN

Office of Admissions, Houston, TX 77002-1001
Phone: 713-221-8522 • **Financial Aid Phone:** 713-221-8041
E-mail: uhdadmit@uhd.edu
Fax: 713-221-8157 • **Website:** www.uhd.edu

This public school was founded in 1974.

RATINGS
Admissions Selectivity Rating: 64   **Fire Safety Rating:** 60*   **Green Rating:** 61

STUDENTS AND FACULTY
Enrollment: 13,549. **Student Body:** 60% female, 40% male, 0% out-of-state, 5% international (65 countries represented). Asian 8%, African American 27%, Caucasian 19%, Hispanic 38%.
Retention and Graduation: 67% freshmen return for sophomore year. 1% freshmen graduate within 4 years. **Faculty:** Student/faculty ratio 20:1. 337 full-time faculty, 84% hold PhDs, 32% are members of minority groups, 49% are women. 0% of classes are taught by teaching assistants.

ACADEMICS
Degrees: bachelor's, master's. **Classes:** Most classes have 20–29 students. Most lab/discussion sessions have 20–29 students. **Majors with Highest Enrollment:** accounting; criminal justice/safety studies; finance. **Special Study Options:** cooperative education program, distance learning, double major, dual enrollment, English as a Second Language (ESL), honors program, independent study, internships, study abroad, teacher certification program, weekend college.

FACILITIES
Computers: Students can register for classes online. Administrative functions (other than registration) can be performed online.

CAMPUS LIFE
Environment: Metropolis. **Activities:** drama/theater, jazz band, literary magazine, student government, student newspaper 52 registered organizations, 3 honor societies, 2 religious organizations. 4 fraternities, 4 sororities. **Athletics (Intercollegiate):** *Men:* badminton, basketball, bowling, football, soccer, softball, tennis, volleyball, weight lifting. *Women:* badminton, basketball, bowling, soccer, softball, tennis, volleyball, weight lifting. **On-Campus Highlights:** Special Events Center, O' Kane Gallery, Food court and adjoining Coffee House, Jesse H. Jones Student Life Center, O' Kane Theatre.

ADMISSIONS
Freshman Academic Profile: Average high school GPA 7% in top 10% of high school class, 27% in top 25% of high school class, 63% in top 50% of high school class. 86% from public high schools. SAT Math middle 50% range 410-500. SAT Critical Reading middle 50% range 370-470. SAT Writing middle 50% range 370-460. ACT middle 50% range 16-20. Minimum web-based TOEFL 80. Minimum paper TOEFL 550. **Basis for Candidate Selection: Freshman Admission Requirements:** High school diploma is required and GED is accepted. *Academic units recommended.* **Freshman Admission Statistics:** 4,194 applied, 91% admitted, 38% enrolled. **Transfer Admission Requirements:** college transcript(s), Lowest grade transferable C. **General Admission Information:** Application Fee $35. Regular application deadline 7/1. Nonfall registration accepted. Admission may be deferred for a maximum of text. Credit offered for CEEB Advanced Placement tests.

COSTS AND FINANCIAL AID
Annual in-state tuition $4,875. Annual out-of-state tuition $15,405. Room and board Required fees $1,122. **Required Forms and Deadlines:** FAFSA. **Notification of Awards:** Applicants will be notified of awards on a rolling basis beginning 4/1. **Types of Aid:** *Need-based scholarships/grants:* Federal Pell, SEOG, state scholarships/grants, private scholarships, the school's own gift aid. *Loans:* Subsidized Stafford, Unsubsidized Stafford, PLUS, state loans. **Student Employment: Financial Aid Statistics:** 86% freshmen, 84% undergrads receive need-based scholarship or grant aid. 19% freshmen, 17% undergrads receive non-need-based scholarship or grant aid. 46% freshmen, 66% undergrads receive need-based self-help aid. 80% freshmen, 78% undergrads receive any aid. **Criteria for awarding institutional aid:** Non-need-based: academics, leadership, state/district residency.

UNIVERSITY OF HOUSTON—VICTORIA

Admissions and Records, Victoria, TX 77901-4450
Phone: 361-570-4110 • **Financial Aid Phone:** 316-570-4131
E-mail: admissions@uhv.edu
Fax: 361-570-4114

This public school was founded in 1973.

RATINGS
Admissions Selectivity Rating: 61   **Fire Safety Rating:** 60*   **Green Rating:** 60*

STUDENTS AND FACULTY
Enrollment: 1,779. **Student Body:** 70% female, 30% male, 1% out-of-state, 2% international (20 countries represented). Asian 7%, African American 12%, Caucasian 57%, Hispanic 21%, Native American 1%.

Retention and Graduation: Faculty: Student/faculty ratio 15:1. 106 full-time faculty, 92% hold PhDs, 38% are members of minority groups, 45% are women. 0% of classes are taught by teaching assistants.

ACADEMICS

Degrees: bachelor's, master's, post-bachelor's certificate, post-master's certificate. **Classes:** Most classes have 20–29 students. **Majors with Highest Enrollment:** business/commerce; education; multi-/interdisciplinary studies, other. **Special Study Options:** distance learning, double major, honors program, independent study, internships, study abroad, teacher certification program. **Disability Services:** Special programs offered to physically disabled students include note-taking services, tutors. **Career services:** alumni services, career/job search classes, career assessment, internships.

FACILITIES

Housing: Coed dorms. 100% of campus accessible to physically disabled. **Special Academic Facilities/Equipment:** Museum of Coastal Bend. **Computers:** Students can register for classes online. Administrative functions (other than registration) can be performed online.

CAMPUS LIFE

Environment: City. **Activities:** student government, International Student Organization. **Athletics (Intercollegiate):** *Men:* baseball. *Women:* softball.

ADMISSIONS

Freshman Academic Profile: Minimum paper TOEFL 550. **Basis for Candidate Selection: Freshman Admission Requirements:** High school diploma is required and GED is accepted. **Transfer Admission Requirements:** college transcript(s), standardized test scores, minimum college GPA of 2.0 required. Lowest grade transferable C. **General Admission Information:** Nonfall registration accepted.

COSTS AND FINANCIAL AID

Annual in-state tuition $7,470. Annual out-of-state tuition $14,940. Room and board $7,071. Required fees $1,600. Average book expense $1,090. **Required Forms and Deadlines:** FAFSA. **Notification of Awards:** Applicants will be notified of awards on a rolling basis beginning 5/1. **Types of Aid:** *Need-based scholarships/grants:* Federal Pell, SEOG, state scholarships/grants, private scholarships, the school's own gift aid. *Loans:* Subsidized Stafford, Unsubsidized Stafford, PLUS, Federal Nursing, state loans. **Student Employment:** Federal Work-Study Program available. Institutional employment available. Off-campus job opportunities are good. **Financial Aid Statistics:** 27% undergrads borrow to pay for school. Average cumulative indebtedness $47,989. **Criteria for awarding institutional aid:** Non-need-based: academics, athletics, leadership, state/district residency.

UNIVERSITY OF IDAHO

UI Admissions Office, Moscow, ID 83844-4264
Phone: 208-885-6326 • **Financial Aid Phone:** 208-885-6312
E-mail: admissions@uidaho.edu • **CEEB Code:** 4843
Fax: 208-885-9119 • **Website:** www.uihome.uidaho.edu/uihome/
ACT Code: 928

This public school was founded in 1889. It has a 12500-acre campus.

RATINGS

Admissions Selectivity Rating: 78   **Fire Safety Rating:** 77   **Green Rating:** 83

STUDENTS AND FACULTY

Enrollment: 8,785. **Student Body:** 46% female, 54% male, 26% out-of-state, 3% international (73 countries represented). Asian 2%, African American 1%, Caucasian 81%, Hispanic 8%, Native American 1%.
Retention and Graduation: 23% freshmen graduate within 4 years. **Faculty:** Student/faculty ratio 18:1. 545 full-time faculty, 85% hold PhDs, 12% are members of minority groups, 34% are women. 9% of classes are taught by teaching assistants.

ACADEMICS

Degrees: bachelor's, certificate, master's, post-bachelor's certificate, post-master's certificate. **Classes:** Most classes have 20–29 students. Most lab/discussion sessions have 10–19 students. **Majors with Highest Enrollment:** elementary education and teaching; mechanical engineering; psychology. **Special Study Options:** Accelerated program, cooperative education program, cross-regis-

tration, distance learning, double major, dual enrollment, English as a Second Language (ESL), exchange student program (domestic), honors program, independent study, internships, student-designed major, study abroad, teacher certification program. **Honors programs:** Established in 1983, the University Honors Program offers a stimulating course of study and the advantages of an enriched learning community for over 500 students from all colleges and majors. **Disability Services:** Special programs offered to physically disabled students include note-taking services, reader services, tape recorders, tutors. **Career services:** Alumni network, alumni services, career/job search classes, career assessment, internships, regional alumni. Career services highlights include Internships.

FACILITIES

Housing: Coed dorms, special housing for disabled students, men's dorms, special housing for international students, women's dorms, fraternity/sorority housing, apartments for married students, apartments for single students. 85% of campus accessible to physically disabled. **Special Academic Facilities/Equipment:** On-campus preschool, experimental forest, electron microscope. **Computers:** 100% of classrooms, 100% of dorms, 100% of libraries, 100% of dining areas, 100% of student union, have wireless network access. Students can register for classes online. Administrative functions (other than registration) can be performed online.

CAMPUS LIFE

Environment: Town. **Activities:** Choral groups, concert band, dance, drama/theater, jazz band, marching band, music ensembles, musical theater, opera, pep band, radio station, student government, student newspaper, student-run film society, symphony orchestra, television station, Campus Ministries, International Student Organization 190 registered organizations, 13 honor societies, 20 religious organizations. 18 fraternities, 9 sororities. **Athletics (Intercollegiate):** *Men:* basketball, cross-country, football, golf, track/field (outdoor), track/field (indoor). *Women:* basketball, cross-country, golf, soccer, swimming, track/field (outdoor), track/field (indoor), volleyball. **On-Campus Highlights:** Idaho Commons - food and meeting rooms, 18 hole golf course, Kibbie Dome - athletics, Student Recreation Center, Borah Theater, 6. Rec Center/Outdoors Program 7. Frisbee Golf Course 8. Religious Centers See our campus live with web cams at http://www.uidaho.edu/webcams. **Environmental Initiatives:** $35 mil ESCO for energy conservation projects currently underway Built institutional infrastructure: launched a Sustainability Center, formed committees, task forces, passed a student fee of $5/semester to support sustainability, etc. to assess and develop long-term plans for sustainability issues Converted steam plant to a biomass boiler

ADMISSIONS

Freshman Academic Profile: Average high school GPA 3.4. 18% in top 10% of high school class, 44% in top 25% of high school class, 77% in top 50% of high school class. 90% from public high schools. SAT Math middle 50% range 490-600. SAT Critical Reading middle 50% range 480-590. SAT Writing middle 50% range 460-570. ACT middle 50% range 20-26. Minimum web-based TOEFL 79. Minimum paper TOEFL 550. **Basis for Candidate Selection:** *Very important factors considered include:* academic GPA, standardized test scores. *Other factors considered include:* recommendation(s). **Freshman Admission Requirements:** High school diploma is required and GED is accepted. *Academic units required:* 4 English, 3 mathematics, 3 science, (1 science labs), 1 foreign language. *Academic units recommended:* 4 English, 3 mathematics, 3 science, (1 science labs), 1 foreign language. **Freshman Admission Statistics:** 7,467 applied, 66% admitted, 33% enrolled. **Transfer Admission Requirements:** college transcript(s), minimum college GPA of 2.0 required. Lowest grade transferable D. **General Admission Information:** Application Fee $40. Regular application deadline 8/1. Nonfall registration accepted. Credit and/or placement offered for CEEB Advanced Placement tests.

COSTS AND FINANCIAL AID

Annual in-state tuition $4,230. Annual out-of-state tuition $17,018. Room and board $7,682. Required fees $1,982. Average book expense $1,474. **Required Forms and Deadlines:** FAFSA. **Notification of Awards:** Applicants will be notified of awards on a rolling basis beginning 3/30. **Types of Aid:** *Need-based scholarships/grants:* Federal Pell, SEOG, state scholarships/grants, private scholarships, the school's own gift aid. *Loans:* Direct Subsidized Stafford, Direct Unsubsidized Stafford, Direct PLUS, Federal Perkins, college/university loans from institutional funds. **Student Employment:** Federal Work-Study Program available. Institutional employment available. Off-campus job opportunities are good. **Financial Aid Statistics:** 74% freshmen, 71% undergrads receive need-based scholarship or grant aid. 93% freshmen, 87% undergrads receive non-need-based scholarship or grant aid. 78% freshmen, 83% undergrads receive need-based self-help aid. 2% freshmen, 3% undergrads receive athletic scholarships. 88% freshmen, 81% undergrads receive any aid. 66% undergrads borrow to pay for school. Average cumulative indebtedness $26,809. **Criteria for awarding institutional aid:** Non-need-based: academics, alumni affiliation, art, athletics, leadership, minority status, music/drama, state/district residency.

UNIVERSITY OF ILLINOIS AT CHICAGO

Office of Admissions & Records, Chicago, IL 60680-5220
Phone: 312-996-4350 • **Financial Aid Phone:** 312-996-3126
E-mail: uicadmit@uic.edu • **CEEB Code:** 1851
Fax: 312-413-7628 • **Website:** www.uic.edu • **ACT Code:** 1155

This public school was founded in 1965. It has a 218-acre campus.

RATINGS
Admissions Selectivity Rating: 82   **Fire Safety Rating:** 94   **Green Rating:** 87

STUDENTS AND FACULTY
Enrollment: 16,593. **Student Body:** 51% female, 49% male, 2% out-of-state, 2% international (84 countries represented). Asian 22%, African American 8%, Caucasian 40%, Hispanic 24%.
Retention and Graduation: 78% freshmen return for sophomore year. 23% grads go on to further study within 1 year. **Faculty:** Student/faculty ratio :1. 1201 full-time faculty, 74% hold PhDs, 21% are members of minority groups, 47% are women.

ACADEMICS
Degrees: bachelor's, doctoral, master's, post-bachelor's certificate, post-master's certificate. **Classes:** Most classes have 20–29 students. Most lab/discussion sessions have 20–29 students. **Majors with Highest Enrollment:** biology/biological sciences; business administration and management; psychology. **Special Study Options:** Accelerated program, cooperative education program, distance learning, double major, dual enrollment, exchange student program (domestic), honors program, independent study, internships, student-designed major, study abroad, teacher certification program. **Combined degree programs:** BA/MD, BA/DDS. **Disability Services:** Special programs offered to physically disabled students include note-taking services, reader services, tape recorders, tutors. **Career services:** Alumni network, alumni services, career/job search classes, career assessment, internships, regional alumni. Career services highlights include The Entrepreneurship Consulting Program provides an opportunity for teams of students to work with a professional consultant to solve real business problems for entrepreneurial firms. Also, we are equally proud because this year we received a National Award for Excellence from the National (Global) Consortium of Entrepreneurship Centers, held at Syracuse University. It was for founding (1997) and growing the national Collegiate Entrepreneurs" Organization (CEO), one of our UIC programs. We have student entrepreneurship clubs on more than 140 university campuses and the Annual CEO Conference attracted 1300 students (and faculty).

FACILITIES
Housing: Coed dorms, special housing for disabled students, apartments for single students, honors floor, Presidential Awards House. 80% of campus accessible to physically disabled. **Computers:** 95% of classrooms, 100% of dorms, 100% of libraries, 100% of dining areas, 100% of student union, have wireless network access. Students can register for classes online. Administrative functions (other than registration) can be performed online.

CAMPUS LIFE
Environment: Metropolis. **Activities:** Choral groups, concert band, drama/theater, jazz band, literary magazine, music ensembles, pep band, radio station, student government, student newspaper, International Student Organization 370 registered organizations, 10 honor societies, 33 religious organizations. 13 fraternities, 15 sororities. **Athletics (Intercollegiate):** *Men:* baseball, basketball, cross-country, diving, gymnastics, soccer, swimming, tennis, track/field (outdoor). *Women:* basketball, cross-country, diving, gymnastics, softball, swimming, tennis, track/field (outdoor), volleyball. **On-Campus Highlights:** Student Center East, Student Center West, UIC Pavilion, Student Services Building, Student Recreation Facility. **Environmental Initiatives:** establishment of Office of Sustainability Preparation of a climate action plan and work to improve energy efficiency and test new green technologies. Undertaking a Sustainability Strategic Thinking and Planning Process

ADMISSIONS
Freshman Academic Profile: Average high school GPA 3.3. 23% in top 10% of high school class, 59% in top 25% of high school class, 93% in top 50% of high school class. 58% from public high schools. SAT Math middle 50% range 510-640. SAT Critical Reading middle 50% range 470-630. SAT Writing middle 50% range 490-620. ACT middle 50% range 21-26. Minimum paper TOEFL 520. **Basis for Candidate Selection:** *Very important factors considered include:* Class rank, application essay, academic GPA, rigor of secondary school record, standardized test scores. *Other factors considered include:* recommendation(s), character/personal qualities, extracurricular activities. **Freshman Admission Requirements:** High school diploma is required and GED is accepted. *Academic units required:* 4 English, 3 mathematics, 3 science, 2 foreign language, 3 social studies. *Academic units recommended:* 4 Eng-

lish, 3 mathematics, 3 science, 2 foreign language, 3 social studies. **Freshman Admission Statistics:** 14,380 applied, 64% admitted, 63% enrolled. **Transfer Admission Requirements:** college transcript(s), minimum college GPA of 2.5 required. **General Admission Information:** Application Fee $40. Regular application deadline 1/15. Notification on a rolling basis, beginning on or about 11/30. Nonfall registration not accepted. Credit and/or placement offered for CEEB Advanced Placement tests.

COSTS AND FINANCIAL AID
Annual in-state tuition $10,232. Annual out-of-state tuition $22,622. Room and board $10,399. Required fees $2,890. Average book expense $1,400. **Required Forms and Deadlines:** FAFSA. **Notification of Awards:** Applicants will be notified of awards on a rolling basis beginning 3/15. **Types of Aid:** *Need-based scholarships/grants:* Federal Pell, SEOG, state scholarships/grants, private scholarships, the school's own gift aid. *Loans:* Direct Subsidized Stafford, Direct Unsubsidized Stafford, Direct PLUS, Federal Perkins, Federal Nursing, state loans, college/university loans from institutional funds, Alternative loans. **Student Employment:** Federal Work-Study Program available. Institutional employment available. Off-campus job opportunities are good. **Financial Aid Statistics:** 80% freshmen, 79% undergrads receive need-based scholarship or grant aid. 3% freshmen, 2% undergrads receive non-need-based scholarship or grant aid. 75% freshmen, 75% undergrads receive need-based self-help aid. 1% freshmen, 1% undergrads receive athletic scholarships. 76% freshmen, 73% undergrads receive any aid. 64% undergrads borrow to pay for school. Average cumulative indebtedness $22,256. **Criteria for awarding institutional aid:** Non-need-based: academics, art, music/drama.

UNIVERSITY OF ILLINOIS AT SPRINGFIELD

One University Plaza, Springfield, IL 62703-5407
Phone: 217-206-4847 • **Financial Aid Phone:** 217-206-6724
E-mail: admissions@uis.edu • **CEEB Code:** 834
Fax: 217-206-6620 • **ACT Code:** 1137

This public school was founded in 1969. It has a 746-acre campus.

RATINGS
Admissions Selectivity Rating: 82   **Fire Safety Rating:** 68   **Green Rating:** 80

STUDENTS AND FACULTY
Enrollment: 2,976. **Student Body:** 51% female, 49% male, 11% out-of-state, 2% international (35 countries represented). Asian 3%, African American 13%, Caucasian 69%, Hispanic 6%.
Retention and Graduation: 72% freshmen return for sophomore year. 29% freshmen graduate within 4 years. **Faculty:** Student/faculty ratio 13:1. 213 full-time faculty, 82% hold PhDs, 23% are members of minority groups, 44% are women.

ACADEMICS
Degrees: bachelor's, master's, post-bachelor's certificate, post-master's certificate. **Classes:** Most classes have 20–29 students. Most lab/discussion sessions have 10–19 students. **Majors with Highest Enrollment:** business administration and management; computer science; psychology. **Special Study Options:** distance learning, double major, English as a Second Language (ESL), honors program, independent study, internships, study abroad, teacher certification program. **Honors programs:** Interdisciplinary four-year baccalaureate experience for highly qualified freshman. **Combined degree programs:** BA/MA. **Disability Services:** Special programs offered to physically disabled students include note-taking services, reader services, tape recorders. **Career services:** Alumni network, alumni services, career/job search classes, career assessment, internships, regional alumni.

FACILITIES
Housing: Coed dorms, special housing for disabled students, special housing for international students, apartments for married students, apartments for single students, Wellness Housing, Theme Housing, Family Housing. 99% of campus accessible to physically disabled. **Special Academic Facilities/Equipment:** Norris L. Brookens Library, Sangamon Auditorium, Observatory **Computers:** 100% of classrooms, 100% of dorms, 100% of libraries, 100% of dining areas, 100% of student union, 100% of common outdoor areas have wireless network access. Students can register for classes online. Administrative functions (other than registration) can be performed online.

CAMPUS LIFE
Environment: City. **Activities:** Choral groups, concert band, dance, drama/theater, jazz band, music ensembles, pep band, student government, student newspaper, student-run film society, Campus Ministries, International Student Organization, Model UN. 76 registered organizations. **Athletics (Intercolle-**

giate): *Men:* basketball, golf, soccer, tennis. *Women:* basketball, cheerleading, golf, soccer, softball, tennis, volleyball. **On-Campus Highlights:** University Hall, Public Affairs Center. **Environmental Initiatives:** Construction of a residence hall with a "green roof." With the support of a grant from the State of Illinois, the university has expanded the recycling program from only academic buildings to include housing. The university has committed 1.95 million dollars to retrofit old single glazed windows in one campus building with double-glazed windows for energy conservation.

ADMISSIONS

Freshman Academic Profile: Average high school GPA 3.4. 19% in top 10% of high school class, 42% in top 25% of high school class, 73% in top 50% of high school class. 86% from public high schools. ACT middle 50% range 20–26. Minimum paper TOEFL 500. **Basis for Candidate Selection:** *Very important factors considered include:* application essay, academic GPA, rigor of secondary school record. *Important factors considered include:* standardized test scores. *Other factors considered include:* Class rank, recommendation(s), extracurricular activities, first generation, level of applicant's interest, work experience. **Freshman Admission Requirements:** High school diploma is required and GED is accepted. *Academic units required:* 4 English, 3 mathematics, 3 science, (2 science labs), 2 foreign language, 2 social studies, 2 history, 2 visual/performing arts. *Academic units recommended:* 4 English, 3 mathematics, 3 science, (2 science labs), 2 foreign language, 2 social studies, 2 history, 2 visual/performing arts. **Freshman Admission Statistics:** 1,506 applied, 56% admitted, 32% enrolled. **Transfer Admission Requirements:** college transcript(s), minimum college GPA of 2.0 required. Lowest grade transferable D. **General Admission Information:** Application Fee $40. Nonfall registration not accepted. Admission may be deferred for a maximum of 1 year. Credit and/or placement offered for CEEB Advanced Placement tests.

COSTS AND FINANCIAL AID

Required Forms and Deadlines: FAFSA. **Notification of Awards:** Applicants will be notified of awards on a rolling basis beginning 1/1. **Types of Aid:** *Need-based scholarships/grants:* Federal Pell, SEOG, state scholarships/grants, private scholarships, the school's own gift aid. *Loans:* Direct Subsidized Stafford, Direct Unsubsidized Stafford, Direct PLUS, Federal Perkins, college/university loans from institutional funds. **Student Employment: Financial Aid Statistics:** 94% freshmen, 85% undergrads receive need-based scholarship or grant aid. 21% freshmen, 12% undergrads receive non-need-based scholarship or grant aid. 88% freshmen, 90% undergrads receive need-based self-help aid. 3% freshmen, 2% undergrads receive athletic scholarships. 67% undergrads borrow to pay for school. Average cumulative indebtedness $21,057. **Criteria for awarding institutional aid:** Non-need-based: academics, alumni affiliation, art, athletics, job skills, leadership, minority status, music/drama, state/district residency.

UNIVERSITY OF ILLINOIS
AT URBANA-CHAMPAIGN

Best 378

901 West Illinois Street, Urbana, IL 61801
Phone: 217-333-0302 • **Financial Aid Phone:** 217-333-0100
E-mail: ugradadmissions@illinois.edu • **CEEB Code:** 4607
Fax: 217-244-0903 • **Website:** illinois.edu • **ACT Code:** 1154

This public school was founded in 1867. It has a 4,724-acre campus.

RATINGS

Admissions Selectivity Rating: 90   **Fire Safety Rating:** 68   **Green Rating:** 99

STUDENTS AND FACULTY

Enrollment: 31,350. **Student Body:** 45% female, 55% male, 15% out-of-state, 12% international (123 countries represented). Asian 14%, African American 6%, Caucasian 59%, Hispanic 77%.
Retention and Graduation: 94% freshmen return for sophomore year. 66% freshmen graduate within 4 years. 82% freshmen graduate within 6 years. 26% grads go on to further study within 1 year. 18% grads pursue arts and sciences degrees. 3% grads pursue law degrees. 2% grads pursue business degrees. 3% grads pursue medical degrees. **Faculty:** Student/faculty ratio 18:1. 1872 full-time faculty 92% hold PhDs, 25% are are members of minority groups, 32% are women. 26% of classes are taught by teaching assistants.

ACADEMICS

Degrees: bachelor's, certificate, first professional, master's, post-bachelor's certificate, post-master's certificate. **Classes:** Most classes have 20–29 students. Most lab/discussion sessions have 20–29 students. **Majors with Highest Enrollment:** cell/cellular and molecular biology; political science and government; psychology. **Special Study Options:** Accelerated program, cooperative education program, cross-registration, distance learning, double major, dual enrollment, English as a Second Language (ESL), exchange student program (domestic), honors program, independent study, internships, liberal arts/career combination, student-designed major, study abroad, teacher certification program, , Jonathan Baldwin Turner Honors program, Campus Honors, Illinois Leadership & Entrepreneurial Programs. **Honors programs:** Campus Honors Program, James Scholars Program **Combined degree programs:** BA/MEng, MD/PhD **Disability Services:** Special programs offered to physically disabled students include note-taking services, reader services, tape recorders, tutors. **Career services:** Alumni network, alumni services, career/job search classes, career assessment, internships, regional alumni.

FACILITIES

Housing: Coed dorms, special housing for disabled students, men's dorms, special housing for international students, women's dorms, fraternity/sorority housing, apartments for married students, cooperative housing, apartments for single students, Living and Learning Communities housed within the residence halls; Private Certified Housing. 100% of campus accessible to physically disabled. Special **Academic Facilities/Equipment:** Art, cultural and natural history museums, performing arts center, National Center for Supercomputing Applications, Beckman Institute, Siebel Computer Science Center, University Library (37 separate libraries and centers on campus), Japan House and Gardens, Assembly Hall for large concerts, Allerton Park and Conference Center, Arboretum, and the Illini Student Union. **Computers:** 85% of classrooms, 100% of dorms, 100% of libraries, 100% of dining areas, 100% of student union, 1% of common outdoor areas have wireless network access. Students can register for classes online. Administrative functions (other than registration) can be performed online.

CAMPUS LIFE

Environment: City. **Activities:** Choral groups, concert band, dance, drama/theater, jazz band, literary magazine, marching band, music ensembles, musical theater, opera, pep band, radio station, student government, student newspaper, student-run film society, symphony orchestra, television station, yearbook, Campus Ministries, International Student Organization, Model UN. 1,000 registered organizations, 30 honor societies, 95 religious organizations. 60 fraternities, 36 sororities. **Athletics (Intercollegiate):** *Men:* baseball, basketball, cheerleading, cross-country, football, golf, gymnastics, tennis, track/field (outdoor), wrestling. *Women:* basketball, cheerleading, cross-country, diving, golf, gymnastics, soccer, softball, swimming, tennis, track/field (outdoor), volleyball. **On-Campus Highlights:** Campus Town restaurants and shops, Krannert Center for Performing Arts, Assembly Hall, Multiple Campus Recreation Centers, Illini Student Union, On-campus Arboretum; The Japan House; extensive athletic facilities; historic round barns; Siebel Computer Science Center; spacious green space at the Central and Bardeen Quads; Papa Dels Pizza and Za's Italian Cafe. **Environmental Initiatives:** The state-of-the-art Business Instructional Facility at the University of Illinois has earned the world's highest honor for sustainable, environmentally friendly construction and design. The year-old building is the first business facility at a public university anywhere in the world to earn platinum certification. Illinois has recently completed a Sustainability Vision process and is now implementing steps that will infuse sustainability into education, research, outreach and operations. The university's retrocommissioning team has completed nearly 2 million square feet of upgrades to campus buildings, resulting in ~10% energy reduction in 2 years.

ADMISSIONS

Freshman Academic Profile: 52% in top 10% of high school class, 90% in top 25% of high school class, 99% in top 50% of high school class. 75% from public high schools. SAT Math middle 50% range 690–780. SAT Critical Reading middle 50% range 540–660. SAT Writing middle 50% range 590–680. ACT middle 50% range 26–31. Minimum web-based TOEFL 79. Minimum paper TOEFL 550. **Basis for Candidate Selection:** Very important factors considered include: Class rank, application essay, academic GPA, rigor of secondary school record, standardized test scores. Important factors considered include: character/personal qualities, extracurricular activities, first generation, talent/ability, volunteer work, work experience. Other factors considered include: geographical residence, racial/ethnic status, state residency. **Freshman Admission Requirements:** High school diploma is required and GED is accepted. **Academic units required:** 4 English, 3 mathematics, 2 science, (2 science labs), 2 foreign language, 2 social studies, 2 academic electives, 3.5 years of mathematics including trigonometry are required in the following programs: Agricultural. **Academic units required:** 4 English, 3 mathematics, 2 science, (2 science labs), 2 foreign language, 2 social studies, 2 academic electives, 3.5 years of mathematics including trigonometry are required in the following programs: Agricultural. **Freshman Admission Statistics:** $28,751 applied, 68% admitted,

37% enrolled. **Transfer Admission Requirements:** college transcript(s), essay or personal statement. Lowest grade transferable D. **General Admission Information:** Application Fee $40. Regular application deadline 1/2. Regular notification 12/14. Nonfall registration not accepted. Admission may be deferred for a maximum of 12 months. Credit and/or placement offered for CEEB Advanced Placement tests.

COSTS AND FINANCIAL AID
Annual in-state tuition $10,386. Annual out-of-state tuition $24,528. Room and board $10,080. Required fees $3,310. Average book expense $1,200. **Required Forms and Deadlines:** FAFSA. **Types of Aid:** Need-based scholarships/grants: Federal Pell, SEOG, state scholarships/grants, private scholarships, the school's own gift aid, United Negro College Fund. Loans: Direct Subsidized Stafford, Direct Unsubsidized Stafford, Direct PLUS, Federal Perkins, college/university loans from institutional funds. Student Employment: Federal Work-Study Program available. Institutional employment available. Highest amount earned per year from on-campus jobs $13,377. Off-campus job opportunities are excellent. **Financial Aid Statistics:** 77% freshmen, 76% undergrads receive need-based scholarship or grant aid. 17% freshmen, 9% undergrads receive non-need-based scholarship or grant aid. 86% freshmen, 87% undergrads receive need-based self-help aid. 1% freshmen, 1% undergrads receive athletic scholarships. 69% freshmen, 72% undergrads receive any aid. 52% undergrads borrow to pay for school. Average cumulative indebtedness $22,975. **Criteria for awarding institutional aid:** Non-need-based: academics, alumni affiliation, art, athletics, leadership, music/drama, state/district residency.

See page 1258.

UNIVERSITY OF INDIANAPOLIS

1400 East Hanna Avenue, Indianapolis, IN 46227-3697
Phone: 317-788-3216 • **Financial Aid Phone:** 317-788-3217
E-mail: admissions@uindy.edu • **CEEB Code:** 1321
Fax: 317-788-3300 • **Website:** www.uindy.edu • **ACT Code:** 1204

This private school, affiliated with the Methodist Church, was founded in 1902. It has a 65-acre campus.

RATINGS
Admissions Selectivity Rating: 70   **Fire Safety Rating:** 63   **Green Rating:** 61

STUDENTS AND FACULTY
Enrollment: 4,138. **Student Body:** 68% female, 32% male, 9% out-of-state, 5% international (47 countries represented). Asian 1%, African American 13%, Caucasian 73%, Hispanic 2%.
Retention and Graduation: 74% freshmen return for sophomore year. 36% freshmen graduate within 4 years. 52% freshmen graduate within 6 years.
Faculty: Student/faculty ratio 15:1. 218 full-time faculty, 76% hold PhDs, 6% are members of minority groups, 57% are women. 0% of classes are taught by teaching assistants.

ACADEMICS
Degrees: associate, bachelor's, master's. **Classes:** Most classes have 10–19 students. Most lab/discussion sessions have 20–29 students. **Majors with Highest Enrollment:** business/commerce; education; nursing/registered nurse (rn, asn, bsn, msn). **Special Study Options:** Accelerated program, cross-registration, double major, dual enrollment, English as a Second Language (ESL), honors program, independent study, internships, liberal arts/career combination, student-designed major, study abroad, teacher certification program, Spring Term Session (4-4-1). **Disability Services:** Special programs offered to physically disabled students include note-taking services, reader services, tape recorders, tutors.

FACILITIES
Housing: Coed dorms, women's dorms, apartments for married students, apartments for single students. 90% of campus accessible to physically disabled. **Special Academic Facilities/Equipment:** Developmental preschool, art gallery, observatory. **Computers:** 100% of classrooms, 100% of dorms, 100% of libraries, 100% of dining areas, 100% of student union, 100% of common outdoor areas have wireless network access.

CAMPUS LIFE
Environment: Metropolis. **Activities:** Choral groups, concert band, dance, drama/theater, jazz band, literary magazine, music ensembles, musical theater, opera, pep band, radio station, student government, student newspaper, television station, yearbook, Campus Ministries, International Student Organization 53 registered organizations, 14 honor societies, 4 religious organizations. **Athletics (Intercollegiate):** *Men:* baseball, basketball, cross-country, diving, football, golf, soccer, swimming, tennis, track/field (outdoor), wrestling. *Women:*

basketball, cross-country, diving, golf, soccer, softball, swimming, tennis, track/field (outdoor), volleyball. **On-Campus Highlights:** Ruth Lilly Fitness Center, Schwitzer Center, Krannert Memorial Library, Christel Dehaan Fine Arts Center, Martin Hall.

ADMISSIONS
Freshman Academic Profile: Average high school GPA 3.4. 27% in top 10% of high school class, 56% in top 25% of high school class, 88% in top 50% of high school class. SAT Math middle 50% range 460-570. SAT Critical Reading middle 50% range 450-560. SAT Writing middle 50% range 440-550. ACT middle 50% range 19-25. Minimum paper TOEFL 500. **Basis for Candidate Selection:** *Very important factors considered include:* academic GPA, rigor of secondary school record. *Important factors considered include:* Class rank, standardized test scores. *Other factors considered include:* recommendation(s), extracurricular activities, interview. **Freshman Admission Requirements:** High school diploma is required and GED is accepted. *Academic units required:* 4 English, 3 mathematics, 3 science, (2 science labs), 2 foreign language, 1 social studies, 1 history, 1 academic electives. *Academic units recommended:* 4 English, 3 mathematics, 3 science, (2 science labs), 2 foreign language, 1 social studies, 1 history, 1 academic electives. **Freshman Admission Statistics:** 5,396 applied, 79% admitted, 19% enrolled. **Transfer Admission Requirements:** High school transcript, college transcript(s), standardized test scores, statement of good standing from prior institution(s). Minimum college GPA of 2.0 required. Lowest grade transferable C–. **General Admission Information:** Application Fee $25. Notification on a rolling basis, beginning on or about 9/1. Nonfall registration accepted. Admission may be deferred for a maximum of N/A. Credit offered for CEEB Advanced Placement tests.

COSTS AND FINANCIAL AID
Annual tuition $23,590. Room and board $9,090. Required fees $240. Average book expense $1,076. **Required Forms and Deadlines:** FAFSA, institution's own financial aid form. **Notification of Awards:** Applicants will be notified of awards on a rolling basis beginning 3/1. **Types of Aid:** *Need-based scholarships/grants:* Federal Pell, SEOG, state scholarships/grants, private scholarships, the school's own gift aid. *Loans:* Subsidized Stafford, Unsubsidized Stafford, PLUS, Federal Perkins. **Student Employment:** Federal Work-Study Program available. Institutional employment available. Off-campus job opportunities are good. **Financial Aid Statistics:** 57% freshmen, 68% undergrads receive need-based scholarship or grant aid. 99% freshmen, 70% undergrads receive non-need-based scholarship or grant aid. 78% freshmen, 79% undergrads receive need-based self-help aid. 8% freshmen, 8% undergrads receive athletic scholarships. 99% freshmen, 98% undergrads receive any aid. 79% undergrads borrow to pay for school. Average cumulative indebtedness $31,731. **Criteria for awarding institutional aid:** Non-need-based: academics, alumni affiliation, art, athletics, job skills, leadership, music/drama, religious affiliation, state/district residency.

UNIVERSITY OF IOWA

107 Calvin Hall, Iowa City, IA 52242
Phone: 319-335-3847 • **Financial Aid Phone:** 319-335-1450
E-mail: admissions@uiowa.edu • **CEEB Code:** 6681
Fax: 319-333-1535 • **Website:** www.uiowa.edu • **ACT Code:** 1356

This public school was founded in 1847. It has a 1900-acre campus.

RATINGS
Admissions Selectivity Rating: 77   **Fire Safety Rating:** 79   **Green Rating:** 87

STUDENTS AND FACULTY
Enrollment: 21,320. **Student Body:** 52% female, 48% male, 39% out-of-state, 9% international (104 countries represented). Asian 3%, African American 3%, Caucasian 74%, Hispanic 5%.
Retention and Graduation: 86% freshmen return for sophomore year. 46% freshmen graduate within 4 years. 67% freshmen graduate within 6 years.
Faculty: Student/faculty ratio 16:1. 1555 full-time faculty, 97% hold PhDs, 17% are members of minority groups, 33% are women.

ACADEMICS
Degrees: bachelor's, certificate, master's, post-master's certificate. **Classes:** Most classes have 10–19 students. Most lab/discussion sessions have 20–29 students. **Majors with Highest Enrollment:** business/commerce; engineering; psychology. **Special Study Options:** Accelerated program, cooperative

education program, distance learning, double major, dual enrollment, English as a Second Language (ESL), exchange student program (domestic), external degree program, honors program, independent study, internships, liberal arts/career combination, student-designed major, study abroad, teacher certification program. **Honors programs:** The University of Iowa Honors Program is dedicated to the academic and personal enrichment of its students. This enrichment is accomplished through special academic opportunities and programs that are sponsored by the Honors Program and open to all Honors students. **Combined degree programs:** BA/MA, BA/DDS, BA/MEng, BBA/BA,BS BSE/BA, BS BSN/BA,BS. **Disability Services:** Special programs offered to physically disabled students include note-taking services, reader services, tape recorders, tutors. **Career services:** Alumni network, alumni services, career/job search classes, career assessment, internships, regional alumni. Career services highlights include The University of Iowa Pomerantz Career Center is a world-class facility with a national reputation for excellence. The Center directly serves more than 20,000 students from the Henry B. Tippie College of Business, the College of Engineering, and the College of Liberal Arts and Sciences.

FACILITIES
Housing: Coed dorms, special housing for disabled students, fraternity/sorority housing, apartments for married students, apartments for single students, Wellness Housing, Theme HousingQuiet Houses available. Living-Learning Communities for the following interests: Honors; Iowa Writers; Health Sciences; Business and Entrepreneurship, Women in Science and Engineering; Men in Engineering; performing arts; international interests; citizenship and service; Law Study and Legal Careers, Sustainability, Career Leadership Academy, Healthy Living Network, Hispanic Culture and Language. 98% of campus accessible to physically disabled. **Special Academic Facilities/Equipment:** National Advanced Driving Simulator, electron microscope, laser facility, Oakdale Research park, UI Hygienic Lab, UI Center for Biocatalysis & Bioprocessing, UI Research Foundation, survey research facilities natural history museum, Medical Museum, Old Capitol Museum, Main Library and 10 departmental libraries, information arcade, newspaper production lab, TV lab, UI Technology Innovation Center, and Project Art. **Computers:** 100% of classrooms, 25% of dorms, 100% of libraries, 25% of dining areas, 90% of student union, 15% of common outdoor areas have wireless network access. Students can register for classes online. Administrative functions (other than registration) can be performed online.

CAMPUS LIFE
Environment: City. **Activities:** Choral groups, concert band, dance, drama/theater, jazz band, literary magazine, marching band, music ensembles, musical theater, opera, pep band, radio station, student government, student newspaper, student-run film society, symphony orchestra, television station, Campus Ministries, International Student Organization 488 registered organizations, 21 honor societies, 24 religious organizations. 18 fraternities, 18 sororities. **Athletics (Intercollegiate): Men:** baseball, basketball, cheerleading, cross-country, diving, football, golf, gymnastics, swimming, tennis, track/field (outdoor), track/field (indoor), wrestling. **Women:** basketball, cheerleading, crew/rowing, cross-country, diving, field hockey, golf, gymnastics, soccer, softball, swimming, tennis, track/field (outdoor), track/field (indoor), volleyball. **On-Campus Highlights:** Kinnick Stadium/Carver Hawkeye Arena, The University of Iowa Museum of Natural History, UI Recreational Services, Hawkeye Hall of Fame, UIHC Project Art. **Environmental Initiatives:** The University of Iowa has established seven 2020 Sustainability Targets that include goals for energy conservation, renewable energy, waste diversion, reduced carbon impact of transportation, increasing student opportunities to learn and practice sustainability principles, support sustainability research and develop partnerships to advance collaborative initiatives. The UI was the first certified Tree Campus in Iowa.The number of LEED-Accredited Professionals on staff in Facilities Management tripled to total 17. The University of Iowa has established a sustainability partnership with EPA Region 7 to "address climate change, as well as sustain air, water and land resources." The UI is recognized by the US EPA as one of the Top 20 on-site green power producers (for both 2009 and 2010), the only university to be listed in the top 20. The University of Iowa is integrating sustainability into its academic and research mission through the creation of ten new interdisciplinary faculty positions and the development of a sustainability studies certificate. Over 130 studeents are now enrolled in the certificate program. A new sustainable living/learning community has been established.

ADMISSIONS
Freshman Academic Profile: Average high school GPA 3.6. 24% in top 10% of high school class, 55% in top 25% of high school class, 91% in top 50% of high school class. 90% from public high schools. SAT Math middle 50% range 550-690. SAT Critical Reading middle 50% range 470-630. SAT Writing middle 50% range 490-610. ACT middle 50% range 22-28. Minimum web-based TOEFL 80. Minimum paper TOEFL 530. **Basis for Candidate Selection:** *Very important factors considered include:* Class rank, academic GPA, rigor of secondary school record, standardized test scores. *Other factors considered include:* recommendation(s), character/personal qualities, state residency, talent/ability. **Freshman Admission Requirements:** High school diploma is required and GED is accepted. *Academic units required:* 4 English,

3 mathematics, 3 science, 2 foreign language, 3 social studies. *Academic units recommended:* 4 English, 3 mathematics, 3 science, 2 foreign language, 3 social studies. **Freshman Admission Statistics:** 19,430 applied, 78% admitted, 29% enrolled. **Transfer Admission Requirements:** High school transcript, college transcript(s), minimum college GPA of 2.5 required. Lowest grade transferable D. **General Admission Information:** Application Fee $40. Regular application deadline 4/1. Notification on a rolling basis, beginning on or about 9/15. Nonfall registration accepted. Admission may be deferred for a maximum of 12. Credit and/or placement offered for CEEB Advanced Placement tests.

COSTS AND FINANCIAL AID
Annual in-state tuition $6,678. Annual out-of-state tuition $24,900. Room and board $9,170. Required fees $1,379. Average book expense $1,090. **Required Forms and Deadlines:** FAFSA, institution's own financial aid form. **Notification of Awards:** Applicants will be notified of awards on a rolling basis beginning 3/15. **Types of Aid:** *Need-based scholarships/grants:* Federal Pell, SEOG, state scholarships/grants, private scholarships, the school's own gift aid. *Loans:* Direct Subsidized Stafford, Direct Unsubsidized Stafford, Direct PLUS, Federal Perkins, Federal Nursing, college/university loans from institutional funds, Short term. **Student Employment:** Federal Work-Study Program available. Institutional employment available. Highest amount earned per year from on-campus jobs $7,200. Off-campus job opportunities are good. **Financial Aid Statistics:** 65% freshmen, 64% undergrads receive need-based scholarship or grant aid. 61% freshmen, 41% undergrads receive non-need-based scholarship or grant aid. 78% freshmen, 83% undergrads receive need-based self-help aid. 2% freshmen, 2% undergrads receive athletic scholarships. 79% freshmen, 72% undergrads receive any aid. 55% undergrads borrow to pay for school. Average cumulative indebtedness $28,554. **Criteria for awarding institutional aid:** Non-need-based: academics, alumni affiliation, art, athletics, leadership, minority status, music/drama.

UNIVERSITY OF KANSAS

Office of Admissions, Lawrence, KS 66045-7576
Phone: 785-864-3911 • **Financial Aid Phone:** 785-864-4700
E-mail: adm@ku.edu • **CEEB Code:** 6871
Fax: 785-864-5017 • **Website:** www.ku.edu/ • **ACT Code:** 1470

This public school was founded in 1866. It has a 1100-acre campus.

RATINGS
Admissions Selectivity Rating: 71   Fire Safety Rating: 84   Green Rating: 76

STUDENTS AND FACULTY
Enrollment: 18,812. **Student Body:** 50% female, 50% male, 22% out-of-state, 5% international (107 countries represented). Asian 4%, African American 4%, Caucasian 76%, Hispanic 6%, Native American 1%.
Retention and Graduation: 79% freshmen return for sophomore year. 37% freshmen graduate within 4 years. 64% freshmen graduate within 6 years. 32% grads go on to further study within 1 year. **Faculty:** Student/faculty ratio 19:1. 1324 full-time faculty, 91% hold PhDs, 18% are members of minority groups, 39% are women. 20% of classes are taught by teaching assistants.

ACADEMICS
Degrees: bachelor's, master's, post-master's certificate. **Classes:** Most classes have 20–29 students. Most lab/discussion sessions have 10–19 students. **Majors with Highest Enrollment:** biology/biological sciences; business/commerce; psychology. **Special Study Options:** Accelerated program, cooperative education program, distance learning, double major, dual enrollment, English as a Second Language (ESL), honors program, independent study, internships, liberal arts/career combination, study abroad, teacher certification program, Off Campus Study: Washington DC semester; Study abroad in over 60 countries. **Honors programs:** The University Honors Program gives outstanding and creative students opportunities for intellectual growth and achievement through its small, challenging classes. web site at www.honors.ku.edu **Disability Services:** Special programs offered to physically disabled students include note-taking services, reader services, tape recorders, tutors. **Career services:** career/job search classes, career assessment, internships Career services highlights include Alternative Breaks, In the Streets Week, Center for Community Outreach.

FACILITIES
Housing: Coed dorms, women's dorms, fraternity/sorority housing, apartments for married students, cooperative housing, apartments for single students. 95%

of campus accessible to physically disabled. **Special Academic Facilities/ Equipment:** 12 libraries (including art and architecture, engineering, law, medical, music and dance, rare research materials, special collections, and science), performing arts center, organ recital hall, museums (art, anthropology, classical, entomology, invertebrate paleontology, and natural history), film studio, student operated radio and television stations, public radio station, herbarium, space technology center, observatory, Robert J. Dole Institute for Politics, Hall Center for the Humanities, Center for International Business Education and Research, ecological reserves, Biological Survey, Geological Survey, Information and Telecommunication Technology Center, energy research center, flight research lab, Transportation Research Center, 400+ bed hospital for clinical learning, Hoglund Brain Imaging Center, Center on Aging.

CAMPUS LIFE

Environment: City. **Activities:** Choral groups, concert band, dance, drama/ theater, jazz band, literary magazine, marching band, music ensembles, musical theater, opera, pep band, radio station, student government, student newspaper, symphony orchestra, television station, International Student Organization 476 registered organizations, 14 honor societies, 39 religious organizations. 27 fraternities, 16 sororities. **Athletics (Intercollegiate):** *Men:* baseball, basketball, cross-country, football, golf, track/field (outdoor), track/field (indoor). *Women:* basketball, crew/rowing, cross-country, diving, golf, soccer, softball, swimming, tennis, track/field (outdoor), track/field (indoor), volleyball. **On-Campus Highlights:** Spencer Museum of Art, Kansas Union and Bookstore, Natural History Museum, Athletic Hall of Fame, Robert J. Dole Institute of Politics, Beautiful campus to walk around. **Environmental Initiatives:** In fall 2011, the University of Kansas released its campus sustainability plan, Building Sustainable Traditions, which establishes a vision for a more sustainable campus and outlines specific strategies for achieving the goals of the plan. Action steps are focused in 9 key areas: administration, research & curriculum, student life, energy, built environment, campus grounds, procurement, waste, and transportation. (http://www.sustainability.ku.edu/Plan/) Three of four research initiatives included in the strategic plan, Bold Aspirations, have a sustainability connection: "Sustaining the Planet, Powering the World", "Promoting Well-Being, Fining Cures", and "Building Communities, Expanding Opportunities". These themes represent the highest priorities for research investment for the next 5 years. Summits on each of the themes were held in 2011 and 2012 to help form research networks, identify funding opportunities and faculty leaders, strategize about needed infrastructure, and inform priorities for future faculty hiring. In 2011, KU opened its Center for Design Research, an incubator for design innovation, in what will likely be the first commercial certified passive building in North America. It is also the fourth LEED Platinum building completed by Studio 804, an architecture design-build course that focuses on sustainable design and construction. The building features solar panels and a wind turbine, a green roof and living wall, an electrochromic curtainwall that controls the amount of sunlight - and therefore heat - entering the windows, and bricks that were hand-cut by students from limestone tailings

ADMISSIONS

Freshman Academic Profile: Average high school GPA 3.5. 26% in top 10% of high school class, 53% in top 25% of high school class, 86% in top 50% of high school class. ACT middle 50% range 22-28. **Basis for Candidate Selection:** *Very important factors considered include:* Class rank, academic GPA, standardized test scores. **Freshman Admission Requirements:** High school diploma is required and GED is accepted. *Academic units required:* 4 English, 3 mathematics, 3 science, 3 social studies. *Academic units recommended:* 4 English, 3 mathematics, 3 science, 3 social studies. **Freshman Admission Statistics:** 12,389 applied, 92% admitted, 33% enrolled. **Transfer Admission Requirements:** college transcript(s), minimum college GPA of 2.5 required. Lowest grade transferable C. **General Admission Information:** Application Fee $30. Regular application deadline 4/1. Notification on a rolling basis, beginning on or about 9/1. Nonfall registration accepted. Credit and/or placement offered for CEEB Advanced Placement tests.

COSTS AND FINANCIAL AID

Annual in-state tuition $8,000. Annual out-of-state tuition $20,843. Room and board $7,258. Required fees $888. Average book expense $900. **Required Forms and Deadlines:** FAFSA. **Notification of Awards:** Applicants will be notified of awards on a rolling basis beginning 4/1. **Types of Aid:** *Need-based scholarships/grants:* Federal Pell, SEOG, state scholarships/grants, private scholarships, the school's own gift aid. *Loans:* Direct Subsidized Stafford, Direct Unsubsidized Stafford, Direct PLUS, Subsidized Stafford, Unsubsidized Stafford, PLUS, Federal Perkins, college/university loans from institutional funds. **Student Employment:** Federal Work-Study Program available. Institutional employment available. Highest amount earned per year from on-campus jobs $4,800. Off-campus job opportunities are excellent. **Financial Aid Statistics:** 63% freshmen, 65% undergrads receive need-based scholarship or grant aid. 45% freshmen, 30% undergrads receive non-need-based scholarship or grant aid. 74% freshmen, 81% undergrads receive need-based self-help aid. 3% freshmen, 2% undergrads receive athletic scholarships. 66% freshmen, 56%

undergrads receive any aid. 51% undergrads borrow to pay for school. Average cumulative indebtedness $23,468. **Criteria for awarding institutional aid:** Non-need-based: academics, alumni affiliation, art, athletics, leadership, minority status, music/drama, state/district residency.

UNIVERSITY OF KENTUCKY

100 Funkhouser Building, Lexington, KY 40506
Phone: 859-257-2000 • **Financial Aid Phone:** 859-257-3172
E-mail: admissions@uky.edu • **CEEB Code:** 1837
Fax: 859-257-3823 • **Website:** www.uky.edu • **ACT Code:** 1554

This public school was founded in 1865. It has a 687-acre campus.

RATINGS
Admissions Selectivity Rating: 79   **Fire Safety Rating:** 88   **Green Rating:** 60*

STUDENTS AND FACULTY
Enrollment: 19,709. **Student Body:** 49% female, 51% male, 20% out-of-state, 2% international (117 countries represented). Asian 2%, African American 7%, Caucasian 81%, Hispanic 2%.
Retention and Graduation: 82% freshmen return for sophomore year. 34% freshmen graduate within 4 years. **Faculty:** Student/faculty ratio 18:1. 1375 full-time faculty, 93% hold PhDs, 18% are members of minority groups, 36% are women. 20% of classes are taught by teaching assistants.

ACADEMICS
Degrees: bachelor's, certificate, first professional, master's. **Classes:** Most classes have 20–29 students. Most lab/discussion sessions have 20–29 students. **Special Study Options:** Accelerated program, cooperative education program, distance learning, double major, English as a Second Language (ESL), exchange student program (domestic), honors program, independent study, internships, study abroad, teacher certification program, weekend college. **Combined degree programs:** BA/MA, JD/MBA. **Disability Services:** Special programs offered to physically disabled students include note-taking services, reader services.

FACILITIES
Housing: Coed dorms, special housing for disabled students, men's dorms, special housing for international students, women's dorms, fraternity/sorority housing, apartments for married students, apartments for single students. 95% of campus accessible to physically disabled. **Special Academic Facilities/ Equipment:** Anthropology and art museums, center for the humanities, centers for equine research, cancer research, and robotics, pharmacy manufacturing lab. **Computers:** 30% of classrooms, 10% of dorms, 100% of libraries, 80% of dining areas, 70% of student union, 50% of common outdoor areas have wireless network access. Students can register for classes online. Administrative functions (other than registration) can be performed online.

CAMPUS LIFE
Environment: City. **Activities:** Choral groups, concert band, dance, drama/ theater, jazz band, literary magazine, marching band, music ensembles, musical theater, opera, pep band, radio station, student government, student newspaper, symphony orchestra, yearbook, International Student Organization 348 registered organizations, 28 honor societies, 20 religious organizations. 19 fraternities, 16 sororities. **Athletics (Intercollegiate):** *Men:* baseball, basketball, cheerleading, cross-country, diving, football, golf, riflery, soccer, swimming, tennis, track/field (outdoor), track/field (indoor). *Women:* basketball, cheerleading, cross-country, diving, golf, gymnastics, riflery, soccer, softball, swimming, tennis, track/field (outdoor), track/field (indoor), volleyball. **On-Campus Highlights:** W.T. Young Library, Johnson Fitness Center, Memorial Coliseum, Arboretum, Memorial Hall.

ADMISSIONS
Freshman Academic Profile: Average high school GPA 3.5. 33% in top 10% of high school class, 62% in top 25% of high school class, 88% in top 50% of high school class. SAT Math middle 50% range 500-630. SAT Critical Reading middle 50% range 490-610. SAT Writing middle 50% range 470-600. ACT middle 50% range 23-28. Minimum paper TOEFL 527. **Basis for Candidate Selection:** *Very important factors considered include:* academic GPA, rigor of secondary school record, standardized test scores. *Other factors considered include:* Class rank, application essay, recommendation(s), alumni/ae relation, character/personal qualities, extracurricular activities, first generation,

geographical residence, interview, racial/ethnic status, talent/ability, volunteer work. **Freshman Admission Requirements:** High school diploma is required and GED is accepted. *Academic units required:* 4 English, 3 mathematics, 3 science, 2 foreign language, 3 social studies, 5 academic electives, 2 Fine or Performing Arts (1), Health (.5), and Physical Ed. (.5). *Academic units recommended:* 4 English, 3 mathematics, 3 science, 2 foreign language, 3 social studies, 5 academic electives, 2 Fine or Performing Arts (1), Health (.5), and Physical Ed. (.5) **Freshman Admission Statistics:** 15,153 applied, 68% admitted, 40% enrolled. **Transfer Admission Requirements:** college transcript(s), minimum college GPA of 2.0 required. Lowest grade transferable D. **General Admission Information:** Application Fee $50. Regular application deadline 2/15. Notification on a rolling basis, beginning on or about 10/1. Nonfall registration accepted. Admission may be deferred for a maximum of 1 year. Credit and/or placement offered for CEEB Advanced Placement tests.

COSTS AND FINANCIAL AID
Annual in-state tuition $8,610. Annual out-of-state tuition $18,798. Room and board $10,192. Required fees $1,066. Average book expense $800. **Required Forms and Deadlines:** FAFSA. **Notification of Awards:** Applicants will be notified of awards on a rolling basis beginning 4/1. **Types of Aid:** *Need-based scholarships/grants:* Federal Pell, SEOG, state scholarships/grants, private scholarships, the school's own gift aid. *Loans:* Direct Subsidized Stafford, Direct Unsubsidized Stafford, Direct PLUS, Subsidized Stafford, Unsubsidized Stafford, PLUS, Federal Perkins, state loans, college/university loans from institutional funds. **Student Employment:** Federal Work-Study Program available. **Financial Aid Statistics:** 46% freshmen, 49% undergrads receive need-based scholarship or grant aid. 90% freshmen, 73% undergrads receive non-need-based scholarship or grant aid. 60% freshmen, 70% undergrads receive need-based self-help aid. 3% freshmen, 3% undergrads receive athletic scholarships. 40% freshmen, 38% undergrads receive any aid. 40% undergrads borrow to pay for school. Average cumulative indebtedness $21,774. **Criteria for awarding institutional aid:** Non-need-based: academics, alumni affiliation, art, athletics, job skills, leadership, minority status, music/drama, state/district residency.

UNIVERSITY OF KING'S COLLEGE

Registrars Office, Halifax, NS B3H 2A1
Phone: 902-422-1271
E-mail: admissions@ukings.ns.ca
Fax: 902-423-3357 • **Website:** www.ukings.ca

This public school was founded in 1789. It has a 3-acre campus.

RATINGS
Admissions Selectivity Rating: 63   **Fire Safety Rating:** 60*   **Green Rating:** 60*

STUDENTS AND FACULTY
Enrollment: 1,137. **Student Body:** 57% female, 43% male, 53% out-of-state, (6 countries represented).
Retention and Graduation: Faculty: Student/faculty ratio 25:1. 51 full-time faculty, 71% hold PhDs, 31% are women. 0% of classes are taught by teaching assistants.

ACADEMICS
Degrees: bachelor's. **Classes: Majors with Highest Enrollment:** English language and literature; psychology; sociology. **Special Study Options:** cooperative education program, double major, honors program, internships, study abroad. **Career services:** career/job search classes, career assessment.

FACILITIES
Housing: Coed dorms, men's dorms, women's dorms. **Computers:** Students can register for classes online. Administrative functions (other than registration) can be performed online.

CAMPUS LIFE
Environment: Metropolis. **Activities:** Choral groups, dance, drama/theater, literary magazine, radio station, student government, student newspaper, student-run film society, yearbook **Athletics (Intercollegiate):** *Men:* badminton, basketball, soccer, volleyball. *Women:* badminton, basketball, soccer, volleyball. **On-Campus Highlights:** The Pit, The Wardroom, The Manning Room, The Library, The Quad.

ADMISSIONS
Freshman Academic Profile: Minimum paper TOEFL 580. **Basis for Candidate Selection:** *Very important factors considered include:* rigor of secondary school record, standardized test scores. **Freshman Admission Requirements:** High school diploma is required and GED is not accepted. **Freshman Admission Statistics:** 1,043 applied, 41% admitted, 83% enrolled. **Transfer**

Admission Requirements: college transcript(s), Lowest grade transferable C. **General Admission Information:** Application Fee $45. Regular application deadline 6/1. Notification on a rolling basis, beginning on or about 3/1. Nonfall registration not accepted. Admission may be deferred for a maximum of One year.

COSTS AND FINANCIAL AID
Room and board Required fees Average book expense $1,000. **Required Forms and Deadlines: Notification of Awards: Types of Aid:** *Need-based scholarships/grants: Loans:* **Student Employment:** Off-campus job opportunities are good.

UNIVERSITY OF LA VERNE

1950 Third Street, La Verne, CA 91750
Phone: 909-392-2800 • **Financial Aid Phone:** 1-800-649-0160
E-mail: admission@laverne.edu • **CEEB Code:** 4381
Fax: 909-392-2714 • **Website:** www.laverne.edu • **ACT Code:** 295

This private school was founded in 1891. It has a 38-acre campus.

RATINGS
Admissions Selectivity Rating: 90   **Fire Safety Rating:** 92   **Green Rating:** 84

STUDENTS AND FACULTY
Enrollment: 2,487. **Student Body:** 60% female, 40% male, 5% out-of-state, 4% international (15 countries represented). Asian 6%, African American 5%, Caucasian 28%, Hispanic 50%.
Retention and Graduation: 85% freshmen return for sophomore year. 40% freshmen graduate within 4 years. 59% freshmen graduate within 6 years.
Faculty: Student/faculty ratio 12:1. 225 full-time faculty, 80% hold PhDs, 23% are members of minority groups, 51% are women. 0% of classes are taught by teaching assistants.

ACADEMICS
Degrees: associate, bachelor's, certificate, master's, post-bachelor's certificate. **Classes:** Most classes have 10–19 students. Most lab/discussion sessions have fewer than 10 students. **Majors with Highest Enrollment:** business/commerce; liberal arts and sciences/liberal studies; psychology. **Special Study Options:** distance learning, double major, English as a Second Language (ESL), exchange student program (domestic), honors program, independent study, internships, liberal arts/career combination, student-designed major, study abroad, teacher certification program, weekend college. **Honors programs:** For students who have demonstrated exceptional academic achievement and motivation, the ULV Honors Program offers increased opportunities for intellectual and personal growth. The Honors Center, available to Honors Program students, offers a study lounge, computer laboratory, and a seminar room. **Combined degree programs:** JD/MBA. **Disability Services:** Special programs offered to physically disabled students include note-taking services, reader services, tape recorders, tutors. **Career services:** career/job search classes, career assessment, internships, Career services highlights include numerous internship listings in all career fields.

FACILITIES
Housing: Coed dorms, special housing for disabled students, women's dorms. 95% of campus accessible to physically disabled. **Special Academic Facilities/ Equipment:** Greenhouse and Animal Care Facility; Montana Field Station— Magpie Ranch; Jeagar science specimen Museum; Photography and Art galleries **Computers:** 100% of classrooms, 100% of dorms, 100% of libraries, 100% of dining areas, 100% of student union, 100% of common outdoor areas have wireless network access. Students can register for classes online. Administrative functions (other than registration) can be performed online.

CAMPUS LIFE
Environment: Town. **Activities:** Choral groups, dance, drama/theater, literary magazine, music ensembles, musical theater, radio station, student government, student newspaper, student-run film society, television station, Campus Ministries, International Student Organization, Model UN. 40 registered organizations, 2 honor societies, 1 religious organizations. 3 fraternities, 6 sororities. **Athletics (Intercollegiate):** *Men:* baseball, basketball, cross-country, diving, football, golf, soccer, swimming, tennis, track/field (outdoor), water polo. *Women:* basketball, cross-country, diving, soccer, softball, swimming, tennis, track/field (outdoor), volleyball, water polo. **On-Campus Highlights:** Campus Center, Sneaky Park (outdoor events), Davenport Dining Hall, Dailey Theater (Fine Arts Performances), University Quad. **Environmental Initiatives:** Total Recycling Program; Energy Management: dual Central Chillers for HVAC; lighting fixture replacement; Water Conservation: plumbing fixtures; irrigation; xeriscaping.

ADMISSIONS

Freshman Academic Profile: Average high school GPA 3.5. 24% in top 10% of high school class, 61% in top 25% of high school class, 88% in top 50% of high school class. SAT Math middle 50% range 470-580. SAT Critical Reading middle 50% range 460-550. SAT Writing middle 50% range 460-560. ACT middle 50% range 20-25. Minimum web-based TOEFL 80. Minimum paper TOEFL 550. **Basis for Candidate Selection:** *Very important factors considered include:* application essay, academic GPA, recommendation(s), rigor of secondary school record, standardized test scores, character/personal qualities. *Important factors considered include:* Class rank, extracurricular activities. *Other factors considered include:* alumni/ae relation, first generation, interview, level of applicant's interest, racial/ethnic status, talent/ability, volunteer work, work experience. **Freshman Admission Requirements:** High school diploma is required and GED is accepted. *Academic units required:* 4 English, 3 mathematics, 2 science, (1 science labs), 2 social studies, 3 history. *Academic units recommended:* 4 English, 3 mathematics, 2 science, (1 science labs), 2 social studies, 3 history. **Freshman Admission Statistics:** 6,989 applied, 39% admitted, 23% enrolled. **Transfer Admission Requirements:** college transcript(s), essay or personal statement, minimum college GPA of 2.7 required. Lowest grade transferable C–. **General Admission Information:** Application Fee $50. Notification on a rolling basis, beginning on or about 12/1. Nonfall registration accepted. Admission may be deferred for a maximum of 1 Year. Credit and/or placement offered for CEEB Advanced Placement tests.

COSTS AND FINANCIAL AID

Annual tuition $32,096. Room and board $11,660. Required fees $1,254. Average book expense $1,656. **Required Forms and Deadlines:** FAFSA, state aid form. **Notification of Awards:** Applicants will be notified of awards on a rolling basis beginning 3/17. **Types of Aid:** *Need-based scholarships/grants:* Federal Pell, SEOG, state scholarships/grants, private scholarships, the school's own gift aid. *Loans:* Subsidized Stafford, Unsubsidized Stafford, PLUS, Federal Perkins, college/university loans from institutional funds, Private Alternative Loans **Student Employment:** Federal Work-Study Program available. **Financial Aid Statistics:** 93% freshmen, 94% undergrads receive need-based scholarship or grant aid. 99% freshmen, 95% undergrads receive non-need-based scholarship or grant aid. 89% freshmen, 93% undergrads receive need-based self-help aid. 88% freshmen, 85% undergrads receive any aid. 78% undergrads borrow to pay for school. Average cumulative indebtedness $30,566. **Criteria for awarding institutional aid:** Non-need-based: academics, alumni affiliation, art, leadership, minority status, music/drama, religious affiliation.

UNIVERSITY OF LOUISIANA AT LAFAYETTE

P.O. Drawer 41210, Lafayette, LA 70504
Phone: 337-482-6553 • **Financial Aid Phone:** 337-482-6506
E-mail: enroll@louisiana.edu • **CEEB Code:** 6672
Fax: 337-482-1112 • **Website:** www.louisiana.edu • **ACT Code:** 1612

This public school was founded in 1898. It has a 1375-acre campus.

RATINGS
Admissions Selectivity Rating: 74   **Fire Safety Rating:** 86   **Green Rating:** 60*

STUDENTS AND FACULTY
Enrollment: 14,796. **Student Body:** 56% female, 44% male, 4% out-of-state, 2% international (101 countries represented). Asian 2%, African American 21%, Caucasian 70%, Hispanic 3%.
Retention and Graduation: 74% freshmen return for sophomore year. 12% freshmen graduate within 4 years. 42% freshmen graduate within 6 years. **Faculty:** Student/faculty ratio 23:1. 584 full-time faculty, 73% hold PhDs, 17% are members of minority groups, 44% are women.

ACADEMICS
Degrees: bachelor's, doctoral, master's, post-master's certificate. **Classes:** Most classes have 20–29 students. **Majors with Highest Enrollment:** biology/biological sciences; business administration and management; nursing/registered nurse (rn, asn, bsn, msn). **Special Study Options:** Accelerated program, cooperative education program, cross-registration, distance learning, double major, dual enrollment, exchange student program (domestic), honors program, independent study, internships, student-designed major, study abroad, teacher certification program. **Honors programs:** Honors Baccalaureate degree is available. **Disability Services:** Special programs offered to physically disabled

students include note-taking services, reader services, tape recorders, tutors. **Career services:** career/job search classes, career assessment.

FACILITIES
Housing: men's dorms, women's dorms, fraternity/sorority housing, apartments for married students, apartments for single students. 85% of campus accessible to physically disabled. **Special Academic Facilities/Equipment:** Art museum, experimental farm, primate center, CAD/CAM laboratory, marine research facility, on campus restaurant and hotel with instructional facilities, 2 nuclear accelerators, 2 electron microscopes, radio station and television production studio, nursery school laboratory, Louisiana Emersive Technologies Enterprise **Computers:** Students can register for classes online. Administrative functions (other than registration) can be performed online.

CAMPUS LIFE
Environment: City. **Activities:** Choral groups, concert band, dance, drama/theater, jazz band, literary magazine, marching band, music ensembles, musical theater, opera, radio station, student government, student newspaper, symphony orchestra, yearbook, Campus Ministries, International Student Organization 155 registered organizations, 14 honor societies, 8 religious organizations. 11 fraternities, 9 sororities. **Athletics (Intercollegiate):** *Men:* baseball, basketball, cheerleading, cross-country, football, golf, tennis, track/field (outdoor), track/field (indoor). *Women:* basketball, cheerleading, cross-country, soccer, softball, tennis, track/field (outdoor), track/field (indoor), volleyball. **On-Campus Highlights:** University Museum, Student Center, Cajun Field, Cajundome, Dupre Library.

ADMISSIONS
Freshman Academic Profile: Average high school GPA 3.2. 17% in top 10% of high school class, 42% in top 25% of high school class, 73% in top 50% of high school class. ACT middle 50% range 20-24. Minimum paper TOEFL 525. **Basis for Candidate Selection:** *Very important factors considered include:* Class rank, academic GPA, rigor of secondary school record, standardized test scores. *Other factors considered include:* state residency. **Freshman Admission Requirements:** High school diploma is required and GED is accepted. *Academic units required:* 4 English, 4 mathematics, 3 science, (0 science labs), 2 foreign language, 1 social studies, 2 history, 1 visual/performing arts, 1 Computer Science/Literacy. *Academic units recommended:* 4 English, 4 mathematics, 3 science, (0 science labs), 2 foreign language, 1 social studies, 2 history, 1 visual/performing arts, 1 Computer Science/Literacy **Freshman Admission Statistics:** 9,062 applied, 68% admitted, 50% enrolled. **Transfer Admission Requirements:** college transcript(s), Lowest grade transferable D. **General Admission Information:** Application Fee $25. Nonfall registration accepted. Admission may be deferred for a maximum of 1 semester. Credit and/or placement offered for CEEB Advanced Placement tests.

COSTS AND FINANCIAL AID
Annual in-state tuition $3,440. Annual out-of-state tuition $12,062. Room and board $8,236. Required fees $1,417. Average book expense $1,200. **Required Forms and Deadlines:** FAFSA. **Notification of Awards:** Applicants will be notified of awards on a rolling basis beginning 4/1. **Types of Aid:** *Need-based scholarships/grants:* Federal Pell, SEOG, state scholarships/grants, private scholarships, the school's own gift aid, Federal Nursing Scholarships. *Loans:* Subsidized Stafford, Unsubsidized Stafford, PLUS, Federal Perkins, Federal Nursing. **Student Employment:** Federal Work-Study Program available. Institutional employment available. Off-campus job opportunities are good. **Financial Aid Statistics:** 94% freshmen, 88% undergrads receive need-based scholarship or grant aid. 14% freshmen, 10% undergrads receive non-need-based scholarship or grant aid. 43% freshmen, 57% undergrads receive need-based self-help aid. 2% freshmen, 2% undergrads receive athletic scholarships. 87% freshmen, 72% undergrads receive any aid.

UNIVERSITY OF LOUISVILLE

Admissions Office, Louisville, KY 40292
Phone: 502-852-6531 • **Financial Aid Phone:** 502-852-5511
E-mail: admitme@louisville.edu
Fax: 502-852-4776 • **Website:** www.louisville.edu • **ACT Code:** 1556

This public school was founded in 1798. It has a 274-acre campus.

RATINGS
Admissions Selectivity Rating: 76   **Fire Safety Rating:** 60*   **Green Rating:** 92

STUDENTS AND FACULTY
Enrollment: 14,854. **Student Body:** 52% female, 48% male, 15% out-of-state, 1% international (countries represented). Asian 3%, African American 12%, Caucasian 77%, Hispanic 3%.

Retention and Graduation: Faculty: Student/faculty ratio 17:1. 802 full-time faculty, 89% hold PhDs, 18% are members of minority groups, 37% are women.

ACADEMICS

Degrees: associate, bachelor's, certificate, diploma, doctoral, master's, post-bachelor's certificate, post-master's certificate, terminal associate, transfer associate. **Classes:** Most classes have 20–29 students. **Special Study Options:** Accelerated program, cooperative education program, cross-registration, distance learning, double major, dual enrollment, English as a Second Language (ESL), honors program, independent study, internships, student-designed major, study abroad, teacher certification program. **Combined degree programs:** , BS-BA/MBA. **Disability Services:** Special programs offered to physically disabled students include note-taking services, reader services, tape recorders, tutors.

FACILITIES

Housing: Coed dorms, special housing for disabled students, fraternity/sorority housing, apartments for married students, cooperative housing, apartments for single students, Theme Housing. 100% of campus accessible to physically disabled. **Special Academic Facilities/Equipment:** Natural history and art museums, planetarium, numerous institutes and centers. **Computers:** Administrative functions (other than registration) can be performed online.

CAMPUS LIFE

Environment: Metropolis. **Activities:** Choral groups, concert band, dance, drama/theater, jazz band, literary magazine, marching band, music ensembles, musical theater, opera, pep band, radio station, student government, student newspaper, symphony orchestra, Campus Ministries, International Student Organization 237 registered organizations, 7 honor societies, 18 religious organizations. 13 fraternities, 10 sororities. **Athletics (Intercollegiate):** *Men:* baseball, basketball, cheerleading, cross-country, diving, football, golf, soccer, swimming, tennis, track/field (outdoor). *Women:* basketball, cheerleading, crew/rowing, cross-country, diving, field hockey, golf, lacrosse, soccer, softball, swimming, tennis, track/field (outdoor), volleyball. **On-Campus Highlights:** Student Activity Center, J.B. Speed Art Museum **Environmental Initiatives:** Unlimited free public transit ride contract for all UofL students, staff and faculty and Commute Green campaign: http://louisville.edu/parking/commute-green. html Local food purchasing and promotion: New campus garden; Community Supported Agriculture (CSA) program on campus; campus Farmers' Market (Gray Street); Minimum 15% local requirement in dining contract with Sodexo; Promoting catering services offering local foods. Brownfield redevelopment: Smart campus growth through the redevelopment of surrounding brownfields has helped enhance environmental quality, revitalize neighborhoods, and reduce vehicle miles traveled by creating a campus environment where people want to live. UofL has been involved in the remediation and reclamation of over 200 acres of brownfield's in Louisville.

ADMISSIONS

Freshman Academic Profile: Average high school GPA 3.5. SAT Math middle 50% range 510-640. SAT Critical Reading middle 50% range 500-620. ACT middle 50% range 22-28. Minimum paper TOEFL 550. **Basis for Candidate Selection:** *Very important factors considered include:* academic GPA, rigor of secondary school record, standardized test scores. *Other factors considered include:* Class rank, recommendation(s), extracurricular activities, racial/ethnic status, state residency, talent/ability, volunteer work, work experience. **Freshman Admission Requirements:** High school diploma is required and GED is accepted. *Academic units required:* 4 English, 3 mathematics, 3 science, (1 science labs), 2 foreign language, 3 social studies, 1 visual/performing arts, 5 academic electives, 5 5 electives must be rigorous; History is included in Social Studies. *Academic units recommended:* 4 English, 3 mathematics, 3 science, (1 science labs), 2 foreign language, 3 social studies, 1 visual/performing arts, 5 academic electives, 5 5 electives must be rigorous; History is included in Social Studies **Freshman Admission Statistics:** 8,441 applied, 76% admitted, 42% enrolled. **Transfer Admission Requirements:** college transcript(s), minimum college GPA of 2.0 required. Lowest grade transferable D. **General Admission Information:** Application Fee $40. Regular application deadline 8/25. Nonfall registration accepted. Credit and/or placement offered for CEEB Advanced Placement tests.

COSTS AND FINANCIAL AID

Annual in-state tuition $8,424. Annual out-of-state tuition $20,424. Room and board $6,602. Average book expense $1,000. **Required Forms and Deadlines; Notification of Awards; Types of Aid:** *Need-based scholarships/grants: Loans:* **Student Employment: Financial Aid Statistics:** 96% freshmen, 88% undergrads receive need-based scholarship or grant aid. 16% freshmen, 11% undergrads receive non-need-based scholarship or grant aid. 57% freshmen, 67% undergrads receive need-based self-help aid. 4% freshmen, 3% undergrads receive athletic scholarships. 47% undergrads borrow to pay for school. Average cumulative indebtedness $18,713.

UNIVERSITY OF MAINE

5713 Chadbourne Hall, Orono, ME 04469-5713
Phone: 207-581-1561 • **Financial Aid Phone:** 207-581-1324
E-mail: um-admit@maine.edu • **CEEB Code:** 3916
Fax: 207-581-1213 • **Website:** www.umaine.edu • **ACT Code:** 1664

This public school was founded in 1865. It has a 660-acre campus.

RATINGS

Admissions Selectivity Rating: 70   **Fire Safety Rating:** 86   **Green Rating:** 87

STUDENTS AND FACULTY

Enrollment: 8,228. **Student Body:** 48% female, 52% male, 17% out-of-state, 2% international (67 countries represented). Asian 1%, African American 2%, Caucasian 82%, Hispanic 2%, Native American 1%.
Retention and Graduation: 76% freshmen return for sophomore year. 36% freshmen graduate within 4 years. 60% freshmen graduate within 6 years. 29% grads go on to further study within 1 year. **Faculty:** Student/faculty ratio 15:1. 533 full-time faculty, 76% hold PhDs, 14% are members of minority groups, 35% are women. 11% of classes are taught by teaching assistants.

ACADEMICS

Degrees: bachelor's, doctoral, master's, post-master's certificate. **Classes:** Most classes have 10–19 students. Most lab/discussion sessions have 10–19 students. **Majors with Highest Enrollment:** business/commerce; education; engineering. **Special Study Options:** Accelerated program, cooperative education program, distance learning, double major, dual enrollment, English as a Second Language (ESL), honors program, independent study, internships, liberal arts/career combination, study abroad, teacher certification program. **Honors programs:** The Honors College at The University of Maine provides a unique opportunity for a community of five hundred motivated students to investigate diverse academic areas of the University, to be challenged in a supportive intellectual environment, and to critically engage fellow students and enthusiastic, distinguished faculty in thoughtful, provocative discussion. The benefits and rewards are substantial, and the program is flexible enough to be tailored precisely to the individual student's needs and interests. **Combined degree programs:** BA/MD, BA/MA, BA/DO. **Disability Services:** Special programs offered to physically disabled students include note-taking services, reader services, tape recorders, tutors. **Career services:** Alumni network, alumni services, career/job search classes, career assessment, internships, regional alumni. Career services highlights include Visit us at http://www.umaine.edu/career/coop.html for information about these programs.

FACILITIES

Housing: Coed dorms, special housing for disabled students, special housing for international students, fraternity/sorority housing, apartments for married students, apartments for single students, Wellness Housing, Theme Housing-Honor's College Housing; Graduate Student Housing; Smoke free; chem free; clusters for engineering and science majors. First Year Residential Experience (FYRE). 90% of campus accessible to physically disabled. **Special Academic Facilities/Equipment:** Laboratory for Advanced Surface Science and Technology (LASST), Advanced Manufacturing Center, Anthropology museum, Digital Media Lab, folklore and oral history museum, art museum, Canadian-American center, social sciences research institute, exceptional child research lab, preschool, experimental farms, land/water resources center, center for marine studies, planetarium/observatory, electron microscopes, farm museum, papermaking machine, aquaculture production facility, woodland preserve, botanical garden, arts center, Franco-American Center **Computers:** 100% of classrooms, 10% of dorms, 100% of libraries, 100% of dining areas, 100% of student union, 50% of common outdoor areas have wireless network access. Students can register for classes online. Administrative functions (other than registration) can be performed online.

CAMPUS LIFE

Environment: Village. **Activities:** Choral groups, concert band, dance, drama/theater, jazz band, literary magazine, marching band, music ensembles, musical theater, opera, pep band, radio station, student government, student newspaper, student-run film society, symphony orchestra, television station, yearbook, Campus Ministries, International Student Organization 224 registered organizations, 42 honor societies, 7 religious organizations. 13 fraternities, 6 sororities. **Athletics (Intercollegiate):** *Men:* baseball, basketball, cross-country, diving, football, ice hockey, soccer, swimming, track/field (outdoor), track/field (indoor). *Women:* basketball, cross-country, diving, field hockey, ice hockey, soccer, softball, swimming, track/field (outdoor), track/field (indoor), volleyball. **On-Campus Highlights:** Collins Center for the Arts, Alfond Arena, Market Place - Memorial Union, Student Recreation Center, The Mall. **Environmental Initiatives:** UMaine has developed a master plan centered on sustainability, restoring habitat, avoiding sprawl, maximizing solar orientation, and reducing carbon emissions. Major efficiency upgrades and fuel switching (No. 6 fuel oil replaced with natural gas) at the university's central heating plant, including the installation of a back-pressure turbine and a new high-efficiency boiler. An institutional commitment (including a $300,000 Green Loan Fund supported by the University of Maine Foundation) to support sustainability, energy efficiency and renewable energy projects on campus. The institution has a huge research focus on renewable energy and sustainability programs, including the Advanced Structures & Composites Center's DeepCWind project, the Climate Change Institute, Sustainability Solutions Initiative, Forest Bioproducts Research Initiative, and interdisciplinary tidal power research. There has also been a push to add curriculum, including UMaine's new renewable energy minors; a sustainability track in the M.B.A. program; an M.A. in global policy with a concentration in international environmental policy; and a planned major in climate change and culture.

ADMISSIONS

Freshman Academic Profile: Average high school GPA 3.4. 18% in top 10% of high school class, 48% in top 25% of high school class, 82% in top 50% of high school class. N/A% from public high schools. SAT Math middle 50% range 480-600. SAT Critical Reading middle 50% range 470-590. SAT Writing middle 50% range 460-570. ACT middle 50% range 20-25. Minimum web-based TOEFL 71. Minimum paper TOEFL 530. **Basis for Candidate Selection:** *Very important factors considered include:* Class rank, academic GPA, rigor of secondary school record, standardized test scores. *Important factors considered include:* application essay, recommendation(s). *Other factors considered include:* character/personal qualities, extracurricular activities, geographical residence, interview, talent/ability, volunteer work, work experience. **Freshman Admission Requirements:** High school diploma is required and GED is accepted. *Academic units required:* 4 English, 3 mathematics, 2 science, (2 science labs), 2 foreign language, 2 social studies, 4 academic electives, 1 Physical education for Education Majors. *Academic units recommended:* 4 English, 3 mathematics, 2 science, (2 science labs), 2 foreign language, 2 social studies, 4 academic electives, 1 Physical education for Education Majors **Freshman Admission Statistics:** 8,306 applied, 81% admitted, 29% enrolled. **Transfer Admission Requirements:** High school transcript, college transcript(s), essay or personal statement, minimum college GPA of 2.0 required. Lowest grade transferable C . **General Admission Information:** Application Fee $40. Notification on a rolling basis, beginning on or about 2/1. Nonfall registration accepted. Admission may be deferred for a maximum of 2 semesters. Credit offered for CEEB Advanced Placement tests.

COSTS AND FINANCIAL AID

Annual in-state tuition $8,370. Annual out-of-state tuition $25,230. Room and board $8,848. Required fees $2,224. Average book expense $1,000. **Required Forms and Deadlines:** FAFSA. **Notification of Awards:** Applicants will be notified of awards on a rolling basis beginning 3/15. **Types of Aid:** *Need-based scholarships/grants:* Federal Pell, SEOG, state scholarships/grants, private scholarships, the school's own gift aid. *Loans:* Subsidized Stafford, Unsubsidized Stafford, PLUS, Federal Perkins, state loans. **Student Employment:** Federal Work-Study Program available. Institutional employment available. Highest amount earned per year from on-campus jobs $4,000. Off-campus job opportunities are good. **Financial Aid Statistics:** 93% freshmen, 85% undergrads receive need-based scholarship or grant aid. 6% freshmen, 4% undergrads receive non-need-based scholarship or grant aid. 86% freshmen, 89% undergrads receive need-based self-help aid. 1% freshmen, 1% undergrads receive athletic scholarships. 81% freshmen, 80% undergrads receive any aid. 78% undergrads borrow to pay for school. Average cumulative indebtedness $32,438. **Criteria for awarding institutional aid:** Non-need-based: academics, alumni affiliation, art, athletics, job skills, leadership, minority status, music/drama, religious affiliation, state/district residency.

See page 1260.

246 Main Street, Farmington, ME 4938
Phone: 207-778-7050 • **Financial Aid Phone:** 207-778-7100
E-mail: umfadmit@maine.edu • **CEEB Code:** 3506
Fax: 207-778-8182 • **Website:** www.farmington.edu • **ACT Code:** 1640

This public school was founded in 1863. It has a 55-acre campus.

RATINGS
Admissions Selectivity Rating: 68   **Fire Safety Rating:** 99   **Green Rating:** 86

STUDENTS AND FACULTY
Enrollment: 2,198. **Student Body:** 65% female, 35% male, 12% out-of-state, 0% international (7 countries represented). Asian 1%, African American 1%, Caucasian 81%, Hispanic 1%.
Retention and Graduation: 74% freshmen return for sophomore year. 41% freshmen graduate within 4 years. 20% grads go on to further study within 1 year. 15% grads pursue arts and sciences degrees. 1% grads pursue law degrees. 3% grads pursue business degrees. 1% grads pursue medical degrees. **Faculty:** Student/faculty ratio 15:1. 120 full-time faculty, 93% hold PhDs, 8% are members of minority groups, 53% are women. 0% of classes are taught by teaching assistants.

ACADEMICS
Degrees: bachelor's, master's. **Classes:** Most classes have 10–19 students. Most lab/discussion sessions have 10–19 students. **Majors with Highest Enrollment:** elementary education and teaching; multi-/interdisciplinary studies, other; psychology. **Special Study Options:** cooperative education program, cross-registration, double major, dual enrollment, exchange student program (domestic), honors program, independent study, internships, liberal arts/career combination, student-designed major, study abroad, teacher certification program, SALT, Documentary Field Study in Portland,ME, National Student Exchange, Service Learning. **Honors programs:** UMF Honors Program **Disability Services:** Special programs offered to physically disabled students include note-taking services, reader services. **Career services:** career assessment Career services highlights include Student Teaching programs.

FACILITIES
Housing: Coed dorms, special housing for international students, women's dorms, Wellness Housing, Theme Housing, Housing for students maintaining a certain GPA, medical rooms, quiet floors, wellness community, international community, independent living environment housing available. 75% of campus accessible to physically disabled. **Special Academic Facilities/Equipment:** Art gallery, health and fitness center, computer center, Mantor Library, Alumni theater, Nordica Auditorium, observatory **Computers:** 100% of classrooms, 100% of dorms, 100% of libraries, 100% of dining areas, 100% of student union, 100% of common outdoor areas have wireless network access. Students can register for classes online. Administrative functions (other than registration) can be performed online.

CAMPUS LIFE
Environment: Village. **Activities:** Choral groups, concert band, dance, drama/theater, literary magazine, music ensembles, musical theater, radio station, student government, student newspaper, yearbook, International Student Organization 52 registered organizations, 3 honor societies, 3 religious organizations. **Athletics (Intercollegiate):** *Men:* baseball, basketball, cross-country, golf, soccer. *Women:* basketball, cross-country, field hockey, soccer, softball, volleyball. **On-Campus Highlights:** Recreation and Fitness Center, Landing, Computer Center, Education Center, Student Center. **Environmental Initiatives:** Completion of two LEED-certified buildings and commitment to new construction and major renovations at the LEED silver level. ACUPCC signatory with completion of GHG inventory and Climate Action Plan as of January 2010. Energy conservation resulting in an energy footprint 20% below national average for comparable colleges.

ADMISSIONS
Freshman Academic Profile: 11% in top 10% of high school class, 38% in top 25% of high school class, 78% in top 50% of high school class. 88% from public high schools. SAT Math middle 50% range 440-540. SAT Critical Reading middle 50% range 440-570. SAT Writing middle 50% range 430-550. Minimum paper TOEFL 550. **Basis for Candidate Selection:** *Very important factors considered include:* Class rank, rigor of secondary school record, extracurricular activities. *Important factors considered include:* application essay, academic GPA, recommendation(s), character/personal qualities, interview, talent/ability, volunteer work, work experience. *Other factors considered include:* alumni/ae relation, first generation, geographical residence, level of applicant's interest, racial/ethnic status, state residency. **Freshman Admission Requirements:** High school diploma is required and GED is accepted. *Academic units required:* 4

English, 3 mathematics, 2 science, (2 science labs), 2 foreign language, 2 social studies. *Academic units recommended:* 4 English, 3 mathematics, 2 science, (2 science labs), 2 foreign language, 2 social studies. **Freshman Admission Statistics:** 1,580 applied, 82% admitted, 37% enrolled. **Transfer Admission Requirements:** High school transcript, college transcript(s), essay or personal statement, minimum college GPA of 2.5 required. Lowest grade transferable c. **General Admission Information:** Application Fee $40. Notification on a rolling basis, beginning on or about 12/15. Nonfall registration accepted. Admission may be deferred for a maximum of one year. Credit and/or placement offered for CEEB Advanced Placement tests.

COSTS AND FINANCIAL AID
Annual in-state tuition $8,352. Annual out-of-state tuition $17,440. Room and board $8,168. Required fees $990. Average book expense $832. **Required Forms and Deadlines:** FAFSA. **Notification of Awards:** Applicants will be notified of awards on a rolling basis beginning 3/15. **Types of Aid:** *Need-based scholarships/grants:* Federal Pell, SEOG, state scholarships/grants, private scholarships, the school's own gift aid, Native American scholarships and waivers. *Loans:* Direct Subsidized Stafford, Direct Unsubsidized Stafford, Direct PLUS, Subsidized Stafford, Unsubsidized Stafford, PLUS, Federal Perkins, state loans, college/university loans from institutional funds, Teachers for Maine Loans. **Student Employment:** Federal Work-Study Program available. Institutional employment available. Highest amount earned per year from on-campus jobs $5,530. Off-campus job opportunities are fair. **Financial Aid Statistics:** 90% freshmen, 87% undergrads receive need-based scholarship or grant aid. 12% freshmen, 14% undergrads receive non-need-based scholarship or grant aid. 99% freshmen, 99% undergrads receive need-based self-help aid. 96% freshmen, 94% undergrads receive any aid. 87% undergrads borrow to pay for school. Average cumulative indebtedness $20,990. **Criteria for awarding institutional aid:** Non-need-based: academics, leadership, minority status, state/district residency.

UNIVERSITY OF MAINE AT MACHIAS

Office of Admissions, Machias, ME 4654
Phone: 207-255-1318 • **Financial Aid Phone:** 207-255-1203
E-mail: ummadmissions@maine.edu • **CEEB Code:** 3956
Fax: 207-255-1363 • **Website:** www.umm.maine.edu • **ACT Code:** 1666

This public school was founded in 1909. It has a 42-acre campus.

RATINGS
Admissions Selectivity Rating: 65   **Fire Safety Rating:** 68   **Green Rating:** 67

STUDENTS AND FACULTY
Enrollment: 554. **Student Body:** 65% female, 35% male, 24% out-of-state, 4% international (18 countries represented). Asian 1%, African American 1%, Caucasian 88%, Hispanic 2%, Native American 4%.
Retention and Graduation: 12% freshmen graduate within 4 years. 42% freshmen graduate within 6 years. **Faculty:** Student/faculty ratio 15:1. 30 full-time faculty, 73% hold PhDs, 3% are members of minority groups, 33% are women. 0% of classes are taught by teaching assistants.

ACADEMICS
Degrees: bachelor's. **Classes:** Most classes have 10–19 students. Most lab/discussion sessions have 10–19 students. **Majors with Highest Enrollment:** elementary education and teaching; marine biology and biological oceanography; parks, recreation and leisure facilities management. **Special Study Options:** cooperative education program, distance learning, double major, dual enrollment, honors program, independent study, internships, student-designed major, study abroad, teacher certification program. **Disability Services:** Special programs offered to physically disabled students include reader services, tape recorders, tutors. **Career services:** career assessment, internships.

FACILITIES
Housing: Coed dorms. 85% of campus accessible to physically disabled.
Special Academic Facilities/Equipment: Art Gallery Book Arts Print Shop Geographic Information Systems Laboratory and Service Center **Computers:** 100% of classrooms, 100% of dorms, 100% of libraries, 100% of dining areas, 100% of student union, 100% of common outdoor areas have wireless network access. Students can register for classes online. Administrative functions (other than registration) can be performed online.

CAMPUS LIFE
Environment: Rural. **Activities:** Choral groups, dance, drama/theater, literary magazine, music ensembles, musical theater, pep band, radio station, student government, Campus Ministries 38 registered organizations, 2 religious organizations. 5 fraternities, 4 sororities. **Athletics (Intercollegiate):** *Men:* basket-

ball, soccer. *Women:* basketball, soccer, volleyball. **On-Campus Highlights:** Aquatics/Fitness Center/Gymnasium, Residence Halls, Wireless Computer Lab/Classroom, Performing Arts Center, Early Care and Education Center, The Portal - multi-media center, Marine Biology lab facilities, Campus Radio Station, Art Studios and Gallery, Bookstore, Book Arts Print Shop, Kilburn Commons, The Galley. **Environmental Initiatives:** Green Council Recycle-Mania

ADMISSIONS
Freshman Academic Profile: 13% in top 10% of high school class, 24% in top 25% of high school class, 63% in top 50% of high school class. SAT Math middle 50% range 400-530. SAT Critical Reading middle 50% range 440-530. ACT middle 50% range 15-25. Minimum paper TOEFL 500. **Basis for Candidate Selection:** *Very important factors considered include:* application essay, recommendation(s), rigor of secondary school record, interview. *Important factors considered include:* Class rank, standardized test scores, extracurricular activities. *Other factors considered include:* character/personal qualities, talent/ability, volunteer work, work experience. **Freshman Admission Requirements:** High school diploma is required and GED is accepted. *Academic units required:* 4 English, 3 mathematics, 2 science, (2 science labs), 2 social studies. *Academic units recommended:* 4 English, 3 mathematics, 2 science, (2 science labs), 2 social studies. **Freshman Admission Statistics:** 381 applied, 92% admitted, 32% enrolled. **Transfer Admission Requirements:** High school transcript, college transcript(s), statement of good standing from prior institution(s). Minimum college GPA of 2.0 required. Lowest grade transferable C–. **General Admission Information:** Application Fee $40. Regular application deadline 8/15. Nonfall registration accepted. Admission may be deferred for a maximum of 1 year. Credit offered for CEEB Advanced Placement tests.

COSTS AND FINANCIAL AID
Annual in-state tuition $6,410. Annual out-of-state tuition $16,550. Room and board $6,574. Average book expense $650. **Required Forms and Deadlines:** FAFSA. **Notification of Awards:** Applicants will be notified of awards on a rolling basis beginning 3/1. **Types of Aid:** *Need-based scholarships/grants:* Federal Pell, SEOG, state scholarships/grants, private scholarships, the school's own gift aid. *Loans:* Subsidized Stafford, Unsubsidized Stafford, PLUS, Federal Perkins. **Student Employment:** Federal Work-Study Program available. Institutional employment available. Highest amount earned per year from on-campus jobs $1,200. Off-campus job opportunities are good. **Financial Aid Statistics:** 97% freshmen, 87% undergrads receive need-based scholarship or grant aid. 9% freshmen, 6% undergrads receive non-need-based scholarship or grant aid. 81% freshmen, 81% undergrads receive need-based self-help aid. 82% freshmen, 74% undergrads receive any aid. 69% undergrads borrow to pay for school. Average cumulative indebtedness $16,127. **Criteria for awarding institutional aid:** Non-need-based: academics, alumni affiliation, art, leadership, minority status, music/drama, state/district residency.

UNIVERSITY OF MAINE—AUGUSTA

46 University Drive, Augusta, ME 4330
Phone: 207-621-3465 • **Financial Aid Phone:** 207-621-3455
E-mail: umaadm@maine.edu • **CEEB Code:** 3929
Fax: 207-621-3333 • **Website:** www.uma.edu • **ACT Code:** 1641

This public school was founded in 1965. It has a 159-acre campus.

RATINGS
Admissions Selectivity Rating: 61   **Fire Safety Rating:** 60*   **Green Rating:** 79

STUDENTS AND FACULTY
Enrollment: 4,466. **Student Body:** 74% female, 26% male, 2% out-of-state, 0% international (5 countries represented). Asian 1%, African American 1%, Caucasian 83%, Hispanic 1%, Native American 3%.
Retention and Graduation: 55% freshmen return for sophomore year. 40% grads go on to further study within 1 year. **Faculty:** Student/faculty ratio 18:1. 99 full-time faculty, 48% hold PhDs, 0% are members of minority groups, 60% are women. 0% of classes are taught by teaching assistants.

ACADEMICS
Degrees: associate, bachelor's, certificate, post-bachelor's certificate, terminal associate, transfer associate. **Classes:** Most classes have 10–19 students. Most lab/discussion sessions have 10–19 students. **Majors with Highest Enrollment:** business/commerce; health services/allied health/health sciences; social sciences. **Special Study Options:** cross-registration, distance learning, double major, dual enrollment, honors program, independent study, internships, liberal arts/career combination, student-designed major, study abroad. **Honors programs:** UMA Honors Program - augments a student's academic and co-curricular experience **Disability Services:** Special programs offered to physically

disabled students include note-taking services. **Career services:** career/job search classes, career assessment.

FACILITIES
Housing: 99% of campus accessible to physically disabled. **Special Academic Facilities/Equipment:** Jewett Gallery, Katz Library, Student Center **Computers:** 100% of classrooms, 100% of libraries, 100% of dining areas, 100% of student union, 100% of common outdoor areas have wireless network access. Students can register for classes online. Administrative functions (other than registration) can be performed online.

CAMPUS LIFE
Environment: Village. **Activities:** drama/theater, jazz band, music ensembles, pep band, student government, student newspaper, International Student Organization 23 registered organizations, 1 honor societies, 1 religious organizations. **Athletics (Intercollegiate):** *Men:* basketball, golf. *Women:* basketball, golf, soccer. **On-Campus Highlights:** Katz Library, Student Center, Campus Center at UCB, Huskins Lounge at UCB. **Environmental Initiatives:** Reduce - Reuse - Recycle program in place since 1990. Energy policy states UMA will purchase at least 15% of its electicity from renewable sources. All new facilities over 5000 sq. ft. and major capital renovations over 50% of building replacement value will seek LEED silver rating or equivalent.

ADMISSIONS
Freshman Academic Profile: 95% from public high schools. Minimum paper TOEFL 500. **Basis for Candidate Selection:** *Important factors considered include:* Class rank, academic GPA, rigor of secondary school record. *Other factors considered include:* application essay, recommendation(s), standardized test scores, character/personal qualities, interview, level of applicant's interest, talent/ability, volunteer work, work experience. **Freshman Admission Requirements:** High school diploma is required and GED is accepted. *Academic units recommended:* **Freshman Admission Statistics:** 971 applied, 94% admitted, 64% enrolled. **Transfer Admission Requirements:** college transcript(s), minimum college GPA of 2.0 required. Lowest grade transferable C. **General Admission Information:** Application Fee $40. Regular application deadline 8/30. Nonfall registration accepted. Admission may be deferred for a maximum of 12 months. Credit offered for CEEB Advanced Placement tests.

COSTS AND FINANCIAL AID
Room and board $0. **Required Forms and Deadlines:** FAFSA. **Notification of Awards:** Applicants will be notified of awards on a rolling basis beginning 3/15. **Types of Aid:** *Need-based scholarships/grants:* Federal Pell, SEOG, state scholarships/grants, private scholarships, the school's own gift aid. *Loans:* Direct Subsidized Stafford, Direct Unsubsidized Stafford, Subsidized Stafford, Unsubsidized Stafford, PLUS, Federal Perkins, Federal Nursing, state loans. **Student Employment:** Federal Work-Study Program available. Institutional employment available. Highest amount earned per year from on-campus jobs $3,800. Off-campus job opportunities are fair. **Financial Aid Statistics:** 87% freshmen, 85% undergrads receive need-based scholarship or grant aid. 83% freshmen, 87% undergrads receive need-based self-help aid. 64% freshmen, 72% undergrads receive any aid. 66% undergrads borrow to pay for school. Average cumulative indebtedness $21,218. **Criteria for awarding institutional aid:** Non-need-based: academics, athletics, leadership, music/drama, state/district residency.

UNIVERSITY OF MAINE—FORT KENT

23 University Drive, Fort Kent, ME 4774
Phone: 888-879-8635 • **Financial Aid Phone:** 207-834-7605
E-mail: umfkadm@maine.maine.edu • **CEEB Code:** 3393
Fax: 207-834-7609 • **Website:** www.umfk.maine.edu • **ACT Code:** 1642

This public school was founded in 1878. It has a 52-acre campus.

RATINGS
Admissions Selectivity Rating: 75   **Fire Safety Rating:** 98   **Green Rating:** 78

STUDENTS AND FACULTY
Enrollment: 836. **Student Body:** 62% female, 38% male, 6% out-of-state, 7% international (countries represented). Asian 0%, African American 3%, Caucasian 82%, Hispanic 1%, Native American 2%.
Retention and Graduation: 64% freshmen return for sophomore year. 39% freshmen graduate within 4 years. 51% freshmen graduate within 6 years. 5% grads go on to further study within 1 year. 3% grads pursue arts and sciences degrees. **Faculty:** Student/faculty ratio 18:1. 30 full-time faculty, 93% hold PhDs, 7% are members of minority groups, 40% are women. 0% of classes are taught by teaching assistants.

ACADEMICS
Degrees: associate, bachelor's. **Classes:** Most classes have 10–19 students. Most lab/discussion sessions have fewer than 10 students. **Majors with Highest Enrollment:** business/commerce; elementary education and teaching; nursing/registered nurse (rn, asn, bsn, msn). **Special Study Options:** cross-registration, distance learning, double major, English as a Second Language (ESL), honors program, independent study, internships, liberal arts/career combination, student-designed major, teacher certification program, Distance learning within entire UMaine system. **Disability Services:** Special programs offered to physically disabled students include note-taking services, reader services, tape recorders, tutors. **Career services:** alumni services, career/job search classes, career assessment, internships,

FACILITIES
Housing: Coed dorms, special housing for disabled students, men's dorms, women's dorms. 80% of campus accessible to physically disabled. **Computers:** 100% of classrooms, 100% of dorms, 100% of libraries, 100% of dining areas, 100% of student union, 100% of common outdoor areas have wireless network access. Students can register for classes online. Administrative functions (other than registration) can be performed online.

CAMPUS LIFE
Environment: Rural. **Activities:** Choral groups, drama/theater, student government 25 registered organizations, 1 honor societies, 1 religious organizations. 1 sororities. **Athletics (Intercollegiate):** *Men:* basketball, cross-country, golf, skiing (downhill/alpine), skiingnordiccross-country, soccer. *Women:* basketball, cross-country, golf, skiing (downhill/alpine), skiingnordiccross-country, soccer, volleyball. **On-Campus Highlights:** Bengal's Lair, The Lodge (res hall), Library

ADMISSIONS
Freshman Academic Profile: Average high school GPA 3.0. 2% in top 10% of high school class, 15% in top 25% of high school class, 55% in top 50% of high school class. 96% from public high schools. SAT Math middle 50% range 400-500. SAT Critical Reading middle 50% range 410-500. SAT Writing middle 50% range 380-490. ACT middle 50% range 17-21. Minimum paper TOEFL 500. **Basis for Candidate Selection:** *Very important factors considered include:* level of applicant's interest. *Important factors considered include:* Class rank, application essay, academic GPA, recommendation(s), rigor of secondary school record, character/personal qualities, first generation, geographical residence, state residency, talent/ability, volunteer work. *Other factors considered include:* standardized test scores, alumni/ae relation, extracurricular activities, interview, work experience. **Freshman Admission Requirements:** High school diploma is required and GED is accepted. *Academic units required:* 4 English, 2 mathematics, 2 science, (2 science labs). *Academic units recommended:* 4 English, 2 mathematics, 2 science, (2 science labs). **Freshman Admission Statistics:** 561 applied, 57% admitted, 57% enrolled. **Transfer Admission Requirements:** High school transcript, college transcript(s), essay or personal statement, Lowest grade transferable C-. **General Admission Information:** Application Fee $40. Notification on a rolling basis, beginning on or about 12/1. Nonfall registration accepted. Credit and/or placement offered for CEEB Advanced Placement tests.

COSTS AND FINANCIAL AID
Annual in-state tuition $6,600. Annual out-of-state tuition $16,560. Room and board $7,400. Required fees $975. Average book expense $1,000. **Required Forms and Deadlines:** FAFSA, institution's own financial aid form, CSS/Financial Aid PROFILE, state aid form. **Notification of Awards: Types of Aid:** *Need-based scholarships/grants:* Federal Pell, SEOG, state scholarships/grants, private scholarships, the school's own gift aid, Federal Nursing Scholarships. *Loans:* Direct Subsidized Stafford, Direct Unsubsidized Stafford, Direct PLUS, Subsidized Stafford, Unsubsidized Stafford, PLUS, Federal Perkins, Federal Nursing, state loans, college/university loans from institutional funds. **Student Employment:** Federal Work-Study Program available. Institutional employment available. Highest amount earned per year from on-campus jobs $1,500. Off-campus job opportunities are good. **Financial Aid Statistics:** 99% freshmen, 92% undergrads receive need-based scholarship or grant aid. 2% freshmen, 4% undergrads receive non-need-based scholarship or grant aid. 90% freshmen, 92% undergrads receive need-based self-help aid. 95% freshmen, 94% undergrads receive any aid. 65% undergrads borrow to pay for school. Average cumulative indebtedness $9,506. **Criteria for awarding institutional aid:** Non-need-based: academics, alumni affiliation, job skills, leadership, state/district residency.

UNIVERSITY OF MAINE—PRESQUE ISLE

Office of Admissions, Presque Isle, ME 4769
Phone: 207-768-9532 • **Financial Aid Phone:** 207-768-9510
E-mail: adventure@umpi.maine.edu • **CEEB Code:** 3008
Fax: 207-768-9777 • **Website:** www.umpi.edu • **ACT Code:**

This public school was founded in 1903. It has a 150-acre campus.

RATINGS
Admissions Selectivity Rating: 64   **Fire Safety Rating:** 76   **Green Rating:** 60*

STUDENTS AND FACULTY
Enrollment: 1,111. **Student Body:** 60% female, 40% male, 2% out-of-state, 18% international (5 countries represented). Asian 1%, African American 2%, Caucasian 79%, Hispanic 1%, Native American 5%.
Retention and Graduation: 55% freshmen return for sophomore year. **Faculty:** Student/faculty ratio 20:1. 49 full-time faculty, 88% hold PhDs, 8% are members of minority groups, 47% are women. 0% of classes are taught by teaching assistants.

ACADEMICS
Degrees: associate, bachelor's, certificate. **Classes:** Most classes have 10–19 students. Most lab/discussion sessions have 10–19 students. **Majors with Highest Enrollment:** elementary education and teaching; liberal arts and sciences/liberal studies; social work. **Special Study Options:** Accelerated program, cooperative education program, cross-registration, distance learning, double major, exchange student program (domestic), honors program, independent study, internships, student-designed major, study abroad, teacher certification program. **Honors programs:** HON 300 Honors Seminar HON/HTY 401 Oral History HON 421 Honors Senior Year Project **Disability Services:** Special programs offered to physically disabled students include note-taking services, reader services, tape recorders, tutors. **Career services:** alumni services, career/job search classes, career assessment, internships.

FACILITIES
Housing: Coed dorms, apartments for married students. 100% of campus accessible to physically disabled. **Special Academic Facilities/Equipment:** Museumn and Art Gallery, Gentile Hall **Computers:** Students can register for classes online. Administrative functions (other than registration) can be performed online.

CAMPUS LIFE
Environment: Village. **Activities:** drama/theater, radio station, student government, student newspaper 27 registered organizations, 1 honor societies, 1 religious organizations. 1 fraternities, 1 sororities. **Athletics (Intercollegiate):** *Men:* baseball, basketball, cross-country, golf, skiingnordiccross-country, soccer. *Women:* basketball, cross-country, skiingnordiccross-country, soccer, softball, volleyball. **On-Campus Highlights:** Caroline D. Gentile Hall, Campus Center, Library, Fitness Center, Owl's Nest, Caroline D. Gentile Hall, the newest building at the University of Maine at Presque Isle, will officially open to the public on January 21, 2006. Named in honor of the University's longest serving faculty member, Gentile Hall features a large multipurpose court, fitness center, pool, elevated track, and climbing wall. The facility will support the University's academic programs and student body, but the community will also be welcomed and encouraged to use its resources.

ADMISSIONS
Freshman Academic Profile: Average high school GPA 3.0. 8% in top 10% of high school class, 23% in top 25% of high school class, 51% in top 50% of high school class. SAT Math middle 50% range 390-500. SAT Critical Reading middle 50% range 390-530. Minimum paper TOEFL 550. **Basis for Candidate Selection:** *Very important factors considered include:* Class rank, application essay, academic GPA, recommendation(s), rigor of secondary school record. *Important factors considered include:* interview. *Other factors considered include:* standardized test scores, alumni/ae relation, character/personal qualities, extracurricular activities, racial/ethnic status, state residency, talent/ability, volunteer work, work experience. **Freshman Admission Requirements:** High school diploma is required and GED is accepted. *Academic units recommended:* **Freshman Admission Statistics:** 507 applied, 95% admitted, 44% enrolled. **Transfer Admission Requirements:** High school transcript, college transcript(s), essay or personal statement, statement of good standing from prior institution(s). Minimum college GPA of 2.0 required. Lowest grade transferable C–. **General Admission Information:** Application Fee $40. Nonfall registration accepted. Admission may be deferred for a maximum of up to one year. Credit offered for CEEB Advanced Placement tests.

COSTS AND FINANCIAL AID
Annual in-state tuition $4,290. Annual out-of-state tuition $10,680. Room and board $5,246. Required fees $530. Average book expense $800. **Required**

Forms and Deadlines: FAFSA. **Notification of Awards:** Applicants will be notified of awards on a rolling basis beginning 3/1. **Types of Aid:** *Need-based scholarships/grants:* Federal Pell, SEOG, state scholarships/grants, private scholarships, the school's own gift aid. *Loans:* Direct Subsidized Stafford, Direct Unsubsidized Stafford, Direct PLUS, Federal Perkins, state loans, college/university loans from institutional funds. **Student Employment: Financial Aid Statistics:** 78% freshmen, 83% undergrads receive need-based scholarship or grant aid. 7% freshmen, 5% undergrads receive non-need-based scholarship or grant aid. 68% freshmen, 76% undergrads receive need-based self-help aid. 89% freshmen, 89% undergrads receive any aid. 33% undergrads borrow to pay for school. Average cumulative indebtedness $11,181. **Criteria for awarding institutional aid:** Non-need-based: academics, alumni affiliation, art, job skills, leadership, minority status, music/drama, state/district residency.

UNIVERSITY OF MANITOBA

424 University Centre, Winnipeg, Mb R3T 2N2
Phone: 204-474-8808 • **Financial Aid Phone:** 204-474-9531
E-mail: umanitoba.ca/ask
Fax: 204-474-7554 • **Website:** www.umanitoba.ca

This public school was founded in 1877.

RATINGS
Admissions Selectivity Rating: 60*   **Fire Safety Rating:** 60*   **Green Rating:** 60*

STUDENTS AND FACULTY
Student/faculty ratio 18:1. 1,129 full-time faculty, 32% are women.

ACADEMICS
Degrees: bachelor's, certificate, diploma, master's. **Disability Services:** Special programs offered to physically disabled students include note-taking services, reader services, tape recorders, tutors.

FACILITIES
Housing: Coed dorms. 100% of campus accessible to physically disabled.

CAMPUS LIFE
Environment: City. **Activities:** Choral groups, concert band, dance, drama/theater, jazz band, literary magazine, music ensembles, musical theater, opera, pep band, radio station, student government, student newspaper, Campus Ministries, International Student Organization.

ADMISSIONS
Freshman Admission Requirements: High school diploma is required and GED is accepted. **General Admission Information:** Application Fee $60. Regular application deadline 8/14. Nonfall registration accepted.

UNIVERSITY OF MARY

7500 University Drive, Bismarck, ND 58504
Phone: 701-255-7500
E-mail: suerood@umary.edu • **CEEB Code:** 6428
Fax: 701-255-7687 • **Website:** www.umary.edu • **ACT Code:** 3201

This private school, affiliated with the Roman Catholic Church, was founded in 1959. It has a 107-acre campus.

RATINGS
Admissions Selectivity Rating: 65   **Fire Safety Rating:** 60*   **Green Rating:** 60*

STUDENTS AND FACULTY
Enrollment: 1,722.
Retention and Graduation: 70% freshmen return for sophomore year. 1% grads pursue arts and sciences degrees. 2% grads pursue law degrees. 4% grads pursue business degrees. **Faculty:** Student/faculty ratio 17:1.

ACADEMICS
Degrees: associate, bachelor's, master's. **Majors with Highest Enrollment:** business/commerce; health services/allied health/health sciences; nursing/registered nurse (rn, asn, bsn, msn). **Special Study Options:** Accelerated program, cooperative education program, distance learning, double major, dual enrollment, external degree program, honors program, independent study, internships, study abroad, teacher certification program. **Combined degree programs:** BA/MA. **Disability Services:** Special programs offered to physi-

cally disabled students include tape recorders, tutors. **Career services:** alumni services, career/job search classes, career assessment, internships.

FACILITIES
Housing: men's dorms, women's dorms, apartments for single students. 75% of campus accessible to physically disabled. **Special Academic Facilities/Equipment:** Art gallery.

CAMPUS LIFE
Environment: Village. **Activities:** Choral groups, concert band, drama/theater, jazz band, literary magazine, music ensembles, musical theater, pep band, radio station, student government, student newspaper, television station, yearbook 50 registered organizations, 5 honor societies, 6 religious organizations. **Athletics (Intercollegiate):** *Men:* baseball, basketball, cross-country, football, golf, soccer, tennis, track/field (outdoor), track/field (indoor), wrestling. *Women:* basketball, cheerleading, cross-country, golf, soccer, softball, tennis, track/field (outdoor), track/field (indoor), volleyball.

ADMISSIONS
Freshman Academic Profile: ACT middle 50% range 19-24. Minimum paper TOEFL 500. **Basis for Candidate Selection:** *Very important factors considered include:* standardized test scores. *Important factors considered include:* Class rank, recommendation(s), rigor of secondary school record. *Other factors considered include:* application essay, character/personal qualities, interview. **Freshman Admission Requirements:** High school diploma is required and GED is accepted. *Academic units recommended:* **Freshman Admission Statistics:** 943 applied, 95% admitted, 48% enrolled. **Transfer Admission Requirements:** college transcript(s), minimum college GPA of 2.0 required. Lowest grade transferable D. **General Admission Information:** Application Fee $15. Regular application deadline 8/23. Notification on a rolling basis, beginning on or about 9/2. Nonfall registration accepted. Admission may be deferred for a maximum of 12. Credit and/or placement offered for CEEB Advanced Placement tests.

COSTS AND FINANCIAL AID
Annual tuition $9,200. Room and board $3,540. Required fees $300. Average book expense $610. **Required Forms and Deadlines:** FAFSA. **Notification of Awards: Types of Aid:** *Need-based scholarships/grants:* Federal Pell, SEOG, state scholarships/grants, private scholarships, the school's own gift aid. *Loans:* Subsidized Stafford, Unsubsidized Stafford, PLUS, Federal Perkins, Federal Nursing. **Student Employment:** Federal Work-Study Program available. Institutional employment available. Highest amount earned per year from on-campus jobs $1,000. Off campus job opportunities are good. **Financial Aid Statistics:** 100% freshmen, 100% undergrads receive need-based scholarship or grant aid. 77% undergrads borrow to pay for school. Average cumulative indebtedness $18,000.

UNIVERSITY OF MARY HARDIN-BAYLOR

UMHB Box 8004, Belton, TX 76513
Phone: 254-295-4520 • **Financial Aid Phone:** 254-295-4517
E-mail: admissions@umhb.edu • **CEEB Code:**
Fax: 254-295-5049 • **Website:** www.umhb.edu • **ACT Code:**

This private school, affiliated with the Baptist Church, was founded in 1845. It has a 170-acre campus.

RATINGS
Admissions Selectivity Rating: 79   **Fire Safety Rating:** 65   **Green Rating:** 60*

STUDENTS AND FACULTY
Enrollment: 2,921. **Student Body:** 61% female, 39% male, 2% out-of-state, 2% international (18 countries represented). Asian 1%, African American 14%, Caucasian 64%, Hispanic 15%, Native American 1%.
Retention and Graduation: 68% freshmen return for sophomore year. 27% freshmen graduate within 4 years. 46% freshmen graduate within 6 years. **Faculty:** Student/faculty ratio 16:1. 146 full-time faculty, 69% hold PhDs, 12% are members of minority groups, 58% are women. 0% of classes are taught by teaching assistants.

ACADEMICS
Degrees: bachelor's, doctoral, master's. **Classes:** Most classes have 10–19 students. Most lab/discussion sessions have 10–19 students. **Majors with Highest Enrollment:** elementary education and teaching; nursing/registered nurse (rn, asn, bsn, msn); psychology. **Special Study Options:** Accelerated program, double major, dual enrollment, English as a Second Language (ESL), honors program, independent study, internships, student-designed major, study abroad, teacher certification program, Tuition exchange program with other partici-

pating universities. Undergrads may take grad level classes. Military degree completion programs. Servicemember Opportunity Colleges (SOCS) programs. **Honors programs:** Lower Level Honors Program—approximately the top 10% of UMHB's entering freshman class. Freshman year offerings include English and religion, and sophomore year offerings are interdisciplinary courses in the humanities and social sciences. Upper Level Honors Program—Minimum requirements for completion of this program is the completion of three upper level courses designated as honors level and the completion of HNRS 3110 "Great Books and Ideas" and HNRS 3120 "living Issues". Successful completion of these requirements will allow the student to graduate with the cum laude designation. To receive the higher designations of magna cum laude or summa cum laude, the student must also successfully complete an Honors Research Project. This project must include original research and both written and oral presentations of that research to the Honors Committee. **Combined degree programs:** , BBA/MBA; 3-1 Clinical Lab Science with local hospital. **Disability Services:** Special programs offered to physically disabled students include note-taking services, reader services, tape recorders, tutors. **Career services:** Alumni network, alumni services, career/job search classes, career assessment, internships, regional alumni. Career services highlights include The UMHB Career Development Center offers an array of self assessments, exploration, document preparation, and career planning opportunities. The most used and results-generated career program is the one on one Resume Clinic which involves an interactive session with our students drafting a successful career document. Many times this is their first resume, and the new confidence that is reflective by the student after completing this document is most exciting. Additional popular programs and workshops include, Show Me the Money: salary negotiations; Facebook, My Space and My Future Employer; and the President"s Senior Etiquette Dinner Program.

FACILITIES
Housing: special housing for disabled students, men's dorms, women's dorms, apartments for single students. 85% of campus accessible to physically disabled. **Special Academic Facilities/Equipment:** Language lab **Computers:** 100% of classrooms, 100% of dorms, 100% of libraries, 100% of dining areas, 100% of student union, 80% of common outdoor areas have wireless network access. Students can register for classes online. Administrative functions (other than registration) can be performed online.

CAMPUS LIFE
Environment: City. **Activities:** Choral groups, concert band, drama/theater, jazz band, literary magazine, marching band, music ensembles, musical theater, opera, pep band, student government, student newspaper, symphony orchestra, yearbook, Campus Ministries, International Student Organization 51 registered organizations, 5 honor societies, 7 religious organizations. **Athletics (Intercollegiate):** *Men:* baseball, basketball, football, golf, soccer, tennis. *Women:* basketball, golf, soccer, softball, tennis, volleyball. **On-Campus Highlights:** SUB (Student Union Building), Sportsplex or ANY sporting event, Millennium Oaks Park (gazebo, pond), Mayborn Center exercise/fitness facilities, Quad area.

ADMISSIONS
Freshman Academic Profile: SAT Math middle 50% range 470-570. SAT Critical Reading middle 50% range 440-550. SAT Writing middle 50% range 430-530. ACT middle 50% range 19-25. **Basis for Candidate Selection:** *Very important factors considered include:* Class rank, standardized test scores. *Important factors considered include:* academic GPA, level of applicant's interest. *Other factors considered include:* application essay, recommendation(s), rigor of secondary school record, alumni/ae relation, character/personal qualities, extracurricular activities, first generation, geographical residence, interview, racial/ethnic status, religious affiliation/commitment, state residency, talent/ability, volunteer work, work experience. **Freshman Admission Requirements:** High school diploma is required and GED is accepted. *Academic units required:* 4 English, 3 mathematics, 3 science, 2 foreign language, 3 social studies. *Academic units recommended:* 4 English, 3 mathematics, 3 science, 2 foreign language, 3 social studies. **Freshman Admission Statistics:** 8,847 applied, 36% admitted, 20% enrolled. **Transfer Admission Requirements:** college transcript(s), minimum college GPA of 2.0 required. Lowest grade transferable C. **General Admission Information:** Application Fee $35. Nonfall registration accepted. Admission may be deferred for a maximum of no set limit. Credit offered for CEEB Advanced Placement tests.

COSTS AND FINANCIAL AID
Annual tuition $21,900. Room and board $6,620. Required fees $2,250. Average book expense $1,200. **Required Forms and Deadlines:** FAFSA, institution's own financial aid form. **Notification of Awards:** Applicants will be notified of awards on a rolling basis beginning 2/1. **Types of Aid:** *Need-based scholarships/grants:* Federal Pell, SEOG, state scholarships/grants, private scholarships, the school's own gift aid, Federal Nursing Scholarships. , federal work study, Texas state work study, UMHB work duty. *Loans:* Direct Subsidized Stafford, Direct Unsubsidized Stafford, Subsidized Stafford, Unsubsidized Stafford, PLUS, Federal Perkins, state loans, college/university loans from institutional funds. **Student Employment:** Federal Work-Study Program available. Institutional

employment available. Highest amount earned per year from on-campus jobs $3,500. Off-campus job opportunities are good. **Financial Aid Statistics:** 100% freshmen, 99% undergrads receive need-based scholarship or grant aid. 4% freshmen, 4% undergrads receive non-need-based scholarship or grant aid. 87% freshmen, 85% undergrads receive need-based self-help aid. 98% freshmen, 89% undergrads receive any aid. 77% undergrads borrow to pay for school. Average cumulative indebtedness $37,890. **Criteria for awarding institutional aid:** Non-need-based: academics, art, leadership, music/drama, religious affiliation.

UNIVERSITY OF MARY WASHINGTON

1301 College Avenue, Fredericksburg, VA 22401
Phone: 540-654-2000 • **Financial Aid Phone:** 540-654-2468
E-mail: admit@umw.edu • **CEEB Code:** 5398
Fax: 540-654-1857 • **Website:** www.umw.edu • **ACT Code:** 4414

This public school was founded in 1908. It has a 176-acre campus.

RATINGS

Admissions Selectivity Rating: 75   **Fire Safety Rating:** 93   **Green Rating:** 65

STUDENTS AND FACULTY

Enrollment: 4,388. **Student Body:** 64% female, 36% male, 13% out-of-state, 0% international (23 countries represented). Asian 5%, African American 6%, Caucasian 63%, Hispanic 6%.
Retention and Graduation: 83% freshmen return for sophomore year. 69% freshmen graduate within 4 years. 76% freshmen graduate within 6 years. 36% grads go on to further study within 1 year. 59% grads pursue arts and sciences degrees. 3% grads pursue law degrees. 1% grads pursue business degrees. 2% grads pursue medical degrees. **Faculty:** Student/faculty ratio 15:1. 244 full-time faculty, 89% hold PhDs, 14% are members of minority groups, 46% are women. 0% of classes are taught by teaching assistants.

ACADEMICS

Degrees: bachelor's, certificate, master's, post-bachelor's certificate. **Classes:** Most classes have 20–29 students. Most lab/discussion sessions have 20–29 students. **Majors with Highest Enrollment:** business administration and management; English language and literature; psychology. **Special Study Options:** Accelerated program, distance learning, double major, independent study, internships, student-designed major, study abroad, teacher certification program. **Combined degree programs:** , BA/BS & M.S. elementary education, BS computer science & MSMIS, MBA/MSMIS. **Disability Services:** Special programs offered to physically disabled students include note-taking services, reader services, tape recorders. **Career services:** Alumni network, alumni services, career/job search classes, career assessment, internships, regional alumni. Career services highlights include Our academic credit internship program allows students to take up to 12 experiential credits toward graduation. Most experiences are graded and in many cases count toward the major.

FACILITIES

Housing: Coed dorms, special housing for disabled students, men's dorms, special housing for international students, women's dorms, apartments for single students, Wellness Housing, Theme Housing, Substance-Free. 63% of campus accessible to physically disabled. **Special Academic Facilities/Equipment:** Two art galleries, Center for Historic Preservation, language labs, Leidecker Center for Asian Studies, cartography lab, greenhouse. **Computers:** 100% of classrooms, 100% of dorms, 100% of libraries, 100% of dining areas, 100% of student union, 5% of common outdoor areas have wireless network access. Students can register for classes online. Administrative functions (other than registration) can be performed online.

CAMPUS LIFE

Environment: City. **Activities:** Choral groups, concert band, dance, drama/theater, jazz band, literary magazine, music ensembles, musical theater, opera, radio station, student government, student newspaper, student-run film society, symphony orchestra, yearbook, Campus Ministries, International Student Organization, Model UN. 120 registered organizations, 23 honor societies, 10 religious organizations. **Athletics (Intercollegiate):** *Men:* baseball, basketball, crew/rowing, cross-country, equestrian sports, lacrosse, soccer, swimming, tennis, track/field (outdoor), track/field (indoor). *Women:* basketball, crew/rowing, cross-country, equestrian sports, field hockey, lacrosse, soccer, softball, swim-

ming, tennis, track/field (outdoor), track/field (indoor), volleyball. **On-Campus Highlights:** Woodard Campus Center, Battleground Athletic facilities/Fitness Center, Palmieri Plaza Fountain, Ball Circle, Lee Hall. **Environmental Initiatives:** In July 2010, UMW adopted sustainability policies and practices committing to reducing solid waste, conserving energy and water,encouraging the purchasing of products to promote sustainability and promote alternative methods of transportation. In 2009, the President's Council on Sustainability was formed as an advisory committee to the University's President and Cabinet on how the university can best act and articulate the institutions commitment to sustainability and environmental stewardship as outlined in the Strategic Plan. The committee is directly responsible to the Executive Vice President for Administration and Finance and the Provost. UMW has a significant University-wide recycling program in place for aluminum, paper, newspaper, cardboard, plastic, motor oil, oil filters, printer cartridges, antifreeze, tires, auto parts, refrigerators, freon, latex paint, computer monitors, CPUs without hard drives, printers and fluorescent tubes. Waste reduction includes composting of yard waste and re-use of wood chips from tree removal. second annual RECY-CLEMANIA at http://sustainability.umw.edu/recycling/umw-recyclemania/

ADMISSIONS

Freshman Academic Profile: Average high school GPA 3.5. 23% in top 10% of high school class, 58% in top 25% of high school class, 94% in top 50% of high school class. 85% from public high schools. SAT Math middle 50% range 510-600. SAT Critical Reading middle 50% range 520-630. SAT Writing middle 50% range 510-610. ACT middle 50% range 22-27. Minimum web-based TOEFL 88. Minimum paper TOEFL 570. **Basis for Candidate Selection:** *Very important factors considered include:* academic GPA, rigor of secondary school record. *Important factors considered include:* Class rank, application essay, recommendation(s), standardized test scores, extracurricular activities. *Other factors considered include:* alumni/ae relation, character/personal qualities, first generation, geographical residence, racial/ethnic status, state residency, talent/ability, volunteer work, work experience. **Freshman Admission Requirements:** High school diploma is required and GED is accepted. *Academic units required:* 4 English, 3 mathematics, 3 science, (3 science labs), 2 foreign language, 2 social studies, 1 history, 0. *Academic units recommended:* 4 English, 3 mathematics, 3 science, (3 science labs), 2 foreign language, 2 social studies, 1 history, 0 **Freshman Admission Statistics:** 4,847 applied, 77% admitted, 26% enrolled. **Transfer Admission Requirements:** High school transcript, college transcript(s), essay or personal statement, statement of good standing from prior institution(s). Minimum college GPA of 2.0 required. Lowest grade transferable C. **General Admission Information:** Application Fee $50. Regular application deadline 2/1. Regular notification 4/1. Nonfall registration accepted. Admission may be deferred for a maximum of 2 semesters. Credit offered for CEEB Advanced Placement tests.

COSTS AND FINANCIAL AID

Annual in-state tuition $6,468. Annual out-of-state tuition $18,782. Room and board $8,840. Required fees $2,778. Average book expense $1,100. **Required Forms and Deadlines:** FAFSA, institution's own financial aid form. **Notification of Awards:** Applicants will be notified of awards on or about 4/15. **Types of Aid:** *Need-based scholarships/grants:* Federal Pell, SEOG, state scholarships/grants, private scholarships, the school's own gift aid, Unendowed gifts. *Loans:* Subsidized Stafford, Unsubsidized Stafford, PLUS, Federal Perkins. **Student Employment:** Federal Work-Study Program available. Institutional employment available. Highest amount earned per year from on-campus jobs $5,200. Off-campus job opportunities are good. **Financial Aid Statistics:** 41% freshmen, 46% undergrads receive need-based scholarship or grant aid. 38% freshmen, 23% undergrads receive non-need-based scholarship or grant aid. 81% freshmen, 64% undergrads receive need-based self-help aid. 58% freshmen, 61% undergrads receive any aid. 45% undergrads borrow to pay for school. Average cumulative indebtedness $23,300. **Criteria for awarding institutional aid:** Non-need-based: academics, alumni affiliation, art, leadership, music/drama, state/district residency.

See page 1262.

UNIVERSITY OF MARYLAND
UNIVERSITY COLLEGE

3501 University Blvd. East, Adelphi, MD 20783
Phone: 301-985-7000 • **Financial Aid Phone:**
E-mail: umucinfo@nova.umuc.edu • **CEEB Code:**
Fax: 301-985-7364 • **Website:** www.umuc.edu • **ACT Code:** 20097

This public school was founded in 1947.

RATINGS
Admissions Selectivity Rating: 61   **Fire Safety Rating:** 60*   **Green Rating:** 60*

STUDENTS AND FACULTY
Enrollment: 17,527. **Student Body:** 58% female, 42% male, 31% out-of-state. **Faculty:** Student/faculty ratio 24:1. 119 full-time faculty, 66% hold PhDs, 38% are women.

ACADEMICS
Degrees: associate, bachelor's, certificate, master's, post-bachelor's certificate. **Classes:** Most classes have 20–29 students. **Majors with Highest Enrollment:** business/commerce; information science/studies; multi-/interdisciplinary studies, other. **Special Study Options:** Accelerated program, cooperative education program, cross-registration, distance learning, double major, dual enrollment, external degree program, teacher certification program, weekend college. **Disability Services:** Special programs offered to physically disabled students include note-taking services, reader services, tape recorders, tutors. **Career services:** alumni services, career/job search classes, career assessment.

FACILITIES
Housing: 85% of campus accessible to physically disabled. **Computers:** Students can register for classes online. Administrative functions (other than registration) can be performed online.

CAMPUS LIFE
Environment: Village.

ADMISSIONS
Freshman Academic Profile: Minimum paper TOEFL 550. **Basis for Candidate Selection; Freshman Admission Requirements:** High school diploma is required and GED is accepted. **Freshman Admission Statistics:** 994 applied, 100% admitted, 53% enrolled. **Transfer Admission Requirements:** High school transcript, college transcript(s), minimum college GPA of 2.0 required. Lowest grade transferable D. **General Admission Information:** Application Fee $30. Nonfall registration accepted. Admission may be deferred for a maximum of 24 months. Credit and/or placement offered for CEEB Advanced Placement tests.

COSTS AND FINANCIAL AID
Annual in-state tuition $5,208. Annual out-of-state tuition $9,576. Required fees $120. Average book expense $1,362. **Required Forms and Deadlines:** FAFSA, institution's own financial aid form. **Notification of Awards:** Applicants will be notified of awards on a rolling basis beginning 5/1. **Types of Aid:** *Need-based scholarships/grants:* Federal Pell, SEOG, state scholarships/grants, private scholarships, the school's own gift aid. *Loans:* Direct Subsidized Stafford, Direct Unsubsidized Stafford, Direct PLUS, Federal Perkins. **Student Employment:** Off-campus job opportunities are good. **Financial Aid Statistics:** 50% freshmen, 60% undergrads receive need-based scholarship or grant aid. 3% undergrads receive non-need-based scholarship or grant aid. 84% freshmen, 88% undergrads receive need-based self-help aid. **Criteria for awarding institutional aid:** Non-need-based: academics, leadership.

UNIVERSITY OF MARYLAND,
BALTIMORE COUNTY

1000 Hilltop Circle, Baltimore, MD 21250
Phone: 410-455-2291 • **Financial Aid Phone:** 410-455-2387
E-mail: admissions@umbc.edu • **CEEB Code:** 5835
Fax: 410-455-1094 • **Website:** www.umbc.edu • **ACT Code:** 1751

This public school was founded in 1966. It has a 530-acre campus.

RATINGS
Admissions Selectivity Rating: 88   **Fire Safety Rating:** 94   **Green Rating:** 79

STUDENTS AND FACULTY
Enrollment: 10,838. **Student Body:** 45% female, 55% male, 6% out-of-state, 4% international (96 countries represented). Asian 20%, African American 16%, Caucasian 47%, Hispanic 5%. **Retention and Graduation:** 49% grads go on to further study within 1 year. 30% grads pursue arts and sciences degrees. 1% grads pursue law degrees. 2% grads pursue business degrees. 5% grads pursue medical degrees. **Faculty:** Student/faculty ratio 20:1. 497 full-time faculty, 86% hold PhDs, 22% are members of minority groups, 44% are women. 2% of classes are taught by teaching assistants.

ACADEMICS
Degrees: bachelor's, master's, post-bachelor's certificate. **Classes:** Most classes have 20–29 students. Most lab/discussion sessions have 10–19 students. **Majors with Highest Enrollment:** biology/biological sciences; computer and information sciences; psychology. **Special Study Options:** Accelerated program, cooperative education program, cross-registration, double major, dual enrollment, English as a Second Language (ESL), exchange student program (domestic), honors program, independent study, internships, student-designed major, study abroad, teacher certification program. **Honors programs:** UMBC Honors College, Merehoff (Science, Technology, Engineering, and Mathematics), Scholars Program, Sherman Teacher Education Scholars Program, Sondheim Scholars Programs, Center for Women and Information Technology (CWIT) Scholars Program, Humanities Scholars Program, Lineman Scholars Program. **Combined degree programs:** BA/MA, BA/MEng, biochemistry, chemistry, economics, info. systems. **Disability Services:** Special programs offered to physically disabled students include note-taking services, reader services, tape recorders, tutors. **Career services:** Alumni network, alumni services, career/job search classes, career assessment, internships, regional alumni. Career services highlights include UMBC Career Services is proud of many of the programs and stellar customer service that it delivers to multiple constituents. Collaboration is high with internal and external partners and a primary example of this type of collaboration is demonstrated by the development of Career Path, a website that is intended to help students understand what they can do with their major within a variety of industries, access current jobs and hear the stories of UMBC alumni. We are also extremely proud of consistent and continual employer recruitment activities and presence on campus despite a downturn in the economy. Our graduates continue to report very good job offers.

FACILITIES
Housing: Coed dorms, special housing for disabled students, apartments for single students, Theme Housing, Same sex floors, honors floors, quiet lifestyle, Substance-free, and living-learning communities: Center for Women and Information Technology, Emergency Health Services, Exploratory Majors, Honors College, Humanities Floor, Intercultural Living Exchange, Shriver Living Learning Center, Visual and Performing Arts Floor, and Women Involved in Learning and Leadership, gender neutral. 95% of campus accessible to physically disabled. **Special Academic Facilities/Equipment:** Albin O. Kuhn Library and Gallery, Center for Art and Visual Culture, Women's Center, Center for Environmental Science, Center for Photonics Technology, Center for Women and Information Technology, Center on Research and Teaching in Social Work, Howard Hughes Medical Institute at UMBC, Imaging Research Center, Institute for Global Electronic Commerce, Joint Center for Earth Systems Technology, Laboratory for Healthcare Informatics, Maryland Center for Telecommunications Research, Maryland Institute for Policy Analysis and Research, bwtech@umbc Research and Technology Park and Incubator and Accelerator, Shriver Center, UMBC Technology Center, Goddard Earth Science and Technology Center. **Computers:** 100% of classrooms, 80% of dorms, 100% of libraries, 100% of dining areas, 100% of student union, 40% of common outdoor areas have wireless network access. Students can register for classes online. Administrative functions (other than registration) can be performed online.

CAMPUS LIFE

Environment: Metropolis. **Activities:** Choral groups, dance, drama/theater, jazz band, literary magazine, music ensembles, musical theater, pep band, radio station, student government, student newspaper, student-run film society, symphony orchestra, Campus Ministries, International Student Organization, Model UN. 230 registered organizations, 8 honor societies, 20 religious organizations. 11 fraternities, 12 sororities. **Athletics (Intercollegiate):** *Men:* baseball, basketball, cheerleading, cross-country, diving, lacrosse, soccer, swimming, tennis, track/field (outdoor), track/field (indoor). *Women:* basketball, cheerleading, cross-country, diving, lacrosse, soccer, softball, swimming, tennis, track/field (outdoor), track/field (indoor), volleyball. **On-Campus Highlights:** Albin O. Kuhn Library and Gallery, The Commons (Student Center), Center for Art , Design and Visual Cultu, Howard Hughes Medical Institute Lab, Retriever Activities Center, Students attend, and take part in, a world of excellent theatre, music and dance performances on campus. They go to art openings and lectures, start clubs and exchange ideas through the campus paper and literary magazines. **Environmental Initiatives:** Climate Commitment Task Force (students, faculty, staff) will commence implementation of its Climate Action Plan and reduce our carbon footprint. Implement energy performance contract. Pursuing a minimum of LEED Silver certification for all new construction and major renovations, including the new Performing Arts and Humanities Building and the Patapsco Hall Addition.

ADMISSIONS

Freshman Academic Profile: Average high school GPA 3.7. 29% in top 10% of high school class, 56% in top 25% of high school class, 85% in top 50% of high school class. NA% from public high schools. SAT Math middle 50% range 580-670. SAT Critical Reading middle 50% range 550-650. SAT Writing middle 50% range 530-640. ACT middle 50% range 24-29. Minimum web-based TOEFL 48. Minimum paper TOEFL 460. **Basis for Candidate Selection:** *Very important factors considered include:* academic GPA, rigor of secondary school record, standardized test scores. *Important factors considered include:* Class rank, application essay, recommendation(s), talent/ability. *Other factors considered include:* character/personal qualities, extracurricular activities. **Freshman Admission Requirements:** High school diploma is required and GED is accepted. *Academic units required:* 4 English, 3 mathematics, 3 science, 2 foreign language, 3 social studies, 3 Social Studies & History. *Academic units recommended:* 4 English, 3 mathematics, 3 science, 2 foreign language, 3 social studies, 3 Social Studies & History **Freshman Admission Statistics:** 8,514 applied, 60% admitted, 30% enrolled. **Transfer Admission Requirements:** college transcript(s), statement of good standing from prior institution(s). Minimum college GPA of 2.5 required. Lowest grade transferable D. **General Admission Information:** Application Fee $50. Regular application deadline 2/1. Notification on a rolling basis, beginning on or about 12/15. Nonfall registration accepted. Admission may be deferred for a maximum of one year. Credit and/or placement offered for CEEB Advanced Placement tests.

COSTS AND FINANCIAL AID

Annual in-state tuition $9,764. Annual out-of-state tuition $20,825. Room and board $10,866. Average book expense $1,200. **Required Forms and Deadlines:** FAFSA. **Notification of Awards:** Applicants will be notified of awards on a rolling basis beginning 3/15. **Types of Aid:** *Need-based scholarships/grants:* Federal Pell, SEOG, state scholarships/grants, private scholarships, the school's own gift aid. *Loans:* Direct Subsidized Stafford, Direct Unsubsidized Stafford, Direct PLUS, Federal Perkins. **Student Employment:** Federal Work-Study Program available. Institutional employment available. Off-campus job opportunities are excellent. **Financial Aid Statistics:** 72% freshmen, 75% undergrads receive need-based scholarship or grant aid. 25% freshmen, 9% undergrads receive non-need-based scholarship or grant aid. 62% freshmen, 73% undergrads receive need-based self-help aid. 3% freshmen, 2% undergrads receive athletic scholarships. 70% freshmen, 64% undergrads receive any aid. 53% undergrads borrow to pay for school. Average cumulative indebtedness $22,600. **Criteria for awarding institutional aid:** Non-need-based: academics, alumni affiliation, art, athletics, music/drama.

See page 1264.

UNIVERSITY OF MARYLAND—COLLEGE PARK

Mitchell Building, College Park, MD 20742-5235
Phone: 301-314-8385 • **Financial Aid Phone:** 301-314-9000
E-mail: um-admit@uga.umd.edu • **CEEB Code:** 5814
Fax: 301-314-9693 • **Website:** www.maryland.edu • **ACT Code:** 1746

This public school was founded in 1856. It has a 1382-acre campus.

RATINGS

Admissions Selectivity Rating: 94   **Fire Safety Rating:** 75   **Green Rating:** 91

STUDENTS AND FACULTY

Enrollment: 25,831. **Student Body:** 47% female, 53% male, 23% out-of-state, 3% international (96 countries represented). Asian 15%, African American 12%, Caucasian 56%, Hispanic 8%.
Retention and Graduation: 94% freshmen return for sophomore year. 63% freshmen graduate within 4 years. **Faculty:** Student/faculty ratio 18:1. 1677 full-time faculty, 92% hold PhDs, 22% are members of minority groups, 36% are women. 12% of classes are taught by teaching assistants.

ACADEMICS

Degrees: bachelor's, certificate, master's, post-bachelor's certificate, post-master's certificate. **Classes:** Most classes have 20–29 students. Most lab/discussion sessions have 20–29 students. **Majors with Highest Enrollment:** criminology; economics; political science and government. **Special Study Options:** Accelerated program, cooperative education program, cross-registration, distance learning, double major, dual enrollment, English as a Second Language (ESL), exchange student program (domestic), external degree program, honors program, independent study, internships, liberal arts/career combination, student-designed major, study abroad, teacher certification program, Living-Learning programs including Gemstone Program, Honors, First-Year Focus, Jiminez-Porter Writers House, Civicus, College Park Scholars, and others. **Honors programs:** Gemstones, Honors, Honors Humanities **Combined degree programs:** BA/JD, BA/MA, BA/MBA. **Disability Services:** Special programs offered to physically disabled students include note-taking services, reader services, tape recorders, tutors. **Career services:** internships.

FACILITIES

Housing: Coed dorms, special housing for disabled students, special housing for international students, women's dorms, fraternity/sorority housing, cooperative housing, apartments for single students, Wellness Housing, Theme Housing. Living/Learning program housing includes Gemstone program, College Park Scholars, Language House, Beyond the Classroom, Civicus, Hinman CEOs, Global Communities, Jimenz-Porter Writer's House, Honors, International House, Honors Humanities, SmokFree/Alcohol-Free. **Special Academic Facilities/Equipment:** Aerospace buoyancy lab, art gallery, international piano archives, center for architectural design and research, model nuclear reactor, wind tunnel. **Computers:** 100% of classrooms, 100% of dorms, 100% of libraries, 100% of dining areas, 100% of student union, 100% of common outdoor areas have wireless network access. Students can register for classes online. Administrative functions (other than registration) can be performed online.

CAMPUS LIFE

Environment: Metropolis. **Activities:** Choral groups, concert band, dance, drama/theater, jazz band, literary magazine, marching band, music ensembles, musical theater, opera, pep band, radio station, student government, student newspaper, student-run film society, symphony orchestra, television station, yearbook, Campus Ministries, International Student Organization, Model UN. 574 registered organizations, 53 honor societies, 55 religious organizations. 36 fraternities, 27 sororities. **Athletics (Intercollegiate):** *Men:* baseball, basketball, cross-country, football, golf, lacrosse, soccer, swimming, tennis, track/field (outdoor), track/field (indoor), wrestling. *Women:* basketball, cheerleading, cross-country, field hockey, golf, gymnastics, lacrosse, soccer, softball, swimming, tennis, track/field (outdoor), track/field (indoor), volleyball, water polo. **On-Campus Highlights:** Clarice Smith Performing Arts Center, Adele H. Stamp Student Union, Eppley Recreation Center, Chevy Chase Bank Field at Byrd Stadium, Comcast Center, 6. Memorial Chapel 7. Riggs Alumni Center. **Environmental Initiatives:** The University of Maryland reduced its carbon footprint 10.5 percent between 2005 and 2009 and is on track for meeting its Climate Action Plan goals. University of Maryland and Johnson Controls have begun implementation of the $20,000,000 energy conservation project. The project is designed to save nearly $2,000,000 a year in energy and reduce the CO_2 emissions by over 4,200 tons per year. The campus aims to reduce stormwater runoff - which is damaging local rivers and the Chesapeake Bay - through multiple projects including three new green roofs, two large rainwater cisterns, rain gardens, low-mow meadows, and the use of permiable pavers.

ADMISSIONS

Freshman Academic Profile: Average high school GPA 4.1. SAT Math middle 50% range 610-720. SAT Critical Reading middle 50% range 580-690. **Basis for Candidate Selection:** *Very important factors considered include:* academic GPA, rigor of secondary school record, standardized test scores. *Important factors considered include:* Class rank, application essay, recommendation(s), first generation, state residency, talent/ability. *Other factors considered include:* alumni/ae relation, character/personal qualities, extracurricular activities, geographical residence, racial/ethnic status, volunteer work, work experience. **Freshman Admission Requirements:** High school diploma is required and GED is accepted. *Academic units required:* 4 English, 3 mathematics, 3 science, (2 science labs), 2 foreign language, 3 social studies. *Academic units recommended:* 4 English, 3 mathematics, 3 science, (2 science labs), 2 foreign language, 3 social studies. **Freshman Admission Statistics:** 25,255 applied, 47% admitted, 33% enrolled. **Transfer Admission Requirements:** college transcript(s), essay or personal statement, statement of good standing from prior institution(s). Lowest grade transferable C. **General Admission Information:** Application Fee $55. Regular application deadline 1/20. Nonfall registration accepted. Admission may be deferred for a maximum of 1 year. Credit and/or placement offered for CEEB Advanced Placement tests.

COSTS AND FINANCIAL AID

Annual in-state tuition $7,175. Annual out-of-state tuition $25,554. Room and board $9,893. Required fees $1,733. Average book expense $1,130. **Required Forms and Deadlines:** FAFSA. **Notification of Awards:** Applicants will be notified of awards on a rolling basis beginning 4/1. **Types of Aid:** *Need-based scholarships/grants:* Federal Pell, SEOG, state scholarships/grants, private scholarships, the school's own gift aid. *Loans:* Subsidized Stafford, Unsubsidized Stafford, PLUS, Federal Perkins. **Student Employment:** Federal Work-Study Program available. Institutional employment available. Off-campus job opportunities are good. **Financial Aid Statistics:** 59% freshmen, 60% undergrads receive need-based scholarship or grant aid. 52% freshmen, 39% undergrads receive non-need-based scholarship or grant aid. 84% freshmen, 90% undergrads receive need-based self-help aid. 1% freshmen, 1% undergrads receive athletic scholarships. 86% freshmen, 71% undergrads receive any aid. 46% undergrads borrow to pay for school. Average cumulative indebtedness $25,276. **Criteria for awarding institutional aid:** Non-need-based: academics, art, athletics.

UNIVERSITY OF MASSACHUSETTS—BOSTON

100 Morrissey Boulevard, Boston, MA 02125-3393
Phone: 617-287-6000 • **Financial Aid Phone:** 617-287-6300
E-mail: enrollment.info@umb.edu • **CEEB Code:** 3924
Fax: 617-287-5999 • **Website:** www.umb.edu

This public school was founded in 1964. It has a 177-acre campus.

RATINGS

Admissions Selectivity Rating: 81   **Fire Safety Rating:** 60*   **Green Rating:** 89

STUDENTS AND FACULTY

Enrollment: 11,457. **Student Body:** 57% female, 43% male, 5% out-of-state, 6% international (143 countries represented). Asian 10%, African American 14%, Caucasian 41%, Hispanic 10%.
Retention and Graduation: 79% freshmen return for sophomore year. 13% freshmen graduate within 4 years. 38% freshmen graduate within 6 years. **Faculty:** Student/faculty ratio 15:1. 587 full-time faculty, 98% hold PhDs, 21% are members of minority groups, 49% are women. 0% of classes are taught by teaching assistants.

ACADEMICS

Degrees: bachelor's, certificate, master's, post-bachelor's certificate, post-master's certificate. **Classes:** Most classes have 20–29 students. Most lab/discussion sessions have fewer than 10 students. **Majors with Highest Enrollment:** management science; nursing/registered nurse (rn, asn, bsn, msn); psychology. **Special Study Options:** cooperative education program, cross-registration, distance learning, double major, dual enrollment, English as a Second Language (ESL), exchange student program (domestic), honors program, independent study, internships, liberal arts/career combination, student-designed major, study abroad, teacher certification program. **Honors programs:** The University Honors Program seeks to meet the needs of students who thrive on intellectual challenge by offering special interdisciplinary academic opportunities outside the major. **Combined degree programs:** BA/MA, BA/MBA BA/MA Applied Science BA/MA Sociology. **Disability Services:** Special programs offered to physically disabled students include note-taking services, reader services, tape recorders, tutors. **Career services:** Alumni network, alumni services, career/job search classes, career assessment, internships, regional alumni.

FACILITIES

Housing: University housing referral service. 100% of campus accessible to physically disabled. **Special Academic Facilities/Equipment:** Art gallery, tropical greenhouse, observatory, adaptive computer lab. **Computers:** 100% of classrooms, 100% of libraries, 100% of dining areas, 100% of student union, have wireless network access. Students can register for classes online. Administrative functions (other than registration) can be performed online.

CAMPUS LIFE

Environment: Metropolis. **Activities:** Choral groups, concert band, dance, drama/theater, jazz band, literary magazine, music ensembles, radio station, student government, student newspaper, student-run film society, symphony orchestra, yearbook, Campus Ministries, International Student Organization, Model UN. 75 registered organizations, 1 honor societies. **Athletics (Intercollegiate):** *Men:* baseball, basketball, cross-country, ice hockey, lacrosse, soccer, tennis, track/field (outdoor), track/field (indoor). *Women:* basketball, cross-country, ice hockey, soccer, softball, tennis, track/field (outdoor), track/field (indoor), volleyball. **On-Campus Highlights:** New Campus Center, Clark Athletic Center, Waterfront area and weekly boat tours, Greenhouse, Healey Library. **Environmental Initiatives:** 1. Comprehensive sustainability program, toxics use reduction program, energy conservation and management efforts, master planning. UMB awarded MA Sustainable Campus of the Year in 2004. 2. Signing Tailories and ACUPCC commitments - only public university in Boston to do so. Academic program with environmental focus in both graduate and undergraduate levels - in many colleges within the university.

ADMISSIONS

Freshman Academic Profile: Average high school GPA 3.2. SAT Math middle 50% range 490-600. SAT Critical Reading middle 50% range 470-570. Minimum web-based TOEFL 70. Minimum paper TOEFL **Basis for Candidate Selection:** *Very important factors considered include:* academic GPA, rigor of secondary school record, standardized test scores, character/personal qualities. *Important factors considered include:* application essay, recommendation(s). *Other factors considered include:* extracurricular activities, first generation, interview, level of applicant's interest, talent/ability, volunteer work, work experience. **Freshman Admission Requirements:** High school diploma is required and GED is accepted. *Academic units required:* 4 English, 3 mathematics, 3 science, (2 science labs), 2 foreign language, 1 social studies, 1 history, 2 academic electives. *Academic units recommended:* 4 English, 3 mathematics, 3 science, (2 science labs), 2 foreign language, 1 social studies, 1 history, 2 academic electives. **Freshman Admission Statistics:** 7,876 applied, 61% admitted, 37% enrolled. **Transfer Admission Requirements:** college transcript(s), essay or personal statement, statement of good standing from prior institution(s). Minimum college GPA of 2.5 required. Lowest grade transferable C–. **General Admission Information:** Application Fee $40. Regular application deadline 6/1. Nonfall registration accepted. Admission may be deferred for a maximum of 1 year. Credit offered for CEEB Advanced Placement tests.

COSTS AND FINANCIAL AID

Annual in-state tuition $1,714. Annual out-of-state tuition $9,758. Required fees $10,252. Average book expense **Required Forms and Deadlines:** FAFSA. **Notification of Awards:** Applicants will be notified of awards on a rolling basis beginning 3/21. **Types of Aid:** *Need-based scholarships/grants:* Federal Pell, SEOG, state scholarships/grants, private scholarships, the school's own gift aid, Federal Nursing Scholarships. *Loans:* Direct Subsidized Stafford, Direct Unsubsidized Stafford, Direct PLUS, Federal Perkins. **Student Employment:** Off-campus job opportunities are excellent. **Financial Aid Statistics:** 93% freshmen, 87% undergrads receive need-based scholarship or grant aid. 4% freshmen, 2% undergrads receive non-need-based scholarship or grant aid. 95% freshmen, 96% undergrads receive need-based self-help aid. 74% undergrads borrow to pay for school. Average cumulative indebtedness $25,499. **Criteria for awarding institutional aid:** Non-need-based: academics, leadership, state/district residency.

UNIVERSITY OF MASSACHUSETTS AMHERST

Best 378

University Admissions Center, Amherst, MA 01003-9291
Phone: 413-545-0222 • **Financial Aid Phone:** 413-545-0801
E-mail: mail@admissions.umass.edu • **CEEB Code:** 3917
Fax: 413-545-4312 • **Website:** www.umass.edu • **ACT Code:** 1924

This public school was founded in 1863. It has a 1463-acre campus.

RATINGS
Admissions Selectivity Rating: 87   **Fire Safety Rating:** 83   **Green Rating:** 99

STUDENTS AND FACULTY
Enrollment: 21,448. **Student Body:** 49% female, 51% male, 21% out-of-state, 2% international (69 countries represented). Asian 8%, African American 4%, Caucasian 68%, Hispanic 5%.
Retention and Graduation: 54% freshmen graduate within 4 years. 23% grads go on to further study within 1 year. **Faculty:** Student/faculty ratio 18:1. 1217 full-time faculty, 94% hold PhDs, 21% are members of minority groups, 40% are women.

ACADEMICS
Degrees: associate, bachelor's, certificate, doctoral, master's, post-bachelor's certificate, post-master's certificate. **Classes:** Most classes have 20–29 students. Most lab/discussion sessions have 20–29 students. **Majors with Highest Enrollment:** biology/biological sciences; business administration and management; psychology. **Special Study Options:** cooperative education program, cross-registration, distance learning, double major, dual enrollment, English as a Second Language (ESL), exchange student program (domestic), honors program, independent study, internships, liberal arts/career combination, student-designed major, study abroad, teacher certification program. **Honors programs:** Commonwealth Honors College offers the advantages of a small honors college, but also the wide-ranging opportunities of a nationally recognized research university. There are approximately 2,800 academically talented students in the Commonwealth College, all experiencing the challenges of a dynamic curriculum that includes interdisciplinary seminars, enriched honors courses, colloquia, independent study, service learning, a "culminating experience" and an honors thesis or project, as well as the option of special living-learning accommodations. **Disability Services:** Special programs offered to physically disabled students include note-taking services, reader services, tape recorders, tutors. **Career services:** Alumni network, alumni services, career/job search classes, career assessment, internships, regional alumni. Career services highlights include We are very proud of the comprehensive career planning services we provide to the students at the University. There is no program that we feel is better than the others.

FACILITIES
Housing: Coed dorms, special housing for disabled students, men's dorms, special housing for international students, women's dorms, fraternity/sorority housing, apartments for married students, apartments for single students, Wellness Housing, Theme Housing, first year housing. **Special Academic Facilities/Equipment:** Computer Science Complex, Polymer Research Institute, Herter (Art) Gallery, University Art Gallery, Natural History Museum, Fine Arts Center, Mullins Center (sports and entertainment arena, Learning Commons **Computers:** 97% of classrooms, 10% of dorms, 100% of libraries, 100% of dining areas, 100% of student union, 20% of common outdoor areas have wireless network access. Students can register for classes online. Administrative functions (other than registration) can be performed online.

CAMPUS LIFE
Environment: Town. **Activities:** Choral groups, concert band, dance, drama/theater, jazz band, literary magazine, marching band, music ensembles, musical theater, opera, pep band, radio station, student government, student newspaper, student-run film society, symphony orchestra, television station, Campus Ministries, International Student Organization, Model UN. 291 registered organizations, 30 honor societies, 14 religious organizations. 21 fraternities, 15 sororities. **Athletics (Intercollegiate):** *Men:* baseball, basketball, cross-country, diving, football, ice hockey, lacrosse, soccer, swimming, track/field (outdoor), track/field (indoor). *Women:* basketball, crew/rowing, cross-country, diving, field hockey, lacrosse, soccer, softball, swimming, tennis, track/field (outdoor), track/field (indoor). **On-Campus Highlights:** The Campus Center / Student Union, The Learning Commons, Recreation Center, The Mullins Center, The Fine Arts Center, http://www.umass.edu/umhome/visit_campus/. **Environmental Initiatives:** Central Heating Plant: Our new Central Heating Plant now allows us to produce roughly 70% of our campus' energy through co-generation. The

Central Heating Plant is fueled by mostly natural gas with some oil in the winter time. Climate Action Plan: The development of our campus' Climate Action Plan is our most recent success that will help UMass Amherst move toward a more sustainable future. Our Climate Action Plan not only lists what UMass Amherst has done, but how we plan to recude our greenhouse gas emissions and other negative environmental impacts in important areas such as energy conservation, green building, transportation, etc. Student Involvement: UMass Amherst is dedicated to not only reducing our greenhouse gas emissions and other environmental impacts through infrastructural changes, but also through actively involving student sin all parts of its sustainability initiative. The UMass Amherst Eco-Rep Program is one of the largest in the country with upwards of 70 Eco-Reps working to educate their peers about environmental issues that they can have a positive impact on as college students. Also, UMass Amherst has just hired its first seven Sustainability Interns to aid the Sustainability Coordinator and our Environmental Performance Advisory Committee in carrying out the Climate Action Plan.

ADMISSIONS
Freshman Academic Profile: Average high school GPA 3.7. 27% in top 10% of high school class, 66% in top 25% of high school class, 95% in top 50% of high school class. SAT Math middle 50% range 560-660. SAT Critical Reading middle 50% range 530-630. ACT middle 50% range 24-28. Minimum web-based TOEFL 80. Minimum paper TOEFL 550. **Basis for Candidate Selection:** *Very important factors considered include:* academic GPA, rigor of secondary school record. *Important factors considered include:* Class rank, standardized test scores. *Other factors considered include:* application essay, recommendation(s), character/personal qualities, extracurricular activities, first generation, geographical residence, level of applicant's interest, racial/ethnic status, state residency, talent/ability, volunteer work, work experience. **Freshman Admission Requirements:** High school diploma is required and GED is accepted. *Academic units required:* 4 English, 3 mathematics, 3 science, (2 science labs), 2 foreign language, 2 social studies, 2 academic electives. *Academic units recommended:* 4 English, 3 mathematics, 3 science, (2 science labs), 2 foreign language, 2 social studies, 2 academic electives. **Freshman Admission Statistics:** 34,326 applied, 63% admitted, 21% enrolled. **Transfer Admission Requirements:** college transcript(s), essay or personal statement, minimum college GPA of 2.5 required. Lowest grade transferable C–. **General Admission Information:** Regular application deadline 1/15. Nonfall registration accepted. Admission may be deferred for a maximum of 1 year. Credit and/or placement offered for CEEB Advanced Placement tests.

COSTS AND FINANCIAL AID
Annual in-state tuition $12,612. Annual out-of-state tuition $25,400. Room and board $10,310. Average book expense $1,000. **Required Forms and Deadlines:** FAFSA. **Notification of Awards:** Applicants will be notified of awards on a rolling basis beginning 3/1. **Types of Aid:** *Need-based scholarships/grants:* Federal Pell, SEOG, state scholarships/grants, private scholarships, the school's own gift aid. *Loans:* Direct Subsidized Stafford, Direct Unsubsidized Stafford, Direct PLUS, Federal Perkins, state loans. **Student Employment:** Federal Work-Study Program available. Institutional employment available. Off-campus job opportunities are good. **Financial Aid Statistics:** 87% freshmen, 82% undergrads receive need-based scholarship or grant aid. 6% freshmen, 5% undergrads receive non-need-based scholarship or grant aid. 81% freshmen, 87% undergrads receive need-based self-help aid. 1% freshmen, 1% undergrads receive athletic scholarships. 89% freshmen, 83% undergrads receive any aid. 71% undergrads borrow to pay for school. Average cumulative indebtedness $27,945. **Criteria for awarding institutional aid:** Non-need-based: academics, art, athletics, music/drama, state/district residency.

UNIVERSITY OF MASSACHUSETTS DARTMOUTH

285 Old Westport Road, N Dartmouth, MA 02747-2300
Phone: 508-999-8605 • **Financial Aid Phone:** 508-999-8857
E-mail: admissions@umassd.edu • **CEEB Code:** 3786
Fax: 508-999-8755 • **Website:** www.umassd.edu/ • **ACT Code:** 1906

This public school was founded in 1895. It has a 710-acre campus.

RATINGS
Admissions Selectivity Rating: 74   **Fire Safety Rating:** 78   **Green Rating:** 88

STUDENTS AND FACULTY
Enrollment: 7,326. **Student Body:** 48% female, 52% male, 4% out-of-state, 1% international (52 countries represented). Asian 2%, African American 8%, Caucasian 57%, Hispanic 4%.
Retention and Graduation: 32% freshmen graduate within 4 years. 50% freshmen graduate within 6 years. **Faculty:** Student/faculty ratio 18:1. 375 full-

time faculty, 85% hold PhDs, 24% are members of minority groups, 44% are women. 3% of classes are taught by teaching assistants.

ACADEMICS

Degrees: bachelor's, doctoral, master's, post-bachelor's certificate, post-master's certificate. **Classes:** Most classes have 20–29 students. Most lab/discussion sessions have 20–29 students. **Majors with Highest Enrollment:** business administration and management; nursing; other; psychology. **Special Study Options:** cooperative education program, cross-registration, distance learning, double major, dual enrollment, exchange student program (domestic), honors program, independent study, internships, student-designed major, study abroad, teacher certification program. **Honors programs:** Honors Program **Combined degree programs:** BA/JD, BA/MA, B.S./M.S. chemistry, biology, engineering, and Nursing; BS/MAT and BA/MAT. **Disability Services:** Special programs offered to physically disabled students include note-taking services, reader services, tape recorders, tutors. **Career services:** Alumni network, career/job search classes, internships.

FACILITIES

Housing: Coed dorms, special housing for disabled students, apartments for single students, Apartments for upperclassmen and graduate students. Program dedicated suites. 97% of campus accessible to physically disabled. **Special Academic Facilities/Equipment:** Art gallery, language center, center for Jewish culture, Robert F. Kennedy assassination archives, electron microscope, observatory, marine research vessels, Advanced Manufacturing and Technology Center, School of Marine Science and Technology **Computers:** 100% of classrooms, 100% of dorms, 100% of libraries, 100% of dining areas, 100% of student union, 100% of common outdoor areas have wireless network access. Students can register for classes online. Administrative functions (other than registration) can be performed online.

CAMPUS LIFE

Environment: Town. **Activities:** Choral groups, concert band, dance, drama/theater, jazz band, literary magazine, music ensembles, musical theater, pep band, radio station, student government, student newspaper, symphony orchestra, yearbook, International Student Organization 103 registered organizations, 5 honor societies, 6 religious organizations. 5 fraternities, 3 sororities. **Athletics (Intercollegiate): Men:** baseball, basketball, cross-country, diving, football, golf, ice hockey, lacrosse, soccer, swimming, tennis, track/field (outdoor), track/field (indoor). **Women:** basketball, cheerleading, cross-country, diving, equestrian sports, field hockey, golf, lacrosse, soccer, softball, swimming, tennis, track/field (outdoor), track/field (indoor), volleyball. **On-Campus Highlights:** Underground Cafe, Tripp Athletic Center, Woodlawn Commons, MacLean Campus Center, Observatory. **Environmental Initiatives:** Large scale energy performance. Lighting, heating, AC, water, sewer LEED Silver Library Forest Stewardship FSC.

ADMISSIONS

Freshman Academic Profile: Average high school GPA 3.2. 17% in top 10% of high school class, 40% in top 25% of high school class, 78% in top 50% of high school class. 91% from public high schools. SAT Math middle 50% range 490–590. SAT Critical Reading middle 50% range 470–570. SAT Writing middle 50% range 460–560. ACT middle 50% range 21-25. Minimum web-based TOEFL 68. Minimum paper TOEFL 520. **Basis for Candidate Selection:** *Very important factors considered include:* academic GPA, rigor of secondary school record, standardized test scores. *Other factors considered include:* Class rank, application essay, recommendation(s), alumni/ae relation, character/personal qualities, extracurricular activities, first generation, talent/ability, volunteer work, work experience. **Freshman Admission Requirements:** High school diploma is required and GED is accepted. *Academic units required:* 4 English, 3 mathematics, 3 science, (2 science labs), 2 foreign language, 1 social studies, 1 history, 2 academic electives. *Academic units recommended:* 4 English, 3 mathematics, 3 science, (2 science labs), 2 foreign language, 1 social studies, 1 history, 2 academic electives. **Freshman Admission Statistics:** 8,063 applied, 72% admitted, 25% enrolled. **Transfer Admission Requirements:** college transcript(s), essay or personal statement, minimum college GPA of 2.5 required. Lowest grade transferable C–. **General Admission Information:** Application Fee $40. Early decision application deadline 11/15. Notification on a rolling basis, beginning on or about 12/15. Nonfall registration accepted. Admission may be deferred for a maximum of 2 semesters. Credit and/or placement offered for CEEB Advanced Placement tests.

COSTS AND FINANCIAL AID

Annual in-state tuition $1,417. Annual out-of-state tuition $8,099. Room and board $10,235. Required fees $10,264. Average book expense $1,200. **Required Forms and Deadlines:** FAFSA. **Notification of Awards:** Applicants will be notified of awards on a rolling basis beginning 3/25. **Types of Aid:** *Need-based scholarships/grants:* Federal Pell, SEOG, state scholarships/grants, private scholarships, the school's own gift aid. *Loans:* Direct Subsidized Stafford, Direct Unsubsidized Stafford, Direct PLUS, Federal Perkins, Federal Nursing, state loans. **Student Employment:** Federal Work-Study Program available.

Institutional employment available. Off-campus job opportunities are excellent. **Financial Aid Statistics:** 89% freshmen, 84% undergrads receive need-based scholarship or grant aid. 5% freshmen, 3% undergrads receive non-need-based scholarship or grant aid. 94% freshmen, 95% undergrads receive need-based self-help aid. 74% freshmen, 71% undergrads receive any aid. 76% undergrads borrow to pay for school. Average cumulative indebtedness $32,349. **Criteria for awarding institutional aid:** Non-need-based: academics, minority status, state/district residency.

UNIVERSITY OF MASSACHUSETTS—LOWELL

Office of Undergrad Admissions, Lowell, MA 01854-5104
Phone: 978-934-3931 • **Financial Aid Phone:** 978-934-4237
E-mail: admissions@uml.edu • **CEEB Code:** 3911
Fax: 978-934-3086 • **Website:** www.uml.edu • **ACT Code:** 1854

This public school was founded in 1894. It has a 150-acre campus.

RATINGS

Admissions Selectivity Rating: 81   **Fire Safety Rating:** 94   **Green Rating:** 80

STUDENTS AND FACULTY

Enrollment: 11,025. **Student Body:** 39% female, 61% male, 8% out-of-state, 1% international (58 countries represented). Asian 9%, African American 7%, Caucasian 68%, Hispanic 9%.
Retention and Graduation: 79% freshmen return for sophomore year. 30% freshmen graduate within 4 years. 50% freshmen graduate within 6 years. **Faculty:** Student/faculty ratio 14:1. 434 full-time faculty, 92% hold PhDs, 20% are members of minority groups, 38% are women. 0% of classes are taught by teaching assistants.

ACADEMICS

Degrees: associate, bachelor's, master's, post-master's certificate. **Classes:** Most classes have 20–29 students. Most lab/discussion sessions have 10–19 students. **Majors with Highest Enrollment:** business/commerce; electrical, electronics and communications engineering; nursing; other. **Special Study Options:** Accelerated program, cooperative education program, cross-registration, distance learning, double major, dual enrollment, honors program, internships, liberal arts/career combination, study abroad, teacher certification program, Teacher Certification program for Education is Graduate only. **Honors programs:** The Honors Program at UMass Lowell offers high-achieving students individualized instruction in small groups, often in seminar format; opportunities for undergraduate research; special "Commonwealth Honors Program Scholar" designation on transcripts and diplomas - upon completion of program requirements; opportunity to live on one of the Honors floors in the residence halls; and Honors Program social events. LEARN PROGRAM - With the Fall 2004 entering class, all first year students will participate in the LEARN Program. LEARN, which stands for Living Education and Resource Networking, links academic, residential and personal development experiences by clustering offices, labs and classrooms among residence hall rooms, and offering a year-long schedule of programs that address a range of pertinent social and personal issues. BA/MA, BA/MEng. **Disability Services:** Special programs offered to physically disabled students include note-taking services, reader services, tape recorders, tutors. **Career services:** Alumni network, alumni services, career/job search classes, career assessment, internships, regional alumni.

FACILITIES

Housing: Coed dorms, special housing for disabled students, apartments for married students, cooperative housing, apartments for single students. 80% of campus accessible to physically disabled. **Special Academic Facilities/Equipment:** Language lab, media center, audio-visual department, Centers for Learning, Center for field studies, Center for Performing and Visual Arts, Center for Health Promotion, Research Nuclear Reactor. New $19.5 million recreation center which includes multi court gymnasium, 1/8 mile indoor elevated track, aerobics room, game rooms, locker rooms, and a sauna. Also included are meeting rooms and an indoor/outdoor food court. **Computers:** 50% of classrooms, 90% of dorms, 100% of libraries, 100% of dining areas, 100% of student union, 75% of common outdoor areas have wireless network access. Students can register for classes online. Administrative functions (other than registration) can be performed online.

CAMPUS LIFE

Environment: City. **Activities:** Choral groups, concert band, dance, drama/theater, jazz band, literary magazine, marching band, music ensembles, pep band, radio station, student government, student newspaper, student-run film society, symphony orchestra, yearbook, International Student Organization 100 registered organizations, 16 honor societies, 4 religious organizations. **Athletics**

(Intercollegiate): *Men:* baseball, basketball, crew/rowing, cross-country, golf, ice hockey, soccer, track/field (outdoor), track/field (indoor). *Women:* basketball, crew/rowing, cross-country, field hockey, soccer, softball, track/field (outdoor), track/field (indoor), volleyball. **On-Campus Highlights:** Campus Recreation Center, South Campus Quad, McGauvran Student Center, Fox Multi-purpose Room, Southwick Lounge, New updated state of the art dining facility in the Southwick Lounge. **Environmental Initiatives:** Zero sort university wide recycling program Energy conservation & submetering utilities Pursuing renewable energy programs - PV Solar

ADMISSIONS
Freshman Academic Profile: Average high school GPA 3.3. 17% in top 10% of high school class, 43% in top 25% of high school class, 82% in top 50% of high school class. 87% from public high schools. SAT Math middle 50% range 520-620. SAT Critical Reading middle 50% range 480-590. Minimum web-based TOEFL 213. Minimum paper TOEFL 550. **Basis for Candidate Selection:** *Very important factors considered include:* application essay, academic GPA, rigor of secondary school record, standardized test scores. *Important factors considered include:* recommendation(s), first generation, level of applicant's interest. *Other factors considered include:* Class rank, character/personal qualities, extracurricular activities, interview, talent/ability, volunteer work, work experience. **Freshman Admission Requirements:** High school diploma is required and GED is accepted. *Academic units required:* 4 English, 3 mathematics, 3 science, (2 science labs), 2 foreign language, 2 social studies, 2 academic electives. *Academic units recommended:* 4 English, 3 mathematics, 3 science, (2 science labs), 2 foreign language, 2 social studies, 2 academic electives. **Freshman Admission Statistics:** 7,720 applied, 65% admitted, 29% enrolled. **Transfer Admission Requirements:** college transcript(s), minimum college GPA of 2.0 required. Lowest grade transferable C–. **General Admission Information:** Application Fee $60. Notification on a rolling basis, beginning on or about 12/1. Nonfall registration accepted. Admission may be deferred for a maximum of 12 months. Credit offered for CEEB Advanced Placement tests.

COSTS AND FINANCIAL AID
Annual in-state tuition $1,454. Annual out-of-state tuition $8,567. Room and board $9,520. Required fees $9,668. Average book expense $1,200. **Required Forms and Deadlines:** FAFSA. **Notification of Awards:** Applicants will be notified of awards on a rolling basis beginning 3/25. **Types of Aid:** *Need-based scholarships/grants:* Federal Pell, SEOG, state scholarships/grants, private scholarships. *Loans:* Direct Subsidized Stafford, Direct Unsubsidized Stafford, Direct PLUS, Federal Perkins. **Student Employment:** Federal Work-Study Program available. Institutional employment available. Highest amount earned per year from on-campus jobs $4,000. Off-campus job opportunities are good. **Financial Aid Statistics:** 90% freshmen, 84% undergrads receive need-based scholarship or grant aid. 6% freshmen, 3% undergrads receive non-need-based scholarship or grant aid. 92% freshmen, 95% undergrads receive need-based self-help aid. 2% freshmen, 2% undergrads receive athletic scholarships. 72% freshmen, 72% undergrads receive any aid. 75% undergrads borrow to pay for school. Average cumulative indebtedness $27,620. **Criteria for awarding institutional aid:** Non-need-based: academics, alumni affiliation, art, athletics, job skills, leadership, minority status, music/drama, religious affiliation, state/district residency.

See page 1266.

UNIVERSITY OF MIAMI

P.O. Box 248025, Coral Gables, FL 33124-4616
Phone: 305-284-4323 • **Financial Aid Phone:** 305-284-5212
E-mail: admission@miami.edu • **CEEB Code:** 5815
Fax: 305-284-6605 • **Website:** www.miami.edu • **ACT Code:** 760

This private school was founded in 1925. It has a 260-acre campus.

RATINGS
Admissions Selectivity Rating: 96 **Fire Safety Rating:** 84 **Green Rating:** 87

STUDENTS AND FACULTY
Enrollment: 10,237. **Student Body:** 51% female, 49% male, 52% out-of-state, 12% international (113 countries represented). Asian 6%, African American 7%, Caucasian 44%, Hispanic 23%.
Retention and Graduation: 91% freshmen return for sophomore year. 69% freshmen graduate within 4 years. 81% freshmen graduate within 6 years. 33%

grads go on to further study within 1 year. 9% grads pursue arts and sciences degrees. 6% grads pursue law degrees. 2% grads pursue business degrees. 6% grads pursue medical degrees. **Faculty:** Student/faculty ratio 11:1. 1043 full-time faculty, 87% hold PhDs, 30% are members of minority groups, 38% are women. 7% of classes are taught by teaching assistants.

ACADEMICS
Degrees: bachelor's, certificate, master's, post-bachelor's certificate, post-master's certificate. **Classes:** Most classes have 10–19 students. Most lab/discussion sessions have 10–19 students. **Special Study Options:** Accelerated program, distance learning, double major, dual enrollment, English as a Second Language (ESL), honors program, independent study, internships, liberal arts/career combination, student-designed major, study abroad, teacher certification program, weekend college. **Honors programs:** Honors Program in Medicine (HPM) BA/MD, BA/JD, BA/MEng. **Disability Services:** Special programs offered to physically disabled students include note-taking services, reader services, tutors. **Career services:** Alumni network, alumni services, career/job search classes, career assessment, internships, regional alumni.

FACILITIES
Housing: Coed dorms, special housing for disabled students, fraternity/sorority housing, apartments for single students, Theme Housing. **Special Academic Facilities/Equipment:** Lowe Art Museum, Gusman Concert Hall, Jerry Herman Ring Theatre, Bill Cosford Cinema, Convocation Center, Wellness Center. **Computers:** 100% of classrooms, 100% of dorms, 100% of libraries, 100% of dining areas, 100% of student union, 100% of common outdoor areas have wireless network access. Students can register for classes online. Administrative functions (other than registration) can be performed online.

CAMPUS LIFE
Environment: Town. **Activities:** Choral groups, concert band, dance, drama/theater, jazz band, literary magazine, marching band, music ensembles, musical theater, opera, pep band, radio station, student government, student newspaper, student-run film society, symphony orchestra, television station, yearbook, Campus Ministries, International Student Organization, Model UN. **Athletics (Intercollegiate):** *Men:* baseball, basketball, cheerleading, cross-country, football, tennis, track/field (outdoor), track/field (indoor). *Women:* basketball, cheerleading, crew/rowing, cross-country, diving, golf, soccer, swimming, tennis, track/field (outdoor), track/field (indoor), volleyball. **On-Campus Highlights:** Lowe Art Museum, Jerry Herman Ring Theater, Bank United Center, Mark Light Stadium (Baseball), Gusman Concert Hall & Recording Studio, University Center Breezeway/ Student Union, The Rock (free speech area). **Environmental Initiatives:** The President signed the ACUPCC and the Talloires Declaration. The University also hired a sustainability coordinator. The University has implemented new building standards for new construction and major renovations to meet or exceed USGBC LEED Silver certification. The University has signed the Panama Pact: a collaboration on a world-class education and research facility addressing present and 22nd century challenges focusing on technologies that are sustainable.

ADMISSIONS
Freshman Academic Profile: Average high school GPA 4.2. 69% in top 10% of high school class, 90% in top 25% of high school class, 96% in top 50% of high school class. 62% from public high schools. SAT Math middle 50% range 630-720. SAT Critical Reading middle 50% range 600-700. SAT Writing middle 50% range 590-690. ACT middle 50% range 28-32. Minimum web-based TOEFL 80. Minimum paper TOEFL 550. **Basis for Candidate Selection:** *Very important factors considered include:* Class rank, application essay, academic GPA, recommendation(s), rigor of secondary school record, standardized test scores, extracurricular activities. *Important factors considered include:* volunteer work. *Other factors considered include:* alumni/ae relation, character/personal qualities, first generation, geographical residence, racial/ethnic status, talent/ability, work experience. **Freshman Admission Requirements:** High school diploma is required and GED is accepted. *Academic units recommended:* **Freshman Admission Statistics:** 27,757 applied, 40% admitted, 18% enrolled. **Transfer Admission Requirements:** college transcript(s), statement of good standing from prior institution(s). Lowest grade transferable C. **General Admission Information:** Application Fee $65. Early decision application deadline 11/1. Regular application deadline 1/15. Regular notification 4/15. Nonfall registration accepted. Admission may be deferred for a maximum of 1 year. Credit and/or placement offered for CEEB Advanced Placement tests.

COSTS AND FINANCIAL AID
Required Forms and Deadlines: FAFSA. **Notification of Awards:** Applicants will be notified of awards on a rolling basis beginning 3/1. **Types of Aid:** *Need-based scholarships/grants:* Federal Pell, SEOG, state scholarships/grants, private scholarships, the school's own gift aid, Federal Nursing Scholarships. , Federal Academic Competitiveness Grant Federal SMART Grant. *Loans:* Subsidized Stafford, Unsubsidized Stafford, PLUS, Federal Perkins, Federal Nursing, college/university loans from institutional funds, Private Alternative Education Loans. **Student Employment:** Federal Work-Study Program avail-

ab[...]nal employment available. Highest amount earned per year from [...] $3,000. Off-campus job opportunities are excellent. **Financial** [...]% freshmen, 96% undergrads receive need-based scholarship [...]% freshmen, 33% undergrads receive non-need-based scholar- [...] aid. 80% freshmen, 85% undergrads receive need-based self-help [...]% freshmen, 2% undergrads receive athletic scholarships. 77% freshmen, [...]% undergrads receive any aid. 45% undergrads borrow to pay for school. Average cumulative indebtedness $26,786. **Criteria for awarding institutional aid:** Non-need-based: academics, athletics, music/drama.

UNIVERSITY OF MICHIGAN—ANN ARBOR

Best 378

1220 Student Activities Building, Ann Arbor, MI 48109-1316
Phone: 734-764-7433 • **Financial Aid Phone:** 734-763-6600
CEEB Code: 1839
Fax: 734-936-0740 • **Website:** www.umich.edu • **ACT Code:** 2062

This public school was founded in 1817. It has a 3177-acre campus.

RATINGS
Admissions Selectivity Rating: 96   **Fire Safety Rating:** 93   **Green Rating:** 98

STUDENTS AND FACULTY
Enrollment: 27,774. **Student Body:** 49% female, 51% male, 34% out-of-state, 6% international (127 countries represented). Asian 12%, African American 4%, Caucasian 65%, Hispanic 4%.
Retention and Graduation: 97% freshmen return for sophomore year. 39% grads go on to further study within 1 year. **Faculty:** Student/faculty ratio 16:1. 2569 full-time faculty, 91% hold PhDs, 25% are members of minority groups, 39% are women. 38% of classes are taught by teaching assistants.

ACADEMICS
Degrees: bachelor's, doctoral, master's, post-bachelor's certificate, post-master's certificate. **Classes:** Most classes have 10–19 students. Most lab/discussion sessions have 20–29 students. **Majors with Highest Enrollment:** business administration and management; mechanical engineering; psychology. **Special Study Options:** Accelerated program, cooperative education program, cross-registration, distance learning, double major, dual enrollment, English as a Second Language (ESL), exchange student program (domestic), external degree program, honors program, independent study, internships, liberal arts/career combination, student-designed major, study abroad, teacher certification program, weekend college. **Honors programs:** LSA Honors Program; departmental honors programs **Combined degree programs:** BA/MA, BA/MEng, BA/M. Arch.; BS/M.S.B.E.; BA Ling/M.A. Info; BS/M.P.H. **Disability Services:** Special programs offered to physically disabled students include note-taking services, reader services, tape recorders, tutors. **Career services:** Alumni network, alumni services, career/job search classes, career assessment, internships Career services highlights include The University of Michigan is equally proud of all its cooperative, experiential, and internship learning opportunities.

FACILITIES
Housing: Coed dorms, special housing for disabled students, women's dorms, fraternity/sorority housing, apartments for married students, cooperative housing, apartments for single students, Wellness Housing, Theme Housing: Living/learning communities; substance free dorms. 97% of campus accessible to physically disabled. **Special Academic Facilities/Equipment:** Anthropology, archaeology, art, natural science, paleontology, and zoology museums; audiovisual center, planetarium, electron microscope, biology station, geology camp, athletic campus, medical center, nuclear lab, botanical garden, herbarium, arboretum. **Computers:** 85% of classrooms, 40% of dorms, 80% of libraries, 95% of dining areas, 80% of student union, 10% of common outdoor areas have wireless network access. Students can register for classes online. Administrative functions (other than registration) can be performed online.

CAMPUS LIFE
Environment: City. **Activities:** Choral groups, concert band, dance, drama/theater, jazz band, literary magazine, marching band, music ensembles, musical theater, opera, pep band, radio station, student government, student newspaper, student-run film society, symphony orchestra, television station, yearbook, Campus Ministries, International Student Organization, Model UN. 1000 registered organizations, 13 honor societies, 67 religious organizations. 39 fraternities, 27

sororities. **Athletics (Intercollegiate):** *Men:* baseball, basketball, cheerleading, cross-country, diving, football, golf, gymnastics, ice hockey, swimming, tennis, track/field (outdoor), track/field (indoor), wrestling. *Women:* basketball, cheerleading, crew/rowing, cross-country, diving, field hockey, golf, gymnastics, soccer, softball, swimming, tennis, track/field (outdoor), track/field (indoor), volleyball, water polo. **On-Campus Highlights:** Michigan Stadium, Museum of Natural History, Museum of Art, Margaret Dow Towsley Sports Museum **Environmental Initiatives:** Formal announcement of Campus Sustainability goals. http://sustainability.umich.edu/news/leadership-voice-president-colemans-speech-about-going-green-staying-blue-sustainability-michig Campus Sustainability Integrated Assessment. http://sustainability.umich.edu/news/campus-sustainability-integrated-assessment-principles-and-goals Planet Blue Operations Teams - a comprehensive campus energy reduction program that combines intensive technical assessment and building occupant involvement. http://opsteams.plantops.umich.edu/

ADMISSIONS
Freshman Academic Profile: Average high school GPA 3.8. SAT Math middle 50% range 650-760. SAT Critical Reading middle 50% range 610-700. SAT Writing middle 50% range 620-720. ACT middle 50% range 28-32. Minimum web-based TOEFL 88. Minimum paper TOEFL 570. **Basis for Candidate Selection:** *Very important factors considered include:* rigor of secondary school record. *Important factors considered include:* application essay, academic GPA, recommendation(s), standardized test scores, character/personal qualities, first generation. *Other factors considered include:* Class rank, alumni/ae relation, extracurricular activities, geographical residence, level of applicant's interest, state residency, talent/ability, volunteer work, work experience. **Freshman Admission Requirements:** High school diploma is required and GED is accepted. *Academic units required:* 4 English, (1 science labs), 3 social studies, 3 history, 1 academic electives. *Academic units recommended:* 4 English, (1 science labs), 3 social studies, 3 history, 1 academic electives. **Freshman Admission Statistics:** 42,544 applied, 37% admitted, 40% enrolled. **Transfer Admission Requirements:** High school transcript, college transcript(s), essay or personal statement, statement of good standing from prior institution(s). Minimum college GPA of 3.0 required. Lowest grade transferable C. **General Admission Information:** Application Fee $40. Regular application deadline 2/1. Notification on a rolling basis, beginning on or about 11/1. Nonfall registration accepted. Admission may be deferred for a maximum of 1 year. Credit and/or placement offered for CEEB Advanced Placement tests.

COSTS AND FINANCIAL AID
Annual in-state tuition $13,625. Annual out-of-state tuition $40,302. Room and board $9,752. Required fees $194. Average book expense $1,048. **Required Forms and Deadlines:** FAFSA, CSS/Financial Aid PROFILE. **Notification of Awards:** Applicants will be notified of awards on a rolling basis beginning 3/14. **Types of Aid:** *Need-based scholarships/grants.* Federal Pell, SEOG, state scholarships/grants, private scholarships, the school's own gift aid, Academic Competitive Grant (ACG); National SMART; DC Tag Program; Byrd; Teach Grant. *Loans.* Direct Subsidized Stafford, Direct Unsubsidized Stafford, Direct PLUS, Federal Perkins, Federal Nursing, college/university loans from institutional funds, Direct Loan Grad Plus; Health Professional Student Loans. **Student Employment:** Federal Work-Study Program available. Institutional employment available. Off-campus job opportunities are excellent. **Financial Aid Statistics:** 69% freshmen, 73% undergrads receive need-based scholarship or grant aid. 58% freshmen, 58% undergrads receive non-need-based scholarship or grant aid. 80% freshmen, 84% undergrads receive need-based self-help aid. 2% freshmen, 2% undergrads receive athletic scholarships. 41% freshmen, 39% undergrads receive any aid. 44% undergrads borrow to pay for school. Average cumulative indebtedness $27,815. **Criteria for awarding institutional aid:** Non-need-based: academics, alumni affiliation, art, athletics, leadership, music/drama, religious affiliation, state/district residency.

UNIVERSITY OF MICHIGAN—DEARBORN

4901 Evergreen Road, Dearborn, MI 48128-1491
Phone: 313-593-5100 • **Financial Aid Phone:** 734-763-6600
E-mail: admissions@umd.umich.edu
Fax: 313-436-9167 • **Website:** www.umd.umich.edu

This is a public school.

RATINGS
Admissions Selectivity Rating: 78   **Fire Safety Rating:** 60*   **Green Rating:** 60*

STUDENTS AND FACULTY
Enrollment: 5,895. **Student Body:** 53% female, 47% male, 2% out-of-state, 1% international (countries represented). Asian 6%, African American 7%, Caucasian 75%, Hispanic 2%, Native American 1%.

Retention and Graduation: 79% freshmen return for sophomore year. **Faculty:** Student/faculty ratio 15:1. 259 full-time faculty, 89% hold PhDs, 23% are members of minority groups, 31% are women.

ACADEMICS
Degrees: bachelor's, master's, post-bachelor's certificate. **Classes:** Most classes have 20–29 students. Most lab/discussion sessions have 10–19 students. **Special Study Options:** Accelerated program, cooperative education program, cross-registration, distance learning, double major, dual enrollment, honors program, independent study, internships, liberal arts/career combination, student-designed major, study abroad, teacher certification program.

FACILITIES
Housing: fraternity/sorority housing.

CAMPUS LIFE
Environment: Activities: drama/theater, literary magazine, radio station, student government, student newspaper, student-run film society, television station

ADMISSIONS
Freshman Academic Profile: Average high school GPA 3.4. 25% in top 10% of high school class, 60% in top 25% of high school class, 94% in top 50% of high school class. 84% from public high schools. ACT middle 50% range 21-26. Minimum web-based TOEFL 80. Minimum paper TOEFL 550. **Basis for Candidate Selection:** *Very important factors considered include:* rigor of secondary school record, standardized test scores. *Other factors considered include:* Class rank, application essay, recommendation(s), interview. **Freshman Admission Requirements:** High school diploma is required and GED is accepted. *Academic units recommended:* **Freshman Admission Statistics:** 2,334 applied, 65% admitted, 47% enrolled. **Transfer Admission Requirements:** High school transcript, college transcript(s), Lowest grade transferable C. **General Admission Information:** Application Fee $30. Nonfall registration accepted. Admission may be deferred for a maximum of no limit. Credit and/or placement offered for CEEB Advanced Placement tests.

COSTS AND FINANCIAL AID
Annual in-state tuition $13,625. Annual out-of-state tuition $40,302. Room and board $9,752. Required fees $194. Average book expense $1,048. **Required Forms and Deadlines:** FAFSA. **Notification of Awards:** Applicants will be notified of awards on a rolling basis beginning 5/1. **Types of Aid:** *Need-based scholarships/grants:* Federal Pell, SEOG, state scholarships/grants, private scholarships, the school's own gift aid. *Loans:* Direct Subsidized Stafford, Direct Unsubsidized Stafford, Direct PLUS, Federal Perkins, state loans, college/university loans from institutional funds. **Student Employment:** Federal Work-Study Program available. Institutional employment available. Off-campus job opportunities are excellent. **Financial Aid Statistics:** 72% freshmen, 70% undergrads receive need-based scholarship or grant aid. 72% freshmen, 24% undergrads receive non-need-based scholarship or grant aid. 28% freshmen, 67% undergrads receive need-based self-help aid. 2% freshmen, 1% undergrads receive athletic scholarships. 41% freshmen, 39% undergrads receive any aid. 27% undergrads borrow to pay for school. Average cumulative indebtedness $14,673. **Criteria for awarding institutional aid:** Non-need-based: academics, alumni affiliation, art, athletics, job skills, leadership, minority status, music/drama, state/district residency.

UNIVERSITY OF MICHIGAN—FLINT

303 E. Kearsley St., Flint, MI 48502
Phone: 810-762-3300 • **Financial Aid Phone:** 810-762-3444
E-mail: admissions@umflint.edu • **CEEB Code:** 1853
Fax: 810-762-3272 • **Website:** www.umflint.edu • **ACT Code:** 2063

This public school was founded in 1956. It has a 72-acre campus.

RATINGS
Admissions Selectivity Rating: 76   **Fire Safety Rating:** 97   **Green Rating:** 73

STUDENTS AND FACULTY
Enrollment: 6,677. **Student Body:** 61% female, 39% male, 1% out-of-state, 4% international (42 countries represented). Asian 2%, African American 12%, Caucasian 70%, Hispanic 4%, Native American 1%.
Retention and Graduation: 74% freshmen return for sophomore year. 10% freshmen graduate within 4 years. 36% freshmen graduate within 6 years.
Faculty: Student/faculty ratio 16:1. 287 full-time faculty, 70% hold PhDs, 22% are members of minority groups, 51% are women. 0% of classes are taught by teaching assistants.

ACADEMICS
Degrees: bachelor's, master's. **Classes:** Most classes have 20–29 students. Most lab/discussion sessions have 20–29 students. **Majors with Highest Enrollment:** business administration and management; elementary education and teaching; nursing/registered nurse (rn, asn, bsn, msn). **Special Study Options:** cooperative education program, distance learning, double major, dual enrollment, English as a Second Language (ESL), honors program, independent study, internships, student-designed major, study abroad, teacher certification program. **Honors programs:** 4-yr University Honors Scholar Program 2-yr Junior/Senior University Honors Scholar Program **Combined degree programs:** , BBA/MBA. **Disability Services:** Special programs offered to physically disabled students include note-taking services, reader services, tape recorders, tutors. **Career services:** career/job search classes, career assessment, internships.

FACILITIES
Housing: Coed dorms. 97% of campus accessible to physically disabled. **Special Academic Facilities/Equipment:** Frances Willson Thompson Library **Computers:** 100% of classrooms, 100% of dorms, 100% of libraries, 100% of dining areas, 100% of student union, have wireless network access. Students can register for classes online. Administrative functions (other than registration) can be performed online.

CAMPUS LIFE
Environment: City. **Activities:** Choral groups, concert band, dance, drama/theater, jazz band, literary magazine, music ensembles, musical theater, student government, student newspaper, television station, International Student Organization 99 registered organizations, 7 honor societies, 6 religious organizations. 4 fraternities, 5 sororities. **On-Campus Highlights:** Recreation Center, University Center/Student Union, University Pavilion/Food Court/Bookstore, Resident's Hall, Frances Willson Thompson Library. **Environmental Initiatives:** Recycling and Waste Minimization Energy Conservation and use of biodegradable paper dinning products Protecton of Campus' Natural Resources.

ADMISSIONS
Freshman Academic Profile: Average high school GPA 3.3. 19% in top 10% of high school class, 44% in top 25% of high school class, 79% in top 50% of high school class. 83% from public high schools. SAT Math middle 50% range 408-750. SAT Critical Reading middle 50% range 460-640. SAT Writing middle 50% range 490-565. ACT middle 50% range 19-25. Minimum web-based TOEFL 61. Minimum paper TOEFL 500. **Basis for Candidate Selection:** *Very important factors considered include:* academic GPA, rigor of secondary school record, standardized test scores. *Important factors considered include:* extracurricular activities. *Other factors considered include:* Class rank, application essay, recommendation(s), interview, talent/ability. **Freshman Admission Requirements:** High school diploma is required and GED is accepted. *Academic units required:* 4 English, 3 mathematics, 2 science, 3 social studies. *Academic units recommended:* 4 English, 3 mathematics, 2 science, 3 social studies. **Freshman Admission Statistics:** 2,638 applied, 74% admitted, 32% enrolled. **Transfer Admission Requirements:** High school transcript, college transcript(s), minimum college GPA of 2.0 required. Lowest grade transferable 2. **General Admission Information:** Application Fee $30. Notification on a rolling basis, beginning on or about 12/1. Nonfall registration accepted. Admission may be deferred for a maximum of 1 Year. Credit and/or placement offered for CEEB Advanced Placement tests.

COSTS AND FINANCIAL AID
Annual in-state tuition $9,102. Annual out-of-state tuition $17,754. Room and board $7,506. Required fees $412. Average book expense $1,000. **Required Forms and Deadlines:** FAFSA, institution's own financial aid formInstitution's own financial aid form used in Spring/Summer Sessions only. **Notification of Awards:** Applicants will be notified of awards on a rolling basis beginning 3/15. **Types of Aid:** *Need-based scholarships/grants:* Federal Pell, SEOG, state scholarships/grants, private scholarships, the school's own gift aid. *Loans:* Direct Subsidized Stafford, Direct Unsubsidized Stafford, Direct PLUS, Federal Perkins, state loans. **Student Employment:** Federal Work-Study Program available. Institutional employment available. Off-campus job opportunities are poor. **Financial Aid Statistics:** 65% freshmen, 72% undergrads receive need-based scholarship or grant aid. 57% freshmen, 56% undergrads receive non-need-based scholarship or grant aid. 84% freshmen, 87% undergrads receive need-based self-help aid. 64% freshmen, 70% undergrads receive any aid. 71% undergrads borrow to pay for school. Average cumulative indebtedness $26,899. **Criteria for awarding institutional aid:** Non-need-based: academics, art, leadership, minority status, music/drama.

UNIVERSITY OF MINNESOTA DULUTH

25 Solon Campus Center, Duluth, MN 55812-3000
Phone: 218-726-7171 • **Financial Aid Phone:** 218-726-8000
E-mail: umdadmis@d.umn.edu • **CEEB Code:** 6873
Fax: 218-726-7040 • **Website:** www.d.umn.edu • **ACT Code:** 2157

This public school was founded in 1947. It has a 247-acre campus.

RATINGS
Admissions Selectivity Rating: 76   **Fire Safety Rating:** 89   **Green Rating:** 87

STUDENTS AND FACULTY
Enrollment: 9,422. **Student Body:** 47% female, 53% male, 11% out-of-state, 1% international (42 countries represented). Asian 3%, African American 1%, Caucasian 90%, Hispanic 1%, Native American 1%. **Retention and Graduation:** 81% freshmen return for sophomore year. 16% grads go on to further study within 1 year. **Faculty:** Student/faculty ratio 21:1. 463 full-time faculty, 75% hold PhDs, 19% are members of minority groups, 43% are women.

ACADEMICS
Degrees: bachelor's, master's, post-bachelor's certificate. **Classes:** Most classes have 20–29 students. Most lab/discussion sessions have 10–19 students. **Majors with Highest Enrollment:** biology/biological sciences; business administration and management; elementary education and teaching. **Special Study Options:** Accelerated program, cross-registration, distance learning, double major, dual enrollment, exchange student program (domestic), honors program, independent study, internships, liberal arts/career combination, study abroad, teacher certification program, weekend college. **Honors programs:** The Honors Program offers motivated students who are serious about their intellectual and personal growth a variety of special classes enhanced by cultural events and activities, as well as leadership and research opportunities. **Disability Services:** Special programs offered to physically disabled students include note-taking services, reader services, tape recorders, tutors. **Career services:** alumni services, career/job search classes, career assessment, internships.

FACILITIES
Housing: Coed dorms, special housing for disabled students, men's dorms, women's dorms. 100% of campus accessible to physically disabled. **Special Academic Facilities/Equipment:** Art museum, planetarium, music performance hall, theatre. **Computers:** 100% of classrooms, 100% of libraries, 100% of dining areas, 100% of student union, have wireless network access. Students can register for classes online. Administrative functions (other than registration) can be performed online.

CAMPUS LIFE
Environment: Village. **Activities:** Choral groups, concert band, dance, drama/theater, jazz band, literary magazine, marching band, music ensembles, musical theater, opera, pep band, radio station, student government, student newspaper, student-run film society, symphony orchestra, Campus Ministries, International Student Organization, Model UN. 150 registered organizations, 10 honor societies, 7 religious organizations. 2 fraternities, 2 sororities. **Athletics (Intercollegiate):** *Men:* baseball, basketball, cross-country, football, ice hockey, track/field (outdoor), track/field (indoor). *Women:* basketball, cross-country, ice hockey, soccer, softball, tennis, track/field (outdoor), track/field (indoor), volleyball. **On-Campus Highlights:** Solon Campus Center, Library, Residence Halls, Kirby Student Center Food Court, Sports and Health Center. **Environmental Initiatives:** LEED Stormwater Management Plan Energy Conservation Projects.

ADMISSIONS
Freshman Academic Profile: 16% in top 10% of high school class, 42% in top 25% of high school class, 85% in top 50% of high school class. 94% from public high schools. SAT Math middle 50% range 480-620. SAT Critical Reading middle 50% range 480-590. SAT Writing middle 50% range 460-580. ACT middle 50% range 20-26. Minimum web-based TOEFL 80. Minimum paper TOEFL 550. **Basis for Candidate Selection:** *Very important factors considered include:* Class rank, standardized test scores. *Important factors considered include:* rigor of secondary school record. *Other factors considered include:* application essay, academic GPA, recommendation(s), alumni/ae relation, extracurricular activities, first generation, geographical residence, racial/ethnic status, state residency, talent/ability. **Freshman Admission Requirements:** High school diploma is required and GED is accepted. *Academic units required:* 4 English, 3 mathematics, 3 science, 2 foreign language, 2 social studies, 1 history. *Academic units recommended:* 4 English, 3 mathematics, 3 science, 2 foreign language, 2 social studies, 1 history. **Freshman Admission Statistics:** 7,936 applied, 71% admitted, 37% enrolled. **Transfer Admission Requirements:** High school transcript, college transcript(s), minimum college GPA of 2.0

required. Lowest grade transferable D. **General Admission Information:** Application Fee $35. Regular application deadline 8/1. Notification on a rolling basis, beginning on or about 9/17. Nonfall registration accepted. Admission may be deferred for a maximum of 3 semesters. Credit and/or placement offered for CEEB Advanced Placement tests.

COSTS AND FINANCIAL AID
Annual in-state tuition $8,230. Annual out-of-state tuition $10,230. Room and board $6,078. Required fees $2,030. Average book expense $1,248. **Required Forms and Deadlines:** FAFSA. **Notification of Awards:** Applicants will be notified of awards on or about 3/1. **Types of Aid:** *Need-based scholarships/grants:* Federal Pell, SEOG, state scholarships/grants, private scholarships, the school's own gift aid. *Loans:* Direct Subsidized Stafford, Direct Unsubsidized Stafford, Direct PLUS, Federal Perkins, state loans, college/university loans from institutional funds. **Student Employment:** Federal Work-Study Program available. Institutional employment available. Off-campus job opportunities are excellent. **Financial Aid Statistics:** 100% freshmen, 97% undergrads receive need-based scholarship or grant aid. 25% freshmen, 27% undergrads receive non-need-based scholarship or grant aid. 84% freshmen, 87% undergrads receive need-based self-help aid. 85% freshmen, 81% undergrads receive any aid. 72% undergrads borrow to pay for school. Average cumulative indebtedness $27,921. **Criteria for awarding institutional aid:** Non-need-based: academics, alumni affiliation, art, athletics, leadership, minority status, music/drama, state/district residency.

UNIVERSITY OF MINNESOTA, CROOKSTON

University of Minnesota, Crookston, Crookston, MN 56716-5001
Phone: 218-281-8569 • **Financial Aid Phone:** 218-281-8563
E-mail: UMCinfo@umn.edu
Fax: 218-281-8575 • **Website:** www.crk.umn.edu/ • **ACT Code:** 2129

This public school was founded in 1966. It has a 237-acre campus.

RATINGS
Admissions Selectivity Rating: 71   **Fire Safety Rating:** 98   **Green Rating:** 78

STUDENTS AND FACULTY
Enrollment: 1,802. **Student Body:** 49% female, 51% male, 27% out-of-state, 7% international (17 countries represented). Asian 2%, African American 7%, Caucasian 76%, Hispanic 2%, Native American 1%. **Retention and Graduation:** 73% freshmen return for sophomore year. 31% freshmen graduate within 4 years. 47% freshmen graduate within 6 years. **Faculty:** Student/faculty ratio 19:1. 73 full-time faculty, 45% hold PhDs, 7% are members of minority groups, 47% are women. 0% of classes are taught by teaching assistants.

ACADEMICS
Degrees: bachelor's, certificate. **Classes:** Most classes have 10–19 students. Most lab/discussion sessions have 10–19 students. **Majors with Highest Enrollment:** business administration and management; equestrian/equine studies; natural resources/conservation. **Special Study Options:** cross-registration, distance learning, double major, dual enrollment, English as a Second Language (ESL), honors program, independent study, internships, student-designed major, study abroad, teacher certification program. **Honors programs:** The University of Minnesota, Crookston Honor"s Program was developed to inspire and transform the students" writing, discussion and critical thinking skills that reflect high expectations for academically successful students. Students will be nurtured and challenged to explore ideas, assess values and develop leadership skills. Honors coursework will address the diverse and global atmosphere in which we live. In addition, students in the Honors Program will have the opportunity for various social outings outside of the normal campus experience. ° Designed for academically highly-motivated students who want more than a degree. ° Small class sizes ensure one-on-one time with faculty, who invest in your success. ° Flexible curriculum helps you meet career goals while meeting discipline and honors specific requirements. ° Innovative program structure involves honor courses, student led discussion groups and individual studies in discipline specific courses. ° You will develop and conduct an original scholarly project as a senior to satisfy final program requirements. ° Exposure to culturally-rich experiences will enable you to develop a global perspective and leadership skills. **Disability Services:** Special programs offered to physically disabled students include note-taking services, reader services, tape recorders, tutors. **Career services:** alumni services, career/job search classes, career assessment, internships Career services highlights include Internships that provide experiential learning and on-the-job training for all students.

FACILITIES

Housing: Coed dorms, special housing for disabled students, apartments for single students, Theme Housing. 90% of campus accessible to physically disabled. **Special Academic Facilities/Equipment:** Red River Valley Natural History Area; Northwest Research and Outreach Center; UMC Horse Riding Arena; Valley Technology Park **Computers:** 20% of classrooms, 100% of dorms, 100% of libraries, 75% of dining areas, 100% of student union, 25% of common outdoor areas have wireless network access. Students can register for classes online. Administrative functions (other than registration) can be performed online.

CAMPUS LIFE

Environment: Village. **Activities:** Choral groups, drama/theater, pep band, radio station, student government, Campus Ministries, International Student Organization 38 registered organizations, 1 honor societies, 2 religious organizations. 1 fraternities, 1 sororities. **Athletics (Intercollegiate):** *Men:* baseball, basketball, football, golf, ice hockey. *Women:* basketball, equestrian sports, golf, soccer, softball, tennis, volleyball. **On-Campus Highlights:** Sargeant Student Center, University Teaching and Outreach Center, Sports Center, Bergland Laboratory, Centennial Hall Student Apartments, Campus Mall Dairy Barns Kiehle Auditorium. **Environmental Initiatives:** The 2008-09 Crookston Student Association committed campus sustainability efforts; formation of Crookston Students for Sustainable Development (CSSD), new residence hall LEED certified, to increased recycling on campus, passage of Green Fee to fund student sustainability assistants. January 8, 2008, President Robert Bruininks signed ACUPCC on behalf of U of MN; subsequently the Crookston campus completed a Greenhouse Gas Inventory and approved an Action Plan for Climate Neutrality and Sustainability. Crookston campus Mission-Vision-Core Values states: "The University of Minnesota, Crookston serving as a regional hub for. innovation, entrepreneurism, and regional sustainability." As part of that implementation, Chancellor Charles Casey established Center for Sustainability on 1 July 2009.

ADMISSIONS

Freshman Academic Profile: Average high school GPA 3.2. 11% in top 10% of high school class, 37% in top 25% of high school class, 71% in top 50% of high school class. SAT Math middle 50% range 460-560. SAT Critical Reading middle 50% range 450-560. SAT Writing middle 50% range 440-510. ACT middle 50% range 20-25. Minimum web-based TOEFL 68. Minimum paper TOEFL 520. **Basis for Candidate Selection:** *Very important factors considered include:* Class rank, academic GPA, rigor of secondary school record, standardized test scores. *Other factors considered include:* application essay, recommendation(s). **Freshman Admission Requirements:** High school diploma is required and GED is accepted. *Academic units required:* 4 English, 3 mathematics, 3 science, (2 science labs), 3 social studies. *Academic units recommended:* 4 English, 3 mathematics, 3 science, (2 science labs), 3 social studies. **Freshman Admission Statistics:** 650 applied, 73% admitted, 51% enrolled. **Transfer Admission Requirements:** college transcript(s), minimum college GPA of 2.0 required. Lowest grade transferable D. **General Admission Information:** Application Fee $30. Notification on a rolling basis, beginning on or about 9/1. Nonfall registration accepted. Admission may be deferred for a maximum of 1 year. Credit and/or placement offered for CEEB Advanced Placement tests.

COSTS AND FINANCIAL AID

Annual in-state tuition $10,034. Annual out-of-state tuition $10,034. Room and board $7,018. Required fees $1,402. Average book expense $1,000. **Required Forms and Deadlines:** FAFSA. **Notification of Awards:** Applicants will be notified of awards on a rolling basis beginning 3/1. **Types of Aid:** *Need-based scholarships/grants:* Federal Pell, SEOG, state scholarships/grants, private scholarships, the school's own gift aid, Federal Academic Competitiveness Grant and SMART Grant. *Loans:* Direct Subsidized Stafford, Direct Unsubsidized Stafford, Direct PLUS, Federal Perkins, state loans, Private loans. **Student Employment:** Federal Work-Study Program available. Institutional employment available. Highest amount earned per year from on-campus jobs $2,000. Off-campus job opportunities are fair. **Financial Aid Statistics:** 93% freshmen, 90% undergrads receive need-based scholarship or grant aid. 18% freshmen, 10% undergrads receive non-need-based scholarship or grant aid. 88% freshmen, 90% undergrads receive need-based self-help aid. 74% freshmen, 70% undergrads receive any aid. 73% undergrads borrow to pay for school. Average cumulative indebtedness $27,608. **Criteria for awarding institutional aid:** Non-need-based: academics, alumni affiliation, athletics, leadership, minority status, music/drama, state/district residency.

UNIVERSITY OF MINNESOTA, MORRIS

600 E 4th St, Morris, MN 56267
Phone: 320-589-6035 • **Financial Aid Phone:** 800-992-8863
E-mail: admissions@morris.umn.edu • **CEEB Code:** 6890
Fax: 320-589-6051 • **Website:** www.morris.umn.edu • **ACT Code:** 2155

This public school was founded in 1959. It has a 130-acre campus.

RATINGS

Admissions Selectivity Rating: 87   **Fire Safety Rating:** 99   **Green Rating:** 95

STUDENTS AND FACULTY

Enrollment: 1,788. **Student Body:** 54% female, 46% male, 10% out-of-state, 10% international (16 countries represented). Asian 3%, African American 2%, Caucasian 67%, Hispanic 2%, Native American 6%.
Retention and Graduation: 47% freshmen graduate within 4 years. 48% grads go on to further study within 1 year. 30% grads pursue arts and sciences degrees. 11% grads pursue law degrees. 3% grads pursue business degrees. 4% grads pursue medical degrees. **Faculty:** Student/faculty ratio 15:1. 118 full-time faculty, 81% hold PhDs, 8% are members of minority groups, 41% are women. 0% of classes are taught by teaching assistants.

ACADEMICS

Degrees: bachelor's, certificate. **Classes:** Most classes have 10–19 students. Most lab/discussion sessions have 10–19 students. **Majors with Highest Enrollment:** biology; elementary education and teaching; psychology. **Special Study Options:** Accelerated program, cooperative education program, distance learning, double major, exchange student program (domestic), honors program, independent study, internships, student-designed major, study abroad, teacher certification program. **Honors programs:** The purpose of the Honors Program is to provide a distinctive, academically challenging, intellectual experience that amplifies and complements the liberal arts mission of UMM for motivated and high-achieving students. It does this by relying upon an interdisciplinary curriculum that is team-taught by UMM's finest faculty. The program consists of a core course, "Traditions in Human Thought." This course explores significant works from history, literature, philosophy, and science from an interdiscplinary perspective. Following the core course, students choose from a variety of interdisciplinary honors courses, participate in service learning and volunteer programs, and complete a senior honors project. **Disability Services:** Special programs offered to physically disabled students include note-taking services, reader services, tape recorders, tutors. **Career services:** alumni services, career/job search classes, career assessment, internships Career services highlights include The Undergraduate Research Opportunities Program (UROP) is a competitive, merit-based program that provides student stipends and expense allowances for students to partner with a faculty member on research, scholarly, or creative projects in laboratories, studios, libraries, and field sites. Students develop detailed knowledge of research methods and may choose to work with faculty members from UMM or from other University of Minnesota campuses, thus giving students access to the University's wide range of faculty and research facilities.

FACILITIES

Housing: Coed dorms, special housing for disabled students, men's dorms, women's dorms, apartments for single students. 70% of campus accessible to physically disabled. **Special Academic Facilities/Equipment:** HFA Art Gallery, conservatory, observatory **Computers:** Students can register for classes online. Administrative functions (other than registration) can be performed online.

CAMPUS LIFE

Environment: Rural. **Activities:** Choral groups, concert band, dance, drama/theater, jazz band, literary magazine, music ensembles, musical theater, radio station, student government, student newspaper, symphony orchestra, television station 90 registered organizations, 5 honor societies, 12 religious organizations. **Athletics (Intercollegiate):** *Men:* baseball, basketball, football, golf, tennis, track/field (outdoor), track/field (indoor). *Women:* basketball, cross-country, diving, golf, soccer, softball, swimming, tennis, track/field (outdoor), track/field (indoor), volleyball. **On-Campus Highlights:** Student Center — KUMM, cafe, Louis' Lower Level, Regional Fitness Center — Outdoor Center, pools, Science Center — completed '02, Humanities Fine Arts Center — gallery, recitals, The Mall — outdoor recreation area. **Environmental Initiatives:** Morris is actively working to become a sustainable and low-carbon community, and renewable energy research and demonstration is a big part of that effort. Morris receives power from a 1.65 MW University of Minnesota wind turbine. Another large turbine was installed in spring 2011. We have an on-campus biomass gasification research and demonstration platform. We have solar thermal and solar PV projects on campus. And we have completed a multi-million dollar energy service contract to retrofit the campus for conservation. Morris has a commitment to developing healthy, local and sustainable food systems. We are a founding partner in Pride of the Prairie. Our student are actively engaged in food projects and research on campus, including a small organic garden. Morris is currently engaged in a new project called the Morris Healthy Eating initiative, a community-wide program working to improve access and knowledge about healthy foods. Morris supports the evolving campus sustainability movement and sustainability reporting initiatives. We are members of ACUPCC, AASHE STARS. Campus leaders, including students, staff, faculty and administrators are involved in helping to create this vision for a sustainable community, set goals, and drive change.

ADMISSIONS

Freshman Academic Profile: 32% in top 10% of high school class, 60% in top 25% of high school class, 92% in top 50% of high school class. 92% from public high schools. SAT Math middle 50% range 540-670. SAT Critical Reading middle 50% range 510-650. SAT Writing middle 50% range 560-620. ACT middle 50% range 23-28. Minimum web-based TOEFL 79. Minimum paper TOEFL 550. **Basis for Candidate Selection:** *Very important factors considered include:* Class rank, rigor of secondary school record, standardized test scores. *Important factors considered include:* application essay, recommendation(s), character/personal qualities, extracurricular activities, talent/ability, volunteer work, work experience. *Other factors considered include:* alumni/ae relation, interview, racial/ethnic status. **Freshman Admission Requirements:** High school diploma is required and GED is accepted. *Academic units required:* 4 English, 3 mathematics, 3 science, (2 science labs), 2 foreign language, 4 social studies, 4 history. *Academic units recommended:* 4 English, 3 mathematics, 3 science, (2 science labs), 2 foreign language, 4 social studies, 4 history. **Freshman Admission Statistics:** 2,349 applied, 60% admitted, 29% enrolled. **Transfer Admission Requirements:** college transcript(s), essay or personal statement, statement of good standing from prior institution(s). Minimum college CPA of 2.5 required. Lowest grade transferable D. **General Admission Information:** Application Fee $35. Regular application deadline 3/15. Regular notification 4/1. Notification on a rolling basis, beginning on or about 9/1. Non-fall registration accepted. Admission may be deferred for a maximum of 1 year. Credit and/or placement offered for CEEB Advanced Placement tests.

COSTS AND FINANCIAL AID

Room and board Required fees Average book expense **Required Forms and Deadlines:** FAFSA. **Notification of Awards:** Applicants will be notified of awards on a rolling basis beginning 3/15. **Types of Aid.** *Need based scholarships/grants:* Federal Pell, SEOG, state scholarships/grants, private scholarships, the school's own gift aid. *Loans:* Direct Subsidized Stafford, Direct Unsubsidized Stafford, Direct PLUS, Federal Perkins, state loans. **Student Employment:** Federal Work-Study Program available. Institutional employment available. Highest amount earned per year from on-campus jobs $2,343. Off-campus job opportunities are good. **Financial Aid Statistics:** 94% freshmen, 95% undergrads receive need-based scholarship or grant aid. 33% freshmen, 31% undergrads receive non-need-based scholarship or grant aid. 76% freshmen, 80% undergrads receive need-based self-help aid. 91% freshmen, 93% undergrads receive any aid. 66% undergrads borrow to pay for school. Average cumulative indebtedness $25,124. **Criteria for awarding institutional aid:** Non-need-based: academics, alumni affiliation, leadership, minority status, music/drama, state/district residency.

UNIVERSITY OF MINNESOTA—TWIN CITIES

240 Williamson Hall, Minneapolis, MN 55455-0213
Phone: 612-625-2008 • **Financial Aid Phone:** 612-624-1111
CEEB Code: 6874
Fax: 612-626-1693 • **Website:** www.umn.edu • **ACT Code:** 2156

This public school was founded in 1851. It has a 2000-acre campus.

RATINGS
Admissions Selectivity Rating: 93 **Fire Safety Rating:** 84 **Green Rating:** 97

STUDENTS AND FACULTY
Enrollment: 30,375. **Student Body:** 51% female, 49% male, 26% out-of-state, 8% international (136 countries represented). Asian 8%, African American 4%, Caucasian 72%, Hispanic 3%.
Retention and Graduation: 91% freshmen return for sophomore year. 50% freshmen graduate within 4 years. 73% freshmen graduate within 6 years.

Faculty: 1906 full-time faculty, 79% hold PhDs, 17% are members of minority groups, 40% are women.

ACADEMICS
Degrees: bachelor's, certificate, diploma, master's, post-bachelor's certificate, post-master's certificate. **Classes:** Most classes have 20–29 students. Most lab/discussion sessions have 10–19 students. **Majors with Highest Enrollment:** biology/biological sciences; journalism; psychology. **Special Study Options:** Accelerated program, cooperative education program, cross-registration, distance learning, double major, dual enrollment, English as a Second Language (ESL), exchange student program (domestic), external degree program, honors program, independent study, internships, liberal arts/career combination, student-designed major, study abroad, teacher certification program, Minors offered in most majors. Students may register in the College of Continuing Education and take courses in any division for B.A. or B.S. degrees. Programs in Foreign Service and pre-social work. Phi Beta Kappa. Pass/fail grading option. Internships. Qualified undergraduates may take graduate level classes. Pre-professional programs in law, medicine, veterinary science, pharmacy, dentistry, architecture, biology, education, journalism, landscape architecture, management, medical technology, mortuary science, nursing, and occupational/physical therapy. **Honors programs:** Honors, Undergraduate Research Opportunities Program **Disability Services:** Special programs offered to physically disabled students include note-taking services, reader services, tape recorders, tutors. **Career services:** Alumni network, alumni services, career/job search classes, career assessment, internships, regional alumni. Career services highlights include Very unique experiential classes described below. Intern program described below. New business hatchery in which 17 undergraduate students receive pro bono legal support, advice from entrepreneurs-in-residence and access to seed funding.

FACILITIES
Housing: Coed dorms, special housing for disabled students, special housing for international students, fraternity/sorority housing, apartments for married students, cooperative housing, apartments for single students, Honors housing, residential college (academic programs in residence). Eight conventional residence halls, plus three new apartment style residence halls. Housing application, $25 non-refundable residence hall application fee, and $100 residence hall advance payment (refundable), required by May 1 for guaranteed freshman housing. Off-campus housing office provides off-campus housing listings. **Special Academic Facilities/Equipment:** Frederick R. Weisman Art Museum, Bell Museum of Natural History, Ted Mann Concert Hall, Recreational Sports Center, Civil Engineering Building, Basic Sciences/Biomedical Engineering Building, Coffman Memorial Union, West Bank Arts Quarter, Goldstein Gallery, Arboretum. **Computers:** Students can register for classes online. Administrative functions (other than registration) can be performed online.

CAMPUS LIFE
Environment: Metropolis. **Activities:** Choral groups, concert band, dance, drama/theater, jazz band, literary magazine, marching band, music ensembles, musical theater, opera, pep band, radio station, student government, student newspaper, student-run film society, symphony orchestra, television station, International Student Organization 600 registered organizations, 10 religious organizations. 22 fraternities, 12 sororities. **Athletics (Intercollegiate):** *Men:* baseball, basketball, cross-country, diving, football, golf, gymnastics, ice hockey, swimming, tennis, track/field (outdoor), track/field (indoor), wrestling. *Women:* basketball, cheerleading, cross-country, diving, golf, gymnastics, ice hockey, soccer, softball, swimming, tennis, track/field (outdoor), track/field (indoor), volleyball. **On-Campus Highlights:** Weisman Art Museum, McNamara Alumni Center, TCF Bank Stadium, Goldstein Gallery, Northrup Memorial Auditorium, Coffman Memorial Union, Mariucci Arena, University Theater, Rarig Center. **Environmental Initiatives:** It All Adds Up Energy Conservation Campaign was kicked off by President Bruninks and Vice President O'Brien on Beautiful U Day in April 2009. Through the campaign the University set a 5% energy use reduction goal by end of fiscal year 2010 " targeting $2.25 Million and 25,000 tons CO2 emissions. Over 10,000 individuals pledged to take action to reduce energy use. Student groups joined together as the Energy Efficiency Student Alliance to work with staff to audit offices and help engage building occupants through building blitzes during recommissioning. The campus achieved the energy reduction goal three months early. The campaign has set a goal of achieving another 5% energy reduction during fisacl year 2011 and a goal of diverting an additional 5% of the waste stream by 2012. More info: http://www1.umn.edu/italladdsup/index.php Welcome Week coordinators worked with staff and students to integrate sustainability awareness into the events, workshops and presentations for 5000 incoming freshmen. Fall 2010 Welcome Week events included: 1. Encouraging reducing waste by providing reusable water containers and zero waste lunches. 2. Promoting alternative transportation through use of the campus transit connector during events and providing bike courtesy/safety info. 3. Encouraging behavior changes through awareness presentations on energy use and campus sustainability, energy pledge booths and student workshop on living green on campus. 4. Increasing awareness of

research, education and engagement opportunities through an open house at the Institute on the Environment which included the Sustainability Minor, and numerous student groups. Education and Research Opportunities on campus: The Sustainability Minor - one of the first Sustainability Minor programs in the country (open to all majors) has grown to over 300 students. The Sustainability minor capstone class offers opportunities to work with staff on campus on real operational problems. Student teams worked on behavior change research to support energy, transportation and recycling departments and also developed an office guide for sustainability. An internship class was also formed to provide opportunities for in depth experience in sustainability projects on campus and with partnerships off campus. Students applied for and were awarded grants through CFANS to work on land care and other projects to green the St. Paul campus - partnering with staff to evaluate the projects. Student Engineers without Borders were funded $50,000 through the Institute on the Environment. Education, Research and Outreach are key guiding principles in the Sustainability policy and are included in the Sustainability Goals for the University System. http://sustainabilitystudies.umn.edu/ http://www.environment.umn.edu/

ADMISSIONS

Freshman Academic Profile: 44% in top 10% of high school class, 80% in top 25% of high school class, 100% in top 50% of high school class. SAT Math middle 50% range 620-740. SAT Critical Reading middle 50% range 540-690. SAT Writing middle 50% range 560-670. ACT middle 50% range 25-30. Minimum paper TOEFL 550. **Basis for Candidate Selection:** *Very important factors considered include:* Class rank, academic GPA, rigor of secondary school record, standardized test scores. *Other factors considered include:* alumni/ae relation, character/personal qualities, extracurricular activities, first generation, geographical residence, racial/ethnic status, talent/ability, volunteer work, work experience. **Freshman Admission Requirements:** High school diploma is required and GED is accepted. *Academic units required:* 4 English, 3 mathematics, 3 science, 2 foreign language, 3 social studies, 1 history. *Academic units recommended:* 4 English, 3 mathematics, 3 science, 2 foreign language, 3 social studies, 1 history. **Freshman Admission Statistics:** 38,174 applied, 50% admitted, 29% enrolled. **Transfer Admission Requirements:** college transcript(s), minimum college GPA of 2.0 required. Lowest grade transferable D. **General Admission Information:** Application Fee $45. Nonfall registration accepted. Admission may be deferred for a maximum of 1 Year. Neither credit nor placement offered for CEEB Advanced Placement tests.

COSTS AND FINANCIAL AID

Required Forms and Deadlines: FAFSA, institution's own financial aid form. **Notification of Awards:** Applicants will be notified of awards on a rolling basis beginning 2/15. **Types of Aid:** *Need-based scholarships/grants:* Federal Pell, SEOG, state scholarships/grants, private scholarships, the school's own gift aid, Federal Nursing Scholarships. *Loans:* Direct Subsidized Stafford, Direct Unsubsidized Stafford, Direct PLUS, Federal Perkins, Federal Nursing, state loans, college/university loans from institutional funds. **Student Employment:** Federal Work-Study Program available. Institutional employment available. **Financial Aid Statistics:** 83% freshmen, 86% undergrads receive need-based scholarship or grant aid. 14% freshmen, 11% undergrads receive non-need-based scholarship or grant aid. 88% freshmen, 88% undergrads receive need-based self-help aid. 63% undergrads borrow to pay for school. Average cumulative indebtedness $29,702. **Criteria for awarding institutional aid:** Non-need-based: academics, art, athletics, job skills, leadership, minority status, music/drama, state/district residency.

UNIVERSITY OF MISSISSIPPI

145 Martindale, University, MS 38677
Phone: 662-915-7226 • **Financial Aid Phone:** 800-891-4596
E-mail: admissions@olemiss.edu • **CEEB Code:** 1840
Fax: 662-915-5869 • **Website:** www.olemiss.edu • **ACT Code:** 2250

This public school was founded in 1844. It has a 2500-acre campus.

RATINGS
Admissions Selectivity Rating: 71   **Fire Safety Rating:** 60*   **Green Rating:** 84

STUDENTS AND FACULTY
Enrollment: 15,791. **Student Body:** 55% female, 45% male, 37% out-of-state, 1% international (countries represented). Asian 2%, African American 17%, Caucasian 76%, Hispanic 3%.

Retention and Graduation: 81% freshmen return for sophomore year. 37% freshmen graduate within 4 years. 58% freshmen graduate within 6 years. **Faculty:** Student/faculty ratio 19:1. 798 full-time faculty, 82% hold PhDs, 18% are members of minority groups, 42% are women.

ACADEMICS
Degrees: bachelor's, certificate, master's. **Classes:** Most classes have 10–19 students. Most lab/discussion sessions have 20–29 students. **Majors with Highest Enrollment:** accounting; elementary education and teaching; marketing/marketing management. **Special Study Options:** Accelerated program, cooperative education program, distance learning, double major, dual enrollment, English as a Second Language (ESL), honors program, independent study, internships, study abroad, teacher certification program. **Honors programs:** Sally McDonnell-Barksdale Honors College **Disability Services:** Special programs offered to physically disabled students include note-taking services, reader services, tape recorders.

FACILITIES
Housing: men's dorms, special housing for international students, women's dorms, fraternity/sorority housing, apartments for married students, apartments for single students, Graduate/Older Students, intensive study floors, special interest, substance free, environmental interest housing available. **Special Academic Facilities/Equipment:** Sally McDonnell-Barksdale Honors College, Croft Institute for International Studies, National Food Service Management Institute, Mississippi Center for Supercomputing Research,Art and archaeology museums, women's studies center, Center for Study of Southern Culture,William Faulkner home, Marine Minerals Research Institute, National Center for Physical Acoustics, National Center for Natural Products Research, Biological Field Station, Barksdale Reading Institute, Ford Center for the Performing Arts, William Winter Institutue for Racial Reconciliation, Paris-Yates Chapel, Trent Lott Leadership Institute, Living Blues Archive, Student Media Center **Computers:** 30% of classrooms, 100% of dorms, 100% of libraries, 80% of dining areas, 100% of student union, 30% of common outdoor areas have wireless network access. Students can register for classes online. Administrative functions (other than registration) can be performed online.

CAMPUS LIFE
Environment: Village. **Activities:** Choral groups, concert band, dance, drama/theater, jazz band, marching band, music ensembles, musical theater, opera, pep band, radio station, student government, student newspaper, symphony orchestra, television station, yearbook, Campus Ministries, International Student Organization 250 registered organizations, 25 honor societies, 21 religious organizations. 18 fraternities, 13 sororities. **Athletics (Intercollegiate):** *Men:* baseball, basketball, cheerleading, cross-country, football, golf, tennis, track/field (outdoor), track/field (indoor). *Women:* basketball, cheerleading, cross-country, golf, riflery, soccer, softball, tennis, track/field (outdoor), track/field (indoor), volleyball. **On-Campus Highlights:** Lyceum, Gertrude C. Ford Center for the Performing Arts, Intramural Sports Practice Facility, Student Union, Business School, INFORMATION SESSIONS at 9 am, 11 am, 1pm, 2 pm; TOURS-10 am, and 3 pm (Please register by phone, email, or online); RED/BLUE PREVIEWS-select Saturdays 8:30-1:00 pm (Register online); Fall and Spring Visit Days-8 am to noon (No advanced registration required): **Environmental Initiatives:** UM is installing SmartMeters on the majority of campus buildings. All new construction on campus must be built to meet LEED Silver certification. UM is in the process of major improvements to its recycling infrastructure.

ADMISSIONS
Freshman Academic Profile: Average high school GPA 3.4. 25% in top 10% of high school class, 47% in top 25% of high school class, 76% in top 50% of high school class. SAT Math middle 50% range 470-590. SAT Critical Reading middle 50% range 460-590. ACT middle 50% range 20-27. Minimum paper TOEFL 550. **Basis for Candidate Selection:** *Very important factors considered include:* academic GPA, rigor of secondary school record. *Important factors considered include:* Class rank, standardized test scores. *Other factors considered include:* alumni/ae relation, state residency, talent/ability. **Freshman Admission Requirements:** High school diploma is required and GED is accepted. *Academic units required:* 4 English, 3 mathematics, 3 science, (2 science labs), 1 foreign language, 1 social studies, 2 history, 1 academic electives. *Academic units recommended:* 4 English, 3 mathematics, 3 science, (2 science labs), 1 foreign language, 1 social studies, 2 history, 1 academic electives. **Freshman Admission Statistics:** 13,321 applied, 79% admitted, 34% enrolled. **Transfer Admission Requirements:** college transcript(s), minimum college GPA of 2.0 required. Lowest grade transferable D. **General Admission Information:** Application Fee $25. Regular application deadline 7/20. Notification on a rolling basis, beginning on or about 10/1. Nonfall registration accepted. Credit offered for CEEB Advanced Placement tests.

COSTS AND FINANCIAL AID
Required Forms and Deadlines: FAFSA. **Notification of Awards:** Applicants will be notified of awards on a rolling basis beginning 4/1. **Types of Aid:**

Need-based scholarships/grants: Federal Pell, SEOG, state scholarships/grants, private scholarships, the school's own gift aid. *Loans:* Subsidized Stafford, Unsubsidized Stafford, PLUS, Federal Perkins, college/university loans from institutional funds. **Student Employment:** Federal Work-Study Program available. Institutional employment available. Off-campus job opportunities are fair. **Financial Aid Statistics:** 85% freshmen, 85% undergrads receive need-based scholarship or grant aid. 14% freshmen, 9% undergrads receive non-need-based scholarship or grant aid. 72% freshmen, 77% undergrads receive need-based self-help aid. 1% freshmen, 1% undergrads receive athletic scholarships. 81% freshmen, 83% undergrads receive any aid. 47% undergrads borrow to pay for school. Average cumulative indebtedness $23,986. **Criteria for awarding institutional aid:** Non-need-based: academics, alumni affiliation, art, athletics, leadership, minority status, music/drama, state/district residency.

UNIVERSITY OF MISSOURI

230 Jesse Hall, Columbia, MO 65211
Phone: 573-882-7786 • **Financial Aid Phone:** 573-882-7506
E-mail: MU4U@missouri.edu
Fax: 573-882-7887 • **Website:** www.missouri.edu • **ACT Code:** 2382

This public school was founded in 1839. It has a 1372-acre campus.

RATINGS
Admissions Selectivity Rating: 75   **Fire Safety Rating:** 88   **Green Rating:** 91

STUDENTS AND FACULTY
Enrollment: 26,590. **Student Body:** 52% female, 48% male, 21% out-of-state, 2% international (120 countries represented). Asian 2%, African American 8%, Caucasian 80%, Hispanic 3%.
Retention and Graduation: 85% freshmen return for sophomore year. **Faculty:** Student/faculty ratio 20:1. 1369 full-time faculty, 93% hold PhDs, 19% are members of minority groups, 38% are women.

ACADEMICS
Degrees: bachelor's, doctoral, master's, post-master's certificate. **Classes:** Most classes have 10–19 students. Most lab/discussion sessions have 20–29 students. **Majors with Highest Enrollment:** biological and biomedical sciences, other, business/commerce. **Special Study Options:** Accelerated program, cooperative education program, cross-registration, distance learning, double major, dual enrollment, English as a Second Language (ESL), exchange student program (domestic), external degree program, honors program, independent study, internships, student-designed major, study abroad, teacher certification program, Evening College, MU Direct. **Honors programs:** Honors College **Combined degree programs:** BA/MA, Accounting. **Disability Services:** Special programs offered to physically disabled students include note-taking services, reader services, tape recorders, tutors. **Career services:** Alumni network, alumni services, career/job search classes, career assessment, internships, regional **alumni. Career services highlights include Our new recruitment** Website: www.HireMizzouGrads.com.

FACILITIES
Housing: Coed dorms, men's dorms, women's dorms, fraternity/sorority housing, apartments for married students, Freshmen Interest Groups and unique learning communities allow students to live in coed residence halls and share in exploring the same academic area of interest. 100% of campus accessible to physically disabled. **Special Academic Facilities/Equipment:** Life Sciences Center for Research TigerPlace- licensed care facility Department of Nursing James B Nutter Family Information Commons - Ellis Library Museum of Anthropology Museum of Art and Archeology World's most powerful univesity research reactor for Nuclear Medicine one of 15 European Union Centers on college campuses. **Computers:** 100% of classrooms, 10% of dorms, 100% of libraries, 100% of dining areas, 100% of student union, 10% of common outdoor areas have wireless network access. Students can register for classes online. Administrative functions (other than registration) can be performed online.

CAMPUS LIFE
Environment: City. **Activities:** Choral groups, concert band, dance, drama/theater, jazz band, literary magazine, marching band, music ensembles, musical theater, opera, pep band, radio station, student government, student newspaper, student-run film society, symphony orchestra, television station, yearbook, Campus Ministries, International Student Organization, Model UN. 598 registered

organizations, 25 honor societies, 47 religious organizations. 32 fraternities, 19 sororities. **Athletics (Intercollegiate):** *Men:* baseball, basketball, cross-country, diving, football, golf, swimming, track/field (outdoor), track/field (indoor), wrestling. *Women:* basketball, cheerleading, cross-country, diving, golf, gymnastics, soccer, softball, swimming, tennis, track/field (outdoor), track/field (indoor), volleyball. **On-Campus Highlights:** Student Recreation Center - amazing recr, Mizzou Arena - home of Tiger Basketball, Memorial Stadium - home of Tiger Football, Jesse Hall - home to administ and various concerts, Life Sciences Center -home of research a, Renovation and construction on campus- Life Sciences Center, Mizzou Arena, James B Nutter Family Infomration Center in Ellis Library, Virginia Avenue Housing and Dining Expansion. **Environmental Initiatives:** Signatory to ACUPCC climate change commitment. Recent purchase of 100% biomass boiler that will reduce greenhouse gas emissions by up to 30% by 2016. Major commitment to energy conservation for the past 20 years, currently saves MU over six million dollars annually. We have an ongoing goal to save an additional 1% cost each year.

ADMISSIONS
Freshman Academic Profile: 26% in top 10% of high school class, 56% in top 25% of high school class, 86% in top 50% of high school class. SAT Math middle 50% range 530-650. SAT Critical Reading middle 50% range 510-640. ACT middle 50% range 23-28. Minimum web-based TOEFL 61. Minimum paper TOEFL 500. **Basis for Candidate Selection:** *Very important factors considered include:* Class rank, academic GPA, standardized test scores. *Important factors considered include:* rigor of secondary school record. *Other factors considered include:* application essay, recommendation(s), first generation, level of applicant's interest, racial/ethnic status, talent/ability, volunteer work, work experience. **Freshman Admission Requirements:** High school diploma is required and GED is accepted. *Academic units required:* 4 English, 4 mathematics, 3 science, (1 science labs), 2 foreign language, 3 social studies, 1 fine arts. *Academic units recommended:* 4 English, 4 mathematics, 3 science, (1 science labs), 2 foreign language, 3 social studies, 1 fine arts **Freshman Admission Statistics:** 20,564 applied, 81% admitted, 39% enrolled. **Transfer Admission Requirements:** college transcript(s), minimum college GPA of 2.5 required. **General Admission Information:** Application Fee $45. Notification on a rolling basis, beginning on or about 1/15. Nonfall registration accepted. Admission may be deferred for a maximum of 1 year. Credit and/or placement offered for CEEB Advanced Placement tests.

COSTS AND FINANCIAL AID
Annual in-state tuition $8,082. Annual out-of-state tuition $22,101. Room and board $8,944. Required fees $1,175. Average book expense $930. **Required Forms and Deadlines:** FAFSA. **Notification of Awards:** Applicants will be notified of awards on a rolling basis beginning 4/1. **Types of Aid:** *Need-based scholarships/grants:* Federal Pell, SEOG, state scholarships/grants, private scholarships, the school's own gift aid, outside. *Loans:* Direct Subsidized Stafford, Direct Unsubsidized Stafford, Direct PLUS, PLUS, Federal Perkins, Federal Nursing, state loans, college/university loans from institutional funds, outside or 3rd party. **Student Employment:** Federal Work-Study Program available. Institutional employment available. Off-campus job opportunities are excellent. **Financial Aid Statistics:** 87% freshmen, 81% undergrads receive need-based scholarship or grant aid. 6% freshmen, 4% undergrads receive non-need-based scholarship or grant aid. 77% freshmen, 80% undergrads receive need-based self-help aid. 3% freshmen, 4% undergrads receive athletic scholarships. 59% undergrads borrow to pay for school. Average cumulative indebtedness $23,588. **Criteria for awarding institutional aid:** Non-need-based: academics, alumni affiliation, art, athletics, leadership, minority status, music/drama, state/district residency.

UNIVERSITY OF MISSOURI—KANSAS CITY

5100 Rockhill Road, Kansas City, mo 64114
Phone: 816-235-1111 • **Financial Aid Phone:** 816-235-1154
E-mail: admit@umkc.edu • **CEEB Code:** 6872
Fax: 816-235-5544 • **Website:** www.umkc.edu • **ACT Code:** 2380

This private school was founded in 1929. It has a 191-acre campus.

RATINGS
Admissions Selectivity Rating: 85   **Fire Safety Rating:** 74   **Green Rating:** 96

STUDENTS AND FACULTY
Enrollment: 8,447. **Student Body:** 58% female, 42% male, 22% out-of-state, 4% international (61 countries represented). Asian 6%, African American 17%, Caucasian 58%, Hispanic 6%.
Retention and Graduation: 69% freshmen return for sophomore year. 22% freshmen graduate within 4 years. 49% freshmen graduate within 6 years.

Faculty: Student/faculty ratio 13:1. 759 full-time faculty, 85% hold PhDs, 22% are members of minority groups, 45% are women. 0% of classes are taught by teaching assistants.

ACADEMICS
Degrees: bachelor's, master's, post-master's certificate. **Classes:** Most classes have 10–19 students. Most lab/discussion sessions have 10–19 students. **Special Study Options:** Accelerated program, distance learning, double major, dual enrollment, English as a Second Language (ESL), honors program, independent study, internships, liberal arts/career combination, student-designed major, study abroad, teacher certification program. **Honors programs:** UMKC Honors Program **Combined degree programs:** BA/MD, BA/JD, BA/DDS, BLA/MD, BA/MPA, BBA/MBA. **Disability Services:** Special programs offered to physically disabled students include note-taking services, reader services, tape recorders, tutors. **Career services:** Alumni network, alumni services, career/job search classes, career assessment, internships Career services highlights include Cooperative Learning Programs.

FACILITIES
Housing: Coed dorms, special housing for disabled students, fraternity/sorority housing, apartments for married students, apartments for single students, University owned houses. 98% of campus accessible to physically disabled. **Special Academic Facilities/Equipment:** Art gallery, professional theater, geosciences museums, language lab, observatory. **Computers:** 90% of classrooms, 100% of dorms, 100% of libraries, 100% of dining areas, 100% of student union, have wireless network access. Students can register for classes online. Administrative functions (other than registration) can be performed online.

CAMPUS LIFE
Environment: Metropolis. **Activities:** Choral groups, concert band, dance, drama/theater, jazz band, literary magazine, music ensembles, musical theater, opera, pep band, student government, student newspaper, symphony orchestra, Campus Ministries, International Student Organization, Model UN. 200 registered organizations, 32 honor societies, 13 religious organizations. 6 fraternities, 7 sororities. **Athletics (Intercollegiate):** *Men:* basketball, cheerleading, cross-country, golf, riflery, soccer, tennis, track/field (outdoor). *Women:* basketball, cheerleading, cross-country, golf, riflery, softball, tennis, track/field (outdoor), volleyball. **On-Campus Highlights:** Muddy's Coffee Shop, Nelson Atkins Museum, Sweeney Recreation Center, Minsky's restaurant, Planet Sub restaurant. **Environmental Initiatives:** Recycling Energy Management Building Design

ADMISSIONS
Freshman Academic Profile: Average high school GPA 3.3. 28% in top 10% of high school class, 54% in top 25% of high school class, 81% in top 50% of high school class. SAT Math middle 50% range 520-700. SAT Critical Reading middle 50% range 530-680. ACT middle 50% range 20-27. Minimum web-based TOEFL 61. Minimum paper TOEFL 500. **Basis for Candidate Selection:** *Very important factors considered include:* Class rank, academic GPA, rigor of secondary school record, standardized test scores. *Other factors considered include:* application essay, recommendation(s), character/personal qualities, extracurricular activities, first generation, interview, talent/ability, volunteer work, work experience. **Freshman Admission Requirements:** High school diploma is required and GED is accepted. *Academic units required:* 4 English, 4 mathematics, 3 science, (1 science labs), 2 foreign language, 3 social studies, 1 Fine Arts. *Academic units recommended:* 4 English, 4 mathematics, 3 science, (1 science labs), 2 foreign language, 3 social studies, 1 Fine Arts **Freshman Admission Statistics:** 4,452 applied, 68% admitted, 37% enrolled. **Transfer Admission Requirements:** college transcript(s), minimum college GPA of 2.0 required. Lowest grade transferable D. **General Admission Information:** Application Fee $45. Nonfall registration accepted. Admission may be deferred for a maximum of 2 semesters. Credit offered for CEEB Advanced Placement tests.

COSTS AND FINANCIAL AID
Annual in-state tuition $7,968. Annual out-of-state tuition $20,502. Room and board $11,428. Required fees $1,252. Average book expense $1,180. **Required Forms and Deadlines:** FAFSA. **Notification of Awards:** Applicants will be notified of awards on a rolling basis beginning 4/15. **Types of Aid:** *Need-based scholarships/grants:* Federal Pell, SEOG, state scholarships/grants, private scholarships, the school's own gift aid, United Negro College Fund, Federal Nursing Scholarships. *Loans:* Direct Subsidized Stafford, Direct Unsubsidized Stafford, Direct PLUS, Federal Perkins, Federal Nursing, state loans, college/university loans from institutional funds. **Student Employment:** Federal Work-Study Program available. Institutional employment available. Highest amount earned per year from on-campus jobs $5,700. Off-campus job opportunities are excellent. **Financial Aid Statistics:** 94% freshmen, 84% undergrads receive need-based scholarship or grant aid. 3% freshmen, 1% undergrads receive non-need-based scholarship or grant aid. 76% freshmen, 83% undergrads receive need-based self-help aid. 2% freshmen, 1% undergrads receive athletic scholarships. 93% freshmen, 69% undergrads receive any aid. 64% undergrads borrow to pay for school. Average cumulative indebtedness $24,326.

Criteria for awarding institutional aid: Non-need-based: academics, alumni affiliation, art, athletics, leadership, minority status, music/drama, state/district residency.

UNIVERSITY OF MISSOURI—SAINT LOUIS

351 Millenium Student Center, Saint Louis, MO 63121-4400
Phone: 314-516-5451 • **Financial Aid Phone:** 314-516-5526
E-mail: admissions@umsl.edu • **CEEB Code:** 6889
Fax: 314-516-5310 • **Website:** www.umsl.edu • **ACT Code:** 2383

This public school was founded in 1963. It has a 475-acre campus.

RATINGS
Admissions Selectivity Rating: 78   **Fire Safety Rating:** 79   **Green Rating:** 69

STUDENTS AND FACULTY
Enrollment: 8,984. **Student Body:** 57% female, 43% male, 10% out-of-state, 4% international (69 countries represented). Asian 4%, African American 20%, Caucasian 62%, Hispanic 2%.
Retention and Graduation: 78% freshmen return for sophomore year. 25% freshmen graduate within 4 years. 18% grads go on to further study within 1 year. 37% grads pursue arts and sciences degrees. 3% grads pursue law degrees. 27% grads pursue business degrees. **Faculty:** Student/faculty ratio 16:1. 483 full-time faculty, 75% hold PhDs, 20% are members of minority groups, 53% are women. 21% of classes are taught by teaching assistants.

ACADEMICS
Degrees: bachelor's, doctoral, master's, post-bachelor's certificate, post-master's certificate. **Classes:** Most classes have 10–19 students. Most lab/discussion sessions have 10–19 students. **Majors with Highest Enrollment:** accounting; business/commerce; psychology. **Special Study Options:** Accelerated program, cooperative education program, cross-registration, distance learning, double major, dual enrollment, English as a Second Language (ESL), exchange student program (domestic), honors program, independent study, internships, student-designed major, study abroad, teacher certification program, Engineering UMSL/WU, 2+3 B.S./M.A. Program in Economics, 2+3 B.A./B.S.-Ed and M.A. Program in History, 2+3 B.A./M.A. Program in Philosophy, 2+3 B.A./M.A. Program in Political Science, 2+3 B.A. in Psychology and M.S. in Gerontology Program, 2+3 B.A./M.A. Program in Sociology, Art and Art History 3+4 Program for School of Architecture at Washington University, Biology 3+4 Program for UMSL College of Optometry, Physics and Astronomy 3+4 Program for UMSL College of Optometry, Biology 3+3 Program for Logan Chiropractic College. **Honors programs:** Pierre Laclede Honors College offers a four-year (for freshmen) and a two-year (for internal and external transfers) honors program through which students can meet their General Education and some other graduation requirements (e.g., advanced composition, global awareness, cultural diversity). Most instruction is in small seminars (average enrollment is 13). There is a six-hour independent study requirement, and a writing program engages all students. **Combined degree programs:** BA/MA, BA/DOPT; BS/DOPT. **Disability Services:** Special programs offered to physically disabled students include note-taking services, reader services, tape recorders. **Career services:** alumni services, career assessment, internships Career services highlights include Experiential learning-as it includes our Internship and Cooperative Education programs.

FACILITIES
Housing: Coed dorms, special housing for disabled students, special housing for international students, fraternity/sorority housing, apartments for married students, apartments for single students, Theme HousingHousing for graduate students and students over 21 in apartments; other themed communities. 100% of campus accessible to physically disabled. **Special Academic Facilities/Equipment:** Art galleries, language, writing labs,math labs Mercantile Library, and observatory,radio station **Computers:** 68% of classrooms, 90% of dorms, 90% of libraries, 100% of dining areas, 90% of student union, 60% of common outdoor areas have wireless network access. Students can register for classes online. Administrative functions (other than registration) can be performed online.

CAMPUS LIFE
Environment: Metropolis. **Activities:** Choral groups, dance, drama/theater, jazz band, literary magazine, music ensembles, musical theater, opera, pep band, radio station, student government, student newspaper, student-run film society, Campus Ministries, International Student Organization, Model UN. 125 registered organizations, 24 honor societies, 9 religious organizations. 3 fraternities, 3 sororities. **Athletics (Intercollegiate):** *Men:* baseball, basketball, golf, soccer, tennis. *Women:* basketball, golf, soccer, softball, tennis, volleyball. **On-Campus Highlights:** Millennium Student Center, Touhill Performing Arts

Center, Mark Twain Athletic Complex, Gallery 210, Pilot House. **Environmental Initiatives:** Energy Conservation Waste Management and Recycling Pollution Prevention.

ADMISSIONS

Freshman Academic Profile: 3.4. 31% in top 10% of high school class, 56% in top 25% of high school class, 83% in top 50% of high school class. 78% from public high schools. SAT Math middle 50% range 480-660. ACT middle 50% range 22-27. Minimum paper TOEFL 500. **Basis for Candidate Selection:** *Very important factors considered include:* Class rank, academic GPA, rigor of secondary school record, standardized test scores. *Other factors considered include:* application essay, recommendation(s). **Freshman Admission Requirements:** High school diploma is required and GED is accepted. *Academic units required:* 4 English, 4 mathematics, 3 science, (1 science labs), 2 foreign language, 3 social studies, 1 Fine Arts. *Academic units recommended:* 4 English, 4 mathematics, 3 science, (1 science labs), 2 foreign language, 3 social studies, 1 Fine Arts **Freshman Admission Statistics:** 1,936 applied, 69% admitted, 41% enrolled. **Transfer Admission Requirements:** college transcript(s), minimum college GPA of 2.0 required. Lowest grade transferable D. **General Admission Information:** Application Fee $35. Regular application deadline 8/23. Notification on a rolling basis, beginning on or about 10/1. Nonfall registration accepted. Credit and/or placement offered for CEEB Advanced Placement tests.

COSTS AND FINANCIAL AID

Required Forms and Deadlines: FAFSA. **Notification of Awards:** Applicants will be notified of awards on a rolling basis beginning 4/1. **Types of Aid:** *Need-based scholarships/grants:* Federal Pell, SEOG, state scholarships/grants, private scholarships, the school's own gift aid, Federal Nursing Scholarships. , Federal ACG and SMART grants. *Loans:* Subsidized Stafford, Unsubsidized Stafford, PLUS, Federal Perkins, Federal Nursing, Federal Teach Grants. **Student Employment:** Federal Work-Study Program available. Institutional employment available. Highest amount earned per year from on-campus jobs $8,000. Off-campus job opportunities are good. **Financial Aid Statistics:** 87% freshmen, 78% undergrads receive need-based scholarship or grant aid. 26% freshmen, 13% undergrads receive non-need-based scholarship or grant aid. 69% freshmen, 88% undergrads receive need-based self-help aid. 2% freshmen, 1% undergrads receive athletic scholarships. 94% freshmen, 77% undergrads receive any aid. 60% undergrads borrow to pay for school. Average cumulative indebtedness $24,077. **Criteria for awarding institutional aid:** Non-need-based: academics, alumni affiliation, art, athletics, music/drama, state/district residency.

UNIVERSITY OF MOBILE

5735 College Parkway, Mobile, AL 36613-2842
Phone: 251-442-2273 • **Financial Aid Phone:** 251-442-2222
E-mail: adminfo@mail.umobile.edu • **CEEB Code:** 1515
Fax: 251-442-2498 • **Website:** www.umobile.edu • **ACT Code:** 29

This private school, affiliated with the Southern Baptist Church, was founded in 1961. It has a 830-acre campus.

RATINGS

Admissions Selectivity Rating: 72   Fire Safety Rating: 84   Green Rating: 61

STUDENTS AND FACULTY

Enrollment: 1,550. **Student Body:** 69% female, 31% male, 20% out-of-state, 2% international (26 countries represented). Asian 1%, African American 24%, Caucasian 62%, Hispanic 1%, Native American 2%.
Retention and Graduation: 73% freshmen return for sophomore year. 30% freshmen graduate within 4 years. **Faculty:** Student/faculty ratio 12:1. 88 full-time faculty, 57% hold PhDs, 3% are members of minority groups, 50% are women. 0% of classes are taught by teaching assistants.

ACADEMICS

Degrees: associate, bachelor's, master's. **Classes:** Most classes have 10–19 students. Most lab/discussion sessions have 10–19 students. **Majors with Highest Enrollment:** business administration and management; elementary education and teaching; nursing/registered nurse (rn, asn, bsn, msn). **Special Study Options:** Accelerated program, double major, honors program, independent study, internships, teacher certification program. **Honors programs:** Exploring the great books and the enduring questions; join a community of enthusiastic students like yourself; take courses designed not to make you do more work, but do the kind of work that will help you become a thinking leader; earn the "Honors Scholar" designation and seal on your diploma and transcript; participate in special events, such as an annual honor dinner hosted by President Foley; have

frequent access to honors faculty; benefit from honors roundtable designed to help students prepare for and apply to graduate school, seek grants and scholarships, and pursue post-graduate career opportunities. **Combined degree programs:** , BS/MBA. **Disability Services:** Special programs offered to physically disabled students include tutors. **Career services:** alumni services, career/job search classes, career assessment, internships.

FACILITIES

Housing: men's dorms, women's dorms. 100% of campus accessible to physically disabled. **Special Academic Facilities/Equipment:** Art gallery, forest learning center **Computers:** 10% of classrooms, 100% of dorms, 100% of libraries, 50% of dining areas, 100% of student union, 20% of common outdoor areas have wireless network access. Students can register for classes online. Administrative functions (other than registration) can be performed online.

CAMPUS LIFE

Environment: City. **Activities:** Choral groups, concert band, jazz band, music ensembles, musical theater, opera, pep band, student government, Campus Ministries 52 registered organizations, 12 honor societies, 3 religious organizations. **Athletics (Intercollegiate):** *Men:* baseball, basketball, cross-country, golf, soccer, tennis. *Women:* basketball, cheerleading, cross-country, golf, soccer, softball, tennis, volleyball. **On-Campus Highlights:** Ram Hall- State of the Art Auditorium, Newly renovated dining hall, Martin Hall — Donald Art Gallery, New Dorms—Faulkner and Samford Halls, Baseball Field/Swimming Pool. **Environmental Initiatives:** Recycling Wildlife conservation Green Energy 4.Sanitary Underground Injection System.

ADMISSIONS

Freshman Academic Profile: Average high school GPA 3.5. 23% in top 10% of high school class, 52% in top 25% of high school class, 80% in top 50% of high school class. SAT Math middle 50% range 470-690. SAT Critical Reading middle 50% range 437-608. ACT middle 50% range 20-25. Minimum web-based TOEFL 61. Minimum paper TOEFL 500. **Basis for Candidate Selection.** *Very important factors considered include:* academic GPA, standardized test scores. *Other factors considered include:* Class rank, recommendation(s), rigor of secondary school record, character/personal qualities, extracurricular activities, level of applicant's interest, talent/ability. **Freshman Admission Requirements:** High school diploma is required and GED is accepted. *Academic units recommended:* **Freshman Admission Statistics:** 789 applied, 80% admitted, 36% enrolled. **Transfer Admission Requirements:** college transcript(s), minimum college GPA of 2.75 required. Lowest grade transferable C. **General Admission Information:** Application Fee $50. Regular application deadline 8/1. Nonfall registration accepted. Admission may be deferred for a maximum of 1 year. Credit offered for CEEB Advanced Placement tests.

COSTS AND FINANCIAL AID

Annual tuition $17,110. Room and board $8,650. Required fees $630.
Required Forms and Deadlines: FAFSA, state aid form. **Types of Aid:** *Need-based scholarships/grants:* Federal Pell, SEOG, state scholarships/grants, private scholarships, the school's own gift aid, Federal Nursing Scholarships. *Loans:* Subsidized Stafford, Unsubsidized Stafford, PLUS, Federal Perkins. **Student Employment:** Federal Work-Study Program available. Institutional employment available. Highest amount earned per year from on-campus jobs $1,855. Off-campus job opportunities are fair. **Financial Aid Statistics:** 62% freshmen, 63% undergrads receive need-based scholarship or grant aid. 100% freshmen, 90% undergrads receive non-need-based scholarship or grant aid. 19% freshmen, 7% undergrads receive need-based self-help aid. 2% freshmen, 1% undergrads receive athletic scholarships. 91% freshmen, 91% undergrads receive any aid. 91% undergrads borrow to pay for school. Average cumulative indebtedness $29,474. **Criteria for awarding institutional aid:** Non-need-based: academics, alumni affiliation, athletics, music/drama, religious affiliation.

THE UNIVERSITY OF MONTANA

Lommasson Center 103, Missoula, MT 59812
Phone: 406-243-6266 • **Financial Aid Phone:** 406-243-5373
E-mail: admiss@umontana.edu • **CEEB Code:** 4489
Fax: 406-243-5711 • **Website:** www.umontana.edu • **ACT Code:** 2422

This public school was founded in 1893. It has a 220-acre campus.

RATINGS
Admissions Selectivity Rating: 76   **Fire Safety Rating:** 80   **Green Rating:** 90

STUDENTS AND FACULTY
Enrollment: 13,237. Student Body: 53% female, 47% male, 27% out-of-state, 2% international (65 countries represented). Asian 1%, African American 1%, Caucasian 83%, Hispanic 3%, Native American 3%. Retention and Graduation: 72% freshmen return for sophomore year. 22% freshmen graduate within 4 years. 48% freshmen graduate within 6 years. 26% grads go on to further study within 1 year. Faculty: Student/faculty ratio 19:1. 572 full-time faculty, 79% hold PhDs, 13% are are members of minority groups, 39% are women. 9% of classes are taught by teaching assistants.

ACADEMICS
Degrees: associate, bachelor's, certificate, first professional, master's, post-master's certificate, terminal associate. Classes: Most classes have 10–19 students. Most lab/discussion sessions have 20–29 students. Majors with Highest Enrollment: business administration and management; education; psychology. Special Study Options: cooperative education program, cross-registration, distance learning, double major, English as a Second Language (ESL), exchange student program (domestic), external degree program, honors program, independent study, internships, study abroad, teacher certification program, Bachelor of Nursing in Missoula in cooperation with Montana State Univeristy-Bozeman. Honors programs: The Davidson Honors College offers talented and motivated students an academic and social community as an important part of their undergraduate experience at The University of Montana, regardless of their major disciplines. Honors courses are taught by many of the best scholars on campus and are generally limited to twenty students. The Honors College encourages its students to participate in community service activities, international educational experiences and undergraduate research. Combined degree programs: JD/MBA, MBA/PharmD, JD/MPA. Disability Services: Special programs offered to physically disabled students include note-taking services, reader services, tape recorders, tutors. Career services: Alumni network, alumni services, career/job search classes, career assessment, internships, regional alumni.

FACILITIES
Housing: Coed dorms, special housing for disabled students, men's dorms, special housing for international students, women's dorms, fraternity/sorority housing, apartments for married students, apartments for single students, Theme Housing, Apartments for students and families; Honors floors, International floors, and quiet floors in dorms; activity dorms; personal development housing. Special Academic Facilities/Equipment: On main campus: clinical psychology center; environmental studies lab; geology field camp; several biological, biomedical, kinesiology, physiology, forestry-related, and other research labs or centers; art galleries; broadcast media center (public radio and television) and performing arts-radio-television building; practical ethics center; extensive presentation technology equipment and services, and others. Other locations: biological station, experimental forest, two-year college of technology (two locations), Fort Missoula field research center, and others. Computers: 20% of classrooms, 100% of libraries, 60% of dining areas, 100% of student union, 5% of common outdoor areas have wireless network access. Students can register for classes online. Administrative functions (other than registration) can be performed online.

CAMPUS LIFE
Environment: City. Activities: Choral groups, concert band, dance, drama/theater, jazz band, literary magazine, marching band, music ensembles, musical theater, opera, pep band, radio station, student government, student newspaper, symphony orchestra, television station 150 registered organizations, 5 fraternities, 4 sororities. Athletics (Intercollegiate): Men: basketball, cheerleading, cross-country, football, tennis, track/field (outdoor), track/field (indoor). Women: basketball, cheerleading, cross-country, golf, soccer, tennis, track/field (outdoor), track/field (indoor), volleyball. On-Campus Highlights: Adams Event Center (basketball, shows, etc.), Washington-Grizzly Stadium (football, other), Campus Recreation Center (student recreation), University Center (student center, movie theater), Performing Arts-RadioTV Center (public radio-TV), 2. Washington-Grizzly Stadium also used for MAJOR events, like Pearl Jam concert a few years ago (kicking off their annual tour), the Rolling Stones concert Oct 2006, and Elton John concerts (2007 and 2008). Environmental Initiatives: Climate Action Plan to reach carbon neutrality by 2020 and biannual Greenhouse Gas Inventories are completed by a full-time Sustainability Coordinator and the Sustainable Campus Committee. UM is currently developing an on-campus biomass plant that will replace 70 percent of natural gas used with locally sourced wood waste. (http://umt.edu/biomassplant/) Farm to College Program provides locally sourced food for on-campus dining services and at events. (http://ordway.umt.edu/sa/UDS/index.cfm/name/Overview)

ADMISSIONS
Freshman Academic Profile: Average high school GPA 3.3. 18% in top 10% of high school class, 41% in top 25% of high school class, 74% in top 50% of high school class. % from public high schools. SAT Math middle 50% range 490-590. SAT Critical Reading middle 50% range 490-600. SAT Writing middle 50% range 470-580. ACT middle 50% range 21-26. Minimum paper TOEFL 500. Basis for Candidate Selection: Very important factors considered include: Class rank, academic GPA, rigor of secondary school record, standardized test scores. Important factors considered include: extracurricular activities, talent/ability. Other factors considered include: application essay, recommendation(s). Freshman Admission Requirements: High school diploma is required and GED is accepted. Academic units required: 4 English, 3 mathematics, 2 science, (2 science labs), 3 social studies, 2 history. Academic units recommended: 4 English, 3 mathematics, 2 science, (2 science labs), 3 social studies, 2 history, Freshman Admission Statistics: 5,634 applied, 51% admitted, 81% enrolled. Transfer Admission Requirements: college transcript(s), Minimum college GPA of 2.0 required. Lowest grade transferable D. General Admission Information: Application Fee $30. Notification on a rolling basis, beginning on or about 9/15. Nonfall registration accepted. Admission may be deferred for a maximum of 1 year. Credit and/or placement offered for CEEB Advanced Placement tests.

COSTS AND FINANCIAL AID
Annual in-state tuition $4,604. Annual out-of-state tuition $20,194. Room and board $7,262. Required fees $1,612. Average book expense $950. Required Forms and Deadlines: FAFSAUM Supplemental Information Sheet. Notification of Awards: Applicants will be notified of awards on a rolling basis beginning 4/1. Types of Aid: Need-based scholarships/grants: Federal Pell, SEOG, state scholarships/grants, private scholarships, the school's own gift aid. Loans: Subsidized Stafford, Unsubsidized Stafford, PLUS, Federal Perkins. Student Employment: Federal Work-Study Program available. Institutional employment available. Off-campus job opportunities are good. Financial Aid Statistics: 64% freshmen, 70% undergrads receive need-based scholarship or grant aid. 44% freshmen, 27% undergrads receive non-need-based scholarship or grant aid. 82% freshmen, 87% undergrads receive need-based self-help aid. 3% freshmen, 2% undergrads receive athletic scholarships. 63% freshmen, 59% undergrads receive any aid. 57% undergrads borrow to pay for school. Average cumulative indebtedness $20,532. Criteria for awarding institutional aid: Non-need-based: academics, alumni affiliation, athletics, leadership, music/drama, state/district residency.

UNIVERSITY OF MONTEVALLO

Station 6030, Montevallo, AL 35115
Phone: 205-665-6030 • **Financial Aid Phone:** 205-665-6050
E-mail: admissions@montevallo.edu • **CEEB Code:** 1004
Fax: 205-665-6032 • **Website:** www.montevallo.edu/

This public school was founded in 1896. It has a 160-acre campus.

RATINGS
Admissions Selectivity Rating: 67   **Fire Safety Rating:** 67   **Green Rating:** 71

STUDENTS AND FACULTY
Enrollment: 2,589. **Student Body:** 65% female, 35% male, 5% out-of-state, 2% international (23 countries represented). Asian 1%, African American 14%, Caucasian 73%, Hispanic 3%, Native American 1%. **Retention and Graduation:** 78% freshmen return for sophomore year. **Faculty:** Student/faculty ratio 16:1. 131 full-time faculty,13% are members of minority groups, 49% are women. 0% of classes are taught by teaching assistants.

ACADEMICS
Degrees: bachelor's, master's, post-master's certificate. **Classes:** Most classes have 10–19 students. Most lab/discussion sessions have 20–29 students. **Majors with Highest Enrollment:** business administration and management; elementary education and teaching; health and physical education. **Special Study Op-**

tions: Accelerated program, cross-registration, double major, dual enrollment, exchange student program (domestic), honors program, independent study, internships, study abroad, teacher certification program, Advanced placement credit; Academic remediation; and Learning disabilities services. **Honors programs:** Honors History; Honors Composition; Honors Literature; Honors Thesis **Combined degree programs:** , 3-2 engineering program with U of Alabama at Birmi. **Disability Services:** Special programs offered to physically disabled students include note-taking services, reader services, tape recorders, tutors. **Career services:** alumni services, career assessment Career services highlights include The Career Center assists students through all aspects of the career-planning process. Career counseling, including career assessments is available to all enrolled students. Other services include employability skills training, job postings, internship information, on-campus interviewing, career events and seminars and graduate school information.

FACILITIES

Housing: Coed dorms, men's dorms, women's dorms, fraternity/sorority housing, apartments for married students. **Special Academic Facilities/Equipment:** Art gallery, child development, speech and hearing, traffic safety, and undergraduate liberal studies centers, mass communications center with cable TV broadcasting capabilities. **Computers:** 98% of classrooms, 85% of dorms, 100% of libraries, 100% of dining areas, 100% of student union, 75% of common outdoor areas have wireless network access. Students can register for classes online. Administrative functions (other than registration) can be performed online.

CAMPUS LIFE

Environment: Rural. **Activities:** Choral groups, concert band, dance, drama/theater, jazz band, literary magazine, music ensembles, musical theater, student government, student newspaper, television station, yearbook 93 registered organizations, 26 honor societies, 8 religious organizations. 7 fraternities, 8 sororities. **Athletics (Intercollegiate):** *Men:* baseball, basketball, golf, soccer. *Women:* basketball, cross-country, golf, soccer, tennis, volleyball. **On-Campus Highlights:** Cafeteria, Student Activity Center, Main Quad, University of Montevallo Student Lake, Intramural Fields. **Environmental Initiatives:** Campus lighting retrofit to energy saving bulbs. Campus-wide retrofit of all toilets, showers and faucets to low use fixtures. An aggressive energy management program. Installed new high efficient 800 ton chiller. Re-designed chilled water loop operation, including VFD's.

ADMISSIONS

Freshman Academic Profile: 3.3. 90% from public high schools. SAT Math middle 50% range 465-562. SAT Writing middle 50% range 570-695. ACT middle 50% range 20-26. Minimum web-based TOEFL 71. Minimum paper TOEFL 525. **Basis for Candidate Selection:** *Very important factors considered include:* rigor of secondary school record, standardized test scores. *Other factors considered include:* Class rank, recommendation(s), alumni/ae relation, character/personal qualities, extracurricular activities, interview, talent/ability, work experience. **Freshman Admission Requirements:** High school diploma is required and GED is accepted. *Academic units required:* 4 English, 2 mathematics, 2 science, 2 social studies, 2 history, 4 academic electives. *Academic units recommended:* 4 English, 2 mathematics, 2 science, 2 social studies, 2 history, 4 academic electives. **Freshman Admission Statistics:** 1,385 applied, 87% admitted, 46% enrolled. **Transfer Admission Requirements:** college transcript(s), minimum college GPA of 2.0 required. Lowest grade transferable D. **General Admission Information:** Application Fee $25. Regular application deadline 8/1. Notification on a rolling basis, beginning on or about 9/1. Nonfall registration accepted. Admission may be deferred for a maximum of 2 years.

COSTS AND FINANCIAL AID

Annual in-state tuition $8,790. Annual out-of-state tuition $17,580. Room and board $5,522. Required fees $490. Average book expense $1,200. **Required Forms and Deadlines:** FAFSA. **Notification of Awards:** Applicants will be notified of awards on a rolling basis beginning 4/20. **Types of Aid:** *Need-based scholarships/grants:* Federal Pell, SEOG, state scholarships/grants, private scholarships, the school's own gift aid. *Loans:* Subsidized Stafford, Unsubsidized Stafford, PLUS, Federal Perkins. **Student Employment:** Federal Work-Study Program available. Institutional employment available. Highest amount earned per year from on-campus jobs $3,100. Off-campus job opportunities are good. **Financial Aid Statistics:** 89% freshmen, 82% undergrads receive need-based scholarship or grant aid. 24% freshmen, 29% undergrads receive non-need-based scholarship or grant aid. 80% freshmen, 85% undergrads receive need-based self-help aid. 5% freshmen, 4% undergrads receive athletic scholarships. 87% freshmen, 77% undergrads receive any aid. 54% undergrads borrow to pay for school. Average cumulative indebtedness $16,581. **Criteria for awarding institutional aid:** Non-need-based: academics, art, athletics, leadership, minority status, music/drama.

UNIVERSITY OF MOUNT UNION

1972 Clark Avenue, Alliance, OH 44601-3993
Phone: 330-823-2590 • **Financial Aid Phone:** 877-543-9185
E-mail: admission@mountunion.edu • **CEEB Code:** 1492
Fax: 330-823-5097 • **Website:** www.mountunion.edu

This private school, affiliated with the Methodist Church, was founded in 1846. It has a 115-acre campus.

RATINGS

Admissions Selectivity Rating: 73　　**Fire Safety Rating:** 78　　**Green Rating:** 84

STUDENTS AND FACULTY

Enrollment: 2,141. **Student Body:** 49% female, 51% male, 14% out-of-state, 3% international (16 countries represented). Asian 0%, African American 6%, Caucasian 84%, Hispanic 1%.
Retention and Graduation: 76% freshmen return for sophomore year. 54% freshmen graduate within 4 years. 65% freshmen graduate within 6 years. 26% grads go on to further study within 1 year. 23% grads pursue arts and sciences degrees. 11% grads pursue law degrees. 8% grads pursue business degrees. 26% grads pursue medical degrees. **Faculty:** Student/faculty ratio 14:1. 128 full-time faculty, 89% hold PhDs, 13% are members of minority groups, 41% are women. 0% of classes are taught by teaching assistants.

ACADEMICS

Degrees: bachelor's, master's. **Classes:** Most classes have 10–19 students. Most lab/discussion sessions have fewer than 10 students. **Majors with Highest Enrollment:** business administration and management; early childhood education and teaching; sport and fitness administration/management. **Special Study Options:** cooperative education program, double major, dual enrollment, English as a Second Language (ESL), honors program, independent study, internships, liberal arts/career combination, student-designed major, study abroad, teacher certification program. **Honors programs:** Four honors programs are offered. Honors in Liberal Arts, Honors in the Major, First Year in Honors and Latin Honors. A qualified student may participate in any program and may discontinue honors study without penalty. Students must declare their intent to participate in an honors program no later than the first semester of their junior year. **Disability Services:** Special programs offered to physically disabled students include note-taking services, reader services, tape recorders, tutors. **Career services:** Alumni network, alumni services, career/job search classes, career assessment, internships, regional alumni. Career services highlights include Employment success results/report.

FACILITIES

Housing: Coed dorms, special housing for disabled students, men's dorms, special housing for international students, women's dorms, fraternity/sorority housing, apartments for single students, Theme Housing. Small, single-sex, college-owned residential homes converted to college housing. 85% of campus accessible to physically disabled. **Special Academic Facilities/Equipment:** Art gallery, ecological center, observatory, educational media center. **Computers:** 100% of classrooms, 90% of dorms, 100% of libraries, 100% of dining areas, 100% of student union, 50% of common outdoor areas have wireless network access. Students can register for classes online. Administrative functions (other than registration) can be performed online.

CAMPUS LIFE

Environment: Village. **Activities:** Choral groups, concert band, dance, drama/theater, jazz band, literary magazine, marching band, music ensembles, musical theater, pep band, radio station, student government, student newspaper, television station, yearbook, Campus Ministries, International Student Organization, Model UN. 80 registered organizations, 16 honor societies, 10 religious organizations. 4 fraternities, 4 sororities. **Athletics (Intercollegiate):** *Men:* baseball, basketball, cross-country, diving, football, golf, soccer, swimming, tennis, track/field (outdoor), track/field (indoor), wrestling. *Women:* basketball, cheerleading, cross-country, diving, golf, soccer, softball, swimming, tennis, track/field (outdoor), track/field (indoor), volleyball. **On-Campus Highlights:** Hoover Price Campus Center, Kolenbrander Harter Information Center, McPherson Athletic Building, Dewald Chapel, Bracy Hall Science Building, Welcome Center. **Environmental Initiatives:** Sustainability (Climate Action) Plan 54 KW Solar Panel LEED certified welcome center.

ADMISSIONS

Freshman Academic Profile: Average high school GPA 3.2. 12% in top 10% of high school class, 39% in top 25% of high school class, 73% in top 50% of high school class. 75% from public high schools. SAT Math middle 50% range 480-590. SAT Critical Reading middle 50% range 440-550. ACT middle 50% range 20-27. Minimum web-based TOEFL 79. Minimum paper TOEFL 550. **Basis for Candidate Selection:** *Very important factors considered include:*

Class rank, academic GPA, rigor of secondary school record, standardized test scores. *Important factors considered include:* recommendation(s). *Other factors considered include:* application essay, alumni/ae relation, character/personal qualities, extracurricular activities, racial/ethnic status, talent/ability, volunteer work, work experience. **Freshman Admission Requirements:** High school diploma is required and GED is accepted. *Academic units recommended:* **Freshman Admission Statistics:** 2,774 applied, 72% admitted, 32% enrolled. **Transfer Admission Requirements:** High school transcript, college transcript(s), essay or personal statement, statement of good standing from prior institution(s). Minimum college GPA of 2.0 required. Lowest grade transferable C. **General Admission Information:** Notification on a rolling basis, beginning on or about 10/1. Nonfall registration accepted. Admission may be deferred for a maximum of one semester. Credit and/or placement offered for CEEB Advanced Placement tests.

COSTS AND FINANCIAL AID

Annual tuition $26,350. Room and board $8,480. Required fees $300. Average book expense $1,100. **Required Forms and Deadlines:** FAFSA. **Types of Aid:** *Need-based scholarships/grants:* Federal Pell, SEOG, state scholarships/grants, the school's own gift aid. *Loans:* Subsidized Stafford, Unsubsidized Stafford, PLUS, Federal Perkins, college/university loans from institutional funds. **Student Employment:** Federal Work-Study Program available. Institutional employment available. Highest amount earned per year from on-campus jobs $2,600. Off-campus job opportunities are fair. **Financial Aid Statistics:** 100% freshmen, 99% undergrads receive need-based scholarship or grant aid. 6% freshmen, 6% undergrads receive non-need-based scholarship or grant aid. 94% freshmen, 93% undergrads receive need-based self-help aid. 90% freshmen, 87% undergrads receive any aid. 93% undergrads borrow to pay for school. Average cumulative indebtedness $34,586. **Criteria for awarding institutional aid:** Non-need-based: academics, alumni affiliation, art, job skills, minority status, music/drama, state/district residency.

UNIVERSITY OF NEBRASKA AT KEARNEY

905 West 25th, Kearney, NE 68849
Phone: 800-532-7639
E-mail: admissionsug@unk.edu • **CEEB Code:** 6467
Fax: 308-865-8987 • **Website:** www.unk.edu • **ACT Code:** 2468

This public school was founded in 1903. It has a 235-acre campus.

RATINGS
Admissions Selectivity Rating: 61   **Fire Safety Rating:** 60*   **Green Rating:** 60*

STUDENTS AND FACULTY
Enrollment: 5,886. **Student Body:** 56% female, 44% male, 6% out-of-state, 3% international (countries represented). Asian 1%, African American 1%, Caucasian 88%, Hispanic 2%.

ACADEMICS
Degrees: bachelor's, master's. **Special Study Options:** distance learning, double major, English as a Second Language (ESL), exchange student program (domestic), external degree program, honors program, internships, study abroad, teacher certification program. **Combined degree programs:** 3-1 Medical technology program. **Disability Services:** Special programs offered to physically disabled students include note-taking services, reader services, tape recorders, tutors. **Career services:** career assessment, internships.

FACILITIES
Housing: Coed dorms, men's dorms, women's dorms, fraternity/sorority housing, apartments for married students, apartments for single students. **Special Academic Facilities/Equipment:** Art gallery, language lab, museum of Nebraska art.

CAMPUS LIFE
Environment: Village. **Activities:** Choral groups, concert band, dance, drama/theater, jazz band, literary magazine, marching band, music ensembles, musical theater, opera, pep band, radio station, student government, student newspaper, symphony orchestra, television station, 1 religious organizations. 10 fraternities, 6 sororities. **Athletics (Intercollegiate):** *Men:* baseball, basketball, cross-country, diving, football, golf, soccer, softball, swimming, tennis, volleyball. *Women:* basketball, cross-country, diving, football, golf, soccer, softball, swimming, tennis, volleyball.

ADMISSIONS
Freshman Academic Profile: 90% from public high schools. Minimum paper TOEFL 520. **Basis for Candidate Selection:** *Very important factors considered include:* Class rank, rigor of secondary school record, standardized

test scores. *Other factors considered include:* religious affiliation/commitment, talent/ability. **Freshman Admission Requirements:** High school diploma is required and GED is accepted. *Academic units required:* 4 English, 3 mathematics, 3 science, (1 science labs), 2 foreign language, 1 social studies, 2 history, 1 academic electives. *Academic units recommended:* 4 English, 3 mathematics, 3 science, (1 science labs), 2 foreign language, 1 social studies, 2 history, 1 academic electives. **Freshman Admission Statistics:** 2,672 applied. **Transfer Admission Requirements:** High school transcript, college transcript(s), minimum college GPA of 2.0 required. Lowest grade transferable C. **General Admission Information:** Application Fee $25. Regular application deadline 8/1. Notification on a rolling basis, beginning on or about 10/1. Nonfall registration accepted. Credit and/or placement offered for CEEB Advanced Placement tests.

COSTS AND FINANCIAL AID

Annual in-state tuition $2,715. Annual out-of-state tuition $5,550. Room and board $4,156. Required fees $498. Average book expense $700. **Required Forms and Deadlines:** FAFSA, institution's own financial aid formC. **Notification of Awards:** Applicants will be notified of awards on or about 5/1. **Types of Aid:** *Need-based scholarships/grants:* Federal Pell, SEOG, state scholarships/grants, private scholarships, the school's own gift aid. *Loans:* Subsidized Stafford, Unsubsidized Stafford, PLUS, Federal Perkins. **Student Employment:** Federal Work-Study Program available. Institutional employment available. Off-campus job opportunities are excellent. **Financial Aid Statistics:** 43% undergrads borrow to pay for school. Average cumulative indebtedness $13,400. **Criteria for awarding institutional aid:** Non-need-based: academics, art, athletics, leadership, music/drama.

UNIVERSITY OF NEBRASKA AT OMAHA

Office of Admissions, Omaha, NE 68182
Phone: 402-554-2393 • **Financial Aid Phone:** 402-554-2327
E-mail: unoadmissions@unomaha.edu • **CEEB Code:** 6420
Fax: 402-554-3472 • **Website:** www.unomaha.edu • **ACT Code:** 2464

This public school was founded in 1908. It has a 472-acre campus.

RATINGS
Admissions Selectivity Rating: 69   **Fire Safety Rating:** 96   **Green Rating:** 70

STUDENTS AND FACULTY
Enrollment: 11,871. **Student Body:** 52% female, 48% male, 7% out-of-state, 3% international (76 countries represented). Asian 3%, African American 7%, Caucasian 74%, Hispanic 7%. **Retention and Graduation:** 72% freshmen return for sophomore year. 13% freshmen graduate within 4 years. 45% freshmen graduate within 6 years. 21% grads go on to further study within 1 year. **Faculty:** Student/faculty ratio 17:1. 505 full-time faculty, 84% hold PhDs, 18% are members of minority groups, 45% are women. 4% of classes are taught by teaching assistants.

ACADEMICS
Degrees: bachelor's, master's, post-bachelor's certificate, post-master's certificate. **Classes:** Most classes have 20–29 students. Most lab/discussion sessions have 20–29 students. **Majors with Highest Enrollment:** biology/biological sciences; elementary education and teaching; psychology. **Special Study Options:** cooperative education program, cross-registration, distance learning, double major, dual enrollment, English as a Second Language (ESL), exchange student program (domestic), honors program, independent study, internships, student-designed major, study abroad, teacher certification program, Business, Engineering. **Honors programs:** UNO Honors Program includes many opportunities such as Early Registration, Honors-only courses, Honors-priority Housing, Honors domestic and international semesters, Honors internships, and a Washington Center affiliation. **Combined degree programs:** , MPA/MSW in Public Administration and Social Work. **Disability Services:** Special programs offered to physically disabled students include note-taking services, reader services, tape recorders, tutors. **Career services:** career/job search classes, career assessment, internships Career services highlights include The Internships are a UNO strength.

FACILITIES
Housing: Coed dorms, leased Apartment dwellings. 99% of campus accessible to physically disabled. **Special Academic Facilities/Equipment:** Center for Afghanistan studies, physical education facility, Strauss Performing Arts Center, Speech Center, Writing Center, Math/Science Center, Peter Kiewit Information Technology Building, and Career Center. **Computers:** 100% of classrooms, 100% of dorms, 100% of libraries, 100% of dining areas, 100% of student union, 85% of common outdoor areas have wireless network access. Students can

register for classes online. Administrative functions (other than registration) can be performed online.

CAMPUS LIFE
Environment: Metropolis. **Activities:** Choral groups, concert band, dance, drama/theater, jazz band, literary magazine, marching band, music ensembles, musical theater, opera, pep band, radio station, student government, student newspaper, student-run film society, symphony orchestra, television station, Campus Ministries, International Student Organization, Model UN. 127 registered organizations, 23 honor societies, 14 religious organizations. 6 fraternities, 8 sororities. **Athletics (Intercollegiate):** *Men:* baseball, basketball, football, ice hockey, wrestling. *Women:* basketball, cross-country, diving, golf, soccer, softball, swimming, tennis, track/field (outdoor), track/field (indoor), volleyball. **On-Campus Highlights:** University Library, Strauss Performing Arts Center, Milo Bail Student Center, Durham Science Center, Peter Kiewit Institute. **Environmental Initiatives:** To identify sustainability opportunities and to develop a recommended action plan for each To integrate sustainability with campus operations, education and outreach, wherever and whenever prudence dictates To engage the campus in an ongoing dialogue about sustainability

ADMISSIONS
Freshman Academic Profile: Average high school GPA 3.4. 15% in top 10% of high school class, 39% in top 25% of high school class, 73% in top 50% of high school class. 90% from public high schools. ACT middle 50% range 19-26. Minimum web-based TOEFL 61. Minimum paper TOEFL 500. **Basis for Candidate Selection:** *Very important factors considered include:* Class rank, rigor of secondary school record, standardized test scores. *Other factors considered include:* character/personal qualities. **Freshman Admission Requirements:** High school diploma is required and GED is accepted. *Academic units required:* 4 English, 3 mathematics, 3 science, (1 science labs), 2 foreign language, 1 social studies, 2 history, 1 academic electives. *Academic units recommended:* 4 English, 3 mathematics, 3 science, (1 science labs), 2 foreign language, 1 social studies, 2 history, 1 academic electives **Freshman Admission Statistics:** 4,536 applied, 80% admitted, 49% enrolled. **Transfer Admission Requirements:** college transcript(s), statement of good standing from prior institution(s). Minimum college GPA of 2.0 required. Lowest grade transferable C–. **General Admission Information:** Application Fee $45. Regular application deadline 8/1. Nonfall registration accepted.

COSTS AND FINANCIAL AID
Annual in-state tuition $5,240. Annual out-of-state tuition $15,250. Room and board $8,465. Required fees $1,270. Average book expense $1,000. **Required Forms and Deadlines:** FAFSA. **Notification of Awards:** Applicants will be notified of awards on a rolling basis beginning 4/15. **Types of Aid:** *Need-based scholarships/grants:* Federal Pell, SEOG, state scholarships/grants, private scholarships, the school's own gift aid. *Loans:* Subsidized Stafford, Unsubsidized Stafford, PLUS, Federal Perkins, college/university loans from institutional funds. **Student Employment:** Federal Work-Study Program available. Institutional employment available. Highest amount earned per year from on-campus jobs $15,600. Off-campus job opportunities are excellent. **Financial Aid Statistics:** 53% freshmen, 56% undergrads receive need-based scholarship or grant aid. 9% freshmen, 12% undergrads receive non-need-based scholarship or grant aid. 47% freshmen, 59% undergrads receive need-based self-help aid. 80% freshmen, 81% undergrads receive any aid. 56% undergrads borrow to pay for school. Average cumulative indebtedness $23,500. **Criteria for awarding institutional aid:** Non-need-based: academics, alumni affiliation, art, athletics, leadership, minority status, music/drama, state/district residency.

UNIVERSITY OF NEBRASKA MEDICAL CENTER

984230 Nebr Med Ctr, Omaha, NE 68198-4230
Phone: 402-559-6864 • **Financial Aid Phone:** 402-559-4109
E-mail: ttonjes@unmc.edu
Fax: 402-559-6796 • **Website:** www.unmc.edu/

This public school was founded in 1902.

RATINGS
Admissions Selectivity Rating: 61   **Fire Safety Rating:** 60*   **Green Rating:** 60*

STUDENTS AND FACULTY
Enrollment: 812. **Student Body:** 88% female, 12% male, 12% out-of-state, 1% international (countries represented). Asian 1%, African American 1%, Caucasian 93%, Hispanic 3%, Native American 1%.
Retention and Graduation: Faculty: Student/faculty ratio :1. 768 full-time faculty, 90% hold PhDs, 14% are members of minority groups, 39% are women.

ACADEMICS
Degrees: bachelor's, first professional, master's, post-bachelor's certificate, post-master's certificate. **Classes: Majors with Highest Enrollment:** medicine (md); nursing/registered nurse (rn, asn, bsn, msn); pharmacy (pharmd [usa], pharmd or bs/bpharm [canada]). **Special Study Options:** Accelerated program, distance learning, honors program, independent study. **Disability Services:** Special programs offered to physically disabled students include note-taking services, tutors.

CAMPUS LIFE
Environment: Metropolis. **Activities:** student government, student newspaper.

ADMISSIONS
Freshman Academic Profile: Minimum paper TOEFL 551. **Transfer Admission Requirements:** college transcript(s), Lowest grade transferable c. **General Admission Information:** Nonfall registration not accepted.

COSTS AND FINANCIAL AID
Annual in-state tuition $6,450. Annual out-of-state tuition $18,900. Required fees $310. Average book expense $950. **Required Forms and Deadlines:** FAFSA, institution's own financial aid form. **Notification of Awards:** Applicants will be notified of awards on or about 4/1. **Types of Aid:** *Need-based scholarships/grants:* Federal Pell, SEOG, state scholarships/grants, private scholarships, the school's own gift aid. *Loans:* Subsidized Stafford, Unsubsidized Stafford, PLUS, Federal Perkins, Federal Nursing, state loans. **Student Employment:** Federal Work-Study Program available. Institutional employment available. Off-campus job opportunities are fair. **Financial Aid Statistics:** 79% undergrads receive need-based scholarship or grant aid. 4% undergrads receive non-need-based scholarship or grant aid. 90% undergrads receive need-based self-help aid. **Criteria for awarding institutional aid:** Non-need-based: academics, leadership, minority status.

UNIVERSITY OF NEBRASKA—LINCOLN

1410 Q Street, Lincoln, NE 68588-0417
Phone: 402-472-2023 • **Financial Aid Phone:** 402-472-2030
E-mail: admissions@unl.edu • **CEEB Code:** 6877
Fax: 402-472-0670 • **Website:** www.unl.edu • **ACT Code:** 2482

This public school was founded in 1869. It has a 617-acre campus.

RATINGS
Admissions Selectivity Rating: 88   **Fire Safety Rating:** 77   **Green Rating:** 66

STUDENTS AND FACULTY
Enrollment: 19,345. **Student Body:** 46% female, 54% male, 16% out-of-state, 4% international (127 countries represented). Asian 2%, African American 2%, Caucasian 82%, Hispanic 4%.
Retention and Graduation: 84% freshmen return for sophomore year. 32% freshmen graduate within 4 years. 28% grads go on to further study within 1 year. **Faculty:** Student/faculty ratio 21:1. 1045 full-time faculty, 97% hold PhDs, 20% are members of minority groups, 30% are women.

ACADEMICS
Degrees: associate, bachelor's, first professional, master's, post-bachelor's certificate, post-master's certificate, terminal associate. **Classes:** Most classes have 20–29 students. Most lab/discussion sessions have 20–29 students. **Majors with Highest Enrollment:** business administration and management; finance; psychology. **Special Study Options:** Accelerated program, cooperative education program, cross-registration, distance learning, double major, dual enrollment, English as a Second Language (ESL), exchange student program (domestic), honors program, independent study, internships, liberal arts/career combination, student-designed major, study abroad, teacher certification program. **Honors programs:** University Honors Program: Acceptance into the program is based on a comprehensive evaluation of student's potential by the Honors Program Faculty Committee. A special notation is made on the transcript and diploma upon graduation. J.D. Edwards Honors Program: Purpose is to produce top quality graduates who combine business knowledge and computing fundamentals for enterprise information and software systems. **Disability Services:** Special programs offered to physically disabled students include note-taking services, reader services, tape recorders, tutors. **Career services:** alumni services, career/job search classes, career assessment.

FACILITIES

Housing: Coed dorms, special housing for disabled students, men's dorms, special housing for international students, women's dorms, fraternity/sorority housing, apartments for married students, cooperative housing, apartments for single students. 85% of campus accessible to physically disabled. **Special Academic Facilities/Equipment:** Art gallery, performing arts center, food industries complex, planetarium, center for mass spectrometry, natural science museum, animal science complex, veterinary animal research/diagnosis center. **Computers:**

CAMPUS LIFE

Environment: City. **Activities:** Choral groups, concert band, dance, drama/theater, jazz band, literary magazine, marching band, music ensembles, musical theater, opera, pep band, radio station, student government, student newspaper, student-run film society, symphony orchestra, television station, yearbook, Campus Ministries, International Student Organization, Model UN. 335 registered organizations, 57 honor societies, 25 religious organizations. 27 fraternities, 18 sororities. **Athletics (Intercollegiate):** *Men:* baseball, basketball, cross-country, football, golf, gymnastics, rodeo, tennis, track/field (outdoor), track/field (indoor), wrestling. *Women:* basketball, bowling, cross-country, diving, golf, gymnastics, riflery, rodeo, soccer, softball, swimming, tennis, track/field (outdoor), track/field (indoor), volleyball. **On-Campus Highlights:** Student Union, Student Recreation, Library, Memorial Stadium and Hewitt Center, Residence Halls. **Environmental Initiatives:** Recycling of paper, plastic, aluminum and many other materials 'Green' new construction; must meet LEED Silver standards Energy conservation measures.

ADMISSIONS

Freshman Academic Profile: 26% in top 10% of high school class, 53% in top 25% of high school class, 84% in top 50% of high school class. SAT Math middle 50% range 520-670. SAT Critical Reading middle 50% range 510-660. ACT middle 50% range 22-28. Minimum web-based TOEFL 70. Minimum paper TOEFL 523. **Basis for Candidate Selection:** *Very important factors considered include:* Class rank, standardized test scores. *Important factors considered include:* rigor of secondary school record. *Other factors considered include:* academic GPA, recommendation(s), first generation, talent/ability. **Freshman Admission Requirements:** High school diploma is required and GED is accepted. *Academic units required:* 4 English, 4 mathematics, 3 science, (1 science labs), 2 foreign language, 3 social studies. *Academic units recommended:* 4 English, 4 mathematics, 3 science, (1 science labs), 2 foreign language, 3 social studies. **Freshman Admission Statistics:** 10,022 applied, 59% admitted, 69% enrolled. **Transfer Admission Requirements:** High school transcript, college transcript(s), minimum college GPA of 2.0 required. Lowest grade transferable D. **General Admission Information:** Application Fee $45. Regular application deadline 5/1. Notification on a rolling basis, beginning on or about 9/1. Nonfall registration accepted. Neither credit nor placement offered for CEEB Advanced Placement tests.

COSTS AND FINANCIAL AID

Annual in-state tuition $6,480. Annual out-of-state tuition $19,230. Room and board $8,648. Required fees $1,417. Average book expense $1,050. **Required Forms and Deadlines:** FAFSA. **Notification of Awards:** Applicants will be notified of awards on a rolling basis beginning 4/1. **Types of Aid:** *Need-based scholarships/grants:* Federal Pell, SEOG, state scholarships/grants, private scholarships, the school's own gift aid. *Loans:* Direct Subsidized Stafford, Direct Unsubsidized Stafford, Direct PLUS, Subsidized Stafford, Unsubsidized Stafford, PLUS, Federal Perkins, college/university loans from institutional funds. **Student Employment:** Federal Work-Study Program available. Institutional employment available. Off-campus job opportunities are excellent. **Financial Aid Statistics:** 82% freshmen, 78% undergrads receive need-based scholarship or grant aid. 11% freshmen, 8% undergrads receive non-need-based scholarship or grant aid. 71% freshmen, 76% undergrads receive need-based self-help aid. 3% freshmen, 4% undergrads receive athletic scholarships. 83% freshmen, 68% undergrads receive any aid. 62% undergrads borrow to pay for school. Average cumulative indebtedness $21,604. **Criteria for awarding institutional aid:** Non-need-based: academics, alumni affiliation, art, athletics, leadership, minority status, music/drama, state/district residency.

UNIVERSITY OF NEVADA, LAS VEGAS

4505 Maryland Parkway, Las Vegas, NV 89154-1021
Phone: 702-774-8658
E-mail: Undergraduate.Recruitment@ccmail.nevada.edu • **CEEB Code:** 4861
Fax: 702-774-8008 • **Website:** www.unlv.edu • **ACT Code:** 2496

This public school was founded in 1957. It has a 337-acre campus.

RATINGS

Admissions Selectivity Rating: 69 **Fire Safety Rating:** 60* **Green Rating:** 60*

STUDENTS AND FACULTY

Enrollment: 20,607. **Student Body:** 56% female, 44% male, 22% out-of-state, 4% international (84 countries represented). Asian 14%, African American 8%, Caucasian 53%, Hispanic 11%, Native American 1%. **Retention and Graduation:** 73% freshmen return for sophomore year. 12% freshmen graduate within 4 years. 42% freshmen graduate within 6 years. **Faculty:** Student/faculty ratio 20:1. 776 full-time faculty, 90% hold PhDs, 18% are members of minority groups, 33% are women. 11% of classes are taught by teaching assistants.

ACADEMICS

Degrees: bachelor's, certificate, first professional, master's, post-bachelor's certificate, post-master's certificate. **Classes:** Most classes have 20–29 students. Most lab/discussion sessions have 20–29 students. **Majors with Highest Enrollment:** elementary education and teaching; hospitality administration/management; psychology. **Special Study Options:** Accelerated program, cooperative education program, cross-registration, distance learning, double major, dual enrollment, English as a Second Language (ESL), exchange student program (domestic), honors program, independent study, internships, student-designed major, study abroad, teacher certification program. **Combined degree programs:** , interdisciplinary program in environmental science. **Disability Services:** Special programs offered to physically disabled students include note-taking services, reader services, tape recorders, tutors. **Career services:** Alumni network, alumni services, career/job search classes, career assessment, internships, regional alumni.

FACILITIES

Housing: Coed dorms. **Special Academic Facilities/Equipment:** Art galleries, national supercomputing center for energy and environment, natural history museum, arboretum, 3 theaters, concert hall, law school, dental school, international gaming institute, professional practice school for teachers. **Computers:** Students can register for classes online. Administrative functions (other than registration) can be performed online.

CAMPUS LIFE

Environment: Metropolis. **Activities:** Choral groups, concert band, dance, drama/theater, jazz band, literary magazine, marching band, music ensembles, musical theater, opera, pep band, radio station, student government, student newspaper, student-run film society, symphony orchestra, television station 24 honor societies, 14 religious organizations. 8 fraternities, 6 sororities. **Athletics (Intercollegiate):** *Men:* baseball, basketball, football, golf, soccer, swimming, tennis. *Women:* basketball, cross-country, equestrian sports, golf, soccer, softball, swimming, tennis, track/field (outdoor), volleyball. **On-Campus Highlights:** Lied Library, Artemus W. Ham Concert Hall, Moyer Student Union, Judy Bailey Theatre, Student Services Complex; Thomas and Mack and Cox Pavilion Event Centers, Lied Athletic Complex, Tonopah Residence Complex.

ADMISSIONS

Freshman Academic Profile: Average high school GPA 3.3. 18% in top 10% of high school class, 47% in top 25% of high school class, 82% in top 50% of high school class. SAT Math middle 50% range 450-580. SAT Critical Reading middle 50% range 440-560. ACT middle 50% range 18-24. Minimum paper TOEFL 500. **Basis for Candidate Selection:** *Very important factors considered include:* rigor of secondary school record, standardized test scores. *Other factors considered include:* recommendation(s). **Freshman Admission Requirements:** High school diploma is required and GED is accepted. *Academic units required:* 4 English, 3 mathematics, 3 science, (2 science labs), 3 social studies. *Academic units recommended:* 4 English, 3 mathematics, 3 science, (2 science labs), 3 social studies. **Freshman Admission Statistics:** 7,042 applied, 81% admitted, 58% enrolled. **Transfer Admission Requirements:** college transcript(s), minimum college GPA of 2.0 required. Lowest grade transferable D-. **General Admission Information:** Application Fee $60. Regular application deadline 4/1. Notification on a rolling basis, beginning on or about 11/1. Nonfall registration accepted. Admission may be deferred for a maximum of 1 year. Credit and/or placement offered for CEEB Advanced Placement tests.

COSTS AND FINANCIAL AID

Required Forms and Deadlines: FAFSA, institution's own financial aid form. **Notification of Awards:** Applicants will be notified of awards on a rolling basis beginning 4/1. **Types of Aid:** *Need-based scholarships/grants:* Federal Pell, SEOG, state scholarships/grants, private scholarships, the school's own gift aid. *Loans:* Direct Subsidized Stafford, Direct Unsubsidized Stafford, Direct PLUS, Federal Perkins, state loans, college/university loans from institutional funds. **Student Employment:** Federal Work-Study Program available. Institutional employment available. Highest amount earned per year from on-campus jobs $3,680. Off-campus job opportunities are excellent. **Financial Aid Statistics:** 42% freshmen, 57% undergrads receive need-based scholarship or grant aid. 62% freshmen, 36% undergrads receive non-need-based scholarship or grant aid. 34% freshmen, 51% undergrads receive need-based self-help aid. 4% freshmen, 3% undergrads receive athletic scholarships. 39% undergrads borrow to pay for school. Average cumulative indebtedness $12,818. **Criteria for awarding institutional aid:** Non-need-based: academics, alumni affiliation, art, athletics, job skills, leadership, minority status, music/drama, state/district residency.

UNIVERSITY OF NEVADA—RENO

Mail Stop 120, Reno, NV 89557
Phone: 775-784-4700
E-mail: asknevada@unr.edu • **CEEB Code:** 4844
Fax: 775-784-4283 • **Website:** www.unr.edu • **ACT Code:** 2497

This public school was founded in 1864. It has a 200-acre campus.

RATINGS

Admissions Selectivity Rating: 68   **Fire Safety Rating:** 60*   **Green Rating:** 60*

STUDENTS AND FACULTY

Enrollment: 11,605. **Student Body:** 55% female, 45% male, 18% out-of-state, 3% international (56 countries represented). Asian 7%, African American 2%, Caucasian 73%, Hispanic 7%, Native American 1%. **Retention and Graduation:** 76% freshmen return for sophomore year. 15% freshmen graduate within 4 years. 47% freshmen graduate within 6 years. **Faculty:** Student/faculty ratio 15:1. 682 full-time faculty, 88% hold PhDs, 14% are members of minority groups, 35% are women.

ACADEMICS

Degrees: bachelor's, first professional, first professional certificate, master's, post-bachelor's certificate, post-master's certificate. **Classes:** Most classes have 20–29 students. Most lab/discussion sessions have 20–29 students. **Special Study Options:** distance learning, double major, dual enrollment, English as a Second Language (ESL), exchange student program (domestic), honors program, independent study, internships, study abroad, teacher certification program. **Disability Services:** Special programs offered to physically disabled students include note-taking services, reader services, tutors. **Career services:** alumni services, career/job search classes, career assessment, internships.

FACILITIES

Housing: Coed dorms, special housing for disabled students, men's dorms, women's dorms, apartments for married students, apartments for single students.

CAMPUS LIFE

Environment: Activities: Choral groups, concert band, dance, drama/theater, jazz band, literary magazine, marching band, music ensembles, musical theater, opera, pep band, radio station, student government, student newspaper, yearbook. **Athletics (Intercollegiate):** *Men:* basketball, cross-country, diving, softball, swimming, tennis, track/field (outdoor), volleyball. *Women:* basketball, cross-country, diving, soccer, softball, swimming, tennis, track/field (outdoor), volleyball.

ADMISSIONS

Freshman Academic Profile: Average high school GPA 3.4. SAT Math middle 50% range 480-600. SAT Critical Reading middle 50% range 470-590. ACT middle 50% range 20-25. Minimum paper TOEFL **Basis for Candidate Selection:** *Very important factors considered include:* rigor of secondary school record. *Other factors considered include:* standardized test scores. **Freshman Admission Requirements:** High school diploma is required and GED is not accepted. *Academic units required:* 4 English, 3 mathematics, 3 science, (2 science labs), 3 social studies. *Academic units recommended:* 4 English, 3 mathematics, 3 science, (2 science labs), 3 social studies. **Freshman Admission Statistics:** 4,024 applied, 88% admitted, 59% enrolled. **Transfer Admission Requirements:** college transcript(s), minimum college GPA of 2.0

required. Lowest grade transferable D-. **General Admission Information:** Application Fee $60. Nonfall registration accepted. Admission may be deferred for a maximum of 1 year. Credit and/or placement offered for CEEB Advanced Placement tests.

COSTS AND FINANCIAL AID

Required Forms and Deadlines: FAFSA. **Notification of Awards:** Applicants will be notified of awards on a rolling basis beginning 4/1. **Types of Aid:** *Need-based scholarships/grants:* Federal Pell, SEOG, private scholarships, the school's own gift aid. *Loans:* Subsidized Stafford, Unsubsidized Stafford, PLUS, Federal Perkins, college/university loans from institutional funds. **Student Employment:** Federal Work-Study Program available. Institutional employment available. Highest amount earned per year from on-campus jobs $3,000. Off-campus job opportunities are excellent. **Financial Aid Statistics:** 44% freshmen, 53% undergrads receive need-based scholarship or grant aid. 89% freshmen, 63% undergrads receive non-need-based scholarship or grant aid. 45% freshmen, 66% undergrads receive need-based self-help aid. 3% freshmen, 4% undergrads receive athletic scholarships. 44% undergrads borrow to pay for school. Average cumulative indebtedness $15,548.

UNIVERSITY OF NEW ENGLAND

11 Hills Beach Road, Biddeford, ME 04005-9599
Phone: 207-602-2297 • **Financial Aid Phone:** 207-602-2342
E-mail: admissions@une.edu • **CEEB Code:** 3751
Fax: 207-602-5900 • **Website:** www.une.edu • **ACT Code:** 3751

This private school was founded in 1831. It has a 550-acre campus.

RATINGS

Admissions Selectivity Rating: 67   **Fire Safety Rating:** 84   **Green Rating:** 60*

STUDENTS AND FACULTY

Enrollment: 1,698. **Student Body:** 77% female, 23% male, 59% out-of-state, 0% international (11 countries represented). Asian 1%, African American 1%, Caucasian 91%, Hispanic 1%. **Retention and Graduation:** 75% freshmen return for sophomore year. 49% freshmen graduate within 4 years. 57% freshmen graduate within 6 years. **Faculty:** Student/faculty ratio 11:1. 137 full-time faculty, 85% hold PhDs, 4% are members of minority groups, 49% are women. 0% of classes are taught by teaching assistants.

ACADEMICS

Degrees: associate, bachelor's, certificate, diploma, first professional, master's, post-bachelor's certificate, post-master's certificate, terminal associate. **Classes:** Most classes have 20–29 students. Most lab/discussion sessions have 10–19 students. **Majors with Highest Enrollment:** athletic training/trainer; biomedical sciences; marine biology and biological oceanography. **Special Study Options:** cross-registration, distance learning, double major, English as a Second Language (ESL), honors program, independent study, internships, student designed major, study abroad, teacher certification program, Advanced standing options are available for qualified undergraduates to both our Physician Assistant and Doctor of Osteopathic Medicine graduate programs. **Honors programs:** The College of Arts and Sciences offers and honors program to qualified applicants. **Combined degree programs:** , DO/MPH and DO/PhD. **Disability Services:** Special programs offered to physically disabled students include note-taking services, reader services, tutors. **Career services:** Alumni network, career/job search classes, career assessment, internships.

FACILITIES

Housing: Coed dorms, women's dorms. 85% of campus accessible to physically disabled. **Special Academic Facilities/Equipment:** Payson Art Gallery; Maine Women Writers Collection; Marine Science Education and Research Center; Marine Animal Rehabilitation Center (MARC); Performance Enhancement and Evaluation Center for health sciences (PEEC); Center for Health Ethics, Law and Policy; Center for Transcultural Health; and New England Institute of Cognitive Science and Evolutionary Psychology. **Computers:** Students can register for classes online.

CAMPUS LIFE

Environment: Village. **Activities:** Choral groups, dance, literary magazine, music ensembles, student government, student newspaper, yearbook 36 registered organizations, 3 honor societies, 1 religious organizations. **Athletics (Intercollegiate):** *Men:* basketball, cross-country, golf, lacrosse, soccer. *Women:* basketball, cross-country, field hockey, golf, lacrosse, soccer, softball, swimming, volleyball. **On-Campus Highlights:** Marine Science and Research Center, Alfond Health Science Center, UNE Beach (on Atlantic Ocean and Saco River), The Point Picnic Area, Campus Center.

ADMISSIONS

Freshman Academic Profile: Average high school GPA 3.2. 17% in top 10% of high school class, 49% in top 25% of high school class, 86% in top 50% of high school class. SAT Math middle 50% range 470–580. SAT Critical Reading middle 50% range 540–570. Minimum paper TOEFL 550. **Basis for Candidate Selection:** *Very important factors considered include:* academic GPA, rigor of secondary school record. *Important factors considered include:* Class rank, interview. *Other factors considered include:* application essay, recommendation(s), standardized test scores, alumni/ae relation, character/personal qualities, extracurricular activities, geographical residence, level of applicant's interest, talent/ability, volunteer work, work experience. **Freshman Admission Requirements:** High school diploma is required and GED is accepted. *Academic units required:* 4 English, 3 mathematics, 3 science, (2 science labs), 2 social studies, 2 history. *Academic units recommended:* 4 English, 3 mathematics, 3 science, (2 science labs), 2 social studies, 2 history. **Freshman Admission Statistics:** 2,055 applied, 92% admitted, 25% enrolled. **Transfer Admission Requirements:** college transcript(s), minimum college GPA of 2.0 required. Lowest grade transferable C–. **General Admission Information:** Application Fee $40. Notification on a rolling basis, beginning on or about 12/15. Nonfall registration accepted. Admission may be deferred for a maximum of 12. Credit and/or placement offered for CEEB Advanced Placement tests.

COSTS AND FINANCIAL AID

Annual tuition $22,940. Room and board $9,255. Required fees $850. Average book expense $1,000. **Required Forms and Deadlines:** FAFSA Tax returns, verification worksheet. **Notification of Awards:** Applicants will be notified of awards on a rolling basis beginning 3/15. **Types of Aid:** *Need-based scholarships/grants:* Federal Pell, SEOG, state scholarships/grants, private scholarships, the school's own gift aid. *Loans:* Subsidized Stafford, Unsubsidized Stafford, PLUS, Federal Perkins, Federal Nursing. **Student Employment:** Federal Work-Study Program available. Institutional employment available. Highest amount earned per year from on-campus jobs $2,000. Off-campus job opportunities are good. **Financial Aid Statistics:** 100% freshmen, 100% undergrads receive need-based scholarship or grant aid. 11% freshmen, 7% undergrads receive non-need-based scholarship or grant aid. 86% freshmen, 91% undergrads receive need-based self-help aid. 93% freshmen, 94% undergrads receive any aid. 88% undergrads borrow to pay for school. Average cumulative indebtedness $37,507. **Criteria for awarding institutional aid:** Non-need-based: academics, alumni affiliation, leadership.

See page 1268.

UNIVERSITY OF NEW HAMPSHIRE

UNH Office of Admissions, Durham, NH 3824
Phone: 603-862-1360 • **Financial Aid Phone:** 603-862-3600
E-mail: admissions@unh.edu • **CEEB Code:** 3918
Fax: 603-862-0077 • **Website:** www.unh.edu • **ACT Code:** 2524

This public school was founded in 1866. It has a 2600-acre campus.

RATINGS

Admissions Selectivity Rating: 73   **Fire Safety Rating:** 92   **Green Rating:** 95

STUDENTS AND FACULTY

Enrollment: 12,565. **Student Body:** 54% female, 46% male, 40% out-of-state, 1% international (65 countries represented). Asian 2%, African American 1%, Caucasian 83%, Hispanic 2%.
Retention and Graduation: 86% freshmen return for sophomore year. 65% freshmen graduate within 4 years. 35% grads go on to further study within 1 year. 10% grads pursue arts and sciences degrees. 1% grads pursue law degrees. 3% grads pursue business degrees. 1% grads pursue medical degrees. **Faculty:** Student/faculty ratio 20:1. 596 full-time faculty, 88% hold PhDs, 10% are members of minority groups, 39% are women. 1% of classes are taught by teaching assistants.

ACADEMICS

Degrees: associate, bachelor's, doctoral, master's, post-bachelor's certificate, post-master's certificate, terminal associate. **Classes:** Most classes have 20–29 students. Most lab/discussion sessions have 20–29 students. **Majors with Highest Enrollment:** business administration and management; English

language and literature; psychology. **Special Study Options:** Accelerated program, cooperative education program, cross-registration, distance learning, double major, English as a Second Language (ESL), exchange student program (domestic), honors program, independent study, internships, student-designed major, study abroad, teacher certification program, weekend college, Research/Creative Projects, Learning Communities, Experiential Learning, Senior Capstone, Service Learning, Work Study, Honors. **Honors programs:** The UNH honors program offers small and dynamic classes, opportunities for research and study overseas, individualized advising and a close and supportive community. **Combined degree programs:** BA/MA, BS/MS OT, BA/BS and MBA, BS/MS Account, BA/BS and MEduc, BS/MS in biochem. **Disability Services:** Special programs offered to physically disabled students include note-taking services, reader services, tape recorders, tutors. **Career services:** Alumni network, alumni services, career/job search classes, career assessment, internships, regional alumni. Career services highlights include UNH's Washington Internship Program through the Washington Internship Program allows UNH students to earn academic credit while working and living in Washington, DC. Recent internships for UNH students have included the US Senate, State Department, US Attorney Generals Office, Environmental Protection Agency, Smithsonian Museum, public interest law firms, lobbyists, and non-profit organizations.

FACILITIES

Housing: Coed dorms, special housing for international students, fraternity/sorority housing, apartments for married students, apartments for single students, Theme Housing. There are 11 theme dorms. for only freshman and 11 others for all students. Four "small halls" of 45 to 50 people in mostly single rooms are also available. 85% of campus accessible to physically disabled. **Special Academic Facilities/Equipment:** Journalism laboratory, Milne Special Collections Archives and Museum, optical observatory, marine research laboratory, experiential learning center, child development center,language lab, art gallery, agricultural and equine facilities, electron microscope, sawmill, nature preserves and trails, survey center, radio station **Computers:** 5% of classrooms, 100% of dorms, 100% of libraries, 100% of student union, 2% of common outdoor areas have wireless network access. Students can register for classes online. Administrative functions (other than registration) can be performed online.

CAMPUS LIFE

Environment: Village. **Activities:** Choral groups, concert band, dance, drama/theater, jazz band, literary magazine, marching band, music ensembles, musical theater, pep band, radio station, student government, student newspaper, student-run film society, symphony orchestra, television station, yearbook, Campus Ministries, International Student Organization, Model UN. 187 registered organizations, 18 honor societies, 10 religious organizations. 10 fraternities, 7 sororities. **Athletics (Intercollegiate):** *Men:* basketball, cross-country, football, ice hockey, skiing (downhill/alpine), skiing nordic cross-country, soccer, track/field (outdoor), track/field (indoor). *Women:* basketball, cross-country, diving, field hockey, gymnastics, ice hockey, lacrosse, skiing (downhill/alpine), skiing nordic cross-country, soccer, swimming, track/field (outdoor), track/field (indoor), volleyball. **On-Campus Highlights:** Dimond Library, Whittemore Center, Hamel Recreation Center, Student Union/Holloway Commons, College Woods, Other spots include Dairy Bar/Train Station, Art Gallery, Thompson Hall, Morse Hall. **Environmental Initiatives:** 1. The UNH USustainability Academy (UNHSA) is the oldest endowed sustainability program in higher education in the U.S. and has worked with the larger campus community over nearly 15 years to develop UNH's unique sustainable learning community model and to foster sustainability locally, statewide, and regionally. www.sustainableunh.unh.edu Under our comprehensive Climate Education Initiative and as a key component of its climate action plan, WildCAP and signature to the American College and University Presidents Climate Commitment, UNH has committed to cut its greenhouse gas emission 50% by 2020 and 80% by 2050 on the road to carbon neutrality by 2100. We also use processed landfill gas from the EcoLine project, a landfill gas-to-energy project that uses methane gas from a nearby landfill, as the primary fuel for our on-campus cogeneration plan. By selling the renewable energy credits associate with EcoLine we are able to help finance this project and invest in more energy efficiency on campus via a new revolving energy efficiency fund. More info at www.sustainableunh.unh.edu/ecoline, www.sustainableunh.unh.edu/cei and http://www.sustainableunh.unh.edu/wildcap Responding to a need by farmers for scientific research to support organic dairy efforts, UNH is the first land grant university to have an organic dairy farm and education/research center. The organic dairy is a research center for organic production and management and an education center for organic dairy farmers, farmers considering the transition to organic, and students of sustainable agriculture. The organic dairy research farm is part of UNH's broader Food & Society Initiative (FAS) through which UNH meets its commitment to being a sustainable food community. Other efforts include a Dual Major in EcoGastronomy for undergraduate students and a Local Harvest Initiative in the dining halls. More info at www.sustainableunh.unh.edu/fas

ADMISSIONS

Freshman Academic Profile: 18% in top 10% of high school class, 50% in top 25% of high school class, 90% in top 50% of high school class. 75% from public high schools. SAT Math middle 50% range 500-610. SAT Critical Reading middle 50% range 490-590. SAT Writing middle 50% range 500-600. ACT middle 50% range 22-27. Minimum web-based TOEFL 80. Minimum paper TOEFL 550. **Basis for Candidate Selection:** *Very important factors considered include:* Class rank, rigor of secondary school record. *Important factors considered include:* academic GPA, recommendation(s). *Other factors considered include:* application essay, standardized test scores, alumni/ae relation, character/personal qualities, extracurricular activities, first generation, geographical residence, racial/ethnic status, state residency, talent/ability, volunteer work, work experience. **Freshman Admission Requirements:** High school diploma is required and GED is accepted. *Academic units required:* 4 English, 3 mathematics, 3 science, (2 science labs), 2 foreign language, 3 social studies. *Academic units recommended:* 4 English, 3 mathematics, 3 science, (2 science labs), 2 foreign language, 3 social studies. **Freshman Admission Statistics:** 17,234 applied, 78% admitted, 22% enrolled. **Transfer Admission Requirements:** High school transcript, college transcript(s), essay or personal statement, interview, standardized test scores, minimum college GPA of 2.8 required. Lowest grade transferable C. **General Admission Information:** Application Fee $50. Regular application deadline 2/1. Notification on a rolling basis, beginning on or about 2/1. Nonfall registration accepted. Admission may be deferred for a maximum of 1 year. Credit and/or placement offered for CEEB Advanced Placement tests.

COSTS AND FINANCIAL AID

Annual in-state tuition $13,670. Annual out-of-state tuition $26,130. Room and board $9,764. Required fees $2,752. Average book expense $1,200. **Required Forms and Deadlines:** FAFSA. **Notification of Awards:** Applicants will be notified of awards on a rolling basis beginning 3/1. **Types of Aid:** *Need-based scholarships/grants:* Federal Pell, SEOG, state scholarships/grants, private scholarships, the school's own gift aid, Veterans Educational Benefits. *Loans:* Subsidized Stafford, Unsubsidized Stafford, PLUS, Federal Perkins, college/university loans from institutional funds. **Student Employment:** Federal Work-Study Program available. Institutional employment available. Highest amount earned per year from on-campus jobs $25,487. Off-campus job opportunities are excellent. **Financial Aid Statistics:** 68% freshmen, 65% undergrads receive need-based scholarship or grant aid. 7% freshmen, 5% undergrads receive non-need-based scholarship or grant aid. 96% freshmen, 96% undergrads receive need-based self-help aid. 1% freshmen, 1% undergrads receive athletic scholarships. 86% freshmen, 81% undergrads receive any aid. 78% undergrads borrow to pay for school. Average cumulative indebtedness $35,168. **Criteria for awarding institutional aid:** Non-need-based: academics, art, athletics, leadership, music/drama, religious affiliation.

UNIVERSITY OF NEW HAMPSHIRE AT MANCHESTER

400 Commercial Street, Manchester, NH 3101
Phone: 603-641-4150
E-mail: unhm.admissions@unh.edu • **CEEB Code:** 2094
Fax: 603-641-4125 • **Website:** www.unh.edu/unhm/ • **ACT Code.**

This public school was founded in 1985.

RATINGS

Admissions Selectivity Rating: 71   **Fire Safety Rating:** 60*   **Green Rating:** 60*

STUDENTS AND FACULTY

Enrollment: 704. **Student Body:** 64% female, 36% male, 1% out-of-state, 1% international (5 countries represented). Asian 1%, African American 2%, Caucasian 94%, Hispanic 1%.
Retention and Graduation: Faculty: Student/faculty ratio 18:1. 23 full-time faculty, 78% hold PhDs, 52% are women. 3% of classes are taught by teaching assistants.

ACADEMICS

Degrees: associate, bachelor's. **Classes:** Most classes have 10–19 students. **Special Study Options:** cross-registration, double major, English as a Second Language (ESL), exchange student program (domestic), independent study, internships, study abroad, teacher certification program. **Disability Services:** Special programs offered to physically disabled students include note-taking services, reader services, tape recorders, tutors. **Career services:** alumni services, career/job search classes, career assessment, internships.

FACILITIES

Housing: 85% of campus accessible to physically disabled.

CAMPUS LIFE

Activities: student government.

ADMISSIONS

Freshman Academic Profile: SAT Math middle 50% range 440-550. SAT Critical Reading middle 50% range 460-550. Minimum web-based TOEFL 75. Minimum paper TOEFL 550. **Basis for Candidate Selection:** *Very important factors considered include:* rigor of secondary school record. *Important factors considered include:* Class rank, application essay, recommendation(s), standardized test scores. *Other factors considered include:* alumni/ae relation, character/personal qualities, extracurricular activities, interview, racial/ethnic status, state residency, talent/ability, volunteer work, work experience. **Freshman Admission Requirements:** High school diploma is required and GED is accepted. *Academic units required:* 4 English, 3 mathematics, (3 science labs), 2 foreign language, 2 social studies. *Academic units recommended:* 4 English, 3 mathematics, (3 science labs), 2 foreign language, 2 social studies. **Freshman Admission Statistics:** 218 applied, 74% admitted, 66% enrolled. **Transfer Admission Requirements:** High school transcript, college transcript(s), essay or personal statement, statement of good standing from prior institution(s). Minimum college GPA of 2.5 required. Lowest grade transferable C. **General Admission Information:** Application Fee $50. Regular application deadline 6/15. Notification on a rolling basis, beginning on or about 1/31. Nonfall registration accepted. Admission may be deferred for a maximum of 2 Semesters. Credit offered for CEEB Advanced Placement tests.

COSTS AND FINANCIAL AID

Annual in-state tuition $4,630. Annual out-of-state tuition $12,190. Required fees $54. Average book expense $700. **Required Forms and Deadlines:** FAFSA, noncustodial PROFILE, business/farm supplement. **Notification of Awards:** Applicants will be notified of awards on a rolling basis beginning 4/1. **Types of Aid:** *Need-based scholarships/grants:* Federal Pell, SEOG, state scholarships/grants, private scholarships, the school's own gift aid. *Loans:* Subsidized Stafford, Unsubsidized Stafford, PLUS, Federal Perkins, Outside Loans. **Student Employment:** Federal Work-Study Program available. Institutional employment available. Off-campus job opportunities are excellent. **Financial Aid Statistics:** **Criteria for awarding institutional aid:** Non-need-based: academics, minority status.

UNIVERSITY OF NEW HAVEN

300 Boston Post Road, West Haven, CT 6516
Phone: 203-932-7319 • **Financial Aid Phone:** 203-932-7315
E-mail: adminfo@newhaven.edu • **CEEB Code:** 3663
Fax: 203-931-6093 • **Website:** www.newhaven.edu • **ACT Code:** 576

This private school was founded in 1920. It has a 78-acre campus.

RATINGS

Admissions Selectivity Rating: 79   **Fire Safety Rating:** 67   **Green Rating:** 60*

STUDENTS AND FACULTY

Enrollment: 4,159. **Student Body:** 50% female, 50% male, 47% out-of-state, 7% international (19 countries represented). Asian 1%, African American 7%, Caucasian 42%, Hispanic 6%.
Retention and Graduation: 72% freshmen return for sophomore year. 37% freshmen graduate within 4 years. 53% freshmen graduate within 6 years.
Faculty: Student/faculty ratio 16:1. 203 full-time faculty, 78% hold PhDs, 11% are members of minority groups, 31% are women.

ACADEMICS

Degrees: associate, bachelor's, certificate, master's, post-bachelor's certificate. **Classes:** Most classes have 10–19 students. Most lab/discussion sessions have 10–19 students. **Majors with Highest Enrollment:** business/commerce; criminal justice/law enforcement administration; engineering. **Special Study Options:** Accelerated program, cooperative education program, cross-registration, double major, dual enrollment, English as a Second Language (ESL), honors program, independent study, internships, student-designed major, study abroad. **Combined degree programs:** , BS/MS in environmental science. **Disability Services:** Special programs offered to physically disabled students include note-taking services, reader services, tape recorders, tutors. **Career services:** Alumni network, alumni services, career/job search classes, career assessment, internships.

FACILITIES

Housing: Coed dorms, apartments for single students. 82% of campus accessible to physically disabled. **Special Academic Facilities/Equipment:** Art gallery, forensic science lab, radio station, tv station, theater Orchestra New England, music and sound recording studio. **Computers:**

CAMPUS LIFE

Environment: Village. **Activities:** Choral groups, dance, drama/theater, music ensembles, musical theater, pep band, radio station, student government, student newspaper, television station, yearbook 50 registered organizations, 5 honor societies, 1 religious organizations. 2 fraternities, 3 sororities. **Athletics (Intercollegiate):** *Men:* baseball, basketball, cross-country, golf, lacrosse, soccer, track/field (outdoor), track/field (indoor), volleyball. *Women:* basketball, cheerleading, cross-country, lacrosse, soccer, softball, tennis, volleyball. **On-Campus Highlights:** Bartel's Student Union, Student Run Dance Hall, Coffe Shop

ADMISSIONS

Freshman Academic Profile: Average high school GPA 3.3. SAT Math middle 50% range 480-580. SAT Critical Reading middle 50% range 470-570. SAT Writing middle 50% range 470-560. ACT middle 50% range 20-25. **Basis for Candidate Selection:** *Very important factors considered include:* rigor of secondary school record, standardized test scores. *Important factors considered include:* Class rank, application essay, recommendation(s). *Other factors considered include:* alumni/ae relation, character/personal qualities, extracurricular activities, interview, talent/ability, volunteer work, work experience. **Freshman Admission Requirements:** High school diploma is required and GED is accepted. *Academic units required:* 4 English, 3 mathematics, 2 science, 2 history, 3 academic electives. *Academic units recommended:* 4 English, 3 mathematics, 2 science, 2 history, 3 academic electives. **Freshman Admission Statistics:** 8,618 applied, 62% admitted, 19% enrolled. **Transfer Admission Requirements:** High school transcript, college transcript(s), minimum college GPA of 2.5 required. Lowest grade transferable C. **General Admission Information:** Application Fee $50. Notification on a rolling basis, beginning on or about 9/15. Nonfall registration accepted. Admission may be deferred for a maximum of 1 year. Credit and/or placement offered for CEEB Advanced Placement tests.

COSTS AND FINANCIAL AID

Required Forms and Deadlines: FAFSA, institution's own financial aid formtax returns. **Notification of Awards:** Applicants will be notified of awards on a rolling basis beginning 3/15. **Types of Aid:** *Need-based scholarships/grants:* Federal Pell, SEOG, state scholarships/grants, private scholarships, the school's own gift aid. *Loans:* Subsidized Stafford, Unsubsidized Stafford, PLUS, Federal Perkins. **Student Employment:** Federal Work-Study Program available. Institutional employment available. Highest amount earned per year from on-campus jobs $900. Off-campus job opportunities are excellent. **Financial Aid Statistics:** 100% freshmen, 100% undergrads receive need-based scholarship or grant aid. 12% freshmen, 9% undergrads receive non-need-based scholarship or grant aid. 83% freshmen, 88% undergrads receive need-based self-help aid. 53% undergrads borrow to pay for school. Average cumulative indebtedness $40,911. **Criteria for awarding institutional aid:** Non-need-based: academics, athletics.

See page 1270.

UNIVERSITY OF NEW MEXICO

Office of Admissions, Albuquerque, NM 87196-4895
Phone: 505-277-2446 • **Financial Aid Phone:** 505-277-8900
E-mail: apply@unm.edu • **CEEB Code:** 4845
Fax: 505-277-6686 • **Website:** www.unm.edu • **ACT Code:** 2650

This public school was founded in 1889. It has a 769-acre campus.

RATINGS

Admissions Selectivity Rating: 79   **Fire Safety Rating:** 70   **Green Rating:** 87

STUDENTS AND FACULTY

Enrollment: Student Body: 10% out-of-state, (92 countries represented). **Retention and Graduation:** 74% freshmen return for sophomore year. **Faculty:** Student/faculty ratio 23:1. 949 full-time faculty, 82% hold PhDs, 24% are members of minority groups, 46% are women.

ACADEMICS

Degrees: associate, bachelor's, certificate, first professional, master's, post-master's certificate. **Classes:** Most classes have 20–29 students. Most lab/discussion sessions have 10–19 students. **Majors with Highest Enrollment:** biology/biological sciences; business administration and management; psychology. **Special Study Options:** Accelerated program, cooperative education program, distance learning, double major, dual enrollment, English as a Second Language (ESL), exchange student program (domestic), honors program, independent study, internships, student-designed major, study abroad, teacher certification program, weekend college. **Honors programs:** The University Honors Program offers the chance to explore major contemporary ideas and values in small interdisciplinary seminars with the additional benefits of personal interaction with outstanding UNM faculty, opportunities for upper-division independent research, social and cultural events, lecture series, and opportunities to participate in regional and national honors conferences. UHP students do not major in University Honors. They graduate with a degree from one of UNM's degree-granting colleges or schools. **Combined degree programs:** BA/MD, 3-2 Latin American Studies/mba. **Disability Services:** Special programs offered to physically disabled students include note-taking services, reader services, tape recorders, tutors. **Career services:** Alumni network, alumni services, career/job search classes, career assessment, internships, regional alumni.

FACILITIES

Housing: Coed dorms, fraternity/sorority housing, apartments for married students, apartments for single students, Special living options include graduate and senior housing, academic floors, scholars wing, and outdoor/wellness units. Computer Science and Engineering unit also available. 100% of campus accessible to physically disabled. **Special Academic Facilities/Equipment:** Museums of art, anthropology, geology, and Southwestern biology, lithography institute, meteoritics institute, electron and electron scanning microscopes, nuclear reactor, robotics lab, observatory, planetarium, Science and Technology Park. **Computers:** 100% of classrooms, 100% of dorms, 100% of libraries, 100% of dining areas, 100% of student union, 85% of common outdoor areas have wireless network access. Students can register for classes online. Administrative functions (other than registration) can be performed online.

CAMPUS LIFE

Environment: Metropolis. **Activities:** Choral groups, concert band, dance, drama/theater, jazz band, literary magazine, marching band, music ensembles, musical theater, opera, pep band, radio station, student government, student newspaper, student-run film society, symphony orchestra, television station 375 registered organizations, 20 honor societies, 23 religious organizations. 9 fraternities, 10 sororities. **Athletics (Intercollegiate):** *Men:* baseball, basketball, cross-country, football, golf, skiing (downhill/alpine), skiingnordiccross-country, soccer, tennis, track/field (outdoor), track/field (indoor). *Women:* basketball, cross-country, diving, golf, skiing (downhill/alpine), skiingnordiccross-country, soccer, softball, swimming, tennis, track/field (outdoor), track/field (indoor), volleyball. **On-Campus Highlights:** SUB (Student Union Building), Duck Pond, Zimmerman Library, Popejoy Hall - Performing Arts Center, Residency Halls, Maxwell Museum, Trolly Tour of Campus for new and prospective students. **Environmental Initiatives:** In November 2009 UNM submitted its first Climate Action Plan to the American College and University Presidents Climate Commitment website and set a climate neutrality target date of year 2050. UNM will use a multi-tiered approach to reducing our greenhouse gas emissions. The tiers are behavior- based energy conservation, technological improvements in utilities production and consumption, renewable energy, and alternative transportation. UNM has won two Energy Star awards from the U.S. Environmental Protection Agency. In November 2007 the Physical Plant Department received the Energy Star Combined Heat and Power award for the Ford Utilities Center cogeneration unit, which met the criteria for energy efficiency and fuel savings. In November 2009 University Hospital became the first academic hospital to be presented with an Energy Star award. In collaboration with over 100 community partners, the Research Service Learning Program (RSLP) under the direction of Dr. Dan Young has offered UNM students 31 courses related to sustainability, food security, and social development since the summer of 2006. During the fall 2009 semester RSLP students in wrote a Guide to Green Living at UNM and developed an Eco Rep Program for the resident halls. The Eco Reps serve as sustainability advocates to their peers in each dorm providing guidance and leadership in recycling, energy conservation, alternative transportation, and purchasing locally grown, organic foods. In fall 2010, the RSLP will partner with Sustainability Studies on a Sustainability Living and Learning Center for 12 - 20 freshmen in the dorms.

ADMISSIONS

Freshman Academic Profile: Average high school GPA 3.3. SAT Math middle 50% range 470-590. SAT Critical Reading middle 50% range 470-600. ACT middle 50% range 19-25. Minimum web-based TOEFL 68. Minimum paper TOEFL 520. **Basis for Candidate Selection:** *Very important factors considered include:* academic GPA, rigor of secondary school record. *Important factors considered include:* Class rank, standardized test scores. *Other factors* *considered include:* application essay, recommendation(s), character/personal qualities, extracurricular activities, first generation, volunteer work, work experience. **Freshman Admission Requirements:** High school diploma is required and GED is accepted. *Academic units required:* 4 English, 3 mathematics, 2 science, (1 science labs), 2 foreign language, 1 social studies, 1 history. *Academic units recommended:* 4 English, 3 mathematics, 2 science, (1 science labs), 2 foreign language, 1 social studies, 1 history. **Freshman Admission Statistics:** 11,410 applied, 64% admitted, 46% enrolled. **Transfer Admission Requirements:** college transcript(s), minimum college GPA of 2.0 required. Lowest grade transferable C. **General Admission Information:** Application Fee $20. Regular application deadline 6/15. Nonfall registration accepted. Admission may be deferred for a maximum of 1 year. Credit and/or placement offered for CEEB Advanced Placement tests.

COSTS AND FINANCIAL AID
Average book expense $958. **Required Forms and Deadlines:** FAFSA. **Notification of Awards:** Applicants will be notified of awards on a rolling basis beginning 4/15. **Types of Aid:** *Need-based scholarships/grants:* Federal Pell, SEOG, state scholarships/grants, private scholarships, the school's own gift aid, United Negro College Fund, Federal Nursing Scholarships. *Loans:* Direct Subsidized Stafford, Direct Unsubsidized Stafford, Direct PLUS, Federal Perkins, Federal Nursing, state loans, college/university loans from institutional funds. **Student Employment:** Federal Work-Study Program available. **Financial Aid Statistics: Criteria for awarding institutional aid:** Non-need-based: academics, alumni affiliation, art, athletics, job skills, leadership, minority status, music/drama, religious affiliation, state/district residency.

UNIVERSITY OF NEW ORLEANS

Best 378

University of New Orleans Admissions, New Orleans, LA 70148
Phone: 504-280-6595 • **Financial Aid Phone:** 504-280-6603
E-mail: http://www.uno.edu/Admissions • **CEEB Code:** 6379
Fax: 504-280-5522 • **Website:** www.uno.edu • **ACT Code:** 1591

This public school was founded in 1956. It has a 195-acre campus.

RATINGS
Admissions Selectivity Rating: 84   **Fire Safety Rating:** 66   **Green Rating:** 61

STUDENTS AND FACULTY
Enrollment: 8,028. **Student Body:** 49% female, 51% male, 4% out-of-state, 4% international (75 countries represented). Asian 7%, African American 16%, Caucasian 55%, Hispanic 8%, Native American 1%. **Retention and Graduation:** 67% freshmen return for sophomore year. 17% freshmen graduate within 4 years. **Faculty:** Student/faculty ratio 20:1. 368 full-time faculty, 97% hold PhDs, 17% are members of minority groups, 39% are women. 5% of classes are taught by teaching assistants.

ACADEMICS
Degrees: bachelor's, master's, post-bachelor's certificate. **Classes:** Most classes have 20–29 students. **Majors with Highest Enrollment:** business administration and management; general studies; psychology. **Special Study Options:** cooperative education program, cross-registration, distance learning, double major, dual enrollment, English as a Second Language (ESL), exchange student program (domestic), honors program, independent study, internships, student-designed major, study abroad, teacher certification program, weekend college. **Disability Services:** Special programs offered to physically disabled students include note-taking services, reader services, tape recorders, tutors. **Career services:** alumni services, career assessment, internships.

FACILITIES
Housing: Coed dorms, special housing for disabled students, apartments for married students, apartments for single students. 100% of campus accessible to physically disabled. **Special Academic Facilities/Equipment:** Performing arts center, audiovisual center, TV studio, Eisenhower leadership studies center, child care center, Louisiana collection. **Computers:** 100% of libraries, 100% of student union, have wireless network access. Students can register for classes online. Administrative functions (other than registration) can be performed online.

CAMPUS LIFE
Environment: Metropolis. **Activities:** Choral groups, concert band, dance, drama/theater, jazz band, literary magazine, music ensembles, musical theater,

opera, pep band, radio station, student government, student newspaper, student-run film society, Campus Ministries, International Student Organization 120 registered organizations, 7 religious organizations. 9 fraternities, 8 sororities. **Athletics (Intercollegiate):** *Men:* baseball, basketball, diving, golf, swimming, tennis. *Women:* basketball, diving, swimming, tennis, volleyball. **On-Campus Highlights:** Recreation and Fitness Center, The University Center, The Homer L. Hitt Alumni and Visitors Ce, Earl K. Long Library.

ADMISSIONS
Freshman Academic Profile: Average high school GPA 3.0. 12% in top 10% of high school class, 30% in top 25% of high school class, 61% in top 50% of high school class. 62% from public high schools. SAT Math middle 50% range 460-590. SAT Critical Reading middle 50% range 480-590. ACT middle 50% range 19-24. Minimum web-based TOEFL 71. Minimum paper TOEFL 525. **Basis for Candidate Selection:** *Very important factors considered include:* Class rank, academic GPA, rigor of secondary school record, standardized test scores. *Other factors considered include:* recommendation(s), geographical residence, state residency. **Freshman Admission Requirements:** High school diploma is required and GED is accepted. *Academic units required:* 4 English, 3 mathematics, 3 science, 2 foreign language, 1 social studies, 2 history, 1 visual/performing arts. *Academic units recommended:* 4 English, 3 mathematics, 3 science, 2 foreign language, 1 social studies, 2 history, 1 visual/performing arts. **Freshman Admission Statistics:** 3,353 applied, 56% admitted, 59% enrolled. **Transfer Admission Requirements:** college transcript(s), minimum college GPA of 2.25 required. Lowest grade transferable D. **General Admission Information:** Application Fee $40. Regular application deadline 8/20. Notification on a rolling basis, beginning on or about 10/1. Nonfall registration accepted. Admission may be deferred for a maximum of 1 year. Credit and/or placement offered for CEEB Advanced Placement tests.

COSTS AND FINANCIAL AID
Annual in-state tuition $5,164. Annual out-of-state tuition $17,176. Room and board $8,310. Required fees $631. Average book expense $1,300. **Required Forms and Deadlines:** FAFSA. **Notification of Awards:** Applicants will be notified of awards on a rolling basis beginning 4/20. **Types of Aid:** *Need-based scholarships/grants:* Federal Pell, SEOG, state scholarships/grants, private scholarships, the school's own gift aid. *Loans:* Direct Subsidized Stafford, Direct Unsubsidized Stafford, Direct PLUS, Subsidized Stafford, Unsubsidized Stafford, PLUS, Federal Perkins, college/university loans from institutional funds. **Student Employment:** Federal Work-Study Program available. Institutional employment available. Highest amount earned per year from on campus jobs $23,920. **Financial Aid Statistics:** 76% freshmen, 63% undergrads receive need-based scholarship or grant aid. 57% freshmen, 39% undergrads receive non-need-based scholarship or grant aid. 44% freshmen, 51% undergrads receive need-based self-help aid. 1% freshmen, 1% undergrads receive athletic scholarships. 78% freshmen, 65% undergrads receive any aid. 19% undergrads borrow to pay for school. Average cumulative indebtedness $18,106. **Criteria for awarding institutional aid:** Non-need-based: academics, athletics.

UNIVERSITY OF NORTH ALABAMA

UNA Box 5011, Florence, AL 35632-0001
Phone: 256-765-4318 • **Financial Aid Phone:** 256-765-4278
E-mail: admissions@una.edu
Fax: 256-765-4329 • **Website:** www.una.edu/

This public school was founded in 1830. It has a 130-acre campus.

RATINGS
Admissions Selectivity Rating: 66   **Fire Safety Rating:** 65   **Green Rating:** 60*

STUDENTS AND FACULTY
Enrollment: 5,235. **Student Body:** 57% female, 43% male, 19% out-of-state, 9% international (67 countries represented). Asian 1%, African American 10%, Caucasian 70%, Hispanic 1%, Native American 1%. **Retention and Graduation:** 68% freshmen return for sophomore year. 55% freshmen graduate within 6 years. **Faculty:** Student/faculty ratio 21:1. 247 full-time faculty, 63% hold PhDs, 14% are members of minority groups, 47% are women. 0% of classes are taught by teaching assistants.

ACADEMICS
Degrees: bachelor's, master's, post-master's certificate. **Classes:** Most classes have fewer than 10 students. Most lab/discussion sessions have 20–29 students. **Majors with Highest Enrollment:** business/commerce; nursing/registered nurse (rn, asn, bsn, msn); secondary education and teaching. **Special Study Options:** Accelerated program, cooperative education program, distance learning, double major, dual enrollment, English as a Second Language (ESL), hon-

ors program, independent study, internships, student-designed major, teacher certification program, weekend college. **Disability Services:** Special programs offered to physically disabled students include tutors.

FACILITIES

Housing: Coed dorms, men's dorms, special housing for international students, women's dorms, fraternity/sorority housing, apartments for married students, apartments for single students. 99% of campus accessible to physically disabled. **Special Academic Facilities/Equipment:** On-campus lab school (N-6), planetarium, observatory, art gallery. **Computers:** Students can register for classes online.

CAMPUS LIFE

Environment: Town. **Activities:** Choral groups, concert band, drama/theater, jazz band, literary magazine, marching band, music ensembles, musical theater, pep band, radio station, student government, student newspaper, yearbook 98 registered organizations. **Athletics (Intercollegiate):** *Men:* baseball, basketball, cross-country, football, golf, tennis. *Women:* basketball, cross-country, soccer, softball, tennis, volleyball. **On-Campus Highlights:** Guillot University Center, Academic Resource Center, Entertainment Industry Center, Recreation Center, Flowers Hall.

ADMISSIONS

Freshman Academic Profile: Average high school GPA 3.0. 44% in top 25% of high school class, 76% in top 50% of high school class. 99% from public high schools. ACT middle 50% range 18-24. Minimum paper TOEFL 500. **Basis for Candidate Selection:** *Very important factors considered include:* Class rank, academic GPA, standardized test scores. *Important factors considered include:* rigor of secondary school record, character/personal qualities. **Freshman Admission Requirements:** High school diploma is required and GED is accepted. *Academic units required:* 4 English, 2 mathematics, 2 science, 2 foreign language, 3 social studies. *Academic units recommended:* 4 English, 2 mathematics, 2 science, 2 foreign language, 3 social studies. **Freshman Admission Statistics:** 2,227 applied, 84% admitted, 54% enrolled. **Transfer Admission Requirements:** college transcript(s), minimum college GPA of 2.0 required. Lowest grade transferable C. **General Admission Information:** Application Fee $25. Notification on a rolling basis, beginning on or about 6/15. Nonfall registration accepted. Admission may be deferred for a maximum of 1 semester. Credit offered for CEEB Advanced Placement tests.

COSTS AND FINANCIAL AID

Annual in-state tuition $3,768. Annual out-of-state tuition $7,536. Room and board $4,372. Required fees $883. Average book expense $830. **Required Forms and Deadlines:** FAFSA. **Notification of Awards:** Applicants will be notified of awards on a rolling basis beginning 5/31. **Types of Aid:** *Need-based scholarships/grants:* Federal Pell, SEOG, state scholarships/grants, private scholarships, the school's own gift aid. *Loans:* Subsidized Stafford, Unsubsidized Stafford, PLUS, Federal Perkins. **Student Employment: Financial Aid Statistics:** 63% freshmen, 61% undergrads receive need-based scholarship or grant aid. 81% freshmen, 57% undergrads receive non-need-based scholarship or grant aid. 61% freshmen, 76% undergrads receive need-based self-help aid. 5% freshmen, 5% undergrads receive athletic scholarships. 47% undergrads borrow to pay for school. Average cumulative indebtedness $18,245. **Criteria for awarding institutional aid:** Non-need-based: academics, art, athletics, leadership, minority status, music/drama, state/district residency.

THE UNIVERSITY OF NORTH CAROLINA AT ASHEVILLE

Best 378

CPO #1320, Asheville, NC 28804-8502
Phone: 828-251-6481 • **Financial Aid Phone:** 828-251-6535
E-mail: admissions@unca.edu • **CEEB Code:** 5013
Fax: 828-251-6482 • **Website:** www.unca.edu • **ACT Code:** 3064

This public school was founded in 1927. It has a 265-acre campus.

RATINGS
Admissions Selectivity Rating: 85   **Fire Safety Rating:** 94   **Green Rating:** 77

STUDENTS AND FACULTY
Enrollment: 3,259. Student Body: 57% female, 43% male, 12% out-of-state, 0% international (23 countries represented). Asian 1%, African American 3%, Caucasian 85%, Hispanic 4%, Native American 0%

Retention and Graduation: 78% freshmen return for sophomore year. 32% freshmen graduate within 4 years. 55% freshmen graduate within 6 years. 20% grads go on to further study within 1 year. 17% grads pursue arts and sciences degrees. 1% grads pursue law degrees. 1% grads pursue business degrees. 1% grads pursue medical degrees. Faculty: Student/faculty ratio 14:1. 213 full-time faculty, 84% hold PhDs, 15% are are members of minority groups, 45% are women. 0% of classes are taught by teaching assistants.

ACADEMICS

Degrees: bachelor's, master's, post-bachelor's certificate. Classes: Most classes have 10–19 students. Most lab/discussion sessions have 20–29 students. Majors with Highest Enrollment: English language and literature; psychology; sociology. Special Study Options: cross-registration, distance learning, double major, dual enrollment, exchange student program (domestic), honors program, independent study, internships, liberal arts/career combination, student-designed major, study abroad, teacher certification program. Honors programs: University Honors Program - Designed for talented and motivated students, the Honors curriculum complements the General Education and major curricula. Successful completion of the Honors Program enables the student to graduate with Distinction as a University Scholar. (See http://www.unca.edu/honors/ for further information.) Undergraduate Research Program - The Undergraduate Research Program at UNCA seeks to encourage the establishment of faculty/student research pairs who work together on a project of mutual interest. Research may be performed in any discipline on campus. Students who have made oral presentations at symposia and have had their work reviewed and published can receive recognition as University Research Scholars. (See http://www.unca.edu/urp/ for more information.) . Disability Services: Special programs offered to physically disabled students include note-taking services, reader services, tape recorders, tutors. Career services: Alumni network, alumni services, career/job search classes, career assessment, internships, regional alumni.

FACILITIES

Housing: Coed dorms, special housing for disabled students, men's dorms, women's dorms, substance-free dorms, 24 hour quiet dorms. 95% of campus accessible to physically disabled. Special Academic Facilities/Equipment: Undergraduate Research Center, Steelcase Teleconference Center, Music Recording Center, Asheville Botanical Gardens, NC Arboretum, Center for Creative Retirement Computers: 1% of classrooms, 100% of libraries, 100% of dining areas, 90% of student union, have wireless network access. Students can register for classes online. Administrative functions (other than registration) can be performed online.

CAMPUS LIFE

Environment: Town. Activities: Choral groups, concert band, dance, drama/theater, jazz band, literary magazine, music ensembles, musical theater, pep band, radio station, student government, student newspaper, Campus Ministries, International Student Organization 82 registered organizations, 14 honor societies, 10 religious organizations. 1 fraternities, 2 sororities. Athletics (Intercollegiate): Men: baseball, basketball, cheerleading, cross-country, soccer, tennis, track/field (outdoor). Women: basketball, cheerleading, cross-country, soccer, tennis, track/field (outdoor), volleyball. On-Campus Highlights: Health and Fitness Center, Main Campus Quadrangle, Highsmith University Union, Asheville Botanical Gardens, Cafe Ramsey in Ramsey Library, . Environmental Initiatives: Examples: The Wilma M. Sherrill Center, home to the North Carolina Center for Health & Wellness, is a new, 162,000 square-foot, multi-purpose facility, completed in 2011. It provides classroom, dance and exercise studios, offices, laboratory, test kitchen and a healthy-choice cafe space as well as an indoor venue for commencement ceremonies and other events.

ADMISSIONS

Freshman Academic Profile: Average high school GPA 4.1. 22% in top 10% of high school class, 62% in top 25% of high school class, 96% in top 50% of high school class. 87% from public high schools. SAT Math middle 50% range 550-640. SAT Critical Reading middle 50% range 550-650. SAT Writing middle 50% range 520-620. ACT middle 50% range 23-27. Minimum web-based TOEFL 79. Minimum paper TOEFL 550. Basis for Candidate Selection: Very important factors considered include: Class rank, academic GPA, rigor of secondary school record. Important factors considered include: application essay, recommendation(s), standardized test scores. Other factors considered include: alumni/ae relation, extracurricular activities, first generation, geographical residence, interview, level of applicant's interest, racial/ethnic status, state residency, talent/ability, volunteer work, work experience. Freshman Admission Requirements: High school diploma is required and GED is not accepted. Academic units required: 4 English, 4 mathematics, 3 science, (1 science labs), 2 foreign language, 1 social studies, 1 history. Academic units recommended: 4 English, 4 mathematics, 3 science, (1 science labs), 2 foreign language, 1 social studies, 1 history. Freshman Admission Statistics: 3,018 applied, 64% admitted, 29% enrolled. Transfer Admission Requirements: college transcript(s), Minimum college GPA of 2.50 required. Lowest grade transferable C. General Admission Information: Application Fee $50. Regular application deadline

2/15. Regular notification 4/1. Nonfall registration accepted. Admission may be deferred for a maximum of 1 year. Credit and/or placement offered for CEEB Advanced Placement tests.

COSTS AND FINANCIAL AID
Annual in-state tuition $3,476. Annual out-of-state tuition $17,292. Room and board $7,584. Required fees $2,440. Average book expense $950. Required Forms and Deadlines: FAFSA. Notification of Awards: Applicants will be notified of awards on a rolling basis beginning 3/15. Types of Aid: Need-based scholarships/grants: Federal Pell, SEOG, state scholarships/grants, private scholarships, the school's own gift aid. Loans: Direct Subsidized Stafford, Direct Unsubsidized Stafford, Direct PLUS, Federal Perkins, state loans, college/university loans from institutional funds. Student Employment: Federal Work-Study Program available. Institutional employment available. Off-campus job opportunities are good. Financial Aid Statistics: 94% freshmen, 95% undergrads receive need-based scholarship or grant aid. 11% freshmen, 12% undergrads receive non-need-based scholarship or grant aid. 72% freshmen, 76% undergrads receive need-based self-help aid. 3% freshmen, 2% undergrads receive athletic scholarships. 73% freshmen, 69% undergrads receive any aid. 58% undergrads borrow to pay for school. Average cumulative indebtedness $17,696. Criteria for awarding institutional aid: Non-need-based: academics, alumni affiliation, art, athletics, job skills, leadership, minority status, music/drama, state/district residency.

THE UNIVERSITY OF NORTH CAROLINA AT CHAPEL HILL

Best 378

CB# 2200, Chapel Hill, NC 27599-2200
Phone: 919-966-3621 • **Financial Aid Phone:** 919-962-8396
E-mail: unchelp@admissions.unc.edu • **CEEB Code:** 5816
Fax: 919-962-3045 • **Website:** www.unc.edu • **ACT Code:** 3162

This public school was founded in 1789. It has a 729-acre campus.

RATINGS
Admissions Selectivity Rating: 97   **Fire Safety Rating:** 87   **Green Rating:** 96

STUDENTS AND FACULTY
Enrollment: 17,918. Student Body: 58% female, 42% male, 18% out-of-state, 3% international (94 countries represented). Asian 8%, African American 9%, Caucasian 66%, Hispanic 8%, Native American 1%.
Retention and Graduation: 77% freshmen graduate within 4 years. 28% grads go on to further study within 1 year. 16% grads pursue arts and sciences degrees. 3% grads pursue law degrees. 1% grads pursue business degrees. 2% grads pursue medical degrees. Faculty: Student/faculty ratio 14:1. 1671 full-time faculty, 92% hold PhDs, 24% are are members of minority groups, 43% are women. % of classes are taught by teaching assistants.

ACADEMICS
Degrees: bachelor's, certificate, doctoral, master's, post-bachelor's certificate, post-master's certificate. Most classes have 10–19 students. Most lab/discussion sessions have 10–19 students. Majors with Highest Enrollment: biology/biological sciences; business administration and management; psychology. Special Study Options: cross-registration, distance learning, double major, dual enrollment, honors program, independent study, internships, student-designed major, study abroad, teacher certification program. Honors programs: see http://www.honors.unc.edu/ . Disability Services: Special programs offered to physically disabled students include note-taking services, reader services, tape recorders. Career services: Alumni network, alumni services, career/job search classes, career assessment, internships, regional alumni. Career services highlights include The eight networking nights we do each year. For each night we bring in 20-30 professionals deep in one career area that is very difficult to break into for internships and full-time jobs. This gives students multiple opportunities to make contacts that they can follow up with to gain a '"foot in the door"' in fields/industries where it is hard to find an internship/job.

FACILITIES
Housing: Coed dorms, special housing for disabled students, men's dorms, special housing for international students, women's dorms, fraternity/sorority housing, apartments for married students, apartments for single students, , WellnessHousing, ThemeHousingSpecial Options in Housing '– Learning

Communities such as RELIC - Religion as Explorative Learning Integrated in our Community, Language Houses, The Carolina Experience, Men@Carolina, W.E.L.L. - Women's Experiences: Learning and Leadership, Connected Learning Program, Service and Leadership, Substance Free Environments, Sustainability, UNITAS. 98% of campus accessible to physically diasbled. Special Academic Facilities/Equipment: Art museum, Folklore council, Institute of Folk Music, communications center, Basketball Museum, Institute of Latin American Studies, Institute of fisheries research, Sitterson Hall Computer Museum, Institute of Natural Science, Research Laboratory of Anthropology, Hayden Planetarium, Paul Green Theatre, Playmakers Theater, Memorial Hall. Computers: 75% of classrooms, 15% of dorms, 100% of libraries, 100% of dining areas, 100% of student union, 50% of common outdoor areas have wireless network access. Students can register for classes online. Administrative functions (other than registration) can be performed online. Undergraduates are required to own a computer.

CAMPUS LIFE
Environment: Town. Activities: Choral groups, concert band, dance, drama/theater, jazz band, literary magazine, marching band, music ensembles, musical theater, opera, pep band, radio station, student government, student newspaper, student-run film society, symphony orchestra, television station, yearbook, Campus Ministries, International Student Organization, Model UN 635 registered organizations, 19 honor societies, 42 religious organizations. 35 fraternities, 23 sororities. Athletics (Intercollegiate): Men: baseball, basketball, cross-country, diving, fencing, football, golf, lacrosse, soccer, swimming, tennis, track/field (outdoor), track/field (indoor), wrestling. Women: basketball, crew/rowing, cross-country, diving, fencing, field hockey, golf, gymnastics, lacrosse, soccer, softball, swimming, tennis, track/field (outdoor), track/field (indoor), volleyball. On-Campus Highlights: The Pit, McCorkle Place, Polk Place, Dean Smith Center, Student Union, Old Well, Coker Arboretum, Morehead Planetarium, Ackland Art Museum, Kenan Stadium. Environmental Initiatives: Partnered with Orange (County) Water and Sewer Authority (OWASA) to install a water reclamation and reuse system that replaced 100 million gallons of potable water in FY 2011. This system reduces total daily water demand in the OWASA service territory by ~10%. Started in summer 2009, the system provides makeup water at all campus cooling towers, irrigates athletic fields, and flushes toilets in new buildings adjacent to the distribution network. 32 MW Cogeneration Facility, district heating and cooling, and 5 million gallon thermal storage facility. Currently testing biomass fuel sources. Constructing a generator to run on landfill gas. Real time energy dashboards for 157 buildings that meter steam, electricity, and chilled water. Fare Free Transit and Commuter Alternatives Program. More than 7 million free bus rides provided annually. UNC contributes more than $6 million annually to fund Chapel Hill Transit.

ADMISSIONS
Freshman Academic Profile: Average high school GPA 4.5. 79% in top 10% of high school class, 97% in top 25% of high school class, 100% in top 50% of high school class. 79% from public high schools. SAT Math middle 50% range 610-710. SAT Critical Reading middle 50% range 590-690. SAT Writing middle 50% range 580-690. ACT middle 50% range 27-32. Minimum web-based TOEFL 100. Minimum paper TOEFL 600. Basis for Candidate Selection: Very important factors considered include: Class rank, application essay, academic GPA, recommendation(s), rigor of secondary school record, standardized test scores, character/personal qualities, extracurricular activities, state residency, talent/ability. Important factors considered include: alumni/ae relation, first generation, racial/ethnic status, volunteer work, work experience. . Freshman Admission Requirements: High school diploma is required and GED is not accepted. Academic units required: 4 English, 4 mathematics, 3 science, (1 science labs), 2 foreign language, 1 social studies, 1 history. 4 English, 4 mathematics, 3 science, (1 science labs), 2 foreign language, 1 social studies, 1 history. Freshman Admission Statistics: 28,437 applied, 28% admitted, 50% enrolled. Transfer Admission Requirements: High school transcript, college transcript(s), essay or personal statement, statement of good standing from prior institution(s). Minimum college GPA of 2.0 required. Lowest grade transferable C. General Admission Information: Application Fee $70. Regular application deadline 1/15. Nonfall registration not accepted. Admission may be deferred for a maximum of 1 year. Credit and/or placement offered for CEEB Advanced Placement tests.

COSTS AND FINANCIAL AID
Annual in-state tuition $5,823. Annual out-of-state tuition $26,575. Room and board $9,734. Required fees $1,870. Average book expense $1,182. Required Forms and Deadlines: FAFSA, CSS/Financial Aid PROFILE. Notification of Awards: Applicants will be notified of awards on a rolling basis beginning 3/15. Types of Aid: Need-based scholarships/grants: Federal Pell, SEOG, state scholarships/grants, private scholarships, the school's own gift aid, State Grants. Loans: Subsidized Stafford, Unsubsidized Stafford, PLUS, Federal Perkins, state loans, college/university loans from institutional funds, Alternative Loans. Student Employment: Federal Work-Study Program available. Institutional employment available. Off-campus job opportunities are good. Financial Aid Statistics: 94% freshmen, 96% undergrads receive need-based scholarship or

grant aid. 11% freshmen, 6% undergrads receive non-need-based scholarship or grant aid. 66% freshmen, 70% undergrads receive need-based self-help aid. 2% freshmen, 1% undergrads receive athletic scholarships. 69% freshmen, 64% undergrads receive any aid. 35% undergrads borrow to pay for school. Average cumulative indebtedness $16,983. Criteria for awarding institutional aid: Non-need-based: academics, alumni affiliation, art, athletics, leadership, music/drama, religious affiliation, state/district residency.

UNIVERSITY OF NORTH CAROLINA— CHARLOTTE

9201 University City Boulevard, Charlotte, NC 28223-0001
Phone: 704-687-2213 • **Financial Aid Phone:** 704-687-2461
E-mail: unccadm@uncc.edu • **CEEB Code:** 5105
Fax: 704-687-6483 • **Website:** www.uncc.edu/ • **ACT Code:** 3163

This public school was founded in 1946. It has a 1000-acre campus.

RATINGS
Admissions Selectivity Rating: 76   **Fire Safety Rating:** 90   **Green Rating:** 80

STUDENTS AND FACULTY
Enrollment: 21,085. **Student Body:** 49% female, 51% male, 7% out-of-state, 2% international (136 countries represented). Asian 5%, African American 17%, Caucasian 61%, Hispanic 7%.
Retention and Graduation: 77% freshmen return for sophomore year. 26% freshmen graduate within 4 years. 53% freshmen graduate within 6 years. 14% grads go on to further study within 1 year. **Faculty:** Student/faculty ratio 19:1. 1021 full-time faculty, 84% hold PhDs, 17% are members of minority groups, 44% are women.

ACADEMICS
Degrees: bachelor's, master's, post-master's certificate. **Classes:** Most classes have 20–29 students. Most lab/discussion sessions have 10–19 students. **Majors with Highest Enrollment:** finance; psychology. **Special Study Options:** Accelerated program, cooperative education program, cross-registration, distance learning, double major, dual enrollment, English as a Second Language (ESL), honors program, independent study, internships, study abroad, teacher certification program, weekend college, Wilderness Exploration Program. **Disability Services:** Special programs offered to physically disabled students include note-taking services, reader services, tape recorders, tutors. **Career services:** career/job search classes, career assessment, internships.

FACILITIES
Housing: Coed dorms, special housing for disabled students, special housing for international students, women's dorms, fraternity/sorority housing, apartments for single students, Rooms for students with disabilities limited, apply early. Graduate and older non-traditional student housing and substance free housing available upon request. 95% of campus accessible to physically disabled. **Special Academic Facilities/Equipment:** Urban studies and community service institute, mock court room, applied research center, language lab, 63-acre ecological reserve, botanical and horticultural complex, tropical rainforest conservatory. **Computers:** 10% of classrooms, 10% of dorms, 30% of libraries, 70% of dining areas, 30% of student union, 10% of common outdoor areas have wireless network access. Students can register for classes online. Administrative functions (other than registration) can be performed online.

CAMPUS LIFE
Environment: Metropolis. **Activities:** Choral groups, concert band, dance, drama/theater, jazz band, literary magazine, music ensembles, musical theater, opera, pep band, student government, student newspaper, television station, yearbook, Campus Ministries 222 registered organizations, 25 honor societies, 22 religious organizations. 14 fraternities, 10 sororities. **Athletics (Intercollegiate):** *Men:* baseball, basketball, cross-country, golf, soccer, tennis, track/field (outdoor). *Women:* basketball, cross-country, soccer, softball, tennis, track/field (outdoor), volleyball. **On-Campus Highlights:** Bonnie E. Cone University Center, James H. Barnhardt Student Activity Center, J. Murrey Atkins Library, UNCC Botanical Gardens and Greenhouse, Ritazza Coffee Shop, After Hours at the Rathskeller, Robinson Hall Theatre. **Environmental Initiatives:** Recycling Alternative Fuel Vehicles Student Green Energy initiative (just starting).

ADMISSIONS
Freshman Academic Profile: Average high school GPA 3.7. 19% in top 10% of high school class, 53% in top 25% of high school class, 88% in top 50% of high school class. 88% from public high schools. SAT Math middle 50% range 500-600. SAT Critical Reading middle 50% range 480-560. SAT Writing middle 50% range 470-550. ACT middle 50% range 20-25. Minimum web-based

TOEFL 64. Minimum paper TOEFL 507. **Basis for Candidate Selection:** *Very important factors considered include:* academic GPA, rigor of secondary school record, standardized test scores. *Other factors considered include:* character/personal qualities, extracurricular activities, geographical residence, level of applicant's interest, state residency, talent/ability. **Freshman Admission Requirements:** High school diploma is required and GED is accepted. *Academic units required:* 4 English, 4 mathematics, 3 science, (1 science labs), 2 foreign language, 2 social studies. *Academic units recommended:* 4 English, 4 mathematics, 3 science, (1 science labs), 2 foreign language, 2 social studies. **Freshman Admission Statistics:** 13,742 applied, 69% admitted, 38% enrolled. **Transfer Admission Requirements:** High school transcript, college transcript(s), statement of good standing from prior institution(s). Minimum college GPA of 2.0 required. Lowest grade transferable C. **General Admission Information:** Application Fee $50. Regular application deadline 7/1. Notification on a rolling basis, beginning on or about 11/1. Nonfall registration accepted. Credit and/or placement offered for CEEB Advanced Placement tests.

COSTS AND FINANCIAL AID
Annual in-state tuition $3,453. Annual out-of-state tuition $15,982. Room and board $8,130. Required fees $2,420. Average book expense $1,200. **Required Forms and Deadlines:** FAFSA. **Notification of Awards:** Applicants will be notified of awards on a rolling basis beginning 3/15. **Types of Aid:** *Need-based scholarships/grants:* Federal Pell, SEOG, state scholarships/grants, private scholarships, the school's own gift aid. *Loans:* Subsidized Stafford, Unsubsidized Stafford, PLUS, Federal Perkins, college/university loans from institutional funds. **Student Employment:** Highest amount earned per year from on-campus jobs $2,000. Off-campus job opportunities are good. **Financial Aid Statistics:** 90% freshmen, 86% undergrads receive need-based scholarship or grant aid. 5% freshmen, 7% undergrads receive non-need-based scholarship or grant aid. 87% freshmen, 84% undergrads receive need-based self-help aid. 3% freshmen, 2% undergrads receive athletic scholarships. 47% freshmen, 75% undergrads receive any aid. **Criteria for awarding institutional aid:** Non-need-based: academics, athletics, leadership, music/drama.

THE UNIVERSITY OF NORTH CAROLINA AT GREENSBORO

1400 Spring Garden Street, Greensboro, NC 27402-6170
Phone: 336-334-5243 • **Financial Aid Phone:** 336-334-5702
E-mail: admissions@uncg.edu • **CEEB Code:** 5913
Fax: 336-334-4180 • **Website:** www.uncg.edu • **ACT Code:** 3166

This public school was founded in 1891. It has a 357-acre campus.

RATINGS
Admissions Selectivity Rating: 80   **Fire Safety Rating:** 75   **Green Rating:** 72

STUDENTS AND FACULTY
Enrollment: 14,275. Student Body: 67% female, 33% male, 7% out-of-state, 1% international (12 countries represented). Asian 4%, African American 24%, Caucasian 65%, Hispanic 5%, Native American 0%
Retention and Graduation: 77% freshmen return for sophomore year. 29% freshmen graduate within 4 years. 53% freshmen graduate within 6 years. Faculty: Student/faculty ratio 17:1. 838 full-time faculty, 73% hold PhDs, 14% are are members of minority groups, 50% are women.

ACADEMICS
Degrees: bachelor's, master's, post-bachelor's certificate, post-master's certificate. Classes: Most classes have 20–29 students. Most lab/discussion sessions have 20–29 students. Majors with Highest Enrollment: biology/biological sciences; business administration and management; nursing/registered nurse (rn, asn, bsn, msn). Special Study Options: Accelerated program, cross-registration, distance learning, double major, dual enrollment, honors program, independent study, internships, study abroad, teacher certification program, Evening University. Combined degree programs: BA/MA, Accounting, Mathematics, Chem, various BA and MBA. Disability Services: Special programs offered to physically disabled students include note-taking services, reader services, tape recorders, tutors. Career services: alumni services, career/job search classes, career assessment, internships.

FACILITIES

Housing: Coed dorms, special housing for international students, women's dorms, apartments for single students. Special Academic Facilities/Equipment: 42-acre recreational site, art gallery, 45,000 sq.ft. Student Center, New Music Building, New Science Building. Computers: 90% of dorms, 35% of libraries, have wireless network access. Students can register for classes online. Administrative functions (other than registration) can be performed online.

CAMPUS LIFE

Environment: City. Activities: Choral groups, concert band, dance, drama/theater, jazz band, literary magazine, music ensembles, musical theater, opera, pep band, radio station, student government, student newspaper, student-run film society, symphony orchestra, International Student Organization 200 registered organizations, 23 honor societies, 13 religious organizations. 11 fraternities, 11 sororities. Athletics (Intercollegiate): Men: baseball, basketball, cross-country, golf, soccer, tennis, wrestling. Women: basketball, cross-country, golf, soccer, softball, tennis, volleyball. On-Campus Highlights: Elliott University Center, Student Rec Center, Weatherspoon Art Museum, Peabody Park, UNCG Theatre.

ADMISSIONS

Freshman Academic Profile: Average high school GPA 3.6. 18% in top 10% of high school class, 48% in top 25% of high school class, 86% in top 50% of high school class. 95% from public high schools. SAT Math middle 50% range 460-560. SAT Critical Reading middle 50% range 460-560. SAT Writing middle 50% range 440-550. Minimum web-based TOEFL 79. Minimum paper TOEFL 550. Basis for Candidate Selection: Very important factors considered include: academic GPA, rigor of secondary school record. Important factors considered include: standardized test scores. Other factors considered include: recommendation(s). Freshman Admission Requirements: High school diploma is required and GED is not accepted. Academic units required: 4 English, 4 mathematics, 3 science, (1 science labs), 2 foreign language, 2 social studies. 4 English, 4 mathematics, 3 science, (1 science labs), 2 foreign language, 2 social studies. Freshman Admission Statistics: 11,574 applied, 58% admitted, 38% enrolled. Transfer Admission Requirements: High school transcript, college transcript(s), standardized test scores, statement of good standing from prior institution(s). Minimum college GPA of 2.0 required. Lowest grade transferable 2. General Admission Information: Application Fee $45. Regular application deadline 3/1. Notification on a rolling basis, beginning on or about 12/15. Nonfall registration accepted. Admission may be deferred for a maximum of 1 semester. Credit and/or placement offered for CEEB Advanced Placement tests.

COSTS AND FINANCIAL AID

Annual in-state tuition $3,454. Annual out-of-state tuition $15,979. Room and board $5,580. Required fees $1,821. Average book expense $1,000. Required Forms and Deadlines: FAFSA. Notification of Awards: Applicants will be notified of awards on a rolling basis beginning 3/15. Types of Aid: Need-based scholarships/grants: Federal Pell, SEOG, state scholarships/grants, private scholarships, the school's own gift aid. Loans: Direct Subsidized Stafford, Direct Unsubsidized Stafford, Direct PLUS, Subsidized Stafford, Unsubsidized Stafford, PLUS, Federal Perkins, college/university loans from institutional funds. Student Employment: Federal Work-Study Program available. Institutional employment available. Off-campus job opportunities are good. Financial Aid Statistics: 58% freshmen, 59% undergrads receive need-based scholarship or grant aid. 75% freshmen, 72% undergrads receive non-need-based scholarship or grant aid. 60% freshmen, 64% undergrads receive need-based self-help aid. 1% freshmen, 1% undergrads receive athletic scholarships. 77% freshmen, 71% undergrads receive any aid. 67% undergrads borrow to pay for school. Average cumulative indebtedness $23,772. Criteria for awarding institutional aid: Non-need-based: academics, alumni affiliation, art, athletics, music/drama, state/district residency.

THE UNIVERSITY OF NORTH CAROLINA AT WILMINGTON

601 South College Rd, Wilmington, NC 28403-5904
Phone: 910-962-3243 • Financial Aid Phone: 910-962-3177
E-mail: admissions@uncw.edu • CEEB Code: 5907
Fax: 910-962-3038 • Website: www.uncw.edu • ACT Code: 3174

This public school was founded in 1947. It has a 656-acre campus.

RATINGS

Admissions Selectivity Rating: 89   Fire Safety Rating: 88   Green Rating: 74

STUDENTS AND FACULTY

Enrollment: 12,060. Student Body: 60% female, 40% male, 16% out-of-state, 1% international (62 countries represented). Asian 2%, African American 5%, Caucasian 82%, Hispanic 6%, Native American 1%
Retention and Graduation: 86% freshmen return for sophomore year. 49% freshmen graduate within 4 years. 68% freshmen graduate within 6 years.
Faculty: Student/faculty ratio 16:1. 639 full-time faculty, 86% hold PhDs, 17% are are members of minority groups, 46% are women.

ACADEMICS

Degrees: bachelor's, certificate, master's, post-bachelor's certificate, post-master's certificate. Classes: Most classes have 20–29 students. Most lab/discussion sessions have 20–29 students. Majors with Highest Enrollment: business/managerial economics; elementary education and teaching; psychology. Special Study Options: Accelerated program, cooperative education program, cross-registration, distance learning, double major, dual enrollment, English as a Second Language (ESL), exchange student program (domestic), honors program, independent study, internships, study abroad, teacher certification program, 2+2 Pre-Engineering Program. Honors programs: The HONORS SCHOLARS PROGRAM at UNCW is designed to offer academically talented students challenging and exciting experiences both in and out of the classroom. A student may begin with general honors in the first two years, and then go on to departmental honors in their major. Disability Services: Special programs offered to physically disabled students include note-taking services, reader services, tape recorders, tutors. Career services: Alumni network, alumni services, career assessment, internships, regional alumni. Career services highlights include The UNCW Virtual Career Center is nationally recognized for it's comprehensive web site.

FACILITIES

Housing: Coed dorms, special housing for international students, women's dorms, apartments for single students, Wellness Housing, Theme Housing. 95% of campus accessible to physically disabled. Special Academic Facilities/Equipment: Upperman African American Cultural Arts Center, N.C. Teachers Legacy Hall, Ev-Henwood Nature Preserve, Center for Marine Science at Myrtle Grove, Almkuist-Nixon Sports Medicine Building, Museum of World Cultures, Claude Howell Gallery, UNCW Library Archives and Special Collections Computers: 100% of classrooms, 100% of dorms, 100% of libraries, 100% of dining areas, 100% of student union, 50% of common outdoor areas have wireless network access. Students can register for classes online. Administrative functions (other than registration) can be performed online.

CAMPUS LIFE

Environment: City. Activities: Choral groups, concert band, dance, drama/theater, jazz band, literary magazine, music ensembles, pep band, radio station, student government, student newspaper, student-run film society, symphony orchestra, television station, Campus Ministries, International Student Organization, Model UN. 173 registered organizations, 8 honor societies, 14 religious organizations. 11 fraternities, 11 sororities. Athletics (Intercollegiate): Men: baseball, basketball, cheerleading, cross-country, diving, golf, soccer, swimming, tennis, track/field (outdoor). Women: basketball, cheerleading, cross-country, diving, golf, soccer, softball, swimming, tennis, track/field (outdoor), volleyball. On-Campus Highlights: Fisher Student Center, William Randall Library, UNCW Student Recreation Center, Trask Coliseum, Cultural Arts Building. Environmental Initiatives: 1) All vegetable oil in Hawk's Nest is recycyled as bio-diesel. 2) Trayless dining and recyclable to-go containers at campus dining facilities. 3) UNCW Carpool Program LEED certification for new housing and parking development.

ADMISSIONS

Freshman Academic Profile: Average high school GPA 4.0. 26% in top 10% of high school class, 65% in top 25% of high school class, 95% in top 50% of high school class. SAT Math middle 50% range 560-630. SAT Critical Reading middle 50% range 540-620. SAT Writing middle 50% range 520-600. ACT middle 50% range 22-26. Minimum web-based TOEFL 71. Minimum paper

TOEFL 525. **Basis for Candidate Selection:** Very important factors considered include: application essay, academic GPA, recommendation(s), rigor of secondary school record, standardized test scores. Important factors considered include: Class rank. Other factors considered include: alumni/ae relation, character/personal qualities, extracurricular activities, first generation, geographical residence, level of applicant's interest, racial/ethnic status, state residency, talent/ability, volunteer work, work experience. **Freshman Admission Requirements:** High school diploma is required and GED is accepted. **Academic units required:** 4 English, 4 mathematics, 3 science, (1 science labs), 2 foreign language, 2 social studies, 1 history. **Academic units recommended:** 4 English, 4 mathematics, 3 science, (1 science labs), 2 foreign language, 2 social studies, 1 history. **Freshman Admission Statistics:** 11,184 applied, 54% admitted, 42% enrolled. **Transfer Admission Requirements:** High school transcript, college transcript(s), essay or personal statement, minimum college GPA of 2.5 required. Lowest grade transferable C. **General Admission Information:** Application Fee $60. Regular application deadline 2/1. Regular notification 4/1. Nonfall registration accepted. Admission may be deferred for a maximum of 1 year. Credit and/or placement offered for CEEB Advanced Placement tests.

COSTS AND FINANCIAL AID

Annual in-state tuition $3,743. Annual out-of-state tuition $15,846. Room and board $9,620. Required fees $2,456. Average book expense $985. **Required Forms and Deadlines:** FAFSA. **Notification of Awards:** Applicants will be notified of awards on a rolling basis beginning 4/1. **Types of Aid:** Need-based scholarships/grants: Federal Pell, SEOG, state scholarships/grants, private scholarships, the school's own gift aid. Loans: Direct Subsidized Stafford, Direct Unsubsidized Stafford, Direct PLUS, Subsidized Stafford, Unsubsidized Stafford, PLUS, Federal Perkins, state loans, college/university loans from institutional funds. Student Employment: Federal Work-Study Program available. Institutional employment available. Off-campus job opportunities are good. **Financial Aid Statistics:** 100% freshmen, 99% undergrads receive need-based scholarship or grant aid. 21% freshmen, 15% undergrads receive non-need-based scholarship or grant aid. 100% freshmen, 99% undergrads receive need-based self-help aid. 2% freshmen, 1% undergrads receive athletic scholarships. 45% freshmen, 47% undergrads receive any aid. 58% undergrads borrow to pay for school. Average cumulative indebtedness $25,821. **Criteria for awarding institutional aid:** Non-need-based: academics, alumni affiliation, art, athletics, leadership, music/drama, state/district residency.

UNIVERSITY OF NORTH DAKOTA

205 Twamley Hall 264 Centennial Drive St, Grand Forks, ND 58202-8357
Phone: 800-225-5863 • **Financial Aid Phone:** 701-777-3121
E-mail: enrollmentservices@und.edu • **CEEB Code:** 6878
Fax: 701-777-3367 • **Website:** www.und.edu • **ACT Code:** 3218

This public school was founded in 1883. It has a 549-acre campus.

RATINGS
Admissions Selectivity Rating: 75   **Fire Safety Rating:** 73   **Green Rating:** 83

STUDENTS AND FACULTY
Enrollment: 11,522. **Student Body:** 45% female, 55% male, 57% out-of-state, 6% international (60 countries represented). Asian 1%, African American 2%, Caucasian 81%, Hispanic 2%, Native American 2%.
Retention and Graduation: 77% freshmen return for sophomore year. 28% grads go on to further study within 1 year. 7% grads pursue arts and sciences degrees. 1% grads pursue law degrees. 4% grads pursue business degrees. 2% grads pursue medical degrees. **Faculty:** Student/faculty ratio 19:1. 638 full-time faculty, 79% hold PhDs, 7% are members of minority groups, 41% are women.

ACADEMICS
Degrees: bachelor's, certificate, diploma, master's, post-bachelor's certificate. **Classes:** Most classes have 20–29 students. Most lab/discussion sessions have fewer than 10 students. **Majors with Highest Enrollment:** airline/commercial/professional pilot and flight crew; nursing/registered nurse (rn, asn, bsn, msn); psychology. **Special Study Options:** Accelerated program, cooperative education program, cross-registration, distance learning, double major, dual enrollment, English as a Second Language (ESL), exchange student program (domestic), external degree program, honors program, independent study, internships, liberal arts/career combination, student-designed major, study abroad, teacher certification program, weekend college. **Honors programs:**

Students may participate in the Honors Program throughout their undergraduate career.Students in any college of the University may enroll in the Honors Program.Most students graduate from the Program as "Scholars in the Honors Program" while also fulfilling a major in the Colleges, but the Honors Program also offers the option of creating an individually designed program of study through Honors.This option may result in either a B.A. or a B.S. degree earned through the College of Arts and Sciences. **Combined degree programs:** , http://www.und.edu/dept/registrar/catalogs/catalog. **Disability Services:** Special programs offered to physically disabled students include note-taking services, reader services, tape recorders. **Career services:** Alumni network, alumni services, career/job search classes, career assessment, internships Career services highlights include Cooperative Learning. Internships. Students work closely with entrepreneur practitioners.

FACILITIES
Housing: Coed dorms, special housing for disabled students, men's dorms, women's dorms, fraternity/sorority housing, apartments for married students, apartments for single students, Wellness Housing, Theme Housing 99% of campus accessible to physically disabled. **Special Academic Facilities/Equipment:** Hughes Fine Arts Center, Burtness Theatre, North Dakota Museum of Art, Chester Fritz Auditorium, mining/mineral resources research institute/ energy research center, remote sensing institute, aviation facilities, meteorology data center,Ralph Engelstad Arena. **Computers:** 70% of classrooms, 100% of dorms, 100% of libraries, 50% of dining areas, 100% of student union, have wireless network access. Students can register for classes online. Administrative functions (other than registration) can be performed online.

CAMPUS LIFE
Environment: Town. **Activities:** Choral groups, concert band, dance, drama/theater, jazz band, literary magazine, marching band, music ensembles, musical theater, opera, pep band, radio station, student government, student newspaper, student-run film society, symphony orchestra, television station, Campus Ministries, International Student Organization 230 registered organizations, 42 honor societies, 3 religious organizations. 13 fraternities, 7 sororities. **Athletics (Intercollegiate):** *Men:* baseball, basketball, cross-country, diving, football, golf, ice hockey, swimming, track/field (outdoor), track/field (indoor). *Women:* basketball, cross-country, diving, golf, ice hockey, soccer, softball, swimming, tennis, track/field (outdoor), track/field (indoor), volleyball. **On-Campus Highlights:** Engelstad Arena, Memorial Union, Archives Coffee shop, International Centre, North Dakota Museum of Art. **Environmental Initiatives:** Energy Conservation Programs Presidential Climate Committment Recycling.

ADMISSIONS
Freshman Academic Profile: Average high school GPA 3.4. 14% in top 10% of high school class, 42% in top 25% of high school class, 73% in top 50% of high school class. 92% from public high schools. ACT middle 50% range 21-26. Minimum paper TOEFL 525. **Basis for Candidate Selection:** *Very important factors considered include:* academic GPA, standardized test scores. *Other factors considered include:* Class rank, rigor of secondary school record. **Freshman Admission Requirements:** High school diploma is required and GED is accepted. *Academic units required:* 4 English, 3 mathematics, 3 science, (3 science labs), 3 social studies. *Academic units recommended:* 4 English, 3 mathematics, 3 science, (3 science labs), 3 social studies. **Freshman Admission Statistics:** 4,857 applied, 71% admitted, 61% enrolled. **Transfer Admission Requirements:** college transcript(s), minimum college GPA of 2.0 required. **General Admission Information:** Application Fee $35. Notification on a rolling basis, beginning on or about 9/1. Nonfall registration accepted. Admission may be deferred for a maximum of 1 Semester. Credit and/or placement offered for CEEB Advanced Placement tests.

COSTS AND FINANCIAL AID
Annual in-state tuition $5,793. Annual out-of-state tuition $15,468. Room and board $6,100. Required fees $1,298. Average book expense $800. **Required Forms and Deadlines:** FAFSA. **Notification of Awards:** Applicants will be notified of awards on a rolling basis beginning 5/15. **Types of Aid:** *Need-based scholarships/grants:* Federal Pell, SEOG, state scholarships/grants, private scholarships, the school's own gift aid, Federal Nursing Scholarships. *Loans:* Subsidized Stafford, Unsubsidized Stafford, PLUS, Federal Perkins, Federal Nursing, Alternative Commercial Loans. **Student Employment:** Federal Work-Study Program available. Institutional employment available. Highest amount earned per year from on-campus jobs $2,071. Off-campus job opportunities are excellent. **Financial Aid Statistics:** 79% freshmen, 73% undergrads receive need-based scholarship or grant aid. 2% freshmen, 1% undergrads receive non-need-based scholarship or grant aid. 91% freshmen, 92% undergrads receive need-based self-help aid. 4% freshmen, 3% undergrads receive athletic scholarships. 84% freshmen, 65% undergrads receive any aid. 85% undergrads borrow to pay for school. Average cumulative indebtedness $31,959. **Criteria for awarding institutional aid:** Non-need-based: academics, alumni affiliation, art, athletics, job skills, leadership, music/drama, religious affiliation.

The Princeton Review's Complete Book of Colleges

UNIVERSITY OF NORTH FLORIDA

1 UNF Drive, Jacksonville, FL 32224-7699
Phone: 904-620-5555 • **Financial Aid Phone:** 904-620-2698
E-mail: admissions@unf.edu • **CEEB Code:** 9841
Fax: 904-620-2414 • **Website:** www.unf.edu • **ACT Code:** 5490

This public school was founded in 1965. It has a 1300-acre campus.

RATINGS
Admissions Selectivity Rating: 91   **Fire Safety Rating:** 71   **Green Rating:** 79

STUDENTS AND FACULTY
Enrollment: 14,103. **Student Body:** 56% female, 44% male, 3% out-of-state, 1% international (116 countries represented). Asian 5%, African American 10%, Caucasian 73%, Hispanic 8%.
Retention and Graduation: Faculty: Student/faculty ratio 20:1. 537 full-time faculty, 78% hold PhDs, 13% are members of minority groups, 46% are women. 0% of classes are taught by teaching assistants.

ACADEMICS
Degrees: associate, bachelor's, master's, post-bachelor's certificate, post-master's certificate, terminal associate, transfer associate. **Classes:** Most classes have 20–29 students. Most lab/discussion sessions have 20–29 students. **Majors with Highest Enrollment:** business administration and management; mass communication/media studies; psychology. **Special Study Options:** Accelerated program, cooperative education program, distance learning, double major, dual enrollment, English as a Second Language (ESL), exchange student program (domestic), honors program, independent study, internships, student-designed major, study abroad, teacher certification program, weekend college, Learning Communities. **Honors programs:** The Honors Program at the University of North Florida offers talented and ambitious students a unique approach to higher education. Honors Classes are limited to 20 students, combining active and experiential learning in an interdisciplinary setting. The goal is to build a community of learners who have the ability to take their learning outside the classroom and into the real world helping to bridge the gap between education and experience. The honors program is a limited access program and spaces are filled on a first-come-first-serve basis. **Disability Services:** Special programs offered to physically disabled students include note-taking services, reader services, tape recorders. **Career services:** alumni services, career/job search classes, internships.

FACILITIES
Housing: Coed dorms, special housing for disabled students, apartments for single students, Suite style housing. **Special Academic Facilities/Equipment:** Art gallery, bird sanctuary, Fine Arts Center. **Computers:** 100% of classrooms, 50% of dorms, 100% of libraries, 50% of dining areas, 100% of student union, 100% of common outdoor areas have wireless network access. Students can register for classes online. Administrative functions (other than registration) can be performed online.

CAMPUS LIFE
Environment: Metropolis. **Activities:** Choral groups, concert band, dance, drama/theater, jazz band, literary magazine, music ensembles, pep band, radio station, student government, student newspaper, television station, Campus Ministries, International Student Organization 140 registered organizations, 8 honor societies, 29 religious organizations. 14 fraternities, 10 sororities. **Athletics (Intercollegiate):** *Men:* baseball, basketball, cheerleading, cross-country, golf, soccer, tennis, track/field (outdoor), track/field (indoor). *Women:* basketball, cheerleading, cross-country, diving, soccer, softball, swimming, tennis, track/field (outdoor), track/field (indoor), volleyball. **On-Campus Highlights:** Student Union, Bookstore, Art Gallery, Nature Trails, Campus skate park, Greek Affairs, Earth Music Festival, Athletics NCAA I, Free movies on Campus, Jazz Program (nationally recognized), Division I sports. **Environmental Initiatives:** Requiring LEED Silver or comparable compliance Establishing sustainability committee and programs through Environmental Center, including Recyclemania and Garbage on the Green A three-hundred acre natural area on campus was designated as a preserve in May 2006 by UNF President John Delaney.

ADMISSIONS
Freshman Academic Profile: Average high school GPA 3.7. 27% in top 10% of high school class, 60% in top 25% of high school class, 88% in top 50% of high school class. SAT Math middle 50% range 530-620. SAT Critical Reading middle 50% range 530-620. ACT middle 50% range 23-26. Minimum web-based TOEFL 61. Minimum paper TOEFL 500. **Basis for Candidate Selection:** *Very important factors considered include:* academic GPA, rigor of secondary school record, standardized test scores. *Other factors considered include:* Class rank, application essay, recommendation(s), extracurricular activi-

ties, level of applicant's interest, talent/ability, volunteer work, work experience. **Freshman Admission Requirements:** High school diploma is required and GED is accepted. *Academic units required:* 4 English, 3 mathematics, 3 science, (1 science labs), 2 foreign language, 3 social studies, 4 academic electives. *Academic units recommended:* 4 English, 3 mathematics, 3 science, (1 science labs), 2 foreign language, 3 social studies, 4 academic electives. **Freshman Admission Statistics:** 11,053 applied, 49% admitted, 32% enrolled. **Transfer Admission Requirements:** college transcript(s), minimum college GPA of 2.0 required. Lowest grade transferable D. **General Admission Information:** Application Fee $30. Regular application deadline 6/11. Regular notification 12/11. Notification on a rolling basis, beginning on or about 11/13. Nonfall registration accepted. Admission may be deferred for a maximum of 2 Semesters. Credit offered for CEEB Advanced Placement tests.

COSTS AND FINANCIAL AID
Annual in-state tuition $4,229. Annual out-of-state tuition $18,688. Room and board $8,190. Required fees $2,006. Average book expense $1,200. **Required Forms and Deadlines:** FAFSAFinancial aid transcript for transfer students. **Notification of Awards:** Applicants will be notified of awards on a rolling basis beginning 3/15. **Types of Aid:** *Need-based scholarships/grants:* Federal Pell, SEOG, state scholarships/grants, private scholarships, the school's own gift aid, 2-2 Scholarships jointly sponsored with Florida Community College at Jacksonville. *Loans:* Subsidized Stafford, Unsubsidized Stafford, PLUS, Federal Perkins. **Student Employment:** Federal Work-Study Program available. Institutional employment available. Highest amount earned per year from on-campus jobs $3,750. Off-campus job opportunities are good. **Financial Aid Statistics:** 67% freshmen, 65% undergrads receive need-based scholarship or grant aid. 94% freshmen, 56% undergrads receive non-need-based scholarship or grant aid. 38% freshmen, 55% undergrads receive need-based self-help aid. 3% freshmen, 2% undergrads receive athletic scholarships. 95% freshmen, 77% undergrads receive any aid. 43% undergrads borrow to pay for school. Average cumulative indebtedness $16,572. **Criteria for awarding institutional aid:** Non-need-based, academics, athletics, leadership, minority status, music/drama, state/district residency.

UNIVERSITY OF NORTH TEXAS

1155 Union Circle #311277, Denton, TX 76203
Phone: 940-565-2681 • **Financial Aid Phone:** 940-565-3901
E-mail: undergrad@unt.edu • **CEEB Code:** 6481
Fax: 940-565-2408 • **Website:** www.unt.edu • **ACT Code:** 4136

This public school was founded in 1890. It has a 850-acre campus.

RATINGS
Admissions Selectivity Rating: 79   **Fire Safety Rating:** 91   **Green Rating:** 95

STUDENTS AND FACULTY
Enrollment: 28,956. **Student Body:** 52% female, 48% male, 4% out-of-state, 3% international (162 countries represented). Asian 5%, African American 13%, Caucasian 56%, Hispanic 19%, Native American 1%.
Retention and Graduation: 22% freshmen graduate within 4 years. **Faculty:** Student/faculty ratio 23:1. 985 full-time faculty, 80% hold PhDs, 28% are members of minority groups, 30% are women. 34% of classes are taught by teaching assistants.

ACADEMICS
Degrees: bachelor's, master's, post-bachelor's certificate. **Classes:** Most classes have 20-29 students. Most lab/discussion sessions have 20-29 students. **Majors with Highest Enrollment:** criminal justice/safety studies; education; sociology. **Special Study Options:** Accelerated program, cooperative education program, cross-registration, distance learning, double major, dual enrollment, English as a Second Language (ESL), honors program, independent study, internships, study abroad, teacher certification program, weekend college. **Honors programs:** University of North Texas Honors College **Combined degree programs:** BA/MD, BA/JD, BA/MA, BA/DDS, BA/MEng. **Disability Services:** Special programs offered to physically disabled students include note-taking services, reader services, tape recorders, tutors. **Career services:** Alumni network, alumni services, career/job search classes, career assessment, internships, regional alumni. Career services highlights include We offer our Alumni Services to our alumni at no cost (very important in these times especially), and have developed some very strong programs for the alumni to help them in their transition.

FACILITIES
Housing: Coed dorms, special housing for disabled students, women's dorms, fraternity/sorority housing, apartments for married students, cooperative hous-

ing, apartments for single students, Theme Housing 90% of campus accessible to physically disabled. **Special Academic Facilities/Equipment:** laser, observatory, accelerators, recreational facility, music facilities, environmental sciences, planetarium, art galleries. **Computers:** 75% of classrooms, 30% of dorms, 100% of libraries, 100% of dining areas, 100% of student union, 10% of common outdoor areas have wireless network access. Students can register for classes online. Administrative functions (other than registration) can be performed online.

CAMPUS LIFE

Environment: City. **Activities:** Choral groups, concert band, dance, drama/theater, jazz band, literary magazine, marching band, music ensembles, musical theater, opera, pep band, radio station, student government, student newspaper, student-run film society, symphony orchestra, television station, Campus Ministries, International Student Organization 330 registered organizations, 40 honor societies, 34 religious organizations. 23 fraternities, 16 sororities. **Athletics (Intercollegiate):** *Men:* basketball, cross-country, football, golf, softball, track/field (indoor). *Women:* basketball, cross-country, diving, golf, soccer, softball, swimming, tennis, track/field (indoor), volleyball. **On-Campus Highlights:** University Union, Student Recreation Center, Library Mall and pavilion, Murchison Performing Arts Center, Eagle Student Services Center, Chestnut Hall. **Environmental Initiatives:** 3 x 100 kW Community-scale Wind Turbines at UNT Eagle Point Campus. Approved by Board of Regents and funded by $2.2 million federal stimulus grant via State Energy Conervation Office program. The project is in progress to be completed by Fall 2011. Energy Performance Contract with Sneider Electric. The project, funded by UNT, will save $3.2 million/year in energy costs over the next 20 years, and will reduce greenhouse gases to below 1990 levels within 5 years. http://smartenergy.unt.edu LEED Buildings at UNT. The Life Sciences Complex opened fall 2010, Silver. The New Football Stadium (seeking platinum) and Business Leadership Building (seeking Gold) will both open in fall 2011. http://www.sustainable.unt.edu/commitments.php

ADMISSIONS

Freshman Academic Profile: 17% in top 10% of high school class, 47% in top 25% of high school class, 89% in top 50% of high school class. 95% from public high schools. SAT Math middle 50% range 500-610. SAT Critical Reading middle 50% range 480-600. SAT Writing middle 50% range 460-570. ACT middle 50% range 20-26. Minimum web-based TOEFL 79. Minimum paper TOEFL 550. **Basis for Candidate Selection:** *Very important factors considered include:* Class rank, academic GPA, standardized test scores. *Important factors considered include:* application essay, recommendation(s), rigor of secondary school record. *Other factors considered include:* character/personal qualities, extracurricular activities, first generation, geographical residence, level of applicant's interest, talent/ability, volunteer work, work experience. **Freshman Admission Requirements:** High school diploma is required and GED is accepted. *Academic units required:* 4 English, 3 mathematics, 3 science, (3 science labs), 2 foreign language, 2 social studies, 2 history, 3 academic electives. *Academic units recommended:* 4 English, 3 mathematics, 3 science, (3 science labs), 2 foreign language, 2 social studies, 2 history, 3 academic electives. **Freshman Admission Statistics:** 14,853 applied, 64% admitted, 36% enrolled. **Transfer Admission Requirements:** college transcript(s), statement of good standing from prior institution(s). Minimum college GPA of 2.5 required. Lowest grade transferable D. **General Admission Information:** Application Fee $40. Regular application deadline 8/1. Notification on a rolling basis, beginning on or about 10/15. Nonfall registration accepted. Credit and/or placement offered for CEEB Advanced Placement tests.

COSTS AND FINANCIAL AID

Annual in-state tuition $6,488. Annual out-of-state tuition $17,018. Room and board $7,150. Required fees $2,590. Average book expense $1,000. **Required Forms and Deadlines:** FAFSA. **Notification of Awards:** Applicants will be notified of awards on a rolling basis beginning 4/1. **Types of Aid:** *Need-based scholarships/grants:* Federal Pell, SEOG, state scholarships/grants, private scholarships, the school's own gift aid. *Loans:* Direct Subsidized Stafford, Direct Unsubsidized Stafford, Direct PLUS, Federal Perkins, state loans. **Student Employment:** Federal Work-Study Program available. Institutional employment available. Highest amount earned per year from on-campus jobs $8,726. Off-campus job opportunities are excellent. **Financial Aid Statistics:** 79% freshmen, 75% undergrads receive need-based scholarship or grant aid. 60% freshmen, 31% undergrads receive non-need-based scholarship or grant aid. 76% freshmen, 84% undergrads receive need-based self-help aid. 1% freshmen, 1% undergrads receive athletic scholarships. 90% freshmen, 71% undergrads receive any aid. **Criteria for awarding institutional aid:** Non-need-based: academics.

UNIVERSITY OF NORTHERN COLORADO

UNC Admissions Office, Greeley, CO 80639
Phone: 970-351-2881 • **Financial Aid Phone:** 970-351-2502
E-mail: admissions@unco.edu • **CEEB Code:** 4074
Fax: 970-351-2984 • **Website:** www.unco.edu • **ACT Code:** 502

This public school was founded in 1890. It has a 243-acre campus.

RATINGS

Admissions Selectivity Rating: 67   **Fire Safety Rating:** 95   **Green Rating:** 68

STUDENTS AND FACULTY

Enrollment: 9,975. **Student Body:** 62% female, 38% male, 10% out-of-state, 1% international (49 countries represented). Asian 2%, African American 4%, Caucasian 70%, Hispanic 12%, Native American 1%.
Retention and Graduation: 70% freshmen return for sophomore year.
Faculty: Student/faculty ratio 19:1. 498 full-time faculty, 10% are members of minority groups, 50% are women.

ACADEMICS

Degrees: bachelor's, master's, post-master's certificate. **Classes:** Most classes have 20–29 students. Most lab/discussion sessions have 20–29 students. **Majors with Highest Enrollment:** business administration and management; kinesiology and exercise science; multi-/interdisciplinary studies, other. **Special Study Options:** cooperative education program, cross-registration, distance learning, double major, English as a Second Language (ESL), exchange student program (domestic), external degree program, honors program, independent study, internships, student-designed major, study abroad, teacher certification program. **Honors programs:** The University Honors Program is designed to offer exceptional students both the resources of a comprehensive university and the individual attention traditionally associated with a small college. It asks that they be alive to the life of the mind and pushes them to raise the expectations they have for themselves and their education. It seeks to involve them in learning, heighten their critical awareness, and encourage their independent thinking and research. **Disability Services:** Special programs offered to physically disabled students include note-taking services, reader services, tape recorders, tutors. **Career services:** alumni services, career/job search classes, career assessment, internships.

FACILITIES

Housing: Coed dorms, special housing for disabled students, women's dorms, fraternity/sorority housing, apartments for married students, apartments for single students. 100% of campus accessible to physically disabled. **Special Academic Facilities/Equipment:** Art Museum, Music Library, James A. Michener Collection **Computers:** 100% of classrooms, 100% of dorms, 100% of libraries, 100% of dining areas, 100% of student union, 5% of common outdoor areas have wireless network access. Students can register for classes online. Administrative functions (other than registration) can be performed online.

CAMPUS LIFE

Environment: City. **Activities:** Choral groups, concert band, dance, drama/theater, jazz band, literary magazine, marching band, music ensembles, musical theater, opera, pep band, radio station, student government, student newspaper, student-run film society, symphony orchestra, television station, Campus Ministries, International Student Organization 137 registered organizations, 9 honor societies, 18 religious organizations. 9 fraternities, 8 sororities. **Athletics (Intercollegiate):** *Men:* baseball, basketball, football, golf, tennis, track/field (outdoor), wrestling. *Women:* basketball, cross-country, diving, golf, soccer, softball, swimming, tennis, track/field (outdoor), volleyball. **On-Campus Highlights:** University Center, James Michener Library, Recreation Center, Cultural Centers **Environmental Initiatives:** Performance Contracting Recycling Non-Potable Water Usage for Irrigation

ADMISSIONS

Freshman Academic Profile: Average high school GPA 3.2. 14% in top 10% of high school class, 38% in top 25% of high school class, 70% in top 50% of high school class. SAT Math middle 50% range 450-580. SAT Critical Reading middle 50% range 460-580. ACT middle 50% range 19-25. Minimum web-based TOEFL 80. Minimum paper TOEFL 550. **Basis for Candidate Selection:** *Very important factors considered include:* Class rank, academic GPA, standardized test scores. *Important factors considered include:* recommendation(s). *Other factors considered include:* rigor of secondary school record, character/personal qualities, extracurricular activities, interview, racial/ethnic status, state residency, talent/ability, work experience. **Freshman Admission Requirements:** High school diploma is required and GED is accepted. *Academic units required:* 4 English, 3 mathematics, 3 science, (2 science labs), 3 social studies, 2 academic electives. *Academic units recommended:* 4 English, 3 mathematics, 3 science, (2 science labs), 3 social studies, 2 academic electives. **Freshman Admission Statistics:** 6,410 applied, 88% admitted, 40% enrolled. **Transfer Admission Requirements:** college transcript(s), statement of good standing from prior institution(s). Minimum college GPA of 2.4 required. Lowest grade transferable C. **General Admission Information:** Application Fee $45. Nonfall registration accepted. Admission may be deferred for a maximum of 3 semesters. Credit offered for CEEB Advanced Placement tests.

COSTS AND FINANCIAL AID
Annual in-state tuition $5,300. Annual out-of-state tuition $16,822. Room and board $9,750. Required fees $1,323. Average book expense $1,325. **Required Forms and Deadlines:** FAFSA. **Notification of Awards:** Applicants will be notified of awards on a rolling basis beginning 4/15. **Types of Aid:** *Need-based scholarships/grants:* Federal Pell, SEOG, state scholarships/grants, private scholarships, the school's own gift aid. *Loans:* Subsidized Stafford, Unsubsidized Stafford, PLUS, Federal Perkins, college/university loans from institutional funds. **Student Employment:** Federal Work-Study Program available. Institutional employment available. Highest amount earned per year from on-campus jobs $4,726. Off-campus job opportunities are fair. **Financial Aid Statistics:** 71% freshmen, 67% undergrads receive need-based scholarship or grant aid. 70% freshmen, 45% undergrads receive non-need-based scholarship or grant aid. 89% freshmen, 90% undergrads receive need-based self-help aid. 2% freshmen, 2% undergrads receive athletic scholarships. **Criteria for awarding institutional aid:** Non-need-based: academics, athletics, music/drama.

UNIVERSITY OF NORTHERN IOWA

1227 West 27th Street, Cedar Falls, IA 50614-0018
Phone: 319-273-2281 • **Financial Aid Phone:** 319-273-2701
E-mail: admissions@uni.edu • **CEEB Code:** 6307
Fax: 319-273-2885 • **Website:** www.uni.edu • **ACT Code:** 1322

This public school was founded in 1876. It has a 910-acre campus.

RATINGS
Admissions Selectivity Rating: 70   **Fire Safety Rating:** 76   **Green Rating:** 95

STUDENTS AND FACULTY
Enrollment: 10,513. **Student Body:** 57% female, 43% male, 5% out-of-state, 3% international (57 countries represented). Asian 1%, African American 3%, Caucasian 88%, Hispanic 3%.
Retention and Graduation: 38% freshmen graduate within 4 years. 16% grads go on to further study within 1 year. 8% grads pursue arts and sciences degrees. 2% grads pursue business degrees. 2% grads pursue medical degrees.
Faculty: Student/faculty ratio 16:1. 602 full-time faculty, 76% hold PhDs, 14% are members of minority groups, 45% are women. 2% of classes are taught by teaching assistants.

ACADEMICS
Degrees: bachelor's, doctoral, master's. **Classes:** Most classes have 20–29 students. Most lab/discussion sessions have 10–19 students. **Majors with Highest Enrollment:** business administration and management; elementary education and teaching; marketing/marketing management. **Special Study Options:** Accelerated program, cooperative education program, distance learning, double major, dual enrollment, English as a Second Language (ESL), exchange student program (domestic), external degree program, honors program, independent study, internships, liberal arts/career combination, student-designed major, study abroad, teacher certification program, weekend college, Combined Bachelors/Masters degree programs (BA/MA, BS/MS, BA/MS); undergraduate Dual Degree Majors; 2+2 Programs; undergraduate and graduate certificates. **Honors programs:** University Honors Program - includes all 5 colleges and is open to all majors. www.uni.edu/honors **Combined degree programs:** BA/MA, BA/MS,BA/MAcc,Biology,Chemistry,Technlgy. **Disability Services:** Special programs offered to physically disabled students include note-taking services, reader services, tape recorders, tutors. **Career services:** alumni services, career/job search classes, career assessment, internships Career services highlights include UNI has had over 10,000 students conduct internships for credit over the past 30 years, with thousands more participating in an internship for no credit.

FACILITIES
Housing: Coed dorms, men's dorms, women's dorms, fraternity/sorority housing, apartments for married students, apartments for single students, Facilities accessible by persons with disabilities. 90% of campus accessible to physically disabled. **Special Academic Facilities/Equipment:** Natural history museum, art gallery, greenhouse and biological preserves, Lakeside biology lab and field lab for conservation problems, Tallgrass Prairie Center, Educational Technology

Center, curriculum lab, on-campus school for student teachers, NASA Regional Teacher Resource Center, speech and hearing clinic, Small Business Development Center, Iowa Waste Reduction Center, Center for Applied Research in Metal Casting. Iowa Communications Network provides two-way audio/video link between classrooms across the state. Satellite video production truck with three cameras. Performing Arts Center. **Computers:** 80% of classrooms, 75% of libraries, 100% of dining areas, 100% of student union, have wireless network access. Students can register for classes online. Administrative functions (other than registration) can be performed online.

CAMPUS LIFE
Environment: Town. **Activities:** Choral groups, concert band, dance, drama/theater, jazz band, literary magazine, marching band, music ensembles, musical theater, opera, pep band, radio station, student government, student newspaper, symphony orchestra, yearbook, Campus Ministries, International Student Organization, Model UN. 278 registered organizations, 18 honor societies, 21 religious organizations. 5 fraternities, 4 sororities. **Athletics (Intercollegiate):** *Men:* basketball, cross-country, football, golf, track/field (outdoor), track/field (indoor), wrestling. *Women:* basketball, cross-country, diving, golf, soccer, softball, swimming, tennis, track/field (outdoor), track/field (indoor), volleyball. **On-Campus Highlights:** Wellness Recreation Center, Gallagher-Bluedorn Performing Arts Center, Piazza and Rialto Dining Centers, Maucker University Union, UNI-DOME and McLeod Center. **Environmental Initiatives:** UNI was a charter member of the AASHE STARS program. UNI's rating of Gold was the first gold rating in the Midwest. Sustainability was outlined as one of eight core institutional values in the most recent university strategic plan. Three UNI students were supported during the last year as EPA onCampus EcoAmbassadors. These students not only represented UNI, but the entire EPA Region Seven.

ADMISSIONS
Freshman Academic Profile: Average high school GPA 3.2. 19% in top 10% of high school class, 48% in top 25% of high school class, 84% in top 50% of high school class. ACT middle 50% range 21-25. Minimum web-based TOEFL 79. Minimum paper TOEFL 550. **Basis for Candidate Selection:** *Very important factors considered include:* Class rank, academic GPA, rigor of secondary school record, standardized test scores. *Other factors considered include:* application essay, recommendation(s), first generation, interview, talent/ability. **Freshman Admission Requirements:** High school diploma is required and GED is accepted. *Academic units required:* 4 English, 3 mathematics, 3 science, 3 social studies, 2 academic electives. *Academic units recommended:* 4 English, 3 mathematics, 3 science, 3 social studies, 2 academic electives. **Freshman Admission Statistics:** 4,322 applied, 78% admitted, 51% enrolled. **Transfer Admission Requirements:** college transcript(s), Lowest grade transferable D. **General Admission Information:** Application Fee $40. Regular application deadline 8/15. Notification on a rolling basis, beginning on or about 9/1. Nonfall registration accepted. Admission may be deferred for a maximum of indefinitely. Credit and/or placement offered for CEEB Advanced Placement tests.

COSTS AND FINANCIAL AID
Annual in-state tuition $6,648. Annual out-of-state tuition $15,734. Room and board $7,597. Required fees $987. Average book expense $1,054. **Required Forms and Deadlines:** FAFSA. **Notification of Awards:** Applicants will be notified of awards on a rolling basis beginning 3/1. **Types of Aid:** *Need-based scholarships/grants:* Federal Pell, SEOG, state scholarships/grants, private scholarships, the school's own gift aid. *Loans:* Direct Subsidized Stafford, Direct Unsubsidized Stafford, Direct PLUS, Federal Perkins, Private, Alternative Loans. **Student Employment:** Federal Work-Study Program available. Institutional employment available. Highest amount earned per year from on-campus jobs $5,872. Off-campus job opportunities are good. **Financial Aid Statistics:** 49% freshmen, 53% undergrads receive need-based scholarship or grant aid. 67% freshmen, 40% undergrads receive non-need-based scholarship or grant aid. 83% freshmen, 88% undergrads receive need-based self-help aid. 3% freshmen, 2% undergrads receive athletic scholarships. 91% freshmen, 84% undergrads receive any aid. 77% undergrads borrow to pay for school. Average cumulative indebtedness $23,575. **Criteria for awarding institutional aid:** Non-need-based: academics, alumni affiliation, art, athletics, leadership, minority status, music/drama, state/district residency.

UNIVERSITY OF NOTRE DAME

220 Main Building, Notre Dame, IN 46556
Phone: 574-631-7505 • **Financial Aid Phone:** 574-631-6436
E-mail: admissions@nd.edu • **CEEB Code:** 1841
Fax: 574-631-8865 • **Website:** www.nd.edu • **ACT Code:** 1252

This private school, affiliated with the Roman Catholic Church, was founded in 1842. It has a 1250-acre campus.

RATINGS
Admissions Selectivity Rating: 98   **Fire Safety Rating:** 92   **Green Rating:** 83

STUDENTS AND FACULTY
Enrollment: 8,466. **Student Body:** 47% female, 53% male, 92% out-of-state, 4% international (87 countries represented). Asian 7%, African American 3%, Caucasian 72%, Hispanic 10%.
Retention and Graduation: 90% freshmen graduate within 4 years. 32% grads go on to further study within 1 year. 12% grads pursue arts and sciences degrees. 5% grads pursue law degrees. 3% grads pursue business degrees. 9% grads pursue medical degrees. **Faculty:** Student/faculty ratio 11:1. 1082 full-time faculty, 90% hold PhDs, 16% are members of minority groups, 30% are women. 9% of classes are taught by teaching assistants.

ACADEMICS
Degrees: bachelor's, first professional, master's. **Classes:** Most classes have 10–19 students. Most lab/discussion sessions have 10–19 students. **Majors with Highest Enrollment:** finance; political science and government; psychology. **Special Study Options:** Accelerated program, cross-registration, double major, dual enrollment, exchange student program (domestic), honors program, independent study, internships, liberal arts/career combination, student-designed major, study abroad, teacher certification program, Teacher Certification only available through Cross Registration with St. Mary's College. **Combined degree programs:** , B.S. Engr./MBA. **Disability Services:** Special programs offered to physically disabled students include note-taking services, reader services, tape recorders. **Career services:** Alumni network, alumni services, career/job search classes, career assessment, internships Career services highlights include Please describe the program above of which you are proudest: Employer Development and Alumni Networking: To continue forming and growing relationships with employers during difficult economic times, The Career Center has increased it efforts and outreach to employers to identify career opportunities for students. The importance of networking continues to grow given the current state of the economy. Also recognizing that building and maintaining professional networking relationships will be critical to the hiring process this year. The Career Center has several programs planned for the spring semester that will help students network. ° The Career Center sent emails to 24,000 alumni in select industries to identify opportunities for Notre Dame students. As a result, employers including IBM, Skanska USA, Switch-Fast, Radio Flyer, Fidelity, Bristol Myers Squibb, Lockheed Martin, Draftfcb, and Societe Generale registered for the Winter Career Fair and/or posted job opportunities for our students. ° Career Counselors have received additional training on searching for jobs within the federal government and public service, a key sector of employment opportunities. ° The Career Center has successfully developed recruiting relationships with small, mid-sized, and family-owned companies to post jobs and internships. ° The Career Center will host a special program in NYC with ND alumni working in private equity and banking, to expand placement opportunities and internships on Wall Street. Also arranging two-week unpaid externships on Wall Street to help students gain experience in a very tough job market. ° The Career Center has added DirectEmployers Association to its Employer Advisory Board and gained instant access to 420 Fortune 500 employers ° The Career Center is working with Alumni Clubs to help seniors find jobs in or near their hometowns ° The Career Center is networking with GradStaff.com, CityStaff.com, Adecco and other professional organizations to help students connect to short-term, paid, professional jobs to gain experience with Fortune 500 companies. ° The Career Center has also implemented distance interviewing with Skype, and Polycam technology as an additional service for employers who cannot travel to campus to interview. ° A Notre Dame Alumni Group has been established on LinkedIn and currently has over 8,200 members. ° The Career Center launched a Job Shadow Program in Fall 2008 with over 1,200 alumni volunteering to host students at their companies for a one day networking visit ° The Career Center also has an agreement with the ND Alumni Association to grant seniors access to Irish Online, the online community of the Notre Dame Alumni Association. Senior students can create an

account on this website before graduation and find alumni contacts. Additionally, networking workshops are being offered, providing students with access to Irish Online that will enable them to find key contacts for career development. Additional programs and information: ° Confirmed 1,475 internships for ND students documented in the Intern Survey for the Summer of 2008 ° Raised funding to reimburse students $200 for travel to the Big East Career Fair in March 2008 and March 2009.

FACILITIES
Housing: men's dorms, women's dorms. 95% of campus accessible to physically disabled. **Special Academic Facilities/Equipment:** Art Museum Theater Germ-free research facility Radiation laboratory **Computers:** Students can register for classes online. Administrative functions (other than registration) can be performed online.

CAMPUS LIFE
Environment: City. **Activities:** Choral groups, concert band, dance, drama/theater, jazz band, literary magazine, marching band, music ensembles, musical theater, opera, pep band, radio station, student government, student newspaper, student-run film society, symphony orchestra, yearbook, Campus Ministries, International Student Organization, Model UN. 299 registered organizations, 10 honor societies, 11 religious organizations. **Athletics (Intercollegiate):** *Men:* baseball, basketball, cross-country, diving, fencing, football, golf, ice hockey, lacrosse, soccer, swimming, tennis, track/field (outdoor). *Women:* basketball, crew/rowing, cross-country, diving, fencing, golf, lacrosse, soccer, softball, swimming, tennis, track/field (outdoor), volleyball. **On-Campus Highlights:** Grotto, The Dome (Main Building), Basilica of the Sacred Heart, Notre Dame Stadium, Eck Center. **Environmental Initiatives:** Expansion of Office of Sustainability to include 3 full time staff and 7 interns; development of metrics and quantitative goals in 7 key sustainability areas Investment of $4 million this year to improve lighting and/or HVAC efficiency in 24 campus buildings Continuous utilization of $2 million Green Loan Fund to support capital projects that save energy and natural resources.

ADMISSIONS
Freshman Academic Profile: 89% in top 10% of high school class, 97% in top 25% of high school class, 100% in top 50% of high school class. 42% from public high schools. SAT Math middle 50% range 680-770. SAT Critical Reading middle 50% range 660-750. SAT Writing middle 50% range 650-750. ACT middle 50% range 31-34. Minimum web-based TOEFL 100. Minimum paper TOEFL 560. **Basis for Candidate Selection:** *Very important factors considered include:* rigor of secondary school record. *Important factors considered include:* Class rank, application essay, academic GPA, recommendation(s), standardized test scores, alumni/ae relation, character/personal qualities, extracurricular activities, talent/ability, volunteer work. *Other factors considered include:* first generation, level of applicant's interest, racial/ethnic status, religious affiliation/commitment, work experience. **Freshman Admission Requirements:** High school diploma is required and GED is not accepted. *Academic units required:* 4 English, 3 mathematics, 2 science, (2 science labs), 2 foreign language, 2 history, 3 academic electives. *Academic units recommended:* 4 English, 3 mathematics, 2 science, (2 science labs), 2 foreign language, 2 history, 3 academic electives. **Freshman Admission Statistics:** 16,957 applied, 23% admitted, 51% enrolled. **Transfer Admission Requirements:** High school transcript, college transcript(s), essay or personal statement, standardized test scores, statement of good standing from prior institution(s). Minimum college GPA of 3.0 required. Lowest grade transferable C. **General Admission Information:** Application Fee $65. Regular application deadline 12/31. Regular notification 4/10. Nonfall registration accepted. Admission may be deferred for a maximum of 12 months.

COSTS AND FINANCIAL AID
Annual tuition $42,464. Room and board $11,394. Required fees $507. Average book expense $950. **Required Forms and Deadlines:** FAFSA, CSS/Financial Aid PROFILE, business/farm supplement. **Notification of Awards:** Applicants will be notified of awards on or about 4/1. **Types of Aid:** *Need-based scholarships/grants:* Federal Pell, SEOG, state scholarships/grants, private scholarships, the school's own gift aid, Federal ACG and SMART Grants. *Loans:* Subsidized Stafford, Unsubsidized Stafford, PLUS, Federal Perkins, Private Student Loans. **Student Employment:** Highest amount earned per year from on-campus jobs $6,300. Off-campus job opportunities are fair. **Financial Aid Statistics:** 95% freshmen, 95% undergrads receive need-based scholarship or grant aid. 51% freshmen, 46% undergrads receive non-need-based scholarship or grant aid. 77% freshmen, 83% undergrads receive need-based self-help aid. 5% freshmen, 5% undergrads receive athletic scholarships. 73% freshmen, 82% undergrads receive any aid. 51% undergrads borrow to pay for school. Average cumulative indebtedness $29,480. **Criteria for awarding institutional aid:** Non-need-based: athletics.

UNIVERSITY OF OKLAHOMA

Best 378

1000 Asp Aveune, Norman, OK 73019-4076
Phone: 405-325-2252 • **Financial Aid Phone:** 405-325-5505
E-mail: admrec@ou.edu • **CEEB Code:** 6879
Fax: 405-325-7124 • **Website:** www.ou.edu • **ACT Code:** 3442

This public school was founded in 1890. It has a 3914-acre campus.

RATINGS
Admissions Selectivity Rating: 81   **Fire Safety Rating:** 93   **Green Rating:** 83

STUDENTS AND FACULTY
Enrollment: 21,572. **Student Body:** 51% female, 49% male, 30% out-of-state, 3% international (127 countries represented). Asian 5%, African American 5%, Caucasian 64%, Hispanic 7%, Native American 5%.
Retention and Graduation: Faculty: Student/faculty ratio 18:1. 1470 full-time faculty, 80% hold PhDs, 19% are members of minority groups, 42% are women. 17% of classes are taught by teaching assistants.

ACADEMICS
Degrees: bachelor's, certificate, master's, post-bachelor's certificate, post-master's certificate. **Classes:** Most classes have 10–19 students. Most lab/discussion sessions have 20–29 students. **Majors with Highest Enrollment:** journalism; management science; psychology. **Special Study Options:** Accelerated program, cooperative education program, distance learning, double major, dual enrollment, English as a Second Language (ESL), external degree program, honors program, independent study, internships, liberal arts/career combination, student-designed major, study abroad, teacher certification program, weekend college. **Honors programs:** Honors at Oxford: This summer program enables students to study at Oxford (while living at Brasenose College). While there, students work in private tutorials with distinguished Oxford dons. Students can earn up to 6 hours of honors credit in one of our four classes that are offered. Honors in Italy: Honors in Italy is built around a three-hours course called "'Imagining Italy'" which is taught in the Tuscan town of Arezzo and includes side trips to Florence, Venice, and Rome where students are led on walking tours of the art and history of Italy. The focus is on how Italian culture has influenced writers, filmmakers, and artists from John Adams to Henry James and from Mark Twain to Martin Scorsese. Honors in Germany (new for summer 2010): Honors students and other OU students travel to Leipzig, Germany in June, live at the University of Leipzig, study German, and take a course on German-American literary relations (American writers who wrote in Germany about German culture.) Additionally, students focus on experiencing and exploring major sites for the history and memory of WWII in Germany by taking day trips from Leipzig to major WWII-related sites in Germany. The course will be for six hours credit and will be offered each summer. Honors Undergraduate Research Assistant Program: Honors Undergraduate Research Assistant Program provides undergraduates the opportunity to work with professors as research assistants on specific projects. Student assistants are expected to work 10 hours a week for 10 weeks for $6 an hour. Honors College students with at least 15 hours of college credit and a 3.4+ GPA are eligible to apply. Medical Humanities Scholars Program: The Honors College and the University of Oklahoma College of Medicine have created a special pathway (through a bachelor of arts degree leading to a medical doctorate) for up to five high school students each year who wish to study the humanistic aspects of medicine as undergraduates. Through a special admissions process, the Medical Humanities Scholars are accepted at the medical school as part of their application to OU's undergraduate honors program. The Honors College has also created a Medical Humanities Minor open to all honors students wishing to study medicine from the perspectives of history, sociology, anthropology, bioethics, literature, and economics. Honors Undergraduate Writing Assistant Program: The Honors Undergraduate Writing Assistant Program includes assistants who receive a stipend to work as writing assistants for the required freshman American Perspectives courses. Students who wish to be writing assistants apply to the program and, if they are selected, participate in a required upper-division preparatory course that focuses on composition pedagogy, research and writing skills, and strategies for commenting and conferencing on students writing. Honors Undergraduate Research Opportunities Program: The Undergraduate Research Opportunities Program is open to all undergraduates at OU. Each semester the Honors College awards more than $12,500 to undergraduate students and their faculty mentors for research and creative activity. Undergraduate Research Day: Each spring the college hosts an Undergraduate Research Day, in which scholars, Honors students or not, share their research with the peers. The

Honors College, Phi Beta Kappa and Phi Kappa Phi give cash awards to the best presentations in various categories. Conversations with the Dean: Each week the Dean of the Honors College has in a distinguished professor, author, diplomat, politician, or some other important community or intellectual figure to discuss world events. With the Dean as moderator, students are encouraged to participate in vibrant discussion with the week"s important guest. Honors College Reading Groups: The Dean and Honors College faculty assign a book of their individual choosing to students who voluntarily join an Honors College Reading Group. Limited to 15 students per group, the books are provided free of charge to participants who then meet as a group, one hour a week, to discuss the assigned pages with the professor. There is no charge for this activity, there are no grades, and students may come and go as they please. The aim is to encourage students to read, think, and discuss with other Honors College students important topics of mutual interest, whether fiction or non-fiction. The Honors Undergraduate Research Journal: The Honors Undergraduate Research Journal is a forum in which Honors students of all majors have the opportunity to have their work published. A panel of Honors College professors who annually appoint an editorial board of about eight Honors students advises THURJ. The board accepts research papers, poetry, and short stories of which the top submissions are published every spring. Freshman Summer Reading Series: Each summer all incoming freshmen receive a free, theme-based book chosen by the faculty. The students are encouraged to actively engage the material (the book arrives at the student"s home in late June), which provides the incoming class with a common intellectual experience that the faculty and students can build on during their first semester in order to develop and nurture a collective intellectual community. **Combined degree programs:** BA/MA, BA/MEng, BAC/MAC. **Disability Services:** Special programs offered to physically disabled students include note-taking services, reader services, tutors. **Career services:** Alumni network, alumni services, career/job search classes, career assessment, internships Career services highlights include Alumni Network- Alumni provide career mentoring to currently enrolled students.

FACILITIES
Housing: Coed dorms, special housing for disabled students, men's dorms, special housing for international students, women's dorms, fraternity/sorority housing, apartments for married students, apartments for single students, Honors House, Cultural Housing, National Merit, and Scholastics floors. 92% of campus accessible to physically disabled. **Special Academic Facilities/Equipment:** Fred Jones Museum of Art, Sam Noble Museum of Natural History, National Weather Center, National Severe Storms Library, OU Biological Station, History of Science Collection, Western History Collection, Oklahoma Geological Survey **Computers:** 60% of classrooms, 80% of dorms, 100% of libraries, 75% of dining areas, 100% of student union, 80% of common outdoor areas have wireless network access. Students can register for classes online. Administrative functions (other than registration) can be performed online.

CAMPUS LIFE
Environment. City. **Activities:** Choral groups, concert band, dance, drama/theater, jazz band, literary magazine, marching band, music ensembles, musical theater, opera, pep band, radio station, student government, student newspaper, student-run film society, symphony orchestra, television station, yearbook, Campus Ministries, International Student Organization, Model UN. 388 registered organizations, 17 honor societies, 39 religious organizations. 30 fraternities, 20 sororities. **Athletics (Intercollegiate):** *Men:* baseball, basketball, cross-country, football, golf, gymnastics, tennis, track/field (outdoor), track/field (indoor), wrestling. *Women:* basketball, crew/rowing, cross-country, golf, gymnastics, soccer, softball, tennis, track/field (outdoor), track/field (indoor), volleyball. **On-Campus Highlights:** Fred Jones Jr. Museum of Art, The Gaylord Family Oklahoma Memorial Sta, Sam Noble Ok. Museum of Natural History, Oklahoma Memorial Union, Lloyd Noble Center. **Environmental Initiatives:** Membership in the Chicago Climate Exchange Joining with the University Presidents' Campus Climate Challenge Operation of the Academic Department for Interdisciplinary Perspectives on the Environment and creation of the Department of Geography and Environmental Sustainability.

ADMISSIONS
Freshman Academic Profile: Average high school GPA 3.6. 33% in top 10% of high school class, 66% in top 25% of high school class, 93% in top 50% of high school class. SAT Math middle 50% range 540-660. SAT Critical Reading middle 50% range 510-640. ACT middle 50% range 23-29. Minimum web-based TOEFL 79. Minimum paper TOEFL 550. **Basis for Candidate Selection:** *Very important factors considered include:* Class rank, academic GPA, rigor of secondary school record, standardized test scores. *Other factors considered include:* application essay, recommendation(s), state residency. **Freshman Admission Requirements:** High school diploma is required and GED is accepted. *Academic units required:* 4 English, 3 mathematics, 3 science, (3 science labs), 2 social studies, 1 history, 2 academic electives. *Academic units recommended:* 4 English, 3 mathematics, 3 science, (3 science labs), 2 social studies, 1 history, 2 academic electives. **Freshman Admission Statistics:** 11,650 applied, 79% admitted, 45% enrolled. **Transfer Admission Require-**

ments: college transcript(s), Lowest grade transferable D. **General Admission Information:** Application Fee $40. Regular application deadline 4/1. Nonfall registration accepted. Credit and/or placement offered for CEEB Advanced Placement tests.

COSTS AND FINANCIAL AID

Annual in-state tuition $3,957. Annual out-of-state tuition $15,594. Room and board $8,382. Required fees $3,384. Average book expense $1,200. **Required Forms and Deadlines:** FAFSA. **Notification of Awards:** Applicants will be notified of awards on a rolling basis beginning 3/15. **Types of Aid:** *Need-based scholarships/grants:* Federal Pell, SEOG, state scholarships/grants, private scholarships, the school's own gift aid, United Negro College Fund. *Loans:* Subsidized Stafford, Unsubsidized Stafford, PLUS, Federal Perkins, Federal Nursing, college/university loans from institutional funds. **Student Employment:** Federal Work-Study Program available. Institutional employment available. Highest amount earned per year from on-campus jobs $3,108. Off-campus job opportunities are excellent. **Financial Aid Statistics:** 54% freshmen, 61% undergrads receive need-based scholarship or grant aid. 62% freshmen, 44% undergrads receive non-need-based scholarship or grant aid. 71% freshmen, 76% undergrads receive need-based self-help aid. 1% freshmen, 1% undergrads receive athletic scholarships. 83% freshmen, 91% undergrads receive any aid. 55% undergrads borrow to pay for school. Average cumulative indebtedness $26,574. **Criteria for awarding institutional aid:** Non-need-based: academics, alumni affiliation, art, athletics, leadership, music/drama, religious affiliation.

UNIVERSITY OF OREGON

1217 University of Oregon, Eugene, OR 97403-1217
Phone: 541-346-3201 • **Financial Aid Phone:** 800-760-6953
E-mail: uoadmit@uoregon.edu • **CEEB Code:** 4846
Fax: 541-346-5815 • **Website:** www.uoregon.edu • **ACT Code:**

This public school was founded in 1876. It has a 295-acre campus.

RATINGS

Admissions Selectivity Rating: 79   **Fire Safety Rating:** 71   **Green Rating:** 92

STUDENTS AND FACULTY

Enrollment: 20,464. **Student Body:** 52% female, 48% male, 35% out-of-state, 10% international (95 countries represented). Asian 5%, African American 2%, Caucasian 67%, Hispanic 7%, Native American 1%.
Retention and Graduation: 85% freshmen return for sophomore year. 44% freshmen graduate within 4 years. 68% freshmen graduate within 6 years.
Faculty: Student/faculty ratio 19:1. 1039 full-time faculty, 95% hold PhDs, 22% are members of minority groups, 44% are women. 21% of classes are taught by teaching assistants.

ACADEMICS

Degrees: bachelor's, master's, post-bachelor's certificate. **Classes:** Most classes have 20–29 students. Most lab/discussion sessions have 20–29 students. **Majors with Highest Enrollment:** business/commerce; journalism; psychology. **Special Study Options:** cross-registration, distance learning, double major, English as a Second Language (ESL), exchange student program (domestic), honors program, independent study, internships, liberal arts/career combination, student-designed major, study abroad, teacher certification program, Semester at Sea program; Professional distinctions program, a certificate program in which students gain direct professional preparation through internships, special courses, a professional mentor program, and the development of an electronic resume and portfolio. There is also a dual enrollment program that allows you to enroll in both UO and Lane Community College or UO and Southwestern Oregon Community College (differs from CDS definition in that it is not a high school dual enrollment program). **Honors programs:** Robert D. Clark Honors College, College of Arts and Sciences Society of College Scholars, Professional Distinctions program, Dean's List, Junior Scholars. **Disability Services:** Special programs offered to physically disabled students include note-taking services, reader services, tape recorders, tutors. **Career services:** Alumni network, alumni services, career/job search classes, career assessment, internships, regional alumni. Career services highlights include Career Assessment Program: This is a free opportunity available to all students that assists them in assessing values, interests, preferences and strengths. Through this process students gain confidence and self direction which helps them gain insight in major selection and career direction.

FACILITIES

Housing: Coed dorms, fraternity/sorority housing, apartments for married students, cooperative housing, apartments for single students, Wellness Housing, Theme HousingMost residence halls have separate men's and women's floors; Graduate Student Housing. 95% of campus accessible to physically disabled. **Special Academic Facilities/Equipment:** Jordan Schnitzer Museum of Art; Museum of Natural and Cultural History; James Warsaw Sports Marketing Center; Lundquist Center for Entrepreneurship; University of Oregon Many Nations Longhouse; Green Chemistry Laboratory and Alice C. Tyler Instrumentation Center; Future Music Oregon, a computer music center in the School of Music; Pine Mountain Observatory (Bend, Oregon); Oregon Institute of Marine Biology (Oregon Coast); Central Oregon programs affiliated with the Oregon University System Cascades Campus (Bend, Oregon); Urban Architecture program and BetterBricks Daylighting Laboratory at the University of Oregon Portland Center (Portland, Oregon). **Computers:** 95% of classrooms, 35% of dorms, 100% of libraries, 100% of dining areas, 100% of student union, 30% of common outdoor areas have wireless network access. Students can register for classes online. Administrative functions (other than registration) can be performed online.

CAMPUS LIFE

Environment: City. **Activities:** Choral groups, concert band, dance, drama/theater, jazz band, literary magazine, marching band, music ensembles, musical theater, opera, pep band, radio station, student government, student newspaper, student-run film society, symphony orchestra, Campus Ministries, International Student Organization 250 registered organizations, 22 honor societies, 20 religious organizations. 12 fraternities, 10 sororities. **Athletics (Intercollegiate):** *Men:* baseball, basketball, cross-country, football, golf, tennis, track/field (outdoor). *Women:* basketball, cross-country, golf, gymnastics, lacrosse, soccer, softball, tennis, track/field (outdoor), volleyball. **On-Campus Highlights:** University of Oregon Duckstore, Knight Library, Erb Memorial Union, Laverne Krauss Gallery in Lawrence Hall, Watch sports at Autzen, Hayward, or Mac Court, The University of Oregon's 295-acre, park-like campus is home to more than 500 varieties of trees, various private spots to study or simply stare at the sky, and tons of quick stops where you can grab a bite between classes. With a wealth of campus resources to make your life as a student easier, the UO campus feeds the mind, body, and spirit. On average, each course you take at the UO will have a person from another country, six people from different states, and several people with religious, cultural, and ethnic heritage different from your own. You'll thrive because this diversity pushes you to see the world differently. You'll listen to new ideas, and maybe even change the world because you changed your mind. **Environmental Initiatives:** Created the Oregon Model for Sustainable Development which puts a cap on building energy consumption. Massive energy efficiency upgrades; lighting retrofits, building upgrades Sustainable Cities Initiative is a unique service-learning program. Twenty-five faculty teach 500 students across twenty-eight courses which results in 80,000 hours of service for an Oregon city working to improve its sustainability performance.

ADMISSIONS

Freshman Academic Profile: Average high school GPA 3.6. 28% in top 10% of high school class, 63% in top 25% of high school class, 94% in top 50% of high school class. SAT Math middle 50% range 502-616. SAT Critical Reading middle 50% range 489-608. Minimum web-based TOEFL 61. Minimum paper TOEFL 500. **Basis for Candidate Selection:** *Very important factors considered include:* academic GPA, rigor of secondary school record. *Other factors considered include:* Class rank, application essay, recommendation(s), standardized test scores, extracurricular activities, first generation, geographical residence, racial/ethnic status, state residency, talent/ability, volunteer work, work experience. **Freshman Admission Requirements:** High school diploma is required and GED is accepted. *Academic units required:* 4 English, 3 mathematics, 2 science, 2 foreign language, 3 social studies. *Academic units recommended:* 4 English, 3 mathematics, 2 science, 2 foreign language, 3 social studies. **Freshman Admission Statistics:** 21,263 applied, 74% admitted, 37% enrolled. **Transfer Admission Requirements:** college transcript(s), minimum college GPA of 2.25 required. Lowest grade transferable D-. **General Admission Information:** Application Fee $50. Regular application deadline 1/15. Notification on a rolling basis, beginning on or about 12/15. Nonfall registration accepted. Credit and/or placement offered for CEEB Advanced Placement tests.

COSTS AND FINANCIAL AID

Annual in-state tuition $8,010. Annual out-of-state tuition $27,360. Room and board $10,580. Required fees $1,300. Average book expense $1,050. **Required Forms and Deadlines:** FAFSA. **Notification of Awards:** Applicants will be notified of awards on a rolling basis beginning 4/15. **Types of Aid:** *Need-based scholarships/grants:* Federal Pell, SEOG, state scholarships/grants, private scholarships, the school's own gift aid. *Loans:* Direct Subsidized Stafford, Direct Unsubsidized Stafford, Direct PLUS, Federal Perkins, college/university loans from institutional funds. **Student Employment:** Federal Work-Study Program available. Institutional employment available. Off-campus job opportunities are good. **Financial Aid Statistics:** 49% freshmen, 57% undergrads receive need-based scholarship or grant aid. 50% freshmen, 34% undergrads receive non-need-based scholarship or grant aid. 89% freshmen, 87% undergrads receive need-based self-help aid. 2% undergrads receive athletic scholarships. 73% freshmen, 68% undergrads receive any aid. 53% undergrads borrow to pay for school. Average cumulative indebtedness $22,736. **Criteria for awarding institutional aid:** Non-need-based: academics, art, athletics, leadership, minority status, music/drama, state/district residency.

See page 1272.

UNIVERSITY OF THE PACIFIC

3601 Pacific Avenue, Stockton, CA 95211
Phone: 209-946-2211 • **Financial Aid Phone:** 209-946-2421
E-mail: admissions@pacific.edu • **CEEB Code:** 4065
Fax: 209-946-2413 • **Website:** web.pacific.edu • **ACT Code:** 240

This private school was founded in 1851. It has a 175-acre campus.

RATINGS

Admissions Selectivity Rating: 94   **Fire Safety Rating:** 90   **Green Rating:** 95

STUDENTS AND FACULTY

Enrollment: 3,872. Student Body: 55% female, 45% male, 10% out-of-state, % international (66 countries represented). Asian %, African American %, Caucasian %, Hispanic %, Native American %
Retention and Graduation: 37% freshmen graduate within 4 years. 69% freshmen graduate within 6 years. Faculty: Student/faculty ratio 13:1. 453 full-time faculty, 92% hold PhDs, 21% are are members of minority groups, 41% are women. % of classes are taught by teaching assistants.

ACADEMICS

Degrees: bachelor's, master's. Classes: Most classes have fewer than 10 students. Most lab/discussion sessions have 10–19 students. Majors with Highest Enrollment: biology/biological sciences; business/commerce; engineering. Special Study Options: Accelerated program, double major, dual enrollment, English as a Second Language (ESL), exchange student program (domestic), honors program, independent study, internships, liberal arts/career combination, student-designed major, study abroad, teacher certification program, , minors, practicum, thematic minors, undergraduate research, ethnic studies, environmental science, gender studies, service learning. Combined degree programs: BA/DDS, BA or BS/MBA, BA or BS/DDS, BS/Pharm.D. Disability Services: Special programs offered to physically disabled students include note-taking services, reader services, tape recorders, tutors. Career services: Alumni network, alumni services, career/job search classes, career assessment, internships.

FACILITIES

Housing: Coed dorms, fraternity/sorority housing, apartments for single students. 90% of campus accessible to physically diasbled. Special Academic Facilities/Equipment: John Muir Collection, Dave and Iola Brubeck Collection, Brubeck Institute for Jazz Studies, Reynolds Art Gallery Computers: 100% of classrooms, 90% of dorms, 100% of libraries, 100% of dining areas, 100% of student union, 30% of common outdoor areas have wireless network access. Students can register for classes online. Administrative functions (other than registration) can be performed online.

CAMPUS LIFE

Environment: City. Activities: Choral groups, concert band, dance, drama/theater, jazz band, literary magazine, music ensembles, musical theater, opera, pep band, radio station, student government, student newspaper, student-run film society, symphony orchestra, yearbook, Campus Ministries, International Student Organization, Model UN 100 registered organizations, 14 honor societies, 10 religious organizations. 8 fraternities, 7 sororities. Athletics (Intercollegiate): Men: baseball, basketball, golf, swimming, tennis, volleyball, water polo. Women: basketball, cross-country, field hockey, soccer, softball, swimming, tennis, volleyball, water polo. On-Campus Highlights: Brubeck Istitute for Jazz Studies, John Muir Collection and Center, Alex Spanos Center, Reynolds Art Gallery, Pharmacy and Health Sciences Bldg, . Environmental Initiatives: Natural Resource Institute Calaveras River Restoration Project LEED Certification of New Student Center

ADMISSIONS

Freshman Academic Profile: Average high school GPA 3.5. 38% in top 10% of high school class, 69% in top 25% of high school class, 92% in top 50% of high school class. 82% from public high schools. SAT Math middle 50% range 540-688. SAT Critical Reading middle 50% range 510-630. SAT Writing middle 50% range 500-630. ACT middle 50% range 23-29. Minimum web-based TOEFL 52. Minimum paper TOEFL 475. Basis for Candidate Selection: Very important factors considered include: rigor of secondary school record. Important factors considered include: application essay, academic GPA, recommendation(s), standardized test scores, extracurricular activities, first generation. Other factors considered include: Class rank, alumni/ae relation, character/personal qualities, geographical residence, level of applicant's interest, talent/ability, volunteer work, work experience. Freshman Admission Requirements: High school diploma is required and GED is accepted. . Academic units recommended: Freshman Admission Statistics: 21,230 applied, 36% admitted, 12% enrolled. Transfer Admission Requirements: college transcript(s), statement of good standing from prior institution(s). Minimum college GPA of 3.0 required. Lowest grade transferable C. General Admission Information: Application Fee $60. Regular application deadline 1/15. Notification on a rolling basis, beginning on or about 3/15. Nonfall registration accepted. Admission may be deferred for a maximum of 1 year. Credit and/or placement offered for CEEB Advanced Placement tests.

COSTS AND FINANCIAL AID

Annual tuition $37,800. Room and board $12,038. Required fees $520. Average book expense $1,665. Required Forms and Deadlines: FAFSA. Notification of Awards: Applicants will be notified of awards on a rolling basis beginning 3/15. Types of Aid: Need-based scholarships/grants: Federal Pell, SEOG, state scholarships/grants, private scholarships, the school's own gift aid, ACG, SMART. Loans: Direct Subsidized Stafford, Direct Unsubsidized Stafford, Direct PLUS, Subsidized Stafford, Unsubsidized Stafford, PLUS, Federal Perkins, Direct Graduate/Professional PLUS Loans. Student Employment. Financial Aid Statistics: 97% freshmen, 96% undergrads receive need-based scholarship or grant aid. 91% freshmen, 94% undergrads receive need-based self-help aid. 3% freshmen, 3% undergrads receive athletic scholarships. 91% freshmen, 83% undergrads receive any aid. Criteria for awarding institutional aid: Non-need-based: academics, athletics, leadership, music/drama, religious affiliation.

UNIVERSITY OF PENNSYLVANIA

1 College Hall, Philadelphia, PA 19104
Phone: 215-898-7507 • **Financial Aid Phone:** 215-898-1988
E-mail: info@admissions.ugao.upenn.edu • **CEEB Code:** 2926
Fax: 215-898-9670 • **Website:** www.upenn.edu • **ACT Code:** 3732

This private school was founded in 1740. It has a 279-acre campus.

RATINGS

Admissions Selectivity Rating: 99   **Fire Safety Rating:** 75   **Green Rating:** 85

STUDENTS AND FACULTY

Enrollment: 9,779. **Student Body:** 51% female, 49% male, 84% out-of-state, 11% international (126 countries represented). Asian 19%, African American 7%, Caucasian 46%, Hispanic 8%.
Retention and Graduation: 87% freshmen graduate within 4 years. 96% freshmen graduate within 6 years. 20% grads go on to further study within 1 year. 5% grads pursue arts and sciences degrees. 4% grads pursue law degrees. 1% grads pursue business degrees. 5% grads pursue medical degrees. **Faculty:** Student/faculty ratio 6:1. 1397 full-time faculty, 100% hold PhDs, 18% are members of minority groups, 36% are women. 5% of classes are taught by teaching assistants.

ACADEMICS

Degrees: associate, bachelor's, certificate, first professional, first professional certificate, master's, post-bachelor's certificate, post-master's certificate, terminal associate. **Classes:** Most classes have 10–19 students. **Majors with Highest Enrollment:** business administration and management; finance; nursing/registered nurse (rn, asn, bsn, msn). **Special Study Options:** Accelerated program, cross-registration, double major, dual enrollment, English as a Second Language (ESL), exchange student program (domestic), honors program, independent study, internships, liberal arts/career combination, student-designed major, study abroad, teacher certification program, Joint degree programs among schools. Accelerated degree programs. Opportunities for preprofessional programs in predentistry, prelaw, premedicine, and preveterinary studies (not actual majors). Washington semester. **Honors programs:** Penn's general honors program is called the Benjamin Franklin Scholars program, although the honors program for students in business is called Joseph Wharton Scholars. There are specialized honors programs including Fisher Program in Management and Technology, the Huntsman Program in International Studies and Business, the Vagelos Scholars Program in Molecular Life Sciences, and the Civic Scholars Program which offers opportunities to integrate community service and academics. The University Scholars Program is open to already matriculated students who are interested in engaging in high-level research. **Combined degree programs:** BA/JD, BA/MA, BA/DDS, BA/MEng, 4-yr. BSE/BS, BSE/MBA, BA/MS Ed., BAS/MS Ed. **Disability Services:** Special programs offered to physically disabled students include note-taking services, reader services, tape recorders, tutors. **Career services:** Alumni network, alumni services, career assessment, internships, regional alumni. Career services highlights include In addition to a full on-campus recruiting program (over 13,000 interviews conducted annually), Career Services sponsors the following career days for undergraduates: CareerLink (business fair), Engineering Career Day, Government and Public Policy Career Day, International Opportunities Fair, Nursing Career Day, and a Spring Career Fair for non-profits and just in time opportunities as well as internships.

FACILITIES

Housing: Coed dorms, special housing for disabled students, fraternity/sorority housing, apartments for married students, apartments for single students, Wellness Housing private off-campus. 92% of campus accessible to physically disabled. **Special Academic Facilities/Equipment:** Art gallery, anthropology museum, institute for contemporary art, language lab, large animal research center, primate research center, arboretum, observatory, wind tunnel, electron microscope. **Computers:** 85% of classrooms, 100% of dorms, 100% of libraries, 85% of dining areas, 100% of student union, 25% of common outdoor areas have wireless network access. Students can register for classes online. Administrative functions (other than registration) can be performed online.

CAMPUS LIFE

Environment: Metropolis. **Activities:** Choral groups, concert band, dance, drama/theater, jazz band, literary magazine, marching band, music ensembles, musical theater, opera, pep band, radio station, student government, student newspaper, student-run film society, symphony orchestra, television station, yearbook, Campus Ministries, International Student Organization, Model UN. 350 registered organizations, 9 honor societies, 29 religious organizations. 35 fraternities, 13 sororities. **Athletics (Intercollegiate):** *Men:* baseball, basketball, crew/rowing, cross-country, diving, fencing, football, golf, lacrosse, light weight football, soccer, squash, swimming, tennis, track/field (outdoor), track/field (indoor), wrestling. *Women:* basketball, crew/rowing, cross-country, diving, fencing, field hockey, golf, gymnastics, lacrosse, soccer, softball, squash, swimming, tennis, track/field (outdoor), track/field (indoor), volleyball. **On-Campus Highlights:** University of Pennsylvania Museum, Institute of Contemporary Art, Walnut Street shops and restuarants, Annenberg Center, Franklin Field. **Environmental Initiatives:** 1) Continued purchase of Renewable Energy Credits in the form of wind-generated electricity. Penn is the nation's leader in wind-energy purchase, with over 45% of our electricity (192,727 MWH) being offset by Renewable Energy Credits. 2) Building optimization implementation, a program to optimize building systems in high-energy-use buildings to reduce their utility use and carbon footprint. 3) Signing on the Presidents Climate Commitment, with ongoing planning for publication of a Climate Action Plan by September 2009.

ADMISSIONS

Freshman Academic Profile: Average high school GPA 3.9. 96% in top 10% of high school class, 99% in top 25% of high school class, 100% in top 50% of high school class. 60% from public high schools. SAT Math middle 50% range 690-780. SAT Critical Reading middle 50% range 660-750. SAT Writing middle 50% range 670-770. ACT middle 50% range 30-34. **Basis for Candidate Selection:** *Very important factors considered include:* recommendation(s), rigor of secondary school record, character/personal qualities. *Important factors considered include:* Class rank, application essay, academic GPA, standardized test scores, extracurricular activities, work experience. *Other factors considered include:* alumni/ae relation, first generation, geographical residence, interview, racial/ethnic status, talent/ability, volunteer work. **Freshman Admission Requirements:** High school diploma or equivalent is not required. *Academic units required:* 4 English, 4 mathematics, 3 science, (3 science labs), 4 foreign language, 3 history. *Academic units recommended:* 4 English, 4 mathematics, 3 science, (3 science labs), 4 foreign language, 3 history. **Freshman Admission Statistics:** 31,663 applied, 12% admitted, 63% enrolled. **Transfer Admission Requirements:** High school transcript, college transcript(s), essay or personal statement, standardized test scores, statement of good standing from prior institution(s). Lowest grade transferable C. **General Admission Information:** Application Fee $75. Early decision application deadline 11/1. Regular applica-

tion deadline 1/1. Regular notification 4/1. Nonfall registration not accepted. Admission may be deferred for a maximum of 1 year. Credit and/or placement offered for CEEB Advanced Placement tests.

COSTS AND FINANCIAL AID

Annual tuition $39,088. Room and board $12,368. Required fees $4,650. Average book expense $1,210. **Required Forms and Deadlines:** FAFSA, institution's own financial aid form, CSS/Financial Aid PROFILE, noncustodial PROFILE, business/farm supplement. Parents' and student's most recently completed income tax. **Notification of Awards:** Applicants will be notified of awards on or about 4/1. **Types of Aid:** *Need-based scholarships/grants:* Federal Pell, SEOG, state scholarships/grants, private scholarships, the school's own gift aid. *Loans:* Subsidized Stafford, Unsubsidized Stafford, PLUS, Federal Perkins, Federal Nursing, college/university loans from institutional funds, Supplemental 3rd Party Loans guaranteed by institution. **Student Employment:** Federal Work-Study Program available. Institutional employment available. Off-campus job opportunities are excellent. **Financial Aid Statistics:** 97% freshmen, 98% undergrads receive need-based scholarship or grant aid. 100% freshmen, 100% undergrads receive need-based self-help aid. 47% freshmen, 45% undergrads receive any aid. 43% undergrads borrow to pay for school. Average cumulative indebtedness $17,891.

UNIVERSITY OF PHOENIX

4035 S. Riverpoint Parkway, Phoenix, AZ 85040
Phone: 480-446-4600 • **Financial Aid Phone:** 1-800-921-1904
Website: www.phoenix.edu

This proprietary school was founded in 1976.

RATINGS

Admissions Selectivity Rating: 60*   **Fire Safety Rating:** 60*   **Green Rating:** 61

STUDENTS AND FACULTY

Enrollment: 332,377. **Student Body:** 69% female, 31% male, 3% international (countries represented). Asian 2%, African American 17%, Caucasian 36%, Hispanic 8%, Native American 1%.
Retention and Graduation: 1% freshmen graduate within 4 years. 9% freshmen graduate within 6 years. **Faculty:** Student/faculty ratio 43:1. 1410 full-time faculty, 23% hold PhDs, 19% are members of minority groups, 46% are women. 0% of classes are taught by teaching assistants.

ACADEMICS

Degrees: associate, bachelor's, certificate, master's, post-bachelor's certificate, post-master's certificate, transfer associate. **Majors with Highest Enrollment:** accounting; business administration and management; health/health care administration/management. **Special Study Options:** Accelerated program, distance learning, independent study, Evening courses meeting 4 hours per night, one night per week for 5 weeks at the bachelor level and 6 weeks at the master level. **Disability Services:** Special programs offered to physically disabled students include tape recorders. **Career services:** Alumni network.

FACILITIES

Housing: 100% of campus accessible to physically disabled. **Computers:** Students can register for classes online. Administrative functions (other than registration) can be performed online.

CAMPUS LIFE

Environment: Metropolis. **Activities:** 2 honor societies.

ADMISSIONS

Freshman Academic Profile: Minimum paper TOEFL 550. **Basis for Candidate Selection:** *Very important factors considered include:* work experience. *Other factors considered include:* recommendation(s). **Freshman Admission Requirements:** High school diploma is required and GED is accepted. **Transfer Admission Requirements:** college transcript(s). **General Admission Information:** Nonfall registration accepted. Neither credit nor placement offered for CEEB Advanced Placement tests.

UNIVERSITY OF PITTSBURGH AT BRADFORD

Office of Admissions - Hanley Library, Bradford, PA 16701
Phone: 814-362-7555 • **Financial Aid Phone:** 814-362-7550
E-mail: Admissions@upb.pitt.edu • **CEEB Code:** 2935
Fax: 814-362-5150 • **Website:** www.upb.pitt.edu • **ACT Code:** 3731

This public school was founded in 1963. It has a 317-acre campus.

RATINGS
Admissions Selectivity Rating: 66   **Fire Safety Rating:** 86   **Green Rating:** 71

STUDENTS AND FACULTY
Enrollment: 1,495. **Student Body:** 55% female, 45% male, 16% out-of-state, 3% international (12 countries represented). Asian 3%, African American 9%, Caucasian 76%, Hispanic 3%.
Retention and Graduation: 72% freshmen return for sophomore year. 29% freshmen graduate within 4 years. 49% freshmen graduate within 6 years. 20% grads go on to further study within 1 year. 12% grads pursue arts and sciences degrees. 2% grads pursue law degrees. 2% grads pursue business degrees. 2% grads pursue medical degrees. **Faculty:** Student/faculty ratio 17:1. 71 full-time faculty, 73% hold PhDs, 14% are members of minority groups, 35% are women. 0% of classes are taught by teaching assistants.

ACADEMICS
Degrees: associate, bachelor's, terminal associate, transfer associate. **Classes:** Most classes have 20–29 students. Most lab/discussion sessions have 10–19 students. **Majors with Highest Enrollment:** business/commerce; elementary education and teaching; nursing/registered nurse (rn, asn, bsn, msn). **Special Study Options:** cross-registration, distance learning, double major, dual enrollment, external degree program, honors program, independent study, internships, study abroad, teacher certification program. **Honors programs:** The University of Pittsburgh at Bradford offers the Scholars Program which is designed to create a learning community for outstanding students at Pitt-Bradford. **Disability Services:** Special programs offered to physically disabled students include note-taking services, reader services, tape recorders, tutors. **Career services:** Alumni network, alumni services, career assessment, internships, regional alumni. Career services highlights include Career Messenger is a monthly newsletter that will be distributed via e-mail. To receive this newsletter you must subscribe.

FACILITIES
Housing: Coed dorms, special housing for disabled students, apartments for single students. 99% of campus accessible to physically disabled. **Special Academic Facilities/Equipment:** Ceramics Studio, Biodiesel Lab, Television and Radio Broadcast Labs. **Computers:** 100% of classrooms, 100% of dorms, 90% of libraries, 90% of dining areas, 100% of student union, 50% of common outdoor areas have wireless network access. Students can register for classes online. Administrative functions (other than registration) can be performed online.

CAMPUS LIFE
Environment: Village. **Activities:** Choral groups, dance, drama/theater, literary magazine, radio station, student government, student newspaper, Campus Ministries 54 registered organizations, 8 honor societies, 1 religious organizations. 3 fraternities, 3 sororities. **Athletics (Intercollegiate):** *Men:* baseball, basketball, cross-country, golf, soccer, swimming, tennis. *Women:* basketball, cross-country, golf, soccer, softball, swimming, tennis, volleyball. **On-Campus Highlights:** Sport and Fitness Center, The Commons, Student apartments, Blaisdell Hall (Fine Arts Building), Smart classrooms. **Environmental Initiatives:** Campus Wide Recycling Initiative Building Upgrades HVAC Waste Reduction, Develop sustainability committee of faculty, staff & students.

ADMISSIONS
Freshman Academic Profile: Average high school GPA 3.3. 8% in top 10% of high school class, 27% in top 25% of high school class, 64% in top 50% of high school class. 91% from public high schools. SAT Math middle 50% range 440-550. SAT Critical Reading middle 50% range 420-530. SAT Writing middle 50% range 410-520. ACT middle 50% range 18-23. Minimum paper TOEFL 550. **Basis for Candidate Selection:** *Very important factors considered include:* level of applicant's interest. *Important factors considered include:* academic GPA, rigor of secondary school record, standardized test scores, interview. *Other factors considered include:* Class rank, application essay, recommendation(s), character/personal qualities, extracurricular activities, talent/ability, volunteer work, work experience. **Freshman Admission Requirements:** High school diploma is required and GED is accepted. *Academic units required:* 4 English, 2 mathematics, 1 science, (1 science labs), 2 foreign language, 0 social studies, 1 history, 5 academic electives. *Academic units recommended:* 4 English, 2 mathematics, 1 science, (1 science labs), 2 foreign language, 0 social studies, 1 history, 5 academic electives. **Freshman Admission Statistics:** 940 applied,

85% admitted, 47% enrolled. **Transfer Admission Requirements:** college transcript(s), statement of good standing from prior institution(s). Minimum college GPA of 2.0 required. Lowest grade transferable C–. **General Admission Information:** Application Fee $45. Notification on a rolling basis, beginning on or about 11/1. Nonfall registration accepted. Admission may be deferred for a maximum of 1 year. Credit and/or placement offered for CEEB Advanced Placement tests.

COSTS AND FINANCIAL AID
Annual in-state tuition $11,970. Annual out-of-state tuition $22,366. Room and board $8,088. Required fees $840. Average book expense $1,132. **Required Forms and Deadlines:** FAFSA. **Notification of Awards:** Applicants will be notified of awards on a rolling basis beginning 4/1. **Types of Aid:** *Need-based scholarships/grants:* Federal Pell, SEOG, state scholarships/grants, private scholarships, the school's own gift aid. *Loans:* Subsidized Stafford, Unsubsidized Stafford, PLUS, Federal Perkins. **Student Employment:** Federal Work-Study Program available. Institutional employment available. Off-campus job opportunities are fair. **Financial Aid Statistics:** 95% freshmen, 93% undergrads receive need-based scholarship or grant aid. 24% freshmen, 27% undergrads receive non-need-based scholarship or grant aid. 96% freshmen, 98% undergrads receive need-based self-help aid. 86% freshmen, 82% undergrads receive any aid. 85% undergrads borrow to pay for school. Average cumulative indebtedness $30,415. **Criteria for awarding institutional aid:** Non-need-based: academics, alumni affiliation, state/district residency.

UNIVERSITY OF PITTSBURGH AT JOHNSTOWN

157 Blackington Hall, Johnstown, PA 15904
Phone: 814-269-7050 • **Financial Aid Phone:** 814-269-7045
E-mail: upjadmit@pitt.edu • **CEEB Code:** 2934
Fax: 814-269-7044 • **Website:** www.upj.pitt.edu

This public school was founded in 1927. It has a 650-acre campus.

RATINGS
Admissions Selectivity Rating: 66   **Fire Safety Rating:** 83   **Green Rating:** 60*

STUDENTS AND FACULTY
Enrollment: 2,956. **Student Body:** 46% female, 54% male, 2% out-of-state, 1% international (20 countries represented). Asian 1%, African American 3%, Caucasian 90%, Hispanic 2%.
Retention and Graduation: 74% freshmen return for sophomore year. 39% freshmen graduate within 4 years. 60% freshmen graduate within 6 years. 8% grads pursue arts and sciences degrees. 1% grads pursue law degrees. 1% grads pursue business degrees. 2% grads pursue medical degrees.

ACADEMICS
Degrees: associate, bachelor's, certificate. **Classes:** Most classes have 20–29 students. Most lab/discussion sessions have 10–19 students. **Special Study Options:** Accelerated program, cooperative education program, cross-registration, distance learning, double major, dual enrollment, independent study, internships, liberal arts/career combination, student-designed major, study abroad, teacher certification program. **Honors programs:** President's Scholars Program. **Disability Services:** Special programs offered to physically disabled students include tutors. **Career services:** Alumni network, alumni services, internships.

FACILITIES
Housing: Coed dorms, special housing for disabled students, fraternity/sorority housing, apartments for single students, Theme Housing, Townhouses, Lodges, Single-sex residence upon request. 100% of campus accessible to physically disabled. **Special Academic Facilities/Equipment:** Art museum, performing arts center, language lab. **Computers:** 75% of classrooms, 100% of libraries, 50% of dining areas, 100% of student union, 50% of common outdoor areas have wireless network access. Administrative functions (other than registration) can be performed online.

CAMPUS LIFE
Environment: City. **Activities:** Choral groups, concert band, dance, drama/theater, literary magazine, music ensembles, musical theater, pep band, radio station, student government, student newspaper, television station, yearbook, Campus Ministries, Model UN. 70 registered organizations, 11 honor societies, 3 religious organizations. 5 fraternities, 3 sororities. **Athletics (Intercollegiate):** *Men:* baseball, basketball, golf, soccer, wrestling. *Women:* basketball, cheerleading, cross-country, golf, soccer, track/field (outdoor), volleyball. **On-Campus Highlights:** Student Union Building, Sports Center, Cafeteria, Living/Learning Center, Performing Arts Center.

ADMISSIONS

Freshman Academic Profile: Average high school GPA 3.4. 11% in top 10% of high school class, 34% in top 25% of high school class, 71% in top 50% of high school class. SAT Math middle 50% range 460-560. SAT Critical Reading middle 50% range 450-540. SAT Writing middle 50% range 430-530. ACT middle 50% range 20-24. Minimum web-based TOEFL 80. Minimum paper TOEFL 550. **Basis for Candidate Selection:** *Very important factors considered include:* Class rank, academic GPA, rigor of secondary school record. *Important factors considered include:* application essay, recommendation(s), standardized test scores, extracurricular activities, interview, level of applicant's interest, talent/ability, volunteer work, work experience. *Other factors considered include:* character/personal qualities, racial/ethnic status. **Freshman Admission Requirements:** High school diploma is required and GED is accepted. *Academic units required:* 4 English, 2 mathematics, 2 science, (1 science labs), 2 foreign language, 4 social studies. *Academic units recommended:* 4 English, 2 mathematics, 2 science, (1 science labs), 2 foreign language, 4 social studies. **Freshman Admission Statistics:** 1,613 applied, 88% admitted, 53% enrolled. **Transfer Admission Requirements:** High school transcript, college transcript(s), minimum college GPA of 2.0 required. Lowest grade transferable C. **General Admission Information:** Application Fee $45. Notification on a rolling basis, beginning on or about 9/1. Nonfall registration accepted. Admission may be deferred for a maximum of 12 months. Credit and/or placement offered for CEEB Advanced Placement tests.

COSTS AND FINANCIAL AID

Average book expense $1,030. **Required Forms and Deadlines:** FAFSA, state aid form. **Notification of Awards:** Applicants will be notified of awards on a rolling basis beginning 3/15. **Types of Aid:** *Need-based scholarships/ grants:* Federal Pell, SEOG, state scholarships/grants, private scholarships, the school's own gift aid. *Loans:* Subsidized Stafford, Unsubsidized Stafford, PLUS, Federal Perkins. **Student Employment:** Federal Work-Study Program available. Institutional employment available. Off-campus job opportunities are good. **Financial Aid Statistics:** 72% freshmen, 69% undergrads receive need-based scholarship or grant aid. 34% freshmen, 31% undergrads receive non-need-based scholarship or grant aid. 90% freshmen, 88% undergrads receive need-based self-help aid. 5% freshmen, 5% undergrads receive athletic scholarships. 80% freshmen, 80% undergrads receive any aid. 83% undergrads borrow to pay for school. Average cumulative indebtedness $27,905. **Criteria for awarding institutional aid:** Non-need-based: academics, athletics, leadership, minority status, state/district residency.

UNIVERSITY OF PITTSBURGH—GREENSBURG

150 Finoli Drive, Greensburg, PA 15601
Phone: 724-836-9880 • **Financial Aid Phone:** 724-836-9881
E-mail: upgadmit@pitt.edu • **CEEB Code:** 2936
Fax: 724-836-7471 • **Website:** www.greensburg.pitt.edu • **ACT Code:** 3733

This public school was founded in 1963. It has a 217-acre campus.

RATINGS

Admissions Selectivity Rating: 67   **Fire Safety Rating:** 60*   **Green Rating:** 60*

STUDENTS AND FACULTY

Enrollment: 1,840. **Student Body:** 49% female, 51% male, 2% out-of-state, 1% international (countries represented). Asian 2%, African American 5%, Caucasian 80%, Hispanic 3%.
Retention and Graduation: 80% freshmen return for sophomore year. 52% freshmen graduate within 6 years. 21% grads go on to further study within 1 year. 15% grads pursue arts and sciences degrees. 1% grads pursue law degrees. 4% grads pursue business degrees. 1% grads pursue medical degrees. **Faculty:** Student/faculty ratio 18:1. 74 full-time faculty, 84% hold PhDs, 15% are members of minority groups, 51% are women. 0% of classes are taught by teaching assistants.

ACADEMICS

Degrees: bachelor's, certificate. **Classes:** Most classes have 30–39 students. Most lab/discussion sessions have 20–29 students. **Majors with Highest Enrollment:** biology/biological sciences; management information systems; psychology. **Special Study Options:** cross-registration, double major, dual enrollment, exchange student program (domestic), independent study, internships, liberal arts/career combination, student-designed major, study abroad. **Disability Services:** Special programs offered to physically disabled students include note-taking services, reader services, tape recorders, tutors. **Career services:** Alumni network, alumni services, career/job search classes, career assessment, internships, regional alumni.

FACILITIES

Housing: Coed dorms, Theme Housing. 95% of campus accessible to physically disabled. **Computers:** 100% of libraries, 100% of dining areas, 100% of student union, have wireless network access. Students can register for classes online. Administrative functions (other than registration) can be performed online.

CAMPUS LIFE

Environment: Village. **Activities:** Choral groups, dance, drama/theater, literary magazine, musical theater, radio station, student government, student newspaper, Campus Ministries, International Student Organization 25 registered organizations, 8 honor societies, 3 religious organizations. **Athletics (Intercollegiate):** *Men:* baseball, basketball, cross-country, golf, soccer, tennis. *Women:* basketball, cross-country, golf, soccer, softball, volleyball. **On-Campus Highlights:** Academic Villages, Exchange - Coffee House, Fireside Lounge, Wagner Dining Hall, Ferguson Theater.

ADMISSIONS

Freshman Academic Profile: Average high school GPA 3.5. 12% in top 10% of high school class, 38% in top 25% of high school class, 80% in top 50% of high school class. 95% from public high schools. SAT Math middle 50% range 470-573. SAT Critical Reading middle 50% range 460-550. SAT Writing middle 50% range 440-540. ACT middle 50% range 20-24. Minimum paper TOEFL 550. **Basis for Candidate Selection:** *Very important factors considered include:* Class rank, academic GPA, rigor of secondary school record, standardized test scores. *Other factors considered include:* application essay, recommendation(s), character/personal qualities, extracurricular activities, interview, level of applicant's interest, talent/ability, volunteer work. **Freshman Admission Requirements:** High school diploma is required and GED is accepted. *Academic units required:* 4 English, 2 mathematics, 1 science, (1 science labs), 3 foreign language, 2 social studies, 2 history, 1 academic electives. *Academic units recommended:* 4 English, 2 mathematics, 1 science, (1 science labs), 3 foreign language, 2 social studies, 2 history, 1 academic electives. **Freshman Admission Statistics:** 1,468 applied, 86% admitted, 36% enrolled. **Transfer Admission Requirements:** High school transcript, college transcript(s), statement of good standing from prior institution(s). Minimum college GPA of 2.0 required. Lowest grade transferable C. **General Admission Information:** Application Fee $45. Notification on a rolling basis, beginning on or about 9/15. Nonfall registration accepted. Admission may be deferred for a maximum of 12 months. Credit and/or placement offered for CEEB Advanced Placement tests.

COSTS AND FINANCIAL AID

Required Forms and Deadlines: FAFSA, state aid form. **Notification of Awards:** Applicants will be notified of awards on a rolling basis beginning 3/15. **Types of Aid:** *Need-based scholarships/grants:* Federal Pell, SEOG, state scholarships/grants, private scholarships, the school's own gift aid, United Negro College Fund. *Loans:* Subsidized Stafford, Unsubsidized Stafford, PLUS, Federal Perkins, college/university loans from institutional funds. **Student Employment:** Federal Work-Study Program available. Institutional employment available. Off-campus job opportunities are good. **Financial Aid Statistics:** 98% freshmen, 98% undergrads receive need-based scholarship or grant aid. 54% freshmen, 42% undergrads receive non-need-based scholarship or grant aid. 67% freshmen, 73% undergrads receive need-based self-help aid. 85% undergrads borrow to pay for school. Average cumulative indebtedness $26,291. **Criteria for awarding institutional aid:** Non-need-based: academics, leadership, minority status.

UNIVERSITY OF PITTSBURGH— PITTSBURGH CAMPUS

4227 Fifth Avenue, Pittsburgh, PA 15260
Phone: 412-624-7488 • **Financial Aid Phone:** 412-624-7488
E-mail: oafa@pitt.edu • **CEEB Code:** 2927
Fax: 412-648-8815 • **Website:** www.pitt.edu • **ACT Code:** 3734

This public school was founded in 1787. It has a 132-acre campus.

RATINGS
Admissions Selectivity Rating: 93   **Fire Safety Rating:** 78   **Green Rating:** 87

STUDENTS AND FACULTY
Enrollment: 18,105. **Student Body:** 50% female, 50% male, 25% out-of-state, 3% international (45 countries represented). Asian 6%, African American 6%, Caucasian 78%, Hispanic 2%.
Retention and Graduation: 93% freshmen return for sophomore year. 62% freshmen graduate within 4 years. 79% freshmen graduate within 6 years.

ACADEMICS
Degrees: bachelor's, certificate, doctoral, master's, post-bachelor's certificate, post-master's certificate. **Classes:** Most classes have 10–19 students. Most lab/discussion sessions have 20–29 students. **Majors with Highest Enrollment:** marketing/marketing management; psychology; speech and rhetorical studies. **Special Study Options:** Accelerated program, cooperative education program, cross-registration, distance learning, double major, dual enrollment, English as a Second Language (ESL), exchange student program (domestic), external degree program, honors program, independent study, internships, liberal arts/career combination, student-designed major, study abroad, teacher certification program, weekend college. **Honors programs:** University Honors College. **Combined degree programs:** BA/MD, BA/DMD. **Disability Services:** Special programs offered to physically disabled students include note-taking services, reader services, tape recorders. **Career services:** Alumni network, alumni services, career/job search classes, career assessment, internships, regional alumni. Career services highlights include The Pitt Career Network is an extremely valuable tool to which Pitt students have access. This is a database of over 6,000 alumni volunteers worldwide searchable by students. They also provide job shadowing opportunities nationwide. The Office of Student Employment and Placement Assistance (SEPA) hosted its first Career Kickoff event this past fall. The theme for this event was "On the Road With SEPA", since this was an event that would be held in multiple locations and the tag line was "Amp Up Your Career" to tie into the road/concert theme. Career Kickoff was created as a weeklong event held in various locations throughout campus making it convenient for students to stop by in between classes. The goal of this event was to provide students with valuable information before the career fair. We gave seniors and juniors a CD filled with valuabe information such as resume templates, sample cover letters, and acceptance letters. We also gave students a long-sleeved American Eagle t-shirt that listed every career related event and date on the back of the shirt (similar to a concert t-shirt to tie into the "On the Road" theme.), magnets with the dates of the career-related events, networking tips, career fair tips, and an opportunity to win a pair of donated Cirque du Soleil tickets. Several components made this event unique. While most schools host a career week prior to their career fairs in their offices, we were in a different location each day making it convenient for students to attend. We also invited various regional employers to participate reviewing student resumes, discussing career opportunities in their companies, and providing students tips on networking with employers. Students had the opportunity to hear first hand from an employer tips on improving their resume. Students also had the opportunity to discuss possible positions with employers prior to the career fair, giving them a competitive edge in their job search. This event was extremely successful attacting over 2,300 students, making this the largest non-career fair event in our office.

FACILITIES
Housing: Coed dorms, special housing for disabled students, women's dorms, fraternity/sorority housing, apartments for single students, Wellness Housing, Theme Housing. 90% of campus accessible to physically disabled. **Special Academic Facilities/Equipment:** Stephen Foster Memorial, observatory. **Computers:** 100% of classrooms, 25% of dorms, 100% of libraries, 100% of dining areas, 100% of student union, 50% of common outdoor areas have wireless network access. Students can register for classes online. Administrative functions (other than registration) can be performed online.

CAMPUS LIFE
Environment: Metropolis. **Activities:** Choral groups, concert band, dance, drama/theater, jazz band, literary magazine, marching band, music ensembles, pep band, radio station, student government, student newspaper, student-run film society, television station, yearbook, Campus Ministries, International Student Organization, Model UN. 395 registered organizations, 17 honor societies, 20 fraternities, 16 sororities. **Athletics (Intercollegiate):** *Men:* baseball, basketball, cross-country, diving, football, soccer, swimming, track/field (outdoor), wrestling. *Women:* basketball, cross-country, diving, gymnastics, soccer, softball, swimming, tennis, track/field (outdoor), volleyball. **On-Campus Highlights:** Cathedral of Learning, William Pitt Union, Heinz Chapel, Peterson Event Center, Sennott Square. **Environmental Initiatives:** NEW STATE-OF-THE-ART STEAM PLANT: The University recently constructed and began operation of a new steam plant housing six 100,000 pound per hour natural gas boilers. The Carrillo Street Steam Plant provides approximately 50% of the steam service for both the University and the University of Pittsburgh Medical Center, with the remainder of the steam load expected to be transferred to the plant over the next several years. Transfer of Pitt's steam production from the original steam provider to the new facility is projected to ultimately reduce steam-related greenhouse gas emissions by approximately 47% (over 39,000 metric tons of CO_2 per year). The new plant is equipped with state of the art emission control technology and ultra-low NOx burners whcih emit less than 9 parts per million (ppm) NOx. To our knowledge, the University of Pittsburgh is the only University in the country to own a plant permitted at 9 ppm NOx. In a concurrent effort, the Bellefield Boiler Plant, which continues to serve approximately 50% of the University's/UPMC's load, converted from primarily coal-fired operation to all natural gas in July, 2009. ENERGY CONSERVATION AND GREEN CONSTRUCTION: The University has invested extensively in energy conservation and green construction. Pitt's comprehensive building automation/energy management system provides automatic control of building temperatures and operating schedules, allowing for setbacks during unoccupied periods and automated curtailment during peak periods. Significant investments have been made in energy conservation measures, including lighting upgrades, occupancy sensors, sub-metering of electric, steam, and chilled water consumption, retrocommissioning of HVAC systems, and the expansion of the University's central steam and chilled water infrastructure. Pitt has also converted selected buildings from constant volume to variable air volume systems and has installed heat recovery systems in recent laboratory upgrades. Over the past 15 years, an estimated cost avoidance of over $35.6 million has been achieved via energy management and conservation projects. The University pursues LEED certification for most large construction and renovation projects. The McGowan Institute for Regenerative Medicine was the first laboratory building in Pennsylvanie to achieve LEED Gold certification. Two new projects achieved LEED Gold certification in December, 2011 - the Benedum Hall Phase I Renovation and the Addition/Renovation to Benedum Hall for the Mascaro Center for Sustainable Innovation. An additional ten projects currently in design or construction are pursuing LEED certification. The University has incorporated many sustainable design standards into its Professional Design Manual. Examples include occupancy sensors, direct digital controls, energy efficient lighting, premium efficiency motors, carpet with recycled content, low or no VOC paints and adhesives and VAV controls, among many others. MASCARO CENTER FOR SUSTAINABLE INNOVATION: The Mascaro Center for Sustainable Innovation at the University of Pittsburgh is a center of excellence in sustainable engineering focusing on the design of sustainable neighborhoods. The Center encourages and nurtures new collaborative projects based on strong and innovative research, translating the fundamental science of sustainability into real products and processes. MCSI's goal is to create innovations that positively impact the environment and improve quality of life. Research includes projects on greening the built environment, more sustainable use of water, and the design of distributed power systems. Other specific areas of interest include Green Building Design and Construction, infrastructure, and sustainable materials (www.mascarocenter.pitt.edu/research/).

ADMISSIONS
Freshman Academic Profile: Average high school GPA 3.9. 52% in top 10% of high school class, 86% in top 25% of high school class, 99% in top 50% of high school class. SAT Math middle 50% range 600-680. SAT Critical Reading middle 50% range 570-660. SAT Writing middle 50% range 560-660. ACT middle 50% range 26-30. Minimum web-based TOEFL 80. Minimum paper TOEFL 550. **Basis for Candidate Selection:** *Very important factors considered include:* academic GPA, rigor of secondary school record. *Important factors considered include:* standardized test scores. *Other factors considered include:* Class rank, application essay, recommendation(s), character/personal qualities, extracurricular activities, first generation, geographical residence, interview, level of applicant's interest, racial/ethnic status, talent/ability, volunteer work, work experience. **Freshman Admission Requirements:** High school diploma is required and GED is not accepted. *Academic units required:* 4 English, 3 mathematics, 3 science, (3 science labs), 2 foreign language, 2 social studies, 3 academic electives. *Academic units recommended:* 4 English, 3 mathematics, 3 science, (3 science labs), 2 foreign language, 2 social studies, 3 academic

electives. **Freshman Admission Statistics:** 24,871 applied, 56% admitted, 26% enrolled. **Transfer Admission Requirements:** High school transcript, college transcript(s), essay or personal statement, Lowest grade transferable C. **General Admission Information:** Application Fee $45. Notification on a rolling basis, beginning on or about 10/1. Nonfall registration accepted. Credit offered for CEEB Advanced Placement tests.

COSTS AND FINANCIAL AID

Annual in-state tuition $15,730. Annual out-of-state tuition $25,420. Room and board $9,870. Required fees $860. Average book expense $1,132. **Required Forms and Deadlines:** FAFSA. **Notification of Awards:** Applicants will be notified of awards on a rolling basis beginning 3/15. **Types of Aid:** *Need-based scholarships/grants:* Federal Pell, SEOG, state scholarships/grants, private scholarships, the school's own gift aid, Federal Nursing Scholarships. *Loans:* Subsidized Stafford, Unsubsidized Stafford, PLUS, Federal Perkins, Federal Nursing, college/university loans from institutional funds. **Student Employment:** Federal Work-Study Program available. Institutional employment available. Off-campus job opportunities are excellent. **Financial Aid Statistics:** 75% freshmen, 69% undergrads receive need-based scholarship or grant aid. 8% freshmen, 6% undergrads receive non-need-based scholarship or grant aid. 85% freshmen, 88% undergrads receive need-based self-help aid. 2% freshmen, 2% undergrads receive athletic scholarships. 63% freshmen, 59% undergrads receive any aid. 67% undergrads borrow to pay for school. Average cumulative indebtedness $33,662. **Criteria for awarding institutional aid:** Non-need-based: academics, athletics.

UNIVERSITY OF PORTLAND

5000 North Willamette Blvd., Portland, OR 97203-7147
Phone: 503-943-7147 • **Financial Aid Phone:** 503-943-7311
E-mail: admissions@up.edu • **CEEB Code:** 4847
Fax: 503-943-7315 • **Website:** www.up.edu • **ACT Code:** 3500

This private school, affiliated with the Roman Catholic Church, was founded in 1901. It has a 130-acre campus.

RATINGS
Admissions Selectivity Rating: 85   **Fire Safety Rating:** 73   **Green Rating:** 87

STUDENTS AND FACULTY
Enrollment: 3,374. **Student Body:** 59% female, 41% male, 65% out-of-state, 3% international (32 countries represented). Asian 10%, African American 1%, Caucasian 67%, Hispanic 9%.
Retention and Graduation: 18% grads go on to further study within 1 year. **Faculty:** Student/faculty ratio 13:1. 213 full-time faculty, 90% hold PhDs, 3% are members of minority groups, 45% are women. 0% of classes are taught by teaching assistants.

ACADEMICS
Degrees: bachelor's, master's, post-master's certificate. **Classes:** Most classes have 20–29 students. Most lab/discussion sessions have 10–19 students. **Majors with Highest Enrollment:** biology/biological sciences; finance; nursing/registered nurse (rn, asn, bsn, msn). **Special Study Options:** cross-registration, double major, honors program, independent study, internships, liberal arts/career combination, study abroad, teacher certification program. **Honors programs:** The honors program provides an exciting intellectual challenge for highly motivated students whit above average high school records. The program is designed to facilitate learning through special small classes which permit a high level of student-faculty interaction. Honors students may be enrolled in any major. **Disability Services:** Special programs offered to physically disabled students include note-taking services, reader services, tutors. **Career services:** Alumni network, alumni services, career/job search classes, career assessment, internships, regional alumni.

FACILITIES
Housing: Coed dorms, men's dorms, women's dorms, Theme Housing, Rental housing. 80% of campus accessible to physically disabled. **Special Academic Facilities/Equipment:** Art gallery, observatory. **Computers:** 100% of classrooms, 100% of dorms, 100% of libraries, 100% of dining areas, 100% of student union, 100% of common outdoor areas have wireless network access. Students can register for classes online. Administrative functions (other than registration) can be performed online.

CAMPUS LIFE
Environment: Metropolis. **Activities:** Choral groups, concert band, dance, drama/theater, jazz band, literary magazine, music ensembles, musical theater, pep band, radio station, student government, student newspaper, student-run film society, symphony orchestra, yearbook, Campus Ministries, Interna-

tional Student Organization 40 registered organizations, 15 honor societies, 9 religious organizations. **Athletics (Intercollegiate):** *Men:* baseball, basketball, cross-country, golf, soccer, tennis, track/field (outdoor). *Women:* basketball, cross-country, golf, soccer, tennis, track/field (outdoor), volleyball. **On-Campus Highlights:** The Cove, St. Mary's Lounge, Howard Recreation Hall **Environmental Initiatives:** Portland host and active participant of Focus the Nation, January 30, 2008 Promotion and availability of alternative transportation sources for students New building construction meet LEED standards

ADMISSIONS
Freshman Academic Profile: Average high school GPA 3.6. 45% in top 10% of high school class, 75% in top 25% of high school class, 95% in top 50% of high school class. 60% from public high schools. SAT Math middle 50% range 550-640. SAT Critical Reading middle 50% range 540-650. Minimum web-based TOEFL 71. Minimum paper TOEFL 525. **Basis for Candidate Selection:** *Very important factors considered include:* academic GPA, rigor of secondary school record, standardized test scores. *Important factors considered include:* Class rank, application essay, recommendation(s), extracurricular activities, talent/ability, volunteer work. *Other factors considered include:* alumni/ae relation, character/personal qualities, first generation, geographical residence, interview, level of applicant's interest, racial/ethnic status, religious affiliation/commitment, work experience. **Freshman Admission Requirements:** High school diploma is required and GED is accepted. *Academic units required:* 3 English, 2 mathematics, 2 science, 2 social studies, 2 history, 7 academic electives. *Academic units recommended:* 3 English, 2 mathematics, 2 science, 2 social studies, 2 history, 7 academic electives. **Freshman Admission Statistics:** 8,696 applied, 67% admitted, 15% enrolled. **Transfer Admission Requirements:** college transcript(s), essay or personal statement, minimum college GPA of 2.5 required. Lowest grade transferable C. **General Admission Information:** Application Fee $50. Regular application deadline 6/1. Notification on a rolling basis, beginning on or about 10/1. Nonfall registration accepted. Credit and/or placement offered for CEEB Advanced Placement tests.

COSTS AND FINANCIAL AID
Annual tuition $35,120. Room and board $12,238. Required fees $140. Average book expense $1,200. **Required Forms and Deadlines:** FAFSA. **Notification of Awards:** Applicants will be notified of awards on a rolling basis beginning 3/15. **Types of Aid:** *Need-based scholarships/grants:* Federal Pell, SEOG, state scholarships/grants, private scholarships, the school's own gift aid. *Loans:* Subsidized Stafford, Unsubsidized Stafford, PLUS, Federal Perkins, Federal Nursing, college/university loans from institutional funds. **Student Employment:** Federal Work-Study Program available. Highest amount earned per year from on-campus jobs $1,377. Off-campus job opportunities are good. **Financial Aid Statistics:** 82% freshmen, 83% undergrads receive need-based scholarship or grant aid. 94% freshmen, 86% undergrads receive non-need-based scholarship or grant aid. 76% freshmen, 80% undergrads receive need-based self-help aid. 2% freshmen, 3% undergrads receive athletic scholarships. 96% freshmen, 95% undergrads receive any aid. 70% undergrads borrow to pay for school. Average cumulative indebtedness $26,957. **Criteria for awarding institutional aid:** Non-need-based: academics, alumni affiliation, athletics, music/drama, religious affiliation.

UNIVERSITY OF PRINCE EDWARD ISLAND

Office of the Registrar, Charlottetown, PE C1A 4P3
Phone: 902-566-0439 • **Financial Aid Phone:** 902-566-0358
E-mail: registrar@upei.ca
Fax: 902-566-0795 • **Website:** www.upei.ca

This public school was founded in 1969. It has a 130-acre campus.

RATINGS
Admissions Selectivity Rating: 63   **Fire Safety Rating:** 60*   **Green Rating:** 60*

STUDENTS AND FACULTY
Student Body: 15% out-of-state, (50 countries represented).
Faculty: Student/faculty ratio 12:1. 244 full-time faculty.

ACADEMICS
Degrees: bachelor's, certificate, diploma, first professional, master's. **Classes:** Most classes have 20–29 students. Most lab/discussion sessions have fewer than 10 students. **Special Study Options:** Accelerated program, cooperative education program, distance learning, double major, English as a Second Language (ESL), exchange student program (domestic), honors program, internships, study abroad, teacher certification program. **Disability Services:** Special programs offered to physically disabled students include tutors.

FACILITIES

Housing: Coed dorms, special housing for disabled students, men's dorms, women's dorms, apartments for single students. **Computers:** Students can register for classes online. Administrative functions (other than registration) can be performed online.

CAMPUS LIFE

Environment: Town. **Activities:** Choral groups, concert band, drama/theater, music ensembles, radio station, student government, student newspaper, yearbook 25 registered organizations, 3 religious organizations. **Athletics (Intercollegiate):** *Men:* basketball, ice hockey, soccer. *Women:* basketball, field hockey, ice hockey, rugby, soccer, volleyball. **On-Campus Highlights:** Chi-Wan Young Sports Centre, W.A. Murphy Student Centre, MacLauchlan Arena and Aquatic Centre, Atlantic Veterinary College, Robertson Library.

ADMISSIONS

Freshman Academic Profile: 90% from public high schools. Minimum paper TOEFL 550. **Basis for Candidate Selection:** *Very important factors considered include:* academic GPA, rigor of secondary school record. *Important factors considered include:* Class rank, recommendation(s). *Other factors considered include:* standardized test scores. **Freshman Admission Requirements: Freshman Admission Statistics:** 1,044 applied, 61% admitted, 91% enrolled. **Transfer Admission Requirements:** college transcript(s), statement of good standing from prior institution(s). **General Admission Information:** Application Fee $50. Regular application deadline 8/1. Regular notification 8/31. Nonfall registration accepted. Admission may be deferred for a maximum of one semester. Neither credit nor placement offered for CEEB Advanced Placement tests.

COSTS AND FINANCIAL AID

Average book expense $500.

UNIVERSITY OF PUGET SOUND

1500 North Warner Street CMB 1062, Tacoma, WA 98416-1062
Phone: 253-879-3211 • **Financial Aid Phone:** 253-879-3214
E-mail: admission@pugetsound.edu • **CEEB Code:** 4067
Fax: 253-879-3993 • **Website:** www.pugetsound.edu • **ACT Code:** 4450

This private school was founded in 1888. It has a 97-acre campus.

RATINGS

Admissions Selectivity Rating: 92   **Fire Safety Rating:** 73   **Green Rating:** 93

STUDENTS AND FACULTY

Enrollment: 2,577. **Student Body:** 57% female, 43% male, 76% out of state, 1% international (13 countries represented). Asian 7%, African American 2%, Caucasian 74%, Hispanic 7%, Native American 1%.
Retention and Graduation: 80% freshmen return for sophomore year. 69% freshmen graduate within 4 years. 23% grads go on to further study within 1 year. **Faculty:** Student/faculty ratio 12:1. 228 full-time faculty, 87% hold PhDs, 8% are members of minority groups, 46% are women. 0% of classes are taught by teaching assistants.

ACADEMICS

Degrees: bachelor's, first professional, master's, post-master's certificate. **Classes:** Most classes have 10–19 students. Most lab/discussion sessions have 10–19 students. **Majors with Highest Enrollment:** business/commerce; English language and literature; psychology. **Special Study Options:** cooperative education program, double major, honors program, independent study, internships, student-designed major, study abroad, teacher certification program, 1 year of study in Asia, 3-2 engineering program, Business Leadership Program. **Honors programs:** Business Leadership Program; Honors Program **Disability Services:** Special programs offered to physically disabled students include note-taking services, reader services, tape recorders, tutors. **Career services:** Alumni network, alumni services, career/job search classes, career assessment, internships, regional alumni. Career services highlights include Internship Seminar 497/8, 1.0 Unit. In this seminar students examine issues related to work and its meaning in individual and collective life. Among the requirements are the completion of 120 hours of field experience at a site prearranged in consultation with the internship coordinator. The seminar provides the context to reflect on concrete experiences at the site and link them to political, psychological, social, economic and intellectual forces that shape our views on work and its meaning.

FACILITIES

Housing: Coed dorms, special housing for disabled students, women's dorms, fraternity/sorority housing, Small residential houses, theme floors in halls. 85% of campus accessible to physically disabled. **Special Academic Facilities/Equipment:** Art gallery, natural history museum, concert hall, transmission and scanning electron microscopes, spectrometers, exercise science lab, observatory, paleomagnetic and X-ray lab, physiology labs, and DNA Sequencer **Computers:** 30% of classrooms, 30% of dorms, 95% of libraries, 95% of dining areas, 85% of student union, 10% of common outdoor areas have wireless network access. Students can register for classes online. Administrative functions (other than registration) can be performed online.

CAMPUS LIFE

Environment: City. **Activities:** Choral groups, concert band, dance, drama/theater, jazz band, literary magazine, music ensembles, musical theater, opera, radio station, student government, student newspaper, student-run film society, symphony orchestra, yearbook 77 registered organizations, 2 honor societies, 12 religious organizations. 4 fraternities, 4 sororities. **Athletics (Intercollegiate):** *Men:* baseball, basketball, crew/rowing, cross-country, football, golf, soccer, swimming, tennis, track/field (outdoor), track/field (indoor). *Women:* basketball, crew/rowing, cross-country, golf, lacrosse, soccer, softball, swimming, tennis, track/field (outdoor), track/field (indoor), volleyball. **On-Campus Highlights:** 3-story Dale Chihuly glass sculpture in Wyatt Hall, Harned Hall, new state-of-the-art science facility, Diversions Caf, 97 acres of rolling lawns, native fir groves, and Tudor Gothic architecture, Music and theater productions directed by faculty and students on campus. **Environmental Initiatives:** In 2005 President Thomas established the Sustainability Advisory Committee (SAC), which reports to the president through the Vice President of Student Affairs and the Vice President for Finance and Administration. The president empowered the committee to advise on and implement sustainability policies and programs on campus and collaboratively with our regional community. The committee addresses sustainability across the institution and in partnership with external organizations. In 2010 SAC reorganized itself around STARS to facilitate comprehensive sustainability management. SAC is using STARS to assess Puget Sound's sustainability status, to identify priorities, and to establish objectives. SAC created subcommittees to manage overall sustainability and all aspects of STARS. Sustainability has been adopted across Puget Sound's curriculum. Sustainability-focused courses concentrate on the concept of sustainability, including its social, economic, and environmental dimensions. They also examine an issue or topic using sustainability as a lens. Sustainability-related courses incorporate sustainability as a distinct course component or module, or concentrate on a single sustainability principle or issue. Using the rubric of seven sustainability principles adopted by the AASHE Sustainability Learning Objective Group, a sustainability-focused course concentrates on the concept of sustainability or uses sustainability as a lens if it engages at least three of the seven sustainability principles in this rubric (using educational goals and learning outcomes in the rubric that match course content to determine "engaging the principles"). A sustainability related course engages at least one but not more than two of the seven principles (using educational goals and learning outcomes in the rubric that match course content to determine "engaging the principles"). Based upon a 2010 comprehensive course survey, Puget Sound offered 923 total courses, 98 of which were sustainability focused and 307 of which were sustainability related. Of 34 academic departments, 32 offered at least one sustainability related or focused course. Sustainability research focuses on a key principle of sustainability (such as social equity or environmental stewardship); addresses a sustainability challenge (such as climate change or poverty); or furthers understanding of the interconnectedness of societal and environmental challenges. Sustainability research leads toward solutions that support economic prosperity, social wellbeing, and ecological health. We use the rubric of seven sustainability principles adopted by the AASHE Sustainability Learning Objective Group to inform analysis of research focus. Based upon a 2010 survey, 353 faculty members were involved in research, 153 of whom engaged in sustainability research. Of 33 departments engaged in research, 32 had at least one faculty member involved in sustainability research.

ADMISSIONS

Freshman Academic Profile: Average high school GPA 3.5. 36% in top 10% of high school class, 67% in top 25% of high school class, 93% in top 50% of high school class. 72% from public high schools. SAT Math middle 50% range 580-660. SAT Critical Reading middle 50% range 570-688. SAT Writing middle 50% range 560-670. ACT middle 50% range 26-30. Minimum web-based TOEFL 79. Minimum paper TOEFL 550. **Basis for Candidate Selection:** *Very important factors considered include:* academic GPA, rigor of secondary school record, standardized test scores. *Important factors considered include:* application essay, recommendation(s), alumni/ae relation, character/personal qualities, extracurricular activities, racial/ethnic status, talent/ability. *Other factors considered include:* Class rank, first generation, interview, level of applicant's interest, volunteer work, work experience. **Freshman Admission Requirements:** High school diploma is required and GED is accepted. *Academic units recommended:* **Freshman Admission Statistics:** 6,878 applied, 54% admitted, 17% enrolled. **Transfer Admission Requirements:** college transcript(s), essay or personal statement, statement of good standing from prior institution(s). Minimum college GPA of 2.0 required. Lowest grade transferable D. **General Admission Information:** Application Fee $40. Early decision application deadline 11/15. Regular application deadline 2/15. Regular notification 4/1. Nonfall registration accepted. Admission may be deferred for a maximum of 1 year. Credit and/or placement offered for CEEB Advanced Placement tests.

COSTS AND FINANCIAL AID
Annual tuition $40,040. Room and board $10,390. Required fees $210. Average book expense $1,000. **Required Forms and Deadlines:** FAFSA. **Notification of Awards:** Applicants will be notified of awards on a rolling basis beginning 3/15. **Types of Aid:** *Need-based scholarships/grants:* Federal Pell, SEOG, state scholarships/grants, private scholarships, the school's own gift aid. *Loans:* Subsidized Stafford, Unsubsidized Stafford, PLUS, Federal Perkins. **Student Employment:** Federal Work-Study Program available. Institutional employment available. Highest amount earned per year from on-campus jobs $2,650. Off-campus job opportunities are excellent. **Financial Aid Statistics:** 100% freshmen, 99% undergrads receive need-based scholarship or grant aid. 16% freshmen, 9% undergrads receive non-need-based scholarship or grant aid. 73% freshmen, 79% undergrads receive need-based self-help aid. 89% freshmen, 90% undergrads receive any aid. 58% undergrads borrow to pay for school. Average cumulative indebtedness $28,923. **Criteria for awarding institutional aid:** Non-need-based: academics, alumni affiliation, art, leadership, music/drama, religious affiliation.

UNIVERSITY OF REDLANDS

1200 E. Colton Avenue, Redlands, CA 92373
Phone: 909-335-4074 • **Financial Aid Phone:** 909-748-8047
E-mail: admissions@redlands.edu • **CEEB Code:** 4848
Fax: 909-335-4089 • **Website:** www.redlands.edu • **ACT Code:** 464

This private school was founded in 1907. It has a 160-acre campus.

RATINGS
Admissions Selectivity Rating: 81   **Fire Safety Rating:** 75   **Green Rating:** 77

STUDENTS AND FACULTY
Enrollment: 3,346. **Student Body:** 56% female, 44% male, 24% out-of-state, 1% international (17 countries represented). Asian 5%, African American 5%, Caucasian 49%, Hispanic 25%, Native American 1%.
Retention and Graduation: 61% freshmen graduate within 4 years. 72% freshmen graduate within 6 years. 25% grads go on to further study within 1 year. 6% grads pursue law degrees. 6% grads pursue business degrees. 5% grads pursue medical degrees. **Faculty:** Student/faculty ratio 14:1. 198 full-time faculty, 90% hold PhDs, 20% are members of minority groups, 47% are women. 0% of classes are taught by teaching assistants.

ACADEMICS
Degrees: associate, bachelor's, certificate, master's, post-bachelor's certificate, post-master's certificate. **Classes:** Most classes have 10–19 students. **Majors with Highest Enrollment:** business/commerce; liberal arts and sciences/liberal studies; psychology. **Special Study Options:** cross-registration, double major, dual enrollment, exchange student program (domestic), honors program, independent study, internships, liberal arts/career combination, student-designed major, study abroad, teacher certification program. **Honors programs:** The Johnston Center for Integrative Studies allows students to design their own majors in consultation with faculty advisors. Students write contracts for their courses and receive narrative evaluations in lieu of traditional grades. The center has received national acclaim for its innovative approaches to education. **Disability Services:** Special programs offered to physically disabled students include note-taking services, reader services, tutors. **Career services:** alumni services, career/job search classes, regional alumni.

FACILITIES
Housing: Coed dorms, special housing for disabled students, men's dorms, women's dorms, fraternity/sorority housing, apartments for single students, Abroad Programming. Apartments for students with dependent children. 75% of campus accessible to physically disabled. **Special Academic Facilities/Equipment:** Art gallery, Far East art collection, Southwest collection, center

for communicative disorders, language lab, Helen and Vernon Farquar Anthropology Lab, Physics Laser Photonics Lab, Irvine Map Library, Geographic Information System lab. **Computers:** 100% of classrooms, 100% of dorms, 100% of libraries, 100% of dining areas, 100% of student union, 100% of common outdoor areas have wireless network access. Students can register for classes online. Administrative functions (other than registration) can be performed online.

CAMPUS LIFE
Environment: Town. **Activities:** Choral groups, concert band, dance, drama/theater, jazz band, literary magazine, music ensembles, musical theater, opera, radio station, student government, student newspaper, student-run film society, symphony orchestra, yearbook 105 registered organizations, 8 honor societies, 8 religious organizations. 5 fraternities, 5 sororities. **Athletics (Intercollegiate):** *Men:* baseball, basketball, cross-country, diving, football, golf, soccer, swimming, tennis, track/field (outdoor), water polo. *Women:* basketball, cross-country, diving, golf, lacrosse, soccer, softball, swimming, tennis, track/field (outdoor), volleyball, water polo. **On-Campus Highlights:** Armacost Library, Peppers Art Center, Currier Gymnasium/Fitness Center, Chapel, Post Office, Other popular places on campus: Math and Physics Building, Aquatic Center, Football Stadium, Jasper's Corner, and Plaza Cafe. **Environmental Initiatives:** Co-Generation facility to provide power to much of the campus Lewis Hall — a high performance earth-sheltered green building that houses the department of Environmental Studies, the GIS program, and the Resdlands Institute Art & Theater Center LEED (green) building

ADMISSIONS
Freshman Academic Profile: Average high school GPA 3.6. 28% in top 10% of high school class, 64% in top 25% of high school class, 91% in top 50% of high school class. SAT Math middle 50% range 530-620. SAT Critical Reading middle 50% range 520-620. SAT Writing middle 50% range 510-610. ACT middle 50% range 22-26. Minimum paper TOEFL 550. **Basis for Candidate Selection:** *Very important factors considered include:* academic GPA, recommendation(s), rigor of secondary school record, character/personal qualities, talent/ability. *Important factors considered include:* application essay, standardized test scores. *Other factors considered include:* alumni/ae relation, extracurricular activities, first generation, geographical residence, interview, racial/ethnic status, volunteer work, work experience. **Freshman Admission Requirements:** High school diploma is required and GED is accepted. *Academic units required:* 4 English, 3 mathematics, 2 science, (1 science labs), 2 foreign language, 2 social studies, 0. *Academic units recommended:* 4 English, 3 mathematics, 2 science, (1 science labs), 2 foreign language, 2 social studies, 0 **Freshman Admission Statistics:** 4,501 applied, 69% admitted, 24% enrolled. **Transfer Admission Requirements:** High school transcript, college transcript(s), essay or personal statement, minimum college GPA of 2.5 required. Lowest grade transferable C. **General Admission Information:** Application Fee $30. Regular application deadline 6/1. Notification on a rolling basis, beginning on or about 11/1. Nonfall registration accepted. Admission may be deferred for a maximum of 12 months. Credit and/or placement offered for CEEB Advanced Placement tests.

COSTS AND FINANCIAL AID
Annual tuition $39,038. Room and board $11,924. Required fees $300. Average book expense $1,650. **Required Forms and Deadlines:** FAFSA, state aid formGPA Verification form for California Residents. **Notification of Awards:** Applicants will be notified of awards on a rolling basis beginning 2/28. **Types of Aid:** *Need-based scholarships/grants:* Federal Pell, SEOG, state scholarships/grants, private scholarships, the school's own gift aid. *Loans:* Subsidized Stafford, Unsubsidized Stafford, PLUS, Federal Perkins, college/university loans from institutional funds. **Student Employment:** Federal Work-Study Program available. Highest amount earned per year from on-campus jobs $2,000. Off-campus job opportunities are fair. **Financial Aid Statistics:** 99% freshmen, 98% undergrads receive need-based scholarship or grant aid. 19% freshmen, 9% undergrads receive non-need-based scholarship or grant aid. 86% freshmen, 90% undergrads receive need-based self-help aid. 94% freshmen, 94% undergrads receive any aid. 68% undergrads borrow to pay for school. Average cumulative indebtedness $32,035. **Criteria for awarding institutional aid:** Non-need-based: academics, art, music/drama.

UNIVERSITY OF RHODE ISLAND

Newman Hall, Kingston, RI 2881
Phone: 401-874-7100 • **Financial Aid Phone:** 401-874-7530
E-mail: admission@uri.edu • **CEEB Code:** 3919
Fax: 401-874-5523 • **Website:** www.uri.edu • **ACT Code:** 3818

This public school was founded in 1892. It has a 1300-acre campus.

RATINGS
Admissions Selectivity Rating: 71   **Fire Safety Rating:** 79   **Green Rating:** 95

STUDENTS AND FACULTY
Enrollment: 13,149. **Student Body:** 55% female, 45% male, 39% out-of-state, 1% international (57 countries represented). Asian 3%, African American 5%, Caucasian 70%, Hispanic 8%.
Retention and Graduation: 81% freshmen return for sophomore year. 42% freshmen graduate within 4 years. 63% freshmen graduate within 6 years.
Faculty: Student/faculty ratio 16:1. 645 full-time faculty, 89% hold PhDs, 10% are members of minority groups, 43% are women. 4% of classes are taught by teaching assistants.

ACADEMICS
Degrees: bachelor's, first professional, master's, post-bachelor's certificate. **Classes:** Most classes have 20–29 students. Most lab/discussion sessions have 10–19 students. **Majors with Highest Enrollment:** communication studies/speech communication and rhetoric; nursing/registered nurse (rn, asn, bsn, msn); psychology. **Special Study Options:** distance learning, double major, dual enrollment, exchange student program (domestic), honors program, independent study, internships, study abroad, teacher certification program, weekend college. **Honors programs:** The Honors Program at URI features small classes, a nationally renowned Honors Colloquium, National Scholarship for upper class students, advising and honors housing for upper class students. **Combined degree programs:** , MCP/JD, MPA/MDS, PH.D/MMA, MS/JD, MA/MLIS, MMA/JD, PharmD/MBA, MPA/MLIS, MP. **Disability Services:** Special programs offered to physically disabled students include note-taking services, tape recorders. **Career services:** Alumni network, alumni services, career assessment, internships, regional alumni. Career services highlights include Career assessments and job search assistance.

FACILITIES
Housing: Coed dorms, special housing for disabled students, fraternity/sorority housing, apartments for married students, cooperative housing, apartments for single students, Wellness Housing, Theme HousingLearning communities for undecided majors, honor program, health sciences, engineering, college environment and health sciences majors, and nursing. 100% of campus accessible to physically disabled. **Special Academic Facilities/Equipment:** Center for robotic research, animal science farm, planetarium, Watson House Museum, Narragansett Bay Campus for Marine Sciences, American historic textiles museum, aquaculture center, fisheries and marine technology laboratory, center for biotechnology and life sciences, human performance laboratory. **Computers:** 50% of classrooms, 100% of dorms, 100% of libraries, 75% of dining areas, 100% of student union, 25% of common outdoor areas have wireless network access. Students can register for classes online. Administrative functions (other than registration) can be performed online.

CAMPUS LIFE
Environment: Village. **Activities:** Choral groups, concert band, dance, drama/theater, jazz band, literary magazine, marching band, music ensembles, musical theater, pep band, radio station, student government, student newspaper, student-run film society, television station, yearbook, Campus Ministries, International Student Organization 100 registered organizations, 40 honor societies, 5 religious organizations. 11 fraternities, 9 sororities. **Athletics (Intercollegiate):** *Men:* baseball, basketball, cheerleading, cross-country, football, golf, soccer, track/field (outdoor), track/field (indoor). *Women:* basketball, cheerleading, crew/rowing, cross-country, diving, soccer, softball, swimming, tennis, track/field (outdoor), track/field (indoor), volleyball. **On-Campus Highlights:** Ryan Center and Boss Ice Arena, Ballentine Hall (Business building), Memorial Student Union, Multi-Cultural Center in heart of campus, Hope Dining Commons, Center for Biotechnology and Life Sciences - LEED certified and the focal point of a statewide effort to build a new, knowledge-based economy for Rhode Island. Green Hall - historic building houses Registrar, Financial Aid and Bursar, as well as Administrative Offices. **Environmental Initiatives:** Development of a sustainability component to the general education requirements for all undergraduate students Reduction of energy use through staff/faculty/student behavior change program Reduction of single-occupancy vehicles driven to/from campus via increasing public transportation awareness, promoting car share and car pooling.

ADMISSIONS
Freshman Academic Profile: Average high school GPA 3.3. 17% in top 10% of high school class, 48% in top 25% of high school class, 83% in top 50% of high school class. SAT Math middle 50% range 500-600. SAT Critical Reading middle 50% range 490-580. SAT Writing middle 50% range 490-590. ACT middle 50% range 21-26. Minimum web-based TOEFL 79. Minimum paper TOEFL 550. **Basis for Candidate Selection:** *Very important factors considered include:* rigor of secondary school record. *Important factors considered include:* Class rank, application essay, academic GPA, standardized test scores. *Other factors considered include:* recommendation(s), alumni/ae relation, character/personal qualities, extracurricular activities, first generation, geographical residence, level of applicant's interest, racial/ethnic status, state residency, talent/ability, volunteer work, work experience. **Freshman Admission Requirements:** High school diploma is required and GED is accepted. *Academic units required:* 4 English, 3 mathematics, 2 science, (1 science labs), 2 foreign language, 2 social studies, 5 academic electives. *Academic units recommended:* 4 English, 3 mathematics, 2 science, (1 science labs), 2 foreign language, 2 social studies, 5 academic electives. **Freshman Admission Statistics:** 20,637 applied, 77% admitted, 21% enrolled. **Transfer Admission Requirements:** college transcript(s), essay or personal statement, statement of good standing from prior institution(s). Minimum college GPA of 2.5 required. Lowest grade transferable C. **General Admission Information:** Application Fee $65. Regular application deadline 2/1. Regular notification 3/31. Notification on a rolling basis, beginning on or about 12/1. Nonfall registration accepted. Credit and/or placement offered for CEEB Advanced Placement tests.

COSTS AND FINANCIAL AID
Annual in-state tuition $10,878. Annual out-of-state tuition $26,444. Room and board $11,160. Required fees $1,572. Average book expense $1,200. **Required Forms and Deadlines:** FAFSA. **Notification of Awards:** Applicants will be notified of awards on a rolling basis beginning 3/31. **Types of Aid:** *Need-based scholarships/grants:* Federal Pell, SEOG, state scholarships/grants, private scholarships, the school's own gift aid. *Loans:* Direct Subsidized Stafford, Direct Unsubsidized Stafford, Direct PLUS, Federal Perkins, Federal Nursing, state loans, college/university loans from institutional funds. **Student Employment:** Federal Work-Study Program available. Institutional employment available. Highest amount earned per year from on-campus jobs $2,000. Off-campus job opportunities are good. **Financial Aid Statistics:** 87% freshmen, 80% undergrads receive need-based scholarship or grant aid. 11% freshmen, 8% undergrads receive non-need-based scholarship or grant aid. 93% freshmen, 94% undergrads receive need-based self-help aid. 78% freshmen, 81% undergrads receive any aid. 77% undergrads borrow to pay for school. Average cumulative indebtedness $30,387. **Criteria for awarding institutional aid:** Non-need-based: academics, alumni affiliation, art, athletics, music/drama.

UNIVERSITY OF RICHMOND

Brunet Memorial Hall: 28 Westhampton Way, University of Richmond, VA 23173
Phone: 804-289-8640 • **Financial Aid Phone:** 804-289-8438
E-mail: admissions@richmond.edu • **CEEB Code:** 5569
Fax: 804-287-6003 • **Website:** www.richmond.edu • **ACT Code:** 4410

This private school was founded in 1830. It has a 350-acre campus.

RATINGS
Admissions Selectivity Rating: 96   **Fire Safety Rating:** 81   **Green Rating:** 93

STUDENTS AND FACULTY
Enrollment: 2,960. **Student Body:** 55% female, 45% male, 79% out-of-state, 8% international (71 countries represented). Asian 6%, African American 8%, Caucasian 58%, Hispanic 6%.
Retention and Graduation: 93% freshmen return for sophomore year. 77% freshmen graduate within 4 years. 24% grads go on to further study within 1 year. 4% grads pursue arts and sciences degrees. 4% grads pursue law degrees. 2% grads pursue business degrees. 4% grads pursue medical degrees. **Faculty:** Student/faculty ratio 9:1. 320 full-time faculty, 92% hold PhDs, 12% are members of minority groups, 41% are women. 0% of classes are taught by teaching assistants.

ACADEMICS

Degrees: associate, bachelor's, certificate, diploma, master's, post-bachelor's certificate. **Classes:** Most classes have 10–19 students. Most lab/discussion sessions have 10–19 students. **Majors with Highest Enrollment:** business administration and management; English language and literature; political science and government. **Special Study Options:** Accelerated program, cross-registration, distance learning, double major, English as a Second Language (ESL), exchange student program (domestic), honors program, independent study, internships, student-designed major, study abroad, teacher certification program, Notes on above: Summer English Language Institute is for accepted International Students only. Distance Learning offered through School of Continuing Studies. **Career services:** Alumni network, alumni services, career/job search classes, career assessment, internships Career services highlights include Spider Road Trips. Trips include Spiders on Wall Street to visit Wall Street firms; Spiders in Media and Communications to New York City; Spiders for the Common Good to public service organizations in Washington D.C. and day trips to selected organizations in the Richmond area. Accompanied by staff, groups of approximately 25 students are given the opportunity to see the operations and hear speakers in different organizations.

FACILITIES

Housing: Coed dorms, special housing for disabled students, men's dorms, women's dorms, apartments for single students, Theme Housing: Global House, Outdoor House, and Civic Engagement represent co-ed housing. Other housing options include: Spinning your Web (for first-year males) and Ready for Moore (for first-year females). 90% of campus accessible to physically disabled. **Special Academic Facilities/Equipment:** Art gallery, mineral museum, Virginia Baptist archives, language lab, Neuroscience lab, Speech Center, Music Technology lab, Jepson School of Leadership, Center for Civic Engagement **Computers:** 100% of classrooms, 100% of dorms, 100% of libraries, 100% of dining areas, 100% of student union, 100% of common outdoor areas have wireless network access. Students can register for classes online. Administrative functions (other than registration) can be performed online.

CAMPUS LIFE

Environment: Metropolis. **Activities:** Choral groups, concert band, dance, drama/theater, jazz band, literary magazine, music ensembles, musical theater, pep band, radio station, student government, student newspaper, student-run film society, symphony orchestra, Campus Ministries, International Student Organization, Model UN. 208 registered organizations, 28 honor societies, 17 religious organizations. 6 fraternities, 8 sororities. **Athletics (Intercollegiate):** *Men:* baseball, basketball, cross-country, football, golf, soccer, tennis, track/field (outdoor), track/field (indoor). *Women:* basketball, cross-country, diving, field hockey, golf, lacrosse, soccer, swimming, tennis, track/field (outdoor), track/field (indoor). **On-Campus Highlights:** Tyler Haynes Commons, Robins Center (Athletic Center), Boatwright Memorial Library and Coffee Shop, Stern Plaza (Weinstein Hall, Jepson Hall, etc.), Westhampton Green (Modlin Center for the Arts). **Environmental Initiatives:** Signing the ACUPCC and completing the Climate Action Plan in December 2010. Initiated a LEED Silver minimum requirement on all new construction. Continuing waste diversion initiatives. Energy conservation and efficiency projects.

ADMISSIONS

Freshman Academic Profile: 59% in top 10% of high school class, 89% in top 25% of high school class, 99% in top 50% of high school class. 56% from public high schools. SAT Math middle 50% range 620-720. SAT Critical Reading middle 50% range 580-700. SAT Writing middle 50% range 590-690. ACT middle 50% range 28-32. Minimum web-based TOEFL 80. Minimum paper TOEFL 550. **Basis for Candidate Selection:** *Very important factors considered include:* academic GPA, rigor of secondary school record. *Important factors considered include:* Class rank, application essay, standardized test scores, character/personal qualities, first generation, talent/ability. *Other factors considered include:* recommendation(s), alumni/ae relation, extracurricular activities, geographical residence, interview, racial/ethnic status, state residency, volunteer work, work experience. **Freshman Admission Requirements:** High school diploma is required and GED is accepted. *Academic units required:* 4 English, 3 mathematics, 2 science, (2 science labs), 2 foreign language, 2 history. *Academic units recommended:* 4 English, 3 mathematics, 2 science, (2 science labs), 2 foreign language, 2 history. **Freshman Admission Statistics:** 10,232 applied, 30% admitted, 25% enrolled. **Transfer Admission Requirements:** High school transcript, college transcript(s), essay or personal statement, statement of good standing from prior institution(s). Minimum college GPA of 2.0 required. Lowest grade transferable C. **General Admission Information:** Application Fee $50. Early decision application deadline 11/15. Regular application deadline 1/15. Regular notification 4/1. Nonfall registration not accepted. Admission may be deferred for a maximum of 12 months. Credit and/or placement offered for CEEB Advanced Placement tests.

COSTS AND FINANCIAL AID

Annual tuition $45,320. Room and board $10,270. Average book expense $1,050. **Required Forms and Deadlines:** FAFSA, institution's own financial

aid form. **Notification of Awards:** Applicants will be notified of awards on or about 4/1. **Types of Aid:** *Need-based scholarships/grants:* Federal Pell, SEOG, state scholarships/grants, private scholarships, the school's own gift aid. *Loans:* Direct Subsidized Stafford, Direct Unsubsidized Stafford, Direct PLUS, Federal Perkins. **Student Employment:** Federal Work-Study Program available. Institutional employment available. Off-campus job opportunities are excellent. **Financial Aid Statistics:** 98% freshmen, 99% undergrads receive need-based scholarship or grant aid. 23% freshmen, 14% undergrads receive non-need-based scholarship or grant aid. 74% freshmen, 82% undergrads receive need-based self-help aid. 6% freshmen, 6% undergrads receive athletic scholarships. 60% freshmen, 69% undergrads receive any aid. 43% undergrads borrow to pay for school. Average cumulative indebtedness $21,825. **Criteria for awarding institutional aid:** Non-need-based: academics, art, athletics, leadership, minority status, music/drama.

See page 1274.

UNIVERSITY OF RIO GRANDE

218 North College Avenue, Rio Grande, OH 45774
Phone: 740-245-7206 • **Financial Aid Phone:** 740-245-7219
E-mail: admissions@rio.edu • **CEEB Code:** 1663
Fax: 740-245-7260 • **Website:** rio.edu • **ACT Code:** 3324

This private school was founded in 1876. It has a 68-acre campus.

RATINGS

Admissions Selectivity Rating: 63   **Fire Safety Rating:** 79   **Green Rating:** 73

STUDENTS AND FACULTY

Enrollment: 1,451. **Student Body:** 63% female, 37% male, 6% out-of-state, 1% international (countries represented). Asian 0%, African American 7%, Caucasian 81%, Hispanic 1%.
Retention and Graduation: 54% freshmen return for sophomore year. 17% freshmen graduate within 4 years. 47% freshmen graduate within 6 years.
Faculty: Student/faculty ratio 16:1. 93 full-time faculty, 54% hold PhDs, 8% are members of minority groups, 46% are women. 0% of classes are taught by teaching assistants.

ACADEMICS

Degrees: associate, bachelor's, certificate, master's. **Classes:** Most classes have fewer than 10 students. Most lab/discussion sessions have 20–29 students. **Majors with Highest Enrollment:** business/office automation/technology/data entry; elementary education and teaching; nursing/registered nurse (rn, asn, bsn, msn). **Special Study Options:** Accelerated program, cooperative education program, distance learning, double major, dual enrollment, English as a Second Language (ESL), honors program, independent study, internships, liberal arts/career combination, student-designed major, study abroad, teacher certification program. **Combined degree programs:** , 2-2 programs: nursing, business, industrial tech. **Disability Services:** Special programs offered to physically disabled students include note-taking services, reader services, tape recorders, tutors. **Career services:** alumni services, career assessment, internships.

FACILITIES

Housing: Coed dorms, special housing for disabled students, men's dorms, women's dorms, Wellness Housing, Private housing owned and operated by university available to responsible students. 75% of campus accessible to physically disabled. **Special Academic Facilities/Equipment:** Archives of local and college history, art museum, fine woodworking, theater, art annex. **Computers:** 75% of classrooms, 100% of dorms, 100% of libraries, 100% of dining areas, 100% of student union, 25% of common outdoor areas have wireless network access. Students can register for classes online. Administrative functions (other than registration) can be performed online.

CAMPUS LIFE

Environment: Rural. **Activities:** Choral groups, concert band, dance, drama/theater, jazz band, literary magazine, music ensembles, musical theater, pep band, radio station, student government, student newspaper, television station 34 registered organizations, 4 honor societies, 3 religious organizations. 4 fraternities, 5 sororities. **Athletics (Intercollegiate):** *Men:* baseball, basketball, cross-country, soccer, track/field (outdoor), track/field (indoor). *Women:* basketball, cheerleading, cross-country, soccer, softball, track/field (outdoor), track/field (indoor), volleyball. **On-Campus Highlights:** Food Court, Red Zone, Basketball Court **Environmental Initiatives:** Recycling program, some solar powered equipment, energy usage reduction program, trayless Tuesdays in the cafeteria.

ADMISSIONS

Freshman Academic Profile: Average high school GPA 2.9. 3% in top 10% of high school class, 22% in top 25% of high school class, 51% in top 50% of high school class. 95% from public high schools. Minimum paper TOEFL 400. **Basis for Candidate Selection:** *Other factors considered include:* Class rank, academic GPA, standardized test scores. **Freshman Admission Requirements:** High school diploma is required and GED is accepted. *Academic units required:* 4 English, 3 mathematics, 3 science, (1 science labs), 3 social studies, 7 academic electives. *Academic units recommended:* 4 English, 3 mathematics, 3 science, (1 science labs), 3 social studies, 7 academic electives. **Freshman Admission Statistics:** 5,039 applied, 44% admitted, 26% enrolled. **Transfer Admission Requirements:** High school transcript, college transcript(s), statement of good standing from prior institution(s). Minimum college GPA of 0 required. Lowest grade transferable D. **General Admission Information:** Application Fee $25. Nonfall registration accepted. Credit and/or placement offered for CEEB Advanced Placement tests.

COSTS AND FINANCIAL AID

Annual tuition $19,720. Room and board $8,640. Required fees $150. Average book expense $1,200. **Required Forms and Deadlines:** FAFSA, institution's own financial aid form. **Notification of Awards:** Applicants will be notified of awards on a rolling basis beginning 1/15. **Types of Aid:** *Need-based scholarships/grants:* Federal Pell, SEOG, state scholarships/grants, private scholarships, the school's own gift aid. *Loans:* Direct Subsidized Stafford, Direct Unsubsidized Stafford, Direct PLUS, Subsidized Stafford, PLUS, Federal Perkins, Federal Nursing, college/university loans from institutional funds. **Student Employment:** Off-campus job opportunities are fair. **Financial Aid Statistics:** 74% freshmen, 85% undergrads receive need-based scholarship or grant aid. 4% freshmen, 39% undergrads receive non-need-based scholarship or grant aid. 66% freshmen, 80% undergrads receive need-based self-help aid. 10% freshmen, 10% undergrads receive athletic scholarships. 78% freshmen, 77% undergrads receive any aid. 78% undergrads borrow to pay for school. Average cumulative indebtedness $22,633. **Criteria for awarding institutional aid:** Non-need-based: academics, alumni affiliation, athletics, leadership, music/drama, state/district residency.

UNIVERSITY OF ROCHESTER

300 Wilson Blvd, Rochester, NY 14627
Phone: 585-275-3221 • **Financial Aid Phone:** 585-275-3226
E-mail: admit@admissions.rochester.edu • **CEEB Code:** 2928
Fax: 585-461-4595 • **Website:** www.rochester.edu • **ACT Code:** 2980

This private school was founded in 1850. It has a 655-acre campus.

RATINGS

Admissions Selectivity Rating: 97   **Fire Safety Rating:** 81   **Green Rating:** 84

STUDENTS AND FACULTY

Enrollment: 5,606. **Student Body:** 51% female, 49% male, 54% out-of-state, 13% international (94 countries represented). Asian 11%, African American 5%, Caucasian 56%, Hispanic 6%, Native American 0%
Retention and Graduation: 96% freshmen return for sophomore year. 74% freshmen graduate within 4 years. 85% freshmen graduate within 6 years. 34% grads go on to further study within 1 year. 64% grads pursue arts and sciences degrees. 7% grads pursue law degrees. 5% grads pursue business degrees. 15% grads pursue medical degrees. **Faculty:** Student/faculty ratio 10:1. 567 full-time faculty, 93% hold PhDs.

ACADEMICS

Degrees: bachelor's, master's, post-bachelor's certificate, post-master's certificate. **Classes:** Most classes have 10—19 students. **Majors with Highest Enrollment:** biology/biological sciences; economics; psychology. **Special Study Options:** Accelerated program, cooperative education program, cross-registration, double major, dual enrollment, English as a Second Language (ESL), honors program, independent study, internships, liberal arts/career combination, student-designed major, study abroad, teacher certification program, "Take 5" a fifth year tuition free to supplement regular requirements; Washington Semester Program; Rochester Curriculum (clusters); Quest Courses. **Combined Degree Programs:** BA/MD, BA/MA, Medicine, Business, Education, Engineering. **Disability Services:** Special programs offered to physically disabled students include note-taking services, reader services,

tape recorders, tutors. **Career Services:** Alumni network, alumni services, career assessment, internships Career services highlights include Rochester students pursue internship, externship, research and volunteer experiences at a high rate. Many are involved in programs directed by other organizations, including 67 study abroad programs in which the University is a partner. The campus career center guides individualized plans for student career development and enjoys extraordinary success. A partial listing of the programs the University has created and manages on its own: internships at the Parliament in London, Parlement in France or the European Parliament in Brussels; "Art New York," a semester spent living in New York City working at galleries or museums; REU programs at Rochester in Chemistry, Engineering, and Medicine; similar programs at Fermilab in Chicago, at NIH and NASA in the DC area; the Urban Scholars summer program in Rochester, now extended as a fifth Rochester Youth Year; a fifth Kaufmann Entrepreneurial Year in which students as individuals or in groups create and manage a new enterprise; the Malawi Immersion Seminar, a summer program centering on a 10-day homestay in a rural African village; a guided summer investigation of Italian architecture, archaeology and engineering, which is now the capstone experience in a new major; intensive in-country immersion language programs for several foreign languages; earth sciences research expeditions in the Arctic and South Africa each year; numerous developmental programs in music and in clinical medical research; the Mt. Hope Family Clinic in developmental and social psychology; engineering industry practicum opportunities with Google, Apple, Microsoft, Kodak, Xerox, IBM etc.; cognitive research with the use of an academic MRI facility on the undergraduate campus; undergraduate study and research programs at Rochester's Laboratory for Laser Energetics, home of the Omega EP laser system, one of the world's most powerful.

FACILITIES

Housing: Coed dorms, special housing for disabled students, men's dorms, special housing for international students, women's dorms, fraternity/sorority housing, apartments for married students, apartments for single students, wellness housing, theme housing. Freshman housing; Special interest housing; Suite style living. 90% of campus accessible to physically disabled. **Special Academic Facilities/Equipment:** Art center and gallery, African and African-American studies institute, center for women's studies, visual science and space science centers, institute of optics, observatory, laser energetics and nuclear structure research labs, electron microscopes. Judaic studies center, political economy institute, sign language research center, biomedical ultrasound center, Polish and central European studies center, electronic imaging systems center, center for future health. **Computers:** 100% of classrooms, 30% of dorms, 100% of libraries, 100% of dining areas, 100% of student union, have wireless network access. Students can register for classes online. Administrative functions (other than registration) can be performed online.

CAMPUS LIFE

Environment: Metropolis. **Activities:** Choral groups, concert band, dance, drama/theater, jazz band, literary magazine, music ensembles, musical theater, opera, pep band, radio station, student government, student newspaper, student-run film society, symphony orchestra, television station, International Student Organization, Model UN 224 registered organizations, 6 honor societies, 14 religious organizations. 17 fraternities, 13 sororities. **Athletics (Intercollegiate):** *Men:* baseball, basketball, cross-country, diving, football, golf, soccer, squash, swimming, tennis, track/field (outdoor), track/field (indoor). *Women:* basketball, crew/rowing, cross-country, diving, field hockey, golf, lacrosse, soccer, softball, swimming, tennis, track/field (outdoor), track/field (indoor), volleyball. **On-Campus Highlights:** Eastman Theater, Memorial Art Gallery, Rush Rhees Library, Interfaith Chapel, Robert B. Goergen Athletic Center, Recent New Buildings on Campus: * Robert B. Goergen Hall for Biomedical Engineering and Optics - A five-story facility that pairs biomedical engineering and optics in an environment of teaching laboratories, high-tech demonstration areas, and gathering spaces for collaboration. * The Gleason Library - A collaborative study space, designed with student input, which features an open floor plan and lightweight furniture that students are encouraged to reconfigure. Riverview Student Apartments - A five-building, 120-unit dormitory complex. The waterfront building features fully furnished apartments and offers amenities not found in other on-campus housing, including air conditioning, kitchens and separate living rooms. Each of the three- and four-story buildings is equipped with laundry and vending facilities. * University Health Services Building -The new facility brings together UHS medical care services, physical therapy, health promotion, administrative offices, and the University Counseling Center. The UHS building is the primary health-care stop for Arts, Sciences & Engineering students, as well as faculty, staff, and other members of the University community. **Environmental Initiatives:** The University's first LEED certified building opened its doors in May. The University's newly dedicated Saunders Research Building, which houses the Clinical and Translational Science Institute, is the first on campus to formally receive LEED (Leadership in Energy and Environmental Design) status. The College of Arts, Sciences & Engineering introduces a minor in sustainability. The Wilson Commons makeover: good looking, good tasting, and green! Step into the Wilson Commons space formerly known as the Pit, and it is immediately clear that sweeping change came to the University's central dining center over the summer of 2010.

ADMISSIONS

Freshman Academic Profile: Average high school GPA 3.8. 77% in top 10% of high school class, 93% in top 25% of high school class, 100% in top 50% of high school class. 74% from public high schools. SAT Math middle 50% range 640-740. SAT Critical Reading middle 50% range 600-700. SAT Writing middle 50% range 600-700. ACT middle 50% range 28-32. Minimum web-based TOEFL 100. Minimum paper TOEFL 600. **Basis for Candidate Selection:** *Very important factors considered include:* recommendation(s), rigor of secondary school record, character/personal qualities. *Important factors considered include:* application essay, academic GPA, standardized test scores, extracurricular activities, interview, talent/ability. *Other factors considered include:* Class rank, alumni/ae relation, first generation, geographical residence, level of applicant's interest, racial/ethnic status, volunteer work, work experience. **Freshman Admission Requirements:** High school diploma is required and GED is accepted. **Freshman Admission Statistics:** 14,987 applied, 36% admitted, 23% enrolled. **Transfer Admission Requirements:** college transcript(s), essay or personal statement, Lowest grade transferable C. **General Admission Information:** Application Fee $60. Early decision application deadline 11/1. Regular application deadline 1/1. Regular notification 4/1. Nonfall registration accepted. Admission may be deferred for a maximum of 1. Credit and/or placement offered for CEEB Advanced Placement tests.

COSTS AND FINANCIAL AID

Annual tuition $42,890. Room and board $12,618. Required fees $776. Average book expense $1,290. **Required Forms and Deadlines:** FAFSA, CSS/Financial Aid PROFILE, state aid form, noncustodial PROFILE, business/farm supplement. **Notification of Awards:** Applicants will be notified of awards on or about 4/1. **Types of Aid:** *Need-based scholarships/grants:* Federal Pell, SEOG, state scholarships/grants, the school's own gift aid. *Loans:* Direct Subsidized Stafford, Direct Unsubsidized Stafford, Direct PLUS, Federal Perkins, Federal Nursing, college/university loans from institutional funds. **Student Employment:** Federal Work-Study Program available. Institutional employment available. Off-campus job opportunities are excellent. **Financial Aid Statistics:** 100% freshmen, 99% undergrads receive need-based scholarship or grant aid. 22% freshmen, 11% undergrads receive non-need-based scholarship or grant aid. 78% freshmen, 89% undergrads receive need-based self-help aid. 83% freshmen, 83% undergrads receive any aid. 53% undergrads borrow to pay for school. Average cumulative indebtedness $27,601. **Criteria for awarding institutional aid:** *Non-need-based:* academics, alumni affiliation, leadership, music/drama.

UNIVERSITY OF SAINT JOSEPH

1678 Asylum Avenue, West Hartford, CT 6117
Phone: 860-231-5216 • **Financial Aid Phone:** 860-231-5223
E-mail: admissions@sjc.edu • **CEEB Code:**
Fax: 860-231-5744 • **Website:** www.sjc.edu

This private school, affiliated with the Roman Catholic Church, was founded in 1932. It has a 84-acre campus.

RATINGS
Admissions Selectivity Rating: 69   **Fire Safety Rating:** 60*   **Green Rating:** 60*

STUDENTS AND FACULTY

Enrollment: 1,001. **Student Body:** 99% female, 1% male, 6% out-of-state, 0% international. Asian 2%, African American 10%, Caucasian 53%, Hispanic 11%, Native American 0%
Retention and Graduation: 75% freshmen return for sophomore year. 43% freshmen graduate within 4 years. 56% freshmen graduate within 6 years.
Faculty: Student/faculty ratio 12:1. 108 full-time faculty, 92% hold PhDs, 16% are members of minority groups, 71% are women. 0% of classes are taught by teaching assistants.

ACADEMICS

Degrees: bachelor's, certificate, master's, post-bachelor's certificate. **Classes:** Most classes have 10—19 students. Most lab/discussion sessions have 10—19 students. **Majors with Highest Enrollment:** nursing/registered nurse (rn, asn, bsn, msn); psychology; social work. **Special Study Options:** Accelerated program, cross-registration, distance learning, double major, honors program, independent study, internships, liberal arts/career combination, student-designed major, study abroad, teacher certification program, weekend college. **Combined Degree Programs:** BA/MA. **Career Services:** alumni services, career/job search classes, career assessment, internships.

FACILITIES

Housing: special housing for disabled students, women's dorms, Suite living (double rooms with shared common area and kitchen). **Computers:** Students can register for classes online.

CAMPUS LIFE

Environment: Town. **Activities:** Choral groups, dance, drama/theater, music ensembles, student government, student newspaper, yearbook, Campus Ministries, International Student Organization. **Athletics (Intercollegiate):** *Women:* basketball, cross-country, diving, lacrosse, soccer, softball, swimming, tennis, volleyball.

ADMISSIONS

Freshman Academic Profile: Average high school GPA 3.3. 17% in top 10% of high school class, 49% in top 25% of high school class, 88% in top 50% of high school class. SAT Math middle 50% range 450-540. SAT Critical Reading middle 50% range 450-550. ACT middle 50% range 22-23. Minimum paper TOEFL 530. **Basis for Candidate Selection:** *Very important factors considered include:* academic GPA, standardized test scores. *Other factors considered include:* Class rank, application essay, recommendation(s), rigor of secondary school record, alumni/ae relation, character/personal qualities, extracurricular activities, first generation, geographical residence, interview, level of applicant's interest, racial/ethnic status, religious affiliation/commitment, state residency, talent/ability, volunteer work, work experience. **Freshman Admission Requirements:** High school diploma is required and GED is accepted. *Academic units required:* 4 English, 3 mathematics, 3 science, 3 foreign language, 3 social studies. *Academic units recommended:* 4 English, 3 mathematics, 3 science, 3 foreign language, 3 social studies. **Freshman Admission Statistics:** 1,335 applied, 78% admitted, 15% enrolled. **Transfer Admission Requirements:** High school transcript, college transcript(s), Lowest grade transferable C. **General Admission Information:** Application Fee $50. Notification on a rolling basis, beginning on or about 10/1. Nonfall registration accepted.

COSTS AND FINANCIAL AID

Average book expense $1,100. **Required Forms and Deadlines:** FAFSA. **Notification of Awards:** Applicants will be notified of awards on a rolling basis beginning 3/1. **Types of Aid:** *Need-based scholarships/grants:* Federal Pell, SEOG, state scholarships/grants, private scholarships, the school's own gift aid, Federal Nursing Scholarships. *Loans:* Direct Subsidized Stafford, Direct Unsubsidized Stafford, Direct PLUS, Subsidized Stafford, Unsubsidized Stafford, PLUS, Federal Perkins, state loans. **Student Employment:** Off-campus job opportunities are good. **Financial Aid Statistics:** 100% freshmen, 99% undergrads receive need-based scholarship or grant aid. 8% freshmen, 7% undergrads receive non-need-based scholarship or grant aid. 90% freshmen, 90% undergrads receive need-based self-help aid. 94% undergrads borrow to pay for school. **Criteria for awarding institutional aid:** *Non-need-based:* academics.

See page 1276.

UNIVERSITY OF SAINT MARY (KS)

4100 South Fourth Street Trafficway, Leavenworth, KS 66048
Phone: 913-758-6118
E-mail: admis@hub.smcks.edu • **CEEB Code:** 6630
Fax: 913-758-6140 • **Website:** www.stmary.edu • **ACT Code:** 1455

This private school, affiliated with the Roman Catholic Church, was founded in 1923. It has a 240-acre campus.

RATINGS
Admissions Selectivity Rating: 84   **Fire Safety Rating:** 60*   **Green Rating:** 60*

STUDENTS AND FACULTY

Enrollment: 787. **Student Body:** 62% female, 38% male, 52% out-of-state, 1% international. Asian 2%, African American 12%, Caucasian 59%, Hispanic 6%, Native American 1%
Retention and Graduation: 28% freshmen graduate within 4 years. 37% freshmen graduate within 6 years. **Faculty:** Student/faculty ratio 10:1. 50 full-time faculty, 60% hold PhDs, 4% are members of minority groups, 54% are women. 0% of classes are taught by teaching assistants.

ACADEMICS

Degrees: associate, bachelor's, master's, transfer associate. **Classes:** Most classes have fewer than 10 students. **Majors with Highest Enrollment:** business/commerce; elementary education and teaching; psychology. **Special Study Options:** Accelerated program, distance learning, double major, dual enrollment, honors program, independent study, internships, student-designed major, study abroad, teacher certification program, Semester-away programs available.

Disability Services: Special programs offered to physically disabled students include note-taking services, tutors.

FACILITIES
Housing: Coed dorms. **Special Academic Facilities/Equipment:** Lincoln Library Collection Art Gallery Bible Collection **Computers:** Students can register for classes online. Administrative functions (other than registration) can be performed online.

CAMPUS LIFE
Environment: Town. **Activities:** Choral groups, concert band, drama/theater, literary magazine, music ensembles, musical theater, pep band, student government, Campus Ministries 22 registered organizations, 2 honor societies, 2 religious organizations. **Athletics (Intercollegiate):** *Men:* baseball, basketball, football, soccer. *Women:* basketball, soccer, softball, volleyball.

ADMISSIONS
Freshman Academic Profile: 80% from public high schools. SAT Math middle 50% range 430-550. SAT Critical Reading middle 50% range 440-500. ACT middle 50% range 19-25. Minimum paper TOEFL 500. **Basis for Candidate Selection:** *Very important factors considered include:* academic GPA, rigor of secondary school record, character/personal qualities. *Important factors considered include:* standardized test scores, extracurricular activities, interview, talent/ability, volunteer work. *Other factors considered include:* Class rank, application essay, recommendation(s), alumni/ae relation, work experience. **Freshman Admission Requirements:** High school diploma is required and GED is accepted. *Academic units required:* 4 English, 2 mathematics, 2 science, 2 history. *Academic units recommended:* 4 English, 2 mathematics, 2 science, 2 history. **Freshman Admission Statistics:** 733 applied, 47% admitted, 34% enrolled. **Transfer Admission Requirements:** college transcript(s), Minimum college GPA of 2.0 required. Lowest grade transferable C. **General Admission Information:** Application Fee $25. Nonfall registration accepted. Admission may be deferred for a maximum of 1 semester. Credit and/or placement offered for CEEB Advanced Placement tests.

COSTS AND FINANCIAL AID
Annual tuition $21,500. Room and board $7,020. Required fees $480. Average book expense $1,200. **Required Forms and Deadlines:** FAFSA. **Notification of Awards:** Applicants will be notified of awards on a rolling basis beginning 2/1. **Types of Aid:** *Need-based scholarships/grants:* Federal Pell, SEOG, state scholarships/grants, private scholarships, the school's own gift aid. *Loans:* Subsidized Stafford, Unsubsidized Stafford, PLUS, Federal Perkins. **Student Employment:** Highest amount earned per year from on-campus jobs $1,500. **Financial Aid Statistics:** 95% freshmen, 88% undergrads receive need-based scholarship or grant aid. 89% freshmen, 93% undergrads receive need-based self-help aid. 61% freshmen, 55% undergrads receive athletic scholarships. 96% undergrads borrow to pay for school. Average cumulative indebtedness $22,914. **Criteria for awarding institutional aid:** *Non-need-based:* academics, art, athletics, leadership, music/drama.

UNIVERSITY OF SAINT THOMAS (MN)

2115 Summit Avenue, St. Paul, MN 55105-1096
Phone: 651-962-6150 • **Financial Aid Phone:** 651-962-6550
E-mail: admissions@stthomas.edu • **CEEB Code:** 6110
Fax: 651-962-6160 • **Website:** www.stthomas.edu • **ACT Code:** 2102

This private school, affiliated with the Roman Catholic Church, was founded in 1885. It has a 78-acre campus.

RATINGS
Admissions Selectivity Rating: 73   **Fire Safety Rating:** 89   **Green Rating:** 82

STUDENTS AND FACULTY
Enrollment: 6,237. **Student Body:** 46% female, 54% male, 19% out-of-state, 3% international (countries represented). Asian 4%, African American 3%, Caucasian 82%, Hispanic 4%, Native American 0%
Retention and Graduation: 88% freshmen return for sophomore year. 63% freshmen graduate within 4 years. **Faculty:** Student/faculty ratio 15:1. full-time faculty. 0% of classes are taught by teaching assistants.

ACADEMICS
Degrees: bachelor's, certificate, master's, post-bachelor's certificate, post-master's certificate. **Classes:** Most classes have 20—29 students. Most lab/discussion sessions have 10—19 students. **Special Study Options:** cross-registration, double major, English as a Second Language (ESL), exchange student program (domestic), honors program, independent study, internships, student-designed major, study abroad, teacher certification program. **Honors Programs:** The

Aquinas Scholars Program is the undergraduate honors program. Its purpose is to provide opportunities for motivated and curious students to deepen and enrich their undergraduate education. **Combined Degree Programs:** BA/MEng. **Disability Services:** Special programs offered to physically disabled students include note-taking services, reader services, tape recorders, tutors. **Career Services:** Alumni network, alumni services, career assessment, internships, regional alumni.

FACILITIES
Housing: men's dorms, special housing for international students, women's dorms, apartments for single studentsChemical-free lifestyle, women in science house, first year experience houses, Catholic women's and Catholic men's communities. **Special Academic Facilities/Equipment:** Seminary. **Computers:** 100% of classrooms, 100% of dorms, 100% of libraries, 100% of dining areas, 100% of student union, 100% of common outdoor areas have wireless network access. Students can register for classes online. Administrative functions (other than registration) can be performed online.

CAMPUS LIFE
Environment: Metropolis. **Activities:** Choral groups, concert band, dance, drama/theater, jazz band, literary magazine, music ensembles, pep band, radio station, student government, student newspaper, television station, yearbook, Campus Ministries, International Student Organization, Model UN 114 registered organizations, 7 religious organizations. 1 fraternities. **Athletics (Intercollegiate):** *Men:* baseball, basketball, cross-country, diving, football, golf, ice hockey, soccer, swimming, tennis, track/field (outdoor), track/field (indoor). *Women:* basketball, cross-country, diving, golf, ice hockey, soccer, softball, swimming, tennis, track/field (outdoor), track/field (indoor), volleyball. **On-Campus Highlights:** O'Shaughnessy - Frey Library, Scooters non-alcoholic pub and restaurant, Koch Commons (workout facility residence hall area), Frey Science and Engineering Center, Chapel of St. Thomas Aquinas. **Environmental Initiatives:** Climate Action Plan approved by President's Staff June 24, 2010 Anderson Student Center opened 17 Jan 2012; LEED Silver status certification application submitted. www.stthomas.edu/openingdoors/studentCenter Campus Sustainability Fund established awarding in the initial year $50,000 to three on-campus sustainability projects Nov 2011.

ADMISSIONS
Freshman Academic Profile: Average high school GPA 3.6. 24% in top 10% of high school class, 54% in top 25% of high school class, 88% in top 50% of high school class. 60% from public high schools. SAT Math middle 50% range 530-650. SAT Critical Reading middle 50% range 530-660. ACT middle 50% range 23-28. Minimum web-based TOEFL 80. Minimum paper TOEFL 550. **Basis for Candidate Selection:** *Very important factors considered include:* academic GPA, rigor of secondary school record, standardized test scores. *Important factors considered include:* Class rank, application essay. *Other factors considered include:* recommendation(s), alumni/ae relation, character/personal qualities, extracurricular activities, geographical residence, racial/ethnic status, talent/ability, volunteer work. **Freshman Admission Requirements:** High school diploma is required and GED is accepted. *Academic units required:* 3 mathematics, 2 science. *Academic units recommended:* 3 mathematics, 2 science. **Freshman Admission Statistics:** 5,362 applied, 87% admitted, 31% enrolled. **Transfer Admission Requirements:** High school transcript, college transcript(s), essay or personal statement, statement of good standing from prior institution(s). Minimum college GPA of 2.3 required. Lowest grade transferable C-. **General Admission Information:** Notification on a rolling basis, beginning on or about 10/1. Nonfall registration accepted. Credit and/or placement offered for CEEB Advanced Placement tests.

COSTS AND FINANCIAL AID
Annual tuition $33,040. Room and board $9,082. Required fees $747. Average book expense $4,085. **Required Forms and Deadlines:** FAFSA. **Notification of Awards:** Applicants will be notified of awards on a rolling basis beginning 3/1. **Types of Aid:** *Need-based scholarships/grants:* Federal Pell, SEOG, state scholarships/grants, private scholarships, the school's own gift aid. *Loans:* Direct Subsidized Stafford, Direct Unsubsidized Stafford, Direct PLUS, Federal Perkins, state loans, private loans. **Student Employment:** Federal Work-Study Program available. Institutional employment available. Off-campus job opportunities are fair. **Financial Aid Statistics:** 99% freshmen, 97% undergrads receive need-based scholarship or grant aid. 15% freshmen, 11% undergrads receive non-need-based scholarship or grant aid. 82% freshmen, 85% undergrads receive need-based self-help aid. 99% freshmen, 94% undergrads receive any aid. 69% undergrads borrow to pay for school. Average cumulative indebtedness $36,077. **Criteria for awarding institutional aid:** *Non-need-based:* academics, music/drama.

UNIVERSITY OF SAN DIEGO

5998 Alcala Park, San Diego, CA 92110-2492
Phone: 619-260-4506 • **Financial Aid Phone:** 619-260-4514
E-mail: admissions@sandiego.edu • **CEEB Code:** 4849
Fax: 619-260-6836 • **Website:** www.sandiego.edu • **ACT Code:** 394

This private school, affiliated with the Roman Catholic Church, was founded in 1949. It has a 180-acre campus.

RATINGS

Admissions Selectivity Rating: 93   **Fire Safety Rating:** 76   **Green Rating:** 98

STUDENTS AND FACULTY

Enrollment: 5,368. **Student Body:** 55% female, 45% male, 38% out-of-state, 5% international (68 countries represented). Asian 6%, African American 3%, Caucasian 57%, Hispanic 18%, Native American 0%
Retention and Graduation: 90% freshmen return for sophomore year. 65% freshmen graduate within 4 years. 14% grads go on to further study within 1 year. 2% grads pursue arts and sciences degrees. 3% grads pursue law degrees. 2% grads pursue business degrees. 1% grads pursue medical degrees. **Faculty:** Student/faculty ratio 16:1. 400 full-time faculty, 95% hold PhDs, 18% are members of minority groups, 47% are women. 0% of classes are taught by teaching assistants.

ACADEMICS

Degrees: bachelor's, master's, post-bachelor's certificate, post-master's certificate. **Classes:** Most classes have 30—39 students. Most lab/discussion sessions have 10—19 students. **Majors with Highest Enrollment:** business administration and management; communication studies/speech communication and rhetoric; finance. **Special Study Options:** double major, English as a Second Language (ESL), honors program, independent study, internships, liberal arts/career combination, study abroad, teacher certification program. **Honors Programs:** Phi Beta Kappa, Honors Program **Combined Degree Programs:** BS/MSN, MBA/JD. **Career Services:** Alumni network, alumni services, career/job search classes, career assessment, internships, regional alumni.

FACILITIES

Housing: Coed dorms, special housing for disabled students, men's dorms, women's dorms, apartments for married students, apartments for single students, wellness housing, theme housing. 85% of campus accessible to physically disabled. **Special Academic Facilities/Equipment:** Art gallery, peace and justice institute, child development center, language labs. **Computers:** 100% of classrooms, 100% of dorms, 100% of libraries, 100% of dining areas, 100% of student union, 100% of common outdoor areas have wireless network access. Students can register for classes online. Administrative functions (other than registration) can be performed online.

CAMPUS LIFE

Environment: Metropolis. **Activities:** Choral groups, dance, drama/theater, jazz band, literary magazine, music ensembles, musical theater, pep band, radio station, student government, student newspaper, symphony orchestra, television station, yearbook, Campus Ministries, International Student Organization, Model UN 129 registered organizations, 20 honor societies, 2 religious organizations. 5 fraternities, 6 sororities. **Athletics (Intercollegiate):** *Men:* baseball, basketball, crew/rowing, cross-country, football, golf, soccer, tennis. *Women:* basketball, cheerleading, crew/rowing, cross-country, diving, soccer, softball, swimming, tennis, track/field (outdoor), volleyball. **On-Campus Highlights:** Aromas Coffee House, Donald P. Shiley Center for Science and Technology, Jenny Craig Pavilion (Sporting/concert venue), Joan B. Kroc Institute for Peace and Justice, Student Life Pavilion. **Environmental Initiatives:** USD opened a full time electronic waste collection center, the first of its kind on a college campus, has collected over 100,000 pounds in the first six months of operation. The university's efficiency savings from ˜10-11 includes 6 million kilowatts of electricity (20%) and 15 million gallons of water (15%). University has the largest rooftop solar installation on a college campus in the country with a 1.23 MW solar system.

ADMISSIONS

Freshman Academic Profile: Average high school GPA 3.9. 46% in top 10% of high school class, 77% in top 25% of high school class, 95% in top 50% of high school class. 58% from public high schools. SAT Math middle 50% range 570-670. SAT Critical Reading middle 50% range 550-650. SAT Writing middle 50% range 560-660. ACT middle 50% range 25-30. Minimum web-based TOEFL 80. Minimum paper TOEFL 550. **Basis for Candidate**

Selection: *Very important factors considered include:* academic GPA, rigor of secondary school record, standardized test scores, religious affiliation/commitment. *Important factors considered include:* Class rank, application essay, recommendation(s), character/personal qualities, extracurricular activities, talent/ability, volunteer work. *Other factors considered include:* alumni/ae relation, first generation, geographical residence, level of applicant's interest, racial/ethnic status, work experience. **Freshman Admission Requirements:** High school diploma is required and GED is accepted. *Academic units required:* 4 English, 3 mathematics, 3 science, (2 science labs), 2 foreign language, 3 social studies. *Academic units recommended:* 4 English, 3 mathematics, 3 science, (2 science labs), 2 foreign language, 3 social studies. **Freshman Admission Statistics:** 16,578 applied, 43% admitted, 15% enrolled. **Transfer Admission Requirements:** High school transcript, college transcript(s), essay or personal statement, Minimum college GPA of 3.0 required. Lowest grade transferable C. **General Admission Information:** Application Fee $55. Regular application deadline 3/1. Regular notification 4/15. Nonfall registration accepted. Admission may be deferred for a maximum of one year. Credit and/or placement offered for CEEB Advanced Placement tests.

COSTS AND FINANCIAL AID

Annual tuition $39,486. Room and board $11,910. Required fees $484. Required **Forms and Deadlines:** FAFSA. **Notification of Awards:** Applicants will be notified of awards on a rolling basis beginning 3/1. **Types of Aid:** *Need-based scholarships/grants:* Federal Pell, SEOG, state scholarships/grants, private scholarships, the school's own gift aid, Federal Nursing Scholarships. *Loans:* Subsidized Stafford, Unsubsidized Stafford, PLUS, Federal Perkins, college/university loans from institutional funds. **Student Employment:** Federal Work-Study Program available. Institutional employment available. Off-campus job opportunities are good. **Financial Aid Statistics:** 96% freshmen, 93% undergrads receive need-based scholarship or grant aid. 61% freshmen, 44% undergrads receive non-need-based scholarship or grant aid. 78% freshmen, 83% undergrads receive need-based self-help aid. 2% freshmen, 2% undergrads receive athletic scholarships. 80% freshmen, 71% undergrads receive any aid. 47% undergrads borrow to pay for school. Average cumulative indebtedness $29,874. **Criteria for awarding institutional aid:** *Non-need-based:* academics, athletics, leadership, music/drama, religious affiliation.

UNIVERSITY OF SAN FRANCISCO

2130 Fulton Street, San Francisco, CA 94117
Phone: 415-422-6563 • **Financial Aid Phone:**
E-mail: admission@usfca.edu • **CEEB Code:** 4850
Fax: 415-422-2217 • **Website:** www.usfca.edu • **ACT Code:**

This private school, affiliated with the Roman Catholic Church,, affiliated with the Jesuit Church, was founded in 1855. It has a 55-acre campus.

RATINGS

Admissions Selectivity Rating: 84   **Fire Safety Rating:** 60*   **Green Rating:** 77

STUDENTS AND FACULTY

Enrollment: 5,571. **Student Body:** 64% female, 36% male, 27% out-of-state, 13% international (74 countries represented). Asian 19%, African American 3%, Caucasian 37%, Hispanic 18%, Native American 0%
Retention and Graduation: 58% freshmen graduate within 4 years. 70% freshmen graduate within 6 years. 1% grads pursue medical degrees. **Faculty:** Student/faculty ratio 16:1. 406 full-time faculty, 91% hold PhDs, 28% are members of minority groups, 48% are women. 0% of classes are taught by teaching assistants.

ACADEMICS

Degrees: bachelor's, certificate, first professional, master's, post-master's certificate. **Classes:** Most classes have 10—19 students. Most lab/discussion sessions have 10—19 students. **Majors with Highest Enrollment:** business/commerce; nursing/registered nurse (rn, asn, bsn, msn); psychology. **Special Study Options:** Accelerated program, cross-registration, distance learning, double major, English as a Second Language (ESL), exchange student program (domestic), external degree program, honors program, independent study, internships, liberal arts/career combination, student-designed major, study abroad, teacher certification program. **Combined Degree Programs:** BA/JD, BA/MA, BA/MEng. **Disability Services:** Special programs offered to physically disabled students include note-taking services, reader services, tape recorders, tutors. **Career Services:** career/job search classes, career assessment, internships.

FACILITIES
Housing: Coed dorms, women's dorms, apartments for single students, Several off campus buildings with flats have been purchased and converted into multiple student housing units. 100% of campus accessible to physically disabled. **Special Academic Facilities/Equipment:** Rare Book Room, Ricci Institute for Chinese-Western Cultural History **Computers:** 25% of classrooms, 25% of dorms, 25% of dining areas, 75% of student union, 25% of common outdoor areas have wireless network access. Students can register for classes online. Administrative functions (other than registration) can be performed online.

CAMPUS LIFE
Environment: Metropolis. **Activities:** Choral groups, dance, drama/theater, literary magazine, music ensembles, musical theater, pep band, radio station, student government, student newspaper, television station, yearbook 90 registered organizations, 14 honor societies, 4 fraternities, 4 sororities. **Athletics (Intercollegiate):** *Men:* baseball, basketball, cross-country, golf, riflery, soccer, tennis, track/field (outdoor). *Women:* basketball, cross-country, golf, riflery, soccer, tennis, track/field (outdoor), volleyball. **On-Campus Highlights:** Koret Health and Recreation Center, War Memorial Gym, St. Ignatius Church, Geschke Learning Resourse Center, Loan Mountain Campus. **Environmental Initiatives:** Sustainability. Placed 5th in National competition in Recyclemania. Currently, USF's co-generation plant produces about half of lower campus' peak energy needs. Located in the basement of Gleeson Library, the plant converts natural gas into electricity. Although the conversion of natural gas to energy does produce some emissions, natural gas is considered the cleanest of the fossil fuels. The plant gets its co-generation designation because it also captures heat lost during the conversion process and uses that to provide some of the heat lower campus uses. The plant provides about 38 percent of lower campus' heating needs. Additionally, the university uses thermal panels on top of Phelan, Gillson, and Hayes-Healy halls. The panels differ from solar panels in that they heat water directly rather than producing electricity, providing some of the hot water needed in those halls. LEED Goals on new projects Incorporation of "green" building practices in construction, including the renovation of Kalmanovitz Hall (formerly Campion Hall). London said USF will try to achieve LEED certification for the new Integrated Science Center, currently being designed. Awarded by the U.S. Green Building Council, LEED provides a suite of standards for environmentally sustainable construction. If the Integrated Science Center receives the certification, it would be the first such building on campus. Installation of Photovoltaic panels. As part of that process, USF is installing new solar panels on top of the Koret Health and Recreation Center, University Center, Cowell Hall, and Kalmanovitz Hall. Together with the solar panels already on Gleeson Library, the panels will produce about 16 percent of lower campus' peak electricity needs.

ADMISSIONS
Freshman Academic Profile: Average high school GPA 3.6. 29% in top 10% of high school class, 63% in top 25% of high school class, 92% in top 50% of high school class. 48% from public high schools. SAT Math middle 50% range 520-630. SAT Critical Reading middle 50% range 510-620. SAT Writing middle 50% range 520-630. ACT middle 50% range 23-27. Minimum web-based TOEFL 79. Minimum paper TOEFL 550. **Basis for Candidate Selection:** *Very important factors considered include:* academic GPA, recommendation(s), rigor of secondary school record, standardized test scores. *Important factors considered include:* Class rank, application essay. *Other factors considered include:* alumni/ae relation, character/personal qualities, extracurricular activities, interview, talent/ability, volunteer work. **Freshman Admission Requirements:** High school diploma is required and GED is accepted. **Freshman Admission Statistics:** 8,485 applied, 64% admitted, 19% enrolled. **Transfer Admission Requirements:** college transcript(s), essay or personal statement, Minimum college GPA of 2.5 required. Lowest grade transferable C. **General Admission Information:** Application Fee $55. Regular notification 4/1. Nonfall registration accepted. Admission may be deferred for a maximum of 1 semester. Credit offered for CEEB Advanced Placement tests.

COSTS AND FINANCIAL AID
Annual tuition $38,490. Room and board $12,640. Required fees $394. Average book expense $1,500. **Required Forms and Deadlines:** FAFSA. **Notification of Awards:** Applicants will be notified of awards on a rolling basis beginning 4/1. **Types of Aid:** *Need-based scholarships/grants:* Federal Pell, SEOG, state scholarships/grants, private scholarships, the school's own gift aid, Federal Nursing Scholarships. *Loans:* Direct Subsidized Stafford, Direct Unsubsidized Stafford, Direct PLUS, Subsidized Stafford, Unsubsidized Stafford, PLUS, Federal Perkins, Federal Nursing, college/university loans from institutional funds, Note: Loans are for Graduate students only. **Student Employment:** Federal Work-Study Program available. Institutional employment available. Highest amount earned per year from on-campus jobs $2,000. Off-campus job opportunities are excellent. **Financial Aid Statistics:** 95% freshmen, 92% undergrads receive need-based scholarship or grant aid. 73% freshmen, 31%

undergrads receive non-need-based scholarship or grant aid. 86% freshmen, 90% undergrads receive need-based self-help aid. 2% freshmen, 2% undergrads receive athletic scholarships. 63% undergrads receive any aid. 64% undergrads borrow to pay for school. Average cumulative indebtedness $26,886. **Criteria for awarding institutional aid:** *Non-need-based:* academics, athletics.

See page 1278.

UNIVERSITY OF SCIENCE & ARTS OF OKLAHOMA

1727 West Alabama, Chickasha, OK 73018
Phone: 405-574-1357 • **Financial Aid Phone:** 405-574-1240
E-mail: usao-admissions@usao.edu • **CEEB Code:** 6544
Fax: 405-574-1220 • **Website:** www.usao.edu • **ACT Code:** 3418

This public school was founded in 1908. It has a 75-acre campus.

RATINGS
Admissions Selectivity Rating: 87   **Fire Safety Rating:** 93   **Green Rating:** 60*

STUDENTS AND FACULTY
Enrollment: 947. **Student Body:** 65% female, 35% male, 8% out-of-state, 6% international (19 countries represented). Asian 1%, African American 4%, Caucasian 70%, Hispanic 5%, Native American 13%
Retention and Graduation: 28% freshmen graduate within 4 years. 41% freshmen graduate within 6 years. 15% grads go on to further study within 1 year. **Faculty:** Student/faculty ratio 13:1. 55 full-time faculty, 85% hold PhDs, 9% are members of minority groups, 40% are women. 0% of classes are taught by teaching assistants.

ACADEMICS
Degrees: bachelor's. **Classes:** Most classes have 10—19 students. Most lab/discussion sessions have 10—19 students. **Majors with Highest Enrollment:** business administration and management; elementary education and teaching; psychology. **Special Study Options:** Accelerated program, double major, dual enrollment, honors program, independent study, internships, student-designed major, study abroad, teacher certification program. **Disability Services:** Special programs offered to physically disabled students include note-taking services, tutors. **Career Services:** career/job search classes, career assessment, internships.

FACILITIES
Housing: Coed dorms, apartments for single students. 95% of campus accessible to physically disabled. **Special Academic Facilities/Equipment:** Language labs, speech and hearing clinic, multiple computer labs, herbarium **Computers:** 100% of classrooms, 85% of dorms, 100% of libraries, 100% of dining areas, 100% of student union, 100% of common outdoor areas have wireless network access.

CAMPUS LIFE
Environment: Village. **Activities:** Choral groups, concert band, drama/theater, jazz band, literary magazine, music ensembles, musical theater, pep band, student government, student newspaper, television station, Campus Ministries 24 registered organizations, 7 honor societies, 4 religious organizations. 1 fraternities, 1 sororities. **Athletics (Intercollegiate):** *Men:* baseball, basketball, cheerleading, soccer. *Women:* basketball, cheerleading, soccer, softball. **On-Campus Highlights:** Lawson Court, Nash Library, Student Center, Bill Smith Ballpark, Scooter's Grill.

ADMISSIONS
Freshman Academic Profile: Average high school GPA 3.4. 21% in top 10% of high school class, 55% in top 25% of high school class, 81% in top 50% of high school class. 90% from public high schools. SAT Math middle 50% range 410-540. SAT Critical Reading middle 50% range 850-1040. SAT Writing middle 50% range 430-520. ACT middle 50% range 20-25. Minimum web-based TOEFL 61. Minimum paper TOEFL 500. **Basis for Candidate Selection:** *Very important factors considered include:* Class rank, academic GPA, rigor of secondary school record, standardized test scores. *Important factors considered include:* talent/ability. *Other factors considered include:* recommendation(s), character/personal qualities. **Freshman Admission Requirements:** High school diploma is required and GED is accepted. *Academic units required:* 4 English, 3 mathematics, 3 science, (3 science labs), 2 social studies, 1 history, 2 academic electives. *Academic units recommended:* 4 English, 3 mathematics, 3 science, (3 science labs), 2 social studies, 1 history, 2 academic electives. **Freshman Admission Statistics:** 597 applied, 39% admitted, 81% enrolled. **Transfer Admission Requirements:** college transcript(s), Minimum college

GPA of 2.0 required. Lowest grade transferable D. **General Admission Information:** Application Fee $25. Regular application deadline 9/1. Notification on a rolling basis, beginning on or about 2/10. Nonfall registration accepted. Admission may be deferred for a maximum of NA. Credit offered for CEEB Advanced Placement tests.

COSTS AND FINANCIAL AID

Average book expense $1,200. **Required Forms and Deadlines:** FAFSA, institution's own financial aid form. **Notification of Awards:** Applicants will be notified of awards on a rolling basis beginning 3/15. **Types of Aid:** *Need-based scholarships/grants:* Federal Pell, SEOG, state scholarships/grants, private scholarships, the school's own gift aid. *Loans:* Subsidized Stafford, Unsubsidized Stafford, PLUS, Federal Perkins, college/university loans from institutional funds. **Student Employment:** Federal Work-Study Program available. Institutional employment available. Highest amount earned per year from on-campus jobs $8,600. Off-campus job opportunities are good. **Financial Aid Statistics:** 93% freshmen, 89% undergrads receive need-based scholarship or grant aid. 9% freshmen, 7% undergrads receive non-need-based scholarship or grant aid. 60% freshmen, 68% undergrads receive need-based self-help aid. 13% freshmen, 9% undergrads receive athletic scholarships. 93% freshmen, 89% undergrads receive any aid. 58% undergrads borrow to pay for school. Average cumulative indebtedness $18,378. **Criteria for awarding institutional aid:** *Non-need-based:* academics, art, athletics, leadership, music/drama, state/district residency.

UNIVERSITY OF THE SCIENCES
IN PHILADELPHIA

600 South 43rd Street, Philadelphia, PA 19104-4495
Phone: 215-596-8810 • **Financial Aid Phone:** 215)596-8894
E-mail: admit@usciences.edu • **CEEB Code:** 2663
Fax: 215-596-8821 • **ACT Code:** 3671

This private school was founded in 1821. It has a 35-acre campus.

RATINGS

Admissions Selectivity Rating: 88   **Fire Safety Rating:** 68   **Green Rating:** 61

STUDENTS AND FACULTY

Enrollment: 2,425. **Student Body:** 61% female, 39% male, 56% out-of-state, 2% international (38 countries represented). Asian 36%, African American 5%, Caucasian 46%, Hispanic 3%, Native American 0%
Retention and Graduation: 84% freshmen return for sophomore year. 65% freshmen graduate within 4 years. 74% freshmen graduate within 6 years.
Faculty: Student/faculty ratio 11:1. 187 full-time faculty, 83% hold PhDs, 17% are members of minority groups, 53% are women. 0% of classes are taught by teaching assistants.

ACADEMICS

Degrees: bachelor's, master's, post-bachelor's certificate, post-master's certificate. **Classes:** Most classes have 20—29 students. Most lab/discussion sessions have 20—29 students. **Majors with Highest Enrollment:** biology/biological sciences; pharmacy (pharmd [usa], pharmd or bs/bpharm [canada]); physical therapy/therapist. **Special Study Options:** distance learning, double major, English as a Second Language (ESL), honors program, internships, liberal arts/career combination, teacher certification program, academic remediation, advanced placement credit, learning disabilities services, off-campus study.
Honors Programs: The Honors Program at University of the Sciences offers exceptional students the opportunity for specialized, intensive learning experiences both inside and outside the classroom. As an honors student, you will take part in special honors classes and recitations. The workload for these classes is not harder than others at University of the Sciences, but different. For example you may do smaller, more advanced experiments in a lab course. You may tour historic sites for a history class, or meet with a visiting author in your writing class. You will work in smaller classes and have more independent and group projects. **Combined Degree Programs:** PharmD/MBA;BSHS/MOT;BSHS/MPT;BSHS/DPT. **Disability Services:** Special programs offered to physically disabled students include note-taking services, reader services, tape recorders, tutors. **Career Services:** alumni services, career/job search classes, career assessment, internships Career services highlights include USP Alumni Career Panels.

FACILITIES

Housing: Coed dorms, fraternity/sorority housing, apartments for single students, wellness housing, honor halls in certain dormitories, upper level floor for upper level students. 90% of campus accessible to physically disabled. **Special**

Academic Facilities/Equipment: Pharmacy museum, electron microscope. **Computers:** 80% of classrooms, 100% of dorms, 100% of libraries, 100% of dining areas, 40% of common outdoor areas have wireless network access. Students can register for classes online. Administrative functions (other than registration) can be performed online.

CAMPUS LIFE

Environment: Metropolis. **Activities:** Choral groups, concert band, dance, drama/theater, literary magazine, musical theater, student government, student newspaper, yearbook 66 registered organizations, 6 honor societies, 6 religious organizations. 2 fraternities, 2 sororities. **Athletics (Intercollegiate):** *Men:* baseball, basketball, cross-country, golf, riflery, tennis. *Women:* basketball, cross-country, golf, riflery, softball, tennis, volleyball. **On-Campus Highlights:** McNeil Science and Technology Center, Athletic Recreation Center, Wilson Hall, Marvin Sampson Museum, Griffith Hall, More than 80 state-of-the-art laboratories, including the Center for Advanced Pharmacy Studies (CAPS), the first laboratory of its kind at any college of pharmacy nationwide. In September 2003, USP opened a new 78,000-square-foot athletic/recreation center that provides exercise and practice space for varsity and intramural sports as well as general recreational facilities. The new building, part of a $30 million campus expansion and beautification project, contains a 3,500-square-foot, three-lane swimming pool; additional classrooms and faculty offices; and space for student organizations to meet and for students to gather informally. In August 2006, USP opened the McNeil Science and Technology Center, a three-story, 77,000-square-foot leading edge facility that reflects the University's commitment to its innovative curriculum. The Center's research laboratories and state-of-the-art-equipped support spaces will accommodate more undergraduate, graduate, post-doctoral, and faculty researchers in biology, microbiology, physics, and other scientific fields. The Center features a 400-seat auditorium, classrooms, computer workrooms and other flexible space that supports innovative teaching and learning through multi-media technology. The Center's two-story, light-filled commons provides a comfortable space for students to relax and study. **Environmental Initiatives:** All "On the Go" containers are fully recyclable. Five meal periods a week are trayless to conserve water and reduce chemical use. We have an Eco-Clam Shell program where a guest can purchase a re-usable fully recyclable clam shell and trade it in for a clean one at each meal period.

ADMISSIONS

Freshman Academic Profile: Average high school GPA 3.6. 46% in top 10% of high school class, 79% in top 25% of high school class, 97% in top 50% of high school class. SAT Math middle 50% range 560-660. SAT Critical Reading middle 50% range 520-600. SAT Writing middle 50% range 520-630. ACT middle 50% range 23-27. Minimum paper TOEFL 550. **Basis for Candidate Selection:** *Very important factors considered include:* Class rank, academic GPA, rigor of secondary school record, standardized test scores. *Important factors considered include:* character/personal qualities, level of applicant's interest. *Other factors considered include:* application essay, recommendation(s), alumni/ae relation, extracurricular activities, interview, talent/ability, volunteer work, work experience. **Freshman Admission Requirements:** High school diploma is required and GED is accepted. *Academic units required:* 4 English, 3 mathematics, 3 science, (3 science labs), 1 foreign language, 1 social studies, 1 history, 4 academic electives. *Academic units recommended:* 4 English, 3 mathematics, 3 science, (3 science labs), 1 foreign language, 1 social studies, 1 history, 4 academic electives. **Freshman Admission Statistics:** 4,307 applied, 56% admitted, 20% enrolled. **Transfer Admission Requirements:** college transcript(s), standardized test scores, Minimum college GPA of 3.0 required. Lowest grade transferable C. **General Admission Information:** Application Fee $45. Notification on a rolling basis, beginning on or about 10/1. Nonfall registration not accepted. Admission may be deferred for a maximum of 12 months. Credit offered for CEEB Advanced Placement tests.

COSTS AND FINANCIAL AID

Annual tuition $31,774. Room and board $13,054. Required fees $1,632. Average book expense $1,050. **Required Forms and Deadlines:** FAFSA. **Notification of Awards:** Applicants will be notified of awards on a rolling basis beginning 1/15. **Types of Aid:** *Need-based scholarships/grants:* Federal Pell, SEOG, state scholarships/grants, private scholarships, the school's own gift aid. *Loans:* Subsidized Stafford, Unsubsidized Stafford, PLUS, Federal Perkins, college/university loans from institutional funds. **Student Employment:** Federal Work-Study Program available. Institutional employment available. Highest amount earned per year from on-campus jobs $4,899. **Financial Aid Statistics:** 100% freshmen, 59% undergrads receive need-based scholarship or grant aid. 96% freshmen, 90% undergrads receive non-need-based scholarship or grant aid. 87% freshmen, 80% undergrads receive need-based self-help aid. 2% freshmen, 5% undergrads receive athletic scholarships. 100% freshmen, 89% undergrads receive any aid. 82% undergrads borrow to pay for school. Average cumulative indebtedness $10,620. **Criteria for awarding institutional aid:** *Non-need-based:* academics, athletics.

UNIVERSITY OF SCRANTON

Best 378

800 Linden Street, Scranton, PA 18510-4699
Phone: 570-941-7540 • **Financial Aid Phone:** 570-941-7700
E-mail: admissions@scranton.edu • **CEEB Code:** 2929
Fax: 570-941-5928 • **Website:** www.scranton.edu • **ACT Code:** 3736

This private school, affiliated with the Roman Catholic-Jesuit Church, was founded in 1888. It has a 50-acre campus.

RATINGS
Admissions Selectivity Rating: 82   **Fire Safety Rating:** 89   **Green Rating:** 67

STUDENTS AND FACULTY
Enrollment: 3,927. **Student Body:** 55% female, 45% male, 58% out-of-state, 0% international (17 countries represented). Asian 3%, African American 2%, Caucasian 81%, Hispanic 7%, Native American 0%
Retention and Graduation: 87% freshmen return for sophomore year. 76% freshmen graduate within 4 years. 84% freshmen graduate within 6 years. 39% grads go on to further study within 1 year. 15% grads pursue arts and sciences degrees. 2% grads pursue law degrees. 3% grads pursue business degrees. 8% grads pursue medical degrees. **Faculty:** Student/faculty ratio 15:1. 272 full-time faculty, 75% hold PhDs, 11% are members of minority groups, 42% are women. 0% of classes are taught by teaching assistants.

ACADEMICS
Degrees: associate, bachelor's, certificate, master's, post-bachelor's certificate, post-master's certificate. **Classes:** Most classes have 10—19 students. Most lab/discussion sessions have 10—19 students. **Majors with Highest Enrollment:** biology/biological sciences; elementary education and teaching; marketing/marketing management. **Special Study Options:** Accelerated program, cross-registration, distance learning, double major, dual enrollment, English as a Second Language (ESL), exchange student program (domestic), honors program, independent study, internships, study abroad, teacher certification program, Baccalaureate/masters degree program. **Combined Degree Programs:** BA/MA, BS/MA, MS/MHA, BS/MS, BS/MDA. **Disability Services:** Special programs offered to physically disabled students include note-taking services, reader services, tape recorders, tutors.

FACILITIES
Housing: Coed dorms, men's dorms, women's dorms, apartments for single students, theme housing. 100% of campus accessible to physically disabled. **Special Academic Facilities/Equipment:** Art gallery, fine arts facility, theatre, center for music groups, language lab, microbiology institute, electron microscope, greenhouse. **Computers:** 40% of classrooms, 100% of dorms, 100% of libraries, 100% of dining areas, 100% of student union, 90% of common outdoor areas have wireless network access. Students can register for classes online. Administrative functions (other than registration) can be performed online.

CAMPUS LIFE
Environment: City. **Activities:** Choral groups, concert band, dance, drama/theater, jazz band, literary magazine, music ensembles, radio station, student government, student newspaper, television station, yearbook, Campus Ministries, International Student Organization 50 registered organizations, 32 honor societies, 14 religious organizations. **Athletics (Intercollegiate):** *Men:* baseball, basketball, cross-country, golf, ice hockey, lacrosse, soccer, swimming, tennis, wrestling. *Women:* basketball, cross-country, field hockey, lacrosse, soccer, softball, swimming, tennis, volleyball. **On-Campus Highlights:** Brennan Hall (Home of the Kania School of Management), DeNaples Campus Center, The Harry and Jeanette Weiberg Memorial Library, The Murray Room (work-out facility). **Environmental Initiatives:** The ongoing infusion of sustainability across the curriculum:http://matrix.scranton.edu/sustainability/done-academics.shtml In addition we have a long standing and internationally known program/commitment to Green(sustainable) chemistry: http://academic.scranton.edu/faculty/CANNM1/greenchemistry.html Physical Plant http://matrix.scranton.edu/sustainability/done-plant.shtml Community Awareness: http://matrix.scranton.edu/sustainability/done-community.shtml Evetns on Campus include: Local Organic Foods Dinner; Sustainability Fair: Climate Change Lectures/Movies.

ADMISSIONS
Freshman Academic Profile: Average high school GPA 3.4. 29% in top 10% of high school class, 64% in top 25% of high school class, 92% in top 50% of high school class. SAT Math middle 50% range 530-620. SAT Critical Reading middle 50% range 510-600. ACT middle 50% range 22-26. Minimum web-based TOEFL 61. Minimum paper TOEFL 550. **Basis for Candidate**

Selection: *Very important factors considered include:* Class rank, academic GPA, rigor of secondary school record, standardized test scores. *Important factors considered include:* extracurricular activities. *Other factors considered include:* application essay, recommendation(s), alumni/ae relation, character/personal qualities, interview, level of applicant's interest, talent/ability, volunteer work, work experience. **Freshman Admission Requirements:** High school diploma is required and GED is accepted. *Academic units required:* 4 English, 3 mathematics, 3 science, (1 science labs), 2 foreign language, 2 social studies, 2 history, 4 academic electives. *Academic units recommended:* 4 English, 3 mathematics, 3 science, (1 science labs), 2 foreign language, 2 social studies, 2 history, 4 academic electives. **Freshman Admission Statistics:** 9,672 applied, 69% admitted, 15% enrolled. **Transfer Admission Requirements:** High school transcript, college transcript(s), Minimum college GPA of 2.75 required. Lowest grade transferable C. **General Admission Information:** Regular application deadline 3/1. Notification on a rolling basis, beginning on or about 12/15. Nonfall registration accepted. Admission may be deferred for a maximum of 12 MONTHS. Credit and/or placement offered for CEEB Advanced Placement tests.

COSTS AND FINANCIAL AID
Annual tuition $37,106. Room and board $12,804. Required fees $350. Average book expense $1,200. **Required Forms and Deadlines:** FAFSA. **Notification of Awards:** Applicants will be notified of awards on a rolling basis beginning 3/15. **Types of Aid:** *Need-based scholarships/grants:* Federal Pell, SEOG, state scholarships/grants, private scholarships, the school's own gift aid. *Loans:* Direct Subsidized Stafford, Direct Unsubsidized Stafford, Direct PLUS, Federal Perkins, Federal Nursing. **Student Employment:** Federal Work-Study Program available. Institutional employment available. Off-campus job opportunities are good. **Financial Aid Statistics:** 96% freshmen, 96% undergrads receive need-based scholarship or grant aid. 9% freshmen, 6% undergrads receive non-need based scholarship or grant aid. 84% freshmen, 89% undergrads receive need-based self-help aid. 90% freshmen, 89% undergrads receive any aid. 75% undergrads borrow to pay for school. Average cumulative indebtedness $34,260. **Criteria for awarding institutional aid:** *Non-need-based:* academics.

UNIVERSITY OF SOUTH ALABAMA

Meisler Hall, Room 2500, Mobile, AL 36688-0002
Phone: 251-460-6141 • **Financial Aid Phone:** 251-460-6231
E-mail: admiss@usouthal.edu • **CEEB Code:** 1880
Fax: 251-460-7876

This public school was founded in 1963. It has a 1215-acre campus.

RATINGS
Admissions Selectivity Rating: 67   **Fire Safety Rating:** 60*   **Green Rating:** 60*

STUDENTS AND FACULTY
Enrollment: 11,054. **Student Body:** 56% female, 44% male, 18% out-of-state, 4% international (87 countries represented). Asian 3%, African American 22%, Caucasian 64%, Hispanic 3%, Native American 1%
Retention and Graduation: 66% freshmen return for sophomore year. 14% freshmen graduate within 4 years. **Faculty:** Student/faculty ratio 21:1. 529 full-time faculty, 77% hold PhDs, 13% are members of minority groups, 49% are women.

ACADEMICS
Degrees: bachelor's, certificate, master's, post-bachelor's certificate, post-master's certificate. **Special Study Options:** Accelerated program, cooperative education program, distance learning, double major, dual enrollment, English as a Second Language (ESL), honors program, independent study, internships, student-designed major, study abroad, teacher certification program, weekend college. **Honors Programs:** Honor Program . **Disability Services:** Special programs offered to physically disabled students include note-taking services, reader services, tape recorders, tutors.

FACILITIES
Housing: Coed dorms, special housing for disabled students, men's dorms, women's dorms, fraternity/sorority housing, apartments for married students, apartments for single students. **Special Academic Facilities/Equipment:** Museum/gallery complex, three hospitals, center for clinical education in health programs, engineering labs. **Computers:** Students can register for classes online. Administrative functions (other than registration) can be performed online. Undergraduates are required to own a computer.

CAMPUS LIFE
Environment: City. **Activities:** Choral groups, concert band, dance, drama/theater, jazz band, literary magazine, marching band, music ensembles, musical

theater, opera, student government, student newspaper, student-run film society, symphony orchestra, television station, Campus Ministries 185 registered organizations, 2 honor societies, 1 religious organizations. 8 fraternities, 8 sororities. **Athletics (Intercollegiate):** *Men:* baseball, basketball, cross-country, football, golf, tennis, track/field (outdoor). *Women:* basketball, cross-country, golf, soccer, softball, tennis, track/field (outdoor), volleyball. **On-Campus Highlights:** Mitchell Center (arena), Stanky Field, John W. Laidlaw Performing Arts Center, Intramural Field Complex

ADMISSIONS

Freshman Academic Profile: 3.4. SAT Math middle 50% range 440-580. SAT Critical Reading middle 50% range 445-570. SAT Writing middle 50% range 440-555. ACT middle 50% range 20-25. Minimum web-based TOEFL 61. **Basis for Candidate Selection:** *Very important factors considered include:* rigor of secondary school record, standardized test scores. **Freshman Admission Requirements:** High school diploma is required and GED is accepted. **Freshman Admission Statistics:** 4,770 applied, 87% admitted, 47% enrolled. **Transfer Admission Requirements:** college transcript(s), Minimum college GPA of 2.0 required. Lowest grade transferable D. **General Admission Information:** Application Fee $35. Regular application deadline 9/10. Nonfall registration accepted. Admission may be deferred for a maximum of N/A. Credit and/or placement offered for CEEB Advanced Placement tests.

COSTS AND FINANCIAL AID

Annual in-state tuition $7,950. Annual out-of-state tuition $15,900. Room and board $7,150. Average book expense $1,200. **Required Forms and Deadlines:** FAFSA, institution's own financial aid form, state aid form. **Notification of Awards:** Applicants will be notified of awards on a rolling basis beginning 5/15. **Types of Aid:** *Need-based scholarships/grants:* Federal Pell, SEOG, state scholarships/grants, private scholarships, the school's own gift aid. *Loans:* Subsidized Stafford, Unsubsidized Stafford, PLUS, Federal Perkins, college/university loans from institutional funds. **Student Employment:** Federal Work-Study Program available. **Financial Aid Statistics:** 89% freshmen, 80% undergrads receive need-based scholarship or grant aid. 89% freshmen, 80% undergrads receive non-need-based scholarship or grant aid. 94% freshmen, 95% undergrads receive need-based self-help aid. 4% freshmen, 4% undergrads receive athletic scholarships. 82% freshmen, 61% undergrads receive any aid. **Criteria for awarding institutional aid:** *Non-need-based:* academics, alumni affiliation, art, athletics, minority status, music/drama.

UNIVERSITY OF SOUTH CAROLINA AIKEN

471 University Parkway, Aiken, SC 29801
Phone: 803-641-3366 • **Financial Aid Phone:** 803-641-3476
E-mail: admit@usca.edu • **CEEB Code:** 5840
Fax: 803-641-3727 • **Website:** web.usca.edu • **ACT Code:** 3879

This public school was founded in 1961. It has a 453-acre campus.

RATINGS

Admissions Selectivity Rating: 65   **Fire Safety Rating:** 88   **Green Rating:** 86

STUDENTS AND FACULTY

Enrollment: 2,876. **Student Body:** 64% female, 36% male, 10% out-of-state, 2% international (24 countries represented). Asian 1%, African American 28%, Caucasian 60%, Hispanic 4%, Native American 0%
Retention and Graduation: 21% freshmen graduate within 4 years. 43% freshmen graduate within 6 years. **Faculty:** Student/faculty ratio 16:1. 142 full-time faculty, 74% hold PhDs, 16% are members of minority groups, 46% are women. 0% of classes are taught by teaching assistants.

ACADEMICS

Degrees: bachelor's, master's. **Classes:** Most classes have 20—29 students. Most lab/discussion sessions have 20—29 students. **Majors with Highest Enrollment:** business/commerce; education; nursing/registered nurse (rn, asn, bsn, msn). **Special Study Options:** cooperative education program, distance learning, double major, dual enrollment, English as a Second Language (ESL), honors program, independent study, internships, student-designed major, study abroad, teacher certification program. **Honors Programs:** The USCA Honors Program is designed to increase the educational opportunities for the academically well qualified and highly motivated student. Designed in accordance with the principles of the National Collegiate Honors Council, the USC Aiken Honors Program provides an enriched academic experience, both in and out of the classroom, for outstanding students committed to reaching their highest potential as scholars and creative thinkers. For details on our Honors Program or the other high quality academic opportunities awaiting you at USC Aiken, please call on our Office of Admissions toll free at 888.WOW.USCA or locally at 803.641.3366. The Honors Director may be reached at 803.641.3226.

Disability Services

Disability Services: Special programs offered to physically disabled students include note-taking services, reader services, tape recorders. **Career Services:** Alumni network, alumni services, career/job search classes, career assessment, internships, regional alumni.

FACILITIES

Housing: Coed dorms, special housing for disabled students, apartments for single students, wellness housing, theme housing. 100% of campus accessible to physically disabled. **Special Academic Facilities/Equipment:** Ruth Patrick Science Education Center Etherredge Center (Fine Arts Center) Wellness Center Planetarium **Computers:** 100% of classrooms, 100% of dorms, 100% of libraries, 100% of dining areas, 100% of student union, 100% of common outdoor areas have wireless network access. Students can register for classes online. Administrative functions (other than registration) can be performed online.

CAMPUS LIFE

Environment: Town. **Activities:** concert band, dance, drama/theater, music ensembles, musical theater, pep band, student government, student newspaper, symphony orchestra, yearbook, Campus Ministries, International Student Organization 89 registered organizations, 12 honor societies, 7 religious organizations. 5 fraternities, 7 sororities. **Athletics (Intercollegiate):** *Men:* baseball, basketball, cheerleading, golf, soccer, tennis. *Women:* basketball, cheerleading, cross-country, soccer, softball, tennis, volleyball. **On-Campus Highlights:** DuPont Planetarium in the Ruth Patrick Science Education Center, The Etherredge Center for Visual and Performing Arts, The Wellness Center and Natatorium, The Alan B. Miller Nursing Building, Pacer Commons Student Housing, Roberto Hernandez Baseball Stadium USC Aiken Convocation Center. **Environmental Initiatives:** Obtain State Energy Department stimulus funding approval to "jump start' significant energy conservation actions with a goal of completion by 2012. The energy conservation projects will reduce each building's energy use (kWh) by 18% - reducing the carbon footprint from purchased electricity by at least 20%. Expand energy management system to include all main campus heating/cooling units and monitor energy usage continuously in 15 minute intervals using SCE&G usage monitoring software. The goal is to keep usage below 22 KW and significantly reduce the August/September KW peak for main campus by using load shedding and energy alert usage reduction campus-wide. Educate and involve students, faculty and staff in sustainability and carbon footprint reduction actions with training and planned USCA carbon footprint reduction web site. Continue to inform, challenge and involve everyone in carbon footprint reduction (ongoing).

ADMISSIONS

Freshman Academic Profile: Average high school GPA 3.6. 13% in top 10% of high school class, 41% in top 25% of high school class, 77% in top 50% of high school class. 91% from public high schools. SAT Math middle 50% range 440-540. SAT Critical Reading middle 50% range 430-540. SAT Writing middle 50% range 410-520. ACT middle 50% range 18-23. Minimum web-based TOEFL 80. Minimum paper TOEFL 550. **Basis for Candidate Selection:** *Very important factors considered include:* Class rank, academic GPA, rigor of secondary school record, standardized test scores. **Freshman Admission Requirements:** High school diploma is required and GED is accepted. *Academic units required:* 4 English, 4 mathematics, 3 science, (3 science labs), 2 foreign language, 2 social studies, 1 history, 4 academic electives, 1 1 elective must be PE or ROTC. *Academic units recommended:* 4 English, 4 mathematics, 3 science, (3 science labs), 2 foreign language, 2 social studies, 1 history, 4 academic electives, 1 1 elective must be PE or ROTC **Transfer Admission Requirements:** college transcript(s), statement of good standing from prior institution(s). Minimum college GPA of 2.0 required. Lowest grade transferable C. **General Admission Information:** Application Fee $45. Regular application deadline 8/1. Notification on a rolling basis, beginning on or about 9/1. Nonfall registration accepted. Credit and/or placement offered for CEEB Advanced Placement tests.

COSTS AND FINANCIAL AID

Annual in-state tuition $8,734. Annual out-of-state tuition $17,490. Room and board $6,780. Required fees $290. Average book expense $1,100. **Required Forms and Deadlines:** FAFSA. **Notification of Awards:** Applicants will be notified of awards on a rolling basis beginning 4/20. **Types of Aid:** *Need-based scholarships/grants:* Federal Pell, SEOG, state scholarships/grants, private scholarships, the school's own gift aid. *Loans:* Direct Subsidized Stafford, Direct Unsubsidized Stafford, Direct PLUS, Subsidized Stafford, Unsubsidized Stafford, PLUS, Federal Perkins, state loans. **Student Employment:** Federal Work-Study Program available. Institutional employment available. Off-campus job opportunities are fair. **Financial Aid Statistics:** 95% freshmen, 85% undergrads receive need-based scholarship or grant aid. 14% freshmen, 8% undergrads receive non-need-based scholarship or grant aid. 84% freshmen, 91% undergrads receive need-based self-help aid. 4% freshmen, 5% undergrads receive athletic scholarships. 75% freshmen, 70% undergrads receive any aid. 85% undergrads borrow to pay for school. Average cumulative indebtedness $22,677. **Criteria for awarding institutional aid:** *Non-need-based:* academics, alumni affiliation, art, athletics, leadership, minority status, music/drama, state/district residency.

UNIVERSITY OF SOUTH CAROLINA BEAUFORT

1 University Boulevard, Bluffton, SC 29909
Phone: 843-208-8000 • **Financial Aid Phone:** 843-521-3104
E-mail: admissions@uscb.edu • **CEEB Code:** 5845
Fax: 843-208-8290 • **Website:** www.uscb.edu • **ACT Code:** 3835

This public school was founded in 1959. It has a 213-acre campus.

RATINGS
Admissions Selectivity Rating: 61   **Fire Safety Rating:** 60*   **Green Rating:** 60*

STUDENTS AND FACULTY
Enrollment: 1,773. **Student Body:** 63% female, 37% male, 22% out-of-state, (14 countries represented).
Faculty: Student/faculty ratio 18:1. 59 full-time faculty, 76% hold PhDs, 15% are members of minority groups, 47% are women.

ACADEMICS
Degrees: associate, bachelor's, post-bachelor's certificate, transfer associate.
Classes: Most classes have 10—19 students. **Majors with Highest Enrollment:** business administration and management; psychology; social sciences.
Special Study Options: cooperative education program, cross-registration, distance learning, dual enrollment, independent study, internships, study abroad, teacher certification program, weekend college. **Disability Services:** Special programs offered to physically disabled students include note-taking services, reader services, tape recorders, tutors. **Career Services:** career/job search classes, internships.

FACILITIES
Housing: Coed dorms, special housing for disabled students, apartments for single students. **Computers:** Students can register for classes online. Administrative functions (other than registration) can be performed online.

CAMPUS LIFE
Environment: Village. **Activities:** Choral groups, drama/theater, literary magazine, musical theater, student government, student newspaper 11 registered organizations. **Athletics (Intercollegiate), Men:** baseball, cross-country, golf, track/field (outdoor). **On-Campus Highlights:** Sandbar Cafe, Campus Center Gym, Library.

ADMISSIONS
Freshman Academic Profile: Minimum paper TOEFL 550. **Basis for Candidate Selection:** *Very important factors considered include:* academic GPA, standardized test scores. *Important factors considered include:* Class rank, rigor of secondary school record. **Freshman Admission Requirements:** High school diploma is required and GED is accepted. *Academic units required:* 4 English, 3 mathematics, 3 science, (3 science labs), 2 foreign language, 2 social studies, 1 history, 4 academic electives, 1 physical education. *Academic units recommended:* 4 English, 3 mathematics, 3 science, (3 science labs), 2 foreign language, 2 social studies, 1 history, 4 academic electives, 1 physical education. **Transfer Admission Requirements:** college transcript(s), Minimum college GPA of 2.0 required. Lowest grade transferable C–. **General Admission Information:** Application Fee $40. Notification on a rolling basis, beginning on or about 2/1. Nonfall registration accepted. Credit offered for CEEB Advanced Placement tests.

COSTS AND FINANCIAL AID
Required Forms and Deadlines: FAFSA. **Notification of Awards:** Applicants will be notified of awards on a rolling basis beginning 5/31. **Types of Aid:** *Need-based scholarships/grants:* Federal Pell, SEOG, state scholarships/grants, private scholarships, the school's own gift aid. *Loans:* Subsidized Stafford, Unsubsidized Stafford, PLUS, state loans. **Student Employment: Financial Aid Statistics:** 35% freshmen, 65% undergrads receive any aid. **Criteria for awarding institutional aid:** *Non-need-based:* academics, state/district residency.

UNIVERSITY OF SOUTH CAROLINA COLUMBIA

Office of Undergraduate Admissions, Columbia, SC 29208
Phone: 803-777-7700 • **Financial Aid Phone:** 803-777-8134
E-mail: admissions-ugrad@sc.edu • **CEEB Code:** 5818
Fax: 803-777-0101 • **Website:** www.sc.edu • **ACT Code:** 3880

This public school was founded in 1801. It has a 384-acre campus.

RATINGS
Admissions Selectivity Rating: 88   **Fire Safety Rating:** 88   **Green Rating:** 98

STUDENTS AND FACULTY
Enrollment: 23,028. **Student Body:** 54% female, 46% male, 31% out-of-state, 1% international (115 countries represented). Asian 3%, African American 11%, Caucasian 78%, Hispanic 4%, Native American 0%
Retention and Graduation: 53% freshmen graduate within 4 years. 72% freshmen graduate within 6 years.

ACADEMICS
Degrees: associate, bachelor's, doctoral, master's, post-bachelor's certificate, post-master's certificate. **Classes:** Most classes have 20—29 students. Most lab/discussion sessions have 20—29 students. **Majors with Highest Enrollment:** experimental psychology; nursing/registered nurse (rn, asn, bsn, msn); sport and fitness administration/management. **Special Study Options:** Accelerated program, cooperative education program, cross-registration, distance learning, double major, dual enrollment, English as a Second Language (ESL), exchange student program (domestic), external degree program, honors program, independent study, internships, student-designed major, study abroad, teacher certification program, weekend college, Alternative Spring Break, Dobson Internship Program, Volunteer Service Program, International Program for Students, Undergraduate Research. **Honors Programs:** The Honors College is a small college of about 1,000 students, all of whom excel in academics. What makes the Honors College different is its ability to weave engaging, exciting course offerings into any undergraduate major. You choose your major and set up your course schedule just like any other student at the University. But your choices include classes especially for Honors College students over 100 courses each semester. **Combined Degree Programs:** BA/MEng. **Disability Services:** Special programs offered to physically disabled students include note-taking services, reader services, tape recorders. **Career Services:** alumni services, career/job search classes, career assessment, internships Career services highlights include Experiential learning through consulting with and assisting with startup of new businesses.

FACILITIES
Housing: Coed dorms, special housing for disabled students, men's dorms, special housing for international students, women's dorms, fraternity/sorority housing, apartments for married students, apartments for single students, wellness housing, honors housing (first year freshman and upperclass), Preston Residential College, Pre-Medical (first year and upperclass), Pre-Law, Engineering and Computing Community, Athletic, Greek, Teaching Fellows, Global, Green, Magellan Explorers, Capstone Scholars, Bridge Community, Journalism, Music, French House, Spanish Language, other Special Interest. 95% of campus accessible to physically disabled. **Special Academic Facilities/Equipment:** Art gallery, movie theater, McKissick Museum, South Caroliniana Library, Melton Observatory, Gibbes Planetarium, Melton Observatory, Filtration Research Engineering Demonstration Unit, Belser Arboretum, A.C. Moore Gardens. **Computers:** Students can register for classes online. Administrative functions (other than registration) can be performed online.

CAMPUS LIFE
Environment: City. **Activities:** Choral groups, concert band, dance, drama/theater, jazz band, literary magazine, marching band, music ensembles, musical theater, opera, pep band, radio station, student government, student newspaper, symphony orchestra 300 registered organizations, 25 honor societies, 32 religious organizations. 20 fraternities, 14 sororities. **Athletics (Intercollegiate):** *Men:* baseball, basketball, diving, football, golf, racquetball, soccer, softball, swimming, tennis, track/field (outdoor). *Women:* basketball, cross-country, diving, equestrian sports, golf, racquetball, soccer, softball, swimming, tennis, track/field (outdoor), volleyball. **On-Campus Highlights:** Strom Thurmond Wellness & Fitness Center, Russell House, Greek Village, Williams Brice Stadium, Historic Horseshoe. **Environmental Initiatives:** Sustainable Carolina represents all the sustainability efforts on campus and utilizes over 40 student interns to implement the campus sustainability plan. The program is based on

leadership development and allows students to apply sustainability practices on campus. Last year students put in nearly 20,000 hours working, learning and training on sustainability issues. Campus has committed to converting 100% of its fleet to alternative fuel vehicles by 2015, which will eliminate 2,000 tons of CO_2 emissions/year. The new Darla Moore School of Business is being designed as the largest net zero energy building in the country. Additionally, the campus efficiency upgrades have reduced energy and water consumption in over 2/3rds of the campus buildings. The campus energy consumption has been reduced by 33% and water consumption by 44% since 2004 producing upto $5 million/year in savings.

ADMISSIONS

Freshman Academic Profile: Average high school GPA 4.0. 30% in top 10% of high school class, 67% in top 25% of high school class, 94% in top 50% of high school class. SAT Math middle 50% range 560-650. SAT Critical Reading middle 50% range 540-640. ACT middle 50% range 24-29. Minimum web-based TOEFL 77. Minimum paper TOEFL 550. **Basis for Candidate Selection:** *Very important factors considered include:* academic GPA, rigor of secondary school record, standardized test scores. *Important factors considered include:* Class rank. *Other factors considered include:* application essay, recommendation(s), alumni/ae relation, character/personal qualities, extracurricular activities, first generation, racial/ethnic status, state residency, talent/ability, volunteer work, work experience. **Freshman Admission Requirements:** High school diploma is required and GED is accepted. *Academic units required:* 4 English, 4 mathematics, 3 science, (3 science labs), 2 foreign language, 2 social studies, 1 history, 1 academic electives, 2 PE or ROTC and fine arts. *Academic units recommended:* 4 English, 4 mathematics, 3 science, (3 science labs), 2 foreign language, 2 social studies, 1 history, 1 academic electives, 2 PE or ROTC and fine arts. **Freshman Admission Statistics:** 23,429 applied, 61% admitted, 33% enrolled. **Transfer Admission Requirements:** college transcript(s), Minimum college GPA of 2.25 required. Lowest grade transferable C–. **General Admission Information:** Application Fee $50. Regular application deadline 12/1. Notification on a rolling basis, beginning on or about 3/15. Nonfall registration accepted. Credit and/or placement offered for CEEB Advanced Placement tests.

COSTS AND FINANCIAL AID

Annual in-state tuition $10,088. Annual out-of-state tuition $27,244. Room and board $8,459. Required fees $400. Average book expense $978. **Required Forms and Deadlines:** FAFSA. **Notification of Awards:** Applicants will be notified of awards on a rolling basis beginning 1/4. **Types of Aid:** *Need-based scholarships/grants:* Federal Pell, SEOG, state scholarships/grants, private scholarships, the school's own gift aid, United Negro College Fund, Federal Nursing Scholarships., USC Opportunity Grant—Institutional Gamecock Guarantee. *Loans:* Subsidized Stafford, Unsubsidized Stafford, PLUS, Federal Perkins, Federal Nursing. **Student Employment:** Federal Work-Study Program available. Institutional employment available. Off-campus job opportunities are good. **Financial Aid Statistics:** 44% freshmen, 51% undergrads receive need-based scholarship or grant aid. 89% freshmen, 64% undergrads receive non-need-based scholarship or grant aid. 90% freshmen, 91% undergrads receive need-based self-help aid. 3% freshmen, 3% undergrads receive athletic scholarships. 96% freshmen, 87% undergrads receive any aid. 46% undergrads borrow to pay for school. Average cumulative indebtedness $25,022. **Criteria for awarding institutional aid:** *Non-need-based:* academics, alumni affiliation, art, athletics, job skills, leadership, minority status, music/drama, religious affiliation, state/district residency.

UNIVERSITY OF SOUTH CAROLINA UPSTATE

800 University Way, Spartanburg, SC 29303
Phone: 864-503-5246
E-mail: dstewart@uscs.edu • **CEEB Code:** 5850
Fax: 864-503-5727 • **Website:** www.uscs.edu • **ACT Code:** 3889

This public school was founded in 1967. It has a 298-acre campus.

RATINGS
Admissions Selectivity Rating: 83   **Fire Safety Rating:** 62   **Green Rating:** 60*

STUDENTS AND FACULTY
Enrollment: 4,237. **Student Body:** 65% female, 35% male, 7% out-of-state, 2% international (30 countries represented). Asian 3%, African American 26%, Caucasian 64%, Hispanic 1%, Native American 0%
Retention and Graduation: 67% freshmen return for sophomore year. 17% freshmen graduate within 4 years. 37% freshmen graduate within 6 years. 20% grads go on to further study within 1 year. **Faculty:** Student/faculty ratio 17:1. 179 full-time faculty, 79% hold PhDs, 54% are women. 0% of classes are taught by teaching assistants.

ACADEMICS

Degrees: associate, bachelor's, master's, terminal associate. **Classes:** Most classes have 20—29 students. Most lab/discussion sessions have 20—29 students. **Majors with Highest Enrollment:** business/commerce; education; nursing/registered nurse (rn, asn, bsn, msn). **Special Study Options:** Accelerated program, cross-registration, distance learning, double major, exchange student program (domestic), honors program, independent study, internships, student-designed major, study abroad, teacher certification program. **Disability Services:** Special programs offered to physically disabled students include note-taking services, reader services, tape recorders, tutors. **Career Services:** alumni services, career/job search classes, career assessment, internships.

FACILITIES

Housing: Coed dorms, apartments for single students. 100% of campus accessible to physically disabled. **Special Academic Facilities/Equipment:** Campus Life Center; performing arts building, including 450 seat theater; arts studies film theater; recital hall; language laboratory; Quality Institute. **Computers:** Students can register for classes online. Administrative functions (other than registration) can be performed online.

CAMPUS LIFE

Environment: Activities: Choral groups, dance, drama/theater, jazz band, literary magazine, music ensembles, musical theater, student government, student newspaper 61 registered organizations, 5 religious organizations. 2 fraternities, 3 sororities. **Athletics (Intercollegiate):** *Men:* baseball, basketball, cross-country, soccer, tennis. *Women:* basketball, cross-country, soccer, softball, tennis, volleyball. **On-Campus Highlights:** Campus Life Center, Aboretum.

ADMISSIONS

Freshman Academic Profile: Average high school GPA 3.4. 11% in top 10% of high school class, 37% in top 25% of high school class, 68% in top 50% of high school class. SAT Math middle 50% range 450-540. SAT Critical Reading middle 50% range 440-530. ACT middle 50% range 18-21. Minimum paper TOEFL 500. **Basis for Candidate Selection:** *Very important factors considered include:* rigor of secondary school record, standardized test scores. **Freshman Admission Requirements:** High school diploma is required and GED is accepted. *Academic units required:* 4 English, 3 mathematics, 3 science, (2 science labs), 2 foreign language, 2 social studies, 1 history, 4 academic electives, 1 physical education or rotc. *Academic units recommended:* 4 English, 3 mathematics, 3 science, (2 science labs), 2 foreign language, 2 social studies, 1 history, 4 academic electives, 1 physical education or rotc **Freshman Admission Statistics:** 1,904 applied, 49% admitted, 75% enrolled. **Transfer Admission Requirements:** college transcript(s), statement of good standing from prior institution(s). Minimum college GPA of 2.0 required. Lowest grade transferable C. **General Admission Information:** Application Fee $35. Notification on a rolling basis, beginning on or about 9/15. Nonfall registration accepted. Admission may be deferred for a maximum of 1 year. Credit offered for CEEB Advanced Placement tests.

COSTS AND FINANCIAL AID

Annual in-state tuition $5,310. Annual out-of-state tuition $10,936. Room and board $4,940. Required fees $226. Average book expense $700. **Required Forms and Deadlines:** FAFSAScholarship Application. **Notification of Awards: Types of Aid:** *Need-based scholarships/grants:* Federal Pell, SEOG, state scholarships/grants, private scholarships, the school's own gift aid, Non-need-based (college-administered): Academic merit Athletic State scholarships/grants ROTC scholarships. *Loans:* Subsidized Stafford, Unsubsidized Stafford, PLUS, Federal Perkins, Federal Nursing, state loans. **Student Employment:** Federal Work-Study Program available. Institutional employment available. Off-campus job opportunities are excellent. **Financial Aid Statistics:** 59% freshmen, 63% undergrads receive need-based scholarship or grant aid. 67% freshmen, 25% undergrads receive non-need-based scholarship or grant aid. 57% freshmen, 80% undergrads receive need-based self-help aid. 3% freshmen, 3% undergrads receive athletic scholarships. 64% undergrads borrow to pay for school. Average cumulative indebtedness $15,779. **Criteria for awarding institutional aid:** *Non-need-based:* academics, athletics, minority status, state/district residency.

THE UNIVERSITY OF SOUTH DAKOTA

414 East Clark, Vermillion, SD 57069
Phone: 605-677-5434 • **Financial Aid Phone:** 605-677-5446
E-mail: admissions@usd.edu • **CEEB Code:** 6881
Fax: 605-677-6323 • **Website:** www.usd.edu • **ACT Code:** 3928

This public school was founded in 1862. It has a 273-acre campus.

RATINGS
Admissions Selectivity Rating: 68   **Fire Safety Rating:** 93   **Green Rating:** 75

STUDENTS AND FACULTY
Enrollment: 6,424. **Student Body:** 63% female, 37% male, 32% out-of-state, 1% international (41 countries represented). Asian 1%, African American 2%, Caucasian 88%, Hispanic 3%, Native American 2%
Retention and Graduation: 75% freshmen return for sophomore year. 27% freshmen graduate within 4 years. 52% freshmen graduate within 6 years. 48% grads go on to further study within 1 year. 27% grads pursue arts and sciences degrees. 15% grads pursue law degrees. 9% grads pursue business degrees. 11% grads pursue medical degrees. **Faculty:** Student/faculty ratio 17:1. 436 full-time faculty, 85% hold PhDs, 14% are members of minority groups, 50% are women. 5% of classes are taught by teaching assistants.

ACADEMICS
Degrees: associate, bachelor's, certificate, doctoral, master's, post-bachelor's certificate, post-master's certificate, terminal associate. **Classes:** Most classes have 10—19 students. Most lab/discussion sessions have 20—29 students. **Majors with Highest Enrollment:** business/commerce; education; psychology. **Special Study Options:** Accelerated program, cross-registration, distance learning, double major, dual enrollment, English as a Second Language (ESL), exchange student program (domestic), external degree program, honors program, independent study, internships, liberal arts/career combination, student-designed major, study abroad, teacher certification program. **Honors Programs:** University Honors Program. The program has its own core curriculum that replaces the University's general education requirements. Thesis Scholars Program, Alumni Student Scholars Program, Law Honors Scholars Program **Combined Degree Programs:** BA/MA. **Disability Services:** Special programs offered to physically disabled students include note-taking services, reader services, tape recorders, tutors. **Career Services:** Alumni network, alumni services, career/job search classes, career assessment, internships Career Services highlights include USD, as the flagship liberal arts institution in the state, provides the framework for an extraordinary education and includes the Interdisciplinary Education & Action or "IdEA" Program. The U. has purposefully designed a contemporary liberal arts education that includes a solid foundation of knowledge, exposure to many different academic disciplines, immersion in interdisciplinary and diverse ways of thinkingt, and understanding of service and citizenship. All students at the U. follow a flexible course of study that first exposes them to great ideas, but ultimately challenges them to integrate their knowledge in ways that serve their own careers and other citizens. (http://catalog.usd.edu/content.php?catoid=3&navoid=34). The integration component of this education is found in the IdEA Program, which invites USD students to explore interdisciplinary approaches to questions that matter in a global, contemporary society. It occurs when juniors and seniors are experiencing the conclusion of their academic careers at USD and at a time when individuals are moving beyond their immediate and personal identities and defining their roles and responsibilities in a wider social, political, economic and physical environments. It provides key liberal learning outcomes such as critical thinking, integrative approaches and active citizenship.

FACILITIES
Housing: Coed dorms, special housing for disabled students, fraternity/sorority housing, apartments for married students, apartments for single students, Apartments for students with dependent children. Brand new state of the art apartment style housing currently under construction with a new wellness center being constructed due to open in 2010. 98% of campus accessible to physically disabled. **Special Academic Facilities/Equipment:** W.H. Over Museum, The National Music Museum, Oscar Howe Art Gallery, Center for Instructional Design and Delivery, Institute of American Indian Studies, Native American Cultural Center, Disaster Mental Health Institute, Neuharth Center for Excellence in Journalism, Missouri Rive Institute. **Computers:** 60% of classrooms, 100% of libraries, 100% of dining areas, 100% of student union, have wireless network access. Students can register for classes online. Administrative functions (other than registration) can be performed online.

CAMPUS LIFE
Environment: Village. **Activities:** Choral groups, concert band, dance, drama/theater, jazz band, literary magazine, marching band, music ensembles, musical theater, opera, pep band, radio station, student government, student newspaper, symphony orchestra, television station, Campus Ministries, International Student Organization 120 registered organizations, 6 honor societies, 6 religious organizations. 8 fraternities, 3 sororities. **Athletics (Intercollegiate):** *Men:* basketball, cross-country, diving, football, golf, swimming, track/field (outdoor), track/field (indoor). *Women:* basketball, cross-country, diving, golf, soccer, softball, swimming, tennis, track/field (outdoor), track/field (indoor), volleyball. **On-Campus Highlights:** Al Neuharth Media Center, The National Music Museum, The Dakota Dome, Belbus Student Service Center, Coyote Student Center,. **Environmental Initiatives:** Creation of the Sustainability Task Force for evaluation, monitoring and policy creation. Facility Management efforts to increase efficiency and decrease energy use. All new construction buildings comply with LEED Silver standards. Faculty, student and administration involvement in sustainability projects including recycling, climate commitment and public outreach.

ADMISSIONS
Freshman Academic Profile: Average high school GPA 3.4. 14% in top 10% of high school class, 33% in top 25% of high school class, 71% in top 50% of high school class. 75% from public high schools. SAT Math middle 50% range 460-620. SAT Critical Reading middle 50% range 460-610. SAT Writing middle 50% range 460-600. ACT middle 50% range 21-26. Minimum web-based TOEFL 81. Minimum paper TOEFL 550. **Basis for Candidate Selection:** *Very important factors considered include:* Class rank, academic GPA, rigor of secondary school record, standardized test scores. *Important factors considered include:* alumni/ae relation. *Other factors considered include:* application essay, recommendation(s), character/personal qualities, extracurricular activities, geographical residence, racial/ethnic status, state residency, talent/ability, volunteer work, work experience. **Freshman Admission Requirements:** High school diploma is required and GED is accepted. *Academic units required:* 4 English, 3 mathematics, 3 science, (3 science labs), 3 social studies, 1 fine arts. *Academic units recommended:* 4 English, 3 mathematics, 3 science, (3 science labs), 3 social studies, 1 fine arts. **Freshman Admission Statistics:** 3,443 applied, 89% admitted, 44% enrolled. **Transfer Admission Requirements:** High school transcript, college transcript(s), Minimum college GPA of 2.0 required. Lowest grade transferable D. **General Admission Information:** Application Fee $20. Notification on a rolling basis, beginning on or about 9/10. Nonfall registration accepted. Admission may be deferred for a maximum of One Semester. Credit and/or placement offered for CEEB Advanced Placement tests.

COSTS AND FINANCIAL AID
Annual in-state tuition $3,897. Annual out-of-state tuition $5,843. Room and board $6,648. Required fees $3,807. Average book expense $1,100. **Required Forms and Deadlines:** FAFSA. **Notification of Awards:** Applicants will be notified of awards on a rolling basis beginning 3/1. **Types of Aid:** *Need-based scholarships/grants:* Federal Pell, SEOG, private scholarships, the school's own gift aid, Federal Nursing Scholarships. *Loans:* Subsidized Stafford, Unsubsidized Stafford, PLUS, Federal Perkins, Federal Nursing, college/university loans from institutional funds. **Student Employment:** Federal Work-Study Program available. Institutional employment available. Highest amount earned per year from on-campus jobs $3,300. Off-campus job opportunities are good. **Financial Aid Statistics:** 48% freshmen, 53% undergrads receive need-based scholarship or grant aid. 84% freshmen, 56% undergrads receive non-need-based scholarship or grant aid. 94% freshmen, 95% undergrads receive need-based self-help aid. 8% freshmen, 6% undergrads receive athletic scholarships. 94% freshmen, 81% undergrads receive any aid. 75% undergrads borrow to pay for school. Average cumulative indebtedness $0. **Criteria for awarding institutional aid:** *Non-need-based:* academics, art, athletics, leadership, minority status, music/drama.

UNIVERSITY OF SOUTH FLORIDA

4202 East Fowler Avenue, Tampa, FL 33620-9951
Phone: 813-974-3350 • **Financial Aid Phone:** 813-974-4700
E-mail: admissions@admin.usf.edu • **CEEB Code:** 5828
Fax: 813-974-9689 • **Website:** www.usf.edu • **ACT Code:** 761

This public school was founded in 1956. It has a 1797-acre campus.

RATINGS
Admissions Selectivity Rating: 93   **Fire Safety Rating:** 81   **Green Rating:** 99

STUDENTS AND FACULTY
Enrollment: 29,232. **Student Body:** 56% female, 44% male, 4% out-of-state, 2% international (141 countries represented). Asian 6%, African American 12%, Caucasian 58%, Hispanic 18%, Native American 0%
Retention and Graduation: 89% freshmen return for sophomore year. 20% grads go on to further study within 1 year. **Faculty:** Student/faculty ratio 27:1. 1089 full-time faculty, 81% hold PhDs, 27% are members of minority groups, 43% are women. 17% of classes are taught by teaching assistants.

ACADEMICS
Degrees: associate, bachelor's, master's. **Classes:** Most classes have 20—29 students. Most lab/discussion sessions have 20—29 students. **Majors with Highest Enrollment:** biomedical sciences; business/commerce; psychology. **Special Study Options:** Accelerated program, cooperative education program, cross-registration, distance learning, double major, dual enrollment, exchange student program (domestic), honors program, internships, study abroad, teacher certification program, weekend college, Honors undergraduate research majors. **Honors Programs:** Honors College: http://honors.usf.edu/ **Combined Degree Programs:** BA/MD, BA/MA, BA/MEng. **Disability Services:** Special programs offered to physically disabled students include note-taking services, reader services, tutors. **Career Services:** alumni services, career/job search classes, career assessment, internships.

FACILITIES
Housing: Coed dorms, special housing for disabled students, men's dorms, special housing for international students, women's dorms, fraternity/sorority housing, apartments for married students, cooperative housing, apartments for single students, Grad students only; Medical students only. 100% of campus accessible to physically disabled. **Special Academic Facilities/Equipment:** Art museum and galleries, contemporary art museum, graphic studio, anthropology museum, fitness center, par course. **Computers:** 80% of classrooms, 35% of dorms, 100% of libraries, 50% of dining areas, 100% of student union, 50% of common outdoor areas have wireless network access. Students can register for classes online. Administrative functions (other than registration) can be performed online.

CAMPUS LIFE
Environment: Metropolis. **Activities:** Choral groups, concert band, dance, drama/theater, jazz band, literary magazine, marching band, music ensembles, musical theater, opera, pep band, radio station, student government, student newspaper, student-run film society, symphony orchestra, television station 507 registered organizations, 33 honor societies, 42 religious organizations. 16 fraternities, 22 sororities. **Athletics (Intercollegiate):** *Men:* baseball, basketball, cheerleading, cross-country, football, golf, sailing, soccer, tennis, track/field (outdoor), track/field (indoor). *Women:* basketball, cheerleading, cross-country, golf, sailing, soccer, softball, tennis, track/field (outdoor), track/field (indoor), volleyball. **On-Campus Highlights:** Marshall Center, The Tampa Campus Library, Contemporary Art Museum, Botanical Gardens, Sun Dome. **Environmental Initiatives:** USF's 2008 Going Green Tampa Bay sustainability EXPO which drew over 3,000 visitors Our USF Sustainability Initiative and 14 subcommittees. Our rapidly expanding Recycling program or Our Campus Transportation program or We have incorporated sustainability into our USF Strategic Plan

ADMISSIONS
Freshman Academic Profile: Average high school GPA 3.8. 32% in top 10% of high school class, 60% in top 25% of high school class, 73% in top 50% of high school class. 95% from public high schools. SAT Math middle 50% range 540-630. SAT Critical Reading middle 50% range 520-620. SAT Writing middle 50% range 500-600. ACT middle 50% range 23-27. Minimum paper TOEFL 550. **Basis for Candidate Selection:** *Very important factors considered include:* academic GPA, rigor of secondary school record. *Important factors considered include:* standardized test scores, first generation. *Other factors considered include:* Class rank, application essay, recommendation(s),

character/personal qualities, extracurricular activities, geographical residence, state residency, talent/ability, volunteer work, work experience. **Freshman Admission Requirements:** High school diploma is required and GED is accepted. *Academic units required:* 4 English, 4 mathematics, 3 science, (2 science labs), 2 foreign language, 3 social studies, 3 academic electives. *Academic units recommended:* 4 English, 4 mathematics, 3 science, (2 science labs), 2 foreign language, 3 social studies, 3 academic electives. **Freshman Admission Statistics:** 29,194 applied, 38% admitted, 30% enrolled. **Transfer Admission Requirements:** college transcript(s), statement of good standing from prior institution(s). Minimum college GPA of 2.3 required. Lowest grade transferable D. **General Admission Information:** Application Fee $30. Regular application deadline 4/15. Regular notification 4/15. Notification on a rolling basis, beginning on or about 10/1. Nonfall registration accepted. Credit and/or placement offered for CEEB Advanced Placement tests.

COSTS AND FINANCIAL AID
Annual in-state tuition $5,732. Annual out-of-state tuition $14,920. Room and board $9,032. Required fees $74. Average book expense $1,500. **Required Forms and Deadlines:** FAFSA. **Notification of Awards:** Applicants will be notified of awards on a rolling basis beginning 3/15. **Types of Aid:** *Need-based scholarships/grants:* Federal Pell, SEOG, state scholarships/grants, private scholarships, the school's own gift aid. *Loans:* Subsidized Stafford, Unsubsidized Stafford, PLUS, Federal Perkins, college/university loans from institutional funds. **Student Employment:** Federal Work-Study Program available. Institutional employment available. Off-campus job opportunities are good. **Financial Aid Statistics:** 65% freshmen, 13% undergrads receive need-based scholarship or grant aid. 95% freshmen, 5% undergrads receive non-need-based scholarship or grant aid. 56% freshmen, 65% undergrads receive need-based self-help aid. 1% freshmen, 1% undergrads receive athletic scholarships. 80% freshmen, 86% undergrads receive any aid. 55% undergrads borrow to pay for school. Average cumulative indebtedness $21,784. **Criteria for awarding institutional aid:** *Non-need-based:* academics, alumni affiliation, art, athletics, job skills, leadership, minority status, music/drama, religious affiliation, state/district residency.

UNIVERSITY OF SOUTHERN CALIFORNIA

Office of Admission/ John Hubbard Hall, Los Angeles, CA 90089-0911
Phone: 213-740-1111 • **Financial Aid Phone:** 213-740-1111
E-mail: admitusc@usc.edu • **CEEB Code:** 4852
Fax: 213-821-0200 • **Website:** www.usc.edu

This private school was founded in 1880. It has a 155-acre campus.

RATINGS
Admissions Selectivity Rating: 98   **Fire Safety Rating:** 94   **Green Rating:** 90

STUDENTS AND FACULTY
Enrollment: 17,994. **Student Body:** 51% female, 49% male, 32% out-of-state, 12% international (94 countries represented). Asian 23%, African American 4%, Caucasian 40%, Hispanic 13%, Native American 0%
Retention and Graduation: 97% freshmen return for sophomore year. 74% freshmen graduate within 4 years. 90% freshmen graduate within 6 years. **Faculty:** Student/faculty ratio 9:1. 1768 full-time faculty, 90% hold PhDs, 27% are members of minority groups, 36% are women. 0% of classes are taught by teaching assistants.

ACADEMICS
Degrees: bachelor's, doctoral, master's, post-bachelor's certificate, post-master's certificate. **Classes:** Most classes have 10—19 students. Most lab/discussion sessions have 20—29 students. **Majors with Highest Enrollment:** business administration and management; communication studies/speech communication and rhetoric; psychology. **Special Study Options:** cooperative education program, distance learning, double major, English as a Second Language (ESL), exchange student program (domestic), honors program, independent study, internships, liberal arts/career combination, student-designed major, study abroad, Learning communities, Thematic Option, Undergraduate Research, and Freshman Seminars. **Honors Programs:** Thematic Option Program Multimedia Scholarship **Combined Degree Programs:** BA/MD, BA/MA, BA/MEng, BS/MA, BS/MS. **Disability Services:** Special programs offered to physically disabled students include note-taking services, reader services, tape recorders, tutors. **Career Services:** Alumni network, alumni services, career assessment, internships, regional alumni. Career services highlights include

Joint Educational Project, a service learning program that provides an interface between USC and the local community.

FACILITIES

Housing: Coed dorms, special housing for disabled students, special housing for international students, fraternity/sorority housing, apartments for married students, apartments for single students, wellness housing, theme housing, special interest floors. 97% of campus accessible to physically disabled. **Special Academic Facilities/Equipment:** USC Fisher Museum of Art; Hancock Memorial Museum; specialized architecture and fine arts galleries, studios and labs; media labs; cinema scoring sound stage; recording studios; theatres and recital halls; exercise physiology lab; specialized engineering laboratories; biomedical imaging labs; Center for Electron Microscopy and Microanalysis; genomic research facilities; GIS research lab; USC Shoah Foundation Institute visual history archive; Archival Research Center; High-Performance Computing Center; public computing centers and labs; extensive wireless access to the USC network; classrooms outfitted with multiple webcams and microphones **Computers:** 15% of classrooms, 10% of dorms, 100% of libraries, 100% of dining areas, 100% of student union, 90% of common outdoor areas have wireless network access. Students can register for classes online. Administrative functions (other than registration) can be performed online.

CAMPUS LIFE

Environment: Metropolis. **Activities:** Choral groups, concert band, dance, drama/theater, jazz band, literary magazine, marching band, music ensembles, musical theater, opera, pep band, radio station, student government, student newspaper, student-run film society, symphony orchestra, television station, yearbook, Campus Ministries, International Student Organization, Model UN 676 registered organizations, 49 honor societies, 74 religious organizations. 41 fraternities, 23 sororities. **Athletics (Intercollegiate):** *Men:* baseball, basketball, diving, football, golf, swimming, tennis, track/field (outdoor), volleyball, water polo, *Women:* basketball, crew/rowing, cross-country, diving, golf, soccer, swimming, tennis, track/field (outdoor), volleyball, water polo. **On-Campus Highlights:** USC Fisher Museum of Art, Galen Center (event & training pavilion), Leavey Library (open 24 hours), Heritage Hall (athletic awards), Tutor Campus Center (opens fall 2010), USC's University Park campus '– located three miles south of downtown Los Angeles, adjacent to the museums and recreational facilities of historic Exposition Park '– is an urban oasis, offering a park-like atmosphere and rich architectural history. **Environmental Initiatives:** Energy Efficiency & Innovation. USC employs a full time Director of Energy Services to manage energy programs including lighting retrofits, equipment upgrades, and a recent retrofit of chillers, cooling towers, and pumps throughout the University, including a three million gallon centralized thermal energy storage tank installed below ground. The 3 million-gallon thermal energy water storage (TES) system was built 40 feet below ground. It is estimated that the new system conserves about 4,500 megawatt-hours of electricity a year by circulating chilled water to air conditioning systems throughout the University Park Campus, significantly expanding the capacity of the campus' existing chilled-water system while reducing utility use. The warmer water coming back through pipes has a chance to chill overnight before it is recirculated which allows USC to shift much of the kilowatt-hour usage to off-peak hours when electricity is more available. The entire system was conceived in 2001 and completed in 2005. Transportation Initiatives: USC counts on the services of a full time Rideshare Coordinator to ensure that transportation programs are available to all members of the University community. In 2006 USC achieved an Average Vehicle Ridership (AVR) of 1.69, exceeding the target of 1.50 established by the South Coast Air Quality Management District (SCAQMD). Seventeen strategies are used to achieve this AVR, most notably: a carpool/vanpool program; transit and parking charge subsidies; telecommuting; various incentives and raffles; availability of compressed work weeks; bicycle accessibility; and various support strategies like providing transit information and ridesharing assistance. There are five primary ride sharing options available to the USC community. Students, Staff, and Faculty are encouraged to ride the MTA Bus Lines, DASH Bus Lines, Metrolink Trains, or participate in carpools and vanpools. Eligible full time employees of USC who participate in the programs receive a subsidy of $30 as a benefit for not purchasing a parking pass. The subsidies provided to employees may be applied to the purchase of monthly passes for Metro (light rail or bus), LADOT, Metrolink, or other services not sold through the Transportation Office. In order to facilitate participation in the carpool program, employees are encouraged to participate in L.A. County's ridematch program to find potential carpool partners. The online database matches potential rideshare partners from the five county regions of Los Angeles, San Bernardino, Orange, Ventura, and Riverside. In addition, USC's Rideshare Office conducts an annual rideshare survey to generate a customized rideguide to match potential carpoolers in a given area. Trojan Transportation has three alternative fuel trams that run on biodiesel which provide service to off-campus housing, between campuses, and to Union Train Station. Recently purchased electric-powered, three-wheeled vehicles and bicycles are now used daily to patrol the campus by the Department of Public Safety. Eight of the three wheeled carts are used daily and offer a green alternative to gasoline powered patrol cars. In addition,

the Facilities Management Services organization counts on a fleet of electric and hybrid vehicles for campus use. Also of note, USC has partnered with Flexcar, a unique car-sharing service that offers members affordable hourly access to vehicles, thus reducing the need for vehicles on campus. The service is available to everyone in the USC community. Sustainability Steering Committee: The Sustainability Steering Committee's core intent is to help USC maintain its current needs without compromising the ability of future generations to do the same. Specific responsibilities of this oversight committee include: a. Benchmarking trends in institutional sustainability and identifying the best economic, social, environmental opportunities on which USC can act; b. Identifying USC's strengths and opportunities relative to advancing sustainability in the areas of campus operations, and community outreach; c. Communicating USC's sustainability initiatives and their benefits to the university community; and d. Making recommendations to the Senior Vice President of Administration detailing specific actions and resources required to best allow USC administrative functions to operationalize sustainable practices. The Sustainability Steering Committee consists of at least 12 voting members appointed by the Senior Vice President, Administration and General Counsel. Members are drawn from a group of senior level administrators, staff, students, and faculty representatives who are knowledgeable of and/or play a potentially large role in the area of sustainability. Sub-committees (such as the Operations Sustainability Steering Committee, which is overseen by the Sustainability Steering Committee) are used as needed to carry out individual initiatives. Committee created the sustainability program manager position to launch new program and has guided the recent establishment of the Sustainability Office. Beginning in 2009, USC's Sustainability Steering Committee set forth to develop a greenhouse gas emissions report that would establish a baseline for the university. This commitment was a significant milestone for the many students, faculty, and staff who have dedicated efforts to promote sustainability initiatives on campus. The completed report establishes USC's greenhouse gas emissions baseline for the years 2001 through 2009, accounting for emissions generated from USC's consumption of electricity, natural gas, refrigerants, and gasoline/diesel fuels. The report can be accessed, along with building-specific energy dashboards, on the USC Sustainability web page located at: http://green.usc.edu/ghg.

ADMISSIONS

Freshman Academic Profile: Average high school GPA 3.7. 56% from public high schools. SAT Math middle 50% range 650-760. SAT Critical Reading middle 50% range 620-720. SAT Writing middle 50% range 640-740. ACT middle 50% range 29-33. **Basis for Candidate Selection:** *Very important factors considered include:* application essay, academic GPA, recommendation(s), rigor of secondary school record, standardized test scores. *Important factors considered include:* extracurricular activities, talent/ability. *Other factors considered include:* Class rank, alumni/ae relation, character/personal qualities, first generation, interview, racial/ethnic status, volunteer work, work experience. **Freshman Admission Requirements:** High school diploma is required and GED is not accepted. *Academic units required:* 4 English, 3 mathematics, 2 science, (2 science labs), 2 foreign language, 2 social studies, 3 academic electives. *Academic units recommended:* 4 English, 3 mathematics, 2 science, (2 science labs), 2 foreign language, 2 social studies, 3 academic electives. **Freshman Admission Statistics:** 46,104 applied, 20% admitted, 49% enrolled. **Transfer Admission Requirements:** High school transcript, college transcript(s), essay or personal statement, Lowest grade transferable C–. **General Admission Information:** Application Fee $65. Regular application deadline 1/10. Regular notification 4/1. Nonfall registration accepted. Credit and/or placement offered for CEEB Advanced Placement tests.

COSTS AND FINANCIAL AID

Required **Forms and Deadlines:** FAFSA, CSS/Financial Aid PROFILEParent and student Federal Income Tax form with all schedules and W-2's. USC Non-filing Forms for those not required to file. **Notification of Awards:** Applicants will be notified of awards on a rolling basis beginning 3/15. **Types of Aid:** *Need-based scholarships/grants:* Federal Pell, SEOG, state scholarships/grants, private scholarships, the school's own gift aid. *Loans:* Subsidized Stafford, Unsubsidized Stafford, PLUS, Federal Perkins, "Credit Ready" and Credit Based loans. **Student Employment:** Federal Work-Study Program available. Institutional employment available. Off-campus job opportunities are excellent. **Financial Aid Statistics:** 87% freshmen, 89% undergrads receive need-based scholarship or grant aid. 62% freshmen, 45% undergrads receive non-need-based scholarship or grant aid. 91% freshmen, 94% undergrads receive need-based self-help aid. 3% freshmen, 2% undergrads receive athletic scholarships. 71% freshmen, 67% undergrads receive any aid. 45% undergrads borrow to pay for school. Average cumulative indebtedness $28,575. **Criteria for awarding institutional aid:** *Non-need-based:* academics, alumni affiliation, art, athletics, leadership, music/drama.

UNIVERSITY OF SOUTHERN INDIANA

8600 University Boulevard, Evansville, IN 47712
Phone: 812-464-1765 • **Financial Aid Phone:** 812-464-1767
E-mail: enroll@usi.edu • **CEEB Code:** 1335
Fax: 812-465-7154 • **Website:** www.usi.edu • **ACT Code:** 1207

This public school was founded in 1965. It has a 330-acre campus.

RATINGS
Admissions Selectivity Rating: 71   **Fire Safety Rating:** 70   **Green Rating:** 73

STUDENTS AND FACULTY
Enrollment: 9,322. **Student Body:** 60% female, 40% male, 12% out-of-state, 3% international (37 countries represented). Asian 1%, African American 5%, Caucasian 86%, Hispanic 1%, Native American 0%
Retention and Graduation: 67% freshmen return for sophomore year. 16% freshmen graduate within 4 years. 5% grads go on to further study within 1 year. 50% grads pursue arts and sciences degrees. 6% grads pursue law degrees. 9% grads pursue business degrees. 13% grads pursue medical degrees. **Faculty:** Student/faculty ratio 17:1. 332 full-time faculty, 67% hold PhDs, 13% are members of minority groups, 55% are women. 0% of classes are taught by teaching assistants.

ACADEMICS
Degrees: associate, bachelor's, certificate, master's, post-bachelor's certificate, terminal associate, transfer associate. **Classes:** Most classes have 20—29 students. Most lab/discussion sessions have 20—29 students. **Majors with Highest Enrollment:** business administration and management; elementary education and teaching; health/health care administration/management. **Special Study Options:** cooperative education program, distance learning, double major, dual enrollment, English as a Second Language (ESL), honors program, independent study, internships, study abroad, teacher certification program. **Combined Degree Programs:** RN/MSN. **Disability Services:** Special programs offered to physically disabled students include note-taking services, reader services, tape recorders, tutors. **Career Services:** Alumni network, alumni services, career/job search classes, career assessment, internships.

FACILITIES
Housing: Coed dorms, special housing for disabled students, fraternity/sorority housing, apartments for married students, apartments for single students, wellness housing, theme housing. 95% of campus accessible to physically disabled. **Computers:** 100% of classrooms, 100% of dorms, 100% of libraries, 100% of dining areas, 100% of student union, 100% of common outdoor areas have wireless network access. Students can register for classes online. Administrative functions (other than registration) can be performed online.

CAMPUS LIFE
Environment: City. **Activities:** Choral groups, dance, drama/theater, jazz band, literary magazine, pep band, radio station, student government, student newspaper, Campus Ministries, International Student Organization, Model UN 102 registered organizations, 6 honor societies, 7 religious organizations. 7 fraternities, 4 sororities. **Athletics (Intercollegiate):** *Men:* baseball, basketball, cross-country, golf, soccer, tennis, track/field (outdoor), track/field (indoor). *Women:* basketball, cross-country, golf, soccer, softball, tennis, track/field (outdoor), track/field (indoor), volleyball. **On-Campus Highlights:** Eagle's Nest, The Loft, Recreation and Fitness Center, Rice Library **Environmental Initiatives:** Established environmental stewardship committee Being more conscious of sustainable materials such as CFL lighting and reducing energy consumption Highlight starter program to recycle materials from new construction and renovation projects. To dovetail with our ongoing recycling of paper, cardboard, plastic, aluminum, and metals recycling.

ADMISSIONS
Freshman Academic Profile: Average high school GPA 3.2. 11% in top 10% of high school class, 25% in top 25% of high school class, 74% in top 50% of high school class. SAT Math middle 50% range 450-560. SAT Critical Reading middle 50% range 440-550. SAT Writing middle 50% range 420-530. ACT middle 50% range 19-24. Minimum web-based TOEFL 71. Minimum paper TOEFL 525. **Basis for Candidate Selection:** *Important factors considered include:* Class rank, academic GPA, standardized test scores. *Other factors considered include:* application essay, recommendation(s), rigor of secondary school record, alumni/ae relation, character/personal qualities, extracurricular activities, interview, talent/ability, work experience. **Freshman Admission Requirements:** High school diploma is required and GED is accepted. **Freshman Admission Statistics:** 6,279 applied, 72% admitted, 42% enrolled. **Transfer Admission Requirements:** High school transcript, college transcript(s), Minimum college GPA of 2.0 required. Lowest grade transferable C–. **General Admission Information:** Application Fee $25. Regular application deadline 8/15. Notification on a rolling basis, beginning on or about 7/1. Nonfall registra-

tion accepted. Credit and/or placement offered for CEEB Advanced Placement tests.

COSTS AND FINANCIAL AID
Annual in-state tuition $6,085. Annual out-of-state tuition $14,485. Room and board $7,498. Required fees $240. Average book expense $1,100. **Required Forms and Deadlines:** FAFSA, institution's own financial aid form. **Notification of Awards:** Applicants will be notified of awards on a rolling basis beginning 4/1. **Types of Aid:** *Need-based scholarships/grants:* Federal Pell; SEOG, state scholarships/grants, private scholarships, the school's own gift aid, Federal Nursing Scholarships. *Loans:* Direct Subsidized Stafford, Direct Unsubsidized Stafford, Direct PLUS. **Student Employment:** Federal Work-Study Program available. Institutional employment available. Off-campus job opportunities are good. **Financial Aid Statistics:** 77% freshmen, 24% undergrads receive need-based scholarship or grant aid. 7% freshmen, 5% undergrads receive non-need-based scholarship or grant aid. 90% freshmen, 91% undergrads receive need-based self-help aid. 1% freshmen, 1% undergrads receive athletic scholarships. 87% freshmen, 85% undergrads receive any aid. **Criteria for awarding institutional aid:** *Non-need-based:* academics, art, athletics, leadership, music/drama, state/district residency.

UNIVERSITY OF SOUTHERN MAINE

PO Box 9300, Portland, ME 4104
Phone: 207-780-5670 • **Financial Aid Phone:** 207-780-5250
E-mail: usmadm@usm.maine.edu • **CEEB Code:** 3691
Fax: 207-780-5640 • **Website:** www.usm.maine.edu • **ACT Code:** 1644

This public school was founded in 1878. It has a 144-acre campus.

RATINGS
Admissions Selectivity Rating: 68   **Fire Safety Rating:** 78   **Green Rating:** 70

STUDENTS AND FACULTY
Enrollment: 6,461. **Student Body:** 56% female, 44% male, 19% out-of-state, 1% international (19 countries represented). Asian 2%, African American 3%, Caucasian 81%, Hispanic 2%, Native American 1%
Retention and Graduation: 64% freshmen return for sophomore year. 10% freshmen graduate within 4 years. 31% freshmen graduate within 6 years. **Faculty:** Student/faculty ratio 15:1. 357 full-time faculty, 83% hold PhDs, 6% are members of minority groups, 45% are women. 0% of classes are taught by teaching assistants.

ACADEMICS
Degrees: bachelor's, certificate, master's, post-master's certificate. **Classes:** **Majors with Highest Enrollment:** perioperative/operating room and surgical nurse/nursing; psychology. **Special Study Options:** Accelerated program, cooperative education program, cross-registration, distance learning, double major, English as a Second Language (ESL), exchange student program (domestic), honors program, independent study, internships, liberal arts/career combination, student-designed major, study abroad, teacher certification program, weekend college, Preengineering program with University of Maine at Orono, living/learning scholars program, Greater Portland Alliance - cross registration with University of New England, St. Joseph's (Maine), Southern Maine Technical College, and Maine College of Art. **Honors Programs:** Russell Scholars - living/learning community, USM honors program . **Disability Services:** Special programs offered to physically disabled students include note-taking services, tape recorders, tutors. **Career Services:** career/job search classes, internships.

FACILITIES
Housing: Coed dorms, special housing for disabled students, fraternity/sorority housing, apartments for married students, apartments for single students, Fine Arts House, Russell Scholars (living/learning), Chemical Free Floor 24 Hour Quiet Floor, Community Living program. 100% of campus accessible to physically disabled. **Special Academic Facilities/Equipment:** Southworth Planetarium, Osher Map Collection and Smith Center for Cartographic Education, WMPG (radio station), GTV (cable t.v. station), Free Press (campus newspaper), various art galleries on all three campuses, and **Computers:** Students can register for classes online. Administrative functions (other than registration) can be performed online.

CAMPUS LIFE
Environment: Town. **Activities:** Choral groups, concert band, dance, drama/theater, jazz band, literary magazine, music ensembles, musical theater, opera, radio station, student government, student newspaper, symphony orchestra, television station, yearbook, International Student Organization 100 registered organizations, 2 honor societies, 3 religious organizations. 4 fraternities, 4

sororities. **Athletics (Intercollegiate):** *Men:* baseball, basketball, cheerleading, cross-country, golf, ice hockey, lacrosse, soccer, tennis, track/field (outdoor), track/field (indoor), wrestling. *Women:* basketball, cheerleading, cross-country, field hockey, golf, ice hockey, lacrosse, soccer, softball, tennis, track/field (outdoor), track/field (indoor), volleyball. **On-Campus Highlights:** Art Gallery, Costello Sports Complex, Russell Theater and Concert Hall, Southworth Planetarium, TV/Radio Station.

ADMISSIONS

Freshman Academic Profile: 3.0. 10% in top 10% of high school class, 33% in top 25% of high school class, 69% in top 50% of high school class. SAT Math middle 50% range 440-560. SAT Critical Reading middle 50% range 450-550. SAT Writing middle 50% range 440-540. ACT middle 50% range 20-25. Minimum web-based TOEFL 80. **Basis for Candidate Selection:** *Very important factors considered include:* Class rank, rigor of secondary school record, standardized test scores. *Important factors considered include:* application essay, recommendation(s). *Other factors considered include:* academic GPA, alumni/ae relation, character/personal qualities, extracurricular activities, geographical residence, interview, level of applicant's interest, racial/ethnic status, state residency, talent/ability, volunteer work, work experience. **Freshman Admission Requirements:** High school diploma is required and GED is accepted. *Academic units required:* 4 English, 3 mathematics, 2 science, (2 science labs), 2 foreign language, 2 social studies, 2 history. *Academic units recommended:* 4 English, 3 mathematics, 2 science, (2 science labs), 2 foreign language, 2 social studies, 2 history. **Freshman Admission Statistics:** 3,900 applied, 83% admitted, 27% enrolled. **Transfer Admission Requirements:** High school transcript, college transcript(s), essay or personal statement, Minimum college GPA of 2.0 required. Lowest grade transferable C–. **General Admission Information:** Application Fee $40. Notification on a rolling basis, beginning on or about 1/1. Nonfall registration accepted. Admission may be deferred for a maximum of 1 year. Credit and/or placement offered for CEEB Advanced Placement tests.

COSTS AND FINANCIAL AID

Annual in-state tuition $7,590. Annual out-of-state tuition $19,950. Room and board $9,130. Required fees $1,310. Average book expense $1,346. **Required Forms and Deadlines:** FAFSA. **Notification of Awards:** Applicants will be notified of awards on a rolling basis beginning 3/15. **Types of Aid:** *Need-based scholarships/grants:* Federal Pell, SEOG, state scholarships/grants, private scholarships, the school's own gift aid. *Loans:* Subsidized Stafford, Unsubsidized Stafford, PLUS, Federal Perkins, Federal Nursing, state loans. **Student Employment:** Federal Work-Study Program available. Off-campus job opportunities are excellent. **Financial Aid Statistics:** 76% freshmen, 74% undergrads receive need-based scholarship or grant aid. 49% freshmen, 28% undergrads receive non-need-based scholarship or grant aid. 95% freshmen, 95% undergrads receive need-based self-help aid. 88% undergrads borrow to pay for school. **Criteria for awarding institutional aid:** *Non-need-based:* academics, music/drama, state/district residency.

UNIVERSITY OF SOUTHERN MISSISSIPPI

118 College Drive #5166, Hattiesburg, MS 39406
Phone: 601-266-5000 • **Financial Aid Phone:** 601-266-4774
E-mail: admissions@usm.edu • **CEEB Code:** 1479
Fax: 601-266-5148 • **Website:** www.usm.edu • **ACT Code:** 2218

This public school was founded in 1910. It has a 1090-acre campus.

RATINGS
Admissions Selectivity Rating: 77   **Fire Safety Rating:** 78   **Green Rating:** 79

STUDENTS AND FACULTY
Enrollment: 13,460. **Student Body:** 62% female, 38% male, 12% out-of-state, 1% international. Asian 1%, African American 31%, Caucasian 59%, Hispanic 3%, Native American 0%.
Retention and Graduation: 75% freshmen return for sophomore year. 27% freshmen graduate within 4 years. 50% freshmen graduate within 6 years.
Faculty: Student/faculty ratio 18:1. 687 full-time faculty, 76% hold PhDs, 16% are members of minority groups, 48% are women.

ACADEMICS
Degrees: bachelor's, certificate, doctoral, master's, post-master's certificate.
Classes: Most classes have 10—19 students. Most lab/discussion sessions have 10—19 students. **Majors with Highest Enrollment:** elementary education and teaching; nursing/registered nurse (rn, asn, bsn, msn); psychology. **Special Study Options:** distance learning, double major, dual enrollment, honors program, independent study, internships, study abroad, teacher certification program. **Disability Services:** Special programs offered to physically disabled

students include note-taking services, reader services, tape recorders, tutors.
Career Services: alumni services, career/job search classes, career assessment, internships Career services highlights include Career Assesmen, Individualized counselors and 24/7 online career center.

FACILITIES
Housing: special housing for disabled students, men's dorms, women's dorms, fraternity/sorority housing, apartments for married students, theme housing.
Special Academic Facilities/Equipment: Museum of Art **Computers:** 100% of classrooms, 100% of dorms, 100% of libraries, 100% of dining areas, 100% of student union, 30% of common outdoor areas have wireless network access. Students can register for classes online. Administrative functions (other than registration) can be performed online.

CAMPUS LIFE
Environment: City. **Activities:** Choral groups, concert band, dance, drama/theater, jazz band, literary magazine, marching band, music ensembles, musical theater, opera, pep band, radio station, student government, student newspaper, student-run film society, symphony orchestra, yearbook, Campus Ministries, International Student Organization 8 honor societies, 20 religious organizations. 15 fraternities, 11 sororities. **Athletics (Intercollegiate):** *Men:* baseball, basketball, football, golf, tennis, track/field (outdoor), track/field (indoor). *Women:* basketball, cross-country, golf, soccer, softball, tennis, track/field (outdoor), track/field (indoor), volleyball. **On-Campus Highlights:** Starbucks, Thad Cochran Center, Barnes & Nobles Bookstore **Environmental Initiatives:** Recycling (12+ years) Energy Conservation LEED certification on new buildings. Pursuing use of green seal cleaning products and organic grounds maintenance.

ADMISSIONS
Freshman Academic Profile: Average high school GPA. 88% from public high schools. SAT Math middle 50% range 460-570. SAT Critical Reading middle 50% range 453-580. ACT middle 50% range 19-25. Minimum web-based TOEFL 71. Minimum paper TOEFL 525. **Basis for Candidate Selection:** *Very important factors considered include:* academic GPA, standardized test scores. *Other factors considered include:* Class rank. **Freshman Admission Requirements:** High school diploma is required and GED is accepted. *Academic units required:* 4 English, 3 mathematics, 3 science, 3 social studies, 2 academic electives. *Academic units recommended:* 4 English, 3 mathematics, 3 science, 3 social studies, 2 academic electives. **Freshman Admission Statistics:** 7,076 applied, 65% admitted, 42% enrolled. **Transfer Admission Requirements:** college transcript(s), statement of good standing from prior institution(s). Minimum college GPA of 2.0 required. Lowest grade transferable D. **General Admission Information:** Application Fee $35. Notification on a rolling basis, beginning on or about 9/1. Nonfall registration accepted. Credit and/or placement offered for CEEB Advanced Placement tests.

COSTS AND FINANCIAL AID
Required Forms and Deadlines: FAFSA, institution's own financial aid form. **Notification of Awards:** Applicants will be notified of awards on a rolling basis beginning 4/1. **Types of Aid:** *Need-based scholarships/grants:* Federal Pell, SEOG, state scholarships/grants, private scholarships, the school's own gift aid. *Loans:* Direct Subsidized Stafford, Direct Unsubsidized Stafford, Direct PLUS, Subsidized Stafford. **Student Employment:** Federal Work-Study Program available. Institutional employment available. Highest amount earned per year from on-campus jobs $3,668. Off-campus job opportunities are good. **Financial Aid Statistics:** 67% freshmen, 70% undergrads receive need-based scholarship or grant aid. 65% freshmen, 50% undergrads receive non-need-based scholarship or grant aid. 74% freshmen, 67% undergrads receive need-based self-help aid. 5% freshmen, 3% undergrads receive athletic scholarships. 62% freshmen, 63% undergrads receive any aid. 62% undergrads borrow to pay for school. Average cumulative indebtedness $29,502.

UNIVERSITY OF THE SOUTHWEST

6610 Lovington Highway, Hobbs, NM 88240
Phone: 505-392-6563 • **Financial Aid Phone:** 505-392-6561
E-mail: admissions@csw.edu • **CEEB Code:** 4116
Fax: 505-392-6006 • **Website:** www.csw.edu • **ACT Code:** 2633

This private school was founded in 1962. It has a 162-acre campus.

RATINGS
Admissions Selectivity Rating: 89   **Fire Safety Rating:** 77   **Green Rating:** 60*

STUDENTS AND FACULTY
Enrollment: 430. **Student Body:** 64% female, 36% male, 39% out-of-state, 1% international (12 countries represented). Asian 1%, African American 4%, Caucasian 52%, Hispanic 39%, Native American 2%

Retention and Graduation: 32% freshmen return for sophomore year. 10% freshmen graduate within 4 years. 29% freshmen graduate within 6 years. 30% grads go on to further study within 1 year. 30% grads pursue arts and sciences degrees. **Faculty:** Student/faculty ratio 11:1. 20 full-time faculty, 60% hold PhDs, 10% are members of minority groups, 45% are women. 0% of classes are taught by teaching assistants.

ACADEMICS

Degrees: bachelor's, master's. **Classes:** Most classes have fewer than 10 students. Most lab/discussion sessions have fewer than 10 students. **Majors with Highest Enrollment:** business/commerce; criminal justice/police science; elementary education and teaching. **Special Study Options:** distance learning, double major, internships, teacher certification program. **Disability Services:** Special programs offered to physically disabled students include tutors.

FACILITIES

Housing: men's dorms, women's dorms. 90% of campus accessible to physically disabled.

CAMPUS LIFE

Environment: Town. **Activities:** Choral groups, drama/theater, literary magazine, student government, student newspaper 3 honor societies, 1 religious organizations. **Athletics (Intercollegiate):** *Men:* baseball, cross-country, golf, rodeo, soccer, track/field (outdoor). *Women:* cross-country, golf, rodeo, soccer, softball, track/field (outdoor), volleyball. **On-Campus Highlights:** Residential Halls-East and West, Scarborough Memorial Library, Mabee Southwest Heritage Center, Jack Williams Baseball Field, Joan M. Tucker Center for Business Leadership, 6. The Mabee Teaching and Learning Center 7. Fadke Arts and Science Building 8. Bill Danies Campus Center.

ADMISSIONS

Freshman Academic Profile: Average high school GPA 3.1. 1% in top 10% of high school class, 16% in top 25% of high school class, 69% in top 50% of high school class. SAT Math middle 50% range 340-500. SAT Critical Reading middle 50% range 340-470. SAT Writing middle 50% range 330-460. ACT middle 50% range 14-20. Minimum paper TOEFL 550. **Basis for Candidate Selection:** *Very important factors considered include:* Class rank, academic GPA, standardized test scores. **Freshman Admission Requirements:** High school diploma is required and GED is accepted. **Freshman Admission Statistics:** 2,207 applied, 23% admitted, 10% enrolled. **Transfer Admission Requirements:** college transcript(s), Minimum college GPA of 2.0 required. Lowest grade transferable D. **General Admission Information:** Application Fee $25. Notification on a rolling basis, beginning on or about 10/5. Nonfall registration accepted. Credit offered for CEEB Advanced Placement tests.

COSTS AND FINANCIAL AID

Annual tuition $11,700. Room and board $5,400. Average book expense $800. **Required Forms and Deadlines:** FAFSA, institution's own financial aid form. **Notification of Awards:** Applicants will be notified of awards on or about 4/2. **Types of Aid:** *Need-based scholarships/grants:* Federal Pell, SEOG, state scholarships/grants, private scholarships, the school's own gift aid. *Loans:* Subsidized Stafford, Unsubsidized Stafford, PLUS. **Student Employment:** Highest amount earned per year from on-campus jobs $3,000. **Financial Aid Statistics:** 36% freshmen, 77% undergrads receive need-based scholarship or grant aid. 12% freshmen, 74% undergrads receive non-need-based scholarship or grant aid. 12% freshmen, 18% undergrads receive need-based self-help aid. 12% freshmen, 26% undergrads receive athletic scholarships. 75% freshmen, 77% undergrads receive any aid. 85% undergrads borrow to pay for school. Average cumulative indebtedness $12,420. **Criteria for awarding institutional aid:** *Non-need-based:* academics, athletics, job skills, leadership, music/drama, religious affiliation, state/district residency.

UNIVERSITY OF ST. FRANCIS

500 Wilcox Street, Joliet, IL 60435
Phone: 815-740-2270 • **Financial Aid Phone:** 866-890-8331
E-mail: admissions@stfrancis.edu • **CEEB Code:** 1130
Fax: 815-740-5078 • **Website:** www.stfrancis.edu • **ACT Code:** 1000

This private school, affiliated with the Roman Catholic Church, was founded in 1920. It has a 22-acre campus.

RATINGS

Admissions Selectivity Rating: 81   **Fire Safety Rating:** 86   **Green Rating:** 73

STUDENTS AND FACULTY

Enrollment: 1,412. **Student Body:** 68% female, 32% male, 6% out-of-state, 1% international. Asian 2%, African American 8%, Caucasian 72%, Hispanic 14%, Native American 0%

Retention and Graduation: 79% freshmen return for sophomore year. 34% freshmen graduate within 4 years. 56% freshmen graduate within 6 years. 20% grads go on to further study within 1 year. **Faculty:** Student/faculty ratio 12:1. 91 full-time faculty, 69% hold PhDs, 15% are members of minority groups, 58% are women. 0% of classes are taught by teaching assistants.

ACADEMICS

Degrees: bachelor's, master's, post-master's certificate. **Classes:** Most classes have 10—19 students. Most lab/discussion sessions have 10—19 students. **Majors with Highest Enrollment:** business administration and management; elementary education and teaching; nursing/registered nurse (rn, asn, bsn, msn). **Special Study Options:** cross-registration, distance learning, double major, honors program, independent study, internships, student-designed major, study abroad, teacher certification program. **Honors Programs:** Duns Scotus Fellow/Scholars Program is designed to create a learning community of motivated students who are challenged to excel academically. **Combined Degree Programs:** BBA/MBA. **Disability Services:** Special programs offered to physically disabled students include note-taking services, reader services, tape recorders, tutors. **Career Services:** Alumni network, alumni services, career/job search classes, career assessment, internships, regional alumni.

FACILITIES

Housing: Coed dorms, apartments for single students, wellness housing. 100% of campus accessible to physically disabled. **Special Academic Facilities/Equipment:** Rialto City Center Campus, new home of the Art & Design Department; Student Center/Bistro in the Motherhouse; Abbey in Marian Residence Hall; Moser Performing Arts Center **Computers:** 100% of classrooms, 100% of dorms, 100% of libraries, 100% of dining areas, 100% of student union, 100% of common outdoor areas have wireless network access. Students can register for classes online. Administrative functions (other than registration) can be performed online.

CAMPUS LIFE

Environment: City. **Activities:** Choral groups, dance, drama/theater, literary magazine, music ensembles, musical theater, opera, radio station, student government, student newspaper, symphony orchestra, television station, Campus Ministries, International Student Organization 29 registered organizations, 13 honor societies, 1 religious organizations. **Athletics (Intercollegiate):** *Men:* baseball, basketball, cross-country, football, golf, soccer, tennis, track/field (outdoor), track/field (indoor). *Women:* basketball, cheerleading, cross-country, golf, soccer, softball, tennis, track/field (outdoor), track/field (indoor), volleyball. **On-Campus Highlights:** Rialto City Center Campus, Student Center/Bistro in Motherhouse, Abbey (in Marian Residence Hall), Moser Performing Arts Center **Environmental Initiatives:** Campus-wide recycling Energy efficient lighting Water conservation.

ADMISSIONS

Freshman Academic Profile: Average high school GPA 3.4. 17% in top 10% of high school class, 50% in top 25% of high school class, 79% in top 50% of high school class. 86% from public high schools. SAT Math middle 50% range 440-560. SAT Critical Reading middle 50% range 410-520. SAT Writing middle 50% range 410-550. ACT middle 50% range 21-25. Minimum web-based TOEFL 79. Minimum paper TOEFL 550. **Basis for Candidate Selection:** *Very important factors considered include:* Class rank, academic GPA, rigor of secondary school record, standardized test scores. *Other factors considered include:* application essay, recommendation(s), interview. **Freshman Admission Requirements:** High school diploma is required and GED is accepted. *Academic units required:* 4 English, 3 mathematics, 2 science, (1 science labs), 2 social studies, 3 academic electives, 3 units from 2 areas: language, computer science, music, or art. *Academic units recommended:* 4 English, 3 mathematics, 2 science, (1 science labs), 2 social studies, 3 academic electives, 3 units from 2 areas: language, computer science, music, or art. **Freshman Admission Statistics:** 1,718 applied, 52% admitted, 25% enrolled. **Transfer Admission Requirements:** college transcript(s), statement of good standing from prior institution(s). Minimum college GPA of 2.5 required. **General Admission Information:** Application Fee $30. Regular application deadline 8/1. Notification on a rolling basis, beginning on or about 9/15. Nonfall registration accepted. Admission may be deferred for a maximum of 12 months. Credit and/or placement offered for CEEB Advanced Placement tests.

COSTS AND FINANCIAL AID

Annual tuition $26,374. Room and board $8,268. Required fees $450. Average book expense $800. **Required Forms and Deadlines:** FAFSA, institution's own financial aid form. **Notification of Awards:** Applicants will be notified of awards on a rolling basis beginning 2/15. **Types of Aid:** *Need-based scholarships/grants:* Federal Pell, SEOG, state scholarships/grants, private scholarships, the school's own gift aid, Federal Nursing Scholarships, Federal ACG and SMART funds. *Loans:* Direct Subsidized Stafford, Direct Unsubsidized Stafford, Direct PLUS, Federal Perkins. **Student Employment:** Federal Work-Study Program available. Institutional employment available. Highest amount earned per year from on-campus jobs $9,350. Off-campus job opportunities are good. **Financial Aid Statistics:** 66% freshmen, 73% undergrads receive need-based scholarship or grant aid. 95% freshmen, 96% undergrads receive non-need-based scholarship or grant aid. 74% freshmen, 80% undergrads receive need-based self-help aid. 5% undergrads receive athletic scholarships. 100% freshmen, 98% undergrads receive any aid. Average cumulative indebtedness $28,267. **Criteria for awarding institutional aid:** *Non-need-based:* academics, alumni affiliation, art, athletics, leadership, music/drama, religious affiliation, state/district residency.

UNIVERSITY OF ST. THOMAS

3800 Montrose Boulevard, Houston, TX 77006-4696
Phone: 713-525-3500 • **Financial Aid Phone:** 713-525-2151
E-mail: admissions@stthom.edu • **CEEB Code:** 6880
Fax: 713-525-3558 • **Website:** www.stthom.edu • **ACT Code:** 4238

This private school, affiliated with the Roman Catholic Church, was founded in 1947. It has a 20-acre campus.

RATINGS
Admissions Selectivity Rating: 73   **Fire Safety Rating:** 95   **Green Rating:** 61

STUDENTS AND FACULTY
Enrollment: 1,552. **Student Body:** 61% female, 39% male, 4% out-of-state, 8% international (58 countries represented). Asian 12%, African American 5%, Caucasian 34%, Hispanic 37%, Native American 0%
Retention and Graduation: 79% freshmen return for sophomore year, 32% freshmen graduate within 4 years. **Faculty:** Student/faculty ratio 11:1. 153 full-time faculty, 93% hold PhDs, 22% are members of minority groups, 39% are women. 0% of classes are taught by teaching assistants.

ACADEMICS
Degrees: bachelor's, diploma, master's. **Classes:** Most classes have 10—19 students. Most lab/discussion sessions have 10—19 students. **Majors with Highest Enrollment:** accounting; biology/biological sciences; psychology. **Special Study Options:** Accelerated program, distance learning, double major, dual enrollment, honors program, independent study, internships, liberal arts/career combination, student-designed major, study abroad, teacher certification program, weekend college. **Honors Programs:** The Honors Program at the University of St. Thomas is a four-year interdisciplinary program for students of exceptional intellectual ability, motivation, and curiosity. It is designed not simply to provoke students to master specific disciplines such as philosophy, history, mathematics, and natural science but to offer an experience which integrates, on the deepest and most profound level, the intellectual, cultural and spiritual foundations of a liberal arts education. **Combined Degree Programs:** BBA/MBA. **Disability Services:** Special programs offered to physically disabled students include note-taking services, reader services, tape recorders, tutors. **Career Services:** career/job search classes, career assessment, internships.

FACILITIES
Housing: Coed dorms, apartments for single students. **Special Academic Facilities/Equipment:** Learning and Writing Center, Chapel of St. Basil, Doherty Library **Computers:** 100% of classrooms, 100% of libraries, 100% of dining areas, 100% of common outdoor areas have wireless network access. Students can register for classes online. Administrative functions (other than registration) can be performed online.

CAMPUS LIFE
Environment: Metropolis. **Activities:** Choral groups, dance, drama/theater, jazz band, literary magazine, music ensembles, musical theater, student government, student newspaper, Campus Ministries, International Student Organization 69 registered organizations, 22 honor societies, 5 religious organizations. **Athletics (Intercollegiate):** *Men:* basketball, soccer. *Women:* volleyball. **On-Campus Highlights:** Jerabeck Activity and Athletic Center, Crooker Student Center, Chapel of St. Basil, The Lounge, Academic Mall. **Environmental Initiatives:** Campus Recycling of glass, aluminum, plastic & paper

ADMISSIONS
Freshman Academic Profile: Average high school GPA 3.6. 53% in top 10% of high school class, 60% in top 25% of high school class, 71% in top 50% of high school class. 75% from public high schools. SAT Math middle 50% range 520-630. SAT Critical Reading middle 50% range 500-608. SAT Writing middle 50% range 490-610. ACT middle 50% range 23-28. Minimum web-based TOEFL 79. Minimum paper TOEFL 550. **Basis for Candidate Selection:** *Very important factors considered include:* Class rank, application essay, academic GPA, rigor of secondary school record, standardized test scores. *Other factors considered include:* recommendation(s), character/personal qualities, extracurricular activities, interview, level of applicant's interest, talent/ability,

volunteer work, work experience. **Freshman Admission Requirements:** High school diploma is required and GED is accepted. *Academic units required:* 4 English, 3 mathematics, 3 science, (2 science labs), 2 foreign language, 2 social studies, 1 history, 3 electives in college preparatory classes. *Academic units recommended:* 4 English, 3 mathematics, 3 science, (2 science labs), 2 foreign language, 2 social studies, 1 history, 3 electives in college preparatory classes **Freshman Admission Statistics:** 863 applied, 80% admitted, 39% enrolled. **Transfer Admission Requirements:** college transcript(s), Minimum college GPA of 2.50 required. Lowest grade transferable C. **General Admission Information:** Application Fee $25. Regular application deadline 5/1. Notification on a rolling basis, beginning on or about 11/15. Nonfall registration accepted. Admission may be deferred for a maximum of 1 year. Credit and/or placement offered for CEEB Advanced Placement tests.

COSTS AND FINANCIAL AID
Annual tuition $26,550. Room and board $7,900. Required fees $340. Average book expense $1,078. **Required Forms and Deadlines:** FAFSA. **Notification of Awards:** Applicants will be notified of awards on a rolling basis beginning 3/22. **Types of Aid:** *Need-based scholarships/grants:* Federal Pell, SEOG, state scholarships/grants, private scholarships, the school's own gift aid, ACG Grant, SMART grant. *Loans:* Subsidized Stafford, Unsubsidized Stafford, PLUS, Federal Perkins, state loans. **Student Employment:** Federal Work-Study Program available. Off-campus job opportunities are excellent. **Financial Aid Statistics:** 99% freshmen, 98% undergrads receive need-based scholarship or grant aid. 12% freshmen, 10% undergrads receive non-need-based scholarship or grant aid. 62% freshmen, 66% undergrads receive need-based self-help aid. 2% freshmen, 2% undergrads receive athletic scholarships. 90% freshmen, 74% undergrads receive any aid. 58% undergrads borrow to pay for school. Average cumulative indebtedness $33,936. **Criteria for awarding institutional aid:** *Non-need-based:* academics, athletics.

THE UNIVERSITY OF TAMPA

401 West Kennedy Boulevard, Tampa, FL 33606-1490
Phone: 813-253-6211 • **Financial Aid Phone:** 813-253-6219
E-mail: admissions@ut.edu • **CEEB Code:** 5819
Fax: 813-258-7398 • **Website:** www.ut.edu • **ACT Code:** 762

This private school was founded in 1931. It has a 100-acre campus.

RATINGS
Admissions Selectivity Rating: 88   **Fire Safety Rating:** 90   **Green Rating:** 60*

STUDENTS AND FACULTY
Enrollment: 6,123. **Student Body:** 56% female, 44% male, 61% out-of-state, 10% international (114 countries represented). Asian 1%, African American 6%, Caucasian 61%, Hispanic 11%, Native American 0%
Retention and Graduation: 47% freshmen graduate within 4 years. 57% freshmen graduate within 6 years. 15% grads go on to further study within 1 year. 7% grads pursue arts and sciences degrees. 3% grads pursue law degrees. 7% grads pursue business degrees. 1% grads pursue medical degrees. **Faculty:** Student/faculty ratio 16:1. 270 full-time faculty, 89% hold PhDs, 14% are members of minority groups, 41% are women. 0% of classes are taught by teaching assistants.

ACADEMICS
Degrees: associate, bachelor's, certificate, master's, post-master's certificate. **Classes:** Most classes have 20—29 students. Most lab/discussion sessions have 10—19 students. **Majors with Highest Enrollment:** business administration and management; communication studies/speech communication and rhetoric; psychology. **Special Study Options:** double major, dual enrollment, exchange student program (domestic), honors program, independent study, internships, liberal arts/career combination, study abroad, teacher certification program, Certificate in International Studies program. **Honors Programs:** UT's Honors Program offers special classes that are developed to enhance creative thinking processes while meeting general distribution requirements. **Combined Degree Programs:** MSN-MBA; BS Chemistry-MBA; RN-MSN. **Disability Services:** Special programs offered to physically disabled students include note-taking services, reader services, tutors. **Career Services:** Alumni network, alumni services, career/job search classes, career assessment, internships Career services highlights include From their first day on campus, students are supported and involved. They are rewarded with an unlimited array of

opportunities that take them to the edge of their imaginations and beyond. All students have opportunities to balance "learning by thinking" with "learning by doing." Both in-class hands on projects and out-of-classroom learning activities help students integrate classroom theory with real world practices. Interactive learning activities such as case studies, behavioral and computer simulations, internships, performances, exhibitions, research, service learning, study abroad, etc., are offered across the curriculum.

FACILITIES

Housing: Coed dorms, special housing for disabled students, apartments for single students, theme housing. 100% of campus accessible to physically disabled. **Special Academic Facilities/Equipment:** Victorian art and furniture museum, theatres, studios, music center, language lab, fully equipped research vessel for marine science, H.B.Plant Museum, marine science research center on Tampa Bay. **Computers:** 50% of classrooms, 25% of dorms, 100% of libraries, 80% of dining areas, 100% of student union, 80% of common outdoor areas have wireless network access. Students can register for classes online. Administrative functions (other than registration) can be performed online.

CAMPUS LIFE

Environment: Metropolis. **Activities:** Choral groups, concert band, dance, drama/theater, jazz band, literary magazine, music ensembles, musical theater, pep band, radio station, student government, student newspaper, student-run film society, symphony orchestra, television station, yearbook, Campus Ministries, International Student Organization, Model UN 145 registered organizations, 13 honor societies, 8 religious organizations. 9 fraternities, 10 sororities. **Athletics (Intercollegiate):** *Men:* baseball, basketball, cross-country, golf, soccer, swimming. *Women:* basketball, crew/rowing, cross-country, soccer, softball, swimming, tennis, volleyball. **On-Campus Highlights:** Vaughn Student Center, Plant Hall, Stadium Center, Vaughn Center Courtyard, Martinez Sports Center.

ADMISSIONS

Freshman Academic Profile: Average high school GPA 3.3. 18% in top 10% of high school class, 46% in top 25% of high school class, 85% in top 50% of high school class. 73% from public high schools. SAT Math middle 50% range 500-590. SAT Critical Reading middle 50% range 480-570. SAT Writing middle 50% range 480-570. ACT middle 50% range 22-26. Minimum web-based TOEFL 79. Minimum paper TOEFL 550. **Basis for Candidate Selection:** *Very important factors considered include:* academic GPA, rigor of secondary school record, standardized test scores. *Important factors considered include:* application essay, recommendation(s), talent/ability. *Other factors considered include:* Class rank, alumni/ae relation, character/personal qualities, extracurricular activities, first generation, interview, level of applicant's interest, volunteer work, work experience. **Freshman Admission Requirements:** High school diploma is required and GED is accepted. *Academic units required:* 4 English, 3 mathematics, 3 science, (2 science labs), 2 foreign language, 3 social studies, 3 academic electives. *Academic units recommended:* 4 English, 3 mathematics, 3 science, (2 science labs), 2 foreign language, 3 social studies, 3 academic electives. **Freshman Admission Statistics:** 14,704 applied, 47% admitted, 22% enrolled. **Transfer Admission Requirements:** college transcript(s), Minimum college GPA of 2.2 required. Lowest grade transferable C. **General Admission Information:** Application Fee $40. Notification on a rolling basis, beginning on or about 10/1. Nonfall registration accepted. Admission may be deferred for a maximum of 1 term. Credit and/or placement offered for CEEB Advanced Placement tests.

COSTS AND FINANCIAL AID

Annual tuition $23,520. Room and board $9,116. Required fees $1,702. Average book expense $1,050. **Required Forms and Deadlines:** FAFSA, state aid form. **Notification of Awards:** Applicants will be notified of awards on a rolling basis beginning 2/1. **Types of Aid:** *Need-based scholarships/grants:* Federal Pell, SEOG, state scholarships/grants, private scholarships, the school's own gift aid. *Loans:* Subsidized Stafford, Unsubsidized Stafford, PLUS, Federal Perkins, college/university loans from institutional funds. **Student Employment:** Federal Work-Study Program available. Institutional employment available. Off-campus job opportunities are fair. **Financial Aid Statistics:** 78% freshmen, 71% undergrads receive need-based scholarship or grant aid. 99% freshmen, 98% undergrads receive non-need-based scholarship or grant aid. 89% freshmen, 85% undergrads receive need-based self-help aid. 3% freshmen, 4% undergrads receive athletic scholarships. 93% freshmen, 90% undergrads receive any aid. 5% undergrads borrow to pay for school. Average cumulative indebtedness $30,338. **Criteria for awarding institutional aid:** *Non-need-based:* academics, alumni affiliation, art, athletics, leadership, music/drama, state/district residency.

See page 1280.

THE UNIVERSITY OF TENNESSEE AT CHATTANOOGA

615 McCallie Avenue, Chattanooga, TN 37403
Phone: 423-425-4662 • **Financial Aid Phone:** 423-425-4677
E-mail: Yancy-Freeman@utc.edu • **CEEB Code:** 1831
Fax: 423-425-4157 • **Website:** www.utc.edu • **ACT Code:** 4022

This public school was founded in 1886. It has a 120-acre campus.

RATINGS

Admissions Selectivity Rating: 71   **Fire Safety Rating:** 77   **Green Rating:** 80

STUDENTS AND FACULTY

Enrollment: 10,015. **Student Body:** 55% female, 45% male, 6% out-of-state, 1% international (50 countries represented). Asian 2%, African American 12%, Caucasian 74%, Hispanic 3%, Native American 0%
Retention and Graduation: 67% freshmen return for sophomore year. 13% freshmen graduate within 4 years. 36% grads go on to further study within 1 year. **Faculty:** Student/faculty ratio 18:1. 438 full-time faculty, 71% hold PhDs, 14% are members of minority groups, 46% are women. 5% of classes are taught by teaching assistants.

ACADEMICS

Degrees: bachelor's, certificate, master's, post-bachelor's certificate, post-master's certificate. **Classes:** Most classes have 20—29 students. Most lab/discussion sessions have 20—29 students. **Majors with Highest Enrollment:** business administration and management; kinesiology and exercise science; psychology. **Special Study Options:** cooperative education program, cross-registration, distance learning, double major, dual enrollment, English as a Second Language (ESL), honors program, independent study, internships, study abroad, teacher certification program. **Honors Programs:** The University Honors curriculum is a 37-hour sequence of specially designed and enhanced seminar courses in the humanities, the fine arts, cultural perspectives, the history of science, and the social sciences, culminating in a senior-year departmental honors project. These seminars fulfill all of the student's general education course requirements except mathematics and laboratory science. http://www.utc.edu/Academic/UniversityHonors/ . **Disability Services:** Special programs offered to physically disabled students include note-taking services, reader services, tape recorders, tutors. **Career Services:** Alumni network, alumni services, internships.

FACILITIES

Housing: Coed dorms, fraternity/sorority housing, apartments for married students, apartments for single students. 95% of campus accessible to physically disabled. **Special Academic Facilities/Equipment:** Walker Teaching Resource Center; Jones Observatory; Institute of Archaeology; Odor Research Center; SIM Center; Challenger Center; Center for Applied Social Research; The Ochs Center for Metropolitan Studies. **Computers:** 90% of classrooms, 100% of libraries, 100% of dining areas, 100% of student union, 60% of common outdoor areas have wireless network access. Students can register for classes online. Administrative functions (other than registration) can be performed online.

CAMPUS LIFE

Environment: City. **Activities:** Choral groups, concert band, dance, drama/theater, jazz band, literary magazine, marching band, music ensembles, opera, pep band, radio station, student government, student newspaper, student-run film society, symphony orchestra, television station, Campus Ministries, International Student Organization, Model UN 130 registered organizations, 34 honor societies, 8 religious organizations. 7 fraternities, 7 sororities. **Athletics (Intercollegiate):** *Men:* basketball, cross-country, football, golf, tennis, track/field (outdoor), wrestling. *Women:* basketball, cross-country, golf, soccer, softball, tennis, track/field (outdoor), volleyball. **On-Campus Highlights:** Challenger Center, University Center, The Aquatic and Recreation Center (ARC), The Crossroads **Environmental Initiatives:** Recycling Energy conservation LEED Certified Building Design (new UTC Library)

ADMISSIONS

Freshman Academic Profile: Average high school GPA 3.4. 43% in top 25% of high school class, 85% in top 50% of high school class. 75% from public high schools. SAT Math middle 50% range 450-580. SAT Critical Reading middle 50% range 450-570. ACT middle 50% range 21-25. Minimum web-based TOEFL 61. Minimum paper TOEFL 500. **Basis for Candidate Selection:** *Very important factors considered include:* academic GPA, rigor of secondary school record, standardized test scores. *Important factors considered include:* character/personal qualities. *Other factors considered include:* application essay, recommendation(s), extracurricular activities, talent/ability, volunteer work, work experience. **Freshman Admission Requirements:** High school diploma is required and GED is accepted. *Academic units required:* 4 English, 3 mathematics, 2 science, (2 science labs), 2 foreign language, 1 social studies, 1 history, 1 visual/performing arts. *Academic units recommended:* 4 English, 3 mathematics, 2 science, (2 science labs), 2 foreign language, 1 social studies, 1 history, 1 visual/performing arts. **Freshman Admission Statistics:** 7,677 applied, 76% admitted, 39% enrolled. **Transfer Admission Requirements:** college transcript(s), Minimum college GPA of 2.0 required. Lowest grade transferable D. **General Admission Information:** Application Fee $30. Regular application deadline 8/1. Nonfall registration accepted. Admission may be deferred for a maximum of 1 semester. Credit and/or placement offered for CEEB Advanced Placement tests.

COSTS AND FINANCIAL AID

Annual in-state tuition $5,722. Annual out-of-state tuition $20,068. Room and board $8,300. Required fees $1,490. Average book expense $1,400. **Required Forms and Deadlines:** FAFSA, institution's own financial aid form. **Notification of Awards:** Applicants will be notified of awards on a rolling basis beginning 3/1. **Types of Aid:** *Need-based scholarships/grants:* Federal Pell, SEOG, state scholarships/grants, private scholarships, the school's own gift aid, United Negro College Fund. *Loans:* Subsidized Stafford, Unsubsidized Stafford, PLUS, Federal Perkins, college/university loans from institutional funds. **Student Employment:** Federal Work-Study Program available. Institutional employment available. Highest amount earned per year from on-campus jobs $19,500. Off-campus job opportunities are good. **Financial Aid Statistics:** 59% freshmen, 55% undergrads receive any aid. **Criteria for awarding institutional aid:** *Non-need-based:* academics, alumni affiliation, art, athletics, job skills, leadership, minority status, music/drama, religious affiliation, state/district residency.

THE UNIVERSITY OF TENNESSEE AT KNOXVILLE

Best 378

320 Student Service Building, Knoxville, TN 37996-0230
Phone: 865-974-2184 • **Financial Aid Phone:** 865-974-3131
E-mail: admissions@utk.edu • **CEEB Code:** 1843
Website: www.utk.edu • **ACT Code:** 4026

This public school was founded in 1794. It has a 520-acre campus.

RATINGS

Admissions Selectivity Rating: 89   **Fire Safety Rating:** 87   **Green Rating:** 83

STUDENTS AND FACULTY

Enrollment: 20,963. **Student Body:** 49% female, 51% male, 9% out-of-state, 1% international (82 countries represented). Asian 3%, African American 7%, Caucasian 82%, Hispanic 3%, Native American 0%
Retention and Graduation: 34% freshmen graduate within 4 years. 63% freshmen graduate within 6 years. **Faculty:** Student/faculty ratio 15:1. 1641 full-time faculty, 85% hold PhDs, 16% are members of minority groups, 41% are women.

ACADEMICS

Degrees: bachelor's, doctoral, master's, post-master's certificate. **Classes:** Most classes have 20—29 students. Most lab/discussion sessions have 20—29 students. **Majors with Highest Enrollment:** business administration and management; journalism; psychology. **Special Study Options:** Accelerated program, cooperative education program, cross-registration, distance learning, double major, dual enrollment, English as a Second Language (ESL), exchange student program (domestic), external degree program, honors program, independent study, internships, liberal arts/career combination, student-designed major, study abroad, teacher certification program. **Honors Programs:** 1. Chancellor's Honors Program 2. Haslam Scholars Program 3. College Scholars Program 4. Global Leadership Scholars Program 5. College of Engineering Honors Program 6. College of Agricultural and Natural Resources Honors Program 7. College of Social Work Honors Program 8. Howard H. Baker Jr. Center for Public Policy's Baker Scholars Program 9. The Math Honors Program 10. Additional departmental Honors Programs. **Combined Degree Programs:** JD/MBA, JD/MPA. **Disability Services:** Special programs offered to physically disabled students include note-taking services, reader services, tape recorders, tutors. **Career Services:** Alumni network, alumni services, career/job search classes, career assessment, internships Career services highlights include Office of Professional Practice in Engineering's Cooperative Education Program.

This program matches students with employers to ensure a real world work experience that significantly enhances the students chances for quality work opportunities at graduation. Approximately 250 students participate in this program annually.

FACILITIES

Housing: Coed dorms, special housing for disabled students, men's dorms, special housing for international students, women's dorms, fraternity/sorority housing, apartments for married students, apartments for single students, theme housing, transfer student floors. 95% of campus accessible to physically disabled. **Special Academic Facilities/Equipment:** Comprehensive museum of anthropology, archaeology, art, geology, natural history, and medicine, theatre-in-the-round, livestock farms, robotics research center, electron microscope, McClung Museum **Computers:** 100% of classrooms, 100% of dorms, 100% of libraries, 100% of dining areas, 100% of student union, 25% of common outdoor areas have wireless network access. Students can register for classes online.

CAMPUS LIFE

Environment: City. **Activities:** Choral groups, concert band, dance, drama/theater, jazz band, literary magazine, marching band, music ensembles, musical theater, opera, pep band, radio station, student government, student newspaper, student-run film society, symphony orchestra, television station, yearbook, Campus Ministries, International Student Organization, Model UN 450 registered organizations, 90 honor societies, 30 religious organizations. 23 fraternities, 18 sororities. **Athletics (Intercollegiate):** *Men:* baseball, basketball, cheerleading, cross-country, diving, football, golf, swimming, tennis, track/field (outdoor), track/field (indoor). *Women:* basketball, cheerleading, crew/rowing, cross-country, diving, golf, soccer, softball, swimming, tennis, track/field (outdoor), track/field (indoor), volleyball. **On-Campus Highlights:** Ayres Hall and the Hill, Neyland Stadium, Hodges Library, Rec Sports Center, Howard Baker, Jr. Ctr. for Public Policy, McClung Museum, Alumni Memorial Building and Cox Auditorium, Thompson-Boling Arena. **Environmental Initiatives:** Climate Action Plan "Switch Your Thinking" and "Chancellor's Challenge" energy conservation campaigns Game day recycling program

ADMISSIONS

Freshman Academic Profile: Average high school GPA 3.9. 44% in top 10% of high school class, 88% in top 25% of high school class, 100% in top 50% of high school class. SAT Math middle 50% range 530-640. SAT Critical Reading middle 50% range 520-640. ACT middle 50% range 24-29. Minimum web-based TOEFL 70. Minimum paper TOEFL 523. **Basis for Candidate Selection:** *Very important factors considered include:* academic GPA, rigor of secondary school record, standardized test scores. *Other factors considered include:* Class rank, application essay, recommendation(s), alumni/ae relation, character/personal qualities, extracurricular activities, first generation, geographical residence, level of applicant's interest, racial/ethnic status, state residency, talent/ability, volunteer work, work experience. **Freshman Admission Requirements:** High school diploma is required and GED is accepted. *Academic units required:* 4 English, 3 mathematics, 2 science, (1 science labs), 2 foreign language, 1 social studies, 1 history, 1 visual/performing arts. *Academic units recommended:* 4 English, 3 mathematics, 2 science, (1 science labs), 2 foreign language, 1 social studies, 1 history, 1 visual/performing arts. **Freshman Admission Statistics:** 13,768 applied, 70% admitted, 44% enrolled. **Transfer Admission Requirements:** High school transcript, college transcript(s), statement of good standing from prior institution(s). Minimum college GPA of 2.0 required. Lowest grade transferable C. **General Admission Information:** Application Fee $30. Regular application deadline 12/1. Regular notification 3/15. Nonfall registration accepted. Credit offered for CEEB Advanced Placement tests.

COSTS AND FINANCIAL AID

Annual in-state tuition $7,224. Annual out-of-state tuition $24,066. Room and board $8,480. Required fees $1,172. Average book expense $1,448. **Required Forms and Deadlines:** FAFSA. **Notification of Awards:** Applicants will be notified of awards on a rolling basis beginning 3/15. **Types of Aid:** *Need-based scholarships/grants:* Federal Pell, SEOG, state scholarships/grants, private scholarships, the school's own gift aid, Federal Nursing Scholarships. *Loans:* Subsidized Stafford, Unsubsidized Stafford, PLUS, Federal Perkins, college/university loans from institutional funds. **Student Employment:** Federal Work-Study Program available. Off-campus job opportunities are fair. **Financial Aid Statistics:** 98% freshmen, 90% undergrads receive need-based scholarship or grant aid. 55% freshmen, 63% undergrads receive need-based self-help aid. 2% freshmen, 2% undergrads receive athletic scholarships. 61% freshmen, 58% undergrads receive any aid. 50% undergrads borrow to pay for school. Average cumulative indebtedness $20,926. **Criteria for awarding institutional aid:** *Non-need-based:* academics, art, athletics, leadership, minority status, music/drama, state/district residency.

THE UNIVERSITY OF TENNESSEE AT MARTIN

200 Hall-Moody, Martin, TN 38238
Phone: 731-881-7020 • Financial Aid Phone: 731-881-7040
E-mail: admitme@utm.edu
Fax: 731-881-7029 • Website: www.utm.edu • ACT Code: 4032

This public school was founded in 1900. It has a 930-acre campus.

RATINGS
Admissions Selectivity Rating: 68   **Fire Safety Rating:** 78   **Green Rating:** 73

STUDENTS AND FACULTY
Enrollment: 6,703. **Student Body:** 58% female, 42% male, 4% out-of-state, 2% international (18 countries represented). Asian 0%, African American 17%, Caucasian 77%, Hispanic 2%, Native American 0%
Retention and Graduation: 76% freshmen return for sophomore year. 22% freshmen graduate within 4 years. 49% freshmen graduate within 6 years. 25% grads go on to further study within 1 year. **Faculty:** Student/faculty ratio 18:1. 290 full-time faculty, 71% hold PhDs, 9% are members of minority groups, 45% are women. 0% of classes are taught by teaching assistants.

ACADEMICS
Degrees: bachelor's, master's. **Classes:** Most classes have 10—19 students. Most lab/discussion sessions have 10—19 students. **Majors with Highest Enrollment:** biology/biological sciences; multi-/interdisciplinary studies, other; nursing/registered nurse (rn, asn, bsn, msn). **Special Study Options:** Accelerated program, cooperative education program, cross-registration, distance learning, double major, dual enrollment, English as a Second Language (ESL), exchange student program (domestic), honors program, independent study, internships, student-designed major, study abroad, teacher certification program, 3-1 programs in pharmacy, veterinary medicine, dentistry, medicine, optometry, podiatry and chiropractory. **Honors Programs:** University Scholars Honors Seminar . **Disability Services:** Special programs offered to physically disabled students include note-taking services, reader services, tape recorders, tutors. **Career Services:** Alumni network, alumni services, career/job search classes, internships, regional alumni. Career services highlights include erecruiting.com allows our students faster and more significant information on employers and job openings from their computers.

FACILITIES
Housing: Coed dorms, special housing for disabled students, men's dorms, special housing for international students, women's dorms, fraternity/sorority housing, apartments for married students, apartments for single students, theme housing. 100% of campus accessible to physically disabled. **Special Academic Facilities/Equipment:** Paul Meek Library contains Houston Gordon University Museum **Computers:** 100% of classrooms, 50% of dorms, 100% of libraries, 100% of dining areas, 100% of student union, 100% of common outdoor areas have wireless network access. Students can register for classes online. Administrative functions (other than registration) can be performed online.

CAMPUS LIFE
Environment: Rural. **Activities:** Choral groups, concert band, dance, drama/theater, jazz band, literary magazine, marching band, music ensembles, opera, pep band, radio station, student government, student newspaper, television station, yearbook, Campus Ministries, International Student Organization 100 registered organizations, 27 honor societies, 11 religious organizations. 12 fraternities, 8 sororities. **Athletics (Intercollegiate):** *Men:* baseball, basketball, cross-country, football, golf, riflery, rodeo. *Women:* basketball, cheerleading, cross-country, equestrian sports, riflery, rodeo, soccer, softball, tennis, volleyball. **On-Campus Highlights:** Boling University Center, Paul Meek Library, Fitness Center, Elam Center and Intramural facilities, Quad, Captain's Coffee in Paul Meek Library Student Life Center. **Environmental Initiatives:** Establishing a Recycling Facility to collect campus and community recyclables. The campus recycles its paper, cardboard, cans and plastic bottles. Purchasing green products such as carpet made from recycled materials and recycled paper products. Retrofit lighting with new, more energy-efficient lamps and ballasts, updating HVAC controls, and installing low flush toilets and urinals and occupancy lighting sensors.

ADMISSIONS
Freshman Academic Profile: Average high school GPA 3.5. 19% in top 10% of high school class, 50% in top 25% of high school class, 85% in top 50% of high school class. 90% from public high schools. ACT middle 50% range 19-24. Minimum web-based TOEFL 61. Minimum paper TOEFL 500. **Basis for Candidate Selection:** *Very important factors considered include:* academic GPA, rigor of secondary school record, standardized test scores. **Freshman Admission Requirements:** High school diploma is required and GED is accepted. *Academic units required:* 4 English, 3 mathematics, 2 science, (1 science labs), 2 foreign language, 2 history, 1 visual/performing arts. *Academic units recommended:* 4 English, 3 mathematics, 2 science, (1 science labs), 2 foreign language, 2 history, 1 visual/performing arts. **Freshman Admission Statistics:** 3,512 applied, 80% admitted, 47% enrolled. **Transfer Admission Requirements:** High school transcript, college transcript(s), Minimum college GPA of 2.0 required. Lowest grade transferable D. **General Admission Information:** Application Fee $30. Regular application deadline 8/1. Notification on a rolling basis, beginning on or about 9/1. Nonfall registration accepted. Admission may be deferred for a maximum of rolling. Credit and/or placement offered for CEEB Advanced Placement tests.

COSTS AND FINANCIAL AID
Required **Forms and Deadlines:** FAFSA. **Notification of Awards:** Applicants will be notified of awards on a rolling basis beginning 4/1. **Types of Aid:** *Need-based scholarships/grants:* Federal Pell, SEOG, state scholarships/grants, private scholarships, the school's own gift aid. *Loans:* Subsidized Stafford, Unsubsidized Stafford, PLUS, Federal Perkins. **Student Employment:** Federal Work-Study Program available. Institutional employment available. Highest amount earned per year from on-campus jobs $9,668. Off-campus job opportunities are fair. **Financial Aid Statistics:** 70% freshmen, 70% undergrads receive need-based scholarship or grant aid. 89% freshmen, 56% undergrads receive non-need-based scholarship or grant aid. 54% freshmen, 67% undergrads receive need-based self-help aid. 6% freshmen, 4% undergrads receive athletic scholarships. 96% freshmen, 81% undergrads receive any aid. 65% undergrads borrow to pay for school. Average cumulative indebtedness $12,436. **Criteria for awarding institutional aid:** *Non-need-based:* academics, art, athletics, leadership, music/drama, state/district residency.

THE UNIVERSITY OF TEXAS AT ARLINGTON

Office of Admissions, Arlington, TX 76019-0111
Phone: 817-272-6287 • Financial Aid Phone: 817-272-3561
E-mail: admissions@uta.edu • CEEB Code: 6013
Fax: 817-272-3435 • Website: www.uta.edu • ACT Code: 4200

This public school was founded in 1895. It has a 394-acre campus.

RATINGS
Admissions Selectivity Rating: 77   **Fire Safety Rating:** 95   **Green Rating:** 70

STUDENTS AND FACULTY
Enrollment: 25,092. **Student Body:** 56% female, 44% male, 2% out-of-state, 4% international (88 countries represented). Asian 11%, African American 15%, Caucasian 43%, Hispanic 22%, Native American 0%
Retention and Graduation: 74% freshmen return for sophomore year. 1% freshmen graduate within 4 years. 42% freshmen graduate within 6 years. **Faculty:** Student/faculty ratio 23:1. 899 full-time faculty, 27% are members of minority groups, 41% are women. 16% of classes are taught by teaching assistants.

ACADEMICS
Degrees: bachelor's, master's, post-bachelor's certificate, post-master's certificate. **Classes:** Most classes have 20—29 students. **Majors with Highest Enrollment:** biology/biological sciences; business administration and management; nursing/registered nurse (rn, asn, bsn, msn). **Special Study Options:** cross-registration, distance learning, double major, dual enrollment, English as a Second Language (ESL), honors program, independent study, internships, student-designed major, study abroad, teacher certification program. **Honors Programs:** We have the only Honors College in N. Texas. Freshmen interest groups, honors study abroad. **Combined Degree Programs:** BA/MD, BS/MBA. **Disability Services:** Special programs offered to physically disabled students include note-taking services, reader services, tape recorders, tutors. **Career Services:** alumni services, career/job search classes, career assessment, internships.

FACILITIES
Housing: Coed dorms, men's dorms, women's dorms, fraternity/sorority housing, apartments for married students, apartments for single students, Family housing (priority given to students with dependent children). 95% of campus accessible to physically disabled. **Special Academic Facilities/Equipment:** Cartographic history library, maps collection, minority cultures collection, library of Texana and Mexican war. Continuing Education Work Force Development Center. material, planetarium, Automation and Robotics Research institute, Wave Scattering Research Center **Computers:** Students can register for classes online. Administrative functions (other than registration) can be performed online.

CAMPUS LIFE

Environment: Metropolis. **Activities:** Choral groups, concert band, dance, drama/theater, jazz band, literary magazine, marching band, music ensembles, opera, radio station, student government, student newspaper, student-run film society, symphony orchestra, Campus Ministries, International Student Organization 459 registered organizations, 30 honor societies, 27 religious organizations. 12 fraternities, 13 sororities. **Athletics (Intercollegiate):** *Men:* baseball, basketball, cross-country, golf, tennis, track/field (outdoor). *Women:* basketball, cross-country, softball, tennis, track/field (outdoor), volleyball. **On-Campus Highlights:** Click Cafe in Library, E. H. Herford University Center, Activities Bldg., Library Mall/Free speech area, Architectue courtyard. **Environmental Initiatives:** Sustainability is prominent component of master plan (http://www.uta.edu/masterplan/ut_arlington_master_plan.pdf); sustainable design guidelines (e.g., LEED Silver Engineering Research Building now being designed); energy conservation (via energy performance contracts) is prominent component of Capital Improvement Plan ($30+ million invested in energy conservation since 1973, much of it since 2005) Formation of President's Sustainability Committee, 2007, comprising 40+ administrative staff, faculty, grad students, undergrad students, and community/NGO representatives (http://blog.uta.edu/sustainability), leading to: launch of sustainability web page (http://www.uta.edu/sustainability); formation of 10 working groups focusing on every aspect of campus life (http://blog.uta.edu/sustainability/contacts/work-groups-related-resources/); active generation and deliberation of extensive set of sustainability recommendations (http://mavspace.uta.edu/xythoswfs/webui/_xy-575263_4) Partnering with City of Arlington on sustainability grants (e.g., for $125,000 composting unit) and sustainability initiatives such as carbon footprint analysis undertaken in 2008 (http://blog.uta.edu/sustainability/2008/01/18/ut-arlington-carbon-footprint-analysis/)

ADMISSIONS

Freshman Academic Profile: 26% in top 10% of high school class, 71% in top 25% of high school class, 93% in top 50% of high school class. SAT Math middle 50% range 500-610. SAT Critical Reading middle 50% range 460-580. ACT middle 50% range 20-25. Minimum web-based TOEFL 79. Minimum paper TOEFL 550. **Basis for Candidate Selection:** *Very important factors considered include:* Class rank, academic GPA, standardized test scores. *Important factors considered include:* rigor of secondary school record. *Other factors considered include:* application essay, recommendation(s), character/personal qualities, extracurricular activities, first generation, level of applicant's interest, talent/ability, volunteer work, work experience. **Freshman Admission Requirements:** High school diploma is required and GED is not accepted. *Academic units required:* 4 English, 3 mathematics, 3 science, 2 foreign language, 3 social studies, 5 academic electives, 5 physical education 1.5; health 0.5; computer proficiency 1; fine arts 1; music, theater, art 1. *Academic units recommended:* 4 English, 3 mathematics, 3 science, 2 foreign language, 3 social studies, 5 academic electives, 5 Physical Education 1.5; Health 0.5; Computer proficiency 1; Fine Arts 1; Music, Theater, Art 1 **Freshman Admission Statistics:** 9,550 applied, 69% admitted, 40% enrolled. **Transfer Admission Requirements:** High school transcript, college transcript(s), Minimum college GPA of 2.25 required. Lowest grade transferable C. **General Admission Information:** Application Fee $35. Nonfall registration accepted. Admission may be deferred for a maximum of 1 year. Credit offered for CEEB Advanced Placement tests.

COSTS AND FINANCIAL AID

Annual in-state tuition $8,878. Annual out-of-state tuition $18,268. Room and board $7,554. Average book expense $908. **Required Forms and Deadlines:** FAFSA. **Notification of Awards:** Applicants will be notified of awards on a rolling basis beginning 4/1. **Types of Aid:** *Need-based scholarships/grants:* Federal Pell, SEOG, state scholarships/grants, private scholarships, the school's own gift aid, United Negro College Fund. *Loans:* Subsidized Stafford, Unsubsidized Stafford, PLUS, Federal Perkins, college/university loans from institutional funds. **Student Employment:** Federal Work-Study Program available. Institutional employment available. Off-campus job opportunities are excellent. **Financial Aid Statistics:** 79% freshmen, 80% undergrads receive need-based scholarship or grant aid. 51% freshmen, 29% undergrads receive non-need-based scholarship or grant aid. 93% freshmen, 95% undergrads receive need-based self-help aid. 70% freshmen, 68% undergrads receive any aid. 59% undergrads borrow to pay for school. Average cumulative indebtedness $22,146.

THE UNIVERSITY OF TEXAS AT AUSTIN

P.O. Box 8058, Austin, TX 78713-8058
Phone: 512-475-7440 • **Financial Aid Phone:** 512-475-6203 • **CEEB Code:** 6882
Fax: 512-475-7478 • **Website:** www.utexas.edu • **ACT Code:** 4240

This public school was founded in 1883. It has a 350-acre campus.

RATINGS
Admissions Selectivity Rating: 93   **Fire Safety Rating:** 77   **Green Rating:** 93

STUDENTS AND FACULTY
Enrollment: 37,725. **Student Body:** 51% female, 49% male, 4% out-of-state, 5% international (99 countries represented). Asian 18%, African American 5%, Caucasian 50%, Hispanic 20%, Native American 0%
Retention and Graduation: 53% freshmen graduate within 4 years. 81% freshmen graduate within 6 years. **Faculty:** Student/faculty ratio 18:1. 2688 full-time faculty, 90% hold PhDs, 21% are members of minority groups, 38% are women.

ACADEMICS
Degrees: bachelor's, first professional, master's. **Classes:** Most classes have 10—19 students. Most lab/discussion sessions have 10—19 students. **Majors with Highest Enrollment:** biology/biological sciences; business/commerce; liberal arts and sciences/liberal studies. **Special Study Options:** Accelerated program, cooperative education program, distance learning, double major, dual enrollment, English as a Second Language (ESL), honors program, independent study, internships, liberal arts/career combination, student-designed major, study abroad, teacher certification program. **Disability Services:** Special programs offered to physically disabled students include note-taking services, reader services. **Career Services:** Alumni network, career/job search classes, career assessment, internships, regional alumni. Career Services highlights include Internships- All BBA students must complete at least one internship in order to graduate. Our internship programs allow our BBAs to compete on a national level.

FACILITIES
Housing: Coed dorms, men's dorms, women's dorms, apartments for married students, apartments for single students, Honors Residence, Living Learning Centers (First-time Freshmen). 98% of campus accessible to physically disabled. **Special Academic Facilities/Equipment:** Blanton Museum of Art, Lyndon Baines Johnson Presidential Library/Museum, Performing Arts Center, Texas Memorial Museum, Harry Ransom Humanities Research Center. **Computers:** Students can register for classes online. Administrative functions (other than registration) can be performed online.

CAMPUS LIFE
Environment: Metropolis. **Activities:** Choral groups, concert band, dance, drama/theater, jazz band, literary magazine, marching band, music ensembles, musical theater, opera, pep band, radio station, student government, student newspaper, student-run film society, symphony orchestra, television station, yearbook, Campus Ministries, International Student Organization 900 registered organizations, 15 honor societies, 95 religious organizations. 26 fraternities, 22 sororities. **Athletics (Intercollegiate):** *Men:* baseball, basketball, cross-country, diving, football, golf, swimming, tennis, track/field (outdoor). *Women:* basketball, crew/rowing, cross-country, diving, golf, soccer, softball, swimming, tennis, track/field (outdoor), volleyball. **On-Campus Highlights:** Texas Union, Frank Erwin Special Events Center, Performing Arts Center, Harry Ransom Humanities Research Center, Blanton Museum of Art,. **Environmental Initiatives:** Adoption of the Campus Sustainability Policy/ Creation of the President's Sustainability Steering Committee. Creation of the Academic Sustainability Directory, an interactive website dedicated to organizing and presenting sustainability-related education and research at UT Austin. The Directory inventories sustainability-related faculty/staff, research/initiatives, courses, degree plans & curriculum, and centers/institutes across campus. Adoption of the student green fee - $503,000 per year allocated by a majority student committee. Fee was passed via student referendum in 2010 and the first fees were collected in Fall 2011. The current referendum has a five-year cycle.

ADMISSIONS
Freshman Academic Profile: 73% in top 10% of high school class, 91% in top 25% of high school class, 98% in top 50% of high school class. SAT Math middle 50% range 580-710. SAT Critical Reading middle 50% range 540-670. SAT Writing middle 50% range 540-680. ACT middle 50% range 25-31. Minimum web-based TOEFL 79. Minimum paper TOEFL 550. **Basis for Candidate**

Selection: *Very important factors considered include:* Class rank, rigor of secondary school record. *Important factors considered include:* application essay, standardized test scores, extracurricular activities, talent/ability, volunteer work, work experience. *Other factors considered include:* recommendation(s), character/personal qualities, first generation, level of applicant's interest, racial/ethnic status, state residency. **Freshman Admission Requirements:** High school diploma is required and GED is accepted. *Academic units required:* 4 English, 3 mathematics, 2 science, (2 science labs), 2 foreign language, 3 social studies. *Academic units recommended:* 4 English, 3 mathematics, 2 science, (2 science labs), 2 foreign language, 3 social studies. **Freshman Admission Statistics:** 32,589 applied, 47% admitted, 47% enrolled. **Transfer Admission Requirements:** college transcript(s), essay or personal statement, Minimum college GPA of 3.0 required. Lowest grade transferable C. **General Admission Information:** Application Fee $60. Regular application deadline 12/15. Nonfall registration accepted. Credit and/or placement offered for CEEB Advanced Placement tests.

COSTS AND FINANCIAL AID
Annual in-state tuition $9,792. Annual out-of-state tuition $33,060. Room and board $10,946. Average book expense $904. **Required Forms and Deadlines:** FAFSA. **Notification of Awards:** Applicants will be notified of awards on a rolling basis beginning 3/15. **Types of Aid:** *Need-based scholarships/grants:* Federal Pell, SEOG, state scholarships/grants, private scholarships, the school's own gift aid. *Loans:* Subsidized Stafford, Unsubsidized Stafford, PLUS, Federal Perkins, state loans. **Student Employment:** Federal Work-Study Program available. Off-campus job opportunities are fair. **Financial Aid Statistics:** 92% freshmen, 80% undergrads receive need-based scholarship or grant aid. 47% freshmen, 26% undergrads receive non-need-based scholarship or grant aid. 66% freshmen, 77% undergrads receive need-based self-help aid. 49% undergrads borrow to pay for school. Average cumulative indebtedness $25,227. **Criteria for awarding institutional aid:** *Non-need-based:* academics, art, athletics, leadership, music/drama, state/district residency.

THE UNIVERSITY OF TEXAS AT BROWNSVILLE

80 Fort Brown, Brownsville, TX 78520
Phone: 956-882-8295 • **Financial Aid Phone:** 956-882-8814
E-mail: admissions@utb.edu • **CEEB Code:** 6825
Fax: 956-882-7810 • **Website:** www.utb.edu

This public school was founded in 1926.

RATINGS
Admissions Selectivity Rating: 60*   **Fire Safety Rating:** 60*   **Green Rating:** 60*

STUDENTS AND FACULTY
Enrollment: 10,145. **Student Body:** 60% female, 40% male, 4% out-of-state, 4% international (21 countries represented). Asian 0%, African American 0%, Caucasian 5%, Hispanic 90%, Native American 0%
Faculty: 366 full-time faculty, 59% hold PhDs, 46% are members of minority groups, 43% are women. 0% of classes are taught by teaching assistants.

ACADEMICS
Degrees: associate, bachelor's, certificate, master's, terminal associate, transfer associate. **Majors with Highest Enrollment:** business/commerce; multi-/interdisciplinary studies, other; psychology. **Special Study Options:** cooperative education program, distance learning, double major, dual enrollment, English as a Second Language (ESL), independent study, internships, teacher certification program. **Disability Services:** Special programs offered to physically disabled students include note-taking services, reader services, tape recorders, tutors.

FACILITIES
Housing: Coed dorms, special housing for disabled students, men's dorms, women's dorms, apartments for single students. **Computers:** Students can register for classes online. Administrative functions (other than registration) can be performed online.

CAMPUS LIFE
Environment: City. **Activities:** Choral groups, concert band, dance, drama/theater, jazz band, music ensembles, opera, radio station, student government, student newspaper 56 registered organizations, 6 honor societies. **Athletics (Intercollegiate):** *Men:* baseball, golf. *Women:* golf, volleyball.

ADMISSIONS
Freshman Academic Profile: Average high school GPA 2.6. 10% in top 10% of high school class, 27% in top 25% of high school class, 57% in top 50% of high school class. 95% from public high schools. **Freshman Admission Requirements:** High school diploma or equivalent is not required. *Academic*

units required: 4 English, 2 mathematics, 2 science, (2 science labs), 2 foreign language, 4 social studies, 2 history, 1 academic electives, 3. *Academic units recommended:* 4 English, 2 mathematics, 2 science, (2 science labs), 2 foreign language, 4 social studies, 2 history, 1 academic electives, 3 **Freshman Admission Statistics:** 3,174 applied, 100% admitted, 57% enrolled. **Transfer Admission Requirements:** High school transcript, college transcript(s), Minimum college GPA of 2.0 required. Lowest grade transferable C. **General Admission Information:** Regular application deadline 7/1. Nonfall registration accepted. Admission may be deferred for a maximum of 1 year. Credit offered for CEEB Advanced Placement tests.

COSTS AND FINANCIAL AID
Average book expense $615. **Required Forms and Deadlines:** FAFSA. **Notification of Awards:** Applicants will be notified of awards on or about 5/1. **Types of Aid:** *Need-based scholarships/grants:* Federal Pell, SEOG, state scholarships/grants, private scholarships, the school's own gift aid. *Loans:* Subsidized Stafford, Unsubsidized Stafford, PLUS, college/university loans from institutional funds. **Criteria for awarding institutional aid:** *Non-need-based:* academics, art, athletics, leadership, music/drama.

THE UNIVERSITY OF TEXAS AT DALLAS

800 West Campbell Road, Richardson, TX 75080
Phone: 972-883-2270 • **Financial Aid Phone:** 972-883-2941
E-mail: interest@utdallas.edu • **CEEB Code:** 6897
Fax: 972-883-2599 • **Website:** www.utdallas.edu • **ACT Code:** 4243

This public school was founded in 1969. It has a 500-acre campus.

RATINGS
Admissions Selectivity Rating: 92   **Fire Safety Rating:** 88   **Green Rating:** 87

STUDENTS AND FACULTY
Enrollment: 11,749. **Student Body:** 44% female, 56% male, 4% out-of-state, 5% international (99 countries represented). Asian 25%, African American 6%, Caucasian 43%, Hispanic 16%, Native American 0%
Retention and Graduation: 85% freshmen return for sophomore year. 45% freshmen graduate within 4 years. 64% freshmen graduate within 6 years. **Faculty:** Student/faculty ratio 21:1. 664 full-time faculty, 94% hold PhDs, 28% are members of minority groups, 29% are women. 5% of classes are taught by teaching assistants.

ACADEMICS
Degrees: bachelor's, master's, post-bachelor's certificate. **Classes:** Most classes have 10—19 students. Most lab/discussion sessions have 20—29 students. **Majors with Highest Enrollment:** biology/biological sciences; business/commerce; electrical, electronics and communications engineering. **Special Study Options:** Accelerated program, cooperative education program, cross-registration, distance learning, double major, dual enrollment, English as a Second Language (ESL), honors program, independent study, internships, liberal arts/career combination, student-designed major, study abroad, teacher certification program, 3-2 Engineering programs, 2-2 Transfer programs. **Honors Programs:** Collegium V offers small classes, innovative instruction, world class faculty, bright and inquisitive colleagues, and an array of extracurricular events to provide special opportunities for professional and personal growth. **Combined Degree Programs:** BA/MA, BS/MS, BA/MPA, BS/MPA, MS/PhD. **Disability Services:** Special programs offered to physically disabled students include note-taking services, reader services, tape recorders, tutors. **Career Services:** career/job search classes, career assessment, internships.

FACILITIES
Housing: Coed dorms, apartments for married students, apartments for single students, Living Learning communities for freshmen. 100% of campus accessible to physically disabled. **Special Academic Facilities/Equipment:** McDermott Library Special Collections which includes History of Aviation Collection, Wineburgh Philatelic Research Library and Louise B. Belsterling Botanical Library. **Computers:** 80% of classrooms, 100% of dorms, 100% of libraries, 100% of student union, 5% of common outdoor areas have wireless network access. Students can register for classes online.

CAMPUS LIFE
Environment: Metropolis. **Activities:** Choral groups, concert band, dance, drama/theater, jazz band, literary magazine, music ensembles, musical theater,

pep band, radio station, student government, student newspaper, student-run film society, symphony orchestra, television station, International Student Organization 142 registered organizations, 8 honor societies, 9 religious organizations. 9 fraternities, 6 sororities. **Athletics (Intercollegiate):** *Men:* baseball, basketball, cross-country, golf, soccer, tennis. *Women:* basketball, cross-country, golf, soccer, softball, tennis, volleyball. **On-Campus Highlights:** The Pub (coffeehouse), Comet Cafe, Student Union, Activity Center, University Village clubhouses,. **Environmental Initiatives:** Campus recycling program DART shuttle program Free DART passes for students, faculty, staff

ADMISSIONS

Freshman Academic Profile: Average high school GPA 3.9. 42% in top 10% of high school class, 73% in top 25% of high school class, 92% in top 50% of high school class. 90% from public high schools. SAT Math middle 50% range 600-710. SAT Critical Reading middle 50% range 560-680. SAT Writing middle 50% range 540-650. ACT middle 50% range 26-31. Minimum web-based TOEFL 80. Minimum paper TOEFL 550. **Basis for Candidate Selection:** *Very important factors considered include:* Class rank, academic GPA, rigor of secondary school record, standardized test scores. *Important factors considered include:* application essay, extracurricular activities. *Other factors considered include:* recommendation(s), character/personal qualities, first generation, geographical residence, level of applicant's interest, state residency, talent/ability, volunteer work, work experience. **Freshman Admission Requirements:** High school diploma is required and GED is accepted. *Academic units required:* 4 English, 4 mathematics, 3 science, (3 science labs), 2 foreign language, 3 social studies. *Academic units recommended:* 4 English, 4 mathematics, 3 science, (3 science labs), 2 foreign language, 3 social studies. **Freshman Admission Statistics:** 7,079 applied, 52% admitted, 42% enrolled. **Transfer Admission Requirements:** college transcript(s), Minimum college GPA of 2.5 required. Lowest grade transferable C. **General Admission Information:** Application Fee $50. Regular application deadline 7/1. Nonfall registration accepted. Admission may be deferred for a maximum of One year. Credit and/or placement offered for CEEB Advanced Placement tests.

COSTS AND FINANCIAL AID

Annual in-state tuition $11,592. Annual out-of-state tuition $29,266. Room and board $9,050. Average book expense $1,200. **Required Forms and Deadlines:** FAFSA. **Notification of Awards:** Applicants will be notified of awards on a rolling basis beginning 3/1. **Types of Aid:** *Need-based scholarships/grants:* Federal Pell, SEOG, state scholarships/grants, private scholarships, the school's own gift aid. *Loans:* Subsidized Stafford, Unsubsidized Stafford, PLUS, Federal Perkins, state loans, college/university loans from institutional funds. **Student Employment:** Federal Work-Study Program available. Institutional employment available. Highest amount earned per year from on-campus jobs $15,318. Off-campus job opportunities are excellent. **Financial Aid Statistics:** 91% freshmen, 86% undergrads receive need-based scholarship or grant aid. 19% freshmen, 7% undergrads receive non-need-based scholarship or grant aid. 76% freshmen, 59% undergrads receive need-based self help aid. 81% freshmen, 70% undergrads receive any aid. 36% undergrads borrow to pay for school. Average cumulative indebtedness $17,516. **Criteria for awarding institutional aid:** *Non-need-based:* academics.

See page 1282.

THE UNIVERSITY OF TEXAS AT EL PASO

500 W. University Ave., El Paso, TX 79968-0510
Phone: 915-747-5890
E-mail: futureminer@utep.edu • **CEEB Code:** 6829
Fax: 915-747-8893 • **Website:** www.utep.edu/ • **ACT Code:** 4223

This public school was founded in 1913. It has a 330-acre campus.

RATINGS

Admissions Selectivity Rating: 64   **Fire Safety Rating:** 67   **Green Rating:** 60*

STUDENTS AND FACULTY

Enrollment: 19,078. **Student Body:** 54% female, 46% male, 3% out-of-state, 5% international (65 countries represented). Asian 1%, African American 3%, Caucasian 8%, Hispanic 81%, Native American 0%
Retention and Graduation: 72% freshmen return for sophomore year. **Faculty:** Student/faculty ratio 21:1. 2% of classes are taught by teaching assistants.

ACADEMICS

Degrees: bachelor's, master's. **Classes:** Most classes have 20—29 students. Most lab/discussion sessions have 10—19 students. **Majors with Highest Enrollment:** criminal justice/safety studies; multi-/interdisciplinary studies, other; psychology. **Special Study Options:** Accelerated program, cooperative education program, cross-registration, distance learning, double major, dual enrollment, English as a Second Language (ESL), exchange student program (domestic), honors program, independent study, internships, study abroad, teacher certification program, weekend college. **Combined Degree Programs:** BA/MA. **Disability Services:** Special programs offered to physically disabled students include note-taking services, reader services, tape recorders. **Career Services:** alumni services, career assessment, internships.

FACILITIES

Housing: special housing for disabled students, apartments for single students. 90% of campus accessible to physically disabled. **Special Academic Facilities/ Equipment:** Cross-cultural ethnic study center, natural history and cultural museum, solar pond and solar house, electron microscope, atmospheric and acoustic research lab, seismic observatory. **Computers:** Students can register for classes online. Administrative functions (other than registration) can be performed online.

CAMPUS LIFE

Environment: Metropolis. **Activities:** Choral groups, concert band, dance, drama/theater, jazz band, literary magazine, marching band, music ensembles, musical theater, opera, pep band, radio station, student government, student newspaper, student-run film society, symphony orchestra 1 honor societies, 1 religious organizations. 6 fraternities, 4 sororities. **Athletics (Intercollegiate):** *Men:* basketball, cross-country, football, golf, track/field (outdoor), track/field (indoor). *Women:* basketball, cross-country, golf, riflery, soccer, softball, tennis, track/field (outdoor), track/field (indoor), volleyball.

ADMISSIONS

Freshman Academic Profile: Average high school GPA 3.2. 17% in top 10% of high school class, 40% in top 25% of high school class, 69% in top 50% of high school class. 94% from public high schools. SAT Math middle 50% range 420-530. SAT Critical Reading middle 50% range 390-500. ACT middle 50% range 17-22. **Basis for Candidate Selection:** *Very important factors considered include:* Class rank, rigor of secondary school record. *Important factors considered include:* standardized test scores, state residency. *Other factors considered include:* recommendation(s), alumni/ae relation, character/personal qualities, extracurricular activities, geographical residence, interview, talent/ability, volunteer work, work experience. **Freshman Admission Requirements:** High school diploma is required and GED is accepted. **Freshman Admission Statistics:** 6,240 applied, 100% admitted, 70% enrolled. **Transfer Admission Requirements:** college transcript(s), Minimum college GPA of 2.0 required. Lowest grade transferable D. **General Admission Information:** Regular application deadline 7/31. Nonfall registration accepted. Admission may be deferred for a maximum of 1 semester.

COSTS AND FINANCIAL AID

Annual in-state tuition $5,565. Annual out-of-state tuition $16,095. Room and board $8,924. Required fees $1,649. Average book expense $1,160. **Required Forms and Deadlines:** institution's own financial aid form, **Notification of Awards:** Applicants will be notified of awards on or about 6/30. **Types of Aid:** *Need-based scholarships/grants:* Federal Pell, SEOG, state scholarships/ grants, private scholarships, the school's own gift aid, United Negro College Fund, Federal Nursing Scholarships. *Loans:* Subsidized Stafford, Unsubsidized Stafford, PLUS, Federal Perkins, state loans, college/university loans from institutional funds. **Student Employment:** Federal Work-Study Program available. Institutional employment available. Off-campus job opportunities are good. **Financial Aid Statistics:** 88% freshmen, 88% undergrads receive need-based scholarship or grant aid. 26% freshmen, 14% undergrads receive non-need-based scholarship or grant aid. 82% freshmen, 86% undergrads receive need-based self-help aid. 1% freshmen, 1% undergrads receive athletic scholarships. 77% freshmen, 65% undergrads receive any aid. 61% undergrads borrow to pay for school. Average cumulative indebtedness $21,123. **Criteria for awarding institutional aid:** *Non-need-based:* academics, alumni affiliation, art, athletics, job skills, leadership, minority status, music/drama, religious affiliation, state/ district residency.

THE UNIVERSITY OF TEXAS HEALTH SCIENCE CENTER AT HOUSTON

PO Box 20036, Houston, TX 77225
Phone: 713-500-3361
E-mail: admissions@uth.tmc.edu
Fax: 713-500-3356 • **Website:** www.uth.tmc.edu

This public school was founded in 1972.

RATINGS
Admissions Selectivity Rating: 60*   **Fire Safety Rating:** 60*   **Green Rating:** 60*

STUDENTS AND FACULTY
Enrollment: 381. **Student Body:** 88% female, 12% male, 2% international. Asian 17%, African American 7%, Caucasian 58%, Hispanic 15%, Native American 1%
Faculty: 985 full-time faculty, 41% are women.

ACADEMICS
Degrees: bachelor's, certificate, first professional, master's, post-master's certificate.

FACILITIES
Housing: University owns an apartment complex which is located approximately 1 1/2 miles from campus. It is competitvively priced with other apartment complexes in the area and does not cater exclusively to students. 100% of campus accessible to physically disabled. **Special Academic Facilities/Equipment:** The student's learning experience takes place in the heart of the Texas Medical Center. Among state of the art hospitals and research facilites. **Computers:** Students can register for classes online. Administrative functions (other than registration) can be performed online. Undergraduates are required to own a computer.

CAMPUS LIFE
Activities: student government.

ADMISSIONS
Freshman Academic Profile: Minimum paper TOEFL 565. **Transfer Admission Requirements:** college transcript(s), interview, standardized test scores, statement of good standing from prior institution(s). Minimum college GPA of 2.8 required. Lowest grade transferable C. **General Admission Information:** Application Fee $30. Regular application deadline 1/1. Nonfall registration not accepted.

COSTS AND FINANCIAL AID
Required Forms and Deadlines: FAFSA, institution's own financial aid form**Types of Aid:** *Need-based scholarships/grants:* Federal Pell, SEOG, state scholarships/grants, the school's own gift aid, Federal Nursing Scholarships, outside Scholarships. *Loans:* Subsidized Stafford, Unsubsidized Stafford, PLUS, Federal Perkins, Federal Nursing, college/university loans from institutional funds, Outside Loans. **Student Employment:** Off-campus job opportunities are excellent. **Financial Aid Statistics:** 71% undergrads receive need-based scholarship or grant aid. 82% undergrads receive need-based self-help aid90% undergrads borrow to pay for school. Average cumulative indebtedness $14,361.

THE UNIVERSITY OF TEXAS MEDICAL BRANCH AT GALVESTON

301 University Boulevard, Galveston, TX 77555-1305
Phone: 409-772-1215 • **Financial Aid Phone:** 409-772-1215
E-mail: enrollment.services@utmb.edu • **CEEB Code:** 6887
Fax: 409-772-4466 • **Website:** www.utmb.edu

This public school was founded in 1891. It has a 85-acre campus.

RATINGS
Admissions Selectivity Rating: 61   **Fire Safety Rating:** 60*   **Green Rating:** 60*

STUDENTS AND FACULTY
Enrollment: 492. **Student Body:** 80% female, 20% male, 1% out-of-state, 2% international (34 countries represented). Asian 18%, African American 18%, Caucasian 42%, Hispanic 14%, Native American 1%

ACADEMICS
Degrees: bachelor's, master's, post-master's certificate. **Majors with Highest Enrollment:** clinical laboratory science/medical technology/technologist; nursing/registered nurse (rn, asn, bsn, msn); respiratory care therapy/therapist. **Special Study Options:** distance learning, independent study, internships. **Combined Degree Programs:** MD/PhD. **Disability Services:** Special programs offered to physically disabled students include note-taking services, reader services, tape recorders, tutors. **Career Services:** Alumni network, alumni services, internships.

FACILITIES
Housing: Coed dorms, fraternity/sorority housing, apartments for married students, apartments for single students. 100% of campus accessible to physically disabled. **Special Academic Facilities/Equipment:** Moody Medical Library **Computers:** Students can register for classes online. Administrative functions (other than registration) can be performed online.

CAMPUS LIFE
Environment: Town. **Activities:** student government, student newspaper, yearbook 94 registered organizations, 4 honor societies, 7 religious organizations. 5 fraternities. **On-Campus Highlights:** Joe Jamail Student Center, Rosenberg House, Ashbel Smith Building, Alumni Field House, Moody Medical Library.

ADMISSIONS
Freshman Academic Profile: Minimum paper TOEFL 550. **Transfer Admission Requirements:** college transcript(s), Minimum college GPA of 2.0 required. Lowest grade transferable C. **General Admission Information:** Neither credit nor placement offered for CEEB Advanced Placement tests.

COSTS AND FINANCIAL AID
Required Forms and Deadlines: FAFSA. **Notification of Awards: Types of Aid:** *Need-based scholarships/grants:* Federal Pell, SEOG, state scholarships/grants, private scholarships, the school's own gift aid. *Loans:* Direct Subsidized Stafford, Direct Unsubsidized Stafford, Direct PLUS, Federal Perkins, Federal Nursing, college/university loans from institutional funds. **Student Employment:** Federal Work-Study Program available. Institutional employment available. Off-campus job opportunities are good. **Financial Aid Statistics: Criteria for awarding institutional aid:** *Non-need-based:* academics, minority status, state/district residency.

THE UNIVERSITY OF TEXAS—PAN AMERICAN

1201 West University Drive, Edinburg, TX 78539-2999
Phone: 956-665-2999 • **Financial Aid Phone:** 956-381-2501
E-mail: admissions@utpa.edu • **CEEB Code:** 6570
Fax: 956-665-2212 • **Website:** www.utpa.edu • **ACT Code:** 4142

This public school was founded in 1927. It has a 330-acre campus.

RATINGS
Admissions Selectivity Rating: 74   **Fire Safety Rating:** 70   **Green Rating:** 61

STUDENTS AND FACULTY
Enrollment: 16,731. **Student Body:** 55% female, 45% male, 1% out-of-state, 2% international (47 countries represented). Asian 1%, African American 1%, Caucasian 3%, Hispanic 91%, Native American 0%
Retention and Graduation: 75% freshmen return for sophomore year. 18% freshmen graduate within 4 years. **Faculty:** Student/faculty ratio 22:1. 640 full-time faculty, 83% hold PhDs, 46% are members of minority groups, 39% are women.

ACADEMICS
Degrees: bachelor's, master's, post-bachelor's certificate. **Classes:** Most classes have 30—39 students. Most lab/discussion sessions have 20—29 students. **Majors with Highest Enrollment:** business administration and management; multi-/interdisciplinary studies, other; speech and rhetorical studies. **Special Study Options:** Accelerated program, cooperative education program, distance learning, double major, dual enrollment, English as a Second Language (ESL), exchange student program (domestic), honors program, independent study, internships, study abroad, teacher certification program, weekend college. **Honors Programs:** PRE-MEDICAL HONORS COLLEGE with Baylor College of Medicine. **Disability Services:** Special programs offered to physically disabled students include note-taking services, reader services, tape recorders, tutors. **Career Services:** alumni services, career assessment, internships.

FACILITIES

Housing: Coed dorms, men's dorms, women's dorms, apartments for married students, apartments for single students. 100% of campus accessible to physically disabled. **Computers:** Students can register for classes online. Administrative functions (other than registration) can be performed online.

CAMPUS LIFE

Environment: Town. **Activities:** Choral groups, concert band, dance, drama/theater, jazz band, music ensembles, musical theater, pep band, student government, student newspaper, symphony orchestra, Campus Ministries, International Student Organization 80 registered organizations, 9 honor societies, 7 religious organizations. 4 fraternities, 1 sororities. **Athletics (Intercollegiate):** *Men:* baseball, basketball, cross-country, golf, tennis, track/field (outdoor). *Women:* basketball, cross-country, golf, tennis, track/field (outdoor), volleyball. **On-Campus Highlights:** Visitors Center, Science Courtyard, Residence Halls, Student Union **Environmental Initiatives:** The direction of disposal of hazardous waste streams toward recycling or reuse. The use of environmentally friendly (low water) landscaping materials The upgrade of lighting fixtures, energy management system components, and chiller systems for energy reduction and emissions friendlier to the environment.

ADMISSIONS

Freshman Academic Profile: 21% in top 10% of high school class, 53% in top 25% of high school class, 83% in top 50% of high school class. 99% from public high schools. SAT Math middle 50% range 440-540. SAT Critical Reading middle 50% range 410-510. SAT Writing middle 50% range 400-500. ACT middle 50% range 18-21. Minimum web-based TOEFL 61. Minimum paper TOEFL 500. **Basis for Candidate Selection:** *Very important factors considered include:* standardized test scores. *Important factors considered include:* Class rank, academic GPA, rigor of secondary school record. **Freshman Admission Requirements:** High school diploma is required and GED is accepted. *Academic units required:* 4 English, 3 mathematics, 3 science, 2 foreign language. *Academic units recommended:* 4 English, 3 mathematics, 3 science, 2 foreign language. **Freshman Admission Statistics:** 9,313 applied, 62% admitted, 54% enrolled. **Transfer Admission Requirements:** college transcript(s), Minimum college GPA of 2.0 required. Lowest grade transferable D. **General Admission Information:** Regular application deadline 8/11. Nonfall registration accepted. Credit and/or placement offered for CEEB Advanced Placement tests.

COSTS AND FINANCIAL AID

Required **Forms and Deadlines:** FAFSA. **Notification of Awards:** Applicants will be notified of awards on or about 3/15. **Types of Aid:** *Need-based scholarships/grants:* Federal Pell, SEOG, state scholarships/grants, private scholarships, the school's own gift aid. *Loans:* Subsidized Stafford, Unsubsidized Stafford, PLUS, Federal Perkins, state loans. **Student Employment:** Federal Work-Study Program available. Institutional employment available. Off-campus job opportunities are good. **Financial Aid Statistics:** 97% freshmen, 96% undergrads receive need-based scholarship or grant aid. 2% freshmen, 1% undergrads receive non-need-based scholarship or grant aid. 38% freshmen, 56% undergrads receive need-based self-help aid. 1% undergrads receive athletic scholarships. 87% freshmen, 87% undergrads receive any aid. 62% undergrads borrow to pay for school. Average cumulative indebtedness $15,257. **Criteria for awarding institutional aid:** *Non-need-based:* academics, alumni affiliation, art, athletics, leadership, music/drama.

THE UNIVERSITY OF TEXAS AT SAN ANTONIO

One UTSA Circle, San Antonio, TX 78249-0617
Phone: 210-458-8000 • **Financial Aid Phone:** 210-458-8000
E-mail: prospects@utsa.edu • **CEEB Code:** 6919
Fax: 210-458-2001 • **Website:** www.utsa.edu/ • **ACT Code:** 4239

This public school was founded in 1969. It has a 600-acre campus.

RATINGS

Admissions Selectivity Rating: 72   **Fire Safety Rating:** 60*   **Green Rating:** 67

STUDENTS AND FACULTY

Enrollment: 25,344. **Student Body:** 47% female, 53% male, 3% out-of-state, 4% international (92 countries represented). Asian 5%, African American 10%, Caucasian 29%, Hispanic 47%, Native American 0%
Retention and Graduation: 63% freshmen return for sophomore year. 9% freshmen graduate within 4 years. 28% freshmen graduate within 6 years.
Faculty: Student/faculty ratio 24:1. 948 full-time faculty, 73% hold PhDs, 36% are members of minority groups, 42% are women.

ACADEMICS

Degrees: bachelor's, doctoral, master's, post-bachelor's certificate. **Classes:** Most classes have 20—29 students. Most lab/discussion sessions have 10—19

students. **Majors with Highest Enrollment:** biology/biological sciences; multi-/interdisciplinary studies, other; psychology. **Special Study Options:** Accelerated program, cooperative education program, distance learning, double major, dual enrollment, English as a Second Language (ESL), exchange student program (domestic), honors program, independent study, internships, study abroad, teacher certification program. **Honors Programs:** The mission of the Honors College is to provide enhanced educational opportunities for selected, motivated, enthusiastic, diverse, and inquisitive students and to foster the pursuit of excellence in undergraduate, higher education. The underlying philosophy of the program is that well-educated individuals should understand broad, interdisciplinary perspectives while demonstrating expertise in their chosen field. The Honors College is open to students from all academic disciplines. Members of the Honors College pursue a rigorous academic program which satisfies all requirements of their academic departments and Colleges and goes beyond those requirements to provide the basis for outstanding achievement and appropriate recognition for that achievement. The Honors College offers small classes with greater opportunities for student participation, increased student-faculty contact, greater individual attention, lively discussions of important issues, special interdisciplinary seminars, community service opportunities, and supervised research experiences, all designed to challenge talented students. **Disability Services:** Special programs offered to physically disabled students include note-taking services, reader services, tape recorders.

FACILITIES

Housing: Coed dorms, special housing for disabled students, apartments for married students, apartments for single students. 100% of campus accessible to physically disabled. **Special Academic Facilities/Equipment:** Art gallery, audiovisual center, Institute of Texan Cultures Museum. **Computers:** Students can register for classes online. Administrative functions (other than registration) can be performed online.

CAMPUS LIFE

Environment: Metropolis. **Activities:** Choral groups, concert band, dance, drama/theater, jazz band, literary magazine, music ensembles, opera, pep band, student government, student newspaper, symphony orchestra, yearbook, Campus Ministries, International Student Organization 140 registered organizations, 40 honor societies, 9 religious organizations. 10 fraternities, 9 sororities. **Athletics (Intercollegiate):** *Men:* baseball, basketball, cross-country, golf, tennis, track/field (outdoor), track/field (indoor). *Women:* basketball, cross-country, soccer, softball, tennis, track/field (outdoor), track/field (indoor), volleyball.

ADMISSIONS

Freshman Academic Profile: 13% in top 10% of high school class, 51% in top 25% of high school class, 89% in top 50% of high school class. SAT Math middle 50% range 490-590. SAT Critical Reading middle 50% range 450-570. SAT Writing middle 50% range 440-540. ACT middle 50% range 20-25. Minimum web-based TOEFL 79. Minimum paper TOEFL 550. **Basis for Candidate Selection:** *Very important factors considered include:* Class rank, academic GPA, standardized test scores. *Other factors considered include:* recommendation(s). **Freshman Admission Requirements:** High school diploma is required and GED is accepted. **Freshman Admission Statistics:** 15,239 applied, 73% admitted, 40% enrolled. **Transfer Admission Requirements:** college transcript(s), Minimum college GPA of 2.0 required. Lowest grade transferable D. **General Admission Information:** Application Fee $40. Regular application deadline 7/1. Regular notification 9/1. Nonfall registration accepted. Credit and/or placement offered for CEEB Advanced Placement tests.

COSTS AND FINANCIAL AID

Annual in-state tuition $5,928. Annual out-of-state tuition $16,458. Room and board $9,693. Required fees $2,491. **Required Forms and Deadlines:** FAFSA, institution's own financial aid form. **Notification of Awards:** Applicants will be notified of awards on a rolling basis beginning 4/1. **Types of Aid:** *Need-based scholarships/grants:* Federal Pell, SEOG, state scholarships/grants, private scholarships, the school's own gift aid. *Loans:* Direct Subsidized Stafford, Direct Unsubsidized Stafford, Direct PLUS, Subsidized Stafford, Unsubsidized Stafford, PLUS, Federal Perkins, state loans, college/university loans from institutional funds. **Student Employment:** Financial Aid Statistics:** 92% freshmen, 87% undergrads receive need-based scholarship or grant aid. 23% freshmen, 17% undergrads receive non-need-based scholarship or grant aid. 74% freshmen, 80% undergrads receive need-based self-help aid. 2% freshmen, 2% undergrads receive athletic scholarships. 65% undergrads borrow to pay for school. Average cumulative indebtedness $25,140. **Criteria for awarding institutional aid:** *Non-need-based:* academics, alumni affiliation, art, athletics, job skills, leadership, music/drama, state/district residency.

THE UNIVERSITY OF TEXAS AT TYLER

3900 University Blvd., Tyler, TX 75799
Phone: 903-566-7202 • **Financial Aid Phone:** 903-566-7180
E-mail: admissions@mail.uttyl.edu
Fax: 903-566-7068 • **Website:** www.uttyler.edu

This public school was founded in 1971. It has a 204-acre campus.

RATINGS
Admissions Selectivity Rating: 72   **Fire Safety Rating:** 93   **Green Rating:** 60*

STUDENTS AND FACULTY
Enrollment: 4,700. **Student Body:** 60% female, 40% male, 2% out-of-state, 1% international (45 countries represented). Asian 2%, African American 10%, Caucasian 79%, Hispanic 6%, Native American 1%
Retention and Graduation: 59% freshmen return for sophomore year. 41% freshmen graduate within 6 years. 14% grads go on to further study within 1 year. **Faculty:** Student/faculty ratio 21:1. 234 full-time faculty, 70% hold PhDs, 12% are members of minority groups, 49% are women.

ACADEMICS
Degrees: bachelor's, master's. **Classes:** Most classes have 20—29 students. **Majors with Highest Enrollment:** business/managerial economics; multi-/interdisciplinary studies, other; nursing/registered nurse (rn, asn, bsn, msn). **Special Study Options:** cooperative education program, distance learning, double major, English as a Second Language (ESL), exchange student program (domestic), independent study, internships, student-designed major, study abroad, teacher certification program, weekend college. **Disability Services:** Special programs offered to physically disabled students include note-taking services, reader services. **Career Services:** career/job search classes, career assessment

FACILITIES
Housing: Coed dorms, apartments for married students, apartments for single students, Univ Pines Apts-384 beds, Patriot Village Apts - 200 beds. Residence Hall Project underway, will be five stories with 268 beds, expected to open in fall 2006. http://www.uttyler.edu/housing. **Computers:** Students can register for classes online. Administrative functions (other than registration) can be performed online.

CAMPUS LIFE
Environment: City. **Activities:** Choral groups, concert band, drama/theater, jazz band, literary magazine, music ensembles, musical theater, opera, pep band, student government, student newspaper, student-run film society 73 registered organizations, 6 honor societies, 4 fraternities, 4 sororities. **Athletics (Intercollegiate):** *Men:* baseball, basketball, cheerleading, cross-country, golf, soccer, tennis. *Women:* basketball, cheerleading, cross-country, golf, soccer, tennis, volleyball. **On-Campus Highlights:** Herrington Patriot Center, Riter Tower and Plaza, Cowan Fine and Performing Art Center, Bill Ratliff Engineering and Science Complex, University Center,.

ADMISSIONS
Freshman Academic Profile: SAT Math middle 50% range 480-580. SAT Critical Reading middle 50% range 470-570. ACT middle 50% range 20-25. Minimum paper TOEFL 550. **Basis for Candidate Selection:** *Very important factors considered include:* Class rank, academic GPA, standardized test scores. *Important factors considered include:* rigor of secondary school record, extracurricular activities, first generation, volunteer work, work experience. **Freshman Admission Requirements:** High school diploma is required and GED is accepted. *Academic units required:* 4 English, 3 mathematics, 3 science, (1 science labs), 2 foreign language, 3 social studies. *Academic units recommended:* 4 English, 3 mathematics, 3 science, (1 science labs), 2 foreign language, 3 social studies. **Freshman Admission Statistics:** 1,823 applied, 76% admitted, 46% enrolled. **Transfer Admission Requirements:** college transcript(s), Minimum college GPA of 2.0 required. Lowest grade transferable C. **General Admission Information:** Application Fee $25. Notification on a rolling basis, beginning on or about 9/1. Nonfall registration accepted. Admission may be deferred for a maximum of 1 year.

COSTS AND FINANCIAL AID
Required Forms and Deadlines: FAFSA, institution's own financial aid form. **Notification of Awards:** Applicants will be notified of awards on a rolling basis beginning 4/15. **Types of Aid:** *Need-based scholarships/grants:* Federal Pell, SEOG, state scholarships/grants, private scholarships, the school's own gift aid, Texas Grant Program, Teach for Texas Conditional Program. *Loans:* Subsidized Stafford, Unsubsidized Stafford, PLUS, Federal Perkins, state loans. **Student Employment: Financial Aid Statistics:** 84% freshmen, 81% undergrads receive need-based scholarship or grant aid. 14% freshmen, 6% undergrads receive non-need-based scholarship or grant aid. 84% freshmen, 91% undergrads

receive need-based self-help aid 44% undergrads borrow to pay for school. Average cumulative indebtedness $11,286. **Criteria for awarding institutional aid:** *Non-need-based:* academics, art, music/drama.

THE UNIVERSITY OF TOLEDO

2801 West Bancroft, Toledo, OH 43606
Phone: 419-530-8700 • **Financial Aid Phone:** 419-530-8700
E-mail: enroll@utnet.utoledo.edu • **CEEB Code:** 1845
Fax: 419-530-5713 • **Website:** www.utoledo.edu • **ACT Code:** 3344

This public school was founded in 1872. It has a 400-acre campus.

RATINGS
Admissions Selectivity Rating: 70   **Fire Safety Rating:** 60*   **Green Rating:** 60*

STUDENTS AND FACULTY
Enrollment: 15,288. **Student Body:** 49% female, 51% male, 8% out-of-state, 1% international (108 countries represented). Asian 2%, African American 13%, Caucasian 76%, Hispanic 3%, Native American 0%
Retention and Graduation: 69% freshmen return for sophomore year. 17% freshmen graduate within 4 years. 43% freshmen graduate within 6 years. **Faculty:** Student/faculty ratio 18:1. 813 full-time faculty, 73% hold PhDs, 17% are members of minority groups, 35% are women.

ACADEMICS
Degrees: associate, bachelor's, certificate, first professional, master's, post-bachelor's certificate, post-master's certificate. **Majors with Highest Enrollment:** education; engineering; marketing/marketing management. **Special Study Options:** Accelerated program, cooperative education program, cross-registration, distance learning, double major, dual enrollment, exchange student program (domestic), honors program, independent study, internships, liberal arts/career combination, student-designed major, study abroad, teacher certification program, weekend college. **Disability Services:** Special programs offered to physically disabled students include note-taking services, reader services, tutors.

FACILITIES
Housing: Coed dorms, special housing for disabled students, men's dorms, special housing for international students, women's dorms, fraternity/sorority housing. 95% of campus accessible to physically disabled. **Special Academic Facilities/Equipment:** Language lab, arboretum, planetariums, two observatories, electron microscope. **Computers:** Students can register for classes online.

CAMPUS LIFE
Environment: City. **Activities:** Choral groups, concert band, dance, drama/theater, jazz band, literary magazine, marching band, music ensembles, musical theater, opera, pep band, radio station, student government, student newspaper, student-run film society, symphony orchestra, television station 200 registered organizations, 14 fraternities, 13 sororities. **Athletics (Intercollegiate):** *Men:* baseball, basketball, cheerleading, cross-country, diving, football, golf, lacrosse, softball, swimming, tennis, track/field (outdoor), track/field (indoor), volleyball. *Women:* basketball, cheerleading, cross-country, diving, golf, lacrosse, softball, swimming, tennis, track/field (outdoor), track/field (indoor), volleyball.

ADMISSIONS
Freshman Academic Profile: Average high school GPA 3.1. 16% in top 10% of high school class, 37% in top 25% of high school class, 64% in top 50% of high school class. SAT Math middle 50% range 460-600. SAT Critical Reading middle 50% range 450-570. ACT middle 50% range 19-25. Minimum paper TOEFL 500. **Basis for Candidate Selection:** *Very important factors considered include:* rigor of secondary school record, standardized test scores, state residency. **Freshman Admission Requirements:** High school diploma is required and GED is accepted. *Academic units required:* 4 English, 3 mathematics, 3 science, 3 social studies. *Academic units recommended:* 4 English, 3 mathematics, 3 science, 3 social studies. **Freshman Admission Statistics:** 8,126 applied, 80% admitted, 49% enrolled. **Transfer Admission Requirements:** college transcript(s), statement of good standing from prior institution(s). Minimum college GPA of 2.0 required. Lowest grade transferable C. **General Admission Information:** Application Fee $40. Notification on a rolling basis, beginning on or about 10/1. Nonfall registration accepted. Admission may be deferred for a maximum of 12 months. Credit and/or placement offered for CEEB Advanced Placement tests.

COSTS AND FINANCIAL AID
Annual in-state tuition $6,430. Annual out-of-state tuition $15,242. Room and board $8,213. Required fees $1,091. Average book expense $690. **Required Forms and Deadlines:** FAFSA. **Notification of Awards:** Applicants will be

notified of awards on a rolling basis beginning 4/1. **Types of Aid:** *Need-based scholarships/grants:* Federal Pell, SEOG, state scholarships/grants, private scholarships, the school's own gift aid. *Loans:* Direct Subsidized Stafford, Direct Unsubsidized Stafford, Direct PLUS, Federal Perkins, state loans. **Student Employment:** Federal Work-Study Program available. **Financial Aid Statistics:** 70% freshmen, 70% undergrads receive need-based scholarship or grant aid. 22% freshmen, 26% undergrads receive non-need-based scholarship or grant aid. 81% freshmen, 84% undergrads receive need-based self-help aid. 55% undergrads receive any aid. 65% undergrads borrow to pay for school. Average cumulative indebtedness $20,859. **Criteria for awarding institutional aid:** *Non-need-based:* academics, art, athletics, minority status, music/drama, state/district residency.

UNIVERSITY OF TORONTO

172 St. George Street, Toronto, ON M5R 0A3
Phone: 416-978-2190
E-mail: admissions.help@utoronto.ca • **CEEB Code:** 982
Fax: 416-978-7022 • **Website:** www.utoronto.ca

This public school was founded in 1827. It has a 1767-acre campus.

RATINGS
Admissions Selectivity Rating: 62   **Fire Safety Rating:** 70   **Green Rating:** 69

STUDENTS AND FACULTY
Enrollment: 64,962. **Student Body:** 56% female, 44% male, 8% out-of-state, 13% international (166 countries represented).
Retention and Graduation: 82% freshmen graduate within 6 years. **Faculty:** Student/faculty ratio 10:1. 5381 full-time faculty.

ACADEMICS
Degrees: bachelor's, certificate, diploma, master's. **Special Study Options:** cooperative education program, double major, English as a Second Language (ESL), exchange student program (domestic), honors program, internships, study abroad, teacher certification program. **Combined Degree Programs:** JD/MBA, JD/MA, JD/PhD/, JD/MISt, JD/MSW. **Disability Services:** Special programs offered to physically disabled students include note-taking services, reader services, tape recorders, tutors. **Career Services:** career/job search classes

FACILITIES
Housing: Coed dorms, men's dorms, women's dorms, apartments for married students, cooperative housing. **Computers:** Students can register for classes online. Administrative functions (other than registration) can be performed online.

CAMPUS LIFE
Environment: Metropolis. **Activities:** Choral groups, concert band, dance, drama/theater, jazz band, literary magazine, music ensembles, opera, radio station, student government, student newspaper, student-run film society, symphony orchestra 200 registered organizations, 49 religious organizations. **Athletics (Intercollegiate):** *Men:* badminton, baseball, basketball, crew/rowing, cross-country, curling, fencing, football, golf, ice hockey, lacrosse, mountain biking, rugby, skiingnordiccross-country, soccer, squash, swimming, tennis, track/field (outdoor), track/field (indoor), volleyball, water polo, wrestling. *Women:* badminton, basketball, crew/rowing, cross-country, curling, fencing, field hockey, ice hockey, lacrosse, mountain biking, rugby, skiingnordiccross-country, soccer, squash, swimming, tennis, track/field (outdoor), track/field (indoor), volleyball, water polo, wrestling. **On-Campus Highlights:** Hart House, The Athletic Centre, Justine Barnike Gallery, Thomas Fisher Rare Book Library, Convocation Hall.

ADMISSIONS
Freshman Academic Profile: Minimum paper TOEFL 600. **Basis for Candidate Selection:** *Very important factors considered include:* academic GPA, standardized test scores. **Freshman Admission Requirements:** High school diploma is required and GED is accepted. **Freshman Admission Statistics:** 67,955 applied, 69% admitted, 18% enrolled. **Transfer Admission Requirements:** High school transcript, college transcript(s), standardized test scores. **General Admission Information:** Application Fee $80. Regular application deadline 3/1. Notification on a rolling basis, beginning on or about 3/15. Nonfall registration not accepted.

COSTS AND FINANCIAL AID
Required Forms and Deadlines: OSAP.

THE UNIVERSITY OF TULSA

800 South Tucker Drive, Tulsa, OK 74104
Phone: 918-631-2307 • **Financial Aid Phone:** 918-631-2526
E-mail: admission@utulsa.edu • **CEEB Code:** 6883
Fax: 918-631-5003 • **Website:** www.utulsa.edu • **ACT Code:** 3444

This private school, affiliated with the Presbyterian Church, was founded in 1894. It has a 209-acre campus.

RATINGS
Admissions Selectivity Rating: 95   **Fire Safety Rating:** 84   **Green Rating:** 80

STUDENTS AND FACULTY
Enrollment: 3,117. **Student Body:** 43% female, 57% male, 42% out-of-state, 22% international (68 countries represented). Asian 3%, African American 5%, Caucasian 58%, Hispanic 4%, Native American 4%
Retention and Graduation: 88% freshmen return for sophomore year. 46% freshmen graduate within 4 years. 66% freshmen graduate within 6 years. 41% grads go on to further study within 1 year. 17% grads pursue arts and sciences degrees. 2% grads pursue law degrees. 7% grads pursue business degrees. 5% grads pursue medical degrees. **Faculty:** Student/faculty ratio 11:1. 316 full-time faculty, 96% hold PhDs, 16% are members of minority groups, 32% are women. 4% of classes are taught by teaching assistants.

ACADEMICS
Degrees: bachelor's, master's, post-bachelor's certificate. **Classes:** Most classes have 10—19 students. Most lab/discussion sessions have 10—19 students. **Majors with Highest Enrollment:** marketing/marketing management; petroleum engineering; psychology. **Special Study Options:** Accelerated program, double major, English as a Second Language (ESL), honors program, independent study, internships, liberal arts/career combination, student-designed major, study abroad, teacher certification program. **Honors Programs:** The Honors Program is a four-year course of study consisting of 21 hours of academic credit. In small classes and individual tutorials, students pursue a critical examination of the moral and political commitments, scientific achievments, and artistic sensibilities that have shaped the modern world. The program culminates in the senior year with students designing and executing individual research projects. The Tulsa Undergraduate Research Challenge (TURC) is an innovative program that enables undergraduates to take challenging courses and conduct advanced research with the guidance of top professors. Its aim is to create leaders in scholarship, research, and public life. The centerpiece of the program is research; the goal of such research may be to deliver papers at academic conferences, to produce publishable articles, or to initiate meaningful community projects. **Combined Degree Programs:** BA/JD, Bachelor's and MBA. **Disability Services:** Special programs offered to physically disabled students include note-taking services, reader services, tape recorders, tutors. **Career Services:** Alumni network, alumni services, career/job search classes, career assessment, internships, regional alumni. Career Services highlights include Internships provide students with the opportunity to supplement classroom training with real-world experience in a position related to their major or career goals. Students may be paid or may receive academic credit or a combination of pay and credit.

FACILITIES
Housing: Coed dorms, special housing for disabled students, men's dorms, women's dorms, fraternity/sorority housing, apartments for married students, apartments for single students, Honors House. 80% of campus accessible to physically disabled. **Special Academic Facilities/Equipment:** Alexandre Hogue Art Gallery, Biotechnology Institute, Center for Communicative Disorders, Charge-Coupled Camera Microscope, Donald W. Reynolds Center (site of a state-of-the-art athletic training program), Education Technology Lab, Electron Microscopes, Kendall Theatre, McFarlin Library Special Collections (focus on American, British, and Irish Literature of the late 19th and early 20th centuries, and on Native American History and Law), Multimedia "boardroom" style classrooms (3), ONEOK Multimedia Auditorium, Sadie Adwan Communication Lab, Sidney Born Technical Library (contains an outstanding collection concerning energy, most notably petroleum), Sun Computer Work Stations, World's largest research flow-loop in Petroleum Engr. **Computers:**

100% of classrooms, 100% of dorms, 100% of libraries, 100% of dining areas, 100% of student union, 100% of common outdoor areas have wireless network access. Students can register for classes online. Administrative functions (other than registration) can be performed online.

CAMPUS LIFE

Environment: Metropolis. **Activities:** Choral groups, concert band, dance, drama/theater, jazz band, literary magazine, marching band, music ensembles, musical theater, opera, pep band, radio station, student government, student newspaper, symphony orchestra, television station, yearbook, Campus Ministries, International Student Organization, Model UN 245 registered organizations, 40 honor societies, 21 religious organizations. 7 fraternities, 9 sororities. **Athletics (Intercollegiate):** *Men:* basketball, cheerleading, cross-country, football, golf, soccer, tennis, track/field (outdoor), track/field (indoor). *Women:* basketball, cheerleading, crew/rowing, cross-country, golf, soccer, softball, tennis, track/field (outdoor), track/field (indoor), volleyball. **On-Campus Highlights:** Collins Fitness Center, Reynolds Center, McFarlin Library, Allen Chapman Activity Center, Fraternity/Sorority Row, (6.) Collins College of Business (7.) The College of Engineering and Natural Sciences (8.) Chapman Hall - The College of Arts and Sciences (9.) Phillips Hall - School of Art (10.) Kendall Hall Theatre (11.) Collins Hall - Visitors Center and Office of Admission (12.) H.A. Chapman Stadium. **Environmental Initiatives:** All campus shuttles run on compressed natural gas Recycling program includes events and all buildings, and covers plastics, aluminum, paper, and glass in targeted areas. Earth Day Week - trayless meals in dining halls, and distribution of recycling bags and totes to students and campus organizations.

ADMISSIONS

Freshman Academic Profile: Average high school GPA 3.8. 72% in top 10% of high school class, 86% in top 25% of high school class, 98% in top 50% of high school class. 77% from public high schools. SAT Math middle 50% range 590-700. SAT Critical Reading middle 50% range 570-710. ACT middle 50% range 25-31. Minimum web-based TOEFL 61. Minimum paper TOEFL 500. **Basis for Candidate Selection:** *Very important factors considered include:* Class rank, academic GPA, rigor of secondary school record, standardized test scores, interview, level of applicant's interest. *Important factors considered include:* application essay, recommendation(s), character/personal qualities, extracurricular activities, talent/ability. *Other factors considered include:* alumni/ae relation, first generation, racial/ethnic status, volunteer work, work experience. **Freshman Admission Requirements:** High school diploma is required and GED is accepted. **Freshman Admission Statistics:** 6,984 applied, 41% admitted, 28% enrolled. **Transfer Admission Requirements:** college transcript(s), essay or personal statement, statement of good standing from prior institution(s). Minimum college GPA of 2.5 required. Lowest grade transferable C. **General Admission Information:** Application Fee $35. Notification on a rolling basis, beginning on or about 10/1. Nonfall registration accepted. Admission may be deferred for a maximum of 1 year. Credit and/or placement offered for CEEB Advanced Placement tests.

COSTS AND FINANCIAL AID

Annual tuition $33,382. Room and board $10,476. Required fees $320. Average book expense $1,200. **Required Forms and Deadlines:** FAFSA, institution's own financial aid form. **Notification of Awards:** Applicants will be notified of awards on a rolling basis beginning 3/1. **Types of Aid:** *Need-based scholarships/grants:* Federal Pell, SEOG, state scholarships/grants, private scholarships, the school's own gift aid. *Loans:* Subsidized Stafford, Unsubsidized Stafford, PLUS, Federal Perkins. **Student Employment:** Federal Work-Study Program available. Institutional employment available. Highest amount earned per year from on-campus jobs $4,700. Off-campus job opportunities are good. **Financial Aid Statistics:** 61% freshmen, 53% undergrads receive need-based scholarship or grant aid. 99% freshmen, 96% undergrads receive non-need-based scholarship or grant aid. 68% freshmen, 76% undergrads receive need-based self-help aid. 11% freshmen, 13% undergrads receive athletic scholarships. 91% freshmen, 88% undergrads receive any aid. **Criteria for awarding institutional aid:** *Non-need-based:* academics, alumni affiliation, art, athletics, leadership, minority status, music/drama, religious affiliation.

See page 1284.

UNIVERSITY OF UTAH

201 South 1460 East, Salt Lake City, UT 84112
Phone: 801-581-7281 • **Financial Aid Phone:** 801-581-6211
E-mail: admissions@sa.utah.edu • **CEEB Code:** 4853
Fax: 801-585-7864 • **Website:** www.utah.edu • **ACT Code:** 4274

This public school was founded in 1850. It has a 1535-acre campus.

RATINGS

Admissions Selectivity Rating: 72   **Fire Safety Rating:** 83   **Green Rating:** 93

STUDENTS AND FACULTY

Enrollment: 20,972. **Student Body:** 51% female, 49% male, 18% out-of-state, 7% international (135 countries represented). Asian 6%, African American 1%, Caucasian 84%, Hispanic 10%, Native American 1%
Retention and Graduation: 88% freshmen return for sophomore year. 22% freshmen graduate within 4 years. **Faculty:** Student/faculty ratio 13:1. 1506 full-time faculty, 80% hold PhDs, 10% are members of minority groups, 42% are women. 12% of classes are taught by teaching assistants.

ACADEMICS

Degrees: bachelor's, doctoral, master's, post-bachelor's certificate, post-master's certificate. **Classes:** Most classes have 20—29 students. Most lab/discussion sessions have 10—19 students. **Majors with Highest Enrollment:** biology/biological sciences; business/commerce; economics. **Special Study Options:** Accelerated program, cooperative education program, cross-registration, distance learning, double major, dual enrollment, English as a Second Language (ESL), exchange student program (domestic), honors program, independent study, internships, liberal arts/career combination, student-designed major, study abroad, teacher certification program. **Honors Programs:** The Honors Program promotes an enriched academic environment for talented and highly motivated students. We foster values of social responsibility, inclusiveness and academic quality - in short a community of excellence. The Honors Program provides talented students with an enhanced undergraduate experience through a number of opportunities. Honors students typically enroll in one or two Honors classes each semester during their first two years. This will put students in contact with other students who set high goals for themselves, like to be challenged and are highly motivated. Rather than the large auditorium classes so many freshmen or sophomore students take, honors classes will be small and students will get to know their professors well. Students will have personal, intense advising at key moments in the next four years that will help them plan for graduation with the Honors degree at each step along the way. **Combined Degree Programs:** BA/MEng, Neuroscience MD/Phd. **Disability Services:** Special programs offered to physically disabled students include note-taking services, reader services, tape recorders, tutors. **Career Services:** Alumni network, alumni services, career/job search classes, career assessment, internships.

FACILITIES

Housing: Coed dorms, special housing for disabled students, special housing for international students, fraternity/sorority housing, apartments for married students, theme housing: Limited Visitation, 24-hour Quiet, First Year Students only. 100% of campus accessible to physically disabled. **Special Academic Facilities/Equipment:** Museums of natural history and fine arts, government institute, environmental biological research facilities, human genetics lab. **Computers:** 100% of classrooms, 100% of dorms, 100% of libraries, 100% of dining areas, 100% of student union, 60% of common outdoor areas have wireless network access. Students can register for classes online. Administrative functions (other than registration) can be performed online.

CAMPUS LIFE

Environment: Metropolis. **Activities:** Choral groups, concert band, dance, drama/theater, jazz band, literary magazine, marching band, music ensembles, musical theater, opera, pep band, radio station, student government, student newspaper, student-run film society, symphony orchestra, television station, Campus Ministries, International Student Organization, Model UN 238 registered organizations, 41 honor societies, 9 religious organizations. 7 fraternities, 6 sororities. **Athletics (Intercollegiate):** *Men:* baseball, basketball, cheerleading, diving, football, golf, skiing (downhill/alpine), skiingnordiccross-country, swimming, tennis. *Women:* basketball, cheerleading, cross-country, diving, gymnastics, skiing (downhill/alpine), skiingnordiccross-country, soccer, softball, swimming, tennis, track/field (outdoor), track/field (indoor), volleyball. **On-Campus Highlights:** Rice Eccles Stadium, Jon M. Huntsman Center, Huntsman Cancer Institute, Utah Museum of Fine Arts, Utah Museum of Natural History, Marriott Library Red Butte Gardens Olympic Cauldron Park Fort Douglas Museum and Cemetery Kingsbury Hall/Gardner Hall. **Environmental Initiatives:** 1. Transportation: Free public transportation (Ed-Pass) for all students, staff and faculty; gas-electric hybrid, biodiesel, and natural gas-powered campus vehicles. 2. Energy Initiatives: Offset more than 10% of our electricity consumption with windpower purchases; new co-generation plant under construction will cut outside energy purchases by another 10%, ongoing building retrofits for lighting, HVAC, and other efficiency gains. 3. Student Involvement: campus as a sustainability learning lab for courses; numerous on-campus green groups; environmental service opportunities with Bennion Community Service Center, student internships available through the Office of Sustainability, and also the greater community through Environmental Studies and Master's in Science and Technology programs.

ADMISSIONS

Freshman Academic Profile: Average high school GPA 3.6. 24% in top 10% of high school class, 48% in top 25% of high school class, 82% in top 50% of high school class. 95% from public high schools. SAT Math middle 50% range 510-560. SAT Critical Reading middle 50% range 510-620. SAT Writing middle 50% range 490-610. ACT middle 50% range 21-27. Minimum web-based TOEFL 80. Minimum paper TOEFL 550. **Basis for Candidate Selection:** *Very important factors considered include:* academic GPA, rigor of secondary school record, standardized test scores. *Important factors considered include:* talent/ability. *Other factors considered include:* Class rank, recommendation(s), extracurricular activities, interview, racial/ethnic status. **Freshman Admission Requirements:** High school diploma is required and GED is accepted. *Academic units required:* 4 English, 2 mathematics, 3 science, (1 science labs), 2 foreign language, 1 history, 4 academic electives. *Academic units recommended:* 4 English, 2 mathematics, 3 science, (1 science labs), 2 foreign language, 1 history, 4 academic electives. **Freshman Admission Statistics:** 11,118 applied, 83% admitted, 38% enrolled. **Transfer Admission Requirements:** college transcript(s), statement of good standing from prior institution(s). Minimum college GPA of 2.6 required. Lowest grade transferable D-. **General Admission Information:** Application Fee $45. Regular application deadline 4/1. Nonfall registration accepted. Credit and/or placement offered for CEEB Advanced Placement tests.

COSTS AND FINANCIAL AID

Annual in-state tuition $6,275. Annual out-of-state tuition $21,974. Room and board $7,155. Required fees $938. Average book expense $590. **Required Forms and Deadlines:** FAFSA, institution's own financial aid form. **Notification of Awards:** Applicants will be notified of awards on a rolling basis beginning 4/15. **Types of Aid:** *Need-based scholarships/grants:* Federal Pell, SEOG, state scholarships/grants, private scholarships, the school's own gift aid, Federal Nursing Scholarships., ACG, National SMART Grant, and TEACH Grant. *Loans:* Subsidized Stafford, Unsubsidized Stafford, PLUS, Federal Perkins, Federal Nursing, college/university loans from institutional funds, Private Alternative Loans. **Student Employment:** Federal Work-Study Program available. Institutional employment available. Highest amount earned per year from on-campus jobs $8,800. Off-campus job opportunities are excellent. **Financial Aid Statistics:** 81% freshmen, 81% undergrads receive need-based scholarship or grant aid. 7% freshmen, 2% undergrads receive non-need-based scholarship or grant aid. 85% freshmen, 92% undergrads receive need-based self-help aid. 1% undergrads receive athletic scholarships. 42% freshmen, 48% undergrads receive any aid. 50% undergrads borrow to pay for school. Average cumulative indebtedness $20,796. **Criteria for awarding institutional aid:** *Non-need based:* academics, alumni affiliation, art, athletics, leadership, minority status, music/drama, state/district residency.

UNIVERSITY OF VERMONT

University of Vermont Admissions, Burlington, VT 05401-3596
Phone: 802-656-3370 • **Financial Aid Phone:** 802-656-5700
E-mail: admissions@uvm.edu • **CEEB Code:** 3920
Fax: 802-656-8611 • **Website:** www.uvm.edu • **ACT Code:** 4322

This public school was founded in 1791. It has a 460-acre campus.

RATINGS

Admissions Selectivity Rating: 79   **Fire Safety Rating:** 89   **Green Rating:** 94

STUDENTS AND FACULTY

Enrollment: 10,192. **Student Body:** 56% female, 44% male, 67% out-of-state, 2% international (46 countries represented). Asian 2%, African American 1%, Caucasian 84%, Hispanic 4%, Native American 0%
Retention and Graduation: 85% freshmen return for sophomore year. 65% freshmen graduate within 4 years. 23% grads go on to further study within 1 year. 8% grads pursue arts and sciences degrees. 2% grads pursue law degrees. 1% grads pursue business degrees. 3% grads pursue medical degrees. **Faculty:** Student/faculty ratio 17:1. 606 full-time faculty, 87% hold PhDs, 15% are members of minority groups, 47% are women. 2% of classes are taught by teaching assistants.

ACADEMICS

Degrees: bachelor's, master's, post-bachelor's certificate, post-master's certificate. **Classes:** Most classes have fewer than 10 students. Most lab/discussion sessions have 20—29 students. **Majors with Highest Enrollment:** biology/biological sciences; business administration and management; psychology. **Special Study Options:** cooperative education program, distance learning, double major, dual enrollment, exchange student program (domestic), honors program, independent study, internships, liberal arts/career combination, student-designed major, study abroad, teacher certification program, Evening University option in several programs. **Honors Programs:** University wide Honors College, a residential learning community where students live together and take classes in one of UVM's newest residence halls. Honors College students are simultaneously enrolled in one of seven other UVM undergraduate colleges or schools. Honors College courses comprise approximately 20% of a students overall coursework and include a year-long common first year seminar, a choice of a variety of sophomore seminars, a junior year thesis prep course, and a senior year thesis, creative project or practicum. Upon graduation program completers are designated as Honors College Scholars. **Combined Degree Programs:** BA/JD, BS/DVM with Tufts University, BA/BS-DPT. **Disability Services:** Special programs offered to physically disabled students include note-taking services, reader services, tape recorders, tutors. **Career Services:** alumni services, career assessment, internships Career services highlights include Dollar Enterprise, an award winning service learning activity in which students are provided with $1 of working capital and develop and run a campus based entrepreneurial activity for one week. The activity is done for one week. All profits are donated to a charity of the group's choice.

FACILITIES

Housing: Coed dorms, fraternity/sorority housing, apartments for married students, apartments for single students, wellness housing, theme housing. 90% of campus accessible to physically disabled. **Special Academic Facilities/Equipment:** Art/ethnography museum, chemistry/physics library, medical library, on-campus preschool, government research and world affairs centers, agricultural experiment station, horse farm, multinuclear magnetic resonance spectrometers, mass spectrometer. **Computers:** 10% of classrooms, 15% of dorms, 100% of libraries, 100% of dining areas, 100% of student union, 5% of common outdoor areas have wireless network access. Students can register for classes online. Administrative functions (other than registration) can be performed online.

CAMPUS LIFE

Environment: Town. **Activities:** Choral groups, concert band, dance, drama/theater, jazz band, literary magazine, music ensembles, musical theater, pep band, radio station, student government, student newspaper, student-run film society, symphony orchestra, television station, Campus Ministries, International Student Organization 140 registered organizations, 30 honor societies, 10 religious organizations. 9 fraternities, 6 sororities. **Athletics (Intercollegiate):** *Men:* basketball, cross-country, ice hockey, lacrosse, skiing (downhill/alpine), skiingnordiccross-country, soccer, track/field (outdoor), track/field (indoor). *Women:* basketball, cross-country, diving, field hockey, ice hockey, lacrosse, skiing (downhill/alpine), skiingnordiccross-country, soccer, swimming, track/field (outdoor), track/field (indoor). **On-Campus Highlights:** Davis Student Center, Fleming Museum, Campus Green, Athletic Complex/Fitness Center, Spear Street Research Farm and Equine Center. **Environmental Initiatives:** Office of Sustainability supports infusion of sustainability into operations, student life, curriculum, and communications Eco-Reps Program provides peer education in residence halls, supports campus-wide events, develops student leaders, and connects them with key administrative, faculty, and community leaders LEED Silver minimum has changed thinking on campus; energy efficiency investments have yielded millions of dollars in avoided costs; Clean Energy Fund is teaching us about renewable energy.

ADMISSIONS

Freshman Academic Profile: 34% in top 10% of high school class, 71% in top 25% of high school class, 96% in top 50% of high school class. 70% from public high schools. SAT Math middle 50% range 550-650. SAT Critical Reading middle 50% range 540-640. SAT Writing middle 50% range 540-650. ACT middle 50% range 24-29. Minimum paper TOEFL 550. **Basis for Candidate Selection:** *Very important factors considered include:* rigor of secondary school record. *Important factors considered include:* Class rank, application essay, academic GPA, standardized test scores, character/personal qualities, state residency. *Other factors considered include:* recommendation(s), alumni/ae relation, extracurricular activities, first generation, geographical residence, interview, level of applicant's interest, racial/ethnic status, talent/ability, volunteer work, work experience. **Freshman Admission Requirements:** High school diploma is required and GED is accepted. *Academic units required:* 4 English, 3 mathematics, 2 science, (1 science labs), 2 foreign language, 3 social studies. *Academic units recommended:* 4 English, 3 mathematics, 2 science, (1 science labs), 2 foreign language, 3 social studies. **Freshman Admission Statistics:** 21,808 applied, 77% admitted, 14% enrolled. **Transfer Admission Requirements:** High school transcript, college transcript(s), essay or personal statement, Minimum college GPA of 2.5 required. Lowest grade transferable C. **General Admission Information:** Application Fee $45. Regular application deadline 1/15. Regular notification 3/31. Nonfall registration accepted. Admission may be deferred for a maximum of 12 months. Credit and/or placement offered for CEEB Advanced Placement tests.

COSTS AND FINANCIAL AID
Annual in-state tuition $13,344. Annual out-of-state tuition $33,672. Room and board $10,064. Required fees $1,940. Average book expense $1,200. **Required Forms and Deadlines:** FAFSA. **Notification of Awards:** Applicants will be notified of awards on a rolling basis beginning 3/15. **Types of Aid:** *Need-based scholarships/grants:* Federal Pell, SEOG, state scholarships/grants, private scholarships, the school's own gift aid, Federal Nursing Scholarships. *Loans:* Subsidized Stafford, Unsubsidized Stafford, PLUS, Federal Perkins, Federal Nursing, college/university loans from institutional funds. **Student Employment:** Federal Work-Study Program available. Institutional employment available. Off-campus job opportunities are good. **Financial Aid Statistics:** 96% freshmen, 96% undergrads receive need-based scholarship or grant aid. 6% freshmen, 4% undergrads receive non-need-based scholarship or grant aid. 76% freshmen, 79% undergrads receive need-based self-help aid. 2% freshmen, 2% undergrads receive athletic scholarships. 89% freshmen, 82% undergrads receive any aid. 59% undergrads borrow to pay for school. Average cumulative indebtedness $27,588. **Criteria for awarding institutional aid:** *Non-need-based:* academics, art, athletics.

UNIVERSITY OF THE VIRGIN ISLANDS

2 John Brewers Bay, St. Thomas, VI 00802-9990
Phone: 340-693-1150
E-mail: admissions@uvi.edu • **CEEB Code:** 879
Fax: 340-693-1220 • **Website:** www.uvi.edu

This public school was founded in 1962.

RATINGS
Admissions Selectivity Rating: 66   **Fire Safety Rating:** 60*   **Green Rating:** 60*

STUDENTS AND FACULTY
Enrollment: 1,972. **Student Body:** 80% female, 20% male, 36% out-of-state, 7% international. Asian 1%, African American 71%, Caucasian 2%, Hispanic 3%, Native American 0%
Retention and Graduation: **Faculty:** Student/faculty ratio 14:1. 99 full-time faculty, 68% hold PhDs, 53% are members of minority groups, 44% are women.

ACADEMICS
Degrees: associate, master's. **Special Study Options:** cooperative education program, distance learning, dual enrollment, exchange student program (domestic), independent study, internships, teacher certification program.

FACILITIES
Housing: men's dorms, women's dorms. **Computers:** Administrative functions (other than registration) can be performed online.

CAMPUS LIFE
Environment: Village. **Activities:** Choral groups, concert band, dance, drama/theater, jazz band, music ensembles, student government, student newspaper, yearbook 27 registered organizations, 2 honor societies, 2 religious organizations. 1 fraternities, 3 sororities. **Athletics (Intercollegiate):** *Men:* basketball, soccer, swimming, tennis, volleyball. *Women:* basketball, swimming, tennis, volleyball.

ADMISSIONS
Freshman Academic Profile: SAT Math middle 50% range 330-450. SAT Critical Reading middle 50% range 360-470. **Basis for Candidate Selection:** *Very important factors considered include:* rigor of secondary school record. *Other factors considered include:* standardized test scores, state residency.

Freshman Admission Requirements: High school diploma is required and GED is accepted. **Freshman Admission Statistics:** 854 applied, 73% admitted, 45% enrolled. **Transfer Admission Requirements:** High school transcript, college transcript(s), statement of good standing from prior institution(s). Minimum college GPA of 2.0 required. Lowest grade transferable C. **General Admission Information:** Application Fee $20. Regular application deadline 4/30. Nonfall registration accepted. Admission may be deferred for a maximum of not specific.

COSTS AND FINANCIAL AID
Annual in-state tuition $1,500. Annual out-of-state tuition $4,500. Room and board $2,715. Required fees $133. Average book expense $400.

UNIVERSITY OF VIRGINIA

Office of Admission, Charlottesville, VA 22906
Phone: 434-982-3200 • **Financial Aid Phone:** 434-982-6000
E-mail: undergradadmission@virginia.edu • **CEEB Code:** 5820
Fax: 434-924-3587 • **Website:** www.virginia.edu • **ACT Code:** 4412

This public school was founded in 1819. It has a 1167-acre campus.

RATINGS
Admissions Selectivity Rating: 98   **Fire Safety Rating:** 74   **Green Rating:** 96

STUDENTS AND FACULTY
Enrollment: 14,640. **Student Body:** 55% female, 45% male, 26% out-of-state, 6% international (138 countries represented). Asian 12%, African American 7%, Caucasian 61%, Hispanic 6%, Native American 0%
Retention and Graduation: 97% freshmen return for sophomore year. 87% freshmen graduate within 4 years. 93% freshmen graduate within 6 years. **Faculty:** Student/faculty ratio 16:1. 1243 full-time faculty, 91% hold PhDs, 14% are members of minority groups, 34% are women. 11% of classes are taught by teaching assistants.

ACADEMICS
Degrees: bachelor's, master's, post-master's certificate. **Classes:** Most classes have 10—19 students. Most lab/discussion sessions have 20—29 students. **Majors with Highest Enrollment:** business/commerce; economics; history. **Special Study Options:** Accelerated program, cooperative education program, double major, English as a Second Language (ESL), exchange student program (domestic), honors program, independent study, internships, liberal arts/career combination, student-designed major, study abroad, teacher certification program, Special January term (during Winter Break) where students can take one course. Semester at Sea option of spending an academic semester on board a ship travelling to multiple countries. **Honors Programs:** Jefferson Scholars: Full scholarship given to approximately 30 students per year. Special lectures and discussions with distinguished University faculty; all first year Jefferson Scholars take part in an outdoor leadership experience; all rising-second year Jefferson Scholars, prior to the beginning of school, participate in a two-week Institute for Leadership and Citizenship designed to foster a deeper understanding of the art of leadership and the importance of citizenship. Additionally, all Jefferson Scholars are granted an opportunity to travel and study abroad between their second and third year. Scholars may elect to spend three weeks of study at either Regent's College in England or the Erasmus Institute in Tuscany, Italy. Following the structured tutorial, each Scholar designs and completes two weeks of travel and independent inquiry. Echols Scholars-School of Arts and Sciences. Separate dormitory, with Rodman Scholars, for first-year students. Flexible degree requirements; exemption from some requirements; preference for courses. Rodman Scholars-School of Engineering and Applied Sciences. Separate dormitory, with Echols Scholars, for first-year students. Special courses designed only for Rodman Scholars in first two years. **Combined Degree Programs:** 5-year B.A./M.Teaching. **Disability Services:** Special programs offered to physically disabled students include note-taking services, reader services, tape recorders, tutors. **Career Services:** Alumni network, alumni services, career/job search classes, career assessment, internships, regional alumni. Career services highlights include (a tie) (1) on-grounds interviewing because, for our size school, we not only have an exceedingly robust program (7,000 to 10,000 individual student interviews per year; and most of the top tier organizations you'd find listed in the Fortune 100), but also because student interviews here are very often evenly distributed among the College, Commerce, and SEAS (Engineering School); and, (2) the dramatic growth and popularity of our

internship programs among our students -- not only corporate internships, but also non-profit/public policy/community service internships, an initiative you rarely find on a large public university campus.

FACILITIES

Housing: Coed dorms, special housing for international students, fraternity/sorority housing, apartments for married students, apartments for single students, theme housing: French, German, Spanish and Russian houses, a multi-lingual house, and three residential colleges. 100% of campus accessible to physically disabled. **Special Academic Facilities/Equipment:** 15 libraries, art museum, experimental farm, biological station, observatory/planetarium, nuclear information center, media center (multimedia editing). **Computers:** 100% of classrooms, 100% of dorms, 100% of libraries, 100% of dining areas, 100% of student union, 26-50% of common outdoor areas have wireless network access. Students can register for classes online. Administrative functions (other than registration) can be performed online.

CAMPUS LIFE

Environment: City. **Activities:** Choral groups, concert band, dance, drama/theater, jazz band, literary magazine, marching band, music ensembles, musical theater, opera, pep band, radio station, student government, student newspaper, student-run film society, symphony orchestra, television station, Campus Ministries, International Student Organization, Model UN 7 honor societies, 44 religious organizations. 28 fraternities, 15 sororities. **Athletics (Intercollegiate):** *Men:* baseball, basketball, cross-country, diving, football, golf, lacrosse, soccer, swimming, tennis, track/field (outdoor), track/field (indoor), wrestling. *Women:* basketball, crew/rowing, cross-country, diving, field hockey, golf, lacrosse, soccer, softball, swimming, tennis, track/field (outdoor), track/field (indoor), volleyball. **On-Campus Highlights:** Rotunda/Academical Village (orig campus), Alderman and Clemons Libraries, John Paul Jones Arena, Football and Soccer Stadiums, Aquatic and Fitness Center, Location of the future "arts precinct;" new library housing original rare and early American manuscripts; Birdwood Golf Course; Observatory; Old Cabell Hall (music performances); Culbreth Theatre (drama); Newcomb Hall (student services building); University of Virginia Bookstore. **Environmental Initiatives:** Academics: The University of Virginia offers 70+ courses in 8 different schools with significant focus on sustainability, including a global sustainability course, a new course model cross listed and taught jointly by faculty from Engineering, Architecture, and Commerce. In Spring 2011, the University created the interdisciplinary Global Sustainability minor. Sustainable Design and Construction: The University's policy to achieve LEED certification on all new buildings and major renovations has led to 30 projects registered with the US Green Building Council, with 10 of these complete and certified (3 Gold, 4 Silver, 3 Certified). Ongoing efficiency and conservation efforts, including: award winning recycling and stormwater management program, extensive building retro-commissioning team, Environmental Management System implementation across multiple departments, and Green Dining that include composting, reusable to-go containers, and local farm relationships.

ADMISSIONS

Freshman Academic Profile: Average high school GPA 4.2. 93% in top 10% of high school class, 98% in top 25% of high school class, 99% in top 50% of high school class. 72% from public high schools. SAT Math middle 50% range 640-740. SAT Critical Reading middle 50% range 620-720. SAT Writing middle 50% range 630-730. ACT middle 50% range 28-32. **Basis for Candidate Selection:** *Very important factors considered include:* Class rank, academic GPA, recommendation(s), rigor of secondary school record, alumni/ae relation, first generation, racial/ethnic status, state residency. *Important factors considered include:* application essay, standardized test scores, character/personal qualities, extracurricular activities, talent/ability. *Other factors considered include:* geographical residence, volunteer work, work experience. **Freshman Admission Requirements:** High school diploma is required and GED is accepted. *Academic units required:* 4 English, 4 mathematics, 2 science, 2 foreign language, 1 social studies. *Academic units recommended:* 4 English, 4 mathematics, 2 science, 2 foreign language, 1 social studies. **Freshman Admission Statistics:** 27,193 applied, 30% admitted, 42% enrolled. **Transfer Admission Requirements:** High school transcript, college transcript(s), essay or personal statement, standardized test scores, statement of good standing from prior institution(s). Minimum college GPA of 2.0 required. Lowest grade transferable C. **General Admission Information:** Application Fee $60. Regular application deadline 1/1. Regular notification 4/1. Nonfall registration not accepted. Admission may be deferred for a maximum of 1 year. Credit and/or placement offered for CEEB Advanced Placement tests.

COSTS AND FINANCIAL AID

Annual in-state tuition $9,622. Annual out-of-state tuition $34,952. Room and board $9,419. Required fees $2,384. Average book expense $1,220. **Required Forms and Deadlines:** FAFSA, institution's own financial aid form. **Notification of Awards:** Applicants will be notified of awards on or about 4/5. **Types of Aid:** *Need-based scholarships/grants:* Federal Pell, SEOG, state scholarships/grants, private scholarships, the school's own gift aid, Federal Nursing Scholar-

ships. *Loans:* Subsidized Stafford, Unsubsidized Stafford, PLUS, Federal Perkins, Federal Nursing, college/university loans from institutional funds, Alternative / Private Loans. **Student Employment:** Federal Work-Study Program available. Institutional employment available. **Financial Aid Statistics:** 84% freshmen, 83% undergrads receive need-based scholarship or grant aid. 12% freshmen receive non-need-based scholarship or grant aid. 56% freshmen, 58% undergrads receive need-based self-help aid. 3% freshmen, 3% undergrads receive athletic scholarships. 54% freshmen, 53% undergrads receive any aid. 36% undergrads borrow to pay for school. Average cumulative indebtedness $21,591. **Criteria for awarding institutional aid:** *Non-need-based:* academics, athletics, leadership, minority status, music/drama, state/district residency.

UNIVERSITY OF VIRGINIA'S COLLEGE AT WISE

1 College Avenue, Wise, VA 24293
Phone: 276-328-0102
E-mail: admissions@uvawise.edu • **CEEB Code:** 5124
Fax: 276-328-0251 • **Website:** www.uvawise.edu • **ACT Code:** 4343

This public school was founded in 1954. It has a 367-acre campus.

RATINGS

Admissions Selectivity Rating: 67   **Fire Safety Rating:** 60*   **Green Rating:** 60*

STUDENTS AND FACULTY

Enrollment: 1,629. **Student Body:** 52% female, 48% male, 5% out-of-state, 0% international. Asian 1%, African American 7%, Caucasian 90%, Hispanic 2%, Native American 0%
Retention and Graduation: 73% freshmen return for sophomore year. 25% freshmen graduate within 4 years. 44% freshmen graduate within 6 years. 14% grads go on to further study within 1 year. 7% grads pursue arts and sciences degrees. 6% grads pursue law degrees. 4% grads pursue business degrees. 1% grads pursue medical degrees. **Faculty:** Student/faculty ratio 16:1. 91 full-time faculty, 29% hold PhDs, 13% are members of minority groups, 41% are women. 0% of classes are taught by teaching assistants.

ACADEMICS

Degrees: bachelor's. **Classes:** Most classes have 10—19 students. Most lab/discussion sessions have 10—19 students. **Special Study Options:** Accelerated program, cooperative education program, distance learning, double major, dual enrollment, honors program, independent study, internships, student-designed major, study abroad, teacher certification program. **Disability Services:** Special programs offered to physically disabled students include note-taking services, reader services, tape recorders, tutors. **Career Services:** alumni services, career/job search classes, career assessment, internships.

FACILITIES

Housing: Coed dorms, special housing for disabled students, men's dorms, women's dorms, apartments for single students. 95% of campus accessible to physically disabled. **Computers:** Administrative functions (other than registration) can be performed online.

CAMPUS LIFE

Environment: Rural. **Activities:** Choral groups, concert band, dance, drama/theater, literary magazine, music ensembles, musical theater, pep band, radio station, student government, student newspaper, television station, yearbook 40 registered organizations, 3 honor societies, 3 religious organizations. 3 fraternities, 2 sororities. **Athletics (Intercollegiate):** *Men:* baseball, basketball, cross-country, football, golf, tennis, track/field (outdoor). *Women:* basketball, cross-country, softball, tennis, track/field (outdoor), volleyball.

ADMISSIONS

Freshman Academic Profile: Average high school GPA 3.3. 18% in top 10% of high school class, 40% in top 25% of high school class, 78% in top 50% of high school class. 99% from public high schools. SAT Math middle 50% range 430-530. SAT Critical Reading middle 50% range 420-530. SAT Writing middle 50% range 16-21. ACT middle 50% range 16-21. Minimum paper TOEFL 550. **Basis for Candidate Selection:** *Very important factors considered include:* Class rank, rigor of secondary school record. *Important factors considered include:* standardized test scores, talent/ability. *Other factors considered include:* application essay, recommendation(s), character/personal qualities, extracurricular activities, interview, racial/ethnic status, volunteer work, work experience. **Freshman Admission Requirements:** High school diploma is required and GED is accepted. *Academic units required:* 4 English, 3 mathematics, 2 science, (2 science labs), 2 foreign language, 1 social studies, 1 history, 5 academic electives. *Academic units recommended:* 4 English, 3 mathematics, 2 science, (2 science labs), 2 foreign language, 1 social studies, 1 history, 5 academic electives. **Freshman Admission Statistics:** 1,084 applied, 81% admitted, 45%

enrolled. **Transfer Admission Requirements:** college transcript(s), Minimum college GPA of 2.3 required. Lowest grade transferable C–. **General Admission Information:** Application Fee $25. Regular application deadline 8/1. Notification on a rolling basis, beginning on or about 9/15. Nonfall registration accepted. Admission may be deferred for a maximum of 1 year. Credit and/or placement offered for CEEB Advanced Placement tests.

COSTS AND FINANCIAL AID

Required Forms and Deadlines: FAFSA. **Notification of Awards:** Applicants will be notified of awards on a rolling basis beginning 4/1. **Types of Aid:** *Need-based scholarships/grants:* Federal Pell, SEOG, state scholarships/grants, private scholarships, the school's own gift aid. *Loans:* Subsidized Stafford, Unsubsidized Stafford, PLUS, Federal Perkins, state loans, college/university loans from institutional funds. **Student Employment:** Federal Work-Study Program available. Institutional employment available. Highest amount earned per year from on-campus jobs $900. Off-campus job opportunities are fair. **Criteria for awarding institutional aid:** *Non-need-based:* academics, alumni affiliation, art, athletics, job skills, leadership, music/drama, state/district residency.

UNIVERSITY OF WASHINGTON

Best 378

1410 NE Campus Parkway, Seattle, WA 98195-5852
Phone: 206-543-9686 • **Financial Aid Phone:** 206-543-6101 • **CEEB Code:** 4854
Fax: 206-685-3655 • **Website:** www.washington.edu • **ACT Code:** 4484

This public school was founded in 1861. It has a 700-acre campus.

RATINGS

Admissions Selectivity Rating: 95   **Fire Safety Rating:** 93   **Green Rating:** 99

STUDENTS AND FACULTY

Enrollment: 27,836. **Student Body:** 52% female, 48% male, 14% out-of-state, 5% international (107 countries represented). Asian 14%, African American 1%, Caucasian 26%, Hispanic 3%, Native American 1%
Retention and Graduation: 93% freshmen return for sophomore year. 56% freshmen graduate within 4 years. 80% freshmen graduate within 6 years.
Faculty: Student/faculty ratio 13:1. 2818 full-time faculty, 87% hold PhDs, 38% are women..

ACADEMICS

Degrees: bachelor's, first professional, first professional certificate, master's, post-master's certificate. **Classes:** Most classes have 20—29 students. Most lab/discussion sessions have 20—29 students. **Majors with Highest Enrollment:** economics; political science and government; psychology. **Special Study Options:** cooperative education program, distance learning, double major, English as a Second Language (ESL), exchange student program (domestic), honors program, independent study, internships, student-designed major, study abroad, teacher certification program, Friday Harbor Labs. **Honors Programs:** We have a University Honors Program, as well as departmental honors options. **Disability Services:** Special programs offered to physically disabled students include note-taking services, reader services, tape recorders, tutors. **Career Services:** Alumni network, alumni services, career/job search classes, career assessment, internships, regional alumni.

FACILITIES

Housing: Coed dorms, special housing for disabled students, special housing for international students, fraternity/sorority housing, apartments for married students, apartments for single students, theme housing. 100% of campus accessible to physically disabled. **Special Academic Facilities/Equipment:** Multiple art galleries, an anthropology and natural history museum, arboretum, closed-circuit TV studio. **Computers:** 100% of dorms, 100% of libraries, 100% of student union, have wireless network access. Students can register for classes online. Administrative functions (other than registration) can be performed online.

CAMPUS LIFE

Environment: Metropolis. **Activities:** Choral groups, concert band, dance, drama/theater, jazz band, literary magazine, marching band, music ensembles, musical theater, opera, pep band, radio station, student government, student newspaper, student-run film society, symphony orchestra, television station, Campus Ministries, International Student Organization, Model UN 711 registered organizations, 13 honor societies, 52 religious organizations. 31 fraternities, 16 sororities. **Athletics (Intercollegiate):** *Men:* baseball, basketball,

crew/rowing, cross-country, football, golf, soccer, tennis, track/field (outdoor). *Women:* basketball, crew/rowing, cross-country, golf, gymnastics, soccer, softball, tennis, track/field (outdoor), volleyball. **On-Campus Highlights:** Henry Art Gallery, Burke Museum, Meany Hall for Performing Arts, football games at Husky Stadium, Waterfront Activities Center (WAC). **Environmental Initiatives:** College of the Environment http://coenv.washington.edu/ Environmental Stewardship and Sustainability Office F2 Administration/Strategy Management Finance and Facilities http://green.washington.edu Campus Sustainability Fund, a student-led fee for sustainability projects http://csf.washington.edu This office supports the Environmental Stewardship Committee (ESAC) http://f2.washington.edu/ess/inform/esac Charter signatory of the American College & University Presidents Climate Commitment (ACUPCC); development and submission of a Climate Action Plan http://f2.washington.edu/ess/inform/uw-climate-action-plan

ADMISSIONS

Freshman Academic Profile: Average high school GPA 3.8. 92% in top 10% of high school class, 98% in top 25% of high school class, 100% in top 50% of high school class. 73% from public high schools. SAT Math middle 50% range 580-710. SAT Critical Reading middle 50% range 520-650. SAT Writing middle 50% range 450-650. ACT middle 50% range 24-30. Minimum web-based TOEFL 76. Minimum paper TOEFL 540. **Basis for Candidate Selection:** *Very important factors considered include:* application essay, academic GPA, rigor of secondary school record. *Important factors considered include:* standardized test scores, character/personal qualities, extracurricular activities, first generation, talent/ability, volunteer work, work experience. *Other factors considered include:* state residency. **Freshman Admission Requirements:** High school diploma or equivalent is not required. *Academic units required:* 4 English, 3 mathematics, 2 science, (1 science labs), 2 foreign language, 3 social studies,. *Academic units recommended:* 4 English, 3 mathematics, 2 science, (1 science labs), 2 foreign language, 3 social studies,. **Freshman Admission Statistics:** 26,138 applied, 59% admitted, 39% enrolled. **Transfer Admission Requirements:** High school transcript, college transcript(s), essay or personal statement, Minimum college GPA of 2.5 required. **General Admission Information:** Application Fee $50. Regular application deadline 1/15. Regular notification 4/15. Notification on a rolling basis, beginning on or about 11/1. Nonfall registration accepted. Credit and/or placement offered for CEEB Advanced Placement tests.

COSTS AND FINANCIAL AID

Annual in-state tuition $11,305. Annual out-of-state tuition $28,860. Room and board $10,689. Required fees $1,078. **Required Forms and Deadlines:** FAFSA. **Notification of Awards:** Applicants will be notified of awards on or about 3/31. **Types of Aid:** *Need-based scholarships/grants:* Federal Pell, SEOG, state scholarships/grants, private scholarships, the school's own gift aid. *Loans:* Direct Subsidized Stafford, Direct Unsubsidized Stafford, Direct PLUS, Federal Perkins, Federal Nursing, college/university loans from institutional funds. **Student Employment:** Federal Work-Study Program available. Institutional employment available. Off-campus job opportunities are excellent. **Financial Aid Statistics:** 73% freshmen, 73% undergrads receive need-based scholarship or grant aid. 19% freshmen, 11% undergrads receive non-need-based scholarship or grant aid. 57% freshmen, 65% undergrads receive need-based self-help aid. 1% freshmen, 1% undergrads receive athletic scholarships. 50% freshmen, 50% undergrads receive any aid. 50% undergrads borrow to pay for school. Average cumulative indebtedness $16,800. **Criteria for awarding institutional aid:** *Non-need-based:* academics, alumni affiliation, art, athletics, leadership, music/drama.

UNIVERSITY OF WEST ALABAMA

Station 4, Livingston, AL 35470
Phone: 888-636-8800
E-mail: admissions@uwa.edu • **CEEB Code:** 1737
Fax: 205-652-3522 • **Website:** www.uwa.edu/

This public school was founded in 1835. It has a 600-acre campus.

RATINGS

Admissions Selectivity Rating: 86   **Fire Safety Rating:** 60*   **Green Rating:** 60*

STUDENTS AND FACULTY

Enrollment: 1,945. **Student Body:** 61% female, 39% male, 19% out-of-state, 0% international. Asian 0%, African American 47%, Caucasian 36%, Hispanic 1%, Native American 0%
Retention and Graduation: 15% grads go on to further study within 1 year. 12% grads pursue arts and sciences degrees. 1% grads pursue law degrees. 1% grads pursue business degrees. 1% grads pursue medical degrees. **Faculty:**

Student/faculty ratio 19:1. 116 full-time faculty, 79% hold PhDs, 16% are members of minority groups, 47% are women. 0% of classes are taught by teaching assistants.

ACADEMICS

Degrees: associate, bachelor's, master's. **Classes:** Most classes have fewer than 10 students. Most lab/discussion sessions have 10—19 students. **Special Study Options:** Accelerated program, cooperative education program, distance learning, double major, dual enrollment, exchange student program (domestic), honors program, independent study, internships, teacher certification program. **Combined Degree Programs:** BA/MEng, 2-yr transfer program in fisheries and wildlife ma. **Disability Services:** Special programs offered to physically disabled students include tutors. **Career Services:** alumni services, career assessment.

FACILITIES

Housing: Coed dorms, men's dorms, women's dorms, apartments for married students, apartments for single students. 100% of campus accessible to physically disabled. **Computers:** Administrative functions (other than registration) can be performed online.

CAMPUS LIFE

Environment: Rural. **Activities:** Choral groups, concert band, dance, drama/theater, marching band, student government, student newspaper, television station, yearbook, Campus Ministries, International Student Organization 30 registered organizations, 8 honor societies, 5 religious organizations. 7 fraternities, 6 sororities. **Athletics (Intercollegiate):** *Men:* baseball, basketball, cheerleading, cross-country, football, rodeo. *Women:* basketball, cheerleading, cross-country, rodeo, softball, volleyball.

ADMISSIONS

Freshman Academic Profile: 88% from public high schools. ACT middle 50% range 18-34. Minimum paper TOEFL 500. **Basis for Candidate Selection:** *Very important factors considered include:* rigor of secondary school record, standardized test scores. **Freshman Admission Requirements:** High school diploma is required and GED is accepted. *Academic units required:* 3 English, 3 mathematics, 3 science, 3 social studies, 3 academic electives. 3 English, 3 mathematics, 3 science, 3 social studies, 3 academic electives. **Freshman Admission Statistics:** 690 applied, 61% admitted, 73% enrolled. **Transfer Admission Requirements:** college transcript(s), statement of good standing from prior institution(s). Minimum college GPA of 2.0 required. Lowest grade transferable C. **General Admission Information:** Application Fee $50. Nonfall registration accepted. Admission may be deferred for a maximum of 1 year. Credit and/or placement offered for CEEB Advanced Placement tests.

COSTS AND FINANCIAL AID

Annual in-state tuition $5,060. Annual out-of-state tuition $10,120. Room and board $3,748. Required fees $360. Average book expense $900. **Required Forms and Deadlines:** FAFSA. **Notification of Awards:** Applicants will be notified of awards on a rolling basis beginning 6/1. **Types of Aid:** *Need-based scholarships/grants:* Federal Pell, SEOG, state scholarships/grants, the school's own gift aid. *Loans:* Subsidized Stafford, Unsubsidized Stafford, PLUS, Federal Perkins, Stafford Federal Loan Teacher Loan Forgiveness. **Student Employment:** Federal Work-Study Program available. Highest amount earned per year from on-campus jobs $1,317. Off-campus job opportunities are good. **Financial Aid Statistics:** 67% freshmen, 84% undergrads receive need-based scholarship or grant aid. 77% freshmen, 76% undergrads receive non-need-based scholarship or grant aid. 78% freshmen, 44% undergrads receive need-based self-help aid. 8% freshmen, 7% undergrads receive athletic scholarships. 54% undergrads borrow to pay for school. Average cumulative indebtedness $3,846. **Criteria for awarding institutional aid:** *Non-need-based:* academics, alumni affiliation, athletics, leadership, music/drama, state/district residency.

UNIVERSITY OF WEST FLORIDA

11000 University Parkway, Pensacola, FL 32514-5750
Phone: 850-474-2230 • **Financial Aid Phone:** 850-474-2400
E-mail: admissions@uwf.edu • **CEEB Code:** 5833
Fax: 850-474-3360 • **Website:** uwf.edu • **ACT Code:** 771

This public school was founded in 1963. It has a 1600-acre campus.

RATINGS

Admissions Selectivity Rating: 76   **Fire Safety Rating:** 84   **Green Rating:** 82

STUDENTS AND FACULTY

Enrollment: 9,948. **Student Body:** 57% female, 43% male, 10% out-of-state, 1% international (97 countries represented). Asian 3%, African American 12%, Caucasian 70%, Hispanic 8%, Native American 1%

Retention and Graduation: 23% freshmen graduate within 4 years. 48% freshmen graduate within 6 years. **Faculty:** Student/faculty ratio 24:1. 300 full-time faculty, 14% are members of minority groups, 43% are women. 4% of classes are taught by teaching assistants.

ACADEMICS

Degrees: associate, bachelor's, doctoral, master's, post-master's certificate. **Classes:** Most classes have 20—29 students. Most lab/discussion sessions have 20—29 students. **Majors with Highest Enrollment:** elementary education and teaching; mass communication/media studies; psychology. **Special Study Options:** cooperative education program, distance learning, dual enrollment, exchange student program (domestic), honors program, independent study, internships, study abroad, teacher certification program, Learning disability services. **Combined Degree Programs:** BS/MS Biology,Chemistry - called Fast Track. **Disability Services:** Special programs offered to physically disabled students include note-taking services, reader services, tape recorders, tutors. **Career Services:** career assessment Career services highlights include UWF is an accredited cooperative education school. We offer the Myers Briggs Type Indicator and Strong Interest Inventory as career assessments.

FACILITIES

Housing: Coed dorms, fraternity/sorority housing, apartments for married students, apartments for single students, Special dorm rooms for disabled students. 80% of campus accessible to physically disabled. **Special Academic Facilities/Equipment:** Archeology museum,instructional media center, biology, chemistry, physics, and psychology labs, property on the Gulf of Mexico for marine and ecology research. **Computers:** 100% of classrooms, 100% of libraries, 100% of dining areas, 100% of student union, 100% of common outdoor areas have wireless network access. Students can register for classes online. Administrative functions (other than registration) can be performed online.

CAMPUS LIFE

Environment: City. **Activities:** Choral groups, concert band, dance, drama/theater, jazz band, music ensembles, musical theater, radio station, student government, student newspaper, symphony orchestra, television station 157 registered organizations, 15 honor societies, 17 religious organizations. 10 fraternities, 7 sororities. **Athletics (Intercollegiate):** *Men:* baseball, basketball, cross-country, golf, soccer, tennis. *Women:* basketball, cross-country, golf, soccer, softball, tennis, volleyball. **On-Campus Highlights:** The Commons (has cafeteria and bookstore), Fitness Facilities, Center for Fine and Performing Arts, Nature Trails, Library, Archeology Institute Artifact Display. **Environmental Initiatives:** All new buildings must be at least L.E.E.D Silver Certified Energy Reduction Program Environmentally Friendly/Green Purchasing Initiative Recycling.

ADMISSIONS

Freshman Academic Profile: Average high school GPA. 9% in top 10% of high school class, 35% in top 25% of high school class, 76% in top 50% of high school class. 90% from public high schools. SAT Math middle 50% range 450-540. SAT Critical Reading middle 50% range 450-550. SAT Writing middle 50% range 430-530. ACT middle 50% range 20-25. Minimum paper TOEFL 550. **Basis for Candidate Selection:** *Very important factors considered include:* academic GPA, rigor of secondary school record, standardized test scores, state residency. *Other factors considered include:* Class rank, application essay, recommendation(s), alumni/ae relation, character/personal qualities, extracurricular activities, first generation, geographical residence, level of applicant's interest, talent/ability, volunteer work, work experience. **Freshman Admission Requirements:** High school diploma is required and GED is accepted. *Academic units required:* 4 English, 3 mathematics, 3 science, (2 science labs), 2 foreign language, 3 social studies, 4 academic electives. *Academic units recommended:* 4 English, 3 mathematics, 3 science, (2 science labs), 2 foreign language, 3 social studies, 4 academic electives. **Freshman Admission Statistics:** 5,744 applied, 63% admitted, 37% enrolled. **Transfer Admission Requirements:** college transcript(s), Minimum college GPA of 2.0 required. Lowest grade transferable D. **General Admission Information:** Application Fee $30. Regular application deadline 6/30. Notification on a rolling basis, beginning on or about 10/1. Nonfall registration accepted. Admission may be deferred for a maximum of one year. Credit offered for CEEB Advanced Placement tests.

COSTS AND FINANCIAL AID

Annual in-state tuition $3,742. Annual out-of-state tuition $16,010. Room and board $8,574. Required fees $1,683. Average book expense $1,200. **Required Forms and Deadlines:** FAFSA, institution's own financial aid form. **Notification of Awards:** Applicants will be notified of awards on a rolling basis beginning 2/1. **Types of Aid:** *Need-based scholarships/grants:* Federal Pell, SEOG, state scholarships/grants, private scholarships, the school's own gift aid. *Loans:* Direct Subsidized Stafford, Direct Unsubsidized Stafford, Direct PLUS, Federal Perkins, college/university loans from institutional funds. **Student Employment:** Federal Work-Study Program available. Institutional employment available. Off-campus job opportunities are good. **Criteria for awarding institutional aid:** *Non-need-based:* academics, alumni affiliation, art, athletics, minority status, music/drama.

UNIVERSITY OF WEST GEORGIA

1601 Maple Street, Carrollton, GA 30118
Phone: 678-839-4000 • **Financial Aid Phone:** 678-839-6421
E-mail: admiss@westga.edu • **CEEB Code:** 5900
Fax: 678-839-4747 • **Website:** www.westga.edu • **ACT Code:** 878

This public school was founded in 1906. It has a 645-acre campus.

RATINGS
Admissions Selectivity Rating: 78   **Fire Safety Rating:** 76   **Green Rating:** 61

STUDENTS AND FACULTY
Enrollment: 9,963. **Student Body:** 61% female, 39% male, 3% out-of-state, 1% international (66 countries represented). Asian 1%, African American 31%, Caucasian 54%, Hispanic 4%, Native American 0%
Retention and Graduation: 15% freshmen graduate within 4 years. 36% freshmen graduate within 6 years. **Faculty:** Student/faculty ratio 19:1. 453 full-time faculty, 77% hold PhDs, 19% are members of minority groups, 53% are women. 0% of classes are taught by teaching assistants.

ACADEMICS
Degrees: bachelor's, certificate, doctoral, master's, post-bachelor's certificate, post-master's certificate. **Classes:** Most classes have 20—29 students. Most lab/discussion sessions have 20—29 students. **Majors with Highest Enrollment:** biology/biological sciences; elementary education and teaching; nursing/registered nurse (rn, asn, bsn, msn). **Special Study Options:** Accelerated program, cooperative education program, distance learning, double major, dual enrollment, external degree program, honors program, independent study, internships, study abroad, teacher certification program. **Disability Services:** Special programs offered to physically disabled students include note-taking services, reader services, tape recorders, tutors. **Career Services:** alumni services, internships.

FACILITIES
Housing: Coed dorms, special housing for disabled students, women's dorms, fraternity/sorority housing. 85% of campus accessible to physically disabled. **Special Academic Facilities/Equipment:** Archaelolgical laboratory, art gallery, electron microscope, observatory, preschool, performing arts center, TV studio. **Computers:** 20% of classrooms, 10% of dorms, 100% of libraries, 100% of dining areas, 100% of student union, 80% of common outdoor areas have wireless network access. Students can register for classes online. Administrative functions (other than registration) can be performed online.

CAMPUS LIFE
Environment: City. **Activities:** Choral groups, concert band, dance, drama/theater, jazz band, literary magazine, marching band, music ensembles, musical theater, opera, pep band, radio station, student government, student newspaper, television station, Campus Ministries, International Student Organization 131 registered organizations, 32 honor societies, 17 religious organizations. 14 fraternities, 8 sororities. **Athletics (Intercollegiate):** *Men:* baseball, basketball, cheerleading, cross-country, football, golf. *Women:* basketball, cheerleading, cross-country, golf, soccer, softball, volleyball. **On-Campus Highlights:** Technology Learning Center (TLC), Bookstore, Ingram Library, Football Stadium, Campus Recreation Center, University Community Center, Coliseum, and Campus Visitor's Center.

ADMISSIONS
Freshman Academic Profile: Average high school GPA 3.1. 95% from public high schools. SAT Math middle 50% range 430-510. SAT Critical Reading middle 50% range 440-520. SAT Writing middle 50% range 420-510. ACT middle 50% range 18-21. Minimum web-based TOEFL 69. Minimum paper TOEFL 523. **Basis for Candidate Selection:** *Very important factors considered include:* academic GPA, rigor of secondary school record, standardized test scores. **Freshman Admission Requirements:** High school diploma is required and GED is not accepted. *Academic units required:* 4 English, 4 mathematics, 3 science, (2 science labs), 2 foreign language, 1 social studies, 2 history. *Academic units recommended:* 4 English, 4 mathematics, 3 science, (2 science labs), 2 foreign language, 1 social studies, 2 history. **Freshman Admission Statistics:** 6,435 applied, 56% admitted, 58% enrolled. **Transfer Admission Requirements:** college transcript(s), Minimum college GPA of 2.0 required. Lowest grade transferable D. **General Admission Information:** Application Fee $30. Regular application deadline 6/1. Notification on a rolling basis, beginning on or about 8/1. Nonfall registration accepted. Credit and/or placement offered for CEEB Advanced Placement tests.

COSTS AND FINANCIAL AID
Annual in-state tuition $4,852. Annual out-of-state tuition $17,128. Room and board $7,482. Required fees $1,858. Average book expense $1,300. **Required Forms and Deadlines:** FAFSA. **Notification of Awards:** Applicants will be notified of awards on a rolling basis beginning 6/1. **Types of Aid:** *Need-based scholarships/grants:* Federal Pell, SEOG, state scholarships/grants, private scholarships, the school's own gift aid, United Negro College Fund, Federal Nursing Scholarships. *Loans:* Direct Subsidized Stafford, Direct Unsubsidized Stafford, Direct PLUS, Federal Perkins, state loans, college/university loans from institutional funds. **Student Employment:** Federal Work-Study Program available. Institutional employment available. Highest amount earned per year from on-campus jobs $5,220. **Financial Aid Statistics:** 88% freshmen, 81% undergrads receive need-based scholarship or grant aid. 91% freshmen, 10% undergrads receive non-need-based scholarship or grant aid. 92% freshmen, 91% undergrads receive need-based self-help aid. 3% freshmen, 3% undergrads receive athletic scholarships. 64% freshmen, 73% undergrads receive any aid. 65% undergrads borrow to pay for school. Average cumulative indebtedness $18,539. **Criteria for awarding institutional aid:** *Non-need-based:* academics, alumni affiliation, art, athletics, leadership, minority status, music/drama, religious affiliation, state/district residency.

UNIVERSITY OF WINDSOR

Office of the Registrar, Windsor, ON N9B3P4
Phone: 519-253-3000 • **Financial Aid Phone:** 519-253-3000
E-mail: registrar@uwindsor.ca
Fax: 519-971-3653 • **Website:** www.uwindsor.ca

This public school was founded in 1857. It has a 125-acre campus.

RATINGS
Admissions Selectivity Rating: 62   **Fire Safety Rating:** 79   **Green Rating:** 72

STUDENTS AND FACULTY
Enrollment: 13,916. **Student Body:** 54% female, 46% male, (99 countries represented).
Faculty: Student/faculty ratio 24:1. 584 full-time faculty, 81% hold PhDs, 40% are women.

ACADEMICS
Degrees: bachelor's, certificate, master's. **Majors with Highest Enrollment:** business/commerce; engineering; social sciences; other. **Special Study Options:** cooperative education program, distance learning, double major, English as a Second Language (ESL), exchange student program (domestic), honors program, independent study, internships, study abroad, teacher certification program, MBA for Managers and Professionals, which is offered on weekends (Centre for Executive Education). **Honors Programs:** As a comprehensive university we have distinguished ourselves at many levels. **Combined Degree Programs:** BA (French)/BEd, BA/BEd/ECE, BScBEd, BMath/BEd, BCS/BEd, JD/LLB. **Disability Services:** Special programs offered to physically disabled students include note-taking services, reader services, tape recorders, tutors. **Career Services:** career/job search classes, career assessment, internships Career services highlights include The Centre for Career Education contributes to the holistic education of students and complements academic programs of study by supporting a wide range of career-related programs and resources with an emphasis on excellence in learning from experience. We guide students through the career development process including the exploration of personal workplace preferences and strengths, the development of career competencies, and the construction of a career plan.

FACILITIES
Housing: Coed dorms, special housing for disabled students, special housing for international students, fraternity/sorority housing, apartments for married students, cooperative housing, apartments for single students, off campus housing lists for tenants and landlords. 100% of campus accessible to physically disabled. **Special Academic Facilities/Equipment:** Centre for Engineering Innovation (completion date 2011) C.A.R.E. (Centre for Automotive Research and Education) GLIER (Great Lakes Institute for Environemntal Research) Jackman Dramatic Art Centre (Theatrical space) Bio-Learning Centre (BLC) Biotechnology Laboratory **Computers:** 100% of classrooms, 100% of dorms, 100% of libraries, 100% of dining areas, 100% of student union, 100% of common outdoor areas have wireless network access. Students can register for classes online. Administrative functions (other than registration) can be performed online.

CAMPUS LIFE
Environment: City. **Activities:** Choral groups, dance, drama/theater, jazz band, literary magazine, music ensembles, musical theater, radio station, student government, student newspaper, student-run film society, Campus Ministries, International Student Organization 116 registered organizations, 1 honor societies, 13 religious organizations. 3 fraternities, 3 sororities. **Athletics (Intercollegiate):** *Men:* basketball, cross-country, football, ice hockey, soccer,

track/field (outdoor), track/field (indoor), volleyball. *Women:* basketball, cross-country, ice hockey, soccer, track/field (outdoor), track/field (indoor), volleyball. **On-Campus Highlights:** CAW Student Centre, Forge Fitness facility, The Basement Pub, St. Denis Athletic Centre/University Sta, Leddy Library, Odette Sculpture Garden which includes a scenic 5km waterfront trail. Many students will exercise or study/relax by the water. **Environmental Initiatives:** LEEDS Certified Buildings - Medical School will qualify after completion of the third floor. LEEDS Certified Bldg. $113 Million Centre for Engineering Innovation forthcoming. Consistent internationally recognized research from The Great Lakes Institute for Environmental Research,and many other areas on campus.

ADMISSIONS

Basis for Candidate Selection: *Very important factors considered include:* academic GPA, rigor of secondary school record. *Other factors considered include:* recommendation(s), standardized test scores, extracurricular activities, geographical residence, interview. **Freshman Admission Requirements:** High school diploma is required and GED is not accepted. **Freshman Admission Statistics:** 9,375 applied, 88% admitted, 25% enrolled. **Transfer Admission Requirements:** college transcript(s). **General Admission Information:** Application Fee $75. Notification on a rolling basis, beginning on or about 1/1. Nonfall registration accepted.

COSTS AND FINANCIAL AID

Required Forms and Deadlines: institution's own financial aid formOntario Student Assistance Program (OSAP). **Notification of Awards:** Applicants will be notified of awards on a rolling basis beginning 6/1. **Types of Aid:** *Need-based scholarships/grants:* the school's own gift aid. *Loans:* Ontario Student Assistance Program (OSAP). **Student Employment:** Off-campus job opportunities are good. **Criteria for awarding institutional aid:** *Non-need-based:* academics, art, athletics, leadership, minority status, music/drama, state/district residency.

UNIVERSITY OF WISCONSIN—EAU CLAIRE

105 Garfield Avenue, Eau Claire, WI 54701
Phone: 715 836 5415 • **Financial Aid Phone:** 715-836-3373
E-mail: admissions@uwec.edu • **CEEB Code:** 1913
Fax: 715-836-2409 • **Website:** www.uwec.edu • **ACT Code:** 4670

This public school was founded in 1916. It has a 333-acre campus.

RATINGS

Admissions Selectivity Rating: 77   **Fire Safety Rating:** 73   **Green Rating:** 83

STUDENTS AND FACULTY

Enrollment: 10,269. **Student Body:** 58% female, 42% male, 23% out-of-state, 2% international (39 countries represented). Asian 3%, African American 1%, Caucasian 90%, Hispanic 2%, Native American 0%
Retention and Graduation: 83% freshmen return for sophomore year. 26% freshmen graduate within 4 years. 66% freshmen graduate within 6 years. 14% grads go on to further study within 1 year. **Faculty:** Student/faculty ratio 22:1. 432 full-time faculty, 83% hold PhDs, 15% are members of minority groups, 47% are women.

ACADEMICS

Degrees: associate, bachelor's, certificate, master's, post-bachelor's certificate, post-master's certificate, terminal associate, transfer associate. **Classes:** Most classes have 20—29 students. Most lab/discussion sessions have 20—29 students. **Majors with Highest Enrollment:** biology/biological sciences; elementary education and teaching; nursing/registered nurse (rn, asn, bsn, msn). **Special Study Options:** Accelerated program, cooperative education program, cross-registration, distance learning, double major, dual enrollment, English as a Second Language (ESL), exchange student program (domestic), external degree program, honors program, independent study, internships, student-designed major, study abroad, teacher certification program, Collaborative programs in Early Childhood Education. **Disability Services:** Special programs offered to physically disabled students include note-taking services, reader services, tutors. **Career Services:** Alumni network, alumni services, career/job search classes, career assessment, internships, regional alumni.

FACILITIES

Housing: Coed dorms, men's dorms, women's dorms, apartments for single students. 80% of campus accessible to physically disabled. **Special Academic Facilities/Equipment:** Art gallery, human development center, bird museum, field station, planetarium. **Computers:** 50% of classrooms, 10% of dorms, 100% of libraries, 100% of dining areas, 100% of student union, 100% of common outdoor areas have wireless network access. Students can register for classes online. Administrative functions (other than registration) can be performed online.

CAMPUS LIFE

Environment: Town. **Activities:** Choral groups, concert band, dance, drama/theater, jazz band, literary magazine, marching band, music ensembles, musical theater, opera, pep band, radio station, student government, student newspaper, student-run film society, symphony orchestra, television station, Campus Ministries, International Student Organization, Model UN 240 registered organizations, 30 honor societies, 16 religious organizations. 2 fraternities, 3 sororities. **Athletics (Intercollegiate):** *Men:* basketball, cross-country, diving, football, golf, ice hockey, swimming, tennis, track/field (outdoor), track/field (indoor), wrestling. *Women:* basketball, cross-country, diving, golf, gymnastics, ice hockey, soccer, softball, swimming, tennis, track/field (outdoor), track/field (indoor), volleyball. **On-Campus Highlights:** Chippewa River Footbridge, Davies Center (Student Center/Union), McPhee Center (Athletic Facility), Hass Fine Arts Center, Higher Ground (Recreational Facility). **Environmental Initiatives:** Creation of an energy performance contract to provide $3.4 million in energy conservation measures across campus, including heating and ventilation, lighting, water conservation, etc. Initiation of a "green fee" and organization of the Student Office of Sustainability to administer it, with an annual budget of approximately $220,000 for sustainability initiatives on campus. Approval for hiring three new faculty members into the interdisciplinary Watershed Institute for Collaborative Environmental Studies; they will develop new courses in sustainability and environmental studies for general education and for environmental studies minors.

ADMISSIONS

Freshman Academic Profile: 20% in top 10% of high school class, 34% in top 25% of high school class, 96% in top 50% of high school class. SAT Math middle 50% range 510-630. SAT Critical Reading middle 50% range 530-650. ACT middle 50% range 22-26. Minimum web-based TOEFL 79. Minimum paper TOEFL 550. **Basis for Candidate Selection:** *Very important factors considered include:* Class rank, rigor of secondary school record. *Important factors considered include:* standardized test scores. *Other factors considered include:* application essay, academic GPA, recommendation(s), character/personal qualities, extracurricular activities, first generation, interview, level of applicant's interest, racial/ethnic status, talent/ability, volunteer work, work experience. **Freshman Admission Requirements:** High school diploma is required and GED is accepted. *Academic units required:* 4 English, 3 mathematics, 3 science, 2 foreign language, 3 social studies, 2 academic electives. *Academic units recommended:* 4 English, 3 mathematics, 3 science, 2 foreign language, 3 social studies, 2 academic electives. **Freshman Admission Statistics:** 6,625 applied, 76% admitted, 41% enrolled. **Transfer Admission Requirements:** High school transcript, college transcript(s), statement of good standing from prior institution(s). Minimum college GPA of 2.0 required. Lowest grade transferable D-. **General Admission Information:** Application Fee $44. Notification on a rolling basis, beginning on or about 9/15. Nonfall registration accepted. Credit and/or placement offered for CEEB Advanced Placement tests.

COSTS AND FINANCIAL AID

Annual in-state tuition $7,361. Annual out-of-state tuition $14,934. Room and board $6,300. Required fees $1,330. Average book expense $470. **Required Forms and Deadlines:** FAFSA. **Notification of Awards:** Applicants will be notified of awards on a rolling basis beginning 4/15. **Types of Aid:** *Need-based scholarships/grants:* Federal Pell, SEOG, state scholarships/grants, private scholarships, the school's own gift aid, Federal Nursing Scholarships., Academic Competetiveness Grant, SMART Grant, BIA Excellence in Math/Comp. Science, EMAC, Student Support Services Grant. *Loans:* Direct Subsidized Stafford, Direct Unsubsidized Stafford, Direct PLUS, Federal Perkins, state loans, college/university loans from institutional funds, Private. **Student Employment:** Federal Work-Study Program available. Institutional employment available. Highest amount earned per year from on-campus jobs $10,023. Off-campus job opportunities are fair. **Financial Aid Statistics:** 79% freshmen, 72% undergrads receive need-based scholarship or grant aid. 4% freshmen, 2% undergrads receive non-need-based scholarship or grant aid. 94% freshmen, 95% undergrads receive need-based self-help aid. 80% freshmen, 73% undergrads receive any aid. 70% undergrads borrow to pay for school. Average cumulative indebtedness $23,825. **Criteria for awarding institutional aid:** *Non-need-based:* academics, art, leadership, minority status, music/drama, state/district residency.

UNIVERSITY OF WISCONSIN—GREEN BAY

2420 Nicolet Drive, Green Bay, WI 53411-7001
Phone: 920-465-2111 • **Financial Aid Phone:** 920)465-2075
E-mail: admissions@uwgb.edu • **CEEB Code:** 1859
Fax: 920-465-5754 • **Website:** www.uwgb.edu/ • **ACT Code:** 4688

This public school was founded in 1965. It has a 700-acre campus.

RATINGS
Admissions Selectivity Rating: 77   **Fire Safety Rating:** 75   **Green Rating:** 89

STUDENTS AND FACULTY
Enrollment: 6,073. **Student Body:** 65% female, 35% male, 7% out-of-state, 1% international (27 countries represented). Asian 3%, African American 1%, Caucasian 88%, Hispanic 3%, Native American 1%
Retention and Graduation: 74% freshmen return for sophomore year. 22% freshmen graduate within 4 years. 51% freshmen graduate within 6 years. 15% grads go on to further study within 1 year. 7% grads pursue arts and sciences degrees. 1% grads pursue law degrees. 3% grads pursue business degrees. 1% grads pursue medical degrees. **Faculty:** Student/faculty ratio 23:1. 187 full-time faculty, 85% hold PhDs, 19% are members of minority groups, 46% are women. 0% of classes are taught by teaching assistants.

ACADEMICS
Degrees: associate, bachelor's, master's, post-bachelor's certificate. **Classes:** Most classes have 20—29 students. Most lab/discussion sessions have 20—29 students. **Majors with Highest Enrollment:** biological and biomedical sciences, other; business/commerce; psychology. **Special Study Options:** cross-registration, distance learning, double major, exchange student program (domestic), external degree program, independent study, internships, liberal arts/career combination, student-designed major, study abroad, teacher certification program. **Combined Degree Programs:** BS/MS Environmental Science/Env Science & Policy. **Disability Services:** Special programs offered to physically disabled students include note-taking services, reader services, tape recorders. **Career Services:** Alumni network, alumni services, career/job search classes, internships.

FACILITIES
Housing: Coed dorms, apartments for single students, Suites w/ private bedrooms. 99% of campus accessible to physically disabled. **Special Academic Facilities/Equipment:** 290-acre arboretum, Herbarium, regional Performing Arts Center **Computers:** 75% of classrooms, 100% of dorms, 100% of libraries, 100% of dining areas, 100% of student union, 10% of common outdoor areas have wireless network access. Students can register for classes online. Administrative functions (other than registration) can be performed online.

CAMPUS LIFE
Environment: City. **Activities:** Choral groups, concert band, dance, drama/theater, jazz band, literary magazine, music ensembles, musical theater, pep band, radio station, student government, student newspaper, student-run film society, television station, Campus Ministries, International Student Organization 100 registered organizations, 7 honor societies, 5 religious organizations. 2 fraternities, 2 sororities. **Athletics (Intercollegiate):** *Men:* basketball, cheerleading, cross-country, diving, golf, skiingnordiccross-country, soccer, swimming, tennis. *Women:* basketball, cheerleading, cross-country, diving, golf, skiingnordiccross-country, soccer, softball, swimming, tennis, volleyball. **On-Campus Highlights:** Mary Ann Cofrin Hall - State-of-the-art academic bldg., Kress Event Center -recently remodeled, Weidner Center for Performing Arts, Lambeau Cottage on the shores of Green B, Student Union-recently remodeled. **Environmental Initiatives:** Building integrated photovoltaics in Mary Ann Cofrin Hall (http://www.buildingsolar.com/index.html) Historically strong academic programs in environmental science and environmental policy and planning at both bachelor's and master's level. Campus design connects buildings with energy efficient underground tunnels.

ADMISSIONS
Freshman Academic Profile: Average high school GPA 3.3. 95% from public high schools. ACT middle 50% range 21-25. Minimum web-based TOEFL 61. Minimum paper TOEFL 500. **Basis for Candidate Selection:** *Very important factors considered include:* academic GPA, rigor of secondary school record, standardized test scores, extracurricular activities. *Important factors considered include:* application essay, level of applicant's interest, volunteer work, work experience. *Other factors considered include:* recommendation(s), character/personal qualities, geographical residence, interview, racial/ethnic status, state residency, talent/ability. **Freshman Admission Requirements:** High school diploma is required and GED is accepted. *Academic units required:* 4 English, 3 mathematics, 3 science, (1 science labs), 3 social studies, 4 academic electives. *Academic units recommended:* 4 English, 3 mathematics, 3 science, (1 science labs), 3 social studies, 4 academic electives. **Freshman Admission Statistics:** 3,298 applied, 64% admitted, 44% enrolled. **Transfer Admission Requirements:** college transcript(s), Minimum college GPA of 2.0 required. Lowest grade transferable D. **General Admission Information:** Application Fee $44. Notification on a rolling basis, beginning on or about 9/15. Nonfall registration accepted. Admission may be deferred for a maximum of 1 year. Credit and/or placement offered for CEEB Advanced Placement tests.

COSTS AND FINANCIAL AID
Annual in-state tuition $6,298. Annual out-of-state tuition $13,871. Room and board $7,076. Required fees $1,350. Average book expense $800. **Required Forms and Deadlines:** FAFSA. **Notification of Awards:** Applicants will be notified of awards on a rolling basis beginning 1/1. **Types of Aid:** *Need-based scholarships/grants:* Federal Pell, SEOG, state scholarships/grants, private scholarships, the school's own gift aid. *Loans:* Subsidized Stafford, Unsubsidized Stafford, PLUS, Federal Perkins. **Student Employment:** Federal Work-Study Program available. Institutional employment available. Off-campus job opportunities are good. **Financial Aid Statistics:** 60% freshmen, 69% undergrads receive need-based scholarship or grant aid. 20% freshmen, 12% undergrads receive non-need-based scholarship or grant aid. 80% freshmen, 80% undergrads receive need-based self-help aid. 1% freshmen, 1% undergrads receive athletic scholarships. 87% freshmen, 77% undergrads receive any aid. 70% undergrads borrow to pay for school. Average cumulative indebtedness $23,650. **Criteria for awarding institutional aid:** *Non-need-based:* academics, art, athletics, leadership, minority status, music/drama.

UNIVERSITY OF WISCONSIN—LA CROSSE

1725 State Street, La Crosse, WI 54601-3742
Phone: 608-785-8939 • **Financial Aid Phone:** 608-785-8604
E-mail: admissions@uwlax.edu • **CEEB Code:** 1914
Fax: 608-785-8940 • **Website:** www.uwlax.edu • **ACT Code:** 4672

This public school was founded in 1909. It has a 120-acre campus.

RATINGS
Admissions Selectivity Rating: 79   **Fire Safety Rating:** 61   **Green Rating:** 60*

STUDENTS AND FACULTY
Enrollment: 9,191. **Student Body:** 58% female, 42% male, 16% out-of-state, 2% international (29 countries represented). Asian 2%, African American 1%, Caucasian 89%, Hispanic 3%, Native American 0%
Retention and Graduation: 86% freshmen return for sophomore year. 36% freshmen graduate within 4 years. 71% freshmen graduate within 6 years. **Faculty:** Student/faculty ratio 20:1. 457 full-time faculty, 75% hold PhDs, 9% are members of minority groups, 50% are women. 0% of classes are taught by teaching assistants.

ACADEMICS
Degrees: associate, bachelor's, certificate, master's, post-bachelor's certificate. **Classes:** Most classes have 20—29 students. Most lab/discussion sessions have 20—29 students. **Majors with Highest Enrollment:** elementary education and teaching; kinesiology and exercise science; marketing/marketing management. **Special Study Options:** cooperative education program, cross-registration, distance learning, double major, dual enrollment, English as a Second Language (ESL), honors program, independent study, internships, liberal arts/career combination, study abroad, teacher certification program, Weekend college: grad only. **Honors Programs:** University Honors Program lt;http://www.uwlax.edu/honors/gt; **Combined Degree Programs:** BS/MSPT; BS/MSOT. **Disability Services:** Special programs offered to physically disabled students include note-taking services, reader services, tape recorders, tutors.

FACILITIES
Housing: Coed dorms, special housing for international students, wellness housing, First Year Experience. 98% of campus accessible to physically disabled. **Special Academic Facilities/Equipment:** Greenhouse, planetarium, Health Science Center,Mississippi Valley Archaeology Center, River Studies center, Business Development Center, La Crosse Exercise and Health Program **Computers:** Students can register for classes online. Administrative functions (other than registration) can be performed online.

CAMPUS LIFE
Environment: City. **Activities:** Choral groups, concert band, drama/theater, jazz band, marching band, music ensembles, pep band, radio station, student government, student newspaper, symphony orchestra, International Student Organization 180 registered organizations, 13 honor societies, 10 religious organizations. 4 fraternities, 2 sororities. **Athletics (Intercollegiate):** *Men:* baseball, basketball, cross-country, diving, football, swimming, tennis, track/field (outdoor), track/field (indoor), wrestling. *Women:* basketball, cross-country,

diving, gymnastics, soccer, softball, swimming, tennis, track/field (outdoor), track/field (indoor), volleyball. **On-Campus Highlights:** Recreation Eagle Center, Cyber Cafe, Archaeology Museum, Murphy Library, Wing Technology Computer Lab, The 119 acre campus has 32 buildings, including 19 used for instruction, academic support and administrative purposes; 10 residence halls and three student centers.

ADMISSIONS
Freshman Academic Profile: 26% in top 10% of high school class, 77% in top 25% of high school class, 98% in top 50% of high school class. SAT Math middle 50% range 520-643. SAT Writing middle 50% range 473-600. ACT middle 50% range 23-28. Minimum web-based TOEFL 73. Minimum paper TOEFL 550. **Basis for Candidate Selection:** *Very important factors considered include:* Class rank, academic GPA, rigor of secondary school record, standardized test scores. *Important factors considered include:* application essay, extracurricular activities, level of applicant's interest, volunteer work. *Other factors considered include:* recommendation(s), alumni/ae relation, character/personal qualities, first generation, geographical residence, interview, racial/ethnic status, state residency, talent/ability, work experience. **Freshman Admission Requirements:** High school diploma is required and GED is accepted. *Academic units required:* 4 English, 3 mathematics, 3 science, (2 science labs), 3 social studies, 4 academic electives. *Academic units recommended:* 4 English, 3 mathematics, 3 science, (2 science labs), 3 social studies, 4 academic electives. **Freshman Admission Statistics:** 6,908 applied, 71% admitted, 38% enrolled. **Transfer Admission Requirements:** college transcript(s), statement of good standing from prior institution(s). Minimum college GPA of 3.0 required. Lowest grade transferable D-. **General Admission Information:** Application Fee $44. Notification on a rolling basis, beginning on or about 9/15. Nonfall registration accepted. Credit and/or placement offered for CEEB Advanced Placement tests.

COSTS AND FINANCIAL AID
Annual in-state tuition $7,585. Annual out-of-state tuition $15,158. Room and board $6,000. Required fees $1,170. Average book expense $300. **Required Forms and Deadlines:** FAFSA. **Notification of Awards:** Applicants will be notified of awards on a rolling basis beginning 4/1. **Types of Aid:** *Need-based scholarships/grants:* Federal Pell, SEOG, state scholarships/grants, private scholarships, the school's own gift aid. *Loans:* Subsidized Stafford, Unsubsidized Stafford, PLUS, Federal Perkins. **Student Employment:** Highest amount earned per year from on campus jobs $7,020. **Financial Aid Statistics:** 42% freshmen, 53% undergrads receive need-based scholarship or grant aid. 61% freshmen, 29% undergrads receive non-need-based scholarship or grant aid. 81% freshmen, 87% undergrads receive need-based self-help aid. 71% undergrads borrow to pay for school. Average cumulative indebtedness $24,863. **Criteria for awarding institutional aid:** *Non need-based:* academics, art, athletics, leadership, music/drama.

UNIVERSITY OF WISCONSIN—MADISON

702 West Johnson Street, Suite 101, Madison, WI 53715
Phone: 608-262-3961 • **Financial Aid Phone:** 608-262-3060
E-mail: onwisconsin@admissions.wisc.edu • **CEEB Code:** 1846
Fax: 608-262-7706 • **Website:** www.wisc.edu • **ACT Code:** 4656

This public school was founded in 1848. It has a 933-acre campus.

RATINGS
Admissions Selectivity Rating: 92   **Fire Safety Rating:** 71   **Green Rating:** 82

STUDENTS AND FACULTY
Enrollment: 29,118. **Student Body:** 52% female, 48% male, 34% out-of-state, 7% international (144 countries represented). Asian 5%, African American 2%, Caucasian 78%, Hispanic 4%, Native American 0%
Retention and Graduation: 95% freshmen return for sophomore year. 54% freshmen graduate within 4 years. 83% freshmen graduate within 6 years.
Faculty: Student/faculty ratio 17:1. 2350 full-time faculty, 91% hold PhDs, 17% are members of minority groups, 36% are women. 21% of classes are taught by teaching assistants.

ACADEMICS
Degrees: bachelor's, doctoral, master's, post-master's certificate. **Classes:** Most classes have 10—19 students. Most lab/discussion sessions have 20—29 students. **Majors with Highest Enrollment:** biology/biological sciences; economics; political science and government. **Special Study Options:** Accelerated program, cooperative education program, distance learning, double major, dual enrollment, English as a Second Language (ESL), exchange student program (domestic), honors program, independent study, internships, liberal arts/career combination, student-designed major, study abroad, teacher certification program. **Disability Services:** Special programs offered to physically disabled students include note-taking services, reader services, tape recorders, tutors. **Career Services:** Alumni network, career/job search classes, career assessment, internships Career services highlights include This question is difficult to answer. We have multiple career placement centers for different schools and colleges. Futhermore, we have all of the services above, but they are not all offered through a career placement center. For example, internships are generally organized through academic departments and alumni services are provided through our alumni association.

FACILITIES
Housing: Coed dorms, men's dorms, special housing for international students, women's dorms, fraternity/sorority housing, apartments for married students, cooperative housing, apartments for single students, theme housing, Residential Learning Communities. 80% of campus accessible to physically disabled. **Special Academic Facilities/Equipment:** Art, physics, and geology museums, nuclear reactor, arboretum, botanical gardens, observatory, campus dairy store (campus-made ice cream and cheese), american indian burial mounds **Computers:** 100% of classrooms, 25% of dorms, 100% of libraries, 100% of dining areas, 100% of student union, 100% of common outdoor areas have wireless network access. Students can register for classes online. Administrative functions (other than registration) can be performed online.

CAMPUS LIFE
Environment: City. **Activities:** Choral groups, concert band, dance, drama/theater, jazz band, literary magazine, marching band, music ensembles, musical theater, opera, pep band, radio station, student government, student newspaper, student-run film society, symphony orchestra, television station, yearbook, International Student Organization 685 registered organizations, 27 honor societies, 26 fraternities, 11 sororities. **Athletics (Intercollegiate):** *Men:* basketball, cheerleading, crew/rowing, cross-country, football, golf, ice hockey, soccer, swimming, tennis, track/field (outdoor), wrestling. *Women:* basketball, cheerleading, crew/rowing, cross-country, golf, ice hockey, soccer, softball, swimming, tennis, track/field (outdoor), volleyball. **On-Campus Highlights:** Allen Centennial Gardens, Kohl Center, Memorial Union Terrace, Chazen Museum of Art, Babcock Hall Dairy Plant and Store, http://www.visit.wisc.edu/todo.html. **Environmental Initiatives:** Our conservation efforts in the last four years have reduced campus energy consumption by over 1 trillion BTUs and water consumption by 178,000,000 gallons annually. Investment of over $70 million in energy conservation since 2001. Integrating research, teaching, and operations arms of the University to maximize sustainability culture change in the university.

ADMISSIONS
Freshman Academic Profile: Average high school GPA 3.8. 56% in top 10% of high school class, 94% in top 25% of high school class, 100% in top 50% of high school class. SAT Math middle 50% range 630-750. SAT Critical Reading middle 50% range 530-650. SAT Writing middle 50% range 570-670. ACT middle 50% range 26-30. Minimum web-based TOEFL 80. Minimum paper TOEFL 550. **Basis for Candidate Selection:** *Very important factors considered include:* Class rank, academic GPA, rigor of secondary school record. *Important factors considered include:* application essay, standardized test scores, state residency. *Other factors considered include:* recommendation(s), alumni/ae relation, character/personal qualities, extracurricular activities, first generation, level of applicant's interest, racial/ethnic status, talent/ability, volunteer work, work experience. **Freshman Admission Requirements:** High school diploma is required and GED is accepted. *Academic units required:* 4 English, 3 mathematics, 3 science, 2 foreign language, 3 social studies, 2 academic electives. *Academic units recommended:* 4 English, 3 mathematics, 3 science, 2 foreign language, 3 social studies, 2 academic electives. **Freshman Admission Statistics:** 30,034 applied, 53% admitted, 40% enrolled. **Transfer Admission Requirements:** High school transcript, college transcript(s), essay or personal statement, Lowest grade transferable D. **General Admission Information:** Application Fee $44. Regular application deadline 2/1. Notification on a rolling basis, beginning on or about 10/1. Nonfall registration accepted. Admission may be deferred for a maximum of 1 year. Credit and/or placement offered for CEEB Advanced Placement tests.

COSTS AND FINANCIAL AID
Annual in-state tuition $9,273. Annual out-of-state tuition $25,523. Room and board $8,080. Required fees $1,111. Average book expense $1,190. **Required Forms and Deadlines:** FAFSA, institution's own financial aid form. **Notification of Awards:** Applicants will be notified of awards on a rolling basis beginning 4/1. **Types of Aid:** *Need-based scholarships/grants:* Federal Pell, SEOG, state scholarships/grants, private scholarships, the school's own gift aid. *Loans:* Subsidized Stafford, Unsubsidized Stafford, PLUS, Federal Perkins, Federal Nursing, state loansWe are transitioning to direct lending within the next year. **Student Employment:** Federal Work-Study Program available. Institutional

employment available. Off-campus job opportunities are excellent. **Financial Aid Statistics:** 61% freshmen, 70% undergrads receive need-based scholarship or grant aid. 62% freshmen, 42% undergrads receive non-need-based scholarship or grant aid. 79% freshmen, 83% undergrads receive need-based self-help aid. 1% freshmen, 2% undergrads receive athletic scholarships. 51% freshmen, 48% undergrads receive any aid. 49% undergrads borrow to pay for school. Average cumulative indebtedness $24,700. **Criteria for awarding institutional aid:** *Non-need-based:* academics, alumni affiliation, art, athletics, job skills, leadership, minority status, music/drama, religious affiliation, state/district residency.

UNIVERSITY OF WISCONSIN—MILWAUKEE

PO Box 749, Milwaukee, WI 53201
Phone: 414-229-2222 • **Financial Aid Phone:** 414-229-4541
E-mail: uwmlook@uwm.edu • **CEEB Code:** 1473
Fax: 414-229-6940 • **Website:** www4.uwm.edu • **ACT Code:** 4658

This public school was founded in 1956. It has a 93-acre campus.

RATINGS
Admissions Selectivity Rating: 71   **Fire Safety Rating:** 95   **Green Rating:** 93

STUDENTS AND FACULTY
Enrollment: 22,685. **Student Body:** 50% female, 50% male, 6% out-of-state, 2% international (81 countries represented). Asian 6%, African American 8%, Caucasian 73%, Hispanic 7%, Native American 0%
Retention and Graduation: 69% freshmen return for sophomore year. **Faculty:** Student/faculty ratio 20:1. 1073 full-time faculty, 63% hold PhDs, 22% are members of minority groups, 46% are women.

ACADEMICS
Degrees: bachelor's, certificate, master's, post-bachelor's certificate, post-master's certificate. **Classes:** Most classes have 20—29 students. Most lab/discussion sessions have 20—29 students. **Special Study Options:** Accelerated program, cooperative education program, cross-registration, distance learning, double major, dual enrollment, English as a Second Language (ESL), external degree program, honors program, independent study, internships, liberal arts/career combination, student-designed major, study abroad, teacher certification program. **Disability Services:** Special programs offered to physically disabled students include note-taking services, reader services, tape recorders, tutors. **Career Services:** career assessment, internships Career services highlights include LaMacchia Enterprises Entrepreneur Internship.

FACILITIES
Housing: Coed dorms, special housing for disabled students, apartments for single students. **Special Academic Facilities/Equipment:** Art and geology museums, childhood education center, foreign language resource center, Great Lakes research facility and environmental studies field station, planetarium.

CAMPUS LIFE
Activities: Choral groups, concert band, dance, drama/theater, jazz band, literary magazine, marching band, music ensembles, musical theater, pep band, radio station, student government, student newspaper, student-run film society, symphony orchestra, Campus Ministries, International Student Organization, Model UN 250 registered organizations, 1 honor societies, 4 religious organizations. 8 fraternities, 4 sororities. **Athletics (Intercollegiate):** *Men:* baseball, basketball, cross-country, diving, soccer, swimming, track/field (outdoor). *Women:* basketball, cross-country, soccer, swimming, tennis, track/field (outdoor), volleyball. **Environmental Initiatives:** Energy Matters- UWM is undergoing performance contracting to reduce energy consumption by 25% by 2013. 1/5 of the campus has been completed and the rest of campus is under construction and planning. Current trends are showing an actual 38% savings. Stormwater Management and "Green Roof" projects. The campus currently has 7 green roofs, one green parking lot that filters 1.5 acres of campus, including the recently completed construction on its largest green roof, 50,000 sq ft, on the Golda Meir Library, which also included an integrated 30 kW solar pv system. Recycling Commitment, including increased recycling, composting, E-Waste recycling, techno trash recycling, and a Construction & Demolition Debris recycling program.

ADMISSIONS
Freshman Academic Profile: Average high school GPA 3.1. 10% in top 10% of high school class, 29% in top 25% of high school class, 68% in top 50% of high school class. ACT middle 50% range 20-24. Minimum paper TOEFL 520. **Basis for Candidate Selection:** *Very important factors considered include:* academic GPA, rigor of secondary school record. *Important factors considered include:* Class rank, standardized test scores, talent/ability. *Other factors consid-*

ered include: application essay, recommendation(s), character/personal qualities, extracurricular activities, first generation, geographical residence, interview, level of applicant's interest, racial/ethnic status, state residency, volunteer work, work experience. **Freshman Admission Requirements:** High school diploma is required and GED is accepted. *Academic units required:* 4 English, 3 mathematics, 3 science, (1 science labs), 3 social studies, 2 academic electives, 2 From the above areas, computer science, fine arts, or other appropriate courses. *Academic units recommended:* 4 English, 3 mathematics, 3 science, (1 science labs), 3 social studies, 2 academic electives, 2 From the above areas, computer science, fine arts, or other appropriate courses **Freshman Admission Statistics:** 10,667 applied, 71% admitted, 45% enrolled. **Transfer Admission Requirements:** High school transcript, college transcript(s), Minimum college GPA of 2.0 required. Lowest grade transferable D-. **General Admission Information:** Application Fee $44. Regular application deadline 7/1. Notification on a rolling basis, beginning on or about 9/15. Nonfall registration accepted. Admission may be deferred for a maximum of 1 semester. Credit offered for CEEB Advanced Placement tests.

COSTS AND FINANCIAL AID
Required Forms and Deadlines: FAFSA. **Notification of Awards:** Applicants will be notified of awards on a rolling basis beginning 3/10. **Types of Aid:** *Need-based scholarships/grants:* Federal Pell, SEOG, state scholarships/grants, private scholarships, the school's own gift aid, Federal Nursing Scholarships. *Loans:* Subsidized Stafford, Unsubsidized Stafford, PLUS, Federal Perkins, Federal Nursing, state loans, Alternative Loans. **Student Employment:** Federal Work-Study Program available. Institutional employment available. Off-campus job opportunities are good. **Financial Aid Statistics:** 54% freshmen, 51% undergrads receive need-based scholarship or grant aid. 6% freshmen, 16% undergrads receive non-need-based scholarship or grant aid. 85% freshmen, 83% undergrads receive need-based self-help aid. 1% freshmen, 4% undergrads receive athletic scholarships. 70% freshmen, 67% undergrads receive any aid. 72% undergrads borrow to pay for school. Average cumulative indebtedness $32,371. **Criteria for awarding institutional aid:** *Non-need-based:* academics, art, athletics, music/drama.

UNIVERSITY OF WISCONSIN—OSHKOSH

Dempsey Hall 135, Oshkosh, WI 54901
Phone: 920-424-0202 • **Financial Aid Phone:** 920-424-4025
E-mail: oshadmuw@uwosh.edu • **CEEB Code:** 1916
Fax: 920-424-1098 • **Website:** www.uwosh.edu/home • **ACT Code:** 4674

This public school was founded in 1871. It has a 192-acre campus.

RATINGS
Admissions Selectivity Rating: 73   **Fire Safety Rating:** 60*   **Green Rating:** 98

STUDENTS AND FACULTY
Enrollment: 10,771. **Student Body:** 57% female, 43% male, 3% out-of-state, 1% international (32 countries represented). Asian 4%, African American 2%, Caucasian 88%, Hispanic 3%, Native American 1%
Retention and Graduation: 75% freshmen return for sophomore year. 13% freshmen graduate within 4 years. **Faculty:** Student/faculty ratio 22:1. 416 full-time faculty, 84% hold PhDs, 12% are members of minority groups, 47% are women. 0% of classes are taught by teaching assistants.

ACADEMICS
Degrees: associate, bachelor's, certificate, master's. **Classes:** Most classes have 20—29 students. Most lab/discussion sessions have 20—29 students. **Majors with Highest Enrollment:** business/commerce; elementary education and teaching; nursing/registered nurse (rn, asn, bsn, msn). **Special Study Options:** Accelerated program, cooperative education program, cross-registration, distance learning, double major, dual enrollment, English as a Second Language (ESL), exchange student program (domestic), honors program, independent study, internships, liberal arts/career combination, student-designed major, study abroad, teacher certification program, weekend college. **Disability Services:** Special programs offered to physically disabled students include note-taking services, reader services, tape recorders, tutors.

FACILITIES
Housing: Coed dorms, special housing for disabled students, men's dorms, women's dorms, fraternity/sorority housing **Special Academic Facilities/Equipment:** Art gallery, ceramics lab, electron microscope. **Computers:** Students can register for classes online.

CAMPUS LIFE
Environment: Village. **Activities:** Choral groups, concert band, dance, drama/theater, jazz band, literary magazine, music ensembles, pep band, radio station,

student government, student newspaper, student-run film society, television station, Campus Ministries, International Student Organization, Model UN 175 registered organizations, 15 honor societies, 6 religious organizations. 8 fraternities, 5 sororities. **Athletics (Intercollegiate):** *Men:* baseball, basketball, cross-country, diving, football, soccer, swimming, tennis, track/field (outdoor), track/field (indoor), wrestling. *Women:* basketball, cross-country, diving, golf, gymnastics, soccer, softball, swimming, tennis, track/field (outdoor), track/field (indoor), volleyball. **Environmental Initiatives:** Leadership in adopting renewable energy, from 2003 as the largest purchaser of renewable electricity in the State of Wisconsin to the recent construction of the first commercial-scale dry anerobic biodigester in the Western Hemisphere. Adopting LEED Gold as the goal for future construction and renovation; 2 buildings are in review for certification and a third is under construction. General education reform listing an essential learning outcome of understanding sustainability and its applications.

ADMISSIONS

Freshman Academic Profile: Average high school GPA 3.3. 10% in top 10% of high school class, 37% in top 25% of high school class, 84% in top 50% of high school class. 90% from public high schools. ACT middle 50% range 20-24. Minimum web-based TOEFL 70. Minimum paper TOEFL 525. **Basis for Candidate Selection:** *Very important factors considered include:* rigor of secondary school record. *Important factors considered include:* Class rank, academic GPA, standardized test scores. *Other factors considered include:* application essay, recommendation(s), alumni/ae relation, character/personal qualities, extracurricular activities, first generation, racial/ethnic status, talent/ability, volunteer work, work experience. **Freshman Admission Requirements:** High school diploma is required and GED is accepted. *Academic units required:* 4 English, 3 mathematics, 3 science, (3 science labs), 3 social studies, 4 academic electives. *Academic units recommended:* 4 English, 3 mathematics, 3 science, (3 science labs), 3 social studies, 4 academic electives. **Freshman Admission Statistics:** 6,052 applied, 66% admitted, 44% enrolled. **Transfer Admission Requirements:** college transcript(s), Minimum college GPA of 2.50 required. Lowest grade transferable D. **General Admission Information:** Application Fee $44. Regular application deadline 8/1. Notification on a rolling basis, beginning on or about 9/15. Nonfall registration accepted. Admission may be deferred for a maximum of 12. Credit offered for CEEB Advanced Placement tests.

COSTS AND FINANCIAL AID

Annual in-state tuition $7,360. Annual out-of-state tuition $14,934. Room and board $6,026. Average book expense $1,000. **Required Forms and Deadlines:** FAFSA. **Notification of Awards:** Applicants will be notified of awards on or about 4/15. **Types of Aid:** *Need-based scholarships/grants:* Federal Pell, SEOG, state scholarships/grants, private scholarships, the school's own gift aid, Federal Nursing Scholarships. *Loans:* Subsidized Stafford, Unsubsidized Stafford, PLUS, Federal Perkins, Federal Nursing, state loans, college/university loans from institutional funds. **Student Employment:** Federal Work-Study Program available. Institutional employment available. **Financial Aid Statistics:** 53% freshmen, 55% undergrads receive need-based scholarship or grant aid. 35% freshmen, 20% undergrads receive non-need-based scholarship or grant aid. 29% freshmen, 20% undergrads receive need-based self-help aid. 66% undergrads borrow to pay for school. Average cumulative indebtedness $25,343. **Criteria for awarding institutional aid:** *Non-need-based:* academics, art, job skills, leadership, minority status, music/drama, state/district residency.

UNIVERSITY OF WISCONSIN—PARKSIDE

Box 2000, Kenosha, WI 53141-2000
Phone: 262-595-2355 • **Financial Aid Phone:** 262-595-2574
E-mail: matthew.jensen@uwp.edu • **CEEB Code:** 1860
Fax: 262-595-2008 • **Website:** www.uwp.edu • **ACT Code:** 4690

This public school was founded in 1968. It has a 700-acre campus.

RATINGS

Admissions Selectivity Rating: 64   **Fire Safety Rating:** 62   **Green Rating:** 60*

STUDENTS AND FACULTY

Enrollment: 4,590. **Student Body:** 57% female, 43% male, 7% out-of-state. 1% international (28 countries represented). Asian 3%, African American 8%, Caucasian 69%, Hispanic 6%, Native American 1%
Retention and Graduation: 65% freshmen return for sophomore year. 9% freshmen graduate within 4 years. 28% freshmen graduate within 6 years.

Faculty: Student/faculty ratio 18:1. 181 full-time faculty, 74% hold PhDs, 22% are members of minority groups, 45% are women. 0% of classes are taught by teaching assistants.

ACADEMICS

Degrees: bachelor's, certificate, master's. **Classes:** Most classes have fewer than 10 students. Most lab/discussion sessions have 20—29 students. **Majors with Highest Enrollment:** business/commerce; criminal justice/law enforcement administration; sociology. **Special Study Options:** Accelerated program, distance learning, double major, dual enrollment, exchange student program (domestic), honors program, independent study, internships, liberal arts/career combination, study abroad, teacher certification program, weekend college, Cooperative nursing program with University of Wisconsin: Milwaukee. **Disability Services:** Special programs offered to physically disabled students include note-taking services, reader services, tape recorders. **Career Services:** alumni services, career/job search classes, career assessment, internships.

FACILITIES

Housing: Coed dorms, special housing for disabled students, special housing for international students, apartments for single students. 99% of campus accessible to physically disabled. **Special Academic Facilities/Equipment:** Language lab, electron microscope. **Computers:** Students can register for classes online. Administrative functions (other than registration) can be performed online.

CAMPUS LIFE

Environment: City. **Activities:** Choral groups, concert band, dance, drama/theater, jazz band, literary magazine, music ensembles, musical theater, pep band, radio station, student government, student newspaper, symphony orchestra 48 registered organizations, 5 honor societies, 1 religious organizations. 3 fraternities, 3 sororities. **Athletics (Intercollegiate):** *Men:* baseball, basketball, cross-country, golf, soccer, track/field (outdoor), track/field (indoor), wrestling. *Women:* basketball, cross-country, soccer, softball, track/field (outdoor), track/field (indoor), volleyball. **On-Campus Highlights:** Wyllie Library/Main Place, Communication Arts Building, Student Union, Student Activities Center, Molinaro Hall.

ADMISSIONS

Freshman Academic Profile: 5% in top 10% of high school class, 23% in top 25% of high school class, 56% in top 50% of high school class. 92% from public high schools. ACT middle 50% range 18-22. Minimum paper TOEFL 525. **Basis for Candidate Selection:** *Very important factors considered include:* Class rank, academic GPA, rigor of secondary school record, standardized test scores. *Other factors considered include:* application essay, recommendation(s), alumni/ae relation, character/personal qualities, extracurricular activities, first generation, interview, level of applicant's interest, racial/ethnic status, talent/ability, volunteer work, work experience. **Freshman Admission Requirements:** High school diploma is required and GED is accepted. *Academic units required:* 4 English, 3 mathematics, 3 science, 3 social studies, 4 academic electives. *Academic units recommended:* 4 English, 3 mathematics, 3 science, 3 social studies, 4 academic electives. **Freshman Admission Statistics:** 1,868 applied, 92% admitted, 51% enrolled. **Transfer Admission Requirements:** High school transcript, college transcript(s), statement of good standing from prior institution(s). Minimum college GPA of 2.0 required. Lowest grade transferable D-. **General Admission Information:** Application Fee $35. Regular application deadline 8/1. Notification on a rolling basis, beginning on or about 9/15. Nonfall registration accepted. Admission may be deferred for a maximum of 1 year. Credit and/or placement offered for CEEB Advanced Placement tests.

COSTS AND FINANCIAL AID

Annual in-state tuition $4,277. Annual out-of-state tuition $14,323. Room and board $5,550. Required fees $720. Average book expense $784. **Required Forms and Deadlines:** FAFSA. **Notification of Awards:** Applicants will be notified of awards on a rolling basis beginning 4/1. **Types of Aid:** *Need-based scholarships/grants:* Federal Pell, SEOG, state scholarships/grants, private scholarships, the school's own gift aid, Federal Nursing Scholarships. *Loans:* Subsidized Stafford, Unsubsidized Stafford, PLUS, Federal Perkins, state loans. **Student Employment:** Federal Work-Study Program available. Institutional employment available. Off-campus job opportunities are excellent. **Financial Aid Statistics:** 81% freshmen, 79% undergrads receive need-based scholarship or grant aid. 29% freshmen, 15% undergrads receive non-need-based scholarship or grant aid. 66% freshmen, 63% undergrads receive need-based self-help aid. 56% undergrads borrow to pay for school. Average cumulative indebtedness $17,158. **Criteria for awarding institutional aid:** *Non-need-based:* academics, art, athletics, minority status, music/drama, state/district residency.

UNIVERSITY OF WISCONSIN—PLATTEVILLE

1 University Plaza, Platteville, WI 53818
Phone: 608)342-1125 • Financial Aid Phone: 608-342-1836
E-mail: admit@uwplatt.edu • CEEB Code: 1917
Fax: 608)342-1122 • Website: www.uwplatt.edu • ACT Code: 4676

This public school was founded in 1866. It has a 820-acre campus.

RATINGS

Admissions Selectivity Rating: 67   Fire Safety Rating: 66   Green Rating: 60*

STUDENTS AND FACULTY

Enrollment: 5,631. **Student Body:** 38% female, 62% male, 10% out-of-state, 0% international (20 countries represented). Asian 1%, African American 1%, Caucasian 95%, Hispanic 1%, Native American 0%
Retention and Graduation: 76% freshmen return for sophomore year. **Faculty:** Student/faculty ratio 20:1. 249 full-time faculty, 83% hold PhDs, 16% are members of minority groups, 31% are women. 0% of classes are taught by teaching assistants.

ACADEMICS

Degrees: associate, bachelor's, certificate, diploma, master's, transfer associate. **Classes:** Most classes have fewer than 10 students. Most lab/discussion sessions have 20—29 students. **Majors with Highest Enrollment:** business administration and management; criminal justice/safety studies; mechanical engineering. **Special Study Options:** cooperative education program, distance learning, double major, dual enrollment, English as a Second Language (ESL), exchange student program (domestic), external degree program, honors program, independent study, internships, liberal arts/career combination, student-designed major, study abroad, teacher certification program. **Honors Programs:** UW-Platteville has a University Honors Program that provides exceptional students with opportunities to study the problems, ideas, and methods of the liberal arts with an intensity, depth, and perspective that cannot usually be achieved in regular courses. **Disability Services:** Special programs offered to physically disabled students include note-taking services, reader services, tape recorders, tutors.

FACILITIES

Housing: Coed dorms, men's dorms, women's dorms, fraternity/sorority housing. 100% of campus accessible to physically disabled. **Special Academic Facilities/Equipment:** Electron microscope Nohr Art Gallery The Wisconsin Room **Computers:** Students can register for classes online. Administrative functions (other than registration) can be performed online.

CAMPUS LIFE

Environment: Village. **Activities:** Choral groups, concert band, drama/theater, jazz band, literary magazine, marching band, music ensembles, musical theater, pep band, radio station, student government, student newspaper, symphony orchestra, television station 180 registered organizations, 15 honor societies, 9 religious organizations. 9 fraternities, 5 sororities. **Athletics (Intercollegiate):** *Men:* baseball, basketball, cross-country, football, soccer, track/field (outdoor), track/field (indoor), wrestling. *Women:* basketball, cross-country, golf, soccer, softball, track/field (outdoor), track/field (indoor), volleyball. **On-Campus Highlights:** Pioneer Student Center, Resident Halls, Field House, Ullrich Hall, New Athletic Fields, Check out our virtual tour at http://www.uwplatt.edu/university/vtour/.

ADMISSIONS

Freshman Academic Profile: 12% in top 10% of high school class, 35% in top 25% of high school class, 77% in top 50% of high school class. 94% from public high schools. ACT middle 50% range 20-25. Minimum paper TOEFL 550. **Basis for Candidate Selection:** *Very important factors considered include:* Class rank, rigor of secondary school record, standardized test scores. *Important factors considered include:* geographical residence, state residency. *Other factors considered include:* academic GPA, recommendation(s), extracurricular activities, interview, talent/ability. **Freshman Admission Requirements:** High school diploma is required and GED is accepted. *Academic units required:* 4 English, 3 mathematics, 3 science, (2 science labs), 3 social studies, 4 academic electives. *Academic units recommended:* 4 English, 3 mathematics, 3 science, (2 science labs), 3 social studies, 4 academic electives. **Freshman Admission Statistics:** 3,075 applied, 85% admitted, 46% enrolled. **Transfer Admission Requirements:** college transcript(s), statement of good standing from prior institution(s). Minimum college GPA of 2.0 required. Lowest grade transferable D. **General Admission Information:** Application Fee $35. Notification on a rolling basis, beginning on or about 9/15. Nonfall registration accepted. Admission may be deferred for a maximum of 1 semester. Credit offered for CEEB Advanced Placement tests.

COSTS AND FINANCIAL AID

Annual in-state tuition $4,277. Annual out-of-state tuition $14,323. Room and board $4,654. Required fees $848. Average book expense $320. **Required Forms and Deadlines:** FAFSA. **Notification of Awards:** Applicants will be notified of awards on a rolling basis beginning 4/15. **Types of Aid:** *Need-based scholarships/grants:* state scholarships/grants. *Loans:* Subsidized Stafford, Unsubsidized Stafford, PLUS, Federal Perkins. **Student Employment: Financial Aid Statistics:** 60% undergrads borrow to pay for school. Average cumulative indebtedness $10,030. **Criteria for awarding institutional aid:** *Non-need-based:* academics, leadership.

UNIVERSITY OF WISCONSIN—RIVER FALLS

410 South Third Street, River Falls, WI 54022
Phone: 715-425-3500 • Financial Aid Phone: 715-425-3141
E-mail: admit@uwrf.edu • CEEB Code: 1918
Fax: 715-425-0676 • Website: www.uwrf.edu • ACT Code: 4678

This public school was founded in 1874. It has a 225-acre campus.

RATINGS

Admissions Selectivity Rating: 65   Fire Safety Rating: 60*   Green Rating: 60*

STUDENTS AND FACULTY

Enrollment: 5,880. **Student Body:** 58% female, 42% male, 42% out-of-state, (18 countries represented).
Retention and Graduation: 26% freshmen graduate within 4 years. 55% freshmen graduate within 6 years. 17% grads go on to further study within 1 year. **Faculty:** Student/faculty ratio 22:1. 241 full-time faculty, 9% are members of minority groups, 42% are women. 0% of classes are taught by teaching assistants.

ACADEMICS

Degrees: bachelor's, master's, post-bachelor's certificate, post-master's certificate. **Classes:** Most classes have 20—29 students. Most lab/discussion sessions have 10—19 students. **Majors with Highest Enrollment:** animal sciences; biological and physical sciences; business/commerce. **Special Study Options:** Accelerated program, cooperative education program, distance learning, double major, dual enrollment, exchange student program (domestic), honors program, independent study, internships, student-designed major, study abroad, teacher certification program. **Honors Programs:** The UW-River Falls Honors Program is designed to meet the educational needs of students who have an outstanding record of academic achievement and a true sense of intellectual adventure. It allows students to experience a variety of course types and educationally related experiences while gaining academic credit. Students enrolled in the program may choose Honors sections of many general education classes, take introductory and advanced Honors seminars, participate in Honors colloquia, complete an Honors thesis/project, enroll in a service-learning experience for credit and receive credits for participation in the intellectual and creative life of the UW-RF community and elsewhere. All of these experiences are gained while still keeping within the major and minor requirements of an Honors student's academic program. **Disability Services:** Special programs offered to physically disabled students include note-taking services, reader services, tape recorders, tutors. **Career Services:** Alumni network, alumni services, career/job search classes, career assessment, internships, regional alumni. Career services highlights include Professional staff are available for one hour appointments to help you with placement, resume writing, portfolio help, licensing, etc.

FACILITIES

Housing: Coed dorms, women's dorms, fraternity/sorority housing, apartments for single students. 95% of campus accessible to physically disabled. **Special Academic Facilities/Equipment:** Local history museum, 20-inch reflecting telescope, observatory, electron microscope, greenhouse, lab farms, educational technology center. **Computers:** Students can register for classes online. Administrative functions (other than registration) can be performed online.

CAMPUS LIFE

Environment: Village. **Activities:** Choral groups, concert band, dance, drama/theater, jazz band, literary magazine, music ensembles, musical theater, pep band, radio station, student government, student newspaper, symphony orchestra, television station 120 registered organizations, 9 honor societies, 12 religious organizations. 5 fraternities, 4 sororities. **Athletics (Intercollegiate):** *Men:* basketball, cross-country, football, ice hockey, swimming, track/field (outdoor), track/field (indoor). *Women:* basketball, cross-country, golf, ice hockey, soccer, softball, swimming, tennis, track/field (outdoor), track/field (indoor), volleyball. **On-Campus Highlights:** University Student Center, Leadership

Center, Knowles/Hunt Recreation Complex, Chalmer Davee Library, Educational Technology Center, Swenson Sundial (world's largest), Carillon, Fine Arts performing complex, Two campus laboratory farms, and Kansas City Chiefs summer camp.

ADMISSIONS

Freshman Academic Profile: 95% from public high schools. ACT middle 50% range 18-24. Minimum paper TOEFL 500. **Basis for Candidate Selection:** *Very important factors considered include:* Class rank, rigor of secondary school record, standardized test scores. *Other factors considered include:* academic GPA, recommendation(s). **Freshman Admission Requirements:** High school diploma is required and GED is accepted. *Academic units required:* 4 English, 3 mathematics, 3 science, 3 social studies, 4 academic electives. *Academic units recommended:* 4 English, 3 mathematics, 3 science, 3 social studies, 4 academic electives. **Freshman Admission Statistics:** 2,886 applied, 91% admitted, 49% enrolled. **Transfer Admission Requirements:** college transcript(s), statement of good standing from prior institution(s). Minimum college GPA of 2.6 required. Lowest grade transferable D. **General Admission Information:** Application Fee $44. Notification on a rolling basis, beginning on or about 9/15. Nonfall registration accepted. Admission may be deferred for a maximum of 12 months. Credit and/or placement offered for CEEB Advanced Placement tests.

COSTS AND FINANCIAL AID

Annual in-state tuition $6,220. Annual out-of-state tuition $13,793. Room and board $5,106. Average book expense $300. **Required Forms and Deadlines:** FAFSA, institution's own financial aid form. **Notification of Awards:** Applicants will be notified of awards on a rolling basis beginning 4/1. **Types of Aid:** *Need-based scholarships/grants:* Federal Pell, SEOG, state scholarships/grants, private scholarships, the school's own gift aid. *Loans:* Subsidized Stafford, Unsubsidized Stafford, PLUS, Federal Perkins. **Student Employment:** Federal Work-Study Program available. Institutional employment available. Off-campus job opportunities are good. **Financial Aid Statistics:** 89% freshmen, 70% undergrads receive need-based scholarship or grant aid. 14% freshmen, 9% undergrads receive non-need-based scholarship or grant aid. 90% undergrads receive need-based self-help aid.

UNIVERSITY OF WISCONSIN—STEVENS POINT

102 Student Services Center, Stevens Point, WI 54481
Phone: 715-346-2441 • **Financial Aid Phone:** 715-346-4771
E-mail: admiss@uwsp.edu • **CEEB Code:** 1919
Fax: 715-346-3296 • **Website:** www.uwsp.edu • **ACT Code:** 4680

This public school was founded in 1894. It has a 335-acre campus.

RATINGS
Admissions Selectivity Rating: 74   **Fire Safety Rating:** 74   **Green Rating:** 99

STUDENTS AND FACULTY
Enrollment: 9,118. **Student Body:** 52% female, 48% male, 9% out-of-state, 2% international (31 countries represented). Asian 2%, African American 1%, Caucasian 90%, Hispanic 2%, Native American 0%
Retention and Graduation: 82% freshmen return for sophomore year. 22% freshmen graduate within 4 years. 21% grads go on to further study within 1 year. 26% grads pursue arts and sciences degrees. 1% grads pursue business degrees. **Faculty:** Student/faculty ratio 21:1. 413 full-time faculty, 79% hold PhDs, 7% are members of minority groups, 41% are women. 0% of classes are taught by teaching assistants.

ACADEMICS
Degrees: associate, bachelor's, master's, terminal associate. **Classes:** Most classes have 20—29 students. Most lab/discussion sessions have 20—29 students. **Majors with Highest Enrollment:** biological and physical sciences; business/commerce; elementary education and teaching. **Special Study Options:** Accelerated program, distance learning, double major, dual enrollment, English as a Second Language (ESL), independent study, internships, student-designed major, study abroad, teacher certification program. **Disability Services:** Special programs offered to physically disabled students include note-taking services, reader services, tape recorders, tutors. **Career Services:** Alumni network, career/job search classes, career assessment, internships.

FACILITIES
Housing: Coed dorms, men's dorms, women's dorms, wellness housing, theme housing, Freshman Interest Groups. 100% of campus accessible to physically disabled. **Special Academic Facilities/Equipment:** Art galleries, costume and goblet collections, museum of natural history, early childhood study institute, communicative disorders center, map center, observatory, planetarium,

Foucault pendulum, nature preserve, environmental station, groundwater center, herbarium, aviary, wellness institute. **Computers:** 100% of classrooms, 10% of dorms, 100% of libraries, 100% of dining areas, 100% of student union, have wireless network access. Students can register for classes online. Administrative functions (other than registration) can be performed online.

CAMPUS LIFE
Environment: Town. **Activities:** Choral groups, concert band, dance, drama/theater, jazz band, literary magazine, music ensembles, musical theater, opera, pep band, radio station, student government, student newspaper, student-run film society, symphony orchestra, television station, Campus Ministries, International Student Organization, Model UN 185 registered organizations, 12 honor societies, 9 religious organizations. 4 fraternities, 3 sororities. **Athletics (Intercollegiate):** *Men:* baseball, basketball, cross-country, diving, football, ice hockey, swimming, track/field (outdoor), wrestling. *Women:* basketball, cross-country, diving, golf, ice hockey, soccer, softball, swimming, tennis, track/field (outdoor), volleyball. **On-Campus Highlights:** University Center/Brewhouse, Schmeeckle Reserve/Wisconsin Conservation Hall of, Health Enhancement Center, Allen Recreation Center, Fine Arts Building. The University Center houses the Information Center, Student Activities and Involvement Center, the university bookstore, meeting rooms, study lounges, Multicultural Center, and several dining options. The Schmeeckle Reserve is a 265-acre reserve available for educational and recreational use by students and community alike. The reserve includes a 24-acre lake and a 2 1/2 mile trail system used for recreational purposes. The Health Enhancement Center houses athletics, facilities for physical education programs, an Olympic-sized swimming pool, 7,500 square foot weight room, state-of-the-art training room, 8-lane indoor track with an infield for 6 tennis courts or 4 full-sized basketball courts, a fieldhouse and the Berg Gym. Allen Recreation Center provides a cardio-fitness facility, massage rooms, and a recreation center with rental equipment available for students. The Fine Arts Center houses the departments of Art and Design, Music, and Theatre and Dance. Concerts and drama productions are scheduled throughout the year in its two theatres. The Carlsten Art Gallery is also located here. Other highlights on campus include a huge mosaic on the outer, south wall of the College of Natural Resources building; a planetarium located in the Science Building; the Learning Resources Center which contains Instructional Media Services, the library, and the Museum of Natural History; and the Communication Arts Center which houses the student radio station, student newspaper and several television studios. **Environmental Initiatives:** "Focused Research Effort for Sustainable Habits" - "FRESH" is a current research effort taking place on campus to implement and study a chemical recycling process for PLA plastics; PLA is polyactic acid, a material used to make a type of bio-based plastic for disposable food containers. The UWSP Sustainable Commute Project is working to estimate UWSP commuting patterns, costs, and emissions while raising awareness and identifying opportunities for change. UWSP is in the pre-design phase of a Chemistry & Biology science building. Energy performance and sustainability goal setting workshops are being conducted to work towards a LEED Gold building. Certification is in the final stages for a LEED NC residence hall and a LEED EB residence hall.

ADMISSIONS
Freshman Academic Profile: Average high school GPA 3.4. 16% in top 10% of high school class, 47% in top 25% of high school class, 89% in top 50% of high school class. SAT Math middle 50% range 468-605. SAT Critical Reading middle 50% range 498-595. SAT Writing middle 50% range 460-595. ACT middle 50% range 21-25. Minimum web-based TOEFL 70. **Basis for Candidate Selection:** *Very important factors considered include:* Class rank, academic GPA, rigor of secondary school record, standardized test scores. *Important factors considered include:* application essay, recommendation(s). *Other factors considered include:* character/personal qualities, extracurricular activities, first generation, level of applicant's interest, racial/ethnic status, talent/ability, volunteer work, work experience. **Freshman Admission Requirements:** High school diploma is required and GED is accepted. *Academic units required:* 4 English, 3 mathematics, 3 science, 3 social studies, 4 academic electives, 4 Additional 2 units from English, mathematics, social sciences, sciences, or foreign language and 2 units from above areas or other academic areas. *Academic units recommended:* 4 English, 3 mathematics, 3 science, 3 social studies, 4 academic electives, 4 Additional 2 units from English, mathematics, social sciences, sciences, or foreign language and 2 units from above areas or other academic areas. **Freshman Admission Statistics:** 4,915 applied, 75% admitted, 45% enrolled. **Transfer Admission Requirements:** High school transcript, college transcript(s), statement of good standing from prior institution(s). Minimum college GPA of 2.25 required. Lowest grade transferable D. **General Admission Information:** Application Fee $44. Nonfall registration accepted. Admission may be deferred for a maximum of semester. Credit and/or placement offered for CEEB Advanced Placement tests.

COSTS AND FINANCIAL AID
Annual in-state tuition $6,298. Annual out-of-state tuition $13,781. Room and board $6,538. Required fees $1,207. Average book expense $500. **Required Forms and Deadlines:** FAFSA. **Notification of Awards:** Applicants will be

notified of awards on a rolling basis beginning 5/1. **Types of Aid:** *Need-based scholarships/grants:* Federal Pell, SEOG, state scholarships/grants, private scholarships, the school's own gift aid. *Loans:* Subsidized Stafford, Unsubsidized Stafford, PLUS, Federal Perkins. **Student Employment:** Federal Work-Study Program available. Institutional employment available. Off-campus job opportunities are good. **Financial Aid Statistics:** 51% freshmen, 55% undergrads receive need-based scholarship or grant aid. 8% freshmen, 10% undergrads receive non-need-based scholarship or grant aid. 91% freshmen, 91% undergrads receive need-based self-help aid. 75% freshmen, 74% undergrads receive any aid. 75% undergrads borrow to pay for school. Average cumulative indebtedness $24,054. **Criteria for awarding institutional aid:** *Non-need-based:* academics, alumni affiliation, art, music/drama.

UNIVERSITY OF WISCONSIN—STOUT

Admissions UW-Stout, Menomonie, WI 54751
Phone: 715-232-1411 • **Financial Aid Phone:** 715-232-1363
E-mail: admissions@uwstout.edu • **CEEB Code:** 1740
Fax: 715-232-1667 • **Website:** www.uwstout.edu • **ACT Code:** 4652

This public school was founded in 1891. It has a 110-acre campus.

RATINGS
Admissions Selectivity Rating: 68   **Fire Safety Rating:** 61   **Green Rating:** 60*

STUDENTS AND FACULTY
Enrollment: 8,067. **Student Body:** 48% female, 52% male, 32% out-of-state, 2% international (28 countries represented). Asian 3%, African American 1%, Caucasian 89%, Hispanic 1%, Native American 0%
Retention and Graduation: 70% freshmen return for sophomore year. 18% freshmen graduate within 4 years. 9% grads go on to further study within 1 year.
Faculty: Student/faculty ratio 19:1. 402 full-time faculty, 11% are members of minority groups, 44% are women. 0% of classes are taught by teaching assistants.

ACADEMICS
Degrees: bachelor's, certificate, master's, post-bachelor's certificate, post-master's certificate. **Classes:** Most classes have 20—29 students. Most lab/discussion sessions have 20—29 students. **Majors with Highest Enrollment:** business/commerce; design and applied arts, other; hospitality administration/management. **Special Study Options:** Accelerated program, cooperative education program, cross-registration, distance learning, double major, dual enrollment, exchange student program (domestic), external degree program, honors program, independent study, internships, study abroad, teacher certification program. **Honors Programs:** The University Honors Program (UHP) is designed to enhance the education of students challenging them to think in more depth and detail and to provide the opportunity to meet other students while doing so. **Disability Services:** Special programs offered to physically disabled students include note-taking services, reader services, tutors. **Career Services:** alumni services, career/job search classes, internships Career services highlights include Our Co-op Program now exceeds 676 co-op students per year.

FACILITIES
Housing: Coed dorms, special housing for disabled students, apartments for single students, freshmen housing, smoke-free housing, upperclass/graduate housing, alcohol-free housing. 100% of campus accessible to physically disabled. **Special Academic Facilities/Equipment:** Specialized labs support degree programs throughout the campus. Furlong Art Gallery in Micheal's Hall. **Computers:** Students can register for classes online. Administrative functions (other than registration) can be performed online. Undergraduates are required to own a computer.

CAMPUS LIFE
Environment: Village. **Activities:** Choral groups, concert band, dance, drama/theater, jazz band, literary magazine, marching band, music ensembles, musical theater, pep band, radio station, student government, student newspaper, student-run film society, Campus Ministries, International Student Organization, Model UN 120 registered organizations, 1 honor societies, 12 religious organizations. 5 fraternities, 3 sororities. **Athletics (Intercollegiate):** *Men:* baseball, basketball, cross-country, football, ice hockey, track/field (outdoor). *Women:* basketball, cross-country, gymnastics, soccer, softball, tennis, track/field (outdoor), volleyball. **On-Campus Highlights:** Millenium Hall, Athletic Complex, Ropes Course- Climbing Wall- In-line Skating, Student Center, Micheels Hall.

ADMISSIONS
Freshman Academic Profile: Average high school GPA 3.1. 8% in top 10% of high school class, 26% in top 25% of high school class, 68% in top 50% of high

school class. ACT middle 50% range 20-24. Minimum paper TOEFL 500. **Basis for Candidate Selection:** *Very important factors considered include:* Class rank, standardized test scores. *Important factors considered include:* application essay, rigor of secondary school record. *Other factors considered include:* academic GPA, recommendation(s), alumni/ae relation, character/personal qualities, extracurricular activities, first generation, interview, level of applicant's interest, racial/ethnic status, talent/ability, volunteer work, work experience. **Freshman Admission Requirements:** High school diploma is required and GED is accepted. *Academic units required:* 4 English, 3 mathematics, 3 science, 3 social studies, 4 academic electives. *Academic units recommended:* 4 English, 3 mathematics, 3 science, 3 social studies, 4 academic electives. **Freshman Admission Statistics:** 3,388 applied, 80% admitted, 54% enrolled. **Transfer Admission Requirements:** college transcript(s), statement of good standing from prior institution(s). Minimum college GPA of 2.5 required. Lowest grade transferable D-. **General Admission Information:** Application Fee $44. Notification on a rolling basis, beginning on or about 9/15. Nonfall registration accepted. Credit offered for CEEB Advanced Placement tests.

COSTS AND FINANCIAL AID
Annual in-state tuition $7,014. Annual out-of-state tuition $14,760. Room and board $6,054. Required fees $1,930. Average book expense $384. **Required Forms and Deadlines:** FAFSA. **Notification of Awards:** Applicants will be notified of awards on a rolling basis beginning 4/1. **Types of Aid:** *Need-based scholarships/grants:* Federal Pell, SEOG, state scholarships/grants, private scholarships, the school's own gift aid. *Loans:* Subsidized Stafford, Unsubsidized Stafford, PLUS, Federal Perkins, Alternative Educational Loans. **Student Employment:** Federal Work-Study Program available. Institutional employment available. Highest amount earned per year from on-campus jobs $948. Off-campus job opportunities are good. **Financial Aid Statistics:** 35% freshmen, 38% undergrads receive need-based scholarship or grant aid. 40% freshmen, 19% undergrads receive non-need-based scholarship or grant aid. 91% freshmen, 94% undergrads receive need-based self-help aid. 71% freshmen, 74% undergrads receive any aid. 68% undergrads borrow to pay for school. Average cumulative indebtedness $29,879. **Criteria for awarding institutional aid:** *Non-need-based:* academics.

UNIVERSITY OF WISCONSIN—SUPERIOR

Belknap and Catlin, P.O. Box 2000, Superior, WI 54880-4500
Phone: 715-394-8230 • **Financial Aid Phone:** 715-394-8200
E-mail: admissions@uwsuper.edu • **CEEB Code:** 1920
Fax: 715-394-8407 • **Website:** www.uwsuper.edu • **ACT Code:** 4682

This public school was founded in 1893. It has a 230-acre campus.

RATINGS
Admissions Selectivity Rating: 69   **Fire Safety Rating:** 66   **Green Rating:** 60*

STUDENTS AND FACULTY
Enrollment: 2,460. **Student Body:** 57% female, 43% male, 46% out-of-state, 6% international (30 countries represented). Asian 1%, African American 2%, Caucasian 84%, Hispanic 2%, Native American 2%
Retention and Graduation: 72% freshmen return for sophomore year. 18% freshmen graduate within 4 years. 35% freshmen graduate within 6 years. **Faculty:** Student/faculty ratio 14:1. 136 full-time faculty, 63% hold PhDs, 13% are members of minority groups, 51% are women. 0% of classes are taught by teaching assistants.

ACADEMICS
Degrees: associate, bachelor's, certificate, master's, post-master's certificate. **Classes:** Most classes have 10—19 students. Most lab/discussion sessions have 10—19 students. **Majors with Highest Enrollment:** biology/biological sciences; business administration and management; elementary education and teaching. **Special Study Options:** cooperative education program, cross-registration, distance learning, double major, dual enrollment, English as a Second Language (ESL), exchange student program (domestic), external degree program, independent study, internships, liberal arts/career combination, student-designed major, study abroad, teacher certification program. **Combined Degree Programs:** 3-2 Forestry program w/ Michigan Tech U. **Disability Services:** Special programs offered to physically disabled students include note-taking services, tape recorders, tutors. **Career Services:** Alumni network, career/job search classes, career assessment, internships.

FACILITIES
Housing: Coed dorms, special housing for disabled students, women's dorms, apartments for married students, apartments for single students, 90% of campus accessible to physically disabled. **Special Academic Facilities/Equipment:** TV, radio, and film facilities, observatory, greenhouse, two art galleries,

The Princeton Review's Complete Book of Colleges

recital hall, four theaters, modern health and wellness center. Major Library renovations to be completed and major student center renovation in works. **Computers:** 40% of classrooms, 100% of libraries, 100% of dining areas, 100% of student union, 20% of common outdoor areas have wireless network access. Students can register for classes online. Administrative functions (other than registration) can be performed online.

CAMPUS LIFE
Environment: City. **Activities:** Choral groups, concert band, dance, drama/theater, jazz band, literary magazine, music ensembles, musical theater, pep band, radio station, student government, student newspaper, student-run film society, symphony orchestra, television station, Campus Ministries, International Student Organization 70 registered organizations, 1 honor societies, 5 religious organizations. 1 sororities. **Athletics (Intercollegiate):** *Men:* baseball, basketball, cross-country, ice hockey, soccer, track/field (outdoor), track/field (indoor). *Women:* basketball, cross-country, golf, ice hockey, soccer, softball, track/field (outdoor), track/field (indoor), volleyball. **On-Campus Highlights:** New Health and Wellness Center, Coffee Nook, Snack Bar, Rothwell Student Center Student Lounge, Multicultural Center, Health and Wellness Center is a new $17 million facility complete with running track, climbing wall, raquetball courts and much more. Library renovations underway, new student center renovations starting soon. **Environmental Initiatives:** LEED certification for new buildings that are now in the planning/construction process.

ADMISSIONS
Freshman Academic Profile: 12% in top 10% of high school class, 28% in top 25% of high school class, 71% in top 50% of high school class. 90% from public high schools. ACT middle 50% range 19-24. Minimum web-based TOEFL 61. Minimum paper TOEFL 500. **Basis for Candidate Selection:** *Very important factors considered include:* rigor of secondary school record. *Important factors considered include:* Class rank, standardized test scores. *Other factors considered include:* application essay, recommendation(s), character/personal qualities, extracurricular activities, first generation, interview, level of applicant's interest, racial/ethnic status, talent/ability, volunteer work, work experience. **Freshman Admission Requirements:** High school diploma is required and GED is accepted. *Academic units required:* 4 English, 3 mathematics, 3 science, 3 social studies, 4 academic electives. *Academic units recommended:* 4 English, 3 mathematics, 3 science, 3 social studies, 4 academic electives. **Freshman Admission Statistics:** 1,001 applied, 76% admitted, 48% enrolled. **Transfer Admission Requirements:** college transcript(s), Minimum college GPA of 2.0 required. Lowest grade transferable D. **General Admission Information:** Application Fee $44. Notification on a rolling basis, beginning on or about 10/1. Nonfall registration accepted. Admission may be deferred for a maximum of 1 year. Credit offered for CEEB Advanced Placement tests.

COSTS AND FINANCIAL AID
Annual in-state tuition $6,535. Annual out-of-state tuition $14,108. Room and board $5,992. Required fees $1,369. Average book expense $820. **Required Forms and Deadlines:** FAFSA. **Notification of Awards:** Applicants will be notified of awards on a rolling basis beginning 3/15. **Types of Aid:** *Need-based scholarships/grants:* Federal Pell, SEOG, state scholarships/grants, private scholarships, the school's own gift aid. *Loans:* Direct Subsidized Stafford, Direct Unsubsidized Stafford, Direct PLUS, Federal Perkins, state loans, college/university loans from institutional funds. **Student Employment:** Federal Work-Study Program available. Institutional employment available. Highest amount earned per year from on-campus jobs $11,000. Off-campus job opportunities are good. **Financial Aid Statistics:** 54% freshmen, 67% undergrads receive need-based scholarship or grant aid. 42% freshmen, 27% undergrads receive non-need-based scholarship or grant aid. 86% freshmen, 91% undergrads receive need-based self-help aid. 67% freshmen, 70% undergrads receive any aid. 76% undergrads borrow to pay for school. Average cumulative indebtedness $26,486. **Criteria for awarding institutional aid:** *Non-need-based:* academics, alumni affiliation, art, leadership, minority status, music/drama, state/district residency.

UNIVERSITY OF WISCONSIN—WHITEWATER

800 West Main Street, Whitewater, WI 53190-1791
Phone: 262-472-1440 • **Financial Aid Phone:** 262-472-1130
E-mail: uwwadmit@uww.edu • **CEEB Code:** 1921
Fax: 262-472-1515 • **Website:** www.uww.edu/ • **ACT Code:** 4684

This public school was founded in 1868. It has a 385-acre campus.

RATINGS
Admissions Selectivity Rating: 64   **Fire Safety Rating:** 71   **Green Rating:** 60*

STUDENTS AND FACULTY
Enrollment: 8,999. **Student Body:** 50% female, 50% male, 4% out-of-state, 0% international (69 countries represented). Asian 2%, African American 4%, Caucasian 90%, Hispanic 2%, Native American 0%
Retention and Graduation: 74% freshmen return for sophomore year. 21% freshmen graduate within 4 years. **Faculty:** Student/faculty ratio 22:1. 392 full-time faculty, 85% hold PhDs, 18% are members of minority groups, 44% are women. 0% of classes are taught by teaching assistants.

ACADEMICS
Degrees: associate, bachelor's, master's. **Classes:** Most classes have 30—39 students. **Majors with Highest Enrollment:** elementary education and teaching; journalism; physical education teaching and coaching. **Special Study Options:** Accelerated program, cooperative education program, cross-registration, distance learning, double major, dual enrollment, English as a Second Language (ESL), exchange student program (domestic), external degree program, honors program, independent study, internships, liberal arts/career combination, student-designed major, study abroad, teacher certification program, weekend college. **Honors Programs:** General academic honors program . **Disability Services:** Special programs offered to physically disabled students include note-taking services, reader services, tape recorders, tutors. **Career Services:** career/job search classes, career assessment, internships. Career services highlights include Internships.

FACILITIES
Housing: Coed dorms, special housing for disabled students, special housing for international students, women's dorms. 100% of campus accessible to physically disabled. **Special Academic Facilities/Equipment:** Two electron microscopes, State of the Art Theater/Auditorium. **Computers:** Students can register for classes online. Administrative functions (other than registration) can be performed online.

CAMPUS LIFE
Environment: Village. **Activities:** Choral groups, concert band, dance, drama/theater, jazz band, literary magazine, marching band, music ensembles, musical theater, opera, radio station, student government, student newspaper, symphony orchestra, television station 130 registered organizations, 4 honor societies, 8 religious organizations. 9 fraternities, 8 sororities. **Athletics (Intercollegiate):** *Men:* baseball, basketball, cross-country, diving, football, soccer, swimming, tennis, track/field (outdoor), track/field (indoor), wrestling. *Women:* basketball, bowling, cross-country, diving, golf, gymnastics, soccer, softball, swimming, tennis, track/field (outdoor), track/field (indoor), volleyball. **On-Campus Highlights:** New Kachel Field House, University Center, Underground Dance Club, Ritazza Coffee Shop, Warhawk Room.

ADMISSIONS
Freshman Academic Profile: 9% in top 10% of high school class, 32% in top 25% of high school class, 77% in top 50% of high school class. 90% from public high schools. SAT Math middle 50% range 480-600. SAT Writing middle 50% range 470-610. ACT middle 50% range 20-24. Minimum paper TOEFL 500. **Basis for Candidate Selection:** *Very important factors considered include:* Class rank, rigor of secondary school record, standardized test scores. *Other factors considered include:* application essay, academic GPA, recommendation(s), character/personal qualities, extracurricular activities, first generation, geographical residence, interview, level of applicant's interest, racial/ethnic status, state residency, talent/ability, volunteer work, work experience. **Freshman Admission Requirements:** High school diploma is required and GED is accepted. *Academic units required:* 4 English, 3 mathematics, 3 science, (1 science labs), 3 social studies, 4 academic electives. *Academic units recommended:* 4 English, 3 mathematics, 3 science, (1 science labs), 3 social studies, 4 academic electives. **Transfer Admission Requirements:** High school transcript, college transcript(s), Minimum college GPA of 2.0 required. Lowest grade transferable D-. **General Admission Information:** Application Fee $35. Notification on a rolling basis, beginning on or about 9/15. Nonfall registration accepted. Admission may be deferred for a maximum of 3 terms or 1. Credit offered for CEEB Advanced Placement tests.

COSTS AND FINANCIAL AID

Annual in-state tuition $5,568. Annual out-of-state tuition $13,042. Room and board $4,322. Required fees $710. Average book expense $170. **Required Forms and Deadlines:** FAFSA. **Notification of Awards:** Applicants will be notified of awards on a rolling basis beginning 4/1. **Types of Aid:** *Need-based scholarships/grants:* Federal Pell, SEOG, state scholarships/grants, private scholarships, the school's own gift aid. *Loans:* Direct Subsidized Stafford, Direct Unsubsidized Stafford, Direct PLUS, Federal Perkins, college/university loans from institutional funds, Alternative Loans. **Student Employment:** Highest amount earned per year from on-campus jobs $3,000. **Financial Aid Statistics:** 38% freshmen, 44% undergrads receive need-based scholarship or grant aid. 28% freshmen, 14% undergrads receive non-need-based scholarship or grant aid. 90% freshmen, 89% undergrads receive need-based self-help aid. 52% freshmen, 42% undergrads receive any aid. 65% undergrads borrow to pay for school. Average cumulative indebtedness $15,602. **Criteria for awarding institutional aid:** *Non-need-based:* academics, alumni affiliation, art, leadership, minority status, music/drama, state/district residency.

UNIVERSITY OF WYOMING

Dept 3435, Laramie, WY 82071
Phone: 307-766-5160 • **Financial Aid Phone:** 307-766-2116
E-mail: admissions@uwyo.edu • **CEEB Code:** 4855
Fax: 307-766-4042 • **Website:** www.uwyo.edu • **ACT Code:** 5006

This public school was founded in 1886. It has a 785-acre campus.

RATINGS

Admissions Selectivity Rating: 67   **Fire Safety Rating:** 83   **Green Rating:** 79

STUDENTS AND FACULTY

Enrollment: 9,993. **Student Body:** 52% female, 48% male, 29% out-of-state, 3% international (91 countries represented). Asian 1%, African American 1%, Caucasian 81%, Hispanic 5%, Native American 1%
Retention and Graduation: 73% freshmen return for sophomore year. 23% freshmen graduate within 4 years. **Faculty:** Student/faculty ratio 14:1. 749 full-time faculty, 85% hold PhDs, 9% are members of minority groups, 38% are women. 10% of classes are taught by teaching assistants.

ACADEMICS

Degrees: bachelor's, certificate, doctoral, master's, post-bachelor's certificate, post-master's certificate. **Classes:** Most classes have 20—29 students. Most lab/discussion sessions have 20—29 students. **Majors with Highest Enrollment:** elementary education and teaching; nursing/registered nurse (rn, asn, bsn, msn); psychology. **Special Study Options:** Accelerated program, distance learning, double major, English as a Second Language (ESL), exchange student program (domestic), external degree program, honors program, independent study, internships, student-designed major, study abroad. **Honors Programs:** The University Honors Program provides highly motivated students a series of curricular and extracurricular opportunities. Most students are selected for the program prior to their freshman year, although the program welcomes UW and transfer students up to the beginning of the junior year. Each year the Honors Program awards scholarships to qualifying students who are beginning their undergraduate education or who are entering the University as transfer students. The honors students organize extracurricular activities, have a student lounge and computers for their use, and have the option of living on one of the honors floors in the residence halls or in the Honors House. Courses offered in the honors program are restricted to honors program students; exceptions must be approved by the Honors program office. **Disability Services:** Special programs offered to physically disabled students include note-taking services, reader services, tape recorders, tutors. **Career Services:** Alumni network, alumni services, career/job search classes, career assessment, internships, regional alumni.

FACILITIES

Housing: Coed dorms, special housing for disabled students, fraternity/sorority housing, apartments for married students, apartments for single students, Floor specific living plans in the residence halls; Health Sciences Living house. 95% of campus accessible to physically disabled. **Special Academic Facilities/Equipment:** Art gallery, Geology museum, American Heritage Center, Rocky Mountain Herbarium, Solheim Mycology Herbarium, art museum, planetarium, environmental biology lab, anthropology museum, on-site elementary school, state veterinary lab, infrared telescope observatory, lysimeter lab, insect

museum and gallery room, Wyoming Geographic Information Science Center, Writing Center, Wyoming Cooperative Fishery and Wildlife Research Unit **Computers:** 75% of classrooms, 20% of dorms, 100% of libraries, 5% of dining areas, 100% of student union, 10% of common outdoor areas have wireless network access. Students can register for classes online. Administrative functions (other than registration) can be performed online.

CAMPUS LIFE

Environment: Town. **Activities:** Choral groups, concert band, dance, drama/theater, jazz band, literary magazine, marching band, music ensembles, musical theater, opera, pep band, radio station, student government, student newspaper, symphony orchestra, television station, Campus Ministries, International Student Organization, Model UN 223 registered organizations, 41 honor societies, 17 religious organizations. 8 fraternities, 6 sororities. **Athletics (Intercollegiate):** *Men:* basketball, cheerleading, cross-country, diving, football, golf, swimming, track/field (outdoor), track/field (indoor), wrestling. *Women:* basketball, cheerleading, cross-country, diving, golf, soccer, swimming, tennis, track/field (outdoor), track/field (indoor), volleyball. **On-Campus Highlights:** Student Union, American Heritage Center and Art Museum, Geology Museum, Fine Arts Center, Half-Acre Gym. **Environmental Initiatives:** Campus Sustainability Committee College of Business Sustainable Business Program Presidents Climate Commitment.

ADMISSIONS

Freshman Academic Profile: Average high school GPA 3.5. 21% in top 10% of high school class, 51% in top 25% of high school class, 79% in top 50% of high school class. SAT Math middle 50% range 490-630. SAT Critical Reading middle 50% range 490-600. ACT middle 50% range 22-27. Minimum web-based TOEFL 76. Minimum paper TOEFL 540. **Basis for Candidate Selection:** *Very important factors considered include:* academic GPA, rigor of secondary school record, standardized test scores. *Important factors considered include:* level of applicant's interest. *Other factors considered include:* application essay, recommendation(s), character/personal qualities, extracurricular activities, interview, state residency, talent/ability. **Freshman Admission Requirements:** High school diploma is required and GED is accepted. *Academic units required:* 4 English, 3 mathematics, 3 science, (3 science labs), 3 Cultural Context Electives - Recomended - 3 behavioral or social sciences, 3 visual or performing arts, 3 humanities or earth/space sciences. *Academic units recommended:* 4 English, 3 mathematics, 3 science, (3 science labs), 3 Cultural Context Electives - Recomended - 3 behavioral or social sciences, 3 visual or performing arts, 3 humanities or earth/space sciences **Freshman Admission Statistics:** 3,883 applied, 96% admitted, 41% enrolled. **Transfer Admission Requirements:** college transcript(s), Minimum college GPA of 2.0 required. Lowest grade transferable D. **General Admission Information:** Application Fee $40. Regular application deadline 8/10. Nonfall registration accepted. Admission may be deferred for a maximum of 1 year. Credit and/or placement offered for CEEB Advanced Placement tests.

COSTS AND FINANCIAL AID

Annual in-state tuition $3,180. Annual out-of-state tuition $12,330. Room and board $9,084. Required fees $1,098. Average book expense $1,200. **Required Forms and Deadlines:** FAFSA. **Notification of Awards:** Applicants will be notified of awards on a rolling basis beginning 3/15. **Types of Aid:** *Need-based scholarships/grants:* Federal Pell, SEOG, state scholarships/grants, private scholarships, the school's own gift aid. *Loans:* Subsidized Stafford, Unsubsidized Stafford, PLUS, Federal Perkins. **Student Employment:** Federal Work-Study Program available. Institutional employment available. Off-campus job opportunities are good. **Financial Aid Statistics:** 64% freshmen, 67% undergrads receive need-based scholarship or grant aid. 83% freshmen, 65% undergrads receive non-need-based scholarship or grant aid. 55% freshmen, 65% undergrads receive need-based self-help aid. 5% freshmen, 4% undergrads receive athletic scholarships. 85% freshmen, 87% undergrads receive any aid. 47% undergrads borrow to pay for school. Average cumulative indebtedness $23,341. **Criteria for awarding institutional aid:** *Non-need-based:* academics, alumni affiliation, art, athletics, leadership, minority status, music/drama, religious affiliation, state/district residency.

UPPER IOWA UNIVERSITY

Parker Fox Hall Box 1859, Fayette, IA 52142-1859
Phone: 800-553-4150 • **Financial Aid Phone:** 563-425-5274
E-mail: admission@uiu.edu
Fax: 319-425-5277 • **ACT Code:** 1360

This private school was founded in 1857. It has a 80-acre campus.

RATINGS
Admissions Selectivity Rating: 76   **Fire Safety Rating:** 72   **Green Rating:** 72

STUDENTS AND FACULTY
Enrollment: 4,531. **Student Body:** 60% female, 40% male, 55% out-of-state, 3% international (19 countries represented). Asian 1%, African American 17%, Caucasian 66%, Hispanic 4%, Native American 1%
Retention and Graduation: 19% freshmen graduate within 4 years. 45% freshmen graduate within 6 years. 25% grads go on to further study within 1 year. **Faculty:** Student/faculty ratio 19:1. 80 full-time faculty, 70% hold PhDs, 8% are members of minority groups, 54% are women. 0% of classes are taught by teaching assistants.

ACADEMICS
Degrees: associate, bachelor's, certificate, master's, terminal associate, transfer associate. **Classes:** Most classes have 10—19 students. Most lab/discussion sessions have 10—19 students. **Majors with Highest Enrollment:** elementary education and teaching; marketing/marketing management; natural resources/conservation. **Special Study Options:** Accelerated program, distance learning, double major, dual enrollment, English as a Second Language (ESL), external degree program, independent study, internships, liberal arts/career combination, student-designed major, study abroad, teacher certification program. **Disability Services:** Special programs offered to physically disabled students include reader services, tape recorders, tutors. **Career Services:** alumni services, career/job search classes, career assessment, internships.

FACILITIES
Housing: Coed dorms, men's dorms, women's dorms, Apartment-style housing. 70% of campus accessible to physically disabled. **Computers.** 100% of classrooms, 100% of dorms, 100% of libraries, 100% of dining areas, 100% of student union, 33% of common outdoor areas have wireless network access. Students can register for classes online. Administrative functions (other than registration) can be performed online.

CAMPUS LIFE
Environment: Rural. **Activities:** Choral groups, pep band, student government, student newspaper, Campus Ministries, International Student Organization 40 registered organizations, 1 honor societies, 1 religious organizations. 4 fraternities, 5 sororities. **Athletics (Intercollegiate):** *Men:* baseball, basketball, cross-country, football, golf, soccer, wrestling. *Women:* basketball, cross-country, golf, soccer, softball, tennis, volleyball. **On-Campus Highlights:** Rec Center, Grill 151, Dorman Gym, Andres Center for Business and Education, Cafeteria, We have 3 new buildings that will be opening in 2010. A new student center, liberal arts building and new housing unit. **Environmental Initiatives:** Geothermal Heating/Cooling Lighting Retrofit Daylight Harvesting

ADMISSIONS
Freshman Academic Profile: Average high school GPA 3.2. 16% in top 10% of high school class, 35% in top 25% of high school class, 65% in top 50% of high school class. ACT middle 50% range 19-25. Minimum web-based TOEFL 61. Minimum paper TOEFL 500. **Basis for Candidate Selection:** *Very important factors considered include:* standardized test scores. *Important factors considered include:* academic GPA. *Other factors considered include:* Class rank, recommendation(s), rigor of secondary school record, alumni/ae relation, first generation. **Freshman Admission Requirements:** High school diploma is required and GED is accepted. **Freshman Admission Statistics:** 1,160 applied, 62% admitted, 27% enrolled. **Transfer Admission Requirements:** High school transcript, college transcript(s), Lowest grade transferable D-. **General Admission Information:** Application Fee $15. Regular application deadline 8/23. Nonfall registration accepted. Admission may be deferred for a maximum of one term. Credit and/or placement offered for CEEB Advanced Placement tests.

COSTS AND FINANCIAL AID
Annual tuition $24,400. Room and board $7,290. Average book expense $1,400. **Required Forms and Deadlines:** FAFSA. **Notification of Awards: Types of Aid:** *Need-based scholarships/grants:* Federal Pell, SEOG, state scholarships/grants, private scholarships, the school's own gift aid. *Loans:* Subsidized Stafford, Unsubsidized Stafford, PLUS, Federal Perkins, Alternative Loans. **Student Employment:** Federal Work-Study Program available. Highest amount earned per year from on-campus jobs $1,860. Off-campus job op-

portunities are fair. **Financial Aid Statistics:** 65% freshmen, 68% undergrads receive need-based scholarship or grant aid. 100% freshmen, 100% undergrads receive non-need-based scholarship or grant aid. 71% freshmen, 73% undergrads receive need-based self-help aid. 17% freshmen, 1% undergrads receive athletic scholarships. 100% freshmen, 91% undergrads receive any aid. 91% undergrads borrow to pay for school. Average cumulative indebtedness $27,361. **Criteria for awarding institutional aid:** *Non-need-based:* academics, alumni affiliation, athletics.

URSINUS COLLEGE

Best 378

Ursinus College, Collegeville, PA 19426
Phone: 610-409-3200 • **Financial Aid Phone:** 610-409-3600
E-mail: admissions@ursinus.edu • **CEEB Code:** 2931
Fax: 610-409-3662 • **Website:** www.ursinus.edu • **ACT Code:** 3738

This private school was founded in 1869. It has a 170-acre campus.

RATINGS
Admissions Selectivity Rating: 83   **Fire Safety Rating:** 85   **Green Rating:** 85

STUDENTS AND FACULTY
Enrollment: 1,741. **Student Body:** 53% female, 47% male, 50% out-of-state, 1% international (13 countries represented). Asian 4%, African American 6%, Caucasian 76%, Hispanic 4%, Native American 0%
Retention and Graduation: 89% freshmen return for sophomore year. 75% freshmen graduate within 4 years. **Faculty:** Student/faculty ratio 11:1. 0% of classes are taught by teaching assistants.

ACADEMICS
Degrees: bachelor's. **Classes:** Most classes have fewer than 10 students. Most lab/discussion sessions have 10—19 students. **Majors with Highest Enrollment:** biology/biological sciences; economics; psychology. **Special Study Options:** double major, dual enrollment, English as a Second Language (ESL), honors program, independent study, internships, student-designed major, study abroad, teacher certification program, Howard University Semester. **Honors Programs:** The Ursinus Summer Fellows program provides stipends to rising juniors and seniors to live on campus and do faculty mentored research over the summer months. Fellows' projects often lead to senior honors projects. **Combined Degree Programs:** BA/MD, BA/MEng, Early Assurance-Drexel Univ. College of Medicine. **Disability Services:** Special programs offered to physically disabled students include note-taking services, reader services, tape recorders, tutors. **Career Services:** Alumni network, alumni services, career/job search classes, career assessment, internships, regional alumni. Career services highlights include Our internship opportunities are exceptional and numerous and have taken our students on all sorts of adventures: to nearby pharmaceutical labs, to U.S. embassies overseas, to the summer stock stages of the Berkshires, and to a marine mammal rescue station at the Jersey Shore. Internships are available to students in every major, and even to those studying abroad. With a full range of staffing and Internet resources to find, match and place students in internships that are right for them, Ursinus has a high percentage of students who participate in these experiences.

FACILITIES
Housing: Coed dorms, men's dorms, special housing for international students, women's dorms, Ursinus features the Residential Village, a cluster of 25 restored Victorian-era houses. Theme houses include: Musser International, Unity, Wellness, Language, Biology, Service, Zwingli Literary House and Wicks Honors House. 40 percent of Ursinus students reside in these houses. 95% of campus accessible to physically disabled. **Special Academic Facilities/Equipment:** The Kaleidoscope (performing arts center)
; New field house <br/>;new 143-bed dormitory
; Berman Museum of Art
;6 new telescopes
; scanning electron microscope
;Bruker 300 MHz NMR
; Perkin Elmer Spectrum 1000 FTIR
; LKB Isothermal Calorimeter
; an assortment of spectrometers and an HPLC
; recently-renovated Pfahler Hall of Science. **Computers:** 100% of classrooms, 100% of libraries, 100% of dining areas, 100% of student union, 50% of common outdoor areas have wireless network access. Students can register for classes online. Administrative functions (other than registration) can be performed online. Undergraduates are required to own a computer.

CAMPUS LIFE

Environment: City. **Activities:** Choral groups, concert band, dance, drama/theater, jazz band, literary magazine, music ensembles, musical theater, pep band, radio station, student government, student newspaper, student-run film society, television station, yearbook 88 registered organizations, 27 honor societies, 4 religious organizations. 7 fraternities, 7 sororities. **Athletics (Intercollegiate):** *Men:* baseball, basketball, cross-country, football, golf, lacrosse, soccer, swimming, tennis, track/field (outdoor), track/field (indoor), wrestling. *Women:* basketball, cross-country, field hockey, golf, gymnastics, lacrosse, soccer, softball, swimming, tennis, track/field (outdoor), track/field (indoor), volleyball. **On-Campus Highlights:** The Kaleidoscope Performing Arts Centerl, Berman Museum of Art lt;brgt;, Pfahler Hall of Science lt;brgt;, Richter-North Hall (new dormitory) lt;br, Bakes Center (field house and fitness ce, Wismer Center houses campus bookstore and dining facilities. Victorian dormitories along Main Street and traditional campus buildings give Ursinus a classic college ambience. **Environmental Initiatives:** Energy efficient enhancements and Energy Dashboard Food waste recycling UCGreen Fellows student sustainability leadership and professional development program.

ADMISSIONS

Freshman Academic Profile: 33% in top 10% of high school class, 70% in top 25% of high school class, 94% in top 50% of high school class. 61% from public high schools. SAT Math middle 50% range 560-670. SAT Critical Reading middle 50% range 550-650. SAT Writing middle 50% range 540-640. ACT middle 50% range 25-30. Minimum paper TOEFL 500. **Basis for Candidate Selection:** *Very important factors considered include:* Class rank, rigor of secondary school record, extracurricular activities. *Important factors considered include:* application essay, academic GPA, recommendation(s), standardized test scores, alumni/ae relation, racial/ethnic status, talent/ability, volunteer work, work experience. *Other factors considered include:* character/personal qualities, first generation, geographical residence, interview, level of applicant's interest. **Freshman Admission Requirements:** High school diploma is required and GED is accepted. *Academic units required:* 4 English, 3 mathematics, 1 science, (1 science labs), 2 foreign language, 1 social studies. *Academic units recommended:* 4 English, 3 mathematics, 1 science, (1 science labs), 2 foreign language, 1 social studies. **Freshman Admission Statistics:** 3,851 applied, 70% admitted, 16% enrolled. **Transfer Admission Requirements:** High school transcript, college transcript(s), essay or personal statement, standardized test scores, Minimum college GPA of 3.0 required. Lowest grade transferable C. **General Admission Information:** Application Fee $50. Early decision application deadline 1/15. Regular application deadline 2/15. Regular notification 4/1. Nonfall registration accepted. Admission may be deferred for a maximum of 1 year. Credit and/or placement offered for CEEB Advanced Placement tests.

COSTS AND FINANCIAL AID

Required Forms and Deadlines: FAFSA, institution's own financial aid form, CSS/Financial Aid PROFILE. **Notification of Awards:** Applicants will be notified of awards on or about 4/1. **Types of Aid:** *Need-based scholarships/grants:* Federal Pell, SEOG, state scholarships/grants, private scholarships, the school's own gift aid. *Loans:* Subsidized Stafford, Unsubsidized Stafford, PLUS, Federal Perkins. **Student Employment:** Federal Work-Study Program available. Institutional employment available. Highest amount earned per year from on-campus jobs $1,200. Off-campus job opportunities are excellent. **Financial Aid Statistics:** 100% freshmen, 100% undergrads receive need-based scholarship or grant aid. 27% freshmen, 24% undergrads receive non-need-based scholarship or grant aid. 77% freshmen, 83% undergrads receive need-based self-help aid. 92% freshmen, 91% undergrads receive any aid. 75% undergrads borrow to pay for school. Average cumulative indebtedness $21,171. **Criteria for awarding institutional aid:** *Non-need-based:* academics, alumni affiliation, art, music/drama.

URSULINE COLLEGE

2550 Lander Road, Pepper Pike, OH 44124-4398
Phone: 440-449-4203 • **Financial Aid Phone:** 440-646-8309
E-mail: admission@ursuline.edu • **CEEB Code:** 1848
Fax: 440-684-6138 • **Website:** www.ursuline.edu

This private school, affiliated with the Roman Catholic Church, was founded in 1871. It has a 110-acre campus.

RATINGS

Admissions Selectivity Rating: 65   **Fire Safety Rating:** 84   **Green Rating:** 61

STUDENTS AND FACULTY

Enrollment: 1,017. **Student Body:** 91% female, 9% male, 3% out-of-state, 1% international (19 countries represented). Asian 1%, African American 27%, Caucasian 67%, Hispanic 2%, Native American 0%

Retention and Graduation: 62% freshmen return for sophomore year. 31% freshmen graduate within 4 years. 43% freshmen graduate within 6 years. **Faculty:** Student/faculty ratio 8:1. 70 full-time faculty, 64% hold PhDs, 7% are members of minority groups, 86% are women. 0% of classes are taught by teaching assistants.

ACADEMICS

Degrees: bachelor's, certificate, master's, post-bachelor's certificate, post-master's certificate. **Classes:** Most classes have 10—19 students. Most lab/discussion sessions have 10—19 students. **Majors with Highest Enrollment:** early childhood education and teaching; nursing/registered nurse (rn, asn, bsn, msn); psychology. **Special Study Options:** Accelerated program, cooperative education program, cross-registration, double major, independent study, internships, teacher certification program. **Disability Services:** Special programs offered to physically disabled students include note-taking services, reader services, tape recorders, tutors. **Career Services:** career assessment, internships Career services highlights include our e-recruiting program that assists students in their search.

FACILITIES

Housing: Coed dorms, women's dorms. 98% of campus accessible to physically disabled. **Special Academic Facilities/Equipment:** Fritsche Gallery (Art) Fitness Center Swimming Pool. **Computers:** 100% of classrooms, 100% of libraries, 100% of dining areas, have wireless network access.

CAMPUS LIFE

Environment: City. **Activities:** Choral groups, drama/theater, literary magazine, student government, Campus Ministries 21 registered organizations, 4 honor societies. **Athletics (Intercollegiate):** *Women:* basketball, bowling, cross-country, golf, soccer, softball, swimming, tennis, track/field (outdoor), volleyball. **On-Campus Highlights:** Bishop Anthony M. Pilla Student Learning Center, Florence O'Donnell Wasmer Gallery, Matthew J. O'Brien Campus Center, Joseph J. Mullen Academic Center, Ralph M. Besse Library. **Environmental Initiatives:** Increased Recycling Energy Conservation Renewable Energy.

ADMISSIONS

Freshman Academic Profile: Average high school GPA 3.2. 11% in top 10% of high school class, 36% in top 25% of high school class, 76% in top 50% of high school class. 80% from public high schools. SAT Math middle 50% range 490-520. SAT Critical Reading middle 50% range 400-500. SAT Writing middle 50% range 350-430. ACT middle 50% range 18-23. Minimum web-based TOEFL 60. Minimum paper TOEFL 500. **Basis for Candidate Selection:** *Very important factors considered include:* academic GPA, standardized test scores. *Important factors considered include:* application essay, recommendation(s). *Other factors considered include:* Class rank, rigor of secondary school record, alumni/ae relation, interview. **Freshman Admission Requirements:** High school diploma is required and GED is accepted. **Freshman Admission Statistics:** 172 applied, 90% admitted, 54% enrolled. **Transfer Admission Requirements:** college transcript(s), essay or personal statement, Minimum college GPA of 2.5 required. Lowest grade transferable c. **General Admission Information:** Application Fee $25. Nonfall registration accepted. Admission may be deferred for a maximum of 1 year. Credit and/or placement offered for CEEB Advanced Placement tests.

COSTS AND FINANCIAL AID

Average book expense $1,125. **Required Forms and Deadlines:** FAFSA. **Notification of Awards:** Applicants will be notified of awards on a rolling basis beginning 2/20. **Types of Aid:** *Need-based scholarships/grants:* Federal Pell, SEOG, state scholarships/grants, private scholarships, the school's own gift aid, Federal Nursing Scholarships. *Loans:* Subsidized Stafford, Unsubsidized Stafford, PLUS, Federal Perkins, state loans, college/university loans from institutional funds. **Student Employment:** Federal Work-Study Program available. Off-campus job opportunities are good. **Financial Aid Statistics:** 100% freshmen, 89% undergrads receive need-based scholarship or grant aid. 6% freshmen, 3% undergrads receive non-need-based scholarship or grant aid. 95% freshmen, 96% undergrads receive need-based self-help aid. 8% freshmen, 2% undergrads receive athletic scholarships. 99% freshmen, 86% undergrads receive any aid. 91% undergrads borrow to pay for school. Average cumulative indebtedness $25,242. **Criteria for awarding institutional aid:** *Non-need-based:* academics, alumni affiliation, art, athletics, leadership, religious affiliation.

UTAH STATE UNIVERSITY

0160 Old Main Hill, Logan, UT 84322-0160
Phone: 435-797-1079 • **Financial Aid Phone:** 435-797-0173
E-mail: admit@usu.edu
Fax: 435-797-3708 • **Website:** www.usu.edu • **ACT Code:** 4276

This public school was founded in 1888. It has a 400-acre campus.

RATINGS
Admissions Selectivity Rating: 67   **Fire Safety Rating:** 74   **Green Rating:** 93

STUDENTS AND FACULTY
Enrollment: 21,129. **Student Body:** 54% female, 46% male, 23% out-of-state, 2% international (83 countries represented). Asian 1%, African American 1%, Caucasian 82%, Hispanic 5%, Native American 2%
Retention and Graduation: 32% grads go on to further study within 1 year. **Faculty:** Student/faculty ratio 22:1. 870 full-time faculty, 80% hold PhDs, 7% are members of minority groups, 34% are women. 7% of classes are taught by teaching assistants.

ACADEMICS
Degrees: associate, bachelor's, certificate, master's, post-bachelor's certificate, post-master's certificate, terminal associate, transfer associate. **Classes:** Most classes have 20—29 students. Most lab/discussion sessions have 10—19 students. **Majors with Highest Enrollment:** accounting; information science/ studies; marketing/marketing management. **Special Study Options:** Accelerated program, cooperative education program, cross-registration, distance learning, double major, dual enrollment, English as a Second Language (ESL), exchange student program (domestic), honors program, independent study, internships, liberal arts/career combination, student-designed major, study abroad, teacher certification program, weekend college. **Honors Programs:** The Honors Program is a community of scholars whose curiosity, creativity, and enthusiasm for learning foster educational achievement and personal growth. Our students are going places--graduate school, professional school, terrific jobs. Honors offers undergraduate students intensive seminars, experimental and interdisciplinary courses, writing projects, leadership opportunities, artistic and social activities. Our classes are smaller, allowing students to get to know professors and encouraging classroom interaction and discussion. We allow students to define their own interests and pursue them through "contracts" with professors, fostering close contact with professors. Other advantages include priority registration, an Honors-only computer lab, the Honors lounge and study areas. Starting in Fall 2005, Honors expects to offer housing. **Disability Services:** Special programs offered to physically disabled students include reader services, tape recorders. **Career Services:** Alumni network, career/job search classes, career assessment, internships.

FACILITIES
Housing: Coed dorms, special housing for disabled students, men's dorms, special housing for international students, women's dorms, fraternity/sorority housing, apartments for married students, apartments for single students, theme housing, Mobile Home Park. 96% of campus accessible to physically disabled. **Special Academic Facilities/Equipment:** Art gallery, agricultural and engineering experiment station, water research lab, wildlife and fishery research unit, on-campus school, intermountain herbarium, electron microscope, space dynamics lab. **Computers:** 99% of classrooms, 95% of dorms, 99% of libraries, 99% of dining areas, 99% of student union, 50% of common outdoor areas have wireless network access. Students can register for classes online. Administrative functions (other than registration) can be performed online.

CAMPUS LIFE
Environment: Town. **Activities:** Choral groups, concert band, dance, drama/ theater, jazz band, marching band, music ensembles, musical theater, opera, pep band, radio station, student government, student newspaper, student-run film society, symphony orchestra, television station, Campus Ministries, International Student Organization 194 registered organizations, 32 honor societies, 8 religious organizations. 5 fraternities, 3 sororities. **Athletics (Intercollegiate):** *Men:* basketball, cross-country, football, golf, tennis, track/field (outdoor), track/ field (indoor). *Women:* basketball, cross-country, gymnastics, soccer, softball, tennis, track/field (outdoor), track/field (indoor), volleyball. **On-Campus Highlights:** Outdoor Recreation Center, Nora Eccles Jones Art Museum, Fieldhouse athletic facility, Taggart Student Center, The quad. **Environmental Initiatives:** Increased energy efficiency in buildings Recycling Aggie Blue Bikes

ADMISSIONS
Freshman Academic Profile: Average high school GPA 3.5. 19% in top 10% of high school class, 43% in top 25% of high school class, 74% in top 50% of high school class. SAT Math middle 50% range 490-630. SAT Critical Reading middle 50% range 480-610. ACT middle 50% range 20-27. Minimum web-based TOEFL 71. Minimum paper TOEFL 525. **Basis for Candidate Selection:** *Very important factors considered include:* academic GPA, standardized test scores. *Important factors considered include:* rigor of secondary school record. *Other factors considered include:* Class rank, recommendation(s). **Freshman Admission Requirements:** High school diploma is required and GED is accepted. *Academic units required:* 4 English, 3 mathematics, 3 science, (1 science labs), 1 history, 4 academic electives. *Academic units recommended:* 4 English, 3 mathematics, 3 science, (1 science labs), 1 history, 4 academic electives. **Freshman Admission Statistics:** 9,052 applied, 97% admitted, 44% enrolled. **Transfer Admission Requirements:** college transcript(s), Minimum college GPA of 2.2 required. Lowest grade transferable D. **General Admission Information:** Application Fee $40. Nonfall registration accepted. Admission may be deferred for a maximum of 2 years+ one semeste. Credit and/or placement offered for CEEB Advanced Placement tests.

COSTS AND FINANCIAL AID
Annual in-state tuition $5,021. Annual out-of-state tuition $16,168. Room and board $5,490. Required fees $910. Average book expense $1,220. **Required Forms and Deadlines:** FAFSA. **Notification of Awards:** Applicants will be notified of awards on a rolling basis beginning 4/1. **Types of Aid:** *Need-based scholarships/grants:* Federal Pell, SEOG, state scholarships/grants, private scholarships, the school's own gift aid. *Loans:* Subsidized Stafford, Unsubsidized Stafford, PLUS, Federal Perkins, college/university loans from institutional funds. **Student Employment:** Federal Work-Study Program available. Institutional employment available. Highest amount earned per year from on-campus jobs $10,200. Off-campus job opportunities are excellent. **Financial Aid Statistics:** 85% freshmen, 85% undergrads receive need-based scholarship or grant aid. 55% freshmen, 38% undergrads receive non-need-based scholarship or grant aid. 67% freshmen, 69% undergrads receive need-based self-help aid. 1% undergrads receive athletic scholarships. 52% freshmen, 56% undergrads receive any aid. 47% undergrads borrow to pay for school. Average cumulative indebtedness $18,900. **Criteria for awarding institutional aid:** *Non-need-based:* academics, alumni affiliation, art, athletics, leadership, minority status, music/drama, religious affiliation, state/district residency.

UTICA COLLEGE

1600 Burrstone Road, Utica, NY 13502-4892
Phone: 315-792-3006 • **Financial Aid Phone:** 315-792-3179
E-mail: admiss@utica.edu • **CEEB Code:** 2932
Fax: 315-792-3003 • **Website:** www.utica.edu • **ACT Code:** 2932

This private school was founded in 1946. It has a 128-acre campus.

RATINGS
Admissions Selectivity Rating: 67   **Fire Safety Rating:** 87   **Green Rating:** 70

STUDENTS AND FACULTY
Enrollment: 2,690. **Student Body:** 59% female, 41% male, 16% out-of-state, 3% international (23 countries represented). Asian 2%, African American 11%, Caucasian 71%, Hispanic 8%, Native American 0%
Retention and Graduation: 67% freshmen return for sophomore year. 33% freshmen graduate within 4 years. 47% freshmen graduate within 6 years. 46% grads go on to further study within 1 year. 1% grads pursue medical degrees. **Faculty:** Student/faculty ratio 11:1. 143 full-time faculty, 49% are women. 0% of classes are taught by teaching assistants.

ACADEMICS
Degrees: bachelor's, certificate, master's, post-bachelor's certificate. **Classes:** Most classes have 10—19 students. Most lab/discussion sessions have 10—19 students. **Majors with Highest Enrollment:** business/commerce; corrections and criminal justice, other; health services/allied health/health sciences. **Special Study Options:** Accelerated program, cooperative education program, cross-registration, distance learning, double major, dual enrollment, exchange student program (domestic), honors program, independent study, internships, liberal arts/career combination, study abroad, teacher certification program, weekend college, BS Health Studies/ MS OT weekend program; ECI online program for undergraduate transfer students. **Honors Programs:** http://www.utica.edu/ academic/opportunities/honors.cfm **Combined Degree Programs:** BS(Health Studies)/MS OT; BS(Health Stud.) Disability Services:** Special programs offered to physically disabled students include note-taking services, reader services, tape recorders, tutors. **Career Services:** Alumni network, alumni services, career/job search classes, career assessment, internships.

FACILITIES
Housing: Coed dorms, special housing for disabled students, apartments for single students, Women's floors Men's floors. 85% of campus accessible to

physically disabled. **Special Academic Facilities/Equipment:** Edith Langley Barrett Art Gallery **Computers:** 95% of classrooms, 10% of dorms, 100% of libraries, 100% of dining areas, 100% of student union, have wireless network access. Students can register for classes online. Administrative functions (other than registration) can be performed online.

CAMPUS LIFE

Environment: City. **Activities:** Choral groups, concert band, dance, drama/theater, literary magazine, radio station, student government, student newspaper, student-run film society, yearbook 80 registered organizations, 8 honor societies, 4 religious organizations. 5 fraternities, 4 sororities. **Athletics (Intercollegiate):** *Men:* baseball, basketball, cross-country, diving, football, golf, ice hockey, lacrosse, soccer, swimming, tennis, track/field (outdoor). *Women:* basketball, cross-country, diving, field hockey, ice hockey, lacrosse, soccer, softball, swimming, tennis, track/field (outdoor), volleyball, water polo. **On-Campus Highlights:** Strebel Student Center and Lounge, Pioneer Cafe, Clark Athletic Center, Romano Hall Lounge, Library Cafe. **Environmental Initiatives:** Committee on sustainability formed in 2007. Extensive recycling program. Partnership in co-generation electrical generation plant.

ADMISSIONS

Freshman Academic Profile: Average high school GPA 3.0. 9% in top 10% of high school class, 29% in top 25% of high school class, 65% in top 50% of high school class. SAT Math middle 50% range 430-540. SAT Critical Reading middle 50% range 420-520. SAT Writing middle 50% range 410-510. ACT middle 50% range 18-24. Minimum paper TOEFL 525. **Basis for Candidate Selection:** *Very important factors considered include:* academic GPA, rigor of secondary school record. *Important factors considered include:* application essay, recommendation(s), character/personal qualities, extracurricular activities, interview, talent/ability, volunteer work, work experience. *Other factors considered include:* Class rank, standardized test scores, alumni/ae relation, first generation, level of applicant's interest. **Freshman Admission Requirements:** High school diploma is required and GED is accepted. *Academic units required:* 4 English, 3 mathematics, 3 science, 2 foreign language, 3 social studies, 1 academic electives. *Academic units recommended:* 4 English, 3 mathematics, 3 science, 2 foreign language, 3 social studies, 1 academic electives. **Freshman Admission Statistics:** 3,260 applied, 81% admitted, 19% enrolled. **Transfer Admission Requirements:** college transcript(s), essay or personal statement, Minimum college GPA of 2.50 required. Lowest grade transferable C. **General Admission Information:** Application Fee $40. Notification on a rolling basis, beginning on or about 9/1. Nonfall registration accepted. Admission may be deferred for a maximum of one year. Credit and/or placement offered for CEEB Advanced Placement tests.

COSTS AND FINANCIAL AID

Average book expense $1,180. **Required Forms and Deadlines:** FAFSA. **Notification of Awards:** Applicants will be notified of awards on a rolling basis beginning 2/1. **Types of Aid:** *Need-based scholarships/grants:* Federal Pell, SEOG, state scholarships/grants, private scholarships, the school's own gift aid, Federal Nursing Scholarships. *Loans:* Direct Subsidized Stafford, Direct Unsubsidized Stafford, Direct PLUS, Federal Perkins, Alternative loans. **Student Employment:** Federal Work-Study Program available. Institutional employment available. Off-campus job opportunities are good. **Financial Aid Statistics:** 100% freshmen, 99% undergrads receive need-based scholarship or grant aid. 4% freshmen, 4% undergrads receive non-need-based scholarship or grant aid. 95% freshmen, 94% undergrads receive need-based self-help aid. 84% freshmen, 84% undergrads receive any aid. 83% undergrads borrow to pay for school. Average cumulative indebtedness $42,303. **Criteria for awarding institutional aid:** *Non-need-based:* academics.

VALDOSTA STATE UNIVERSITY

1500 North Patterson Street, Valdosta, GA 31698
Phone: 229-333-5791 • **Financial Aid Phone:** 229-333-5935
E-mail: admissions@valdosta.edu • **CEEB Code:** 5855
Fax: 229-333-5482 • **Website:** www.valdosta.edu/ • **ACT Code:** 874

This public school was founded in 1906. It has a 178-acre campus.

RATINGS

Admissions Selectivity Rating: 79   **Fire Safety Rating:** 63   **Green Rating:** 68

STUDENTS AND FACULTY

Enrollment: 10,638. **Student Body:** 60% female, 40% male, 4% out-of-state, 1% international (73 countries represented). Asian 1%, African American 34%, Caucasian 54%, Hispanic 4%, Native American 0%

Retention and Graduation: 67% freshmen return for sophomore year. 17% freshmen graduate within 4 years. 43% freshmen graduate within 6 years. **Faculty:** Student/faculty ratio 23:1. 489 full-time faculty, 77% hold PhDs, 15% are members of minority groups, 48% are women. 2% of classes are taught by teaching assistants.

ACADEMICS

Degrees: associate, bachelor's, master's, post-master's certificate. **Classes:** Most classes have 20—29 students. Most lab/discussion sessions have 20—29 students. **Majors with Highest Enrollment:** biology/biological sciences; early childhood education and teaching; nursing/registered nurse (rn, asn, bsn, msn). **Special Study Options:** cooperative education program, distance learning, double major, dual enrollment, English as a Second Language (ESL), external degree program, honors program, independent study, internships, study abroad, teacher certification program, weekend college. **Honors Programs:** Honors Program . **Disability Services:** Special programs offered to physically disabled students include note-taking services, reader services, tape recorders, tutors. **Career Services:** alumni services, career/job search classes, career assessment, internships.

FACILITIES

Housing: Coed dorms, special housing for disabled students, men's dorms, special housing for international students, women's dorms, apartments for married students, apartments for single students, wellness floors and honors floors. 100% of campus accessible to physically disabled. **Special Academic Facilities/Equipment:** Planetarium; Herbarium; Art Gallery; VSU Archives **Computers:** Students can register for classes online. Administrative functions (other than registration) can be performed online.

CAMPUS LIFE

Environment: City. **Activities:** Choral groups, concert band, dance, drama/theater, jazz band, literary magazine, marching band, music ensembles, pep band, radio station, student government, student newspaper, symphony orchestra, television station 140 registered organizations, 22 honor societies, 11 religious organizations. 12 fraternities, 10 sororities. **Athletics (Intercollegiate):** *Men:* baseball, basketball, cross-country, football, golf, tennis. *Women:* basketball, cheerleading, cross-country, softball, tennis, volleyball. **On-Campus Highlights:** Student Recreation Center, Game Room, Internet Cafe, The Loop, Palms Dining Center and quad. **Environmental Initiatives:** Recycling Faculty and Student Environmental Advocacy Groups.

ADMISSIONS

Freshman Academic Profile: Average high school GPA 3.1SAT Math middle 50% range 460-540. SAT Critical Reading middle 50% range 470-540. SAT Writing middle 50% range 450-530. ACT middle 50% range 20-23. Minimum paper TOEFL 523. **Basis for Candidate Selection:** *Very important factors considered include:* standardized test scores. *Important factors considered include:* Class rank, academic GPA, rigor of secondary school record. **Freshman Admission Requirements:** High school diploma is required and GED is not accepted. *Academic units required:* 4 English, 4 mathematics, 3 science, (2 science labs), 2 foreign language, 3 social studies. *Academic units recommended:* 4 English, 4 mathematics, 3 science, (2 science labs), 2 foreign language, 3 social studies. **Freshman Admission Statistics:** 7,950 applied, 58% admitted, 48% enrolled. **Transfer Admission Requirements:** college transcript(s), Minimum college GPA of 2.0 required. Lowest grade transferable D. **General Admission Information:** Application Fee $40. Regular application deadline 7/1. Notification on a rolling basis, beginning on or about 8/1. Nonfall registration accepted. Admission may be deferred for a maximum of 2 years. Credit and/or placement offered for CEEB Advanced Placement tests.

COSTS AND FINANCIAL AID

Annual in-state tuition $3,644. Annual out-of-state tuition $13,224. Room and board $6,850. Required fees $1,910. Average book expense $1,200. **Required Forms and Deadlines:** FAFSA. **Notification of Awards:** Applicants will be notified of awards on a rolling basis beginning 5/15. **Types of Aid:** *Need-based scholarships/grants:* Federal Pell, SEOG, state scholarships/grants, private scholarships, the school's own gift aid, LEAP, ACG SMART Grant. *Loans:* Direct Subsidized Stafford, Direct Unsubsidized Stafford, Direct PLUS, Subsidized Stafford, Unsubsidized Stafford, PLUS. **Student Employment:** Federal Work-Study Program available. Institutional employment available. Highest amount earned per year from on-campus jobs $4,000. Off-campus job opportunities are good. **Financial Aid Statistics:** 89% freshmen, 82% undergrads receive need-based scholarship or grant aid. 6% freshmen, 5% undergrads receive non-need-based scholarship or grant aid. 87% freshmen, 77% undergrads receive need-based self-help aid. 1% freshmen, % undergrads receive athletic scholarships. 76% freshmen, 70% undergrads receive any aid. 66% undergrads borrow to pay for school. Average cumulative indebtedness $21,166. **Criteria for awarding institutional aid:** *Non-need-based:* academics, art, athletics, leadership, music/drama, state/district residency.

VALLEY CITY STATE UNIVERSITY

101 College St. SW, Valley City, ND 58072
Phone: 701-845-7101 • **Financial Aid Phone:** 701-845-7412
E-mail: enrollment.services@vcsu.edu
Fax: 701-845-7299 • **Website:** www.vcsu.edu • **ACT Code:** 3216

This public school was founded in 1890. It has a 55-acre campus.

RATINGS
Admissions Selectivity Rating: 66   **Fire Safety Rating:** 64   **Green Rating:** 60*

STUDENTS AND FACULTY
Enrollment: 1,013. **Student Body:** 53% female, 47% male, 28% out-of-state, 5% international (7 countries represented). Asian 0%, African American 2%, Caucasian 89%, Hispanic 1%, Native American 2%
Retention and Graduation: 64% freshmen return for sophomore year. **Faculty:** Student/faculty ratio 18:1. 55 full-time faculty, 36% hold PhDs, 0% are members of minority groups, 51% are women. 0% of classes are taught by teaching assistants.

ACADEMICS
Degrees: bachelor's, master's. **Classes: Majors with Highest Enrollment:** computer and information sciences and support services, other; elementary education and teaching. **Special Study Options:** Accelerated program, cooperative education program, distance learning, double major, dual enrollment, internships, liberal arts/career combination, student-designed major, teacher certification program. **Disability Services:** Special programs offered to physically disabled students include note-taking services, reader services, tape recorders, tutors **Career Services:** career/job search classes, career assessment, internships.

FACILITIES
Housing: Coed dorms, special housing for disabled students, men's dorms, women's dorms, fraternity/sorority housing, apartments for married students, Apts. for students with dependant children. 85% of campus accessible to physically disabled. **Special Academic Facilities/Equipment:** Planetarium. **Computers:** Students can register for classes online. Administrative functions (other than registration) can be performed online.

CAMPUS LIFE
Environment: Rural. **Activities:** Choral groups, concert band, drama/theater, jazz band, music ensembles, musical theater, pep band, student government, student newspaper, yearbook 16 registered organizations, 5 honor societies, 3 religious organizations. 1 fraternities, 1 sororities. **Athletics (Intercollegiate):** *Men:* baseball, basketball, football. *Women:* basketball, cheerleading, softball, volleyball. **On-Campus Highlights:** Planetarium, Medicine Wheel, Fieldhouse, Vangstad Auditorium, Student Center.

ADMISSIONS
Freshman Academic Profile: Average high school GPA 3.0. 6% in top 10% of high school class, 22% in top 25% of high school class, 54% in top 50% of high school class. 98% from public high schools. SAT Math middle 50% range 450-570. SAT Critical Reading middle 50% range 450-580. ACT middle 50% range 18-23. Minimum paper TOEFL 525. **Basis for Candidate Selection:** *Very important factors considered include:* rigor of secondary school record. *Other factors considered include:* Class rank, standardized test scores. **Freshman Admission Requirements:** High school diploma is required and GED is accepted. *Academic units required:* 4 English, 3 mathematics, 3 science, (3 science labs), 3 social studies. *Academic units recommended:* 4 English, 3 mathematics, 3 science, (3 science labs), 3 social studies. **Freshman Admission Statistics:** 256 applied, 94% admitted, 73% enrolled. **Transfer Admission Requirements:** college transcript(s), statement of good standing from prior institution(s). Minimum college GPA of 2.0 required. Lowest grade transferable D. **General Admission Information:** Application Fee $35. Nonfall registration accepted. Admission may be deferred for a maximum of indefinete. Neither credit nor placement offered for CEEB Advanced Placement tests.

COSTS AND FINANCIAL AID
Annual in-state tuition $3,536. Annual out-of-state tuition $9,761. Room and board $4,694. Required fees $1,504. Average book expense $700. **Required Forms and Deadlines:** FAFSA. **Notification of Awards:** Applicants will be notified of awards on a rolling basis beginning 1/15. **Types of Aid:** *Need-based scholarships/grants:* Federal Pell, SEOG, state scholarships/grants. *Loans:* Subsidized Stafford, Unsubsidized Stafford, PLUS, Federal Perkins. **Student Employment:** Financial Aid Statistics: 51% freshmen, 55% undergrads receive need-based scholarship or grant aid. 74% freshmen, 55% undergrads receive non-need-based scholarship or grant aid. 87% freshmen, 91% undergrads receive need-based self-help aid. 6% freshmen, 5% undergrads receive athletic scholarships. 93% freshmen, 86% undergrads receive any aid. 36% undergrads

borrow to pay for school. Average cumulative indebtedness $18,209. **Criteria for awarding institutional aid:** *Non-need-based:* academics, alumni affiliation, athletics, leadership, minority status, music/drama.

VALPARAISO UNIVERSITY

Office of Admission, Kretzmann Hall, Valparaiso, IN 46383
Phone: 219-464-5011 • **Financial Aid Phone:** 219-464-5015
E-mail: undergrad.admission@valpo.edu • **CEEB Code:** 1874
Fax: 219-464-6898 • **Website:** valpo.edu • **ACT Code:** 1256

This private school, affiliated with the Lutheran Church, was founded in 1859. It has a 320-acre campus.

RATINGS
Admissions Selectivity Rating: 81   **Fire Safety Rating:** 71   **Green Rating:** 74

STUDENTS AND FACULTY
Enrollment: 2,930. **Student Body:** 53% female, 47% male, 59% out-of-state, 7% international (60 countries represented). Asian 2%, African American 5%, Caucasian 76%, Hispanic 7%, Native American 0%
Retention and Graduation: 62% freshmen graduate within 4 years. 74% freshmen graduate within 6 years. 27% grads go on to further study within 1 year. 17% grads pursue arts and sciences degrees. 3% grads pursue law degrees. 2% grads pursue business degrees. 1% grads pursue medical degrees. **Faculty:** Student/faculty ratio 13:1. 267 full-time faculty, 91% hold PhDs, 8% are members of minority groups, 41% are women. 0% of classes are taught by teaching assistants.

ACADEMICS
Degrees: associate, bachelor's, certificate, master's, post-bachelor's certificate, post-master's certificate, terminal associate. **Classes:** Most classes have 10—19 students. Most lab/discussion sessions have 10—19 students. **Majors with Highest Enrollment:** nursing/registered nurse (rn, asn, bsn, msn); political science and government; psychology. **Special Study Options:** Accelerated program, cooperative education program, cross-registration, distance learning, double major, English as a Second Language (ESL), exchange student program (domestic), honors program, independent study, internships, liberal arts/career combination, student-designed major, study abroad, teacher certification program. **Honors Programs:** Christ College, VU's honors college, provides an honors-level liberal arts curriculum dedicated to the study and practice of the basic arts of inquiry and committed to educational processes that enable students to achieve a measure of intellectual independence. **Combined Degree Programs:** BA/JD, BA/MA, JD/MA, JD/MBA, JD/MALS, JD/MS, BSN/MSN, BA/EdS. **Disability Services:** Special programs offered to physically disabled students include note-taking services, reader services, tape recorders, tutors. **Career Services:** Alumni network, alumni services, career/job search classes, career assessment, internships, regional alumni.

FACILITIES
Housing: Coed dorms, women's dorms, fraternity/sorority housing, apartments for single students, theme housing, residence hall for German language students. 86% of campus accessible to physically disabled. **Special Academic Facilities/Equipment:** Art museum, galleries, language lab, planetarium, electron microscope, observatory, TV Studio, weather station, Virtual Nursing Learning Center, VisBox, non-linear video editing, Christopher Center for Learning and Information Resources, Doppler Radar facility **Computers:** 60% of classrooms, 100% of dorms, 100% of libraries, 100% of dining areas, 100% of student union, 15% of common outdoor areas have wireless network access. Students can register for classes online. Administrative functions (other than registration) can be performed online.

CAMPUS LIFE
Environment: Town. **Activities:** Choral groups, concert band, dance, drama/theater, jazz band, literary magazine, music ensembles, musical theater, pep band, radio station, student government, student newspaper, symphony orchestra, yearbook, Campus Ministries, International Student Organization 94 registered organizations, 33 honor societies, 7 religious organizations. 9 fraternities, 7 sororities. **Athletics (Intercollegiate):** *Men:* baseball, basketball, cross-country, diving, football, golf, soccer, swimming, tennis, track/field (outdoor), track/field (indoor). *Women:* basketball, bowling, cross-country, diving, golf, soccer, softball, swimming, tennis, track/field (outdoor), track/field (indoor), volleyball. **On-Campus Highlights:** Harre Union, Christopher Center for Library & Infor., VU Center for the Arts, Brauer Art Museum, Athletics-Recreation Center, Kallay-Christopher Hall Kade Duesenberg German House Grinder's Cafe. **Environmental Initiatives:** In addition to previous years, this year the College of Engineering received partial funding from the Dept. of Energy to construct a solar furnace. In addition to previous years, an addition to the

College of Engineering completed & seeking LEED platinum certification. A new building nearly complete & seeking LEED Silver certification. Sustainability subcommittee worked with 3 student groups to provide programming for Earthweek (awareness, collection of electronics, batteries, and clothing). The battery recycling program has now been extended on an ongoing basis to a number of buildings. For 2012, we are launching the US Energy Stars Checklist completion program.

ADMISSIONS

Freshman Academic Profile: Average high school GPA 3.6. 35% in top 10% of high school class, 66% in top 25% of high school class, 93% in top 50% of high school class. SAT Math middle 50% range 510-620. SAT Critical Reading middle 50% range 500-600. SAT Writing middle 50% range 480-580. ACT middle 50% range 23-29. Minimum web-based TOEFL 80. Minimum paper TOEFL 550. **Basis for Candidate Selection:** *Very important factors considered include:* academic GPA, rigor of secondary school record. *Important factors considered include:* Class rank, standardized test scores, alumni/ae relation, character/personal qualities, extracurricular activities, talent/ability. *Other factors considered include:* application essay, recommendation(s), first generation, interview, level of applicant's interest, racial/ethnic status, religious affiliation/ commitment, volunteer work. **Freshman Admission Requirements:** High school diploma is required and GED is accepted. *Academic units required:* 4 English, 3 mathematics, 2 science, (2 science labs), 2 foreign language, 2 history, 3 academic electives. *Academic units recommended:* 4 English, 3 mathematics, 2 science, (2 science labs), 2 foreign language, 2 history, 3 academic electives. **Freshman Admission Statistics:** 5,555 applied, 80% admitted, 17% enrolled. **Transfer Admission Requirements:** college transcript(s), essay or personal statement, statement of good standing from prior institution(s). Minimum college GPA of 2.0 required. Lowest grade transferable C−. **General Admission Information:** Application Fee $30. Regular application deadline 8/15. Notification on a rolling basis, beginning on or about 10/1. Nonfall registration accepted. Admission may be deferred for a maximum of 1 year. Credit and/or placement offered for CEEB Advanced Placement tests.

COSTS AND FINANCIAL AID

Annual tuition $31,170. Room and board $9,164. Required fees $1,080. Average book expense $1,200. **Required Forms and Deadlines:** FAFSA. **Notification of Awards:** Applicants will be notified of awards on a rolling basis beginning 3/1. **Types of Aid:** *Need-based scholarships/grants:* Federal Pell, SEOG, state scholarships/grants, private scholarships, the school's own gift aid. *Loans:* Direct Subsidized Stafford, Direct Unsubsidized Stafford, Direct PLUS, Federal Perkins, college/university loans from institutional funds, Private/alternative education loans if credit standards are met. **Student Employment:** Federal Work-Study Program available. Institutional employment available. Highest amount earned per year from on-campus jobs $5,481. Off-campus job opportunities are good. **Financial Aid Statistics:** 100% freshmen, 100% undergrads receive need-based scholarship or grant aid. 19% freshmen, 27% undergrads receive non-need-based scholarship or grant aid. 85% freshmen, 86% undergrads receive need-based self-help aid. 3% freshmen, 3% undergrads receive athletic scholarships. 98% freshmen, 96% undergrads receive any aid. 72% undergrads borrow to pay for school. Average cumulative indebtedness $31,957. **Criteria for awarding institutional aid:** *Non-need-based:* academics, alumni affiliation, art, athletics, leadership, music/drama, religious affiliation, state/district residency.

VANDERBILT UNIVERSITY

Best 378

2305 West End Avenue, Nashville, TN 37203
Phone: 615-322-2561 • **Financial Aid Phone:** 800-288-0204
E-mail: admissions@vanderbilt.edu • **CEEB Code:** 1871
Fax: 615-343-7765 • **Website:** www.vanderbilt.edu • **ACT Code:** 4036

This private school was founded in 1873. It has a 323-acre campus.

RATINGS
Admissions Selectivity Rating: 99   **Fire Safety Rating:** 95   **Green Rating:** 96

STUDENTS AND FACULTY
Enrollment: 6,753. **Student Body:** 50% female, 50% male, 87% out-of-state, 5% international (96 countries represented). Asian 8%, African American 8%, Caucasian 63%, Hispanic 8%, Native American 0%.
Retention and Graduation: 96% freshmen return for sophomore year. 87% freshmen graduate within 4 years. 46% grads go on to further study within 1

year. 11% grads pursue arts and sciences degrees. 6% grads pursue law degrees. 1% grads pursue business degrees. 7% grads pursue medical degrees. **Faculty:** Student/faculty ratio 8:1. 919 full-time faculty, 97% hold PhDs, 14% are members of minority groups, 37% are women.

ACADEMICS
Degrees: bachelor's, doctoral, master's. **Classes:** Most classes have 10—19 students. Most lab/discussion sessions have 10—19 students. **Majors with Highest Enrollment:** engineering science; psychology; sociology. **Special Study Options:** Accelerated program, cooperative education program, cross-registration, distance learning, double major, dual enrollment, English as a Second Language (ESL), honors program, independent study, internships, liberal arts/career combination, student-designed major, study abroad, teacher certification program. **Honors Programs:** Psychology, Child Development, Cognitive Studies, and Child Studies, Biomedical Engineering, Biological Sciences **Combined Degree Programs:** BA/MBA, MBA/JD, MBA/MD,JD/ MDIV, JD/MTS. **Disability Services:** Special programs offered to physically disabled students include note-taking services, reader services, tape recorders, tutors. **Career Services:** Alumni network, alumni services, career/job search classes, career assessment, internships, regional alumni.

FACILITIES
Housing: Coed dorms, special housing for disabled students, men's dorms, special housing for international students, women's dorms, apartments for married students, apartments for single students, theme housing. The Commons is a community of first-yar students, residential faculty, and professional staff. 95% of campus accessible to physically disabled. **Special Academic Facilities/Equipment:** Art galleries, center for research on education and human development, multimedia classrooms, teaching center, observatories, free-electron laser, electron microscope. **Computers:** 100% of classrooms, 100% of dorms, 100% of libraries, 100% of dining areas, 100% of student union, 100% of common outdoor areas have wireless network access. Students can register for classes online. Administrative functions (other than registration) can be performed online.

CAMPUS LIFE
Environment: Metropolis. **Activities:** Choral groups, concert band, dance, drama/theater, jazz band, literary magazine, marching band, music ensembles, musical theater, opera, pep band, radio station, student government, student newspaper, student-run film society, symphony orchestra, television station, yearbook, Campus Ministries, International Student Organization, Model UN 329 registered organizations, 20 honor societies, 18 religious organizations. 19 fraternities, 12 sororities. **Athletics (Intercollegiate):** *Men:* baseball, basketball, cross-country, football, golf, tennis. *Women:* basketball, cross-country, golf, lacrosse, soccer, tennis, track/field (outdoor). **On-Campus Highlights:** The Commons, Jean and Alexander Heard Library, Student Recreation Center, Student Life Center, Sarratt Student Center. **Environmental Initiatives:** American Studies Sustainability Project " In Fall 2011, Vanderbilt's program in American Studies initiated the Sustainability Project (http://www.vanderbilt. edu/americanstudies/sustainability/index.php), which aims to encourage campus-wide dialogue that will promote and further the university's sustainability efforts. Programming part of this effort includes over 30 sustainability-themed course offerings, a speaker's series, a green bag luncheon workshop series, film series, symposia, art installations, and educational road trips. Additionally, Vanderbilt's Center for Teaching sponsored the Cumberland Project (http:// cumberland.vanderbilt.edu/) in May 2011, a two-day workshop intended to mirror the success of the Piedmont Project and foster an interdisciplinary teaching and learning community around sustainability themes at Vanderbilt. Due to the success of the initial workshop, a second workshop is planned for May 2012. Water Conservation Efforts - One of the student-initiated utility conservation projects funded by the Vanderbilt's newly created Green Fund is a water conservation project known as Water Drop. This project proposed the installation of simple hourglass-style shower timers in an effort to reduce shower times in residential halls on campus. The first phase of the project aims to demonstrate proof of concept behind the shower timers. Three first-year student residence halls are capable of metering water consumption at the building level. One residence hall will serve as the control; one residence hall will receive regular water conservation education; and the final residence hall will receive water conservation education coupled with the provision of shower timers. Normalized monthly water consumption will be reported and used to evaluate the success of shower timer installation and use. Non-potable water from underground utility tunnels continues to be captured and reused to irrigate the athletic fields and in the on-campus cogeneration power plant cooling towers. By capturing this water and redirecting it, Vanderbilt is reducing water purchases from Metro Water and sewer by over 50 million gallons a year and saving an estimated $140,000 each year in reduced water purchases. Additionally, Vanderbilt has committed to water conservation through investments in low flow no touch faucets, low flow toilets, dual flush toilets, and waterfree urinals in many facilities on campus. Vanderbilt's Plumbing Shops have retrofitted over 2,500 water-saving bathroom fixtures, conserving over 31.5 million gallons of water and saving over

$175,000 each year. Such retrofits have contributed to significant reductions in water use " overall water consumption at Vanderbilt has decreased 47.7% since 2006. Visit http://www.vanderbilt.edu/sustainvu/what-we-do/water/ for more information on water conservation efforts at Vanderbilt. Recycling - Vanderbilt has 2 full-time recycling coordinators, 2 full-time recycling technicians, and 10 student recycling workers. VU has a central recycling center and additional outdoor recycling facilities for the collection of traditional materials. In 2011, Vanderbilt recycled over 3 million pounds, or 1,500 tons, of cardboard, paper, confidential paper, plastic and aluminum. In 2011, Vanderbilt also recycled over 8,150 tons of non-traditional items, such as coal ash, scrap metals, lawn and leaf waste/compost, solvents, batteries, electronics and computers, light bulbs, ink and toner cartridges, cell phones, and pens and mechanical pencils. Recycling is also available at numerous campus events, including all home football, basketball, and baseball games, move-in, move-out, and Commencement. The community is also encouraged to utilize Vandy FreeSwap, an online, Vanderbilt-hosted forum for the trading of free items among VU employees and students: http://www.vanderbilt.edu/sustainvu/vandy-freeswap/. For more information about recycling at Vanderbilt visit http://www.vanderbilt.edu/sustainvu/what-we-do/waste-and-recycling/.

ADMISSIONS

Freshman Academic Profile: Average high school GPA 3.8. 90% in top 10% of high school class, 98% in top 25% of high school class, 100% in top 50% of high school class. 58% from public high schools. SAT Math middle 50% range 710-790. SAT Critical Reading middle 50% range 690-770. SAT Writing middle 50% range 670-770. ACT middle 50% range 32-34. Minimum paper TOEFL 570. **Basis for Candidate Selection:** *Very important factors considered include:* Class rank, application essay, academic GPA, rigor of secondary school record, standardized test scores, character/personal qualities, extracurricular activities. *Important factors considered include:* recommendation(s), talent/ability. *Other factors considered include:* alumni/ae relation, first generation, geographical residence, interview, racial/ethnic status, state residency, volunteer work, work experience. **Freshman Admission Requirements:** High school diploma is required and GED is accepted. *Academic units required:* 4 English, 3 mathematics, 3 science, (2 science labs), 2 foreign language, 2 social studies, 1 history, 3 academic electives. *Academic units recommended:* 4 English, 3 mathematics, 3 science, (2 science labs), 2 foreign language, 2 social studies, 1 history, 3 academic electives. **Freshman Admission Statistics:** 28,348 applied, 14% admitted, 40% enrolled. **Transfer Admission Requirements:** college transcript(s), essay or personal statement, statement of good standing from prior institution(s). Lowest grade transferable C. **General Admission Information:** Application Fee $50. Early decision application deadline 11/1. Regular application deadline 1/3. Regular notification 4/1. Nonfall registration not accepted. Admission may be deferred for a maximum of 1 year. Credit and/or placement offered for CEEB Advanced Placement tests.

COSTS AND FINANCIAL AID

Annual tuition $41,088. Room and board $13,818. Required fees $1,030. Average book expense $1,370. **Required Forms and Deadlines:** FAFSA, CSS/Financial Aid PROFILE. **Notification of Awards:** Applicants will be notified of awards on or about 4/1. **Types of Aid:** *Need-based scholarships/grants:* Federal Pell, SEOG, state scholarships/grants, private scholarships, the school's own gift aid. *Loans:* Subsidized Stafford, Unsubsidized Stafford, PLUS, Federal Perkins, Federal Nursing, college/university loans from institutional funds, Undergrad Education Loan. **Student Employment:** Federal Work-Study Program available. Institutional employment available. Highest amount earned per year from on-campus jobs $2,000. Off-campus job opportunities are excellent. **Financial Aid Statistics:** 88% freshmen, 93% undergrads receive need-based scholarship or grant aid. 52% freshmen, 41% undergrads receive non-need-based scholarship or grant aid. 38% freshmen, 50% undergrads receive need-based self-help aid. 4% freshmen, 4% undergrads receive athletic scholarships. 63% freshmen, 62% undergrads receive any aid. 34% undergrads borrow to pay for school. Average cumulative indebtedness $17,349. **Criteria for awarding institutional aid:** *Non-need-based:* academics, athletics, leadership, minority status, music/drama, state/district residency.

See page 1286.

VANDERCOOK COLLEGE OF MUSIC

3140 South Federal Street, Chicago, IL 60616-3886
Phone: 312-225-6288 x230 • **Financial Aid Phone:** 312-225-6288 ext 233
E-mail: admissions@vandercook.edu • **CEEB Code:** 1872
Fax: 312-225-5211 • **Website:** www.vandercook.edu • **ACT Code:** 1156

This private school was founded in 1909. It has a 1-acre campus.

RATINGS
Admissions Selectivity Rating: 86   **Fire Safety Rating:** 74   **Green Rating:** 60*

STUDENTS AND FACULTY
Enrollment: 110. **Student Body:** 54% female, 46% male, 25% out-of-state, 3% international (4 countries represented). Asian 0%, African American 4%, Caucasian 59%, Hispanic 9%, Native American 0%. **Retention and Graduation:** 90% freshmen return for sophomore year. 44% freshmen graduate within 4 years. 52% freshmen graduate within 6 years. **Faculty:** Student/faculty ratio 9:1. 9 full-time faculty, 56% hold PhDs, 33% are members of minority groups, 56% are women. 0% of classes are taught by teaching assistants.

ACADEMICS
Degrees: bachelor's, master's. **Special Study Options:** independent study, teacher certification program.

FACILITIES
Housing: Coed dorms, men's dorms, women's dorms, fraternity/sorority housing.

CAMPUS LIFE
Environment: Metropolis. **Activities:** Choral groups, concert band, jazz band, music ensembles, musical theater, student newspaper 5 registered organizations, 1 fraternities.

ADMISSIONS
Freshman Academic Profile: Average high school GPA 3.3. 8% in top 10% of high school class, 35% in top 25% of high school class, 81% in top 50% of high school class. SAT Math middle 50% range 538-627, SAT Critical Reading middle 50% range 630-670. SAT Writing middle 50% range 553-597. ACT middle 50% range 20-28. Minimum web-based TOEFL 70. Minimum paper TOEFL 500. **Basis for Candidate Selection:** *Very important factors considered include:* interview, talent/ability. *Important factors considered include:* application essay, rigor of secondary school record, extracurricular activities. *Other factors considered include:* Class rank, recommendation(s), standardized test scores, alumni/ae relation, character/personal qualities, volunteer work, work experience. **Freshman Admission Requirements:** High school diploma is required and GED is accepted. *Academic units required:* 3 English, 2 mathematics, 2 science, 2 foreign language, 3 social studies, 3 academic electives. 3 English, 2 mathematics, 2 science, 2 foreign language, 3 social studies, 3 academic electives. **Freshman Admission Statistics:** 54 applied, 65% admitted, 77% enrolled. **Transfer Admission Requirements:** High school transcript, college transcript(s), essay or personal statement, interview, standardized test scores, Minimum college GPA of 2.5 required. Lowest grade transferable C. **General Admission Information:** Application Fee $35. Regular application deadline 5/1. Nonfall registration accepted. Admission may be deferred for a maximum of case by case. Credit offered for CEEB Advanced Placement tests.

COSTS AND FINANCIAL AID
Annual tuition $22,776. Room and board $10,626. Required fees $1,340. Average book expense $1,900. **Required Forms and Deadlines:** FAFSA. **Notification of Awards: Types of Aid:** *Need-based scholarships/grants:* state scholarships/grants. *Loans:* Subsidized Stafford, PLUS. **Student Employment: Financial Aid Statistics:** 71% freshmen, 74% undergrads receive need-based scholarship or grant aid. 100% freshmen, 90% undergrads receive non-need-based scholarship or grant aid. 100% freshmen, 92% undergrads receive need-based self-help aid. 100% freshmen, 93% undergrads receive any aid. 86% undergrads borrow to pay for school. Average cumulative indebtedness $31,553.

VANGUARD UNIVERSITY OF SOUTHERN CALIFORNIA

55 Fair Drive, Costa Mesa, CA 92626
Phone: 714-556-3610 • **Financial Aid Phone:** 714-556-3610
E-mail: admissions@vanguard.edu • **CEEB Code:** 4701
Fax: 714-966-5471 • **Website:** www.vanguard.edu • **ACT Code:** 432

This private school, affiliated with the Assemblies of God Church, was founded in 1920. It has a 38-acre campus.

RATINGS
Admissions Selectivity Rating: 68   **Fire Safety Rating:** 79   **Green Rating:** 60*

STUDENTS AND FACULTY
Enrollment: 1,847. **Student Body:** 63% female, 37% male, 14% out-of-state, 1% international (17 countries represented). Asian 4%, African American 3%, Caucasian 66%, Hispanic 17%, Native American 1%
Retention and Graduation: 76% freshmen return for sophomore year. 37% freshmen graduate within 4 years. 49% freshmen graduate within 6 years. **Faculty:** Student/faculty ratio 16:1. 66 full-time faculty, 77% hold PhDs, 14% are members of minority groups, 39% are women. 0% of classes are taught by teaching assistants.

ACADEMICS
Degrees: bachelor's, master's. **Classes:** Most classes have 10—19 students. Most lab/discussion sessions have fewer than 10 students. **Majors with Highest Enrollment:** business/commerce; education; psychology. **Special Study Options:** Accelerated program, cooperative education program, cross-registration, double major, dual enrollment, external degree program, independent study, internships, study abroad, teacher certification program. **Disability Services:** Special programs offered to physically disabled students include note-taking services, tutors.

FACILITIES
Housing: special housing for disabled students, men's dorms, women's dorms, apartments for married students, apartments for single students, One dorm is coed (Floors 1, 2, 4 for males; floor 3 for females). 95% of campus accessible to physically disabled. **Special Academic Facilities/Equipment:** Lyceum Theater;Computer Lab;Communications Lab **Computers:** Students can register for classes online. Administrative functions (other than registration) can be performed online.

CAMPUS LIFE
Environment: City. **Activities:** Choral groups, concert band, dance, drama/theater, jazz band, music ensembles, musical theater, opera, pep band, student government, student newspaper, symphony orchestra, yearbook 50 registered organizations, 5 honor societies, 25 religious organizations. **Athletics (Intercollegiate):** *Men:* baseball, basketball, cross-country, soccer, tennis, track/field (outdoor), track/field (indoor). *Women:* basketball, cross-country, soccer, softball, tennis, track/field (outdoor), track/field (indoor), volleyball. **On-Campus Highlights:** Cove-Student Union, The Library, The Pit-our gymnasium, Heath Academic Center, The Dining Commons.

ADMISSIONS
Freshman Academic Profile: Average high school GPA 3.4. 22% in top 10% of high school class, 49% in top 25% of high school class, 78% in top 50% of high school class. 73% from public high schools. SAT Math middle 50% range 430-560. SAT Critical Reading middle 50% range 450-570. ACT middle 50% range 19-24. Minimum paper TOEFL 550. **Basis for Candidate Selection:** *Very important factors considered include:* application essay, academic GPA, recommendation(s), rigor of secondary school record, character/personal qualities. *Important factors considered include:* standardized test scores, religious affiliation/commitment. *Other factors considered include:* extracurricular activities, interview, level of applicant's interest, talent/ability, volunteer work, work experience. **Freshman Admission Requirements:** High school diploma is required and GED is accepted. **Freshman Admission Statistics:** 899 applied, 83% admitted, 53% enrolled. **Transfer Admission Requirements:** college transcript(s), essay or personal statement, Minimum college GPA of 2.0 required. Lowest grade transferable C–. **General Admission Information:** Application Fee $45. Notification on a rolling basis, beginning on or about 1/15. Nonfall registration accepted. Credit offered for CEEB Advanced Placement tests.

COSTS AND FINANCIAL AID
Annual tuition $22,466. Room and board $7,270. Required fees $520. Average book expense $1,314. **Required Forms and Deadlines:** FAFSA, state aid form. **Notification of Awards:** Applicants will be notified of awards on a rolling basis beginning 4/1. **Types of Aid:** *Need-based scholarships/grants:* Federal

Pell, SEOG, state scholarships/grants, private scholarships, the school's own gift aid. *Loans:* Subsidized Stafford, Unsubsidized Stafford, PLUS, Federal Perkins. **Student Employment:** Federal Work-Study Program available. Institutional employment available. Highest amount earned per year from on-campus jobs $6,000. Off-campus job opportunities are excellent. **Financial Aid Statistics:** 80% freshmen, 67% undergrads receive need-based scholarship or grant aid. 90% freshmen, 85% undergrads receive non-need-based scholarship or grant aid. 81% freshmen, 91% undergrads receive need-based self-help aid. 2% freshmen, 2% undergrads receive athletic scholarships. 94% freshmen, 99% undergrads receive any aid. 76% undergrads borrow to pay for school. Average cumulative indebtedness $16,979. **Criteria for awarding institutional aid:** *Non-need-based:* academics, athletics, music/drama.

VASSAR COLLEGE

Best 378

124 Raymond Avenue, Poughkeepsie, NY 12604
Phone: 845-437-7300 • **Financial Aid Phone:** 845-437-5320
E-mail: admissions@vassar.edu • **CEEB Code:** 2956
Fax: 845-437-7063 • **Website:** www.vassar.edu • **ACT Code:** 2982

This private school was founded in 1861. It has a 1000-acre campus.

RATINGS
Admissions Selectivity Rating: 97   **Fire Safety Rating:** 89   **Green Rating:** 85

STUDENTS AND FACULTY
Enrollment: 2,408. **Student Body:** 58% female, 42% male, 73% out-of-state, 6% international (43 countries represented). Asian 9%, African American 5%, Caucasian 67%, Hispanic 9%, Native American 0%
Retention and Graduation: 96% freshmen return for sophomore year. 90% freshmen graduate within 4 years. 93% freshmen graduate within 6 years. 23% grads go on to further study within 1 year. 11% grads pursue arts and sciences degrees. 3% grads pursue law degrees. 3% grads pursue medical degrees. **Faculty:** Student/faculty ratio 8:1. 279 full-time faculty, 89% hold PhDs, 23% are members of minority groups, 47% are women. 0% of classes are taught by teaching assistants.

ACADEMICS
Degrees: bachelor's, master's. **Classes:** Most classes have 10—19 students. Most lab/discussion sessions have 10—19 students. **Majors with Highest Enrollment:** English language and literature; political science and government; psychology. **Special Study Options:** cooperative education program, cross-registration, double major, exchange student program (domestic), independent study, internships, liberal arts/career combination, student-designed major, study abroad, teacher certification program. **Combined Degree Programs:** BA/MA. **Disability Services:** Special programs offered to physically disabled students include note-taking services, reader services, tape recorders. **Career Services:** Alumni network, alumni services, career/job search classes, career assessment, internships, regional alumni.

FACILITIES
Housing: Coed dorms, special housing for disabled students, special housing for international students, women's dorms, apartments for married students, cooperative housing, apartments for single students, wellness housing, quiet housing. 69% of campus accessible to physically disabled. **Special Academic Facilities/Equipment:** Art center, theatres, nursery school, environmental field station, geology museum, electron microscope, observatory, Skinner Music Hall, Fitness Center **Computers:** 100% of classrooms, 100% of dorms, 100% of libraries, 100% of dining areas, 100% of student union, 80% of common outdoor areas have wireless network access. Students can register for classes online. Administrative functions (other than registration) can be performed online.

CAMPUS LIFE
Environment: Town. **Activities:** Choral groups, concert band, dance, drama/theater, jazz band, literary magazine, marching band, music ensembles, musical theater, opera, radio station, student government, student newspaper, student-run film society, symphony orchestra, television station, yearbook, Campus Ministries, International Student Organization, Model UN 105 registered organizations, 2 honor societies, 11 religious organizations. **Athletics (Intercollegiate):** *Men:* baseball, basketball, crew/rowing, cross-country, diving, fencing, lacrosse, soccer, squash, swimming, tennis, track/field (outdoor), volleyball. *Women:* basketball, crew/rowing, cross-country, diving, fencing, field hockey, golf, lacrosse,

soccer, squash, swimming, tennis, track/field (outdoor), volleyball. **On-Campus Highlights:** Library, Shakespeare Garden, Class of 1951 Observatory, Frances Lehman Loeb Art Center, Center for Drama and Film. **Environmental Initiatives:** composting nearly 100% of food waste on site purchasing local food. 30% locally grown or purchased shared bicycle program.

ADMISSIONS

Freshman Academic Profile: Average high school GPA 3.8. 65% in top 10% of high school class, 96% in top 25% of high school class, 100% in top 50% of high school class. 63% from public high schools. SAT Math middle 50% range 640-720. SAT Critical Reading middle 50% range 670-740. SAT Writing middle 50% range 660-750. ACT middle 50% range 29-32. Minimum web-based TOEFL 100. Minimum paper TOEFL 600. **Basis for Candidate Selection:** *Very important factors considered include:* rigor of secondary school record. *Important factors considered include:* Class rank, application essay, academic GPA, recommendation(s), standardized test scores, extracurricular activities, talent/ability. *Other factors considered include:* alumni/ae relation, character/personal qualities, first generation, geographical residence, interview, level of applicant's interest, racial/ethnic status, volunteer work, work experience. **Freshman Admission Requirements:** High school diploma is required and GED is accepted. *Academic units required:* 4 English, 4 mathematics, 4 science, (3 science labs), 3 foreign language, 2 social studies, 2 history, 4 academic electives. *Academic units recommended:* 4 English, 4 mathematics, 4 science, (3 science labs), 3 foreign language, 2 social studies, 2 history, 4 academic electives. **Freshman Admission Statistics:** 7,822 applied, 24% admitted, 36% enrolled. **Transfer Admission Requirements:** High school transcript, college transcript(s), essay or personal statement, standardized test scores, statement of good standing from prior institution(s). Minimum college GPA of 3.0 required. Lowest grade transferable C. **General Admission Information:** Application Fee $60. Early decision application deadline 11/15, Regular application deadline 1/1. Regular notification 4/1. Nonfall registration not accepted. Admission may be deferred for a maximum of 12 months. Credit and/or placement offered for CEEB Advanced Placement tests.

COSTS AND FINANCIAL AID

Annual tuition $45,580. Room and board $10,800. Required fees $655. Average book expense $860. **Required Forms and Deadlines:** FAFSA, CSS/Financial Aid PROFILE, noncustodial PROFILE, business/farm supplement. **Notification of Awards.** Applicants will be notified of awards on or about 3/30. **Types of Aid:** *Need-based scholarships/grants:* Federal Pell, SEOG, state scholarships/grants, private scholarships, the school's own gift aid. *Loans:* Direct Subsidized Stafford, Direct Unsubsidized Stafford, Direct PLUS, Federal Perkins, Loans for Non-citizens with need. **Student Employment:** Federal Work-Study Program available. Institutional employment available. Highest amount earned per year from on-campus jobs $4,350. Off-campus job opportunities are fair. **Financial Aid Statistics:** 100% freshmen, 99% undergrads receive need-based scholarship or grant aid. 100% freshmen, 100% undergrads receive need-based self-help aid. 64% freshmen, 63% undergrads receive any aid. 49% undergrads borrow to pay for school. Average cumulative indebtedness $18,153.

VAUGHN COLLEGE OF AERONAUTICS AND TECHNOLOGY

86-01 23rd Avenue, Flushing, NY 11369
Phone: 718-429-6600 • **Financial Aid Phone:** 718-429-6600
E-mail: admitme@vaughn.edu • **CEEB Code:** 2001
Fax: 718-779-2231 • **Website:** www.vaughn.edu

This private school was founded in 1932. It has a 6-acre campus.

RATINGS

Admissions Selectivity Rating: 67   **Fire Safety Rating:** 95   **Green Rating:** 60*

STUDENTS AND FACULTY

Enrollment: 1,796. **Student Body:** 13% female, 87% male, 11% out-of-state, 2% international. Asian 8%, African American 19%, Caucasian 17%, Hispanic 38%, Native American 1%
Retention and Graduation: 80% freshmen return for sophomore year. 35% freshmen graduate within 4 years. **Faculty:** Student/faculty ratio 15:1. 41 full-time faculty, 54% hold PhDs, 39% are members of minority groups, 12% are women. 0% of classes are taught by teaching assistants.

ACADEMICS

Degrees: associate, bachelor's, certificate, master's. **Classes:** Most classes have 20—29 students. Most lab/discussion sessions have 20—29 students. **Majors with Highest Enrollment:** airframe mechanics and aircraft maintenance tech-

nology/technician; business/commerce; transportation/transportation management. **Special Study Options:** Accelerated program, distance learning, double major, independent study, internships, liberal arts/career combination. **Career Services:** Alumni network, alumni services, career/job search classes, career assessment, internships Career services highlights include Internship program.

FACILITIES

Housing: Coed dorms. **Computers:** 100% of classrooms, 100% of dorms, 100% of libraries, 100% of dining areas, 100% of common outdoor areas have wireless network access. Administrative functions (other than registration) can be performed online.

CAMPUS LIFE

Environment: City. **Activities:** dance, drama/theater, student government, yearbook, International Student Organization 21 registered organizations, 1 honor societies. **Athletics (Intercollegiate):** *Men:* basketball, soccer. *Women:* tennis. **On-Campus Highlights:** Complex of six flight simulators, Laboratories, Observation Tower, Cafeteria, Library.

ADMISSIONS

Freshman Academic Profile: 84.2. SAT Math middle 50% range 468-574. SAT Critical Reading middle 50% range 434-520. ACT middle 50% range 18-24. Minimum web-based TOEFL 80. Minimum paper TOEFL 580. **Basis for Candidate Selection:** *Very important factors considered include:* rigor of secondary school record. *Important factors considered include:* academic GPA, standardized test scores, level of applicant's interest. *Other factors considered include:* application essay, recommendation(s), character/personal qualities, extracurricular activities, first generation, interview, talent/ability, volunteer work, work experience. **Freshman Admission Requirements:** High school diploma is required and GED is accepted. *Academic units required:* 4 English, 3 mathematics, 2 science, (2 science labs), 1 social studies,. *Academic units recommended:* 4 English, 3 mathematics, 2 science, (2 science labs), 1 social studies,. **Freshman Admission Statistics:** 723 applied, 85% admitted, 52% enrolled. **Transfer Admission Requirements:** college transcript(s), Minimum college GPA of 2.0 required. Lowest grade transferable C. **General Admission Information:** Application Fee $40. Notification on a rolling basis, beginning on or about 10/1. Nonfall registration accepted. Admission may be deferred for a maximum of 1 year. Credit and/or placement offered for CEEB Advanced Placement tests.

COSTS AND FINANCIAL AID

Annual tuition $19,850. Room and board $11,880. Required fees $400. Average book expense $2,100. **Required Forms and Deadlines:** FAFSA, state aid form. **Notification of Awards.** Applicants will be notified of awards on a rolling basis beginning 4/15. **Types of Aid:** *Need-based scholarships/grants:* Federal Pell, SEOG, state scholarships/grants, private scholarships, the school's own gift aid. *Loans:* Subsidized Stafford, Unsubsidized Stafford, PLUS. **Student Employment:** Federal Work-Study Program available. Institutional employment available. Off-campus job opportunities are excellent. **Financial Aid Statistics:** 86% freshmen, 87% undergrads receive need-based scholarship or grant aid. 39% freshmen, 41% undergrads receive non-need-based scholarship or grant aid. 85% freshmen, 94% undergrads receive need-based self-help aid. 95% undergrads borrow to pay for school. Average cumulative indebtedness $32,500. **Criteria for awarding institutional aid:** *Non-need-based:* academics, alumni affiliation, job skills, leadership.

See page 1288.

VERMONT TECHNICAL COLLEGE

PO Box 500, Randolph Center, VT 5061
Phone: 802-728-1242
E-mail: Admissions@vtc.edu
Fax: 802-728-1321 • **Website:** www.vtc.edu/

This is a public school.

RATINGS

Admissions Selectivity Rating: 77   **Fire Safety Rating:** 60*   **Green Rating:** 60*

STUDENTS AND FACULTY

Enrollment: 1,378. **Student Body:** 40% female, 60% male, 21% out-of-state.
Retention and Graduation: 65% freshmen return for sophomore year.
Faculty: Student/faculty ratio 12:1. 79 full-time faculty, 80% hold PhDs, 47% are women.

ACADEMICS

Degrees: associate, bachelor's, certificate, diploma. **Classes:** Most classes have 10—19 students. Most lab/discussion sessions have 10—19 students. **Special Study Options:** distance learning, double major, dual enrollment, internships.

FACILITIES

Housing: Coed dorms.

CAMPUS LIFE

Activities: radio station, student government, television station, yearbook.

ADMISSIONS

Freshman Academic Profile: 8% in top 10% of high school class, 27% in top 25% of high school class, 60% in top 50% of high school class. SAT Math middle 50% range 450-560. SAT Critical Reading middle 50% range 410-520. SAT Writing middle 50% range 410-520. **Basis for Candidate Selection:** *Very important factors considered include:* academic GPA, rigor of secondary school record. *Important factors considered include:* recommendation(s), standardized test scores, interview. *Other factors considered include:* application essay, alumni/ae relation, character/personal qualities, extracurricular activities, first generation, volunteer work, work experience. **Freshman Admission Requirements:** High school diploma is required and GED is accepted. *Academic units required:* 4 English, 3 mathematics, 2 science, (1 science labs), 2 social studies, 2 history. *Academic units recommended:* 4 English, 3 mathematics, 2 science, (1 science labs), 2 social studies, 2 history. **Freshman Admission Statistics:** 920 applied, 58% admitted, 54% enrolled. **Transfer Admission Requirements:** college transcript(s), statement of good standing from prior institution(s). Lowest grade transferable C−. **General Admission Information:** Application Fee $36. Notification on a rolling basis, beginning on or about 10/1. Nonfall registration accepted.

COSTS AND FINANCIAL AID

Student Employment: Financial Aid Statistics: 80% freshmen, 74% undergrads receive need-based scholarship or grant aid. 3% freshmen, 5% undergrads receive non-need-based scholarship or grant aid. 85% freshmen, 84% undergrads receive need-based self-help aid.

VILLA MARIA COLLEGE OF BUFFALO

240 Pine Ridge Road, Buffalo, NY 14225
Phone: 716-961-1805 • **Financial Aid Phone:** 716-961-1850
E-mail: admissions@villa.edu
Fax: 716-896-0705 • **ACT Code:** 2983

This private school, affiliated with the Roman Catholic Church, was founded in 1960. It has a 9-acre campus.

RATINGS

Admissions Selectivity Rating: 65   **Fire Safety Rating:** 60*   **Green Rating:** 60*

STUDENTS AND FACULTY

Enrollment: 408. **Student Body:** 62% female, 38% male, 2% out-of-state, 0% international (0 countries represented). Asian 1%, African American 17%, Caucasian 73%, Hispanic 5%, Native American 0%
Retention and Graduation: 70% freshmen return for sophomore year. 25% freshmen graduate within 4 years. 33% freshmen graduate within 6 years.
Faculty: Student/faculty ratio 8:1. 30 full-time faculty, 47% hold PhDs, 7% are members of minority groups, 60% are women. 0% of classes are taught by teaching assistants.

ACADEMICS

Degrees: associate, bachelor's. **Classes:** Most classes have 10—19 students. Most lab/discussion sessions have 10—19 students. **Majors with Highest Enrollment:** interior design; music management and merchandising; visual and performing arts. **Special Study Options:** cooperative education program, cross-registration, dual enrollment, internships, liberal arts/career combination, study abroad, Selected courses are offered in evening modules primarily with non-traditional students in mind. These offerings are limited. **Disability Services:** Special programs offered to physically disabled students include tutors. **Career Services:** alumni services, career/job search classes, career assessment, internships.

FACILITIES

Housing: apartments for married students, apartments for single students-Housing is available at Collegiate Village (college affiliated) which is a mile off-campus; however van service to campus is available. There is no on-campus housing. 100% of campus accessible to physically disabled. **Special Academic Facilities/Equipment:** Art Gallery, Music Building, Recording Studio, Student Center, Athletic Center, Art Shop **Computers:** 100% of libraries, 100% of dining areas, have wireless network access. Students can register for classes online. Administrative functions (other than registration) can be performed online.

CAMPUS LIFE

Environment: City. **Activities:** Choral groups, jazz band, literary magazine, music ensembles, student government, student newspaper, Campus Ministries 1 honor societies. **On-Campus Highlights:** Athletic/Student Center, Recording Studio .

ADMISSIONS

Freshman Academic Profile: Average high school GPA 3.0. 5% in top 10% of high school class, 11% in top 25% of high school class, 41% in top 50% of high school class. 96% from public high schools. SAT Math middle 50% range 300-500. SAT Critical Reading middle 50% range 350-500. ACT middle 50% range 17-26. Minimum paper TOEFL 450. **Basis for Candidate Selection:** *Very important factors considered include:* application essay, academic GPA, interview, talent/ability. *Important factors considered include:* level of applicant's interest. *Other factors considered include:* recommendation(s), rigor of secondary school record, standardized test scores, volunteer work, work experience. **Freshman Admission Requirements:** High school diploma is required and GED is accepted. **Freshman Admission Statistics:** 243 applied, 81% admitted, 38% enrolled. **Transfer Admission Requirements:** college transcript(s), interview, Lowest grade transferable C. **General Admission Information:** Nonfall registration accepted. Admission may be deferred for a maximum of 2 semesters. Credit and/or placement offered for CEEB Advanced Placement tests.

COSTS AND FINANCIAL AID

Required Forms and Deadlines: FAFSA. **Notification of Awards:** Applicants will be notified of awards on a rolling basis beginning 2/15. **Types of Aid:** *Need-based scholarships/grants:* Federal Pell, SEOG, state scholarships/grants, private scholarships, the school's own gift aid. *Loans:* Subsidized Stafford, Unsubsidized Stafford, PLUS. **Student Employment:** Federal Work-Study Program available. Off-campus job opportunities are fair. **Financial Aid Statistics:** 42% freshmen, 9% undergrads receive need-based scholarship or grant aid. 38% freshmen, 22% undergrads receive non-need-based scholarship or grant aid. 99% freshmen, 92% undergrads receive any aid. 43% undergrads borrow to pay for school. Average cumulative indebtedness $30,353. **Criteria for awarding institutional aid:** *Non-need-based:* academics, alumni affiliation, art, leadership, minority status, music/drama.

VILLANOVA UNIVERSITY

Best 378

Austin Hall, 800 Lancaster Avenue, Villanova, PA 19085
Phone: 610-519-4000 • **Financial Aid Phone:** 610-519-4010
E-mail: gotovu@villanova.edu • **CEEB Code:** 2959
Fax: 610-519-6450 • **Website:** www.villanova.edu • **ACT Code:** 3744

This private school, affiliated with the Roman Catholic Church, was founded in 1842. It has a 254-acre campus.

RATINGS

Admissions Selectivity Rating: 95   **Fire Safety Rating:** 88   **Green Rating:** 93

STUDENTS AND FACULTY

Enrollment: 6,899. **Student Body:** 51% female, 49% male, 75% out-of-state, 3% international (52 countries represented). Asian 6%, African American 4%, Caucasian 75%, Hispanic 7%, Native American 0%
Retention and Graduation: 94% freshmen return for sophomore year. 85% freshmen graduate within 4 years. 23% grads go on to further study within 1 year. 7% grads pursue arts and sciences degrees. 5% grads pursue law degrees. 1% grads pursue business degrees. 2% grads pursue medical degrees. **Faculty:** Student/faculty ratio 12:1. 598 full-time faculty, 86% hold PhDs, 14% are members of minority groups, 38% are women. 1% of classes are taught by teaching assistants.

ACADEMICS

Degrees: associate, bachelor's, master's, post-bachelor's certificate, post-master's certificate. **Classes:** Most classes have 10—19 students. Most lab/discussion sessions have 10—19 students. **Majors with Highest Enrollment:** communication studies/speech communication and rhetoric; finance; nursing/registered nurse (rn, asn, bsn, msn). **Special Study Options:** Accelerated program, cooperative education program, cross-registration, distance learning, double major, dual enrollment, English as a Second Language (ESL), exchange student program (domestic), honors program, independent study, internships, liberal arts/career combination, study abroad, teacher certification program. **Honors Programs:** Honors at Villanova is a comprehensive four-year program that offers challenging seminars, research opportunities, service projects, and cultural and social events designed to bring together superior students and dedicated faculty. Honors courses and co-curricular activities enrich and complement the academic experience inherent in a Villanova education. The Honors Program also works closely with the University's Center for Undergraduate Grants and Awards, which administers the Presidential Scholarship program for incoming students; Connelly-Delouvrier International Scholarships for study abroad; and Villanova's support for students pursuing prestigious national fellowships. The Villanova University Honors Program is an active member of both the National Collegiate Honors Council and the Northeast Region of the National Collegiate Honors Council. **Combined Degree Programs:** BS/MD, BS/OD, BS/MS, BS/DDM. **Disability Services:** Special programs offered to physically disabled students include note-taking services, reader services, tape recorders, tutors. **Career Services:** Alumni network, alumni services, career/job search classes, career assessment, internships, regional alumni. Career services highlights include Hundreds of companies recruit Villanova students for internships--either on campus or via job boards--each year. Many internships ultimately lead to full-time job offers.

FACILITIES

Housing: Coed dorms, men's dorms, women's dorms, apartments for single students, wellness housing, theme housing, Learning Communities. 100% of campus accessible to physically disabled. **Special Academic Facilities/Equipment:** Driscoll Hall, home of the Villanova College of Nursing; the Villanova School of Business Applied Finance Lab; the Structural Engineering Teaching and Research Laboratory; the Augustinian Historical Museum, and the Villanova Observatory. **Computers:** 90% of classrooms, 90% of dorms, 100% of libraries, 100% of dining areas, 100% of student union, 10% of common outdoor areas have wireless network access. Students can register for classes online. Administrative functions (other than registration) can be performed online. Undergraduates are required to own a computer.

CAMPUS LIFE

Environment: Village. **Activities:** Choral groups, concert band, dance, drama/theater, jazz band, literary magazine, marching band, music ensembles, musical theater, pep band, radio station, student government, student newspaper, student run film society, symphony orchestra, television station, yearbook, Campus Ministries, International Student Organization, Model UN 250 registered organizations, 34 honor societies, 15 religious organizations. 9 fraternities, 9 sororities. **Athletics (Intercollegiate):** Men: baseball, basketball, cheerleading, cross-country, diving, football, golf, lacrosse, soccer, swimming, tennis, track/field (outdoor), track/field (indoor). Women: basketball, cheerleading, crew/rowing, cross-country, diving, field hockey, lacrosse, soccer, softball, swimming, tennis, track/field (outdoor), track/field (indoor), volleyball, water polo. **On-Campus Highlights:** St. Thomas of Villanova Church, Davis Center for Athletics and Fitness, Villanova University Shop, Connelly Center and Cinema, Bartley Hall Exchange. **Environmental Initiatives:** Academic programs: The master's degree in sustainable engineering; the first-year environmental leadership learning community; bachelor's degrees in environmental science and environmental studies; an undergraduate minor in sustainability; a biology master's degree, graduate certificate, and advanced graduate certificate with a concentration in ecology, evolution, and organismal biology; a master's degree in water resources and environmental engineering, and a graduate certificate in urban water resources design. Non-academic programs: In addition to the contributions of academic departments, several groups of students, faculty, and staff are working together to strengthen Villanova's commitment to the environment. These groups include the President's Environmental Sustainability Committee, the Villanova Environmental Group, the Villanova Ecological Society, Business Without Borders, Engineers Without Borders, and Engineers for a Sustainable World. In Fall 2010, the Student Government Association (SGA) at Villanova established a sustainability subcommittee designed to promote sustainable practices on campus. Villanova has a green dorm, as well as an ongoing dorm energy conservation competition. The Sustainable Endowments Institute awarded Villanova an "A" in several categories in its most recent Green Report Card, including Food & Recycling. The Institute also considers Villanova to be an "Endowment Sustainability Leader," a title given to only a few colleges that earned an average grade of A- or better on three endowment management categories: transparency, investment priorities, and shareholder engagement. Lastly, the University implements green building practices, with features that include green roofs, extensive natural lighting and other energy-conserving building features, efficient plumbing, and a 90% construction waste diversion rate. Villanova has committed to achieving a minimum of LEED Silver, and is especially pleased to have received LEED Gold for the two buildings most recently constructed. Dining services: Villanova has implemented a comprehensive composting initiative, and has transitioned one of its locations into a green facility, reducing its trash volume by two thirds. In addition, Villanova Dining Services (VDS) purchases a large percentage of its food from local and organic sources. Since August 2006, VDS has been purchasing and serving organic

produce, organic fruits and organic groceries. VDS, through its partnership with Primo Produce, is purchasing local produce and vegetables from approximately 63 farms located in Pennsylvania, New York, New Jersey, Maryland, and Delaware. Primo Produce contracts with local farmers throughout New Jersey and Pennsylvania to purchase fruits, vegetables and herbs in season; their total purchases in local produce (PA, NJ, NY, MD, DE, and OH) are 27% of their total produce purchases. Primo Produce is dedicated to supplying produce grown with good stewardship. Primo has dedicated to partner with growers whose mission as good stewards is to grow the finest quality fruits and vegetables, using the natural resources entrusted to them, without compromising the ability of future generations to do the same. Finally, VDS supports local dairies by purchasing all University dairy products exclusively from a local dairy. The largest retail food outlet on campus operated by VDS, the Belle Air Terrace, features a totally organic salad bar. On the operations side, VDS offers a large selection and variety of organic groceries and healthy products (including Chelten House products, United Natural Food products, and Earth Bound Organic products) in convenience stores on campus, and serves organic and fair-trade coffee. Villanova Dining Services partnered with local consortia to bring a farmer's market to campus on Earth Day in both April 2010 and 2011. Villanova partners with the Monterey Bay Aquarium, following the Seafood Watch program (exclusively purchasing and serving seafood which is abundant, and caught or farmed in environmentally-friendly ways). Finally, 100% of the resident dining halls are trayless and have complete vegetarian options available.

ADMISSIONS

Freshman Academic Profile: Average high school GPA 3.9. 58% in top 10% of high school class, 87% in top 25% of high school class, 97% in top 50% of high school class. 55% from public high schools. SAT Math middle 50% range 610-710. SAT Critical Reading middle 50% range 590-680. SAT Writing middle 50% range 590-690. ACT middle 50% range 28-31. Minimum paper TOEFL 550. **Basis for Candidate Selection:** *Very important factors considered include:* Class rank, academic GPA, rigor of secondary school record, standardized test scores. *Important factors considered include:* application essay, recommendation(s), character/personal qualities, extracurricular activities, talent/ability, volunteer work, work experience. *Other factors considered include:* alumni/ae relation, first generation, geographical residence, level of applicant's interest, racial/ethnic status, state residency. **Freshman Admission Requirements:** High school diploma is required and GED is accepted. *Academic units required:* 4 English, 4 mathematics, 4 science, (2 science labs), 2 foreign language, 2 academic electives. *Academic units recommended:* 4 English, 4 mathematics, 4 science, (2 science labs), 2 foreign language, 2 academic electives. **Freshman Admission Statistics:** 14,901 applied, 46% admitted, 24% enrolled. **Transfer Admission Requirements:** High school transcript, college transcript(s), essay or personal statement, standardized test scores, statement of good standing from prior institution(s). Lowest grade transferable C. **General Admission Information:** Application Fee $75. Regular application deadline 1/7. Regular notification 4/1. Nonfall registration not accepted. Admission may be deferred for a maximum of 1 year. Credit and/or placement offered for CEEB Advanced Placement tests.

COSTS AND FINANCIAL AID

Annual tuition $42,150. Room and board $11,393. Required fees $590. Average book expense $988. **Required Forms and Deadlines:** FAFSA, institution's own financial aid form. **Notification of Awards:** Applicants will be notified of awards on or about 4/1. **Types of Aid:** *Need-based scholarships/grants:* Federal Pell, SEOG, state scholarships/grants, private scholarships, the school's own gift aid. *Loans:* Subsidized Stafford, Unsubsidized Stafford, PLUS, Federal Perkins, Federal Nursing. **Student Employment:** Federal Work-Study Program available. Institutional employment available. Off-campus job opportunities are excellent. **Financial Aid Statistics:** 91% freshmen, 88% undergrads receive need-based scholarship or grant aid. 26% freshmen, 29% undergrads receive non-need-based scholarship or grant aid. 90% freshmen, 91% undergrads receive need-based self-help aid. 2% freshmen, 3% undergrads receive athletic scholarships. 66% freshmen, 69% undergrads receive any aid. 53% undergrads borrow to pay for school. Average cumulative indebtedness $35,297. **Criteria for awarding institutional aid:** *Non-need-based:* academics, alumni affiliation, athletics, leadership, minority status, religious affiliation.

VIRGINIA COMMONWEALTH UNIVERSITY

821 West Franklin Street, Richmond, VA 23284
Phone: 804-828-1222 • **Financial Aid Phone:** 804-828-7372
E-mail: upgrad@vcu.edu • **CEEB Code:** 5570
Fax: 804-828-1899 • **Website:** www.vcu.edu

This public school was founded in 1838. It has a 143-acre campus.

RATINGS

Admissions Selectivity Rating: 83   **Fire Safety Rating:** 80   **Green Rating:** 98

STUDENTS AND FACULTY

Enrollment: 22178. **Student Body:** 57% female, 43% male, 7% out-of-state, 3% international (110 countries represented). Asian 12%, African American 18%, Caucasian 52%, Hispanic 7%.
Retention and Graduation: 85% freshmen return for sophomore year.
Faculty: Student/faculty ratio 18:1. 2048 full-time faculty, % hold PhDs, 20% are are members of minority groups, 43% are women. % of classes are taught by teaching assistants.

ACADEMICS

Degrees: bachelor's, certificate, master's, post-bachelor's certificate, post-master's certificate. **Classes:** Most classes have 10–19 students. Most lab/discussion sessions have 20–29 students. **Special Study Options:** Accelerated program, cooperative education program, distance learning, double major, dual enrollment, English as a Second Language (ESL), honors program, independent study, internships, liberal arts/career combination, student-designed major, study abroad, teacher certification program. **Honors programs:** Mentorship Programs: All first year students are invited to participate in this program. In this program upper classmen volunteer to serve as mentors offering support and assistance to new honors students during their first semester. **Combined degree programs:** BA/MD, BA/DDS, Pharmacy (PharmD) as a part of Honors Program. **Disability Services:** Special programs offered to physically disabled students include note-taking services, reader services, tape recorders, tutors. **Career services:** Alumni network, alumni services, career/job search classes, career assessment, internships.

FACILITIES

Housing: Coed dorms, special housing for disabled students, apartments for single students. 90% of campus accessible to physically disabled. **Special Academic Facilities/Equipment:** Anderson Gallery, Student Art Gallery, Larrick Student Center, Shafer Ct. Dining Facilities, Student Commons, Siegel Center, Cabell Library, Biotech Research Bldgs., Tompkins McCaw Library and VCU Bookstores **Computers:** 75% of classrooms, 100% of dorms, 100% of libraries, 100% of dining areas, 100% of student union, 25% of common outdoor areas have wireless network access. Students can register for classes online. Administrative functions (other than registration) can be performed online. Undergraduates are required to own a computer.

CAMPUS LIFE

Environment: Metropolis. **Activities:** Choral groups, concert band, dance, drama/theater, jazz band, literary magazine, musical theater, pep band, radio station, student government, student newspaper, television station, yearbook, Campus Ministries, International Student Organization. 377 registered organizations, 30 religious organizations. 22 fraternities, 13 sororities. **Athletics (Intercollegiate):** Men: baseball, basketball, cross-country, golf, soccer, tennis, track/field (outdoor). Women: basketball, cross-country, field hockey, soccer, tennis, track/field (outdoor), volleyball. **On-Campus Highlights:** Student Commons, Cabell Library, Siegel Center, Anderson Gallery, Shafer Court Dining Facility, Cary Street Recreation Complex. **Environmental Initiatives:** Annual GHG Emissions Inventory and VCU Climate Action Plan's annual GHG reduction goal of 3,000 to 4,000 MTCDE to achieve climate neutrality by 2050 and inclusion of sustainability in VCU strategic plan, Quest for Distinction, in May 2011. VCU successfully secured $3.1 million in federal funds for solar energy projects and in 2011 installed solar arrays on two parking decks, three pole-mounted solar trackers and a 750-gallon solar thermal water heater, which together will eliminate 371 metric tons of carbon dioxide equivalents (MTCDE) per year. Installation of 19 building energy dashboards and 22 solar trash compactors.

ADMISSIONS

Freshman Academic Profile: Average high school GPA 3.6 20% in top 10% of high school class, 53 88% in top 50% of high school class. SAT Math middle 50% range 500-600. SAT Critical Reading middle 50% range 500-610. SAT Writing middle 50% range 490-590. ACT middle 50% range 21-26. Minimum web-based TOEFL 80. Minimum paper TOEFL 550. **Basis for Candidate Selection:** Very important factors considered include: academic GPA, rigor of secondary school record. Important factors considered include: standard-

ized test scores, talent/ability. Other factors considered include: Class rank, application essay, recommendation(s), extracurricular activities, first generation, volunteer work, work experience. **Freshman Admission Requirements:** High school diploma is required and GED is accepted. **Academic units required:** 4 English, 3 mathematics, 3 science, (1 science labs), 2 foreign language, 1 social studies, 2 history. **Academic units recommended:** 4 English, 3 mathematics, 3 science, (1 science labs), 2 foreign language, 1 social studies, 2 history. **Freshman Admission Statistics:** 15,750 applied, 60% admitted, 38% enrolled. **Transfer Admission Requirements:** college transcript(s), Minimum college GPA of 2.25 required. Lowest grade transferable C. **General Admission Information:** Application Fee $40. Notification on a rolling basis, beginning on or about 12/1. Nonfall registration accepted. Admission may be deferred for a maximum of 1 semester. Credit offered for CEEB Advanced Placement tests.

COSTS AND FINANCIAL AID

Annual in-state tuition $7,860. Annual out-of-state tuition $21,275. Room and board $8,748. Required fees $2,025. Average book expense $1,319. **Required Forms and Deadlines:** FAFSA. **Notification of Awards:** Applicants will be notified of awards on a rolling basis beginning 4/1. **Types of Aid:** Need-based scholarships/grants: Federal Pell, SEOG, state scholarships/grants, private scholarships, the school's own gift aid. Loans: Direct Subsidized Stafford, Direct Unsubsidized Stafford, Direct PLUS, Federal Perkins, Federal Nursing. Student Employment: Federal Work-Study Program available. Institutional employment available. Off-campus job opportunities are good. **Financial Aid Statistics:** 77% freshmen, 73% undergrads receive need-based scholarship or grant aid. 29% freshmen, 17% undergrads receive non-need-based scholarship or grant aid. 84% freshmen, 87% undergrads receive need-based self-help aid. 1% freshmen receive athletic scholarships. 72% freshmen, 66% undergrads receive any aid. 63% undergrads borrow to pay for school. Average cumulative indebtedness $28,889. **Criteria for awarding institutional aid:** Non-need-based: academics, alumni affiliation, art, athletics, leadership, music/drama.

See page 1290.

VIRGINIA INTERMONT COLLEGE

1013 Moore Street, Bristol, VA 24201-4298
Phone: 276-466-7856 • **Financial Aid Phone:** 276-466-7872
E-mail: viadmit@vic.edu • **CEEB Code:** 5857
Fax: 276-466-7855 • **ACT Code:** 4416

This private school, affiliated with the Baptist Church, was founded in 1884. It has a 27-acre campus.

RATINGS

Admissions Selectivity Rating: 78   **Fire Safety Rating:** 78   **Green Rating:** 60*

STUDENTS AND FACULTY

Enrollment: 885. **Student Body:** 69% female, 31% male, 68% out-of-state, 8% international. Asian 1%, African American 7%, Caucasian 78%, Hispanic 2%, Native American 1%
Retention and Graduation: 74% freshmen return for sophomore year. 10% grads go on to further study within 1 year. 3% grads pursue arts and sciences degrees. 1% grads pursue law degrees. 2% grads pursue business degrees. 1% grads pursue medical degrees. **Faculty:** Student/faculty ratio 12:1. 44 full-time faculty, 61% hold PhDs, 5% are members of minority groups, 41% are women. 0% of classes are taught by teaching assistants.

ACADEMICS

Degrees: associate, bachelor's. **Classes:** Most classes have fewer than 10 students. Most lab/discussion sessions have fewer than 10 students. **Majors with Highest Enrollment:** business/commerce; equestrian/equine studies; photography. **Special Study Options:** Accelerated program, cross-registration, distance learning, double major, English as a Second Language (ESL), honors program, independent study, internships, study abroad, teacher certification program. **Honors Programs:** Honors program available for students who meet the necessary academic requirements. **Disability Services:** Special programs offered to physically disabled students include note-taking services, reader services, tape recorders, tutors. **Career Services:** alumni services, career/job search classes, internships.

FACILITIES

Housing: Coed dorms, special housing for disabled students, men's dorms, women's dorms, apartments for married students, apartments for single students. 25% of campus accessible to physically disabled. **Special Academic Facilities/Equipment:** Museum/gallery, 129-acre riding center for equestrian program. Newly constructed Fine Arts Center. **Computers:** Students can register for classes online. Administrative functions (other than registration) can be performed online.

CAMPUS LIFE

Environment: Town. **Activities:** Choral groups, dance, drama/theater, musical theater, student government, yearbook 26 registered organizations, 4 honor societies, 2 religious organizations. **Athletics (Intercollegiate):** *Men:* baseball, basketball, cross-country, equestrian sports, golf, soccer, tennis, track/field (outdoor), track/field (indoor). *Women:* basketball, cheerleading, cross-country, equestrian sports, soccer, softball, tennis, track/field (outdoor), track/field (indoor), volleyball. **On-Campus Highlights:** Fine Arts Gallery, Van Dyke Davis Alumni House, President's Home, Equestrian Center, Bell Tower.

ADMISSIONS

Freshman Academic Profile: Average high school GPA 3.2. 8% in top 10% of high school class, 20% in top 25% of high school class, 58% in top 50% of high school class. 85% from public high schools. SAT Math middle 50% range 410-540. SAT Critical Reading middle 50% range 410-530. ACT middle 50% range 17-25. Minimum paper TOEFL 500. **Basis for Candidate Selection:** *Very important factors considered include:* academic GPA, rigor of secondary school record, standardized test scores. *Other factors considered include:* Class rank, application essay, recommendation(s), alumni/ae relation, character/personal qualities, extracurricular activities, first generation, interview, level of applicant's interest, talent/ability, work experience. **Freshman Admission Requirements:** High school diploma is required and GED is accepted. *Academic units required:* 4 English, 2 mathematics, 1 science, (1 science labs), 2 social studies, 6 academic electives. *Academic units recommended:* 4 English, 2 mathematics, 1 science, (1 science labs), 2 social studies, 6 academic electives. **Freshman Admission Statistics:** 624 applied, 55% admitted, 44% enrolled. **Transfer Admission Requirements:** college transcript(s), essay or personal statement, statement of good standing from prior institution(s). Minimum college GPA of 2.0 required. Lowest grade transferable C. **General Admission Information:** Application Fee $25. Nonfall registration accepted. Admission may be deferred for a maximum of 2 terms. Credit and/or placement offered for CEEB Advanced Placement tests.

COSTS AND FINANCIAL AID

Annual tuition $16,895. Room and board $6,095. Required fees $950. Average book expense $900. **Required Forms and Deadlines:** FAFSA, state aid form. **Notification of Awards:** Applicants will be notified of awards on a rolling basis beginning 2/15. **Types of Aid:** *Need-based scholarships/grants:* Federal Pell, SEOG, state scholarships/grants, private scholarships, the school's own gift aid. *Loans:* Subsidized Stafford, Unsubsidized Stafford, PLUS, Federal Perkins. **Student Employment:** Federal Work-Study Program available. Highest amount earned per year from on-campus jobs $1,500. Off-campus job opportunities are good. **Financial Aid Statistics:** 98% freshmen, 93% undergrads receive need-based scholarship or grant aid. 8% freshmen, 5% undergrads receive non-need based scholarship or grant aid. 76% freshmen, 86% undergrads receive need-based self-help aid. 14% freshmen, 10% undergrads receive athletic scholarships. 65% freshmen, 73% undergrads receive any aid. 79% undergrads borrow to pay for school. Average cumulative indebtedness $20,051. **Criteria for awarding institutional aid:** *Non-need-based:* academics, alumni affiliation, art, athletics, minority status, music/drama, religious affiliation, state/district residency.

VIRGINIA MILITARY INSTITUTE

VMI Office of Admissions, Lexington, VA 24450-0304
Phone: 540-464-7211 • **Financial Aid Phone:** 540-464-7208
E-mail: admissions@vmi.edu • **CEEB Code:** 5858
Fax: 540-464-7746 • **Website:** www.vmi.edu • **ACT Code:** 4418

This public school was founded in 1839. It has a 140-acre campus.

RATINGS

Admissions Selectivity Rating: 88   **Fire Safety Rating:** 78   **Green Rating:** 60*

STUDENTS AND FACULTY

Enrollment: 1,428. **Student Body:** 41% out-of-state, 2% international (9 countries represented). Asian 4%, African American 6%, Caucasian 84%, Hispanic 4%, Native American 0%
Retention and Graduation: 8% grads go on to further study within 1 year. 3% grads pursue arts and sciences degrees. 2% grads pursue law degrees. 1% grads pursue business degrees. 1% grads pursue medical degrees. **Faculty:** Student/faculty ratio 10:1. 120 full-time faculty, 98% hold PhDs, 7% are members of minority groups, 19% are women. 0% of classes are taught by teaching assistants.

ACADEMICS

Degrees: bachelor's. **Classes:** Most classes have 10—19 students. **Majors with Highest Enrollment:** business/managerial economics; history; mechanical

engineering. **Special Study Options:** Accelerated program, double major, exchange student program (domestic), honors program, independent study, internships, study abroad, teacher certification program, Summer Transition Program: Optional for incoming freshman. **Honors Programs:** Institute Honors Program, departmental Honors Programs. **Career Services:** Alumni network, career/job search classes, career assessment, internships.

FACILITIES

Housing: Barracks (3-5 students/room). 50% of campus accessible to physically disabled. **Special Academic Facilities/Equipment:** VMI Museum George C. Marshall Museum **Computers:** Students can register for classes online. Administrative functions (other than registration) can be performed online.

CAMPUS LIFE

Environment: Village. **Activities:** Choral groups, concert band, drama/theater, jazz band, literary magazine, marching band, music ensembles, musical theater, pep band, student government, student newspaper, yearbook 50 registered organizations, 11 honor societies, 3 religious organizations. **Athletics (Intercollegiate):** *Men:* baseball, basketball, cross-country, football, golf, lacrosse, riflery, soccer, swimming, track/field (outdoor), track/field (indoor), wrestling. *Women:* cross-country, riflery, soccer, swimming, track/field (outdoor), track/field (indoor). **On-Campus Highlights:** VMI Museum, George C. Marshall Museum

ADMISSIONS

Freshman Academic Profile: Average high school GPA 3.4. 10% in top 10% of high school class, 40% in top 25% of high school class, 82% in top 50% of high school class. 84% from public high schools. SAT Math middle 50% range 530-620. SAT Critical Reading middle 50% range 510-620. SAT Writing middle 50% range 480-590. ACT middle 50% range 21-26. Minimum paper TOEFL 500. **Basis for Candidate Selection:** *Very important factors considered include:* Class rank, rigor of secondary school record, standardized test scores, character/personal qualities. *Important factors considered include:* extracurricular activities, interview, racial/ethnic status, state residency, volunteer work. *Other factors considered include:* recommendation(s), alumni/ae relation, geographical residence, talent/ability. **Freshman Admission Requirements:** High school diploma is required and GED is not accepted. *Academic units required:* 4 English, 3 mathematics, 3 science, (3 science labs), 3 foreign language. *Academic units recommended:* 4 English, 3 mathematics, 3 science, (3 science labs), 3 foreign language. **Freshman Admission Statistics:** 1,600 applied, 54% admitted, 48% enrolled. **Transfer Admission Requirements:** High school transcript, college transcript(s), standardized test scores. Minimum college GPA of 2.0 required. Lowest grade transferable C. **General Admission Information:** Application Fee $35. Early decision application deadline 11/15. Regular application deadline 2/15. Notification on a rolling basis, beginning on or about 1/1. Nonfall registration not accepted. Credit and/or placement offered for CEEB Advanced Placement tests.

COSTS AND FINANCIAL AID

Required Forms and Deadlines: FAFSA, institution's own financial aid form. **Notification of Awards:** Applicants will be notified of awards on a rolling basis beginning 3/15. **Types of Aid:** *Need-based scholarships/grants:* Federal Pell, SEOG, state scholarships/grants, private scholarships, the school's own gift aid. *Loans:* Direct Subsidized Stafford, Direct Unsubsidized Stafford, Direct PLUS, Federal Perkins. **Student Employment:** Highest amount earned per year from on-campus jobs $850. **Financial Aid Statistics:** 75% freshmen, 75% undergrads receive need-based scholarship or grant aid. 27% freshmen, 28% undergrads receive non-need-based scholarship or grant aid. 43% freshmen, 48% undergrads receive need-based self-help aid. 11% freshmen, 7% undergrads receive athletic scholarships. 85% freshmen, 82% undergrads receive any aid. 52% undergrads borrow to pay for school. Average cumulative indebtedness $19,114. **Criteria for awarding institutional aid:** *Non-need-based:* academics, alumni affiliation, athletics, leadership, music/drama.

VIRGINIA STATE UNIVERSITY

One Hayden Drive, Petersburg, VA 23806
Phone: 804-524-5902 • **Financial Aid Phone:** 804-524-5990
E-mail: admiss@vsu.edu • **CEEB Code:** 5860
Fax: 804-524-5055 • **Website:** www.vsu.edu • **ACT Code:** 4424

This public school was founded in 1882. It has a 246-acre campus.

RATINGS

Admissions Selectivity Rating: 64   **Fire Safety Rating:** 60*   **Green Rating:** 60*

STUDENTS AND FACULTY

Enrollment: 5,181. **Student Body:** 60% female, 40% male, 32% out-of-state, 0% international (29 countries represented). Asian 0%, African American 85%, Caucasian 2%, Hispanic 2%, Native American 0%

Retention and Graduation: 71% freshmen return for sophomore year. 21% freshmen graduate within 4 years. 40% freshmen graduate within 6 years. **Faculty:** Student/faculty ratio 16:1. 280 full-time faculty, 43% are women. 0% of classes are taught by teaching assistants.

ACADEMICS

Degrees: associate, bachelor's, certificate, master's, post-master's certificate. **Classes: Majors with Highest Enrollment:** liberal arts and sciences/liberal studies; physical education teaching and coaching; sociology. **Special Study Options:** cooperative education program, double major, dual enrollment, exchange student program (domestic), honors program, independent study, internships, teacher certification program. **Disability Services:** Special programs offered to physically disabled students include note-taking services, reader services, tutors. **Career Services:** Alumni network, internships.

FACILITIES

Housing: Coed dorms, men's dorms, women's dorms, apartments for single students. Note: Coed dorm - students required to have a 3.0 GPA and a record of leadership and service. (Honors Co-educational Residence Facility). 90% of campus accessible to physically disabled. **Computers:** Administrative functions (other than registration) can be performed online.

CAMPUS LIFE

Environment: Town. **Activities:** Choral groups, concert band, dance, drama/theater, jazz band, literary magazine, marching band, music ensembles, pep band, radio station, student government, student newspaper, television station, yearbook, Campus Ministries 70 registered organizations, 6 honor societies, 4 religious organizations. 5 fraternities, 4 sororities. **Athletics (Intercollegiate):** *Men:* baseball, basketball, cheerleading, cross-country, football, golf, tennis, track/field (outdoor), track/field (indoor). *Women:* basketball, bowling, cheerleading, cross-country, golf, softball, tennis, track/field (outdoor), track/field (indoor), volleyball.

ADMISSIONS

Freshman Academic Profile: Average high school GPA 2.8. 5% in top 10% of high school class, 21% in top 25% of high school class, 59% in top 50% of high school class. SAT Math middle 50% range 390-460. SAT Critical Reading middle 50% range 390-460. SAT Writing middle 50% range 380-450. ACT middle 50% range 15-19. Minimum paper TOEFL 500. **Basis for Candidate Selection:** *Very important factors considered include:* application essay, recommendation(s), rigor of secondary school record, standardized test scores. *Important factors considered include:* academic GPA. *Other factors considered include:* Class rank, alumni/ae relation, character/personal qualities, extracurricular activities, geographical residence, state residency, talent/ability, volunteer work, work experience. **Freshman Admission Requirements:** High school diploma is required and GED is accepted. *Academic units required:* 4 English, 3 mathematics, 2 science, (1 science labs), 2 social studies. *Academic units recommended:* 4 English, 3 mathematics, 2 science, (1 science labs), 2 social studies. **Transfer Admission Requirements:** college transcript(s), essay or personal statement, statement of good standing from prior institution(s). Minimum college GPA of 2.0 required. Lowest grade transferable C. **General Admission Information:** Application Fee $25. Regular application deadline 5/1. Notification on a rolling basis, beginning on or about 11/1. Nonfall registration accepted. Credit offered for CEEB Advanced Placement tests.

COSTS AND FINANCIAL AID

Required Forms and Deadlines: FAFSA, institution's own financial aid form. **Notification of Awards:** Applicants will be notified of awards on a rolling basis beginning 5/1. **Types of Aid:** *Need-based scholarships/grants:* Federal Pell, SEOG, state scholarships/grants, private scholarships, the school's own gift aid. *Loans:* Direct Subsidized Stafford, Direct Unsubsidized Stafford, Direct PLUS, PLUS, Federal Perkins, college/university loans from institutional funds. **Student Employment:** Federal Work-Study Program available. Institutional employment available. **Financial Aid Statistics:** 80% freshmen, 80% undergrads receive need-based scholarship or grant aid. 22% freshmen, 22% undergrads receive non-need-based scholarship or grant aid. 72% freshmen, 72% undergrads receive need-based self-help aid. 3% freshmen, 3% undergrads receive athletic scholarships. 90% undergrads borrow to pay for school. Average cumulative indebtedness $28,250. **Criteria for awarding institutional aid:** *Non-need-based:* academics, alumni affiliation, art, job skills, leadership, music/drama, religious affiliation.

Undergraduate Admissions, Blacksburg, VA 24061
Phone: 540-231-6267 • **Financial Aid Phone:** 540-231-5179
E-mail: vtadmiss@vt.edu • **CEEB Code:** 5859
Fax: 540-231-3242 • **Website:** www.vt.edu • **ACT Code:** 4420

This public school was founded in 1872. It has a 2600-acre campus.

RATINGS
Admissions Selectivity Rating: 91   **Fire Safety Rating:** 80   **Green Rating:** 98

STUDENTS AND FACULTY
Enrollment: 23,823. **Student Body:** 41% female, 59% male, 24% out-of-state, 3% international (113 countries represented). Asian 8%, African American 3%, Caucasian 73%, Hispanic 5%, Native American 0%
Retention and Graduation: 83% freshmen graduate within 6 years. 27% grads go on to further study within 1 year. **Faculty:** Student/faculty ratio 16:1. 1422 full-time faculty, 90% hold PhDs, 17% are members of minority groups, 33% are women.

ACADEMICS
Degrees: associate, bachelor's, master's, post-master's certificate. **Classes:** Most classes have 20—29 students. Most lab/discussion sessions have 20—29 students. **Majors with Highest Enrollment:** biology/biological sciences; engineering. **Special Study Options:** Accelerated program, cooperative education program, distance learning, double major, dual enrollment, English as a Second Language (ESL), honors program, independent study, internships, study abroad, teacher certification program. **Combined Degree Programs:** BA/MA. **Disability Services:** Special programs offered to physically disabled students include note-taking services, reader services, tape recorders, tutors. **Career Services:** Alumni network, alumni services, career/job search classes, career assessment, internships.

FACILITIES
Housing: Coed dorms, special housing for disabled students, men's dorms, special housing for international students, women's dorms, fraternity/sorority housing, wellness housing, theme housing, housing for Corps of Cadets and athletes. The World--a cross cultural environment The W.E.L.L.--a personal health/development community. Foreign language hall and academic success hall available. The Wing--a transitional/orientation community for freshmen. Residential Leadership Community Biological and Life Sciences Learning Community Virginia Tech Design Collaborative. 60% of campus accessible to physically disabled. **Special Academic Facilities/Equipment:** Art gallery, digital music facilities, multimedia labs, Black Cultural Center, television studio, anaerobic lab, CAD-CAM labs, observatory, wind tunnel, farms, Math Emporium, the CAVE (virtual reality learning facility). Virtual Reality Cave **Computers:** Students can register for classes online. Administrative functions (other than registration) can be performed online. Undergraduates are required to own a computer.

CAMPUS LIFE
Environment: Town. **Activities:** Choral groups, concert band, dance, drama/theater, jazz band, literary magazine, marching band, music ensembles, musical theater, pep band, radio station, student government, student newspaper, yearbook 600 registered organizations, 32 honor societies, 53 religious organizations. 31 fraternities, 12 sororities. **Athletics (Intercollegiate):** *Men:* baseball, basketball, cheerleading, cross-country, diving, football, golf, soccer, swimming, tennis, track/field (outdoor), track/field (indoor), ultimate frisbee, water polo. *Women:* basketball, cheerleading, cross-country, diving, lacrosse, soccer, softball, swimming, tennis, track/field (outdoor), track/field (indoor), ultimate frisbee, volleyball, water polo. **Environmental Initiatives:** I. THE VIRGINIA TECH CLIMATE ACTION COMMITMENT AND SUSTAINABILITY PLAN IMPLEMENTATION On June 1, 2009 the Virginia Tech Board of Visitors unanimously approved The Virginia Tech Climate Action Commitment and accepted the accompanying Sustainability Plan. See: http://www.facilities.vt.edu/documents/sustainability/sustPlan.pdf The Sustainability Plan contains six topical areas: administrative structure and governance, facilities infrastructure, facilities operations, transportation, behavior and campus life, and academic programs. Each topical area identifies actions and measures to be conducted in the immediate term (2009-2012), in the midterm (2013-2025), or in the long term (2026-2050). The Office of Energy and Sustainability has the responsibility for overseeing the implementation of the Sustainability Plan and reporting progress. The Virginia Tech Climate Action Commitment and Sustainability Plan Status Report contains over 80 sustainabil-

ity actions and measures in the immediate term. See: http://www.facilities.vt.edu/documents/sustainability/vtcac_status.pdf Virginia Tech's Sustainability Plan Implementation was the recipient of the 2011 Governor's Environmental Excellence Gold Award in the Environmental Program Category which was presented at the 22nd Annual Environment Virginia Symposium at the Virginia Military Institute in Lexington. See: http://www.vtnews.vt.edu/articles/2011/04/040811-facilities-excellenceaward.html Virginia Tech achieved a Silver Rating from the Association for the Advancement of Sustainability in Higher Education (AASHE) for sustainability performance in the Sustainability Tracking, Assessment & Rating System (STARS) program. The STARS program provides a common standard of measurement for 135 separate sustainability topics which are organized into three primary categories: Education & Research; Operations; and Planning, Administration and Engagement. The STARS program serves as an excellent framework for universities to objectively and transparently assess their sustainability efforts. STARS has been a very useful tool in benchmarking our progress towards a more sustainable campus. Virginia Tech earned a Silver Rating for sustainability performance in the STARS program, with an overall score of 61.94 points (just 3.06 points shy of the 65 points needed for gold rating). To view Virginia Tech's STARS submission, please visit: https://stars.aashe.org/institutions/virginia-tech-va/report/2011-08-02/ ENERGY REDUCTION, EFFICIENCY AND CONSERVATION MEASURES 1. In accordance with the Campus Energy and Water Policy 5505, significant energy reduction has been achieved through the implementation of temperature settings (68 degrees Fahrenheit for the heating season and 74 degrees Fahrenheit for the cooling season). These measures have resulted in substantial energy savings, cost savings, and reductions in greenhouse gas emissions. 2. Significant energy reduction has been achieved through the select shutdown of building air handlers during periods of reduced occupancy using the Building Automation System. Substantial energy savings, cost savings, and reductions in greenhouse gas emissions have been realized. 3. Implementation of the use of the free cooling during the winter months for campus chilled water systems has provided energy savings, cost savings, and reductions in greenhouse gas emissions. 4. Completion of a $28 million capital project significantly enhanced the Central Steam Plant efficiency and campus-wide steam distribution infrastructure. 5. A $5.3 million Energy Performance Contract was recently executed for Energy Service Company (ESCO) Pepco Energy Services, Inc. to complete an energy conservation measure package for five major buildings to include: the Central Steam Plant, Cassell Coliseum (Athletics), Dietrick Dining Hall, McBryde Hall (Academic), and Hahn Hall-South (Research). Implementation is scheduled to begin in January 2012, and is expected to be completed by the end of calendar year 2012. 6. The Virginia Tech Climate Action Commitment Resolution point #6 states the university will pursue LEED Silver Certification or better for all new buildings and major renovations. Fifteen new construction and major renovation capital projects totaling 1,050,222 gross square feet (GSF) are registered in the Leadership in Energy and Environmental Design (LEED) program with the U.S. Green Building Council. Recently certified buildings include the Henderson Hall Renovation & Theatre 101 Addition " LEED Gold (38,750 GSF), Addition to the Football Locker Room " LEED Silver (42,145 GSF), and the Institute for Critical Technology & Applied Sciences II " LEED Gold (42,190 GSF). 7. The Energy and Sustainability Committee recently revised campus policies on energy and water to incorporate additional energy use, water use, waste reduction, transportation, and travel guidelines and directives. The revision to the campus policy is entitled, University Policy 5505 Campus Energy, Water, and Waste Reduction. In accordance with Policy 5505, the Office of Energy and Sustainability successfully developed the Comprehensive Waste Management Plan for Virginia Tech. The plan was completed on July 15, 2011 and included stakeholders from all major campus units. See: http://facilities.vt.edu/documents/sustainability/unlinked/Comprehensive_Waste_Mangement_Plan_Virginia_Tech_7_15_2011_Final.pdf III. STUDENT SUSTAINABILITY INTERN PROGRAM Program Overview: Developed and coordinated by the first sustainability intern in the Office of Energy and Sustainability, an extremely innovative student sustainability internship program is being implemented at Virginia Tech with a focus on student development. What makes this program unique is the emphasis on interdisciplinary collaboration between all of the layers of the university and its focus on the synergy between project based and classroom based learning outcomes. The projects chosen for the program allow interns to apply the concepts and skills learned in the classroom to real world challenges that exist right here on campus to gain experience working with their peers in different career fields. Students are charged to develop creative solutions to on campus sustainability challenges while being provided with structure to understand the project itself and skills based workshops that offer individual and professional development opportunities. Started in the spring of 2010, this program just completed its third cohort and will be expanding to a year-long program starting in the fall of 2012. Program Mission & Vision: Our current undergraduate and graduate students are the sustainability professionals of tomorrow. They will enter the working world with a new set of challenges and parameters that will define the work that they can and will do, regardless of their field. Because of this, it is critical that

we, as an institution of higher education, prepare our students for the world that they will soon be leading by providing them with the critical skills and a learning environment that will prepare them to be the inventors of a sustainable future. With the foundations in collaborative research and interdisciplinary teamwork to tackle campus sustainability, this project and classroom based learning experience will train students to be able to understand and address society's most pressing challenges. Examples of Current and Past Projects: a. Campus Sustainability Web Portal Development The purpose of this project is to create an information portal for the Virginia Tech community to streamline, connect, and organize all sustainability related activities. Interns will focus on the development and coding of a dynamic web portal, in collaboration with the existing Ensemble CMS framework, to organize existing information and details gathered (including all STARS credits data) to facilitate communication and collaboration on sustainability projects on campus. The portal will continually evolve each year and can be accessed at www.sustainability.vt.edu b. Football Game Best Practices Toolkit Student interns conducted original research in collaboration with a panel of technical experts from across the country and major national campus sustainability organizations. The findings were presented in a toolkit outlining best practices and case studies of some of the most successful programs in the nation. The toolkit was extremely well received and can be downloaded from the College and University Recycling Coalition (CURC) • Website: http://curc3r.org/images/pdfs/collegiate_football_smm_guide_final.pdf See toolkit article: http://www.vtnews.vt.edu/articles/2011/10/102111-facilities-toolkit.html

ADMISSIONS

Freshman Academic Profile: Average high school GPA 4.0. 44% in top 10% of high school class, 84% in top 25% of high school class, 99% in top 50% of high school class. SAT Math middle 50% range 570-670. SAT Critical Reading middle 50% range 540-640. Minimum paper TOEFL 550. **Basis for Candidate Selection:** *Very important factors considered include:* academic GPA, rigor of secondary school record, standardized test scores. *Other factors considered include:* recommendation(s), alumni/ae relation, character/personal qualities, extracurricular activities, first generation, geographical residence, racial/ethnic status, state residency, talent/ability, volunteer work, work experience. **Freshman Admission Requirements:** High school diploma is required and GED is accepted. *Academic units required:* 4 English, 3 mathematics, 2 science, (2 science labs), 1 social studies, 1 history, 4 academic electives. *Academic units recommended:* 4 English, 3 mathematics, 2 science, (2 science labs), 1 social studies, 1 history, 4 academic electives. **Freshman Admission Statistics:** 20,191 applied, 70% admitted, 39% enrolled. **Transfer Admission Requirements:** High school transcript, college transcript(s), Minimum college GPA of 3.0 required. Lowest grade transferable C. **General Admission Information:** Application Fee $50. Early decision application deadline 11/1. Regular application deadline 1/15. Regular notification 4/1. Nonfall registration accepted. Admission may be deferred for a maximum of 1 year. Credit and/or placement offered for CEEB Advanced Placement tests.

COSTS AND FINANCIAL AID

Annual in-state tuition $9,187. Annual out-of-state tuition $23,575. Room and board $7,254. Required fees $1,736. Average book expense $1,100. **Required Forms and Deadlines:** FAFSA General Scholarship Application. **Notification of Awards:** Applicants will be notified of awards on a rolling basis beginning 3/30. **Types of Aid:** *Need-based scholarships/grants:* Federal Pell, SEOG, state scholarships/grants, private scholarships, the school's own gift aid, cadet scholarships/grants. *Loans:* Direct Subsidized Stafford, Direct Unsubsidized Stafford, Direct PLUS, Federal Perkins, college/university loans from institutional funds. **Student Employment:** Federal Work-Study Program available. Off-campus job opportunities are excellent. **Financial Aid Statistics:** 65% freshmen, 70% undergrads receive need-based scholarship or grant aid. 52% freshmen, 37% undergrads receive non-need-based scholarship or grant aid. 72% freshmen, 79% undergrads receive need-based self-help aid. 2% freshmen, 2% undergrads receive athletic scholarships. 77% freshmen, 75% undergrads receive any aid. 54% undergrads borrow to pay for school. Average cumulative indebtedness $25,759. **Criteria for awarding institutional aid:** *Non-need-based:* academics, art, athletics, leadership, minority status, music/drama, state/district residency.

VIRGINIA WESLEYAN COLLEGE

Best 378

1584 Wesleyan Drive, Norfolk/Virginia Beach, VA 23502-5599
Phone: 757-455-3208 • **Financial Aid Phone:** 757-455-3345
E-mail: admissions@vwc.edu • **CEEB Code:** 5867
Fax: 757-461-5238 • **Website:** www.vwc.edu • **ACT Code:** 4429

This private school, affiliated with the Methodist Church, was founded in 1961. It has a 300-acre campus.

RATINGS
Admissions Selectivity Rating: 67   **Fire Safety Rating:** 70   **Green Rating:** 89

STUDENTS AND FACULTY
Enrollment: 1,385. **Student Body:** 64% female, 36% male, 25% out-of-state, 1% international (7 countries represented). Asian 1%, African American 23%, Caucasian 59%, Hispanic 7%, Native American 0%
Retention and Graduation: 42% freshmen graduate within 4 years. 48% freshmen graduate within 6 years. 32% grads go on to further study within 1 year. 1% grads pursue law degrees. 1% grads pursue business degrees. **Faculty:** Student/faculty ratio 12:1. 91 full-time faculty, 89% hold PhDs, 10% are members of minority groups, 48% are women. 0% of classes are taught by teaching assistants.

ACADEMICS
Degrees: bachelor's. **Classes:** Most classes have 10—19 students. **Majors with Highest Enrollment:** business administration and management; communication studies/speech communication and rhetoric; criminal justice/safety studies. **Special Study Options:** double major, honors program, independent study, internships, liberal arts/career combination, student-designed major, study abroad, teacher certification program, Externships; PORTfolio, a 4-year competitive program designed to integrate liberal arts and experiential learning. **Honors Programs:** Wesleyan Scholars is an honors program which is designed for applicants with superior high school achievement records. The Honors and Scholars program, including Wesleyan Scholars, offers academically challenging honors courses and stimulating co-curricular experiences. Program enhancement is also offered through PORTfolio, a selective program designed to integrate the liberal arts with experiential learning opportunities available in Hampton Roads. **Combined Degree Programs:** 2-2 program in business/accounting with Tidewater. **Disability Services:** Special programs offered to physically disabled students include note-taking services, reader services, tape recorders, tutors. **Career Services:** Alumni network, career/job search classes, internships, regional alumni.

FACILITIES
Housing: Coed dorms, special housing for disabled students, special housing for international students, women's dorms, fraternity/sorority housing, apartments for single students, wellness housing, Townhouses, Honors and Scholars Hall, Wellness Hall-a substance free hall which provides special programs focusing on social, physical, spiritual, emotional, and intellectual wellness. 90% of campus accessible to physically disabled. **Special Academic Facilities/Equipment:** Greenhouse, language lab, teleconferencing facility, social science teach. and learn. lab, radio station, TV studio, Barclay Sheaks Art Gallery, computerized classrooms, Internet access all classrooms, 24-hr. computer lab, Lambuth M. Clarke Hall with state-of-the-art teaching technologies, three academic villages combining residences and campus offices and services. **Computers:** 20% of classrooms, 100% of libraries, 100% of student union, have wireless network access. Students can register for classes online. Administrative functions (other than registration) can be performed online.

CAMPUS LIFE
Environment: Metropolis. **Activities:** Choral groups, dance, drama/theater, literary magazine, music ensembles, musical theater, radio station, student government, student newspaper, yearbook, Campus Ministries, International Student Organization, Model UN 60 registered organizations, 19 honor societies, 4 religious organizations. 3 fraternities, 4 sororities. **Athletics (Intercollegiate):** *Men:* baseball, basketball, cross-country, golf, lacrosse, soccer, tennis, track/field (outdoor), track/field (indoor). *Women:* basketball, cheerleading, cross-country, field hockey, lacrosse, soccer, softball, tennis, track/field (outdoor), track/field (indoor), volleyball. **On-Campus Highlights:** The Marlin Restaurant, Jane P. Batten Student Center, Village III, Trinder Athletic Center **Environmental Initiatives:** Green Roof Recycling Sustainable Purchasing

ADMISSIONS
Freshman Academic Profile: Average high school GPA 3.3. 13% in top 10% of high school class, 42% in top 25% of high school class, 80% in top 50% of high school class. 86% from public high schools. SAT Math middle 50% range 440-550. SAT Critical Reading middle 50% range 450-560. SAT Writing middle 50% range 440-540. ACT middle 50% range 19-24. Minimum paper TOEFL 550. **Basis for Candidate Selection:** *Very important factors considered include:* academic GPA, rigor of secondary school record, level of applicant's interest. *Important factors considered include:* application essay, recommendation(s), standardized test scores, extracurricular activities. *Other factors considered include:* alumni/ae relation, character/personal qualities, first generation, interview, talent/ability, volunteer work, work experience. **Freshman Admission Requirements:** High school diploma is required and GED is accepted. *Academic units required:* 4 English, 3 mathematics, 2 science, (2 science labs), 2 foreign language, 1 history, 1 computer science. *Academic units recommended:* 4 English, 3 mathematics, 2 science, (2 science labs), 2 foreign language, 1 history, 1 computer science. **Freshman Admission Statistics:** 3,890 applied, 86% admitted, 13% enrolled. **Transfer Admission Requirements:** High school transcript, college transcript(s), essay or personal statement, statement of good standing from prior institution(s). Minimum college GPA of 2.5 required. Lowest grade transferable C. **General Admission Information:** Application Fee $40. Notification on a rolling basis, beginning on or about 9/15. Nonfall registration accepted. Credit and/or placement offered for CEEB Advanced Placement tests.

COSTS AND FINANCIAL AID
Annual tuition $30,348. Room and board $8,188. Required fees $650. Average book expense $1,000. **Required Forms and Deadlines:** FAFSA, state aid form. **Notification of Awards:** Applicants will be notified of awards on a rolling basis beginning 2/1. **Types of Aid:** *Need-based scholarships/grants:* Federal Pell, SEOG, state scholarships/grants, private scholarships, the school's own gift aid, Virginia Coalition for Independent Colleges; United Methodist Greater Higher Education Board. *Loans:* Subsidized Stafford, Unsubsidized Stafford, PLUS, Federal Perkins, state loans, Private Alternative Loan Program. **Student Employment:** Federal Work-Study Program available. Institutional employment available. Highest amount earned per year from on-campus jobs $1,200. Off-campus job opportunities are good. **Financial Aid Statistics:** 100% freshmen, 99% undergrads receive need-based scholarship or grant aid. 18% freshmen, 16% undergrads receive non-need-based scholarship or grant aid. 84% freshmen, 82% undergrads receive need-based self-help aid. 99% freshmen, 98% undergrads receive any aid. 85% undergrads borrow to pay for school. Average cumulative indebtedness $36,445. **Criteria for awarding institutional aid:** *Non-need-based:* academics, alumni affiliation, leadership, religious affiliation, state/district residency.

VITERBO UNIVERSITY

900 Viterbo Drive, La Crosse, WI 54601
Phone: 608-796-3010 • **Financial Aid Phone:** 608-496-3900
E-mail: admission@viterbo.edu • **CEEB Code:** 1878
Fax: 608-796-3020 • **ACT Code:** 4662

This private school, affiliated with the Roman Catholic Church, was founded in 1890. It has a 25-acre campus.

RATINGS
Admissions Selectivity Rating: 66   **Fire Safety Rating:** 63   **Green Rating:** 60*

STUDENTS AND FACULTY
Enrollment: 1,922. **Student Body:** 71% female, 29% male, 19% out-of-state, 1% international (15 countries represented). Asian 1%, African American 1%, Caucasian 93%, Hispanic 1%, Native American 1%
Retention and Graduation: 74% freshmen return for sophomore year. 30% freshmen graduate within 4 years. 48% freshmen graduate within 6 years. 7% grads go on to further study within 1 year. 4% grads pursue arts and sciences degrees. 1% grads pursue law degrees. 2% grads pursue medical degrees. **Faculty:** Student/faculty ratio 13:1. 110 full-time faculty, 56% hold PhDs, 4% are members of minority groups, 56% are women. 0% of classes are taught by teaching assistants.

ACADEMICS
Degrees: associate, bachelor's, master's, post-bachelor's certificate, terminal associate, transfer associate. **Classes:** Most classes have 10—19 students. Most lab/discussion sessions have 10—19 students. **Majors with Highest Enrollment:** business administration and management; elementary education and teaching; nursing/registered nurse (rn, asn, bsn, msn). **Special Study Options:** Accelerated program, cross-registration, distance learning, double major, dual

enrollment, honors program, independent study, internships, liberal arts/career combination, student-designed major, study abroad, teacher certification program, weekend college, Weekend college is basically for our Master's level programs. **Honors Programs:** The mission of the Viterbo University Honors Program is to provide a supportive, enriched learning environment responsive to the educational needs of highly able and exceptionally motivated undergraduate students who are committed to achieving academic excellence. The program provides honors sections of regular, general education courses, honors credit within regular sections, interdisciplinary Honors Capstone courses, oversight of senior honors projects, and increased opportunity for undergraduate research and creative activity. The program complements and enhances the Liberal Arts mission of the university. Together, honors students and faculty constitute a community of scholars. **Combined Degree Programs:** chiropractic. **Disability Services:** Special programs offered to physically disabled students include note-taking services, reader services, tape recorders, tutors. **Career Services:** Alumni network, alumni services, career/job search classes, career assessment, internships, regional alumni. Career services highlights include We have been very successful placing our students in internships that have not only assisted the student but the larger La Crosse community.

FACILITIES

Housing: Coed dorms, apartments for single students, theme floors in dorms. and university owned theme houses. 90% of campus accessible to physically disabled. **Special Academic Facilities/Equipment:** Fine Arts Center; Center for Ethics, Science and Technology with distance education labs and video conferencing; Nursing center with labs and simulated equipment; new recreation and education center co-sponsored by Viterbo University and the Boys and Girls Club **Computers:** Students can register for classes online. Administrative functions (other than registration) can be performed online.

CAMPUS LIFE

Environment: Town, **Activities:** Choral groups, dance, drama/theater, literary magazine, music ensembles, musical theater, opera, pep band, student government, student newspaper 22 registered organizations, 2 honor societies, 2 religious organizations. **Athletics (Intercollegiate):** *Men:* baseball, basketball, golf, soccer. *Women:* basketball, golf, soccer, softball, volleyball. **On-Campus Highlights:** Reinhart Center for Ethics, Science and Technology, Fine Arts Center, Amie Mathy Center for Recreation and Education, Student Activity Center, Dancing Francis, --Center for Ethics, Science and Technology opened the Fall of 2003. --Center for Recreation and Wellness opens Fall 2005 is sponsored by Viterbo and the Boys/Girls club --Dancing Francis is a bronze sculpture of Francis of Assisi by Paul Granland --Fine Arts Center is home of performing arts in the region --Student Activity Center is home to the V-Hawks as well as fitness center for all students.

ADMISSIONS

Freshman Academic Profile: Average high school GPA 3.3. 13% in top 10% of high school class, 39% in top 25% of high school class, 73% in top 50% of high school class. 97% from public high schools. ACT middle 50% range 20-24. Minimum paper TOEFL 550. **Basis for Candidate Selection:** *Very important factors considered include:* academic GPA, rigor of secondary school record, standardized test scores, character/personal qualities, level of applicant's interest. *Important factors considered include:* Class rank, interview, talent/ability. *Other factors considered include:* application essay, recommendation(s), alumni/ae relation, extracurricular activities, first generation, volunteer work. **Freshman Admission Requirements:** High school diploma is required and GED is accepted. *Academic units required:* 3 English, 2 mathematics, 2 science, 2 social studies, 5 academic electives. *Academic units recommended:* 3 English, 2 mathematics, 2 science, 2 social studies, 5 academic electives. **Freshman Admission Statistics:** 1,148 applied, 88% admitted, 36% enrolled. **Transfer Admission Requirements:** High school transcript, college transcript(s), statement of good standing from prior institution(s). Minimum college GPA of 2.0 required. Lowest grade transferable C–. **General Admission Information:** Application Fee $25. Nonfall registration accepted. Admission may be deferred for a maximum of Two years. Credit offered for CEEB Advanced Placement tests.

COSTS AND FINANCIAL AID

Annual tuition $18,170. Room and board $6,140. Required fees $420. Average book expense $800. **Required Forms and Deadlines:** FAFSA, institution's own financial aid form. **Notification of Awards:** Applicants will be notified of awards on a rolling basis beginning 4/1. **Types of Aid:** *Need-based scholarships/grants:* Federal Pell, SEOG, state scholarships/grants, private scholarships, the school's own gift aid. *Loans:* Subsidized Stafford, Unsubsidized Stafford, PLUS, Federal Perkins, Federal Nursing, state loans. **Student Employment:** Federal Work-Study Program available. Institutional employment available. Highest amount earned per year from on-campus jobs $2,500. Off-campus job opportunities are good. **Financial Aid Statistics:** 98% freshmen, 97% undergrads receive need-based scholarship or grant aid. 6% freshmen, 6% undergrads receive non-need-based scholarship or grant aid. 94% freshmen, 93% undergrads receive need-based self-help aid. 1% undergrads receive athletic scholarships.

98% freshmen, 89% undergrads receive any aid. 86% undergrads borrow to pay for school. Average cumulative indebtedness $15,703. **Criteria for awarding institutional aid:** *Non-need-based:* academics, alumni affiliation, art, athletics, leadership, minority status, music/drama.

VOORHEES COLLEGE

P.O. BOX 678, Denmark, SC 29042
Phone: 803-703-7111
E-mail: white@voorhees.edu • **CEEB Code:** 5863
Fax: 803-793-1117 • **Website:** www.voorhees.edu • **ACT Code:** 3882

This private school, affiliated with the Episcopal Church, was founded in 1897. It has a 350-acre campus.

RATINGS

Admissions Selectivity Rating: 78   **Fire Safety Rating:** 62   **Green Rating:** 60*

STUDENTS AND FACULTY

Enrollment: 738. **Student Body:** 64% female, 36% male, 30% out-of-state, 1% international. Asian 0%, African American 98%, Caucasian 1%, Hispanic 0%, Native American 0%

Retention and Graduation: 70% freshmen return for sophomore year. 100% freshmen graduate within 4 years. 25% grads go on to further study within 1 year. 17% grads pursue arts and sciences degrees. 2% grads pursue law degrees. 5% grads pursue business degrees. 4% grads pursue medical degrees. **Faculty:** Student/faculty ratio 20:1. 43 full-time faculty, 44% hold PhDs, 91% are members of minority groups, 37% are women. 0% of classes are taught by teaching assistants

ACADEMICS

Degrees: bachelor's, terminal associate. **Special Study Options:** cooperative education program, honors program, internships, weekend college. **Disability Services:** Special programs offered to physically disabled students include tape recorders, tutors. **Career Services:** Alumni network, career/job search classes, internships.

FACILITIES

Housing: men's dorms, women's dorms, fraternity/sorority housing, Faculty + Staff Apartments Housing for Single Mothers. **Computers:** Administrative functions (other than registration) can be performed online.

CAMPUS LIFE

Environment: Rural. **Activities:** Choral groups, drama/theater, literary magazine, pep band, radio station, student government, student newspaper, yearbook 33 registered organizations, 2 honor societies, 3 religious organizations. 4 fraternities, 4 sororities. **Athletics (Intercollegiate):** *Men:* baseball, basketball, cheerleading, cross-country. *Women:* basketball, cheerleading, cross-country, softball, volleyball.

ADMISSIONS

Freshman Academic Profile: Average high school GPA 2.0. 1% in top 10% of high school class, 44% in top 25% of high school class, 50% in top 50% of high school class. 95% from public high schools. SAT Math middle 50% range 390-410. SAT Critical Reading middle 50% range 300-400. ACT middle 50% range 11-18. Minimum paper TOEFL 500. **Basis for Candidate Selection:** *Very important factors considered include:* Class rank, rigor of secondary school record, standardized test scores. *Important factors considered include:* recommendation(s), alumni/ae relation, character/personal qualities, talent/ability. *Other factors considered include:* extracurricular activities. **Freshman Admission Requirements:** High school diploma is required and GED is accepted. *Academic units required:* 4 English, 3 mathematics, 2 science, 2 foreign language, 1 social studies, 1 history, 7 academic electives. *Academic units recommended:* 4 English, 3 mathematics, 2 science, 2 foreign language, 1 social studies, 1 history, 7 academic electives. **Freshman Admission Statistics:** 3,511 applied, 37% admitted, 19% enrolled. **Transfer Admission Requirements:** college transcript(s), statement of good standing from prior institution(s). Minimum college GPA of 2.0 required. Lowest grade transferable c. **General Admission Information:** Application Fee $25. Notification on a rolling basis, beginning on or about 1/1. Nonfall registration accepted. Admission may be deferred for a maximum of 2 years. Credit offered for CEEB Advanced Placement tests.

COSTS AND FINANCIAL AID

Annual tuition $6,460. Room and board $3,516. Required fees $170. Average book expense $2,500. **Required Forms and Deadlines:** FAFSA, institution's own financial aid form. **Notification of Awards:** Applicants will be notified of awards on a rolling basis beginning 5/1. **Types of Aid:** *Need-based scholarships/*

grants: Federal Pell, SEOG, state scholarships/grants, private scholarships, the school's own gift aid, United Negro College Fund. *Loans:* Subsidized Stafford, Unsubsidized Stafford, PLUS, Federal Perkins. **Student Employment:** Federal Work-Study Program available. Institutional employment available. Off-campus job opportunities are poor. **Financial Aid Statistics:** 93% freshmen, 89% undergrads receive need-based scholarship or grant aid. 1% freshmen, 1% undergrads receive non-need-based scholarship or grant aid. 90% freshmen, 92% undergrads receive need-based self-help aid. 70% undergrads borrow to pay for school. Average cumulative indebtedness $8,939. **Criteria for awarding institutional aid:** *Non-need-based:* academics, art, athletics, leadership.

WABASH COLLEGE

PO Box 352, Crawfordsville, IN 47933
Phone: 765-361-6225 • **Financial Aid Phone:** 765-361-6370
E-mail: admissions@wabash.edu • **CEEB Code:** 1895
Fax: 765-361-6437 • **Website:** www.wabash.edu • **ACT Code:** 1260

This private school was founded in 1832. It has a 60-acre campus.

RATINGS
Admissions Selectivity Rating: 85   **Fire Safety Rating:** 86   **Green Rating:** 65

STUDENTS AND FACULTY
Enrollment: 901. **Student Body:** 0% female, 100% male, 26% out-of-state, 7% international (12 countries represented). Asian 1%, African American 6%, Caucasian 76%, Hispanic 5%, Native American 1%
Retention and Graduation: 86% freshmen return for sophomore year. 69% freshmen graduate within 4 years. 73% freshmen graduate within 6 years. 25% grads go on to further study within 1 year. 11% grads pursue arts and sciences degrees. 6% grads pursue law degrees. 7% grads pursue medical degrees. **Faculty:** Student/faculty ratio 10:1. 91 full-time faculty, 96% hold PhDs, 13% are members of minority groups, 35% are women. 0% of classes are taught by teaching assistants.

ACADEMICS
Degrees: bachelor's. **Classes:** Most classes have 10—19 students. Most lab/discussion sessions have fewer than 10 students. **Majors with Highest Enrollment:** history; psychology; religion/religious studies. **Special Study Options:** double major, independent study, internships, liberal arts/career combination, study abroad, teacher certification program, Student designed majors, minors, or areas of concentration. Immersion Learning courses are offered, which involve travel domestically and abroad. **Combined Degree Programs:** BA/JD, BA/MEng, Columbia University School of Law. **Disability Services:** Special programs offered to physically disabled students include note-taking services, reader services, tape recorders, tutors. **Career Services:** Alumni network, alumni services, career/job search classes, career assessment, internships, regional alumni. Career services highlights include Our brand new (beginning Fall 09)Wabash Business Leaders Program: Co-curricular program, designed to provide a comprehensive background in business, regardless of major. Couples our Business Sequence with experiential learning through internships, immersion programs, case studies, and speaker events.

FACILITIES
Housing: special housing for disabled students, men's dorms, fraternity/sorority housing, College-owned houses and apartments. 80% of campus accessible to physically disabled. **Special Academic Facilities/Equipment:** Malcolm X Institute of Black Studies, two art galleries, language lab, electron microscope, atomic absorption, nuclear and infrared spectrometers, Beowulf Supercomputer, Center of Inquiry in the Liberal Arts, Wabash Center for Teaching and Learning in Theology and Religion, Ramsey Archival Center **Computers:** 100% of classrooms, 100% of dorms, 100% of libraries, 100% of dining areas, 100% of student union, 100% of common outdoor areas have wireless network access. Administrative functions (other than registration) can be performed online.

CAMPUS LIFE
Environment: Village. **Activities:** Choral groups, concert band, drama/theater, jazz band, literary magazine, music ensembles, pep band, radio station, student government, student newspaper, student-run film society, symphony orchestra, yearbook, Campus Ministries, International Student Organization, Model UN 65 registered organizations, 7 honor societies, 5 religious organizations. 9 fra-

ternities. **Athletics (Intercollegiate):** *Men:* baseball, basketball, cross-country, diving, football, golf, soccer, swimming, tennis, track/field (outdoor), track/field (indoor), wrestling. **On-Campus Highlights:** Allen Athletics and Recreation Center, Wabash Chapel, New Science Building, Hays Hall, Trippet Hall, Lilly Library, Malcolm X Institute of Black Studies. **Environmental Initiatives:** Printing Quota that saved 240,000 sheets of paper in the first semester (among 900 students) New, state-of-the-art, energy efficient boilers A commitment to purchasing locally grown and raised food for use by our food service partner, and the establishment of a Community Garden

ADMISSIONS
Freshman Academic Profile: Average high school GPA 3.6. 37% in top 10% of high school class, 70% in top 25% of high school class, 94% in top 50% of high school class. 91% from public high schools. SAT Math middle 50% range 530-655. SAT Critical Reading middle 50% range 510-620. SAT Writing middle 50% range 480-590. ACT middle 50% range 22-28. Minimum paper TOEFL 550. **Basis for Candidate Selection:** *Very important factors considered include:* Class rank, academic GPA, rigor of secondary school record. *Important factors considered include:* recommendation(s), standardized test scores, extracurricular activities, interview, level of applicant's interest, talent/ability. *Other factors considered include:* application essay, alumni/ae relation, character/personal qualities, first generation, geographical residence, racial/ethnic status, volunteer work, work experience. **Freshman Admission Requirements:** High school diploma is required and GED is accepted. **Freshman Admission Statistics:** 1,331 applied, 67% admitted, 28% enrolled. **Transfer Admission Requirements:** High school transcript, college transcript(s), essay or personal statement, standardized test scores, statement of good standing from prior institution(s). Lowest grade transferable C. **General Admission Information:** Application Fee $40. Early decision application deadline 11/15. Notification on a rolling basis, beginning on or about 11/15. Nonfall registration accepted. Admission may be deferred for a maximum of 1 year. Credit and/or placement offered for CEEB Advanced Placement tests.

COSTS AND FINANCIAL AID
Annual tuition $35,000. Room and board $8,510. Required fees $650. Average book expense $1,000. **Required Forms and Deadlines:** FAFSA, CSS/Financial Aid PROFILE, noncustodial PROFILEFederal tax returns and W-2 statements. **Notification of Awards:** Applicants will be notified of awards on or about 3/31. **Types of Aid:** *Need-based scholarships/grants:* Federal Pell, state scholarships/grants, private scholarships, the school's own gift aid. *Loans:* Direct Subsidized Stafford, Direct Unsubsidized Stafford, Direct PLUS, college/university loans from institutional funds. **Student Employment:** Institutional employment available. Highest amount earned per year from on-campus jobs $3,000. Off-campus job opportunities are good. **Financial Aid Statistics:** 99% freshmen, 97% undergrads receive need-based scholarship or grant aid. 17% freshmen, 16% undergrads receive non-need-based scholarship or grant aid. 89% freshmen, 87% undergrads receive need-based self-help aid. 83% freshmen, 81% undergrads receive any aid. 76% undergrads borrow to pay for school. Average cumulative indebtedness $28,919. **Criteria for awarding institutional aid:** *Non-need-based:* academics, art, job skills, music/drama.

WAGNER COLLEGE

Pape Admissions Building, Staten Island, NY 10301-4495
Phone: 718-390-3411 • **Financial Aid Phone:** 718-390-3183
E-mail: adm@wagner.edu • **CEEB Code:** 2966
Fax: 718-390-3105 • **Website:** www.wagner.edu • **ACT Code:** 2984

This private school was founded in 1883. It has a 110-acre campus.

RATINGS
Admissions Selectivity Rating: 81   **Fire Safety Rating:** 95   **Green Rating:** 69

STUDENTS AND FACULTY
Enrollment: 1,840. **Student Body:** 64% female, 36% male, 48% out-of-state, 2% international (31 countries represented). Asian 2%, African American 6%, Caucasian 70%, Hispanic 8%, Native American 0%
Retention and Graduation: 79% freshmen return for sophomore year. 63% freshmen graduate within 4 years. 50% grads go on to further study within 1 year. 27% grads pursue arts and sciences degrees. 4% grads pursue law degrees. 34% grads pursue business degrees. 2% grads pursue medical degrees. **Faculty:** Student/faculty ratio 14:1. 96 full-time faculty, 90% hold PhDs, 9%

are members of minority groups, 50% are women. 0% of classes are taught by teaching assistants.

ACADEMICS
Degrees: bachelor's, master's, post-bachelor's certificate. **Classes:** Most classes have 10—19 students. Most lab/discussion sessions have 10—19 students. **Majors with Highest Enrollment:** biology/biological sciences; business/commerce; psychology. **Special Study Options:** double major, exchange student program (domestic), honors program, independent study, internships, study abroad, teacher certification program, Learning Communities. **Combined Degree Programs:** BA/DDS, 7-year dental program with New York University. **Disability Services:** Special programs offered to physically disabled students include note-taking services, reader services, tape recorders, tutors. **Career Services:** Alumni network, alumni services, internships Career services highlights include The Wagner Plan for the Practical Liberal Arts involves both of the above.

FACILITIES
Housing: Coed dorms, fraternity/sorority housing, apartments for single students, theme housing. **Special Academic Facilities/Equipment:** Art gallery, early childhood center, nursing resource center, planetarium, two electron microscopes, solar energy project. **Computers:** 90% of classrooms, 100% of dorms, 100% of libraries, 100% of dining areas, 100% of student union, 50% of common outdoor areas have wireless network access. Students can register for classes online. Administrative functions (other than registration) can be performed online.

CAMPUS LIFE
Environment: Metropolis. **Activities:** Choral groups, dance, drama/theater, jazz band, literary magazine, music ensembles, musical theater, pep band, radio station, student government, student newspaper, yearbook, Campus Ministries, International Student Organization, Model UN 66 registered organizations, 11 honor societies, 4 religious organizations. 5 fraternities, 4 sororities. **Athletics (Intercollegiate):** *Men:* baseball, basketball, cross-country, football, golf, lacrosse, tennis, track/field (outdoor), track/field (indoor). *Women:* basketball, cross-country, golf, lacrosse, soccer, softball, swimming, tennis, track/field (outdoor), track/field (indoor), water polo. **On-Campus Highlights:** Coffee House, Spiro Sports Center, Wagner Student Union, Main Hall Theatre, Foundation Hall, Hawk's Nest. **Environmental Initiatives:** competing in Recylemania, Spring 2009 going trayless in all dining venues

ADMISSIONS
Freshman Academic Profile: 89.0. 14% in top 10% of high school class, 71% in top 25% of high school class, 91% in top 50% of high school class. SAT Math middle 50% range 520-640. SAT Critical Reading middle 50% range 530-610. SAT Writing middle 50% range 520-630. ACT middle 50% range 22-28. Minimum web-based TOEFL 17. Minimum paper TOEFL 550. **Basis for Candidate Selection:** *Very important factors considered include:* Class rank, academic GPA, rigor of secondary school record. *Important factors considered include:* application essay, recommendation(s), standardized test scores, extracurricular activities, interview. *Other factors considered include:* character/personal qualities, geographical residence, level of applicant's interest, talent/ability, volunteer work, work experience. **Freshman Admission Requirements:** High school diploma is required and GED is accepted. *Academic units required:* 4 English, 3 mathematics, 2 science, (1 science labs), 2 foreign language, 1 social studies, 3 history, 6 academic electives. *Academic units recommended:* 4 English, 3 mathematics, 2 science, (1 science labs), 2 foreign language, 1 social studies, 3 history, 6 academic electives. **Freshman Admission Statistics:** 3,001 applied, 69% admitted, 23% enrolled. **Transfer Admission Requirements:** college transcript(s), essay or personal statement, statement of good standing from prior institution(s). Minimum college GPA of 3.0 required. Lowest grade transferable C. **General Admission Information:** Application Fee $50. Early decision application deadline 1/1. Regular application deadline 2/15. Regular notification 3/1. Nonfall registration accepted. Admission may be deferred for a maximum of 1 year. Credit offered for CEEB Advanced Placement tests.

COSTS AND FINANCIAL AID
Annual tuition $37,240. Room and board $11,160. Required fees $200. Average book expense $781. **Required Forms and Deadlines:** FAFSA, institution's own financial aid form, state aid form. **Notification of Awards:** Applicants will be notified of awards on a rolling basis beginning 3/1. **Types of Aid:** *Need-based scholarships/grants:* Federal Pell, SEOG, state scholarships/grants, private scholarships. *Loans:* Subsidized Stafford, Unsubsidized Stafford, PLUS, Federal Perkins, Federal Nursing, Alternative Loans. **Student Employment:** Federal Work-Study Program available. Institutional employment available. Highest amount earned per year from on-campus jobs $1,000. Off-campus job opportunities are good. **Financial Aid Statistics:** 100% freshmen, 99% undergrads receive need-based scholarship or grant aid. 82% freshmen, 83% undergrads receive need-based self-help aid. 5% freshmen, 5% undergrads receive athletic scholarships. 95% freshmen, 90% undergrads receive any aid. 56% undergrads borrow to pay for school. Average cumulative indebtedness

$40,110. **Criteria for awarding institutional aid:** *Non-need-based:* academics, athletics, music/drama.

WAKE FOREST UNIVERSITY

P.O. Box 7305, Winston Salem, NC 27109
Phone: 336-758-5201 • **Financial Aid Phone:** 336)758-5154
E-mail: admissions@wfu.edu • **CEEB Code:** 5885
Fax: 336-758-4324 • **Website:** www.wfu.edu • **ACT Code:** 3168

This private school was founded in 1834. It has a 340-acre campus.

RATINGS
Admissions Selectivity Rating: 96   **Fire Safety Rating:** 86   **Green Rating:** 77

STUDENTS AND FACULTY
Enrollment: 4,801. **Student Body:** 52% female, 48% male, 77% out-of-state, 3% international (27 countries represented). Asian 5%, African American 7%, Caucasian 76%, Hispanic 5%, Native American 0%
Retention and Graduation: 94% freshmen return for sophomore year. 83% freshmen graduate within 4 years. 32% grads go on to further study within 1 year. 28% grads pursue arts and sciences degrees. 16% grads pursue law degrees. 36% grads pursue business degrees. 17% grads pursue medical degrees. **Faculty:** Student/faculty ratio 11:1. 534 full-time faculty, 92% hold PhDs, 14% are members of minority groups, 40% are women. 0% of classes are taught by teaching assistants.

ACADEMICS
Degrees: first professional, master's, post-bachelor's certificate. **Classes:** Most classes have 10—19 students. Most lab/discussion sessions have 10—19 students. **Majors with Highest Enrollment:** business/commerce; political science and government; psychology. **Special Study Options:** cross-registration, double major, dual enrollment, honors program, independent study, internships, study abroad, teacher certification program. **Honors Programs:** For highly qualified students, a series of interdisciplinary honors courses are offered. Additionally, for students especially talented in individual areas of study, most departments in the College offer special studies leading to graduation with honors in a particular discipline. **Combined Degree Programs:** BS/MS in accountancy. **Disability Services:** Special programs offered to physically disabled students include note-taking services, reader services, tape recorders, tutors. **Career Services:** Alumni network, alumni services, career/job search classes, career assessment, internships, regional alumni.

FACILITIES
Housing: Coed dorms, fraternity/sorority housing, apartments for single students, wellness housing, theme housing. Wellness = Substance Free. **Special Academic Facilities/Equipment:** Museum of Anthropology; Charlotte and Philip Hanes Art Gallery; Scales Fine Arts Center; Reynolda House, Museum of American Art; Laser and Electron Microscope Labs. **Computers:** 100% of classrooms, 100% of dorms, 100% of libraries, 100% of dining areas, 100% of student union, 5% of common outdoor areas have wireless network access. Students can register for classes online. Administrative functions (other than registration) can be performed online. Undergraduates are required to own a computer.

CAMPUS LIFE
Environment: City. **Activities:** Choral groups, concert band, dance, drama/theater, jazz band, literary magazine, marching band, music ensembles, pep band, radio station, student government, student newspaper, student-run film society, symphony orchestra, television station, yearbook, Campus Ministries, International Student Organization, Model UN 168 registered organizations, 16 honor societies, 16 religious organizations. 14 fraternities, 9 sororities. **Athletics (Intercollegiate):** *Men:* baseball, basketball, cheerleading, cross-country, football, golf, soccer, tennis, track/field (outdoor), track/field (indoor). *Women:* basketball, cheerleading, cross-country, field hockey, golf, soccer, tennis, track/field (outdoor), track/field (indoor), volleyball. **On-Campus Highlights:** Charlotte and Philip Hanes Art Gallery, Museum of Anthropology, The Z. Smith Reynolds Library, Wait Chapel, Benson University Center. **Environmental Initiatives:** Campus Master Plan: Wake Forest has completed a new campus master plan that will guide development over the next 50 years. Heavily integrated into that plan are tenents for sustainable design (e.g. LEED) as well as stormwater management and biohabitat protection. This new master plan will guide the campus

in integrating sustainability within the built and natural environments for the years ahead. Energy management: the university has a robust Energy Management software system to conserve energy during normal operating periods and to cycle down energy use to minimal levels during low- or no-occupancy periods. Also, energy reduction projects are underway in FY09 - lighting retro-fits, motor replacements, central plant upgrades, etc. Also, new capital projects are designed to achieve energy savings in excess of 30% greater than ASHRAE requirements. Recycling: Approximately 30 percent of the WFU waste stream is diverted from the landfill as either recycled or reused. A renewed emphasis on recycling - to include deskside capture and more functional campus collection containers - is seeing significant success.

ADMISSIONS

Freshman Academic Profile: 79% in top 10% of high school class, 94% in top 25% of high school class, 99% in top 50% of high school class. 65% from public high schools. SAT Math middle 50% range 630-710. SAT Critical Reading middle 50% range 620-700. ACT middle 50% range 29-31. Minimum paper TOEFL 600. **Basis for Candidate Selection:** *Very important factors considered include:* Class rank, application essay, academic GPA, rigor of secondary school record, character/personal qualities. *Important factors considered include:* recommendation(s), extracurricular activities, interview, talent/ability. *Other factors considered include:* standardized test scores, alumni/ae relation, first generation, geographical residence, level of applicant's interest, racial/ethnic status, religious affiliation/commitment, state residency, volunteer work. **Freshman Admission Requirements:** High school diploma is required and GED is accepted. *Academic units required:* 4 English, 3 mathematics, 1 science, 2 foreign language, 2 social studies. *Academic units recommended:* 4 English, 3 mathematics, 1 science, 2 foreign language, 2 social studies. **Freshman Admission Statistics:** 11,407 applied, 34% admitted, 32% enrolled. **Transfer Admission Requirements:** High school transcript, college transcript(s), essay or personal statement, statement of good standing from prior institution(s). Minimum college GPA of 2.0 required. Lowest grade transferable C. **General Admission Information:** Application Fee $50. Early decision application deadline 11/15. Regular application deadline 1/15. Regular notification 4/1. Nonfall registration not accepted. Admission may be deferred for a maximum of 1 year. Credit and/or placement offered for CEEB Advanced Placement tests.

COSTS AND FINANCIAL AID

Annual tuition $42,700. Room and board $11,660. Required fees $500. **Required Forms and Deadlines:** FAFSA, CSS/Financial Aid PROFILE, state aid form, noncustodial PROFILE. **Notification of Awards:** Applicants will be notified of awards on a rolling basis beginning 4/1. **Types of Aid:** *Need-based scholarships/grants:* Federal Pell, SEOG, state scholarships/grants, private scholarships, the school's own gift aid. *Loans:* Subsidized Stafford, Unsubsidized Stafford, PLUS, Federal Perkins, state loans, college/university loans from institutional funds. **Student Employment:** Federal Work-Study Program available. Institutional employment available. Highest amount earned per year from on-campus jobs $2,495. Off-campus job opportunities are excellent. **Financial Aid Statistics:** 97% freshmen, 95% undergrads receive need-based scholarship or grant aid. 49% freshmen, 70% undergrads receive non-need-based scholarship or grant aid. 81% freshmen, 89% undergrads receive need-based self-help aid. 6% freshmen, 4% undergrads receive athletic scholarships. 39% freshmen, 34% undergrads receive any aid. 39% undergrads borrow to pay for school. Average cumulative indebtedness $35,070. **Criteria for awarding institutional aid:** *Non-need-based:* academics, alumni affiliation, art, athletics, leadership, music/drama, religious affiliation, state/district residency.

WALDORF COLLEGE

106 South 6th St., Forest City, IA 50436
Phone: 641-585-8112
E-mail: admissions@waldorf.edu
Fax: 641-585-8125 • **Website:** www.waldorf.edu • **ACT Code:** 1895

This private school, affiliated with the Lutheran Church, was founded in 1903. It has a 40-acre campus.

RATINGS
Admissions Selectivity Rating: 63   **Fire Safety Rating:** 61   **Green Rating:** 60*

STUDENTS AND FACULTY
Enrollment: 573. **Student Body:** 53% female, 47% male, 17% out-of-state, 6% international. Asian 1%, African American 4%, Caucasian 99%, Hispanic 1%, Native American 0%
Faculty: Student/faculty ratio 15:1. 64 full-time faculty, 25% hold PhDs. 0% of classes are taught by teaching assistants.

ACADEMICS
Degrees: associate, bachelor's. **Classes:** Most classes have 10—19 students. Most lab/discussion sessions have fewer than 10 students. **Majors with Highest Enrollment:** business, management, marketing, and related support services, other; communication, journalism, and related programs, other; computer and information sciences and support services, other. **Special Study Options:** Accelerated program, cooperative education program, double major, English as a Second Language (ESL), honors program, internships, student-designed major, study abroad, teacher certification program. **Combined Degree Programs:** BA/MD. **Disability Services:** Special programs offered to physically disabled students include note-taking services, reader services, tutors. **Career Services:** Alumni network, alumni services, career/job search classes, career assessment, internships. Career services highlights include internships.

FACILITIES
Housing: Coed dorms, special housing for disabled students, Suites, Special Interest Housing, Townhouses. **Computers:** Administrative functions (other than registration) can be performed online.

CAMPUS LIFE
Environment: Rural. **Activities:** dance, drama/theater, jazz band, student government, student newspaper, Campus Ministries. **Athletics (Intercollegiate):** *Men:* baseball, basketball, football, golf, soccer, wrestling. *Women:* basketball, cheerleading, golf, soccer, softball, volleyball. **On-Campus Highlights:** Walucks (coffee/snacks), Wellness Center, Video-Production Studio, Library (new), Breen Hall.

ADMISSIONS
Freshman Academic Profile: Average high school GPA 3.0. 95% from public high schools. Minimum paper TOEFL 500. **Basis for Candidate Selection:** *Very important factors considered include:* recommendation(s), rigor of secondary school record, standardized test scores. *Important factors considered include:* extracurricular activities, talent/ability. *Other factors considered include:* Class rank, alumni/ae relation, character/personal qualities, interview, racial/ethnic status, religious affiliation/commitment. **Freshman Admission Requirements:** High school diploma is required and GED is accepted. **Freshman Admission Statistics:** 584 applied, 67% admitted, 50% enrolled. **Transfer Admission Requirements:** High school transcript, college transcript(s), standardized test scores, statement of good standing from prior institution(s). Minimum college GPA of 2.0 required. Lowest grade transferable C–. **General Admission Information:** Notification on a rolling basis, beginning on or about 10/4. Nonfall registration not accepted. Admission may be deferred for a maximum of 1 year.

WALLA WALLA UNIVERSITY

Office of Admissions, College Place, WA 99324-1198
Phone: 480-527-2615 • **Financial Aid Phone:** 509-527-2815
E-mail: info@wallawalla.edu • **CEEB Code:** 4940
Fax: 509-527-2253 • **Website:** www.wallawalla.edu • **ACT Code:** 4486

This private school, affiliated with the Seventh Day Adventist Church, was founded in 1892. It has a 77-acre campus.

RATINGS
Admissions Selectivity Rating: 62   **Fire Safety Rating:** 61   **Green Rating:** 60*

STUDENTS AND FACULTY
Enrollment: 1,549. **Student Body:** 50% female, 50% male, 59% out-of-state, 2% international (30 countries represented). Asian %, African American 2%, Caucasian 60%, Hispanic 8%, Native American 1%
Retention and Graduation: 78% freshmen return for sophomore year. 23% freshmen graduate within 4 years. **Faculty:** Student/faculty ratio :1. 112 full-time faculty, 69% hold PhDs, 6% are members of minority groups, 39% are women. 0% of classes are taught by teaching assistants.

ACADEMICS
Degrees: associate, bachelor's, master's. **Classes:** Most classes have fewer than 10 students. Most lab/discussion sessions have fewer than 10 students. **Majors with Highest Enrollment:** business/commerce; engineering; social work. **Special Study Options:** cooperative education program, distance learning, double major, honors program, independent study, internships, liberal arts/career combination, study abroad, teacher certification program. **Disability Services:** Special programs offered to physically disabled students include note-taking services, reader services, tape recorders, tutors. **Career Services:** Alumni network, career/job search classes, career assessment, internships Career services highlights include All of our accounting and management students participate in internships.

FACILITIES

Housing: special housing for disabled students, men's dorms, women's dorms, apartments for married students, apartments for single students, wellness housing. 75% of campus accessible to physically disabled. **Special Academic Facilities/Equipment:** Marine station on the Rosario Strait of the Puget Sound in Washington state. **Computers:** Students can register for classes online.

CAMPUS LIFE

Environment: Town. **Activities:** Choral groups, concert band, drama/theater, literary magazine, music ensembles, radio station, student government, student newspaper, symphony orchestra, television station, yearbook, Campus Ministries, International Student Organization 33 registered organizations, 7 honor societies, 6 religious organizations. **Athletics (Intercollegiate):** *Men:* basketball, golf, soccer, volleyball. *Women:* basketball, softball, volleyball. **On-Campus Highlights:** The Dairy Express, Peterson Memorial Library, The Student Association Center, Winter Educational Complex: gym/climbing wall/pool, The College Store, Clyde and Mary Harris Gallery.

ADMISSIONS

Freshman Academic Profile: Minimum paper TOEFL 550. **Basis for Candidate Selection:** *Very important factors considered include:* academic GPA, recommendation(s), rigor of secondary school record. *Important factors considered include:* character/personal qualities, level of applicant's interest. *Other factors considered include:* Class rank, standardized test scores, extracurricular activities, talent/ability. **Freshman Admission Requirements:** High school diploma is required and GED is accepted. *Academic units required:* 4 English, 3 mathematics, 2 science, (2 science labs), 2 history. *Academic units recommended:* 4 English, 3 mathematics, 2 science, (2 science labs), 2 history. **Freshman Admission Statistics:** 626 applied, 89% admitted, 54% enrolled. **Transfer Admission Requirements:** college transcript(s), Minimum college GPA of 2.0 required. Lowest grade transferable D . **General Admission Information:** Application Fee $40. Notification on a rolling basis, beginning on or about 9/25. Nonfall registration accepted. Admission may be deferred for a maximum of 1 year. Credit and/or placement offered for CEEB Advanced Placement tests.

COSTS AND FINANCIAL AID

Annual tuition $23,670. Room and board $5,655. Required fees $528. Average book expense $1,068. **Required Forms and Deadlines:** FAFSA, institution's own financial aid form. **Notification of Awards:** Applicants will be notified of awards on a rolling basis beginning 3/15. **Types of Aid:** *Need-based scholarships/grants:* Federal Pell, SEOG, state scholarships/grants, private scholarships, the school's own gift aid, Federal Nursing Scholarships. *Loans:* Subsidized Stafford, Unsubsidized Stafford, PLUS, Federal Perkins, Federal Nursing, college/university loans from institutional funds. **Student Employment:** Federal Work-Study Program available. Institutional employment available. Off-campus job opportunities are good. **Financial Aid Statistics:** 79% freshmen, 79% undergrads receive need-based scholarship or grant aid. 99% freshmen, 80% undergrads receive non-need-based scholarship or grant aid. 89% freshmen, 93% undergrads receive need-based self-help aid. 84% freshmen, 83% undergrads receive any aid. 70% undergrads borrow to pay for school. Average cumulative indebtedness $32,697. **Criteria for awarding institutional aid:** *Non-need-based:* academics, leadership, music/drama.

WALSH COLLEGE

3838 Livernois Road, Troy, MI 48007-7006
Phone: 248-689-8282 • **Financial Aid Phone:** 248-823-1285
E-mail: admissions@walshcollege.edu
Fax: 248-689-0938

This private school was founded in 1922. It has a 20-acre campus.

RATINGS

Admissions Selectivity Rating: 61   **Fire Safety Rating:** 60*   **Green Rating:** 61

STUDENTS AND FACULTY

Enrollment: 984. **Student Body:** 55% female, 45% male, 1% out-of-state, 4% international (46 countries represented). Asian 3%, African American 5%, Caucasian 65%, Hispanic 1%, Native American 0%
Retention and Graduation: Faculty: Student/faculty ratio 17:1. 18 full-time faculty, 72% hold PhDs, 6% are members of minority groups, 44% are women. 0% of classes are taught by teaching assistants.

ACADEMICS

Degrees: bachelor's, master's, post-bachelor's certificate, post-master's certificate. **Classes:** Most classes have 20—29 students. **Majors with Highest**

Enrollment: liberal arts and sciences/liberal studies; pharmacy (pharmd [usa], pharmd or bs/bpharm [canada]); psychology. **Special Study Options:** distance learning, double major, dual enrollment, independent study, internships. **Disability Services:** Special programs offered to physically disabled students include note-taking services, reader services, tape recorders, tutors. **Career Services:** Alumni network, alumni services, career/job search classes, career assessment, internships.

FACILITIES

Housing: 100% of campus accessible to physically disabled. **Computers:** 100% of classrooms, 100% of libraries, 100% of dining areas, have wireless network access. Students can register for classes online. Administrative functions (other than registration) can be performed online.

CAMPUS LIFE

Environment: City. **Activities:** student government, student newspaper, student-run film society 6 registered organizations, 1 honor societies. **On-Campus Highlights:** Barry Center.

ADMISSIONS

Freshman Academic Profile: Minimum web-based TOEFL 79. Minimum paper TOEFL 550. **Transfer Admission Requirements:** college transcript(s), Minimum college GPA of 2.0 required. Lowest grade transferable C. **General Admission Information:** Application Fee $25.

COSTS AND FINANCIAL AID

Required Forms and Deadlines: FAFSA. **Types of Aid:** *Need-based scholarships/grants:* Federal Pell, SEOG, state scholarships/grants, the school's own gift aid. *Loans:* Subsidized Stafford, Unsubsidized Stafford, state loans. **Student Employment:** Federal Work-Study Program available. Off-campus job opportunities are fair. **Financial Aid Statistics:** 64% undergrads receive need-based scholarship or grant aid. 18% undergrads receive non-need-based scholarship or grant aid. 100% undergrads receive need-based self-help aid 61% undergrads borrow to pay for school. Average cumulative indebtedness $12,367. **Criteria for awarding institutional aid:** *Non-need-based:* academics.

WALSH UNIVERSITY

2020 East Maple St, North Canton, OH 44720-3396
Phone: 330-490-7172 • **Financial Aid Phone:** 330-490-7367
E-mail: admissions@walsh.edu • **CEEB Code:** 1926
Fax: 330-490-7165 • **Website:** www.walsh.edu • **ACT Code:** 3349

This private school, affiliated with the Roman Catholic Church, was founded in 1958. It has a 140-acre campus.

RATINGS

Admissions Selectivity Rating: 70   **Fire Safety Rating:** 85   **Green Rating:** 61

STUDENTS AND FACULTY

Enrollment: 2,292. **Student Body:** 63% female, 37% male, 3% out-of-state, 1% international (20 countries represented). Asian 0%, African American 3%, Caucasian 64%, Hispanic 1%, Native American 0%
Retention and Graduation: 74% freshmen return for sophomore year. 14% grads go on to further study within 1 year. 1% grads pursue arts and sciences degrees. 2% grads pursue law degrees. 5% grads pursue business degrees. 1% grads pursue medical degrees. **Faculty:** Student/faculty ratio 14:1. 128 full-time faculty, 64% hold PhDs, 6% are members of minority groups, 52% are women. 0% of classes are taught by teaching assistants.

ACADEMICS

Degrees: associate, bachelor's, master's. **Classes:** Most classes have 10—19 students. Most lab/discussion sessions have fewer than 10 students. **Majors with Highest Enrollment:** biological and physical sciences; business/commerce; nursing/registered nurse (rn, asn, bsn, msn). **Special Study Options:** Accelerated program, double major, dual enrollment, English as a Second Language (ESL), exchange student program (domestic), external degree program, honors program, independent study, internships, liberal arts/career combination, study abroad, teacher certification program, Combined bachelor's/master's degree programs CCSA College Consortium for Study Abroad Rome Experience. **Honors Programs:** Honors Program students may pursue any major and have opportunity annually to attend the national honors conference, where Walsh students frequently present their research. **Combined Degree Programs:** BA/MA, 3-1 med-tech, 3-4 dentistry. **Disability Services:** Special programs offered to physically disabled students include reader services, tape recorders, tutors. **Career Services:** Alumni network, alumni services, career assessment, internships, regional alumni.

FACILITIES

Housing: Coed dorms, special housing for disabled students, special housing for international students, apartments for single students, wellness housing, apartment-style residence hall with kitchens. 100% of campus accessible to physically disabled. **Special Academic Facilities/Equipment:** bioinformatics lab, Hoover Museum, human cadaver lab (prosection for undergrad), Gathering Garden for Education activities with schoolchildren, Religious Education Center **Computers:** 10% of classrooms, 12% of dorms, 100% of libraries, 100% of dining areas, 100% of student union, 5% of common outdoor areas have wireless network access. Students can register for classes online. Administrative functions (other than registration) can be performed online.

CAMPUS LIFE

Environment: City. **Activities:** Choral groups, dance, drama/theater, literary magazine, music ensembles, pep band, radio station, student government, student newspaper, Campus Ministries, International Student Organization 30 registered organizations, 10 honor societies, 3 religious organizations. **Athletics (Intercollegiate):** *Men:* baseball, basketball, cheerleading, cross-country, football, golf, soccer, tennis, track/field (outdoor), track/field (indoor). *Women:* basketball, cheerleading, cross-country, golf, soccer, softball, tennis, track/field (outdoor), track/field (indoor), volleyball. **On-Campus Highlights:** David Campus Center, Alumni Arena, University Apartments, Barrette Business and Community Center, Wellness Center. **Environmental Initiatives:** HVAC & electrical managament system recycling program for paper, plastic, and aluminum ink cartridge recycle system.

ADMISSIONS

Freshman Academic Profile: Average high school GPA 3.4. 18% in top 10% of high school class, 43% in top 25% of high school class, 76% in top 50% of high school class. 74% from public high schools. SAT Math middle 50% range 470-580. SAT Critical Reading middle 50% range 440-560. ACT middle 50% range 20-25. Minimum web-based TOEFL 61. Minimum paper TOEFL 500. **Basis for Candidate Selection:** *Very important factors considered include:* academic GPA, rigor of secondary school record, standardized test scores. *Important factors considered include:* recommendation(s), character/personal qualities. *Other factors considered include:* Class rank, application essay, interview, volunteer work. **Freshman Admission Requirements:** High school diploma is required and GED is accepted. **Freshman Admission Statistics:** 1,621 applied, 78% admitted, 39% enrolled. **Transfer Admission Requirements:** High school transcript, college transcript(s), Minimum college GPA of 2.0 required. Lowest grade transferable C. **General Admission Information:** Application Fee $25. Regular application deadline 8/15. Notification on a rolling basis, beginning on or about 10/1. Nonfall registration accepted. Admission may be deferred for a maximum of 1 year. Credit offered for CEEB Advanced Placement tests.

COSTS AND FINANCIAL AID

Annual tuition $23,550. Room and board $8,940. Required fees $1,140. Average book expense $1,104. **Required Forms and Deadlines:** FAFSA, institution's own financial aid form. **Notification of Awards:** Applicants will be notified of awards on a rolling basis beginning 2/15. **Types of Aid:** *Need-based scholarships/grants:* Federal Pell, SEOG, state scholarships/grants, private scholarships, the school's own gift aid. *Loans:* Direct Subsidized Stafford, Direct Unsubsidized Stafford, Direct PLUS, Federal Perkins, state loans. **Student Employment:** Federal Work-Study Program available. Institutional employment available. Highest amount earned per year from on-campus jobs $3,000. **Financial Aid Statistics:** 86% freshmen, 79% undergrads receive need-based scholarship or grant aid. 100% freshmen, 100% undergrads receive non-need-based scholarship or grant aid. 94% freshmen, 69% undergrads receive need-based self-help aid. 16% freshmen, 16% undergrads receive athletic scholarships. 99% freshmen, 93% undergrads receive any aid. 87% undergrads borrow to pay for school. Average cumulative indebtedness $23,895. **Criteria for awarding institutional aid:** *Non-need-based:* academics, alumni affiliation, athletics, music/drama, religious affiliation, state/district residency.

WARNER PACIFIC COLLEGE

Office of Admissions, Portland, OR 97215
Phone: 503-517-1020 • **Financial Aid Phone:** 503-517-1091
E-mail: admissions@warnerpacific.edu • **CEEB Code:** 4595
Fax: 503-517-1540 • **Website:** www.warnerpacific.edu

This private school, affiliated with the Church of God Church, was founded in 1937. It has a 15-acre campus.

RATINGS

Admissions Selectivity Rating: 79   **Fire Safety Rating:** 62   **Green Rating:** 60*

STUDENTS AND FACULTY

Enrollment: 551. **Student Body:** 58% female, 42% male, 33% out-of-state, (12 countries represented). Asian 5%, African American 8%, Caucasian 67%, Hispanic 9%, Native American 1%
Retention and Graduation: 66% freshmen return for sophomore year. 41% freshmen graduate within 4 years. **Faculty:** Student/faculty ratio 11:1. 27 full-time faculty, 63% hold PhDs, 15% are members of minority groups, 44% are women. 0% of classes are taught by teaching assistants.

ACADEMICS

Degrees: associate, bachelor's, certificate, master's. **Classes:** Most classes have 10—19 students. **Special Study Options:** cooperative education program, double major, independent study, internships, student-designed major, study abroad, teacher certification program, weekend college, Adult Degree Program. **Disability Services:** Special programs offered to physically disabled students include note-taking services, reader services, tape recorders, tutors. **Career Services:** career assessment, internships.

FACILITIES

Housing: men's dorms, women's dorms, apartments for married students, apartments for single students. 50% of campus accessible to physically disabled. **Special Academic Facilities/Equipment:** Early learning center, electron microscopes. **Computers:** 100% of classrooms, 10% of dorms, 100% of libraries, 100% of dining areas, 100% of student union, 50% of common outdoor areas have wireless network access.

CAMPUS LIFE

Environment: Metropolis. **Activities:** Choral groups, concert band, dance, drama/theater, jazz band, literary magazine, music ensembles, musical theater, student government, student newspaper, yearbook, Campus Ministries, International Student Organization 20 registered organizations, 2 religious organizations. **Athletics (Intercollegiate):** *Men:* basketball, cross-country, golf, soccer, track/field (outdoor), track/field (indoor). *Women:* basketball, cross-country, golf, soccer, track/field (outdoor), track/field (indoor), volleyball. **On-Campus Highlights:** Tabor Grind Coffee Shop, Dining Hall, Student Union Building, Otto F. Linn Library, A.F. Gray lawn.

ADMISSIONS

Freshman Academic Profile: 3.2. 6% in top 10% of high school class, 38% in top 25% of high school class, 79% in top 50% of high school class. SAT Math middle 50% range 410-540. SAT Critical Reading middle 50% range 450-580. SAT Writing middle 50% range 440-560. ACT middle 50% range 17-24. Minimum web-based TOEFL 71. Minimum paper TOEFL 525. **Basis for Candidate Selection:** *Important factors considered include:* application essay, academic GPA, standardized test scores. *Other factors considered include:* Class rank, recommendation(s), rigor of secondary school record. **Freshman Admission Requirements:** High school diploma is required and GED is accepted. **Freshman Admission Statistics:** 966 applied, 58% admitted, 17% enrolled. **Transfer Admission Requirements:** college transcript(s), essay or personal statement, Minimum college GPA of 2.5 required. Lowest grade transferable d. **General Admission Information:** Application Fee $50. Early decision application deadline 6/1. Nonfall registration accepted. Admission may be deferred for a maximum of 1 year. Credit offered for CEEB Advanced Placement tests.

COSTS AND FINANCIAL AID

Annual tuition $18,370. Room and board $7,690. Required fees $660. Average book expense $1,300. **Required Forms and Deadlines:** FAFSA. **Notification of Awards:** Applicants will be notified of awards on a rolling basis beginning 3/1. **Types of Aid:** *Need-based scholarships/grants:* Federal Pell, SEOG, state scholarships/grants, private scholarships, the school's own gift aid. *Loans:* Direct Subsidized Stafford, Direct Unsubsidized Stafford, Direct PLUS, Subsidized Stafford, Unsubsidized Stafford, PLUS, Federal Perkins. **Student Employment:** Federal Work-Study Program available. Institutional employment available. Highest amount earned per year from on-campus jobs $4,000. **Financial Aid Statistics:** 91% freshmen, 89% undergrads receive need-based scholarship or grant aid. 94% freshmen, 88% undergrads receive non-need-based scholarship or grant aid. 91% freshmen, 92% undergrads receive need-based self-help aid. 20% freshmen, 24% undergrads receive athletic scholarships. 96% freshmen, 97% undergrads receive any aid. 91% undergrads borrow to pay for school. Average cumulative indebtedness $33,035. **Criteria for awarding institutional aid:** *Non-need-based:* academics, alumni affiliation, athletics, leadership, music/drama, religious affiliation.

WARNER SOUTHERN COLLEGE

13985 Hwy. 27, Lake Wales, FL 33859
Phone: 863-638-7212 • **Financial Aid Phone:** 863-638-7203
E-mail: admissions@warner.edu • **CEEB Code:** 5883
Fax: 863-638-7290 • **ACT Code:** 777

This private school, affiliated with the Church of God Church, was founded in 1968. It has a 320-acre campus.

RATINGS
Admissions Selectivity Rating: 72   **Fire Safety Rating:** 69   **Green Rating:** 60*

STUDENTS AND FACULTY
Enrollment: 937. **Student Body:** 58% female, 42% male, 1% international (20 countries represented). Asian 1%, African American 17%, Caucasian 56%, Hispanic 8%, Native American 0%
Retention and Graduation: 26% freshmen graduate within 4 years. 34% freshmen graduate within 6 years. **Faculty:** Student/faculty ratio 13:1. 34 full-time faculty, 59% hold PhDs, 12% are members of minority groups, 38% are women. 0% of classes are taught by teaching assistants.

ACADEMICS
Degrees: associate, bachelor's, certificate, master's, terminal associate. **Classes:** Most classes have 10—19 students. **Majors with Highest Enrollment:** business/commerce; education; pastoral studies/counseling. **Special Study Options:** Accelerated program, distance learning, double major, dual enrollment, English as a Second Language (ESL), independent study, internships, study abroad, teacher certification program.

FACILITIES
Housing: men's dorms, women's dorms. 80% of campus accessible to physically disabled.

CAMPUS LIFE
Environment: Rural. **Activities:** Choral groups, music ensembles, student government, student newspaper 2 registered organizations, 6 honor societies, 1 religious organizations. 2 fraternities, 2 sororities. **Athletics (Intercollegiate):** *Men:* baseball, basketball, cheerleading, cross-country, golf, soccer, tennis, track/field (outdoor), track/field (indoor). *Women:* basketball, cheerleading, cross-country, golf, soccer, softball, tennis, track/field (outdoor), track/field (indoor), volleyball. **On-Campus Highlights:** Lion's Den, Turner Athletic Center, Pontious Learning Resource Center, Caffe Cristiano.

ADMISSIONS
Freshman Academic Profile: Average high school GPA 3.0. 11% in top 10% of high school class, 23% in top 25% of high school class, 66% in top 50% of high school class. 90% from public high schools. SAT Math middle 50% range 351-613. SAT Critical Reading middle 50% range 342-580, ACT middle 50% range 15-24. Minimum paper TOEFL 500. **Basis for Candidate Selection:** *Important factors considered include:* Class rank, academic GPA, recommendation(s), standardized test scores, level of applicant's interest. *Other factors considered include:* application essay, rigor of secondary school record, alumni/ae relation, character/personal qualities, extracurricular activities, interview, talent/ability, volunteer work. **Freshman Admission Requirements:** High school diploma is required and GED is accepted. **Freshman Admission Statistics:** 363 applied, 66% admitted, 47% enrolled. **Transfer Admission Requirements:** college transcript(s), essay or personal statement, statement of good standing from prior institution(s). Minimum college GPA of 2.0 required. Lowest grade transferable D. **General Admission Information:** Application Fee $20. Notification on a rolling basis, beginning on or about 9/1. Nonfall registration accepted. Admission may be deferred for a maximum of No time set. Neither credit nor placement offered for CEEB Advanced Placement tests.

COSTS AND FINANCIAL AID
Annual tuition $13,600. Room and board $5,730. Required fees $150. Average book expense $1,000. **Required Forms and Deadlines:** FAFSA, state aid formVerification Form. **Notification of Awards:** Applicants will be notified of awards on a rolling basis beginning 1/15. **Types of Aid:** *Need-based scholarships/grants:* Federal Pell, SEOG, state scholarships/grants, private scholarships, the school's own gift aid. *Loans:* Subsidized Stafford, Unsubsidized Stafford, PLUS, Federal PerkinsAlternative Loans. **Student Employment:**

Federal Work-Study Program available. Institutional employment available. Highest amount earned per year from on-campus jobs $1,200. Off-campus job opportunities are good. **Financial Aid Statistics:** 79% freshmen, 66% undergrads receive need-based scholarship or grant aid. 100% freshmen, 98% undergrads receive non-need-based scholarship or grant aid. 81% freshmen, 89% undergrads receive need-based self-help aid. 66% freshmen, 34% undergrads receive athletic scholarships. 100% freshmen, 93% undergrads receive any aid. **Criteria for awarding institutional aid:** *Non-need-based:* academics, alumni affiliation, athletics, leadership, minority status, music/drama, religious affiliation, state/district residency.

WARREN WILSON COLLEGE

PO Box 9000, Asheville, NC 28815-9000
Phone: 800-934-3536 • **Financial Aid Phone:** 828-771-2082
E-mail: admit@warren-wilson.edu • **CEEB Code:** 5886
Fax: 828-298-1440 • **Website:** www.warren-wilson.edu • **ACT Code:** 3170

This private school, affiliated with the Presbyterian Church, was founded in 1894. It has a 1100-acre campus.

RATINGS
Admissions Selectivity Rating: 70   **Fire Safety Rating:** 63   **Green Rating:** 97

STUDENTS AND FACULTY
Enrollment: 903. **Student Body:** 62% female, 38% male, 84% out-of-state, 3% international (12 countries represented). Asian 2%, African American 2%, Caucasian 85%, Hispanic 3%, Native American 0%
Retention and Graduation: 64% freshmen return for sophomore year. 30% freshmen graduate within 4 years. 45% freshmen graduate within 6 years. 30% grads go on to further study within 1 year. 30% grads pursue arts and sciences degrees. 1% grads pursue business degrees. **Faculty:** Student/faculty ratio 13:1. 65 full-time faculty, 92% hold PhDs, 11% are members of minority groups, 40% are women. 0% of classes are taught by teaching assistants.

ACADEMICS
Degrees: bachelor's, master's. **Classes:** Most classes have 10—19 students. Most lab/discussion sessions have 10—19 students. **Majors with Highest Enrollment:** parks, recreation, leisure, and fitness studies, other; psychology. **Special Study Options:** cross-registration, double major, dual enrollment, English as a Second Language (ESL), exchange student program (domestic), honors program, independent study, internships, liberal arts/career combination, student-designed major, study abroad. **Disability Services:** Special programs offered to physically disabled students include tape recorders. **Career Services:** career assessment, internships, regional alumni.

FACILITIES
Housing: Coed dorms, men's dorms, women's dorms, apartments for married students, cooperative housing, apartments for single students. 100% of campus accessible to physically disabled. **Special Academic Facilities/Equipment:** 300-acre farm,700-acre forest, community gardens, archaeological dig on campus, organically managed garden, GIS lab, photomicroscopy lab.

CAMPUS LIFE
Environment: Village. **Activities:** Choral groups, dance, drama/theater, jazz band, literary magazine, music ensembles, musical theater, student government, student newspaper, yearbook 25 registered organizations, 5 religious organizations. **Athletics (Intercollegiate):** *Men:* basketball, cross-country, diving, kayaking, mountain biking, soccer, swimming, ultimate frisbee. *Women:* basketball, cross-country, diving, kayaking, mountain biking, soccer, swimming, ultimate frisbee. **On-Campus Highlights:** Sage Caf, Pond, Witherspoon/Morse Science Center, Dogwood-a short hike to this great view, Cow Pie Caf. **Environmental Initiatives:** Climate Action Plan to achieve 80% reduction in emissions campus wide by 2020 includes our formal climate change partnership with city of Asheville;quarterly emissions reports to support changes;college solar array KW's sold to NC Green Power for sustainability outreach to community to influence reduction in GHG's; 100% renewable energy wind credits purchased each year equal to total campus electric use;INSULATE! weatherization program in region for people in poverty where faculty/students and staff to do a house a weekend to provide assistance and reduce regional GHG emissions. Curriculum of our Triad of academics, work and service: Environmental studies largest major on campus (since '70's)with 6 concentrations using on campus

living laboratory of farm, garden and forest; new inter-disciplinary sustainability curriculum focusing on energy; service learning curriculum focused on regional study of food security for the academic year; work crew supervisors (all students work 15 hours a week to run the campus) now evaluate students on adherence to sustainability principles; Sustainability Recognition Program established for programs that engage Triad in environmental sustainability education; the Sustainability Speaker Series for the campus has hosted Bill McKibben, Lester Brown, Peter Raven, Wendell Berry, and others over the past 3 semesters. Built environment: more than 30% of core campus buildings are either LEED Gold(4), LEED EB platinum(1) or green (1); 3 existing buildings (dorm, office and classroom) have undergone energy efficient retrofits that have included installation of geothermal HVAC systems; Campus energy usage measured monthly for all buildings; use of digital controls underway to reduce energy use; one campus building serves as case study for sustainable practices for rest of campus.

ADMISSIONS

Freshman Academic Profile: Average high school GPA 3.2. 14% in top 10% of high school class, 42% in top 25% of high school class, 78% in top 50% of high school class. 71% from public high schools. SAT Math middle 50% range 490-590. SAT Critical Reading middle 50% range 540-660. SAT Writing middle 50% range 510-630. ACT middle 50% range 22-28. Minimum paper TOEFL 550. **Basis for Candidate Selection:** *Very important factors considered include:* application essay, rigor of secondary school record, standardized test scores, character/personal qualities, interview, volunteer work, work experience. *Important factors considered include:* Class rank, recommendation(s). *Other factors considered include:* alumni/ae relation, extracurricular activities, state residency, talent/ability. **Freshman Admission Requirements:** High school diploma is required and GED is accepted. *Academic units required:* 4 English, 3 mathematics, 2 science, (2 science labs), 3 history. *Academic units recommended:* 4 English, 3 mathematics, 2 science, (2 science labs), 3 history. **Freshman Admission Statistics:** 986 applied, 93% admitted, 25% enrolled. **Transfer Admission Requirements:** High school transcript, college transcript(s), standardized test scores, Minimum college GPA of 3.0 required. Lowest grade transferable C. **General Admission Information:** Early decision application deadline 11/15. Regular application deadline 2/15. Nonfall registration accepted. Admission may be deferred for a maximum of 1. Credit and/or placement offered for CEEB Advanced Placement tests.

COSTS AND FINANCIAL AID

Annual tuition $27,740. Room and board $8,566. Required fees $300. Average book expense $920. **Required Forms and Deadlines:** FAFSA, institution's own financial aid form, state aid form. **Notification of Awards:** Applicants will be notified of awards on a rolling basis beginning 3/2. **Types of Aid:** *Need-based scholarships/grants:* Federal Pell, SEOG, state scholarships/grants, the school's own gift aid. *Loans:* Subsidized Stafford, Unsubsidized Stafford, PLUS, Federal Perkins, college/university loans from institutional funds. **Student Employment:** Highest amount earned per year from on-campus jobs $3,144. Off-campus job opportunities are good. **Financial Aid Statistics:** 91% freshmen, 91% undergrads receive need-based scholarship or grant aid. 24% freshmen, 17% undergrads receive non-need-based scholarship or grant aid. 100% freshmen, 100% undergrads receive need-based self-help aid. 90% freshmen, 90% undergrads receive any aid. 44% undergrads borrow to pay for school. Average cumulative indebtedness $17,533. **Criteria for awarding institutional aid:** *Non-need-based:* academics, art, leadership, state/district residency.

WARTBURG COLLEGE

100 Wartburg Blvd., Waverly, IA 50677-0903
Phone: 319-352-8264 • **Financial Aid Phone:** 319-352-8262
E-mail: admissions@wartburg.edu • **CEEB Code:** 6926
Fax: 319-352-8579 • **Website:** www.wartburg.edu • **ACT Code:** 1364

This private school, affiliated with the Lutheran Church, was founded in 1852. It has a 118-acre campus.

RATINGS

Admissions Selectivity Rating: 73   **Fire Safety Rating:** 68   **Green Rating:** 69

STUDENTS AND FACULTY

Enrollment: 1,755. **Student Body:** 52% female, 48% male, 25% out-of-state, 5% international (38 countries represented). Asian 2%, African American 5%, Caucasian 82%, Hispanic 1%, Native American 0%
Retention and Graduation: 82% freshmen return for sophomore year. 61% freshmen graduate within 4 years. 64% freshmen graduate within 6 years. 23% grads go on to further study within 1 year. 11% grads pursue arts and sciences degrees. 1% grads pursue law degrees. 2% grads pursue business degrees. 6%

grads pursue medical degrees. **Faculty:** Student/faculty ratio 12:1. 109 full-time faculty, 84% hold PhDs, 5% are members of minority groups, 48% are women. 0% of classes are taught by teaching assistants.

ACADEMICS

Degrees: bachelor's. **Classes:** Most classes have 20—29 students. Most lab/discussion sessions have 20—29 students. **Majors with Highest Enrollment:** biology/biological sciences; business, management, marketing, and related support services, other; communication studies/speech communication and rhetoric. **Special Study Options:** Accelerated program, double major, dual enrollment, honors program, independent study, internships, student-designed major, study abroad, teacher certification program. **Honors Programs:** Scholars Program - features small seminar classes, distinguished speaker series, sophomore-year program of lectures, concerts, and performances, student involvement in designing courses and activities, variety of social and travel opportunities, student-designed senior project **Combined Degree Programs:** 2-2 nursing, 3-1 occup. therapy, 3-2 phys therapy. **Disability Services:** Special programs offered to physically disabled students include note-taking services, reader services, tutors. **Career Services:** Alumni network

FACILITIES

Housing: Coed dorms, men's dorms, women's dorms, apartments for single students, theme housing, suite-style living. 85% of campus accessible to physically disabled. **Special Academic Facilities/Equipment:** Art gallery, fine arts center, institute for leadership education, planetarium, prairie preserve, state-of-the-art library, center for community engagement, wellness center **Computers:** 30% of classrooms, 10% of dorms, 100% of libraries, 100% of dining areas, 100% of student union, 10% of common outdoor areas have wireless network access. Students can register for classes online. Administrative functions (other than registration) can be performed online.

CAMPUS LIFE

Environment: Village. **Activities:** Choral groups, concert band, dance, drama/theater, jazz band, literary magazine, music ensembles, musical theater, opera, pep band, radio station, student government, student newspaper, student-run film society, symphony orchestra, television station, yearbook, Campus Ministries, International Student Organization 90 registered organizations, 12 honor societies, 9 religious organizations. **Athletics (Intercollegiate):** *Men:* baseball, basketball, cross-country, football, golf, soccer, tennis, track/field (outdoor), track/field (indoor), wrestling. *Women:* basketball, cross-country, golf, soccer, softball, tennis, track/field (outdoor), track/field (indoor), volleyball. **On-Campus Highlights:** Konditorei Coffee Shop/Vogel Library, Sports and Wellness Center (new 2007), Saemann Student Center (renovated 2004), Walston-Hoover Stadium (new 2001), Old Main (on National Historic Registry), $31 million Sports and Wellness Center. **Environmental Initiatives:** LEED requirements for new Sports and Wellness Center Partnership with Waverly Light and Power on wind generation to offset-carbon-based energy in new Sports and Wellness Center Trayless dining; use of front load washers to reduce water and energy use

ADMISSIONS

Freshman Academic Profile: Average high school GPA 3.5. 28% in top 10% of high school class, 56% in top 25% of high school class, 84% in top 50% of high school class. SAT Math middle 50% range 470-610. SAT Critical Reading middle 50% range 420-600. SAT Writing middle 50% range 410-570. ACT middle 50% range 21-27. Minimum web-based TOEFL 55. Minimum paper TOEFL 480. **Basis for Candidate Selection:** *Very important factors considered include:* Class rank, academic GPA, recommendation(s), rigor of secondary school record, standardized test scores. *Important factors considered include:* character/personal qualities, interview. *Other factors considered include:* application essay, extracurricular activities, level of applicant's interest, racial/ethnic status, talent/ability, volunteer work, work experience. **Freshman Admission Requirements:** High school diploma is required and GED is accepted. **Freshman Admission Statistics:** 2,278 applied, 73% admitted, 29% enrolled. **Transfer Admission Requirements:** High school transcript, college transcript(s), standardized test scores, statement of good standing from prior institution(s). Minimum college GPA of 2.0 required. Lowest grade transferable C-. **General Admission Information:** Notification on a rolling basis, beginning on or about 7/1. Nonfall registration accepted. Admission may be deferred for a maximum of 1 year. Credit and/or placement offered for CEEB Advanced Placement tests.

COSTS AND FINANCIAL AID

Required **Forms and Deadlines:** FAFSA. **Notification of Awards:** Applicants will be notified of awards on a rolling basis beginning 3/21. **Types of Aid:** *Need-based scholarships/grants:* Federal Pell, SEOG, state scholarships/grants, private scholarships, the school's own gift aid. *Loans:* Subsidized Stafford, Unsubsidized Stafford, PLUS, Federal Perkins, Alternative. **Student Employment:** Federal Work-Study Program available. Institutional employment available. Highest amount earned per year from on-campus jobs $8,435. Off-campus job opportunities are good. **Financial Aid Statistics:** 100% freshmen,

100% undergrads receive need-based scholarship or grant aid. 19% freshmen, 15% undergrads receive non-need-based scholarship or grant aid. 79% freshmen, 84% undergrads receive need-based self-help aid. 99% freshmen, 98% undergrads receive any aid. 81% undergrads borrow to pay for school. Average cumulative indebtedness $27,225. **Criteria for awarding institutional aid:** *Non-need-based:* academics, alumni affiliation, leadership, music/drama, religious affiliation.

WASHBURN UNIVERSITY

1700 SW College Ave, Topeka, KS 66621
Phone: 785-670-1030
E-mail: admissions@washburn.edu
Fax: 785-670-1113 • **Website:** www.washburn.edu

This is a public school.

RATINGS
Admissions Selectivity Rating: 65   **Fire Safety Rating:** 60*   **Green Rating:** 60*

STUDENTS AND FACULTY
Enrollment: 5,626. **Student Body:** 59% female, 41% male, 7% out-of-state.
Retention and Graduation: 67% freshmen return for sophomore year. **Faculty:** Student/faculty ratio 15:1. 265 full-time faculty, 87% hold PhDs, 15% are members of minority groups, 51% are women.

ACADEMICS
Degrees: associate, bachelor's, certificate, first professional, first professional certificate, master's, post-bachelor's certificate. **Classes:** Most classes have 20—29 students. Most lab/discussion sessions have 10—19 students. **Special Study Options:** cooperative education program, cross-registration, distance learning, double major, dual enrollment, English as a Second Language (ESL), honors program, independent study, internships, liberal arts/career combination, student-designed major, study abroad, teacher certification program, Transformational Experience.

FACILITIES
Housing: Coed dorms, fraternity/sorority housing, apartments for single students, Wellness housing Special interest housing.

CAMPUS LIFE
Environment: Activities: Choral groups, concert band, dance, drama/theater, jazz band, literary magazine, marching band, music ensembles, musical theater, pep band, student government, student newspaper, student-run film society, symphony orchestra, television station, yearbook, Campus Ministries, International Student Organization, Model UN.

ADMISSIONS
Freshman Academic Profile: Average high school GPA 3.3. 16% in top 10% of high school class, 37% in top 25% of high school class, 67% in top 50% of high school class. 96% from public high schools. ACT middle 50% range 19-24. Minimum paper TOEFL 450. **Basis for Candidate Selection:** *Very important factors considered include:* academic GPA, rigor of secondary school record, standardized test scores. **Freshman Admission Requirements:** High school diploma is required and GED is accepted. **Freshman Admission Statistics:** 1,916 applied, 96% admitted, 48% enrolled. **Transfer Admission Requirements:** college transcript(s), statement of good standing from prior institution(s). Minimum college GPA of 2.0 required. Lowest grade transferable 1. **General Admission Information:** Application Fee $20. Regular application deadline 8/1. Notification on a rolling basis, beginning on or about 9/1. Nonfall registration accepted. Credit and/or placement offered for CEEB Advanced Placement tests.

COSTS AND FINANCIAL AID
Annual in-state tuition $6,750. Annual out-of-state tuition $15,270. Room and board $6,216. Required fees $86. Average book expense $1,000. **Required Forms and Deadlines:** FAFSA, Admission/Scholarship Application. **Notification of Awards:** Applicants will be notified of awards on a rolling basis beginning 3/15. **Types of Aid:** *Need-based scholarships/grants:* Federal Pell, SEOG, state scholarships/grants, private scholarships, the school's own gift aid. *Loans:* Direct Subsidized Stafford, Direct Unsubsidized Stafford, Direct PLUS, Federal Perkins, college/university loans from institutional funds, Alternative Loans. **Financial Aid Statistics:** 68% freshmen, 66% undergrads receive need-based scholarship or grant aid. 58% freshmen, 44% undergrads receive non-need-based scholarship or grant aid. 84% freshmen, 88% undergrads receive need-based self-help aid. 3% freshmen, 3% undergrads receive athletic scholarships. 59% undergrads borrow to pay for school. Average cumulative indebtedness $17,970. **Criteria for awarding institutional aid:** *Non-need-based:* academ-

ics, alumni affiliation, art, athletics, job skills, leadership, minority status, music/drama, religious affiliation, state/district residency.

WASHINGTON BIBLE COLLEGE

6511 Princess Garden Parkway, Lanham, MD 20706-3599
Phone: 301-552-1400
E-mail: admissions@bible.edu
Fax: 301-552-2775 • **Website:** www.bible.edu • **ACT Code:** 1462

This private school was founded in 1938. It has a 63-acre campus.

RATINGS
Admissions Selectivity Rating: 63   **Fire Safety Rating:** 60*   **Green Rating:** 60*

STUDENTS AND FACULTY
Enrollment: 352. **Student Body:** 42% female, 58% male.
Retention and Graduation: 10% freshmen graduate within 4 years. 60% freshmen graduate within 6 years. **Faculty:** 70% of classes are taught by teaching assistants.

ACADEMICS
Degrees: associate, bachelor's, certificate. **Special Study Options:** English as a Second Language (ESL), independent study, internships. **Career Services:** alumni services.

FACILITIES
Housing: men's dorms, women's dorms, apartments for married students. 60% of campus accessible to physically disabled.

CAMPUS LIFE
Environment: Village. **Activities:** Choral groups, music ensembles, student government, yearbook 1 honor societies. **Athletics (Intercollegiate):** *Men:* basketball, soccer. *Women:* basketball, cheerleading, volleyball.

ADMISSIONS
Freshman Academic Profile: Minimum paper TOEFL 550. **Basis for Candidate Selection:** *Very important factors considered include:* application essay, recommendation(s), religious affiliation/commitment. *Important factors considered include:* Class rank, rigor of secondary school record, standardized test scores, character/personal qualities. *Other factors considered include:* alumni/ae relation, extracurricular activities, interview, talent/ability, volunteer work. **Freshman Admission Requirements:** High school diploma is required and GED is accepted. **Freshman Admission Statistics:** 56 applied, 29% admitted. **Transfer Admission Requirements:** college transcript(s), essay or personal statement, statement of good standing from prior institution(s). Minimum college GPA of 2.0 required. Lowest grade transferable C. **General Admission Information:** Application Fee $25. Regular application deadline 8/1. Nonfall registration accepted. Admission may be deferred for a maximum of 36.

COSTS AND FINANCIAL AID
Annual tuition $10,140. Room and board $4,180. Required fees $100. Average book expense $300. **Required Forms and Deadlines:** FAFSA, institution's own financial aid formV. **Notification of Awards:** Applicants will be notified of awards on a rolling basis beginning 1/30. **Types of Aid:** *Need-based scholarships/grants:* Federal Pell, SEOG, state scholarships/grants, private scholarships, the school's own gift aid. *Loans:* Subsidized Stafford, Unsubsidized Stafford, PLUS. **Student Employment:** Federal Work-Study Program available. Institutional employment available. Highest amount earned per year from on-campus jobs $3,000. Off-campus job opportunities are excellent. **Financial Aid Statistics:** 38% freshmen, 17% undergrads receive need-based scholarship or grant aid. 20% freshmen, 6% undergrads receive non-need-based scholarship or grant aid. 80% freshmen, 100% undergrads receive need-based self-help aid. 20% undergrads borrow to pay for school. Average cumulative indebtedness $13,000. **Criteria for awarding institutional aid:** *Non-need-based:* academics, leadership, minority status, music/drama.

WASHINGTON COLLEGE

300 Washington Avenue, Chestertown, MD 21620
Phone: 410-778-7700 • **Financial Aid Phone:** 410-778-7214
E-mail: adm.off@washcoll.edu • **CEEB Code:** 5888
Fax: 410-778-7287 • **Website:** www.washcoll.edu • **ACT Code:** 1754

This private school was founded in 1782. It has a 144-acre campus.

RATINGS
Admissions Selectivity Rating: 85   **Fire Safety Rating:** 97   **Green Rating:** 63

STUDENTS AND FACULTY
Enrollment: 1,458. **Student Body:** 58% female, 42% male, 49% out-of-state, 4% international (30 countries represented). Asian 2%, African American 3%, Caucasian 82%, Hispanic 4%, Native American 0%
Retention and Graduation: 85% freshmen return for sophomore year. 66% freshmen graduate within 4 years. 50% grads go on to further study within 1 year. 12% grads pursue arts and sciences degrees. 4% grads pursue law degrees. 8% grads pursue business degrees. 3% grads pursue medical degrees. **Faculty:** Student/faculty ratio 12:1. 91 full-time faculty, 93% hold PhDs, 12% are members of minority groups, 41% are women. 0% of classes are taught by teaching assistants.

ACADEMICS
Degrees: bachelor's, master's. **Classes:** Most classes have 10—19 students. Most lab/discussion sessions have fewer than 10 students. **Majors with Highest Enrollment:** business administration and management; English language and literature; psychology. **Special Study Options:** cross-registration, double major, dual enrollment, exchange student program (domestic), honors program, independent study, internships, liberal arts/career combination, student-designed major, study abroad, teacher certification program. **Honors Programs:** The Douglass Cater Society of Junior Fellows is the College's flagship academic enrichment program--one that rewards creativity, initiative and intellectual curiosity with competitive grants to support self-directed undergraduate research and scholarship anywhere in the world. The intent is to bring together the best and brightest in what founder Douglass Cater called "a companionship of learning." **Combined Degree Programs:** 3+2 nursing. **Career Services:** Alumni network, alumni services, career assessment, internships, regional alumni. Career services highlights include The Washington Center has over 35,000 alumni, many of whom are leaders in numerous professions and nations around the world. Based in the nation's capitol it offers exceptional experiential learning opportunities in various government and public service sectors.

FACILITIES
Housing: Coed dorms, special housing for disabled students, men's dorms, special housing for international students, women's dorms, fraternity/sorority housing, wellness housing, theme housing. 90% of campus accessible to physically disabled. **Special Academic Facilities/Equipment:** Language lab, computer classroom, C.V. Starr Center for the Study of the American Experience, The Center for the Environment and Society, O'Neil Literary House **Computers:** Administrative functions (other than registration) can be performed online.

CAMPUS LIFE
Environment: Rural. **Activities:** Choral groups, concert band, dance, drama/theater, jazz band, literary magazine, music ensembles, radio station, student government, student newspaper, yearbook, Campus Ministries, International Student Organization, Model UN 50 registered organizations, 13 honor societies, 4 religious organizations. 4 fraternities, 3 sororities. **Athletics (Intercollegiate):** *Men:* baseball, basketball, crew/rowing, lacrosse, sailing, soccer, swimming, tennis. *Women:* basketball, crew/rowing, field hockey, lacrosse, sailing, soccer, softball, swimming, tennis, volleyball. **On-Campus Highlights:** Miller Library, Johnson Lifetime Fitness Center, Gibson Center for the Arts, O'Neill Literary House, Hodson Commons Student Center, Hynson Pavillion and Washington College Boathouse providing water access and kayaks, sail boats, pantoons, canoes, motor boats, wakeboarding boats, etc. **Environmental Initiatives:** George Goes Green (G3) is Washington College's initiative for stewardship and sustainability. Situated on Maryland's Eastern Shore, the College is surrounded by the coastal and inland waters of the Chesapeake Bay, which informs our sense of history, our sense of self, and our sense of place. Our benefactor George Washington promoted sustainable economic cycles by advocating compost as a method to amend damaged soils. Today, Washington College is nationally renowned for promoting sustainability. Green at a Glance: Chesapeake Semester composting recycling environmentally-friendly products

local foods native plant landscaping green facilities Recycling is now available in every building on campus. On campus, we recycle plastic and glass bottles, aluminum and tin cans, cardboard, and most types of paper. In the academic buildings, bottles and cans can be recycled in the blue bins, while paper can be recycled in the tall green bins or the locked blue paper bins where they are available. Student Environmental Alliance: The Washington College Student Environmental Alliance (SEA) is a student-run organization on campus. It promotes sustainability on campus and within the community, and works with various outside organizations to help promote sustainable practices. SEA welcomes all majors and disciplines to join at weekly meetings and events. SEA primarily focuses on: Promoting awareness of local, national, and international environmental issues and concerns Environmental education Keeping a record of accomplishments to provide for future SEA generations Providing a group that fosters personal environmental well-being Positively impacting the Washington College, Chestertown, and outside communities through its environmental initiatives

ADMISSIONS
Freshman Academic Profile: Average high school GPA 3.5. 35% in top 10% of high school class, 65% in top 25% of high school class, 90% in top 50% of high school class. 68% from public high schools. SAT Math middle 50% range 530-620. SAT Critical Reading middle 50% range 540-630. SAT Writing middle 50% range 520-620. ACT middle 50% range 23-27. **Basis for Candidate Selection:** *Very important factors considered include:* academic GPA, rigor of secondary school record, interview. *Important factors considered include:* Class rank, standardized test scores, level of applicant's interest, work experience. *Other factors considered include:* application essay, recommendation(s), alumni/ae relation, character/personal qualities, extracurricular activities, first generation, geographical residence, racial/ethnic status, state residency, talent/ability, volunteer work. **Freshman Admission Requirements:** High school diploma is required and GED is accepted. *Academic units required:* 4 English, 3 mathematics, 3 science, (2 science labs), 2 foreign language, 2 social studies, 2 history. *Academic units recommended:* 4 English, 3 mathematics, 3 science, (2 science labs), 2 foreign language, 2 social studies, 2 history. **Freshman Admission Statistics:** 4,484 applied, 66% admitted, 13% enrolled. **Transfer Admission Requirements:** High school transcript, college transcript(s), essay or personal statement, statement of good standing from prior institution(s). **General Admission Information:** Application Fee $55. Early decision application deadline 11/1. Regular application deadline 3/1. Notification on a rolling basis, beginning on or about 10/15. Nonfall registration accepted. Admission may be deferred for a maximum of 0ne year. Credit and/or placement offered for CEEB Advanced Placement tests.

COSTS AND FINANCIAL AID
Annual tuition $39,208. Room and board $8,824. Required fees $736. Average book expense $1,250. **Required Forms and Deadlines:** FAFSA, institution's own financial aid form. **Notification of Awards:** Applicants will be notified of awards on a rolling basis beginning 2/15. **Types of Aid:** *Need-based scholarships/grants:* Federal Pell, SEOG, state scholarships/grants, private scholarships, the school's own gift aid. *Loans:* Subsidized Stafford, Unsubsidized Stafford, PLUS, Federal Perkins. **Student Employment:** Federal Work-Study Program available. Institutional employment available. Highest amount earned per year from on-campus jobs $2,000. Off-campus job opportunities are good. **Financial Aid Statistics:** 100% freshmen, 98% undergrads receive need-based scholarship or grant aid. 32% freshmen, 17% undergrads receive non-need-based scholarship or grant aid. 86% freshmen, 87% undergrads receive need-based self-help aid. 94% freshmen, 88% undergrads receive any aid. 66% undergrads borrow to pay for school. Average cumulative indebtedness $34,208. **Criteria for awarding institutional aid:** *Non-need-based:* academics.

See page 1292.

WASHINGTON & JEFFERSON COLLEGE

Best 378

60 South Lincoln Street, Washington, PA 15301
Phone: 724-223-6025 • **Financial Aid Phone:** 724-223-6019
E-mail: admission@washjeff.edu • **CEEB Code:** 2967
Fax: 724-223-6534 • **Website:** www.washjeff.edu • **ACT Code:** 3746

This private school was founded in 1781. It has a 60-acre campus.

RATINGS
Admissions Selectivity Rating: 92   **Fire Safety Rating:** 84   **Green Rating:** 81

STUDENTS AND FACULTY
Enrollment: 1,394. **Student Body:** 51% female, 49% male, 27% out-of-state, 1% international (19 countries represented). Asian 2%, African American 3%, Caucasian 83%, Hispanic 3%, Native American 1%
Retention and Graduation: 70% freshmen graduate within 4 years. 35% grads go on to further study within 1 year. 19% grads pursue arts and sciences degrees. 14% grads pursue law degrees. 8% grads pursue medical degrees. **Faculty:** Student/faculty ratio 11:1. 113 full-time faculty, 91% hold PhDs, 13% are members of minority groups, 44% are women. 0% of classes are taught by teaching assistants.

ACADEMICS
Degrees: bachelor's. **Classes:** Most classes have 10—19 students. Most lab/discussion sessions have 10—19 students. **Majors with Highest Enrollment:** accounting; business/commerce; psychology. **Special Study Options:** Accelerated program, double major, dual enrollment, honors program, independent study, internships, student-designed major, study abroad, teacher certification program, Advanced placement credit. **Combined Degree Programs:** BA/MD, BA/JD, BA/MEng, 3/3 law, 3/4 podiatry, 3/4 optometry. **Disability Services:** Special programs offered to physically disabled students include tutors. Career Services: Alumni network, alumni services, career/job search classes, career assessment, internships, regional alumni. Career services highlights include While we are proud of many programs, we especially appreciate the support of the alumni of the college, particularly with hosting interns. Many of these experiences result in full time employment.

FACILITIES
Housing: Coed dorms, special housing for disabled students, men's dorms, women's dorms, fraternity/sorority housing, apartments for single students, wellness housing, theme housing, on-campus suites. 48% of campus accessible to physically disabled. **Special Academic Facilities/Equipment:** Microplate Reader, Cell Culture Labs, Isolator Lab, X-Ray Diffraction Unit, Neuropsychology Lab, Atomic Absorption Unit, Nuclear Magnetic Resonance (NMR) Lab, Refrigerated Centrifuge, Global Learning Unit, Language Lab, Spectrometers, Laser Scanning Confocal Microscope Facility, Abernathy Field Station **Computers:** 100% of classrooms, 100% of dorms, 100% of libraries, 100% of dining areas, 100% of student union, 95% of common outdoor areas have wireless network access. Students can register for classes online. Administrative functions (other than registration) can be performed online.

CAMPUS LIFE
Environment: Village. **Activities:** Choral groups, concert band, dance, drama/theater, jazz band, literary magazine, music ensembles, musical theater, pep band, radio station, student government, student newspaper, student-run film society, symphony orchestra, yearbook, Campus Ministries, International Student Organization, Model UN 94 registered organizations, 21 honor societies, 4 religious organizations. 6 fraternities, 4 sororities. **Athletics (Intercollegiate):** *Men:* baseball, basketball, cheerleading, cross-country, diving, football, golf, lacrosse, soccer, swimming, tennis, track/field (outdoor), track/field (indoor), water polo, wrestling. *Women:* basketball, cheerleading, cross-country, diving, field hockey, golf, lacrosse, soccer, softball, swimming, tennis, track/field (outdoor), track/field (indoor), volleyball, water polo. **On-Campus Highlights:** The Hub (Student Center), Swanson Wellness Center, Monticellos Coffee House, Burnett (for meetings/studying), Ski Lodge/Barista in the Commons. **Environmental Initiatives:** American College & University Presidents' Climate Commitment Silver LEED Certification for new Science building Food service sustainability initiatives. Food service at W&J purchases 20% of their products locally, recycles fryer grease into bio-diesel fuel and uses it in their delivery trucks, became trayless, recycles all of their cardboard, and uses bio-degradable to go packaging, recycled paper, napkins made from recycled materials, and paper cups.

ADMISSIONS
Freshman Academic Profile: Average high school GPA 3.3. 32% in top 10% of high school class, 57% in top 25% of high school class, 91% in top 50% of high school class. 83% from public high schools. SAT Math middle 50% range 520-620. SAT Critical Reading middle 50% range 520-610. ACT middle 50% range 23-28. Minimum web-based TOEFL 90. Minimum paper TOEFL 577. **Basis for Candidate Selection:** *Very important factors considered include:* Class rank, application essay, academic GPA, recommendation(s), rigor of secondary school record, character/personal qualities, interview. *Important factors considered include:* standardized test scores, extracurricular activities. *Other factors considered include:* alumni/ae relation, geographical residence, level of applicant's interest, racial/ethnic status, state residency, talent/ability, volunteer work, work experience. **Freshman Admission Requirements:** High school diploma is required and GED is accepted. *Academic units required:* 3 English, 3 mathematics, 2 foreign language, 1 history, 6 Six or more academic courses from English, Mathematics, Foreign Language, History (Social or Natural. 3 English, 3 mathematics, 2 foreign language, 1 history, 6 Six or more academic courses from English, Mathematics, Foreign Language, History (Social or Natural **Freshman Admission Statistics:** 6,504 applied, 41% admitted, 14% enrolled. **Transfer Admission Requirements:** High school transcript, college transcript(s), essay or personal statement, standardized test scores, statement of good standing from prior institution(s). Minimum college GPA of 2.50 required. Lowest grade transferable C. **General Admission Information:** Application Fee $25. Early decision application deadline 12/1. Regular application deadline 3/1. Notification on a rolling basis, beginning on or about 10/1. Nonfall registration accepted. Admission may be deferred for a maximum of 1 Year. Credit and/or placement offered for CEEB Advanced Placement tests.

COSTS AND FINANCIAL AID
Annual tuition $37,850. Room and board $10,162. Required fees $460. Average book expense $800. **Required Forms and Deadlines:** FAFSA. **Notification of Awards:** Applicants will be notified of awards on a rolling basis beginning 3/1. **Types of Aid:** *Need-based scholarships/grants:* Federal Pell, SEOG, state scholarships/grants, private scholarships, the school's own gift aid, ACG and SMART Grants. *Loans:* Subsidized Stafford, Unsubsidized Stafford, PLUS, Federal Perkins, college/university loans from institutional funds. **Student Employment:** Federal Work-Study Program available. Institutional employment available. Highest amount earned per year from on-campus jobs $3,440. Off-campus job opportunities are good. **Financial Aid Statistics:** 86% freshmen, 85% undergrads receive need-based scholarship or grant aid. 96% freshmen, 87% undergrads receive non-need-based scholarship or grant aid. 91% freshmen, 90% undergrads receive need-based self-help aid. 99% freshmen, 98% undergrads receive any aid. 70% undergrads borrow to pay for school. **Criteria for awarding institutional aid:** *Non-need-based:* academics, alumni affiliation.

WASHINGTON AND LEE UNIVERSITY

Letcher Avenue, Lexington, VA 24450-0303
Phone: 540-458-8710
E-mail: admissions@wlu.edu • **CEEB Code:** 5887
Fax: 540-458-8062 • **Website:** www2.wlu.edu • **ACT Code:** 4430

This private school was founded in 1749. It has a 322-acre campus.

RATINGS
Admissions Selectivity Rating: 97   **Fire Safety Rating:** 60*   **Green Rating:** 60*

STUDENTS AND FACULTY
Enrollment: 1,747. **Student Body:** 49% female, 51% male, 85% out-of-state, 4% international (47 countries represented). Asian 3%, African American 4%, Caucasian 86%, Hispanic 1%, Native American 0%
Retention and Graduation: 94% freshmen return for sophomore year. 84% freshmen graduate within 4 years. 86% freshmen graduate within 6 years. 24% grads go on to further study within 1 year. 6% grads pursue arts and sciences degrees. 9% grads pursue law degrees. 1% grads pursue business degrees. 5% grads pursue medical degrees. **Faculty:** Student/faculty ratio 10:1. 215 full-time faculty, 94% hold PhDs, 7% are members of minority groups, 30% are women. 0% of classes are taught by teaching assistants.

ACADEMICS
Degrees: bachelor's, first professional, master's. **Classes:** Most classes have 10—19 students. Most lab/discussion sessions have fewer than 10 students. **Majors with Highest Enrollment:** business/commerce; economics; history. **Special Study Options:** double major, exchange student program (domestic), honors program, independent study, internships, liberal arts/career combination, student-designed major, study abroad, teacher certification program. **Honors Programs:** University Scholars, Bonner Scholars **Combined Degree**

Programs: BA/JD, 3-3 JD with Washington and Lee School of Law. **Career Services:** Alumni network, career/job search classes, career assessment, internships, regional alumni.

FACILITIES

Housing: Coed dorms, special housing for international students, fraternity/sorority housing, apartments for single students, Outing Club House, Spanish House, Chavis House. 80% of campus accessible to physically disabled. **Special Academic Facilities/Equipment:** History and porcelain museums performing arts center communications labs nuclear science lab scanning electron microscope **Computers:** Students can register for classes online. Administrative functions (other than registration) can be performed online.

CAMPUS LIFE

Environment: Village. **Activities:** Choral groups, dance, drama/theater, jazz band, literary magazine, music ensembles, radio station, student government, student newspaper, student-run film society, symphony orchestra, television station, yearbook 90 registered organizations, 5 honor societies, 11 religious organizations. 14 fraternities, 5 sororities. **Athletics (Intercollegiate):** *Men:* baseball, basketball, cross-country, equestrian sports, football, golf, lacrosse, soccer, swimming, tennis, track/field (outdoor), track/field (indoor), wrestling. *Women:* basketball, cheerleading, cross-country, equestrian sports, field hockey, lacrosse, soccer, swimming, tennis, track/field (outdoor), track/field (indoor), volleyball. **On-Campus Highlights:** Lee Chapel, Elrod University Commons, Lenfest Center for the Arts, Doremus Fitness Center, Reeves Center and Watson Pavillion.

ADMISSIONS

Freshman Academic Profile: 81% in top 10% of high school class, 98% in top 25% of high school class, 100% in top 50% of high school class. SAT Math middle 50% range 650-730. SAT Critical Reading middle 50% range 660-730. ACT middle 50% range 28-31. **Basis for Candidate Selection:** *Very important factors considered include:* Class rank, rigor of secondary school record, standardized test scores, character/personal qualities, extracurricular activities. *Important factors considered include:* recommendation(s), interview. *Other factors considered include:* application essay, alumni/ae relation, geographical residence, racial/ethnic status, state residency, talent/ability, volunteer work, work experience. **Freshman Admission Requirements:** High school diploma or equivalent is not required. *Academic units required:* 4 English, 3 mathematics, 1 science, (1 science labs), 3 foreign language, 1 social studies, 1 history, 4 academic electives. *Academic units recommended:* 4 English, 3 mathematics, 1 science, (1 science labs), 3 foreign language, 1 social studies, 1 history, 4 academic electives. **Freshman Admission Statistics:** 4,215 applied, 27% admitted, 39% enrolled. **Transfer Admission Requirements:** High school transcript, college transcript(s), essay or personal statement, standardized test scores, statement of good standing from prior institution(s). Minimum college GPA of 2.0 required. Lowest grade transferable C. **General Admission Information:** Application Fee $50. Early decision application deadline 11/15. Regular application deadline 1/15. Regular notification 4/1. Nonfall registration not accepted. Admission may be deferred for a maximum of 1 year. Credit and/or placement offered for CEEB Advanced Placement tests.

COSTS AND FINANCIAL AID

Annual tuition $27,960. Room and board $7,225. Required fees $675. Average book expense $1,500. **Required Forms and Deadlines:** FAFSA, CSS/Financial Aid PROFILE, noncustodial PROFILE, business/farm supplement. **Notification of Awards:** Applicants will be notified of awards on or about 4/6. **Types of Aid:** *Need-based scholarships/grants:* Federal Pell, SEOG, state scholarships/grants, private scholarships, the school's own gift aid. *Loans:* Subsidized Stafford, Unsubsidized Stafford, PLUS, Federal Perkins, college/university loans from institutional funds. **Student Employment:** Federal Work-Study Program available. Institutional employment available. Off-campus job opportunities are fair. **Financial Aid Statistics:** 84% freshmen, 80% undergrads receive need-based scholarship or grant aid. 27% freshmen, 31% undergrads receive non-need-based scholarship or grant aid. 36% freshmen, 42% undergrads receive need-based self-help aid. 25% undergrads borrow to pay for school. Average cumulative indebtedness $17,105. **Criteria for awarding institutional aid:** *Non-need-based:* academics.

WASHINGTON STATE UNIVERSITY

PO Box 641067, Pullman, WA 99164-1067
Phone: 509-335-5586 • **Financial Aid Phone:** 509-335-9711
E-mail: admiss2@wsu.edu • **CEEB Code:** 4705
Fax: 509-335-4902 • **Website:** www.wsu.edu • **ACT Code:** 4482

This public school was founded in 1890. It has a 1745-acre campus.

RATINGS

Admissions Selectivity Rating: 73   **Fire Safety Rating:** 85   **Green Rating:** 92

STUDENTS AND FACULTY

Enrollment: 22,814. **Student Body:** 50% female, 50% male, 7% out-of-state, 4% international (96 countries represented). Asian 5%, African American 3%, Caucasian 68%, Hispanic 9%, Native American 1%
Retention and Graduation: 82% freshmen return for sophomore year. 39% freshmen graduate within 4 years. 67% freshmen graduate within 6 years. 22% grads go on to further study within 1 year. **Faculty:** Student/faculty ratio 15:1. 1224 full-time faculty, 89% hold PhDs, 15% are members of minority groups, 38% are women. 8% of classes are taught by teaching assistants.

ACADEMICS

Degrees: bachelor's, certificate, master's, post-bachelor's certificate, post-master's certificate. **Classes:** Most classes have 20—29 students. **Majors with Highest Enrollment:** business administration and management; communication, journalism, and related programs, other; social sciences. **Special Study Options:** Accelerated program, cooperative education program, cross-registration, distance learning, double major, dual enrollment, English as a Second Language (ESL), exchange student program (domestic), external degree program, honors program, independent study, internships, liberal arts/career combination, student-designed major, study abroad, teacher certification program. **Honors Programs:** Now in its fiftieth year, the Honors College is one of the oldest and most highly regarded public university honors colleges in the country. It attracts top students in all majors from throughout the United States and around the world. The Honors College curriculum emphasizes global awareness and international impact. It immerses students in the study of international issues, builds their proficiency in a second language, and encourages them to study abroad. Instead of lecturing, professors teach courses interactively, inspiring discussions among students. Honors students conduct research as undergraduates, exploring an academic question of importance to them, documenting their analysis and conclusions, and orally presenting their work to faculty. The Honors College deepens students' intellectual curiosity and builds a lifelong love of learning, as well as skills in critical thinking, writing, public presentation, and information literacy. Graduates emerge with the tools required to become leaders in their fields. **Disability Services:** Special programs offered to physically disabled students include note-taking services, reader services, tape recorders, tutors. **Career Services:** Alumni network, alumni services, career/job search classes, career assessment, internships Career services highlights include Experiential Learning opportunities and Internships. The Internship Program at The Center for Advising and Career Development provides comprehensive career counseling and services to help students integrate educational experiences with internships in the government, business, industry and non-profit sectors. The program is free for participants. The program is also a resource to WSU faculty, staff and employers. It provides faculty/staff assistance regarding internship concerns and issues. The program assists employers with creating internship programs, recruiting for interns, and connecting with faculty/staff and students. On average, 1600 students participate in internships per academic year.

FACILITIES

Housing: Coed dorms, special housing for disabled students, men's dorms, special housing for international students, women's dorms, fraternity/sorority housing, apartments for married students, apartments for single students, wellness housing, theme housing, freshman focus-living/learning communities. 90% of campus accessible to physically disabled. **Special Academic Facilities/Equipment:** Anthropology museum; arboretum; art museum; audio labs; bear research center; beef center; behavioral lab; cadaver anatomy laboratory; child development laboratory; composite materials and engineering center; creamery, culinary lab and teaching kitchen; dairy center; ecological reserve; electronic piano/music computer lab; electronic trading room; engineering and teaching research laboratory; feed preparation laboratory; food sensory evaluation laboratory; geological collections; greenhouses; historic textiles and costume collection; horticultural orchard and organic farm; entomological collection; natural history museum; observatory; oil and gas processing laboratory; planetarium;

       The Princeton Review's Complete Book of Colleges

herbarium and mycological herbarium; soil monolith collection; veterinary anatomy teaching museum; laboratory for atmospheric research; laboratory for biotechnology and bioanalysis; electron microscopy center; environmental research center; geoanalytical laboratory; music listening library; music recording studio; nuclear radiation center; planetarium; public and student-run television stations; student-run radio stations; social and economic sciences research center; state of Washington water research center; center for spectroscopy; speech and hearing clinic; center for teaching, learning and technology; TV production studios and editing suites; vet teaching hospital; vertebrate zoology museum **Computers:** 100% of classrooms, 100% of dorms, 100% of libraries, 100% of dining areas, 100% of student union, 25% of common outdoor areas have wireless network access. Students can register for classes online. Administrative functions (other than registration) can be performed online.

CAMPUS LIFE

Environment: Town. **Activities:** Choral groups, concert band, dance, drama/ theater, jazz band, literary magazine, marching band, music ensembles, musical theater, opera, pep band, radio station, student government, student newspaper, student-run film society, symphony orchestra, television station, yearbook, Campus Ministries, International Student Organization, Model UN 300 registered organizations, 36 honor societies, 19 religious organizations. 26 fraternities, 13 sororities. **Athletics (Intercollegiate):** *Men:* baseball, basketball, cross-country, football, golf, track/field (outdoor). *Women:* basketball, crew/rowing, cross-country, golf, soccer, swimming, tennis, track/field (outdoor), volleyball. **On-Campus Highlights:** Compton Union Building (CUB), Terrell Friendship Mall, Student Recreation Center, Beasley Performing Arts Coliseum, Martin Stadium, The newly renovated CUB stands at the heart of student leadership, engagement, and culture on campus. It is home to offices for student government and many student services. The building houses a selection of food vendors, the campus bookstore, banks, and a post office. Both wired and wireless Internet services serve students and faculty. Ballrooms, meeting rooms, and a surround-sound auditorium host a variety of events. A passage through the CUB gives students 24-hour access to the library. The whole student body comes together on Glenn Terrell Friendship Mall. Located at the heart of campus, the Mall is where culture, ideas, and lively dialogue are exchanged daily. It is the site of many outdoor events, including frequent live performances by student musicians. Students gather here as they walk to and from the library, the Compton Union Building (student union), and academic buildings, often staking out favorite spots to talk, relax, study, or catch a bite to eat. The 160,000-square-foot Student Recreation Center features the largest student weight and cardio center in the country; basketball and volleyball courts, indoor soccer, a four-lane indoor track, racquetball and squash courts, roller hockey, badminton, and much more. Swimmers enjoy the five-lane lap pool, leisure pool, and 53-person spa. Big crowds pack Beasley Performing Arts Coliseum for Pac-10 Cougar men's and women's basketball games and for big name entertainment for Dad's and Mom's Weekends. WSU students turn out for entertainment ranging from pop music concerts to ballet to wresting. Located in the center of campus, Martin Stadium is home to the Pac-10 Cougars. 2008 stadium renovations include a north-side concourse, additional concession and restroom areas, and a state-of-the-art scoreboard. Still to come are the addition of more seats and premium seating, slated for completion by fall of 2012. **Environmental Initiatives:** Sustainability & Environment Committee, established by the President of WSU. Meets monthly and has campus-wide representation. Greenhouse Gas Inventory for the Pullman campus Ongoing Environmental Management System Implementation.

ADMISSIONS

Freshman Academic Profile: Average high school GPA 3.3. 26% in top 10% of high school class, 46% in top 25% of high school class, 78% in top 50% of high school class. 99% from public high schools. SAT Math middle 50% range 470-600. SAT Critical Reading middle 50% range 460-570. SAT Writing middle 50% range 450-550. ACT middle 50% range 20-25. Minimum web-based TOEFL 68. Minimum paper TOEFL 520. **Basis for Candidate Selection:** *Very important factors considered include:* academic GPA, standardized test scores. *Important factors considered include:* Class rank, application essay, rigor of secondary school record. *Other factors considered include:* recommendation(s), character/personal qualities, extracurricular activities, talent/ability, volunteer work, work experience. **Freshman Admission Requirements:** High school diploma is required and GED is accepted. *Academic units required:* 4 English, 3 mathematics, 2 science, (3 science labs), 1 One unit of fine, visual, or performing arts, or one additional unit of academic elective. *Academic units recommended:* 4 English, 3 mathematics, 2 science, (3 science labs), 1 One unit of fine, visual, or performing arts, or one additional unit of academic elective. **Freshman Admission Statistics:** 14,825 applied, 76% admitted, 39% enrolled. **Transfer Admission Requirements:** college transcript(s), Minimum college GPA of 2.5 required. Lowest grade transferable D. **General Admission Information:** Application Fee $50. Notification on a rolling basis, beginning on or about 11/1. Nonfall registration accepted. Credit offered for CEEB Advanced Placement tests.

COSTS AND FINANCIAL AID

Annual in-state tuition $10,874. Annual out-of-state tuition $23,966. Room and board $10,524. Required fees $1,426. Required **Forms and Deadlines:** FAFSA. **Notification of Awards:** Applicants will be notified of awards on a rolling basis beginning 4/15. **Types of Aid:** *Need-based scholarships/grants:* Federal Pell, SEOG, state scholarships/grants, private scholarships, the school's own gift aid, United Negro College Fund, Federal Nursing Scholarships. *Loans:* Subsidized Stafford, Unsubsidized Stafford, PLUS, Federal Perkins, Federal Nursing. **Student Employment:** Federal Work-Study Program available. Institutional employment available. Highest amount earned per year from on-campus jobs $8,517. Off-campus job opportunities are good. **Financial Aid Statistics:** 63% freshmen, 65% undergrads receive need-based scholarship or grant aid. 56% freshmen, 36% undergrads receive non-need-based scholarship or grant aid. 80% freshmen, 84% undergrads receive need-based self-help aid. 1% freshmen, 2% undergrads receive athletic scholarships. 79% freshmen, 67% undergrads receive any aid. 57% undergrads borrow to pay for school. Average cumulative indebtedness $23,433. **Criteria for awarding institutional aid:** *Non-need-based:* academics, alumni affiliation, art, athletics, job skills, leadership, minority status, music/drama, religious affiliation, state/district residency.

WASHINGTON UNIVERSITY IN ST. LOUIS

Campus Box 1089, St. Louis, MO 63130-4899
Phone: 314-935-6000 • **Financial Aid Phone:** 888-547-6670
E-mail: admissions@wustl.edu • **CEEB Code:** 6929
Fax: 314-935-4290 • **Website:** wustl.edu • **ACT Code:** 2386

This private school was founded in 1853. It has a 169-acre campus.

RATINGS

Admissions Selectivity Rating: 99   Fire Safety Rating: 91   Green Rating: 96

STUDENTS AND FACULTY

Enrollment: 6,702. **Student Body:** 51% female, 49% male, 93% out-of-state, 7% international (90 countries represented). Asian 17%, African American 6%, Caucasian 56%, Hispanic 5%, Native American 0%. **Retention and Graduation:** 96% freshmen return for sophomore year. 88% freshmen graduate within 4 years. 94% freshmen graduate within 6 years. 33% grads go on to further study within 1 year. **Faculty:** Student/faculty ratio 7:1. 953 full-time faculty, 97% hold PhDs, 37% are women.

ACADEMICS

Degrees: bachelor's, certificate, doctoral, master's, post-bachelor's certificate, post-master's certificate. **Classes:** Most classes have fewer than 10 students. Most lab/discussion sessions have 10—19 students. **Majors with Highest Enrollment:** biology/biological sciences; finance; psychology. **Special Study Options:** Accelerated program, cooperative education program, cross-registration, double major, dual enrollment, English as a Second Language (ESL), exchange student program (domestic), independent study, internships, liberal arts/career combination, student-designed major, study abroad, teacher certification program, The University Scholars Program at Washington University gives selected students the opportunity to be admitted to undergraduate study and a graduate program at the same time. **Combined Degree Programs:** BA/MA, BA/MEng, 5 year BA/BFA 3/2 AB/MSOT. **Disability Services:** Special programs offered to physically disabled students include note-taking services, reader services, tape recorders, tutors. **Career Services:** Alumni network, alumni services, career/job search classes, career assessment, internships, regional alumni. Career services highlights include Opportunities are provided for cooperative education programs in Engineering. Internships are available in most areas including business, communications, social service, and many others. Internships and study abroad are available in numerous foreign countries.

FACILITIES

Housing: Coed dorms, fraternity/sorority housing, apartments for married students, cooperative housing, apartments for single students, wellness housing, special interest suites, upper-class housing, single sex floors in coed buildings, on-campus transfer-specific housing, and small-group housing for students who share common interests and goals. 95% of campus accessible to physically disabled. **Special Academic Facilities/Equipment:** Art gallery, business/economics experimental lab, botanical garden, NASA planetary imaging facility, TAP reactor system, triple monochromator, Computer Automated Radioactive Particle Tracking and gamma ray Computed Tomography, Observatory, EADS learning center, Student Enterprise Zone, Edison Theatre, lab science building, outdoor Tyson Research Center. **Computers:** Students can register for classes online. Administrative functions (other than registration) can be performed online.

CAMPUS LIFE

Environment: City. **Activities:** Choral groups, concert band, dance, drama/theater, jazz band, literary magazine, music ensembles, musical theater, opera, pep band, radio station, student government, student newspaper, student-run film society, symphony orchestra, television station, Campus Ministries, International Student Organization, Model UN 200 registered organizations, 18 honor societies, 19 religious organizations. 12 fraternities, 6 sororities. **Athletics (Intercollegiate):** *Men:* baseball, basketball, cross-country, diving, football, soccer, swimming, tennis, track/field (outdoor), track/field (indoor). *Women:* basketball, cross-country, diving, golf, soccer, softball, swimming, tennis, track/field (outdoor), track/field (indoor), volleyball. **On-Campus Highlights:** Gallery of Art, Edison Theatre, Ursa's Cafe, Francis Gymnasium and Francis Field, Residence Halls. **Environmental Initiatives:** Washington University banned the sale of bottled water on campus beginning January 1, 2009, and was the first North American university to have done so. This includes vending machines and campus dining locations. Washington University has a strong commitment to green building, having constructed 16 buildings to LEED specifications, of which 14 have been certified and 2 are awaiting certification. The majority of the projects have been rated at the Gold level. In addition, Washington University constructed the world's first Living Building in 2009, designed to meet the stringent energy and environmental design specifications of the Living Building Challenge, authored by the International Living Building Institute. It received formal designation as a Living Building following its certification in spring 2011. The 2010 Strategic Plan for Environmentally Sustainable Operations, our guiding document for sustainability, outlined the $46 million that the university has committed over the next 10 years to reducing our carbon footprint through energy efficiency improvements on campus. This represents a substantial investment for the university and a major focus of our administration. You can find details of it at http://sustain.wustl.edu

ADMISSIONS

Freshman Academic Profile: 96% in top 10% of high school class, 100% in top 25% of high school class, 100% in top 50% of high school class. 57% from public high schools. SAT Math middle 50% range 720-790. SAT Critical Reading middle 50% range 700-770. SAT Writing middle 50% range 690-780. ACT middle 50% range 32-34. **Basis for Candidate Selection:** *Very important factors considered include:* Class rank, application essay, academic GPA, recommendation(s), rigor of secondary school record, standardized test scores, character/personal qualities, extracurricular activities, talent/ability, volunteer work, work experience. *Other factors considered include:* alumni/ae relation, first generation, interview, level of applicant's interest, racial/ethnic status. **Freshman Admission Requirements:** High school diploma is required and GED is accepted. **Freshman Admission Statistics:** 27,265 applied, 18% admitted, 34% enrolled. **Transfer Admission Requirements:** college transcript(s), essay or personal statement, statement of good standing from prior institution(s). Lowest grade transferable C. **General Admission Information:** Application Fee $55. Early decision application deadline 11/15. Regular application deadline 1/15. Regular notification 4/1. Nonfall registration not accepted. Admission may be deferred for a maximum of 24 months. Credit and/or placement offered for CEEB Advanced Placement tests.

COSTS AND FINANCIAL AID

Annual tuition $44,100. Room and board $13,977. Required fees $741. Average book expense $940. **Required Forms and Deadlines:** FAFSA, CSS/Financial Aid PROFILE, noncustodial PROFILEStudent and parent 1040 tax return or signed waiver if there is no tax return. **Notification of Awards:** Applicants will be notified of awards on or about 4/1. **Types of Aid:** *Need-based scholarships/grants:* Federal Pell, SEOG, state scholarships/grants, private scholarships, the school's own gift aid, United Negro College Fund, Federal Academic Competitive Grant, Federal SMART Grant. *Loans:* Direct Subsidized Stafford, Direct Unsubsidized Stafford, Direct PLUS, Subsidized Stafford, Unsubsidized Stafford, PLUS, Federal Perkins, state loans, college/university loans from institutional funds. **Student Employment:** Federal Work-Study Program available. Institutional employment available. Highest amount earned per year from on-campus jobs $2,000. Off-campus job opportunities are excellent. **Financial Aid Statistics:** 93% freshmen, 96% undergrads receive need-based scholarship or grant aid. 12% freshmen, 7% undergrads receive non-need-based scholarship or grant aid. 76% freshmen, 68% undergrads receive need-based self-help aid. 41% freshmen, 40% undergrads receive any aid. 35% undergrads borrow to pay for school. **Criteria for awarding institutional aid:** *Non-need-based:* academics.

WATKINS COLLEGE OF ART, DESIGN & FILM

2298 Rosa L Parks Blvd, Nashville, TN 37228
Phone: 615-277-7418 • **Financial Aid Phone:** 615-277-7421
E-mail: admissions@watkins.edu
Fax: 615-383-4849 • **Website:** www.watkins.edu • **ACT Code:** 4027

This private school was founded in 1895. It has a 13-acre campus.

RATINGS
Admissions Selectivity Rating: 68 **Fire Safety Rating:** 97 **Green Rating:** 60*

STUDENTS AND FACULTY
Student Body: 30% out-of-state, (4 countries represented).
Retention and Graduation: 67% freshmen graduate within 6 years. 10% grads go on to further study within 1 year. 10% grads pursue arts and sciences degrees. **Faculty:** Student/faculty ratio 7:1. 20 full-time faculty, 60% hold PhDs, 0% are members of minority groups, 50% are women. 0% of classes are taught by teaching assistants.

ACADEMICS
Degrees: bachelor's, post-bachelor's certificate. **Classes:** Most classes have 10—19 students. **Majors with Highest Enrollment:** film/cinema studies; fine/studio arts; graphic design. **Special Study Options:** dual enrollment, independent study, internships, study abroad. **Disability Services:** Special programs offered to physically disabled students include note-taking services, reader services, tape recorders, tutors. **Career Services:** Alumni network, alumni services, career/job search classes, career assessment, internships Career services highlights include Internships available in all majors.

FACILITIES
Housing: Coed dorms, special housing for disabled students, women's dorms, apartments for single students. 100% of campus accessible to physically disabled. **Special Academic Facilities/Equipment:** Brownlee O. Currey Gallery **Computers:** 100% of classrooms, 100% of dorms, 100% of libraries, 100% of dining areas, 100% of student union, 50% of common outdoor areas have wireless network access. Administrative functions (other than registration) can be performed online.

CAMPUS LIFE
Environment: Metropolis. **Activities:** student newspaper, student-run film society. **Environmental Initiatives:** Recycling Program Filtered Water Bottle filling stations Sustainability classes in certain majors

ADMISSIONS
Freshman Academic Profile: 60% from public high schools. ACT middle 50% range 20-25. Minimum web-based TOEFL 60. Minimum paper TOEFL 340. **Freshman Admission Requirements: Freshman Admission Statistics:** 113 applied, 83% admitted, 61% enrolled. **Transfer Admission Requirements:** college transcript(s), essay or personal statement, Minimum college GPA of 3.0 required. Lowest grade transferable C. **General Admission Information:**

COSTS AND FINANCIAL AID
Annual tuition $18,900. Room and board $6,200. Required fees $1,560. Average book expense $1,500. **Student Employment:** Federal Work-Study Program available. Institutional employment available. Off-campus job opportunities are excellent. **Financial Aid Statistics:** 68% freshmen, 83% undergrads receive need-based scholarship or grant aid. 37% freshmen, 10% undergrads receive non-need-based scholarship or grant aid. 100% freshmen, 83% undergrads receive need-based self-help aid. 50% freshmen, 40% undergrads receive any aid. 50% undergrads borrow to pay for school. Average cumulative indebtedness $20,000.

WAYLAND BAPTIST UNIVERSITY

1900 West 7th Street, Plainview, TX 79072
Phone: 806-291-3500 • **Financial Aid Phone:** 806-291-3520
E-mail: admityou@wbu.edu
Fax: 806-291-1963 • **ACT Code:** 4246

This private school, affiliated with the Southern Baptist Church, was founded in 1908. It has a 80-acre campus.

RATINGS
Admissions Selectivity Rating: 64 **Fire Safety Rating:** 84 **Green Rating:** 60*

STUDENTS AND FACULTY

Enrollment: 1,255. **Student Body:** 44% female, 56% male, 13% out-of-state, 3% international (22 countries represented). Asian 1%, African American 14%, Caucasian 44%, Hispanic 29%, Native American 1%
Retention and Graduation: 48% freshmen return for sophomore year. 22% freshmen graduate within 4 years. 36% freshmen graduate within 6 years. **Faculty:** Student/faculty ratio 11:1. 103 full-time faculty, 69% hold PhDs, 18% are members of minority groups, 30% are women. 0% of classes are taught by teaching-assistants.

ACADEMICS

Degrees: associate, bachelor's, master's, transfer associate. **Classes:** Most classes have 10—19 students. **Majors with Highest Enrollment:** business/commerce; christian studies; elementary education and teaching. **Special Study Options:** Accelerated program, distance learning, double major, dual enrollment, external degree program, honors program, internships, study abroad, teacher certification program. **Honors Programs:** The Honors Program offered by Wayland is designed to challenge the academically superior student to develop initiative and abilities beyond what is expected in a normal course of study. Electing an Honors program offers breadth and depth of content through independent study and research, aiding the student in preparation for entering a career upon graduation or attending graduate school in a field of choice. Honors work represents the highest level of academic work available at Wayland on the undergraduate level. **Disability Services:** Special programs offered to physically disabled students include note-taking services, reader services, tutors. **Career Services:** career assessment.

FACILITIES

Housing: men's dorms, women's dorms, apartments for married students. 100% of campus accessible to physically disabled. **Special Academic Facilities/Equipment:** Llano Estacado Museum. **Computers:** 80% of classrooms, 80% of dorms, 100% of libraries, 100% of dining areas, have wireless network access. Students can register for classes online. Administrative functions (other than registration) can be performed online.

CAMPUS LIFE

Environment: Town. **Activities:** Choral groups, concert band, drama/theater, marching band, music ensembles, musical theater, pep band, radio station, student government, student newspaper, television station, yearbook, Campus Ministries 34 registered organizations, 4 honor societies, 7 religious organizations. **Athletics (Intercollegiate):** *Men:* baseball, basketball, cheerleading, cross-country, golf, soccer, track/field (outdoor), track/field (indoor). *Women:* basketball, cheerleading, cross-country, golf, soccer, track/field (outdoor), track/field (indoor), volleyball. **On-Campus Highlights:** McClung University Center, Mabee Learning Resource Center, Gates Hall, Hutcherson Gymnasium, Harral Auditorium, Pete and Nelda Laney Activities Center. **Environmental Initiatives:** Installed energy efficient lighting in major buildings across campus.

ADMISSIONS

Freshman Academic Profile: Average high school GPA 3.2. 9% in top 10% of high school class, 28% in top 25% of high school class, 57% in top 50% of high school class. SAT Math middle 50% range 400-560. SAT Critical Reading middle 50% range 400-530. SAT Writing middle 50% range 380-490. ACT middle 50% range 18-23. Minimum web-based TOEFL 61. Minimum paper TOEFL 500. **Basis for Candidate Selection:** *Very important factors considered include:* Class rank, standardized test scores. *Important factors considered include:* rigor of secondary school record. **Freshman Admission Requirements:** High school diploma is required and GED is accepted. *Academic units required:* 3 English, 2 mathematics, 2 science, 2 history. *Academic units recommended:* 3 English, 2 mathematics, 2 science, 2 history. **Freshman Admission Statistics:** 556 applied, 97% admitted, 68% enrolled. **Transfer Admission Requirements:** college transcript(s), statement of good standing from prior institution(s). Minimum college GPA of 2.0 required. Lowest grade transferable D. **General Admission Information:** Application Fee $35. Notification on a rolling basis, beginning on or about 3/1. Nonfall registration accepted. Credit offered for CEEB Advanced Placement tests.

COSTS AND FINANCIAL AID

Annual tuition $13,650. Room and board $4,158. Required fees $980. Average book expense $1,300. **Required Forms and Deadlines:** FAFSA, institution's own financial aid form Tax returns/Verification worksheet. **Notification of Awards:** Applicants will be notified of awards on a rolling basis beginning 2/15. **Types of Aid:** *Need-based scholarships/grants:* Federal Pell, SEOG, state scholarships/grants, private scholarships, the school's own gift aid. *Loans:* Subsidized Stafford, Unsubsidized Stafford, PLUS, Federal Perkins, state loans. **Student Employment:** Federal Work-Study Program available. Institutional employment available. Off-campus job opportunities are fair. **Financial Aid Statistics:** 98% freshmen, 97% undergrads receive need-based scholarship or grant aid. 6% freshmen, 8% undergrads receive non-need-based scholarship or grant aid. 78% freshmen, 79% undergrads receive need-based self-help aid. 7% freshmen, 7% undergrads receive athletic scholarships. 57% freshmen, 58%

undergrads receive any aid. 82% undergrads borrow to pay for school. Average cumulative indebtedness $21,981. **Criteria for awarding institutional aid:** *Non-need-based:* academics, alumni affiliation, art, athletics, music/drama, religious affiliation.

WAYNE STATE COLLEGE

1111 Main Street, Wayne, NE 68787
Phone: 402-375-7234 • **Financial Aid Phone:** 402-375-7230
E-mail: admit1@wsc.edu • **CEEB Code:** 6469
Fax: 402-375-7204 • **Website:** www.wsc.edu • **ACT Code:** 2472

This public school was founded in 1909. It has a 128-acre campus.

RATINGS

Admissions Selectivity Rating: 64   **Fire Safety Rating:** 60*   **Green Rating:** 61

STUDENTS AND FACULTY

Enrollment: 2,967. **Student Body:** 57% female, 43% male, 14% out-of-state, 0% international (21 countries represented). Asian 0%, African American 3%, Caucasian 81%, Hispanic 6%, Native American 1%
Retention and Graduation: 70% freshmen return for sophomore year. **Faculty:** Student/faculty ratio 20:1. 123 full-time faculty, 83% hold PhDs, 5% are members of minority groups, 45% are women.

ACADEMICS

Degrees: bachelor's, master's, post-master's certificate. **Classes:** Most classes have 20—29 students. Most lab/discussion sessions have 30—39 students. **Majors with Highest Enrollment:** business administration and management; criminal justice/safety studies; elementary education and teaching. **Special Study Options:** cooperative education program, distance learning, double major, dual enrollment, honors program, independent study, internships, student-designed major, study abroad, teacher certification program, Learning Communities; First-Year Experience; Service Learning. **Disability Services:** Special programs offered to physically disabled students include note-taking services, reader services, tape recorders, tutors. **Career Services:** Alumni network, alumni services, career/job search classes, career assessment, internships,

FACILITIES

Housing: Coed dorms. **Special Academic Facilities/Equipment:** Art gallery, fine arts center, planetarium, recreation center, telecommunications network. **Computers:** 100% of classrooms, 100% of dorms, 100% of libraries, 100% of dining areas, 100% of student union, 40% of common outdoor areas have wireless network access. Students can register for classes online. Administrative functions (other than registration) can be performed online.

CAMPUS LIFE

Environment: Rural. **Activities:** Choral groups, concert band, dance, drama/theater, jazz band, literary magazine, marching band, music ensembles, musical theater, pep band, radio station, student government, student newspaper, television station, Campus Ministries, International Student Organization 96 registered organizations, 18 honor societies, 7 religious organizations. 2 fraternities, 3 sororities. **Athletics (Intercollegiate):** *Men:* baseball, basketball, cross-country, football, golf, track/field (outdoor), track/field (indoor). *Women:* basketball, cross-country, golf, soccer, softball, track/field (outdoor), track/field (indoor), volleyball. **Environmental Initiatives:** Recycling Program Gray Water Project.

ADMISSIONS

Freshman Academic Profile: Average high school GPA 3.2. 9% in top 10% of high school class, 24% in top 25% of high school class, 57% in top 50% of high school class. ACT middle 50% range 18-24. Minimum paper TOEFL 550. **Freshman Admission Requirements:** High school diploma is required and GED is accepted. **Freshman Admission Statistics:** 2,278 applied, 100% admitted, 31% enrolled. **Transfer Admission Requirements:** college transcript(s), Minimum college GPA of 2.0 required. Lowest grade transferable C–. **General Admission Information:** Application Fee $30. Regular application deadline 8/24. Notification on a rolling basis, beginning on or about 9/15. Nonfall registration accepted. Admission may be deferred for a maximum of 1 semester. Credit and/or placement offered for CEEB Advanced Placement tests.

COSTS AND FINANCIAL AID

Required Forms and Deadlines: FAFSA. **Notification of Awards:** Applicants will be notified of awards on a rolling basis beginning 3/1. **Types of Aid:** *Need-based scholarships/grants:* Federal Pell, SEOG, state scholarships/grants, private scholarships, the school's own gift aid. *Loans:* Subsidized Stafford, Unsubsidized Stafford, PLUS, Federal Perkins. **Student Employment:** Federal

Work-Study Program available. Institutional employment available. Off-campus job opportunities are fair. **Financial Aid Statistics:** 73% freshmen, 68% undergrads receive need-based scholarship or grant aid. 70% freshmen, 60% undergrads receive non-need-based scholarship or grant aid. 84% freshmen, 83% undergrads receive need-based self-help aid. 2% freshmen, 2% undergrads receive athletic scholarships. **Criteria for awarding institutional aid:** *Non-need-based:* academics, art, athletics, leadership, minority status, music/drama, religious affiliation, state/district residency.

WAYNE STATE UNIVERSITY

42 West Warren, Detroit, MI 48202
Phone: 313-577-3577 • **Financial Aid Phone:** 313-577-3378
E-mail: Admissions@wayne.edu • **CEEB Code:** 1898
Fax: 313-577-7536 • **Website:** www.wayne.edu • **ACT Code:** 2064

This public school was founded in 1868. It has a 219-acre campus.

RATINGS
Admissions Selectivity Rating: 68   Fire Safety Rating: 74   Green Rating: 60*

STUDENTS AND FACULTY
Enrollment: 18,532. **Student Body:** 57% female, 43% male, 1% out-of-state, 2% international (90 countries represented). Asian 8%, African American 23%, Caucasian 50%, Hispanic 3%, Native American 0%
Retention and Graduation: 75% freshmen return for sophomore year. 10% freshmen graduate within 4 years. **Faculty:** Student/faculty ratio 16:1. 1026 full-time faculty, 27% are members of minority groups, 44% are women.

ACADEMICS
Degrees: bachelor's, first professional, master's, post-bachelor's certificate, post-master's certificate. **Majors with Highest Enrollment:** elementary education and teaching; nursing/registered nurse (rn, asn, bsn, msn); psychology. **Special Study Options:** Accelerated program, cooperative education program, cross-registration, distance learning, double major, dual enrollment, English as a Second Language (ESL), external degree program, honors program, independent study, internships, liberal arts/career combination, study abroad, teacher certification program, weekend college. **Disability Services:** Special programs offered to physically disabled students include note-taking services, reader services, tape recorders, tutors. **Career Services:** career/job search classes, career assessment, internships.

FACILITIES
Housing: Coed dorms, special housing for disabled students, fraternity/sorority housing, apartments for married students, apartments for single students. 100% of campus accessible to physically disabled. **Special Academic Facilities/Equipment:** Detroit Institute of Arts; Detroit Historical Museum; Detroit Science Museum; Charles H Wright Museum of African American History **Computers:** Students can register for classes online. Administrative functions (other than registration) can be performed online.

CAMPUS LIFE
Environment: Metropolis. **Activities:** Choral groups, concert band, dance, drama/theater, jazz band, literary magazine, music ensembles, musical theater, opera, pep band, student government, student newspaper, student-run film society, symphony orchestra, yearbook 166 registered organizations, 4 honor societies, 12 religious organizations. 7 fraternities, 8 sororities. **Athletics (Intercollegiate):** *Men:* baseball, basketball, cross-country, diving, fencing, football, golf, ice hockey, swimming, tennis. *Women:* basketball, cross-country, diving, fencing, ice hockey, softball, swimming, tennis, volleyball. **On-Campus Highlights:** Recreation and Fitness Center, Student Center Building, Subway, Starbucks, Residence Halls.

ADMISSIONS
Freshman Academic Profile: 3.3. 24% in top 10% of high school class, 53% in top 25% of high school class, 81% in top 50% of high school class. ACT middle 50% range 18-26. Minimum paper TOEFL 550. **Basis for Candidate Selection:** *Very important factors considered include:* rigor of secondary school record, standardized test scores. *Other factors considered include:* Class rank, extracurricular activities. **Freshman Admission Requirements:** High school diploma is required and GED is accepted. **Freshman Admission Statistics:** 10,249 applied, 81% admitted, 28% enrolled. **Transfer Admission Requirements:** college transcript(s), Minimum college GPA of 2.0 required. Lowest grade transferable C. **General Admission Information:** Application Fee $30. Regular application deadline 8/1. Nonfall registration accepted. Admission may be deferred for a maximum of One Year. Credit and/or placement offered for CEEB Advanced Placement tests.

COSTS AND FINANCIAL AID
Annual in-state tuition $9,747. Annual out-of-state tuition $22,373. Room and board $8,504. Required fees $1,242. Average book expense $1,122. **Required Forms and Deadlines:** FAFSA. **Notification of Awards:** Applicants will be notified of awards on a rolling basis beginning 4/1. **Types of Aid:** *Need-based scholarships/grants:* Federal Pell, SEOG, state scholarships/grants, private scholarships, the school's own gift aid. *Loans:* Subsidized Stafford, Unsubsidized Stafford, PLUS, Federal Perkins, Federal Nursing, state loans, college/university loans from institutional funds. **Student Employment:** Institutional employment available. Off-campus job opportunities are fair. **Financial Aid Statistics:** 82% freshmen, 81% undergrads receive need-based scholarship or grant aid. 42% freshmen, 35% undergrads receive non-need-based scholarship or grant aid. 95% freshmen, 94% undergrads receive need-based self-help aid. 1% freshmen, 1% undergrads receive athletic scholarships. 57% undergrads borrow to pay for school. Average cumulative indebtedness $22,420. **Criteria for awarding institutional aid:** *Non-need-based:* academics, art, athletics, leadership, music/drama.

WAYNESBURG UNIVERSITY

51 West College Street, Waynesburg, PA 15370
Phone: 724-852-3248 • **Financial Aid Phone:** 724-852-3208
E-mail: admissions@waynesburg.edu • **CEEB Code:** 2969
Fax: 724-627-8124 • **ACT Code:** 3748

This private school, affiliated with the Presbyterian Church, was founded in 1849. It has a 30-acre campus.

RATINGS
Admissions Selectivity Rating: 70   Fire Safety Rating: 92   Green Rating: 61

STUDENTS AND FACULTY
Enrollment: 1,501. **Student Body:** 59% female, 41% male, 18% out-of-state, 0% international (4 countries represented). Asian 0%, African American 4%, Caucasian 92%, Hispanic 1%, Native American 0%
Retention and Graduation: 83% freshmen return for sophomore year. 54% freshmen graduate within 4 years. 60% freshmen graduate within 6 years. **Faculty:** Student/faculty ratio 16:1. 76 full-time faculty, 71% hold PhDs, 8% are members of minority groups, 47% are women. 0% of classes are taught by teaching assistants.

ACADEMICS
Degrees: associate, bachelor's, master's. **Classes:** Most classes have 10—19 students. Most lab/discussion sessions have 10—19 students. **Majors with Highest Enrollment:** business, management, marketing, and related support services, other; communication studies/speech communication and rhetoric; nursing/registered nurse (rn, asn, bsn, msn). **Special Study Options:** Accelerated program, distance learning, double major, dual enrollment, English as a Second Language (ESL), honors program, independent study, internships, liberal arts/career combination, study abroad, teacher certification program, 3-2 program in engineering with Penn State University in State College, PA and Washington University in Saint Louis, MO, 3-1 program in marine bioloy with Florida Institute of Technology; 3-3 law program with Duquesne University. **Combined Degree Programs:** BA/JD, 3/2 Pre-Law -Waynesburg and Duquense. **Disability Services:** Special programs offered to physically disabled students include tutors. **Career Services:** Alumni network, alumni services, career/job search classes, career assessment, internships, regional alumni. Career services highlights include Professional Development course for second semester juniors and seniors.

FACILITIES
Housing: Coed dorms, men's dorms, women's dorms. 90% of campus accessible to physically disabled. **Special Academic Facilities/Equipment:** Geology, biology, archaeology, and ceramics museum, arboretum, 174-acre farm, Center for Research and Economic Development. **Computers:** 95% of classrooms, 95% of libraries, 100% of dining areas, 100% of student union, 20% of common outdoor areas have wireless network access. Students can register for classes online. Administrative functions (other than registration) can be performed online.

CAMPUS LIFE
Environment: Village. **Activities:** Choral groups, concert band, dance, drama/theater, literary magazine, marching band, music ensembles, musical theater, pep band, radio station, student government, student newspaper, television station, yearbook 40 registered organizations, 16 honor societies, 7 religious organizations. **Athletics (Intercollegiate):** *Men:* baseball, basketball, cross-country, football, golf, soccer, tennis, track/field (outdoor), wrestling. *Women:* basketball,

cross-country, golf, lacrosse, soccer, softball, tennis, track/field (outdoor), volleyball. **On-Campus Highlights:** Communication Department, Stover Campus Center, Museum, Alumni Hall/Chapel, New Residence Halls.

ADMISSIONS

Freshman Academic Profile: Average high school GPA 3.5. 18% in top 10% of high school class, 44% in top 25% of high school class, 80% in top 50% of high school class. SAT Math middle 50% range 460-560. SAT Critical Reading middle 50% range 450-550. ACT middle 50% range 20-26. Minimum web-based TOEFL 83. Minimum paper TOEFL 557. **Basis for Candidate Selection:** *Very important factors considered include:* Class rank, academic GPA, rigor of secondary school record, standardized test scores, interview. *Important factors considered include:* extracurricular activities. *Other factors considered include:* application essay, recommendation(s), alumni/ae relation, character/personal qualities, level of applicant's interest, volunteer work, work experience. **Freshman Admission Requirements:** High school diploma is required and GED is accepted. *Academic units required:* 4 English, 3 mathematics, 2 science, 2 social studies, 5 academic electives. *Academic units recommended:* 4 English, 3 mathematics, 2 science, 2 social studies, 5 academic electives. **Freshman Admission Statistics:** 1,827 applied, 76% admitted, 25% enrolled. **Transfer Admission Requirements:** High school transcript, college transcript(s), statement of good standing from prior institution(s). Minimum college GPA of 2.5 required. Lowest grade transferable C. **General Admission Information:** Application Fee $20. Nonfall registration accepted. Credit offered for CEEB Advanced Placement tests.

COSTS AND FINANCIAL AID

Annual tuition $19,450. Room and board $8,250. Required fees $360. Average book expense $1,300. **Required Forms and Deadlines:** FAFSA. **Notification of Awards:** Applicants will be notified of awards on a rolling basis beginning 2/15. **Types of Aid:** *Need-based scholarships/grants:* Federal Pell, SEOG, state scholarships/grants, private scholarships, the school's own gift aid. *Loans:* Subsidized Stafford, Unsubsidized Stafford, PLUS, Federal Perkins, Federal Nursing, Private Alternative Loans. **Student Employment:** Federal Work-Study Program available. Institutional employment available. Highest amount earned per year from on-campus jobs $3,000. Off-campus job opportunities are good. **Financial Aid Statistics:** 100% freshmen, 97% undergrads receive need-based scholarship or grant aid. 12% freshmen, 9% undergrads receive non-need-based scholarship or grant aid. 86% freshmen, 86% undergrads receive need-based self-help aid. 94% freshmen, 85% undergrads receive any aid. 03% undergrads borrow to pay for school. Average cumulative indebtedness $27,625. **Criteria for awarding institutional aid:** *Non-need-based:* academics, alumni affiliation, art, job skills, leadership, minority status, music/drama, religious affiliation, state/district residency.

WEBB INSTITUTE

298 Crescent Beach Road, Glen Cove, NY 11542
Phone: 516-674-9838 • **Financial Aid Phone:** 516-671-2213
E-mail: admissions@webb-institute.edu • **CEEB Code:** 2970
Fax: 516-674-9838 • **Website:** www.webb-institute.edu • **ACT Code:** 2987

This private school was founded in 1889. It has a 26-acre campus.

RATINGS

Admissions Selectivity Rating: 96   **Fire Safety Rating:** 68   **Green Rating:** 60*

STUDENTS AND FACULTY

Enrollment: 81. **Student Body:** 16% female, 84% male, 70% out-of-state, 0% international (0 countries represented). Asian 9%, African American 0%, Caucasian 86%, Hispanic 2%, Native American 0%
Retention and Graduation: 83% freshmen return for sophomore year. 80% freshmen graduate within 4 years. 80% freshmen graduate within 6 years. 30% grads go on to further study within 1 year. **Faculty:** Student/faculty ratio 7:1. 11 full-time faculty, 64% hold PhDs, 0% are members of minority groups, 9% are women. 0% of classes are taught by teaching assistants.

ACADEMICS

Degrees: bachelor's. **Classes:** Most classes have 20—29 students. **Special Study Options:** double major, independent study, internships. **Career Services:** Alumni network, career/job search classes, internships, regional alumni. Career services highlights include Winter Work program. All students are

required to work in the industry for 2 months of each academic year. Freshmen work in shipyards; Sophomore work onboard ships; Juniors and Seniors work in engineering design offices.

FACILITIES

Housing: Coed dorms, men's dorms, women's dorms. 70% of campus accessible to physically disabled. **Special Academic Facilities/Equipment:** Towing tank for model testing, marine engineering lab. **Computers:** 100% of classrooms, 100% of dorms, 100% of libraries, 100% of dining areas, 100% of student union, 100% of common outdoor areas have wireless network access.

CAMPUS LIFE

Environment: Village. **Activities:** Choral groups, drama/theater, music ensembles, student government, yearbook 2 registered organizations. **Athletics (Intercollegiate):** *Men:* basketball, cross-country, sailing, soccer, tennis, volleyball. *Women:* basketball, cross-country, sailing, soccer, tennis, volleyball. **On-Campus Highlights:** Stevenson Taylor Hall, Brockett Pub, Waterfront Facility.

ADMISSIONS

Freshman Academic Profile: Average high school GPA 3.9. 63% in top 10% of high school class, 88% in top 25% of high school class, 100% in top 50% of high school class. 78% from public high schools. SAT Math middle 50% range 695-740. SAT Critical Reading middle 50% range 640-700. SAT Writing middle 50% range 620-720. **Basis for Candidate Selection:** *Very important factors considered include:* Class rank, academic GPA, rigor of secondary school record, standardized test scores, character/personal qualities, interview, level of applicant's interest. *Important factors considered include:* recommendation(s), extracurricular activities. *Other factors considered include:* talent/ability, volunteer work, work experience. **Freshman Admission Requirements:** High school diploma is required and GED is not accepted. *Academic units required:* 4 English, 4 mathematics, 2 science, (2 science labs), 2 social studies, 4 academic electives. *Academic units recommended:* 4 English, 4 mathematics, 2 science, (2 science labs), 2 social studies, 4 academic electives. **Freshman Admission Statistics:** 72 applied, 44% admitted, 56% enrolled. **Transfer Admission Requirements:** High school transcript, college transcript(s), interview, standardized test scores, Minimum college GPA of 3.5 required. **General Admission Information:** Application Fee $25. Early decision application deadline 10/15. Regular application deadline 2/15. Notification on a rolling basis, beginning on or about 4/15. Nonfall registration not accepted. Neither credit nor placement offered for CEEB Advanced Placement tests.

COSTS AND FINANCIAL AID

Room and board $13,200. Average book expense $950. **Required Forms and Deadlines:** FAFSA. **Notification of Awards:** Applicants will be notified of awards on or about 8/1. **Types of Aid:** *Need-based scholarships/grants:* Federal Pell, state scholarships/grants, private scholarships, the school's own gift aid. *Loans:* Subsidized Stafford, Unsubsidized Stafford, PLUS. **Student Employment:** Off-campus job opportunities are fair. **Financial Aid Statistics:** 50% freshmen receive need-based scholarship or grant aid. 17% freshmen, 25% undergrads receive any aid. 33% undergrads borrow to pay for school. Average cumulative indebtedness $4,500. **Criteria for awarding institutional aid:** *Non-need-based:* academics.

WEBBER INTERNATIONAL UNIVERSITY

PO Box 96, Babson Park, FL 33827
Phone: 863-638-2910 • **Financial Aid Phone:** 863-638-2930
E-mail: admissions@webber.edu • **CEEB Code:** 5893
Fax: 863-638-1591 • **Website:** www.webber.edu • **ACT Code:** 773

This private school was founded in 1927. It has a 110-acre campus.

RATINGS

Admissions Selectivity Rating: 78   **Fire Safety Rating:** 82   **Green Rating:** 60*

STUDENTS AND FACULTY

Enrollment: 666. **Student Body:** 33% female, 67% male, 11% out-of-state, 26% international (45 countries represented). Asian 1%, African American 21%, Caucasian 41%, Hispanic 8%, Native American 0%
Retention and Graduation: 51% freshmen return for sophomore year. 29% freshmen graduate within 4 years. 7% grads go on to further study within 1 year. 2% grads pursue law degrees. 5% grads pursue business degrees. **Faculty:** Student/faculty ratio 22:1. 21 full-time faculty, 62% hold PhDs, 10% are members of minority groups, 43% are women. 0% of classes are taught by teaching assistants.

ACADEMICS

Degrees: associate, bachelor's, master's. **Classes:** Most classes have 20—29 students. **Majors with Highest Enrollment:** business administration and management; business/commerce; parks, recreation and leisure facilities management. **Special Study Options:** cooperative education program, cross-registration, distance learning, double major, dual enrollment, English as a Second Language (ESL), exchange student program (domestic), external degree program, independent study, internships, study abroad, weekend college. **Career Services:** career/job search classes, career assessment, internships Career services highlights include As a Career Counselor I am most proud of the experiential learning in the classroom in classes like Career Development where we engage the learner at a more personal level by addressing the needs of the individual. In career development each student is treated as an individual and the learning process is individual not necessarily as a group. Students are given individual personality assessments and must demonstrate goal setting abilities while observing different occupations, in hands on setting and finally presenting the occupation they have chosen as a career. I am also very proud of our internship program which gives students a valuable learning tooland hands-on opportunity in the field they are most intersted in.

FACILITIES

Housing: men's dorms, women's dorms. 70% of campus accessible to physically disabled. **Computers:** Administrative functions (other than registration) can be performed online.

CAMPUS LIFE

Environment: Rural. **Activities:** marching band, pep band, student government, student newspaper, International Student Organization 6 registered organizations. **Athletics (Intercollegiate):** *Men:* baseball, basketball, bowling, cheerleading, cross-country, football, golf, soccer, tennis, track/field (outdoor). *Women:* basketball, bowling, cheerleading, cross-country, golf, soccer, softball, tennis, track/field (outdoor), volleyball. **On-Campus Highlights:** Student Union, Fitness Center, Computer Lab, Career Center.

ADMISSIONS

Freshman Academic Profile: Average high school GPA 3.1. 5% in top 10% of high school class, 15% in top 25% of high school class, 48% in top 50% of high school class. 75% from public high schools. SAT Math middle 50% range 440-520. SAT Critical Reading middle 50% range 415-500. ACT middle 50% range 17-21. Minimum paper TOEFL 500. **Basis for Candidate Selection:** *Very important factors considered include:* academic GPA, standardized test scores. *Important factors considered include:* rigor of secondary school record. *Other factors considered include:* Class rank, application essay, recommendation(s), alumni/ae relation, character/personal qualities, interview. **Freshman Admission Requirements:** High school diploma is required and GED is accepted. *Academic units required:* 4 English, 2 mathematics, 1 science, 2 social studies, 2. *Academic units recommended:* 4 English, 2 mathematics, 1 science, 2 social studies, 2 **Freshman Admission Statistics:** 525 applied, 55% admitted, 48% enrolled. **Transfer Admission Requirements:** college transcript(s), statement of good standing from prior institution(s). Minimum college GPA of 2.0 required. Lowest grade transferable C. **General Admission Information:** Application Fee $35. Regular application deadline 8/1. Notification on a rolling basis, beginning on or about 12/1. Nonfall registration accepted. Admission may be deferred for a maximum of 1 semester. Credit offered for CEEB Advanced Placement tests.

COSTS AND FINANCIAL AID

Annual tuition $20,418. Room and board $7,900. Required fees $1,993. Average book expense $1,050. **Required Forms and Deadlines:** FAFSA, state aid form. **Notification of Awards:** Applicants will be notified of awards on a rolling basis beginning 4/1. **Types of Aid:** *Need-based scholarships/grants:* Federal Pell, SEOG, state scholarships/grants, private scholarships, the school's own gift aid. *Loans:* Subsidized Stafford, Unsubsidized Stafford, PLUS, Federal Perkins. **Student Employment:** Federal Work-Study Program available. Institutional employment available. Highest amount earned per year from on-campus jobs $1,950. Off-campus job opportunities are good. **Financial Aid Statistics:** 100% freshmen, 70% undergrads receive need-based scholarship or grant aid. 100% freshmen, 54% undergrads receive non-need-based scholarship or grant aid. 100% freshmen, 96% undergrads receive need-based self-help aid. 31% freshmen, 33% undergrads receive athletic scholarships. 97% freshmen, 96% undergrads receive any aid. 81% undergrads borrow to pay for school. Average cumulative indebtedness $27,121. **Criteria for awarding institutional aid:** *Non-need-based:* academics, alumni affiliation, athletics, leadership, state/district residency.

See page 1294.

1137 University Circle, Ogden, UT 84408-1137
Phone: 801-626-6743 • **Financial Aid Phone:** 801-626-6586
E-mail: admissions@weber.edu • **CEEB Code:** 4941
Fax: 801-626-6747 • **Website:** weber.edu/ • **ACT Code:** 4282

This public school was founded in 1889. It has a 526-acre campus.

RATINGS

Admissions Selectivity Rating: 64   **Fire Safety Rating:** 86   **Green Rating:** 96

STUDENTS AND FACULTY

Enrollment: 18,461. **Student Body:** 51% female, 49% male, 9% out-of-state, 2% international (48 countries represented). Asian 2%, African American 2%, Caucasian 72%, Hispanic 7%, Native American 1%
Retention and Graduation: 71% freshmen return for sophomore year.
Faculty: Student/faculty ratio 22:1. 463 full-time faculty, 72% hold PhDs, 10% are members of minority groups, 44% are women. 0% of classes are taught by teaching assistants.

ACADEMICS

Degrees: associate, bachelor's, certificate, master's, post-bachelor's certificate, terminal associate, transfer associate. **Classes:** Most classes have 10—19 students. Most lab/discussion sessions have 10—19 students. **Majors with Highest Enrollment:** business administration and management; elementary education and teaching; nursing/registered nurse (rn, asn, bsn, msn). **Special Study Options:** Accelerated program, cooperative education program, distance learning, double major, dual enrollment, English as a Second Language (ESL), exchange student program (domestic), external degree program, honors program, independent study, internships, student-designed major, study abroad, teacher certification program, First Year Experience. **Disability Services:** Special programs offered to physically disabled students include note-taking services, reader services, tape recorders, tutors. **Career Services:** Alumni network, alumni services, career/job search classes, career assessment, internships, regional alumni.

FACILITIES

Housing: special housing for disabled students, men's dorms, women's dorms, apartments for married students, apartments for single students. 99% of campus accessible to physically disabled. **Special Academic Facilities/Equipment:** Art gallery, language lab, TV studio, communication arts/technologies facilities, natural science museum, herbarium, planetarium, aerospace technology equipment for developing satellite projects, dental hygiene clinic. **Computers:** 50% of classrooms, 50% of dorms, 100% of libraries, 100% of dining areas, 100% of student union, 100% of common outdoor areas have wireless network access. Students can register for classes online. Administrative functions (other than registration) can be performed online.

CAMPUS LIFE

Environment: Town. **Activities:** Choral groups, concert band, dance, drama/theater, jazz band, literary magazine, marching band, music ensembles, musical theater, opera, pep band, radio station, student government, student newspaper, student-run film society, symphony orchestra, television station 100 registered organizations, 1 honor societies, 4 religious organizations. 2 fraternities, 3 sororities. **Athletics (Intercollegiate):** *Men:* basketball, cheerleading, cross-country, football, golf, tennis, track/field (outdoor), track/field (indoor). *Women:* basketball, cheerleading, cross-country, golf, soccer, tennis, track/field (outdoor), track/field (indoor), volleyball. **On-Campus Highlights:** Health and Physical Education Center, Bowling Alley and Arcade, Student Union Building, Kimball Visual Arts Building, Val A. Browning Center, Student Union Building is under renovation, West side is completed, the East side will be completed summer 2008. Pool tables and games have been moved to Promontory Tower for the time being. Bowling has been contracted out to a local alley. **Environmental Initiatives:** Weber State University is in the process of upgrading all interior and exterior campus lighting to high-efficiency flourescents, CLFs and LEDs in some applications. This project began last year and will continue for another 3 years. Weber State University is in the process of upgrading its vast system of steam tunnel pipes to make them more energy and water efficient. Expansion joints and steam traps will be replaced, isolation valves will be added, and the entire network of pipes will be re-insulated with aerogel. Aerogel is a high performance thermal insulator that has been used by NASA to insulate the Mars Rover and spacesuits. All new construction at Weber State University must meet LEED silver standards. Our two newest buildings, Elizabeth Hall and the Hurst Center, have both been LEED silver certified.

ADMISSIONS

Freshman Academic Profile: 99% from public high schools. ACT middle 50% range 18-24. **Basis for Candidate Selection:** *Important factors consid-*

ered include: rigor of secondary school record, standardized test scores. *Other factors considered include:* character/personal qualities, extracurricular activities, interview. **Freshman Admission Requirements:** High school diploma is required and GED is accepted. **Freshman Admission Statistics:** 55% enrolled. **Transfer Admission Requirements:** college transcript(s), Minimum college GPA of 2.0 required. Lowest grade transferable C. **General Admission Information:** Application Fee $45. Regular application deadline 8/22. Nonfall registration accepted. Admission may be deferred for a maximum of 1 year. Placement offered for CEEB Advanced Placement tests.

COSTS AND FINANCIAL AID
Annual in-state tuition $3,773. Annual out-of-state tuition $11,485. Room and board $4,600. Required fees $775. Average book expense $1,200. **Required Forms and Deadlines:** FAFSA, institution's own financial aid form. **Notification of Awards:** Applicants will be notified of awards on a rolling basis, beginning 3/15. **Types of Aid:** *Need-based scholarships/grants:* Federal Pell, SEOG, state scholarships/grants, private scholarships, the school's own gift aid. *Loans:* Subsidized Stafford, Unsubsidized Stafford, PLUS, Federal Perkins, Short-term Tuition Loan. **Student Employment:** Federal Work-Study Program available. Institutional employment available. Off-campus job opportunities are good. **Financial Aid Statistics:** 83% freshmen, 82% undergrads receive need-based scholarship or grant aid. 70% freshmen, 36% undergrads receive non-need-based scholarship or grant aid. 55% freshmen, 62% undergrads receive need-based self-help aid. 3% freshmen, 3% undergrads receive athletic scholarships. 60% freshmen, 58% undergrads receive any aid. **Criteria for awarding institutional aid:** *Non-need-based:* academics, alumni affiliation, art, athletics, job skills, leadership, minority status, music/drama, state/district residency.

WEBSTER UNIVERSITY

470 East Lockwood Avenue, Saint Louis, MO 63119-3194
Phone: 314-968-6991 • **Financial Aid Phone:** 314-968-6992
E-mail: admit@webster.edu • **CEEB Code:** 6933
Fax: 314-968-7115 • **Website:** www.webster.edu • **ACT Code:** 2388

This private school was founded in 1915. It has a 47-acre campus.

RATINGS
Admissions Selectivity Rating: 89   **Fire Safety Rating:** 91   **Green Rating:** 74

STUDENTS AND FACULTY
Enrollment: 3,249. **Student Body:** 57% female, 43% male, 21% out-of-state, 2% international (48 countries represented). Asian 2%, African American 11%, Caucasian 69%, Hispanic 3%, Native American 0%
Retention and Graduation: 51% freshmen graduate within 4 years. 65% freshmen graduate within 6 years. 21% grads go on to further study within 1 year. **Faculty:** Student/faculty ratio 13:1. 184 full-time faculty, 80% hold PhDs, 10% are members of minority groups, 47% are women. 0% of classes are taught by teaching assistants.

ACADEMICS
Degrees: bachelor's, certificate, master's, post-bachelor's certificate, post-master's certificate. **Classes:** Most classes have 10—19 students. **Majors with Highest Enrollment:** business/commerce; computer science; education. **Special Study Options:** Accelerated program, cooperative education program, cross-registration, distance learning, double major, dual enrollment, English as a Second Language (ESL), exchange student program (domestic), independent study, internships, liberal arts/career combination, student-designed major, study abroad, teacher certification program, Certificate Programs, Combination bachelor's/master's degree in many subject areas, Independent study, Student Leadership Development Program. In addition to the programs offered at its four St. Louis area campuses, Webster University offers undergraduate degree completion programs at the following extended campus locations in the United States: Charleston, SC, Columbia, SC, Greenville, SC, Kansas City, MO, Orlando, FL, Irvine, CA, San Diego, CA, Geneva, Switzerland, Leiden, The Netherlands, Vienna, Austria. **Combined Degree Programs:** BA/MA, 3/4 BA-BFA/MS w/ Washington Univ. in Architecture. **Disability Services:** Special programs offered to physically disabled students include note-taking services, reader services, tape recorders, tutors. **Career Services:** Alumni network, alumni services, career assessment, internships.

FACILITIES
Housing: Coed dorms, special housing for international students, women's dorms, apartments for married students, apartments for single students. 85% of campus accessible to physically disabled. **Special Academic Facilities/Equipment:** Loretto-Hilton Center for Performing Arts (Houses St. Louis Repertory company, Opera Theatre of St. Louis, and Webster Symphony); Community

Music School of Webster University. **Computers:** 10% of classrooms, 12% of dorms, 50% of libraries, 100% of dining areas, 100% of student union, 60% of common outdoor areas have wireless network access. Students can register for classes online. Administrative functions (other than registration) can be performed online.

CAMPUS LIFE
Environment: Metropolis. **Activities:** Choral groups, dance, drama/theater, jazz band, literary magazine, music ensembles, musical theater, opera, radio station, student government, student newspaper, student-run film society, symphony orchestra, television station, yearbook, Campus Ministries 62 registered organizations, 1 honor societies, 1 religious organizations. 1 fraternities. **Athletics (Intercollegiate):** *Men:* baseball, basketball, cross-country, golf, soccer, tennis, track/field (outdoor). *Women:* basketball, cross-country, soccer, softball, tennis, track/field (outdoor), volleyball. **On-Campus Highlights:** University Center, The Quadrangle, Emerson Library, Fitness Center, Marletto's Marketplace (dining hall). **Environmental Initiatives:** Recycling program.

ADMISSIONS
Freshman Academic Profile: Average high school GPA 3.5. 24% in top 10% of high school class, 55% in top 25% of high school class, 83% in top 50% of high school class. 77% from public high schools. SAT Math middle 50% range 460-630. SAT Critical Reading middle 50% range 520-650. ACT middle 50% range 21-28. Minimum paper TOEFL 550. **Basis for Candidate Selection:** *Very important factors considered include:* academic GPA, standardized test scores, talent/ability. *Important factors considered include:* Class rank, application essay, recommendation(s), rigor of secondary school record, level of applicant's interest. *Other factors considered include:* extracurricular activities, geographical residence, interview, racial/ethnic status, volunteer work. **Freshman Admission Requirements:** High school diploma is required and GED is accepted. **Freshman Admission Statistics:** 1,584 applied, 52% admitted, 60% enrolled. **Transfer Admission Requirements:** college transcript(s), essay or personal statement. Minimum college GPA of 2.5 required. Lowest grade transferable C. **General Admission Information:** Application Fee $35. Regular application deadline 6/1. Notification on a rolling basis, beginning on or about 9/1. Nonfall registration accepted. Admission may be deferred for a maximum of 12 months. Credit offered for CEEB Advanced Placement tests.

COSTS AND FINANCIAL AID
Required Forms and Deadlines: FAFSA, institution's own financial aid form. **Notification of Awards:** Applicants will be notified of awards on a rolling basis beginning 2/1. **Types of Aid:** *Need-based scholarships/grants:* Federal Pell, SEOG, state scholarships/grants, private scholarships, the school's own gift aid. *Loans:* Subsidized Stafford, Unsubsidized Stafford, PLUS, Federal Perkins. **Student Employment:** Federal Work-Study Program available. Institutional employment available. Off-campus job opportunities are good. **Financial Aid Statistics:** 87% freshmen, 83% undergrads receive need-based scholarship or grant aid. 84% freshmen, 73% undergrads receive non-need-based scholarship or grant aid. 93% freshmen, 93% undergrads receive need-based self-help aid. 95% freshmen, 68% undergrads receive any aid. 53% undergrads borrow to pay for school. Average cumulative indebtedness $22,598. **Criteria for awarding institutional aid:** *Non-need-based:* academics, art, music/drama, state/district residency.

WELLESLEY COLLEGE

Board of Admission, Wellesley, MA 02481-8203
Phone: 781-283-2270 • **Financial Aid Phone:** 781-283-2360
E-mail: admission@wellesley.edu • **CEEB Code:** 3957
Fax: 781-283-3678 • **Website:** www.wellesley.edu • **ACT Code:** 1926

This private school was founded in 1870. It has a 500-acre campus.

RATINGS
Admissions Selectivity Rating: 97   **Fire Safety Rating:** 92   **Green Rating:** 83

STUDENTS AND FACULTY
Enrollment: 2,364. **Student Body:** 84% out-of-state, 12% international (93 countries represented). Asian 21%, African American 6%, Caucasian 44%, Hispanic 10%, Native American 0%
Retention and Graduation: 97% freshmen return for sophomore year. 84% freshmen graduate within 4 years. 92% freshmen graduate within 6 years. 80%

grads go on to further study within 1 year. 40% grads pursue arts and sciences degrees. 14% grads pursue law degrees. 3% grads pursue business degrees. 12% grads pursue medical degrees. **Faculty:** Student/faculty ratio 8:1. 275 full-time faculty, 95% hold PhDs, 23% are members of minority groups, 55% are women. 0% of classes are taught by teaching assistants.

ACADEMICS

Degrees: bachelor's. **Classes:** Most classes have 10—19 students. Most lab/discussion sessions have 10—19 students. **Majors with Highest Enrollment:** economics; political science and government; psychology. **Special Study Options:** cross-registration, double major, dual enrollment, exchange student program (domestic), honors program, independent study, internships, student-designed major, study abroad, teacher certification program. **Combined Degree Programs:** BA/MA, Brandeis MA ief (International Economics and Finance). **Disability Services:** Special programs offered to physically disabled students include note-taking services, reader services, tape recorders, tutors. **Career Services:** Alumni network, alumni services, career/job search classes, career assessment, internships, regional alumni. Career services highlights include Wellesley College funded at least one internship for more than half the class of 2009. This included grants of up $3,500 for what otherwise would have been unpaid internships over the summer.

FACILITIES

Housing: women's dorms, cooperative housing, apartments for single students, wellness housing, theme housing. 85% of campus accessible to physically disabled. **Special Academic Facilities/Equipment:** Clapp Library Davis Museum and Cultural Center Harambee House Houghton Memorial Chapel Hunnewell Arboretum, Alexandra Botanic Gardens, and Ferguson Greenhouses Jewett Art Museum Keohane Sports Center Knapp Media and Technology Center Knapp Social Science Center Lake Waban Pforzheimer Learning and Teaching Center Ruth Nagel Jones Theatre Science Center, including NMR Spectrometers Slater International Center Wang Campus Center Wellesley Centers for Women Whitin Observatory, including 3 telescopes **Computers:** 100% of classrooms, 100% of dorms, 100% of libraries, 100% of dining areas, 100% of student union, 5% of common outdoor areas have wireless network access. Students can register for classes online. Administrative functions (other than registration) can be performed online.

CAMPUS LIFE

Environment: Town. **Activities:** Choral groups, dance, drama/theater, jazz band, literary magazine, music ensembles, radio station, student government, student newspaper, student-run film society, symphony orchestra, yearbook, Campus Ministries, International Student Organization 160 registered organizations, 7 honor societies, 30 religious organizations. **Athletics (Intercollegiate):** *Women:* basketball, crew/rowing, cross-country, diving, fencing, field hockey, golf, lacrosse, soccer, softball, squash, swimming, tennis, track/field (outdoor), track/field (indoor), volleyball. **On-Campus Highlights:** Wang Campus Center, Davis Museum and Cultural Center, Clapp Library and Knapp Media Center, Science Center, Lake Waban. **Environmental Initiatives:** 1. The College has made a large difference in improving the landscape by turning two significant brown field sites into green space. This effort reduced paved surfaces by 5.7 acres, greatly improved storm water management and quality, and reduced potable water consumption. This initiative also resulted in the planting of thousands of trees and shrubs. 2. We have greatly increased the recycling program over the past several years. We are recycling more than 10% of all solid waste. Wellesley College has a strong focus on reduction in consumption of materials while maintaining a strong recycling program. 3. Wellesley has been a leader in the efficient utilization of energy in many areas of the campus for nearly 30 years. Since 2003, we have reduced electrical consumption by 12% even though a new, highly programmed, 50,000 square foot building was brought on line during that period. In this effort, we are implementing additional practices and equipment to further reduce electrical use.

ADMISSIONS

Freshman Academic Profile: 59% from public high schools. SAT Math middle 50% range 640-740. SAT Critical Reading middle 50% range 650-740. SAT Writing middle 50% range 650-750. ACT middle 50% range 29-32. **Basis for Candidate Selection:** *Very important factors considered include:* application essay, academic GPA, recommendation(s), rigor of secondary school record, standardized test scores, character/personal qualities. *Important factors considered include:* Class rank, extracurricular activities. *Other factors considered include:* alumni/ae relation, first generation, geographical residence, interview, level of applicant's interest, racial/ethnic status, state residency, talent/ability, volunteer work, work experience. **Freshman Admission Requirements:** High school diploma or equivalent is not required. High school diploma is required and GED is not accepted. **Freshman Admission Statistics:** 4,478 applied, 30% admitted, 43% enrolled. **Transfer Admission Requirements:** High school transcript, college transcript(s), essay or personal statement, interview, standardized test scores, statement of good standing from prior institution(s). Lowest grade transferable C. **General Admission Information:** Application Fee $50. Early decision application deadline 11/1. Regular application deadline

1/15. Regular notification 4/1. Nonfall registration not accepted. Admission may be deferred for a maximum of 1 year. Credit and/or placement offered for CEEB Advanced Placement tests.

COSTS AND FINANCIAL AID

Annual tuition $41,824. Room and board $13,032. Average book expense $800. **Required Forms and Deadlines:** FAFSA, CSS/Financial Aid PROFILE, noncustodial PROFILE, business/farm supplement. Business taxes, if applicable. **Notification of Awards:** Applicants will be notified of awards on or about 4/1. **Types of Aid:** *Need-based scholarships/grants:* Federal Pell, SEOG, state scholarships/grants, private scholarships, the school's own gift aid, ACG Grant and SMART Grant. *Loans:* Direct Subsidized Stafford, Direct Unsubsidized Stafford, Direct PLUS, Federal Perkins, state loans, college/university loans from institutional funds. **Student Employment:** Federal Work-Study Program available. Institutional employment available. Off-campus job opportunities are excellent. **Financial Aid Statistics:** 96% freshmen, 97% undergrads receive need-based scholarship or grant aid. 83% freshmen, 89% undergrads receive need-based self-help aid. 58% freshmen, 60% undergrads receive any aid. 54% undergrads borrow to pay for school. Average cumulative indebtedness $14,189.

WELLS COLLEGE

Route 90, Aurora, NY 13026
Phone: 315-364-3264 • **Financial Aid Phone:** 315-364-3289
E-mail: admissions@wells.edu • **CEEB Code:** 2971
Fax: 315-364-3227 • **Website:** www.wells.edu • **ACT Code:** 2971

This private school was founded in 1868. It has a 365-acre campus.

RATINGS

Admissions Selectivity Rating: 80   **Fire Safety Rating:** 81   **Green Rating:** 70

STUDENTS AND FACULTY

Enrollment: 552. **Student Body:** 71% female, 29% male, 32% out-of-state, 2% international (13 countries represented). Asian 2%, African American 6%, Caucasian 67%, Hispanic 4%, Native American 1%
Retention and Graduation: 53% freshmen graduate within 4 years. 51% freshmen graduate within 6 years. 25% grads go on to further study within 1 year. 18% grads pursue arts and sciences degrees. 4% grads pursue law degrees. 1% grads pursue business degrees. 2% grads pursue medical degrees. **Faculty:** Student/faculty ratio 10:1. 39 full-time faculty, 95% hold PhDs, 18% are members of minority groups, 54% are women. 0% of classes are taught by teaching assistants.

ACADEMICS

Degrees: bachelor's. **Classes:** Most classes have 10—19 students. **Majors with Highest Enrollment:** English language and literature; molecular biology; psychology. **Special Study Options:** Accelerated program, cross-registration, double major, English as a Second Language (ESL), independent study, internships, student-designed major, study abroad, teacher certification program, Cross registration with Cornell University, Ithaca College, and Cayuga Community College. **Combined Degree Programs:** BA/MBA, BA/MPH, BA/DVM, BA/M.Ed. **Disability Services:** Special programs offered to physically disabled students include tutors. **Career Services:** Alumni network, alumni services, career assessment, internships, regional alumni. Career services highlights include Wells College's ability to connect our students to the real world, through the use of internships, study abroad and experiential learning makes us unlike any other.

FACILITIES

Housing: Coed dorms, women's dorms, Off campus college affiliated housing as well as an Environmental Science theme house. 58% of campus accessible to physically disabled. **Special Academic Facilities/Equipment:** Two greenhouses, environmentally regulated animal room, the college theatre (Phillips Auditorium), recital hall, electronic music studio, 15 pianos, a Dowd harpsichord, an early instrument collection, a sculpture and ceramics studio, dark rooms, painting and drawing studio, a Book Arts Center, lithography presses, an extensive art library, art gallery, general and specialized clusters for the social sciences, foreign languages, and natural and mathematical sciences. **Computers:** 10% of classrooms, 90% of dorms, 100% of libraries, 100% of student union, have wireless network access. Students can register for classes online. Administrative functions (other than registration) can be performed online.

CAMPUS LIFE

Environment: Rural. **Activities:** Choral groups, dance, drama/theater, literary magazine, music ensembles, student government, student newspaper, yearbook, Model UN 35 registered organizations, 2 honor societies, 2 religious organizations. **Athletics (Intercollegiate):** *Men:* basketball, cross-country, golf, lacrosse, soccer, swimming. *Women:* basketball, cross-country, field hockey, golf, lacrosse, soccer, softball, swimming, tennis. **On-Campus Highlights:** Sommer Center, Boat House, Schwartz Student Union, Macmillan Hall, Main Building.

ADMISSIONS

Freshman Academic Profile: Average high school GPA 3.5. 31% in top 10% of high school class, 65% in top 25% of high school class, 91% in top 50% of high school class. 88% from public high schools. SAT Math middle 50% range 480-600. SAT Critical Reading middle 50% range 500-630. SAT Writing middle 50% range 480-590. ACT middle 50% range 22-27. Minimum paper TOEFL 550. **Basis for Candidate Selection:** *Very important factors considered include:* academic GPA, recommendation(s), rigor of secondary school record, standardized test scores, extracurricular activities. *Important factors considered include:* application essay, interview. *Other factors considered include:* Class rank, alumni/ae relation, character/personal qualities, level of applicant's interest, talent/ability, volunteer work, work experience. **Freshman Admission Requirements:** High school diploma is required and GED is accepted. *Academic units required:* 4 English, 3 mathematics, 2 science, (2 science labs), 1 social studies, 3 history, 2 academic electives. *Academic units recommended:* 4 English, 3 mathematics, 2 science, (2 science labs), 1 social studies, 3 history, 2 academic electives. **Freshman Admission Statistics:** 1,673 applied, 71% admitted, 12% enrolled. **Transfer Admission Requirements:** High school transcript, college transcript(s), essay or personal statement, standardized test scores, statement of good standing from prior institution(s). Minimum college GPA of 2.0 required. Lowest grade transferable C–. **General Admission Information:** Application Fee $40. Early decision application deadline 12/15. Regular application deadline 3/1. Regular notification 4/1. Nonfall registration accepted. Admission may be deferred for a maximum of 12 months. Credit and/or placement offered for CEEB Advanced Placement tests.

COSTS AND FINANCIAL AID

Annual tuition $30,680. Room and board $11,400. Required fees $1,500. Average book expense $800. **Required Forms and Deadlines:** FAFSA, CSS/Financial Aid Profile for Early Decision Applicants only. **Notification of Awards:** Applicants will be notified of awards on a rolling basis beginning 3/1. **Types of Aid:** *Need-based scholarships/grants:* Federal Pell, SEOG, state scholarships/grants, private scholarships, the school's own gift aid. *Loans:* Subsidized Stafford, Unsubsidized Stafford, PLUS, Federal Perkins. **Student Employment:** Federal Work-Study Program available. Institutional employment available. Highest amount earned per year from on-campus jobs $1,600. Off-campus job opportunities are poor. **Financial Aid Statistics:** 93% freshmen, 93% undergrads receive need-based scholarship or grant aid. 13% freshmen, 15% undergrads receive non-need-based scholarship or grant aid. 75% freshmen, 70% undergrads receive need-based self-help aid. 96% freshmen, 95% undergrads receive any aid. 90% undergrads borrow to pay for school. Average cumulative indebtedness $26,207. **Criteria for awarding institutional aid:** *Non-need-based:* academics, alumni affiliation, leadership.

See page 1296.

WENTWORTH INSTITUTE OF TECHNOLOGY

550 Huntington Avenue, Boston, MA 02115-5998
Phone: 617-989-4000 • **Financial Aid Phone:** 617-989-4174
E-mail: admissions@wit.edu • **CEEB Code:** 3958
Fax: 617-989-4010 • **Website:** www.wit.edu • **ACT Code:**

This private school was founded in 1904. It has a 35-acre campus.

RATINGS

Admissions Selectivity Rating: 81	**Fire Safety Rating:** 87	**Green Rating:** 82

STUDENTS AND FACULTY

Enrollment: 3,972. **Student Body:** 18% female, 82% male, 36% out-of-state, 4% international (49 countries represented). Asian 6%, African American 5%, Caucasian 61%, Hispanic 4%, Native American 0%.
Retention and Graduation: 82% freshmen return for sophomore year. 47% freshmen graduate within 4 years. 64% freshmen graduate within 6 years. 26% grads go on to further study within 1 year. 23% grads pursue arts and sciences degrees. 2% grads pursue business degrees. **Faculty:** Student/faculty ratio 16:1. 145 full-time faculty, 61% hold PhDs, 13% are members of minority groups, 26% are women. 0% of classes are taught by teaching assistants.

ACADEMICS

Degrees: associate, bachelor's, master's, terminal associate. **Classes:** Most classes have 20—29 students. Most lab/discussion sessions have 10—19 students. **Majors with Highest Enrollment:** architecture (barch, ba/bs, march, ma/ms, phd); construction management; mechanical engineering/mechanical technology/technician. **Special Study Options:** cooperative education program, cross-registration, distance learning, study abroad, Cross registration available through the Colleges of the Fenway Consortium with member colleges: Simmons College, Emmanuel College, Wheelock College, Massachusetts College of Pharmacy and Health Sciences, Massachusetts College of Art, and Wentworth Institute of Technology. **Disability Services:** Special programs offered to physically disabled students include note-taking services, reader services, tape recorders, tutors. **Career Services:** Alumni network, career/job search classes, internships Career services highlights include Active for over 30 years, WIT's co-op program is one of the largest and most comprehensive cooperative education programs of its kind in the nation. Co-op is a requirement for all majors. 100% of WIT's co-op placements are directly related to the student's field of study.

FACILITIES

Housing: Coed dorms. 75% of campus accessible to physically disabled. **Computers:** 100% of classrooms, 100% of dorms, 100% of libraries, 100% of dining areas, have wireless network access. Students can register for classes online. Administrative functions (other than registration) can be performed online.

CAMPUS LIFE

Environment: Metropolis. **Activities:** Choral groups, dance, drama/theater, music ensembles, musical theater, radio station, student government, student newspaper, student-run film society, yearbook, International Student Organization 50 registered organizations, 3 honor societies, 1 religious organizations. **Athletics (Intercollegiate):** *Men:* baseball, basketball, golf, ice hockey, lacrosse, riflery, soccer, tennis, volleyball. *Women:* basketball, golf, riflery, soccer, softball, tennis, volleyball. **On-Campus Highlights:** 550 Huntington Ave (newest residence hall), Beatty Hall (cafe, library, student activities), Computer Info Systems Networking Lab (, Tansey Gymnasium, Annex (architecture and design studios), Daily tours and info sessions, fall Open Houses, spring Special Events, see website www.wit.edu (under Prospective Students) for details. **Environmental Initiatives:** Cogeneration System High Efficient Boilers Lighting Upgrade

ADMISSIONS

Freshman Academic Profile: Average high school GPA 3.0. 12% in top 10% of high school class, 40% in top 25% of high school class, 76% in top 50% of high school class. SAT Math middle 50% range 520-620. SAT Critical Reading middle 50% range 470-570. SAT Writing middle 50% range 450-560. ACT middle 50% range 21-26. Minimum web-based TOEFL 71. Minimum paper TOEFL 525. **Basis for Candidate Selection:** *Important factors considered include:* application essay, recommendation(s), rigor of secondary school record, standardized test scores. *Other factors considered include:* academic GPA, alumni/ae relation, character/personal qualities, extracurricular activities, first generation, geographical residence, level of applicant's interest, talent/ability, volunteer work, work experience. **Freshman Admission Requirements:** High school diploma is required and GED is accepted. *Academic units required:* 4 English, 3 mathematics, 2 science, (1 science labs), 1 social studies. academic electives. 3 college-preparatory math,1 physics recommended for many programs.&4 years of mathmematics for some. *Academic units recommended:* 4 English, 3 mathematics, 2 science, (1 science labs), 1 social studies. academic electives. 3 college-preparatory math,1 physics recommended for many programs.&4 years of mathmematics for some. **Freshman Admission Statistics:** 5,650 applied, 61% admitted, 30% enrolled. **Transfer Admission Requirements:** High school transcript, college transcript(s), essay or personal statement, Lowest grade transferable C. **General Admission Information:** Application Fee $50. Notification on a rolling basis, beginning on or about 10/30. Nonfall registration accepted. Admission may be deferred for a maximum of 12 months. Credit offered for CEEB Advanced Placement tests.

COSTS AND FINANCIAL AID

Annual tuition $25,900. Room and board $11,900. Average book expense $1,500. **Required Forms and Deadlines:** FAFSA. **Notification of Awards:** Applicants will be notified of awards on a rolling basis beginning 3/15. **Types of Aid:** *Need-based scholarships/grants:* Federal Pell, SEOG, state scholarships/grants, private scholarships, the school's own gift aid. *Loans:* Subsidized Stafford, Unsubsidized Stafford, PLUS, Federal Perkins, state loans. **Student Employment:** Federal Work-Study Program available. Institutional employment available. Highest amount earned per year from on-campus jobs $875. Off-campus job opportunities are good. **Financial Aid Statistics:** 70% freshmen, 63% undergrads receive need-based scholarship or grant aid. 100% freshmen, 93% undergrads receive non-need-based scholarship or grant aid. 84% freshmen, 84% undergrads receive need-based self-help aid. 71% freshmen, 62% undergrads receive any aid. 82% undergrads borrow to pay for school. Average cumulative indebtedness $33,968. **Criteria for awarding institutional aid:** *Non-need-based:* academics, leadership, state/district residency.

See page 1298.

WESLEY COLLEGE (DE)

120 North State Street, Dover, DE 19901-3875
Phone: 302-736-2400
E-mail: admissions@wesley.edu • **CEEB Code:** 1433
Fax: 302-736-2382 • **Website:** www.wesley.eud • **ACT Code:** 636

This private school, affiliated with the Methodist Church, was founded in 1873. It has a 40-acre campus.

RATINGS
Admissions Selectivity Rating: 68   **Fire Safety Rating:** 67   **Green Rating:** 60*

STUDENTS AND FACULTY
Enrollment: 1,605. **Student Body:** 52% female, 48% male, 63% out-of-state, 1% international. Asian 2%, African American 22%, Caucasian 72%, Hispanic 3%, Native American 1%
Retention and Graduation: 82% freshmen return for sophomore year. 34% freshmen graduate within 4 years. 50% freshmen graduate within 6 years. 30% grads go on to further study within 1 year. 2% grads pursue arts and sciences degrees. 1% grads pursue law degrees. 10% grads pursue business degrees. **Faculty:** Student/faculty ratio 19:1. 66 full-time faculty, 79% hold PhDs, 11% are members of minority groups, 50% are women. 0% of classes are taught by teaching assistants.

ACADEMICS
Degrees: associate, bachelor's, certificate, master's, post-bachelor's certificate. **Classes:** Most classes have 20—29 students. Most lab/discussion sessions have fewer than 10 students. **Majors with Highest Enrollment:** business/commerce; elementary education and teaching; psychology. **Special Study Options:** double major, honors program, independent study, internships, liberal arts/career combination, teacher certification program. **Disability Services:** Special programs offered to physically disabled students include tape recorders, tutors. **Career Services:** internships.

FACILITIES
Housing: Coed dorms, men's dorms, women's dorms, apartments for single students. 80% of campus accessible to physically disabled. **Special Academic Facilities/Equipment:** 1 **Computers:** Students can register for classes online. Administrative functions (other than registration) can be performed online.

CAMPUS LIFE
Environment: Town. **Activities:** Choral groups, drama/theater, literary magazine, music ensembles, radio station, student government, student newspaper, yearbook 30 registered organizations, 2 honor societies, 2 religious organizations. 3 fraternities, 3 sororities. **Athletics (Intercollegiate):** *Men:* baseball, basketball, cheerleading, cross-country, football, golf, lacrosse, soccer, tennis. *Women:* baseball, basketball, cheerleading, cross-country, field hockey, golf, lacrosse, soccer, softball, tennis.

ADMISSIONS
Freshman Academic Profile: Average high school GPA 3.0. 24% in top 10% of high school class, 56% in top 25% of high school class, 78% in top 50% of high school class. 80% from public high schools. SAT Math middle 50% range 400-500. SAT Critical Reading middle 50% range 499-490. SAT Writing middle 50% range 390-490. Minimum paper TOEFL 550. **Basis for Candidate Selection:** *Very important factors considered include:* academic GPA. *Important factors considered include:* Class rank, rigor of secondary school record, standardized test scores. *Other factors considered include:* application essay, recommendation(s), alumni/ae relation, character/personal qualities, extracurricular activities, interview, level of applicant's interest, talent/ability, volunteer work, work experience. **Freshman Admission Requirements:** High school diploma is required and GED is accepted. **Freshman Admission Statistics:** 2,633 applied, 76% admitted, 25% enrolled. **Transfer Admission Requirements:** High school transcript, college transcript(s), Minimum college GPA of 2.0 required. Lowest grade transferable C. **General Admission Information:** Application Fee $25. Nonfall registration accepted. Admission may be deferred for a maximum of 2 sems (1 yr). Credit and/or placement offered for CEEB Advanced Placement tests.

COSTS AND FINANCIAL AID
Annual tuition $16,750. Room and board $7,800. Required fees $829. Average book expense $1,000. **Required Forms and Deadlines:** FAFSA, institution's own financial aid form. **Notification of Awards:** Applicants will be notified of

awards on a rolling basis beginning 1/1. **Types of Aid:** *Need-based scholarships/grants:* Federal Pell, SEOG, state scholarships/grants, private scholarships. *Loans:* Direct PLUS, Subsidized Stafford, Unsubsidized Stafford, PLUS, Federal Perkins. **Student Employment:** Highest amount earned per year from on-campus jobs $2,550. **Financial Aid Statistics:** 78% freshmen, 87% undergrads receive need-based scholarship or grant aid. 46% freshmen, 50% undergrads receive non-need-based scholarship or grant aid. 100% freshmen, 100% undergrads receive need-based self-help aid. 95% freshmen, 95% undergrads receive any aid. 93% undergrads borrow to pay for school. **Criteria for awarding institutional aid:** *Non-need-based:* academics, alumni affiliation, religious affiliation.

WESLEYAN COLLEGE

Best 378

4760 Forsyth Road, Macon, GA 31210-4462
Phone: 478-477-1110 • **Financial Aid Phone:** 478-757-5205
E-mail: admissions@wesleyancollege.edu • **CEEB Code:** 5895
Fax: 478-757-4030 • **Website:** www.wesleyancollege.edu • **ACT Code:** 876

This private school, affiliated with the Methodist Church, was founded in 1836. It has a 200-acre campus.

RATINGS
Admissions Selectivity Rating: 84   **Fire Safety Rating:** 85   **Green Rating:** 78

STUDENTS AND FACULTY
Enrollment: 648. **Student Body:** 63% out-of-state, 18% international (27 countries represented). Asian 1%, African American 19%, Caucasian 24%, Hispanic 3%, Native American 0%
Retention and Graduation: 83% freshmen return for sophomore year. 26% grads go on to further study within 1 year. 6% grads pursue arts and sciences degrees. 1% grads pursue law degrees. 10% grads pursue business degrees. 4% grads pursue medical degrees. **Faculty:** Student/faculty ratio 10:1. 51 full-time faculty, 84% hold PhDs, 12% are members of minority groups, 57% are women. 0% of classes are taught by teaching assistants.

ACADEMICS
Degrees: bachelor's, master's. **Classes:** Most classes have 10—19 students. **Majors with Highest Enrollment:** business administration, management and operations, other; international business/trade/commerce; psychology. **Special Study Options:** Accelerated program, cross-registration, double major, dual enrollment, exchange student program (domestic), honors program, independent study, internships, liberal arts/career combination, student-designed major, study abroad, teacher certification program, weekend college, Dual degree engineering(3/2) with Georgia Tech, Auburn University and Mercer University. **Honors Programs:** Honors Program **Combined Degree Programs:** 3-2 eng. prg. w/ Auburn U, Georgia Tech, Mercer. **Disability Services:** Special programs offered to physically disabled students include note-taking services, tutors. **Career Services:** Alumni network, career/job search classes, career assessment, internships Career services highlights include Internships are required for all graduating seniors.

FACILITIES
Housing: special housing for disabled students, women's dorms, apartments for single studentsStudents required to live on campus unless married or living with family in the local area. 70% of campus accessible to physically disabled. **Special Academic Facilities/Equipment:** Art and history museums, special collection of Georgiana and Americana, on-campus equestrian center. **Computers:** 80% of classrooms, 100% of libraries, 100% of dining areas, 100% of student union, 50% of common outdoor areas have wireless network access. Students can register for classes online. Administrative functions (other than registration) can be performed online.

CAMPUS LIFE
Environment: City. **Activities:** Choral groups, dance, drama/theater, literary magazine, music ensembles, student government, student newspaper, yearbook, Campus Ministries, International Student Organization, Model UN 40 registered organizations, 10 honor societies, 5 religious organizations. **Athletics (Intercollegiate):** *Women:* basketball, cross-country, equestrian sports, soccer, softball, tennis, volleyball. **On-Campus Highlights:** Historic quad of buildings Georgian brick design, Equestrian and Fitness Centers, Lake, Residence Halls, Art Galleries. **Environmental Initiatives:** We are currently renovating one

of our main teaching buildings to achieve LEED Silver Certification. We have established an Energy Star purchasing policy in accordance with the President's Climate Commitment. We have begun a campus-wide recycling program.

ADMISSIONS

Freshman Academic Profile: 3.4. 0% in top 10% of high school class, 1% in top 25% of high school class, 13% in top 50% of high school class. 81% from public high schools. SAT Math middle 50% range 420-540. SAT Critical Reading middle 50% range 450-575. SAT Writing middle 50% range 445-570. ACT middle 50% range 17-22. Minimum web-based TOEFL 80. Minimum paper TOEFL 550. **Basis for Candidate Selection:** *Very important factors considered include:* rigor of secondary school record. *Important factors considered include:* Class rank, academic GPA, recommendation(s), standardized test scores, extracurricular activities, interview, talent/ability. *Other factors considered include:* application essay, alumni/ae relation, level of applicant's interest, volunteer work, work experience. **Freshman Admission Requirements:** High school diploma is required and GED is accepted. *Academic units required:* 4 English, 3 mathematics, 3 science, (2 science labs), 2 foreign language, 3 social studies. *Academic units recommended:* 4 English, 3 mathematics, 3 science, (2 science labs), 2 foreign language, 3 social studies. **Freshman Admission Statistics:** 699 applied, 50% admitted, 35% enrolled. **Transfer Admission Requirements:** college transcript(s), essay or personal statement, statement of good standing from prior institution(s). Minimum college GPA of 2.5 required. Lowest grade transferable C. **General Admission Information:** Application Fee $30. Early decision application deadline 11/15. Regular application deadline 6/1. Notification on a rolling basis, beginning on or about 10/1. Nonfall registration accepted. Admission may be deferred for a maximum of 1 year. Credit and/or placement offered for CEEB Advanced Placement tests.

COSTS AND FINANCIAL AID

Annual tuition $19,000. Room and board $8,400. Average book expense $1,500. **Required Forms and Deadlines:** FAFSA, institution's own financial aid form, state aid form. **Notification of Awards:** Applicants will be notified of awards on a rolling basis beginning 3/1. **Types of Aid:** *Need-based scholarships/grants:* Federal Pell, SEOG, state scholarships/grants, private scholarships, the school's own gift aid. *Loans:* Subsidized Stafford, Unsubsidized Stafford, PLUS, Federal Perkins, state loans, college/university loans from institutional funds, CitiAssist, Wells FARGO,Collegiate Loans, Key Alternative Loans. **Student Employment.** Federal Work Study Program available. Highest amount earned per year from on-campus jobs $1,500. Off-campus job opportunities are good. **Financial Aid Statistics:** 100% freshmen, 98% undergrads receive need-based scholarship or grant aid. 13% freshmen, 12% undergrads receive non-need-based scholarship or grant aid. 79% freshmen, 81% undergrads receive need-based self-help aid. 97% freshmen, 67% undergrads receive any aid. 71% undergrads borrow to pay for school. Average cumulative indebtedness $34,368. **Criteria for awarding institutional aid:** *Non-need-based:* academics, alumni affiliation, art, job skills, leadership, minority status, music/drama, religious affiliation, state/district residency.

WESLEYAN UNIVERSITY

70 Wyllys Avenue, Middletown, CT 06459-0265
Phone: 860-685-3000 • **Financial Aid Phone:** 860-685-2800
E-mail: admissions@wesleyan.edu • **CEEB Code:** 3959
Fax: 860-685-3001 • **Website:** www.wesleyan.edu • **ACT Code:** 614

This private school was founded in 1831. It has a 240-acre campus.

RATINGS

Admissions Selectivity Rating: 97   **Fire Safety Rating:** 81   **Green Rating:** 93

STUDENTS AND FACULTY

Enrollment: 2,870. **Student Body:** 51% female, 49% male, 92% out-of-state, 8% international (46 countries represented). Asian 8%, African American 7%, Caucasian 53%, Hispanic 10%, Native American 0%
Retention and Graduation: 94% freshmen return for sophomore year. 87% freshmen graduate within 4 years. 92% freshmen graduate within 6 years.
Faculty: Student/faculty ratio 9:1. 339 full-time faculty, 94% hold PhDs, 18% are members of minority groups, 45% are women. 0% of classes are taught by teaching assistants.

ACADEMICS

Degrees: bachelor's, master's, post-master's certificate. **Classes:** Most classes have 10—19 students. Most lab/discussion sessions have 20—29 students. **Majors with Highest Enrollment:** English language and literature; political science and government; psychology. **Special Study Options:** cross-registration, double major, dual enrollment, exchange student program (domestic), honors program, independent study, student-designed major, study abroad. **Combined Degree Programs:** BA/MA. **Disability Services:** Special programs offered to physically disabled students include note-taking services, reader services, tape recorders, tutors.

FACILITIES

Housing: Coed dorms, special housing for disabled students, fraternity/sorority housing, apartments for married students, apartments for single students, wellness housing, theme housing, 14 Residence halls, 32 program houses, 139 woodframe houses. **Special Academic Facilities/Equipment:** Art center, art galleries, Center for Afro-American studies, East Asian Studies Center, Cinema Archives, concert hall, public affairs center, language lab, electron microscope, observatory, nuclear magnetic resonance spectrometers. **Computers:** 90% of classrooms, 100% of dorms, 90% of libraries, 90% of dining areas, 100% of student union, 90% of common outdoor areas have wireless network access. Students can register for classes online. Administrative functions (other than registration) can be performed online.

CAMPUS LIFE

Environment: Town. **Activities:** Choral groups, concert band, dance, drama/theater, jazz band, literary magazine, music ensembles, musical theater, pep band, radio station, student government, student newspaper, student-run film society, symphony orchestra, yearbook, Campus Ministries 220 registered organizations, 2 honor societies, 10 religious organizations. 9 fraternities, 4 sororities. **Athletics (Intercollegiate):** *Men:* baseball, basketball, crew/rowing, cross-country, diving, football, golf, ice hockey, lacrosse, soccer, squash, swimming, tennis, track/field (outdoor), track/field (indoor), wrestling. *Women:* basketball, crew/rowing, cross-country, diving, field hockey, ice hockey, lacrosse, soccer, softball, squash, swimming, tennis, track/field (outdoor), track/field (indoor), volleyball. **On-Campus Highlights:** Center for the Arts, Freeman Athletic Center, Center for Film Studies, Olin Memorial Library, Van Vleck Observatory, Freeman East Asian Studies Center. **Environmental Initiatives:** Energy conservation activities resulting in a 28% reduction of energy consumption campus wide and the construction of a PV solar system with a combined output of 215 kW. Education of campus community on Wesleyan's Carbon footprint and the steps required to meet the 2020 and 2050 goals towards carbon neutrality. Campus community commitment to climate change and education of personal impact on global climate change starting with your home and office.

ADMISSIONS

Freshman Academic Profile: Average high school GPA 3.8. 66% in top 10% of high school class, 88% in top 25% of high school class, 99% in top 50% of high school class. 54% from public high schools. SAT Math middle 50% range 660-740. SAT Critical Reading middle 50% range 640-740. SAT Writing middle 50% range 660-750. ACT middle 50% range 29-33. Minimum web-based TOEFL 100. Minimum paper TOEFL 600. **Basis for Candidate Selection:** *Very important factors considered include:* rigor of secondary school record. *Important factors considered include:* Class rank, application essay, academic GPA, recommendation(s), standardized test scores, character/personal qualities, first generation, racial/ethnic status, talent/ability. *Other factors considered include:* alumni/ae relation, extracurricular activities, geographical residence, interview, volunteer work, work experience. **Freshman Admission Requirements:** High school diploma is required and GED is accepted. **Freshman Admission Statistics:** 9,658 applied, 24% admitted, 35% enrolled. **Transfer Admission Requirements:** High school transcript, college transcript(s), essay or personal statement, standardized test scores, statement of good standing from prior institution(s). Lowest grade transferable C–. **General Admission Information:** Application Fee $55. Early decision application deadline 11/15. Regular application deadline 1/1. Regular notification 4/1. Nonfall registration not accepted. Admission may be deferred for a maximum of 1 year. Credit and/or placement offered for CEEB Advanced Placement tests.

COSTS AND FINANCIAL AID

Annual tuition $43,404. Room and board $13,678. Required fees $300. **Required Forms and Deadlines:** FAFSA, CSS/Financial Aid PROFILE, state aid form, noncustodial PROFILE. **Notification of Awards:** Applicants will be notified of awards on or about 4/1. **Types of Aid:** *Need-based scholarships/grants:* Federal Pell, SEOG, state scholarships/grants, private scholarships, the school's own gift aid. *Loans:* Direct Subsidized Stafford, Direct Unsubsidized Stafford, Direct PLUS, Federal Perkins, college/university loans from institutional funds. **Student Employment:** Federal Work-Study Program available. Institutional employment available. Off-campus job opportunities are good. **Financial Aid Statistics:** 93% freshmen, 93% undergrads receive need-based scholarship or grant aid. 97% freshmen, 97% undergrads receive need-based self-help aid. 47% freshmen, 48% undergrads receive any aid. 47% undergrads borrow to pay for school. Average cumulative indebtedness $25,864. **Criteria for awarding institutional aid:** *Non-need-based:* academics.

WEST CHESTER UNIVERSITY OF PENNSYLVANIA

Messikomer Hall, West Chester, PA 19383
Phone: 610-436-3411 • **Financial Aid Phone:** 610-436-2627
E-mail: ugadmiss@wcupa.edu • **CEEB Code:** 3328
Fax: 610-436-2907 • **Website:** www.wcupa.edu

This public school was founded in 1871. It has a 403.4-acre campus.

RATINGS
Admissions Selectivity Rating: 87   **Fire Safety Rating:** 95   **Green Rating:** 79

STUDENTS AND FACULTY
Enrollment: 13,053. **Student Body:** 59% female, 41% male, 12% out-of-state, 0% international (72 countries represented). Asian 2%, African American 9%, Caucasian 82%, Hispanic 5%, Native American 0%
Retention and Graduation: 43% freshmen graduate within 4 years. 69% freshmen graduate within 6 years. **Faculty:** Student/faculty ratio 18:1. 605 full-time faculty, 83% hold PhDs, 14% are members of minority groups, 54% are women. 0% of classes are taught by teaching assistants.

ACADEMICS
Degrees: bachelor's, master's, post-bachelor's certificate, post-master's certificate. **Classes:** Most classes have 20—29 students. **Majors with Highest Enrollment:** elementary education and teaching; history; psychology. **Special Study Options:** cooperative education program, cross-registration, distance learning, double major, dual enrollment, English as a Second Language (ESL), exchange student program (domestic), honors program, independent study, internships, liberal arts/career combination, student-designed major, study abroad, teacher certification program. **Honors Programs:** See the Honors College section of the WCU. **Disability Services:** Special programs offered to physically disabled students include note-taking services, reader services, tape recorders, tutors. **Career Services:** Alumni network, alumni services, career/job search classes, career assessment, internships, regional alumni. Career services highlights include Student Teaching.

FACILITIES
Housing: Coed dorms, special housing for disabled students, men's dorms, special housing for international students, women's dorms, fraternity/sorority housing, apartments for single students, wellness housing. 95% of campus accessible to physically disabled. **Special Academic Facilities/Equipment:** McKinney Gallery, Long Gallery, Emile K. Asplundh Concert Hall, Swope Auditorium, EO Bull Main Stage, Sykes Theater, Frances Harvey Green Library, Presser Music Library, Darlington Herbarium, Geology Museum, Speech and Hearing Clinic, Philips Autograph Library, Farrell Stadium, Hollinger Fieldhouse, Schmucker Science Center, The Center for Advanced Scientific Imaging and the Materials Research Center, WCU Planetarium, WCU Observatory, Robert B. Gordon Natural Area for Environmental Studies, The Children's Center, Southeastern PA Autism Resource Center, Geography and Planning Geographic Informatino Systems Lab, Philips Auditorium, Main Hall Auditorium, Schmucker Auditorium, Boucher Lecture Hall, Center for Government and Community Affairs, The Poetry Center. **Computers:** 100% of classrooms, 20% of dorms, 100% of libraries, 100% of dining areas, 100% of student union, 100% of common outdoor areas have wireless network access. Students can register for classes online. Administrative functions (other than registration) can be performed online.

CAMPUS LIFE
Environment: Village. **Activities:** Choral groups, concert band, dance, drama/theater, jazz band, literary magazine, marching band, music ensembles, musical theater, opera, pep band, radio station, student government, student newspaper, symphony orchestra, television station, yearbook, Campus Ministries, International Student Organization 233 registered organizations, 26 honor societies, 12 religious organizations. 12 fraternities, 13 sororities. **Athletics (Intercollegiate):** *Men:* baseball, basketball, cross-country, diving, football, golf, soccer, swimming, tennis, track/field (outdoor). *Women:* basketball, cheerleading, cross-country, diving, field hockey, golf, gymnastics, lacrosse, rugby, soccer, softball, swimming, tennis, track/field (outdoor), volleyball. **On-Campus Highlights:** Emilie K. Asplundh Concert Hall, E.O. Bull Main Stage, Farrell Stadium, Sykes Student Union Building, Educational Center for Earth Observation Systems, Please see our website for a campus events calendar: http://www.wcupa.edu/_INFORMATION/events/. **Environmental Initiatives:** Construction of

new buildings and the renovation of existing buildings are done so that they could meet LEED Silver if the necessary paper work was filed and fees paid. Geothermal heating and cooling used for new residence halls, renovations, and buildings. Also, all buildings undergoing lifecycle renovations and some old existing buildings are having their HVAC systems changed out to geothermal systems. University vehicle fleet includes some that use compressed natural gas.

ADMISSIONS
Freshman Academic Profile: Average high school GPA 3.5. 12% in top 10% of high school class, 42% in top 25% of high school class, 85% in top 50% of high school class. 84% from public high schools. SAT Math middle 50% range 500-590. SAT Critical Reading middle 50% range 490-570. SAT Writing middle 50% range 480-570. Minimum web-based TOEFL 80. Minimum paper TOEFL 550. **Basis for Candidate Selection:** *Very important factors considered include:* Class rank, academic GPA, rigor of secondary school record. *Important factors considered include:* standardized test scores. *Other factors considered include:* application essay, character/personal qualities, extracurricular activities, racial/ethnic status, talent/ability, volunteer work, work experience. **Freshman Admission Requirements:** High school diploma is required and GED is accepted. *Academic units required:* 4 English, 3 mathematics, 2 science, (1 science labs), 2 social studies, 2 history, 1 academic electives. *Academic units recommended:* 4 English, 3 mathematics, 2 science, (1 science labs), 2 social studies, 2 history, 1 academic electives. **Freshman Admission Statistics:** 14,356 applied, 50% admitted, 33% enrolled. **Transfer Admission Requirements:** college transcript(s), essay or personal statement, Minimum college GPA of 2.0 required. Lowest grade transferable C. **General Admission Information:** Application Fee $35. Notification on a rolling basis, beginning on or about 10/1. Nonfall registration accepted. Admission may be deferred for a maximum of Varies. Credit and/or placement offered for CEEB Advanced Placement tests.

COSTS AND FINANCIAL AID
Annual in-state tuition $6,428. Annual out-of-state tuition $16,070. Room and board $7,922. Required fees $2,192. Average book expense $1,500. **Required Forms and Deadlines:** FAFSA. **Notification of Awards:** Applicants will be notified of awards on or about 4/1. **Types of Aid:** *Need-based scholarships/grants:* Federal Pell, SEOG, state scholarships/grants, the school's own gift aid. *Loans:* Subsidized Stafford, Unsubsidized Stafford, PLUS, Federal Perkins, Federal Nursing. **Student Employment:** Federal Work-Study Program available. Institutional employment available. Off-campus job opportunities are good. **Financial Aid Statistics:** 46% freshmen, 53% undergrads receive need-based scholarship or grant aid. 18% freshmen, 13% undergrads receive non-need-based scholarship or grant aid. 87% freshmen, 88% undergrads receive need-based self-help aid. 1% freshmen, 1% undergrads receive athletic scholarships. 75% freshmen, 72% undergrads receive any aid. 71% undergrads borrow to pay for school. Average cumulative indebtedness $30,345.

WEST LIBERTY STATE COLLEGE

PO Box 295, West Liberty, WV 26074
Phone: 304-336-8076 • **Financial Aid Phone:** 304-336-8016
E-mail: wladmsn1@wlsc.edu • **CEEB Code:** 5901
Fax: 304-336-8403 • **Website:** www.wlsc.edu • **ACT Code:** 4534

This public school was founded in 1837. It has a 290-acre campus.

RATINGS
Admissions Selectivity Rating: 64   **Fire Safety Rating:** 60*   **Green Rating:** 60*

STUDENTS AND FACULTY
Enrollment: 2,305. **Student Body:** 55% female, 45% male, 28% out-of-state, 1% international. Asian 0%, African American 3%, Caucasian 95%, Hispanic 1%, Native American 0%
Retention and Graduation: 43% grads go on to further study within 1 year. 6% grads pursue arts and sciences degrees. 1% grads pursue law degrees. 1% grads pursue business degrees. 1% grads pursue medical degrees. **Faculty:** Student/faculty ratio 18:1. 98 full-time faculty, 45% hold PhDs, 5% are members of minority groups, 40% are women. 0% of classes are taught by teaching assistants.

ACADEMICS
Degrees: associate, bachelor's. **Classes:** Most classes have 10—19 students. Most lab/discussion sessions have 10—19 students. **Majors with Highest Enrollment:** business/commerce; criminal justice/safety studies; elementary education and teaching. **Special Study Options:** Accelerated program, double major, external degree program, honors program, independent study, internships, student-designed major, teacher certification program. **Honors**

Programs: The goal of the Honors Program is to foster excellence through personal endeavors. These are original challenging studies, experiemnts, or other creative accomplishments which students wish to pursue in order to enhance their intellectual development. **Disability Services:** Special programs offered to physically disabled students include note-taking services, reader services, tape recorders, tutors.

FACILITIES

Housing: Coed dorms, men's dorms, women's dorms, apartments for married studentsHonors Dorm. 90% of campus accessible to physically disabled. **Special Academic Facilities/Equipment:** Book museums, language lab, clinical lab sciences and dental hygiene labs. clinical lab sciences and dental hygiene labs.

CAMPUS LIFE

Environment: Rural. **Activities:** Choral groups, concert band, drama/theater, jazz band, literary magazine, marching band, music ensembles, musical theater, pep band, radio station, student government, student newspaper, television station 50 registered organizations, 10 honor societies, 4 religious organizations. 5 fraternities, 4 sororities. **Athletics (Intercollegiate):** *Men:* baseball, basketball, cheerleading, cross-country, football, golf, swimming, tennis, track/field (outdoor), wrestling. *Women:* basketball, cheerleading, cross-country, golf, softball, swimming, tennis, track/field (outdoor), volleyball.

ADMISSIONS

Freshman Academic Profile: Average high school GPA 3.1. 5% in top 10% of high school class, 32% in top 25% of high school class, 58% in top 50% of high school class. 88% from public high schools. SAT Math middle 50% range 390-490. SAT Critical Reading middle 50% range 400-500. ACT middle 50% range 17-22. Minimum paper TOEFL 500. **Basis for Candidate Selection:** *Very important factors considered include:* rigor of secondary school record, standardized test scores. **Freshman Admission Requirements:** High school diploma is required and GED is accepted. *Academic units required:* 4 English, 2 mathematics, 2 science, (2 science labs), 2 social studies, 1 history. *Academic units recommended:* 4 English, 2 mathematics, 2 science, (2 science labs), 2 social studies, 1 history. **Freshman Admission Statistics:** 1,202 applied, 98% admitted, 38% enrolled. **Transfer Admission Requirements:** college transcript(s), Minimum college GPA of 2.0 required. Lowest grade transferable D. **General Admission Information:** Notification on a rolling basis, beginning on or about 10/1. Nonfall registration accepted. Credit offered for CEEB Advanced Placement tests.

COSTS AND FINANCIAL AID

Annual in-state tuition $3,138. Annual out-of-state tuition $7,790. Room and board $4,730. Average book expense $800. **Required Forms and Deadlines:** FAFSA. **Notification of Awards:** Applicants will be notified of awards on a rolling basis beginning 2/15. **Types of Aid:** *Need-based scholarships/grants:* Federal Pell, SEOG, state scholarships/grants, private scholarships, the school's own gift aid. *Loans:* Direct Subsidized Stafford, Direct Unsubsidized Stafford, Direct PLUS, Federal Perkins, Federal Nursing. **Student Employment:** Off-campus job opportunities are good. **Financial Aid Statistics:** 78% freshmen, 63% undergrads receive need-based scholarship or grant aid. 78% freshmen, 32% undergrads receive non-need-based scholarship or grant aid. 72% freshmen, 88% undergrads receive need-based self-help aid. 64% undergrads borrow to pay for school. Average cumulative indebtedness $13,800. **Criteria for awarding institutional aid:** *Non-need-based:* state/district residency.

WEST SUBURBAN COLLEGE OF NURSING

3 Erie Court, Oak Park, IL 60302
Phone: 708-763-6530 • **Financial Aid Phone:** 708-763-1426
E-mail: admission@wscn.edu
Fax: 708-763-1531 • **Website:** www.wscn.edu

This private school, affiliated with the Roman Catholic Church, was founded in 1914.

RATINGS

Admissions Selectivity Rating: 60*   **Fire Safety Rating:** 60*   **Green Rating:** 60*

STUDENTS AND FACULTY

Enrollment: 236. **Student Body:** 86% female, 14% male, 0% international. Asian 24%, African American 10%, Caucasian 40%, Hispanic 13%, Native American 0%
Faculty: Student/faculty ratio 10:1. 23 full-time faculty, 17% hold PhDs, 17% are members of minority groups, 100% are women. 0% of classes are taught by teaching assistants.

ACADEMICS

Degrees: bachelor's, master's. **Classes:** Most classes have 10—19 students. Most lab/discussion sessions have fewer than 10 students. **Special Study Options:** Accelerated program, WSCN offers an Evening & Weekend program. There is also a Master of Science in Nursing program, which offers four separate majors. **Career Services:** alumni services, career assessment.

FACILITIES

Computers: 100% of classrooms, 100% of libraries, 100% of dining areas, have wireless network access. Students can register for classes online. Administrative functions (other than registration) can be performed online. Undergraduates are required to own a computer.

CAMPUS LIFE

Environment: Metropolis. **Activities:** student government 2 registered organizations.

ADMISSIONS

Freshman Admission Requirements: High school diploma is required and GED is accepted. **Transfer Admission Requirements:** college transcript(s), essay or personal statement, standardized test scores, Minimum college GPA of 2.75 required. Lowest grade transferable C. **General Admission Information:** Application Fee $30. Regular application deadline 4/1. Admission may be deferred for a maximum of.1 semester.

COSTS AND FINANCIAL AID

Types of Aid: *Need-based scholarships/grants:* Federal Pell, SEOG, state scholarships/grants, private scholarships, the school's own gift aid, Federal Nursing Scholarships. *Loans:* Subsidized Stafford, Unsubsidized Stafford, PLUS, college/university loans from institutional funds. **Student Employment:** Federal Work-Study Program available. Institutional employment available. Highest amount earned per year from on-campus jobs $5,353. Off-campus job opportunities are good. **Financial Aid Statistics:** 100% undergrads receive need-based scholarship or grant aid. 18% undergrads receive non need-based scholarship or grant aid. 79% undergrads receive need-based self-help aid. 86% undergrads receive any aid. 86% undergrads borrow to pay for school. **Criteria for awarding institutional aid:** *Non-need-based:* academics.

WEST TEXAS A&M UNIVERSITY

PO Box 60907, Canyon, TX 79016-0001
Phone: 806-651-2020 • **Financial Aid Phone:** 806-651-2055
E-mail: admissions@mail.wtamu.edu • **CEEB Code:** 3665
Fax: 806-651-5268 • **Website:** www.wtamu.edu • **ACT Code:** 4250

This public school was founded in 1910. It has a 135-acre campus.

RATINGS

Admissions Selectivity Rating: 72   **Fire Safety Rating:** 73   **Green Rating:** 60*

STUDENTS AND FACULTY

Enrollment: 6,535. **Student Body:** 55% female, 45% male, 10% out-of-state, 2% international (37 countries represented). Asian 1%, African American 5%, Caucasian 65%, Hispanic 23%, Native American 1%
Retention and Graduation: 24% freshmen graduate within 4 years. 43% freshmen graduate within 6 years. **Faculty:** Student/faculty ratio 20:1. 266 full-time faculty, 71% hold PhDs, 12% are members of minority groups, 42% are women. 4% of classes are taught by teaching assistants.

ACADEMICS

Degrees: bachelor's, diploma, master's. **Classes:** Most classes have 20—29 students. Most lab/discussion sessions have 20—29 students. **Majors with Highest Enrollment:** business/commerce; multi-/interdisciplinary studies, other; nursing/registered nurse (rn, asn, bsn, msn). **Special Study Options:** cooperative education program, distance learning, double major, English as a Second Language (ESL), honors program, independent study, internships, liberal arts/career combination, study abroad, teacher certification program. **Honors Programs:** The Honors Program at West Texas AandM University is committed to providing exceptional students with challenging academic studies, innovative approaches to instruction; increased opportunities for improving skills in critical thinking, research, developing creative works and writing; expanded cultural knowledge; and the opportunity to interact closely with faculty and similarly motivated students. **Combined Degree Programs:** BBA/MPA. **Disability Services:** Special programs offered to physically disabled students include note-taking services, reader services, tape recorders, tutors. **Career Services:** Alumni network, alumni services, career/job search classes, career assessment, internships, regional alumni.

FACILITIES

Housing: Coed dorms, special housing for disabled students, men's dorms, women's dorms, fraternity/sorority housing, Honors Program. 100% of campus accessible to physically disabled. **Special Academic Facilities/Equipment:** Regional History Museum, Research Center, Panhandle Plains Historical Museum, Killgore Research Center. **Computers:** Students can register for classes online. Administrative functions (other than registration) can be performed online.

CAMPUS LIFE

Environment: Village. **Activities:** Choral groups, concert band, dance, drama/theater, jazz band, literary magazine, marching band, music ensembles, musical theater, opera, radio station, student government, student newspaper, symphony orchestra, Campus Ministries, International Student Organization 110 registered organizations, 15 honor societies, 13 religious organizations. 5 fraternities, 5 sororities. **Athletics (Intercollegiate):** *Men:* baseball, basketball, cross-country, football, golf, soccer. *Women:* basketball, cheerleading, cross-country, equestrian sports, golf, soccer, softball, volleyball. **On-Campus Highlights:** Panhandle-Plains Historical Museum, Jack B. Kelley Student Center, Virgil Henson Activities Center, Old Main (first building built on campus), WTAMU Horse Center, Panhandle-Plains Historical Museum is the largest historical museum in the State of Texas.

ADMISSIONS

Freshman Academic Profile: 15% in top 10% of high school class, 43% in top 25% of high school class, 78% in top 50% of high school class. 97% from public high schools. SAT Math middle 50% range 450-550. SAT Critical Reading middle 50% range 410-530. ACT middle 50% range 18-23. Minimum web-based TOEFL 190. Minimum paper TOEFL 520. **Basis for Candidate Selection:** *Very important factors considered include:* Class rank, academic GPA, standardized test scores. *Important factors considered include:* rigor of secondary school record. *Other factors considered include:* recommendation(s). **Freshman Admission Requirements:** High school diploma is required and GED is accepted. *Academic units required:* 4 English, 3 mathematics, 3 science. *Academic units recommended:* 4 English, 3 mathematics, 3 science. **Freshman Admission Statistics:** 4,109 applied, 69% admitted, 42% enrolled. **Transfer Admission Requirements:** college transcript(s), Minimum college GPA of 2.0 required. Lowest grade transferable C. **General Admission Information:** Application Fee $25. Notification on a rolling basis, beginning on or about 9/1. Nonfall registration accepted. Admission may be deferred for a maximum of 1 term. Credit offered for CEEB Advanced Placement tests.

COSTS AND FINANCIAL AID

Annual in-state tuition $6,440. Annual out-of-state tuition $15,562. Room and board $6,864. Average book expense $1,000. **Required Forms and Deadlines:** FAFSA. **Notification of Awards:** Applicants will be notified of awards on a rolling basis beginning 2/1. **Types of Aid:** *Need-based scholarships/grants:* Federal Pell, SEOG, state scholarships/grants, private scholarships, the school's own gift aid. *Loans:* Subsidized Stafford, Unsubsidized Stafford, PLUS, Federal Perkins, state loans. **Student Employment:** Highest amount earned per year from on-campus jobs $5,850. **Financial Aid Statistics:** 76% freshmen, 76% undergrads receive need-based scholarship or grant aid. 64% freshmen, 43% undergrads receive non-need-based scholarship or grant aid. 86% freshmen, 97% undergrads receive need-based self-help aid. 2% freshmen, 1% undergrads receive athletic scholarships. 52% freshmen, 53% undergrads receive any aid. 63% undergrads borrow to pay for school. Average cumulative indebtedness $19,774. **Criteria for awarding institutional aid:** *Non-need-based:* academics, art, athletics, leadership, music/drama, state/district residency.

WEST VIRGINIA STATE UNIVERSITY

106 Ferrell Hall, Institute, WV 25112
Phone: 304-766-3033 • **Financial Aid Phone:** 304-766-3131
E-mail: admissions@wvstateu.edu • **CEEB Code:** 5903
Fax: 304-766-5182 • **Website:** www.wvstateu.edu • **ACT Code:** 4538

This public school was founded in 1891. It has a 95-acre campus.

RATINGS

Admissions Selectivity Rating: 61   **Fire Safety Rating:** 60*   **Green Rating:** 60*

STUDENTS AND FACULTY

Enrollment: 3,455. **Student Body:** 59% female, 41% male, 8% out-of-state, 0% international (8 countries represented). Asian 1%, African American 15%, Caucasian 81%, Hispanic 1%, Native American 0%
Retention and Graduation: 6% grads go on to further study within 1 year. 3% grads pursue arts and sciences degrees. 1% grads pursue law degrees. 1% grads pursue business degrees. 1% grads pursue medical degrees.

ACADEMICS

Degrees: bachelor's, master's. **Majors with Highest Enrollment:** business administration and management; elementary education and teaching; general studies. **Special Study Options:** cooperative education program, off-campus study: Washington, DC. **Disability Services:** Special programs offered to physically disabled students include tutors.

FACILITIES

Housing: Coed dorms, men's dorms, women's dorms, apartments for married students. **Special Academic Facilities/Equipment:** On-campus day-care center, art gallery, ROTC Hall of Fame, Sports Hall of Fame.

CAMPUS LIFE

Environment: Village. **Activities:** Choral groups, concert band, jazz band, literary magazine, marching band, music ensembles, radio station, student government, student newspaper, television station, yearbook 4 honor societies, 2 religious organizations. 6 fraternities, 3 sororities. **Athletics (Intercollegiate):** *Men:* baseball, basketball, cross-country, football, softball, tennis, track/field (outdoor), volleyball. *Women:* basketball, cross-country, softball, tennis, track/field (outdoor), volleyball.

ADMISSIONS

Freshman Academic Profile: 99% from public high schools. **Freshman Admission Requirements:** High school diploma is required and GED is accepted.High school diploma is required and GED is not accepted. *Academic units required:* 4 English, 2 mathematics, 2 science, 2 foreign language, 3 social studies, 1 history. *Academic units recommended:* 4 English, 2 mathematics, 2 science, 2 foreign language, 3 social studies, 1 history. **Transfer Admission Requirements:** college transcript(s), Minimum college GPA of 2.0 required. Lowest grade transferable D. **General Admission Information:** Regular application deadline 8/22. Nonfall registration accepted. Credit and/or placement offered for CEEB Advanced Placement tests.

COSTS AND FINANCIAL AID

Annual in-state tuition $2,116. Annual out-of-state tuition $5,150. Room and board $3,550. Required fees $125. Average book expense $500. **Required Forms and Deadlines:** FAFSA, institution's own financial aid form. **Types of Aid:** *Need-based scholarships/grants: Loans:* Subsidized Stafford, PLUS. **Student Employment:** Highest amount earned per year from on-campus jobs $1,300.

WEST VIRGINIA UNIVERSITY

Admissions Office, Morgantown, WV 26506-6009
Phone: 304-293-2121 • **Financial Aid Phone:** 304-293-5242
E-mail: go2wvu@mail.wvu.edu • **CEEB Code:** 5904
Fax: 304-293-3080 • **Website:** www.wvu.edu • **ACT Code:** 4540

This public school was founded in 1867.

RATINGS

Admissions Selectivity Rating: 69   **Fire Safety Rating:** 91   **Green Rating:** 86

STUDENTS AND FACULTY

Enrollment: 22,292. **Student Body:** 45% female, 55% male, 47% out-of-state, 3% international. Asian 2%, African American 4%, Caucasian 84%, Hispanic 3%, Native American 0%
Retention and Graduation: 77% freshmen return for sophomore year. 34% freshmen graduate within 4 years. 56% freshmen graduate within 6 years.
Faculty: Student/faculty ratio 23:1. 1004 full-time faculty, 84% hold PhDs, 13% are members of minority groups, 42% are women.

ACADEMICS

Degrees: bachelor's, master's. **Classes:** Most classes have 20—29 students. Most lab/discussion sessions have 20—29 students. **Majors with Highest Enrollment:** business/commerce; engineering; health professions and related clinical sciences, other. **Special Study Options:** Accelerated program, cooperative education program, distance learning, double major, English as a Second Language (ESL), exchange student program (domestic), external degree program, honors program, independent study, internships, student-designed major, study abroad, teacher certification program, weekend college. **Honors Programs:** Honors Leadership Academy **Combined Degree Programs:** BA/MA, BA/MA in Ed.,BSBAd/BA Lang,BA/MOT,BA/MPT,MPA/BSW. **Disabil-**

ity Services: Special programs offered to physically disabled students include note-taking services, reader services, tape recorders, tutors. **Career Services:** Alumni network, alumni services, career/job search classes, career assessment, internships.

FACILITIES

Housing: Coed dorms, special housing for disabled students, men's dorms, special housing for international students, women's dorms, fraternity/sorority housing, apartments for married students, cooperative housing, apartments for single students, (Special interest "floors" available, Operation Jump Start places faculty residence hall leaders adjacent to residence halls allowing frequent opportunities for faculty-student interaction outside classroom. This program mandatory for freshmen). 90% of campus accessible to physically disabled. **Special Academic Facilities/Equipment:** Art galleries, creative arts center, arboretum, herbarium, planetarium, concurrent engineering research center, discovery lab (for inventors), Appalachian hardwood center, small business development center, pharmacy museum, coal and energy museum, center for economic research, fluidization center, center for software development. **Computers:** 80% of classrooms, 75% of dorms, 100% of libraries, 40% of dining areas, 100% of student union, 10% of common outdoor areas have wireless network access. Students can register for classes online. Administrative functions (other than registration) can be performed online.

CAMPUS LIFE

Environment: Town. **Activities:** Choral groups, concert band, dance, drama/theater, jazz band, literary magazine, marching band, music ensembles, musical theater, pep band, radio station, student government, student newspaper, symphony orchestra, television station, yearbook, Campus Ministries, International Student Organization 370 registered organizations, 31 honor societies, 28 religious organizations. 14 fraternities, 9 sororities. **Athletics (Intercollegiate):** *Men:* baseball, basketball, diving, football, riflery, soccer, swimming, wrestling. *Women:* basketball, crew/rowing, cross country, diving, gymnastics, riflery, soccer, swimming, tennis, track/field (outdoor), track/field (indoor), volleyball. **On-Campus Highlights:** New State of the Art Student Recreation Center, Mountainlair (Student Union), Personal Rapid Transit (PRT), Mountaineer Field, Historic Woodburn Circle, Core Arboretum. **Environmental Initiatives:** 1. Energy performance management and emissions reduction through a performance contract (approx. $30 million) between WVU and Siemens Inc. 2. Dining: Trayless dining in four dining halls, cage free shell eggs served in all dining halls, and food donations to local charities. 3. Alt. Transportation offerings such as car-sharing (Zipcar), carpool (Zimride), Vanpool (VSNI), occasional parking program, Mountain Line Bus, and PRT.

ADMISSIONS

Freshman Academic Profile: Average high school GPA 3.4. 17% in top 10% of high school class, 41% in top 25% of high school class, 75% in top 50% of high school class. SAT Math middle 50% range 470-580. SAT Critical Reading middle 50% range 460-560. ACT middle 50% range 21-26. Minimum web-based TOEFL 61. Minimum paper TOEFL 550. **Basis for Candidate Selection:** *Very important factors considered include:* academic GPA, standardized test scores. *Important factors considered include:* rigor of secondary school record, level of applicant's interest, state residency. *Other factors considered include:* recommendation(s), extracurricular activities, talent/ability, volunteer work. **Freshman Admission Requirements:** High school diploma is required and GED is accepted. *Academic units required:* 4 English, 4 mathematics, 3 science, (3 science labs), 2 foreign language, 3 social studies, 1 visual/performing arts. *Academic units recommended:* 4 English, 4 mathematics, 3 science, (3 science labs), 2 foreign language, 3 social studies, 1 visual/performing arts. **Freshman Admission Statistics:** 15,815 applied, 85% admitted, 37% enrolled. **Transfer Admission Requirements:** college transcript(s), Minimum college GPA of 2.0 required. Lowest grade transferable D. **General Admission Information:** Application Fee $25. Regular application deadline 8/1. Notification on a rolling basis, beginning on or about 10/1. Nonfall registration accepted. Admission may be deferred for a maximum of 1 year. Credit and/or placement offered for CEEB Advanced Placement tests.

COSTS AND FINANCIAL AID

Annual in-state tuition $6,090. Annual out-of-state tuition $18,868. Room and board $8,508. Average book expense $1,050. **Required Forms and Deadlines:** FAFSA, state aid form. **Notification of Awards:** Applicants will be notified of awards on a rolling basis beginning 3/15. **Types of Aid:** *Need-based scholarships/grants:* Federal Pell, SEOG, state scholarships/grants, private scholarships, the school's own gift aid. *Loans:* Direct Subsidized Stafford, Direct Unsubsidized Stafford, Direct PLUS, Federal Perkins, college/university loans from institutional funds. **Student Employment:** Federal Work-Study Program available. Institutional employment available. Highest amount earned per year from on-campus jobs $2,500. Off-campus job opportunities are good. **Financial Aid Statistics:** 52% freshmen, 48% undergrads receive need-based scholarship or grant aid. 82% freshmen, 65% undergrads receive non-need-based scholarship or grant aid. 55% freshmen, 61% undergrads receive need-based self-help aid. 2% freshmen, 1% undergrads receive athletic scholarships. 72% freshmen,

75% undergrads receive any aid. 59% undergrads borrow to pay for school. Average cumulative indebtedness $27,511. **Criteria for awarding institutional aid:** *Non-need-based:* academics, alumni affiliation, art, athletics, job skills, leadership, minority status, music/drama, state/district residency.

WEST VIRGINIA UNIVERSITY INSTITUTE OF TECHNOLOGY

Box 10 Old Main, Montgomery, WV 25136
Phone: 304-442-3167
E-mail: admissions@wvutech.edu
Fax: 304-442-3097 • **Website:** www.wvutech.edu

This is a public school.

RATINGS
Admissions Selectivity Rating: 69   **Fire Safety Rating:** 60*   **Green Rating:** 60*

STUDENTS AND FACULTY
Enrollment: 2,001. **Student Body:** 39% female, 61% male, 6% out-of-state, 4% international. Asian 1%, African American 8%, Caucasian 87%, Hispanic 1%, Native American 0%
Retention and Graduation: 62% freshmen return for sophomore year. **Faculty:** Student/faculty ratio 16:1. 119 full-time faculty, 47% hold PhDs, 18% are members of minority groups, 28% are women.

ACADEMICS
Degrees: associate, bachelor's, certificate, master's. **Classes:** Most classes have 10—19 students. Most lab/discussion sessions have 20—29 students. **Special Study Options:** cooperative education program, distance learning, double major, dual enrollment, internships, student-designed major.

FACILITIES
Housing: Coed dorms, men's dorms, women's dorms, fraternity/sorority housing.

CAMPUS LIFE
Environment: Activities: Choral groups, concert band, drama/theater, jazz band, marching band, music ensembles, pep band, student government, student newspaper.

ADMISSIONS
Freshman Academic Profile: Average high school GPA 3.2. 20% in top 10% of high school class, 21% in top 25% of high school class, 43% in top 50% of high school class. 88% from public high schools. SAT Math middle 50% range 400-580. SAT Critical Reading middle 50% range 380-530. ACT middle 50% range 17-23. Minimum paper TOEFL 500. **Basis for Candidate Selection:** *Very important factors considered include:* rigor of secondary school record, standardized test scores. *Other factors considered include:* Class rank, recommendation(s), alumni/ae relation, character/personal qualities, extracurricular activities, interview, state residency, talent/ability, volunteer work. **Freshman Admission Requirements:** High school diploma is required and GED is accepted. *Academic units required:* 4 English, 2 mathematics, 2 science, (2 science labs), 3 social studies. *Academic units recommended:* 4 English, 2 mathematics, 2 science, (2 science labs), 3 social studies. **Freshman Admission Statistics:** 1,191 applied, 74% admitted, 47% enrolled. **Transfer Admission Requirements:** college transcript(s), Minimum college GPA of 1.7 required. Lowest grade transferable D. **General Admission Information:** Notification on a rolling basis, beginning on or about 9/30. Nonfall registration accepted. Admission may be deferred for a maximum of 1 semester. Credit offered for CEEB Advanced Placement tests.

COSTS AND FINANCIAL AID
Annual in-state tuition $3,200. Annual out-of-state tuition $8,400. Room and board $4,896. Average book expense $800. **Required Forms and Deadlines:** FAFSA, institution's own financial aid form. **Notification of Awards:** Applicants will be notified of awards on a rolling basis beginning 3/3. **Types of Aid:** *Need-based scholarships/grants:* Federal Pell, SEOG, state scholarships/grants, private scholarships, the school's own gift aid. *Loans:* Direct Subsidized Stafford, Direct Unsubsidized Stafford, Direct PLUS, Subsidized Stafford, Unsubsidized Stafford, PLUS, Federal Perkins. **Student Employment: Financial Aid Statistics:** 78% freshmen, 78% undergrads receive need-based scholarship or grant aid. 70% freshmen, 48% undergrads receive non-need-based scholarship or grant aid. 59% freshmen, 70% undergrads receive need-based self-help aid. 2% freshmen, 6% undergrads receive athletic scholarships. 47% undergrads borrow to pay for school. Average cumulative indebtedness. **Criteria for awarding institutional aid:** *Non-need-based:* academics, alumni affiliation, art, athletics, music/drama.

WEST VIRGINIA WESLEYAN COLLEGE

59 College Avenue, Buckhannon, WV 26201
Phone: 304-473-8510 • **Financial Aid Phone:** 304-473-8080
E-mail: admission@wwc.edu • **CEEB Code:** 5905
Fax: 304-473-8108 • **Website:** www.wvwc.edu • **ACT Code:** 4544

This private school, affiliated with the Methodist Church, was founded in 1890. It has a 120-acre campus.

RATINGS
Admissions Selectivity Rating: 68   **Fire Safety Rating:** 60*   **Green Rating:** 67

STUDENTS AND FACULTY
Enrollment: 1,349. **Student Body:** 53% female, 47% male, 38% out-of-state, 5% international (12 countries represented). Asian 1%, African American 10%, Caucasian 78%, Hispanic 2%, Native American 0%
Retention and Graduation: 67% freshmen return for sophomore year. 42% freshmen graduate within 4 years. 35% grads go on to further study within 1 year. 57% grads pursue arts and sciences degrees. 11% grads pursue law degrees. 16% grads pursue business degrees. 6% grads pursue medical degrees. **Faculty:** Student/faculty ratio 13:1. 78 full-time faculty, 74% hold PhDs, 1% are members of minority groups, 50% are women. 0% of classes are taught by teaching assistants.

ACADEMICS
Degrees: bachelor's, master's. **Classes:** Most classes have 10—19 students. Most lab/discussion sessions have 10—19 students. **Majors with Highest Enrollment:** biology/biological sciences; business administration and management; elementary education and teaching. **Special Study Options:** double major, English as a Second Language (ESL), exchange student program (domestic), honors program, independent study, internships, liberal arts/career combination, student-designed major, study abroad, teacher certification program. **Honors Programs:** The Honors Program is offered to recognize and challenge the College's most academically talented students. Participation is voluntary for all qualified students. **Combined Degree Programs:** BA/MA. **Disability Services:** Special programs offered to physically disabled students include note-taking services, reader services, tape recorders, tutors. **Career Services:** Alumni network, alumni services, career/job search classes, internships.

FACILITIES
Housing: Coed dorms, special housing for disabled students, men's dorms, women's dorms, fraternity/sorority housing. **Computers:** Students can register for classes online. Undergraduates are required to own a computer.

CAMPUS LIFE
Environment: Village. **Activities:** Choral groups, dance, drama/theater, jazz band, literary magazine, music ensembles, musical theater, opera, radio station, student government, student newspaper, yearbook, Campus Ministries, International Student Organization 75 registered organizations, 31 honor societies, 6 religious organizations. 6 fraternities, 5 sororities. **Athletics (Intercollegiate):** *Men:* baseball, basketball, cross-country, football, golf, soccer, softball, swimming, tennis, track/field (outdoor), track/field (indoor). *Women:* basketball, cross-country, golf, lacrosse, soccer, swimming, tennis, track/field (outdoor), track/field (indoor), volleyball. **On-Campus Highlights:** Cat's Claw (alternate dining facility), Sunny Bucks (Convenience Store), Wesley Chapel, Sleeth Art Gallery, Atkinson Theatre.

ADMISSIONS
Freshman Academic Profile: Average high school GPA 3.4. 22% in top 10% of high school class, 49% in top 25% of high school class, 79% in top 50% of high school class. 88% from public high schools. SAT Math middle 50% range 440-550. SAT Critical Reading middle 50% range 410-520. SAT Writing middle 50% range 390-520. ACT middle 50% range 20-26. Minimum paper TOEFL 500. **Basis for Candidate Selection:** *Very important factors considered include:* rigor of secondary school record. *Important factors considered include:* Class rank, academic GPA, standardized test scores, alumni/ae relation, character/personal qualities, extracurricular activities, first generation, interview, level of applicant's interest, talent/ability, volunteer work. *Other factors considered include:* application essay, recommendation(s), geographical residence, religious affiliation/commitment, state residency, work experience. **Freshman Admission Requirements:** High school diploma is required and GED is accepted. **Freshman Admission Statistics:** 1,743 applied, 78% admitted, 30% enrolled. **Transfer Admission Requirements:** High school transcript, college transcript(s), statement of good standing from prior institution(s). Minimum college GPA of 2.50 required. Lowest grade transferable C–. **General Admission Information:** Application Fee $35. Notification on a rolling basis, beginning on or about 9/15. Nonfall registration accepted. Admission may be deferred for a maximum of 1 yr. Credit offered for CEEB Advanced Placement tests.

COSTS AND FINANCIAL AID
Annual tuition $24,790. Room and board $7,510. Required fees $1,024. Average book expense $2,500. **Types of Aid:** *Need-based scholarships/grants:* ACG and SMART Grants. *Loans:* **Student Employment:** Federal Work-Study Program available. Institutional employment available. Highest amount earned per year from on-campus jobs $1,000. Off-campus job opportunities are fair. **Financial Aid Statistics:** 100% freshmen, 99% undergrads receive need-based scholarship or grant aid. 17% freshmen, 16% undergrads receive non-need-based scholarship or grant aid. 75% freshmen, 77% undergrads receive need-based self-help aid. 7% freshmen, 9% undergrads receive athletic scholarships. 99% freshmen, 98% undergrads receive any aid. 68% undergrads borrow to pay for school. Average cumulative indebtedness $24,155.

See page 1300.

WESTERN CAROLINA UNIVERSITY

102 Camp Building, Cullowhee, NC 28723
Phone: 828-227-7317 • **Financial Aid Phone:** 828-227-7290
E-mail: admiss@email.wcu.edu • **CEEB Code:** 5897
Fax: 828-227-7319 • **Website:** www.wcu.edu • **ACT Code:** 3172

This public school was founded in 1889. It has a 682-acre campus.

RATINGS
Admissions Selectivity Rating: 90   **Fire Safety Rating:** 88   **Green Rating:** 90

STUDENTS AND FACULTY
Enrollment: 7,796. **Student Body:** 53% female, 47% male, 7% out-of-state, 1% international (28 countries represented). Asian 1%, African American 7%, Caucasian 83%, Hispanic 3%, Native American 1%
Retention and Graduation: 28% freshmen graduate within 4 years. **Faculty:** Student/faculty ratio 16:1. 478 full-time faculty, 75% hold PhDs, 5% are members of minority groups, 47% are women. 1% of classes are taught by teaching assistants.

ACADEMICS
Degrees: bachelor's, master's, post-bachelor's certificate, post-master's certificate. **Classes:** Most classes have 20—29 students. Most lab/discussion sessions have 10—19 students. **Majors with Highest Enrollment:** criminal justice/safety studies; elementary education and teaching; nursing/registered nurse (rn, asn, bsn, msn). **Special Study Options:** cooperative education program, distance learning, double major, dual enrollment, English as a Second Language (ESL), exchange student program (domestic), honors program, independent study, internships, student-designed major, study abroad, teacher certification program. **Honors Programs:** Western has a residential Honors College designed to enhance the academic and social university experience for high-achieving students. The college consists of honors courses throughout liberal studies with an emphasis on special projects and undergraduate research in the major. Also, special housing, academic, leadership and social programs are available for honors students. **Disability Services:** Special programs offered to physically disabled students include note-taking services, reader services, tape recorders, tutors. **Career Services:** Alumni network, alumni services, career assessment, internships Career services highlights include Co-op and internship experiences are very common among WCU students. Some departments require them for degree completion. Intern and co-op opportunities are available domestically and internationally.

FACILITIES
Housing: Coed dorms, special housing for disabled students, men's dorms, women's dorms, fraternity/sorority housing, apartments for married students, wellness housing, theme housing. 89% of campus accessible to physically disabled. **Special Academic Facilities/Equipment:** Fine Arts Gallery, Mountain Heritage Center, Reading Center, North Carolina Center for the Advancement of Teaching, Speech/Hearing Center, Center for Applied Technology, CATA Lab (high technology computer lab), Fine and Performing Arts Center, Institute for the Economy and the Future, Public Policy Institute **Computers:** 90% of classrooms, 10% of dorms, 100% of libraries, 70% of dining areas, 100% of student union, 50% of common outdoor areas have wireless network access. Students can register for classes online. Administrative functions (other than registration) can be performed online. Undergraduates are required to own a computer.

CAMPUS LIFE
Environment: Rural. **Activities:** Choral groups, concert band, dance, drama/theater, jazz band, literary magazine, marching band, music ensembles, musi-

cal theater, pep band, radio station, student government, student newspaper, student-run film society, television station, Campus Ministries, International Student Organization, Model UN 103 registered organizations, 7 honor societies, 12 religious organizations. 11 fraternities, 8 sororities. **Athletics (Intercollegiate):** *Men:* baseball, basketball, cheerleading, cross-country, football, golf, track/field (outdoor), track/field (indoor). *Women:* basketball, cheerleading, cross-country, golf, soccer, softball, tennis, track/field (outdoor), track/field (indoor), volleyball. **On-Campus Highlights:** University Center, Campus Recreation Center, Hunter Library, Fine & Performing Arts Center, Ramsey Regional Activity Center, Courtyard Dining Hall is a new facility that opened in summer 2009. It provides students with the following options: All-you-can-eat, foodcourt with 4 restaurants, McAlisters Deli, Starbucks, and a C-store. **Environmental Initiatives:** Currently have two buildings under construction that will be LEED certified and completed in 2012. Continuing the development of our Carbon Paw Print program. Our largest efforts this year are Sustainability Council, Recyclmania 2012, Campus Conservation Nationals Energy Competition 2012, Earth and Wellness Celebration and the Wild and Scenic Film Festival In 2010-11 we achieved a 32% btu/sq ft. reduction in energy consumption using 2002-03 as the baseline year.

ADMISSIONS

Freshman Academic Profile: Average high school GPA 3.6. 13% in top 10% of high school class, 39% in top 25% of high school class, 78% in top 50% of high school class. SAT Math middle 50% range 480-570. SAT Critical Reading middle 50% range 460-560. SAT Writing middle 50% range 440-530. ACT middle 50% range 20-24. Minimum web-based TOEFL 79. Minimum paper TOEFL 550. **Basis for Candidate Selection:** *Very important factors considered include:* academic GPA, rigor of secondary school record, standardized test scores, level of applicant's interest, talent/ability. *Important factors considered include:* Class rank, application essay, recommendation(s), character/personal qualities, extracurricular activities, volunteer work, work experience. *Other factors considered include:* alumni/ae relation, first generation, geographical residence, interview, state residency. **Freshman Admission Requirements:** High school diploma is required and GED is accepted. *Academic units required:* 4 English, 4 mathematics, 3 science, (3 science labs), 2 foreign language, 2 social studies, 1 history, 4 academic electives. *Academic units recommended:* 4 English, 4 mathematics, 3 science, (3 science labs), 2 foreign language, 2 social studies, 1 history, 4 academic electives. **Freshman Admission Statistics:** 15,234 applied, 38% admitted, 27% enrolled. **Transfer Admission Requirements:** college transcript(s), statement of good standing from prior institution(s). Minimum college GPA of 2.0 required. Lowest grade transferable C. **General Admission Information:** Application Fee $45. Regular application deadline 3/1. Notification on a rolling basis, beginning on or about 1/15. Nonfall registration accepted. Credit and/or placement offered for CEEB Advanced Placement tests.

COSTS AND FINANCIAL AID

Annual in-state tuition $3,397. Annual out-of-state tuition $12,994. Room and board $6,932. Required fees $2,528. Average book expense $758. **Required Forms and Deadlines:** FAFSA, institution's own financial aid form. **Notification of Awards:** Applicants will be notified of awards on a rolling basis beginning 4/1. **Types of Aid:** *Need-based scholarships/grants:* Federal Pell, SEOG, state scholarships/grants, private scholarships, the school's own gift aid. *Loans:* Direct Subsidized Stafford, Direct Unsubsidized Stafford, Direct PLUS, Subsidized Stafford, Unsubsidized Stafford, PLUS, Federal Perkins. **Student Employment:** Federal Work-Study Program available. Institutional employment available. Off-campus job opportunities are fair. **Financial Aid Statistics:** 97% freshmen, 95% undergrads receive need-based scholarship or grant aid. 3% freshmen, 3% undergrads receive non-need-based scholarship or grant aid. 73% freshmen, 78% undergrads receive need-based self-help aid. 5% freshmen, 4% undergrads receive athletic scholarships. **Criteria for awarding institutional aid:** *Non-need-based:* academics, art, athletics, leadership, music/drama, state/district residency.

WESTERN CONNECTICUT STATE UNIVERSITY

Undergraduate Admissions Office, Danbury, CT 06810-6855
Phone: 203-837-9000 • **Financial Aid Phone:** 203-837-8588
E-mail: admissions@wcsu.edu • **CEEB Code:** 3350
Fax: 203-837-8338 • **Website:** www.wcsu.edu • **ACT Code:** 558

This public school was founded in 1903. It has a 364-acre campus.

RATINGS

Admissions Selectivity Rating: 76   **Fire Safety Rating:** 94   **Green Rating:** 67

STUDENTS AND FACULTY

Enrollment: 5,467. **Student Body:** 55% female, 45% male, 8% out-of-state, 0% international (7 countries represented). Asian 3%, African American 8%, Caucasian 73%, Hispanic 12%, Native American 0%
Retention and Graduation: 72% freshmen return for sophomore year. 16% freshmen graduate within 4 years. 23% grads go on to further study within 1 year. 10% grads pursue arts and sciences degrees. 2% grads pursue law degrees. 3% grads pursue business degrees. 1% grads pursue medical degrees. **Faculty:** Student/faculty ratio 16:1. 226 full-time faculty, 84% hold PhDs, 13% are members of minority groups, 51% are women. 0% of classes are taught by teaching assistants.

ACADEMICS

Degrees: associate, bachelor's, certificate, master's. **Classes:** Most classes have 20—29 students. Most lab/discussion sessions have 20—29 students. **Majors with Highest Enrollment:** criminal justice/police science; elementary education and teaching; nursing/registered nurse (rn, asn, bsn, msn). **Special Study Options:** cooperative education program, cross-registration, distance learning, double major, dual enrollment, English as a Second Language (ESL), honors program, independent study, internships, student-designed major, study abroad, teacher certification program. **Honors Programs:** University Scholars Program . **Disability Services:** Special programs offered to physically disabled students include note-taking services, reader services, tape recorders, tutors. **Career Services:** career/job search classes, career assessment, internships Career services highlights include Career assessment utilizes career software, "SIG13", which assesses career interests, maintains an extensive career library which offers a large collection of literature on career fields, job search, company profiles, and graduate/professional school information; and hosts a major Career Fair each year.

FACILITIES

Housing: Coed dorms, women's dorms, apartments for single students, On campus housing assigned on a first-come, first-served basis. 100% of campus accessible to physically disabled. **Special Academic Facilities/Equipment:** Language lab, observatory, electron microscope, nature preserve, computer-enhanced classrooms, business library, Jane Goodall Institute. **Computers:** 50% of classrooms, 80% of dorms, 100% of libraries, 100% of dining areas, 100% of student union, have wireless network access. Students can register for classes online. Administrative functions (other than registration) can be performed online.

CAMPUS LIFE

Environment: City. **Activities:** Choral groups, concert band, dance, drama/theater, jazz band, literary magazine, music ensembles, musical theater, opera, pep band, radio station, student government, student newspaper, symphony orchestra, yearbook, Campus Ministries, International Student Organization 40 registered organizations, 8 honor societies, 3 religious organizations. 3 fraternities, 4 sororities. **Athletics (Intercollegiate):** *Men:* baseball, basketball, football, lacrosse, soccer, tennis. *Women:* basketball, field hockey, lacrosse, soccer, softball, swimming, tennis, volleyball. **On-Campus Highlights:** Student Centers (Midtown and Westside), O'Neill Center, Science Building, White Hall, Ancell Classroom Building. **Environmental Initiatives:** "Think Green: Go Blue" recycling efforts (with distribution campus wide of an instruction brochure). Building Automation. Controls monitoring.

ADMISSIONS

Freshman Academic Profile: Average high school GPA 2.8. 5% in top 10% of high school class, 20% in top 25% of high school class, 61% in top 50% of high school class. 91% from public high schools. SAT Math middle 50% range 450-540. SAT Critical Reading middle 50% range 450-540. Minimum web-based TOEFL 79. Minimum paper TOEFL 550. **Basis for Candidate Selection:** *Very important factors considered include:* rigor of secondary school record, standardized test scores, talent/ability. *Important factors considered include:* Class rank, extracurricular activities. *Other factors considered include:* application essay, recommendation(s), alumni/ae relation, character/personal qualities, interview, racial/ethnic status, state residency, volunteer work, work experience. **Freshman Admission Requirements:** High school diploma is required and

GED is accepted. *Academic units required:* 4 English, 3 science, (2 science labs), 2 foreign language, 1 social studies, 1 history. *Academic units recommended:* 4 English, 3 mathematics, 2 science, (2 science labs), 2 foreign language, 1 social studies, 1 history. **Freshman Admission Statistics:** 4,157 applied, 62% admitted, 34% enrolled. **Transfer Admission Requirements:** college transcript(s), Minimum college GPA of 2.0 required. Lowest grade transferable C–. **General Admission Information:** Application Fee $50. Notification on a rolling basis, beginning on or about 12/1. Nonfall registration accepted. Admission may be deferred for a maximum of 1 year. Credit offered for CEEB Advanced Placement tests.

COSTS AND FINANCIAL AID

Required **Forms and Deadlines:** FAFSA, institution's own financial aid form. **Notification of Awards:** Applicants will be notified of awards on a rolling basis beginning 4/15. **Types of Aid:** *Need-based scholarships/grants:* Federal Pell, SEOG, state scholarships/grants, private scholarships, the school's own gift aid. *Loans:* Direct Subsidized Stafford, Direct Unsubsidized Stafford, Direct PLUS, Subsidized Stafford, Unsubsidized Stafford, PLUS, Federal Perkins. **Student Employment:** Highest amount earned per year from on-campus jobs $1,500. Off-campus job opportunities are excellent. **Financial Aid Statistics:** 87% freshmen, 86% undergrads receive need-based scholarship or grant aid. 21% freshmen, 15% undergrads receive non-need-based scholarship or grant aid. 88% freshmen, 88% undergrads receive need-based self-help aid. 63% freshmen, 61% undergrads receive any aid. 66% undergrads borrow to pay for school. Average cumulative indebtedness $26,348. **Criteria for awarding institutional aid:** *Non-need-based:* academics.

WESTERN ILLINOIS UNIVERSITY

1 University Circle, Macomb, IL 61455-1390
Phone: 309-298-3157 • **Financial Aid Phone:** 309-298-2446
E-mail: wiuadm@wiu.edu • **CEEB Code:** 1900
Fax: 309-298-3111 • **Website:** www.wiu.edu • **ACT Code:** 1158

This public school was founded in 1899. It has a 1050-acre campus.

RATINGS

Admissions Selectivity Rating: 71   **Fire Safety Rating:** 75   **Green Rating:** 78

STUDENTS AND FACULTY

Enrollment: 10,518. **Student Body:** 48% female, 52% male, 6% out-of-state, 1% international (61 countries represented). Asian 1%, African American 14%, Caucasian 72%, Hispanic 6%, Native American 0%
Retention and Graduation: 71% freshmen return for sophomore year. 30% freshmen graduate within 4 years. 53% freshmen graduate within 6 years. 19% grads go on to further study within 1 year. 12% grads pursue arts and sciences degrees. 1% grads pursue law degrees. 6% grads pursue business degrees. 1% grads pursue medical degrees. **Faculty:** Student/faculty ratio 16:1. 666 full-time faculty, 72% hold PhDs, 16% are members of minority groups, 45% are women. 5% of classes are taught by teaching assistants.

ACADEMICS

Degrees: bachelor's, doctoral, master's, post-bachelor's certificate. **Classes:** Most classes have 20—29 students. Most lab/discussion sessions have 10—19 students. **Majors with Highest Enrollment:** business administration and management; criminal justice/law enforcement administration; elementary education and teaching. **Special Study Options:** distance learning, double major, dual enrollment, English as a Second Language (ESL), external degree program, honors program, independent study, internships, student-designed major, study abroad, teacher certification program, weekend college. **Honors Programs:** Illinois Centennial Honors College. **Disability Services:** Special programs offered to physically disabled students include note-taking services, reader services, tape recorders, tutors.

FACILITIES

Housing: Coed dorms, men's dorms, special housing for international students, women's dorms, fraternity/sorority housing, apartments for married students, wellness housing. 95% of campus accessible to physically disabled. **Special Academic Facilities/Equipment:** Art gallery, electron microscope **Computers:** 100% of classrooms, 100% of dorms, 100% of libraries, 100% of dining areas, 100% of student union, 100% of common outdoor areas have wireless network access. Students can register for classes online. Administrative functions (other than registration) can be performed online.

CAMPUS LIFE

Environment: Village. **Activities:** Choral groups, concert band, dance, drama/theater, jazz band, marching band, music ensembles, musical theater, pep band, radio station, student government, student newspaper, symphony orchestra,

television station, yearbook, Campus Ministries, International Student Organization 200 registered organizations, 25 honor societies, 12 religious organizations. 14 fraternities, 11 sororities. **Athletics (Intercollegiate):** *Men:* baseball, basketball, cross-country, diving, football, golf, soccer, swimming, tennis, track/field (outdoor), track/field (indoor). *Women:* basketball, cheerleading, cross-country, diving, golf, soccer, softball, swimming, tennis, track/field (outdoor), track/field (indoor), volleyball. **On-Campus Highlights:** University Union, Student Recreation Center, Leslie Malpass Library **Environmental Initiatives:** n the last year Western has received two Illinois Clean Energy Community Foundation grants for energy efficient lighting upgrades. The most recent award of $59,262 is for an energy-efficient lighting upgrade in Morgan Hall consisting of retrofitting existing fluorescent lighting fixtures with high efficiency electronic ballasts and lamps that use 35 percent less energy than the original 35-year-old equipment. The University recently completed work from a previous Clean Energy Foundation grant to upgrade the lighting in Stipes Hall. The $83,680 project grant is projected to save nearly $15,000 a year in energy costs due to more efficient lighting Western students have been involved in campus beautification through the Litter Patrol, the Adopt-a-Street Program and the We Care Program to keep the campus and community clean and attractive.

ADMISSIONS

Freshman Academic Profile: Average high school GPA 3.0. 8% in top 10% of high school class, 26% in top 25% of high school class, 57% in top 50% of high school class. ACT middle 50% range 18-23. Minimum web-based TOEFL 79. Minimum paper TOEFL 550. **Basis for Candidate Selection:** *Very important factors considered include:* Class rank, academic GPA, rigor of secondary school record, standardized test scores. **Freshman Admission Requirements:** High school diploma is required and GED is accepted. **Freshman Admission Statistics:** 9,731 applied, 66% admitted, 31% enrolled. **Transfer Admission Requirements:** college transcript(s), Minimum college GPA of 2.0 required. Lowest grade transferable D. **General Admission Information:** Application Fee $30. Regular application deadline 5/15. Nonfall registration accepted. Admission may be deferred for a maximum of none. Credit offered for CEEB Advanced Placement tests.

COSTS AND FINANCIAL AID

Average book expense $1,200. **Required Forms and Deadlines:** FAFSA. **Notification of Awards:** Applicants will be notified of awards on a rolling basis beginning 1/15. **Types of Aid:** *Need-based scholarships/grants:* Federal Pell, SEOG, state scholarships/grants, private scholarships, the school's own gift aid. *Loans:* Subsidized Stafford, Unsubsidized Stafford, PLUS, Federal Perkins, college/university loans from institutional funds. **Student Employment:** Federal Work-Study Program available. Institutional employment available. Highest amount earned per year from on-campus jobs $6,500. Off-campus job opportunities are fair. **Financial Aid Statistics:** 76% freshmen, 70% undergrads receive need-based scholarship or grant aid. 95% freshmen, 95% undergrads receive need-based self-help aid. 4% freshmen, 3% undergrads receive athletic scholarships. 87% freshmen, 84% undergrads receive any aid. Average cumulative indebtedness $23,227. **Criteria for awarding institutional aid:** *Non-need-based:* academics, alumni affiliation, art, athletics, leadership, minority status, music/drama.

WESTERN KENTUCKY UNIVERSITY

Potter Hall 117, Bowling Green, KY 42101-1020
Phone: 270-745-2551 • **Financial Aid Phone:** 270-745-2755
E-mail: admission@wku.edu • **CEEB Code:** 1901
Fax: 270-745-6133 • **Website:** www.wku.edu • **ACT Code:** 1562

This public school was founded in 1906. It has a 235-acre campus.

RATINGS

Admissions Selectivity Rating: 66   **Fire Safety Rating:** 95   **Green Rating:** 86

STUDENTS AND FACULTY

Enrollment: 16,351. **Student Body:** 57% female, 43% male, 16% out-of-state, 3% international (50 countries represented). Asian 1%, African American 12%, Caucasian 79%, Hispanic 2%, Native American 0%
Retention and Graduation: 27% freshmen graduate within 4 years. 50% freshmen graduate within 6 years. **Faculty:** Student/faculty ratio 19:1. 785 full-time faculty, 70% hold PhDs, 19% are members of minority groups, 50% are women. 2% of classes are taught by teaching assistants.

ACADEMICS

Degrees: associate, bachelor's, certificate, master's, post-bachelor's certificate, post-master's certificate. **Classes:** Most classes have 20—29 students. Most lab/discussion sessions have 10—19 students. **Majors with Highest Enrollment:**

biology/biological sciences; business administration and management; elementary education and teaching. **Special Study Options:** cooperative education program, distance learning, double major, dual enrollment, English as a Second Language (ESL), exchange student program (domestic), honors program, independent study, internships, study abroad, teacher certification program, Gatton Academy of Math and Science, Learning Communities/Block Scheduling, Honors College, American Democracy Project. **Honors Programs:** University Honors College Gatton Academy of Mathematics and Science . **Disability Services:** Special programs offered to physically disabled students include note-taking services, reader services, tape recorders, tutors. **Career Services:** Alumni network, alumni services, career/job search classes, career assessment, internships.

FACILITIES

Housing: Coed dorms, men's dorms, special housing for international students, women's dorms, fraternity/sorority housing, theme housing, Gatton Academy, Learning Communities, Themed Living options - Fit,Honors, Mosiac Communities. **Special Academic Facilities/Equipment:** Kentucky Museum, University Farm, Hardin Planetarium, Media and Technology Hall **Computers:** 100% of classrooms, 68% of dorms, 100% of libraries, 100% of dining areas, 100% of student union, have wireless network access. Students can register for classes online. Administrative functions (other than registration) can be performed online.

CAMPUS LIFE

Environment: Town. **Activities:** Choral groups, concert band, dance, drama/theater, jazz band, literary magazine, marching band, music ensembles, musical theater, opera, pep band, radio station, student government, student newspaper, student-run film society, symphony orchestra, television station, yearbook, Campus Ministries, International Student Organization 360 registered organizations, 28 honor societies, 23 religious organizations. 18 fraternities, 13 sororities. **Athletics (Intercollegiate):** *Men:* baseball, basketball, cross-country, diving, football, golf, riflery, swimming, tennis, track/field (outdoor), track/field (indoor). *Women:* basketball, cross-country, diving, golf, riflery, soccer, swimming, tennis, track/field (outdoor), track/field (indoor), volleyball. **On-Campus Highlights:** Downing University Center, Preston Health and Activities Center, E.A. Diddle Arena and L.T. Smith Stadium, Mass Media and Technology Hall, Guthrie Tower, Please visit www.wku.edu/tour.html for further information and an interactive tour of the university. **Environmental Initiatives:** Sustainability-oriented staff positions and Sustainability Committee, Education for Sustainability resolution adopted 2010, Sustainability in operations, services, and academics included in 2010-2012 University Strategic Plan. Creation of comprehensive Energy Policy that guides purchasing, building operation, building design and construction, transportation, and personal energy use more responsibly. Commitment to LEED guidelines for all new building and renovation.

ADMISSIONS

Freshman Academic Profile: Average high school GPA 3.1. 22% in top 10% of high school class, 44% in top 25% of high school class, 70% in top 50% of high school class. SAT Math middle 50% range 420-570. SAT Critical Reading middle 50% range 410-580. ACT middle 50% range 18-25. Minimum web-based TOEFL 71. Minimum paper TOEFL 525. **Basis for Candidate Selection:** *Very important factors considered include:* academic GPA, standardized test scores. **Freshman Admission Requirements:** High school diploma is required and GED is accepted. *Academic units required:* 4 English, 3 mathematics, 3 science, (1 science labs), 2 foreign language, 3 social studies, 1 1/2 credits each: Health and PE, History, Performing Arts. *Academic units recommended:* 4 English, 3 mathematics, 3 science, (1 science labs), 2 foreign language, 3 social studies, 1 1/2 credits each: Health and PE, History, Performing Arts **Freshman Admission Statistics:** 8,526 applied, 92% admitted, 43% enrolled. **Transfer Admission Requirements:** college transcript(s), statement of good standing from prior institution(s). Minimum college GPA of 2.0 required. Lowest grade transferable D°. **General Admission Information:** Application Fee $40. Regular application deadline 8/1. Nonfall registration accepted. Admission may be deferred for a maximum of N/A. Credit and/or placement offered for CEEB Advanced Placement tests.

COSTS AND FINANCIAL AID

Annual in-state tuition $8,472. Annual out-of-state tuition $21,000. Room and board $7,320. Average book expense $1,000. **Required Forms and Deadlines:** FAFSA. **Notification of Awards:** Applicants will be notified of awards on a rolling basis beginning 3/1. **Types of Aid:** *Need-based scholarships/grants:* Federal Pell, SEOG, state scholarships/grants, private scholarships, the school's own gift aid, United Negro College Fund. *Loans:* Subsidized Stafford, Unsubsidized Stafford, PLUS, Federal Perkins, Alternative private loans, Federal Parent Plus Loans. **Student Employment:** Federal Work-Study Program available. Institutional employment available. Off-campus job opportunities are good. **Financial Aid Statistics:** 70% freshmen, 70% undergrads receive need-based scholarship or grant aid. 86% freshmen, 60% undergrads receive non-need-based scholarship or grant aid. 71% freshmen, 77% undergrads receive need-based self-help aid. 3% freshmen, 3% undergrads receive athletic

scholarships. 95% freshmen, 89% undergrads receive any aid. 59% undergrads borrow to pay for school. Average cumulative indebtedness $26,110. **Criteria for awarding institutional aid:** *Non-need-based:* academics, alumni affiliation, art, athletics, job skills, leadership, minority status, music/drama, religious affiliation, state/district residency.

WESTERN MICHIGAN UNIVERSITY

1903 W. Michigan Avenue, Kalamazoo, MI 49008-5211
Phone: 269-387-2000 • Financial Aid Phone: 269-387-6000
E-mail: ask-wmu@wmich.edu • CEEB Code: 1902
Fax: 269-387-2096 • Website: www.wmich.edu • ACT Code: 2066

This public school was founded in 1903. It has a 1200-acre campus.

RATINGS

Admissions Selectivity Rating: 67   Fire Safety Rating: 77   Green Rating: 90

STUDENTS AND FACULTY

Enrollment: 19,044. **Student Body:** 50% female, 50% male, 7% out-of-state, 3% international (95 countries represented). Asian 1%, African American 11%, Caucasian 76%, Hispanic 4%, Native American 0%
Retention and Graduation: 73% freshmen return for sophomore year. **Faculty:** Student/faculty ratio 18:1. 913 full-time faculty, 80% hold PhDs, 17% are members of minority groups, 42% are women. 13% of classes are taught by teaching assistants.

ACADEMICS

Degrees: bachelor's, master's, post-bachelor's certificate, post-master's certificate. **Classes:** Most classes have 20—29 students. Most lab/discussion sessions have 20—29 students. **Majors with Highest Enrollment:** elementary education and teaching; management science; nursing/registered nurse (rn, asn, bsn, msn). **Special Study Options:** Accelerated program, cross-registration, distance learning, double major, dual enrollment, English as a Second Language (ESL), exchange student program (domestic), honors program, independent study, internships, student designed major, study abroad, teacher certification program. **Honors Programs:** The Lee Honors College The mission of the Carl and Winifred Lee Honors College is to provide a lively, rigorous undergraduate program for bright, highly motivated, and active students. **Combined Degree Programs:** BA/MA, BA/MEng, Computer; Music. **Disability Services:** Special programs offered to physically disabled students include note-taking services, reader services, tape recorders, tutors. **Career Services:** Alumni network, alumni services, career/job search classes, career assessment, internships, regional alumni.

FACILITIES

Housing: Coed dorms, special housing for disabled students, men's dorms, special housing for international students, women's dorms, fraternity/sorority housing, apartments for married students, apartments for single students, wellness housing, theme housing. Each hall has a special thematic concept that is developed through programming and student involvment. Examples are: Community Service, Honors, Arts and Athletics, First Year Initiative, Upper Class Students, Diversity. 85% of campus accessible to physically disabled. **Special Academic Facilities/Equipment:** Pilot plant for manufacturing and printing of paper and for fiber recovery, behavior research and development center, nuclear accelerator, center for electron microscopy, particle accelerator lab, Library Department of Special Collections: Cistercian and Monastic Studies Collections, Medieval Studies Collections, Carol Ann Haenicke American Women's Poetry Collection, Nineteenth and Twentieth Century Literature and History Collection, Book Arts Collections: Paper and Fine Printing; Aviation **Computers:** 100% of classrooms, 25% of dorms, 100% of libraries, 100% of dining areas, 100% of student union, 100% of common outdoor areas have wireless network access. Students can register for classes online. Administrative functions (other than registration) can be performed online.

CAMPUS LIFE

Environment: City. **Activities:** Choral groups, concert band, dance, drama/theater, jazz band, literary magazine, marching band, music ensembles, musical theater, opera, pep band, radio station, student government, student newspaper, student-run film society, symphony orchestra, Campus Ministries, International Student Organization 300 registered organizations, 7 honor societies, 21 religious organizations. 16 fraternities, 11 sororities. **Athletics (Intercollegiate):** *Men:* baseball, basketball, football, ice hockey, soccer, tennis. *Women:* basketball, cross-country, golf, gymnastics, soccer, softball, tennis, track/field (outdoor), track/field (indoor), volleyball. **On-Campus Highlights:** Bernhard Center, Waldo Library, University Recreation Center, Miller Auditorium, Gilmore Theatre Complex, Lawson Ice Arena and Gabel Natatorium provide swimming and skating facilities including lessons and family activities. **Environmental Initiatives:** Strategic Planning for Sustainability"including the creation of our new Office for Sustainability (Sept. 2010), ED for Campus Sustainability (Sept. 2010), and Sustainability Across the Curriculum Initiative (May 2010). Student Engagement"WMU's Student Sustainability Fee was approved in April 2010. Subsequently, we have created a $50,000 Student Sustainability Grants Program (decisions made totally by students), a Sustainability Intern Program with 30-40 interns/yr., the Camps Beet (student run café initiative), a bike coop initiative, a peer-to-peer sustainability education program in the Residence Halls (Wesustain Ambassadors),and a student farm initiative among many other initiatives and research projects. Sustainable Operations"including GHG reduction, green cleaning, water reduction, comprehensive storm water management (no net discharge), xeriscaping, waste reduction, green building, purchasing, etc.

ADMISSIONS

Freshman Academic Profile: Average high school GPA 3.3. 10% in top 10% of high school class, 31% in top 25% of high school class, 70% in top 50% of high school class. ACT middle 50% range 19-25. Minimum web-based TOEFL 80. Minimum paper TOEFL 550. **Basis for Candidate Selection:** *Very important factors considered include:* academic GPA. *Important factors considered include:* rigor of secondary school record, standardized test scores. *Other factors considered include:* application essay, recommendation(s). **Freshman Admission Requirements:** High school diploma is required and GED is accepted. *Academic units required:* 4 English, 3 mathematics, 2 science, (1 science labs), 2 social studies, 1 history, 2 academic electives. *Academic units recommended:* 4 English, 3 mathematics, 2 science, (1 science labs), 2 social studies, 1 history, 2 academic electives. **Freshman Admission Statistics:** 13,985 applied, 83% admitted, 26% enrolled. **Transfer Admission Requirements:** college transcript(s), Minimum college GPA of 2.0 required. Lowest grade transferable C. **General Admission Information:** Application Fee $35. Regular application deadline 8/1. Notification on a rolling basis, beginning on or about 7/1. Nonfall registration accepted. Admission may be deferred for a maximum of 1 semester. Credit and/or placement offered for CEEB Advanced Placement tests.

COSTS AND FINANCIAL AID

Annual in-state tuition $9,138. Annual out-of-state tuition $22,418. Room and board $8,414. Required fees $844. Average book expense $1,040. **Required Forms and Deadlines:** FAFSA. **Notification of Awards:** Applicants will be notified of awards on a rolling basis beginning 3/15. **Types of Aid:** *Need-based scholarships/grants:* Federal Pell, SEOG, state scholarships/grants, private scholarships, the school's own gift aid. *Loans:* Direct Subsidized Stafford, Direct Unsubsidized Stafford, Direct PLUS, Federal Perkins, Alternative Loans. **Student Employment:** Federal Work-Study Program available. Institutional employment available. Highest amount earned per year from on-campus jobs $5,000. Off-campus job opportunities are excellent. **Financial Aid Statistics:** 68% freshmen, 68% undergrads receive need-based scholarship or grant aid. 44% freshmen, 34% undergrads receive non-need-based scholarship or grant aid. 98% freshmen, 97% undergrads receive need-based self-help aid. 2% freshmen, 2% undergrads receive athletic scholarships. 79% freshmen, 76% undergrads receive any aid. 62% undergrads borrow to pay for school. Average cumulative indebtedness $30,867. **Criteria for awarding institutional aid:** *Non-need-based:* academics, alumni affiliation, art, athletics, minority status, music/drama, state/district residency.

WESTERN NEW ENGLAND UNIVERSITY

Admissions Office, Springfield, MA 1119
Phone: 413-782-1321 • **Financial Aid Phone:** 413-796-2080
E-mail: learn@wne.edu • **CEEB Code:** 3962
Fax: 413-782-1777 • **Website:** • **ACT Code:** 1930

This private school was founded in 1919. It has a 215-acre campus.

RATINGS
Admissions Selectivity Rating: 71   **Fire Safety Rating:** 63   **Green Rating:** 61

STUDENTS AND FACULTY
Enrollment: 2,671. **Student Body:** 39% female, 61% male, 57% out-of-state, 1% international (12 countries represented). Asian 3%, African American 5%, Caucasian 79%, Hispanic 7%, Native American 0%.
Retention and Graduation: 75% freshmen return for sophomore year. 51% freshmen graduate within 4 years. **Faculty:** Student/faculty ratio 13:1. 220 full-time faculty, 90% hold PhDs, 13% are members of minority groups, 41% are women. 0% of classes are taught by teaching assistants.

ACADEMICS
Degrees: bachelor's, certificate, master's, terminal associate. **Classes:** Most classes have 20—29 students. Most lab/discussion sessions have 10—19 students. **Majors with Highest Enrollment:** business/commerce; criminal justice/safety studies; psychology. **Special Study Options:** Accelerated program, cross-registration, distance learning, double major, dual enrollment, exchange student program (domestic), honors program, independent study, internships, liberal arts/career combination, student-designed major, study abroad, teacher certification program, 3+3 law program with Western New England College School of Law. Washington Semester Program. 5 Yr BSBS/MBA and Engr/MBA. 6 Yr BSBE/Law and 6 Yr BiomedEngr/Law. 5 yr BSEM/MSEM. **Honors Programs:** The Honors Program at Western New England College gives academically qualified and motivated students the opportunity to join a community of like students and participate in challenging courses taught by some of the College's best faculty. Honors students generally take one honors course per semester for their first three years and work on a senior honors project during their final year. **Combined Degree Programs:** BA/JD. **Disability Services:** Special programs offered to physically disabled students include note-taking services, reader services, tape recorders, tutors. **Career Services:** Alumni network, career assessment, internships.

FACILITIES
Housing: Coed dorms, special housing for disabled students, apartments for single students. 90% of campus accessible to physically disabled. **Special Academic Facilities/Equipment:** Art Gallery; Math, Writing Science Centers **Computers:** Students can register for classes online. Administrative functions (other than registration) can be performed online.

CAMPUS LIFE
Environment: City. **Activities:** Choral groups, concert band, dance, drama/theater, jazz band, literary magazine, music ensembles, pep band, radio station, student government, student newspaper, yearbook, Campus Ministries, International Student Organization 60 registered organizations, 8 honor societies. **Athletics (Intercollegiate):** *Men:* baseball, basketball, cross-country, football, golf, ice hockey, lacrosse, soccer, tennis, wrestling. *Women:* basketball, cross-country, field hockey, lacrosse, soccer, softball, swimming, tennis, volleyball. **On-Campus Highlights:** Alumni Healthful Living Center, St Germain Campus Center, D'Amour Library, Computer Labs, Rock Cafe.

ADMISSIONS
Freshman Academic Profile: Average high school GPA 3.3. 13% in top 10% of high school class, 43% in top 25% of high school class, 80% in top 50% of high school class. SAT Math middle 50% range 490-600. SAT Critical Reading middle 50% range 460-570. ACT middle 50% range 22-26. Minimum web-based TOEFL 79. Minimum paper TOEFL 550. **Basis for Candidate Selection:** *Very important factors considered include:* academic GPA, recommendation(s), standardized test scores. *Other factors considered include:* Class rank, application essay, rigor of secondary school record, alumni/ae relation, character/personal qualities, extracurricular activities, interview, level of applicant's interest, racial/ethnic status, talent/ability, volunteer work, work experience. **Freshman Admission Requirements:** High school diploma is required and GED is accepted. *Academic units required:* 4 English, 2 mathematics, 1 science, (1 science labs), 1 social studies, 1 history. *Academic units recommended:* 4 English, 2 mathematics, 1 science, (1 science labs), 1 social studies, 1 history. **Freshman Admission Statistics:** 6,057 applied, 79% admitted, 17% enrolled. **Transfer Admission Requirements:** High school transcript, college transcript(s), Minimum college GPA of 2.3 required. Lowest grade transferable C–. **General Admission Information:** Application Fee $50. Notification on a rolling basis, beginning on or about 12/1. Nonfall registration accepted. Admission may be deferred for a maximum of 12 months. Credit and/or placement offered for CEEB Advanced Placement tests.

COSTS AND FINANCIAL AID
Annual tuition $29,738. Room and board $12,144. Required fees $2,174. Average book expense $1,200. **Required Forms and Deadlines:** FAFSAstudent and parent 1040; W-2s. **Notification of Awards:** Applicants will be notified of awards on a rolling basis beginning 3/15. **Types of Aid:** *Need-based scholarships/grants:* Federal Pell, SEOG, state scholarships/grants, private scholarships, the school's own gift aid, ACG, Smart Grants. *Loans:* Direct Subsidized Stafford, Direct Unsubsidized Stafford, Direct PLUS, PLUS, Federal Perkins, state loans, Private loan programs. **Student Employment:** Federal Work-Study Program available. Institutional employment available. Off-campus job opportunities are good. **Financial Aid Statistics:** 100% freshmen, 99% undergrads receive need-based scholarship or grant aid. 8% freshmen, 7% undergrads receive non-need-based scholarship or grant aid. 88% freshmen, 89% undergrads receive need-based self-help aid. 98% freshmen, 96% undergrads receive any aid. **Criteria for awarding institutional aid:** *Non-need-based:* academics.

WESTERN OREGON UNIVERSITY

345 N Monmouth Avenue, Monmouth, OR 97361
Phone: 503-838-8211 • **Financial Aid Phone:** 503-838-8475
E-mail: wolfgram@wou.edu • **CEEB Code:** 4585
Fax: 503-838-8067 • **Website:** www.wou.edu • **ACT Code:** 3480

This public school was founded in 1856. It has a 157-acre campus.

RATINGS
Admissions Selectivity Rating: 65　　**Fire Safety Rating:** 92　　**Green Rating:** 67

STUDENTS AND FACULTY
Enrollment: 5,287. **Student Body:** 59% female, 41% male, 5% international (19 countries represented). Asian 2%, African American 3%, Caucasian 73%, Hispanic 11%, Native American 2%
Retention and Graduation: 70% freshmen return for sophomore year. 20% freshmen graduate within 4 years. **Faculty:** Student/faculty ratio 20:1. 191 full-time faculty, 77% hold PhDs, 11% are members of minority groups, 46% are women. 0% of classes are taught by teaching assistants.

ACADEMICS
Degrees: associate, bachelor's, master's, post-bachelor's certificate. **Classes:** Most classes have 10—19 students. Most lab/discussion sessions have 20—29 students. **Majors with Highest Enrollment:** business/commerce; social sciences; teacher education, multiple levels. **Special Study Options:** distance learning, double major, dual enrollment, English as a Second Language (ESL), honors program, independent study, internships, study abroad, teacher certification program. **Honors Programs:** WOU Honors Program . **Disability Services:** Special programs offered to physically disabled students include note-taking services, reader services, tape recorders, tutors. **Career Services:** career/job search classes, internships.

FACILITIES
Housing: Coed dorms, special housing for disabled students, apartments for married students, apartments for single students. 95% of campus accessible to physically disabled. **Special Academic Facilities/Equipment:** Jensen Arctic Museum **Computers:** 70% of classrooms, 90% of dorms, 100% of libraries, 90% of dining areas, 90% of student union, 20% of common outdoor areas have wireless network access. Students can register for classes online. Administrative functions (other than registration) can be performed online.

CAMPUS LIFE
Environment: Village. **Activities:** Choral groups, concert band, dance, drama/theater, jazz band, literary magazine, music ensembles, musical theater, student government, student newspaper, symphony orchestra, Campus Ministries, International Student Organization 50 registered organizations, 4 honor societies, 6 religious organizations. **Athletics (Intercollegiate):** *Men:* baseball, basketball, cheerleading, cross-country, football, track/field (outdoor). *Women:* basketball, cheerleading, cross-country, soccer, softball, track/field (outdoor), volleyball. **On-Campus Highlights:** Wayne and Lynn Hamersly Library, Neal Werner University Center, Paul Jensen Arctic Museum, Campbell Hall Art Gallery, Arbor Park Apartments. **Environmental Initiatives:** paper recyling.

ADMISSIONS
Freshman Academic Profile: Average high school GPA 3.2. 11% in top 10% of high school class, 32% in top 25% of high school class, 68% in top 50% of high school class. 95% from public high schools. SAT Math middle 50% range 420-550. SAT Critical Reading middle 50% range 410-540. SAT Writing middle 50% range 390-510. ACT middle 50% range 17-22. Minimum paper TOEFL 500. **Basis for Candidate Selection:** *Very important factors considered include:* academic GPA, rigor of secondary school record, standardized test scores. *Important factors considered include:* Class rank. *Other factors considered include:* recommendation(s), alumni/ae relation, racial/ethnic status, talent/ability. **Freshman Admission Requirements:** High school diploma is required and GED is accepted. *Academic units required:* 4 English, 3 mathematics, 2 science, 2 foreign language, 2 social studies, 1 history. *Academic units recommended:* 4 English, 3 mathematics, 2 science, 2 foreign language, 2 social studies, 1 history. **Freshman Admission Statistics:** 2,841 applied, 88% admitted, 41% enrolled. **Transfer Admission Requirements:** college transcript(s), Minimum college GPA of 2.0 required. Lowest grade transferable D-. **General Admission Information:** Application Fee $50. Notification on a rolling basis, beginning on or about 1/1. Nonfall registration accepted. Admission may be deferred for a maximum of 0. Credit and/or placement offered for CEEB Advanced Placement tests.

COSTS AND FINANCIAL AID
Annual in-state tuition $4,725. Annual out-of-state tuition $15,750. Room and board $7,675. Required fees $1,143. Average book expense $1,125. **Required Forms and Deadlines:** FAFSA. **Notification of Awards:** Applicants will be notified of awards on a rolling basis beginning 2/28. **Types of Aid:** *Need-based scholarships/grants:* Federal Pell, SEOG, state scholarships/grants, private scholarships, the school's own gift aid. *Loans:* Direct Subsidized Stafford, Direct Unsubsidized Stafford, Direct PLUS, Federal Perkins, college/university loans from institutional funds. **Student Employment:** Federal Work-Study Program available. Highest amount earned per year from on-campus jobs $5,000. Off-campus job opportunities are good. **Financial Aid Statistics:** 86% freshmen, 82% undergrads receive need-based scholarship or grant aid. 3% freshmen, 2% undergrads receive non-need-based scholarship or grant aid. 91% freshmen, 91% undergrads receive need-based self-help aid. 1% freshmen, 1% undergrads receive athletic scholarships. 18% freshmen, 29% undergrads receive any aid. **Criteria for awarding institutional aid:** *Non-need-based:* academics, alumni affiliation, art, athletics, leadership, music/drama.

WESTERN STATE COLLEGE OF COLORADO

600 N. Adams, Gunnison, CO 81231
Phone: 970-943-2119 • **Financial Aid Phone:** 970-943-3085
E-mail: admissions@western.edu • **CEEB Code:** 4946
Fax: 970-943-2363 • **Website:** www.western.edu • **ACT Code:** 536

This public school was founded in 1911. It has a 228-acre campus.

RATINGS
Admissions Selectivity Rating: 75　　**Fire Safety Rating:** 92　　**Green Rating:** 88

STUDENTS AND FACULTY
Enrollment: 2,071. **Student Body:** 39% female, 61% male, 24% out-of-state, 0% international (7 countries represented). Asian 0%, African American 2%, Caucasian 79%, Hispanic 4%, Native American 1%
Retention and Graduation: 60% freshmen return for sophomore year. 18% freshmen graduate within 4 years. 36% freshmen graduate within 6 years. 15% grads go on to further study within 1 year. **Faculty:** Student/faculty ratio 17:1. 105 full-time faculty, 82% hold PhDs, 3% are members of minority groups, 42% are women. 0% of classes are taught by teaching assistants.

ACADEMICS
Degrees: bachelor's. **Classes:** Most classes have 10—19 students. **Majors with Highest Enrollment:** parks, recreation and leisure studies. **Special Study Options:** distance learning, double major, dual enrollment, honors program, independent study, internships, liberal arts/career combination, study abroad, teacher certification program. **Honors Programs:** Honors Program--based on the National Collegiate Honors Council-modeled City of Text explores urban environments, while the Partners in the Parks: Black Canyon of the Gunnison course immerses students in the ecosystems of one of America's most amazing national parks. **Disability Services:** Special programs offered to physically disabled students include note-taking services, reader services, tape recorders, tutors. **Career Services:** Alumni network, alumni services, career/job search classes, career assessment, internships, regional alumni.

FACILITIES
Housing: Coed dorms, men's dorms, women's dorms, apartments for married students, apartments for single students, theme housing. 80% of campus accessible to physically disabled. **Computers:** 100% of classrooms, 50% of dorms, 100% of libraries, 100% of dining areas, 100% of student union, have wireless network access. Students can register for classes online. Administrative functions (other than registration) can be performed online.

CAMPUS LIFE
Environment: Rural. **Activities:** Choral groups, concert band, dance, drama/theater, jazz band, literary magazine, music ensembles, pep band, radio station, student government, student newspaper, student-run film society, symphony orchestra, television station, Campus Ministries, International Student Organization 60 registered organizations, 8 honor societies, 5 religious organizations. **Athletics (Intercollegiate):** *Men:* basketball, cross-country, football, track/field (outdoor), track/field (indoor), wrestling. *Women:* basketball, cross-country, track/field (outdoor), track/field (indoor), volleyball. **On-Campus Highlights:** College Center--new student center, Hurst Hall -- renovated science building, Kelley Hall--renovated social sciences, Gym -- Highest Elevation NCAA basketball Court, Borick Business--new business building, College Center, Borick, Business Building and Kelley Hall are either LEED certified or seeking LEED certification. Kelley also features solar panels for energy efficiency. The new College Center features campus dining and a first-run movie theatre. **Environmental Initiatives:** President's Climate Committment--which is a significant challenge for one of the coldest locations in the nation and the isolated nature of Gunnison Bio Mass boiler system and LEED certified buildings. 4th construction project seeking will be underway in spring 2010 with biomass

bioler which has received a competitive NEED grant food purchasing, pulping and composting.

ADMISSIONS

Freshman Academic Profile: Average high school GPA 3.0. 9% in top 10% of high school class, 25% in top 25% of high school class, 54% in top 50% of high school class. SAT Math middle 50% range 460-550. SAT Critical Reading middle 50% range 450-550. SAT Writing middle 50% range 450-550. ACT middle 50% range 19-24. Minimum paper TOEFL 550. **Basis for Candidate Selection:** *Very important factors considered include:* Class rank, rigor of secondary school record, standardized test scores. *Other factors considered include:* application essay, recommendation(s), alumni/ae relation, character/personal qualities, extracurricular activities, first generation, interview, talent/ability, volunteer work. **Freshman Admission Requirements:** High school diploma is required and GED is accepted. *Academic units required:* 4 English, 4 mathematics, 3 science, (2 science labs), 1 foreign language, 2 social studies, 2 history, 3 academic electives. *Academic units recommended:* 4 English, 4 mathematics, 3 science, (2 science labs), 1 foreign language, 2 social studies, 2 history, 3 academic electives. **Freshman Admission Statistics:** 1,928 applied, 66% admitted, 38% enrolled. **Transfer Admission Requirements:** college transcript(s), Minimum college GPA of 2.0 required. Lowest grade transferable C. **General Admission Information:** Application Fee $40. Regular application deadline 8/1. Notification on a rolling basis, beginning on or about 11/1. Nonfall registration accepted. Admission may be deferred for a maximum of 1 year. Credit and/or placement offered for CEEB Advanced Placement tests.

COSTS AND FINANCIAL AID

Average book expense $1,500. **Required Forms and Deadlines:** FAFSA. **Notification of Awards:** Applicants will be notified of awards on a rolling basis beginning 4/1. **Types of Aid:** *Need-based scholarships/grants:* Federal Pell, SEOG, state scholarships/grants, the school's own gift aid. *Loans:* Direct Subsidized Stafford, Direct Unsubsidized Stafford, Direct PLUS, Federal Perkins. **Student Employment:** Federal Work-Study Program available. Institutional employment available. Highest amount earned per year from on-campus jobs $1,500. Off-campus job opportunities are good. **Financial Aid Statistics:** 43% freshmen, 43% undergrads receive need-based scholarship or grant aid. 13% freshmen, 20% undergrads receive non-need-based scholarship or grant aid. 90% freshmen, 90% undergrads receive need-based self-help aid. 30% freshmen, 30% undergrads receive athletic scholarships. 82% freshmen, 80% undergrads receive any aid. 75% undergrads borrow to pay for school. Average cumulative indebtedness $17,750. **Criteria for awarding institutional aid:** *Non-need-based:* academics, art, athletics, leadership, music/drama.

WESTERN UNIVERSITY

Western Student Services Bldg., RM 3140, London, ON N6A 3K7
Phone: 519-661-2100 • **Financial Aid Phone:** 519-661-2100
E-mail: reg-admissions@uwo.ca
Fax: 519-661-3710 • **Website:** www.uwo.ca

This public school was founded in 1878. It has a 1178-acre campus.

RATINGS

Admissions Selectivity Rating: 60*   **Fire Safety Rating:** 73   **Green Rating:** 89

STUDENTS AND FACULTY

Student Body: (100 countries represented).
Retention and Graduation: 50% freshmen graduate within 4 years. 78% freshmen graduate within 6 years. **Faculty:** Student/faculty ratio 20:1. 1408 full-time faculty, 33% are women.

ACADEMICS

Degrees: bachelor's, certificate, diploma, doctoral, master's. **Majors with Highest Enrollment:** biology/biological sciences; health services/allied health/health sciences; social sciences, other. **Special Study Options:** Accelerated program, cooperative education program, cross-registration, distance learning, double major, dual enrollment, English as a Second Language (ESL), exchange student program (domestic), honors program, independent study, internships, liberal arts/career combination, student-designed major, study abroad, teacher certification program. **Honors Programs:** Scholar's Electives **Combined Degree Programs:** BESc/MD, BESc/LLB, LLB/MBA, BSc/LLB, HBA/BMSc. **Disability Services:** Special programs offered to physically disabled students include note-taking services, reader services, tape recorders. **Career Services:** Alumni network, alumni services, career/job search classes, career assessment, internships, regional alumni. Career services highlights include Western's Internship Program www.career.uwo.ca/wip Backpack2briefcase http://www.alumni.uwo.ca/b2b/ Interview Stream - Online mock interview tool! Career Week/Job Fairs.

FACILITIES

Housing: Coed dorms, special housing for disabled students, men's dorms, special housing for international students, women's dorms, apartments for married students, apartments for single students. 92% of campus accessible to physically disabled. **Special Academic Facilities/Equipment:** McIntosh Gallery Hume Cronyn Memorial Observatory Student Recreation Centre **Computers:** 100% of libraries, 100% of student union, have wireless network access. Students can register for classes online. Administrative functions (other than registration) can be performed online.

CAMPUS LIFE

Environment: City. **Activities:** Choral groups, concert band, dance, drama/theater, jazz band, marching band, music ensembles, musical theater, opera, pep band, radio station, student government, student newspaper, student-run film society, symphony orchestra, television station, Campus Ministries, International Student Organization, Model UN 189 registered organizations, 14 fraternities, 5 sororities. **Athletics (Intercollegiate):** *Men:* badminton, baseball, basketball, crew/rowing, cross-country, curling, fencing, football, golf, ice hockey, rugby, soccer, squash, swimming, tennis, track/field (outdoor), track/field (indoor), volleyball, water polo, wrestling. *Women:* badminton, basketball, crew/rowing, cross-country, curling, fencing, field hockey, golf, ice hockey, lacrosse, rugby, soccer, squash, swimming, tennis, track/field (outdoor), track/field (indoor), volleyball, wrestling. **On-Campus Highlights:** University Community Centre, Student Recreation Centre, TD Waterhouse Stadium, Von Kuster Hall, McIntosh Gallery, McIntosh Gallery - Oldest university art gallery in Canada. **Environmental Initiatives:** Annual Green Awards, recognizing iniatives of staff, faculty, and students. Greenhouse gas inventory with action items. (Ongoing - beginning 2009) LEED Building - All new construction and major renovation will be LEED Silver Certified or better.

ADMISSIONS

Freshman Academic Profile: Minimum web-based TOEFL 83. Minimum paper TOEFL 550. **Basis for Candidate Selection:** *Very important factors considered include:* academic GPA, standardized test scores. *Important factors considered include:* rigor of secondary school record. *Other factors considered include:* Class rank, application essay, recommendation(s), alumni/ae relation, character/personal qualities, extracurricular activities, talent/ability, volunteer work, work experience. **Freshman Admission Requirements:** High school diploma is required and GED is accepted. *Academic units required:* 4 English, 3 mathematics, 3 science, 2 foreign language, 3 social studies. *Academic units recommended:* 4 English, 3 mathematics, 3 science, 2 foreign language, 3 social studies. **Transfer Admission Requirements:** High school transcript, college transcript(s), Lowest grade transferable C. **General Admission Information:** Application Fee $50. Notification on a rolling basis, beginning on or about 11/1. Nonfall registration accepted. Admission may be deferred for a maximum of 1 year.

COSTS AND FINANCIAL AID

Annual in-state tuition $5,633. Required fees $1,175.

WESTERN WASHINGTON UNIVERSITY

Mail Stop 9009, Bellingham, WA 98225-9009
Phone: 360-650-3440 • **Financial Aid Phone:** 360-650-3470
E-mail: admit@cc.wwu.edu • **CEEB Code:** 4947
Fax: 360-650-7369 • **Website:** www.wwu.edu/ • **ACT Code:** 4490

This public school was founded in 1893. It has a 300-acre campus.

RATINGS

Admissions Selectivity Rating: 73   **Fire Safety Rating:** 81   **Green Rating:** 90

STUDENTS AND FACULTY

Enrollment: 13,801. **Student Body:** 55% female, 45% male, 8% out-of-state, 1% international (30 countries represented). Asian 6%, African American 2%, Caucasian 76%, Hispanic 6%, Native American 1%
Retention and Graduation: 36% freshmen graduate within 4 years. 69% freshmen graduate within 6 years. 14% grads go on to further study within 1 year. **Faculty:** Student/faculty ratio 21:1. 516 full-time faculty, 90% hold PhDs, 13% are members of minority groups, 46% are women. 2% of classes are taught by teaching assistants.

ACADEMICS

Degrees: bachelor's, certificate, master's, post-bachelor's certificate, post-master's certificate. **Classes:** Most classes have 20—29 students. Most lab/discussion sessions have 10—19 students. **Majors with Highest Enrollment:** political science and government; pre-medicine/pre-medical studies; psychology. **Special Study Options:** distance learning, double major, English as a Second Language (ESL), exchange student program (domestic), honors program, independent study, internships, student-designed major, study abroad, teacher certification program. **Honors Programs:** Honors Program features small classes and interaction between students and faculty. It is an exciting opportunity for accomplished students who would like a more intimate college experience within the setting of a larger institution. Honors students are welcome to pursue any academic major, and all students complete a self-designed capstone senior project. **Disability Services:** Special programs offered to physically disabled students include note-taking services, reader services, tape recorders, tutors. **Career Services:** Alumni network, career/job search classes, career assessment, internships, regional alumni.

FACILITIES

Housing: Coed dorms, special housing for disabled students, apartments for married students, apartments for single students, theme housing, wellness floors, multicultural floors available. 100% of campus accessible to physically disabled. **Special Academic Facilities/Equipment:** Outdoor art museum, planetarium, electronic music studio, air pollution lab, motor vehicle research lab, marine lab, wind tunnel, electron microscope, neutron generator lab. **Computers:** 100% of classrooms, 100% of dorms, 100% of libraries, 100% of dining areas, 100% of student union, 100% of common outdoor areas have wireless network access. Students can register for classes online. Administrative functions (other than registration) can be performed online.

CAMPUS LIFE

Environment: City. **Activities:** concert band, dance, drama/theater, jazz band, literary magazine, marching band, music ensembles, musical theater, opera, pep band, radio station, student government, student newspaper, symphony orchestra, television station, Campus Ministries, International Student Organization 200 registered organizations, 4 honor societies, 18 religious organizations. **Athletics (Intercollegiate):** *Men:* basketball, cheerleading, crew/rowing, cross-country, golf, soccer, track/field (outdoor), track/field (indoor). *Women:* basketball, cheerleading, crew/rowing, cross-country, golf, soccer, softball, track/field (outdoor), track/field (indoor), volleyball. **On-Campus Highlights:** Viking Union Student Center, Red Square, Performing Arts Center, Sehome Arboretum, Student Recreation Center. **Environmental Initiatives:** WWU Green Energy Fee The GEF pays for purchase of Renewable Energy Credits to offset 100% of WWU's CO2 emissions from electrical energy consumption, and pays for approximately $260,000 per year of on-campus sustainability projects. Due to our purchase of Renewable Energy Credits, WWU is ranked 17th by the EPA for largest higher ed. purchase of renewable energy in the US. This year's projects include a $167,000 solar array, high-speed hand driers, conversion of parking lot lights to high-efficiency LEDs, a paper towel composting system, and water bottle refilling stations. 10x12 Program The 10x12 Program is a partnership between Facilities Management and the OS aimed at goal of a 10% reduction in utility consumption in academic buildings by the end of 2012. This program includes changes in building operations (set points, building operating hours), energy conservation retrofits electricity, NG, and water), a departmental behavior change campaign (via Departmental Conservation Coordinators), and reinvestment of utility savings. Total savings of all current projects is estimated at 3 to 3.5 million dollars in savings over twelve years as well as a 5% drop in carbon emissions. Sustainability in the Curriculum Approximately 30 faulty are currently and actively invested in the Faculty Sustainability Academy, organizing Western's sustainability programs and developing methods for furthering sustainability education. A series of surveys distributed between 2008 and 2011 indicate approximately 120 additional faculty members either teach sustainability curriculum in their classes or have professional interest in sustainability education. Between 2009 and 2011 SII, the Academy, and students successfully launched a three-part General Education course sequence titled Sustainability Literacy and drafted curriculum concepts for several minors and majors in Sustainability. Survey data shows that over 900 WWU classes contain some sustainability information, while 20-25 classes are sustainability focused. WWU offers six environmentally-themed majors and one minor. The College of Business and Economics has been recognized for its efforts to integrate sustainability into the MBA program by ranking 74th globally within the 2010 Beyond Grey Pinstripes list of green business schools from the Aspen Institute.

ADMISSIONS

Freshman Academic Profile: Average high school GPA 3.5. 23% in top 10% of high school class, 55% in top 25% of high school class, 89% in top 50% of high school class. 90% from public high schools. SAT Math middle 50% range 510-610. SAT Critical Reading middle 50% range 510-620. SAT Writing middle 50% range 480-600. ACT middle 50% range 22-28. Minimum web-based TOEFL 80. Minimum paper TOEFL 550. **Basis for Candidate Selection:** *Very important factors considered include:* rigor of secondary school record. *Important factors considered include:* application essay, academic GPA, standardized test scores, level of applicant's interest. *Other factors considered include:* Class rank, recommendation(s), character/personal qualities, extracurricular activities, first generation, geographical residence, state residency, talent/ability,

volunteer work, work experience. **Freshman Admission Requirements:** High school diploma is required and GED is accepted. *Academic units required:* 4 English, 3 mathematics, 2 science, (1 science labs), 2 foreign language, 3 social studies. *Academic units recommended:* 4 English, 3 mathematics, 2 science, (1 science labs), 2 foreign language, 3 social studies. **Freshman Admission Statistics:** 9,791 applied, 80% admitted, 34% enrolled. **Transfer Admission Requirements:** college transcript(s), statement of good standing from prior institution(s). Minimum college GPA of 2.0 required. Lowest grade transferable D-. **General Admission Information:** Application Fee $50. Regular application deadline 3/1. Notification on a rolling basis, beginning on or about 11/1. Nonfall registration accepted. Admission may be deferred for a maximum of 1 year. Credit and/or placement offered for CEEB Advanced Placement tests.

COSTS AND FINANCIAL AID

Required **Forms and Deadlines:** FAFSA. **Notification of Awards:** Applicants will be notified of awards on a rolling basis beginning 3/20. **Types of Aid:** *Need-based scholarships/grants:* Federal Pell, SEOG, state scholarships/grants, private scholarships, the school's own gift aid. *Loans:* Direct Subsidized Stafford, Direct Unsubsidized Stafford, Direct PLUS, Federal Perkins, state loans, Private Loans. **Student Employment:** Institutional employment available. Highest amount earned per year from on-campus jobs $2,690. Off-campus job opportunities are good. **Financial Aid Statistics:** 78% freshmen, 74% undergrads receive need-based scholarship or grant aid. 5% freshmen, 2% undergrads receive non-need-based scholarship or grant aid. 81% freshmen, 86% undergrads receive need-based self-help aid. 1% freshmen, 1% undergrads receive athletic scholarships. 75% freshmen, 64% undergrads receive any aid. 55% undergrads borrow to pay for school. Average cumulative indebtedness $20,473. **Criteria for awarding institutional aid:** *Non-need-based:* academics, alumni affiliation, art, athletics, job skills, leadership, minority status, music/drama, state/district residency.

WESTFIELD STATE UNIVERSITY

Westfield State University, Westfield, MA 1086
Phone: 413-572-5218 • **Financial Aid Phone:** 413-572-5218
E-mail: admissions@westfield.ma.edu • **CEEB Code:** 3523
Fax: 413-572-0520 • **Website:** www.westfield.ma.edu • **ACT Code:** 1912

This public school was founded in 1838. It has a 227-acre campus.

RATINGS
Admissions Selectivity Rating: 76   **Fire Safety Rating:** 83   **Green Rating:** 73

STUDENTS AND FACULTY
Enrollment: 5,191. **Student Body:** 53% female, 47% male, 7% out-of-state, 1% international (15 countries represented). Asian 1%, African American 4%, Caucasian 81%, Hispanic 6%, Native American 0%
Retention and Graduation: 44% freshmen graduate within 4 years. 14% grads go on to further study within 1 year. 5% grads pursue arts and sciences degrees. 1% grads pursue business degrees. **Faculty:** Student/faculty ratio 17:1. 223 full-time faculty, 89% hold PhDs, 15% are members of minority groups, 49% are women. 0% of classes are taught by teaching assistants.

ACADEMICS
Degrees: bachelor's, master's, post-bachelor's certificate, post-master's certificate. **Classes:** Most classes have 20—29 students. Most lab/discussion sessions have 10—19 students. **Special Study Options:** cooperative education program, cross-registration, distance learning, double major, dual enrollment, exchange student program (domestic), honors program, independent study, internships, student-designed major, study abroad, teacher certification program. **Disability Services:** Special programs offered to physically disabled students include note-taking services, reader services, tape recorders, tutors. **Career Services:** career/job search classes, career assessment.

FACILITIES
Housing: Coed dorms, special housing for disabled students, apartments for single students, Living/Learning Unit (Honors/Academic Intensive) Quiet Living Section All Women Section Designated smoking Section(other housing smoke free) Movement Science Student Section. **Special Academic Facilities/Equipment:** Art gallery, language lab, electron microscope.

CAMPUS LIFE
Environment: Village. **Activities:** Choral groups, concert band, drama/theater, jazz band, literary magazine, music ensembles, musical theater, pep band, radio station, student government, student newspaper, television station, yearbook. **Athletics (Intercollegiate):** *Men:* baseball, basketball, cross-country, football, golf, soccer, track/field (outdoor). *Women:* basketball, cheerleading, cross-country, field hockey, soccer, softball, swimming, volleyball. **Environmental**

Initiatives: RecycleMania: placed 4th in the targeted paper competition in 2011 Environmental Science program Solar panels: http://www.westfield.ma.edu/news/solar-panels-a-sea-of-green/

ADMISSIONS

Freshman Academic Profile: Average high school GPA 3.1. 6% in top 10% of high school class, 27% in top 25% of high school class, 72% in top 50% of high school class. SAT Math middle 50% range 470-560. SAT Critical Reading middle 50% range 460-550. SAT Writing middle 50% range 450-540. ACT middle 50% range 20-24. Minimum web-based TOEFL 79. Minimum paper TOEFL 550. **Basis for Candidate Selection:** *Very important factors considered include:* rigor of secondary school record, standardized test scores. *Important factors considered include:* extracurricular activities, talent/ability. *Other factors considered include:* application essay, recommendation(s), character/personal qualities, racial/ethnic status, volunteer work, work experience. **Freshman Admission Requirements:** High school diploma is required and GED is accepted. *Academic units required:* 4 English, 3 mathematics, 3 science, (2 science labs), 2 foreign language, 1 social studies, 1 history, 2 academic electives. *Academic units recommended:* 4 English, 3 mathematics, 3 science, (2 science labs), 2 foreign language, 1 social studies, 1 history, 2 academic electives. **Freshman Admission Statistics:** 4,941 applied, 64% admitted, 31% enrolled. **Transfer Admission Requirements:** college transcript(s), Minimum college GPA of 2.0 required. Lowest grade transferable C–. **General Admission Information:** Application Fee $25. Regular application deadline 3/1. Nonfall registration accepted. Admission may be deferred for a maximum of 1 semester. Credit and/or placement offered for CEEB Advanced Placement tests.

COSTS AND FINANCIAL AID

Annual in-state tuition $970. Annual out-of-state tuition $7,050. Room and board $9,233. Required fees $7,327. Average book expense $958. **Required Forms and Deadlines:** FAFSA. **Notification of Awards:** Applicants will be notified of awards on or about 4/15. **Types of Aid:** *Need-based scholarships/grants:* Federal Pell, SEOG, state scholarships/grants, private scholarships, the school's own gift aid. *Loans:* Subsidized Stafford, Unsubsidized Stafford, PLUS, Federal Perkins, state loans. **Student Employment:** Federal Work-Study Program available. Highest amount earned per year from on-campus jobs $1,000. Off-campus job opportunities are good. **Financial Aid Statistics:** 62% freshmen, 62% undergrads receive need-based scholarship or grant aid. 31% freshmen, 15% undergrads receive non-need-based scholarship or grant aid. 88% freshmen, 89% undergrads receive need-based self-help aid. 68% freshmen, 71% undergrads receive any aid. 76% undergrads borrow to pay for school. Average cumulative indebtedness $24,825.

WESTMINSTER CHOIR COLLEGE
OF RIDER UNIVERSITY

101 Walnut Lane, Princeton, NJ 08540-3899
Phone: 800-962-4647 • **CEEB Code:** 2758
Fax: 609-921-8829 • **Website:** www.rider.edu • **ACT Code:** 2590

This private school was founded in 1926. It has a 23-acre campus.

RATINGS
Admissions Selectivity Rating: 75   **Fire Safety Rating:** 60*   **Green Rating:** 60*

STUDENTS AND FACULTY
Enrollment: 328. **Student Body:** 64% female, 36% male, 56% out-of-state, 4% international. Asian 2%, African American 7%, Caucasian 75%, Hispanic 4%, Native American 1%
Retention and Graduation: 79% freshmen return for sophomore year.

ACADEMICS
Degrees: bachelor's, master's. **Majors with Highest Enrollment:** accounting; business/commerce; elementary education and teaching.

FACILITIES
Housing: Coed dorms.

CAMPUS LIFE
Environment: Town. **Activities:** Choral groups, concert band, dance, jazz band, music ensembles, opera 8 registered organizations, 4 honor societies.

ADMISSIONS
Freshman Academic Profile: Average high school GPA 3.4. SAT Math middle 50% range 490-610. SAT Critical Reading middle 50% range 490-620. Minimum paper TOEFL 563. **Basis for Candidate Selection:** *Very important factors considered include:* application essay, academic GPA, recommendation(s), rigor of secondary school record, standardized test scores.

Important factors considered include: level of applicant's interest. *Other factors considered include:* Class rank, alumni/ae relation, character/personal qualities, extracurricular activities, geographical residence, interview, state residency, talent/ability, volunteer work, work experience. **Freshman Admission Requirements:** High school diploma is required and GED is accepted. *Academic units required:* 4 English, 3 mathematics. *Academic units recommended:* 4 English, 3 mathematics. **Freshman Admission Statistics:** 206 applied, 76% admitted, 56% enrolled. **General Admission Information:** Application Fee $45.

COSTS AND FINANCIAL AID
Annual tuition $22,910. Room and board $9,200. Required fees $560. Average book expense $1,000.

WESTMINSTER COLLEGE (MO)

Champ Auditorium, Westminster College, Fulton, MO 65251
Phone: 573-592-5251 • **Financial Aid Phone:** 800-475-3361
E-mail: admissions@westminster-mo.edu • **CEEB Code:** 6937
Fax: 573-592-5255 • **Website:** www.westminster-mo.edu/ • **ACT Code:** 2392

This private school, affiliated with the Presbyterian Church, was founded in 1851. It has a 86-acre campus.

RATINGS
Admissions Selectivity Rating: 71   **Fire Safety Rating:** 67   **Green Rating:** 61

STUDENTS AND FACULTY
Enrollment: 1,080. **Student Body:** 44% female, 56% male, 26% out-of-state, 11% international (66 countries represented). Asian 1%, African American 5%, Caucasian 52%, Hispanic 3%, Native American 2%
Retention and Graduation: 83% freshmen return for sophomore year. 59% freshmen graduate within 4 years. 30% grads go on to further study within 1 year. 10% grads pursue arts and sciences degrees. 4% grads pursue law degrees. 6% grads pursue business degrees. 3% grads pursue medical degrees. **Faculty:** Student/faculty ratio 14:1. 64 full-time faculty, 91% hold PhDs, 0% are members of minority groups, 41% are women. 0% of classes are taught by teaching assistants.

ACADEMICS
Degrees: bachelor's. **Classes:** Most classes have 10—19 students. **Majors with Highest Enrollment:** biology/biological sciences; business/commerce; political science and government. **Special Study Options:** cooperative education program, cross-registration, double major, dual enrollment, exchange student program (domestic), honors program, independent study, internships, liberal arts/career combination, student-designed major, study abroad, teacher certification program, Urban Studies Program (Chicago). Other off-campus study opportunities supported through Office of International Programs. Coursework and certification are also available through the Center of Leadership and the Remley Women's Center. **Combined Degree Programs:** BA/MEng, BA/MEng - University of Missouri-Columbia. **Disability Services:** Special programs offered to physically disabled students include note-taking services, reader services, tape recorders, tutors. **Career Services:** career/job search classes, career assessment, internships, regional alumni.

FACILITIES
Housing: Coed dorms, special housing for disabled students, men's dorms, women's dorms, fraternity/sorority housing, apartments for single students, theme housing. 70% of campus accessible to physically disabled. **Special Academic Facilities/Equipment:** Winston Churchill Memorial Museum, Coulter Science Center, language lab, NMR spectrometer, laser equipment. **Computers:** 100% of classrooms, 100% of libraries, 100% of dining areas, 100% of student union, 40% of common outdoor areas have wireless network access. Students can register for classes online. Administrative functions (other than registration) can be performed online.

CAMPUS LIFE
Environment: Village. **Activities:** Choral groups, dance, drama/theater, literary magazine, music ensembles, pep band, student government, student newspaper, yearbook, Campus Ministries, International Student Organization, Model UN 49 registered organizations, 15 honor societies, 2 religious organizations. 6 fraternities, 3 sororities. **Athletics (Intercollegiate):** *Men:* baseball, basketball, cheerleading, cross-country, football, golf, soccer, tennis, track/field (outdoor). *Women:* basketball, cheerleading, cross-country, golf, soccer, softball, tennis, track/field (outdoor), volleyball. **On-Campus Highlights:** Coulter Science Center, Johnson College Inn (student center), Hunter Activity Center, Library, Wetterau Athletic Facility.

ADMISSIONS

Freshman Academic Profile: Average high school GPA 3.4. 23% in top 10% of high school class, 43% in top 25% of high school class, 75% in top 50% of high school class. 70% from public high schools. SAT Math middle 50% range 470-610. SAT Critical Reading middle 50% range 390-550. SAT Writing middle 50% range 420-530. ACT middle 50% range 21-27. Minimum paper TOEFL 550. **Basis for Candidate Selection:** *Very important factors considered include:* rigor of secondary school record, standardized test scores, character/personal qualities. *Important factors considered include:* Class rank, academic GPA, recommendation(s), extracurricular activities, volunteer work. *Other factors considered include:* application essay, alumni/ae relation, interview, talent/ability, work experience. **Freshman Admission Requirements:** High school diploma is required and GED is accepted. *Academic units required:* 4 English, 3 mathematics, 2 science, (2 science labs). *Academic units recommended:* 4 English, 3 mathematics, 2 science, (2 science labs). **Freshman Admission Statistics:** 1,420 applied, 72% admitted, 26% enrolled. **Transfer Admission Requirements:** college transcript(s), Lowest grade transferable C. **General Admission Information:** Notification on a rolling basis, beginning on or about 10/1. Nonfall registration accepted. Admission may be deferred for a maximum of 12 months. Credit and/or placement offered for CEEB Advanced Placement tests.

COSTS AND FINANCIAL AID

Annual tuition $19,750. Room and board $8,450. Required fees $1,100. Average book expense $1,100. **Required Forms and Deadlines:** FAFSA. **Notification of Awards:** Applicants will be notified of awards on a rolling basis beginning 3/15. **Types of Aid:** *Need-based scholarships/grants:* Federal Pell, SEOG, state scholarships/grants, private scholarships, the school's own gift aid. *Loans:* Subsidized Stafford, Unsubsidized Stafford, PLUS, Federal Perkins. **Student Employment:** Federal Work-Study Program available. Institutional employment available. Highest amount earned per year from on-campus jobs $2,500. Off-campus job opportunities are good. **Financial Aid Statistics:** 100% freshmen, 100% undergrads receive need-based scholarship or grant aid. 86% freshmen, 87% undergrads receive need-based self-help aid. 98% freshmen, 98% undergrads receive any aid. 64% undergrads borrow to pay for school. Average cumulative indebtedness $26,723. **Criteria for awarding institutional aid:** *Non-need-based:* academics, alumni affiliation, leadership, minority status, music/drama, religious affiliation.

WESTMINSTER COLLEGE (PA)

319 South Market Street, New Wilmington, PA 16172
Phone: 724-946-7100
E-mail: admis@westminster.edu • **CEEB Code:** 2975
Fax: 724-946-7171 • **Website:** www.westminster.edu • **ACT Code:** 2975

This private school, affiliated with the Presbyterian Church, was founded in 1852. It has a 350-acre campus.

RATINGS

Admissions Selectivity Rating: 75   **Fire Safety Rating:** 96   **Green Rating:** 60*

STUDENTS AND FACULTY

Enrollment: 1,387. **Student Body:** 64% female, 36% male, 21% out-of-state, 0% international (1 countries represented). Asian 0%, African American 3%, Caucasian 80%, Hispanic 1%, Native American 0%
Retention and Graduation: 83% freshmen return for sophomore year. 65% freshmen graduate within 4 years. 76% freshmen graduate within 6 years. 21% grads go on to further study within 1 year. 3% grads pursue law degrees. 2% grads pursue business degrees. 3% grads pursue medical degrees. **Faculty:** Student/faculty ratio 12:1. 100 full-time faculty, 83% hold PhDs, 5% are members of minority groups, 44% are women. 0% of classes are taught by teaching assistants.

ACADEMICS

Degrees: bachelor's, master's. **Classes:** Most classes have 10—19 students. Most lab/discussion sessions have 10—19 students. **Majors with Highest Enrollment:** biology/biological sciences; business/commerce; education. **Special Study Options:** double major, exchange student program (domestic), honors program, independent study, internships, liberal arts/career combination, student-designed major, study abroad, teacher certification program. **Combined Degree Programs:** BA/JD, BA/MA. **Disability Services:** Special programs offered to physically disabled students include tutors.

FACILITIES

Housing: special housing for disabled students, men's dorms, women's dorms, fraternity/sorority housing. We offer townhouses for upperclass men and women. 90% of campus accessible to physically disabled. **Special Academic Facilities/Equipment:** On-campus preschool, Moeller pipe organs, planetarium, observatory, electron microscopes, X-ray diffractor, spectrometer. **Computers:** Administrative functions (other than registration) can be performed online.

CAMPUS LIFE

Environment: Village. **Activities:** Choral groups, concert band, dance, drama/theater, jazz band, literary magazine, marching band, music ensembles, musical theater, pep band, radio station, student government, student newspaper, television station, yearbook 60 registered organizations, 21 honor societies, 3 religious organizations. 5 fraternities, 5 sororities. **Athletics (Intercollegiate):** *Men:* baseball, basketball, cheerleading, cross-country, football, golf, soccer, swimming, tennis, track/field (outdoor), track/field (indoor). *Women:* basketball, cheerleading, cross-country, golf, soccer, softball, swimming, tennis, track/field (outdoor), track/field (indoor), volleyball.

ADMISSIONS

Freshman Academic Profile: Average high school GPA 3.4. 20% in top 10% of high school class, 55% in top 25% of high school class, 87% in top 50% of high school class. 90% from public high schools. SAT Math middle 50% range 480-590. SAT Critical Reading middle 50% range 470-570. ACT middle 50% range 20-25. Minimum paper TOEFL 550. **Basis for Candidate Selection:** *Very important factors considered include:* rigor of secondary school record, standardized test scores, interview. *Important factors considered include:* Class rank, application essay, recommendation(s), character/personal qualities. *Other factors considered include:* alumni/ae relation, extracurricular activities, racial/ethnic status, talent/ability, volunteer work, work experience. **Freshman Admission Requirements:** High school diploma is required and GED is accepted. *Academic units required:* 4 English, 3 mathematics, 2 science, (2 science labs), 2 foreign language, 2 social studies, 1 history, 3 academic electives. *Academic units recommended:* 4 English, 3 mathematics, 2 science, (2 science labs), 2 foreign language, 2 social studies, 1 history, 3 academic electives. **Freshman Admission Statistics:** 1,368 applied, 71% admitted, 32% enrolled. **Transfer Admission Requirements:** High school transcript, college transcript(s), essay or personal statement, interview, standardized test scores, Minimum college GPA of 2.5 required. Lowest grade transferable c. **General Admission Information:** Application Fee $35. Regular application deadline 4/15. Notification on a rolling basis, beginning on or about 9/1. Nonfall registration not accepted. Admission may be deferred for a maximum of 1 year. Credit and/or placement offered for CEEB Advanced Placement tests.

COSTS AND FINANCIAL AID

Annual tuition $29,150. Room and board $9,200. Required fees $1,160. Average book expense $1,000. **Required Forms and Deadlines:** FAFSA, institution's own financial aid formF. **Notification of Awards:** Applicants will be notified of awards on a rolling basis beginning 11/1. **Types of Aid:** *Need-based scholarships/grants:* Federal Pell, SEOG, state scholarships/grants, private scholarships, the school's own gift aid. *Loans:* Subsidized Stafford, Unsubsidized Stafford, PLUS, Federal Perkins, Resource Loans. **Student Employment:** Highest amount earned per year from on-campus jobs $1,300. **Financial Aid Statistics:** 100% freshmen, 98% undergrads receive need-based scholarship or grant aid. 11% freshmen, 13% undergrads receive non-need-based scholarship or grant aid. 55% freshmen, 81% undergrads receive need-based self-help aid. 80% undergrads borrow to pay for school. Average cumulative indebtedness $28,262. **Criteria for awarding institutional aid:** *Non-need-based:* academics, alumni affiliation, leadership, minority status, music/drama.

WESTMINSTER COLLEGE (UT)

Best 378

1840 South 1300 East, Salt Lake City, UT 84105
Phone: 801-832-2200 • **Financial Aid Phone:** 801-832-2502
E-mail: admission@westminstercollege.edu • **CEEB Code:** 4948
Fax: 801-832-3101 • **Website:** www.westminstercollege.edu • **ACT Code:** 4284

This private school was founded in 1875. It has a 27-acre campus.

RATINGS
Admissions Selectivity Rating: 79   **Fire Safety Rating:** 98   **Green Rating:** 95

STUDENTS AND FACULTY
Enrollment: 2,387. **Student Body:** 54% female, 46% male, 38% out-of-state, 5% international (41 countries represented). Asian 3%, African American 1%, Caucasian 70%, Hispanic 10%, Native American 1%
Retention and Graduation: 78% freshmen return for sophomore year. 40% freshmen graduate within 4 years. 57% freshmen graduate within 6 years. 13% grads go on to further study within 1 year. 3% grads pursue arts and sciences degrees. 1% grads pursue law degrees. 2% grads pursue business degrees. 1% grads pursue medical degrees. **Faculty:** Student/faculty ratio 10:1. 155 full-time faculty, 95% hold PhDs, 8% are members of minority groups, 47% are women. 0% of classes are taught by teaching assistants.

ACADEMICS
Degrees: bachelor's, master's, post-bachelor's certificate. **Classes:** Most classes have 10—19 students. Most lab/discussion sessions have 10—19 students.
Majors with Highest Enrollment: business/commerce; nursing/registered nurse (rn, asn, bsn, msn); social sciences. **Special Study Options:** Accelerated program, cooperative education program, distance learning, double major, dual enrollment, English as a Second Language (ESL), honors program, independent study, internships, liberal arts/career combination, student-designed major, study abroad, teacher certification program, weekend college. **Honors Programs:** http://www.westminstercollege.edu/honors/ . **Disability Services:** Special programs offered to physically disabled students include note-taking services, reader services, tape recorders, tutors. **Career Services:** alumni services, career/job search classes, career assessment, internships Career services highlights include Internship Program.

FACILITIES
Housing: Coed dorms, men's dorms, women's dorms, apartments for single students. 98% of campus accessible to physically disabled. **Special Academic Facilities/Equipment:** Emma Ecceles Jones Conservatory, Gore school of Business, Giovale Library, Dick Science Building, Climbing Wall, Converse Hall, Dolores Dore Eccles Health, Wellness, and Athletic Center **Computers:** 100% of classrooms, 100% of dorms, 100% of libraries, 100% of dining areas, 100% of student union, 25% of common outdoor areas have wireless network access. Students can register for classes online. Administrative functions (other than registration) can be performed online.

CAMPUS LIFE
Environment: Metropolis. **Activities:** Choral groups, dance, drama/theater, jazz band, literary magazine, music ensembles, musical theater, student government, student newspaper, student-run film society, symphony orchestra, Campus Ministries, International Student Organization 55 registered organizations, 4 honor societies, 4 religious organizations. **Athletics (Intercollegiate):** *Men:* basketball, cross-country, golf, lacrosse, skiing (downhill/alpine), snowboarding, soccer, track/field (outdoor), track/field (indoor). *Women:* basketball, cross-country, golf, lacrosse, skiing (downhill/alpine), snowboarding, soccer, track/field (outdoor), track/field (indoor), volleyball. **On-Campus Highlights:** Shaw Student Center, Giovale Library, Emma Eccles Jones Conservatory, Dolores Dore Eccles Health, Wellness, and Athletic, Residential Village. **Environmental Initiatives:** With guidance from the Environmental Center, students completed the STARS assessment in 2010, achieving a Silver rating. Westminster scored particularly well in co-curricular and curricular sustainability efforts. Campus as a Sustainability Teaching Tool: New LEED Platinum Meldrum Science Center was completed in 2010. Demonstration gardens, organic vegetable garden, and residence hall energy monitoring also all contribute to transforming campus itself into a sustainability demonstration and laboratory. American College & University Presidents' Climate Commitment charter signatory with a target climate neutrality date of 2030.

ADMISSIONS
Freshman Academic Profile: Average high school GPA 3.5. 22% in top 10% of high school class, 56% in top 25% of high school class, 87% in top 50% of high school class. 75% from public high schools. SAT Math middle 50% range 500-620. SAT Critical Reading middle 50% range 500-613. ACT middle 50% range 22-27. Minimum web-based TOEFL 79. Minimum paper TOEFL 550. **Basis for Candidate Selection:** *Very important factors considered include:* academic GPA, rigor of secondary school record. *Important factors considered include:* Class rank, application essay, standardized test scores, interview. *Other factors considered include:* recommendation(s), alumni/ae relation, character/personal qualities, extracurricular activities, geographical residence, talent/ability. **Freshman Admission Requirements:** High school diploma is required and GED is accepted. *Academic units required:* 4 English, 2 mathematics, 3 science, 2 foreign language, 2 social studies, 1 history, 2 academic electives. *Academic units recommended:* 4 English, 2 mathematics, 3 science, 2 foreign language, 2 social studies, 1 history, 2 academic electives. **Freshman Admission Statistics:** 3,764 applied, 70% admitted, 19% enrolled. **Transfer Admission Requirements:** High school transcript, college transcript(s), essay or personal statement, Minimum college GPA of 2.5 required. Lowest grade transferable C–. **General Admission Information:** Application Fee $40. Notification on a rolling basis, beginning on or about 9/1. Nonfall registration accepted. Admission may be deferred for a maximum of 1 year. Credit and/or placement offered for CEEB Advanced Placement tests.

COSTS AND FINANCIAL AID
Annual tuition $27,720. Room and board $7,890. Required fees $490. Average book expense $1,000. **Required Forms and Deadlines:** FAFSA. **Notification of Awards:** Applicants will be notified of awards on a rolling basis beginning 3/1. **Types of Aid:** *Need-based scholarships/grants:* Federal Pell, SEOG, state scholarships/grants, private scholarships, the school's own gift aid. *Loans:* Subsidized Stafford, Unsubsidized Stafford, PLUS, Federal Perkins. **Student Employment:** Federal Work-Study Program available. Institutional employment available. Highest amount earned per year from on-campus jobs $6,934. Off-campus job opportunities are excellent. **Financial Aid Statistics:** 99% freshmen, 96% undergrads receive need-based scholarship or grant aid. 5% freshmen, 10% undergrads receive non-need-based scholarship or grant aid. 87% freshmen, 90% undergrads receive need-based self-help aid. 2% freshmen, 2% undergrads receive athletic scholarships. 97% freshmen, 95% undergrads receive any aid. 54% undergrads borrow to pay for school. Average cumulative indebtedness $28,323. **Criteria for awarding institutional aid:** *Non-need-based:* academics, alumni affiliation, art, athletics, leadership, minority status, music/drama, religious affiliation.

WESTMONT COLLEGE

955 La Paz Road, Santa Barbara, CA 93108
Phone: 805-565-6200 • **Financial Aid Phone:** 888-963-4624
E-mail: admissions@westmont.edu • **CEEB Code:** 4950
Fax: 805-565-6234 • **Website:** www.westmont.edu • **ACT Code:** 478

This private school, affiliated with the Christian (Nondenominational) Church, was founded in 1937. It has a 133-acre campus.

RATINGS
Admissions Selectivity Rating: 81   **Fire Safety Rating:** 60*   **Green Rating:** 60*

STUDENTS AND FACULTY
Enrollment: 1,333. **Student Body:** 61% female, 39% male, 31% out-of-state, 1% international (8 countries represented). Asian 9%, African American 2%, Caucasian 69%, Hispanic 10%, Native American 2%
Retention and Graduation: 87% freshmen return for sophomore year. 65% freshmen graduate within 4 years. 69% freshmen graduate within 6 years. **Faculty:** Student/faculty ratio 12:1. 93 full-time faculty, 89% hold PhDs, 11% are members of minority groups, 31% are women. 0% of classes are taught by teaching assistants.

ACADEMICS
Degrees: bachelor's, post-bachelor's certificate. **Classes:** Most classes have 10—19 students. Most lab/discussion sessions have 10—19 students. **Majors with Highest Enrollment:** cell/cellular and molecular biology; English/language arts teacher education. **Special Study Options:** Accelerated program, double major, exchange student program (domestic), honors program, independent study, internships, student-designed major, study abroad, teacher certification program. **Honors Programs:** Some general education courses are designated as honors courses. **Combined Degree Programs:** 3/2 Engineering Program. **Disability Services:** Special programs offered to physically disabled students include note-taking services, reader services, tape recorders, tutors. **Career Services:** career/job search classes, career assessment, internships,

FACILITIES

Housing: Coed dorms, apartments for single students, The Coed dorms. are segregated by floors and/or suites. Men and women do not share hallways and bathrooms. There are selected visiting hours for members of the opposite sex. 65% of campus accessible to physically disabled. **Special Academic Facilities/Equipment:** Reynolds Art Gallery features the gallery, art studios and classrooms; Carroll Observatory houses a 24-inch reflector telescope; Mericos Whittier Science facility includes state of the art technical equipment such as ultracentrifuge, Fouriertransform NMR spectrometer, etc., as well as the pre-med center; Voskuyl Library holds over 150,000 bound volumes; the physics department is developing advanced experiments for the lab; Ellen Porter Hall of Fine Arts showcases ten to twenty live musical and theatrical performances each year; Physiology Lab and Fitness Center for Kinesiology studies. **Computers:** Administrative functions (other than registration) can be performed online.

CAMPUS LIFE

Environment: City. **Activities:** Choral groups, dance, drama/theater, jazz band, literary magazine, music ensembles, musical theater, radio station, student government, student newspaper, student-run film society, symphony orchestra, yearbook, Campus Ministries 50 registered organizations, 7 honor societies, 40 religious organizations. **Athletics (Intercollegiate):** *Men:* baseball, basketball, cross-country, soccer, tennis, track/field (outdoor). *Women:* basketball, cross-country, soccer, tennis, track/field (outdoor), volleyball.

ADMISSIONS

Freshman Academic Profile: Average high school GPA 3.8. 45% in top 10% of high school class, 79% in top 25% of high school class, 96% in top 50% of high school class. 70% from public high schools. SAT Math middle 50% range 540-660. SAT Critical Reading middle 50% range 540-650. SAT Writing middle 50% range 540-650. ACT middle 50% range 24-28. Minimum paper TOEFL 560. **Basis for Candidate Selection:** *Very important factors considered include:* academic GPA, standardized test scores, character/personal qualities, religious affiliation/commitment. *Important factors considered include:* application essay, recommendation(s), rigor of secondary school record, extracurricular activities, interview, racial/ethnic status, talent/ability. *Other factors considered include:* Class rank, alumni/ae relation, first generation, geographical residence, level of applicant's interest, state residency, volunteer work, work experience. **Freshman Admission Requirements:** High school diploma is required and GED is accepted. *Academic units required:* 4 English, 3 mathematics, 3 science, (2 science labs), 2 foreign language, 2 social studies, 4 academic electives. *Academic units recommended:* 4 English, 3 mathematics, 3 science, (2 science labs), 2 foreign language, 2 social studies, 4 academic electives. **Freshman Admission Statistics:** 1,651 applied, 73% admitted, 32% enrolled. **Transfer Admission Requirements:** High school transcript, college transcript(s), essay or personal statement, statement of good standing from prior institution(s). Lowest grade transferable C-. **General Admission Information:** Application Fee $50. Notification on a rolling basis, beginning on or about 4/1. Nonfall registration accepted. Credit and/or placement offered for CEEB Advanced Placement tests.

COSTS AND FINANCIAL AID

Annual tuition $30,422. Room and board $9,622. Required fees $790. Average book expense $1,386. **Required Forms and Deadlines:** FAFSA, Cal Grant GPA Verification Form (if student is a California resident). **Notification of Awards:** Applicants will be notified of awards on a rolling basis beginning 4/1. **Types of Aid:** *Need-based scholarships/grants:* Federal Pell, SEOG, state scholarships/grants, private scholarships, the school's own gift aid. *Loans:* Subsidized Stafford, Unsubsidized Stafford, PLUS, Federal Perkins, college/university loans from institutional funds, Work-Study. **Student Employment:** Federal Work-Study Program available. Institutional employment available. **Financial Aid Statistics:** 100% freshmen, 99% undergrads receive need-based scholarship or grant aid. 9% freshmen, 8% undergrads receive non-need-based scholarship or grant aid. 83% undergrads receive need-based self-help aid. 4% freshmen, 5% undergrads receive athletic scholarships. 85% undergrads receive any aid. 53% undergrads borrow to pay for school. Average cumulative indebtedness $25,008. **Criteria for awarding institutional aid:** *Non-need-based:* academics, art, athletics, leadership, minority status, music/drama.

WHEATON COLLEGE (IL)

501 College Avenue, Wheaton, IL 60187
Phone: 630-752-5005 • **Financial Aid Phone:** 630-752-5021
E-mail: admissions@wheaton.edu • **CEEB Code:** 1905
Fax: 630-752-5285 • **Website:** www.wheaton.edu • **ACT Code:** 1160

This private school was founded in 1860. It has a 80-acre campus.

RATINGS
Admissions Selectivity Rating: 93   **Fire Safety Rating:** 86   **Green Rating:** 74

STUDENTS AND FACULTY
Enrollment: 2,477. **Student Body:** 51% female, 49% male, 74% out-of-state, 2% international (37 countries represented). Asian 8%, African American 2%, Caucasian 81%, Hispanic 4%, Native American 0%
Retention and Graduation: 76% freshmen graduate within 4 years. 27% grads go on to further study within 1 year. 16% grads pursue arts and sciences degrees. 1% grads pursue law degrees. 6% grads pursue medical degrees. **Faculty:** Student/faculty ratio 12:1. 197 full-time faculty, 97% hold PhDs, 11% are members of minority groups, 33% are women. 0% of classes are taught by teaching assistants.

ACADEMICS
Degrees: bachelor's, master's, post-bachelor's certificate. **Classes:** Most classes have 10—19 students. Most lab/discussion sessions have 10—19 students. **Majors with Highest Enrollment:** business/managerial economics; English language and literature; health services/allied health/health sciences. **Special Study Options:** cross-registration, double major, exchange student program (domestic), independent study, internships, liberal arts/career combination, student-designed major, study abroad, teacher certification program. **Honors Programs:** Some departments offer qualified students to submit an honors project. **Combined Degree Programs:** Liberal Arts/Engineering; Liberal Arts/N. **Disability Services:** Special programs offered to physically disabled students include note-taking services, reader services, tape recorders, tutors. **Career Services:** Alumni network, alumni services, career/job search classes, career assessment, internships, regional alumni.

FACILITIES
Housing: Coed dorms, men's dorms, women's dorms, apartments for married students, cooperative housing, apartments for single students, Housing for disabled provided as needed. 97% of campus accessible to physically disabled. **Special Academic Facilities/Equipment:** World evangelism museum, language lab, observatory, Collection of works/papers of seven British authors, Billy Graham Center Museum **Computers:** 10% of classrooms, 100% of dorms, 100% of libraries, 100% of dining areas, 100% of student union, 75% of common outdoor areas have wireless network access. Students can register for classes online. Administrative functions (other than registration) can be performed online.

CAMPUS LIFE
Environment: Town. **Activities:** Choral groups, concert band, dance, drama/theater, jazz band, literary magazine, music ensembles, musical theater, opera, pep band, radio station, student government, student newspaper, student-run film society, symphony orchestra, television station, yearbook, Campus Ministries, International Student Organization, Model UN 85 registered organizations, 13 honor societies, 12 religious organizations. **Athletics (Intercollegiate):** *Men:* baseball, basketball, cross-country, football, golf, soccer, swimming, tennis, track/field (outdoor), track/field (indoor), wrestling. *Women:* basketball, cross-country, golf, soccer, softball, swimming, tennis, track/field (outdoor), track/field (indoor), volleyball, water polo. **On-Campus Highlights:** Billy Graham Center - archive, museum, Wade Center - collection of English auth, New Science Building opens Fall 2010, Todd M. Beamer Student Center, J. Dennis Hastert Center. **Environmental Initiatives:** Environmental Studies Major LEED Certifications Recycling

ADMISSIONS
Freshman Academic Profile: Average high school GPA 3.7. 58% in top 10% of high school class, 84% in top 25% of high school class, 97% in top 50% of high school class. 53% from public high schools. SAT Math middle 50% range 610-700. SAT Critical Reading middle 50% range 600-720. SAT Writing middle 50% range 600-710. ACT middle 50% range 27-32. Minimum web-based TOEFL 95. Minimum paper TOEFL 587. **Basis for Candidate Selection:** *Very important factors considered include:* application essay, academic GPA,

recommendation(s), rigor of secondary school record, standardized test scores, character/personal qualities, interview, religious affiliation/commitment. *Important factors considered include:* extracurricular activities, talent/ability, volunteer work, work experience. *Other factors considered include:* Class rank, alumni/ae relation, first generation, geographical residence, level of applicant's interest, racial/ethnic status, state residency. **Freshman Admission Requirements:** High school diploma is required and GED is accepted. **Freshman Admission Statistics:** 1,959 applied, 69% admitted, 44% enrolled. **Transfer Admission Requirements:** High school transcript, college transcript(s), essay or personal statement, Minimum college GPA of 3.0 required. Lowest grade transferable C–. **General Admission Information:** Application Fee $50. Regular application deadline 1/10. Regular notification 4/1. Nonfall registration not accepted. Admission may be deferred for a maximum of 1 year. Credit and/or placement offered for CEEB Advanced Placement tests.

COSTS AND FINANCIAL AID

Annual tuition $30,120. Room and board $8,560. Average book expense $816. **Required Forms and Deadlines:** FAFSA, institution's own financial aid form. **Notification of Awards:** Applicants will be notified of awards on a rolling basis beginning 3/1. **Types of Aid:** *Need-based scholarships/grants:* Federal Pell, SEOG, state scholarships/grants, the school's own gift aid. *Loans:* Subsidized Stafford, Unsubsidized Stafford, PLUS, Federal Perkins. **Student Employment:** Federal Work-Study Program available. Institutional employment available. Off-campus job opportunities are excellent. **Financial Aid Statistics:** 99% freshmen, 98% undergrads receive need-based scholarship or grant aid. 35% freshmen, 32% undergrads receive non-need-based scholarship or grant aid. 81% freshmen, 81% undergrads receive need-based self-help aid. 78% freshmen, 72% undergrads receive any aid. 59% undergrads borrow to pay for school. Average cumulative indebtedness $24,067. **Criteria for awarding institutional aid:** *Non-need-based:* academics, alumni affiliation, art, minority status, music/drama.

WHEATON COLLEGE (MA)

Office of Admission, Norton, MA 2766
Phone: 508-286-8251 • **Financial Aid Phone:** 508-286-8232
E-mail: admission@wheatoncollege.edu • **CEEB Code:** 3963
Fax: 508-286-8271 • **Website:** wheatoncollege.edu • **ACT Code:** 1932

This private school was founded in 1834. It has a 400-acre campus.

RATINGS
Admissions Selectivity Rating: 90   **Fire Safety Rating:** 78   **Green Rating:** 79

STUDENTS AND FACULTY
Enrollment: 1,622. **Student Body:** 64% female, 36% male, 65% out-of-state, 8% international (41 countries represented). Asian 2%, African American 5%, Caucasian 74%, Hispanic 7%, Native American 0%
Retention and Graduation: 86% freshmen return for sophomore year. 73% freshmen graduate within 4 years. 77% freshmen graduate within 6 years. 56% grads go on to further study within 1 year. 35% grads pursue arts and sciences degrees. 5% grads pursue law degrees. 1% grads pursue business degrees. 2% grads pursue medical degrees. **Faculty:** Student/faculty ratio 11:1. 139 full-time faculty, 88% hold PhDs, 19% are members of minority groups, 50% are women. 0% of classes are taught by teaching assistants.

ACADEMICS
Degrees: bachelor's. **Classes:** Most classes have 10—19 students. Most lab/discussion sessions have 10—19 students. **Majors with Highest Enrollment:** economics; English language and literature; psychology. **Special Study Options:** Accelerated program, cross-registration, double major, dual enrollment, exchange student program (domestic), honors program, independent study, internships, liberal arts/career combination, student-designed major, study abroad, teacher certification program. **Combined Degree Programs:** BA/MA, BA/MEng, BA/MBA; BA/BFA;BA/BS;BA/Doctor of Optometry. **Disability Services:** Special programs offered to physically disabled students include note-taking services, reader services, tape recorders, tutors. **Career Services:** Alumni network, alumni services, career/job search classes, career assessment, internships, regional alumni., Career services highlights include Wheaton provides stipends ranging from $3,000 to $6,000 for at least 60% of our students to partcipate in unpaid internships, research opportunities and other out of classroom learning opportunities.

FACILITIES
Housing: Coed dorms, special housing for disabled students, men's dorms, special housing for international students, women's dorms, wellness housing, theme housing, quiet house. 50% of campus accessible to physically disabled. **Special Academic Facilities/Equipment:** Art gallery,language lab, photography darkrooms,dance studio,on-campus nursery school, media center, observatory. **Computers:** 100% of classrooms, 100% of dorms, 100% of libraries, 100% of dining areas, 100% of student union, have wireless network access. Students can register for classes online. Administrative functions (other than registration) can be performed online.

CAMPUS LIFE
Environment: Village. **Activities:** Choral groups, dance, drama/theater, jazz band, literary magazine, music ensembles, musical theater, pep band, radio station, student government, student newspaper, student-run film society, symphony orchestra, yearbook, International Student Organization, Model UN 60 registered organizations, 8 honor societies, 4 religious organizations. **Athletics (Intercollegiate):** *Men:* baseball, basketball, cross-country, diving, lacrosse, soccer, swimming, tennis, track/field (outdoor), track/field (indoor). *Women:* basketball, cross-country, diving, field hockey, lacrosse, soccer, softball, swimming, synchronized swimming, tennis, track/field (outdoor), track/field (indoor), volleyball. **On-Campus Highlights:** Mars Arts and Humanities:a$20 million arts facility, Haas Athletic Center, Lyon's Den - coffee house, Mary Lyon Hall - college's oldest building, Balfour-Hood Student Center. **Environmental Initiatives:** Modeling Sustainability: Construction of the new Mars Science Center is LEED certified Silver. See http://wheatoncollege.edu/news/2010/04/15/science-rising Two new committees, the President's Steering Committee on Sustainability and the Student Government Association's Green Initiative Committee (G.I.C.), both established in 2009 to expand the reach of the student-initiated Sustainability Committee. Numerous sustainability activities (farmers' market, energy competitions, expanded sustainability clubs) have grown under this new infrastructure for sustainability. Dining Services: The Director and staff of Wheaton's dining services, Aramark, is a regular member of the Sustainability Committee and is fully engaged in the community. http://www.campusdish.com/en-US/CSNE/Wheaton/Sustainability/

ADMISSIONS
Freshman Academic Profile: Average high school GPA 3.5. 42% in top 10% of high school class, 29% in top 25% of high school class, 98% in top 50% of high school class. 64% from public high schools. SAT Math middle 50% range 580-660. SAT Critical Reading middle 50% range 580-680. ACT middle 50% range 26-30. Minimum web-based TOEFL 90. **Basis for Candidate Selection:** *Very important factors considered include:* application essay, academic GPA, rigor of secondary school record, character/personal qualities, extracurricular activities, first generation, talent/ability. *Important factors considered include:* Class rank, recommendation(s), alumni/ae relation, interview, volunteer work, work experience. *Other factors considered include:* geographical residence, level of applicant's interest, racial/ethnic status, state residency. **Freshman Admission Requirements:** High school diploma is required and GED is accepted. **Freshman Admission Statistics:** 3,448 applied, 60% admitted, 21% enrolled. **Transfer Admission Requirements:** High school transcript, college transcript(s), essay or personal statement, statement of good standing from prior institution(s). Minimum college GPA of 3.0 required. Lowest grade transferable C. **General Admission Information:** Application Fee $55. Early decision application deadline 11/15. Regular application deadline 1/15. Regular notification 4/1. Nonfall registration accepted. Admission may be deferred for a maximum of 1 year. Credit and/or placement offered for CEEB Advanced Placement tests.

COSTS AND FINANCIAL AID
Annual tuition $43,480. Room and board $11,160. Required fees $294. Average book expense $940. **Required Forms and Deadlines:** FAFSA, CSS/Financial Aid PROFILE, noncustodial PROFILE, business/farm supplement. Parent and Student Federal Tax Returns and W2's. **Notification of Awards:** Applicants will be notified of awards on or about 4/1. **Types of Aid:** *Need-based scholarships/grants:* Federal Pell, SEOG, state scholarships/grants, private scholarships, the school's own gift aid. *Loans:* Subsidized Stafford, Unsubsidized Stafford, PLUS, Federal Perkins. **Student Employment:** Federal Work-Study Program available. Institutional employment available. Highest amount earned per year from on-campus jobs $2,528. Off-campus job opportunities are good. **Financial Aid Statistics:** 95% freshmen, 95% undergrads receive need-based scholarship or grant aid. 2% freshmen, 2% undergrads receive non-need-based scholarship or grant aid. 96% freshmen, 97% undergrads receive need-based self-help aid83% freshmen, 76% undergrads receive any aid. 59% undergrads borrow to pay for school. Average cumulative indebtedness $25,778. **Criteria for awarding institutional aid:** *Non-need-based:* academics.

WHEELING JESUIT UNIVERSITY

316 Washington Avenue, Wheeling, WV 26003
Phone: 304-243-2359 • **Financial Aid Phone:** 304-243-2304
E-mail: admiss@wju.edu • **CEEB Code:** 5906
Fax: 304-243-2397 • **Website:** www.wju.edu • **ACT Code:** 4546

This private school, affiliated with the Roman Catholic Church, was founded in 1954. It has a 70-acre campus.

RATINGS
Admissions Selectivity Rating: 77   **Fire Safety Rating:** 97   **Green Rating:** 66

STUDENTS AND FACULTY
Enrollment: 1,034. **Student Body:** 58% female, 42% male, 68% out-of-state, 3% international (16 countries represented). Asian 2%, African American 4%, Caucasian 67%, Hispanic 2%, Native American 0%
Retention and Graduation: 72% freshmen return for sophomore year. 49% freshmen graduate within 4 years. 60% freshmen graduate within 6 years. 26% grads go on to further study within 1 year. 10% pursue arts and sciences degrees. 4% grads pursue law degrees. 8% grads pursue business degrees. 4% grads pursue medical degrees. **Faculty:** Student/faculty ratio 11:1. 90 full-time faculty, 69% hold PhDs, 4% are members of minority groups, 48% are women. 0% of classes are taught by teaching assistants.

ACADEMICS
Degrees: bachelor's, master's. **Classes:** Most classes have 10—19 students. Most lab/discussion sessions have 10—19 students. **Majors with Highest Enrollment:** business, management, marketing, and related support services, other; nursing/registered nurse (rn, asn, bsn, msn); psychology. **Special Study Options:** distance learning, double major, English as a Second Language (ESL), honors program, independent study, internships, liberal arts/career combination, student-designed major, study abroad, teacher certification program, Off-campus study: Washington, DC. **Honors Programs:** The Laut Honors program which is designed to introduces students to aspects of the arts and sciences that are not available in the regular curriculum in order to inspire and awaken curiosity through a variety of enriching experiences offered. **Combined Degree Programs:** 3-2 engineering program with Case Western Reserve. **Disability Services:** Special programs offered to physically disabled students include note-taking services, reader services, tutors. **Career Services:** Alumni network, alumni services, career/job search classes, career assessment, internships, regional alumni

FACILITIES
Housing: Coed dorms, special housing for disabled students, men's dorms, special housing for international students, women's dorms, apartments for married students. 85% of campus accessible to physically disabled. **Special Academic Facilities/Equipment:** Center for Educational Technologies (NASA). **Computers:** 10% of classrooms, 100% of libraries, 100% of dining areas, 100% of student union, 10% of common outdoor areas have wireless network access. Students can register for classes online. Administrative functions (other than registration) can be performed online.

CAMPUS LIFE
Environment: Town. **Activities:** Choral groups, dance, drama/theater, literary magazine, musical theater, pep band, radio station, student government, student newspaper, television station, yearbook, Campus Ministries, International Student Organization 30 registered organizations, 9 honor societies, 6 religious organizations. **Athletics (Intercollegiate):** *Men:* baseball, basketball, cross-country, golf, lacrosse, soccer, swimming, track/field (outdoor), track/field (indoor). *Women:* basketball, cross-country, golf, soccer, softball, swimming, track/field (outdoor), track/field (indoor), volleyball. **On-Campus Highlights:** Coffee Shop- located in Swint Hall, McDonough Fitness Center, Creek Bank surrounding campus, Rathskeller- Pub on campus, McDonough indoor swimming pool and racqu. **Environmental Initiatives:** Faculty/student research related to environmental topics. New sustainability major available Fall 2012 with student-led projects. Appalachian Institute's collaborative programs with Appalachian communities, including education/research/advocacy related to environmental issues.

ADMISSIONS
Freshman Academic Profile: Average high school GPA 3.4. 20% in top 10% of high school class, 46% in top 25% of high school class, 77% in top 50% of high school class. 73% from public high schools. SAT Math middle 50% range 470-550. SAT Critical Reading middle 50% range 480-550. SAT Writing middle 50% range 450-540. ACT middle 50% range 20-25. Minimum web-based TOEFL 80. Minimum paper TOEFL 550. **Basis for Candidate Selection:** *Very important factors considered include:* academic GPA, standardized test scores. *Important factors considered include:* application essay,

rigor of secondary school record, interview. *Other factors considered include:* recommendation(s), character/personal qualities, extracurricular activities, level of applicant's interest, talent/ability, volunteer work, work experience. **Freshman Admission Requirements:** High school diploma is required and GED is accepted. *Academic units required:* 4 English, 2 mathematics, 1 science, (1 science labs), 2 social studies, 2 history, 6 academic electives. *Academic units recommended:* 4 English, 2 mathematics, 1 science, (1 science labs), 2 social studies, 2 history, 6 academic electives. **Freshman Admission Statistics:** 1,401 applied, 63% admitted, 32% enrolled. **Transfer Admission Requirements:** college transcript(s), Minimum college GPA of 2.3 required. Lowest grade transferable C. **General Admission Information:** Application Fee $25. Regular notification 8/15. Notification on a rolling basis, beginning on or about 9/1. Nonfall registration accepted. Admission may be deferred for a maximum of 1 semester. Credit and/or placement offered for CEEB Advanced Placement tests.

COSTS AND FINANCIAL AID
Annual tuition $24,650. Room and board $9,028. Required fees $990. Average book expense $1,300. **Required Forms and Deadlines:** FAFSA. **Notification of Awards:** Applicants will be notified of awards on a rolling basis beginning 3/15. **Types of Aid:** *Need-based scholarships/grants:* Federal Pell, SEOG, state scholarships/grants, private scholarships, the school's own gift aid. *Loans:* Direct Subsidized Stafford, Direct Unsubsidized Stafford, Direct PLUS, Subsidized Stafford, Unsubsidized Stafford, PLUS, Federal Perkins, Federal Nursing, Private Alternative Loans. **Student Employment:** Federal Work-Study Program available. Institutional employment available. Highest amount earned per year from on-campus jobs $2,200. Off-campus job opportunities are good. **Financial Aid Statistics:** 66% freshmen, 68% undergrads receive need-based scholarship or grant aid. 83% freshmen, 90% undergrads receive non-need-based scholarship or grant aid. 72% freshmen, 73% undergrads receive need-based self-help aid. 34% freshmen, 31% undergrads receive athletic scholarships. 97% freshmen, 98% undergrads receive any aid. 79% undergrads borrow to pay for school. Average cumulative indebtedness $30,516. **Criteria for awarding institutional aid:** *Non-need-based:* academics, alumni affiliation, athletics, leadership, music/drama.

WHEELOCK COLLEGE

200 The Riverway, Boston, MA 2215
Phone: 617-879-2206 • **Financial Aid Phone:** 617-879-2206
E-mail: undergrad@wheelock.edu • **CEEB Code:** 3964
Fax: 617-879-2449 • **Website:** www.wheelock.edu • **ACT Code:** 1934

This private school was founded in 1888. It has a 6-acre campus.

RATINGS
Admissions Selectivity Rating: 71   **Fire Safety Rating:** 90   **Green Rating:** 60*

STUDENTS AND FACULTY
Enrollment: 871. **Student Body:** 90% female, 10% male, 48% out-of-state, 0% international (6 countries represented). Asian 2%, African American 12%, Caucasian 61%, Hispanic 11%, Native American 0%
Retention and Graduation: 69% freshmen return for sophomore year. 58% freshmen graduate within 6 years. 25% grads go on to further study within 1 year. 12% grads pursue arts and sciences degrees. 1% grads pursue law degrees. **Faculty:** Student/faculty ratio 9:1. 65 full-time faculty, 89% hold PhDs, 29% are members of minority groups, 75% are women. 0% of classes are taught by teaching assistants.

ACADEMICS
Degrees: bachelor's, master's, post-bachelor's certificate, post-master's certificate. **Classes:** Most classes have 10—19 students. **Majors with Highest Enrollment:** elementary education and teaching; human development, family studies, and related services, other; social work. **Special Study Options:** cross-registration, double major, honors program, independent study, internships, liberal arts/career combination, study abroad, teacher certification program. **Combined Degree Programs:** BA/MA. **Disability Services:** Special programs offered to physically disabled students include note-taking services, reader services, tape recorders, tutors. **Career Services:** Alumni network, career/job search classes, career assessment, internships.

FACILITIES
Housing: Coed dorms, men's dorms, women's dorms, Wellness Floor, First Year Floors. 67% of campus accessible to physically disabled. **Special Academic Facilities/Equipment:** Art studio, resource center with fully equipped workshop for creating and developing original curriculum tools.

CAMPUS LIFE

Environment: Metropolis. **Activities:** Choral groups, dance, drama/theater, music ensembles, musical theater, student government, symphony orchestra 20 registered organizations, 1 honor societies, 1 religious organizations. **Athletics (Intercollegiate):** *Men:* basketball, tennis. *Women:* basketball, diving, field hockey, soccer, softball, swimming. **On-Campus Highlights:** The Wheelock Family Theater, The Student Center, The Library, Brookline Campus - Hawes Street, The Resource Center.

ADMISSIONS

Freshman Academic Profile: Average high school GPA 3.0. 7% in top 10% of high school class, 36% in top 25% of high school class, 63% in top 50% of high school class. 85% from public high schools. SAT Math middle 50% range 430-520. SAT Critical Reading middle 50% range 440-540. SAT Writing middle 50% range 450-550. ACT middle 50% range 17-22. Minimum paper TOEFL 500. **Basis for Candidate Selection:** *Very important factors considered include:* application essay, academic GPA, rigor of secondary school record. *Important factors considered include:* Class rank, recommendation(s), character/personal qualities, extracurricular activities, volunteer work. *Other factors considered include:* standardized test scores, alumni/ae relation, interview, talent/ability, work experience. **Freshman Admission Requirements:** High school diploma is required and GED is accepted. *Academic units required:* 4 English, 3 mathematics, 2 science, (1 science labs), 2 social studies. academic electives. Child Development Classes. *Academic units recommended:* 4 English, 3 mathematics, 2 science, (1 science labs), 2 social studies. academic electives. Child Development Classes **Freshman Admission Statistics:** 1,537 applied, 71% admitted, 21% enrolled. **Transfer Admission Requirements:** High school transcript, college transcript(s), essay or personal statement, Minimum college GPA of 2.0 required. Lowest grade transferable C. **General Admission Information:** Application Fee $35. Regular application deadline 3/1. Notification on a rolling basis, beginning on or about 1/1. Nonfall registration accepted. Admission may be deferred for a maximum of 1 year. Credit offered for CEEB Advanced Placement tests.

COSTS AND FINANCIAL AID

Annual tuition $29,860. Room and board $12,800. Required fees $1,095. Average book expense $880. **Required Forms and Deadlines:** FAFSA. **Notification of Awards:** Applicants will be notified of awards on a rolling basis beginning 3/5. **Types of Aid:** *Need-based scholarships/grants:* Federal Pell, SEOG, state scholarships/grants, the school's own gift aid, Merit scholarships are available for all freshmen applicants with a 3.0 G.P.A.(or higher) and SAT scores of 1050(or higher). Scholarhips range from $3000 to $12,000. *Loans:* Subsidized Stafford, Unsubsidized Stafford, PLUS, Federal Perkins, college/university loans from institutional funds. **Student Employment:** Federal Work-Study Program available. Institutional employment available. Highest amount earned per year from on-campus jobs $2,000. Off-campus job opportunities are good. **Financial Aid Statistics:** 100% freshmen, 99% undergrads receive need-based scholarship or grant aid. 7% freshmen, 8% undergrads receive non-need-based scholarship or grant aid. 92% freshmen, 90% undergrads receive need-based self-help aid. 85% freshmen, 81% undergrads receive any aid. 97% undergrads borrow to pay for school. Average cumulative indebtedness $45,391. **Criteria for awarding institutional aid:** *Non-need-based:* academics, leadership.

WHITMAN COLLEGE

345 Boyer Ave, Walla Walla, WA 99362
Phone: 509-527-5176 • **Financial Aid Phone:** 509-527-5178
E-mail: admission@whitman.edu • **CEEB Code:** 4951
Fax: 509-527-4967 • **Website:** www.whitman.edu • **ACT Code:** 4492

This private school was founded in 1883. It has a 117-acre campus.

RATINGS

Admissions Selectivity Rating: 95   **Fire Safety Rating:** 83   **Green Rating:** 89

STUDENTS AND FACULTY

Enrollment: 1,525. **Student Body:** 57% female, 43% male, 66% out-of-state, 3% international (52 countries represented). Asian 8%, African American 1%, Caucasian 72%, Hispanic 6%, Native American 1%
Retention and Graduation: 94% freshmen return for sophomore year. 80% freshmen graduate within 4 years. **Faculty:** Student/faculty ratio 9:1. 146 full-time faculty, 95% hold PhDs, 15% are members of minority groups, 48% are women. 0% of classes are taught by teaching assistants.

ACADEMICS

Degrees: bachelor's. **Classes:** Most classes have 10—19 students. Most lab/discussion sessions have 20—29 students. **Majors with Highest Enrollment:** biology/biological sciences; history; political science and government. **Special Study Options:** Accelerated program, cooperative education program, cross-registration, double major, dual enrollment, exchange student program (domestic), honors program, independent study, liberal arts/career combination, student-designed major, study abroad, Undergraduate research conference. **Combined Degree Programs:** BA/JD, BA/MA, 3-2 Forest./Duke; 3-2 Ocean./Bio. or Geo. **Disability Services:** Special programs offered to physically disabled students include note-taking services, reader services, tape recorders, tutors. **Career Services:** Alumni network, alumni services, career assessment

FACILITIES

Housing: Coed dorms, special housing for international students, women's dorms, fraternity/sorority housing, apartments for single students, theme housing, interest houses. 85% of campus accessible to physically disabled. **Special Academic Facilities/Equipment:** Art gallery, Asian art collection, anthropology museum, planetarium, outdoor observatory, two electron microscopes, outdoor sculpture walk, technology/video-conferencing center, indoor and outdoor rock-climbing walls, organic garden. **Computers:** 100% of classrooms, 100% of dorms, 100% of libraries, 100% of dining areas, 100% of student union, 40% of common outdoor areas have wireless network access. Students can register for classes online. Administrative functions (other than registration) can be performed online.

CAMPUS LIFE

Environment: Town. **Activities:** Choral groups, concert band, dance, drama/theater, jazz band, literary magazine, music ensembles, musical theater, radio station, student government, student newspaper, student-run film society, symphony orchestra, Campus Ministries, International Student Organization, Model UN 80 registered organizations, 3 honor societies, 7 religious organizations. 4 fraternities, 3 sororities. **Athletics (Intercollegiate):** *Men:* baseball, basketball, cross-country, golf, soccer, swimming, tennis. *Women:* basketball, cross-country, golf, soccer, swimming, tennis, volleyball. **On-Campus Highlights:** Reid Campus Center, Penrose Library, Baker Ferguson Fitness Center, Sheehan Art Gallery, Olin Hall, Harper Joy Theatre. **Environmental Initiatives:** Installed 21kW Solar Panels on roof of Bratton Tennis Center. Installed industrial vermicomposting system on campus which can accommodate 600 pounds of food waste each week. All resulting compost is used for on-campus landscaping. Creation of a Sustainability Revolving Loan Fund, a $50,000 line of credit that is designated for campus improvements that significantly benefit Whitman's sustainability efforts by conserving resources and improving efficiency.

ADMISSIONS

Freshman Academic Profile: Average high school GPA 3.8. 62% in top 10% of high school class, 89% in top 25% of high school class, 100% in top 50% of high school class. 75% from public high schools. SAT Math middle 50% range 610-700. SAT Critical Reading middle 50% range 610-740. SAT Writing middle 50% range 620-710. ACT middle 50% range 29-32. Minimum web-based TOEFL 85. Minimum paper TOEFL 560. **Basis for Candidate Selection:** *Very important factors considered include:* application essay, academic GPA, rigor of secondary school record, character/personal qualities. *Important factors considered include:* recommendation(s), standardized test scores, extracurricular activities, racial/ethnic status, talent/ability. *Other factors considered include:* Class rank, alumni/ae relation, first-generation, geographical residence, interview, level of applicant's interest, state residency, volunteer work, work experience. **Freshman Admission Requirements:** High school diploma is required and GED is accepted. **Freshman Admission Statistics:** 2,854 applied, 49% admitted, 28% enrolled. **Transfer Admission Requirements:** High school transcript, college transcript(s), essay or personal statement, statement of good standing from prior institution(s). Lowest grade transferable C–. **General Admission Information:** Application Fee $50. Early decision application deadline 11/15. Regular application deadline 1/15. Regular notification 4/1. Nonfall registration accepted. Admission may be deferred for a maximum of 1 year. Credit and/or placement offered for CEEB Advanced Placement tests.

COSTS AND FINANCIAL AID

Annual tuition $41,790. Room and board $10,560. Required fees $336. Average book expense $1,400. **Required Forms and Deadlines:** FAFSA, CSS/Financial Aid PROFILE. **Notification of Awards:** Applicants will be notified of awards on a rolling basis beginning 12/20. **Types of Aid:** *Need-based scholarships/grants:* Federal Pell, SEOG, state scholarships/grants, private scholarships, the school's own gift aid. *Loans:* Subsidized Stafford, Unsubsidized Stafford, PLUS, Federal Perkins, state loans, Alternative student loans. **Student Employment:** Federal Work-Study Program available. Institutional employment available. Highest amount earned per year from on-campus jobs $2,463. Off-campus job opportunities are good. **Financial Aid Statistics:** 100% freshmen, 100% undergrads receive need-based scholarship or grant aid. 50% freshmen, 32% undergrads receive non-need-based scholarship or grant aid. 84% freshmen, 85% undergrads receive need-based self-help aid. 78% freshmen, 81% undergrads receive any aid. 48% undergrads borrow to pay for school. Average cumulative indebtedness $15,042. **Criteria for awarding institutional aid:** *Non-need-based:* academics, art, leadership, minority status, music/drama.

WHITTIER COLLEGE

Best 378

13406 Philadelphia Street, Whittier, CA 90608
Phone: 562-907-4238 • **Financial Aid Phone:** 562-907-4285
E-mail: admission@whittier.edu • **CEEB Code:** 4952
Fax: 562-907-4870 • **Website:** www.whittier.edu • **ACT Code:** 480

This private school was founded in 1887. It has a 75-acre campus.

RATINGS
Admissions Selectivity Rating: 74   **Fire Safety Rating:** 84   **Green Rating:** 71

STUDENTS AND FACULTY
Enrollment: 1,361. **Student Body:** 53% female, 47% male, 27% out-of-state, 2% international (24 countries represented). Asian 9%, African American 6%, Caucasian 41%, Hispanic 30%, Native American 1%
Retention and Graduation: 55% freshmen graduate within 4 years. 61% freshmen graduate within 6 years. 18% grads go on to further study within 1 year. 7% grads pursue arts and sciences degrees. 2% grads pursue law degrees. 3% grads pursue business degrees. 1% grads pursue medical degrees. **Faculty:** Student/faculty ratio 13:1. 96 full-time faculty, 99% hold PhDs, 27% are members of minority groups, 47% are women. 0% of classes are taught by teaching assistants.

ACADEMICS
Degrees: bachelor's, master's. **Classes:** Most classes have 10—19 students. Most lab/discussion sessions have 20—29 students. **Majors with Highest Enrollment:** biology/biological sciences; business administration and management; psychology. **Special Study Options:** double major, independent study, internships, liberal arts/career combination, student-designed major, study abroad, teacher certification program. **Combined Degree Programs:** BA/JD, 3-2 engineering programs. **Disability Services:** Special programs offered to physically disabled students include note-taking services, reader services, tape recorders. **Career Services:** Alumni network, alumni services, career/job search classes, career assessment, internships, regional alumni. Career services highlights include Backpack to Briefcase: The Office of Career Services and the Office of Alumni Relations have teamed up to present a series of workshops throughout the school year to enable students to learn and develop practical career skills and explore diverse career paths, and at the same time showcase Whittier College alumni professionals, who serve as volunteer mentors and workshop leaders.

FACILITIES
Housing: Coed dorms, special housing for international students, living and learning community; special interest housing. 60% of campus accessible to physically disabled. **Special Academic Facilities/Equipment:** Performing arts center, on-campus pre-school/ elementary school, image processing lab, state-of-the-art nightclub, on-air radio studio and production room, video production room **Computers:** 100% of classrooms, 100% of dorms, 100% of libraries, 100% of dining areas, 100% of student union, have wireless network access. Students can register for classes online. Administrative functions (other than registration) can be performed online.

CAMPUS LIFE
Environment: City. **Activities:** Choral groups, dance, drama/theater, jazz band, literary magazine, music ensembles, musical theater, radio station, student government, student newspaper, student-run film society, yearbook, Campus Ministries, International Student Organization, Model UN 60 registered organizations, 17 honor societies, 6 religious organizations. 4 fraternities, 5 sororities. **Athletics (Intercollegiate):** *Men:* baseball, basketball, cross-country, diving, football, golf, lacrosse, soccer, swimming, tennis, track/field (outdoor), water polo. *Women:* basketball, cross-country, diving, lacrosse, soccer, softball, swimming, tennis, track/field (outdoor), volleyball, water polo. **On-Campus Highlights:** The Campus Center, Bonnie Bell Wardman Library, Donald Graham Athletics Center, Ruth B. Shannon Center for the Performing Arts, the Rock (campus icon), The recently renovated Campus Center houses

the student services division, campus dining, The Spot (campus cafe), student organization offices, KPOET radio, student newspaper Quaker Campus, and an outdoor amphitheatre. **Environmental Initiatives:** Climate Commitment signatory EnergyStar purchasing policy Waste minimization program

ADMISSIONS
Freshman Academic Profile: Average high school GPA 3.1. 30% in top 10% of high school class, 42% in top 25% of high school class, 82% in top 50% of high school class. SAT Math middle 50% range 470-590. SAT Critical Reading middle 50% range 470-580. SAT Writing middle 50% range 470-570. ACT middle 50% range 19-25. Minimum paper TOEFL 550. **Basis for Candidate Selection:** *Very important factors considered include:* application essay, rigor of secondary school record. *Important factors considered include:* academic GPA, recommendation(s), standardized test scores, character/personal qualities, extracurricular activities, interview, talent/ability, volunteer work. *Other factors considered include:* Class rank, alumni/ae relation, first generation, geographical residence, racial/ethnic status, state residency, work experience. **Freshman Admission Requirements:** High school diploma is required and GED is accepted. *Academic units required:* 3 English, 2 mathematics, 1 science, (1 science labs), 2 foreign language, 1 social studies. *Academic units recommended:* 3 English, 2 mathematics, 1 science, (1 science labs), 2 foreign language, 1 social studies. **Freshman Admission Statistics:** 2,263 applied, 72% admitted, 22% enrolled. **Transfer Admission Requirements:** High school transcript, college transcript(s), essay or personal statement, Lowest grade transferable C–. **General Admission Information:** Application Fee $50. Notification on a rolling basis, beginning on or about 12/30. Nonfall registration accepted. Admission may be deferred for a maximum of 1 year. Credit and/or placement offered for CEEB Advanced Placement tests.

COSTS AND FINANCIAL AID
Annual tuition $36,632. Room and board $10,428. Required fees $360. Average book expense $1,638. **Required Forms and Deadlines:** FAFSA, institution's own financial aid form. **Notification of Awards:** Applicants will be notified of awards on a rolling basis beginning 2/15. **Types of Aid:** *Need-based scholarships/grants:* Federal Pell, SEOG, state scholarships/grants, private scholarships, the school's own gift aid. *Loans:* Direct PLUS, Subsidized Stafford, Unsubsidized Stafford, PLUS, Federal Perkins, Alternative Financing Loans. **Student Employment:** Federal Work-Study Program available. Highest amount earned per year from on-campus jobs $1,250. Off-campus job opportunities are good. **Financial Aid Statistics:** 89% freshmen, 92% undergrads receive need-based scholarship or grant aid. 10% freshmen, 7% undergrads receive non-need-based scholarship or grant aid. 87% freshmen, 89% undergrads receive need-based self-help aid. 92% freshmen, 89% undergrads receive any aid. 67% undergrads borrow to pay for school. Average cumulative indebtedness $24,687. **Criteria for awarding institutional aid:** *Non-need-based:* academics, alumni affiliation, art, music/drama.

WHITWORTH COLLEGE

300 West Hawthorne Road, Spokane, WA 99251
Phone: 509-777-4786 • **Financial Aid Phone:** 509-777-4306
E-mail: admission@whitworth.edu • **CEEB Code:** 4953
Fax: 509-777-3758 • **ACT Code:** 4494

This private school, affiliated with the Presbyterian Church, was founded in 1890. It has a 200-acre campus.

RATINGS
Admissions Selectivity Rating: 86   **Fire Safety Rating:** 84   **Green Rating:** 60*

STUDENTS AND FACULTY
Enrollment: 2,233. **Student Body:** 61% female, 39% male, 37% out-of-state, 1% international (15 countries represented). Asian 4%, African American 3%, Caucasian 86%, Hispanic 2%, Native American 1%
Retention and Graduation: 89% freshmen return for sophomore year. 59% freshmen graduate within 4 years. 74% freshmen graduate within 6 years. 50% grads go on to further study within 1 year. **Faculty:** Student/faculty ratio 12:1. 123 full-time faculty, 74% hold PhDs, 10% are members of minority groups, 42% are women. 0% of classes are taught by teaching assistants.

ACADEMICS
Degrees: bachelor's, master's. **Classes:** Most classes have 10—19 students. Most lab/discussion sessions have 10—19 students. **Majors with Highest Enrollment:** business/commerce; elementary education and teaching; English language and literature. **Special Study Options:** cooperative education program, cross-registration, double major, dual enrollment, English as a Second Language (ESL), exchange student program (domestic), honors program, in-

dependent study, internships, liberal arts/career combination, student-designed major, study abroad, teacher certification program. **Disability Services:** Special programs offered to physically disabled students include note-taking services, reader services, tape recorders.

FACILITIES

Housing: Coed dorms, men's dorms, women's dorms, theme houses within walking distance to the campus. 80% of campus accessible to physically disabled. **Special Academic Facilities/Equipment:** Language laboratory, art gallery, computer labs **Computers:** Students can register for classes online. Administrative functions (other than registration) can be performed online.

CAMPUS LIFE

Environment: City. **Activities:** Choral groups, concert band, dance, drama/theater, jazz band, music ensembles, musical theater, pep band, radio station, student government, student newspaper, symphony orchestra, yearbook 50 registered organizations, 5 honor societies. **Athletics (Intercollegiate):** *Men:* baseball, basketball, cheerleading, cross-country, football, golf, soccer, swimming, tennis, track/field (outdoor). *Women:* basketball, cheerleading, cross-country, golf, soccer, softball, swimming, tennis, track/field (outdoor), volleyball. **On-Campus Highlights:** Hixon Union Building (Student Union) - cafe, Weyerhauser Hall (Teaching Theatre), Boppell Hall - new dormitory for upperclass man, Athletic Complex, Library.

ADMISSIONS

Freshman Academic Profile: Average high school GPA 3.7. 41% in top 10% of high school class, 74% in top 25% of high school class, 92% in top 50% of high school class. 87% from public high schools. SAT Math middle 50% range 540-650. SAT Critical Reading middle 50% range 540-660. SAT Writing middle 50% range 530-640. ACT middle 50% range 23-28. Minimum paper TOEFL 550. **Basis for Candidate Selection:** *Very important factors considered include:* Class rank, application essay, recommendation(s), rigor of secondary school record, standardized test scores. *Important factors considered include:* alumni/ae relation, character/personal qualities, extracurricular activities, geographical residence, interview, talent/ability. *Other factors considered include:* racial/ethnic status, religious affiliation/commitment, volunteer work. **Freshman Admission Requirements:** High school diploma is required and GED is accepted. **Freshman Admission Statistics:** 2,686 applied, 63% admitted, 28% enrolled. **Transfer Admission Requirements:** High school transcript, college transcript(s), essay or personal statement, standardized test scores, statement of good standing from prior institution(s). Minimum college GPA of 2.5 required. Lowest grade transferable C–. **General Admission Information:** Regular application deadline 3/1. Notification on a rolling basis, beginning on or about 12/20. Nonfall registration accepted. Admission may be deferred for a maximum of 12. Credit offered for CEEB Advanced Placement tests.

COSTS AND FINANCIAL AID

Annual tuition $31,830. Room and board $8,918. Required fees $314. Average book expense $860. **Required Forms and Deadlines:** FAFSA. **Notification of Awards:** Applicants will be notified of awards on a rolling basis beginning 4/1. **Types of Aid:** *Need-based scholarships/grants:* Federal Pell, SEOG, state scholarships/grants, private scholarships, the school's own gift aid. *Loans:* Direct Subsidized Stafford, Direct Unsubsidized Stafford, Direct PLUS, Federal Perkins, college/university loans from institutional funds. **Student Employment:** Highest amount earned per year from on-campus jobs $2,500. **Financial Aid Statistics:** 99% freshmen, 99% undergrads receive need-based scholarship or grant aid. 10% freshmen, 9% undergrads receive non-need-based scholarship or grant aid. 85% freshmen, 84% undergrads receive need-based self-help aid. 93% freshmen, 90% undergrads receive any aid. 66% undergrads borrow to pay for school. Average cumulative indebtedness $22,540. **Criteria for awarding institutional aid:** *Non-need-based:* academics, alumni affiliation, art, music/drama, religious affiliation.

WICHITA STATE UNIVERSITY

1845 Fairmount, Wichita, KS 67260
Phone: 316-978-3085 • **Financial Aid Phone:** 800-522-2978
E-mail: admissions@wichita.edu • **CEEB Code:** 6884
Fax: 316-978-3174 • **Website:** www.wichita.edu • **ACT Code:** 1472

This public school was founded in 1895. It has a 330-acre campus.

RATINGS

Admissions Selectivity Rating: 66   **Fire Safety Rating:** 79   **Green Rating:** 73

STUDENTS AND FACULTY

Enrollment: 11,149. **Student Body:** 54% female, 46% male, 4% out-of-state, 5% international (90 countries represented). Asian 7%, African American 7%, Caucasian 65%, Hispanic 8%, Native American 1%

Retention and Graduation: 70% freshmen return for sophomore year. 17% freshmen graduate within 4 years. **Faculty:** Student/faculty ratio 20:1. 459 full-time faculty, 81% hold PhDs, 17% are members of minority groups, 40% are women. 10% of classes are taught by teaching assistants.

ACADEMICS

Degrees: associate, bachelor's, certificate, diploma, doctoral, master's, post-bachelor's certificate, post-master's certificate, terminal associate, transfer associate. **Classes:** Most classes have 10—19 students. Most lab/discussion sessions have 20—29 students. **Majors with Highest Enrollment:** accounting; elementary education and teaching; psychology. **Special Study Options:** Accelerated program, cooperative education program, cross-registration, distance learning, double major, dual enrollment, English as a Second Language (ESL), exchange student program (domestic), honors program, independent study, internships, study abroad, teacher certification program. **Honors Programs:** Emory Lindquist Honors Program. The Honors Program offers freshman/sophomore seminars, lower division regular classes, honors colloquia, and honors upper division sections of regular classes. Students can also choose to do independent study projects. The Honors Program also offers a Senior Project, which is an opportunity for students to earn special honors recognition in a student's academic major. **Disability Services:** Special programs offered to physically disabled students include note-taking services, reader services, tape recorders, tutors. **Career Services:** Alumni network, alumni services, career/job search classes, career assessment, internships, regional alumni. Career services highlights include To empower our clients (students, alumni, faculty, staff and community members) with the skills, knowledge and resources necessary for effective career development, and to build partnerships with employers to expand client career opportunities.

FACILITIES

Housing: Coed dorms, fraternity/sorority housing, apartments for married students, apartments for single students, Some dorm floors are reserved for students majoring in Fine Arts, Health Professions, and for students in the Emory Lindquist Honors Program. 98% of campus accessible to physically disabled. **Special Academic Facilities/Equipment:** Art museum, performance hall, media resource center, observatory, national institute of aviation research, supersonic wind tunnels, 24-hour study room in library, outdoor sculpture collection. **Computers:** Students can register for classes online. Administrative functions (other than registration) can be performed online.

CAMPUS LIFE

Environment: Metropolis. **Activities:** Choral groups, concert band, dance, drama/theater, jazz band, literary magazine, music ensembles, musical theater, opera, pep band, radio station, student government, student newspaper, student-run film society, symphony orchestra, television station, Campus Ministries, International Student Organization, Model UN 140 registered organizations, 11 honor societies, 10 religious organizations. 11 fraternities, 10 sororities. **Athletics (Intercollegiate):** *Men:* baseball, basketball, bowling, cheerleading, cross-country, golf, rugby, swimming, tennis, track/field (outdoor). *Women:* basketball, bowling, cheerleading, cross-country, golf, softball, swimming, tennis, track/field (outdoor), volleyball. **On-Campus Highlights:** Rhatigan Student Center, Ulrich Museum of Art, Heskett Center, outdoor sculpture collection, Charles Koch arena, Wichita State University, founded in 1895 as a Congregational institution, is distinguished from other state supported schools in Kansas by its urban setting. Wichita State's location in the largest city in Kansas enhances the traditional classroom experience by providing students greater opportunities in resources, contacts with business and government leaders, employment, and internships. **Environmental Initiatives:** Recycle Program

ADMISSIONS

Freshman Academic Profile: Average high school GPA 3.4. 22% in top 10% of high school class, 47% in top 25% of high school class, 77% in top 50% of high school class. SAT Math middle 50% range 460-595. SAT Critical Reading middle 50% range 435-570. ACT middle 50% range 20-26. Minimum web-based TOEFL 72. Minimum paper TOEFL 530. **Basis for Candidate Selection:** *Very important factors considered include:* Class rank, academic GPA, rigor of secondary school record, standardized test scores. **Freshman Admission Requirements:** High school diploma is required and GED is accepted. *Academic units required:* 4 English, 4 mathematics, 3 science, 3 social studies, 1 computer proficiency. *Academic units recommended:* 4 English, 4 mathematics, 3 science, 3 social studies, 1 computer proficiency **Freshman Admission Statistics:** 3,515 applied, 95% admitted, 41% enrolled. **Transfer Admission Requirements:** college transcript(s), Minimum college GPA of 2.0 required. Lowest grade transferable C. **General Admission Information:** Application Fee $30. Nonfall registration accepted. Admission may be deferred for a maximum of 2 years. Credit and/or placement offered for CEEB Advanced Placement tests.

COSTS AND FINANCIAL AID

Annual in-state tuition $5,205. Annual out-of-state tuition $13,239. Room and board $6,460. Required fees $1,237. Required **Forms and Deadlines:** FAFSA.

Notification of Awards: Applicants will be notified of awards on a rolling basis beginning 3/15. Types of Aid: *Need-based scholarships/grants:* Federal Pell, SEOG, state scholarships/grants, private scholarships, the school's own gift aid, Bureau of Indian Affairs. *Loans:* Subsidized Stafford, Unsubsidized Stafford, PLUS, Federal Perkins. Student Employment: Federal Work-Study Program available. Institutional employment available. Highest amount earned per year from on-campus jobs $14,224. Off-campus job opportunities are excellent. Financial Aid Statistics: 72% freshmen, 67% undergrads receive need-based scholarship or grant aid. 58% freshmen, 34% undergrads receive non-need-based scholarship or grant aid. 65% freshmen, 81% undergrads receive need-based self-help aid. 4% freshmen, 3% undergrads receive athletic scholarships. 83% freshmen, 75% undergrads receive any aid. 53% undergrads borrow to pay for school. Average cumulative indebtedness $21,068. Criteria for awarding institutional aid: *Non-need-based:* academics, alumni affiliation, art, athletics, leadership, music/drama.

WIDENER UNIVERSITY

One University Place, Chester, PA 19013
Phone: 610-499-4126 • Financial Aid Phone: 610-499-4152
E-mail: admissions.office@widener.edu • CEEB Code: 2642
Fax: 610-499-4676 • Website: www.widener.edu • ACT Code: 3652

This private school was founded in 1821. It has a 110-acre campus.

RATINGS
Admissions Selectivity Rating: 76   Fire Safety Rating: 60*   Green Rating: 60*

STUDENTS AND FACULTY
Enrollment: 3,209. Student Body: 57% female, 43% male, 40% out-of-state, 3% international (38 countries represented). Asian 3%, African American 16%, Caucasian 71%, Hispanic 3%, Native American 0%. Retention and Graduation: 71% freshmen return for sophomore year. 43% freshmen graduate within 4 years. 55% freshmen graduate within 6 years. 20% grads go on to further study within 1 year. Faculty: Student/faculty ratio 12:1. 317 full-time faculty, 90% hold PhDs, 14% are members of minority groups, 53% are women. 0% of classes are taught by teaching assistants.

ACADEMICS
Degrees: associate, bachelor's, certificate, master's. Classes: Most classes have 10–19 students. Most lab/discussion sessions have fewer than 10 students. Majors with Highest Enrollment: business/commerce; civil engineering; nursing/registered nurse (rn, asn, bsn, msn). Special Study Options: Accelerated program, cooperative education program, distance learning, double major, English as a Second Language (ESL), honors program, independent study, internships, liberal arts/career combination, student-designed major, study abroad, teacher certification program, weekend college. Honors Programs: Honors Program in General Education Combined Degree Programs: BA/MD, BA/MA, BA/MEng. Disability Services: Special programs offered to physically disabled students include note-taking services, reader services, tape recorders, tutors. Career Services: Alumni network, alumni services, career/job search classes, career assessment, regional alumni.

FACILITIES
Housing: Coed dorms, men's dorms, women's dorms, fraternity/sorority housing, cooperative housing, apartments for single students, wellness housing, theme housing. Special Academic Facilities/Equipment: Art gallery, restaurant lab, child development center education lab, recording studio, commercial graphics lab, physical therapy lab, science labs, engineering labs, nursing labs, multimedia classrooms, Media Center Computers: Students can register for classes online. Administrative functions (other than registration) can be performed online.

CAMPUS LIFE
Environment: Town. Activities: Choral groups, concert band, dance, drama/theater, jazz band, literary magazine, music ensembles, pep band, radio station, student government, student newspaper, student-run film society, television station, yearbook, Campus Ministries, International Student Organization 80 registered organizations, 29 honor societies, 3 religious organizations. 7 fraternities, 3 sororities. Athletics (Intercollegiate): *Men:* baseball, basketball, cross-country, football, golf, lacrosse, soccer, swimming, tennis, track/field (outdoor), track/field (indoor). *Women:* basketball, cheerleading, cross-country, field hockey, lacrosse, soccer, softball, swimming, tennis, track/field (outdoor), track/field (indoor), volleyball. On-Campus Highlights: University Center, Java City and Residential Restaurant, Schwartz Athletic Center, Greek Row, Art Gallery, PMC Museum, Media Center, Observatory.

ADMISSIONS
Freshman Academic Profile: Average high school GPA 3.4. 12% in top 10% of high school class, 35% in top 25% of high school class, 72% in top 50% of high school class. 55% from public high schools. SAT Math middle 50% range 460-570. SAT Critical Reading middle 50% range 450-550. ACT middle 50% range 19-24. Minimum paper TOEFL 500. Basis for Candidate Selection: *Very important factors considered include:* Class rank, academic GPA, rigor of secondary school record, standardized test scores. *Other factors considered include:* application essay, recommendation(s), alumni/ae relation, character/personal qualities, extracurricular activities, interview, level of applicant's interest, talent/ability, volunteer work. Freshman Admission Requirements: High school diploma is required and GED is accepted. *Academic units required:* 4 English, 3 mathematics, 3 science, 2 foreign language, 3 social studies, 3 academic electives. *Academic units recommended:* 4 English, 3 mathematics, 3 science, 2 foreign language, 3 social studies, 3 academic electives. Freshman Admission Statistics: 4,863 applied, 66% admitted, 23% enrolled. Transfer Admission Requirements: college transcript(s), Minimum college GPA of 2.0 required. Lowest grade transferable C. General Admission Information: Application Fee $35. Notification on a rolling basis, beginning on or about 10/1. Nonfall registration accepted. Admission may be deferred for a maximum of 1 academic year. Credit offered for CEEB Advanced Placement tests.

COSTS AND FINANCIAL AID
Annual tuition $35,764. Room and board $12,248. Required fees $618. Average book expense $1,200. Required Forms and Deadlines: FAFSA. Notification of Awards: Applicants will be notified of awards on a rolling basis beginning 3/15. Types of Aid: *Need-based scholarships/grants:* Federal Pell, SEOG, state scholarships/grants, private scholarships, the school's own gift aid, Federal Nursing Scholarships. *Loans:* Subsidized Stafford, Unsubsidized Stafford, PLUS, Federal Perkins. Student Employment: Federal Work-Study Program available. Institutional employment available. Off-campus job opportunities are good. Financial Aid Statistics: 76% freshmen, 78% undergrads receive need-based scholarship or grant aid. 90% freshmen, 85% undergrads receive non-need-based scholarship or grant aid. 82% freshmen, 84% undergrads receive need-based self-help aid. 99% freshmen, 90% undergrads receive any aid. 88% undergrads borrow to pay for school. Average cumulative indebtedness $40,460. Criteria for awarding institutional aid: *Non-need-based:* academics, leadership, music/drama.

WILBERFORCE UNIVERSITY

1055 N. Bickett Road, Wilberforce, OH 45384
Phone: 800-367-8568
E-mail: kchristm@shorter.wilberforce • CEEB Code: 1906
Fax: 937-376-4751 • Website: www.wilberforce.edu • ACT Code: 3360

This private school was founded in 1856. It has a 125-acre campus.

RATINGS
Admissions Selectivity Rating: 64   Fire Safety Rating: 60*   Green Rating: 60*

STUDENTS AND FACULTY
Enrollment: 1,180. Student Body: 60% female, 40% male, 39% out-of-state, 0% international (2 countries represented). Asian 0%, African American 90%, Caucasian 5%, Hispanic 1%, Native American 0%. Retention and Graduation: Faculty: Student/faculty ratio 17:1. 49 full-time faculty, 67% are members of minority groups, 45% are women.

ACADEMICS
Degrees: bachelor's. Special Study Options: Accelerated program, cooperative education program, cross-registration, distance learning, double major, external degree program, honors program, independent study, internships, liberal arts/career combination, student-designed major, study abroad. Career Services: career/job search classes, career assessment, internships.

FACILITIES
Housing: Coed dorms, men's dorms, women's dorms, apartments for married students. Special Academic Facilities/Equipment: African Methodist Church archives.

CAMPUS LIFE
Environment: Activities: Choral groups, concert band, dance, jazz band, literary magazine, music ensembles, radio station, student government, student newspaper, yearbook 4 religious organizations. 4 fraternities, 4 sororities.

ADMISSIONS
Freshman Academic Profile: Minimum paper TOEFL 500. Freshman Admission Requirements: High school diploma is required and GED is

accepted. *Academic units required:* 4 English, 2 mathematics, 2 science, 2 social studies, 5 academic electives. *Academic units recommended:* 4 English, 2 mathematics, 2 science, 2 social studies, 5 academic electives. **Freshman Admission Statistics:** 2,405 applied, 22% admitted, 36% enrolled. **Transfer Admission Requirements:** college transcript(s), Minimum college GPA of 2.0 required. Lowest grade transferable C. **General Admission Information:** Application Fee $20. Regular application deadline 6/1. Nonfall registration accepted. Credit and/or placement offered for CEEB Advanced Placement tests.

COSTS AND FINANCIAL AID

Annual tuition $9,720. Room and board $5,320. Required fees $1,060. Average book expense $1,000. **Required Forms and Deadlines:** FAFSA, institution's own financial aid form, state aid form. **Notification of Awards: Types of Aid:** *Need-based scholarships/grants:* United Negro College Fund. *Loans:* Subsidized Stafford, PLUS. **Student Employment:** Federal Work-Study Program available. Highest amount earned per year from on-campus jobs $2,000. Off-campus job opportunities are good.

WILKES UNIVERSITY

84 W South St, Wilkes-Barre, PA 18766
Phone: 570-408-4400 • **Financial Aid Phone:** 570-408-2000
E-mail: admissions@wilkes.edu • **CEEB Code:** 2977
Fax: 570-408-4904 • **Website:** www.wilkes.edu • **ACT Code:** 3756

This private school was founded in 1933. It has a 27-acre campus.

RATINGS

Admissions Selectivity Rating: 72 **Fire Safety Rating:** 76 **Green Rating:** 67

STUDENTS AND FACULTY

Enrollment: 2,196. **Student Body:** 49% female, 51% male, 17% out-of-state, 5% international (21 countries represented). Asian 3%, African American 4%, Caucasian 80%, Hispanic 4%, Native American 0%
Retention and Graduation: 80% freshmen return for sophomore year. 49% freshmen graduate within 4 years. 61% freshmen graduate within 6 years.
Faculty: Student/faculty ratio 14:1. 160 full-time faculty, 88% hold PhDs, 10% are members of minority groups, 47% are women. 0% of classes are taught by teaching assistants.

ACADEMICS

Degrees: bachelor's, doctoral, master's. **Classes:** Most classes have 10—19 students. Most lab/discussion sessions have 10—19 students. **Majors with Highest Enrollment:** business administration and management; nursing/registered nurse (rn, asn, bsn, msn); pharmacy (pharmd [usa], pharmd or bs/bpharm [canada]). **Special Study Options:** cooperative education program, cross-registration, distance learning, double major, dual enrollment, English as a Second Language (ESL), external degree program, honors program, independent study, internships, student-designed major, study abroad, teacher certification program, weekend college. **Disability Services:** Special programs offered to physically disabled students include note-taking services, reader services, tape recorders, tutors. **Career Services:** Alumni network, alumni services, career/job search classes, career assessment, internships, regional alumni.

FACILITIES

Housing: Coed dorms, men's dorms, women's dorms, apartments for single students. **Special Academic Facilities/Equipment:** Art gallery, performing arts center, electron microscope, television studio. **Computers:** Students can register for classes online. Administrative functions (other than registration) can be performed online.

CAMPUS LIFE

Environment: City. **Activities:** Choral groups, dance, drama/theater, jazz band, literary magazine, music ensembles, musical theater, pep band, radio station, student government, student newspaper, television station, yearbook, Campus Ministries, International Student Organization 65 registered organizations, 19 honor societies. **Athletics (Intercollegiate):** *Men:* baseball, basketball, cross-country, football, golf, soccer, tennis, wrestling. *Women:* basketball, cross-country, field hockey, lacrosse, soccer, softball, tennis, volleyball.

ADMISSIONS

Freshman Academic Profile: 25% in top 10% of high school class, 53% in top 25% of high school class, 87% in top 50% of high school class. SAT Math middle 50% range 480-600. SAT Critical Reading middle 50% range 470-570. SAT Writing middle 50% range 450-560. Minimum web-based TOEFL 61. Minimum paper TOEFL 500. **Basis for Candidate Selection:** *Very important factors considered include:* Class rank, rigor of secondary school record. *Important factors considered include:* academic GPA, standardized test scores, character/

personal qualities, extracurricular activities. *Other factors considered include:* recommendation(s), alumni/ae relation, interview, talent/ability, volunteer work, work experience. **Freshman Admission Requirements:** High school diploma is required and GED is accepted. **Freshman Admission Statistics:** 2,998 applied, 76% admitted, 26% enrolled. **Transfer Admission Requirements:** college transcript(s), statement of good standing from prior institution(s). Minimum college GPA of 2.0 required. Lowest grade transferable C. **General Admission Information:** Application Fee $40. Notification on a rolling basis, beginning on or about 9/1. Nonfall registration accepted. Admission may be deferred for a maximum of 12 months. Credit and/or placement offered for CEEB Advanced Placement tests.

COSTS AND FINANCIAL AID

Annual tuition $27,908. Room and board $12,034. Required fees $1,418. Average book expense $1,500. **Required Forms and Deadlines:** FAFSA. **Notification of Awards:** Applicants will be notified of awards on a rolling basis beginning 3/1. **Types of Aid:** *Need-based scholarships/grants:* Federal Pell, SEOG, state scholarships/grants, private scholarships, the school's own gift aid. *Loans:* Subsidized Stafford, Unsubsidized Stafford, PLUS, Federal Perkins, Federal Nursing, state loans, college/university loans from institutional funds. **Student Employment:** Federal Work-Study Program available. Institutional employment available. Off-campus job opportunities are good. **Financial Aid Statistics:** 99% freshmen, 96% undergrads receive need-based scholarship or grant aid. 83% freshmen, 82% undergrads receive non-need-based scholarship or grant aid. 89% freshmen, 87% undergrads receive need-based self-help aid. 95% freshmen, 93% undergrads receive any aid. 86% undergrads borrow to pay for school. Average cumulative indebtedness $38,442. **Criteria for awarding institutional aid:** *Non-need-based:* academics, leadership, minority status, music/drama.

WILLAMETTE UNIVERSITY

900 State Street, Salem, OR 97301
Phone: 503-370-6303 • **Financial Aid Phone:** 503-370-6273
E-mail: libarts@willamette.edu • **CEEB Code:** 4954
Fax: 503-375-5363 • **Website:** www.willamette.edu • **ACT Code:** 3504

This private school, affiliated with the Methodist Church, was founded in 1842. It has a 72-acre campus.

RATINGS

Admissions Selectivity Rating: 92 **Fire Safety Rating:** 96 **Green Rating:** 78

STUDENTS AND FACULTY

Enrollment: 1,967. **Student Body:** 56% female, 44% male, 70% out-of-state, 1% international (41 countries represented). Asian 6%, African American 2%, Caucasian 64%, Hispanic 6%, Native American 1%
Retention and Graduation: 88% freshmen return for sophomore year. 70% freshmen graduate within 4 years. 20% grads go on to further study within 1 year. 5% grads pursue arts and sciences degrees. 3% grads pursue law degrees. 4% grads pursue business degrees. 2% grads pursue medical degrees. **Faculty:** Student/faculty ratio 10:1. 246 full-time faculty, 94% hold PhDs, 13% are members of minority groups, 47% are women. 0% of classes are taught by teaching assistants.

ACADEMICS

Degrees: bachelor's, first professional, first professional certificate, master's. **Classes:** Most classes have 10—19 students. **Majors with Highest Enrollment:** biology/biological sciences; economics; psychology. **Special Study Options:** Accelerated program, cross-registration, double major, dual enrollment, exchange student program (domestic), independent study, internships, student-designed major, study abroad, teacher certification program. **Honors Programs:** Our challenging curriculum includes a variety of opportunities for individualized honors study, for example: Presidential Scholars (senior year), Carson Undergraduate Research Program, Science Collaborative Research Program, various departmental Honors Programs. **Combined Degree Programs:** BA/JD, 5 year (BA/MBA);4-2 program in eng(BA/MS). **Disability Services:** Special programs offered to physically disabled students include note-taking services, reader services, tape recorders, tutors. **Career Services:** Alumni network, career/job search classes, career assessment, internships Career services highlights include Willamette University has a long tradition of academic internships. Three internship programs are in place: to explore career choices

(Insight Internship), to gain deeper knowledge of a chosen field (Major Program Internship), or a program which places an emphasis on bridging the gap between liberal arts study and professional responsibilities (Professional Internship). Generally these internships offer one course credit as part of the student's regular academic load though some one-half and two credit internships are available. Internships are an effective means to selecting an interesting, sustaining career; helping students assign meaning and context to their course work; and smoothing the transition from college to work or graduate study. Interns are regularly placed with agencies of the Oregon state government, the Salem city government and the Oregon State Legislature. Other facilities include the Oregon School for the Blind, the Oregon State Hospital and the Salem public schools. Majors in economics, politics, sociology and psychology frequently undertake internships at such sites. Rhetoric and media studies majors may intern with local radio and television stations; English majors intern with the local newspaper or with art organizations; exercise science majors with parks and recreation programs; and others in a variety of settings. Students seeking an internship opportunity will find it at Willamette! Sites in the Salem area which have hosted Willamette interns: • Legislative internships are available with many senators and representatives at the Oregon State Capitol – located across the street from campus. • Historic Deepwood Estate offers a variety of projects geared toward students majoring in the humanities; the gardens and nature trails provide opportunities for biology and environmental science majors as well. • Auburn Elementary School in Salem offers an internship focusing on issues facing children and how they are addressed in the school system. • Marion County Children's Mental Health Services offers internships in counseling. • SAIF Corporation offers internships in industrial psychology. • Silver Falls Soccer Club offers internships in coaching. • The District Attorney's office offers internships in victim's assistance. Internships are available at distant sites as well. These programs often occur during the summer, in which case the academic credit is completed on campus with the assistance of the on-campus supervisor. Some of the organizations which have recently served as internship sites are: • Oregon Public Broadcasting in Portland, Ore. - summer internship for students studying journalism and telecommunications • Albany Police Department, Albany, Ore. - experience in the criminal justice system • Conari Press in Berkeley, Calif. - editing • Hart Crowser, environmental consulting firm in Lake Oswego, Ore. - site assessment and remedial technologies • Olympic National Forest in Olympia, Wash. - watershed restoration and geology • Corporate Realty Advisors/CRESA in Portland, Ore. - summer research and marketing internship in commercial real estate • The Taylor Family Foundation in Lafayette, Calif. - corporate fundraising • TCI Media Services in Seattle, Wash. - advertising and communication For further information please refer to http://www.willamette.edu/cla/intern/index.html.

FACILITIES

Housing: Coed dorms, fraternity/sorority housing, apartments for single students, Substance-free Residence, Environmental Residence (Terra House), Intensive Study (24 hour quiet study) Residence. 95% of campus accessible to physically disabled. **Special Academic Facilities/Equipment:** Student Art purchased annually,and displayed in all public access buildings, Hallie Ford Museum of Art,Collections and papers of Congressional leaders from Oregon,Electron Microscope Lab (scanning and transmission), Herbarium, Japanese and Botanical Gardens, Carnegie Library(fully restored) **Computers:** 100% of classrooms, 100% of dorms, 100% of libraries, 100% of dining areas, 100% of student union, 50% of common outdoor areas have wireless network access. Students can register for classes online. Administrative functions (other than registration) can be performed online.

CAMPUS LIFE

Environment: City. **Activities:** Choral groups, concert band, dance, drama/theater, jazz band, literary magazine, music ensembles, musical theater, opera, student government, student newspaper, student-run film society, symphony orchestra, yearbook, Campus Ministries, International Student Organization, Model UN 107 registered organizations, 7 honor societies, 5 religious organizations. 4 fraternities, 3 sororities. **Athletics (Intercollegiate):** *Men:* baseball, basketball, crew/rowing, cross-country, football, golf, soccer, swimming, tennis, track/field (outdoor), track/field (indoor). *Women:* basketball, crew/rowing, cross-country, golf, soccer, softball, swimming, tennis, track/field (outdoor), track/field (indoor), volleyball. **On-Campus Highlights:** Hallie Ford Museum of Art, Montag Student Center, Sparks Sports and Recreation Center, Willamette Bistro, Mill Stream on campus. **Environmental Initiatives:** Kaneko Commons Residential Hall Ford Hall-Academic Building Purchased Zena Forest-nearby 308 Acre Sustainable forest for research and teaching New Construction Achieved LEED Gold status in 2007. Photo Voltaic panels, solar hot water heating, rainwater reclamation for flushing toilets, FSC wood products, Indoor Air Quality measures, low/no VOC materials and products, sustainability educational signage, high recycled content materials, energy efficient boilers, lighting control system, Energy Management System controls, 50% reduction in irrigation, low flow plumbing fixtures, use of plate to plate heat exchangers, sun shades, 95% recycle of construction waste, reflective roof coatings, use of local materials & labor, FSC cert furnishings, Fat Spaniel PV panel monitoring, elec-

trical use monitoring, FLEX CAR program initiated, purchase of Green Power, energy star appliances, and more. Development and approval of a sustainability law certificate program in the University Law School (2007), and planning for a sustainable MBA tract in the MBA program and sustainability concentration in the undergraduate curriculum (2008). Active work groups integrated with curriculum in Law, MBA and undergraduate that research and seek solutions to campus sustainaibility objectives. 2009-2010 projects include Efficacy of purchasing Carbon Offsets (Law), efficacy of Solar Panels on Campus(MBA, Wind Generation (CLA) Solutions for green and post consumer Waste (MBA). President M. Lee Pelton has done much to institutionalize sustainability in both our infrastructure and our educational mission. He created the university wide Sustainability Council in November of 2004, with representation throughout the university, including staff, students, faculty, and administrators. The Sustainability Council is charged with promoting sustainability and environmental literacy, advancing strategic initiatives and best practices on campus (including all new construction and renovations), and enhancing sustainability beyond the campus.Please see http://www.willamette.edu/about/sustainability/ for more details. In 2007, President Pelton created the Willamette Center for Sustainable Communities (CSC). The CSC is charged with advancing the faculty research and teaching in the area of sustainability, developing meaningful research and learning opportunities for students, and encouraging the adoption of sustainability both on campus and beyond. For more information, see http://www.willamette.edu/centers/csc/

ADMISSIONS

Freshman Academic Profile: Average high school GPA 3.5. 41% in top 10% of high school class, 74% in top 25% of high school class, 100% in top 50% of high school class. 80% from public high schools. SAT Math middle 50% range 540-650. SAT Critical Reading middle 50% range 560-670. SAT Writing middle 50% range 540-650. ACT middle 50% range 26-30. Minimum paper TOEFL 550. **Basis for Candidate Selection:** *Very important factors considered include:* Class rank, application essay, academic GPA, rigor of secondary school record, standardized test scores *Important factors considered include:* recommendation(s), interview. *Other factors considered include:* alumni/ae relation, character/personal qualities, extracurricular activities, first generation, geographical residence, racial/ethnic status, talent/ability. **Freshman Admission Requirements:** *Academic units required:* 4 English, 4 mathematics, 3 science, (3 science labs), 1 foreign language, 2 social studies. *Academic units recommended:* 4 English, 4 mathematics, 3 science, (3 science labs), 1 foreign language, 2 social studies. **Freshman Admission Statistics:** 8,175 applied, 57% admitted, 13% enrolled. **Transfer Admission Requirements:** High school transcript, college transcript(s), essay or personal statement, statement of good standing from prior institution(s). Lowest grade transferable C. **General Admission Information:** Application Fee $50. Notification on a rolling basis, beginning on or about 10/1. Nonfall registration accepted. Admission may be deferred for a maximum of 1 year. Credit and/or placement offered for CEEB Advanced Placement tests.

COSTS AND FINANCIAL AID

Annual tuition $40,560. Room and board $9,820. Required fees $214. Average book expense $948. **Required Forms and Deadlines:** FAFSA. **Notification of Awards:** Applicants will be notified of awards on a rolling basis beginning 4/1. **Types of Aid:** *Need-based scholarships/grants:* Federal Pell, SEOG, state scholarships/grants, private scholarships, the school's own gift aid. *Loans:* Subsidized Stafford, Unsubsidized Stafford, PLUS, Federal Perkins. **Student Employment:** Federal Work-Study Program available. Institutional employment available. Highest amount earned per year from on-campus jobs $2,000. Off-campus job opportunites are excellent. **Financial Aid Statistics:** 99% freshmen, 99% undergrads receive need-based scholarship or grant aid. 37% freshmen, 22% undergrads receive non-need-based scholarship or grant aid. 73% freshmen, 81% undergrads receive need-based self-help aid. 99% freshmen, 97% undergrads receive any aid. 67% undergrads borrow to pay for school. Average cumulative indebtedness $25,932. **Criteria for awarding institutional aid:** *Non-need-based:* academics, alumni affiliation, leadership, minority status, m

WILLIAM JEWELL COLLEGE

Best 378

500 College Hill, Liberty, MO 64068
Phone: 816-781-7700 • **Financial Aid Phone:** 816-415-5975
E-mail: admission@william.jewell.edu • **CEEB Code:** 6941
Fax: 816-415-5040 • **Website:** www.jewell.edu • **ACT Code:** 2394

This private school was founded in 1849. It has a 200-acre campus.

RATINGS
Admissions Selectivity Rating: 88   **Fire Safety Rating:** 81   **Green Rating:** 64

STUDENTS AND FACULTY
Enrollment: 1,060. **Student Body:** 59% female, 41% male, 34% out-of-state, 3% international (12 countries represented). Asian 2%, African American 4%, Caucasian 82%, Hispanic 4%, Native American 1%
Retention and Graduation: 75% freshmen return for sophomore year. 58% freshmen graduate within 4 years. 63% freshmen graduate within 6 years. 27% grads go on to further study within 1 year. 5% grads pursue arts and sciences degrees. 2% grads pursue law degrees. 2% grads pursue business degrees. 3% grads pursue medical degrees. **Faculty:** Student/faculty ratio 11:1. 67 full-time faculty, 78% hold PhDs, 3% are members of minority groups, 52% are women. 0% of classes are taught by teaching assistants.

ACADEMICS
Degrees: bachelor's, certificate. **Classes:** Most classes have fewer than 10 students. Most lab/discussion sessions have 30—39 students. **Majors with Highest Enrollment:** business/commerce; nursing/registered nurse (rn, asn, bsn, msn); psychology. **Special Study Options:** Accelerated program, double major, dual enrollment, honors program, independent study, internships, liberal arts/career combination, student-designed major, study abroad, teacher certification program, Pryor Leadership Studies. **Honors Programs:** The Oxbridge Honors Program combines British tutorial methods of instruction with opportunities for a year of study in Oxford or Cambridge. **Career Services:** Alumni network, alumni services, career/job search classes, career assessment, internships, regional alumni. Career services highlights include The Pryor Leadership Program requires 2 internships - one in service; one career-related. Over 50% of Jewell students participate in some form of internship or similar experiential learning opportunity.

FACILITIES
Housing: Coed dorms, men's dorms, women's dorms, fraternity/sorority housing, Off-campus housing utilized like residence halls. ADA compliant housing available for disabled students. 80% of campus accessible to physically disabled. **Special Academic Facilities/Equipment:** Radio station, art gallery, observatory, language and computer labs, high-ropes course, Teleconferencing center. **Computers:** 80% of classrooms, 20% of dorms, 25% of libraries, 80% of dining areas, 90% of student union, have wireless network access. Students can register for classes online. Administrative functions (other than registration) can be performed online.

CAMPUS LIFE
Environment: Town. **Activities:** Choral groups, concert band, dance, drama/theater, jazz band, literary magazine, music ensembles, pep band, radio station, student government, student newspaper, symphony orchestra, Campus Ministries 70 registered organizations, 13 honor societies, 7 religious organizations. 4 fraternities, 4 sororities. **Athletics (Intercollegiate):** *Men:* baseball, basketball, cheerleading, cross-country, football, golf, soccer, tennis, track/field (outdoor), track/field (indoor). *Women:* basketball, cheerleading, cross-country, golf, soccer, softball, tennis, track/field (outdoor), track/field (indoor), volleyball. **On-Campus Highlights:** The Perch--campus coffee shop, Mabee Center - athletic facility, The Quad - central campus quadrangle, Yates College Union - student union buil, Ely Triangle - first-year residence hall, Fitness Center. **Environmental Initiatives:** Campus recycling program Food composting Community garden.

ADMISSIONS
Freshman Academic Profile: Average high school GPA 3.7. 25% in top 10% of high school class, 59% in top 25% of high school class, 91% in top 50% of high school class. 90% from public high schools. SAT Math middle 50% range 520-620. SAT Critical Reading middle 50% range 490-640. ACT middle 50% range 23-28. Minimum web-based TOEFL 80. Minimum paper TOEFL 550. **Basis for Candidate Selection:** *Very important factors considered include:* rigor of secondary school record. *Important factors considered include:* Class rank, academic GPA, recommendation(s), standardized test scores. *Other factors considered include:* application essay, alumni/ae relation, character/personal qualities, extracurricular activities, first generation, interview, talent/ability, volunteer work, work experience. **Freshman Admission Requirements:** High school diploma is required and GED is accepted. *Academic units required:* 4 English, 3 mathematics, 3 science, (1 science labs), 2 foreign language, 3 social studies. *Academic units recommended:* 4 English, 3 mathematics, 3 science, (1 science labs), 2 foreign language, 3 social studies. **Freshman Admission Statistics:** 3,333 applied, 54% admitted, 15% enrolled. **Transfer Admission Requirements:** college transcript(s), statement of good standing from prior institution(s). Minimum college GPA of 2.5 required. Lowest grade transferable C–. **General Admission Information:** Application Fee $25. Regular application deadline 8/15. Notification on a rolling basis, beginning on or about 9/15. Nonfall registration accepted. Admission may be deferred for a maximum of 1 year, w/ a. Credit and/or placement offered for CEEB Advanced Placement tests.

COSTS AND FINANCIAL AID
Average book expense $1,200. **Required Forms and Deadlines:** FAFSA. **Notification of Awards:** Applicants will be notified of awards on a rolling basis beginning 2/15. **Types of Aid:** *Need-based scholarships/grants:* Federal Pell, SEOG, state scholarships/grants, the school's own gift aid. *Loans:* Subsidized Stafford, Unsubsidized Stafford, PLUS, Federal Perkins, Federal Nursing, Non-Federal Private Loans. **Student Employment:** Federal Work-Study Program available. Institutional employment available. Highest amount earned per year from on-campus jobs $1,300. Off-campus job opportunities are excellent. **Financial Aid Statistics:** 100% freshmen, 98% undergrads receive need-based scholarship or grant aid. 93% freshmen, 92% undergrads receive non-need-based scholarship or grant aid. 79% freshmen, 81% undergrads receive need-based self-help aid. 8% freshmen, 9% undergrads receive athletic scholarships. 99% freshmen, 96% undergrads receive any aid. 63% undergrads borrow to pay for school. Average cumulative indebtedness $29,444. **Criteria for awarding institutional aid:** *Non-need-based:* academics, alumni affiliation, art, athletics, music/drama.

WILLIAM PATERSON UNIVERSITY

Admissions Hall, Wayne, NJ 7470
Phone: 973-720-2125 • **Financial Aid Phone:** 973-720-2202
E-mail: admissions@wpunj.edu • **CEEB Code:** 2518
Fax: 973-720–2910 • **Website:** ww2.wpunj.edu • **ACT Code:** 2584

This public school was founded in 1855. It has a 370-acre campus.

RATINGS
Admissions Selectivity Rating: 72   **Fire Safety Rating:** 94   **Green Rating:** 73

STUDENTS AND FACULTY
Enrollment: 9,921. **Student Body:** 55% female, 45% male, 2% out-of-state, 1% international (37 countries represented). Asian 7%, African American 14%, Caucasian 50%, Hispanic 22%, Native American 0%
Retention and Graduation: 76% freshmen return for sophomore year. 19% freshmen graduate within 4 years. 47% freshmen graduate within 6 years. 27% grads go on to further study within 1 year. 18% grads pursue arts and sciences degrees. 15% grads pursue business degrees. **Faculty:** Student/faculty ratio 16:1. 389 full-time faculty, 92% hold PhDs, 33% are members of minority groups, 51% are women. 0% of classes are taught by teaching assistants.

ACADEMICS
Degrees: bachelor's, master's, post-bachelor's certificate, post-master's certificate. **Classes:** Most classes have 10—19 students. **Majors with Highest Enrollment:** business/commerce; communication studies/speech communication and rhetoric; psychology. **Special Study Options:** Accelerated program, cross-registration, distance learning, double major, dual enrollment, English as a Second Language (ESL), exchange student program (domestic), honors program, independent study, internships, study abroad, teacher certification program, Cluster courses (a program that provides opportunities for students and faculty to study and learn together in courses grouped in interdisciplinary clusters of three. Three faculty members teach these courses that meet together once every week to help students see the interdisciplinary connections). University Honors Program (Honors major tracks are available, and "honors" general education courses are offered.) International exchange program. **Honors Programs:** University Honors Program offers honors major tracks as well as honors general education courses. For more information please visit our Honors College Homepage at: http://www.wpunj.edu/icip/honors/default.htm . **Disability Services:** Special programs offered to physically disabled students include note-taking services, reader services, tape recorders, tutors. **Career**

Services: alumni services, career/job search classes, career assessment Career services highlights include Career Counseling and job search assistance. Unique combination of career services for all students as well as advisement services for undeclared and transfer students.

FACILITIES

Housing: Coed dorms, special housing for disabled students, apartments for single students. A floor for women is available in one of the residence halls. Apartment style housing is available in groups of single students. who are 21 or older or are 20 with 58 or more credits. Academic interest housing is available; High Mountain East is freshmen scholars and High Mountain West houses upperclass students who maintain a 2.5 GPA or better. One residence hall is reserved for students who are 21 or older. 88% of campus accessible to physically disabled. **Special Academic Facilities/Equipment:** Art galleries; Collection of NJ State Documents; Collection of William Paterson's private papers; Interactive television classroom; Neurobiology facility;E-Trading Campus Network with ATM technology; Center for Computer Art and Animation; State-of-the-art electron microscopy facility; Teleconference Center with uplink and downlink capabilities; 44,000 square foot, state-of-the-art studio art facility; Center for Electro-Acoustic Music (CEM); E-Trade Financial Learning Center, a real-time simulated trading and financial educational facility; Russ Berrie Institute for Professional Sales including real-time Sales Laboratory **Computers:** Students can register for classes online. Administrative functions (other than registration) can be performed online.

CAMPUS LIFE

Environment: Metropolis. **Activities:** Choral groups, concert band, dance, drama/theater, jazz band, literary magazine, music ensembles, student government, student newspaper, student-run film society, television station, yearbook, Campus Ministries, International Student Organization, Model UN 61 registered organizations, 21 honor societies, 4 religious organizations. 11 fraternities, 10 sororities. **Athletics (Intercollegiate):** *Men:* baseball, basketball, football, soccer, swimming. *Women:* basketball, cheerleading, field hockey, soccer, softball, swimming, volleyball. **On-Campus Highlights:** Student Center: Coffee Cafe (Starbucks), College of Business E-Trading Center, Power Art Gallery, Atrium Lobby, Library, New Student Center Facility, New Center for Student Services. **Environmental Initiatives:** ACUPCC NJHEPS challenge LEED Standard adoption.

ADMISSIONS

Freshman Academic Profile: 11% in top 10% of high school class, 31% in top 25% of high school class, 64% in top 50% of high school class. 86% from public high schools. SAT Math middle 50% range 460-550. SAT Critical Reading middle 50% range 440-550. Minimum web-based TOEFL 79. Minimum paper TOEFL 550. **Basis for Candidate Selection:** *Very important factors considered include:* Class rank, rigor of secondary school record, standardized test scores. *Important factors considered include:* academic GPA, level of applicant's interest. *Other factors considered include:* application essay, recommendation(s), alumni/ae relation, character/personal qualities, extracurricular activities, geographical residence, interview, talent/ability, volunteer work. **Freshman Admission Requirements:** High school diploma is required and GED is accepted. *Academic units required:* 4 English, 3 mathematics, 2 science, (2 science labs), 2 social studies, 5 5 Additional college preparatory courses (in Advanced Math, Literature, Foreign Language and Social Science) are also required. *Academic units recommended:* 4 English, 3 mathematics, 2 science, (2 science labs), 2 social studies, 5 5 Additional college preparatory courses (in Advanced Math, Literature, Foreign Language and Social Science) are also required. **Freshman Admission Statistics:** 10,059 applied, 71% admitted, 20% enrolled. **Transfer Admission Requirements:** college transcript(s), Minimum college GPA of 2.00 required. Lowest grade transferable C. **General Admission Information:** Application Fee $50. Regular application deadline 5/1. Notification on a rolling basis, beginning on or about 10/1. Nonfall registration accepted. Admission may be deferred for a maximum of 1 semester. Credit and/or placement offered for CEEB Advanced Placement tests.

COSTS AND FINANCIAL AID

Annual in-state tuition $6,967. Annual out-of-state tuition $14,131. Room and board $9,540. Required fees $8,832. Average book expense $1,600. **Required Forms and Deadlines:** FAFSA. **Notification of Awards:** Applicants will be notified of awards on a rolling basis beginning 3/15. **Types of Aid:** *Need-based scholarships/grants:* Federal Pell, SEOG, state scholarships/grants, the school's own gift aid. *Loans:* Subsidized Stafford, Unsubsidized Stafford, PLUS, Federal Perkins, state loans. **Student Employment:** Federal Work-Study Program available. Institutional employment available. Highest amount earned per year from on-campus jobs $3,200. Off-campus job opportunities are good. **Financial Aid Statistics:** 60% freshmen, 63% undergrads receive need-based scholarship or grant aid. 28% freshmen, 17% undergrads receive non-need-based scholarship or grant aid. 86% freshmen, 88% undergrads receive need-based self-help aid. 82% freshmen, 83% undergrads receive any aid. 70% undergrads borrow to pay for school. Average cumulative indebtedness $29,314. **Criteria for awarding institutional aid:** *Non-need-based:* academics, music/drama.

WILLIAM PEACE UNIVERSITY

15 East Peace Street, Raleigh, NC 27604
Phone: 919-508-2000 • **Financial Aid Phone:** 325-674-2300
E-mail: admissions@peace.edu
Fax: 325-674-2130 • **Website:** www.peace.edu

This private school, affiliated with the Presbyterian Church, was founded in 1857.

RATINGS
Admissions Selectivity Rating: 60*   **Fire Safety Rating:** 60*   **Green Rating:** 60*

STUDENTS AND FACULTY
Enrollment: 760. Student Body: 96% female, 4% male, 9% out-of-state. Retention and Graduation: 72% freshmen return for sophomore year. 22% freshmen graduate within 4 years. 29% freshmen graduate within 6 years. Faculty: Student/faculty ratio 11:1. 52 full-time faculty, 54% are women.

CAMPUS LIFE
Environment: City.

ADMISSIONS
Freshman Academic Profile: 4% in top 10% of high school class, 23% in top 25% of high school class, 57% in top 50% of high school class. SAT Math middle 50% range 420-520. SAT Critical Reading middle 50% range 420-510. ACT middle 50% range 18-23. Freshman Admission Statistics: 1,217 applied, 53% admitted, 26% enrolled.

COSTS AND FINANCIAL AID
Annual tuition $25,890. Room and board $8,900. Average book expense $1,300.

See page 1302.

WILLIAM PENN UNIVERSITY

201 Trueblood Avenue, Oskaloosa, IA 52577
Phone: 641-673-1012
E-mail: admissions@wmpenn.edu • **CEEB Code:** 6943
Fax: 641-673-2113 • **Website:** www.wmpenn.edu • **ACT Code:** 1372

This private school, affiliated with the Quaker Church, was founded in 1873. It has a 53 acre campus.

RATINGS
Admissions Selectivity Rating: 63   **Fire Safety Rating:** 60*   **Green Rating:** 60*

STUDENTS AND FACULTY
Enrollment: 1,528. **Student Body:** 48% female, 52% male, 28% out-of-state. **Faculty:** Student/faculty ratio 14:1. 35 full-time faculty, 49% hold PhDs, 3% are members of minority groups, 29% are women. 0% of classes are taught by teaching assistants.

ACADEMICS
Degrees: associate, bachelor's, transfer associate. **Classes:** Most classes have fewer than 10 students. **Majors with Highest Enrollment:** business/commerce; education; psychology. **Special Study Options:** cooperative education program, double major, English as a Second Language (ESL), independent study, internships, study abroad, teacher certification program, College for Working Adults. **Disability Services:** Special programs offered to physically disabled students include tape recorders, tutors. **Career Services:** alumni services, career/job search classes, internships.

FACILITIES
Housing: Coed dorms, women's dorms, apartments for married students, apartments for single students. 75% of campus accessible to physically disabled. **Special Academic Facilities/Equipment:** Foyer Gallery, Mid-East art and artifact collection.

CAMPUS LIFE
Environment: Rural. **Activities:** Choral groups, drama/theater, jazz band, literary magazine, music ensembles, musical theater, radio station, student government, student newspaper, yearbook 34 registered organizations, 3 honor societies, 4 religious organizations. 3 fraternities, 3 sororities. **Athletics (Intercollegiate):** *Men:* baseball, basketball, cheerleading, cross-country, football, golf, soccer, track/field (outdoor), wrestling. *Women:* basketball, cheerleading, cross-country, soccer, softball, track/field (outdoor), volleyball.

ADMISSIONS

Freshman Academic Profile: 14% in top 25% of high school class, 47% in top 50% of high school class. 97% from public high schools. Minimum web-based TOEFL 61. Minimum paper TOEFL 500. **Basis for Candidate Selection:** *Very important factors considered include:* rigor of secondary school record. *Important factors considered include:* Class rank, standardized test scores, character/personal qualities. *Other factors considered include:* application essay, recommendation(s), alumni/ae relation, extracurricular activities, interview, talent/ability, volunteer work, work experience. **Freshman Admission Requirements:** High school diploma is required and GED is accepted. **Freshman Admission Statistics:** 841 applied, 54% admitted, 53% enrolled. **Transfer Admission Requirements:** college transcript(s), Minimum college GPA of 2.0 required. Lowest grade transferable D. **General Admission Information:** Application Fee $20. Notification on a rolling basis, beginning on or about 10/1. Nonfall registration accepted. Credit offered for CEEB Advanced Placement tests.

COSTS AND FINANCIAL AID

Annual tuition $22,840. Room and board $5,472. Required fees $370. Average book expense $1,150. **Required Forms and Deadlines:** FAFSA. **Notification of Awards:** Applicants will be notified of awards on a rolling basis beginning 1/1. **Types of Aid:** *Need-based scholarships/grants:* Federal Pell, SEOG, state scholarships/grants, private scholarships, the school's own gift aid. *Loans:* Subsidized Stafford, Unsubsidized Stafford, PLUS, Federal Perkins. **Student Employment:** Federal Work-Study Program available. Institutional employment available. Off-campus job opportunities are excellent. **Financial Aid Statistics:** 74% undergrads borrow to pay for school. Average cumulative indebtedness $18,624. **Criteria for awarding institutional aid:** *Non-need-based:* academics, alumni affiliation, athletics, leadership, music/drama, religious affiliation.

WILLIAM TYNDALE COLLEGE

35700 W. Twelve Mile Road, Farmington Hills, MI 48331-3147
Phone: 800-483-0707
E-mail: admissions@williamtyndale.edu • **CEEB Code:** 1167
Fax: 248-553-5963 • **Website:** www.williamtyndale.edu • **ACT Code:** 2252

This private school was founded in 1945. It has a 28-acre campus.

RATINGS
Admissions Selectivity Rating: 86   **Fire Safety Rating:** 60*   **Green Rating:** 60*

STUDENTS AND FACULTY

Enrollment: 278. **Student Body:** 45% female, 55% male, 7% out-of-state, 3% international (6 countries represented). Asian 1%, African American 31%, Caucasian 63%, Hispanic 0%, Native American 1%
Retention and Graduation: 66% freshmen return for sophomore year. 21% freshmen graduate within 4 years. **Faculty:** Student/faculty ratio 8:1. 4 full-time faculty, 50% hold PhDs, 0% are members of minority groups, 50% are women. 0% of classes are taught by teaching assistants.

ACADEMICS

Degrees: associate, bachelor's, certificate. **Classes:** Most classes have fewer than 10 students. **Majors with Highest Enrollment:** business/commerce; counseling psychology; religion/religious studies, other. **Special Study Options:** Accelerated program, distance learning, double major, dual enrollment, independent study, internships. **Disability Services:** Special programs offered to physically disabled students include note-taking services, tutors..

FACILITIES

Housing: Coed dorms. 100% of campus accessible to physically disabled.

CAMPUS LIFE

Environment: Village. **Activities:** Choral groups, drama/theater, music ensembles, student government, student newspaper 2 registered organizations, 2 honor societies. **On-Campus Highlights:** Billy T's Cafe.

ADMISSIONS

Freshman Academic Profile: Average high school GPA 3.3. 20% in top 10% of high school class, 60% in top 25% of high school class, 40% in top 50% of high school class. 76% from public high schools. ACT middle 50% range 23-24. Minimum paper TOEFL 500. **Basis for Candidate Selection:** *Very important factors considered include:* rigor of secondary school record, standardized test scores. *Other factors considered include:* application essay, recommendation(s), character/personal qualities, interview, religious affiliation/commitment. **Freshman Admission Requirements:** High school diploma is required and GED is accepted. **Freshman Admission Statistics:** 40 applied, 50% admitted, 80% enrolled. **Transfer Admission Requirements:** High school transcript, college

transcript(s), statement of good standing from prior institution(s). Minimum college GPA of 2.0 required. Lowest grade transferable C. **General Admission Information:** Nonfall registration accepted. Admission may be deferred for a maximum of 12 months. Credit and/or placement offered for CEEB Advanced Placement tests.

COSTS AND FINANCIAL AID

Annual tuition $8,550. Room and board $3,520. Required fees $100. Average book expense $1,328. **Student Employment:** Federal Work-Study Program available. Institutional employment available. Highest amount earned per year from on-campus jobs $1,500. Off-campus job opportunities are good.

WILLIAM WOODS UNIVERSITY

One University Avenue, Fulton, MO 65251
Phone: 573-592-4221 • **Financial Aid Phone:** 573-592-4236
E-mail: admissions@williamwoods.edu
Fax: 573-592-1146 • **Website:** www.williamwoods.edu • **ACT Code:** 2396

This private school, affiliated with the Disciples of Christ Church, was founded in 1870. It has a 170-acre campus.

RATINGS
Admissions Selectivity Rating: 74   **Fire Safety Rating:** 77   **Green Rating:** 60*

STUDENTS AND FACULTY

Enrollment: 1,118. **Student Body:** 75% female, 25% male, 19% out-of-state, 4% international. Asian 0%, African American 3%, Caucasian 87%, Hispanic 2%, Native American 1%
Retention and Graduation: 76% freshmen return for sophomore year. 39% freshmen graduate within 4 years. 48% freshmen graduate within 6 years. **Faculty:** Student/faculty ratio 13:1. 50 full-time faculty, 4% are members of minority groups, 52% are women. 0% of classes are taught by teaching assistants.

ACADEMICS

Degrees: associate, bachelor's, master's, post-master's certificate. **Classes:** Most classes have fewer than 10 students. Most lab/discussion sessions have fewer than 10 students. **Majors with Highest Enrollment:** animal sciences; business/commerce; education. **Special Study Options:** Accelerated program, cross-registration, double major, dual enrollment, honors program, independent study, internships, liberal arts/career combination, student-designed major, study abroad, teacher certification program, Hollywood semester. **Disability Services:** Special programs offered to physically disabled students include note-taking services, reader services, tape recorders, tutors. **Career Services:** career/job search classes, career assessment.

FACILITIES

Housing: Coed dorms, special housing for disabled students, men's dorms, special housing for international students, women's dorms, fraternity/sorority housing, apartments for single students. 80% of campus accessible to physically disabled. **Special Academic Facilities/Equipment:** Weitzman Court Room Mildred Cox Gallery Gladys Woods Kemper Center for the Arts ASL Interpreting Lab Equestrian Facilities **Computers:** Administrative functions (other than registration) can be performed online.

CAMPUS LIFE

Environment: Village. **Activities:** Choral groups, dance, drama/theater, literary magazine, musical theater, radio station, student government, student newspaper 42 registered organizations, 3 honor societies, 1 religious organizations. 2 fraternities, 4 sororities. **Athletics (Intercollegiate):** *Men:* baseball, golf, soccer. *Women:* basketball, golf, soccer, softball, volleyball. **On-Campus Highlights:** Center for Human Performance, McNutt Student Center

ADMISSIONS

Freshman Academic Profile: Average high school GPA 3.3. 15% in top 10% of high school class, 40% in top 25% of high school class, 77% in top 50% of high school class. SAT Math middle 50% range 420-570. SAT Critical Reading middle 50% range 455-575. ACT middle 50% range 19-25. Minimum paper TOEFL 550. **Basis for Candidate Selection:** *Very important factors considered include:* Class rank, academic GPA, rigor of secondary school record. *Important factors considered include:* recommendation(s), standardized test scores, extracurricular activities. *Other factors considered include:* character/personal qualities, interview. **Freshman Admission Requirements:** High school diploma is required and GED is accepted. *Academic units required:* 3 English, 3 mathematics. *Academic units recommended:* 3 English, 3 mathematics. **Freshman Admission Statistics:** 792 applied, 68% admitted, 43% enrolled. **Transfer Admission Requirements:** college transcript(s), statement of good standing from prior institution(s). Minimum college GPA of 2.5 required.

Lowest grade transferable C. **General Admission Information:** Application Fee $25. Notification on a rolling basis, beginning on or about 9/1. Nonfall registration accepted. Admission may be deferred for a maximum of 1. Credit and/or placement offered for CEEB Advanced Placement tests.

COSTS AND FINANCIAL AID

Annual tuition $14,700. Room and board $5,900. Required fees $420. Average book expense $1,000. **Required Forms and Deadlines:** FAFSA, institution's own financial aid form. **Notification of Awards:** Applicants will be notified of awards on a rolling basis beginning 3/15. **Types of Aid:** *Need-based scholarships/grants:* Federal Pell, SEOG, state scholarships/grants, private scholarships, the school's own gift aid. *Loans:* Subsidized Stafford, Unsubsidized Stafford, PLUS, Federal Perkins, college/university loans from institutional funds. **Student Employment:** Federal Work-Study Program available. Institutional employment available. Highest amount earned per year from on-campus jobs $800. Off-campus job opportunities are good. **Financial Aid Statistics:** 100% freshmen, 95% undergrads receive need-based scholarship or grant aid. 23% freshmen, 18% undergrads receive non-need-based scholarship or grant aid. 75% freshmen, 79% undergrads receive need-based self-help aid. 2% freshmen, 3% undergrads receive athletic scholarships. 100% freshmen, 95% undergrads receive any aid. 85% undergrads borrow to pay for school. Average cumulative indebtedness $13,865. **Criteria for awarding institutional aid:** *Non-need-based:* academics, alumni affiliation, art, athletics, leadership, music/drama, religious affiliation, state/district residency.

WILLIAMS COLLEGE

PO BOX 487, Williamstown, MA 1267
Phone: 413-597-2211 • **Financial Aid Phone:** 413-597-4181
E-mail: admission@williams.edu • **CEEB Code:** 3965
Fax: 413-597-4052 • **Website:** www.williams.edu • **ACT Code:** 1936

This private school was founded in 1793. It has a 450-acre campus.

RATINGS
Admissions Selectivity Rating: 99   **Fire Safety Rating:** 92   **Green Rating:** 86

STUDENTS AND FACULTY
Enrollment: 2,011. **Student Body:** 52% female, 48% male, 86% out-of-state, 6% international (79 countries represented). Asian 11%, African American 8%, Caucasian 58%, Hispanic 12%, Native American 0%
Retention and Graduation: 96% freshmen return for sophomore year. 91% freshmen graduate within 4 years. 96% freshmen graduate within 6 years.
Faculty: Student/faculty ratio 7:1. 273 full-time faculty, 97% hold PhDs, 21% are members of minority groups, 42% are women. 0% of classes are taught by teaching assistants.

ACADEMICS
Degrees: bachelor's, master's. **Classes:** Most classes have fewer than 10 students. Most lab/discussion sessions have 10—19 students. **Majors with Highest Enrollment:** economics; English language and literature/letters, other; visual and performing arts. **Special Study Options:** cross-registration, double major, independent study, internships, student-designed major, study abroad. **Combined Degree Programs:** Combined program in liberal arts and eng. **Disability Services:** Special programs offered to physically disabled students include note-taking services, reader services, tape recorders, tutors. **Career Services:** Alumni network, alumni services, career/job search classes, internships, regional alumni.

FACILITIES
Housing: Coed dorms, cooperative housing. **Special Academic Facilities/ Equipment:** Hopkins Observatory; Williams College Museum of Art; Adams Memorial Theatre; Chapin Rare Books Library; Spencer Studio Art Building, '62 Center for Theatre and Dance, Hopkins Experimental Forest **Computers:** 100% of classrooms, 100% of dorms, 100% of libraries, 100% of dining areas, 100% of student union, 100% of common outdoor areas have wireless network access. Students can register for classes online. Administrative functions (other than registration) can be performed online.

CAMPUS LIFE
Environment: Village. **Activities:** Choral groups, dance, drama/theater, literary magazine, music ensembles, radio station, student government, student newspaper, student-run film society, symphony orchestra, yearbook, Interna-

tional Student Organization 110 registered organizations, 3 honor societies, 8 religious organizations. **Athletics (Intercollegiate):** *Men:* baseball, basketball, crew/rowing, cross-country, diving, football, golf, ice hockey, lacrosse, skiing (downhill/alpine), skiingnordiccross-country, soccer, squash, swimming, tennis, track/field (outdoor), track/field (indoor), wrestling. *Women:* basketball, crew/ rowing, cross-country, diving, field hockey, golf, ice hockey, lacrosse, skiing (downhill/alpine), skiing(nordiccross-country), soccer, softball, squash, swimming, tennis, track/field (outdoor), track/field (indoor), volleyball. **On-Campus Highlights:** Paresky Student Center, Schow Science Library, Williams College Museum of Art, '62 Center for Theatre and Dance, Chandler Gymnasium. **Environmental Initiatives:** Completed installation of real-time energy metering in all main campus buildings Infrastructure Improvements: Undertaking $1.5 million in energy conservation projects " lighting, motors, lab hood improvements, etc. Installed real time electricity meters in almost all campus buildings, and make data available on the sustainability webpage. Buildings: LEED certification of new academic buildings.

ADMISSIONS
Freshman Academic Profile: 92% in top 10% of high school class, 97% in top 25% of high school class, 100% in top 50% of high school class. 57% from public high schools. SAT Math middle 50% range 660-780. SAT Critical Reading middle 50% range 670-780. SAT Writing middle 50% range 680-780. ACT middle 50% range 30-34. **Basis for Candidate Selection:** *Very important factors considered include:* application essay, academic GPA, recommendation(s), rigor of secondary school record, standardized test scores. *Important factors considered include:* Class rank, extracurricular activities, talent/ability. *Other factors considered include:* alumni/ae relation, character/personal qualities, first generation, geographical residence, racial/ethnic status, volunteer work, work experience. **Freshman Admission Requirements:** High school diploma or equivalent is not required. **Freshman Admission Statistics:** 7,069 applied, 17% admitted, 45% enrolled. **Transfer Admission Requirements:** High school transcript, college transcript(s), essay or personal statement, standardized test scores, statement of good standing from prior institution(s) Minimum college GPA of 3.5 required. Lowest grade transferable C–. **General Admission Information:** Application Fee $60. Early decision application deadline 11/10. Regular application deadline 1/1. Regular notification 4/1. Nonfall registration not accepted. Admission may be deferred for a maximum of negotiable. Placement offered for CEEB Advanced Placement tests.

COSTS AND FINANCIAL AID
Required **Forms and Deadlines:** FAFSA, CSS/Financial Aid PROFILE, noncustodial PROFILE, business/farm supplement. Parent and Student federal taxes and W2s. **Notification of Awards:** Applicants will be notified of awards on or about 4/1. **Types of Aid:** *Need-based scholarships/grants:* Federal Pell, SEOG, state scholarships/grants, private scholarships, the school's own gift aid. *Loans:* Direct Subsidized Stafford, Direct Unsubsidized Stafford, Direct PLUS, Federal Perkins, college/university loans from institutional funds. **Student Employment:** Federal Work-Study Program available. Institutional employment available. **Financial Aid Statistics:** 100% freshmen, 100% undergrads receive need-based scholarship or grant aid. 100% freshmen, 100% undergrads receive need-based self-help aid. 53% freshmen, 53% undergrads receive any aid. 31% undergrads borrow to pay for school. Average cumulative indebtedness $12,749.

WILLISTON STATE COLLEGE

PO Box 1326, Williston, ND 58802-1326
Phone: 701-774-4210
E-mail: Lacey.Madison@wsc.nodak.edu
Fax: 701-774-4211 • **Website:** www.wsc.nodak.edu

This public school was founded in 1961. It has a 80-acre campus.

RATINGS
Admissions Selectivity Rating: 64   **Fire Safety Rating:** 60*   **Green Rating:** 60*

STUDENTS AND FACULTY
Enrollment: 937. **Student Body:** 71% female, 29% male, 19% out-of-state, 2% international (2 countries represented). Asian 0%, African American 1%, Caucasian 91%, Hispanic 1%, Native American 4%
Retention and Graduation: Faculty: Student/faculty ratio 12:1. 38 full-time faculty, 39% are women. 0% of classes are taught by teaching assistants.

ACADEMICS
Degrees: associate, certificate, diploma, terminal associate, transfer associate. **Special Study Options:** cooperative education program, distance learning, dual enrollment, external degree program, independent study, internships, liberal arts/career combination. **Disability Services:** Special programs offered

to physically disabled students include note-taking services, reader services, tape recorders, tutors.

FACILITIES
Housing: Coed dorms, special housing for disabled students, men's dorms, women's dorms, Athletic Housing units Married/Family Housing units. 90% of campus accessible to physically disabled.

CAMPUS LIFE
Environment: Rural. **Activities:** Choral groups, drama/theater, literary magazine, pep band, student government 18 registered organizations, 1 honor societies, 1 religious organizations. **Athletics (Intercollegiate): Men:** baseball, basketball, golf. *Women:* basketball, golf, volleyball.

ADMISSIONS
Freshman Academic Profile: Average high school GPA 2.8. 12% in top 10% of high school class, 22% in top 25% of high school class, 71% in top 50% of high school class. ACT middle 50% range 16-22. Minimum paper TOEFL 330. **Freshman Admission Requirements:** High school diploma is required and GED is accepted. **Transfer Admission Requirements:** college transcript(s), statement of good standing from prior institution(s). Lowest grade transferable D. **General Admission Information:** Application Fee $35. Notification on a rolling basis, beginning on or about 1/1. Nonfall registration accepted. Credit and/or placement offered for CEEB Advanced Placement tests.

COSTS AND FINANCIAL AID
Required Forms and Deadlines: FAFSA. **Notification of Awards:** Applicants will be notified of awards on a rolling basis beginning 5/15. **Types of Aid:** *Need-based scholarships/grants:* Federal Pell, SEOG, state scholarships/grants, private scholarships, the school's own gift aid. *Loans:* Subsidized Stafford, Unsubsidized Stafford, PLUS, Federal Perkins. **Student Employment:** Federal Work-Study Program available. Institutional employment available. Off-campus job opportunities are good. **Criteria for awarding institutional aid:** *Non-need-based:* academics, athletics, minority status.

WILMINGTON COLLEGE (DE)

320 Dupont Highway, New Castle, DE 19720
Phone: 302-328-9401
E-mail: mlee@wilmcoll.edu • **CEEB Code:** 5925
Fax: 302-328-5902 • **Website:** www.wilmcoll.edu • **ACT Code:** 635

This private school was founded in 1967. It has a 15-acre campus.

RATINGS
Admissions Selectivity Rating: 61   **Fire Safety Rating:** 60*   **Green Rating:** 60*

STUDENTS AND FACULTY
Enrollment: 4,399. **Student Body:** 53% female, 47% male, 3% out-of-state, 0% international. Asian 1%, African American 14%, Caucasian 64%, Hispanic 2%, Native American 0%
Retention and Graduation: 87% freshmen return for sophomore year. 50% grads go on to further study within 1 year. 9% grads pursue arts and sciences degrees. 10% grads pursue law degrees. 80% grads pursue business degrees. 1% grads pursue medical degrees. **Faculty:** Student/faculty ratio 18:1. 0% of classes are taught by teaching assistants.

ACADEMICS
Degrees: associate, bachelor's, certificate, master's, post-master's certificate. **Classes: Majors with Highest Enrollment:** business/commerce; education. **Special Study Options:** Accelerated program, cooperative education program, distance learning, double major, independent study, internships, teacher certification program, weekend college. **Disability Services:** Special programs offered to physically disabled students include tutors. **Career Services:** alumni services, career/job search classes, career assessment, internships.

FACILITIES
Housing: All housing is off campus.

CAMPUS LIFE
Environment: Village. **Activities:** student government 1 honor societies. **Athletics (Intercollegiate):** *Men:* baseball, basketball, cross-country, soccer. *Women:* basketball, softball.

ADMISSIONS
Freshman Academic Profile: Minimum paper TOEFL 500. **Basis for Candidate Selection:** *Important factors considered include:* recommendation(s), rigor of secondary school record. **Freshman Admission Requirements:** High school diploma is required and GED is accepted.High school diploma is re-

quired and GED is not accepted. **Transfer Admission Requirements:** college transcript(s), Minimum college GPA of 2.0 required. Lowest grade transferable C. **General Admission Information:** Application Fee $25. Nonfall registration accepted. Admission may be deferred for a maximum of 12 months. Credit offered for CEEB Advanced Placement tests.

COSTS AND FINANCIAL AID
Annual tuition $6,060. Required fees $50. Average book expense $500. **Required Forms and Deadlines:** FAFSA. **Student Employment:** Federal Work-Study Program available. Highest amount earned per year from on-campus jobs $1,000. Off-campus job opportunities are excellent.

WILMINGTON COLLEGE (OH)

1870 Quaker Way, Wilmington, OH 45177
Phone: 937-382-6661 • **CEEB Code:** 1909
Fax: • **Website:** www.wilmington.edu • **ACT Code:** 3362

This private school, affiliated with the Quaker Church, was founded in 1870. It has a 65-acre campus.

RATINGS
Admissions Selectivity Rating: 79   **Fire Safety Rating:** 60*   **Green Rating:** 60*

STUDENTS AND FACULTY
Enrollment: 1,274. **Student Body:** 56% female, 44% male, 6% out-of-state, 1% international. Asian 0%, African American 11%, Caucasian 73%, Hispanic 1%, Native American 1%
Retention and Graduation: 67% freshmen return for sophomore year. 46% freshmen graduate within 4 years. **Faculty:** Student/faculty ratio 14:1. 66 full-time faculty. 0% of classes are taught by teaching assistants.

ACADEMICS
Degrees: bachelor's, master's. **Classes:** Most classes have 10—19 students. **Majors with Highest Enrollment:** bible/biblical studies. **Special Study Options:** cross-registration, double major, dual enrollment, honors program, independent study, internships, liberal arts/career combination, student-designed major, study abroad, teacher certification program, weekend college. **Disability Services:** Special programs offered to physically disabled students include note-taking services, reader services, tape recorders, tutors. **Career Services:** alumni services, internships.

FACILITIES
Housing: Coed dorms, women's dorms, fraternity/sorority housing, apartments for single students. 100% of campus accessible to physically disabled. **Special Academic Facilities/Equipment:** Hiroshima-Nagasaki memorial collection and peace resource center, education lab, language lab, three farms, observatory, electron microscope.

CAMPUS LIFE
Environment: Rural. **Activities:** Choral groups, drama/theater, literary magazine, music ensembles, musical theater, student government, student newspaper, yearbook, Campus Ministries, International Student Organization 48 registered organizations, 3 honor societies, 3 religious organizations. 6 fraternities, 5 sororities. **Athletics (Intercollegiate):** *Men:* baseball, basketball, cheerleading, cross-country, football, golf, soccer, swimming, tennis, track/field (outdoor), wrestling. *Women:* basketball, cheerleading, cross-country, golf, soccer, softball, swimming, tennis, track/field (outdoor), volleyball. **On-Campus Highlights:** Residence Hall room, Athletic Center, Student Center/Dining Hall, Computer labs, Class room.

ADMISSIONS
Freshman Academic Profile: Average high school GPA 3.2. 11% in top 10% of high school class, 36% in top 25% of high school class, 70% in top 50% of high school class. SAT Math middle 50% range 420-550. SAT Critical Reading middle 50% range 440-560. ACT middle 50% range 18-23. Minimum paper TOEFL 500. **Basis for Candidate Selection:** *Very important factors considered include:* academic GPA. *Important factors considered include:* Class rank, rigor of secondary school record, standardized test scores, alumni/ae relation, character/personal qualities, talent/ability. *Other factors considered include:* recommendation(s), extracurricular activities, interview, level of applicant's interest, volunteer work. **Freshman Admission Requirements:** High school diploma is required and GED is accepted. *Academic units required:* 4 English, 2 mathematics, 2 science, (2 science labs). *Academic units recommended:* 4 English, 2 mathematics, 2 science, (2 science labs). **Freshman Admission Statistics:** 1,651 applied, 28% admitted, 45% enrolled. **Transfer Admission Requirements:** college transcript(s), statement of good standing from prior institution(s). Minimum college GPA of 2.0 required. Lowest grade transferable

C–. General Admission Information: Application Fee $25. Regular application deadline 8/1. Notification on a rolling basis, beginning on or about 12/1. Nonfall registration accepted. Admission may be deferred for a maximum of 1 year. Credit and/or placement offered for CEEB Advanced Placement tests.

COSTS AND FINANCIAL AID

Annual tuition $25,214. Room and board $8,520. Required fees $500. **Student Employment:** Federal Work-Study Program available. Institutional employment available. Off-campus job opportunities are excellent.

WILSON COLLEGE

1015 Philadelphia Avenue, Chambersburg, PA 17201
Phone: 717-262-2002 • **Financial Aid Phone:** 717-262-2016
E-mail: admissions@wilson.edu • **CEEB Code:** 2979
Fax: 717-262-2546 • **ACT Code:** 3758

This private school, affiliated with the Presbyterian Church, was founded in 1869. It has a 300-acre campus.

RATINGS

Admissions Selectivity Rating: 84   **Fire Safety Rating:** 76   **Green Rating:** 75

STUDENTS AND FACULTY

Enrollment: 515. **Student Body:** 92% female, 8% male, 24% out-of-state, 4% international (10 countries represented). Asian 0%, African American 5%, Caucasian 76%, Hispanic 3%, Native American 0%
Retention and Graduation: 57% freshmen return for sophomore year. 43% freshmen graduate within 4 years. 56% freshmen graduate within 6 years. 30% grads go on to further study within 1 year. 6% grads pursue arts and sciences degrees. 9% grads pursue law degrees. 8% grads pursue business degrees. 8% grads pursue medical degrees. **Faculty:** Student/faculty ratio 10:1. 45 full-time faculty, 82% hold PhDs, 7% are members of minority groups, 56% are women. 0% of classes are taught by teaching assistants.

ACADEMICS

Degrees: associate, bachelor's, master's. **Classes:** Most classes have 10—19 students. Most lab/discussion sessions have 10—19 students. **Majors with Highest Enrollment:** business/commerce; elementary education and teaching; veterinary/animal health technology/technician and veterinary assistant. **Special Study Options:** cooperative education program, cross-registration, double major, English as a Second Language (ESL), honors program, independent study, internships, liberal arts/career combination, student-designed major, study abroad, teacher certification program. **Honors Programs:** Wilson Scholars Program . **Disability Services:** Special programs offered to physically disabled students include note-taking services, reader services, tape recorders, tutors. **Career Services:** Alumni network, alumni services, career/job search classes, career assessment, internships Career services highlights include I am proudest of the variety of services we offer and the increased # of services. An alum commented last week on how much more we offer in the Career Development Center.

FACILITIES

Housing: women's dorms. Students of junior standing or above are guaranteed single residence hall room. We also offer women with children housing, maximum of 2 children. 70% of campus accessible to physically disabled. **Special Academic Facilities/Equipment:** Archives, Bogigian Art gallery, Dance Studio, Helen M. Beach '24 Veterinary Medical Center, Penn Hall Equestrian Center, Natural History Museum, electron microscope, NMR spectrometer. **Computers:** 50% of classrooms, 100% of dining areas, 100% of student union, 15% of common outdoor areas have wireless network access. Students can register for classes online. Administrative functions (other than registration) can be performed online.

CAMPUS LIFE

Environment: Village. **Activities:** Choral groups, dance, drama/theater, literary magazine, music ensembles, radio station, student government, student newspaper, yearbook, Campus Ministries, International Student Organization 35 registered organizations, 1 honor societies, 4 religious organizations. **Athletics (Intercollegiate):** *Women:* basketball, field hockey, gymnastics, lacrosse, soccer, softball, tennis. **On-Campus Highlights:** Penn Hall Equestrian Center, Helen M. Beach '24 Veterinary Medical Center, Complex for Science, Math & Technology, Prentis Hall Women with Children Residence, Lenfest Commons with Fitness Center and Coffee House. **Environmental Initiatives:** Organic farm Alternative Energy Production Environmental Sustainability mission statement of college.

ADMISSIONS

Freshman Academic Profile: Average high school GPA 3.4. 22% in top 10% of high school class, 50% in top 25% of high school class, 82% in top 50% of high school class. 84% from public high schools. SAT Math middle 50% range 430-550. SAT Critical Reading middle 50% range 450-570. SAT Writing middle 50% range 430-550. ACT middle 50% range 21-23. Minimum web-based TOEFL 61. Minimum paper TOEFL 500. **Basis for Candidate Selection:** *Very important factors considered include:* rigor of secondary school record. *Important factors considered include:* Class rank, academic GPA, recommendation(s). *Other factors considered include:* application essay, standardized test scores, alumni/ae relation, character/personal qualities, extracurricular activities, interview, talent/ability, volunteer work, work experience. **Freshman Admission Requirements:** High school diploma is required and GED is accepted. *Academic units required:* 4 English, 3 mathematics, 2 science, (2 science labs), 2 foreign language, 4 social studies. *Academic units recommended:* 4 English, 3 mathematics, 2 science, (2 science labs), 2 foreign language, 4 social studies. **Freshman Admission Statistics:** 563 applied, 50% admitted, 33% enrolled. **Transfer Admission Requirements:** High school transcript, college transcript(s), essay or personal statement, Minimum college GPA of 2.0 required. Lowest grade transferable C. **General Admission Information:** Application Fee $35. Notification on a rolling basis, beginning on or about 9/15. Nonfall registration accepted. Admission may be deferred for a maximum of 12 Months. Credit and/or placement offered for CEEB Advanced Placement tests.

COSTS AND FINANCIAL AID

Annual tuition $28,745. Room and board $9,710. Required fees $595. Average book expense $1,000. **Required Forms and Deadlines:** FAFSA, institution's own financial aid form, state aid form. **Notification of Awards:** Applicants will be notified of awards on a rolling basis beginning 2/15. **Types of Aid:** *Need based scholarships/grants:* Federal Pell, SEOG, state scholarships/grants, private scholarships, the school's own gift aid. *Loans:* Subsidized Stafford, Unsubsidized Stafford, PLUS, Federal Perkins, college/university loans from institutional funds. **Student Employment:** Federal Work-Study Program available. Institutional employment available. Highest amount earned per year from on-campus jobs $1,500. Off-campus job opportunities are fair. **Financial Aid Statistics:** 100% freshmen, 99% undergrads receive need-based scholarship or grant aid. 11% freshmen, 9% undergrads receive non-need-based scholarship or grant aid. 83% freshmen, 81% undergrads receive need-based self-help aid. 99% freshmen, 97% undergrads receive any aid, 81% undergrads borrow to pay for school. Average cumulative indebtedness $36,021. **Criteria for awarding institutional aid:** *Non-need-based:* academics, alumni affiliation, religious affiliation, state/district residency.

See page 1304.

WINGATE UNIVERSITY

Campus Box 3059, Wingate, NC 28174
Phone: 704-233-8200 • **Financial Aid Phone:** 704-233-8209
E-mail: admit@wingate.edu • **CEEB Code:** 5908
Fax: 704-233-8110 • **Website:** www.wingate.edu • **ACT Code:** 3176

This private school, affiliated with the Baptist Church, was founded in 1896. It has a 390-acre campus.

RATINGS

Admissions Selectivity Rating: 72   **Fire Safety Rating:** 75   **Green Rating:** 60*

STUDENTS AND FACULTY

Enrollment: 1,713. **Student Body:** 54% female, 46% male, 18% out-of-state, 4% international (21 countries represented). Asian 3%, African American 13%, Caucasian 61%, Hispanic 2%, Native American 1%
Retention and Graduation: 75% freshmen return for sophomore year. 41% freshmen graduate within 4 years. 53% freshmen graduate within 6 years. 20% grads go on to further study within 1 year. 9% grads pursue arts and sciences degrees. 2% grads pursue law degrees. 8% grads pursue business degrees. 1% grads pursue medical degrees. **Faculty:** Student/faculty ratio 14:1. 126 full-time faculty, 94% hold PhDs, 2% are members of minority groups, 52% are women. 0% of classes are taught by teaching assistants.

ACADEMICS

Degrees: bachelor's, first professional, master's. **Classes:** Most classes have 20—29 students. Most lab/discussion sessions have 10—19 students. **Majors with Highest Enrollment:** biology/biological sciences; business/commerce; sport and fitness administration/management. **Special Study Options:** cross-registration, double major, dual enrollment, honors program, independent study, internships, study abroad, teacher certification program, A Bachelor in Liberal Arts is offered to non-traditional students looking to complete a degree. This programs is offered at the Wingate Metro Center in Matthews, NC. **Honors Programs:** Our University Honors program offers students 18 hours of honors courses covering a spectrum of disciplines. Students may travel to New York City as part of the program. **Disability Services:** Special programs offered to physically disabled students include note-taking services, tape recorders, tutors.

FACILITIES

Housing: men's dorms, women's dorms, apartments for single students. 95% of campus accessible to physically disabled. **Special Academic Facilities/ Equipment:** Douglas Helms Art Gallery, outdoor recreation lab, Batte Fine Arts Center **Computers:** Administrative functions (other than registration) can be performed online.

CAMPUS LIFE

Environment: Village. **Activities:** Choral groups, drama/theater, jazz band, literary magazine, music ensembles, musical theater, student government, student newspaper, television station, yearbook 45 registered organizations, 10 honor societies, 8 religious organizations. 4 fraternities, 4 sororities. **Athletics (Intercollegiate):** *Men:* baseball, basketball, cheerleading, cross-country, football, golf, lacrosse, soccer, swimming, tennis. *Women:* basketball, cheerleading, cross-country, golf, soccer, softball, swimming, tennis, volleyball. **On-Campus Highlights:** George A. Batte Jr. Fine Arts Center, Kondike Grill, Irwin Belk Football Stadium, Ehtel's Cafe (in the Ethel K. Smith Library), Jefferson Clubhouse, - Batte Fine Arts Center, a 44,000 sq. foot facility provides a venue foe musicians, singers, actors, and artists. The center features a 554 theatre, among other facilities. - Ethel's Cafe provides a quiet environment to study while enjoying coffee, pastries, and other refreshments. -Jefferson Clubhouse, houses a convinience store, gym, swinmming pool, Health Services, and the offices of Greek Life.

ADMISSIONS

Freshman Academic Profile: Average high school GPA 3.7. 25% in top 10% of high school class, 58% in top 25% of high school class, 90% in top 50% of high school class. 85% from public high schools. SAT Math middle 50% range 470-580. SAT Critical Reading middle 50% range 440-540. SAT Writing middle 50% range 430-540. ACT middle 50% range 19-24. Minimum paper TOEFL 550. **Basis for Candidate Selection:** *Very important factors considered include:* Class rank, rigor of secondary school record. *Important factors considered include:* academic GPA, recommendation(s), standardized test scores. *Other factors considered include:* character/personal qualities, extracurricular activities, talent/ability. **Freshman Admission Requirements:** High school diploma is required and GED is accepted. **Freshman Admission Statistics:** 4,049 applied, 81% admitted, 16% enrolled. **Transfer Admission Requirements:** High school transcript, college transcript(s), statement of good standing from prior institution(s). Minimum college GPA of 2.0 required. Lowest grade transferable C. **General Admission Information:** Application Fee $30. Notification on a rolling basis, beginning on or about 9/15. Nonfall registration accepted. Admission may be deferred for a maximum of 1 year. Credit and/or placement offered for CEEB Advanced Placement tests.

COSTS AND FINANCIAL AID

Annual tuition $22,540. Room and board $9,320. Required fees $1,305. Average book expense $1,100. **Required Forms and Deadlines:** FAFSA. **Notification of Awards:** Applicants will be notified of awards on a rolling basis beginning 3/1. **Types of Aid:** *Need-based scholarships/grants:* Federal Pell, SEOG, state scholarships/grants, private scholarships, the school's own gift aid. *Loans:* Direct Subsidized Stafford, Direct Unsubsidized Stafford, Direct PLUS, Subsidized Stafford, Unsubsidized Stafford, PLUS. **Student Employment:** Federal Work-Study Program available. Institutional employment available. Highest amount earned per year from on-campus jobs $1,200. Off-campus job opportunities are good. **Financial Aid Statistics:** 96% freshmen, 97% undergrads receive need-based scholarship or grant aid. 20% freshmen, 18% undergrads receive non-need-based scholarship or grant aid. 78% freshmen, 83% undergrads receive need-based self-help aid. 18% freshmen, 11% undergrads receive athletic scholarships. 97% freshmen, 96% undergrads receive any aid. 59% undergrads borrow to pay for school. Average cumulative indebtedness $24,298. **Criteria for awarding institutional aid:** *Non-need-based:* academics, alumni affiliation, art, athletics, leadership, music/drama, religious affiliation, state/district residency.

WINONA STATE UNIVERSITY

175 Mark Street, Winona, MN 55987
Phone: 507-457-5100 • **Financial Aid Phone:** 507-457-5090
E-mail: admissions@winona.edu • **CEEB Code:** 6680
Fax: 507-457-5620 • **Website:** www.winona.edu • **ACT Code:** 2162

This public school was founded in 1858. It has a 40-acre campus.

RATINGS

Admissions Selectivity Rating: 75   **Fire Safety Rating:** 85   **Green Rating:** 86

STUDENTS AND FACULTY

Enrollment: 8,223. **Student Body:** 61% female, 39% male, 32% out-of-state, 2% international (53 countries represented). Asian 2%, African American 2%, Caucasian 89%, Hispanic 2%, Native American 0%
Retention and Graduation: 78% freshmen return for sophomore year. 26% freshmen graduate within 4 years. 15% grads go on to further study within 1 year. 10% grads pursue arts and sciences degrees. 1% grads pursue law degrees. 6% grads pursue business degrees. 1% grads pursue medical degrees. **Faculty:** Student/faculty ratio 22:1. 293 full-time faculty, 67% hold PhDs, 12% are members of minority groups, 29% are women. 0% of classes are taught by teaching assistants.

ACADEMICS

Degrees: associate, bachelor's, master's, post-bachelor's certificate, post-master's certificate. **Classes:** Most classes have 20—29 students. Most lab/discussion sessions have 20—29 students. **Majors with Highest Enrollment:** business administration and management; elementary education and teaching; nursing/registered nurse (rn, asn, bsn, msn). **Special Study Options:** Accelerated program, cross-registration, distance learning, double major, dual enrollment, English as a Second Language (ESL), external degree program, independent study, internships, student-designed major, study abroad, teacher certification program. **Disability Services:** Special programs offered to physically disabled students include note-taking services, reader services, tape recorders. **Career Services:** alumni services, career assessment, internships Career services highlights include While we do not offer career/job search 'classes,' we do provide nearly 150 workshops and presentations annually reaching an average of 5000 students; we also have podcasts on a variety of topics available online 24/7.

FACILITIES

Housing: Coed dorms, special housing for disabled students, men's dorms, women's dorms, apartments for single students, Residential College-Residence halls with classrooms and faculty offices. 100% of campus accessible to physically disabled. **Special Academic Facilities/Equipment:** Paul Watkins Art Gallery. **Computers:** 100% of classrooms, 50% of dorms, 100% of libraries, 100% of dining areas, 100% of student union, 85% of common outdoor areas have wireless network access. Students can register for classes online. Administrative functions (other than registration) can be performed online. Undergraduates are required to own a computer.

CAMPUS LIFE

Environment: Town. **Activities:** Choral groups, concert band, dance, drama/ theater, jazz band, literary magazine, music ensembles, musical theater, pep band, radio station, student government, student newspaper, student-run film society, symphony orchestra, television station, Campus Ministries, International Student Organization, Model UN 208 registered organizations, 14 honor societies, 10 religious organizations. 2 fraternities, 3 sororities. **Athletics (Intercollegiate):** *Men:* baseball, basketball, cross-country, football, golf. *Women:* basketball, cross-country, golf, gymnastics, soccer, softball, tennis, track/field (outdoor), track/field (indoor), volleyball. **On-Campus Highlights:** The Library, Lourdes Hall - Residential College, Central Courtyard and Clock Tower, The Smaug - Kryzsko Commons, Wabasha Hall Fitness Center. **Environmental Initiatives:** Sustainable buildings Local Foods Transportation.

ADMISSIONS

Freshman Academic Profile: Average high school GPA 3.3. 8% in top 10% of high school class, 32% in top 25% of high school class, 76% in top 50% of high school class. 68% from public high schools. SAT Math middle 50% range 420-570. SAT Critical Reading middle 50% range 420-570. SAT Writing middle 50% range 440-440. ACT middle 50% range 21-25. Minimum web-based TOEFL 68. Minimum paper TOEFL 520. **Basis for Candidate Selection:** *Very important factors considered include:* Class rank, rigor of secondary school record, standardized test scores. *Important factors considered include:* academic GPA. *Other factors considered include:* recommendation(s). **Freshman Admission Requirements:** High school diploma is required and GED is accepted. *Academic units required:* 4 English, 3 mathematics, 3 science, (3 science labs), 2 foreign language, 2 social studies, 1 history, 1 academic electives. *Academic units recommended:* 4 English, 3 mathematics, 3 science, (3 science labs), 2 foreign language, 2 social studies, 1 history, 1 academic electives. **Freshman Admission Statistics:** 7,361 applied, 62% admitted, 39% enrolled. **Transfer Admission Requirements:** college transcript(s), Minimum college GPA of 2.4 required. Lowest grade transferable D. **General Admission Information:** Application Fee $20. Regular application deadline 3/1. Notification on a rolling basis, beginning on or about 9/1. Nonfall registration accepted. Admission may be deferred for a maximum of 12 months. Credit and/or placement offered for CEEB Advanced Placement tests.

COSTS AND FINANCIAL AID
Annual in-state tuition $6,660. Annual out-of-state tuition $11,780. Room and board $7,540. Required fees $1,860. Average book expense $1,200. **Required Forms and Deadlines:** FAFSA. **Notification of Awards:** Applicants will be notified of awards on a rolling basis beginning 3/1. **Types of Aid:** *Need-based scholarships/grants:* Federal Pell, SEOG, state scholarships/grants, private scholarships, the school's own gift aid. *Loans:* Subsidized Stafford, Unsubsidized Stafford, PLUS, Federal Perkins, state loans, college/university loans from institutional funds. **Student Employment:** Federal Work-Study Program available. Institutional employment available. Highest amount earned per year from on-campus jobs $2,200. Off-campus job opportunities are fair. **Financial Aid Statistics:** 48% freshmen, 51% undergrads receive need-based scholarship or grant aid. 58% freshmen, 33% undergrads receive non-need-based scholarship or grant aid. 86% freshmen, 87% undergrads receive need-based self-help aid. 53% freshmen, 29% undergrads receive athletic scholarships. 77% freshmen, 72% undergrads receive any aid. 76% undergrads borrow to pay for school. Average cumulative indebtedness $31,275. **Criteria for awarding institutional aid:** *Non-need-based:* academics, alumni affiliation, art, athletics, minority status, music/drama, state/district residency.

WINSTON-SALEM STATE UNIVERSITY

601 MLK, Jr. Drive, Winston-Salem, NC 27110
Phone: 336-750-2070
E-mail: admissions@wssu1.adp.wssu.edu • **CEEB Code:** 5909
Fax: 336-750-2079 • **Website:** www.wssu.edu • **ACT Code:** 3178

This public school was founded in 1892. It has a 94-acre campus.

RATINGS
Admissions Selectivity Rating: 62   **Fire Safety Rating:** 60*   **Green Rating:** 60*

STUDENTS AND FACULTY
Enrollment: 5,254. **Student Body:** 70% female, 30% male, 6% out-of-state, 0% international. Asian 1%, African American 84%, Caucasian 12%, Hispanic 1%, Native American 0%
Retention and Graduation: 72% freshmen return for sophomore year. 14% freshmen graduate within 6 years. **Faculty:** Student/faculty ratio 16:1. 275 full-time faculty, 63% hold PhDs, 62% are women.

ACADEMICS
Degrees: bachelor's, master's, post-bachelor's certificate, post-master's certificate. **Classes:** Most classes have fewer than 10 students. **Special Study Options:** cooperative education program, double major, dual enrollment, exchange student program (domestic), honors program, independent study, liberal arts/career combination, study abroad, teacher certification program. **Disability Services:** Special programs offered to physically disabled students include tutors. **Career Services:** alumni services, internships.

FACILITIES
Housing: Coed dorms, men's dorms, women's dorms. **Special Academic Facilities/Equipment:** Art gallery.

CAMPUS LIFE
Environment: Activities: Choral groups, jazz band, marching band, music ensembles, radio station, student government, student newspaper, yearbook. **On-Campus Highlights:** CLEON Thompson Student Center, Fitness Center, O'Kelly Library.

ADMISSIONS
Basis for Candidate Selection: *Very important factors considered include:* Class rank, rigor of secondary school record, standardized test scores. *Other factors considered include:* alumni/ae relation, character/personal qualities, extracurricular activities, interview, talent/ability. **Freshman Admission Statistics:** 1,353 applied, 80% admitted, 46% enrolled. **Transfer Admission Requirements:** college transcript(s), Lowest grade transferable C. **General Admission Information:** Application Fee $20. Nonfall registration accepted.

COSTS AND FINANCIAL AID
Annual in-state tuition $1,575. Annual out-of-state tuition $7,868. **Required Forms and Deadlines:** FAFSA. **Notification of Awards:** Applicants will be notified of awards on or about 5/15. **Types of Aid:** *Need-based scholarships/grants:* Federal Pell, SEOG, state scholarships/grants, private scholarships, the school's own gift aid, Federal Nursing Scholarships. *Loans:* Subsidized Stafford, Unsubsidized Stafford, PLUS, Federal Perkins, state loans, college/university loans from institutional funds. **Student Employment:** Federal Work-Study Program available. Institutional employment available. Highest amount earned per year from on-campus jobs $800. Off-campus job opportunities are good. **Financial Aid Statistics:** 83% freshmen, 92% undergrads receive need-based scholarship or grant aid. 13% freshmen, 7% undergrads receive non-need-based scholarship or grant aid. 90% freshmen, 91% undergrads receive need-based self-help aid. 7% freshmen, 5% undergrads receive athletic scholarships.

WINTHROP UNIVERSITY

, Rock Hill, SC 29733
Phone: 803-323-2137 • **Financial Aid Phone:** 803-323-4857
E-mail: admissions@winthrop.edu • **CEEB Code:** 5910
Fax: 803-323-2137 • **Website:** www.winthrop.edu • **ACT Code:** 3884

This public school was founded in 1886. It has a 418-acre campus.

RATINGS
Admissions Selectivity Rating: 75   **Fire Safety Rating:** 86   **Green Rating:** 80

STUDENTS AND FACULTY
Enrollment: 4,747. **Student Body:** 67% female, 33% male, 8% out-of-state, 3% international (37 countries represented). Asian 1%, African American 31%, Caucasian 60%, Hispanic 2%, Native American 0%
Retention and Graduation: 73% freshmen return for sophomore year. 33% freshmen graduate within 4 years. 53% freshmen graduate within 6 years. 11% grads go on to further study within 1 year. 20% grads pursue arts and sciences degrees. 3% grads pursue law degrees. 25% grads pursue business degrees. 5% grads pursue medical degrees. **Faculty:** Student/faculty ratio 15:1. 286 full-time faculty, 87% hold PhDs, 14% are members of minority groups, 53% are women. 0% of classes are taught by teaching assistants.

ACADEMICS
Degrees: bachelor's, master's, post-bachelor's certificate. **Classes:** Most classes have 20—29 students. Most lab/discussion sessions have 20—29 students. **Majors with Highest Enrollment:** biology/biological sciences; business/commerce; design and visual communications. **Special Study Options:** cooperative education program, cross-registration, distance learning, double major, exchange student program (domestic), honors program, independent study, internships, study abroad, teacher certification program. **Disability Services:** Special programs offered to physically disabled students include note-taking services, reader services, tape recorders. **Career Services:** Alumni network, alumni services, career assessment, internships, regional alumni.

FACILITIES
Housing: Coed dorms, men's dorms, women's dorms, fraternity/sorority housing, apartments for married students, apartments for single students. 85% of campus accessible to physically disabled. **Special Academic Facilities/Equipment:** Art gallery, on-campus nursery and kindergarten. **Computers:** 25% of classrooms, 10% of dorms, 100% of libraries, 100% of dining areas, 100% of student union, 10% of common outdoor areas have wireless network access. Students can register for classes online. Administrative functions (other than registration) can be performed online.

CAMPUS LIFE
Environment: Town. **Activities:** Choral groups, concert band, dance, drama/theater, jazz band, literary magazine, music ensembles, musical theater, opera, pep band, radio station, student government, student newspaper, yearbook, Campus Ministries, International Student Organization, Model UN 184 registered organizations, 23 honor societies, 10 religious organizations. 8 fraternities, 9 sororities. **Athletics (Intercollegiate):** *Men:* baseball, basketball, cross-country, golf, soccer, tennis, track/field (outdoor). *Women:* basketball, cross-country, golf, soccer, softball, tennis, track/field (outdoor), volleyball. **On-Campus Highlights:** Java City, Winthrop Coliseum, Frisbee-Golf Course **Environmental Initiatives:** Very strong recycling program. Commitment to have all new buildings be green certified or green features. Outstanding record of reducing energy use by upgrading historic buildings (electrical, windows, etc.)

ADMISSIONS
Freshman Academic Profile: Average high school GPA 3.8. 19% in top 10% of high school class, 83% in top 50% of high school class. SAT Math middle 50%

range 470-570. SAT Critical Reading middle 50% range 460-580. ACT middle 50% range 20-25. Minimum web-based TOEFL 68. Minimum paper TOEFL 520. **Basis for Candidate Selection:** *Very important factors considered include:* rigor of secondary school record. *Important factors considered include:* Class rank, academic GPA, standardized test scores. *Other factors considered include:* application essay, recommendation(s), extracurricular activities, interview, talent/ability, volunteer work. **Freshman Admission Requirements:** High school diploma is required and GED is accepted. *Academic units required:* 4 English, 3 mathematics, 3 science, (3 science labs), 2 foreign language, 2 social studies, 1 history, 4 academic electives, 1 P.E. or ROTC. *Academic units recommended:* 4 English, 3 mathematics, 3 science, (3 science labs), 2 foreign language, 2 social studies, 1 history, 4 academic electives, 1 P.E. or ROTC **Freshman Admission Statistics:** 4,316 applied, 71% admitted, 37% enrolled. **Transfer Admission Requirements:** college transcript(s), statement of good standing from prior institution(s). Minimum college GPA of 2.0 required. Lowest grade transferable C. **General Admission Information:** Application Fee $40. Regular application deadline 5/1. Notification on a rolling basis, beginning on or about 12/1. Nonfall registration accepted. Admission may be deferred for a maximum of 1 semester. Credit offered for CEEB Advanced Placement tests.

COSTS AND FINANCIAL AID

Annual in-state tuition $13,026. Annual out-of-state tuition $24,476. Room and board $7,384. Average book expense $1,200. **Required Forms and Deadlines:** FAFSA. **Notification of Awards:** Applicants will be notified of awards on a rolling basis beginning 3/15. **Types of Aid:** *Need-based scholarships/grants:* Federal Pell, SEOG, state scholarships/grants, private scholarships, the school's own gift aid. *Loans:* Direct Subsidized Stafford, Direct Unsubsidized Stafford, PLUS, Federal Perkins. **Student Employment:** Federal Work-Study Program available. Institutional employment available. Highest amount earned per year from on-campus jobs $1,750. Off-campus job opportunities are fair. **Financial Aid Statistics:** 98% freshmen, 86% undergrads receive need-based scholarship or grant aid. 17% freshmen, 10% undergrads receive non-need-based scholarship or grant aid. 76% freshmen, 83% undergrads receive need-based self-help aid. 3% freshmen, 3% undergrads receive athletic scholarships. 70% freshmen, 83% undergrads receive any aid. 70% undergrads borrow to pay for school. Average cumulative indebtedness $27,735. **Criteria for awarding institutional aid:** *Non-need-based:* academics, art, athletics, job skills, music/drama.

WISCONSIN LUTHERAN COLLEGE

8800 West Bluemound Road, Milwaukee, WI 53226
Phone: 414-443-8811 • **Financial Aid Phone:** 414-443-8856
E-mail: admissions@wlc.edu • **CEEB Code:** 1513
Fax: 414-443-8514 • **Website:** www.wlc.edu • **ACT Code:** 4699

This private school, affiliated with the Lutheran Church, was founded in 1973. It has a 21-acre campus.

RATINGS
Admissions Selectivity Rating: 72   **Fire Safety Rating:** 67   **Green Rating:** 61

STUDENTS AND FACULTY
Enrollment: 707. **Student Body:** 56% female, 44% male, 23% out-of-state, 2% international (9 countries represented). Asian 2%, African American 4%, Caucasian 89%, Hispanic 2%, Native American 0%.
Retention and Graduation: 76% freshmen return for sophomore year. 51% freshmen graduate within 4 years. 66% freshmen graduate within 6 years.
Faculty: Student/faculty ratio 10:1. 60 full-time faculty, 67% hold PhDs, 33% are women. 0% of classes are taught by teaching assistants.

ACADEMICS
Degrees: bachelor's. **Classes:** Most classes have 10—19 students. Most lab/discussion sessions have fewer than 10 students. **Majors with Highest Enrollment:** biology/biological sciences; communication studies/speech communication and rhetoric; psychology. **Special Study Options:** double major, dual enrollment, English as a Second Language (ESL), independent study, internships, student-designed major, study abroad, teacher certification program. **Disability Services:** Special programs offered to physically disabled students include note-taking services, reader services, tape recorders, tutors. **Career Services:** Alumni network, career assessment, internships.

FACILITIES
Housing: men's dorms, women's dorms, apartments for single students. 90% of campus accessible to physically disabled. **Special Academic Facilities/Equipment:** Center for Arts and Performance, Science Hall **Computers:** Students can register for classes online.

CAMPUS LIFE
Environment: Metropolis. **Activities:** Choral groups, concert band, dance, jazz band, music ensembles, pep band, student government, student newspaper, Campus Ministries, International Student Organization 31 registered organizations. **Athletics (Intercollegiate):** *Men:* baseball, basketball, cross-country, football, golf, soccer, tennis, track/field (outdoor), track/field (indoor). *Women:* basketball, cross-country, golf, soccer, softball, tennis, track/field (outdoor), track/field (indoor), volleyball. **On-Campus Highlights:** Residence Halls, Center for Arts and Performance, Chapel, The Warrior Underground, The Recreation Complex, Science Hall, Warrior Fields.

ADMISSIONS
Freshman Academic Profile: Average high school GPA 3.3. 18% in top 10% of high school class, 43% in top 25% of high school class, 77% in top 50% of high school class. ACT middle 50% range 21-26. Minimum paper TOEFL 550. **Basis for Candidate Selection:** *Important factors considered include:* academic GPA, recommendation(s), rigor of secondary school record, standardized test scores, character/personal qualities, level of applicant's interest, religious affiliation/commitment. *Other factors considered include:* Class rank, application essay, alumni/ae relation, extracurricular activities, first generation, interview, racial/ethnic status, talent/ability, volunteer work, work experience. **Freshman Admission Requirements:** High school diploma is required and GED is accepted. *Academic units required:* 4 English, 3 mathematics, 2 science, (1 science labs), 2 foreign language, 2 history, 3 academic electives. *Academic units recommended:* 4 English, 3 mathematics, 2 science, (1 science labs), 2 foreign language, 2 history, 3 academic electives. **Freshman Admission Statistics:** 646 applied, 76% admitted, 46% enrolled. **Transfer Admission Requirements:** college transcript(s), statement of good standing from prior institution(s). Minimum college GPA of 2.5 required. Lowest grade transferable CD. **General Admission Information:** Application Fee $20. Notification on a rolling basis, beginning on or about 9/1. Nonfall registration accepted. Admission may be deferred for a maximum of 1 semester. Credit and/or placement offered for CEEB Advanced Placement tests.

COSTS AND FINANCIAL AID
Annual tuition $21,040. Room and board $7,700. Required fees $140. Average book expense $700. **Required Forms and Deadlines:** FAFSA, institution's own financial aid form, business/farm supplement. **Notification of Awards:** Applicants will be notified of awards on a rolling basis beginning 3/15. **Types of Aid:** *Need-based scholarships/grants:* Federal Pell, SEOG, state scholarships/grants, private scholarships, the school's own gift aid. *Loans:* Subsidized Stafford, Unsubsidized Stafford, PLUS, state loans, Private Educational Loans. **Student Employment:** Federal Work-Study Program available. Institutional employment available. Highest amount earned per year from on-campus jobs $2,800. Off-campus job opportunities are excellent. **Financial Aid Statistics:** 100% freshmen, 99% undergrads receive need-based scholarship or grant aid. 11% freshmen, 10% undergrads receive non-need-based scholarship or grant aid. 91% freshmen, 91% undergrads receive need-based self-help aid. 100% freshmen, 98% undergrads receive any aid. 71% undergrads borrow to pay for school. Average cumulative indebtedness $17,596. **Criteria for awarding institutional aid:** *Non-need-based:* academics, art, leadership, music/drama.

WITTENBERG UNIVERSITY

PO Box 720, Springfield, OH 45501
Phone: 937-327-6314 • **Financial Aid Phone:** 937-327-7321
E-mail: admission@wittenberg.edu • **CEEB Code:** 1922
Fax: 937-327-6379 • **Website:** www.wittenberg.edu • **ACT Code:** 3364

This private school, affiliated with the Lutheran Church, was founded in 1845. It has a 71-acre campus.

RATINGS
Admissions Selectivity Rating: 75   **Fire Safety Rating:** 96   **Green Rating:** 72

STUDENTS AND FACULTY
Enrollment: 1,720. **Student Body:** 55% female, 45% male, 27% out-of-state, 2% international (23 countries represented). Asian 1%, African American 8%, Caucasian 87%, Hispanic 3%, Native American 0%.
Retention and Graduation: 78% freshmen return for sophomore year. 65% freshmen graduate within 6 years. 27% grads go on to further study within 1 year. 13% grads pursue arts and sciences degrees. 4% grads pursue law degrees.

2% grads pursue business degrees. 7% grads pursue medical degrees. **Faculty:** Student/faculty ratio 11:1. 141 full-time faculty, 96% hold PhDs, 11% are members of minority groups, 42% are women. 0% of classes are taught by teaching assistants.

ACADEMICS

Degrees: bachelor's, master's. **Classes:** Most classes have 10—19 students. Most lab/discussion sessions have 10—19 students. **Majors with Highest Enrollment:** biology/biological sciences; business/commerce; education. **Special Study Options:** cross-registration, double major, dual enrollment, honors program, independent study, internships, liberal arts/career combination, student-designed major, study abroad, teacher certification program. **Honors Programs:** Honors Program, 3-2 Engineering Program, Pre-Health Programs. **Disability Services:** Special programs offered to physically disabled students include note-taking services, reader services, tape recorders, tutors. **Career Services:** Alumni network, alumni services, career/job search classes, career assessment, internships, regional alumni. Career services highlights include Lutheran College Washington Semester.

FACILITIES

Housing: Coed dorms, special housing for international students, women's dorms, fraternity/sorority housing, apartments for married students, apartments for single students, University owned houses around campus. 81% of campus accessible to physically disabled. **Special Academic Facilities/Equipment:** Language lab, electron microscope, observatory. **Computers:** 50% of classrooms, 100% of libraries, 100% of dining areas, 100% of student union, 100% of common outdoor areas have wireless network access. Students can register for classes online. Administrative functions (other than registration) can be performed online.

CAMPUS LIFE

Environment: Town. **Activities:** Choral groups, concert band, dance, drama/theater, jazz band, literary magazine, music ensembles, musical theater, opera, pep band, radio station, student government, student newspaper, student-run film society, symphony orchestra, yearbook, Campus Ministries, International Student Organization 126 registered organizations, 24 honor societies, 10 religious organizations. 6 fraternities, 5 sororities. **Athletics (Intercollegiate):** *Men:* baseball, basketball, cross-country, diving, football, golf, lacrosse, soccer, swimming, tennis, track/field (outdoor), track/field (indoor). *Women:* basketball, cheerleading, cross-country, diving, field hockey, golf, lacrosse, soccer, softball, swimming, tennis, track/field (outdoor), track/field (indoor), volleyball. **On-Campus Highlights:** HPERC Athletic Center, Benham Prince Student Center, Chakers Theatre, Weaver Observatory, Thomas Library. **Environmental Initiatives:** Campus-wide recycling. Commitment to make construction projects LEED equivalent. A revolving loan fund to support improvements in energy efficiency.

ADMISSIONS

Freshman Academic Profile: Average high school GPA 3.4. 23% in top 10% of high school class, 48% in top 25% of high school class, 79% in top 50% of high school class. 80% from public high schools. SAT Math middle 50% range 500-620. SAT Critical Reading middle 50% range 500-620. ACT middle 50% range 23-28. Minimum paper TOEFL 550. **Basis for Candidate Selection:** *Very important factors considered include:* Class rank, academic GPA, rigor of secondary school record. *Important factors considered include:* application essay, recommendation(s), character/personal qualities, extracurricular activities, talent/ability, volunteer work. *Other factors considered include:* standardized test scores, alumni/ae relation, first generation, interview, work experience. **Freshman Admission Requirements:** High school diploma is required and GED is accepted. *Academic units required:* 4 English, 3 mathematics, 3 science, (2 science labs), 2 foreign language, 2 history. *Academic units recommended:* 4 English, 3 mathematics, 3 science, (2 science labs), 2 foreign language, 2 history. **Freshman Admission Statistics:** 4,887 applied, 91% admitted, 11% enrolled. **Transfer Admission Requirements:** college transcript(s), Minimum college GPA of 2.0 required. Lowest grade transferable C. **General Admission Information:** Application Fee $40. Early decision application deadline 11/15. Notification on a rolling basis, beginning on or about 1/1. Nonfall registration accepted. Admission may be deferred for a maximum of 12 months. Credit and/or placement offered for CEEB Advanced Placement tests.

COSTS AND FINANCIAL AID

Annual tuition $37,230. Room and board $9,736. Required fees $800. Average book expense $1,000. **Required Forms and Deadlines:** FAFSA. **Notification of Awards:** Applicants will be notified of awards on a rolling basis beginning 3/1. **Types of Aid:** *Need-based scholarships/grants:* Federal Pell, SEOG, state scholarships/grants, private scholarships, the school's own gift aid. *Loans:* Subsidized Stafford, Unsubsidized Stafford, PLUS, Federal Perkins, college/university loans from institutional funds, Private "alternative" loans. **Student Employment:** Federal Work-Study Program available. Institutional employment available. Off-campus job opportunities are excellent. **Financial Aid Statistics:** 100% freshmen, 100% undergrads receive need-based scholarship

or grant aid. 92% freshmen, 92% undergrads receive need-based self-help aid. 100% freshmen, 99% undergrads receive any aid. 71% undergrads borrow to pay for school. Average cumulative indebtedness $31,712. **Criteria for awarding institutional aid:** *Non-need-based:* academics, alumni affiliation, art, leadership, minority status, music/drama, religious affiliation, state/district residency.

See page 1306.

WOFFORD COLLEGE

429 North Church Street, Spartanburg, SC 29303-3663
Phone: 864-597-4130 • **Financial Aid Phone:** 864-597-4160
E-mail: admission@wofford.edu • **CEEB Code:** 5912
Fax: 864-597-4147 • **Website:** www.wofford.edu • **ACT Code:** 3886

This private school, affiliated with the Methodist Church, was founded in 1854. It has a 170-acre campus.

RATINGS

Admissions Selectivity Rating: 92   **Fire Safety Rating:** 80   **Green Rating:** 77

STUDENTS AND FACULTY

Enrollment: 1,568. **Student Body:** 48% female, 52% male, 42% out-of-state, 2% international (15 countries represented). Asian 3%, African American 8%, Caucasian 81%, Hispanic 3%, Native American 0%
Retention and Graduation: 79% freshmen graduate within 4 years. 84% freshmen graduate within 6 years. 46% grads go on to further study within 1 year. 16% grads pursue arts and sciences degrees. 13% grads pursue law degrees. 2% grads pursue business degrees. 13% grads pursue medical degrees. **Faculty:** Student/faculty ratio 11:1. 128 full-time faculty, 91% hold PhDs, 9% are members of minority groups, 40% are women. 0% of classes are taught by teaching assistants.

ACADEMICS

Degrees: bachelor's. **Classes:** Most classes have 10—19 students. Most lab/discussion sessions have 20—29 students. **Majors with Highest Enrollment:** biology/biological sciences; business/managerial economics; finance. **Special Study Options:** Accelerated program, cross-registration, double major, dual enrollment, independent study, internships, student-designed major, study abroad, teacher certification program, Presidential International Scholar program; "Success Initiative, " Bonner Scholars, Community of Scholars, Learning Communities and Creative Writing Concentration. **Combined Degree Programs:** BA/MEng. **Disability Services:** Special programs offered to physically disabled students include note-taking services, reader services, tape recorders, tutors. **Career Services:** Alumni network, alumni services, career/job search classes, career assessment, internships, regional alumni. Career services highlights include Institute for Professional Development.

FACILITIES

Housing: Coed dorms, apartments for single students, wellness housing. 85% of campus accessible to physically disabled. **Special Academic Facilities/Equipment:** Campus is an Arboretum, Art galleries, Franklin W. Olin Building (teaching technology center), Milliken Science Center. **Computers:** 100% of classrooms, 10% of dorms, 100% of libraries, 100% of dining areas, 100% of student union, 40% of common outdoor areas have wireless network access. Students can register for classes online. Administrative functions (other than registration) can be performed online.

CAMPUS LIFE

Environment: City. **Activities:** Choral groups, concert band, dance, drama/theater, literary magazine, music ensembles, pep band, student government, student newspaper, yearbook, Campus Ministries 105 registered organizations, 10 honor societies, 8 religious organizations. 8 fraternities, 4 sororities. **Athletics (Intercollegiate):** *Men:* baseball, basketball, cross-country, football, golf, riflery, soccer, tennis, track/field (outdoor), track/field (indoor). *Women:* basketball, cross-country, golf, riflery, soccer, tennis, track/field (outdoor), track/field (indoor), volleyball. **On-Campus Highlights:** The Roger Milliken Arboretum, Roger Milliken Science Center/Great Oaks, Main Building/Leonard Auditorium, Franklin W. Olin Building, Village Student Housing, Gibbs Stadium Richardson Physical Activities Building Russell C. King Field and Switzer Stadium Joe E. Taylor Athletic Center. **Environmental Initiatives:** Establishment of an innovative and inter-disciplinary Environmental Studies program (a BS/BA major are offered through this program). Wofford "houses its Environmental Studies field studies, research, and community outreach programs in the state-of-the-art, LEED Platinum, historically significant Goodall Environmental Studies Center, situated eight miles from campus. The facility substantiates Wofford's commitment to real life, engaged learning. Wofford students, faculty, and staff, as well as area K-12 educators and community members all benefit from the Center's status as a living-learning laboratory for sustainability and environmental literacy." The college has a director for the environmental studies program. Santee Cooper Lecture Series on Sustainability & Energy. This endowed two-year series is designed to introduce the campus and Spartanburg community to preeminent experts from the field of sustainability. For more information, go to http://www.wofford.edu/newsroom/story.aspx?id=60490 As of 2011-2012, the Wofford College Board of Trustees has formed a formal Committee on Conservation and Sustainability.

ADMISSIONS
Freshman Academic Profile: Average high school GPA 4.1. 55% in top 10% of high school class, 79% in top 25% of high school class, 98% in top 50% of high school class. 65% from public high schools. SAT Math middle 50% range 590-680. SAT Critical Reading middle 50% range 570-670. SAT Writing middle 50% range 470-630. ACT middle 50% range 23-28. Minimum web-based TOEFL 80. Minimum paper TOEFL 550. **Basis for Candidate Selection:** *Very important factors considered include:* academic GPA, rigor of secondary school record. *Important factors considered include:* Class rank, application essay, standardized test scores, character/personal qualities, extracurricular activities, talent/ability, volunteer work. *Other factors considered include:* recommendation(s), alumni/ae relation, first generation, geographical residence, interview, racial/ethnic status, work experience. **Freshman Admission Requirements:** High school diploma is required and GED is accepted. **Freshman Admission Statistics:** 3,197 applied, 63% admitted, 22% enrolled. **Transfer Admission Requirements:** High school transcript, college transcript(s), essay or personal statement, standardized test scores, statement of good standing from prior institution(s). Minimum college GPA of 2.5 required. Lowest grade transferable C. **General Admission Information:** Application Fee $35. Early decision application deadline 11/15. Regular application deadline 2/1. Regular notification 3/15. Nonfall registration accepted. Admission may be deferred for a maximum of 1 year. Credit and/or placement offered for CEEB Advanced Placement tests.

COSTS AND FINANCIAL AID
Annual tuition $34,555. Room and board $9,920. Average book expense $1,200. **Required Forms and Deadlines:** FAFSA. **Notification of Awards:** Applicants will be notified of awards on or about 3/31. **Types of Aid:** *Need-based scholarships/grants:* Federal Pell, SEOG, state scholarships/grants, the school's own gift aid. *Loans:* Subsidized Stafford, Unsubsidized Stafford, PLUS, Federal Perkins. **Student Employment:** Federal Work-Study Program available. Institutional employment available. Highest amount earned per year from on-campus jobs $1,940. Off-campus job opportunities are good. **Financial Aid Statistics:** 91% freshmen, 63% undergrads receive need-based scholarship or grant aid. 29% freshmen, 31% undergrads receive non-need-based scholarship or grant aid. 57% freshmen, 54% undergrads receive need-based self-help aid. 10% freshmen, 9% undergrads receive athletic scholarships. 95% freshmen, 93% undergrads receive any aid. 50% undergrads borrow to pay for school. Average cumulative indebtedness $22,118. **Criteria for awarding institutional aid:** *Non-need-based:* academics, athletics, leadership, music/drama, religious affiliation, state/district residency.

ACADEMICS
Degrees: bachelor's, master's. **Classes:** Most classes have 10—19 students. **Majors with Highest Enrollment:** architecture and related services, other; business administration and management; fashion/apparel design. **Special Study Options:** Accelerated program, double major, dual enrollment, English as a Second Language (ESL), exchange student program (domestic), independent study, internships, liberal arts/career combination, student-designed major, study abroad, weekend college. **Disability Services:** Special programs offered to physically disabled students include note-taking services, tape recorders, tutors. **Career Services:** alumni services, career assessment, internships.

FACILITIES
Housing: Coed dorms, off-campus overflow apartments. 90% of campus accessible to physically disabled. **Special Academic Facilities/Equipment:** Art Gallery; Architecture Gallery; **Computers:** 100% of classrooms, 100% of libraries, 100% of dining areas, have wireless network access. Students can register for classes online. Administrative functions (other than registration) can be performed online. Undergraduates are required to own a computer.

CAMPUS LIFE
Environment: City. **Activities:** student government 20 registered organizations, 3 honor societies, 2 fraternities, 2 sororities.

ADMISSIONS
Freshman Academic Profile: SAT Math middle 50% range 400-530. SAT Critical Reading middle 50% range 390-520. ACT middle 50% range 16-23. Minimum paper TOEFL 500. **Basis for Candidate Selection:** *Very important factors considered include:* academic GPA, rigor of secondary school record, standardized test scores. *Other factors considered include:* Class rank, application essay, recommendation(s), alumni/ae relation, extracurricular activities, first generation, interview, level of applicant's interest, volunteer work, work experience. **Freshman Admission Requirements:** High school diploma is required and GED is accepted. **Freshman Admission Statistics:** 514 applied, 41% admitted, 61% enrolled. **Transfer Admission Requirements:** college transcript(s), Minimum college GPA of 2.5 required. Lowest grade transferable C. **General Admission Information:** Application Fee $50. Notification on a rolling basis, beginning on or about 11/1. Nonfall registration accepted. Admission may be deferred for a maximum of 2 years. Credit offered for CEEB Advanced Placement tests.

COSTS AND FINANCIAL AID
Annual tuition $28,465. Room and board $9,293. Required fees $390. Average book expense $1,700. **Required Forms and Deadlines:** FAFSA, institution's own financial aid form. **Notification of Awards:** Applicants will be notified of awards on a rolling basis beginning 3/15. **Types of Aid:** *Need-based scholarships/grants:* Federal Pell, SEOG, state scholarships/grants, private scholarships, the school's own gift aid. *Loans:* Subsidized Stafford, Unsubsidized Stafford, PLUS, Federal Perkins. **Student Employment:** Federal Work-Study Program available. Institutional employment available. Off-campus job opportunities are good. **Financial Aid Statistics:** 98% freshmen, 96% undergrads receive need-based scholarship or grant aid. 4% freshmen, 3% undergrads receive non-need-based scholarship or grant aid. 91% freshmen, 93% undergrads receive need-based self-help aid. 79% freshmen, 86% undergrads receive any aid. 91% undergrads borrow to pay for school. Average cumulative indebtedness $47,059. **Criteria for awarding institutional aid:** *Non-need-based:* academics.

WOODBURY UNIVERSITY

7500 Glenoaks Boulevard, Burbank, CA 91510-7846
Phone: 818-767-0888 • **Financial Aid Phone:** 818-767-0888
E-mail: admissions@woodbury.edu • **CEEB Code:** 4955
Fax: 818-767-7520 • **ACT Code:** 481

This private school was founded in 1884. It has a 22-acre campus.

RATINGS
Admissions Selectivity Rating: 85   **Fire Safety Rating:** 63   **Green Rating:** 60*

STUDENTS AND FACULTY
Enrollment: 1,269. **Student Body:** 53% female, 47% male, 10% international (41 countries represented). Asian 10%, African American 5%, Caucasian 41%, Hispanic 33%, Native American 0%
Retention and Graduation: 80% freshmen return for sophomore year.
Faculty: Student/faculty ratio 11:1. 59 full-time faculty, 83% hold PhDs, 12% are members of minority groups, 56% are women. 0% of classes are taught by teaching assistants.

WORCESTER POLYTECHNIC INSTITUTE

Best 378

Admissions Office, Bartlett Center, Worcester, MA 1609
Phone: 508-831-5286 • **Financial Aid Phone:** 508-831-5469
E-mail: admissions@wpi.edu • **CEEB Code:** 3969
Fax: 508-831-5875 • **Website:** www.wpi.edu • **ACT Code:** 1942

This private school was founded in 1865. It has a 80-acre campus.

RATINGS
Admissions Selectivity Rating: 94   **Fire Safety Rating:** 82   **Green Rating:** 81

STUDENTS AND FACULTY
Enrollment: 3,746. **Student Body:** 31% female, 69% male, 53% out-of-state, 11% international (80 countries represented). Asian 5%, African American 3%, Caucasian 69%, Hispanic 8%, Native American 0%

Retention and Graduation: 95% freshmen return for sophomore year. 64% freshmen graduate within 4 years. 76% freshmen graduate within 6 years. 25% grads go on to further study within 1 year. 2% grads pursue law degrees. 2% grads pursue business degrees. 2% grads pursue medical degrees. **Faculty:** Student/faculty ratio 14:1. 288 full-time faculty, 90% hold PhDs, 15% are members of minority groups, 24% are women. 0% of classes are taught by teaching assistants.

ACADEMICS

Degrees: bachelor's, master's, post-bachelor's certificate, post-master's certificate. **Classes:** Most classes have fewer than 10 students. Most lab/discussion sessions have 20—29 students. **Majors with Highest Enrollment:** computer science; electrical, electronics and communications engineering; mechanical engineering. **Special Study Options:** Accelerated program, cooperative education program, cross-registration, distance learning, double major, dual enrollment, English as a Second Language (ESL), honors program, independent study, liberal arts/career combination, student-designed major, study abroad, teacher certification program, Completion of degree-required projects at off-campus locations (international and domestic) supervised by WPI faculty. This program requires the students to reside at the site for 2 months after having prepared for the experience for two months while on campus. **Honors Programs:** Chemistry and Biochemistry Scholars Program: Students selected for this highly competitive program will be given the opportunity to participate in faculty research within these departments beginning in the freshman year. In addition to the scholars program, each CBSP Scholar receives an academic merit scholarship. Scholarship amounts will vary, but typically range between $12,500 and $25,000, and are renewable for four years. **Combined Degree Programs:** BS/MS, BS/MBA, BS/MEng. **Disability Services:** Special programs offered to physically disabled students include note-taking services, reader services, tape recorders, tutors. **Career Services:** Alumni network, alumni services, career/job search classes, career assessment, internships, regional alumni. Career services highlights include Two hands-on, professional-level projects that are the equivalent of three courses each are a requirement in our curriculum. They provide students with the opportunity to apply theory to practice through real-world problems and to find solutions that can be implemented by the project sponsors. As an example, one company implemented eight of nine student recommendations and saved $35,000 a day!.

FACILITIES

Housing: Coed dorms, special housing for disabled students, special housing for international students, fraternity/sorority housing, apartments for single students, 4 co-ed residential houses/special interest housing. 90% of campus accessible to physically disabled. **Special Academic Facilities/Equipment:** Several off-campus project centers, TV studio, robotics lab, CAD-CAM lab, laser labs, electron microscopes, wind tunnel, manufacturing engineering applications center, VLSI design lab, nuclear reactor. **Computers:** 100% of classrooms, 100% of dorms, 100% of libraries, 100% of dining areas, 100% of student union, 100% of common outdoor areas have wireless network access. Students can register for classes online. Administrative functions (other than registration) can be performed online.

CAMPUS LIFE

Environment: City. **Activities:** Choral groups, concert band, dance, drama/theater, jazz band, literary magazine, marching band, music ensembles, musical theater, pep band, radio station, student government, student newspaper, student-run film society, symphony orchestra, yearbook, International Student Organization 200 registered organizations, 20 honor societies, 4 religious organizations. 13 fraternities, 3 sororities. **Athletics (Intercollegiate):** *Men:* baseball, basketball, crew/rowing, cross-country, diving, football, soccer, swimming, track/field (outdoor), track/field (indoor), wrestling. *Women:* basketball, crew/rowing, cross-country, diving, field hockey, soccer, softball, swimming, track/field (outdoor), track/field (indoor), volleyball. **On-Campus Highlights:** Student invented fountain, Campus Center, Robotics Lab, Wind Tunnels, Fire Protection Engineering Lab, - New biomedical and life sciences research center at Gateway Park - New pub-style restaurant on-campus - New apartment-style residence hall will open in summer 2008 - New Sports and Recreation Center Opening in 2012. **Environmental Initiatives:** Creation of the President's Task Force on Sustainability, the creation of a Sustainability Coordinator position, and the creation of a Student Sustainability Coordination position. In 2007, WPI's Board of Trustees adopted a policy for all future buildings to be designed to meet LEED certification. And the newly formed Institute for Energy and Sustainability, collaboration between WPI and other institutions and businesses, funded by a grant from the Massachusetts Clean Energy Center is working to develop jobs in the clean energy sector.

ADMISSIONS

Freshman Academic Profile: Average high school GPA 3.8. 65% in top 10% of high school class, 93% in top 25% of high school class, 100% in top 50% of high school class. 66% from public high schools. SAT Math middle 50% range 640-730. SAT Critical Reading middle 50% range 560-670. SAT Writing middle 50% range 560-660. ACT middle 50% range 27-31. Minimum web-based

TOEFL 79. Minimum paper TOEFL 550. **Basis for Candidate Selection:** *Very important factors considered include:* academic GPA, rigor of secondary school record. *Important factors considered include:* Class rank, application essay, recommendation(s), standardized test scores, character/personal qualities, extracurricular activities. *Other factors considered include:* alumni/ae relation, first generation, geographical residence, interview, level of applicant's interest, talent/ability, volunteer work, work experience. **Freshman Admission Requirements:** High school diploma is required and GED is accepted. *Academic units required:* 4 English, 4 mathematics, 2 science, (2 science labs). *Academic units recommended:* 4 English, 4 mathematics, 2 science, (2 science labs). **Freshman Admission Statistics:** 7,049 applied, 57% admitted, 25% enrolled. **Transfer Admission Requirements:** college transcript(s), essay or personal statement, statement of good standing from prior institution(s). Minimum college GPA of 3.0 required. Lowest grade transferable C. **General Admission Information:** Application Fee $60. Regular application deadline 2/1. Regular notification 4/1. Nonfall registration accepted. Admission may be deferred for a maximum of 1 year. Credit and/or placement offered for CEEB Advanced Placement tests.

COSTS AND FINANCIAL AID

Annual tuition $40,790. Room and board $12,650. Required fees $590. Average book expense $1,000. **Required Forms and Deadlines:** FAFSA, CSS/Financial Aid PROFILE, noncustodial PROFILE. **Notification of Awards:** Applicants will be notified of awards on or about 4/1. **Types of Aid:** *Need-based scholarships/grants:* Federal Pell, SEOG, state scholarships/grants, private scholarships, the school's own gift aid. *Loans:* Subsidized Stafford, Unsubsidized Stafford, PLUS, Federal Perkins, state loans, college/university loans from institutional funds. **Student Employment:** Federal Work-Study Program available. Institutional employment available. Off-campus job opportunities are good. **Financial Aid Statistics:** 99% freshmen, 94% undergrads receive need-based scholarship or grant aid. 36% freshmen, 27% undergrads receive non-need-based scholarship or grant aid. 59% freshmen, 61% undergrads receive need-based self-help aid. 99% freshmen, 95% undergrads receive any aid. **Criteria for awarding institutional aid:** *Non-need-based:* academics, leadership, minority status.

See page 1308.

WORCESTER STATE UNIVERSITY

486 Chandler Street, Worcester, MA 01602-2597
Phone: 508-929-8040 • **Financial Aid Phone:** 508-929-8058
E-mail: admissions@worcester.edu • **CEEB Code:** 3524
Fax: 508-929-8183 • **Website:** www.worcester.edu • **ACT Code:** 1914

This public school was founded in 1874. It has a 58-acre campus.

RATINGS

Admissions Selectivity Rating: 73   **Fire Safety Rating:** 90   **Green Rating:** 80

STUDENTS AND FACULTY

Enrollment: 4,808. **Student Body:** 60% female, 40% male, 3% out-of-state, 1% international (17 countries represented). Asian 3%, African American 5%, Caucasian 64%, Hispanic 6%, Native American 0%.
Retention and Graduation: 78% freshmen return for sophomore year. 33% freshmen graduate within 4 years. 51% freshmen graduate within 6 years. **Faculty:** Student/faculty ratio 18:1. 196 full-time faculty, 80% hold PhDs, 19% are members of minority groups, 59% are women. 0% of classes are taught by teaching assistants.

ACADEMICS

Degrees: bachelor's, certificate, master's, post-bachelor's certificate, post-master's certificate. **Classes:** Most classes have 20—29 students. Most lab/discussion sessions have 10—19 students. **Majors with Highest Enrollment:** business administration and management; criminal justice/safety studies; psychology. **Special Study Options:** cross-registration, distance learning, double major, English as a Second Language (ESL), exchange student program (domestic), honors program, independent study, internships, liberal arts/career combination, study abroad, teacher certification program, Foreign Exchange Student Program. **Honors Programs:** Commonwealth Honors Program: The mission of the honors program at Worcester State College is to offer all qualified students an outstanding undergraduate experience through courses that emphasize innovative pedagogy and the values of liberal learning. Honors classes are small (often fewer than 20 students) and are designed to encourage active and lifelong learning. Small classes and extracurricular programs provide honors students with greater interaction between their peers and a select core of dedicated faculty members. In addition to stimulating classes, honors students also enjoy campus speakers, field trips to cultural centers, occasional luncheons with faculty members, and an annual dinner with the college president. Founded in 1996, the program currently enrolls 150 students and recently earned accreditation as a Commonwealth Honors Program from the Massachusetts Board of Higher Education. **Combined Degree Programs:** BA/MA, Occupational Therapy. **Disability Services:** Special programs offered to physically disabled students include note-taking services, reader services, tape recorders, tutors. **Career Services:** Alumni network, alumni services, career/job search classes, career assessment, internships, regional alumni. Career services highlights include Sustainability Fair, Green Work.

FACILITIES

Housing: Coed dorms, special housing for disabled students, men's dorms, women's dorms. 100% of campus accessible to physically disabled. **Special Academic Facilities/Equipment:** Art Studio **Computers:** 100% of classrooms, 100% of dorms, 100% of libraries, 100% of dining areas, 100% of student union, 100% of common outdoor areas have wireless network access. Students can register for classes online. Administrative functions (other than registration) can be performed online. Undergraduates are required to own a computer.

CAMPUS LIFE

Environment: City. **Activities:** Choral groups, concert band, dance, drama/theater, jazz band, music ensembles, radio station, student government, student newspaper, television station, yearbook, Campus Ministries, International Student Organization 39 registered organizations, 17 honor societies, 1 religious organizations. **Athletics (Intercollegiate):** *Men:* baseball, basketball, cheerleading, cross-country, football, golf, ice hockey, soccer, track/field (outdoor), track/field (indoor). *Women:* basketball, cheerleading, cross-country, field hockey, lacrosse, soccer, softball, tennis, track/field (outdoor), track/field (indoor), volleyball. **On-Campus Highlights:** Wasylean Hall, Student Center Living Room, Science and Technology Building, Food Court, Campus Bookstore. **Environmental Initiatives:** 100 KW photovoltaic installation (solar panels) Single stream recycling process Presidents climate commitment

ADMISSIONS

Freshman Academic Profile: Average high school GPA 3.1. SAT Math middle 50% range 460-550. SAT Critical Reading middle 50% range 440-540. SAT Writing middle 50% range 440-530. ACT middle 50% range 19-23. Minimum web-based TOEFL 79. Minimum paper TOEFL 550. **Basis for Candidate Selection:** *Very important factors considered include:* academic GPA, rigor of secondary school record, standardized test scores. *Important factors considered include:* Class rank, character/personal qualities. *Other factors considered include:* application essay, recommendation(s), alumni/ae relation, extracurricular activities, first generation, geographical residence, racial/ethnic status, state residency, talent/ability, volunteer work, work experience. **Freshman Admission Requirements:** High school diploma is required and GED is accepted. *Academic units required:* 4 English, 3 mathematics, 3 science, (1 science labs), 2 foreign language, 1 social studies, 1 history, 2 academic electives. *Academic units recommended:* 4 English, 3 mathematics, 3 science, (1 science labs), 2 foreign language, 1 social studies, 1 history, 2 academic electives. **Freshman Admission Statistics:** 3,434 applied, 68% admitted, 34% enrolled. **Transfer Admission Requirements:** High school transcript, college transcript(s), statement of good standing from prior institution(s). Minimum college GPA of 2.5 required. Lowest grade transferable C–. **General Admission Information:** Application Fee $40. Regular application deadline 5/1. Notification on a rolling basis, beginning on or about 12/1. Nonfall registration accepted. Admission may be deferred for a maximum of 1 year. Credit and/or placement offered for CEEB Advanced Placement tests.

COSTS AND FINANCIAL AID

Required **Forms and Deadlines:** FAFSA. **Notification of Awards:** Applicants will be notified of awards on a rolling basis beginning 3/1. **Types of Aid:** *Need-based scholarships/grants:* Federal Pell, SEOG, state scholarships/grants, private scholarships, the school's own gift aid. *Loans:* Subsidized Stafford, Unsubsidized Stafford, PLUS, Federal Perkins, state loans. **Student Employment:** Federal Work-Study Program available. Institutional employment available. Highest amount earned per year from on-campus jobs $17,184. Off-campus job opportunities are good. **Financial Aid Statistics:** 90% freshmen, 79% undergrads receive need-based scholarship or grant aid. 47% freshmen, 30% undergrads receive non-need-based scholarship or grant aid. 98% freshmen, 94% undergrads receive need-based self-help aid. 58% freshmen, 49% undergrads receive any aid. 74% undergrads borrow to pay for school. Average cumulative indebtedness $20,449. **Criteria for awarding institutional aid:** *Non-need-based:* academics.

WRIGHT STATE UNIVERSITY

3640 Colonel Glenn Highway, Dayton, OH 45435
Phone: 937-775-5700 • **Financial Aid Phone:** 937-775-5721
E-mail: admissions@wright.edu • **CEEB Code:** 1179
Fax: 937-775-5795 • **Website:** www.wright.edu • **ACT Code:** 3295

This public school was founded in 1964. It has a 557-acre campus.

RATINGS

Admissions Selectivity Rating: 73   **Fire Safety Rating:** 95   **Green Rating:** 80

STUDENTS AND FACULTY

Enrollment: 12,602. **Student Body:** 53% female, 47% male, 3% out-of-state, 4% international (66 countries represented). Asian 2%, African American 14%, Caucasian 73%, Hispanic 3%, Native American 0%
Retention and Graduation: 56% freshmen return for sophomore year. 19% freshmen graduate within 4 years. 40% freshmen graduate within 6 years. **Faculty:** Student/faculty ratio 22:1. 642 full-time faculty, 14% are members of minority groups, 45% are women. 13% of classes are taught by teaching assistants.

ACADEMICS

Degrees: associate, bachelor's, certificate, doctoral, master's, post-master's certificate, terminal associate, transfer associate. **Classes:** Most classes have 20—29 students. Most lab/discussion sessions have fewer than 10 students. **Majors with Highest Enrollment:** elementary education and teaching; nursing/registered nurse (rn, asn, bsn, msn); psychology. **Special Study Options:** cooperative education program, cross-registration, distance learning, double major, dual enrollment, English as a Second Language (ESL), honors program, independent study, internships, student-designed major, study abroad, teacher certification program, weekend college. **Honors Programs:** Honors Program. **Disability Services:** Special programs offered to physically disabled students include note-taking services, reader services, tape recorders, tutors. **Career Services:** Alumni network, alumni services, career/job search classes, career assessment, internships Career services highlights include WSU has a very flexible set of programs that meet the needs of our students.

FACILITIES

Housing: Coed dorms, special housing for disabled students, apartments for married students, apartments for single students, Honors Dorm. 100% of campus accessible to physically disabled. **Special Academic Facilities/Equipment:** Art gallery located in the Creative Arts Center **Computers:** 100% of classrooms, 100% of dorms, 100% of libraries, 100% of dining areas, 100% of student union, have wireless network access. Students can register for classes online. Administrative functions (other than registration) can be performed online.

CAMPUS LIFE

Environment: City. **Activities:** Choral groups, concert band, dance, drama/theater, jazz band, literary magazine, music ensembles, musical theater, opera, pep band, radio station, student government, student newspaper, symphony orchestra, television station, Campus Ministries, Model UN 145 registered organizations, 22 honor societies, 9 religious organizations. 8 fraternities, 8 sororities. **Athletics (Intercollegiate):** *Men:* baseball, basketball, cheerleading, cross-country, diving, golf, soccer, swimming, tennis. *Women:* basketball, cheerleading, cross-country, diving, soccer, softball, swimming, tennis, track/field (outdoor), volleyball. **On-Campus Highlights:** Student Union, Garden of the Senses, Rec Center, Fitness Center, Nutter Center. **Environmental Initiatives:** Matthew O. Diggs III Laboratory for Life Sciences Research achieved LEED Gold status, the first laboratory in Ohio to achieve LEED-NC Gold status. Recycling (38% increase 2010-2011 in RecycleMania competition) Energy Efficiency (20% savings by 2014).

ADMISSIONS

Freshman Academic Profile: Average high school GPA 3.1. 14% in top 10% of high school class, 33% in top 25% of high school class, 65% in top 50% of high school class. 85% from public high schools. SAT Math middle 50% range 430-580. SAT Critical Reading middle 50% range 430-570. SAT Writing middle 50% range 420-540. ACT middle 50% range 18-24. Minimum web-based TOEFL 61. **Basis for Candidate Selection:** *Very important factors considered include:* academic GPA, rigor of secondary school record, standardized test scores. *Important factors considered include:* Class rank. *Other factors considered include:* recommendation(s), state residency. **Freshman Admission Requirements:** High school diploma is required and GED is accepted. *Academic units required:* 4 English, 3 mathematics, 3 science, (3 science labs), 2 foreign language, 3 social studies, 1 visual/performing arts. *Academic units recommended:* 4 English, 3 mathematics, 3 science, (3 science labs), 2 foreign language, 3 social studies, 1 visual/performing arts. **Freshman Admission Statistics:** 8,112 applied, 69% admitted, 41% enrolled. **Transfer Admission**

Requirements: college transcript(s), Minimum college GPA of 2.0 required. Lowest grade transferable D. **General Admission Information:** Application Fee $30. Notification on a rolling basis, beginning on or about 10/1. Nonfall registration accepted. Admission may be deferred for a maximum of Four Quarters. Credit offered for CEEB Advanced Placement tests.

COSTS AND FINANCIAL AID

Annual in-state tuition $8,354. Annual out-of-state tuition $16,182. Room and board $8,629. Average book expense $1,392. **Required Forms and Deadlines:** FAFSA. **Notification of Awards:** Applicants will be notified of awards on a rolling basis beginning 3/15. **Types of Aid:** *Need-based scholarships/grants:* Federal Pell, SEOG, state scholarships/grants, private scholarships, the school's own gift aid, United Negro College Fund, Federal Nursing Scholarships., Choose Ohio First Scholarships. *Loans:* Subsidized Stafford, Unsubsidized Stafford, PLUS, Federal Perkins, Federal Nursing, state loans, college/university loans from institutional funds, Private Loans. **Student Employment:** Federal Work-Study Program available. Institutional employment available. Off-campus job opportunities are good. **Financial Aid Statistics:** 85% freshmen, 79% undergrads receive need-based scholarship or grant aid. 6% freshmen, 4% undergrads receive non-need-based scholarship or grant aid. 95% freshmen, 96% undergrads receive need-based self-help aid. 1% freshmen, 1% undergrads receive athletic scholarships. 83% freshmen, 76% undergrads receive any aid. 83% undergrads borrow to pay for school. Average cumulative indebtedness $28,349. **Criteria for awarding institutional aid:** *Non-need-based:* academics, alumni affiliation, art, athletics, leadership, minority status, music/drama.

XAVIER UNIVERSITY (OH)

3800 Victory Parkway, Cincinnati, OH 45207-5311
Phone: 513 745-3301 • **Financial Aid Phone:** 513-745-3142
E-mail: xuadmit@xavier.edu • **CEEB Code:** 1965
Fax: 513-745-4319 • **Website:** www.xavier.edu • **ACT Code:** 3366

This private school, affiliated with the Roman Catholic-Jesuit Church, was founded in 1831. It has a 146-acre campus.

RATINGS

Admissions Selectivity Rating: 79   **Fire Safety Rating:** 79   **Green Rating:** 87

STUDENTS AND FACULTY

Enrollment: 4,351. **Student Body:** 54% female, 46% male, 44% out-of-state, 2% international (45 countries represented). Asian 2%, African American 9%, Caucasian 79%, Hispanic 4%, Native American 0%
Retention and Graduation: 80% freshmen return for sophomore year. 71% freshmen graduate within 4 years. 78% freshmen graduate within 6 years. 51% grads go on to further study within 1 year. **Faculty:** Student/faculty ratio 12:1. 342 full-time faculty, 78% hold PhDs, 18% are members of minority groups, 51% are women. 0% of classes are taught by teaching assistants.

ACADEMICS

Degrees: associate, bachelor's, certificate, master's, terminal associate. **Classes:** Most classes have 20—29 students. Most lab/discussion sessions have 20—29 students. **Majors with Highest Enrollment:** business/commerce; liberal arts and sciences/liberal studies; nursing/registered nurse (rn, asn, bsn, msn). **Special Study Options:** cooperative education program, cross-registration, double major, dual enrollment, English as a Second Language (ESL), honors program, independent study, internships, study abroad, teacher certification program, weekend college, Service Learning Semester. **Honors Programs:** University Scholars Progam Philosophy, Politics and the Public Honors AB **Combined Degree Programs:** BSBA/MBA in Accounting. **Disability Services:** Special programs offered to physically disabled students include note-taking services, reader services, tape recorders, tutors. **Career Services:** Alumni network, alumni services, career/job search classes, career assessment, internships, regional alumni. Career services highlights include Our premier programs include our Executive Mentor Program in which students are matched with a business executive in their sophomore year to guide, advise and serve as a sounding board on career, academic and life issues. Additionally our Business Profession Program, an intentional four-year career development program for business undergraduates has received national attention.

FACILITIES

Housing: Coed dorms, special housing for disabled students, apartments for single students, theme housing. 95% of campus accessible to physically disabled. **Special Academic Facilities/Equipment:** Student-run art gallery, Montessori lab school. **Computers:** 100% of classrooms, 100% of dorms, 100% of libraries, 100% of dining areas, 100% of student union, 100% of common outdoor areas have wireless network access. Students can register for classes online. Administrative functions (other than registration) can be performed online.

CAMPUS LIFE

Environment: Metropolis. **Activities:** Choral groups, concert band, dance, drama/theater, jazz band, literary magazine, music ensembles, musical theater, opera, pep band, radio station, student government, student newspaper, student-run film society, symphony orchestra, television station, Campus Ministries, International Student Organization 124 registered organizations, 10 honor societies, 11 religious organizations. **Athletics (Intercollegiate):** *Men:* baseball, basketball, cheerleading, cross-country, golf, soccer, swimming, tennis, track/field (outdoor), track/field (indoor). *Women:* basketball, cheerleading, cross-country, golf, soccer, swimming, tennis, track/field (outdoor), track/field (indoor), volleyball. **On-Campus Highlights:** Cintas Center basketball arena and conce, McDonald Library, The Gallagher Student Center, O'Conner Sports Center, Bellarmine Chapel. **Environmental Initiatives:** New construction will be required to be LEED Silver. Active participation in Recyclemania and recycling of the waste stream throughout the year. Investment in large central plant hot-cold water high-efficiency equipment to provide heating and cooling for the majority of the building on campus, resulting in lower carbon generation and lower expenses.

ADMISSIONS

Freshman Academic Profile: 3.6. 23% in top 10% of high school class, 53% in top 25% of high school class, 86% in top 50% of high school class. 48% from public high schools. SAT Math middle 50% range 500-600. SAT Critical Reading middle 50% range 500-600. SAT Writing middle 50% range 479-600. ACT middle 50% range 23-28. Minimum web-based TOEFL 71. **Basis for Candidate Selection:** *Very important factors considered include:* rigor of secondary school record. *Important factors considered include:* Class rank, application essay, academic GPA, recommendation(s), standardized test scores, character/personal qualities. *Other factors considered include:* alumni/ae relation, extracurricular activities, first generation, level of applicant's interest, talent/ability, volunteer work, work experience **Freshman Admission Requirements:** High school diploma is required and GED is accepted. **Freshman Admission Statistics:** 11,232 applied, 68% admitted, 14% enrolled. **Transfer Admission Requirements:** High school transcript, college transcript(s), statement of good standing from prior institution(s). Minimum college GPA of 2.0 required. Lowest grade transferable C–. **General Admission Information:** Application Fee $35. Regular application deadline 2/1. Notification on a rolling basis, beginning on or about 10/15. Nonfall registration accepted. Admission may be deferred for a maximum of 1 year. Credit and/or placement offered for CEEB Advanced Placement tests.

COSTS AND FINANCIAL AID

Annual tuition $30,230. Room and board $11,730. Required fees $930. Average book expense $1,000. **Required Forms and Deadlines:** FAFSA. **Notification of Awards:** Applicants will be notified of awards on a rolling basis beginning 2/15. **Types of Aid:** *Need-based scholarships/grants:* Federal Pell, SEOG, state scholarships/grants, private scholarships, the school's own gift aid. *Loans:* Subsidized Stafford, Unsubsidized Stafford, PLUS, Federal Perkins. **Student Employment:** Federal Work-Study Program available. Institutional employment available. Highest amount earned per year from on-campus jobs $4,900. Off-campus job opportunities are excellent. **Financial Aid Statistics:** 98% freshmen, 95% undergrads receive need-based scholarship or grant aid. 16% freshmen, 13% undergrads receive non-need-based scholarship or grant aid. 79% freshmen, 79% undergrads receive need-based self-help aid. 3% freshmen, 4% undergrads receive athletic scholarships. 100% freshmen, 90% undergrads receive any aid. 71% undergrads borrow to pay for school. Average cumulative indebtedness $29,575. **Criteria for awarding institutional aid:** *Non-need-based:* academics, alumni affiliation, art, athletics, leadership, music/drama, religious affiliation.

XAVIER UNIVERSITY OF LOUISIANA

One Drexel Drive, New Orleans, LA 70125
Phone: 504-520-7388 • **Financial Aid Phone:** 504-520-7835
E-mail: apply@xula.edu • **CEEB Code:** 6975
Fax: 504-520-7941 • **Website:** www.xula.edu • **ACT Code:** 1618

This private school, affiliated with the Roman Catholic Church, was founded in 1915. It has a 29-acre campus.

RATINGS

Admissions Selectivity Rating: 76   **Fire Safety Rating:** 77   **Green Rating:** 60*

STUDENTS AND FACULTY

Enrollment: 2,725. **Student Body:** 71% female, 29% male, 57% out-of-state, 2% international (8 countries represented). Asian 9%, African American 79%, Caucasian 4%, Hispanic 2%, Native American 0%
Retention and Graduation: 69% freshmen return for sophomore year. 35% freshmen graduate within 4 years. 31% grads go on to further study within 1 year. **Faculty:** Student/faculty ratio 13:1. 240 full-time faculty, 85% hold PhDs, 50% are members of minority groups, 49% are women. 0% of classes are taught by teaching assistants.

ACADEMICS

Degrees: bachelor's, master's, post-master's certificate. **Classes:** Most classes have 10—19 students. Most lab/discussion sessions have 20—29 students. **Majors with Highest Enrollment:** pre-medicine/pre-medical studies; pre-pharmacy studies; psychology. **Special Study Options:** Accelerated program, cooperative education program, cross-registration, double major, dual enrollment, exchange student program (domestic), honors program, independent study, internships, study abroad, African American Studies Minor; Women Studies. **Disability Services:** Special programs offered to physically disabled students include note-taking services, reader services, tape recorders, tutors. **Career Services:** career/job search classes, career assessment, internships.

FACILITIES

Housing: Coed dorms, special housing for disabled students, men's dorms, women's dorms. 99% of campus accessible to physically disabled. **Computers:** 100% of classrooms, 100% of dorms, 100% of libraries, 100% of dining areas, 100% of student union, 100% of common outdoor areas have wireless network access. Students can register for classes online. Administrative functions (other than registration) can be performed online.

CAMPUS LIFE

Environment: Metropolis. **Activities:** Choral groups, concert band, dance, drama/theater, jazz band, literary magazine, music ensembles, opera, student government, student newspaper, symphony orchestra, television station, yearbook, Campus Ministries, International Student Organization 88 registered organizations, 8 honor societies, 1 religious organizations. 4 fraternities, 4 sororities. **Athletics (Intercollegiate):** *Men:* basketball, cross-country, tennis, track/field (outdoor), track/field (indoor). *Women:* basketball, cross-country, tennis, track/field (outdoor), track/field (indoor), volleyball. **On-Campus Highlights:** New University Center, Gymnasium (The Barn), Library, University Quadrangle, Historic Administration Building.

ADMISSIONS

Freshman Academic Profile: Average high school GPA 3.3. 29% in top 10% of high school class, 55% in top 25% of high school class, 82% in top 50% of high school class. SAT Math middle 50% range 430-540. SAT Critical Reading middle 50% range 430-540. SAT Writing middle 50% range 410-520. ACT middle 50% range 19-24. Minimum paper TOEFL 550. **Basis for Candidate Selection:** *Very important factors considered include:* academic GPA, recommendation(s), rigor of secondary school record, standardized test scores. *Important factors considered include:* Class rank, application essay. *Other factors considered include:* alumni/ae relation, character/personal qualities, extracurricular activities, interview, talent/ability, volunteer work, work experience. **Freshman Admission Requirements:** High school diploma is required and GED is accepted. *Academic units required:* 4 English, 2 mathematics, 1 science, 1 social studies, 8 academic electives. *Academic units recommended:* 4 English, 2 mathematics, 1 science, 1 social studies, 8 academic electives. **Freshman Admission Statistics:** 4,463 applied, 64% admitted, 27% enrolled. **Transfer Admission Requirements:** college transcript(s), Minimum college GPA of 2.00 required. Lowest grade transferable C. **General Admission Information:** Application Fee $25. Regular application deadline 7/1. Regular

notification 10/15. Nonfall registration accepted. Credit and/or placement offered for CEEB Advanced Placement tests.

COSTS AND FINANCIAL AID

Annual tuition $17,700. Room and board $7,600. Required fees $1,000. Average book expense $1,200. **Required Forms and Deadlines:** FAFSA. **Notification of Awards:** Applicants will be notified of awards on a rolling basis beginning 4/1. **Types of Aid:** *Need-based scholarships/grants:* Federal Pell, SEOG, state scholarships/grants, private scholarships, the school's own gift aid, United Negro College Fund. *Loans:* Direct Subsidized Stafford, Direct Unsubsidized Stafford, Direct PLUS, Subsidized Stafford, Unsubsidized Stafford, PLUS, Federal Perkins. **Student Employment:** Federal Work-Study Program available. Institutional employment available. Highest amount earned per year from on-campus jobs $1,000. Off-campus job opportunities are good. **Financial Aid Statistics:** 74% freshmen, 73% undergrads receive need-based scholarship or grant aid. 88% freshmen, 75% undergrads receive non-need-based scholarship or grant aid. 98% freshmen, 97% undergrads receive need-based self-help aid. 3% freshmen, 3% undergrads receive athletic scholarships. 94% freshmen, 24% undergrads receive any aid. 83% undergrads borrow to pay for school. Average cumulative indebtedness $26,106. **Criteria for awarding institutional aid:** *Non-need-based:* music/drama.

YALE UNIVERSITY

PO Box 208234, New Haven, CT 06520-8234
Phone: 203-432-9300 • **Financial Aid Phone:** 203-432-2700
E-mail: student.questions@yale.edu • **CEEB Code:** 3987
Fax: 203-432-9392 • **Website:** www.yale.edu • **ACT Code:** 618

This private school was founded in 1701. It has a 320-acre campus.

RATINGS

Admissions Selectivity Rating: 99   **Fire Safety Rating:** 61   **Green Rating:** 95

STUDENTS AND FACULTY

Enrollment: 5,296. **Student Body:** 50% female, 50% male, 94% out-of-state, 10% international (108 countries represented). Asian 14%, African American 6%, Caucasian 47%, Hispanic 9%, Native American 0%
Retention and Graduation: 99% freshmen return for sophomore year. 89% freshmen graduate within 4 years. 96% freshmen graduate within 6 years. 27% grads go on to further study within 1 year. 9% grads pursue arts and sciences degrees. 6% grads pursue law degrees. 8% grads pursue medical degrees. **Faculty:** Student/faculty ratio 6:1. 1158 full-time faculty, 91% hold PhDs, 18% are members of minority groups, 33% are women. 3% of classes are taught by teaching assistants.

ACADEMICS

Degrees: bachelor's, master's, post-master's certificate. **Classes:** Most classes have 10—19 students. **Majors with Highest Enrollment:** economics; history; political science and government. **Special Study Options:** Accelerated program, distance learning, double major, English as a Second Language (ESL), honors program, independent study, internships, liberal arts/career combination, student-designed major, study abroad, teacher certification program. **Combined Degree Programs:** BA/MA, BA/MM in Music, BA/MA, BS/MS. **Disability Services:** Special programs offered to physically disabled students include note-taking services, reader services, tape recorders, tutors. **Career Services:** Alumni network, alumni services, career/job search classes, internships, regional alumni. Career services highlights include In coordination with the Yale Undergraduate Career Services department, the university helps place hundreds of students in internships across the country and around the world every year. UCS utilizes a vast array of resources, including alumni, private firms and research fellowships to place students in a wide variety of internships.

FACILITIES

Housing: Coed dorms, special housing for disabled students, Students are randomly assigned to 1 of 12 residential colleges where they live,eat,socialize,and pursue various academic and extracurricular activities. All undergraduate housing is provided through residential college system. **Special Academic Facilities/Equipment:** Art and history museums, observatory, electron microscopes, nuclear accelerators, center for international and areas studies, child study center, marsh botanical gardens, center for parallel supercomputing. **Computers:** 100% of classrooms, 100% of dorms, 100% of libraries, 100% of dining areas,

100% of student union, 100% of common outdoor areas have wireless network access. Students can register for classes online. Administrative functions (other than registration) can be performed online.

CAMPUS LIFE

Environment: City. **Activities:** Choral groups, concert band, dance, drama/theater, jazz band, literary magazine, marching band, music ensembles, musical theater, opera, pep band, radio station, student government, student newspaper, student-run film society, symphony orchestra, television station, yearbook, Campus Ministries, International Student Organization, Model UN 350 registered organizations. **Athletics (Intercollegiate):** *Men:* baseball, basketball, crew/rowing, cross-country, diving, fencing, football, golf, ice hockey, lacrosse, sailing, soccer, squash, swimming, tennis, track/field (outdoor), track/field (indoor). *Women:* basketball, crew/rowing, cross-country, diving, fencing, field hockey, golf, gymnastics, ice hockey, lacrosse, sailing, soccer, softball, squash, swimming, tennis, track/field (outdoor), track/field (indoor), volleyball. **On-Campus Highlights:** Old Campus, Sterling Memorial Library, Yale British Art Center, Beinecke Rare Book and Manuscript Library, Payne-Whitney Gymnasium, http://www.yale.edu/admit/visit/index.html. **Environmental Initiatives:** Greenhouse gas commitment of 43% below 2005 levels by 2020 40% of food served in the dining halls is local/organic LEED Silver for all new construction

ADMISSIONS

Freshman Academic Profile: 97% in top 10% of high school class, 100% in top 25% of high school class, 100% in top 50% of high school class. 55% from public high schools. SAT Math middle 50% range 710-790. SAT Critical Reading middle 50% range 700-800. SAT Writing middle 50% range 710-800. ACT middle 50% range 32-35. Minimum web-based TOEFL 100. Minimum paper TOEFL 600. **Basis for Candidate Selection:** *Very important factors considered include:* Class rank, application essay, academic GPA, recommendation(s), rigor of secondary school record, standardized test scores, character/personal qualities, extracurricular activities, talent/ability. *Other factors considered include:* alumni/ae relation, first generation, geographical residence, interview, level of applicant's interest, racial/ethnic status, state residency, volunteer work, work experience. **Freshman Admission Requirements:** High school diploma or equivalent is not required. **Freshman Admission Statistics:** 25,869 applied, 8% admitted, 66% enrolled. **Transfer Admission Requirements:** High school transcript, college transcript(s), essay or personal statement, standardized test scores, statement of good standing from prior institution(s). Lowest grade transferable C. **General Admission Information:** Application Fee $75. Regular application deadline 12/31. Regular notification 4/1. Nonfall registration not accepted. Admission may be deferred for a maximum of one year. Placement offered for CEEB Advanced Placement tests.

COSTS AND FINANCIAL AID

Annual tuition $42,300. Room and board $13,000. Average book expense $1,000. **Required Forms and Deadlines:** FAFSA, CSS/Financial Aid PROFILE, noncustodial PROFILE, business/farm supplement. Parent Tax returns. **Notification of Awards:** Applicants will be notified of awards on or about 4/1. **Types of Aid:** *Need-based scholarships/grants:* Federal Pell, SEOG, state scholarships/grants, private scholarships, the school's own gift aid, United Negro College Fund. *Loans:* Subsidized Stafford, Unsubsidized Stafford, PLUS, Federal Perkins, state loans, college/university loans from institutional funds. **Student Employment:** Institutional employment available. **Financial Aid Statistics:** 100% freshmen, 100% undergrads receive need-based scholarship or grant aid. 70% freshmen, 83% undergrads receive need-based self-help aid. 58% freshmen, 52% undergrads receive any aid. 31% undergrads borrow to pay for school. Average cumulative indebtedness $10,717.

YESHIVA UNIVERSITY

500 West 185th Street, New York, NY 10033-3299
Phone: 212-960-5277
E-mail: yuadmit@yu.edu • **CEEB Code:** 2990
Fax: 212-960-0086 • **Website:** www.yu.edu • **ACT Code:** 2992

This private school was founded in 1886. It has a 12-acre campus.

RATINGS

Admissions Selectivity Rating: 91   **Fire Safety Rating:** 60*   **Green Rating:** 60*

STUDENTS AND FACULTY

Enrollment: 2,866. **Student Body:** 46% female, 54% male, 35% out-of-state, 12% international (53 countries represented). Asian 0%, African American 0%, Caucasian 83%, Hispanic 2%, Native American 0%
Retention and Graduation: 90% freshmen return for sophomore year. 49% freshmen graduate within 4 years. **Faculty:** Student/faculty ratio 7:1. 0% of classes are taught by teaching assistants.

ACADEMICS

Degrees: bachelor's, master's. **Classes:** Most classes have 10—19 students. Most lab/discussion sessions have 10—19 students. **Majors with Highest Enrollment:** jewish/judaic studies; political science and government; psychology. **Special Study Options:** double major, honors program, independent study, internships, student-designed major, study abroad, teacher certification program. **Combined Degree Programs:** BA/MA, 3-2 and 4-2 engineering programs with Columbia U. **Career Services:** career/job search classes, career assessment, internships.

FACILITIES

Housing: men's dorms, women's dorms, apartments for married students, apartments for single students. **Special Academic Facilities/Equipment:** Archives and rare book collection, museum of Jewish art, architecture, history, and culture.

CAMPUS LIFE

Activities: Choral groups, concert band, drama/theater, jazz band, literary magazine, music ensembles, musical theater, radio station, student government, student newspaper, yearbook. **Athletics (Intercollegiate):** *Men:* basketball, tennis, volleyball. *Women:* basketball, tennis.

ADMISSIONS

Freshman Academic Profile: Average high school GPA 3.5. 48% in top 10% of high school class, 77% in top 25% of high school class, 95% in top 50% of high school class. SAT Math middle 50% range 550-680. SAT Critical Reading middle 50% range 550-690. ACT middle 50% range 22-28. Minimum paper TOEFL 500. **Basis for Candidate Selection:** *Important factors considered include:* application essay, academic GPA, rigor of secondary school record, standardized test scores, extracurricular activities, interview, talent/ability. *Other factors considered include:* volunteer work, work experience. **Freshman Admission Requirements:** High school diploma is required and GED is accepted. **Freshman Admission Statistics:** 2,027 applied, 63% admitted, 65% enrolled. **Transfer Admission Requirements:** High school transcript, college transcript(s), essay or personal statement, interview, standardized test scores, Lowest grade transferable 75. **General Admission Information:** Application Fee $40. Regular application deadline 2/15. Regular notification 4/1. Nonfall registration accepted. Credit and/or placement offered for CEEB Advanced Placement tests.

COSTS AND FINANCIAL AID

Annual tuition $31,594. Room and board $10,380. Required fees $500. Average book expense $1,224. **Required Forms and Deadlines:** FAFSA, institution's own financial aid form, CSS/Financial Aid PROFILE, state aid form, noncustodial PROFILE, business/farm supplement. **Notification of Awards: Types of Aid:** *Need-based scholarships/grants:* Federal Pell, SEOG, state scholarships/grants, private scholarships, the school's own gift aid. *Loans:* Subsidized Stafford, Unsubsidized Stafford, PLUS, Federal Perkins, college/university loans from institutional funds. **Student Employment:** Federal Work-Study Program available. Institutional employment available. Highest amount earned per year from on-campus jobs $500. Off-campus job opportunities are good. **Financial Aid Statistics:** 89% freshmen, 85% undergrads receive need-based scholarship or grant aid. 14% freshmen, 10% undergrads receive non-need-based scholarship or grant aid. 80% freshmen, 77% undergrads receive need-based self-help aid. **Criteria for awarding institutional aid:** *Non-need-based:* academics.

YORK COLLEGE

1125 E. 8th Street, York, NE 68467
Phone: 402-363-5627 • **Financial Aid Phone:** 402-363-5625
E-mail: enroll@york.edu
Fax: 402-363-5623 • **Website:** www.york.edu • **ACT Code:** 2484

This private school, affiliated with the Church of Christ Church, was founded in 1890. It has a 200-acre campus.

RATINGS

Admissions Selectivity Rating: 81   **Fire Safety Rating:** 98   **Green Rating:** 60*

STUDENTS AND FACULTY

Enrollment: 385. **Student Body:** 51% female, 49% male, 69% out-of-state, 1% international (6 countries represented). Asian 2%, African American 5%, Caucasian 72%, Hispanic 4%, Native American 0%
Retention and Graduation: 55% freshmen return for sophomore year.
Faculty: Student/faculty ratio 7:1. 33 full-time faculty, 36% hold PhDs, 3% are members of minority groups, 27% are women. 0% of classes are taught by teaching assistants.

ACADEMICS

Degrees: associate, bachelor's, transfer associate. **Classes:** Most classes have fewer than 10 students. **Majors with Highest Enrollment:** business administration and management; education; psychology. **Special Study Options:** double major, dual enrollment, internships, student-designed major, teacher certification program. **Career Services:** Alumni network, career assessment, Career services highlights include Most degrees require students to serve in some type of internship before graduation.

FACILITIES

Housing: special housing for disabled students, men's dorms, women's dorms, apartments for married students. 60% of campus accessible to physically disabled. **Computers:** 100% of libraries, 100% of student union, have wireless network access.

CAMPUS LIFE

Environment: Village. **Activities:** Choral groups, drama/theater, literary magazine, music ensembles, musical theater, student government, student newspaper, yearbook, Campus Ministries 12 registered organizations, 2 honor societies, 1 religious organizations. 4 fraternities, 4 sororities. **Athletics (Intercollegiate):** *Men:* baseball, basketball, soccer, wrestling. *Women:* basketball, soccer, softball, volleyball. **On-Campus Highlights:** Mackey Center, Prayer Chapel, Spiritual Life Center/Coffee Shop, Gurganus Hall, Freeman Center.

ADMISSIONS

Freshman Academic Profile: Average high school GPA 3.4. 13% in top 10% of high school class, 25% in top 25% of high school class, 60% in top 50% of high school class. SAT Math middle 50% range 440-560. SAT Critical Reading middle 50% range 450-590. ACT middle 50% range 18-26. Minimum paper TOEFL 500. **Basis for Candidate Selection:** *Very important factors considered include:* Class rank, academic GPA, rigor of secondary school record, standardized test scores. *Other factors considered include:* application essay, recommendation(s), alumni/ae relation, character/personal qualities, extracurricular activities, first generation, level of applicant's interest, religious affiliation/commitment, talent/ability, volunteer work. **Freshman Admission Requirements:** High school diploma is required and GED is accepted. *Academic units required:* 3 English, 2 mathematics, 2 science, 1 social studies, 1 history. *Academic units recommended:* 3 English, 2 mathematics, 2 science, 1 social studies, 1 history. **Freshman Admission Statistics:** 531 applied, 57% admitted, 30% enrolled. **Transfer Admission Requirements:** High school transcript, college transcript(s), Minimum college GPA of 2 required. Lowest grade transferable 1. **General Admission Information:** Application Fee $20. Regular application deadline 8/31. Nonfall registration accepted.

COSTS AND FINANCIAL AID

Annual tuition $12,500. Room and board $4,500. Required fees $1,500. Average book expense $1,500. **Required Forms and Deadlines:** FAFSA. **Notification of Awards:** Applicants will be notified of awards on a rolling basis beginning 3/1. **Types of Aid:** *Need-based scholarships/grants:* Federal Pell, SEOG, state scholarships/grants, private scholarships, the school's own gift aid. *Loans:* Direct Subsidized Stafford, Direct Unsubsidized Stafford, Direct PLUS, Subsidized Stafford, Unsubsidized Stafford, PLUS, Federal Perkins, Federal Nursing, college/university loans from institutional funds. **Student Employment:** Federal Work-Study Program available. Off-campus job opportunities are good. **Financial Aid Statistics:** 89% freshmen, 89% undergrads receive any aid. 89% undergrads borrow to pay for school. **Criteria for awarding institutional aid:** *Non-need-based:* academics, athletics, leadership, music/drama.

YORK COLLEGE OF PENNSYLVANIA

Country Club Road, York, PA 17403-3651
Phone: 717-849-1600 • **Financial Aid Phone:** 717-849-1682
E-mail: admissions@ycp.edu • **CEEB Code:** 2991
Fax: 717-849-1607 • **Website:** www.ycp.edu • **ACT Code:** 3762

This private school was founded in 1787. It has a 190-acre campus.

RATINGS

Admissions Selectivity Rating: 74   **Fire Safety Rating:** 91   **Green Rating:** 61

STUDENTS AND FACULTY

Enrollment: 5,011. **Student Body:** 56% female, 44% male, 40% out-of-state, 0% international (32 countries represented). Asian 1%, African American 5%, Caucasian 84%, Hispanic 5%, Native American 0%
Retention and Graduation: 73% freshmen return for sophomore year. 41% freshmen graduate within 4 years. 59% freshmen graduate within 6 years.
Faculty: Student/faculty ratio 16:1. 189 full-time faculty, 81% hold PhDs, 4%

are members of minority groups, 43% are women. 0% of classes are taught by teaching assistants.

ACADEMICS

Degrees: associate, bachelor's, master's. **Classes:** Most classes have 20—29 students. Most lab/discussion sessions have 10—19 students. **Majors with Highest Enrollment:** biology/biological sciences; business administration and management; nursing/registered nurse (rn, asn, bsn, msn). **Special Study Options:** Accelerated program, cooperative education program, double major, dual enrollment, honors program, independent study, internships, liberal arts/career combination, student-designed major, study abroad, teacher certification program. **Honors Programs:** Honors Program includes coursework, special academic and career advising and extracurricular enrichment activities. **Combined Degree Programs:** BS/MBA. **Disability Services:** Special programs offered to physically disabled students include tape recorders, tutors. **Career Services:** Alumni network, alumni services, career/job search classes, career assessment, internships, regional alumni. We are very proud of the experiential education opportunities that all of our students enjoy. Credit-based experiential learning is available in all academic programs and provides reflective learning and practical application of skills. Experiential education offerings vary based upon the academic program, and include internships, independent research, service-learning, course based projects, practica, student teaching, clinical rotations, and many other special learning opportunities. Co-ops are exclusive to our three engineering programs, and students are required to participate in 3 before graduating as well as a number of other hands-on experiences and projects.

FACILITIES

Housing: Coed dorms, men's dorms, women's dorms, fraternity/sorority housing, apartments for single students, wellness housing, theme housing. 98% of campus accessible to physically disabled. **Special Academic Facilities/Equipment:** Museum, telecommunications center, science and foreign language labs. All of campus is wired to the computer network. **Computers:** 50% of classrooms, 35% of dorms, 100% of libraries, 100% of dining areas, 80% of student union, 65% of common outdoor areas have wireless network access. Students can register for classes online. Administrative functions (other than registration) can be performed online.

CAMPUS LIFE

Environment: City. **Activities:** Choral groups, concert band, drama/theater, jazz band, literary magazine, music ensembles, musical theater, radio station, student government, student newspaper, symphony orchestra, television station, Campus Ministries, International Student Organization, Model UN 80 registered organizations, 7 honor societies, 4 religious organizations. 9 fraternities, 7 sororities. **Athletics (Intercollegiate):** *Men:* baseball, basketball, cheerleading, cross-country, golf, lacrosse, soccer, swimming, tennis, track/field (outdoor), wrestling. *Women:* basketball, cheerleading, cross-country, field hockey, lacrosse, soccer, softball, swimming, tennis, track/field (outdoor), volleyball. **On-Campus Highlights:** Student Union Spart's Den, TV and Radio Studios, Bookstore, York College Art Galleries, Tyler Run Walking Path.

ADMISSIONS

Freshman Academic Profile: Average high school GPA 3.5. 8% in top 10% of high school class, 35% in top 25% of high school class, 76% in top 50% of high school class. SAT Math middle 50% range 500-600. SAT Critical Reading middle 50% range 490-570. SAT Writing middle 50% range 470-560. ACT middle 50% range 20-24. Minimum web-based TOEFL 72. Minimum paper TOEFL 530. **Basis for Candidate Selection:** *Very important factors considered include:* academic GPA, rigor of secondary school record. *Important factors considered include:* Class rank, standardized test scores, character/personal qualities. *Other factors considered include:* application essay, recommendation(s), alumni/ae relation, extracurricular activities, interview, level of applicant's interest, talent/ability, volunteer work, work experience. **Freshman Admission Requirements:** High school diploma is required and GED is accepted. *Academic units required:* 4 English, 3 mathematics, 3 science, 2 foreign language, 3 social studies. *Academic units recommended:* 4 English, 3 mathematics, 3 science, 2 foreign language, 3 social studies. **Freshman Admission Statistics:** 9,283 applied, 74% admitted, 17% enrolled. **Transfer Admission Requirements:** college transcript(s), Minimum college GPA of 2.0 required. Lowest grade transferable C. **General Admission Information:** Application Fee $30. Notification on a rolling basis, beginning on or about 10/1. Nonfall registration accepted. Admission may be deferred for a maximum of 12 months. Credit and/or placement offered for CEEB Advanced Placement tests.

COSTS AND FINANCIAL AID

Annual tuition $15,350. Room and board $9,580. Required fees $1,660. Average book expense $1,200. **Required Forms and Deadlines:** FAFSA. **Notification of Awards:** Applicants will be notified of awards on a rolling basis beginning 3/1. **Types of Aid:** *Need-based scholarships/grants:* Federal Pell, SEOG, state scholarships/grants, private scholarships, the school's own gift aid. *Loans:* Direct Subsidized Stafford, Direct Unsubsidized Stafford, Direct PLUS, Subsidized Stafford, Unsubsidized Stafford, PLUS, Federal Perkins, Federal Nursing, college/university loans from institutional funds. **Student Employment:** Federal Work-Study Program available. Institutional employment available. Highest amount earned per year from on-campus jobs $12,022. Off-campus job opportunities are good. **Financial Aid Statistics:** 63% freshmen, 70% undergrads receive need-based scholarship or grant aid. 98% freshmen, 68% undergrads receive non-need-based scholarship or grant aid. 85% freshmen, 90% undergrads receive need-based self-help aid. 99% freshmen, 89% undergrads receive any aid. 77% undergrads borrow to pay for school. Average cumulative indebtedness $35,297. **Criteria for awarding institutional aid:** *Non-need-based:* academics, alumni affiliation, music/drama.

YORK UNIVERSITY

Bennett Centre for Student Services, Toronto, ON M3J 1P3
Phone: 416-736-5000 • **Financial Aid Phone:** 416-872-9675
E-mail: intlenq@yorku.ca • **CEEB Code:** 894
Fax: 416-736-5536 • **Website:** www.yorku.ca

This public school was founded in 1959. It has a 550-acre campus.

RATINGS
Admissions Selectivity Rating: 60*   **Fire Safety Rating:** 61   **Green Rating:** 60*

STUDENTS AND FACULTY
Enrollment: 48,589. **Student Body:** 59% female, 41% male, 0% international (170 countries represented).
Retention and Graduation: Faculty: Student/faculty ratio 19:1. 1475 full-time faculty, 45% are women.

ACADEMICS
Degrees: bachelor's, certificate, diploma, doctoral, master's, post-bachelor's certificate. **Majors with Highest Enrollment:** psychology. **Special Study Options:** Accelerated program, distance learning, double major, English as a Second Language (ESL), exchange student program (domestic), honors program, independent study, internships, student-designed major, study abroad, teacher certification program. **Combined Degree Programs:** MBA/LLB,BA/BEd,BSc/BEd,BFA/BEd,MES/LLB,MBA/MFA. **Disability Services:** Special programs offered to physically disabled students include note-taking services, reader services, tape recorders, tutors. **Career Services:** career/job search classes, career assessment, internships, Career services highlights include The York University International Internship Program (YIIP) provides both York undergraduate and graduate students a non-credit opportunity to apply their academic knowledge to an international work environment and enhance their job-related skills in an international and intercultural setting.

FACILITIES
Housing: Coed dorms, special housing for disabled students, men's dorms, special housing for international students, women's dorms, apartments for married students, apartments for single students, theme housing. **Special Academic Facilities/Equipment:** 5 museums with more than 4.4 million items. Observatory with 2 telescopes. Robotics laboratory. 2 professionally staffed art galleries. 6 student-run art exhibition spaces. 3 theatres. 2 cinemas. 1 screening room. Wide-variety professional standard film and video production facilities. **Computers:** Students can register for classes online. Administrative functions (other than registration) can be performed online.

CAMPUS LIFE
Environment: Metropolis. **Activities:** Choral groups, concert band, dance, drama/theater, jazz band, music ensembles, pep band, radio station, student government, student newspaper, symphony orchestra, yearbook, International Student Organization, Model UN 259 registered organizations, 35 religious organizations. **Athletics (Intercollegiate):** *Men:* badminton, basketball, cross-country, fencing, football, ice hockey, soccer, swimming, tennis, track/field (outdoor), volleyball, water polo. *Women:* badminton, basketball, cross-country, fencing, field hockey, ice hockey, rugby, soccer, swimming, tennis, track/field (outdoor), volleyball, water polo. **On-Campus Highlights:** York Lanes: on-campus mall, Tait McKenzie Centre: sports complex, Student Centre: food court/lounge/club, Accolade East: theatre, art gallery, Central Square: Scott library, food court.

ADMISSIONS
Freshman Academic Profile: Minimum web-based TOEFL 83. Minimum paper TOEFL 560. **Basis for Candidate Selection:** *Very important factors considered include:* academic GPA, rigor of secondary school record. *Important factors considered include:* standardized test scores. *Other factors considered include:* Class rank, interview. **Freshman Admission Requirements:** High school diploma is required and GED is not accepted. **Transfer Admission Requirements:** college transcript(s), Minimum college GPA of 2.5 required.

Lowest grade transferable C. **General Admission Information:** Application Fee $90. Regular application deadline 2/1. Notification on a rolling basis, beginning on or about 1/1. Nonfall registration accepted. Admission may be deferred for a maximum of 1 year. Credit offered for CEEB Advanced Placement tests.

COSTS AND FINANCIAL AID
Annual in-state tuition $6,523. Annual out-of-state tuition $6,523. Room and board $7,784. Average book expense $1,000. **Required Forms and Deadlines:** FAFSAS. **Notification of Awards: Types of Aid:** *Need-based scholarships/grants: Loans:* Subsidized Stafford, Unsubsidized Stafford, PLUS, Federal Perkins, Institutionally administered bursaries and international work study positions available on a limited basis. Canadian Student Loans and Provincial Student Loans (for Canadian citizens only). **Student Employment:** Institutional employment available. Off-campus job opportunities are good. **Criteria for awarding institutional aid:** *Non-need-based:* academics, art, music/drama.

SCHOOL SAYS . . .

In this section you'll find hundreds of colleges with extended listings describing admissions, curriculum, internships, and much more. This is your chance to get in-depth information on colleges that interest you. The Princeton Review charges each school a small fee to be listed, and the editorial responsibility is solely that of the college.

ALVERNIA UNIVERSITY

AT A GLANCE

Located in Berks County, Pennsylvania, Alvernia University offers all the best features of an outstanding university—specialized professional programs, experiential learning, internships, and a variety of leadership opportunities—in the personal setting of a college environment. A private Franciscan institution rooted in the Catholic and liberal arts tradition, the core institutional values—service, humility, peacemaking, contemplation, and collegiality—are as relevant today as they were in 1958 when the school was founded. Students appreciate the small class sizes and breadth of academic programs offered, all taught by faculty who are experts in their fields and equally committed to their students' success. Graduates are prepared to achieve their personal dreams and professional success, and to be engaged citizens and lifelong learners. Alvernia has been honored by the Templeton Foundation as one of the top 100 character-building colleges in the nation and a model of excellence in education. Alvernia was also named a Military Friendly School for 2013 by G.I. Jobs magazine. In addition, the University is regularly named to the President's Higher Education Community Service Honor Roll for its commitment to and achievement in community service.

The University's 3,000 total students (1,500 traditional undergraduates) can choose from more than 600 courses and 50 majors and minors in the College of Arts and Sciences and College of Professional Programs. Programs are geared toward real-world learning and preparing students for a rewarding career. Study abroad, internships, and international service trips make learning come alive and allow students to develop practical, valuable skills.

Master's degrees are awarded in occupational therapy, business administration, nursing, community counseling, education, and liberal studies. A Ph.D. program in leadership is also available.

LOCATION AND ENVIRONMENT

Situated on a scenic 121-acre suburban campus, Alvernia is bordered by a park that features hiking trails, a picnic grove, and a nine-hole disk-golf course. When students want to explore big city life, Philadelphia (60 miles), New York, Baltimore, and Washington, D.C. are all just a short drive away.

OFF-CAMPUS OPPORTUNITIES

The Washington Center experience is a popular way for students to expand their education beyond the classroom. Earning college credit while spending a semester in Washington D.C., students serve as interns in a congressional office, government agency, major corporation, newspaper, news network, or nonprofit group, or an agency devoted to legal affairs, international relations, or business and economics.

Study abroad has become increasingly popular. In recent years, Alvernia students have studied in Great Britain, Germany, Italy, Spain, and in the Semester-at-Sea program.

MAJORS AND DEGREES OFFERED

Alvernia offers a breadth of academic programs with a boundary-free learning approach. Bachelor's degrees are awarded in the following majors: accounting, athletic training, behavioral health, biochemistry, biology, biology–medical technology, chemistry, chemistry–medical technology, communication, criminal justice administration, education (concentrations in early childhood, early childhood and special, middle school, and secondary), English, forensic science, general science, healthcare science, history, human resource management, liberal studies, marketing, management, mathematics, nursing, occupational therapy, philosophy, political science, psychology, social work, sport management, theater, and theology.

Pre-professional programs are available in dentistry, law, medicine, and veterinary studies. Alvernia also offers minors and certificate programs.

Since 1967, the Middle States Association of Colleges and Schools has granted Alvernia accreditation. The education program curriculum is approved by the Pennsylvania State Department of Education. The occupational therapy program is fully accredited by the American Occupational Therapy Association. The Bachelor of Science in Nursing has approval by the Pennsylvania State Board of Nursing and is accredited by the Commission on Collegiate Nursing Education. The athletic training program is accredited by the Commission on Accreditation of Athletic Training Education. The social work program is accredited by the Council on Social Work Education. The behavioral health program is certified by the Pennsylvania Certification Board. The business department is accredited by the Accreditation Council for Business Schools and Programs.

ACADEMIC PROGRAMS

Alvernia offers a range of academic programs with a learning approach grounded in the real world. With a foundation in the liberal arts tradition, the curriculum and instruction is designed to help students develop critical thinking skills and explore their own ideas. This approach produces well-rounded individuals who are ready to succeed no matter what path they choose.

Qualified students may participate in the Honors Program, which assists students of outstanding intellectual promise and high motivation that seek a more challenging program and are interested in pursuing future graduate or professional studies. The program encourages students to achieve, often letting them work at their own pace. It facilitates a stimulating exchange of ideas and information between students' varied interests and different disciplines.

In order to earn a bachelor's degree from Alvernia, students must complete a minimum of 123 credits, with 54 credits in the liberal arts. Additional requirements vary by major.

CAMPUS FACILITIES AND EQUIPMENT

Alvernia has recently invested in several additions to campus including a new laser laboratory to support science programs, state-of-the-art learning suites developed for the criminal justice and counseling programs, an educational technology center that supports all majors, and a new theater and recital hall.

On-campus housing includes traditional residence halls, apartments, suites, and town houses. All residential facilities are clean, spacious and equipped with laundry, cable TV, and phones with voice mail.

The recently completed Campus Commons houses a fitness center; dance/aerobics studio; and a campus "living room," complete with a fireplace, for leisure activities, study, and programs.

Alvernia's campus is fully networked. Students have access to the academic information network and the Internet from their residence hall rooms, as well as from other campus locations including classrooms, the library, and labs. All students may connect personal computers through the University's secure system. Network access and Alvernia email accounts are available to all students.

TUITION, ROOM, BOARD AND FEES

For the 2013–14 academic year, tuition is $28,500 and room and board is $10,190 (an approximate cost based on Veronica Hall residence and an all-you-can-eat meal plan).

FINANCIAL AID

Ninety-nine percent of students receive some form of financial aid. Financial aid is offered to students whose personal and family resources are insufficient to meet the full cost of an education. Aid usually comes in the form of scholarships, grants, loans, and work-study arrangements. Depending upon their academic record, incoming first-year students may be eligible for one of three merit-based scholarships: the Presidential Scholarship ($14,000), the Trustee's Scholarship ($12,000), and the Veronica Founder's Scholarship ($10,000). Applicants interested in financial aid should submit the FAFSA as soon as possible after January 1.

STUDENT ORGANIZATIONS AND ACTIVITIES

Alvernia encourages students to take advantage of learning opportunities outside the classroom by participating in any of the more than fifty-five groups including intramural and intercollegiate sports, academic clubs, honor societies, student government, and faith-based environmental and service clubs. Campus organizations offer opportunities to suit the interests of all students, to meet new people, to learn various skills, and to develop leadership abilities.

Athletics are a proud and integral part of the educational mission. Students may participate in intercollegiate, intramural, and club-level programs. Intercollegiate teams compete at the NCAA Division III level. Alvernia is part of the highly competitive Middle Atlantic States Athletic Conference (MAC), and is also a member of the Eastern Collegiate Athletic Conference.

The Office of Student Activities works with the many student organizations to provide a calendar of social, cultural, and other co-curricular activities. The Student Government Association provides an opportunity for leadership through the exercise of personal and group responsibility. All students complete approved community service hours as part of Alvernia's commitment to peace, justice, and the dignity of life. This helps foster devotion to service of others, especially the materially and spiritually disadvantaged of the local and global community.

ADMISSIONS PROCESS

Admission requirements normally include a high school diploma with 16 Carnegie units in the following subjects: English, 4 units; mathematics, 2 units; science, 2 units; social studies, 2 units; and modern languages, 2 units. The remaining units may be made up of academic electives. The University is willing to consider good students whose preparation does not include all of these subjects. Nursing students must fulfill the admission requirements established by the Pennsylvania State Board of Nurse Examiners. The State High School Equivalency Diploma is generally recognized as fulfilling the minimum entrance requirements. Applicants are required to take the SAT; the ACT is also acceptable. Outstanding candidates are considered for entrance to Alvernia at the end of their junior year of high school on the basis of requests made by the candidate and the school. With the approval of their school officials, students may also be admitted to certain courses during their senior year, simultaneously earning credit toward their high school diploma and a college degree.

APPLICATION AND INFORMATION

Many factors are considered for admission, including academic performance, standardized test scores, class rank, extracurricular activities, and community involvement. Application and admission notification is on a rolling basis; however, applicants are encouraged to submit the admission application as early as possible. In addition to their transcripts and SAT or ACT scores, nursing applicants must also submit two letters of recommendation.

Alvernia accepts and/or offers special programs for accelerated high school students, nontraditional students (older than 24), transfer students, students with disabilities, veterans, and international students.

Applicants should submit an application for admission and enclose a nonrefundable $25 processing fee. The application form may be obtained from the Office of Admissions or the University's website at www.alvernia.edu/admissions/undergraduate/apply.html. Applicants should have an official copy of their high school record sent to the Office of Admissions, along with the official results of the SAT or ACT.

Because Alvernia has a rolling admission policy, the Director of Admissions notifies an applicant of acceptance shortly after the necessary credentials are on file and have been reviewed, generally within one month. To reserve a place in the freshman class, all students must make a $300 deposit by May 1. This deposit is credited to the student's account for the first semester but is not refunded if the student fails to attend. Transfer students should have a grade point average of 2.0 or higher on a 4.0 scale and should be aware that only grades of C or better are eligible for credit transfer. Alvernia accepts a maximum of 75 transfer credits; at least 45 credits that are required for graduation must be earned at Alvernia and must satisfy all graduation requirements. A detailed analysis of credits to be transferred is done only after the University has accepted students.

The best way to get to know Alvernia is through a campus visit and tour. Applicants and those considering the school are strongly encouraged to come for an individual campus visit, which will be personalized to match each student's unique interests. Alvernia also hosts information sessions and open houses throughout the year that allow prospective freshmen or transfers to meet current students, talk to admissions and financial aid counselors, and meet faculty and coaches. Overnight and shadow visits are also available.

For more information or to schedule a visit, students should contact:

Director of Admissions

Alvernia University

Reading, Pennsylvania 19607

Phone: 888-ALVERNIA (258-3764, toll-free)

Fax: 610-790-2873

E-mail: admissions@alvernia.edu

Website: http://www.alvernia.edu

http://on.fb.me/Alvernia_University (Facebook)

http://twitter.com/alverniauniv (Twitter)

ARCADIA UNIVERSITY

AT A GLANCE

Founded in 1853, Arcadia is a top-ranked private university in metropolitan Philadelphia offering bachelor's, master's, and doctoral degrees to more than 4,000 students. Undergraduate and graduate students choose from among 80 fields of study and enjoy personal attention in the classroom with an average class size of 15 and a 14:1 student to faculty ratio.

The University's diverse student population represents a cross section of cultural and socioeconomic backgrounds and, at present, Arcadia students come from 46 states and 21 countries. With 77 percent of all full-time undergraduate students residing on campus, Arcadia offers a variety of activities including Division III athletics and more than 90 clubs and organizations.

Arcadia's commitment to students includes opportunities to explore global perspectives, integrate theory with real-world experiences, and benefit from the personal attention that is the hallmark of Arcadia's learning community. Known as the Arcadia Promise, this commitment affirms that students will have a distinctively global, integrative and personal learning experience that prepares them to contribute and prosper in a diverse and dynamic world.

In 2012, the Institute of International Education's Open Doors Report ranked Arcadia #1 in the nation for undergraduate participation in study abroad.

U.S. News & World Report ranks Arcadia University among the top master's universities in the North, as one of the top study abroad programs in the nation.

LOCATION AND ENVIRONMENT

Located in metropolitan Philadelphia, Arcadia features a beautiful rolling campus built around the historic landmark Grey Towers Castle. The University is 12 miles from Center City Philadelphia and only 90 minutes from the Jersey shore and Pennsylvania's Pocono Mountains. Students have access to dozens of museums, galleries, performing arts centers, nightspots, and historic, government, and commercial sites.

OFF-CAMPUS OPPORTUNITIES

Arcadia University, top-ranked in the nation by U.S. News & World Report, offers more than 100 study abroad programs around the world. Students can spend a summer, semester, or full year abroad for approximately the same cost as remaining on the Glenside campus. Through Arcadia's highly innovative Undergraduate Curriculum, students have many pathways to study away while remaining on track to complete their degree in four years.

Arcadia offers two distinct opportunities for students to study abroad during their first year of college. The University's Preview program enables first-year students in good academic standing to earn 2 credits while spending their spring break in China, Cuba, England, Ireland, Mexico, Scotland, Spain, and other countries. The First Year Study Abroad Experience (FYSAE) gives select incoming students the chance to spend their first or second semester studying abroad. Arcadia's FYSAE and Preview programs have been recognized as among the most innovative international programs in the country by the Princeton Review, the American Council on Education, and U.S. News & World Report.

Arcadia offers seven different Majors Abroad Programs (MAPs). Students in these majors spend a year (two semesters) abroad, taking general courses as well as major-related courses at an overseas institution.

Off-campus study in the Philadelphia area includes internships, clinical experiences and fieldwork in most majors.

MAJORS AND DEGREES OFFERED

Arcadia offers Bachelor of Arts degrees in accounting, acting, art and design (art education, art history, ceramics, graphic design, interior design, metals and jewelry, painting, photography, pre-art therapy, printmaking, studio art), biology (allied health, biological basis of behavior, biomedical, conservation, forensics, molecular), business (economics, international economics, international finance, international human resources, international marketing, marketing), chemistry (biochemistry, chemical professions, forensics, health professions), communications (cinema studies, corporate, international cinema, print, video), computer science, computing technology (design, technical), criminal justice, cultural anthropology, digital media/global media, education (art education, elementary and early childhood, middle level, secondary, special education), engineering, English (creative writing, professional writing), environmental studies, fashion studies, forensic science, French studies, global legal studies, global security and emergency management, health administration, history, interdisciplinary science, international business and culture, international peace and conflict resolution, international studies (globalization, development and human rights; modern Mediterranean world; global public health), Italian studies, liberal studies (applied social science for the global citizen, individualized), mathematics (actuarial science), media industries, modern languages, optometry, philosophy, physical therapy, physician assistant, political science (international politics, pre-law and political theory, U.S. politics and policy), pre-dentistry, pre-medicine, pre-nursing, pre-veterinary medicine, psychology (pre-art therapy, human resources), scientific illustration, sociology (human services), sound and music, Spanish, Spanish cultural studies, special education, sport psychology, sports management and theater arts and English. Bachelor of Science degrees are offered in accounting, business administration, chemistry, chemistry and business, computer science, international finance, marketing, and mathematics. Bachelor of Fine Arts degrees are awarded to students majoring in acting or studio arts with concentrations in ceramics, graphic design, interior design, metals and jewelry, painting, photography, and printmaking. Preparation for certification in art education is offered in conjunction with the B.F.A. program, as is preparation for graduate study in art therapy. A five-year program combines the Bachelor of Arts in education with a Master of Education in special education.

Arcadia's physician assistant studies 4+2 program provides a four-year undergraduate degree in a related field, followed by two years of graduate study in the Physician Assistant Program at Arcadia. Arcadia undergraduates who satisfy the prerequisites are assured admission to the program. The University also offers a combined undergraduate and graduate (4+2.5) program leading to the Doctor of Physical Therapy, with assured admission for undergraduates who meet established criteria. The International Peace and Conflict Resolution Program provides a four-year undergraduate degree followed by two years of study in the Master of Arts in international peace and conflict resolution. The forensic science program provides a four-year undergraduate program in a related field followed by two years in the Master of Science in Forensic Science (M.S.F.S.) program.

Arcadia offers a number of accelerated degree programs for high achieving students. A three-year undergraduate degree is offered in Business Administration, Communications, International Business & Culture, International Studies and Psychology. 3+2 programs are offered in Forensic Science and International Peace and Conflict Resolution and a 3+3 program is offered in Physical Therapy.

Arcadia offers several five-year combined programs in education. These include master's degrees in special education, environmental education, literacy education/reading, literacy education/ESL, technology education, and library science.

A dual-degree (3+2) program in engineering is offered in conjunction with Columbia University. An accelerated (3+4) program with Salus University leads to Bachelor of Arts and Doctor of Optometry degrees. A 3+2 program in environmental studies leads to a B.A. in biology and a Master of Arts in Education in environmental education. Pre-professional preparation is offered for dentistry, law, medicine, nursing, optometry, veterinary medicine, and other areas. A 3+3 Pre-Law program leads to a B.A. in political science and a J.D. from Drexel University.

ACADEMIC PROGRAMS

The academic programs at Arcadia University take a personalized approach to education and emphasize critical thinking and collaborative learning, and promote each student's unique intellectual and personal growth. Close interaction with faculty, including the ability to be a part of research both in the United States and abroad, further allows students to apply their classroom learning in real-world settings.

Arcadia operates on a two semester academic calendar.

CAMPUS FACILITIES AND EQUIPMENT

The campus includes historical buildings as well as extensive modern facilities. A prime academic resource on campus is Landman Library, which offers students increased technology and access to resources both on campus and around the globe. Easton Hall academic building features smart classrooms with the latest technology, a cafe and an outdoor patio and waterfall, which make great places for students, faculty, and staff to interact.

Arcadia's Kuch Recreation and Athletic Center features the Alumni Gymnasium, which seats 1,500 and includes basketball and volleyball courts. The Lenox Pool is a six-lane wave-resistant swimming pool with adjacent jacuzzi. The Kuch Center also includes the newly renovated fitness center, an indoor track that overlooks the gym, an aerobics/dance studio, locker rooms, saunas and first aid/training rooms. The University Commons student center, featuring lounges, dining areas, meeting rooms, and more, opened in 2012.

Wireless Internet access is available everywhere on campus and extends to each room in the residence halls. Computer labs-including a Mac lab-are available for student use.

TUITION, ROOM, BOARD, AND FEES

For 2012-2013, undergraduate tuition is $36,150 and room and board charges are $12,560 per year. Annual student fees are $660.

FINANCIAL AID

Arcadia believes that a qualified student should not have to choose their college based on financial factors alone. With this philosophy in mind, Arcadia University helps qualified students find the financial assistance they need to attend college. On average, 99 percent of students at Arcadia receive financial aid, and over 98 percent receive grants and scholarships.

Aid is awarded on the basis of need, as determined by the Free Application for Federal Student Aid (FAFSA) and the Arcadia University Financial Aid Application, and is available in the form of grants, loans, and part-time campus employment or some combination of the three. Scholarships are presented annually to entering first-year and transfer students who have achieved academic distinction or have been recognized for outstanding extracurricular accomplishments. In 2012, Distinguished Scholarships, ranging up to $84,000 over four years, and Achievement Awards, ranging up to $56,000 over four years, recognize academic excellence, leadership, and extracurricular accomplishments. A limited number of full-tuition scholarships are available to the top entering first-year undergraduates in the applicant pool. To receive full consideration for financial aid, students should complete their applications and submit the FAFSA and the Arcadia University Financial Aid Application by March 1.

A financial aid calculator for students considering full-time undergraduate enrollment is available at www.arcadia.edu/calculator. This calculator allows students to estimate their eligibility for federal, state, and Arcadia University financial aid (including merit scholarships).

STUDENT ORGANIZATIONS AND ACTIVITIES

With more than 90 clubs and organizations at Arcadia, it's easy to get involved in campus life. Clubs and organizations give students the opportunity to meet people with similar interests and to develop leadership, organizational and management skills. Options include participating in student government, religious and cultural organizations, musical, academic and media-related groups, community service organizations; and athletics.

Arcadia is a member of the National Collegiate Athletic Association (NCAA) Division III and Middle Atlantic States Collegiate Athletic Corporation (MAC), the largest Division III Conference holding NCAA membership. Student-athletes compete in 17 intercollegiate sports. Men's sports include baseball, basketball, golf, lacrosse, soccer, swimming, and tennis. Women's sports include basketball, field hockey, golf, lacrosse, soccer, softball, swimming, tennis, and volleyball. The equestrian club team is coed and competes in the Intercollegiate Horse Show Association (IHSA). Cheerleading is also offered as club sport, while intramural sports offer other athletic opportunities.

ADMISSIONS PROCESS

Prospective students are evaluated on the basis of their academic preparation, intellectual achievement, and potential for success. The admissions staff evaluates each application individually. The most important factors in an admissions decision are the student's academic transcript, including the quality of his or her secondary school program, GPA, and class rank. Arcadia also looks closely at standardized test scores, recommendations, and the student's involvement in extracurricular or community activities.

Prospective freshmen must submit a secondary school transcript, official scores from the SAT or ACT, a personal essay, and recommendations from a high school teacher and guidance counselor. The Priority Deadline for freshman applicant review for admission and Arcadia's premier scholarship programs is January 15 for the subsequent fall term.

Students are encouraged to follow a strong high school program of at least 19 academic units. Though not required, it is recommended that students visit the campus. Visit opportunities are varied and include large Open Houses, small frequent info sessions each day and on Saturday by appointment, and one-on-one meetings during the application process. Students applying for transfer admission may apply for the fall or spring semester, and must submit college transcripts from each school they have attended. Transfer students with fewer than 30 college credits are also required to submit their high school transcript and standardized test scores.

ASSUMPTION COLLEGE

AT A GLANCE

Established in 1904 by the Augustinians of the Assumption, Assumption College is a coeducational institution known for its classic liberal arts curriculum and strong academic programs in business and professional studies. Our 2,050 undergraduates choose among 40 majors and 45 minors, gaining the depth and breadth of knowledge that is the foundation of lifelong success.

The educational experience is grounded in the rich Catholic intellectual tradition, which cultivates both the intellect and personal values students need to meet the demands of a constantly changing world. Undergraduates and graduate students closely interact with faculty members and staff in a thriving community that forms graduates known for critical intelligence, thoughtful citizenship and compassionate service.

The academic atmosphere is marked by individual attention and the quest for personal excellence. With a student/faculty ratio of just 12:1, Assumption's professors serve as mentors who challenge students to ask questions, find their own answers, and grow — intellectually, socially, and spiritually. Students are encouraged to gain professional experience at internships and to participate in individual research projects. Ninety-five percent of Assumption graduates are employed or in graduate school within six months of graduation.

Located on 185 acres, the Assumption campus is situated in a beautiful, residential neighborhood just minutes from downtown Worcester, Massachusetts. The college also has its own campus in the heart of Rome, offering an educational experience especially developed for sophomores. At Assumption, 90 percent of the undergraduates live on campus and housing is guaranteed for all four years. The campus is lively seven days a week with academic programming, activities sponsored by student clubs and organizations, community service opportunities, campus ministry programs and intercollegiate, intramural, and club sports. The College's state-of-the-art recreation center supports the well-being of all students.

LOCATION AND ENVIRONMENT

Worcester, the second-largest city in New England, is a college town that is home to more than 30,000 students. Assumption has established an array of internship opportunities in virtually every field, and a great network for career placements. Students enjoy a variety of local restaurants, cultural venues and programs, retail and entertainment options, and professional sports teams. In addition, Boston and Providence are only an hour's drive away, and there is regular commuter rail service to Boston.

The Rome campus is close to the metro and walking distance to Vatican City. The newly renovated facility accommodates up to 25 students a semester.

OFF-CAMPUS OPPORTUNITIES

Assumption encourages students to expand their horizons. In addition to the Rome campus, undergraduates can spend a semester or a year studying abroad -- from France and England, to Japan, the Czech Republic and Australia, to name a few locations. Many students also augment their education and hone professional skills through local, regional, national and international internships. Assumption students have worked at diverse organizations around the globe, from the Department of Commerce, Central America Bureau and the Department of State (NAFTA Agreement), to Smith Barney, Fidelity, Morgan Stanley, ABC News, and the Alliance Francaise in Paris.

As a member of the Colleges of Worcester Consortium, an association of 12 higher education institutions in the Worcester region, Assumption students can register for courses at the other colleges and participate in their social and cultural events.

MAJORS AND DEGREES OFFERED

The College offers 40 different majors. Some of the most popular academic programs include English (concentrations in literature or writing and mass communications), history, political science, psychology and the natural sciences -- biology, biotechnology and molecular biology, chemistry and environmental science. Other popular academic programs include education, human services and rehabilitation studies, and business - accounting, international business, management, marketing and organizational communication. Minors are offered in 45 areas.

Pre-professional preparation is available for dentistry, medicine, and law. Assumption has partnered with prestigious colleges and universities. Eligible students can attend Assumption for three years and then go on to law school at Duquesne, Vermont or Western New England Law Schools. There is guaranteed admission to specific graduate programs in the health and natural sciences for eligible students. There is also a 3 + 2 engineering degree with University of Notre Dame. In addition, Assumption College offers graduate degrees in business, special education, school counseling, counseling psychology and rehabilitation counseling.

ACADEMIC PROGRAMS

The College's classic liberal arts curriculum promotes the lively discussion of the books, ideas, people and events that have shaped civilization. Faculty and students explore the rich Catholic intellectual tradition as they seek "truth" and the nature of the world. In all areas of academic study, students learn not only how to ask questions, but also how to find the answers. That is why so many classes at Assumption are discussions, not lectures, and why the faculty assign cooperative projects and frequent writing and hands-on assignments. The curriculum is designed to teach the student how to think, not simply memorize.

Assumption also offers academic programs and courses that help students achieve their full potential. The College's first-year program engages new students with linked courses from two disciplines and coordinated activities that complement classroom experiences. The same 20 students take courses in the fall and spring semesters, enabling them to make important intellectual connections while also getting to know other students. The Honors Program and the Fortin and Gonthier Foundations of Western Civilization Program encourage students to challenge themselves intellectually. Students broaden their world view and their practical experiences through study abroad and internships. Cross-registration through the Colleges of Worcester Consortium enables Assumption students to take classes at Clark, WPI and Holy Cross, among others. Air Force and Army ROTC are also available.

Assumption College follows a traditional two-semester calendar, from late August to mid-May, as well as an optional January intersession. Graduate Studies programs and the Center for Continuing and Career Education also offer two summer sessions for students.

In order to earn their degrees, undergraduates must have 120 credit hours, and a minimum of 38 courses. Assumption liberal arts core curriculum requires all students complete courses in English, philosophy, theology, humanities, history, social sciences, and some select courses in art, music or theater, mathematics, laboratory science, and/or foreign language.

CAMPUS FACILITIES AND EQUIPMENT

Assumption offers first-rate facilities for learning and living and virtually all the campus is wireless. Key facilities include:

The Information Technology Center has computer labs, and classrooms used for collaborative projects, multimedia presentations, foreign language work and leading-edge software and computer systems.

The Richard and Janet Testa Science Center houses the Department of Natural Sciences and features multi-use classrooms with state-of-the-art technology; 10 teaching laboratories, seven laboratories dedicated for faculty and student research; a working greenhouse, conference rooms and student lounge areas.

The Emmanuel d'Alzon Library is an ideal location to study, research and relax. The professional library staff, the collection of 200,000 volumes, 1,125 journal subscriptions and extensive access to local, regional and national library networks and databases are vital resources for students and faculty.

Assumption's Multi-Sport Stadium, a lighted, synthetic turf field with seating for 1,200 is the home of Assumption's intercollegiate field hockey, football, men's and women's lacrosse and men's and women's soccer teams and the College's extensive outdoor intramural programs. The Plourde Recreation Center features a swimming pool, exercise and wellness classes, courts, and a fitness facility that is accessible to all students, faculty and staff.

A variety of housing options are available to accommodate the 90 percent of under-graduates who live on campus. Traditional residence halls, the living/learning center, suites and apartments with full kitchens provide housing options for all four years. All resident students have individual hard-wired and wireless high speed Internet access in their rooms, as well as in the computer labs.

TUITION, ROOM, BOARD AND FEES

For 2012 - 2013, tuition was $33,390; room and board was $10,590 and student fees were $415. The board plan is required for all first-year residential students.

FINANCIAL AID

This past year, Assumption awarded more than $32 million in financial assistance to students. The College offers need-based financial aid, as well as merit-based assistance. All students who apply for admission are considered for merit scholar-ships ranging from $2,500 - $22,000 annually and recipients are chosen based on their academic excellence and demonstrated student leadership. To qualify for need-based financial aid, students must submit the Free Application for Federal Student Aid (FAFSA) by February 1.

STUDENT ORGANIZATIONS AND ACTIVITIES

The 2,050 undergraduates at Assumption come from 25 states and 28 countries. Ninety percent of the students reside on campus and housing is guaranteed for all four years. Numerous social, athletic, recreational and cultural activities are offered on- and off- campus and make Assumption a dynamic place to live.

Assumption College has 60+ clubs and organizations that seek to complement the educational process and offer opportunities for students to develop their interests and talents. Students can participate in academic/professional clubs, arts and entertainment groups, student publications, politics and student government, service projects, special interest groups, or spiritual activities. These groups also give students opportunities to develop their leadership and team-building skills.

The various student clubs and organizations plan a wide range of events. This includes many large-scale programs, such as Family Weekend, Siblings Weekend, Welcome Week, Midnight Madness and the Spring Concert. Other more frequent events include comedians, coffeehouses, films, lectures, off-campus trips, and many special events.

Assumption offers 23 intercollegiate teams, as well as 8 club and 21 intramural sports. The College is a charter member of the Northeast-10 Conference and competes as an NCAA Division II institution. The intercollegiate sports for men include: baseball, basketball, cross country, football, golf, hockey, lacrosse, soccer, tennis and track & field (indoor and outdoor). Women's sports include: basketball, cross country, field hockey, lacrosse, rowing, soccer, softball, swimming, tennis, track & field (indoor and outdoor) and volleyball.

ADMISSIONS PROCESS

Assumption College admits students who demonstrate an active intellect and self-motivation and who have compiled a solid academic record and completed all prescribed high school requirements.

The College encourages prospective students to schedule a campus visit prior to applying for admission. During the summer months, high school students are en-couraged to attend group information sessions, tours and interviews Monday-Friday. In the fall semester, prospective students may attend group information sessions, including some Saturdays, or schedule a campus visit during the week.

APPLICATION AND INFORMATION

To apply, students are required to submit the Common Application, a $50 application fee, official high school transcripts, and a letter of recommendation. Assumption is test-score optional, so SAT or ACT scores are not required. Applications, including all supporting documents and recommendations, must be received in the Office of Admissions by February 15. Students who want to be considered for Early Action must apply by November 1 and for Early Action II by December 15.

For more information, please contact:

Assumption College

Office of Admissions

500 Salisbury Street

Worcester, MA 01609

Telephone: 866-477-7776 (toll free) or 508-767-7285

Web: www.assumption.edu

E-mail: admiss@assumption.edu

BABSON COLLEGE

AT A GLANCE

Babson College is the educator, convener, and thought leader for Entrepreneurship of All Kinds™. As the only school to teach Entrepreneurial Thought and Action®, Babson shapes the leaders our world needs most: those with strong functional knowledge and the skills and vision to navigate change, accommodate ambiguity, surmount complexity, and motivate teams in a common purpose. Every day, Babson students, faculty, alumni, and staff address real-world business and societal problems, creating sustainable economic and social value in today's fast-paced global economy.

LOCATION AND ENVIRONMENT

This 370-acre suburban campus is located in Wellesley, Massachusetts. This is the ideal charming New England town, a classic setting for a college environment. A mere 14 miles outside of Boston, students here are sure to experience the best of both worlds: the quaintness of small town life bordering the cultural and social excitement of the big city. Although Boston is accessible by means of public transportation, approximately half of all students have cars.

MAJORS AND DEGREES OFFERED

At Babson College, concentrations are an optional way for you to organize your advanced studies, and certify that your focus of study is on your final transcript. Students may choose to plan their course of study around one of twenty-six optional concentrations in both business and liberal arts disciplines.

ACADEMIC PROGRAMS

Our academic program with an emphasis on hands-on experiential learning is uniquely designed for students who want to study business and learn about the world around them. Babson shapes the leaders our world needs most: those who can envision and navigate change, understand global perspectives, and motivate teams in a common purpose to create economic and social value. Our focus on Entrepreneurial Thought and Action® enables students to discover their strengths, pursue their passions, and create their own path to success. Babson offers additional academic programs including field-based learning programs, a first-year seminar, independent study, an honors program, a student-managed endowment fund and much more. Also, all students develop, launch, manage and liquidate their own businesses with money loaned by Babson during their first year as part of Foundations of Management and Entrepreneurship. Students also have the opportunity to work as consultants to external organizations as part of the Management Consulting Field Experience.

CAMPUS FACILITIES AND EQUIPMENT

Babson's contemporary facilities provide students with access to dynamic academic and social resources. Students frequent the Donald W. Reynolds Campus Center, the Richard W. Sorenson Family Visual Arts Center, the Richard W. Sorenson Center for the Arts, the Webster Athletic Center, the Glavin Family Chapel, and the Arthur M. Blank Center for Entrepreneurship. These centers offer students a state-of-the-art campus experience.

Horn Library houses an extensive business collection of print, media, and computerized information resources. Students have campus-wide access to newspapers, journals, investment analyst reports, corporate records, directories, and international information. They also benefit from numerous electronic research and news services that supplement a selection of the best business and liberal arts books, newspapers, journals, CD-ROMs, audiocassettes, videocassettes, and videodiscs. It also holds the Sir Isaac Newton Collection, archives, and a museum. The school is a member of a library consortium, which allows students to borrow books from other libraries.

The Stephen D. Cutler Center for Investments and Finance, a joint venture between the Finance Division and Horn Library, exemplifies Babson College's innovative, real-world approach to business education and applied research. It is the hub for investment education programs, finance-related student organizations and a forum for thought leadership where industry practitioners, faculty and students collaborate, exchange ideas and learn from one another. The Center's programs and resources enhance understanding of the importance of investments and finance in funding the growth engines of the global economy.

Wireless access is available everywhere on campus. Every incoming Babson undergraduate student receives a leased laptop computer with integrated Wi-Fi wireless. After their sophomore year, Babson students return their laptops and receive brand new ones, which are then returned at the end of their senior year. When students graduate, they have the option to purchase a new one at Babson's discounted rate. Babson provides microcomputer accounts for student use complete with Internet access and email.

FINANCIAL AID

Babson is committed to educating students from diverse backgrounds, and we will do all we can to make it financially possible for any student to attend Babson. In 2013-2014, Babson is awarding $30 million from its own funds to undergraduate students. Federal and state grants, loans, and work-study are awarded based on financial need. Students who wish to apply for financial aid should submit the CSS/Financial Aid PROFILE and FAFSA by February 15.

STUDENT ORGANIZATIONS AND ACTIVITIES

Babson offers students an extensive variety of student activities. These extracurriculars include 22 NCAA Division III (11 men's and 11 women's) intercollegiate athletic teams. Intramural sports are also popular student activities. More than 95 student-run clubs, organizations, and publishing opportunities are available across every interest spectrum. Some of these activities include: dance groups, theater, literary magazine, cultural groups, music ensembles, radio station, student government, student news source, the yearbook, and much, much more. The school also has four fraternities and three sororities. Approximately 15 percent of students are involved in Greek life.

ADMISSIONS PROCESS

Babson College bases its acceptance of students on both academic and nonacademic factors. The academic factors include high school record, recommendations, standardized test scores, and essays. The nonacademic factors include extracurricular activities, shown leadership, character/personal qualities, volunteer work, work experience, creativity and enthusiasm and a willingness to contribute to the Babson community in meaningful ways. Graduation from secondary school is required for admission. The most competitive students have taken approximately 5 solid academic courses per year at the highest available level (Honors, Advanced Placement or International Baccalaureate). The SAT I or ACT with writing is required for admission. The TOEFL or IELTS is required for students who are nonnative English speakers.

APPLICATION AND INFORMATION

Babson offers several application programs. Students may apply Early Decision (binding process), Early Action or Regular Decision. The deadline for Early Decision and Early Action is November 1. The Regular Decision Deadline is January 1. Transfer students may apply for September entrance by April 1 and for January entrance by November 1.

BARNARD COLLEGE

AT A GLANCE

Founded in 1889, Barnard College was one of the first colleges to offer young women the chance to earn a college degree. Today, Barnard College remains committed to the education of over 2,390 undergraduate women from more than 40 countries and nearly 50 states. Partnered with Columbia University since 1900, under an agreement unique in the world of higher education, Barnard is an independent college for women, maintaining its own Board of Trustees, campus, curriculum, faculty, staff, and admissions process. Barnard also operates from its own endowment, while Columbia University confers degrees to Barnard students. The fully residential campus features countless, independent resources and facilities; students at Barnard also have academic and extra-curricular access to the Columbia campus across the street, including cross-registration for courses, and benefit from both an all women and a coeducational experience. Additionally, Barnard women complete alongside Columbia students on 16 NCAA Division I athletic teams as part of the Ivy League conference. The small, personal, and close-knit character of Barnard is augmented by the resources of a large research university.

LOCATION AND ENVIRONMENT

Barnard is located in New York City and offers students endless cultural, academic, and professional opportunities. New York is an extension of our classrooms and students make use of its resources for both study and exploration. Barnard's Office of Career Development lists over 2,500 student internships throughout New York City each year and classes often incorporate visits to museums, tours of historic neighborhoods, or participation in civic engagement projects. Barnard's location in the neighborhood of Morningside Heights offers a retreat from the fast pace of Mid-town Manhattan and is often referred to as an educational Mecca with students, staff and faculty from a number of institutions of higher education all calling the Heights "home." Institutions neighboring the Barnard campus, in addition to Columbia University, include the Manhattan School of Music, Teachers College, Bank Street College of Education, Union Theological Seminary, and the Jewish Theological Seminary. New York City is the ultimate college town, drawing more than 500,000 college students each year.

OFF-CAMPUS OPPORTUNITIES

There are numerous opportunities for Barnard students to explore academics beyond the Barnard gates. Barnard students have full access to Columbia resources including more than 30 libraries and collections, research facilities, and courses which complement the Barnard curriculum, even at a graduate or professional level. The Jewish Theological Seminary allows Barnard students to enroll in courses for credit and the Juilliard School and the Manhattan School of Music allow highly qualified Barnard musicians to enroll in a selective lesson exchange program.

Barnard students also explore academics beyond both New York and the United States through over 150 study-abroad programs in more than 50 countries including, but not limited to: Argentina, Australia, China, Costa Rica, Czech Republic, Egypt, Greece, Ireland, Israel, Kenya, Panama, Peru, Russia, Scotland, and Tibet. Programs focus on cultural immersion, advanced or independent study, and field-based or experiential learning and may include a single semester or a full year of study. Many students also enroll in programs in Beijing, Kyoto, Berlin, or Paris via our partnership with Columbia University. Other Barnard students enroll in a variety of programs offered through other universities, consortiums, and international organizations. Atlanta's Spelman College and Washington, D.C.'s Howard University offer domestic exchange programs with Barnard.

MAJORS AND DEGREES OFFERED

Barnard offers the bachelor of arts (BA) degree, and students choose from more than 50 majors, including Africana studies, American studies, ancient studies, anthropology, architecture, art history (including visual arts), Asian and Middle Eastern cultures, biochemistry, biological studies, chemistry, classics (Greek and Latin), comparative literature, computer science, dance, economics, education, English (including creative writing), environmental science and policy, European studies, film studies, French, German, history, human rights studies, Italian, Jewish studies, mathematics, Medieval and Renaissance studies, music, neuroscience and behavior, philosophy, physics and astronomy, political science (including international politics), psychology, religion, Slavic studies, sociology, Spanish and Latin American cultures, statistics, theatre, urban studies, and women's studies. With this foundation in the liberal arts and sciences, Barnard women succeed in a variety of career fields, including business, communications, health and public service, and are well prepared for global and diverse settings.

Opportunities for double and joint degrees are also available at Barnard in conjunction with other schools within Columbia University. One option is the five-year AB/MIA or AB/MPA program where Barnard students also earn their masters from Columbia's School of International and Public Affairs. Barnard may also nominate juniors with outstanding records for early admission to Columbia Law School under the Accelerated Program in Interdisciplinary Legal Education and may recommend candidates for an accelerated degree with Columbia's School of Oral and Dental Surgery. Students interested in both the liberal arts and engineering may earn the AB/BS degrees in a five-year (3-2) program with Columbia's Fu Foundation School of Engineering and Applied Science. Advanced music students can apply and audition for the Juilliard School's five-year (3-2) program, earning their AB from Barnard and the MM degree from Julliard. Finally, students may earn an AB from Barnard and a BA from the nearby Jewish Theological Seminary's List College, if admitted to the double degree program.

ACADEMIC PROGRAMS

A Barnard education seeks to provide women with the tools and techniques necessary to think critically and act effectively in the world today. Barnard requires students to complete 122 points of course work (including First-Year English, First-Year Seminar, and two semesters of physical education) in addition to a major for the Bachelor of Arts (AB) degree. Barnard believes that a successful liberal arts education revolves around central "ways of knowing" the world. This philosophy forms the basis of the general education requirements within Nine Ways of Knowing, organized in the following categories: ethics and value, social analysis, cultures in comparison, language, laboratory science, historical studies, literature, visual and performing arts, and quantitative reasoning. To allow for flexibility within this framework, a student chooses among the designated courses, typically 40-100 choices in each area, that fulfill the nine requirements. Thus, each student will shape her own academic program by electing a combination of wide-ranging introductory courses and more specialized upper level courses.

The College has a long-standing commitment to prepare students sufficiently in a subject so that they may undertake a semester- or year-long thesis or project, usually during the senior year, on a topic related to their major. Students are encouraged to explore internships in their field, thereby acquiring information and experience that complement what is learned through formal study. A student may major in two fields by satisfying all the major requirements prescribed by each department.

CAMPUS FACILITIES AND EQUIPMENT

Barnard's Campus covers four acres of prime New York real estate stretching from 116th to 120th Street along Broadway with 15 buildings comprising Barnard's cozy campus. Milbank Hall, a nationally registered historic landmark, contains offices, classrooms, a cutting-edge greenhouse, and the Minor Latham Playhouse. Fourteen-story Altschul Hall houses state-of-the-art science research facilities and equipment, along with classrooms, offices, and laboratories. A full gymnasium is located on the first floor of Barnard Hall, facing the college's main entrance. Barnard Hall is also the home of the Barnard Center for Research on Women in addition to the Athena Center for Leadership Studies. Brooks, Reid, and Sulzberger Halls along with Hewitt, make up the Quad, the residence life complex serving first-year students situated at the southern end of campus. Campus housing is guaranteed to continuously enrolled first-years for four years and housing options include opportunities for coeducational living. The heart of student life is the Diana Center, the student center which opened January of 2010, where students have access to many amenities which augment academic life, including an art gallery, black box theatre, event and dining spaces, art and architecture studios, music practice rooms, and more. Finally, Wollman Library offers three floors of study space and along with Columbia's libraries, with more than 10 million volumes, over 100,000 current journals and serials, and an extensive collection of electronic resources, manuscripts, rare books, microforms, and other non-print formats, provides access to one of the top five academic library systems in the nation

TUITION, ROOM, BOARD AND FEES

Tuition and fees for 2013-14 are $44,790. Room and board is an additional $14,210.

FINANCIAL AID

Financial aid at Barnard is strictly need-based. A student's need is determined using criteria established by both the federal government and Barnard's institutional analysis. The financial aid awarded by Barnard supplements a family's own financial resources, while Barnard meets 100 percent of the remaining demonstrated need. Financial aid awards typically consist of grants, work study jobs, and student loans. Students who are awarded Barnard College grants should expect grants throughout their four years at Barnard, providing the students' families maintain their level of need and the students maintain their academic standing. 53% of first-year students received some form of financial aid during the 2012-2013 school year and the average total grant (including state and federal funds) was $35,320. Need plays no role in the Barnard admissions process for US citizens and permanent residents; admission for first-year students is need-blind, and admissibility is evaluated solely on merit.

STUDENT ORGANIZATIONS AND ACTIVITIES

The Barnard College community offers numerous activities and opportunities to an active student body. The Office of Student Life engages each student and promotes active and involved citizenship through leadership development, multicultural education, and a foundation in social justice. More than 80 Barnard student-run organizations are available to Barnard students, a sampling include: Asian American Alliance, Barnard Bulletin, Gospel Choir, Community Impact, Late Nite Theatre, Model United Nations, Mujeres, McIntosh Activities Council, Orchesis Dance Troupe, Russian Cultural Association, Students Against Silence, and Women's International Business Council. Barnard and Columbia students take part in organizations and activities on both campuses; and Barnard women take leadership roles in many of several hundred additional Columbia-sponsored clubs. Women's intercollegiate, intramural, and club athletics are also popular. Barnard's varsity athletes compete at the NCAA Division I level alongside their Columbia peers as part of the Ivy League conference through the Barnard/Columbia Athletic Consortium. The 16 intercollegiate teams include archery, basketball, crew, cross-country, fencing, field hockey, golf, indoor and outdoor track and field, lacrosse, soccer, softball, squash, swimming and diving, tennis, and volleyball. Intramural and club sports include cycling, equestrian, ice hockey, martial arts, rugby, and sailing.

ADMISSIONS PROCESS

High school transcripts, letters of recommendation, standardized test scores, personal attributes and achievements all play a role in Barnard's highly selective and holistic admissions process. The College seeks women with strong academic records who exhibit the capacity and desire to grow intellectually and personally. While there is not a set group of criteria that an applicant must match, the successful applicant will have completed a rigorous college preparatory program or its equivalent, with a recommended 4 years of English, 3 or more years of math, 3 or more years of a foreign language, 3 or more years of laboratory science, and 3 or more years of history at minimum. Every applicant is evaluated on both the qualities that she personally espouses and her potential for success at Barnard. Applicants must submit the following test scores: either the ACT with writing, or the SAT Reasoning Test and two SAT Subject Tests. Students for whom English is not their primary language of instruction or who have been in the United States for less than 4 years must submit results from the TOEFL or IELTS exams. Interviews, available only for first-year applicants, are optional.

BECKER COLLEGE

AT A GLANCE

Becker College has been named one of the best institutions for undergraduate education by The Princeton Review. Becker is a private, independent, co-educational four-year institution with undergraduate (associate's and bachelor's) degrees, and adult education degrees (associate's and bachelor's) and certificate programs. The College offers some of the country's best educational experiences in programs such as nursing, veterinary studies, and video game design.

The Becker College nursing program ranks as one of the best in Massachusetts. In May 2011, 99 percent of graduates passed the National Licensure Examination.

Becker College is #1in New England and among the top-15 producers nationally among four-year private institutions in awarding undergraduate animal studies degrees in 2011-2012. Nationally, Becker is one of the 10 largest producers of undergraduate veterinary technology degrees among four-year private institutions, and one of only two private colleges in New England to offer AVMA-accredited undergraduate programs in veterinary technology.

The Princeton Review has named Becker among the top 10 colleges in the U.S. and Canada for video game design for three consecutive years.

Becker is home of the Massachusetts Digital Games Institute (MassDiGI), a first-in-the-nation, statewide center that creates opportunities for industry-leading game design companies to work with faculty and students on game development projects and curriculum enhancements, which ensure Becker graduates have the skills for success upon graduation.

The Becker College student experience focuses on preparation for global citizenship, supporting the belief that students must be prepared to thrive in a world that is increasingly more global. The "three pillars" of global citizenship—academic excellence, social responsibility, and creative expression—provide the contextual framework for student life programming. These experiences include academic study, community service and leadership experiences, internships, personal connections, and activities that make each student's education an engaging and enriching experience. Through these experiences, students are encouraged not only to transform themselves into educated people, but also to consider how they can make a positive impact on others in ways that transform lives and communities.

Students thrive on campuses that foster the College's core values of excellence, accountability, community and diversity, social responsibility, integrity, and creative expression. There is a connectedness between students and faculty that enhances learning and student success and provides each student with personal attention and a close-knit, family atmosphere.

A nurturing environment for every student

CAREER-FOCUSED FOUR-YEAR ACADEMIC PROGRAMS

Outstanding record for job placement

Choice of two campuses (urban/rural)

Numerous community service/volunteer opportunities

A wide range of student clubs and organizations

Athletics and intramural programs

Innovative Learning Experience

Our professors care about the success of each student and are committed to providing one-on-one attention and support. Full-time and adjunct professors bring extensive academic, career, and life experience to the classroom. Their focus is on helping students excel, both inside the classroom and beyond.

Our academic programs combine rigorous course work and experiential learning into an innovative curriculum that prepares graduates for career success.

Courses in each major have been designed to give students the required knowledge base and hands-on practical experience to rise to the top of their chosen professions.

Students engage in outreach programs, internships, externships, practica, clinical field work, preceptorships, and other career-developing opportunities, to develop the knowledge and skills needed for graduate school or entry into careers.

The Massachusetts Digital Games Institute (MassDiGI), which is housed at Becker College, improves the talent pipeline between higher education and the digital games industry through its Reverse Sabbatical Program, Virtual Production Laboratory, and Summer Innovation Program—all of which were created to allow Becker College computer game design students and others from across the country to develop new game content under the direction of industry professionals.

LOCATION AND ENVIRONMENT

Becker College traces its history to 1784—one of the nation's top-25 oldest institutions of higher learning—with a founding charter signed by John Hancock and Samuel Adams. The College evolved from the union of two Massachusetts educational institutions: Leicester Academy—the third preparatory school in Massachusetts, the first in central Massachusetts, and the first in the Commonwealth to accept female students—and Becker's Business School, a Worcester school that offered career preparation for men and women. Today more than 2,000 students from across the nation and around the world live and learn on these two distinctively New England campuses, located six miles apart, in the heart of Massachusetts.

The Worcester campus is situated in the Elm Park neighborhood of Worcester—New England's second largest urban center, with a population of approximately 180,000. With its quiet tree-lined streets and historic Victorian-style homes, the Worcester Campus is only a short walk from the downtown business district. The greater Worcester area is home to more than 30,000 students at 13 colleges.

The Leicester Campus is situated in a quintessential New England country town, adjacent to an historic village green. This rural setting provides space for Becker's Division III athletic team facilities and for the animal studies programs. The College provides students with a free shuttle service, which enables them to move easily between campuses.

Becker College is less than an hour drive from Boston, three hours from New York City, and 70 miles or less from three major international airports.

OFF-CAMPUS OPPORTUNITIES

Worcester offers a wide array of social, cultural, and recreational opportunities, including entertainment and sports arenas, semi-professional sports teams—the Worcester Sharks (ice hockey) and Worcester Tornadoes (baseball)—first-class museums, the Hanover Theatre, outdoor recreation areas, and a wide range of shopping and dining options. Because we are a member of the Colleges of Worcester Consortium, made up of 12 other Worcester-area colleges, our students have access to each member's facilities, events, and activities.

Becker College offers study abroad options through its partnerships with the Center for International Studies (CIS) and Semester at Sea.

MAJORS AND DEGREES OFFERED

Becker College offers some of the country's leading programs in animal studies, business, criminal justice and legal studies, design, education and psychology, liberal arts and biology, nursing, and exercise science.

All majors listed below are bachelor's degree programs except where associate's degree is indicated.

Animal Studies: Animal care (associate's degree), Equine studies, Laboratory animal management, Pre-veterinary, Veterinary science/clinical medicine and laboratory animal medicine, Veterinary technology (associate's degree); Business: Business administration; Computer information systems; Equine management; Management; Marketing; Sports management; Criminal Justice and Legal Studies: Criminal justice; Forensic science/crime scene processing concentration; Design: Communications design; Graphic design; Interactive Media Design: Game Design; Interactive Media Design: Game Development and Programming; Education and Psychology: Early childhood education; Elementary education (B.A. in liberal arts); Forensic psychology; Psychology; Psychology/ applied behavior analysis (ABA); Liberal Arts and Biology: Biology; Liberal arts; Nursing and Exercise Science: Exercise science (health and fitness); Nursing (associate's degree); Nursing (4-year BSN); Nursing RN-BSN; Minors: Addictions counseling (LADC-II); American studies; Creative Writing; English; Equine studies; Exercise science; Film and literature; Health and fitness; Psychology.

ACADEMIC PROGRAMS

With a student-to-faculty ratio of 16 to 1, Becker's intimacy fosters a connectedness between students and faculty that enhances learning and student success.

The academic programs at Becker College prepare students for a wide range of future professional opportunities while providing the necessary competencies to lead in a global society. Courses in each major have been designed to impart the required knowledge base and hands-on practical experience for students to rise to the top of their chosen professions. Our strong liberal arts program provides balanced exposure to major achievements in the arts, sciences, humanities, and social sciences. Core curriculum is designed so students develop an appreciation of the philosophical, ethical, and aesthetic issues that have evolved throughout human history.

In addition to our core curriculum programs, Becker College provides students with numerous opportunities to participate in internships and practical experiences in rural, suburban, and inner-city settings. State-of-the-art teaching facilities include the nursing program's simulation laboratory and the College's on-campus animal clinic. Upon graduation, our students are ready to step into career-targeted jobs and make valuable contributions from day one.

CAMPUS FACILITIES AND EQUIPMENT

A variety of housing options are available for those students who choose to live on campus. The Worcester Campus offers housing in historic homes, and the Leicester Campus offers both historic homes and contemporary residences. Both campuses offer all-female, all-male, co-ed, over 21, and all-freshman living spaces. In addition, there is a Living and Learning community. Each campus has its own dining hall, library, campus center, and fitness facility.

Students in the equine programs are involved in the daily maintenance and care of horses at the Becker College Equestrian Center, located on a beautiful expansive site in Paxton. The center contains an indoor and outdoor riding arena, indoor and outdoor pens, round pen, and pastures and turnout areas. The Becker College Lenfest Animal Health Center houses the College's veterinary clinic, which sees more than 1,000 patients annually. The center also includes teaching facilities for laboratory animals, grooming, dog obedience, and laboratories for animal care and veterinary technology students.

TUITION, ROOM, BOARD, AND FEES

The current tuition for the year 2013-2014 is $30,000. Room and board for the year is $11,500.

FINANCIAL AID

Financial aid is available for all eligible students through federal, state, and Becker College programs.

STUDENT ORGANIZATIONS AND ACTIVITIES

The Becker College community is an active one. Opportunities abound for on- and off-campus involvement to enrich each student's learning and personal development. Regardless of personal interests, it's easy to be active, social, and connected with the pulse of campus life.

The Student Government Association (SGA) serves as the official voice of all Becker College students. The SGA protects and promotes the best interests and rights of the student body, serves as the liaison between the students and the College administration, and works with student groups to enhance the overall student experience.

The intramural program promotes fun and healthy competition, with programs geared to student interest. Numerous clubs and organizations promote indoor and outdoor activities, cultural interests, the arts, and more. In addition, students are involved in community service and volunteer activities with such organizations as the American Red Cross, the Animal Rescue League, the United Way, schools, and others, which give students ample opportunities to be active and passionate about helping others.

Close to 75 percent of Becker students participate in varsity or intramural sports. More than one-third of student-athletes are annually recognized for achieving a GPA of 3.0 or higher. Becker competes at the NCAA Division III level and is a member of the following:

Eastern Collegiate Athletic Conference-Northeast (men's ice hockey)

New England Collegiate Conference (baseball, softball, men's tennis, women's tennis, men's basketball, women's basketball, field hockey, men's soccer, women's soccer, golf, volleyball)

Great Northeast Athletic Conference (men's lacrosse)

New England Women's Lacrosse Alliance (women's lacrosse)

Eastern Collegiate Football Conference (football)

Intercollegiate Horse Show Association (equestrian)

Becker College offers the following sports. Men's Varsity Sports: baseball, ice hockey, basketball, lacrosse, football, soccer, golf, tennis. Women's Varsity Sports: basketball, softball, field hockey, tennis, Lacrosse, volleyball, soccer. Co-Ed Sports: cheerleading, equestrian.

APPLICATION AND INFORMATION

To learn more about Becker College call 877.523.2537, email admissions@becker.edu, or visit www.becker.edu.

Becker College

61 Sever Street

Worcester, MA 01609

BELMONT UNIVERSITY

AT A GLANCE

Belmont University sits on 75 historic acres in the heart of Nashville, Tennessee, a thriving metropolis known worldwide as Music City USA. Belmont University is among the fastest growing Christian universities in the nation with approximately 6,700 students hailing from every state and 25 countries. Belmont University is accredited by the Commission on Colleges of the Southern Association of Colleges and Schools to award baccalaureate, master's, and doctoral degrees. Belmont offers over 75 undergraduate majors, 20 graduate master's and six doctoral programs through its eight colleges and one school: Arts & Sciences, Business Administration, Mike Curb College of Entertainment and Music Business, Gordon E. Inman College of Health Sciences & Nursing, Law, Pharmacy, Religion, University College, and Visual & Performing Arts.

ACADEMICS

Intent on being a leader among teaching universities, Belmont brings together the best of liberal arts and professional education in a Christian community of learning and service. Belmont was ranked seventh on the U.S. News & World Report listing of "Best Universities" in the South in the master's category for the 2013 edition of America's Best Colleges, making Belmont the highest ranked university in Tennessee in this category. In addition, Belmont was named a most cited "School to Watch," a high honor that indicates the strength of the university's reputation and innovations.

Both Rolling Stone and Time magazines have hailed Belmont's Mike Curb College of Entertainment & Music Business as one of the best music business programs in the country. The Jack C. Massey Graduate School of Business has been named the best MBA program in the region, while Belmont's business administration and accounting programs have been accredited by AACSB International, the premier accrediting agency in that arena. Moreover, for the second year in a row, Belmont University's undergraduate School of Business achieved a Top 100 national ranking in BusinessWeek's annual report on the "The Best Undergrad B-Schools" in the U.S. Belmont's Entrepreneurship major was even named National Model Undergraduate Program of the Year by the United States Association of Small Business and Entrepreneurship. Belmont's Enactus team won the 2012 National Championship and captured the World Cup for the United States.

Located in the heart of Music City USA, one of Belmont's consistent success stories is its world-renowned music and music business programs, including songwriting. Several big names in the music industry started their careers at Belmont including "American Idol" finalist Melinda Doolittle, Christian recording artists Ginny Owens and Steven Curtis Chapman, and country stars Trisha Yearwood, Lee Ann Womack, Brad Paisley and Josh Turner. The annual "Christmas at Belmont" concert showcases performing ensembles from many different genres and has been broadcast nationwide on PBS for several years.

Students who have passions outside of the music industry also have a home at Belmont. From international business and accounting to education, sport administration, nursing, journalism and the humanities, Belmont provides avenues of learning for almost any interest. Recent program additions include interdisciplinary studies in Social Entrepreneurship and Asian Studies as well as a doctoral degree in Pharmacy, a program that is already gaining acclaim for its four-pillared approach to educating pharmacists for an ever-evolving health care environment. Belmont's also received attention for its innovative, year-long programming around the university's hosting of the 2008 Town Hall Presidential Debate. "

Belmont faculty members display a consistent commitment to excellence as well. Multiple professors have been awarded Fulbright awards, including a nursing professor who spent a year recently in Uganda as a guest lecturer while conducting research on how standards of nursing are adapted to austere conditions. Also, five Belmont professors from four different schools--Finance, Psychology, Spanish and Philosophy--have been chosen as Tennessee Professor of the Year by CASE/Carnegie Foundation since 2000.

Belmont's boundaries extend beyond the Nashville campus through its Cool Springs campus and organized programs such as the Washington Center program and music business' Belmont West in Los Angeles and Belmont East in New York City. Study-abroad programs place students in China, Costa Rica, Great Britain, France, Germany, Italy, Russia, South Africa and Spain, among other foreign nations. Also, Belmont serves as a regional site for the East-West Center for the Development of Asian Studies and is the host institution for the Cooperative Center for Study Abroad, a higher education consortium of 24 colleges and universities.

CAMPUS FACILITIES AND EQUIPMENT

Recent construction includes the new home to the College of Law, the Baskin Center, which opened in 2012, as well the two new residence halls in 2012 and 2013, respectively. Another new residence hall is under construction. The McAfee Concert Hall opened in 2012, and a new 160,000+ square feet academic building – home to the arts and sciences as well as religion – will open in 2014. Ground was broken in 2013 on a new dining center and academic facility that will open in 2015, including 1,000 additional underground parking spaces.

Previously, the Gordon E. Inman Center opened in 2006, providing a state-of-the-art $22.5 million facility that houses Belmont's nursing, social work, occupational therapy and physical therapy programs and also serves as the temporary home of the School of Pharmacy. The School of Nursing was recognized by Laerdal Medical Corporation as a Center of Educational Excellence in part due to the advanced training the school's multiple simulation models offer to its students. In fall 2010, the university opened a second Health Sciences building adjacent to the first. The $30 million structure is a model, 21st century academic facility, providing a venue where students and faculty resources can intersect to help meet the needs of the community and the world. The 90,000-square-foot building emphasizes integrated, "hands-on" experiential learning components through medical simulation spaces and a licensed, state-of-the-art pharmacy.

Belmont's intimate theater complex opened in 2007, featuring the 350-seat Bill and Carole Troutt proscenium theater, a Black Box theater and scene shop. The complex now plays host to numerous student productions as well as collaborative efforts with local professional ensembles, including the Nashville Children's Theatre, Actors Bridge Ensemble, Nashville Shakespeare Festival and the Nashville Ballet. In 2008, the university opened Maple Hall, a residence facility to accommodate 190 freshmen students. Opened in 2010 is a new 103,000 square foot residence hall that provides additional housing for 400 freshmen, creating a unique living-learning community for first-year students in the heart of campus.

In addition to celebrating academic excellence and phenomenal growth, Belmont boasts 17 intercollegiate sports teams. The Belmont Bruins men's basketball team won the Ohio Valley Conference Championship in 2013 and made its sixth appearance in the NCAA National Tournament. Both Belmont cross country teams and the volleyball team have earned Conference titles, and the cross country teams have earned multiple conference titles. Belmont student-athletes excel in the classroom, too, as Belmont has won the Conference All-Academic Trophy multiple years.

A Christian Community of Learning and Service

Belmont is a student-focused, Christian community of learning and service where students hear from their first visit to campus until the day they graduate that they are created for a purpose in life. The Belmont faculty and staff dedicate themselves to preparing and empowering students to find their passion and use it to change the world. The university seeks to show every student how the love of Christ can compel them to lead lives of disciplined intelligence, compassion, courage and faith.

In fact, Belmont students, faculty and staff are consistently challenged to look at the hardest circumstances and ask, "What can we do?" Students are encouraged to engage and transform the world, locally and globally, by participation in disaster relief trips to everywhere from the tsunami-stricken areas of Southeast Asia to the Gulf Coast after Hurricane Katrina. Students serve locally at various relief and community organizations in Nashville throughout the year, and student-athletes take part annually in sports evangelism mission trips to South Africa, Ukraine and Brazil. Others have taken advantage of what they're learning at Belmont, incorporating their major studies into various service projects around the world, including working with orphans in India and assisting with physical therapy needs in Guatemala.

TUITION, ROOM, BOARD AND FEES

The total cost of attending Belmont is only 80 percent of the national average for a private college. For a full-time student living on campus the total cost for the 2013-14 academic year is approximately $37,000 which included tuition, fees, room, and board.

FINANCIAL AID

The financial aid program at Belmont combines merit-based assistance with need-based assistance to make the university education affordable. Institutional merit awards range from full-tuition Presidential Scholarships to various levels of partial merit awards. Athletic and artistic scholarships are also available. Belmont also administers traditional state and federal financial aid programs. Campus employment is available. Parents may arrange monthly tuition payments through an outside vendor. To apply for financial assistance, the student must complete the Free Application for Federal Student Aid (FAFSA). FAFSA Code: 003479

ADMISSIONS PROCESS

Belmont's Admissions Committee considers applications based on the total picture that a student's credentials present. High school students will be considered competitive for admission if they present a rigorous course of college-preparatory, academic studies. Students should have an above-average academic and cumulative grade point average and rank in the top half of their graduating class. Any college-level work is also expected to be at the above-average level. A strong correlation between high school grades and entrance examination scores is expected. The personal supplemental information, résumé of activities, and recommendations are also strongly considered as indicators of success at Belmont. Additional requirements such as portfolios or auditions are considered in conjunction with the academic credentials for those programs that require them. Each application is considered on an individual basis. No two applicants will present the same credentials or the same "fit" with the university. Our desire is to work with each student to determine the likelihood of that student to enroll in, graduate from, and use the benefits of the Belmont educational experience.

APPLICATION AND INFORMATION

For more information, contact:

Office of Admissions

Belmont University

1900 Belmont Boulevard

Nashville, TN 37212

615-460 6785

800-56ENROLL

Fax: 615-460-5434

admissions@belmont.edu

www.belmont.edu

CEEB Code: 1058

ACT Code: 3946

BELOIT COLLEGE

AT A GLANCE

Beloit College is a four-year, independent, national college of liberal arts and sciences where the focus is on great teaching and mentoring, and where students put what they've learned into practice by conducting independent research, pursuing fieldwork, internships, and capstone projects, and collaborating with peers and professors. Beloit's residential campus engages students in an uncommonly diverse community where cliques, stereotypes, and exclusivity are left behind. The flexible curriculum crosses traditional academic boundaries, emphasizes the importance of putting theory into practice, and teaches students to develop global perspectives on wide-ranging issues. Beloit's 1,250 students come from nearly every state and more than 40 countries. With an incredible breadth of opportunities, a historic campus with modern facilities, a nationally recognized faculty, and creative, motivated students, Beloit is a college that changes lives. It was so named by education editor Loren Pope in his landmark book Colleges That Change Lives: 40 Schools That Will Change the Way You Think About Colleges. Beloit is also Wisconsin's first college, founded in 1846 to serve a frontier society.

LOCATION AND ENVIRONMENT

Beloit's 40-acre campus is located on the Wisconsin-Illinois state line, 90 miles northwest of Chicago, 50 miles south of Madison, and 70 miles southwest of Milwaukee in a small city that noted anthropologist Margaret Mead called "American Society in a microcosm." Students take advantage of the resources offered by the three major metropolitan areas, as well as those offered by the city itself. Beloit's hospital, clinics, industry, and civic and service organizations provide numerous internship, job shadowing, enrichment, and community outreach opportunities. Beloit's academic buildings cluster around lawns dotted with ancient Indian burial mounds, while across campus, residence halls form a tight-knit community of their own. Beloit's Center for the Sciences, a platinum LEED-certified green building, opened at the center of campus in 2008, offering students a sustainable facility designed for 21st century approaches to teaching and learning in the sciences. The Hendricks Center for the Arts, a historic building in Beloit's nearby downtown, was completely renovated, expanded, and opened in 2010, offering students new studios for music, dance, and theatre, a state-of-the-art film classroom, and set design and staging labs. A 25-acre athletic field and Strong Stadium, featuring a new turf field and track, are located just a few blocks east of the main campus.

OFF-CAMPUS OPPORTUNITIES

On average, more than half of any Beloit College class has studied off campus, in either international or domestic programs. Beloit students study worldwide through a combination of Beloit College programs, programs offered by other institutions and providers, and direct enrollment in universities. Locations include China, Ecuador, Estonia, Germany, Hong Kong, Hungary, Japan, Morocco, Russia, Senegal, and Turkey. Off-campus study programs in North America include semesters in Chicago focused on the arts, humanities, business, science, and urban studies; the American University Programs in Washington, D.C.; and environmental science at the Marine Biological Laboratory in Woods Hole, Mass. The college's Liberal Arts in Practice Center connects community needs with students interested in pursuing internships, field terms, and special projects.

MAJORS AND DEGREES OFFERED

Beloit is an undergraduate college that confers bachelor of arts and bachelor of science degrees. There are more than 50 fields of study in 19 departments.

Majors: anthropology, art history, art (studio), biochemistry, biology (ecology, evolution, and behavioral; environmental; mathematical; molecular, cellular, and integrative), business economics, chemistry (applied, biological, environmental), Chinese language and culture, classical civilization, classical philology, comparative literature, computer science, economics, education and youth studies, English (creative writing and literary studies), environmental studies, French, geology (environmental), German, health and society, history, interdisciplinary studies (self-designed), international relations, international political economy, Japanese language and culture, mathematics, modern languages and literatures, music, philosophy, physics, political science, psychology, religious studies, Russian, science for elementary teaching, sociology, Spanish, theatre (dance, media studies, performance, and production), and women's and gender studies.

Education certification (BA, BS): Children & schools (grades 1-8), Adolescents & schools (grades 9-12). Minors: African studies, American studies, ancient Mediterranean studies, anthropology, art & art history, Asian studies, biology, chemistry, computer science, computational visualization & modeling, English, environmental studies, European studies, geology, health & society, history, interdisciplinary studies, journalism, Latin American & Caribbean studies, legal studies, mathematics, medieval studies, modern languages and literatures, museum studies, music, performing arts, philosophy, physics, political science, religious studies, Russian studies, women's and gender studies.

Pre-professional programs: Special engineering programs; forestry and environmental management program; pre-law; and medical professions programs.

ACADEMIC PROGRAMS

Study abroad is transformative at Beloit, with courses that prepare students before they leave, Cities in Transitions courses that engage students in studying urban change in select locations abroad, and courses that help students integrate what they've learned once they return. Beloit offers a variety of programs that supplement the academic curriculum. First-Year Initiatives links each student to an experienced professor and a group of peers in an interdisciplinary seminar that investigates the nature of learning. The Advising Practicum, a full-day series of workshops and discussions held every semester before advising week, is designed to help students reflect on Beloit's educational opportunities and develop and academic plan tailored to individual interests and goals. Through the Initiatives Program, Venture Grants are available to students the summer after their second academic year, allowing students to pursue intellectually challenging activities that are self-testing or will benefit others and the campus community. The Upton Programs expose both economics majors and non-majors alike to the work of leading economic thinkers and then brings those economists to campus for an annual residency. The Center for Language Studies offers intensive summer language instruction in Chinese, Japanese, Russian, and Arabic. The anthropology field training program has taken students to excavation sites from Colorado to Chile, and geology field expeditions include trips to Iceland, New Zealand, and Scotland. Further experiential opportunities exist through Beloit's memberships in the Keck Consortium in Geology, and the Pew Midstates Science and Mathematics Consortium. Each spring, students present their research at the Student Symposium; the fall International Symposium Day is a forum for research that students have conducted abroad. Beloit students sit on the editorial board of the Beloit Fiction Journal. The Lois and Willard Mackey Chair in Creative Writing brings well-known writers to campus to conduct writing workshops in residency. The Center for Entrepreneurship in Liberal Education at Beloit (CELEB) serves as an incubator for student ventures in a variety of fields, with special emphasis on entrepreneurship in the fine arts.

CAMPUS FACILITIES AND EQUIPMENT

Student organizations have offices in the Jeffris-Wood Campus Center, Pearsons Hall, along with the radio station (WBCR), snack bar, coffee house, mail center, and an all-night study lounge. Turtle Creek, the Beloit College bookstore, features 10,000 square feet of books, supplies, and clothing, and is located just two blocks from campus in downtown Beloit.

Beloit's sports and recreation facilities reflect that 70 percent of the students participate in club, intramural, and varsity athletics. The Sports Center includes the Flood Arena, with three collegiate basketball/volleyball courts; the Marvin Field House, with indoor facilities for soccer, tennis, track, golf, baseball, and softball; a fitness center; dance studio; handball and racquetball courts; and a six-lane swimming pool. The 25-acre field complex offers the 3,500-seat Strong Stadium for football and soccer, fields for softball, lacrosse, and baseball, and six all-weather surface tennis courts.

The Colonel Robert H. Morse Library holdings include over a quarter million books, periodicals, and government documents, and the facility is home to the college archives, computer labs, group study rooms, and extensive listening and viewing areas designed for individual use of audio/video materials.

Beloit is noteworthy for its two teaching museums on campus. The Logan Museum of Anthropology holds more than 300,000 archaeological and 15,000 ethnographic objects from 126 countries and nearly 500 cultural groups. The Wright Museum of Art holds a permanent collection of 5,000 works of art, including significant works of American impressionism, modernist paintings, 19th century plaster casts, German expressionism, and Japanese modern prints. Both offer students opportunities to do the work of the museums in collaboration with faculty and staff.

The Beloit College campus has been transformed by the new LEED-certified, environmentally sustainable Center for the Sciences. The innovative design of classroom and laboratory spaces supports new approaches to teaching and learning. Besides its spectacular four-story open foyer, roof garden, and rain garden, it features student offices and space for studio format and inquiry-based courses that integrate class, laboratory, and collaborative group work. The building encourages interdisciplinary learning, critical for today's science students to take a leadership role in 21st century science. Special facilities include a visualization lab, a 1,900 square-foot greenhouse with three climate zones, an herbarium, and a rooftop small-telescope astronomy area. Major scientific equipment includes a scanning electron microscope with EDS elemental analysis system, a nuclear magnetic resonance spectrometer, circular dichroism fluorescence spectrophotometer, digital polarized light microscope systems, and more. Off-campus facilities include Chamberlin Springs, 50 acres of oak and hickory woods and wildlife northwest of the city; the Smith Limnology Lab, a small boat launch and aquatic station on the Rock River; and the Newark Road Prairie, a 32.5 acre virgin prairie with more than 300 species of flowering plants.

The Laura Aldrich Neese Performing Arts theatre complex features a large thrust stage theater built to Equity standards, a black box theater with flexible staging, a scenic design studio, costume shop, make-up rooms, dressing rooms, and a greenroom.

TUITION, ROOM, BOARD AND FEES

Costs for the 2012-13 academic year are as follows:

Tuition and fees: $38,474

Room: $3,854

Board: $4,008

Total: $46,336

FINANCIAL AID

More than 85% of students receive financial aid in the form of merit scholarships, grants, loans, and campus employment. Students may qualify for financial aid on the basis of financial need, scholastic ability and achievement, and personal qualities. The Early Action Plan is strongly advised for students who wish to be considered for merit scholarships.

STUDENT ORGANIZATIONS AND ACTIVITIES

Beloit students are eclectic, defy definition, and place a premium on individual expression. Beloit students serve on college governance and search committees, establish their own organizations, orchestrate events such as the annual Folk 'n' Blues music festival, and host their own radio and cable TV shows, for example. The college has more than 60 active student clubs ranging in focus from ballroom dance to Ultimate Frisbee to yoga. As an NCAA Division III school, Beloit offers numerous varsity and club sports. Men's varsity sports include baseball, basketball, cross country, football, lacrosse, soccer, swimming, and track. Women's varsity sports include basketball, cross country, lacrosse, soccer, softball, swimming, tennis, track, and volleyball. Intramural and club sports include basketball, fencing, flag football, floor hockey, indoor soccer, lacrosse, martial arts, racquetball, rowing, Frisbee golf, Ultimate Frisbee, volleyball, water polo, rock climbing, scuba, ski/snowboarding, and triathlon.

ADMISSIONS PROCESS

Beloit offers two non-binding Early Action plans with deadlines of either November 1 or December 1; notification is December 15 and January 15 respectively. The Regular Decision priority application deadline is January 15, with notification beginning in March. Applications received after January 15 will be given full consideration as space remains available. Admitted students have until May 1 to reply to Beloit. A complete application includes the Common Application & Supplement (available at www.beloit.edu/apply), personal essay, secondary school report, high school transcript, SAT or ACT test scores, TOEFL or IELTS scores for international students, and a teacher recommendation. Interviews are not required, but are recommended.

BENTLEY UNIVERSITY

AT A GLANCE

Bentley is an internationally recognized business university, dedicated to preparing the next generation of smart, nimble and compassionate leaders. Located on a classic New England campus minutes from Boston, Bentley combines an advanced business curriculum with the best of the arts and sciences, educates using the latest technology by a faculty that collaborates across disciplines. Bentley offers a wide variety of majors and minors, as well as optional Liberal Studies and Business Studies majors designed to create a modern intersection of the arts and sciences and business that's unique in higher education. Bentley students are highly sought after by today's leading organizations because of their professionalism, exposure to state-of-the-art research tools, and diverse, real-world experience.

LOCATION AND ENVIRONMENT

Bentley's location in Waltham, Massachusetts—just minutes west of Boston—puts the city within easy reach. As the country's ultimate university town, Boston's options range from theater to art exhibits, dance clubs to concerts, and championship sports to world-class shopping. Bentley's free shuttle makes regular trips to Harvard Square in Cambridge, just a subway ride from Boston. Boston also offers many opportunities for internships and jobs after graduation.

The more than 4,250 undergraduates who attend Bentley live and learn in an environment that reflects and prepares them for a multicultural world. Students come from across the United States and nearly 100 countries. The topic of diversity is not only addressed in courses but is also a vibrant facet of campus life. Offices such as the Center for International Students and Scholars, Center for Women in Business, Multicultural Center, Spiritual Life Center, and Women's Center support the university's commitment to cultural awareness.

OFF-CAMPUS OPPORTUNITIES

Hands-on experience is emphasized across the Bentley curriculum. Internships, study abroad, service–learning projects, corporate partnerships, and other opportunities allow students to apply classroom theory in the workplace and community.

More than 90 percent of Bentley students complete at least one internship, building useful work experience and valuable networking connections. Past internship employers include the Cannes Film Festival, CBS News, Converse, Fidelity Investments, MTV Networks, the TJX Companies, Liberty Mutual, Bain & Company, and all of the Big Four accounting firms.

Bentley students can gain insight into different countries and cultures by studying abroad. Programs take place in more than 25 countries and vary in length from one week to a full academic year.

Through Bentley's Service–Learning Center, students build valuable skills in business, communication and teamwork while assisting nonprofit and community-based organizations, both locally and internationally.

In 2012, Bentley was ranked 16th in the nation by the Princeton Review for best career services. The Miller Center for Career Services offers resources including an on-campus recruiting program involving 1,000 national and international companies, an online job and internship database, career fairs, workshops on topics such as interviewing and networking, and a newly developed Career Development Seminar (CDI 101) for first-year students.

In addition, students can develop a customized four-year development plan, which contributes to the university's outstanding placement rates. In 2012, more than 95 percent of students found employment or enrolled in graduate school within six months of graduation. Their median annual salary was $50,000.

MAJORS AND DEGREES OFFERED

Bentley's curriculum, focusing on business, technology and the arts and sciences, provides students with options for shaping an academic program that fits their skills, interests and career goals.

Bachelor of Science (B.S.) degree programs enable students to gain in-depth knowledge and skills in specific business disciplines: accountancy, actuarial science, computer information systems, corporate finance and accounting, economics–finance, finance, information design and corporate communication, information systems audit and control, management, managerial economics, marketing, and mathematical sciences.

Bentley also offers Bachelor of Arts (B.A.) degree programs with majors in global studies, health sciences, history, liberal arts, media and culture, philosophy, public policy, Spanish studies, and sustainable science. All Bachelor of Arts students gain business experience through either the Business Studies major (BSM) or minor. All students can also choose from minors such as entrepreneurial studies, law and sports management.

The Liberal Studies major (LSM), an optional double major, can be combined with any business program. It provides students with a competitive edge by building meaningful connections across and within disciplines. To complete the LSM, students do not need to take any extra courses beyond those normally required. It allows students to add another credential to their degree, helping them stand out to employers. LSM concentrations include American studies; earth, environment, and global sustainability; ethics and social responsibility; global perspectives; health and industry; media arts and society; and quantitative perspectives.

ACADEMIC PROGRAMS

The Bentley curriculum is an integration of business and the arts and sciences. The university's undergraduate students benefit from an incredible breadth of programs and the ability to specialize and combine subjects to best fit their interests. Whether students are interested in creating ad campaigns, managing a health-care organization, or working on Wall Street, Bentley gives them the tools to prepare them for professional success.

A Bentley education also focuses on gaining hands-on experience in the classroom. Students benefit from classes where they partner with outside companies to solve current business problems and present their solutions directly to company executives. Bentley also offers top applicants a chance to enroll in the Honors Program. Participants select honors-level courses each semester that offer extra intellectual challenge in a seminar atmosphere.

The Five-Year Master's Candidate program enables students to earn a Bachelor of Business Administration degree and either an Emerging Leaders M.B.A. or Master of Science (M.S.) degree.

CAMPUS FACILITIES AND EQUIPMENT

Concepts taught in the classroom are put to use in several high-tech learning laboratories.

Bentley's financial Trading Room combines state-of-the-art technology and real-time data to offer first-hand exposure to financial concepts in simulated trading sessions. Resources include Bloomberg, FactSet, Datastream, Thomson One Analytics, Capital IQ, Portfolio Analysis, Matlab, SNP Compustat and Worldscope.

The Center for Marketing Technology plays an integral role in marketing programs. Students gain a full grasp of software options, familiarity with research tools and techniques, and knowledge of new digital marketing frameworks.

The Accounting Center for Electronic Learning and Business Management (ACELAB) introduces cutting-edge technologies that are reshaping the accounting profession. Students have access to auditing and tax preparation software as well as other professional applications from industry leaders such as SAP and Oracle.

The Center for Languages and International Collaboration (CLIC) is a key resource for language courses, international studies majors, and students with an interest in global issues. The center promotes collaboration among Bentley students and their counterparts overseas.

The Media and Culture Labs and Studio feature resources for video production and editing as well as digital photography. The lab provides students with industry-standard software programs for screenwriting, sound mixing, graphic design and DVD authoring.

The Design and Usability Center (DUC) features labs ideal for usability testing. Students use the applications employed by technical communicators, Web developers, user-interface designers and usability specialists.

The brand-new CIS Learning and Technology Sandbox is a collaborative space for learning new technologies. Its resources include Google TVs, Xbox 360 with Kinect, study spaces, large-screen TVs, a smart board, specialized networking equipment and tools such as Windows 8, Linux and Android development software.

The Bentley Library is outfitted with computer workstations, group study rooms and wireless network access. It also has an exceptional number of online database resources. In 2010, Bentley was ranked 14th on the Princeton Review's list of best college libraries.

TUITION, ROOM, BOARD AND FEES

Tuition for resident and nonresident students during the 2013–14 academic year is $39,600. Room and board (double room, meal plan) costs are $13,445. Additional expenses include books, supplies, technology fee, and personal and travel expenses.

FINANCIAL AID

Bentley's financial aid program includes both scholarships based on academic achievement, which are awarded through the admission process, as well as grants based on financial need. Bentley administered over $96 million in aid to undergraduate students last year. Well over half of that amount came in the form of grants and scholarships directly from Bentley. Significant institutional resources are committed each year so that all academically qualified students have access to a Bentley education regardless of their financial resources. Currently, more than 70 percent of undergraduates receive some type of financial assistance—including grants, scholarships, loans and/or work study.

STUDENT ORGANIZATIONS AND ACTIVITIES

Approximately 98 percent of freshmen live on campus. Twenty-three residence halls provide a range of housing options: dorms, suites and apartments. Housing is provided for all four years and all residence halls are air-conditioned and typically include study lounges, exercise facilities, TV lounges and game rooms. In 2010, the Princeton Review ranked Bentley 18th on its list of Dorms Like Palaces.

Students live and learn in a multicultural environment that prepares them to thrive in today's diverse world. International students representing nearly 100 countries represent a large percentage of the student body and bring valuable perspectives to Bentley community.

Supporting Bentley's commitment to diversity are offices such as the Multicultural Center, Spiritual Life Center, Center for International Students and Scholars, Center for Women in Business and the Women's Center.

The Student Center is the hub of campus activity and is home to Seasons Dining Room and more than 100 student organizations. These groups represent academics, the arts, media, fraternity and sorority life, and cultural interests.

Athletic programs are a Bentley hallmark and include intramurals, recreational sports and more than 20 varsity teams in NCAA Divisions I and II. The Dana Athletic Center houses a weight and fitness complex, food court, locker rooms, a gym, a basketball court, volleyball and racquetball courts, a competition-size pool with a diving tank, and saunas. Outdoor facilities include soccer and baseball fields, a track and tennis courts.

ADMISSIONS PROCESS

Students applying for admission are encouraged to complete a competitive university preparatory program. Recommendations include four years of English, four years of mathematics (preferably algebra I and II, geometry, and pre-calculus or its equivalent), and at least three each of history, laboratory science and a foreign language.

APPLICATION AND INFORMATION

Bentley University accepts the Common Application. Along with the application, students must submit a secondary school transcript, letters of recommendation from a teacher and a counselor, and official scores of either the SAT or ACT, including the ACT writing test. The university has special applications for international students and transfer students. Applicants who are non-native speakers of English must also supply official scores of the Test of English as a Foreign Language (TOEFL) or the International English Language Testing Systems (IELTS) exam. Please visit bentley.edu/undergraduate/applying for application information and deadlines.

Office of Undergraduate Admission

Bentley University

175 Forest Street

Waltham, Massachusetts 02452-4705

United States

Phone: 781-891-2244

800-523-2354 (toll-free)

Fax: 781-891-3414

E-mail: ugadmission@bentley.edu

Website: http://bentley.edu/undergraduate

Facebook: http://www.facebook.com/bentleyadmission

YouTube: http://www.youtube.com/discoverbentleyu

Twitter: http://twitter.com/bentleyu

BETHANY COLLEGE (WV)

AT A GLANCE

Bethany, a small college of national distinction, was founded March 2, 1840. For more than 170 years, Bethany College has been a highly contemporary institution based in the tradition of the liberal arts.

The College's program of classical liberal arts education prepares students for a lifetime of work and a life of significance. Teaching and learning form the mission of Bethany College. Central to this broad purpose is providing a liberal arts education for students, including the preparation of professionals, in an atmosphere of study, work, and service.

Bethany College is an academic community founded on the close interaction between students and faculty in the educational process. Bethany College values intellectual rigor and freedom, diversity of thought and lifestyle, personal growth within a community context, and responsible engagement with public issues.

Founded by Alexander Campbell, who provided the land and funds for the first building and served as the first president, Bethany has been a four-year private liberal arts college affiliated with the Christian Church (Disciples of Christ) since its inception. This religious body, of which Campbell was one of the principal founders, continues to support and encourage the College, but exercises no sectarian control. Students from virtually every religious community attend Bethany.

LOCATION AND ENVIRONMENT

Bethany's 1,300-acre campus is located only 39 miles from America's Most Livable City, Pittsburgh, and is a 40-minute drive from the Pittsburgh International Airport. Situated in the beautiful foothills of the Allegheny Mountains in the northern panhandle of West Virginia, Wheeling, West Virginia and Washington, Pennsylvania, are less than a half-hour away.

MAJORS AND DEGREES OFFERED

The College offers a wide array of studies, awarding Bachelor of Science, Bachelor of Arts, and Master of Arts in Teaching degrees. Students may choose from more than 25 departmental and 6 interdisciplinary majors, many with options for emphasis. Students also have the option of including one or more of 35 optional minors as part of their programs.

ACADEMIC PROGRAMS

Accounting, Biology, Business Administration, Chemistry, Communications and Media Arts, Computer Science, Computer Science and Accounting (Dual Major), Economics, Economics and Mathematics (Dual Major), Education, English, Environmental Science (Interdisciplinary), Equine Studies, History, International Economics with Study Abroad (Interdisciplinary), International Relations (Interdisciplinary), Mathematics, Music, Physical Education and Sports Studies, Pre-Engineering/Physical Science, Political Science, Psychology, Psychology and Education (Interdisciplinary), Psychology and Social Work (Dual Major), Religious Studies, Social Studies (Interdisciplinary), Social Work, Spanish, Theatre, Visual Arts.

Pre-Professional Studies

Pre-Dentistry, Pre-Engineering, Pre-Law, Pre-Medical, Pre-Ministry, Pre-Physical Therapy, Pre-Veterinary.

CAMPUS FACILITIES AND EQUIPMENT

The campus features rolling wooded hills and a lush, green academic mall. Facilities include beautiful historic landmarks, modern well-equipped classrooms, spacious sports/recreational areas, indoor and outdoor theaters, art galleries, an equestrian center, a teaching greenhouse and more. The College operates the Mountainside Conference Center, which includes Gresham Inn, and also the Campbell Mansion and Museum.

The 31,140 square-foot Mary Cutlip Center for Library and Information Services contains computers, collaborative learning spaces, and a multi-media area. Its holdings include more than 200,000 bound volumes, 50,000 electronic books, 2,000 periodical subscriptions, and nearly 100,000 microforms along with numerous online information resources. The library also contains two extensive special collections. The College is a partner in the Bowen Central Library of Appalachia, a widely acclaimed research library collaborative of the 36 Appalachian College Association institutions. Bethany is also one of seven colleges in three states participating in the Independent College Enterprise, a state-of-the-art collaborative addressing academic computing.

The Thomas Phillips Johnson Health and Recreation Center includes Hummel Fieldhouse (Nutting Gymnasium), three-court multi-use gymnasium (Sandwen Arena), Knight Natatorium (Olympic-size pool), two racquetball courts, a free-weight exercise fitness center with cardiovascular equipment, and an indoor jogging track. The Cummins Community Center is a state-of-the-art, 24-hour fitness center.

Outdoor Facilities: A multi-purpose stadium (Bison Stadium) with artificial turf and lights that primarily serves football, lacrosse, women's field hockey, and track and field, Hoag Soccer Field, John Cunningham Soccer Complex, equestrian center, 6 tennis courts, baseball and softball fields, football practice fields, and additional playing fields for intramural and club sports. The equestrian team trains at the Oglebay Stables.

More than 90 percent of students live in spacious on-campus apartments, residential halls or fraternity/sorority houses, which include Internet, cable TV and voice-mail access. Computer labs with Internet and library access, e-mail, digital media labs, rehearsal halls, research and language labs, The McCann Learning Center for academic support, and other amenities are provided.

TUITION, ROOM, BOARD AND FEES

The 2013-14 costs for resident students enrolled in the Fall 2013 semester were:

Tuition $24,828

Fees $1,145

Room and Board $9, 346 to $9,746 (depending on option)

Books and Supplies (est) $1,200

Personal/Transportation (est) $2,100

Total $38,619 (approximate)

° Total cost may vary depending on housing option.

FINANCIAL AID

Bethany College is committed to making a financial commitment to our students. If your desire is to receive a Bethany education, our financial aid office will do everything we can to make it affordable for you and your family.

The College awards scholarships based on academic performance, leadership capability and other academic factors.

Additionally, need-based aid is awarded to all eligible students in accordance with FAFSA results. Financial aid packages generally consist of loans, grants, scholarships and student employment.

STUDENT ORGANIZATIONS AND ACTIVITIES

Bethany's 22 varsity athletic teams (11 women's and 11 men's) compete in the NCAA Division III Presidents Athletic Conference (PAC) and the Eastern College Athletic Association (ECAC).

Bethany also offers more than 50 student organizations: scholastic and honorary, government, special interest and departmental.

The Stampede, Bethany College's new Marching Band, will make its debut during the 2013 fall semester.

Greek organizations include Phi Kappa Tau, Delta Tau Delta, Phi Mu, Alpha Xi Delta, Alpha Sigma Phi, Zeta Tau Alpha, Beta Theta Pi, Sigma Nu.

Student Clubs and Service/Philanthropic Organizations include: Alpha Phi Omega, American Chemical Society (ACS), Amnesty International, Baseball Club, Bethanians for Life, Big Brothers/Big Sisters, Circle K, Collegiate Middle Level Association (CMLA), Drama Club, Economics and Business Club, Environmental Science Club, Equestrian Club, Film Club, Fire and Rescue Club, French Club, Gay Straight Alliance (GSA), German Club, International Relations Club, International Students Association (ISA), Japanese Club, Judo Club, Math and Computer Science Club (MCSC), Men's Lacrosse, National Broadcasting Society (NBS) (Alpha Epsilon Rho), Outdoors Club, Photography Club, Physical Education Club, Political Awareness Society, Psychology Club, Public Relations Student Society of America (PRSSA), Soccer Club, Social Awareness, Society of Physics Students (SPS), Society of Collegiate Journalists (SCJ), Softball Club, Spanish Club, Special Education Club, Student Activities Council (SAC), Student Art Guild, Student Athletic Advisory Committee (SAAC), Student Literacy Association, Student National Education Association (SNEA), Tri Beta, Writers Club

Campus Media include: Bethany Political Journal, Bethanian Yearbook, Folio Magazine, Harbinger, Tower Online, WTVX TV-3, WVBC Online

ADMISSIONS PROCESS

Bethany College specializes in a personalized admission process for each student. As a small college, our enrollment counselors evaluate each applicant individually – because of this, we are not limited by designated 'cut-offs.'

Enrollment Fast Facts

Application Deadline: Rolling

Interview Required: No, but strongly recommended

SAT average: 1060

ACT average: 23.2

Average GPA: 3.30

Enrollment Toll Free Number: (800) 922-7611

Enrollment E-mail: enrollment@bethanywv.edu

BOSTON UNIVERSITY

AT A GLANCE

Is Boston University the right place for you? At BU, you'll be taught by Pulitzer Prize winners, Nobel Laureates, Fulbright Scholars, and MacArthur Fellows. With an average class size of 28 students and a faculty-to-student ratio of 13:1, your professors will not only know you by name, they'll want to hear what you have to say. They're looking for students who are original thinkers and who embrace academic challenges. If hands-on research is what interests you, we have more than 2,000 laboratories on campus and hundreds of research opportunities across all areas of study – even for freshmen! And if you're not sure what your academic interests are yet, BU offers more than 250 programs of study for you to choose from, and you don't have to declare a major until the end of your sophomore year. So you can take classes in subjects as varied as biology, broadcast journalism, business, computer engineering, elementary education, film, international relations, physical therapy, psychology, and theatre, just to name a few. Offering thousands of extracurricular activities and social opportunities, and surrounded by the exciting city of Boston, you'll never experience a dull moment as a student at BU. We dare you to discover what a great school Boston University is.

LOCATION AND ENVIRONMENT

Boston provides an environment rich in intellectual and cultural stimuli; no other city in the world can compete with Boston's remarkable concentration of history, higher education institutions, and culture. The city provides many opportunities for internship and research positions as well. The Undergraduate Research Opportunities Program (UROP) helps students locate research positions both within and beyond the university; BU's Center for Career Development works to provide students with the resources they need to get internships or part-time jobs in any number of fields. Boston is a world-class center for attractions including numerous museums, libraries, major league baseball at Fenway Park, the Boston Symphony Orchestra, and a thriving theater district. The city has an atmosphere of learning and excitement. In fact, students make up 20 percent of Boston's population during the academic year.

OFF-CAMPUS OPPORTUNITIES

Boston University has one of the world's most extensive study abroad programs, providing opportunities for students to work and study all over the world. Among the University's study abroad offerings are language and liberal arts programs; programs that combine studies with internships; fieldwork programs for students wishing to pursue academic or scientific research; and summer programs. Programs are available in Argentina, Australia, China, Denmark, Ecuador, England, France, Germany, Guatemala, Ireland, Israel, Italy, Japan, Lebanon, Morocco, New Zealand, Peru, Singapore, South Korea, Spain, Switzerland, Syria, and Turkey. There are also programs available in Washington, D.C. and Los Angeles.

MAJORS AND DEGREES OFFERED

The university awards the BA, BS, BSBA, BLS, MusB, and BFA undergraduate degrees. Nine of Boston University's 16 colleges and schools have undergraduate study programs. The listing below shows the wide variety of study options available to undergraduates.

College of Arts & Sciences students may pursue degrees in American studies; Ancient Greek; Ancient Greek and Latin; anthropology; anthropology and religion; archaeology; architectural studies; astronomy; astronomy and physics; biochemistry and molecular biology; biology; biology with a specialization in behavioral biology; biology with a specialization in cell biology, molecular biology, and genetics; biology with a specialization in ecology and conservation; biology with a specialization in neurobiology; biology with a specialization in quantitative biology; chemistry; chemistry: biochemistry; chemistry: teaching; Chinese language and literature; classical civilization; classics and philosophy; classics and religion; comparative literature; computer science; earth sciences; East Asian studies; economics; economics and mathematics; English; environmental analysis and policy; environmental science; European studies; French and linguistics; French studies; geography with specialization in human geography; geography with specialization in physical geography; geophysics and planetary sciences; German language and literature; Hispanic language and literatures; history; history of art and architecture; international relations; Italian and linguistics; Italian studies; Japanese and linguistics; Japanese language and literature; Latin; Latin American studies; linguistics; linguistics and philosophy; marine science; mathematics (includes statistics); mathematics and computer science; mathematics and mathematics education; mathematics and philosophy; music (nonperformance); neuroscience; philosophy, philosophy and physics; philosophy and political science; philosophy and psychology; philosophy and religion; physics; political science; psychology; religion; Russian language and literature; sociology; and Spanish and linguistics. Special curricula are also available, including the Boston University Dual Degree program (allowing you to earn two degrees), seven-year Accelerated Medical and Accelerated Dental programs, the Modular Medical Integrated Curriculum (MMEDIC), and a variety of combined BA/MA degree programs. Pre-medical, pre-veterinary, and pre-dental studies are supported through the College of Arts & Sciences with nearly any major.

Through the College of Communication, students can pursue majors in communication (includes advertising, public relations and communication), film and television (includes production, writing and management), and journalism (includes news-editorial, broadcast, magazine, online, and photojournalism).

At the College of Engineering, students may choose from programs in biomedical, computer, electrical, mechanical, mechanical with specialization in aerospace, and mechanical with specialization in manufacturing engineering. Cutting-edge minors in nano-technology, energy technologies, and technology innovation are also offered.

The School of Education allows students to pursue bilingual education (includes TESOL), deaf studies, early childhood education, elementary education, English education, Latin and classical studies education, mathematics education, modern foreign languages education, science education, social studies education, and special education. There is also a five-year Double Degree Program which allows students to earn degrees simultaneously in the School of Education and the College of Arts & Sciences.

The School of Hospitality Administration's intense curriculum trains students in the management of hotels, restaurants, food and beverage service, travel and tourism, and entertainment.

The School of Management allows students to pursue concentrations in accounting, entrepreneurship, finance, general management, international management, business law, management information systems, marketing, operations and technology management, and organizational behavior.

At the College of Fine Arts, students may pursue studies in the School of Music (composition theory, music education, musicology, and performance), the School of Theatre (conservatory-style acting, theatre arts, design, stage management, production), and the School of Visual Arts (art education, graphic design, painting, and sculpture). There is also a five-year BFA/BA Double Degree program which allows students to earn degrees simultaneously in the College of Fine Arts and the College of Arts & Sciences.

At the College of Health & Rehabilitation Sciences: Sargent College, students may pursue concentrations in athletic training; behavior and health; health science; human physiology; nutrition; and speech, language, and hearing sciences. Also available are six-year combined programs in physical therapy (BS/DPT) and athletic training/physical therapy (AD/DPT) (not open to transfer students).

The College of General Studies offers a two-year, general education program centered on an interdisciplinary curriculum. The program is designed for students to continue their studies in one of the university's degree-granting schools and colleges in their junior year. CGS also offers the January Program in Boston and London, which offers students an interdisciplinary and global curriculum for their freshman year beginning in the spring semester and ending with a summer term abroad in London.

ACADEMIC PROGRAMS

Boston University is committed to providing outstanding instruction, combining a strong liberal arts program with superior preparation for the professional job market. The Kilachand Honors College provides exceptional students with a challenging and innovative interdisciplinary curriculum in the arts, sciences, social sciences, and professions. Outstanding sophomores in the School of Management are invited to apply to participate in an honors program that offers specialized colloquia and seminars.

CAMPUS FACILITIES AND EQUIPMENT

Boston University's academic and athletic facilities are some of the best in the country. The Life Sciences and Engineering building includes 41 laboratories for faculty-led research, while the 235,000 square-foot Photonics Center houses state-of-the-art laboratories devoted to developing new light-based technologies. The Student Village provides students with first-rate recreation, athletics, living, dining, and outdoor spaces. In addition to high-rise residences and a Track and Tennis Center, the Village includes the ultramodern Fitness and Recreation Center and the state-of-the-art Agganis Arena, offering space for University sporting events as well as concerts and family shows. The University also offers a 106,000-square-foot Center for Student Services, which houses the Center for Career Development, Educational Resource Center, Pre-Professional Advising Offices, and Marciano Commons, a two-story dining hall.

TUITION, ROOM, BOARD AND FEES

Tuition for the 2013-2014 academic year is $43,970; standard room and board is $13,620. Additional mandatory fees are $940. Allowances for the cost of books, supplies, travel, and other incidental expenses brings the total cost of attendance for a student to $61,476.

FINANCIAL AID

Boston University Financial Assistance offers comprehensive services to help students and their families finance the cost of a BU education. The University offers a wide variety of financial assistance programs and provides resources to help inform students and their families about payment strategies and financing options. Merit and scholarship awards, need-based scholarships, loans, student employment, and a payment plan are all offered.

Because Boston University believes scholars should be encouraged and recognized for their efforts and abilities, the University is committed to offering a variety of scholarships to selected freshmen. University need-based scholarships are offered based on several factors, including calculated financial eligibility, academic achievement, and the availability of funds for a student's program of study. While every effort is made to assist students with limited resources, the university does not have sufficient funds to offer a grant award to every admitted student who has calculated financial eligibility. Those who present the strongest academic credentials are most likely to be offered grant or scholarship aid.

STUDENT ORGANIZATIONS AND ACTIVITIES

Boston University students are extremely engaged, participating in academic clubs, cultural or religious organizations, cutting-edge research, community service groups, and professional internships. There are approximately 500 student organizations and more than 50 intramural and club sports that students can participate in throughout the year. You can choose to get involved with organizations such as Alianza Latina, Holistic Yoga Society, Boston University Habitat for Humanity, the Debate Society, or the Alpine Ski Team. A separate student government exists at each school and college to manage student affairs, and the Student Union, the governing body that presides over all of the university's student governments, includes members who represent all schools and colleges within the university.

ADMISSIONS PROCESS

The Board of Admissions evaluates each prospective student individually. The Board's main focus centers on the merits of a student's high school record, but required standardized test scores (SAT and ACT Plus Writing), personal qualities and integrity, interests, teacher and counselor references, and other relevant attributes are also considered carefully. All candidates must have graduated from high school or earned an equivalency diploma to be considered. For admission to the College of Fine Arts students must either audition or submit a portfolio (some programs also require pre-screening). A few select programs require interviews.

Students should consult the Boston University website at www.bu.edu/admissions for additional information. Boston University also considers students with transferable credit from other institutions for admission. Boston University considers applicants for September or January admission, depending on the program of interest.

Boston University offers early decision (which is a binding agreement) and regular decision programs. All applications for early decision must be submitted by November 1 and applications for regular decision must be submitted by January 1. Accelerated program applications must be submitted by November 15. Nominations and/or applications for admission to qualify for the Presidential or Trustee Scholarships must be submitted by December 1.

Transfer students seeking January admission must submit their application forms by November 1. Those seeking September admission must submit their application forms by March 1.

Transfer students cannot be admitted to the Accelerated Liberal Arts Medical or Dental Programs; or the six-year, combined AT/DPT and DPT programs in the College of Health & Rehabilitation Sciences: Sargent College. Transfer students may not apply for January admission to the School of Theatre in the College of Fine Arts. They also cannot apply as "undeclared" to any school or college.

Boston University accepts qualified applicants regardless of age, color, disability, national origin, race, religion, sexual orientation, or gender to all of its activities and programs.

BRYANT UNIVERSITY

AT A GLANCE

Bryan delivers an exceptional education for success in an age of unlimited global opportunity. The undergraduate curriculum is nationally recognized for innovation. From the very first semester, you'll find that Bryant's interdisciplinary studies and engaged learning are designed with your success in mind. Princeton Review notes that Bryant faculty are "good at teaching, but even better at providing real working knowledge."

You'll take notes from an industry expert in one class and be on site doing service learning in the next. Our world-class faculty integrate theoretical and applied concepts in a broad range of majors from accounting to sociology, all complemented by rich co-curricular opportunities.

Proven success. A Bryant education speaks for itself – 98% of our students are employed or enrolled in graduate school within six months of Commencement. The median starting salary for a Bryant grad is $50,160.

Academics and Majors

Bryant's student-centered learning community will inspire you to discover your passion and create your own path as you develop the knowledge, skills, credentials, and qualities of character to become an active contributor who thinks in a global context.

Uniquely dedicated to the integration of business and the liberal arts, and committed to the creation of an educational experience which blends knowledge and practice.

Bryant cultivates in our students the qualities of character vital for leadership and essential to the health of a democratic society.

We have nearly 100 courses of study to choose from, ranging from traditional courses like Actuarial Mathematics, Finance, and Marketing to contemporary ones like Social Entrepreneurship, Forensic Science, and the distinguished International Business program.

Bryant's Graduate School of Business offers one-year or two-year Master of Business Administration (MBA) programs; a Master of Science in Taxation (MST); and a Master of Professional Accountancy (MPAc).

The College of Arts and Sciences offers graduate programs from the Master of Arts in Communication (MACom), to the Master of Science in Global Environmental Studies (MSGES), to the Master of Arts in Teaching (MAT).

ADMISSION

Bryan's great strentgh in education is our attention to each individual student. And that begins before you even apply.

Bryant's applicants have taken a strong college preparatory curriculum in high school. But we know that you are more than your grades and test scores.

We want to know you - what makes you laugh out loud, what inspires you, what makes you want to dig deeper. We're looking for great students who want to belong to a dynamic community with an atmosphere of purpose.

Do you want to graduate with the knowledge, skills, credentials, and qualities of character to lead and succeed in an age of unlimited global opportunity?

STUDENT BODY

Who is a Bryant student? He or she is hard working, motivated and driven to succeed. Willing to go the extra mile, Bryant students learn as much inside the classroom as they do out of it.

From attending a Bulldogs football game to practicing for a business competition, Bryant students have access to more than 90 clubs and organizations to keep them entertained, physically fit, and intellectually stimulated.

Most of our students, nearly 90%, choose to reside on campus to take advantage of the rich campus life. Whether it's a show by the Bryant Players, working late at the student-run WJMF radio station, or preparing with your team for the national xTAX finals, the campus is a safe, vibrant place even after dark.

Bryant students come from a variety of backgrounds – 85% of our students are from out of state, and 6.32% are international students from 55 countries around the world.

CAMPUS FACILITIES AND EQUIPMENT

Our stunning, 428-acre campus in Smithfield, Rhode Island, is just 15 minutes from downtown Providence, an hour from Boston, and three hours from New York City.

Our strategic location provides students with a a plethora of internship and employment opportunities within driving distance of the campus.

Providence, a small city that's home to nearly 50,000 college students and features a thriving arts and culture scene, is close to the headquarters of large corporations such as GTECH, CVS, and Hasbro, as well as many small businesses.

The "Tupper campus"

Over the past decade, our campus has been transformed, incorporating the latest technological capabilities, new facilities, and strategic renovations that support Bryant's tradition of innovation.

The impressive Elizabeth and Malcolm Chace Wellness and Athletic Center features a spacious and sunny fitness center, six-lane swimming pool, circuit-training equipment and free weights, and a group exercise room.

The Douglas and Judith Krupp Library is one of the most comprehensive business library collections in the region, and the C.V. Starr Financial Markets Center receives real-time data through live feeds from Reuters 3000, the leading information service for finance professionals.

Bryant is also home to the John H. Chafee Center for International Business, which houses the World Trade Center Rhode Island, the Confucius Institute, the Rhode Island Export Assistance Center, and the U.S.-China Institute.

TUITION AND FINANCIAL AID

MORE THAN 85% of the incoming first-year students in Fall 2012 received financial aid. The average aid package exceeded $19,000.

Tuition, 2012-2013: $35,591

*Includes a new laptop

Room and board: $12,982

Student activity fee: $349

The value of a Bryant education is measured in the academic, professional, cultural, and personal growth and opportunities available to help you create your path, expand your world, and achieve success that will long outlast tuition payments.

However, we understand that financing your education is a vital part of the decision about which college you will attend.

For the upcoming academic year, Bryant will offer more than $10 million to incoming students alone in institutional grants and merit scholarships. For more information about cost and financial aid, please visit http://www.bryant.edu/admissions/cost-and-financial-aid/

VISITING AND CONTACT INFORMATION

Visit Bryant to experience what it is like to live and learn in our close-knit, friendly community. You might even run into our Bulldog mascot, Tupper, who often appears at football games and visits with students during class breaks in the main lobby.

According to Barron's Best Buys in College Education, "At Bryant University, 12 miles outside Providence, Rhode Island, seeing is believing...."

A campus visit is the best way to make an informed decision about college. Prospective students who visit Bryant's campus usually apply — evidence that our friendly atmosphere, beautiful campus and high-quality academics are best experienced in person.

Bryant offers several options for visiting campus, including:

Student-guided tours

Information Sessions presented by an admission staff member

Day With Class

Bryant is located on Route 7, just off Route 295 in Smithfield, RI.

BUCKNELL UNIVERSITY

AT A GLANCE

With academic programs in the arts, engineering, humanities, management, and social and natural sciences – and broad opportunities outside of class – Bucknell University prepares its students for professional and personal success.

Bucknell University offers academic programs in the arts, engineering, humanities, management, and social and natural sciences, and many opportunities beyond the classroom. The University's 3,500 undergraduates can choose from more than 50 majors and 65 minors, all taught in the tradition of the liberal arts, through which students gain the broad, multidisciplinary knowledge that employers seek. Student satisfaction at the University is extremely high: 95 percent of first-year students entering in the Class of 2015 returned for their sophomore year. Likewise, students consistently graduate on time, with Bucknell having an 85 percent four-year graduation rate for the Class of 2012 – a rate among the highest of all four-year colleges. According to the 2012–13 PayScale College Salary Survey, Bucknell ranks thirty-seventh among private colleges and universities and tenth among liberal arts institutions for alumni mid-career salary. Each entering class consists of about 925 students.

LOCATION AND ENVIRONMENT

With its green spaces, red brick buildings and striking vistas, Bucknell's 400-acre campus is a quintessential college environment in the heart of scenic central Pennsylvania. The shops of historic downtown Lewisburg – including the new Barnes & Noble at Bucknell University and the newly renovated historic Campus Theatre – lie within walking distance of campus. The University is located within three to four hours of New York City, Washington, D.C., Philadelphia, and Pittsburgh by car. For more information about Bucknell's location, see www.bucknell.edu/explore.

OFF-CAMPUS OPPORTUNITIES

Bucknell is a residential university, so nearly all of students live on campus, but learning, service, research and recreation extend off campus. Students frequently volunteer as close as the local nursing home, community center and sustainable farm, and as far away as New Orleans and Nicaragua. Every year, students also travel off campus to conduct research with faculty mentors. Destinations range from Alaska, Suriname, and the American southwest to the Sudan.

Many students explore their career options and network with alumni through summer internships with corporations, government organizations and non-profits locally and nationally. An externship program provides job shadowing opportunities for sophomores.

More than 45 percent of students spend a summer, semester, or year abroad through one of university's own "in" programs or 160 other approved programs in Africa, Asia, Australia, the Caribbean, Europe, and South America.

Throughout a student's time at Bucknell and even after graduation, the university offers career services including advising, networking, mock interviews, internship and externship support, and employer fairs to students. The placement rate is consistently high: 94.5 percent of the Class of 2011 was employed, in graduate school or volunteering within nine months of graduation.

MAJORS AND DEGREES OFFERED

Bucknell's 3,500 undergraduates can choose from more than 50 majors and 65 minors. Students can build robots, write and perform in their own plays or debate solutions to global issues. Engineers can make art, artists can analyze DNA and philosophers can make music. Each student chooses his or her own pathway, but what unites everyone is a shared enthusiasm for learning and a desire to achieve deeper levels of understanding about life and the world.

The College of Arts and Sciences offers bachelor's degrees in science, arts, music and education. Master's degrees are available in select disciplines.

The School of Management offers bachelor of science degrees in business administration with four new majors in accounting and financial management; global management; managing for sustainability; and markets, innovation and design.

The College of Engineering offers a bachelor of science degree in seven majors, a five-year dual degree in engineering and management, a five-year dual degree in engineering and the liberal arts, and a five-year combined bachelor's and master's degree. As one of a select group of private colleges and universities admitted to the Kern Entrepreneurship Education Network, Bucknell offers its engineers even more resources to build entrepreneurial spirit and become technical leaders.

For details about any academic program, see www.bucknell.edu/catalog.

ACADEMIC PROGRAMS

Bucknell's academic programs are enlivening and inspiring, largely because of the professors. They encourage free-flowing ideas and stimulating discussions across campus, getting to know students personally and challenging them to do their best. The professors are also dedicated scholars who frequently receive awards and grants for their work. Often, they engage students in research and creative projects outside of class. By doing so, they provide students with mentorship and guidance for the future. The student-faculty ratio is 10:1.

In addition to the faculty, visiting scholars and speakers come to Bucknell regularly. Recent visitors include Arianna Huffington, Robert F. Kennedy Jr., author Edwidge Danticat and choreographer Twyla Tharp.

Distinctive programs that complement the curriculum include, but are not limited to:

Residential Colleges – http://www.bucknell.edu/rescolleges

Theme-based living and learning environments that combine classroom learning with the residential experience

Themes: Arts, Discovery, Environmental, Global, Humanities, Languages and Cultures, Social Justice, Society and Technology

Participating first-year students take a class together and join in programs and social activities that complement their classroom learning

Bucknell University Environmental Center – http://www.bucknell.edu/environmentalcenter

Faculty, staff, and students collaborate on environmental and nature-related learning, teaching, scholarship and service

Initiatives: Campus Greening, Place Studies, Marcellus Shale, Susquehanna River

Civic Engagement – www.bucknell.edu/civicengagement

Educational experiences link academic course work with efforts to meet a community need

Opportunities include Bucknell Brigade to Nicaragua, Katrina Recovery Trips, Alternative Spring Break trips, tutoring in local schools and international service

Institute for Leadership in Technology and Management – www.bucknell.edu/iltm

This two-summer program bridges the disciplines of engineering and management for select students in engineering, management and the liberal arts

CAMPUS FACILITIES AND EQUIPMENT

Bucknell's campus includes facilities for art, engineering, music, the sciences, theatre and dance, and a 1,200-seat performance hall. Bertrand Library holds nearly 833,000 volumes, provides access to more than 35,000 periodicals and nearly 300 databases and offers a video-editing lab, thousands of audiovisual materials and multimedia equipment. Computer labs are available across campus, and most of campus is wireless-accessible. Classrooms are equipped with projectors and computers, some with computers for each student. All student residences are connected to the residential network, which features a high-speed data connection and digital television programming, for each student. Science and engineering programs offer sophisticated instrumentation available for student use, including a structural testing lab, an atomic force microscope and a nuclear magnetic resonance spectrometer.

The campus also boasts a poetry center, writing center, observatory, 18-hole golf course and Olympic-sized pool. A new Film/Media Production Clinic gives students with opportunities to partner with nonprofit organizations and produce broadcast-quality content. Bucknell also is moving forward with plans for new buildings that support excellence in learning. The first of these facilities, called Academic West, will add 70,000 square feet of classrooms, offices, laboratories and meeting areas to campus. The building will be complete by 2013.

TUITION, ROOM, BOARD, AND FEES

For the 2013-14 academic year, tuition and fees are set at:

Tuition and student activity fees: $46,902

Room and Board: $11,258

Total Comprehensive Fee: $58,160

FINANCIAL AID

The Bucknell Office of Financial Aid works closely with students and families who need aid. The University offers a range of financial aid options to students with demonstrated financial need as calculated by the university. These include scholarships, grants, loans and student employment. Bucknell considers each family's situation on an individual basis and re-evaluates cases annually to accommodate families' changes in financial resources.

About 50 percent of students receive financial aid from Bucknell, and 62 percent receive financial aid of some form.

The average financial aid award for first-year students with financial need in the fall of 2012 was about $28,000, including scholarships, loans, and work study.

The average loan total upon graduation is about $21,000.

With its unique combination of professional programs and the liberal arts, Bucknell offers an education that provides lifelong personal and career benefits. Consider it an investment worth making.

Important Note: If you are applying for financial aid, you must submit your CSS PROFILE by November 15 for Early Decision I and January 15 for Early Decision II and Regular Decision applications.

STUDENT ORGANIZATIONS AND ACTIVITIES

Outside of class, students participate in more than 150 student-run clubs and organizations. These groups focus on anything from social and environmental causes to cultural awareness, poetry slams, dance, pottery, video games or politics. Bucknell offers Division I athletics along with intramural and club sports. Students can enrich their religious and spiritual lives through multiple university and student-led faith organizations. About half of sophomore, juniors and seniors participate in Greek life.

ADMISSIONS PROCESS

Bucknell seeks dynamic, well-rounded students who embrace challenge, ask provocative questions and take advantage of the rich opportunities we offer. Bucknell encourages prospective students and their families to visit campus to determine whether Bucknell is a good fit. View visit options at www.bucknell.edu/visitbucknell.

The university focuses on academic achievement, evidence of significant talent or ability, personal character and leadership skills. Grades and recommendations are extremely important, but Bucknell also values applicants who cultivate passions outside of the classroom and contribute to their schools and communities in thoughtful and unique ways. Students who are willing to take healthy intellectual risks in both their academic and personal endeavors are also well suited to join Bucknell's community.

To apply for admission, fill out and submit the Common Application as well as the Bucknell Application Supplement. You can do this on the Common Application website: www.commonapp.org. There is a $60 required application fee. Early Decision students should also complete an Early Decision Form.

Deadlines

For students seeking to begin college in the fall, Regular Decision applications should be filed before January 15 for notification by April 1.

SAT and/or ACT results must be submitted before March 1.

Early Decision candidates may apply for Early Decision I consideration by November 15 or Early Decision II consideration by January 15.

Transfer student information is available on our website. Applications for transfer students should be submitted by March 15 for studies beginning the following fall and by November 1 for the spring semester.

To request application information by mail, please call 570-577-3000.

For detailed information about admissions at Bucknell, go to www.bucknell.edu/admissions.

CABRINI COLLEGE

AT A GLANCE

Cabrini College is a co-educational Catholic college that welcomes students of all faiths and cultures. Founded in 1957 by the Missionary Sisters of the Sacred Heart of Jesus, Cabrini is located on 112 acres in the Main Line suburb of Radnor, Pennsylvania. Cabrini has 1,298 full-time undergraduate students and more than 800 reside on-campus.

The top majors at Cabrini are as follows: Education (Early Childhood, Elementary, Special Education, and Secondary Education), English, Communication, Business, Biology/Pre-Med, Graphic Design, and Psychology. The College operates on a Rolling Admissions Basis. There is a two-week turnaround time once a prospective student has submitted the application, application fee, official copy of their high school transcript, and an official copy of their SAT or ACT scores. Merit based scholarships are awarded to students whose SAT/ACT and G.P.A. meet the academic criteria. The average SAT score for an incoming Cabrini student is a combined Math and Verbal score of 930 and the average G.P.A. is a 3.1. The average class size at Cabrini is 17 with a student/teacher ratio of 16:1.

Cabrini offers a foundation for career success. There are more than 30 majors and professional programs, co-op educational experiences and internships, academically focused living and learning communities, and an honors program. Within 10 months of graduation, 95 percent of Cabrini graduates are employed or in graduate school.

Cabrini's commitment to social justice spans more than two decades: it was among the first in higher education to implement community service into the curriculum, and the first in Pennsylvania to require community service of all undergraduates. In 2005, Cabrini signed a formal agreement with Catholic Relief Services (CRS) to support global service initiatives.

The National Survey of Student Engagement consistently shows that Cabrini first-year students and seniors score higher than those at more than 700 colleges and universities in several benchmarks of effective educational practice, such as level of academic challenge, student-faculty interaction, enriching educational experiences, and supportive campus environment.

A Division III school, Cabrini students are able to participate in sports while maintaining excellent grades. Cabrini College has earned more conference championships than any other school in the Colonial States Athletic Conference (CSAC).

LOCATION AND ENVIRONMENT

Cabrini College is located on a beautiful campus setting in Radnor, Pennsylvania, just 30 minutes from downtown Philadelphia, a city brimming with great food, museums, music, and professional sports teams. The King of Prussia Mall is located less than 10 minutes from campus and minutes from downtown Wayne, which boasts a movie theater, restaurants, and shops. Cabrini is located only a few hours from New York, Washington, D.C., and Harrisburg.

OFF-CAMPUS OPPORTUNITIES

Internship opportunities are readily available with easy access to companies such as Vanguard, Unisys, Pfizer, Merck, ING, KPMG, CHOP, ABC, NBC, and numerous other places where Cabrini students gain valuable hands-on experience.

MAJORS AND DEGREES OFFERED

Cabrini students can earn a Bachelor of Arts, Bachelor of Science, Bachelor of Science in Education, or a Bachelor of Science in Social Work by majoring in any one of the Programs offered at Cabrini. At the graduate level, the College offers a Master of Education, Teacher Certifications, and Master of Science in Leadership.

ACADEMIC PROGRAMS

The benefit of a liberal arts education is that Cabrini offers various Majors and Minors so students can find the right one for them.

ACADEMIC MAJORS

Business (Accounting, Business Administration, Finance, Human Resources Management, Marketing); Communication; Criminology; Education (Early Childhood Education, Educational Studies, Elementary Education, Secondary Education Certification, Special Education);English; Exercise Science and Health Promotion; Graphic Design; History and Political Science (American Studies, History, Political Science); Individualized Major; Information Science and Technology (Computer Information Science, Information Systems); Mathematics; Philosophy & Liberal Studies; Psychology; Religious Studies; Romance Languages and Literatures (French, Italian, Spanish); Science (Non Degree Granting) (Pre-Nursing, Pre-Occupational Therapy, Pre-Pharmacy, Pre-Physical Therapy); Social Work; Sociology

CAMPUS FACILITIES AND EQUIPMENT

Located in suburban Philadelphia, Cabrini's wireless 112-acre campus features state-of-the-art academic and athletic resources. The centerpiece of Cabrini is its turn-of-the-century Mansion, a National Historic Landmark. The Antoinette Iadarola Center for Science, Education, and Technology has state-of-the-art science labs and research tools for students. It also houses the Center for Teaching and Learning, a learning commons that provides individualized support for students in math, writing and specific subjects. The Communications Center is a campus-based professional style media center, home to the campus television studio, award-winning radio station (WYBF), and newsroom. Cabrini's Dixon Field, an artificial turf surface with seating for 700 fans, is located beside the Dixon Center, which houses the pool, squash courts, basketball courts, workout gym, and exercise science lab.

STUDENT ORGANIZATIONS AND ACTIVITIES

With over 50 student-run clubs and organizations at Cabrini, it's easy to get involved in campus life. Students have opportunities to meet others who have similar interests and are encouraged to start their own club or organization.

Cabrini students participate in almost 60 clubs and organizations, ranging from intramural sports like dodge ball and volleyball, to professional organizations like the Accounting Association and the American Institute for Graphic Arts. Students are active in religious, musical and academic clubs as well as community service organizations and athletics.

Cabrini is a member of the National Collegiate Athletic Association (NCAA) Division III and Colonial States Athletic Conference (CSAC). Men's sports include basketball, cross country, golf, lacrosse, soccer, swimming, and tennis. Women's sports include basketball, cross country, field hockey, lacrosse, soccer, softball, swimming, tennis, and volleyball.

ADMISSIONS PROCESS

The Admissions Process is Rolling Admissions, where students can apply until the class is full. To be considered for admission, students must submit the following: Application, Application Fee, Official High School Transcript, and an Official Copy of the SAT or ACT scores. Students whose files are complete will hear back from an admissions representative within two weeks. Merit scholarships are awarded based on SAT/ACT scores and the high school G.P.A.

CALIFORNIA COLLEGE OF THE ARTS

AT A GLANCE

California College of the Arts. Empowering students to make art that makes a difference.

California College of the Arts (CCA), founded in 1907, offers studies in 21 undergraduate and 11 graduate majors in the areas of fine art, architecture, design, and writing. The college has world-class facilities at its two campuses in San Francisco and Oakland. More than 500 highly regarded artists and scholars instruct a population of approximately 1,450 undergraduate and 467 graduate students. The average class size is 15.

Students at CCA discover cross-disciplinary opportunities, innovative courses with real-world applications, outstanding faculty, successful alumni, and a world-class campus environment. Wherever their art takes them—producing an experimental film, painting outside the canvas, designing sustainable products, or working in the community—CCA offers an ideal environment to make it happen. Students develop competencies that will serve them well, both while they are in school and long after they graduate. Our alumni have been successful in all kinds of creative endeavors.

CCA students begin making their mark well before graduation day. Just in the past year: A typeface designed by one of our Graphic Design students was used by both presidential candidates' campaigns. Another student won both the $15,000 Windgate Fellowship, one of the nation's largest art and design awards, and the Wilsonart Design Challenge, a student competition held at the International Contemporary Furniture Fair (ICFF) in New York. An Interior Design student won the prestigious Angelo Donghia Foundation Student Scholarship, which comes with $30,000 to complete one's senior year. And a Fashion Design senior was offered a prestigious internship with the New York fashion designer Rubin Singer.

LOCATION AND ENVIRONMENT

CCA is located in the San Francisco Bay Area, near Silicon Valley and tech giants such as Google, Yahoo, Facebook, and Twitter. The region is known for creative and technological innovation, environmental leadership, and thriving art and design communities. It is home to world-class museums and alternative gallery spaces as well as active scenes in theater, music, dance, film, and literature. Close by are beaches, hiking and biking trails, the Napa Valley, Mendocino, Monterey, Lake Tahoe, the Sierra Nevada mountains, and Yosemite National Park.

CCA's Oakland campus occupies four acres in the residential Rockridge neighborhood, three miles from UC Berkeley. The San Francisco campus spans a city block in Potrero Hill, near Mission Bay and the design district. Both campuses are easily accessible via bus and train. CCA also operates a shuttle between its campuses and residence halls.

OPPORTUNITIES

Artist talks, lectures, and other special events take place on both campuses almost every day.

Internships (required by some programs, and encouraged by all) allow students to gain practical experience and make professional connections while earning academic credit.

CCA's Center for Art and Public Life organizes a wide range of programs that put students into direct contact with the diverse communities of the Bay Area and beyond. Three of its notable initiatives are: ENGAGE at CCA, a family of courses embedded throughout the college's curriculum in which students work with outside experts to find solutions to community issues; the IMPACT Social Entrepreneurship Awards, which give $10,000 to interdisciplinary teams of students so that they may undertake large projects over the course of a summer, anywhere in the world; and CCA Connects, a community-based internship experience.

Sponsored studio courses, offered throughout the year, enable students to work directly with professional practitioners from globally distinguished firms such as Gensler, Intel, and IDEO.

Through the International Exchange Program, students may spend a semester at one of more than 30 colleges of art and design around the globe. CCA also offers summer study-abroad courses.

Qualified upper-division students may spend a semester at one of 32 other art schools throughout the United States through the Association of Independent Colleges of Art and Design (AICAD). Students may cross-register at Mills College or Holy Names University, both in Oakland.

The CCA Wattis Institute for Contemporary Arts, housed on the San Francisco campus, presents several exhibitions every year featuring internationally prominent contemporary artists.

MAJORS AND DEGREES OFFERED

CCA offers the bachelor of fine arts (BFA) degree in Animation, Ceramics, Community Arts, Fashion Design, Film, Furniture, Glass, Graphic Design, Illustration, Industrial Design, Interaction Design, Interior Design, Jewelry/Metal Arts, Painting/Drawing, Photography, Printmaking, Sculpture, and Textiles. The college offers the bachelor of arts (BA) degree in Writing and Literature and Visual Studies. CCA also offers a bachelor of architecture (BArch) degree, a five-year program.

CCA offers the master of architecture (MArch), master of advanced architectural design (MAAD), and master of architecture in urban design and landscape (MAUDL) degrees; the master of business administration (MBA) in Design Strategy; the master of fine arts (MFA) in Comics, Design, Film, Fine Arts, and Writing; and the master of arts (MA) in Curatorial Practice and Visual and Critical Studies. Graduate Fine Arts students can choose to concentrate in studio practice or social practice. There are also several dual-degree options for graduate students.

ACADEMIC PROGRAMS

CCA's curriculum emphasizes inter-disciplinarity, community engagement, and professional practice. Undergraduates begin with a core curriculum, which introduces a variety of artistic media, principles, and processes as well as humanities courses in writing, literature, art history, and critical theory.

The college runs on a two-semester academic calendar with a six-week summer session. Summer programs include the Pre-College Program for high school students (participants earn college credit). Various summer art and design programs that emphasize English skills are available to international students entering in the fall. Extension courses are offered throughout the year.

FACILITIES AND EQUIPMENT

CCA offers outstanding facilities for making art. There are 14 dedicated computer labs, wireless access, and media centers with equipment for checkout. <The labs have Intel-based Mac computers and a complete range of software. There is a rapid prototyping studio for 3-D printing.>

OAKLAND CAMPUS

The Oakland campus is home to the First Year Program and the programs in Animation, Ceramics, Community Arts, Glass, Jewelry / Metal Arts, Photography, Printmaking, Sculpture, Textiles, Visual Studies, and Writing and Literature. (Painting/Drawing courses are held on both campuses.)

Animation students have dedicated studios and equipment for digital video, film, and sound production. The ceramics facilities include numerous gas and electric kilns. Sculpture facilities include a bronze foundry, a wax-working area, a plaster and mold-making room, a metal fabrication studio, and a woodshop. Textiles facilities include a computerized weaving lab, a digital Jacquard TC-1 loom, and a fiber sculpture studio. For printmaking there are lithography presses, a 40x60 American French Tool etching press, a silkscreening and papermaking complex, and a letterpress lab. The two-floor photography center supports analog and digital processes.

SAN FRANCISCO CAMPUS

The San Francisco campus houses the programs in Architecture, Fashion Design, Film, Furniture, Graphic Design, Illustration, Industrial Design, Interaction Design, and Interior Design as well as all of the graduate programs.

There is a state-of-the-art digital production facility and stage. The studio and shop facilities include a furniture studio, model making studio, alternative materials studio, rapid prototyping studio, hybrid lab, welding studio, plaster room, sanding room, and spray booth. The MFA Program in Writing has its own building.

LIBRARIES

CCA's libraries (one on each campus) specialize in art and design. The collections include more than 55,000 book and audiovisual titles, 240 current periodical subscriptions, more than 4,000 online journals, and a growing number of digital artifacts. The library maintains several special research collections and is a charter member of ARTstor. On the San Francisco campus there is also a materials library (one of very few such libraries at an educational institution) that contains thousands of material samples.

GALLERIES

The college has several dedicated on-campus spaces for exhibitions of student work, and individual departments and courses frequently present off-campus shows of student work. Many of these exhibitions are organized by the students themselves, giving them valuable hands-on gallery experience. Student exhibitions on both campuses change weekly.

TUITION, ROOM, BOARD, AND FEES

Tuition for the 2013–14 academic year is $39,984 for full-time undergraduate students and $1,666 per unit for part-time students. Tuition is the same for California and out-of-state residents. Campus housing costs an additional $8,000. Total costs for 2013–14 are approximately $56,134 per year, which includes $40,334 in tuition and fees, $10,850 for room and board, $1,500 for books and supplies, and $3,450 for miscellaneous expenses.

FINANCIAL AID

In 2011–12, 87 percent of CCA students received financial aid from some source. Approximately 76 percent of CCA students received CCA scholarship assistance. The college offers financial aid in the form of scholarships, grants, loans, and work-study programs. There are both need-based and merit-based awards. For an estimate of your scholarship and financial aid, see the net-cost calculator at cca.edu/financialaid.

Students applying for merit scholarships must complete their admission application by February 1. Students applying for financial assistance should submit the Free Application for Federal Student Aid (FAFSA) by March 1. CCA will continue to award aid to applicants after March 1 as funding permits. Students can apply for Federal Pell Grants and Federal Direct Loans throughout the year. CCA is approved for veterans who wish to attend under the Veterans Administration Educational Benefits Program. In addition to financial awards, CCA offers an interest-free payment plan.

STUDENT ORGANIZATIONS AND ACTIVITIES

At CCA, education takes place both inside and outside the classroom. About 80 percent of first-year students live on campus. Throughout the year, the residential-life staff hosts social and educational programs ranging from movie nights and barbecues to museum trips and professional lectures.

Students are encouraged to join existing clubs and organizations or to form new ones. Clubs and activities range in focus from community building to politics to physical fitness. Students may also choose to get involved in student government. The Student Council sponsors a range of activities throughout the year, including dinners, films, and shuttles to San Francisco galleries.

Our students are active in many pre-professional groups that are affiliated with corresponding Bay Area professional chapters: American Institute of Architecture Students (AIAS), American Institute of Graphic Arts (AIGA), Industrial Designers Society of America (IDSA), and International Interior Design Association (IIDA).

Student services include counseling, tutoring, advising, disability services, fitness classes, stress relief, and safety workshops. There are many services specifically for international students, including dedicated staff, special workshops, social events, and exhibitions.

ADMISSIONS PROCESS

Applications are reviewed on an individualized basis, taking into account academic achievements, creative abilities, individual achievements and activities, a personal essay, recommendations, and a portfolio. Undergraduate applicants must have a high school diploma or the equivalent. First-year applicants should follow a college preparatory program in high school, including courses in studio art and art history whenever possible.

Undergraduates interested in applying for merit scholarships should submit their applications by February 1. The priority deadline for all other undergraduate applicants is March 1. The priority deadline for spring undergraduate applicants is October 1. Students who meet the admissions priority deadlines receive first consideration for housing, financial aid, and course selection. Admissions decisions are made on a rolling basis; this means that applications are reviewed in the order they are received. There is a nonrefundable application fee of $60. It is possible to register for courses as a non-degree student (on a space-available basis).

You can schedule a campus visit, request information, and apply online at cca.edu/admissions. For additional information please contact

Office of Enrollment Services

California College of the Arts

1111 Eighth Street

San Francisco CA 94107-2247

800.447.1ART

cca.edu

enroll@cca.edu

CALIFORNIA UNIVERSITY OF PENNSYLVANIA

AT A GLANCE

The mission of California University of Pennsylvania is to build character and careers for our students. Although building careers may be expected of universities, building character is less often their focus. But the rationale for building character, as well as careers, is best seen in these words by Theodore Roosevelt: "To educate a person in mind but not in morals is to educate a menace to society."

Since 1852, eager students have seized the opportunity to develop their character and careers at California University of Pennsylvania. In so doing, they have improved their lives and the lives of those around them.

To achieve its mission, the University relies upon committed faculty, motivated students, challenging programs and exceptional facilities. We invite you to meet our faculty and students, to evaluate our academic offerings, and to tour our classrooms, laboratories and residence halls.

Cal U is a student-centered university that is committed above all to academic excellence and intellectual rigor in the context of personal and institutional integrity, civility and responsibility. We provide a welcoming, family atmosphere. Cal U is large enough to offer a variety of programs, yet small enough that most students are known by name.

LOCATION AND ENVIRONMENT

California University of Pennsylvania is nestled in western Pennsylvania's beautiful Monongahela Valley, in a bend of the scenic Monongahela River. The main campus 98 beautifully maintained acres, with a nationally recognized arboretum at its heart. The 98-acre George H. Roadman University Park, just one mile to the south, includes Adamson Stadium and a variety of sports fields and recreation facilities. The adjacent SAI Farm adds another 98 acres of green space for recreation and features a farmhouse that is being renovated for student meetings. The south campus also is home to Vulcan Village, a garden-style apartment complex for students.

OFF-CAMPUS OPPORTUNITIES

In the southwestern corner of Pennsylvania, the University is a short drive from camping, hiking, fishing, hunting, whitewater rafting, canoeing and skiing. Students have easy access to the Pittsburgh metropolitan area, located only 35 miles from campus.

MAJORS AND DEGREES OFFERED

Students may choose from more than 120 four-year degree options and concentrations. The University requires a minimum of 120 semester credits, including satisfactory completion of all required credits, for graduation. Students in all curricula must complete a minimum of 30 credits of their last 60 credits at California University of Pennsylvania.

ACADEMIC PROGRAMS

The College of Education and Human Services carries on the University's long tradition of excellence in teacher education and offers a variety of other professional programs, as well. Other programs in the College include athletic training, gerontology, physical therapist assistant, sport management studies and professional golf management. Also available is a B.S. Ed. in communication disorders, a pre-professional degree that prepares students for future graduate training before employment as a speech-language pathologist, and social work, which provides career opportunities in a variety of human service settings.

The College of Liberal Arts offers a diverse array of major and minor programs of study, including anthropology, art, criminology, English, justice studies, history, political science, psychology, sociology, theater and more. In addition, a broad, general education course of study, based on the liberal arts, encourages students to explore a variety of course offerings and to become aware of the ways many different disciplines understand and view the world.

The Eberly College of Science and Technology offers associate and bachelor's degree programs that prepare students to meet current and future requirements of specific professions and/or to undertake advanced studies. Programs include biology, chemistry, earth sciences and mathematics, as well as a variety of technology-based programs. Environmental studies, computer science, robotics engineering technology and business administration programs also are housed in this College. Each program in the Eberly College includes both general and professional education components to ensure that students receive a well-rounded education as well as the technical training required for a successful career.

CAMPUS FACILITIES AND EQUIPMENT

Residence Life

California University offers a variety of residence life options for students, designed to fit freshman through graduate students. Six suite-style residence halls house students on the main campus, and a garden-style apartment complex is located on the south campus at Vulcan Village. All housing is air-conditioned and furnished. Most students on the main campus share a bathroom with only one other person; many apartments at Vulcan Village have private baths for each suitemate.

Students who live on the main campus must purchase a food service plan, but Vulcan Village apartments have fully equipped kitchens, so a meal plan is optional. All student rooms have free Internet, cable and phone access.

Manderino Library

The Louis L. Manderino Library offers a physical collection of more than 276,000 print titles, 330,000 print volumes, 7,000 electronic books, 18,000 government documents and 4,000 Pennsylvania documents. Through the library's website, users have 24-hour-a-day access to more than 50,000 online books and reference resources, over 36,000 online full-text periodical titles, and numerous electronic databases. PILOT, the library's online public access catalog, is a user-friendly resource that can be used to locate books and other resources in the library's collection. Manderino Library also offers public access computers, wireless Internet connectivity on all floors, and wireless laptop computers that students can borrow for use in the library. The Manderino Library Gallery hosts a series of Smithsonian Institution Traveling Exhibition Service programs year-round.

Other Services

Computer labs are available in many departments, in all residence halls, and in special locations such as the Media Access Center (MAC) Lab in the Natali Student Center and the Instructional Computing Facility in Noss Hall.

Career Services assists students in developing, evaluating and effectively implementing career plans — services offered free to alumni, as well. An Internship Center offers students an opportunity to acquire college-level knowledge and skills outside a traditional classroom setting through affiliations with community organizations, governmental agencies or private businesses.

TUITION, ROOM, BOARD AND FEES
Tuition

California University is a member of the Pennsylvania State System of Higher Education, and the Board of Governors of the State System sets its tuition. Tuition usually is set in July for the academic year that begins in August.

The 2011-2012 tuition for a resident of Pennsylvania attending full-time (12 to 18 credits) was $3,120 per semester. For a full-time nonresident, tuition was $4,992 per semester. Room costs per semester for 2011-12 ranged from $3,049 to $4,448. Board prices ranged from $1,281 to $1,743 per semester. Based on a full-time, in-state student schedule, fees for 2011-2012 included a $15 per credit technology fee, an $85 service fee, a $270 Student Association fee, a $148 student union building fee, an $84 student center operations and maintenance fee, a $158 Herron Recreation and Fitness Center Fee, a $37 Leadership Program fee and a $330 academic support fee. The cost of books, materials, and supplies varies with each program. A current list of all charges and fees is listed on our website, www.calu.edu.

FINANCIAL AID
There are several types of financial available. Grants and scholarships are considered "gift aid" because they do not have to be repaid. Loans and work-study employment are considered "self help aid" because loans have to be repaid and by working, students earn money for educational expenses. Loans are by far the largest source of financial aid for the majority of students and families. Most grants, some loans (Subsidized Stafford and the Perkins Loan), and Federal Work-Study are need-based financial aid programs. The Unsubsidized Stafford and the Parent Loan for Undergraduate Students (PLUS) are considered non-need-based. Scholarships can be based upon merit, financial need or both.

Approximately 93 percent of all students attending California University receive some type of financial aid. The Free Application for Federal Student Aid (FAFSA), along with the cost of education, will determine whether a student has financial need. To receive financial aid, students must complete the FAFSA or Renewal FAFSA. The forms can be obtained from high school guidance counselors, public libraries, or the financial aid office of a college or university, including the Financial Aid Office at California University.

STUDENT ORGANIZATIONS AND ACTIVITIES
More than 120 clubs and student organizations are offered through academic departments and the Student Association Inc. These groups provide social, educational, community service and leadership opportunities for students. Their range is as varied as the interests of the student members.

ADMISSIONS PROCESS
To be considered for admission as a degree-seeking student at California University, applicants must submit the following:

1. Completed application form

2. Application fee

3. Official high school transcript that includes class rank if applicable (or GED certificate and scores)

4. SAT or ACT scores (may be waived for applicants who have been out of high school for a least two years or who have an associate, R.N. or baccalaureate degree)

Transfer students must submit official transcripts from all colleges and universities attended.

Students can apply and pay their application fee online by visiting www.calu.edu. All applications are individually evaluated. As soon as applications are complete, decisions are reached and applicants are notified. This process usually takes less than two weeks.

Admission standards have been established by the university to select those students who will be most likely to succeed.

1. Academics. An applicant must be a graduate of an approved or accredited secondary school or have an equivalent preparation as determined by any state's Department of Education.

2. Assessment and Ability Standards. An ability to do work in higher education should be evident from an assessment examination such as the SAT. In certain circumstances, other kinds of evidence may be used to determine the ability to do such work.

3. Character and Personality. Applicants must be able to demonstrate that they possess the personality traits, interests, attitudes and personal characteristics necessary for higher education. Recommendation letters are welcomed.

4. Admission to Special Curricula. A student seeking admission to a special curriculum may be required to complete additional requirements or have earned specific credentials.

The Admissions Office considers as many variables as possible in making admission decisions: class rank, cumulative grade-point average, type of curriculum completed in relation to proposed major, guidance counselor or other recommendations, on-campus interview, standardized test scores, activities and maturity. Each of these variables contributes to the overall assessment of individual applicants.

CENTRAL CONNECTICUT STATE UNIVERSITY

AT A GLANCE

Central Connecticut State University (CCSU) is a comprehensive public university dedicated to learning in the liberal arts and sciences and to education for the professions. Comprising five schools—Carol Ammon School of Arts & Sciences, Business, Education & Professional Studies, Engineering & Technology, and Graduate Studies—CCSU offers full- and part-time undergraduate programs in more than 100 areas of study.

Conveniently located in New Britain, CCSU's innovative undergraduate curriculum inspires student learning in a wide range of fields, while extensive internship and co-op opportunities help students prepare for rewarding careers. The University's Division I athletics teams provide exciting opportunities to play or watch.

LOCATION AND ENVIRONMENT

CCSU is located in suburban New Britain, conveniently located in the center of Connecticut, approximately 2 hours from Boston or New York. The campus has been recently renovated. The University is surrounded by a pleasant neighborhood, with shopping and dining facilities nearby.

OFF-CAMPUS OPPORTUNITIES

CCSU's Center for Advising and Career Exploration coordinates a comprehensive Co-op Education Program as well as internships at local and area corporations, agencies, and government offices. Annual career fairs bring some 200 area and regional businesses to campus. CCSU Co-op students annually earn $4 million, and more than 65% are offered full-time career starting jobs with their Co-op employers.

The School of Education has many connections to area schools, including several Professional Development Schools, which provide CCSU students nearly unique opportunities to perfect their teaching skills in a full range of elementary and secondary classrooms.

The School of Engineering & Technology offers a wide array of internship opportunities in area engineering, manufacturing, and technology businesses.

The George R. Muirhead Center for International Education, nationally recognized for the quality of its Study Abroad programs, offers students a rich variety of study-abroad opportunities at more than 40 locations throughout the world and provides academic and cultural programs that promote a better understanding of peoples and cultures.

And the University and the New Britain Museum of American Art (an internationally acclaimed museum) have a partnership allowing students and faculty to visit the museum for free.

MAJORS AND DEGREES OFFERED

CCSU is accredited by the New England Association of Schools and Colleges (NEASC). The University operates on a two-semester calendar and offers four summer sessions plus one winter session. Undergraduate programs include: Accounting; Anthropology; Art (Art History); Athletic Training; Biochemistry; Biology (Ecology; Biodiversity; Evolutionary; Environmental Science; General); Biomolecular Sciences; Chemistry; Civil Engineering; Civil Engineering Technology; Communication (Broadcast Journalism; Media Studies; Organizational Communications; Promotion/Public Relations); Computer Engineering Technology; Computer Science; Construction Management; Criminology; Design (Graphic/Information); Earth Sciences; Economics (General; Operations Research); Education (Elementary; K-12; Secondary; Special Education); Electronics Technology; Engineering &Technology Education; Engineering Technology; English; Entrepreneurship; Exercise Science; Finance; French; Geography (Environmental; General Regional; Planning; Geographic Information Science; Tourism); German; History; Hospitality & Tourism; Industrial Technology (Electro-Mechanical Technology; Environmental & Occupational Safety; Graphics Technology; Manufacturing; Networking Technology; Technology Management); Interdisciplinary Science (Environmental Interpretation; Physical Sciences); International Business; International Studies; Italian; Journalism; Management (Entrepreneurship; Human Resource); Management Information Systems; Manufacturing Engineering Technology; Marketing; Mathematics (Actuarial; Statistics); Mechanical Engineering; Mechanical Engineering Technology; Music; Nursing (BSN & RN to BSN); Philosophy; Physical Education (Exercise Science & Health Promotion); Physics; Political Science (General; Public Administration); Psychology; Social Sciences; Social Work; Sociology; Spanish; Theatre.

Degrees: BA, BFA (Theatre); BS; BSN; BS-RN, Teacher Certification (elementary; secondary; k-12)

ACADEMIC PROGRAMS

CCSU also offers a number of interdisciplinary programs as well as independently designed majors. The Honors Program, a challenging interdisciplinary program of study for academically qualified students, offers half- and full-tuition merit scholarships and a variety of other benefits and resources, including a new Honors Lab.

CAMPUS FACILITIES AND EQUIPMENT

CCSU offers an attractive campus with new and renovated buildings adding to the classic collegiate style of its historical architecture. The academic buildings feature technologically state-of-the-art "smart classrooms" and seminar rooms, and the entire campus offers wireless access. The Student Center provides lounges, dining services, conference and game rooms, information services, and a range of other support services. Three theatres offer space for plays, concerts, and guest lectures. The S.T. Chen Art Gallery hosts shows by student, faculty, and visiting artists. The Student Technology Center features 250 computers plus printers and scanners for student use. Campus-based TV and radio stations provide exciting entertainment as well as opportunities to learn about the professions. The Elihu Burritt Library provides access to over 2 million books through an online catalog, a wide array of electronic databases and online resources, and special collections ranging from the unparalleled collection of Polish American materials to the Equity Archive. The University also offers many new athletic facilities, including an Olympic-sized swimming pool, modern exercise equipment, a state-of-the-art fitness center, a weight-training room, and an athletic training center. In the Kaiser Annex students can walk, jog, and play tennis or a pickup basketball game. CCSU recently opened new football, soccer, softball, and baseball fields to complement its basketball and volleyball arena. The residence halls and classrooms are fully networked. Approximately 20% of the students live on campus in nine residence halls.

TUITION, ROOM, BOARD AND FEES

Expenses for the 2012-13 academic year include tuition (in-state: $8,322; out-of-state: $19,353), room and board ($9,800 [approx.]); expenses for books, transportation, fees, and other expenses range from $5000 (in residence) to $6000 (off-campus residence).

FINANCIAL AID

Approximately 75% of CCSU full-time students receive some form of financial aid. CCSU's office of Financial Aid works with students to help them meet educational expenses from their first year until graduation. To apply for financial aid students must complete the FAFSA form. For more information, call 860-832-2200, e-mail FinancialAid3@ccsu.edu, or on the Web at www.ccsu.edu/finaid.

STUDENT ORGANIZATIONS AND ACTIVITIES

There are 120 student clubs and organizations, which cover a broad range of interests: academic--such as the Anthropology or the Investment clubs; athletic--such as the crew or flying clubs; cultural--for example, the art club, the jazz band, and other musical organizations; ethnic--such as the Black Student Union, Latin American Students Organization, and the Muslim Student Association; religious— such as Hillel and the Newman Club; and such honors organizations as Delta Mu Delta, Lambda Delta, and Kappa Delta Pi. On-campus entertainment is wide and varied, including, most recently, "Devils Den@ 10"—student-run entertainment on Thursday evenings

ADMISSIONS PROCESS

CCSU is a learning community of students with a broad range of abilities, interests, and backgrounds. We value excellence and achievement in academic scholarship, community involvement, and extracurricular activities. Our admissions process evaluates the readiness of applicants to succeed based on past demonstrations of academic and personal successes. The preferred deadlines for best consideration are May 1 (for Fall semester) and December 1 (for Spring).

First-year applicants are considered on the basis of performance in college preparatory classes, rank in class, SAT or ACT test scores, recommendations, and community and extracurricular involvement and leadership. A personal essay is required. For some applicants an interview with a representative of the Office of Recruitment & Admissions may be necessary. If the applicant ranks in the top 20% of his/her class, is an A-B student, and has SAT scores of 1100 or higher, the student should consider finding out about CCSU's Honors Program by calling 860-832-2938 for details. CCSU accepts most Advanced Placement (AP) courses for college credit, provided the minimum CCSU required score is achieved. Check with Admissions for the required scores.

Admission criteria include graduation from a regionally accredited secondary school. High school work should include college preparatory courses in: English (four years); Mathematics (covering algebra I, geometry, and algebra II); Science (two years including one-year lab science); Social sciences (two to three years including U.S. history). Coursework in foreign language is recommended (at least three consecutive years of the same foreign language up through the third level will satisfy the foreign language proficiency required of all CCSU-enrolled students). Students whose preparation does not follow this pattern may still qualify for admission if, in the judgment of the Director of Recruitment and Admissions, there is strong evidence that they have the potential to complete a degree program or if they meet other established criteria as authorized by the University President under authority delegated by the Board of Trustees of the Connecticut State University System. Applicants who are not graduates of a secondary school should submit their secondary school transcript up to the time of withdrawal and a copy of their high school equivalency diploma and scores.

Students interested in enrolling part-time on a non-degree basis should contact Continuing Education at (860) 832-2255.

The most important thing for the applicant to remember is to provide as much information as possible—achievements, awards, and examples of leadership—when applying.

APPLICATION AND INFORMATION

Students are encouraged to apply online at www.ccsu.edu/apply. For paper applications, please provide the Office of Recruitment & Admissions with 1) completed application for undergraduate admission 2) official high school transcript, SAT or ACT test scores, recommendations, and essay and 3) a non-refundable application fee of $50. All correspondence should be sent to the Office of Recruitment and Admissions, CCSU, P.O. Box 4010, 1615 Stanley Street, New Britain, CT 06050-4010.

Tours and information sessions may be arranged by calling 860.832.2289 or via e-mail at: admissions@ccsu.edu.

CHAPMAN UNIVERSITY

AT A GLANCE

During its 151-year history, Chapman University has evolved from a small, traditional liberal arts college into a comprehensive university distinguished for its extraordinary blend of liberal arts, science, and professional programs. Film and television production, business and economics, theatre, dance, music, education, and the natural and applied sciences — Chapman boasts a breadth of fields usually only found at larger institutions. Chapman University's mission is to develop global citizen-leaders who are distinctively prepared to improve their community and their world.

With beautiful grounds and stately buildings, Chapman is one of the oldest schools on the West Coast, yet its park-like campus is also one of the most modern. More than a dozen buildings have been built or renovated in just the last two decades, with four more on the drawing board. Architecturally impressive residence halls and apartment buildings offer students exciting lifestyle amenities within a vibrant Southern California setting.

With its central Orange County, California, location and more than 7,000 undergraduate, graduate, and professional school students, the University environment is alive with activity. In addition to the temperate climate, Chapman students enjoy a dynamic, eclectic, and outdoor-oriented lifestyle, both on campus and off. Students come from all walks of life; from across the country and from all over the world, each student brings his or her own unique view of what makes a true global citizen. Over the past five years, Chapman students have been named Truman Scholars, Coro Fellows, USA Today All-USA College Academic Team members, NCAA All-Americans, and NCAA Academic All-Americans.

Chapman's academic preparation and wide breadth of excellence is evidenced by the University's accomplished alumni, who include Loretta Sanchez ('88), member of Congress; David Bonior ('85), member of Congress and former house minority whip; Jose Gomez ('75) member of the Panamanian National Assembly; television and film producers John Copeland ('73), Jon Garcia ('90), and John David Currey ('98); cinematographer Gene Jackson ('70); St. John's University men's basketball coach Steve Lavin ('88); Tony Award nominee and Broadway star of Showboat Michel Bell ('68); Indy car racing star Jacques Lazier ('93); former major league baseball stars Tim Flannery ('80), Marty Castillo ('80), Gary Lucas ('76), and Randy Jones ('72); and George L. Argyros ('65), philanthropist and former U.S. Ambassador to Spain.

LOCATION AND ENVIRONMENT

Orange County, California, has been rated by Places Rated Almanac as "the #1 place to live in North America," citing superior climate and cultural, recreational, educational, and career-entree opportunities. Orange County's central location between two major cities means there is never a lack of entertainment choices. It is, in fact, home to the happiest place on Earth — Disneyland is literally minutes from campus.

The Segerstrom Center for the Arts, Major League Baseball's Los Angeles Angels of Anaheim, and the National Hockey League's Anaheim Ducks are all nearby Chapman's campus in Old Towne Orange. Pristine West Coast beaches are less than 10 miles from the campus, and seasonal snow skiing is 90 minutes away. The average year-round temperature on campus is 71°F, and the daily sea breeze from the nearby Pacific Ocean keeps the air cool, clean, and smog free.

On campus, Chapman students take part in the dynamic student activities program. There are over 100 student run clubs, including community service organizations, 17 national fraternities and sororities, 19 NCAA D-III intercollegiate athletic programs, an active intramural sports program, and music, art, and theatre productions.

OFF-CAMPUS OPPORTUNITIES

Chapman's Career Development Center provides a variety of services to students, graduates, and former students. These include internship opportunities, an on-campus recruiting program, full-time job postings and computer-networked job listings, individual career counseling and career assessment, a career resource library, job search and resume writing skills development, interview coaching, and an alumni mentor program. The center will assist teachers in establishing a self-managed educational placement file.

Chapman students are encouraged to participate in study abroad programs in many academic fields in almost every part of the world. Students studying abroad through Chapman-approved programs are enrolled in a full course of study at the host institution, but receive academic credit from Chapman. The study abroad program directly supports Chapman's emphasis on encouraging students to recognize and develop their roles as global citizens in an increasingly interdependent world.

MAJORS AND DEGREES OFFERED

Chapman University confers degrees in the following field of study: Accounting, Art, Art History, Athletic Training, Biochemistry and Molecular Biology, Biological Sciences, Business Administration, Chemistry, Communication Studies, Computer Information Systems, Computer Science, Creative Producing, Creative Writing, Dance, Dance Performance, Digital Arts, Economics, English, Environmental Science and Policy, Film Production, Film Studies, French, Graphic Design, Health Sciences, History, Integrated Educational Studies (teaching), Mathematics, Mathematics and Civil Engineering, Music, Music Composition, Music Education, Music Performance, Peace Studies, Philosophy, Physics and Computational Science, Political Science, Pre-Health, Pre-Law, Psychology, Public Relations and Advertising, Religious Studies, Screen Acting, Screenwriting, Sociology, Spanish, Strategic and Corporate Communication, Television and Broadcast Journalism, Theatre, Theatre Performance

ACADEMIC PROGRAMS

Chapman University strives to provide every student with a comprehensive, liberal arts-based course of study, which will result in producing an engaging, articulate, and communicative world citizen with specific skills to offer. Chapman University's academic structure includes the Wilkinson College of Humanities and Social Sciences; the Dodge College of Film and Media Arts; the AACSB International–accredited Argyros School of Business and Economics; the CTC-approved College of Educational Studies; the ABA-accredited School of Law; the Schmid College of Science and Technology; and the College of Performing Arts, which includes the NASM-accredited Hall-Musco Conservatory of Music, the NAST-accredited Department of Theatre, and the NASD-accredited Department of Dance.

CAMPUS FACILITIES AND EQUIPMENT

Chapman's stunning campus continues to grow by leaps and bounds. Major additions to the campus over the past few years include the 100,000-square-foot Leatherby Libraries complex, housing eight discipline-specific individual libraries, a cyber courtyard, and a 24-hour study commons and coffee bar. The Oliphant Hall addition to the Conservatory of Music is a 24,000-square-foot space featuring fourteen teaching studios, a 60-seat lecture hall, music therapy laboratory, and orchestra hall. In addition to the Conservatory of Music's Bertea and Oliphant Halls, the College of Performing Arts facilities include the Moulton Fine Arts Complex featuring the 250-seat repertory-style Waltmar Theatre, a black box theater, the Guggenheim Art Gallery, and the Partridge Dance Center. The Fish Interfaith Center features the 12,500-square-foot Wallace All-Faiths Chapel, recognized by Architectural Digest for innovation in design. The 200,000-square-foot Sandhu Residence and Conference center houses the primary on-campus dining facility for resident students, as well as a conference center and residence hall. The 90,000-square-foot Argyros Forum includes the newly expanded student union with additional campus dining options, as well as conference and classroom facilities. The 800-seat Memorial Auditorium is the primary performance and assembly venue on campus and is listed on the National Register of Historic Places. Athletic facilities include the 2,500-seat Hutton Sports Center; the 2,000-seat Ernie Chapman Stadium for football, lacrosse, and soccer; and the 500-seat Allred Aquatics Center swim stadium/Olympic pool complex. Beckman Hall is the center for business and information technology — the newly opened Janes Financial Center with its eleven Bloomberg terminals is housed there. The Hashinger Science Center features laboratories for nuclear science, radiation, crystallography, genetics, food science, physics, and computational sciences.

TUITION, ROOM, BOARD AND FEES

Undergraduate tuition (annual, 12-18 semester credits), room, board, and fees for the 2012-2013 academic are as follows:

Annual tuition: $41,040

Accident/Sickness plan: $380

Associated students fee: $120

Wellness Center fee: $244

Total tuition/fees: $41,784

Room/board cost for academic year 2010-2011:

Room & Board: $12,060

Parking fee: $300

Total room/board: $12,360

FINANCIAL AID

More than 85 percent of Chapman students benefit from some form of need based aid, merit, or talent scholarship. Awards are made through a combination of grants, scholarships, loans, and work-study programs. Awards may be renewed throughout a student's term of study. A student's financial needs are usually met through a combination of internal assets and federal and state funding. Chapman awards merit scholarships, regardless of financial need, to all eligible admitted new students using a standardized test score/entering grade point average-driven formula. Chapman also offers talent scholarships in areas such as art, music, dance, theatre, writing, film and television, and science awarded regardless of financial need. Audition, submission of portfolio, or supplemental application materials will be required to be considered for talent awards.

STUDENT ORGANIZATIONS AND ACTIVITIES

More than 100 clubs and organizations are recognized on campus, many with commitments to a wide range of community service efforts. Chapman's Greek system includes nine nationally chartered fraternities for men and eight nationally chartered sororities for women. Intramural sports, on-campus intercollegiate athletic events, as well as music, art, and theater productions provide students with plenty to do outside of class.

Chapman's long and distinguished heritage in intercollegiate athletics includes five NCAA national championships in baseball, tennis, and softball. The Panthers compete in the NCAA Division III Southern California Intercollegiate Athletic Conference (SCIAC) and field teams in baseball, basketball, crew, cross-country, football, golf, lacrosse, soccer, softball, swimming, tennis, track and field, volleyball, and water polo. Approximately 20 percent of Chapman's student body participates in intercollegiate athletics.

ADMISSIONS PROCESS

Admission to Chapman is selective. In 2012, admission was granted to 41 percent of the applicant pool. The University is interested in admitting students whose prior records indicate that they will be successful in a competitive collegiate environment. Freshman applicants are considered for admission based primarily on the nature and sequence of their high school course work, grade point average achieved, their results on either the SAT or ACT examination, co-curricular involvements, and personal characteristics. Transfer candidates are considered for admission on the basis of their course work and cumulative grade point average earned at other regionally accredited postsecondary institutions, their co-curricular involvements, and personal characteristics.

Chapman University exclusively uses the Common Application (http://www.commonapp.org), as well as a Chapman-specific supplement to the Common Application and departmental applications for those applying to the art, dance, film, music, or theater programs. Candidates are strongly encouraged to visit and tour the campus and participate in an information session led by an admission officer. Arrangements for a group information session and campus tour can be made through the Office of Admission.

Students may request more information by contacting:

Office of Admission

Chapman University

One University Drive

Orange, CA 92866

Telephone: 714- 997-6711 or 888-CUAPPLY (toll free)

Fax: 714-997-6713

E-mail: admit@chapman.edu

CHESTNUT HILL COLLEGE

AT A GLANCE

A college of distinction, Chestnut Hill College is a four-year Catholic, coed, liberal arts college located in Philadelphia, Pennsylvania. Founded in 1924 by the Sisters of St. Joseph, it is situated on a 75-acre campus overlooking Wissahickon Creek. Since opportunities for leadership and self-expression are frequent, the Chestnut Hill College graduate can enter a competitive world well prepared for success. Students come from 28 states, 31 countries, and every imaginable background. In addition to its undergraduate degrees, Chestnut Hill College awards the M.Ed., M.A., and M.S. in five fields, including Education, Clinical and Counseling Psychology, Administration of Human Services, Holistic Spirituality, and Instructional Technology.

When it comes to student activities, students enthusiastically engage in the many clubs and organizations available. The College is NCAA Division II and competes in softball, baseball, MW golf, W volleyball, MW cross country, MW soccer, MW lacrosse, MW tennis, and MW basketball. A swimming pool, gymnasium, soccer/lacrosse field, softball field, fitness center, outdoor volleyball and basketball courts and six tennis courts provide excellent athletic facilities for Chestnut Hill College students.

LOCATION AND ENVIRONMENT

Located in an historic area of Philadelphia, Chestnut Hill College's beautiful campus is bordered by Fairmount Park, yet is a quick train or car ride away from bustling downtown Philadelphia. One of the mid-Atlantic's premiere cities, Philadelphia offers a wide variety of restaurants, sports, and cultural and recreational activities. In particular, Philadelphia is home to a number of world-class museums, including the Philadelphia Museum of Art, the Rodin Museum, and the Franklin Institute. An historic city, the atmosphere and architecture around Independence Hall, Society Hill, and Penn's Landing are gems of colonial architecture and atmosphere. In addition to the city's cultural resources, Philadelphia is home to 25 colleges and universities, creating a vibrant collegiate environment for study and social life.

While students at Chestnut Hill College have access to cosmopolitan Philadelphia, the college is set in a lovely suburban neighborhood in the northwest corner of the city. The charming colonial area of Chestnut Hill is just a mile from campus. Well known in and beyond Philadelphia, Chestnut Hill gives students easy access to shopping and cultural events, as well as convenient transportation downtown.

MAJORS AND DEGREES OFFERED

The Bachelor of Arts and Bachelor of Science degrees are offered with majors in: Accounting, Biology, Biochemistry, Chemistry, Communications, Communications and Technology, Computer and Information Sciences, Computer and Information, Technology, Criminal Justice, Early Education (Pre-K to 4), English Literature, English Literature and Communications, Environmental Sciences, Forensic Biology, Forensic Chemistry, French, History, Human Services, Individualized, International Business, Language and Culture, Management, Marketing, Mathematical and Computer Sciences, Mathematics, Middle-level Education (Grades 4-8), Molecular Biology, Music (Performance), Music Education, Political Science, Psychology, Sociology, Spanish.

ACADEMIC PROGRAMS

Chestnut Hill College's core curriculum is designed to provide students with a meaningful education that is rooted in college's mission. Steeped in the liberal arts, the curriculum recognizes the impact of the information-age revolution and addresses career demands of the twenty-first century, while at the same time providing an unparalleled holistic education to all of the college's students. The core curriculum consists of fundamental requirements, Ways of Knowing perspectives, proficiencies, and free electives. In addition, students fulfill all of the requirements specified in a major program of study.

Focused on six perspectives (Historical, Literary, Artistic, Scientific, Behavioral, and Problem-Solving and Analysis), the Ways of Knowing component of the Core Curriculum is designed to introduce students to different learning methodologies and strategies for interpreting and understanding the world in which we live.

Students may be approved to pursue a degree simultaneously within two major disciplines. Students who wish to double major must discuss their proposed course of study with the chair of each department and submit a proposal to the Dean of the College. To earn a dual degree, students must satisfy the individual requirements of both department programs.

Select students have the opportunity to participate in the challenging Interdisciplinary Honors Program (IDHP). The courses in the IDHP consist of seminars co-taught by two faculty members from different disciplines. In these reading- and writing-intensive seminars, learning is achieved through active discussion involving students and professors alike. Each is interdisciplinary to promote the integration of knowledge. An atmosphere of cooperation replaces competition for grades, fostering in students their own unique potential and enthusiasm for learning.

Chestnut Hill College's faculty is accomplished in research, publication, and travel, but are teachers first and foremost. The undergraduate college faculty consists of 170 faculty members, 65 of whom are full-time. Over 75 percent of faculty members hold doctoral or terminal degrees in their subject area. Chestnut Hill College instructors take teaching seriously, and with an excellent student/faculty ratio of 11:1, students have ample opportunity to work individually with professors. Chestnut Hill's distinguished instructors have earned degrees from such premiere institutions as the University of Oxford in England, the University of Paris, the University of Budapest, Catholic University of America, Middlebury College, Bryn Mawr College, Columbia University, the University of Notre Dame, the University of Pennsylvania, Duke University, New York University, the New School for Social Research, Purdue University, Temple University, and the University of Minnesota.

STUDENT ORGANIZATIONS AND ACTIVITIES

The Student Activities Office organizes and hosts weekly campus events, off campus trips, and late night programming on every Friday night. The office also coordinates large campus wide events such as Griffin Days, Orientation, and Family Weekend. Events hosted by clubs and organizations receive the support of the Activities Office in order to achieve success throughout the year. Student Activities also offers leadership development programs such as workshops, conferences, and more.

Each student at Chestnut Hill College is part of the most influential organization on campus, the Student Government Association (SGA). SGA commits itself to actively representing the student body while striving to serve the school community with leadership, equality, dedication, loyalty, and responsibility. Moreover, by preserving the traditions of the College, SGA encourages an appreciation and awareness of the College and the world at-large.

Student Activities serves as the home for many academic interest groups, drama and music groups, cultural organizations, yearbook and newspaper staffs, and community action groups. While not comprehensive, this list includes: Accounting Club, Adventure Club, AAAS (African-American Awareness Society), APA (Association for Performing Arts), Aurelian (yearbook), Biology Club, Brazilian Jiu Jitsu Club, CEC (Council for Exceptional Children), Chamber Singers, CHAT (Chestnut Hill Activities Team), Commuter Appreciation Club, Computer Club, Crown the King Chess Club, Dance Club, FADD (Fighting Against Dangerous Decisions), Fishing Club, Gospel Choir, The Griffin (newspaper), Griffins for Paws, GRN (Griffin Radio Network), GSA (Gay Straight Alliance), History Club, Improv Comedy Club, International Society, Japanese Culture Club, La Voz Latina, Link, Mask and Foil Drama Club, Phi Beta Lambda (business society), Photography Club, Psychology Club, Students Political Science Association.

CAMPUS FACILITIES AND EQUIPMENT

CHC's Logue Library affords students wireless internet connectivity, access to 130,000 books, 450 periodicals, subscriptions to scholarly research databases, a rare book room that contains first editions and special editions, the Gruber Theater, the fine Curriculum Library for elementary education, and an Irish literature collection. Well equipped science laboratories, a math center, a multimedia technology center, a writing enrichment center, individual practice rooms for music students, a spacious art studio, a planetarium, and an observatory are among the many other outstanding facilities on campus. Opened in the fall of 2000, Martino Hall houses a performance center, gymnasium, and convocation center. The second and third floors house cutting-edge, "smart" classrooms. Fitzsimmons Hall opened in fall 2006 and houses 150 students in suite style living. The newest addition to the college can be found on the adjacent Sugarloaf Campus; facilities include a residence hall and Sugarloaf Mansion which provides additional classrooms as well as gathering space for students.

OFF-CAMPUS OPPORTUNITIES

Chestnut Hill College participates in a consortium arrangement with eight colleges throughout the nation, founded by the Sisters of St. Joseph. As participants, students can study at any other member institution for a semester or a year, while maintaining status as a full-time Chestnut Hill student. Chestnut Hill College is also a member of SEPCHE (Southeastern Pennsylvania Consortium for Higher Education); the collaboration allows Chestnut Hill College the ability to learn best practices surrounding student life, academics, and technology. SEPCHE membership also allows students to share various resources at other member institutions.

An average of B or above and approval of the academic dean allow an upper class student to pursue organized study in another country. The major department must approve the course of study. In recent years, Chestnut Hill College students have enrolled in institutions in London, Rome, Madrid, Vienna, Salzburg, and other European centers.

The Office of Career Development at Chestnut Hill College provides information and guidance on careers, professions, employment, and graduate school opportunities for current and prospective students as well as alumni. Additionally, the Office of Career Development coordinates the College's experiential education program. In today's competitive job market, there is a growing need for students to acquire on-the-job experience while still in college. Through credit-bearing experiential education opportunities like internships and co-ops, students are able to link the world of learning with the world of work, synthesizing academic theory with practice.

TUITION, ROOM, BOARD AND FEES

Over 75 percent of students at Chestnut Hill College receive financial aid. Chestnut Hill College offers financial aid in the form of scholarships, loans, work-study, federal grants, and Chestnut Hill College grants. Each package is tailored to suit a student's needs and abilities. All prospective students applying for aid must file the Free Application for Federal Student Aid (FAFSA). In addition to need-based awards, Chestnut Hill awards merit-based scholarships; the average merit-based award is $11,500. Tuition for 2012-2013 is $29,995 plus additional estimated room and board cost of $9,616.

ADMISSIONS PROCESS

CHC seeks accomplished students prepared to benefit from a challenging undergraduate curriculum. Admissions counselors review all applications and evaluate students on their intellectual ability and academic achievement. To be considered for admission, students must submit an application, a nonrefundable application fee, an official high school transcript, and scores from the SAT or ACT. A personal statement and letters of recommendation are strongly encouraged. Though usually not required, a personal interview is recommended.

Prospective transfer students are required to submit an official transcript of all college or university work. International students may be required to submit additional materials to support English proficiency.

Admissions decisions are made on a rolling basis. To set up an interview or request more information about academics or admissions, students may contact:

Office of Undergraduate Admissions

Chestnut Hill College

9601 Germantown Avenue

Philadelphia, PA 19118

Telephone: 215-248-7001

800-248-0052 (toll free)

E-mail: admissions@chc.edu

Website: www.chc.edu

THE CITY COLLEGE OF NEW YORK

AT A GLANCE

What do you want to be? Where do you want to go? You have so many choices – we'd like to show you why City may be the right choice for you.

City is an old school with new ideas. Founded in 1847, we take pride in our tradition, eagerly embrace the present, and ride the cutting edge of the future. The College, with one of the most diverse student bodies in any college of America, is a mirror image of New York City. Our mission emphasizes access and excellence in undergraduate and graduate education and research, and opportunities for internships and study abroad abound. Whether you are looking for preparation for an exciting career or graduate and doctoral studies, City College offers the path to your future. We offer over 100 undergraduate and graduate degrees in architecture, education, engineering, the arts and humanities, the social sciences and science, as well as a unique BS/MD program.

Visit Us!

Come discover the diversity of our college community, the beauty of our campus and the academic excellence that is City College. Join us for a general campus tour that combines a walk through history and a peek into the future. Reservations are required and can only be made by joining our on-line community, here: https://cunyccny.askadmissions.net/Vip/Default.aspx

Graduate students looking to schedule a tour of CCNY should visit http://www.ccny.cuny.edu/admissions/graduate-campus-tours.cfm for more information about Graduate Tours.

GROUP TOURS

If you are a school counselor or group organizer looking to bring a group of 10 or more for a campus tour you must make a reservation. Reservations for group visits can be made by contacting the Tour Line at tours@ccny.cuny.edu or by calling (212) 650-6476.

Our group tours fill up quickly so we recommend that reservations be made at least 4 weeks prior to the desired visit date.

OUR ILLUSTRIOUS HISTORY

This year the City College of New York celebrates the 166th anniversary of its founding. The need for an institution like The City College was recognized as early as 1847, when the State Legislature authorized a local referendum to determine whether a public college should be established in the City of New York; at the time, the city had a population of a half a million people and two private colleges, which had high tuition and only 247 pupils. The vote was overwhelmingly in favor of the proposition, and the Free Academy was established in a new building at Lexington Avenue and 23rd Street. The doors to its first entering class opened in January, 1849, and a class of seventeen young men graduated in 1853; with friends and family members, that first commencement was too large for the chapel at the Free Academy, so it was celebrated in Biblo's beer garden.

In 1866 the name of the Free Academy was changed by legislative act to The College of the City of New York. Since then, it has been called CCNY — an unofficial designation the College retained even after its name was again changed in 1929 to The City College. Students, alumni and friends call the College, simply, "City." The college colors, lavender and black, were chosen by the student body in 1866. The beaver, symbol of intelligence, industry and determination, was voted to be the College's official athletics' mascot by a student-wide poll in 1934.

The governing body of the College, originally the Board of Education, was replaced in 1900 by a separate Board of Trustees appointed by the Mayor. In 1926, the Board of Higher Education was established to govern both City and Hunter College (founded in 1870), and subsequently the entire City University system, established in 1961. After primary responsibility for funding the University became that of New York State rather than New York City, an enlarged Board of Trustees, appointed by the Governor and the Mayor, assumed control in 1980.

The City College of New York, originally limited to undergraduate programs in classical and practical courses of study, has continually enlarged both the breadth and the depth of its offerings. Today it offers more than fifty undergraduate programs and majors and more than forty graduate programs, including Ph.D. programs in six disciplines.

The City College moved to its present location in 1907, and now occupies a thirty-five acre Neo-Gothic and modern campus on historic St. Nicholas Heights. It is really a small university, with a College of Liberal Arts and Science and four professional schools — the School of Architecture, Urban Design and Landscape Architecture, the School of Engineering, the School of Education, and the Sophie Davis School of Biomedical Education.

The City College is the nation's flagship institution of public higher education, predating the Midwestern state and land-grant colleges by two decades. For more than 165 years it has been a primary avenue of advancement for generations of New Yorkers who might not have had the chance to attend college. Today it continues to fulfill the aim of its founder, Townsend Harris, who said; "Open the doors to all — Let the children of the rich and the poor take their seats together and know of no distinction save that of industry, good conduct and intellect."

CLEMSON UNIVERSITY

AT A GLANCE

One of the country's most selective public research universities, Clemson was founded in 1889 with a mission to be a "high seminary of learning" dedicated to teaching, research, and service. Today, these three concepts remain at the heart of the University and provide the framework for an exceptional educational experience.

At Clemson University, professors take the time to get to know students and explore innovative ways of teaching. Exceptional teaching is one reason Clemson's retention and graduation rates rank among the highest in the country for public universities.

Exceptional teaching is also why Clemson continues to attract an increasingly talented student body. In 2012, more than half of the entering freshmen were ranked in the top 10 percent of their high school classes, and the freshman class averaged 1246 on the critical reading and math sections of the SAT.

Clemson is committed to world-class research, with externally funded research expenditures totaling $101.5 million in 2011–12. New awards to Clemson totaled more than $99 million in 2011–12.

The University is also invested in the success of its students. In the 2011–12 academic year, Clemson's student retention rate was more than 91 percent. Much of this is due to the Academic Success Center (ASC), established in 2001 and recognized nationally and internationally for its programs in tutoring, supplemental instruction, and collegiate learning. The ASC moved into a new facility in 2012 where it offers free one-on-one tutoring services for more than 80 courses as well as for additional courses as the need arises. Supplemental instruction, academic skills workshops, and academic counseling are also available—free to all Clemson students. It is estimated that more than 50 percent of freshmen use ASC services during their first semester.

Clemson has also received national recognition for its innovative Communication Across the Curriculum (CAC) program, ranking ninth on the U.S.News & World Report list of public colleges and universities identified as making writing across all curriculums a priority. At Clemson, CAC has become a standard teaching method used in nearly every department to provide real-life challenges that require students to think and communicate effectively.

From cheering the Tigers at a football game to socializing at the Hendrix Student Center, Clemson students can participate in a wide variety of activities outside the classroom. The more than 400 campus clubs and organizations include fraternities and sororities, as well as honorary, international, military, performing arts, political, professional, religious, service, social interest, special interest, sports and fitness, and student media.

With nineteen intercollegiate sports, Clemson offers exciting spectator sports year-round. Clemson is a charter member of the Atlantic Coast Conference and is an NCAA Division I school. Admission to regular-season home events is included in University fees for full-time students.

Admissions:

864-656-2287

clemson.edu/admissions/undergraduate

Campus Tours:

864-656-4789

clemson.edu/visitors

LOCATION AND ENVIRONMENT

Clemson University is located in Clemson, S.C., a town of about 14,000 located in the middle of the I-85 corridor between Atlanta, Ga., and Charlotte, N.C. The 1,400-acre campus borders the shores of Hartwell Lake and the foothills of the Blue Ridge Mountains.

OFF-CAMPUS OPPORTUNITIES

Study Abroad

Clemson students are strongly encouraged to incorporate a study-abroad experience in their overall Clemson journey. Programs are available on six continents for all disciplines and interests. These include faculty-led programs, exchange programs, and programs available through Clemson's partnerships with study-abroad providers and institutions. Students in a variety of majors also have opportunities at Clemson campuses in South Carolina and around the world, including the Archbold Center in Dominica; the Daniel Center in Genoa, Italy; and the Brussels Center in Belgium.

Cooperative Education

The Cooperative Education program provides an opportunity for students to alternate periods of academic study with semesters of paid, career-related, engaged-learning experiences to bridge the gap between academic study and its application in professional practice. Clemson's Michelin® Career Center helps to pair students with companies seeking interns or co-op students. Internships are also available on campus where students can work part- or full-time, with many in full-time positions having the option of earning credit. Clemson is ranked among the top 10 universities that produced the largest percentage of interns among the class of 2011, according to U.S. News & World Report's "The Short List."

Community Service

An important aspect of Clemson is its dedication to improving the world through public service. In a typical year, more than 10,000 Clemson students contribute about 73,000 service hours, earning the University national recognition on the President's Higher Education Community Service Honor Roll. Opportunities to make a difference are available through student service organizations, ongoing service projects, and one-time service events —on campus, in the community, across the nation, or around the world.

MAJORS AND DEGREES

Students can select from more than 80 undergraduate and 110 graduate degree programs offered by five colleges: Agriculture, Forestry and Life Sciences; Architecture, Arts and Humanities; Business and Behavioral Science; Engineering and Science; and Health, Education and Human Development. To find out what majors are available go to: clemson.edu/majors.

Clemson University is accredited by the Commission on Colleges of the Southern Association of Colleges and Schools to award bachelor's, master's, specialist, and doctoral degrees. Questions about the accreditation of Clemson University can be directed to the Commission on Colleges at 1866 Southern Lane, Decatur, Georgia 30033-4097; phone: 404-679-4500.

Honors College

Calhoun Honors College is a University-wide program that combines the strengths of a public, land-grant university with those of a highly selective small college. Calhoun Scholars may choose to pursue departmental honors within their specific academic discipline. In addition, EUREKA! (Experiences in Undergraduate Research, Exploration, and Knowledge Advancement) is a unique and exciting program that enables honors students to pursue research and scholarly activities with faculty members across all disciplines. The advantages of membership in the Honors College include priority registration, extended library loan privileges, honors research grants, and a special living-learning community.

The National Scholars Program is a highly selective program for exceptional students who strive to meet their highest intellectual potential. One of its goals is to develop the interests and talents students need to compete for Rhodes, Marshall, and Truman scholarships; Fulbright Grants; National Science Foundation Graduate Fellowships; and other prestigious international fellowships. In 2012, eleven Clemson students received National Science Foundation Graduate Fellowships and six others received honorable mentions. Four recent Clemson graduates received Fulbright grants to conduct research or teach abroad.

Undergraduate Research

Clemson's Creative Inquiry (CI) program allows undergraduate students to engage in research about problems that spring from their own curiosity, from a professor's challenge, or from the pressing needs of the world around them. Team-based investigations are led by a faculty mentor and typically span two to four semesters. Students take ownership of their projects and take the risks necessary to solve problems and get answers. This invaluable experience produces exceptional graduates, capable of thinking critically, solving problems as a team, and communicating and presenting their ideas to others.

Programs for Educational Enrichment and Retention

Clemson's nationally recognized Programs for Educational Enrichment and Retention (PEER) is committed to improving the academic performance of underrepresented students in engineering and science. According to a 2012 survey by the magazine Diverse: Issues In Higher Education, Clemson ranks eighth among the nation's universities in graduating African-American students in engineering.

Living-Learning Communities

Living-learning communities offer the chance for students to live and work with others who have similar interests and goals. There are living options for students interested in business, engineering and science, civics and service, honors courses, professional golf management, and much more. Recognized as a national model, the communities are designed to help students be more successful by offering on-site advising and academic support, common course assignments, guest speakers, service opportunities, and a variety of social activities.

CAMPUS FACILITIES

Information Technology

The University's wireless networking capability lets students communicate with professors and classmates, read online course materials, check e-mail, and conduct research—all from their own laptops. Students are required to complete an electronic portfolio prior to graduation, allowing them the opportunity to present themselves through a creative venue to prospective employers and graduate schools.

Housing

Located within a 10- to 15-minute walk to class, Clemson's 22 residence halls and five apartment complexes offer a vast selection of living arrangements.

Fike Recreation Center

Fike is a 200,000-square-foot recreation center that features a fitness atrium complete with a suspended running track that overlooks the indoor courts. It's also equipped with indoor swimming facilities, fitness studios, racquetball courts, state-of-the-art cardio equipment, weights, locker rooms, and a climbing wall.

Hendrix Student Center

The Hendrix Center is the hub of campus activity and is located a step away from most housing. Here you can find people taking a yoga class or enjoying a meal at the food court. It's home to the University Bookstore and offers plenty of quiet places to stop and study. It has a movie theater, ice cream parlor, and much more.

Health Center

Redfern Health Center provides medical services, counseling and psychological services, and health-related programs like alcohol and drug education. It's one of the nation's few on-campus accredited health centers.

TUITION, ROOM, BOARD, AND FEES

2012-13 Academic Year

S.C Resident Full Time

Tuition and Fees°: $13,076

Room and Board (approximate): $ 7,914

Books and Supplies (approximate): $ 1,098

Total: $22,088

Nonresident Full Time

Tuition and Fees°: $30,004

Room and Board (approximate): $ 7,914

Books and Supplies (approximate: $1,098

Total: $39,016

Other Expenses

Estimated Personal and Transportation Expenses: $3,698

One-time computer cost°°: $1,700

°Assumes health and other mandatory fees (required for all full-time students) and average lab and loan fees.

°°All students are required to own a laptop computer. For details, go to clemson.edu/laptop.

FINANCIAL AID

Each year Clemson awards $225 million in financial aid in the form of grants, scholarships, loans, and part-time employment to more than 15,000 students. Over half of first-year students receive scholarships ranging from $500 to all-inclusive cost coverage. All financial aid is awarded annually, and FAFSA applications for the next year are available in January. Entering freshmen are evaluated on a competitive basis for scholarships using the admission application.

ADMISSION REQUIREMENTS

In 2012, the University received about 18,500 applications for a fall freshman class of more than 3,400. Transfer applications were received from about 2,300 students, 1,160 of whom enrolled.

For freshman applicants, the following factors are considered: class standing, standardized test scores (SAT or ACT), high school curriculum, grades, and choice of major. All entering freshmen must have completed 4 credits of English, 3 credits of mathematics, 3 credits of laboratory science, 3 credits of a foreign language (in the same language), 3 credits of social sciences, 1 credit of U.S. history, 1 credit of physical education or ROTC, and 1 credit of fine arts.

To be considered for transfer admission, candidates must have completed a full year of college study (a minimum of 30 semester hours or 45 quarter hours of transferable work), earned a cumulative GPA of at least 2.5 on a 4.0 scale (3.0 preferred), and completed freshman-level courses in English, science, and mathematics for their intended major at Clemson.

Application deadlines for freshman admissions are December 1 (priority date for fall semester), May 1 (fall semester), and December 15 (spring semester). For transfer admissions, the application deadlines are July 1 (fall semester) and December 15 (spring semester).

THE COLLEGE OF NEW JERSEY

AT A GLANCE

The College of New Jersey (TCNJ) has created a culture of constant questioning. In small classes, students and faculty members collaborate in a rewarding process. They seek to understand fundamental principles, apply key concepts, reveal new problems and pursue lines of inquiry to gain a fluency of thought in their disciplines. This transformative process is at the core of the educational experience at the College.

Many students extend their classroom work by participating in research with faculty members or studying abroad. Often, professors and students co-author papers published in academic journals. The mentor relationship helps students discuss career options and land pertinent fellowships, internships, and summer research positions.

TCNJ admits a diverse class each year full of ambitious students, eager to build on their earlier education and plunge into new topics. In finding a home away from home, ninety-five percent of first year students return their second year. The most successful admits are prepared to steer their own academic pursuits toward post-graduation goals of graduate school, professional training, or satisfying careers.

Prestigious graduate schools, including the University of Pennsylvania, Georgetown Law School, Maxwell School at Syracuse University, NYU Law School, and Harvard, Yale, and Northwestern Universities, routinely welcome TCNJ alumni into their ranks. Eighty-five percent of TCNJ students who apply to medical school are accepted.

Many top corporations recruit TCNJ graduates, providing avenues into rewarding jobs directly after graduation. Other barometers of student success include the 100 percent pass rate of education majors taking the state teacher preparation test and the 85 percent three-year pass rate for nursing students going for their license. The variety of learning opportunities at the College prepare students to prosper in any arena after leaving the campus.

LOCATION AND ENVIRONMENT

Neoclassical Georgian Colonial architecture, meticulous landscaping and thoughtful design merge to meet the evolving needs of TCNJ students. Students enjoy a campus with 289 acres of trees, lakes, and open spaces within the suburban setting of Ewing Township, New Jersey. Two out of three undergraduate students live in campus residence halls. The residence halls vary in configuration from the freshman towers to suites and townhouse arrangements for upper class students. An on-campus 600-bed apartment complex is the most recent addition. The College ensures that on-campus housing is available to all students in their first two years.

More that 200 student organizations flourish at the College. Anyone can find an intramural sports team, Greek organization, cultural club, or academic group to suit his or her interests. Many students make friends and enjoy their leisure time participating in one of these groups. In addition, the College Union Board organizes events, including concerts, performances, and comedy nights. The College's highly successful Division III teams also provide an opportunity to socialize and cheer on fellow classmates. Nearby cities, such as Princeton, Trenton, Philadelphia, and New York, allow for abundant entertainment, employment, and social options. Many courses incorporate field trips to New York City or Washington DC.

OFF-CAMPUS OPPORTUNITIES

TCNJ administers an extensive international study program, featuring exchange programs in locations as diverse as Johannesburg, London and the University of Santiago. Some students choose to attend one of the 131 available institutions in the U.S., while others venture to one of the 33 countries offering full-year or semester-long programs.

Student internships, both on and off campus, expose students to career options as they gain professional skills. With the college's location in the center of corporate activity close to New York and Philadelphia, many internships are available - some with pay and some for credit.

Faculty members lend their advice and help students locate and procure appropriate opportunities including fellowships, research positions and internships. Students may also use resources at the Career Center to find positions in New York, Philadelphia, or any of the corporations, government agencies, or research organizations closer to campus.

MAJORS AND DEGREES OFFERED

The College of New Jersey hosts seven schools: the Arts and Communication; Business; Humanities and Social Sciences; Education; Engineering; Nursing, Health & Exercise Science; Science. The College offers programs leading to the Bachelor of Arts, Bachelor of Fine Arts, Bachelor of Music, Bachelor of Science, and Bachelor of Science in Nursing.

TCNJ grants degrees in the following majors: accountancy, art°, art history, digital arts, fine arts, graphic design, interactive multimedia, biology°, business administration (specializations: finance, general business, international business, management, marketing), chemistry°, communication studies, computer science, economics°, early childhood education°, education of the deaf and hard of hearing°, elementary education°, health and exercise science°, special education°, urban education, engineering (biomedical engineering, computer engineering, electrical engineering, mechanical engineering, and civil engineering), English° (options: liberal arts, journalism, professional writing), history°, international studies, criminology, mathematics° (option: statistics), music°, nursing, philosophy, physics°, political science, psychology, sociology, Spanish°, technology education°, and women's and gender studies°.

(° programs in which students may prepare for teacher certification)

Students may also choose to complete a minor, in one of the previously mentioned fields or another subject area, such as African American studies, classical studies, comparative literature, religion, public administration, French, Italian, and Spanish.

Joint degrees are also available at TCNJ. In conjunction with UMDNJ, students can pursue a seven-year combined BS/MD degree. A seven-year combined BS/OD degree program is also available through the State University of New York College of Optometry. Students can study for five years to receive their dual certification in the education of the deaf and hard of hearing and elementary education/master of arts in teaching. Other five-year programs include special education, urban education, school counseling and English.

ACADEMIC PROGRAMS

A Liberal Learning Curriculum ensures that all students are grounded in the values of civic responsibility, intellectual and scholarly growth, and that they receive a well-rounded education in the liberal arts.

In 2004, the College completed a transformation of its curriculum requiring fewer, more in-depth courses. All courses have been transformed and contain a significant out-of-class requirement that provides for even more student and faculty interaction.

The small classes enable dialog between students, and every class at TCNJ is taught by a professor, not a graduate student. The College shapes its curricula and educational experiences around the concept of the accomplished and engaged learner.

The required First-Year Seminar, the cornerstone of the new Liberal Learning program, introduces students to the habits of mind and the methodologies of research; it's seminar format of no more than 15 students reinforces the message that students are not to be passive recipients of knowledge but rather active contributors to their own learning. Requirements are grouped as diversity and community engagement goals that can be self designed or designated interdisciplinary concentrations.

Top students may enroll in TCNJ's honors program, designed to provide a core curriculum with additional challenges and opportunities for individualized work. Most honors classes take an interdisciplinary approach to the history of civilizations, its accomplishments, and its problems. Independent study arrangements fall easily within the parameters of the honors program, as well.

CAMPUS FACILITIES AND EQUIPMENT

Learning, like everything else, is contextual. The surroundings in which students learn and the tools they use influence their experience. Not surprisingly, the college supports its educational aspirations with careful attention to the quality of its facilities. In the first decade of the 21st century, more than $250 million in ongoing and new facilities construction is ensuring that TCNJ students continue to have an environment that not only meets their academic, athletic, social and living needs but extends their reach—resulting in higher scholarship, better health and fitness, closer community, and greater comfort.

TUITION, ROOM, BOARD AND FEES

Because TCNJ is a public institution, costs are lower than most equivalent private institutions. The tuition and fees for undergraduates in the 2011-2012 academic year are as follow:

In-state tuition and fees: $14,187.00

Out-of-state tuition and fees: $23,996

Room and board (all students): $10,120

FINANCIAL AID

Close to 50 percent of full-time undergraduates benefit from financial aid, which can come in the form of merit-based scholarships, work-study programs, loans, or government or institutional grants. All students seeking financial aid must submit the Free Application for Federal Student Aid (FAFSA) form or renewal FAFSA to apply. The Title IV FAFSA Code for The College is 002642.

Students may compete for the College's merit scholarships, which are funded by the state, as well as corporate and private donors. These awards are offered to those applicants with top SAT/ACT scores and class rankings. Over the last six years, TCNJ has given scholarships totaling more than $30 million.

STUDENT ORGANIZATIONS AND ACTIVITIES

Classroom learning at TCNJ is complemented by an extensive and acclaimed Leadership Development Program. Life outside the classroom is not something our students do on the side. It's an extension of the learning experience. At every turn from the first year on, students blur the boundary between living and learning, closing the gap between "student" and "life."

For fun or experience, students can participate in any of the more than 200 TCNJ clubs, catering to interests as diverse as theater, professional training, writing, fraternities and sororities, and athletics. TCNJ teams play in the NCAA Division III, as non-scholarship student athletes. The men field teams in 11 sports and the women compete in 10. The College holds the record for championship and runner-up titles since Division III was started in 1979.

For those looking for something a little less competitive, intramural sports, including flag football, volleyball, softball, floor hockey, and basketball, have thriving coed leagues of their own. Intramural teams play in state, regional, and national tournaments. The college was proud to send its top-ten flag football team to the recent championship in New Orleans.

TCNJ students administer both the Student Finance Board and College Union Board. They organize popular student events, bringing people to the campus such as Matt Nathanson, Ludacris, Third Eye Blind, John Leguizamo, Ann Coulter, Angela Davis, Cory Booker, Jack Dorsey, Eddie Palmieri, Bo Burnham, and Chris Hardwick.

ADMISSIONS PROCESS

The admissions committee at TCNJ accepts a class of motivated, ambitious, and highly talented students. Most successful applicants have taken 16 college-preparatory units in high school. They also show impressive class ranks and SAT/ACT scores. Most students admitted fall within the top 10 percent of their graduating class. The committee also considers extracurricular involvement, individual pursuits, and community participation. Students applying to the art and music departments are evaluated on additional criteria specific to their intended course of study.

Those applying for September admission must have their applications submitted by January 15th. TCNJ offers an early-decision program to those who know the College is their first choice: applications received by November 15th, for this program, will receive a response by December 15th. A small number of students begin classes in January, and they must apply by November 1st. For further information, please contact:

Office of Admissions

The College of New Jersey

PO Box 7718

Ewing, NJ 08628-0718

Telephone: 609-771-2132

E-mail: tcnjinfo@tcnj.edu

Visit us at: tomorrow@tcnj

COLUMBIA COLLEGE (MO)

AT A GLANCE

Columbia College opens doors for its students to experience new discoveries, new relationships and new areas of knowledge that can be explored through thought-provoking, honest dialogue, both in and out of the classroom. Academics are strong, grounded in the liberal arts and sciences and offered in a learning environment characterized by civility and respect. Students feel at home on the beautiful campus, located in Columbia, Mo., thanks to the private college's close-knit community where opportunities to get involved are plentiful.

Each year, more than 1,000 students attend the traditional Day Campus and represent more than 22 states and 44 countries. At Columbia College, students choose from 50+ outstanding majors and pre-professional programs. Undergraduate and graduate degrees are offered at the home campus in Columbia, Mo., as well as at 34 locations across the nation and online. Our worldwide alumni network of 64,000-strong helps students find internships and jobs after graduation.

Personal service and attention have been hallmarks at the institution since it was founded in 1851 — traditions that can be seen and felt with a student-faculty ratio of 11-to-1 and meaningful relationships with professors and classmates. More than 80 percent of our faculty have earned the highest academic degrees possible in their fields.

Whether you're an athlete or a fan, you'll appreciate Cougar Athletics with award-winning NAIA varsity sports in men's and women's basketball, men and women's soccer, men and women's golf, men and women's cross country and women's volleyball and softball.

Columbia College welcomes students of all religious affiliations, while maintaining a covenant with the Christian Church (Disciples of Christ). The covenant dates back to our founding as Christian Female College, the first women's college west of the Mississippi River to be chartered by a state legislature. In 1970, the college opened its doors to both women and men and changed its name to Columbia College.

LOCATION AND ENVIRONMENT

At Columbia College, you have the best of both worlds when it comes to experiences. You'll live on a campus of 30 beautiful acres, where you'll bump into friends and faculty everywhere you go. You'll also be part of an exciting city life as you share the neighborhood with more than 30,000 other college students from Stephens College and the University of Missouri, which is why Columbia is often referred to as Collegetown, U.S.A. Plus, the city has consistently been ranked among the best places to live in the nation by national publications and offers a surprisingly afford-able cost of living, ideal for the needs and budgets of its large student population. You can walk downtown and experience the fascinating cuisines, eclectic entertainment, excellent shopping, outdoor adventures at the Devil's Ice Box, Rock Bridge State Park, MKT Trail and a variety of cultural events such as the True/False Film Festival, Roots & Blues Festival and more.

OFF-CAMPUS OPPORTUNITIES

Many of our students can list one or more real-world professional experiences on their résumés by the time they graduate. Our students have presented cutting-edge research to a prestigious professional gathering, landed internships with the FBI and at Walt Disney World, volunteered at a local elementary school and traveled to New York, England and China as members of the Jane Froman Singers. Our students also have the opportunity to explore new cultures through study abroad programs to countries like England, Japan, Australia, New Zealand, Italy and France.

MAJORS AND DEGREES OFFERED

Columbia College awards the Associate in Arts, Associate in General Studies, Associate in Science, Bachelor of Science, Bachelor of Arts, Bachelor of Arts in General Studies, Bachelor of Fine Arts, Master of Business Administration, Master of Arts in Teaching, Master of Education, Master of Human Services, Master of Science in Criminal Justice and Master of Arts in Military Studies. Students can major in accounting, American studies, art, art history, studio art, biology, business administration, ceramics, chemistry, computer information systems, computer science, criminal justice administration, criminology, education certification, English, environmental studies, ethics, philosophy and religious studies, financial services, fire service administration, forensic science, , geography, graphic design, healthcare management, history, human resource management, human services, international business, international relations, management, management information systems, marketing, mathematics, printing and drawing, photography, political science, printmaking, psychology, public administration, sociology, speech communication and sports management. The college also offers an outstanding teacher education program.

Students can minor in art history, art studio, criminology, education, environmental science, ethics, philosophy and religious studies, geography, international relations, legal studies, music, ROTC, Spanish and women's studies. Columbia College also offers pre-professional programs in dental, engineering, law, medicine and veterinary.

ACADEMIC PROGRAMS

If you are a first-time freshman confident in the major you have chosen, the college will commit to offering you all the classes you require to graduate in four years through the Four-Year Graduation Plan.

Columbia College also offers a unique program for teachers. Students can earn a Bachelor of Arts, Master of Arts in Teaching and teacher certification in a little more than four years through the DAYSTAR teacher education program. Graduates are eligible to be certified to teach at the elementary, middle or secondary school level anywhere in the state of Missouri.

CAMPUS FACILITIES AND EQUIPMENT

We hear time and again about the beauty of our campus from students, parents and visitors. Our campus is a wonderful mix of historic and contemporary buildings situated on 30 park-like acres. Yet all the buildings are within a five-minute walk no matter where you are located on campus. We take great pride in preserving our historic buildings, many of which are 100-150 years old. We are also proud of our new buildings, such as the Atkins-Holman Student Commons and the Southwell Athletic Complex, which are designed to tastefully blend in with the existing historic structures. The college also is pleased to host the Larson Art Gallery, featuring artwork from students and professionals year-round. The college continues to thrive and is in the process of developing plans and raising funds for a new science building.

We have three residence halls; Banks, Hughes and Miller, along with upperclassmen apartments. Each residence hall features extra-spacious rooms; individually controlled heating and air conditioning; voicemail, e-mail and Internet services; cable television; computer labs with printers; study lounges; free laundry facilities; and access to a kitchenette with a microwave station. Banks Hall also includes a Wellness Floor exclusively reserved for students committed to a substance-free lifestyle.

TUITION, ROOM, BOARD AND FEES

Making financial plans for college isn't always easy. Many colleges increase their tuition every year, sometimes drastically and unexpectedly. This can have a serious effect on your financial situation and your ability to pay for your education.

At Columbia College, we believe that you should be able to plan your finances with confidence. That's why we've removed the uncertainty over tuition increases by introducing our fixed rate tuition program. From the fall of 2013, the tuition rate charged for your first academic year at the college will remain fixed for five consecutive years. For the 2013-2014 academic year, tuition is $19,386; and room and board is $6,254. The room & board rates are based on a double-room rate and a standard 20-meal plan.

FINANCIAL AID

The Student Guide to America's 100 Best College Scholarships ranked Columbia College as one of the nation's most affordable top-rated colleges in the country. In addition to maintaining competitive tuition costs, Columbia College also awards more than $4 million in financial aid and scholarships every year. The majority of our students receive financial aid in one form or another.

STUDENT ORGANIZATIONS AND ACTIVITIES

As a Columbia College student, you'll quickly discover that your initiative and involvement are key to your own success. Maybe that's why nearly 100 percent of our Day Campus students are involved in at least one of the 50 student clubs and organizations offered.

At Columbia College, you'll have the opportunity to become a respected voice on the Student Government Association, an admired actor in the Elysium Players, a responsible resident assistant, or an inspiring leader from the Emerging Leaders Institute, just to name a few of the possibilities. Other student interest groups include student government, mock trial, international club, honorary clubs and organizations, academic clubs and organizations, social clubs and service clubs. It's also easy to start your own club or organization with assistance from Campus Life.

Columbia College also offers competitive athletic programs with ten NAIA sports which are men's and women's basketball, men and women's soccer, men and women's golf, men and women's cross country and women's volleyball and softball. Every one of our athletic programs has produced All-Americans and All-America Scholar-Athletes in the past 10 years. Our women's volleyball team has brought home the NAIA national championship title three times. In 2012-2013, the men's basketball team was ranked 1st in the NAIA and finished their season undefeated. And for eight of the past 10 years two or more Columbia College coaches have been recognized as conference or regional coach of the year. In 2012, head men's basketball coach Bob Burchard was inducted into the NAIA Hall of Fame and in 2013 was named NAIA/NABC National Coach of the Year.

ADMISSIONS PROCESS

While Columbia College is selective about admission, students with a minimum high school cumulative GPA of 2.5 who rank in the top half of their graduating class, or score at 21 or above on the ACT, SAT I or GED generally can expect to be admitted to the college. We also welcome transfer students who have maintained a minimum cumulative grade point average of 2.0. We accept college credits from previous accredited college-level coursework, as well as from programs like CLEP, Advanced Placement, International Baccalaureate, dual credit, proficiency exams and DANTES.

With more than 3,000 colleges and universities in the country, it can be a challenge to find the school that best fits you. There's no better way to make a final decision than to visit the colleges on your short list. Columbia College offers three Preview Days, 2 Departmental Showcases and three Scholarship Days, where students can compete for one of 10 full ride scholarships, each year, or you can contact the Admissions Office at (800) 231-2391, ext. 7352, to schedule an individual campus visit that's convenient for you. Columbia College accepts applications throughout the year and the non-refundable application fee is $35. The fee is waived for applications received by Jan. 1 for the following fall semester. Plan a visit today and learn about the opportunities that await you.

COLUMBIA COLLEGE CHICAGO

AT A GLANCE

Columbia College Chicago is the largest and most diverse private non-profit arts and media college in the nation. We offer a four-year liberal arts education specifically tailored for a community of gifted, highly motivated students who want to turn their creative talents into rewarding careers. Our student body is comprised of approximately 11,200 students who come from all 50 states and more than 40 foreign countries. The College admits students after a holistic review of their entire application – not just their test scores or class rank – and then provides them with the rigorous academics and unparalleled resources necessary to be successful in a highly competitive 21st century marketplace.

We offer Bachelor's degrees in more than 120 programs of study in the arts, media, and communications. Our curriculum is designed to provide students with practical, real-world understandings of their chosen fields and to prepare them to meet professional expectations. Columbia's faculty members are industry insiders (artists, designers, executives, writers, filmmakers, marketers, journalists, musicians, entrepreneurs, dancers) with national reputations. They are experienced, award-winning instructors who share their first-hand knowledge with students both in and out of the classroom. Interaction with faculty members who are practicing professionals themselves provides our students with access to valuable expertise, insight, viewpoints, and industry-current aesthetics.

LOCATION AND ENVIRONMENT

Columbia is an eclectic, urban environment located in the city's historic South Loop neighborhood. Close by are several other colleges and universities, Navy Pier, the Adler Planetarium, the Art Institute, the Field Museum, the Chicago Symphony, the Museum of Contemporary Art, the Harold Washington Library, and the Goodman Theatre. Convenient public transportation allows Columbia's faculty and students to utilize the whole city as a social, cultural, educational, and professional resource —effectively turning the entire city into our campus.

Because Columbia believes that residence centers should extend the supportive philosophies of the College's creative learning environment, all four residence halls were designed specifically with creative students in mind. They offer a variety of apartment and suite-style housing options with a range of amenities that may include: study rooms, drawing and painting studios, full kitchens, music practice space, fitness rooms, a swimming pool, a graffiti room, and views of Lake Michigan. Apartments, suites, and rooms are fully furnished. All facilities are conveniently located steps from the main campus buildings and are close to public transportation. All students also have access to student health and counseling services.

The College hosts close to 700 on-campus events each year and when students aren't showing at campus galleries, publishing in our award-winning newspaper, performing on stage, attending screenings, freestyling at poetry slams, producing shows for our television and radio stations, or taking an active role in the college's 85+ social and academic clubs and organizations, they are interacting with the larger Chicago community around them. The presence of Columbia's students can be felt in theaters, bookstores, nightclubs, concert venues, museums, and media outlets throughout the city, and every spring Columbia returns the favor by inviting Chicago to its doorstep for Manifest, the city's largest student arts exhibition.

MAJORS AND DEGREES OFFERED

Columbia College offers Bachelors (BA, BFA, BS, BMus) and Masters (MA, MFA, MAM, MAT) degrees in the following areas.

Acoustics, Advertising Art Direction, American Sign Language English Interpretation, Art & Design, Art & Materials Conservation, Art History, Arts Management, Advanced Management, concentrations in:, Live & Performing Arts, Media Management, Music Business Management, Sports Management, Visual Arts Management, Audio Arts & Acoustics, concentrations in:, Audio Design & Production, Audio for Visual Media, Live & Installed Sound, Creative Writing: Nonfiction, Creative Writing: Poetry, Cultural Studies, Dance, Early Childhood Education, Fashion Business, Fashion Design, Fiction Writing, Film & Video, concentrations in:, Animation, Cinema Studies, Cinematography, Directing, Documentary, Post-Production, Producing, Screenwriting, Sound for Cinema, Fine Arts, concentrations in:, Game Design, Game Art, Game Development, Sound Design, Game Programming, Graphic Design, Illustration, Interactive Arts and Media, Interior Architecture, Journalism, concentrations in:, Broadcast Journalism/Radio, Broadcast Journalism/Television, Magazine Writing & Editing, News Reporting & Writing, News Reporting & Writing/Sports, Science Journalism, Marketing Communication, concentrations in:, Advertising, Marketing, Public Relations, Mobile Media Programming, Music, concentrations in:, Composition, Contemporary Urban & Popular Music, Instrumental Jazz, Instrumental Performance, Vocal Performance, Photography, concentrations in:, Commercial, Fine Art, Photojournalism, Playwriting, Product Design, Radio, Television, concentrations in:, Internet Mobile Media, Post-Production Effects, Production/Directing, Writing/Producing, Theatre, concentrations in:, Acting, Comedy Writing & Performance, Directing, Musical Theatre, Technical Theatre, Theatre Design

ACADEMIC PROGRAMS

Honors Program-The Honors Program offers motivated, high-achieving students the opportunity to pursue deeper intellectual and creative challenges through a rich array of specially designed courses that emphasize more active and applied learning, independent research, and enhanced academic rigor.

Comedy Studies-Comedy Studies is a full-time, semester-long program of immersive study in comedic literature, history, writing, and performance with the comedy experts at Chicago's famed Second City.

Study Abroad-Some Columbia programs include international study as a component of the curriculum but for those wishing to explore additional options, the International Programs office assists students in accessing independent study abroad options worldwide.

Portfolio Center-The Portfolio Center helps our students pull out the best of the best from what they've done in and out of class. They not only help students put together professional-grade portfolios, resumes, press kits, demo reels, tapes, and web sites, they also connect them with professionals who will give feedback on their work and how to best present it to meet current industry standards.

Semester in L.A.-SiLA is a full-credit, five-week immersion program open to any Columbia College Chicago student who wants to gain first-hand experience in the entertainment industry. SiLA instructors come from every facet of the show business industry – producers, screenwriters, casting agents, directors, actors, designers – and have years of experience.

Learning Studio-The Learning Studio helps Columbia students reach their academic goals by offering a variety of academic support programs to all students, at all achievement levels, in order to enhance student success both in and out of the classroom.

Industry Night - Industry Night is where our seniors showcase their talents and make real connections with industry leaders like Saks Fifth Avenue, Pitchfork Media, DraftFCB, Leo Burnett, SPIN Magazine, CBS 2 Chicago, and McDonald's Creative Services.

CAMPUS FACILITIES AND EQUIPMENT

The Columbia College Chicago campus is comprised of 23 buildings that house advanced facilities for television, art, computer graphics, photography, radio, interactive multimedia, fashion design, and film. They are state-of-the-industry and include professionally equipped color and black-and-white darkrooms, digital imaging computer facilities, photography and film stages, film and video editing suites, and studios for painting, drawing, and 3-D design. The campus also includes the Museum of Contemporary Photography (one of only two such facilities in the United States), and the Audio Technology Center, a recording production and research facility. The dance, music, and theater departments each have separate centers that are designed for their program's individual needs. Additionally, Columbia has extensive computer facilities for use by students as well as dedicated computer resources geared for specific departmental needs.

In 2010, Columbia opened the Media Production Center, a state-of-the-art facility including two film production soundstages, a motion-capture studio, digital labs, animating suites, a fabrication shop, and classrooms. Considered the first educational complex of its kind anywhere, the Media Production Center was designed from the ground up to foster cross-disciplinary collaboration in arts and media education.

TUITION, ROOM, BOARD, AND FEES

COSTS AND FINANCIAL AID for 2012-2013 academic year

Undergraduate in-state tuition (academic year): $21,200

Undergraduate out-of-state tuition (academic year): $21,200

Room and Board (academic year): average cost $11,000

Scholarships: Yes

Grants: Yes

Loans: Yes

Work-study programs: Yes

Co-ops/internships: Yes

FINANCIAL AID

Our Student Financial Services department is available to assist all students in the research of funding sources, including scholarships, grants, and loans. Visit http://www.colum.edu/Student_Financial_Services/ for comprehensive information.

Regarding scholarships, in 2012, nearly 48% of new freshmen received scholarship support from Columbia College with awards averaging $5,000–$10,000 per student. Scholarship awards were based on the student's admission application date, merit, and receipt of the student's FAFSA. The earlier you apply, the better.

STUDENT ORGANIZATIONS AND ACTIVITIES

ShopColumbia: ShopColumbia is our student art boutique offering products and designs created and produced by our student body. Spanning all media and disciplines, ShopColumbia is defined by what Columbia students are making right now, both inside and outside the classroom.

Internships: Columbia is very proud of its robust internship programs. Each academic department has its own internship coordinator, ensuring that students get placed in internships that offer real opportunities and experience.

Student Organizations: With 85+ student clubs and organizations, Columbia College Chicago offers students myriad opportunities to independently organize events, clubs, and initiatives that give voice to their passions and creative interests.

Manifest: Our annual urban arts festival, Manifest, takes place each May. Showcasing the free-for-all creativity and innovation of our seniors and graduate students, this highly-anticipated festival has become the talk of Chicago's arts scene, turning Chicago's South Loop neighborhood into an interactive gallery for thrilling performances and one-of-a-kind performances.

COLUMBIA UNIVERSITY SCHOOL OF GENERAL STUDIES

AT A GLANCE

The School of General Studies (GS) of Columbia University is one of the finest liberal arts colleges in the United States created specifically for returning and nontraditional students seeking a rigorous, traditional, Ivy League undergraduate degree full- or part-time. Most students at GS have, for personal or professional reasons, interrupted their education, never attended college, or are only able to attend part time. GS is unique among colleges of its type, because its students are fully integrated into the Columbia undergraduate curriculum: they take the same courses with the same faculty members and earn the same degree as all other Columbia undergraduates.

GS students come from varied backgrounds and all walks of life. Many students work full time while pursuing a degree, and many have family responsibilities; others attend classes full time and experience Columbia's more traditional college life. In the classroom, the diversity and varied personal experience of the student body promote discussion and debate, fostering an environment of academic rigor and intellectual development. GS has approximately 1,600 undergraduate degree candidates and more than 500 Postbaccalaureate Premedical students. The average age of a GS student is 29. More than 60 percent of GS students attend classes full time.

In addition to its bachelor's degree program, GS offers combined undergraduate/graduate degree programs with Columbia's Schools of Social Work, International and Public Affairs, Law, Business, Dental Medicine, Teachers College, and the College of Physicians and Surgeons, and undergraduate dual-degree programs with the Columbia School of Engineering and Applied Science the Jewish Theological Seminary, and the Dual BA Program Between Columbia University and the French University Sciences Po.. More than 70 percent of the students go on to earn advanced degrees after graduation.

GS is home to the oldest and largest Postbaccalaureate Premedical Program in the United States. In recent years, the acceptance rate for GS Postbaccalaureate Premedical Program students applying to U.S. medical schools is up to 90 percent.

LOCATION AND ENVIRONMENT

Columbia University is located in Morningside Heights, on the Upper West Side of Manhattan. The University's neighbors include the Union Theological Seminary, the Jewish Theological Seminary, the Manhattan School of Music, St. Luke's Hospital, Women's Hospital, Riverside Church, and the Cathedral of St. John the Divine. The diversity of intellectual and social activities offered by these institutions is one of Columbia's great assets as a university; another is its location in New York City, which offers students at Columbia a rich and almost boundless variety of social, cultural, and recreational opportunities that are themselves an education.

OFF-CAMPUS OPPORTUNITIES

Columbia students may enhance their academic experiences through various study-abroad programs around the world. For example, students may spend a term at the Reid Hall Program in the Montparnasse district of Paris, the Berlin Consortium for German Studies, Kyoto Consortium for Japanese Studies, or the Language Program in Beijing, China. Additionally, students may apply to participate in one of the Columbia approved study abroad programs located in countries all over the world.

MAJORS AND DEGREES OFFERED

The School of General Studies grants the B.A. and B.S. degrees and offers more than 70 majors and concentrations, which include : African studies; African-American studies; American studies; ancient studies; anthropology; applied mathematics; archaeology; architecture; architecture, history and theory; art history; art history–visual arts; astronomy; astrophysics; biochemistry; biology; biophysics; chemical physics; chemistry; classical studies; classics; comparative literature and society; computer science; computer science–mathematics; creative writing; dance; drama and theater arts; earth science; East Asian studies; East Central European studies; economics; economics–mathematics; economics–operations research; economics–philosophy; economics–political science; economics–statistics; English and comparative literature; environmental biology; environmental chemistry; environmental science; evolutionary biology of the human species; film studies; financial economics; French; French and Francophone studies; German literature and cultural history; Hispanic studies; history; human rights; information science, Italian cultural studies; Italian language and literature; Latin American and Caribbean studies; mathematics; mathematics–statistics; Middle Eastern, South Asian, and African studies; music; neuroscience and behavior; philosophy; physics; political science; political science-statistics; psychology; regional studies; religion; Russian language and culture; Russian literature and culture; Slavic studies; sociology; statistics; sustainable development; urban studies; visual arts; women's and gender studies; and Yiddish studies. Individually designed majors are also available.

In addition, Columbia University School of General Studies offers undergraduate dual-degree programs with the Columbia School of Engineering and Applied Science the Jewish Theological Seminary, Hong Kong's City University and the Dual BA Program Between Columbia University and the French University Sciences Po.

The Dual BA Program is an intensive, transatlantic course of study in which undergraduate students earn bachelor's degrees from both Sciences Po and Columbia University in four years. Students will spend two years at one of three Sciences Po campuses, each of which is devoted to a particular region of the world and offers a heavy linguistic and cultural focus. After completing Sciences Po's interdisciplinary social-sciences curriculum, Dual BA students will matriculate at GS to complete the requirements for a major, as well as fulfill core distribution requirements in a variety of disciplines, including literature, art, music, science, and the humanities. Upon graduation, Dual BA Program students are eligible for guaranteed admission to a graduate program at Sciences Po. Admission to the program is highly competitive, and high school seniors are eligible to apply.

ACADEMIC PROGRAMS

The School of General Studies offers a traditional liberal arts education designed to provide students with the broad knowledge and intellectual skills that foster continued education and growth in the years after college, as well as providing a sound foundation for positions of responsibility in the professional world. Requirements for the bachelor's degree comprise three elements: (1) core requirements, intended to develop in students the ability to write and communicate clearly; to understand the modes of thought that characterize the humanities, social sciences, and sciences; to gain familiarity with central cultural ideas through literature, fine arts, and music; and to acquire a working proficiency in a foreign language; (2) major requirements, designed to give students sustained and coherent exposure to a particular discipline in an area of strong intellectual interest; and (3) elective courses, in which students pursue particular interests and skills for their own personal growth or for their relationship to future professional or personal objectives. Students are required to complete a minimum of 124 credits for the bachelor's degree; 60 of these may be in transfer credit, but at least 64 credits (including the last 30 credits) must be completed at Columbia. In addition to the usual graduation honors (cum laude, magna cum laude, and summa cum laude), honors programs for superior students are available in a majority of the University's departments.

ACADEMIC FACILITIES

The Columbia University libraries constitute the nation's sixth-largest academic library system, with a collection of more than 10.4 million volumes, more than 6.4 million microform pieces, and 26 million manuscript items and 979,000 rare books. Of the twenty-two libraries in the system, five are designated Distinctive Collections because of their unusual depth and nationally recognized excellence.

All library divisions are available to GS students. The University's Computer Center is one of the largest and most powerful university installations in the world and has remote units and terminals in several parts of the campus to enhance its accessibility.

The Fairchild Life Science Building houses research facilities, laboratories, electron microscopes, and a vast amount of biochemical equipment used for teaching and research. The University's physics building has been the scene of many important developments in the recent history of physics, including the invention of the laser and the first U.S. demonstration of nuclear fission.

TUITION, ROOM, BOARD AND FEES

For the 2012-2013 academic year, tuition was $1,454 per credit, fees were approximately $1900 not including the one-time orientation and transcript fees; living (room and board) and personal expenses (books, local commuting costs, and miscellaneous expenses) were $22,045 for the year.

FINANCIAL AID

The School of General Studies awards financial aid based upon need and academic ability. Approximately 70 percent of General Studies degree candidates receive some form of financial aid, including Federal Pell Grants, New York State TAP Grants, Federal Stafford and unsubsidized Stafford Loans, Federal Perkins Loans, General Studies Scholarships, and Federal Work-Study Program awards. The average award of the GS Scholarship is $7,500-$9,000. Priority application deadlines for new students are June 1 for the fall semester and October 15 for the spring semester.

STUDENT ORGANIZATIONS AND ACTIVITIES

One student represents GS students in the University Senate, a decision-making body comprised of students, faculty and administrative staff members from each division of the University. In addition, two GS students sit as voting members on the Committee on Instruction, which oversees the curriculum of the School. The General Studies Student Council elects officers each year and sponsors activities for students. The Observer, the School's student-run magazine, is published several times each year. The Premedical Association (PMA) sponsors events related to the medical school admissions process.

Additionally, students are eligible to participate in any of the more than 500 student organizations on campus.

ADMISSIONS PROCESS

The GS admission policy is geared to the maturity and varied backgrounds of its students. Aptitude and motivation are considered along with past academic performance, standardized test scores, and employment history. The School's admission decisions are based on a careful review of each application and reflect the Admissions Committee's considered judgment of the applicant's maturity, academic potential, and present ability to undertake course work at Columbia.

Admission requirements include a completed application form; a 1,500- to 2,000-word autobiographical statement describing the applicant's past educational history and work experience, present situation, and future plans; two letters of recommendation from academic or professional evaluators; an official high school transcript; official transcripts from all colleges and universities attended; official SAT or ACT scores (applicants may take the General Studies Admissions Examination); and a nonrefundable application fee of $80.

Students from outside the United States may apply to the School of General Studies to start or complete a baccalaureate degree. In addition to the materials described above, international applicants must submit official TOEFL scores or take the Columbia University American Language Program Essay Exam.

For more information, please contact:

Office of Admissions and Educational Financing

School of General Studies

408 Lewisohn Hall

2970 Broadway

Columbia University, Mail Code 4101

New York, New York 10027

United States

Phone: 212-854-2772

E-mail: gsdegree@columbia.edu

Website: http://www.gs.columbia.edu

CONNECTICUT COLLEGE

AT A GLANCE

One of the nation's premiere liberal arts colleges, Connecticut College is a small, highly selective, residential, private institution drawing national and international students.

Chartered in 1911, Connecticut College was founded in the spirit of political and social equality, self-determination, and shared governance. The College actively seeks out students who are not only smart and intellectually curious, but who also bring a wide range of life experiences and perspectives that enable this spirit to endure within the College community. The College's near century-old Honor Code defines campus life and is observed by all students, faculty, and staff. Intellectually and academically, the Honor Code inspires students to challenge themselves and their peers to see the world from diverse perspectives, to remain receptive to new ideas and experiences, and, by instilling a sense of mutual respect, to consider how their actions and education may ultimately better the common good. The College offers over 47 majors and minors and participates in the NCAA Division III New England Small College Athletic Conference (NESCAC.) The College is nationally known for career and internship placement and has been called a "college with a conscience," as one of the top schools sending students to Teach for America or the Peace Corps. Enrollment at the College for 2012-13 is 1,900. In the past six years, thirty-two Connecticut College students have been awarded Fulbright Scholarships.

LOCATION AND ENVIRONMENT

Connecticut College is located two hours from Boston and two and a half hours from New York City, in historic New London, Connecticut, a small city (pop. 28,000) founded in 1646. The College's 750-acre campus, which is maintained as an Arboretum, features a centralized series of granite and limestone buildings adjacent to wooded trails. At the heart of the campus, Tempel Green sweeps down to offer commanding views of Long Island Sound. The College's athletic and fitness center is located along the Thames River.

OFF-CAMPUS OPPORTUNITIES

The College is located convenient to shopping and to the New London transportation center, which features train, bus, and ferry service to points along the eastern seaboard. New London is a diverse community home to numerous restaurants and cafes, galleries, and historic sites. The city also serves as the region's legal, medical, and social service center. The College operates a shuttle service for students to area locations and provides two ZipCars for students, although students are permitted to have cars on campus. A student environmental initiative begun in 2010, however, prohibits freshmen from having cars on campus. The College's career and volunteer offices work closely with students to arrange for volunteer or internship opportunities. Many students volunteer in local schools or afterschool programs and may, in conjunction with coursework, receive teaching certification for elementary or secondary education.

MAJORS AND DEGREES OFFERED

Connecticut College offers over 47 majors and 42 minors, including self-designed study, as part of a liberal-arts curriculum designed for intellectual breadth, critical thinking, and acquisition of the fundamental skills and habits of a mind conducive to lifelong inquiry. Courses lead toward a Bachelor of Arts degree. Students complete General Education Requirements to ensure broad engagement with the range of disciplines that constitute the liberal arts. Connecticut College students launch their inquiry across disciplines and geographic boundaries and consider the campus and course catalogue open to them in this pursuit. The College, for example, offers free music lessons to all students. Through a course of study, students in a variety of majors may become certified for elementary, secondary, or private school education or receive a certificate demonstrating experience in Museum Studies. The most popular majors at the College are economics, government, English, psychology, international relations, and biological sciences. The College's dance program is internationally reputed, as is its theater program, which offers students the opportunity to study at the Eugene O'Neill Theater Center in Waterford, Connecticut and/or the Eugene O'Neill Moscow Art Theater in Russia.

ACADEMIC PROGRAMS

Students benefit from small classes that foster discussion and lead to personalized relationships with professors who serve as teacher-scholars. Professors frequently spark the interest that will inspire a student for their lifetime. The faculty to student ratio is 1 to 9. Average class size is 18. First-year students enroll in a seminar course (in which maximum enrollment is 16.) Ninety percent of full-time faculty members have a PhD or other terminal degree.

More than half of all students study away in a variety of domestic or international programs. Study away is a crucial component of a Connecticut College education, as it complements and informs a liberal arts curriculum (students who choose to study away do so primarily through the College's affiliation with institutions in over 40 countries.) The College also maintains domestic affiliations, including those with the Williams-Mystic Seaport Program, the Maritime Biological Laboratory Ecosystems Center at Woods Hole, and the Twelve College Exchange. In addition, students study away through Connecticut College's Study Away-Teach Away (SATA) program, in which a group of 10 to 15 students and one or two professors travel overseas and affiliate with a foreign university. SATA programs have been conducted in the Czech Republic, Cuba, China, Peru, Egypt, Ghana, Greece, India, Italy, Mexico, Morocco, South Africa, Spain, Tanzania, and Vietnam.

To ensure that students consider the practical application of their study, the College provides each student with $3,000 to fund an internship or research project between their junior and senior year. About 80 percent of all students attend a series of seminars and work in conjunction with professors and career services to become eligible for the funding. One in five students conducts their internship overseas. Recent internships have been conducted with such organizations as The Field Museum of Chicago, Google, J.P. Morgan, Azafady in Madagascar, Vera Wang, New Line Cinema, and, CBS Sports.

To illustrate how several areas of study may be fused to best equip a student to understand and resolve complex issues, the College operates a series of interdisciplinary centers. The Centers are certificate-granting programs within the College that serve as an intellectual commons to bring together professors, students, and outside experts. There are five Centers, each with their own focus: The Toor Cummings Center for International Studies and the Liberal Arts; The Ammerman Center for Arts and Technology; The Holleran Center for Community Action and Public Policy; The Goodwin-Niering Center for Environmental Studies; and, the Center for the Comparative Study of Race and Ethnicity. Students combine their coursework with an integrated project and a paid overseas or domestic internship organized through the Center to receive a certificate from their chosen Center.

CAMPUS FACILITIES AND EQUIPMENT

Connecticut College occupies 750 acres (all of which is included in the Connecticut College Arboretum) on a hill overlooking the Thames River and Long Island Sound. The Arboretum's diverse acreage includes the landscaped grounds of the campus as well as the surrounding plant collections and natural areas. The resources of the Arboretum support the College's mission of preparing the next generation of citizen leaders to craft a sustainable relationship with the natural world. The symbiosis of the Environmental Studies major and the Goodwin-Niering Center provides an outstanding model of an ethically and environmentally sound community and places the College in a singular environment which offers a quality of life unique among liberal arts institutions.

Located at the center of the campus, the Charles E. Shain Library consists of more than 616,000 books and bound periodicals, 151,000 media and computing materials, and 5,599 subscriptions to periodicals. The collection is augmented through a consortium with Trinity College and Wesleyan University that provides fast access to more than 2.2 million items.

Other key buildings, include: Hale Laboratory; the Frank Loomis Palmer Auditorium; the F.W. Olin Science Center; Dayton Arena; the College Athletic Center; the Lyn and David Silfen Track and Field; and, Cummings Arts Center, which includes the Greer Music Library.

In the fall of 2009, the College opened a new $8 million fitness center overlooking the Thames River. The center more than triples the amount of exercise and wellness space at the College.

In the fall of 2012, the College completed a $20 million renovation and expansion of New London Hall, which transformed the historic building into a state-of-the-art home for life and computer sciences. The new facility is designed to achieve LEED certification. An $11 million gift to the College has led to creation of a new Academic Resource Center, which will dramatically expand and unify academic and career advising, student support services, peer-to-peer learning, and student-faculty relationships.

TUITION, ROOM, BOARD, AND FEES

Tuition, fees, room, and board cost $56,790 for 2012-2013. Housing is guaranteed for all students for four years. Ninety-nine percent of students live on campus. There is no Greek system.

FINANCIAL AID

Connecticut College offers need-based financial aid and meets 100 percent of demonstrated need. In 2012-13, the College awarded $31.9 million in institutional grants. Forty-eight percent of students received some form of institutional aid. The average aid award was $35,249.

In 2006, Connecticut College began replacing or reducing need-based loan eligibility with institutional grants for students whose family income was less than $75,001 and contribution was less than $15,001.

STUDENT ORGANIZATIONS AND ACTIVITIES

As a small, residential liberal arts college, Connecticut College encourages students to pursue many interests outside the classroom, with the Crozier-Williams Student Center serving as the main hub for extracurricular activity as the site of club offices, WCNI-FM radio station, the weekly College Voice newspaper, and forums for live music, debate, dance, and poetry. Galleries, student run cafes, and performance spaces are found throughout campus. The Tansill Theater, a blackbox theater, is frequently home to student written productions. Students participate in dozens of clubs and organizations, including the Pegotty Investment Club, the Connecticut College Asian/Asian-American Student Association, Hillel, and Habitat for Humanity. Students compete in a range of varsity, club, and intramural sports. The campus LGBTQ Center and Women's Center both host events focused on issues of sexuality, equity, and gender, while Unity House is the campus multicultural center and works with the Director of Unity House to host events focused on issues of race.

ADMISSIONS PROCESS

Connecticut College is one of the nation's most highly selective colleges. In 2013, 35 percent of applicants were offered a place in the class of 2017. The College requires the Common Application and Member Page. An interview is recommended but not required. The submission of standardized tests (SAT Reasoning, SAT II, or ACT) is optional, although students whose primary language is not English are required to submit TOEFL scores or an equivalent. The College expects applicants will have taken the most appropriately rigorous courses available.

Application deadlines: Early Decision I, Nov. 15 for all ED1 application materials, Early Decision II and Regular Decision, Jan. 1 for all application materials. Financial Aid application dates: ED I, Nov. 15; ED II, Jan. 15; Regular Decision, Feb. 1.

CURRY COLLEGE

AT A GLANCE

Curry College is a private, four-year, liberal arts-based institution located on a wooded 137-acre campus in Milton, MA just seven miles from downtown Boston. Curry College today offers 20 undergraduate majors, as well as four graduate programs. The college serves a combined enrollment of approximately 4,000 students, consisting of over 2,000 traditional students from over 40 states and 32 countries; 1,600 continuing education students; and 400 graduate students. More than 1,400 of its students reside on the Curry campus.

Under the leadership of President Kenneth K. Quigley, there's a culture of excellence that exists at Curry College as it continues to rise to a place of prominence and great promise among New England's finest colleges. As we enter our 133nd year, we invite you to meet the people of Curry on the Web or at an upcoming campus event to truly experience excellence in action.

LOCATION AND ENVIRONMENT

The wooded, 137-acre Milton campus is one of the most attractive small college campuses in New England. Right on campus, you'll have at your fingertips the resources to help you excel academically, socially, and physically and find endless sources of entertainment, action, and challenge.

Unlike other isolated suburban or rural campuses, Curry is just a stone's throw away from Boston, one of the most exciting cities in the world. As a result, Curry can offer its students an exceptional advantage through access to Boston's cultural and educational institutions. The opportunity for internships and entertainment in this New England capital is a significant part of the Curry experience.

Curry's location has yet another advantage: it is less than two miles from the scenic Blue Hills, a natural reservation which offers skiing, hiking, horseback riding, and a range of resources for environmental education and recreation. The Milton campus is a beautiful retreat in the woods, with the excitement of the City waiting right outside.

Back on campus, students also enjoy the comfort Curry's tight-knit, friendly community and the security services provided by the Department of Public Safety, which administers a highly professional system for the enforcement of rules and regulations designed to promote the general safety and security of persons and properties on the campus.

Curry College is home to a caring and committed community where visitors are always welcome. We invite you to visit our interactive campus map online to learn about our campus facilities and to consider visiting Curry in person. We hope to see you on campus soon!

MAJORS AND DEGREES OFFERED

At Curry, we recognize the potential in all of our students. We take a personalized approach to education that allows you to build on your dreams while you simultaneously explore new ideas and uncover talents, strengths, and abilities you never thought you had. A Curry education will lead you to a level of excellence that will touch all facets of your life. You can select from 20 majors and 65-plus minors and concentrations ranging from biology to theatre. Challenge yourself with the Curry Honors Program as well as support through the Program for Advancement of Learning. You can choose from a wide array of extracurricular activities ranging from 14 NCAA Division III athletic teams — seven men's team and seven female teams — to an outstanding theater program. The Curry College experience is as unique as you are and the opportunities are endless. At Curry, you can achieve excellence in the classroom—and beyond.

OFF-CAMPUS OPPORTUNITIES

As an alumnus/alumna of Curry College, you are always welcome to use the Office of Career Services. We recognize that you have different challenges than current students, whether it's undertaking a career change, dealing with a job loss, or brushing up on your job search skills. You have free access to individual career counseling, including skills/interests assessments, career exploration, and job search planning; assistance in selecting and applying to graduate school; resume and cover letter reviews; online and print resources; and job postings.

CAMPUS FACILITIES AND EQUIPMENT

In the fall of 2009, Curry College opened a new student center. The 84,000 square foot facility is full of state-of-the-art areas for dinning, studying, athletics, student activities, or simply lounging around. The student center has become a place to study between classes, to meet up with friends for dinner, work out or even take on your roommate in a game of billiards or foosball.

The Gertrude M. Webb Learning Center is a unique, Tudor-style building with several thousand square feet of space dedicated to PAL students. The architecture of the learning center is based in the earlier part of this century and features majestic touches including cathedral ceilings and ornate fireplaces. The Kennedy Academic Center, located on South Campus, houses many of Curry's classrooms as well as PC and MAC computer labs. The John S. Hafer Academic Building, erected in 1965, is located on the Academic Quadrangle on North Campus and houses many of Curry's classrooms. The Hafer Building is also a popular location on campus for hosting cultural activities and guest speakers. In 2001, our state-of-the art television studio, the Hirsh Communication Center, complete with full TV production facilities, was added to the facility. In August 2006, the Academic and Performance Center, opened to the College community. The new three-story, 30,000 square-foot building has eight classrooms, including an amphitheatre-style lecture hall and a stock trading classroom, faculty office suites, a student lounge, conference and breakout meeting rooms, and a two-story atrium with a smart-café offering quick and healthy eating options. In addition, the building includes a 229-seat multi-purpose auditorium, the first dedicated performance space for Curry College students.

TUITION, ROOM, BOARD, AND FEES

Annual Tuition and Fees 2012–2013

  Tuition: $31,900

  Fees: $1,565

  Room: $7,160

  Board: $5,600

Total (exclusive of PAL)

  Resident: $46,225 °°

  Commuter: $33,465

  PAL Fee (if applicable): $6,550

°°The total cost for resident students is based on 14 meals per week and a multiple occupancy room. The plan including 17 meals per week would increase the cost by $590. The 10 meals per week plan would decrease the total cost by $1,330. A single occupancy room would increase the total cost by $1,960. Additional fees may apply.

FINANCIAL AID

Recognizing that meeting the total cost of a higher education today can be challenging for students and families, Curry College provides a variety of financing options and participates in federal and state financial aid programs. The Student Financial Services staff is committed to helping you create a financial plan that will allow you to reach your enrollment goals. In order to be considered for need-based financial aid, students must complete a FAFSA annually. You can fill out a FAFSA online at www.fafsa.ed.gov or use the paper application. If you would like us to mail you a paper FAFSA application, please contact our office and we would be happy to mail one to you. FAFSA forms are also available at any high school. Financial aid comes in three forms: grants and scholarships; loans; and student employment. Curry College provides students with millions of dollars in financial aid each year. The college uses its own endowment funds, gifts from friends, foundations and corporations, alumni, parents, and other donors to be able to provide this funding to our students. We believe in the potential of every Curry College student and realize that financing a student's education can be a difficult task for a family. Curry also receives substantial funding from the various state and federal financial aid programs.

STUDENT ORGANIZATIONS AND ACTIVITIES

College is a time for making lifelong connections—with new people, new interests, and passions—a time of endless possibilities. It's a time to go beyond life as you know it now and do the things you've always dreamed of doing. At Curry College, you'll instantly become part of a unique, upbeat community with all the resources to help you excel academically, socially, and physically. Whether you're a resident student or commuter student, we'll help you find your niche. Right on campus you'll find countless sources of entertainment, action, and challenge. You can unwind at the Colonel's Corner snack bar over a game of pool, meet friends at a movie night, take a turn behind the mic, or just listen, at a coffeehouse or comedy night. Work out in the weight room or exercise your voice in the Currier Times newspaper or campus chorale. Join one of the many student clubs and organizations or volunteer for community service projects.

Life as a Curry student extends beyond the campus, too. You can hike or ski in the nearby Blue Hills Reservation, and will have easy access to big city excitement and resources just seven miles away in downtown Boston. The staff in the offices of Student Affairs—Student Activities, Residence Life, Public Safety, Health and Counseling, and the Chaplaincy—are all committed to helping you develop your personal goals and establish relationships within the Curry College community. We encourage your involvement and leadership in all aspects of college life.

ADMISSIONS PROCESS

As you explore enrollment at Curry College, the Office of Admission encourages you to visit the campus and meet with an Admission Counselor. To be considered for admission to Curry College, we require you to submit the following:

A completed application with a nonrefundable fee of $50

An official high school transcript

Results of the SAT or ACT

A letter of recommendation from a guidance counselor or high school teacher

A college essay

D'YOUVILLE COLLEGE

AT A GLANCE

Focused on professional studies and the liberal arts, D'Youville College is a private institution with a coed student body of 3,200. Founded in 1908, D'Youville has a proud history: The College was the first in western New York to grant undergraduate degrees to female students. Today, D'Youville offers degrees in over thirty-five different undergraduate and graduate programs. The College's holistic approach to education, as well as the 14:1 student-faculty ratio, encourages personal development alongside of academic pursuits.

D'Youville hosts one of the nation's biggest four-year, private nursing programs. The multiple-option Nursing Degree Program allows students to also choose an RN to BSN course of study. Students can also undertake a five-year programs resulting in a combined bachelor's/master's (BS/MS) degree in the areas of accounting, education, occupational therapy, international business, physician assistant and dietetics. Those seeking master's degrees may apply in childhood, adolescent, special education, community health nursing, MBA, occupational therapy, international business, and health services administration. There is also a 7 year, bachlor's and doctorate of chiropractic and 6 year, bachelor's and doctorate of physical therapy and a 6 year Doctorate of Pharmacy. Upon graduating from D'Youville, 96 percent of students either secure jobs in their chosen field or go on to graduate school.

The College's location by the Niagara River and Lake Erie provides breathtaking vistas, enjoyed by students living in Marguerite Hall. The Koessler Administration Building houses the president's offices as well as the offices of admissions, financial aid, student accounts, and the registrar. The Learning Center and Kavinoky Theatre also share that building. When it's time to relax, students head to the Student Center, outfitted with a gymnasium, swimming pool, weight-training room, dance studio, general recreation center, pub, and dining facilities.

Campus life thrives thanks to student organizations including social groups, academic clubs, and the College newspaper. For athletes of any persuasion, the ski club, intramural teams, and NCAA Division III intercollegiate sports (baseball, basketball, volleyball, golf, cross-country, crew, soccer, softball, and club hockey) provide athletic activities.

LOCATION AND ENVIRONMENT

Located in Buffalo, the D'Youville campus enjoys a residential setting. The downtown shopping center, the Kleinhans Music Hall, the Albright-Knox Art Gallery, two museums, and several theaters are all nearby. Toronto, a mere 90 miles away, offers additional metropolitan attractions, and Niagara Falls can be reached in just 25 minutes. Skiers can make it to Holiday Valley in about an hour. Buffalo can be reached via the New York State Thruway, Amtrak, Greyhound and Trailways bus lines, and most major airlines.

D'Youville connects itself to the community by forging relationships with local schools, hospitals, and social groups. Buffalo is home to more than 60,000 college students in all.

Specific departments affiliate with the appropriate area organizations. For instance, the nursing program works with 13 local hospitals and public health agencies. Nearby elementary, junior high, and secondary schools, as well as special education centers, are available for student teaching assignments for those in the education program. D'Youville students pursuing degrees in occupational therapy, physical therapy, and the physician assistant program can get hands-on experience at clinics across the country. D'Youville also maintains its own Chiropractic Clinic.

MAJORS AND DEGREES OFFERED

D'Youville students can pursue the degrees of Bachelor of Arts (BA), Bachelor of Science (BS), Bachelor of Science in Nursing (BSN), five-year, two-degree, BS+MS programs, and combined BS+DC or BS +DPT programs. In 2010 D'Youville started accepting applications for the new 6 year, Pharmacy Program. Students choose from majors including bachelor degrees in Accounting, Biology, Biology, Chemistry, English, Exercise and Sports Studies, Global Studies, Health Services Management, History, Liberal Studies for Education, Mathematics, Business Management, Nursing, Pharmacy, Philosophy, Pre-Professional, science (pre-medical, pre-dental, pre-veterinary, pre-law), Psychology, Sociology. For the BS+MS programs, achieved over five years, these include accounting (BS) + international business(MS), dietetics, international business, occupational therapy, physician assistant, and education.

Additionally, there is a 6 year, BS+ DPT, physical therapy program, a 7 year, BS + DC, chiropractic program, and a 6 year Doctorate in Pharmacy program with an early assurance program.

We are now offering a doctoral degree, Ed.D. in Health Policy and Health Education, Doctor of Nursing Practice, Physical Therapy, and Chiropractic.

ACADEMIC PROGRAMS

Students select a major based on their interests and career goals. Any area of study provides a solid background for post-college pursuits. In order to graduate, students must fulfill the requirements of their department, complete the core requirements, pass a total of 120 credit hours, and maintain a minimum grade point average of 2.0. The core requirements cover humanities, 24 hours; social science, 12 hours; science, 7 hours; mathematics/computer science, 6 hours; and electives, 9 hours. Most students take five or six classes, approximately 16 credit hours, each semester. Internships can compliment classroom experiences in any course of study.

Students who are undecided regarding their major can benefit from participation in the Career Discovery Program. Over the course of two years, students explore career options through classes and internships.

The academic year is divided into two fifteen-week semesters. Students complete the final exams for the first semester prior to winter break. Summer programs, lasting eight weeks, are also available for certain classes.

In order to better prepare for D'Youville courses, students can find assistance at the College Learning Center. For help in a specific subject, the Tutor Bank provides trained peer tutors.

CAMPUS FACILITIES AND EQUIPMENT

Living on campus is a great way to make the most of your college years. A D'Youville education extends further than the classroom, and being a campus resident is a major part of that education. Living on campus, students often make friendships that last a lifetime. Close proximity to the labs and library makes it easier to use free moments for study. Living on campus also puts you closer to campus events.

Marguerite Hall, a twelve-story co-ed residence hall, is home to up to 308 students. Each floor in Marguerite houses approximately 28 students. Students can select from several options including single gender floors, coed floors, intensive study floors, and an over-21 floor. Based on availability, students may select a single, double or triple room. Singles are not available for freshmen.

The new Student Apartment Complex has one and four, fully furnished bedroom apartments with cooking facilities. These are available to upperclassmen.

Twenty-four-hour security coverage is provided in the residence halls. All visitors must sign in and be accompanied by their student host. Limited campus parking is available to residence students.

Computer and Network Services (CANS) provides the infrastructure and technical support necessary for many services on campus including email, web access, file and print sharing, and application support for distance learning, the library and administrative offices. We take pride in being a wired campus, providing high-speed network access in our offices, classrooms and dorms. Dialup and VPN access is also provided on a limited basis, and technical support is available free of charge to the college community.

TUITION, ROOM, BOARD AND FEES

In 2013-2014, tuition totaled $22,480 annually, and $10,520 for room and board. A mandatory College fee is assessed according to the number of credit hours a student enrolls in. There is a $55 Student Association fee, which defrays the costs of concerts, yearbooks, guest lectures, and other activities. Additionally, there is a $25 orientation fee and $20 liability insurance fee.

FINANCIAL AID

Financial aid is intended to ensure that D'Youville is financially accessible to students of all backgrounds. The allocations of grants, loans, and work-study opportunities are determined by review of the Free Application for Federal Student Aid.

Ninety percent of D'Youville freshmen receive financial aid. This includes nearly $2,000,000 in grants and scholarships. Grants include: Federal Pell Grants and Supplemental Education Opportunity Grants, New York State Tuition Assistance Program, and Aid for Part-Time Study Federal Work-Study programs, federally insured loans, and flexible payment plans are also available.

All applicants are reviewed for academic scholarships at the time of acceptance. Notifications of awards are made upon acceptance. Awards include: Presidential Honors Scholarships, Academic Initiative Scholarships, Achievement Scholarships and Transfer Achievement Scholarships. These scholarships are based on academic performance and could be worth up to $67,500.

All continuing students may apply for thousands of dollars from endowed and restricted scholarships.

Canadian students receive a 20-percent tuition waiver unless the student receives a RN Nursing waiver. All undergraduate Canadian students are eligible for academic scholarships.

Nursing students in the BSN completion program for RNs receive a 50% tuition-only waiver.

D'Youville is a member of the Council of Independent Colleges Tuition Exchange Program, the Tuition Exchange Program, Inc, and The Catholic Cooperative Tuition Exchange Program. All are tuition remission programs.

STUDENT ORGANIZATIONS AND ACTIVITIES

Student representatives elected to the Student Association (SA) work with the administration and faculty to make decisions regarding the College's academic, social, and moral life. The SA comprises the executive council and student senate, and any D'Youville attendees can run for a position or participate in any of the 17 related academic and social organizations.

Extracurricular activities are an important part of college life and at D'Youville we want your academic experience to be safe, successful and fun. Several key services and programs will help you meet your goals and enjoy your time outside of the classroom.

Our intercollegiate program is a Division III member of the National Collegiate Athletic Association, competing in the Allegheny Mountain Collegiate Conference. A variety of recreational activities are available as well as a fitness center, swimming pool and game room.

Students can also join academic, cultural, and recreational clubs, serve on campus wide committees, contribute to student publications, perform in the arts, attend special events, and take advantage of many volunteer opportunities.

As a new student, you will be invited to attend an orientation program for freshmen, families, transfers, certificate or graduate students. Here you'll learn about program requirements, course selection with an academic advisor, registration, and information seminars.

The D'Youville Freshman Experience (DFX) is designed to help make your first year exciting, fun and challenging. At orientation, you'll be assigned a college mentor and registered for the FOCUS Freshmen Seminar. There are also activities and leadership opportunities (D'Youville Leads) as well as a Peer Mentor Program coordinated through the Leadership Development Institute.

ADMISSIONS PROCESS

Admission to D'Youville College is moderately competitive. Our selection process identifies those qualified men and women who will benefit most from the programs the college offers. In making admissions decisions, we consider grades, class rank, standardized test scores, recommendations, and any additional information you can provide.

To apply you'll need to submit a completed application along with, official high school transcripts or, if you're a transfer student, official transcripts from all colleges previously attended. High school only graduates must also submit SAT I or ACT scores and letters of recommendation. Review the admission requirements for the major of your choice on our website.

Applications are reviewed on a rolling basis for all programs except the Physicians Assistant program. You can expect to receive an admissions decision within three weeks of the time we receive all the necessary forms, test scores, and transcripts. The sooner you complete your application, the sooner you'll receive a decision.

Admission to D'Youville College is granted without regard to age, race, gender, national origin, religious affiliation, or disability.

DAEMEN COLLEGE

AT A GLANCE

Located just outside of Buffalo, New York, Daemen College is a private college offering strong liberal arts majors, exceptional professional degrees, and widely acclaimed Graduate programs. Daemen is distinguished by a low student/faculty ratio and consistently small class sizes, which encourage students to interact with professors and grow as individuals. Daemen students have their education enriched by challenging opportunities that engage them in learning experiences through international education programs, collaborative research with faculty, clinical and field experiences, internships for credit, and service learning positions. Daemen students embrace an academically challenging atmosphere where they are encouraged to develop a strong repertoire of knowledge and skills. Daemen College meets the individual goals and needs of each student, preparing them for leadership and professional life in a global economy.

LOCATION AND ENVIRONMENT

Daemen's beautiful 39-acre campus is located in Amherst, New York, a peaceful suburb of Buffalo. Due to its proximity to Buffalo, Daemen's campus is close to many major rail, plane, and motor routes. While the campus setting is tranquil and residential, Buffalo is a vibrant cultural city, bustling with world-class entertainment, such as the Philharmonic Orchestra, the Albright-Knox Art Gallery, and the Shea's Theater. The greater Buffalo area is rich with sports and recreational activities all year round, whether it be skiing and swimming, or watching our professional sports teams. Niagara Falls is only 30 minutes away and the attractive, international city of Toronto is just two hours by car. On campus, the numerous trees and open green spaces create a lovely environment to work and study.

OFF-CAMPUS OPPORTUNITIES

Daemen's office of Global Programs operates and coordinates distinctive study abroad opportunities designed to facilitate students' professional aspirations. In today's global economy, it makes sense to learn all you can about different cultures, political systems, and histories. International study is a staple of the Daemen experience. There are several options when looking at the amount of time students want to study abroad – whether it's a week, semester, or even a year!

Daemen's Career Service Office provides students and graduates with a wide variety of services specially geared to the vocational and self-development needs of the College community before and after graduation. Career Services helps students find an internship or co-op position so that they can gain real-world experience in their area of interest. Students often express how prepared they feel to have had the chance to experience what careers in their fields are really like. An added bonus, internship employers sometimes offer Daemen interns full-time positions after graduation. The opportunities are local, national, or international – including excellent opportunities with the Washington Internship Institute.

Daemen believes in "learning through service." Each academic year, nearly 500 Daemen students contribute more than 30,000 volunteer service hours to make a difference in the lives of youth, families and communities. In the process, Daemen students serve, learn, and gain the leadership, cross-cultural, and communication skills necessary to become civic-minded individuals prepared to participate in a democratic society. Students can choose from a variety of service-learning courses and site placements in settings that include Boys & Girls Clubs, community centers, soup kitchens, housing rehabilitation and refugee resettlement agencies, shelters for the homeless, nursing homes, and many other health and human service agencies.

MAJORS AND DEGREES OFFERED

Daemen College offers BA, BFA, BS, MS, DNP and DPT programs.

Majors offered at Daemen include: Accounting BS/MS, Animation, Art; Applied Design/Printmaking, Applied Theater, Drawing, Graphic Design, Illustration, Painting, Sculpture, Visual Arts Education K-12, Arts Administration BA/MS, Athletic Training BS/MS, Biology; Adolescence Education 7-12, Environmental Studies, Biochemistry; Pre-Professional, Business Administration; Human Resource Management, International Business, Management Information Systems, Marketing, Sport Management, Education; Childhood Education 1-6, Childhood Education/ Special Education1-6, Early Childhood Education/Special Education B-12, English; Adolescence Education 7-12, Communications/Public Relations, French; Adolescence Education 7-12, Health Care Studies; Community Health, Complementary and Alternative Health Care Practices, Health and Fitness Training, History, History and Government; Adolescence Education 7-12, Environmental Studies, Mathematics; Adolescence Education 7-12, Natural Sciences; Environmental Studies, Forensic Science, Health Science, Individualized Studies, Nursing, Paralegal, Physical Therapy BS,NS/DPT, Physician Assistant BS/MS, Political Science, Psychology, Religious Studies, Social Work, Spanish; Adolescence Education 7-12, Sustainability (Global and Local) Interdisciplinary studies; Environmental Studies, Health Care Studies, Individualized Study, and Pre-Professional Programs; Pre-Dentistry, Pre-Law, Pre-Medicine, and Pre-Veterinary.

Graduate MS programs include Accounting; Professional Accountancy BS/MS, Athletic Training BS/MS, Arts Administration BS/MS, Education; Adolescence Education 7-12, Childhood Education 1-6, Special Education 1-6, Executive Leadership and Change, Global Business, Nursing; Adult Nurse Practitioner, Nursing Education, Nursing Executive Leadership and Physician Assistant.

Doctorate programs include Doctor of Nursing Practice and Direct Entry Doctor of Physical Therapy. In addition Physical Therapy offers an Orthopedic Manual Physical Therapy Fellowship Program.

ACADEMIC PROGRAMS

Daemen College is committed to complimenting the depth of study in a major field with a well-rounded academic understanding in the liberal arts. The College's core curriculum ensures that every student graduates with the following seven core competencies: critical thinking and creative problem solving; communication skills; information and literacy; civic responsibility; contextual competency; affective awareness; and moral and ethical discernment. This innovative core curriculum competes with those of Ivy League Institutions and prepares the student in a holistic manner which not only makes them more marketable upon graduation, but instructs them on alternative ways of approaching education and learning.

Daemen provides students with small classes and a caring and committed faculty, allowing for a personalized educational experience. Academics at Daemen will challenge you to test your knowledge, raise your expectations, and think critically and creatively. Daemen's core competencies, honors program, academic exchanges, global programs, and undergraduate research are just a few examples of what makes the College challenging and distinctive.

Daemen students are well prepared for professional success. The vast majority of them obtain a position of choice or admission to Graduate study in less than a year after graduation. They are leaders in their communities, with a strong dedication to the improvement of the communities in which they live.

CAMPUS FACILITIES AND EQUIPMENT

Modern apartment-style residence halls provide separate housing for male and female students, in addition to our existing five-story residence hall. All residence halls have kitchens, laundry facilities, lounges, and in-room phone/Internet connections.

Full-service meals are served in the main dining hall, with an a la carte selection in the snack bar. The recreation room and Cyber Cafe are popular spots for socializing and relaxing during the day or evening

The Research and Information Commons has transformed the campus, both aesthetically and academically. This is a technological showcase that has become the hub of academic research, as well as the academic and social heart of the campus.

The new Center for Visual and Performing Arts is equipped with an interactive performance/lecture space with seating for 50, featuring high-resolution projection and state-of-the-art smart board technology. The Center features flexible studio space allowing for studio instruction and theatrical space, with moveable walls making it possible to transform one large studio into three smaller ones. A second floor, dedicated to Graphic Design, houses a large, open production space as well as computer labs and faculty offices.

TUITION, ROOM, BOARD AND FEES

Tuition for the 2012-2013 academic year is $23,130, with additional room and board fees of $10,700. (Cost varies according to meal plan and residence facility.)

FINANCIAL AID

Learning to navigate the financial aid system can be a daunting task. That's why Daemen has trained professionals on hand to assist you every step of the way. Their Admissions Staff and Financial Aid Counselors are available to assist you and your family with the financial aid application process, and to ensure that you understand the necessary paperwork and deadlines required in order for you to receive the best financial aid package available.

Daemen strives to create individualized financial aid packages for you and your family that will meet your needs and enable you to get the most out of your college education. With this philosophy in mind, Daemen College offers merit-based and need-based financial assistance, as well as aid based on a combination of financial need and academic achievement. More than 92% of current Daemen students receive some form of financial assistance. In addition to the College's own scholarships, Daemen College participates in all federal and state programs.

STUDENT ORGANIZATIONS AND ACTIVITIES

Student activities provide for the development of the whole person outside of the classroom. The Director of Student Activities on campus helps students participate in recognized organizations, form new ones, and plan events. With over 50 student organizations the possibilities for involvement at Daemen are limitless. Whether your interests are in art or skiing, there is bound to be something that grabs your interest and introduces you to students who share similar passions. Daemen believes that now is the time to discover exactly who you are; cultivating your hidden talents, taking new risks and challenging yourself to grow are all part of the Daemen experience. Daemen encourages all of their students to become actively engaged in the campus community.

Daemen College has enjoyed a tremendous amount of recent success from its athletic programs. They have won thirteen American Mideast Conference North titles in the past ten years. The Wildcats are currently transitioning from the National Association of Intercollegiate Athletics (NAIA) to Division II National Collegiate Athletic Association (NCAA). Daemen is currently in year 1 of the NCAA Division II membership process which will take three years to complete. In 2013-2014, the Wildcats will join the East Coast Conference of NCAA Division II. Our student athletes work hard to achieve success on the field and in the classroom, with 45 student-athletes having been recognized as All-American Scholar-Athletes in the last 10 years.

Daemen College Intercollegiate Athletics include:

Men's: Basketball, Cross Country, Track and Field (indoor and outdoor), Golf, Soccer, Tennis

Women's: Basketball, Cross Country, Track and Field (indoor and outdoor), Soccer, Volleyball, Tennis

More casual athletes take part in club or intramural sports and keep fit in the exercise and weight rooms.

ADMISSIONS PROCESS

Daemen College offers a test optional policy. Applicants are not required to submit standardized test scores (SAT, ACT) as part of the admission application. Our decision to make test scores optional reflects our commitment to enrolling students who reflect intellectual curiosity, persistence in reaching a goal, talent, motivation, and determination to make a difference in their lives and the lives of others. We rely on high school GPA, transcripts (including grade performance and rigor of courses selected), extracurricular activities, class rank, and counselor or teacher recommendations in making our admission decisions. We value strong writing skills, a solid secondary school program, and a student's potential for making an important contribution to our campus community. We will also give careful consideration to applications from students whose preparation is unusual and who can provide strong recommendations as to their ability to succeed in a college program of study. We encourage an on campus interview and any other information a prospective student wishes to provide.

Daemen has a rolling admissions policy. However, due to program and residence-hall capacity limits, we highly encourage you to send your deposit as soon as you have made your decision.

The best way to get to know Daemen is in person. On your visit, we'll take you on a campus tour, arrange for you to meet professors and current students, and plan a one-on-one meeting with an Admissions Counselor.

To schedule your appointment, contact the Office of Admissions at 800-462-7652 or register inline at www.daemen.edu/admissions. You may make an individual visit Mon-Sat, attend our Fall and Spring Open Houses, or join us for many of our other special admissions events. We hope to see you on campus soon!

DENISON UNIVERSITY

AT A GLANCE

Founded in 1831, Denison University has long been recognized as a leader among national liberal arts institutions. Denison is a highly selective, four-year, independent, and fully residential undergraduate college located in the Village of Granville, Ohio, a central Ohio suburb located east of Columbus, the state capital and 16th-largest city in the U.S.

The college enrolls some 2,100 outstanding students from across the country and around the world and offers 48 courses of study in the divisions of the Sciences, Humanities, Social Sciences and Fine Arts. Through an intentional learning process that spans academic, residential and experiential spheres, Denison prepares students with the knowledge, ability, vision and resolve to lead through both thought and action in all walks of life.

Denison has an impressive history, but it is also a college that challenges the status quo and refuses to rest on its laurels. As one of 40 Colleges That Change Lives, it is described as a place that "has become even more of its new and better self." Author Loren Pope wrote:

"Ralph Waldo Emerson said an institution is the lengthening shadow of one man—or woman. What has happened and is happening at Denison proves it. The change in ambience and ethos is palpable. It is a place where good things are happening and a new spirit is in the air ... It is first rate."

Following this arc of achievement, the men and women who currently learn and grow at Denison make up the most diverse and highest achieving student body in the school's history. They come for a transformative, liberating education that demands profound reflection, spirited debate and active engagement. In small classes, they learn directly from—and collaborate with—an accomplished and involved faculty. They put that knowledge into motion, building bridges to the world and applying their liberal arts foundations in research, creativity, innovation entrepreneurship and service. At the core of this experience is a set of rock-solid ideals: integrity, reason, scholarship, community, diversity, intellect, dignity and respect.

THE STUDENTS

Denison takes seriously its commitment not only to attracting a high quality and diverse student body, but also to making this extraordinary education accessible to them. The college's forward-thinking admissions program includes a paperless, highly personal, SAT-optional application process. Admissions at Denison are need-blind. Thanks to strong financial resources, fully 94 percent of current students receive need-based financial aid and/or merit-based scholarships. Denison consistently ranks among the top institutions nationally, and best in Ohio, for the lowest average student debt following graduation. In addition, the default rate on federal student loans is the lowest among all Ohio colleges and universities.

Denison is a fully residential college where 99 percent of the students live on campus, the few exceptions being those with homes nearby. The learning environment extends beyond classrooms, labs and studios into the residence halls, social spaces and recreational facilities. Principles of human dignity and ethical integrity are paramount.

Denison students have unusual opportunities to participate in research, creative projects, and scholarship in all academic disciplines, as well as through service to others, student organizations, Greek life, campus governance, and athletics and recreation.

All told, amid Denison's robust intellectual environment, students participate in 23 varsity athletics programs, 55 intramural clubs, and 170 student organizations representing a wide array of cultural, social, political and professional interests, and offering more than 600 leadership positions. The result, by design, is a lively, participatory campus culture.

Denison is a member of the North Coast Athletic Conference and the National Collegiate Athletic Association's Division III. Its athletes recently completed what some are calling their "best year ever," with a record-setting 12th NCAC All-Sports Championship and a number of individual and team honors, including the 2011 national championship and second-place finish respectively for the men's and women's swimming and diving teams. Denison's scholar-athletes excel in academics as well; their ranks include 44 NCAA Postgraduate Scholars, the third most among all Division III institutions.

THE FACULTY

A Denison education may be tracked according to the breadth and depth of its liberal arts curriculum, but it comes to life in the mutually enriching relationships that develop between students and Denison's 219 full-time faculty. These men and women, holding the most advanced degrees in their fields, are selected on the basis of teaching and scholarly ability. They are highly active within their respective academic and creative disciplines, and they are committed to their roles as scholars, teachers, advisors and mentors, guiding the intellectual and personal growth of their students.

Denison's professors are loyal to the mission of a residential liberal arts college, and that dedication is widely evident beyond their teaching and research. They thrive on collaboration with their students through joint research, small seminars and lively discussions in and outside the classroom. They give immense thought and energy to stewarding the curriculum, assuring its relevance and rigor, and vision for the future. They develop interdisciplinary opportunities such as team-teaching courses, or specially focused courses that relate to the Spectrum Series, which introduces an intellectual theme to each year's campus-wide discourse. They advise individual students and student organizations, and they contribute to small-group dialogue programs with students and staff. They are enthusiastic participants in community service endeavors, and they support student scholars, artists and athletes at academic, cultural and sports events. And they maintain friendships with their students well beyond the college years. By virtue of talent, hard work and dedication, Denison's professors truly are the heart and soul of the college.

THE LIBERAL ARTS

Denison is committed to an exclusively undergraduate liberal arts education and awards three different degrees: Bachelor of Arts, Bachelor of Science and Bachelor of Fine Arts.

Denison boasts generations of students who can attest to the college's impact on their lives. Each could cite something different, and they would all be correct, because Denison's liberal arts tradition and residential community create a world of endless personal possibilities. At Denison, students have to step up—there is no hiding in the back of a large lecture hall, no anonymity, no flying under the radar. Students matter as individuals, and they are prepared for lives of consequence by an outstanding and committed faculty.

Denison has a reputation for challenging academics, but energetic, discussion-oriented classes and dedicated professors are just part of what distinguishes its programs. The college combines outstanding classroom experiences and provocative interdisciplinary approaches to teaching creativity with opportunities to test knowledge in the world beyond campus. Independent research and close collaboration with professors and fellow students are hallmarks of a Denison education. In addition to a hands-on learning model across the curriculum, specific programs foster independent and collaborative research, including Denison's extraordinary Summer Scholars Program, with paid research opportunities in the arts and sciences for more than 100 students each year. Off-campus study also is an important aspect of a Denison education. About half of each class participates in off-campus academic study, either abroad or domestically.

The William Howard Doane Library, along with its adjacent Seeley G. Mudd Learning Center, is a hub of teaching and learning at Denison. The number and range of library resources available have grown dramatically in recent years, in part due to partnerships with colleges and universities in Ohio (OhioLINK) and with local liberal arts colleges (CONSORT). Several significant grants, particularly a Five Colleges of Ohio Information Literacy grant from the Andrew W. Mellon Foundation, have provided opportunities for innovation and improvements in instruction and managing information.

The John W. Alford Center for Service Learning engages students in programs and activities through the Denison Community Association, America Reads, Curricular Service Learning, and the college's Service Orientation. Denison has been duly recognized for its student service by being selected for the Carnegie Foundation's Community Engagement Classification and the President's Higher Education Community Service Honor Roll.

THE ALUMNI

Denison graduates have a voice. They can speak, write, listen, persuade, collaborate, innovate, create, perform, take responsibility, solve, adapt and lead. Currently numbering more than 31,500, the alumni of Denison illustrate leadership and impact in virtually every walk of life.

Moreover, the alumni show a remarkable penchant for staying connected with each other and involved with their alma mater. Individual departments, programs and organizations commonly cultivate ties among former students. Meanwhile, the Office of Alumni Relations engages the entire alumni body in a mutually beneficial, lifelong connection to each other and to Denison. The office helps constituents maintain the friendships, associations and interests they formed as students and fosters giving to the college. Sponsored events include: class reunions every summer; Big Red Weekend for alumni, parents and friends in the fall; regional club and affinity group gatherings throughout the year; and a number volunteer activities.

As students prepare for post-graduate life, they work closely with the Office of Career Exploration and Development, which helps them integrate a liberal arts education into lifetimes of personal and professional fulfillment. And as alumni, they work with the office to provide internships to students and jobs to new graduates.

THE CAMPUS

As a residential campus, Denison provides an education that is rooted in a strong sense of place. The campus is situated on and around a hilltop overlooking Granville, a charming New England-style village where 3,500 residents provide a supportive and friendly community for students and faculty. Established in 1805 by pioneers from Massachusetts, Granville provides a beautiful and safe environment in which to live and learn, with all the big-city energy of Columbus just down the road.

The residential character of Denison's campus is more than a convenience. It is an intentionally shared enterprise where students, drawn together from diverse backgrounds and perspectives, must learn how to live and learn together as engaged citizens, striving toward ideals of integrity, intellect, diversity, and respect for one another and the environment.

The 900-acre campus, designed by the famed architectural landscape firm of Frederick Law Olmsted and Sons, is pedestrian friendly and exceptionally well suited for the college's academic mission. The buildings are arranged in quadrangles, and pathways encourage the kind of chance meetings and casual conversations among students, faculty and staff that advance learning and build relationships. State-of-the-art buildings for both the arts and the sciences have been constructed to the United States Green Building Council's LEED specifications, and many historic buildings have been renovated to the same standards.

All buildings are within walking distance of one another, which helps build a sense of community. Denison's campus includes a 550-acre Biological Reserve on contiguous sections of land that are within walking distance of campus.

With numerous lectures, concerts, theatrical and dance performances, film screenings and exhibitions by students, faculty and visiting artists, including events sponsored by the Vail Series and a number of endowed lecture series, Denison attracts not only campus members, but the Granville and greater Columbus communities to its many and varied cultural offerings throughout the year.

DESALES UNIVERSITY

AT A GLANCE

DeSales University is a medium-sized, Catholic liberal arts university for men and women administered by the Oblates of St. Francis de Sales.

Founded in 1964, DeSales University is a Catholic liberal arts university that offers courses in a wide range of disciplines. DeSales provides personal attention, small class size, and a feeling of community. The University uses a holistic approach to help students develop a "sense of self," enabling every student to reach their personal and academic potential. This student-centered philosophy is conveyed by an enthusiastic, accessible faculty.

LOCATION AND ENVIRONMENT

DeSales University' suburban campus is located 15 minutes south of Bethlehem and Allentown, Pa., and only 1 hour from Philadelphia, 90 minutes from Scranton and Wilkes-Barre, Pa., less than 2 hours from New York City, and 3 hours from Baltimore. The campus is 500 acres with more than 16 major buildings.

OFF-CAMPUS OPPORTUNITIES

Allentown and Bethlehem are a short 15-minute drive from campus and offer many dining, shopping, and outdoor activities, including the Promenade Shops at Saucon Valley, just minutes from campus. The Lehigh Valley, aka 'College Valley,' boasts beautiful hiking and biking trails, historic sites, museums, cultural festivals, and Dorney Park and Wildwater Kingdom. Skiing at nearby Blue Mountain and other Pocono resorts is just a short drive away. The Poconos also offer white water rafting trips down the Lehigh and Delaware Rivers.

MAJORS AND DEGREES OFFERED

DeSales University offers 37 bachelor's degrees including 10 pre-professional programs, and seven graduate programs through the divisions of business, liberal arts and social sciences, performing arts, and science and health care. Our more popular majors include criminal justice, theatre, medical studies, and business administration.

ACADEMIC PROGRAMS

DeSales University defines "global competence" as using an open, inquisitive mind to understand the norms and expectations of other cultures, and using this acquired knowledge to communicate and to work effectively outside of one's usual environment in the promotion of human solidarity. DeSales University presents opportunities for students to enlarge their world view, from activities and concerts to short- and long-term study abroad programs.

Study abroad programs through DeSales present the opportunity for our students to live and work in this vibrantly interdependent world and range from semester long study to short stay travel of 10 days. Our students can spend semesters in England, Greece, Italy, Ireland, Switzerland, France, and Monte Carlo . More importantly, DeSales is employing a new model of intensive hands on engagement through short-stay co-curricular trips of students, faculty, and staff. Trips to Ireland, Germany, Peru, and South Africa for short stay intensive travel have been combined with academic courses, the activities of student organizations or out of season competition for our athletic teams.

Freshman students are asked to participate in the Character U program, a self-assessment program based on the Golden Counsels of St. Francis de Sales. Each month, University programming addresses one of these Golden Counsels or traits including patience, trust and cooperation, and perseverance. The DeSales Experience offers opportunities to learn and lead outside the classroom.

The University's Academic Resource Center can offer assistance in reading comprehension, study skills, time management and effective writing techniques. Additionally they can help find a tutor if you need it or provide you with the opportunity to become a peer tutor.

CAMPUS FACILITIES AND EQUIPMENT

Trexler Library has a collection of more than 500,000 items and there are electronic databases of newspapers, journal articles, and the Oxford Dictionary of National Biography. There are computer and multimedia labs and a staff who will help with any research topic. Trexler Library has wireless access both with personal laptops or laptops that can be borrowed to use in the building. The Library's resources can be accessed from anywhere on campus. There is online access to databases and full text journal articles. Students can also instant message a librarian with a question.

The DeSales University Center features many menu choices—especially for healthy eaters—in a food court setting. The University Center also has wireless laptop capability so you can eat and surf, as well as see panoramic views of campus.

The Priscilla Payne Hurd Science Center, a 37,500 square foot facility, is equipped with up-to-date computers, labs, and medical equipment. The Hurd Science Center also features a sterile molecular/cell biology suite, complete with a freezer room, bench room, support room, dark room, and instrument room. An ecology/environmental lab with a growing chamber, an analytical/physical chemistry/inorganic laboratory, and a bioinformatics/physics lab also inhabit the two-story building.

The University just opened a 77,000 square foot academic building that houses the school's business division and health care majors. The Gambet Center for Business and Health Care Education features a simulated trading room for business and finance majors, standardized patient areas, and a gross anatomy lab.

TUITION, ROOM, BOARD, AND FEES

Tuition and Fees (2012-13): $29,000

Room and Board: $10,970

Student & Technology Fee: $1,150

Total: $41,120

FINANCIAL AID

Nine out of ten DeSales University students receive financial aid in the form of grants, scholarships, work study, and loans. About 85 percent of the students receive grants directly from DeSales University, and funds are also available from federal and state programs to those who qualify. The amount of aid received and the composition of an aid package will depend on financial need and on academic achievement and potential.

Academic scholarships are also available through DeSales University. All applicants for admission are automatically considered for each of the scholarships offered by the University.

STUDENT ORGANIZATIONS AND ACTIVITIES

DeSales University has more than 31 campus organizations, including the Student Activities crew, which helps plan student events, bus trips, and on-campus performances. Recent renovations to the McShea Student Center include a student activities lounge open to students for entertainment and socializing, and Café McShea, an internet café with late night hours. Both new areas are just the beginning of increased special events such as independent movie nights, comedians, music acts, and expanded space for programs sponsored by various student organizations.

DeSales University has 16 intercollegiate varsity sports teams and all are members of the NCAA Division III, Middle Atlantic States Collegiate Athletic Corporation (MAC) Freedom Conference, and the Eastern College Athletic Conference (ECAC).

The University's men's sports are baseball, basketball, cross-country, golf, lacrosse, soccer, and indoor and outdoor track and field. Women's sports are basketball, cross-country, field hockey, soccer, softball, indoor and outdoor track & field, and volleyball. The University also has seven club sports: cheerleading, cycling, disc golf, equestrian, ice hockey, tennis, and men's volleyball

There are intramural sports for all seasons, or student can visit the state-of-the-art Billera Hall fitness center, which offers aerobic, Nautilus, and free-weight training.

ADMISSIONS PROCESS

To Apply for Admission you need to:

Complete a DeSales University application and submit it with a nonrefundable $30 fee to our Admissions Office.

Have your high school guidance department send your official high school transcript to our Admissions Office.

Have your standardized test scores (SAT or ACT) sent to our Admissions Office. Our code number for SAT scores is 2021.

Have a guidance counselor and teacher complete the recommendation forms and send to our Admissions Office.

DRAKE UNIVERSITY

AT A GLANCE

Drake University provides a thriving intellectual environment offering more than 70 majors, covering subjects from the liberal arts to professional and pre-professional programs. The University employs professors who demonstrate a dedication to students along with academic prowess. Students benefit from the low 12:1 student-faculty ratio, and they never take classes from graduate students or teaching assistants. Drake enrolls a heterogeneous group of nearly 5,600 students, from 49 states and more than 50 foreign countries. Drake prides itself on alumni success, noting that 97.3% percent of 2011 Drake graduates embarked on careers or started graduate programs during their first six months out of school.

Drake grants master's degrees in: accounting, business administration, communication leadership, education, financial management, and public administration. Students may also pursue their Doctor of Pharmacy, Doctor of Jurisprudence, and Doctor of Education degrees. Joint degrees are also available in MBA/JD, MPA/JD, MBA/PharmD, MPA/PharmD, and PharmD/JD.

LOCATION AND ENVIRONMENT

Students take advantage of Drake's location in Des Moines, Iowa, the state capital and a thriving business center. Internships are available in fields such as government, banking, insurance, publishing, nonprofit organizations, and health care, and nearly 80 percent of students participate in at least one internship during their four years at the University.

OFF-CAMPUS OPPORTUNITIES

Many students take advantage of overseas studies options offered through January Term options or the Center for International Programs and Services. Through the Center's work with international institutions and consortia, semester- and yearlong programs are offered in more than 60 countries.

MAJORS AND DEGREES OFFERED

Those studying in the College of Arts and Sciences receive a classic liberal arts education, preparing them for futures in science, mathematics, politics, and the arts, among many other areas. Students may earn their Bachelor of Arts and Bachelor of Science degrees in the following areas: anthropology and sociology; astronomy; biochemistry, cell and molecular biology; biology; chemistry; computer science; English; environmental policy; environmental science; history; international relations; law, politics, and society; mathematics; mathematics education (secondary); neuroscience; philosophy; physics; politics; psychology; religion; rhetoric and communication studies; sociology; study of culture and society; and writing. Some students design their own majors, while others opt for open enrollment and do not immediately declare a major. The University also administers pre-professional study in dentistry, engineering, law, medicine and veterinary medicine. Concentrations are available in anthropology, geography, Latin American studies, primate studies, women's studies and most fields that offer majors.

Students who attend the School of Fine Arts pursue their Bachelor of Arts, Bachelor of Fine Arts, Bachelor of Music, and Bachelor of Music Education degrees. The available fields include art, music, and theatre arts with a dual focus on teaching excellence and artistic creativity. Holding accreditation from by the National Association of Schools of Art and Design, Drake's Department of Art and Design offers instruction in art history, graphic design, and studio art (drawing, painting, printmaking, and sculpture). Students in the Department of Music select from degrees in applied music (instrumental, piano or vocal music performance) and music education. Other alternatives exist, such as a Bachelor of Arts degree with a music major, a Bachelor of Music degree with elective studies in business, and a Bachelor of Music with a jazz studies concentration. Those who wish to study theatre, acting, directing, theatre design, musical theatre, and theatre education enroll in the Department of Theatre Arts.

Students enrolled in the Drake University College of Business and Public Administration complete their undergraduate degree of Bachelor of Science in Business Administration in four years. Available majors include accounting, actuarial science, economics, entrepreneurial management, finance, general business, information systems, international business, management, and marketing. Concentrations in insurance and law and business are also available. The College allows interdisciplinary majors, combinations of majors, and open business (undeclared) status. The College is accreditation by the AACSB International—The International Association to Advance Collegiate Schools of Business.

First-year students admitted directly to the PharmD program in the College of Pharmacy and Health Sciences complete a two-year pre-pharmacy program then are guaranteed consideration for admission into a four-year PharmD program. A health sciences major with three tracks — clinical and applied sciences, health services management, and pharmaceutical sciences — is also available. The College is accredited by the Accreditation Council for Pharmacy Education and belongs to the American Association of Colleges of Pharmacy.

Students who wish to pursue Bachelor of Arts majors in advertising (management and creative tracks), electronic media (broadcast news and radio/television), magazines, news/Internet, and public relations study in the School of Journalism and Mass Communication. The School allows an open enrolled (undeclared) option and holds accreditation from the Accrediting Council on Education in Journalism and Mass Communication.

Interdisciplinary concentrations are offered in behavior analysis of developmental disabilities, global public health and comparative studies and human resources management.

In addition, the College of Arts and Sciences, the College of Business and Public Administration, and the School of Journalism offer combined 3+3 programs with the Drake University Law School. Students in this program can obtain their undergraduate degrees in three years in one of the aforementioned colleges or schools, then pursue a law degree for the next three years at the Law School.

Programs at the School of Education lead to degrees in elementary or secondary education. Students may earn a Bachelor of Science or Bachelor of Arts degree that is tailored to prepare graduates for employment in elementary or secondary schools. Other options include adding middle school and coaching endorsements to teaching credentials. Drake University has belonged to the American Association of Colleges for Teacher Education since the association's founding.

ACADEMIC PROGRAMS

From their first classes on the Drake campus, students have the chance to learn in an individualized, challenging, and supportive environment. Research opportunities abound; students work closely with their professors and often publish their findings. With more than 160 student-run organizations on campus, there is an outlet for students to investigate career paths and network with professionals in their field.

Students benefit from a combination of liberal arts training and professional preparation. Through the Drake Curriculum, all students take interactive classes that develop their critical thinking and expressive skills. Students also receive personalized academic advising. At the end of their four years, students undertake the Senior Capstone, which is a research project, thesis, or other major work that shows the concepts and skills the student has acquired at Drake. Drake's Honors Program is open to top students who wish to undertake a rigorous, interdisciplinary course of study.

CAMPUS FACILITIES AND EQUIPMENT

Students have access to the Cowles Library and its more than more than 600,000 books and journals, 100,000 federal and state government documents, 777,000 microform records, 118 electronic databases, and approximately 22,000 scholarly online journals. The collections also include DVDs and music CDs, as well as a digital repository of scholarship and historical material unique to Drake. In addition, many classes utilize the resources in specialized collections in the Law School, College of Pharmacy and Health Sciences, Center for Teacher Education, and School of Fine Arts. Between the Dwight D. Opperman Hall and Law Library, there are 330,000 volumes, along with computer labs and study facilities. The Studio Theater, the Monroe Recital Hall, and the Hall of the Performing Arts are housed in the Harmon Fine Arts Center. Another performance hall, Sheslow Auditorium with a capacity of 755 seats, is located in Old Main. The Bell Center offers a gym, pool, aerobic dance room, fitness room, basketball, volleyball, and badminton courts. A student-only fitness facility is also located in the student union. Additional athletic facilities are available in the Knapp Center, such as racquetball, volleyball and basketball courts, a jogging track, and a weight room. More than 7,000 people can congregate in Knapp for major events. Basketball courts and a track are available at the Fieldhouse, while the Tennis Center provides six indoor and six outdoor tennis courts.

TUITION, ROOM, BOARD AND FEES

2013-14 tuition, room and board costs, and student fees total $39,880.

FINANCIAL AID

More than 98 percent of full-time students at Drake have their education financed to some degree with the help of financial aid. In the 2011-12 school year, students enrolling directly from high school received on average $14,600 in grants and scholarships. More than 5,000 awards, worth $48 million, are given annually, in the form of need- or merit-based grants and scholarships.

STUDENT ORGANIZATIONS AND ACTIVITIES

With more than 160 organizations operating on campus, students can always find activities that suit their interests. Elected student representatives run the Student Senate. Students also hold seats on some committees in the Faculty Senate. The Student Activities Board is charged with putting on special events, including cultural celebrations, social functions, guest speakers, and concerts. Drake also maintains the Residence Hall Association, composed of students who manage the logistics and activities surrounding residential life.

ADMISSIONS PROCESS

While admission is selective, Drake University considers the full record of each candidate for admission. Since the University prefers students with varied talents and interests, there is no single and inflexible set of admission standards applied to all candidates for admission. The admission process involves a comprehensive review of a student s academic background (courses and grades), standardized test scores (ACT or SAT), personal essay, recommendations, and activities both in high school and the community. Drake University does not discriminate on the basis of age, sex, sexual orientation, race, religion, color, national or ethnic origin, or disability.

A completed application for first-year admission contains the following items: a completed application form, the $25 nonrefundable application fee (the fee is waived for those who apply online), the High School Report and Counselor Recommendation Form, an official high school transcript, and ACT or SAT scores and a personal essay. Students applying to transfer to Drake are required to submit official transcripts for all previous college-level coursework.

Application for admission to undergraduate degree programs, except pre-pharmacy, may be made for any fall, spring, or summer term. Beginning October 15, students are notified of the admission decision within four to six weeks of the date that all materials are received. March 1 is the priority deadline for consideration for admission and merit- and need-based financial aid. Freshman applicants to the pre-pharmacy program in the College of Pharmacy and Health Sciences must submit a completed application by the December 1 deadline. Transfer students are only admitted to the professional PharmD program.

Candidates should contact:

Drake University

Office of Admission

2507 University Avenue

Des Moines, IA 50311

800-44-DRAKE, x3181 or 1-800-443-7253 x 3181

515-271-3181 (locally and outside the U.S)

Fax: 515-271-2831

www.drake.edu

admission@drake.edu

ELMHURST COLLEGE

AT A GLANCE

A private liberal arts college in the heart of metropolitan Chicago, Elmhurst College ranks in the top tier of its category, according to U.S.News & World Report. With a student-faculty ratio of only 13:1, Elmhurst offers a personal approach where every student counts. All classes at Elmhurst are taught by professors, not teaching assistants, and about 84 percent of the College's 151 full-time faculty hold the highest degree in their field.

The College is located in Elmhurst, Illinois, a quiet suburb that ranks Number 1 in a Chicago magazine survey of the "best places to live." Downtown Chicago is a 30-minute train ride away, offering a wealth of professional, cultural, and recreational opportunities.

Students come to Elmhurst from many states and countries, and from nearly every religious, racial, and ethnic background. The student body comprises more than 3,000 undergraduates and nearly 300 graduate students.

LOCATION AND ENVIRONMENT

Elmhurst College is located 16 miles west of downtown Chicago in the quiet suburb of Elmhurst, a community of 43,000 that has been called "the quintessential Chicago suburb." Within walking distance from campus are two art museums, a library, an eight-screen movie house, lots of great restaurants, and more.

The College is just a short train ride from downtown Chicago, where students enjoy unlimited access to world-class cultural and professional opportunities--from internships to sporting events to concerts of all kinds.

Elmhurst looks like a college ought to look, with big trees, broad lawns and classic red-brick buildings. A 48-acre arboretum, the campus boasts nearly 800 trees and shrubs—and all the modern facilities required of scholarship today.

OFF-CAMPUS OPPORTUNITIES

Elmhurst offers international education experiences in many countries, including Spain, the Netherlands, Poland, Germany, Bulgaria, and England. Students can go abroad for a semester, a year or a month during the College's distinctive January Term.

Other off-campus opportunities include a wealth of internship and job-shadowing experiences. One student recently shadowed a renowned neurosurgeon in San Francisco, for example; another worked on staff at the Mayo Clinic in Rochester, Minnesota. A third traveled to New York to participate in a high-level discussion of medical ethics.

MAJORS AND DEGREES OFFERED

Elmhurst offers more than 50 majors, ranging from accounting to exercise science to jazz studies. Students may complete a double major, add a minor or create their own interdisciplinary major. The Honors Program provides extra opportunities for students who are especially talented, curious and motivated. We also offer a range of pre-professional programs leading to graduate study in health care, law and more. Ten graduate programs lead to the master's degree.

ACADEMIC PROGRAMS

Elmhurst is a private, four-year college in the liberal arts tradition. The curriculum combines self-formation and early professional preparation to prepare students for lives of meaningful work and personal fulfillment.

Academic programs at Elmhurst are characterized by their real-world connections. Students conduct research and defend their results. They analyze data, think critically, solve problems collaboratively, study and write across the disciplines, and learn to formulate new ideas and to convey them with maximum impact.

All classes at Elmhurst are taught by professors, not teaching assistants, and about 84 percent of the College's 151 full-time faculty hold the highest degree in their field. With a student-faculty ratio of only 13:1, faculty members get to know their students as individuals.

CAMPUS FACILITIES AND EQUIPMENT

Elmhurst's facilities include a recently renovated student center and an excellent library and computer center. At the Speech-Language-Hearing Clinic, student clinicians practice their skills and treat patients. Old Main, built in 1879, is on the National Register of Historic Places. The Tyrrell Fitness Center offers more than 6,000 square feet of weight training and physical fitness equipment. Facilities are open throughout the day and evening and are readily accessible to all students.

TUITION, ROOM, BOARD AND FEES

Full-time tuition for 2012-2013 is $31,450; standard room & board is $8,838. Need-based financial aid and merit-based scholarships are available.

FINANCIAL AID

Elmhurst provides financial aid to about 85 percent of entering students. Financial aid programs include scholarships (based on academic merit), and grants, loans and student employment (based on financial need). Many students work on campus through our work-study program. The College makes admission decisions independently from any consideration of financial need.

STUDENT ORGANIZATIONS AND ACTIVITIES

Students come to Elmhurst from many states and countries, and from nearly every religious, racial and ethnic background. The student body comprises more than 3,000 undergraduates and nearly 300 graduate students.

Life at Elmhurst is active and creative. Students get involved in more than 100 activities, from theatre to intramurals to the Mock Trial Team. The student newspaper wins awards; the radio station has been on the air since 1947. The campus regularly hosts performances, art exhibits and an array of nationally known guest speakers.

Elmhurst's 19 varsity sports teams compete in the CCIW, one of the top conferences in NCAA Division III athletics. We're big enough to offer a wide choice of sports, but small enough that you can really contribute to your team's success. Bluejay teams have won conference championships in a variety of sports. And they compete in first-rate facilities.

Admission Process

Rolling admission begins on October 1 and continues until all spaces are filled.

Here's how to apply:

First, complete the application for admission. It's available online at www.elmhurst.edu or by mail from the Elmhurst Admission Office.

Next, submit your high school transcript, your ACT or SAT scores, and a recommendation from a teacher or counselor. (An essay and a campus interview are recommended but not required.)

If you're applying as a transfer student, also submit an official transcript from all colleges or universities you've attended.

ELMIRA COLLEGE

AT A GLANCE

Founded in 1855, Elmira College is a private, coeducational, liberal arts college. Elmira, a city of 35,000, is located in the beautiful Finger Lakes Region of Upstate New York.

Campus: 42 historic acres which include 7 classroom buildings, 12 dormitories, 2 administrative office buildings, library, health center, campus center, President's Home and Mark Twain Study. A major athletic facility completes the total campus. Eight college buildings are listed on the National Register of Historic Places.

Academic calendar: Two twelve-week terms followed in April and May by a unique six-week Term III devoted to travel, field experience, research, independent study, and innovative courses.

Enrollment: 1,200 students, thirteen percent of whom are valedictorians or salutatorians of their high schools or prep schools, from 35 states and 31 foreign countries.

Faculty: All have earned the Ph.D. or the highest degree in their field required for undergraduate instruction; 12:1 student faculty ratio. No classes are taught by teaching assistants.

Average Class Size: 16 students per class; 90% of all offerings have 25 or fewer students; 35% have fewer than 12 students. Elmira ranks in the Top Five colleges in the eleven Northern states for small class size.

Athletics: NCAA Division III in men's and women's intercollegiate sports. Member of the Eastern College Athletic Conference, the New York State Women's Collegiate Athletic Association, and the Empire 8 Conference.

LOCATION AND ENVIRONMENT

Elmira, a city of 35,000, is located in the beautiful Finger Lakes Region of Upstate New York. Nestled in the lush, rolling hills of the southern Finger Lakes region, Elmira is a thriving, forward-thinking American community, with fresh air and wide-open spaces in harmony with the modern amenities of a larger city. Nearby, you can attend superb, live entertainment; soar back into American aviation's lofty past; tour historic neighborhoods; investigate Mark Twain's imagination or visit the beautiful lakes that give this region its name.

Within a ten-block radius of the Elmira College campus, there are many restaurants, a performing arts center, a fine arts museum, and shopping. There are about 60 churches, serving most denominations, within walking distance of campus.

Elmira is the place that many scholars say Samuel Clemens (Mark Twain) did his best work, penning the American literary classic The Adventures of Huckleberry Finn and many other works in his study. In 1870, Clemens married Elmira College alumna Olivia Langdon of the Class of 1864. In 1983, the Langdon family gave the study and the historic Quarry Farm to Elmira College. Now Quarry Farm is used as a residence for visiting Twain scholars from all over the world. The Center for Mark Twain Studies at Quarry Farm offers year-round educational programs.

OFF-CAMPUS OPPORTUNITIES

Elmira College offers a wide range of exciting off-campus opportunities. During the Spring Term, for instance, Elmira College students have traveled with faculty to San Salvador in the Bahamas, Spain, France, Russia, England, Italy, Germany, China, Scotland, Japan, Peru, Egypt, Belgium, Greece, Mexico, Australia, the American West, Alaska, and Hawaii.

The highly selective and competitive Junior Year Abroad (JYA) program facilitates the study of foreign language and cultures. Generally, financial aid applies to the JYA program; however, tuition exchange programs do not apply. Interested students apply in the Fall Term of their sophomore year.

All Elmira College students participate in a community service activity for a minimum of 60 hours. This service is an academic course required for graduation. New students register for Community Service before beginning their first term at Elmira, with the expectation that they will complete the requirement by the end of their first year. Many find the experience so rewarding that they continue volunteering to help others all four years.

MAJORS AND DEGREES OFFERED

Elmira College offers majors in more than 35 academic areas, but our range of program options is even greater. In ten of these subjects you may pursue either a Bachelor of Science or a Bachelor of Arts degree. While the B.S. degree encourages specialization in a specific area, the B.A. degree offers a broader education in the liberal arts and sciences.

Students must earn a stipulated number of credits in the major--with a passing grade--as well as complete the General Degree Requirements.

Academic Majors Include:

Accounting

American Studies

Anthropology and Sociology

Art

Biology

Biology - Chemistry

Business Administration

Chemistry

Classical Studies

Criminal Justice

Economics

Education

Educational Studies

Engineering-Chemical

English Literature

Environmental Studies

Foreign Languages

History

Human Services

Individualized Studies

International Studies

Mathematics

Medical Technology

Music

Nursing

Philosophy & Religion

Political Science

Pre-Medical

Psychology

Public Affairs

Social Studies

Sociology and Anthropology

Speech & Hearing

Speech and Language Disabilities

Theatre

ACADEMIC PROGRAMS

With a faculty-student ratio of 12:1, you will have the chance to express your ideas in class. Debate the nature of the universe with fellow students and professors. And learn from each other: well over half our students are from beyond New York State, representing 35 states, six Canadian provinces and 31 foreign countries. You will end up discussing your future one-on-one with people, who are committed to your success.

The requirements for baccalaureate degrees granted by Elmira College have been established by members of the faculty so that each graduate receives a broad general education, explores different fields of knowledge, examines one or more of those fields intensively, and applies the knowledge acquired in the classroom to realistic and appropriate work experiences.

SPECIAL ACADEMIC PROGRAMS:

Interested in becoming a doctor or lawyer? Elmira College offers a variety of academic programs that will prepare students for a range of career choices. Special Academic Programs include: Chemical Engineering, Army & Air Force ROTC, Pre-Law, Pre-Professional Programs, English as a Second Language, a 4+1 MBA Program, and Athletic Coaching Certificate.

Our Distinctive Academic Programs make the Elmira College experience unique. Required community service and internships allow students to grow and gain practical experience in a workplace dynamic. Encore, the College's performing arts appreciation requirement, and off-campus opportunities, such as, the Junior Year Abroad program expose students to a diversity of experiences not always found in a traditional classroom. The six-week Term III provides students with an exceptional opportunity to immerse themselves into one or two subjects intensely. Additionally (as you probably know by now), Elmira College is one of the best places in the world to study the work and life of Mark Twain.

TUITION, ROOM, BOARD AND FEES

2010-2011 Full time Student Charges

Dorm Students°

Tuition: $34,500

Room & Board: $11,150

Required Fees: $1,400

° Elmira College is a residential campus. All Undergraduate students, except those who live with parents locally, are required to live on campus.

Town Students

Tuition: $34,500

Required Fees: $1,400

FINANCIAL AID

Elmira College Financial Aid is based on need and merit. Free Application for Federal Student Aid (FAFSA) is required and Financial Aid PROFILE is accepted. Grants and distinctive Honor Scholarships are awarded to students based on academic achievement, leadership activity, and financial need. Awards start at $10,000 per year and range up to full tuition for Valedictorians and Salutatorians. Students may also be eligible for federal and state grants, loans, and work on campus.

-No student has ever paid the full cost of an Elmira College education since its founding in 1855.

-Elmira College awards more than $11 million each year in academic scholarships and awards.

-100% of students demonstrating need receive financial assistance.

-Elmira College administers more than $38 million each year in scholarships and awards, grants, loans and work study programs.

STUDENT ORGANIZATIONS AND ACTIVITIES

Students are welcome to join one of more than 100 clubs or organizations any time during the academic year. During Summer Registration, new students can browse our Club and Organization Guide and sign up to receive more information from club officers. Two Activities Fairs, one during Fall Orientation and another in mid-September, offer the opportunity to meet current club members, ask questions, and see photos of past events and projects.

Some of our clubs and organizations include: Classics Society, Equestrian Club, French Club, Political Science Club, Silent Voices, Spanish Club, College Republicans, Circle K, Compeer, College Democrats, EC Ambassadors, Orientation Leaders, Red Cross Club, Work for a Cure, Relay for Life, Christian Fellowship, Hillel - Jewish Student Association, and the Ski Club.

National Honor Societies include: Phi Beta Kappa, Psi Chi, Kappa Delta Pi, Phi Eta Sigma, Phi Alpha Theta, Alpha Phi Sigma, Omicron Delta Kappa, Beta Beta Beta, Sigma Beta Delta, Lambda Iota Tau, National Residence Hall Honorary, Pi Sigma Alpha, Sigma Theta Tau, Lambda Alpha, Pi Gamma Mu, and Alpha Sigma Lambda.

Elmira is an NCAA Division III college, as well as a member of the Eastern College Athletic Conference, the New York State Women's Collegiate Athletic Association, United Volleyball Conference, and the Empire 8 Conference. We field varsity teams in men's and women's basketball, cheerleading, field hockey, men's and women's golf, men's and women's ice hockey, men's and women's lacrosse, men's and women's soccer, softball, men's and women's tennis, and men's and women's volleyball. National rankings and post-season tournaments have become annual traditions for the Soaring Eagles.

Elmira College offers its students the chance to compete in collegiate athletics at many levels. The goal of the Junior Varsity and Intramural program is to offer students a chance to participate in athletics without the focus on skill level. Intramural sports range anywhere from flag football to ultimate frisbee. The success of our intramural program can be seen every Term III as our students softball teams compete daily.

ADMISSIONS PROCESS

We offer two admissions plans for freshmen applicants. Early Decision and Regular Admission.

International students may apply only under the Regular Admission program.

Regular Admission

If you are applying to several colleges, here is what you do for Elmira College:

1. Submit a completed application to Elmira College. You can fill out an application online, or print an application that you can send in. We also accept the Common Application and Universal Application.

2. Have your college counselor send your official transcript, including senior year courses and grades to date. Have your official SAT I or ACT scores sent to Elmira College.

3. Have at least one letter of recommendation sent to the college.

4. Write a great essay.

5. While not required, we strongly suggest you sit down with an Elmira College admissions counselor for an interview. You can schedule your interview by calling the Office of Admissions at 800-935-6472.

Early Decision

If Elmira College is your first choice college, Early Decision is the program for you. We'll make a decision on your application as soon as it is complete, but you do have to meet the deadlines. There are two Early Decision programs; the first deadline is November 15, and the second is January 15. We promise to notify you of our decision by December 15 for Early Decision I applicants and by January 31 for Early Decision II applicants.

ELMIRA COLLEGE

AT A GLANCE

Founded in 1855, Elmira College is a private, coeducational, liberal arts college. Elmira, a city of 35,000, is located in the beautiful Finger Lakes Region of Upstate New York.

Campus: 55 historic acres which include 7 classroom buildings, 12 dormitories, 2 administrative office buildings, library, health center, campus center, President's Home and Mark Twain Study. A major athletic facility completes the total campus. Eight college buildings are listed on the National Register of Historic Places.

Academic calendar: Two twelve-week terms followed in April and May by a unique six-week Term III devoted to travel, field experience, research, independent study, and innovative courses.

Enrollment: 1,200 students, thirteen percent of whom are valedictorians or salutatorians of their high schools or prep schools, from 35 states and 31 foreign countries.

Faculty: All have earned the Ph.D. or the highest degree in their field required for undergraduate instruction; 11:1 student faculty ratio. No classes are taught by teaching assistants.

Average Class Size: 16 students per class; 90% of all offerings have 25 or fewer students; 35% have fewer than 12 students. Elmira ranks in the Top Five colleges in the eleven Northern states for small class size.

Athletics: NCAA Division III in men's and women's intercollegiate sports. Member of the Eastern College Athletic Conference, the United Volleyball Conference, and the Empire 8 Conference.

LOCATION AND ENVIRONMENT

Elmira, a city of 35,000, is located in the beautiful Finger Lakes Region of Upstate New York. Nestled in the lush, rolling hills of the southern Finger Lakes region, Elmira is a thriving, forward-thinking American community, with fresh air and wide-open spaces in harmony with the modern amenities of a larger city. Nearby, you can attend superb, live entertainment; soar back into American aviation's lofty past; tour historic neighborhoods; investigate Mark Twain's imagination or visit the beautiful lakes that give this region its name.

Within a ten-block radius of the Elmira College campus, there are many restaurants, a performing arts center, a fine arts museum, and shopping. There are about 60 churches, serving most denominations, within walking distance of campus.

Elmira is the place that many scholars say Samuel Clemens (Mark Twain) did his best work, penning the American literary classic The Adventures of Huckleberry Finn and many other works in his study. In 1870, Clemens married Elmira College alumna Olivia Langdon of the Class of 1864. In 1983, the Langdon family gave the study and the historic Quarry Farm to Elmira College. Now Quarry Farm is used as a residence for visiting Twain scholars from all over the world. The Center for Mark Twain Studies at Quarry Farm offers year-round educational programs.

OFF-CAMPUS OPPORTUNITIES

Elmira College offers a wide range of exciting off-campus opportunities. During the Spring Term, for instance, Elmira College students have traveled with faculty to San Salvador in the Bahamas, Spain, France, Russia, England, Italy, Germany, China, Scotland, Japan, Peru, Egypt, Belgium, Greece, Mexico, Australia, the American West, Alaska, and Hawaii.

The highly selective and competitive Junior Year Abroad (JYA) program facilitates the study of foreign language and cultures. Generally, financial aid applies to the JYA program; however, tuition exchange programs do not apply. Interested students apply in the Fall Term of their sophomore year for an experience during their junior year.

All Elmira College students participate in a community service activity for a minimum of 60 hours. This service is an academic course required for graduation. New students register for Community Service before beginning their second term at Elmira, with the expectation that they will complete the requirement by the end of their second year. Many find the experience so rewarding that they continue volunteering to help others all four years.

MAJORS AND DEGREES OFFERED

Elmira College offers majors in more than 35 academic areas, but our range of program options is even greater. In ten of these subjects you may pursue either a Bachelor of Science or a Bachelor of Arts degree. While the B.S. degree encourages specialization in a specific area, the B.A. degree offers a broader education in the liberal arts and sciences. EC offers signature programs in Education, Business Administration, the Sciences, and Nursing.

Students must earn a stipulated number of credits in the major--with a passing grade--as well as complete the General Degree Requirements.

Academic Majors Include: Accounting, American Studies, Anthropology and Sociology, Art, Biology, Biology – Chemistry, Business Administration, Chemistry, Classical Studies, Criminal Justice, Economics, Education, Educational Studies, English Literature, Environmental Studies, Foreign Languages, History, Human Services, Individualized Studies, International Studies, Mathematics, Medical Technology, Music, Nursing, Philosophy & Religion, Political Science, Pre-Medical, Psychology, Public Affairs, Social Studies, Sociology and Anthropology, Speech & Hearing, Speech and Language Disabilities, Theatre.

ACADEMIC PROGRAMS

With a faculty-student ratio of 11:1, you will have the chance to express your ideas in class. Debate the nature of the universe with fellow students and professors. And learn from each other: well over half our students are from beyond New York State, representing 35 states, six Canadian provinces and 31 foreign countries. You will end up discussing your future one-on-one with people, who are committed to your success.

The requirements for baccalaureate degrees granted by Elmira College have been established by members of the faculty so that each graduate receives a broad general education, explores different fields of knowledge, examines one or more of those fields intensively, and applies the knowledge acquired in the classroom to realistic and appropriate work experiences.

Special Academic Programs:

Interested in becoming a doctor or lawyer? Elmira College offers a variety of academic programs that will prepare students for a range of career choices. Special Academic Programs include: Chemical Engineering, Army & Air Force ROTC, Pre-Law, Pre-Professional Programs, English as a Second Language, a 4+1 MBA Program, and Athletic Coaching Certificate.

Our Distinctive Academic Programs make the Elmira College experience unique. Required community service and internships allow students to grow and gain practical experience in a workplace dynamic. Encore, the College's performing arts appreciation requirement, and off-campus opportunities, such as, the Junior Year Abroad program expose students to a diversity of experiences not always found in a traditional classroom. The six-week Term III provides students with an exceptional opportunity to immerse themselves into one or two subjects intensely. Additionally (as you probably know by now), Elmira College is one of the best places in the world to study the work and life of Mark Twain.

TUITION, ROOM, BOARD AND FEES

2013-2014 Full-time Student Charges

Dorm Students°

Tuition: $36,600

Room & Board: $11,800

Required Fees: $1,500

° Elmira College is a residential campus. All Undergraduate students, except those who live with parents locally, are required to live on campus.

Town Students

Tuition: $36,600

Required Fees: $1,700

FINANCIAL AID

Elmira College Financial Aid is based on need and merit. Free Application for Federal Student Aid (FAFSA) is required and Financial Aid PROFILE is accepted. Grants and distinctive Honor Scholarships are awarded to students based on academic achievement, leadership activity, and financial need. Awards start at $13,000 per year and range up to full tuition for Valedictorians and Salutatorians of their high school classes. Students may also be eligible for federal and state grants, loans, and work on campus.

-No student has ever paid the full cost of an Elmira College education since its founding in 1855.

-Elmira College awards more than $14 million each year in academic scholarships and awards.

-100% of students demonstrating need receive financial assistance.

-Elmira College administers more than $40 million each year in scholarships and awards, grants, loans and work study programs.

STUDENT ORGANIZATIONS AND ACTIVITIES

Students are welcome to join one of more than 100 clubs or organizations any time during the academic year. During Summer Registration, new students can browse our Club and Organization Guide and sign up to receive more information from club officers. Two Activities Fairs, one during Fall Orientation and another in mid-September, offer the opportunity to meet current club members, ask questions, and see photos of past events and projects.

Some of our clubs and organizations include: Classics Society, Equestrian Club, French Club, Political Science Club, Silent Voices, Spanish Club, College Republicans, Circle K, College Democrats, EC Ambassadors, Orientation Leaders, Red Cross Club, Work for a Cure, Relay for Life, Christian Fellowship, Hillel - Jewish Student Association, and the Ski Club.

National Honor Societies include: Phi Beta Kappa, Psi Chi, Kappa Delta Pi, Phi Eta Sigma, Phi Alpha Theta, Alpha Phi Sigma, Omicron Delta Kappa, Beta Beta Beta, Sigma Beta Delta, Lambda Iota Tau, National Residence Hall Honorary, Pi Sigma Alpha, Sigma Theta Tau, Lambda Alpha, Pi Gamma Mu, and Alpha Sigma Lambda.

Elmira is an NCAA Division III college, as well as a member of the Eastern College Athletic Conference, United Volleyball Conference, and the Empire 8 Conference. We field varsity teams in men's and women's basketball, cheerleading, field hockey, men's and women's golf, men's and women's ice hockey, men's and women's lacrosse, men's and women's soccer, softball, men's and women's tennis, and men's and women's volleyball. National rankings and post-season tournaments have become annual traditions for the Soaring Eagles. Baseball and Women's Cross Country will be added beginning in the Fall of 2014.

Elmira College offers its students the chance to compete in collegiate athletics at many levels. The goal of the Junior Varsity and Intramural program is to offer students a chance to participate in athletics without the focus on skill level. Intramural sports range anywhere from flag football to ultimate frisbee. The success of our intramural program can be seen every Term III as our students softball teams compete daily.

ADMISSIONS PROCESS

We offer two admissions plans for freshmen applicants. Early Decision and Regular Admission.

International students may apply only under the Regular Admission program.

Regular Admission

If you are applying to several colleges, here is what you do for Elmira College:

1. Submit a completed application to Elmira College. You can fill out an application online, or print an application that you can send in. We also accept the Common Application.

2. Have your college counselor send your official transcript, including senior year courses and grades to date. Have your official SAT I or ACT scores sent to Elmira College.

3. Have at least one letter of recommendation sent to the college.

4. Write a great and memorable essay.

5. While not required, we strongly suggest you sit down with an Elmira College admissions counselor for an interview. You can schedule your interview by calling the Office of Admissions at 800-935-6472.

Early Decision

If Elmira College is your first choice college, Early Decision is the program for you. We'll make a decision on your application as soon as it is complete, but you do have to meet the deadlines. There are two Early Decision programs; the first deadline is November 15, and the second is January 15. We promise to notify you of our decision by December 15 for Early Decision I applicants and by January 31 for Early Decision II applicants.

EMMANUEL COLLEGE

AT A GLANCE

Emmanuel College, founded by the Sisters of Notre Dame de Namur in 1919, is a coed, residential, Catholic liberal arts and sciences college located in the city of Boston. The College's student body includes 1,800 undergraduate students from 35 countries and 33 states; its neighbors include the world-class surgeons of the Longwood Medical and Academic Area, the Monets and Gauguins of the Museum of Fine Arts and 250,000 college students at institutions across the city. With a history of providing high-quality, values-based academic programs, Emmanuel offers opportunities to learn, teach, explore and research in more than 40 areas of study. Through a supportive learning environment that fosters academic excellence, intellectual integrity and a strong social conscience, Emmanuel students develop the skills and confidence to succeed and make a difference in an ever-changing world.

LOCATION AND ENVIRONMENT

Residing in Boston's Fenway neighborhood, Emmanuel students are encouraged to view Boston as their extended classroom. Its unique location enables students and faculty to explore real-world experiences through internships, research and strategic partnerships in and around the city. Within a few steps from campus students can find: The Emerald Necklace, a system of parks that connects throughout Boston; the Longwood Medical and Academic Area, one of the most prestigious medical, academic and research districts in the world; the Museum of Fine Arts and Isabella Stewart Gardner Museum, and Fenway Park - the home of the Boston Red Sox.

The College's campus is a vibrant community alive with energy of teaching and learning, of exploration and research. Emmanuel is the only college in the country to boast a 12-story, 300,000 square-foot private research facility right on campus: Merck Research Laboratories-Boston. In the last three years, the College opened the Maureen Murphy Wilkens Science Center, completed renovations on its Administration Building and Art Department, and restored nearby Roberto Clemente Field, which serves as home field for Emmanuel athletics.

OFF-CAMPUS OPPORTUNITIES

At Emmanuel, internships are considered an integral component of a student's education experience - in fact, the majority of our departments require an internship. The College's location in the city of Boston gives students access to some of the most renowned financial, cultural, medical and academic institutions in the world. Nearly 90% of Emmanuel students, from across all academic disciplines, participate in internships to apply the knowledge they have gained in the classroom within a professional environment, to enhance their skills, and to build a network of professional contacts.

At the core of Emmanuel College's mission is a commitment to social justice and service to the community. Students have ample opportunities to participate in community service, including programs like Alternative Spring Break and service-learning courses. The three main branches of community service outreach available at Emmanuel are the Jean Yawkey Center for Community Leadership, the Carolyn A. Lynch Institute and the Campus Ministry Office. The College also offers service opportunities through partnering agencies in the city of Boston.

Emmanuel is part of the Colleges of the Fenway (COF) consortium, which allows students to cross-register for courses at neighboring colleges, take advantage of shared resources, participate in intramurals and play in the COF orchestra. COF schools include: Emmanuel College, Massachusetts College of Art and Design, Massachusetts College of Pharmacy and Health Sciences, Simmons College, Wentworth Institute of Technology and Wheelock College.

MAJORS AND DEGREES OFFERED

Emmanuel offers opportunities in the pursuit of learning, teaching, exploration and research in more than 40 areas of study. Students are also encouraged to pursue an individualized major by tailoring a course of study from the College's offerings.

Areas of Study: Accounting, American Politics and Government, American Studies, Art History, Art Therapy, Biochemistry, Biology, Biostatistics, Catholic Studies, Chemistry, Communication, Media and Cultural Studies, Counseling and Health, Crime and Justice, Developmental Psychology, Diplomacy and Security, Economics, Education - Elementary and Secondary, English, Forensic Science, Gender and Women's Studies, Graphic Design and Technology, Health Sciences, History, Human Services, International Relations and Comparative Politics, International Studies, Latin American Studies, Literature, Management, Mathematics, Middle East Studies, Neuroscience, Organizational Leadership, Philosophy, Photography, Political Science, Psychology, Social Inequality and Social Justice, Sociology, Spanish, Sport Management, Studio Art, Sustainability and Global Justice, Theology and Religious Studies, Writing and Literature.

Other Academic Opportunities: Pre-Professional Preparation, Pre-Medical, Pre-Veterinary, Pre-Dental, Pre-Law.

ACADEMIC PROGRAMS

Emmanuel offers a rigorous liberal arts and sciences curriculum supported by an individualized approach. The academic requirements of Emmanuel College have been established and designed to ensure that every student experiences the range of skills and content that is implied by the liberal arts mission of the College. Through required courses drawn from a cross-section of the liberal arts disciplines, students are exposed to models of analytical reasoning, symbolic thinking, observation, creativity, critical thinking, moral reasoning, self-knowledge, and significant intellectual content from the fields of history, literature, the arts, philosophy, religion, the social sciences, the natural sciences and the study of cultures outside the United States. Additionally, such courses require student work that enhances the ability of students to comprehend and to function intellectually in the variety of disciplinary modes that constitute the liberal arts.

Emmanuel College's Office of Academic Advising provides students with the support needed to attain their academic goals and serves as a model of the Emmanuel experience. All first-year students receive an academic advisor who assists them in navigating the first few semesters of college, helping them to understand the liberal arts and sciences curriculum and its value, and to develop a unique academic plan.

All new students are also required to take a first-year seminar of his or her choice in the fall. In small classes, working closely with each other and a member of the faculty, students are introduced to the academic traditions of the liberal arts and sciences, and to the expectations and values of Emmanuel College's academic community.

Each year, students who demonstrate superior academic ability and promise are invited to participate in Emmanuel College's Honors Program. This four-year academic and co-curricular program combines a rigorous, discussion-based curriculum with complementary opportunities such as cultural activities, faculty-directed research projects and service in the community. The program begins with the yearlong Honors Colloquium for first-year students and includes four interdisciplinary, writing-intensive seminars, a service-learning component, and an independent research project.

For those students who are uncertain of a major or are exploring majors, Emmanuel College offers the Majors Exploration Program (MEP), which helps students explore careers that will be satisfying and subsequently determine an appropriate major for that career path. Through MEP, students complete the online career tool, FOCUS, which teaches students about themselves and their career ideas through questions about their own interests, values, personality, skills and extracurricular activities.

Additionally, students have access to Emmanuel's Academic Resource Center (ARC), which offers specially designed programs to help students meet their academic goals, and one-on-one guidance from the Office of Internships and Career Development.

CAMPUS FACILITIES AND EQUIPMENT

The Maureen Murphy Wilkens Science Center expands opportunities for interactive teaching and learning, enabling the College to better prepare students in the sciences and enhance the academic experience for students and faculty in all fields. The center includes teaching laboratories for biology, chemistry, biochemistry, physics, psychology/neuroscience; faculty research space and offices; student study areas; and new classrooms for all disciplines.

The College's Jean Yawkey Center gymnasium is home to the Saints for both practice and competition. The Center includes one NCAA regulation-sized basketball court or two full-size practice courts with bleacher seating for up to 1,400, an updated fitness center, training room, locker room facilities, and athletic staff offices and conference rooms. The facility also houses the Jean Yawkey Center for Community Leadership, which is dedicated to developing service opportunities and leadership skills for Emmanuel students and providing programs for young people in Boston-area schools and community organizations. Through the Jean Yawkey Center for Community Leadership, Emmanuel students volunteer in schools throughout the city as mentors and tutors.

Recently, Emmanuel College partnered with the city of Boston on a comprehensive restoration of Roberto Clemente Field, located across the street from campus. The upgraded facility, which serves as home field for the Emmanuel softball, men's and women's soccer and men's and women's lacrosse teams, includes a 120,000 sq. ft. NCAA-regulation synthetic turf field, a three-lane rubberized track, practice facilities for expanded track and field events, and new MUSCO lighting.

Since Merck Research Laboratories-Boston opened its doors on Emmanuel's campus in October 2004, the College's students have gained access and opportunity to a world few undergraduates ever get to see. This unique partnership gives Emmanuel access to cutting-edge research equipment, supports faculty-student research initiatives, and provides student stipends for summer research projects. Through the Merck Scholars Program, Emmanuel students are awarded scholarships based on outstanding academic performance in the sciences.

TUITION, ROOM, BOARD, AND FEES

Emmanuel College is committed to providing students with a quality education at an affordable cost. And we offer billing options and payment plans to ensure that you're able to pay for college in the most convenient way for you.

2013-2014 Tuition and Fees

Tuition: $34,450

Room and Board: $13,315 (double occupancy)

Fees: $500 (includes one-time Orientation fee of $280)

Estimated Student Health Insurance: $1,637

FINANCIAL AID

Emmanuel College is committed to making a liberal arts and sciences education affordable for our students and their families. We understand that financing a quality private education can be a challenge. That is why we believe that paying for an education is a partnership between the student, their family and the College.

At Emmanuel, financial assistance programs include a combination of scholarships, institutional grants, federal and state grants, federal loans and part-time employment. Merit scholarships are based on a combination of students' high school academic achievement and extracurricular activities.

To apply for financial aid, students must complete the Free Application for Federal Student Aid (FAFSA). Once a FAFSA is completed, students are automatically considered for Emmanuel College grant aid. Some students will also be eligible to receive federal, state and other grant or scholarship funding. These funds may be awarded in addition to merit or other scholarship funds students receive from Emmanuel. Students who complete a FAFSA may also receive low-interest student loans, including the Federal Stafford Loan and Federal Work Study.

For more information, visit www.emmanuel.edu and click on "Tuition and Aid."

ADMISSIONS PROCESS

For more information or to apply for admission, please visit www.emmanuel.edu and click on "Admissions." We require the Common Application (available online), an essay, a secondary school transcript, first quarter grades, two letters of recommendation (one from a guidance counselor, one from an academic teacher) and official SAT or ACT test scores. Students whose native language is not English should submit the TOEFL.

EMORY & HENRY COLLEGE

AT A GLANCE

Founded in 1836, Emory & Henry is the oldest college in Southwest Virginia. It is one of the few Southern colleges to have operated more than 175 years under the same name and with the same affiliation: the United Methodist Church. The campus and surrounding village is home to students as well as E&H professors, administrators and retired college employees. It is an academic environment that underscores the broad dedication within the community to each student's enlightenment and success.

Noted for its exceptional beauty, Emory & Henry remains firmly grounded in its 175-year commitment to excellence in liberal arts education. Dedicated to creating informed minds and global citizens, Emory & Henry translates an emphasis on civic virtues to active service learning. A hallmark of the College's civic engagement is its leadership in advancing a pragmatic understanding of sustainable communities and practices.

LOCATION AND ENVIRONMENT

Emory & Henry is located in Emory, Virginia, which is approximately 25 miles north of Bristol, a city that offers large shopping areas, movies, and restaurants. The area surrounding Emory is known for its scenic beauty, recreational opportunities, and talented craftsmen. Within an hour's drive are slopes for snow skiing, lakes for waterskiing, the Appalachian Trail for hiking, and locations for horseback riding, canoeing, and many other sports. The historic town of Abingdon, Virginia, which lies just 7 miles south of Emory, is the home of the renowned Barter Theatre, the oldest professional theater in the United States. Abingdon's downtown district includes shopping areas, movie theaters, restaurants, and museums. The city also hosts the annual Virginia Highlands Festival, bringing together musicians, artists, and craftsmen for exhibitions and competition.

ACADEMICS

Emory & Henry College is a transformative academic community. Our education is distinguished by progress – sometimes sudden, sometimes gradual – toward an expanded sense of personal potential and an enlightened sense of civic responsibility. This transformation, this increase in excellence, is the foundation of our campus culture. Its impact is lasting and profound. Emory & Henry offers a liberal arts program with an emphasis on writing, reasoning, value inquiry, and knowledge of global concerns. All students complete a core curriculum that integrates classroom work with study and research beyond the classroom – and the campus, ultimately contributing to a deep understanding of regional and cultural differences and challenges. The core curriculum includes an emphasis on student proficiencies in writing, communication, quantitative literacy, ethical reasoning and critical thinking. Undergraduate programs of study include art, athletic training, biology, business administration, chemistry, computer information management, economics, education, English, geography, history, languages, mass communications, mathematics, music, philosophy, physical education, physics, political science, psychology, religion, sociology and anthropology, and theater. Special and interdisciplinary programs of study offered are environmental studies, international studies, pre-engineering, pre-law, pre-medicine, and public policy and community service. Emory & Henry operates on a semester calendar from late August to mid-December and from mid-January to mid-May. A summer session runs from late May to early July. First-year students typically carry a four-course load of 13 to 14 credit hours per semester. Upperclass students carrying a full load complete five courses (14 to 15 credit hours) each semester. Thirty-eight courses are required for graduation. Classes meet on Monday-Wednesday-Friday or Tuesday-Thursday schedules. One important feature of the Emory & Henry curriculum is its dedication to helping students make a smooth transition from high school to college. The Powell Resource Center provides academic support, advising, career services, and personal counseling. The Writing Center helps students in every department to use writing for effective communication.

ADMISSIONS

Emory & Henry maintains a rolling admissions policy, but applicants are encouraged to apply to the College as early as possible. Prospective undergraduate students may apply online using the College's online application or by submitting the Common Application. Emory & Henry offers a binding, early decision option for students who have given considerable thought to their college choice. To apply for admission, students should submit the basic application form, their high school transcripts, scores from either the SAT or ACT, an essay, and at least one letter of recommendation. Transfer applicants must submit a transcript from any college previously attended and a Dean's Certificate from the last college in which they were enrolled. A rolling admission policy allows notification of a decision within two weeks after a file has been completed. Admission to Emory & Henry is determined on the basis of both academic achievement and personal qualifications. Strong emphasis also is placed on involvement and leadership in extracurricular and community activities. Merit-based scholarships are offered to students need-blind. Eligibility for need-based grants are determined by submitting the Free Application for Federal Student Aid (FAFSA) as soon as possible after Jan. 1. Indicate that you want results sent to Emory & Henry College, code 003709. Virginia residents need to submit the Virginia Tuition Assistance Grant (VTAG) application by July 31.

CAMPUS FACILITIES AND EQUIPMENT

McGlothlin-Street Hall is a 70,000-square-foot academic center that houses the Departments of Biology, Business, Chemistry, Education, Environmental Studies, Geography, International Studies, and Psychology; a 104-seat auditorium; and a tiered sixty-seat auditorium. Classrooms and laboratories in McGlothlin-Street Hall are equipped with the most current technological equipment. Miller-Fulton Hall contains computerized classrooms used for instruction in such fields as accounting and computer science. Science departments located in Miller-Fulton and McGlothlin-Street Halls feature a variety of equipment, such as a microcomputer-based laboratory for physics students, computerized chromatography for chemistry students, a DNA sequencer in the Biology Department, and biofeedback equipment. In 2013, the College finished construction on the latest of several attractive, modern residence halls. Hickory Hall includes 117 beds in double-occupancy rooms, each of which has its own bathroom. Hickory is the first large-scale residence hall in the nation to be built with passive energy design. Other new residence halls include Elm Hall, which includes 116 beds in double occupancy rooms, each with its own bathroom, and two modern, small-scale student residence halls located in the Emory village a few blocks from the main campus. The newly renovated Byars Hall houses three stories of classrooms, seminar rooms, choir and ensemble rehearsal halls, a digital art lab, a dark room, two large art studios, practice rooms for instrumental music, and a theatre support room. The collections of Kelly Library consist of more than 350,000 items, including books, periodicals, government documents, audio and videotapes, compact discs, DVDs, and electronic databases. The library contains a group of computers reserved for library research, an open computer lab, and a computer classroom.

CAMPUS LIFE

Students at Emory & Henry are encouraged to take part in campus decision making. They have voting representatives on nearly every faculty committee and on the Board of Trustees. The central body in campus government is the Student Senate, which brings together representatives of the student body, faculty, and administration. Students have opportunities for involvement in a variety of campus activities: service clubs, Christian fellowship, fraternities, sororities, sports clubs, honor groups, and multicultural groups. Student staffs produce a yearbook, an online magazine, and a literary magazine; others operate a 9,000-watt FM public radio station with a coverage area that extends some 40 miles beyond the campus. Musically talented students have opportunities to participate in a choral program and a pep band. The prestigious Concert Choir has toured throughout the United States and in parts of Europe. The Barter Theatre, a professional theater in nearby Abingdon, works with Emory & Henry College to provide a theater education program that integrates college-level drama study with the benefits of experience on a professional stage.

MAJORS AND DEGREES

Emory & Henry College offers programs of study in art, athletic training, biology, business administration, chemistry, computer information management, economics, education (early childhood through high school, including many subject-area options), English, environmental studies, geography, history, international studies (East Asia, European community, or Middle Eastern and Islamic studies), languages, mass communications, mathematics, music, philosophy, physical education, physics, political science, psychology, public policy and community service; religion, sociology and anthropology, and theater (in association with the Barter Theatre, the state theatre of Virginia). Preprofessional preparation in dentistry, law, medicine, and veterinary medicine may be completed within several of the programs. The Bachelor of Arts degree is awarded in all programs of study and the Bachelor of Science degree in selected areas. Individualized programs of study may be developed in consultation with a faculty adviser.

OFF-CAMPUS OPPORTUNITIES

The Appalachian Center for Community Service is available for students committed to community service and integrates service learning into many classes. The King Health and Physical Education Center includes a new fitness center and enhances the College athletics program. Varsity sports for men are baseball, basketball, cross-country, football, golf, soccer, and tennis; women compete in basketball, cross-country, soccer, softball, swimming, tennis, and volleyball. Several sports are played on a club basis. A large percentage of E&H students engage in community projects that often involve policy research and advocacy aimed at benefitting the region. An aggressive internship program provides on-the-job opportunities for students in most of the College's programs, providing academic credit for off-campus work in community agencies and businesses. Many students have completed internships in the surrounding communities, while others have opted for internships outside the region, including several in Washington, D.C., in positions related to the Congress or the federal government. Emory & Henry students participate in a wide variety of study-abroad programs. From Rome to Beijing and from Eastern Europe to East Asia, Emory & Henry students experience cultures and people in a way that enriches their perspective on their studies, their lives, and their futures. Emory & Henry helps students prepare for these experiences through language study and with courses offered through a comprehensive international studies program. The College has exchange agreements with colleges and universities in Asia, Europe, and Central and South America. Students who desire other types of travel/study are assisted by the E&H International Education Program in locating suitable programs.

TUITION AND AID

Our Financial Aid Office works to ensure students receive an Emory & Henry education with a minimal amount of debt. Compared to other private colleges, our annual out-of-pocket expenses are among the lowest in Virginia. The average award to our incoming first-year students including only grants and scholarships is $24,322. Approximately 98 percent of all students receive financial aid. Virginia residents may qualify for the Tuition Assistance Grant (TAG), currently a $2,650 value. In recent years, the rate of alumni giving has been among the highest among colleges and universities in the nation. This percentage of giving says volumes about the high degree of satisfaction Emory & Henry graduates have with their education. This level of giving also has translated into tremendous support for scholarships that are offered to Emory & Henry students.

TUITION AND FEES

For 2012-13, Tuition per semester is $14,061 and $28,122 annually. Room for the academic year is $4,782 and board is $4,644 (19 meals per week with $140 in flex dollars).

THE FASHION INSTITUTE OF TECHNOLOGY

AT A GLANCE

The Fashion Institute of Technology (FIT), a leader in career-oriented education, is a college of art and design, business and technology of the State University of New York (SUNY).

FIT has been a leader in career education in art, design, business, and technology for nearly 70 years. With a curriculum that provides its 10,000 students with a singular blend of hands-on, practical experience, classroom study, and a firm grounding in the liberal arts, FIT offers a wide range of outstanding programs that are affordable and relevant to today's rapidly changing industries. The college grants AAS, BFA, BS, MA, MFA, and MPS degrees, and offers more than 45 majors in fields ranging from marketing and textiles to toy design and entrepreneurship, preparing students for professional success and leadership in the global marketplace.

FIT's special brand of education reflects the college's close ties to industry. Top executives serve as curriculum advisors, faculty, and mentors to students; industry members and leading companies provide scholarships, internships, and support for critical FIT initiatives. Relationships with industry enable the college to offer students experiences that mirror the marketplace and give them a competitive edge.

LOCATION AND ENVIRONMENT

Occupying an entire tree-lined block in Manhattan's dynamic Chelsea neighborhood, FIT's campus places students at the heart of the fashion, advertising, visual arts, design, business, and communications industries. Approximately 2,300 students live on campus, in accommodations ranging from traditional dorm-style rooms with meal plans to apartment-style suites with kitchens, and from single to quad occupancy.

OFF-CAMPUS OPPORTUNITIES

FIT draws on its New York City location to provide a vibrant, creative environment for our college community. Students enjoy a wealth of opportunities to learn, to play, and to explore the city's abundant resources. A wide range of cultural and entertainment options—from museums to dining to theater—are available within walking distance of the campus, which also offers convenient access to subway and bus lines and major rail and bus transportation hubs. One of New York's most dynamic neighborhoods, Chelsea boasts a lively gallery scene, exotic restaurants, a wide variety of retail outlets, and historic landmarks.

MAJORS AND DEGREES OFFERED

FIT offers programs leading to the AAS, BFA, BS, MFA, MA, and MPS degrees. Undergraduates choose from among 39 majors and 16 liberal arts minors. The School of Graduate Studies offers seven master's degree programs.

SCHOOL OF ART AND DESIGN

Accessories Design, Advertising Design, Communication Design Foundation, Computer Animation and Interactive Media, Fabric Styling, Fashion Design, Fine Arts, Graphic Design, Illustration, Interior Design, Jewelry Design, Menswear, Packaging Design, Photography, Textile/Surface Design, Toy Design, and Visual Presentation and Exhibition Design.

Jay and Patty Baker School of Business and Technology

Advertising and Marketing Communications, Cosmetics and Fragrance Marketing, Direct and Interactive Marketing, Entrepreneurship for the Fashion and Design Industries, Fashion Merchandising Management, Home Products Development, International Trade and Marketing for the Fashion Industries, Production Management: Fashion and Related Industries, Technical Design, and Textile Development and Marketing.

SCHOOL OF LIBERAL ARTS

Art History and Museum Professions and liberal arts minors (subject-based and interdisciplinary minors are offered).

SCHOOL OF GRADUATE STUDIES

Art Market: Principles and Practices; Cosmetics and Fragrance Marketing and Management; Exhibition Design; Fashion and Textile Studies: History, Theory, Museum Practice; Global Fashion Management; Illustration; and Sustainable Interior Environments

ACADEMIC PROGRAMS

FIT's programs offer a vibrant learning environment, combining the practical and the theoretical. Each provides hands-on instruction, each is supported by a focused liberal arts curriculum, and each draws on a faculty of dedicated working professionals who are influential in their fields. The School of Liberal Arts offers the opportunity to minor in a variety of liberal arts areas in two forms: subject-based minors and interdisciplinary minors unique to the FIT liberal arts curriculum. Minors include film and media, economics, Latin American studies, and sustainability.

The Presidential Scholars honors program, open to academically exceptional students in all disciplines, offers special liberal arts courses, projects, colloquiums, and cultural and community service activities designed to broaden horizons and stimulate discourse.

Internships are an essential part of many majors. The college's extensive internship program provides students with vital experience in their field. The Career and Internship Center helps students with career planning and offers lifetime placement services to graduates.

The study-abroad experience allows students to immerse themselves in diverse cultures and prepares them to live and work in a global community. FIT offers programs in Italy—in Florence and Milan—where students study fashion design or fashion merchandising management and gain firsthand experience in the dynamics of European fashion. Australia, China, England, France, and Mexico are a few of the other countries where FIT offers semester-long programs. Students can also study abroad during the winter or summer sessions.

The School of Continuing Education and Professional Studies provides evening and weekend credit and noncredit classes to students and working professionals who want to pursue a degree or certificate or just gain skills and knowledge. FIT also offers a wide range of classes for high school students on weekends and in the summer.

Online courses are offered on a wide variety of subjects. An AAS degree in Fashion Merchandising Management and a BS in International Trade and Marketing are available fully online.

CAMPUS FACILITIES AND EQUIPMENT

Students have access to state-of-the-art technology and equipment in FIT's studios and labs. Facilities include art, printmaking, display design, and photography studios, a model-making workshop, a graphics printing service bureau, a toy design lab, and a textile testing lab. A computer-aided design and communications facility allows students to explore the latest advancements in technology and their integration in design, photography, and computer graphics and animation. The Annette Green Fragrance Foundation Studio, a professionally equipped fragrance development lab, is the only one of its kind on a U.S. college campus. Cutting and sewing labs offer the most advanced apparel production machinery among educational facilities in the nation. Other facilities include a lighting laboratory, broadcast studio, knitting and weaving labs, and a multimedia foreign language lab.

The Museum at FIT is New York City's only museum dedicated to fashion. Students, designers, and historians use it for research and inspiration. The museum, which is accredited by the American Alliance of Museums, operates year-round, and its exhibitions are free and open to the public. The Gladys Marcus Library provides more than 300,000 volumes of print, non-print, and electronic materials. The newspaper and periodicals collection includes 500 current subscriptions. Online resources include more than 90 searchable databases. The library also offers specialized resources, such as clipping files, fashion and trend forecasting services, and sketch collections.

Also on campus are three multimedia venues—the Katie Murphy Amphitheatre, the Morris W. and Fannie B. Haft Auditorium, and the John E. Reeves Great Hall—used for fashion shows, exhibitions, student presentations, industry panels, conferences, and special events.

TUITION, ROOM, BOARD, AND FEES

For 2012–13, the associate level tuition per semester was $2,100 for in-state residents and $6,300 for nonresidents. Baccalaureate-level tuition per semester was $2,884 for in-state residents and $7,715 for nonresidents. Housing costs ranged from $6,119 to $6,299 per semester for traditional residence hall accommodations with mandatory meal plan and from $5,241 to $9,521 for apartment-style accommodations. Meal plans varied from $1,643 to $2,105 per semester. Textbook costs and other nominal fees, such as locker rental or laboratory use, vary per program. Costs are subject to change.

FINANCIAL AID

FIT attempts to remove financial barriers to college entrance by providing scholarships, grants, loans, and part-time employment based on available funds for students with financial need. The Free Application for Federal Student Aid (FAFSA) is the core application for all financial aid programs.

STUDENT ORGANIZATIONS AND ACTIVITIES

The college is home to more than 70 student organizations, including merit societies, athletic teams, major-related organizations, and clubs based on areas of interest. Concerts, dances, field trips, films, flea markets, and other events are regularly scheduled. Student-run publications include a campus newspaper, a literary and art magazine, and the FIT yearbook.

FIT has intercollegiate teams in cross-country, half marathon, track and field, dance, table tennis, tennis, soccer, swimming and diving, and volleyball. Athletics and Recreation offers students group fitness classes at no extra cost. Open gym activities allow students to participate in team and individual sports.

The David Dubinsky Student Center houses lounges, a game room, a dining hall, a student radio station, a student-run boutique, student government and club offices, health services, gyms, a dance studio, a fitness center, a counseling center, studios, and laboratories.

ADMISSIONS PROCESS

For applicants to undergraduate programs, the admissions committee considers academic accomplishments that predict success on the college level, as well as students' demonstrated talent. For transfer applicants, overall grade point average and performance in liberal arts courses are also considered. All applicants, whether to a full-time day program or evening/weekend program, must meet the same admissions standards.

All applicants are required to submit a personal essay indicating why they selected their major, and highlighting all activities and accomplishments. FIT believes that creative and leadership abilities are revealed through activities in various fields, such as a governing organization or student club, or the visual or performing arts.

Applicants to the School of Art and Design must submit a portfolio that demonstrates their artistic and creative ability. Fashion Design applicants should be versed in both art and garment construction. Applicants to the School of Business and Technology programs must demonstrate the ability to work with others, leadership, and sound mathematical skills.

First-year students must apply for the two-year Associate in Applied Science Degree. Upon completing the AAS degree, students may enter a bachelor's program. Transfer applicants may qualify for a one-year AAS or bachelor's degree program depending on their previous college coursework and intended major.

In evaluating candidates, the School of Graduate Studies considers factors such as academic preparation, communication skills, professional experience, maturity, passion for knowledge, and potential for growth, as well as the degree to which the candidate's and the program's goals coincide.

All prospective students are invited to attend an information session with an admissions counselor and take a student-led campus tour. For more information and to make a reservation for a campus visit, please go to fitnyc.edu/visitfit.

Admission Dates and Deadlines for Undergraduate Study

Fall semester	Spring semester
Application deadline: January 1	Application deadline: October 1
Notification date: April 1	Notification date: November 1
Tuition deposit due: May 1	Tuition deposit due: December 1

Please visit fitnyc.edu for information on the admissions process and deadlines for applicants to FIT's graduate programs.

FIVE TOWNS COLLEGE

AT A GLANCE

Nestled in the rolling hills of Long Island's North Shore, Five Towns College offers students the opportunity to study in a suburban environment that is within easy access of New York City. Founded in 1972 by a group of educators and community leaders who wished to provide students with an alternative to the large university atmosphere, Five Towns College is a nonsectarian, coeducational institution that places its emphasis on the student as an individual. Many students are drawn to Five Towns College because of its strong programs in music and music-related fields. Five Towns College is an institution of higher learning that offers two-year, four-year, master and doctoral degree programs.

From as far away as England and Japan and from as close as Long Island and New York City, the 1,000 full-time students who attend the College reflect a rich cultural diversity. The College's enrollment is currently 60 percent men and 40 percent women; there is a minority population of approximately 30 percent. The College's music programs are contemporary in nature although classical musicians are also part of this creative community.

Coeducational living accommodations are available on campus. Each Residence hall contains single and double occupancy rooms equipped with private bathrooms, broadband Internet access, cable television and other amenities.

The College serves the cause of business, education, and the performing arts with emphasis on Jazz/Commercial music. The most popular programs are audio recording technology, broadcasting, journalism, music performance, music business, music and elementary education, theatre, and film/video production.

The College seeks to foster, in those who participate in its intimate community, a noble commitment to ethical, intellectual, and social values and seeks to encourage and stimulate the pursuit of lifelong learning. It encourages its students to respect the differences of others as well as to develop their own unique talents to the fullest. To ensure that students place such high demands upon themselves, the College seeks out for its faculty, men and women who are committed to excellence in teaching, guidance, and scholarship.

Five Towns College, in its recruitment and retention of individuals for membership in our college community, maintains an openness to all qualified persons.

LOCATION AND ENVIRONMENT

The College's serene 40-acre campus, located in the wooded countryside of Dix Hills in the town of Huntington, New York, provides students with a park-like refuge where they can pursue their studies. Just off campus is Long Island's bustling Route 110 corridor, the home of numerous national and multinational corporations.

New York City, with everything from Lincoln Center to Broadway is just a train ride away and provides students with some of the best cultural advantages in the world. Closer to campus, the many communities of Long Island abound with the cultural and recreational opportunities. The College is located within the historic town of Huntington, which is home to the Cinema Arts Center, InterMedia Arts Center, Hecksher Museum, Vanderbilt Museum, numerous restaurants, coffeehouses, and quaint shops. The nearby shores of Jones Beach State Park and the Fire Island National Seashore are world renowned for their white, sandy beaches.

OFF-CAMPUS OPPORTUNITIES

Off-campus internship opportunities are available for all Five Towns College students who have fulfilled the necessary prerequisites, including a cumulative GPA of at least 3.0, with a 2.5 in their major. In recent semesters, students have obtained valuable field experience interning for major corporations such as MTV, Atlantic Records, Polygram Records, CBS Records, EMI Records, MCA Records, Cablevision, Channel 12 News, The Power Station, SONY Records, Pyramid Recording Studios, and many others.

MAJORS AND DEGREES OFFERED

2-Year Associate Degree Programs:

Associate in Arts (A.A.) in Liberal Arts

Teaching Assistant

Literature

Associate in Science (A.S.) in Business Administration

Business Administration

Associate in Applied Science (A.A.S.) in Business Management

Audio Recording Technology

Business Management

Music Business

Associate in Applied Science (A.A.S.) in Jazz/Commercial Music

Music Performance

4-Year Bachelor Degree Programs:

Bachelor of Music (Mus.B.) in Jazz/Commercial Music

Music Performance

Composition/Songwriting

Musical Theater

Audio Recording Technology

Music Business

Bachelor of Music (Mus.B.) in Music Education

Music Education

Bachelor of Professional Studies (B.P.S.) in Business Management

Audio Recording Technology

Music Business

Bachelor of Fine Arts (B.F.A.) in Theatre Arts

Bachelor of Fine Arts (B.F.A.) in Film/Video

Bachelor of Science (B.S.) in Childhood Education

Bachelor of Science (B.S.) in Mass Communication

Broadcasting

Journalism

Graduate Degree Programs:

Master of Music (Mus.M.) in Jazz/Commercial Music Concentrations:

Music Performance

Composition/Arranging

Music History

Music Technology

Master of Music (Mus.M.) in Music Education:

Music Education

Master of Education (M.S. Ed.)

Childhood Education

Doctor of Musical Arts (D.M.A.)

Music Performance

Composition and Arranging

Music Education

Music History and Literature

ACADEMIC PROGRAMS

The comprehensive program in Jazz/Commercial Music provides both a common core of technical studies and a foundation for specialized courses in the student's major are of concentration.

The Audio Recording Technology includes the study of the theory of sound, recording electronics, engineering procedures, music production techniques, and audio/video post production in a sequence of courses designed to develop practical and technical skills.

The Composition/Songwriting concentration provides intensive instruction in harmony, orchestration, counterpoint, MIDI, songwriting, keyboard techniques, form and analysis, commercial arranging and composition.

In the Music Business concentration, the coursework includes the technical, legal, production, management, and merchandising and licensing aspects of the music business.

The Musical Theatre/Vocal concentration includes coursework in music, movement, acting, voice, general education, and musical theatre production.

The Performance concentration provides a foundation of specialized courses such as music history, harmony, counterpoint, improvisation, ensemble performance and private instruction.

The Music Education program leads to New York State provisional certification in grades K-12.

The Business Management program is designed for students planning to pursue careers as business management/marketing executives with firms in the area of record and music production, broadcasting, concert promotion, radio, television, theatre and communications.

The Childhood Education program fulfills the New York State Education Department requirements for the Initial Certificate in Childhood Education (1-6).

The Film/Video program is designed to provide the knowledge and technical expertise required to succeed in the wide range of career paths this interesting and expanding field has to offer; including cinematography, motion picture editing, and multi-camera television production.

The Broadcasting students explore the technical, legal, programming, and marketing issues that guide mass media companies. In the Journalism concentration, students explore a variety of different journalistic styles, including news, script, feature, magazine, editorial and review writing.

The Theatre Arts Program is designed for students interested in a career in the performing arts field as an actor, entertainer, director, stage managers, lighting or sound technician or any other related aspect of the dynamic and rapidly expanding entertainment industry.

CAMPUS FACILITIES AND EQUIPMENT

The Five Towns College campus is equipped with the latest information technology and a wide variety of facilities that support the College's instructional program, student services, and extracurricular activities.

These state-of-the-art facilities include three Audio Recording Studios, a Film/Television Studio, Piano Lab, MIDI Lab hosted by Apple iMacs, Computer Graphics/Video Editing Lab hosted by Apple iMacs, PC Lab, as well as the College Library, Learning Center, Music Rooms and Music Studios, Studio Theatres, Upbeat Cafe, Performing Arts Center and the College Bookstore.

Five Towns College is licensed by the Federal Communication Commission to operate commercial radio station WFTU (1570 AM). The main broadcast studio is located on the college campus at Dix Hills. The radio station is also streamed on the web.

The College Library has more than 35,000 print and non-print materials. These includes nearly 30,000 books and print items, 500 periodical subscriptions, and approximately 4,500 records, 3,000 DVD's, and more than 3,000 CD's. Through its membership in the Long Island Library Resource Council (LILRC), students have access to other libraries around the country.

Multi-strand Fiber optic cabling is the College's backbone for its Local Area Network (LAN). A 50Mbps Ethernet hand off provides access to the World Wide Web. All students have access to this network and are provided with an e-mail account.

TUITION, ROOM, BOARD AND FEES

For the 2012-2013 academic year, the tuition at Five Towns College was $19,800. Miscellaneous fees are approximately $600, and books are about $1,000. Private instruction fees for music students are $810 per semester. For information regarding on-campus room and board charges, contact the Five Towns College Admissions Office.

FINANCIAL AID

Although Five Towns College is a modestly priced private institution, we recognize that tuition and fees is beyond the reach of many students. Five Towns College responds to the needs of these students with a comprehensive Financial Aid program.

Approximately 81% of all FTC students receive some financial assistance. The Financial Aid Office administers several million dollars of student aid monies every year. FTC students are eligible to participate in all Title IV Student Financial Assistance programs, including Pell, FSEOG, FCWS, and the Direct Student Loan Program. New York State Residents may also participate in the Tuition Assistance Program (TAP). Five Towns College also administers approximately $3,000,000 in grants and scholarships to deserving students.

For applications and specific program requirements for each Financial Aid Program, students should contact the Five Towns College Financial Aid Office at (631) 656-2164 as early as possible.

ADMISSIONS PROCESS

Five Towns College seeks students who are generally able to benefit from the programs of study available at the College and who will enrich the lives of their fellow students by actively participating in the academic process and debate. Although all applicants are considered, the College encourages applications from students who have attained a minimum high school grade point average of 80 percent, and SAT scores of approximately 980 (old version) or 1350 (new version). Prospective students must submit a completed application and an official high school transcript. Transfer students must also submit official transcripts of all college-level work attempted. International students must present a TOEFL score of at least 520 (paper test) or its equivalent. The Admissions Office will consider the entirety of a candidate's application before rendering a decision on admissions. Students submitting GED scores of at least 2500 are also invited to apply for admission. Students may be admitted for deferred entrance or advanced standing. The College does accept students on an early admissions basis, although early decision is available.

Admission into the Bachelor of Music program is contingent upon passing an audition demonstrating skill in performance on a major instrument or vocally. Applicants for the Theatre program are also auditioned. An interview may be required. Students are accepted on a rolling admission basis and are notified shortly after all required documents have been filed with the admissions office. New students may begin their studies at the start of either the fall semester or the spring semester. There is an application fee of $35.

For further information, students should contact:

Five Towns College

Director of Admissions

305 North Service Road

Dix Hills, NY 11746-5871

Telephone: 631-656-2110

World Wide Web: www.ftc.edu

FLORIDA ATLANTIC UNIVERSITY

ACADEMICS

Florida Atlantic University's colleges include the College for Design and Social Inquiry, the Dorothy F. Schmidt College of Arts and Letters, the College of Business, Charles E. Schmidt College of Medicine, the College of Education, the College of Engineering and Computer Science, the Graduate College, the Christine E. Lynn College of Nursing, the Charles E. Schmidt College of Science. Together, these colleges offer over 170 different academic degree programs. In 1999, FAU opened the Harriet L. Wilkes Honors College, which provides a unique and challenging liberal arts curriculum for the brightest students from Florida and across the nation.

ADMISSIONS

Admission to the University as an undergraduate is limited to applicants who have graduated from regionally accredited high schools or who hold a General Equivalency Degree (GED). Evaluation is based on the academic course grade point average combined with acceptable results on the Scholastic Aptitude Test (SAT) or the American College Test (ACT). Candidates for admission should have 18 academic high school units, including 4 units of English, 4 units of mathematics, 3 units of natural science, 3 units of social science, 2 units of one foreign language in sequence, and 2 academic electives. Score reports will be accepted directly from the testing agency. FAU's SAT school code number is 5229. FAU's ACT school code number is 0729. Applicants who have completed the GED (General Educational Development) should request official high school transcripts (if applicable) and an official GED score report from the Florida Department of Education. The Florida Department of Education GED Division can be reached at 1-877-352-4331. Admission for freshman students requires an application for admission, a non-refundable $30.00 application fee, official transcripts from an accredited high school, and the results of the SAT or ACT administrations. All admitted freshmen must confirm their intention to enroll and secure their place with the freshman class by submitting a required $200.00 admissions tuition deposit. Please contact the Office of Undergraduate Admissions for details or visit our website: www.fau.edu/admissions. Admission into FAU as a transfer with fewer than 60 transferable credits requires the applicant to be in good academic standing at their previous, regionally accredited colleges or universities, the applicant must present a cumulative GPA of 2.5 or higher, and must meet all freshman admissions requirements. Please submit an application for admission, a non-refundable $30.00 application fee, official transcripts from high school and previously attended colleges, and the results of the SAT or ACT administrations. For students with 60 or more transferable credits, please submit an application for admission, a non-refundable $30.00 application fee, and official transcripts from each previously attended college or university. Please note that meeting the minimum admission requirements does not guarantee admission into the university. For application deadlines or further information, please contact:

Office of Undergraduate Admissions, Florida Atlantic University, 777 Glades Road Boca Raton, FL 33431. Telephone: 561-297-3040. Fax: 561-297-2758.

World Wide Web: www.fau.edu/admissions.

AT A GLANCE

Florida Atlantic University is a public research university with multiple campuses along the southeast Florida coast serving a uniquely diverse community. With 46 percent of its student body classified as minority or international students, FAU ranks as the most racially, ethnically and culturally diverse institution in Florida's State University System. The student-to-faculty ratio is just 20:1, an advantage normally offered by small, private colleges. Similarly, classes are taught primarily by the University's full-time faculty rather than by graduate students or part-time instructors. It promotes academic and personal development, discovery, and lifelong learning. FAU fulfills its mission through excellence and innovation in teaching, outstanding research, public engagement, and distinctive scientific alliances; all within an environment that fosters inclusiveness. Florida Atlantic University was established by the Florida State Legislature in 1961 as the fifth university in the state system. When it originally opened in 1964, FAU was the first university in the country to offer only upper-division and graduate-level work, on the theory that freshmen and sophomores could be served by the community college system. Located in rapidly growing Southeast Florida, the University responded to the need to provide increased access to educational opportunities by opening its doors to freshmen in 1984. It offers a comprehensive array of undergraduate and graduate programs, and enrolls students who reflect the rich cultural diversity of the region. FAU has Eminent Scholar Chairs in multiple disciplines and is the home of nationally recognized research centers. The University's burgeoning research parks are facilitating exciting new research and learning initiatives by bringing high-tech industries into close collaboration with faculty and students. In recognition of the University's research funding and doctoral programs, the Division of Colleges and Universities of the Florida Board of Education has designated FAU as a research university. Additionally, FAU has been classified as a "Research University - High Research Activity" by the Carnegie Foundation for the Advancement of Teaching. Florida Atlantic University is a member of the Southern Association of Colleges and Schools, the National Association of State Universities and Land-Grant Colleges, and the Council of Graduate Schools in the United States.

Campus Life

By joining one of FAU's 300 student clubs and organizations, students have the opportunity to make new acquaintances outside of the classroom. Getting involved on campus helps students develop leadership, management, and interpersonal skills while contributing to the FAU community. Students are welcome to participate in Academic Organizations, Honor Societies, Spiritual/Religious Organizations, Personal Interest Clubs, Diversity Association Organizations, Service Organizations, Sports Clubs, and Greek Life.

LOCATION AND ENVIRONMENT

The University's campus locations along the Florida Gold and Treasure coasts, which boast a temperate climate and beautiful beaches, innovative industry, and unique cultural opportunities, provide a stimulating environment for its outstanding scholars and researchers. FAU's main campus in Boca Raton is on an 850-acre site located only three miles from the Atlantic Ocean. The campus is conveniently located half way between West Palm Beach and Fort Lauderdale and offers a broad range of academic programs, activities, and services. Students attending FAU- Boca Raton have some honored guests: burrowing owls. In fact, the Audubon Society has named the site a burrowing owl sanctuary and FAU varsity athletic teams are known as the Owls in their honor. Our campuses throughout South Florida can be conveniently reached from Interstate 95 or from the Florida Turnpike.

MAJORS AND DEGREES OFFERED:

Florida Atlantic University prepares its undergraduate students to be productive and thoughtful citizens by offering a broad liberal education coupled with the development of competency in fields of special interest. FAU encourages students to think creatively and critically and provides intellectual tools needed for lifelong learning. A variety of curricular and extracurricular opportunities enables students to appreciate the rich diversity that characterizes their region and world.

Florida Atlantic University's 10 colleges include the College for Design and Social Inquiry, the Dorothy F. Schmidt College of Arts and Letters, the College of Business, Charles E. Schmidt College of Medicine, the College of Education, the College of Engineering and Computer Science, the Graduate College, the Christine E. Lynn College of Nursing, the Charles E. Schmidt College of Science and the Harriet L. Wilkes Honors College in Jupiter, Florida.

Through its partnerships with other educational institutions, local businesses, industries, and other and cultural organizations, FAU enhances the economic, human, and cultural development of the surrounding communities and beyond.

Students at Florida Atlantic University may participate in a work-study program that coincides their classroom learning with hands-on experience. Many local businesses and government laboratories participate in the program each year. Students who wish to study overseas can become involved in FAU international programs in various locations across the globe from Asia to the Caribbean.

TUITION, ROOM, BOARD AND FEES:

Undergraduate tuition is $199.54 per semester credit for Florida residents and $718.09 per semester credit for non-Florida residents (subject to change). Graduate tuition is $369.82 per semester credit for Florida residents and $1,024.81 for non-Florida residents. In addition, the estimated nine-month budget for room and board on campus is $11,353; books and supplies cost approximately $1,203

FINANCIAL AID

FAU distributes more than $177 million in scholarships, grants, loans and work study annually, based on the policies of the College Scholarship Service of the College Board. Aid packages may be adjusted over the course of a student's academic career, but assistance can be earned from the first year of attendance all the way through graduate study.

Students seeking need-based aid must submit the Free Application for Federal Student Aid (FAFSA). It is recommended that students planning on fall admission turn in their FAFSA forms by the previous January, though the deadline for priority applications is March 1. Typically, the application procedure takes six to eight weeks. Students are notified about their financial aid packages after they are informed of their acceptance to the University.

Limited merit-based scholarships are also available for outstanding students. Funding is reserved for top performers in academics, athletics, and the arts. For further information, please refer to the FAU catalog under Financial Assistance.

FROSTBURG STATE UNIVERSITY

AT A GLANCE

Frostburg State University is a leader in preparing students to live, work and lead in a global environment. FSU's learner-centered academic environment emphasizes teaching and real-world experience.

Frostburg State University is a leader in preparing students to live, work and lead in a global environment. FSU offers a learner-centered academic environment created by a low student-faculty ratio and an emphasis on teaching and real-world experience. A diverse student body connects with the world at large through study abroad, internships, research alongside mentor faculty and nationally acclaimed community service programs. The University offers more than distinctive undergraduate programs and 17 high-quality, competitively priced applied graduate programs. Frostburg has been recognized by Colleges of Distinction and designated a Military Friendly School by G.I. Jobs magazine. FSU's online MBA has been recognized as a "Best Buy " among AACSB-accredited programs by GetEducated.com. FSU promotes civic responsibility, sustainability and wellness and prepares future leaders to meet the challenges of a complex and changing global society.

LOCATION AND ENVIRONMENT

Located in the beautiful mountains of Western Maryland, Frostburg is within minutes of plenty of outdoor fun and just over two hours away from Baltimore, Pittsburgh and Washington, D.C. All the buildings on FSU's campus are within easy walking distance of one another, but shuttles are available, too.

If you love the outdoors, you should know that within minutes from campus, you can:

Downhill and cross-country ski, snowboard, whitewater raft, kayak, sail, swim, fish and camp at Garrett County's Deep Creek Lake, Wisp Resort or New Germany State Park (41 minutes or less)

Camp, swim, fish and boat at Rocky Gap State Park (20 minutes)

Hike or bike on the Great Allegheny Passage (2 minutes) or the C&O Canal Towpath (10 minutes)

See the views from Dan's Rock. Go at sunrise and prepare to be amazed. (15 minutes)

The mountains are fantastic, and yes, we have snow in the winter. You'll love it.

OFF-CAMPUS OPPORTUNITIES

FSU is in the historic town of Frostburg, Md. Main Street is within walking distance from campus and features stores, pubs, cafes, pizza shops, convenience stores and restaurants to suit most tastes and budgets. Bus service, free to students, is available to nearby larger communities for more shopping, food, recreation and entertainment. Opportunities for outdoor recreation are close and numerous.

MAJORS AND DEGREES OFFERED

Frostburg offers more than 40 undergraduate majors – some traditional, some unique – in business, education, the performing and visual arts, humanities, natural and social sciences, technology and engineering. Frostburg offers high-quality applied graduate programs at the master's and doctoral levels.

Bachelor's Degree Programs

Accounting (combined BS/MBA option)

Applied Physics (bachelor's/master's collaborative program; dual-degree program)

Art and Design (teaching certification option)

Athletic Training

Biology (pre-health professions option; concentrations in biotechnology and environmental science; teaching certification option)

Business Administration (concentrations in finance, general management, human resource management, integrated business, marketing and small business/entrepreneurship)

Chemistry (track in traditional chemistry; concentrations in professional chemistry and biochemistry; teaching certification option)

Communication Studies

Computer Information Systems

Computer Science

Early Childhood/Elementary Education

Earth Science (concentration in environmental science; teaching certification option)

Economics (concentrations in business economics, public policy economics and quantitative economics)

Elementary Education

Engineering (concentrations in electrical engineering, materials engineering, industrial chemistry and engineering management)

English (concentrations in literature, creative writing and professional writing; teaching certification option)

Environmental Analysis and Planning

Ethnobotany

Exercise and Sports Science

Foreign Languages and Literature (concentrations in French and Spanish; teaching certification option)

Geography (concentrations in mapping sciences and global systems analysis)

Health and Physical Education (major with teaching certification)

History (concentrations in international history and history of the Americas)

Information Technology

Information Technology Management

International Studies (concentrations in international business, international politics, international economics and international development)

Interpretive Biology and Natural History

Law: Bachelor/Juris Doctor Program (dual-degree program)

Law and Society (concentrations in criminal justice and legal studies)

Liberal Studies

Mass Communication

Mathematics (teaching certification option)

Mechanical Engineering (collaborative program)

Music (concentrations in vocal performance and music management; teaching certification option; track in instrumental performance)

Nursing (R.N. to B.S.N. completion program, online)

Philosophy

Physics (tracks in traditional physics and engineering physics; teaching certification option)

Political Science

Psychology (certificate in child and family psychology)

Recreation and Parks Management (concentrations in adventure sports, community program delivery, hospitality management and tourism and therapeutic recreation)

Secure Computing and Information Assurance

Social Science (teaching certification option)

Social Work

Sociology (tracks in general sociology and applied social research; option in data analysis)

Theatre (tracks in acting, directing, production/design and general theatre)

Urban and Regional Planning

Wildlife and Fisheries

ACCREDITATION

In addition to regional accreditation by the Middle States Commission on Higher Education, several individual FSU programs and colleges have also earned accreditation:

College of Business (AACSB International)

College of Education's teacher education programs (NCATE, with recognition by 14 professional content associations for compliance with national standards, and the Maryland State Department of Education)

Athletic Training Education (CAAHEP)

Recreation and Parks Management (NRPA/AALR)

Social Work (Council on Social Work Education)

Mechanical Engineering collaborative program (ABET)

M.S. in Counseling Psychology (sMPAC)

Commission on Collegiate Nursing Education (CCNE)

FSU's Counseling and Psychological Services office is recognized by the International Association of Counseling Services, and the Brady Health Center is recognized by the Accreditation Association for Ambulatory Health Care.

ACADEMIC PROGRAMS

Learning communities are offered for freshmen, who study a handful of themed courses with a group of students who share similar interests. Lifelong friendships often start here.

The FSU Honors Program is set up for promising and motivated students (3.50 high school GPA or minimum 1800 SAT score) to receive research stipends, special courses and housing options.

Frostburg State University believes that living and learning go hand in hand, so out-of-classroom experiences are well-integrated into the academic life of the University. There are opportunities to conduct research alongside faculty mentors, to act, dance, perform music or exhibit your art; to compete in sports; to learn about and work toward environmental sustainability; to serve the community; and to lead. Internships are available in almost every major, and there are short- and long-term study abroad opportunities on almost every continent.

There is also plenty of academic support available, including assistance with writing, peer and group tutoring, placement testing and help with study skills and techniques.

CAMPUS FACILITIES AND EQUIPMENT

Frostburg State University boasts:

Advanced facilities (including a new science center with a variety of specialized labs and an impressive performing arts center) and the latest technology – which undergraduate students actually get to use.

A new Center for Communications and Information Technology will open in early 2014, boasting a TV and radio station, advanced video and audio studios and a multimedia learning center featuring a planetarium.

The Sustainable Energy Research Facility (SERF), which is entirely off of the power grid, offers opportunities to do hands-on research on a variety of renewable energy techniques and technologies.

A newly renovated student center featuring a fitness center, a "smart lounge" game room, computer lab, food court, coffee bar and enhanced entertainment, meeting and bookstore space.

Wireless and fiber optics networks, computer labs, including one open 24/7.

Residence halls with single- and double-room occupancy available. Residence halls feature high-speed Internet, cable TV, laundry – and all of it included for free. If you live on campus, bring your car and park it for free, too.

Edgewood Commons, a privately run student apartment community on campus, comprised of two- and four-bedroom units.

A library with a wealth of research and reference materials, including more than half a million items, including books, periodicals, audiovisual materials, maps, art

prints and U.S. and Maryland government information resources. In addition, the library subscribes to 60 electronic databases providing access to 20,000 full-text electronic journals. You also have access to the resources of all the libraries in the University System of Maryland through catalogUSMAI.

TUITION, ROOM, BOARD, AND FEES

Frostburg's costs are competitive with other public institutions, so you won't leave college with a mountain of debt.

Full-time undergraduate tuition for Maryland State residents for the 2012-13 school year is $5,464. Tuition for students residing in contiguous counties in Pennsylvania, Virginia and West Virginia is $11,698 per year. All other out-of-state tuition is $15,652 per year.

Mandatory fees (such as technology, athletics, activities, etc.) are $1,972 per year per student. Room fees range from $3,652 to $5,290 per year. Meal plans range from $3,228 to $4,422 per year.

Other fees may apply based on academic program or specialized activities.

FINANCIAL AID

In addition to institutional and private scholarships, a number of state and federal programs are available to reduce the cost of attending Frostburg. The FSU Financial Aid Office works closely with each student to help him or her meet educational requirements.

STUDENT ORGANIZATIONS AND ACTIVITIES

Whatever your interests are, we bet you can find like-minded students at Frostburg. FSU's major organizations include Student Government Association, Black Student Alliance, University Programming Council, and a number of nationally affiliated fraternities and sororities. There are academic clubs for many majors and specific interest clubs like creative writing and poetry, leadership, community service, entrepreneurship, wildlife, fashion, even stage combat.

Frostburg offers 21 NCAA Division III intercollegiate sports, most teams participating in the Capital Athletic Conference (Empire 8 for football), under the regional umbrella of the Eastern College Athletic Conference. There are also a number of club and intramural sports.

Chances are you'll find something for you in FSU's list of 90+ clubs and organizations. And if you don't find a specific club of interest, we encourage you to start your own.

ADMISSIONS PROCESS

Frostburg State University operates on a rolling admission basis, although we may have to close admissions when no further space for students is available. Applicants from high school should apply in the fall or early winter of the senior year. Beginning on Sept. 15, the admissions office will start accepting applications for the fall semester of the following year. Early Decision application deadline is Dec.15.

Admission for the spring semester is granted on a space-available basis. Applications will be considered if received no later than Dec. 1 for the subsequent spring semester. The University does accept applications from first-year students who would like to begin in the spring semester.

Freshmen applicants must complete the FSU Online Application, which includes an essay (gobobcats.frostburg.edu), and submit it with a $30 non-refundable application fee (by mail or provide credit card information). The Request for Academic Record should be given to the guidance counselor or other appropriate official at your high school. SAT scores are required for most freshman applicants.

Transfer applicants must also complete the entire FSU Online Application and submit it with a $30 non-refundable application fee, with official transcripts from each institution of higher education attended. If currently enrolled, an official transcript of the final grades must be submitted. If the applicant has less than 24 transferable credits, the student must also submit an official high school transcript and SAT or ACT scores.

GEORGIA COLLEGE

AT A GLANCE

As Georgia's designated Public Liberal Arts University, Georgia College is committed to combining the educational experiences typical of esteemed private liberal arts colleges with the affordability of public higher education. The faculty is dedicated to challenging students and fostering excellence in the classroom and beyond. Georgia College seeks to endow its graduates with a passion for achievement, a lifelong curiosity and exuberance for learning.

Georgia College was chartered in 1889 as Georgia Normal and Industrial College. The institution had several name changes over the years and became coeducational in 1967. In August of 1996, the Board of Regents approved a new name, Georgia College & State University, and a change of mission which designated the university to serve the entire state of Georgia as the public liberal arts university.

Recent national recognition of Georgia College involves its selection as the only public school in Georgia to be included in "Colleges of Distinction" and being named in the annual report on "America's 100 Best College Buys."

LOCATION AND ENVIRONMENT

Milledgeville is approximately 100 miles southeast of Atlanta, and 30 miles northeast of Macon. The town, which is the former capital of Georgia, has a population of over 20,000 and is a center of history and culture featuring beautiful homes and historic buildings. Located on the fall line in a setting of rolling hills and recreational lakes, Milledgeville's natural beauty is among its most appealing assets.

The university is an integral part Milledgeville's downtown environment and it enhances the town with its architectural blending of majestic buildings of red brick and white Corinthian columns. Georgia's Old Governor's Mansion, one of the finest examples of Greek revival architecture in the United States, is the founding building of the university. "West Campus," comprised of the athletic complex and the Village at West Campus apartment community, is located on a 546-acre site one mile away from the main campus.

OFF-CAMPUS OPPORTUNITIES

Service Learning allows students to apply classroom knowledge to the benefit of others under the auspices of nonprofit agencies with the particular experience tailored to a specific class or major. Participation in community service allows students to gain important experience in implementation of various projects and tasks, reveals a sense of commitment and responsibility, and offers wide-ranging leadership opportunities. Participation in study abroad programs provides experience and understanding of the global context of the society in which we live. Cross-cultural experiences help students appreciate and respect cultural diversity and develop an important sense of the role Americans play around the world. Internships offer paid and unpaid practical work experience directly related to a student's major. Not only do internships enhance skills and knowledge first gained in the classroom, but such experiences provide important networking advantages for students preparing to graduate and seeking career opportunities. Participation in undergraduate research resulting in presentations or publication, such as in Georgia College's own Corinthian, indicates a student's commitment to critical thinking, development of analytical skills, self-motivation and thirst for knowledge.

MAJORS AND DEGREES OFFERED

The College of Arts and Sciences provides academic programs in the fine and applied arts; the humanities; the behavioral and social sciences; the physical, biological, and mathematical sciences; and various professional fields. Students may choose from over 50 different degree programs at the undergraduate and graduate levels. There are a variety of opportunities for students to participate in internships, field placements, research projects and study abroad.

The John H. Lounsbury College of Education offers teacher education programs that are accredited by the National Council for the Accreditation of Teacher Education (NCATE) and is the recipient of the 2007 Wisniewski Award for "singularly significant contributions to the theory and practice of teacher education." Most of the undergraduate initial certification programs at Georgia College are nationally recognized by specialty program areas. Early Childhood, Middle Grades, and Special Education-Interrelated comprise the undergraduate degrees. Initial certification for Secondary Education is offered at the master's level. Music Education and Health Education are located in their respective departments in the College of Arts and Sciences (Music) and College of Health Sciences (Kinesiology).

The student who enrolls in the J. Whitney Bunting College of Business is first provided with educational opportunities in the broad areas of arts and humanities, natural sciences, and the social sciences. During the junior and senior years, there is an opportunity for in-depth understanding of the entire field of business, as well as for the selection of a major and/or minor field of study that is consistent with the individual's career objectives. The J. Whitney Bunting College of Business is nationally accredited by and is a member of AACSB International, the Association to Advance Collegiate Schools of Business.

The mission of the College of Health Sciences is to provide undergraduate and graduate programs in disciplines that emphasize health education, promotion, maintenance, and restoration. By engaging in the university's liberal arts experience, College of Health Sciences graduates attain intellectual integrity, appreciation of diversity, and commitment to the best for self, family, society, and the world. Students emerge with a world view that promotes leadership, initiative, accountability, stewardship, ethical respect for self and others, and the ability to effect change in a dynamic society.

ACADEMIC PROGRAMS

The Center for Student Success has a strong commitment to the retention of Georgia College students through the first-year experience programs, each of which seek to establish a solid base of academic success skills. Focus is directed to academic advisement at Georgia College that is a faculty-based system that assures each student contact with a faculty member who can guide a student's course selection and assist in career preparation.

Our Residential Learning Communities bridge the gap between learning inside and outside of the classroom. Incoming students have the ability to apply to one of seven living-learning communities based upon their interests. Activities are designed to provide participants with experiences beneficial to their personal development while at Georgia College.

The Georgia Education Mentorship (GEM) program matches outstanding Georgia College students with exemplary leaders in fields such as business, education, politics, healthcare, law and industry. These executives serve as mentors for participating students, promoting their personal and professional growth by providing opportunities for them to identify and understand the principles and practices of leadership and success that benefit both the professional world and the community.

The Georgia College Honors Program is an integrated program of learning that presents challenging opportunities for students with proven academic strength. The program promotes student interaction with faculty through small group discussion, supervised projects, internships, interdisciplinary studies and service learning. Through capstone experiences such as a senior thesis, a creative project or an internship, the Honors extends study into the student's academic major.

CAMPUS FACILITIES AND EQUIPMENT

Approximately 150 million dollars of construction has transformed the Georgia College campus in the last 10 years. New campus venues include the Wellness and Recreation Center (a student fitness facility providing state-of-the-art fitness facilities and programs), a student activities center with a top-notch student lounge, campus bookstore and black box theatre (adapted from a old movie theatre in downtown Milledgeville), completely renovated dining facilities and a complete replacement of all campus housing — creating on-campus suites and off-campus apartments.

One of the most impressive additions to campus is the renovation and expansion of the Library and Information Technology Center. Now one of the largest library complexes in Georgia, the Georgia College Library and Information Technology Center houses close to 200,000 volumes and holds subscriptions to more than 23,000 serials. The library also possesses several special collections, including the Flannery O'Connor Collection, the Georgia College Horology Collection and Senator Paul Coverdell's papers. The library is a selective depository of United States Government Documents.

Georgia College infuses a strong emphasis on technology into its liberal arts environment. The comprehensive wireless system frees faculty and students to surf the web from virtually anywhere on campus. Georgia College has also received national acclaim for its innovative partnership and programs utilizing Apple Computer products and creative uses of Apple's iPod to enhance learning environments.

TUITION, ROOM, BOARD AND FEES

For the 2010-2011 year, freshman tuition and fees for a full-time Georgia resident equal $3,926 per semester. Full-time out-of-state freshman tuition and fees total $12,445 per semester. Current housing and meal plan rates vary and can be reviewed at the Georgia College website.

FINANCIAL AID

Through financial aid programs, Georgia College makes every effort to assure that no qualified student will be denied the opportunity to attend school because of lack of funds.

Financial aid awards at Georgia College are based on scholastic ability, financial need, contribution to the campus community, or a combination thereof. Students may receive aid in the form of scholarships, grants, loans, or work opportunities. All students are encouraged to apply by using the Free Application for Federal Student Aid (FAFSA). First consideration will be given to any student whose file is complete by March 1. Students must have a complete file by July 1 to guarantee aid will be available at the beginning of the fall term.

STUDENT ORGANIZATIONS AND ACTIVITIES

Georgia College students may participate in a variety of activities that are coordinated or organized through the Office of Student Activities. Such activities include concerts, drama productions, comedians, intramurals, movies and more. More than 200 registered student organizations include club sports, special interest groups, academic organizations, honor societies, student media, student government, and Greek organizations. The intramural program provides team as well as individual sports. The university offers a number of indoor and outdoor campus facilities for student use as well.

ADMISSIONS PROCESS

The successful freshman applicant will demonstrate his or her potential for success by completing a rigorous college preparatory curriculum with a competitive grade point average, show strong SAT or ACT score results, and provide a well-developed personal essay. The middle 50% of admitted students for Fall 2012 had SAT total scores ranging from 1100 to 1240 (CR + M subscores only), and high school grade point averages ranging from 3.21 to 3.74 (calculated on academic courses only). These numbers are provided only as guidelines.

Admissions decisions are based on the total student portfolio and demonstrated potential for contribution to the university and probability for success in the unique environment of Georgia College.

Freshmen applicants must submit to the Office of Admissions, Campus Box 23, Milledgeville, GA 31061, the following documents for admission consideration, no later than April 1 (November 1 for Early Action):

1. Application for admission

2. Application fee

3. Official high school transcript

4. Official SAT and/or ACT score report, including Writing sample(s) –Georgia College school codes are 5252 (SAT) and 0828 (ACT)

5. Official transcripts from all colleges attended, if any

6. Personal Essay

7. While not mandatory, a resume of activities and a teacher recommendation letter are encouraged.

GONZAGA UNIVERSITY

AT A GLANCE

Gonzaga University, founded in 1887, is an independent, comprehensive university with a distinguished background in the Catholic, Jesuit, and humanistic tradition. Gonzaga emphasizes the moral and ethical implications of learning, living, and working in today's global society. Through the University Core Curriculum, each student develops a strong liberal arts foundation, which many alumni cite as a most valuable asset. In addition, students specialize in any of more than 75 academic programs and majors. Gonzaga enrolls approximately 4,800 undergraduates and 3,000 graduate and law students.

Gonzaga's 131-acre campus combines the old and new: College Hall, the original administration building, and DeSmet Residence Hall with the modern architectural structures of Foley Library, Hughes Life Sciences Building, Jundt Art Center and Museum, and the PACCAR Center for Applied Science. The campus is characterized by sprawling green lawns and majestic evergreen trees. Towering above the campus are the stately spires of St. Aloysius Church, the well-recognized landmark featured in the University logo.

Gonzaga encompasses five undergraduate schools: Arts and Sciences, Business Administration, Education, Engineering and Applied Science, and Professional Studies. The University offers the BA, BBA, BEd, BS, BSCE, BSCpE, BSCS, BSEE, BSEM, BSME, and BSN degrees.

Gonzaga offers several unique options for students. The Honors Program provides a rigorous liberal arts curriculum for intellectually curious students who thrive in a competitive academic environment. Business leaders mentor the Hogan Entrepreneurial Leadership Program students, and internships are an integral part of the program. The award-winning Gonzaga Alumni Mentor Program (GAMP) connects current students and recent graduates with alumni in their professional areas of interest. Students in the Comprehensive Leadership Program take a leadership certificate curriculum that may be combined with any major, and they participate in valuable, interactive leadership experiences. The Army ROTC unit prepares select women and men as leaders in service for their communities and their country. Gonzaga's nationally ranked debate team includes all skill levels. The Mock Trial Team competes nationally and involves students majoring in many different areas of study. Internships, research with faculty, and community service learning enhance class time while providing students first-hand experience.

LOCATION AND ENVIRONMENT

As the hub of the Inland Northwest, Spokane plays a vital role in shaping the University's character. While offering urban advantages such as museum exhibits, shopping, symphony, Broadway and ballet performances, Spokane still maintains an intimate, friendly, and community atmosphere. Used for running and cycling, part of the 37-mile Centennial Trail, runs through campus and to Coeur d' Alene, Idaho. Within a short distance of campus, students snow and water ski, hike, cycle, rock climb, swim, camp, and golf. With an average rainfall of only 16.7 inches per year, outdoor activities are easily accessible.

The 24 residence halls and apartments on campus, both single-sex and coed, house 40 to 360 students each. Freshmen and sophomores are required to live on campus. The ZagNet network provides students round-the-clock electronic access to email, Internet, campus intranet, and library holdings, all directly from residence hall rooms. Additionally, the whole campus is wireless. Resident Directors and Assistants, along with a Resident Chaplain, provide a fun, secure, and nurturing environment.

OFF-CAMPUS OPPORTUNITIES

Recognizing the importance of an international perspective for learning, Gonzaga offers study abroad programs in Argentina, Australia, Austria, Belgium, Benin, Chile, China, Costa Rica, Denmark, Ecuador, El Salvador, England, France, Ghana, India, Ireland, Italy, Japan, Jordan, Mexico, the Netherlands, New Zealand, Peru, Scotland (Honors Program students), South Africa, Spain, Taiwan, Thailand, Turkey, Turks and Caicos, and Zambia. Gonzaga's campus in Florence, Italy is the most popular option.

MAJORS AND DEGREES OFFERED

Gonzaga offers the following areas of study in the five undergraduate schools. The College of Arts and Sciences offers applied communication studies, art, biochemistry, biology (research option), broadcast and electronic media studies, chemistry, classical civilizations, criminal justice, economics, English (writing concentration), environmental studies, French, history, integrated studies, international studies (including international relations and Asian, European, and Latin American studies), Italian studies, journalism, mathematics, mathematics/computer science, music (including emphases in composition, general studies, and performance and minors in conducting and jazz performance), music education, philosophy (Kossel Track option), physics, political science, psychology, public relations, religious studies, sociology, Spanish, and theatre arts (performance and technical tracks). Additionally, the School offers minors in advertising (for communication arts majors), Catholic studies, dance, German, Italian, Native American studies, and women's and gender studies. Students interested in the following areas take tracks of classes respectively in pre-dentistry, pre-law, pre-medicine, pre-physical therapy, and pre-veterinary studies. The School of Business Administration offers majors in accounting or business administration (with concentrations in economics, entrepreneurship and innovation, finance, human resource management, individualized study, international business, law and public policy, management information systems, marketing, and operations and supply chain management). As well as granting teacher certification on both the elementary and secondary levels, the School of Education offers degrees in physical education, special education, and sport management. The School of Engineering and Applied Science offers computer science and civil, computer, electrical, and mechanical engineering degrees, as well as an engineering management degree and a 5-year BSEM/MBA option. Also, The School of Professional Studies offers human physiology and nursing degrees. Advanced degrees in accounting, business, education, engineering, law, leadership studies, nursing, philosophy, religious studies, and teaching English as a second language are also offered.

ACADEMIC PROGRAMS

The core curriculum (a basic set of courses in thought and expression, philosophy, religious studies, mathematics, and English literature) is at the foundation of every student's academic experience at Gonzaga. In keeping with the Jesuit ethos of the University, all students share a framework of 31 credits: a trio block of thought and expression courses including English composition, critical thinking, and speech communication; three additional courses in philosophy; three religious studies courses; and one course each in math and English literature. Various schools in the University add courses that complement the core such as modern/classical language requirements, history and science classes, additional math courses, etc. Often, classes at Gonzaga require oral presentations or use of the written and discussion-based communication skills emphasized in the core curriculum.

CAMPUS FACILITIES AND EQUIPMENT

The Foley Library contains more than 800,000 volumes and microform titles, with two special collections of material especially rich in the areas of philosophy and classical civilization, as well as the nation's most extensive collection of works concerning the famous Jesuit poet Gerard Manley Hopkins. The historic College Hall houses the recently-renovated Harry & Colleen Magnuson Theatre, a 24-hour computer lab, a Florentine-style University Chapel, and numerous classrooms and faculty offices.

Students are able to produce sophisticated multimedia presentations and research hundreds of libraries across the country from their own residence hall rooms, by accessing campus-wide wireless, or from one of the 10 labs on campus. The Communications Building offers an arts lab for the Bulletin (the weekly student-published newspaper), KAGU, the University's radio station, and GUTV, a state-of-the-art TV production station where students learn all aspects of broadcast and electronic media studies. The Herak Center for Engineering offers state-of-the-art CAD/CAM, electronic, digital, microwave, and calibration labs, and the PACCAR Center for Applied Science, which received a "Gold" certification rating from the Leadership in Energy and Environmental Design (LEED), adds more classroom space, a robotics lab, a computer science lab with a high-speed cluster computer array, and the rapidly growing Electric Utility Transmission & Distribution program.

The Martin Athletic Centre boasts a 13,000 sq. ft. state-of-the-art fitness center, and next door, the 6000-seat McCarthey Athletic Center houses the men's and women's basketball games as well as concerts and events throughout the year. Washington Trust Field at Patterson Baseball Complex hosts the Gonzaga baseball program.

Gonzaga has committed that any new buildings on campus will seek "Silver" LEED certification, and as a signatory of the Presidents' Climate Commitment, Gonzaga has created a Climate Action Plan to reduce its carbon footprint by 20% by 2020 and 50% by 2035 (from 2009 levels).

TUITION, ROOM, BOARD AND FEES

Tuition for the 2013-2014 academic year is $34,570; room and board is estimated at $9,120. Including tuition, room and board, books, fees, transportation, and living expenses, Gonzaga estimates $48,595 as the total cost of attendance for the 2013-2014 year.

FINANCIAL AID

Over 96% percent of students receive financial aid. The average package for 2011-2012 was $23,694 awarded in the form of grants, scholarships, loans, and campus employment. A number of merit-based, merit/need-based, athletic, music, debate, and other program scholarships are awarded to students each year. Students should file the Free Application for Federal Student Aid (FAFSA) by the priority date of February 1 and check the website for scholarship information and applications. Gonzaga is committed to working with students and families to finance their investment in a quality education.

STUDENT ORGANIZATIONS AND ACTIVITIES

GU students enjoy a wide variety of activities on and off campus. The Gonzaga Student Body Association (GSBA) oversees over one hundred academic, social, and cultural clubs and provides the structure of student government. Some of the most popular clubs include the Outdoors Club, THIRST (a non-denominational worship group), GUTS (an improvisational comedy team), and the Hawaii Pacific Islanders Club. GSBA organizes service and conservation projects, dances, and countless other activities to channel and challenge the talents and passions of motivated men and women who seek to make a difference.

As the leading provider of service hours in the entire city of Spokane, Gonzaga University encourages students to volunteer their services at any of the area non-profit organizations. University Ministry, the Gonzaga Student Body Association, Unity Multicultural Education Center, and the Center for Community Action and Service Learning (CCASL) provide organized projects through which students become involved in the greater Spokane community.

Division I, West Coast Conference sports include baseball (men), basketball, crew, cross-country/track, golf, soccer, tennis, and volleyball (women). Approximately 85% of students participate in intramural and club sports such as ultimate frisbee and rugby. The Harry & Colleen Magnuson Theatre hosts main-stage plays (including musicals), dance recitals, GUTS, and numerous one-acts and student directed scenes. Gonzaga's musical groups include a nationally recognized University Choir, a Chorale, the GU Symphony, the Jazz Ensemble, the Gonzaga Bulldog Band, The Big Bing Theory an a cappella group, the Boone Street Band, and numerous other ensembles. GU's students also host programs on Gonzaga's TV and radio stations. Additionally, many students participate in University Ministry events, such as retreats, the annual Pilgrimage hike, THIRST, Masses, Christian Life Communities, and interdenominational and/or interfaith services.

ADMISSIONS PROCESS

The University seeks diligent, inquisitive applicants with diverse backgrounds who will benefit from the rigorous Jesuit instruction at Gonzaga as well as enhance the University environment. A Common Application (www.commonapp.org) and the Gonzaga supplement, SAT I (Writing Section not used universally) or ACT scores (Writing Section not required), a transcript, a teacher recommendation, a school report, an activities list or resume, and an essay are required. Transfer students and students with any college credit must submit official transcripts from all colleges. Transfer students must also complete the Common Application for Transfers, including the College Official's Report. International students must also submit official transcripts from all colleges attended. Additionally, international students must submit official results of their TOEFL examination. The Non-binding Early Action application deadline for freshmen is November 15th (postmarked). The main advantages of the Early Action Program are early communication of admission and potential scholarship notice (by January 15th). The Regular Decision application date for freshmen is February 1 (postmarked). Students applying Regular Decision by this date will receive an admission decision by the beginning of April. After February 1, applications will be accepted only if space is available.

GRACELAND UNIVERSITY

AT A GLANCE

There is always something great going on at Graceland University's main campus in Lamoni, Iowa, (founded in 1895) and our Independence, Missouri, campus (1999). Graceland students and faculty are on the go, both on our campuses and around the world.

Graceland University creates and maintains high academic standards of excellence by prioritizing a close student/faculty learning environment, providing nurturing communities that foster intellectual engagement and curiosity, and embracing the philosophy that learning is not confined to the classroom. Graceland integrates a strong tradition in the liberal arts with targeted professional learning.

LOCATION AND ENVIRONMENT

Situated on 170 acres of rolling hills and trees, our main campus in Lamoni, Iowa, is home to about 1,000 students. It's a short, one-hour drive to Des Moines, Iowa, or two hours to Kansas City, MO. We offer a beautiful, safe residential campus where diversity of thought and culture are celebrated. You are warmly welcomed at Graceland and in Lamoni from the minute you arrive. You instantly have friends and become a valued member in your home away from home.

At Graceland, we integrate learning inside and outside of the classroom and provide limitless opportunities for involvement in educational service, leadership and entertainment activities. The Independence Campus offers online learning opportunities—both graduate and undergraduate--in nursing, religion, education and more.

Life at Graceland includes forums and guest speakers on the hot issues of the day; community service projects; poetry readings at a downtown coffee house; world-class entertainment; and quiet time in a relaxed, countryside setting.

OFF-CAMPUS OPPORTUNITIES

Lamoni is a small, friendly town with a big heart. There's an old-fashioned pizza place, a bustling coffee house, a university-owned movie theatre, called the Coliseum, and a night spot, called Choices--all just a five-minute walk from campus. It's easy to venture into the Lamoni community. You can hike around a beautiful nearby lake or use new, city bike trails. Popular lakes at Slip Bluff County Park and Nine Eagles State Park offer swimming, boating, fishing and camping, and both are only a few miles away. There are close bonds between Graceland and the small, but vibrant town of Lamoni, home to 2,500 residents.

MAJORS AND DEGREES OFFERED

Bachelor's Degrees

Accounting

Agricultural Business

Art: Studio°

Art: Visual Communication

Athletic Training

Basic Science°

Biology°

Business Administration

Chemistry°

Communications°

Computer Science and Information Technology

Criminal Justice

Economics

Elementary Education

English°

Film, Theatre, and Performance Studies°

Health°

Health Care Management

History°

Human Services

International Studies

Liberal Studies

Mathematics°

Music°

Nursing

Organizational Leadership

Physical Education°

Psychology

Publication Writing and Design

Recreation

Religion and Philosophy

Sport Management

Web Design

Wellness Program Management

°Secondary teacher education program offered.

Pre-Professional Programs

Pre-Chiropractic

Pre-Dentistry

Pre-Forensic Science

Pre-Law

Pre-Medicine

Pre-Optometry

Pre-Pharmacy

Pre-Physical Therapy

Pre-Veterinary Medicine

Masters Programs

Master of Arts in Religion

Master of Education

Master of Science in Nursing

Doctorate Program

Doctor of Nurse Practice

ACADEMIC PROGRAMS

From day one at Graceland, students learn in an individualized, challenging, yet supportive environment, with a 15:1 student/faculty ratio. Students immediately meet key professors in "First Year Experience" classes. The university offers over 50 academic majors and programs. Students will work closely with professors who are both teachers and scholars. Most of our professors hold a doctorate or the highest degree in their field. Our Honors Program, highly acclaimed by participants, is designed for motivated students who want to expand their learning beyond the regular curriculum. The program takes annual cultural trips to big cities (for example, Chicago) and gives students the opportunity to present at regional Honors conferences.

Our Enactus team participates in national and international service efforts. The team has won regional championships 11 times of the last 12 years. Our 80-strong Enactus team placed first in the U.S. and second in the world (at the competition in Paris) in 2006.

Winter Term at Graceland separates the two traditional semesters and allows students to interact with faculty in action-oriented learning experiences on campus and around the world. Winter Term takes students abroad where they are building stoves in Nicaragua, touring European art museums and teaching in Zambian schools.

Your Graceland Experience will combine a personalized education and an ongoing adventure. Both will stay with you for the rest of your life. We know, "Once a Gracelander, always a Gracelander." Our graduates go on to stellar careers in the sciences, the arts, nursing, education, business, athletics and human services. Our alumni will tell you that the Graceland Experience helped focus their passions and shape their futures.

In addition to traditional programs, Graceland offers many options for distance learners. Programs offered online by our renowned School of Nursing include the Bachelor in Healthcare Management, R.N.-B.S.N., R.N.-M.S.N. and M.S.N. programs. The M.S.N. program has two tracks: family nurse practitioner and nurse educator. The School of Education offers a Master of Education with six different emphases. The Master of Education program is offered in Cedar Rapids, Des Moines, and Lamoni, Iowa; Independence, Missouri; and online. The Community of Christ Seminary at Graceland offers a Master of Arts in Religion in a blended delivery system.

CAMPUS FACILITIES AND EQUIPMENT

In 2012, Graceland finished construction of the $1.6 million Fitzgerald Fitness Center, a new student wellness center with a group exercise area and a variety of weight and cardio equipment.

Graceland also re-introduced the Shaw Center in the fall of 2012 after the $16 million expansion and renovation project. The new Shaw Center features JR Theatre, a state-of-the-art black box facility; Carol Hall, an acoustically perfect recital hall; the Shaw Family Auditorium, with over 500 seating capacity; the outdoor Amphitheatre for spring jazz concerts and more. The new Shaw Center is one of the most remarkable performing arts venues in southern Iowa.

Our Resch Science and Technology Hall was dedicated in 2009. It provides state-of-the-art sciences and math facilities. Nearly everything, including the computer science equipment, is new and industry-standard in Resch Hall. The Helene Center for the Visual Arts (2004) includes 29,000 square feet of classrooms, studios and exhibit space. It is regarded by artists as "the perfect place to get creative."

Campus computer facilities include three microcomputer labs and industry-standard equipment for desktop publishing and graphic design. Graceland's Enter.Net.C@fe provides 24-hour computer and printing access in a cozy atmosphere.

Our Closson Athletic Center boasts an indoor track and field facility, a beautiful hardwood basketball and volleyball court, and an indoor pool. We have a new FieldTurf, an artificial turf football field (the envy of other universities), a wonderful outdoor track facility, and a top soccer complex, home to our perennial conference champion men's and women's teams. Our men's soccer team won the NAIA National Championship in 2006, and our women's team won the Conference Championship eight years in a row.

The Frederick Madison Smith Library uses the latest technologies to provide information services to accommodate student needs. Ten fully networked computer workstations offer access to the Internet and many research databases, including seven reference databases and more than 45 periodical databases, many providing access to full-text articles. Access to LIBBIE, the library's online catalog, and to the online reference sources, is available to all patrons. Articles and books may be ordered from a worldwide network of research libraries.

TUITION, ROOM, BOARD, AND FEES

Graceland University has been named a "Best College in the Midwest" by The Princeton Review. We are committed to managing our costs, now and in the future, while maintaining the quality of education we provide every student. Costs for traditional students for the 2013-2014 academic year are listed below. Online program costs vary.

	Annual	Semester
Tuition	$23,180	$11,590
Room	$3,230	$1,615
Board	$4,660	$2,330
Activity Fee	$350	$175
Total Direct Costs	$31,420	$15,710

FINANCIAL AID

Student Financial Aid is available for those students who qualify. All aid is based upon financial need, academic achievement, and/or meritorious performance. Financial aid is viewed as a supplement to the effort of the family to finance their student's college education. In order to receive federal or state financial aid, students must file a Free Application for Federal Student Aid (FAFSA) each year (add Graceland's code: 001866), and maintain satisfactory academic progress. Institutional Scholarships and Grants may be awarded to full-time students for academics, athletics, performing arts, and for Community of Christ students. When Graceland University receives all documents needed to complete a Financial Aid Package, an award notice will be sent to the student for review. More than 98 percent of Graceland students receive some form of financial aid.

STUDENT ORGANIZATIONS AND ACTIVITIES

Graceland sponsors more than 50 student clubs and organizations. We boast 19 varsity and numerous junior varsity sports and a variety of performing arts groups. Anyone who wants to play or perform at Graceland has ample opportunities to do so.

The basic residential and social unit of student life is known as a "House." The house system at GU is a unique program that started in the 1960s and is based on the principle of inclusion. The importance of each student is recognized. Unlike fraternities and sororities, every student is involved in the House system. Members of each House elect a leadership council that plans social events and represents students in Student Government. By cooperative effort, the House organizes its own social, religious and intramural programs. Each student determines the extent of his/her participation in all House activities. Our students love this community approach to residential life.

Our students hail from more than 40 states and 40 countries. At Graceland, you will meet students from China, Kosovo, Belize and many other countries. We are also committed to providing an environment that is free of alcohol and tobacco. Graceland cares about your spiritual life as well. Whatever your faith tradition, your spiritual life will be nurtured as much as you desire while you are at Graceland.

ADMISSIONS PROCESS

To be considered for acceptance at Graceland, you must meet two of the three following criteria: rank in the upper 50 percent of your high school class, have a 2.5 grade point average (based on a 4.0 system) and a minimum composite ACT score of 21, or a minimum combined SAT score of 960. International students also need to score at or above 550 on TOEFL and prove ability to cover expenses while enrolled. Transfer students need a minimum 2.0 GPA on previous college coursework.

HAVERFORD COLLEGE

AT A GLANCE

Haverford is a coeducational, residential liberal arts college located 8 miles west of center city Philadelphia. Haverford was founded in 1833 by members of the Religious Society of Friends (Quakers). While the College is no longer formally affiliated with any religious body, the values of academic strength, intellectual freedom, individual worth, and tolerance upon which it was founded remain central to its character.

Haverford's 1,200 students represent a wide variety of interests, backgrounds, and talents. They come from public and independent schools from all 50 States, DC, Puerto Rico, and more than 30 countries around the world.

Extensive cooperation with nearby Bryn Mawr College adds an important dimension to the resources available at Haverford. Educational opportunities are further enhanced by cooperation with Swarthmore College and the University of Pennsylvania.

The academic experience at Haverford revolves around opportunities for students to be directly engaged with their education on the highest levels. Special emphasis is placed on collaborative work and research, and three academic centers – the Center for Peace and Global Citizenship, the Hurford Humanities Center, and the Koshland Integrated Natural Sciences Center – support student and faculty engagement beyond the boundaries of the traditional classroom. And Haverford is one of the very few institutions where all students produce a senior thesis or final project.

Although students choose Haverford because of its academic excellence, a strong sense of community participation informs the Haverford College experience both inside the classroom and out. Haverford is well known for its emphasis on self-governance, and students work together through the arts and cultural activities, service programs, athletic programs, and day-to-day campus life.

The Honor Code, affirmed by the student body each year, embodies the philosophy of conduct within the College. Students are expected to maintain a strong sense of individual responsibility as well as intellectual integrity, honesty, and genuine concern for others.

Haverford College offers an atmosphere of intellectual and personal challenge, excitement, and growth in a close-knit community that is dedicated to encouraging humane values during the undergraduate years and for a lifetime.

LOCATION AND ENVIRONMENT

Originally landscaped by the English gardener William Carvill, the park-like, 204-acre campus includes more than 400 species of trees and shrubs, a nature walk, and a duck pond. The varied architectural styles of campus buildings, representing more than 150 years of architectural evolution, give the campus a unique character and charm. Just 8 miles away from Haverford are the cultural and educational resources of Philadelphia. Frequent train service to and from the city add to campus resources and enhance student opportunities.

OFF-CAMPUS OPPORTUNITIES

In addition to course offerings at Swarthmore, Bryn Mawr and the University of Pennsylvania, there are numerous opportunities for internships and volunteer service in the surrounding communities and in Philadelphia. If students want to go farther afield they may participate in one of over 50 study abroad programs supported by Haverford. Domestic study away programs include exchanges with Claremont McKenna, Spellman, and Fiske Colleges.

MAJORS AND DEGREES OFFERED

Haverford College offers the Bachelor of Arts Degree in the following areas:

In the Natural Sciences: astronomy, biology, chemistry, computer science, geology, mathematics, physics.

In the Social Sciences: anthropology, archaeology, East Asian studies, economics, growth and structure of cities, history, political science, psychology, sociology.

In the Humanities: Chinese, classics, comparative literature, English, fine arts, French, German, history of art, Italian, Japanese, music, philosophy, religion, Russian, Spanish.

Science majors have the option of choosing a Bachelor of Science.

ACADEMIC PROGRAMS

Haverford offers the following academic programs, in addition to the majors and minors named above, as Concentrations: Africana and African studies, biochemistry and biophysics, creative writing, dance, education, environmental studies, gender and sexuality studies, Hebrew and Judaic studies, Hispanic and Hispanic American studies, international economic relations, Latin American and Iberian studies, mathematical economics, neural and behavioral sciences, peace and conflict studies, 3/2 liberal arts and engineering, and theater studies.

Students may pursue pre-medical, pre-law or pre-business intentions through any major; special advising is offered in these areas.

CAMPUS FACILITIES AND EQUIPMENT

A listing of facilities and equipment would fill several pages. Please visit Haverford's website at www.haverford.edu for a campus tour and an overview of the College's facilities. The newest facilities are the Koshland Integrated Natural Sciences Center, completed in 2002, with state of the art laboratories, computer workrooms, faculty offices and classrooms, and, completed in fall 2005, the Gardner Integrated Athletic Center, a 100,000 square foot athletic complex serving the entire College community.

Tuition, Room, Board and Fees

For the 2010-2011 School Year, tuition for Haverford College is as follows: For Tuition, the cost is $40,280, for Room and Board $12,346. In addition, there is an activity fee of $364, and an orientation fee of $200 (new students only).

FINANCIAL AID

Haverford has always sought to enroll the most qualified students regardless of their financial circumstances. To that end, the admission staff admits students without regard to their financial need. An application for financial aid will have no bearing on admission decisions for all US citizens and permanent residents.

Financial aid decisions are made solely according to a need-based allocation formula developed by the College. In other words, Haverford does not offer any financial aid on the basis of academic, musical, athletic, or other evaluation of merit. For many years, Haverford has provided aid to all admitted students who were judged eligible according to the College's formula and procedures. Beginning with the Class of 2012, Haverford no longer includes loans as part of a student's financial aid package, replacing this form of aid with additional College grant funds.

Applicants are required to fill and submit the FAFSA and the PROFILE application if they want to be considered for financial aid. Regular Decision candidates must register for the PROFILE by January 1 of the senior year of high school and submit by January 31. The FAFSA should be mailed to the federal government with Haverford's Federal Code (003274) by January 31. Early Decision candidates are held to different deadlines; please visit www.haverford.edu/financialaid/dates.php for further details.

STUDENT ORGANIZATIONS AND ACTIVITIES

There are more than 150 student organizations on campus. Musicians, athletes, writers, actors, rock climbers, gourmet cooks, feminists, political activists . . . everyone finds ways to pursue their extracurricular passions at Haverford. There are 11 varsity sports for women and 12 for men, including the only varsity cricket team in the nation. In addition, the students support a host of club sports and intramural teams.

ADMISSIONS PROCESS

The admission process at Haverford is conducted as a comprehensive review, treating each application personally and individually and with extraordinary care and attention to detail. We aim to provide you with the opportunity to convey the broadest sense possible of who you are, what you have achieved during your secondary school experience, and how you will both contribute to and grow from a Haverford education.

Our primary consideration in the evaluation process is academic excellence. Haverford is interested in students who demonstrate ability and interest in achieving at the highest levels of scholarship and service; who will engage deeply and substantively with the community; and who are intent on growing deeply both intellectually and personally. To this end, we consider:

-Secondary school transcript

-Standardized tests

-Teacher and counselor recommendations

-Quality of writing as demonstrated in your essays, testing, and recommendations

-Potential for contribution to the campus community

-Interview

Students may begin their studies in the fall semester only. The College uses the Common Application, along with a Supplement, both of which can be obtained and submitted on-line or by mail. All applications should be accompanied by a non-refundable $60 application fee payable to Haverford College. Decisions are announced before April 1. Students are required to submit all forms and supporting documents included in the application. In addition, they must also have their official SAT or ACT scores and two SAT II test scores sent to Haverford.

HAWAI'I PACIFIC UNIVERSITY

AT A GLANCE

Hawai'i Pacific University (HPU) is a private, nonprofit university with an international student population of approximately 8,200 students. HPU is one of the most culturally diverse universities in America with students from all 50 U.S. states and more than 100 countries. Founded in 1965, HPU prides itself on maintaining strong academic programs,...Hawai'i Pacific University (HPU) is the state's leading, private, nonprofit university with a student population of more than 8,000 students. HPU is one of the most culturally diverse universities in America with students from all 50 states and more than 100 countries. Founded in 1965, HPU prides itself on maintaining strong academic programs, small class sizes, individual attention to students, and a diverse faculty and student population. HPU offers more than 50 acclaimed undergraduate programs and 14 distinguished graduate programs.

Hawai'i Pacific University is consistently ranked among the best institutions of high education in the nation. HPU is regionally recognized as a "Best in the West" college by both The Princeton Review and the U.S. News and World Report, and a "Best Buy" by Barron's business magazine. Bloomberg Businessweek also recognized HPU for having the "Best Undergraduate Return on Investment" among any College or University in the state of Hawai'i, based on tuition costs and earnings of alumni. HPU is accredited by the Western Association of Schools and Colleges (WASC). The Nursing program is approved by the Hawai'i Board of Nursing, and accredited by the National League for Nursing Accrediting Commission (NLNAC) and the Commissions on Collegiate Nursing Education (CCNE). The Social Work Program is accredited by the Council on Social Work Education (CSWE), and the University is recognized by the Hawaii Commission on Postsecondary Education.

HPU is proud to offer more than 600 full and part-time faculty members from around the world with outstanding academic and business credentials. Faculty range from top-level executives at Fortune 500 companies, to state government leaders that enliven the learning experience with real-world knowledge. Our student-centered approach and low student-faculty ratio of 15:1 naturally results in personal attention and one-on-one guidance. HPU puts a priority on teaching. There are no teaching assistants; only highly qualified faculty in the classrooms. Even with more than 8,000 students, our average class size is under 25. This means you'll enjoy all of the technological and academic resources expected at a large university, delivered within the atmosphere of a small school.

The diversity of HPU's student body stimulates learning about other cultures firsthand, both inside and outside of the classroom. Students are encouraged to examine the values, customs, traditions, and principles of others to gain a clearer understanding of their own perspectives. HPU students develop friendships with students from throughout the world and form important connections for success in the global economy.

HPU has NCAA Division II intercollegiate sports. Men's athletic programs include baseball, basketball, cross-country, golf, soccer, and tennis. Women's athletics include basketball, cross-country, soccer, softball, tennis, golf, and volleyball. HPU's women's softball team as well as its cheerleading squad and dance team have received numerous national championship titles.

The housing office at HPU offers many services and living options for students. Residence halls with cafeteria service are available on the windward Hawai'i Loa campus, while off-campus apartments are available in the Honolulu and Waikiki areas for those seeking more independent living arrangements.

Visiting and Contact Information

1164 Bishop Street Suite 200

Honolulu, HI 96813

United States

(808) 544-0238

Toll-free: 1-800-CALL-HPU

Fax: 808-544-1136

Website: www.hpu.edu

ACADEMIC PROGRAMS

HPU offers more than 50 acclaimed undergraduate programs and 14 distinguished graduate programs, with liberal arts at the heart of the curriculum. Baccalaureate students must complete at least 124 semester hours of credit. Of these credits, 45 provide the student with a strong foundation in the liberal arts and sciences, with the remaining credits composed of appropriate upper-division classes in the student's major and related areas. HPU's academic year consists of standard fall and spring semesters. HPU also has other available terms so that students can take courses year round. HPU offers a 5 week winter intersession, two accelerated sessions (fall and spring), and three summer sessions. By attending these supplemental sessions, a student may accelerate the completion of their Baccalaureate degree program in three years.

MAJORS AND DEGREES OFFERED

Hawai'i Pacific University offers programs that lead to the undergraduate degrees of Bachelor of Arts (B.A.), Bachelor of Education (B.Ed.), Bachelor of Science (B.S.), Bachelor of Science in Business Administration (B.S.B.A.), Bachelor of Science in Nursing (B.S.N.), and Bachelor of Social Work (B.S.W.).

Undergraduate programs include:

Accounting, Advertising/Public Relations , Anthropology, Asian Studies, Biochemistry, Biology (concentrations in General Biology and Human and Health Science), Business (General), Business Economics, Chemistry, Communication, Computer Information Systems, Computer Science, Diplomacy and Military Studies , Economics, Secondary Education (concurrent program), Elementary Education, English, Entrepreneurial Studies, Environmental Science, Environmental Studies, Finance, Health Science, History, Human Resource Development, Human Resource Management, Humanities (concentrations in Art History, East West Classical Studies, Philosophy, Religious Studies), International Business, International Studies (concentrations in Globalization and Social Change, International Relations and Security, International Political Economy and Development), Journalism, Justice Administration , Management, Marine Biology, Marketing, Mathematics (concentrations in Applied Math, 3-2 Engineering, Mathematics Education, Pure Math), Multimedia (concentrations in Cinematic Production or Integrated Multimedia), Nursing , Oceanography, Political Science, Pre-Chiropractic, Pre-Health Professions Programs , Pre-Physical Therapy, Psychology, Public Administration, Social Science, Social Work, Sociology, Teaching English to Speakers of other Languages, Theatre (individualized), Travel Industry Management

Dual degrees, double majors, and minors are also offered.

ADMISSIONS

Hawai'i Pacific University utilizes a holistic approach during the admissions process. HPU considers not just your GPA, but also the strength of your class schedule, SAT I and/or ACT results, extracurricular activities, the personal statement you provide and your academic area of interest. An admissions decision is made based on all of these factors.

Hawai'i Pacific University seeks students who are motivated and show academic promise. The Admissions Office requires that applicants complete and forward the admission application and their high school transcripts. Transfer students should also submit college transcripts. SAT and/or ACT scores should be submitted if these scores are not posted in ...Hawai'i Pacific University seeks students who are motivated and show academic promise. The Admissions Office requires that applicants complete and forward the admission application and their high school transcripts. Transfer students should also submit college transcripts. SAT and/or ACT scores should be submitted if these scores are not posted in their transcripts. First-time freshmen have an average GPA of 3.30 (on a 4.0 scale). HPU recommends that students complete 4 years of English, 4 years of history or social science, 3 years of math, and 2 years of science. Transfer students with 24 or more postsecondary credits have an average GPA of 2.75. For students with less than 24 credits, a combination of college and high school GPA is used. Transfer students must demonstrate ability in science and math at the college level. The Marine Science and Environmental Science Programs require 3 years of science, including biology, chemistry (physics is recommended), as well as mathematics through trigonometry (calculus is recommended). Students not meeting the above criteria are encouraged to enroll at HPU without declaring a major to demonstrate the ability to do college-level work in science and math.

APPLICATION INFORMATION

Our priority deadline for the fall semester is March 1st; however, applications are accepted on a rolling basis, year-round. Candidates are notified of admission decisions usually within two weeks of receipt of application materials. Early entrance and deferred entrance are available.

For further information and for application materials, students should contact:

OFFICE OF ADMISSIONS

Hawai'i Pacific University

1164 Bishop Street, Suite 200

Honolulu, Hawai'i 96813

Phone: 808-544-0238 / 866-CALL-HPU (toll-free in U.S. and Canada)

Fax: 808-544-1136

E-mail: admissions@hpu.edu

Website: www.hpu.edu/princetonreview

STUDENT BODY

With more than 8,200 students from all 50 states and more than 100 countries, HPU is one of the most culturally diverse universities in the world. HPU is consistently ranked as one of the best international institutions of higher education by Open Doors, the annual publication on international student enrollment in the U.S. and around the world. The diversity of HPU's student body is a unique asset that stimulates learning about other cultures firsthand, both inside and outside of the classroom. Students are encouraged to examine the values, customs, traditions, and principles of others to gain a clearer understanding of their own perspectives.

Below are some statistics regarding HPU's student body (Fall 2012):

Total Enrollment:	8,071
Undergraduates:	6740
Graduates:	1331
Full-time:	6,171
Part-time:	1,900
Male:	45%
Female:	55%

The Center for Student Life and First-Year Programs holds regular on-campus activities and events to enhance the college experience at HPU. Students can look forward to the following organized events: Movie on the Mall, Music on the Mall, intramural sports tournaments, and recreational activities. Some annual events include Club Carnival, Welcome Week, Da Freakshow, Pa'ina on the Pier, Halloween Hoopla, and more. HPU students can join one of more than 50 student clubs; run for office in the Associated Students of Hawai'i Pacific University (ASHPU), the University's governing body; participate in Army or Air Force ROTC; write for the student newspaper, Kalamalama; edit the school's literary journal, Hawai'i Pacific Review; or join HPU's stage and pep band, the cheer and dance team, or the International Choral program.

CAMPUS AND FACILITIES

Hawai'i Pacific University's main campus in downtown Honolulu provides a fast-paced, exciting urban environment in the heart of the business community. The downtown campus comprises six buildings in the center of Honolulu's business district and is home to the College of Business Administration and the College of Humanities & Social Sciences. The ...Hawai'i Pacific University's downtown campus in provides a fast-paced, exciting urban environment in the heart of Honolulu's business community. The downtown campus is comprised of six buildings in the center of Honolulu's business district and is home to the College of Business Administration and the College of Humanities & Social Sciences. This campus location makes it convenient for students to commute to, find, and maintain internship opportunities at neighboring businesses. At this campus you can find the offices of Admissions, Academic Advising, Financial Aid, Student Life and First Year Programs, the Graduate Center, and Career Services.

Eight miles away, on the windward side of the island, the 135-acre Hawaii Loa campus is set in the lush foothills of the Ko'olau Mountains. This campus is home to the College of Nursing & Health Sciences and the College of Natural & Computational Sciences. The Hawai'i Loa campus has residence halls, a dining commons, the Educational Technology Center, a student center, and outdoor recreational facilities including a soccer field, tennis courts, a softball field, and an exercise room.

HPU is also affiliated with the Oceanic Institute, a major research center specializing in marine biology, marine aquaculture, biotechnology and ocean resource management. It is located on a 56-acre site at Makapu'u Point on the southeastern coast of O'ahu. Learning, internship and research opportunities for graduates and undergraduates abound in this hands-on learning environment. All three sites are conveniently linked by free shuttle.

TUITION, ROOM, BOARD AND FEES

For the 2013-2014 academic year, tuition for most majors is $19,980. Other expenses including books, supplies, and health insurance cost approximately $3,480. Tuition for junior- or senior-year nursing majors is $25,650. The cost to live in on-campus residence halls or off-campus apartments is comparable; estimated room and board are $12,550 for a double occupancy room. There is an additional $500 refundable security deposit required for residence halls and off-campus apartments.

FINANCIAL AID

HPU offers most forms of federal financial aid, including student grant and loan programs, as well as loans for parents of dependent students. Over 75 percent of the University's students benefit from federal financial aid programs, or a wide range of institutional scholarships. Students should complete the Free Application for Federal Student Aid (FAFSA) to be considered for federal aid programs. While aid can be awarded throughout the academic year, students should complete the application prior to the March 1 priority deadline to be considered for all available funding. Visit www.hpu.edu/financialaid for current Financial Aid and Scholarship information.

HILLSDALE COLLEGE

AT A GLANCE

Hillsdale College is a private, coeducational, nonsectarian institution of higher learning founded in 1844 by men and women "grateful to God for the inestimable blessings resulting from the prevalence of civil and religious liberty and intelligent piety in the land, and believing that the diffusion of sound learning is essential to the perpetuity of these blessings." The College maintains independence from direct and indirect state and federal government aid. Far-reaching private support from a national constituency has enabled Hillsdale to continue its trusteeship of the intellectual and spiritual inheritance derived from the Judeo-Christian faiths and Greco-Roman cultures.

The undergraduate enrollment for fall 2012 was 1,400, of whom 47 percent were men. The College draws students from 47 states and 8 foreign countries. Approximately 40 percent of students are from Michigan. The entering freshman class in 2012 had an average high school grade-point average of 3.81 and mean test scores—ACT 29 and SAT 1980—well above the national averages.

The Hillsdale faculty is in a 10-to-1 ratio to students and is comprised of 117 full-time members. Each student has a faculty advisor for core and major coursework who directs the program of study and provides academic and career counseling. While teaching is their first priority, faculty members also engage in research and scholarly writing supported by summer and sabbatical leaves funded by the College, and are often invited to comment on the national scene.

Special student services provided by the College include a career services office, academic tutoring, and a health service staffed by a physician and a resident nurse.

LOCATION AND ENVIRONMENT

Located in rural southern Michigan, the nearly 400-acre stately Hillsdale College campus includes both modern and historic buildings. The Indiana and Ohio turnpikes are each 30 minutes away, and the College is within close reach of metropolitan areas as large as Detroit and Chicago. The town of Hillsdale is a county seat with a population of 10,000. Stores, churches, restaurants and movie theaters are all within walking distance of the campus.

OFF-CAMPUS OPPORTUNITIES

For 40 years, the Washington Hillsdale Internship Program (WHIP) has provided students the opportunity to participate in full-time, academically intensive internships in the nation's capital. The program has been significantly bolstered with the 2008 establishment of the Hillsdale College Allan P. Kirby, Jr. Center for Constitutional Studies and Citizenship in Washington, D.C. In addition to study opportunities in D.C., Hillsdale students also take advantage of programs in England with Oxford University and Regent's College, as well as the University of St. Andrews in Scotland. Science students benefit from Hillsdale's 685-acre field research laboratory in northern Michigan, as well as from a marine biology program in the Florida Keys, internship opportunities with the Omaha Zoo, and a summer research program in South Africa. Foreign language students frequently study abroad in Argentina, France, Germany, and Spain.

MAJORS AND DEGREES OFFERED

Hillsdale awards Bachelor of Arts and Bachelor of Science degrees in accounting, art, biochemistry, biology, chemistry, classical studies, computational mathematics, economics, education, English, exercise science, financial management, French, German, Greek, history, Latin, marketing/management, mathematics, music, philosophy, physical education, physics, politics, psychology, religion, Spanish, speech, sport management, sport psychology and theatre. Interdisciplinary majors in American studies, Christian studies, comparative literature, European studies, international studies in business and foreign language, political economy, and sociology and social thought are also available. Pre-professional programs are offered in allied health services (including optometry, physical therapy, nursing, and medical technology), dentistry, engineering, environmental sciences, forestry, law, medicine, osteopathy, theology, and veterinary medicine. Hillsdale also offers 2-2 and 3-2 cooperative programs in engineering.

ACADEMIC PROGRAMS

Hillsdale operates on a two-semester schedule. Two three-week summer sessions are also offered.

The College believes that a sound classical liberal arts education includes study in the humanities, natural sciences and social sciences, and each student is required to complete a structured core of courses in these areas. All students declare a major by the end of the sophomore year. To graduate, students must complete at minimum 124 hours of course work and fulfill the requirements of at least one major field. Each baccalaureate program is based on the completion of four years of study in the liberal arts. The B.A. program includes a foreign language proficiency requirement. The B.S. program requires additional studies in mathematics and the natural sciences.

The Honors Program enables exceptionally talented students interested in an interdisciplinary community of learning to develop their intellectual potential through an accelerated college core and Honors seminars in the junior and senior years. Discussions, guest lectures and travel opportunities contribute to the social cohesiveness of the group. All Honors students complete a senior thesis on an interdisciplinary topic of their choosing.

The Center for Constructive Alternatives conducts four weeklong symposia during the academic year and is one of the largest college lecture series in America. Each brings to the campus distinguished scholars and public figures of national and international renown in a diverse range of fields. All students are required to enroll in two full seminars for credit prior to graduation.

CAMPUS FACILITIES

The Hillsdale College Mossey Library maintains a collection of more than 952,000 volumes. In addition to the main study and research collections, the Library also contains a number of rare and special holdings. Connected to other Michigan libraries through MelCat, and with college libraries nationwide via interlibrary loan, students have access to most any material necessary for on-campus research.

Lane and Kendall Halls at the front of campus serve as the primary academic facilities in the humanities and contain classroom space and faculty offices, as well as a special laboratory for experimental psychology. The Strosacker Science Center houses the departments of biology, chemistry and physics. The Joseph H. Moss Family Laboratory Wing, completed in 2008, is a 17,000-square-foot addition that includes a microbiology/cell biology lab, anatomy/physiology lab with human cadaver access, conservation genetics lab, water lab, greenhouse, and organic/general chemistry labs. The 32,000-square-foot Herbert Henry Dow Science Building provides additional classrooms, research laboratories and a computer lab. The Mary Randall Preschool is a circular laboratory school in which nursery school children are taught by students specializing in early childhood education and psychology. The Hillsdale Academy, a K–12 private model school, provides additional opportunities for classroom observation.

The Roche Sports Complex is a facility available to varsity athletes and the general student body alike. The building houses the 60,000-square-foot Jesse Philips Arena, which features a six-lane, 200-meter running track and basketball/volleyball court. The building also houses the John "Jack" McAvoy Natatorium, a combination pool/diving area; an exercise physiology and sports medicine facility; three racquetball courts; extensive locker room space; and a weight/fitness room. Adjacent is the 7,000-seat capacity Frank "Muddy" Waters Stadium, which features a Pro Grass Artificial Surface football field and all-weather, Olympic-quality Mondo™ eight-lane running track, along with outdoor tennis courts and fields for soccer, baseball and women's softball. The new Margot V. Biermann Athletic Center houses a six-lane track and four tennis courts.

The Sage Center for the Arts is home to the departments of art, theatre and speech. This 47,000-square-foot facility contains studios, classroom space, an exhibition gallery, a prop and scene-construction shop, a sound studio, a dance studio, graphics lab, Black Box theatre, and Markel Auditorium, a 353-seat performance hall (with orchestra pit). Completed in 2003, the 32,809-square-foot Howard Music Hall houses office, studio, classroom, rehearsal and performance space for the John E.N. and Dede Howard Department of Music. Notable features include the McNamara Rehearsal Hall, Conrad Recital Hall, and studio space for percussion and jazz studies. Lower-level practice rooms are available to students during business hours without reservation.

Dedicated in January 2008, the 53,000-square-foot Grewcock Student Union is the center of student life. The two-story structure houses the cafeteria, bookstore, student mail center, offices for student activities and publications, a 100" flat screen television lounge, formal lounge and conference room, AJ's Café, and game area. The entire building is wireless, and any student with an ID can check out a laptop at the main desk.

Tuition, Room, Board & Fees

Annual tuition for 2012-13 academic year is $21,390, room is $4,290, board is $4,350, and mandatory fees are $540. Books, supplies, and personal expenses (including travel, recreation, and clothing) are estimated at $3,000 per year.

FINANCIAL AID

Financial aid at Hillsdale is available in many forms. Academic scholarships are awarded on a competitive basis; the application for admission also serves as the application for merit-based aid. The priority deadline for academic scholarship consideration is January 1. Athletic scholarships are also available on a competitive basis in men's baseball and football, men's and women's basketball, track and cross-country, and women's swimming and volleyball. The departments of art and music award a select number of scholarships based on strength of portfolio/audition. To apply for aid on the basis of financial need, students are required to file Hillsdale's Confidential Family Financial Statement (CFFS) in January or February of the year of prospective enrollment at Hillsdale. Grants and loans are available from the College. Students may defer payment of up to $500 per semester while working on campus.

STUDENT ORGANIZATIONS AND ACTIVITIES

Hillsdale's Charger athletes compete in 12 intercollegiate NCAA Division II varsity sports as part of the Great Lakes Intercollegiate Athletic Conference (GLIAC). Since 1998, the College has produced 94 athletic All-Americans and 28 conference champions, and Hillsdale teams have qualified for national tournaments 17 times. Thirty-one athletes have earned national academic honors in their respective sports as well. An active intramural program is also available. Four national fraternities, three national sororities, and more than 70 other social, academic, spiritual and service organizations provide Hillsdale students with a diverse array of co-curricular opportunities. A resident drama troupe and dance company, a concert choir and chamber chorale, a jazz program with big band and combos, instrumental chamber ensembles from string quartets to percussion ensemble, and a College-community orchestra and band constitute the College's performing arts organizations.

ADMISSIONS PROCESS

Admission is a privilege extended to students who will benefit from and contribute to the academic, social and spiritual environments of the College. Students may apply any time after the completion of the junior year of high school. A formal application includes a completed application form, writing samples in the form of essays, a resume of extra-curricular activities, official score reports from the ACT or SAT examination, official transcripts from high schools and colleges from which students have received academic credit, two letters of recommendation, and a nonrefundable application fee of $35 (free if submitted online). An on-campus interview is highly encouraged. Application plans include Early Decision (November 15), Early Action (December 15), and Regular Decision (February 15). Hillsdale College has been distinguished since its founding by voluntarily adhering to a nondiscriminatory policy regarding race, religion, sex, and national or ethnic origin—long before the government began regulating such matters. Transfer applications are evaluated similarly to non-transfers; students must submit a transfer form from the Dean of Students at the college most recently attended. International applicants follow regular entrance procedures in addition to demonstrating a proficiency in English by satisfactory performance on the Test of English as a Foreign Language (TOEFL) or the Michigan Test of English Proficiency.

All records and forms should be directed to:

Admissions Office

Hillsdale College

33 E. College Street

Hillsdale, Michigan 49242-1298

United States

Phone: (517) 607-2327

Fax: (517) 607-2223

E-mail: admissions@hillsdale.edu

Online: hillsdale.edu

HOFSTRA UNIVERSITY

AT A GLANCE

At Hofstra University, our students learn and grow on a campus that offers engaging classes, exceptional facilities and resources, dedicated faculty, and a supportive network of peers and mentors. We inspire students to discover their strengths and find their passion through career-enhancing, life-shaping experiences. At Hofstra, students find opportunity, pride and purpose.

A UNIVERSITY OF DISTINCTION

Hofstra University is the largest private college on Long Island, New York. Since its founding in 1935, Hofstra has evolved into an internationally renowned university that continues to achieve recognition as an institution of academic excellence. Hofstra is consistently recognized on the Best College lists of U.S. News & World Report, The Princeton Review, Fiske, Washington Monthly, and Forbes.

Among other private Long Island colleges, Hofstra is the only university that grants the Phi Beta Kappa distinction, and it has the largest number of students and professionals going on to pursue graduate and postgraduate programs of study. In addition to the myriad opportunities available on Hofstra's lively campus, students benefit from easy access to the academic, cultural, media and career opportunities of nearby New York City.

AND THAT'S NOT ALL.

The Hofstra North Shore-LIJ School of Medicine at Hofstra University welcomed its second class of students in August 2012. Incoming medical school students train as emergency medical technicians by working shifts on North Shore-LIJ Health System ambulances.

In addition, Hofstra recently established a School of Engineering and Applied Science with an innovative co-op and cross-disciplinary education program, and a School of Health Sciences and Human Services dedicated to educating students to become effective and compassionate clinicians, evidence-based practitioners, policy makers, managers and advocates who promote health equity.

THE BEST AND BRIGHTEST

Every day on Hofstra's vibrant campus, our students enrich, enlighten and challenge one another, both inside and outside the classroom. Hofstra's diverse and driven student body of more than 11,000 – who come from 50 U.S. states and territories and more than 60 countries – bring with them a wealth of knowledge, views and experiences, thus enhancing the Hofstra experience for the entire campus community. And with an average undergraduate class size of 21 and a student-to-faculty ratio of 14-to-1, Hofstra students are challenged and encouraged to debate, question, research, discuss and think critically in an open and broad-minded learning environment.

Our hardworking, ambitious students are taught by Guggenheim Fellows and Fulbright scholars; Emmy Award recipients; prize-winning scientists; leaders in business, education and the health sciences; and knowledgeable and insightful thinkers. Our 1,135 faculty members, of whom 517 are full-time, are experts in their fields and are dedicated to and focused on providing the foundation and tools you need to succeed. Hofstra's faculty affirm the value of education – 93 percent of our full-time faculty hold the highest degree attainable in their fields. Plus, unlike many other schools, students at Hofstra learn from faculty – not graduate students.

DIVERSE ACADEMIC OFFERINGS ... ONE JUST FOR YOU

Hofstra students can discover their strengths and find their passions in about 140 undergraduate program options in liberal arts and sciences, business, engineering and applied science, communication, education, and health sciences and human services. At Hofstra, students can explore majors as diverse as criminology, engineering science, Hebrew, music performance, physician assistant studies, urban ecology, film studies/production, finance, and community health. In addition, Hofstra offers more than 100 dual degree programs, including the B.A.-B.S./M.D., B.A./J.D. and Physician Assistant Studies programs , giving you the opportunity to earn both a graduate and undergraduate degree in less time than if each degree was pursued separately – while saving the cost of one or more semesters of tuition.

Explore the possibilities at hofstra.edu/academics or hofstra.edu/dualdegree

PROGRAM OPTIONS

Accounting; African Studies; American Studies; Anthropology; Applied Physics; Art History; Asian Studies; Athletic Training; Biochemistry; Biology – Cell and Molecular; Ecology and Evolution; Marine; Pre-Allied Medical Professions; Pre-Dental; Pre-Medical/Pre-Health; Pre-Veterinary; Secondary Education; Business Economics; Chemistry; Chinese; Chinese Studies; Classics; Community Health; Comparative Literature and Languages; Computer Engineering; Computer Science; Computer Science and Mathematics (dual major); Criminology; Dance; Dance Education; Drama; Early Childhood and Childhood Education (with dual major in liberal arts discipline); Early Childhood Education (with dual major in liberal arts discipline); Economics; Electrical Engineering; Elementary Education (with dual major in liberal arts discipline); Engineering Science – Biomedical; Civil; Production and Manufacturing; English – Creative Writing and Literature; English and American Literature; Publishing Studies and Literature; English Education (with dual major in liberal arts discipline); Entrepreneurship; Environmental Resources; Exercise Science; Film Studies and Production; Finance; Fine Arts – Ceramics; Design; Painting; Photography; Sculpture-Industrial Design; Fine Arts Education; Foreign Language Education – French; German; Italian; Russian; Spanish (with dual major in liberal arts discipline); Forensic Science; French; Geography; Geology; German; Global Studies; Health Education; Health Science; Hebrew; History; Ibero-American Studies; Individually Designed Major; Industrial Engineering; Information Technology; International Business; Italian; Jewish Studies; Journalism; Labor Studies; Latin; Latin American and Caribbean Studies; Legal Studies in Business; Liberal Arts; Linguistics; Management; Mass Media Studies; Mathematical Business Economics; Mathematical Economics; Mathematics – Mathematics; Actuarial Science; Applied Mathematics; Chemistry; Computer Science; Engineering; Physics; Mathematics Education (with dual major in liberal arts discipline); Mechanical Engineering; Music – History/Literature; Jazz and Commercial Music; Music Merchandising; Performance; Theory and Composition; Music Education (with dual major in liberal arts discipline); Philosophy; Physical Education; Physics; Political Science; Psychology; Public Relations; Radio Production and Studies; Religion; Russian; Science Education – Biology; Chemistry; Geology; Physics (with dual major in liberal arts discipline); Social Studies Education (with dual major in liberal arts discipline); Sociology; Spanish; Speech Communication and Rhetorical Studies; Speech-Language-Hearing Sciences; STEM (Science, Technology, Engineering and Math) as co-major for Elementary Education; Supply Chain Management; Sustainability Studies; Theater Arts – Performance Sequence; Production Sequence; Urban Ecology; Video/Television; Video/Television and Business; Video/Television and Film; Women's Studies; Where You'll Learn and Grow

Hofstra University, which blends longstanding traditions with 21st-century resources, is home to both ivy-covered classroom buildings and modern, elegant facilities. On our campus, you will find exceptional and technologically advanced classrooms, six theaters, a state-of-the-art fitness center, an accredited museum, modern athletic facilities, and an impressive 10-floor library that offers nearly one-million print volumes and 24/7 electronic access to more than 125,000 journals and books.

C.V. Starr Hall, home to the Frank G. Zarb School of Business, features the Martin B. Greenberg Trading Room, which has the largest number of Bloomberg Professional terminals among all academic trading rooms in the United States and around the world. The School of Communication's Dempster Hall contains one of the largest broadcast facilities in the northeastern United States as well as a converged newsroom and multimedia classroom. Plus, our students benefit from real-world experience at our on-campus radio station, WRHU 88.7FM (Radio Hofstra University), which has a 35-mile broadcast range and is webcast at wrhu.org. Hagedorn Hall, where the School of Education is located, features a technologically robust learning environment complete with interactive whiteboards, computer-driven instructor stations and wireless communication.

The David S. Mack Sports and Exhibition Complex, a 93,000-square-foot facility, is home to the Hofstra Pride men's and women's basketball teams and wrestling, and is also the site for events such as commencements, exhibitions, trade shows, televised political events, and concerts. Other recreational and athletic facilities include an indoor, Olympic-sized swimming pool, and various athletic fields.

Here at Hofstra, it's all about choice. Students may choose to live and learn in one of our 37 residence halls, each with a unique flair, community and life of its own. We also offer eight living/learning communities, which give students the opportunity to live with many of the same students they are in classes with, and well as students who share the same passion for leadership, health sciences, or the visual or performing arts. In addition, Hofstra students can choose from 18 on-campus dining facilities, including Starbucks, Nathan's, Subway, and Au Bon Pain, as well as sushi and vegetarian and kosher options. It's no wonder our students view Hofstra as their "home away from home."

MUCH MORE THAN ACADEMICS

Hofstra students are engaged, driven and motivated, and we provide them with the knowledge, experiences and opportunities they need to grow academically, personally and professionally.

Hofstra University hosts hundreds of social, academic and cultural events each year, drawing together scholars, business leaders, authors, celebrities, health care professionals, politicians, and journalists from across the nation and around the world. These events help foster that connection between in-classroom work and extracurricular interests we know you're looking for. In addition, Hofstra offers 17 intercollegiate athletic programs that compete at the NCAA Division I level and more than 200 academic, fraternal/sororal, media, multicultural, performance, pre-professional, religious, social, social/political, and sports clubs and organizations. You can join clubs as diverse as Organization of Commuter Students, Accounting Society, Nonsense humor magazine, The Pride Network, Hofstra Quidditch and Ski Snowboard Club. Exciting and enriching experiences beyond the classroom ... there's definitely something for everyone.

SUCCESSFUL ALUMNI IN VIRTUALLY EVERY FIELD

At Hofstra, you will join a network of almost 124,000 graduates. Our outstanding alumni include Academy Award-winning film director and producer Francis Ford Coppola; best-selling author Nelson DeMille; vascular surgeon Dr. Donna Mendes; president of the New York Yankees Randy Levine; from Everybody Loves Raymond, creator, executive producer and writer Philip Rosenthal and actress Monica Horan; president of H.J. Kalikow & Company and former MTA chairman Peter S. Kalikow; actresses Lainie Kazan and Susan Sullivan; and New York State Comptroller Thomas P. DiNapoli. These prominent and successful individuals began their life's work here at Hofstra. You can too.

A WORLD OF RESOURCES ... A WORLD OF OPPORTUNITY

At Hofstra, we provide students with the tools they need to reach their career aspirations. Each year, Hofstra is visited by more than 400 employers who recognize just how much our students have to offer. In addition to the plentiful networking opportunities on campus, you may choose to do an internship at a top company on Long Island or in New York City, thus gaining critical work experience that will give you an edge in a competitive job market.

And we will help you at every turn. The Career Center, just one example of the world-class resources here at Hofstra, provides students and alumni with professional programs and services such as career-related workshops, counseling, job/internship search coaching, and networking events. All this doesn't start at graduation – it begins the moment you step onto campus.

APPLYING TO HOFSTRA

Hofstra University seeks to enroll talented first-year and transfer students from diverse backgrounds and locations, with varied interests. Applications are accepted for fall and spring admission. The Admission Committee reviews each application individually to assess academic achievement, curricular rigor, leadership potential, depth of extracurricular activities, standardized test scores and overall interest in attending Hofstra University. The application process provides an opportunity for the applicant to share information that may not be apparent on a transcript or through a test score. For more information about the admission process, visit hofstra.edu/admission

SEE FOR YOURSELF

Opportunity, knowledge, and confidence. Hofstra offers all you want and need from the college experience. We invite you to visit and explore our dynamic campus. See the energy, focus and drive of our students. Meet our award-winning and prestigious faculty. Your journey begins at hofstra.edu.

HUNTER COLLEGE (CITY UNIVERSITY OF NEW YORK)

AT A GLANCE

Hunter College is a liberal arts college serving over 21,000 undergraduate and graduate students of all racial, ethnic, and cultural backgrounds. Wide offerings in the liberal arts and sciences and three professional schools—education, health sciences, and social work, makes Hunter the largest senior college in the CUNY system.

LOCATION AND ENVIRONMENT

Located on the Upper East Side in New York City, Hunter College has been in existence since 1870, long enough to have the nearby subway station named after it. With such easy access to every museum, theater, library, business, and cultural resource in New York City, it's no wonder that Hunter College students regularly intern at places like the Metropolitan Museum of Art and CNN, as well as city and state government offices.

OFF-CAMPUS OPPORTUNITIES

Hunter College taps Manhattan to allow innumerable internships. Hosts have included Atlantic Records, CNN, the Council on Foreign Relations, DreamWorks SKG, Madison Square Garden, Metropolitan Museum of Art, New York City Council, Simon & Schuster, and many more. Interns perform curatorial and administrative work in museums, research and production work on TV news shows and newspapers, design work in commercial graphics, and booking, managing, and technical work in theaters.

MAJORS AND DEGREES OFFERED

Hunter College offers bachelor's and master's degrees in the arts and sciences, education, health professions, nursing, and social work, along with several combined (B.A./M.A. or B.A./M.S.) degrees. The following programs of study are available: accounting, Africana and Puerto Rican/Latino studies, anthropology, archaeology, art history, biological sciences, chemistry, Chinese language and literature, classical studies, community health education, comparative literature, computer science, dance, economics, elementary education, environmental studies, English, English language arts, film, French, geography, German, Greek, Hebrew, history, honors curriculum, Italian, Jewish social studies, Latin, Latin American and Caribbean Studies, Latin and Greek, mathematics, media studies, medical laboratory sciences, music, nursing, nutrition and food science, philosophy, physics, political science, psychology, religion, Romance languages, Russian, secondary education, sociology, Spanish, statistics, studio art, theater, urban studies, and women's studies. Secondary education programs are for grades 7–12 unless otherwise noted and include biology, chemistry, Chinese, dance (pre-K–12), English, French, German, Hebrew, Italian, mathematics, music (pre-K–12, accelerated B.A./M.A. program only), physics, Russian, social studies, and Spanish.

Special programs in anthropology, biological sciences/environmental and occupational health sciences, biopharmacology, biotechnology, economics, English, history, mathematics, music, physics, sociology/social research, and statistics and applied mathematics lead to the combined bachelor's/master's degree, enabling highly qualified students to earn both degrees more quickly.

Hunter College also provides pre-professional advisement and preparation for advanced study in chiropractic, dentistry, engineering, law, medicine, optometry, osteopathy, pharmacy, podiatry, and veterinary medicine.

ACADEMIC PROGRAMS

Hunter instills a rich and informed sense of the possibilities of humanity in its students and expects them to carry their liberal arts education forward in their careers, their public responsibilities, and their personal lives.

The College trains its students in the sciences, the humanities, and a number of professional fields. As they strive to achieve their career goals, students are expected to perceive their chosen fields of study as only a part of a wider realm of knowledge. Undergraduate programs of study at Hunter consist of five parts, totaling 120 credits: a general education requirement, a pluralism and diversity requirement, a concentration of in-depth study and elective courses.

Undergraduate students at Hunter who exhibit intellectual curiosity and exceptional ability may apply to the Thomas Hunter Scholars Program, an interdisciplinary program that individualizes study according to needs and interests and grants a Bachelor of Arts degree.

Students may earn sophomore standing (up to 30 credits) if they score well on the College-Level Examination Program (CLEP) subject tests, the Advanced Placement examinations of the College Board, and the Regents College Examination (RCE) Program of New York State.

CAMPUS FACILITIES AND EQUIPMENT

The College is made up of five sites in Manhattan. The largest, a modern complex of buildings connected by skywalks at 68th Street and Lexington Avenue, sits above a convenient subway stop. This campus offers programs in the arts and sciences and in teacher education.

Our Brookdale Campus is located downtown on East 25th Street and houses the Division of the Schools of the Health Professions, which includes the Hunter-Bellevue School of Nursing, one of the nation's largest nursing programs, and the School of Health Sciences.

Uptown on East 119th Street is the Silberman School of Social Work at Hunter College. This campus also encompasses Hunter's programs in Public Health, Nutrition and Community Health. Downtown, on Manhattan's West Side, Hunter's brand new Studio Art Building houses a 7,000-square-foot gallery and provides M.F.A. students with individual studios that are among the best in the city.

At East 94th Street, the Campus Schools house an elementary school and a high school for the intellectually gifted that are renowned, as is the College itself, for a long tradition of academic excellence.

The collections of the Hunter College libraries are housed in the Jacqueline Grennan Wexler Library and the Art Slide Library (located at the main campus), as well as at the branch libraries at the Brookdale Campus and the School of Social Work. The libraries hold 750,000 volumes, 2,300 periodicals, a nonprint collection of more than 1 million microforms, and 250,000 art slides in addition to records, tapes, scores, music CDs, and videos. Recently, Hunter installed new computer, multimedia, and Internet labs and its first CD-ROM network. The CD-ROM network provides access to indexes, abstracts, and complete texts and multimedia resources, and Internet labs make the World Wide Web accessible.

Our sports complex features two large gyms, a fitness and weight training room, a combative gym for martial arts and wrestling, 5 racquetball courts, a pool and an aerobics and fencing studio.

TUITION, ROOM, BOARD, AND FEES

Hunter College is affordable. In 2112, New York State residents enrolled as full-time, matriculated students paid $2865 per semester ($245 per credit part-time). Nonresidents enrolled as full-time, matriculated students paid $510 per credit. All students paid a Student Activity Fee ($84.50 per semester for full-time students and $54.45 per semester for part-time students) and a $15-per-semester Consolidated Fee.

FINANCIAL AID

Hunter College participates in all state and federal financial aid programs. Financial aid is available to matriculated students in the form of grants, loans, and work-study. Grants provide funds that do not have to be repaid. Loans must be repaid in regular installments over a prescribed period of time. Work-study consists of part-time employment, either on campus or in an outside agency. More information is available from the Office of Financial Aid at 212-772-4820.

Entering freshmen whose high school records indicate a high level of academic achievement may apply to the CUNY Honors College at Hunter College. This prestigious program offers a generous financial aid package, including a full academic scholarship, as well as extensive benefits, including a free room at the Hunter College Residence Hall. In addition, other scholarships are offered.

STUDENT ORGANIZATIONS AND ACTIVITIES

Hunter College has a thriving student life, with over 100 chartered clubs, Greek letter organizations, and a student government that is actively involved in both college and New York City issues. Hunter has its own radio station and diverse publications, including the Envoy, the college's student newspaper for the last 50-odd years.

ADMISSIONS PROCESS

Hunter's profile for the Fall 2012 was the following:

Average high school academic grade point average: 88.7

Average SAT Score: 1220 (Math & Verbal only)

All applicants must fill out a CUNY application, which must be filed online. Any personal computer or laptop can be used to complete the online application. The website to begin the process is http://www.cuny.edu/admissions/apply.html

The deadlines are as follows: Fall Deadline: February 1 and Spring Deadline: September 15 Iona College

IONA COLLEGE

AT A GLANCE

Located on 45 acres just 20 miles north of Midtown Manhattan in the suburb of New Rochelle, N.Y., Iona was founded by the Congregation of Christian Brothers in 1940. Iona has just over 3,000 degree-seeking undergraduate students and a total campus population of roughly 3,800. Housing is guaranteed for students during their four years of study, and there are five residence halls on campus, along with one apartment complex. Approximately 1,300 total students reside on campus, including 70 percent of the first-year class. As part of the College's mission statement, students are encouraged to integrate the spiritual, intellectual, emotional and physical dimensions of their lives and are immersed in a community where ethical decisions and service to others are primary considerations. Approximately 28 percent of the undergraduate student body represents diversity.

ACADEMICS

Iona College is one of the most highly accredited colleges in the state of New York and holds several prestigious national accreditations in business (AACSB), social work (CSWE), teacher education (NCATE), computer science (ABET), journalism and mass communication (ACEJMC), psychology (NASP), chemistry (ACS) and marriage and family therapy (COAMFTE). In addition, Iona's Samuel Rudin Academic Resource Center is accredited by the National Tutoring Association and by the College Reading and Learning Association.

Iona College offers more than 45 undergraduate majors (BA, BS and BBA degrees), over 35 minors, and more than 30 graduate programs. An honors program is available for the most academically gifted students -- the course of study is designed to develop intellectual curiosity, analytic abilities, and awareness of ethical and civic responsibilities. The faculty/student ratio is 15:1 and classes are taught by professors, never teaching assistants. Ninety percent of Iona's professors have earned the highest degree in their field, and 76 percent of classes have fewer than 30 students. Combined five-year bachelor's/master's programs are available in computer science, criminal justice, English, history, psychology, chemistry/education and chemistry/computer science. A fast-track MBA program is structured to enable students to earn the degree in 13-15 months.

ADMISSIONS

Prospective students benefit from the services of a personal admissions counselor and a personal financial aid counselor. Admission decisions at Iona are based on a wide range of criteria. Most important is an applicant's academic record including the level of curriculum and grades earned. Also considered are SAT I or ACT scores, grade trends, a writing sample, activities and recommendations. Iona has a non-binding Early Action program (applications due December 1) and a preferred regular admissions date of February 15, but does review first-year applications through at least May 1. Campus visits are available on most weekdays and on selected Saturdays; appointments are recommended. Campus Visit Days and other special visit programs, are offered on a regular basis. To schedule a visit, please contact our Campus Visit Center at (914) 633-2622 or visit www.iona.edu/visit.

CAMPUS FACILITIES AND EQUIPMENT

In recent years, Iona College has undertaken an ambitious multi-million dollar renovation and building campaign that has transformed the campus. East Hall, a new residence hall, was dedicated in fall 2012. The campus features four dining areas, two libraries and two gyms. The newly dedicated LaPenta-Lynch Trading Floor in the Hagan School of Business was dedicated in October 2011. An expanded and renovated main library -- with multimedia seminar room, group study facilities, digital archive room, classrooms with dual-boot Apple computers, Smartboards and other interactive equipment, and refurbished auditorium -- opened in fall 2009. The Hynes Athletics Center has seen new construction and updates, including modern workout equipment, an aerobic/dance studio, a pool, rowing tank and more. Other new residence halls, an arts center and student union -- with a radio station, extensive room for clubs, comfortable lounges, bookstore, a food court and café -- complete the recent changes.

CAMPUS LIFE

The Office of Student Development organizes and oversees hundreds of on- and off-campus events throughout the year, and students can participate in more than 80 student-run organizations. Iona College encourages students to broaden their educational experience through study abroad and sponsors summer, semester and intersession programs in Australia, England, France, Ireland, Italy and Spain. Campus Ministries provides multiple opportunities for students to engage in service and ministry projects, while Iona in Mission offers students the chance to travel to aid the less fortunate in the United States and abroad. The College has a vibrant athletics program with more than 400 student-athletes in Iona's 21 NCAA Division I teams in the Metro Atlantic Athletic Conference (MAAC).

COLLEGE BASICS

Iona College is a diverse community of learners and scholars dedicated to academic excellence in the tradition of the Christian Brothers and American Catholic Higher Education.

LOCATION AND ENVIRONMENT

Iona is located just 20 miles north of Midtown Manhattan and two miles from the shore of the Long Island Sound and its many parks, and provides students with exceptional cultural, educational, internship and career opportunities. Recruiters from top Fortune 500 companies participate in Iona's Internship/Career Expo every year and students have held internships at some of the best-known corporations in New York City and the surrounding area.

MAJORS AND DEGREES

Iona College offers over 45 majors and over 35 minors including accounting, biochemistry, biology (general, pre-professional), business administration, chemistry, computer science, criminal justice, economics, education (childhood, adolescence), English, environmental science, environmental studies, finance, foreign languages (French, Italian, Spanish), history, information systems, interdisciplinary studies, interdisciplinary science, international business, international studies, management, marketing, mass communication (advertising, journalism, public relations, TV/video), mathematics, philosophy, physics, political science, psychology, public policy, religious studies, social work, sociology, speech communication studies, and speech/language pathology and audiology. Combined five-year bachelor's/master's programs are available in computer science, criminal justice, English, history, psychology, chemistry/education and chemistry/computer science. Pre-professional dental, medicine, physical therapy and veterinary programs are available in conjunction with a selected major. Additional minors include film studies, fine and performing arts, peace and justice studies, pre-law, sports and entertainment studies, women's studies, and writing. A number of programs offer a business minor.

On the graduate level, the College offers Master of Arts, Science and Business Administration degrees as well as certificates and post-master's/advanced certificates. Graduate students in the School of Arts and Science can choose to study computer science, counseling (experimental/industrial and organizational; mental health counseling; school psychology; and marriage and family therapy), criminal justice, education (teaching, literacy education, educational leadership, educational technology), English, history, psychology, public relations and Spanish. Through the AACSB-accredited Hagan School of Business, students seeking to earn an MBA can concentrate on financial management, information systems, management, human resource management, marketing, general accounting, public accounting and health care management. Master of Science programs are available in accounting, finance, financial services and international finance.

Advanced certificates in business continuity and risk management, sports and entertainment management, infrastructure management, e-commerce, health care information systems, health care management, long-term care services, general and public accounting, project management and international business are offered.

OFF-CAMPUS OPPORTUNITIES

Students are encouraged to attend events and in Westchester County and in nearby New York City, where entertainment, sporting, cultural and internship opportunities abound. With the creation of the Office of Off-Campus Housing, programs have been created to involve and inform neighbors about student initiatives and events. The Center for Campus Ministries actively seeks student involvement for its outreach programs such as partnerships with Habitat for Humanity, Project Sunshine, Midnight Runs and more.

TUITION AND FEES

Undergraduate tuition and fees for the 2013-2014 academic year is $32,770. Room and board is an additional $13,175.

FINANCIAL AID

Iona offers academic scholarships in combination with need-based financial aid to help make a private education affordable. Merit scholarship consideration is part of the standard admissions process, with no separate scholarship application required. Honors Program candidates may apply for additional scholarships, and athletes are considered for athletic awards in consultation with the coaching staff. Sibling and alumni legacy programs are also available, as our scholarships for the College's award-winning pipe band. For 2011-2012 academic year, 94 percent of undergraduates received some financial aid. To apply for financial aid, students must file the Free Application for Federal Student Aid (FAFSA).

JOHNS HOPKINS UNIVERSITY

AT A GLANCE

The Johns Hopkins undergraduate experience is all about exploration and discovery, for all students in every major.

Ever since its founding in 1876, Johns Hopkins has made the undergraduate experience all about exploration and discovery. We believe in learning through hands-on investigation for anyone in any major. Our students work in every discipline and with every subject imaginable, from Beowulf to bioengineering. And they do it all with the resources of Baltimore and Washington, D.C., at their fingertips, from the comfort of an active and close-knit campus community. You'll have the opportunity to make your own discoveries and receive the guidance you need to get there: in groups; through faculty mentorships; and through internships, study abroad, and the cultural connections of one of the most exciting cities around.

ACADEMICS

Classes are small here, and the resources are big. That means you get to know your professors and classmates the way you would at a small liberal arts college, but you have all of the opportunities of a major research institution with a global reach, right at your fingertips as an undergraduate. Many students complete independent projects with professors, mentors, and teams. Lots more take advantage of study abroad, internships, semesters in Washington, D.C., and advanced graduate study. Johns Hopkins has schools, centers, and affiliates all over the Baltimore area—and they are often linked by free shuttle bus—in Washington, D.C., across the country, and around the world. Cross registration, independent projects, and internships are all encouraged options. Several generous awards—such as the Provost's Undergraduate Research Awards and the Woodrow Wilson Undergraduate Research Fellowships—are available to give participants the chance to complete projects of their own design under the guidance of a faculty mentor. Instead of a rigid core of compulsory courses, Johns Hopkins leaves you free to concentrate on what you love, or to explore more broadly. Academic and faculty advisers, career advisers, and pre-professional advisers help you chart the waters.

ADMISSIONS

Each year we review more than 20,000 applications, from which we must select a freshman class of around 1,250. Also each year, we welcome transfer students from other colleges and universities. Transfer students apply for entrance during their sophomore or junior years. Each application we receive represents an individual, and the Admissions Committee considers each one individually. High school students should inquire by the fall term of senior year and complete and submit applications by January 1 (by November 1 for Early Decision). We accept both the Universal College Application and the Common Application; both require a Johns Hopkins supplement. To apply, complete either application and the Johns Hopkins supplement and submit them as soon as possible, but no later than the deadline, with your $70 nonrefundable application fee. Supporting materials may be received at any time up until the application deadline. Essays and two teacher recommendations are also required parts of the application. Visit http://apply.jhu.edu/apply/application.htmlfor detailed information about the application process.

PLEASE NOTE this important policy: Students wishing to enroll in the biomedical engineering (BME) major must indicate BME as their first-choice major on their application. Students are admitted specifically into the BME major, based on evaluation of credentials and space available. Students can be admitted to the university without acceptance to the BME major. No separate application is required. Notification of acceptance into the BME major is given at the time of decision notification.

STANDARDIZED TEST REQUIREMENTS

Applicants must submit scores from all SAT tests, including Subject Tests, or ACT tests taken. For freshmen, the SAT Reasoning Test or the ACT with Writing Test are required. For those submitting SAT scores, Johns Hopkins strongly encourages submitting SAT Subject Test scores, and if submitted, requests results from three tests. For transfer students, SAT Reasoning Test scores are optional; SAT Subject Tests are not required. For international students, the TOEFL is required of applicants who do not speak English at home AND have not attended an English-language school for five years or longer. All other international applicants are not required to submit TOEFL scores but may do so to supplement their application.

Applicants should score a minimum of 600 (written test) or 250 (computer test). Applicants taking the Internet-based TOEFL (iBT) should have minimum sub-scores of 26 (Reading), 26 (Listening), 22 (Writing), and 25 (Speaking). A Critical Reading SAT score of 670 or higher waives for the TOEFL requirement for all students.

CAMPUS FACILITIES AND EQUIPMENT

Student life is centered around the 140 acres of the Homewood campus. A park-like setting within the city of Baltimore, our campus has had many renovations in recent years. The Mattin Center offers space for student groups and artistic endeavors. The center features a theater, café, art studios, darkrooms, music practice rooms, dance studios, the Digital Media Center, multipurpose rooms, and meeting spaces. The Ralph S. O'Connor Recreation Center, open for use by all students, houses basketball and volleyball courts, a rock-climbing wall, a weight room, and fitness training and aerobics areas, as well as access to the Athletic Center's swimming facilities. Popular fitness classes include yoga, pilates, kickboxing, step aerobics, spinning, West African dance, and sports conditioning. Charles Commons, a two-building residential complex, features suites with single rooms, kitchenettes, and in many cases, living rooms. The complex is also home to a number of student amenities and common areas. The recently renovated Gilman Hall, located in the heart of campus, is home to the humanities departments and also features the Hutzler Reading Room, or "the Hut," a popular spot for quiet study or group projects; a glass-ceilinged atrium; the Johns Hopkins Archaeological Museum, and a coffee bar. Our campus is also home to many academic resources, including the Baltimore Museum of Art, the Homewood Museum, a world-class archaeological collection, and the six-story Milton S. Eisenhower Library that contains over 3 million books.

Surrounding the campus is Baltimore's vibrant Charles Village community, home to many shops, restaurants, some student housing, and the Barnes and Noble bookstore. Students can often be found here, grabbing lunch or coffee at sub shops or local spots; using services like banks and dry cleaners; and grocery shopping.

CAMPUS LIFE

There are at least 370 student groups and organizations on campus. All Johns Hopkins student groups are governed and managed by students, and there is literally something for everybody, from theater and performing arts groups, to political, special interest, and cultural groups, to publications, student government, and religious groups. Published since 1896, the News-Letter is one of the oldest student papers in the country. In 122 years of competition, the men's lacrosse team has won 44 national championships, including the 2005 and 2007 NCAA Division I National Championship, and twice represented the United States in the Olympic Games. For the past 10 years, the women's lacrosse team has also competed in Division I. Outside of lacrosse, one out of six Johns Hopkins students participates in one of our twenty Division III teams or club athletics, and more than half participate in the popular intramural program.

TUITION AND FEES

Tuition: $42,280

Room and Board: $12,962°

Matriculation Fee: $500 (onetime fee only)

Books and Supplies: $1,200 (estimated)

Personal Expenses: $1,000 (estimated)

°°University room and board charges are based on type of room selected, location, and meal plan. Shown above is an estimate for a typical double room and an anytime dining plan.

JOHNSON & WALES UNIVERSITY

AT A GLANCE

Johnson & Wales University (JWU), founded in 1914, is a nonprofit, private, accredited institution with campuses in Providence, R.I.; North Miami, Fla.; Denver, Colo.; and Charlotte, N.C. An innovative educational leader, JWU offers a broad range of undergraduate and graduate degree programs that inspire professional success and lifelong personal and intellectual growth by integrating arts & sciences and experiential education with leadership and personal development opportunities.

A recognized leader in career education, we offer degrees in business, hospitality, culinary arts, technology, counseling psychology and education to more than 17,000 graduate and undergraduate students, representing 50 states and more than 90 countries.

The university's 517 full-time and 294 part-time undergraduate faculty members (all campuses) are oriented toward instruction rather than research. Many are chosen for their professional experience in business, culinary arts, hospitality, technology, counseling psychology or education. The student-faculty ratio university wide is 26:1. The academic focus of the university is on degree programs in business, culinary arts, hospitality, technology, and counseling psychology. JWU offers an MBA with optional concentrations in accounting, enhanced accounting, hospitality, and information technology, as well as an M.S. in Criminal Justice Management. M.A.T. programs in teaching include elementary education and secondary special education; elementary education and elementary special education; elementary education and elementary/secondary special education; business education and secondary special education; and food service education. The university also offers a doctoral program in educational leadership. The university maintains 26 residence halls throughout its four campuses. Student services include academic counseling and testing, a tutorial center, and health services. The university's Experiential Education & Career Services office provides extensive career planning and placement services. Our more than 89,000 alumni pursue careers around the world. Johnson & Wales is accredited by the New England Association of Schools and Colleges.

LOCATION AND ENVIRONMENT

The location of each of the university's campuses enables students to take advantage of a variety of internship and part-time work activities. The urban setting of the Providence Campus provides students proximity to the city's many cultural and recreational facilities. The North Miami Campus is a short trip from the sun and fun of Fort Lauderdale and the culture and diversity of Miami. The Denver Campus offers students great opportunities as Forbes rates Denver a "top city in America to live and work." The Charlotte Campus is located in a vibrant urban setting that combines commercial and residential life. More than 250 Fortune 500 companies have offices in Charlotte, which is known as the second largest financial center in the U.S.

OFF-CAMPUS OPPORTUNITIES

Many of our majors offer internships at university-owned facilities to expand learning beyond the classroom. The hotel and restaurant management programs feature an internship at the Johnson & Wales Inn, Radisson Airport Hotel, or the Double-Tree Hotel by Hilton Hotel Charlotte—Gateway Village; all are full-service hotel complexes owned and/or operated by the university (the Radisson and DoubleTree are corporate franchises). For all majors optional selective career internships are available throughout the U.S. and worldwide. All internships are offered for course credit. Most internships are one term in duration and carry 13.5 quarter hours of credit. Study abroad programs are also offered.

MAJORS AND DEGREES OFFERED

The degree programs described below are for the 2013-2014 academic year and are subject to change. Students may pursue concentrations related to their program of study to further tailor their degrees to their specific interests and career goals. They also have the opportunity to take concentrations through the School of Arts & Sciences.

The Providence Campus offers degree programs in

accounting, advertising & marketing communications, baking & pastry arts, baking & pastry arts and food service management, business administration, counseling psychology, criminal justice, culinary arts, culinary arts and food service management, culinary nutrition, electronics engineering, engineering design & configuration management, entrepreneurship, equine business management, equine business management/riding, fashion merchandising & retail marketing, finance, food service entrepreneurship, graphic design & digital media, hotel & lodging management, international business, international hotel and tourism management, management, , marketing, network engineering, restaurant, food & beverage management, risk management, software engineering, sports/entertainment/event management, and travel-tourism & hospitality management.

The university also offers two online bachelor's degree programs in baking & pastry and food service management, and culinary arts and food service management. These programs are open to applicants who hold an associate degree in either baking & pastry arts or culinary arts. In its Adult & Continuing Education division, JWU's Providence Campus offers associate and bachelor degrees in business, culinary arts, hospitality and technology.

The North Miami Campus offers degree programs in baking & pastry arts, business administration, criminal justice, culinary arts, culinary arts and food service management, fashion merchandising & retail marketing, hotel & lodging management, management, marketing, pastry arts and food service management, restaurant, food & beverage management, sports/entertainment/event management, and travel-tourism & hospitality management.

The Denver Campus offers degree programs in baking & pastry arts, baking & pastry arts and food service management, business administration, criminal justice, culinary arts, culinary arts and food service management, culinary nutrition, fashion merchandising & retail marketing, hotel & lodging management, pastry arts and food service management, restaurant, food & beverage management, and sports/entertainment/event management. In its Adult & Continuing Education division, JWU's Denver Campus offers associate degrees in culinary arts or baking & pastry arts.

The Charlotte Campus offers degree programs in accounting, baking & pastry arts, baking & pastry arts and food service management, business administration, culinary arts, culinary arts and food service management, fashion merchandising & retail marketing, hotel & lodging management, management, marketing, restaurant, food & beverage management, and sports/entertainment/event management.

ACADEMIC PROGRAMS

Johnson & Wales University offers its programs within an academic structure of three 11-week terms. The university's "upside-down" curriculum provides immediate focus in the student's chosen major. Many programs include laboratory studies as well as formal internship requirements. Special advanced placement programs are featured for high school seniors with exceptional skills in culinary arts or baking and pastry arts. In addition, the university awards credit for certain courses based on the successful completion of Challenge, CLEP or Portfolio Assessments. All degree candidates must successfully complete the required number of courses and/or quarter credit hours, as prescribed in the various curricula.

CAMPUS FACILITIES AND EQUIPMENT

The facilities of the Providence Campus are located throughout the intimate state of Rhode Island and in nearby Massachusetts. The Downcity Campus is home to the university's College of Business, The Hospitality College, the School of Technology, and the John Hazen White School of Arts & Sciences. The Harborside Campus, located nearby in Providence, houses the university's College of Culinary Arts. This campus has five student residence halls as well as classrooms and laboratories, production kitchens, bakeshops, dining rooms, a storeroom, and meat-cutting facilities. Most of these are located in the new Cuisinart Center for Culinary Excellence, an 82,000 square-foot LEED-certified facility. This campus is also home to the Alan Shawn Feinstein Graduate School and the School of Education. Other facilities at this campus include the University Recreation and Athletic Center and a dining center. The North Miami Campus is located in the heart of North Miami, between Miami and Ft. Lauderdale. Facilities include classrooms, production/demonstration kitchens, a bakeshop, residence halls and a conference center. The Denver Campus, located in the Park Hill neighborhood, combines stately turn-of-the-century buildings and newer student centers in a quiet park landscape. The campus has computers in every classroom and laboratory. The Charlotte Campus is located in the heart of Gateway Village in Uptown Charlotte. The academic center is home to a 200-seat auditorium with a production kitchen; top-of-the-line culinary laboratories, classrooms, seminar rooms and computer labs.

TUITION, ROOM, BOARD AND FEES

Tuition at all campuses for 2012-2013 is $26,112. Basic room and board plans range from $9,750 to $12,000. These vary at each campus. There is also an orientation fee of $300 for new students. Books and supplies are estimated at $800-$900 per year, depending upon the program.

FINANCIAL AID

Johnson & Wales students are eligible to apply for a variety of financial aid programs, including Federal programs, university-based student scholarship programs and state-supported grants and scholarships. In the past, more than 90 percent of the university's entering students have received some sort of financial assistance. Students must submit the Free Application for Federal Student Aid (FAFSA) to the Federal Student Aid Processor after January 1 to be considered for financial aid. Early application is strongly suggested for full consideration.

STUDENT ORGANIZATIONS AND ACTIVITIES

Students are involved in a variety of extracurricular activities. Nearly 25 percent of the students at the university are members of national student organizations such Business Professionals of America, DECA, Future Business Leaders of America, Family, Career, Community Leaders of America, National FFA, SkillsUSA and TSA. The Student Activities office and fraternities and sororities are among the many groups that schedule social functions throughout the academic year. Sports and fitness programs include aerobics, baseball, basketball, sailing, soccer, tennis, golf, wrestling, ice hockey, and volleyball.

ADMISSIONS PROCESS

Johnson & Wales University prepares driven students who are seeking a competitive advantage in the global economy. Academic qualifications are important, but an applicant's motivation and interest in doing well are given special consideration. Graduation from high school or equivalent credentials are required for admission. It is recommended that students applying for admission into the culinary arts and baking & pastry arts programs have some prior education or experience in food service. Although no tests are required for most programs, all applicants are encouraged to submit scores from the SAT or ACT. Students who wish to apply for the Honors Program must have taken a college prep curriculum, maintained an average of B or better, placed in the top 25 percent of their high school graduating class and submitted SAT/ACT scores above the national average. High school juniors may apply for early admission under the Early Enrollment Program (EEP). Transfer students are required to submit official high school and college transcripts and to have a minimum GPA of 2.0 for most programs. Credits to be transferred from other institutions are evaluated on the basis of their equivalent at Johnson & Wales. Johnson & Wales does not require an application fee. After submitting the application, the student is responsible for requesting that appropriate transcripts be forwarded to the Admissions Office of the university. While there is no deadline, students are advised to apply as early as possible before the intended date of enrollment to ensure full consideration of their application. Applications are accepted for terms beginning in September, December, and March and for the summer sessions. Inquiries and applications should be addressed to: Kenneth DiSala, Senior Vice President of Enrollment Management, Johnson & Wales University, 8 Abbott Park Place, Providence, Rhode Island 02903, Telephone: 401-598-1000 1-800-DIAL-JWU (toll-free) Fax: 401-598-4901 E-mail: jwu@admissions.jwu.edu.

KETTERING UNIVERSITY

AT A GLANCE

Where do you want to go? What do you want to be? No college helps students answer these questions better than Kettering University.

There isn't another college like us. Kettering is a highly-acclaimed, private university located in Flint, Michigan, that combines innovative, hands-on programs in engineering, math, science, and business with a ground-breaking experiential learning and professional cooperative education program. What that means: students in all degree programs alternate between study terms and work terms. During study terms, students learn exciting material in small classes taught by professors, not teaching assistants. During work terms, they gain professional experience at corporations related to their studies and interests.

More importantly, Kettering students graduate with up to 2 ½ years of real world experience and envy-worthy resumes. Our students have done everything from testing ballistic systems and re-engineering crowd management to designing biomedical tools. And since students can go to work their first year, they learn early what they like to do – and what they never want to do again.

All of this experience pays off. Research shows that students who participate in co-op and experiential learning programs are more mature, better problem solvers, and more technically knowledgeable. Employers know that Kettering students are the cream of the crop – our students typically graduate with job offers or grad school acceptances in hand, and frequently start their positions at a higher salary than their peers from other schools.

Those who know Kettering students agree – tomorrow's business and industry leaders are at Kettering today. At Kettering, students earn a degree for the real world. Any university will take you places. Kettering will take you farther.

LOCATION AND ENVIRONMENT

Flint is located in east-central Michigan, just 60 miles west of Lake Huron and the Canadian border, and 60 miles north of Detroit. Flint has approximately 117,00 residents and has a metropolitan area of 450,000. The College Cultural Center Complex is located just one-and-a-half miles from campus and houses a museum, a performing arts auditorium, a planetarium, and the Flint Public Library. The proximity to outdoor activities, city culture, and Flint's own distinctive resources provides students with access to a wide range of activities and opportunities.

OFF-CAMPUS OPPORTUNITIES

More than half of a Kettering student's time is spent off campus, fulfilling professional co-op and experiential work requirements outside the Flint area. On average, students spend 11 academic semesters working for their employer and nine academic semesters in the classroom. The corporations and agencies that employ Kettering students are located throughout North America, Europe and Asia. Approximately 70 percent of students work for a corporation located in their hometown, which allows them to live at home during the work experience portion of their education. On average, students earn between $40,000 and $65,000 over the entire professional co-op program.

MAJORS AND DEGREES OFFERED

The four and a half year professional cooperative education program allows students to earn designated Bachelor of Science degrees in: Applied Biology, Applied Mathematics, Applied Physics, Biochemistry, Bioinformatics, Business Administration, Chemical Engineering, Chemistry, Computer Engineering, Computer Science, Electrical Engineering, Engineering Physics, Industrial Engineering, Mechanical Engineering.

Kettering also offers more than 50 minors, concentrations, specialties, courses of study and dual degrees, in areas such as Fuel Cell, Applied Optics, Pre-Law, Computer Gaming and Data Security, and Pre-Med. Additionally, the school offers seven Master's Degrees, including an accredited MBA program. Please visit our website for more details on these programs.

ACADEMIC PROGRAMS

The unique structure of Kettering's program allows students to fulfill the academic requirements of 160 credit hours throughout a four and a half year period. This is completed over nine academic semesters and up to 11 co-op work semesters. Students also complete a capstone thesis project on behalf of their co-op employer during their senior year for credit toward the 160 required hours. The academic year consists of two 11-week academic terms on-campus in Flint and two 12-week academic terms working for the corporate employer; students alternate their time between Flint and the employer's site. On average, a freshman student who spends 24 weeks during the academic year working for the professional co-op employer earns $11,000.

CAMPUS FACILITIES AND EQUIPMENT

Kettering University opened its $42 million Mechanical Engineering & Chemistry Center in 2003. This state-of-the-art facility is loaded with hands-on learning laboratories such as automotive labs with several unique test cells and the most advanced chemistry labs around! Engineering and chemistry facilities of this caliber are usually found only in graduate-level programs.

The Academic Building houses more classrooms, laboratories, and department offices. More than 100,000 square feet of this facility is dedicated to labs, which are stocked with equipment to demonstrate and experiment with methods in the engineering industry, from basic machining to emerging technologies. The entire campus, including residence hall rooms, campus apartments, and labs, is networked, providing each student with 24-hour access to computer resources and the Internet.

The library contains more than 118,000 volumes, more than 390 periodicals, and various online services. Special facilities include a microfilm area, database search services, record and tape listening- and videotape viewing-facilities, and a special collection of SAE, SME, and ASME technical papers.

TUITION, ROOM, BOARD AND FEES*

Tuition for the 2012 – 2013 academic year: $33,946 – Fixed Tuition Guarantee, students making normal progress towards their degree will pay the same tuition rates for their entire college career.

Room Rate: $4,150

Board, including 19 meals per week: $2,610

*Please remember that tuition and fees are subject to change at any time.

FINANCIAL AID

Kettering University offers all the traditional need and merit-based financial aid, including a generous merit scholarship program. All Kettering students also benefit from the substantial co-op salaries that they earn throughout their years in school. The average range of salaries over the entire period is from $40,000 to $65,000. About 70 percent of students are able to live at home during their work experience terms, and are then able to contribute more of their salaries to their educational expenses. Many students win scholarships from agencies and organizations from their local communities. The primary purpose of Kettering's financial aid program is to supplement students' financial need after co-op earnings and parents' contributions. Aid is given as grants, scholarships, loans, and work-study awards. Students who wish to apply for financial aid should complete the FAFSA.

STUDENT ORGANIZATIONS AND ACTIVITIES

Kettering students enjoy the activities and participate in the organizations that make college exciting and unique.

College is a place to get to know people, and to make contacts students will have throughout their professional lives. Students can make these vital connections at Kettering University by participating in one of the more than 50 clubs and organizations represented on campus. Whatever their social or professional interests, there are opportunities to work together with other students who share those interests, planning and organizing activities, and perfecting essential leadership and teamwork skills.

Outside of class, students will find plenty of ways to enjoy their free time at Kettering. The following list represents just a few of Kettering's many clubs and organizations:

Firebirds (autocross club),Student Government, International Club, Aquaneers (scuba diving club), Campus Crusade for Christ, Christians In Action (CIA),Cycling Club, Bulldog Band, Outdoors Club, SADD, Tech Sailors, Hockey Club, Karate Club, Black Unity Congress, Political Awareness Club (PAC), Intramural Sports (including basketball, cross country, golf, soccer, swimming, tennis and volleyball), and Swing Club

Kettering also has one of the largest student chapters of the Society of Automotive Engineers (SAE), and their Delta Epsilon Chi Chapter (college version of DECA) annually wins top awards in state and national competitions.

Students compete in an intense intramural athletic program and are involved in clubs and professional organizations. Approximately a third of Kettering students join the 13 national fraternities and five sororities that are represented on campus. The school's active student government produces programs to develop peers' leadership skills, self-confidence, interpersonal relations, and organizational operations. Because enrolled students represent approximately 48 states and 18 countries, they have a lot to share with and learn from one another.

ADMISSIONS PROCESS

Admission to Kettering University is competitive and based on scholastic achievement and extracurricular interests, activities, and achievements. Applicants are required to have completed the following courses (one credit represents two semesters or one year of study): two credits algebra, one credit geometry, a half credit trigonometry, two credits laboratory science (one of these credits must be from physics or chemistry, and both are strongly recommended), and three credits English. A minimum of 16 credits is required, but 20 credits are strongly encouraged. Applicants must submit SAT or ACT scores. Most Kettering University students rank at or near the top 10 percent of their high school class.

Although applications are accepted all year long, prospective students are encouraged to file their application early in their senior year. Early application significantly improves students' chances for early co-op employment. Kettering University also accepts transfer students. Admission decisions for transfer applicants are based on college records for those who have completed at least 30 credits. Interested students can apply online at www.kettering.edu/apply.

KING'S COLLEGE (PA)

AT A GLANCE

King's College is a liberal arts Catholic college that offers growth and personal development in a welcoming and supportive environment. Founded in 1946 by the Congregation of Holy Cross from the University of Notre Dame, we're located on a small urban campus in Wilkes-Barre, Pennsylvania.

At King's, we offer 37 majors in Business, Humanities, Social Sciences, Education, Sciences and Allied Health programs, 7 pre-professional programs and 11 special concentrations. With over 50 clubs and activities and 19 NCAA Division III athletic programs for men and women, there is plenty to do outside the classroom.

Small classes and labs allow for meaningful interaction with professors. Our average class size is 18 students, average lab size is 13 students, and the student/faculty ratio is 14:1. This personal attention translates into better graduation rates than at institutions with larger classroom environments.

King's consistently ranks high in the top college national review issues of major publications:

• For 18 straight years, King's has been ranked in the top tier of the U.S.News & World Report's list of Best Colleges in the United States.

• Barron's Best Buys in College Education selected King's among the nation's top 10% of colleges for its tenth consecutive edition.

• Forbes ranked King's amongst the United States' best colleges and universities in its America's Best Colleges 2012 listing.

• The President's Higher Education Community Service Honor Roll recognized King's innovative and effective community service and service-learning programs for the sixth consecutive year.

• For the second consecutive year, King's College was recognized as among the best master's degree granting institutions in the country in a national ranking by Washington Monthly magazine, which recognizes higher learning institutions for service to the community and social mobility of the student body.

• The American Association of Colleges and Universities' Greater Expectations Initiative named King's as one of only 16 "Leadership Institutions" nationwide for visionary innovations in undergraduate education.

• The John Templeton Foundation Honor Roll for Character-Building Colleges recognized King's in its select group of 100 colleges nationwide.

In addition, many of our individual academic programs are accredited by several highly respected organizations.

• The Association to Advance Collegiate Schools of Business for the William G. McGowan School of Business, one of only 42 undergraduate schools of business nationwide

• The National Council for the Accreditation of Teacher Education (one of only 20 colleges in Pennsylvania with this accreditation)

• The Accreditation Review Commission on Education for Physician Assistants

• The Commission on Accreditation of Athletic Training Education

• The Chemistry program is accredited by the American Chemical Society

LOCATION AND ENVIRONMENT

King's College is ideally situated in northeastern Pennsylvania within driving distance to New York City, Philadelphia, Washington, D.C. and other east coast attractions. Our atmosphere is friendly and inviting, with a strong sense of community. Our campus is easy to navigate and has impressive facilities, equal to those at much larger institutions. Our student/faculty ratio is 14:1 allowing for personal interaction with professors, which translates into better graduation rates than at institutions with larger classroom environments.

OFF-CAMPUS OPPORTUNITIES

It's not all limited to campus, we've got malls, theatres and restaurants minutes away as well as specialty shops, cultural events, ethnic celebrations and festivals. Our bookstore is located in a Barnes & Noble/Starbucks Café and is the centerpiece of a bustling South Main Street.

MAJORS AND DEGREES OFFERED

William G. McGowan School of Business: Accounting, Finance, Health Care Administration (five-year master's), Human Resource Management, International Business, Management, Marketing.

Humanities and Social Sciences: Computers and Information Systems, Criminal Justice, Economics, Engineering – Dual Degree Program with the University of Notre Dame, English – Literature, English – Professional Writing, Environmental Studies, French, History, Mass Communications, Philosophy, Political Science, Physics, Psychology, Sociology, Spanish, Theatre, Theology.

Education: Pre-school-Grade 4 (Special Education included), Secondary Certification (Special Education certification offered), Special Education

Sciences: Biology, Chemistry, Computer Science, Environmental Science, General Science, Mathematics, Neuroscience

Allied Health: Athletic Training Education, Clinical Laboratory Science/Medical Technology, Physician Assistant (five-year master's)

7 Pre-Professional Programs

11 Special Concentrations

CAMPUS FACILITIES AND EQUIPMENT

We offer a state-of-the-art sports medicine clinic for our athletic training program. New science labs and equipment enable hands-on research. We have a radio and television station on campus and offer audio and video editing equipment for those interested in communications or media. The D. Leonard Corgan Library offers an amazing collection of books, periodicals and catalogs to provide students with the informational resources they need to enhance their skills.

Residence halls offer a variety of living arrangements from single rooms to apartments. There are 24-hour computer labs in several residence halls and each lounge features cable television. These facilities are all secure, accessible either by student ID card or by the desk attendant on staff 24-hours a day. King's takes pride in our campus security efforts and can assure you that safety is a top priority here.

ATHLETICS FACILITIES

The 33-acre Robert L. Betzler Fields at McCarthy Stadium is one of the finest facilities in the MAC for football, field hockey, baseball, softball, soccer and lacrosse.

The 13,000 square-foot John J. Dorish Field House features locker rooms, an equipment room with laundry facilities, as well as a sports medicine treatment center.

The William S. Scandlon Physical Education Center features the Robert McGrane Basketball Arena, which just underwent a complete bleacher replacement and air-conditioning installation. The center also includes a sports medicine clinic, swimming pool, handball and racquetball courts, wrestling room, and new locker rooms. In addition, the recently completed gym expansion project has added a new facility to the Scandlon Center, including three multi-purpose courts as well as new offices, meeting rooms, and additional sports medicine facilities.

The Intermetro Welness Center includes 25,000 pounds of free weights, five full rack stations with platforms for strength lifting, 6,000 pounds of dumbbells, eight Hammer Strength units, and a number of weight training machines. The top floor consists of nearly 30 cardiovascular exercise machines, including treadmills, stationary bikes, elliptical and rowing machines.

The tennis teams play on the newly-surfaced courts at Kirby Park, one of the top facilities in the MAC. (The Kingston Indoor Tennis Center is utilized during the winter.)

The golf team plays at the Wyoming Valley Country Club, a par 72, 6,391-yard course that is only 10 minutes from campus.

TUITION, ROOM, BOARD AND FEES

When determining the cost of a college education, one should also take into consideration the value. In August 2011, the Morning Call newspaper published an article about which college graduates earn the highest salaries in the nation. "Pennsylvania's biggest success story may be King's College in Wilkes-Barre, where graduates start out small — $34,000, No. 939 in the nation — but grow to earn $91,100, the 88th-highest."

Approximately 97% of all full-time students attending King's College receive financial assistance. Last year, our average financial aid was $22,303, taking a significant amount of the financial obligation away from the student and their family. The average net cost of tuition, room and board for 2012-2013 was $17,891. We encourage every student to apply for financial aid no matter what their family circumstances are. Only after you have applied and been considered for all available assistance will you have a true idea of what your costs will be.

King's offers deferred payment plans, which allows families to make monthly payments on the balance of tuition, fees, room and board less any financial aid received.

FINANCIAL AID

Applicants for financial aid will be considered for all need-based programs which include private, state and federal grants (gifts), loans and work study programs. King's even has financial aid programs specific to transfer students, so all applicants should take the time to review their options.

Federal campus-based work program allows students to earn money through employment to help pay for educational costs. FAFSA must be filed each year by May 1 to be considered.

The Office of Financial Aid is here to educate you about the various financial aid programs available and to answer your questions. We'll make the application process as simple and painless as possible because our goal is have you join us at King's. Contact us at 1-888-KINGS-PA or finaid@kings.edu.

STUDENT ORGANIZATIONS AND ACTIVITIES

King's recognizes that involvement in student clubs and organizations is an important part of your educational experience. King's offers the opportunity to participate in clubs in the following general areas:

ACADEMIC

Accounting Association, Economics and International Business Club, Finance & Investment Association, King's College Chapter of The Society for Human Resource Management (SHRM)/Human Resources Management Association, Marketing and Management Association, Pre-Health Professions Society

HEALTH RELATED ORGANIZATIONS

Lester Saidman Student Society (PA Club), Pre Professional Physician Assistant Society, Sports Medicine Society

ARTS & SCIENCES ORGANIZATIONS

Academy of Biological Sciences (Biology Club), Chemical Society (Chemistry Club), Criminal Justice Association, Education Club, History Society, Mathematics & Computer Sciences Club, Neuroscience Club, Pre-Law Society, Psychology Club

INTERNATIONAL

Multicultural/International Club

MEDIA & DESIGN

Media Club, The Crown (student newspaper), Regis (yearbook), WRKC (radio station), KCTV (television station), InHouse Design Club

MUSIC AND ARTS

Campion Society, King's Players, Monarch Dancers, Music Ensembles at King's, SCOP (fine arts magazine)

SERVICE

Blood Council, Circle K Club, Columbiettes, Emergency Response Team (ERT), Knights of Columbus, Monarch Ambassadors, Oxfam America, Sigma Kappa Sigma (EKE-men), Sigma Kappa Tau (EKT-women)

SPECIAL INTEREST

Coding Club, Commuter Life Association, Environmental Awareness and Outdoors Club, Questions and Answers, Residence Hall Council, ROTC, Ski and Snowboard Club, Ultimate Frisbee

ADMISSIONS PROCESS

APPLYING TO KING'S FOR FRESHMAN

The Office of Admission offers two methods for candidates to apply for admission: The SAT/ACT Traditional Choice and the Standardized Test Option/ Essay Choice. Applicants are required to state their preference prior to the application review and the decision is non-reversible.

SAT/ACT Traditional Choice:

Completed application

Official high school transcripts

SAT I or ACT scores

Guidance counselor recommendation

Essay

$30 Application fee (waived if done online)

Standardized Test Option/Essay Choice:

Completed application

Official high school transcripts

Official graded writing sample from either junior or senior year submitted and notarized by the high school guidance office

Guidance counselor recommendation

Essay

$30 Application fee (waived if done online)

General Guidelines

While each application for admission is reviewed individually, here are some general guidelines:

The most important criteria in the admission decision are a student's four-year academic record, GPA, strength of curriculum and overall rank in class. Recommendations, the personal statement, co-curricular activities, leadership and community service help to complete your profile. March 1 is the preferred application deadline for first-year students. Applications may be submitted after September 1 and are reviewed on a rolling admission basis. Decisions are released in mid-October. Once we have received your application materials, we will notify you with a decision in two to three weeks. Students choosing the standardized test option are required to notify the Office of Admission on the application. A students' decision is non-reversible and must be made prior to application review.

APPLYING FOR TRANSFER STUDENTS

Transferring to King's could not be easier, especially if you're transferring from LCCC. King's offers generous financial assistance packages so don't let cost be a deterrent.

Individual Admission Counselor information sessions, campus walking tours, and shuttle tours of the Wilkes-Barre area may be scheduled Monday through Friday throughout the year. Group information sessions and campus tours are offered on Saturdays during the academic year.

KNOX COLLEGE

AT A GLANCE

We are Knox – an academically challenging, diverse, and connected community of scholar-teachers and students who embrace the Freedom to Flourish, and work together to open minds, make a statement, and make a difference.

Veritas, meaning "truth," is the motto of Knox College – a top ranked, private liberal arts college in Galesburg, Illinois. Established in 1837 by social reformers from upstate New York, Knox has stayed true to its Mission of Access: that those truly wanting a liberal arts education should be free to achieve it – regardless of race, gender, cultural background, or economic standing.

In this spirit, Abraham Lincoln chose Knox's Old Main as his platform to advocate for unity, equality, and freedom during the historic Lincoln-Douglas debates.

Today, Knox's egalitarian spirit lives on in our commitment to give every student a voice and an education that enables lifelong learning and the Freedom to Flourish. A student-established Honor Code guides academic and intellectual integrity.

Knox also celebrates one of the most culturally diverse campuses in the U.S. with 1,392 students from 48 states and 46 countries, including 21% U.S. students of color and 7% international students.

As independent thinkers, Knox students actively plan their own program of study. More than 80% complete hands-on work through research, independent study, internships, creative projects, and off-campus study. Knox devotes much of its resources toward developing and supporting experiential learning opportunities.

Knox follows a 3-3 calendar – 3 terms with 3 classes per term. Popular programs include: Biology, Business, Chemistry, Computer Science, Creative Writing, Economics, English, International Relations, Mathematics, Neuroscience, Physics, Political Science, Pre-Law, Pre-Med, and Psychology – as well as internships and study abroad.

Classes are taught by distinguished scholar-teachers, 96% of whom have a Ph.D. or the highest degree in their field – more than 60% have been published or publicly honored in the past 3 years. A 12:1 student-faculty ratio and small classes averaging 17 students allow for one-on-one student-professor interaction.

Knox students embrace extracurricular activities for fun, athletics, and social causes – the College has more than 100 clubs and organizations. Our radio station, WVKC, has been ranked as one of the top 10 nationwide. And our internationally acclaimed Catch is the country's oldest collegiate literary magazine.

Knox athletic programs include 21 NCAA Division III teams, and 11 club and intramural sports teams. The Prairie Fire is the official moniker of Knox's sports teams.

Named one of the Colleges That Change Lives by former New York Times education editor Loren Pope, Knox is consistently ranked as one of the best values among U.S. liberal arts colleges.

LOCATION AND ENVIRONMENT

Under the open skies of west-central Illinois sits the 82-acre Knox campus. Built on prairieland, its broad lawns and big trees offer plenty of prime spots to study, play or simply relax and enjoy. Days are generally clear and sunny, with warm springs and colorful falls. Knox's nearby Green Oaks Biological Field Station offers an additional 700 acres of restored prairie, woods, and waterways to explore.

Campus buildings are a blend of histories, old and new. The stone hewn, wood-paneled Seymour Library is a favorite study spot. Old Main, with its working bell, well-worn marble steps, and grand Alumni Room (featuring Lincoln's chair) is Knox's oldest building. Students, faculty, and staff also "hang out" at Seymour Union – in the Gizmo café, on the boardwalk patio, or in the new student lounge, with its game room and stage.

Life at Knox encompasses a deeply woven sense of community, where professors and students can freely meet and share ideas. Most faculty live nearby and nearly all seniors have been to their professor's home.

More than 95% of Knox students live on campus in a unique array of historic houses, apartments, suites and traditional residence halls. Fraternity houses and theme houses such as International House, Casa Latina, ABLE Center for Black Culture, Jazz House, and Eco House are fixtures.

Joining the Knox community means meeting everyone – before your first day of class. That's when Knox holds its Pumphandle tradition. Students, faculty, and staff gather at Old Main to meet one another, eventually forming a meandering line on the lawn (and through buildings) as everyone shakes hands with everyone else.

Off-Campus Opportunities

Galesburg was established by the founders of Knox in 1837, and shares the College's roots of diversity and freedom – it was a key center for the Underground Railroad in Illinois. In town you'll find the same Midwest generosity that gives the Knox campus such an easy-going atmosphere.

The city's many historic charms include brick streets and an abundance of Victorian and Craftsman architecture. Within walking distance from campus, downtown Galesburg offers shops, restaurants, and many venues for live entertainment. Its historic Seminary Street district features quaint cafés and boutiques – and the train station with daily Amtrak service to and from Chicago.

The arts and culture scene has always thrived in Galesburg, and includes the award-winning Knox-Galesburg Symphony, Prairie Players Civic Theatre, Discovery Depot Children's Museum, Civic Art Center, and restored Orpheum Theatre. The city's daily newspaper, The Register Mail, is near campus.

Knox students also work closely with the community in volunteer and internship capacities for schools, hospitals, and neighborhood agencies.

About 45 minutes in either direction are the urban centers of Peoria and Moline, with access to airports, shopping, museums, galleries – and attractions on the Illinois and Mississippi rivers.

Majors and Degrees Offered

The Knox bachelor's program provides a balanced curriculum in the arts, humanities, sciences, and social sciences. Knox's 3-3 academic calendar – 3 terms (fall, winter, and spring), 3 courses per term – allows students to fully explore course subject matter and fulfill research expectations.

Knox offers 39 majors, 48 minors, 10 cooperative degree programs, and 30-plus off-campus and study abroad programs – in addition to grant-sponsored hands-on research and internship opportunities. Self-designed majors are also popular.

Knox graduates enjoy one of the highest acceptance rates to post-graduate and professional school programs. The College is in the top 3% of institutions producing successful Ph.D. candidates, and ranks 11th for post-graduate math and science degree candidates.

ACADEMIC PROGRAMS

Experiential learning is a cornerstone of Knox's curriculum and the College offers many hands-on opportunities.

Research, Honors, & Independent Study: Knox provides more than $250,000 in grants and funding for graduate-style research, Honors research, and creative projects. Nearly 90% of Knox students complete independent study courses or projects, where they're encouraged to explore interests, generate ideas, and pursue a well-planned course of study under the guidance of a faculty member.

Immersion Experiences: Knox's unique and exciting immersion terms allow students to fully explore specific subjects in real world style. Clinical Psychology Term involves courses and fieldwork as a clinical psychology intern. During the interdisciplinary Green Oaks Term, students live at Green Oaks Biological Field Station, conducting scientific and historical research, and working on creative projects. Japan Term students fully explore Japanese language, history, and philosophy, followed by a two-week trip to Japan. Open Studio Term allows students to work independently as full-time artists and concludes in a Senior Show. Repertory Theatre Term teaches students how to run a repertory theatre and culminates in the staging of two major theatrical productions.

Off-Campus & Study Abroad: More than 30 off-campus study and study abroad programs are available in the U.S. and 20 different countries through the Center for Global Studies.

Public Service: Knox is the first college or university in the country to offer an official Peace Corps Program. Knox also provides opportunities for community, national, and international internships, and volunteer work.

CAMPUS FACILITIES AND EQUIPMENT

Knox College provides about $250,000 annually to support independent study, creative projects, and Honors projects, as well as student access to superior research resources and equipment.

Libraries: Knox College maintains three libraries: Seymour Library, the Science-Mathematics Library, and the Ford Center for Fine Arts music library. Seymour, the main library, houses more than 350,000 volumes, and the Special Collections and Archives – which contains primary source materials used by students, faculty, and researchers from around the world.

Arts: Ford Center for the Fine Arts – a comprehensive facility for the visual arts, theatre, dance, and music – features the 600-seat Harbach theatre with its rotating stage and the 325-seat Kresge Recital Hall. Other resources include the Studio Theatre, the 360-degree Art Gallery and Round Room, and numerous art and music studios.

Science: Major grants from the National Science Foundation, National Institutes of Health, and Howard Hughes Medical Institute, help Knox continue to expand an equipment roster that includes electron microscopes, NMR, ESR, GC-MS, other spectrometers and chromatographs, X-ray, laser labs, experimental psychology labs, four computer labs, and a greenhouse.

Green Oaks Biological Field Station, near the Spoon River about 20 miles east of Knox, encompasses 700 acres of forest, aquatic habitat, and North America's second-oldest restored tall-grass prairie.

Athletics: The 50,000 sq. ft. Fleming Fieldhouse provides an indoor six-lane 200-meter track, and court space for numerous activities. Andrew Fitness Center offers separate cardio/weight machine, and free-weight floors. Knosher Bowl, a true bowl stadium, features artificial turf and one of the best playing surfaces in Division III football. Blodgett Field, a pro-level baseball diamond, features its own sprinkler system and special soil composition. Knox also maintains a main gym and basketball court, a 6-lane outdoor track, softball and soccer fields, tennis courts, a wrestling complex, and natatorium. Golf is played at a nearby private 18-hole course.

TUITION, ROOM, BOARD, AND FEES

Expenses per academic year:

Tuition:	$34,110
Room:	$3,750
Board:	$3,738
Fees:	$354
Total:	$41,952

Average cost for books and supplies: $900

FINANCIAL AID

Knox is committed to ensuring that cost is not a barrier to a high-caliber college education. The College offers a wide variety of merit-based scholarships and need-based financial aid to help cover expenses. Writer's, Visual and Performing Arts, Social Concerns, and Regional scholarships are also available.

For more information on scholarships or financial aid, visit www.knox.edu, or contact us at 800-678-KNOX.

STUDENT ORGANIZATIONS AND ACTIVITIES

Student Clubs and Organizations: The more than 100 student-run organizations on campus provide an outlet for everything from academics, such as chemistry or physics, to the arts – 13 music and dance ensembles – to social and community concerns to national fraternities and sororities. Clubs such as Common Ground, Model United Nations, Alliance for Peaceful Action, Asian Student Association, and Intervarsity Christian Fellowship, focus on identity, culture, and politics. Knox is the national headquarters of the Association of Black Culture Centers (ABCC).

Prairie Fire Athletics: The Athletic Program at Knox has been building a winning tradition for more than a century. Knox is a member of the NCAA Division III and the Midwest Conference (MWC), one of the oldest conferences in the nation. Competition in the conference is intense and spirited, including the local rivalry between Knox and Monmouth College – the sixth-oldest athletic rivalry in the country. As a Knox student-athlete, you'll train in some of the best athletic facilities, and your coaches will challenge you to grow and achieve at even higher levels than you might have expected.

Club and Intramural Sports: Intramural sports are organized in student-directed leagues. Regular offerings include volleyball, basketball, indoor soccer, dodgeball, and softball. Our competitive club sports include co-ed and women's water polo (the team placed 10th in national competition); men's and women's lacrosse; fencing; and co-ed, men's, and women's Ultimate Frisbee.

Student Governance: Getting involved is a key principle of a Knox liberal arts education. Knox prides itself on an active and self-governing student body – students sit on all committees. The Honor Code, initiated by students in 1951, continues to anchor the sense of responsibility and self-direction that is central to intellectual life at Knox.

Admissions Process

Visiting Knox is the best way to get to know us. Visits include a student-guided tour of campus and an opportunity to meet with your admission counselor, professors, and coaches, and to sit in on classes. We also offer open houses throughout the year for prospective students and their families.

Knox uses the Common Application. Deadlines for first-year admission are November 1 for Early Action I, December 1 for Early Action II, and February 1 for Regular Decision. We also accept transfer applications for Fall, Winter, and Spring terms.

For more information please visit admission online or contact us directly.

Office of Admission

Knox College

2 East South Street

Galesburg, Illinois 61401-4999

United States

Phone: 800-678-KNOX or 309-341-7100

Fax: 309-341-7070

E-mail: admission@knox.edu

Web: www.knox.edu

LA ROCHE COLLEGE

AT A GLANCE

La Roche College is a private, Catholic, four-year institution located 20 minutes north of downtown Pittsburgh. The College is fully accredited by the Middle States Association of Colleges.

La Roche College prepares students for active, successful participation in a thriving global marketplace. A total of 1,465 students are currently enrolled.

Dedicated to fostering a global outlook, La Roche welcomes students of all religions, ethnic origins, socioeconomic backgrounds and talents. The College's Pacem In Terris Institute invites students from all over the world to its campus, including those from conflict, post-conflict and developing nations. La Roche currently hosts students from 14 states, one territory and 30 countries. This diverse campus encourages transcultural awareness and prepares students for working in a fast-paced global economy.

For the past 50 years, La Roche College has established itself as a reputable institution of higher learning, ranking 29th on the U.S. News list of Best Regional Colleges. The Princeton Review also has listed La Roche as one of the Best Northeastern Colleges for the past seven years. The College has been recognized as one of the safest four-year, private college campuses.

LOCATION AND ENVIRONMENT

Located on an 80-acre, secluded campus in McCandless Township, a northern suburb of Pittsburgh, La Roche provides students just the right blend of suburban and metropolitan life. Students have the advantage of a safe, supportive environment with big city amenities. The small campus also enhances learning by allowing devoted faculty to provide personalized attention to all students.

Pittsburgh is the second-largest city in Pennsylvania and is the headquarters of several of the largest U.S. corporations, including 84 Lumber, Alcoa, American Eagle Outfitters, Bayer, Calgon Carbon, H.J. Heinz Company, PNC, PPG Industries, U.S. Airways and Westinghouse. Forbes has ranked Pittsburgh as the nation's most livable city more than once, and The Economist named Pittsburgh a Top U.S. City in its list of the world's most livable cities in 2011.

OFF-CAMPUS OPPORTUNITIES

With downtown Pittsburgh so nearby, students have access to the city's outstanding facilities and attractions. This convenient location deepens the college experience, exposing students to Pittsburgh's rich and historic culture.

Pittsburgh's thriving cultural district includes the Benedum Center for the Performing Arts, the Pittsburgh Symphony, the Civic Light Opera, the Andy Warhol Museum, Pittsburgh Public Theater, Carnegie Music Hall, Carnegie Museums of Pittsburgh and Heinz Hall for the Performing Arts. Pittsburgh also is home to three professional sports teams: the Pittsburgh Steelers, Pittsburgh Pirates and Pittsburgh Penguins. Aside from recreational benefits, the large metropolitan area offers students a number of internship and career opportunities.

MAJORS AND DEGREES OFFERED

La Roche offers more than 50 undergraduate majors and 20 undergraduate majors, including the top 10 most popular among today's college students.

Majors currently offered include: Accounting; Athletic Training; Biology; Biology/Forensic Science; Chemistry; Chemistry/Chemical Engineering; Chemistry/Environmental Science and Management; Chemistry/Forensic Science; Child and Family Studies; Communication, Media and Technology; Computer Science; Computer Science/Industrial Engineering; Criminal Justice; Education; English Studies: Professional Writing; English Studies: Language and Literature; Film, Video and Media; Finance; Graphic & Communication Design; Health Science; History; Information Technology; Interior Design; International Affairs; International Management; Liberal Studies; Management; Management Information Systems; Marketing; Mathematics; Mathematics/Industrial Engineering; National Security Studies; Nursing – Associate of Science; Nursing – BSN Completion Degree; Occupational Therapy; Performing Arts – Dance; Physical Therapy; Physician Assistant; Political Science; Psychology; Radiologic Technology – Associate of Science; Religious Studies; Self-Designed; Sociology; Speech and Language Pathology; and Undeclared.

The College offers master's degrees in four high-demand employment areas, providing adult learners with the necessary skills, training and professional guidance to succeed in today's competitive job market. La Roche's graduate programs include Nursing, Accounting, Human Resources Management and Health Sciences.

La Roche faculty members are an acclaimed group of scholars who work closely with students to challenge and encourage them. Seventy-seven percent of the College's full-time faculty members hold terminal degrees or have completed the highest level of study in their fields. Many faculty members also have earned distinguished honors. These highly trained and experienced professionals engage in research and spend time in classrooms, laboratories and studios. Faculty imparts wisdom and encourages students to reach beyond the classroom to achieve their academic goals.

ACADEMIC PROGRAMS

La Roche College offers a blend of liberal arts studies and professional preparation, enabling students to develop broad perspectives while acquiring career skills.

Students have the opportunity to strive for even greater academic achievement through the La Roche College Honors Institute. Designed to recognize and promote academic excellence, the program offers demanding classes taught by top La Roche faculty who are experts in their fields. The Honors Institute combines classroom learning with distinctive co-curricular activities, allowing students to engage in group discussion and independent inquiry research.

The College's Study Abroad+Study USA program offers the value-added component of studying abroad at little or no cost. This unique opportunity is offered to qualified La Roche students who want to broaden their horizons and marketability in an ever-expanding global workplace. After completing 60 La Roche credits and meeting all eligibility requirements, students may apply for a Study Abroad+Study USA course to travel internationally or domestically. Students only are responsible for incidentals, passport costs, visas and spending money. Traditional study-abroad programs also are available.

CAMPUS FACILITIES AND EQUIPMENT

With renovated classrooms and facilities, the College offers students a unique combination of 21st-century education and advanced technology in an intimate setting.

The Office of Academic Counseling & Tutoring provides free academic support services, such as individualized and group tutoring sessions, supplemental instruction, mentoring services and one-on-one appointments with an academic counselor. Students also may visit The Writers' Center on campus, which is a free service for students who need assistance at any stage of the writing process.

After a recent series of renovations, The John J. Wright Library earned a state-of-the-art status. The library is a valuable resource on campus, with a collection of more than 70,000 volumes, 80,000 electronic books, 44 electronic databases, 500 periodical subscriptions and access to 30,000 government documents through a United States Government Depository Library. As a member of the Pennsylvania Academic Library Consortium, Inc., the library also offers Interlibrary Loan and EZ-Borrow services. With the Providence World Café housed within the library, students enjoy the comfortable setting of a local coffee house.

TUITION, ROOM, BOARD AND FEES

Full-time tuition for the 2012-13 academic year is $23,328. Room and board costs are $9,732. Student support and development has a $400 annual fee, and the curricular learning support tech fee is $330.

La Roche encourages students to live on campus in one of five residence halls. The College's two freshman residence hall rooms are large and include their own private bathrooms, and the three apartment-style-suites promote group interaction and a sense of community. All residence hall rooms are wired for Internet access and come fully equipped with microwave and refrigerator units. Resident students also have access to the free, on-site laundry facilities.

Under the guidance of a residence life director, resident assistants help to plan a variety of programs, including recreational events, off-campus events, hosting guest speakers and other social activities.

FINANCIAL AID

La Roche provides quality education at an affordable cost by awarding grants, scholarships, loans, several repayment plans and work-study employment. Nearly 75 percent of our students receive financial aid, and the average financial aid package is approximately $21,893 per student. All students who intend to apply for financial aid must submit the Free Application for Federal Student Aid (FAFSA) after Jan. 1 of their senior year in high school. Students who live outside of Pennsylvania should submit their own state grant form, if applicable. La Roche encourages all students to submit the proper forms as soon as possible after Jan. 1 so that they are processed prior to the College's May 1 priority deadline.

STUDENT ORGANIZATIONS AND ACTIVITIES

Campus life is active and exciting, with more than 35 clubs and organizations and 12 NCAA Div. III athletic teams – including basketball, cross country and soccer. La Roche combines quality education with sports, student activities and community-based events.

Student organizations tailor many interests, including nursing, chemistry, graphic design and skiing. The Student Government Association (SGA) is a central and vital organization at the College. This legislative body is responsible for all areas of student life and represents all students who are enrolled at the College. Students also are represented on various administrative committees within the College, including the College Cabinet and the Academic Senate.

The Office of Mission and Service offers the Service Learning Club for students who are interested in volunteer work within the community. The club participates in a variety of service projects that acknowledge children, the disabled, the environment and issues of health care and human rights. Every year, the club travels to a select location for Alternative Spring Break. In March of 2013, the group traveled to Union Beach, N.J. to help with Hurricane Sandy recovery.

ADMISSIONS PROCESS

La Roche College, which is selective in its admission process, seeks students who have a clear commitment to personal growth and achievement and demonstrate a strong desire to fulfill their academic potential.

The admission committee reviews each applicant individually, assessing personal and academic strengths in light of a student's background. Committee members carefully examine high school records, including course work, grade point average and SAT or ACT scores. SAT and ACT scores should be sent directly to the Office of Admissions at La Roche. (La Roche's code numbers are SAT: 2379 and ACT: 3607).

Candidates should submit a completed application and a copy of their high school transcript. Nursing majors are required to provide an essay explaining why the student wants to be a nurse, along with two letters of recommendation.

Each paper application requires a $50 nonrefundable fee. Applications also may be completed online at www.laroche.edu for free. Application fees are waived for students who visit the college for a personal campus visit and tour, a Saturday visit or an open house.

La Roche adheres to a rolling admissions system, meaning students receive decisions once their application credentials are complete.

To ensure appropriate financial aid and preferred housing opportunities, students should apply as soon as possible, preferably before March 31 for the fall semester and Dec. 31 for the spring semester.

For more information regarding the La Roche College admission process, prospective students should contact:

OFFICE OF ADMISSIONS

La Roche College

9000 Babcock Boulevard

Pittsburgh, Pennsylvania 15237

United States

Phone: 412-536-1272

800-838-4572 (toll-free)

Fax: 412-847-1820

E-mail: admissions@laroche.edu

Web site: www.laroche.edu

LAKE FOREST COLLEGE

AT A GLANCE

Founded in 1857, Lake Forest College has a long tradition of academic excellence and is known for its innovative curriculum. In addition to majors in the humanities, social sciences, and natural sciences, the College features programs of study in pre-law, pre-medicine, communication, business, finance, computer science, and still other practical areas. Lake Forest prepares students to lead successful lives, and many go on to competitive graduate programs and top jobs. Abundant internships, research opportunities, personal guidance from professors, and connections to nearby Chicago also set the Lake Forest apart.

Students learn in a rigorous academic environment in small class settings where professors do all the teaching and also serve as advisors and mentors. Professors are accomplished scholars, published authors, and recipients of prestigious grants. Many have come from some of the top PhD programs in the country.

Students represent 47 states and 79 countries around the world and international and ethnic minorities make up more than 25 percent of the student body. Together they comprise a learning community that prepares them to succeed in a global society.

More than fifty student groups provide a host of extracurricular opportunities that develop leadership skills and enhance students' campus experience and post-college prospects. Lake Forest College offers recreational music, art, and theater programs, as well as 17 varsity sports and intramural and club sports. It competes in NCAA Division III.

LOCATION AND ENVIRONMENT

Just an hour's train ride to Chicago, the College is located in the town of Lake Forest, Illinois, 30 miles north of the city along the shores of Lake Michigan. The 107-acre residential campus is a safe academic home in a beautiful wooded suburban setting within walking distance to the train to downtown Chicago, historic Lake Forest, and the beaches of Lake Michigan.

The College is only 25 miles from O'Hare International Airport and is also served by Midway Airport and Mitchell International Airport in Milwaukee.

The campus is surrounded by lush wooded neighborhoods, ravines, natural prairies, the beautiful beaches along Lake Michigan, and an extensive network of bike and running trails. Nearby Chicago boasts nearly 70 world-class museums, more than 200 theaters, seven major league sports teams, and one of the nation's top opera companies. Chicago is known for its cleanliness, abundant green space, good transportation system, and friendly people.

OFF-CAMPUS OPPORTUNITIES

Lake Forest encourages students to take advantage of study, internship, and research opportunities in Chicago, around the United States, and abroad. Internship opportunities are plentiful in the Chicago area and students have interned at places such as the Art Institute of Chicago, Chicago Blackhawks, Chicago Board of Trade, Chicago Council on Global Affairs, Edelman Public Relations Worldwide, Morgan Stanley, NBC Chicago, Second City, and the John G. Shedd Aquarium, among others.

In addition to a well-established internship program, Lake Forest College provides students with a wide variety of opportunities for off-campus study. Semester-long options in the United States include the "Lake Forest College in the Loop" Chicago Semester Program, Chicago Arts Program, Oak Ridge Science Semester, Chicago Urban Studies Program, Chicago Program in Business and Society, Newberry Library Program in the Humanities, and the Washington Semester Program at American University.

There are many options for international study, such as Lake Forest's own international internship programs in Paris, France and Granada, Spain; the Ancient Civilizations Program in Greece, which uses historical and archaeological sites and museums to study the ancient Aegean world; the Border Studies Program in Mexico and the U.S.; as well as a semester-long program in China and New Zealand. As a member of the Associated Colleges of the Midwest, Lake Forest also offers programs in Botswana, Costa Rica, England, India, Italy, Japan, Russia, and Tanzania. The off-campus program director works with students to facilitate participation in other approved off-campus study programs.

MAJORS AND DEGREES OFFERED

The academic calendar is based on two 15-week semesters, beginning in August and January. Students normally take four course credits per semester (the equivalent of 16 semester hours).

There are no teaching assistants at the College. Courses are taught in small classroom settings by professors who are experts in their fields and who also serve students as one-on-one advisors. In addition to classroom studies, students are encouraged to complete an internship, conduct original research, and study abroad for a semester.

A Lake Forest graduate will have studied a broad range of ideas; developed real competence in writing, speaking, and quantitative skills; and gained significant experience in humanities, natural sciences and mathematics, and social sciences while completing requirements for a major in an academic department or interdisciplinary program. The College's General Education Curriculum, advising system, and major requirements are designed to support these educational ideals.

Lake Forest awards the Bachelor of Arts (BA) degree in both traditional academic departments and interdisciplinary programs. Areas of study include: African American studies, American studies, anthropology, area studies, studio art, art history, art education, Asian studies, biology, border studies, business, chemistry, cinema studies, classical studies, communication, computer science, economics, education (elementary and secondary), engineering (dual degree), English (literature and writing), environmental studies, finance, history, international relations, Islamic world studies, Latin American studies, legal studies, mathematics, media design and technology, metropolitan studies, modern languages and literatures (Arabic, Chinese, French, German, Italian, Japanese, Russian, and Spanish), media studies, music, music education, neuroscience, philosophy, physics, politics, psychology, religion, rhetoric, social justice, sociology, theater, women's and gender studies. Lake Forest also offers pre-professional programs in law, medicine, dentistry, and veterinary medicine.

Accelerated and dual-degree programs are offered. Three-year degree programs are available in communication and philosophy. Dual-degree programs are available in law, international studies, pharmacy, and engineering. Lake Forest is affiliated with several competitive law schools that allow students to complete a bachelor's degree and a law degree in a total of six years, rather than the usual seven. Qualified Lake Forest College students may be admitted to the Monterey Institute of International Studies with accelerated status, and can complete their master's degrees with 48 credits as opposed to the 60 normally required. A dual-degree program has been arranged, leading to a Bachelor of Arts Degree in Biology from Lake Forest College and a Doctor of Pharmacy from the Rosalind Franklin University of Medicine and Science. The engineering program is in cooperation with the Sever Institute of Technology at Washington University (St. Louis).

ACADEMIC PROGRAMS

The First-Year Studies Program (FIYS)

First-year studies classes are small in size to encourage interaction and discussion. The FIYS professors also serve as the students' primary academic advisors and help them navigate the College's academic offerings during their first year. With more than twenty topics to choose from, first-year studies courses cover a wide range of academic interests from music, art, and politics to neuroscience, terrorism and religion, many with a focus on Chicago or directly utilizing the resources available there. Chicago plays an integral role in the FIYS program. Students travel to the city with their class during orientation week, providing a first-hand introduction to how the educational, cultural, and social resources of Chicago will influence their coursework and experiences during their four years at Lake Forest.

Honors Fellow Program

As part of the first-year student admission application process, select students are invited to apply to the Honors Fellow Program.

The Richter Apprentice Scholars Program

This program provides students, early in their academic careers, with the opportunity to conduct independent, individual research with Lake Forest faculty. In the summer after their first year, each student in the Richter Program is employed for a ten-week period and does independent research one-on-one with a faculty member.

The Independent Scholar Program

This program allows students to develop an academic major of their own, working closely with a faculty advisor, culminating in a thesis or a creative project.

CAMPUS FACILITIES AND EQUIPMENT

A new 230-bed residence hall will open in August 2013 and features doubles, suites, and super suites with living rooms, lounges, kitchen, and a multipurpose room for group events.

A new recreation, sports, and fitness facility opened in April 2010 and includes three new multipurpose courts, a suspended running track, an aerobic and dance studio, a batting/golf cage, strength, cardio, and fitness spaces, among other amenities.

The Donnelley and Lee Library is a twenty-first century library and information technology center incorporating the latest learning and technological innovations while providing a comfortable environment for collaboration and study. Features include wireless network; 24-hour computing labs; numerous study spaces and workstations; a production and rhetoric room; "smart" classrooms, and a cafe.

The Mohr Student Center is a student-centered social space that is the hub of social activity on campus. It features pool tables and other games, stage and performance space, large-screen TVs, lounges, deli/snack bar, and an outdoor terrace with seating.

CENTER FOR CHICAGO PROGRAMS

Chicago provides a hands-on resource for student learning through research, internships, study, and fun. At the Center for Chicago Programs on campus, students can plan visits to the city and professors can get help incorporating Chicago resources into their classrooms. The Center also brings well-known Chicagoans to the College for lectures and performances.

TUITION, ROOM, BOARD AND FEES

2012 -2013

Tuition: $37,660.00

Room: $4,440.00

Board: $4,610.00

Fees: $640.00

FINANCIAL AID

Lake Forest College provides an affordable, high-quality education through maintaining a strong commitment to supporting each student's demonstrated financial need.

The College offers academic scholarships ranging from $5,000 to $16,000 and talent scholarships ranging from $1,000 to $5,000 for recognized dedication in the fine arts, foreign languages, leadership, music, sciences (including math and computers), theater, or writing.

The College offers an In-State Scholarship in the amount of $12,000 for students living in Illinois who have graduated from an Illinois high school.

STUDENT ORGANIZATIONS AND ACTIVITIES

Lake Forest College is a place to study, work, and live. With the diversity of the student body there is an eclectic mix of activities and opportunities outside the classroom.

Student organizations include student government, international interest groups, Greek Life, academic honor societies, community service, publications and media, music and performance, spiritual and religious groups, and many others.

Students have a voice in how the College is run and are actively involved in governance committees such as the College Council and have representation on the Board of Trustees. Student writers and performers can showcase their talents on stage with the Garrick Players, by hosting a show on "WMXM," the College's FM radio station, or through the student newspaper, literary magazines, chorus and instrumental ensembles. Academic honor societies enjoy active student participation as do the community service groups and many special-interest clubs. The College provides and maintains a comprehensive intramural and intercollegiate athletic program. There are two national fraternities and five national sororities, all housed within the residence halls. All students have equal opportunity to take advantage of the richness of the College's programs.

Lake Forest College competes in the NCAA Division III fielding nine women's and eight men's intercollegiate varsity teams. Women's teams include basketball, cross-country, handball, ice hockey, soccer, softball, swimming and diving, tennis, and volleyball. Men's teams include basketball, cross-country, football, handball, ice hockey, soccer, swimming and diving, and tennis. The College also offers an extensive roster of intramural and club sports.

The College's Center for Chicago Programs facilitates engagement with the resources of Chicago which often complements programs for student organizations as well as provides students with information on cultural and social activities happening downtown. The train to Chicago is a short walk from campus and students enjoy traveling to the city for fun and entertainment. The College shuttle provides service seven days a week to popular shopping areas and destinations around campus.

ADMISSIONS PROCESS

The criteria used for selection include assessment of a student's program of study, academic achievement, aptitude, intellectual curiosity, qualities of character and personality, and activities.

Standardized test scores (ACT/SAT) are optional, except for international or home-schooled candidates, and those applying for some academic scholarships. A personal interview is required for students who do not submit scores.

LANDMARK COLLEGE

AT A GLANCE

Landmark College offers two and four-year degree options and is a global leader in integrated teaching methods for capable students with learning disabilities, including dyslexia, ADHD and ASD.

Established in 1985, Landmark College in Putney, Vermont, was the first degree-granting institution of higher education dedicated to serving students with diagnosed learning disability (LD), including dyslexia, attention deficit hyperactivity disorder (ADHD), and autism spectrum disorder (ASD). Our renowned faculty and resource-intensive programs make Landmark College the best place for students who learn differently to gain skills and strategies for success. Our program is designed for students to develop and practice academic skills and strategies in a way that builds from semester to semester. The innovative programs— developed over 25 years of working with students who learn differently— make Landmark College a global leader. Studies lead to an associate's or a bachelor's degree, and integrate traditional college level coursework with Landmark College's signature use of proven learning strategies and the latest in educational technology. Landmark College's rigorous curriculum prepares students to best pursue a bachelor's, master's or professional degree.

LOCATION AND ENVIRONMENT

Landmark College's campus is located in beautiful southern Vermont, in the town of Putney.

Putney is just nine miles from historic Brattleboro, which was named one of the Top 10 Small Towns in America. In summer and spring, activities include hiking, running, mountain biking, and swimming. During the winter, students find an atmosphere perfect for snowboarding, cross-country and downhill skiing, and winter camping. For those who prefer something more urban, Boston is 2-hours by car and New York City is only 4 hours.

OFF-CAMPUS OPPORTUNITIES

Students enjoy exploring the diverse social and cultural offerings in the local Vermont towns of Putney and Brattleboro, and in Massachusetts, Northampton and Amherst. These areas have bustling downtowns with shops, restaurants, and entertainment. Brattleboro has a vibrant arts community with galleries, music, and theater. Northampton and Amherst are home to elite institutions and a thriving creative culture. Larger cities like Boston, Montreal, and New York are close enough for day and weekend trips.

At Landmark College, students have the opportunity to study at locations around the world, including Africa, England, Ireland, Greece, and Costa Rica. These study abroad options enable students to experience other cultures first-hand. While expanding their horizons, students are engaged in rigorous college courses taught by Landmark College faculty members.

MAJORS AND DEGREES OFFERED

Landmark College offers a Bachelor of Arts, Associate of Arts and Associate of Science degree options in the following areas of study:
B. A. in Liberal Studies

A.A. in Business Administration

A.A. in Business Studies

A.A. in General Studies

A.A. in Liberal Arts

A.S. in Life Sciences

A.S. in Computer Science/Gaming

ACADEMIC PROGRAMS

While many colleges offer special programs for students with learning disabilities, Landmark College is one of the only accredited colleges in the United States designed exclusively for students with dyslexia, attention deficit hyperactivity disorder (ADHD), autism spectrum disorder (ASD) and other specific learning disabilities.

Why does Landmark College's approach succeed? Students learn the skills and strategies necessary for success in college and the workforce. That's why they succeed.

Bright students who learn differently can thrive and achieve their goals—that is a core belief at the College. Designed through research and practice, Landmark College's innovative educational model helps all students become confident, self-empowered, and independently successful learners.

Students at Landmark College experience more personal, directed assistance than at other colleges and universities. Each student receives individualized attention from faculty in classes tailored to meet his or her individual learning style. A wide variety of courses are offered for skills development, college credit, and Bachelor's and Associate's Degree Programs. Experienced advisors meet frequently with students to review and guide progress. All faculty are trained professional educators, not teaching assistants or peer tutors.

Landmark College also offers several summer and January-Term programs:

Three-Week High School Summer Programs for Rising Juniors & Seniors

This program is designed for rising juniors and seniors in high school, and it includes a new Social Pragmatics Track.

Two-Week Transition to College Program for College-Bound Seniors

This program immerses recent high school graduates in an actual living/learning college experience.

Five-Week Visiting College Student Summer Program

This program teaches effective learning skills and strategies for college-level studies. Students have the opportunity to earn up to five college credits.

Three-Week Visiting College Student January-Term Program

This program is designed to provide maximum opportunity for intense learning and focuses on enriching the mind and body connection. Students may earn up to five college credits.

CAMPUS FACILITIES AND EQUIPMENT

The campus includes several multi-purpose classroom buildings, five traditional residence halls, two apartment and condominium-style residential buildings, and a fine arts building housing two theaters. The main campus was designed by noted architect Edward Durrell Stone, known for his design of the Kennedy Center in Washington, D.C.

The campus library houses a growing print, audiovisual, and digital materials collection as well as specialized areas for research, instruction, LD research, and media production. Other campus facilities include the Drake Center for Academic Support, a Women's Resource Center, the Click Sports Center and the Strauch Family Student Center.

TUITION, ROOM, BOARD, AND FEES

Fees for 2013 -2014 Academic Year

$49,500 Tuition

$5,300 Room Fee

$5,000 Board Fee

$300 Damage Deposit

$1,500 Health Insurance

$130 Technology Fee (International students: $1,000)

$61,730 Total

Note: Landmark College's tuition and fees may qualify as a medical tax deduction.

FINANCIAL AID

Most Landmark College students qualify to receive federal loans and grants, as well as vocational rehabilitation grants. In addition, the College offers these institutionally-funded programs:

Landmark College Scholarships: $5,000 to $35,000 (based on need)

Landmark College Recognition Scholarships: $5,000 to $10,000 (based on leadership, character and talent)

Landmark Endowment Scholarships: $500 to $8,000 (based on need and other criteria)

Total Financial Aid Awarded: $7.4 million

Average Grant Award: $20,276

Number of Scholarships Awarded:

166 (new students)

197 (returning students)

STUDENT ORGANIZATIONS AND ACTIVITIES

Students who come to Landmark College have the opportunity to learn and grow into self-assured, contributing community members. Educators across the College believe that there's more to education than just what can be found in textbooks and classrooms. Students are supported and encouraged to grow in all areas of life: body, mind, and spirit.

The Division of Student Affairs helps students to get involved by providing numerous opportunities, programs, and services. These opportunities are designed to enhance intellectual, social, ethical, physical, and cultural development. Students find their favorite pastimes and discover new activities. At Landmark College, students build the self-direction needed for maximum individual accomplishment.

At Landmark College, faculty, staff, and fellow students understand many of the challenges and triumphs of living with an LD. Surrounded by understanding, students can relax in an atmosphere where their capabilities are recognized. We want learners to strive toward success at everything they try. Why? Because we know they can do it. This is borne out in fact by the success of our graduates.

From the faculty and staff to the president of the College, Landmark endeavors to work with and for students. We encourage students to become involved in the campus community and to take leadership roles here and in the world. The friendships, experiences, and connections that students make at Landmark College create an exciting environment in which to live and learn. Our goal is to provide the widest possible range of activities, and to offer something that will appeal to every student.

ADMISSIONS PROCESS

Our Admissions Process is as straightforward as we can make it. Here is a brief overview (full details are in the application package or visit our website: www.landmark.edu).

What We Consider

We are looking for students who meet two essential criteria:

Average to superior intellectual potential, and

Diagnosis of dyslexia, ADHD, ASD and/or other specific learning disability
The Steps We Follow

The Admissions Process has three steps:

1. Applicant completes the application and personal statement (preferably in own handwriting) and submits these to the Admissions Office with the application fee.

2. Applicant ensures that all required records and recommendations get to Landmark College in time for consideration by the Admissions Committee.

3. Our Admissions Committee reviews the completed application package and determines whether to:

Request further documentation

Invite applicant for an interview

Decline the application

Admit applicant directly to Landmark College

LAWRENCE TECHNOLOGICAL UNIVERSITY

AT A GLANCE

Lawrence Technological University is a private, personally focused university providing students a rigorous, high-quality education – an education that pays off. Most Lawrence Tech students are employed within one month of graduating and according to a Bloomberg Businessweek survey, the earning power of a Lawrence Tech bachelor's degree ranks in the top 20 percent of U.S. universities. This means Lawrence Tech grads tend to earn more during their careers than other college graduates.

The University, including its graduate programs, is accredited by the Higher Learning Commission and is a member of the North Central Association of Colleges and Schools. LTU placed in the top tier category of Best University-Masters-Midwest in the U.S. News and World Report's 2013 America's Best Colleges rankings. Other honors include the designation as a Military Friendly School by G.I. Jobs. Lawrence Tech's online bachelor's degree program is ranked first in the nation for student engagement, and sixth overall, in the 2013 survey by U.S. News & World Report.

Lawrence Tech's honors program is available for highly motivated and qualified students, as well as Quest, which encourages students to go above and beyond their studies and explore their interests on a deeper level. A scholars program is also available, designed to ease the transition from high school to college by providing support services. The unique Leadership Program, integrated into all bachelor's degrees, helps students gain critical thinking, teamwork, and communication skills.

LTU's student-faculty ratio is 11:1. Most undergraduate classes have 19 or fewer students, and less than 1 percent of the classes enroll more than 50. More than 500 students live in University Housing. Women make up 25 percent of the student body, and 28 states and 43 nations are represented on campus.

LOCATION AND ENVIRONMENT

The University is located in Southfield, a dynamic suburb of more than 72,000 people in Oakland County, Michigan, home to hundreds of Fortune 500 and international companies. According to a report by TechAmerica, Michigan is leading the nation in technology-related job growth. Southeastern Michigan also offers a rich variety of recreational and cultural activities, with public transportation making most areas accessible to students. Hundreds of major research, manufacturing, scientific, and business enterprises are located nearby, aiding students who work full- or part-time while attending classes, as well as those in co-op and internships. The campus is close to major freeways and about a 30-minute drive north of downtown Detroit and Detroit Metro Airport.

OFF-CAMPUS OPPORTUNITIES

Students can participate in applied research partnerships that offer remarkable hands-on experience. Professional organizations provide additional opportunities to network with industry leaders.

Lawrence Tech's Detroit Studio and Innovation Center allows students to explore community-based architectural, urban design, and community development projects. Architecture students regularly build homes for Habitat for Humanity.

The Global Engineering Program arranges for engineering students to work and study abroad. The Study-Abroad Program is open to all students.

The University also maintains relationships with universities in Asia, Canada, Europe, Mexico, and the Middle East.

MAJORS AND DEGREES OFFERED

LTU is a 4,500-student university offering over 100 undergraduate, master's, and doctoral programs in Colleges of Architecture and Design, Arts and Sciences, Engineering, and Management. Most programs are available days or evenings; many are offered on weekends and online. Dual majors and customized degree programs combining either associate and bachelor's programs or bachelor's and master's programs also are available. Pre-professional preparation includes pre-dental, pre-law, and pre-medical programs, as well as a post-baccalaureate certificate in premedical studies.

The College of Architecture and Design offers bachelor's degrees in architecture, game art, graphic design, industrial design, interaction design, interior architecture, and transportation design. Lawrence Tech enrolls more architectural students than any other school in Michigan, and is one of the top 10 largest architecture schools in the nation.

The College of Arts and Sciences offers bachelor's degrees in chemical biology, chemistry, computer science (business software development, game software development, network software development, and scientific software development), English and communication arts, environmental chemistry, humanities, mathematics, mathematics and computer science, media communication, molecular and cell biology, physics, physics and computer science, and psychology (clinical psychology, industrial/organizational psychology, and pre-med/biobehavioral psychology).

Bachelor's degrees offered by the College of Engineering are architectural engineering (combined bachelor's and master's program), audio engineering technology, biomedical engineering, biomedical engineering technology, civil engineering, computer engineering, construction management, electrical engineering (electrical energy systems and electronics engineering), engineering technology, industrial operations engineering, and mechanical engineering (alternative energy, automotive engineering, manufacturing engineering, mechanical system design, robotics engineering, and thermo-fluids).

The College of Management offers undergraduate degrees in business administration (general business, information technology, and marketing) and a minor in business.

Minors include aeronautical engineering, biology, business management, chemistry, computer science, economics, energy engineering, English, general sciences, history, mathematics, media communication, philosophy, physics, psychology, Spanish, technical and professional communication, and television and video production.

Associate degrees are offered in chemical technology, communications engineering technology, construction engineering technology, general studies, manufacturing engineering technology, mechanical engineering technology, and radio and television broadcasting.

Undergraduate certificates can be earned in alternative energy engineering technology, animation, biochemical engineering, bioelectronics, biomechanics, building information modeling and computer visualization, computer science, electrical power systems, embedded systems, entrepreneurial skills, entrepreneurial strategy, industrial/organizational psychology, set design, technical and professional communication, and television and video production.

THEORY AND PRACTICE

LTU provides students the tools they need to compete and succeed within their chosen profession. Whether inside or outside of the classroom, the University's theory and practice approach to learning gives opportunities to combine practical knowledge with real-world applications.

Lawrence Tech is the recipient of numerous grants and awards for the development and implementation of innovative materials and practices that are expected to double the lifespan of concrete bridges and new armor protection for soldiers.

Student engineering teams design, build, and race hybrid, Baja, and Formula-style vehicles. Students also compete in bridge building and assembling, designing zero energy homes, and in airplane design, robotics, and concrete canoe competitions.

CAMPUS FACILITIES AND EQUIPMENT

Lawrence Tech's modern 102-acre campus includes a variety of academic, recreational, and housing facilities.

All undergraduates are provided high-end personal laptops, tablets, or devices that are customized with the software they need to succeed – a unique benefit valued up to $15,000. Lawrence Tech is Michigan's first wireless laptop computer campus and is ranked among the nation's top 50 "unwired" universities.

The University has two residence halls, featuring one- and two-bedroom apartment-style suites that accommodate two to four students. Single rooms also are available. All utilities, wireless Internet access, basic cable TV, and individual telephone lines and voicemail are included.

The library offers a wide selection of print and electronic materials, including numerous online databases, visual resources, digital images, and full-text periodical titles accessible on and off campus. Librarians provide research guidance and instruction. As a key part of the research community in Michigan, the library participates in the reciprocal borrowing and sharing of resources with many other institutions.

LTU's full-service 102-acre campus offers a variety of academic, recreational, housing, and food service options. Students use advanced, leading edge facilities, including the acclaimed Center for Innovative Materials Research; the region's only environmental scanning microscope; architectural and design studios; a structural testing lab; a wind tunnel; wood, metal, and model shops; a 4 x 4 chassis dynamometer; and labs for alternative energy, robotics, biomedical research, graphics, and much more.

The A. Alfred Taubman Student Services Center consolidates all student support services – from admissions through career services – into a convenient one-stop center. This innovative 42,000-square-foot building, which utilizes many energy-efficient and environmentally friendly features and technologies, serves as a "living laboratory" and is part of a region-wide storm water management effort. The Center for Innovative Materials Research is a state-of-the-art laboratory for the research, development, and testing of materials for defense and infrastructure applications. Students participate in related research projects as part of their academic programs.

The Automotive Engineering Institute provides students opportunities to conduct sponsored research on a unique 4 x 4 vehicle chassis dynamometer, which measures many areas of vehicle performance.

TUITION, ROOM, BOARD, AND FEES

Tuition for all undergrads includes a laptop, tablet or device with all requied software. The 2012–13 tuition for students majoring in arts and sciences was $770 per credit hour for basic studies courses and $840 for other arts and sciences and management courses. Sophomores in arts and sciences and management paid $890 per credit hour, while the tuition for juniors and seniors in the two majors was $935 per credit hour. In architecture and design and engineering, tuition for freshmen and sophomores was $930 to $935 per credit hour; for juniors and seniors, it was $955 per credit hour.

A normal course load is 12–17 credit hours per semester. The undergraduate registration fee is $135 each semester. International students on temporary visas must have sufficient funds to pay for an entire year of tuition, room and board, and books at the time of first registration. Additional fees for specific labs and studio courses vary.

Room costs vary, but average $6,000 per year. Average board is $1,620, with a variety of meal plans available.

FINANCIAL AID

Approximately 71 percent of students receive financial assistance and the University awards more than $43 million in scholarships, grants, loans, and work-study funds each academic year. The average annual, need-based financial aid package is $21,796. Many privately funded scholarships are awarded to qualified students, based on need and/or scholastic performance. Part-time employment is available at the University on a first-come, first-served basis for full-time students. Student loans are also available from a variety of sources – state, federal, and private. Prospective students are urged to contact the Office of Financial Aid for information on deadlines and requirements for eligibility (ltu.edu/financial_aid).

STUDENT ORGANIZATIONS AND ACTIVITIES

More than 60 student clubs and organizations, including fraternities, sororities, honor societies, and student chapters of professional groups are active on campus and sponsor a variety of activities during the year. The Student Government sponsors and supports a variety of campus activities.

A member of the National Association of Intercollegiate Athletics, Lawrence Tech offers Blue Devil varsity sports in men's and women's basketball, soccer, cross-country, and lacrosse; men's bowling; and women's volleyball and dance team. The men's hockey team plays in the American Collegiate Hockey Association (ACHA Division III). Intramural sports leagues and tournaments in badminton, basketball, billiards, dodge ball, flag football, golf, racquetball, soccer, softball, table tennis, tennis, volleyball, and wallyball are active throughout the academic year. Club sports include lacrosse, mixed martial arts, and biking. The Don Ridler Field House is open to all students and features a fitness track, gymnasium, racquetball courts, game room, saunas, and weight and conditioning room.

ADMISSIONS PROCESS

Admissions decisions are based on a student's recalculated GPA, ACT/SAT scores, essay, and letters of recommendation. Strong emphasis is placed on grade trends as well as the strength of the curriculum and rigor of a student's senior schedule. A portfolio is required for transportation design, industrial design, and game art majors.

Lawrence Tech's ACT code is 2020 and SAT is 1399. Required high school courses vary with the curriculum, and LTU offers a number of basic studies courses designed to augment incoming students' backgrounds if deficiencies exist.

Programs start in August and January. An optional summer semester begins in May. Entry in the fall semester is advised but not required. Students must submit transcripts from all schools attended, along with a nonrefundable $30 application fee. Students may also fill out a brief survey and apply free at ltu.edu/applyfree. To view a digital viewbook and an application form, visit www.ltu.edu or contact:

Lawrence Technological University

Office of Admissions

21000 West Ten Mile Road

Southfield, MI 48075-1058

800.225.5588 or 248.204.3160

admissions@ltu.edu

www.ltu.edu

LE MOYNE COLLEGE

AT A GLANCE

Le Moyne College is a four-year, coeducational Jesuit College of approximately 2,500 full-time undergraduate students that uniquely balances a comprehensive liberal arts education with preparation for specific career paths or graduate study.

Founded by the Society of Jesus in 1946, Le Moyne is the second youngest of the twenty-eight Jesuit colleges and universities in the United States. Its emphasis is on the education of the whole person and on the search for meaning and value as integral parts of an intellectual life. Learning, leadership and service are the hallmarks of a Le Moyne College education. Those values are evident in the College's undergraduate majors in more than 30 areas of study, as well as in its pre-professional studies and graduate programs in business administration, education, nursing and physician assistant studies.

Le Moyne's personal approach to education is reflected in the quality of contact between students and faculty members. With approximately 150 full-time faculty members, Le Moyne has a student-faculty ratio of 13:1 and an average class size of 21.

LOCATION AND ENVIRONMENT

Le Moyne's 160-plus acre, tree-lined campus is located in a residential setting 10 minutes from downtown Syracuse, the heart of New York state, whose metropolitan population is about 700,000. Just a few miles outside the city are the rolling hills, picturesque lakes, and miles of open country for which central New York is renowned.

Off Campus Opportunities

Syracuse is convenient to most major cities throughout the Northeast, New England, and Canada and offers a wide array of shopping centers and restaurants, many near Le Moyne. Syracuse offers year-round entertainment in the form of rock concerts at the Landmark Theatre, professional baseball and hockey, the Bristol Omni-theatre, the Syracuse Stage, the Everson Museum of Art, and the Armory Square district downtown, which offers one-of-a-kind eateries, pubs, and coffeehouses in addition to a wide variety of social and cultural events. Central New York is home to an extensive network of state and county parks, recreational areas, and other facilities that offer an abundance of recreational opportunities, including swimming, boating, hiking, downhill and cross-country skiing, snowboarding, and golf.

Majors and Degrees

Le Moyne College awards the Bachelor of Arts degree in biological sciences, communication (advertising, filmmaking, journalism, music industry, music journalism, music and culture, media studies, public relations, television/radio), computer science, criminology (human services, international affairs, law enforcement, research), economics, English (creative writing, literature), French, history, mathematics (actuarial science, pure mathematics, statistics), peace and global studies, philosophy, physics, political science, psychology, religious studies, sociology (anthropology, criminology, human services, research and theory), Spanish, and theatre arts. The Bachelor of Science degree is awarded in biochemistry, biological sciences (health professions, molecular biology, neurobiology), chemistry, economics, environmental science systems, environmental studies, general science, physics, and psychology. The Bachelor of Science in business is awarded in accounting, business analytics, finance, information systems, management and leadership, and marketing. A Bachelor of Science in nursing is also offered.

Students may minor in arts administration, Catholic studies, classical humanities, film, gender and women's studies, health information systems, human resource management, Irish literature, Italian, Latin, legal studies, management information systems, medieval studies, music, urban and regional studies, or visual arts as well as most of the major fields of study offered. Pre-professional programs are offered in dentistry, law, medicine, optometry, physical therapy, physician assistant studies, podiatry, and veterinary science. Students may prepare for teaching careers through certification programs in adolescent education, dual adolescent/special education, dual childhood/special education, and TESOL.

Le Moyne College and the L. C. Smith College of Engineering and Computer Science at Syracuse University have a dual-degree program in which students may earn a bachelor's degree from Le Moyne and a master's degree in engineering from Syracuse University in as few as five years. Concentrations include aerospace, chemical, electrical, and mechanical engineering, as well as computer science and other fields of engineering.

Formal accelerated 3-4 programs are offered in dentistry, optometry, and podiatry in cooperation with the State University of New York at Buffalo School of Dental Medicine, Pennsylvania College of Optometry, and the New York College of Podiatric Medicine. Pre-dental students may also participate in an early assurance program with the State University of New York at Buffalo School of Dental Medicine. Cooperative 3-2 dual-degree programs in engineering are available with Clarkson University, Manhattan College, and University of Detroit Mercy.

SUNY Upstate Medical University in Syracuse offers students pursuing careers in the health-related professions an accelerated 3-3 doctoral-level transfer program in physical therapy as well as two-year cooperative transfer programs in medical technology and respiratory care. Pre-medical students at Le Moyne are also offered the opportunity to participate in a medical school early assurance program. An early assurance program for premedical students is also available through the State University of New York at Buffalo School of Medicine.

ACADEMIC PROGRAMS

While each major department has its own sequence requirements for the minimum 120 credit hours needed for the Le Moyne degree, the College is convinced that there is a fundamental intellectual discipline that should characterize the graduate of a superior liberal arts college. Le Moyne's core curriculum provides this foundation by including studies of English language and literature, philosophy, history, religious studies, natural science, and social science.

For exceptional students, Le Moyne offers an integral honors program that includes an interdisciplinary humanities sequence as well as departmental honors courses.

The study-abroad program allows qualified students to spend a semester or year in numerous countries around the world. Le Moyne College has study-abroad programs or affiliations in Czech Republic, Dominican Republic, Germany, Ireland, Scotland, Spain, and England. Students can also use partner programs to study in locations such as Australia, Costa Rica, Egypt, France, Italy, Japan, and South Africa. Le Moyne is a participant in the sixty-member New York State Visiting Student Program.

As part of the mission of preparing future leaders, Le Moyne College places a strong emphasis on career preparation through internships and other forms of experiential education. Academic departments and the Office of Career Services both provide programs and services for students interested in interning part time and full time, both locally and in major cities such as New York and Washington, D.C. The Offices of Service Learning and the Academic Deans are also involved in experiential education to promote learning outside the classroom. In the sciences, students take part in campus research with faculty mentors. Others receive assistance in pursuing outstanding opportunities off campus in leading research laboratories and health-care settings. Through the College's long-standing relationship with The Washington Center for Internships and Academic Seminars, students from all majors complete full-time semester-long internships in Washington, D.C., with government, business, or major nonprofit organizations. Faculty members in the Department of Political Science assist students interested in opportunities in Albany, NY, the state's seat of government, with either the State Senate or Assembly. Finally, the education programs at Le Moyne put students into school classrooms starting immediately as freshmen and continuing each year until graduation.

Le Moyne students may enroll in Army and Air Force ROTC programs in conjunction with Syracuse University.

CAMPUS FACILITIES AND EQUIPMENT

Le Moyne students benefit from an ongoing commitment to technological excellence. The College's 49 buildings are equipped with accounting, biological sciences, chemistry, computer science, physics, psychology, and statistics laboratories. The W. Carroll Coyne Center for the Performing Arts houses generous production, performance, and classroom space; the latest light and sound technology; scene and costume shops; an aerobics and dance studio; and rehearsal rooms for instrumental and choral music. Academic facilities also include an extensively renovated color television studio, a radio/recording studio; a receiver-antenna satellite dish; transmission and scanning electron microscopes; a nuclear magnetic resonance spectrometer; a gas chromatograph/mass spectrophotometer; a 240,000-volume, open-stack library; and extensive on-site computer facilities. A wireless network allows students easy access to the campus network and Internet. All classrooms are smart classrooms, with multimedia capabilities that expand and enrich the learning process. Le Moyne students have access to other libraries through the Central New York Library Resources Council, and the campus Academic Support Center is available to students for instructional support. Athletic facilities include a new soccer/lacrosse turf field; a new softball field; baseball field, tennis, basketball, and racquetball courts; a weight-training and fitness center; practice fields; and two gymnasiums. A recreation center houses an Olympic-size indoor swimming pool, jogging track, indoor tennis and volleyball courts, and additional basketball, racquetball, and fitness areas. In 2010, the College opened a new plaza, which houses its bookstore, a café and a pizzeria; the new Dolphin Den, which features a food court and a convenience store and has quickly become a popular space for students to meet, have a bite to eat, or just spend a quiet moment relaxing; and a multi-use turf field, home to four of the College's 17 NCAA teams. In addition, a 48,000-square-foot, state-of-the-art addition to Le Moyne's existing science complex was completed and opened at the beginning of the 2012 spring semester.

Tuition, Room, Board and Fees

For 2013–14, Le Moyne's tuition is $29,470. Room and board charges are $11,740. Additional fees amount to approximately $990, and books and supplies cost approximately $700.

FINANCIAL AID

Financial aid is offered to a large percentage of Le Moyne's students through scholarships, grants, loans, and work-study assignments. Le Moyne offers a generous program of merit-based academic and athletic scholarships as well as financial aid based on a student's need and academic promise. Federal funds are available through the Federal Pell Grant, Federal Work-Study, Federal Supplemental Educational Opportunity Grant, and Federal Perkins Loan programs. A student's eligibility for need-based financial aid is determined from both the Free Application for Federal Student Aid (FAFSA) and the Le Moyne Financial Aid Application Form. It is recommended that these forms be mailed by February 1.

STUDENT ORGANIZATIONS AND ACTIVITIES

A wide range of student-directed activities, athletics, clubs, and service organizations complement the academic experience. Intramural sports are very popular with Le Moyne students; nearly 85 percent of the students participate. Le Moyne also has seventeen NCAA intercollegiate teams (eight for men and nine for women). More than 80 percent of students live in residence halls, apartments, and town houses on campus. The Residence Hall Councils and the Le Moyne Student Programming Board organize a variety of campus activities, including concerts, dances, a weekly film series, student talent programs, and special lectures as well as off-campus trips and skiing excursions.

The College encourages student leadership in all activities with positions open to students in all class years. Students are represented by a Student Government Association and have formal representation through the senate on most College-wide committees involved in decision making and policy formation.

ADMISSIONS PROCESS

Le Moyne seeks qualified students who are well prepared for serious academic study. Secondary school preparation must have included at least 17 college-preparatory high school units, 4 of which must be in English, 4 in social studies, 3–4 in mathematics, 3–4 in foreign language, and 3–4 in science. It is also recommended that prospective science and mathematics majors complete 4 units of mathematics and science. Submitting scores from standardized tests is optional for admission to Le Moyne, but scores from the SAT or ACT will be considered if students choose to submit them. However, to be considered for the more prestigious scholarships (Presidential, Dean, Ignatian or Loyola), standardized test scores are required. Campus visits are strongly recommended, as the admission process is a personal one. As bases for selection, academic achievement and secondary school recommendations are of primary importance. Out-of-state students are encouraged to apply.

The Admission Committee reviews applications and mails decisions on a rolling admission cycle beginning December 1. The priority deadline for applications is February 1; all students who wish to be considered for academic merit scholarships should have a completed application on file in the Office of Admission before this date. Transfer students are encouraged to apply before June 1 for the fall semester and December 1 for the spring semester. Orientation programs for incoming freshmen and transfer students take place in midsummer.

LEWIS & CLARK COLLEGE

AT A GLANCE

On a stunning campus in one of the most exciting and progressive cities anywhere, the next generation of global thinkers gathers to discard conventional thinking, civic complacency, and outmoded preconceptions. Leaders, visionaries, and problem-solvers, we come together to explore new ways of knowing through classic liberal learning and innovative collaboration.

At Lewis & Clark College in Portland, Oregon, we welcome all who are alive to inquiry, open to diversity, and eager to shape the new global century. Through our undergraduate programs in the arts, humanities, and sciences, and through our graduate and professional studies in education, counseling, and law, we undertake original research, interdisciplinary studies, and community service. We push beyond what is known in order to discover something new every day.

Reflecting the College's national and global reach, approximately 79 percent of Lewis & Clark's 2,150 undergraduate students come from outside Oregon, representing forty-seven states plus the District of Columbia and 72 countries.

LOCATION AND ENVIRONMENT

Founded in 1867, Lewis & Clark College moved to its present location in Portland's southwest hills in 1942. The 137- acre campus sits on a wooded hilltop just six miles from Portland's exciting downtown, offering stunning views of snow-covered Mount Hood.

Portland is a very livable city with an excellent public transportation system that includes buses, light-rail, and the Portland Street Car. In addition, a free College shuttle runs frequently into the heart of the city and back to campus. The scenic Willamette River bisects Metropolitan Portland, which is home to approximately 2 million people. There are endless things to do in Portland: 10,477 acres of parks, 33 music groups, 35 theater and dance companies, 90 galleries and museums, and more than 1,000 restaurants. The city also offers professional hockey, soccer, and the NBA's Portland Trailblazers. Our students take advantage of the many internship and service opportunities available in the Portland metro area.

Just 50 miles east of campus rises Mount Hood and its 10-month-a-year skiing and snow-boarding. The rugged Oregon coastline is just 90 miles to the west. Throughout the state lie innumerable hiking, climbing, and backpacking opportunities.

OFF-CAMPUS OPPORTUNITIES

Overseas and off-campus study programs have been a big part of Lewis & Clark for 50 years. Each year, about 300 students participate in approximately 30 programs abroad and in selected areas of the United States. During the next few years, programs will be offered in the Arizona Borderlands, Australia, Chile, China, Cuba, Dominican Republic, East Africa, Ecuador, England, France, Germany, Greece, India, Ireland, Italy, Japan, Morocco, New York, New Zealand, Russia, Scotland, Senegal, Spain, Vietnam and Washington, D.C.

Whether their off-campus study is domestic or abroad, students earn credit (equivalent to a full semester or year) for their academic work. Depending on the specific program content, it is possible to earn General Education and/or major credit during these programs. Typically, over 50% of students participate in one of these programs prior to graduating from Lewis & Clark. Students can use Lewis & Clark's financial aid and scholarships for assistance in these programs.

MAJORS AND DEGREES OFFERED

The College offers one degree: the Bachelor of Arts. Students have a wide selection of majors from which to choose: art (studio), art history, biochemistry and molecular biology, biology, chemistry, classics, computer science, computer science and mathematics, East Asian studies, economics (international, management, public policy, and theory), English, environmental studies, foreign languages, French, German, Hispanic studies, history, international affairs, mathematics, music, philosophy, physics, political science, psychology, rhetoric and media studies, religious studies, sociology/anthropology, and theater. Students may also design their own major, pursue a double major, or select from 25 minors. Pre-professional preparation is available in the fields of law and medicine. Dual degree (3-2 or 4-2) programs in engineering are available in conjunction with Columbia University in New York, Washington University in St. Louis, the University of Southern California in Los Angeles, and Oregon Health and Science University in Portland. A dual degree, 4-2 B.A/M.B.A. program is available in conjunction with the Simon Graduate School of Business at the University of Rochester. A dual degree, 4-1 B.A/M.A.T program is available in conjunction with Lewis & Clark's Graduate School of Education and Counseling. In addition, there is a guaranteed admission agreement with Lewis &Clark's Law School for students meeting certain criteria.

ACADEMIC PROGRAMS

A liberal arts education at Lewis & Clark connects classical learning with fresh inquiry and exciting research that pushes the frontiers of knowledge. Lewis & Clark considers the following elements essential to a liberal arts education:

1. Mastery of the fundamental techniques of intellectual inquiry: effective writing and speaking, active reading, and critical and imaginative thinking.

2. Exposure to the major assumptions, knowledge, and approaches in the fine arts, humanities, natural sciences and social sciences.

3. Critical understanding of important contemporary and historical issues.

4. Awareness of international and cross-cultural issues and gender relations.

5. Application of theory and knowledge to the search for informed, thoughtful and responsible solutions to important human problems.

The curriculum combines structure and freedom. Depth and breadth of subject matter are highly valued, but equally important are creativity and critical thinking. There are many opportunities for students to take their learning to a higher level, such as honors projects within academic departments, independent research, and internships.

Two 15-week semesters make up the academic year, and each semester students normally take four 4-semester-hour courses, and one or more activity courses. The average student course load is 16 credits per semester. The requirement for graduation is 128 semester hours - approximately eight classes each year.

CAMPUS FACILITIES AND EQUIPMENT

Located on Palatine Hill on a former estate, Lewis & Clark offers students a campus of unmatched physical beauty, along with academic and residential buildings designed to support a rigorous academic environment and strong sense of community.

The academic buildings include: the Aubrey R. Watzek library, which is open 24 hours on weekdays during the school year and houses over 740,000 items including books, documents, audiovisual materials, microforms, and periodicals. Through the Summit catalog, access to approximately 28 million items from 36 member institutions in the Pacific Northwest. Also houses the most extensive collection of printed materials known to exist on the Lewis and Clark Expedition. Evans Music Center, which includes a 410-seat recital hall equipped with an orchestra pit and stage elevator, 22 practice rooms, 43 pianos, two harpsichords, four pipe organs including an 85-rank Casavant pipe organ, a Baroque organ, Javanese gamelan, and an electronic music studio with CD production capability; Fir Acres Theatre, which houses a 225-seat Main Stage performance/teaching theatre and a black-box experimental theatre (also used as dance studio) along with a scene shop, costume room, green room and design lab; the Olin Center (physics and chemistry), the Biology-Psychology building, and BoDine (mathematical sciences), which all house well-equipped classrooms and extensive laboratory spaces for our natural sciences. Among our notable science facilities are a scanning electron microscope, a molecular modeling lab, a gas chromatograph/mass spectrometer, a high-pressure liquid chromatograph, 300 MHz FTNRM spectrometer, inert spectrophotometers, infrared spectrometers, observatory with Newtonian and solar telescopes, computer-enhanced optical microscope, a solid-state physics lab with variable temperature cryostat and superconducting magnet, a lab for studying the biomechanics of animal locomotion, an astrophysics lab and a lab for studying parallel computing. Nearby Tryon Creek State Park and the Columbia River Gorge are frequently used as laboratories for field courses in biology and geology.

Among other academic buildings are the Fields Center, which includes studio facilities for drawing, painting, sculpture, ceramics, computer graphics, graphic design, and photography; the Miller Center and Howard Hall are home to the humanities and social sciences with state-of-the-art classrooms, small auditoriums, and the Keck Interactive Language Lab.

Computer facilities include several public computer labs around campus available for student use. These labs house more than 130 Macintosh and Microsoft Windows computers, along with peripherals such as scanners, color and black & white laser printer, and digital video editing equipment. Other equipment including digital still and video cameras, digital audio recorders and more are available for checkout. All residence halls have wireless network. The institution has an 800 Mbps (Megabits per second) connection to the internet.

TUITION, ROOM, BOARD AND FEES

2013-14 tuition and fees are $41, 928, and room and board are $10,636.

FINANCIAL AID

During the 2011-12 academic year approximately 82 percent of Lewis & Clark students received some form of financial assistance. Individual aid packages ranged from $1000 to $55,491. Institutional, state, and federal resources including grants, loans and work-study may be part of an aid package. Eligibility for need-based funds is based primarily on an analysis of the income and asset information submitted on the Free Application for Federal Student Aid (FAFSA) and the College Board's CSS/Financial Aid PROFILE. Household size and the number of students in college (excluding parents) are also considered in the analysis. Students must submit the FAFSA and PROFILE by February 15 in order to get priority consideration for financial aid.

STUDENT ORGANIZATIONS AND ACTIVITIES

With over 50 student organizations, there's never a lack of things to do at Lewis & Clark. Cultural events include lectures, symposia, art exhibits, plays, musical events, and dance performances. Athletics play an important role on campus, where 19 varsity teams, eight club teams, and numerous intramural sports keep students physically active. Nature-lovers will enjoy the College Outdoors Program, which offers activities such as hiking, backpacking, rafting, skiing, and kayaking in the wilderness of the Pacific Northwest. There are also plenty of opportunities for volunteering in and around the Portland area.

Lewis & Clark is committed to residential education, to creating a community dedicated to the exploration of ideas, values, beliefs and backgrounds, to the discovery of lifelong friendships; and to collaboration, both formal and informal, with peers, faculty, and staff. There is no Greek system at Lewis & Clark.

About 70 percent of undergraduates live on campus in residence halls; most of our residential space is co-ed. Along with personal living space (usually shared by two to four students) are several community venues within the residence halls, including coffee houses, convenience stores, art centers, outdoor basketball courts, recreation and fitness centers, lounges, and game rooms. A variety of themed communities within the residence halls are also available (visual and performing arts, multicultural, outdoor pursuits, environmental action and service, wellness).

ADMISSIONS PROCESS

Commitment to academic excellence and personal and intellectual growth is imperative for successful Lewis & Clark applicants. Lewis & Clark is very selective, and every part of the application matters: academic records, essays, involvement in activities at school and in the community, leadership, and the strength of recommendations. Students are encouraged to visit our campus. Interviews are available but not required. The best-prepared applicants will have had four years of English, four years of mathematics, three to four years of history or social sciences, three years of laboratory sciences, two to three years of a foreign language, and one year of fine arts. Required credentials include: an essay; an official transcript including senior grades from first semester; a counselor recommendation; and one academic teacher recommendation. Lewis & Clark requires the SAT or ACT, except if the student is applying via the test-optional Portfolio Path (see www.lclark.edu for details). Students apply using either the on-line or paper version of the Common Application. The $50 application fee is waived for students applying on-line. Keep in mind these deadlines: First-year applicants - November 1 for non-binding Early Action (notification, January 1) and January 15 for Regular Decision (notification, April 1). Transfer applicants are reviewed on a rolling basis.

LIM COLLEGE

AT A GLANCE

LIM College is where business meets fashion. The campus is comprised of four buildings nestled in the Midtown East neighborhood of New York City – the undisputed fashion capital of the world. Our state of the art residence hall is located on the Upper East Side of Manhattan, just a few blocks from Central Park.

LIM College is accredited by the Commission on Higher Education of the Middle States Association of Colleges and Schools and the Accreditation Council for Business Schools and Programs (ACBSP).

The LIM College curriculum stresses both professional and academic preparation, a combination which empowers student success. Students at LIM College receive highly individualized attention as they study the fashion industry. The student body consists of approximately 1500 undergraduates. This College's small size ensures that students have access to instructors, staff, and administrators. The average class size is 17 and the student-faculty ratio is 8:1.

The curriculum requires students to complete a core set of courses in fashion, business, and the liberal arts, and also emphasizes the importance of hands-on experience. This unique approach opens numerous options to graduates, whom the College prepares for work in management, marketing, and merchandising in both the traditional fashion world and fashion-related businesses.

The Department of Experiential Education & Career Management is one of LIM College's chief assets. Every student receives extensive career assistance throughout their time at the College, beginning in the first semester. This counseling helps direct students to positions within their field of study. LIM College is extremely proud of its placement record- students seeking employment from the 2011 graduating class had 97% employment rate within one year of graduation.

LIM College's housing is currently located at the 1760 Third Avenue Residence Hall on Manhattan's Upper East Side. It's just minutes away from fantastic restaurants and shopping, the remarkable sights and sounds of Museum Mile and Central Park, and two blocks from the subway. A trained live-in staff and 24-hour security ensure students' safety and comfort. Double and triple furnished rooms offer private bathrooms and a flat-screen TV with DVD player transmitting over 100 digital cable stations, as well as a refrigerator and microwave. Each student receives free local telephone service with their own voicemail, as well as high-speed Internet service. This state-of-the-art building also features a game room, a fully-equipped 3,500 sq. ft. fitness center, and a computer center.

LIM College welcomes all who are interested to attend its Open House program. This program allows students and their families to tour the College with current students, learn about career opportunities in the fashion industry, explore academic programs and financing options, and meet with faculty and administrators. LIM College also offers many other opportunities to visit including weekly Information Sessions, Transfer Services Days, Webinars, Mock Classes, and other special events.

LIM College's student body is diverse, but they have one thing in common: a passion for fashion. As of Fall 2012, approximately 1500 undergraduate students were enrolled at LIM College. About 76% of the student body is from the Tri-State area (NY, NJ, and CT). 23% of students live in LIM College housing. 93% of students are female. 81% of students received some form of financial aid during the 2011-2012 school year.

LOCATION AND ENVIRONMENT

LIM College students benefit from an amazing location in the heart of New York City. World-famous sights, including St. Patrick's Cathedral, Central Park, the Museum of Modern Art, the Garment District, and Rockefeller Center are all a short walk away from the College.

The fashion universe waits just beyond LIM College's front door. New York City is the center of many fashion and fashion-related industries, including cosmetics, textiles, visual merchandising, styling, and fashion publishing. The College's location and prestige facilitates students' interaction with many principals in these areas. Additionally, the curriculum frequently incorporates New York City's vast resources. For example, a student taking the College's Fashion Magazines course could visit showrooms and magazine offices, meet designers, and enjoy other similar experiences. No other city offers the breadth of experiences and fashion-related opportunities that New York does.

ACADEMICS

Students learn in a variety of settings at LIM College. Classroom instruction is supplemented by required internships performed under the supervision of industry professionals. The entire curriculum is aimed at preparing students for entry-level executive positions throughout the fashion industry.

LIM College offers four-year programs in fashion merchandising, management, marketing, and visual merchandising, leading to a Bachelor of Business Administration (B.B.A.) or a Bachelor of Professional Studies (B.P.S.) degree, and a two-year program in fashion merchandising leading to the Associate in Applied Sciences (A.A.S.) degree. The fashion merchandising program has tracks in either the traditional apparel & accessories or the new home fashions track. LIM College also offers two graduate programs: the Master of Business Administration (M.B.A.) in either entrepreneurship or fashion management and the Master of Professional Studies (M.P.S.) in Merchandising and Retail Management.

LIM College also offers concentrations within its majors. The current list of concentrations includes: Fashion Merchandising, Visual Merchandising, Styling, Event Planning, Cosmetics, Fashion Publishing, Entrepreneurship, International Marketing, Retailing, Fashion Communications, and Digital Business Strategy.

Experiential learning is an integral part of the LIM College curriculum. One of our experiential programs is our internship program that helps students become truly prepared for successful careers within fashion and fashion related industries. All students are required to take three internships to earn their Bachelor's Degree at LIM College. Each internship has a prerequisite seminar attached to it that includes activities such as field trips, guest speakers, and portfolio building that help our students to network with industry professionals and develop into dynamic business leaders. The Industry Exploration Internship focuses on understanding the nature of the fashion industry through a retail experience, while the Career Pathing internship allows students to explore potential career fields, such as management, publishing, cosmetics, advertising, public relations, or fashion forecasting. Both of these internships dovetail with academic courses the students have taken during previous semesters. The third and final internship is the semester-long Senior Co-op, which is a required four-day-a-week placement in a field related to the student's chosen area of specialization. Co-ops may lead students to positions at fashion magazines, public relations firms, buying offices, or other essential areas of the fashion industry. The Senior Co-op serves as the ideal culmination of the academic experience and a perfect transition into the business world, preparing undergraduates for the challenge and excitement of their future careers.

LIM College operates on a two-semester calendar and students may enter in either semester.

The Fashion Lab is a pre-college program for both high school and visiting transfer students who are looking to explore both LIM College and the fashion industry. Courses are offered on Saturdays in the fall and spring, and during the week in the summer. Examples of classes include Fashion Magazines, Fashion Show Production, Event Planning, Fashion Photography, Marketing Communications, Fashion Buying, and Fashion Styling, and combine traditional coursework with hands-on activities. Summer Fashion Lab students have the option to stay in our state of the art residence hall during classes.

CAMPUS FACILITIES AND EQUIPMENT

LIM College is situated in four buildings in Midtown Manhattan, on 45th, 53rd, 54th Streets and on 5th Avenue. All facilities house a blend of classrooms, administrative offices, computer labs, studios, and student lounges.

The Adrian G. Marcuse Library contains approximately 98,000 volumes pertaining to the liberal arts, fashion merchandising and related fields, as well as 240 periodical subscriptions. The Library also offers access to an extensive array of online databases worldwide.

Personal computers are available for use throughout the College. The student/computer ratio is 4:1. LIM College also offers wireless internet throughout all four of its academic buildings.

The Math and Writing Centers offer peer tutoring and special programs to supplement and reinforce classroom learning and further develop students' skills in those areas.

TUITION, ROOM, BOARD AND FEES

Tuition for the 2013-2014 academic year is $23,070 and mandatory fees are $575. Students normally spend $1200 to $2,000 for transportation, depending on commuting distance. The LIM College residence hall is comprised of double and triple rooms costing $15,850 and board is approximately $4000 for the academic year. Students should also budget about $1,500 per year for personal expenses.

FINANCIAL AID

LIM College wants every student it admits to be able to attend the College and works hard to make its education affordable to all. Admissions decisions are made independently of financial aid considerations. About 81 percent of LIM College's students received some form of financial aid during the 2011-12 school year. Financial assistance is offered in many forms: grants, scholarships, loans, and work-study were made available to students who qualified.

Students should submit the Free Application for Federal Student Aid (FAFSA) by March 1 to receive priority consideration for financial assistance. Aid in all forms is available on a need basis. LIM College offers merit scholarships to both incoming freshmen and transfer students. The College gives these awards to candidates who demonstrate exceptional academic ability in high school or college. Merit scholarships are awarded to those with high academic achievement and other significant talents, regardless of financial need.

Please consult our website to learn about other need and non-need based scholarships. You can also contact Student Financial Services for more details.

STUDENT ORGANIZATIONS AND ACTIVITIES

The mission of the Office of Student Life is to develop student leaders. Student Life provides a supportive social environment and a wealth of cultural opportunities that cultivate personal and academic growth. Club advisors are experienced in their field and can help students connect with key people in the industry. Students can meet friends, build a resume, and make the most of your college experience by joining a student club.

Co-curricular organizations include the Student Council, the Fashion Club, the Styling Club, Dance Club, Fashion Sense magazine, and various other clubs formed by students to serve special needs and interests. Students create the annual yearbook (called LIMLIGHT), produce the annual fashion show (which hosted over 1000 guests last year), and organize cultural and social activities. Eligible students may be nominated for Sigma Beta Delta, the national honor society. Each year, LIM College students participate in several different volunteer activities including the Revlon Run/Walk for Women's Cancers and the school Blood Drive.

Study Abroad Opportunities

Fashion is a notably international industry, and LIM College recognizes and appreciates that through its off-campus opportunities, all offered for academic credit. For students who are interested in seeing the broad scope of European fashion, there is a short-term study abroad each January. This tour highlights European fashion hot-spots as well as figures and companies in each of the locations (which are determined on an annual basis).

LIM College has two summer programs at American University in Rome and a field trip to China, including stops in Beijing, Hong Kong, and Shanghai.

LIM College offers two full semester study abroad programs that are available to students during their junior year. The first option, offered during the spring semester, is at the University of Westminster in London, England. Participating students will take 3-4 classes (with an optional internship) in Westminster's Merchandise Management program. The second full semester option is at the Royal Melbourne Institute of Technology in Australia, where students will have the opportunity to take both fashion and business classes. Check the LIM College website for more exciting opportunities in Paris, Milan, and Barcelona.

Admissions

LIM College has a rolling admissions policy. All students are required to submit the LIM College application for admission, an essay, a $40 fee, SAT or ACT scores, two letters of recommendation and official high school transcripts from all high schools attended. After receipt of academic transcripts and test scores some applicants may be asked to complete a personal interview. LIM College strongly suggests all applicants submit an activity sheet or resume. Freshmen applicants will be considered for Early Action Admission if all application requirements are complete by November 15th.

Transfer students must also submit official transcripts from all colleges attended. The SAT/ACT requirement is waived for transfer students with more than 30 credit hours. International students must also submit TOEFL, IELTS, or PTE scores. Please check our International Admissions website for more details.

LIMESTONE COLLEGE

AT A GLANCE

Founded in 1845, Limestone is a fully accredited, private, coeducational liberal arts college. The College maintains a small student body and a well-qualified faculty in order to create an atmosphere in which each student develops intellectually, physically, and socially. The College endeavors to help students prepare for a satisfying, useful life through effective communication skills, responsible decision-making abilities, meaningful leisure-time activities, and lifelong aspirations. In addition to its programs on campus, Limestone offers several of its academic majors in an accelerated format called The Extended Campus.

Extracurricular activities play a vital part in the development of all students at Limestone College. Among these activities are intercollegiate athletics in baseball, basketball, cross-country, field hockey, golf, lacrosse, soccer, softball, swimming, tennis, track and field, volleyball, wrestling, and our brand new Football program starting in 2014. Music and theater programs are also available.

The 125 acre Limestone campus is well laid out for pleasant college living. The classrooms, library, laboratories, auditorium, bookstore, post office, and administrative offices are housed in buildings that border the central and circular drives, making each easily accessible to the others. The back campus has a plaza of five dormitories, a student center, and our dining hall. The Timken Center is a physical education complex that houses the gymnasium, an AAU-size swimming pool, fitness/dance studio, 2 racquetball courts, and an auxillary gym. The Walt Griffin Physical Education Center houses the athletic training education program, a fitness center, three classrooms, and a wrestling practice facility. The College also has eight-lighted tennis courts, a baseball field, a softball field, a soccer/lacrosse field, a field hockey field, and several practice fields.

LOCATION AND ENVIRONMENT

Limestone College is located in the Piedmont region of South Carolina in the city of Gaffney. Rich in culture and tradition, Gaffney, a city of 25,000 people, is a beautiful place, picturesque with its historic homes and large trees. Gaffney has numerous restaurants, grocery stores and discount shopping such as Premium Outlets, an outlet shopping mall with more than 80 stores.

Whereas the distractions associated with a large city are absent from daily life, the cultural programs and services offered in Charlotte, North Carolina and Spartanburg/Greenville, South Carolina are all within a 50-mile radius of the campus. Interstate 85 connects all to Gaffney.

MAJORS AND DEGREES OFFERED

Limestone College offers the Bachelor of Arts, Bachelor of Science, and Bachelor of Social Work degrees with majors in art (concentrations in studio art, and graphic design), athletic training, biology, business administration (concentrations in accounting, computer science , E-Business, economics, finance, general business,, human resource management, management, and marketing), chemistry, computer science (concentrations in computer and information systems security, internet management, information technology, and programming), criminal justice, early childhood education, elementary education, English, health care administration, history, liberal studies, mathematics, music, professional communication, physical education (concentrations in athletic training and strength and conditioning), pre-professional programs, psychology, social work, sport management, and theater. Majors approved for South Carolina teacher certification are early childhood education, elementary education, English education, mathematics education, music education, physical education, and secondary education.

The Associate of Arts degree is offered with majors in business administration, computer science, and liberal studies.

The Master of Business Administration is offered through an online format with three on-campus learning sessions.

ACADEMIC PROGRAMS

The course of study leading to the B.A., B.S., B.S.W., or A.A. degree consists of four elements: requirements in communication and quantitative skills; a general liberal arts program, involving five different subject groups; courses in the major; and appropriate electives. The baccalaureate degree programs require the completion of a minimum of 123 semester hours. The associate degree programs require the completion of a minimum of 62 semester hours.

Advanced placement and credit are given for scores of 3 or higher on the Advanced Placement examinations of the College Board.

An Honors Program involving special courses, seminars, and lectures is available for exceptional students. Admission to this program is contingent upon outstanding high school grades and scores on the SAT I of the College Board, the completion of a special application, and an interview. Almost 10 percent of all Limestone students are enrolled in this rigorous academic program.

A Program for Alternative Learning Styles (PALS) is available for qualified students with certified learning disabilities.

The Developmental Studies Program recognizes that some students have special needs in such areas as reading, writing, and mathematics. For this reason, a number of courses are offered to help students improve his/her basic skills.

CAMPUS FACILITIES AND EQUIPMENT

The CAREER SERVICES CENTER staff provides direction in defining career goals and directing academic preparation toward those goals. The A.J. EASTWOOD LIBRARY houses over 136,000 volumes. The library is accessible online at http://www.limestone.edu/library.The CARROLL FINE ARTS BUILDING houses a music technology lab, practice rooms, classrooms, and a formal recital hall. An addition has been made this past year with the adding of Downtown Campus which provides more rehearsal space for our Marching Band and Music majors. The COMPUTER LABS at Limestone offer a wide array of the latest data processing and data communication technology. The DOBSON STUDENT CENTER houses the Academic Success Center, Health Center, Limestone Dixie Cafeand the Mail Center. It also has a game room, sitting areas with televisions and vending machines. FULLERTON AUDITORIUM, an acoustically excellent hall, with a seating capacity of 975, serves for drama and musical productions and is one of the finest such facilities in the state of South Carolina. The Limestone Center is a state of the art facility that houses the majority of Limestone athletic offices and it is home to the college's Theatre Department. Recently, Limestone College has also added the DANIEL HOUSE, which is the home of our new Football offices. We also have purchased two sets of apartments, WALTON RIDGE and the CEDARS, located above the Walt Griffen Physical Education Center that will be used as residence halls. The ACADEMIC SUCCESS CENTER offers tutorial services in all academic subjects, as well as specially trained tutors for writing and math.

ATHLETIC TEAMS consist of Men's Baseball, Basketball, Cross Country, Golf, Lacrosse, Soccer, Swimming, Tennis, Track &Field, Volleyball, Wrestling, and our newest addition, Football. Women's Basketball, Cheerleading, Competitive Dance, Cross Country, Field Hockey, Golf, Lacrosse, Soccer, Softball, Swimming, Tennis, Track & Field, and Volleyball

ATHLETIC FACILITIES include the Saints Game Field, the Bob Prevatte Baseball Field, the Emmie Evans Rector Tennis Pavilion, the softball field, the field hockey field, three practice fields, the Limestone Center, Timken Center, and the Walt Griffin Physical Education Center.

A registered nurse is available in the HEALTH CENTER for all non-emergency situations. The school MAIL CENTER offers convenience for students to receive letters and care packages from home and to mail packages from campus. RESIDENCE HALLS are equipped with laundry facilities and vending machines. Each room provides a phone, cable, and internet access.The SIB COLLINS COUNSELING CENTER provides services to students struggling with academic,

social and psychological issues.

Tuition, Room, Board and Fees

The direct cost for a student at Limestone College for the 2013-2014 school year is $ $29,880; the tuition is, $22,080, and room and board costs are $7,800.

FINANCIAL AID

Limestone College, one of the least costly private colleges in South Carolina, endeavors to meet the financial need of any qualified student through scholarships, grants, loans, work-study opportunities, or a combination of these. Limestone offers merit scholarships to students with outstanding academic, leadership, or athletic abilities as well as to those who have exceptional talents in such areas as art, music, and theater.

More than 90 percent of Limestone College day students receive some type of financial aid. Because institutional financial aid is limited, students are urged to submit their applications for admission and financial aid as early as possible.

Student Organizations and Activities

ACADEMIC INTEREST GROUPS: Alpha Chi Honor Society, Alpha Phi Sigma, Art League, Chi Alpha Sigma, Athletic Training Student Org., Criminal Justice Student Org., International Business Club, Limestone Activities Board, Limestone College Research Group, Limestone College Outdoor Recreation and Education Club, Music Educators National Conf., Phi Alpha Theta, Student Organization of Social Workers, Students in Free Enterprise. CAMPUS PUBLICATIONS: The Calciid Annual, The Candelabra Literary Magazine. LEADERSHIP: Student Alumni Leadership Council, Student Government Association. MUSICAL GROUPS: Brass Ensemble, Community Chorus, Ipan Steel Band Ensemble, Jazz Ensemble, Joyful Saints

Marching Band, Saxophone Quartet, Show Choir, Wind Ensemble. RELIGIOUS: Christian Education and Leadership Program, Fellowship of Christian Athletes. INTRAMURAL TOURNAMENTS: Basketball, Bowling, Flag Football, Spades, Table Tennis, Tennis, Sand Volleyball. STUDENT ACTIVITIES: Alcohol Awareness Week, Alumni Weekend, Campus Cookouts, Christian Mission Trips, Christmas Luminaries, Comedians, Diversity Awareness Week, Earth Day Celebration, Exam Breaks, Faculty/Student Athletic Games, Family Weekend, Hypnotist, Homecoming Activities, Live Bands, Mid-Term Madness Events, Spirit Week, Spring Fling Week, Theme Dinners.

ADMISSIONS PROCESS

Limestone College does not discriminate on the basis of race, color, creed, national origin, financial need, or physical handicap. Each candidate for admission is evaluated as an individual. The College recommends that applicants have the following high school preparation: English, 4 units; social science, 3 units; mathematics, 3 units; and science, 2 units.

Applicants must submit an official transcript of the secondary school record, scores on the SAT I or ACT, and a nonrefundable $25 application fee. The application fee is waived if the student applies online at www.limestone.edu or visits campus.. Transfer applications are encouraged.

Completed application forms for admission and for financial aid should be sent to the Office of Admissions at Limestone College. It is recommended that applications be submitted by May 1. Any admission applications received after that date are considered on a space-available basis. The College practices a rolling admissions policy. As soon as the application, high school transcript, and test scores have been received, the applicant is notified of his or her status. Upon acceptance, a student is required to submit a $100 tuition deposit.

LOYOLA UNIVERSITY CHICAGO

AT A GLANCE

Committed to preparing people to lead extraordinary lives, Loyola University Chicago is the largest Jesuit Catholic university in the U.S., with 15,720 students. Loyola has three campuses in the Chicago area, and one in Rome, Italy.

Consistently ranked a "Best National University" and a "Great School, Great Price" by U.S. News &World Report, Loyola University Chicago continues to advance the 450-year-old Jesuit tradition of rigorous academic study firmly grounded in the liberal arts.

Loyola is the largest Jesuit Catholic university in the United States, enrolling 15,720 students from 50 states and 82 countries. Loyola offers more than 70 undergraduate majors and more than 140 graduate, professional, and graduate-level certificate programs as well as three professional programs in law, medicine, and nursing.

Loyola helps students prepare for meaningful careers with top academic programs in business, the sciences, and numerous other disciplines, along with opportunities for internships throughout the city of Chicago and beyond. Loyola's well-rounded, transformative education will help you develop as a whole person—intellectually, socially, physically, and spiritually.

LOCATION AND ENVIRONMENT

Loyola gives students the best of campus and city life with diverse living and learning opportunities in the world-class city of Chicago. Located off North Michigan Avenue, Chicago's Magnificent Mile, Loyola's dynamic Water Tower Campus is home to the Schools of Business Administration, Communication, Continuing and Professional Studies, Education, Law, and Social Work and connects students to myriad internship, job, and service opportunities. Loyola's Lake Shore Campus, home to the College of Arts and Sciences, the Graduate School, and the Marcella Niehoff School of Nursing, is located on the picturesque shore of Lake Michigan and offers students the comforts of a traditional residential campus. The Stritch School of Medicine is housed at the Medical Sciences Campus in west suburban Maywood, Illinois.

Exposure to Loyola's three Chicago campuses gives students three diverse experiences: a vibrant urban environment, the comfort of a more traditional collegiate setting, and the bustle of a professional medical environment. At each campus, students have access to computers, study areas, and dining halls, as well as a network of student groups and activities. A free intercampus shuttle is available between the Lake Shore and Water Tower Campuses, and an intracampus shuttle is available at the Medical Sciences Campus.

Students may also study abroad at Loyola's fourth campus, the John Felice Rome Center in Italy; or they may attend The Beijing Center for Chinese Studies or choose from one of 100 other study abroad programs in 55 countries.

MAJORS AND DEGREES OFFERED

Loyola students may choose from more than 70 majors and 70 minors. Undergraduate degrees offered include the Bachelor of Arts (BA), BA Classics, Bachelor of Science (BS), Bachelor of Business Administration (BBA), Bachelor of Science in Education (BSEd), Bachelor of Science in Nursing (BSN), and the Bachelor of Social Work (BSW) degrees.

The College of Arts and Sciences offers undergraduate majors in anthropology, art history, biochemistry, bioinformatics, biology, biophysics, Black world studies, chemistry, classical civilization, communications networks and security, computer science, criminal justice and criminology, dance, economics, English, environmental science (chemistry), environmental studies, forensic science, French, Greek (ancient), history, human services, information technology, international studies, Italian, Latin, mathematics, mathematics and computer science, music, philosophy, physics, physics and computer science, political science, psychology, religious studies, sociology, sociology and anthropology, software development, Spanish, statistics, studio art, theater, theology, theoretical physics and applied mathematics, visual communication, and women's studies and gender studies (as a second major only).

The School of Business Administration offers majors in accounting, economics, entrepreneurship, finance, human resource management, information systems, international business, management, marketing, operations management, and sport management.

The School of Communication offers majors in advertising and public relations, communication studies, film and digital media, and journalism.

The School of Education offers majors in bilingual/bicultural education, early childhood/special education, elementary education, mathematics education, science education, and special education, along with an expanded secondary education dual-degree program.

The Marcella Niehoff School of Nursing offers the Bachelor of Science in Nursing, a Bachelor of Science in Health Systems Management, exercise science, and an accelerated BSN program, which is available to students who have already completed a baccalaureate degree.

The School of Social Work offers an undergraduate major in social work and a combined bachelor's and master's degree in social work, which may be completed in five years.

ACADEMIC PROGRAMS

The Core Curriculum is the foundation of Loyola's liberal arts education. Core courses are aimed at increasing students' understanding of themselves and the world while they explore diverse subjects and cultivate new interests. Courses provide a strong base of knowledge, skills, and values that will help students achieve academic, professional, and personal success throughout their lives.

Exceptionally well-qualified students may apply to the Interdisciplinary Honors Program.

Other special academic opportunities include pre-professional programs for law and health professions; 19 five-year (bachelor's/master's) degree programs; 18 interdisciplinary programs; a six-year, early admission to Loyola's School of Law; early assurance to Loyola's Stritch School of Medicine; and the Loyola/Midwestern University Dual-Acceptance Pharmacy Program.

CAMPUS FACILITIES AND EQUIPMENT

Not only is the recently completed Cuneo Hall a state-of-the-art building with a cutting-edge academic center—but it also uses sustainable technologies to reduce its ecological footprint. Cuneo is LEED Gold certified and will use approximately 60% less energy than comparable academic buildings.

Last summer, the renovated Mundelein Center reopened with new options for fine arts programming. For plays and theatre are the new Newhart Family Theatre and the Underground Laboratory Theatre.

Mundelein Music Hall was completely renovated as well. These new spaces give students an opportunity to hone their craft in contemporary surroundings.

Completed this spring, the new Damen Student Union spans 70,000 square feet and includes a food court, fireplace, WLUW radio station, student workspaces, pool hall, game room, worship spaces, and more.

The new School of Communication is in the heart of Chicago's creative and business communities. Located at the Water Tower Campus, the building features generously equipped computer labs, state-of-the-art classrooms and offices, and on-site production facilities, including street-side lab with a TV studio and radio interview sets.

The Information Commons, which opened in Spring 2008, is a new four-story lakeside research facility that provides individual and group study space for students, as well as state-of-the-art technology with 222 computers, wireless internet connections, and a lakefront café.

Loyola's Michael R. and Marilyn C. Quinlan Life Sciences Education and Research Center provides numerous opportunities for undergraduates to engage in the latest scientific research alongside their professors in modern labs for biology, bioinformatics, chemistry, ecology, and other life sciences.

The Loyola University Museum of Art (LUMA) showcases permanent and rotating exhibitions of professional and student work. The Sullivan Center for Student Services consolidates a dozen student services offices into one convenient location.

Recently opened residence halls include: seven-story Regis Hall, located at the Lake Shore Campus; and the 25-story Baumhart Hall and Terry Student Center at the Water Tower Campus, in the heart of Chicago's Magnificent Mile, which provides upper-class student housing and a fitness center, study lounge, food court, outdoor terrace, and wireless internet access.

For more information about campus facilities, visit LUC.edu/undergrad/whatsnew.shtml.

TUITION, ROOM, BOARD, AND FEES

Tuition for 2012-2013 entering students (per year): $33,810

Room and board (per year): Room and board cost is dependent on students' selection of residence hall and meal plan (average is $12,010).

Tuition part-time (per credit hour): $675

FINANCIAL AID

At Loyola, we're committed to making a high-quality education affordable. Our office of Student Financial Assistance works with students and families to address each student's specific situation and needs. Our expert staff evaluates financial aid eligibility for resources such as grants, scholarships, and loans to help make a Loyola education a possibility for students.

Approximately 96% of Loyola freshmen receive some form of financial aid. Students are encouraged to file the Free Application for Federal Student Aid (FAFSA) by February 15 in order to meet Loyola's March 1 priority processing date.

In addition to the many scholarships awarded with admission, students may also explore more than 75 types of additional scholarships. For more information, visit LUC.edu/finaid/scholarships.

STUDENT ORGANIZATIONS AND ACTIVITIES

Loyola offers students the chance to develop leadership and social skills by participating in any of its more than 185 academic, athletic, cultural, hobby, media, political, social, and spiritual student-run organizations.

ADMISSIONS PROCESS

Students seeking admission to Loyola are evaluated on their overall academic record, including ACT or SAT scores. The freshman class entering in Fall 2012 had middle 50% ACT score ranges between 25 and 29, middle 50% range on the SAT Verbal between 550 and 650, middle 50% range on the SAT Math between 540 and 650, and an average GPA of 3.76. Most Loyola students rank in the upper quarter of their graduating class, but consideration is given to students in the upper half.

Transfer students with 20 credit hours or more are evaluated on the basis of their college work only. The minimum acceptable GPA varies from 2.0 to 2.5, depending upon academic interest. Candidates must also be in good standing at the last college attended.

Loyola notifies applicants four to six weeks after the application, supporting credentials, and secondary school counselor or teacher recommendation are received. The application is only available online and there is no application fee at LUC.edu/applyluc.

Prospective students are encouraged to visit campus by arranging individual appointments and campus tours up to two weeks in advance. Arrange a visit at LUC.edu/visit.

To obtain an application, get more information, or arrange a visit, contact:

Undergraduate Admission Office

Loyola University Chicago

820 North Michigan Avenue

Chicago, IL 60611

Telephone: 312.915.6500 or 800.262.2373 (toll-free)

E-mail: admission@luc.edu

Web site: LUC.edu/undergrad

LYNN UNIVERSITY

AT A GLANCE

At Lynn University, all styles are welcome. Our hands-on, experiential and tailored learning will allow you to discover your style and passion.

Lynn University is a private, non-profit liberal arts-focused institution located in Boca Raton, Florida. Since its founding in 1962, Lynn has been focused on preparing students for success in the world. That means every student's education is customized to their style of learning. This isn't mass market; it's a boutique education. With 24 undergraduate majors and ten graduate degrees, Lynn offers a school for every interest, passion and style. Lynn's student body of 1,657 undergraduate and 440 graduate students hails from 45 states and 87 nations. Over 23 percent of Lynn's student body is international, making Lynn a hub for global citizenship. In fact, Lynn is ranked fourth in the United States for the highest concentration of international students by U.S. News & World Report. Lynn also provides an array of athletic opportunities, academic organizations, cultural clubs, sororities and fraternities, special interest groups, and religious organizations. The vision of Lynn University is to be considered one of the most innovative, international, and individualized universities in America.

LOCATION AND ENVIRONMENT

Lynn University is located in Boca Raton, Florida. At Lynn, you're surrounded by a lush, green campus that you can enjoy year-round. It's a mild 76° in January and February. Our five lakes, fountains, patios and courtyards make every day on campus paradise. At Lynn, you're just three miles from the beach, 45 miles from Miami, midway between Fort Lauderdale and West Palm Beach, and centrally located in the heart of sunny South Florida.

OFF-CAMPUS OPPORTUNITIES

There's so much to experience just minutes off campus. Boca Raton and the South Florida region are known for pristine beaches (70 miles of them), parks and golf courses – in fact, there are 152 golf courses in Palm Beach County alone. That means you can fish, play tennis, Jet Ski, water ski, surf, snorkel, and dive year-round. Some of the best shopping and dining in the country is just minute's way. Las Olas Boulevard in Fort Lauderdale is another popular spot for eating, shopping, entertainment, and people watching.

South Florida is one of only ten metropolitan areas in the United States that has all four major league sports: Miami Dolphins football, Miami Heat basketball, Florida Panthers hockey, and the Miami Marlins baseball team. National golf and tennis tournaments are held in the region during the winter.

Another perk of living in South Florida is year-round outdoor concerts at Mizner Park Amphitheater in downtown Boca Raton or the Cruzan Amphitheater in West Palm Beach. Students can also catch big-name music acts and cultural life at the BB&T Center in Sunrise, American Airlines Arena in Miami, or Performing Arts centers of West Palm Beach, Fort Lauderdale and Miami.

Boca Raton is right in the heart of South Florida's booming business community, home to over 800 multinational companies, providing students ample internship and networking opportunities.

So, whether you're into surfing, shopping, sports, or a concert under the stars, there's something here for you.

MAJORS AND DEGREES OFFERED

Lynn University is accredited by the Southern Association of Colleges and Schools Commission on Colleges to award baccalaureate, masters and doctorate degrees. At Lynn you skills and career goals will come together in remarkable ways.

UNDERGRADUATE MAJORS

College of Liberal Education

Biology , Criminal Justice, Environmental Studies, Forensic Science, Political Science, Psychology

College of Business and Management

Aviation Management, Entrepreneurship, Event Management, Fashion and Retail, Hospitality Management, International Business Management, Investment Management, Marketing, Sports Management

College of Education

Elementary Education Grades K-6

  Pre K/Primary (Age 3 – Grade 3)

  Exceptional Student Education

Independent Schools Elementary Education

College of International Communication

Advertising and Public Relations, Communication and Emerging Media, Drama, Film, Multimedia Design, Multimedia Journalism

Conservatory of Music

Composition, Performance

ACADEMIC PROGRAMS

Lynn University offers a variety of special academic programs and student services.

As of fall 2013, all new freshmen and transfer students with less than 30 credit hours will receive a brand new iPad mini to learn on, study with, upgrade, and keep forever. The iPad is used to enhance classroom discussions through interactive lessons, instant access to information, study guide, and productivity tools.

The Conservatory of Music is one of only twelve conservatories of music in the United States and the only one in the South.

Lynn 3.0 allows qualified students to complete their undergraduate degree in just three years, enabling students to enroll in Lynn 3+1 and receive a graduate degree in one additional year.

Lynn University offers several notable programs:

Based upon their academic and/or career interests, each incoming student is assigned a faculty advisor that educates students on academic programs and strategies for success.

The Dialogues of Learning is an innovative core curriculum that blends liberal arts and professional study and spans all four years.

The Dialogues of Innovation and the Citizenship Project: All students are required to participate in a domestic or international, two-and-a-half week academic program in January, also called the January term.

The Center for Learning Abroad helps internationalize the student experience through short-and-long-term education abroad opportunities and off-campus January Term academic programs.

The Institute for Achievement and Learning (IAL) offers internationally recognized programs for students with learning differences.

CAMPUS FACILITIES AND EQUIPMENT

Lynn University provides its students first-class facilities, right on campus.

Lynn offers a variety of food options right on campus – the dining hall, Knights' Court Grill and Christine's Coffee House give students exactly what they are looking for.

Lynn University also has culinary and biology laboratories conveniently located on campus. The Lynn Library has services and resources that will assist you with your courses and research projects.

The Keith C. and Elaine Johnson Wold Performing Arts Center is a state of the art facility that houses Lynn's world-renowned Conservatory of Music.

The de Hoernle Sports and Cultural Center is home to men and women's basketball as well as women's volleyball. Lynn's campus is also equipped with multiple tennis courts, baseball fields and swimming pools. Bobby Campbell Stadium will be completed in the spring of 2014 and will house the men's and women's soccer teams as well as men's lacrosse.

TUITION, ROOM, BOARD, AND FEES

Lynn University's tuition and fees are competitive when compared to similar universities in the state of Florida. The tuition for the 2013-2014 academic year is $31,900. At Lynn we minimize the cost of tuition and fees by offering financial aid through scholarships, grants, loans and work-study opportunities.

Total room and board costs for 2013-2014 are estimated at $10,900. First year students typically live in double or triple rooms with a community bath or private bath. Returning students participate in a Housing Selection Process and can choose whether they want to live in a private or double room. Students that meet the March 31 deposit deadline will receive the housing option of their choice, based on availability. Lynn offers meal plans that include "flex dollars," which can be used on campus at Knights' Court Grill and Christine's Coffee House.

International students and those participating in the Institute for Achievement and Learning and flight academy programs are charged additional fees to cover costs unique to their needs or programs.

All undergraduate students pay a $1,000 annual student service fee. New freshmen and transfer students with less than 30 credit hours pay a $700 technology fee if residing on campus; commuters pay $350.

FINANCIAL AID

Lynn University is committed to helping students meet the challenge of funding a college education by offering an array of financial aid opportunities. To make Lynn even more affordable, our Financial Aid staff will help you find the scholarships, grants, loans and work-study opportunities you need to make your college dreams a reality. We work individually with each student to determine exactly what you're eligible for.

STUDENT ORGANIZATIONS AND ACTIVITIES

Lynn students take their campus involvement and social lives pretty seriously. So no matter what your style is, you'll find plenty of things to keep you busy and make for a unique experience at Lynn University. If your style is athletic, Lynn offers popular intramural and club sports like flag football, soccer, basketball, and ping pong. Students can also get involved in fitness classes and field trips. If your style is adventurous, popular off-campus trips include the Miami Heat, Florida Panthers, Universal Studios, or Disney World. Or spend a break, summer, semester or year aboard in countries like Japan, China, and South Africa. If your style is to give back through community service, join Knights in the Community (KIC).

ADMISSION PROCESS

Lynn University works closely with students to make the application process as easy as possible. Here are the steps of how to apply:

Fill out an application and include:

A letter of recommendation from a high school counselor or teacher (freshmen)

Dean of Students Recommendation Form (transfer students)

A personal statement or essay

Submit $45 nonrefundable application fee (waived for veterans)

Submit official transcripts from all previous schools you attended

Submit your official SAT/ACT scores (freshmen only)

Applicants to the Conservatory of Music also need to audition and fill out an additional section of the undergraduate application. Applicants to the Comprehensive Support Program should submit WISC or WAIS scores taken within the last three years.

International students and Transfer students have additional requirements for admission. Your admission counselor at Lynn will assist in ensuring all additional requirements are submitted.

Once your file is complete, it will be evaluated for an admission decision. It can take from one to three weeks for an application to be processed.

Deadlines:

The Fall 2014 priority deadline for applications is March 31, 2014. Applications received after March 31, 2014 will be reviewed on a rolling basis. Be sure to submit your application in advance to take advantage of the priority deadline for deposit.

By meeting the March 31, 2014 deposit deadline, you will:

Get the housing option of your choice, based on availability

Get first choice of classes

Receive an early financial aid estimate

MANHATTAN COLLEGE

AT A GLANCE

Manhattan College is an independent, coeducational Catholic college in the Lasallian tradition. Manhattan offers more than 40 major fields of study in programs of arts, business, education, engineering and science.

Manhattan College is a Lasallian educational institution founded in 1853 by the De La Salle Christian Brothers, a Catholic teaching order established by Saint John Baptist De La Salle.

Today, these same ideals ring true at Manhattan College, where students embody the core Lasallian principles of an inclusive community, concern for the poor and social justice, respect for all people, all while obtaining a quality education.

There are some 40 major fields of study within five undergraduate schools, guided by an internationally recognized faculty, sought-after leaders and real-world consultants in their fields, 96 percent of whom hold doctoral degrees. Students have opportunities to study abroad in more than 30 countries.

Manhattan College participates in Division I sports as part of the MAAC, there are 18 teamsEvery year brings excitement to the courts, fields and track as the Jaspers compete. The College is known for its student-athletes, having many ranking among the MAAC All Academic teams.

LOCATION AND ENVIRONMENT

Manhattan College is located in the Riverdale section of New York City, giving students a beautiful tree-lined neighborhood, just a short distance from the heart of Manhattan. The campus' 22 acres provide students with a peaceful environment, with the knowledge that all cultural, business and educational experiences New York City has to offer is a quick subway, bus or car ride away.

The student body of 3,000 hails from 39 states and 59 countries. With a four-year guarantee of resident housing, 82 percent of freshmen choose to live on campus. Throughout the academic year, there are many activities offered at the College, which creates a family atmosphere for the entire student body.

OFF-CAMPUS OPPORTUNITIES

Manhattan College students actively define their commitment toward community around the city, country and world.

Each year, Campus Ministry and Social Action (CMSA) runs its L.O.V.E. program (Lasallian Outreach Volunteer Experience), which gives students the chance to participate in service experiences allowing them to travel to areas such as New Orleans, Kenya, Ecuador, the Dominican Republic and West Virginia, and volunteer with people of very different socio-economic backgrounds.

Many students also participate in local community service projects. These include Habitat for Humanity, , work with the elderly in nearby nursing homes, volunteering in soup kitchens, tutoring at the local schools , the Annual Toy Drive, blood drives, the American Cancer Society's Relay for Life and more. New projects are regularly developed in response to students' interests.

Each year mor than 300 students find internships in their field of study. Students participate in internships throughout the metropolitan area, gaining experience in the fields they are studying. With so many college alumni living in the tri-state area, networking opportunities are in every profession.

MAJORS AND DEGREES OFFERED

Manhattan College offers more than 40 major fields of study in the programs of arts, business, education, engineering and science, and graduate degrees are also offered in education, engineering and business . The College's professional schools are externally accredited by the following accrediting organizations: school of business, Association to Advance Collegiate Schools of Business (AACSB); school of education, Teacher Education Accrediting Council (TEAC); and individual school of engineering programs are accredited by the Engineering Accreditation Commission (EAC) of ABET, Inc. Within these programs, Manhattan College is able to provide students with the knowledge they need to succeed in the classroom and in the workforce.

The Arts students may major in: Art History, Communication, Economics, English, French, Government, History, International Studies, Labor Studies, Peace Studies, Philosophy, Psychology, Religious Studies, Sociology, Spanish, Urban Affairs and General Studies.

The Business students may choose from: Accounting, Computer Information Systems, Economics, Finance, Global Business Studies, Management and Marketing.

In addition, Manhattan College also offers the following graduate programs: the Bachelor of Science in Professional Accounting / Master of Business Administration Program and the Bachelor of Science in Business / Master of Business Administration Program, which offers students an option to complete a five-year multiple award program.

The Education program offers three options for undergraduate students interested in earning a bachelor's degree in teaching including: Early Childhood Education, Childhood Education, Dual: Childhood/Special Education and Adolescent Education. In addition, the program features two undergraduate majors in the department of Physical Education and Human Performance in Physical Education Teaching (grades K-12) or Exercise Science.

Another option is the Five-Year Childhood/Special Education Program, which combines baccalaureate and graduate work, allowing the student to receive a bachelor's and master's degree with eligibility to pursue certification for grades 1-6 in regular and special education. The school of education also offers master's degrees and professional diplomas in school counseling, mental health counseling, special education and school building leadership.

The Radiological and Health Professions Program is also part of the school of education and is available to students pursuing a Bachelor of Science with three major selections: Nuclear Medicine Technology, Radiation Therapy Technology or Allied Health.

The Engineering program offers programs leading to the baccalaureate degree in five disciplines: Chemical Engineering, Civil Engineering, Computer Engineering, Electrical Engineering and Mechanical Engineering. Graduate study at the master's level is also available in: Chemical Engineering, Civil Engineering, Computer Engineering, Electrical Engineering, Environmental Engineering and Mechanical Engineering.

Graduate Certificate programs currently available to engineering students are: Engineering Management, Environmental Management, Engineering Law, Engineering Mathematics, Biochemical Engineering, Manufacturing/Systems, HVAC (Heating, Ventilation and Air Conditioning), Construction Management, Electrical Power Engineering, Computer Engineering and Energy Management.

The Science program offers students the chance to major in the following areas: Biology, Biochemistry, Chemistry, Computer Science, Mathematics and Physics.

ACADEMIC PROGRAMS

Manhattan College is one of the few American colleges to have chapters of all five of these distinguished national honor societies: Beta Gamma Sigma, Kappa Delta Pi, Phi Beta Kappa, Sigma Xi and Tau Beta Pi.

Manhattan College is one of 276 institutions in the United States with a chapter of Phi Beta Kappa, the nation's oldest and most widely known academic honor society, which celebrates and advocates excellence in the liberal arts and sciences.

Other programs at Manhattan College:

The National Model United Nations offers a unique opportunity for students to better understand the inner workings of the United Nations and other international organizations while building skills in diplomacy and compromise.

The Branigan Fellowships program promotes undergraduate research in the humanities by awarding several grants per year in excess of $3,000 each for student-initiated projects.

The Fellowships Committee works with students and alumni to encourage graduate study and help work through sometimes challenging application processes.

The Pre-Law Advisory Committee works with students interested in pursuing law.

There are several study abroad options open to students. Students can choose to study abroad for a semester, an academic year, a month-long summer program or a seven-week summer program.

Manhattan's Mentorship program provides opportunities for students to gain insight into their intended careers by being paired with professionals, generally Manhattan alumni in those careers.

The College's Internship program allows students to complete at the minimum of one internship within their four years of study.

Manhattan's Finance and Economics club organizes student preparation and participation in the Volunteer Income Tax Assistance Program (VITA) and other service activities.

CAMPUS FACILITIES AND EQUIPMENT

O'Malley Library is home to a number of new features and services, including more than 100 computer workstations, a round-the-clock Internet Café, a media center equipped with teleconferencing capabilities, and many group study rooms scattered throughout the five-story layout.

Both commuters and residents can take advantage of the Fitness Center and newly renovated cafeterias. There are a variety of dining options, as well as spaces to relax and enjoy a snack while watching large screen televisions. The Commuter Lounge serves as a crossroads for students between classes while on campus.

The College is currently in the building phase of a new student center, which will include a 1200 square foot fitness center, cafeterias, lounges, offices for student clubs and much more.

TUITION, ROOM, BOARD, AND FEES

A. Full Time Students, 2012-2013

Full time students register for 12 or more credits per semester.

Tuition Charges per Semester

New Students entering 2012-2013: $ 15,050

Continuing students: $15,050

Program Fees per Semester

Arts, Education: 600

Business: $710

Science: $765

Engineering: $1,200

Over credit Charges per credit hour B. Part Time Students, 2012-2013

Part time students in day, evening or special (January and Summer) sessions register for less than 12 credits per semester.

FINANCIAL AID

Manhattan College provides the maximum financial aid available to qualified students to make their attendance at Manhattan financially possible.

New Students: Students admitted to the College and demonstrating financial need will receive a financial aid assistance offer in the form of a financial aid award letter from the Office of Admissions and Financial Aid, which is based on an assessment of your financial need.

Continuing Eligibility: All financial aid is renewable on a yearly basis provided the student remains eligible.

Manhattan College Programs:

Presidential Scholarships: Non-need based scholarships awarded to extraordinary applicants. Eligibility is based on exceptional SAT or ACT scores, secondary school grade point average, and rank in class.

Dean's Award: Dean's Awards are offered to academically gifted students who fall slightly below Presidential Scholarship requirements.

Manhattan College Grant-in-Aid: Manhattan College awards grants-in-aid to accepted students who demonstrate financial need.

Manhattan College Campus Employment Program: Manhattan offers its own campus work program to students who need employment to meet college expenses but are not eligible for Federal Work Study

Athletic Grants: The Manhattan College Athletics department may fund athletic grants to students who, by the possession of certain athletic skills, can add to the community spirit and morale of the campus.

Resident Assistant Grants: These grants are awarded to students selected to serve as Resident Assistants in the dormitories.

Dollars for Scholars: As a collegiate partner, Manhattan College matches Scholarship of America awards up to $500 a year.

Other programs: Veterans Administration Educational Benefits, Post-9/11 GI Bill Participant, Tuition Remission, Tuition Exchange Scholarship

The school also awards endowed and special category scholarships as part of the existing financial aid package.

STUDENT ORGANIZATIONS AND ACTIVITIES

Manhattan College offers many events and activities for students to participate in with more than 60 clubs and organizations on campus.

Cultural Groups: Asian Culture Club, Association for Black Culture, Gaelic Society, International Student Association and the Multicultural Student Union

Special Interest Groups: Christ in Your Life, Lasallian Outreach Volunteer Experience (L.O.V.E.), Electronics Club, Fashion Student Association, Just Peace, LaSallian Collegians (service group), New York Water Environmental Association, Relay for Life and Student Government.

Club Sports: Cheerleading & Crew

Social Leisure Clubs: Games Club, Outdoors Club, Steppers

Performing Arts: Bagpipers, Jasper Dancers, Jasper Band, Jazz Band, Orchestra, Players, Scatterbomb and Singers.

Communication: Manhattanite (yearbook), MCTV, Quadrangle (college newspaper), WRCM radio station

Social Fraternities & Sororities

Co-curricular clubs: Accounting Society, American Advertising Federation, American Chemistry Society, American Institute of Biological Science, American Institute of Chemical Engineers, American Society of Mechanical Engineers, Amnesty International, Association for Supervision and Curriculum Development, Biological Engineering Student Society, Communications Club, Economics and Finance Society, Italian Club, Information Technology Club, Institute of Electronic and Electrical Engineers, French Club, Manhattan Magazine, Mini Baja, National Society of Black Engineers, Phi Delta Epsilon, Psychology Club, Radiological Science Society, Society of Civil Engineers, Society of Hispanic Professional Engineers, Society of Mechanical Engineers, Society of Women Engineers, St. Thomas More Law Society.

ADMISSIONS PROCESS

Course Selection and Performance: Most emphasis is placed upon student course selection on the secondary level and grades earned in those subjects.

SAT and/or ACT Scores

Recommendations

Personal Statement

General Equivalency Diploma (G.E.D.)

Students who are transferring without an associate degree or with an A.A.S. degree must submit:

A high school transcript

Official college transcripts

A list of courses presently being taken

College catalogs from all institutions previously attended

Financial aid transcripts from all collegiate institutions previously attended (even if you only took one or two courses while in high school)

MARLBORO COLLEGE

AT A GLANCE

Marlboro College is a liberal arts college known for the rigor of its self-directed academic program. The philosophy at Marlboro is that of self-governance and empowering 300 students who value learning for its own sake. The curriculum combines wide exploration in many courses within the first two years with more focused research and independent study in the second two years, culminating in a major body of work known as the Plan of Concentration. Marlboro College also offers numerous opportunities to study abroad through the World Studies Program, Asian Studies and other faculty-led programs.

LOCATION AND ENVIRONMENT

Nestled in the foothills of southern Vermont, Marlboro College offers the benefits of living in the country, with more urban areas nearby. The campus is situated on the side of Potash Hill in the town of Marlboro, Vermont. Most of the 350-acre campus is deliberately preserved as natural forest with trails and streams running through the property. Our location serves to both inspire and inform the unique nature of our undergraduate experience.

OFF-CAMPUS OPPORTUNITIES

With the nearby locations of Brattleboro, a town of 12,000, just 10 miles away and Northampton, Massachusetts, 45 minutes away, Marlboro students have access to many resources, activities, and cultural life in central New England and New York. Vans run from the college into Brattleboro multiple times a day and trips to Northeastern cities such as Boston, New York and Montreal occur several weekends each semester.

MAJORS AND DEGREES OFFERED

Marlboro College provides a liberal arts education where students are able to work independently and at the same time closely with their teachers to achieve their academic goals. The college offers more than 30 degree fields in the Arts, the Humanities, the Natural Sciences and the Social Sciences. In developing their own courses of study, students are encouraged, though not required, to draw from more than one area and design an interdisciplinary Plan of Concentration. Degrees offered include Bachelor of Arts, Bachelor of Science and, through the World Studies Program, Bachelor of Arts or Science in International Studies.

American Studies, Anthropology, Art History, Asian Studies, Astronomy, Biochemistry, Biology, Ceramics, Chemistry, Classics, Computer Science, Cultural History, Dance, Economics, Environmental Studies, Film/Video Studies, Foreign Languages, History, Literature, Mathematics, Music, Painting, Philosophy, Photography, Physics, Political Science, Psychology, Religion, Sociology, Theater, Visual Arts, World Studies Program, Writing.

ACADEMIC PROGRAMS

The first two years at Marlboro are designed to give students the opportunity to study broadly in many different courses and areas. With the approval of their faculty advisor, students choose their own course schedules incorporating course work from all four areas of the curriculum: arts, humanities, sciences, and social sciences. The one requirement every student must meet within their first three semesters is the Clear Writing Program. When a student moves from the sophomore to the junior year, it is referred to as going "on Plan."

The Plan of Concentration is what sets Marlboro's curriculum apart from other colleges and is Marlboro's alternative to traditional majors. Plans are often interdisciplinary and self-designed with faculty sponsors. In the junior year, Plan students spend time strengthening their knowledge in the particular areas of study on which they are focusing. In the senior year, students complete a great deal of independent study and research. Throughout the whole process of working on their Plan, students benefit from the close academic sponsorship they receive from faculty members. Ultimately, evaluators from outside the college who are considered experts in their field are also included in the final assessment of a student's "Plan of Concentration".

The World Studies Program (WSP) integrates the best traditions of liberal arts learning and international studies with a six-to-eight-month working internship in a foreign culture. Students use their experiences abroad in their Plan of Concentration work. Students in the WSP design and carry out their internships in numerous fields, including photojournalism, business, education, relief work, development, anthropology, and scientific research, to name just a few. Graduates of the program have been accepted to many prestigious graduate schools, and more than two-thirds of the program's graduates now work or study in international fields. The World Studies Program operates in conjunction with the School for International Training in Brattleboro, Vermont, about 15 miles away from Marlboro's campus.

CAMPUS FACILITIES AND EQUIPMENT

Many of the campus buildings were originally farmhouses and barns renovated by the first students who attended Marlboro. These include Dalrymple Hall, which is the main classroom building; the dining hall; the admissions building; Mather, the administrative building. Over many years the College added more buildings, including residence halls, student cabins and cottages, the Whittemore Theater, the Rice-Aron Library, and a post-and-beam campus center, which the students and faculty built through a joint effort. The College has winterized its auditorium and built an art gallery, an art studio, a photography darkroom, an integrated science lab, a DNA lab, and a new residence hall. The new Total Health Center opened in 2008. The Serkin Center for the Performing Arts is an outstanding new facility providing performance and rehearsal space, in support of all performing arts programs..

TUITION, ROOM, BOARD, AND FEES

For the 2011-2012 academic year, the fees are as follows:

Tuition: $35,250

Fees: $1,310

Room: $5,310

Board: $4,330

Total: $46,200

FINANCIAL AID

Students should not refrain from applying to Marlboro College because of perceived inability to meet costs. Marlboro College is committed to helping every student who qualifies for financial aid to assemble the resources necessary to attend. More than 80 percent of all Marlboro students receive financial aid. Applicants should contact the Financial Aid Office directly to request a financial aid packet, which includes step-by-step instructions. The deadline for completing the Free Application for Federal Student Aid (FAFSA) is March 1. After that date, the College cannot promise a full financial aid package. The financial aid office can be reached at 802-258-9312 or finaid@marlboro.edu.

STUDENT ORGANIZATIONS AND ACTIVITIES

One particularly unique feature of Marlboro College is the college-wide Town Meeting held every three weeks during each semester. On these Wednesday afternoons, the whole College community, including students, faculty, and staff, gathers after lunch to discuss and debate any variety of college issues. Town Meeting's all-inclusive nature distinguishes it from more traditional student body governments.

Marlboro College is not the type of college that has a football team, unless you count a pick-up game of tag football. Instead, one of the most heavily used student activities is the Outdoor Program, OP for short. The OP offers a variety of activities from week-long orientation trips for new students to weekend mini trips, to winter- and spring-break trips in tropical climates. Some of the popular activities have been rock climbing, hiking, rafting, kayaking, camping, yoga, intramural soccer, broomball and Ultimate Frisbee. The College also has an indoor climbing wall and regular intramural activities.

Marlboro College has no fraternities or sororities. Students enjoy a wide range of social, artistic, and cultural activities. A sampling of student activities in one semester would include performances by rock, folk, jazz, and ethnic bands; dances; lectures; poetry readings; recitals; plays; and concerts. Annual events that are considered traditions are Convocation, Cabaret, Broomball Tournament, Community and International Dinners, Gender Bender Ball and Apple Days.

ADMISSIONS PROCESS

Marlboro College seeks students with intellectual promise, a high degree of motivation, self-discipline, creativity, social concern, and the ability and desire to contribute to the College community. The admissions committee assesses student preparedness and academic potential in the unique context of each applicant's personal experience without the confines of G.P.A or standardized test score minimums.

Students may apply to Marlboro under three different application plans.

Early Decision: Deadline-November 15; Notification-December 1

Early Action: Deadline-January 15; Notification-February 1

Regular Admission: Priority Deadline-March 1; Notification-April 1

Please note that if you are applying for financial aid it is important to file the FAFSA by March 1.

In order to be considered for admission, please submit the following: a completed Common Application and Marlboro College Supplement with the "Why Marlboro?" personal statement, the $50 nonrefundable application fee, all high school and college transcript(s), an analytic writing sample, and two letters of recommendation (teacher and general). Submission of SAT or ACT scores is optional.

MARQUETTE UNIVERSITY

AT A GLANCE

As Wisconsin's largest private university, Marquette University offers countless opportunities: the chance to live, study, and play in the heart of a dynamic city; access to nationally known programs and powerhouse faculty; and a Catholic and Jesuit tradition that emphasizes ethics and lifelong values across all disciplines. For more than 130 years, we have inspired students to Be the Difference in their professional and personal lives.

Our almost 12,000 undergraduate and graduate students come from all 50 states and 69 countries to create a vibrant, diverse, residential learning experience. They learn from professors who believe in the reality of a student-centered university that conducts world-class research.

Marquette's rigorous academic programs are recognized for challenging students to grow intellectually, socially, and spiritually. Our demanding core curriculum is grounded in the humanities, social sciences, and natural sciences; this liberal arts core, coupled with a student's academic major, provides the balance of knowledge a student will need to succeed as a professional — and a person.

At Marquette, you'll be taught and mentored by some of the nation's most successful professors who frequently win international awards and grants, publish influential works, and conduct cutting-edge research. And you won't just hear about that research; you'll have the chance to participate in research with faculty mentors yourself, helping to advance your field while gaining unrivaled experience.

You will have a diverse experience. As one of more than 8,000 undergraduates, you will meet students who look, think, and act very much like you — and more who don't. More than 90 percent of freshmen live on campus, so you're sure to find your niche in the Marquette family.

We'll ask you tough questions: "What do you believe in?" "What do you stand for?" "Why?" You will be challenged to lead a thoughtful, reflective life.

You will be encouraged to find God in all things. Through retreats, religious services, prayers, and conversations within the university community, Marquette fosters an environment that nurtures spiritual growth for students of all faiths.

U.S. News & World Report ranks Marquette 83rd in the 2013 edition of "America's Best Colleges"; Marquette is one of only 50 universities recognized in the "Best Value Schools" category. In other rankings, The Princeton Review named Marquette one of the country's "Best 376 Colleges" for 2012; the Fiske Guide to Colleges named the university a "Best Buy School," one of only 49 in its 2012 edition; and Kiplinger's Personal Finance listed the university among its "Best Values in Private Colleges for 2011–12." But Marquette is more than rankings. In 2010, the university was the 10th higher education institution bestowed the Changemaker Campus title by the Ashoka Institute, a leader in social entrepreneurship — the practice of applying sustainable business models to solve social problems. And Marquette was named to the 2013 President's Higher Education Community Service Honor Roll by the Corporation for National and Community Service.

LOCATION AND ENVIRONMENT

With a metro population of almost 1 million, Milwaukee has all the bonuses you'd expect from a big city — like proximity to the arts, professional sports, fantastic restaurants, and shopping — with fewer of the hassles. And right at the heart of the city is Marquette's 90-acre campus, giving you easy access to everything Milwaukee has to offer, including internships, service opportunities, and social activities. Your Marquette education will extend from campus classrooms to the larger, more expansive classroom that is the city. It's a place where you can connect what you're learning with what you do.

Off-campus Opportunities

Your education doesn't need to be limited to Milwaukee. Each year, many Marquette students grab their passports, pack their bags, and head off to distant lands to study for a few weeks, a semester, or a year. The experience is life-changing. Marquette offers study abroad and exchange program opportunities on every continent but Antarctica. And if you want to go there, we can probably arrange something for you.

If you prefer to stay in the states, Marquette's Les Aspin Center for Government in Washington, D.C., is one of the country's top legislative internship programs. For a semester or a summer, you can live, learn, and work on Capitol Hill. Take an active role in the legislative process while you work as an intern or aide in the House of Representatives, the Senate, or various federal agencies. You'll also take unique courses, meet with government officials and dignitaries, and become well-connected in a city where connections are everything.

MAJORS AND DEGREES OFFERED

The Carnegie Foundation classifies Marquette as a research university that offers a wide variety of degrees and maintains high research activity. Marquette offers rigorous academic programs in nearly 80 undergraduate majors, as well as excellent advanced education in 38 master's degree programs, 17 doctoral programs, and 37 graduate certificate programs. Marquette is also home to the state's only School of Dentistry and a Law School with a reputation as a forum for public policy debate in state-of-the-art Eckstein Hall.

ACADEMIC PROGRAMS

At the heart of all Marquette academic programs is the University Core of Common Studies. You'll take courses in nine knowledge areas designed to teach you how to examine, engage, and evaluate the world; these areas include rhetoric, mathematical reasoning, individual and social behavior, diverse cultures, literature, history of cultures and societies, science and nature, human nature and ethics, and theology. The courses within the University Core will teach you how to understand and be understood, to act responsibly, and to think for yourself.

Marquette is a direct-entry university, meaning students can begin work in their majors right away. Because you can deepen your interest, knowledge, and expertise early, you'll practice what you've learned through internships in and beyond Milwaukee. If you are undecided about a major, your academic adviser can help find the right fit for your passions and abilities.

CAMPUS FACILITIES AND EQUIPMENT

More than 90 percent of Marquette's freshmen and sophomores live in nine on-campus residence halls; most juniors and seniors live immediately off campus in university-owned or independent apartments and houses. The high concentration of residential students gives Marquette a vitality not often found in urban universities. The Raynor Memorial Libraries offer areas for quiet and group study, as well as wireless Internet access and a coffee shop. When students aren't studying, you can find them enjoying our two recreation centers and campus green spots.

TUITION, ROOM, BOARD, AND FEES

Full-time tuition for the 2013–14 academic year is $34,200. Room and board averages about $10,730, depending on housing preference and meal plan.

FINANCIAL AID

We recognize that Marquette is a great place, but we also know that private school tuition can be rather expensive. That's why the university offers a variety of partial to full-tuition, merit-based scholarships. To apply for need-based financial aid, Marquette requests that you file the Free Application for Federal Student Aid (FAFSA). Financial need that is demonstrated on this form determines our ability to award federal, state, and university-funded grants and loans, as well as some forms of student employment. More than 90 percent of Marquette undergraduates receive financial assistance in the form of scholarships, grants, loans, and/or student employment.

STUDENT ORGANIZATIONS AND ACTIVITIES

With upwards of 270 student organizations vying for your time, you won't be bored at Marquette. And because most of our students spend their weekends on campus, there's plenty to do here and around the city. Also, our students don't hesitate to get out in the community; 90 percent of undergraduates participate in service through a wide range of programs, student organizations, service-learning classes, and one-day projects.

Are you a sports fan? If so, you're looking in the right place. Whether you're a big-time intercollegiate athlete or a die-hard spectator, Marquette offers a huge variety of opportunities, including 14 varsity teams that compete in the NCAA Division I Big East Conference. If club and recreational sports are more your speed, we have about 50 coed, men's, or women's clubs and intramural teams.

ADMISSIONS PROCESS

For all academic programs, Marquette has a priority admission deadline of December 1 (postmark date). Applications postmarked after December 1 will be considered on a space-available basis for admission and scholarships. Admission decisions are based on a thorough review of high school course selection, academic performance (grade point average), class rank (when applicable), ACT and/or SAT scores, essay quality, and extracurricular activities. Visit marquette.edu/explore for more information about deadlines and requirements.

MARYMOUNT UNIVERSITY

AT A GLANCE

Marymount is a comprehensive Catholic university offering undergraduate, graduate, and certificate programs through four schools: Arts and Sciences, Business Administration, Education and Human Services, and the Malek School of Health Professions. The University is located in Arlington, Virginia, just across the Potomac River from Washington, DC, providing students with unparalleled access to all the resources of the nation's capital.

Marymount's undergraduate programs combine a strong liberal arts foundation with solid career preparation. Small classes and professors who take a personal interest in student success provide a supportive academic environment.

ACADEMICS

Marymount puts an emphasis on intellectual curiosity. Critical thinking and student research are highlighted across the curriculum and through the DISCOVER Program. Discover 101, a first-year experience course taken by all freshmen, introduces new students to the excitement of inquiry learning with wide-ranging topics such as "CSI Marymount," "Green Computing," and "Who's Dow Jones?" From the freshman seminar to the senior capstone course, Marymount students are encouraged to explore topics of interest more deeply through original research and creative projects. The DISCOVER Program also coordinates the annual Student Research Conference, student conference travel support, and the Summer Research Program for students and faculty mentors.

The selective Honors Program draws on all facets of the curriculum to offer highly motivated students extra opportunities for academic enrichment. Program benefits include substantial scholarship support, one-one-faculty mentoring, and special seminar and field-trip opportunities.

All Marymount undergraduates are required to complete an internship or research experience related to their field of study, and the DC region offers unique opportunities. Internships provide invaluable hands-on experience in exciting locations in and around the nation's capital, including Capitol Hill, the National Institutes of Health, the Smithsonian museums, and international businesses. Marymount faculty incorporate DC resources into the curriculum, so that students learn to take advantage of all that the city offers.

In addition, distinguished speakers of national and international stature are frequent visitors to campus; Marymount guests have included Nobel Laureate Desmond Tutu, Secretary of Defense Chuck Hagel, Pulitzer Prize-winning author Jennifer Egan, and fashion designer Michael Kors.

SERVICE

In the rich tradition of Catholic higher education, Marymount is also known for its commitment to service, and students embrace opportunities to make a difference in the local community and beyond. As part of orientation, freshmen are introduced to service options at Volunteer Service Day. Throughout the academic year, the Campus Ministry Association, student organizations, and athletic teams sponsor a variety of service activities. In addition, many courses include a service component.

WORLD VIEW

Gaining a global perspective is increasingly important in an interconnected world. Marymount's Center for Global Education provides the chance to live, study, and even complete an internship in virtually any corner of the world. Both short-term and semester-long programs are offered. On campus, Marymount promotes global awareness and understanding through guest speakers, interfaith forums, and the celebration of the university's diverse campus community. Marymount students represent more than 40 states and 63 countries, and they are of all faiths and backgrounds. Marymount is a welcoming community where each individual is respected and diverse perspectives enrich the learning experience.

VIBRANT COMMUNITY

Marymount's student life offers something for everyone: athletics, student government, volunteer service programs, and more than 40 clubs address diverse interests and provide opportunities for involvement. An NCAA Division III school, Marymount fields men's and women's basketball, cross-country, lacrosse, soccer, and swimming, plus men's golf and women's volleyball. In fall 2013, Marymount will add men's volleyball and men and women's triathlon teams to the roster. Baseball comes to Marymount in 2014.

CAMPUS VISITS

Visit Marymount and see for yourself all that the University has to offer! Join us for one of the Campus Visit Days held in the fall and spring, or arrange for your own visit. A student ambassador will guide you on a campus tour and answer questions about college life. An admissions counselor will provide details on the admissions process, financial aid and scholarship opportunities, and academic requirements. You can also arrange to talk with faculty or coaches.

Marymount's Main Campus is located at 2807 North Glebe Road in Arlington, Virginia. To schedule a visit or learn more about Marymount University, call (800) 548-7638;

e-mail prospectivestudents@marymount.edu, or visit us online at www.marymount.edu.

LOCATION AND ENVIRONMENT

Marymount's Main Campus and Ballston Center are located in Arlington, Virginia, just minutes from Washington, DC. The public Metrorail system connects the University with the entire greater Washington, DC, region. Marymount also maintains a free shuttle service that connects the Main Campus, Ballston Center, and the Ballston-MU Metro station. Students have easy access to national landmarks, cultural sites, restaurants, and shopping. Marymount's Reston Center is located in western Fairfax County.

OFF-CAMPUS OPPORTUNITIES

University faculty and students takes full advantage of the resources in and around the nation's capital. Popular internship sites include Congressional offices, the Smithsonian museums, the White House, major media outlets, international businesses, and prestigious health care institutions. Students also have access to incredible research facilities like the Library of Congress.

Marymount students take advantage of the opportunity to fully experience Washington, DC, and many of the activities are free! Sit in on a Congressional hearing or view the latest exhibit at the National Gallery of Art. For sports fans, DC is home to professional football, basketball, baseball, soccer, and ice hockey teams. Culture, history, world-class museums, restaurants, theatre, sports and music are all just across the Potomac River from Marymount.

MAJORS AND DEGREES OFFERED

The University offers a strong liberal arts education combined with solid career preparation. The following is a listing of Marymount's majors and degree programs:

Bachelor of Arts (B.A.): Art with tracks in Art Management and Pre-Art Therapy; Communication with emphasis areas in Journalism/Broadcasting, Public/Corporate Communication, Speech Communication, and Visual/Media Communication; Criminal Justice; Economics in Society; English with tracks in Literature, Media and Performance Studies and Writing; Fashion Design; Fashion Merchandising; Graphic Design, History, Interior Design, Liberal Studies; Multidisciplinary Studies (B.A. with teaching licensure for Elementary Education grades PK-6, and Special Education, grades K-12); Philosophy; Politics; Psychology; Sociology; Theology and Religious Studies

Bachelor of Science (B.S.) Biology with tracks in General Biology, Molecular and Cellular Biology, and Pre-Med Studies; Biochemistry; Criminal Justice; Criminal Justice with a concentration in Forensic Science; Health Information Management; Health Sciences (B.S., B.S./M.S.) with emphasis areas in Health Promotion and Pre-Physical Therapy; Information Technology (B.S., B.S./M.S.) with specialty areas in Applied IT, Computer Science, Forensic Computing, Health IT, Information Systems, and Interactive Media; Mathematics

Bachelor of Business Administration (B.B.A., B.B.A./M.B.A): Business Administration with specialties in Accounting, Business Law, Finance, General Business, Hospitality Management, International Business, Management, Marketing, and Sport Management

Nursing (B.S.N.): traditional four-year program; hybrid online R.N.-to B.S.N.; accelerated B.S.N. program for students with a previous bachelor's degree in another field.

MINORS

Art History, Biology, Business Administration, Business Law, Communication, Computer Science, Criminal Justice, Economics, English, Fashion Design, Fashion Merchandising, Forensic Computing, French, Graphic Design, Health Information Technology, Health Sciences, History, Illustration, Interdisciplinary Studies – Media and Performance Studies, Interdisciplinary Studies – Gender and Society, Studio Art, Mathematics, Physical Science, Psychology, Public History, Public Health, Philosophy, Politics, Social Entrepreneurship, Social Justice, Sociology, Spanish, Studio Art, Sustainability, Theology and Religious Studies, Web Design, Writing

Pre-Professional Studies: Pre-Law, Pre-Medicine, Pre-Physical Therapy

Undergraduate Certificates: Computer Networking and Cybersecurity, Criminal Justice/Forensic Science, Web Design

Undergraduate Teaching Licensure Programs

Art Education — grades K-12 (B.A. in Art); Elementary Education — grades PK-6 (B.A. in Multidisciplinary Study); Secondary Education — grades 6-12, Biology (B.S. in Biology), English (B.A. in English), History/Social Science (B.A. in History), Mathematics (B.S. in Mathematics); Special Education, General Curriculum — grades K-12 (B.A. in Multidisciplinary Studies)

CAMPUS FACILITIES AND EQUIPMENT

Marymount University has two locations in Arlington, Virginia - the Main Campus and the Ballston Center. Marymount's Reston Center, located in western Fairfax County, focuses on meeting the educational needs of adult learners.

Facilities on the Main Campus consist of the Main House, the Emerson G. Reinsch Library, the Barry Art Gallery, and academic and residential halls. The Lee University Center is the hub of student activities on Main Campus and houses the Verizon sports arena, the collegiate swimming facility, Bernie's Café, and the University bookstore.

Marymount's Ballston Center, located in the Ballston professional district, is home to Marymount's School of Business Administration. It is just minutes from the Main Campus, and students travel to and from both locations on free Marymount shuttles.

The Reston Center is located in northern Virginia's business and technology corridor.

Tuition, Room, Board and Fees

The undergraduate tuition and fees for 2013-14 is $26,100 per academic year; room and board starts at $11,550 per academic year for double occupancy.

FINANCIAL AID

Marymount has an extensive scholarship and grant program and participates in federal and state aid programs. To be considered for aid, students must file the Free Application for Federal Student Aid (FAFSA). Financial aid may come in the form of scholarships, grants, and loans from a variety of public and private sources. The University offers numerous scholarships based on academic accomplishment, volunteer service, and financial need. In fall 2011, 86% of full-time degree-seeking undergraduates received financial assistance.

STUDENT ORGANIZATIONS AND ACTIVITIES

Athletics, student government, volunteer opportunities, and lots of campus activities mean there's always plenty to do at Marymount. More than 40 clubs and organizations are active on campus. An NCAA Division III institution, Marymount fields men's and women's teams in basketball, lacrosse, soccer, swimming, and cross country, as well as women's volleyball and men's golf. In fall 2013, Marymount will add men and women's triathlon and men's volleyball to the team roster. Baseball comes to Marymount in 2014.

The Activities Programming Board, composed of Marymount students and staff, plans and implements ongoing social activities, both on-and-off campus. Major annual events that Marymount students plan, participate in, and enjoy include International Week, a recognition of the global cultures represented by Marymount students; SpringFest, a week-long celebration of the arts; HalloweenFest, a trick-or-treat extravaganza for disadvantaged children; and the Special Olympics Basketball Tournament, a community outreach program organized and staffed by Marymount volunteers.

ADMISSIONS PROCESS

The Admissions team reviews the strength of an applicant's academic record, national test scores, breadth of academic preparation, and letters of recommendation. Applicants to the freshman class are considered if a student's high school grade point average in academic courses is 2.5 or better on a 4.0 scale, the combined SAT score is within 100 points of the national average or better, and the student's academic preparation, recommendations, and character indicate that he or she is qualified to undertake Marymount programs. A campus interview is not required, but is strongly recommended. It gives students a chance to see if Marymount would be a good fit. The University holds Campus Visit Days in the fall and spring. Visitors are welcome at any time, and appointments with Admissions staff may be made in advance.

Application Information

High school students seeking admission are advised to apply early during their senior year. They should submit an application (which can be completed online), a nonrefundable fee of $40, a high school transcript, SAT or ACT scores, evidence of expected graduation from an accredited high school, and a recommendation from a high school counselor or an appropriate school official. The University has a rolling admission policy and notifies applicants soon after the application process is completed and a decision on admission has been made.

MERCER UNIVERSITY

AT A GLANCE

Mercer University (founded in 1833) offers more than 70 undergraduate, graduate and professional degree programs. The University consists of 11 colleges and schools: the College of Liberal Arts; the Eugene W. Stetson School of Business and Economics; the School of Engineering; the Tift College of Education; the Townsend School of Music; the Walter F. George School of Law; the School of Medicine; the College of Pharmacy and Health Sciences; the Georgia Baptist College of Nursing; the James & Carolyn McAfee School of Theology; and the College of Continuing and Professional Studies.

Mercer University, with campuses in Macon, Atlanta, and Savannah, Georgia and regional centers around the state, receives its accreditation from the Commission on Colleges of the Southern Association of Colleges and Schools. U.S. News and World Report has ranked Mercer among the leading universities in the South, both for value and quality of education, for 18 consecutive years.

Mercer's exceptional reputation springs from its sound academic programs, excellent faculty, and modern facilities. Tradition, however, is also a central component of this institution's unique identity. Mercer's commitment to Judeo-Christian values and its dedication to intellectual and religious freedom truly distinguish the University.

Mercer enrolls over 8,300 students in its 11 schools. With 2,500 undergraduates studying at the main campus, undergraduates enjoy small classes (average class size is 21) made possible by the 13:1 student/faculty ratio (an unusually low ratio for a university of its size). While a majority of Mercer students come from the Southeast, the student body is representative of at least 48 states and 24 countries. All students gain from Mercer's friendly atmosphere, excellent teaching (by faculty members only, never by teaching assistants), and small classes. Mercer instructors hold degrees from some of the most prestigious institutions in the world; they excel in both their research and teaching abilities. Nearly all hold Ph.D.s or the equivalent terminal degree in their fields.

Undergraduates may choose from a range of housing options, including conventional dormitories, apartment-style residences, and Greek houses. Mercer is an active campus, home to more than 120 clubs and organizations; among their number are academic clubs, honor societies, performing arts organizations, special interest groups, and religious groups. Ten fraternities and seven sororities play a central role in the community, providing social outlets and performing a wide assortment of community services. ROTC is another option available to Mercer undergraduates.

Mercer's athletic teams compete in Division I of the NCAA and the Atlantic Sun Conference. The University fields teams in men's baseball, basketball, cross-country, golf, lacrosse, tennis, and soccer, and women's basketball, cross-county, golf, sand volleyball, soccer, softball, tennis, and court volleyball. Football rejoins the roster in Fall 2013! The school also offers a variety of intramural and club sport competition.

LOCATION AND ENVIRONMENT

The 130-acre Macon campus is a blend of tradition and innovation. Students walk among hundred-year-old trees, yet state-of-the-art learning technology is at their fingertips. The 230,000-square-foot University Center is a hub for campus activity. From enjoying a lingering cup of mocha at the Coffee Shop to jogging laps around the indoor track to attending a concert or Division I basketball game in the arena, students make memories in this facility that enhance their college experience.

Macon is a vibrant community with a rich arts and musical heritage. Centrally located in the heart of the state, the campus allows easy access to the Georgia coast, Florida beaches and the Blue Ridge Mountains. Grand antebellum homes along the tree-lined streets contrast with the new convention center and premier shopping centers. Downtown Macon, site of the renovated Douglass Theatre, the Grand Opera House, and the Georgia Sports Hall of Fame, is a lively shopping and visitors district located not far from the campus.

UNDERGRADUATE MAJORS AND DEGREES OFFERED

The College of Liberal Arts offers the following undergraduate degrees: Bachelor of Arts; Bachelor of Science. Available majors and concentrations include: Africana Studies, Anthropology, Art, Biology, Biochemistry and Molecular Biology, Chemistry, Christianity, Classical Foreign Languages - Latin, Greek, Classical Studies, Communication Studies, Computational Science, Computer Science, Criminal Justice, Earth and Environmental Science, English - Creative Writing, English – Literature, Global Health Studies, Health Physics, History, Information Science & Technology, International Affairs, Journalism, Mathematics, Media Studies, Modern Foreign Languages - French, German, Spanish, Natural Science, Philosophy, Photography, Physics, Political Science, Psychology, Social Entrepreneurship, Sociology, Southern Studies, Theatre, Women's & Gender Studies. Pre-professional tracks are available in pre-dentistry, pre-law, pre-medicine, pre-nursing, pre-pharmacy, pre-physician assistant, pre-physical therapy, pre-veterinary medicine, and pre-theology.

The School of Business and Economics offers the Bachelor of Business Administration degree. Students may study administration, accounting, economics, finance, marketing, management, and sports management. A strong emphasis is placed on practical experience gained through internships and group projects. Faculty advisors work closely with each student to match appropriate industry experiences and complementary courses offered through Mercer's other schools and colleges.

The School of Engineering offers programs leading to the Bachelor of Science in Engineering degree. Students may specialize in biomedical, computer, electrical, industrial, mechanical, and environmental engineering. The School also offers the Bachelor of Science degree, with majors in industrial management and technical communication.

The College of Education offers the Bachelor of Science in Education degree in early childhood/special education and middle level education. The school offers secondary/grade certification in art, English, foreign languages, history, mathematics, music, broad field science, and broad field social science.

The School of Music offers the Bachelor of Arts, Bachelor of Music Education, and Bachelor of Music Performance. The school is also home to the Robert McDuffie Center for Strings.

The College of Nursing offers the Bachelor of Science in Nursing. After completing their pre-nursing requirements through the College of Liberal Arts, students may elect to finish their nursing degree on Mercer's Macon or Atlanta campus.

ACADEMIC PROGRAMS

Undergraduates at Mercer may choose between two academic tracks. The first, the General Education Program, requires study in a number of areas and leads to a broad-based education. General Education students investigate the major fields of human accomplishment and learning. This track, which is completed by the end of sophomore year, establishes a base from which students can continue a lifetime of study in many fields. General Education students spend their junior and senior years specializing in a major field and completing upper-division courses.

The second track, the Great Books Program, immerses students in the classic works of Western civilization. Students probe the writings of Plato, Socrates, Milton, and Freud in order to learn more about our society and its intellectual lineage. The Great Books Program is an eight-course sequence that is not completed until the first semester of the student's final year.

Exceptional students are eligible to participate in Mercer's Honors Program, which helps academically superior students reach their maximum learning potential by undertaking more challenging assignments and coursework. Qualified students in the College of Liberal Arts, School of Business and Economics, College of Education, and School of Engineering, are eligible to enter the Honors Program.

All students at Mercer University must complete a major. However, the University also encourages undergraduates to investigate fields outside their majors. Options for independent reading, independent research, and course work in special topics exists in many departments. The University also allows undergraduates to design independent majors, with the consultation of an academic advisor and the approval of the college dean and a faculty committee.

Most students in the College of Liberal Arts, the Stetson School of Business and Economics, the Tift College of Education, and Townsend School of Music undertake 15 hours of coursework (five courses) per semester. Students in the School of Engineering generally undertake 15 to 18 hours of coursework (five to six courses) per semester. Students who wish to take an extra course must have a GPA of 3.0 or better and receive permission from their academic advisor. Up to 30 hours of course credit can be earned through the College-Level Examination Program (CLEP) or International Baccalaureate (IB). Students who take Advanced Placement exams (College Board) and receive scores of 3 or better usually receive credit for the equivalent coursework.

CAMPUS FACILITIES AND EQUIPMENT

Mercer's commitment to its students may also be seen through the numerous additions to campus over the past few years. Most recently, the University opened its new Science and Engineering building, bringing to campus one of the finest and most accommodating research facilities in the South. The Lofts at Mercer Village opened in 2011, with three floors of loft-style apartments for students and retail and dining space on the ground level. Phase II of the Lofts at Mercer Village is under construction. The second phase will house Mercer's new Center for Collaborative Journalism on the first floor of the building.

TUITION, ROOM, BOARD AND FEES

Tuition for the 2011-2012 school year is $31,248; room and board is an additional $10,408. On average, students spend $1,200 on books and supplies each year.

FINANCIAL AID

Mercer offers generous financial assistance to all qualified undergraduates through grants, scholarships, loans, and work-study opportunities. Mercer students are also eligible for a variety of federal, state, and local assistance, which in combination bring a Mercer education within any student's financial means. All financial assistance applicants should submit the Free Application for Federal Student Aid (FAFSA). Georgia residents may also be eligible for the Georgia Tuition Equalization Grant and the HOPE Scholarship. Students who qualify for scholarships are notified by the University by letter after they have been accepted to the school.

STUDENT ORGANIZATIONS AND ACTIVITIES

The Student Government Association sponsors and manages numerous student activities at the University. Each year, elections are held in the spring to select the SGA president, vice president, secretary-treasurer, and freshman advisor, as well as representatives of each of the four classes plus one at-large representative. Students also elect the editors of major student publications and members of the student activities board, QuadWorks. Most school committees include student representatives from the liberal arts, business, engineering, music, and education divisions.

Mercer students participate in more than 120 clubs and 17 national fraternities and sororities. A small sampling includes: the Shakespearean Society, Mercer Cycling, Mac-Town Breakers, Indian Cultural Exchange, the Society of Women Engineers, Up 'Til Dawn, Animercer, and Students For Environmental Action. With so many options, getting involved is easy.

ADMISSIONS PROCESS

Students seeking admission to the freshman class should be on track to complete (or have already completed) a college preparatory high-school curriculum including at least 4 units each of English and mathematics; 3 units each of laboratory science and social science, and 2 units of foreign language. For this work, they should have received a minimum B average (3.0 GPA). Applicants should submit standardized test scores reflecting a minimum combined SAT I score of 1000 or its equivalent ACT composite score. Furthermore, students seeking admission to computer science, engineering, mathematics, pre-health sciences (medicine, pharmacy, nursing, dentistry, etc.) or natural sciences programs must score at least a 550 on the SAT I math test (or its equivalent on the ACT). Applicants must be in good academic and disciplinary standing at the school currently, or most recently, attended.

Students seeking admission to Mercer should submit an application; an official high school transcript that clearly identifies academic coursework (admitted students must submit a completed transcript at the end of their senior year to finalize their admission to Mercer); and, an official standardized test score report (SAT I or ACT) (Scores on official high school transcripts are accepted). A résumé of high school and community activities, as well as work experience, is encouraged, but not required.

Students seeking admission in the fall should submit applications before May 1. Applicants should submit all necessary materials as early as possible for premier scholarship consideration. Contact the Office of University Admissions with all inquiries.

More information is available by contacting:

Office of University Admissions

Mercer University

1400 Coleman Avenue

Macon, GA 31207

Telephone. 478-301-2650

800-840-8577 (toll free)

E-mail: admissions@mercer.edu

World Wide Web: mercer.edu/admissions

MICHIGAN TECHNOLOGICAL UNIVERSITY

AT A GLANCE

Michigan Technological University (www.mtu.edu) is a leading public research university developing new technologies and preparing students to create the future for a prosperous and sustainable world.

Undergraduate involvement in research is a common part of a Michigan Tech education, and recent examples include prosthetic feet, a human-powered hovercraft, and noise-monitoring devices. In our Enterprise Program and other special opportunities, students can invest real money in the stock market; create better satellites, snowboards, and video games; and journey to foreign nations to help the less-fortunate with engineering and other projects.

LOCATION AND ENVIRONMENT

Our rural setting in the Upper Peninsula allows us to provide an excellent education in a beautiful location. Recreational opportunities include our own ski hill, golf course, and 600 acres of on-campus recreational forest and trails for cross country running, skiing, hiking, and biking.

The Ford Forest, in nearby Alberta, Michigan, is a 4,000-acre research forest managed by our School of Forest Resources and Environmental Science

OFF-CAMPUS OPPORTUNITIES

The entire local area is great for outdoor enthusiasts, with easy access to rivers, lakes, woods and trails. Also, downtown Houghton and Hancock (combined population 14,000) offer coffee shops, theaters, stores, restaurants and more. Major retailers are just outside of Houghton, a short drive or bus ride from campus. All in all, it's a great combination: a world-class education in a beautiful location.

MAJORS AND DEGREES OFFERED

Michigan Tech offers more than 130 undergraduate and graduate degree programs in engineering; forest resources; computing; technology; business; economics; natural, physical and environmental sciences; arts; humanities; and social sciences.

The environmental, geological/mining, and mechanical engineering programs rank in the top fifteen nationally in enrollment and degrees awarded. Our scientific and technical communication program is also among the nation's largest.

Our newest academic programs include the BS in Engineering Management, the BA in History, and MS in Medical Informatics.

ACADEMIC PROGRAMS

The Enterprise Program involves nearly 800 students on twenty-eight teams from all across campus and allows them to solve real problems for industry. Currently, students are working on projects related to EcoCAR, natural resources, better bicycles, IT, and homeland security, to name just a few.

The Pavlis Institute for Global Technological Leadership has embarked on projects as far away as Ghana. Its future enrollment is expected to exceed 300: truly the next generation of leaders.

Through the International Scholars Program, every Michigan Tech student can participate in a meaningful international experience via this certificate program.

The Honors Institute has grown from 87 to 337 students in just six years, and these best and brightest students have added much to our campus and community.

The Applied Portfolio Management Program has won the RISE national investment competition in the value category three times. This is especially impressive in today's nerve-wracking financial climate. They also have their own space, the LSGI Trading Room.

Dedicated to prosperity by design, the D80 Center aims to assist the most vulnerable 80 percent of humanity in meeting their most basic needs. Programs include Engineers Without Borders, Aqua Terra Tech Enterprise, International Sustainable Development Engineering Certificate and Research Experiences, International Senior Design, the nation's largest Peace Corps Master's International Program, and the newest group, Global City at Michigan Tech.

The Senior Design program connects students and industry through open-ended, industrial projects. Students gain the skills and experience that can launch them into successful careers, while industry partners gain access to tomorrow's engineers—today. As they say, it is not their last class; in many respects, it is their first job.

Approximately 350 companies recruit students on campus annually, ensuring an average of five job interviews per student, and within six months of graduation 95 percent of those reporting got jobs, entered graduate school, or joined the armed forces.

CAMPUS FACILITIES AND EQUIPMENT

State of the art laboratories and classrooms permeate the campus, and wireless networking is everywhere. On the waterfront, our new Great Lakes Research Center will advance our expertise in environmental studies and our proximity to Lake Superior.

More than twenty research centers and institutes allow Michigan Tech faculty, staff, and students to focus on a broad range of inquiry, from climate change to transportation, from power and energy to computational science. The newest research center looks at precollege outreach innovations, stressing our science and engineering strengths.

Our athletic campus has recently upgraded Sherman Field, our football and soccer stadium, with state-of-the-art playing surface. Our MacInnes Student Ice Arena features skyboxes, new ice plant, and, soon, a high-tech videoboard.

TUITION, ROOM, BOARD, AND FEES

Annual Tuition

Undergraduate (in-state)	$13,095°
Room and Board	$8,865
Graduate Tuition	$744/credit hour

°Tuition is based on 15 credit hours per semester, with a per-credit cost of $436.50 for Michigan residents and $900 for non-Michigan residents.

FINANCIAL AID

Scholarships are the most familiar and sought-after type of financial aid. All admitted students are automatically considered for most merit-based scholarships; a special application form is not required, except for the Michigan Tech Leading Scholars Award and career interest scholarships.

Grants are gift aid based on financial need and are available to US citizens and permanent residents. Accepted students are automatically considered for grant programs if their FAFSA results are released to Michigan Tech. Students must apply for grant renewal each year.

Loans consist of borrowed funds, which must be repaid. They are available to most US citizens and permanent residents. Each loan program has certain maximum limits for borrowing; however, students may not borrow more than the cost of attendance, less any other financial aid received. Accepted students are automatically considered for loans if their FAFSA results are released to Michigan Tech and they have indicated on the FAFSA an interest in receiving loans. Students must apply for loan renewal each year and make progress in obtaining their degree according to the Satisfactory Progress Policy.

Part-time employment on campus is available through government-funded and University-funded programs. Students who complete the FAFSA and indicate they would like to work on campus are automatically considered for work-study employment.

FEDERAL WORK-STUDY PROGRAM

These programs provide funds to students for part-time employment who are US citizens or permanent residents and who have financial need. Students must reapply for work-study each year and meet the Satisfactory Progress Policy requirements.

Specific departmental work-study assignments are made by the Financial Aid Office. Students normally work eight to ten hours per week. The hourly rate paid is equivalent to at least minimum wage.

UNIVERSITY-FUNDED STUDENT EMPLOYMENT

University-funded, on-campus employment is available to students, regardless of need. Students may apply directly to the desired departments. On average, 2,000 to 2,500 students are employed on campus each year. Nearly every department utilizes students as employees.

STUDENT ORGANIZATIONS AND ACTIVITIES

More than 180 student organizations offer leadership opportunities in many different categories: Academic/Honors, Arts and Culture, Club Sports, Governance, Greeks, Programming/Social, Religious, and Service.

Our traditions include Winter Carnival with massive snow statues and broomball; Parade of Nations, celebrating more than sixty nations and cultures represented here; K-Day on Lake Superior's shore; and Spring Fling on campus.

ADMISSIONS PROCESS

Applying to college doesn't have to be stressful. In fact, Michigan Tech makes it pretty easy. You don't need to get teacher recommendations or even apply for scholarships with a separate form. Just submit your application for admission, official high school and/or college transcripts, and official ACT or SAT test scores to us.

Additional application materials are required for students applying for admission into the following degree programs: Audio Production and Technology, Sound Design, Theatre and Electronic Media Performance, and Theatre and Entertainment Technology.

Apply by January 15 of the year you plan to enroll for priority consideration for admission, financial aid, and scholarships.

We'll review your high school transcript (including your freshman year) and evaluate the courses you took in high school and the grades you received. The cumulative GPA provided by your high school is used in the admissions process. We do not recalculate your GPA.

MOLLOY COLLEGE

AT A GLANCE

At Molloy College, students gain that "I will" attitude they need to make a difference in our fast-paced, ever changing world.

Located in Rockville Centre, NY, Molloy offers students a rich and multidimensional educational experience. Our faculty is accomplished, yet approachable, leading small classes where students are encouraged to think critically and explore creatively.

Through our Global-Learning Program, students study abroad, traveling to such exotic and enriching destinations as India, Thailand, Spain, Italy, Belgium, and even Australia.

Molloy's campus provides for abundant opportunities to explore new interests, pursue career goals, and enrich our community:

Molloy opened its first residence hall in September 2011, which houses more than 150 students. Additionally, in November of 2011 the College opened a new performing arts center, with comedian Martin Short, former Yankees great Bernie Williams and other world-class artists making appearances at Molloy.

Whether it's participating in a music ensemble, writing for a campus publication, or serving as a student government representative, with more than 40 clubs and honor societies, Molloy has something for each and every student.

For those who choose to combine athletic with scholastic success, Molloy offers a number of winning programs. Students participate competitively in the East Coast Conference (ECC), which is NCAA Division II.

Students have exciting opportunities to "fast track" their careers. With dual bachelor's/master's degree program offerings in Accounting, Business Management, Criminal Justice, Music Therapy and Education, Molloy students can complete a dual degree in five years.

Students are encouraged to make a difference in local communities and many become involved in Molloy-sponsored service projects such as BoxTown, a simulation program that educates students about homelessness.

The College also provides forums welcoming regional, national, and international leaders such as Secretary of State Gen. Colin Powell, the late Prime Minister of Pakistan Benazir Bhutto, and editor of Newsweek International Fareed Zakaria.

Molloy College has built a rich, dynamic, and diverse educational environment over the past 50 years. It is within this welcoming yet challenging environment that Molloy College students develop that all-important confidence, that strong, "I will" attitude that enables them to succeed in their careers, and more importantly, to make a difference in our world.

LOCATION AND ENVIRONMENT

Molloy College is located on the South Shore of Long Island in Rockville Centre. Our proximity to New York City allows for our students to benefit from the cultural and social opportunities that Manhattan has to offer – and it's just a short train ride away from our 30-acre campus.

Molloy College also offers off campus locations for study at the Suffolk Center in East Farmingdale, just off of the Rt. 110 corridor. In addition, the College offers courses at area hospitals and schools – all designed to provide convenience for our graduate and continuing education students.

OFF-CAMPUS OPPORTUNITIES

You can stay local – but still go far – with the Global-Learning Program available at Molloy College. At Molloy you can study what you want, where you want, for as long as you want.

Molloy College also offers students the opportunity to combine job experience and classroom exposure through its internship program. At Molloy, students are encouraged to participate in internships so that they can gain first-hand knowledge and experience in their future career path.

MAJORS AND DEGREES OFFERED

Molloy College offers the AA degree in liberal arts; the AAS degree in cardiovascular technology, nuclear medicine technology and respiratory care; and the BA or BS degree in accounting, art, biology, business management, communications, computer science, computer information systems, criminal justice, education, English, earth and environmental studies, health service leadership, history, interdisciplinary studies, mathematics, music, music therapy, nuclear medicine technology, nursing, philosophy, political science, psychology, sociology, Spanish, speech language pathology/audiology, and theology; and the BSW in Social Work; and the BFA in art and music. Teacher certification programs are available in childhood (1-6), adolescence (7-12), special education and birth – grade 2 childhood special education. Masters degree programs are available in Accounting, Business, Criminal Justice, Education, Music Therapy, Nursing, Speech Pathology and Personal Financial Planning, and there is a Ph.D. program in Nursing.

Students interested in pre-dental, pre-law, pre-medical, or pre-veterinary programs are offered special advisement.

ACADEMIC PROGRAMS

A minimum of 128 credit hours is required for a baccalaureate degree; these courses include a strong liberal arts general education curriculum for every major field of study. Students may choose a double major, and many minors are available. Molloy has a 4-1-4 academic calendar.

Students may earn CLEP and CPE credit, and advanced placement credit is granted for a score of 3 or better on the AP exam. Qualified full-time students may participate in the Army ROTC program at Hofstra University or St. John's University on a cross enrolled basis. Molloy students may also elect Air Force ROTC on a cross enrolled basis with New York Institute of Technology.

CAMPUS FACILITIES AND EQUIPMENT

Today, a school's computer facilities are very important to students. They want access to computers, the Internet, e-mail, and good software; this is certainly something that Molloy College provides. Molloy is a wireless campus and our computer labs house more than 325 PCs. Also, many departments have their own computer labs with state-of-the-art equipment.

The James E. Tobin Library is the center of academic research on the Molloy College campus. The library houses 110,000 volumes, as well as 685 journals and periodicals in its collection. On-line access to information is very important. The library subscribes to over 40 subscription databases, including but not limited to EBSCO's Academic Search Premier, ProQuest Direct and Sage's Nursing and Health Sciences database giving students and faculty access to thousands of full-text resources. Also in the library is a "smart" classroom used by the librarians for library instruction classes.

The media center houses an extensive collection of DVD's and videos as well as state of the art digital equipment. There is a Faculty Development / Instructional Technology Lab in the Media Center. The library is a wireless facility.

The Wilbur Arts Center features numerous art and music studios, a cable television studio, and the Lucille B. Hays Theatre. The school also has six science labs, a language lab, the education resource center, two nursing labs, and a behavioral sciences research facility.

TUITION, ROOM, BOARD AND FEES

Fulltime Undergraduate tuition is $ 22, 290. In addition, there is approximately $1,130 in required fees. Students can expect to spend about $1,400 on books and supplies, and approximately $2,400 in miscellaneous expenses.

FINANCIAL AID

Financial aid, which is based on academic achievement and financial need, is awarded to more than 85 percent of the student body. Aid is awarded in the form of scholarships, grants, loans, and Federal Work-Study Program employment. Non-need scholarships and grants are also available. Students are required to complete the FAFSA application every year. Students who graduate from high school with a 95 percent average and a minimum combined score of 1280 on the SAT I critical reading and math sections are considered for the Molloy Scholars' Program, which awards full tuition scholarships. Partial scholarships are available through the following: Dominican Scholarships, Fine and Performing Arts Scholarships, Community Service Awards, and other funded scholarships. The Transfer Scholarship Program awards partial tuition scholarships to students transferring into Molloy College with at least a 3.0 cumulative GPA. Nursing transfers are required to have a 3.3 GPA to be eligible for a transfer scholarship. Athletic grants (Division II only) are awarded to full-time students who show superior athletic ability in baseball, basketball, cross-country, equestrian, lacrosse, soccer, softball, tennis, or volleyball.

STUDENT ORGANIZATIONS AND ACTIVITIES

Molloy students are involved in a highly active life outside the classroom, something that the college administration supports and encourages. Whether you are an athlete, an aspiring journalist, someone with a strong opinion, or just someone with a desire to expand your horizons, you will find a group to join here. Such organizations provide students with the opportunity to interact with fellow students as leaders, as part of a team, or in a social environment.

Student-run publications include the yearbook, a literary magazine, and the school newspaper. Molloy College sponsors a number of varsity sports, including baseball, men's and women's basketball, men's and women's cross country, men's and women's lacrosse, men's and women's soccer, softball, women's tennis and women's volleyball. Recently, women's basketball participated in the NCAA tournament, and the women's softball team was one of eight schools in the country to qualify for the NCAA College World Series. The college is a member of the East Coast Conference (ECC) in NCAA Division II. In addition, they sponsor a club dance team and a co-ed club equestrian team. The equestrian team is part of the Intercollegiate Horse Show Association.

The student government is elected from the Molloy Student Association, made up of every member of the student body. Members of the Molloy Student Government provide their classmates with a leadership that keeps extracurricular activities alive, productive, and practical.

ADMISSIONS PROCESS

Molloy College's admissions committee recommends that applicants meet the following admission qualifications: graduation from a four-year public or private high school or equivalent (GED test) with a minimum of 20.5 units, including 4 in English, 4 in social studies, 3 in a foreign language, 3 in mathematics, and 3 in science. Nursing applicants must have completed biology and chemistry courses. Mathematics applicants must have taken 4 units of math and 2 of science (including chemistry or physics). Biology applicants must have credits in biology, chemistry, and physics and 4 units in math. Art applicants must submit a portfolio; music students must audition. The committee selects candidates based on the following: high school record, SAT I or ACT scores, class rank, and the school's recommendation. Personality and character are considered in admissions decisions, as are talent or ability in a non-curricular field, as well as alumni relationships.

A select group of freshmen are invited to participate in the Molloy College Honors Program. This program offers challenging coursework and encourages reflection and personal growth. Honors students are provided with several special participation incentives such as a laptop computer, and priority registration.

The HEOP and the Albertus Magnus Program, may be options for students not normally eligible for admission.

Early admission is available. Molloy admits students on a rolling basis and students are advised of the admission decision within a few weeks of completion of the application filing process.

Prospective students should submit the following to the admissions office to be considered for enrollment: a completed application for admission, a nonrefundable $30 application fee, an official high school transcript or GED score report, official SAT I or ACT score, and official college transcripts (transfer students only).

MOUNT ALOYSIUS COLLEGE

AT A GLANCE

Mount Aloysius College is a private, comprehensive, Catholic liberal arts college with more than 70 undergraduate academic programs. The College competes in the NCAA Division III with 14 varsity sports.

Mount Aloysius College is a private, comprehensive, Catholic liberal arts college sponsored by the Sisters of Mercy and is one of sixteen Mercy Colleges nationwide. As part of the Mercy College curriculum, students are encouraged to evaluate ethical issues and form a sound character consistent with traditional, Judeo-Christian values. Social growth is seen as a vital element of a complete liberal arts education, encompassing the important ability to relate closely to people. Established in 1853, the College today specializes in both undergraduate and graduate education. Since the founding of the College, more than 14,500 students have become proud Mount Aloysius College graduates. The College is committed to providing a small classroom size and a highly structured environment. Mount Aloysius College students come from the commonwealth of Pennsylvania, but many other states are represented on campus, including Connecticut, Delaware, Maine, Maryland, Missouri, Massachusetts, New Jersey, New York, Rhode Island, Vermont, Virginia, and West Virginia. Approximately sixty-five percent of the College's students are women. There are approximately 2,500 students enrolled (unduplicated headcount).

LOCATION AND ENVIRONMENT

Mount Aloysius College is located in the scenic southern Allegheny Mountains of west-central Pennsylvania, in the small town of Cresson, which is adjacent to U.S. Route 22. The College's 220-acre campus setting is rural, with two midsized cities, Altoona and Johnstown, within a very short distance. The area has warm, beautiful summers; brisk, breathtaking autumns; invigorating, snowy winters; and cool, blooming springs. Facilities in the area are available for outdoor activities, including biking, golfing, swimming, horseback riding, waterskiing and water activities, hiking, spelunking, picnicking, and amusement and water parks.

OFF-CAMPUS OPPORTUNITIES

Situated in the heart of the Allegheny Mountains, Mount Aloysius College is located between Altoona and Johnstown. The College is about one hour and a half from Pittsburgh and approximately three hours from Washington, D.C. and Baltimore, MD. To the east of the College, Harrisburg is approximately two hours away and Philadelphia, three hours.

MAJORS AND DEGREES OFFERED

Mount Aloysius College awards bachelor's and associate degrees in the arts, sciences, and health studies fields in both career-oriented and traditional liberal arts programs. Students may choose from more than 70 programs of study:

Mount Aloysius is a comprehensive college that is fully accredited by the Middle States Association of Colleges and Schools and approved by the Pennsylvania Department of Education. All nursing programs and health studies programs are fully accredited by their professional accrediting bodies, including the National League for Nursing Accrediting Commission, the Commission on Accreditation in Physical Therapy Education, the American Association of Medical Assistants, and the Joint Commission on Accreditation for Programs of Surgical Technology

ACADEMIC PROGRAMS

Whether preparing students for careers upon graduation or for graduate school, Mount Aloysius recognizes the importance of a broad and liberal education. Thus, in addition to receiving solid preparation for a chosen career, every student at the College receives a foundation in the arts, sciences, and humanities through an outstanding core curriculum. Strong emphasis is placed on the specialized courses within each program of study, and many academic programs combine classroom experience with internships and related training at area clinical sites, agencies, and institutions. In addition to its regular academic programs, Mount Aloysius offers independent and directed study with a commitment to service, which is a key ingredient in a Mercy education. The College has an excellent honors program and academic services area. The academic calendar has two traditional semesters and two or three optional summer sessions.

OFF-CAMPUS PROGRAMS

An important feature of many academic programs is off-campus training. The majority of the College's programs of study require credit-yielding practicums, through which students work and receive training at local and regional hospitals, public and private schools, or health or human service agencies. Students in all health programs participate in required on-the-job training during their time at the College.

CAMPUS FACILITIES AND EQUIPMENT

The main building is a picturesque structure dating to 1897; it houses the admissions, financial aid, security, health, and academic offices, along with the Office of the President, classrooms, the nursing Robotics Center, and the Wolf-Kuhn art gallery. Cosgrave Center is the main hub on campus, serving as the Student Union. The building contains the dining hall, snack bar, bookstore, child-care center (part of the elementary education/early childhood program at the College), lounges, recreational rooms, student affairs offices, and meeting rooms. The College's Health and Physical Fitness Center is adjacent to Cosgrave Center. Its main athletic arena has a seating capacity of approximately 2,000 and serves as the home to all Mounties fans. The facility provides space for three basketball courts, three volleyball courts, a tennis court, a weight and exercise room equipped with a sauna, two locker rooms, office areas, changing rooms for sports officials, public restrooms, a lobby, and a vestibule. Alumni Hall, which was recently renovated to twenty-first century standards, is a historic, multipurpose room that is used for College drama, musicals, lectures, and many performing arts events. The College operates twelve months per year and opens its facilities to the outside community as well.

In 1995, Mount Aloysius College opened both a new library and a new era, signifying greater access to information for the College community. This state-of-the-art facility is the campus hub for technology and studying. With a Buhl Electronic Classroom and more than 80,000 print and nonprint titles, the library is an impressive, 31,000-square-foot facility with ample seating space, four group-study rooms, a reading lounge, a law library and classroom, an unparalleled 18,000-volume ecumenical collection that was donated by Pastor Gerald Myers, and additional room for future expansion. This facility is completely automated, with an online catalog and access to remote libraries and the World Wide Web at more than thirty public workstations. Also located in the library is the Information Technology Center, home to fifteen multimedia computer workstations and some of the latest offerings in educational software.

Pierce Hall serves as the science center on campus and is a state-of-the-art, 31,000-square-foot facility that was completed in 1997 and houses all science laboratories, health science centers, and offices of faculty members in the health studies programs. Academic Hall is an impressive facility that is home to the College Honors Program. It also has classrooms, labs, seminar rooms, faculty offices, and electronic rooms. The College is proud of its bridge to the past and its progress in providing twenty-first-century buildings.

The College is also building a $25 million Athletic Facility and Convocation Center that will open in early 2014. It will host all indoor athletic events along with concerts, job fairs and various other campus activities.

TUITION, ROOM, BOARD, AND FEES

Annual tuition and fees for the 2012–13 academic year for full-time students are approximately $18,640, and room and board are approximately $8,450.

Mount Aloysius College provides various contemporary residence halls on campus. Freshmen and sophomores are required to live on-campus unless a student is living with parents or legal guardians within the local area of the College. Housing is only guaranteed until April 1 of each year.

Mount Aloysius offers a variety of residence halls that students live in while taking classes. Ihmsen Halls are key housing facilities for residential students that are located directly across from the student center. Misciagna Residence Hall is a state-of-the-art hall, providing twenty-five suites and private bathrooms. McAuley Hall, situated near athletic facilities and academic buildings, features both double and single rooms. This Hall houses a large multipurpose room as well as study lounges on each of its three floors.

FINANCIAL AID

Mount Aloysius recognizes the expense involved in acquiring a liberal arts education and encourages all students to apply for all available aid. Through the Office of Financial Aid, the College assists students in applying for state and federal grants, loans, work-study awards, and College merit scholarships and grants. The College awards academic monies based on GPA and SAT or ACT scores; these awards are renewable over a four-year period and range from $1000 to $10000 per year. Mount Aloysius College participates in all federal and state programs; 94 percent of the College's students receive some form of financial aid. U.S. News & World Report has ranked Mount Aloysius College as one of the best-priced private liberal arts colleges in the U.S.

All students applying for financial aid must complete the Free Application for Federal Student Aid (FAFSA). Mount Aloysius College offers grants and scholarships to each student as they submit academic credentials to the institution. Pre-awarding takes place as students inquire and submit academic credentials. Mount Aloysius College offers Mercy Presidential Scholarships on a competitive basis. Please refer to the college web site at http://www.mtaloy.edu/scholarships or the scholarship/financial aid pamphlet for more information.

STUDENT ORGANIZATIONS AND ACTIVITIES

Whether you live on campus or commute from home, and no matter your age, you can fully engage in college life at Mount Aloysius College. Student organizations, leadership opportunities, activities and events, facilities to keep you healthy and fit, great places to hang with friends…it's all part of the Mount Aloysius lifestyle.

The College recognizes that student activities play a distinctive role in the total campus educational program. There are approximately 100 organized clubs, groups, honor societies, and intramural sports programs, including a newspaper, residence hall associations, student government, cheerleading, dance team, scholarship-funded theater and choir programs, and a student activities planning board. Student activities include many social events, intramural sports programs, NCAA Division III athletic events, comedians, cultural and educational events, campus forums, and lectures by guest speakers.

Mount Aloysius College is a member of NCAA Division III. The following athletic programs are available to both women and men: basketball, cross-country, golf, soccer and tennis. Men's baseball and women's bowling, softball and volleyball are also offered. Both intercollegiate and intramural athletes benefit from the Ray S. and Louise S. Walker Athletic Field Complex, which includes a softball field, one of the finest soccer fields in the area, and the Calandra-Smith baseball field. A brand new Athletic Facility and Convocation Center will open in early 2014 which will be a great addition to the campus community and athletic programs.

The Student Government Association (SGA) represents students on all issues that concern the College. The SGA appoints student representatives to all student-oriented College committees. The College encourages active student participation in the general governance structure and in other matters concerning the development and implementation of policies on residential student life.

ADMISSIONS PROCESS

Mount Aloysius College reviews files on a rolling admissions basis starting August 1 of the approaching senior year. Students are encouraged to apply as early as possible during their senior year. Nursing, Pre-Nursing and Health Studies applicants are encouraged to apply by January 1 for priority consideration. Health programs fill very quickly.

The College enrolls a freshman class of approximately 350 students, which amounts to a total class of 550 with transfer students. Admission is selective and is based on academic promise, as indicated by a student's secondary school performance and activities, standardized test scores, and special experience and talents. Applicants are required to have, or expect to earn, a diploma from an approved secondary school or a GED diploma. Submission of official transcripts and SAT or ACT scores is required. In addition to the general admission requirements, specific admission requirements exist for the health programs; students should visit the College's Web site (http://www.mtaloy.edu) for further information.

Prospective students are highly encouraged to visit the scenic 220-acre campus. The College is open Monday to Friday from 8:30 to 5 and on select Saturdays.

To apply for admission to Mount Aloysius College, candidates are encouraged to submit their application and $30 application fee to the Office of Undergraduate and Graduate Admissions. In addition, students may apply online. For further information, students should contact:

Office of Undergraduate and Graduate Admissions

Mount Aloysius College

7373 Admiral Peary Highway

Cresson, Pennsylvania 16630

United States

Phone: 814-886-6383

888-823-2220 (toll-free)

Fax: 814-886-6441

E-mail: admissions@mtaloy.edu

Website: http://www.mtaloy.edu

NAZARETH COLLEGE OF ROCHESTER

AT A GLANCE

Nazareth College is an independent coeducational college with undergraduate and graduate studies in the liberal arts and sciences and professional programs in health and human services, education, and management. The College is located on 150 scenic acres in suburban Rochester, New York, and currently enrolls 2,000 undergraduate and 1000 graduate students. Nazareth has a strong commitment to experience-based learning and civic engagement. In the past five years, the College has produced 17 Fulbright recipients and two Pickering Foreign Affairs Fellowships. Nazareth is a member of the New American Colleges and Universities Consortium.

More than 60 undergraduate majors and minors are available. Internship opportunities provide students with participatory experience in their field of study. Nazareth competes at the NCAA Division III level. Its intercollegiate teams include men's and women's basketball, cross-country, equestrian, golf, lacrosse, soccer, swimming, diving, tennis, volleyball, track and field; and women's field hockey, softball and men's ice hockey.

LOCATION AND ENVIRONMENT

The Nazareth campus is a short walk from the village of Pittsford, which offers a selection of restaurants and specialty shops, as well as bike trails and boat rides along the Erie Canal. The campus is seven miles from Rochester, the third largest city in the state of New York. Rich in culture and entertainment, the city serves as corporate headquarters for many companies with both national and international customers. The city offers a broad array of museums, annual festivals, shopping malls, tourist attractions, professional sporting events, and ski resorts. Two internationally renowned museums — the George Eastman House/International Museum of Film and Photography, and Strong National Museum of Play — make their homes in Rochester.

OFF-CAMPUS OPPORTUNITIES

Nazareth students are able to gain valuable work-related experience off campus no matter what their program of study. Student teaching assignments, clinical work with therapy-related programs, social work placements, and business internships are just a few of the opportunities available.

Nazareth students have access to study abroad programs across five continents. In addition to well-known destinations such as France, Italy, Spain, and Germany, students travel to South America, Asia, Africa, Australia, and the Middle East. Programs include traditional academic semesters abroad, as well as those that address special study in nursing, archeology, business, and other topics of interest. The College has institutional relationships with many highly-regarded institutions across the globe, allowing students a myriad of choices.

MAJORS AND DEGREES OFFERED

Nazareth offers Bachelor of Arts, Bachelor of Music, and Bachelor of Science in the following areas: accounting, American studies, anthropology, art (studio), art education (BS/MS), art history, biochemistry, biology, business administration, chemistry, communication sciences and disorders (speech pathology), communication and rhetoric, economics, English, environmental science, French, German, graphics and illustration, history, Inclusive Education, information technology, international business, international studies, Italian, marketing, modern foreign languages, mathematics, music, music/business, music education, music performance, music theatre, music theory, music therapy, nursing, occupational therapy (5-year Masters) peace and justice studies, philosophy, physical therapy (6-year DPT program) political science, psychology, religious studies, social science, social work, sociology, Spanish, and theatre arts and women's studies. New majors include legal studies, Chinese, Asian Studies, and BFA programs in Visual Communication and Design, Acting, Musical Theatre, and Technical Production.

Nazareth offers pre-professional programs in dentistry, legal studies, medicine, and veterinary science. Students may combine education certification with their declared major to earn certification in secondary education (grades 7-12) or double major in Inclusive Education (Elementary and Special Education with a liberal arts major. Nazareth offers certification in art (5 year BS/MS), music, speech and hearing (birth-grade 12). Most majors are also available as academic minors. Students may pursue interdisciplinary minors in American studies, Asian studies, gerontology, multicultural studies, and women's studies.

Graduate degrees include Master of Arts in Liberal Studies; Master of Science in the following areas: accounting, art education, computer education/technology specialist, creative arts therapy (art or music), human resource management, inclusive education (early childhood, childhood, adolescence), literacy, management, music education, speech-language pathology, social work, TESOL; and a Doctoral program in physical therapy.

CAMPUS FACILITIES AND EQUIPMENT

The College's 150-acre campus features more than 20 buildings of contemporary and Gothic design. The Otto A. Shults Community Center houses a full gymnasium, a 25-meter swimming pool, fitness center, the student union, college radio station, and student personnel offices. Classrooms — including many smart rooms — are located in Smyth Hall, the Arts Center, Carroll Hall, and Golisano Academic Center. Computer labs are found throughout campus, and a campus wi-fi system is installed in all major academic buildings. The Golisano Academic Center houses faculty and administrative offices, a full service dining facility, and multi-faith chapel. Peckham Hall, an Integrated Math & Science building opened in 2012.

Nazareth's 11 residence halls include singles, doubles, suites and apartments. A four-story, environmentally friendly residence hall was completed in Fall 08. Approximately 63 percent of the full-time student body lives on campus. French majors have the option of rooming at the La Maison Française. The Casa Hispana and Casa Italiana, as well as a German Cultural Center, serve as social, academic, and cultural centers for students wishing to immerse themselves in Spanish, Italian, and German language and customs.

TUITION, ROOM, BOARD AND FEES

Actual costs for 2012-2013 academic year $39,920 ($28,330 for tuition & fees; $11,590 for room and board;). Books, transportation, and personal expenses are not included in this estimate. Fees may change at any time. For the most current information, contact the Admissions Office.

FINANCIAL AID

Nazareth provides its students with more than $22 million in grant and scholarship assistance; the school is committed to making a Nazareth education affordable for every admitted student. The college also offers an assortment of merit-based awards for those demonstrating excellence in academics, the arts, music and drama. Those seeking aid must submit a completed Free Application for Federal Student Aid (FAFSA), the form should reach the federal processors between January 1 and February 15. Those seeking early decision must submit the CSS Profile by November 1.

STUDENT ORGANIZATIONS AND ACTIVITIES

Nazareth offers a wealth of co-curricular choices for students of all interests and backgrounds. Campus clubs and organizations include Amnesty International, Art Club, Asian Club, Association of Student Social Workers, Campus Ministry Council, Cultural Affairs/CALEB, Dance Team, Economics Club, Environmental Club, French Club, German Club, Gleaner (the student newspaper), History Club, iClub, Italian Club, Inter-ethnic Nazareth Coalition, Lambda Association, Math Club, Music Therapy Club, Nazareth Commuter Association, Nazareth Speech, Hearing, and Language Association, Peer Health Educators, Physical Therapy Club, Pre Med Club, Residence Hall Association, Science Club, Sigilium (yearbook), Spanish Club, Student Activities Council, Theater League, Verity (literary magazine), WNAZ (radio station) and Wilderness Club. The student political voice is heard through the Undergraduate Association.

ADMISSIONS PROCESS

A complete application to Nazareth includes: application form (common app online or paper version mailed), original essay or graded writing sample, letter of recommendation from a teacher or guidance counselor, an official transcript of high school academic achievement, a non-refundable $45 application fee (waived if student visits or submits online application), and Standardized Test scores, if the student decides he/she would like those scores to be used in the admissions process (Nazareth is a Standardized Test Optional college).

Early Decision, Early Action and Regular Decision applications are welcome. The deadline for Early Decision applications is November 1; applicants are notified after December 1; the due date for enrollment deposit is February 1. Those applying for Early Action must submit their application by December 1; notification for Early Action applicants begins January 15; students have until May 1 to make a decision about attending Nazareth. Those applying for Regular Decision are encouraged to file before the final deadline of February 1. Regular Decision applicants receive notification of the College's decision after March 1. Admitted applicants must make a final decision on whether they will attend Nazareth by May 1.

The school recommends that the applicants complete a college-preparatory curriculum including English, Mathematics, Social Studies, Science and Foreign Language. Academic achievement is the primary consideration in admissions decisions, but the Admissions Committee also considers special talent in drama, music and art; it also looks at students' co-curricular activities. A campus tour is recommended in order to familiarize you with the college and all that it has to offer. An interview is not a required part of the application, but highly recommended. You can plan a visit or ask for more information by contacting: Office of Admissions, Nazareth College, 4245 East Avenue, Rochester, NY 14618; Telephone: 585-389-2860; Toll Free Line: 800-462-3944; Email: admissions@naz.edu; World Wide Web: www.naz.edu.

NEW YORK SCHOOL OF INTERIOR DESIGN

AT A GLANCE

The New York School of Interior Design (NYSID) is New York's only private, not-for-profit college devoted to the design of the interior environment. NYSID's guiding principle is that the interior environment is a fundamental element of human welfare.

Situated in the design capital of the world, the New York School of Interior Design has for nearly one hundred years been preparing aspiring interior designers to join one of the most exciting and important design professions. Today, the value of educational credentials is greater than ever, as the need grows for interior spaces that are functional, safe, beautiful, and sustainable. NYSID continues to prepare leaders to face the newest challenges facing the world of the built environment; designing and building interiors in a socially and environmentally conscientious way.

NYSID is the only institution in the New York City metropolitan area dedicated to the advancement of interior design through education, research, programming, professional development, and outreach. Its nationally ranked graduate and undergraduate programs are taught by a faculty of dedicated scholars and practitioners in a state-of-the-art campus. Most importantly, its graduates excel professionally, receiving the recognition they deserve in leading contract and home magazines.

LOCATION AND ENVIRONMENT

The excitement of being in New York City can be matched nowhere else on the planet, and there is no better place to study the dynamic field of interior design than NYSID with its state-of-the-art facilities in two historic buildings in the heart of it all - the city itself is part of a NYSID education!

Our uptown location's neighborhood, the Upper East Side, has long been regarded as one of New York City's finest. Besides having Central Park as its backyard, what makes the neighborhood so popular is its location near New York's greatest museums, including the Metropolitan Museum of Art, the Guggenheim and the Frick Collection, as well as one of Manhattan's finest shopping streets — Madison Avenue. Students love the area for its numerous shops, cafes, nightlife, transportation, and housing options. Interior design students appreciate the area's art and antique dealers and the close proximity to the industry's major trade showrooms. The downtown Graduate Center, situated at Manhattan's design epicenter, is a short subway ride away. New York – It's part of who we are.

OFF-CAMPUS OPPORTUNITIES

NYSID's location is an ideal for those looking for job opportunities. Interior designers are being sought by residential and commercial clients who are building, restoring, and renovating, to address the challenging decisions that face designers today. They are employed by interior design and architectural firms, urban planners, and companies that specialize in restaurant, office, or exhibition design as well as the design of interiors for banks, schools, and hospitals. The career placement service at NYSID facilitates finding work in this competitive and dynamic field by maintaining an active list of job openings.

MAJORS AND DEGREES OFFERED

Whether you seek an undergraduate college degree, a graduate degree, or a basic program to begin your interior design education, NYSID has an academic program in Interior Design to suit your needs.

The college offers two undergraduate interior design degree programs: the professional-level, 132-credit Bachelor of Fine Arts (BFA), and the pre-professional-level, 66-credit Associate in Applied Science (AAS). Both degree programs, in conjunction with the requisite work experience, prepare graduates to sit for the NCIDQ exam leading to state certification. The 120-credit Bachelor of Arts (BA) is a liberal arts degree in the history of the interior and the decorative arts.

A 24-credit nondegree certificate program, Basic Interior Design (BID), is offered for those who need to develop a portfolio in order to apply to the BFA or AAS degree program, or for those seeking personal enrichment and entry-level job opportunities in fields related to interior design.

ACADEMIC PROGRAMS

The focus of the CIDA-accredited BFA program is on the development of the professional interior designer's ability to formulate, propose, and carry out creative design solutions in a safe and pleasing fashion. With the required professional experience, the curriculum satisfies educational requirements for membership in national and local interior design associations and allows candidates to sit for the qualifying exams for interior design certification in many states.

The AAS degree program fulfills the minimum of two years of college-level interior design education that is required along with the requisite work experience to be eligible to become a Certified Interior Designer in the State of New York. Required credits earned in AAS courses may be applied to the BFA upon acceptance into the BFA program.

The nondegree Basic Interior Design (BID) certificate program provides an introduction to interior design with emphasis on fundamental skills and knowledge in interiors, architecture, and the visual and decorative arts. On completion, students can continue by applying to a degree program or pursue jobs in fields related to interior design. Introductory courses focus on drawing, design concepts, and design history, building a foundation-level understanding of the technical and aesthetic principles essential to understanding space planning, color, drafting, and materials and finishes.

Applicants who do not have the portfolio of art and design work that is required for acceptance into the BFA and AAS programs can apply to the BID program in which they can complete most of the courses that are in the first year of a degree program while building a portfolio of work for acceptance into a degree program. Credits earned in Basic Interior Design courses may be applied to the AAS and BFA degree programs upon acceptance into these programs.

The BA in the in the History of the Interior & the Decorative Arts program combines the study of design and material culture from a historical perspective with an introduction to basic studio practice. Graduates of the BA program are eligible to apply to the MFA-1 professional-level graduate program with one year of advanced standing.

CAMPUS FACILITIES AND EQUIPMENT

NYSID is in the design capital of the United States, if not the world – New York City. In many important respects, New York City is our campus. Students have access to some of the most coveted and valuable resources critical to any designer's work: world-class museums and galleries, showrooms filled with the work of leading furniture and materials designers, many of the nation's top design firms, and a dizzying array of architectural styles and design approaches found in the City's thousands of residential and commercial buildings. Here, inspiration abounds.

NYSID's Manhattan location offers everything you would expect from the leader in interior design education: classrooms and labs equipped with CAD and related software, and a one-of-a-kind lighting laboratory; an atelier for independent work that is equipped with computers, a comprehensive materials library, and a high-end digital output center; a library with over 12,000 books, over 100 serial and magazine subscriptions, and access to image and research databases; galleries for the exhibition of student, faculty, and alumni work; and places for students to relax, socialize, study, or grab a quick bite or a cup of coffee.

NYSID offers housing at a state-of-the-art student residential facility at the corner of East 97th Street and Third Avenue. This lively, safe, and easily accessible eastside location makes the NYSID student experience complete. The Residence at 1760 Third Avenue features double-occupancy accommodations, all with their own bathroom, and provides 24-hour security and concierge service. Each student room is equipped with a refrigerator, microwave oven, and 26-inch DVD-equipped, flat-screen TV. There is free cable, free local and national phone service, and free high-speed internet. Rooms come fully furnished (except for bedding), and the facility has on site a full-service gym, game room, common rooms, laundry room, quiet rooms, and computer kiosks.

TUITION, ROOM, BOARD, AND FEES

Undergraduate tuition for the 2012-2013 academic year is $828 per credit (a full-time student can expect to pay approximately $13,248 in tuition per semester). Registration/Technology/Student Activity fees equal $335 per semester.

Housing costs vary depending on room types. Rates for nine months are approximately $11,400

FINANCIAL AID

Most financial aid dollars in the United States, in loans, grants, and work-study, are from federal and state programs. They are awarded to US citizens and permanent residents who qualify according to the financial aid program's criteria. Standards for satisfactory academic progress are measured once per academic year according to federal regulations.

To apply, all applicants must complete the Free Application for Federal Student Aid (online at www.fafsa.ed.gov). If financial need has been established and adequate funding is available, eligible applicants are considered for federal grant, loan, and work-study programs, NYSID institutional aid, and New York State aid, if applicable.

STUDENT ORGANIZATIONS AND ACTIVITIES

Being located in the heart of Manhattan, the opportunities for both professional and recreational activities are endless. NYSID Student Council sponsored events have recently included ice skating in Central Park; trips to Broadway shows; bus trips to historic Hudson River Valley houses and Frank Lloyd Wright's Fallingwater; a masquerade ball; movie nights; and a boat cruise in the harbor. NYSID's student chapter of the American Society of Interior Designers (ASID) offers students the opportunity to prepare for rewarding careers by participating in a wide variety of learning experiences and programs that complement their academic training, such as commercial and residential firm office tours, hotel and showroom visits and lectures. The Contract Club organizes monthly tours to prominent commercial interior design and architecture firms, such as Steelcase, Clodagh, and Swanke, Hayden, Connell Architects.

ADMISSIONS PROCESS

It is simple to apply to NYSID; it can be done either by paper or online. Log-in information will be e-mailed to you once you apply so you may track your application through NYSID's online portal. The requirements include the application form and fee; an essay; transcripts of previous academic work; two letters of recommendation; SAT or ACT scores; and a fine arts portfolio of ten to fifteen pieces (AAS and BFA programs only).

If you are an undergraduate applicant who does not have a portfolio, you may apply to our Basic Interior Design (BID) certificate program. In the BID program you will develop a portfolio from the work you are doing in your first-semester classes. Using that work you may then apply to our AAS or BFA programs. Since the classes in the BID program are required in the AAS and BFA programs, and the AAS program is equivalent to the first two years of our BFA, it is possible – wherever you begin – to "step-up" to the next higher program without wasting time or money.

The recommended date to submit applications for admission for all programs is February 1. After that date, applications will be accepted on a space-available basis.

NEW YORK UNIVERSITY

AT A GLANCE

NYU is the largest independent research university in the United States, yet it also retains a close-knit community that combines the intellectual atmosphere of a small-to medium-sized college with the myriad cultural offerings and research opportunities. The energy and resources of New York City, Abu Dhabi, and Shanghai serve as extensions of our campuses there, providing unique opportunities for research, internships, and job placement. A faculty of world-famous scholars, researchers, and artists teach both undergraduate and graduate courses and foster NYU's intellectual climate. NYU's more than 22,000 undergraduates come from all 50 states and over 130 countries. They choose from thousands of courses in over 230 areas of study.

ACADEMICS

At NYU in New York, students enroll into one of the University's undergraduate schools, colleges, or programs: The College of Arts and Science; the Core Program in Liberal Studies; the Global Liberal Studies Program; the Leonard N. Stern School of Business; the Steinhardt School of Culture, Education, and Human Development; the Tisch School of the Arts; the Gallatin School of Individualized Study; the Silver School of Social Work; the College of Nursing; and the Preston Robert Tisch Center for Hospitality, Tourism, and Sports Management and the Schack Institute of Real Estate, both of which are housed within the School of Continuing and Professional Studies. In addition, the Polytechnic Institute of NYU will soon be the University's new school of science, technology, and engineering.

NYU Abu Dhabi is NYU's second degree-granting campus. Located in the United Arab Emirates, it opened in fall 2010 and offers degrees in the liberal arts and sciences as well as engineering. It is the first campus of its kind and the only comprehensive liberal arts college in the Middle East that is fully operated by and integrated into an American private research university.

NYU Shanghai, NYU's third and newest degree-granting campus in China, welcomes its inaugural class in fall 2013. NYU Shanghai will offer students a strong foundation in the liberal arts and sciences with emphasis in science, technology, engineering, and mathematics, as well as Chinese language and culture. It will support world-class academic research as well as graduate and professional education.

NYU faculty are among the world's leading scholars, and have received Nobel, Crafoord, and Pulitzer Prizes; MacArthur, Guggenheim, and Fulbright Fellowships; and Oscar and Emmy Awards. Faculty members teach undergraduate and graduate courses, allowing undergraduate students to become directly involved in research projects with internationally known professors and experts in their fields.

ADMISSIONS

When choosing a new entering class, the Admissions Committee reviews each application holistically, carefully considering many significant factors, including a comprehensive review of the applicant's academic background, standardized test scores, extracurricular activities, an essay, personal statements, and recommendation letters. Several programs also require the applicant to audition or submit creative materials. Applicants who have successfully completed a broad range of challenging course work throughout high school are the most desirable candidates. Also considered are your unique talents, personal attributes, and future goals.

Applicants are expected to demonstrate their talents and mastery of subject matter to support their applications and to make their best case for admission. As a result, NYU accepts a wide range of national examinations in addition to the SAT, ACT, SAT Subject Tests, AP exams, and IB scores. International students may be required to submit TOEFL, iELTS, or PTE Academic results as proof of English language proficiency. More information about NYU's complete standardized testing requirements can be found online at admissions.nyu.edu.

NYU accepts applications in three separate rounds: Early Decision I, Early Decision II, and Regular Decision.

While NYU does not conduct interviews for admissions purposes, prospective students are strongly encouraged to visit campus and attend an information session. The admissions staff also visits high schools and hosts receptions worldwide. For dates and times, and for reserving a space at our information sessions and campus tours, please go to admissions.nyu.edu/visit.

CAMPUS FACILITIES AND EQUIPMENT

NYU offers an exceptional range of facilities and student services and a range of residence halls, meal plans, and dining locations on each campus. Academic facilities include nine libraries and institutes renowned for their research in applied mathematics, physics, neural science, and fine arts. Foreign language and cultural centers offer lectures, films, and concerts. Students may also access NYU's Wasserman Center for Career Development, and student support offices addressing almost every student need, from health and wellness to academic support and enrichment. The Kimmel Center for Student Life houses dining facilities, student lounges, computers, club spaces, and the Skirball Center for the Performing Arts, lower Manhattan's largest performance space.

CAMPUS LIFE

With NCAA Division III, intramural, and club athletics, over 400 student clubs, and numerous volunteer activities, NYU students are actively involved both on and off campus.

Student-run clubs are as varied as the student body. Whether their interests lie in world languages, politics, ballroom dancing, writing for the Washington Square News or working at NYU's radio station, students will find something (or more likely, a dozen things!) they love to do.

Two gyms – Coles Sports and Recreation Center and the Palladium Athletic Facility – cater to intramurals, recreation classes, and 21 varsity teams. NYU is also partnered with local athletic facilities, including Chelsea Piers in New York City, to provide space for golf, gymnastics, ice-skating, indoor soccer, volleyball, and other sports.

Hundreds of students annually serve communities across the city, country and world through the Office of Student Activities' C-Team, Alternative Breaks Program, student OutReach Program, fraternities and sororities, and student grassroots organizations. Students deliver meals to the needy and homebound, tutor children, paint public schools, clean up parks, rebuild areas devastated by natural disasters, provide healthcare services in underdeveloped areas, and more.

COLLEGE BASICS

New York University is unlike any other institution of higher education in the world. Whether your home campus is in Greenwich Village, Abu Dhabi, or Shanghai, you'll challenge yourself beyond the classroom and around the world—becoming a global-minded, academically confident, and truly independent thinker who stands apart from your peers.

LOCATION AND ENVIRONMENT

At NYU, New York City is the integral backdrop to the undergraduate experience. NYU's Washington Square campus is located in the heart of Greenwich Village, a historic neighborhood and one of the city's most creative communities that has attracted generations of writers, musicians, artists, and intellectuals. The campus surrounds beautiful Washington Square Park, where students gather to study, enjoy musical performances and events, and spend time with friends. Rather than building walls to separate the campus from the community, NYU embraces the city as an essential element of academic life. New York is a world center of finance, media, and art, offering internships, part-time jobs and research experiences that pair course work with practical experience. The city offers the best in theatre, dance, music, film, museums, and galleries. Undergraduates can be found presenting academic papers at annual conferences; winning prizes at film festivals; working on innovative research projects in laboratories; interning on Wall Street; and completing field work in some of the world's best hospitals and schools.

In addition, NYU's newer Abu Dhabi and Shanghai campuses both put students in the center of entrepreneurial hubs of ideas and talent. Abu Dhabi has developed a progressive agenda in health care, the arts, economic and environmental sustainability, and educational human development; Shanghai is the fast-growing, bustling financial and commercial capital of China.

TUITION AND FEES

On average, tuition and fees are approximately $43,000 for two semesters; room and board cost approximately $16,000 per year. Most NYU students receive one or more forms of financial aid to support contributions made by them and their families. (Financial aid information is subject to change; please visit admissions. nyu.edu for the most up-to-date information.)

MAJORS AND DEGREES

NYU students begin their studies at one of NYU's three dynamic urban campuses: in New York City's Greenwich Village, in Abu Dhabi, UAE; or in Shanghai, China. No matter where their home campus is, all graduate with an NYU degree, and may travel throughout the NYU global network as they complete their majors.

In New York, students enroll directly into one of the aforementioned undergraduate schools, colleges, or programs, all of which have earned national recognition in their respective fields.

Among the more than 230 areas of study offered by NYU's three campuses are: Arab Crossroads Studies, Anthropology, Biochemistry, Economics, Dance, Education, Engineering, Environmental Science, Film and Television, Finance, Global Public Health, Hospitality and Tourism Management, Individualized Study, Integrated Digital Media, Marketing, Metropolitan Studies, Nursing, Real Estate, Social Work, Theatre, and Recorded Music.

OFF-CAMPUS OPPORTUNITIES

Students have access to NYU's extensive global network, within which they can pursue their studies and explore new cultures and perspectives while remaining connected to all of the University's academic resources. They may choose from 11 global academic centers—in Accra, Ghana; Berlin, Germany; Buenos Aires, Argentina; Florence, Italy; London, England; Madrid, Spain; Paris, France; Prague, Czech Republic; Sydney, Australia; Tel Aviv, Israel; and Washington, DC—or in one of many exchange programs NYU has with outstanding research universities around the world. Each location provides a rich curriculum in which students—who have access to portable financial aid—can complete some of their general degree requirements and, in many fields, take courses in their major. In fact, a number of NYU's schools, colleges, and programs (like the Global Liberal Studies program and the major in Business and Political Economy) offer specific curricula and majors with an international focus.

TUITION AND AID

Scholarships take into account both financial need and academic merit. NYU is committed to using the vast majority of its scholarship funds to assist students whose families are unable to pay the full cost of tuition. Low-interest education loans are available for both students and parents. NYU also offers or participates in a variety of payment plans, ranging from interest-free prepayment plans to extensive loan programs that allow families to finance the cost of a college education over many years. A financial aid package might include any combination of scholarships, loans, or work-study programs. Approximately 60% of full-time NYU undergraduates receive some form of financial aid.

Students wishing to be considered for financial aid must submit the Free Application for Federal Student Aid (FAFSA) and the CSS/Financial Aid PROFILE (and CSS Noncustodial Parent PROFILE, if applicable), administered by the College Board. The submission deadline for financial aid applications is February 15 for the fall semester and November 1 for the spring semester.

Financial aid information is subject to change; visit admissions.nyu.edu for the most up-to-date information and deadlines.

STUDENT ORGANIZATIONS AND ACTIVITIES

NYU is anything but cookie-cutter—that's one of the best things about being a part of a larger, global network university. Its culture of openness, opportunity, and inclusion allows NYU's community to thrive. There are so many choices here about what to do that no two students make exactly the same selection.

Students at NYU find their niche by doing what they love. With more than 400 student organizations, there are many ways to get involved at NYU—including a dynamic student government, a variety of sports teams, myriad community service opportunities, and much more. You can determine your future as you contribute to university life, and learn to become a leader in the process.

NIAGARA UNIVERSITY

AT A GLANCE

Niagara University (NU), founded in 1856, is a private, independent university rooted in a Catholic and Vincentian tradition. The suburban 160-acre campus combines the old and new; both ivy-covered buildings and modern architectural structures are among its thirty-three buildings. The University is easily accessible from every major city in the eastern and midwestern United States via the New York State Thruway, Buffalo International Airport, and rail and bus service.

There are approximately 3,300 undergraduate and 870 graduate students enrolled at Niagara. A large percentage of these students take advantage of the more than eighty extracurricular and cocurricular activities offered. Volunteer work in the community is popular among the students and enhances community relations. Students work with numerous organizations, including Habitat for Humanity, Big Brothers/Big Sisters, and the Skating Association for the Blind and Handicapped.

University teams compete on the Division I level and are members of the NCAA, the Metro Atlantic Athletic Conference, Atlantic Hockey Conference, and College Hockey America Conference. Intercollegiate sports for men include baseball, basketball, cross-country, golf, ice hockey, soccer, swimming and diving, and tennis. Intercollegiate sports for women include basketball, cross-country, golf, lacrosse, outdoor track & field, soccer, softball, swimming and diving, tennis, and volleyball. Club sports include cheerleading, danceline, hockey, martial arts, rugby, and skiing. The Kiernan Center offers a variety of sports and recreational facilities, including a multipurpose gymnasium, a swimming and diving pool, an indoor track, racquetball courts, free-weight and Nautilus rooms, and aerobics rooms. There are several outdoor athletic fields and basketball and tennis courts.

Additional student services include the Health Center, which provides inpatient and outpatient care during the day; the Learning Center, which provides free tutoring services; and the Career Development Office, which offers professional and career counseling. Other services include counseling, orientation, academic planning, career planning, and job placement.

Niagara University's housing accommodations include five residence halls, a grouping of five small cottages, and a student apartment complex.

The University offers graduate studies in business, counseling, criminal justice, education, interdisciplinary studies, sport management, and a PhD program in leadership & policy.

LOCATION AND ENVIRONMENT

Niagara University's picturesque 160-acre campus is located in the town of Lewiston, New York, 2 minutes off I-190 on Route 104. The campus is situated on Monteagle Ridge overlooking the lower Niagara River, which connects the two Great Lakes of Erie and Ontario. The University's suburban campus setting is just a few miles from the world-famous Niagara Falls, 20 minutes from Buffalo, which offers a variety of cultural events, sports, and entertainment opportunities, and just 90 minutes from Toronto, Canada's largest metropolitan area. In addition, the University is minutes away from the quaint village of Lewiston, New York, and the city of Niagara Falls, New York.

MAJORS AND DEGREES OFFERED

The College of Arts and Sciences offers the Bachelor of Arts degree in art history with museum studies, chemistry, communication studies, English, French, history, international studies, liberal arts, life sciences, mathematics, philosophy, political science, psychology, religious studies, social sciences, sociology, and Spanish. The Bachelor of Science degree is awarded in biochemistry (with a concentration in bioinformatics), biology (with concentrations in bioinformatics and biotechnology), chemistry (with a concentration in computational chemistry), computer and information sciences, criminal justice and criminology, mathematics, nursing, and social work. This division also offers the Bachelor of Fine Arts degree in theater studies (with concentrations in design technology, general theater, and performance). Pre-professional programs are offered in dentistry, law, medicine, pharmacy, veterinary medicine, and Army-ROTC. An Associate of Arts degree is available in general studies. In addition, Niagara offers an environmental studies concentration to supplement a degree in biology, chemistry, or political science. A five-year program is available in criminal justice administration and an accelerated nursing program

for RN's who are seeking a baccalaureate degree. Enrichment courses in fine arts and languages are also available.

In addition to the programs listed above NU offers a number of pre-professional partnerships. These include a 3+4 partnership in pharmacy with the State University of New York at Buffalo (SUNY), a 2+3 partnership in pharmacy with Lake Erie College of Osteopathic Medicine (LECOM), a 3+4 partnership in medicine with LECOM, and a 3+4 partnership in dentistry with SUNY at Buffalo. Qualified premedical Niagara students are eligible to apply for the early assurance program sponsored by the SUNY at Buffalo.

Niagara University's College of Business Administration is accredited by AACSB International—The Association to Advance Collegiate Schools of Business and offers a B.B.A. and a combination B.B.A./M.B.A. degree (five-year program) in accounting. This division offers B.S. degrees in economics, finance, management (with concentrations in human resources, international business, and supply chain management), and marketing. In addition, an A.A.S. degree can be earned in business.

Business students can gain real-world learning experiences through internships, study abroad, cooperative education programs and research that is being conducted in several of our business-focused campus centers. These centers include the Family Business Center, the Center for Supply Chain Management, and the Center for International Accounting.

Holding the highest accreditations possible in both the United States and Canada— the United States National Council for Teacher Education (NCATE) and Canada's Ontario College of Teachers—Niagara University's College of Education provides students with an option of earning dual certification to teach in both countries. The College of Education offers bachelor's degree programs leading to New York State initial certification in early childhood (birth–grade 6), childhood (grades 1–6), childhood and middle childhood (grades 1–9), middle childhood and adolescence (grades 5–12), adolescence (grades 7–12), certification for teaching students with disabilities (grades 1–6 childhood and grades 7–12 adolescence), and in Teaching English to Speakers of Other Languages (TESOL). All education majors pursue an academic concentration to establish expertise in one of the following subject areas: biology, business, chemistry, English, French, liberal arts, mathematics, social studies, and Spanish. Business education is offered only at grades 5–12. The academic concentration in liberal arts can only be pursued in the early childhood and childhood (birth–grade 6), and special education and childhood (grades 1–6). Most other states, and Puerto Rico, have reciprocity agreements with New York, meaning that an NU education would qualify education majors to teach in those states as well. In addition, the Canadian province of Ontario recognizes Niagara graduates as qualified for the Letter of Eligibility to teach in that province.

The College of Hospitality and Tourism Management provides a career-oriented curriculum leading to a B.S. degree in three specific areas: hotel and restaurant management (with concentrations in food and beverage management; luxury hospitality operations; and hotel planning, development, and operations), sport management (with concentrations in sport operations and revenue management), and tourism and recreation management (with concentrations in event and meeting management and tourism destination management). The College of Hospitality and Tourism Management offered the world's first bachelor's degree in tourism. NU's hotel and restaurant program, the second oldest in New York State, has the distinction of being the seventh program nationally to be accredited by the Accreditation Commission for Programs in Hospitality Administration by the Council of Hotel, Restaurant, and Institutional Education. The College introduces students to a comprehensive body of knowledge about the hotel, restaurant, tourism, and recreational areas and applies this knowledge to current industry challenges. The College requires that its students accumulate 800 hours of industry-related experience. These and other practical experiences offer NU students the knowledge necessary to advance in the field. Students work with industry leaders in classroom projects, join academic clubs and professional organizations, and participate in special trips to trade shows and conventions and specially designed study-abroad experiences, making NU a national leader in the area.

For students who are undecided about which major to choose, Niagara University offers an award-winning Academic Exploration Program (AEP). AEP provides a structured opportunity for students to participate in a thorough, organized process of selecting a major that meets their academic talents and career goals.

ACADEMIC PROGRAMS

Niagara University's curricula enable students to pursue their academic preferences and to complete courses that lead to proficiency in other academic areas. Courses that have been considered upper-division courses are available to all students. This provides students with the opportunity to avoid introductory and survey courses and permits motivated students to take advantage of more challenging courses early in their collegiate career. The honors program provides special academic opportunities that stimulate, encourage, and challenge participants. In addition, an accelerated three-year degree program is offered to qualified students.

Students pursuing a bachelor's degree must complete a total of 40 or 42 course units (120 or 126 hours) to meet graduation requirements. Niagara grants credit for successful scores on the Advanced Placement and College-Level Examination Program and the International Baccalaureate tests.

Internships, research, independent study, study abroad, and cooperative education are available in many academic programs. An Army ROTC program is also offered.

NU is fully accredited by the Middle States Association of Colleges and Schools. Its programs in the respective areas are accredited by the National Council for Accreditation of Teacher Education, AACSB International–The Association to Advance Collegiate Schools of Business, and the Council on Social Work Education, and the chemistry department has the approval of the American Chemical Society. The travel, hotel, and restaurant administration program is accredited by the Commission for Programs in Hospitality Administration.

OFF-CAMPUS OPPORTUNITIES

For those students who wish to study abroad, the University offers semester and summer programs in Chile, China, England, France, Ireland, Mexico, Spain Thailand, and many other countries. In fact, students may choose from 150 programs in more than 30 countries available through the university's membership in the American Institute for Foreign Studies, Center for Cross Cultural Studies, College consortium for International Studies, Global Learning Semesters and Semester at Sea.

Campus Facilities

The University's open-stack library exceeds 200,000 books and has more than 22,000 periodical titles as well as reference databases accessible through the Web. The library is housed in a modern facility that includes seating for 500 people, including individual study carrels. The library is affiliated with the Online Computer Library Center (OCLC) network.

The Academic Complex, the home to the College of Education and the College of Business Administration (Bisgrove Hall), is a state-of-the-art learning facility. Dunleavy Hall, outstanding both educationally and architecturally, includes a computerized lecture hall and TV production rooms. The University's facilities also include the Computer Center; DePaul Hall of Science; St. Vincent's Hall; the Kiernan Center, NU's athletic and recreation center; the Elizabeth Ann Clune Center for Theatre; the Castellani Art Museum; the Dwyer Arena, a dual-rink ice hockey complex And the B. Thomas Golisano Center for Integrated Sciences, which is scheduled to open in the Fall of 2013.

Tuition

Tuition for 2012-13 was $26,100 . Room and board (with a choice of meal plans) cost an additional $11,300 per year. Fees were estimated at $1,100 per year. Niagara estimates that an additional $2500 to $3050 per year is adequate for books, laundry, and other essentials, such as travel to and from home.

FINANCIAL AID

Ninety-eight percent of the entering freshmen and transfers received a financial aid package averaging more than $23,000 per year. They receive assistance in the form of merit scholarships, loans, grants, or campus employment. Students seeking financial aid should file the Free Application for Federal Student Aid (FAFSA). New York State residents should also file a Tuition Assistance Program (TAP) application.

Faculty

Niagara University has a dedicated, accessible faculty who genuinely cares about the academic and personal growth of their students. Their commitment to teaching is their primary concern. A student-faculty ratio of 12:1 and an average class size of approximately 24 allow personal attention and classroom interaction.

Student Government

The Student Government represents all parts of the student body equally. It coordinates and legislates all student activities, serving as both liaison to and a participating member of the University. In addition, students serve on all major departmental committees and on the University Senate, which is the major advisory committee to the president and Board of Trustees.

ADMISSIONS PROCESS

The University welcomes men and women who have demonstrated aptitude and academic achievement at the high school level. Either SAT or ACT test scores are required. International students are required to submit the results of their TOEFL examination. Interviews are recommended. Transfer students are accepted in any semester. (Transfer credit is evaluated individually by the dean of each division.) Students who complete high school in less than four years are eligible for early admission. Students may also apply under an early action program. Economically and educationally disadvantaged students from New York State are eligible to apply for admission through the Higher Educational Opportunity Program (HEOP).

Application and Information

Niagara operates on a rolling admission basis and adheres to the College Board Candidates Reply Date. A visit to the campus is encouraged, and overnight accommodations in a residence hall are available through the Niagara Nights program.

Information on all aspects of the University can be obtained by contacting the Office of Admissions or through www.niagara.edu.

Mark Wojnowski

DIRECTOR OF ADMISSIONS

Niagara University

Niagara University, New York 14109-2011

United States

Phone: 716-286-8700

800-462-2111 (toll-free)

Fax: 716-286-8710

E-mail: admissions@niagara.edu

Web site: http://www.niagara.edu

http://www.facebook.com/niagarau

http://twitter.com/niagarauniv

NICHOLS COLLEGE

AT A GLANCE
YOUR SUCCESS IS OUR BUSINESS

Within a supportive community, Nichols College transforms today's students into tomorrow's leaders through a dynamic, career-focused business and professional education.

We transform our students into successful graduates who can respond to challenges, are eager for responsibility, and will assume significant roles in the global economy.

The Nichols experience happens in a welcoming environment where every student is encouraged to learn and grow under the guidance of mentoring faculty and staff committed to student success.

The best way to show you the value of a Nichols degree is to share some statistics from our recent graduating classes.

• Every year, over 90% of our graduates are employed in professional positions within 6 months of graduation

• 4 out of 10 Nichols graduates is a CEO, corporate president, or business owner. That is what we mean by success!

LOCATION AND ENVIRONMENT

Nichols is located in Dudley, Massachusetts, roughly twenty minutes south of Worcester and within an hour's drive of Boston, Springfield, Hartford, and Providence. Set on over 200 acres of rolling hills, we proudly offer top notch facilities in a picturesque setting.

Students can walk to classrooms, the Lombard Dining Hall, Daniels Auditorium, the Library, and the Athletic Center in less than 5 minutes. In addition, you will find that all of our facilities, residence halls, classrooms, and library are equipped with top flight technology to ensure that students are connected everywhere they go.

Please schedule a campus visit with our admissions staff because there is no substitute for seeing it in person.

OFF-CAMPUS OPPORTUNITIES

The greater Worcester area is an active, vibrant, and energetic community. Downtown Worcester is in the midst of a dynamic revitalization effort as over $1 billion is being invested in new development projects including City Square, the Hanover Theatre for the Performing Arts, and the Blackstone Canal District Initiative.

Whether it's catching the latest concert at the DCU Center, sampling the restaurants on Shrewsbury Street, shopping at Blackstone Valley, or watching the Worcester Tornadoes (Can-Am League baseball) or Worcester Sharks (American Hockey League) in thrilling sports action, Worcester is the place to be for fun and exciting attractions.

MAJORS AND DEGREES OFFERED

There are two undergraduate degrees offered:

• Bachelor of Science in Business Administration (B.S.B.A.)

• Bachelor of Arts (B.A.)

The Business Core curriculum offers a firm grounding in key areas of business including accounting, computer information systems, finance, management, and marketing.

In addition to our business core, students complete a modified liberal arts curriculum and 18-27 credits in their area of specialization.

B.S.B.A. Specializations:

• Accounting

• Business Communication

• Criminal Justice Management

• Economics

• Entrepreneurship/Small Business Management

• Finance

• General Business

• Hospitality Management

• Human Resource Management

• International Business

• Management

• Marketing

• Sport Management

Qualified applicants who have maintained a 3.0 or better cumulative GPA in high school may be eligible to participate in our 3 year accelerated B.S.B.A program.

B.A. Programs

Students who pursue one of our Bachelor of Arts programs must complete 120 credit hours. The Liberal Arts core of 12 credit hours includes selected studies in the humanities and world culture. In addition, students complete 30 credits within their program.

B.A. Majors:

• Economics

• English

• History

• Mathematics

• Psychology

EDUCATOR PREPARATION

Nichols College Educator Preparation Program prepares students to teach business, history, English, or mathematics in middle or secondary schools.

Graduate Options

• MBA with concentrations in

Marketing

General Business

International Business

Finance/Accounting

• Master of Organizational Leadership

ACADEMIC PROGRAMS

Professional Development Seminar

Our four-year Professional Development Seminar (PDS) program helps students develop career skills that set them apart. The first year component is designed to help ease the adjustment to college life and help students understand how to be a successful student here at Nichols. The second year component helps students explore career fields as they start to understand where each degree program can lead them.

In the program's 3rd and 4th years, students will increasingly focus on building skills to help them enter the job market. Students will focus on refining interview skills and developing a portfolio that showcases their skill sets.

Students in particular find the mock interview process helpful. They also enjoy the annual "Etiquette Dinner" for seniors and our fashion show that helps them better understand appropriate attire for the modern workplace.

Internship Program

An internship allows students to build their resume of professional experience, develop a work portfolio, and build a network of contacts for future employment opportunities. At Nichols, many of our business specializations require internships. In recent years our students have been placed in top-tier positions with organizations that include Madison Square Garden, Boston Celtics, Sovereign Bank, Abbott Labs, and many more.

CAREER SERVICES

Our Career Services Office is renowned throughout New England. The staff maintains a detailed listing of job opportunities and sponsors one of the largest career fairs in the area. Our staff helps students keep their resume current, develop a strong cover letter, and create a complete list of references to help in the job search.

Honors Program

Our undergraduate students have the opportunity to be recognized for outstanding academic achievement.

To be eligible, a student must maintain a GPA of 3.2 or higher and have earned a minimum of 29 credit hours. Participating students complete additional study requirements to earn an extra fourth credit in 300- or 400-level courses. After achieving a B+ or higher grade in each of the three courses, students are qualified to apply for entrance into a senior-year Honors Scholar Seminar.

Students may select honors courses from across the curriculum. At Commencement, students completing the program with a 3.2 GPA or higher will earn an academic mark of distinction as a Nichols Honors Scholar.

Accelerated Programs

Qualified applicants may be able to take part in one of our unique accelerated programs. Students with above a 3.0 can enter a 3 years B.S.B.A program upon enrollment. In addition to our 3 year degree we also offer a 4+1 M.B.A. option.

CAMPUS FACILITIES AND EQUIPMENT

Our state of the art Athletics Center features an indoor climbing wall, squash courts, racquet ball courts, two fitness rooms, and four locker rooms. There is also an indoor track above the varsity basketball court. Connected to the gym is the Chalmers field house. The field house serves as our indoor practice facility for field sports and houses our sports information staff, training room, varsity weight room, several coaches' offices, and our new athletics lounge.

Once known as the Bison Bowl, Nichols College now plays all of its home football, field hockey, and lacrosse games on the new Michael J. Vendetti Multi-Purpose Field. The men's and women's soccer teams also play some of their home contests on that surface as well as their "soccer exclusive" grass field.

The turf field includes an eight-lane rubberized quarter-mile track surrounding a turf field surface. To facilitate media coverage, there is a new press box with online capabilities and Musco lighting to light the field for night contests.

TUITION, ROOM, BOARD, AND FEES
Tuition: $32,440.00

Room / Board: $11,000.00

Fees: $300

Total: $43,740.00

FINANCIAL AID

Nichols awards merit-based and need-based scholarships and grants. You can supplement your Nichols awards with federal and state grants and/or loans. Students with an unweighted cumulative G.P.A. of 2.5 or higher are eligible to receive merit grants.

At Nichols College, the average full-time student receives in excess of $27,000 in financial aid from all sources. High-need students may receive up to $35,000 in financial aid. We also have numerous financing plans to fit nearly every budget.

Student Organizations and Activities

Nichols proudly boasts a vibrant residential community. Nearly 90% of our student body lives on campus and a vast majority of our students participate in at least one on-campus group.

Getting connected to other students is a huge part of the college experience. We make sure that's easy and fun to do during your admissions process and through our orientation program.

CAMPUS ORGANIZATIONS

Academic Honor Societies

Delta Mu Delta, Mu Kappa Tau, Omicron Delta Epsilon, Phi Alpha Theta, Zeta Alpha Phi

Athletic Honor Societies

The Student Athlete Advisory Council (SAAC), Elbridge Boyden Society

Student Government and Service Organizations

Campus Activities Board (CAB), Campus Ministry Association, The Student Government Association (SGA)

Student Publications and Communications Media

The College Yearbook, The College Literary Magazine, WNRC Radio Station

Club Sports

Paintball Club, Racquetball Club, Men's Ice Hockey Club, Women's Ice Hockey Club, Men's Rugby Club, Women's Volleyball Club

General Interest

Accounting Club, Commuter Club, Criminal Justice Management Club, Economics/Finance Club, History Club, Human Resource Club, Management Club, Marketing Club, MIS Club, Psychology Club, Sport Management Club, Umoja

NCAA Division III Athletics:

Nichols competes in The Commonwealth Coast Conference, New England Football Conference, ECAC Northeast Hockey League, and the ECAC Women's East Hockey League.

ADMISSIONS PROCESS

Nichols College regards each prospective student as an individual, considering each application as it is submitted throughout the academic year. The admissions process is a joint partnership between the applicant and the College. We want to ensure each admitted student is the "right fit," both for the student and for Nichols. Admission candidacy requires that every applicant is either a high school graduate or has earned a high school equivalency diploma (GED). Our typical applicants' credentials vary greatly and many factors go into the admissions decision. We look at the areas of strength and weakness in each candidate and assess the student's ability to succeed at Nichols. Our typical admitted student has a GPA above 2.4, an average SAT score of 1400 (combined verbal, math and essay scores), and a strong desire to succeed.

Proficiency in certain academic areas is a basic requirement for entrance to the College. Successful candidates for admission will follow a college preparatory course of study prior to applying to Nichols. We encourage students to challenge themselves with a rigorous secondary school curriculum. Though there is no specific schedule of courses required, an ideal four-year program includes the following coursework:

English - 4 units , Social Science - 2 units, Laboratory Science - 2 units, Academic Electives - 5 units, Foreign Language - 2 units and College Preparatory Mathematics - 3 units (recommended courses include: Algebra I, Geometry, Algebra II, and Advanced Mathematics)

SAT/ACT Optional

Graduating seniors with an unweighted cumulative GPA of 3.0 (B) or higher can choose to waive their SAT scores when applying to Nichols. This is our way of rewarding a strong high school performance and helping make your application process as smooth as possible.

NORTHEASTERN UNIVERSITY

AT A GLANCE

Founded in 1898, Northeastern University is a private research university located in the heart of Boston. Northeastern is a leader in worldwide experiential learning, urban engagement, and interdisciplinary research that meets global and societal needs. Our broad mix of experience-based education programs—our signature cooperative education program, as well as student research, service learning, and global learning—build the connections that enable students to transform their lives.

Experiential learning, anchored by our signature cooperative education program, lies at the heart of a Northeastern education. Over the past century, the University has perfected the integration of study and practice, creating an unparalleled way to learn.

Our students make an impact on the world – before they graduate – through our signature co-op program, research, civic engagement, and global experience.

These points of real-world engagement-at a university that is a world leader in experiential learning-enrich classroom studies, fuel intellectual and personal growth, and provide students with opportunities to explore their path and discover their passion. It's the world's most powerful learning experience.

The current undergraduate enrollment of 16,685 is made up of students of all backgrounds, interests, and tastes, giving Northeastern its distinctive, urban style. This diversity shows in the range of available activities. Students participate in undergraduate research opportunities, join one of more than 280 student clubs and organizations, tutor local children, workout in one of three fitness facilities, explore the City of Boston, and much more. Students have many opportunities to make friends, try something new, become a leader, or simply have fun. Students can also find quiet corners of the campus that feel far from city streets where they can read or just relax, sprawled on a wooden bench under a shade tree; sip gourmet coffee from a nearby campus café; or listen to a midday jazz performance behind the Curry Student Center amid the art of Northeastern's sculpture park. The 73-acre campus is dynamic and welcoming, a beautiful stretch of leafy green in the heart of Boston. Its compact size lets students get to class on time or rush back for a forgotten book.

LOCATION AND ENVIRONMENT

Northeastern's residential campus lies in the heart of Boston, where the distinctive neighborhoods of the Back Bay, the South End, the Fenway, and Roxbury meet. In the past five years, Northeastern has built a host of new on-campus residence halls, more than doubling the amount of housing available to undergraduates. Upperclass residence halls offer apartment-style living with modern kitchens complete with dishwashers, disposals, and full-sized appliances; cable hookups; and data jacks. Many have amazing views of the Boston skyline.

The Back Bay area, known for its many cultural and educational institutions, is steps from Symphony Hall, the New England Conservatory of Music, the Museum of Fine Arts, and the Isabella Stewart Gardner Museum. The South End is home to elegant Victorian row houses, exciting arts, hidden gardens and some of the finest dining in Boston. The Fenway area, with its beautiful rose garden, bicycle and jogging paths, and Fenway Park (home of the Boston Red Sox), is just a few blocks away.

MAJORS AND DEGREES OFFERED

Northeastern's academic programs are divided among eight undergraduate colleges: the College of Arts, Media and Design, the D'Amore-McKim School of Business, the College of Computer and Information Science, the College of Engineering, the Bouvé College of Health Sciences, the College of Professional Studies, the College of Science, and the College of Social Sciences and Humanities. Top-notch faculty members with a variety of research interests personally guide students through their studies.

The College of Arts, Media and Design awards undergraduate degrees in architecture, art, cinema studies, communication studies, digital art, game design, graphic design, interactive media, journalism, landscape architecture, music history and analysis, music industry, music technology, studio art (in collaboration with the School of the Museum of Fine Arts, Boston), theatre, and theatre performance.

The D'Amore-McKim School of Business offers two tracks: the Bachelor of Science in Business Administration (B.S.B.A.) or the Bachelor of Science in International Business (B.S.I.B.). The B.S.I.B. program includes language instruction and international study and work. The School offers concentrations in accounting, entrepreneurship and innovation, finance, management, management information systems, marketing, and supply-chain management.

The College of Computer and Information Science awards degrees in computer science, cyber operations, and information science, and also offers dual-major degrees combining computer science with business, cognitive psychology, mathematics, physics, biology, multimedia arts, music technology, game design, or digital art.

The College of Engineering offers degrees in chemical, civil, computer, electrical, industrial, and mechanical engineering.

The Bouvé College of Health Sciences awards degrees in health science, nursing, pharmacy, physical therapy, and speech-language pathology and audiology. The college also offers a six-year Doctor of Pharmacy degree and a six-year program leading to a Master of Science in Physical Therapy.

The College of Professional Studies offers undergraduate and graduate degree programs in a wide range of disciplines, with an emphasis on global options. Also, the college is home to the School of Education.

The College of Science awards undergraduate degrees in applied physics, behavioral neuroscience, biochemistry, biology, biomedical physics, chemistry, environmental geology, environmental science, environmental studies, geology, linguistics, marine biology, marine science, mathematics, physics, psychology, surficial processes, and wildlife studies.

The College of Social Sciences and Humanities awards undergraduate degrees in African-American studies, American Sign Language—English interpreting, Asian studies, criminal justice, cultural anthropology, economics, English, history, human services, international affairs, international and comparative politics, Jewish studies and religion, languages, literatures, and cultures, philosophy, political science, public history, public policy and administration, religious studies, sociology, and Spanish.

ACADEMIC PROGRAMS

At the heart of a Northeastern education lies award-winning professors and faculty mentors, rigorous and innovative curriculum, undergraduate research and global experiences that challenge and transform. Innovative programs encompass a wide range of majors, concentrations, combined majors and interdisciplinary studies along with honors, pre-professional, and study-abroad programs.

Northeastern's approach integrates academics with a variety of experiential learning opportunities including research, global experience, civic engagement and our signature cooperative education program (co-op) enabling students to discover their path before they leave college.

Through the internationally known co-op program, after completing their freshman year, students alternate classroom learning with periods of full-time (usually paid) work or other types of practical learning related to their major or interests, earning their bachelor's degree in either four or five years. Graduates accumulate as many as eighteen months of professional experience, professional contacts, and the social confidence that gives them a significant edge in the job market over new graduates without experience. By working in varied jobs and settings, students learn what they like—and do not like—before committing to a permanent position. Many Northeastern students even go to work for a co-op employer after graduation. Co-op is an education in itself. Northeastern students graduate knowing what they only could have learned on the job: how to conduct themselves, what to wear, how to interpret a company's culture, how to get things done, and how to write a resume and interview successfully.

Co-op employers include some of the country's largest and most reputable companies, such as Pfizer, John Hancock, Fidelity Investments, General Electric, Massachusetts General Hospital, and the Boston Globe. Students also enjoy international placements for a semester or a year abroad; co-op employers recruit from Australia, Scotland, Italy, and Spain, among many other countries.

Experiential learning opportunities—including US and international co-op, service-learning, research, and study abroad—are currently available in 92 countries around the world.

The University Honors Program gives students opportunities to participate in enriched educational experiences and offers opportunities that include honors sections of required academic courses, honors seminars, independent research, and study abroad. The University also offers Army, Naval Nursing, and Air Force ROTC. The Disability Resource Center provides many support services that enable students with disabilities to participate fully in the life of the University community.

CAMPUS FACILITIES AND EQUIPMENT

Northeastern is home to 37 research centers, including the Center for Labor Market Studies, the Barnett Institute of Chemical and Biological Analysis, the Center for High-rate Nanomanufacturing, the Institute on Race and Justice, and many others. Students have ample opportunities to work alongside their professors to aid and conduct research on a variety of topics.

The University Libraries system comprises Snell Library, a 240,000 square foot central library on the Boston Campus, the School of Law Library (also on the Boston Campus) and a small supplemental collection at the Nahant Marine Science Center. Total non-law holdings as of June 30, 2011 include 932,999 print volumes, 206,507 e-books, 1,489,153 microfilms, and 70,225 current serials subscriptions, with access to 59,926 electronic journals. In addition, Snell Library houses 23,437 audio, video, and computer software items, and 5,712 linear feet of archival material. The library is a selective depository of federal government publications and currently holds 143,905 printed government documents.

Northeastern University provides a broad range of academic and administrative computer resources available to students and faculty and staff members. Many computing resources are available, including Internet connections for all offices and University-owned residence halls, technology-assisted classrooms, computer labs, and the myNEU portal, which allows student to access many administrative and academic functions online. There is also extensive wireless network access, found in the library, Student Center, and many dorms.

TUITION, BOARD, AND FEES

For 2012–2013, tuition was $39,320, and room and board were $13,140. Whether you choose four or five years for your undergraduate degree, you will only pay tuition for the academic experience (tuition is not charged for the experiential educational periods). If you choose to live on campus during co-op, you will be responsible for room and board charges.

FINANCIAL AID

The University operates a substantial aid program designed to make attendance at Northeastern feasible for all qualified students. By coordinating the resources of the University and various public and private scholarship programs, Northeastern offers more than $180 million in grant and scholarship assistance, participates in all federal aid programs. About 80 percent of the freshman class received some form of financial aid. Financial aid is based on need and academic merit and may consist of grants, loans, work-study employment, or any combination of the three. To apply, students must file a Free Application for Federal Student Aid (FAFSA) and a CSS PROFILE form with the College Scholarship Service by the priority filing date of February 15.

ADMISSION

Admission Requirements:

Students may enter the University with advanced credit on the basis of test scores on Advanced Placement (AP) examinations, the College-Level Examination Program (CLEP), the International Baccalaureate (I.B.), or on successful completion of accredited college-level courses before enrollment at Northeastern. In addition to the application for admission, prospective freshmen must submit official high school transcript(s) (or official GED score reports), including their senior-year grades; official transcripts for any college-level course work taken while a secondary-school student; written recommendations from their secondary school guidance counselor and a teacher; and scores on the SAT (Northeastern's College Board code is 3667) or ACT, including the writing section. Please visit our website for transfer admissions requirements (www.northeastern.edu/admissions/transfer/index.html).

Application and Information

Admission to Northeastern is selective and competitive. For the fall 2013 entering freshman class, the University received more than 47,000 applications for 2,800 places. Northeastern offers approximately 550 additional spots to The N.U.in Program, an international, first semester experience. Students admitted into The N.U.in Program spend their fall semester studying abroad at a partner institution and then join the Boston community in the spring. Students who thrive in a challenging academic environment — one that also challenges you outside the classroom, through our dynamic global experiential learning options — are best suited for a Northeastern education. Experiential learning at Northeastern will expand your initiative, adaptability, confidence, poise, and ability to work collaboratively - the foundations of leadership.

November 1 is the deadline for the early action admission program. Students who have carefully explored their college options and have decided that Northeastern is where they want to enroll may choose to apply under the early action program. The deadline for the regular admission program is January 15. If admitted for the fall semester, either through the early action process or the regular decision process, freshmen are required to send a tuition deposit by May 1 to secure a place in the class. For transfer students, the priority deadline for the fall is May 1. Admission decisions for transfer applicants are made on a space-available, rolling basis. November 1 is the deadline for January transfer admission for both freshman and transfer applicants and for international applicants for January admission. Admission decisions for spring applicants are made on a space-available, rolling basis. Campus tours and group information sessions are held daily and are available without an appointment.

For more information, students should contact:

Office of Undergraduate Admissions

240 West Village F

Northeastern University

360 Huntington Avenue

Boston, Massachusetts 02115

Phone: 617-373-2200

E-mail: admissions@neu.edu

Website: http://www.northeastern.edu/Admissions

NOTRE DAME COLLEGE

AT A GLANCE

Notre Dame College offers stimulating academics, personalized attention, small class sizes, Division II intercollegiate athletics and vibrant student life.

Founded in 1922 by the Sisters of Notre Dame, the College has grown strategically to keep pace with the rapidly changing needs of students and the dramatic changes in higher education. But it has never lost sight of its emphasis on teaching students not only how to make a good living but also how to live a good life.

Under the leadership of President Dr. Andrew P. Roth since 2003, Notre Dame College is rapidly becoming one of the finest small, Catholic, residential, liberal arts colleges in the Great Lakes region. Founded as an all-women's school, the College became coeducational in 2001, and total enrollment has since grown from 875 to 2,150, a remarkable 240-percent increase.

A snapshot of the fall 2012 traditional NDC student population shows: 45% female, 55% male; 55% Catholic; 28% minority; 55% student-athletes; and 53% live on campus. The mosaic of NDC students represents 20 states and 12 foreign countries.

Notre Dame offers quality academic programs in over 30 disciplines including a nationally accredited Education major, a Business major, a Bachelor of Science in Nursing, Intelligence Analysis and Research, and Criminal Justice.

MISSION

A Catholic institution in the tradition of the Sisters of Notre Dame, the College educates a diverse population in the liberal arts for personal, professional and global responsibility. The College believes that truly progressive education selectively blends traditional values with new ideas that represent real growth. Within the scope of a career-oriented liberal arts education, students can grow to meet the challenges of the present and the future.

LOCATION

Located in South Euclid, Ohio, the 53-acre campus is in a residential neighborhood just 25 minutes from downtown Cleveland and all the excitement and cultural wealth of the city, such as the Rock and Roll Hall of Fame and Museum, the Cleveland Metroparks, University Circle, several professional sports teams, and one of the richest cultural, theatrical, entertainment, healthcare, and employment regions in the nation. Only five minutes from Legacy Village and Beachwood Place, Cleveland's lifestyle retail centers, the area combines all the opportunities of a major urban and educational center with the relaxed atmosphere of a suburban setting.

The beautiful campus provides the perfect setting for the Clara Fritzsche Library; the historic Administration Building which houses classrooms, labs and offices; Regina Hall and Regina Auditorium; Connelly Center, the dining hall and student center; Keller Center, the recreational and fitness facility; Falcon Café; and five residence halls, including two newer apartment-style facilities that house 288 upper-class students.

CAMPUS LIFE

A variety of clubs and activities enrich the overall experience of the 2,100+ students. Campus Ministry promotes the spiritual growth of the College community and facilitates community service, and the award-winning FalconCorps service program provides students opportunities to serve at local charities and national programs such as Habitat for Humanity.

Most on-campus events are free, and students often may purchase tickets at reduced rates for off-campus programs such as performances of the world-famous Cleveland Orchestra, the Cleveland Opera, and road shows of Broadway productions at the Cleveland Play House, the Palace Theatre, the State Theatre, and the Ohio Theatre at Playhouse Square.

ATHLETICS

With 22 intercollegiate sports for men and women, Notre Dame is a NCAA Division II institution and an associate member of the Great Lakes Intercollegiate Athletics Conference (GLIAC), a league widely recognized as one of the top Division II conferences.

ACADEMICS

The College awards the Bachelor of Arts degree in accounting (business administration); biology; chemistry; communication; education, including early childhood (pre-K–3), middle childhood (4–9), and young adult education and mild-moderate intervention specialist studies; English; graphic design; history/political science; information systems; international business; management; marketing; mathematics; psychology; public administration; sports management; studio art; and theology.

The Bachelor of Science is awarded in biology, chemistry, and mathematics. A student can also design his or her own major that leads to a Bachelor of Arts or Bachelor of Science degree by combining two or three academic areas, such as graphic design, human resource management, and public relations. Notre Dame College also offers a Bachelor of Science in Nursing program. An RN to B.S.N. completion program is also available.

A Master of Education degree is offered with concentrations available in special education, reading, and critical and creative thinking.

The College launched a Master of Arts in Security Policy Studies in the fall of 2011.

Teacher licensure is available in early childhood education, middle childhood education, adolescent/young adult education, and multiage for mild/moderate intervention specialist studies.

The College is accredited by both the North Central Association of Colleges and Schools and NCATE and is registered for the awarding of State Teachers' Licenses by the State of Ohio Department of Education.

The Associate in Arts degree is awarded at the completion of two-year programs in business management and pastoral ministry.

The Center for Pastoral Theology and Ministry grants a two-year catechetical diploma and the College awards a Bachelor of Arts degree.

For the bachelor's degree, students must earn 128 semester hours of credit, with a minimum cumulative grade point average of 2.0. From 36 to 68 semester hours of credit are required in the major field of study.

Through a cooperative education program, students can earn up to six credit hours for paid or volunteer work experience related to their academic field of study. All students are required to complete a co-op or internship experience.

Advanced Placement credit is awarded to students who have demonstrated the ability to pursue coursework beyond the level of entering freshmen, as indicated by their scores on the Advanced Placement (AP) or College-Level Examination Program (CLEP) tests of the College Board. College credit is given on the basis of a decision made jointly by the academic dean and the department involved.

FACULTY

The College has 57 full-time faculty members, augmented by highly qualified instructors. Faculty members hold advanced degrees from more than 30 universities in the United States, Canada and Europe.

CAMPUS FACILITIES AND EQUIPMENT

Students with documented learning differences, such as Attention Deficit Disorder (ADD), Attention Deficit Hyperactivity Disorder (ADHD), dyslexia, Asperger's Syndrome and Specific Learning Disabilities (SLD) can enroll in our Academic Support Center to receive comprehensive support services. These include tutoring, academic advising and access to a large array of adaptive equipment. In order to be accepted into the Learning Differences Program, students must first meet the admission requirements of Notre Dame College. To participate in the Academic Support Center, students must submit documentation of a learning disability.

The Career Services Center coordinates co-op jobs and internships for students and interacts with faculty to create meaningful programs that link academics to the workplace. It further offers graduate school advising, résumé preparation assistance, interviewing and job search coaching, posting of positions available and a resource library. On-campus recruiting opportunities attract employers to the College to meet with students firsthand.

The Clara Fritzsche Library, housing the modern media center, has a capacity for 100,000 volumes. As a member of OhioLINK, the College also has online access to members throughout the state, with access to more than 31 million library items and more than 90 research databases. The library also houses the smart classroom, a state-of-the-art classroom equipped with laptops for each student and two SMARTBoards.

The Dwyer Success Center consists of an electronic classroom, a student computer lab, a writing lab, a test proctoring room and a tutoring room. The writing lab is staffed by English faculty who provide professional writing assistance to students free of charge. The tutoring room is staffed with graduate assistants and upper-class peer tutors for one-on-one study skills and subject specific assistance.

The multi-media lab for graphic design majors offers PC and Macintosh technology for advanced multimedia production capabilities.

The Finn Center for Adult, Graduate, Online and Professional Programs unifies all aspects of adult education at NDC, providing convenient, flexible programs for educational advancement on days, nights, weekends and the Web. Housing the Office of Adult and Graduate Admissions and the Office of Professional Development, the Finn Center offers professional development classes, associate's degrees, bachelor's degrees, post-baccalaureate programs and master's degrees.

TUITION, ROOM, BOARD AND FEES

For the 2012–13 academic year tuition and fee charges are $25,514. Room and board costs are $8,296 for double occupancy.

FINANCIAL AID

Notre Dame believes that all qualified students should have the opportunity to attend college, and provides need, merit and athletic-based aid to our students. A comprehensive financial assistance program of more than $25 million assists nearly 93 percent of all full-time students. Students applying for aid must submit the Free Application for Federal Student Aid (FAFSA).

ADMISSIONS PROCESS

Notre Dame College admits students who demonstrate potential for success in rigorous academic work. In fulfilling its mission, the College seeks to attract students of diverse religious, racial and economic backgrounds. Candidates for admission as first-time, full-time freshmen are reviewed on an individual basis, and decisions are based on a broad range of criteria. The most important consideration is the candidate's high school performance, as demonstrated by her/his overall grade average, class rank, grade trends and level of courses completed. Aptitude for verbal and mathematical reasoning, as measured by performance on standardized tests, is also considered. In addition, counselor and teacher recommendations are reviewed.

Notre Dame College recommends that students complete at least 16 units of high school credit in academic subjects as a prerequisite for matriculation in the College. The distribution of these subject areas and the units are as follows: English, 4; mathematics, 3 (to include algebra I, geometry and algebra II); science, 3 (with laboratory experience); social studies, 3; foreign language, 2 (from the same language); and fine arts, 1. Applicants should generally rank in the upper half of their high school graduating class and have a minimum average of C+. Either ACT or SAT scores are accepted.

The College has a fair and generous policy on the transfer of academic credit earned within the preceding five years at a regionally accredited college or university. Students wishing to transfer from other regionally accredited colleges and universities are admitted to advanced standing upon presentation of satisfactory evidence of scholarship and character.

Special consideration may be granted to an applicant whose academic preparation is not consistent with the requirements stated above.

Notre Dame College strongly recommends that prospective students schedule an appointment to visit the campus and talk with an admissions counselor.

A free application is available online at NotreDameCollege.edu. The College maintains a rolling admission policy. To apply, students should submit the completed application for undergraduate admission, an official transcript of their high school record and results of the ACT or SAT to:

OFFICE OF ADMISSIONS

Notre Dame College

4545 College Road

South Euclid, Ohio 44121

United States

Telephone: 877.NDC.OHIO ext. 5355 Fax: 216.373.5278

E-mail: admissions@ndc.edu

Web: NotreDameCollege.edu

OLD DOMINION UNIVERSITY

AT A GLANCE

Old Dominion University is Virginia's forward-focused residential research university for high-achieving students who want rigorous and dynamic academic programs and an exceptional student lifestyle in metropolitan Norfolk, Va.

With 24,753 students (5,387 graduate students, 19,367 undergraduates) from more than 113 countries and across the U.S., ODU is a rich and creative fusion of cultures, viewpoints, and life experiences.

Life here is active, energizing, and entrepreneurial. So is our education. It's the kind of learning that gets you involved and engaged, both inside and outside the classroom – internships, research, service learning and fieldwork. Our hands-on style gives you opportunities to challenge yourself and gain leadership experience in a thousand different ways.

Live-action-learning is our trademark – equal parts thought and action, knowledge and skill. ODU is the only doctoral university in the nation that guarantees every student practical career-related experience within their major – and for credit. With 165 different areas of study available in our six colleges, you're sure to find the career path you're looking for.

So it's no accident that ODU graduates routinely launch successful careers directly upon graduation or are accepted to top professional schools throughout the world. Either way, ODU's vast resources will help you every step along the way.

LOCATION AND ENVIRONMENT

ODU offers the best of the best: A dynamic, multicultural campus flowing with energy combined with an opportunity-rich city right outside your door.

The 250-acre campus is located between two rivers in the cultural and commercial crossroads of Norfolk, Virginia, a cosmopolitan area with a population of 1.7 million on the Chesapeake Bay, centrally positioned on the East Coast. The campus is short drive from the Atlantic Ocean and less than 3 miles from Norfolk's city center.

Norfolk is a dynamic city, home to the world's largest U.S. Navy base and to the North Atlantic Treaty Organization's (NATO) North American headquarters. Virginia Beach, a resort with sparkling white-sand beaches, and Colonial Williamsburg, a restored settlement dating from 1632, are close by. The nation's capital, Washington, D.C., is just a three-hour drive north.

Norfolk International Airport, AMTRAK, and Greyhound offer convenient transportation options to major U.S. cities. Locally, ODU students can access all public transportation for free.

The Norfolk climate is ideal for outdoor and recreational activities. Average temperatures range from 86°F in the warm summer months to 41°F during moderate winter months.

OFF-CAMPUS OPPORTUNITIES

Norfolk is at the core of the Hampton Roads area, one of the world's largest natural harbors at the mouth of the Chesapeake Bay. The area is steeped in 400 years of American history and the dozens of historical sites, hundreds of miles of beaches, and outstanding cultural and recreational attractions in the area make it among the top tourism destinations in the world.

All year round, Monarchs enjoy easy access to the nearby oceanfront in Virginia Beach, the museums and sporting events in downtown Norfolk, and the historical attractions of Williamsburg and Busch Gardens.

The Hampton Roads region also boasts thriving cultural, artistic and music scenes, with a wide variety of clubs, restaurants, museums, entertainment venues, and frequent festivals within the region.

And for outdoor enthusiasts, there are plenty of options for hiking, white water rafting, sea kayaking, surfing, or biking on rails-to-trails in Virginia.

MAJORS AND DEGREES OFFERED

Old Dominion University is one of the nation's elite centers for undergraduate, graduate and professional education, research and scholarship. We offer programs in 165 different areas of study, including

69 Bachelor's degrees

54 Master's degrees

42 Doctoral degrees

And a host of certification and licensure options

The degree programs are delivered through six distinguished colleges:

College of Arts and Letters

College of Business and Public Administration

College of Health Sciences

College of Sciences

Darden College of Education

Frank Batten College of Engineering and Technology

In addition, ODU is home to six Fusion Centers, top scientific research centers that are working on solutions to society's challenges in critical areas - Modeling & Simulation, Bioelectric & Plasma Medicine, Nanotechnology, Maritime Health & Systems, Alternative Energies, and Computer Science & Informatics

Some of our rankings and honors:

Princeton Review – A "Best Southern College"

Forbes Magazine – Among "America's Top Colleges"

U.S.News & World Report – "America's Best Colleges" Tier II Carnegie Research Institution

Asian Pacific Journal of Business Administration – 17th in the world among universities with the most prolific authors in leading international business journals

National Science Foundation – 55th in the U.S. for research and development at institutions without a medical school

State Council of Higher Education for Virginia – 26 professors have won the Outstanding Faculty Award

G.I. Jobs magazine – For four years in a row, Old Dominion University has been named a "Military Friendly School"

ACADEMIC PROGRAMS

The benefits of studying at a major doctoral research university are intense.

Our professors are masters in their fields who combine top academic credentials with real-world experience: Authors and creators, thinkers and doers who bring sharply honed expertise, pioneering artistry, and cutting-edge discovery into their classrooms.

Students are engaged both inside the classroom and outside it: Internships, research, service learning, clinical training, co-ops, and fieldwork are standard in most areas of study. From idea to innovation to invention, students and faculty work together to shape the way we interact with the world and to give voice to the human experience.

Our extensive partnerships with leading businesses, industries, civic organizations, and government agencies mean your live-action-learning options grow by 1,000%. We tallied more than 5,600 career-enhancing opportunities for students and alumni last year alone. Take your pick.

Each year, a dozen or more job fairs held at ODU attract hundreds of potential employers offering career-building opportunities through full-time jobs, internships, and co-op positions. And ODU's Career Management Center is a national award-winning service that matches thousands of students and alumni with potential employers each year.

CAMPUS FACILITIES AND EQUIPMENT

ODU's modern buildings and facilities are packed with 21st-century technology connecting students to the world and their professors. Our trading room offers state-of-the-art Bloomberg terminals that integrate real-time financial data from around the world into the classroom

Our one-of-a-kind Learning Commons is an incredible facility that provides high-tech environments for collaboration and teamwork, and also has quiet study spaces and a café for relaxation and refreshment.

And learning today doesn't always involve desks and chairs. In the CAVE virtual environment at ODU, operating room holograms and stethoscopes that simulate real vital signs create life-like surgeries that help medical students become the best caregivers in their fields.

On the housing front, we have 14 different options, including suites, apartments and even condos in the University Village – a campus neighborhood combining offices, apartments, classrooms, restaurants and shops. Campus residences are fully equipped with lounges, wireless Internet, laundry facilities, shared kitchens and air conditioning.

The multi-level, state-of-the-art fitness center is the hub for sports, adventure and wellness. You'll have access to certified personal trainers. The many amenities include:

Indoor swimming pool and multi-lane running track

Outdoor adventure center

Rock climbing wall

State-of-the-art fitness studios, cardio, strength and weights equipment

Basketball, volleyball, racquetball, and multipurpose courts

Equipment rentals: Kayaks, canoes, surfboards, camping gear and bikes

TUITION, ROOM, BOARD, AND FEES

ODU is a state-assisted public institution, so we provide premier academic quality, outstanding campus facilities, and distinctive campus amenities at a fraction of the cost of private institutions. We also offer great opportunities for financial aid.

In-state tuition for most undergraduate programs is based on a cost of approximately $273 per credit hour, while out-of-state tuition is approximately $769 per credit hour (tuition for some courses and degree programs will differ).

Housing and meal costs depend upon which residence option and meal plan you choose.

Calculate your education and housing costs here: http://blue.odu.edu/admissions/calculator/

FINANCIAL AID

Each year, ODU distributes more than $185 million in financial aid packages through a variety of federal, state and private sources in the form of grants, scholarships, loans and work-study programs.

Seventy-two percent of ODU undergraduates receive some form of financial assistance, but to be considered, you have to submit the FAFSA (Free Application for Federal Student Aid). The university's FAFSA priority deadline is February 15.

We award more than 2,280 scholarships each year, including merit-based scholarships, endowed scholarships, need-based scholarships, and outside agency scholarships.

Student Organizations and Activities

You thought you had lots to do before, but this is on a whole different scale. Start with NCAA Division I Monarch athletics, the campus passion! The Monarchs compete in 12 intercollegiate sports:

Football (Men)

Baseball (Men)

Basketball (Men and Women)

Field Hockey (Women)

Golf (Men and Women)

Lacrosse (Women)

Rowing (Women)

Soccer (Men and Women)

Sailing (Men and Women)

Swimming/Diving (Men and Women)

Tennis (Men and Women)

Wrestling (Men)

But it doesn't stop there. Everywhere you go, from the student center to the Quad, the fitness center to the Village, you'll run into people you know and things you can't wait to try. Concerts, club sports, contests, football, Frisbee, basketball, touring artists, debates, lectures and more.

With 300+ student clubs, groups, club sports, teams and organizations to choose from, it's easy to meet new friends, enhance leadership skills, build a résumé, make a difference through volunteerism, try new things, and just have fun! From the honors club to Greek life, investment club to ODU Quidditch, student government to rugby to sailing, student life at ODU is dynamic and energizing, whatever your passion.

No wonder 72% of freshmen choose to live right in the middle of the campus buzz. It all makes for a campus zinging with energy.

ADMISSIONS PROCESS

The best way to get a feel for ODU is to visit. You're welcome any time! Campus tours and information sessions are held weekdays and selected Saturdays throughout the year, and scheduled open houses include presentations by academic units, financial aid, and housing reps, with tours led by student guides.

LEARN MORE ABOUT CAMPUS VISIT OPTIONS AT ODU.EDU/ADMISSION
APPLY ONLINE

Our web-based application simplifies your application experience. Login to create an account and apply: http://www.odu.edu/admission/apply. After you submit your application, you can login and check the status of your application at anytime.

Call (800) 348-7926 to get quick answers to your questions, or visit odu.edu/admission.

Thanks for choosing Old Dominion University!

OHIO WESLEYAN UNIVERSITY

AT A GLANCE

Ohio Wesleyan University, a national liberal arts university with a major international presence, is remarkable for the broad range of its academic and pre-professional programs, the international dimensions of its curriculum, its historic emphasis on community through leadership and service, and its unwavering focus on linking theory to practice in every field of study.

Most notable is the university's Theory-to-Practice initiative, which includes both Travel-Learning Courses that augment classroom study in multiple fields in countries throughout the world and a competitive University-funded grant program that allows students to design and individual research projects, internships, service projects, and cultural immersion wherever in the world their research takes them. Students flock to both of these opportunities, increasing their understanding of academic research and their cultural competence.

OWU's unique Course Connections are networks of courses that allow students to study a topic of interest in depth for a protracted period of time, taking courses from multiple disciplines and University divisions. Classes are rigorous, and a Connection make take two to three semesters to complete.

Approximately 1,850 men and women undergraduates attend OWU. Students hail from nearly every state and more than 45 countries; Ohio Wesleyan has one of the nation's largest percentages of international students among private, liberal arts colleges. Most students live on the lovely 200-acre campus. Residences include six large halls, including Stuyvesant Hall, a University landmark that received a $14 million renovation and reopened for the 2012-2013 academic year; several small/themed living units; three residences primarily for upperclass men and women, including a residence for students in economics disciplines and another for members of the Honors Program, and seven fraternity houses (the school's five sorority houses are nonresidential).

Ohio Wesleyan is widely known for its national and international mission teams (up to 10 each year) and local community service learning. Nearly every student participates in at least one service learning opportunity or philanthropic activity each year; for five consecutive years, the University has been honored with the President's Award for Community Service, with Distinction, and in 2010, the university received the President's Award for Excellence in General Community Service, one of only three colleges in the nation recognized with that honor. Students also publish The Transcript, the nation's oldest independent student newspaper; produce four major theatre productions; and stage a number of concerts featuring OWU's ensembles and other musical groups. Cultural- and ethnic-interest groups are represented by such diverse groups as the Student Union on Black Awareness, Sisters United, VIVA and SANGAM (which promote understanding of Latin American and South Asian cultures, respectively), Hillel, and the Muslim Students Association, among others.

OWU has 23 varsity athletic teams: 11 for men and 12 for women teams. The University is part of the North Coast Athletic Conference, one of Division III's most competitive conferences, and has won national titles in men's soccer, men's basketball, and women's soccer. OWU has captured the NCAC All-Sports Trophy nine times and boasts more team championships and Academic All-America® scholar-athletes than any other school in the conference.

OWU's intramural and club sports programs enjoy wide support. Students find ample facilities for training and fitness in the Branch Rickey Physical Education Center and the Wellness Center. The Meek Aquatics and Recreation Center, which is a "green" building heated and cooled by 90 geothermal wells, offers 10 lanes, a 13-foot diving well, and 1- and 3-meter boards, as well as recreational water sports for the entire student body and the local community. The Delaware area provides opportunities for backpacking, boating, camping, golf, hiking, skiing, and swimming.

LOCATION AND ENVIRONMENT

Hometown Delaware (pop. 34,000) offers OWU students a small-city setting in one of the fastest-growing counties in the nation, only 30 minutes from Columbus, the state capital and the 16th-largest city in the country. Delaware offers Midwest friendliness, but the city is large enough to offer meaningful internship opportunities just steps from campus. Columbus provides students with an array of internships, access to international research projects, cultural events, shopping, and restaurants.

VISITING OHIO WESLEYAN

Transportation:

The Port Columbus International Airport in Columbus is a 45-minute drive from campus.

Driving Instructions:

The campus is located near the junction of US Routes 23 and 36. From Route 36 (William St. in Delaware), head south on Sandusky St. Turn left into the parking lot off Sandusky St. and follow signs to the Admission office.

If you're staying overnight:

Several hotels and motels are located in Delaware and many more can be found in southern Delaware County. Delaware is 20 miles north of downtown Columbus and 120 miles southwest of Cleveland.

OFF-CAMPUS OPPORTUNITIES

The Ohio Wesleyan curriculum strengthens students' awareness of international cultures and issues. Beyond individual study grants and faculty-led travel-learning, OWU offers significant opportunities for traditional study abroad. Study abroad programs are available in more than 20 countries, including Ohio Wesleyan's affiliation programs in Cork, Ireland, and Salamanca, Spain. Students are encouraged take advantage of international study opportunities. Many students also participate in the Wesleyan in Washington, New York Arts, and Philadelphia Center programs, which offer semester-long internships in government, the arts, communication, public service, and more.

MAJORS AND DEGREES OFFERED

Ohio Wesleyan offers 93 majors, sequences, and courses of study and confers the Bachelor of Arts degree in accounting, astronomy, botany, chemistry, classics, computer science, economics (including accounting, international business, and economics with management concentration), education (elementary and secondary licensing in 17 areas), English literature and writing, environmental science, fine arts, French, genetics, geography, geology, German, health and human kinetics, history, humanities, journalism, mathematics, microbiology, music (applied or history/literature), neuroscience, philosophy, physics, planetary science, politics and government, psychology, religion, sociology/anthropology, Spanish, theatre and dance, and zoology. Interdisciplinary majors include black world studies; East Asian Studies; environmental studies; international studies; urban studies; ancient, medieval and Renaissance studies; Latin American studies; and women's and gender studies, as well as pre-dentistry, pre-law, pre-medicine, pre-theology, and pre-veterinary medicine.

The university awards two professional degrees: the Bachelor of Fine Arts and the Bachelor of Music; it offers combined-degree programs in engineering, medical technologies, optometry, and physical therapy.

OWU has 137 full-time faculty members; the student-faculty ratio is approximately 11:1. All full-time tenure-track faculty members have earned the terminal degree in their field of expertise.

ACADEMIC PROGRAMS

Ohio Wesleyan stresses the importance of acquiring a broad general education that fosters insight into our cultural and historical past. The curriculum also emphasizes the value of specialization through its majors. OWU has competency requirements in English composition and foreign language, and distribution requirements in the natural and social sciences, the humanities, and the arts. All majors require students to complete eight to 15 courses.

The University's four-year honors program designates select first-year students as Schubert Scholars and allows them to work one-to-one with faculty advisors on original creative projects, self-designed reading programs, and research. Independent study is encouraged for juniors and seniors. The school is home to chapters of more than 20 scholastic honorary societies, and the University's chapter of Phi Beta Kappa is more than a century old.

CAMPUS FACILITIES AND EQUIPMENT

Ohio Wesleyan's libraries are teaching libraries that actively support the curriculum and research conducted by both students and faculty. The Leon A. Beeghly Library and three branch libraries house more than 550,000 holdings. Special collections include the Archives of the Ohio United Methodism Center, the Ohio Wesleyan University Historical Collection; and the Rare Books, Manuscripts, and Artifacts Collection. Ohio Wesleyan is a member of OhioLINK, which allows students to connect to a consortium of Ohio academic libraries.

The $35-million Schimmel/Conrades Science Center includes an atrium designed to facilitate and showcase student and faculty collaborative research, an expanded science library, improved classrooms, laboratories, state-of-the-art instrumentation, student lounges, and faculty offices. It is home to Ohio Wesleyan's Summer Science Research Program and its accompanying symposium.

Two nature preserves and an observatory allow for hands-on field-work and long-term projects in astronomy and astrophysics.

The Chappelear Drama Center with its two stages, Edgar and Haycock Halls for 2-D and 3-D art, and Sanborn Hall for music studies offer students multiple opportunities to hone their talents in the arts. The Richard M. Ross Art Museum, the Edgar Hall Werner Student Gallery and two additional galleries are part of the campus.

Tuition, Room, Board and Fees

The cost of attending OWU for the 2012-2013 academic year was $ 51,180.

Tuition: $38,890

Mandatory fees $260

Room $ 5,690

Board $ 4,890

Books and personal expenses (average): $1,100 per year.

Additional nominal fees are charged for some studio art courses, off-campus study, student teaching programs, and private music lessons for non-music majors.

FINANCIAL AID

OWU awards financial assistance to almost every entering first-year student who demonstrates need. Aid includes a combination of grants, loans, and employment. Federal and state aid are often part of an aid package. Nearly 70 percent of all undergraduates receive need-based financial assistance; another 25 percent are granted merit-based aid. More than three-quarters of all aid is awarded in the form of grants and scholarships.

The University's Schubert Scholars competition gives selected students the opportunity to increase the value of their base award by coming to campus to complete a writing assignment, meet with panels of professors, and audition (only for music and theatre & dance scholarships.)

The University awards several merit scholarships ranging from $1,000 to full tuition. The school awarded more than 2,000 scholarships to new and prospective students for 2012-2013. Private loan programs and flexible payment plans are available to all students, regardless of demonstrated financial need.

Student Organizations and Activities

The OWU student body is deeply involved in all aspects of campus life. Undergraduates play a major role within the University community. Major departments incorporate the contributions of student academic boards in planning coursework and requirements. The school provides both encouragement and the necessary resources for students to start new organizations.

OWU is home to approximately 100 student clubs and organizations, with each organization managed by its officers and committees. The fraternity and sorority scene is lively, both socially and within the community.

ADMISSIONS PROCESS

Admission to OWU is competitive. Academic record and strength of the student's academic program are the most important factors, followed closely by teacher and counselor recommendations, SAT or ACT scores; many other factors, such as creativity, community service, and leadership are carefully considered. A minimum 16-course preparatory program is required. Four units of English and three each of mathematics, social studies, science, and foreign language are recommended, but variations of this program are considered. SAT Subject Tests may be used for advanced placement but are not required for admission. Candidates for the Bachelor of Music degree must audition (tapes are accepted). OWU offers early action and transfer admission. The University strongly recommends, but does not require, campus interviews. OWU admitted approximately 69 percent of the applicants it reviewed in 2010-2011.

The University encourages students to apply as early as possible in the senior year, particularly if they wish to be considered for merit and/or need-based financial aid. Admission decisions are made on a rolling basis once all application materials (application, transcript, recommendations, and SAT I or ACT scores) are received; the first decisions are delivered in January. Students must notify the school of their decision by May 1. Early Action I deadline is November 30; Early Action II deadline in January 15. Applications arriving after March 1 are considered on a space-available, rolling admission basis.

PACIFIC LUTHERAN UNIVERSITY

AT A GLANCE

PLU's mission is to empower students for lives of thoughtful inquiry, service, leadership and care - for other people, for their communities and for the earth.

PLU was founded in 1890 by a group of mostly Norwegian Lutherans from the Puget Sound region. Currently there are 3,300 undergraduate students and 200 graduates studying at PLU. PLU is a comprehensive university accredited by the Northwest Commission on Colleges and Universities and committed to the integration of liberal arts studies and professional preparation. PLU follows a 4-1-4 calendar that consists of two 15-week semesters bridged by a four-week January Term. Summer consists of three four-week terms

For incoming first-years, the average GPA is 3.61, SAT is 1110 (Math and Critical Reading Only) and ACT is 25. PLU conducts a holistic review of every application for admission and academic merit scholarships.

LOCATION AND ENVIRONMENT

Pacific Lutheran University is located in the beautiful Pacific Northwest in Tacoma, Washington. The 146-acre wooded campus lies in the shadow of the 14,410' Mt. Rainier and is a few miles away from Puget Sound. PLU lies in the bustling Interstate-5 corridor that stretches from the state capital in Olympia to Tacoma and up through Seattle.

OFF-CAMPUS OPPORTUNITIES

PLU is just minutes away from world-class museums, concert venues, parks and downtown Tacoma. Great waterfront activities on Puget Sound and the excitement of Seattle (40 miles north) are also only a short drive or bus ride away. A Pierce Transit Bus Station is two blocks from campus, making downtown Tacoma, Seattle and the airport easily accessible.

PLU's location is ideal for outdoor enthusiasts with the Cascade and Olympic Mountain Ranges and the Pacific Ocean just two hours away from campus. Students can often be found camping, hiking and kayaking at these sites with friends from their classes, residence halls or the popular Outdoor Recreation Club. Closer to home in PLU's Parkland neighborhood, Garfield Street offers a diverse dining experience, great coffee shops and is home to the Garfield Book Company, PLU's community bookstore.

MAJORS AND DEGREES OFFERED

PLU is committed to the integration of liberal arts studies and professional preparation. PLU offers Bachelors degrees through our three divisions in Humanities, Social Sciences and Natural Sciences and through our four professional Schools of The Arts and Communication, Business, Education and Movement Studies and Nursing. PLU has 36 majors and 43 minors available to undergraduate students.

Some of the most popular majors include business administration, pre-professional sciences, communication, education and nursing. In addition to selecting a major, students at PLU complete the liberal arts core by taking general education requirements or enrolling in the International Honors Program.

PLU also offers Master's degrees in six areas: Business Administration, Finance, Creative Writing, Education, Nursing and Marriage and Family Therapy.

ACADEMIC PROGRAMS

All undergraduates enroll in general education requirements or in the International Honors Program to satisfy PLU's liberal arts core requirement. The International Honors Program reviews problems and issues through multiple disciplines asking students to consider the ways in which their unique interests and intellectual gifts can be of service to the international community.

Studying the liberal arts at PLU - such as psychology, history, the natural sciences - prepares students for a lifetime of success in a rapidly changing and highly competitive world. They gain skills in decision making, analysis, communication and reasoning. Our fully accredited professional programs in business, education, nursing, physical education and social work prepare them for careers.

PLU has a First-Year Experience Program which enrolls all first-years in a Writing 101 and Inquiry Seminar course helping prepare them to write a variety of college-level papers and to learn the communication, critical analysis and questioning skills necessary for a small classroom environment.

PLU has long been associated with a strong arts program. The Mary Baker Russell Music Center, plays host to more than 100 annual concerts that feature students, faculty artists and renowned guest performers. The Choir of the West has shown off their talents across the country, and recently in China and Europe. In addition, PLU puts on four main-stage theatrical shows each year, and The Wekell Gallery regularly hosts exhibits from students in current art classes.

Over 40% of PLU's students study away during their years on campus. PLU was recognized with the 2009 Senator Paul Simon Award for Campus Internationalization, a prestigious award that honors outstanding efforts on and off campus to engage the world and the international community. PLU is the first and only private college in the West to have received this honor. In 2008, PLU was also the first university in the U.S. to have students studying on all seven continents simultaneously (again in 2010 and 2012).

CAMPUS FACILITIES AND EQUIPMENT

The Karen Hille Phillips Center for the Performing Arts is being fully restored thanks to a $10 million gift from Karen Hille Phillips and other donors. A black box theatre opened up in the Fall of 2011, while the 630-seat auditorium will be completed in 2013. The Center will host PLU's four main stage productions in addition to many other smaller productions throughout the year.

The new Morken Center for Learning and Technology, the environmentally efficient home to the School of Business, the Department of Mathematics, and the Department of Computer Science and Computer Engineering, features computer equipped classrooms and laboratories, as well as multimedia and electronic labs. The Morken Center is the first building at an independent college in Washington to receive gold-level certification under the U.S. Green Building Council's Leadership in Energy and Environmental Design (LEED) program.

Mary Baker Russell Music Center houses the acoustically acclaimed Lagerquist Concert Hall and the Gottfried and Mary Fuchs Organ, the largest all-mechanical pipe organ in a West Coast university. Twelve choral and instrumental ensembles participate in over 100 concerts each year in Lagerquist, the U.S. and around the globe.

The Rieke Science Center is home to open lab for all students taking natural science courses. Two PLU faculty recently secured a grant to land a nuclear magnetic resonance (NMR) spectrometer, one of the first of its kind located in a West Coast undergraduate institution. Undergraduate students, who usually do not have access to such a powerful instrument, will be able to engage with their professors to use the NMR.

TUITION, ROOM, BOARD, AND FEES

Costs for 2012

Tuition & Fees: $32,800

Room & Board: $ 9,620

Comprehensive Cost: $42,420

FINANCIAL AID

PLU awards both merit and need-based financial aid. Academic merit scholarships are based upon a holistic review of the application. No additional materials other than the application for admission are required to be considered for an academic scholarship. For 2012, these awards ranged from $5,000-$19,000 for first-year students and are renewable for up to 4 years. Students with talents in music, theater, forensics and dance can audition for additional talent scholarships by contacting the respective departments.

First-Year Students can apply for the President's and Regents' Scholarship by December 15th. The President's scholarship was $19,000 in 2012 and was awarded to 150 of about 600 applicants. All President's scholars are then invited to campus to interview with faculty teams for 1 of 15 $24,000 Harstad Founder's Scholarships and 1 of 5 full tuition Regents Scholarships.

In addition to merit scholarships, students are also eligible for need-based aid by completing the FAFSA. Through the FAFSA, students can receive scholarships, grants, work study and loans. On average, students received just over $20,000 in financial aid in 2011.

STUDENT ORGANIZATIONS AND ACTIVITIES

A variety of organizations and activities help keep PLU students busy outside of the classroom. Activities include dance ensemble, theater, speech and debate, newspaper, radio, television, literary magazine. There are over sixty clubs covering many interests including community service, religious, environmental, social justice, political, and cultural/ethnic. Some of the most prominent and active organizations include the Diversity Center, ASPLU (Student Government), Residence Hall Association, GREAN (Sustainability Club) and Outdoor Recreation.

As a part of the Northwest conference within the NCAA Division III, PLU has long been known as a sports powerhouse within. The football team has won four national titles, and more than 400 Lutes in all sports have been named first-team NCAA All-Americans. PLU has won the Northwest All-Sports Trophy 15 times in the award's 27-year history. Women's intercollegiate sports: Soccer, cross-country, volleyball, basketball, swimming, track and field, tennis, crew, golf and softball. Men's intercollegiate sports: Soccer, football, cross country, basketball, swimming, track and field, baseball, crew, golf, and tennis.

ADMISSIONS PROCESS

First-year and transfer students can apply to PLU for free using either PLU's online application or the Common Application. There are no deadlines for admission applications. Application reading dates and admission decisions occur on the 15th of each month from October through February. After February, PLU reviews applications on a rolling basis.

For first-year students, we require the following: application, high school transcripts, SAT or ACT scores, personal essay, activities resume and a letter of recommendation.

For transfer students, we require the following: application, college transcripts, high school transcript, personal essay, transfer statement of good standing, activities resume and a letter of recommendation (SAT or ACT scores are required if transferring less than 30 credits).

For international students we require the following: application, personal essay, one letter of recommendation, Send official transcripts translated to English from all schools you've attended (upper secondary and any schools you are currently attending), the Declaration of Finances form, TOEFL or IELTS or PTE scores if your first language is other than English, and a copy of your passport photo page.

All students are strongly encouraged to contact their respective admission counselors to ask questions about admission and provide additional information pertinent to the admission process. To learn more about PLU, you can take a virtual tour at http://video.realviewtv.com/education/plu/.

PENNSYLVANIA COLLEGE OF TECHNOLOGY

AT A GLANCE

Pennsylvania College of Technology is ranked among the top public colleges in the north and is one of the nation's top 100 associate degree producers.

As a special mission affiliate of Penn State committed to applied technology education, Penn College offers bachelor, associate, and certificate majors in more than 100 career fields ranging from manufacturing, design, transportation, and construction to hospitality, health, business, and natural resources.

Business/industry connections, national corporate sponsors, small classes, industry-standard equipment, and faculty with work experience contribute to strong graduate placement rates.

The College's main campus is located in Williamsport, PA, a city known around the world as the home of Little League Baseball.

LOCATION AND ENVIRONMENT

The main campus is located in Williamsport (Northcentral Pennsylvania), no more than a four-hour drive from major cities including Philadelphia, New York, Pittsburgh, and Washington, D.C.

Air service is provided at the Williamsport Regional Airport.

In addition to the main campus, the College operates an aviation facility at the regional airport and nearby centers for the earth sciences and advanced automotive technologies.

Students benefit from internships, work-based, and other experiences outside of the classroom. For many, these experiences are the first step toward a full-time job after graduation. "I took advantage of almost every opportunity Penn College offered, both academic and professional. I went on the Italy, Ireland, and Japan study abroad opportunities. I also took advantage of an internship opportunity after my freshman year and worked at Tyco Electronics as an injection molding machine operator. The work experience was invaluable as well as the social interaction with my much more experienced co-workers," says Bradley Stroup, Plastics and Polymer Engineering Technology. "I've also attended multiple Student Leadership Conferences and took leadership roles in the Society of Plastic Engineers student organization. The Plastics faculty had a large role in finding these opportunities and supporting me in taking on the challenges. The faculty members are well connected to industry professionals and keep on top of advances and emerging technologies in the plastics industry."

Stroup is currently studying specialized plastics processing techniques at Queen's University in Belfast, Ireland. Upon his return to Penn College, he plans to complete the nanofabrication capstone semester at nearby Penn State and then perform a stint for Raytheon Polar Services in Antarctica – an opportunity that arose after Stroup connected with a Penn College alum while attending a Student Leadership Conference.

MAJORS AND DEGREES OFFERED

Programs include:

Bachelor of Science:

Accounting

Applied Health Studies

Applied Human Services

Automotive Technology Management

Aviation Maintenance Technology

Building Automation Technology

Building Science & Sustainable Design (Architectural Technology, Building Construction Technology)

Business Administration (Banking & Finance, Management, Marketing)

Civil Engineering Technology

Computer-Aided Product Design

Construction Management

Culinary Arts and Systems

Dental Hygiene: Health Policy & Administration

Electronics and Computer Engineering Technology

Graphic Design

Health Information Management

HVAC Technology

Industrial and Human Factors Design

Information Technology Sciences - Gaming and Simulation

Information Technology (Information Assurance and Security, Network Specialist)

Legal Assistant/Paralegal Studies

Manufacturing Engineering Technology

Nursing

Physician Assistant

Plastics and Polymer Engineering Technology

Residential Construction Technology and Management

Software Development & Information Management

Technology Management

Web and Interactive Media

Welding and Fabrication Engineering Technology

Associate of Applied Arts:

Advertising Art

Associate of Arts:

General Studies

Studio Arts

Associate of Applied Science:

Accounting

Architectural Technology

Automated Manufacturing Technology

Automotive Restoration Technology

Automotive Service Sales and Marketing

Automotive Technology (Ford ASSET & Honda PACT)

Aviation Technology

Baking and Pastry Arts

Building Construction Technology

Building Construction Technology: Masonry

Business Management

Civil Engineering Technology

Collision Repair Technology

Computer-Aided Drafting Technology

Culinary Arts Technology

Dental Hygiene

Diesel Technology

Early Childhood Education

Electrical Technology

Electromechanical Maintenance Technology

Electronics and Computer Engineering Technology (Electronics & Computer Engineering, Robotics & Automation)

Emergency Medical Services

Forest Technology

Graphic Communications Technology

Health Arts

Health Arts: Practical Nursing

Health Information Technology

HVAC Technology

Heavy Construction Equipment Technology (Caterpillar Equipment, Operator, Technician)

Hospitality Management

Human Services

Individual Studies

Information Technology: Technical Support Technology

Landscape/Nursery Technology (Landscape, Plant Production)

Legal Assistant/Paralegal

Machine Tool Technology

Nursing

Occupational Therapy Assistant

On-Site Power Generation

Physical Fitness Specialist

Plastics and Polymer Technology

Radiography

Renewable Energy Technologies

Surgical Technology

Surveying Technology

Welding Technology

Certificates.

Automotive Service Technician

Aviation Maintenance Technician

Collision Repair Technician

Diesel Technician

Electrical Occupations

Health Information Coding Specialist

Machinist General

Nurse/Health Care Paralegal Studies

Paramedic Technician

Plumbing

Practical Nursing

Residential Builder

Welding

ACADEMIC PROGRAMS

Classrooms and laboratories offer extensive "hands-on" experiences that prepare graduates for success in the workplace. Applied technology in each major gives students the opportunity to learn the most current advances in their fields of study. To ensure an ever-present connection to the workforce, business, and industry, advisers provide guidance on matters of curriculum, facilities, and equipment.

Small classes (1:17 faculty-to-student ratio) - and no graduate assistants teaching classes - mean students have access to faculty. "I think the most unique thing about Penn College is the awesome student-to-teacher ratio and the interaction we get as students with our instructors. I really like the small class sizes," says Ethan Griffin, Automotive Technology/Honda PACT Emphasis.

School Says . . .

"I love the relationship I can have with my professors," says Amy Vanderwall, nursing. "They do not make me feel like they are superior to me - they make me feel like they are my mentors wanting me to succeed as much as I myself want to succeed."

For those who need alternatives beyond the traditional, on-campus programs of study, Penn College also offers a variety of courses and bachelor-degree completion programs via distance learning. Bachelor's degrees that can be completed through distance learning include: Applied Health Studies, Automotive Technology Management, Dental Hygiene, Health Information Management, Nursing, and Technology Management.

Taking courses online made it possible for Kelly Braun, Dental Hygiene: Health Policy and Administration Concentration, to earn her degree while working full-time as a registered dental hygienist at Geisinger Medical Center. She says that "the online completion was wonderful as it allowed me to work full time while finishing my degree full time."

Bachelor-degree, associate-degree, and certificate majors combine hands-on experience with theory and management education. Among the majors with the most students enrolled in Fall 2012 were Nursing, Welding, Physician Assistant, Building Construction, and Civil Engineering Technology.

Penn College offers associate-degree General Studies and Individual Studies majors for students who are undecided or have specific career goals not addressed in other programs. Counseling and career services also are available to help students find potential occupations or college majors that reflect their interests.

TUITION, ROOM, BOARD, AND FEES

In 2012-13, Pennsylvania residents attending Penn College paid approximately $24,830 per year and out-of-state residents, approximately $28,460 per year. These estimated costs are based upon tuition and fees for an average 15 credits per semester, plus estimated expenses for housing, meals, books, and supplies.

FINANCIAL AID

Four out of five Penn College students receive some form of financial aid. Regardless of family income, students are encouraged to apply for financial aid, including grants, loans, scholarships, and work-study options. For the most current information, visit www.pct.edu/finaid

Student Organizations and Activities

In addition to Greek life, clubs, and organizations - many of which are affiliated with national and professional organizations - Penn College offers intercollegiate athletic teams, various club sports, and intramural sport activities.

"Penn College offers so many different clubs and activities for students to choose from. Whether you want to join a sorority or play on an intramural team, there is something fun for everyone to get involved in on campus," says Jordan Pennypacker, Physical Fitness Specialist. About the campus, she states, "The residence halls are great, and all of the buildings are equipped with everything you need for school. The library is my favorite place! Penn College is a gorgeous campus!"

ADMISSIONS PROCESS

Application deadline for fall is July 1. Submit application and $50 application fee online at www.pct.edu/princeton or contact the Admissions Office for an application.

Applicants for bachelor-degree majors must submit SAT test scores in addition to high school transcripts to be considered for admission.

Applicants must satisfactorily complete placement testing and satisfy other major-specific admission criteria in order to be offered acceptance into a major program of study.

Information on all Penn College majors, as well as details on admissions and enrollment, is offered at www.pct.edu/princeton.

Pennsylvania College of Technology
One College Avenue
Williamsport, PA 17701
800-367-9222 or 570-327-4761
Fax: 570.321.5551
PCTinfo@pct.edu
www.pct.edu/princeton

1173

PITZER COLLEGE

AT A GLANCE

Founded in 1963, Pitzer is a nationally recognized, independent, residential liberal arts college. With a strong emphasis on the five core values of social responsibility, student engagement, environmental sustainability, interdisciplinary studies, and intercultural understanding, Pitzer believes that students should take an active role in their education and their world.

Pitzer was founded in 1963 and today offers forty majors in the arts, humanities, sciences, and social sciences. Majors with the largest enrollments currently include art, biology, English, environmental studies, intercultural and international studies, media studies, organizational studies, political studies, psychology, and sociology. Pitzer students have a great deal of freedom to choose the courses they want to take and even have the opportunity to design their own major.

Pitzer offers the best of both worlds: membership in a small, close-knit academic community and access to the resources of a midsize university through the College's partnership with the Claremont Colleges. The Claremont Colleges are a consortium of five distinct undergraduate colleges (Pitzer, Claremont McKenna, Harvey Mudd, Pomona, and Scripps) and two graduate institutions (Claremont Graduate University and the Keck Institute for Applied Biological Sciences). Each college has its own personality, but all share major facilities such as the library, bookstore, campus security, health services, counseling center, ethnic study centers, queer resource center, and chaplains' offices. The total enrollment of all of the colleges is approximately 6,500 students. Students at Pitzer may enroll in courses offered by the other colleges and consult with professors on all of the adjoining campuses.

In 2012, the first-year class of 256 students represented twenty-eight different states and eight other countries. About 57 percent of the first-year students came from outside of California. Pitzer has had a deep commitment to welcoming members of underrepresented groups since its founding. In 2012, students of color made up approximately 33 percent of the entering class.

Residential life plays a significant role in a student's educational experience. Each of Pitzer's residence halls establishes its own Hall Council to serve as a forum for addressing and meeting the needs of the community. Pitzer students have a long tradition of arranging their living communities based on common interests. All rooms are wired for Internet access, television, and phone service. After opening three new LEED Gold residence halls in 2007, Pitzer proudly opened an additional four LEED Platinum residence halls for sophomores, juniors, and seniors in the fall of 2012. The newest residence halls also house media studies facilities, an art gallery and a demonstration kitchen.

LOCATION AND ENVIRONMENT

We are located in the city of Claremont (population 35,000) at the base of the San Gabriel Mountains, about 35 miles east of Los Angeles and 78 miles west of Palm Springs. Pitzer is a short distance from rock climbing at Joshua Tree National Park, the Getty, Norton Simon and other LA County museums, the beaches of Southern California and skiing at Mt. Baldy and Big Bear. Claremont's quaint village, a short walk from campus, has a wide variety of restaurants, galleries and shops.

OFF-CAMPUS OPPORTUNITIES

Almost 80 percent of Pitzer students participate in study-abroad programs. Pitzer currently approves twelve exchanges with U.S. institutions and over fifty international study options in Argentina, Australia, Botswana, Brazil, Bulgaria, Canada, Chile, China, Costa Rica, Cuba, Denmark, Ecuador, England, France, Germany, Ghana, Hong Kong, Hungary, Iceland, Israel, Italy, Japan, Korea, Mexico, Morocco, Netherlands, Nepal, New Zealand, Singapore, South Africa, Spain, Sweden, Thailand, and Turkey.

MAJORS AND DEGREES OFFERED

Pitzer offers a Bachelor of Arts degree in Africana studies, American studies, anthropology, art, art history, Asian American studies, biochemistry, biology, chemistry, Chicano/Latino studies, classics, dance, economics, English/world literature, environmental analysis, gender and feminist studies, history, human biology, international and intercultural studies, international political economy, linguistics, management engineering, mathematical economics, mathematics, media studies, modern language, literature and cultures: Spanish, molecular biology, music, neuroscience, organismal biology, organizational studies, philosophy, physics, political studies, psychology, religious studies, science and management, science, technology and society, sociology, and theater.

Minors are available in Africana studies, anthropology, art, art history, Asian American studies, biology, classics, dance, economics, English/world literature, environmental analysis, gender and feminist studies, history, linguistics, mathematics, media studies, music, philosophy, science, technology and society, sociology, Spanish, and theater.

ACADEMIC PROGRAMS

To earn their B.A., students are required to complete thirty-two courses with approximately one third of those courses in their major. Students work with faculty advisers to organize a curriculum that meets the educational objectives of the College: breadth of knowledge, understanding in depth, written expression, interdisciplinary and intercultural exploration, and social responsibility and the ethical implications of knowledge and action. Specific course requirements depend on the student's academic interests. Certain concentrations require a senior thesis.

The system of cross-registration at the Claremont Colleges provides Pitzer students with the opportunity to take advantage of the wide range of courses available at each of the other colleges. Students may also enroll in certain courses at Claremont Graduate University with the instructor's approval.

The College observes a semester calendar; classes begin in early September and end in mid-May. There is a study break near the middle of each semester and another break between semesters from mid-December through mid-January.

CAMPUS FACILITIES AND EQUIPMENT

The central services of the Claremont Colleges include the Honnold-Mudd Library, which houses more than 2 million volumes and more than 6,000 serial subscriptions. Other shared facilities include theaters, music halls, music and dance studios, the W. M. Keck Science Center (shared with Claremont McKenna and Scripps Colleges), and a wellness center that includes counseling and health services.

Specialized facilities at Pitzer include a newly renovated auditorium, a television studio, film editing suites, art galleries, social science laboratories, an arboretum, a reading library, and several computing facilities, including a 24-hour computer center.

Tuition, Room, Board and Fees

Costs for the 2012-13 academic year were as follows:

Tuition: 43,136

Room: 8,028

Board: 5,836

Books and personal expenses: $2,000 (estimated)

Travel expenses will vary.

Costs are subject to change for the 2013-14 academic year.

FINANCIAL AID

Approximately 42 percent of Pitzer's students receive aid in the forms of grants, loans, and work-study. Pitzer's financial aid is primarily need-based and in order to apply for aid, students must complete the Free Application for Federal Student Aid (FAFSA) and the CSS/Financial Aid PROFILE. California residents should also apply for California state grants. Students must reapply for aid each spring. Pitzer is committed to meeting 100 percent of the demonstrated need of all accepted students.

STUDENT ORGANIZATIONS AND ACTIVITIES

Opportunities for student engagement abound at Pitzer. Students can participate in a wide variety of sports, clubs, community service programs, and social activities. Currently, more than 150 student organizations allow students to get involved in a wide variety of activities. Pitzer partners with Pomona College to offer NCAA Division III teams in baseball, basketball, cross-country, football, golf, soccer, softball, swimming and diving, tennis, track and field, volleyball, and water polo. Club sports include crew, cycling, lacrosse, rugby, Ultimate (Frisbee), and volleyball. Intramural sports include inner tube water polo, squash, chess, flag football, and table tennis.

Pitzer's governmental structure is distinctive among American colleges. Instead of the traditional college governance style which restricts student participation to limited areas, Pitzer students are represented on all standing committees of the College, including those that deal with the most vital and sensitive issues of the College community. Though this model demands a serious time commitment from those who choose to participate, it offers interested students an active educational experience and the opportunity to make a genuine impact on the life of the College and its students, faculty, and staff.

ADMISSIONS PROCESS

Pitzer has developed a highly personalized admission process. Each applicant is considered on the basis of his or her own strengths. The College seeks students who have performed well in high school, have shown a significant amount of involvement in activities outside of the classroom, are motivated to learn, and are interested in the opportunity to take an active role in planning their education in a liberal arts framework.

Pitzer College offers both Early Decision and Regular Decision for prospective applicants. Students interested in applying early may submit a completed application by November 15 to apply for Early Decision I or by January 1 to apply for Early Decision II. Interviews for Early Decision are required. Regular Decision candidates must submit their applications for admission by January 1 and are notified by April 1. Interviews are not required for Regular Decision candidates but are highly recommended and should be completed by December 15.

All applicants must supply an official transcript of grades, two teacher evaluations, one counselor or school official recommendation, and the application fee of $65 by the necessary deadline. Pitzer accepts the Common Application for first-year students. When submitting the Common Application, students must also complete a supplement, which is available on the Common Application website.

Pitzer's admission process is test optional. Students who have an unweighted GPA of 3.5 or higher or who are in the top 10 percent of their class are exempt from needing to submit any testing. Students who do not fall within one of those ranges have multiple options for the kind of testing they would like to submit. Students can contact the College for further details.

Pitzer exempts students graduating in the top 10 percent of their class, or those who have an unweighted cumulative GPA of 3.50 or higher in academic subjects, from having to submit any standardized tests. Applicants not falling into either one of those categories will be required to submit at least one of the following options:

Pitzer College adheres to the May 1 National Candidate's Reply Date Agreement.

POST UNIVERSITY

AT A GLANCE

Post University is a student-focused, career-driven institution committed to helping students develop the knowledge, personal skills and experience they need to become leaders in their chosen fields. With small classes and dedicated faculty and staff, Post University provides students with the personal attention they need to succeed. Located in Waterbury, Connecticut, we also can offer you the best of all worlds – a small, safe New England campus that's not far from two of the nation's most exciting cities, Boston and New York. We invite you to explore all that Post University has to offer.

Founded in 1890, the mission of Post University is to provide our students with the knowledge, personal skills, and experiences required to become leaders in tomorrow's careers. We prepare each student, every day to be confident, competent, and competitive participants in a global marketplace. Our intimate campus and NCAA Division II athletics provide a lively, challenging and fun environment to help graduates transition into the world of advanced studies and professional careers. Approximately two-thirds of Post University's students live on campus in one of the six residence halls. Over 70 percent of undergraduates participate in activities including student government, campus activities team, clubs and organizations, intramural sports or NCAA Division II athletics. Students also enjoy the nearby cultural and social activities in Waterbury, West Hartford as well as trips to New York City and Boston. Post students participate in a year-round schedule of intercollegiate and intramural athletic activities. The Post University Eagles are members of the National Collegiate Athletic Association (NCAA) Division II and the Central Atlantic Collegiate Conference (CACC). Men's intercollegiate sports teams include baseball, basketball, cross-country, golf, soccer, sprint football, swimming and tennis. Women's athletic teams include basketball, cross-country, lacrosse, soccer, softball, swimming, tennis, and volleyball. Post also sponsors an active, coeducational equestrian team. Intramural sports are diverse, ranging from softball and volleyball to basketball and flag football. Students enjoy the facilities of the Drubner Conference and Fitness Center, including a gymnasium, a swimming pool, tennis and racquetball courts, a fitness club, and weight-training rooms.

ACADEMICS

For the bachelor's degree, students must complete a minimum of 120 credit hours. To receive an associate degree from Post, students must complete a minimum of 60 credit hours. The University has a two-semester calendar.

ADMISSIONS

Post University welcomes applicants who are motivated to succeed academically and professionally. Admission to Post University is based upon an evaluation of the candidate's qualifications and the recommendation of an admissions counselor. All decisions are made without regard to race, creed, color, religion, national origin, handicap, or sexual orientation. Criteria for admission are objective as well as subjective. The applicant's academic experience, standardized test scores, personal qualities, recommendations, and individual characteristics are considered. Post has a rolling admissions policy. The Admissions Committee makes a decision with respect to a candidate's admission to the University as soon as the candidates file is complete. The minimum requirements to make an admissions decision are official high school transcripts, standardized test scores, and the recommendation of an admissions counselor, which is gained through an admissions interview. International students are required to earn a minimum score of 500 on the paper-based version or 173 on the computer-based version of the TOEFL and adhere to the above requirements. Campus visit appointments may be scheduled Monday through Thursday at 1:00 p.m., Friday at 11:00 a.m., 1:00 p.m. or 3:00 p.m., and Saturdays at 11:00 a.m. or 1:00 p.m.. Post periodically offers group information sessions, on-site and off-site open houses. To schedule a campus visit, students should call the Office of Admissions at 800.345.2562 (toll-free) or send an email message to admissions@ Post.edu. Transfer candidates must have a minimum GPA of 2.0 and must file transcripts from all other colleges and universities attended. Grades of C or higher may receive transfer credits. The maximum number of transfer credits allowed for bachelor's candidates is 90; the maximum for associate candidates is 30. To apply, students should submit the application form, the non-refundable $40 application fee, a recommendation, SAT or ACT scores, and the applicable transcripts. A file must be completed before an admissions decision is made. Post employs a system of rolling admissions but a priority freshman application deadline is March 1st. However, each student should attempt to file the application packet as soon as possible. This gives the Admissions Committee the opportunity to carefully review the application and grants the student a chance to begin preparation for life at college. Online applications are available through the university's website. For additional information, students should contact:

Office of Admissions

Post University

800 Country Club Road

P.O. Box 2540

Waterbury, CT 06723-2540

United States

Phone: 203.596.4520 or 800.345.2562 (toll-free)

Fax: 203.756.5810

E-mail: admissions@Post.edu

Website: http://www.Post.edu

CAMPUS LIFE

Students play active roles in the day-to-day functioning of Post University. The student's official voice at the university is the Student Government Association (SGA), which expresses recommendations pertaining to student life, oversees the operations of each active student group, and decides on funding for each group. The Student Activities Committee participates in the scheduling and programming of campus events. A large percentage of Post University's standing committees include student representatives.

COLLEGE BASICS

Founded in 1890, Post University is a student-focused, career-driven university located in Waterbury, Connecticut. Post is known for its quality academic programs, small classes, national award winning student activities, and its NCAA Division II athletic programs.

LOCATION AND ENVIRONMENT

Post University is located midway between New York City and Boston. Post University occupies a 58-acre hilltop residential campus in the suburbs of Waterbury, Connecticut. Post's campus and surrounding community offer a safe, scenic, friendly, and convenient residence. Whether students want to visit museums, shops or the shores of Connecticut, they are in close proximity to a wide variety of cultural and recreational attractions.

TUITION AND FEES

For 2012-13, full-time resident students pay a comprehensive fee of $37,879, covering tuition, room, and board. For commuting students, the comprehensive fee is $26,250 per year. Student Services, technology, equine, laboratory fees, the $40 application fee, and an estimated $1000-$1,500 per year for books and supplies are not included in this basic comprehensive fee.

PRINCETON UNIVERSITY

AT A GLANCE

Princeton combines the strengths of a major research university with the qualities of an outstanding liberal arts college. The University prepares its 5,100 undergraduates for lives of leadership and service.

Chartered in 1746, Princeton is the fourth-oldest college in the nation. It is a private, non-sectarian university that seeks to fulfill its informal motto, first expressed by the University's 13th president, Woodrow Wilson: "Princeton in the nation's service and in the service of all nations."

LOCATION AND ENVIRONMENT

Princeton is a residential campus set on 500 park-like acres located in the town of Princeton (pop: 30,000) in central New Jersey. Known for its beauty and architectural variety, including the famed "Collegiate Gothic" style of architecture, the campus is home to historic landmarks such as Nassau Hall, which was built in 1756 and played an important role during the American Revolution.

Princeton students enjoy convenient transportation options to New York City and Philadelphia, both only about an hour away by car. Other nearby attractions include numerous parks, cultural venues, and commercial hubs. For arts lovers, the McCarter Theatre is a campus treasure within easy walking distance.

ACADEMICS

Princeton undergraduates pursue either the bachelor of arts (A.B.) or the bachelor of science in engineering (B.S.E.) degree. Students in the A.B. degree program choose a concentration (major) in one of 34 departments in the arts, humanities, social sciences, and natural sciences, including undergraduate programs in the Woodrow Wilson School of Public and International Affairs and the School of Architecture. The B.S.E. degree is granted by the School of Engineering and Applied Science, which has six engineering departments.

Princeton offers doctoral programs in a range of subjects in the humanities, natural sciences, social sciences, School of Architecture, School of Engineering and Applied Science, and within the Woodrow Wilson School of Public and International Affairs.

In addition to their major course of study, students are encouraged to enroll in one or more of the University's 46 interdisciplinary certificate programs, which offer diverse fields of study. For example, a student may wish to concentrate in ecology and evolutionary biology while pursuing a certificate in musical performance.

Undergraduates benefit from small class sizes and one-on-one advising with faculty, particularly while working on independent projects such as the junior paper and senior thesis. The University's 1,148 faculty members are leaders in their disciplines, and it is not uncommon for students to receive classroom instruction from a Nobel laureate, Pulitzer Prize winner, or MacArthur fellow. During their freshman year, students are introduced to many of Princeton's notable faculty through the freshman seminars program, which offers small discussion-focused classes on a variety of topics. One such freshman seminar may cover the art and science of motorcycle design; another may explore the qualities that make a poem endure.

Students are encouraged to bring a multidisciplinary approach to their studies, synthesizing what they discover in different classes and through their own research. This approach may be informal, based on a student's particular avenue of study, or it may be more formally structured, such as with the integrated science curriculum that combines the study of physics, mathematics, computer science, and molecular biology.

A global perspective is emphasized across the curriculum, with special opportunities such as the Study Abroad Program and the Princeton Institute for International and Regional Studies. A relatively recent initiative, the Bridge Year Program, allows selected students to delay the start of their freshman year to engage in nine months of University-sponsored service abroad.

FACILITIES AND EQUIPMENT

Academic support services include academic advising centered in each of the six residential colleges (for A.B. students) and in the engineering school (for B.S.E. students); the McGraw Center, which offers workshops and individual consultations with students as they evolve as scholars; and the Writing Program, which strengthens students' writing skills through a required seminar. Ongoing tutoring sessions also are available at the program's Writing Center.

Throughout their undergraduate careers, Princeton students are supported by a range of first-rate academic resources, including libraries, laboratories, and one of the leading university art museums in the country. The largest library on campus, Firestone Library, contains more than 70 miles of shelving and a vast range of electronic resources. The Peter B. Lewis Library, designed by renowned architect Frank Gehry, offers impressive print and digital collections in the sciences. In the past several years, new initiatives in African American studies and neuroscience have resulted in expanded activities.

A new state-of-art and environmentally sustainable science facility houses the chemistry department and provides laboratory space for research and teaching. A new neuroscience and psychology building is scheduled to open soon.

Numerous venues for the arts as well as a range of athletic facilities also are available.

TUITION AND FEES

Estimated cost of attendance for 2012-13

Tuition: $ $38,650

Room charge: $ $6,950

Board rate: $5,680

Estimated miscellaneous expenses (books, supplies, laundry, telephone, recreation, etc.): $3,500

Total: $$54,780

FINANCIAL AID

Princeton offers one of the strongest need-based financial aid programs in the country, ensuring that all qualified students, regardless of financial need, can afford to attend. There is no income cutoff on Princeton's aid application; any family who feels the need for financial assistance is welcome to apply for aid.

Since 2001, when Princeton initiated its landmark no-loan financial aid program, the university has been a leader in changing the face of financial aid policy. Central to the program is Princeton's groundbreaking "no-loan" policy; the university offers every aid recipient a financial aid package that replaces loans with grant aid that students do not pay back.

If admitted, applicants can be confident that their financial need, as determined by Princeton's aid office, will be met. Today, about 60 percent of undergraduates receive aid, compared with 38 percent more than a decade ago. As a result, Princeton has been able to enroll growing numbers of students from low- and middle-income backgrounds. The average aid package for the Class of 2016 was $ $39,700, which exceeds the cost of tuition.

CAMPUS LIFE

Princeton is a residential campus that provides a close-knit living environment for its undergraduates. Through its six residential colleges, students pursue a host of recreational and academic activities. The residential colleges also serve as home base for academic advising for students, who learn about all that the university has to offer from faculty and staff advisers, peer mentors, and fellow students.

With more than 300 student organizations, as well as an extensive calendar of cultural and athletic events, students find it easy to pursue their interests or explore new ones. The Frist Campus Center serves as the hub of campus life, and is home to the Women's Center, the Davis International Center, the LGBT Center, the Pace Center for civic engagement, and the Undergraduate Student Government, as well as many other student clubs and organizations.

For many students, social life at Princeton includes becoming a member of an eating club. The 10 historic eating clubs are open to juniors and seniors and are run independently of the university. Fraternities and sororities are not recognized as official student organizations on campus.

Princeton is an NCAA Division I school. The university offers 38 varsity sports and 36 club teams. Each year more than 1,000 students participate in intercollegiate varsity and junior varsity sports. In any given year, more than half of Princeton's varsity athletic teams compete in national championships. In recent years, Princeton teams have won national titles in lacrosse, rowing, fencing, track and field, and squash.

ADMISSIONS

Princeton's admission process goes beyond simply looking for academically accomplished students. For each freshman class, Princeton brings together a varied mix of high-achieving, intellectually gifted students from diverse backgrounds to create an exceptional learning community. American minorities comprise about 39 percent of the undergraduate student body, and students from nearly 100 countries are represented.

Princeton cares about what students have accomplished in and out of the classroom. The admission process is highly selective. In 2012, the university offered admission to 7.9 percent of applicants for the class of 2016.

Students applying to Princeton are asked to describe their talents, academic accomplishments, and personal achievements. A transcript and recommendations also are required. To be considered for admission to Princeton, students must submit the results of the SAT Reasoning Test or ACT (with Writing, where offered). In addition, all applicants must submit the results of two different SAT Subject Tests. The university accepts both online and paper applications. Princeton does not accept transfer students.

Under Princeton's admission policy, need for financial aid is not in any way a disadvantage. Princeton welcomes applications from talented students of diverse economic backgrounds.

QUINNIPIAC UNIVERSITY

AT A GLANCE

Quinnipiac, founded in 1929, is a private, co-educational, non-sectarian University - a residential campus in a uniquely attractive New England setting. Quinnipiac's mission is to provide a supportive and stimulating environment for the intellectual and personal growth of undergraduate, graduate, and law students.

The university offers broadly based undergraduate programs together with graduate programs in selected professional fields. At the undergraduate level, through integrated liberal arts and professional curricula, programs in Arts and Sciences, Business, Communications, Education, Engineering, Health Sciences and Nursing prepare students for career entry or advanced studies. Graduate programs are designed to provide professional qualifications for success in business, education, engineering, health sciences, nursing, communications, and law.

An education at Quinnipiac embodies the university's commitment to three important values: excellence in education, a student centered campus, and a spirit of community. The entire university shares a service orientation toward students and their needs. Its collegial atmosphere fosters a strong sense of community, identity, and purpose among faculty, staff, and students.

LOCATION AND ENVIRONMENT—THREE SETTINGS, ONE UNIVERSITY

Hamden, Connecticut: 8 miles north of New Haven, 20 miles south of Hartford, midway between Boston and New York City. Quinnipiac is a suburban campus with 600 acres on three sites. The Mount Carmel campus is adjacent to Sleeping Giant State Park, with 1,700 acres of hills and trails for hiking and walking. A picturesque setting provides an enjoyable academic and residential campus experience for 6200 undergraduate and 2300 graduate students. A campus shuttle system provides easy access to theater, shopping, museums, sports, recreation, and a variety of dining and entertainment options in Hamden and New Haven. The nearby York Hill campus is home to the TD Bank Sports Center, plus new apartment and suite-style residence halls with kitchens to accommodate 1500 students, a lodge-inspired student/recreation center, and 2000 car parking garage. The North Haven campus, just 4 miles away, provides the upper level and graduate students in the Schools of Education, Health Sciences, Nursing and Medicine with a state-of-the-art setting on 100 acres.

Students from over 28 states and 15 countries study at Quinnipiac. Ninety-five percent of the incoming 1600 freshmen choose to live on campus. Housing options include traditional residence halls, suites, and suites with full kitchens. Housing is available for all four years.

Driving time to Quinnipiac from Boston or New York City is about two hours. Metro-North railroad from Grand Central Terminal in New York City and Amtrak Northeast Corridor trains also arrive in New Haven. The campus is a 15-minute taxi ride (students can take the campus shuttle) from the station. Bradley Airport (BDL), just north of Hartford is the nearest international airport, about 40 minutes from campus. Students can also arrive at John F. Kennedy, Newark, or LaGuardia airports in the New York area and travel via Connecticut Limousine to New Haven.

All academic programs at Quinnipiac offer an excellent combination of classroom learning with internships or clinical affiliations. Students in the health sciences are placed in clinical affiliations as part of their course work. Students in business, communications, and liberal arts have nearby corporations, health care agencies, or media outlets available for internships.

Career Services, offered by each of the academic schools, can provide excellent assistance in resume writing and job placement. A survey of recent alumni showed that close to 90 percent were either employed or in graduate school within six months of graduation. Each year about half of students in internships are offered permanent jobs as a result of their work.

Students in all majors can also take advantage of study abroad opportunities either during the summer months or during the academic year. Program sites include: Ireland, Australia, Austria, Argentina, Czech Republic, England, France, Spain, Italy, Netherlands, Russia, South Africa, Spain and Independent Programs, and through affiliates such as AIFS, API, and Semester at Sea. Study abroad is an experience of a lifetime allowing you to live a different country for a period of time while earning credits at your home institution. Any student in any major can apply to study abroad with at least a 3.0 GPA.

MAJORS AND DEGREES OFFERED

Undergraduate students can choose from more than 50 majors through the Schools of Business, Communications, Education, Health Sciences and Nursing, and the College of Arts and Sciences. Majors in mechanical, industrial, civil and software engineering were added in Fall 2012. About 30% of all entering freshmen remain at Quinnipiac through their graduate degree program.

Graduate students specialize in law, business, organizational leadership, health management, journalism, interactive communications, public relations, information technology, education and health science programs for physician assistant, pathologist's assistant, medical laboratory sciences, molecular and cell biology, radiologist assistant and a doctorate in nursing practice. Several programs are offered online.

ACADEMIC PROGRAMS

The School of Business and Engineering, which is AACSB accredited, offers majors in: accounting, advertising, biomedical marketing, computer information systems, economics, entrepreneurship, finance, international business, management, marketing and engineering. The Lender School of Business Center has case method classrooms, a high-tech Financial Technology Center 'trading room' and specially designed team study rooms for project work.

The School of Health Science majors include: athletic training/sports medicine, biomedical science, diagnostic imaging, health and science studies, microbiology/molecular biology, occupational therapy (a 5 ½ -year freshmen entry-level BS/MOT Master's program), physician assistant (6-year freshmen entry-level BS/MHS Master's program), physical therapy (a 6- or 7-year freshmen entry-level BS/DPT doctorate). The North Haven facility has state-of-the-art labs including a diagnostic imaging suite, orthopedics lab, a model adaptive apartment, clinical skills labs, intensive care unit, pediatric/neonatal lab, clinical simulation labs and a biomechanics lab. The nursing major is offered through the School of Nursing.

The College of Arts and Sciences majors include: behavioral neuroscience, biology, biochemistry, chemistry, English, computer science, criminal justice, game design and development, gerontology, history, interactive digital design, legal studies, mathematics, philosophy, political science, psychology, social services, sociology, Spanish literature and language, and theater. Independent majors are also offered.

In the School of Communications, majors include: film, video and interactive media, communications/media studies, journalism, and public relations. The Ed McMahon Center for Communications provides a cutting-edge facility with a fully-digital high-definition production studio, a news technology center, audio production studio, editing suites and more.

For those interested in teaching, completion of an undergraduate liberal arts or natural sciences major, combined with junior and senior year courses in the School of Education, ending with a fifth year full-time graduate education program, culminates in the Master of Arts in Teaching degree.

A Pre-Medical Studies program is designed to provide the undergraduate student interested in a career as a health professional the appropriate background necessary to meet the entrance requirements of a variety of different medical schools. The new Frank H. Netter MD School of Medicine will welcome its first class in Fall 2013.

TECHNOLOGY, OPPORTUNITIES AND LIBRARY RESOURCES

Quinnipiac is ranked among the top masters-level universities in the Northeastern region, and this is reflected in its facilities, services and programs. All incoming students must bring or purchase a laptop computer for use in the classroom and in the residence halls. Service is provided through the 'technology center'. The campus is 100% wireless.

Academic life focuses on the Bernhard Library, open 24 x 7 during the fall and spring semesters. Automated library systems and over 100 personal computer workstations and 600 data ports are located throughout the library, along with individual study carrels and team study rooms.

Students seeking to improve their grades use the Learning Center for free tutoring help as well as sessions to improve study techniques, writing skills and research methods. Since 2000, Quinnipiac has adopted a writing-across-the-curriculum approach to teaching writing throughout the University. All undergraduate majors seek to promote good critical thinking and communication skills. We strive to provide our graduates the learning outcomes they need through a coherent, purposeful integration of the full student experience comprised of three intensive University seminars, the University core curriculum, deep engagement in the content and construction of a major and active participation in co-curricular experience.

The Honors Program fosters the needs and interests of our most academically talented and committed students. Service Learning courses integrate meaningful community service with instruction and refection to enrich the learning experience, teach civic responsibility and strengthen communities.

Tuition, Room, Board and Fees

Tuition and Fees for 2012-13 are $39,330. with $14,250. for room and board.

FINANCIAL AID

The Quinnipiac University Office of Financial Aid works with all applicants to assure that they receive the maximum state and federal aid for which they are eligible. Families need to file the FAFSA and the CSS Profile. The University also offers merit-based scholarships to incoming freshmen in the fall semester (admission application deadline February 1st) for which no financial need is required. There is no additional application necessary for scholarship consideration and students are notified by the admissions office. Please visit www.quinnipiac.edu/finaid for more information. School FAFSA code: 001402; CSS code: 3712.

Student Organizations and Activities

Quinnipiac University has more than 100 student clubs and organizations: including student government, newspaper, yearbook, radio station, service organizations, community activities, religious fellowships (Hillel, Christian Fellowship, Muslim Student Society, Branches), cultural awareness (Black Student Union, Latino Cultural Society, Asian and Pacific Islander Association), dance and drama productions, and Greek life, along with numerous recreation activities, providing a balanced college experience. An active Intramural program has league competition in more than 20 sports.

Quinnipiac Bobcats: www.quinnipiacbobcats.com The NCAA Division I athletic program sports include Men: basketball, baseball, cross country, lacrosse, ice hockey, tennis, and soccer. Women: Acrobatics & Tumbling, basketball, softball, cross country and track (indoor and outdoor), field hockey, golf, ice hockey, lacrosse, rugby, soccer, tennis and volleyball. Quinnipiac competes in the Northeast Conference and the ECAC in Men's and Women's Ice Hockey.

The athletic facilities include a multi-purpose gymnasium, locker rooms, training rooms, steam room, and a 24,000-square-foot, fully-equipped recreation and fitness center, with a suspended indoor track, outdoor lighted tennis, plus the TD Bank Sports Center with twin 3500 seat arenas for ice hockey and basketball.

ADMISSIONS PROCESS

High school students should begin applying for admissions early in their senior year. Visit www.quinnipiac.edu/apply for application information. Quinnipiac is a member of the Common Application. A completed application consists of the application form, official high school transcript, SAT I test scores (QU SAT code - 3712) or ACT scores (QU ACT code - 0582) senior year, first-quarter grades, essay, and one letter of recommendation.

Quinnipiac reviews applications on a "rolling admissions" basis but also offers an "Early Decision" option, which is binding, for freshmen applicants in all programs. Early Decision students must file their application by Oct. 15, followed by their application supportive materials, test scores and letter of recommendation, and submit first quarter grades when they are available. Those admitted Early decision will receive their financial aid award based on the information submitted on the CSS Profile form. Admitted students have until May 1 (Feb. 1 for those students admitted under 'Early Decision') to confirm their enrollment. The admissions office begins reviewing applications as soon as they are complete, and begins notifying students of their decisions in early January. Students applying for the physical therapy, nursing and physician assistant programs should apply by November 1st. We recommend February 1st as the deadline for all other applicants. In general, Quinnipiac admits between 55-60% of their applicants.

Transfer students who have or will receive an associate's degree prior to entrance do not need to provide high school transcripts and SAT results. We must receive transcripts of all courses taken at other colleges. Transfer students interested in the physician assistant or physical therapy programs may apply to the graduate program once they complete their bachelor's degree.

To schedule an interview, tour, group information session or register for an open house, go to http://www.quinnipiac.edu/visit . For questions, email admissions@quinnipiac.edu or call us at 800-462-1944, or 203-582-8600. Visit the website at: http://www.quinnipiac.edu.

RAMAPO COLLEGE OF NEW JERSEY

AT A GLANCE

Ramapo College of New Jersey is a comprehensive institution of higher education dedicated to the promotion of teaching and learning within a strong liberal arts based curriculum, thus earning the designation "New Jersey's Public Liberal Arts College." Its curricular emphases include the liberal arts and sciences, social sciences, fine and performing arts, and professional programs such as business, nursing, and teacher certification, within a residential and sustainable living and learning environment.

Ramapo College provides academic excellence through its interdisciplinary curriculum, international education, intercultural understanding and experiential learning opportunities. These four pillars, supported by global partnerships established in Europe, Africa, Asia, South America, the Caribbean, and several Native American tribal communities, have become central themes in Ramapo College's excellence in the teaching and learning continuum.

Ramapo College provides students with individual academic attention and social support within a caring, sensitive and intellectually vigorous community. The College provides service and leadership opportunities for students and faculty through a combination of internships, field placements, community service, study abroad, and cooperative education. These opportunities allow students, faculty and staff to encounter the world beyond the campus.

Ramapo College is committed to maintaining strength and opportunity through diversity of age, race, gender, sexual orientation, ethnicity, and economic background among faculty, staff, and students. Ramapo College is a selective institution committed to providing equal access to under-represented populations. Barrier-free, the College maintains a continuing commitment to persons with disabilities.

Ramapo College provides a rich living and learning environment through over one hundred student organizations, intramural sports, and intercollegiate athletics. The College maintains a strong positive and economic impact on the surrounding communities by partnering with area communities, corporations, schools, service organizations, and governmental entities, while sharing its intellectual and cultural resources and its facilities. Ramapo College of New Jersey is committed to providing service and ethical leadership through international understanding and the creation of 21st century partnerships.

LOCATION AND ENVIRONMENT

Set on approximately 300 wooded acres with a stunning mountain backdrop, the Ramapo College campus is one of the most picturesque suburban environments in American higher education. Enhancing these tranquil surroundings is the knowledge that the campus is approximately 30 miles from the nation's cultural Mecca, New York City.

A magnificent turn-of-the-century mansion sits among state-of-the-art academic buildings, residence halls, and other facilities. The campus is centrally located near county and state parks, skiing and recreation areas, as well as activities such as riding, hiking and camping. Major highways bring you right to Ramapo's doorstep.

Once on campus, Ramapo's barrier-free facilities make accessibility to all buildings, classrooms, residence halls, dining and recreation areas easy.

OFF-CAMPUS OPPORTUNITIES

As a progressive college with a vigilant eye to the future, Ramapo combines a comprehensive curriculum with opportunities for working partnerships in business and industry. It is these factors which help graduates develop the solid foundation of knowledge and skills, abilities and values required to be productive members of tomorrow's society.

The experiential learning component, woven through the Ramapo curriculum, gives students the opportunity to put theory into practice in real world settings. This program also has consistently provided a distinct advantage to Ramapo graduate school applicants and job-seekers. The percentage of Ramapo graduates who obtain entrance to graduate and professional schools has been lauded as comparable to the nation's most elite colleges. Many of these graduates point to the experiential aspect of their college preparation as a principal factor in their admission to highly ranked, prestigious graduate programs. Employers such as American Home Products, Becton Dickinson, IBM, MTV, Withum Smith+Brown, Sanyo, Sharp, and Sony, among thousands of others, seek Ramapo graduates because they know a Ramapo degree represents completion of work experience in the field as well as a rigorous academic curriculum.

MAJORS AND DEGREES OFFERED

The College offers the following degrees: Bachelor of Arts, Bachelor of Science, Bachelor of Social Work, Bachelor of Science in Nursing, Bachelor of Science in Clinical Laboratory Science, Bachelor of Science in Biology/Doctor of Physical Therapy, Bachelor of Science in Biology/Master of Science in Physician Assistant (joint degree programs with UMDNJ), Bachelor of Science/Doctor of Chiropractic (joint degree program with New York Chiropractic College); Bachelor of Science/Doctor of Optometry (join degree program with SUNY College of Optometry), Master of Arts in Liberal Studies, Master of Science in Educational Technology, Master of Arts in Sustainability Studies, Master of Arts in Educational Leadership, Masters in Business Administration, and a Master of Science in Nursing (Nursing Education).

ACADEMIC PROGRAMS

At Ramapo, a "liberating" education means students gain the means to acquire the knowledge, skills, abilities, and values to seek both general and expert knowledge and expand their views of humanity in a multicultural setting.

Ramapo's curriculum provides a balance between practical and theoretical knowledge. The curriculum and support programs foster the acquisition of knowledge and skills related to individual programs of study and, ultimately, to future careers.

To strengthen the college background before concentrating on major courses for a degree, students are required to complete an all-college general education program consisting of courses in English, mathematics, the humanities, social sciences, and natural sciences.

.All students are assigned an academic advisor during their first semester, allowing the choice of major to be made by the end of the sophomore year (with the exception of Nursing and Biology). There is ample time to explore several fields of interest before selecting a major.

CAMPUS FACILITIES AND EQUIPMENT

The campus features new and upgraded facilities that enhance all areas of campus life, including a library with electronic research facilities; a student life building with FM radio station, student offices, cafeteria, and entertainment and meeting rooms; housing for over 3,000 students; and modern academic buildings with 24-hour computer labs and a real-time Global Financial Market Trading Laboratory. The Angelica and Russ Berrie Center for Performing and Visual Arts offers Shakespearean and Broadway theatres, fine arts studios, art galleries, photography suite, and new music recording studio. The Bill Bradley Sports and Recreation Center features a 1,500-seat arena, fitness center, 25-meter pool, climbing wall, jogging track, and locker room facilities. Other key campus facilities include the Salameno Spirituality Center, established in 2009; the Marge Roukema Center for International Education and Entrepreneurship, and the Sharp Sustainability Center. Upcoming construction to create the Adler Center for Nursing Excellence will add new, technologically advanced microbiology labs, classrooms, and student lounge and study areas.

TUITION, ROOM, BOARD AND FEES

Undergraduate tuition and tuition related fees are calculated on a flat rate for full-time (12 or more credits) students. Full-time charges are calculated on a flat rate between 12-18 credits. The flat rate amount is based on 16 credits. If a full-time student takes more than 18 credits, the charges are calculated on the flat rate plus the per credit rate. The rates as follows are for the 2010-2011 academic year:

Per Credit Rate/Semester Flat Rate (In-State): $410.75/$6,572.00

Per Credit Rate/Semester Flat Rate (Out-of-State): $675.75/$10,812.00

Per Credit Rate/Semester Flat Rate (Qualified Rockland County College Graduates): $543.75/$8,700.00

FINANCIAL AID

About 40 percent of Ramapo's students receive more than $15 million in aid. This aid includes grants - funds which the students are awarded but don't have to pay back - and loans, which must be repaid. Students also can receive a work-study job to earn money to help pay for school.

APPLYING FOR FINANCIAL AID:

To apply for aid at Ramapo, students should complete the Free Application for Federal Student Aid (FAFSA) and mail it by March 1. No other application forms are required. By complying with this priority deadline, students will be notified by May 1 about their expected aid package. The FAFSA is usually available from any high school after January 1, or you can call Ramapo's Financial Aid Office at (201) 684-7549 for a copy. Applicants should use Ramapo's school code (009344) when filing.

Transfer students must initiate a school code change on the Student Aid Report (SAR) to ensure that their account will be appropriately credited. Students should begin this process at the time of application. Contact Ramapo's Financial Aid Office at (201) 684-7549.

STUDENT ORGANIZATIONS AND ACTIVITIES

Arriving on campus amid a scenic summer landscape, students quickly realize that life at Ramapo includes a warm environment blending a diverse campus community that serves as a catalyst for study, friendship and discovery.

There is a firm belief that learning occurs both inside and outside the classroom. Both commuting and residential students have a wide variety of activities, organizations, and experiences from which to choose.

Participation enables students to become more involved with the inner workings of the campus community. Serving together with administrators, faculty members and staff, students play direct roles in planning and implementing a variety of college activities. Whatever the interest, Ramapo has an outlet to match it.

ADMISSIONS PROCESS

Each year Ramapo College welcomes about 900 freshmen and 700 transfer students, primarily from the Mid-Atlantic and Northeast regions and from many foreign countries. You may apply online at www.ramapo.edu/admissions/apply.html. Ramapo College is a member of the Common Application and also has its own web based application.

Ramapo College practices a holistic review process. Each application is evaluated individually with emphasis placed on academic achievement in high school and standardized test scores. Students who are applying to the Nursing or Biology program must apply by December 15th. The priority deadline for all majors is also December 15th. The supporting documents and credential deadline (date by which Ramapo College must be receipt of your documents, including transcript, test scores, recommendation letters, and EOF questionnaire, if applicable) is January 15th.

Students wishing to apply for all other majors not for priority admission may apply by March 1st. All supporting documents must be received by March 15th. All decisions will be sent by April 1st.

While there is no Early Action or Early Decision option, Ramapo College does offer Immediate Decision Day for students meeting certain criteria. Please visit our website for more information.

SCHOLARSHIPS

Ramapo College of New Jersey offers a variety of merit based scholarships for students who have excelled academically. Scholarship awards include the Academic Achievement Award ($12,000), the Deans Award ($24,000), Provost's Award ($40,000) and Presidential Scholarship ($72,000) and are disbursed over the duration of four years.

Please note all applications received by December 15th are automatically reviewed for our prestigious academic scholarships. As such, all high school seniors are encouraged to apply early.

APPLICATIONS

A completed application for freshmen admission includes: high school transcript, SAT or ACT scores, at least one letter of recommendation, application, essay, and $60 application fee. Transfer students are encouraged to review our website for application information specific to the amount of credits they hold and program of interest.

If you have a General Equivalency Diploma (GED), you must submit an official copy of your test scores. Prospective full-time students with a GED are still required to take the SAT. The Test of English as a Foreign Language (TOEFL) is required of all international students and is recommended for all students who have resided in the United States fewer than four years.

Ramapo College seeks the very best students for its Educational Opportunity Fund (EOF) Program. If you qualify, you will join a community of achievers who are supported by a partnership between the college and EOF that is outstanding not only in financial assistance to cover your college cost, but also in personal and academic counseling, career planning, and leadership training. Your admission to the Ramapo College EOF program depends upon meeting our financial eligibility requirements and academic standards.

Deadlines

December 15th: Biology, Nursing, Lab Sciences, Scholarships°

March 1st: All other programs

If you have any questions, please e-mail us at admissions@ramapo.edu.

REED COLLEGE

AT A GLANCE

Intellectual. Free-thinking. Rigorous. Laid back. Classical. Iconoclastic. Paradoxical. Liberal. College guides grapple to define the Reed College experience, but they all tend to agree on two points: Reed is one of the most distinctive colleges in the nation and it is not for everyone. Reed attracts serious students, and often brings out the best in them. Always engaged, often engrossed, and occasionally engulfed in a demanding, exhilarating educational adventure, "Reedies" thrive on a mix of classical study, critical analysis, and guided inquiry that rewards creativity, independence, and reflection. Classes are small, faculty make themselves accessible, and students adhere to an honor principle both inside and outside the classroom.

Reed recruits nationally, with strong representation from California, the Pacific Northwest, and the eastern corridor. The student body is also composed of 8 percent international students. Reed ranks second among U.S. liberal arts colleges in percentage of graduates going on to earn doctoral degrees and fourth among all institutions of higher education. The breadth, depth, and rigor of the curriculum provide great preparation for nearly any career. Many Reed alumni found or lead companies and organizations, earn medical or law degrees, write books or create works of art, and work to make life on the planet better for all.

LOCATION AND ENVIRONMENT

Talk about the best of both worlds! Located in a quiet residential neighborhood is a 116-acre campus of verdant lawns, winding paths, statuesque trees, a wooded natural wetland preserve, and a spring-fed lake frequented by migratory birds and other wildlife. Reed is a short bicycle or bus ride from the energy and excitement of downtown Portland, which is widely cited as the nation's most livable urban center. Portland boasts a wealth of diverse cultural, entertainment, shopping, and dining opportunities in an environment characterized by a combination of youthful exuberance and Pacific Northwest reserve. The Oregon Coast is an hour to the west and Mt. Hood an hour to the east where Reed has its own ski cabin.

On the campus itself, century-old brick Tudor gothic buildings are interspersed with newer traditionally designed and remodeled facilities. The library, classrooms, and laboratories resonate with the history of decades of inquiry and discovery, supported with modern technology. Extensive facility expansion and renovation financed by a $112 million development campaign has increased the overall square footage of Reed's buildings by almost 30 percent and added seven acres of contiguous property to the northwest corner of the campus. Five new eco-friendly residence halls opened in 2008, making it possible for 75% of Reed students to live on campus. For those who want it, housing on campus is all but guaranteed for all four years, because a healthy percentage of Reed students enjoy living in Portland neighborhoods near campus.

OFF-CAMPUS OPPORTUNITIES

Reed undergraduates may participate in a number of domestic exchange and study abroad opportunities. Howard University in Washington, D.C.; Sarah Lawrence College in New York; and Sea Education Association in Massachusetts. In addition, Reed provides study-abroad opportunities for students in Australia, Argentina, China, Costa Rica, Cuba, Ecuador, Egypt, France, Germany, Greece, Hungary, Ireland, Morocco, Italy, Kenya, Lebanon, Russia, South Africa, Spain, Turks and Caicos, and the United Kingdom Students may also arrange independent study plans in consultation with appropriate faculty members, the director for off-campus studies, and the registrar.

MAJORS AND DEGREES OFFERED

Reed confers the bachelor of arts degree in a wide selection of fields, both in

traditional academic departments and in interdisciplinary combinations; the approval of such special programs, which link two or more disciplines, is reviewed by the student's adviser and the departments concerned.

Reed offers a number of 3-2 (dual degree) programs; these allow undergraduates to earn a three-year bachelor's degree from Reed, then earn a professional degree from a cooperating institution (Cal Tech, Columbia, Duke, RPI, the University of Washington) in two additional years.

ACADEMIC PROGRAMS

The curriculum at Reed is both demanding and wide-ranging. Through required studies, Reed students receive a solid grounding in the liberal arts and sciences.

All freshmen must complete "Hum 110," a survey of Greek, Roman, and other Mediterranean scholars from Homer to Petronius. Distribution requirements set a substantial portion of a student's curriculum for the first two years at Reed. Freshmen and sophomores must complete two courses in each of the four major divisions of the college. No specific courses are required; students are free to pursue their interests within the strictures of the requirements.

Reed juniors must pass a comprehensive exam in their major, to allow faculty members the chance to determine the student's readiness for his or her senior thesis project. The required senior thesis is the capstone experience of a Reed education. Every senior must produce an original independent research project over the course of the final year.

Reed strongly believes that learning should be undertaken for its own sake, not for the sake of letter grades. Accordingly, students do not receive grade reports unless they wish to. A student's transcript does include letter grades for all courses taken, but students can better gauge their progress through professors' written evaluations of their work and one-on-one meetings with faculty. Most prefer this system, which eliminates competition among students and allows them to focus entirely on the content of their academic work.

CAMPUS FACILITIES AND EQUIPMENT

The Reed College campus was established on a tract of land known in 1910 as Crystal Springs Farm. The social center of the college is the Gray Campus Center. It includes a commons building, student union, kitchen, dining room, private meeting rooms, student activities offices, bookstore, and mail services. In a park-like setting near the heart of the city, the rolling lawns and open spaces of Reed's 116-acre campus include some of the largest and finest specimen trees in the Portland area.

At the center of the campus is the canyon, a beautiful wooded upland surrounding a spring-fed lake and emergent marsh. A walking trail around the lake provides numerous opportunities to observe migratory birds and other woodland wildlife. The college recently built a fish passageway that creates a link from the upper Reed Lake area to the Crystal Springs stream below.

For those interested in the arts, the campus houses studio art facilities that recently saw a $2-million expansion, performing arts facilities, twenty instrumental practice rooms, a computer music laboratory, a recording system, and an 800-seat auditorium. Slated to be complete in time for the Fall 2013 semester, Reed's new $28-million Performing Arts Building represents a major step forward in the College's commitment to the important role the arts have played throughout Reed's first 100 years. For the first time in Reed's history, the departments of music, dance, and theatre will be housed in one building that includes rehearsal and performance space, offices, scene and costume studios, collaborative spaces, and a multimedia lab.

Eight new residence halls have been built since 1997. The eco-friendly cluster of Aspen, Bidwell Sequoia, and Sitka opened in August 2008. A new Spanish House also opened in 2008, completed a language house cluster that includes a Chinese House, French House, German House, and Russian House.

TUITION, ROOM, BOARD AND FEES

Tuition for the 2012-2014 academic year is $44,200. A $260 student body fee is added. Room and board is an additional $11,460, bringing the yearly total cost to $55,920.

FINANCIAL AID

Reed provides financial assistance to roughly 50% of its undergraduates. The college maintains a need-based assistance program that allows students of all economic backgrounds to attend the college; it further guarantees that full need will be met for all continuing students who maintain good academic standing and who meet all other requirements of the aid process (such as application deadlines). The college makes every effort to make admission decisions on a need-blind basis but cannot guarantee that it will have the funds to do so. Each year, approximately half of all first-year and transfer students receive aid packages equaling their full demonstrated need. The college budgeted approximately $22 million for grant aid in 2012-2013. For the 2012-2013 academic year, the average financial aid package, including grants, loans, and work opportunities, was approximately $39,885, , which includes grants, loans, and work opportunities. Reed students' average graduating loan debt for all four years is $19,407, well below the national average. The college is the primary source of grant money for its students. Reed also administers federal grants and a number of other awards. Students may take Perkins Loans and other federally subsidized loans; campus employment and work-study programs also figure into many aid packages.

STUDENT ORGANIZATIONS AND ACTIVITIES

Reed shuns exclusive organizations and activities, so the college has no Greek organizations and no NCAA or NAIA athletic teams (more about sports below). All campus organizations are student-created and student-run. Student organizations must lobby the Student Senate for funding annually, after which the Senate oversees a vote in which the entire student body decides what organizations should be funded. Thus, the number and nature of campus organizations at Reed changes every year to meet current student interests. Reed may not compete at the NCAA or NAIA level, but most students participate in sports on an informal basis. Intramural sports and club sports proliferate in basketball, fencing, rugby, sailing, soccer, squash and ultimate Frisbee. A three-semester physical education requirement demonstrates that the school recognizes the importance of physical fitness and the salutary effects of exercise.

ADMISSIONS PROCESS

Reed seeks students who demonstrate a commitment to learning and to the ideals embodied by a rigorous and stimulating liberal arts education. Freshman and transfer applications are welcome. The admission committee attempts to determine which candidates will benefit most from a Reed education as well as who is most likely to succeed at Reed.

The ideal incoming class is diverse in its range of talents, interests, ethnic and socioeconomic backgrounds, and perspectives, yet constituted of students who share a common passion for academic inquiry. The admission committee places most emphasis on an applicant's record of previous academic accomplishment. Successful applicants have usually pursued a rigorous secondary school curriculum that includes honors and advanced courses and typically includes 4 years of English, at least 3 years of a foreign or classical language, 3 to 4 years of mathematics, 3 to 4 years of science, and 3 to 4 years of history or social studies. Because secondary school curricula vary widely in quality and content, Reed sets no fixed requirements in this area.

With rare exceptions, incoming students have obtained a secondary school diploma prior to enrollment. The admissions committee sets no "cutoff points" for high school grades, college grades (for transfer students), or standardized test scores. Reed seeks candidates who demonstrate excellence of character, motivation, intellectual curiosity, individual responsibility, and social consciousness. The admission committee recognizes the importance of creating a diverse community in which individual differences contribute to the vitality of the campus. Reed strongly recommends a personal interview, especially for early decision candidates, but an interview is not required. Early decision applications should arrive at Reed by November 15 (Option 1) or December 20 (Option 2). Early decision at Reed is binding: students who are accepted under early decision are expected to matriculate. The deadline for regular freshman admission applications is January 15. Transfer candidates should apply no later than March 1.

RIPON COLLEGE

AT A GLANCE

Together with the other members of our tightly-knit learning community, at Ripon you'll learn more deeply, live more fully, and achieve more success. You'll be surprised to discover that here you have more opportunities to be involved, to lead, to speak out, to make a difference, to explore new interests than you would at a college 10 times our size. Through collaborative learning, group living, teamwork, and networking, you'll tap into the power of a community where we all work together to ensure your success at Ripon and beyond.

LOCATION AND ENVIRONMENT

All of the best residential liberal arts colleges strive to be true learning communities like Ripon. We succeed better than most because our enrollment of around 1,000 students is perfect for fostering connections inside and outside the classroom. Our students flourish in this environment of mutual respect, where shared values are elevated and diverse ideas are valued. If you are seeking academic challenge and want to benefit from an environment of personal attention and support then you should take a closer look at Ripon.

In classes that average 20 students, your professors are able to know you, your strengths, and your capabilities extraordinarily well. They'll tailor your course work to make sure you're always challenged to perform at the top of your game. Yet they're always ready to provide extra support when you need it. Faculty collaborate with you on research projects, suggest independent study topics, and connect you with internships and other active learning experiences.

OFF-CAMPUS OPPORTUNITIES

U.S. or abroad? Three weeks, one semester, two semesters? We offer you more than 40 different programs to choose from, each one officially sanctioned by and affiliated with Ripon. Although most programs are connected with a major or minor program, all are open to every Ripon student, regardless of major.

U.S. Programs: Chicago Urban Studies Semester; Fisk University-Ripon Exchange Program; Newberry Seminar in the Humanities; Oak Ridge Science Semester; Washington Semester; Woods Hole Marine Biology.

International Programs: Budapest Semester; Central European Studies Program in the Czech Republic; Cost Rica; Cross-Cultural Study Center in Seville, Spain; Florence Program; France and Spain; Bonn, Germany Program; Global Studies Program in Turkey; India Studies; Japan Study; London and Florence Program in the Arts; Madrid Program; Montpellier, France; Paris, France;; Russia Program; Sea Semester at Woods Hole; Swansea Program; Tanzania; Toledo, Spain; University of Wales in Bangor; Sea Education Association (marine biology abroad).

MAJORS AND DEGREES OFFERED

Majors include anthropology, art, art history, biology, business management, chemistry, chemistry/biology, communication, computer science, economics, educational studies, English, environmental studies, exercise science, foreign languages, French, German, global studies, history, Latin American area studies, mathematics, music, philosophy, physics, politics and government, psychobiology, psychology, religion, sociology, Spanish, theater.

Pre-professional programs include dentistry, journalism, law and government, library and information science, medicine, ministry, optometry, physical therapy, veterinary medicine.

Dual-degree programs include engineering, forestry, allied health sciences/medical technology, and social welfare.

Certification programs include education certification, early childhood, elementary, elementary/middle school, secondary, secondary/middle, music K-12, and physical education K-12.

Programs are also available in leadership studies, women's studies, Army ROTC, national security studies, and sports medicine/athletic training.

ACADEMIC PROGRAMS

Ripon's liberal arts curriculum is designed to introduce you to a wide variety of disciplines. About 40 percent of our students complete double or triple majors, while some create special self-designed majors. Excellent communications skills written and oral as well as critical-thinking and problem-solving skills are the hallmark of a Ripon education, no matter what your major. In addition, our leadership studies program and our ethical leadership program provide a strong foundation for leadership skills.

A Ripon education will take you anywhere! You could study psychology and play basketball at Ripon, and then become a five-time Grammy winner like jazz singer Al Jarreau (1962). You could guide the space shuttle into orbit like Jeff Bantle (1980), a chief flight director with NASA, or become an international opera star like Gail Dobish (1976). Perhaps you'll set records in medical science like neonatologist Dr. John Muraskas (1978), who is on record for saving the world's smallest premature baby... Or perhaps you'll end up studying at Oxford University as a Rhodes Scholar like Zach Morris '02, who also found time to play touch football with former President Bill Clinton and spend an evening at Buckingham Palace with the Queen.

CAMPUS FACILITIES AND EQUIPMENT

Located on 250 tree-lined, rolling acres adjacent to downtown Ripon, the campus looks and feels like a college should. Ripon's 25 first-rate buildings are a striking combination of historic (10 campus structures listed on the national register of historic buildings) and modern architecture. Constant improvements, like a new apartment-style residence hall, a multimillion dollar renovation of one of our main classroom buildings, upgrades to the library, student union, the campus bookstore, our dining facilities, and numerous student activity spaces maintain Ripon's ability to meet the needs of today and tomorrow.

Technology services include high-speed Internet and e-mail, telephone, and video communication. Intranet and Internet services are accessible from systems located throughout the college. Our campus wide network provides access from every room, and several wireless "hot-spots" in key areas let you access the world without tying you down.

Our science labs contain a variety of high-tech instruments, including a 300-Mhz FTNMR Spectrometer, spectrophotometers, an X-ray diffraction instrument, chromatographs, a spectrofluorimeter, modern electroanalytical instrumentation, a HeliumCadmium Laser Lab, transmission and scanning electron microscopes, a super-speed refrigerated centrifuge, a Zeiss universal microscope with digitizing tablet and two Nikon diaphot inverted microscopes. Ripon also houses a small planetarium classroom, but since research is not limited to the lab, Ripon's Ceresco Prairie Conservancy provides the ultimate outdoor classroom_a 130-acre area natural prairie ecosystem where students can not only study science but also become involved in service learning through prairie restoration.

The library staff provides friendly, efficient circulation, reference, instruction, and interlibrary loan services that aid in research. The library also houses the college archives, a computer lab, and more than a dozen online databases. Library holdings include 164,000 volumes, 800 current periodicals, and microfilms.

The C.J. Rodman Center for the Arts is home to a theater with a state-of-the-art computerized lighting system, a recital hall with one of only 50 existing Bedient organs, an art gallery, and a sculpture garden.

The J.M. Storzer Center includes an Olympic-size pool, a first-class gymnasium, tennis and racquetball courts, a dance studio, training facilities, and a weight room. Our outdoor playing fields and courts are the best in their class. In addition, a large, modern exercise facility was recently added in the main student residence area.

TUITION, ROOM, BOARD AND FEES

Education is an investment, but you don't want to mortgage your future. Ripon has been consistently recognized as a best value by all of the national ranking organizations. Nearly 100 percent of Ripon students receive some form of merit-based scholarship and/or need-based grants and loans.

Tuition is $31,327, room and board is $8,815, and fees are $275, for a total cost of $40,417.

FINANCIAL AID

We recognize and reward your success in high school with Ripon's institutionally funded scholarships, based not only on academic merit, but also on special achievements in other areas such as the creative arts. Our scholarships range from $1,000 to full tuition. Ripon participates in all federal and state need-based financial aid programs. Our financial aid counselors will work individually with you and your family to investigate every possible financial resource for which you are eligible.

Student Organizations and Activities

The list of student clubs and organizations is ever-changing, reflecting our students' ever-changing interests. A recent addition is FUERZA Alliance, designed to educate students about Latino cultures and to provide services to the Spanish-speaking community of Ripon. Student initiated and sponsored club sports include Rugby and Lacrosse. These competitive teams travel throughout the Midwest.

Every day at Ripon is packed with a host of activities that include: Concerts we have eight vocal and instrumental groups that perform regularly on campus, as well as many individual student and faculty recitals. The Caestecker Fine Arts Series and the Chamber Music at Ripon Series annually bring national performers to campus. The Theatre Department sponsors two major productions annually, plus a series of student-directed one-acts. Our most recent Ripon Film Festival (an annual showcase for independent films from around the country) included the premiere of a feature-length horror film written, directed by, and starring a Ripon student.

Ripon's NCAA Division III Intercollegiate Teams compete in the Midwest Conference:

Men's varsity sports: baseball, basketball, cross-country, cycling, football, golf, soccer, swimming and diving, tennis, and indoor and outdoor track and field.

Women's varsity sports: basketball, cross-country, cycling, dance, golf, soccer, softball, swimming and diving, tennis, indoor and outdoor track and field, volleyball.

ADMISSIONS PROCESS

Ripon enrolls students who will contribute to and benefit from the academic and residential programs we provide. Ripon does not discriminate on the basis of gender, sexual orientation, race, color, age, religion, national and ethnic origin, or disability in the administration of its educational policies, admission practices, scholarship and loan programs, athletic, and other college-administered programs.

The faculty committee on academic standards establishes the criteria for admission. The school considers a variety of factors, including secondary school record, standardized test scores (SAT or ACT), recommendations, a written essay, and extracurricular or community service activities. Ripon's admission process reflects the personal attention students can expect to receive during their college careers, and applicants are encouraged to provide any additional information that they consider helpful.

For more information contact:

Admission Office

Ripon College

300 Seward Street

PO Box 248

Ripon, WI 54971

Telephone: 800-947-4766

E-mail: adminfo@ripon.edu

ROCHESTER INSTITUTE OF TECHNOLOGY

AT A GLANCE

Whatever your passion, you can master it at RIT. RIT is a place where brilliant minds assemble and collaborate, where they pool together their individual talents across disciplines in service of big projects and big ideas. It is a vibrant community teeming with students collaborating with experts and specialists: a hub of innovation and creativity. As one of the nation's largest private universities, RIT has an unmatched array of specialized, career-oriented academic programs that attracts designers, artists, photographers, journalists, and filmmakers on the one hand, and scientists, engineers, computing scientists, social scientists, and entrepreneurs on the other. It is a launching pad for a brilliant career, and a highly unique state of mind. It is a perfect environment in which to pursue your passion. Here, the future is envisioned each day. And remade each day after.

ACADEMICS

RIT is one of the world's leading career-oriented, technological universities. At RIT, some of the world's most talented, ambitious, and creative students find a remarkable array of academic programs; diverse, talented and accessible faculty; sophisticated facilities; an unusual emphasis on experiential learning; and a vibrant, connected community that is home to students from more than 100 countries. RIT's nine colleges offer more than 90 undergraduate programs in areas such as engineering, computing, information technology, engineering technology, business, hospitality, art, design, science, psychology, public policy, game design, photography, film and animation, health sciences, and biomedical sciences. Excelling in teaching and research, RIT's faculty are passionate about their role in the classroom and in their field. RIT's faculty are diverse, innovative and resourceful, and engage students in the process of personal and professional discovery. To complement their specialized field of study, students select from more than 100 minors available at RIT. Students can also complete a master's degree in five years through one of the university's accelerated BS/MS or 4+1 MBA programs. Since 1912, the hallmark of an RIT has been experiential education. RIT was among the first universities in the world to offer cooperative education, and its co-op program is now one of the largest in the world. Last year more than 3,600 co-op students alternated periods of study on campus with paid employment in nearly 2,000 firms across the United States and overseas. Experiential learning also includes internships, study abroad, and undergraduate research. Regardless of background or academic interest, students find that RIT offers a stimulating environment for intellectual and personal growth.

ADMISSIONS

RIT seeks a diverse and multicultural student body. Entering students come from a variety of geographic, social, cultural, economic, and ethnic backgrounds. Admission to RIT is competitive, but the admission process is a personal one. The university is interested in learning about students' interests, abilities, and goals in order to provide the best information and guidance as they select the college that is right for them. Students applying for freshman admission for the fall semester (September) may apply through an Early Decision Plan or Regular Decision Plan. The Early Decision Plan is designed for students who consider RIT their first-choice college and wish to make an early commitment regarding admission. Early Decision requires that candidates file their applications and supporting documents by December 1 in order to receive admission notification by January 15. Freshmen who choose not to apply for Early Decision are considered under our Regular Decision Plan. Regular Decision applicants who have provided all required application materials by February 1 will receive admission notification by March 15. Applications received after February 1 will be reviewed on a space-available basis, with notification letters mailed four to six weeks after the application is complete. Students interested in being considered for merit-based (academic and extracurricular) scholarships or the RIT Honors program must apply by February 1. All applications for transfer admission are reviewed as they are received, and notification letters are mailed four to six weeks after the application is complete. Factors considered in our admission decisions include, but are not limited to, past high school and/or college performance (particularly in required academic subjects), admission test scores, competitiveness of high school or previous college, and academic program selected. Recommendations from those familiar with your academic performance and interviews with admissions counselors are often influential. Most students applying to RIT choose a specific academic program as part of the admission process. This is important because there are a variety of academic programs, and admission requirements may differ from one program to another. For example, a student applying for admission to our computer science program would present a strong academic record with particular strength in mathematics, while a student applying for a fine art or design major would need to show artistic talent through a required portfolio. For incoming freshmen who wish to explore their options before declaring a major, RIT offers the following undeclared options: University Studies (for students wishing to explore programs in two or more colleges); Undeclared Art & Design; Undeclared Business; Computing Exploration; Undeclared Crafts; Engineering Exploration; Undeclared Engineering Technology; Liberal Arts Exploration; and General Science Exploration.

CAMPUS FACILITIES AND EQUIPMENT

The campus is filled with the latest equipment, software, laboratories, and conveniences to give students the tools they need to excel. RIT offers academic facilities that are rarely matched on other university campuses, and students use the latest technology to solve problems creatively. RIT plays leadership role in academic computing and gives students maximum access to research and information resources via two OC3 connections to the Internet, 20,000 network connections, and an eight-million-foot fiber-optic backbone. RIT is one of a select group of universities with access to the Internet 2 research network.

CAMPUS LIFE

Students take their academic pursuits seriously, but they'll be the first to tell you that they are passionate about life outside of the lectures and labs. RIT is alive with energy and excitement—24/7. It won't take long for you to find your niche in this community because there are so many ways to be involved. The backgrounds and interests of RIT students contribute in many ways to the quality of campus life. With students from all 50 states and more than 100 countries, RIT is a living-learning environment rich in diversity in classrooms, residence halls, and everywhere else on campus. A number of campus organizations and student services focus on the unique needs and interests of minority, deaf, and international students at RIT. You'll have plenty of opportunity to interact with a mind-expanding mix of people. More than 7,100 full-time students live on campus in residence halls or apartments, and our self-contained, suburban location creates a safe and secure atmosphere. Clubs and organizations exist to bring students of similar interest together and provide them with opportunities to become effective leaders. These groups enhance the quality of student life by fostering social interaction, leadership development, school spirit and an affinity to RIT. Clubs and Organizations promote activities, diversity, service and learning outside of the classroom. Currently there are approximately 200 active clubs, 10 Major Student Organizations, and 30 Greek Organizations on campus. Last year, clubs and organizations held nearly 1,300 events on campus.

RIT's intercollegiate teams have a history of excellence, recording many impressive seasons and capturing a number of conference and national championships. The men's and women's hockey teams are Division I. The remainder of the intercollegiate teams competes at Division III. RIT teams are members of the National Collegiate Athletic Association (NCAA), the Eastern College Athletic Conference (ECAC), the Atlantic Hockey Association, the College Hockey America, the Liberty League, and the New York State Women's Collegiate Athletic Association.

COLLEGE BASICS

As one of the world's leading career-oriented, technological universities, RIT's goal is to prepare students for 21st century career success.

LOCATION AND ENVIRONMENT

RIT's 1,300-acre campus is located in the suburbs, about six miles from downtown Rochester, NY. More than 6,800 diverse, creative, ambitious students live on campus in residence halls or apartments, and the self-contained, suburban location gives the campus a safe, residential atmosphere. RIT also maintains campuses in Croatia, Dubai, and Kosovo.

MAJORS AND DEGREES

Few universities provide RIT's variety of career-oriented programs. RIT's nine colleges offer more than 90 undergraduate programs in areas such as engineering, computing, information technology, engineering technology, business, hospitality, art, design, science, psychology, public policy, game design, photography, film and animation, health sciences, and biomedical sciences.

OFF-CAMPUS OPPORTUNITIES

Rochester provides a perfect setting--it's large enough to provide the dining, shopping, and night life opportunities found in a bigger city, yet small and friendly enough to be inviting and accessible. In fact, Rochester was ranked 10th best among large cities in the Northeast in a recent Money magazine Best Places to Live in America survey. The greater Rochester area is home to more than 1 million people, making it the third largest metropolitan area in New York State. Rochester's reputation as an active and inventive community is supported by extensive cultural and intellectual opportunities.

TUITION AND FEES

For 2012-13, tuition and fees cost $32,784; room and board averaged $10,800; and books, transportation, and other expenses averaged $2,025.

FINANCIAL AID

RIT's Office of Financial Aid and Scholarships assists students and their families in identifying sources of financial aid to help meet the cost of a quality education. Currently, more than 12,000 RIT undergraduate and graduate students receive over $291 million dollars in financial assistance from federal, state, and institutional resources, in the form of scholarships, grants, loans, and part-time employment.

SAINT ANSELM COLLEGE

AT A GLANCE

Saint Anselm is a Catholic, Benedictine College providing all its students a distinctive liberal arts education that incorporates opportunities for professional and career preparation. It does so in a learning community that encourages the lifelong pursuit of the truth and fosters intellectual, moral and spiritual growth to sustain and enrich its graduates' personal lives, work, and engagement within local, national, and global communities.

Because democracy depends on active participation of citizens, Saint Anselm College is committed to graduating men and women who view themselves as citizens of their communities and of the world.

ACADEMICS

Students at Saint Anselm College are provided with an outstanding liberal arts education. Students normally take 15+ courses directly related to their major; the remainder of the courses needed to graduate consist of liberal arts core curriculum and a variety of electives. Students in the Honors Program will take honors courses in order to earn their Honors Degree.

Saint Anselm College believes that there are certain things one must know to be an educated person in the 21st century. As freshmen and sophomores, all students take part in Saint Anselm's nationally recognized humanities program. This interdisciplinary program known as "Portraits of Human Greatness" focuses on a series of group seminars, readings and lectures that explore various facets of western civilization.

Saint Anselm College is also home to the New Hampshire Institute of Politics and Political Library (NHIOP). The NHIOP is a place where students of all majors interact with world leaders, members of Congress, scholars, journalists, public policy makers, public officials, and innovators of all types. All Saint Anselm College students will have courses held at the NHIOP. Saint Anselm College is a leader in Civic Engagement and encourages all students to explore what it means to be a citizen in a democratic society.

Saint Anselm takes part in the College Board's Advanced Placement program. Students who earn a score of 3 or greater on most AP examinations may gain credit and advanced placement in the related course of study. Students who have taken examinations through the College-Level Examination Program and International Baccalaureate may be awarded credit and advanced placement if they earn satisfactory scores.

ADMISSIONS

In reviewing applicants to the freshman class, the admission committee considers each prospective student individually and carefully. The committee assesses each applicant's secondary school performance, SAT I or ACT scores (optional for non-nursing majors, nursing major must submit scores), recommendation letters, and the written essay included in the application for admission. Of highest priority is the applicant's secondary school transcript, with a specific focus on both the rigor of course study and the marks received. Saint Anselm invites transfer and international students to apply.

Saint Anselm College has the following admission deadlines:

Early Action, November 15

Nursing Majors, November 15

Regular Decision, February 1

It is highly suggested that all students visit the Saint Anselm College campus for a tour, information session and/or interview.

For more information, students should contact:

OFFICE OF ADMISSION

Saint Anselm College

100 Saint Anselm Drive

Manchester, NH 03102-1310

Telephone: 603-641-7500 or 888-426-7356 (toll-free)

Fax: 603-641-7550

Email: admission@anselm.edu

World Wide Web: www.anselm.edu

MAJORS AND DEGREES OFFERED

At Saint Anselm College, students may pursue the Bachelor of Arts degree in the following academic programs and majors: in accounting, American studies, biochemistry, biology, business, chemistry, classics, classical archaeology, communication, computer science, computer science with business, computer science with mathematics, criminal justice, economics, education (secondary and elementary) English, environmental science, environmental politics and sustainability, financial economics, fine arts, forensic science, French, german studies, history, international business, international relations, liberal studies in the great books, mathematics, mathematics with economics, natural science, peace & justice studies, philosophy, physics, politics, psychology, sociology, Spanish, and theology. A program that leads to the Bachelor of Science in Nursing (BSN) degree is also offered at the College.

Saint Anselm students may pursue pre-professional programs in dentistry, law, medicine, and theology.

A 3-2 engineering program is offered in partnership with the University of Notre Dame, University of Massachusetts-Lowell, Catholic University of America, and Manhattan College.

CAMPUS FACILITIES AND EQUIPMENT

Saint Anselm College has over 60 different campus facilities. The John Maurus Carr Activities Center is a versatile recreational area that includes a new three story fitness center as well as racquetball courts. The Davison Hall dining area, open all day long, provides a spacious and pleasant atmosphere in which students enjoy spending time. Additional facilities include the Academic Resource Center, the Cushing Student Center (where students will find career and academic counseling services), health services, the Multicultural Center, the Meelia Center for Community Service, Stoutenburgh Gymnasium (where varsity games are played), Sullivan Ice Arena, and The New Hampshire Institute of Politics -home of the 1st in the nation Presidential Primary and the largest television studio north of Boston.

Saint Anselm residential housing accommodates more than 1,800 students in various living arrangements, from traditional residence halls to suites, townhouses, and apartments. More than 90 percent of students choose to live on campus and enjoy a balance of academic study, rest and relaxation, and social life.

Housing is guaranteed for all four years to students who enter as freshmen. Each residence hall has a staff of student resident assistants (RAs) and a residence director (RD) who assist students and are responsible for maintaining the College's residence hall regulations.

CAMPUS LIFE

Student government helps to create an atmosphere of camaraderie and unity on campus. Saint Anselm's student government consists of three branches: Campus Activities Board, the Class Councils, and the Student Senate. The student government's primary goal is to ensure that all students have as many educational opportunities open to them as possible. Student government coordinates academic, cultural, and social, functions, all of which are essential to a broad liberal arts education.

There are over 60 organizations catering to a wide variety of interests. Among these are the Abbey Players (theater group), choral groups, the debate group, an economics club, a jazz band, a local Knights of Columbus chapter, a music society, an outing club, a pre-law society, a pre-med society, and the Meelia Center for Community Engagement.

Saint Anselm offers men's intercollegiate sports in baseball, basketball, cross-country, football, golf, ice hockey, lacrosse, skiing, soccer, and tennis and offers women's sports in basketball, cross-country, field hockey, ice hockey, lacrosse, skiing, soccer, softball, tennis, and volleyball. Saint Anselm is an NCAA Division II school and does award athletic scholarships. Intramural sports at the College include basketball, ice hockey, indoor and outdoor soccer, racquetball, softball, tennis, and volleyball. There are men's and women's club sports in Alpine, cycling, ice hockey, rugby, field hockey, lacrosse, softball, ski and snowboard, swimming, synchronized skating and track.

COLLEGE BASICS

Saint Anselm College encourages you not only to challenge yourself academically, but also to lead a life that is both creative and generous. Saint Anselm student are active both in and out of the classroom.

LOCATION AND ENVIRONMENT

Nestled in its breathtaking New Hampshire surroundings, the Saint Anselm campus melds traditional and contemporary architecture to create a beautiful academic environment. Students from 3 countries and 31 states attend the College. Roughly 90 percent of Saint Anselm's students enjoy on-campus housing in apartments, dormitories, suites, and townhouses.

Situated on the outer edge of Manchester, New Hampshire's largest city, Saint Anselm College provides the advantages of a chiefly residential neighborhood in a suburban locale. Manchester has a great deal to offer, including a variety of movie theaters, restaurants, and shopping malls. Furthermore, public transportation runs hourly between Manchester and the campus. Southern New Hampshire provides a perfect atmosphere for students desiring a dynamic college lifestyle. The exciting city of Boston, the majestic mountains, and Hampton Beach on the Atlantic Ocean are all within an hour's drive from campus.

OFF-CAMPUS OPPORTUNITIES

All departments throughout Saint Anselm College offer internship positions to students who wish to apply their classroom knowledge to a real-life work experience. Students normally acquire internship positions as juniors or seniors. Internships are offered in Boston, in and around Manchester, New York City, or in Washington, DC.

Saint Anselm encourages students to consider spending a year, semester, or summer studying in another country (usually during the junior year). Studying abroad presents an invaluable opportunity to gain a more informed perspective on your world, your country, and yourself.

In recent years, students have studied marine biology on Australia's Great Barrier Reef, art history in the museums of Florence, finance in London, language in Spain and France, the culture of peace in Peru and political history in Ireland.

Students' experiences studying abroad often remain the most memorable times of their college careers. In addition to the obvious cultural benefits gained from living abroad, students often make intellectual and personal gains as well. Experience studying abroad is a desirable qualification on your resume

In lieu of participating in study abroad during the academic year, students can sign up for faculty-led programs which include travel to such destinations as France, Greece, Italy, Mexico, Vietnam, China, Berlize and Spain during the summer.

TUITION AND FEES

The 2013-2014 school year tuition is $34,084 and room and board costs are $12,690.

FINANCIAL AID

Saint Anselm provides students with financial aid opportunities through both private and federal aid programs. The College provides financial aid to offset the reasonable monetary investment that the student and family are expected to contribute. 96 percent of the College's undergraduates receive some degree of financial aid. Saint Anselm's financial aid opportunities include grants, loans, scholarships, and employment positions. Merit awards are awarded to outstanding students. Two forms are required in applying for aid: the student must submit the CSS/Financial Aid PROFILE and the Free Application for Federal Student Aid (FAFSA) by March 15.

SAINT FRANCIS UNIVERSITY (PA)

AT A GLANCE

Saint Francis is a private, Catholic, co-ed liberal arts university. Established in 1847, the University is among America's first Franciscan institutions and is the nation's 12th-oldest Catholic institution of higher education. Saint Francis operates under the conventions of the Franciscan Friars of the Third Order Regular. The University is dedicated to providing each student with top-rated academics, a vibrant student life, opportunities for leadership, and unflagging attention from a distinguished faculty. For the past century and a half, Saint Francis University's commitment to academics and student life has embodied two important values: high-quality education and respecting students as individuals.

LOCATION AND ENVIRONMENT

Saint Francis University is located on a 600-acre mountaintop campus in the town of Loretto, Pennsylvania. Just 80 miles east of Pittsburgh and 60 miles east of State College, the campus has its own lake, nature trails and championship golf course. Near to campus are three state parks, four biking/ walking trails and four ski resorts.

OFF-CAMPUS OPPORTUNITIES

Saint Francis University's Center for International Education and Outreach offers a truly unique semester abroad program in the beautiful village of Ambialet, in southern France. Students can experience the adventure, beauty, and history of Europe in the halls of a centuries-old Franciscan monastery. The program includes weekly classroom visits to the University of Albi and also multiple educational and personal excursions to Paris, Barcelona and other European cities.

MAJORS AND DEGREES OFFERED

Integrating distinct learning communities within the University, Saint Francis University has four schools: School of Business; School of Health Science; School of Arts & Letters; and School of Sciences.

Highlighted Majors

Accounting, Arts & Letters, Communications, Criminal Justice, Education, Environmental Engineering, History, Management, Political Science, Pre-Professional Studies, Public Health, Sociology, Aquarium & Zoo Science.

Graduate Programs

Business Administration, Education, Educational Leadership, Human Resource Management, Medical Science, Occupational Therapy, Physician Assistant Science, and Physical Therapy, as well as various online programs. Post-Bachelorette certificates are also available in Paralegal Studies and Education.

ACADEMIC PROGRAMS

Bachelor degrees are typically earned within eight semesters. To graduate, each student is required to complete a course of study that meets with approval from the University Provost. The University operates on a two-semester academic calendar, with three sessions in the summer.

CAMPUS FACILITIES AND EQUIPMENT

Saint Francis offers a totally wireless campus, computer labs, a Macintosh-based computer lab, and 27 Smart Classrooms. The cost of attendance at Saint Francis includes a laptop computer as well as technical support. At the University's Library, students can take advantage of approximately 176,000 volumes, 600 periodicals, a large collection of microfilm, and services for interlibrary loan. Other facilities that complement student learning include well-equipped science labs, on-campus radio and television stations, an auditorium with a 600-person capacity, and the Southern Alleghenies Museum of Art.

At the heart of campus is the DiSepio Institute for Rural Health and Wellness. This 30,000-square-foot education and research center features the DiSepio Center for Rehabilitation, Student Health Services, Fitness Center, Spiritual Wellness Center, Human Performance Laboratory, and Ernest J. Scharpf Family Conference Center. The new Saint Francis University Science Center is scheduled to open in August 2013. The 70,000 square foot building will give our students and faculty the opportunity to study science in a state-of-the-art facility Learn more at francis. edu/science-center

Tuition, Room, Board and Fees

In 2013-2014, costs includes

Tuition $28,942

Technology Fee $1,050

Room/Board $10,346

FINANCIAL AID

Saint Francis University awards financial aid to greater than 90 percent of its student body. Aside from offering aid through federal and state programs, the University's ample grant and scholarship programs provide awards ranging from $1,000 to $16,000 scholarships to students who have demonstrated their academic potential through strong high-school grade point averages and impressive ACT or SAT I (math and critical reading) scores. As a member of the NCAA Division I, scholarships may be granted to athletes in all 22 sports. Students can also receive scholarship money in all sports, Hugh O'Brian Youth Leadership (HOBY), Pep Band, Marching Band, and Cheerleading.

Student Organizations and Activities

The University provides students many opportunities to exercise their interests and talents. For instance, 50-plus on-campus clubs and organizations are active. These range from departmental clubs to volunteer organizations, and include social and service sororities and social, service, and business fraternities. Student-run activities on campus include the Bell Tower yearbook, KSFU-FM radio, New Theatre drama group, the SFU singers, and the Troubadour newspaper. Each year, the Student Activities Organization brings a lively docket of comedians, concerts, films, and lectures to campus. The University is a member of NCAA Division I athletics and maintains a comprehensive program that consists of men's and women's teams. Men may compete in basketball, cross-country, football, golf, soccer, tennis, track (indoor and outdoor), and volleyball. Women may compete in basketball, bowling, cross-country, field hockey, golf, lacrosse, soccer, softball, swimming, tennis, track (indoor and outdoor), and volleyball. Students may also participate in cheerleading, pep band, and marching band.

ADMISSIONS PROCESS

Admission to Saint Francis University is granted on rolling basis. All applicants must submit a completed admissions application including essay, an official high-school transcript, ACT or SAT I (critical reading and math) scores, and a minimum of one recommendation letter. A December 1 deadline applies to the physician assistant program and a January 15 deadline applies to the physical therapy and occupational therapy programs. To learn more about Saint Francis University, students and families are encouraged to call the Office of Admissions at

1-866-DIAL-SFU (toll free).

SAINT LOUIS UNIVERSITY

AT A GLANCE

Saint Louis University is a Catholic, Jesuit university ranked among the top research institutions in the nation. SLU fosters the intellectual and character development of over 14,000 students on campuses in St. Louis and Madrid, Spain. Founded in 1818, it's the oldest university west of the Mississippi River and the second-oldest Jesuit university in the United States. Through teaching, research, health care and community service, Saint Louis University has provided one-of-a-kind education, leadership and service for 194 years.

With nearly 100 undergraduate majors and more than 70 graduate and professional programs, students from all 50 states and nearly 69 countries travel to SLU to pursue a top notch education in a broad range of studies. Students take advantage of SLU's highly ranked programs in business, law and engineering, special opportunities such as direct-entry nursing and health sciences programs, early admission to the University's medical and law schools and an extensive list of study-abroad programs.

SLU education extends far beyond the classroom.

SLU offers students something rare in higher education: the opportunity to study at a place where academic achievement and scientific advancement unite with a commitment to community and Jesuit values. Here, 99 percent of faculty members hold a Ph.D. or the highest degree in their field. SLU students get to do more than just sit in class; they collaborate with premier scholars and researchers and conduct research that will transform their disciplines and the lives of others.

Around the world, SLU students are putting their education into practice. Six months after graduation, 93 percent of our graduates are either working or in graduate or professional school. SLU alumni have written books and produced Broadway musicals, become mayors of major cities, presidents of countries and even worked with Mother Theresa and the Haitian Ambassador to America, Raymond Joseph. Billiken alumni are also highly successful doctors, lawyers, physical therapists, engineers and social workers.

Learn more about SLU at slu.edu and beabilliken.com.

LOCATION AND ENVIRONMENT

At Saint Louis University, students are in the center of everything. SLU's campus in Midtown St. Louis stretches across more than 230 acres of flowers, fountains and lush greenery. Students and visitors alike appreciate the "green oasis" in the middle of a bustling city. Get a taste of campus and schedule your own visit.

The St. Louis metro region boasts nearly 3 million people, with approximately 320,000 residents in the city itself. The city's small-town feel coupled with the amenities of a large city has helped St. Louis garner its ranking as one of the best cities for young professionals. The city is home to the famous Gateway Arch, a number of Fortune 500 and Fortune 1000 companies and a variety of cultural, historical and sporting attractions.

Students don't have to travel far from SLU to experience these great St. Louis attractions. Just steps away from SLU's urban campus is one of the city's esteemed arts districts, rich with theatre and music. Students can also hop onto a light rail train or bus and sample international delicacies in one of the many delicious restaurants before hitting St. Louis' can't-miss concert scenes. With three professional sports teams and a number of independent sports teams, St. Louis is always high on any sports fan's list of must-see cities.

But that's not all SLU has to offer. The University expanded internationally in 1969 by establishing a campus in Madrid, Spain. The Madrid campus has been recognized by Spain's higher education authority as an official foreign university, the first United States institution ever so recognized. Each semester, more than 600 students arrive at the Madrid campus for a study-abroad experience. Attracted by the quality educational reputation of the St. Louis and Madrid campuses, more than 250 universities in the United States send study-abroad students to SLU's Madrid campus.

OFF-CAMPUS OPPORTUNITIES

Midtown St. Louis offers access to affordable living as well as the excitement of the Grand Center arts district, the cultural heart of St. Louis. The booming performing arts neighborhood features opportunities for art, theatre, dance and music just steps away from SLU's campus. Don't miss the historic Fox Theatre with some of the most memorable concerts and Broadway shows or the famous St. Louis Symphony Orchestra in Powell Symphony Hall.

Just minutes away by car, bus or light rail train, you can play in Forest Park, the 1904 World's Fair site that's larger than even New York City's Central Park and home to the city's world-class art museum, zoo, science center and history museum. Check out the Delmar Loop, one of the "10 Great Streets in America," or head to "The Hill," a nationally noted neighborhood for authentic Italian cuisine, including St. Louis' famous toasted ravioli. Or go downtown to catch a professional baseball, hockey, or football game – St. Louis is noted for being one of the nation's best sports cities. Residents root for the St. Louis Cardinals baseball team, St. Louis Blues hockey team, St. Louis Rams football team and a bevy of independent sports teams. In addition, the Saint Louis University Billikens excite the city with 18 NCAA Division I sports as St. Louis' only Division I school.

ACADEMIC PROGRAMS

Saint Louis University offers nearly 100 undergraduate programs of study and more than 70 graduate and professional programs in the following areas:

Doisy College of Health Sciences

Athletic Training °, Clinical Laboratory Science, Cytotechnology, Health Informatics and Information Management , Health Sciences, Investigative and Medical Sciences, Nuclear Medicine Technology, Nutrition and Dietetics (Culinary Emphasis), Occupational Science and Occupational Therapy °, Physical Therapy °, Radiation Therapy, Still Deciding (Health Sciences), Health Management

School of Nursing

Nursing, School of Public Health, Public Health, Emergency Management , Health Management

College of Arts and Sciences

African American Studies, American Studies, Anthropology, Art History, Biochemistry, Biology, Chemistry, Classical Humanities, Communication, Communication Sciences and Disorders, Computer Science, Criminal Justice, Economics (B.A.), English, Environmental Science, Environmental Studies, French, Geology, Geophysics, German, Greek and Latin Languages and Literature, History, International Studies, Italian Studies, Latin American Studies, Mathematics, Meteorology, Music, Philosophy, Physics (B.A.), Political Science, Psychology, Russian, Sociology, Spanish, Still Deciding, Studio Art, Theater, Theological Studies, Women's Studies

John Cook School of Business

Business Administration (Areas of Emphasis:: Accounting, Economics (B.S.), Entrepreneurship, Finance, Information Technology Management, International Business, Leadership and Change Management, Marketing, Sports Business), Still Deciding (Business)

Parks College of Engineering, Aviation and Technology

Aerospace Engineering, Aviation Management, Biomedical Engineering, Civil Engineering, Computer Engineering, Electrical Engineering, Engineering Physics, Flight Science ^ , Interdisciplinary Engineering , Mechanical Engineering, Still Deciding (Engineering), Physics

College of Education and Public Service

Early Childhood Education , Early Childhood Special Education, Elementary Education, Middle School Education, Secondary Education, Special Education for Mild/Moderate Disabilities, Education (without certification)   ,UrbanAffairs, Still Deciding

School of Social Work

Social Work , Still Deciding

College of Philosophy and Letters

Philosophy

School for Professional Studies

Criminal Justice and Security Management, Education , General Studies, Organizational Studies, Aviation Management, Computer Science Technology, Health Information Management, Nursing, Organizational Leadership and Technology, Social Work, Contract Degree Option

School of Law

School of Medicine

Still Deciding"

KEY

° A five-year, direct-entry master's degree program.

^ Students are strongly encouraged to apply by December 1 for the Flight Science program.

° Physical Therapy is a direct-entry doctoral program. Students must apply by December 1 for consideration.

" For students who are "Still Deciding" but have not yet narrowed their interests to a particular college or school at the University.

Students who are "Still Deciding" but have narrowed their interests to either the College of Arts and Sciences, Doisy College of Health Sciences, John Cook School of Business, College of Education and Public Service or Parks College of Engineering, Aviation and Technology should choose the "Still Deciding" program that corresponds with the appropriate college or school.

For the most up-to-date selection of majors and programs offered, visit admissions. slu.edu.

CAMPUS FACILITIES AND EQUIPMENT

Under the leadership of University President Lawrence Biondi, S.J., Saint Louis University continues to fuel the ongoing renaissance of Midtown St. Louis. Saint Louis University improvements and expansions have totaled approximately $850 million since 1987. The University now stretches across more than 230 acres of fountains and lush greenery, appealing to visitors who often say it's the "nicest city campus in the country."

In the past few years, Saint Louis University unveiled the two most significant building projects in its history. The new $82 million Edward A. Doisy Research Center offers SLU's world-class researchers a world-class facility. The $81 million Chaifetz Arena is the new home for Billiken men's and women's basketball, volleyball and hosts concerts, family shows, sporting events, trade shows and other events. The 10,600-seat arena is complete with an athletics practice facility, offices and support facilities for all Division I sports and the athletic department. SLU's next major project will be the relocation of the Law School to a newly renovated facility in downtown St. Louis. The state-of-the art facility plans to open in the Summer of 2013.

Recent campus additions also include a new 40,000-foot expansion to its Simon Recreation Center and a renovated Busch Student Center. The SLU Laclede Park Recreational Complex includes three lakes, walking paths, a picnic area, waterfall, softball field and recreation fields. The campus is also home to the historic Cupples House, a fully restored mansion built in 1890, as well as several unique art galleries and St. Francis Xavier College Church.

Tuition, Room, Board and Fees

Annual tuition for full-time undergraduate students is $34,740. Room and board amounts to approximately $9,612 per student (depending on specific residence hall and board plan). Fees average $506 per year.

FINANCIAL AID

Saint Louis University remains committed to keeping its one-of-a-kind education affordable and understands the sacrifices students and families make for quality education. SLU is dedicated to serving others, in part, by providing financial access to a remarkable education.

For the fiscal year 2011, 97 percent of SLU's first-time freshmen received some sort of scholarship or financial assistance, as did 86.5 percent of all SLU students. The financial aid package for first-time freshman entering in 2010-11 averaged $27,805.

Scholarships are awarded based on academic merit, talents, service, leadership and financial need. In addition to SLU financial aid programs, the state of Missouri and the federal government also provide assistance.

Contact SLU's office of student financial services at (314) 977-2350, (800)SLU-FOR-U or finaid@slu.edu.

Student Organizations and Activities

Students support more than 140 clubs, honor societies and service organizations; 16 NCAA Division I teams; intramural sports; and community service efforts that engage the SLU community in more than 1 million volunteer hours in a typical year.

Talent and commitment matter at SLU, and high levels of energy and dedication exist in everything our students pursue: academic societies, athletics, performing arts and media groups, student government, cultural and political organizations and fraternities and sororities. Students come out in force to support Billiken athletics, and the Simon Recreation Center is popular with both serious and more casual athletes. Co-curricular life extends throughout the campus with numerous lectures, workshops, films, festivals, concerts and plays.

ADMISSIONS PROCESS

For information about the admission process at Saint Louis University or to schedule a campus visit, call the office of admission at (800) SLU-FOR-U, e-mail admission@ slu.edu, or check out visit.slu.edu.

SAINT MICHAEL'S COLLEGE

AT A GLANCE

At Saint Michael's, we believe that a college education should prepare students not only for a meaningful career, but for a meaningful life.

That's why our students start by building a strong liberal studies foundation, then dive deep into their majors. By the time they graduate, they've developed essential skills and knowledge that will help them be successful in any field. And in the meantime, they've also been engaged in service (through our popular MOVE program), in the great outdoors (with our ground-breaking Wilderness Program and Smuggs' Ski Pass), and with the close campus community in meaningful ways that educate the body, mind and spirit.

And happiness matters. At Saint Michael's, you'll find bright, engaged, friendly, happy students and faculty. Our formula for happiness is our close campus community, our perspective-changing exploration of the liberal arts, our legacy of faith and service, and our stunning Vermont location.

All this happiness and engagement underscores Saint Michael's successes: We are among only 280 colleges and universities nationwide to host a prestigious Phi Beta Kappa chapter on campus. Our recent graduates are Rhodes Scholars, Pickering Fellows, medical students, law students, dental students, medical researchers, pharmacists, new media specialists, sports writers, non-profit directors and more. Alumni include a United States Senator, one of the founders of MTV, noted authors, scientists, investment bankers, social workers, teachers, professors and scholars. No matter what career paths they choose, our alumni take with them a solid liberal arts foundation, a strong sense of self and a desire to give back to their communities.

Students at Saint Michael's are seriously involved with life on campus, taking on leadership roles, rallying support for worthy causes and generally making things happen. Because everyone lives on campus (student housing is guaranteed for all four years), there's an incredible sense of community, and you'll always find someone ready for whatever adventures you have in mind, from taking on a research project to rock climbing. Over one third of St. Mike's students study abroad for a semester, an academic year or a summer.

LOCATION AND ENVIRONMENT

Saint Michael's beautiful, safe 440-acre campus is just three miles from Burlington, which is Vermont's largest city. Burlington is a vibrant college town that is home to 14,000 students who attend five local colleges and universities. Downtown Burlington is a thriving city center of businesses that offer great opportunities for hands-on learning through internships. There are tons of shops, restaurants, and cafés, the Church Street Marketplace and a lively local music scene as well as tons of places to ski, skate, kayak and bike. Our Smuggs' pass lets students to take advantage of some of the best skiing in the East, and our renowned Wilderness Program offers dozens of outdoor adventure opportunities. Our Cultural Pass gives students unlimited access to fine arts performances at Burlington's famous Flynn Theater.

The Burlington International Airport, Amtrak station and the Greyhound bus station are all only a 10-minute drive from the campus.

MAJORS AND DEGREES OFFERED

Saint Michael's College offers bachelor's degrees with a liberal arts foundation. We offer 34 majors in the following areas: accounting, American studies, art, art education, biochemistry, biology, business administration, chemistry, classics, computer science, economics, elementary education, engineering (3+2), English, environmental studies, French, gender/women's studies, history, information systems, mathematics, media studies, digital arts & journalism, modern languages and literature, music, philosophy, physics, political science, pre-pharmacy, psychology, religious studies, secondary education, sociology and anthropology, Spanish, and theater. In addition, advising programs for pre-medicine, prelaw, pre-dentistry, and pre-veterinary studies are available. Secondary education licensure is also available in several subject areas. 37 minors, including interdisciplinary areas.

Dual degree program are available in engineering through Clarkson University (Potsdam, New York) and the University of Vermont (Burlington, Vermont); pharmacy through Albany College of Pharmacy's Burlington campus; and physical therapy through the University of Vermont. A 4+1 M.B.A. program is offered in conjunction with Clarkson University.

ACADEMIC PROGRAMS

Saint Michael's prepares its students for life after college with a dynamic liberal arts curriculum designed to foster intellectual curiosity and exploration, including a highly competitive honors program and many opportunities for self-directed study. Our curriculum emphasizes a solid understanding of building blocks of a meaningful life as a well-rounded, thoughtful person: humanities, social sciences, religious studies, philosophy, natural sciences, mathematics and fine arts. Our students develop excellent communication skills through writing intensive courses, and foreign language requirements. And our curriculum pays serious attention to questions of ethics and responsible citizenship.

The Saint Michael's academic year is two semesters and a summer session. The College's focus is on undergraduate instruction, and our small classes support this primary emphasis. Saint Michael's has a strong faculty-student research tradition and provides competitive opportunities for research for academic credit and with faculty during the academic year and over the summer.

Nowhere is Saint Michael's mission more evident than in our service-learning opportunities. Service-learning at Saint Michael's is a credit-bearing, educational experience in which students in an academic course participate in a thoughtfully organized service activity that meets identified community needs. Students reflect on the service activities in ways that develop further understanding of course content, a broader appreciation of the discipline and an enhances sense of civic responsibility.

OFF-CAMPUS OPPORTUNITIES

At Saint Michael's, you can gain hands-on experience in an internship related to your career goals and major. Internships are available both locally and in other selected areas around the U.S. and abroad. Sites include scientific research laboratories, brokerage houses, hospitals, schools, newspapers, and accounting firms.

More than a third of our students study abroad for a semester or an academic year. Unique Saint Michael's programs include study-abroad experiences at University of the Americas, Mexico; College of Ripon and York St. John, England; Kansai Gaidai University, Japan; and a Washington, D.C., semester program. In recent years, many students have studied abroad in locations such as Australia, Botswana, China, France, Ghana, Ireland, Italy, Nepal, Samoa, and Spain.

CAMPUS FACILITIES AND EQUIPMENT

Saint Michael's has a Main Campus and a North Campus. Main Campus is home to almost all academic and administrative buildings. The Jeremiah Durick Library holds 277,000 volumes, 110 research databases, access to articles from more than 82,000 online journals, and 74,000 electronic books, maps, videos, and other items. Students have access to more than 490 computers connected to the College's campus-wide information technology network. This network provides access to PC applications, including Microsoft Office Suite, the Internet, e-mail, and the College library. Most campus areas have wireless internet access.

Cheray Science Center has recently renovated facilities for the study of biochemistry, biology, chemistry, environmental science, and physics.

Saint Edmund's Hall, an impressive academic complex, includes media labs, psychology labs, computer facilities, and language labs, in addition to traditional classroom and lecture hall space.

TUITION, ROOM, BOARD, AND FEES

Tuition and residence fees for the 2013-14 academic year are $48,740. The residence fee includes housing and meals and is based on a standard double room and a standard meal plan. Housing options on campus include traditional residence halls, apartment-style housing, theme housing, and suite-style housing. Some science, journalism, language, and art courses require laboratory fees. Book, personal, and travel expenses vary according to course selection and individual needs.

FINANCIAL AID

Approximately 90 percent of admitted students receive financial aid in the form of loans, grants, and work-study dollars. Students must file the FAFSA by February 15 for fall-semester enrollment.

FACULTY

Saint Michael's faculty are known not only for being experts in their fields but for sharing that expertise effectively with their students. Their doors are always open, too—it's not unusual to join professors for coffee or lunch, or to be invited to their homes for dinner. You'll find them at fundraisers and on the sidelines of athletic games. And chances are excellent that they'll know your name by the end of your first week of class with them. Saint Michael's remarkable faculty include 155 full-time professors, 86 percent whom have the doctoral or terminal degree in their field. Many have been recipients of grants, awards, and honors in recent years. While undergraduate instruction is the focus of the College, faculty members remain active in their field through research and publication, often facilitated through sabbaticals.

STUDENT GOVERNMENT

The Student Association (SA), an active and important part of campus life, is an elected body of students that authorizes and funds most other student activities and organizations. Representatives from the SA sit on many campus-wide committees, including the Curriculum Committee and various committees of the Board of Trustees.

ADMISSION REQUIREMENTS

Successful applicants to Saint Michael's typically rank in the top 25 percent of their high school class and have a strong college-preparatory background. Students should have completed 16 units of courses in English, foreign language, mathematics, science, and social science. SAT or ACT scores are optional for admission purposes. For reference, the average SAT score last year for accepted students ranged between 1600 and 1890, and the average ACT score ranged between 25 and 26. Applicants wishing to be considered for merit based aid are advised to submit test scores for admission. In addition, students should submit a counselor recommendation and any teacher recommendations they choose. Transfer applicants must submit transcripts of all college work in addition to the information required of first-year applicants.

APPLICATION AND INFORMATION

Saint Michael's offers an Early Action admission program deadline of either November 1 or December 1, as well as a Regular Action deadline of February 1. Students should consult the Web site for application deadlines and information. Candidates for the fall semester are notified of their admission decision on or before April 1. A limited number of students may be admitted to the spring semester and should have their applications in by November 1. The College adheres to the Candidates Reply Date of May 1 for the fall semester.

For further information, students should contact:

Office of Admission

Saint Michael's College

One Winooski Park, Box 7

Colchester, Vermont 05439

United States

Phone: 800-762-8000 (toll-free)

Fax: 802-654-2906

E-mail: admission@smcvt.edu

Website: www.smcvt.edu

SAINT PETER'S UNIVERSITY

AT A GLANCE

Saint Peter's University is a Jesuit, coeducational, liberal arts University that seeks to develop the whole person in preparation for a lifetime of learning, leadership, and service in a diverse and global society.

Saint Peter's University's main campus comprises nearly 25 acres in the heart of Jersey City, the second largest city in New Jersey. The University is 12 minutes by train from New York City and seconds from "The Gold Coast," the rejuvenated Jersey City waterfront district that is home to some of the nation's most respected financial, insurance and real estate companies including Goldman, Sachs and Co., American Express, Morgan Stanley, and Deutsche Bank. The University has a branch campus for adults in Englewood Cliffs and courses are also offered at various corporate sites.

The total enrollment at Saint Peter's University in fall 2012 was 2,927 full-time, and part-time undergraduate and graduate students. Currently, a total of 1100 students, about 50 percent of the full-time day session undergraduates, reside on campus. Saint Peter's students, born in at least 32 different countries, reflect the increasing diversity of our nation. Excluding international students, approximately 28 percent full-time undergraduate students identify themselves as Hispanic; 27 percent as African American; and 12 percent as Asian. Saint Peter's University students come from at least 29 states. New Jersey is home to 78 percent of full-time undergraduates; while 18 percent come from other states and 4 percent from foreign countries.

LOCATION AND ENVIRONMENT

The main campus of Saint Peter's University, in Jersey City, is blocks from McGinley Square and Journal Square; our students enjoy the convenience and comforts of an urban-centered campus. Within the past decade Jersey City, located directly across the Hudson River from lower Manhattan, has developed its waterfront area into an impressive hub for business and finance.

Saint Peter's branch campus at Englewood Cliffs in Bergen County is located on the Palisades about 15 miles up the Hudson River from Jersey City. Primarily working adults from nearby corporate parks and medical centers enroll to pursue undergraduate and graduate degrees through evening and weekend study.

OFF-CAMPUS OPPORTUNITIES

Supervised, off-campus cooperative education opportunities and internships are available in all fields. Students in Saint Peter's nationally ranked Cooperative Education Program may earn a maximum of 9 academic credits and up to $10,000. Sixty percent of Saint Peter's undergraduates take advantage of the unique and exciting opportunities afforded by the University's proximity to the nation's business, financial, and media capital, New York City. They work throughout the tri-state area, earning college credit and a salary, with firms such as Atlantic Records, WKTU, Panasonic, Unilever, ABC, HBO, CBS, Univision, MTV Networks, The Rachel Ray Show, L'Oreal USA, CNN, Coach INC., Walgreens, Merrill Lynch, Goldman Sachs, KPMG LLC, PSE&G, Showtime Networks, the National Basketball Association, MLB Network, WBLS Radio, Madison Square Garden, Hackensack University Medical Center, and the NJ Sports and Exposition Authority.

Up to 15 credits are awarded through the Washington Center Program in Washington, D.C., which provides experience working in the nation's capital in a wide range of internship positions. Study abroad is arranged through the International Student Exchange Program, which conducts programs at more than 60 universities in Europe, Asia, Africa, and Latin America.

Students can also take advantage of a center for information and assistance in applying for admission to graduate, law, or medical schools.

MAJORS AND DEGREES OFFERED

The University's academic departments offer more than 50 major programs, a variety of minors, individualized majors, and opportunities to earn credit for internships, service learning and other off-campus learning experiences. As befits a school founded in the classic Jesuit liberal arts tradition, Saint Peter's has a rich and varied range of academic offerings.

Pre–Professional Joint Programs are also offered. These programs allow undergraduate students to begin pursuing a graduate degree as early as their junior year, thereby reducing the overall length of time required to earn both the undergraduate and graduate degree.

For a detailed list of full-time day programs please visit www.saintpeters.edu/academics/areas-of-study/

For a detailed list of part-time/full-time evening programs please visit www.saintpeters.edu/spcs.

ACADEMIC EXCELLENCE

Saint Peter's academic programs are designed to offer students a wide breadth of knowledge along with providing the skills necessary to be successful in their chosen field. Students may pursue a double major by completing requirements for two separate majors or may design a composite major in consultation with the appropriate academic dean.

All students complete a core curriculum requirement consisting of at least 60 credits. The remainder of the academic program is devoted to the major field of specialization. Students must earn 120 credits to graduate.

A four-year honors program provides academically talented students an opportunity to do extensive scholarly research and participate in small seminars that emphasize class discussion. Selected students are invited to join this program and, upon successful completion, are awarded degrees in cursu honorum.

Academic Success Program is a first-year program designed to provide students the opportunity to build college success skills while enrolled full-time at the University. While enrolled students are invited to participate are also invited to a three-week summer program in advance of their first semester at the University.

Saint Peter's is dedicated to supporting students in their effort to complete their academic degrees. Boasting a 1:13 faculty to student ratio students experience individualized attention and guidance. Academic support services include CALL (content-based tutoring) Reading/Writing Lab, and Center for English Language and Culture (CELAC).

CAMPUS FACILITIES

The Theresa and Edward O'Toole Library contains more than 50,000 sq. ft. of space. Students benefit from interlibrary loan arrangements as well as access to the New Jersey state-supported university library system. Students may obtain referral cards to other metropolitan area libraries and have access to the research collections of the New York Public Library and the Science, Industry, and Business Library, both located in midtown Manhattan. The library at the branch campus at Englewood Cliffs offers an additional 25,000 volumes.

The University operates 14 instructional and research labs on campus. In addition to general purpose computer labs distributed throughout the academic buildings, each residential hall has a mini-lab open 24 hours a day, 7 days a week. Saint Peter's also has several specialized computer labs to support learning in specific academic areas. The Fine Arts department operates a networked Graphic Arts lab with Apple and PC computer stations. The Modern Language department has its own computerized language lab and the Psychology department has a dedicated computer instruction lab.

Saint Peter's extends its commitment to integrating state of the art technology with high quality instruction beyond the use of computers. Gannon Hall, the science building, recently underwent an $8 million renovation and now offers sophisticated laboratory support to the University's course offerings in the natural sciences. The University has also implemented smart classroom technologies in all of its facilities, combining fully networked computer systems with powerful multimedia capabilities.

With a $2 million federal grant to establish the nation's first and only center for microplasma research, the University is garnering a national and international reputation for research in this emerging science. The Department of Psychology are recipients of a $500 million dollar research grant from NASA supporting cutting edge research in motion sickness. The College of Nursing's SimLab provides students a hands-on learning experience to practice real life health care scenarios.

The Green Energy Command Center, opened in fall 2012, has provided the University with the facilities to study and track energy use. As a result the University has embarked upon a major effort to "go green."

The Yanitelli Recreational Life Center is a modern multi-million dollar facility offering five indoor tennis courts, a state-of-the-art fitness center with strength training and cardiovascular equipment, an Olympic-sized swimming pool, free weight room, racquetball, squash, indoor track, and three regulation basketball courts. The Center is home to the University's extensive intramural and recreational programs as well as its 19 Division I athletic teams.

The University broke ground in 2012 for the Mac Mahon Student Center. A six-story building dedicated to enhancing the students' experiences. Equipped with the campus dining facilities, Campus Ministry Offices, administrative offices for the Student Development and Life team, student activities offices, student meeting rooms, and the Duncan Family Skyroom (with prime views of the New York City and surrounding New Jersey landscape) the building opened in the spring 2013 and is the epicenter for student-life.

TUITION, ROOM, BOARD AND FEES

Undergraduate tuition and fees for the 2013-2014 school year is a flat rate of $32,420 (12-18 credits per semester). Annual room and board is $13,020. Annual tuition for graduate students is $23,400 (24 credits at $975 per credit).

FINANCIAL AID

97% of full-time undergraduates receive financial assistance from Saint Peter's, with an average total package of more than $20,000. It is recommended that students file the FAFSA by March 15 for fullest consideration of all federal, state (including EOF for eligible NJ residents), and institutional sources available. All applications for admission are reviewed for academic scholarships, athletic scholarships, and need-based grants. Students should call the Office of Student Financial Aid (201-761-6070) for more information.

STUDENT DEVELOPMENT AND LIFE

Academic life at Saint Peter's University is enriched by many programs and services that complement classroom instruction. The Campus Ministry Office offers religious services, seminars, and counseling. Students can also make use of the Office of Community Service and Service Learning. The Office of Campus Activities sponsors annual events on campus featuring popular entertainment, guest lecturers, and social events, both on and off campus. New York City, just a short distance away, offers countless cultural opportunities. Residence Life provides formal and informal opportunities for students to experience community living.

Saint Peter's is a Division I school and competitive member of the Metro Atlantic Athletic Conference. Holding a number conference titles, athletes at Saint Peter's have proven to be outstanding ambassadors of the University contributing to creating a strong community pride.

ADMISSIONS PROCESS

Saint Peter's University considers several factors in the review of candidates for admission. Students are required to have a college preparatory curriculum including:

four years of English

three years of college prep math

two years of social science/history

two years of a foreign language

two years of science, with at least on year of lab science

at least three additional units in any combination of the subject areas listed above.

Students' potential for success is determined by the cumulative academic record as well as utilizing standardized test scores (SAT or ACT). Teacher and counselor recommendations provide information about the student's character and support for pursuit of a college-level education. Notification of the admission decision is made on a rolling basis once the admission file is complete.

Admission to the pre-professional programs (i.e. Pre-nursing, Pharmacy, Medicine, Law, Physician Assistant) are highly selective and often require minimum G.P.A. and SAT/ACT test scores. Contact the Office of Admission for more information about applying to a pre-professional/joint-admission program.

SCHOOL OF THE ART INSTITUTE OF CHICAGO

AT A GLANCE

A leader in educating artists, designers, and scholars since 1866, the School of the Art Institute of Chicago (SAIC) offers nationally accredited undergraduate, graduate, and post-baccalaureate programs to nearly 3,200 students from across the globe. Located in the heart of Chicago, SAIC has an educational philosophy that is built upon an interdisciplinary approach to art and design, giving students unparalleled opportunities to develop their creative and critical abilities, while working with renowned faculty who include many of the leading practitioners in their fields. SAIC's resources include the Art Institute of Chicago and its new Modern Wing; numerous special collections and programming venues provide students with exceptional exhibitions, screenings, lectures, and performances. For more information, please visit www.saic.edu.

SAIC was recognized as "the most influential art school in the nation" in a poll of national art critics conducted by Columbia University. SAIC's Master of Fine Arts program has been ranked for 2013 as the top two graduate fine arts programs in the nation by U.S. News and World Report. SAIC is accredited by the North Central Association of Colleges and Schools and the National Association of Schools of Art and Design.

ACADEMICS

The School of the Art Institute of Chicago (SAIC) offers acclaimed liberal arts-based undergraduate degrees with studio practice at their core. More than ever before, contemporary artists cross media and disciplinary practices and utilize a wide variety of materials and processes to create their work. Through our unique, interdisciplinary curriculum, we prepare our emerging artists designers and visual scholars to work in this manner.

Our students may design their own curricular pathways between multiple areas of interest or may choose to concentrate in a single discipline. Beginning in their first semester with us, students are assigned an academic advisor who helps mentor and guide them to ensure that they are making the most of the courses and opportunities available to them.

Today, more than ever, students of art and design need a firm grounding in the liberal arts to provide not only the critical writing and reading skills needed to write artists' statements, grants, and graduate school applications, but to enrich their knowledge of the world, allowing them to produce well-informed works of art and design that engage the social, political, economic, philosophical, and scientific aspects of our complex world. 30 credits in the liberal arts with offerings including literature, philosophy, theology, anthropology, psychology, history, economics, biology, geology, mathematics and physics are required for completion of all our undergraduate degrees. Additionally, 18 credits of art and design history are required for graduation – the equivalent of a "minor" at most institutions.

In order to prepare students for what is it like to be a creative professional for whom the highest value is placed on the relationship between idea and execution and to allow students to take creative risks, SAIC has a critique-based assessment tool, and a credit/no-credit grading system. Our students also take 6-credits of off campus study – including study trips and internships – to allow them to make "real-world" connections and consider their work in the context of what is happening outside the classroom.

ADMISSIONS

SAIC encourages our students to meet with us on campus, at National Portfolio Days, and SAIC Days around the country to begin a dialogue about your portfolio and the steps needed to complete your application. Our admission counselors, themselves artists and designers, are also available to advise students over the phone and through email.

Undergraduate applicants are required to submit an application; a nonrefundable application fee of $65 for domestic students and a fee of $85 for international students; an electronic portfolio consisting of ten to fifteen examples of recent work; a statement of purpose; transcript(s) from high school(s) or an official copy of the high school equivalency certificate; transcripts from any college previously attended; one letter of recommendation.

Domestic applicants must submit either scores from the SAT or the ACT test. Any transfer applicant who has successfully completed SAIC English requirements and/ or other Liberal Arts coursework at another accredited college may be exempt from standardized test requirements for admission. All international students who are not U.S. citizens, permanent residents or are not native English speakers are required to take either the TOEFL or IELTS.

Prospective students may apply to SAIC through the Immediate Decision Option (IDO) or the traditional admission procedure. IDO Days allow prospective students who have submitted all their application materials an opportunity to receive an admissions decision by the end of the IDO day while on the SAIC campus. All students are required to submit their applications electronically by applying online at http://www.saic.edu/ugapp or via the Common Application.

First-time freshmen may apply through Early Action with a deadline of December 1 or the February 15 merit deadline; transfers may also apply through Early Action or a March 1 merit deadline.

Admissions Office

School of the Art Institute of Chicago

36 South Wabash, suite 1201

Chicago, Illinois 60603

CAMPUS LIFE

SAIC builds a strong sense of community on campus with special activities and programs. The Visiting Artist Program hosts approximately 50 public presentations by artists each year in lectures, symposia, performances and screenings. It showcases artists working in all media including sound, video, performance, poetry, painting, and independent film, in addition to curators, critics, and art historians.

The Student Union Galleries (SUGs) program provides a professional student exhibition space that is operated by students. Students are involved in every facet of the gallery's operation--from administration and program design to the selection of exhibitions, curating, advertising, installation and de-installation.

Student Government is responsible for funding and co-sponsoring events such as a Welcome Back to School Party, All-School Barbecues, Holiday and Spring Art Sales, and the First Thursdays events. In recent history they've implemented a School TV station (EXTV), improved recycling efforts on campus, and developed new programs to improve the sense of community at SAIC. Students may also participate in SAIC's award-winning newspaper, "F Newsmagazine," or Free Radio SAIC, a student-run Internet radio station airing approximately 40 hours of original programming per week.

College Basics

The School of the Art Institute of Chicago provides a leading global vision for the education of artists, designers and others who shape contemporary art practice. SAIC fosters the conceptual and technical education of students in a studio-oriented and academically rigorous environment

TUITION AND FEES

Tuition for the 2012-13 academic year is $38,340 for full-time undergraduate students or $1,278 per credit hour. For 2012-13, student housing costs $10,400 per academic year for a double room.

SEATTLE UNIVERSITY

AT A GLANCE

Seattle University, founded in 1891, is one of 28 Jesuit colleges and universities in the United States. The undergraduate student body numbers 4,589 and includes representatives from 53 states and territories and 89 nations. Seattle University provides an ideal environment for motivated students interested in self-reliance, awareness of different cultures, social justice, and the fulfillment that comes from making a difference. Our location in the center of one of the nation's most diverse and progressive cities attracts a student body, faculty, and staff rich in diversity. Our urban setting promotes the development of leadership skills and independence and provides the opportunity for students to apply what they learn through internships, clinical experiences, and volunteer work.

The student life program includes over 130 extracurricular clubs and organizations. Four residence halls and two on-campus apartment complexes house 1,900 students and undergraduate housing is available all four years. Approximately 92% of freshmen live on campus. The Connolly Athletic Center serves as the major facility for varsity and intramural athletics and recreation. It features the Eisiminger Fitness Center, which opened in fall 2011, two swimming pools, two gymnasiums, and saunas. A 6-acre complex provides fields for outdoor sports.

Seattle University is accredited by the Northwest Commission on Colleges and Universities, the Accreditation Board for Engineering and Technology, AACSB International-Association to Advance Collegiate Schools of Business, the American Chemical Society, the Commission on Accreditation of Allied Health Education Programs, the National Association of Schools of Public Affairs and Administration, the National Council for Accreditation of Teacher Education, Association of Theological Schools, the Commission on Collegiate Nursing Education, Council on Social Work Education, and the American Bar Association.

LOCATION AND ENVIRONMENT

Seattle University is located in a port city of unsurpassed natural beauty. As the Pacific Northwest's largest city (and the 15th largest metropolitan area in the United States), Seattle is a scenic and cultural center in a setting that includes breathtaking mountain views of the Cascades to the east and the Olympics to the west. In addition to being situated along Puget Sound, Seattle also contains Lakes Union and Washington.

The campus is located in the center of the city. Seattle's sights and sounds, rich ethnic diversity, celebrated restaurants, first-run entertainment, major-league athletics, theater, opera, and ballet all enhance campus life.

OFF-CAMPUS OPPORTUNITIES

Seattle University offers a diverse array of short- and long-term international study programs. Some are appropriate for any student interested in study of a particular culture or language, while others are designed to complement specific majors. Short-term programs include opportunities in Brazil, Costa Rica, France, India, Ireland, Italy, Japan, Korea, Mexico, South Africa, and Sweden. Long-term programs, which last an entire academic quarter or more, are available for Austria, Belize, China, Denmark, Ecuador, France, Ghana, Ireland, Japan, Mexico, and Spain. Students also have the opportunity to intern with non-governmental organizations in Asia, Africa, and Latin America through the unique International Development Internship Program (IDIP), which embodies the Jesuit emphasis on social justice and global awareness. Additional study-abroad programs in other nations, in conjunction with other colleges' overseas programs, are also offered. Arrangements are made through the Education Abroad Office.

MAJORS AND DEGREES OFFERED

Seattle University offers the following undergraduate degrees: Bachelor of Arts, Bachelor of Science, Bachelor of Science in Nursing, Bachelor of Social Work, Bachelor of Criminal Justice, and the Bachelor of Arts in Business Administration. The University offers 64 majors and 31 minors in five academic units: The Albers School of Business and Economics; The College of Arts and Sciences; The College of Nursing; The College of Science and Engineering; and The Matteo Ricci College.

Undergraduate Programs include accounting; art history; Asian studies, biochemistry; biology; business administration; business economics; cell & molecular biology; chemistry; clinical laboratory science; communication; computer engineering; computer science; criminal justice; cultural anthropology; diagnostic ultrasound; e-commerce, environmental science; environmental studies; economics; electronic commerce; engineering (civil, computer, electrical, environmental, and mechanical); English/creative writing; exercise science; film studies; finance; fine, applied, and performing arts; French; general science; German; history; humanities; humanities for teaching; international business; international studies; journalism; liberal studies; management; marine & conservation biology; marketing; mathematics; military science/ROTC; music; nursing; philosophy; physics; political science; pre-law; pre-medical/pre-dental; psychology; public affairs; sociology; Spanish; string performance; theology/religious studies; and women and gender studies.

ACADEMIC PROGRAMS

Students at Seattle University take a program of liberal studies called the core curriculum. The University Core curriculum is the "center of gravity" of a Seattle University undergraduate education. The 12-course sequence of courses serves as an important foundation for studies in various majors and minors. Deeply rooted in the 450 year old Jesuit educational tradition and emphasizing rigorous, intentional, and engaging courses, the University Core helps students understand the world deeply, develop strong intellectual skills, and prepare to be thoughtful and empowered leaders for a better world. Students can choose from a wide variety of interesting topics for these courses, which are carefully coordinated to ensure that students develop key knowledge, skills, and values regardless of which section they complete.

Seattle University offers two honors program options for students seeking the greatest possible challenge. The University Honors Program is a small select two year long learning community. It is humanities focused, and its fully integrated curriculum examines the most significant texts and ideas of Western culture. The Core Honors Program involves seminar sections of nine required courses in English, history, philosophy, social science, and theology/religious studies. This option is particularly suited to students in profession oriented majors where participation in University Honors is less feasible due to specific major requirements and scheduling conflicts. Admission is competitive and requires a separate application.

CAMPUS FACILITIES AND EQUIPMENT

The University is located on 50 acres in the First Hill/Capitol Hill neighborhoods in the center of Seattle. There are 28 buildings enhanced by $200 million worth of additions, renovations, and new construction over the last fifteen years. The University endowment is $179 million.

Tuition, Room, Board and Fees

For the 2013-2014 academic year, full-time tuition is $35,865; room and meals are $10,545. The estimate for books, supplies, fees and personal expenses is an additional $6,195. Travel costs vary among students. Costs are subject to change. Seattle University operates on a quarter calendar with fall term beginning in late September.

FINANCIAL AID

Approximately 96 percent of new freshmen in 2012 received financial aid; the average award was $23,757 per year. These awards usually include scholarships, grants, loans, and Federal Work-Study. Last year, Seattle University awarded more than $96.1 million in aid to undergraduates - nearly $49 million of that came from the university's own funds. Students are required to apply for financial aid by February 1, as awards are made early each spring for the following fall quarter. Applications that are received after this deadline will be evaluated in the order received for any remaining aid. Students must submit the Free Application for Federal Student Aid (FAFSA) and be accepted for admission to be considered for financial assistance. There are a number of scholarships for freshmen that are awarded on the basis of academic achievement, extracurricular involvement, and community service. Transfer scholarships are also available.

Student Organizations and Activities

All undergraduates belong to the Student Government of Seattle University (SGSU), the central student organization on campus, which is organized around an elected president, an executive vice president, and an activities vice president. Additionally, a 12-member representative council oversees every facet of the student body and is responsible for policy making, a diverse activities program, and the communication of student needs to the administration and faculty.

ADMISSIONS PROCESS

Seattle University is committed to qualitative decision making based upon evaluations of students as a whole. Decisions are based primarily upon individual course selection, performance, and trends. The expected academic program comprises 16 units of coursework, including 4 years of English, 3 years of social studies or history, 2 years of a foreign language, 3 years of college-preparatory mathematics, and 2 units of lab science (3 are preferred). Laboratory physics and chemistry, as well as 4 units of college-preparatory mathematics are required for engineering; we require laboratory chemistry and biology for admission to the nursing program. Also required for all programs are official scores from either the ACT or the SAT I. The middle 50 percent of enrolling freshmen have secondary school averages of 3.3-3.9 (on a 4.0 scale).

Essays or personal statements are required for admission and are carefully considered during application review. College credit is awarded to those who have successfully earned minimum scores on Advanced Placement or International Baccalaureate examinations.

Applications and information can be obtained by contacting the Admissions Office. Secondary school students who have completed at least six semesters are encouraged to complete the application process no later than January 15 of their senior year, the deadline for regular admission. For those who wish to apply via Early Action, the deadline is November 15. Transfer students must submit official transcripts from all post-secondary institutions attended, regardless of whether course work was completed. The recommended financial aid/admission deadline for transfers is March 1. Applications are accepted after these dates but financial aid funds may no longer be available.

Campus visits can be scheduled Monday through Friday and many Saturdays. Guests can attend a class, meet with faculty, participate in a campus tour, and speak individually with representatives from admissions. Students can apply directly or online via our website, www.seattleu.edu. Seattle University is a member of The Common Application.

SETON HALL UNIVERSITY

AT A GLANCE

As one of the nation's leading Catholic universities, Seton Hall provides over 90 rigorous academic programs that are highly ranked by The Princeton Review, U.S.News & World Report and Bloomberg Businessweek. We offer all the advantages of a large research university — national reputation; challenging academic programs; notable alumni; state-of-the-art facilities; renowned faculty; and extensive opportunities for internships, research and scholarship — with all benefits of a small, supportive and nurturing environment. Our 14:1 student-to-faculty ratio and average class size of 21 students means faculty know more than just your name.

Our accomplished faculty include more than 10 Fulbright Scholars, prominent researchers, authors, artists, filmmakers, former school superintendents and principals, leaders in nursing, former ambassadors, analysts and lawmakers—all of whom are dedicated to their fields and their students. They have graduated from some of the nation's leading institutions, including Seton Hall, Harvard, Columbia, Yale, Princeton and Dartmouth. Each day, our faculty shine in the lecture halls, meet regularly with students outside the classroom and help them learn to think critically.

Seton Hall offers more than 15,000 internship opportunities, and over 75 percent of our students have an internship — or two — on their resume before graduation, this is just one of the reasons our students have an employment rate of 84 percent – almost 20 percent higher than the national average. Our national reputation and stellar academic programs draw over 550 employers to campus each year just to recruit our graduates.

Seton Hall is a Catholic university with a more than 155-year tradition of educational excellence. A welcoming community, Seton Hall embraces students of all faiths and inspires students to become servant leaders who make a difference in the world, that's why our community performs over 30,000 hours of community service annually. You'll feel at home on our campus, where it's easy to make friends and get involved.

LOCATION AND ENVIRONMENT

Nestled in the suburban village of South Orange, New Jersey, Seton Hall provides small-town charm combined with big-city opportunities. The University's suburban, 58-acre park-like campus sits proudly within this picturesque town with tree-lined streets; historic, gracious homes; and quaint shops just 14 miles from New York City – close to all the action, yet not engulfed by it.

Just a five-minute walk from campus lands you in the middle of a bustling town center where you'll find diners and pizzerias, banks, pharmacies, Starbucks, Cold Stone Creamery, Garden of Eden Marketplace, South Orange Performing Arts Center, a movie Theatre, and so much more. You might not ever want to leave this quiet suburbia, but if you do, the train station, right in the center of town, is your direct link to NYC's Penn Station – just 30 minutes away.

We take full advantage of all the Big Apple has to offer—where the worlds of entertainment, art, publishing, global finance, international diplomacy and fashion collide. NYC is also one of the world's largest job markets, brimming with internship and job placement opportunities in a variety of companies. , Seventy-five percent of Seton Hall students have an internship or two on their resume before graduation at leading companies like American Express, The Associated Press, NYSE, United Nations, The New York Times, NBC, Sony Music, JP Morgan Chase and more.

And if all the advantage and opportunity of the Big Apple aren't enough, New Jersey's got you covered. One of the wealthiest states in the nation, New Jersey is brimming with opportunity. Seton Hall's backyard boasts a powerhouse corporate corridor of more than 50 Fortune 500 companies, pharmaceutical giants and major corporations. For you this means networking, internships and career opportunities.

MAJORS AND DEGREES OFFERED

Seton Hall is a place where leaders learn. This is evident in the nearly two dozen student and alumni national scholars and fellows, including ten prestigious Fulbright Scholars since 2009, as well as Rhodes, Udall, Pickering, Marshall, Critical Language and Truman Scholars and the more than 92,000 alumni who are now successful as CEOS, judges, doctors, principals, CFOs, journalists, diplomats and more. About 1,000 Seton Hall graduates have served in executive positions like Presidents, CEOs, CFOs, and Executive Vice Presidents at places like Oppenheim, the Visiting Nurse Service of New York, American Express and Meryl Lynch. They have served our nation as elected officials - in Washington, in Trenton, and in hundreds of town halls throughout the country. In fact, in New Jersey alone, 18 of our state's 120 Assembly and Senate members hold Seton Hall degrees – 15 percent of our Legislature. Seton Hall's commitment to academic excellence is evident in the more than 90 stellar academic programs offered through our six undergraduate schools and colleges.

Majors and Programs

Accounting•, Accounting (5-year B.S./M.S. dual-degree∞), Africana Studies•, American Humanics√, Ancient Greek†, Anthropology•, Applied Scientific Mathematics†, Arabic†, Archaeology†, Art (Art History•, Fine Arts•, Graphic Interactive and Advertising Design•), Asian Studies•, Athletic Training (5-year B.S./M.S. or B.A./M.S. dual-degree)∞, Biochemistry, Biology (B.A. or B.S.), Broadcasting, Visual and Interactive Media•, Business Administration•‡, Catholic Studies•‡, Catholic Theology•, Chemistry•, Classical Culture†, Classical Languages†, Classical Studies•, Communication Studies•, Computer Graphics√, Computer Science•, Creative Writing, Criminal Justice•, Data Visualization and Analysis√, Digital Media and Video√, Digital Media Production for the Web√, Diplomacy and International Relations•, Early Childhood (integrated with elementary and special education), Elementary Education (integrated with early childhood and special education), Education with Speech Language Pathology (6-year B.S.E./M.S. dual- degree)∞, Economics (B.A. or B.S.), Engineering (Biomedical, Chemical, Civil,, Computer, Electrical, Industrial, Mechanical)§, English•, Entrepreneurial Studies√, Environmental Sciences†, Environmental Studies•, Ethics and Applied Ethics†, Finance, French•, Gerontology√, History•, Information Technologies√, Information Technology Management‡, International Business†, Italian•, Italian Studies†, Journalism and Public Relations•, Latin†, Latin America and Latino/Latina Studies•, Law (dual admission program with Seton Hall Law)∞, Legal Studies in Business†, Liberal Studies, Management, Marketing, Mathematics•, M.B.A. (5-year B.S./M.B.A. or B.A./ M.B.A. dual-degree)∞, Modern Languages, Music (Comprehensive Music/ Music Education, Music Performance•), Musical Theatre†, Nonprofit Studies†, Nursing, Occupational Therapy (6-year B.A./M.S. dual-degree)∞, Online Course Development and Management√, Philosophical Theology√, Philosophy•, Physical Therapy (7-year B.S./D.P.T. dual-degree)∞, Physician Assistant (6-year B.S./M.S. dual-degree)∞, Physics (B.A. or B.S.)•, Political Science•, Pre-Dental°, Pre-Law°, Pre-Medical°, Pre-Optometry°, Pre-Veterinary°, Psychology (B.A. or B.S.)•, Religion•, Russian†, Russian and East European Studies†√, Secondary Education (optional integration with special education), Social and Behavioral Sciences, Social Work•, Sociology•, Spanish•, Special Education (integrated with early childhood, elementary, and secondary education), Sport Management•, Supply Chain Management√, Theatre and Performance•, Web Design√, Women and Gender Studies†, Writing†

• Minor also available

† Minor only

√ Certificate program only

‡ Certificate program also available

§ Dual-degree Program with NJIT

∞ Seton Hall dual-degree program

(please contact the Office of

Admissions for details)

° Pre-professional programs (you must also select a major)

CAMPUS FACILITIES AND EQUIPMENT

Seton Hall places a strong emphasis on the use of state-of-the-art technology, facilities and support services to aid in its students' development:

Our award-winning Mobile Computing Program provides all incoming, full-time freshman a new, fully loaded laptop. Two years later, you'll trade it in for a newer, upgraded model, and when you graduate in four years, it is yours to keep.

Seton Hall's Recreation Center serves the recreational and fitness needs of the Seton Hall community. Here students can go for a swim in our Olympic sized pool, run on the indoor track or tear up the six indoor basketball courts. Our new, 2-story, glass atrium fitness center set to open in 2014 features a free-weight center, new cardiovascular equipment, and plasma screen televisions complete with wireless listening capabilities.

The Walsh library is a state-of-the-art research facility complete with a computerized catalog, 200 computer terminals for undergraduates, four electronic multimedia facilities and approximately one million holdings. The library also provides students free access to numerous databases of scholarly research.

The University's newest addition is the McNulty Science and Technology Center, which is home to state-of-the-future biology and chemistry labs, an atrium and auditorium, as well as an observatory and greenhouse.

Unique learning labs like our Mock Trading Room, Patient Simulation Labortory, Market Research Center, student-run radio station, Sport Polling Center and more offer students hands-on experience while on campus.

Tuition, Room, Board and Fees

Seton Hall offers a flat-tuition rate for students taking between 12-18 credit hours. The 2012-13 tuition and fees are $34,750. Room and Board fees range depending on meal plans; however, an average cost is $11,576.

FINANCIAL AID

Paying for college is a major investment. That's why Seton Hall University is committed to providing you with the resources needed to make your dreams a reality. We give over $70 million in aid each year and 97 percent of our students receive some form of financial aid with 93 percent receiving scholarships or grants directly from the University. Most scholarships are automatically awarded upon admission and do not require separate applications. At Seton Hall, all you need to begin the process of applying for need-based financial aid is the completion and submission of the Free Application for Federal Student Aid (FAFSA) form.

STUDENT ORGANIZATIONS AND ACTIVITIES

On campus, Seton Hall leaders learn to put their ideas into action; discover something new; become part of a community; and build trust, spirit and lasting friendships. Here, you'll find activities galore, over 130 clubs and organizations and 22 Greek societies. You can audition for one of the nearly dozen theatre performances cast each year or broadcast at our award-winning, student-run radio station, WSOU-FM, which attracts more than 120,000 listeners a week from the NYC area. Join the Brownson Speech and Debate Team, ranked in the Top 20 college and university forensic teams for years or write for one of our three student newspapers. You won't only makes lots of new friends and have fun, you'll also learn about your leadership style. More than two-thirds of our students participate in clubs and organizations.

You don't have to be a superstar athlete to be part of the game at Seton Hall. Our athletic programs include competition on varsity, intramural and club levels. In fact, almost 50 percent of our students participate in club or intramural sports. Even if you don't know a handball from a handoff, you'll be decked out in blue and cheering your heart out when you attend any one of Seton Hall's 14 NCAA division I athletic events. So grab your friends and catch some Pirate fever!

ADMISSIONS PROCESS

At Seton Hall, we take a holistic approach to reviewing your application. What do your teachers and high school guidance counselors say about you? What does your essay tell us about you?

When we receive your application, we start by considering your academic performance in high school, your grades and the rigor of your curriculum, as well as your standardized SAT and/or ACT scores. These are essential indicators of your ability to succeed at Seton Hall. We also will consider your personal essay, recommendations and extracurricular activities.

The typical student who enter Seton hall last year had an average GPA of 3.4 (B+) and an average SAT score of 1100 on the Critical Reading and Math sections (24 on the ACT).

For more information, contact the Office of Undergraduate Admission:

Website: admissions.shu.edu

Telephone: 1-800-THE-HALL (843-4255)

E-mail: thehall@shu.edu

SIMMONS COLLEGE

AT A GLANCE

Steeped in a tradition of cultivating the intellectual and professional growth of women, Simmons College is a warm and engaging community with a national reputation of academic excellence. Founded in 1899, Simmons was the first college in the United States to offer women a liberal arts education integrated with career preparation. Today, Simmons embraces the opportunity to provide a transformative learning experience for students, linking their passion with lifelong purpose.

Located in the heart of Boston, Simmons is best known for its small classes, access to faculty, and internship and research opportunities. Students say that Simmons's location offers the best of both worlds—an intimate college experience in the heart of a vibrant and bustling city. Simmons's nearly 2,000 undergraduates love the fact that they can easily access the city's rich social and cultural resources but also come home to a safe, friendly campus.

ACADEMICS & MAJORS

Simmons offers more than 40 majors and programs. Popular majors include psychology, nursing, business, political science, and communications. Faculty advisors help each student create a plan that fulfills requirements and satisfies her personal and professional goals. A number of integrated degrees and accelerated programs allow students to go directly from undergraduate study to earning a graduate degree in less time than traditional programs. Students can accelerate to graduate degrees in areas such as business, education, health care, liberal arts, physical therapy, social work, and library science. Simmons also offers individually designed pre-professional programs for dentistry, law, medicine, and veterinary medicine. Simmons students typically declare a major by the end of their sophomore year, and nearly a third choose to double major.

The hallmark of a Simmons education is the independent learning requirement, which students fulfill through internships, fieldwork, and research projects. Science students co-publish research with faculty in nationally recognized academic journals as undergraduate students. Most students take advantage of the abundance of competitive internship opportunities available in Boston. In addition, Simmons's Longwood Medical Area partnerships provide outstanding clinical opportunities at Boston's world-renowned hospitals. On campus, students conduct research using state-of-the-art equipment in areas such as materials science, gene splicing, and computer modeling. Yet the most important aspect of Simmons's approach to hands-on learning is that professors frequently invite undergraduates to collaborate on professional research projects, articles, and presentations, as early as their freshman year.

ADMISSIONS

Admission to Simmons College is highly selective. The admission committee looks for students who have shown academic excellence both in and out of the classroom, and evaluates high school performance, SAT or ACT scores, recommendations, and the application essay. If English is not the applicant's first language, the TOEFL, IELTS, or a comparable exam score is required. Typical high school preparation for entrance includes 4 years of English, 4 years of math, 3-4 years of lab sciences, and 3-4 years of a foreign language. Although not required, an interview and campus visit is strongly recommended.

Simmons welcomes applications from prospective freshmen, transfer students, international students, and students who are beyond the traditional college age.

Students may apply online, using the Common Application, or submit a print application, along with the $55 fee and all supporting credentials. The early action deadline (nonbinding) is December 1. The regular freshman application deadline is February 1. Transfer students are evaluated on a continual basis; the preferred filing date for applications for the fall semester is April 1. All students applying for the spring should submit their application by November 1.

STUDENT BODY

Simmons fosters a student-centered environment and encourages each individual to actively participate in the College community in a way that is right for her. Simmons has more than fifty student organizations, clubs, and academic liaisons, including honor societies, cultural organizations, volunteer programs, a literary magazine, a campus newspaper, and ten NCAA Division III varsity teams. In addition, every academic department has a student liaison that participates in department evaluations and helps promote educational and social activities for students and faculty and staff members.

CAMPUS LIFE/FACILITIES

Simmons's historic, tree-lined campus is located in Boston's eclectic Fenway neighborhood, which is alive with music and fine arts, medical care and research, action and activism, and the resounding cheers of baseball fans at legendary Fenway Park. Considered by many to be the best college town in the nation, Boston has more than 50 colleges and universities, and approximately 300,000 students. Compact, historic, charming, and clean, the city is easy to get around on foot or via the T, Boston's public transportation system.

SPECIAL NEEDS

Simmons College is committed to the full participation of all students in its programs and activities. Although Simmons has no academic program specifically designed for students with disabilities who are otherwise qualified for admission, Simmons is committed to providing support service and reasonable accommodations when requested by students who qualify for them.

The Disability Services staff assist students, both undergraduate and graduate, who have a disability, by reviewing documentation supplied by licensed professionals and by completing Student Accommodation Letters. The Disability Services staff will make referrals for diagnostic services (at student expense), provide advice and personal contact for students with disabilities, and assist with locating needed resources. The Disability Services staff is also available to faculty and staff who have questions regarding a student's accommodation and other issues pertaining to a disability.

Tuition & Aid

Tuition and fees for the 2012-2013 academic year are as follows:

Undergraduate tuition and fees: $33,350

Room and board: $13,140

Total: $47,490

Graduate tuition costs vary by program.

FINANCIAL AID

More than 90 percent of Simmons first-year students receive some form of financial aid. Scholarships, grants, loans, and federal work-study are determined by the Free Application for Federal Student Aid (FAFSA). Simmons also awards academic merit scholarships, ranging from $2000 to full tuition awards, renewable for four years.

For further information, contact:

OFFICE OF UNDERGRADUATE ADMISSION

Simmons College

300 The Fenway

Boston, MA 02115

Telephone: 800-345-8468 (toll free)

Fax: 617-521-3190

E-mail: ugadm@simmons.edu

Website: www.simmons.edu/undergraduate

SKIDMORE COLLEGE

AT A GLANCE

Founded in 1903 and located in Saratoga Springs, N.Y., Skidmore is an independent, coeducational, liberal arts college that prides itself on its creative approaches to just about everything. Hence, the college's core belief that creative thought matters. With a diverse student body of 2,400 from 50 states and 50 countries and a faculty of 250 dedicated teacher-scholars, Skidmore offers more than 50 majors in the humanities, sciences, and social sciences, as well as in career-specific fields such as business, education, exercise science, and social work. Skidmore is known for its interdisciplinary approach to learning, faculty-student collaborative research, off-campus study (60% of students study abroad), and the prominence of the performing and visual arts, enhanced by the unique Tang Teaching Museum and Art Gallery and award-winning Arthur Zankel Music Center. The college's rigorous academic program begins with the foundational First-Year Experience which integrates the curricular, co-curricular, and residential aspects of a student's first year, and gets them connected and involved in the life of the community from day one. Students enjoy close relationships with talented faculty members who have earned recognition through Guggenheim, Pulitzer, and Emmy awards, and fellowships and grants from Fulbright, MacArthur, and the National Science Foundation, among others. Sixty percent of students carry two majors or add a related minor to their major. More than half of Skidmore students pursue advanced degrees within five years of graduation.

ADMISSIONS JOURNAL

Searching for a college experience that will challenge you? Give you virtually unlimited opportunities to create and explore? Then consider Skidmore. Creativity is embodied in all that is Skidmore: academic, co-curricular life, campus setting, and the nature of Saratoga Springs itself. We are a diverse world of thinkers and doers—academics, performing artists, community volunteers, and athletes who come together in the shared belief and commitment that creative thought matters. If you share that belief, consider visiting and applying to Skidmore.

LOCATION AND ENVIRONMENT

Saratoga Springs, 30 miles north of Albany, New York State's capital, is perennially short-listed as one of the most interesting and vibrant small cities in the U.S. Famed for "health, history, and horses"—its mineral waters, Revolutionary War battlefield, and the nation's oldest thoroughbred racetrack—Saratoga is equally renowned as an arts and cultural destination. The Saratoga Performing Arts Center is summer home to the New York City Ballet, Philadelphia Orchestra, and Lake George Opera, and is a performing venue for top rock and jazz musicians. The city's downtown—a 10-minute walk from Skidmore—is brimming with galleries, clubs, museums, shops, coffeehouses, bistros, and restaurants. The city's location near the foothills of the Adirondack Mountains puts an abundance of outdoor recreational opportunities within an hour's drive. Boston, New York City, and Montreal are each approximately 180 miles from the campus.

OFF-CAMPUS OPPORTUNITIES

About sixty percent of Skidmore's students spend a semester or year off campus. In addition to Skidmore programs in China, England, France, and Spain, students can access more than 130 international programs through the college's Approved Programs structure, including programs in Africa, Asia, Europe, Latin America, and Australia. Students can also study at 200 other U.S. campuses, thanks to Skidmore's affiliation with National Student Exchange. All academic majors and minors can be accommodated, and transfer credits are guaranteed for students studying on an approved program. Financial aid is transferable to most off-campus study programs.

The college also offers a Washington Semester (internship in conjunction with American University) and a semester at the Marine Biological Lab in Wood Hole, Mass. Arrangements for student internships (for academic credit) are made through Skidmore's academic departments or Career Development. More than 50% of Skidmore students are involved in volunteer work, much of it in the local community. There are also as many as 50 courses each semester with service-learning components.

MAJORS AND DEGREES OFFERED

Skidmore College grants a Bachelor of Arts degree in American studies, anthropology, Asian studies, biology, chemistry, classics, computer science, economics, English, environmental studies, foreign languages and literatures (French, German, and Spanish), French area studies, gender studies, geosciences, government, history, history of art, international affairs, mathematics, music, neuroscience, philosophy, physics, psychology, religion, and sociology. The Bachelor of Science degree is granted in the following pre-professional areas: business, dance, education, exercise science, social work, studio art, and theater. There is also a self-determined major and more than 10 interdepartmental offerings.

Skidmore offers 3-2 engineering programs with Clarkson and Dartmouth; 4+1 M.B.A. programs with Clarkson, Rochester Institute of Technology, and Union Graduate College; the Whitman MBA Advantage program with Syracuse; 4+1 M.S.A. and M.S.F. programs with Syracuse; a 4+1 Master's in Teaching program at Union College; a 4+1 dual degree program in nursing with New York University's School of Nursing, and 4 +1/4 +2 dual degree programs in physical therapy and occupational therapy at the Sage College Graduate School.

The college also offers a nonresidential program leading to a master of arts in liberal studies (MALS). An external degree program, MALS offers multidisciplinary graduate study to adult learners.

ACADEMIC PROGRAMS

The Skidmore academic journey begins with the First-Year Experience which introduces students to the college's rigorous academic program and overall approach to learning and connects them with a faculty advisor/mentor. Talented but economically disadvantaged students who have been accepted into the Opportunity Program (Higher Education Opportunity Program and Academic Opportunity Program) participate in a month-long summer program. And a small percentage of students apply for entry into Honors Forum, Skidmore's own honors program, on the basis of academic achievement, leadership qualities, and civic commitment. Generally, students choose a major by the end of sophomore year. In the interests of breadth, they are also expected to take 1-2 courses in both quantitative reasoning and expository writing, and at least one course in all of the following: lab science, social science, arts, humanities, and culture. There is plenty of academic support through Student Academic Services. In addition, there are specific programs for pre-law and pre-med students. In their junior and senior years, most students (more than 80%) add value to their courses of study through faculty-student collaborative research, internships, volunteerism, service-learning, and off-campus study.

CAMPUS FACILITIES AND EQUIPMENT

Skidmore's 1,000-acre-plus campus offers buildings that are designed and arranged to blend with the natural surroundings and to foster intellectual and social interaction. The newest academic building, the Arthur Zankel Music Center, features a spectacular 600-seat recital hall and a state-of-the-art recording studio. The beautifully renovated Murray-Aikins Dining Hall boasts a variety of food stations and intimate seating arrangements. On the residential side, phase one of the Sussman Village Apartments was completed in fall 2012. Once the 238-bed project is completed in late 2013, fully 90% of Skidmore's student body will reside on campus. And field hockey, lacrosse, soccer, and softball venues have all been recently outfitted with the latest turf fields.

Skidmore's visual and performing arts space includes the Saisselin Art Building, with studios and the Schick Art Gallery, and Bernhard Theater, with a seating capacity of 350 and an experimental Black Box theater. The Tang Museum, designed by renowned architect Antoine Predock, provides a focal point for cross-disciplinary study through the visual arts and serves as a major cultural resource for Saratoga Springs and the region, attracting nearly 40,000 visitors a year. Dana Science Center offers high-quality teaching and research space, including a greenhouse, specialized labs, and a science machine shop. Dana links the College's science departments to the Department of Mathematics and Computer Science in neighboring Harder Hall, which features a Linux lab of 24 workstations for advanced computer science projects.

TUITION, ROOM, BOARD, AND FEES

Costs 2013–2014: $44,820 tuition; $904 fees; $7,214 room; and $4,988 board. Total: $57,926

FINANCIAL AID

More than half of Skidmore's students receive some form of financial assistance. Aid is awarded on the basis of demonstrated financial need and is provided in the form of a student-aid "package" that usually includes a grant, campus job, and loan.

We encourage any student interested in applying for admission to do so regardless of his/her intention to seek financial aid. The Free Application for Federal Student Aid (FAFSA), a copy of the federal income tax form, and the CSS PROFILE must be filed each year. The application date is January 15 for entering freshmen. The College hosts an annual Filene Music Scholarship Competition to award four $48,000 ($12,000 per year) scholarships on the basis of musical ability without regard to financial need. Five $15,000 scholarships in math and science are also awarded annually ($60,000 over four years). Detailed information concerning scholarships, grants, loans, and/or work awards can be obtained through the Office of Financial Aid.

Student Organizations and Activities

The college's nearly 100 student clubs and organizations run the gamut, including five a capella groups, SkidTV, WSPN Radio, Model European Union, snowboarding, and academic, cultural awareness, and religious groups. Skidmore's 19 intercollegiate teams compete at the NCAA Division III level. Students are active in the intramural sports program and enjoy abundant opportunities for personal fitness and recreation, both on campus and in the nearby Adirondack Mountains.

Skidmore students participate in all aspects of academic and social life on campus. They play a major role in governing the college through the Student Government Association (SGA) and numerous major college committees. Elected faculty members and students serve on three panels: the Academic Integrity Board, the All-College Council, and the Social Integrity Board.

ADMISSIONS PROCESS

Those seeking admission to Skidmore's first-year class should complete a secondary school curriculum that includes at least 16 credits in college-preparatory courses. The Admissions Committee is also pleased to consider applications from qualified high school juniors who plan to accelerate and enter college early. Applicants typically have completed 4 years of English, 4 years of a foreign language, 4 years of mathematics, 4 years of social studies, and 3-4 years of laboratory science. Applicants must provide a secondary school transcript, standardized test scores (SAT I with writing or ACT with writing), letters of recommendation from two teachers of academic subjects, and a report from their guidance counselor. Skidmore recommends that applicants submit scores for three SAT II Subject Tests. The school also strongly recommends a campus visit and interview. Through its participation in the Higher Education Opportunity Program (HEOP), Skidmore enrolls capable, energetic, and ambitious New Yorkers who, because of their academic and financial situations, would not otherwise gain admission to the College under traditional requirements. Skidmore's Academic Opportunity Program (AOP) enrolls similar students who reside out of state and/or whose family income slightly exceeds HEOP guidelines.

An applicant for admission registers by completing the Common Application and submitting it with a $65 fee. All information should be postmarked by January 15. Applications from early decision candidates should be submitted by November 15 for the Round I early decision plan or by January 15 for the Round II early decision plan. Transfer candidates are urged to apply by April 1 for the next fall term and by November 15 for the next spring term.

International students are given special attention throughout the admissions process. Applicants whose first language is not English are encouraged to submit the results of the Test of English as a Foreign Language (TOEFL). There are a limited number of need-based financial-aid awards available for outstanding international students.

Transfer applicants should apply online at www.commonapp.org and return the application (with the $65 application fee or request for a fee waiver from your advisor) by November 15 for admission in January, or by April 1 for admission in September. In addition to a high school transcript and standardized test scores, we require by the appropriate deadlines an official transcript of all college-level work completed, recommendations from two professors, and a statement regarding personal and academic standing from the dean of students at the current college.

ST. JOSEPH'S COLLEGE

AT A GLANCE

Since 1916, St. Joseph's College has provided an affordable liberal arts education to a diverse group of students. Independent and coeducational, St. Joseph's prepares students for lives of integrity, social responsibility and service - lives that are worthy of the College's motto, Esse non videri – "To be and not to seem."

At St. Joseph's College, we believe that qualified students deserve a top quality education for the best value. We've been transforming lives since 1916, consistently earning a place among top colleges in the Region as ranked by U.S.News & World Report. In the Forbes Magazine Best Colleges Guide, St. Josephs ranks as one of the top four-year private colleges in the NY Metro area and first on Long Island. We offer stellar academics, innovative programs, accomplished professors and solid community connections – all while ensuring that tuition costs are reasonable and more than 70 percent of students receive financial aid. The end result: At St. Joseph's College, students earn a top-tier education while paying one of the lowest tuition rates of any private college in New York.

LOCATION AND ENVIRONMENT

Founded in 1916, St. Joseph's College is an independent, private institution with two campuses, one in the Clinton Hill section of Brooklyn (urban setting), New York and the other on Long Island in the town of Patchogue (suburban setting). The Brooklyn campus enrollment has over 1200 students, and the Long Island campus has close to 5,000 students.

OFF-CAMPUS OPPORTUNITIES

Brooklyn Campus

Our campus in Brooklyn is located in the safe Clinton Hill Historic District, home to several prestigious schools and a hub of cultural and intellectual activity. Manhattan career opportunities and cultural attractions lie within easy reach via public transportation. The Brooklyn Campus is surrounded by historic and unique architecture, tree-lined streets and new eateries and shops. The College developed its property on Vanderbilt Avenue into an attractive and attended parking facility.

LONG ISLAND CAMPUS

Located in the Village of Patchogue on Great South Bay, our 27-acre Long Island campus is about 50 miles from Manhattan and 60 miles from Montauk Point in Suffolk County. Patchogue offers fine harbors, shops, restaurants, athletic fields and tennis courts right in the village.

MAJORS AND DEGREES OFFERED

Majors

Accounting

Biology

Business Administration

Chemistry (Only at the Brooklyn Campus)

Child Study (Elementary and Special Education)

Computer Information Systems

Criminal Justice

English

History

Human Relations

Journalism and New Media Studies

Marketing

Mathematics

Medical Technology

Political Science

Psychology

Recreation

Social Sciences

Economics

Sociology

Spanish

Speech Communication

MINORS

Accounting

American Studies

Business Administration

Chemistry

Computer Information Systems

Computer Science

Economics

English

History

Latino Studies

Mathematics

Music

Political Science

Religious Studies

Sociology

Spanish

Speech

Theatre

CERTIFICATE PROGRAMS

No matter what major you choose, you can earn an additional certificate. Certificate programs help you delve deeper into your specific interests, help you focus your career goals and give you a head start when entering the work world. We offer Certificate Programs in:

Criminology/Criminal Justice

Gerontology

Information Technology

Leadership & Supervision

Management

Marketing, Advertising & Public Relations

Religious Studies

Affiliated Programs

Want a fast track to an advanced degree? Try these special affiliated programs at St. Joseph's:

St. Joseph's College Accounting Program

(B.S. plus M.B.A., a five-year program)

Podiatric Medicine: St. Joseph's College/New York College of Podiatric Medicine.

(Leads to a Doctor of Podiatric Medicine, D.P.M.)

ACADEMIC PROGRAMS

St. Joseph's has an outstanding honors program, which offers eligible students the opportunity to participate in a three-semester honors program as part of their bachelor's degree. The program provides an enriched and rigorous academic experience, meeting the special needs of those students who have demonstrated extraordinary academic accomplishment and ability and who are committed to achieving their full potential. In addition, St. Joseph's offers a freshmen year experience to help students make a seamless transition from high school to college. Study abroad opportunities are also available on each campus.

CAMPUS FACILITIES AND EQUIPMENT

Brooklyn Campus Facilities

SJC's Brooklyn Campus offers easy access to transit lines and brings students from every part of the New York Metropolitan area to the College each day. Students enjoy the freedom of campus life, while profiting from the many cultural and educational advantages of being in New York City. The Brooklyn campus provides architecturally stunning halls in the historical Clinton Hill section of Brooklyn, NY. The Brooklyn campus also offers state-of-the art technology, a gymnasium and fitness center, an outdoor theatre and The Dillon Child Study Center, which offers toddler, preschool and kindergarten programs based on the child development approach to the education of young children.

Long Island Campus Facilities

The 27-acre Long Island Campus, located in Patchogue adjacent to Great Patchogue Lake, is an ideal setting for studying, socializing and partaking in extracurricular activities. Just off of Sunrise Highway, the College is easily accessible from all parts of Long Island.

The Long Island Campus features modern, state-of-the-art facilities, including the recent completion of the Business Technology Center, the John A. Danzi Athletic Center, the Clare Rose Playhouse, the ultra-modern Callahan Library, O'Connor Hall (which includes the D'Ecclesiis Auditorium for fine arts and student theater productions) and Gregg Alfano Field as well as the new state-of-the-art athletic fields for soccer, lacrosse, softball and tennis.

TUITION, ROOM, BOARD, AND FEES

Tuition for the Fall 2012 is $19,500 and $635 per credit for NY State and out-of-area residents.

Housing is available for Brooklyn campus students at the St George Residence in nearby Brooklyn Heights. Costs vary by year, to learn more, please contact the admissions office at 718.940.5800 (Brooklyn) or 631.687.4500 (Long Island)

FINANCIAL AID

Students should be sure to consult the St. Joseph's College catalogs for more information concerning financial aid programs, policies and requirements.

Financial aid applications are also available in the Office of Financial Aid on each campus.

FOLLOW THESE INSTRUCTIONS TO APPLY FOR FINANCIAL AID

Complete the Free Application for Federal Student Aid (FAFSA) online designating St. Joseph's College, Brooklyn NY as a recipient. You will be asked to enter St. Joseph's federal Title IV school code, which is 002825 for the Brooklyn Campus.

Complete the New York State Tuition Assistance Program (TAP) application online. Full-time semester students should use code No. 0755. Part-time students should complete the New York State Aid for Part-time Study (APTS) application. The APTS application is available at the Office of Financial Aid. For more information about New York State programs, please visit New York State Higher Education Services Corporation on the Web.

Complete any other requirements as requested by the Office of Financial Aid.

STUDENT ORGANIZATIONS AND ACTIVITIES

St. Joseph's College students have a plethora of extracurricular activity opportunities within reach through our Office of Co-Curricular Programs. Joining the Student Government Association, clubs, athletics, organizations and committees emphasizes leadership, community service and effective communication. We also arrange for a student's health insurance. To learn more about our student life opportunities, please visit our website at www.sjcny.edu.

ADMISSIONS PROCESS

What are the admissions requirements?

St. Joseph's College is a selective institution. Applicants are evaluated on an individual basis. The College enrolls students that are academically talented and diverse. Successful admissions candidates typically have:

a high school diploma or its equivalent

solid grades in a strong college preparatory curriculum

standardized test scores that demonstrate the promise of success in college-level courses

St. Joseph's College offers generous scholarships and financial aid packages to students who qualify. For a listing of our scholarships, please visit our website at http://www.sjcny.edu/Academics/Scholarships/136/

Students can obtain a copy of our application or also apply online, by visiting http://www.sjcny.edu/Admissions/Apply-Now/85/

When should I apply? When is the application deadline?

St. Joseph's College admits students on a rolling basis, there are priority dates though.

For the fall semester, the scholarship priority date is March 15 for freshmen and August 1 for transfer students. For the spring semester, the priority date is January 1 for both freshmen and transfer students.

What else do I need to submit in addition to my application?

Applicants for Brooklyn and Long Island must also submit high school transcripts and SAT or ACT scores. A personal statement/essay and two letters of recommendation are also requested.

Students wishing to transfer to St. Joseph's should file their applications at least three months in advance of the expected date of matriculation. Transfer students must request that official transcripts from all former colleges, marked catalogs of former colleges and a listing of courses in progress be sent to the St. Joseph's College Office of Admissions.

We provide a block transfer of courses (up to 64 credits) for students who have earned an associate in arts, or an associate in science (with science emphasis) degree in a transfer program at an accredited community or junior college.

ST. LAWRENCE UNIVERSITY

AT A GLANCE
St. Lawrence University is a private, independent, non-denominational, university that seeks to provide a stimulating and rigorous liberal arts education to undergraduate students chosen for their intellectual potential and seriousness of purpose. Chartered in 1856, it is New York State's oldest continuously coeducational college or university. St. Lawrence's 2,400 students arrive from 42 states and 50 countries. The school is situated in Canton, New York, midway between the Adirondacks Mountains and Ottawa, Canada's national capital. The University provides unmatched access to social and cultural opportunities, international government, and outdoor recreation.

LOCATION AND ENVIRONMENT
St. Lawrence University provides a distinctive learning environment, offering 36 majors, 37 minors, and 3 graduate programs in education. Its First-Year Program is nationally recognized. St. Lawrence offers international study programs on six continents; it also belongs to the International Student Exchange Program. The University offers four off-campus programs within the United States, including a semester program in the Adirondack wilderness. St. Lawrence is currently undergoing an educational renaissance; bold academic initiatives are underway to maximize the learning potential of each and every student. A major facilities upgrade has been completed to provide expanded resources to undergraduates. A new residence hall project has started in spring 2013; the residence hall is slated to be open for the fall 2014 incoming class.

OFF-CAMPUS OPPORTUNITIES
St. Lawrence University offers international programs in 17 countries: Australia, Austria, Canada, China, Costa Rica, Czech Republic, Denmark, England, France, India, Italy, Japan, Kenya, New Zealand, Spain, Thailand and Trinidad and Tobago; students can also direct-enroll in foreign universities in countries through the International Student Exchange Program (ISEP).

The University also offers four off-campus study programs within the United States. These are located at: American University, Washington, D.C.; Fisk University, Nashville, Tennessee; New York City and the Adirondack Semester, near Tupper Lake, New York.

MAJORS AND DEGREES OFFERED
Students have the following major/minors to choose from:

African Studies, African-American Studies, Anthropology, Art & Art History, Asian Studies, Biochemistry, Biology, Biology-Physics, Canadian Studies, Caribbean and Latin American Studies, Chemistry, Communications, Computer Science, Conservation Biology, Creative Writing, Dance, Economics, Economics-Mathematics, Education, English, Environmental Studies, Estudios Hispanicos (Spanish), European Studies, Exercise Science, Film and Representation Studies, Foreign Languages, Francophone Studies (French), Gender and Sexuality Studies, Geology, Geology-Physics, German Studies, Global Studies, Government, History, International Economics, International Studies, Japanese Studies, Journalism, Languages, Latin American Studies, Mathematics, Modern Languages & Literatures, Multifield (self-designed), Music, Native American Studies, Neuroscience, Outdoor Studies, Peace Studies, Performance and Communication Arts, Philosophy, Physics, Political Science, Psychology, Religious Studies, Sociology, Spanish, Sports Studies and Exercise Science, Statistics, Studio Art, Theatre, Visual Art, and Writing.

ACADEMIC PROGRAMS
The University confers the Bachelor of Arts and Bachelor of Science degrees; it also awards graduate degrees in education.

Thirty-six majors are available, as is the option to declare a double major (see Majors and Degrees Offered.)

The University offers 37 optional minors (see Majors and Degrees Offered.)

Qualified students may pursue five-year programs in business administration (this program leads to the MBA) and engineering, combining coursework at St. Lawrence with work at other institutions.

Specialized advising is available for postgraduate work in dentistry, law, medicine, and veterinary medicine.

The St. Lawrence distribution requirements involve coursework in six areas.

All students are expected to demonstrate writing competence before graduating.

The University provides extensive opportunities for honors projects and independent work.

CAMPUS FACILITIES AND EQUIPMENT
The University's two libraries, the Owen D. Young Library and Launders Science Library, contain more than half a million volumes, electronic resources, and ample space for reading and research.

Students also enjoy an arts center with recital hall, two theaters, and an art gallery as well as a 7,000-piece art collection. The Peterson-Kermani Performance Hall, a 19,000 square-foot space for the performing arts, is part of the campus dedicated to the arts.

St. Lawrence's science complex - including the Gold LEED-certified Johnson Hall of Science - is connected to the science library and computing center.

A 15,000-square-foot Sullivan Student Center is available for student meetings, studying, staff offices and one of the dining areas available on campus.

Recreational facilities include cross-country ski and running trails; a 133-station fitness center; a three-story clombing wall; indoor and outdoor tennis courts; and two gymnasium/fieldhouse complexes, one with a 9-lane/400-meter track and five tennis/basketball courts and the other with a 200-meter track, three tennis courts, and ten squash courts. Facilities also include a pool, ice arena, equestrian center, golf course, indoor golf facility, boathouse, AstroTurf field, baseball, soccer and softball fields.

TUITION, ROOM, BOARD AND FEES
For the 2012-2013 academic year, the comprehensive fee (including tuition, fees, and typical room and board) is $53,740.

Typically, annual personal costs and book expenditures cost an additional $1,650.

FINANCIAL AID

St. Lawrence University offers merit scholarships as well as need-based financial assistance.

The school grants aid in some form to more than 93 percent of its students. Aid packages typically consist of grants, student loans, and campus jobs.

Aid applicants must submit the Free Application for Federal Student Aid (FAFSA) between January 1 and February 1, and request that results be sent to St. Lawrence. Applicants must also submit the CSS PROFILE form.

Student Organizations and Activities:

Undergraduates commence their studies with the First-Year Program, which places approximately 30 first-year students in communities that live and learn together.

Once they achieve upper-class status, students may choose to live in traditional residence halls, interest-based theme suites, theme cottages, Greek houses, or senior townhouses.

St. Lawrence provides a full range of services to students, including comprehensive career planning as well as graduate and professional school guidance

Students seeking co-curricular activities can choose from over 100 organizations, including everything from student government to interest groups to arts and culture.

St. Lawrence boasts 32 intercollegiate teams including NCAA Division I teams in men's and women's ice hockey. All other teams compete in the NCAA's Division III. Club sports are also available, as is participation in a broad range of popular intramural sports.

The University is home to numerous recreational facilities, including: a 133-station fitness center; a three-story climbing wall; cross-country ski and running trails; and indoor and outdoor tennis courts. Students enjoy access to two gymnasium/ fieldhouse complexes; one has a 9-lane/400-meter track as well as five basketball/ tennis courts, while the other has a 200-meter track, ten squash courts, and three tennis courts. Other facilities include an AstroTurf field; baseball, softball, and soccer fields; an equestrian center; a golf course; an indoor golf facility; an ice arena; a boathouse; and a pool.

ADMISSIONS PROCESS

St. Lawrence seeks undergraduates with the capacity to manage a demanding academic regimen successfully. In addition, the ideal student contributes substantially to the quality of community life. The University strives to enroll students who represent the broadest possible range of economic, ethnic, geographic, and social backgrounds. The admissions committee values academic achievement, but ability in athletics, community service, or the creative arts is also considered a strong indicator of a student's capacity to benefit from his or her time at St. Lawrence. The University is test optional for all domestic students; students may choose whether they would like the results of their SAT Reasoning Test and/or ACT used during the evaluation process. Students are strongly encouraged to plan a campus visit; interviews may be scheduled to occur on campus. In certain areas, off-campus interviews are also an option.

The University makes no requirement of applicants' high school curricula; however, successful applicants generally demonstrate extensive preparation in the humanities, mathematics, the natural sciences, and the social sciences. Advanced Placement, IB and honors work are looked upon favorably, as they demonstrate the applicants intellectual curiosity and maturity. These are qualities that are highly sought by the admission committee.

St. Lawrence uses the Common Application exclusively and students are free to use any version of the Common Application. An application supplement is required and is available on-line. The application processing fee is $60. Applicants pursuing regular decision should submit all materials by February 1; they will be notified in March of their decision. Students whose first choice is St. Lawrence may apply for Early Decision: the priority deadline for Early Decision applications begins on November 1. Applicants for transfer to St. Lawrence should submit all application materials by November 1 for the spring semester or March 1 for the fall semester.

To request an application or for more information, students should contact:

Office of Admissions and Financial Aid

St. Lawrence University

Canton, NY 13617

Telephone: 315-229-5261

800-285-1856 (toll free)

admissions@stlawu.edu

www.stlawu.edu

ST. MARY'S COLLEGE OF MARYLAND

AT A GLANCE

St. Mary's College of Maryland is designated the Honors College of the State of Maryland in recognition of the quality of our students, faculty and curriculum. St. Mary's offers an undergraduate, liberal arts education and small-college experience like those found at exceptional private colleges. Home to approximately 2,000 students, the campus is located on the St. Mary's River in the heart of the Chesapeake region, about 70 miles outside of Washington, D.C.

The school shares the hallmarks of private institutions: an outstanding faculty, talented students, high academic standards, a challenging curriculum, small classes, a sense of community, and a spirit of intellectual inquiry. By combining the virtues of public and private education, St. Mary's provides a unique alternative for students and their families. The special identity underpins the College's success and its reputation for excellence.

In 1992, the Maryland legislature designated this public, coeducational institution the state's honors college. Over 98% of the faculty holds the Ph.D. or other terminal degree and 11 of the current faculty have received Fulbright Awards. Although professors are exceptionally active in research and writing, the faculty's primary interest and central concern is teaching. The College is home to the Zeta Chapter of Phi Beta Kappa.

Small classes, dedicated teachers, and an informal atmosphere encourage faculty and students to share in the intellectual life of the College, both in and out of the classroom. Professors serve as academic advisors, work with students in extracurricular programs, involve students in research, and mentor them in individualized projects.

More than 50% of St. Mary's graduates continue on to graduate school. St. Mary's alumni have distinguished themselves in every academic field and creative pursuit. When the State of Maryland surveys graduates of its public colleges and universities, St. Mary's alumni consistently report higher levels of satisfaction with their education than do alumni of other institutions.

ACADEMICS

St. Mary's offers a wide and diverse variety of majors and minors and a Master of Arts in Teaching (M.A.T.) for certification in early childhood, elementary and secondary education. English, biology, psychology, political science, and economics typically enroll the largest numbers of majors.

The cornerstone of a St. Mary's education is the First Year Seminar. These small, discussion-focused classes are taught by professors from every discipline at the college, and introduce students to the richness and complexity of intellectual inquiry in a setting of active learning. Students may choose from dozens of topics — ranging from "A Softer Energy Footprint" to "Math, Music, and the Mind" — in order to cultivate an area of particular interest while building the critical thinking, researching, writing, and speaking skills they will use throughout their time at St. Mary's. The First Year Seminar also has a co-curricular component, which through flexibly structured attendance at campus events helps to integrate first year students into college life. St. Mary's also provides students the opportunity to explore cross-disciplinary studies in African and African Diaspora Studies, Asian Studies, Environmental Studies, Museum Studies, Neurosciences, and Women, Gender and Sexuality Studies. Cross-disciplinary studies can increase intellectual community across disciplines, encourage cohesion in the choice of electives, and promote combinations of methods and materials that challenge the boundaries of knowledge.

Many St. Mary's students consider careers in professional fields such as medicine, law, and business. Our pre-professional programs work with interested students throughout their four years by providing academic advice, career exploration, and help applying to professional programs. These include pre-dentistry, pre-engineering, pre-law, pre-medicine, pre-optometry, pre-pharmacy, and pre-veterinary science.

The Paul H. Nitze Scholars Program is designed for highly motivated students with exceptional academic potential and a proven record of leadership and service. As a small cohort of peers, Nitze Scholars meet some of the components of the core curriculum through a series of thematically organized interdisciplinary courses with special components such as a study-tour abroad and collaborative activities on campus.

The DeSousa-Brent Scholars program builds leadership skills and provides mentorship for students from traditionally underserved populations. The mission of the program is to further cultivate the academic and professional leadership potential of students who are the first in their families to attend college, are from rural and urban communities, are ethnic minorities, are students with disabilities, or are economically disadvantaged. These students bring unique experiences and knowledge to St. Mary's, and the College is committed to ensuring that they shine as campus leaders.

In compliance with St. Mary's College's position as Maryland's public honors college, the St. Mary's Project (SMP) is the senior capstone experience at the College. The project is an eight-credit, independent, sustained endeavor of research or creative expression that is supervised by a faculty mentor and presented in a public forum.

St. Mary's College of Maryland offers semester and year-long international exchange programs, study tours, and internship opportunities. Approximately 45% of students who start college at St. Mary's study abroad at some point before they graduate. From semester and year-long programs, study tours, and international internships, there are many options for students to choose from. Some of the more popular study-abroad sites include the Centre for Medieval and Renaissance Studies at Oxford University (England), the University of The Gambia, the Institute for Central American Development Studies (Costa Rica), and Fudan University (China). Additional international programs and study tours provide opportunities to study in the Gambia, Argentina, Thailand, Ireland, India, Belize, Germany, Greece, and Japan.

St. Mary's operates on a two-semester academic calendar. Students customarily complete four courses, or 16 credits, each semester and must complete 128 credits for graduation. Students do not need to declare a major until the end of their sophomore year.

ADMISSIONS

St. Mary's College is a selective institution. We admit students with records of high academic achievements, personal abilities, and accomplishments of superior quality. High school or college grades, the quality of course selection, standardized test scores, and letters of recommendation provide evidence of academic accomplishment and potential. These measures are supplemented by the required application essay and resume of co-curricular activities. Individual involvement outside the classroom and in the community also is given attention. Activities that have resulted in honors and awards, or other recognition of special talents, should be listed on the application.

At St. Mary's, we are proud to be a public honors college and are looking for students who are ready to be challenged. We are a member of the Common Application (www.commonapp.org), and we accept applications from first-year and transfer students for the fall and spring semesters. Our Early Decision Deadlines are November 1 and January 1. When students apply under the Early Decision option, they are indicating to us that St. Mary's is their top choice and will attend if admitted. Notification of an admissions decision is approximately six weeks past the Early Decision deadline. Regular Decision applicants must apply by January 1 and notification will be no later than April 1. Fall transfer applicants must apply February 1 and spring transfer students must apply by November 1. For details, visit www.smcm.edu/admissions.

Prospective students are strongly encouraged to come to campus for a student-led tour and an information session or interview with an admissions counselor. These visits should be scheduled in advance by calling 800-492-7181.

CAMPUS FACILITIES AND EQUIPMENT

At the crossroads of the campus, the Campus Center offers a wide range of activities and services including dining, meeting rooms and lounges, a café, the campus store, student activity offices, and a movie theater. The library, overlooking St. John's Pond, houses state-of-the-art media and computer centers that serve the needs of students as well as faculty and staff. Academic buildings feature computerized classrooms, modern laboratories, and specialized instructional spaces. To ensure that development preserves the natural beauty and Tidewater charm of the St. Mary's campus, the College has adopted a campus master plan calling for courtyards, walkways, and gardens that enrich the landscape. In addition, the environmental fragility of its waterfront combined with its historic location inspires the College to approach campus development with special sensitivity to the ecology of the Chesapeake Bay watershed and the archaeology of Maryland's 17th-century capital.

CAMPUS LIFE

Almost 85% of our students live on campus all four years, contributing a wonderful and safe learning and living environment. Our students enjoy the options of residence halls, suites, apartments and townhouses, and find living on campus an essential part of their college experience.

When our students are not in the classroom, they are busy doing independent research, traveling abroad, interning, and volunteering in the community. They unwind by enjoying the waterfront recreation, watching movies in Cole Cinema, partaking in our 90 clubs and organizations, and competing in intramural and varsity athletics.

LOCATION AND ENVIRONMENT

A unique aspect of St. Mary's culture is the influence of the river. Our campus is located on 361 acres and sits on a horseshoe bend of the St. Mary's River just upstream from the confluence of the Potomac River and Chesapeake Bay. It is no wonder we have earned 14 national sailing championships. You don't have to be an expert; the waterfront is open to recreational and novice sailors alike. With our unique location, students also swim, kayak, windsurf, row and are drawn to environmental research. Once you see the campus you'll know you have arrived at a college like no other.

TUITION, ROOM, BOARD, AND FEES

Basic educational fees for 2013-2014

Tuition and Fees

$14,865 per year (Maryland Resident)

$28,665 per year (Non-Maryland Resident)

Room: $6,575

Board: $5,060

MAJORS AND DEGREES

Anthropology

Art and Art History

Asian Studies

Biochemistry

Biology

Chemistry

Computer Science

Economics

English

History

International Languages and Cultures (Chinese, French, German, Latin American Studies, Spanish, Courses in Translation)

Mathematics

Music

Natural Science

Philosophy

Physics

Political Science

Psychology

Public Policy Studies

Religious Studies

Sociology

Student Designed Major

Theater, Film and Media Studies

OFF-CAMPUS OPPORTUNITIES

Located about 20 minutes from the College is Solomons Island, a quiet waterfront fishing village offering museums and attractions, shopping, waterfront dining, sailing and other water sports. Historic Leonardtown, located 20 minutes from St. Mary's, boasts one of the state's few preserved town squares. Maryland's state capital, Annapolis, is located 70 miles from the College. The Nation's Capital, Washington, D.C., is 70 miles from the College and the harbor city of Baltimore is approximately 100 miles from campus.

FINANCIAL AID

St. Mary's College believes that qualified students should have an opportunity for a college education. The primary responsibility for paying for the cost of education is the family's. However, as a public institution, St. Mary's College recognizes that students and their families are not always able to fund the full cost of a college education. For this, the school offers a variety of programs designed to assist in meeting college expenses. These programs include scholarships, grants, loans, work opportunities, and a tuition payment plan. In the end, the goal is to ensure that qualified applicants have the opportunity to obtain a liberal arts education at St. Mary's.

To be considered for need-based aid, including federal, state and college grants, loan, and employment programs, students must fill out the Free Application for Federal Student Aid (FAFSA); St. Mary's College's FAFSA filing deadline for fall semester applicants is February 28. In order to be considered for merit-based aid from St. Mary's, students should submit their admissions application by our priority scholarship deadline of November 15. Applicants are automatically reviewed by the Scholarship Review Committee with consideration in the areas of academic record, standardized test scores, strength of curriculum, essay, recommendations, and co-curricular involvement.

ST. NORBERT COLLEGE

AT A GLANCE

With a liberal arts foundation that teaches critical thinking, problem solving and leadership development skills, St. Norbert College offers academic excellence, individual attention and faculty members focused on student success.

St. Norbert is a private, coeducational institution with more than 40 fields of study, including several pre-professional programs, all of which can be enhanced by our honors program, student-faculty collaborative research (as early as your first year), professional internships and our study abroad program. With a four-year graduation guarantee, St. Norbert offers students a true value when considering the personal attention that a St. Norbert education offers, and the high graduate school and career placement that our graduates achieve.

Founded in 1898, St. Norbert has become one of the top-10 Catholic liberal arts colleges in the nation. St. Norbert is open to students of all faiths and committed to a well-rounded education fueled by the Norbertine tradition of communio (a deep-rooted, heartfelt sense of community) and the motto docere verbo et exemplo ("to teach by word and example").

ACADEMICS PROGRAMS

Experiential learning is the norm at St. Norbert. Research fellowships, as early as freshman year, give students hands-on opportunities to experience graduate-level research from Day One. Those opportunities for collaborative research with St. Norbert faculty continue throughout their four years, and students often have the opportunity to present their work at local, regional or national conferences.

Students are also privileged to experience one of the more prolific study abroad programs in the country offering six continents, 37 countries and more than 75 program sites for St. Norbert students to experience a global perspective. In fact, an average of 30 percent of St. Norbert students study abroad each year—more than double the national average.

And that international perspective is part of the fabric at St. Norbert. Our Center for International Education on campus encourages a diverse student body, with more than 100 students representing an average of 30 countries typically on campus. An additional 60+ students are in our English as a Second Language (ESL) program, many who stay to complete their bachelor's degree.

All students are assigned an advisor, who helps them chart their academic career and ensure they can graduate in four years. Students have the option of designing a personal major to help them achieve their academic objectives.

For high-achieving students, a challenging honors program provides plenty of opportunity for academic engagement. Honors students have been particularly fond of participating in the living-learning community of intellectually curious and creative students.

The metropolitan Green Bay area offers students nearly unlimited opportunities for internships. More than just cheese and the Green Bay Packers, the region boasts Fortune 500 companies, hospitals, schools and service organizations that play host to many student internships. Of course, students also regularly intern for the world champion Packers, who hold their summer training camp on campus.

For those students more interested in volunteering, the Norbertine philosophy of self-emptying service is a perfect fit. Local, national and international service opportunities are one of the hallmarks of a St. Norbert education.

MAJORS AND DEGREES OFFERED

We offer Bachelor of Arts (BA), Bachelor of Science (BS), Bachelor of Music (BM) and Bachelor of Business Administration (BBA) undergraduate degrees.

Undergraduate Programs

Accounting

American Studies

Anthropology

Art – fine arts and graphic design

Biology – biomedical and organismal

Business Administration

Chemistry and Biochemistry

Classical Studies

Communication and Media Studies

Computer Science – business information systems and graphic design and implementation

Economics

Education

English and Creative Writing

Environmental Science

French

Geography

Geology

German

History

Human Services (Social Work)

International Business and Language Area Studies

International Studies

Japanese

Leadership Studies

Mathematics

Military Science/ROTC

Modern Languages and Literatures

Music

Natural Sciences

Peace and Justice

Philippine Studies

Philosophy

Physics

Political Science

Pre-Dental

Pre-Engineering

Pre-Law

Pre-Medical

Pre-Nursing

Pre-Veterinary

Psychology

Religious Studies and Youth Ministry

Sociology/Anthropology

Spanish

Teacher Education

Theatre Studies

Women's and Gender Studies

ADMISSIONS PROCESS

Students can apply using either the St. Norbert College online application or the Common Application.

Because St. Norbert reviews applications on a rolling basis and gives preference to students according to the date of admission and enrollment deposit, it benefits students to apply as early as possible during their senior year.

Notification of the admission decision is made on a rolling basis beginning in late September. After St. Norbert receives all of the required admission information, you will receive notification via mail of your admission status within 2-4 weeks. A nonrefundable $350 deposit is required to confirm enrollment.

U.S. applications require a $10.00 online application fee. International applications require a $50.00 application fee.

First year domestic student important dates:

- September 15 – admission office begins reviewing applications

- October 1 – admission office begins notifying students of their application status

- January 1 – apply for financial aid at www.fafsa.ed.gov; St. Norbert's FAFSA school code is 003892

- March 1 – financial aid priority deadline

- May 1 – priority date for enrollment deposit

- June/July – summer orientation

For more information, prospective students are encouraged to contact:

St. Norbert College

Office of Admission

100 Grant Street

De Pere, WI 54115-2099

Phone: 920-403-3005 or 800-236-4878

Fax: 920-403- 4072

E-mail: admit@snc.edu

Web: www.snc.edu

STUDENT BODY

Students quickly adjust to campus with a welcoming community of faculty, students and staff. First Year Experience (FYE) programming helps students acclimate to campus and to college life in general. The Norbertine principle of radical hospitality is immediately evident when arriving on campus.

Students at St. Norbert tend to be very involved. Because it's a residential campus, activities and opportunities are close at hand. The college offers more than 70 student organizations and clubs that provide a rich co-curricular campus environment. Organizations range in type and variety from independent social groups to religious groups and Greek life to intramural sports. St. Norbert College works hard to provide a wide variety of organizations that appeal to all. Students can find opportunities in academic, diversity, ethnic and cultural, Greek, social, special interest, governing, programming and media, recreation, and service and faith organizations. And if students are looking for a particular interest that hasn't found its place on campus yet, they can create a new student organization.

A Division III school, we offer 10 men's and 10 women's varsity sports, and our athletes have been named Academic All-America more times than any other school in the Midwest Conference. Additionally, our men's and women's hockey teams compete in the Northern Collegiate Hockey Association. The Green Knights are frequent conference champions—averaging about three per year. Nearly one quarter of our students are involved in varsity sports, with many others participating in intramurals.

CAMPUS FACILITIES AND EQUIPMENT

Located on the banks of the Fox River in De Pere (a residential community of 23,000) in northeastern Wisconsin, the St. Norbert campus comprises 39 buildings on 93 beautifully landscaped acres. Students also have easy access to the neighboring all-American city of Green Bay and its suburbs, with a metropolitan population of about 230,000. With a safe, supportive atmosphere on campus and a thriving corporate, cultural and entertainment industry close at hand, St. Norbert is a place that students love so much that they often refer to it as "home."

St. Norbert continues to experience great momentum with record high enrollment and increasingly high achieving students. And as the students come, so do the facilities to support them. A new state-of-the-art library was opened in 2009, as well as a new student services building where students have a one-stop-shop. Here they can go to the bookstore, registrar, financial aid, academic advising, campus ministry and many other services, all under one roof.

New in 2010, an outdoor athletics complex serves as the practice and competition venue for Green Knights football, soccer, and track and field. And the most recent additions during the 2011-12 academic year are a remodeled visitor and welcome center, and a $7.7 million completely renovated student dining facility – Michels Commons. Planning is also well underway for a new $40 million state-of-the-art science facility.

A campus center and marina located on the Fox River offers students a relaxing environment to grab a bite to eat, sit out on the deck or in the gazebo, work out in the fitness center or gym, or gather for a concert or movie. The campus coffee shop—Ed's—is another favorite student hangout.

Only a five-minute drive from campus, students can easily access Green Bay and all the restaurants, shopping malls, museums and performing arts opportunities when they've exhausted the shops and boutiques of charming De Pere.

TUITION & AID

Full-time undergraduate students (3 or more full courses/12-18 credits):

$28,935 2011-12 academic year tuition

$ 460   Fees

$ 7,349   Average room and board

Graduate students:

$ 390   Tuition per credit

More than 97 percent of St. Norbert students receive some form of financial aid, with the average award being more than $24,500. To achieve our goal of helping students obtain an affordable and quality college education, St. Norbert College allocates funds each year for distribution to students whose families lack necessary funds. More than $50 million in financial aid is available annually at St. Norbert College in the form of scholarships, grants, student employment and loans. We encourage students to submit the Free Application for Federal Student Aid (FAFSA) as early as possible, and preferably by March 1. The St. Norbert FAFSA code is 003892. Financial aid awards typically go out in mid-March.

STATE UNIVERSITY OF NEW YORK—NEW PALTZ

The State University of New York at New Paltz is a highly selective public university committed to offering high-quality, affordable education to students of all social and economic backgrounds.

AT A GLANCE

New Paltz, a public institution founded in 1828, has an undergraduate enrollment of 6,685 and a graduate enrollment of 1,082. Students of color comprise more than 25 percent of our diverse campus population, and our student body represents 59 foreign countries. With a student-faculty ratio of 16:1, more than 90 percent of classes have less than 40 students, and 73 percent contain less than 30 students.

LOCATION AND ENVIRONMENT

Our 216-acre campus in New York State's beautiful Hudson Valley is situated midway between the capital city of Albany and the most dynamic urban center in the world, New York City. The college's unsurpassed location offers not only superb opportunities for local cultural and recreational enjoyment, but also easy access to the world-class connections of the city. Creativity permeates every aspect of campus life at New Paltz, with an air of imagination and inquiry which bridges all academic endeavors.

OFF-CAMPUS OPPORTUNITIES

New Paltz, named one of National Geographic's Best Places to Live and Play, is a haven for lovers of the outdoors. The nearby Shawangunk and Catskill mountain ranges offers some of the world's best rock climbing, hiking, kayaking and mountain biking conditions. Meanwhile, in the vibrant Village of New Paltz (pop. 14,003), students are treated to a thriving social scene including an array of eclectic restaurants, shops, live entertainment venues, and historic sites.

MAJORS AND DEGREES OFFERED

While most well-known for education and fine and performing arts programs, New Paltz offers 105 undergraduate and 50 graduate degree programs taught by distinguished faculty who are dedicated to empowering their students by developing mentor relationships. As of 2012, our top undergraduate programs were psychology, elementary education, visual arts, English, sociology, biology, accounting, journalism, history, and communication disorders. Our top 10 graduate programs are literacy education (birth through sixth grade), school leadership, communication disorders, electrical engineering, humanistic-multicultural education, English, business administration, music therapy, second language education and computer science.

In 2013, the School of Business at New Paltz became internationally accredited by the Association to Advance Collegiate Schools of Business (AACSB), a distinction held by fewer than five percent of the world's business programs. Our nationally-ranked Master in Fine Arts program consistently garners recognition as one of the top programs of its kind in the entire nation, and the School of Education is accredited by the National Council for Accreditation of Teacher Education (NCATE).

ACADEMIC PROGRAMS

Fifteen percent of New Paltz students participate in Study Abroad programs on six of the seven continents, compared to the national four-year college average of 1 percent.

The First-Year Initiative program at New Paltz is reflective of the living-learning communities that college freshmen are choosing to live in nationwide. The FYI places first-year students in residence halls where half the students in the building are fellow first-year students. These students also take courses in common during the fall semester.

New Paltz features a small Honors program, consisting of about 160 students. Once admitted, Honors students take special interdisciplinary seminars which emphasize dialogue, debate and discussion rather than lecture.

CAMPUS FACILITIES AND EQUIPMENT

The New Paltz Wellness and Recreation program provides a variety of active leisure opportunities for the campus community, as well as programs which foster healthy lifestyles (health assessments, personal training, wellness workshops, etc.). Students have access to a slew of facilities including a pool, tennis courts, gyms, a rock climbing wall, indoor and outdoor track, and much more.

The Sojourner Truth Library at SUNY New Paltz fosters learning and supports scholarship by providing an extensive array of information resources and services. With a collection of more than 500,000 books, 700+ print journals, electronic access to more than 60,000 journals and e-books, a MediaSpace for viewing and group work, plus much more, Sojourner Truth Library promotes and encourages active and effective use of all library services and resources. Our strong partnership with classroom faculty helps to successfully instill information literacy skills in all New Paltz graduates.

TUITION, ROOM, BOARD, AND FEES

According to 2012-2013 figures, undergraduate tuition for New York State residents is $16,842 per year, which includes fees, room, and board. Out-of-state undergraduate tuition, also including fees, room, and board, is $26,092 per year.

New York State resident graduate tuition is $4,685 per semester ($9,370 per year). Non-New York State graduate tuition is $8,340 per semester ($16,680 per year). These figures do not include room, board, or fees.

Tuition for the MBA program for New York State residents is $5,565 per semester ($11,130 per year), excluding room, board, and fees. Non-New York State residents' tuition for the MBA program is $9,160, also excluding room, board, and fees ($18,320 per year).

FINANCIAL AID

Our Financial Aid office can help you see what financing opportunities are available to you, including federal and state aid, payment plans and part-time jobs. Students may submit the Free Application for Federal Student Aid (FASFA) and will be sent a New York State Tuition Assistance Program application after the FASFA has been processed.

STUDENT ORGANIZATIONS AND ACTIVITIES

The activities offered at New Paltz range from NCAA Division II athletics, more than 130 recognized clubs and organizations, Greek life and nationally renowned fine and performing arts programming. There are also more than 800 leadership opportunities for New Paltz students, including the Emerging Leaders program, where students are encouraged to explore what it means to be an effective leader through hands-on activities, discussion groups and self-reflection.

ADMISSIONS PROCESS

Admission to the freshman class at New Paltz is highly selective and based on many factors, including but not limited to quality of high school academic performance; SAT and ACT scores; quality of personal essay; and letter of recommendation from a teacher or guidance counselor. A college preparatory program containing the five core subject areas of English, social studies, math, science and foreign language is strongly recommended.

STERLING COLLEGE

AT A GLANCE

Sterling College is a progressive liberal arts college in northern Vermont that combines liberal arts study and practical training to prepare environmental stewards.

Sterling College is a small and progressive liberal arts college in northern Vermont. Our small size, our environmental focus, and our commitment to grassroots sustainability all make us unique.

Sterling College knows that the most rewarding learning is hands-on learning. Whether offered on campus in a laboratory or seminar room, on the side of a mountain, or in a barn or pasture, classes at Sterling are small and foster experiential learning and deep inquiry through close relationships between faculty and students.

Students will gain insight into theory, integrate research into study, and learn how to use tools such as a chainsaw, a compass, and a tractor as part of daily life.

Sterling College removes the barriers between living one's life and learning. It is for the student who wants to commit to becoming an environmental steward and looks forward to the rigor and challenge of working with both hands and mind.

LOCATION AND ENVIRONMENT

Sterling students love living in Craftsbury Common. The focal point of the village is the "Common" and the quintessential New England white clapboard buildings that border it. This area of Vermont is also a place of innovation, and is an important center for a revolution in rural food systems of farms and enterprises such as Pete's Greens, Hill Farmstead Brewery, High Mowing Seeds, Jasper Hill Cheese, and Vermont Soy, just to name a few.

This region of Vermont is known as the "Northeast Kingdom," and is an international destination for outdoor sports and adventure. There are four ski areas within 45 minutes of the college. When city life beckons, however, Burlington is about an hour or so away.

OFF-CAMPUS OPPORTUNITIES

At Sterling we not only live together, we work to create community together. Sterling College strives to be an educational community in which people of all backgrounds and identities feel at home, where differences are embraced, and where individuals take responsibility for furthering the dignity of all.

Professors at Sterling are united by an affinity for small-town life, ecological awareness, a strong interest in relating human experience to natural resources, and a determination to work with students as whole people.

Sterling is small, and will remain so by design. It is the only college in the nation where the entire community of students and faculty sit together each week for community meeting. Everyone is on a first name basis, including the president, deans, and faculty.

Community life is informal. Sterling College students aren't as interested in the kind of structured events and clubs found on most campuses—they're more likely to enjoy a long weekend of hiking, a lively evening of contra dancing, caring for beehives with friends, snowshoeing at the Craftsbury Outdoor Center, or sitting by a bonfire at the College's lean-tos above the Black River.

MAJORS AND DEGREES OFFERED

Sterling College offers Bachelor of Arts degrees in Ecology, Environmental Humanities, Outdoor Education, and Sustainable Agriculture. Students can also choose to design their own major, and some examples include Agroecology, Environmental Justice, Conservation Education, and International Agriculture and Business.

ACADEMIC PROGRAMS

A Sterling education is both local and global. Through Global Field Studies, students and faculty have the opportunity to travel together to look at issues related to environmental stewardship and to experience rich ecological and cultural diversity. Recent programs have included experiences in the Bahamas, Belize, Canada, Israel, Maine, and the Sierra Nevada.

The typical class size at Sterling is 10, and the student-to-faculty ratio is 7 to 1. Sterling's faculty is composed of 17 full-time members and 17 part-time members. 85 percent of the professors hold an advanced degree. In a continuous attempt to bring learning to life, professors teach in both traditional and experiential ways.

All new students, accompanied by 5 to 6 faculty members, take part in Winter Expedition, a four-day, three-night trek along the ridge of the nearby Lowell Mountain Range. Expedition is a 47 year tradition at Sterling College.

CAMPUS FACILITIES AND EQUIPMENT

Sterling's rural location is one of the college's most prized characteristics. The campus boasts 130 acres, with an additional 300 acres of boreal research forest. The campus has sixteen residential, administrative, and classroom buildings. Facilities include a woodshop, a darkroom, two computer rooms and an environmental science computer lab, two greenhouses, and the Brown Library. Outdoor teaching facilities include a challenge course with a climbing wall, a managed wood lot, recreation and nature trails, large organic gardens, and a diverse livestock farm with solar- and wind-powered barns. Students spend about 40 percent of their class time outside the traditional classroom setting.

TUITION, ROOM, BOARD, AND FEES

Tuition for the 2013-14 academic year is $28,978, room and board is $8498, and fees are $766.

FINANCIAL AID

College is a big investment, but Sterling College offers robust financial aid packages, and the Office of Admission and Financial Aid works closely with students and families to plan an affordable path to graduation. Sterling College also awards over $1 million each year in need and merit based grants and scholarships. All students determined to have financial need receive assistance, and participation in the Work Program earns each student additional funds that help offset the cost of attendance.

STUDENT ORGANIZATIONS AND ACTIVITIES

Students are part of the daily work of the college. Regardless of financial need, all students work on campus, whether in the kitchen, on the farm, in the woodshop, or elsewhere. Sterling College is one of only seven colleges recognized by the federal government as a Work College – a college where student work is an integral and mandatory part of the educational process, as opposed to being an appended requirement. Sterling is also the only Work College in the northeast.

Besides working on campus, a highlight of the Sterling education is a ten-week, 6-credit internship anywhere in the world. Internships in agriculture, cross-cultural education, ecotourism, environmental education, hydrology, land and resource management, outdoor education and leadership, and wildlife rehabilitation and research are popular options.

"I was drawn to Sterling because of the work program. I know that at the end of four years I will walk away from Sterling with a résumé full of work and life experiences that any employer would find of interest. A college education here trains you to be a leader through engaged practice in community living."—Allyson Makuch '15

ADMISSIONS PROCESS

We endeavor to enroll a diverse student population reflecting a broad range of interests and lived experiences. Good students who have demonstrated a commitment to the values that underlie Sterling's mission—a concern for environmental stewardship, social justice, and personal integrity—are strongly encouraged to apply.

Sterling College offers admission to both first-time college applicants and transfer applicants. Application review at Sterling is a highly individualized process, characterized by a personal approach. In arriving at an admission decision, the College looks for evidence of a combination of the following characteristics:

Academic preparation, intellectual curiosity, and creativity

Passion for environmental stewardship and social justice

Enthusiasm for hard work and interest in seeking out challenges

Interest in experiential education and intrepid outlook on learning

Desire to be part of a small community in a rural location

High school seniors who wish to receive an early response to their application may apply for Early Action or Early Decision. For Early Decision, a completed application must be on file by November 15 to be notified of a decision on or before December 15. For Early Action, a completed application must be on file on or before December 15 to be notified of a decision on or before January 15. All other applicants are encouraged to submit applications before June 1 for fall enrollment, January 1 for spring enrollment, and April 1 for summer enrollment. Once completed, an application is reviewed for admission within two weeks.

STEVENS INSTITUTE OF TECHNOLOGY

AT A GLANCE

A strong commitment to discovery, collaboration and mentorship drive the academic culture at Stevens Institute of Technology, known as The Innovation University®. Stevens has built upon a legacy of technological innovation since 1870. Students and faculty collaborate in an interdisciplinary, student-centric, entrepreneurial environment to leverage technology to confront global challenges. Exceptional opportunities for internships, undergraduate research and cooperative education give students the experience and connections to engage in high level intellectual and practical pursuits that prepare students for their futures.

Students choose from more than 30 undergraduate majors in Business, Humanities, Arts, Computer Science, Engineering and the Sciences; many students double major or choose to pursue both bachelor's and master's degrees. Most programs of study culminate in a capstone project often undertaken in collaboration with students from other disciplines, supported and mentored by faculty, and sponsored by industry partners. Graduates are highly skilled in creating solutions at the intersections of disciplines and can lead in today's complex, cross-functional and highly technical environments, and have always fared exceptionally well in career and graduate school placement. Stevens is the nation's fastest-rising college and is consistently ranked among the nation's elite for ROI for students, career services, and mid-career salaries of alumni.

Stevens' 2,549 undergraduate students come from more than 40 states and 28 countries, creating a diverse, dynamic environment. Stevens also boasts an outstanding campus life – students will find more than 100 student clubs and organizations and 26 NCAA Division III athletics teams.

LOCATION AND ENVIRONMENT

Stevens is located in one of the most exciting, cosmopolitan towns in the United States. Hoboken, New Jersey, is a quaint one-mile-square city with old Victorian brownstones and tree-lined streets dotted with great restaurants and trendy shops. Located on Castle Point, a high bank on the majestic Hudson River, the 55-acre campus is home to stretches of deep green lawns, majestic elm and maple trees, and historic classroom buildings. With Manhattan directly across the river, from every point on the Stevens campus, the New York City skyline is breathtaking and appears within reach. This unique location offers more than a great view. The heart of NYC is a mere 10-minute commute away. Stevens students take advantage of being just minutes away from top companies with exciting internships, career placements, and industry partners as well as unlimited cultural experiences and events throughout the year.

Stevens students enjoy a safe and dynamic living environment. Ninety percent of Stevens undergraduate students live on campus, and housing is guaranteed for undergraduates for four years. There are six on-campus resident halls in addition to various on- and off-campus apartments for upperclassmen. Sixteen fraternities and sororities have chapters on campus and most maintain houses where members may live. Stevens also features "affinity housing" in Hammond Hall for students interested in community service and civic engagement, as well as women's special interest housing in the Lore-El Center. The dining program features late night hours to meet students' busy schedules, and many establishments in Hoboken also accept Stevens' Duck Bills, reloadable on students' ID cards.

OFF-CAMPUS OPPORTUNITIES

A Stevens education is more than a curriculum. In addition to rigorous major programs, Stevens cultivates the value of being a world citizen, giving back to the community, building bridges across cultures, and reaching for more than a traditional college experience. In addition to the popular internship, undergraduate research, and cooperative education opportunities offered at Stevens, students take their educational experience across the globe through study abroad, service-oriented organizations, and department-sponsored trips.

Stevens' location is ideal for off-campus activities nearby. Dining, entertainment, and major attractions in exciting Hoboken, New York City, and the surrounding metro area offer numerous artistic, cultural, athletic, and recreational opportunities.

MAJORS AND DEGREES OFFERED

Stevens students are committed to exploring the frontiers of engineering, science, business, the humanities and arts. Undergraduate degrees awarded include the Bachelor of Engineering (BE), Bachelor of Science (BS), and Bachelor of Art (BA) degrees.

BE degree: Biomedical Engineering; Chemical Engineering; Civil Engineering; Computer Engineering; Electrical Engineering; Engineering Management; Environmental Engineering; Mechanical Engineering; and Naval Engineering.

BS degree: Business and Technology; Bioanalytical Chemistry; Bioinformatics; Chemical Biology; Chemistry; Computational Science; Computer Science; Cybersecurity; Engineering Physics; Finance; Information Systems; Management; Marketing; Mathematical Sciences; Physics; Science, Technology and Society; and Quantitative Finance.

BA degree: History; Literature; Music and Technology; Philosophy; Science Communications; Social Sciences; and Visual Arts and Technology.

Many students pursue dual degree options or opt to complete requirements for both bachelor's and master's degrees during their four or five years on campus.

Stevens students may also pursue a pre-professional program in dentistry, medicine, or law.

ACADEMIC PROGRAMS

In addition to its outstanding major and degree programs, Stevens offers unique and challenging educational opportunities that foster innovation and lead students to success. Research projects and summer internships are available for all major fields of study. With a strong emphasis on hands-on, experiential learning, Stevens students are afforded many opportunities to work on sophisticated projects typically reserved for graduate students at other universities.

The Cooperative Education (co-op) program is also distinctive. Co-op students alternate semesters of on-campus study with semesters of paid, professional work experience. A significant number of Stevens undergraduate students, 35 percent, elects to participate in co-op education, and the benefits are excellent. Co-op students graduate with a competitive edge in the job market, having gained a higher level of confidence through development of significant workplace skills.

The Stevens Scholars Program allows exceptional students to participate in honor seminars and summer research. Many take advantage of the option to accelerate their course work and graduate with a bachelor's and master's degree in four years at no additional cost.

Unique to Stevens is its Engineering Design Spine, an eight-course sequence of hands-on design courses that begins in students' freshman year and is closely linked to their engineering and science classes. It culminates in a capstone senior project showcased at the annual Stevens Innovation Expo. The Expo is one of many programs aimed at promoting entrepreneurial thinking at Stevens. In addition to the design project showcase, student inventors present their technologies in a fast-paced and exciting venture-style competition called the Pitch Olympics, where students propose business ideas for their new technologies to a panel of five experts, who evaluate and award the most viable projects with that have the greatest potential for market realization.

Stevens Technical Enrichment Program (STEP) helps broaden the access of minority and economically disadvantaged students to careers in engineering, science, and technology through pre-college and in-college programs and support services.

CAMPUS FACILITIES AND EQUIPMENT

Stevens operates within a technology-centric environment to meet the needs of a technologically fluent campus, offering a variety of centralized, departmental, and individual resources. Facilities include "smart" classrooms, computer-aided design and manufacturing labs, graphics labs, robotic sites, a media arts center, green screen, sound synthesis lab, a computer-aided education lab, and a financial systems center. In addition, Stevens offers its community an extensive wireless networking system with access from anywhere on campus, indoors and out. All new students are given a well-outfitted notebook computer upon entry, which includes the sophisticated software programs used in their classroom work.

There are many specialized laboratory facilities on campus used for academic and research functions, applied research, and educational programs in systems integration that meet and support the needs of government and industry. The Office of Innovation and Entrepreneurship fosters an entrepreneurial culture across the university and engages in the technology transfer that brings new ideas to the marketplace. Creative and entrepreneurial research is central to the mission of the University. Stevens has established key research areas building on existing faculty strengths and synergizing resources to address major interdisciplinary topics of national significance: healthcare and medicine; sustainable energy; financial systems; security; and STEM education. Stevens has earned distinction in several areas, including its selection by the U.S. Department of Homeland Security as a National Center of Excellence in Port Security Research, by the U.S. Department of Defense as a National Center of Excellence in Systems Engineering Research, and the National Security Agency as a National Center of Excellence in Information Assurance Research and Education.

TUITION, ROOM, BOARD, AND FEES

Stevens tuition and fees for 2013-2014 are $44,666. Room and board total $14,214 (typical on-campus, double occupancy/typical meal plan; other plans vary). Student fees consist of a student activity fee, lab fees, technology fee, and freshman orientation fee.

FINANCIAL AID

Stevens is committed to assisting, investing in, and ensuring the highest quality of service to its prospective and current students. The university offers a wide range of institutional need- and merit-based scholarships and grants, and government grant, loan, and work opportunity programs. Stevens encourages students to file the College Scholarship Service (CSS) Profile and Free Application for Federal Student Aid (FAFSA) by February 15 (Early Decision I and II applicants submit the CSS Profile by December 1 or January 15 respectively.) To apply for merit-based scholarships, no other application is needed except for the Stevens Application for Admission.

Student Organizations and Activities

Stevens' 100+ student clubs and organizations include sororities and fraternities, performing arts and athletic groups, student government, ethnic organizations, professional societies, and more. The Alpha Phi Omega service fraternity, Engineers Without Borders, and Habitat for Humanity are service-oriented groups with active student engagement. Campus traditions like Boken and TechFest (campus-wide festivals), the Unity Show, and Midnight Breakfast during finals study periods are among students' favorites.

The Schaefer Athletic and Recreation Center features a NCAA competition-size pool with Jacuzzi, four-court basketball gymnasium, racquetball courts, and a fitness center. DeBaun Field has been surfaced in a state-of the-art, durable, year-round playing surface for varsity and intramural competition. Walker Gym has an elevated indoor track plus a weightlifting facility and dance studios. There are also six outdoor tennis courts with spectacular Manhattan skyline views and a sand volleyball court.

Stevens competes in NCAA Division III sports. For men: baseball, basketball, cross-country, fencing, golf, indoor/outdoor track and field, lacrosse, soccer, swimming, tennis, volleyball and wrestling. For women: basketball, cross-country, equestrian, fencing, field hockey, indoor/outdoor track and field, lacrosse, soccer, swimming, tennis, softball and volleyball. Students may also join a club team or play intramural sports, take health and wellness or fitness classes, or participate in outdoor adventure trips.

ADMISSIONS

Stevens is highly competitive. Undergraduate applicants must submit:

An application for admission; official high school transcript which includes four years of English, four years of mathematics, and a minimum of three years of science; two letters of recommendation; personal statement or essay; standardized test scores as described below.

SAT I or ACT scores are required for all domestic applicants. International applicants can satisfy testing requirements by submitting TOEFL or IELTS scores as well as one of the following options:

Two (2) SAT II Tests – Math and either Chemistry or Physics

Two (2) AP Exams – Calculus and either Chemistry or Physics

International Baccalaureate Degree with two higher level exams scores in math or science.

International students may also submit SAT I scores in lieu of the previous recommendation.

Admissions interviews, while not required, are strongly recommended. Interviews are required for Accelerated Law and Accelerated Medical programs. Additionally, SAT II scores are required for those applying to the Accelerated Medical (at least two SAT II exams, math level I or II and biology or chemistry).

Stevens typically accepts 41% percent of its applicants and enrolls around 720 students each fall; SAT scores range from 1210-1390; and the average high school GPA is 3.9. The application deadline for the fall semester is February 1 (Early Decision I and II deadlines are November 15 and January 15, respectively.)

SWARTHMORE COLLEGE

AT A GLANCE

Swarthmore College, a highly selective college of liberal arts and engineering, celebrates the life of the mind while preparing students with the knowledge, insight, skills, and experience to become leaders for the common good.

Swarthmore, one of the nation's finest institutions of higher learning, is a college like no other. Private, yet open to all regardless of financial need. Global in outlook, the College draws students from around the world and all 50 states. Small, yet with the financial strength to offer students and faculty the resources needed to push their own and the world's understanding of disciplines from Arabic to plasma physics, from microbiology to dance, from engineering to art history.

Swarthmore graduates include CEO patent-holders who bring technology to underserved markets, investment bankers looking for alternative forms of energy, lawyers who become college presidents, doctors who serve in Congress, Nobel Prize winners, educators who establish schools in underserved parts of the world, and artists who use their talents to inspire and empower others.

So much of what Swarthmore stands for, from its commitment to curricular breadth and rigor to its demonstrated interest in facilitating discovery and fostering social responsibility among exceptional young people, lies in the quality and passion of its faculty. Professors at Swarthmore are leading scholars and researchers in their fields, yet remain deeply committed to serving their students as outstanding teachers and mentors. A student/faculty ratio of 8:1 ensures that students have close, meaningful engagement with their professors, preparing them to translate the skills and understanding gained at Swarthmore into the mark they want to make on the world.

Location and Environment

Located 11 miles southwest of Philadelphia, Swarthmore's idyllic, 425-acre campus is an arboretum, complete with rolling lawns, a creek, wooded hills, and hiking trails. From its state-of-the-art L.E.E.D. certified science center to its new residence halls with environmentally responsible design, Swarthmore's buildings and architecture stand as national models of curricular and co-curricular undergraduate facilities.

OFF-CAMPUS OPPORTUNITIES

Swarthmore College is a member of the Tri-College consortium, linking the campus to Bryn Mawr and Haverford Colleges both academically and socially. Students are also able to take courses at the University of Pennsylvania. The College offers shuttles to the other Tri-Co schools, local community service sites, movie theaters and shopping complexes, as well as to the city of Philadelphia. Public transportation is readily available with a train station located on campus; the ride to Philadelphia takes approximately 20 minutes.

MAJORS AND DEGREES OFFERED

Swarthmore College awards two degrees, the Bachelor of Arts and the Bachelor of Science. The following courses of study are offered at the College:

Art and Art History

Asian Studies

Astronomy

Biology

Black Studies

Chemistry and Biochemistry

Classics

Cognitive Science

Comparative Literature

Computer Science

Dance

Economics

Educational Studies

Engineering

English Literature

Environmental Studies

Film and Media Studies

Gender and Sexuality Studies

History

Interpretation Theory

Islamic Studies

Latin American Studies

Linguistics

Mathematics and Statistics

Medieval Studies

Modern Languages and Literatures (including Arabic, Chinese, French, German, Japanese, Russian, and Spanish)

Music

Peace and Conflict Studies

Philosophy

Physics

Political Science

Psychology

Religion

Sociology and Anthropology

Theater

ACADEMIC PROGRAMS

The College offers more than 600 courses a year; an exceptional Honors Program; individual special majors; a program in education that leads to Pennsylvania secondary school certification; and undergraduate research opportunities in the sciences, social sciences, humanities, and engineering.

Swarthmore's Honors Program features faculty working with small groups of dedicated and accomplished students; an emphasis on independent learning; students entering into a dialogue with peers, teachers, and examiners; a demanding program of study in major and minor fields; and an examination at the end of two years' study by outside scholars.

CAMPUS FACILITIES AND EQUIPMENT

The 425-acre campus is an arboretum. Arts resources include an art gallery, dance studios, cinema, and theater performance space. Highlights of Swarthmore's library facilities include the Friends Historical Library and the Peace Collection. The athletics facilities include a lighted stadium complex, a 400-meter dual durometer track, a synthetic grass playing field, fitness center, and indoor tennis courts. The Science Center is L.E.E.D. certified. The College's two newest residence halls feature loft-style rooms and environmentally friendly green roofs.

TUITION, ROOM, BOARD, AND FEES

For 2012–2013, the College charges including tuition, room, board, and student activity fee total $55,750. The activity fee covers not only the usual student services—health, library, laboratory fees, for example—but admission to all social, cultural, and athletic events on campus.

FINANCIAL AID

Swarthmore commits its strong financial aid program to ensuring that all capable students have access to the College. In the coming year, Swarthmore College will award in excess of $30 million in scholarships. For U.S. citizens and permanent residents, a student's financial need will not influence his or her admission decision, as the two decisions are made independently at Swarthmore. Financial aid is also available for international students. All Swarthmore aid awards are loan-free to meet the full demonstrated need for admitted students.

STUDENT ORGANIZATIONS AND ACTIVITIES

With more than 100 student clubs and organizations on campus, dozens of community service groups, 22 varsity athletic teams, free lectures and performances occurring daily on campus, and full academic schedules, Swarthmore students are rarely idle. The student culture encourages involvement and a strong sense of community.

ADMISSIONS PROCESS

In an effort to seek a variety of students leading to a well-rounded class, the admissions staff carefully considers a number of criteria without a rigid emphasis on any one factor in particular. Applicants are evaluated based upon the following:

High school record (as well as strength of curriculum)

Rank in class (if high school ranks)

Standardized tests (SAT with 2 SAT Subject Tests or ACT with Writing)

Extracurricular commitments

Essays (included in application)

Recommendations (two from academic teachers, one from counselor)

Interview (highly recommended but not required)

SWEET BRIAR COLLEGE

AT A GLANCE

Since its founding in 1901, Sweet Briar College has been deeply committed to the education of women. It is consistently ranked as one of the top liberal arts and sciences colleges in the country. For the past several years, Sweet Briar has ranked in the Princeton Review categories that reflect the College's core mission: the accessibility of its faculty, the beauty of the campus, the encouragement of class discussion and the strength of the career placement program.

In the National Survey of Student Engagement (NSSE), a national survey recognized as one of the most reliable assessments of effective practices in higher education, Sweet Briar seniors rated the College above the nation's benchmarks for level of academic challenge, active collaborative learning, student-faculty interaction, enriching educational experiences and being a supportive campus environment.

At Sweet Briar, faculty and staff members are committed to helping each individual young woman reach her full potential. Impressive outcome statistics help demonstrate the effectiveness of this commitment — six-months after graduation, nearly two-thirds of graduates from the Class of 2012 were employed and slightly over one-third were pursuing advanced studies.

About 700 women from across the country and around the world are enrolled at Sweet Briar's Virginia campus; another 120 students are enrolled in Sweet Briar's coed Junior Year in France and Junior Year in Spain programs.

A Sweet Briar education sets in motion the conviction that any goal is achievable, and prepares young women for a lifetime of success. Classes average twelve students, and a student to faculty ratio of 8:1 ensures academic interaction and personal attention.

LOCATION AND ENVIRONMENT

Sweet Briar is located in central Virginia in the foothills of the Blue Ridge Mountains. The spacious campus of 3,250 acres contains hiking trails, nature preserves, and spectacular views. The core buildings, designed by Ralph Adams Cram, form the Sweet Briar College National Historic District.

The College opened a 53,000 square foot Fitness and Athletic Center (FAC) addition to its gymnasium in November 2009, as well as a new "green" residence hall/townhouse facility in August of that year. The FAC includes multiple volleyball/tennis courts, a suspended indoor running track, racquetball courts, lots of student common space, and a movie theater. The "Green Village" is composed of 5 buildings, each with 3 townhomes, providing an independent living option for 60 seniors and juniors. Sweet Briar is the only college in the country with a residential artists' colony on its campus, the Virginia Center for the Creative Arts. The on-campus equestrian center, one of the largest and best-designed college facilities in the country, attracts both competitive and recreational riders.

The community atmosphere of the College is enhanced by the large proportion of faculty and administrators who also live on campus.

The College is 12 miles north of Lynchburg, Virginia; less than an hour south of Charlottesville, Virginia; and about 3 hours southwest of Washington, D.C.

OFF-CAMPUS OPPORTUNITIES

By the time they graduate, more than a third of Sweet Briar students have studied abroad. The Sweet Briar Junior Year in France was the first program in Paris for American students, and students from colleges and universities across the country have participated in the coed program. The successful Junior Year in Spain is recognized as the premier program in Seville. The College has special relationships with the University of St. Andrews in Scotland, Heidelberg University in Germany, Doshisha Women's College in Japan, and the University of Urbino in Italy. Sweet Briar students have also chosen the following destinations for study abroad: Australia, China, the Czech Republic, Denmark, Greece, Holland, Ireland, Jamaica, Korea, Mongolia, Morocco, New Zealand, Vietnam, and Thailand. Off-campus study may also include an Environmental Junior Year, the Washington Semester at American University, and summer programs at St. Anne's College in Oxford, England. Summer programs are also available in Australia; Central America, including Costa Rica; Münster, Germany; Rome and Urbino, Italy; Nepal; and Spain.

Sweet Briar participates in the Tri-College Consortium with Randolph College and Lynchburg College. In addition to taking courses at the other colleges, students can participate in combined social and cultural activities on those campuses.

MAJORS AND DEGREES OFFERED

Sweet Briar awards the Bachelor of Arts, Bachelor of Science, and Bachelor of Fine Arts degrees. The College offers majors in anthropology, art history, biochemistry and molecular biology, biology, business management, chemistry, classics, dance, economics, education, engineering science, English, English and creative writing, environmental science, French, government, history, international affairs, mathematics, modern languages and literatures, music, musical theater, philosophy, physics, psychology, religion, sociology, Spanish, studio art, and theater.

Additional areas of study, minors, and certificate programs include archeology, arts management, equine studies, engineering (3-2 dual degree), journalism, new media and communications, Latin American studies, law and society, medieval and Renaissance studies, pre-law, pre-medicine, and pre-veterinary science. Students may design an interdisciplinary major focused on a topic of special interest or may construct personalized majors.

ACADEMIC PROGRAMS

Sweet Briar's mission is to prepare women to be active, responsible members of a world community. Underscoring every one of the major fields of study is the idea that the best way to learn about the world is to experience it. The curriculum emphasizes hands-on learning, comprehensive understanding, analysis, reflection, creativity, and communication across disciplines. The academic programs are nationally celebrated. To add to this, the College recently adopted a strategic plan that includes emphasis on providing an education that is dynamic, digitally sophisticated, connected, and entrepreneurial. Making the most effective use of Sweet Briar's unique campus as a "landscape for learning," the strategic plan aims at an educational experience that prepares students to engage with today's digital world, be ready to adapt to the dizzying rate of technological change, and encourage entrepreneurial thinking across disciplines.

The general education program has four components—composition and writing, skills requirements, experiences requirements, and knowledge areas requirements—that work together to ensure the development of strong communication and quantitative reasoning skills. Independent studies and seminars are included in most majors, with a culminating senior course or exercise required in most majors. Sweet Briar has a chapter of Phi Beta Kappa and was the first women's college to establish a chapter of the pre-law honorary society Phi Alpha Delta. It also has a four-year honors program that is nationally recognized for its innovative partnering of interdisciplinary academic and co-curricular programs. Honors students may take special tutorials and seminars as well as complete a yearlong research project culminating in an honors thesis on an original topic.

Sweet Briar's two-semester calendar allows students to participate in intensive courses, independent research projects, or internships on campus or throughout the world.

CAMPUS FACILITIES AND EQUIPMENT

Sweet Briar's library collection of over 300,000 print items, nearly 50,000 journals and access to millions of items through electronic databases support high levels of student learning. Strong areas of the collection include art history, the sciences, religion and music. Computer labs running Mac OS and Windows operating systems are open 24 hours a day, and there is wireless and wired high-speed Internet access throughout campus, including many outdoor spaces. The student-computer ratio is 6:1.

A lab for Sweet Briar's engineering department includes a 5-Kip-capacity Universal Test Machine; a United Tru-Blue Rockwell hardness tester; a set of gauged beams and test fixtures for mechanics experiments; eight new computers, each with NI ELVIS and Labview with Protoboards; and a well-equipped machine shop. Students studying science use state-of-the-art equipment that enhances faculty-student collaborative research. Biology equipment includes a scanning electron microscope with digital imaging system, equipment for plant and animal tissue culture, and DNA sequencing equipment. Chemistry students have access to two nuclear magnetic resonance spectrometers (NMR; 400 MHz and 60 MHz), an atomic absorption spectrometer (AAS), a diode array UV/Vis spectrometer, a Fourier-transform infrared spectrometer (FT-IR), a modular LASER laboratory, a gas chromatograph/mass spectrograph (GC/MS), a high-pressure liquid chromatograph (HPLC), and a differential scanning calorimeter (DSC). Physics equipment includes a scanning tunneling microscope, an X-ray crystallography system, and holographic instrumentation.

The environmental studies program occupies two sites. A renovated train station provides classroom and laboratory space equipped with a Rigaku Miniflex powder X-ray diffraction system for mineralogical analysis, a Rocklabs bench-top ring mill for grinding rock and soil samples, a drying oven, a high-temperature muffle furnace, and more. An adjacent caboose car provides office space for faculty members. A water treatment plant was also converted to an education/nature center and environmental lab; equipment includes instrumentation for sampling water, soil, wastewater, and sediment, including N-Con composite samplers, macroinvertebrate samplers, and specialized water-collection devices.

The Babcock Fine Arts Center includes individual practice rooms, an electronic piano lab, dance studios, theaters, and Murchison Lane Auditorium for lectures and performing arts. Two former dairy barns were renovated for classroom and office space to house studio arts, including a ceramics and sculpture studio; four large studios for painting, drawing, and printmaking; and a photo studio and darkroom.

The Academic Resource Center (ARC) provides free of charge to all students academic support services that include assistance with papers and study strategies, a personalized time management system, stress management advice, tutoring information, and one-on-one peer mentoring. The ARC also provides support and learning strategies for students with diagnosed learning differences.

TUITION, ROOM, BOARD AND FEES

For 2013–14, tuition and fees were $33,605 and room and board totaled $11,800. Books and supplies were estimated at $1,200 and personal expenses averaged $1,250.

FINANCIAL AID

A family's financial circumstance does not limit a student's choices at Sweet Briar because of the College's generous financial aid program. More than 95 percent of enrolling students receive financial assistance from the College, including merit scholarships, need-based grants, loans, and work-study awards. Scholarships for international students are also available on a competitive basis.

STUDENT ORGANIZATIONS AND ACTIVITIES

Students who derive the most from the Sweet Briar experience are those who participate in and contribute to community life, striking a good balance between academic work and the rest of life. They recognize that one of the advantages of the College is the unlimited opportunities for women to participate and assume leadership roles in many types of organizations and activities. About fifty campus organizations are available, including honor societies, a literary journal, community service groups, a multicultural club, political groups, a student newspaper, drama and dance clubs, a radio station, and singing groups. Students plan and participate in an extensive array of concerts, films, and dance and theater productions as well as workshops and master classes by visiting scholars and performers. Visitors have included the best-selling novelists Masha Hamilton and Barbara Kingsolver, physicist Brian Greene, food journalist Michael Pollan, environmental attorney Robert F. Kennedy Jr., columnist Christine Brennan, and naturalist E. O. Wilson.

Varsity athletes compete in NCAA Division III field hockey, lacrosse, soccer, softball, swimming, and tennis. Club sports include cross-country, fencing, volleyball, and riding.

ADMISSIONS PROCESS

Sweet Briar seeks talented women who are adventurous, enthusiastic about learning, and want to take an active part in their education. The Admissions Committee looks for qualities such as independent thinking, ethical principles, assertiveness, and an appreciation of diversity. Sweet Briar welcomes students of all economic, ethnic, geographic, religious, and social backgrounds.

Requirements normally include a minimum of 4 units in English, 3 in mathematics, 3 in social studies, 2 sequential years in a foreign language, and 3 units in science, as well as additional units in these subjects to total 16. Most candidates have 20 such academic units. Special attention is given to the difficulty of the applicant's curriculum and her academic achievement in the classroom; scores on the SAT or ACT are required. An interview at the College is strongly encouraged but not required. Candidates who are unable to visit the campus are invited to meet with staff members or talk with alumnae in their hometowns.

Prospective students are encouraged to contact the admissions office for the appropriate application deadlines and options. Sweet Briar will notify each student of acceptance within one month of the date her application becomes complete. A completed application includes a transcript of the candidate's academic work, scores on the required test, recommendations from the guidance counselor and a teacher, and an essay written by the candidate. There is a $40 application fee, which may be waived at the request of the student's guidance counselor if it is deemed to be a financial burden. Sweet Briar also accepts the Common Application (a supplement is required). All materials and requests for information should be sent to the admissions office at the address listed below.

DEAN OF ADMISSIONS

Sweet Briar College

P.O. Box 1052

Sweet Briar, Virginia 24595

Phone: 434-381-6142

800-381-6142 (toll-free)

TEMPLE UNIVERSITY

AT A GLANCE

Temple University attracts the nation's brightest and most motivated minds from all 50 states and 130 foreign countries. Offering the perfect combination of large-school resources and a small-school feel, Temple has something for every kind of student. At home in Philadelphia, Pennsylvania, Temple is nationally recognized for innovative achievements in teaching and research. Students have the opportunity to choose between suburban and city campuses. Temple University strives to instill a sense of global perspective in our students and offers the ability to study at our campuses in Rome, Italy and Tokyo, Japan. On all of our campuses, the Temple faculty includes instructors who are distinguished and active members in their fields. Professors bring the critical perspective of scholars and the practical knowledge of their discipline to their classrooms. With an average class-size of just 27, students have the access they need to thrive within the classroom. Temple is renowned in areas such as Business, Communications, Education, Art, Music, Science, and the Health Professions, and Temple graduates have the know-how and confidence to achieve success and make lasting contributions. Driven by the knowledge that the greatest students are students that are having fun, Temple goes to great lengths to make sure students are never at a loss for things to do. With a campus that is home to more than 25,000 students, activities are as diverse as the student body. In addition to cultural, athletic, and social events on campus, students always have the nation's 6th largest city at their fingertips.

LOCATION AND ENVIRONMENT

The city of Philadelphia is the cornerstone of life at Temple. One of the largest cities on the East Coast, Philadelphia is home to a variety of forward-looking businesses, progressive work in technology and science, and thriving artistic output. While the city is the product of a rich history, it is also a center for 21st century innovation and culture. With plays, concerts, museums, major league sporting events, shopping, clubs, and restaurants, Philadelphia provides students with tremendous opportunities for resources and fun. As an alternative to the urban setting, students can attend Temple University Ambler, set on 187 acres 30 minutes outside of the city. Ambler is a great choice for students who want all the resources of a world-renowned research university in a small and quiet setting. Temple also offers three additional campuses/sites in the Philadelphia region. Free shuttles connect all of our campuses giving Temple students ample opportunities to experience the many sides of Temple University.

OFF-CAMPUS OPPORTUNITIES

For Temple, "off-campus" is synonymous with opportunity. Whether it's hopping the subway to an internship with a Fortune 500 Company, hailing a cab to see priceless works of art at Philadelphia's museums, or flying to one of the dozens of study-abroad programs we have to offer, the world off-campus serves us as a classroom without walls.

Temple students are encouraged to incorporate travel and study into their academic experience. In addition to the tremendous opportunities of Philadelphia, the world abroad presents students with an exciting and affordable way to gain invaluable global perspective. Boasting a list of locales from Scotland to France and from Ghana to Beijing and campuses in Rome and Tokyo, a Temple education becomes more than just books and papers - it's about experience.

MAJORS AND DEGREES OFFERED

Temple University offers 122 undergraduate majors through 13 undergraduate schools and colleges. Temple has become nationally recognized in areas such as business, communications, education, engineering, health professions, liberal arts, science and technology, tourism and hospitality, horticulture, music and the arts.

ACADEMIC PROGRAMS

Academics form the foundation of your college life, and at Temple, GenEd is the heart of that experience. GenEd provides connections through dozens of new courses that are fresh, relevant and exciting – courses like The Jazz Century, Sustainable Environments, The Bionic Human and Global Cities. All have a focus on complex 21st century problems, from global climate change to global terrorism. Many of them will take you into the city through PEX, the Philadelphia passport program, free or discounted admission to cultural events across the city: museums, dance performances, historic buildings, local schools and community centers, green roofs and neighborhood gardens.

Temple University offers an extensive breadth of academic programs that provide graduates with an esteemed education. Temple's mission is to provide students with the resources they need to become leaders in their fields. Whether it's cutting-edge technology, a diverse educational experience, or small classes, Temple succeeds in producing graduates that are critical thinkers in addition to working professionals. By integrating the foundations of a student's field in major coursework with a scholarly approach to conceptual ideas through our general education curriculum, Temple prepares students for the rigors of the workplace and the complexity of the world around them. Temple recognizes that education should be personalized to meet the diverse needs of a diverse student body. First-year students can participate in courses and programs that are designed to meet their unique needs. Additionally, programs like University Honors and Diamond Research Scholars provide tremendous opportunities for students seeking a more rigorous intellectual challenge. Wholly, Temple University's academic programs are founded on a comprehensive and personalized approach to education that enables students to thrive.

CAMPUS FACILITIES AND EQUIPMENT

Temple University's facilities are on the cutting-edge of technology and expose today's students to tomorrow's innovation. Home to the TECH Center, one of the largest student computer labs in the country, Temple students have access to nearly 2,000 computers in over a dozen computer labs across campus. With a campus that is nearly 90% wireless, students have limitless access to information and 24-hour access to their courses through the Temple Blackboard® system. Temple also strives to bring technology into the classroom by outfitting them with "smart" technology as can be seen in Temple's Alter Hall, a state-of-the-art building for our Fox School of Business. Also new to campus, the Tyler School of Art building on Main Campus is one of the finest and most advanced facilities of its kind in the nation. Tyler's new Architecture building opened in fall 2011. The university is currently constructing a new residence hall as well as a Science and Research Center that will open in 2013 and 2014, respectively. On the social scene, Temple's Student Center offers students lounges, a food court, a non-alcoholic nightclub, and a movie theater. Temple's Liacouras Walk is home to restaurants and shops that make campus a city within a city. To stave off that weight from the world-famous Philly cheese steaks, students have access to the Independence Blue Cross Student Recreation Center and the Temple University Fitness (TUF) where they can work out with state-of-the-art equipment, take fitness classes, or run the top-floor indoor track. Also, Temple is the proud home of the 11,000 seat Liacouras Center that serves campus as the state-of-the-art home for men's and women's basketball and a variety of top-ticket concerts throughout the year. Temple has been called a "boomtown" as it continues to make improvements and additions to an already vibrant and modern campus.

TUITION, ROOM, BOARD AND FEES

In 2012-2013, full-time undergraduates that are Pennsylvania residents pay $13,006 per year. Students that are residents of other states pay $22,832 per year. Room and board and annual fees cost an additional $9,300 per year on average. Specific schools and colleges within the university, including the Boyer College of Music and Dance, the Tyler School of Art, the College of Health Professions and Social Work, the College of Engineering, the School of Media and Communication, and the Fox School of Business, may charge slightly different tuitions.

FINANCIAL AID

Those seeking financial aid are asked to submit the Free Application for Federal Student Aid (FAFSA). The deadline for the FAFSA is March 1st. Students transferring to Temple need to submit a financial aid transcript whether they received aid at their previous institution or not. Merit-based scholarships are awarded to top students annually and vary in value from $3000-full tuition. These scholarships may be renewed for each of a student's four years.

STUDENT ORGANIZATIONS AND ACTIVITIES

Temple's campuses are always pulsating with activity. Whether it's a movie night in the residence halls or grabbing a slice of pizza at the campus food court, the Temple experience centers upon living on campus. With 12,000 students that live on or around campus, Temple students never run out of things to do. More than 200 clubs and organizations provide opportunities for socializing, political debate and community service. Temple is also home to 23 NCAA Division I athletics and offers students free tickets to games. For the student who wants to do more than watch, students can get involved with a large variety of intramural sports teams. For students who wish to indulge their cultural side, Temple's prestigious art, music, dance, and theater departments offer over 75 performances and exhibitions annually. Temple University also offers plenty of opportunities for students to take a break from the books with events like "Free Food and Fun Fridays" and an array of low-priced trips to ski resorts, amusements parks, and local attractions. But with downtown Philadelphia less than two miles from campus, Temple students take advantage of the city they call home. With attractions like the Philadelphia Museum of Art, Olde City, South Street, the Italian Market, Main Street Manayunk and the Avenue of the Arts, students find a world of fun to be experienced in their backyard.

ADMISSIONS PROCESS

Temple University takes a holistic approach to the admissions process by taking into consideration every piece of information that a student chooses to provide. Applications are reviewed by the admissions committee in an individualized context. But to standardize the process for all of our applicants, the admissions committee will look at three things specifically. The first and most important piece of information is the student's high school record. Generally, students should have a strong and consistent 3.30 GPA (B+) in academic coursework. Students are required to submit scores from college entrance exams (SAT or ACT). For the SAT, the admissions committee would like to see that a student has a score that is close to Temple's average, which ranges from 500-600 on each section. The Writing section of the SAT is also considered as part of the admissions review process. Temple's average for the ACT is a 23 composite score, and the Writing section of this test is required and considered. Given our holistic approach, Temple also gives consideration to the student's essay, extracurricular activities, recommendation letters and special awards and honors. All applicants are automatically assessed for merit scholarships and the University Honors Program.

The best way to apply to Temple is online at admissions.temple.edu/apply or via the Common Application. Temple's application deadline is November 1st for early action and March 1st for rolling admission. For questions, Temple encourages students to visit our website at admissions.temple.edu, email us at askanowl@temple.edu or find us on Twitter @admissionsTU.

THOMAS MORE COLLEGE

AT A GLANCE

Thomas More College is a small, liberal arts college with a big reputation. Money Magazine ranks Thomas More as one of the "Best College Buys" in higher education. And the Carnegie Foundation for the Advancement of Teaching praises the college as a "selective liberal arts college."

Founded in 1921 by the Benedictine Sisters as Villa Madonna College, Thomas More now serves approximately 1,900 full- and part-time students from across the country and around the world on its beautiful campus. Whether you plan to earn an advanced degree at another university, or pursue your career upon graduation, a degree from Thomas More College prepares you well for your next challenge in life.

LOCATION AND ENVIRONMENT

Thomas More College is ideally located in beautiful Crestview Hills, Kentucky, just 10 minutes from downtown Cincinnati, Ohio.

MAJORS AND DEGREES OFFERED

UNDERGRADUATE

Accountancy°

Art°

Art History°

Biology°

Business Administration°

Chemistry°

Communication°

Computer Information Systems°

Criminal Justice°

Economics°

Education

English°

Environmental Science

Forensic Science

French°°

Gerontology°°

History°

Humanities°

International Studies°

Mathematics°

Medical Laboratory Science

Music°°

Nursing

Philosophy°

Physics°

Political Science°

Pre-Engineering

Pre-Legal Studies°°

Pre-Dental

Pre-Medical

Pre-Pharmacy

Pre-Veterinary

Pre-Occupational or Physical Therapy

Psychology°

Sociology°

Spanish°

Sports Entertainment Marketing

Theatre°

Theology°

°Also offered as a two-year degree program.

°°Only offered as a two-year degree program

CAMPUS FACILITIES

The Thomas More experience begins in the academic building yet transcends the confines of the four walls of a classroom. For a small, private, liberal arts school, Thomas More is packed with big ideas, featured facilities and powerful programs that are sure to make a big impact on your life stretching your mind, feeding your soul, and lifting your spirit.

The main campus of Thomas More College is situated on over 100 beautiful acres within walking distance of the Crestview Towncenter which includes shopping, dining and numerous retail options. Unique features of the campus include the fully-equipped Observatory, the state-of-the-art Library Center, new athletic complex, newly renovated Seiler Commons dining facility, new Chapel and the Student Center. These are just some of the featured cornerstones of excellence and opportunity for Thomas More students.

The Biology Field Station located on the Ohio River provides a unique opportunity for undergraduate research. The field station includes a research center, undergraduate housing for research students, classrooms, conference space and boat docks. Thomas More College works with numerous government agencies in conducting river research and monitoring water quality. These opportunities allow for experiential learning at the undergraduate level and the basis for our students to publish and present at local, regional and national conferences.

CAMPUS LIFE

With more than 35% of our traditional students living on campus in four residence halls, residence life is an important part of the total Thomas More experience. Forming the nucleus of the campus community, resident students experience first-hand the important interaction and life skills that will help shape their lives. Our residence halls create a comfortable and safe living-learning environment, which encourages personal growth and development through a variety of activities and social interaction. Each resident is a 'citizen' in this special community, contributing to an atmosphere of harmony and maturity.

For those who choose not to live on campus, it is easy and convenient to become an active member of the campus community. Student activities, intramural sports, campus ministry, clubs and organizations and Greek life provide a vibrant atmosphere and active social life. Whether as a fan or player, participating in NCAA athletics as a member of the President's Athletic conference provides a wonderful atmosphere on campus.

ATHLETICS

Thomas More College is a member of the Presidents' Athletic Conference (one of the most competitive NCAA

Division III conferences in the country) and sponsors a total of 16 men's and women's varsity athletic teams. The Saints have a rich athletic tradition that includes a national championship, consistent berths in the NCAA tournaments, conference tournament titles and individual honors. For information about athletics at Thomas More College, visit www.thomasmore.edu/athletics

ADMISSIONS PROCESS

The admissions staff at Thomas More offers a personal experience as you navigate the college search process. Never hesitate to contact our staff for assistance, to plan a personalized visit to campus or with questions about Thomas More or the admissions process in general.

The College makes the admission process simple and easy! There are three ways to Apply:

1. Save $25 by applying online at www.thomasmore.edu

2. Complete a paper application and submit by mail with your $25 application fee.

3. Download a paper application from www.thomasmore.edu and submit by mail with your $25 application fee.

Do You Qualify?

Entering students have a high school average of C or better, and a minimum of 20 on the ACT or 940 on the SAT. Transfer students with less than 24 hours of transferable credit must meet the freshman admission criteria, while those with more than 24 hours must have a college GPA of 2.0 or higher. We also look at your extracurricular activities, as well as life or work experience, as important indicators of your ability to succeed at Thomas More.

TUITION, ROOM, BOARD AND FEES

For the school year of 2012-2013 the cost per semester is:

Tuition

Full-Time student 12-18 credit hours: $13,250

Part-Time student 1-11 credit hours: $590 per credit hour

Nursing Differential: $30 per credit hour

Fees

Technology Fee for full-time student: $300

Technology Fee for part-time student: $30/ credit hour, max $300

Student Activity Fee: $60

Reservation Deposit: $100

Orientation Fee (one-time): $125

Room

Housing Security Deposit: $100

Double Occupancy: $1,750

Single Occupancy: $2,110

Two Bedroom Suites: $2,110

Board

19 meal plan with $65 flex dollars: $2,020

14 meal plan with $115 flex dollars: $1,720

10 meal plan with $115 flex dollars: $1,450

FINANCIAL AID

The Office of Financial Aid works to keep tuition affordable for students and their families, while maintaining high standards of quality throughout the College's academic and extracurricular programs. Our track record of helping students experience a high-quality private education at the most affordable price underscores our mission of expanding access to educational opportunities. All Thomas More College students receive financial aid from the institution and the average institutional aid package is $13,000.

TMC3, The Three Year Degree Program at Thomas More College

Thomas More College offers a three year bachelor's degree program as an option in the traditional class track. Students take a challenging course load in the fall and spring semesters for three years, and elective classes in the summer session following the first and second year. The program has a fixed cost that is guaranteed not to increase for the duration of the program. For complete information on program requirements, curriculum and financing, visit www.thomasmore.edu/tmc3

FOR YOUR WHOLE LIFE

Thomas More College offers an experience that you will carry with you For Your Whole Life. Visit the website, www.thomasmore.edu to explore more about how this small, liberal arts Catholic College can meet your needs and provide the opportunities of a lifetime.

TRANSYLVANIA UNIVERSITY

AT A GLANCE

Transylvania, a small, private co-ed liberal arts college of approximately 1,100 students, is consistently ranked among the best small colleges in the nation. With a rich history dating back to its founding in 1780, Transylvania holds the distinction of being the sixteenth oldest college in the nation and the first college founded west of the Allegheny Mountains. Literally meaning "across the woods" in Latin, the university established the first schools of medicine and law in what was then the West and educated the doctors, lawyers, ministers, political leaders, and others who helped shape the young nation. Transylvania also founded the first college literary magazine in the West, The Transylvanian, still published by students today.

Transylvania continues as a pioneer in higher education, preparing future leaders in business, government, education, the sciences, and the arts. Over the past decade, Transylvania faculty members have won six Kentucky professor of the year awards. The excellence of Transylvania faculty is evidenced by the common sight of professors working side by side with students in small classes. None of Transylvania's classes have more than 35 students, and 47 percent of classes have 10 or fewer students. The student-faculty ratio is 11:1, and 97 percent of full-time faculty members hold a doctorate or the highest degree in their fields. Many faculty members are recognized for their scholarship and professional activities, but their central concern is teaching and advising. Due in large part to these small classes and close collaborations with faculty, a high percentage of graduates attend selective medical, law, and other graduate and professional programs.

Transylvania students are an active and involved group, enriching their lives of each of their peers through a vibrant and dynamic campus community. Students benefit from tremendous opportunities for learning outside the classroom and off-campus, oftentimes choosing to participate in campus and community organizations. Many students reach out to the Lexington community by pursuing research projects, internships, and volunteer activities that allow them to grow and learn in a broader context. Also, over two-thirds of students embrace the global community through study abroad programs at Transylvania.

LOCATION AND ENVIRONMENT

Transylvania is located in Lexington, Kentucky, a city of 300,000 and a growing center of commerce, culture, research, and education. Known as the horse capital of the world, rolling green pastures of the famous Bluegrass region of central Kentucky surround the city. The area is also home to over 30,000 college students. Transylvania's park-like campus is just a 5-minute walk from a lively downtown, with easy access to diverse restaurants, shops, and entertainment. The proximity to downtown is also an advantage for students who want convenient part-time jobs and internship opportunities in law offices, financial firms, hospitals, non-profits, and other organizations.

OFF-CAMPUS OPPORTUNITIES

Experiencing diverse cultures through international study is a vital part of a Transylvania liberal arts education. Students are encouraged to study abroad for a summer, a term, or a year. In recent years, Transylvania students have studied in 52 foreign countries. Scholarships are available for both semester-long and summer study abroad programs. Summer study programs, including those in Austria, Brazil, China, Costa Rica, Ecuador, France, Germany, Italy, Japan, Mexico, and Spain, are available through Transylvania's affiliation with the Kentucky Institute for International Studies. Transylvania also cooperates with the English-Speaking Union to offer advanced students scholarships for summer study at Cambridge and Oxford Universities. Students may participate in seminars or internships in Washington, D.C., through the Washington Center and in the Canadian Parliamentary Internship Program in Ottawa. Internships with congressional offices, Kentucky state government, city government, and local firms are easily arranged.

MAJORS AND DEGREES OFFERED

The Bachelor of Arts degree is awarded in the following majors: accounting, anthropology, art history, art studio, biology, business administration (concentrations in finance, hospitality management, management, and marketing), chemistry (concentrations in chemistry and in biochemistry), classics, computer science, drama, economics, education, educational studies, English, exercise science, French, German, history, international affairs, mathematics, music, music technology, neuroscience, PPE (politics, philosophy, and economics), philosophy, physical education, physics, political science, psychology, religion, sociology, Spanish, and writing, rhetoric, and communication. Individually designed majors also may be arranged, and students have the option to double major. Minors are available in most majors and in Asian studies, classical studies, communication, environmental studies, hospitality management, multicultural studies, and women's studies. Advising and undergraduate preparation are provided for pre-professional programs in dentistry, engineering, law, medicine, ministry, pharmacy, physical therapy, and veterinary medicine. A cooperative program in engineering allows students to earn a B.A. in physics or liberal studies from Transylvania in three years and a B.S. in engineering from the University of Kentucky or Vanderbilt University in two years.

ACADEMIC PROGRAMS

The academic year is based on a 4-4-1 academic calendar, with two 14-week terms (fall and winter) and a one-month May term. During the May term, students participate in a variety of programs on or off campus. Students normally take four courses in each of the fall and winter terms and one course in the May term. Thirty-six courses are required to graduate. Freshmen participate in a unique first-year academic experience beginning with August Term. August Term is an innovative three-week experience designed to prepare students for academic success and personal growth. Students learn their way around campus, explore the city of Lexington, and earn a full-course credit in the First Engagements seminar. August Term is followed by a two-term First Year Seminar program, which features small-group discussions with a faculty leader; lectures, films, concerts, and other presentations; and a tutorial program in critical reading, critical thinking, and research skills. Students must complete requirements designed to ensure broad familiarity with the major areas of learning and human endeavor in the humanities and fine arts, social sciences, natural sciences and mathematics, logic, and languages.

CAMPUS FACILITIES

Transylvania University's academic facilities pay homage to its rich historical design while keeping up-to-date with current technology. In all of the academic buildings, students have access to wireless internet. Two Georgian-style buildings combine elegance with high-tech facilities to offer the latest advances in teaching and learning. The Cowgill Center for Business, Economics, and Education includes a multimedia classroom where professors from any discipline can use a large display screen to show the entire class information from one of the twenty-five networked student computers. A specialized area for education majors includes a laboratory classroom for teacher training. The Lucille C. Little Theater, used for faculty- and student-directed productions and drama classes, is a technically innovative facility that includes computerized lighting and sound, flexible staging options, and movable seating. The Frances Carrick Thomas/J. Douglas Gay, Jr. Library offers sophisticated computerized databases, which are invaluable for research and can be accessed from any computer connected to Transylvania's server. The Mitchell Fine Arts Center provides music program facilities, including practice rooms, a recital hall, and an auditorium. It also houses the Career Development Center, which helps students research career options, improve job search skills, arrange internships and part-time jobs, and apply to graduate schools and to professional positions. Mitchell is also home to a state-of-the-art Fine Arts Technology Lab. The Charles L. Shearer Art Building is dedicated to instructional space, student and faculty studios, and a student gallery. Other modern facilities include the newly renovated L. A. Brown Science Center, the Haupt Humanities Building, and the Clive M. Beck Athletic and Recreation Center, which includes a state-of-the-art fitness center.

About 80 percent of students, and 98 percent of first-year students, live on campus in seven residence halls - two for men, one for women, and four for men and women. These include traditional-style accommodations, apartment-style living for upper class students, and suite style rooms. Thomson Hall, opened in fall 2008, was only the second residence hall in the southeast to earn the EPA's Energy Star certification. All rooms are air-conditioned and completely furnished, with access to Transylvania's cable television and computer networks. Each residence hall has ample lounge and study space and easy access to computer labs and recreational facilities. Dining options include a cafeteria, two grills, and a coffee shop. The William T. Young Campus Center offers a competition-size indoor pool, a gymnasium, and other meeting and recreation facilities.

TUITION, ROOM, BOARD AND FEES

Transylvania charges an annual tuition that covers fall, winter, and May terms for a normal full-time schedule of courses. For 2013-14, tuition and fees are $31,560 and room and board (double occupancy) are $8,975.

FINANCIAL AID

Transylvania is committed to providing financial aid to students and their families. Four types of financial assistance are available: scholarships, which are based on academic performance and leadership. Grants, loans, and work-study are based on financial need. Over 90 percent of Transylvania students receive some form of financial assistance, and many receive more than one type of aid. Outstanding entering freshmen may qualify for one of twenty full-tuition William T. Young Scholarships, each worth more than $120,000 over four years. Submission of Transylvania's Application for Admission and Scholarships is all that is necessary to be considered for academic scholarships at Transylvania. Students who are interested in need-based aid must file the Free Application for Federal Student Aid (FAFSA).

STUDENT ORGANIZATIONS AND ACTIVITIES

Transylvania offers more than sixty co-curricular organizations covering a range of student interests. The athletics program, in NCAA Division III, includes nine varsity sports for men, thirteen for women, and more than a dozen intramural sports. Transylvania also has four national sororities and four national fraternities.

ADMISSIONS PROCESS

Each applicant is considered individually on the basis of academic performance, SAT scores and/or ACT scores, activities, interests, essays, and recommendations. Admission is also offered to transfer students, international students and nontraditional students.

Transylvania enrolled approximately 350 new students each academic year. The middle 50 percent composite ACT score for the freshman class iss 24 to 30.. Nearly fifty percent are in the top 10 percent of their high school class.

Submission of a Transylvania Application for Admission and Scholarships or submission of the Common Application is all that is necessary to be considered for admission and academic scholarships at Transylvania. The early action deadline is December 1 for applicants who wish to learn of their admission by January 15 and who want to be considered for all Transylvania scholarships. February 1 is the regular admission and scholarships deadline for applicants who wish to be considered for all Transylvania scholarships except the William T. Young and Trustee Scholarships. Applicants who apply after February 1 are considered on a space-available basis. The deadline for applications for the winter term, which begins in January, is December 1.

Students considering Transylvania are urged to visit the campus, and high school seniors are encouraged to stay overnight in a dorm with a student admissions ambassador. Weekday visits may include a customized campus tour; the opportunity to attend classes; meetings with professors, coaches, students, and admissions and financial aid counselors; and a meal or two on campus. Visits should be arranged with the Office of Admissions, preferably one to two weeks in advance. Preview Days are held in the fall and spring, and special senior visit days are offered in the winter and spring for admitted students.

To request application materials and additional information, contact:

OFFICE OF ADMISSIONS

Transylvania University

300 North Broadway

Lexington, KY 40508-1797

Telephone: (859) 233-8242 or (800) 872-6798

E-mail: admissions@transy.edu

Web site: www.transy.edu

TRINITY COLLEGE (CT)

AT A GLANCE

Trinity College is an independent, nonsectarian liberal arts college located in the historic capital city of Hartford, Connecticut. Founded in 1823, Trinity is one of the oldest colleges in the country, and is consistently ranked among the best. It brings the great tradition of the liberal arts into the 21st century with a dynamic living and learning community where education doesn't stop at the classroom door.

Our 2,200 students work closely with faculty and extend their education through campus activities and organizations. They engage with the city of Hartford through internships and community learning and service, and explore the wider world through study abroad and international initiatives on campus. With a 10 to 1 student-faculty ratio, each student is challenged and encouraged by Trinity's outstanding faculty. Students are offered a rigorous curriculum that is firmly grounded in the traditional liberal arts, but that also incorporates newer fields, an interdisciplinary approach, and urban engagement.

With 38 majors (39 as of the fall 2013 semester) and approximately 900 courses to choose from, students are immersed in a community of learning that is facilitated by a stimulating academic environment, small classes, and exceptional facilities, including fully networked classrooms and dorms. Opportunities to explore the arts abound on campus and students can nurture and hone artistic skills. More than 40 percent of our students play varsity and club sports, and many more participate in intramurals and fitness activities.

As a student at Trinity College, you will explore new worlds, thoughts, and ideas, and become prepared for the challenge and change of a successful, fulfilling life.

LOCATION AND ENVIRONMENT

Trinity is situated on a beautiful, 100-acre campus in Connecticut's capital city of Hartford, midway between Boston and New York. Hartford is a city with a rich history that offers many opportunities for urban engagement. Mark Twain lived here, as did Harriet Beecher Stowe. Dentist Horace Wells discovered anesthesia here. It is the home of the oldest continuously published newspaper in America as well as the oldest public art museum, the Wadsworth Atheneum. Trinity effectively uses the city as a classroom, with access to assets and resources that is matched by few liberal arts colleges of our size.

Anyone who visits the College sees the beauty of the campus, with its hilltop location, mix of historic and contemporary buildings, and abundant trees and lawns. Trinity is one of the earliest examples of "Collegiate Gothic"; many of the original buildings are modeled after the architecture of Oxford and Cambridge and symbolize Trinity's roots in the classical liberal arts. A major campus and community revitalization initiative created the state-of-the-art Raether Library and Information Technology Center on campus and the neighboring innovative Learning Corridor of magnet schools and academic resources, which now also includes the Hartford Magnet Trinity College Academy. Also, in 2006, the award-winning Koeppel Community Sports Center opened its doors as a multi-use athletic facility on the southern edge of campus.

Off campus, the 256-acre field station at Church Farm in Ashford, Connecticut, is dedicated to research in the natural sciences and a wide range of environmental educational endeavors.

As a Trinity student, you have numerous opportunities to engage in internships, research with faculty, community learning projects, and volunteer work,. Many courses – from art history to political science and from economics to neuroscience – incorporate aspects of city life. There are more than 200 internships that allow you to extend classroom learning while exploring career opportunities. And whatever your tastes, there are cultural and entertainment events throughout the city and a shuttle service provided by the College.

OFF-CAMPUS OPPORTUNITIES

Trinity students have a wide variety of opportunities to take advantage of the College's special relationship to the city of Hartford. The Community Learning Initiative comprises nearly 30 courses each year that weave direct contact with local people and institutions directly into the learning process. Such urban engagement builds on Trinity's liberal arts foundation, and for some students, has led to independent studies or collaborative research papers published in scholarly journals.

Trinity offers over 200 internship opportunities that represent excellent preparation for life after college. Students can explore career interests in a wide variety of fields, including law, banking, journalism, communications, health care, engineering, computer science, government, and non-profit organizations. The College's Legislative Internship Program offers students the opportunity to work for a member of the Connecticut General Assembly. Trinity challenges its students to make a difference in the real world - starting with their Hartford community. Students can choose from a wide range of community service activities, from child-mentoring programs to the Boys and Girls Club at Trinity to Habitat for Humanity.

Trinity's study abroad programs provide unforgettable learning experiences that broaden perspectives and deepen understanding. Among the rich menu of study abroad choices are Trinity's own campus in Rome and our seven additional global learning sites, as well as intercollegiate exchange and study abroad programs. Equally valuable are many study-away programs in the U.S., including Trinity/La Mama Performing Arts in New York City, research and internships in Washington D.C., maritime studies at Mystic Seaport, and theater courses at the O'Neill Theater Program. Students can also take advantage of the Twelve College Exchange Program.

Trinity also created the Center for Urban and Global Studies to integrate the College's well-established tradition of urban engagement with its strong global programs. The center, which is the first of its kind at a liberal arts college in the United States, takes advantage of Trinity's location and strengthens the long-standing mutually beneficial relationship between the College and Hartford. Playing off Trinity's global reach, it is expanding new learning and research opportunities in world cities.

MAJORS AND DEGREES OFFERED

Undergraduates completing the necessary requirements receive the Bachelor of Arts or the Bachelor of Science degrees from Trinity College.

Trinity offers approximately 900 courses in 38 majors. Beginning in the fall 2013 semester, the College will offer a new major in urban studies, bringing the total number of majors to 39. Options include cross-disciplinary majors, such as American studies, and self-designed majors, such as environmental studies, as well as interdisciplinary minors, such as human rights. At Trinity, your education is student-centered, and our array of curricular options will provide you with the tools to help you to meet your goals.

Trinity offers majors in: American Studies, Anthropology, Art History, Biochemistry, Biology, Chemistry, Classical Civilization, Classics, Computer Science, Economics, Educational Studies, Engineering, English, Environmental Science, French, German, History, International Studies, Italian, Jewish Studies, Language and Culture Studies (including Arabic, Hebrew, Chinese and Japanese), Mathematics, Music, Neuroscience, Philosophy, Physics, Political Science, Psychology, Public Policy, Religion, Russian, Sociology, Spanish, student-designed interdisciplinary major, Studio Arts, Theater and Dance, and Women, Gender and Sexuality. Beginning in fall 2013, we will offer a new major in urban studies.

As you can see, Trinity's curriculum is both broad and flexible, encouraging you to challenge yourself as you follow your interests and select a major.

ACADEMIC PROGRAMS

At Trinity, the curriculum features the First-Year Seminar Program, where a small group of students and a faculty members explore a topic through critical reading and discussion, analysis, and writing. It's a shared introduction to intellectual life at Trinity and an important way to meet other students and make friends. All first-year students are housed in first-year residence halls and are supported by a student mentor who participates in your seminar.

There are many special curricular options, including the Guided Studies, Interdisciplinary Science, InterArts and Cities Programs, as well as the Trinity/La MaMa Performing Arts Program in New York. Trinity is also home to the first undergraduate Human Rights Program in the United States, as well as the unique Center for Urban and Global Studies.

The key words here are variety and flexibility—if you don't see exactly what you want, that doesn't mean we don't have it. Independent study? Study abroad? Engineering? Neuroscience? Law courses? How about an academic leave of absence to work on a political campaign or hike the Appalachian Trail? Many Trinity students pursue these and other existing opportunities. And it is very easy to work with faculty to create your own opportunities. Your motivation and imagination are your only limits.

CAMPUS FACILITIES AND EQUIPMENT

The campus is fully wired, with every student room connected to the campus network and the Internet. The newly expanded Raether Library and Information Technology Center combines the resources of one of the leading small-college library facilities in the nation with an array of electronic resources, including digital media labs and video-conferencing capabilities. The library houses over one million books, bound collections, and electronic books, as well as approximately 90,000 periodical titles received. It also houses the Watkinson Library rare-book collections.

The science labs offer our undergraduates an opportunity to work hands on with sophisticated equipment, including a research nuclear magnetic resonance spectrometer, a scanning electron microscope, incubators, and climatically controlled growth chambers.

Focal points for the visual arts are the Widener Gallery in the Austin Arts Center and the Broad Street Gallery. In addition to a proscenium theater and a more intimate black box performance space, each art medium has its own studio.

The Ferris Athletic Center houses a fully-equipped fitness center, an Olympic-size pool, premier international-size squash courts, crew tanks, an indoor track, a field house, and basketball and tennis courts. Outdoor features include an all-weather track, soccer fields, softball and baseball diamonds, the Paul D. Assaiante Tennis Center, , an artificial turf field hockey field, and a field turf playing surface for football and lacrosse. In addition, the Koeppel Community Sports Center serves as home-ice for Trinity men's and women's ice hockey teams, as well as a place for community academic and athletic mentoring programs.

TUITION, ROOM, BOARD AND FEES

Estimated college fees for 2012–13 are as follows:

Tuition: $43,570

Room & Board: $11,800

General Fee: $2,160

FINANCIAL AID

Through the generosity of alumni and friends, the College has an endowment sufficient to give our students an education that's worth considerably more than the actual tuition charged. If you decide that Trinity is the right college for you, we are determined not to let money stand in your way. We are committed to making a Trinity education accessible to promising students who are unable to meet the full educational costs. Approximately 40 percent of our students receive need-based financial aid from Trinity, federal, or state funds. If you have any questions about financial aid at Trinity during any point in your college search, you should not hesitate to contact the Office of Student Financial Services at 860-297-2046 or e-mail financial-aid@trincoll.edu.

STUDENT ORGANIZATIONS AND ACTIVITIES

While the number in our student body is relatively small, their interests are incredibly diverse. With over a hundred student organizations on campus, the opportunities for active involvement are wide open – whether continuing something in which you've already been involved or something that is completely new to you. Student organizations include community service organizations, cultural organizations, media groups, such as the College newspaper and radio station, academic clubs, fraternities/sororities, and club sports. And if you have an interest that isn't covered by an existing organization, then start one! It will probably be impossible for you not to find at least one activity that appeals to you, whether on campus or in the city. Academics are the most important part of your education, but they aren't the only part. We encourage you to get involved beyond the classroom. The opportunities are right at hand.

ADMISSIONS PROCESS

Selecting candidates for admission to Trinity is a complex but personalized process. The components of your evaluation include your academic credentials. Your grades are very important, but so is the strength of the academic programs in which you participated. We require one form of standardized test; either the SAT, ACT, or any two SAT Subject Tests. Non-native speakers of English are encouraged to submit the TOEFL.

In addition, two teachers' recommendations and one college counselor recommendation are required. Teachers give us insight into your scholarship, work habits, and classroom contributions. Personal qualities are considered, too. What talents, skills, or qualities can you bring to the life of the campus? What contributions have you made to your school and community? We aren't as concerned with the number of your activities as we are with the quality and depth of them.

If we may be of assistance, please don't hesitate to call upon us in the Office of Admissions at 860-297-2180 or e-mail admissions.office@trincoll.edu.

TRUMAN STATE UNIVERSITY

AT A GLANCE

Truman State University is Missouri's premier liberal arts and sciences university and the only highly selective public institution in the state. As one of the very few publicly funded liberal arts schools in the nation, Truman successfully combines affordability with the type of education and personal attention typically only offered at a private institution.

Truman has established an impeccable reputation in the Midwest and throughout the nation for the high-quality undergraduate programs offered. In fact, for the sixteenth consecutive year, U.S. News & World Report has ranked Truman State University as the number one master's level public institution in the Midwest. A commitment to student achievement and learning is the focus of the University.

LOCATION AND ENVIRONMENT

The Truman campus is beautifully situated on 140 acres in Kirksville, a town of approximately 17,000 located in the northeast corner of Missouri. The historic downtown area is within walking distance of the Truman campus and provides a connection to the Kirksville community with local restaurants, shops, and entertainment.

MAJORS AND DEGREES OFFERED

Undergraduate degrees offered by Truman include the Bachelor of Arts (B.A.), Bachelor of Science (B.S.), Bachelor of Music (B.M.), Bachelor of Fine Arts (B.F.A.), and Bachelor of Science in Nursing (B.S.N.). Truman offers more than forty areas of study in the following disciplines: Accounting, Agricultural Science, Art, Art History, Athletic Training, Biology, Business Administration, Chemistry, Classics, Communication, Communication Disorders, Computer Science, Creative Writing, Economics, English, Exercise Science, French, German, Health Science, History, Interdisciplinary Studies, Justice Systems, Linguistics, Mathematics, Music, Nursing, Philosophy and Religion, Physics, Political Science, Psychology, Romance Languages, Russian, Sociology/Anthropology, Spanish, and Theatre.

Professional paths include but are not limited to dentistry, engineering, law, medicine, optometry, pharmacy, physical therapy, occupational therapy and veterinary medicine.

The teaching degree at Truman is the Master of Arts in Education. Students wishing to pursue a teaching career first complete a bachelor's degree in an academic discipline and then apply for admission into professional study at the master's level. Master's programs in special education, elementary education, middle school education, and secondary education are available.

Truman also offers Master's level degrees in Accountancy (MAc), Biology (MS), Communication Disorders (MA), Counseling (MA), English (MA), Leadership (MA) and Music (MA).

ACADEMIC PROGRAMS

The Liberal Studies Program is the heart of Truman's curriculum and is intended to serve as a foundation for all major programs of study. The philosophy behind the Liberal Studies Program is based upon a commitment that Truman has made to provide students with essential skills needed for lifelong learning, breadth across the traditional liberal arts and sciences through exposure to various discipline-based modes of inquiry, and interconnecting perspectives that stress interdisciplinary thinking and integration as well as linkage to other cultures and experiences.

Students at Truman complete a "capstone," or culminating experience their senior year. This experience prompts seniors to reflect on the knowledge they have gained throughout their learning experience and to integrate the knowledge, skills, and attitudes of liberal learning with an in-depth understanding of the major.

Truman also offers a challenging Honors Scholar Program. Students have the opportunity to select the most rigorous honors courses to satisfy the liberal arts component of their respective programs. Those who successfully complete this program benefit from an even richer academic experience at Truman and receive special recognition at graduation. Departmental honors are also available in several disciplines.

OFF-CAMPUS OPPORTUNITIES

Students at Truman are active both inside and outside of the classroom. More than 400 Truman students participate in enriching and life-changing study abroad experiences each year. Students can participate in programs ranging from a couple weeks to a year in duration, and can choose from numerous destinations worldwide. In recent years, Truman has continued to rank among the top 25 in the nation among master's level institutions for number of students studying abroad, according to the "Open Doors" survey conducted by the Institute of International Education.

Truman offers a wide variety of experiential internships, a required component of some academic programs. The "Truman in Washington" program provides work-experience opportunities in the nation's capitol in such areas as foreign affairs/diplomacy, government affairs, criminal justice, international relations, health and human services, and communications as well as other areas. Truman also offers internship opportunities with the Missouri State Legislature. In recent years, students have completed internships with United States senators, the United States Supreme Court, the governor of Missouri, business and industry managers, advertising agencies, physical therapists, and artists.

STUDENT ORGANIZATIONS AND ACTIVITIES

With approximately 250 student organizations to choose from, encompassing service, Greek, honorary, professional, religious, social, political and recreational influences, Truman students have tremendous opportunities to become involved on campus and in the Kirksville community. Truman student organizations sponsor a number of events throughout the year, such as Truman Live, International Idol, guest speakers, poetry slams, musical performances, dance recitals, volunteering events, and ever-popular food nights.

The Kohlenberg Lyceum Series also provides a variety of cultural programs that interest students throughout the year. Past programs have included brilliant performances by the Peking Acrobats, The 5 Browns, Preservation Hall Jazz Band, and the Russian Festival Ballet.

Truman's Student Activity Board sponsors a variety of entertainment events. Recent SAB concerts include Sara Bareilles, Regina Spektor, B.o.B., and Ben Folds. Comedic acts like Donald Glover and Judah Friedlander have also come to Truman's campus in recent years.

CAMPUS FACILITIES AND EQUIPMENT

Students take advantage of numerous academic resources and facilities available to them. Improvements to campus facilities have included the renovation and expansion of Truman's Science facility, Magruder Hall, which was completed for the spring 2006 semester. Renovations to Barnett Hall include a new Convergence Media Center encompassing facilities for the student-produced newspaper, Midwest travel magazine, radio station, and TV studio. Students also enjoy dining, socializing, and relaxing in the newly renovated Student Union Building.

Just opened for the 2011 fall semester is the Health Sciences Building which houses a speech and hearing clinic for Communication Disorders students, an independent learning center for Nursing students, a Human Performance lab, and the Fontaine C. Piper Movement Analysis lab. Additional facilities include a biofeedback laboratory, an organic chemistry lab, an observatory, a 400-acre university farm, a multicultural affairs center, student health center, and a career center. Athletic facilities include a 5,000-seat football stadium, a 3,000-seat arena with three basketball courts, an Olympic-size swimming pool, soccer and rugby fields, baseball and softball fields, tennis courts, a dance studio, and a Student Recreation Center.

Residence halls also provide comfortable and enriching living environments for students. Most of the halls have been renovated within the last five years. All residence halls offer lounges, kitchenettes, laundry facilities, high-speed internet (including wireless), cable TV, and many other amenities. Students can eat in dining halls or in the food court style dining in the Student Union Building.

TUITION, ROOM, BOARD, AND FEES

Tuition for Missouri residents for the 2012-13 academic year is $6,978; out-of-state tuition is $12,714. The average room and board rate for both Missouri residents and nonresidents is $7,504. Additional fees include a one-time $315 freshman orientation fee, and annual fees including an $84 activities fee, a $100 athletic fee, a $54 Student Health Center fee, a $105 parking fee for those with a vehicle, and costs of books and personal expenses.

FINANCIAL AID

Truman offers automatic scholarships ranging from $500 to $5,000. Competitive scholarship awards vary from $500 up to full tuition, room and board, plus a $4,000 study-abroad stipend. The application for admission also serves as the application for the automatic and competitive scholarship programs, and it is free to apply.

A limited number of scholarships are awarded to students for excellence in fine arts, debate or foreign language. These scholarships are available for instrumental or vocal music; acting or dramatic production; studio art or art history; speech or debate; and foreign languages offered at Truman. Of special interest to piano students is the Truman Piano Fellowship Competition, a February competition offering scholarships to top pianists.

Truman, a National Collegiate Athletic Association Division II member, offers 20 men's and women's sports. The NCAA and the University authorize a limited number of grants to outstanding athletes. The value of this aid may vary with each individual recipient.

ADMISSIONS PROCESS

Truman accepts the Free Application for Federal Student Aid (FASFA) and participates in all Federal Title IV financial aid programs. Financial aid estimates are available upon request.

Each applicant is evaluated for admission based upon academic and co-curricular record, ACT or SAT results, and the admission essay. Truman requires the following high school core: 4 units of English, 3 units of mathematics (4 recommended), 3 units of social studies/history, 3 units of natural science, 1 unit of fine arts and 2 units of the same foreign language.

Students interested in being considered for all scholarships are encouraged to apply by December 1 of their senior year. The recommended final deadline to apply for the fall semester is March 1. There is no application fee. Students may apply online at the website listed below. For further information or to schedule a campus visit, students should contact:

Office of Admission

Truman State University

100 East Normal

Kirksville, Missouri 63501

Telephone: 660.785.4114 or 800.892.7792

Fax: 660.785.7456

E-mail: admissions@truman.edu

http://admissions.truman.edu

UNION COLLEGE (NY)

AT A GLANCE

Union College, chartered by the state of New York in 1795, is one of the nation's oldest and most distinguished liberal arts colleges. Union is a leader in educating students to be engaged, innovative and ethical contributors to a diverse, global and technologically complex society. The curriculum emphasizes collaboration with students and faculty through small classes and undergraduate research, international study and learning through service. The student population of approximately 2,200 full-time undergraduates comes from 37 U.S. states and territories and 37 other countries. Approximately 19 percent of students identify themselves as members of a multicultural group.

LOCATION AND ENVIRONMENT

Union is located on 100 acres in Schenectady, 15 miles from Albany, the capital of New York state. The first planned campus in America, it was designed by noted French architect Joseph Ramée and features many beautiful gardens and natural woodlands. Its centerpiece is the 16-sided Nott Memorial. The city of Schenectady is part of Upstate New York's picturesque Capital-Saratoga Region, which has a population of nearly 1 million. The region has a rich cultural heritage and a thriving high-tech industry that offers many opportunities for internships, job placements and student/faculty research. A 15-minute drive from Albany International Airport, Union College is three hours by car from New York City and Boston, four hours from Montreal, and close to East Coast ski slopes, the Mohawk and Hudson Rivers, and the Adirondack Mountains.

OFF-CAMPUS OPPORTUNITIES

Union offers international study programs in more than 30 countries. They combine elements of entrepreneurship, research or global service with the chance for students to pursue their academic interests and individual passions. About 60 percent of Union students go on terms abroad, one of the highest percentages among U.S. liberal arts colleges. Most programs are led by Union faculty. Students may also design their own program of study, and participate in non-Union and exchange programs. Three-week mini-terms are offered during winter and summer breaks in various U.S. cities and countries.

MAJORS AND DEGREES OFFERED

Union offers more than 40 majors and 55 minors. Students may choose double majors; combine majors and minors; pursue interdepartmental and multidisciplinary concentrations, and area, ethnic and cultural studies programs; or design their own major. Most students take three courses in each of the three 10-week terms that comprise Union's academic calendar system. The average introductory class has 18 students; the average upper level class, 15.

Union offers Bachelor of Arts (B.A.) and Bachelor of Science (B.S.) degrees. Union also offers a five-year Business/Management program with Union Graduate College (B.A. or B.S. and M.B.A.); five-year Education program with Union Graduate College (B.A. or B.S. and M.A.T.); six-year Law and Public Policy program with Albany Law School (B.A. and J.D.); and an eight-year Leadership in Medicine program with Albany Medical College and Union Graduate College (B.S., M.S. or M.B.A., and M.D.). Union's 14 academic honor societies include Phi Beta Kappa, the first chapter established in New York.

ACADEMIC PROGRAMS

Union's interdisciplinary approach to the liberal arts combines the humanities and social sciences with science and engineering, emphasizing the practical application of ideas through hands-on experience. Students must complete a minimum of 36 courses (up to 40 for engineering degrees) and satisfy all departmental and Common Curriculum requirements. These requirements include the First-Year Preceptorial and Sophomore Research Seminar, which promote skills in reading, writing, research and critical thinking. Distribution requirements in the humanities, literature, social sciences, linguistic and cultural competency, quantitative mathematical reasoning and the sciences promote a breadth of knowledge about the social and natural world, and key skills in analysis, literacy and numeracy. Approved interdisciplinary clusters on particular intellectual themes prompt awareness of interdisciplinary connections and understanding of issues from multiple perspectives.

The Union Scholars program provides an enriched experience for academically accomplished students through extensive opportunities for independent study, study abroad, colloquia and departmental honors programs. Union encourages student research in all disciplines. At Steinmetz Symposium each spring, some 400 students present the results of their research, scholarly and creative activities. Many students co-author publications with their professors and present at the National Conference on Undergraduate Research (NCUR). Many participate in businesses, health care, government and social service internships. The Michael Rapaport '59 Ethics Across the Curriculum promotes courses that provide training in everyday ethics. Writing Across the Curriculum requires students to take five designated courses from at least two divisions and one Senior Writing Experience.

CAMPUS FACILITIES AND EQUIPMENT

Union's nearly 100 buildings include the 16-sided Nott Memorial, a National Historic Landmark used for study, lectures, exhibits and special events. The Peter Irving Wold Center is a home for interdisciplinary study, with leading-edge programs in biochemistry, environmental studies, electrical engineering and music research. The facility includes everything from a music production studio to a rooftop renewable energy lab, all for student use. The F.W. Olin Center is a high-technology classroom and laboratory building. The Science and Engineering Center houses the Center for Bioengineering and Computational Biology and contains specialized research tools available for student use, including a nuclear magnetic resonance spectrometer, a Pelletron accelerator and a scanning electron microscope. The Center for Neuroscience in Butterfield Hall, opened in 2012, brings together computer and research labs, classrooms, offices and collaborative spaces for this fast-growing program. The Peschel Computer Center houses the IBM High-Performance Computing Cluster, which offers some of the most advanced computing capabilities among the nation's undergraduate liberal arts schools.

Schaffer Library has 618,000 volumes, some 800 periodicals (paper) and more than 9,000 electronic subscriptions. Three hundred databases provide access to a quarter million printed books, documents and scores. The College Archives, Language Lab, Special Collections and Writing Center are also housed here. Flanking the library are the Humanities Building and the newly renovated Lippman Hall, home to the Social Sciences, including the departments of Economics, History, Political Science and Sociology, and the Religious Studies program. Union's arts facilities include the Mandeville Gallery and Wikoff Student Gallery; the all-Steinway Taylor Music Center, which houses Emerson Auditorium, a music technology studio and the World Musics Room. The Visual Arts Building includes painting, drawing and sculpture studios, darkrooms and the Burns Arts Atrium gallery. The Yulman Theater is home to Mountebanks, the country's oldest student performing group. The Henle Dance Pavilion, to open in May 2013, features a variety of classrooms, rehearsal and performance studios, and other spaces. The Kelly Adirondack Center at Union College, located in nearby Niskayuna, houses one of the largest research collections on the Adirondack region.

Residential options for Union students include traditional dorms, apartment-style housing, theme houses (focusing on everything from arts to spirituality), Minerva Houses, Greek houses and College Park Hall, which houses upper class students. The Reamer Campus Center houses dining facilities, an auditorium, bookstore, radio station, Unity Lounge and multiple spaces for other student activities. Among the athletic facilities are Alumni Gymnasium, which features the Breazzano Fitness Center as well as an eight-lane swimming/diving pool, and dance, aerobics and yoga studios. Other recreational and sports facilities include the 3,000-seat Messa Rink at Achilles Center; the Viniar Athletic Center for basketball and volleyball; and the Travis J. Clark '00 Strength Training Facility for varsity athletes. The men's and women's crew teams train at the College's boathouse on the banks of the Mohawk River. The Wicker Wellness Center, opening next year, will offer an array of health, wellness and counseling services.

The Becker Career Center offers a full range of career planning programs and services, from resume writing and internship searches to career fairs. It also works with employers and alumni to open doors and guide students in competing effectively in today's job market. HireU, the center's internship and job database, contains opportunities from alumni and employers who are looking specifically for Union students.

STUDENT ORGANIZATIONS AND ACTIVITIES

Union has more than 100 campus clubs, including performance and arts clubs; cultural groups; the student newspaper, Concordiensis, and radio station, WRUC; sports clubs; 10 residential Greek organizations; more than a dozen theme houses; academic and honor societies; service groups; and political interest groups. Cultural events include concerts, theater, dance, film and art exhibits. Union's comprehensive athletics program offers 26 varsity intercollegiate sports, organized intramurals, club sports, and recreational and fitness activities. Union is a member of the NCAA, Liberty League and ECAC Hockey. Men's and women's ice hockey compete in NCAA Division I programs; other teams are Division III.

Seven houses in the center of campus make up the student-run Minerva House system. Each student belongs to one of the houses, and all faculty members have house affiliations. This unique program encourages students and faculty members to contribute in a variety of ways to Union's social, cultural, academic and intellectual life. Minerva programs range from book clubs and barbecues to film series, cooking with professors and discussions about current events. The Kenney Community Center connects students with Big Brothers Big Sisters, Habitat for Humanity, tutoring programs and a variety of civic projects. Some 1,200 students each year are involved more than 30 service programs and innumerable other opportunities for service and leadership.

TUITION, ROOM, BOARD AND FEES

Union's comprehensive fee, which includes tuition, room, board, and mandatory fees, is $58,248 for the 2013-14 academic year. The estimated cost for books and personal expenses is $1,900.

FINANCIAL AID

Union is committed to admitting an economically diverse student body and to meeting the full demonstrated need of all admitted students. The College offers $38 million annually in aid. The average Union need-based scholarship is $29,000; the average merit scholarship is $10,000. Families who are unable to pay full tuition and fees are typically covered by a financial aid package consisting of a grant, loan and work opportunity. About half of all applicants apply for financial aid; more than 60 percent of all students receive assistance from the College. Scholarship awards are based on academic performance and financial need. Candidates for aid should complete the Free Application for Federal Student Aid (FAFSA) and the College Scholarship Service's PROFILE form and mail them directly to the appropriate agencies by Feb. 1.

ADMISSION PROCESS

More than 5,000 applicants typically seek first-year class positions; approximately 60 percent are in the top 10 percent of their secondary school class. Admissions counselors look at grades, rigor of courses taken, class rank, teacher recommendations and extracurricular involvement. Typically, 16 units of secondary school preparation are required for admission. These should include credits in such fundamental subjects as English, foreign language, mathematics, social studies and science. It is strongly recommended that students visit Union for an interview and student-guided tour. Alumni interviews may be requested online. A student can choose not to submit his or her SAT or ACT scores for review, except for accelerated programs, which require applicants to submit the SAT and two SAT Subject Tests.

Early decision (ED) candidates have two options. The application deadline (including all supporting credentials) for Option I is Nov. 15, with notification by Dec. 15. Option II has a Jan. 15 deadline (including all supporting credentials) and Feb. 15 notification. Applications for regular decision (RD) admission must be filed by Jan.15; decisions are mailed by April 1. Applications to the Leadership in Medicine program are due no later than Dec. 15, and for Law and Public Policy, by Jan. 1. Those deferred under ED and all regular applicants are given a final decision by April 1. Accepted students have until May 1 to commit.

UNITED STATES AIR FORCE ACADEMY

AT A GLANCE

The Air Force Academy was established in 1954 to train and motivate Air Force cadets pursuing careers in the military. The Academy emphasizes character building, military discipline, physical fitness and academic excellence. An Academy education builds valuable leadership skills in all areas. Approximately 4,000 students attend the Academy, with about 1,100 as entering students (fourth class). The makeup of the student body reflects that of the corps of Air Force Officers: approximately 23 percent women and 26 percent diverse. Cadets arrive from all 50 states and a number of other countries. All cadets must live on campus and wear uniforms. The Academy is accredited by the North Central Association of Colleges and Schools. Engineering programs are approved by the Engineering Accreditation Commission of the Accreditation Board for Engineering and Technology. Computer courses are approved by the Computing Sciences Accreditation Board. The Commission on Professional Training of the American Chemical Society establishes the requirements made of biochemistry and chemistry majors. Cadets are required to engage in club, intramural or intercollegiate athletics each semester. Options for intramural activity include basketball, boxing (men), cross-country, flag football, Flickerball, rugby (men's and women's), soccer, softball, team handball, tennis, ultimate Frisbee, volleyball and wallyball. The Academy fields intercollegiate teams in Division I of the NCAA; its teams compete both regionally and nationally. The men compete in baseball, basketball, boxing, cheerleading, cross-country, diving, fencing, football, golf, gymnastics, ice hockey, lacrosse, rifle, soccer, swimming, tennis, track, water polo and wrestling. Women compete in basketball, cheerleading, cross-country, diving, fencing, gymnastics, rifle, soccer, swimming, tennis, track and volleyball. More than 80 extracurricular activities are available to cadets, including competitive and recreational clubs, hobby clubs, mission support clubs, professional organizations and sports groups. Qualified graduates of the Academy may commence flight training after graduating. About three-quarters of all cadets undertake graduate study within 10 years of graduation. Every year, many graduates of the Academy are granted fellowships and scholarships, including the Rhodes, Fulbright, Marshall, NCAA and National Science Foundation.

LOCATION AND ENVIRONMENT

Located in the foothills of the Rocky Mountains' Rampart Range, the Academy is truly surrounded by natural beauty. The campus sits upon a 7,300-foot mesa; the campus and its immediate area are among the state's most popular tourist attractions. Contemporary architecture is featured on campus; the space age Cadet Chapel, with its seventeen 150-foot aluminum spires, set the tone for the entire cadet area. This modern setting aptly reflects the campus' mission: to educate, train and inspire men and women to become officers of character, motivated to lead the United States Air Force in service to our nation. The campus is located just north of Colorado Springs, a city of over 400,000, which sits at the foot of Pikes Peak (14,100 feet). The state capital, Denver, is just 55 miles to the north. This metropolis of more than 2.5 million offers a plethora of cultural, educational and recreational opportunities. Cadets also enjoy horseback riding, hunting, snowboarding, skiing, whitewater rafting and many other outdoor activities in the nearby mountains and its resorts.

OFF-CAMPUS OPPORTUNITIES

Cadets chosen to participate in a semester-long exchange program may attend the Military Academy, Naval Academy, Coast Guard Academy or foreign Air Force academies in Canada, Chile, France, Germany and Spain. Other international programs are usually one to three weeks in duration visiting one of several countries.

MAJORS AND DEGREES OFFERED

Graduates receive a bachelor of science degree and a commission as second lieutenants in the Air Force. Students may pursue their degree in: aeronautical engineering, astronautical engineering, basic sciences, behavioral sciences, biology, chemistry, civil engineering, computer engineering, computer science, economics, electrical engineering, English, environmental engineering, foreign area studies, general engineering, geospatial science, history, humanities, legal studies, management, mathematical sciences, mechanical engineering, meteorology, military strategic studies, operations research, philosophy, physics, political science, social sciences, space operations, system engineering and system engineering management. Cadets may minor in foreign languages, philosophy and religion studies.

ACADEMIC PROGRAMS

The school year for entering students begins in late June or early July; incoming cadets commence their tenure at the Academy with a rigorous 38-day summer training program designed to test their physical and mental abilities. This training is conducted by upperclass cadets while commissioned officers serve as advisers. Cadets who successfully complete this program are admitted as fourth-class cadets in the cadet wing. Academic courses begin in early August and run through May. Cadets begin by focusing on core curriculum in engineering, humanities, science and the social sciences. Cadets choose a specialized academic major during their second year. Core courses are designed to prepare cadets for a wide range of duties as Air Force Officers. They include courses in academic subjects; military training and leadership; and athletics and physical education. All cadets must also complete the requirements of an academic major. Other graduation requirements include: demonstration of ability to serve and to lead; demonstration of character befitting a member of a professional military; along with maintenance of a minimum Military Performance Average (MPA), Grade Point Average (GPA) and Physical Education Average of 2.0. Cadets have numerous options in selecting elective courses. All cadets must enter as freshmen. Cadets who have previously completed comparable core coursework at other institutions may earn transfer or validation credit for their work. Those who receive transfer credit may take other courses at the Academy in place of their core courses. Advanced study classes are open to cadets who meet academic prerequisites, including a minimum grade point average. Cadets learn all operational procedures of the Air Force through the Academy's aviation program. Optional courses are available in basic flying, navigation, parachuting and soaring. Students who complete these courses may earn pilot or glider certificates issued by the Federal Aviation Administration. Once they have graduated from the academy, select cadets may enter Air Education and Training Command flight programs to train as pilots or navigators. Cadets may pursue summer studies in aviation and military training. These programs prepare them for the responsibilities of an Air Force Officer. A number of optional assignments are available, both at the Air Force Academy and at other military installations.

CAMPUS FACILITIES AND EQUIPMENT

The Air Force Academy has excellent facilities to sustain the academic, athletic and military goals of its programs. Classrooms are designed to accommodate small sessions of 12 to 20 students. A few larger classes meet in lecture halls, as do assemblies. The Academy provides its science students with fully equipped laboratories, as well as an aeronautics laboratory that houses rocket engines, shock tubes and wind tunnels. A LAN links every classroom, dorm room, laboratory and faculty and staff office on campus. All entering cadets are required to purchase microcomputers, which they may use for both academic and personal purposes. The library houses more than 1.5 million volumes, and its collection includes an entire floor designated to historical materials pertaining to aeronautics.

TUITION, ROOM, BOARD AND FEES

The government of the United States bears the entire cost of an Air Force Academy education in exchange for a commitment to serve. There are no charges for tuition, room, board or medical or dental care. Academy cadets earn a monthly salary, with which they are expected to purchase clothing, supplies and personal items. Cadets who manage their money carefully will meet all obligations and have a small sum left over for personal expenses.

FINANCIAL AID

All cadets attend the Air Force Academy on full scholarship, as described above.

STUDENT ORGANIZATIONS AND ACTIVITIES

Cadets learn important leadership skills through their duties in the cadet wing, an organization through which upper-class cadets take responsibility for enforcing the honor system and honor education, leading under-class cadets in military drills and enforcing the human relations, ethics and character development programs of the Academy. Firstclass cadets (fourth-year students) supervise the operations of the cadet wing and they hold the rank of cadet officer and command its groups, squadrons, flights and elements.

ADMISSIONS PROCESS

Every year, young U.S. citizens (both men and women) receive appointments to the Academy. They arrive from all of the nation's states and territories. A limited number of foreign nationals are also admitted. Applicants must be between the ages of 17 and 23 as of July 1 of their projected year of admission, must be unmarried and without dependents. They must be principled individuals and must be physically fit. An official nomination is a required part of any application to the Academy. Most nominations come from members of Congress and are submitted for students living in their districts and states. Representatives and senators nominate high school juniors who have demonstrated academic excellence, who possess leadership qualities (as demonstrated by academic and extracurricular records), who are physically fit, who have the respect of their peers and associates and who desire a career in the military. It is not necessary for applicants to know their congressional representatives personally to receive their nomination. Other categories than congressional exist and interested applicants should consult their guidance counselor or local Admissions Liaison Officer to learn more about other available nomination categories. Students wishing to enter the Academy upon completion of high school should submit applications as soon after March 1 of their junior year as possible. Applicants who receive a nomination must pass a Candidate Fitness Assessment (CFA) and a medical exam. They must also submit standardized test scores (SAT I or ACT). Applicants should visit academyadmissions.com, click on "Apply Now" and carefully read the instructions. These instructions clearly detail the application process. Applicants needing assistance should contact an Admissions Liaison Officer (ALO); there is at least one in every state. Your ALO can be found by visiting academyadmissions.com. Enter your information to find your ALO representative.

Applications are available to high school juniors. To request information, write to:

HQ USAFA/RR

2304 Cadet Dr., Ste. 2300

USAF Academy, CO 80840-5025

United States

Phone: (800) 443-9266

Website: academyadmissions.com

828 West

UNIVERSITY OF ARKANSAS

AT A GLANCE

Founded in 1871, the University of Arkansas is both the major land-grant university for Arkansas and the state's flagship university. It has a proud legacy of internationally significant scientific and intellectual achievements in many academic fields. The U of A boasts one of the most unique traditions found on any college or university campus: Senior Walk, consisting of more than 5 miles of sidewalks crisscrossing campus that are engraved with the names of more than 150,000 graduates, dating back to 1876. It's concrete proof of the University's commitment to students.

The university has 10 colleges and schools offering more than 210 academic programs including bachelor's degrees in 75 fields of study. The U of A is moderate in size among major research institutions with nearly 25,000 students, of which more than 20,000 are undergraduates. Its diverse student population includes nearly 1,200 international students from 120 countries.

LOCATION AND ENVIRONMENT

Fayetteville is routinely considered among the country's finest college towns and the surrounding Northwest Arkansas region is regularly ranked one of the best places to live in the U.S.

Northwest Arkansas is one of the most economically stable regions in the nation and serves as the base of operations for Walmart, Tyson Foods, Inc. and J.B. Hunt Transport Services. Because of their presence, many other corporations have established primary or secondary headquarters in NWA. Their close proximity to the U of A campus, along with their executives' and employees' active involvement in university life, offers students and faculty exceptional opportunities for research partnerships, internships, and post-graduation employment.

The Northwest Arkansas metroplex was ranked in the top fifty by the Milken Report's Best Performing Cities, a report which measures U.S. cities' economic performance. The Fayetteville-Springdale-Rogers area has been ranked by the U.S. Census Bureau as one of the fastest-growing metro areas in the nation.

Nestled among the scenic Ozark Mountains, Fayetteville offers a distinctive mix of thriving business community, scenic outdoor activities, distinct seasons, excellent schools, and an unemployment rate well below national averages. Fayetteville is vibrant with the cultural life that would be expected in any major university town. The area is a haven for both artists and outdoor sports enthusiasts.

OFF-CAMPUS OPPORTUNITIES

The study abroad office works eagerly with students to identify opportunities in virtually any country around the world. Students in all majors are eligible to go abroad and can start as early as the summer following freshman year. Proficiency in a foreign language is not always necessary, as students can study in English-speaking countries or in programs where classes are taught in English. Often students make multiple trips abroad in the course of their college careers.

There are numerous additional scholarships available for study abroad, including a $4 million endowment specifically for undergraduate international study. Scholarships and federal financial aid (including Pell grants and Stafford loans) can be used for study abroad.

MAJORS AND DEGREES OFFERED

Dale Bumpers College of Agricultural, Food and Life Sciences offers Agricultural Business; Agricultural Education, Communications, & Technology; Animal Science; Apparel Studies; Biological Engineering; Crop Management; Environmental, Soil & Water Science; Food, Human Nutrition & Hospitality; Food Science; General Human Environmental Sciences; Horticulture Landscape & Turf Science; Human Development & Family Sciences; and Poultry Science.

The Fay Jones School of Architecture offers Architecture; Architectural Studies; Landscape Architecture; Landscape Architectural Studies; and Interior Design.

J. William Fulbright College of Arts and Sciences offers African and African American Studies; American Studies; Anthropology; Arabic; Art; Asian Studies; Biology; Chemistry; Classical Studies; Communication; Criminal Justice; Drama; English; European Studies; French; Geography; Geology; German; History; International Relations; Journalism; Latin American and Latino Studies; Mathematics; Middle East Studies; Music; Philosophy; Physics; Political Science; Pre-professional Programs; Psychology; Social Work; Sociology; and Spanish.

Sam M. Walton College of Business offers Accounting; Economics; Finance; General Business; Information Systems; International Business; Management; Marketing; Retail; and Supply Chain Management.

College of Education and Health Professions offers Career & Technical Education – Secondary Education; Childhood Education; Communication Disorders; Community Health Promotion; Elementary Education; Human Resource Development; Kinesiology; Nursing (BSN); Recreation & Sport Management; and Teacher Certification through Master of Arts in Teaching (MAT) Program.

College of Engineering offers Biological Engineering; Biomedical Engineering; Chemical Engineering; Civil Engineering; Computer Engineering; Electrical Engineering; Industrial Engineering; and Mechanical Engineering.

The Honors College offers all academic majors to students enrolled concurrently in the home college or school of their academic majors.

Beyond undergraduate programs, the university also maintains a Graduate School, a School of Law, and a variety of continuing education programs.

ACADEMIC PROGRAMS

The school operates on a traditional two-semester academic year schedule, with two regular summer sessions, three two week intersessions, and some special concurrent summer sessions. The majority of undergraduate degree offerings follow a four-year plan requiring from 124 to 136 course hours for graduation; there are some exceptions to this requirement, such as the five-year, design-oriented architecture and landscape architecture programs, which requires 157 hours.

The endowed Honors College enables students to pursue honors programs in any college or department and provides undergraduate research and study abroad opportunities. Requirements vary among programs and schools. More information is available by visiting honorscollege.uark.edu.

The University of Arkansas is the state's only institution classified as having the highest possible level of research by the Carnegie Foundation, placing the University among the top 2% of colleges and universities nationwide. Last year, the university recorded $123 million in research expenditures.

CAMPUS FACILITIES AND EQUIPMENT

The University has made investments of more than $1.3 billion in new construction, major renovations and facilities enhancements across campus since 2000.

The combined holdings of the University Libraries total more than 2 million volumes of books and periodicals and 5.5 million microforms. The Libraries received more than 53,700 serial publications by subscription and gift. Other resources include several thousand maps, numerous pamphlets, manuscripts, sound and video recordings, as well as electronic databases and journals.

The university is a member of Internet2, providing a high speed connection to other national and international research networks. In addition, extensive computing resources are available including e-mail, free internet connections, and Web page development, to all students, faculty and staff.

TUITION, ROOM, BOARD AND FEES

The University is consistently ranked as one of the nation's best public values by multiple sources including:

Kiplinger's Personal Finance — which ranked the U of A 65th on its top 100 'Best Values in Public Colleges' list for 2012-2013.

The Princeton Review — which recognized the University as one of the top 75 schools on its "2013 Best Value Colleges" list.

And Forbes — which ranked the U of A 44th on its "Top 100 Best Buy Colleges" list last year.

Tuition and fees for the 2012-2013 were estimated at $7,554 for Arkansas residents and $18,434 for out-of-state residents. Room and board rates average $8,672 annually. For undergraduate students, the resident tuition rate is $204.70 per credit hour and nonresident tuition is $567.41 per credit hour.

Financial Aid and Academic Scholarships

Undergraduates receive over $145 million in grants, loans, scholarships, and work-study funds. Students need to complete the FAFSA to be considered for federal financial aid. Students interested in freshman scholarships should apply for admission by November 1 and submit the scholarship application by November 15 for priority consideration. The final scholarship deadline is February 1.

Academic scholarships are awarded on a competitive basis and include: Sturgis, Bodenhamer, Boyer, and Honors College Fellowships ($12,500 per year), Chancellor's Scholarships (up to $8,000 per year), Silas Hunt Distinguished Scholarships (up to $8,000 per year), Arkansas Alumni Association Endowed Scholarships ($6,500 per year), Honors College Academy Scholarships ($4,000 per year), Razorback Bridge ($3,500 per year), Leadership Scholarships ($2,000 per year), University Enrichment ($2,000 one-time), Freshman Academic ($1,000 one-time), New Arkansan Nonresident Tuition Award Scholarship (waiver of out-of-state tuition), Transfer Student Scholarships (up to $3,000 per year), Arkansas Alumni Association Scholarships (variable), and Alumni Legacy Scholarships (out-of-state tuition waivers). See scholarships.uark.edu for more information.

NATIONALLY COMPETITIVE

University of Arkansas students have enjoyed much success in nationally competitive award programs. In 2002, the university was named a Truman Honor Institute, an award recognizing high-performing institutions in the Truman Scholarship program. Throughout its history, the university boasts 46 Goldwater Scholars, 58 NSF Graduate Research Fellowships, 46 Fulbright Scholars, 16 Truman Scholars, 6 Marshall Scholars, 4 Madison Scholars, 3 Gates Cambridge Scholars, 6 Udall Scholars, a Pickering Fellow, and 10 Rhodes Scholars. U of A students are consistently named as finalists for national awards and accepted into top graduate, medical, and law programs.

HONORS COLLEGE

The University of Arkansas Honors College offers honors programs in every college tailored to specific majors, and encourages interdisciplinary collaboration. More than fifty percent of Honors College graduates have studied abroad by the time they graduate, and one hundred percent of our graduates have engaged in undergraduate research with a faculty mentor. The Honors College also provides significant financial support to students, annually funding up to 90 freshman fellowships that offer from $50,000 to $70,000 over four years, and from $500,000 to $1 million in study abroad and undergraduate research grants.

STUDENT ORGANIZATIONS AND ACTIVITIES

The university offers a vibrant campus life for its student population. University residence halls accommodate approximately 4,600 students. In addition, Fayetteville offers abundant off-campus housing opportunities, many along university transit routes.

There are more than 350 registered student organizations, including special interest organizations, religious organizations, cultural organizations, honorary and professional service organizations, and student government. Students may also choose to participate in the Greek system, which is made up of 14 sororities and 17 fraternities.

The academic semesters are filled with cultural and intellectual events including musical performances, theatre productions, art exhibits, concerts, poetry readings and visiting speakers - both on campus and at the nearby Walton Arts Center. The University's Distinguished Lecture Series has featured former President George H. W. Bush; the Dalai Lama; Elie Wiesel; Anderson Cooper, a CNN news anchor; Benazir Bhutto, former Pakistani Prime Minister; Ehud Barak, former Israeli Prime Minister; Apollo Ohno, U.S. Olympian; and political commentators James Carville and Mary Matalin. Former President Bill Clinton, a former faculty member at the U of A School of Law, and renowned primatologist Jane Goodall also spoke on campus in 2012.

ADMISSIONS PROCESS

Students interested in applying to the University of Arkansas for the fall semester are urged to apply through the early admission process. By applying prior to November 1, students are able to register for housing and orientation early; however, regular fall applications will be accepted until August 15.

Entering freshmen are advised to prepare for admission in high school by taking 4 units of English, 4 of math, 3 of social studies, 3 of natural sciences, and 2 of electives. A minimum 3.0 high school GPA and an ACT composite score of 20 (930 SAT, combined critical reading and math scores) are required for admission. The ACT code is 0144, and the SAT code is 6866. The average ACT of the 2012 freshman class was 26, and the average G.P.A. was 3.6.

Transfer students need a cumulative GPA of at least 2.0 on all college courses taken and must be in good academic standing when applying for admission. Students completing fewer than 24 transferable hours will need to meet all requirements for freshman admission in addition to those for transfer students.

To apply, complete the application for admission available by visiting apply.uark. edu. The application deadline for the fall semester is August 15; the spring deadline is December 20. The student must also request that official transcripts be mailed to the office of admissions. A preliminary admission is provided for those high school seniors who have a transcript of six or seven semesters, but a final transcript is needed to certify high school graduation. Official ACT or SAT scores no more than 5 years old must be submitted by all entering freshmen and transfer students with fewer than 24 transferable hours.

New freshmen interested in applying for academic scholarships at the University of Arkansas should apply for admission and request a scholarship application on the admissions form. Scholarship applications, transcripts and test scores should be submitted by November 1 for priority consideration or by the February 1 final deadline. More information is available at scholarships.uark.edu.

UNIVERSITY OF THE ARTS

AT A GLANCE

The University of the Arts (UArts) is located in the heart of Philadelphia's vibrant professional arts community. For more than 135 years, UArts has been a leader in educating artists, performers and creative individuals.. More than 2,100 students from forty-three states and twenty-two countries are enrolled in undergraduate and graduate programs in the visual and performing arts, film and design. Comprised of the College of Media, Art and Design (CAMD), the College of Performing Arts (CPA) and the Division of Liberal Arts, the University offers intensive concentration within a major field as well as creative challenges in multidisciplinary exploration.

One quarter of students live in University housing, which provides coed apartment-style accommodations. . Resident advisers live on each floor, and there is 24-hour security. First-time students are guaranteed housing if their contracts are received by May 1. The University also assists students in finding off-campus residences. Dining Services operates several dining locations on campus, which are available to both residential and commuter students.

The graduate programs of the University of the Arts offer an impressive combination of strengths: accomplished faculty members, an individualized and interactive learning environment, access to outstanding facilities and resources, specialized studios, and programs of study that are both focused and flexible. UArts offers graduate degrees in Art Education; Book Arts/Printmaking; Industrial Design; Museum Communication; Museum Education; Museum Exhibition, Planning and Design; Jazz Studies, and Music Education. A Post-Baccalaureate certificate in Crafts is also offered.

LOCATION AND ENVIRONMENT

The University's campus spans the Avenue of the Arts from South Street to Walnut Street and is the cultural hub of Center City Philadelphia. Next door to the University's historic Hamilton Hall is the Kimmel Center for the Performing Arts; in adjacent blocks are the Academy of Music, Wilma Theater, Suzanne Roberts Theater, and the University's historic Merriam Theater, which books touring Broadway shows for the public and hosts UArts student performances. The area also has internationally renowned museums (Philadelphia Museum of Art and Barnes Museum), galleries, superb restaurants, and retail stores. Of historic importance, but also modern and sophisticated, the city is one of the nation's major metropolitan centers as well as a series of small, close-knit neighborhoods. Fairmount Park, one of the country's largest public park systems, provides facilities for sports activities and picnicking. Statistics show that UArts is one of the safest campuses in the city.

MAJORS AND DEGREES OFFERED

Undergraduate Programs

The College of Art, Media and Design confers degrees through its three Schools: Film (BFA in Animation, Film/Video, and Writing for Film and Television): Art (BFA in Crafts, Multidisciplinary Fine Arts, Painting/Drawing, Photography, Printmaking and Sculpture); and Design (BFA in Graphic Design and Web Development and Interaction Design; BS in Industrial Design), as well as in College-Wide Programs (BFA in Illustration and Design, Art & Technology). The College also offers the 5-Year BFA/MAT program, which allows students to complete the requirements for a BFA in studio art and Master of Arts in Teaching in Visual Arts in five years. Undergraduate students with a major in the College may also do a concentration in Art Therapy. The Division of Liberal Arts confers two degrees: a BFA in Creative Writing, and a BA in Film & Media Studies. The School of Music confers BM degrees in Composition, Instrumental Performance and Vocal Performance, as well as a BS in Music Business, Entrepreneurship and Technology. A four-year diploma in music is also available. The School of Dance offers a BFA in Dance. The School of Theater Arts offers BFA degrees in Acting, Musical Theater, Theater Design and Technology, and Directing, Playwriting and Production.

ACADEMIC PROGRAMS

Students are attracted to the University of the Arts because of its dynamic, creative atmosphere, and opportunities for cross-discipline collaboration. Students are encouraged to take elective courses outside their chosen major, and many participate in collaborative projects with students from a range of other programs. All students take 42 credits in liberal arts, providing exposure to humanities, social sciences, and science, and giving students a historical and theoretical framework for their major fields.

Freshmen in the College of Art, Media and Design spend their first year enrolling in courses in the College's Core Studies curriculum, which is designed to expose students to the skills, concepts and techniques necessary for in-depth study of a specific field. Students are not required to declare a major until their sophomore year; the flexibility of the Core Studies curriculum allows highly focused students to begin concentrating on an area of study in their first year, while undecided students benefit from the breadth of topics explored in the curriculum. Core Studies includes courses exploring concepts of Time, Object, Image, and Environment, as well as introductory courses to the various majors within the Schools.

Students who choose a concentration in the School of Film will focus on the sensory bases of moving-image art, cinematic art and story-telling; courses include documentary video, narrative video, screenwriting, film history and video production. The School of Design curriculum challenges students to apply critical-thinking and problem-solving skills to design-oriented endeavors, including mobile web applications, product design, advertising and marketing, and typography. Programs within the School of Art are designed to allow students to pursue a highly-focused study of one area, or have the freedom to combine elements and techniques of various fine arts disciplines. All students within the School are encouraged to develop a well-rounded portfolio as well as their professional practice and research skills.

In the College of Performing Arts, the School of Music program stresses individualized training, with a performance emphasis. In this contemporary jazz-based program, students undergo intensive training in theory and musicianship, supplemented by master classes and ensemble work. Students in the School of Dance begin with two years of intensive studio training in the traditional study of ballet, jazz and modern, as well as emerging and contemporary forms, before choosing an area of emphasis for their junior and senior years. In the Ira Brind School of Theater Arts, students can choose one of four majors: Acting; Musical Theater; Directing, Playwriting and Production, and Theater Design and Technology. All programs emphasize intensive training, with a goal of developing strong professional practices while giving students exposure to all elements of theatrical production.

In the Division of Liberal Arts, the Creative Writing program provides students the opportunity for immersive study in the craft of writing with small, workshop-style classes. Students will choose a concentration in either Fiction or Poetry, but are also able to sample other forms of writing such as creative non-fiction, playwriting, screenwriting and graphic novels. Film & Media Studies is a theory-based program that allows students to explore the critical, historical and aesthetic aspects of cinematic arts through a combination of studio classes and lecture-based seminars.

INTERNSHIPS

Internships in professional settings provide students with real-life experience in the field. A wide variety of internship opportunities are available to qualified students.

STUDY ABROAD

The University of the Arts offers a wide range of International Study Abroad programs. The Provost's Office assists students in finding suitable overseas programs, applying, and arranging financial aid.

CAMPUS FACILITIES AND EQUIPMENT

The University facilities are composed of numerous buildings along Philadelphia's Avenue of the Arts, including residence halls, academic and administrative buildings, studios, galleries and performance venues.

College of Art, Media & Design facilities include the Typography Lab, the Borowsky Center for Publication Arts, digital video editing suites, TV and video production studios, photo/film/animation labs and darkrooms, a scanner lab, an SGI lab, a bronze foundry and plaster workshop, and crafts studios and workshops for ceramics, metals, wood, glassblowing, papermaking, and fibers. Many programs offer individual workstations or studios for upperclassmen. Academic computing resources include more than twenty labs on Macintosh and PC platforms that can be used for animation, digital imaging, 3-D modeling, multimedia, music, CAD, Web page design, and more. The University maintains several public galleries where students may exhibit their work along with curator-managed exhibitions of guest artists' work.

Performance spaces include the 1,800-seat Merriam Theater, the 239-seat Caplan Center for the Performing Arts black box theater and recital hall, the 200-seat Dance Theater, the Arts Bank main theater and cabaret theater, and the Gershman Hall black box theater. Other performing arts facilities include a recording studio; music technology (MIDI) studios; editing suites; practice rooms; dance and movement studios with barres, mirrors, and resilient floors; and acting studios.

Library facilities include Albert M. Greenfield Library, a Picture Resource File; Special Collections, with special strengths in book arts and textiles; a slide library with a collection of more than 140,000 slides of art works and historical images; and a music library with manuscripts, journals, scores, and listening and viewing facilities.

TUITION, ROOM, BOARD AND FEES

Tuition for the 2013-2014 academic year is $36,582. . Accommodations in apartment-style dormitory units start at $8200. The 19 meal per week board plan is $4500.

FINANCIAL AID

Last year, UArts provided nearly $10 million in scholarships and grants to new students alone. About one third went to those demonstrating financial need; the balance was awarded in talent- or merit-based scholarships. Overall, UArts students receive more than $50 million in scholarships, grants, loans, and part-time employment each year. Typically, more than 90 percent of the students enrolled on a full-time basis are eligible for some type of need-based aid. Where need exists, UArts assists in meeting costs within its available resources.

The University funds Trustees Scholarships, Presidential Scholarships, Promising Young Artist Awards and Artist Grants based on artistic potential and academic achievement. Financial aid is also available on the applicant's demonstrated financial need. Applicants must submit the Free Application for Federal Student Aid (FAFSA). March 1 is the suggested filing date. The University administers a full range of Federal Aid programs. Applicants who wish to be considered for scholarships should complete applications for admission and financial aid prior to April 1. Families from many different income levels can qualify for some type of financial assistance. In addition, the University's location in a large, active city provides students with diverse opportunities for part-time employment.

STUDENT ORGANIZATIONS AND ACTIVITIES

The student activities office sponsors a variety of on and off-campus activities to complement academic programs, as well as overseeing student organizations including Student Council, community service organizations, and a student-run gallery.

Admission Process

In addition to submitting a portfolio or auditioning, undergraduate applicants should submit their high school transcript, SAT or ACT scores, one letter of recommendation, and a personal statement of purpose.

The placement of transfer students is made after an evaluation of their portfolio or audition and a determination of their approved college credits. Transfer students may be given advanced standing.

International applicants are required to submit scores on the Test of English as a Foreign Language (TOEFL) or the International English Language Testing System (IELTS). A minimum TOEFL score of 550pbt/80ibt , or an IELTS score of 6.0 is required for undergraduate programs. .Students who do not meet these requirements may receive a conditional admittance pending completion of an ESL course.

The University of the Arts follows rolling admission system. Students are notified of their decisions as their applications are completed. Students are encouraged to submit applications by March 15 for fall admission and December 1 for spring admission. For additional information, students should contact:

Office of Admission

The University of the Arts

320 South Broad Street

Philadelphia, PA 19102

United States

Phone: 215-717-6049

800-616-ARTS (toll-free)

www.uarts.edu/admission

UNIVERSITY OF CENTRAL FLORIDA

AT A GLANCE

The University of Central Florida is a comprehensive research university with over 59,000 students. As one of the nation's fastest growing universities and the 2nd largest in the nation, UCF enrolls a diverse student body representing 50 states and over 120 countries. The University offers educational and research programs that complement the economy, with strong components in aerospace engineering, business, education, film, health, nursing, social sciences, and hospitality management. UCF's programs in communication and the fine arts help to meet the cultural and recreational needs of a growing metropolitan area. The University also offers many graduate programs leading to masters and doctoral degrees.

UCF has established extensive partnerships with businesses and industry in the central Florida area that provide students with exceptional research and learning experiences. These partnerships bring practical learning environments to UCF students through co-op and internship programs. Joint curriculum development strategies are used throughout the university.

The on-campus and campus-affiliated housing facilities include traditional residence halls, apartment-style options, and Greek housing that accommodates approximately 10,000 students. Several thousand students live in apartments located within walking distance of the campus. Approximately 400 students live in on-campus Greek housing.

LOCATION AND ENVIRONMENT

The University of Central Florida: Competitive Advantages

A Focus on Undergraduate Education: We're committed to teaching and providing advising and academic support services for all students. Our undergraduates have access to state-of-the-art wireless buildings, high-tech classrooms and research labs, Web-based classes and an undergraduate Research and Mentoring program.

A Talented Student Body: As one of the fastest growing universities in the southeast, total enrollment has reached over 59,000; 50,000 are undergraduates. Our emphasis on excellence in undergraduate education has produced many rewarding results: a Goldwater Scholarship awardee, a Rhodes Scholarship finalist, a Clarion awardee in Radio/Television, a Zonta International Amelia Earhart fellowship awardee, and a nationally ranked Computer Science programming team.

Career Opportunities: Our Career Services professionals help students gain practical experiences at NASA, schools, hospitals, high-tech companies, local municipalities, and the entertainment industry. UCF faculty sit on boards and planning committees, and our graduates make their mark in engineering, business, computer science, education, health care, science, tourism, film and public service.

An International Presence: With an international focus to our curricula and research programs, we currently enroll international students from 122 nations. Our study abroad programs and other study and research opportunities include agreements with 98 institutions and 36 countries, including Australia, France, Germany, Holland, Italy, Russia, South Africa, Spain and Wales.

A Spacious, Modern Campus, plus Orlando: UCF's 1,415-acre campus provides a safe and serene setting for learning, with natural lakes and woodlands. The university provides housing for 10,000 students on campus and through affiliated housing. The bustle of Orlando lies a short distance away: the Orlando Magic, the Orlando Predators, the Kennedy Space Center, major film studios, Walt Disney World, Universal Orlando, Sea World, and sandy beaches are all nearby.

OFF-CAMPUS OPPORTUNITIES

Career Services and Experiential Learning offers programs in which student's alternate semesters of classroom study with equal periods of paid employment in government, industry, or business. The Department of Foreign Languages offers summer study programs in Canada, Eastern Europe, France, Germany, Italy, Japan, Poland, Spain, Sweden, and Russia. Courses are available in the subject areas of language (all levels), art, and civilization. UCF is also a participant in the National Student Exchange Consortium.

MAJORS AND DEGREES OFFERED

The University offers the degrees of Bachelor of Applied Science, Bachelor of Arts, Bachelor of Arts in Business Administration, Bachelor of Fine Arts, Bachelor of Science, Bachelor of Science in Business Administration, Bachelor of Science in Education, Bachelor of Science in Engineering, Bachelor of Science in Nursing, and Bachelor of Science in Social Sciences.

These degrees are available in the colleges listed below, with majors or areas of specialization as indicated.

The College of Arts and Humanities offers degrees in art, Architecture, digital media, English, film, , French, history, humanities, Latin American Studies, music, philosophy, Photography, Religious Studies, Spanish, and Theatre Studies.

The College of Business Administration offers degrees in accounting, Business Economics, economics, finance, general business administration, management, real estate and marketing. The College also offers a minor in international business.

The College of Education offers degrees in art education, early childhood development and education, elementary education, English language arts education, , foreign language education, mathematics education, science education, sport and exercise science, social science education, and technical education and industry training.

The College of Engineering and Computer Science offers degrees in aerospace engineering, civil engineering, computer engineering, computer science, construction engineering, electrical engineering, environmental engineering, industrial engineering, Information Technology and mechanical engineering.

The College of Health and Public Affairs offers degrees in athletic training, Communication Sciences and Disorders, criminal justice, health Informatics and information management, health services administration, health sciences, legal studies, physical therapy (master's program), public administration, and social work.

The College of Nursing offers degrees in nursing.

The College of Sciences offers degrees in advertising/public relations, anthropology, biology, chemistry, forensic science, International and Global Studies, interpersonal and organizational communications, journalism, mathematics, physics, political science, psychology, radio/television, social sciences, sociology, and statistics.

The Rosen College of Hospitality Management offers degrees in Hospitality Management, Event Management, and in Restaurant and Foodservice Management.

The College of Medicine and the Burnett School of Biomedical Sciences offers degrees in Biotechnology, Medical Laboratory Sciences, and biomedical sciences. Pre-professional programs are offered in chiropractic, medicine, optometry, osteopathy, pharmacy, physical therapy, physical assistant, podiatry, dentistry and veterinary medicine.

Degrees in Interdisciplinary Studies are available through the Office of Undergraduate Studies.

CAMPUS FACILITIES AND EQUIPMENT

In addition to the academic programs offered on the Orlando campus, upper division students can work toward a degree at 10 locations around the central Florida area. These regional campuses work cooperatively with local community colleges to provide all four years of course work in many academic areas. The library houses nearly 1.4 million volumes and subscribes to more than 10,000 periodicals and journals. In addition, students have access to an online computer catalog that provides information on the collections of the State University System libraries. An extensive online network of more than 500 computer terminals and a network of nearly 1,000 IBM PC's cover the campus. The Institute for Simulation and Training gives students the opportunity to pursue undergraduate research. The School of Optics allows faculty members and students to work directly with industrial personnel in conducting basic and applied research at the regional and national level. The Central Florida Research Park, located next to the UCF campus, houses more than ninety important high-technology firms and agencies. This proximity fosters relationships between industry and the University, which strengthens the academic programs at UCF.

TUITION, ROOM, BOARD AND FEES

Approximate Tuition, Health Fee, Room and Board Annual Rates 2012-2013:

	Florida Resident	Non-Florida Resident
Tuition and Fees	$6,247	$22,345
Room	$5,620	$5,620
Board	$3,620	$3,620
Books (estimate)	$800	$800
Approximate Total Annual Cost	$16,287	$32,385

Based on 15 credit hours per semester, double room and meal plan.

FINANCIAL AID

Financial aid is awarded according to each student's demonstrated need in relation to college costs and may include grants, loans, scholarships and part-time employment. Programs based on need include the Federal Perkins Loan, Federal Pell Grant, Florida Student Assistance Grant, Federal Work-Study, Florida College Career Work-Study Program, and Federal Stafford Student Loan. To qualify for these programs, students must complete the Free Application for Federal Student Aid. The priority application deadline is March 1. Approximately 70 percent of UCF students receive some form of financial aid.

STUDENT ORGANIZATIONS AND ACTIVITIES

Students participate in more than 400 organizations, including special interest clubs, multicultural associations, fraternities and sororities, honor societies, and academic and pre-professional organizations. The Office of Student Involvement schedules a wide array of extracurricular programs, including concerts, movies, and guest speakers.

The University of Central Florida is a member of the NCAA and the American Athletic Conference. All teams compete on the NCAA Division 1 Level. UCF's men's teams compete in intercollegiate baseball, basketball, football, golf, soccer, and tennis. Women's teams compete in basketball, cross-country, golf, rowing, soccer, softball, tennis, track and field, and volleyball. Intercollegiate coed club activities include championship cheerleading, crew, and waterskiing teams. The university intramural sports program offers many options including disc golf, flag football, floor hockey, racquetball, soccer, softball, tennis, and volleyball.

ADMISSIONS PROCESS

A freshman applicant is a student with fewer than 12 hours of college coursework after high school graduation. The most important criteria in the admission decision for these applicants is the high school academic record, quality and level of difficulty of courses, grade point average, grade trends, and SAT I or ACT test scores. UCF operates on a rolling admission basis. Students are generally notified of their admission decision within two to three weeks after receipt of the application and all supporting documents. If the number of qualified applicants exceeds the number that the university is permitted to enroll, a waiting list will be established.

All applicants must have earned a minimum of 18 high school academic units (year-long courses that are not remedial in nature). These include 4 units of English (3 must include substantial writing), 4 units of mathematics at or above algebra I, 3 units of natural science (2 must include a laboratory), 3 units of social science, 2 units of one foreign language, and 2 units of academic electives. Grades in honors courses, International Baccalaureate, Advanced Placement, AICE and dual enrollment courses are given additional weight in the GPA computation. Students must meet the Department of Education minimum eligibility to be considered for admission. Applicants should understand that the satisfaction of minimum requirements does not automatically guarantee admission to UCF.

Transfer applicants with fewer than 60 semester hours of college course work must submit official high school transcripts, SAT I or ACT test scores, and all official college transcripts. Transfer students with more than 60 semester hours or who have earned an Associate in Arts degree or a state-wide articulated Associate in Science degree from a Florida public community college need only to submit all official college transcripts. A transfer credit summary evaluation is provided to students once they are offered admission to UCF.

Students are encouraged to apply several months in advance and can apply online at www.admissions.ucf.edu. It is recommended that freshman students apply early during the fall semester of their senior year. Applications are accepted up to one year prior to the start of the term for which entry is desired. Priority application deadlines are May 1 for the fall term (July 1 for transfers), November 1 for the spring term, and March 1 for the summer term.

UNIVERSITY OF CHICAGO

AT A GLANCE

A private university chartered in 1890, the University of Chicago quickly became a world leader in research. In addition, UChicago's coherent program of general education for undergraduates has been replicated throughout the nation. Drawn to theoretical inquiry and open discussion, UChicago's 5,000 undergraduates enjoy small classes and spirited give-and-take discussions where they are free to break down artificial disciplinary barriers and frequently explore research and coursework outside their selected fields. This atmosphere of free and open inquiry not only attracts exceptional students and faculty from around the globe, including at total of 85 Nobel laureates, but has also led to the development of academic disciplines in fields ranging from literary criticism and urban sociology to ecology and the study of religions, as well as world-renowned programs in anthropology, physics, and economics.

The University of Chicago encourages a close-knit learning environment on campus, and promotes this by guaranteeing each student on-campus housing for four years. Chicago's ten residence halls, including modern dorm complexes and neo-Gothic buildings, are distinct communities made up of undergraduate students as well as Resident Heads, who are advanced graduate students or faculty members. These communities are a focal point for campus life and, along with hundreds of clubs and organizations, uphold the traditions of the College.

LOCATION AND ENVIRONMENT

The University's neighborhood, Hyde Park, is a vibrant yet relaxed residential community, seven miles from downtown Chicago. More than 60% of the faculty and their families call Hyde Park home. The University's 211-acre campus is distinguished by its English Gothic style architecture and its designation as a botanic garden. With its stimulating diversity Hyde Park boasts a thriving cultural scene ranging from the Checkerboard Blues Lounge and the Museum of Science and Industry to The Point, a park on a promontory extending into Lake Michigan and a site for sunbathing and barbeques. Hyde Park is home to a community whose common bond is a shared passion for the type of invigorating discussion bred by such close proximity to UChicago's many educational resources.

ACADEMIC PROGRAMS

Bachelor of Arts or Bachelor of Science degrees are awarded in the following programs:

Anthropology

Archeology°

Art History

Astronomy and

Astrophysics°

Big Problems°

Biological Chemistry

Biological Sciences

Chemistry

Chicago Studies°

Cinema and Media Studies

Classical Studies

Comparative Human Development

Comparative Literature

Comparative Race and Ethnic Studies

Computer Science

Computational Neuroscience°

Creative Writing°

Early Christian Literature

East Asian Languages and Civilization

Economics

Education°

English and Creative Writing (minor only)

English Language and Literature

Environmental Studies

Fundamentals: Issues and Texts

Gender Studies

Geographical Studies

Geophysical Sciences

Germanic Studies

History

History, Philosophy, and Social Sciences (HIPS)

Human Rights°

Interdisciplinary Studies in the Humanities

International Studies

Jewish Studies

Latin American Studies

Law, Letters, and Society

Linguistics

Mathematics

Medieval Studies

Music

Near Eastern Languages and Civilizations

Norwegian Studies (minor only)

Philosophy

Physics

Political Science

Psychology

Public Policy Studies

Religion and the Humanities

Religious Studies

Romance Languages and Literatures

Russian Civilization

Slavic Languages and Literatures

Sociology

South Asian Languages and Civilizations

Statistics

Tutorial Studies

Theatre and Performance Studies (tutorial and theatre are out of order)

Visual Arts

°Interdisciplinary option

CAMPUS FACILITIES AND EQUIPMENT

Campus facilities offer a broad array of academic, cultural, and other resources, including the Oriental Institute Museum; the David and Alfred Smart Museum of Art; Court Theatre; the University of Chicago Hospitals; the Ryerson Astronomical Observatory; and the Department of Ecology and Evolution's rooftop greenhouse. The Biological Sciences Learning Center is the most up-to-date biology teaching and medical facility of its kind in the nation. Each student has a college advisor, and other support is offered by staff in the residence halls, counselors in the career and planning office, tutors, and the campus ministries.

TUITION, ROOM, BOARD, AND FEES

For freshmen living on campus, the cost of attending the University of Chicago for the 2012-2013 academic year is $58,955. Of that, tuition amounts to $41,853, and room and board and fees total $12,633. Living expenses and books are estimated to cost $3,539, and a student life fee of $930 supports student programming and campus-wide activities.

STUDENT ORGANIZATIONS AND ACTIVITIES

Chicago students are involved in more than 400 student organizations. Community service, academic interest, and cultural awareness groups provide a wide range of opportunities, perspectives, and support. In addition to three student newspapers, a campus radio station, and music, art, theater, and film organizations, the award-winning Model United Nations Team, Debate Society, and College Bowl Team offer forums for competition. An annual scavenger hunt and the winter festival Kuviasungnerk (from an Eskimo word roughly translated as "pursuit of happiness") are among the traditional "UChicago" events on campus. With one of the most extensive intramural and club sports programs in the country, Chicago students take athletics seriously, and more than 70 percent participate in intramurals. Varsity athletics attract 14 percent of the undergraduate student population, where competition at the NCAA Division III level has resulted in numerous Academic All-American awards plus team league championships in women's cross-country, soccer, softball and tennis, and men's basketball, wrestling, and cross country and national champions in track and field and women's tennis last year.

ADMISSIONS PROCESS

No formula exists for the successful Chicago applicant; all have displayed the capacity to inquire, to contribute to their schools and communities, and to succeed at the tasks before them. Among 1411 students in the Class of 2015 (High School graduation year 2011), approximately 94.5% graduated in the top 10 percent of their high school classes. The middle 50 percent of admitted students had a combined score of between 1420 and 1530 on the SAT-I (out of 1600) or between 31 and 34 on the ACT.

To apply for admission or to obtain more information about the University of Chicago, please write to the Office of College Admissions, The University of Chicago, 1101 East 58th Street, Suite 105, Chicago, Illinois 60637, or call 773-702-8650.

Information can also be obtained on the web from the University of Chicago College Admissions home page at collegeadmissions.uchicago.edu

UNIVERSITY OF THE CUMBERLANDS

AT A GLANCE

Founded in 1889, University of the Cumberlands is committed to providing a superior education in an exceptional Christian atmosphere. The University emphasizes the growth of the individual student and strives to instill in students the desire to be agents of change in the world and to use knowledge for the benefit of others, as well as themselves.

University of the Cumberlands is a four-year, coed liberal arts university offering a broad curriculum with more than 40 programs of study from which to choose. UC serves a diverse body of 1,800 undergraduate students from 42 states and 32 countries. Primarily a residential campus, about 75% of students live in University housing in one of the University's eleven residence halls. A director assisted by student staff members supervises each hall.

Students benefit from such special services as the Career Services Center, Center for Leadership Studies, Academic Resource Center, and free tutorial assistance.

LOCATION AND ENVIRONMENT

University of the Cumberlands is located in Williamsburg, Kentucky, one of the older cities of the state. Located in the southern part of the mountains of Eastern Kentucky, Williamsburg is about two hundred miles south of Cincinnati, about an equal distance from Louisville, about eighty miles north of Knoxville, and about 100 miles south of Lexington.

UC offers a well-kept historical campus which is Antebellum in structure, blending stately old buildings with new ones and has a panoramic view of the Cumberland River Valley. Nestled in the foothills of the Appalachian mountain range, the main campus is situated on three hills which divide it into three distinct parts and afford a magnificent view of the surrounding area. The University's buildings, which are situated on these hills and a viaduct, spanning the south and middle hills, provide an easy and pleasant passageway to each part of the campus.

Within a few miles of campus are Laurel Lake, Cumberland Falls State Park, Cumberland Gap National Park, and the Daniel Boone National Forest.

OFF-CAMPUS OPPORTUNITIES

Study Abroad

Ministry Opportunities

Internships

MAJORS AND DEGREES OFFERED

Major fields of study include accounting, art°, biological science°, biology, business administration, chemistry, church music, Christian ministries, Christian studies, communication arts, communication and theatre arts°, criminal justice, early elementary education°, English°, exercise and sport science°, fitness and sport management, health, health education°, history, history and political science, human services, journalism and public relations, management information systems, mathematics°, middle school education°, missions, music°, philosophy and religion, physical science°, physician assistant studies, physics, political science, psychology, public health, social studies°, Spanish°, special education°, and theatre arts. Minor fields of study include biblical languages, and French°. Pre-professional and special curricula are offered in military science, pre-dentistry, pre-engineering, pre-law, pre-medicine, pre-optometry, pre-pharmacy, pre-physical therapy, pre-physician assistant studies, pre-veterinary medicine, and religious vocations.

°Denotes teacher certification available

University of the Cumberlands is accredited by the Commission of Colleges of the Southern Association of Colleges and Schools to award baccalaureate, master's, and doctoral degrees. Inquiries concerning the accreditation status of the University may be directed to the Commission on Colleges at 1866 Southern Lane, Decatur, Georgia 30033-4097or by calling 404-679-4500. The University's Teacher Education and Certification programs are also approved by the Kentucky State Department of Education

ACADEMIC PROGRAMS

The University remains keenly aware of the importance of a traditional liberal arts education and seeks to provide academic specialization within this broad framework. Providing the foundation for a deeper understanding of advanced studies regardless of the chosen major, 37 semester hours of general studies from the areas of Christian faith and values, cultural and aesthetic values, the English language, humanities, leadership and community service, natural and mathematical sciences, physical education, and social sciences are required. Students must earn 128 semester hours to graduate with a bachelor's degree.

Professors work diligently to arrange internships for students within the community, larger cities around the country, and through study abroad options. Listed as a "Top Tier" institution by US News and World Report, our graduates enjoy a high acceptance rate to graduate and professional schools, particularly in science, business, and education.

University of the Cumberlands is one of the few institutions where all students complete a leadership program, which helps fulfill our mission to prepare students for lives of ethical and responsible leadership. Students gain practical hands-on experience working with established service organizations and designing and implementing community service projects.

The academic year begins in late August, with the first semester ending in mid-December. The second semester runs from early January to early May. Two on line undergraduate and graduate summer sessions are also offered. Orientation, pre-registration, and academic advising by faculty members begin in the summer preceding entrance.

Students may receive credit for passing the College Board Advanced Placement (AP exams), the College-Level Examination Programs (CLEP), and special departmental tests. Highly qualified students have the opportunity to undertake advanced independent study through Presidential Research options.

CAMPUS FACILITIES AND EQUIPMENT

UC's campus contains 36 buildings in the architectural style of the early 1900s. Recent additions to campus include the state-of-the-art Hutton School of Business, a 27,000 square foot addition to the science building, featuring well-equipped labs providing graduate-level research opportunities, a women's residence hall and a baseball complex. The McGaw Music Building contains individual rehearsal and studio areas as well as a recital hall. The Norma Perkins Hagan Memorial Library houses thousands of book titles, current serial subscriptions, and microform titles. Sophisticated computer equipment provides access to millions of items from many of the nation's outstanding libraries. The instructional media center includes a children's library, a computerized language lab, and a listening library.

Other special academic features include a computer center, an art gallery, a word processing center for English composition, a theatre, the Career Services Center, a 600-seat chapel, four large lecture halls, and the Distance Learning laboratory.

TUITION, ROOM, BOARD AND FEES

For 2013-2014, the basic academic year expenses are $20,000 for tuition and fees and $7,500 for room and board. The average cost for books and supplies is approximately $1,000 per academic year. There are no additional fees for out of state students.

FINANCIAL AID

University of the Cumberlands sponsors a large financial aid program that coordinates money from federal, state, private, and University sources. Last year, 95 percent of UC students shared more than $31 million in aid. Academic, athletic and other scholarships are available.

STUDENT ORGANIZATIONS AND ACTIVITIES

Our students bring with them fresh perspectives and diverse experiences. UC students quickly become integral parts of the campus family and are involved with all aspects of campus life from ministry programs, student government and athletics to stimulating academic programs, internships and research opportunities. Whether your interest lies in athletics, creative expression, student government, academic enrichment, community service, spiritual development, or in any combination of these areas, you'll find an outlet here for your energy.

Many academic departments sponsor clubs and academic honor societies for students with a particular interest in the discipline, so be sure to visit the departments that interest you or contact a faculty member in that department for more information.

Each year, University of the Cumberlands hosts numerous guest performers and speakers and celebrates the talents of its students and faculty through a variety of lectures, concerts, art exhibitions, and theatrical productions. Many of these events are free of charge, and most are open to the public.

UC is proud of its competitive athletic program which fields 24 varsity sports for men and women. Competing in the Mid-South Conference, UC is a member of the NAIA and is Division I. Core values of respect, responsibility, integrity, servant leadership and sportsmanship are enhanced by our participation in the Champions of Character program, a national initiative through the NAIA.

The Student Government Association is dedicated to giving students a voice through elected representatives. In addition to promoting student concerns and working as a liaison between students and college administrators, the SGA provides a number of important services, and sponsors a number of student-centered events throughout the year.

ADMISSIONS PROCESS

The purpose of the admission process is to identify applicants who are likely to succeed academically at University of the Cumberlands and at the same time contribute positively to the campus community. The process considers such factors as high school records (including courses taken, grade trends, and rank in class), scores on the American College Test (ACT), or on the Scholastic Aptitude Test (SAT), application essay (not required of all applicants), extracurricular activities and honors, and personal contact.

UNIVERSITY OF DELAWARE

AT A GLANCE

At the center of the East Coast is a classic college campus rich in history and academic offerings. Both public and private, the University of Delaware is unique institution with students from all 50 states and 100+ countries. Our alumni – including U.S. Vice President Joe Biden, NJ Governor Chris Christie, and Super Bowl winning quarterback Joe Flacco – are leaders in their fields. Students choose Delaware for our Study Abroad Program (1st in the U.S.), 145+ majors, and discovery learning experiences that ensure they will graduate with impressive resumes and meaningful degrees.

LOCATION AND ENVIRONMENT

The University of Delaware looks and feels the way many dream a college campus should. A central green mall flanked by Georgian, brick buildings, our medium-sized campus is walkable and historic. UD's Northeast location is enviable -- located minutes from I-95, we are safe, green campus less than two hours between New York City and Washington, D.C., a short drive to Philadelphia International Airport, and steps away from our very own Main Street, a charming strip of shops and restaurants at the center of campus.

OFF-CAMPUS OPPORTUNITIES

University of Delaware graduates are in demand due to the opportunities they take advantage of during their undergraduate years. The University's Career Services Center reports that over 93 percent of Delaware grads go on to graduate schools or full-time jobs within twelve months of leaving the University. Fifteen major career fairs are hosted on campus each year with over 600 employers in attendance. In addition, more than 300 corporations and non-profits participate in the Campus Interview Program and contribute to the 20,000 employment possibilities listed at the Career Services Center.

MAJORS AND DEGREES OFFERED

From Accounting to Wildlife Conservation, students at the University of Delaware can choose from over 145 majors and 100 minors. In fact, close to one-third of Delaware students choose to do more, pursuing double majors and multiple minors. Academic programs of study are found in our seven colleges: Arts & Sciences; Agriculture & Natural Resources; Lerner College of Business & Economics; Earth, Ocean, & Environment; Education and Human Development; Engineering; and Health Sciences. Students can explore the many options with our major finder at http://www.udel.edu/majorfinder/

145+ Majors (and 100 Minors)

Accounting; Agricultural Education; Agriculture & Natural Resources; Animal & Food Sciences ; Anthropology; Anthropology Education; Apparel Design; Applied Nutrition; Art Conservation; Art Interests (includes Fine Arts, BFA or BA, and Visual Communications, BFA); Art History; Asian Studies; Athletic Training; Biochemistry; Biological Science Education; Biological Sciences (includes biotechnology, Cellular & Molecular Biology & Genetics, and Ecology & Organismic Biology); Black American Studies (includes Black Arts, Literature & Cultural Studies, Black Gender Study, and Law, Public Policy & Social Justice)

Business - Undeclared; Chemical Engineering; Chemistry/Environmental Chemistry (BA or BS) ; Chemistry Education; Civil Engineering; Cognitive Science (BS); Communication (includes Interpersonal and Mass); Comparative Literature; Computer Engineering; Computer Science (BA or BS); Criminal Justice (includes Law & Society); Dietetics; Early Childhood Education ; Earth Science Education; Ecology; Economics (BA or BS) (includes Applied Economics and Economic Theory & Econometrics) ; Economics Education; Electrical Engineering; Elementary Teacher Education (with certification options in: Elementary Education, Middle School English, Middle School Mathematics, Middle School Science, Middle School Social Studies, and Special Education); Energy & Environmental Policy; Engineering - Undeclared; English (includes Creative Writing, Drama, Ethnic/Cultural Studies, Film Literary Studies, and Professional Writing); English Education; Entomology; Environmental Engineering; Environmental Science (includes Atmospheric Science, Ecology & Organismal Biology, Environmental Chemistry, Environmental Soil Science, GeoScience, Hydrology, Marine Science, Pollution Control, Sustainable Energy Technology, and Water Resources, Quality, & Technology); Environmental

Soil Science; Environmental Studies (includes Environmental Economics & Resource Policy, International Environmental Politics & Policy, Environmental Law, Policy & Politics, and Environment, Society & Sustainability); European Studies; Exercise Science; Fashion Merchandising; Finance; Food & Agribusiness Marketing & Management; Food Science; Foreign Languages & Literatures (includes ancient Greek & Roman Studies, French Educaiton, French Studies, French/Political Science, German Education, German Studies, German/Political Science, Italian Education, Italian Studies, Latin Educaiton & Classics, Russian Studies, Spanish Education, Spanish/Political Science, Spanish Studies, and Three Languages); Geography; Geography Education; Geology (BA or BS) (includes Coastal & Marine GeoScience, Geophysics, and Paleobiology); Health & Physical Education; Health Behavior Science ; History (includes American, European, and World); History Education; History - Foreign Languages includes Classics, French, German, Russian, and Spanish); Hospitality Industry Studies; Hotel, Restaurant & Institutional Management; Human Services (includes clinical Services and Administration & Family Policy); Information Systems; International Business Studies; International Relations (includes Development, Diplomacy, Political Economy, and U.S. Foreign Policy); Landscape Horticulture & Design (includes Public Horticulture); Latin American & Iberian Studies; Linguistics; Management; Management Information Systems; Marketing; Mathematical Sciences (BA or BS); Mathematics & Economics; Mathematics Education (BA or BS); Mechanical Engineering (includes Aerospace); Medical Laboratory Science (Biomedical Sciences); Music (includes Music Management); Music, Applied - Instrumental; Music, Applied - Piano; Music, Applied - Voice; Music Education - General/Choral; Music Education - Instrumental; Music History & Literature; Music Theory/Composition; Natural Resource Management; Neuroscience; Nursing; Nutritional Sciences; Occupational Therapy (Health Studies); Operations Management; Organizational & Community Leadership; Pharmacy Interest; Philosophy; Physics (BA or BS) (includes Astronomy/Astrophysics); Physics Education; Plant Science (includes Plant Protection); Political Science (includes American Politics, Global Studies, Public Law, and Public Policy & Administration); Political Science Education; Pre-Veterinary Medicine & Animal Biosciences; Psychology (BA or BS); Psychology Education; Public Policy; Quantitative Biology (BS); Resource Economics (includes Environmental Economics and Sustainable Development); Sociology (includes Emergency & Environmental Management, Health Services, Law & Society, and Social Welfare); Sociology Education; Sport Management; Statistics; University Studies - Undeclared; Wildlife Conservation; Women's Studies

ACADEMIC PROGRAMS

Delaware's wealth of academic programs draws students who have more than one academic interest. UD undergrads make the most of their college investment by pursuing multiple majors, minors, and interdisciplinary studies. And they tackle UD's discovery learning requirement through participation in one of more of the following:

University Honors Program

At the intellectual heart of the University is the University Honors Program (UHP). Entrance into the Program is highly selective, with about 450 new freshmen enrolled each year. Advantages of the Honors Program include smaller classes, private music instruction, academic scholarships, superb teaching, special housing options, personal attention, interdisciplinary colloquia, "great books" tutorials, lectures, and student-run activities and field trips.

Service-Learning

Service-Learning at UD allows students to participate in an organized service experience that heightens their academic experience. As part of their course work, students will provide a service to a community - From Newark to Wilmington to Costa Rica to Vietnam - and then reflect on these real-world experiences in light of the academic theories and information being taught in the course.

The Princeton Review's Complete Book of Colleges

STUDY ABROAD

UD founded the first Study Abroad program in 1923 and continues to lead in overseas opportunities. Over 40% of our student body choose to study abroad at least once with 12% (and rising each year) studying abroad more than once. The reasons are compelling: UD credits applicable toward any major; UD faculty; UD's reasonable tuition rate; special study abroad scholarships; & exotic destinations on any of the seven continents including - that's right - Antarctica.

Undergraduate Research

The University of Delaware is recognized as a national leader in fostering undergraduate research by offering research apprenticeships with faculty mentors in a variety of disciplines. Over 1,000 faculty take students (including freshmen) on each year to work alongside them in the frontiers of knowledge.

CAMPUS FACILITIES AND EQUIPMENT

Although the University traces its roots to 1743, it remains firmly planted in the 21st century with continuing construction and enhancements to campus facilities. Within the past 20 years, Delaware students have benefitted from hundreds of millions of dollars worth of improvements and additions to campus including: the Independence Complex, a breathtaking community of residence halls (named in honor of UD's three alumni who signed the Declaration of Independence); the $48 million Roselle Center for the Arts, featuring multiple performance theatres, private study rooms, and a practice space large enough for Delaware's 350-member Marching Band; the Exelon Trading Center, a 2,200-square-foot space designed to replicate the trading floors on Wall Street; newly constructed athletic complex, the Interdisciplinary Science & Engineering Laboratory (ISE Lab) opening in 2013, and recently expanded Science, Technology and Advanced Research (STAR) campus, home to UD's College of Health Sciences and collaborative partners.

Extensive facilities and resources exist to meet the needs of UD students. Over 7,000 students live on campus in one of 65 residence halls and dine in any of more than 16 eateries. Morris Library, a six-acre structure, houses millions of books, journals, and items on microtext, with additional access to over 75 networked databases. Students can plug in their own computers or log on at one of 28 microcomputing sites on campus. Socializing, performing, and engaging in a variety of entertainment options takes place at Perkins Student Center, Trabant University Center, the Roselle Center for the Arts, on the Green, in the residence halls, or at one of the smaller theatres on campus. Athletic facilities abound at the University, including the 23,000-seat Delaware Stadium; 5,000-seat Bob Carpenter Sports/Convocation Center; Rust & Gold Ice Skating Arenas (home of the Ice Skating Development Center and training ground for Olympic skaters); outdoor hockey rink; track, softball, and practice fields; indoor and outdoor swimming pools; Outdoor Recreation Resource Center; and indoor climbing wall, fitness centers, and weight rooms.

TUITION, ROOM, BOARD AND FEES

Delaware Residents

Tuition $ 10,150

Room°° $6,804

Board°° $4,242

Health Service Fee $504

Comprehensive Student Fee $790

Student Center Fee $238

TOTAL $22,728

Cost Per Credit Hour $423

Non-Residents

Tuition $25,940

Room°° $6,804

Board°° $4,242

Health Service Fee $504

Comprehensive Student Fee $790

Student Center Fee $238

TOTAL $9,818

Cost Per Credit Hour $1,135

° Optional Winter and Summer Sessions are charged separately.

°°Actual rates vary owing to different housing arrangements & meal plans.

FINANCIAL AID

The University of Delaware awards more than $100 million annually in aid. Our commitment to making a University of Delaware education affordable is seen in our reasonable tuition for in-state and out-of-state students and in our variety of scholarships, financial aid programs, and financing plans. These include Merit Scholarships, Athletic Scholarships, Music Scholarships, Art Scholarships, Additional Scholarships, Need-based Aid, and Outside Resources.

Additional information can be found online at http://www.udel.edu/finance

STUDENT ORGANIZATIONS AND ACTIVITIES

The Fightin' Blue Hens are a spirited community with the mix of academics, campus activities, and athletics that fit the profile of a national university. UD supports 21 varsity sports, all NCAA Division I members of the Colonial Athletic Association, except women's rowing, which is independent. You could say that athletics are a big part of the UD culture, since over 80% of the undergraduate body participates in intramurals, varsity, club, band, cheerleading, or other sports.

In addition to athletics, the University is home to close to 300 campus organizations covering a spectrum of interests and communities. Visit the Web at www.udel.edu/RSO/ for a complete list. The UD undergraduate experience begins with New Student Orientation and New Student Convocation. Annual events on The Green, at the Bob Carpenter Center, in theatres across campus, and in the Trabant University or Perkins Student Centers keep students entertained and active. Delaware students fill their free time with movie nights; Mallstock; and concerts and performances such as Elton John, Jon Stewart, Common, O.A.R., Margaret Cho, and Dane Cook. In addition, there are 38 Greek letter organizations, including 17 NIC fraternities, 11 NPC sororities, and 5 National PanHellenic Council chapters (traditionally African-American membership).

ADMISSIONS PROCESS

The complete admissions process and requirements can be found on the UD website at www.udel.edu/apply.

THE UNIVERSITY OF FINDLAY

AT A GLANCE

Consistently ranked in the top tier of U.S. News & World Report's "America's Best Colleges" in the Midwest, The University of Findlay offers a wide range of programs and opportunities, while maintaining a small campus feel. Affiliated with the Church of God since being founded in 1882, we are a comprehensive, private university with a liberal arts tradition. UF offers nearly 60 exciting majors, 24 varsity sports, more than 100 clubs and organizations, theater, art, music and so much more — there is something for every type of student! Our most popular majors include animal science/pre-veterinary medicine, equestrian studies, pharmacy, business administration, physical therapy and education.

Our Fall 2012 enrollment of nearly 3,600 students includes full-time and part-time students pursuing associate's, bachelor's or master's degrees, as well as first-professional doctorates in pharmacy and physical therapy. The diverse student body encompasses nearly 1,400 students living on campus. In addition, nearly 300 international students from 31 countries and territories attend Findlay.

Faculty and staff are focused on students, with personal attention, individual academic advising and a caring environment cited by students and alumni as hallmarks of their education at Findlay. Classes are taught by professors, not graduate assistants. Most faculty have worked in their chosen professions, bringing a wealth of experience to the classroom, where their true love is teaching.

Discover who you will be at The University of Findlay!

LOCATION AND ENVIRONMENT

The University of Findlay is located in a small city that is pleasant and progressive. The city of Findlay has been designated as a "dreamtown" by Bizjournals.com, which gave high marks to the community for its strong economy, light traffic and moderate cost of living, with well-educated adults and easy access to big-city attractions. It is the only municipality in Ohio to be selected four times as one of the 100 Best Communities for Young People by America's Promise.

The campus has a great location just 45 minutes from Toledo, Ohio, two hours from Cleveland and Columbus, Ohio, and five hours from Chicago.

OFF-CAMPUS OPPORTUNITIES

The University offers career planning and placement services that assist students in determining career goals, developing job search skills, locating internship, cooperative education and degree-related work experience, in finding paid employment in their fields, and in selecting and applying to graduate programs.

MAJORS AND DEGREES OFFERED

College of Business

The College of Business builds its programs on a strong foundation that promotes problem solving, sound decision-making and the integration of the latest technological applications, and most programs allow you to declare a major in one or two disciplines.

UF also offers a Master of Business Administration degree, available both in a traditional setting and entirely online.

Our business majors are:

Accounting; Business Management; Economics; Entrepreneurship; Finance; Hospitality Management; Human Resource Management; International Business

Marketing; Operations & Logistics; Sport & Event Management

College of Education

UF's teacher education program is constantly evolving to meet the changing requirements of the state and national education systems. Accredited by the National Council for Accreditation of Teacher Education and the Higher Learning Commission, our program emphasizes practical experience, the integration of technology in classrooms and the benefits of service learning.

At UF, you will explore the teaching profession through a combination of general education classes, professional education courses and field experiences. As early as your freshman year, you will be in the schools - observing, participating and learning - to prepare you for an exciting career as an educator.

Findlay also offers a Master of Arts in Education degree, available in traditional classes or entirely online.

Our education programs are:

Adolescent/Young Adult; Early Childhood; Intervention Specialist Education/Mild to Moderate Disabilities; Middle Childhood; Multi-Age

College of Health Professions

Our College of Health Professions is home to some of our most in-demand programs including occupational therapy, physical therapy, and nuclear medicine technology. In the majority of the college's majors, you will gain hands-on experience through clinical training in some of the 1,000 hospitals, outpatient clinics and rehabilitation centers associated with the University.

On the cutting edge in health professions education, UF provides master's degree-level programs in athletic training, health informatics, occupational therapy and physician assistant, as well as a first-professional doctorate in physical therapy.

Health and Physical Education

Health Science; Health Studies; Health Studies; Medical Laboratory Science; Nuclear Medicine Technology; Positron Emission Tomography/Computed Tomography; Pre-Nursing (Non-degree granting course of study in cooperation with Mt. Carmel College of Nursing or Lourdes University); Social Work; Strength & Conditioning

Closely allied with the College of Health Professions is the College of Pharmacy, which offers a six-year program with direct entry from high school. The program offers small classes with excellent faculty, combined with tutoring services, collaboration with other health professions students on campus and state-of-the-art teaching facilities, including specially designed laboratories. All students admitted to pharmacy will graduate from UF with a Pharm.D. as long as all academic and professional standards are met.

College of Liberal Arts

The College of Liberal Arts offers programs that will equip you with the indispensable tools you will need for that first job and for a lifetime of achievements. Our programs range from English and political science to history and theatre.

We also offer a Master of Arts in Teaching English to Speakers of Other Languages (TESOL) and a Master of Rhetoric and Writing.

Our programs are:

Art; Art Management; Children's Book Illustration; Criminal Justice; Criminal Justice; English; English as an International Language; Forensic Science; Graphic Design; History; Japanese; Journalism; Law and the Liberal Arts (Pre-Law); Philosophy/Applied Philosophy; Political Science; Psychology; Public Relations; Religious Studies; Biblical Studies; Comparative Religion Studies; Individualized Studies; Sociology; Spanish; Teaching English to Speakers of Other Languages (TESOL); Theatre

College of Sciences

From environmental management to Internet security, UF's College of Sciences can train you for many of the fastest-growing careers in today's marketplace. At UF, you can observe an equine surgery, study gene replication, develop new computer software, analyze exposure risks to hazardous chemicals and more. Our rigorous academic programs, experienced faculty and focus on hands-on training will prepare you for a successful career in the sciences.

We also offer a Master of Science in Environmental, Safety and Health Management, also available entirely online.

Our majors are:

Animal Science; Animal Science; Biology (recommended for students interested in medical school); Chemistry (recommended for students interested in medical school); Computer Science; Environmental, Safety and Occupational Health Management; Equestrian Studies; Equine Business Management; Mathematics; Pre-Veterinary Medicine, Animal Science

CAMPUS FACILITIES AND EQUIPMENT

The University of Findlay has more than 70 acres at the main campus on North Main Street, which includes major academic, administrative and athletic buildings; residence halls, townhouses, apartment-style cottages and special interest houses; and a number of facilities housing faculty and staff offices and academic units.

In addition, the University operates a 32-acre facility on the east side of Findlay, containing the English equestrian studies program and University Equine Veterinary Services Inc. The University's 152-acre Animal Sciences Center is located eight miles south of campus and houses the western riding and animal science/pre-veterinary medicine programs. A five-acre site on State Route 12 east of Findlay provides hands-on training simulations for the All Hazards Training Center.

In 2009, the University opened a 31,000-square-foot animal science building that combines a working barn with first-rate academic facilities for pre-veterinary medicine.

During 2010, a new Student Recreation Center was installed in the Koehler Fitness and Recreation Complex, featuring basketball, volleyball and tennis courts, a three-lane running/jogging track, a rock climbing wall, racquetball/wallyball court, varsity weight room, golf simulator, game room, student lounge, and juice bar. The second floor already housed a cardio center with treadmills, weight machines, exercise bikes, stair-steppers, and other fitness equipment.

In 2012, UF open a 42,000-square-foot addition to its newest academic building, providing high-technology classrooms and lecture halls, eight cutting edge science laboratories and faculty offices.

STUDENT ORGANIZATIONS AND ACTIVITIES

Extracurricular Activities

Students may participate in any of more than 100 organizations, including special interest clubs, student media, student government, music and theatre groups, service clubs, and academic honorary organizations.

The fine arts flourish on campus with a variety of theatre productions, art exhibits and vocal and instrumental music concerts that offer creative outlets and training for students and serve as a source of cultural enrichment for the community.

Findlay participates in 24 intercollegiate sports and is a member of the National Collegiate Athletic Association (NCAA), Division II, and the Great Lakes Intercollegiate Athletic Conference (GLIAC). Its equestrian teams compete in the Intercollegiate Horse Show Association (IHSA). Women's lacrosse will be added as an NCAA sport for the 2012-13 academic year.

NCAA Sports at The University of Findlay:

Baseball (M)

Basketball (M)

Basketball (W)

Cross country (M)

Cross country (W)

Football

Golf (M)

Golf (W)

Lacrosse (W)

Soccer (M)

Soccer (W)

Softball (W)

Swimming (M)

Swimming (W)

Indoor track (M)

Indoor track (W)

Outdoor track (M)

Outdoor track (W)

Tennis (M)

Tennis (W)

Volleyball (W)

Wrestling (M)

English equestrian (IHSA)

Western equestrian (IHSA)

ADMISSIONS PROCESS

Admission as a first-time, full-time undergraduate student to The University of Findlay requires an earned diploma from an accredited high school in a college preparatory course of study or a GED certificate. Candidates for admission should successfully complete the following requirements: four units of English, three units of mathematics, two units of science, two units of social science and two units of foreign language.

Students who intend to major in equestrian studies, equine business management, animal science-pre-veterinary medicine option or pharmacy are encouraged to complete the application as early as possible, due to limited space available in these programs.

The profile for the Fall 2011 class was: SAT Average of 1566, ACT Average of 23.5, and a GPA average of 3.5.

Application Instructions

Students should complete the Application for Undergraduate Admission after they've finished their junior year course work. Students can apply online at www.findlay.edu or request a paper application from the Office of Undergraduate Admissions. No application fee is required.

Applicants should send an official high school transcript that includes class rank, attendance information, a calculated GPA, and proficiency tests results. Post-secondary option participants should submit transcripts of all college-level work.

Applicants may send the results of the ACT and/or SAT tests directly to The University of Findlay by listing the following codes during test registration: ACT-3272, SAT-1223.

To enroll, all candidates must submit their final transcript after graduation.

Tuition, Room, Board and Fees (2012-13)

Tuition: $14,040/semester

Room and Board: $4,583/semester

Student Fees: $417/semester (includes Activity Fee and General Service Fee)

FINANCIAL AID

To apply for financial aid, the student must complete the Free Application for Federal Student Aid (FAFSA). Eighty-five percent of students attending The University of Findlay receive some form of financial assistance. Students received $33 million in financial aid in 20011-12 through scholarships, work-study grants, and/or government loans.

Scholarships:

If eligible, merit scholarships range from $10,000 to $16,000 per year for 2012-13. These scholarships are deducted from your tuition each year subject to the student remaining in good academic standing.

THE UNIVERSITY OF HARTFORD

AT A GLANCE

The University of Hartford, a fully accredited, independent, nonsectarian institution, is composed of the College of Arts and Sciences; the College of Engineering, Technology and Architecture; the College of Education, Nursing, and Health Professions; Hillyer College; the Barney School of Business; the Hartford Art School; and The Hartt School.

Our full-time undergraduate enrollment of approximately 4,700 men and women includes students from nearly all 50 states and 61 countries. Students participate in about 100 organized student groups, including clubs devoted to special interests or political, professional, religious, or civic activities. Athletics include intercollegiate (NCAA Division I) and intramural sports. These activities, as well as the recreational and fitness needs of the university, are served by a 130,000-square-foot Sports Center. Students are also involved in school publications and AM and FM radio stations, and the Hartt School, the Hartford Art School, and the University Players present a variety of concerts, exhibitions, and theatrical productions each year.

The university's Career Services Center provides career counseling and information on occupations, employers, testing, and graduate schools; serves as a reference and credential source; and provides graduating students with an on-campus recruiting program. Courses, programs, and educational counseling are provided by the Office of Graduate and Adult Academic Services for part-time adult students.

LOCATION AND ENVIRONMENT

The university is located in the peaceful residential suburb of West Hartford. The West Hartford area offers hundreds of shops and restaurants along with many opportunities for students to discover new cultural and intellectual experiences. With museums, theaters, libraries, the XL Center, , a symphony orchestra, shopping, great restaurants, an international airport, and local and intercity transportation systems, the opportunities are plentiful.

Off Campus Opportunities

Through the Hartford Consortium for Higher Education, Hartford students have the opportunity to register for select courses at Saint Joseph College and Trinity College. Opportunities are available to education and health profession majors for field and/or clinical experiences where applicable. The Career Services Center and cooperative education office is available to custom-tailor work experiences within many of the University's programs.

ACADEMICS

The University of Hartford is known nationally for the breadth and depth of its programs. Hartford's seven schools and colleges offer 84 undergraduate majors. The university encourages students to sample a variety of academic areas and enroll in courses in any of the colleges in campus. Students interested in interdisciplinary majors can combine courses from the different schools within the university. Students are assigned academic advisors who help guide them in curriculum choices, career exploration, and the transition to university life. The All-University curriculum was developed in order to help students learn more about how different academic disciplines approach related topics and issues. Courses in different fields of expertise are team taught, and topics are examined from the perspective of several academic disciplines. Students who are undecided on their majors are assisted by a special program at the university. Individual students will also find help in the areas of writing proficiency, reading comprehension, and research and test-taking skills at the reading and writing center, which is available to the entire student body. The Math Tutoring Lab, which is staffed by full-time faculty members and math majors, offers further help for students in math. Selected students are encouraged to participate in the Honors Program. Honors students have the opportunity to graduate with an Honors degree.

MAJORS AND DEGREES OFFERED

The Bachelor of Arts is offered in art history, biology, chemistry, cinema, communication, computer science, criminal justice, drama, economics, English, foreign languages and literatures, history, multimedia and web design & development, international studies, Judaic studies, mathematics, music, performing arts management, philosophy, physics, political economy, politics and government, rhetoric and professional writing, psychology, and sociology.

The Bachelor of Science in secondary education is offered in the fields of English and mathematics.

Students can earn the Bachelor of Fine Arts in ceramics, dance, drawing, illustration, music theater, painting, photography, printmaking, actor training, sculpture, video, and visual communication design.

The Bachelor of Music is offered at the Hartt School with majors in performance (guitar, orchestral instrument, organ, piano, and voice), composition, jazz studies, music education, music history, music management, music production and technology, opera, , and theory.

The Bachelor of Science is awarded in biology, chemistry, chemistry-biology, computer science, early childhood education, elementary education, health sciences (upper division only), mathematics, physics, radiological technology, respiratory therapy, and integrated elementary/special education.

The Bachelor of Science in Business Administration (BSBA) is offered in accounting, economics and finance, entrepreneurial studies, finance and insurance, management, and marketing.

Additional BS programs are offered in the College of Engineering, Technology and Architecture and include ABET-accredited BSEE, BSME, BSCE, BSCMPE, and interdisciplinary BSE options. The most popular BS options are acoustics/music, biomedical engineering, and environmental engineering. Bachelor of Science degrees are also offered in architectural engineering technology, computer engineering technology, electronic engineering technology, and mechanical engineering technology.

Additional special programs include the Doctor of Physical Therapy (freshman entry); Master's degree in prosthetics and orthotics (freshman entry); the five-year music education program; five-year double-major programs; and the Bachelor of Science in Engineering with an acoustics concentration, offered by the College of Engineering.

CAMPUS FACILITIES AND EQUIPMENT

Our suburban West Hartford campus houses the buildings and facilities of our seven colleges and schools.

The newest additions to the campus are the Shaw Center at Hillyer College a 10,000-square-foot addition to Hillyer Hall that provides faculty offices, state-of-the-art classrooms, a dedicated seminar classroom, a conference room, and a large common area; the Handel Center for Performing Arts for students in theater and dance; the Integrated Science, Engineering and Technology Complex, which houses 37,000 square feet of new state-of-the-art classrooms and laboratories as well as a complete renovation of the existing science and engineering facilities; and the Renee Samuels Center which provides state-of-the art digital equipment and studios specifically designed for Media Arts and Photography.

The Harry Jack Gray Center is the home of the Mildred P. Allen Memorial Library; the William H. Mortensen Library; the Museum of American Political Life; the Harry J. Gray Conference Center; the Joseloff Gallery; the University Bookstore; the School of Communication; and studios for art, radio, and television. The library has approximately 572,000 items, including books, musical scores, recordings, periodicals, journals, and microfilm units. The Hartford Consortium for Higher Education, the Hartford Library, and the Interlibrary-Loan systems also offer extensive resources.

The University of Hartford has a Computer Center that houses the central computer systems and operates a high-performance campus wide network that connects student residential housing, all academic buildings on campus, and the university's remote locations. A high-speed T1 line connects the university's network to the Internet. Each student resident has his or her own Ethernet connection to the campus network. The library is connected to the campus network and provides network access in study carrels and study rooms. The library's online systems include the online catalog for book, audio, and video collection, CD-ROM databases and Internet resources, including 1,000 electronic journals. Easy-to-use Web access for many of the library's online resources and electronic reserves are part of the ongoing improvements to the library's systems. Access is available to all of the university network resources--on campus at university facilities and off campus by using computers with modems. Computing labs, used by all students of the university, are provided at three locations around the campus. The labs are equipped with PCs and Macs, computer workstations, and are connected to the campus network and the Internet. Word processing, spreadsheet, database management, and graphics programs are some of the types of software made available to students. On-duty lab assistants are available to help students with any questions or problems. There are also specialized computer facilities for instruction and learning, including the Gilman Center for Communication Technology for English and journalism instruction; Information Technology Center for business students; the Computer Assisted Learning Center; the Center for Computer and Electronic Music; the Computer Aided Design/Computer Aided Manufacturing Laboratory; and the Dana Computer Lab with workstations for computer science. Additional facilities consist of the Hoffman Computer Lab for health professions, the Graphic Design Lab for art instruction, the Educational Computing Lab, and the GIS Computer Lab for engineering instruction.

TUITION, ROOM, BOARD, AND FEES:

Costs for 2013-2014

Tuition $31,804

Double Room (Complexes) $7,328

Freshman Meal Plan $4,920

Fees $1554

Total $45,606

Ninety-three percent of University of Hartford students receive a scholarship or grant from the university. For most students, the cost of a University of Hartford education is significantly reduced by financial assistance.

The average "out of pocket" expense for new students this year was $17,999.

FINANCIAL AID

The university's financial aid program, which administers over $90 million annually including student loans, consists of scholarships, grants, loans, and work-study opportunities provided through the federal government, private agencies, interested individuals, and the University. Factors contributing to disbursal of university funds are the college or school in which the student is enrolled, availability of funds, applicant pool, and competition for funds. About 92 percent of all full-time undergraduate students receive assistance; the average amount is $26,277 per year. Students who have demonstrated outstanding academic achievement are eligible for full and partial-tuition scholarships.

STUDENT BODY

The Student Government Association (SGA) represents all full-time students at the University. Through SGA, students and faculty work together to develop and coordinate the co-curriculars of the university. In addition, students are represented on all major administrative committees, including the Board of Regents.

ADMISSIONS

The admissions decision is based on a combination of the following: quality of the secondary school curriculum, course selection, academic performance in secondary school, recommendations of the secondary school principal or guidance counselor, ACT or SAT scores, evidence of a desire to succeed, and leadership qualities shown by academic and extracurricular activities. Music and art applicants are required to audition, show portfolios, and take other tests depending upon the program to which they are applying.

The University has a rolling admission policy.

For more information, students should contact:

Richard A. Zeiser

Dean of Admission

University of Hartford

West Hartford, CT 06117-0395

Phone: 860-768-4296

Toll free: 800-947-4303

Fax: 860-768-4961

E-mail: admission@hartford.edu

Website: http://admission.hartford.edu

UNIVERSITY OF ILLINOIS AT URBANA-CHAMPAIGN

Please limit to 30 words. If this section is not provided, we will use the first 30 words from the "At a Glance" section that follows. Enter your text below:

The University of Illinois at Urbana-Champaign is among the nation's most prestigious universities. Illinois' tradition of academic excellence, groundbreaking research, and exceptional career preparation is evidence of its renowned standing in higher education.

AT A GLANCE

Established as a land-grant university in 1867, the University of Illinois is committed to teaching, research, and public engagement. Illinois offers unlimited opportunities with 150+ majors, 1,000+ student organizations, 400+ study abroad options, and countless research and leadership experiences. Students also enjoy Division I sports and impressive recreation facilities.

LOCATION AND ENVIRONMENT

Centrally located between Chicago, Indianapolis, and St. Louis, the University of Illinois is a large, public, research institution with 31,000+ undergraduate and 10,500+ graduate students. In-state students comprise about 75% of the undergraduate student body and Illinois is the most diverse public university in the Big Ten. You'll find a traditional college environment where a majority of students live on campus and life is centered on the Quad.

Campustown offers a large assortment of restaurants, shops, cafés, and nightlife. The wide variety of cultural opportunities enhances campus life by providing an inclusive and educational atmosphere. You'll be able to attend so many fantastic events: top performances of nationally touring bands for student-friendly prices at the Assembly Hall and Canopy Club; renowned theatre and dance shows at the Krannert Center for Performing Arts; and hot-topic lectures or rallies from award-winning speakers. As a student at Illinois, you will gain exposure to these types of diverse, exciting, college-focused events because of the University's stature and size.

OFF-CAMPUS OPPORTUNITIES

As an active micro-urban community, Champaign-Urbana maintains an intimate small-town feel while offering big-city advantages. This means that you get a wide variety of delicious culinary options, a diverse live music scene that continually brings in national and independent acts, and an active visual and performing arts community. More than 100,000 people live in C-U, in addition to the University student body. It is the ideal setting for your college education.

Exciting events include:

Roger Ebert's Film Festival – an annual weekend-long festival of movie screenings, actors, and panel discussions, hosted by Roger Ebert, American film critic, screenwriter, and Illinois alumnus

Pygmalion Music Festival – an annual showcase of live music held in multiple locations throughout the downtowns of Champaign and Urbana

Ellnora Guitar Festival – a biennial guitar extravaganza, one of the biggest and most unique festivals in the region, featuring the full spectrum of genres

For more info about Champaign-Urbana, check out:

- www.visitchampaigncounty.org
- www.the217.com
- www.40north.org
- www.smilepolitely.com

MAJORS AND DEGREES OFFERED

The University of Illinois offers Bachelors, Masters, and Doctoral degrees. Undergraduates can choose from over 150 majors, many of which are highly ranked, within 9 undergraduate academic communities: the Colleges of Agricultural, Consumer, and Environmental Sciences; Applied Health Sciences; Business; Education; Engineering; Fine and Applied Arts; Liberal Arts and Sciences; Media; and the School of Social Work. Students can also enter as "undeclared" in the Division of General Studies.

ACADEMIC PROGRAMS

Illinois provides a 145-year tradition of academic excellence and success. By learning from faculty members who are among the best in their fields, participating in undergraduate research, and gaining invaluable hands-on experience, Illinois students receive an education second-to-none.

Study Abroad: Illinois has the 9th largest program among doctorate institutions. All students are encouraged to study abroad and there is a program for any major or interest. With over 400 programs in approximately 60 countries, you can go study in a different country for an academic break, semester, or an entire year. From learning about business at Hong Kong University to cinema studies in London, the opportunities are endless.

Honors Programs: For high-achieving students, Illinois offers interconnected and cooperating honors programs at the campus, college, and departmental levels. Students can complete more than one program over the course of an undergraduate career. Additionally, the National and International Scholarships Program assists high-achieving students in applying for various nationally competitive awards, such as the Rhodes and Fulbright scholarships.

Career Services: One of the most important resources on campus is The Career Center, which acts as an umbrella for 28 college and departmental career centers across campus.

Having a network of centers will greatly benefit you as an Illinois student because not only will you have access to the larger center not affiliated with any particular field, but also a center that specializes in your specific major. The Career Center provides invaluable services like career counseling, pre-health advising, résumé and cover letter reviews, mock interviews, and workshops on salary negotiations and professional etiquette.

Leadership Center: The center's professionals are committed to helping you develop and enhance your leadership skills through active participation in leadership consulting programs, leadership retreats, and a certificate program that involves extended leadership involvement through activities, classes, or employment.

CAMPUS FACILITIES AND EQUIPMENT

Illinois has amazing facilities. You'll find everything from traditional campus classrooms to state-of-the-art research facilities. Highlights:

Student Dining & Residential Programs (SDRP) building: Opened in 2010, SDRP is a dining facility and common area for students to learn and gather. It has been recognized with silver Leadership in Energy and Environmental Design (LEED) certification.

There are three dining areas, including the main hall, which seats over 1,200 and offers delicious and diverse options for each meal, including many choices for vegetarian and vegan dining. You will also find a residential library, study rooms, a fitness area, and a new state-of-the-art residence hall for students with physical disabilities.

Recreational Centers: Both main centers have been remodeled recently and offer abundant options for staying physically active. You have access to a climbing wall, saunas, leisure and swimming pools, running tracks, courts, an instructional kitchen, fitness classes, a wellness center, and so much more. Campus Recreation also provides an ice arena, many additional gyms and pools, and outdoor recreational spaces.

Krannert Center for the Performing Arts: Krannert hosts 4,000 audience members on any given night and over 300 performances each year. Students and professionals showcase their talents here in music, theatre, and dance.

The Library: Illinois is proud to have the 3rd largest academic library in the nation, the largest public university library.

Business Instructional Facility (BIF): BIF has earned the world's highest honor for sustainable, environmentally friendly construction and design with platinum Leadership in Energy and Environmental Design (LEED) certification. It is the first such building at any public university business school in the world and boasts state-of-the-art classrooms, a trading floor, career development and academic counseling centers, student program offices, a recruitment suite, and a 300-seat auditorium.

Beckman Institute for Advanced Science & Technology: This is an interdisciplinary research institute devoted to cutting-edge research in the physical sciences, computation, engineering, biology, behavior, cognition, and neuroscience. More than 600 researchers from 40 University of Illinois departments work in Beckman.

The Institute for Genomic Biology (IGB): IGB houses a microfabrication lab, a plant growth facility, and a microscopy suite. Research at the IGB falls under one of three program areas: Systems Biology, Cellular and Metabolic Engineering, and Genome Technology.

The Student Sustainable Farm: This is a student-run production farm that supplies Illinois residence halls with locally grown, low-input, sustainable food.

TUITION, ROOM, BOARD, AND FEES

Est. Summary of Expenses for 2013 – 2014

Undergraduate students at Illinois are guaranteed the same tuition rate for four continuous academic years.

	Residents	Non-residents	International
Tuition and fees	$15,258-20,178°	$29,640-34,560°	$30,440–$37,360°
Books and supplies	$1,200	$1,200	$1,200
Room and board	$10,636	$10,636	$10,636
Other expenses	$2,500	$2,500	$2,500
TOTAL	$29,594-34,514°	$43,976-48,896°	$44,776 - $51,696°

° The low end of the tuition range indicates the base rate for students initially enrolled after May 2013. Students enrolled in certain programs may be a higher tuition rate up to the high end of the range shown. For tuition details for specific programs, visit www.osfa.illinois.edu/cost.

FINANCIAL AID

The Office of Student Financial Aid (OSFA) assists students by awarding financial aid to help pay for educational expenses. Financial aid is available from federal, state, University and private resources. There are four primary types of financial aid programs: grants, scholarships/waivers, loans, and employment. Last year, over $755 million in financial aid funds were administered and 74% of students received financial aid.

STUDENT ORGANIZATIONS AND ACTIVITIES

As a Big Ten university, Illinois has 19 varsity sports teams. Cheer with other fans as a member of the student-cheering group, Illini Pride, at historic Memorial Stadium or Assembly Hall. Or join a team—there are 40 club sports teams and Campus Recreation organizes over 20 intramural sports for students.

At Illinois there are more than 1,000 Registered Student Organizations, which include clubs that are philanthropic, athletic, political, interest-based, and academic. After reviewing all those choices, if you still can't find one that fits your interest it's easy to create your own.

Illinois also offers one of the largest Greek communities in the nation. There are 59 fraternities and 35 sororities, in which about 22% of all undergraduates participate.

A great advantage of going to Illinois is that you can pick and choose how you'd like to get involved. You can continue your involvement in something important to you, or try something new.

ADMISSIONS PROCESS

Admission is selective. We perform a holistic review of the application in order to form a complete picture of you and how you can benefit from being a part of Illinois. In an admission decision, we consider coursework, academic performance, class rank, ACT and/or SAT scores, application essays, extracurricular activities, volunteer work, work experience, and awards and honors.

Application Dates & Deadlines

Freshmen: The Priority Filing deadline is November 1 with admission decisions announced in mid-December. The final deadline is January 2 with admission decisions announced in mid-February.

Transfers: The deadline for spring applicants is October 15 with admission decisions by mid-December. The deadline for fall applicants is March 1 with admission decisions in mid-April.

Check our website (http://www.admissions.illinois.edu) for details, as dates change slightly each year.

Official ACT composite scores or SAT I (critical reading & math) scores are required for an application to be complete. We do not use the SAT II for any admission purposes.

UNIVERSITY OF MAINE

AT A GLANCE

The University of Maine offers the major research, close-knit community and lauded academics that go beyond your expectations. As Maine's flagship public university, UMaine offers more than 90 undergraduate majors and academic programs, 75 master's programs and 30 doctoral programs. Top students are invited to join UMaine's Honors College — one of the country's oldest and most prestigious.

Ranked in the National Science Foundation's top 100 research universities, UMaine is also included in the top 8 percent of colleges and universities nationwide to be classified by the Carnegie Foundation for the Advancement of Teaching as a "Research University–High Research Activity" institution. The Laboratory for Surface Science and Technology is a hub for cutting-edge sensor and nanotechnology research, and our Advanced Structures and Composites Center is a global leader in deepwater offshore wind energy development.

UMaine students have extraordinary opportunities to garner real-world, immersive experience. SPIFFY, the student investment club, manages a $1.8-million, real-money portfolio. Wildlife ecology majors learn about bear behavior by going out and tagging cubs. Engineering majors secure co-ops and internships that often lead to employment after graduation. Education majors take advantage of urban, rural and international student-teaching opportunities. Marine science undergrads can spend a semester by the sea at our internationally renowned Darling Marine Center.

LOCATION AND ENVIRONMENT

50 minutes from NYC, 50 miles from Acadia National Park

There's no place like Maine, and UMaine students explore the great outdoors whenever they can. There are 15 miles of walking, biking and cross-country skiing trails on campus. Some of the best skiing in the East is located within easy driving distance of campus, as are Bar Harbor, Acadia National Park and Baxter State Park, the northern terminus of the Appalachian Trail.

The Maine Bound adventure center on campus offers a comprehensive outdoor experience for all skill levels. By combining recreation and education, our programs offer adventure opportunities for every lifestyle, instilling safety and survival training. Students can kayak, ski, snowshoe, canoe, hike and even learn about wilderness first aid.

Orono is a classic college town, bounded by the Stillwater and Penobscot rivers, located in the heart of Maine. The University of Maine is 10 minutes from the state's third-largest city, Bangor, and its international airport.

UMaine's 660-acre campus was designed by legendary landscape architect Frederick Law Olmsted, who also designed Central Park in New York City and the U.S. Capitol grounds in Washington, D.C. It is a traditional New England campus, with ivy-covered brick buildings, towering pines and incredible fall foliage.

ACADEMIC PROGRAMS

The UMaine Academic Difference

At UMaine, we provide a comprehensive academic and student experience, yielding graduates who are well-educated, well-adjusted and well-prepared to assume leadership roles in our society. We foster excellence and innovation through inspired, dedicated teaching and the discovery of new knowledge.

UMaine offers more than 90 majors and programs across five colleges — the College of Education and Human Development; the College of Engineering; the College of Liberal Arts and Sciences; the College of Natural Sciences, Forestry, and Agriculture; the Honors College — and the Maine Business School. In addition, the Explorations program is designed to help undecided students identify a major from across UMaine's colleges while making progress toward their degree. The Division of Lifelong Learning offers online classes and distance-learning opportunities for students who need a flexible class schedule.

UMaine's Honors College — one of the country's oldest and most prestigious — provides an in-depth, academically challenging curriculum for qualified students in any major. Honors students take advantage of unique research, academic and cultural opportunities, as well as exclusive housing.

All students at the University of Maine benefit from a solid liberal arts foundation. Here, students develop and refine the qualities they need to more fully engage with the world around them — critical thinking, curiosity, a sense of discovery, a broader perspective — no matter what discipline they choose.

Fogler Library, the state's largest library, houses approximately 1 million volumes, subscribes to more than 4,000 periodicals and serial titles and serves as a depository for more than 2.2 million government documents. In addition, Fogler provides access to countless online documents.

Undergraduate Research Opportunities

At the University of Maine, undergraduate research is a priority and point of pride. Our students publish, travel and work alongside UMaine's world-class scholars and scientists.

The Center for Undergraduate Research was established in 2008 to connect students with faculty projects that suit their interests. For many, research provides an opportunity for a mentor-mentee relationship different from — and often richer than — that of teacher-student. Skills developed through research and scholarship make students more competitive in the workplace and in graduate school.

Accessible Professors

There's a common misconception that if students choose a university rather than a small college, they'll get lost in the shuffle. They'll never see a professor — only teaching assistants — until they're in grad school. But at the University of Maine, the majority of undergraduate classes are taught by professors — and many of those faculty members go on to become friends and mentors to their students. Here, professors are known for having an open-door policy. Our students have opportunities to work alongside some of the most renowned scholars and scientists in the world — whether they're talking civil engineering over pies at Pat's Pizza or traversing an Antarctic ice sheet with researchers from UMaine's Climate Change Institute.

STUDENT ORGANIZATIONS AND ACTIVITIES

So Much to Do

In addition to state-of-the art research and classroom facilities, the University of Maine is also a cultural hub. It is home to the region's premier performing arts center, the Collins Center for the Arts, as well as several museums and galleries. Student Entertainment brings in national acts, such as Janelle Monae, Boys Like Girls and All American Rejects. The New Balance Student Recreation Center is a campus hot spot, and is ranked 7th in Best College Reviews' 25 Most Amazing Campus Student Recreation Centers.

Students can get involved in more than 200 clubs and organizations — academic and social — one of 17 fraternities or seven sororities, Student Government, community service-oriented groups, intramural sports and much, much more. On campus, there are free events including game nights, first-run movies, open mic nights and karaoke. UMaine is the state's only NCAA Division I school, and athletic events — especially hockey — are a big part of student life here. In fact, the Wall Street Journal says Alfond Arena has the best atmosphere in college hockey, and Orono is ranked 29 in The Bleacher Report's Top 50 Hockey Cities in North America.

When UMaine students travel, they can reach New York City in 50 minutes or go global, through study abroad, international volunteerism and the worldwide research opportunities available to undergraduates. In recent semesters, UMaine students have traveled to China to learn more about the country's emerging financial markets, to Italy to explore Renaissance art history at the source, to Turkey to study film and to Brazil to learn about a sensitive and diverse ecosystem.

ADMISSIONS PROCESS

Admission to the University of Maine is a selective process. Successful applicants are those whose scholastic achievement, intellectual curiosity and established study habits promise success in a comprehensive university environment. Space availability in certain programs may also be considered when selecting candidates for admission. Applicants may submit electronic or paper versions of the University of Maine System application, and may also apply through the Common Application.

The University of Maine has an Early Action deadline of December 15. Students whose complete applications are postmarked by December 15 are reviewed by the end of January. Early Action candidates are given first consideration for the Honors College and merit scholarships awarded by the Admissions Office.

All other applicants are encouraged to submit their applications and all supporting documents by February 1, and are notified by rolling admission. An admission decision is typically be made within six weeks from the receipt of the application and all supporting documents.

UNIVERSITY OF MARY WASHINGTON

AT A GLANCE

The University of Mary Washington, a top-ranked public liberal arts and sciences university, attracts talented, intellectually curious students looking for exceptional academics and a supportive community of high integrity.

Founded in 1908, UMW has a rich tradition of academic excellence. We celebrate the fact that everyone thinks differently. It's the reason we keep classes small, dynamic, highly interactive, and it's why every course is taught by a master teacher in the field – no teaching assistants here.

We're consistently ranked as one of the best public liberal arts and sciences universities in the nation in Fiske Guide to Colleges, Peterson's, Princeton Review, Forbes.com, and others.

But don't worry, we make plenty of time for your fun side. This is an incredibly friendly, close-knit campus community, active and energizing, where friends are like family and there's always something exciting going on.

Some quick facts:

4,515 undergrads, 578 graduate students

Student-faculty ratio: 15:1

Average class size is 22 students

Honors Program for high-achieving students

60+ undergraduate majors, minors, and courses of study (or make your own)

140+ student clubs, sports teams, performance ensembles, and volunteer groups

LOCATION AND ENVIRONMENT

We have a drop-dead-gorgeous campus: Trees and greenery, fun gathering spots, hidden places to relax, outstanding facilities, all packaged in an easy-walking, park-like setting. Everywhere you go you'll bump into friends and discover exciting things going on. No wonder 93 percent of freshmen live on campus.

Fredericksburg is picturesque and steeped in American history. George Washington grew up just across the river and the Civil War unfolded all around us. We're home to the President James Monroe Museum and Gari Melchers Home and Studio. Studying in this historic place gives you a unique perspective on the world.

But we're also just a hop and a skip from one of the world's great epicenters of business, technology, biotech, research, and culture – Washington, D.C. It all adds up to great living and the perfect setting for our hands-on, into-the-world style of learning.

But it's the intangibles – the friendly, close-family feel, the camaraderie, the Honor Code, the sense that you can count on anyone at any time – that truly set Mary Washington apart.

OFF-CAMPUS OPPORTUNITIES

You come for the premier academics and career prep. You stay for the friendships and exceptional lifestyle.

We're surrounded by an eclectic mix of recreational and outdoor opportunities. Head west into the Blue Ridge Mountains. Or east toward the Chesapeake Bay and the Atlantic Ocean. Hiking, canoeing, biking, camping, climbing, surfing, ocean-plunging – all close by.

And as for shopping, nightlife, and culture, the Fredericksburg area is known for its quaint shops, cozy coffee houses, charming bistros, and restaurants for every palate. Yet, the state's largest mall is just 30 minutes away. And being so close to both Washington, DC, and Richmond means that there's an endless array of choices.

That proximity also means opportunities to get in on the ground floor with businesses, government agencies, non-profits, and global organizations:

Interning for a congressman on Capitol Hill

Launching an international bank to make micro-loans to the needy in Third-world countries

Conducting research on the effects of a common household chemical on human health

Researching paint chips at George Washington's home in Mount Vernon

Our students have done all these, and more. Learning by doing, the kind of multi-dimension education that gives you an edge in landing a great career. The only question is this: What exciting out-of-the classroom options will you choose during your college career? We'll help you find the right ones:

Internships

Research

Fieldwork

Study abroad

Independent study

Volunteering and service learning

MAJORS AND DEGREES OFFERED

We offer Bachelor of Arts, Bachelor of Science, and Bachelor of Liberal Studies degrees in 60+ areas of study in the physical sciences, business, humanities, fine and performing arts, computer sciences, social sciences, political science, geography and GIS, religious studies, and more.

Or you can go DIY and create a double major or your own one-of-a-kind interdisciplinary major. Our most popular areas:

- Business administration

- English

- Psychology

- Biology

- History

- International affairs

- Political science

- Historic preservation

- Computer science

- Modern foreign languages (French, German, Spanish)

- Geography

Many students also choose pre-med and pre-law programs as the solid foundation for a professional career.

In addition, our College of Education, respected nationwide for combining theory with practice, offers multiple paths to teacher licensure, along with a Master of Science in Elementary Education, Master of Education degrees, and a variety of graduate teaching endorsements and certificates.

The College of Business offers a Master of Business Administration and Master of Science in Management Information Systems, in addition to its undergraduate degrees.

Once you choose your major, you'll join the close-knit professional families in one (or more) of our distinguished Colleges:

- College of Business

- College of Education

- College of Arts and Sciences

ACADEMIC PROGRAMS

Every class at UMW is taught by a passionate, skilled master teacher who believes that education is a journey to be taken with students. You'll partner with them in the lab and in the field and in the classroom, in small groups and one on one. They'll get to know your name and your strengths and interests, too. And they'll become lifelong mentors who are available to you along every step of your career journey.

Honors Program

If you have a strong academic record, the Honors Program offers advanced, seminar-style courses, interdisciplinary seminars, special internships, and mentored research and creative projects.

Study Abroad

We have 17 partner programs and more than a dozen faculty-led travel programs to global destinations. For-credit programs are available over spring/winter breaks, summer, a semester, or an academic year.

Internships and Fieldwork

We'll help you take learning beyond the book. UMW is perfectly positioned for internships in science, technology, industry, business, education, law, health care, media, and the arts.

Student Research

UMW also supports student research and scholarship. Regardless of major, students have access to top-of-the-line equipment and facilities: from the electron microscopes, DNA sequencer, and magnetic resonance spectrometer to the electronic media lab.

The payoff is that you're prepared for career success. Every year, UMW graduates are accepted at top graduate and professional schools. Many others launch successful careers right after graduation. Either way, you'll join an elite network of entrepreneurs, innovators, thinkers, and leaders who have the well-rounded knowledge, skills, and experience to excel in a fast-changing world.

CAMPUS FACILITIES AND EQUIPMENT

First-year students have a choice of seven different campus residences: Live in a vintage 80-year-old hall with high ceilings and elegant parlors or in a modern apartment with granite countertops and stainless steel appliances. Or join friends who share your interests in a Living Learning Community. This is a campus designed for an exceptional student experience.

Eagle Village, a mixed-use facility with upscale student residences, restaurants, shops, offices, a Hyatt hotel (under construction), and classrooms, is a short walk across the pedestrian bridge from campus.

Campus amenities include a mix of restaurants, student lounges, and coffee shops, as well as the 2-story Fitness Center and Goolrick Hall, which have an impressive array of cardiovascular and resistance equipment, free weights, basketball courts, pool, and fitness stations, as well as a Wellness Resource Center.

The Underground, a favorite restaurant and after-hours club, hosts popular Open Mic Comedy Nights, Monday Night Football, and Bingo, Karaoke, and Trivia nights. Another option is The Wash Room, with pool, ping pong, fooshall, and air hockey tables, along with Starbucks, deli restaurant, and computers to catch up on your networking.

The stunning Anderson Center in the heart of campus seats 2,000 for men's and women's varsity sports and seats up to 3,000 for concerts. Coming soon is the innovative Information and Technology Convergence Center, a future-oriented, technology-rich place for student collaboration, slated to open in fall 2014.

Some of our impressive facilities are in the cloud, not on the campus: The groundbreaking Domain of One's Own, for example, provides Web domains and hosting, encouraging you to own and control your own online presence.

TUITION, ROOM, BOARD, AND FEES

UMW offers the exceptional academics of an elite private school, but as a public liberal arts and sciences university, our tuition and fees are 30 percent or less of those typical at the top private colleges in the nation.

No surprise that UMW is a "Best Buy" in higher education. For the 2012-13 academic year, undergraduate tuition and fees for Virginia residents was $9,246; for non-residents, $21,560. Room and board was about $8,900. The cost of graduate school for in-state residents is $426 per credit hour.

FINANCIAL AID

UMW distributes more than $28 million in financial aid through some 450 different awards each year -- scholarships, grants, and financial aid programs from federal, state, internal, and private sources. More than half of UMW's undergraduates receive some form of financial aid.

Work-study jobs are also readily available. In short, UMW's quality-value equation is extraordinary — something you'll learn first-hand when you schedule a visit and talk to current students.

STUDENT ORGANIZATIONS AND ACTIVITIES

From the very first day on campus, you'll find lots of exciting ways to get immersed in student life.

Eagle athletics, for example: With 23 NCAA Division III Eagle sports, everyone is either a player or a fan. One in 10 UMW students suited up as a scholar-athlete last year – incredible!

There's a host of club sports, too, so you're sure to find just what you're looking for – from swimming to horseback riding, field hockey to soccer, boxing to lacrosse… and much more.

Talk about involvement! Students run 140-plus different clubs, organizations, athletics teams, and volunteer groups: Aubade Literary Magazine and The Bullet newspaper; Aikido martial arts and BellA'capella singers; Biology and Humans vs. Zombies. Always something exciting going on.

Students in the group Giant Productions book concerts by top performing artists and bring in provocative thinkers and speakers. Recent bookings: Passion Pit, Taking Back Sunday, the Maine, Bad Rabbits, Ben & Jerry, and Fun. Recent visitors: Anthony Bourdain, Keenan Thompson, Karl Rove, and Michelle Obama.

Another thing to know about UMW is our tradition of putting beliefs into action through civic and social involvement. We've earned our place on the President's Higher Education Community Service Honor Roll 4 years in a row! Thousands of our students have discovered that they can do just a little to change the world through volunteer and service learning projects at homeless shelters, Habitat for Humanity, Head Start, SPCA, churches, and many other worthy groups.

UMW students pitch in. They lead. Give directions. Return the iPhone you left in The Underground. Smile. And donate countless hours to organizations that help people they will never see.

ADMISSIONS PROCESS

Visit

To get the full flavor of the Mary Washington experience, we invite you to visit. During scheduled Discovery Days, you can walk the campus with a student guide, visit residence halls, have lunch, and learn what life here is really like. You'll talk with students and master teachers, ask questions and explore.

Or sign up for a visit on your schedule, and we'll make sure that staff members and students are here to greet you. Campus tours are offered mornings and afternoons, Monday through Friday.

Register for Discovery Days or independent visits at admissions.umw.edu/visit.

Apply

Apply online by visiting umw.edu/apply and clicking on the Common Application link. Choose UMW, and make sure to fill out the UMW Supplement.

Special Application Tips

Pay special attention to extra-curricular activities, community service, recommendations from others, and your personal essay narrative and story. Take time to fill out the free application for Federal Student Aid (FAFSA) as well. You might be very glad you did.

UNIVERSITY OF MARYLAND, BALTIMORE COUNTY

AT A GLANCE

UMBC attracts creative and motivated students and rewards them with the resources and attention they need to succeed. A selective, medium-sized public research university, UMBC provides students with opportunities for hands-on research and liberal arts experience working with professors at the top of their fields. This fall, U.S. News & World Report again ranked UMBC number one among "Up and Coming" national universities, "schools everyone should be watching." UMBC also is tied with Yale on a list of the top national universities "where the faculty has an unusual commitment to undergraduate teaching. UMBC President Freeman A. Hrabowski, III, has been named "one of the 10 best college presidents" and "one of the 100 most influential people in the world" by Time Magazine. Theatre students rank 3rd nationally in invitations to perform at the Kennedy Center American College Theatre Festival. The Carnegie Foundation ranks UMBC in the category of Research Universities with high research activity. UMBC is a two-time winner of the U.S. Presidential Award for Excellence in Science, Mathematics and Engineering Mentoring. The University's academic reputation and industry partnerships help place students in promising careers and leading graduate programs. One-third of UMBC students immediately go on to leading graduate or professional schools such as Harvard, Johns Hopkins, Stanford, and Yale. Three UMBC graduates have received one of the world's most selective academic awards, the Gates Cambridge Fellowship.

Undergraduates have access to the latest technology in areas from geography to art history to chemistry. A new Performing Arts and Humanities building opened in 2012, providing state-of-the-art facilities for several arts and humanities departments and programs. The Goddard Earth Science and Technology Center brings NASA scientists, UMBC professors, and students together to study the earth. Students in UMBC's Imaging Research Center (IRC) gain professional experience with companies such as the Discovery Channel, CNN, and PBS. UMBC also has a Howard Hughes Medical Institute laboratory, a privately sponsored research facility dedicated to the study of the structural building blocks of the AIDS virus. The UMBC climate is friendly and energetic; 10,953 undergraduates have enough ideas and interests to support more than 250 groups, including Greek organizations, recreational sports clubs, community outreach efforts, and campus events. Students enthusiastically follow UMBC NCAA Division I athletic teams and attend games in the UMBC Stadium and Retriever Activities Center. The new book, Higher Education? How Colleges Are Wasting Our Money and Failing Our Kids— and What We Can Do About It, features UMBC as a school where students can receive a first-class undergraduate education at a reasonable price. Approximately 75% of freshman students live on campus, with 14% from out of state. The undergraduate student population is 45% female, 24% Asian American, 12% African American, 4% Hispanic American and Native American. UMBC houses nearly 3,900 students, 1,600 live in UMBC's three new residence suites and apartment communities. Residential communities feature nine living-learning programs, including the Center for Women in Technology; Intercultural Living Exchange; Shriver Living Learning Center.

COLLEGE BASICS

An Honors University with the teaching and student support traditions of a small liberal arts college, UMBC is also among the most rapidly developing and diverse research universities in the nation.

LOCATION AND ENVIRONMENT

Located a few miles south of Baltimore, UMBC is 15 minutes from downtown Baltimore and 30 minutes from Washington, D.C. The Baltimore-Washington area is known for its music, sports, museums, restaurants, and historical traditions. UMBC's 530-acre campus includes more than 40 buildings accessed by a two-mile elliptical drive, with housing and dining facilities on one side and core facilities (classroom/lab buildings, performing arts center, a library, galleries, a student union, a bookstore, a gymnasium, an Olympic-size pool, and tennis courts) surrounding a central walkway. bwtech@UMBC Research and Technology Park, adjacent to the campus, attracts firms in the high-technology fields, including engineering, information technology, and the life sciences.

OFF-CAMPUS OPPORTUNITIES

Surrounded by business, government, and metropolitan centers, UMBC places students in over 1,200 co-ops and internships in more than 500 organizations each year in the Baltimore-Washington area. UMBC matches students with such employers as the federal Centers for Medicare and Medicaid, Bank of America, Silicon Graphics, MBNA, the Smithsonian Institution, NASA, and the National Aquarium. The university encourages students to participate in study abroad experiences during the semester or travel-study opportunities during winter and summer breaks. The Shriver Center links the resources of the campus to urgent social problems, places students in co-ops and internships at hundreds of businesses and organizations, organizes and manages community service projects that bring the resources of the university to people in need, and connects students to a wide range of social service projects.

ACADEMICS

UMBC's academic calendar consists of fall and spring semesters, a four-week mini session in January, and summer sessions from six to eight weeks. To receive a UMBC degree, students complete 120 to 128 credits plus two physical education courses. In addition to the requirements for the chosen major, the general education program (GEP), provides a solid basis for a lifetime of learning. GEP courses encompass humanities and fine arts, mathematics and natural sciences, social sciences, and languages and culture. The Honors College at UMBC is a special option for students seeking a community of like-minded people for whom the quest for knowledge is its own reward. All Honors College students must take at least one honors course per semester. Students choose from honors versions of core courses, special honors seminars, and plenty of other honors courses.

ADMISSIONS

In fall 2012, the average incoming freshman had a 3.71 cumulative GPA, 52% ranked in the top quarter of his or her senior class, and had a combined SAT I score of 1206. Approximately 65% of freshman applicants are admitted each year. Academic performance and curriculum strength play an important part in the decision. An essay is required, and a letter of recommendation is strongly encouraged. Transfer students with at least 30 semester hours of college-level work are admitted based on the strength of college success. A minimum 2.5 GPA is recommended for full consideration. Prospective freshmen are encouraged to submit applications by the early action deadline of November 1. The final deadline is February 1 for full consideration for admission, campus housing, financial aid, and scholarships. The priority deadline for transfer students is March 15 for fall admission and November 1 for spring admission for students seeking admission to special programs or wishing to be considered for campus housing, financial aid, or scholarships. The final deadline for applications is May 31 for fall and December 15 for spring. For further information, students or parents may contact:

Dale Bittinger

Director of Undergraduate Admissions and Orientation

Office of Undergraduate Admissions and Orientation

UMBC

1000 Hilltop Circle

Baltimore, Maryland 21250

Telephone: 410-455-2291 or 800-UMBC-4U2

Fax: 410-455-1094

Web: www.umbc.edu

CAMPUS FACILITIES AND EQUIPMENT

UMBC's landmark building, the Albin O. Kuhn Library and Gallery, contains over 1 million books and bound volumes of journals, an extensive reference collection, 4,200 journal and database subscriptions, more than 200 computers , wireless and wired connections for laptops, and more than 3 million other items, including slides, photographs, maps, musical scores, recordings, and microforms. The Commons, UMBC's state-of-the-art student center, the hub of campus life includes a food court, general lounges, the University bookstore, meeting spaces, a student recreation center, a full-service bank, student organization offices, retail-type spaces, wireless computer connectivity, and Web-accessible kiosks. UMBC students have access to research opportunities and equipment such as conducting AIDS research on one of the world's largest nuclear magnetic resonance spectrometers in the only Howard Hughes Medical Institute lab at a public university in Maryland. Newer facilities include a Public Policy Building and a state-of-the-art Information Technology/Engineering Building. UMBC's a new Performing Arts and Humanities Building houses seven departments and new performance space that showcase the University's strong arts and humanities programs and creates a regional and national appreciation of UMBC as a cultural attraction.

CAMPUS LIFE

The campus climate is friendly and energetic. UMBC's more than 10,973 undergraduates have enough ideas and interests to support more than 250 student groups, including Greek organizations and recreational sports clubs, such as fencing and sailing; community outreach efforts, such as Habitat for Humanity; and campus events, including lectures, films, concerts, and plays. Students enthusiastically follow UMBC NCAA Division I athletic teams, such as basketball, lacrosse, and soccer and attend games in the UMBC Stadium and Retriever Activities Center, which includes a multipurpose gym, auxiliary gym, weight room, and classrooms. Elections are held each year for officers in UMBC's Student Government Association (SGA). The SGA represents the student body on a number of administrative committees, including the Undergraduate Council, the Library Committee, and the Student Health Advisory Committee.

MAJORS AND DEGREES OFFERED

Programs leading to Bachelor of Arts, Bachelor of Fine Arts, and Bachelor of Science degrees: acting, Africana studies, American studies, aging services, ancient studies, Asian studies, biochemistry and molecular biology, bioinformatics and computational biology, biological sciences, business technology administration, chemical engineering, chemistry and biochemistry, chemistry education, computer engineering and computer science, cultural anthropology, dance, economics and financial economics, emergency health services, English, environmental science and environmental studies, gender and women's studies, geography, health administration and policy, history, information systems, innovation and entrepreneurship, interdisciplinary studies, mathematics and statistics, mechanical engineering, media and communication studies, modern languages, linguistics and intercultural communication, music, philosophy, physics education, physics, political science, psychology, social work, sociology, theater, and visual arts. New programs include computer gaming, media and communication studies, Asian studies, global studies and physics education. An interdisciplinary studies program allows students to design their own course of study according to their specific educational and career goals. UMBC offers pre-professional studies programs, including two-and four-year advisement programs to prepare students for clinical training in dental hygiene, medical and research technology, medicine, nursing, pharmacy, physical therapy, and veterinary medicine. Minors include Africana studies, American studies, ancient studies, anthropology, applied politics, art history and theory, astronomy, biological sciences, chemistry, computer science, dance, East Asian history, economics, emergency health services, environmental geography, gender and women's studies, geography, history, international affairs, international economics, Judaic studies, legal policy, literature, mathematics, modern languages and linguistics, music, philosophy, physics, political science, political thought, psychology, public administration, religious studies, social welfare, sociology, statistics, theater, writing, and media and communication studies.

FINANCIAL AID

More than 45% of undergraduates receive some financial aid. UMBC uses the Free Application for Federal Student Aid (FAFSA) to help determine a student's financial need. Aid is awarded to qualified applicants on a first-come, first-served basis. Since aid is awarded only to admitted students, early application for admission is also important. Well-qualified freshmen are automatically considered for general merit scholarships once they are admitted to the University. The Scholars Programs at UMBC provide special opportunities for outstanding entering freshmen who want to focus their education through intense study in their major. Scholars participate in a wide range of academic and cultural enrichment activities, extracurricular travel, or summer study. The selection process for specialty scholarships includes application, an interview, and, in some cases, nomination from a high school official.

Tuition and Fees

Tuition and fees for 2011-2012 are $9,764 for Maryland residents and $20,825 for out-of-state students. Room and board averaged $10,214. Miscellaneous expenses, books, and transportation cost about $1,500 per year.

UNIVERSITY OF MASSACHUSETTS—LOWELL

AT A GLANCE

The University of Massachusetts Lowell is a nationally recognized doctoral-level research university whose graduates are ready for work, for life and for all that the world has to offer.

The University of Massachusetts (UMass) Lowell is a nationally recognized doctoral-level research university. It is ranked in the top tier of U.S. News and World Report's national universities. Founded in 1894, the University has built a tradition of innovation, entrepreneurship and partnerships with industry and the community to advance research, provide public service and enrich the student educational experience. Its graduates are ready to contribute meaningfully in the work place, to build lives around the principles and passions they develop at UMass, and to make a difference in communities anywhere in the world.

The University is part of the five-campus University of Massachusetts system and comprises six colleges: the College of Fine Arts, Humanities and Social Sciences; the College of Sciences; the Francis College of Engineering; the School of Health and Environment; the Manning School of Business; and the Graduate School of Education. Together, the colleges offer more than 120 programs to UMass Lowell's 9,500 undergraduate students. The Graduate School enrolls nearly 4,000 students in 36 master's degree and 23 doctoral programs. The UMass Lowell education focuses on putting the lessons of the classroom into practice. Students have multiple opportunities for co-ops, internships, service-learning activities and undergraduate research, all of which give them relevant hands-on experience in their fields. A real-world focus is reflected in the interdisciplinary nature of many academic initiatives. These include grant-funded projects such as Artbotics and Sound Thinking, which combine the arts and computer science, and interdisciplinary minors such as energy engineering; Asian studies; and technology, society, and human values. All programs are accredited at the highest levels.

UMass Lowell offers dozens of programs that allow students to stay as little as one extra year to earn both a bachelor's and a master's degree, giving them a competitive advantage as they enter the workplace. The undergraduate experience is enhanced by the diverse and international campus community and extensive opportunities for studying abroad. The University has developed more than 90 partnerships with prestigious institutions in 40 countries that reflect the diversity its own community and contemporary geopolitics. UMass Lowell offers a robust honors program for those students who want to achieve at the highest level as well as programs and resources designed to help students succeed. Academic and residential learning communities help first-year students make the transition to college by fostering connections among small groups with similar academic interests. The Centers for Learning offers a range of tutoring and other support programs and the Center for Career Services and Cooperative Education helps students transition to the working world. The University maintains a student-faculty ratio of 14:1.

The University community is ethnically, culturally, and economically diverse. Nearly half of all students, and 83 percent of incoming freshmen, choose to live in University housing, which ranges from traditional residence halls to apartment and suite style housing opening Fall 2013. Students are active in a wide variety of community service activities and in more than 200 campus organizations that range from academic and athletic to recreational and special interest groups. Examples include a marching band, a weekly student newspaper, an FM radio station and the Off-Broadway Players. A vibrant campus life includes rallying for the nationally ranked River Hawks men's ice hockey team, which competes in Hockey East. As of Fall 2013, all 17 varsity teams for men and women will compete in Division I.

LOCATION AND ENVIRONMENT

The University is located in Lowell, a city of 110,000 that has gained national attention by successfully leveraging its history, ethnic diversity, and entrepreneurial spirit to create a vital urban center. The site of a unique, urban National Historical Park that honors the city as the birthplace of the industrial revolution, Lowell is also home to an acclaimed professional theater company, literary and folk festivals, and museums that include the Museum of American Textile History and the Whistler House Museum.

OFF-CAMPUS OPPORTUNITIES

Located 25 miles from the cultural and educational riches of Boston and Cambridge, Lowell is situated within the region's major business corridors, which provide internship and co-op opportunities for students. It is also within an hour of ocean beaches and the lakes and mountains of New Hampshire via major highways and regional train and bus service.

MAJORS AND DEGREES OFFERED

Dual majors are permitted. Dual B.A./B.S. and an array of bachelor's-to-master's degree programs are available in all fields. Pre-dental and pre-medical programs are also available.

The College of Fine Arts, Humanities and Social Sciences offers baccalaureate programs in American studies, art, criminal justice, design, economics, English, environmental studies, history, liberal arts, modern languages, music business, music performance, music studies, peace and conflict studies, philosophy, political science, psychology, sociology, and sound recording technology.

The College of Sciences offers baccalaureate programs in biological sciences; chemistry with an option in forensics science; computer science; environmental, earth, and atmospheric sciences (meteorology); mathematics; and physics.

The James B. Francis College of Engineering offers baccalaureate day programs in chemical, civil and environmental, electrical and computer, mechanical, and plastics engineering. Engineering programs are accredited by the Accreditation Board for Engineering and Technology, Inc. (ABET).

The School of Health and Environment offers baccalaureate day programs in clinical sciences, which is accredited by the National Accrediting Agency for Clinical Laboratory Sciences (NAACLS); community health education; environmental health; exercise physiology; medical technology; nursing, which is accredited by the National League for Nursing Accrediting Commission (NLNAC); and nutritional science.

The Manning School of Business offers baccalaureate day programs, all of which are accredited by AACSB International—The Association to Advance Collegiate Schools of Business—in business administration (B.S.B.A.), with concentrations in accounting, entrepreneurship, finance, international business, management, management information systems, marketing, and supply chain and operations management.

The University's Graduate School of Education offers widely respected master's and doctoral programs, as well as a range of initial certification courses. The school is a partner with the national UTeach program for science, technology, engineering and math majors.

The University's Division of Continuing Studies and Corporate Education offers a wide range of evening programs through all six colleges, delivered on line and on campus.

ACADEMIC PROGRAMS

UMass Lowell's academic programs are infused with opportunities for learning through experience in research labs, industry and campus-based co-ops, internships and service to local communities.

The University operates on a calendar of two semesters, a three-week intersession in January, and a summer term with two sessions. Full-time undergraduates generally take five courses each semester. A minimum of 120 credits is required for baccalaureate degrees; the minimum credits required for professional degree programs are generally higher. A University general education requirement is imposed for all baccalaureate programs. Majors require 30–60 credits. Elective course options vary widely according to the degree program and major area. Professional degree program options and requirements follow specific accreditation guidelines. Maximum curricular freedom is permitted in B.A. programs. The academic climate is both serious and supportive, and requires self-motivation.

The First Year program provides learning communities, a freshman leadership program and an ongoing schedule of educational and recreational activities.

Students who thrive on challenge and like to achieve at a high level can add the distinction of Commonwealth Honors Program Scholar to their résumés. Offerings include a special first-year seminar, honors courses, honors thesis or project, research opportunities and a host of activities and events. Students in Honors housing enjoy special programming and get to know affiliated faculty members outside the classroom setting.

The Centers for Learning and Academic Support Services offers individual and group tutoring in more than 70 subject areas and help with course selection, writing and study skills.

The staff and resources at the Career Services & Cooperative Education Center help students identify career paths, locate internships and co-ops, develop resumes, practice interviewing and prepare for careers after graduation.

The University is committed to helping students develop a global perspective in the belief that it is an important life skill. Students have access to study, work and service opportunities in every corner of the globe. In many cases, students can use financial aid to cover some of the costs associated with studying abroad. UMass Lowell enables students to spend time studying in almost any country in the world during a semester, year, or summer or winter session. Offerings include faculty-led courses, exchanges and third-party affiliate programs. Our more than 90 formal partnerships with universities in 40 countries around the world reflect both the diversity of our own community and contemporary geo-politics.

CAMPUS FACILITIES AND EQUIPMENT

The campus is in the midst of a bold expansion. The Emerging Technologies and Innovation Center, a state-of-the-art facility focused on applications of nanotechnology in manufacturing, defense and medicine, opened this fall and will be followed by a Health and Social Sciences building, two new suite-style residence halls, a student center and business school building. Recent renovations to both libraries have created new learning commons equipped with learning technologies and areas for quiet and group study. Other state-of-the-art academic facilities include six sound recording technology studios, a nursing simulation lab, and a manufacturing lab where engineering and management students team up to produce microelectronic components. The newly renovated Tsongas Center is home to River Hawks hockey and is also a venue that attracts national acts. The Campus Recreation Center provides additional spaces for recreation and fitness instruction.

TUITION, ROOM, BOARD, AND FEES

Total Tuition and fees 2012-13

In-State Residents: $11,847

Out-of-State Residents: $24,896

New England Regional Program: $18,510

Total Room and Board $10,282

The University offers a wide range of merit-based scholarships in addition to financial aid.

FINANCIAL AID

The University is committed to making higher education accessible to all qualified students and participates in federal and state programs, assisting students through grants-in-aid, loans, employment opportunities and scholarships. The amount of a student's financial aid award is determined by need, as indicated by the Free Application for Federal Student Aid (FAFSA), which should be filed by March 1. In fiscal 2012, the campus awarded $120 million in financial aid.

STUDENT ORGANIZATIONS AND ACTIVITIES

The University's diverse and inclusive community is a supportive environment for students. Departments dedicated to residence life, health services, multicultural affairs, and student activities and leadership support a wide range of programs that help students adjust to and make the most of being in college. More than 200 student organizations, recreational sports and intercollegiate athletics teams give students the opportunity to make friends, have fun and develop leadership skills. These include the student-managed weekly newspaper, "The Connector," annual literary magazine, "The Offering," and radio station, WUML 91.5FM. Leadership opportunities are provided in residence halls and student organizations. Students also participate in the disciplinary system and in most University committees.

Seventy-five percent of freshmen and a growing number of upperclassmen choose to live in University housing. Options include traditional residence halls, apartments, suites and a former downtown hotel. In addition to health, dining and security services, the university provides advocacy and resources for people with disabilities.

ADMISSIONS PROCESS

All undergraduate day applicants must have a high school diploma or a general equivalency diploma and satisfactory SAT scores. The incoming freshman class for fall 2012 had an average GPA of 3.29 and the average SAT score (combined reading and math) was 1125. Students whose high school average is below the required minimum may be considered for admission if they present SAT verbal and mathematics scores that are higher than those specified for the admission of degree candidates by the college or program to which they wish to apply.

Transfer students are considered for fall- or spring-semester admissions. Transcripts of completed work must be on file prior to acceptance. Depending on the number of transfer credits and college GPA, transfer students who seek admission as matriculating day students may be asked to provide a high school record and SAT scores.

For day programs, the University admits students through early action, regular admission and transfer admission. Entering freshmen are admitted for the fall or spring semester. The early action deadline for freshman applications is November 15; the deadline for regular admission is February 15. Applicants to the nursing program are encouraged to apply by the early action deadline. The preferred deadline for transfer applications is August 15 for the fall semester and January 7 for the spring semester.

For further information, contact:

Office of Undergraduate Admissions

University of Massachusetts Lowell

883 Broadway Street, Suite 110

Lowell, Massachusetts 01854-5104

United States

Phone: 978-934-3931

admissions@uml.edu

UNIVERSITY OF NEW ENGLAND

AT A GLANCE

The University of New England (UNE) is an independent, coeducational university committed to academic excellence and the enhancement of the quality of life for the people, organizations and communities it serves. UNE is an innovative health sciences university grounded in the liberal arts. The University fosters critical inquiry through a student-centered, academic environment rich in research, scholarship, creative activity, and service while providing opportunities for acquiring and applying knowledge in selected clinical, professional, and community settings.

UNE's 5,587 students are enrolled in a wide variety of academic programs at the undergraduate, graduate, and professional levels in six colleges: the College of Arts and Sciences, the Westbrook College of Health Professions, the College of Pharmacy, the College of Osteopathic Medicine (housing Maine's only medical school), the College of Graduate Studies and the College of Dental Medicine. At the under-graduate level, UNE has approximately 2,790 students enrolled from 35 different states and several foreign countries in more than 40 undergraduate degree programs.

UNE traces its history to 1831 with the founding of Westbrook College, one of Maine's oldest institutions of learning. Today's University represents the joining of three unique higher education institutions through the combining of St. Francis College and the New England College of Osteopathic Medicine in 1978, and Westbrook College in 1996.

LOCATION AND ENVIRONMENT

The University of New England has two campuses located in picturesque southern coastal beach communities in Maine. The 540-acre Biddeford Campus in Bid-deford, home to the College of Arts and Sciences and the College of Osteopathic Medicine, is situated on a beautiful coastal site where the Saco River flows into the Atlantic Ocean and includes more than 4,000 feet of water frontage. Located 20 miles to the north is the Portland Campus, home to the Westbrook College of Health Professions, the College of Pharmacy, the College of Graduate Studies and the College of Dental Medicine. The campus sits on 41 acres in a quiet residential setting in Portland. Students at both campuses enjoy the vibrant social life offered in nearby metropolitan Boston (located 90 miles to the south of Biddeford) as well as Portland and the dynamic outdoor recreational activities that have made Maine a prime tourist destination. Southern Maine is conveniently serviced by a number of airlines at the Portland International Jetport and by bus and train service with stations in Biddeford/Saco and Portland, making both campuses accessible to all areas of the northeastern United States and beyond.

UNE will be opening a third campus in Tangier, Morocco, in 2014. At no additional cost, UNE students may choose to spend a semester or a year at UNE's Tangier campus learning about the culture and languages while taking their college courses in English.

OFF-CAMPUS OPPORTUNITIES

UNE is committed to supplementing the traditional learning process with practical applications. All students are encouraged to participate in cooperative education programs, field placements, and practicums. These experiences provide valuable learning situations and increase a student's exposure to job-related opportunities, and they are required for graduation by most majors. Students also have the op-portunity to arrange a study-abroad experience. For the same cost as a semester on campus in Maine, students can enroll in the UNE semester in Seville, Spain; take courses in Spanish and intercultural communication; and choose from a variety of courses in the sciences, humanities, social sciences, business, and the arts taught in English by the host university. Faculty-led short-term travel courses are another way to study abroad. Students and faculty meet throughout the term to prepare for travel academically and practically through readings, lectures, and coursework

MAJORS AND DEGREES OFFERED

UNE offers highly competitive undergraduate and graduate programs in a variety of areas. The University confers the Bachelor of Arts, Bachelor of Science, Master of Science in Occupational Therapy, Master of Public Health, Master of Science, Master of Science in Education, Master of Science in Nurse Anesthesia, Master of Social Work, Doctor of Dental Medicine, Doctor of Education, Doctor of Os-teopathic Medicine, Doctor of Pharmacy, and Doctor of Physical Therapy degrees along with several post-graduate and graduate certificate programs.

Bachelor degrees are offered in: animal behavior, applied exercise science, aquaculture and aquarium science, art education, athletic training, biochemistry, biological sciences, business administration, chemistry, communications, dental hygiene, elementary education, English, environmental science, environmental studies, health wellness and occupational studies, history, laboratory science, liberal studies (including pre-law), marine sciences, mathematics, medical biology (health and medical sciences tracks for pre-dental, pre-medicine, pre-optometry, pre-physical therapy and pre-veterinary studies), neuroscience, nursing, political science, psychology, psychology and social relations, secondary education, sociology, and sport management.

Various minors, a pre-physical therapy designation, an accelerated pre-physician assistant program, pre-pharmacy, and secondary education certification (Teacher Certification Program) is also available at the undergraduate level.

Masters degree programs are offered in biological sciences, education, marine sci-ences, medical education leadership, nurse anesthesia, occupational therapy, physi-cian assistant, public health, and social work. Doctor degree programs are offered in dental medicine, education, osteopathic medicine, pharmacy, and physical therapy. Graduate certificate programs are offered in medical leadership and public health.

ACADEMIC PROGRAMS

UNE's academic programs ensure that students have plenty of opportunities for extensive fieldwork, clinical experiences, research, internships and global experi-ences at both the undergraduate and graduate levels. All undergraduate programs at UNE have a core curriculum as a common thread. Designed to provide a foun-dation in the liberal arts, the core reflects the values of the college and is designed to prepare students for living informed, thoughtful, and active lives in a complex and changing society.

UNE offers highly competitive undergraduate and graduate programs in a variety of areas. Through its Graduate Pathways to Success (GPS) program, qualified un-dergraduate students can declare their intent to pursue a graduate or professional degree and then move directly into that graduate program as long as the program-matic and progression requirements are met.

UNE's Student Academic Success Center provides a wide-range of services to assist students with health, academic support, educational and career planning, and equal opportunities during their academic experience. The Office of Career Services provides academic and career exploration assistance, assistance in apply-ing to graduate schools, self-assessment and personal interest exploration, resume help, job listings, and job fairs.

CAMPUS FACILITIES AND EQUIPMENT

Both the Biddeford and Portland Campuses feature buildings with a variety of uses to support the needs of the university community. On the Biddeford Campus, classroom and office spaces are housed in several facilities across campus, including the Jack S. Ketchum Library. The Department of Creative and Fine Arts offers a dedicated building that provides faculty offices and studio space for drawing, painting, printmaking, sculpting and photography. Several research facilities are on campus, including the Marine Science Education and Research Center, which includes the Marine Animal Rehabilitation Center; the Harold Alfond Center for Health Sciences, with biology and chemistry labs as well as lecture halls, classrooms, a gross anatomy lab, and UNE's medical school facilities; the Pickus Center for Biomedical Research, and the Peter and Cécile Morgane Hall, a science center providing additional classrooms and an undergraduate teaching laboratory.

On the University's Portland Campus, Ludcke Auditorium is used for a variety of academic programs. Coleman Dental Hygiene Building houses classroom, clinic and faculty space. The Blewett Science Center, home to UNE's nursing program, consists of science labs and classrooms, and the Clinical Simulation Program (CSP), which provides customized training and education for students and health professionals. Proctor Hall is also a classroom building and is home to the Proctor Learning and Career Center. The Josephine S. Abplanalp Library houses study space and computer labs, as well as the Maine Women Writers Collection. The College of Pharmacy is an LEED-certified academic and research facility with teaching and research laboratories and a lecture hall. The College of Dental Medicine has its administration offices in historical Goddard Hall, and the new Patient Care Center will be its clinical and academic home.

Both campuses also provide a variety of facilities in support of community life. The 55,000 square-foot Campus Center on the Biddeford Campus houses both a sports complex and student union. The student union provides multipurpose rooms, snack bar, the University bookstore, and offices. The sports complex includes a gymnasium with indoor track, collegiate swimming pool, fully equipped fitness center, racquetball courts and athletic training room. The Harold Alfond Forum, a 106,000 square-foot facility on the Biddeford Campus, features an ice hockey rink, a basketball court, classroom and lab space, a fitness center, and multipurpose rooms and administrative offices. UNE's Big Blue Turf Field (one of only a handful at colleges in the US) is home to UNE's field hockey and lacrosse teams. The Finley Recreation Center on the Portland Campus provides a variety of fitness, health, wellness, and recreational programs and includes a gymnasium, fitness center, and multi-purpose room.

TUITION, ROOM, BOARD AND FEES

For 2012-2013, full-time (12 to 18 credits) undergraduate comprehensive annual costs are $44,370. This includes:

Full-time tuition $30,750

Room and Board $12,500 (traditional double occupancy)

General Services Fee $1,120

FINANCIAL AID

In 2011-2012, approximately 98% percent of full-time undergraduate students received some form of financial assistance. The average package was $26,000, including scholarships, grants, loans and employment. The University of New England has an extensive academic scholarship program. Merit awards range from $3,000 to $18,000 per year. The Financial Aid Office uses the Free Application for Federal Student Aid (FAFSA) as its primary application for institutional, federal, and state aid programs.

STUDENT ORGANIZATIONS AND ACTIVITIES

Both campuses offer a variety of cultural and social events. The Student Senate plays a vital role in the student life at both campuses and supports various events and programs through funding derived from the General Services Fee.

The university encourages students to become involved in activities, clubs, and sports. Popular interests include scuba diving, skiing, hiking, biking, swimming, surfing, music, theater, photography, community service, and student leadership development programs.

UNE's Department of Athletics operates an NCAA Division III varsity athletics program. Varsity sports for men are basketball, cross-country, golf, ice hockey, lacrosse, soccer. Varsity sports for women are basketball, cross-country, field hockey, golf, ice hockey, lacrosse, soccer, softball, swimming and volleyball. Intramural teams in basketball, floor hockey, softball, skiing, and volleyball are popular.

ADMISSIONS PROCESS

Students applying for admission should submit a completed application, a $40 nonrefundable application fee, transcripts of all academic work (high school and college), and scores on either the ACT or SAT. Students who do not use English as their primary language must submit TOEFL scores. Students applying for admission should have completed a curriculum that includes English, mathematics, science, and social sciences. International students must also complete an International Student Supplemental Application.

The undergraduate freshman admission application deadline is February 15; applications received after that date are reviewed on a space-available basis. There is a nonbinding December 1 early action application deadline with a December 31 notification date. Applications for the spring term are accepted through December 1.

All prospective students are strongly encouraged to visit the campuses of the University of New England for an information session and tour. Tours are held daily Monday through Friday, and Saturday tours are also available. Prospective students can register for a tour at www.une.edu/admissions/undergrad/visits.

UNIVERSITY OF NEW HAVEN

AT A GLANCE

Founded in 1920, the University of New Haven is a private, co-educational institution that offers a wide range of majors in a small, intimate college environment. UNH attracts students who are interested in a Liberal Arts education with an emphasis on career preparation through internships, co-operative education, research, community service, and more! With over 100 different programs of study for 4,300 full-time students, UNH offers a personalized experience that focuses on "experiential learning" reflecting the belief that students learn best if they are actively engaged in real-world applications of what they learn.

LOCATION

The University of New Haven is located in suburban West Haven, Connecticut. UNH is conveniently situated 75 miles from New York City and 135 miles from Boston. Only minutes away from the beautiful beaches along Long Island Sound, the university offers a shuttle to downtown New Haven and other local areas.

FACULTY

UNH has over 225 full-time professors, 90% of whom hold a Ph.D. or other terminal degree. All classes are taught by professors, not graduate students or teaching assistants. Student-to-faculty ratio: 16:1. Average class size: 22. Primary focus is on our students and emphasis is on a solid liberal arts education with experiential education, pre-professional advising, and career preparation as key components. UNH is a proud partner of the National Society of Experiential Education (N.S.E.E.) and has over 50 faculty members certified through N.S.E.E.'s Experiential Education Academy.

FACILITIES

Some of the finest anywhere in the United States. Over $100 million has been invested in facilities and academic programs in just the past five years. Some of these include the 58,000 square-foot David A. Beckerman Recreation Center, the $48 million Soundview Residence Hall for upperclassmen, the Henry C. Lee Institute of Forensic Science, National Crime Scene Training & Technology Center, Levy Family Fire Investigation Laboratory, Laurel Vlock Center for Convergent Media, Samuel Bergami Learning Center for Finance & Technology, TV and Film Production Studio, Digital and Analog Recording Studios, MIDI and Sound Synthesis Lab, Music Practice Rooms, 300-seat addition to our main dining hall, Ralph A. DellaCamera Stadium featuring our Blue & Gold turf field, Solar Testing & Training Laboratory, Hazel Nut Café (student-run coffee shop), and the planned opening of the Robert M. and Linda W. Lee Center for Marine Sciences right on the water in the greater New Haven area.

MAJORS AND DEGREES OFFERED

The University of New Haven mixes traditional degrees along with some unique programs throughout our four academic colleges.

College of Arts and Sciences

The College of Arts and Sciences offers traditional majors like Art, Biology, Biotechnology, Chemistry, Education (BA/MS), English, History, Liberal Studies, Mathematics, Psychology, and Political Science as well as unique majors in the areas of Communication, Mass Communication, Dental Hygiene, Environmental Science, Global Studies, Graphic Design, Digital Art and Design, Interior Design, Interior Design – Pre-Architecture, Marine Biology, Music, Music Industry, Music & Sound Recording, Nutrition & Dietetics, and Theatre Arts. UNH also offers minors in languages such as Arabic, Chinese, Russian and Spanish.

College of Business

The College of Business offers degrees in Business Management, Accounting, Economics, Finance, Management of Sports Industries, Marketing, and Hospitality and Tourism Management with concentrations in Hotel & Resort Management, Foodservice Management, Event & Tourism Management and Spa Management.

Tagliatela College of Engineering

The Tagliatela College of Engineering offers degrees in Chemistry, Sustainability Studies, General Engineering, Chemical Engineering, Civil Engineering, Computer Engineering, Electrical Engineering, Mechanical Engineering, System Engineering, Computer Science, and Information Technology with concentrations in Web & Database Development, and Network & Security Administration.

Henry C. Lee College of Criminal Justice and Forensic Sciences

The Henry C. Lee College of Criminal Justice and Forensic Sciences offers degrees in Criminal Justice, Forensic Science, Fire Science, Legal Studies and National Security Studies. UNH offers eight separate Criminal Justice concentrations in Investigative Services, Crime Analysis, Law Enforcement Administration, International Justice and Security, Forensic Psychology, Juvenile and Family Justice, Victim Services and Corrections. The Henry C. Lee College of Criminal Justice and Forensic Sciences also contains four distinct degrees in the area of Fire Science: Arson Investigation, Fire Science Administration, Fire Science Technology and Fire Protection Engineering. Legal Studies programs are offered in Paralegal Studies, Public Affairs, and Dispute Resolution.

Accreditations and Recognitions

Many of our academic programs have earned further distinction through high-level private accrediting bodies in the respective fields:

A.B.A. (American Bar Association) approves our undergraduate degree in Legal Studies, one of only a few such programs at the undergraduate level in the entire country.

A.B.E.T. (Accreditation Board of Engineering and Technology) accredits six of our undergraduate academic degree programs in the Tagliatela College of Engineering: Civil Engineering, Chemical Engineering, Computer Engineering, Computer Science, Electrical Engineering, and Mechanical Engineering.

A.C.S. (American Chemical Society) certifies our bachelor's degree in Chemistry. We also offer certified options in Environmental Chemistry, Materials Chemistry, and preparation for high school Chemistry teachers.

A.D.A. (American Dietetic Association) the Commission on Accreditation for Dietetics Education (C.A.D.E.) of the American Dietetic Association (A.D.A.) accredits our very popular undergraduate degree in Nutrition and Dietetics, leading many of our students to become Registered Dietitians (R.D.).

F.E.P.A.C. (Forensic Science Accreditation Commission) accredits our nationally renowned Forensic Science program. Only a select number of programs have earned this level of distinction through the American Academy of Forensic Science (A.A.F.S.).

Marvin K. Peterson Library

The Marvin K. Peterson Library offers over 240,000 volumes, 1,400 print journal and newspaper subscriptions, electronic access to over 19,000 full-text journal and newspaper titles, approximately 550,000 pieces of microfiche, 12,000 volumes of microfilm, e-books, 33,000 e-journals and 162,000 paper U.S. Government documents. Students have access to numerous Internet stations and ports throughout the library and a coffee shop and lounge area for students to study and take a break.

STUDY ABROAD

The University of New Haven opened its satellite campus in Tuscany, Italy in the fall of 2012. The course offerings at the Tuscany campus change from semester to semester. Students can take a total of 15 credits (5 courses) during the semester including one mandatory Italian language course. Each semester the university sends full-time faculty to teach UNH courses alongside Italian faculty. Students can study abroad at our Prato, Italy campus as early as first-semester Freshman year. UNH is also a leading provider of study abroad education, offering students over 300 options worldwide. We also offer an intensive study abroad program which offers 2-week abroad sessions with a UNH faculty member during intersession for six credits at a number of locations such as London, Dubai, Rome and more.

ATHLETICS

As a member of the Northeast 10 Conference, UNH competes in 16 Division II varsity sports (7 men's and 9 women's) baseball, basketball, cross-country, football, lacrosse, soccer, softball, tennis, track, and volleyball. Opened in December 2007, the new 58,000-square-foot David A. Beckerman Recreation Center adds another dimension to athletic opportunities at UNH. It features a fitness center with aerobic equipment, weights, and televisions; multi-purpose rooms for yoga, aerobics, Pilates, spinning, and other wellness activities; two basketball/volleyball courts; a multi-sport court for rollerblading, floor hockey, indoor soccer, and other activities; an elevated indoor running track; and lounge areas including a juice bar/café. Recent highlights include our football team finishing the 2012 season with a 10-1 overall record and third straight NE-10 conference title, Women's Volleyball earning a trip to the NCAA Division II Elite Eight with a 30-2 record, and Men's Basketball finishing the 2012-13 season with a 20-9 record and advancing to the second round of the NCAA Division II tournament.

RESIDENTIAL LIFE

UNH has 11 on-campus and 6 off-campus housing options which offers a variety for students to choose from ranging from a traditional residence hall to apartment-style housing with suites of two or more bedrooms. In 2005, UNH started a Living Learning Community (LLC) program where students combine their residence hall and academic experience by interacting with faculty members outside of the classroom and living with students in the same academic area of interest as theirs. Participants also enjoy special trips and opportunities geared towards their major of interest. Currently, UNH offers LLC's in Business, Criminal Justice, Community of the Arts, Engineering, Fire Science, Forensic Science, Health Sciences, Health and Wellness, Marine Biology, Music/Music Industry/Music & Sound Recording, Pre-Law, Honors Program, and ROTC.

STUDENT ORGANIZATIONS AND ACTIVITIES

The Undergraduate Student Government Association (USGA) oversees all aspects of undergraduate life, organizing campus social and cultural activities, supporting the student-run radio station and student-produced publications, and overseeing the budget for all undergraduate organizations.

There are more than 160 campus clubs and organizations, including chapters of several professional societies, religious groups, social clubs, student councils, cultural clubs, and national fraternities and sororities.

TUITION, ROOM, BOARD AND FEES

Cost for the 2012-2013 Academic year is: Tuition & Fees – $33,740 and Room & Board – $14,110.

SCHOLARSHIPS AND FINANCIAL AID

Students are automatically considered for merit-based academic scholarships by simply applying for admission to UNH. Students must complete their admission application by May 1 for the fall semester or by January 2 for the spring semester in order to be eligible for merit-based awards. Merit-based scholarships range from $6,000 to $20,000 per academic year for students who qualify.

To file for need-based aid, the priority deadline for Financial Aid is March 1 for the fall semester and December 1 for the spring semester. Students must fill out the Free Application for Federal Student Aid (FAFSA), which is available online at www.fafsa.ed.gov in order to be considered for need-based aid at UNH. For students who wish to receive a financial aid package earlier than March, the CSS Profile, https://profileonline.collegeboard.com is available to fill out beginning October 1. Please note, that the CSS Profile is not required but recommended for students who would like to get a financial aid package earlier in the process.

ADMISSIONS PROCESS

UNH has an Early Action Admissions Policy; we begin to review applications on September 1st and continue until programs are filled. UNH offers two non-binding admission programs for fall admission. To be considered for certain programs applicants must follow the established timelines and important dates. Early Action Applications are due by December 1, Regular Decision Applications are due after December 1, and Spring Admission Applications are due no later than January 15.

Students may apply using the Common Application. To be considered for admission, candidates must complete the application form and submit it along with a nonrefundable $50 application fee. An application is considered complete once we receive the application, personal essay (250-500 words), transcript(s), standardized test scores (SAT I or ACT), and one letter of recommendation (from an academic source).

VISITING CAMPUS

We encourage all prospective students and their families to visit us and see what the University of New Haven has to offer. UNH offers a variety of campus visits for students and their families to choose from seven days a week! Visits to choose from include daily campus information sessions and tours, Open Houses, Summer Preview Days, Enhanced Visits, Accepted Student Days, Charger Days, Explore UNH Days and much more! To view our campus visit calendar and register for an event, visit our website at www.newhaven.edu/visitunh.

For further information about the University of New Haven and to schedule a campus visit or personal interview, students may contact:

Office of Undergraduate Admissions

Phone: 203-932-7319

Fax: 203-931-6093

Email: adminfo@newhaven.edu

Or visit our website: www.newhaven.edu

UNIVERSITY OF OREGON

AT A GLANCE

At the University of Oregon (UO), you'll be part of a community dedicated to making a difference in the world. Whether you want to change a community, a law, or one person's mind, the UO will provide you with the inspiration and resources you'll need to succeed.

With a student-teacher ratio of 20:1 and a median class size of 20 students, you'll connect easily with faculty members and your peers. You'll also have all the resources of a major research university, with 269 comprehensive academic programs and more than 250 student organizations.

Set in a 295-acre arboretum, the University of Oregon is aesthetically and environmentally green. Academic programs and student activities will bring you to the forests, mountains, and rivers of Oregon's wilderness areas. On campus, many of the UO's buildings get a green thumbs-up, including the cutting-edge Lewis Integrative Science Building, which is on track to earn a "platinum" certification from the U.S. Green Building Council's Leadership in Energy and Environmental Design (LEED) program. In addition to temperature-controlled windows and an innovative waste heat recovery system, red oak trees on the building site were carefully preserved. At the UO, you'll have access to nationally recognized programs in sustainable business, architecture, and technology. In addition, our Campus Recycling Program is a national award winner, and the university recently signed an agreement to eliminate our carbon footprint.

You'll learn to see the world differently, attending classes alongside students from all fifty states, two US territories and ninety-five countries. You'll learn from people with religious, cultural, and ethnic heritages different from your own. Your global degree options include 20 languages, as well as international, ethnic, religious, African, Asian, European, Latin American, Judaic, and Russian, Eurasian, and East European studies. The UO offers 170 study programs in 95 countries. You'll experience the history, arts, social institutions, customs, and beliefs of new cultures while earning credit toward your UO degree. The IE3 Global Internships Program offers you professional experience in internships worldwide.

LOCATION AND ENVIRONMENT

The UO is located in the center of Eugene (metropolitan area population 156,929), a classic college town that's small enough to bike across but large enough to offer diverse art, music, and social venues. The Hult Center for the Performing Arts and the Oregon Bach Festival lure a variety of nationally acclaimed musical acts each year. Rolling Stone included Eugene in its list of top ten college towns that rock.

Eugene loves the outdoors, offering more than 100 city parks, 250 miles of bicycle trails, rock climbing areas, and beautiful public gardens, all within the city limits. Getting here is easy. Eugene is served by several major airlines and is on the main north–south Amtrak artery connecting Seattle and San Diego.

With 18 NCAA Division 1 teams, as well as 45 club sports, you'll have your choice of sports to play or teams to cheer. The excitement begins in the fall, when you'll root for the Ducks' football team at Autzen Stadium. In the winter, the men's and women's basketball teams thrill the crowds at the Matthew Knight Arena. In the spring, UO track stars compete at the world-famous Hayward Field, often the site for NCAA championships and US Olympic Track and Field Trials.

Two campus museums are valuable resources in the sciences and visual arts. The Jordan Schnitzer Museum of Art offers exhibitions of classical and contemporary art. The Museum of Natural and Cultural History features Native American artifacts, archaeological finds, and historically and scientifically significant items. Students appear in music, dance, and theater performances in newly refurbished facilities, including proscenium and "black box" performance spaces. Films, lectures, and cultural events are an everyday part of campus life.

OFF-CAMPUS OPPORTUNITIES

The Career Center offers off-campus internships in fields related to your academic major or extracurricular interests. Both paid and volunteer internships are widely available to all majors.

Pine Mountain Observatory, near Bend, Oregon, offers study options in physics and astronomy. You can participate in an annual Archaeological Field School in central Oregon's Northern Great Basin. The Oregon Institute of Marine Biology on the Pacific coast gives you access to deep sea, coastal watershed, and estuary habitats. The UO Portland Center provides classes in architecture, digital arts, product design, journalism, and business in a vibrant urban center.

Cooperatively run by students, the Outdoor Program takes you beyond campus to Oregon's great outdoors. You can choose from activities like snowboarding, skiing, rock climbing, hiking, surfing, white water rafting, and kayaking.

MAJORS AND DEGREES OFFERED

Undergraduate academic majors, minors, certificates, and preparatory programs offered include:

School of Architecture and Allied Arts

Architecture; art; art history; ceramics; community arts; digital arts; fibers; historic preservation; interior architecture; landscape architecture; material and product studies; metalsmithing and jewelry; multimedia; nonprofit administration; painting; photography; planning, public policy, and management; printmaking; product design; and sculpture.

College of Arts and Sciences

African studies; anthropology; Asian studies; biochemistry; biology; chemistry; Chinese; cinema studies; classics; clinical laboratory science-medical technology;° comics and cartoon studies; comparative literature; computer and information science; computer information technology; creative writing; dentistry;° East Asian studies; economics; engineering;° English; environmental science; environmental studies; ethnic studies; European studies; folklore; forensic science;° French; general science; general social science; geography; geological sciences; German; German studies; Greek; health sciences;° history; humanities; human physiology; international studies; Italian; Japanese; Judaic studies; Latin; Latin American studies; law;° linguistics; marine biology; mathematics; mathematics and computer science; medicine;° medieval studies; nursing;° occupational therapy;° optometry;° peace studies; pharmacy;° philosophy; physical therapy;° physician assistant;° physics; podiatry;° political science; psychology; queer studies; religious studies; Romance languages; Russian and East European studies; Scandinavian; social work;° sociology; South Asian studies; Southeast Asian studies; Spanish; theater arts; veterinary medicine;° women's and gender studies; and writing, speaking, and critical reasoning.

Charles H. Lundquist College of Business

Accounting; business administration with concentrations in entrepreneurship; finance; information systems and operations; management; marketing; sports business; and global management.

College of Education

Communication disorders and sciences; educational foundations; family and human services; special education; and teacher education.°

School of Journalism and Communication

Communication studies; journalism; journalism: advertising; journalism: communication studies; and journalism: public relations.

School of Music and Dance

Dance; music; music composition; music education; music: jazz studies; and music performance.

An ° denotes preparatory programs.

ACADEMIC PROGRAMS

The UO is on a quarter system, and you'll spend about one third of your education on each of three areas of course work: the general education requirements, requirements for your major, and elective credit. Your general education requirements will include courses in the natural sciences, social sciences, and humanities as well as multicultural course work.

Freshman Interest Groups (FIGs) bring together a small group of 25 first-year students interested in the same academic area in three related interdisciplinary courses. Freshman Seminars are small-group discussion courses taught by some of the UO's most outstanding faculty members. These academically rigorous FIG programs provide a helpful transition to college-level course work.

The Robert D. Clark Honors College offers the academic rigor of an outstanding small liberal arts college with all the resources of a major research university. High-achieving students prepare for participation and leadership in society and come to understand the role of knowledge in their lives as global citizens. CHC classes are limited to 19 or fewer students and complement any UO major. The CHC application process is competitive, with 200 spots available each year and applications averaging more than 1,500.

Upon acceptance to the UO, qualified students will be invited to join the College Scholars Program. You'll have access to specialized courses, internship opportunities, and scholarships. Faculty members assist you in developing a plan to achieve department honors or professional distinctions upon graduation.

CAMPUS FACILITIES AND EQUIPMENT

The University of Oregon Libraries, an Association of Research Libraries member, houses the second largest research collection in the northwest, including over 3 million volumes and 90,000 journal subscriptions, both print and electronic.

Wireless internet access is available in all UO buildings, and computer labs are open in the library, residence halls, and academic facilities across campus.

Science facilities at the UO are among the best in the nation. Cutting-edge equipment is housed in the underground Lokey Laboratories, which were designed to minimize vibrations and stray electric fields. The new Lewis Integrative Science Building encourages interdisciplinary research and studies in areas such as nanotechnology, neuroscience, and solar energy.

TUITION, ROOM, BOARD, AND FEES

Resident

Undergraduate tuition and fees for the 2012–13 academic year: $9,258. On-campus residence halls, including room and board: $10,260 per academic year for double occupancy. Books and supplies: $1,050. Personal expenses: $2,430. Total: $22,998.

Nonresident

Undergraduate tuition and fees for the 2012–13 academic year: $28,653. On-campus residence halls, including room and board: $10,260 per academic year for double occupancy. Books and supplies: $1,050. Personal expenses: $2,430. Total: $42,393.

FINANCIAL AID

The UO makes a concerted effort to enable you to attend, regardless of your family's income. Financial aid in the form of grants, loans, and employment is available to qualifying students. The majority of our students receive scholarships and financial aid that are awarded through the federal government, university, and academic departments.

Eligibility information

To apply for financial aid, you must file the Free Application for Federal Student Aid (FAFSA) in early February. The UO's federal school code is 003223.

Incoming freshmen will be considered automatically for Summit, Apex, and General University Scholarships by completing the UO admission application by January 15. The Presidential Scholarship and Diversity Excellence Scholarship require separate applications due January 15. The Stamps scholarship also requires a separate application due November 1. For more information, visit financialaid.uoregon.edu.

Summit and Apex scholarships are awarded each year to academically successful entering freshmen and range from $3,000 to $8,000 per year.

General University Scholarship are awarded each year and range from $1,500 to $2,700 per year.

Presidential Scholarships are awarded each year to Oregon's brightest incoming freshmen in the amount of $9,000 per year, renewable for up to four years of study.

Diversity Excellence Scholarships are tuition-based with awards ranging from partial to full tuition and fee waivers.

Stamps Scholarships, awarded to Oregon residents graduating from an Oregon high school, grant students full tuition, room, and board.

Staton Scholarships in the amount of $5,750 are awarded each year to incoming Oregon students with extraordinary financial need and are renewable for up to four years.

STUDENT ORGANIZATIONS AND ACTIVITIES

The Associated Students of the University of Oregon offers more than 250 student organizations, including cultural organizations, fraternities and sororities, student government, campus ministries, political groups, performing arts groups, international student clubs, and honor societies. Learn more at asuo.uoregon.edu.

The UO Student Vote Coalition led the nation in registering student voters in each of the past three presidential elections. The UO also ranks 8th in the nation for current Peace Corps volunteers.

ADMISSIONS PROCESS

The early notification deadline for fall 2014 is November 1, 2013. The standard admission deadline for fall 2014 is January 15, 2014. To be eligible for freshman admission, you must submit your official high school transcripts, graduate from a standard or accredited high school, submit SAT or ACT scores, and complete an application essay.

We require the following college-preparatory courses: Four years of English in preparatory composition and literature; three years of mathematics including first-year algebra and two additional years of college-preparatory mathematics; three years of science in such areas as biology, chemistry or physics; and three years of social science that could include one year of US history, one year of global studies such as world history or geography, and one elective. Two years of the same second language in high school or two college terms of the same second language are also required.

Other factors considered for admission include the strength of high school GPA, high school course work, grade trend, essay, and senior-year course load. Academic potential and special talents are also considered.

To apply, submit a completed application for admission, transcripts, SAT or ACT scores, essay, and nonrefundable $50 application fee to the Office of Admissions.

For information and an application, contact:

Office of Admissions

1217 University of Oregon

Eugene, OR 97403-1217

USA

Phone: 541-346-3201

Toll-free: 800-BE-A-DUCK

Website: http://admissions.uoregon.edu

Virtual Tour: http://admissions.uoregon.edu/virtualtour

UNIVERSITY OF RICHMOND

AT A GLANCE

The University of Richmond is a private, highly selective, liberal arts university with approximately 3,000 undergraduate students. Founded in 1830, it is characterized by a personalized, interdisciplinary experience for each student.

The University of Richmond emphasizes collaborative learning and research in a cross-disciplinary curriculum that integrates five academic schools—the School of Arts and Sciences, the E. Claiborne Robins School of Business, the Jepson School of Leadership Studies, the University of Richmond School of Law, and the School of Professional and Continuing Studies. In addition to those in their major, students explore a variety of other classes, including many that are team-taught by faculty from different schools. This multidisciplinary lens is at the core of the Richmond experience.

Students benefit from the individual attention of more than 375 full-time faculty thanks to a 9:1 student-faculty ratio and an average class size of 16. No classes are taught by teaching assistants.

Richmond prizes diversity of experience and thought, and is committed to ensuring its opportunities are accessible to talented students of all backgrounds. Current undergraduates hail from 45 states, Washington, D.C., Puerto Rico, and 67 countries. Of 788 incoming first-year students in 2011, 57% come from public high schools, 16% are first-generation college students, 21% are American students of color, and 85% ranked in the top 20% of their high school class. Approximately two-thirds of undergraduates receive financial aid.

LOCATION AND ENVIRONMENT

Located on a 350-acre suburban campus featuring Collegiate Gothic architecture, the University of Richmond is six miles from downtown Richmond, Va., and 90 miles from Washington, D.C.

The city of Richmond is a hotbed of opportunities for hands-on experience, including city and state legislative, executive, and judicial offices, as well as the corporate headquarters of Altria, Dominion Resources, CarMax, Genworth Financial, and Capital One. The legal sector includes state courts and the U.S. Court of Appeals for the Fourth Circuit, and major law firms such as McGuireWoods, Williams Mullen, and Hunton & Williams.

Residents enjoy access to river rapids, mountain peaks, and ocean views. Richmond is the only city in the U.S. with Class IV rapids running through the city limits, begging residents to white-water raft, canoe, kayak, tube, and fish. To the west, the Blue Ridge Mountains and Shenandoah National Park beckon, offering winter sports, camping, hiking, caving, and rafting. Venture east to the Chesapeake Bay and Atlantic Ocean for water sports and beaches.

OFF-CAMPUS OPPORTUNITIES

The University of Richmond recognizes its role in the larger community and offers partnerships that enhance the student experience and engage local organizations. The Bonner Center for Civic Engagement organizes community-based partnership opportunities, internships, and service-learning courses.

UR Downtown, which opened in March 2009, houses community programs in the heart of the city. In its first year, 30 students participated in internships, work study, and clinical courses; 90 undergraduates took community-based courses; 25 clients received assistance from the Family Law Clinic; 25 law students graduated with a pro bono certificate recognizing at least 120 service hours; and nine public schools received $65,000 in grants from Partners in the Arts.

Students quickly learn the lingo of Richmond's neighborhoods and what they add to the University experience. Whether unwinding at a Northside park, tasting the cuisine at a Carytown café, catching a favorite band at The National downtown, checking out Shockoe Bottom nightlife, or exploring the history living in the Fan District, students make the city their own.

Richmond celebrates a thriving arts scene. The University's own Modlin Center for the Arts is a powerhouse venue for world-renowned performing artists. Dozens of art galleries and music venues both large and small mean there's never a dull week. Professional arts organizations and museums abound, including the Richmond Ballet, Richmond Symphony Orchestra, Richmond Jazz Society, Virginia Opera, Virginia Museum of Fine Arts, Science Museum of Virginia, Virginia Historical Society, and Virginia Holocaust Museum.

MAJORS AND DEGREES OFFERED

The University of Richmond offers more than 100 majors, minors, and concentrations including 60 undergraduate majors through its five schools of arts and sciences, business, law, leadership studies, and professional and continuing studies. An integrated learning approach asks students to explore courses in at least two schools outside of the one in which their major resides.

All undergraduates begin in the School of Arts and Sciences, the heart of Richmond's liberal arts curriculum. Courses span the arts, humanities, social sciences, and sciences, and 70% of undergraduates ultimately declare a major in the school.

In the E. Claiborne Robins School of Business—one of the top 15 business programs in the country—students specialize in accounting, business administration, economics, finance, international business, management, or marketing.

The Jepson School of Leadership Studies—the first undergraduate school of its kind in the nation—educates students for and about leadership, including the history and theory of leadership, ethics, and leader-follower relationships.

The Richmond School of Law is home to 500 full-time students pursuing a juris doctorate, or one of several dual-degree programs in business, health administration, social work, urban studies and planning, or public administration.

The School of Professional and Continuing Studies provides educational opportunities to the Greater Richmond community and plays a role in the undergraduate experience. The school runs Summer Study Abroad programs, summer school courses, and a variety of "Think Again" classes aimed at personal enrichment and professional development.

ACADEMIC PROGRAMS

As part of the University of Richmond's emphasis on a distinct experience, the general education curriculum is made up of four main components drawn from across the University. Students choose two First-Year Seminars taught by faculty from each of the five schools, which introduce academic inquiry and the modes of expression that are the heart of a liberal arts education. Students also complete courses in communication skills—including oral communication and foreign language—historical sciences, literary studies, social analysis, visual and performing arts, symbolic reasoning, and natural science. There also is a wellness requirement, which includes an alcohol awareness program and workshops in such topics as nutrition, sexual health, and fitness.

More than half of Richmond students study abroad in one of more than 75 programs in 30 countries.

CAMPUS FACILITIES AND EQUIPMENT

Visitors to the University of Richmond instantly get a traditional campus feel, thanks to the Collegiate Gothic buildings. However, the old-style architecture quickly gives way to modern amenities and forward-thinking construction.

The new Carole Weinstein International Center was planned and constructed to Leadership in Energy and Environmental Design (LEED) standards, an international certification for green building.

The Weinstein Center for Recreation and Wellness offers first-rate facilities and is one of only five U.S. facilities to receive the 2008 National Intramural Recreational Sports Association Outstanding Sports Facility award.

Also award winning is the Heilman Dining Center. Daily fare begins with a full breakfast of made-to-order omelets, Belgian waffles, pastries, and more. Lunch and dinner choices include a Mongolian Grill, pasta station, brick-oven pizza, a Latin American station, homemade soup and salad bar, vegetarian and vegan options, desserts, and a deli.

The Modlin Center for the Arts is considered a work of art, and houses state-of-the-art performance venues, galleries, and studios. Visitors come to attend world-class performing arts events as part of the Modlin Great Performances Series. The theatre and dance department and the University Players present three mainstage productions, and the music department's annual series features 30 free concerts.

No university is complete without a solid library system, and Richmond is no exception. The Boatwright Memorial Library, Parsons Music Library, and William Taylor Muse Law Library house more than 1 million books, journals, and periodicals, and extensive online resources.

Finally, Tyler Haynes Commons, spanning Westhampton Lake, is the center of student life, with meeting rooms for organizations and space for entertainment and dining.

Tuition, Room, Board, and Fees

The estimated undergraduate cost of attendance at the University of Richmond is based on expenses for full-time students living on or off campus for the academic year. In 2010-11, the rates for tuition, room, and board were:

Tuition	$43,170
Room	$4,170
Board	$5,080
Total	$52,420

Additional expenses, such as books, personal expenses and loan fees, bring the estimated cost to $54,520.

Tuition and fees vary for students in the law school and graduate business programs.

FINANCIAL AID

The University of Richmond is committed to being accessible and affordable to students who can most benefit from, and contribute to, the educational environment. The application process is need-blind, meaning a family's finances are never reviewed when making admission decisions. The University meets 100% of demonstrated need. Nearly two-thirds of students receive financial aid, with an average award of $38,700 for students entering in 2011. Virginians with a family income below $40,000 receive full scholarships.

The University also offers merit-based scholarships. Full-tuition scholarships are awarded to Richmond Scholars in recognition of exemplary talents in scholarship and leadership, science and math, visual and performing arts, or academic achievement. Presidential and Trustee scholarships are available for up to $15,000, and National Merit Scholarships, National Achievement Finalists, and National Hispanic Scholarships award $750 to $2,000.

Military personnel may qualify for full-tuition Army ROTC scholarships, and scholarships through the Yellow Ribbon Program in conjunction with the Post 9/11 G.I. Bill.

Financial aid also is available for graduate students in the schools of business, law, and professional and continuing studies.

STUDENT ORGANIZATIONS AND ACTIVITIES

Students at the University of Richmond find a number of paths to building their own life on campus. Nearly 250 student organizations—including 39 sport clubs, 28 honorary societies, 17 religious groups, a student newspaper, and a radio station—mean there's something for every interest. Students also can choose from eight fraternities and seven sororities, but with just over a third of undergraduates affiliated, Greek life doesn't dominate campus life.

Sports provide an outlet for both athletes and spectators. The University's 18 NCAA Division I teams range from basketball and lacrosse, to field hockey, golf, and soccer. In 2008, the football team celebrated a national championship. In 2010, men's basketball won the Atlantic 10 conference and made a run to the NCAA "Sweet Sixteen." Approximately 600 students participate in sport clubs, such as gymnastics, ice hockey, martial arts, Ultimate Frisbee, rugby, and water polo. Many also join intramural teams for three-on-three hoops, swimming, softball, and racquetball.

ADMISSIONS PROCESS

Applications for the standard admission process are due Jan. 15, or Dec. 1 for Richmond Scholars consideration. Acceptance notification is sent April 1.

Fall early decision applications are due Nov. 15, and notification is sent on Dec. 15. The winter early decision deadline is Dec. 1 for Richmond Scholars consideration and Jan. 15 for standard applications. Acceptance and financial aid notification is sent on Feb. 15.

International student applications are due Dec. 1 for Richmond Scholars or Jan. 15 for standard admission, and the CSS profile is due to the College Board for financial aid consideration by Feb. 15. Acceptance notification is sent April 1.

Students applying for spring transfer submit an application by Nov. 1, and notification is sent Dec. 7. Fall transfer students apply by Feb. 15 and notification is sent April 15. A limited number of spaces may be available for applications sent between Feb. 15 and April 15, and notification is sent June 15.

Financial aid consideration for most applicants is due by Feb. 15.

Applicants must complete a minimum of 16 units of secondary school coursework in English, math, history, laboratory science, and foreign language. Competitive candidates typically exceed the minimum requirements.

The University received 9,431 applications for the 2015 class, admitted 3,085, and 788 enrolled. Of those, 36% were Early Decision applicants, 55% were regular decision, and 9% were wait listed.

UNIVERSITY OF SAINT JOSEPH

AT A GLANCE

The University of Saint Joseph combines excellence in liberal arts with career-focused, professional undergraduate education for women, co-educational Programs for Adult Learners, and the co-educational graduate program.

The University of Saint Joseph (USJ) is a comprehensive institution with career-focused undergraduate, graduate, and certificate programs. Enhanced by the intellectual tradition and the values of its founding Sisters of Mercy, the university allows students to thrive in a culture of achievement and collaboration.

As a private, liberal arts college, the university is nationally recognized for the quality of its academic programs. USJ consists of five schools and more than 25 undergraduate and graduate programs, along with pre-professional and certificate programs. USJ serves a diverse, intergenerational student body that is enrolled in the undergraduate programs for women; the Program for Adult Learners, which serves women and men who are completing their bachelor's degrees; and the co-educational graduate programs and professional studies program.

Founded in 1932, USJ offers the student population opportunities to excel - intellectually, socially and ethically. Students can choose from among rigorous academic programs accompanied by local and global internship opportunities that are focused on helping them fulfill their potential.

The core values of compassionate service, Catholic identity and commitment to women through academic excellence are evident in the curriculum and daily life on campus. Students from a multitude of faith traditions and backgrounds are empowered for success. Drawing on its Mercy heritage, the university is a community of 1,000 undergraduate and 1,300 graduate students that promotes the growth of the whole person. This is accomplished in a caring environment that encourages strong ethical values, personal integrity and a sense of responsibility to the needs of society.

LOCATION AND ENVIRONMENT

The university is located on 84 acres in suburban West Hartford, four miles from the state capitol and the city of Hartford's arts and entertainment district. West Hartford Center, just minutes from campus, offers an array of coffee bars, boutiques, restaurants and a beautiful movie theater at Blue Back Square.

The campus consists of seven residence halls, two of which feature apartment-style living. Approximately 75 percent of the first-year students in the undergraduate program live on campus and have access to special services including a free weekend shuttle to off campus shops and restaurants. Amenities in each residence hall include study lounge space, internet access, cable television and free laundry facilities.

Also located on campus is the Gengras Center, a state-approved private special education facility that provides a highly structured, intensive, self-contained special education program for elementary, middle and high school students. Located one block from campus is the renowned School for Young Children, one of the oldest early childhood centers in the state. The Gengras Center and The School for Young Children serve as lab schools for special education and early childhood education teacher training.

OFF-CAMPUS OPPORTUNITIES

University of Saint Joseph students are actively engaged in their local and global communities. Students have the opportunity to participate in cross-registration programs at four different colleges in the local area through the Hartford Consortium for Higher Education. No additional tuition is charged for courses taken through the consortium; credits are transferable and free transportation is provided.

Service initiatives are in abundance on campus and provide students with the opportunity to impact their community. Students may gain practical work experience in fields like nursing, social work and nutrition through volunteer opportunities at the Hartford Wellness Center and other local health care facilities. The university has also established a partnership with the Franciscan Center for Urban Ministry to reach out to its neighboring city and enhance the quality of life of its residents in need.

University of Saint Joseph students are making a global impact through programs such as study abroad. Students can work with the Director of International Studies on campus in planning for an international study experience anywhere in the world. The university offers a specialized program in Guyana, South America through the college's sister hospital. Students also have the chance to travel domestically and work on a number of community service projects through alternative breaks.

MAJORS AND DEGREES OFFERED

The academic programs at the University of Saint Joseph emphasize quality instruction, challenging course work, and close connections between students and faculty in the spirit of collaboration and mentorship. The university offers more than 21 academic majors and six pre-professional programs, plus accelerated bachelor's-to-master's degrees.

The University of Saint Joseph enjoys a strong academic reputation based on a combination of liberal arts and career-focused, professional majors. The university awards B.A. or B.S. degree in accounting, , art history, biochemistry, biology, chemistry, child study, economics, English,, family studies, history, international studies, management, mathematics, nursing, nutrition and dietetics, philosophy, psychology, public health, public policy and advocacy, religious studies, social work, Spanish, special education, and women's studies.

The Education program offers teaching certification in early childhood education, elementary education, secondary education and special education. Research, clinical, and work placements are factored into all majors as an important component of each student's program.

Pre-professional programs are also available for students interested in pre-dental, pre-law, pre-medical, pre-pharmacy, pre-physical therapy and pre-veterinary programs as well as health and biomedical sciences.

In addition to the university's undergraduate programs, Master of Arts and Master of Science degrees are also offered through the graduate school. Master's degree programs are available in autism and applied behavior analysis, biochemistry, biology, chemistry, clinical mental health counseling, early childhood education/special education, education, management, marriage and family therapy, nursing, nutrition, school counseling, special education, and teacher licensure. Graduate certificate programs are offered in applied behavior analysis, autism spectrum disorders, dietetic internship, emerging diseases, healthcare systems management, homeland security management, gerontology, and Latino community practice. USJ also offers a Doctor of Pharmacy and Doctorate of Nursing Practice.

ACADEMIC PROGRAMS

USJ remains committed to providing students with the opportunity to pursue a rigorous academic major while remaining focused on achieving their dreams. Average class size is 14 students with a student-faculty ratio of 12:1, which is ideal for faculty mentorship. Classes are taught by faculty members, not teaching assistants, so students study and work with professors all four years. In accordance with the Founding Sisters' vision of combining professional program applications with broader humanistic studies, the curriculum incorporates themes such as the social/historical contexts of science and technology, global awareness, women's studies, and ethical analysis. Most major fields of study incorporate practical experience and professional opportunity as part of the curriculum. Students are provided internships, mentorship, study abroad programs, and professional networking opportunities.

The Honors Program offers enhanced learning opportunities and a motivated community of learners who excel in and out of the classroom as they combine academics with intensive practical experiences. Many Honors students present research at conferences or publish in periodicals.

Students are given every opportunity to succeed on campus which is evident in our high pass rates on professional exams. The Center for Academic Excellence manages the university's Writing Portfolio Program, which enhances students writing skills. The center also provides tutoring and other academic support services. Students may also design their own major or may develop an interdisciplinary major or minor around a particular theme or problem related to their special talents, personal interests, or career goals.

The university's faculty consists of 108 full-time faculty members, five of whom are Fulbright Scholars. Of the full-time faculty, over 80% percent hold the highest possible degrees in their fields. The faculty and all members of the college community promote the welfare students and help them attain the objectives set forth by the college's mission.

CAMPUS FACILITIES AND EQUIPMENT

The campus is easily accessible and offers ample parking, seven residence halls, dining facilities and bookstore. The Pope Pius XII Library has a collection of more than 134,000 volumes, including computer databases, periodicals, microforms, audiovisuals and OCLC interlibrary loans. The Carol Autorino Center for the Arts and Humanities is the cultural center of campus and features The Bruyette Athenaeum, the 365-seat Hoffman Auditorium and the University of Saint Joseph Art Gallery. Professional performers, speakers, comedians and musicians engage the community in various events held on campus in this facility.

The college's primary technology centers are located in McDonough Hall; internet access is available throughout campus including many WiFi hotspots. The O'Connell Athletic Center features a fitness center, swimming pool, suspended indoor track, dance studio and a gym. The Athletic Complex features an outdoor track, soccer/lacrosse field, softball field and six tennis courts. Division III athletics teams include basketball, cross-country, lacrosse, soccer, softball, swimming and diving, tennis and volleyball.

TUITION, ROOM, BOARD, AND FEES

The tuition and fees for full-time freshmen entering in 2012 are $31,826. Room and board cost is approximately $12,270.

FINANCIAL AID

The goal of the University of Saint Joseph Financial Aid Program is to place a high-quality, private education within the reach of as many qualified students as possible. This goal is achieved by offering need- and merit-based financial aid that includes a combination of grants, loans and on campus employment opportunities. More than 85 percent of full-time undergraduate students receive some form of financial assistance. Merit-based scholarship awards are available to all eligible first-year, transfer and international students. Students are automatically considered for merit-based scholarship awards upon admission and are considered for all additional financial aid after completion of the FAFSA form. Financial Aid counselors are available to assist families with the financial aid process at any time.

STUDENT ORGANIZATIONS AND ACTIVITIES

The University of Saint Joseph is a tight knit community where faculty members and students know one another by name. The college is primarily a residential community and therefore offers many opportunities on campus for students to become involved in life. On campus activities including concerts, performances, multicultural events, dances, service projects and NCAA Division III sports draw guests from the community and surrounding local colleges to campus. Free shuttle transportation to and from campus to West Hartford Center and the West Farms Mall offers students the opportunity to enjoy time in over 140 bustling local restaurants and shops. Students visit Hartford's arts and entertainment district which features galleries, coffee bars, theaters, concert venues and professional sports teams. Bus trips to nearby Boston and New York City, as well as Six Flags and the Big E are very popular.

Student Clubs and organizations available to students reflect the diverse interests of the student body. Some of the more popular organizations on campus include the Students Programming and Events Council (SPEC), the Green Team, Queenye's Compayne (drama/theater club) and the Dance Team. Through clubs and organizations students have an opportunity to be actively engaged in leadership roles on campus. Opportunities for USJ students are focused on empowering action and encouraging students to become involved in every aspect of their college experience.

ADMISSIONS PROCESS

When applying to the University of Saint Joseph, it is important to note that the application deadline is rolling. It is selective, with an acceptance rate of 78.4%. For information about the University of Saint Joseph, or our admissions process, please visit our website: www.usj.edu/admissions.

You can reach the Office of Admissions directly by phone at 860.231.5216 or by e-mail at admissions@usj.edu.

You may also write to:

Office of Admissions

University of Saint Joseph

1678 Asylum Avenue

West Hartford, CT 06117

UNIVERSITY OF SAN FRANCISCO

AT A GLANCE

When the Jesuits founded the University of San Francisco in 1855, it was a one-room schoolhouse. Now, it is one of the West Coast's largest Catholic universities. Some things haven't changed: class size is still small, and student/faculty ratio is still low. USF has been dedicated to helping students learn the skills they need to improve their world for over 150 years. USF's Jesuit education is committed to providing all students with individual attention. Both love of learning and the willingness to face the challenge of serving society are fostered in programs in the arts, the sciences, business, education, nursing, and law.

San Francisco itself is a laboratory for students. The city and its university have interconnected histories, and today, this vibrant partnership gives students the wonderful opportunity to bring classroom theory into real, twenty-first-century life. There are 5,937 undergraduates on the 55-acre residential campus, and these students come from all 50 states and 80 countries. All new undergraduate students admitted with 40 or fewer transfer credits must live on campus for their first two semesters of enrollment, unless they have permanent residence within forty miles of the university. Students have access to facilities including libraries, a health and recreation center with an Olympic-size swimming pool, a coffeehouse, and several dining areas. Right outside is the city of San Francisco, and it has "facilities" of its own: the ballet, opera, museum exhibits, concerts, theater, and sports events. In addition, students have the opportunity to live with their peers in a cozy, laid-back environment within the residence halls. There are traditional residence halls and also University apartment-style facilities on campus. There are laundry facilities, study/computer rooms, and television lounges in every residence hall. Most floors in each dormitory also contain a community kitchen.

There are six dining facilities on campus that are convenient to the residence halls and classrooms. The Market has a dining environment similar to a food court with options for vegans, vegetarians and those who only consume organic or gluten-free foods. Other selections include a student-run coffeehouse, and a convenience store/cafe.

There are over 100 student-run associations for undergraduates at USF, including culturally-focused clubs, leadership and community service organizations, honors and professional societies, and club sports and intramural programs. These associations include the oldest continuously performing theater group west of the Mississippi River: The College Players, a weekly newspaper, and a literary magazine. The Career Services Center is one of the most active offices, aiding students in choosing a career path and learning about employment and internship opportunities. The exciting Koret Health and Recreation Center offers facilities for exercise, racquetball, swimming, court games, and socializing.

There are graduate programs in the arts and sciences, business, education, law, and nursing.

LOCATION AND ENVIRONMENT

The beautiful University of San Francisco campus is 55 acres, and is located in a residential neighborhood. Downtown San Francisco and the Pacific Ocean are just minutes away, and the 1,000-acre Golden Gate Park is only a few blocks away. There are many benefits of an urban campus, and San Francisco's diversity and compact geography allow students to discover research facilities, community involvement options, and work opportunities found in few other cities.

OFF-CAMPUS OPPORTUNITIES

USF students have many opportunities for university-sponsored study abroad programs, such as ones to Sophia University (Tokyo) and Oxford (England) through USF's St. Ignatius Institute, as well as a program at Universidad Iberoamericana in Mexico City. USF is connected to Gonzaga University's study abroad program in Florence (Italy) and to Loyola University of Chicago's program in Rome. The Institute of European and Asian Studies, of which USF is an associate member, offers programs in Durham and London, England; Paris, Dijon, and Nantes, France; Berlin and Freiburg, Germany; Vienna, Austria; Madrid and Salamanca, Spain; Milan, Italy; Tokyo and Nagoya, Japan; Moscow, Russia; Adelaide and Canberra, Australia; Beijing, China; and Singapore. There are many other study abroad opportunities as well. Students receive assistance from USF in all aspects of the program: choosing a location, completing applications, arranging financial matters, registering for academic credit, obtaining a passport and visa, and organizing travel plans.

MAJORS AND DEGREES OFFERED

BA and BS degrees are available through USF. The College of Arts and Sciences offers majors in Advertising, Architecture and Community Design, Arts History/ Arts Management, Asian Studies, Biology, Chemistry, Communication Studies, Comparative Literature and Culture, Computer Science, Design, Economics, English, Environmental Science, Environmental Studies, Fine Arts, French, History, International Studies, Kinesiology, Latin American Studies, Mathematics, Media Studies, Performing Arts and Social Justice, Philosophy, Physics, Politics, Psychology, Sociology, Spanish, Theology and Religious Studies, Undeclared Arts/ Science. The McLaren School of Management offers degrees in Accounting, Business Administration, Entrepreneurship and Innovation, Finance, Hospitality Industry Management, International Business, and Marketing. Qualified high school graduates and second-baccalaureate candidates can pursue a four-year baccalaureate program through the School of Nursing and Health Professions. Students can receive teacher certification at the elementary or secondary level by completing a fifth year of study in the Dual Degree in Teacher Preparation program.

The Pre-Professional Health Committee at USF advises and recommends students to medical, dental, pharmacy, veterinary, podiatry, and optometry professional health schools. The pre-medical or other pre-health science requirements can be taken as part of, or in addition to, the requirements of an academic major. The Pre-Professional Health Committee helps students with the application process, creates a professional file for each student, gathers and sends recommendations to professional schools, gives interviews in preparation for application, and endorses approved candidates through a committee letter of recommendation that is sent to all professional schools the student selects. The University currently has, on average, a 70% acceptance rate to medical school.

ACADEMIC PROGRAMS

It is hoped that students leave USF with a well-rounded education and with a focus and awareness of social justice. A curriculum of 128 credits is required for the degree. Core Curriculum requirements from six particular categories of knowledge make up 44 credits of the curriculum, including a nine-credit block of basic skills courses and 88 credits divided between major requirements and electives. Superior students may be selected for an honors program that provides a high academic challenge.

USF urges qualified high school students to study subjects traditionally reserved for colleges as early as possible. To this end, advanced placement courses, as certified by the College Board's Advanced Placement Program tests, are honored. USF also cooperates with the College-Level Examination Program (CLEP). Students interested in obtaining this credit are required to take the CLEP tests before registering for their freshman courses.

A special program is available through the St. Ignatius Institute. The Institute offers a distinguished Great Books curriculum – a historical sequence of courses based on classical works of literature, theology, and philosophy, from ancient Greece to the contemporary world.

Army ROTC is also available at USF, and qualified applicants and continuing students have access to ROTC scholarships.

Two semesters make up the academic year, and there are also summer sessions and a January intersession.

CAMPUS FACILITIES AND EQUIPMENT

USF students enjoy access to the more than 700,000 volumes at Gleeson Library and access to the Computer Center, the Applied Math Laboratory, the Institute of Chemical Biology, and the Physics Research Laboratories, all in the Harney Science Center. The Instructional Media Center is located in Cowell Hall, along with the home base of nursing classes and the Nursing Skills Laboratory. The headquarters for the School of Management is Malloy Hall, which also holds an additional computer laboratory and special seminar rooms.

TUITION, ROOM, BOARD AND FEES

Estimated cost of tuition for the 2013/2014 school year is $39,840. Room and board are $12,990 for the academic year. An additional $5,454 per year is generally required for books, fees, travel, and other expenses.

FINANCIAL AID

Many scholarships, grants, loans, and work-study programs are available for USF students, and all students must submit the Free Application for Federal Student Aid (FAFSA). Approximately 65% of all University students receive some form of financial assistance. Students have access to many jobs both on and off campus.

New freshman applicants with a minimum cumulative grade point average of 3.8 and a combined SAT I score of 1320 (Critical Reading + Math sections only) or an ACT composite score of 30 can participate in the University Scholars Program. University Scholars receive a non-need-based scholarship that covers a large portion of tuition costs for four years of undergraduate work. Scholars must maintain a GPA of 3.25 to remain eligible. Students eligible for University Scholars are identified during the admission process, and interested students must apply for admission by the January 15 priority application deadline.

The President's Merit Award, the Provost's Merit Award and the Dean's Merit Award, also for new freshmen, are non-need-based awards of $10,000, 8,000 and $6,000 respectively. Awardees are also identified during the admission process, and students must apply by the January 15 priority application deadline to be considered.

STUDENT ORGANIZATIONS AND ACTIVITIES

Every undergraduate student is a member of the Associated Students of the University of San Francisco (ASUSF). There are three purposes to the ASUSF: to represent the official student viewpoint, to recommend policies, and to fund activities and services. There are three branches: the executive branch, the Student Senate, and the Student Court. The main representative body of the undergraduate day students is the Senate, and it monitors the expenditures of the $200,000-plus student budget.

USF offers over 100 different clubs and organizations. They give students opportunities to be involved in leadership and professional organizations, honor societies, culturally focused clubs, fraternities and sororities, club sports and intramurals.

ADMISSIONS PROCESS

Admission is selective, and each application receives an individual review. USF desires a high-quality and diverse student body, and thus encourages applications from men and women of all races, nationalities, and religious beliefs. Prospective students are evaluated on many criteria, including high school grade point average, the application essay, a personal recommendation, extracurricular involvement, and satisfactory test scores. All applicants must take the SAT I or the ACT, and international applicants must take the TOEFL or IELTS. A completed application file is made up of the application form, an essay, all academic transcripts, test scores, and one letter of recommendation. For the fall semester, November 15 is the deadline for early action and January 15 is the deadline for regular action.

For additional information, please contact:

Office of Admission

University of San Francisco

2130 Fulton Street

San Francisco, CA 94117-1046

Telephone: 415-422-6563

800-CALL-USF (toll free outside California)

Fax: 415-422-2217

E-mail: admissions@usfca.edu

World Wide Web: www.usfca.edu

UNIVERSITY OF TAMPA

AT A GLANCE

The University of Tampa is a private, medium-sized, comprehensive university in the heart of Tampa. The university offers exciting learning experiences in over 150 areas of study. All programs offer students a combination of challenging coursework and real world experience. Situated on a beautiful 105 acre campus, the university is adjacent to the Hillsborough River and downtown Tampa. Students enjoy a traditional self-contained campus, only steps away from the excitement and opportunities of the bustling city. At the center of campus lies Plant Hall, once a luxurious hotel for the rich and famous. This historical landmark is complemented by modern surroundings and excellent facilities including a student union, art studios and gallery, theatres, computer resource center, complete athletic facilities, science labs, and new residence halls. Over 6,900 students (6,000 full-time undergraduates) are enrolled at the university. UT students represent 50 states and 125 countries. Students choose from more than 180 different clubs and organizations including honors societies, social clubs, Greek Life, community service and others. The University of Tampa has one of the top NCAA Division II sports programs in the nation, winning twelve national championships including recent championships in Baseball (2006 & 2007), Women's Volleyball (2006), and Women's Soccer (2007).

LOCATION AND ENVIRONMENT

Located on the west central coast of Florida, Tampa has far more to offer than just beautiful beaches and a pleasant climate. Tampa Bay is one of the fastest growing areas in the United States. The city is a leading center for the arts, international business, law, education, media, and health and scientific research. Forbes magazine and Newsweek magazine consistently pick Tampa Bay as one of the best places to live in the United States.

OFF-CAMPUS OPPORTUNITIES

Across the river in downtown Tampa is the Museum of Art, Tampa Bay Center for the Performing Arts, the Florida Aquarium, the Tampa Bay Times Forum, and an outstanding public library. Busch Gardens is only several miles from campus and Walt Disney World and Universal Studios are only 90 minutes away. Tampa International Airport is five miles from campus

Major and Degrees Offered

The University of Tampa offers Bachelor's degrees in accounting, advertising & public relations, applied dance, art, athletic training & sports medicine, biochemistry, biology, chemistry, communication, criminology, digital arts, economics, education (elementary and secondary certification), , English, entrepreneurship, environmental science, exercise science & sport studies, film & media arts, finance, financial services operations & systems, forensic science, government and world affairs, graphic design, history, international business, international & cultural studies, journalism, liberal studies, management, management information systems, marine science (biology and chemistry), marketing, mathematical programming, mathematics, music, music education, music performance, new media production, nursing, painting, performing arts, philosophy, psychology, public health, social sciences, sociology, Spanish, sport management, theatre, and writing. Minors and concentrations are offered in adult fitness, advertising, aerospace studies, art history, arts administration & management, Asian studies, biology/business, biology/molecular, biology/organismal & evolutionary, business administration, , French, humanities, interdisciplinary studies, international studies, law & justice, leadership studies, military science, physical education, physics, recreation, speech/theatre, urban studies, women's studies, and world affairs. Pre-professional programs offered include pre-dentistry, pre-law, pre-medicine, pre-veterinary science, allied health, art therapy, and chemistry. Certificate programs include early childhood education, European studies, French, German, gerontology, Italian, Latin American studies, and Spanish. An undergraduate School of Continuing Studies offers fifteen degree programs designed for adults who want to study part-time. Four summer sessions also offer excellent learning and professional advancement opportunities. At the graduate level, the business school offers the Master of Business Administration degree and Master of Science degrees in accounting, finance, and marketing. A Master of Science in Nursing, Master of Fine Arts in Creative Writing and Master of Arts in Teaching degrees are also offered to students.

ACADEMIC PROGRAMS

The University of Tampa's undergraduate curriculum is designed to give students a broad academic and cultural background as well as a concentrated study in a major. Students complete a comprehensive core curriculum known as the Baccalaureate Experience, which is highlighted by the unique and innovative first year program known as Gateways. Gateways is an extensive orientation program which encourages student development via exploration of global issues, career possibilities, and development of critical thinking and communication skills. International experience has always been a major focus at the University of Tampa. Students are essentially educated and prepared to live and work internationally. Academic opportunities in this area are available to students immediately and in 2013 there are over 20 faculty led study abroad opportunities available to students. For qualifying students, the university has a rigorous and rewarding Honors Program of expanded instruction, student research, and University of Oxford semester.

CAMPUS FACILITIES AND EQUIPMENT

$330 million has been invested in new academic facilities, technology, and residence halls since 1997, making this national historic landmark the model of a modern university. 90% of all residence halls are new within the past 13 years and most of the others have been renovated. The Vaughn Student Center and residence hall complex serves as the hub of student life. Here students find food courts, a two-story cyber cafe, recreational areas, the Reeves Theatre, student office space, Barnes & Noble campus store and a 9th floor conference center with magical views of downtown Tampa. The Frank and Carol Morsani Hall opened in Fall 2007 with state-of-the-art amenities and eight separate dining venues. Other outstanding facilities and resources include the Sykes College of Business, a waterfront Marine Science Field Station and research vessels, the Ferman Music Center, Reeves Theatre, 1,000-seat Falk Theatre, the R.K. Bailey Art Studio, and Sykes Chapel & Center for Faith and Values. The newly renovated Martinez Sports Complex, Naimoli Family Softball Complex, and Naimoli Family Lacrosse Stadium opened during this past year.

TUITION, ROOM, BOARD, AND FEES

The cost for the 2012-2013 academic year is $24,682 for tuition & fees and $9.116 for room & board. The average financial aid award for students at the University of Tampa in 2012 was $17,900 with 92% of students receiving financial assistance.

FINANCIAL AID

A high-quality, private education at the University of Tampa presents students with exceptional value and is not as difficult to finance as some students may think. Each family's situation is evaluated individually for need-based assistance. Academic achievements, leadership potential, athletic skills, and other special talents are also recognized, regardless of need. Academic scholarships are awarded to most entering first year students with a 3.0 unweighted grade point average or above. Transfer, leadership, departmental, Phi Theta Kappa, International Baccalaureate and ROTC scholarships are also available.

STUDENT ORGANIZATIONS AND ACTIVITIES

Students choose from more than 180 student clubs and organizations including honors societies, social clubs, and community service groups amongst many others. Visit The University of Tampa website at www.ut.edu to learn more about student organizations and activities.

ADMISSIONS PROCESS

The University of Tampa is an academically competitive institution that offers several non-binding early action admission dates. Check The University of Tampa website at www.ut.edu for specific admission details.

UNIVERSITY OF TEXAS AT DALLAS, THE

AT A GLANCE

Founded in 1969, UT Dallas has evolved into one of the top research institutions in Texas, and its programs in engineering and the biomedical sciences have gained national attention. With an enrollment of nearly 20,000, The University of Texas at Dallas offers students the close-knit community of a small university with excellent student-faculty ratios of 21:1. However, UT Dallas is also backed by the powerful UT System and is aligned strategically with other institutions to offer advanced research opportunities traditionally found at larger institutions.

As a young, agile and rapidly growing university, The University of Texas at Dallas attracts a unique combination of student and faculty resources to the vibrant, dynamic and globally connected Dallas-Fort Worth area. UT Dallas is ranked in the top 100 by Kiplinger's and in the top 75 by The Princeton Review as a best value among public universities, and Times Higher Education ranks UT Dallas as one of the top 100 universities in the world under 50 years of age.

UT Dallas consistently draws a high caliber of student. The average entering freshman SAT for Fall 2012 was 1270. Nearly 39% of freshmen ranked in the top 10% of their high school class, with 75% in the top 25%. UT Dallas is ranked among the top 100 American universities in the number of National Merit Scholars enrolled, and the University confers a higher percentage of science, engineering and business degrees (84%) than any other Texas public doctoral-granting institutions.

About 65% of our pre-med students are admitted to medical schools, compared to an average national admission rate of 45%. In addition, 86% of students advised through our Pre-Law Advising and Resource Center were admitted to one or more law schools.

LOCATION AND ENVIRONMENT

UT Dallas is located in suburban Richardson, Texas, a prime location that places the University in the second largest state and the fourth largest metropolitan area in the nation. Because of the two local airports, Dallas Love Field and Dallas/Fort Worth International Airport, the Dallas area is an international destination. Richardson, known as The Telecom Corridor, is home to diverse global technology-based companies.

OFF-CAMPUS OPPORTUNITIES

The Dallas-Fort Worth Metroplex is one of the nation's largest urban areas, with shopping, entertainment venues, five major sports teams, museums and art galleries, and places for outdoor running, biking, hiking and skating. Area attractions include the Fort Worth Stockyards, the Dallas and Fort Worth zoos, Fair Park, the Dallas World Aquarium, the Perot Museum of Nature and Science, the Kimbell and Amon Carter museums and the Dallas Arts District. Major sports teams include the Dallas Cowboys and their $1.2 billion stadium, the Dallas Mavericks, the Dallas Stars, the Texas Rangers and the soccer team FC Dallas. Dallas' vibrant music scene covers the spectrum—rock, jazz, blues, country, classical and more.

To get to all these venues, we offer free DART (Dallas Area Rapid Transit) gold passes to all students, giving unlimited access to buses, light rail and the University's own Comet Cruiser line that runs to local businesses and grocery stores near campus.

ACADEMIC PROGRAMS

The University of Texas at Dallas offers 133 academic programs across its seven schools. Undergraduate degrees include:

Accounting; Actuarial Science; American Studies; Art and Performance; Arts and Technology; Biochemistry; Biology; Biomedical Engineering; Business Administration; Chemistry; Child Learning and Development; Cognitive Science; Computer Engineering; Computer Science; Criminology; Economics; Electrical Engineering; Emerging Media and Communication; Finance; Geosciences; Geospatial Information Sciences; Global Business; Healthcare Studies; Historical Studies; Interdisciplinary Studies; International Political Economy; Literary Studies; Management Information Systems; Marketing; Mathematics; Mechanical Engineering; Molecular Biology; Neuroscience; Physics; Political Science; Psychology; Public Affairs; Sociology; Software Engineering; Speech-Language Pathology and Audiology; Supply Chain Management; Telecommunications Engineering

Freshman Year Experience

To help students with the transition to college life, UT Dallas offers two-day orientation programs that include the option to stay overnight in the Freshman Residence Hall. New students are advised on mastering their courses, meeting new friends and learning about advisors. Freshman Convocation, held the day before fall classes begin, provides an official welcome ceremony for all incoming students.

Honors Programs

The University offers a four-year comprehensive program for outstanding students, known as Collegium V. Collegium V includes special seminar-style classes offered by selected University professors as well as a program of extracurricular activities designed to encourage and reward exceptional academic achievement. Each of the University's seven schools also offers qualified students the opportunity to participate in an honors program within their discipline.

Study Abroad

As a research-focused university, we help students seeking study abroad opportunities. Faculty and staff actively help students identify and apply for competitive programs with prestigious international universities. Students secure opportunities as varied as their interests. They have worked with an international research team in Ireland studying Lou Gehrig's disease, conducted a study on cognition and depression in Scotland, and collected public policy data in Zimbabwe. Faculty also lead travel study experiences, using the world as their classroom.

CAMPUS FACILITIES AND EQUIPMENT

NSERL

The Natural Science and Engineering Research Laboratory (NSERL) includes a nanoelectronics materials laboratory. The four-story, 192,000-square-foot, $85 million state-of-the-art facility draws faculty, graduate students and post-doctoral researchers from all disciplines around the world.

Activity Center

Students are able to work out on the latest equipment and participate in athletics and recreational sports. The university's Activity Center features a gym; racquetball, squash and basketball courts; a rock climbing wall; and a 25-yard indoor swimming pool.

Career Center

The Career Center offers a variety of services for students during all stages of their job search. Licensed professional career counselors provide career assessments and mock interview training. A full-time resume editor helps prepare resumes and cover letters, business communications and personal statements. The center also has career workshops and an online job-search database, and helps students find internships for the summer or school year. Because DFW is one of the nation's busiest and fastest growing business regions, UT Dallas graduates are highly recruited by leading local and national companies and receive prestigious graduate fellowships, scholarships and advanced research opportunities. Nearly all of the Fortune 500 companies headquartered in the DFW area recruit UT Dallas students. More than 83% of a recent UT Dallas graduating class reported employment or continuing education upon graduation. Recent graduates have received job offers from corporations that included Amazon, Citigroup, Exxon Mobil, Hewlett Packard, Merrill Lynch, Microsoft, Texas Instruments and Xerox.

Student Success Center

The Student Success Center is part of the Office of Undergraduate Education and is a portal to educational enhancement and success. Our student success team members make every attempt to help students achieve their academic goals, whether it is through individualized tutoring, peer-led team learning, supplemental instruction or coordinated group study. Services include a math lab, writing center, and testing center. Success coaches help with time management, navigating the University and personalized plans for studying.

TUITION, ROOM, BOARD, AND FEES

Estimated Cost of Attendance 2013-2014°

Per Year	Texas Resident	Out of State
Tuition & Fees	$11,806	$30,378
Books & Supplies	$1,200	$1,200
Room & Board	$9,240	$9,240
Total	$22,246	$40,818

Note: For residents of Oklahoma, tuition is the Texas resident rate shown plus $30 per semester credit hour.

FINANCIAL AID

The Financial Aid Office awards scholarships to undergraduate and graduate students based on financial need, residency status and other criteria specific to the scholarship program. UT Dallas participates in all federal and state need-based financial aid programs, including grants, loans and work study.

All first-time college freshman undergraduates are considered for an Academic Excellence Scholarship Award, which range from $3,000 per semester up to complete coverage of tuition and fees.

The Guaranteed Tuition Plan is designed to help new students and their families better plan for the cost of a college education. It gives students a four-year, locked-in rate on up to 15 credit hours per semester.

The Tuition Promise dedicates resources to cover the tuition and mandatory fees for newly enrolling students whose families earn $25,000 or less annually and who meet other specific qualifications.

Transfer students are considered for scholarship awards based on incoming transfer GPA and membership in organizations such as Phi Theta Kappa.

Scholarships offered through private sources are available throughout the academic year. Students apply for these types of scholarships through either a University scholarship committee or the specific donor.

McDermott Scholars, selected from top students across the country, have educational expenses — including tuition and fees, and stipends for living expenses, books, travel and post-graduation preparation — covered for four years. They also participate in a wide variety of cultural and educational enrichment experiences in the Dallas area and beyond.

Terry Scholars are Texas students nominated for their leadership potential and academic ability. The scholarships cover a broad range of student expenses over four years of study, including tuition and fees, housing, books and living expenses. Terry Scholars also have access to a broad range of academic, service, cultural, social and leadership opportunities intended to enhance their undergraduate experience.

Campus Life

Student organizations sponsor a variety of activities for the campus including service projects and community outreach. With more than 200 registered student organizations at UT Dallas, it is easy for students to get connected. UT Dallas is also home to 19 national Greek-letter fraternities and sororities, 13 competitive athletic teams, and 27 club sports. The School of Arts and Humanities presents an average of 50 artistic, musical and theatrical events a year. The UT Dallas chess team has won state, national and international titles and regularly represents the University in the Final Four of Chess.

Our students' ideas and visions for the University have become reality. From writing the alma mater and the fight song to founding the Greek System, the cheerleading squad, the Power Dancers and the student radio station, to helping design the freshman residence hall and campus dining facility, our students are making a difference.

ADMISSIONS PROCESS

To apply to UT Dallas, all students should submit an application for admission, which is available at https://www.applytexas.org. Applicants are required to submit official copies of all past academic transcripts, test scores and other degree specific documentation by the appropriate application deadlines to be considered for admission to The University of Texas at Dallas.

Official transcripts in envelopes sealed by the issuing institution may be delivered to the Office of Admission and Enrollment Services, or may be mailed directly from the educational institution. All materials submitted in the process of making application become the property of the University and will not be returned to the applicant.

Students in good standing from an accredited high school who have an SAT of 1200 (combined math and critical reading) or higher, a composite ACT score of 26 or greater or are in the top 15% of their high school class will be admitted to UT Dallas.

Application Fees and Deadlines

All fees are non-refundable.

The application fee is $50 if your application is submitted on or before the regular application deadline.

If you submit your application after the application deadline but prior to the Completed Application Deadline (application and all required documents) the application fee is $125 in order to process your application for decision in time to register for classes.

Applicants with international academic documents will be assessed an additional foreign credential evaluation fee of $50.

All supporting documents and transcripts, with the exception of courses in progress, must be postmarked by the Completed Application Deadline (see Deadlines for U.S. Citizens and Residents chart below).

A new application must be completed and submitted for consideration for any subsequent semester for all incomplete applications after the Documentation Deadline.

Deadlines for U.S. Citizens and Residents

Fall Full-Term	July 1
Spring Full-Term	November 1
Summer	April 1

International Student Application Fees and Deadlines

All fees are non-refundable.

The application fee is $50 if your application is submitted on or before the regular application deadline.

If you submit your application after the application deadline but prior to the Completed Application Deadline, the application fee is $125 in order to process your application in time to register for classes.

Applicants with international academic documents will be assessed an additional foreign credential evaluation fee of $50.

All supporting documents and transcripts, with the exception of courses in progress, must be postmarked by the Completed Application Deadline (see chart below).

A new application must be completed and submitted for consideration for any subsequent semester for all incomplete applications after the documentation deadline.

Term	Application Deadline
Fall Full-Term	May 1°
Spring Full-Term	September 1°
Summer	March 1°

Questions related to undergraduate admissions should be addressed to:

Office of Admission and Enrollment Services- ROC11

The University of Texas at Dallas

800 West Campbell Road

Richardson, Texas 75080-3021

Telephone (972) 883-2270

Fax (972) 883-2599

THE UNIVERSITY OF TULSA

AT A GLANCE

The University of Tulsa (TU) is a private, comprehensive doctoral-degree-granting university that provides education of the highest quality in the arts, humanities, sciences, engineering, business, education, applied health sciences, and law. TU features three undergraduate colleges: the Henry Kendall College of Arts and Sciences, the Collins College of Business, and the College of Engineering and Natural Sciences, and a College of Law and Graduate School.

TU's 11:1 student/faculty ratio, average class size of 19, and emphasis on individual attention anchor an educational culture where students are rigorously challenged and comprehensively supported.

The University is fully accredited by the North Central Association of Colleges and Universities, and is an NCAA Division IA participant in Conference USA. TU maintains a covenant relationship with the Presbyterian Church (USA).

Extracurricular opportunities include intramural sports, special-interest clubs, pre-professional organizations, national fraternities and sororities, community service organizations, an active student government, departmental honoraries, and campus ministry groups.

Total fall 2012 enrollment was 4,327, with 3,160 undergraduates and 1,167 graduate and law students. The ratio of men to women is 56:44 and 19% are multicultural students. Over half the students are from out of state and international students make up about 26 percent of the student population, with 68 countries represented. U.S. News & World Report ranks The University of Tulsa among the top 100 doctoral national universities.

LOCATION AND ENVIRONMENT

TU features a 216 acre residential campus in midtown Tulsa, OK. Tulsa's prominent industries include energy, telecommunications, high technology, data processing, manufacturing, healthcare, aerospace, transportation, and education which present opportunities for internships and employment after graduation. Tulsa has about 550,000 residents and has been named one of America's most livable cities by Forbes. Cultural assets include the Performing Arts Center, BOK Center (arena), acclaimed ballet and opera companies, symphony, Philbrook Museum, Gilcrease Museum, and cultural festivals. Professional sports in Tulsa include minor league baseball, hockey, and arena football. The popular River Parks development has facilities for outdoor activities and extensive jogging and bicycling trails.

OFF-CAMPUS OPPORTUNITIES

The University is strongly supportive of the study abroad experience and the Office of Global Education helps students locate the perfect program, whether it is for TU credit or an intern/volunteer option. Students choose from hundreds of opportunities offered around the world through direct exchange with an international university, through an affiliate sponsored program, or as part of a faculty led course.

Many students take advantage of the of internship opportunities afforded by the city of Tulsa's business and industry community, as well as in the arts, social services and government agencies.

MAJORS AND DEGREES OFFERED

The Henry Kendall College of Arts and Sciences grants the Bachelor of Arts or Bachelor of Science degree in anthropology, art, art history, arts management, Chinese studies, communication, deaf education, economics, elementary education, English, environmental policy, film studies, French, German, history, music, musical theatre, organizational studies, philosophy, political science, psychology, religion, Russian studies, sociology, Spanish, speech-language pathology, theatre, women's and gender studies, and a self-designed major. Minors include most disciplines as well as advertising, classics, creative writing, dance, early childhood intervention, film scoring, Greek, Latin, and Russian. Secondary teacher certification is available in designated disciplines. Interdisciplinary Certificate programs offer a way for students to focus their interests in Advertising, African American Studies, Classics, Creative Writing, International Studies, Journalism Studies, Judaic Studies, Legal Thought, Museum Studies, and Political Philosophy.

The Collins College of Business awards the Bachelor of Science in Business Administration degree in accounting, economics, energy management, finance, management, management information systems, and marketing and a Bachelor of Science in international business and language. Minors are available in most disciplines plus business administration (for non-majors), coaching, healthcare informatics, and international business. Certificate programs are available in accounting, finance, MIS, not-for-profit administration, and sport administration. Management majors may choose specializations in business law, entrepreneurship and family business management, or human resource management. The college is home to several specialized centers, including the Family Owned Business Institute, the Genave King Rogers Center for Business Law, and the Williams Risk Management Center.

Within the Collins College of Business, the School of Nursing offers the Bachelor of Science degree in athletic training, exercise and sports science, and a Bachelor of Science in Nursing degree program.

The College of Engineering and Natural Sciences offers the Bachelor of Science degree in applied mathematics, biochemistry, biogeosciences, biological science (options in Pre-Medicine, Pre-Dentistry, and Pre-Veterinary), chemical engineering, chemistry, computer science, earth and environmental science, electrical engineering, engineering physics, geology, geophysics, information technology, mathematics, mechanical engineering, petroleum engineering and physics. Minors are available in the science and computational science disciplines. The college features state-of-the-art research facilities, including the Center for Information Security and the Williams Communications Fiber Optic Networking Laboratory. From 1995 to 2011, 48 TU engineering students were named recipients of the prestigious Barry M. Goldwater Scholarship, the nation's premier award for undergraduate students studying engineering, math, or science.

Master of Arts, Master of Science, Master of Business Administration and Ph.D. degrees are offered in each college through the Graduate School and The University of Tulsa College of Law awards the J.D. degree.

ACADEMIC PROGRAMS

The Tulsa Curriculum links a broad, humanities-based core and writing across the curriculum approach for all students with a highly flexible group of majors, minors, concentrations, and certificate programs. TU students can receive an education that is well-rounded, in-depth, and uniquely personalized. Candidates for graduation must complete at least 124 semester hours of course work.

The Honors Program engages students in a critical examination of the major epochs and ideas of Western thought and culture through careful study of primary texts. A separate application is required. The acclaimed Tulsa Undergraduate Research Challenge (TURC) program combines advanced research in most disciplines, scholarship, and community service.

The TU Center for Information Security is developing defenses against cyber-terrorist attacks and information warfare. The center supports the University's National Security Agency (NSA)-accredited certificate program in information assurance, a curriculum that integrates information security with computer law and policy issues. TU has been designated a Center of Excellence in Information Assurance by the NSA and is one of six pioneer institutions selected by the National Science Foundation for the Federal Cyber Service Initiative (Cyber Corps).

Air Force ROTC is available through a satellite program.

Students may receive credit through Advanced Placement testing. Students who complete the International Baccalaureate diploma can receive up to 30 college credits, depending on their test scores.

The University of Tulsa operates on a semester calendar. The fall term begins in late August, the spring term in early January, and the summer session in mid May.

CAMPUS FACILITIES AND EQUIPMENT

Since 2002, The University of Tulsa has added one million square feet of building space and a stunning entrance to its beautifully landscaped campus.

The Lorton Performance Center opened in 2011. Home to the School of Music and the Film Studies Department, the 77,000 square-foot facility includes a 700-seat concert hall, specialized rehearsal and practice rooms and film production suite with post-production editing and scoring capabilities.

In 2012, the College of Engineering & Natural Sciences added to its existing Keplinger Hall, J. Newton Rayzor Hall, a $14-million home for the Computer Science and Electrical Engineering departments with 24 integrated classroom and state of the art teaching/research laboratories, and Stephenson Hall, the new 38,600 square foot home for the Mechanical Engineering department and McDougall School of Petroleum Engineering. Additional research facilities are housed at Tulsa's North Campus where government and industry funded research consortia explore innovations and solve problems faced by the petroleum industry while fostering student learning.

The University of Tulsa's libraries, historic McFarlin Library and Mabee Legal Information Center, house more than 3.6 million items. McFarlin holdings include over 920,000 volumes, 620,000 titles, 120,000 e-books, 40,000 electronic periodicals, 7,500 videos, and 10,000 recordings. McFarlin's Special Collections rare book holdings number over 125,000 volumes and are internationally recognized, particularly in Native American history and law, along with nineteenth and twentieth century Irish, English, and American Literature. McFarlin is home to the papers of 2001 Nobel Laureate V.S. Naipaul. The 12,000 square foot Academic Technology Center annex was dedicated in 2009, adding computer labs, a coffee shop, and restored reading rooms.

Helmerich Hall houses the Collins College of Business building and was recently renovated inside and out with architectural elements to blend with the rest of campus and innovative learning spaces such as the Williams Student Services Center and Studio Blue.

The Mary K. Chapman Center for Communicative Disorders serves the community with its clinical facility and is the learning center for the Department of Communication Disorders. The department has the latest equipment and instrumentation available for use in research, diagnostic, and therapy activities.

Kendall Hall is home to the departments of Theatre and Musical Theatre and features two fully equipped theatres, a scene shop, costume shop and computer design lab.

The Allen Chapman Activity Center features the University Bookstore, student organization offices, the Great Hall for lectures and entertainment, a sports bar, food court, and fast food venues.

The Donald W. Reynolds Center is the campus arena and convocation center. This $28 million facility is the home for the intercollegiate basketball and volleyball programs, and has cutting-edge facilities for video editing and training.

Dedicated in 2007, the 29,000 square foot Case Athletic Complex is home to the Golden Hurricane football program and adjoins the renovated H.A. Chapman Stadium where players enjoy one of the nation's elite college football training and playing environments.

The university's 34-acre sports and recreation complex features a 64,000 square foot student fitness center, competition-grade tennis complex, track, NCAA soccer and softball fields, and intramural fields.

TU manages the acclaimed Gilcrease Museum and the two have embarked on an expansion into Tulsa's Brady Arts District to open the Zarrow Center for Art and Education, providing classes and studio space.

TU students have the option of hundreds of attractive and convenient on-campus apartments, all built within the last 5 – 10 years.

TUITION, ROOM, BOARD AND FEES

In 2013-14, the typical cost for students living on campus is $45,051, including $34,030 for tuition and $10,166 for room and board. Expenses for books average about $1,200 per year.

FINANCIAL AID

In 2012, nearly 90 percent of entering students received some form of financial aid (including grants, scholarships, work-study, and loans). TU offers a limited number of highly competitive Presidential Scholarships which cover full tuition, room, and board. All applicants may be considered for a range of university scholarships based on academic merit. Performance scholarships are available in music and theater by audition. The University of Tulsa participates in National Merit and National Achievement Scholarship Corporation's Finalist program, and the National Hispanic Scholar Program. Applicants for aid should submit the Free Application for Federal Student Aid (FAFSA) by March 1 for priority consideration.

Admission Process

The University of Tulsa seeks students whose academic background indicates potential for success in the university's rigorous academic environment. Performance in high school college-preparatory subjects and scores on the SAT or ACT are key factors in the admission evaluation, but each applicant is reviewed holistically. The counselor recommendation, extracurricular activities, and indicators of leadership, creativity, and focus are all taken into consideration. Campus visits and interviews are highly recommended.

TU has a non-binding, Early Action freshman admission plan with an application deadline of November 1. Decisions are mailed within three weeks. Applications received after November 1 are reviewed under a Rolling Admission process with notifications made on an ongoing basis after mid-December.

An application, official high school transcript, ACT or SAT score results, and a guidance counselor recommendation are required of freshman applicants. TU accepts the Common Application or its own online or paper application form. TU adheres to the national Candidate's Reply Date of May 1.

For additional information, students should contact:

The University of Tulsa

Office of Admission

800 South Tucker Drive

Tulsa, Oklahoma 74104-3189

Telephone: (918) 631-2307 (in Tulsa)

(800) 331-3050 (toll-free)

Fax: (918) 631-5008

E-mail: admission@utulsa.edu

Web: www.utulsa.edu/admission

US Air Force Academy

should go here. Doc is a PDF so it can't be pasted in.

VANDERBILT UNIVERSITY

AT A GLANCE

In 1873, on the heels of the Civil War, Commodore Cornelius Vanderbilt gave $1 million to the university that now bears his name, with the hope that it would "contribute to strengthening the ties which should exist between all sections of our common country." Since then, Vanderbilt has consistently enrolled America's most talented students and challenged them daily to expand their intellectual horizons in an inclusive environment based on open inquiry and respect. Vanderbilt's comprehensive interdisciplinary approach to education allows students to pursue a wide array of academic and curricular interests outside of their main focus of study, and the university's Opportunity Vanderbilt financial aid program assures that it is often cited among the country's best values in national universities.

Consistently ranked among the top 20 universities in the country by U.S. News & World Report, Vanderbilt is a private research university that features four undergraduate schools and six graduate and professional schools. Each year, 1,600 first-year students join the university, bringing the total undergraduate population to approximately 6,800 students, many of whom collaborate with professors on cutting edge research projects and present their findings at professional conferences. Our 8:1 student-faculty ratio gives each student access to faculty members of prominence in every area of academic study. Faculty members provide a challenging, comprehensive education that encourages broad perspectives and critical thinking.

ACADEMICS

Students apply directly to one of Vanderbilt's four undergraduate schools: the College of Arts and Science, the School of Engineering, Peabody College of Education and Human Development, or the Blair School of Music. In all four schools, honors programs and opportunities for research, independent study, and internships are available. Roughly 40 percent of undergraduate students pursue double majors within and across all four undergraduate schools. This leads to some diverse combinations, such as pre-med students who study Spanish, engineers who study violin, math majors who study songwriting, and chemistry majors who study art history.

The College of Arts and Science provides many opportunities to experience a wide range of academic disciplines and subjects. Within the requirements of the AXLE (Achieving eXcellence in Liberal Education) curriculum, students refine their skills in writing, mathematics, foreign language, the humanities, natural sciences, social sciences, history, and culture.

The Blair School of Music offers the Bachelor of Music degree in composition and theory, musical arts, musical arts/teacher education, and performance. Instruction is available in every instrument of the orchestra as well as piano, organ, euphonium, multiple woodwinds, saxophone, classical guitar, and voice. Unlike many schools of music, Blair has no graduate students. The curriculum combines intensive musical training with liberal arts studies. The Blair School also offers a music minor and a wide variety of courses, private instruction, and performing organizations for non-majors.

For more than 125 years, the School of Engineering has educated engineers for careers in industry, government, consulting, teaching, and research. In addition to technical courses, each student's program includes a complement of course work in the humanities and social sciences, resulting in a balanced foundation for future achievement. All programs leading to a Bachelor of Engineering degree are ABET-accredited, and students can earn the Bachelor of Science degree while majoring in Computer Science or Engineering Science.

The top-ranked graduate school of education (according to U.S. News & World Report) for five consecutive years, Peabody College offers degree programs leading to teacher certification and to careers in other areas of education and human development, including child development, child studies, cognitive studies, and human and organizational development. The degree reflects a strong liberal arts foundation combined with a solid program of pre-professional courses and a multitude of internship and practicum opportunities. All undergraduates must complete requirements in communications, the humanities, mathematics, the natural sciences, and the social sciences. Moreover, students have an abundance of field experiences throughout their four years.

ADMISSIONS

Vanderbilt seeks students with high standards of scholarship and character. Admission is based on a holistic review of academic and personal credentials. The typical applicant will have completed 20 or more units in a challenging high school curriculum, including at least two years of foreign language study. School of Engineering applicants should complete at least four units of mathematics; calculus and physics are strongly recommended.

Generally, applicants who are admitted to Vanderbilt have exceptional academic credentials and are highly engaged in their communities, often serving in leadership roles. Admissions decisions are based on strength of high school transcript, standardized test results (either the SAT Reasoning Test or ACT with Writing), personal essays, official recommendations, and extracurricular activities. SAT Subject Tests are not required. In addition to completing standard application materials, candidates for the Blair School of Music must audition on their primary instrument.

Campus visits are recommended, although a student's demonstrated interest in Vanderbilt is not a consideration in admissions decisions. Students should visit admissions.vanderbilt.edu/visit to learn about group information sessions, campus tours, half-and full-day visit programs, and opportunities to attend classes and to "shadow" a current Vanderbilt student. To visit Vanderbilt without traveling, take the virtual tour at admissions.vanderbilt.edu/tour. Vanderbilt does not conduct on-campus interviews, but optional alumni interviews are available in many locations.

Students whose first choice is Vanderbilt may apply under one of Vanderbilt's early decision plans. Application materials must be submitted electronically or postmarked by November 1 for Early Decision I and by January 1 for Early Decision II; notification is made by December 15 for Early Decision I and by February 15 for Early Decision II. Regular Decision applications are due January 1 and students are informed of the admission decision by April 1. To apply, applicants must submit official standardized test scores and all required parts of the Common Application, including the School Report (counselor recommendation and official high school transcript), two academic teacher recommendations, and a $50 application fee.

CAMPUS FACILITIES AND EQUIPMENT

Vanderbilt University sits 1.5 miles southwest of downtown Nashville on a 330-acre, park-like campus that was designated a national arboretum in 1988. The university comprises over 200 buildings, including a world-class medical center and the Jean and Alexander Heard Library, home to over 8 million items. The most recent additions to campus include The Martha Rivers Ingram Commons, a group of 10 new or newly renovated residence houses designed specifically for first-year students. Seven of these buildings have received the gold LEED (Leadership in Energy and Environmental Design) certification. Additionally, two new residential colleges known as College Halls are set to open in August 2014. Each building will house approximately 330 upperclassmen students and will be led by a faculty director and two graduate students in residence.

CAMPUS LIFE

Vanderbilt is recognized for an active campus life. Students can select from among 510+ student-run organizations, including pre-professional, cultural, religious, political, recreational, and social clubs. Elected representatives of Vanderbilt Student Government work in conjunction with other student leaders and faculty to bring noted speakers and events to campus. Vanderbilt also has a thriving college athletics program. A founding member of the SEC, Vanderbilt sponsors 16 Division I teams. Since 2000, Vanderbilt has claimed 12 SEC championships. Vanderbilt athletes succeed on and off the field: the school's teams achieve the highest graduation rate in the SEC and one of the top rates in the country.

LOCATION AND ENVIRONMENT

Vanderbilt is located in the heart of Nashville, home to a diverse population of 1.6 million and marked by its unique blend of cosmopolitan flair and small-town charm. A thriving center of entertainment, publishing, health care, and technology, Nashville is consistently ranked as one of America's friendliest cities and was honored by Rolling Stone as the "Best Music Scene in the Country" in 2011. Nashville sits at the intersection of three major interstates, and the international airport is served by all major airlines.

MAJORS AND DEGREES OFFERED

College of Arts & Science: African American and Diaspora Studies; American Studies; Anthropology; Art; Asian Studies; Biological Sciences; Chemistry; Classical Civilizations; Classical Languages; Classics; Communication of Science and Technology; Communication Studies; Earth and Environmental Sciences; Ecology, Evolution, and Organismal Biology; Economics; Economics and History; English; European Studies; Film Studies; French; French and European Studies; German; German and European Studies; History; History of Art; Italian and European Studies; Jewish Studies; Latin American Studies; Mathematics; Medicine, Health, and Society; Molecular and Cellular Biology; Neuroscience; Philosophy; Physics; Political Science; Psychology; Public Policy Studies; Religious Studies; Russian; Russian and European Studies; Sociology; Spanish; Spanish and European Studies; Spanish and Portuguese; Spanish, Portuguese, and European Studies; Theater; Women's and Gender Studies; and individually designed majors.

Blair School of Music: Composition/Theory; Musical Arts; Musical Arts/Teacher Education; and Performance

School of Engineering: Biomedical Engineering; Chemical Engineering; Civil Engineering; Computer Engineering; Computer Science; Electrical Engineering; Engineering Science; and Mechanical Engineering

Peabody College of Education and Human Development: Child Development; Child Studies; Cognitive Studies; Early Childhood Education; Elementary Education; Human and Organizational Development; Secondary Education; and Special Education

Graduate/Professional Schools: Divinity School; The Graduate School; Law School; Owen Graduate School of Management; School of Medicine; and School of Nursing

Pre-professional advising is available for students interested in pursuing graduate degrees in architecture, business, law and medicine.

OFF-CAMPUS OPPORTUNITIES

Study-abroad programs allow students to immerse themselves in languages and cultures around the world. More than 120 programs are offered in Argentina, Australia, Austria, Chile, China, Costa Rica, the Czech Republic, Denmark, the Dominican Republic, Egypt, England, France, Germany, Israel, Italy, Japan, Russia, Singapore, South Africa, and Spain, among others. Students receive direct credit for their courses, and the cost of tuition is usually the same as for study on campus in Nashville. In addition, any scholarships, grants, or loans a student has been awarded apply to Vanderbilt study-abroad programs. Students may also participate in programs sponsored by other universities by working with an adviser.

Students also take advantage of internships in many industries located in Nashville, including entertainment, business, health-care, government, publishing, and education.

FINANCIAL AID

Through Opportunity Vanderbilt, the university makes three important commitments to ensure that students from many different economic circumstances can enroll as undergraduates at Vanderbilt: the admissions process is need-blind for all U.S. citizens and eligible non-citizens, Vanderbilt meets 100 percent of demonstrated need for admitted students, and Vanderbilt's financial aid packages do not include loans. These three commitments combined place Vanderbilt among a small number of universities to adopt such progressive policies.

More than 60 percent of the University's undergraduate students received some type of financial aid in the 2012/2013 school year. Need-based aid is awarded according to the evaluation of the FAFSA and the CSS/Financial Aid PROFILE.

Vanderbilt also awards merit-based scholarships to select first-year applicants who demonstrate exceptional accomplishment and intellectual promise. Three signature scholarship programs comprise the majority of these merit scholarships: the Ingram Scholarship Program (for students who plan to combine a professional or business career with an exceptional commitment to community service), the Cornelius Vanderbilt Scholarship Program (for students who combine outstanding academic achievements with strong leadership and contributions outside the classroom), and the Chancellor's Scholarship Program (for students who have worked to build strong high school communities by bridging gaps among economically, socially, and racially diverse groups). All three programs require a separate application in addition to the application for admission.

TUITION, ROOM, BOARD, AND FEES

The estimated costs for 2013-2014 include: tuition, $41,928; housing, $9,208; meals, $4,890; books and supplies, $1,370; student activities and recreation fee, $1,054; personal expenses allowance, $2,662; travel allowance varies; first-year experience fee, $690; new student transcript fee, $30; engineering lab fee°, $650; and engineering laptop allowance°, $1,500 °The engineering laptop allowance and laboratory fee are for engineering students only. First-year engineering students are required to provide their own computer that meets published requirements.

VAUGHN COLLEGE OF AERONAUTICS AND TECHNOLOGY

AT A GLANCE

Located in New York City, Vaughn College of Aeronautics and Technology is a private, four-year college committed to providing its students with the excellent education and skills needed to achieve professional success in engineering, technology, management and aviation. Founded in 1932, the College, adjacent to LaGuardia Airport, is a small, high-quality institution where students can experience personal attention as they progress through academic course work.. The College offer master's, bachelor's and associate degree programs in engineering, technology, management and aviation and fosters a culture of excellence in rigorous degree, professional, technical, and certification programs. These programs incorporate the latest technology and meet the universal needs of the industries they serve. The result is well-educated graduates who are successful in their fields. The College's student body of more than 1,700 and its low, 15:1 student-faculty ratio ensure a highly personalized learning environment. More than 92 percent of Vaughn College graduates are employed or continue their educations within one year of obtaining their degrees, and they work in twenty countries and all fifty states. Vaughn College is also committed to making education affordable for students. Vaughn's reasonable tuition can be an important consideration in your decision-making process.

In recent years, opportunities generated by technology have crossed all segments of American industry. There is a high demand for jobs in electronics, engineering firms, computer software companies, fiber-optics communication corporations, local, state and federal government, defense and airport authorities as well as major transportation companies. Recent graduates have pursued advanced degrees at such institutions as Columbia, Stony Brook and Texas A&M, or landed positions at well-known organizations such as Lockheed Martin, The Port Authority of New York and New Jersey, United Technologies, Consolidated Edison, Embraer and JetBlue Airways. Vaughn's master's degree in airport management is uniquely targeted to an industry that contributes significantly to the regional economy.

ACADEMICS

All students in associate and baccalaureate degree programs complete a core curriculum as part of their degree requirements. The core curriculum is derived from the mission of the College and reflects what the institution believes is important and elementary to students' education and development. In general, the core instills in students critical-thinking skills, values appropriate to an educated person and the ability to communicate. It also provides context for advanced learning. The baccalaureate core consists of three components: academic seminars (2 credits, including the freshman year experience and information literacy), the liberal arts (21 credits, including a year of world and American literature), and math and science (16 credits).

ADMISSIONS PROCESS

Vaughn College offers equal educational opportunity to all students without regard to age, citizenship status, color, disability, marital status, national origin, race, religion, creed, veteran status, gender or sexual orientation. High school graduates must submit a completed application (available online at www.vaughn.edu); the $40 application fee; SAT or ACT scores; an official copy of the high school transcript and any college transcripts (if applicable); a copy of the high school diploma (or GED), complete with scores; and immunization records. Some students may need to take a placement exam, while flight operations applicants must pass the FAA Class III physical examination. An interview with an admissions counselor and a financial aid counselor is required for all flight operations applicants and recommended for all others.

Students who have lived in the United States for less than three years and for whom English is a second language, or international applicants from countries where English is not an official language, can substitute results of the TOEFL exam. Students who have completed 24 or more college credits are exempt from the SAT/ACT requirement.

The admissions counseling staff is available to advise applicants and their parents and to provide up-to-date advisement material to high school guidance offices. The admissions office reviews applications on a rolling basis. All applicants are encouraged to file by March 1 for the fall semester and November 15 for the spring semester to best take advantage of scholarship opportunities. For more information, contact the office of admissions at 1.866.6VAUGHN, ext. 118.

CAMPUS FACILITIES AND EQUIPMENT

Each laboratory provides the work/study environment suited to the requirements of each program. This practical, hands-on experience helps qualify students for immediate employment upon graduation. From the new mechatronics laboratory to the CATIA/NASTRAN computer center, the College is committed to providing students with the knowledge and tools they are likely to find in today's businesses. The College's $1-million flight simulator center features Frasca142 and 241 simulators, a Canadair regional jet trainer, and two Redbird simulators. In addition, a revolutionary educational partnership with Redbird Flight Simulations enables students to pursue FAA flight certifications and ratings at Redbird's innovative facility in San Marcos, Texas.

The College has substantially upgraded its technology environment over the past few years. Students have access to more than 200 computers in classrooms and labs, providing software applications for desktop publishing, word processing, spreadsheets, databases, and shared printing services. These computers also afford students the opportunity to interact with industry-leading applications used within their academic programs, including CATIA, SolidWorks, Nastran and Patran. The College's recently created student portal provides online access to tools that enhance and support academic efforts. All of Vaughn's classrooms have updated instructional technologies, including projection, and Internet connectivity to classrooms and labs. Wireless access exists across campus, including within the residential facilities, and each student is provided a vaughn.edu e-mail address. Identification cards provide students with access to secured facilities, laundry payment, dining services, library access, vending and purchasing options, and more.

The College's library offers extensive general, technical, resource, and periodical material totaling more than 125,000 volumes. The real and virtual resources include books, periodicals, videos, and research databases. The video collection consists of subject videos to support the College's curriculum, general-interest videos, and movies. The library houses VHS tapes and DVDs and its research databases contain more than 8,000 full-text periodicals and newspapers. Ten personal computers are available for student use in the reference area. Vaughn is also nearing the construction phase of a new library that will provide students and faculty with a one-stop location for research materials, academic support services, and technology support. This new library, scheduled to open in 2013, triples the size of the current facility and is part of a more than $30-million renovation of Vaughn's campus planned over the next several years.

CAMPUS LIFE

Vaughn recognizes that the college experience also takes place outside the classroom. The College's residence hall features panoramic views of Manhattan and a staff eager to help students take advantage of all that New York City has to offer. An array of clubs and organizations exist, including the Robotics Club, American Association of Airport Executives–Student Chapter and Women in Aviation-International. Vaughn also competes in intercollegiate athletics as a member of the Hudson Valley Men's and Women's Athletic Conferences, a confederation of four-year colleges in the metropolitan area. The seven intercollegiate sports programs are men's and women's basketball, men's soccer, men's and women's cross country, and men's and women's tennis.

LOCATION AND ENVIRONMENT

Located in New York City, the College offers numerous internship opportunities with an array of technology, manufacturing, and aviation companies. The cultural, spiritual, and physical needs of the students are met by the outstanding facilities of New York City. Restaurants are easily accessible, and hospitals and other medical facilities are among the best in the world. New York City's legendary museums focus on arts, natural history, science, and world civilization.

MAJORS AND DEGREES OFFERED

The College awards the Associate of Applied Science (A.A.S.) degree in aeronautical engineering technology, airport management, aviation maintenance, animation and digital technologies, electronic engineering technology–avionics, and flight.

The Bachelor of Science (B.S.) degree is available in general management, airline management, airport management, aviation maintenance, aviation maintenance management, electronic engineering technology–avionics, electronic engineering technology–general electronics, flight, mechatronics engineering, mechanical engineering technology–aeronautical option, and mechanical engineering technology–computer-aided design option. A nondegree course of study in air traffic control, a Federal Aviation Administration Collegiate Training Initiative program (AT-CTI), is also available. The College is one of thirty-six institutions nationwide to offer this program. There is also an aircraft dispatch program offered.

OFF-CAMPUS OPPORTUNITIES

Internships are an important part of a student's learning experience at Vaughn College, and they have led to job offers upon graduation. The department of career services and faculty chairs arrange for internships with top U.S. corporations. As a federally designated Hispanic-serving institution, the College participates with the Hispanic Association of Colleges and Universities (HACU) to place students in internships with various federal agencies year-round. Other active internships and cooperatives include the Boeing Company, Federal Aviation Administration (FAA), Federal Express, Global Air Dispatch, HACU, JetBlue, Lockheed Martin, the Metropolitan Transportation Authority (MTA), the National Broadcasting Company, the Northrop Grumman Corporation, Northwest Airlines, ORBIS, the Port Authority of New York and New Jersey, and Teterboro Airport.

STUDENT ORGANIZATIONS AND ACTIVITIES

Vaughn College supports a variety of student organizations. Activities are moderated by members of the faculty and staff. The Student Government Association (SGA) is primarily concerned with the quality of student life on campus. SGA carries the concerns of its constituency, the student body, to the administration and is the voice of the student body. Serving students as the liaison to the administration, SGA coordinates social programming and provides a system for cocurricular involvement through many clubs and organizations. SGA meets on a regular basis and encourages all students to attend meetings and become involved.

TUITION, ROOM, BOARD AND FEES

In 2012–13, full-time tuition (12 to 18 credits per semester) was $9,450. Students taking 11 credits or fewer paid $600 per credit. The semester fee, which covers the cost of orientation courses, Internet and computer usage, and student-support services, activities, and leadership programs, was $200.

For the 2012–13 academic year, rooms in Vaughn's four-year-old residence hall cost $4,515 for a double room and $5,200 for a single room, per semester. A $250 housing deposit is required. Residents live in either a two-person or a four-person suite with a semi-private bath. The residence hall has laundry, study, and kitchen facilities in a common area within the building. Residence hall rooms are supplied with a bed, dresser, closet, desk, chair, and wastebasket for each student. Each room is also equipped with phone and cable TV hookup and computer port.

FINANCIAL AID

Vaughn College offers federal, state, and institutional funds to help students pay for their education. Ninety percent of students are eligible for some type of financial aid. The first step is to file the Free Application for Federal Student Aid (FAFSA) and, if appropriate, the New York State Tuition Assistance Program (TAP) application. Applications for the fall semester should be filed by March 1. The College recognizes academic excellence by awarding scholarships to high-achieving students pursuing Bachelor of Science degree programs. Applicants must file the FAFSA to be eligible.

Awards for new students include Founders' Scholarships, which are merit-based and range from $500 to $6,000 per year, and the need-based Vaughn College financial grants, which range from $250 to $2,200.

Financial aid is determined by a variety of factors, including income, assets, family size and other family information. Each applicant has unique circumstances and the financial aid office is committed to helping students and their parents through the process. It is strongly recommended that students file for financial assistance as early in the year prior to enrollment as possible.

Financial aid eligibility requires that the student maintain satisfactory academic progress and program pursuit after enrolling.

VIRGINIA COMMONWEALTH UNIVERSITY

AT A GLANCE

At Virginia Commonwealth University, learning extends beyond the classroom. As a premier urban, public research institution, our students confront real-world challenges in unique learning and living environments teeming with culture.

VCU students arrive ready to turn their ambitions into action. Whether your passion lies in the medical field, the visual or performing arts, social work, engineering, education or life sciences, you'll find the tools to answer your calling. Designated by the Carnegie Foundation as a "Community Engaged" institution with "Very High Research Activity" status, VCU has cemented its reputation as one of the nation's leading research universities — with more than $250 million in funded research. As such, you'll find guidance and support from distinguished faculty members always at the forefront of their fields, as well as abundant opportunities to contribute to that constant pursuit of new knowledge through your own research endeavors and creative projects.

LOCATION AND ENVIRONMENT AND OFF-CAMPUS OPPORTUNITIES

Located at the heart of the commonwealth in Richmond, Va., VCU's campus blends into the fabric of the city, offering students a mix of modern amenities, historic buildings and small-town charm. Vibrant cultural districts featuring a variety of galleries, theaters, museums and shops balance the city's thriving business sector, which boasts internship opportunities for students at Fortune 500 and Fortune 1000 companies, as well as local and state agencies. And, just a short walk from campus you'll find the historic James River and more than 550 acres of waterfront parks in which to relax and explore.

MAJORS AND DEGREES OFFERED

VCU offers degrees in 63 baccalaureate, 74 master's and 38 doctoral disciplines, many of which are unique in Virginia, and its academic medical center offers specialized training within VCU's five health sciences schools. With an emphasis on interdisciplinary study, students can use their sculpture training to mold casts for surgical procedures, fashion and engineering students can design and produce environmentally friendly nursing scrubs, and business and mass communications majors can work with scientists, physicians and inventors on product innovation, design and marketing.

Our School of the Arts in Qatar also offers undergraduate degrees in fashion design, graphic design, interior design, and painting and printmaking, as well as a master's degree in design studies, helping to foster creativity, diversity and an open exchange of ideas in the Middle East.

With a full slate of offerings in the humanities and sciences, as well as schools in the disciplines of allied health professions, arts, business, dentistry, education, engineering, government and public affairs, life sciences, mass communications, medicine, nursing, pharmacy, social work and world studies, you're given the flexibility to make the educational experience at VCU your own.

Those pursuing graduate study will find 32 of our programs ranked nationally by U.S. News & World Report, with 12 of those placing in the top 10, but whether graduate, undergraduate, doctoral or first-professional, your VCU degree will mark only the beginning of a life spent making a difference in your field.

ACADEMIC PROGRAMS

At VCU, outstanding academics extend beyond the classroom, and whether your passions cause you to venture out into the city or the far corners of the world, you'll find a wealth of resources to help you on your path.

Our Division of Community Engagement provides students, faculty and staff with opportunities to partner with the community through volunteer work and service-learning courses, and for six straight years, the U.S. Department of Education has admitted VCU to the President's Higher Education Community Service Honor Roll — the highest federal recognition that colleges and universities can achieve for service learning and civic engagement.

Students can seek added challenges through The Honors College, which provides a unique, academically intense environment (coupled with the opportunity to live in honors-only residence halls) and allows those who complete the program to continue their studies in any VCU professional health science or graduate program without competing for admission.

Our University College can advise and work with you to hone your academic skills, and as you continue your studies, our University Career Center can help augment your classroom experience with internship and experiential learning opportunities, as well as assist with all aspects of the job search, so you can effectively market yourself in the field.

Those interested in studying abroad can count on our Global Education Office to help them find the right fit, and prospective international students interested in VCU can learn more and receive guidance from that office as well.

For students interested in transferring to VCU or who have already transferred here, our Transfer Center can help ensure a smooth, efficient and fulfilling process. To help ease military service members in their transition from soldier to student, the Military Student Services Center offers help in applying for aid, managing benefits and future deployments, and scheduling classes to fit family schedules. Similarly, our Office of Multicultural Student Affairs assists traditionally underserved or underrepresented student populations through advising, mentoring, retention and program development.

CAMPUS FACILITIES AND EQUIPMENT

Like Richmond and all of Central Virginia, VCU values its proximity and relationship to the James River, not just for its boundless recreational pursuits, but also for its importance to the health and vitality of our communities. With the creation of our satellite field station, the Inger and Walter Rice Center for Environmental Life Sciences, located on 494 acres along the James midway between Richmond, Va., and Williamsburg, Va., our researchers, students and volunteers work to increase our understanding of river and wetland habitats, as well as influence state and federal resource protection policy.

On campus, we take our impact on our environment just as seriously. Since joining a nationwide coalition to eliminate greenhouse gas emissions from colleges and universities, VCU remains the only institution in Virginia to achieve an A-range rating on the national Green Report Card. With smaller steps such as Dining Services participating in an organic composting program and installing solar trash compacting bins throughout campus, to larger initiatives like our two vegetative rooftop gardens and our solar water heating system at Shafer Court Dining Center — which saves nearly 73,000 kilowatt hours of energy each year — VCU's efforts to go green have set us on a path to be climate-neutral by 2050.

VCU Medical Center has done its share in this arena as well, having eliminated its paper trail through an enhanced electronic medical records system, and stands as the only Level I trauma center in Central Virginia. In 2012, U.S. News & World Report ranked VCU Medical Center the No. 1 hospital in the state.

VCU's continued excellence in medical education will receive a boost with the construction of the $158 million James W. and Frances G. McGlothlin Medical Education Center, scheduled to be complete September 2013. In the next few years, VCU and the city of Richmond will welcome the opening of the $32 million VCU Institute for Contemporary Art, which will host world-class exhibits and performances, as well as studio space for students, strengthening our reputation as an artists' haven.

And, when it comes to living on campus, those artists have a chance to begin informing and inspiring each other's work through residential villages, which allow students in the arts, business and health sciences to live and work together in the same environment, while also enrolling in one shared class. Similarly, our newest residence hall offers apartment living space for 459 upperclassmen, and the first two floors house students in the Academic Scholars Program in Real Environments — ASPiRE — an innovative and comprehensive community engagement-focused living-learning program for sophomores. A second, similar residence hall focused on global education is slated to open in summer 2013.

TUITION, ROOM, BOARD, AND FEES

Undergraduate tuition and fees for the 2012-13 academic year are $9,885.46 for in-state students and $23,912.46 for out-of-state students.

Room rates for both in-state and out-of-state students are $5,292, and board rates for in-state and out-of-state students are $3,456.

FINANCIAL AID

At VCU, we want your focus to be on your community and your passion. Our Office of Financial Aid uses all available funds to help you gain access to a great education and disperses more than $200 million in aid to more than 14,000 students each year. Eligibility depends on a student's academic and financial situation, but most students who enroll at VCU do so with at least some assistance. Additionally, VCU awards numerous scholarships each fall to freshman applicants on the merits of academic performance, community service and artistic talent.

STUDENT ORGANIZATIONS AND ACTIVITIES

With more than 500 student organizations (including 30 sororities and fraternities) hosting more than 600 events each year, you're sure to find the social outlet that's right for you. Still, in the event you don't (or, if you're simply looking for something unique and new) you can start your own with help from the Office for Student Organization Development.

Perhaps the hottest ticket in town is our men's basketball team. Led by coach Shaka Smart, VCU stormed the NCAA Final Four in 2011 and returned to the tournament in 2012. Our 16 NCAA sports teams hold a total of 27 Colonial Athletic Association conference titles over the past 10 years, and, with our recent move to the Atlantic 10 Conference, we're excited to rack up many more against new competition. So, whatever your sports passion, you'll find reason to don black and gold on game days.

For recreational and outdoor fitness enthusiasts, VCU boasts the Cary Street Gym, which was named one of the National Intramural-Recreational Sports Association's outstanding facilities in 2012. There, you'll find an 18,000-square-foot fitness center, two indoor swimming pools, a 38-foot rock-climbing wall and much more.

With the James River just a walk away from campus, and the Blue Ridge Mountains just a short drive, there's also plenty to explore, and the VCU Outing Rental Center can equip you with everything you need for a safe and exhilarating day trip.

ADMISSIONS PROCESS

Applications for undergraduate admission are reviewed based on academic merit, with additional weight given to extracurricular and community engagement, as well as SAT and ACT scores. Students also should have completed at an accredited high school four units of English study and three units each in mathematics, history, social studies or government, science with at least one lab, and foreign language. Students who have taken advanced placement, international baccalaureate or dual enrollment courses may also be eligible for course credit at VCU.

International applicants also must meet the same academic criteria and be able to demonstrate adequate English language proficiency.

Graduate and first-professional applicants will be asked to meet specific requirements pertaining to their chosen discipline.

Through a guaranteed admission agreement with the Virginia Community College System, students who meet the agreement's academic requirements can continue their education at VCU with all transferrable credits earned from the associate degree program accepted.

For more information pertaining to undergraduate, graduate, first-professional, international and transfer application requirements, deadlines and admissions procedures, visit www.vcu.edu/apply.

Key Statistics

Rankings and designations

32 graduate programs ranked by U.S. News & World Report

Carnegie Foundation designation as a "Community Engaged" institution with "Very High Research Activity" status

Top 100 National Science Foundation research institution

VCU Medical Center ranked No. 1 hospital in Virginia by U.S. News & World Report

AT A GLANCE

Year founded: 1838

School Type: Public

Religious Affiliation: No affiliation

Campus Environment: Urban

Enrollment: 31,899 (fall 2011)

Regular Application Deadline: 01/15

Tuition: In-state: $9,885.46/Out-of-state: $23,912.46

Financial Aid Deadline: 03/01

Website: www.vcu.edu

WASHINGTON COLLEGE

AT A GLANCE

The first college chartered for the new nation, Washington College was founded in 1782 to educate citizens for the tasks of the new democracy, and that mission remains central today. The College's rich history helps distinguish it among the nation's selective liberal arts colleges: General George Washington lent his name, donated 50 guineas to our founding and served on our first Board of Visitors and Governors. His example of citizenship and leadership continues to shape our traditions and our high expectations for our students.

We believe that a broad, general education in the liberal arts—one shaped by personal relationships with professors and classmates in a supportive residential community—is not only mentally liberating but also the most effective way to prepare for a successful career and a meaningful life. In your first two years on campus, we will encourage you to explore many interests and try new areas of study, to encounter different perspectives and challenge old ways of thinking. We also will encourage you to pursue creative endeavors, athletic competition, recreational activities and campus leadership roles.

LOCATION AND ENVIRONMENT

The College is set on the scenic Chester River on Maryland's Eastern Shore, between the Atlantic and the Chesapeake, just 75 miles from Washington, D.C. Students benefit greatly from our proximity to the mid-Atlantic's major urban centers, which offer a wealth of distinguished speakers, intern opportunities, institutional partnerships and other opportunities for academic and cultural enrichment. That said, we also take full advantage of our setting in a historic river town close by the Chesapeake Bay. The Eastern Shore becomes an extension of the campus—a personal learning laboratory for intellectual, social and personal growth.

Two centers of special research and programming, The C.V. Starr Center for the Study of the American Experience and the Center for Environment & Society, were developed specifically to take advantage of the region's history, rural and maritime cultures, and natural resources. Founded in 2009, the Chesapeake Semester offered through the Center for Environment & Society is a four-course immersion experience that focuses on the complex issues affecting the health of the Chesapeake Bay and the people whose lives depend on it.

The College maintains a small fleet of boats—including a 46-foot research vessel used as a floating classroom—that supports coursework in underwater archaeology, marine and estuarine biology, environmental chemistry, and environmental studies; the College also boasts nationally ranked programs in rowing and sailing.

Small Campus, Big Opportunities

With a student body of 1,500 undergraduates, the College remains defiantly, confidently small and celebrates the interaction between student and professor. The average class size is 17 students; only one class in seven will have more than 25 students enrolled. Faculty members reach beyond the classroom to challenge and nurture a student's maturing intellect and creativity with collaborative research, independent and self-directed study, and a rigorous senior "capstone" project.

Washington College offers a growing array of internships and field experiences, including fellowships for the study of American history, internships with theaters and museums and model diplomacy programs. Students can participate in a summer archaeology field school, make investment decisions for the $500,000 Alex. Brown Fund, and work at the College-run research center that studies migrating birds and sustainable land management.

Writing Across the Curriculum

Washington College is recognized for its rich literary arts environment—the Rose O'Neill Literary House hosts a steady stream of significant writers and editors supported by the Sophie Kerr Program, and each year, one graduating senior is awarded the Sophie Kerr Prize, the largest undergraduate literary award in the world. (The 2013 winner took home $61,000.) The College is committed to helping all students become better writers, no matter what major they pursue. Writing-intensive courses help students cultivate proficiency in the language arts, as well as stay up-to-date with ever-evolving information technologies.

ACADEMIC ENRICHMENT

The Douglass Cater Society of Junior Fellows is Washington College's flagship academic enrichment program—one that rewards initiative and intellectual curiosity with competitive grants to support self-directed undergraduate research, internships and scholarship anywhere in the world. Membership is open only to rising juniors and seniors, but another important academic opportunity, the Presidential Fellows program, was created with first-year students in mind. An invitation to be a Presidential Fellow puts you on the fast track to academic distinction, including the chance to work with full Cater Fellows as a Cater Apprentice. At the heart of each program are opportunities for intellectual exchange and social outings.

Study Abroad

Washington College offers one of the most extensive study abroad programs of any small liberal arts college. Among more than 40 offerings are summer programs in literature (the celebrated Kiplin Hall program), international business (Germany in 2013), economic development (Tanzania), and environmental studies (Bermuda, Ecuador); yearlong exchanges in Morocco and Ireland; and semesters abroad in Australia, Japan and Argentina.

MAJORS AND DEGREES OFFERED

With 50 majors and academic programs, Washington College provides you the opportunity to shape an academic program that fits your intellectual interests and career aspirations. We operate on a two-semester academic calendar. Students complete four courses, or 16 credits, each semester, and choose a program of study at the end of the sophomore year. We award the degrees of Bachelor of Arts and Bachelor of Science. In addition, the English Department offers a part-time program leading to a master's degree.

Bachelor of Arts degrees can be earned in the following majors:

American Studies
Anthropology
Art and Art History
Business Management
Drama
Economics
English
Environmental Studies
French Studies
German Studies
Hispanic Studies
History
Human Development
Humanities
International Literature and Culture
International Studies
Mathematical Science
Music
Psychology- Clinical/Counseling
Sociology
Bachelor of Science degrees are awarded in the following:
Biology
Chemistry
Physics
Psychology- Behavioral Neuroscience
The College offers interdisciplinary programs of study, minors and/or concentrations in the following:
Accounting and Finance
African Studies
Archaeology
Asian Studies
Biochemistry
Black Studies
Chesapeake Regional Studies
Creative Writing

Dance
Earth and Planetary Science
Elementary Education
Engineering
European Studies
Gender Studies
Geographic Information Systems
Global Business Studies
Information Systems
Justice, Law, and Society
Latin American Studies
Near Eastern Studies
Nursing 3+2
Peace and Conflict Studies
Pharmacy 3+4
Pre-Law Preparation
Premedical Program
Secondary Education Studies
Social Welfare

CAMPUS FACILITIES

Our beautiful campus is a collection of historic redbrick, Georgian-style structures, large shade trees and charming old brick walkways. The oldest buildings, the Hill Dorms, were built in the mid-nineteenth century on the site where an original structure burned to the ground in 1827. New and newly renovated buildings feature expanses of glass that create modern spaces flooded with light.

The Gibson Center for the Arts, opened in August 2009, is a glittering showcase offering several venues where students can learn, rehearse, practice, perform and exhibit their work. The $24 million facility encompasses a main stage, an experimental theater, a music recital hall, and an art gallery, as well as all the latest tools and technology to support professional-caliber theater, concerts and exhibitions.

In late fall of 2009, the College opened Hodson Hall Commons, a new dining hall and student-center complex. In addition to the main dining hall, the contemporary glass-and-brick structure features a large student lounge, an intimate space for meetings and performances, and several specialty eateries.

The Chester and Sassafras residence halls, completed in Summer 2008, were the first buildings on campus to incorporate geothermal heating and cooling. More recently, a major renovation of the campus library included a geothermal system along with a new coffee shop and popular group-study rooms. The latest dramatic facelift took place at the Johnson Fitness Center, where a $2 million renovation added a cardio-fitness area enclosed by a dramatic curving wall of glass.

According to Lacrosse Magazine, our Roy Kirby, Jr. Stadium is among the top ten venues for collegiate lacrosse in the nation. The stadium, completed in 2008, is the only Division III venue to make the cut. In 2009, Athey Park, the College's baseball park, was built to mirror Kirby Stadium.

Scientific Instrumentation and Technology

Advances in technology are incorporated throughout the curriculum, from sequencing DNA in the lab to accessing primary sources for a Shakespeare project via the library's Early English Books Online database. Other examples: The biology department uses a Nuclear Magnetic Spectrometer, the psychology department uses brain mappers and eye trackers to test cognitive function, and archaeology students use a seabed scanning device and a Remotely Operated Vehicle (ROV) to explore underwater wreckage and search the Chester River floor for clues of Native American and colonial settlements.

TUITION, ROOM, BOARD AND FEES
Basic educational fees for 2013-2014

Tuition (full-time) $40,384

Student Service Fee $736

Campus Housing $4,796

Meal Plans per year

19/week $4,646

FINANCIAL AID
Washington College is committed to providing educational excellence and equity for all students. We strive to provide monetary assistance to students who can benefit from a Washington College education, but who, without such assistance, would be unable to attend. Washington College offers several types of financial aid to help qualified students meet their college expenses. College-sponsored tuition scholarships, tuition grants, work/study, and low-interest loans are available. In addition, eligible students can receive assistance from federal, state and independent aid programs.

National Honor Society members who are accepted to Washington College are automatically considered Washington Scholars, qualifying for $50,000 tuition scholarships ($12,500 for four years). Some students receive even more. Since 1996, approximately 50% of all entering freshmen have been NHS members. To qualify, students must be inducted into NHS before March 1 of their senior year.

STUDENT ORGANIZATIONS AND ACTIVITIES
We cherish our residential tradition because it brings round-the-clock opportunities for academic, social and personal growth. Students may choose to go Greek, participate in program-specific honor society activities, or volunteer in the community. There is a club to meet nearly every interest, from the Environmental Alliance and and Writers Union to clubs for Wakeboarding and Wilderness Adventure.

Nearly a third of our students compete in one or more of our 17 varsity sports, and another third participate in club sports and intramurals. The Student Events Board creates a variety of activities that everyone on campus can enjoy, from festivals and quiz nights to the semi-formal George Washington's Birthday Ball. While students reap the benefits of living in one of the best small college towns on the East Coast and the relaxed informality characteristic of the Chesapeake Bay region, they also take advantage of the campus's proximity to three urban centers—Washington, D.C, Baltimore, and Philadelphia.

ADMISSIONS PROCESS
Washington College is a selective institution. In order to assess an applicant's "fit" with the College, the Admission Committee requires the submission of all relevant academic records and test scores, an activity profile, an essay/personal statement, and a letter of recommendation. In some cases, an on-campus interview may also be required.

Prospective applicants are strongly encouraged to come to campus for an information session and tour. These visits should be scheduled in advance by calling 410-778-7700 or visiting www.washcoll.edu/admissions

Prospective students may apply online using the Common Application. Preference in admission and financial aid decisions is given to students who apply on or before February 1. Early Decision applicants have an application deadline of November 15; Early Action applicants have a deadline of December 1, and Regular applicants have a deadline of March 1. Admitted applicants must pay a $500.00 enrollment deposit by May 1. For details, visit www.washcoll.edu/admissions.

WEBBER INTERNATIONAL UNIVERSITY

AT A GLANCE

Webber is a private business university. It is a wonderful educational facility with excellent faculty to student ratios and a sincere caring for our students. Being part of a focused, close-knit environment means being more than just a number.

Webber International University is a four-year independent coeducational university. It was founded in 1927. Webber is accredited by the Southern Association of Colleges and Schools to award Associate and Bachelor of Science degrees and the MBA graduate degree. Webber International University provides an environment that encourages success through academic excellence and hard work.

LOCATION AND ENVIRONMENT

Webber is located on a beautiful 110-acre campus along the shoreline of Crooked Lake in Babson Park, Florida, 45 minutes from Orlando and about an hour from Tampa.

OFF-CAMPUS OPPORTUNITIES

Webber is approximately one-hour driving distance from some of the most popular tourist attractions such as Disney World and Universal Studios. Webber's campus is positioned on a crystal clear lake in central Florida and boasts tennis courts, baseball, softball, beach volleyball and soccer fields that face the lakefront. The town is called Babson Park, named after Roger W. Babson founder of the University. The town's population is very small which provides a nice atmosphere for study.

MAJORS AND DEGREES OFFERED

Webber International University students may pursue bachelors and associate degrees in business administration. The school offers ten majors: accounting, computer information systems management, corporate communications, finance, hospitality and tourism management, management, marketing, pre-law, security management and sport business management. The university also offers the Masters in Business Administration.

CAMPUS FACILITIES AND EQUIPMENT

Consisting of a variety of circulating and reference books and periodicals, a wide array of electronic databases, and group and individual workspaces, The Roger and Grace Babson Library provides ample support for any undergraduate or graduate research project a Webber student might undertake.

Our Programs for Academic Student Success (PASS) Center provides centralized peer tutoring services under the direction of a doctoral qualified English professor. Here you will find tutors who are able to assist with any course offered at Webber.

Webber's computer resources centers are computer labs and teaching facilities whose equipment offers the most up-to-date technology, encouraging outstanding student performance in business, communication, and creativity.

Webber also offers a variety of athletic facilities. They include a baseball stadium, soccer field, softball field, tennis courts, junior Olympic size swimming pool, beach volleyball courts, two training facilities and a gym for basketball and indoor volleyball.

TUITION, ROOM, BOARD, AND FEES

For the 2013-2014 academic year, the annual cost (including tuition and room and board) is $32,654. The annual cost for commuting students is $21,050. These costs are adjusted periodically. Webber International University projects that $1000 is sufficient for books and supplies. Laboratory fees are not included in this amount.

FINANCIAL AID

The Student Financial Aid Department is available to guide and assist students in meeting educational costs. Financial aid is distributed on the basis of academic performance, applicant need, and potential. Roughly 90 percent of undergraduates at the University are awarded financial assistance. Students applying for need-based assistance must file the Free Application for Federal Student Aid (FAFSA). Numerous forms of aid, such as Federal Work-Study awards, grants, loans, and scholarships are employed to meet undergraduate needs. A number of non-need-based scholarships are also offered; these are awarded based on academic achievement, on college and community service, or on athletic performance.

STUDENT ORGANIZATIONS AND ACTIVITIES

At Webber International University, not all learning takes place in the classroom. Active involvement in social programs, recreational activities and personal-growth experiences create special moments. At Webber students have a wide variety of clubs and organizations to choose from. These include, Fellowship of Christian Athletes, Marketing Club, Pep/ Jazz Band, Phi Beta Lambda, Poetry Club, Quality Club, Society of Hosteurs, Society of International Students, Sport Management Club, Student Leadership Association, and The Warrior (campus newspaper).

ADMISSIONS PROCESS

Prospective students must be high school graduates. The majority of prospective students rank in the top half of their graduating class. Applicants must present their SAT or ACT scores before being considered for admission. International applicants are required to present scores on the Test of English as a Foreign Language (TOEFL). Students must submit official transcripts from their high school.

Transfer student applications are welcome, as well as applications from students resuming their education as nontraditional adult students. Transfer students must have satisfactory records at their previous institution. They must also submit transcripts from all previous institutions.

The University operates on a rolling admissions basis. It is strongly suggested that application forms be submitted at the earliest possible date, as on-campus housing is in high demand. (Freshmen must reside in the dormitory unless they share a residence with a parent, guardian, or spouse.)

WELLS COLLEGE

AT A GLANCE

Wells College is a coeducational, private, liberal arts college enrolling 568 students from across the United States and throughout the world. Today, true to its heritage, Wells maintains a national reputation for academic excellence. The College prides itself on offering one of the most collaborative learning environments in higher education today. The top five reasons to consider Wells: (1) Wells offers students a personal education: the average class size is 14 and professors know students by name (2) 90% of Wells faculty members have doctoral degrees and all classes are taught by professors - not teaching assistants (3) Wells students prepare for careers and entrance into top graduate and professional schools through experiential learning: internships, research with faculty members, and community service (4) Wells offers an extensive study abroad program with affiliated programs in 17 different countries (5) All students at Wells benefit from an academic experience similar to honors programs available only to a small number of students at other institutions. Throughout their four years, they work toward a senior thesis that is comparable to graduate-level study. Wells prides itself on offering one of the most collaborative learning environments in higher education.

ACADEMICS

This is not your ordinary education. The Wells experience is deeply personal and intensely focused on superior academic achievement. Wells offers 18 majors and over 40 minors. With one professor for every NINE students, professors really get to know each student. The average class size has FOURTEEN students and is taught seminar-style, with discussions taking precedence over lectures. Fundamental to the Wells curriculum is an interdisciplinary approach to the liberal arts with the opportunity to experience intimate classes and innovative teaching methods. Through the Wells experiential learning program, students have opportunities to participate in quality internships, off campus study programs, and academic research projects. Experiential learning in the curriculum enables students to test theories learned in the classroom with real-life situations intertwined with a rigorous academic program.

ADMISSIONS

Wells students are intellectually curious, open-minded, and creative. They are comfortable expressing themselves, listening to others and sharing ideas. They are caring citizens of the world, eager to travel beyond the campus. Wells students love to learn. If you love learning, you will love the Wells experience.

Candidates for admission are expected to complete a solid college preparatory program throughout their four years in secondary school. The college recommends a program which provides the best background for study at Wells, including four years of English grammar, composition, and literature; four years of history; three years of mathematics; two years of laboratory science; and coursework in a foreign language. Student records are enhanced by the addition of courses such as computer science, art, and music, when appropriate curricular choices are offered. To apply for admission to Wells College candidates must submit completed application forms to the Admissions Office by March 1 of the year of entrance.

In addition, the following credentials are required: a transcript of all secondary school work, including the recommendation of the high school principal or school counselor; scores from either the College Entrance Examination Board Scholastic Aptitude Test (SAT I) or the American College Testing Program (ACT); two letters of recommendation from teachers in academic subject areas. A personal interview is recommended.

Admissions Deadline Options:

Early Decision. December 15: Students whose first choice is Wells College are encouraged to apply under the early decision option. This is a binding admissions option; if admitted; early decision applicants agree to accept Wells offer of admission and agree to withdraw their applications from all other colleges.

Early Action. December 15: Students who would like to receive an early review of their application files are encouraged to apply under the early action option. This is a non-binding admissions option.

Regular Admission. March 1: All other applications to the college should be received by the regular admission deadline. Applications are reviewed after this date and decisions are mailed by April 1.

CAMPUS LIFE

Wells students enjoy all of the advantages of living in a closely-knit community. A well-respected Honor Code shapes the educational and social atmosphere of the campus. Wells supports more than 40 clubs and organizations including a literary magazine and newspaper, music and drama groups, and political organizations, in addition to student-sponsored events, lectures, and performances. Wells is also a member of Division III NCAA. Wells women compete in nine intercollegiate sports: cross country, field hockey, tennis, lacrosse, soccer, softball, basketball, volleyball and swimming. Wells men compete in five intercollegiate sports: basketball, cross country, lacrosse, soccer, volleyball and swimming. Wells campus has a nine-hole golf course where our team of both men and women compete as well.

LOCATION AND ENVIRONMENT

The beautiful 365-acre lakeside campus is situated in the heart of the Finger Lakes Region of New York State. Located in the historical village of Aurora on Cayuga Lake students enjoy phenomenal views and access to our campus boathouse. The campus is 30 minutes from Ithaca, one hour from Syracuse and Rochester, and approximately five hours from New York City.

MAJORS AND DEGREES OFFERED

Wells College offers the Bachelor of Arts degree with majors in the following areas (concentrations within the majors appear in parentheses): American Studies (African-American Studies, American Cultures); Biological and Chemical Sciences (Biochemistry and Molecular Biology, Biology, Chemistry); Economics and Management (Economics, Management); English (Creative Writing, Literature); Environmental Studies (Environmental Policies and Values, Environmental Sciences); Foreign Languages, Literatures, and Cultures (Spanish); History; International Studies; Mathematical and Physical Sciences (Computer Science, Mathematics, Physics, Applied Physics); Performing Arts (Theatre and Dance); Psychology; Public Affairs: Ethics, Politics, and Social Policy (Ethics and Philosophy, Government and Politics); Sociology and Anthropology (Sociology, Anthropology/Cross-cultural Sociology), Visual Arts (Art History, Studio Art); Women and Gender Studies, and Film an Media Studies. In consultation with the dean and faculty, students may also design their own concentrations and majors. In addition, Wells offers programs that lead to provisional certification in elementary and secondary education.

TUITION, ROOM, BOARD, AND FEES

For the 2013-2014 year: Tuition: $34,400; Room and board: $12,300; Fees: $1,500

WENTWORTH INSTITUTE OF TECHNOLOGY

AT A GLANCE

Founded in 1904, Wentworth Institute of Technology is an independent, co-educational, nationally-ranked institution offering career-focused education through 19 bachelor's degree programs in areas such as applied mathematics, architecture, business management, computer science and networking, construction management, design, engineering, and engineering technology. The Institute also offers master's degrees in architecture, construction management, and facility management.

A leader in engineering, technology, design and management education, Wentworth's unique three-part experiential learning model combines class work, laboratory/studio work, and cooperative education (co-op) experience to provide students with a hands-on approach to learning. The co-op program, one of the largest and most comprehensive of its kind in the nation, has been active for more than 35 years and provides Wentworth students the ability to gain the professional work experience needed to succeed in their field. Wentworth is well-known for its academic excellence, community service, and support for the economic growth of the region. For more information, please visit www.wit.edu.

Additionally, Wentworth is a member of one of Boston's largest academic collaborations, the Colleges of the Fenway consortium, which is an association of six Fenway area institutions including Emmanuel College, Massachusetts College of Art and Design, Massachusetts College of Pharmacy and Health Sciences, Simmons College, Wentworth, and Wheelock College,

LOCATION AND ENVIRONMENT

Small school benefits, big city resources.

This private, coeducational college is located on 31 acres in the heart of Boston. With over 3,800 students, it provides the friendliness of a small school, alongside the resources and excitement of the ultimate college town.

When it comes to college towns, there is no place more exciting or full of more opportunities than Boston. The original center of higher education in the U.S., it hosts 50 colleges and universities and draws a quarter of a million students every year, with nearly 20,000 of those students coming from outside the country. Boston is a city with exceptional character. In addition to its rich history, it's also a hub for technology, business and medicine - giving Wentworth students access to educational and career opportunities they would not find elsewhere.

OFF-CAMPUS OPPORTUNITIES

At Wentworth, building professional, paid work experience into the academic program is a priority. Co-op has been a fundamental part of our curriculum for over 35 years, and ours is one of the largest and most comprehensive programs of its kind in the nation. All full-time day bachelor's degree candidates must complete two semesters of co-op, beginning after the first two years of study.

Wentworth's Office of Career Services assists students every step of the way, as they take advantage of opportunities in Boston, in other areas of the US, and abroad.

MAJORS AND DEGREES OFFERED

- Applied Mathematics (three-year program with a four-year option)
- Architecture
- Business Management
- Biomedical Engineering
- Civil Engineering
- Computer Engineering
- Computer Engineering Technology
- Computer Information Systems
- Computer Networking
- Computer Science
- Construction Management
- Electrical Engineering
- Electromechanical Engineering (five-year program)
- Electronic Engineering
- Engineering
- Facility Planning & Management
- Industrial Design
- Interior Design
- Mechanical Engineering

ACADEMIC PROGRAMS

A leader in technology education for over a century, Wentworth offers bachelor's degrees in 19 practical, career-oriented majors. All programs center on Wentworth's distinctive three part experiential learning model, which incorporates classes, labs and studios, and co-op.

As Wentworth is a member of the Colleges of the Fenway, students can cross-register for one course each semester at the participating colleges (Emmanuel, Simmons, and Wheelock Colleges, the Massachusetts College of Art and Design, and the Massachusetts College of Pharmacy and Health Sciences).

CAMPUS FACILITIES AND EQUIPMENT

The Wentworth campus is well-appointed to deliver the top-notch education and living conditions demanded by today's students. Our modernized laboratories are at the vanguard of technology; the equipment mirrors that found in the leading employers in industry. The Institute has spent millions of dollars to upgrade its information technology infrastructure. And the facilities for sleeping are just as impressive as the ones for studying. The Institute operates six residence halls- Evans Way/Tudbury Hall, Edwards/Rodgers Hall, Baker Hall, Louis Prang Apartments, 610 Huntington Avenue, and 555 Huntington Avenue.

Whether you're looking for state-of-the-art computing resources, healthcare you can rely on, or one of any of a number of other services that make campus life better, you can rest assured that Wentworth is working hard to meet your needs.

The Flanagan Campus Center is the hub of student life at Wentworth. The campus center is home to the bookstore, the cafeteria, the Schuman Fitness Center. The Intercultural Center, Wentworth Internet Radio Experience (WIRE), a recreation room, study areas, and the Office of Campus Life.

The Learning Center and The Writing Center provide students with academic support services such as peer and faculty tutoring, computer-based tutorials, and subject study groups. We are dedicated to preparing students for academic success.

Wentworth is committed to helping you make the best use of computers. We offer a range of computing resources including: a wireless campus; labs equipped with the latest hardware and software; and a full-time Office of Information Technology. The result is a highly connected academic and social community where advanced computing is accessible and convenient.

Wentworth subscribes to the policies set forth in the Americans with Disabilities Act and in Section 504 of the Federal Rehabilitation Act of 1973, which mandate equal opportunity in educational programs and activities for students with disabilities.

At Wentworth, we work hard to provide the very best health services. In addition to expert primary medical care, we also offer specialized services including counseling, disability services and comprehensive health education.

In order to make the transition for international students as smooth as possible, Wentworth employs a full-time international student advisor who has extensive experience with international students, and assists them in their personal, social and academic adjustment to Wentworth and the U.S..

Conveniently located at the center of campus, the Wentworth Alumni Library is a valuable resource. The online catalogue includes the holdings of nine other libraries – all available for use by Wentworth students. And, membership in the 14-institution Fenway Library Consortium provides access to more than 2,900,000 volumes and 13,000 periodical titles. Various services are also available through the Alumni Library.

TUITION, ROOM, BOARD AND FEES

Tuition for full-time students (12-20 credits) for 2013-2014 is $27,950 per year. Tuition includes the cost of a laptop computer. Laptops are provided to each student along with the specific software required for their major.

The per credit charge (less than 12 and over 20) is $875 per credit.

Room and Board is approximately $12,550 per year.

Health Insurance, required by Commonwealth of Massachusetts is $1,250 per year (can be waived if student is covered by parent's health insurance).

FINANCIAL AID

We are dedicated to helping you to create a financial plan that allows you and your family to afford a Wentworth education. In cooperation with financial aid specialists, financial services specialists can help discern how best to combine a student's financial aid package with alternative parent or student loans, as well as with Wentworth's monthly payment plan.

More than 88 percent of our students receive financial aid. For the fall of 2012, the average financial aid package for a first-time full time student was $14,391. A typical package is made up of a combination of grants, loans, and work-study earnings. To be considered for financial aid you must complete the Free Application for Federal Student Aid (FAFSA) as early as possible after January 1. You do not have to be an applicant for admission to complete the FAFSA. However, you must be accepted to Wentworth to receive notification of your actual financial aid award.

STUDENT ORGANIZATIONS AND ACTIVITIES

Wentworth participates in 15 NCAA-sponsored varsity sports. More than twenty professional organizations operate on campus, offering unbeatable networking opportunities to students in every field. In addition, there are more than a forty clubs and organizations to help students make productive and fun use of their hours outside the classroom. And if students can't find what they're looking for on the Wentworth campus, they simply visit one of the five neighboring Colleges of the Fenway institutions with which the Institute is affiliated. In addition to Wentworth, the Colleges of the Fenway consist of the Massachusetts College of Art, Massachusetts College of Pharmacy, and Emmanuel, Simmons, and Wheelock Colleges.

Here's the makeup of the student body of Wentworth Institute of Technology during the 2012-2013 academic year:

3,948 students (3,513 day, 435 evening & weekend, 144 Graduate)

738 women (18.6%)

Students from Massachusetts- 63%

Students from other New England states- 23 %

Students from New York, New Jersey, Pennsylvania- 7%

Students from 22 other states and territories- 2%

Students from 60 other countries- 5%

1089: mean SAT score of entering class

77% of new students live in on-campus housing

ADMISSIONS PROCESS

At Wentworth, we look for students who are qualified and motivated to succeed in engineering, technology, design, and management programs. We make our admissions decisions based on:

Academic achievement, measured by official transcripts

Performance on standardized tests (SAT I or ACT)

Personal qualities, such as leadership or creativity, indicated by information in the completed application form

At Wentworth, it's our goal to assist students and their parents as much as possible as they move through the admissions process. In fact, every applicant has a regional admissions counselor they can contact directly with questions.

To apply to Wentworth, you must submit the following materials:

A completed Wentworth application ($50 application fee)

Official high school transcripts

SAT I or ACT scores

A written personal statement

At least one letter of recommendation from a guidance counselor or teacher

TOEFL score, if your native language is not English

Wentworth practices rolling admissions, which means we review each completed application as soon as we receive it -- so you can apply early and get a decision early.

WEST VIRGINIA WESLEYAN COLLEGE

AT A GLANCE

Hello, tomorrow. Founded in 1890, West Virginia Wesleyan is a private four-year co-educational residential college that is affiliated with The United Methodist Church. Small interactive classes and a dedicated and accessible faculty whose priorities are teaching and advising allow students to benefit from a highly personalized educational experience. With its beautiful Georgian campus located in the small town of Buckhannon, West Virginia provides the ideal backdrop for a liberal arts education.

Over 80 percent of Wesleyan's faculty hold the highest degree in their respective teaching field and the student faculty ratio is 14:1. The curriculum foundation begins with a general studies liberal arts program where students complete one-third of their course of study. The College offers over 40 majors and over 40 minors of study, and several additional Master's programs spanning Athletic Training, Business Administration, Education, English (Creative Writing), and Nursing.

West Virginia Wesleyan is accredited by the Commission on Institutions of Higher Education of the North Central Association of Colleges and Schools, and approved by the University Senate of The United Methodist Church. It is a member of the National Association of Schools of Music and is approved by the West Virginia Department of Education and the National Council for the Accreditation of Teacher Education. The College participates in the Interstate Certification Project whereby a number of states certify teachers graduating from Wesleyan's Department of Education. The athletic training program is accredited by the Commission on Accreditation of Allied Health Education Programs. Degree programs offered in business and economics, including the Master of Business Administration program, are accredited by the International Assembly for Collegiate Business Education.

All academic programs either require or strongly encourage the completion of an internship experience. Wesleyan's academic calendar is 4-4-1 that includes an optional May Term in which over 50 students pursue study abroad courses or intensive study curricular offerings. The Advising and Career Center assists students with course scheduling, academic advising, internships and study abroad, resume writing, job searches, and graduate and professional school placement. The Learning Center provides tutoring services as well as comprehensive services for students with diagnosed learning disabilities.

Of the more than 1,400 undergraduate students, 53 percent are from West Virginia, while the other 47 percent originate from 39 states and 19 countries. 15 percent of Wesleyan's American students are minority students. Over 90 percent of Wesleyan's students live on-campus and the College guarantees four years of on-campus housing for all undergraduate students. Housing options include double and single rooms, suites, and apartments. Campus dining is provided and prepared by a contracted professional catering service.

LOCATION AND ENVIRONMENT

Situated in the foothills of the Allegheny Mountains, Wesleyan's beautiful 100-acre campus is located in the quaint, residential town of Buckhannon, West Virginia. Buckhannon has been included in Norman Crampton's book, The Top 100 Best Small Towns in America, a Random House Publication. Many students are drawn to this personal and picturesque setting and the numerous outdoor opportunities located in close proximity to campus. The local community offers movie theatres, coffee houses, department stores, and a wide selection of local and chain restaurants. Wesleyan is a short two-hour drive from Pittsburgh, Pennsylvania, and 90 minutes from Charleston, West Virginia, the state capital.

ACADEMIC PROGRAMS

Wesleyan's liberal arts curriculum begins with a broad base view in a variety of core courses designed to enrich the student's whole view. The classes range from the humanities to contemporary issues and can be intermingled with the courses in the individual's major throughout the four-year program.

Wesleyan's Honors Program is offered for superior students who meet the specific requirements and demonstrate a high quality of academic excellence. Challenging, yet rewarding, classes, along with culturally enriching outings, offer Honors students a diverse and unique educational experience.

MAJORS AND DEGREES OFFERED

West Virginia Wesleyan offers four undergraduate degrees: the Bachelor of Arts; the Bachelor of Music Education; the Bachelor of Science; and the Bachelor of Science in Nursing. The most popular programs of study are in the sciences (biology, physics / engineering, pre-professional studies, etc.); education; business; athletic training; and nursing. Wesleyan also offers a number of master's degree programs.

STUDENT ORGANIZATIONS AND ACTIVITIES

Wesleyan has a balanced and diverse student life program that includes more than 70 campus organizations. Included among these are a campus radio station, newspaper, student government, departmental clubs, national fraternities and sororities, and religious organizations. Over 87 percent of Wesleyan students participate in community service activities that include the complete administration of a youth basketball program to Special Olympics, to tutoring, mentoring, and educational activities to senior citizens programs to more global programs such as hurricane relief and international service trips.

Wesleyan features 19 varsity programs in NCAA Division II. Wesleyan competes in the West Virginia Intercollegiate Athletic Conference. Together the 19 programs have combined to win an unprecedented 163 conference championships.

While Wesleyan is affiliated with The United Methodist Church, students of all faiths are welcome and active. The College holds an optional weekly ecumenical worship service every Tuesday morning and a Catholic Mass each Saturday evening.

OFF-CAMPUS OPPORTUNITIES

Wesleyan encourages all students to expand their education beyond the traditional classroom. Many students have studied abroad in such places as England, Ireland, Wales, Germany, Spain, Kenya, Scotland, and Australia. Professional internships are available in the Buckhannon area, Charleston, WV, Washington, D.C.; New York, NY; Pittsburgh, PA; and other states and countries.

CAMPUS FACILITIES AND EQUIPMENT

Wesleyan's 23 buildings include 10 modern residence hall units, including one brand new residence hall and another completely renovated suite-style residence hall. Located in the center of campus is Wesley Chapel, which chapel serves as a focal point of campus and houses many campus events, both religious and cultural. The hub of the campus, Benedum Campus and Community Center, houses a convenience store, bookstore, swimming pool, campus radio station, student development offices, study lounges, and a cabaret-style restaurant, The Cat's Claw. The Rockefeller Physical Education Center includes a main arena that seats 3,700 spectators, an intramural gymnasium, training rooms, and an indoor astro-turf training area. The multimillion dollar Reemsnyder Research Center was opened in 2009 and boasts state of the art laboratory space for the sciences. Other vital buildings on campus include Christopher Hall of Science; Middleton Hall, which houses Admission as well as the Nursing Department; and the Lynch-Raine Administration Building. In addition, the multimillion dollar Virginia Thomas Law Center for the Performing Arts, opened in 2009, offers the most advanced performing arts facility of its kind in the region. Most recently, a brand new student wellness center was opened in 2012.

Wesleyan's Annie Merner Pfeiffer Library is committed to providing high quality resources and services that empower students for advanced learning. Currently, the number of print and electronic books is nearly equal at 150,000 each, and the nearly 20,000 electronic journal titles far exceed the 300 received in print. In addition to its collections and research services, the Library offers media viewing facilities, areas for group study, and a

quiet place for reading and reflection.

The entire campus has been outfitted with a ubiquitous campus-wide wireless network ensuring access to all students, faculty, and staff from all major campus buildings and every residence hall room.

TUITION, ROOM, BOARD AND FEES

The 2012-2013 total direct costs at Wesleyan are $24,780 for tuition, $7,510 for standard room and board, and $1,024 for student fees, which includes a student activity fee, facilities fee, and a technology fee. These costs do not include books, travel, clothing, the laptop computer, medical insurance, or other personal expenses. Wesleyan offers an interest-free monthly payment plan during the academic year.

FINANCIAL AID

The College offers financial aid on the basis of a variety of criteria: scholastic achievements, special talents and abilities, and financial need. A number of scholarships are available including awards for academics, athletics, performing arts, leadership, community service, and visual arts. Student employment is available in most areas of the College community, financed through a blend of institutional and federal funds. Students may apply for low-cost federal loans. Students should file the Free Application for Federal Student Aid by March 1. Currently, more than 95 percent of all students receive grants or scholarships from Wesleyan.

ADMISSION PROCESS

Students are selected by the Office of Admission on the basis of ability, interests, academic preparation, character, and promise, as indicated by their own statements on the application, as well as by high school or college records, recommendations, and standardized test results. Open without discrimination to all qualified students, the College reserves the right to refuse to admit any applicant who, because of low scholarship or citizenship record, is deemed by the Admission and Academic Standing Council to be unlikely to succeed within the standards the College seeks to maintain.

Persons wishing to be admitted directly from high school should present an application for admission with $35 fee (waived for online applications); a transcript of record from an accredited high school; and a record of either SAT I or ACT scores. Applicants from non-accredited high schools or completing General Educational Development may be considered for admission if satisfactory ability and achievement are demonstrated.

Persons seeking to transfer from another accredited college or university may be admitted to advanced standing upon presentation of an application for admission with $35 fee (waived for on-line applications); an official transcript showing all credits attempted at all post-secondary institutions previously attended; a high school transcript certifying graduation and showing courses pursued and grades earned and, if the cumulative grade point average is less than 2.5, either SAT I or ACT scores.

Wesleyan will accept transfer credit courses compatible with its academic program. Grades and hours so earned shall count toward graduation. The College accepts no more than 60 semester hours of credit from a junior or community college.

Students who transfer to Wesleyan with an associate degree from a regionally accredited community or junior college may be admitted with the degree credited as fulfilling Wesleyan's general studies requirements when the total educational background, including high school record, shows compatibility with Wesleyan's general studies requirements. Deficiencies in general studies requirements, as determined by the Admission and Academic Standing Council, must be satisfied after enrollment at Wesleyan.

Wesleyan participates in the Advanced Placement Program of the College Entrance Examination Board and the International Baccalaureate Diploma Program. Students who have successfully completed AP or IB programs should contact the Office of Admission for credit transfer policies.

WILLIAM PEACE UNIVERSITY

AT A GLANCE

William Peace University located in downtown Raleigh, offers countless clubs and activities as well as innovative academic programs rooted in the liberal arts tradition.

William Peace University students develop an appreciation for lifelong learning, pursuing meaningful careers and building skills for ethical citizenship. The institution was founded in 1857 and named for founding benefactor William Peace, an elder of the First Presbyterian Church of Raleigh.

On average, more than 90% of William Peace University graduates find jobs, or are enrolled in graduate school within a year of graduation.

William Peace University has been ranked among the nation's best in value-added gains in three of the four categories from the Collegiate Learning Assessment. The nationally employed assessment measures the improvement in critical thinking and analytical writing test scores of individual students between their freshman and senior years to determine how much they have learned while enrolled. WPU students also rank the university's academic programs among the best in the nation.

LOCATION AND ENVIRONMENT

William Peace University offers the comfort of a small school with all the possibilities of a big city.

Surrounded by beautiful oak trees and a large front lawn, the historic campus has carved out its own niche in downtown Raleigh. The university is just a short walk from the state capitol, museum, music halls, restaurants, theatres and nightlife.

Students can observe the state legislature in session, dine downtown in popular cafes, attend concerts at the Raleigh Amphitheatre and enjoy live theatre at the REP and NCSU without ever needing a car.

OFF-CAMPUS OPPORTUNITIES

Raleigh is consistently regarded as one of the nation's best places to live for its economic, cultural and professional opportunities. In addition to being named the No. 1 ranking in BusinessWeek's list of America's 50 Best Cities in 2011, Raleigh was ranked one of the top five Hottest Job Markets for Young Adults, a Top 10 Technology Town and a Top 10 City for Singles.

Malls, retail areas and shopping centers complete a lively shopping scene in Raleigh. From the major department stores of Triangle Town Center and Crabtree Valley Mall to the exclusive shops and boutiques of Cameron Village, one can enjoy exceptional shopping in any part of the city.

Raleigh is also home to North Carolina's museums of art, history and natural sciences and every inch of Raleigh is easily accessible from William Peace University. The R-Line, a free downtown bus service with stops on campus, connects you to restaurants, retail and entertainment venues, museums and hotels. The Amtrak train station is less than two miles from campus and RDU International Airport is an easy 20-minute drive.

Whether you are in the mood for a round of golf or edge-of-your-seat football, professional baseball or NHL hockey, the greater Raleigh area has a game for everyone. With several surrounding colleges and universities along Tobacco Road, there is great football and basketball action.

There are also several thriving cities and towns just outside Raleigh, including Chapel Hill, Durham and Cary, and the Research Triangle Park offers a flourishing business landscape for career opportunities before and after graduation.

MAJORS AND DEGREES OFFERED

William Peace University offers Bachelor of Arts degrees in biology, communication, education, English, liberal studies, political science, pre-law, psychology, simulation and gaming design, and theatre.

Bachelor of Science degrees are offered in biology (pre-med, pre-dental, pre-veterinary) and business administration. Additionally a Bachelor of Fine Arts degree in musical theatre is offered.

There are several minors and concentrations in fields such as graphic design, religion, anthropology and global studies to complement and enhance any major.

A new core curriculum includes focusing on ethical decision-making and emphasizing on basic knowledge needed beyond graduation. Additionally, there are mandatory courses in personal financial management, media literacy and four years of writing courses within the English department.

Students are also required to take a series of three classes focusing on career and professional development.

An academic internship related to any major is a requirement with a goal of combining educational theory with job experience. Students are required to complete internships within their field of study during their junior or senior years. Internships are offered in conjunction with classes that include bi-weekly meetings with the faculty. Recent student internships sites include Duke University Medical Center, Mothers Against Drunk Driving and the North Carolina General Assembly.

An average of 60% of William Peace University graduates reported that their internship experience resulted in a job offer.

The student to faculty ratio at William Peace University is 11:1.

William Peace University also offers four evening, online and/or classes on Saturday-only degrees through its School of Professional Studies where students can receive a Bachelor of Arts degree in Education, Liberal Studies or Psychology and a Bachelor of Science degree in Business Administration. Courses are taught by experienced faculty members in seven-week accelerated formats and include many opportunities for individualized academic advising throughout the program. Classes are geared toward meeting the unique needs of non-traditional students and working professionals.

ACADEMIC PROGRAMS

Eligible students have the ability to join several national honors' societies such as Sigma Tau Delta, Alpha Chi, Psi Chi, and TriBeta at William Peace University.

Additionally, students can also join the university's Honor Program that includes academic challenges, enriching experiences outside of the classroom and opportunities to work on undergraduate research. The program is one of the most exciting and prestigious on campus providing academically talented and motivated students to study, conduct research and exchange ideas in a challenging and supportive academic environment. It brings outstanding students and dynamic faculty together in courses that arouse curiosity and promote intellectual discovery and development.

Program members are encouraged to choose from a variety of courses that fulfill liberal education requirements that include psychology, biology, cultural and physical anthropology, literature and public speaking.

Students also have access to the Career Services Office, which provides career counseling, listings of internship options, workshops and a resource library. Students have access to courses and library facilities and on-line databases of other Raleigh colleges and universities through the Cooperating Raleigh Colleges consortium.

International study programs are available in several parts of the world, and opportunities are available annually in a variety of other locations for short-term work or internships or for a semester abroad.

CAMPUS FACILITIES AND EQUIPMENT

William Peace University is a wireless campus.

Computer laboratories, the library and the student publications area are equipped with state-of-the-art computer hardware and software. Other specialized computer laboratories are also available in the biology, media, theatre and visual communication departments.

Student laboratories in the chemistry, general biology and molecular and cellular biology departments are also available. A recital hall, the Leggett Theatre and a studio are available for students in the fine arts department.

The Hermann Athletic Center on campus was recently upgraded and includes state-of-the art fitness center, training room, weight rooms, home and visiting locker rooms, a field house for spring training and intramural space.

The university also offers an expanded student union center that comprises a dining hall, a coffee shop, a student game and lounge space and student government and activity offices.

Residential living at William Peace University is an extended classroom where students have the unique opportunity to learn about different people and new cultures and to experience life on their own in a supportive community.

There are seven residence halls on campus equipped with free wireless Internet and cable services, lounges, study rooms, kitchens, living areas and bedrooms. There are no cost laundry machines that notify students [via a text message] when their laundry is finished.

TUITION, ROOM, BOARD, AND FEES

The 2012-2013 tuition, room, board and fees at William Peace University are:

Tuition	$23,700
Room	$6,186
Board	$2,814
Annual Student Activity Fee	$200 (all students)

The charges are the same for in-state and out-of-state.

FINANCIAL AID

William Peace University strongly believes that everyone should have access to a college education and that's why the university is committed to making it as affordable as possible. We recognize that students and families are struggling to pay for college and therefore, we want to help. In a time where colleges across the country are raising costs, we have actually lowered ours.

Every accepted student is automatically considered for merit and need-based aid (with a submitted FAFSA). We also offer academic awards for the performing arts, community service, leadership, extracurricular activities and more.

Through a combination of financial aid packaging, pursuit of scholarship and grant opportunities and on-campus work-study groups, WPU works to make its educational program available to all qualified students, regardless of financial need. We also provide online information about payment options and the forms you need.

Call 919.508.2394 or email finaid@peace.edu for more information on how to pay for college.

STUDENT ORGANIZATIONS AND ACTIVITIES

There are more than 30 student clubs and organizations, including publications, performance groups and academic honor societies at William Peace University. Some of them include:

Anthropology Club

Cheer/Drill Collaboration

Campus Activities Board (CAB)

Commuter Student Association

Helping Hands

MOSAIC (Multicultural Association)

Peace Times (student newspaper)

Student Government Association (SGA)

Student Recreation Association

Society for Human Resource Management

Spectrum (LGBTQ)

Student Athlete Advisory Committee

William Peace University Singers

ADMISSIONS PROCESS

William Peace University seeks to enroll individuals who will benefit from the academic programs and who will contribute to university life — a community upheld by the honor system, which requires students to maintain academic and personal integrity. The university encourages individuals with varied talents and interests representative of all social, economic, ethnic and racial backgrounds to apply. Admission decisions are made on a rolling basis.

William Peace University does not discriminate in its recruitment and admission of students, regardless of gender, race, creed, color, religion, age, national and ethnic origin, sexual orientation, disability, or veteran status.

Admission requirements/procedures for students are defined by five categories:

Traditional first-year student (high school senior or graduate)

High school student applying as a junior for early entrance

Transfer student

International student

Former student (readmission)

Applications are reviewed individually and decisions are based on the following credentials:

GPA in academic courses

SAT (verbal and math only) or ACT scores

Course selection

Rank in class

Interview with an admissions representative, if requested

Further consideration will be given to an applicant's personal qualifications, co-curricular activities, community involvement and overall potential for success. In addition, consideration of a students' acceptance will be granted upon the discretion of the Vice President for Enrollment.

WILSON COLLEGE

AT A GLANCE
Wilson College offers a personalized education with small classes that give students the opportunity to work closely with dedicated faculty, and teach them to think critically and to communicate with confidence.

Wilson—a coeducational liberal arts college—provides a rigorous academic program with small classes that give students the opportunity to work closely with faculty in a collaborative environment that encourages students to push themselves and to succeed.

The College strives to create an open, welcoming community where relationships formed with classmates and professors can endure throughout their lifetime. Curiosity and enthusiasm to take advantage of all that Wilson offers are essential in preparing students to make a difference in their careers and in their communities.

All Wilson students, faculty and staff adhere to the school's honor principle, which creates a community where personal responsibility and individual success, both in and out of the classroom, are highly valued. Wilson's traditions serve as bonds that join the community together. From Convocation to Commencement, they are an important part of every student's experience.

The College—founded in 1869—is affiliated with the Presbyterian Church, but is open to students of all religions and faiths. The student body in fall 2013 was 746, representing 23 states and 13 foreign countries. Wilson's student-to-faculty ratio is 10-to-1.

LOCATION AND ENVIRONMENT
Wilson College sits on 300 acres in Chambersburg, Pa., located along Interstate 81, approximately 17 miles from the Maryland border. The campus, with its Collegiate Gothic architecture and beautiful grounds is on the National Register of Historic places.

Wilson can be easily accessed from several major cities and airports. Its campus is 1-hour driving distance from Harrisburg; one and 1.5 hours from Washington, D.C.; 2 hours from Baltimore; 3 hours from Philadelphia and Pittsburgh; and 4 hours from New York City.

OFF-CAMPUS OPPORTUNITIES
Founded in 1764, Chambersburg and the surrounding region are steeped in Civil War history. Students can walk to shopping downtown or take a campus shuttle to nearby shopping areas. Hiking, biking and fishing are available on campus and close by, including at Caledonia State Park, only 20 minutes away. Skiing and snowboarding are available at Whitetail Ski area and Ski Liberty. Both are within 30 minutes of the College. Faculty and students regularly visit Washington, D.C., to take advantage of its many offerings.

MAJORS AND DEGREES OFFERED
Students can earn degrees from 28 majors, 18 areas of concentration and 39 minors. Pre-professional programs are offered in health sciences, law, medicine and veterinary medicine. The most popular majors include business, education, English, veterinary medical technology and equestrian studies. A 3 + 1 option allows students to earn a bachelor's degree and a Master of Arts (M.A.) degree in humanities in four years. Wilson also offers a Master of Education (M.Ed.), with a master's degree in accountancy expected to begin fall 2013. In addition, Wilson's Teacher Intern Program (TIP) offers certification for pre-K through 4 education, and secondary education in the areas of biology, chemistry, English, environmental studies, mathematics, social studies and Spanish. The certificate qualifies teachers in 45 states.

Most majors require internships or capstone projects and all majors in the sciences require a three-semester research project. An agreement with Vermont Law School allows qualified Wilson graduates to study environmental law and apply with preference for entrance to the law school

ACADEMIC PROGRAMS
Wilson is a member of Phi Beta Kappa, the nation's oldest and most prestigious and academic honorary society.

Wilson is well-known for its distinctive Women with Children Program, one of only a few in the nation, which provides family-friendly on-campus housing year-round to single mothers and their children (20 months and older) so the mother can pursue a bachelor's degree full time.

Wilson offers many academic options beyond the classroom. From interning in Washington, D.C., and pursuing honors classes to studying abroad.

CAMPUS FACILITIES AND EQUIPMENT
With state-of-the-art classroom, laboratory and research spaces, the Harry R. Brooks Complex for Science, Mathematics and Technology enhances the College's strengths in the sciences at the undergraduate level. The Wilson campus also includes the Fulton Center for Sustainable Living with its organic farm, the Penn Hall Equestrian Center, and the Hankey Center for the Education and Advancement of Women.

Wilson's exceptional Penn Hall Equestrian Center serves as the base for equestrian programs and includes two indoor riding arenas featuring shadowless lighting and sand/sawdust footing. The center also houses an outdoor arena with racetrack sand footing, three pristine barns with 72 stalls, 20 acres of fenced paddocks and pastures, and plenty of space for outdoor riding. Horse boarding is available.

The Fulton Center for Sustainable Living, with its active CSA (community-supported agriculture) program and organic farm, provides options for students in environmental majors or those who are interested in sustainable practices. The center provides internships, service learning and volunteer opportunities.

Wilson will begin a campus renovation in the coming year, starting with a new student center space (scheduled to be completed during the 2013-14 academic year) and updated residence halls. The College is also in the planning stages for a new library with a learning commons that will serve as a hub for academic life on campus.

TUITION, ROOM, BOARD, AND FEES

As part of its commitment to affordable education, Wilson College will lower its tuition rate for the 2014-15 academic year to $23,745. The cost of room and board for the 2014-15 academic year will be determined in fall 2013.

For 2013-14, the tuition rate was held at $28,745 for a second year, with room and board set at $10,393.

Wilson guarantees on-campus housing for all four years, with single-room options available. All students are permitted to have cars on campus and laundry facilities are provided free of charge.

FINANCIAL AID

Wilson College awards more than $12 million in aid every year, with 96 percent of students receiving financial assistance. Wilson also awards a variety of scholarships, from those tied to specific majors to competitive scholarships and more. Merit scholarships, based solely on academic performance, are automatically awarded at the point of admission to the college. These renewable scholarships are based upon the applicant's participation in a college preparatory curriculum in a regionally accredited high school and cumulative grade-point average (GPA). The GPA standards apply to transfer students as well.

Wilson Merit Scholarships 2013-14

Scholarship	Annual Reduction	GPA
Presidential	50% tuition	3.75+
Dean's	35% tuition	3.5 – 3.74
Faculty	25% tuition	3.25 – 3.49

STUDENT ORGANIZATIONS AND ACTIVITIES

Students are encouraged to get involved and meet fellow students on campus by joining any of the many clubs and organizations or participating in intercollegiate athletics or equestrian teams. Wilson has something to satisfy the interests and pursuits of most students, but if they can't find what they want, they can take the lead and start a new club.

Three student organizations carry academic credit for participants: Billboard, the student newspaper, the Wilson College Choir and Orchesis, Wilson's acclaimed modern dance troupe. The Wilson College Government Association (WCGA) is jointly responsible for the rules that govern the college campus, and provides leadership opportunities. Students can also participate in internships, such as the Washington Center program, or complete research projects and study abroad.

Wilson College is part of the National Collegiate Athletic Association (NCAA) Division III and a member of the North Eastern Athletic Conference (NEAC). By 2014, Wilson plans to offer basketball, cross country and golf for men, and have two additional men's sports in place by 2016. Women's sports include basketball, cross country, field hockey, lacrosse, soccer and softball.

Wilson's hunt seat and western equitation teams compete in the Intercollegiate Horse Show Association (IHSA), while the dressage team competes in the Intercollegiate Dressage Association (IDA). Additional equestrian clubs provide students with the opportunity to participate in the eventing team and the mounted drill team.

ADMISSIONS PROCESS

High school students may apply at the beginning of their senior year. High school graduates can apply for admission within a year of their intended semester of enrollment. Wilson operates under a rolling admissions policy, which means the admissions office will review student applications as soon as all the required documents are received.

Wilson seeks students who have completed a college preparatory curriculum that includes four units of English, four units of history, three units of math (algebra 1 and 2 and geometry), two units of the same foreign language, and two units of natural science with labs. Students who have at least a 3.0 GPA in a college preparatory curriculum at a regionally accredited high school are not required to submit SAT or ACT scores. Each applicant will be assigned an admissions counselor, who will assist them with the application process and continue guiding them until classes begin.

Required application documents include:

Application form, either online or paper, or the common application.

Official high school transcripts.

Official college transcripts (transfer students or dual-enrollment students)

Teacher recommendation

Graded English paper (written for a junior or senior English class)

Official SAT or ACT scores (if not applying as test-optional)

SAT code for Wilson College: 2979

ACT code for Wilson College: 3758

Call or email in advance to schedule a personalized tour, tailored to meet your interests. To apply, go online to wilson.edu or contact an admissions officer by phone at 800-421-8402 or email admissions@wilson.edu.

WITTENBERG UNIVERSITY

AT A GLANCE

Wittenberg University offers a highly personal, active and engaged academic experience in a supportive environment that facilitates close interaction with award-winning faculty. Wittenberg enrolls approximately 2,000 full-time students, representing more than 41 states and 19 countries around the world. With most students living on or near campus, Wittenberg's campus is alive with activity.

Founded in 1845 in Springfield, Ohio, Wittenberg is a private, coeducational, liberal arts and sciences college affiliated with the Evangelical Lutheran Church in America. In keeping with its mission, Wittenberg provides an education dedicated to intellectual inquiry and wholeness of person within a diverse residential community. Reflecting its Lutheran heritage, Wittenberg also challenges students to become responsible global citizens, to discover their callings, and to lead personal, professional, and civic lives of creativity, service, compassion, and integrity.

Wittenberg's strong arts and sciences programs, coupled with internships and community service, make its graduates attractive to prominent medical, law, and graduate programs. More than 20 percent of students begin graduate programs immediately after graduation, and 70 percent pursue an advanced degree at some point in their careers. Graduates have enjoyed successful careers in education, business, science, fine and performing arts, politics, medicine, ministry, dentistry, and law.

Wittenberg competes in the nationally renowned Division III North Coast Athletic Conference (NCAC), which consists of 10 academically selective colleges and universities in Ohio, Pennsylvania, and Indiana. The NCAC features championship competition in 23 sports-11 for men and 12 for women. Intramurals are very popular among students, and club sports, including crew, rugby, sailing, skiing, and men's volleyball, are available.

Wittenberg is accredited by the Higher Education Commission of the North Central Association of Colleges and Schools, the American Association of University Women, the American Chemical Society, the National Council for the Accreditation of Teacher Education, and the National Association of Schools of Music.

LOCATION AND ENVIRONMENT

Located in Springfield, Ohio, Wittenberg's campus, ranked as one of the nation's most beautiful, rests on 95 wooded, rolling acres in a residential neighborhood. With a population of 65,000, Springfield offers cultural events and internship opportunities found in larger urban areas, as well as the friendliness and sense of community typical of small towns.

The University's Center for Civic and Urban Engagement celebrates Wittenberg's distinct urban environment and promotes scholarship, service, and collaboration between the university and the greater Springfield area, creating a more vibrant, cohesive community.

Recreational opportunities include an extensive bike trail system and recently constructed kayaking structures on Buck Creek, both of which border the Wittenberg campus. Students also enjoy the nearby Frank Lloyd Wright Westcott House; the Heritage Center, a museum showcasing Springfield's vibrant history; beautiful state parks; and the Springfield Museum of Art, located adjacent to campus.

Springfield's proximity to Dayton (25 miles), Columbus (45 miles), and Cincinnati (75 miles) gives students convenient access to airports and additional social and recreational opportunities, such as concerts, shopping, parks, museums, and sporting events.

OFF-CAMPUS OPPORTUNITIES

Every day Wittenberg students engage in the world around them—and apply what they have learned in the classroom to real-world situations—through community service, internships, and part-time jobs. One of a select few universities requiring community service of all its students, Wittenberg believes students learn more of themselves when they give of themselves. Students contribute thousands of hours annually by tutoring local school children, building homes with Habitat for Humanity, serving the hungry and homeless, working in community gardens, or serving with organizations such as Boy Scouts of America, Girl Scouts, Head Start, and Junior Achievement.

Off-campus academic opportunities include an extensive student-teaching program, a marine biology/freshwater ecology program in the Bahamas, the Local Government Management Program, the Africana Studies/community service program in Lesotho, and the Lutheran College Washington, D.C. Semester Program. Students also have interned with business and non-profits across the country, including the U.S. Library of Congress, ABC Primetime Live, The Children's Museum of Indianapolis, and the National Institutes of Health.

The Office of International Education assists students with selecting study-abroad programs and counsels them on integrating international study with their academic and career goals. Through memberships in several consortia, more than 20 percent of Wittenberg students participate in study-abroad programs at 40 sites in more than 20 countries in Europe, Asia, Africa, and Latin America.

MAJORS AND DEGREES OFFERED

Wittenberg offers five undergraduate degrees: Bachelor of Arts (BA), Bachelor of Science (BS), Bachelor of Music (BMus), Bachelor of Music Education (BME), and Bachelor of Fine Arts (BFA). Wittenberg also offers a Master of Arts in Education.

Thirty-three majors are offered: accounting, American Studies, art, biochemistry & molecular biology, biology, business, chemistry, communication, computer science, dance, earth science, East Asian studies, economics, education, English, financial economics, French, geography, geology, German, history, international studies, mathematics, music, philosophy, physics, political science, psychology, religion, Russian and Central Eurasian studies, sociology, Spanish, and theatre.

In addition to the above, Wittenberg offers minors in African and Diaspora Studies, Chinese, computational science, creative writing, environmental studies, health science, Japanese, journalism, marine science, pre-modern and ancient world studies, Russian, sport management, statistics, technical theatre, theatre performance, urban studies, and women's studies.

ACADEMIC PROGRAMS

A Wittenberg education consists of three parts: a broad base in the liberal arts, an intensive course of study in a major, and an enhanced course of study that makes up a minor or electives. Wittenberg also places considerable emphasis on strong speaking, writing, critical thinking and research skills to ensure that its students are competitive graduate school applicants, outstanding future employees, and global leaders. At the same time, a Wittenberg education provides an in-depth investigation of human behavior and diversity.

Wittenberg students engage in experiential learning, pursue independent studies and honors theses, and collaborate with award-winning faculty on research projects. The Honors Program, which offers special seminars, honors theses or projects, and a variety of academic and cultural activities, is available to outstanding students who want to challenge themselves and enhance their academic program.

The WittEntrepreneurs Program, for both business and non-business majors, combines cutting-edge classes with opportunities for students to launch, operate and manage an enterprise on campus. Popular summer programs include the Screenwriters' Institute, in which award-winning alumni in television and theatre share their professional expertise with students, and the Journalism Institute, during which students create an original magazine.

For students interested in the health professions, more than 45 internships are available each semester through the clinical internship program, which pairs them with area physicians and medical health professionals in ways that offer unprecedented access and hands-on learning opportunities.

Cooperative education programs with other leading research institutions, including Case Western Reserve, Columbia University, Duke University, Johns Hopkins University, and Washington University in St. Louis, are available to help students complete their majors. These special programs include engineering, environmental studies, marine/aquatic biology, nursing, and occupational therapy.

Pre-professional programs include accounting, education, law, theology, and the pre-health fields of pre-medicine, pre-dentistry, pre-veterinary, and pre-optometry. With approval, students may plan interdepartmental majors composed of courses selected from several departments that reflect a unified purpose or theme.

CAMPUS FACILITIES AND EQUIPMENT

Wittenberg's campus consists of 26 major buildings, including nine academic buildings designed to enhance learning and encourage interaction and collaboration among faculty and students. The state-of-the-art Barbara Deer Kuss Science Center contains modern technology and equipment, including new cell and microbiology labs, organic chemistry labs, and neurobiology and physiology labs that provide hands-on learning experiences for all students, regardless of major. Home to the humanities, Hollenbeck Hall houses a 24-hour computer lab, the Math Workshop, the Writing Center, and the Foreign Language Learning Center.

Carnegie Hall houses the Wittenberg Center for Applied Management (WittCAM), through which students serve as consultants to help area businesses and non-profit organizations succeed. The recently renovated Blair Hall, home to the university's nationally recognized education program, earned LEED Gold certification for its green-focused building strategies.

The recently acquired Springfield Center for the Arts at Wittenberg University is the new home for the visual and performing arts and features a blackbox theatre for theatre and dance performances and an art gallery. Students interested in music have access to the John M. Chowning Laboratory for Music and Technology, practice rooms and recital space. Thomas Library, open extensive hours, offers an abundance of both digital and print resources and houses the Oral Communication Center and Research Help Center.

Wittenberg's 23 men's and women's Division III athletics teams compete using outstanding facilities and fields. Athletics facilities include basketball, volleyball, and racquetball courts; a football field and outdoor track; access to nearby baseball fields; a tennis complex; a softball field; a natatorium; a state-of-the-art fitness center; and a weight room.

Seven residence halls offer a variety of living arrangements for freshmen and sophomores in both historic and new buildings, all equipped with computer labs and lounges. Upperclass students can choose to live in the residence halls or on-campus apartments, the Campus Ministries House, or sorority and fraternity houses.

TUITION, ROOM, BOARD AND FEES

Basic costs for full-time undergraduates for the 2012-2013 academic year are:

Tuition: $37,230

Room: $5,056

Board: $4,680

Activity fee: $300

Technology fee: $500

Total: $47,766

FINANCIAL AID

Wittenberg is aggressive in offering different ways to finance an outstanding, affordable education, including both need-based and merit-based assistance. Need-based assistance includes grants, loans, and work-study programs. Approximately 70 percent of Wittenberg students qualify for need-based aid, and the average scholarship and grant financial assistance award is $21,098 per year. To be considered, applicants must file the Free Application for Federal Student Aid (FAFSA) by March 1.

All accepted students are automatically considered for academic scholarships, and special interest awards. To be given priority consideration, students should submit a complete application for admission by December 1.

Accepted students may compete for special interest awards that recognize commitment to community service, superior student leadership experience, or a passion for East Asian business and culture. Fine arts scholarships reward students for talent in art, dance, music, and theatre. Each of these scholarships requires a separate audition/application process.

STUDENT ORGANIZATIONS AND ACTIVITIES

With more than 125 organizations and clubs, students can easily pursue their passions while at the same time develop management and leadership skills. Student groups are formed on topics ranging from cultural and social awareness to recreational to religious involvement and communication. For aspiring leaders, Wittenberg offers the Emerging Leaders program for first-year students.

Approximately 30 percent of the students are involved in Greek life. Many academic departments have major-specific honor societies and clubs. Weekend activities include lectures, art exhibits, concerts, dances, movies, coffeehouses, and comedians. New organizations and activities are created regularly to meet the changing interests of students.

ADMISSIONS PROCESS

Admission to Wittenberg is selective and based on the following information.

high school record, including the strength of the high school and its curriculum,

and trends in the student's academic work; SAT or ACT scores; co-curricular activities and community participation; recommendations; and an essay. Wittenberg is a test optional school. International students and transfer students are encouraged to apply. An on-campus interview is not required but is highly recommended. Students may apply using the free online application at www.wittenberg.edu/apply or the Common Application.

The deadlines for applying are as follows for incoming freshmen:

Early Decision: November 15

Early Action I: December 1

Early Action II: January 15

Regular Action: March 15

Students must apply by December 1 to receive full consideration for merit-based scholarships. Transfer application deadlines are December 1 for spring semester and July 15 for fall semester. The international student application deadline is March 15.

WORCESTER POLYTECHNIC INSTITUTE

AT A GLANCE

You want to be on the first Mars mission, find alternative energy sources, or cure cancer. WPI wants to help you make an impact. Our students do much more than study science and technology. They delve into the arts and humanities. They complete projects on campus and around the globe, connecting what they've learned in the classroom with pressing real-life challenges—from health to the environment to global competitiveness. Students grow - personally, professionally, and intellectually - as they discover how to apply their talents and turn ideas into tangible solutions.

WPI's aim is to educate students broadly, so they achieve greatly. Though WPI has been around for more than 145 years, our approach to education, like our students, is innovative and practical. Small classes, a flexible curriculum, and one-on-one interaction with professors at the top of their fields make learning at WPI an experience unlike any other.

WPI has been widely recognized for its quality. It was the only technological university out of 16 national Leadership Institutions selected by the Association of American Colleges and Universities to serve as models of outstanding practices in liberal education. WPI consistently ranks among the top national universities by U.S. News & World Report and was recently ranked in the top 20 in the nation for Best Career Services and for Happiest Students by the Princeton Review.

LOCATION AND ENVIRONMENT

With its beautiful architecture, grassy quad, and ivy-covered walls, WPI has a traditional New England campus. Students stop and chat with friends and professors on tree-lined paths. They play pool or get a coffee between classes at the Campus Center. They study by the fountain in Reunion Plaza, get a group together for bowling at Gompeiis Gutters, stop and smell the roses in the formal English garden behind Higgins House, or see a student play at the Little Theatre.

Home to 12 other colleges and universities and over 35,000 college students, greater Worcester is a great college town. WPI is a member of the Colleges of Worcester Consortium, through which WPI students may register for courses at other colleges and take advantage of a wide range of cultural programming offered by consortium members. A shuttle provides free transportation between campuses.

Late-night diners, clubs, museums, concert venues, and theaters are right down the hill from WPI in Worcester's vibrant downtown. Boston is less than an hour away by commuter rail if you want to catch Red Sox fever. There's great skiing and boarding at nearby Wachusett Mountain. If you want to go a bit farther, Worcester is centrally located with easy access to Providence, New York City, the Berkshire and White Mountains, and Cape Cod.

OFF-CAMPUS OPPORTUNITIES

In Worcester you'll find:

35,000+ college students at 13 colleges and universities

14,800 seats at the DCU Center for arena concerts and sporting events

5,000 objects of arms and armor at the Higgins Armory Museum

53 parks including the largest urban nature sanctuary in New England and the Olmstead-designed Elm Park

36 galleries and 5,000 years of art at the Worcester Art Museum

20 ski trails at nearby Wachusett Mountain

2 minor league sports teams (Tornadoes, baseball; Sharks, hockey)

1 Gompei the goat (WPI mascot)

MAJORS AND DEGREES OFFERED

WPI offers over 36 areas of study in engineering, science, management, and the liberal arts leading to the Bachelor of Science (B.S.) or Bachelor of Arts (B.A.) degree. Exciting new interdisciplinary programs, driven by real-world demand, include interactive media and game development, environmental engineering, architectural engineering, and the nation's first undergraduate program in robotics engineering.

We offer pre-professional programs (law, medicine, dentistry, and veterinary) and a five-year BS/MS program. You can even create your own major or minor program. Not surprisingly, over 40 percent of students change their major at least once. A comprehensive academic advising program and a wide array of academic support services help students make the right choices and reach their goals.

WPI students have received some of the nation's highest academic honors. Over just the last decade, two students have received the prestigious Marshall Scholarship, 14 have been awarded Goldwater scholarships, five have received the Rotary Ambassadorial Scholarship, three have won National Science Foundation Fellowships, two have been named to the USA Today All-USA College Academic Team, and one has been named an NIH-Oxford/Cambridge Biomedical Research Scholar.

ACADEMIC PROGRAMS

At WPI, learning is about more than just theories and ideas. Students put what they learn into practice through a unique project-enriched curriculum. Each undergraduate complete two projects: one directly related to their major and one in which they work with a team of students to solve a problem at the intersection of society and technology. Students gain valuable professional skills, a talent for teamwork, and the confidence to dive right in—no matter what the challenge.

WPI's academic program is built to be flexible. Students take the equivalent of three courses (as courses or project work) during each of four 7-week terms (two in the fall and two in the spring). It is also designed to encourage collaboration, not competition. Students work closely on projects and in project-oriented classes. Learning to work in teams prepares students to get results and become leaders, no matter what path they take in life.

WPI's award-winning Global Perspective Program, with more than 30 project centers on five continents, is one of the most comprehensive and highly regarded global studies programs in the nation. Most WPI students complete projects off campus; over half complete project work outside the United States in places like Thailand, Namibia, New Zealand, Costa Rica, and Italy. Global project experiences not only give students the chance to work in teams to solve meaningful real-life problems for people around the world, they immerse students in other cultures and give them a powerful sense of self-confidence.

Top-tier employers seek out WPI graduates for their real-world experience and ability to work collaboratively. With a placement rate of over 90 percent, students are recruited by leading organizations such as Pfizer, General Electric, Fidelity Investments, IBM and Google. Not surprisingly, WPI graduates' starting salaries are higher than those of many other college graduates, according to the National Association of Colleges and Employers. Each year, WPI graduates are accepted at many prestigious graduate schools, including MIT, Yale University, Princeton University, Johns Hopkins University and Tufts University Medical School.

CAMPUS FACILITIES AND EQUIPMENT

With all of the amazing things WPI students and faculty do, our outstanding research facilities should come as no surprise.

Our 125,000-square-foot WPI Life Sciences and Bioengineering Center at Gateway Park is a state-of-the-art research center housing faculty from four departments. Our two atomic force microscopes let you see individual atoms on a material's surface. The Fire Science Laboratory enables students and faculty to evaluate fire safety measures in actual fire simulations. Laser holography labs, computer music labs, medical imaging labs, a bioprocess lab – they're all here, and lots more.

Recent additions to WPI's undergraduate teaching facilities include a newly constructed chemistry laboratory center that facilitates team-based work a new $11 million Undergraduate Life Sciences Laboratory Center that is the focal point for undergraduate teaching and research in biology and biotechnology, biomedical engineering, chemistry and biochemistry, and chemical engineering.

WPI also opened a brand new $53 million Sports and Recreation Center in May 2012 including a four-court gymnasium, indoor jogging track, 14,000 sq. ft. of fitness space, racquetball and squash courts, competition pool, workout studios, and rowing tanks.

TUITION, ROOM, BOARD AND FEES

(2012-2013)

Tuition: $42,178.00

Social Fee: $260.00

Health Fee: $340.00

Total: $42,778.00

Typical Room: $7,466.00

Typical Board Plan: $5,616.00

Books and Supplies: $1,000.00

Personal Expenses: $1,200.00

Total: $58,060.00

FINANCIAL AID

It's no secret. A great education costs a lot of money, but think about the return on your investment. College graduates in general earn over the course of their careers at least $1 million more than those without a degree. For WPI graduates, starting salaries frequently exceed the national averages and graduates are able to move quickly up the ranks to positions of influence as a result of their excellent preparation. In fact, WPI was recently ranked No. 4 for the highest average starting salaries among all national universities.

APPLYING FOR FINANCIAL AID

Students should file the FAFSA and CSS Profile on or near their admissions application deadline. WPI should receive all financial aid materials by February 1. Applications after this date will be reviewed subject to funds available.

Most applicants (including early applicants) will receive a financial aid package within two weeks of their acceptance. We'll inform you of the Financial Aid Committee's decision no later than April 15 for regular decision admissions, and you'll have until the Candidates Common Reply Date (May 1) to either accept or decline the offer.

Academic Scholarships

WPI offers academic scholarships to freshman applicants based upon academic performance, standardized test scores, leadership, extracurricular involvement and community service. All admitted applicants are considered and there is no separate application required.

Scholarships vary in amounts, but typically range between $10,000 and $25,000, and are renewable for four years. Valedictorians and Salutatorians are guaranteed a minimum scholarship of $20,000. National Merit, National Achievement, and National Hispanic Recognition Finalists are guaranteed a minimum of $20,000.

STUDENT ORGANIZATIONS AND ACTIVITIES

WPI has 20 varsity (NCAA Division III) athletics teams and 34 club and intramural athletics. WPI won the "Worcester Cup" for the sixth time in seven years, recognizing it as the top collegiate program in Worcester County. WPI has 13 fraternities and five sororities, 20 music and performing arts group, dozens of academic clubs, international organizations, religious groups and other organizations. Overall, there are more than 200 student clubs and activities.

ADMISSIONS PROCESS

WPI Admissions offers a variety of application options. Students can apply using the Common Application (paper or on-line). A $65 application fee is required for all applicants. (WPI endorses the fee waiver policy of the College Board, as well as accepts fee waivers from guidance or college counselors.)

Academic Requirements

four years of math (including pre-calculus)

four years of English

two years of lab science

Other requirements include:

High school transcript

Science or math recommendation

Guidance counselor's recommendation

Personal essay

SAT I or ACT scores or alternate materials through WPI's "Flex Path"

TOEFL, IELTS, or Pearson Exam scores for international students whose first language is not English

Interviews

While interviews are optional, this is your chance to meet one-on-one with an Admissions staff member or a trained Admissions intern. We'll have the chance to learn more about you, and can answer specific questions you may have. Seniors in high school should interview before December 15th of their senior year if they are interested in an interview.

Deadlines

Early Action (Round 1) - Nov. 10

Early Action (Round 2) - Jan. 1

Regular Decision - Feb. 1

January Admission - Transfer Students Only - Nov. 15 (Rolling notification)

Fall Admission - Transfer Students - Apr. 15° (Rolling notification)

INDEXES

INDEXES

ALPHABETICAL INDEX

INDEX BY LOCATION

The Princeton Review's Complete Book of Colleges

VIRGINIA

Averett University	53
Bluefield College	86
Bridgewater College	99
Christendom College	156
Christopher Newport University	157
College of William and Mary, The	193
Eastern Mennonite University	257
Emory and Henry College	270, 1078
George Mason University	306
Hampden-Sydney College	331
Hampton University	333
Hollins University	350
James Madison University	376
Liberty University	418
Longwood University	427
Lynchburg College	437
Mary Baldwin College	453
Marymount University	456, 1142
Old Dominion University	565, 1166
Patrick Henry College	578
Radford University	609
Randolph College	611
Randolph-Macon College	612
Regent University	614
Roanoke College	624
Saint Paul's College	651
Shenandoah University	673
Sweet Briar College	742, 1226
University of Mary Washington	832, 1262
University of Richmond	877, 1274
University of Virginia	908
University of Virginia's College at Wise	909
Virginia Commonwealth University	934, 1290
Virginia Intermont College	934
Virginia Military Institute	935
Virginia State University	935
Virginia Tech	936
Virginia Wesleyan College	938
Washington and Lee University	949

WASHINGTON

Bastyr University	63
Central Washington University	147
City University	159
Cornish College of the Arts	216
Eastern Washington University	260
Evergreen State College, The	276
Gonzaga University	316, 1090
Heritage University	344
Northwest College	543

Pacific Lutheran University	573, 1170
Saint Martin's University	647
Seattle Pacific University	668
Seattle University	668, 1202
Trinity Lutheran College	767
Trinity Western University	768
University of Puget Sound	875
University of Washington	910
Walla Walla University	942
Washington State University	950
Western Washington University	972
Whitman College	980
Whitworth College	981

WEST VIRGINIA

Alderson-Broaddus College	20
Bethany College (WV)	78, 1024
Bluefield State College	87
Concord University	205
Davis & Elkins College	226
Fairmont State University, including Pierpont Community & Technical College	279
Glenville State College	314
Marshall University	452
Mountain State University	510
Ohio Valley University	561
Salem-Teikyo University	656
Shepherd University	673
University of Charleston	799
West Liberty State College	962
West Virginia State University	964
West Virginia University	964
West Virginia University Institute of Technology	965
West Virginia Wesleyan College	966, 1300
Wheeling Jesuit University	979

WISCONSIN

Alverno College	25
Beloit College	69, 1020
Carroll College (WI)	135
Carthage College	136
Concordia University Wisconsin	209
Edgewood College	261
Lawrence University	410

Marian University	448
Marquette University	451, 1140
Milwaukee Institute of Art and Design	484
Milwaukee School of Engineering	484
Mount Mary College	506
Northland College	542
Ripon College	623, 1186
St. Norbert College	712, 1216
University of Wisconsin—Eau Claire	913
University of Wisconsin—Green Bay	914
University of Wisconsin—La Crosse	914
University of Wisconsin—Madison	915
University of Wisconsin—Milwaukee	916
University of Wisconsin—Oshkosh	916
University of Wisconsin—Parkside	917
University of Wisconsin—Platteville	918
University of Wisconsin—River Falls	918
University of Wisconsin—Stevens Point	919
University of Wisconsin—Stout	920
University of Wisconsin—Superior	920
University of Wisconsin—Whitewater	921
Viterbo University	938
Wisconsin Lutheran College	994

WYOMING

Central Wyoming College	148
University of Wyoming	922

INTERNATIONAL

INDEX BY SIZE

California State University,
San Bernardino 124
Central Michigan University 146
City University of New York—Borough of
Manhattan Community College 160
City University of New York—
Hunter College 162, 1102
City University of New York—
New York City College of Technology 164
City University of New York—
Queens College 165
Clemson University 174, 1046
Colorado State University 197
DePaul University 231
Drexel University 247
East Carolina University 252
Eastern Michigan University 257
Florida Atlantic University 285, 1084
George Mason University 306
Georgia Southern University 310
Georgia State University 312
Grand Valley State University 323
Illinois State University 362
Indiana University—Purdue University
Indianapolis 369
James Madison University 376
Kansas State University 388
Kennesaw State University 391
Kent State University—Kent Campus 392
Louisiana State University—Baton Rouge 429
McGill University 463
Middle Tennessee State University 477
Mississippi State University 488
New York University 526, 1156
North Carolina State University 531
Northeastern University 537, 1162
Northern Arizona University 538
Oakland University 552
Ohio University—Athens 560
Oklahoma State University 564
Old Dominion University 565, 1166
Oregon State University 569
Portland State University 599
Sam Houston State University 658
San Diego State University 659
State University of New York—
Stony Brook University 731
State University of New York—
University at Buffalo 733
Thomas Edison State College 757
Towson University 761
Troy University—Troy
(formerly Troy State University) 769
University of Akron, The 780
University of Arkansas—
Fayetteville 785, 1242

University of California—Irvine 791
University of California—Riverside 793
University of California—San Diego 794
University of California—Santa Barbara 795
University of California—Santa Cruz 795
University of Cincinnati 800
University of Connecticut 803
University of Delaware 806, 1252
University of Illinois at Chicago 819
University of Iowa 821
University of Kansas 822
University of Kentucky 823
University of Maryland University
College 833
University of Massachusetts Amherst 836
University of Mississippi 844
University of Nebraska—Lincoln 851
University of Nevada, Las Vegas 852
University of North Carolina
at Chapel Hill, The 859
University of North Carolina—Charlotte 860
University of Oklahoma 867
University of Oregon 868, 1272
University of Pittsburgh—
Pittsburgh Campus 873
University of South Carolina Columbia 887
University of Southern California 890
University of Tennessee at Knoxville 897
University of Texas at El Paso, The 901
University of Texas—Pan American, The 902
University of Toledo 904
University of Utah 906
University of Wisconsin—Milwaukee 916
Utah State University 925
Virginia Commonwealth University 934, 1290
Virginia Tech 936
Washington State University 950
Wayne State University 954
Weber State University 956
West Virginia University 964
Western Kentucky University 968
Western Michigan University 969

25,000–35,000 STUDENTS

Brigham Young University (UT) 101
California State University, Fullerton 121
California State University, Long Beach 121
California State University, Northridge 123
California State University, Sacramento 123
Excelsior College 276
Florida State University 290

Indiana University—Bloomington 365
Iowa State University 373
Northern Illinois University 539
Purdue University—West Lafayette 605
Rutgers, The State University
of New Jersey—New Brunswick 637
San Francisco State University 660
San Jose State University 660
Temple University 746, 1228
Texas State University—San Marcos 753
Texas Tech University 754
University of Alabama
at Tuscaloosa, The 782
University of Arizona 785
University of British Columbia, The 788
University of California—Davis 790
University of California—Los Angeles 792
University of Colorado—Boulder 802
University of Florida 811
University of Georgia 812
University of Houston 816
University of Illinois
at Urbana-Champaign 820, 1258
University of Maryland—College Park 834
University of Michigan—Ann Arbor 839
University of Minnesota—Twin Cities 843
University of Missouri 845
University of North Texas 863
University of South Florida 890
University of Texas at Arlington, The 898
University of Texas at San Antonio, The 903
University of Washington 910
University of Wisconsin—Madison 915

MORE THAN 35,000 STUDENTS

Arizona State University 37
Florida International University 288
Michigan State University 474
Ohio State University—Columbus, The 556
Pennsylvania State University—
University Park 587
Texas A&M University—College Station 748
University of Central Florida 797, 1246
University of Phoenix 870
University of Texas at Austin, The 899
University of Toronto 905
York University 1003

INDEX BY TUITION

Western University	972
Westfield State University	973
Wichita State University	982
Wilberforce University	983
William Paterson University	986
William Tyndale College	988
Wilmington College (DE)	990
Winona State University	992
Winston-Salem State University	993
Wright State University	998
York University	1003

$10,000–$15,000

Andrews University	32
Art Institute of Colorado	43
Atlanta Christian College	46
Avila University	54
Benedict College	71
Bennett College	72
Bethany University	78
Bethune-Cookman College	81
Blessing-Rieman College of Nursing	84
Bob Jones University	88
Brewton-Parker College	98
California State University, Long Beach	121
California State University, Monterey Bay	122
California State University, San Bernardino	124
Central Michigan University	146
Citadel, The Military College of South Carolina, The	158
Claflin University	167
Cleary University	173
Clemson University	174, 1046
College of New Jersey, The	186, 1048
Colorado School of Mines	196
Columbia College—Hollywood	200
Cumberland University	220
DeVry Institute of Technology (Long Island City, NY)	233
DeVry University (Addison, IL)	233
DeVry University (Alpharetta, GA)	234
DeVry University (Chicago, IL)	234
DeVry University (Columbus, OH)	234
DeVry University (Denver, CO)	234
DeVry University (Fremont, CA)	236
DeVry University (Irving, TX)	236
DeVry University (Kansas City, MO)	236
DeVry University (Long Beach, CA)	237
DeVry University (North Brunswick, NJ)	237
DeVry University (Orlando, FL)	238

DeVry University (Phoenix, AZ)	238
DeVry University (Pomona, CA)	238
DeVry University (West Hills, CA)	239
Divine Word College	241
Dominican School of Philosophy and Theology	243
Evangel University	275
Faulkner University	280
Ferris State University	282
Florida College	286
Franciscan University, The	295
Freed-Hardeman University	299
Gallaudet University	302
Gibbs College	314
Goldey-Beacom College	315
Grace Bible College	319
Hampton University	333
Harding University	335
Howard Payne University	355
Husson University	359
Huston-Tillotson University	360
Jewish Theological Seminary, Albert A. List College	378
Judson College (AL)	384
Judson College (IL)	385
Kendall College of Art and Design of Ferris State University	391
Laura and Alvin Siegal College of Judaic Studies	409
Lee University	412
Lenoir-Rhyne College	414
Lincoln Christian College and Seminary	420
Lindenwood University	423
Lindsey Wilson College	424
Lubbock Christian University	434
Marygrove College	453
Massachusetts College of Art and Design	459
Medaille College	465
Medical University of South Carolina	466
Metropolitan College of New York	473
Miami University	474
Michigan State University	474
Michigan Technological University	475, 1146
Mississippi College	487
Missouri Valley College	491
Monroe College	495
Morehouse College	501
Nebraska Methodist College	517
New Jersey City University	522
New Jersey Institute of Technology	522
New World School of the Arts	525
Newman University	528
North Carolina Wesleyan College	532
North Central University	533
Northwest College	543
Oak Hills Christian College	551

Oakland University	552
Ohio University—Athens	560
Ohio Valley University	561
Pacific States University	575
Park University	577
Patten University	579
Pennsylvania College of Technology	579, 1172
Pennsylvania State University—Abington	580
Pennsylvania State University—Altoona	580
Pennsylvania State University—Beaver	581
Pennsylvania State University—Berks	581
Pennsylvania State University—Delaware County	581
Pennsylvania State University—DuBois	582
Pennsylvania State University—Erie, The Behrend College	582
Pennsylvania State University—Fayette, The Eberly Campus	583
Pennsylvania State University—Greater Allegheny	583
Pennsylvania State University—Harrisburg	584
Pennsylvania State University—Hazleton	584
Pennsylvania State University—Lehigh Valley	585
Pennsylvania State University—Mont Alto	585
Pennsylvania State University—New Kensington	586
Pennsylvania State University—Schuylkill	586
Pennsylvania State University—Shenango	587
Pennsylvania State University—Wilkes-Barre	588
Pennsylvania State University—Worthington Scranton	588
Pennsylvania State University—York	589
Pfeiffer University	590
Regent University	614
Rutgers, The State University of New Jersey—New Brunswick	637
Saint Joseph Seminary College	642
Saint Paul's College	651
San Jose State University	660
Southern Vermont College	695
St. Francis College (NY)	705
St. John's College, Department of Nursing (IL)	707
St. Mary's College of Maryland	711, 1214
Temple University	746, 1228
Tennessee Wesleyan College	748
Thomas More College of Liberal Arts	758
Trinity College of Florida	765
Trinity Lutheran College	767
Trinity Western University	768

$20,000–$25,000

Academy of Art University	10
Adrian College	13
Albertus Magnus College	18
Alderson-Broaddus College	20
Alvernia College	24, 1006
American Jewish University	27
Anderson University (SC)	31
Anna Maria College	33
Art Academy of Cincinnati	40
Art Institute of Atlanta, The	41
Art Institute of Las Vegas, The	43
Art Institutes International Minnesota, The	44
Baker University	55
Barton College	62
Benedictine University	72
Bethany College (WV)	78, 1024
Bethel College (KS)	79
Bluffton University	87
Brevard College	97
Briar Cliff University	99
Bryan College	104
Burlington College	108
Cairn University	110
California Institute of Integral Studies	113
Campbellsville University	129
Carlow University	133
Carroll College (MT)	134
Carroll College (WI)	135
Carson-Newman College	135
Cogswell College	177
Coker College	178
College of Idaho, The	183
College of Mount St. Joseph	185
College of New Rochelle, The	186
College of Saint Mary	190
Columbia College (SC)	199
Columbia College Chicago (IL)	200, 1052
Concordia College (NY)	206
Concordia University (OR)	207
Concordia University Chicago	208
Concordia University Irvine	209
Concordia University, Nebraska	210
Corban College	213
Corcoran College of Art and Design	214
Crown College	218
Culver-Stockton College	219
Daemen College	221, 1062
Dallas Baptist University	223
Doane College	241
Dominican College	242
Drury University	248
D'Youville College	251, 1060
Edgewood College	261
Emory and Henry College	270, 1078

Fontbonne University	290
Franklin College	297
Fresno Pacific University	300
Friends University	300
Gardner-Webb University	304
Grace College and Seminary	319
Graceland University	320, 1092
Grand View University	323
Hardin-Simmons University	336
Harrisburg University of Science and Technology	337
Hillsdale College	347, 1098
Holy Family University	351
Hope International University	353
Huntingdon College	357
Huntington University	358
Indiana Wesleyan University	371
John Brown University	379
Kendall College	390
Keuka College	395
Keystone College	396
King College	397
La Roche College	400, 1116
LeTourneau University	415
LIM College	419, 1128
Limestone College	419, 1130
Lipscomb University	425
Lyon College	439
Maharishi University of Management	441
Maine College of Art	441
Malone University	442
Marymount Manhattan College	455
Marymount University	456, 1142
Maryville University of Saint Louis	457
Massachusetts College of Pharmacy and Health Science	459
Memphis College of Art	467
Mercyhurst University	470
MidAmerica Nazarene University	476
Milligan College	480
Molloy College	493, 1148
Montreat College	498
Morningside College	502
Mount Vernon Nazarene University	510
Multnomah Bible College and Biblical Seminary	512
Muskingum College	514
Naropa University	514
Neumann University	518
Neumont University	519
North Park University	536
Nova Southeastern University	551
Ohio Dominican University	555
Oklahoma City University	563
Oral Roberts University	567
Oregon College of Art and Craft	568

Oregon Health Sciences University	569
Ouachita Baptist University	571
Our Lady of the Lake University (OLLU)	572
Palm Beach Atlantic University	576
Point Loma Nazarene University	595
Post University	600, 1176
Quincy University	607
Robert Morris University	625
Robert Morris University (IL)	626
Roberts Wesleyan College	626
Rockford College	628
Rocky Mountain College	629
Russell Sage College	635
Saint Joseph's College of Maine	643
Saint Mary-of-the-Woods College	647
Saint Vincent College	653
Saint Xavier University	654
Schreiner University	666
Soka University of America	681
Spelman College	699
Spring Arbor University	700
St. Mary's University	712
Sterling College (VT)	736, 1220
Stevenson University	738
Texas Lutheran University	752
Thomas Aquinas College	756
Thomas Jefferson University	757
Tiffin University	759
Trinity International University	766
Union University	775
Unity College	779
University of Bridgeport	788
University of Detroit Mercy	808
University of Dubuque	809
University of Hartford	813, 1256
University of Indianapolis	821
University of Mary Hardin-Baylor	831
University of New England	853, 1268
University of Saint Mary (KS)	880
University of Tampa	895, 1280
University of the Arts, The	787, 1244
Upper Iowa University	923
VanderCook College of Music	929
Vanguard University of Southern California	930
Walla Walla University	942
Walsh University	943
Webber International University	955, 1294
West Virginia Wesleyan College	966, 1300
Westminster Choir College of Rider University	974
Wheeling Jesuit University	979
William Penn University	987
Wingate University	991
Wisconsin Lutheran College	994

INDEX BY SELECTIVITY

The Princeton Review's Complete Book of Colleges

NOTES

NOTES

NOTES

NOTES

NOTES

NOTES

NOTES

NOTES

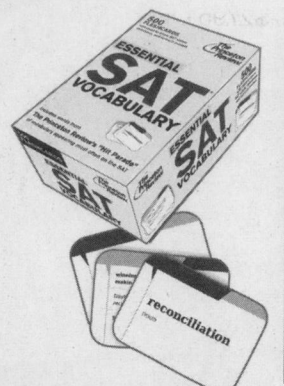

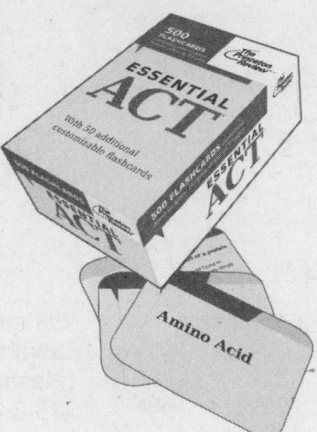